·ALABAMA·COLORADO·ARIZONA·MAINE·TEXAS·UTAH·ALASKA·
·IOWA·LOUISIANA·WISCONSIN·TENNESSEE·IDAHO·

CALIFORNIA·MICHIGAN·MINNESOTA·MISSISSIPPI·MISSOURI·WEST VIRGINIA·NEW YORK·NEVADA
NORTH DAKOTA·PENNSYLVANIA·SOUTH CAROLINA·SOUTH DAKOTA·MARYLAND·ARKANSAS

1817 2019

MISERANDO ATQUE ELIGENDO

The Official Catholic Directory

Anno
Domini
2019

Published Annually by
P. J. Kenedy & Sons

GEORGIA·DELAWARE·ILLINOIS·KANSAS·NORTH CAROLINA·OREGON·NEBRASKA·KENTUCKY
NEW HAMPSHIRE·NEW JERSEY·NEW MEXICO·CONNECTICUT·FLORIDA·MASSACHUSETTS

·INDIANA·OKLAHOMA·RHODE ISLAND·MONTANA·
·HAWAII·WASHINGTON·VIRGINIA·VERMONT·WYOMING·OHIO·

The Official Catholic Directory®
P.J. Kenedy & Sons, Publishers

Robert Docherty
Publisher

FOREWORD

It is with great pleasure that we present the 2019 edition of *The Official Catholic Directory*. For over 200 years, *The Official Catholic Directory* has provided comprehensive coverage of the institutions and clergy of the Catholic Church in the United States. To complement this data, we have included the 2018 Highlights, our annual recap of the key events impacting the U.S. Catholic Church over the past year.

The 2019 volume saw the enhancement of our new online updating system. It is part of our ongoing commitment to improve our service to the Church and provide better, more modern means to do so. We have continued to augment and refine this new database to ensure the best possible user experience and also allow the Church greater access to the important information collected.

Although the U.S. Catholic Church has changed significantly over the past two hundred years, our core mission remains the same: to provide a thorough and accurate portrait of the Catholic Church in America and to continually improve this unique and valuable reference tool. This directory owes a debt of gratitude to the ecclesiastical authorities and diocesan officials who help make *The Official Catholic Directory* possible. We thank them for their cooperation and invaluable assistance.

Sincerely,

Robert J. Docherty
Publisher

430 Mountain Avenue, Suite 403, New Providence, New Jersey 07974 • (908) 517-0780 • (844) 592-4197

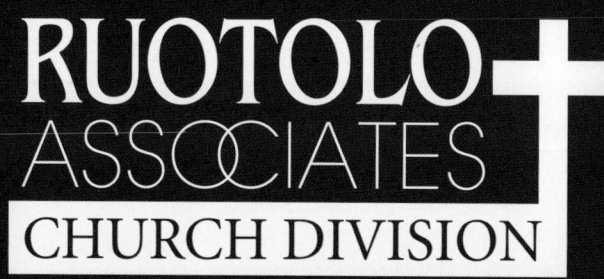

before

"Do not forget the poor!"

- His Holiness Pope Francis

We invite you to partner with Food For The Poor to answer our Holy Father's call. We never forget the poor. We provide critical support to the daily works of mercy of clergy, religious leaders and 102 Catholic Dioceses in primarily 17 countries throughout the Caribbean and Latin America. From building homes to feeding the hungry, Food For The Poor saves lives and renews hope for the destitute. **A large number of parishes in the United States welcome Food For The Poor each year**. Trusting us as partners to help the poor are some of the highest ranking members of the Catholic Church in the regions where we work.

His Eminence Óscar Andrés Cardinal Rodríguez Maradiaga, S.D.B., Coordinator of Pope Francis' Council of Cardinal Advisors is on Food For The Poor's Board of Directors.
"I pray you will partner with us in our ministry to be the hands and feet of Christ to the church in the developing world."

Leopoldo José Cardinal Brenes Solórzano, Archbishop of Managua (Nicaragua)
"I urge my brother Bishops and Archbishops around the world to join Food For The Poor and to open the doors of their dioceses to Food For The Poor. Under this union, they will efficiently respond to the Holy Father's petition of coming together for the good of the poor."

Charles H. Dufour, Archbishop Emeritus of Kingston in Jamaica
"It is quite impossible to find the words to express the appreciation for Food For The Poor, for the invaluable assistance given to all the dioceses I served over the last 37 years in Jamaica."

Archbishop Fortunatus Nwachukwu, Apostolic Nuncio to Trinidad and Tobago, Antilles
"Food For The Poor is evidently a good channel for good-hearted Catholics who wish to learn of the severe needs worldwide, and who seek a reliable channel to exercise their personal giving or prayer and financial support."

Max Leroy Mesidor, Archbishop of Port-au-Prince, Haiti, puts it best:
"If Food For The Poor had not existed, it would be necessary to invent it."

Robin Mahfood, Food For The Poor President/CEO, and his wife, Gail, meet with His Holiness Pope Francis.

Now celebrating its 37th year, Food For The Poor is an interdenominational Christian relief and development organization working primarily in 17 countries in the Caribbean and Latin America.

FOOD FOR THE POOR, INC.
Saving Lives... Transforming Communities... Renewing Hope

6401 Lyons Road • Coconut Creek, FL 33073
877-654-2960, ext. 6419 • www.FoodForThePoor.org

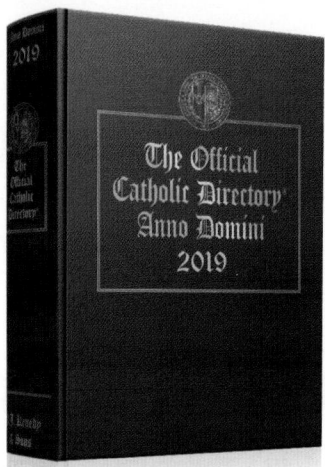

The Seal of P.J. Kenedy & Sons
The Official Catholic Directory

Significance

The shield is the central part of a heraldic device, which is more commonly known as a coat of arms. If that shield is enclosed within a body of text, or other type of surrounding configuration, the device becomes known as a seal, yet it is the shield portion of the design that is the most important, and that which is described technically as the blazon. As the design is examined, it must be remembered that by heraldic tradition the design is described (blazoned) as if being done by the bearer with the shield being worn on the arm. Therefore, the terms dexter and sinister will be reversed as the design is viewed from the front.

The shield of the seal for **The Official Catholic Directory** has been designed to reflect the character and heritage of this publication of P.J. Kenedy & Sons.

The shield is in two major portions. The right half (sinister impalement) is composed of the blue shield on which are seen a silver tree, two candles (in silver or white) in their candleholders (of gold or yellow) and an open book, edged in gold and with a red bookmark. These symbols have been used over the years as the sign of the P.J. Kenedy & Sons publishing organization. These are the traditional symbols of knowledge and learning, so appropriate to a publisher.

The other side of the shield (the dexter impalement) is composed of a silver (white) field on which is seen a red cross, throughout, and a gold eagle. These symbols, combined with the field of the sinister impalement, are represented in the color of the flag of the United States of America and the eagle, the symbol of the United States. The cross represents Christianity and all of this combines to signify that **The Official Catholic Directory** annually reports on the Catholic Church in the United States.

The shield is surrounded by a laurel wreath of excellence and is enclosed within the legend that states the name of the company, the name of the publication and date (1817) of its founding.

— ***Paul J. Sullivan***

2018 Highlights

The Official Catholic Directory®
Digital Flipbook

ALL THE BOOK HAS TO OFFER...NOW DIGITALLY ENHANCED!

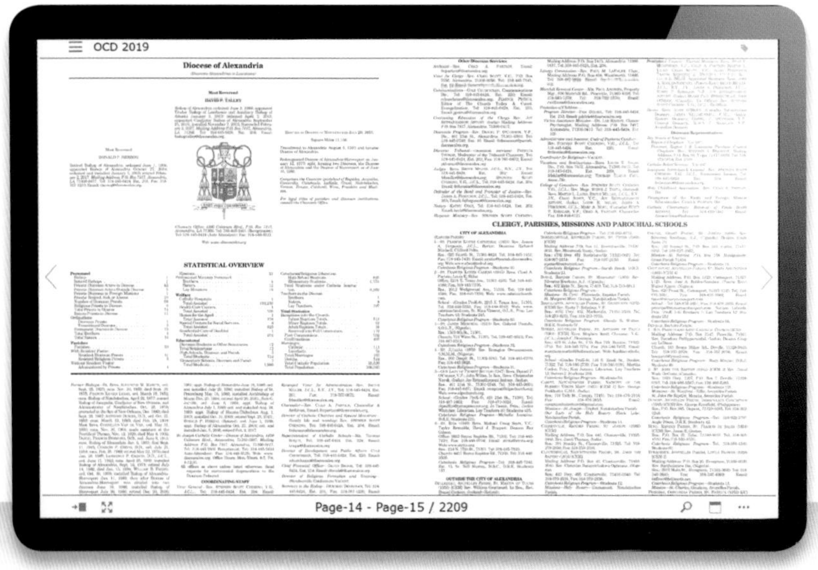

Features

- Accessible with web browsers on a PC and most portable devices (tablets, mobile phones)
- Accessible 24/7 with User Name & Password
- Active Links in Table of Contents for quick/easy navigation

Benefits

- Communicate more efficiently using Email and Phone links
- Quick access to Websites with just one click
- Searchable by a Word and/or Phrase
- Print page(s) for proof of tax-exempt status

View **Sample Digital Flipbook** from our website: www.officialcatholicdirectory.com.

The Official Catholic Directory is the official subordinate listing for verifying the IRS tax-exempt status of U.S. Catholic institutions under the USCCB Group Ruling.

The Official Catholic Directory, 430 Mountain Avenue, Suite 403, New Providence, NJ 07974
www.officialcatholicdirectory.com

PUBLISHED BY P.J. KENEDY & SONS SINCE 1817

U.S. Catholic Church 2018 Highlights

Amid 2018's challenges, Catholics turn to prayer and look ahead

BY CAROL ZIMMERMANN

Although 2018 was a difficult year for the Catholic Church in the United States, as it dealt with allegations of past sexual misconduct and cover-up by its church leaders, it was also a time of renewed soul searching, prayer and discussion for Catholics nationwide and a time of continued efforts to support the dignity of all human life and effectively live out the Gospel message.

The archbishop (Gregory M. Aymond of New Orleans) asked for forgiveness from victims and survivors of abuse, Catholics disillusioned and scandalized by the crisis, and priests, deacons and seminarians who now bear the burden of being "tainted by the sins of others."

From the summer -- when allegations of abuse made headlines -- and through the end of the year, Catholics gathered in cathedrals and parishes across the country to attend healing Masses celebrated by bishops who often prostrated themselves before the altar in postures of repentance. Several bishops issued statements on the crisis and many urged Catholics to pray and fast for the church to find healing and restoration.

Catholics also met in parish halls and other venues to ask church leaders what went wrong and to discuss ways the church should move forward.

Several dioceses held Masses for healing Sept. 14, the feast of the Triumph of the Cross, or Sept. 15, the feast of Our Lady of Sorrows, emphasizing the significance of these dates as appropriate times for penance and seeking God's grace.

During a Mass for healing Aug. 28 at St. Joseph Church in New Orleans, Archbishop Gregory M. Aymond of New Orleans said he was overwhelmed by the number of people who had packed the historic church to join him in prayer and he also made reference to Hurricane Katrina, the day before its 13th anniversary.

Today, "we are hit by another storm," he said.

The archbishop asked for forgiveness from victims and survivors of abuse, Catholics disillusioned and scandalized by the crisis, and priests, deacons and seminarians who now bear the burden of being "tainted by the sins of others."

"We are now called in many ways to move forward, yes, as a wounded church. But as a wounded church, we can move forward. When someone is wounded, they can still walk, and we must move forward, asking for God's mercy and healing," the Clarion Herald, archdiocesan newspaper of New Orleans, reported.

(PEXEL FREE PHOTO/ VANDERLEI LONGO)

Similar pleas came from other bishops at healing Masses nationwide who also urged Catholics to join in more prayer and fasting for healing in the church.

Another prayerful response to the crisis was the renewed recitation of the Prayer to St. Michael the Archangel, taken up by many individual parishes and also dioceses across the country at the end of Masses.

In a Sept. 14 letter to priests, Portland Archbishop Alexander K. Sample urged Catholics to pray the St. Michael Prayer after each Mass and to encourage parishioners to say this prayer daily. He said there are many things to do to purify the church but that "prayer will also be the foremost and most appropriate response, on which all other efforts will build."

Church leaders were not just taking the crisis to prayer. They also met privately with Pope Francis to discuss it. Cardinal Daniel N. DiNardo of Galveston-Houston, president of the U.S. Conference of Catholic Bishops, met privately with the pope in September and again in October, along with Los Angeles Archbishop Jose H. Gomez, USCCB vice president.

The crisis was a focus of the bishops' June meeting in Fort Lauderdale, Florida and was front and center at the bishops' annual fall assembly in Baltimore Nov. 12-14. The meeting, which many hoped would provide a decisive response to the abuse crisis, began with an announcement that the Vatican wanted the bishops to delay any vote on new procedures until after a February meeting with the pope and presidents of bishops' conferences around the world on the issue.

At the Baltimore meeting's end, Cardinal DiNardo said he was more hopeful than he was at the meeting's start.

"We leave this place committed to taking the strongest possible actions at the earliest possible moment," he said, adding: "We will do so in communion with the universal church."

Throughout the year, U.S. Catholics also responded to crises of other kinds including a number of natural disasters. Catholic Charities agencies on the ground provided help to victims of hurricanes in the South, wildfires in California and an earthquake in Hawaii.

The California Camp Fire in November, which began Nov. 8 and burned more than 153,000 acres, destroyed more than 14,000 homes and caused 88 fatalities, had a major impact on St. Thomas More Parish in Paradise, California, where 640 of the parish's 800 families lost their homes in the fire.

Deacon Ray Helgeson from St. Thomas More, said the parish and local community had rallied to support one another throughout the devastation.

"Something like this awakens something within us," he told the Catholic San Francisco, archdiocesan newspaper. "It gives the Lord a chance to pull triggers within us of generosity, of kindness and of gentleness with others."

He said the fire and his faith had forged something new and unexpected in himself and other survivors that he described as "an awareness of being without, but there is also a sweetness to it."

In response to the fire, which scattered local residents far and wide and closed schools for weeks, Catholic schools in the Diocese of Sacramento opened their doors at six elementary schools and a high school to all students

(PEXEL FREE PHOTO/ LUIS NÚÑEZ)

displaced by the fires to attend their schools tuition free for the rest of the year.

Kasia Heinert, principal at St. Thomas the Apostle School in Oroville, 20 miles south of Paradise, said the school's students had been asking: "What can we do?" since the wildfires began and had taken part in clothing drives, serving food and walking shelter dogs during the fires and were happy to welcome displaced students to their small school community.

She said the Catholic school outreach and the response to it from people across the country was inspiring, "especially after everything the Catholic Church has been through in the news lately."

She told Catholic News Service she heard from someone in Florida who had heard about what Sacramento Catholic schools were doing and said: "I am so proud to be Catholic."

Throughout the year, not only in emergencies, U.S. Catholics remained committed to their usual work of prayer and advocacy for social justice and life issues and to deepening their faith.

During Easter Vigil Masses across the country, more than 30,000 people joined the Catholic Church. The Archdiocese of Los Angeles, the largest diocese in the U.S., welcomed 1,700 catechumens and 1,127 candidates.

"The next generation is every bit as committed to life as the current generation. It tells us that the future is very bright."
-Cardinal Donald Wuerl, Former Archbishop of Washington, D.C.

When the Rite of Christian Initiation of Adults process began in February, Detroit Archbishop Allen H. Vigneron, told the catechumens and candidates in his archdiocese that they were joining the history of God's plan to redeem the world from sin.

"It is by communion with Jesus Christ that God's history becomes our history," he said, adding that just as each person's conversion story is unique, the Rite of Election and the Easter Vigil are very much public acts in which one's personal history is joined with the history and gifts of the Catholic Church.

During the year, Catholics responded to the influx of migrants at the U.S.-Mexico border by assisting the efforts of the Diocese of El Paso, Texas and Catholic Charities of the Rio Grande Valley providing food, clothing and temporary shelter. U.S. bishops voiced their support for migrants and their right to seek refuge and in July, top leadership from the USCCB traveled to the border region in Texas to personally meet with immigrants at a Catholic-run temporary shelter and a government detention center.

The year began with thousands of Catholics attending the annual March for Life in Washington and also participating in local rallies and walks showing their opposition to the 1973 Supreme Court decision that legalized abortion.

At the National Prayer Vigil for Life, Jan. 18, the night before the annual march, New York Cardinal Timothy M. Dolan told the thousands gathered at the National Shrine of the Immaculate Conception in Washington that they were there to "advocate and give witness, to advocate for those who cannot yet speak or walk with us."

We are also here to pray, he reminded them.

The next day, the Capital One Arena in Washington was filled with thousands of youth from around the country who attended a Youth Rally and Mass for Life prior to the annual March for Life.

"This is so, so exciting to see this entire arena filled with thousands and thousands of young people," Cardinal Donald Wuerl, then archbishop of Washington, told the Catholic Standard, newspaper of the Washington Archdiocese. "The next generation is every bit as committed to life as the current generation. It tells us that the future is very bright."

Young Catholics, specifically young adult Catholics, were the focus of a month-long synod at the Vatican during the month of October.

The synod, which had delegates and observers from around the world, including the United States, brought together about 300 church leaders -- cardinals, bishops, priests, women religious and laity -- to discuss young people, the faith and vocational discernment.

The focus of the synod's final document was on improving ways to support young Catholics' baptismal call to holiness, to welcome the contributions they make to the church and help them in their process of growing in faith and in deciding the state of life that would best fit what God wants from them.

The first person under 30 to address the Synod of Bishops was Sister Briana Santiago, a 27-year-old member of the Apostles of the Interior Life from San Antonio.

"I think all of us young people need to be listened to first of all and then guided" in discovering God's calling, Sister Santiago told the synod Oct. 4.

Another major Catholic gathering during the year that particularly reflected the changing demographics of the U.S. Catholic Church was the Fifth National Encuentro, a meeting of nearly 3,000 Hispanic Catholic ministry leaders in Texas representing 159 dioceses across the country. Hispanics represent about 40 percent of U.S. Catholics and nearly 60 percent of millennial Catholics, according to research

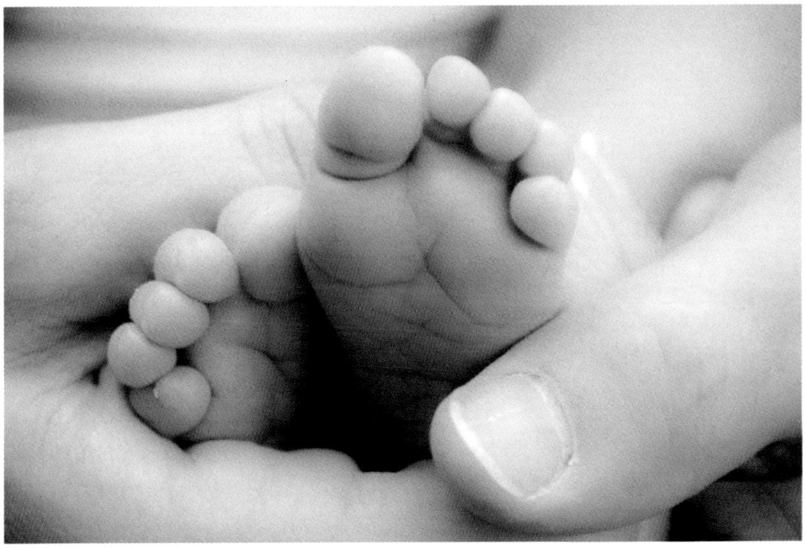

(PEXEL FREE PHOTO/ PIXABAY)

from the Center for Applied Research in the Apostolate.

At the start of the four-day gathering Sept. 20, Archbishop Christophe Pierre, apostolic nuncio to the United States, encouraged Hispanic Catholic leaders and bishops to continue working toward being an evangelizing church by seeking an encounter with Christ and accompanying those on the peripheries.

"The church which 'goes forth' is a community of missionary disciples who take the first step, who are involved and supportive, who bear fruit and rejoice," he said.

During the gathering, which examined how the Catholic Church should respond to Hispanic Catholics in parishes around the country and how to best equip Hispanic Catholics as leaders and missionary disciples, participants took part in a range of listening and dialogue sessions.

Hispanic Catholic leaders are living an important moment in the history of the Catholic church in the U.S. and are called to continue the work of building the church, Los Angeles Archbishop Jose H. Gomez told participants during the closing Mass Sept. 23.

"Jesus entrusted the mission of his church in the New World to a layperson. Not to a priest or a bishop. Nor to a member of a religious order," Archbishop Gomez said. "You are the children of Our Lady of Guadalupe in our present times; you are the spiritual heirs of Juan Diego.

"The mission that was entrusted to him, is now entrusted to you."

And in a closing message that could apply to U.S. Catholics at large, not just those at the National Encuentro gathering, he said: "I believe that this moment in the church -- is the hour of the laity. It is the time for saints." The archbishop urged participants to recognize that God is "calling the lay faithful to work together with the bishops to renew and rebuild his church. Not only in this country, but throughout the continents of the Americas."

CAROL ZIMMERMANN *is an education reporter and feature writer at* Catholic News Service.

"Jesus entrusted the mission of his church in the New World to a layperson. Not to a priest or a bishop... You are the children of Our Lady of Guadalupe...you are the spiritual heirs of Juan Diego."
–Most Rev. Jose H. Gomez, Archbishop of Los Angeles

Table of Contents

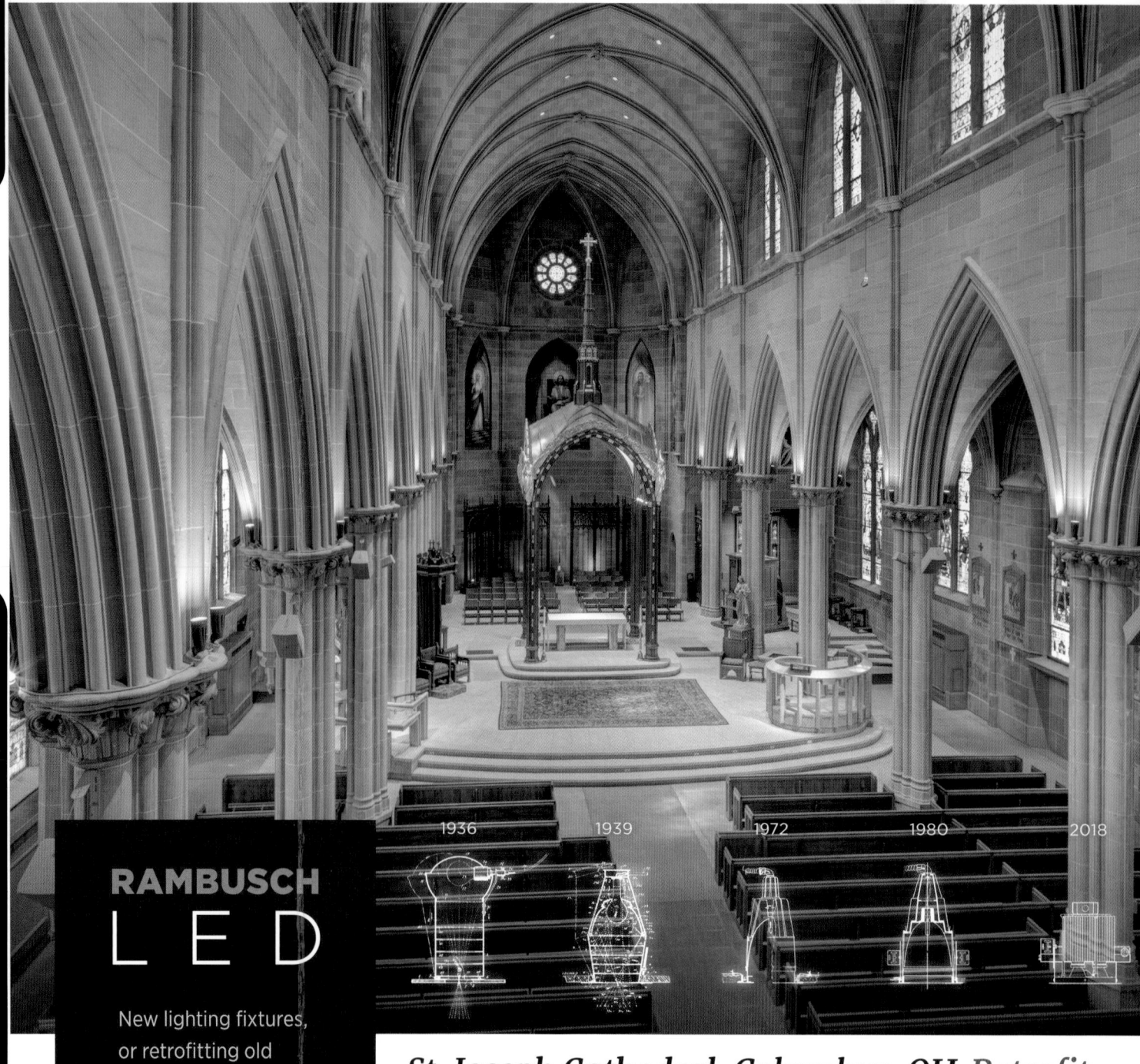

Table of Contents

The Official Catholic Directory

for the Year of Our Lord

2019

GIVING STATUS OF THE CATHOLIC CHURCH AS OF JANUARY 1, 2019

Containing Ecclesiastical Statistics of

THE UNITED STATES, PUERTO RICO,
THE VIRGIN ISLANDS, AGANA, CAROLINE AND MARSHALL ISLANDS,
AND FOREIGN MISSIONARY ACTIVITIES.

THE OFFICIAL CATHOLIC DIRECTORY · P.J. KENEDY & SONS · 1817

P.J. KENEDY & SONS
Publishers of the Holy Apostolic See

For inquiries call: 908-517-0780, or write:
430 Mountain Avenue, Suite 403, New Providence, NJ 07974
To place an order call: 1-844-592-4197

THE OFFICIAL CATHOLIC DIRECTORY®

Published by P.J. Kenedy & Sons in association with NRP Direct

Printed and bound in the United States of America
International Standard Book Number: 978-0-87217-077-3
International Standard Serial Number: 0078-3854
Library of Congress Catalog Card Number: 81-30961

CONTENTS

ARCHDIOCESES AND DIOCESES

APOSTOLATES

PRELATURE OF THE HOLY CROSS AND OPUS DEI

EASTERN CHURCHES

TERRITORIAL SEES

RELIGIOUS INSTITUTION SECTION

THE ARCHDIOCESES AND DIOCESES OF THE UNITED STATES—BY STATES

A—Indicates Archdiocese. The Archdiocese of Washington includes the District of Columbia and five counties of Maryland. Dioceses traverse state lines in the following instances only: Cheyenne includes all of Yellowstone National Park; South Norwich includes Fisher's Island; Wilmington includes the eastern shores of Maryland; and Gallup includes parts of Arizona and New Mexico.

United States Conference of Catholic Bishops

Address—3211 Fourth St., N.E., Washington, DC 20017-1194. Tel: 202-541-3000; Web Site: www.usccb.org.

The United States Conference of Catholic Bishops is a permanent institute composed of Catholic bishops of the United States of America in and through which the bishops exercise in a communal or collegial manner the pastoral mission entrusted to them by the Lord Jesus of sanctification, teaching, and leadership, especially by devising forms and methods of the apostolate suitably adapted to the circumstances of the times. Such exercise is intended to offer appropriate assistance to each bishop in fulfilling his particular ministry in the local Church, to effect a commonality of ministry addressed to the people of the United States of America, and to foster and express communion with the Church in other nations within the Church universal, under the leadership of its chief pastor, the Pope.

OFFICE

President—Cardinal Daniel N. DiNardo
Vice President—Archbishop José H. Gomez
Treasurer—Archbishop Dennis M. Schnurr
Secretary—Archbishop Allen H. Vigneron

GENERAL SECRETARIAT

General Secretary—Rev. Msgr. J. Brian Bransfield, S.T.D.
Associate General Secretary—Rev. Msgr. Jeffrey D. Burrill, S.T.L.
Mr. Anthony R. Picarello, Jr., Esq.
Ms. Theresa Ridderhoff
Assistant General Secretary—Dr. Jonathan J. Reyes
Director of Strategic Planning—Mr. Robert Yates

STAFF OFFICES

Chief Communications Officer—Mr. James L. Rogers
Finance & Accounting—Mrs. Joyce L. Jones
General Counsel—Mr. Anthony R. Picarello, Jr., Esq.
General Services—Mr. Keith Manley
Government Relations—Dr. Jonathan J. Reyes
Human Resources—Ms. Allison McGinn
Information Technology—Mr. John A. Galotta
Child & Youth Protection—Deacon Bernard V. Nojadera

USCCB COMMITTEES

I. EXECUTIVE LEVEL

ADMINISTRATIVE COMMITTEE

Chairman—Cardinal Daniel N. DiNardo
Members—Cardinal Joseph William Tobin, C.Ss.R.
Archbishop Timothy P. Broglio
Archbishop Charles J. Chaput, O.F.M.Cap.
Archbishop Paul D. Etienne
Archbishop José H. Gomez
Archbishop Wilton D. Gregory
Archbishop Joseph E. Kurtz
Archbishop William E. Lori (Region IV)
Archbishop Archbishop George J. Lucas (Region IX)
Archbishop Dennis M. Schnurr
Archbishop Charles C. Thompson (Region VII)
Archbishop Allen H. Vigneron
Bishop Joseph C. Bambera
Bishop Michael C. Barber, S.J.
Bishop Robert Barron
Bishop Michael F. Burbidge
Bishop Liam Cary (Region XII)
Bishop Myron J. Cotta (Region XI)
Bishop Andrew H. Cozzens (Region VIII)
Bishop Edgar M. da Cunha, S.D.V. (Region I)
Bishop Robert P. Deeley
Bishop Frank J. Dewane
Bishop Timothy L. Doherty
Bishop Felipe J. Estevez (Region XIV)
Bishop Shelton J. Fabre (Region V)
Bishop Francis Kalabat (Region XV)
Bishop Gregory John Mansour
Bishop Nelson J. Perez
Bishop Lawrence T. Persico (Region III)
Bishop Kevin C. Rhoades
Bishop Jorge Rodriguez-Novelo (Region XIII)
Bishop Michael J. Sis (Region X)
Bishop Daniel E. Thomas (Region VI)
Bishop Joe S. Vásquez
Archbishop Joseph F. Naumann
Vacant (Region II)
Staff—Rev. Msgr. J. Brian Bransfield
Rev. Msgr. Jeffrey D. Burrill, S.T.L.
Mr. Anthony R. Picarello, Jr., Esq.
Ms. Theresa Ridderhoff
Dr. Jonathan J. Reyes
Mr. James L. Rogers

ADMINISTRATIVE COMMITTEE-REGIONAL ALTERNATES

Alternate (Region I)—Bishop Peter A. Libasci
Alternate (Region II)—Bishop Edward B. Scharfenberger
Alternate (Region III)—Bishop James F. Checchio
Alternate (Region IV)—Bishop Barry C. Knestout
Alternate (Region V)—Bishop William F. Medley
Alternate (Region VI)—Bishop David J. Walkowiak
Alternate (Region VII)—Bishop Donald J. Hying
Alternate (Region VIII)—Bishop Robert D. Gruss
Alternate (Region IX)—Bishop Thomas Zinkula
Alternate (Region X)—Archbishop Paul S. Coakley
Alternate (Region XI)—Bishop Timothy E. Freyer
Alternate (Region XII)—Bishop Eusebio L. Elizondo, M.Sp.S.
Alternate (Region XIII)—Bishop Steven Biegler
Alternate (Region XIV)—Bishop Enrique Delgado
Alternate (Region XV)—Bishop Paul P. Chomnycky, O.S.B.M.

EXECUTIVE COMMITTEE

President—Cardinal Daniel N. DiNardo
Members—Archbishop Charles J. Chaput, O.F.M. Cap.
Vice President—Archbishop José H. Gomez
Treasurer—Archbishop Dennis M. Schnurr
Secretary—Archbishop Allen H. Vigneron
Staff—Rev. Msgr. J. Brian Bransfield
Rev. Msgr. Jeffrey D. Burrill, S.T.L.
Mr. Anthony R. Picarello, Jr., Esq.
Ms. Theresa Ridderhoff

COMMITTEE ON BUDGET AND FINANCE

Chairman—Archbishop Dennis M. Schnurr
Chairman-Elect—Bishop Gregory L. Parkes
Members—Archbishop Paul D. Etienne
Bishop James F. Checchio
Bishop John M. LeVoir
Bishop Michael Mulvey
Consultants—Rev. Msgr. J. Brian Bransfield
Staff—Ms. Karen Acton
Ms. Raquel Dean
Mrs. Joyce L. Jones

Audit Subcommittee

Chairman—Bishop John M. LeVoir
Members—Bishop John T. Folda
Consultant—Bishop Joseph R. Binzer
Staff—Mrs. Karen Acton
Mrs. Joyce L. Jones

COMMITTEE ON PRIORITIES AND PLANS

Chairman—Archbishop Allen H. Vigneron
Vice Chairman—Archbishop Dennis M. Schnurr
Members—Archbishop William E. Lori (Region IV)
Archbishop George J. Lucas (Region IX)
Archbishop Charles C. Thompson (Region VII)
Bishop Liam Cary (Region XII)
Bishop Myron J. Cotta (Region XI)
Bishop Andrew H. Cozzens (Region VIII)
Bishop Edgar M. da Cunha S.D.V. (Region I)
Bishop Felipe J. Estevez (Region XIV)
Bishop Shelton J. Fabre (Region V)
Bishop Francis Kalabat (Region XV)
Bishop Lawrence T. Persico (Region III)
Bishop Jorge Rodriguez-Novelo (Region XIII)
Bishop Edward B. Scharfenberger (Region II)
Bishop Michael J. Sis (Region X)
Bishop Daniel E. Thomas (Region VI)
Consultant—Rev. Msgr. J. Brian Bransfield
Staff—Rev. Msgr. Jeffrey D. Burrill, S.T.L.
Mr. Anthony R. Picarello, Jr. Esq.
Ms. Theresa Ridderhoff
Mrs. Joyce L. Jones
Mr. James L. Rogers
Mr. Robert Yates

II. GENERAL MEMBERSHIP LEVEL STANDING COMMITTEES CANONICAL AFFAIRS AND CHURCH GOVERNANCE

Chairman—Bishop Robert P. Deeley
Members—Archbishop Salvatore J. Cordileone
Archbishop Bernard A. Hebda
Bishop Mark L. Bartchak
Bishop Kurt R. Burnette
Bishop Edward C. Malesic
Bishop Thomas John Paprocki
Bishop Gregory L. Parkes
Bishop Peter L. Smith
Consultants—Rev. Msgr. Ronny E. Jenkins
Rev. Sean Sheridan, T.O.R.
Prof. Kurt Martens
Staff—Rev. David G. Howard
Ms. Siobhan M. Verbeek

CATHOLIC EDUCATION

Chairman—Bishop Michael C. Barber, S.J.
Members—Archbishop Charles C. Thompson
Bishop Thomas A. Daly
Bishop James Massa
Bishop John M. Quinn
Bishop Gerald F. Kicanas
Staff—
Ms. Jennifer Daniels
Dr. Marc DelMonico
Ms. Mary Pat Donoghue
Ms. Barbara Humphrey McCrabb

Subcommittee on Certification for Ecclesial Ministry and Service

Chairman—Bishop Gerald F. Kicanas
Members—Bishop Earl A. Boyea
Bishop Arturo Cepeda
Bishop George J. Rassas
Bishop Robert Reed
Consultants—Rev. Wayne Cavalier, O.P.
Ms. Linda Couri
Sr. Maria Theresa Lara, O.P.
Mr. David A. Lichter
Dr. C. Vanessa White
Staff—Dr. Harry J. Dudley

CLERGY, CONSECRATED LIFE, AND VOCATIONS

Chairman—Cardinal Joseph William Tobin, C.Ss.R.
Chairman-Elect—Bishop James F. Checchio
Members—Archbishop Samuel J. Aquila
Archbishop Charles C. Thompson
Archbishop John C. Wester
Bishop Earl A. Boyea
Bishop Thomas A. Daly
Bishop Michael F. Olson
Consultants—
Deacon Raphael Duplechain
Sr. Sharon A. Euart, R.S.M.
Rev. Msgr. Roberto Garza
Rev. Cletus Kiley
Mrs. Rosemary Sullivan
Staff—Rev. Luke Ballman
Rev. Ralph O'Donnell

COMMUNICATIONS

Chairman—Bishop Michael F. Burbidge
Members—Archbishop John C. Wester
Bishop John Michael Botean
Bishop Daniel E. Flores
Bishop Daniel E. Garcia
Bishop Joel M. Konzen, S.M.
Bishop John J. McIntyre
Bishop Gregory L. Parkes
Bishop Robert Reed
Consultants—Mr. Phil Alongi
Mr. Sean Caine
Ms. Sara McDonald
Ms. Amy S. Mitchell
Staff—Mr. Greg Erlandson
Mr. David Felber
Ms. Patricia Ryan Garcia
Ms. Judy Keane

Ms. Mary McDonald
Mr. James L. Rogers

Subcommittee on the Catholic Communications Campaign
Chairman—(Vacant)
Staff—Ms. Patricia Ryan Garcia
Mr. James L. Rogers

CULTURAL DIVERSITY IN THE CHURCH
Chairman—Bishop Nelson J. Pérez
Members—Archbishop Gustavo Garcia-Siller, M.Sp.S.
Archbishop John C. Wester
Bishop Arturo Cepeda
Bishop Joseph N. Perry
Bishop Oscar Azarcon Solis
Bishop Joseph J. Tyson
Bishop James S. Wall
Bishop Oscar Cantu
Staff—Mr. Alejandro Aguilera-Titus
Rev. Michael Carson
Mr. David Corrales
Ms. Donna Toliver Grimes
Mrs. María del Mar Muñoz-Visoso
Sr. Joanna Okereke, H.H.C.J.
Sr. Myrna Tordillo, M.S.C.S.

Subcommittee on African American Affairs
Chairman—Bishop Joseph N. Perry
Members—Bishop Gerald R. Barnes
Bishop Brendan J. Cahill
Bishop Roy E. Campbell
Bishop Jeffrey Haines
Bishop Barry C. Knestout
Bishop Denis J. Madden
Bishop Mark S. Rivituso
Bishop Guy Sansaricq
Consultants—Rev. Anthony Bozeman, S.S.J.
Rev. Msgr. Vernon Hughley, V.F.
Ms. Valerie Jennings
Mr. Ashley Morris
Rev. Richard Owens, O.F.M. Cap.
Rev. Stephen Thorne
Staff—Ms. Donna Toliver Grimes

Subcommittee on Asian and Pacific Island Affairs
Chairman—Bishop Oscar Azarcon Solis
Members—Bishop Randolph R. Calvo
Bishop William J. Justice
Bishop Witold Mroziewski
Bishop Thanh Thai Nguyen
Bishop Larry Silva
Bishop F. Richard Spencer
Bishop Philipos Mar Stephanos Thottathil
Consultants—Rev. Linh Hoang, O.F.M., Ph.D.
Dr. Jem Sullivan
Staff—Sr. Myrna Tordillo, M.S.C.S.

Subcommittee on Hispanic Affairs
Chairman—Bishop Arturo Cepeda
Members—Bishop John O. Barres
Bishop Andrew H. Cozzens
Bishop Shelton J. Fabre
Bishop Richard E. Pates
Bishop Alberto Rojas
Coadjutor Bishop Oscar Cantu
Consultants—Rev. Joseph Corpora, C.S.C.
Sr. Immaculada Cuesta, C.M.S.
Ms. Jessica Maciel-Hernandez
Mrs. Wanda Vasquez
Staff—Mr. Alejandro Aguilera-Titus

Subcommittee on Native American Affairs
Chairman—Bishop James S. Wall
Members—Bishop Liam Cary
Bishop James D. Conley
Bishop Thomas A. Daly
Bishop John T. Folda
Bishop Robert D. Gruss
Bishop Steven J. Raica
Bishop Chad Zielinski
Consultants—Mr. Robert Barbry, II
Mr. Juanatano Cano
Ms. Shirley Zuni
Rev. Maurice Henry Sands
Staff—Rev. Michael Carson

Subcommittee on Pastoral Care of Migrants, Refugees, and Travelers
Chairman—Bishop Joseph J. Tyson
Members—Archbishop Jerome E. Listecki
Archbishop Thomas G. Wenski
Bishop Brendan J. Cahill
Bishop Fernand Cheri, III, O.F.M.
Bishop Edgar M. da Cunha, S.D.V.
Bishop Frank J. Dewane
Bishop Yousif Habash
Bishop Guy Sansaricq
Bishop Oscar Cantu
Consultants—Rev. Msgr. Anselm Nwaorgu
Rev. Jean Yvon Pierre
Staff—Mr. David Corrales
Sr. Joanna Okereke, H.H.C.J.

DIVINE WORSHIP
Chairman—Archbishop Wilton D. Gregory
Chairman-Elect—Archbishop Leonard P. Blair
Members—Bishop Christopher J. Coyne
Bishop Daniel E. Garcia
Bishop Mark J. Seitz
Bishop Joseph M. Siegel
Bishop Daniel E. Thomas
Bishop Andrzej Zglejszewski
Bishop David A. Zubik
Consultants—Sr. Janet Baxendale, S.C.
Rev. James Bessert
Abbot Jeremy Driscoll, O.S.B.
Rev. Msgr. Kevin W. Irwin
Rev. Jan Michael Joncas
Abbot Gregory J. Polan, O.S.B.
Rev. Juan J. Sosa
Mrs. Rita Thiron
Staff—Ms. Carmen Aguinaco
Rev. Andrew Menke
Rev. Randy Stice

Subcommittee on Divine Worship in Spanish
Chairman—Bishop Daniel E. Garcia
Members—Bishop Octavio Cisneros
Bishop Mario E. Dorsonville-Rodríguez
Bishop Alberto Rojas
Bishop Carlos A. Sevilla, S.J.
Consultants—Sr. Rosanne Belpedio, C.S.J.
Rev. Heliodoro Lucatero
Ms. Dolores Martinez
Rev. Jorge I. Perales
Rev. Juan J. Sosa
Mr. Rogelio Zelada
Staff—Ms. Carmen Aguinaco

DOCTRINE
Chairman—Bishop Kevin C. Rhoades
Members—Bishop Michael C. Barber, S.J.
Bishop Andrew H. Cozzens
Bishop John F. Doerfler
Bishop Daniel E. Flores
Bishop Richard G. Henning
Bishop Steven J. Lopes
Bishop Robert J. McManus
Bishop Michael F. Olson
Consultants—Archbishop William E. Lori
Bishop James Massa
Dr. John C. Cavadini
Rev. Msgr. Michael Heintz
Dr. Margaret McCarthy
Staff—Rev. Michael Fuller
Dr. James LeGrys
Ms. Siobhan M. Verbeek

Subcommittee on Health Care Issues
Chairman—(Vacant)
Staff—Rev. Michael Fuller
Mr. Tom Grenchik
Dr. James LeGrys
Dr. Jonathan J. Reyes
Mr. Greg Schleppenbach
Ms. Siobhan M. Verbeek

Subcommittee on the Translation of Scripture Text
Chairman—(Vacant)
Staff—Rev. Michael Fuller
Dr. James LeGrys

DOMESTIC JUSTICE AND HUMAN DEVELOPMENT
Chairman—Bishop Frank J. Dewane
Chairman-Elect—Archbishop Paul S. Coakley
Members—Archbishop Charles J. Chaput, O.F.M.Cap.
Archbishop Thomas G. Wenski
Bishop Nicholas DiMarzio
Bishop Robert W. McElroy
Bishop Jaime Soto
Bishop Dennis J. Sullivan
Bishop David P. Talley
Consultants—Archbishop Samuel J. Aquila
Bishop Joe S. Vásquez
Bishop David A. Zubik
Coadjutor Bishop Oscar Cantu
Mr. Ray Boshara
Mr. James Ennis
Mr. John H. Garvey
Mr. Jason Hall
Dr. Joseph P. Kaboski
Sr. Carol Keehan, D.C.
Sr. Donna Markham
Dr. Michael J. Naughton
Rev. John Pavlik, O.F.M.Cap.
Ms. Debra Soltis, Esq.
Sr. Joan Marie Steadman, C.S.C.
Sr. Marie Bernadette Thompson, O.P.
Dr. W. Bradford Wilcox
Staff—Ms. Julie M. Bodnar
Mr. Anthony Granado
Mr. Michael O'Rourke
Ms. Jill Rauh
Dr. Jonathan J. Reyes

Subcommittee on the Catholic Campaign for Human Development
Chairman—Bishop David P. Talley
Members—Bishop Donald F. Hanchon
Bishop Robert F. Hennessey
Bishop David G. O'Connell
Bishop Jorge Rodríguez-Novelo
Bishop Jaime Soto
Bishop John Stowe, O.F.M.Conv.
Bishop Michael W. Warfel
Bishop Gerald F. Kicanas
Consultants—Rev. Msgr. Edward B. Branch
Mr. Matthew Brower
Rev. Ty S. Hullinger
Mrs. Danise Jones-Dorsey
Rev. Msgr. Joseph J. Kerrgian, Jr.
Rev. J. Daniel Mindling, O.F.M.Cap.
Dr. Linda Plitt-Donaldson
Staff—Mr. Juan Aranda
Ms. Alexandra Carroll
Mr. Gene Giannotta
Mr. W. Randy Keesler
Mr. Ralph McCloud
Mr. Ian Mitchell
Ms. Jill Rauh
Dr. Jonathan J. Reyes
Mr. Sean Wendlinder

ECUMENICAL AND INTERRELIGIOUS AFFAIRS
Chairman—Bishop Joseph C. Bambera
Members—Bishop Bohdan Danylo
Bishop Steven J. Lopes
Bishop Denis J. Madden
Bishop Robert W. McElroy
Bishop Mitchell Thomas Rozanski
Bishop Peter L. Smith
Bishop David P. Talley
Bishop Michael W. Warfel
Consultants—Cardinal Blase J. Cupich
Cardinal Timothy M. Dolan
Cardinal Seán P. O'Malley, O.F.M.Cap.
Cardinal Joseph William Tobin, C.Ss.R.
Bishop John Michael Botean
Bishop Tod D. Brown
Bishop Howard J. Hubbard
Bishop Thomas J. Olmsted
Bishop Edward B. Scharfenberger
Bishop Richard J. Sklba
Rev. Dennis McManus
Staff—Dr. Anthony Cirelli
Rev. Ronald G. Roberson, C.S.P.

EVANGELIZATION AND CATECHESIS

Chairman—Bishop Robert Barron
Members—Archbishop Leonard P. Blair
Archbishop J. Peter Sartain
Bishop John O. Barres
Bishop Frank J. Caggiano
Bishop Daniel E. Flores
Bishop Richard J. Malone
Bishop David L. Ricken
Cardinal Donald W. Wuerl
Consultants—Archbishop Alfred C. Hughes
Rev. Frank Donio, S.A.C.
Mr. Curtis Martin
Sr. M. Johanna Paruch, F.S.G.M.
Ms. Julianne Stanz
Mr. Brandon Vogt
Staff—Ms. Marie Ferman
Dr. Zachary Keith
Ms. Marylin Santos
Dr. David Spesia
Mr. Carlos Taja

Subcommittee on the Catechism
Chairman—Bishop Frank J. Caggiano
Members—Archbishop Alexander K. Sample
Bishop Christopher J. Coyne
Bishop James Massa
Bishop David L. Ricken
Consultant—Archbishop Alfred C. Hughes
Staff—Dr. Zachary Keith
Ms. Marylin Santos
Dr. David Spesia
Mr. Carlos Taja

INTERNATIONAL JUSTICE AND PEACE

Chairman—Archbishop Timothy P. Broglio
Members—Bishop Michael C. Barber, S.J.
Bishop David J. Malloy
Bishop Robert W. McElroy
Bishop William F. Murphy
Bishop Jaime Soto
Bishop Michael W. Warfel
Bishop Abdallah Elias Zaidan, M.L.M.
Co-Adjutor Bishop Oscar Cantú
Consultants—Archbishop Thomas G. Wenski
Bishop Frank J. Dewane
Bishop Gregory John Mansour
Bishop Michael Mulvey
Bishop Joe S. Vásquez
Ambassador William Burns
Mr. Sean Callahan
Ambassador Mary Ann Glendon
Rev. Msgr. John Kozar
Dr. Maryann Cusimano Love
Dr. Thomas F. Farr
Staff—Mrs. Virginia Farris
Mr. Stephen Hilbert
Mr. Lucas Koach
Mr. Christopher Ljunquist
Ms. Jill Rauh
Dr. Jonathan J. Reyes

LAITY, MARRIAGE, FAMILY LIFE AND YOUTH

Chairman—Archbishop Charles J. Chaput, O.F.M. Cap.
Chairman-Elect— Bishop Salvatore J. Cordileone
Members—Bishop Frank J. Caggiano
Bishop James D. Conley
Bishop David Konderla
Bishop Richard J. Malone
Bishop Thomas John Paprocki
Bishop Joseph N. Perry
Bishop George J. Rassas
Bishop Jorge Rodríguez-Novelo
Consultants—Mrs. Christine Codden
Mrs. Kari Colella
Dr. John S. Grabowski
Mr. Curtis Martin
Mr. Chris Stefanick
Staff—Ms. Julia Dezelski
Mr. Paul Jarzembowski
Mr. Dominic Lombardi
Dr. Theresa Notare
Ms. Sara Perla
Mr. Timothy Roder
Mr. Robert Vega

Subcommittee for the Promotion and Defense of Marriage
Chairman—Bishop James D. Conley
Members—Archbishop William E. Lori
Archbishop Joseph F. Naumann
Bishop Liam Cary
Bishop Andrew H. Cozzens
Bishop Martin D. Holley
Bishop James Massa
Bishop Peter L. Smith
Consultants—Mr. Carl A. Anderson
Mr. Jeffrey Caruso, Esq.
Dr. David Crawford
Ms. Anna Halpine
Dr. Edward Sri
Mr. J.D. Flynn
Staff—Rev. Msgr. Jeffrey D. Burrill, S.T.L.
Mr. Anthony R. Picarello, Jr. Esq.
Mrs. Hillary Byrnes, Esq.
Mr. Dominic Lombardi
Ms. Sara Perla
Mr. Timothy Roder
Mr. Robert Vega

MIGRATION

Chairman—Bishop Joe S. Vásquez
Chairman-Elect—Bishop Mario E. Dorsonville-Rodriguez
Members—Archbishop Thomas G. Wenski
Archbishop John C. Wester
Bishop Nicholas DiMarzio
Bishop Eusebio L. Elizondo, M.Sp.S.
Bishop Martin D. Holley
Bishop David G. O'Connell
Bishop Kevin W. Vann
Consultants—Cardinal Roger M. Mahony
Cardinal Seán P. O'Malley, O.F.M.Cap.
Bishop Ricardo Ramírez, C.S.B.
Ms. Jeanne Atkinson
Rev. Daniel Groody, C.S.C.
Sr. Donna Markham
Mr. William O'Keefe
Ms. Heather Reynolds
Mr. Michael B. Sheedy
Staff—Mr. William Canny
Ms. Ashley Feasley

NATIONAL COLLECTIONS

Chairman—Archbishop Paul D. Etienne
Members—Cardinal Joseph William Tobin, C.Ss.R.
Bishop Octavio Cisneros
Bishop W. Shawn McKnight
Bishop David P. Talley
Rev. Jeffrey M. Monforton
Consultants—Mr. Patrick Markey
Sr. Stephanie Still, P.V.B.M.
Staff—Ms. Mary Mencarini Campbell
Mr. Richard Coll
Ms. Nicole Germain
Mr. Edward Kiely
Ms. Gina Laurent
Rev. Juan J. Molina, O.S.S.T.
Ms. Tetiana Stawnychy

Subcommittee on Catholic Home Missions
Chairman—Bishop W. Shawn McKnight
Staff—Ms. Mary Mencarini Campbell
Mr. Richard Coll
Mr. Kenneth Ong

Subcommittee on the Church in Africa
Chairman—Cardinal Joseph William Tobin, C.Ss.R.
Staff—Ms. Mary Mencarini Campbell
Mr. Edward Kiely

Subcommittee on the Church in Central and Eastern Europe
Chairman—Rev. Jeffrey M. Monforton
Staff—Ms. Mary Mencarini Campbell
Mr. Andrew Kirkpatrick
Ms. Tetiana Stawnychy

Subcommittee on the Church in Latin America
Chairman—Bishop Octavio Cisneros
Staff—Ms. Mary Mencarini Campbell
Mr. Kevin Day
Mr. Jacques Liautaud
Rev. Juan J. Molina, O.S.S.T.

PRO-LIFE ACTIVITIES

Chairman—Archbishop Joseph F. Naumann
Members—Archbishop Paul S. Coakley
Archbishop William E. Lori
Archbishop Alexander K. Sample
Bishop Jacob Angadiath
Bishop James D. Conley
Bishop Felipe J. Estévez
Bishop Shelton J. Fabre
Bishop James V. Johnston, Jr.
Consultants—Cardinal Daniel N. DiNardo
Cardinal Timothy M. Dolan
Cardinal Seán P. O'Malley, O.F.M.Cap.
Archbishop Joseph E. Kurtz
Archbishop Thomas G. Wenski
Bishop Brendan J. Cahill
Bishop Martin D. Holley
Bishop Steven J. Lopes
Bishop Thomas Olmsted
Bishop David L. Ricken
Bishop Mark J. Seitz
Ms. Helen Alvaré
Mr. Carl A. Anderson
Dr. John F. Brehany
Mrs. Colleen Carroll Campbell
Ms. Luisa de Poo
Mother Agnes Mary Donovan, S.V.
Dr. John M. Haas
Mr. Ron Johnson
Ms. Elizabeth Kirk, Esq.
Rev. J. Daniel Mindling, O.F.M.Cap.
Dr. Natasha Wilson
Mr. Patrick Kelly
Dr. Kathleen Raviele
Staff—Ms. Kimberly Baker
Mr. Tom Grenchik
Mrs. Mary McClusky
Ms. Anne McGuire
Mr. Greg Schleppenbach
Ms. Katherine Talalas

PROTECTION OF CHILDREN AND YOUNG PEOPLE

Chairman—Bishop Timothy L. Doherty
Members—Bishop Joy Alappat
Bishop Andrew E. Bellisario, C.M.
Bishop Stephen J. Berg
Bishop Joseph R. Binzer
Bishop Joseph V. Brennan
Bishop Michael J. Fitzgerald
Bishop John T. Folda
Bishop Donald J. Hying
Bishop Barry C. Knestout
Bishop Joseph R. Kopacz
Bishop Terry R. LaValley
Bishop Mark S. Rivituso
Bishop Peter J. Uglietto
Bishop William Wack, C.S.C.
Bishop Patrick J. Zurek
Consultant—Ms. Mary Jane Doerr
Staff—Rev. Msgr. Jeffrey D. Burrill, S.T.L.
Mr. Drew Dillingham
Ms. Judy Keane
Mr. Jeffrey Moon, Esq.
Deacon Bernard V. Nojadera
Mr. James L. Rogers
Ms. Melanie Takinen
Ms. Siobhan M. Verbeek
Rev. Ralph O'Donnell

RELIGIOUS LIBERTY

Chairman—Archbishop Joseph E. Kurtz
Members—Archbishop Timothy P. Broglio
Archbishop Charles J. Chaput, O.F.M.Cap.
Archbishop Joseph F. Naumann
Bishop Robert Barron
Bishop Michael F. Burbidge
Bishop Frank J. Dewane
Bishop Kevin C. Rhoades
Bishop Joe S. Vásquez
Consultants—Archbishop William E. Lori
Bishop Joseph C. Bambera
Bishop James D. Conley
Bishop Robert P. Deeley
Bishop George V. Murry, S.J.

Bishop Nelson J. Pérez
Bishop John M. Quinn
Mr. Jason Adkins, Esq.
Ms. Maria Alvarado
Mr. Carl A. Anderson
Mr. Kevin Baine, Esq.
Ambassador Mary Ann Glendon
Mr. L. Martin Nussbaum, Esq.
Mrs. Gloria Purvis
Mr. Jason Shanks
Mrs. Kim Daniels
Mr. Patrick Kelly
Staff—Rev. Msgr. J. Brian Bransfield
Rev. Msgr. Jeffrey D. Burrill, S.T.L.
Mr. Anthony R. Picarello, Jr., Esq.
Mrs. Hillary Byrnes, Esq.
Rev. Michael Fuller
Mr. Lucas Koach
Mrs. Lauren McCormack
Dr. Jonathan J. Reyes
Mr. James L. Rogers
Mr. Aaron Weldon

NATIONAL ADVISORY COUNCIL

Chairman—Colonel Anita Raines, US Army Ret., Military Archdiocese
Chair-Elect—Mrs. Deborah Amato, Brighton, Michigan
Secretary—Ms. Edith Avila Olea, Joliet, Illinois
Members—
Bishops—Bishop Paul J. Bradley, Diocese of Kalamazoo
Bishop Frank Y. Kalabat, Eparchy of Saint Thomas the Apostle of Detroit (Chaldean)
Bishop Michael F. Olson, Diocese of Fort Worth
Diocesan Priests—Rev. Msgr. Steven Camp, Baldwin, New York, Region II
Rev. David Whitestone, Fairfax, Virginia, Region IV
Rev. Gary Benz, Stanley, North Dakota, Region VIII
Rev. Mario Jose Arroyo, Houston, Texas, Region X
Rev. Vincent Blanco, Anchorage, Alaska, Region XII
Rev. James Boddie, Jr., Jacksonville, Florida, Region XIV
Men Religious—Rev. Brad Milunski, O.F.M.Conv.
Bro. Peter J. O'Loughlin, C.F.C.
Women Religious—Sr. M. Stephanie Belgeri, F.S.G.
Sr. Mary Kathryn Dougherty, O.S.F.
Sr. Jenny Howard, S.P.
Sr. Gilmary Kay, R.S.M.
At Large—Colonel Anita Raines, US Army Ret., Carlisle, PA, Military Archdiocese
Mrs. Bernarda Liriano, Bethlehem, PA, Region III
Ms. Katharina Acosta, Annapolis, MD, Region IV
Ms. Edith Avila Olea, Joliet, IL, Region VII
Mrs. Bridget Yallaly, Madison, WI, Region VII
Mr. Walter Fountain, Green Bay, WI, Region VII
Mr. James Daniel (JD) Flynn, Region VIII
Mrs. Maria de la Luz (Lucy) Rodriguez Cardenas, Laredo, TX, Region X
Deacon Matthew Halbach, Ankeny, IA, Region XI
Mr. Daniel C. Kinsella, Silver City, IA, Region XI
Ms. Renae Bennett, Winter Park, FL, Region XIV
Regional Representatives
Region I—Mr. John E. Kearns, Jr., Fall River, MA
Ms. Paula Moses, Wells, ME
Region II—Mr. Roger Aguinaldo, Rego Park, NY
Ms. Valerie Torres, Bronx, NY
Region III—Mr. James Delaney, Malvern, PA
Mrs. Catherine Jantsch Butel, Scranton, PA
Region IV—(Vacant)
Mrs. Catherine Liberatore, Phoenix, MD
Region V—
Mr. Patrick Potter, Louisville, KY
Ms. Lisa McClain, New Orleans, LA
Region VI—(Vacant)
Mrs. Deborah Amato, Brighton, MI
Region VII—Mr. William F. Becerra Pedraza, Crest Hill, IL
Ms. Shingai Chigwedere, Lombard, IL
Region VIII—Dr. John (Jack) Lane Rochester, MN (Vacant)
Region IX—Mr. Norman Kelly, Esq., Salina, KS
Mrs. Chris McCormick Pries, Bettendorf, IA
Region X—Mr. Luis D. Sanchez, Midland, TX
Ms. Alicia Alvarez Lubbock, TX
Region XI—Mr. Timothy Connors, Atherton, CA
Ms. Maria Cristina Hernandez, Oakland, CA
Region XII—(Vacant)
Ms. Cindy Eultgen Great Falls, MT
Region XIII—The Honorable Manuel Saucedo, Lordsburg, NM
Mrs. Teresa Ornelas, Tempe, AZ
Region XIV—Mr. S. Scott Voynich, Columbus, GA
Ms. Myriam Mezadieu, El Portal, FL
Region XV—Mr. Sadeer Farjo Sterling Heights, MI
Mrs. Maria Freishyn Chirovsky, Pittsburgh, PA
Staff—Ms. Danilsa A. Reyes-Gonzalez
Mrs. Theresa Ridderhoff
Ms. Nancy Wisdo, Consultant
Mrs. Christina Zvir

TASK FORCE ON THE SPANISH LANGUAGE BIBLE

Chairman—Archbishop José H. Gomez
Members—Bishop Eusebio L. Elizondo, MSpS
Bishop Anthony B. Taylor
Bishop Patrick J. Zurek
Consultants—Rev. Msgr. Juan Alfaro
Rev. Juan J. Molina, O.S.S.T.

NORTH AMERICAN COLLEGE, ROME

Chairman—Bishop Robert P. Deeley
Vice Chairman— Archbishop J. Peter Sartain
Members—Archbishop Samuel J. Aquila
Bishop Earl A. Boyea
Bishop William P. Callahan, O.F.M. Conv.
Bishop John R. Gaydos
Bishop Robert D. Gruss
Bishop Salvatore R. Matano
Bishop Michael Mulvey
Bishop Glen J. Provost
Bishop Bernard E. Shlesinger, III
Bishop Kevin W. Vann
Bishop William John Waltersheid
Treasurer—Bishop Kurt R. Burnette
Secretary—Bishop Adam J. Parker
Staff—Rev. Msgr. J. Brian Bransfield
Rev. Kerry M. Abbott, O.F.M.Conv.
Very Rev. Peter C. Harman, S.T.D.
Mr. Mark Randall

BOARD OF DIRECTORS: CATHOLIC LEGAL IMMIGRATION NETWORK, INC.

Chairman—Bishop Kevin W. Vann
Members—Rev. Msgr. J. Brian Bransfield
Archbishop Thomas J. Rodi
Archbishop Thomas G. Wenski
Bishop Roy E. Campbell
Bishop Nicholas DiMarzio
Bishop Eusebio L. Elizondo, M.Sp.S.
Bishop Gregory J. Hartmayer, O.F.M.Conv.
Bishop Joseph A. Pepe
Bishop Jaime Soto
Bishop Joe S. Vásquez
Bishop Gerald F. Kicanas
Mr. William Canny
Sr. Sally Duffy, S.C.
Sr. RayMonda DuVall, C.H.S.
Ms. Marguerite Harmon
Mr. Francis J. Mulcahy
Mr. Vincent Pitta
Mr. D. Taylor
Ms. Carmen M. Vazquez
Vice President—Bishop Mark J. Seitz
Staff—Ms. Anna Marie Gallagher

BOARD OF DIRECTORS: CATHOLIC RELIEF SERVICES

Chairman—Bishop Gregory John Mansour
Members—Mr. Mark Rauenhorst
Archbishop Timothy P. Broglio
Archbishop Paul S. Coakley
Archbishop Bernard A. Hebda
Archbishop Thomas G. Wenski
Bishop Edward J. Burns
Bishop Felipe J. Estévez
Bishop Shelton J. Fabre
Bishop James V. Johnston, Jr.
Bishop Gregory L. Parkes
Bishop Kevin C. Rhoades
Bishop Oscar Azarcon Solis
Ms. Helen Alvare
Ms. Geraldine P. Carolan
Dr. Patricia M. Dinneen
Mr. Christopher J. Policinski
Mrs. Jeri Eckhart Queenan
Mr. Stephen Walsh
Mr. Brian Wenger
Mr. Tom Arndorfer
Archbishop Jerome Listecki
Honorable Risë Jones Pichon
Treasurer—Mrs. Mary Jane Creamer
Secretary—Rev. Msgr. J. Brian Bransfield
Staff—Mr. James Bond
Mr. Sean Callahan
Mr. Mark Melia
Mr. Shawn Mood
Mr. William O'Keefe
Ms. Annemarie Reilly
Mr. Schuyler Thorup

BOARD OF TRUSTEES: CONFRATERNITY OF CHRISTIAN DOCTRINE, INC.

President—Cardinal Daniel N. DiNardo
Members—Archbishop José H. Gomez
Archbishop Dennis M. Schnurr
Archbishop Allen H. Vigneron
Staff—Ms. Mary Elizabeth Sperry

NATIONAL REVIEW BOARD

Chairman—Dr. Francesco Cesareo
Members—RADM (ret) Garry Hall
Ms. Jan Slattery
Ms. Amanda Callanan
Mr. Howard Healy
Ms. Suzanne Healy
Ms. Stacie LeBlanc
Dr. Christopher McManus
Mrs. D. Jean Ortega-Piron
Ms. Eileen Puglisi
Ms. Theresa Simak
Mr. Ernest Stark
Mr. Donald Wheeler
Staff—Deacon Bernard V. Nojadera

AD HOC COMMITTEE AGAINST RACISM

Chairman—Bishop Shelton J. Fabre
Members—Cardinal Timothy M. Dolan
Archbishop Charles J. Chaput, O.F.M.Cap.
Archbishop Gustavo García-Siller, M.Sp.S.
Archbishop José H. Gomez
Archbishop Wilton D. Gregory
Archbishop Thomas J. Rodi
Archbishop Allen H. Vigneron
Bishop Randolph R. Calvo
Bishop Martin D. Holley
Bishop George V. Murry, S.J.
Bishop Thomas J. Tobin
Consultants—Archbishop William E. Lori
Cardinal Blasé J. Cupich
Bishop Joseph C. Bambera
Bishop Frank J. Dewane
Bishop Gregory John Mansour
Bishop John H. Ricard, S.S.J.
Bishop David P. Talley
Bishop Joe S. Vásquez
Ms. Jessica Murdoch, Collegeville, PA
Mr. Carl A. Anderson
Mr. James Ellis
Rev. John I. Jenkins, C.S.C.
Sr. Donna Markham
Dr. Hosffman Ospino
Sr. Norma Pimentel, M.J.
Dr. C. Reynold Verrett
Rev. Maurice Henry Sands
Staff—Ms. Danielle M. Brown, Esq.
Dr. Jonathan J. Reyes

NATIONAL RELIGIOUS RETIREMENT

National Religious Retirement Office
3211 Fourth St. Washington, DC 20017-1194. Tel: 202-541-3215. Email: retirement@usccb.org. Sr. Stephanie Still, P.B.V.M., Exec. Dir. The Mission of the National Religious Retirement Office is to coordinate the National Collection for the

Retirement Fund for Religious and to distribute these monies to eligible religious institutes for their retirement needs. The office also provides retirement planning and educational assistance to religious institutes. The National Religious Retirement Office is sponsored by the Conference of Major Superiors of Men, the Conference of Major Superiors of Women Religious, the Leadership Conference of Women Religious and the United States Conference of Catholic Bishops.

REFUGEE TRAVEL ASSISTANCE PROGRAM LLC

Refugee Travel Assistance Program LLC

3211 Fourth St. NW Washington, DC 20017-1194. Tel: 202-541-3328. LLC's sole member: United States Conference of Catholic Bishops.

Managers—Monsignor J. Brian Bransfield, Archbishop Dennis Schnurr, and Bishop Joe S. Vásquez.

Officers—Monsignor J. Brian Bransfield, William A. Canny, Gregory J. Scott, and Leonard A. Harrod.

The purpose of Refugee Travel Assistance Program LLC is to engage in and conduct any and all activities and transactions necessary, appropriate or incident to the servicing of refugee travel loans, pursuant to a memorandum of understanding with the International Organization for Migration, which are financed by The Bureau of Population, Refugees and Migration, United States Department of State, and made to refugees to assist them in resettling in the United States.

RELATED ORGANIZATIONS

***Catholic Legal Immigration Network, Inc.**

National Office, 8757 Georgia Ave., Ste 850 Silver Spring, MD 20910. Tel: 301-565-4829 Fax: 301-565-4824 Email: jatkinson@cliniclegal.org Web: www.cliniclegal.org

Board of Directors—Bishop Kevin W. Vann, Chm., Bishop Martin D. Holley, Vice Pres., Sr. Sally Duffy, S.C., Treas., Ms. Jeanne Atkinson, Exec. Dir., Rev. Msgr. Brian Bransfield, Gen. Sec., USCCB, William A. Canny, Bishop Edgar M. da Cunha, S.D.V., Bishop Nicholas A. DiMarzio, Sr. RayMonda DuVall, C.H.S., Bishop Eusebio L. Elizondo, M.Sp.S., Bishop Richard J. Garcia, Mr. Emilio Gonzalez, Ms. Marguerite (Peg) Harmon, Bishop Gerald F. Kicanas, Mr. Francis J. Mulcahy, Mr. Javier Palomarez, Bishop Joseph A. Pepe, Mr. Vincent Pitta, Bishop Mark J. Seitz, Bishop Jaime Soto, Mr. D. Taylor, Bishop Joe S. Vasquez, Archbishop Thomas G. Wenski

The Catholic Legal Immigration Network, Inc. (CLINIC), an independent agency founded by the United States Conference of Catholic Bishops (USCCB), operates a legal support agency for a rapidly growing national network of Catholic immigration programs. CLINIC advocates for transparent, fair and generous immigration policies, and expresses the Church's commitment to the full membership of migrants in U.S. society.

Catholic Relief Services

Catholic Relief Services-USCCB *CRS World Headquarters,* 228 W. Lexington St. Baltimore, MD 21201-3413. Tel: 866-608-5978 Web: www.crs.org Mr. Sean Callahan, Pres.

Catholic Relief Services is the official international humanitarian agency of the Catholic community in the United States. CRS alleviates suffering and provides assistance to people in need in nearly 93 countries, without regard to race, religion or nationality.

CRS was founded in 1943 by the bishops of the United States to assist the poor and disadvantaged outside this country — helping people in need for more than 70 years.

CRS is efficient and effective directing more than 92 percent of the agency's expenditures directly to programs that benefit the poor overseas. Our agency touches nearly 100 million lives, by addressing the root causes and effects of poverty, promoting human dignity, and helping to build more just and peaceful societies.

Our relief and development work is accomplished through programs of emergency response, HIV, health, agriculture, education, microfinance and peace building.

We serve Catholics in the United States by inviting them to live out their faith as part of one human family.

For more information, please visit www.crs.org.

Chairman—Bishop Gregory J. Mansour

Members—Mr. Tom Arndorfer, Rev. Msgr. J. Brian Bransfield, S.T.D., Bishop Edward J. Burns, Bishop Paul S. Coakley, Mrs. Mary Jane Creamer, Dr. Patricia M. Dinneen, Bishop Felipe J. Estevez, S.T.D., Mr. Kevin Farrell, Bishop James V. Johnston, Jr., Archbishop Jerome E. Listecki, Archbishop George J. Lucas, Bishop Gregory J. Parkes, Honorable Rise Jones Pichon, Mr. Christopher J. Policinski, Mrs. Jeri Eckhart Queenan, Mr. Mark Rauenhorst, Bishop Kevin C. Rhoades, Hon. Geraldine E. Rivera, Bishop Arthur J. Serratelli, Bishop Joe S. Vasquez, Mr. Stephen A. Walsh, Mrs. Charmaine Warmenhoven, Archbishop Thomas G. Wenski

Staff—Mr. Sean Callahan, Pres. & CEO, Mr. Mark Palmer, Exec. Vice Pres. & Chief Financial Officer, Mr. Mark Melia, Exec. Vice Pres., Charitable Giving, Ms. Joan Rosenhauer, Exec. Vice Pres., U.S. Oper., Mr. Schuyler Thorup, Exec. Vice Pres., Overseas Oper., Ms. Annemarie Reilly, Exec. Vice Pres., Strategy and Organizational Devel., Mr. David Palasits, Acting Exec. Vice Pres., Human Resources

NATIONAL ORGANIZATIONS

Listing in this category is not related to classification under Canon Law as a public juridic person.

American Catholic Correctional Ministries

c/o Deacon John Tomandl, ACCM, 48 Park Ave., Auburn, NY 13021-1928. Tel: 315-729-4668 Fax: 315-252-0336 Email: accmsec@gmail.com. Web: www.tomandl.com/ACCM/htm. Bishop Barry C. Knestout, D.D., V.G., Episcopal Advisor, Deacon John Tomandl, Pres., Rev. Richard A. Deshaies, S.J., Exec. Dir. & Treas., Paul Rogers, Certification Chair, Christine M. Shimrock, Past Pres.

The Board of Directors include the Episcopal Advisor and Elected Officers. Address all Communications to the President or Exec. Director.

ACCM is a nonprofit organization for the purposes of unifying and implementing the Church's corrective and restorative efforts for the spiritual welfare of persons committed to the Catholic ministry in the Criminal Justice system, and to foster a Catholic approach to issues of criminal justice in accord with the principles of Sacred Scripture and Catholic social justice teaching. Affiliated with the Social Development and World Peace Department, USCCB, the International Commission of Catholic Prison Pastoral Care, American Correctional Association, American Correctional Chaplains Association, National Council on Crime and Delinquency and The Catholic University of America, it was established with approval of the American Bishops in 1952. Grants USCCB recognized certification to qualified members.

American Catholic Historical Association (1919)

Fordham University, Dealy Hall, Rm. 637, 441 E. Fordham Bronx, NY 10458. Tel: 718-817-3830 Fax: 718-817-5690 Email: acha@fordham.edu Rev. Richard Gribble, C.S.C., Pres., Rev. R. Bentley Anderson, S.J., Sec. & Treas.

An academic and scholarly organization, founded to promote the study of Catholicism and Roman Catholic history understood in the broad sense.

The American College of the Roman Catholic Church of the United States

3211 Fourth St., N.E., Washington, DC 20017-1194. Tel: 202-541-5411 Fax: 202-722-8804 Email: pnacdc@pnac.org Most Rev. Robert Deeley, J.C.D., Chm., Rev. Peter C. Harman, S.T.D., Rector, Mark Randall, C.F.R.E, Exec. Dir., Institutional Advancement.

The American College is delegated by the Holy See to exercise oversight of the formational activities of the Pontifical North American College in Rome, and its Board of Governors is composed of one Bishop from each of the fifteen USCCB Regions. It was created by a Special Act of the Maryland Legislature in 1886, and its tax status is governed by Section 501(c)(3) of the United States Internal Revenue Code.

Apostleship of the Sea of the United States of America (AOSUSA)

1500 Jefferson Dr. Port Arthur, TX 77642-0646. Tel: 409-985-4545 Fax: 409-985-5945 Email: aosusa@sbcglobal.net Capt. George P. McShea, Jr., Pres., Rev. Sinclair Oubre, J.C.L., Immediate Past Pres., Ms. Doreen M. Badeaux, Sec. Gen.

AOSUSA is an association of the faithful of Catholic maritime chaplains, cruise ship priests, seafarers, deacons, religious, lay ecclesial ministers, and affiliates serving the people of the sea in ports throughout the USA.

Private Association of the Faithful.

Publication: AOS USA Maritime E-News.

Association of Catholic Diocesan Archivists

Archdiocese of St. Louis Office of Archives & Records, 20 Archbishop May Dr., St. Louis, MO 63119-5738 Tel: 314-792-7020 Bishop Thomas J. Paprocki, D.D., J.C.D., S.T.D., Episcopal Moderator, Eric Fair, Pres., Kathryn Periera, Vice Pres. & Pres.-Elect, Angelique Richardson, Treas., Kate Feighery, Sec.

The Association of Catholic Diocesan Archivists first met in 1979 and formally organized the Association of Catholic Diocesan Archivists in 1982. The organization promotes professionalism in the management of diocesan archives in the United States and Canada, and fosters cooperation between diocesan archivists and others on regional, national and international levels. Membership information is available through the above address and telephone number.

Catholic Association of Diocesan Ecumenical and Interreligious Officers (CADEIO)

7600 Old Keene Mill Rd., Springfield, VA 22152. Fax: 703-269-1121 Email: skrehotj@stthom.edu Cell: 281-684-9220 Mrs. Jan Skrehot, M.Div., Pres., Rev. Joseph D. Wallace, B.S., M.Div., M.A., Vice Pres., Mr. Rick Caporali, Treas., Rev. Phil Latronico, Sec.

CADEIO (formerly NADEO) is the Catholic Association of Ecumenical and Interreligious Officers who serve as delegates of dialogue on behalf of their bishops of (Arch)Dioceses and Eparchies in the United States: to promote collaboration which advances the work of Christian unity and interreligious understanding; to arrange programs for continuing formation and education of the membership; and to cooperate with the Bishops' Committee for Ecumenical and Interreligious Affairs of the United States Conference of Catholic Bishops, and with other ecumenical and interreligious networks and agencies.

Catholic Association of Teachers of Homiletics (CATH)

St. Mary's Seminary, 5400 Roland Ave. Baltimore, MD 21210-1994. Email: egriswold@stmarys.edu Rev. Edward Griswold, D.Min., M.Ed., S.T.L., Pres.

Catholic Campus Ministry Association

National Office, 330 W. Vine St. Cincinnati, OH 45215-3149. Tel: 513-842-0167 Fax: 513-842- 0171 Email: info@ccmanet.org Web: www.ccmanetwork.org

Founded in 1969 by the United States Conference of Catholic Bishops, CCMA promotes the mission of the Church in higher education and implements the 1985 Pastoral Letter on Campus Ministry through the training, formation and networking of Catholic campus ministers. Membership is open to individuals involved in the campus ministry field.

Publications: Small Group Field Guide, Catholic Campus Ministry Directory, Ministry Evaluation Instrument, online resources.

Catholic Cemetery Conference

Office Headquarters, 1400 S. Wolf Rd., Bldg. 3 Hillside, IL 60162. Tel: 708-202-1242; Web: www.catholiccemeteryconference.org. David J. LaBarre, M.A., M.S., Exec. Dir., Bishop Gerald F. Kicanas, D.D., Episcopal Moderator

The Conference is an organization of Diocesan Directors of Cemeteries and parish cemetery administrators from throughout the United States, Canada, Australia and Italy. Guided by the principle: "That burial of the dead is one of the Corporal Works of Mercy," the Conference promotes high standards of Catholic cemetery management, development, operation and maintenance consistent with Christian service to the Catholic community; and fosters and promotes the religious, charitable and educational interests of Catholic cemeteries and the people they serve.

Founded in 1949, the Catholic Cemetery Conference (CCC) helps cemetery staff enhance their skills in caring for the deceased and comforting their loved ones through ministry, education, networking and service opportunities.

Publications: monthly magazine, Catholic Cemetery; various booklets on cemetery management & evaluation services; funeral liturgy at the cemetery. Annual Convention; School of Leadership and Management Excellence at the University of Notre Dame, Exploring Catholic Cemetery Operations.

Catholic Charities USA

2050 Ballenger Ave., Ste. 400 Alexandria, VA 22314. Tel: 703-549-1390 Fax: 703-549-1656 Sr. Donna Markham, O.P., Ph.D., Pres. & CEO, Bishop David A. Zubik, Episcopal Liaison

Catholic Charities USA is a national network of more than 160 agencies that provide help and create hope for nearly 9 million people a year regardless of their religious, social, or economic backgrounds.

For more than 280 years, Catholic Charities agencies have been providing a wide range of vital services in their communities ranging from day care, adoption, and refugee resettlement to advocacy, counseling, and emergency food and housing. Today, the Catholic Charities network is made up of more than 70,000 staff and 260,000 volunteers. In addition, more than 5,000 individuals serve as volunteer members of local boards.

The national office, Catholic Charities USA, was founded in 1910 as the National Conference of Catholic Charities by the Most Rev. Thomas J. Shahan and Rt. Rev. Msgr. William J. Kerby in cooperation with lay leaders of the Society of St. Vincent De Paul.

Catholic Charities USA provides its members a national voice, networking opportunities, training and technical assistance, program development, and financial support.

Catholic Charities USA has been commissioned by the U.S. Catholic bishops to represent the Catholic community in times of domestic disaster. Catholic Charities USA also provides disaster preparedness training to dioceses and agencies to mitigate the disruption of business and services consequent to natural disasters.

Publications: Charities USA, a quarterly membership magazine; an annual report; an annual survey of Catholic Charities services nationwide; and various publications on issues of concern to Catholic Charities agencies.

The Catholic Communications Foundation (CCF)

c/o 6363 St. Charles Ave. New Orleans, LA 70118. Dr. William H. Hummell, Board Member & Contact Person

The Catholic Communications Foundation was established and is supported by Catholic Fraternal Benefit Societies. Its mission is to assist the communications apostolates of the Catholic Church in the United States, with particular emphasis at the diocesan level. The Foundation awards religious communications training scholarships.

The Catholic Health Association of the United States (1919)

4455 Woodson Rd. Saint Louis, MO 63134. Tel: 314-427-2500 Fax: 314-427-0029 Web: www. chausa. org Sr. Carol Keehan, D.C., Pres. & CEO, Sr. Mary Haddad, R.S.M., Vice Pres. Sponsorship & Mission Svcs., Lisa Smith, Vice Pres. Advocacy & Public Policy, Rhonda Mueller, Senior Vice Pres. Finance & Opers., Catherine Hurley, Vice Pres. Gen. Counsel, Brian Reardon, Vice Pres. Communications & Mktg., Angela Botticella, Chief of Staff

CHA represents the combined strength of its members, more than 2,000 Catholic healthcare sponsors, systems, facilities, and related organizations.Founded in 1915, CHA unites members to advance selected strategic directions. Presents annual awards recognizing contribution to the health ministry by organizations and individuals. Sponsors continuing education for healthcare personnel.

Service Areas: Planning and Policy Development, Public Policy and Advocacy, Communications, Sponsorship, Ethics and Mission Services. Annual Assembly: Annual assembly and membership meeting for Catholic healthcare leaders.

Publications: 6 times-year, Health Progress; bimonthly Catholic Health World; booklets, books & audiovisual on healthcare, Church-related subjects.

Catholic Kolping Society of America (1849)

(Please direct all correspondence to the National Administrator).

1223 Van Houten Clifton, NJ 07013. Patricia Farkas, Natl. Admin.

The Society was founded by Rev. Adolph Kolping in Cologne, Germany, and established in the United States in 1856. The Catholic Kolping Society of America is a part of the worldwide Kolping movement and belongs to the International Kolping Society. There are 11 branches in principal cities of the United States with a combined membership of approximately 2,000. The membership is open to men and women of all ages. The Society's mission statement reads: We, the members of the Catholic Kolping Society of America, extend the vision of our founder, Blessed Adolph Kolping, by promoting the development of the individual and family; we foster a sense of belonging and friendship through our program of spiritual, educational, charitable and social activities.

Catholic Medical Association

National Headquarters, 29 Bala Ave., Ste. 205, Bala Cynwyd, PA 19004. Tel: 484-270-8002 Fax: 866-666-2319 Email: info@cathmed.org Web: www.cathmed.org

Officers—Mr. Mario Dickerson, M.T.S., Exec. Dir., John A. Schirger, M.D., Pres., Michael S. Parker, M.D., Vice Pres., Craig L. Treptow, M.D., Treas., Michelle K. Stanford, M.D., Sec.

Upholding the principles of the Catholic faith in the science and practice of medicine.

Catholic Volunteer Network

6930 Carroll Ave., Ste. 820 Takoma Park, MD 20912-4423. Tel: 301-270-0900 Tel: 800-543- 5046 Email: info@catholicvolunteernetwork.org Web: www.catholicvolunteernetwork.org Bishop Oscar Solis, Episcopal Advisor

Catholic Volunteer Network promotes, recruits and refers volunteers to missions in the United States and overseas. We represent more than 200 faith-based volunteer programs worldwide and work with the U.S. dioceses, religious communities and the private sector to determine their needs for help. Catholic Volunteer Network (CVN) is committed to the goal that every Catholic man and woman be invited to consider a period of service in the missions, as a vital and important manifestation of the baptismal call of all Catholic people. Currently over 20,000 men and women are serving in CVN member mission programs offering their gifts and abilities in full-time service to people in need and living their Catholic faith more fully. These volunteers are serving domestically for a summer, six months, a year or more, and they are serving internationally for two or more years at a time. They are single and married, recent college graduates and early retirees, doctors and teachers, parish ministers and social workers, community organizers, computer programmers, legal aides and more. Gatherings: Annual Conference; Formation Workshop, Training Seminars.

Publications: annual, Response: Directory of Volunteer Opportunities; monthly, How Can I Help?; quarterly, FaithWorks.

Awards: The Father George Mader Award, given annually to honor organizations and individuals who promote the value of lay mission service. The Bishop Joseph A. Francis Award to honor organizations and individuals who promote community service.

The Catholic Press Association of the United States and Canada, Inc.

205 W. Monroe St., Ste. 470 Chicago, IL 60606. Tel: 312-380-6789 Fax: 312-361-0256 Web: www. catholicpress.org

Board of Directors—Joseph Towalski, Pres., Most Rev. Christopher J. Coyne, Honorary Pres., Mary Anne Castranio, Vice President, Joe Sinasac, Treas., Kerry Weber, Sec., Jennifer Brinker, Editorial Staff Member, Newspaper, Robert DeFrancesco, Regl. Rep., Western, John Feister, Member At Large, Magazine, Amy Kawula, Business Staff Member, Newspaper, Michael La Civita, Business Staff Member, Magazine, Katherine Long, Regl. Rep., Eastern, JD Long-Garcia, Publisher Member, Magazine, Deirdre Mays, Member At Large, Matthew Schiller (Past President), Publisher Member, Newspaper, Tim Walter, Exec. Dir.

The Catholic Press Association of the United States and Canada, Inc., is the trade and professional association of Catholic newspapers, magazines, and general publishers in the U.S. and Canada and their staff personnel. The CPA was established in 1911. It serves a professional Catholic press market of nearly 2,000 persons working in more than 600 publications with a wide promotion and representation of Catholic press interests in social media, education, and professional development.

Catholic Rural Life

University of St. Thomas, 2115 Summit Ave. Mail 4080 St. Paul, MN 55105-1048. Tel: 651-962-5955 Fax: 651-962-5957 Email: info@catholicrurallife. org Web: www.catholicrurallife.org Bishop Paul D. Etienne, D.D., S.T.L., Pres. Bd., Mr. James F. Ennis, Exec. Dir.

Catholic Rural Life is a membership-based organization focused on renewing Catholic faith in rural communities by applying the teachings of Jesus Christ for the social, economic, and spiritual development of rural America. CRL collaborates with dioceses nationwide through three program areas: Rural Ministry and Outreach, Ethical Food and Agriculture, and Stewardship of Creation; strengthening and sustaining the Church in the countryside by training leaders, advocating on behalf of family farmers and rural communities, and educating our membership from a faith-based perspective.

The Catholic Theological Society of America

c/o John Carroll University, 1 John Carroll Blvd. University Heights, OH 44118. Tel: 440-360-0816

Board Members—Paul Lakeland, Pres., Fairfield, CT, Maria Pilar Aquino, Pres.-Elect, San Diego, CA, Christine Firer Hinze, Vice Pres., Bronx, NY; Hosffman Ospino, Sec., Chestnut Hill, MA, John D. Dadosky, S.T.D., Treas., Toronto, ON, Mary E. Hines, Past Pres., Boston, MA, Kevin F. Burke, S.J., Denver, CO, Edmund Chia, East Melbourne, VIC, Julie Hanlon Rubio, Berkeley, CA, Michele Saracino, Riverdale, NY, Mary Jane Ponyik, Exec. Dir., University Heights, OH.

An association of professional theologians. Its purpose is to promote studies and research in theology within the Roman Catholic tradition, to relate theological science to current problems, and to foster a more effective theological education by providing a forum for an exchange of views among theologians and with scholars in other disciplines.

Catholic Youth Foundation USA

415 Michigan Ave., Ste. 40 Washington, DC 20017-4503. Tel: 202-636-3825 Fax: 202-526-7544 Email: info@cyfusa.org Web: nfcym.org Ms. Christine Lamas, MSW, Exec. Dir.

Catholic Youth Foundation USA (CYFUSA) is assuring a faithful future by promoting effective and innovative youth ministry. CYFUSA provides financial support to the National Federation for Catholic Youth Ministry of the Catholic Church. CYFUSA makes the following possible: scholarships for youth and youth leaders to attend the National Catholic Youth Conference and the National Conference for Catholic Youth Ministry and ongoing programing of the National Federation for Catholic Youth Ministry.

Conference for Catholic Facility Management

20 Archbishop May Dr. St. Louis, MO 63119. Tel: 314-792-7002 Email: lbaird@ccfm.net Web: www.ccfm.net. Louis Baird, Exec. Dir., Mary Tichy, Assoc. Dir., Bob Palish, Bd. Pres., Dave Prada, Bd. Vice Pres., Jennifer Hunter, Bd. Treas., Cindy Jacobson, Bd. Sec., Most Rev. Roger Foys, Episcopal Moderator.

Mindful of their special ministry in the Roman Catholic Church in facility and real estate matters, the members of the CCFM united to be of service to the Church in ministry of facility and real estate concerns. In particular, this organization promotes the spiritual growth of its membership; promotes facility and real estate knowledge and expertise in service to the local and national Church, facilitates the exchange of ideas and information through personal contacts, quarterly newsletters and annual meetings.

The Conference of Major Superiors of Men of the United States, Inc.

7300 Hanover Dr., Ste. 304, Greenbelt, MD 20770. Tel: 301-588-4030 Fax: 240-650-3697 Very Rev. Mark Padrez, O.P., Pres., Bro. Larry Schatz, F.S.C., Vice Pres., Very Rev. Timothy P. Kesicki, S.J., Sec. & Treas.

A canonical conference of the major superiors of religious communities and institutes of men for the purpose of promoting the spiritual and apostolic welfare of priests and brothers.

The Confraternity of Christian Doctrine, Inc.

3211 Fourth St., N.E. Washington, DC 20017. Tel: 202-541-3098 Fax: 202-541-3089 Mary Elizabeth Sperry, Assoc. Dir. Email: msperry@usccb.org.

Members—Cardinal Daniel DiNardo, Archbishop Allen H. Vigneron, Archbishop Jose Gomez, Archbishop Dennis Schnurr

The Confraternity is a distinct entity, separately incorporated and directed by a Board of Trustees from the United States Conference of Catholic Bishops. The purpose of the Corporation is to foster and promote the teachings of Christ as understood and handed down by the Roman Catholic Church. To this end it licenses use of the Lectionary for Mass and the New American Bible, translations made from the original languages.

Council of Major Superiors of Women Religious in the United States of America

415 Michigan Ave., N.E., Ste. 420 P.O. Box 4467 Washington, DC 20017-0467. Tel: 202-832-2575 Fax: 202-832-6325 Email executivedirector@cmswr.org Mother Mary McGreevy, R.S.M., Chairperson, Sister Mary Christine Cremin, R.S.M., Exec. Dir.

A canonically erected conference of Major Superiors of women's religious communities established in 1992 to promote mutual support among them and to foster coordination and cooperation with the Bishops' conference and individual Bishops.

Diocesan Fiscal Management Conference

National Office, 4727 E. Bell Rd., Ste. 45-358 Phoenix, AZ 85032-2831. Tel: 602-992-2900 Email: pmarkey@dfmconf.org Bishop Barry C. Knestout, Episcopal Moderator, Mr. Patrick Markey, M.B.A., CPA, Exec. Dir.

The mission of the Diocesan Fiscal Management Conference (DFMC) is to provide leadership in fiscal management to the Catholic Church. Mindful of its special ministry in the Church as the extension of the Diocesan Bishop in fiscal matters, the members of the Diocesan Fiscal Management Conference unite to be of service to the Church in the Ministry of Fiscal Management. In particular, this organization promotes the spiritual growth of its members; encourages the development of professional relationships of its members; facilitates the free exchange of ideas and information; and provides fiscal and administrative expertise and professional services to the local and national Church.

Diocesan Information Systems Conference

National Office, 1250 Connecticut Ave., N.W., Ste. 200 Washington, DC 20036. Tel: 419-214-4908 Email: info@discinfo.org Bishop Jeffrey M. Monforton, Episcopal Moderator, Sharon Landis, Pres., Kory Hopkins, Vice Pres., Carla Haiar, Sec., Debbi Hutchings, Treas.

The members of DISC unite to be of service to the Roman Catholic Church in information systems matters. The DISC organization serves as a liaison among technology managers for Archdioceses, Dioceses and related entities.

In particular, this organization promotes the spiritual growth of its members, provides technical expertise in Information Technology, promotes professional technical services to the local and national church communities, encourages the development of professional relationships among its members and facilitates the free exchange of technical information and ideas.

Federation of Diocesan Liturgical Commissions

FDLC National Office, 415 Michigan Ave., N.E., Ste. 70 Washington, DC 20017. Tel: 202-635-6990 Fax: 202-529-2452 Web: www.FDLC.org Mrs. Rita A. Thiron, Exec. Dir., Rev. James Bessert, Chm., Bd. Dirs., Rev. Michael Poradek, Vice Chair; Ms. Laura Bertone, Treas.

The FDLC was initiated by the Bishops' Committee on the Liturgy (BLC) in October, 1969, in order to assist and develop the liturgical apostolate in the dioceses of the United States of America. The FDLC is a national organization composed of members of diocesan liturgical commissions and directors of worship offices duly appointed by their local bishops. Its members may also include others who support the liturgical life of parishes and other Catholic institutions. As a pastoral and professional organization, the FDLC serves as an official collaborating agent between the local Churches and the BCDW. The Board of Directors is made up of fourteen representatives, one from each of the fourteen episcopal regions. The Executive Director leads the Federation's daily operations. The FDLC serves as a forum through which diocesan liturgy personnel may contribute responsibly and effectively in articulating the concerns of the local Church in liturgical matters; provides formation for parish and diocesan leadership; and aids the full implementation of the liturgical rites as envisioned by the Constitution on the Sacred Liturgy, subsequent post-conciliar documentation, and the praenotanda of the liturgical books.

Instituto Nacional Hispano de Liturgia, Inc.

St. Joseph Catholic Church, 8670 Byron Ave., Miami Beach, FL 33141. Tel: 305-866-6567 Rev. Juan J. Sosa, Pres., Sr. Marilu Covani, S.P., Vice Pres., Mrs. Mary Frances Reza, Sec.

The Instituto is a national organization committed to assisting the bishops of the country in promoting the liturgical reforms mandated by the Second Vatican Council, while it studies, reflects and celebrates more authentically the Catholic faith from the various religious traditions of Hispanics who reside in the United States. Instituto members assist the Church at the national, diocesan and parish levels by providing lectures, translations, and other Spanish and bilingual resources that may meet the liturgical needs of Hispanics whenever they surface. Membership to the organization is open to all persons and institutions interested in liturgy. Board members meet twice a year, members meet annually. National Conference every 2 years and/or symposium on liturgical topics.

International Catholic Migration Commission (ICMC) & ICMC, Inc.

c/o USCCB 3211 Fourth St., N.E. Washington, DC 20017-1194. Peter Sutherland, Pres., Msgr. Robert Vitillo, Sec. Gen., Jane Bloom, U.S. Head of Office

Provides technical assistance and coordination in area of service to migrants and refugees. Nonprofit New York Corporation.

International Catholic Stewardship Council, Inc. (ICSC)

National Office, 26300 Ford Rd., #317, Dearborn Heights, MI 48127. Tel: 800-352-3452 Fax: 313-446-8316 Email: icsc@catholicstewardship.org Web: www.catholicstewardship.com Archbishop Michael Owen Jackels, Archbishop of Dubuque, IA, Michael Murphy, Exec. Dir.

Through its annual conference, Stewardship and Development Institutes, publications and audio materials, ICSC allows people committed to Christian stewardship to gather, share ideas, and learn from each other. At one with the universal church, ICSC fosters solidarity of stewardship as a way of life in parishes and dioceses all over the world. Membership in ICSC is extended to several categories of Christian stewards: (Arch)dioceses, parishes, Catholic associations and professional firms from the United States and around the world. Members receive a number of essential benefits to enable them to live stewardship and bring this way of life to others in their communities and organizations.

ICSC encourages the growing professionalism of diocesan stewardship and development procedures and programs, as well as the development of parish-centered stewardship renewal aimed at increasing the time, talent and treasure contributed by parishioners. These principles of stewardship outlined in the 1992 USCCB Pastoral Letter: Stewardship: A Disciple's Response.

For a complete list of services and publications contact the ICSC office or visit the ICSC Website at www.catholicstewardship.org. Membership information is available upon request.

Jesuit Conference, Inc.

1016 16th St., N.W., Ste. 400 Washington, DC 20036. Tel: 202-462-0400 Fax: 202-328-9212 Very Rev. Timothy P. Kesicki, S.J., Pres., Rev. Sean D. Michaelson, S.J., Ph.D., Socius & Treas.

Ladies of Charity of the United States of America (LCUSA)

National Center, 2816 E. 23ed St., Kansas City, MO 64127. Tel: 816-260-3853 Email: office@ladiesofcharity.us Web: aic.ladiesofcharity.us Bishop David A. Zubik, D.D., Episcopal Chm., Suzanne Johnson, Esq., Pres. 2017-2018, Rev. Richard Gielow, C.M., Spiritual Advisor

Ladies of Charity in the United States of America (R) is a national organization with local associations of Ladies of Charity as its members. The Local Associations are dedicated to the service of poor & frail people in their communities in the spirit of St. Vincent de Paul, St. Louise de Marillac & St. Elizabeth Ann Seton. Nationally about 6,100 members contribute volunteer hours and financial support. LCUSA is a member of the International Association of Charities of St. Vincent de Paul (AIC) which traces its founding to St. Vincent de Paul in 1617. We are women acting together against all forms of poverty through service, education & advocacy.

Publications; triannual: Servicette.

Leadership Conference of Women Religious in the United States of America

Office, 8808 Cameron St. Silver Spring, MD 20910. Tel: 301-588-4955 Fax: 301-587-4575 Sr. Marcia Allen, C.S.J., D.Min., Past Pres., Sr. Mary Pellegrino, C.S.J., B.A., M.S., M.A., Pres., Sr. Teresa Maya, C.C.V.I., B.A., M.A., Ph.D., Pres.-Elect, Sr. Patricia A. Eck, C.B.S., M.A., Treas., Sr. Mary Beth Gianoli, O.S.F., M.A., Sec., Sr. Joan Marie Steadman, C.S.C., B.S., M.A., Exec. Dir.

A conference of leaders of U.S. women religious congregations, founded in 1956, canonically approved in 1959 with a name change in 1972 and canonical approval of revised by-laws in 1972 and 1989, to promote a developing understanding and living of religious life, to assist members to carry out more collaboratively their service of leadership, to provide a vehicle for dialogue with the Bishops' Conference and other ecclesiastical authority, and to collaborate with other groups concerned with the needs of society in continuing the mission of Christ in the world today.

Lithuanian Roman Catholic Federation of America

4545 W. 63rd St. Chicago, IL 60629. Tel: 312-585-9500 Email: svkuprys@gmail.com Bishop Paul Baltakis, O.F.M., Episcopal Advisor, Saulius V. Kuprys, Pres.

A not-for-profit corporation founded in 1906 in Wilkes-Barre, PA, to promote and coordinate religious, educational and charitable activities among Lithuanian American Catholics, their organizations, institutions, religious communities, and parishes (for detailed information regarding religious institutions please refer to the Apostolate for Lithuanians).

Mariological Society of America (1949)

Secretariat: Marian Library, University of Dayton Dayton, OH 45469-1390. Tel: 937-229-4294. MSA Web: http://mariologicalsociety.com MSA Email: cmushenheim1@udayton.edu Rev. Thomas A. Thompson, S.M., Exec. Sec.

The objects and purposes of this organization are to promote interest and research in the theology of the Virgin Mary. Professional and associate membership. Proceedings of annual meeting published in Marian Studies now available at https://ecommons.udayton.edu/marian_studies/. Annual convention in late May or early June.

National Apostolate for Inclusion Ministry NAFIM (1967)

7202 Buchanan Street Landover Hills, MD 20784. Tel: 800-736-1280 Tel: 301-577-1130 Email: info@nafim.org Bishop Mitchell T. Rozanski, D.D., V.G., Episcopal Moderator, Deacon Lawrence R. Sutton, Ph.D., Pres., Barbara J. Lampe, Exec. Dir., Dennis McNulty, E-Journal

Established in 1967 to promote the full participation of persons with intellectual disabilities in the life of the Catholic Church. Formerly known as National Apostolate with Persons with Mental Retardation (NAPMR) 1992-1997, National Apostolate with Mentally Retarded Persons (NAMRP) 1974-1992 and National Apostolate for the Mentally Retarded (NAMR) 1967-1974.

Publications: internet journal; newsletter; pamphlets; training materials.

National Association of Black Catholic Deacons, Inc.

820 18th Ave. Seattle, WA 98122. Deacon Joseph E. Connor, Pres., Seattle, WA, Deacon Larry Chatman, Vice Pres., Oakland, CA, Deacon Alfred Mitchell, Sec., Atlanta, GA, Deacon Jerry M. Lett, Treas., Lithonia, GA, Deacon Paul E. Richardson, Immediate Past Pres. Yellow Springs, OH

Members At Large—Deacon Arthur L. Miller, Windsor, CT, Deacon Jimmie L. Boyd, Sr., Buffalo, NY, Deacon Keith McKnight, Jersey City, NJ, Deacon Ralph Cyrus, Ft. Washington, MD, Deacon Emith Fludd, St. Croix, VI, Deacon Dexter Watson, Chicago, IL, Deacon Oliver Washington, Cincinnati, OH, Deacon Dunn Cumby, Oklahoma City, OK, Deacon A. Stephen Pickett, Lenoir, SC

Wives Representatives—Magnolia Cumby, Oklahoma City, OK, Barbara Connor, Seattle, WA

To establish an organization of Permanent deacons of African heritage ordained in the Roman Catholic Church. To promote unity among deacons of African descent by facilitating effective communication network on a national, regional, and diocesan level. To be a pro-active organization in promoting and contributing to the future of the African American family with emphasis on African American men. To promote justice, peace, equality, an end to racism, and the sharing of resources among all peoples in light of the social teachings of the Roman Catholic Church.

National Association of Catholic Chaplains

National Office, 4915 S. Howell Ave., Ste. 501 Milwaukee, WI 53207-5939. Tel: 414-483-4898 Fax: 414-483-6712 Email: info@nacc.org Web: www.nacc.org Bishop Donald J. Hying, Diocese of Gary, Episcopal Liaison, Jim Letourneau, M.Div., MSW, LCSW BCC, Chair Bd., Mr. David A. Lichter, D.Min., Exec. Dir.

The National Association of Catholic Chaplains advocates for the profession of spiritual care and educates, certifies, and supports chaplains, clinical pastoral educators, and all members who continue the healing ministry of Jesus in the name of the Church.

Publication: 6 times-year, journal-newsletter, Vision; 26 times-year (every other Monday), email newsletter, NACC Now.

The National Association of Catholic Family Life Ministers

P.O. Box 23, Alpha, OH 45301. Tel: 937-431-5443 Fax: 937-431-5443 Email: nacflm@gmail.com Web: www.nacflm.org Dr. Lauri Przybysz, D. Min., Pres., Mike Day, Pres.-Elect

The National Association of Church Personnel Administrators (NACPA)

1727 King St., Ste. 105, Alexandria, VA 22314. Tel: 571-551-6064 Email: nacpa@nacpa.org Web: www.nacpa.org Maureen Fontenot, Bd. Pres., Regina Haney, Ed.D., Exec. Dir.

The National Association of Church Personnel Administrators (NACPA) is a membership association of lay, religious and clergy serving dioceses, parishes, religious congregations and other church-related institutions. The purpose of the Association is to promote justice in the workplace where the Church is the employer through ethical and just standards and to provide programs and resources that assist members in developing competencies in human resource management grounded in gospel values.

National Association of Diaconate Directors (1977)

National Office, 7625 N. High St. Columbus, OH 43235-1499. Tel: 614-985-2276 Email: info@nadd.org Web: www.nadd.org Deacon Raphael Duplechain, Chm., Deacon Christopher M. Ast, Vice Chm., Deacon James D. Caruso, Sec. & Treas., Deacon Thomas R. Dubois, Exec. Dir.

NADD serves formation directors, deacon directors, vicars for deacons, and other diocesan personnel who are responsible to their bishops for the formation of deacon candidates and the continued professional development and education of deacons following ordination. The Association takes a leadership role relating to national and regional issues of the diaconate and serves as a consultant to the USCCB Committee for Clergy, Consecrated Life and Vocations. The Association leadership is comprised of an Executive Director, Executive Committee and a Board of Directors representing each of the 14 USCCB regions. NADD promotes expertise through the National Directory Institute, Ministry and Life Institute, annual conventions, regional meetings, research, newsletters, and by providing consultation teams which evaluate formation programs upon request of the ordinary.

National Association of Pastoral Musicians

National Office, 962 Wayne Ave., Ste. 210 Silver Spring, MD 20910-4461. Tel: 240-247-3000 Fax: 240-247-3001 Email: npmsing@npm.org Web: www.npm.org Mr. Steve Petrunak, Pres. & CEO, Bishop Mark J. Seitz, Episcopal Moderator

The National Association of Pastoral Musicians fosters the art of musical liturgy. The members of NPM serve the Catholic Church in the United States as musicians, clergy, liturgists, and other leaders of prayer. Regular parish membership includes both parish musicians and parish clergy. Individual membership is also available.

NPM programs include an annual national convention for musicians, clergy, and other leaders, as well as institutes for cantors, choir directors, guitarists, and ensemble musicians in addition to programs in pastoral liturgy, chant, music with children, and handbells. Several webinars are held each year on topics of interest and concern to musicians and other liturgical leaders. NPM provides a Job Hotline to assist musicians seeking employment and parishes searching for musicians. The Association also sponsors certification programs for organists, pianists, cantors, and professional directors of music ministries.

The Association is directed by a 5-member Board of Directors, advised by a 40-member NPM Council and served by a 7-person staff. There is a division for professional directors of music ministries as well as special interest sections for cantors, choir directors, organists, clergy, ensemble musicians, pianists, composers, diocesan directors of music, music educators, military musicians, campus ministers, youth, pastoral liturgy, chant, technology, and musicians serving African American parishes, Hispanic communities, Asian Pacific communities, and religious congregations.

Publications include Pastoral Music (five times annually); Pastoral Music Notebook (twice monthly by e-mail); Sunday Word for Pastoral Musicians (weekly by e-mail); The Liturgical Singer (four times annually); as well as e-newsletters for clergy and professional directors of music ministries. The NPM website provides a wealth of free resources, including access to official church documents and downloadable recordings of chants for the Mass. Additionally, online premium resources including a Digital Conservatory, NPM Academy, Planning Calendar, Choral Anthems, and Choral Practice Tracks are available to members.

National Black Catholic Clergy Caucus

Resurrection Catholic Missions, Office, 2815 Forbes Dr. Montgomery, AL 36110.

Board of Directors—Rev. Kenneth Taylor, V.F., Pres., Rev. Clarence Williams, C.PP.S., Vice Pres., Rev. Manuel B. Williams, C.R., Sec., Deacon Jerry M. Lett, Treas., Lithonia, GA, Rev. Anthony M. Bozeman, S.S.J., Immediate Past Pres., Deacon Melvin Tardy, Deacon Larry Chatmon, Rev. Maurice J. Nutt, C.Ss.R., Rev. Norman Fischer, Bro. Douglas McMillan, O.F.M- .Conv., Men Religious Representative, Baltimore, MD, Deacon Joseph Connor, Pres., NABCD, Mr. Kareem Smith, Pres., NBCSA

The National Black Catholic Clergy Caucus serves as a fraternity for Black Catholic Clergy and Religious to support the spiritual, theological, educational and ministerial growth of its members. It is a vehicle to bring the contributions of the Black Community to fruition within the Catholic Church.

National Catholic Committee on Scouting Executive Committee (1934)

1325 W. Walnut Hill Ln. P.O. Box 152079 Irving, TX 75015-2079. Fax: 972-580-2535 Bishop R. Daniel Conlon, Bishop of Joliet, IL, Episcopal Liaison, George Sparks, Past Natl. Chm. (Keller, TX), Edward Martin, Past Natl. Chm. (Medina, OH) Rev. Michael P. Hanifin, Past Natl. Chap. (Yorba Linda, CA), Rev. Kevin Smith, Past Natl. Chap. (Oyster Bay, NY), Jim Weiskircher Natl. Chm. (Spartanburg, SC), Rev. Joseph Powers, Natl. Chap. (Independence, MO)

A voluntary organization of clergy and laymen, members include a chaplain and lay chairman from all of the dioceses in the United States Conferences. It serves as an advisory committee to the Boy Scouts of America. It has the responsibility of promoting and guiding cooperative contracts between the proper authorities of the Catholic Church in the United States and the Boy Scouts of America.

National Catholic Development Conference, Inc. (1968)

734 15th St., N.W., Ste. 700, Washington, DC Tel: 202-637-0470 Web: www.ncdc.org Sr. Georgette Lehmuth, O.S.F., Pres. & CEO, Allison Hewitt, C.F.R.E., CAP, Chair, Ms. Lisa Quist, Vice Chair Mr. Ray Alcaraz, Treas., Ms. Anne Marie Gardiner, Sec.

NCDC leads the Catholic development community toward excellence in the ministry of ethical fundraising through education, resources, networking and advocacy. As the United States' largest association of religious philanthropies, NCDC affirms the mission of each of its members by working for and with them as fundraisers. The hallmark of NCDC is the promotion of the integrity of its member organizations to donors, the media and the general public. To this end, all members are required to fully adhere to the NCDC Code of Stewardship and Ethics and support the Donor Bill of Rights. Central to NCDC's existence are the many services provided to its membership: advocacy, regional seminars, the annual Conference and Exposition, informative publications, educational resources and other specialized services geared to meet member needs.

Publications: Dimensions (4 times a year); E-Newsletters: Newswire, Essentials, Breaking News, Jobs eBulletin, Workshop and Programming; Stewardship for Mission, Toward a Theology of Fundraising; A Call to Accountability: Where Donors and Mission Meet.

National Catholic Educational Association (1904)

National Headquarters, 1005 N. Glebe Ave., Ste. 525 Arlington, VA 22201. Tel: 800-711-6232 Fax: 703-243-0025 Bishop Gerald F. Kicanas, Bd. Chair, Thomas W. Burnford, D.Min., Pres./CEO

The National Catholic Educational Association (NCEA) has been providing leadership to American Catholic educators since 1904. NCEA's institutional and individual memberships represent Catholic school education in a variety of settings: preschools, elementary and secondary schools, diocesan offices and colleges and universities. NCEA is the professional membership organization for Catholic School Educators. The Association's mission is to Lead, Learn and Proclaim. It provides professional development opportunities to its members and hosts an annual convention.

National Catholic Office for the Deaf (1971)

NCOD Office, 7202 Buchanan St. Landover Hills, MD 20784-2236. Tel: 301-577-1684, VP Tel: 301-841-8209 Email: info@ncod.org Web: www.ncod.org. Rev. Shawn Carey, NCOD Bd. Pres. Rev. Msgr. Glenn L. Nelson, V.G., J.C.L.

The NCOD, established by the Catholic pastoral workers of the deaf in 1971 at Trinity College, Washington, DC is devoted to coordinating the Church's pastoral ministry to deaf and hard of hearing persons at the national level; developing special liturgies, catechetical texts and materials; organizing workshops, leadership programs, and national and regional pastoral workers meetings; coordinating a training program for ministers with the deaf; and serving as an information and referral center for all those involved in this special ministry as well as members of the deaf community and their families. Policy is established by a board of directors elected by the members.

Publication: pastoral journal, Vision.

National Catholic Partnership on Disability

415 Michigan Ave., N.E., Ste. 95 Washington, DC 20017-4501. Tel: 202-529-2933; Fax: 202-529-4678 Web: www.ncpd.org; Teletype: 202-529-2934 Ms. Janice L. Benton, O.F.S., Exec. Dir., Marsha Rivas, NCPD Chair.

Works to implement the 1978 *Pastoral Statement of U.S. Catholic Bishops on Persons with Disabilities* in parishes and dioceses across the United States. Collaborates with USCCB staff and other national Catholic organizations in advocating for disability involvement and concerns; works with other ministries of the church to enhance meaningful participation; affirms the culture of life through promoting the giftedness of all people with assorted disabilities at all stages of the life cycle. Mission is promoted through media, consultation, lectures, workshops, and regional gatherings.

National Catholic Student Coalition (1988)

45 Lovett Ave. Newark, DE 19711. Tel: 302-368-4728 Email: ncsc@catholicstudent.org Web: www.catholicstudent.org

The National Catholic Student Coalition (NCSC) is a national coalition of Catholic student communities in institutes of higher education. The coalition provides a platform for Catholic students to reflect, speak, and act on issues within the university, the Church and society. The NCSC promotes the development of campus ministry and Catholic lay and religious leaders for the Church and society. The NCSC is a member of the International Movement of Catholic Students. Membership is open to groups or individuals associated with Catholic student groups in higher education. The NCSC holds an annual leadership conference.

Publication: The Catholic Collegian.

The National Center for Urban Ethnic Affairs (1971)

National Office, P.O. Box 20, Cardinal Station Washington, DC 20064. Tel: 202-319-5128 Tel: 202-319-6188 Dr. John A. Kromkowski, Pres., Rev. Msgr. Salvatore E. Polizzi, Chm.

"The great task incumbent on all men of good will is to restore the relations of the human family in truth, in justice, in love, and in freedom." (Pope John XXIII, Peace on Earth.) The independent program of this nonprofit organization has evolved from the efforts initiated by the former Task Force on Urban Problems of the United States Catholic Conference. Its aims and purposes are to continue the expression of the Catholic Church's concern for the problems facing our urban society. NCUEA promotes the celebration of cultural pluralism in America and bridges the gaps between groups of various ethnic and cultural traditions. The Center disseminates information, conducts research, develops and supports programs concerned with ethnic Americans and urban society. The Center in association with various community and church groups develops workshops, conferences, and programs related to the quality of human life, national priorities and the development of an urban mission strategy. The Center is also associated with public and private agencies in developing urban economic, social, and intercultural programs, etc.

The National Conference for Catechetical Leadership (NCCL)

415 Michigan Ave., N.E., Ste. 110 Washington, DC 20017. Tel: 202-756-5512 Fax: 202-756-5519 Web: www.nccl.org Ken Ogorek, Pres., Margaret Matijasevic, Exec. Dir.

A voluntary organization composed of diocesan and parish catechetical personnel, academics specializing in religious education, and various associate and affiliated members, including publishers of catechetical materials. The Conference operates on three levels: national, regional and provincial. The purpose of the Conference is to promote and develop professional competence within catechetical leadership and to assist its members in their roles as leaders in the Church's catechetical ministry through networking, resource development, research, training, consultation and advocacy. The Conference is committed to collaboration with other national groups concerned with catechesis/religious education as a means of expanding and coordinating a service to catechetical ministry.

National Conference of Catholic Airport Chaplains (NCCAC)

Chicago O'Hare International Airport, P.O. Box 66353 Chicago, IL 60666-0353. Tel: 773-686-2636 Fax: 773-686-0130 Email: office@nccac.us Web: www.nccac.us Rev. Michael G. Zaniolo, S.T.L., C.A.C., Pres. (Chicago O'Hare International Airport), Rev. Canon Philip S. Majka, Vice Pres. (Dulles International Airport), Ms. Susan E. Schneider, C.A.P., Sec. (Chicago O'Hare International Airport), Deacon Ray Oden, Treas. (Houston Bush Intercontinental Airport), Archbishop Jerome E. Listecki, Archbishop of Milwaukee, Episcopal Liaison

This Conference provides support and communication for all Catholics performing pastoral ministry to airport & airline workers, and travelers; in affiliation with USCCB Secretariat of Cultural Diversity in the Church, Subcommittee on Pastoral Care of Migrants, Refugees and Travelers.

National Council of Catholic Women

200 N. Glebe Rd., Ste. 725 Arlington, VA 22203. Tel: 703-224-0990 Fax: 703-224-0991 Email: nccw01@nccw.org Web: www.nccw.org Mary Elizabeth Stewart, Pres., Andrea Cecilli, Admin.

The NCCW consists of Catholic women's organizations in the United States, numbering 4,000+ local, diocesan, national organizations and 2,500+ individual members. It delivers programs through Spirituality, Leadership and Service Commissions and the Annual Convention.

Publications: quarterly, Catholic Woman; monthly, e-newsletter NCCW Connect.

National Federation for Catholic Youth Ministry, Inc. (NFCYM) (1981)

415 Michigan Ave., N.E., Ste. 40 Washington, DC 20017-4502. Tel: 202-636-3825 Email: info@nfcym.org Web: www.nfcym.org Bishop Frank J. Caggiano, D.D., S.T.D., V.G., Episcopal Advisor, Ms. Christina Lamas, MSW, Exec. Dir., Mr. Mark Graveline, Chair.

A membership association of diocesan youth offices and collaborating organizations, founded after a reorganization of the USCC Department of Education and the National CYO Federation. The NFCYM fosters the development of youth ministry in the "United States to, with, by, and for youth." The NFYCM mission is "support and strengthen those who accompany young people as they encounter and follow Jesus Christ". Members of the Federation work through diocesan, regional and national structures to provide national leadership, resources and vision for adults and youth in youth ministry. Key services include the biennial National Conference on Catholic Youth Ministry (for adults working with youth); the biennial National Catholic Youth Conference (for teenagers and their adult chaperones); the development of resources for parish workers; religious recognitions for Catholic Girl Scouts/Camp Fire; position papers on current topics and issues in youth ministry; regional and diocesan consultations and programs for diocesan youth ministry leaders.

National Organization for Continuing Education of Roman Catholic Clergy, Inc. (NOCERCC)

13 Crotona Ct. Timonium, MD 21093. Tel: 410-978-3676 Fax: 410-752-2703 Email: nocercc@nocercc.org Web: www.nocercc.org Rev. Thomas M. Dragga, D.Min., Pres., Rev. Raymond McHenry, M.B.A., Vice Pres. Membership at Large, Rev. James E. Myers, P.S.S., M.Div., Mrs. Karla Cross, M.Ed., Rev. Randy Cuevas, S.T.L., S.T.B., B.A., Mr. Uli Schmitt, M.Div.

Founded in 1973, The National Organization for Continuing Education of Roman Catholic Clergy (NOCERCC) is a membership association of dioceses and religious communities and other interested organizations and individuals committed to the Church's mission to promote and support ongoing formation for priests and presbyterates. Professional and formational services offered include an annual convention; programs that dioceses and religious communities can host for clergy and other pastoral ministers; a monthly newsletter; and other practical resources in diverse media.

Publications: Handbook for Directors of Ongoing Formation of Priests, Renewing Sunday Preaching.

National Pastoral Center for the Chinese Apostolate, Inc.

Sacred Heart of Jesus, 4201 14th St. Plano, TX 75074. Tel: 972-516-8500 Rev. Vincent Lin Yu Ming, Dir.

North American Pastoral Center for Czech Catholics

344 Koch Ave. Placentia, CA 92870-1928. Tel: 714-524-0092 Fax: 714-637-6789 Bishop Peter Esterka, Pres.

The Papal Foundation

Office, 150 Monument Rd., Ste. 609 Bala Cynwyd, PA 19004. Tel: 610-535-6340 Fax: 610-535-6343 Mr. James V. Coffey, M.A., Vice Pres. Advancement

Cardinal Members—Cardinal Donald Wuerl, Chm., Cardinal Samuel Aquila, Cardinal Daniel N. DiNardo, Cardinal Wilton D. Gregory, Cardinal Timothy M. Dolan, Cardinal Roger Mahony, D.D., Cardinal Adam Maida, Cardinal Theodore McCarrick, Cardinal Sean Patrick O'Malley, Cardinal Justin Rigali

Trustees—Archbishop Jose H. Gomez, S.T.D., Bishop Michael J. Bransfield, Pres., Bishop Richard F. Stika, Bishop David Allen Zubik, Frank J. Hanna, III, James Longon, Patricia Lynch, Eustace Mita, Wayne W. Murdy, Treas., James A. Nolen, III, J. Eustace Wolfington

The Parish Evaluation Project

3073 S. Chase Ave., Ste. 320 Milwaukee, WI 53207. Tel: 414-483-7370; 414-520-3465 Fax: 414-483-7380 Email: pep@pitnet.net Web: www.pepparish.org Rev. Thomas P. Sweetser, S.J., Dir.

The Parish Evaluation Project is a nonprofit organization under the laws of Wisconsin, whose purpose is to provide religious and educational services to Catholic parishes in the United States in the areas of surveying, needs assessment, leadership skills, goal setting, evaluation techniques, staff development, pastoral council formation and other resources helpful in parish planning and renewal.

Pax Christi U.S.A., National Catholic Peace Movement

415 Michigan Ave., N.E., Ste. 240, Washington, DC 20017-4502. Tel: 202-635-2741; Email: info@paxchristiusa.org. Sr. Patricia Chappell, Exec. Dir., Sr. Anne-Louise Nadeau, Dir. of Programs, Rachel Schmidt, Communication Coord., Myron Ford, Office Mgr., Robert Shine, Council Chair, Jean Stokan, Vice-Chair, Isaac Chandler, Sec., Brian Ashmankas, Treas., Bishop John Stowe, Bishop Pres.

Pax Christi USA is a national Catholic peace Justice movement, reaching more than half of the Catholics in the U.S. each year. Membership includes: regional groups, local chapters, religious communities, parishes, college campuses, U.S. bishops and clergy. Pax Christi USA is a section of Pax Christi International, with consultative status at the United Nations.

Publications: Peace Current, Advent & Lenten booklets along with peace education materials.

Religious Brothers Conference

National Office, 233 S. Wacker Dr., 84th Fl. Chicago, IL 60606. Tel: 866-339-0371 Fax: 866-339-0371 Email: rbc@todaysbrother.com Web: www.todaysbrother.com

Board of Directors—Bro. Daniel Magner, C.M.F., Bro. Nich Perez, C.S.C., Bro. Andres Rivera, S.T., Bro. Stephen Glodek, S.M., Pres., Bro. David Eubank, M.S., Bro. John Skrodinsky, S.T., Bro. Peter O'Loughlin, C.F.C., Bro. Chris Patino, F.S.C., Bro. William Boslet, O.S.F., Exec. Sec., Bro. Allen Pacquing, S.M., Bro. Albert Rivera, F.M.S.

Publications for members: Archival Editions of: Brothers' Voice; Reflections.

Religious Formation Conference

National Office, 5401 S. Cornell Ave., Ste. 304 Chicago, IL 60615. Tel: 773-675-8362 Fax: 773-675-6187 Sr. Ellen Dauwer, S.C., Ph.D., Exec. Dir., Sr. Noreen Walter, SCL, Chm.

A national Roman Catholic organization which assists women and men religious who are engaged in the ministry of initial and on-going formation in their congregations.

The Resource Center for Religious Institutes

8824 Cameron St. Silver Spring, MD 20910. Tel: 301-589-8143 Fax: 301-589-2897 Email: trcri@trcri.org Web: www.trcri.org Sr. Sharon A. Euart, R.S.M., J.C.D., Exec. Dir.

Serves its members institutes by providing integrated education, advocacy, consultation and collaborative initiatives to support religious institutes in meeting their current and emerging stewardship responsibilities.

The Slovak Catholic Federation (1911)

304 S. Elmer Ave. Sayre, PA 18840. Tel: 570-888-9641 Email: ahvoz87@gmail.com Web: www.slovakcatholicfederation.org Rev. Andrew S. Hvozdovic, M.Div., Pres., Rt. Rev. Gary A. Hoover, O.S.B., Mod., Rev. Msgr. Thomas A. Derzack, M.Div., Spiritual Dir., Dolores M. Evanko, Sec. & Treas.

Founded by Father Joseph Murgas at Wilkes-Barre, Pennsylvania as a nonprofit corporation to promote and coordinate religious and social activities among Slovak Catholic fraternal benefit societies, religious communities, Slovak parishes and individuals in order to address the pastoral needs of Slovak Catholics at home and abroad.

United States Catholic Mission Association

415 Michigan Ave., N.E., Ste. 102 Washington, DC 20017-4502. Tel: 202-832-3112 Fax: 202-832- 3688 Email: uscma@uscatholicmission.org Web: www.uscatholicmission.org Rev. Gregory Gallagher, O.M.I., Pres., Dr. Donald McCrabb, D.Min., Exec. Dir.

The USCMA was juridically established September 1, 1981. Its members include U.S. missioners, mission organizations, diocesan mission offices, and others concerned about the mission of the Church and global solidarity. It provides members opportunities to convene, connect and collaborate on efforts to animate missionary disciples and accompany them through recruitment, preparation, service, integration and leadership. USCMA activities include a national conference that highlights specific mission themes and issues, liaison and cooperation with missionary bodies of other Christian churches. USMA conducts research on mission sending organizations and missionaries for the U.S. Church.

Publications: monthly newsletter; quarterly journal; study guides; educational programs.

NATIONAL ORGANIZATIONS WITH INDIVIDUAL I.R.S. RULINGS

Beginning Experience International Ministry Inc.

395 W. Avon Rd. Avon, CT 06001. Tel: 574-283-0279 Tel: 866-610-8877 Fax: 877-296-0856 Email: imc@beginningexperience.org Web: www.beginningexperience.org Bishop Patrick J. Zurek, D.D., Episcopal Moderator, Yvonne Stoops, Exec. Dir., Brenda Sznaka, Pres., Jay Fredrick, Treas. & Sec.

The Beginning Experience ministry offers a copyrighted weekend program to help divorced, separated and widowed persons, as well as their families, work through the trauma of the loss of their spouse and make a new beginning in life. The program was designed by and for Catholics and has its roots in sound Catholic tradition and the sacramental life of the Church. True to the ecumenical spirit in the Church since Vatican II, it has always been open to persons of all faiths. The Beginning Experience weekend originated in 1974 with the efforts of Sr. Josephine Stewart & Jo Lamia in Fort Worth, TX. It has spread throughout the United States as well as other countries. Trained teams make the Beginning Experience weekend available on a regular basis. The ministry also serves as an informational and materials resource for the establishment of support groups to minister to the needs of the divorced, separated and widowed and their families at various points in their grief process.

Canon Law Society of America

415 Michigan Ave., N.E., Ste. 101 Washington, DC 20017. Tel: 202-832-2350 Fax: 202-832-2331 Email: info@clsa.org. Rev. Msgr. John J.M. Foster, J.C.D., Pres., Zabrina R. Decker, J.C.D., Vice Pres., Timothy Olson, J.C.L., Sec., Nancy Reynolds, S.P., J.C.L., Treas., Rev. Patrick J. Cogan, S.A., J.C.D., Exec. Coord.; Colleen Crawford, Gen. Sec.

A membership association of Bishops, Clergy, Religious and Laity for the purpose of promoting research and professional collaboration in the area of Canon Law.

Catholic Engaged Encounter, Inc.

4239 Shirley Rd. Richmond, VA 23225. Tel: 800-339-9790 Jim Dyk, Sandy Dyk, Rev. Jay Biber

Catholic Library Association

8550 United Plaza Blvd., Ste. 1001 Baton Rouge, LA 70809. Tel: 225-408-4417 Fax: 225-408-4422 Email: cla2@cathla.org Web: www.cathla.org

The Catholic Mutual Relief Society of America

10843 Old Mill Rd. Omaha, NE 68154-2600. Tel: 402-551-8765 Mr. Michael Intrieri, Pres. & CEO, Mr. Paul Peterson, Exec. Vice Pres. & COO

The Catholic Relief Insurance Company of America

76 St. Paul St., Ste. 500 Burlington, VT 05401. Tel: 402-551-8765 Mr. Michael Intrieri, Pres., Mr. Paul Peterson, Vice Pres.

Conference for Pastoral Planning and Council Development

P.O. Box 3523 Schenectady, NY 12303. Tel: 518-859-4506. Email: cppcd@cppcd.org Web: www.cppcd.org. Dr. Catherine Butel, Chair, Debra Trulli-Cassale, Admin. Dir.

National Association for Lay Ministry (NALM)

National Office, 5401 S. Cornell Ave. Chicago, IL 60615. Tel: 773-595-4042 Email: nalm@nalm.org Web: www.nalm.org

The National Association for Lay Ministry (NALM) is a collaborative organization of lay, vowed religious, and ordained ministers that empowers, advocates for, and develops lay pastoral leadership and promotes the growth of lay pastoral ministry in the Catholic Church. The organization also provides a national voice for Catholic lay ministry. NALM's membership is drawn from the more than 40,000 lay ecclesial ministers who devote their lives to the Church by working in parishes and dioceses. Other members are students preparing for ministry. Still others live out their baptismal call as generous volunteers to the Church. NALM has a long tradition of support from bishops, priests, deacons, publishers and academic institutions. Each, in its own way, collaborates with NALM to promote the empowerment of the laity in the Catholic Church.

NALM led the Emerging Models of Pastoral Leadership project. This project was one of the largest research efforts to examine the changing nature of parish life in the United States. In addition, NALM and its partners in the Alliance for the Certification of Lay Ecclesial Ministers, have promulgated and published National Certification Standards for Lay Ecclesial Ministers. In 2012, the Alliance implemented a national certification process for lay ecclesial ministers.

The National Catholic Risk Retention Group, Inc.

National Office, 801 Warrenville Rd., Ste. 175 Lisle, IL 60532-4334. Tel: 630-725-0986 Tel: 877-486-2774 Fax: 630-725-1374 Dennis H. O'Hara, ARM, Pres. & CEO, Rev. Jay C. Haskin, M.Ch.A., Chm.

Bd., Mr. John M. Scholl, C.P.C.U., A.I.M., Vice Pres., Mr. John J. Maxwell, CPA, Treas.

The Company is wholly owned by 52 Catholic (Arch) Dioceses and one Catholic Risk Pooling Trust. It underwrites excess liability insurance for Dioceses and other Church organizations listed in the Official Catholic Directory. Coverage is always subject to a minimum self-insured retention or underlying coverage of $250,000. Maximum limits of coverage available are $14,750,000. The company has the capability to underwrite insurance in all states, Territories and Possessions of the U.S.

National Catholic Young Adult Ministry Association

National Office, 415 Michigan Ave., N.E., Ste. 40 Washington, DC 20017. Email: info@ncyama.org Web: www.ncyama.org Amy McEntee, Exec. Dir.

Founded in 1982, NCYAMA is an organization supporting those who minister to and with single and married people in their late teens, twenties or thirties. We develop and promote programs and resources while providing opportunities for networking and communication. We advocate for the full integration of young adults in the life of the Catholic faith community in order to connect them with Jesus, the Church, the mission of the Church and their peers.

Publication: electronic newsletter.

National Conference of Diocesan Vocation Directors (1962)

National Office, 440 W. Neck Rd. Huntington, NY 11743. Tel: 631-645-8210 Fax: 631-812-0249 Email: office@ncdvd.org Web: www.ncdvd.org Rev. Christopher Martin, Pres., Rev. Michael M. Simone, S.T.L., Treas., Mrs. Rosemary C. Sullivan, Exec. Dir.

NCDVD is a professional organization that supports, educates and provides resources for diocesan vocation directors as they promote all Church vocations, but particularly diocesan priesthood. This organization serves all dioceses associated with the United States Conference of Catholic Bishops.

Online resources; documents of interest & training institutes; Meetings annually for Regional Conferences and a National Convention.

The National Federation of Priests' Councils (1968)

National Office, 333 N. Michigan Ave., Ste. 1114 Chicago, IL 60601-4002. Tel: 312-442-9700 Tel: 888-271-6372 Email: nfpc@nfpc.org Web: www.nfpc. org Rev. Anthony Cutcher, Pres., Mr. Terry Oldes, Financial Dir., Mr. Alan Szafraniec, Mng. Dir., Connie Awrey, Communications Dir.

The NFPC promotes the communion, brotherhood and solidarity of priests and bishops through the arch/diocesan priests' councils, offering services to support and facilitate communication between councils. NFPC is a clearinghouse for arch/dioceses promoting the sharing of knowledge and resources; offers advocacy for priests with the USCCB as a contributing organization to the Clergy, Consecrated Life and Vocations Committee; offers programs and publications on research and best practices; edits, condenses and shares information from Councils' minutes; partners with other national Catholic organizations; and offers an annual National Convocation of Priests to encourage fraternity, idea exchange, fellowship, and rejuvenation. All arch/diocesan priests' councils are members of NFPC; active members support NFPC financially. A Council of Consultors and a Board of Directors determine the direction of the organization, which is implemented by the NFPC President during a 5-year term.

Publications: NFPC This Week e-letter; Touchstone periodical; Income Tax for Priests Clergy (updated each year); and research results: Same Call Different Men and The Laborer is Worthy of His Hire.

National Service Committee of the Catholic Charismatic Renewal of the United States, Inc.

P.O. Box 628 Locust Grove, VA 22508-0628. Mr. Ron Riggins, Chm., Walter Matthews, Exec. Dir.

Our focus is to foster baptism in the Holy Spirit in the life of the Church in the United States and throughout the world, to broaden and deepen the understanding that baptism in the Holy Spirit is the Christian inheritance of all, and to strengthen the Catholic Charismatic Renewal. The National Service Committee has established and supported numerous programs to help further our mission. Some of the activities and programs include the establishment of Chariscenter USA, which serves as the national headquarters for our committee and a national office for the Catholic Charismatic Renewal.

Publications: Magazine, "Pentecost Today"; Leaders' training materials as well as an annual national conference, outreach to young adults & young adult leaders and evangelization training. The NSC has supported the International Catholic Charismatic Renewal Office in Rome.

Worldwide Marriage Encounter

275 W. Hospitality Ln., Ste. 102 San Bernardino, CA 92408. Tel: 909-3332-7309 Fax: 909-332-7409 Email: wwmeoffice1968@gmail.com

Secretariat Team—Rev. Emile Frische, M.H.M., Anthony Witczak, Catherine Witczak

Organized to foster a program of Christian information to instruct married couples in the means to find God's plan and matrimony in their lives, for their own spiritual development and the betterment of all humankind; and to develop, foster and disseminate an adult catechesis supporting, furthering and building upon such instruction. Worldwide Marriage Encounter offers the marriage encounter weekend experience in 150 dioceses in the United States as well as in 88 foreign countries. In the United States over 1,500,000 couples and over 5,000 priests and bishops have experienced the Worldwide weekend.

Publication: EMatrimony online at ematrimony.org.

MISCELLANEOUS

Catholic Committee for Refugees & Children

3211 Fourth St., N.E. Washington, DC 20017-1194. Fax: 202-722-8755 Ambassador Johnny Young, Pres.

Incorporated since 1954, the Catholic Committee for Refugees and Children was founded to counsel and cooperate with European refugees during and after World War II. Since that time its mission has been expanded to include service to refugees worldwide. It has a special mandate from the bishops concerning its work with children through international child welfare, child care or placement, and international adoption. The USCCB Committee on Migration serves as the Board of Directors for CCRC.

Alphabetical List of Places in the United States

This comprehensive list includes all cities and towns in the United States in which a Catholic Institution is located.

The abbreviations identify each city or town to the corresponding Diocese or Archdiocese.

Abbeville, LA	LAF
SC	CHR
Abbott, TX	FWT
Abbottstown, PA	HBG
Aberdeen, MD	BAL
MS	JKS
SD	SFS
WA	SEA
Abernathy, TX	LUB
Abilene, KS	SAL
TX	SAN
Abingdon, IL	PEO
MD	BAL
VA	RIC
Abington, MA	BO
PA	PH
PA	SYM
Abiquiu, NM	SFE
Abita Springs, LA	NO
Absecon, NJ	CAM
Acme, MI	GLD
Acton, MA	BO
ME	PRT
Acushnet, MA	FR
Acworth, GA	ATL
Ada, MI	GR
MN	CR
OH	COL
OK	OKL
Adams, MA	SPR
MN	WIN
NY	OG
WI	LC
Adamsville, AL	BIR
Addison, IL	JOL
NY	ROC
Adel, GA	SAV
IA	DM
Adelanto, CA	SB
Adelphi, MD	WDC
Adena, OH	STU
Adrian, MI	LAN
MN	WIN
Advance, MO	SPC
Affton, MO	STL
Agawam, MA	SPR
Agua Dulce, TX	CC
Aguilar, CO	PBL
Ahoskie, NC	R
Aiea, HI	HON
Aiken, SC	CHR
Ainsworth, NE	GI
Aitkin, MN	DUL
Ajo, AZ	TUC
Akron, CO	DEN
NY	BUF
OH	CLV
OH	SJP
OH	NTN
Alakanuk, AK	FBK
Alameda, CA	OAK
Alamo, TX	BWN
Alamogordo, NM	LSC
Alamosa, CO	PBL
Albany, CA	OAK
GA	SAV
IL	RCK
KY	L
LA	BR
MN	SCL
NY	ALB
OR	P
TX	FWT
Albemarle, NC	CHL
Albers, IL	BEL
Albert Lea, MN	WIN
Albertville, MN	STP
Albia, IA	DAV
Albion, IN	FTW
MI	KAL
NE	OM
NY	BUF
PA	E
RI	PRO
Albuquerque, NM	HPM
NM	SFE
Alburgh, VT	BUR
Alcoa, TN	KNX
Alden, NY	BUF
Aledo, IL	PEO
TX	FWT
Alexander City, AL	BIR
Alexandria, IN	LFT
KY	COV
LA	ALX
MN	SCL
SD	SFS
VA	ARL
VA	WDC
Alexandria Bay, NY	OG
Alfred, ME	PRT
NY	BUF
Algoma, WI	GB
Algona, IA	SC
Algonquin, IL	RCK
Alhambra, CA	LA
Alice, TX	CC
Aliquippa, PA	PBR
PA	PIT
PA	SJP
Aliso Viejo, CA	ORG
Allegan, MI	KAL
Allegany, NY	BUF
Allen, TX	DAL
Allen Park, MI	DET
MI	PRM
Allendale, MI	GR
NJ	NEW
Allenspark, CO	DEN
Allenton, MI	DET
WI	MIL
Allentown, NJ	TR
PA	ALN
PA	OLD
PA	PSC
Alleyton, TX	VIC
Alliance, NE	GI
OH	Y
Allison Park, PA	PIT
Allston, MA	BO
Alma, MI	SAG
Alma Center, WI	LC
Almond, WI	LC
Aloha, OR	P
Alpena, MI	GLD
Alpha, NJ	MET
Alpharetta, GA	ATL
Alpine, AZ	GLP
CA	SD
TX	ELP
Alsip, IL	CHI
Alta Loma, CA	SB
Altadena, CA	LA
Altamont, IL	SFD
NY	ALB
Altamonte Springs, FL	ORL
Alton, IA	SC
IL	SFD
TX	BWN
Altona, NY	OG
Altoona, IA	DM
PA	ALT
PA	SJP
WI	LC
Alturas, CA	SAC
Altus, AR	LR
OK	OKL
Alva, OK	OKL
Alvin, TX	GAL
Alviso, CA	SJ
Ama, LA	NO
Amargosa Valley, NV	LAV
Amarillo, TX	AMA
Ambia, IN	LFT
Ambler, PA	PH
Amboy, IL	RCK
Ambridge, PA	PBR
PA	PIT
PA	SJP
Amelia, LA	HT
OH	CIN
Amenia, NY	NY
American Canyon, CA	SR
American Falls, ID	B
American Fork, UT	SLC
Americus, GA	SAV
Amery, WI	SUP
Ames, IA	DUB
Amesbury, MA	BO
Amherst, MA	SPR
NY	BUF
OH	CLV
VA	RIC
WI	LC
Amite, LA	BR
Amity, OR	P
Amityville, NY	RVC
Amory, MS	JKS
Amsterdam, NY	ALB
NY	STF
OH	STU
Anaconda, MT	HEL
Anacortes, WA	SEA
Anacostia, Washington, DC	WDC
Anadarko, OK	OKL
Anaheim, CA	HPM
CA	ORG
Anahuac, TX	BEA
Anamoose, ND	FAR
Anamosa, IA	DUB
Anchorage, AK	ANC
AK	HPM
Andale, KS	WCH
Andalusia, AL	MOB
IL	PEO
Anderson, CA	SAC
IN	LFT
SC	CHR
TX	GAL
Andover, KS	WCH
MA	BO
NJ	PAT
NY	BUF
OH	Y
Andrews, NC	CHL
TX	SAN
Angels Camp, CA	STO
Angleton, TX	GAL
Angola, IN	FTW
NY	BUF
Angus, MN	CR
Aniak, AK	FBK
Ankeny, IA	DM
Ann Arbor, MI	LAN
MI	OLL
Anna, IL	BEL
OH	CIN
Annandale, MN	STP
NJ	MET
VA	ARL
VA	PSC
Annapolis, MD	BAL
Annawan, IL	PEO
Anniston, AL	BIR
Annville, PA	HBG
Anoka, MN	STP
Anson, TX	LUB
Ansonia, CT	HRT
CT	STF
Anthem, AZ	PHX
Anthony, NM	LSC
Antigo, WI	GB
Antioch, CA	OAK
IL	CHI
TN	NSH
Anton Chico, NM	SFE
Antonito, CO	PBL
Anza, CA	SB
Apache Junction, AZ	TUC
Apalachicola, FL	PT
Apex, NC	R
NC	SYM
Apollo, PA	GBG
Apopka, FL	ORL
FL	SJP
Apple Creek, MO	STL
Apple Valley, CA	SB
Applegate, CA	SAC
Appleton, MN	NU
WI	GB
Appomattox, VA	RIC
Aptos, CA	MRY
Aransas Pass, TX	CC
Arbor Vitae, WI	SUP
Arcade, NY	BUF
Arcadia, CA	LA
FL	VEN
WI	LC
Arcata, CA	SR
Archbald, PA	SCR
Archbold, OH	TOL
Arcola, IL	SFD
Arden, NC	CHL
Ardmore, OK	OKL
PA	PH
Ardsley, NY	NY
PA	PH
Argo, IL	CHI
Argusville, ND	FAR
Argyle, MN	CR
MO	JC
TX	FWT
Arkadelphia, AR	LR
Arkansas City, KS	WCH
Arkansaw, WI	LC
Arlington, MA	BO
MN	NU
SD	SFS
TX	FWT
TX	POC
VA	ARL
VT	BUR
WA	SEA
Arlington Heights, IL	CHI
Arma, KS	WCH
Armada, MI	DET
Armonk, NY	NY
Armour, SD	SFS
Armstrong, IA	SC
Armstrong Creek, WI	GB
Arnaudville, LA	LAF
Arnold, MO	STL
PA	SJP
Arroyo Grande, CA	MRY
Arroyo Seco, NM	SFE
Artesia, CA	LA
NM	LSC
Arvada, CO	DEN
CO	SYM
Arvin, CA	FRS
Asbury Park, NJ	TR
Ash Fork, AZ	PHX
Ashaway, RI	PRO
Ashburn, VA	ARL
Ashburnham, MA	WOR
Ashdown, AR	LR
Asheboro, NC	CHL
Asherton, TX	LAR
Asheville, NC	CHL
Ashford, CT	NOR
Ashfork, AZ	PHX
Ashkum, IL	JOL
Ashland, IL	SFD
KS	DOD
KY	LEX
MA	BO
MT	GF
NE	LIN
OH	CLV
OR	P
PA	ALN
VA	RIC

WI	SUP
Ashland City, TN	NSH
Ashley, PA	SCR
Ashtabula, OH	Y
Ashton, IA	SC
Aspen, CO	DEN
Aspinwall, PA	PIT
Assonet, MA	FR
Assumption, IL	SFD
Aston, PA	PH
Astoria, NY	BRK
OR	P
Atascadero, CA	MRY
CA	NTN
Atchison, KS	KCK
Atco, NJ	CAM
Athens, AL	BIR
GA	ATL
NY	ALB
OH	STU
TN	KNX
TX	TYL
WI	LC
WV	WH
Atherton, CA	SFR
Athol, MA	WOR
Athol Springs, NY	BUF
Atkins, AR	LR
Atkinson, IL	PEO
NE	OM
Atlanta, GA	ATL
GA	NTN
GA	SAM
TX	TYL
Atlantic, IA	DM
Atlantic Beach, FL	STA
Atlantic City, NJ	CAM
Atlantic Highlands, NJ	TR
Atmore, AL	MOB
Attica, IN	LFT
NY	BUF
OH	TOL
Attleboro, MA	FR
Attleboro Falls, MA	FR
Atwater, CA	FRS
Atwood, KS	SAL
Au Sable Forks, NY	OG
AuGres, MI	SAG
Auburn, AL	MOB
CA	SAC
IA	SC
IL	SFD
IN	FTW
KY	OWN
MA	WOR
ME	PRT
MI	SAG
NE	LIN
NH	MAN
NY	ROC
WA	SEA
Auburn Hills, MI	DET
Auburndale, WI	LC
Audubon, IA	DM
PA	PH
Augusta, GA	NTN
GA	SAV
KS	WCH
KY	COV
ME	PRT
MI	KAL
MO	STL
Ault, CO	DEN
Aumsville, OR	P
Auriesville, NY	ALB
Aurora, CO	DEN
IL	JOL
IL	ROM
IL	RCK
IN	IND
MN	DUL
MO	SPC
NE	LIN
NY	ROC
OH	Y
Austin, MN	WIN
TX	AUS
TX	OLL
Austintown, OH	Y
Ava, MO	SPC
Avalon, CA	LA
NJ	CAM
Ave Maria, FL	VEN
Avella, PA	PBR
PA	PIT
Avenal, CA	FRS
Avenel, NJ	MET
Avenue, MD	WDC
Averill Park, NY	ALB
Avilla, IN	FTW
Aviston, IL	BEL

Avoca, IA	DM
PA	SCR
Avon, CT	HRT
MA	BO
MN	SCL
NY	ROC
OH	CLV
Avon By The Sea, NJ	TR
Avon Lake, OH	CLV
Avon Park, FL	VEN
Avondale, AZ	OLD
AZ	PHX
CO	PBL
LA	NO
PA	PH
Avonmore, PA	GBG
Axtell, KS	KCK
Ayrshire, IA	SC
Aztec, NM	GLP
Azusa, CA	LA
Babbitt, MN	DUL
Babylon, NY	RVC
Bad Axe, MI	SAG
Baden, PA	PIT
Bagdad, AZ	PHX
Bagley, MN	CR
Bailey, CO	COS
Baileys Harbor, WI	GB
Baileyville, KS	KCK
Bainbridge, GA	SAV
NY	SY
Bainbridge Island, WA	SEA
Bairdford, PA	PIT
Baker, MT	GF
Baker City, OR	BAK
Bakersfield, CA	FRS
Bakerstown, PA	PIT
Bala Cynwyd, PA	PH
Baldwin, KS	KCK
LA	LAF
MI	GR
NY	RVC
Baldwin City, KS	KCK
Baldwin Park, CA	LA
Baldwinsville, NY	SY
Baldwinville, MA	WOR
Ball, LA	ALX
Ballinger, TX	SAN
Ballston Lake, NY	ALB
Ballston Spa, NY	ALB
Ballwin, MO	STL
Bally, PA	ALN
Balmorhea, TX	ELP
Balsam Lake, WI	SUP
Baltic, CT	NOR
Baltimore, MD	BAL
MD	PHU
MD	POC
MD	SYM
MD	PSC
Bancroft, IA	SC
Bandera, TX	SAT
Bandon, OR	P
Bangor, ME	PRT
MI	KAL
PA	ALN
WI	LC
Banks, OR	P
Bannister, MI	SAG
Banquete, TX	CC
Bantam, CT	HRT
Baptistown, NJ	MET
Bar Harbor, ME	PRT
Baraboo, WI	MAD
Barberton, OH	CLV
OH	PRM
Barbourville, KY	LEX
Bardonia, NY	NY
Bardstown, KY	L
Bardwell, KY	OWN
Barefoot Bay, FL	ORL
Barhamsville, VA	RIC
Bark River, MI	MAR
Barker, NY	BUF
Barling, AR	LR
Barnegat, NJ	TR
Barnesville, MD	WDC
MN	CR
OH	STU
PA	ALN
Barnwell, SC	CHR
Barre, VT	BUR
Barrett Station, TX	GAL
Barrington, IL	CHI
RI	PRO
Barron, WI	SUP
Barrow, AK	FBK
Barryville, NY	NY
Barstow, CA	SB
Bartelso, IL	BEL
Bartlesville, OK	TLS

Bartlett, IL	CHI
TN	MEM
Barton, VT	BUR
Bartonville, IL	PEO
Bartow, FL	ORL
Bascom, OH	TOL
Basehor, KS	KCK
Basile, LA	LAF
Basking Ridge, NJ	MET
Bassfield, MS	BLX
Bastrop, LA	SHP
TX	AUS
Batavia, IL	RCK
NY	BUF
OH	CIN
Batesburg–Leesville, SC	CHR
Batesville, AR	LR
IN	IND
MS	JKS
Bath, NY	ROC
OH	CLV
PA	ALN
Bathgate, ND	FAR
Baton Rouge, LA	BR
LA	LKC
Battle Creek, MI	KAL
NE	OM
Battle Ground, WA	SEA
Battle Lake, MN	SCL
Battle Mountain, NV	RNO
Baudette, MN	CR
Baxley, GA	SAV
Bay City, MI	PRM
MI	SAG
TX	VIC
Bay Head, NJ	TR
Bay Minette, AL	MOB
Bay Point, CA	OAK
Bay Shore, NY	RVC
Bay St. Louis, MS	BLX
Bay Village, OH	CLV
Bayard, NM	LSC
Bayfield, WI	SUP
Bayonne, NJ	NEW
NJ	OLD
NJ	PSC
Bayou La Batre, AL	MOB
Bayport, MN	STP
Bayside, NY	BRK
Baytown, TX	GAL
Bayville, NJ	TR
NY	RVC
Beach, ND	BIS
Beacon, NY	NY
Beacon Falls, CT	HRT
Bear, DE	SYM
DE	WIL
Bear Creek, PA	SCR
Beardsley, MN	NU
Beardstown, IL	SFD
Beatrice, NE	LIN
Beattie, KS	KCK
Beattyville, KY	LEX
Beaufort, SC	CHR
Beaumont, CA	SB
TX	BEA
Beaver, PA	PBR
PA	PIT
Beaver Crossing, NE	LIN
Beaver Dam, AZ	PHX
KY	OWN
WI	MIL
Beaver Falls, PA	PIT
Beaver Island, MI	GLD
Beaver Meadows, PA	PSC
Beavercreek, OH	CIN
Beaverdale, PA	PBR
Beaverton, OR	P
OR	OLL
Beaverville, IL	JOL
Beckemeyer, IL	BEL
Beckley, WV	WH
Bedford, IN	IND
MA	BO
NH	MAN
NY	NY
OH	CLV
OH	PRM
PA	ALT
TX	FWT
VA	RIC
Bee, NE	LIN
Beebe, AR	LR
Beech Grove, IN	IND
Beemer, NE	OM
Beeville, TX	CC
Bel Air, MD	BAL
Bel Aire, KS	WCH
Belchertown, MA	SPR
Belcourt, ND	FAR
Belding, MI	GR

Belen, NM	SFE
Belfield, ND	BIS
ND	STN
Belgrade, MN	SCL
MT	HEL
Bell City, LA	LKC
Bell Gardens, CA	LA
Bella Vista, AR	LR
Bellaire, MI	GLD
OH	STU
Belle, MO	JC
WV	WH
Belle Chasse, LA	NO
Belle Fontaine, AL	MOB
Belle Fourche, SD	RC
Belle Glade, FL	PMB
Belle Harbor, NY	BRK
Belle Plaine, MN	STP
Belle Rose, LA	BR
Belle Vernon, PA	GBG
Belleair, FL	SP
Bellefontaine, OH	CIN
Bellefonte, PA	ALT
Bellerose, NY	BRK
Belleview, FL	ORL
Belleville, IL	BEL
KS	SAL
MI	DET
NJ	NEW
WI	MAD
Bellevue, IA	DUB
KY	COV
NE	OM
OH	TOL
PA	PIT
WA	SEA
Bellflower, CA	LA
Bellingham, MA	BO
WA	SEA
Bellmawr, NJ	CAM
Bellmore, NY	RVC
Bellows Falls, VT	BUR
Bellport, NY	RVC
Bellville, TX	GAL
Bellwood, IL	CHI
IL	SYM
NE	LIN
PA	ALT
Belmar, NJ	TR
Belmont, CA	SFR
MA	BO
MA	OLN
MI	GR
NC	CHL
NH	MAN
NY	BUF
WI	MAD
Beloit, KS	SAL
WI	MAD
WI	MIL
Belpre, KS	DOD
Belt, MT	GF
Belton, MO	KC
TX	AUS
Beltsville, MD	PSC
MD	WDC
Belvidere, IL	RCK
NJ	MET
Belzoni, MS	JKS
Bemidji, MN	CR
Bemus Point, NY	BUF
Ben Bolt, TX	CC
Benavides, TX	CC
Bend, OR	BAK
Bendena, KS	KCK
Benedict, MD	WDC
Benedicta, ME	PRT
Benet Lake, WI	MIL
Benicia, CA	SAC
Benkelman, NE	LIN
Bennington, VT	BUR
Bensalem, PA	PH
Bensenville, IL	JOL
IL	SCL
IL	SYM
Benson, AZ	TUC
MN	NU
Bentleyville, PA	PIT
Benton, AR	LR
IL	BEL
LA	SHP
MO	SPC
TN	KNX
WI	MAD
Benton City, WA	YAK
Benton Harbor, MI	KAL
Bentonville, AR	LR
Benwood, WV	WH
Berea, KY	LEX
OH	CLV
Beresford, SD	SFS

Bergen, NY	BUF
Bergenfield, NJ	NEW
Berkeley, CA	OAK
Berkeley Heights, NJ	NEW
Berkeley Springs, WV	WH
Berkley, MI	DET
MI	SYM
Berlin, MA	WOR
MD	WDC
MD	WIL
NH	MAN
NJ	CAM
WI	MAD
Bernalillo, NM	SFE
Bernardsville, NJ	MET
Berryville, AR	LR
VA	ARL
Berthoud, CO	DEN
Berwick, LA	LAF
PA	HBG
PA	PHU
Berwyn, IL	CHI
IL	SYM
PA	PH
Bessemer, AL	BIR
MI	MAR
Bethalto, IL	SFD
Bethany, MO	KC
WV	WH
Bethany Beach, DE	WIL
Bethel, AK	FBK
CT	BGP
OH	CIN
VT	BUR
Bethel Park, PA	PIT
Bethesda, MD	WDC
Bethlehem, CT	HRT
PA	ALN
PA	PHU
PA	PSC
Bethpage, NY	RVC
Bettendorf, IA	DAV
Beulah, ND	BIS
Beverly, MA	BO
OH	STU
Beverly Hills, CA	LA
CA	SYM
FL	SP
MI	DET
Beverly Shores, IN	GRY
Bicknell, IN	EVN
Biddeford, ME	PRT
Big Bear Lake, CA	LA
CA	SB
Big Bend, WI	MIL
Big Lake, AK	ANC
MN	SCL
TX	SAN
Big Pine Key, FL	MIA
Big Rapids, MI	GR
Big Spring, TX	SAN
Big Stone City, SD	SFS
Big Stone Gap, VA	RIC
Big Sur, CA	MRY
Big Timber, MT	GF
Bigelow, AR	LR
Bigfork, MN	DUL
MT	HEL
Billerica, MA	BO
Billings, MO	SPC
MT	GF
Biloxi, MS	BLX
Binghamton, NY	SY
NY	PSC
Birch Run, MI	SAG
Bird Island, MN	NU
Birmingham, AL	BIR
AL	NTN
AL	OLL
MI	DET
MI	GLD
Birmingham (Hoover), AL	BIR
Birnamwood, WI	GB
Bisbee, AZ	TUC
ND	FAR
Biscoe, NC	CHL
Bishop, CA	FRS
TX	CC
Bismarck, ND	BIS
Bixby, OK	TLS
Black Canyon City, AZ	PHX
Black Creek, WI	GB
Black Diamond, WA	SEA
Black Mountain, NC	CHL
Black River, NY	OG
Black River Falls, WI	LC
Blackfoot, ID	B
Blacksburg, VA	RIC
Blackstone, MA	WOR
VA	RIC
Blackwell, OK	OKL

Blackwood, NJ	CAM
Bladensburg, MD	WDC
Blaine, MN	STP
Blair, NE	OM
Blairstown, NJ	MET
Blairsville, GA	ATL
PA	GBG
Blakely, GA	SAV
Blanco, NM	GLP
TX	AUS
Blasdell, NY	BUF
Blauvelt, NY	NY
NY	CAM
Blenker, WI	LC
Blessing, TX	VIC
Block Island, RI	PRO
Bloomer, WI	LC
Bloomfield, CT	HRT
IN	EVN
NJ	NEW
NJ	PAT
NM	GLP
Bloomfield Hills, MI	DET
Bloomfield Township, MI	EST
Blooming Prairie, MN	WIN
Bloomingdale, IL	JOL
NY	OG
OH	STU
Bloomington, CA	SB
IL	PEO
IN	IND
MN	STP
TX	VIC
WI	MAD
Bloomsburg, PA	HBG
Bloomsbury, NJ	MET
Bloomsdale, MO	STL
Blountstown, FL	PT
Blue Bell, PA	PH
Blue Earth, MN	WIN
Blue Grass, IA	DAV
Blue Island, IL	CHI
Blue Point, NY	RVC
Blue Ridge, GA	ATL
Blue Springs, MO	KC
Bluefield, WV	WH
Bluffton, IN	FTW
MN	SCL
OH	TOL
SC	CHR
Blythe, CA	SB
Blytheville, AR	LR
Blythewood, SC	CHR
Boalsburg, PA	ALT
Boardman, OH	Y
OH	ROM
OH	PBR
OR	BAK
Bobtown, PA	PIT
Boca Grande, FL	VEN
Boca Raton, FL	PMB
Bode, IA	SC
Boerne, TX	SAT
Bogalusa, LA	NO
Bogota, NJ	NEW
Bohemia, NY	RVC
Boise, ID	B
Bokeelia, FL	VEN
Bolingbrook, IL	JOL
Bolivar, MO	SPC
NY	BUF
OH	COL
PA	GBG
TN	MEM
Bolton, CT	NOR
Bolton Landing, NY	ALB
Bonduel, WI	GB
Bonesteel, SD	RC
Bonfield, IL	JOL
Bonham, TX	DAL
Bonifay, FL	PT
Bonita, CA	SD
Bonita Springs, FL	VEN
Bonne Terre, MO	STL
Bonner, MT	HEL
Bonners Ferry, ID	B
Bonnots Mill, MO	JC
Boomer, WV	WH
Boone, IA	SC
NC	CHL
Booneville, AR	LR
MS	JKS
Boonsboro, MD	BAL
Boonton, NJ	PAT
Boonville, IN	EVN
MO	JC
NC	CHL
NY	SY
Boothwyn, PA	PH
Bordelonville, LA	ALX
Bordentown, NJ	TR

Borger, TX	AMA
Borrego Springs, CA	SD
Boscobel, WI	MAD
Bossier City, LA	SHP
Boston, MA	BO
NY	BUF
Boswell, PA	ALT
Bothell, WA	SEA
Botkins, OH	CIN
Bottineau, ND	FAR
Boulder, CO	DEN
MT	HEL
Boulder City, NV	LAV
Boulder Creek, CA	MRY
Boulder Junction, WI	SUP
Bound Brook, NJ	MET
Bountiful, UT	SLC
Bourbonnais, IL	JOL
Bourg, LA	HT
Bovina, TX	AMA
Bowdle, SD	SFS
Bowie, MD	WDC
Bowling Green, KY	OWN
MO	JC
OH	TOL
Bowman, ND	BIS
Bowmansville, NY	BUF
Box Elder, MT	GF
Boyce, LA	ALX
Boyceville, WI	LC
Boyd, WI	LC
Boyertown, PA	ALN
Boylston, MA	WOR
Boyne City, MI	GLD
Boynton Beach, FL	PMB
Boys Town, NE	OM
Bozeman, MT	HEL
Brackettville, TX	SAT
Braddock, PA	PIT
Bradenton, FL	VEN
Bradenville, PA	PBR
Bradford, OH	CIN
PA	E
VT	BUR
Bradley, IL	JOL
Bradley Beach, NJ	TR
Bradshaw, MD	BAL
Brady, TX	SAN
Brady's Bend, PA	GBG
Braham, MN	SCL
Braidwood, IL	JOL
Brainard, NE	LIN
Brainerd, MN	DUL
Braintree, MA	BO
Braithwaite, LA	NO
Branchville, NJ	PAT
Brandenburg, KY	L
Brandon, FL	SP
FL	SYM
MN	SCL
SD	SFS
VT	BUR
Brandywine, MD	WDC
Branford, CT	HRT
Branson, MO	SPC
Brant Beach, NJ	TR
Brasher Falls, NY	OG
Brattleboro, VT	BUR
Brawley, CA	SD
Brazil, IN	IND
Brazoria, TX	GAL
Brea, CA	ORG
Breaux Bridge, LA	LAF
Breckenridge, MN	SCL
TX	FWT
Brecksville, OH	CLV
OH	PRM
Breda, IA	SC
Breese, IL	BEL
Bremen, IN	FTW
OH	COL
Bremerton, WA	SEA
Bremond, TX	AUS
Brenham, TX	AUS
Brentwood, CA	OAK
MO	STL
NY	RVC
TN	NSH
Brevard, NC	CHL
Brewerton, NY	SY
Brewster, MA	FR
MN	WIN
NY	NY
WA	SPK
Brewton, AL	MOB
Briarcliff Manor, NY	NY
Briarwood, NY	BRK
Brick, NJ	TR
Brick Town, NJ	TR
Bridal Veil, OR	P
Bridge City, TX	BEA

Bridgehampton, NY	RVC
Bridgeport, CT	BGP
CT	STF
NE	GI
NY	SY
OH	STU
PA	PHU
PA	POC
TX	FWT
WV	WH
Bridger, MT	GF
Bridgeton, MO	STL
NJ	CAM
Bridgeview, IL	CHI
Bridgeville, PA	PIT
Bridgewater, MA	BO
NJ	MET
SD	SFS
Bridgman, MI	KAL
Bridgton, ME	PRT
Brigantine, NJ	CAM
Briggsville, WI	MAD
Brigham City, UT	SLC
Brighton, CO	DEN
IL	SFD
MA	BO
MA	ROM
MI	DET
MI	LAN
Brillion, WI	GB
Brimfield, IL	PEO
MA	SPR
Brimley, MI	MAR
Brinkley, AR	LR
Bristol, CT	HRT
IN	FTW
PA	PH
PA	PHU
RI	PRO
VA	RIC
VT	BUR
WI	MIL
Bristow, IN	IND
VA	ARL
Britton, SD	SFS
Broad Brook, CT	HRT
Broadalbin, NY	ALB
Broadus, MT	GF
Broadview, IL	CHI
Broadview Heights, OH	CLV
Brockport, NY	ROC
Brockton, MA	BO
MA	SAM
Brockway, PA	E
Brodheadsville, PA	SCR
Broken Arrow, OK	TLS
Broken Bow, NE	GI
Bromley, AL	MOB
Bronson, MI	KAL
Bronx, NY	NY
NY	STF
NY	SYM
NY	CHI
NY	MCE
Bronxville, NY	NY
Brook Park, OH	CLV
Brookeville, MD	WDC
Brookfield, CT	BGP
IL	CHI
MO	JC
WI	MIL
Brookhaven, MS	JKS
PA	PH
Brookings, OR	P
SD	SFS
Brookline, MA	BO
MA	ROM
Brooklyn, CT	NOR
IA	DAV
MI	LAN
NY	NY
NY	BRK
NY	NTN
NY	STF
NY	SAM
OH	CLV
OH	NTN
OH	SJP
Brooklyn Center, MN	STP
Brooklyn Park, MN	STP
Brooksville, FL	SP
FL	SJP
KY	COV
MS	JKS
Brookville, IN	IND
NY	RVC
PA	E
Broomall, PA	PH
Broomfield, CO	DEN
Brooten, MN	SCL
Broussard, LA	LAF

Browerville, MN	SCL
Brown Deer, WI	MIL
Brownfield, TX	LUB
Browning, MT	HEL
Browns Mills, NJ	TR
Browns Valley, MN	SCL
Brownsburg, IN	IND
Brownstown, MI	DET
Brownsville, PA	GBG
PA	PBR
TN	MEM
TX	BWN
Brownville, NY	OG
Brownwood, TX	SAN
Bruce, MS	JKS
Bruno, NE	LIN
Brunswick, GA	SAV
MD	BAL
ME	PRT
MO	JC
OH	CLV
OH	PRM
Brush, CO	DEN
Brushton, NY	OG
Brusly, LA	BR
Brussels, IL	SFD
WI	GB
Bryan, OH	TOL
TX	AUS
Bryant, IN	LFT
Bryantown, MD	WDC
Bryn Mawr, PA	PH
Bryson City, NC	CHL
Buchanan, MI	KAL
NY	NY
Buckeye, AZ	PHX
Buckeye Lake, OH	COL
Buckeystown, MD	BAL
Buckhannon, WV	WH
Buckley, WA	SEA
Buckner, MO	KC
Bucksport, ME	PRT
Bucyrus, KS	KCK
OH	TOL
Buda, TX	AUS
Budd Lake, NJ	PAT
Buena Park, CA	ORG
Buena Vista, CO	COS
Buffalo, IA	DAV
MN	STP
MO	SPC
NY	BUF
NY	STF
SD	RC
TX	TYL
WY	CHY
Buffalo Grove, IL	CHI
Buford, GA	ATL
Buhl, ID	B
MN	DUL
Bulger, PA	PIT
Bullhead City, AZ	PHX
Buna, TX	BEA
Bunkie, LA	ALX
Bunnell, FL	STA
Burbank, CA	LA
IL	CHI
Burgaw, NC	R
Burgettstown, PA	PIT
Burien, WA	SEA
Burkburnett, TX	FWT
Burke, SD	RC
VA	ARL
Burleson, TX	FWT
Burley, ID	B
Burlingame, CA	SFR
Burlington, CO	COS
IA	DAV
KS	KCK
KY	COV
MA	BO
NC	R
NJ	TR
TX	AUS
VT	BUR
WA	SEA
WI	MIL
Burnet, TX	AUS
Burney, CA	SAC
Burnham, IL	CHI
Burns, OR	BAK
Burnsville, MN	STP
Burr Ridge, IL	JOL
Burton, MI	LAN
OH	PRM
Burtonsville, MD	WDC
Bushnell, FL	ORL
IL	PEO
Bushton, KS	WCH
Bushwood, MD	WDC
Butler, AL	MOB
MO	KC
NJ	PAT
PA	PIT
WI	MIL
Butner, NC	R
Butte, MT	HEL
NE	OM
Butternut, WI	SUP
Buttonwillow, CA	FRS
Buxton, NC	R
Buzzards Bay, MA	FR
Byers, CO	DEN
Byron, CA	OAK
IL	RCK
MN	WIN
Byron Center, MI	GR
MI	KAL
Cable, WI	SUP
Cabot, PA	PIT
Cactus, TX	AMA
Cadet, MO	STL
Cadillac, MI	GLD
Cadiz, KY	OWN
OH	STU
Cadyville, NY	OG
Cahokia, IL	BEL
Cairo, IL	BEL
NY	ALB
Calais, ME	PRT
Caldwell, ID	B
KS	WCH
NJ	NEW
OH	STU
TX	AUS
Caledonia, MI	GR
MN	WIN
NY	ROC
WI	MIL
Calexico, CA	SD
Calhan, CO	COS
Calhoun, GA	ATL
KY	OWN
Caliente, NV	LAV
Califon, NJ	MET
California, KY	COV
MO	JC
PA	PIT
California City, CA	FRS
Calimesa, CA	SB
CA	HPM
Calipatria, CA	SD
Calistoga, CA	SR
Callahan, FL	STA
Callaway, MN	CR
Callicoon, NY	NY
Calmar, IA	DUB
Calumet, MI	MAR
Calumet City, IL	CHI
Calvert City, KY	OWN
Camanche, IA	DAV
Camarillo, CA	LA
Camas, WA	SEA
Cambria, CA	MRY
Cambria Heights, NY	BRK
Cambridge, MA	BO
MD	WIL
MN	SCL
NE	LIN
NY	ALB
OH	STU
VT	BUR
WI	MAD
Cambridge City, IN	IND
Cambridge Springs, PA	E
Camden, AL	MOB
AR	LR
ME	PRT
MS	JKS
NJ	CAM
NY	SY
OH	CIN
SC	CHR
TN	MEM
WV	WH
Camdenton, MO	JC
Cameron, LA	LKC
MO	KC
TX	AUS
Camillus, NY	SY
Camp Douglas, WI	LC
Camp Hill, PA	HBG
Camp Springs, KY	COV
MD	WDC
Camp Verde, AZ	PHX
Campbell, CA	SJ
CA	SPA
MO	SPC
NE	LIN
OH	Y
OH	PBR
Campbell Hall, NY	STF
Campbellsport, WI	MIL
Campbellsville, KY	L
Campo, CA	SD
Campti, LA	ALX
Campus, IL	PEO
Canaan, CT	HRT
Canadaigua, NY	ROC
Canadian, TX	AMA
Canal Fulton, OH	Y
Canal Winchester, OH	COL
Canandaigua, NY	ROC
Canaseraga, NY	BUF
Canastota, NY	SY
Canby, MN	NU
OR	P
Candler, FL	ORL
NC	CHL
Cando, ND	FAR
Candor, NC	CHL
Caney, KS	WCH
Canfield, OH	Y
Cankton, LA	LAF
Cannon Falls, MN	STP
Canoga Park, CA	LA
Canon City, CO	PBL
Canonsburg, PA	PBR
PA	PIT
Canterbury, CT	NOR
Canton, GA	ATL
IL	PEO
MA	BO
MI	DET
MI	LAN
MO	JC
MS	JKS
NY	OG
OH	Y
OH	ROM
PA	SCR
SD	SFS
TX	TYL
Cantonment, FL	PT
Canutillo, TX	ELP
Canyon, TX	AMA
Canyon Lake, TX	SAT
Capac, MI	DET
Cape Charles, VA	RIC
Cape Coral, FL	VEN
Cape Elizabeth, ME	PRT
Cape Girardeau, MO	SPC
Cape May, NJ	CAM
Cape May Court House, NJ	CAM
Cape May Point, NJ	CAM
Cape Vincent, NY	OG
Capitola, CA	MRY
Captain Cook, HI	HON
Capulin, CO	PBL
Carbondale, CO	DEN
IL	BEL
PA	PHU
PA	SCR
Cardington, OH	COL
Carefree, AZ	PHX
Carencro, LA	LAF
Carey, OH	TOL
Caribou, ME	PRT
Carle Place, NY	RVC
Carleton, MI	DET
Carlin, NV	RNO
Carlinville, IL	SFD
Carlisle, AR	LR
IA	DM
KY	LEX
MA	BO
PA	HBG
Carlos, MN	SCL
Carlsbad, CA	SD
CA	POC
NM	LSC
TX	SAN
Carlton, MN	DUL
OR	P
Carlyle, IL	BEL
Carmel, CA	MRY
IN	LFT
NY	NY
Carmel Valley, CA	MRY
Carmi, IL	BEL
Carmichael, CA	OLL
CA	SAC
Carmichaels, PA	PIT
Carnegie, PA	PIT
PA	SAM
PA	SJP
Carney's Point, NJ	CAM
Caro, MI	SAG
Carol Stream, IL	JOL
Carolina, RI	PRO
Carpentersville, IL	RCK
Carpinteria, CA	LA
Carrington, ND	FAR
Carrizo Springs, TX	LAR
Carrizozo, NM	LSC
Carroll, IA	SC
Carrollton, GA	ATL
IL	SFD
KY	COV
MI	SAG
MO	KC
OH	STU
TX	DAL
TX	FWT
Carrolltown, PA	ALT
Carson, CA	LA
ND	BIS
Carson City, MI	GR
NV	RNO
Carteret, NJ	MET
NJ	PSC
NJ	PHU
Cartersville, GA	ATL
Carterville, IL	BEL
Carthage, MO	SPC
MS	JKS
NY	OG
TX	TYL
Carthagena, OH	CIN
Caruthersville, MO	SPC
Carver, MA	BO
MN	STP
Cary, IL	RCK
NC	R
NC	PSC
Casa Grande, AZ	TUC
Cascade, CO	COS
IA	DUB
Casco, ME	PRT
WI	GB
Caseville, MI	SAG
Caseyville, IL	BEL
Cashion, AZ	PHX
Cashmere, WA	YAK
Cashton, WI	LC
Casper, WY	CHY
Caspian, MI	MAR
Cass City, MI	SAG
Cass Lake, MN	DUL
Casselberry, FL	ORL
Casselton, ND	FAR
Cassopolis, MI	KAL
Cassville, MO	SPC
WI	MAD
Castle Hayne, NC	R
Castle Rock, CO	COS
WA	SEA
Castleton, VT	BUR
Castleton On Hudson, NY	ALB
Castro Valley, CA	OAK
Castroville, CA	MRY
TX	SAT
Catasauqua, PA	ALN
Catawissa, MO	STL
PA	HBG
Catharine, KS	SAL
Cathedral City, CA	SB
Cato, WI	GB
Catonsville, MD	BAL
Catskill, NY	ALB
Cattaraugus, NY	BUF
Cavalier, ND	FAR
Cave Creek, AZ	PHX
Cayucos, CA	MRY
Cazenovia, NY	SY
WI	LC
Cecil, PA	PIT
WI	GB
Cecilia, LA	LAF
Cedar, MI	GLD
Cedar Bluffs, NE	OM
Cedar City, UT	SLC
Cedar Falls, IA	DUB
Cedar Grove, NJ	NEW
WI	MIL
Cedar Knolls, NJ	PAT
Cedar Lake, IN	GRY
Cedar Park, TX	AUS
Cedar Rapids, IA	DUB
NE	OM
Cedar Springs, MI	GR
Cedarburg, WI	MIL
Cedarhurst, NY	RVC
Cedartown, GA	ATL
Celebration, FL	ORL
Celestine, IN	EVN
Celina, OH	CIN
Centennial, CO	DEN
Center, CO	PBL
ND	BIS
TX	TYL
Center Harbor, NH	MAN
Center Line, MI	MCE
Center Moriches, NY	RVC

Center Ossipee, NH	MAN
Center Ridge, AR	LR
Center Valley, PA	ALN
Centereach, NY	RVC
Centerport, NY	RVC
Centerville, IA	DAV
LA	LAF
MA	FR
MN	STP
OH	CIN
SD	SFS
TN	NSH
TX	TYL
Central City, IA	DUB
KY	OWN
NE	OM
PA	ALT
Central Falls, RI	PRO
Central Islip, NY	RVC
Central Point, OR	P
Central Square, NY	SY
Central Valley, UT	SLC
Centralia, IL	BEL
MO	JC
WA	SEA
Centreville, MD	WIL
VA	SYM
Ceres, CA	SPA
CA	STO
Cerrillos, NM	SFE
Chadds Ford, PA	PH
Chadron, NE	GI
Chadwicks, NY	SY
Chaffee, MO	SPC
Chagrin Falls, OH	CLV
Chalfont, PA	PH
Chalmette, LA	NO
Chama, NM	SFE
Chamberino, NM	LSC
Chamberlain, SD	SFS
Chambersburg, PA	HBG
Chamblee, GA	ATL
Chamois, MO	JC
Champaign, IL	PEO
Champion, MI	MAR
Champlain, NY	OG
Chandler, AZ	PHX
OK	OKL
Chanhassen, MN	STP
Channahon, IL	JOL
Channelview, TX	GAL
Channing, MI	MAR
Chantilly, VA	ARL
Chanute, KS	WCH
Chaparral, NM	LSC
Chapel Hill, NC	R
Chapin, SC	CHR
Chapman, KS	SAL
Chappaqua, NY	NY
Chappell, NE	GI
Chappell Hill, TX	AUS
Chaptico, MD	WDC
Chardon, OH	CLV
Charenton, LA	LAF
Chariton, IA	DM
Charleroi, PA	PBR
PA	PIT
Charles City, IA	DUB
Charles Town, WV	WH
Charleston, AR	LR
IL	SFD
MO	SPC
MS	JKS
SC	CHR
SC	POC
WV	WH
Charlestown, IN	IND
MA	BO
NH	MAN
Charlevoix, MI	GLD
Charlotte, IA	DAV
MI	LAN
NC	CHL
NC	SYM
TX	SAT
VT	BUR
Charlotte Hall, MD	WDC
Charlottesville, VA	RIC
Charlton, MA	WOR
Charlton City, MA	WOR
Chaska, MN	STP
Chataignier, LA	LAF
Chateaugay, NY	OG
Chatfield, MN	WIN
Chatham, IL	SFD
MA	FR
NJ	PAT
NY	ALB
Chatom, AL	MOB
Chatsworth, CA	LA
Chattahoochee, FL	PT
Chattanooga, TN	KNX
Chauvin, LA	HT
Chazy, NY	OG
Chebanse, IL	JOL
Cheboygan, MI	GLD
Cheektowaga, NY	BUF
Chefornak, AK	FBK
Chehalis, WA	SEA
Chelan, WA	YAK
Chelmsford, MA	BO
Chelsea, MA	BO
MI	LAN
Cheltenham, PA	PH
Cheney, WA	SPK
Cheneyville, LA	ALX
Chenoa, IL	PEO
Chepachet, RI	PRO
Cheraw, SC	CHR
Cherokee, IA	SC
Cherokee Village, AR	LR
Cherry, IL	PEO
Cherry Hill, NJ	CAM
NJ	PHU
Cherry Valley, NY	ALB
Cherryvale, KS	WCH
Chesaning, MI	SAG
Chesapeake, OH	STU
VA	RIC
Cheshire, CT	HRT
MA	SPR
Chest Springs, PA	ALT
Chester, CT	NOR
IL	BEL
MD	WIL
MT	GF
NJ	PAT
NY	NY
PA	PH
SC	CHR
VT	BUR
WV	WH
Chesterfield, MO	STL
NJ	TR
VA	RIC
Chesterland, OH	CLV
OH	ROM
Chesterton, IN	GRY
Chestertown, MD	WIL
NY	ALB
Chestnut Hill, MA	BO
Chetek, WI	SUP
Chevak, AK	FBK
Cheverly, MD	WDC
Chewelah, WA	SPK
Cheyenne, WY	CHY
Cheyenne Wells, CO	COS
Chicago, IL	CHI
IL	STN
IL	SYM
IL	LIT
IL	DET
IL	JOL
IL	EST
Chicago Heights, IL	CHI
Chicago Ridge, IL	CHI
Chickasaw, AL	MOB
Chickasha, OK	OKL
Chico, CA	SAC
Chicopee, MA	SPR
Chicora, PA	PIT
Chiefland, FL	STA
Childress, TX	AMA
Childs, MD	WIL
Chillicothe, IL	PEO
MO	KC
OH	COL
Chillum, MD	WDC
Chiloquin, OR	BAK
Chilton, WI	GB
Chimayo, NM	SFE
China, TX	BEA
China Spring, TX	AUS
Chincoteague Island, VA	RIC
Chinle, AZ	GLP
Chino, CA	SB
Chino Hills, CA	SB
Chino Valley, AZ	PHX
Chinook, MT	GF
Chipley, FL	PT
Chippewa Falls, WI	LC
Chisholm, MN	DUL
Chittenango, NY	SY
Chokio, MN	SCL
Choteau, MT	HEL
Chowchilla, CA	FRS
Chrisney, IN	EVN
Christiansburg, VA	RIC
Christopher, IL	BEL
Christoval, TX	SAN
Chula Vista, CA	SD
Church Point, LA	LAF
Churchville, NY	ROC
Churdan, IA	SC
Churubusco, IN	FTW
Cibecue, AZ	GLP
Cicero, IL	CHI
IN	LFT
NY	SY
Cimarron, NM	SFE
Cincinnati, OH	CIN
OH	OLL
Cinnaminson, NJ	TR
Circle, MT	GF
Circleville, OH	COL
Citronelle, AL	MOB
Citrus Heights, CA	SAC
Citrus Springs, FL	SP
Claflin, KS	DOD
Clairton, PA	PBR
PA	PIT
Clanton, AL	BIR
Clara City, MN	NU
Clare, MI	SAG
Claremont, CA	LA
NH	MAN
Claremore, OK	TLS
Clarence, NY	BUF
PA	ALT
Clarendon, TX	AMA
Clarendon Hills, IL	JOL
Clarinda, IA	DM
Clarion, IA	DUB
PA	E
Clarissa, MN	SCL
Clark, NJ	NEW
SD	SFS
Clarkesville, GA	ATL
Clarklake, MI	LAN
Clarks Green, PA	SCR
Clarks Summit, PA	SCR
Clarksburg, CA	SAC
WV	WH
Clarksdale, MS	JKS
Clarkson, KY	OWN
NE	OM
Clarkston, MI	DET
WA	SPK
Clarksville, AR	LR
IN	IND
MD	BAL
PA	PIT
TN	NSH
TX	TYL
VA	RIC
Clawson, MI	DET
Claxton, GA	SAV
Clay Center, KS	SAL
Claymont, DE	WIL
Clayton, GA	ATL
MO	STL
NC	R
NJ	CAM
NM	SFE
NY	OG
Cle Elum, WA	YAK
Clear Lake, IA	DUB
MN	SCL
SD	SFS
Clearfield, PA	E
Clearlake, CA	SR
Clearville, PA	ALT
Clearwater, FL	SP
MN	STP
Clearwater Beach, FL	SP
Cleburne, TX	FWT
TX	POC
Clemmons, NC	CHL
Clemson, SC	CHR
Clermont, FL	ORL
IA	DUB
Cleveland, GA	ATL
MN	STP
MS	JKS
OH	CLV
OH	PRM
OH	SJP
OH	ROM
TN	KNX
TX	BEA
Cleveland Heights, OH	CLV
Clewiston, FL	VEN
Cliffside Park, NJ	NEW
NJ	NTN
Clifton, AZ	TUC
IL	JOL
NJ	PAT
TX	FWT
VA	ARL
Clifton Forge, VA	RIC
Clifton Heights, PA	PH
Clifton Park, NY	ALB
Clifton Springs, NY	ROC
Clint, TX	ELP
Clinton, AR	LR
CT	NOR
IA	DAV
IL	PEO
IN	IND
KY	OWN
MA	WOR
MD	WDC
MO	KC
MS	JKS
NC	R
NY	SY
OH	CLV
OK	OKL
SC	CHR
TN	KNX
WI	MAD
Clinton Township, MI	DET
MI	OLL
MI	PRM
Clintonville, WI	GB
Clintwood, VA	RIC
Clio, AL	MOB
MI	LAN
Cloquet, MN	DUL
Closter, NJ	NEW
Cloudcroft, NM	LSC
Cloutierville, LA	ALX
Cloverdale, CA	SR
OH	TOL
Cloverport, KY	OWN
Clovis, CA	FRS
NM	SFE
Clute, TX	GAL
Clyde, KS	SAL
MO	JC
MO	KC
NY	ROC
OH	TOL
Clymer, NY	BUF
PA	GBG
PA	PBR
Coachella, CA	SB
Coal City, IL	JOL
Coal Township, PA	HBG
Coal Valley, IL	PEO
Coalinga, CA	FRS
Coalport, PA	E
Coalton, WV	WH
Coatesville, PA	PH
PA	PSC
Cobden, IL	BEL
Cobleskill, NY	ALB
Cockeysville, MD	BAL
Cocoa, FL	ORL
Cocoa Beach, FL	ORL
Coconut Creek, FL	PSC
Coconut Grove, FL	MIA
Coden, AL	MOB
Cody, WY	CHY
Coeur d'Alene, ID	B
Coffeyville, KS	WCH
Coggon, IA	DUB
Cohasset, MA	BO
Cohoes, NY	ALB
NY	STF
Colbert, WA	SPK
Colby, KS	SAL
WI	LC
Colchester, CT	NOR
CT	STF
VT	BUR
Cold Spring, KY	COV
MN	SCL
NY	NY
Coldwater, KS	DOD
MI	KAL
OH	CIN
Colebrook, NH	MAN
Coleman, TX	SAN
Colerain, OH	STU
Coleraine, MN	DUL
Colfax, CA	SAC
IA	DAV
IL	PEO
LA	ALX
WA	SPK
College Park, MD	WDC
College Point, NY	BRK
College Station, TX	AUS
Collegeville, MN	SCL
PA	PH
Colleyville, TX	FWT
Collierville, TN	MEM
Collingdale, PA	PH
Collings Lakes, NJ	CAM
Collingswood, NJ	CAM
Collinsville, CT	HRT
IL	SFD
OK	TLS

Collyer, KS SAL
Colma, CA SFR
Colo, IA DUB
Cologne, MN STP
Colon, NE LIN
Colona, IL PEO
Colonia, NJ MET
Colonial Beach, VA ARL
Colonial Heights, VA RIC
Colonie, NY ALB
Colorado City, TX SAN
Colorado Springs, CO COS
CO SYM
Colstrip, MT GF
Colton, CA SB
NY OG
WA SPK
Colts Neck, NJ TR
Columbia, CT NOR
IL BEL
KY L
MD BAL
MO JC
MS BLX
PA HBG
SC CHR
TN NSH
VA RIC
Columbia City, IN FTW
Columbia Falls, MT HEL
Columbia Heights, MN STP
Columbia Station, OH CLV
Columbiana, OH Y
Columbus, GA SAV
IN IND
KS WCH
MS JKS
MT GF
NE OM
OH L
OH COL
OH PRM
OH SYM
TX VIC
WI MAD
Columbus Grove, OH TOL
Columbus Junction, IA DAV
Colusa, CA SAC
Colver, PA ALT
Colville, WA SPK
Colwich, KS WCH
Combined Locks, WI GB
Comfort, TX SAT
Comfrey, MN NU
Commack, NY RVC
Commerce, CA LA
TX DAL
Commerce City, CO DEN
Compton, CA LA
Comstock Park, MI GR
Conception, MO KC
Conception Junction, MO KC
Concord, CA OAK
MA BO
MI LAN
NC CHL
NH MAN
Concord Twp., OH CLV
Concordia, KS SAL
Condon, OR BAK
Conejos, CO PBL
Conemaugh, PA ALT
PA PBR
Congers, NY NY
Congress, AZ PHX
Conifer, CO DEN
Conklin, MI GR
Conneaut, OH Y
Conneaut Lake, PA E
Conneautville, PA E
Connell, WA SPK
Connellsville, PA GBG
Connersville, IN IND
Conrad, MT HEL
Conroe, TX GAL
Conshohocken, PA PH
Constable, NY OG
Constableville, NY OG
Continental, OH TOL
Convent, LA BR
Convent Station, NJ PAT
Converse, TX SAT
Conway, AR LR
MI GLD
MO SPC
PA PIT
SC CHR
Conway Springs, KS WCH
Conyers, GA ATL
GA SJP
Conyngham, PA SCR

Cook, MN DUL
Cookeville, TN NSH
Coolidge, AZ TUC
Coon Rapids, IA SC
MN STP
Coon Valley, WI LC
Cooper City, FL MIA
Coopersburg, PA ALN
Cooperstown, ND FAR
NY ALB
Coopersville, MI GR
Coos Bay, OR P
Copake Falls, NY ALB
Copemish, MI GLD
Copenhagen, NY OG
Copiague, NY RVC
Coplay, PA ALN
Copley, OH CLV
Coppell, TX DAL
TX SYM
Copperas Cove, TX AUS
Copperhill, TN KNX
Copperopolis, CA STO
Copperton, UT SLC
Coquille, OR P
Coral, PA GBG
Coral Gables, FL MIA
Coral Springs, FL MIA
FL SYM
Coralville, IA DAV
Coram, NY RVC
Coraopolis, PA PIT
Corbin, KY LEX
Corcoran, CA FRS
MN STP
Cordele, GA SAV
Cordova, AK ANC
TN MEM
Corfu, NY BUF
Corinth, MS JKS
NY ALB
Cornelius, OR P
Cornell, WI LC
Corning, AR LR
CA SAC
IA DM
KS KCK
NY ROC
OH COL
Cornucopia, WI SUP
Cornwall, NY NY
PA HBG
Cornwall–on–Hudson, NY NY
Corona, CA SB
NY BRK
Coronado, CA SD
Corpus Christi, TX CC
Corrales, NM SFE
Corralitos, CA MRY
Corry, PA E
Corsicana, TX DAL
Cortaro, AZ TUC
Cortez, CO PBL
Cortland, NE LIN
NY SY
OH Y
Cortlandt Manor, NY NY
Corvallis, OR P
Corydon, IN IND
Coshocton, OH COL
Costa Mesa, CA ORG
Cotati, CA SR
Cottage City, MD WDC
Cottage Grove, MN STP
OR P
WI MAD
Cottonport, LA ALX
Cottonwood, AZ PHX
ID B
MN NU
Cotulla, TX LAR
Coudersport, PA E
Council Bluffs, IA DM
Council Grove, KS WCH
Country Club Hills, IL CHI
Countryside, IL CHI
Coushatta, LA SHP
Coventry, CT NOR
RI PRO
Covina, CA LA
Covington, GA ATL
IN LFT
KY COV
LA NO
OH CIN
TN MEM
VA RIC
WA SEA
Coweta, OK TLS
Cowiche, WA YAK
Cox's Creek, KY L

Coxsackie, NY ALB
Cozad, NE GI
Crabtree, PA GBG
Crafton, PA PIT
Craig, CO DEN
Cranberry Township, PA PIT
Cranberry Twp, PA PIT
Crandon, WI GB
WI SUP
Crane, TX SAN
Cranford, NJ NEW
Cranston, RI PRO
RI SAM
Crawford, NE GI
Crawfordsville, IN LFT
Crawfordville, FL PT
Creighton, NE OM
PA PIT
Crescent, PA PIT
Crescent City, CA SR
FL STA
Crescent Springs, KY COV
Cresco, IA DUB
PA PSC
PA SCR
Cresskill, NJ NEW
Cresson, PA ALT
Crest Hill, IL JOL
Crestline, CA SB
OH TOL
Creston, IA DM
Crestone, CO PBL
Crestview, FL PT
Crestview Hills, KY COV
Crestwood, KY L
MO STL
NY NY
Crete, NE LIN
Creve Coeur, MO STL
Crivitz, WI GB
Crockett, CA OAK
TX TYL
Crofton, MD BAL
NE OM
Croghan, NY OG
Cromwell, CT NOR
Crookston, MN CR
Cropwell, AL BIR
Crosby, MN DUL
ND BIS
TX GAL
Cross Plains, WI MAD
Crossett, AR LR
Crosslake, MN DUL
Crossville, TN KNX
Croton–on–Hudson, NY NY
Crow Agency, MT GF
Crowley, LA LAF
TX FWT
Crown, PA E
Crown Point, IN GRY
NY OG
Crownpoint, NM GLP
Crownsville, MD BAL
Croydon, PA PH
Crozet, VA RIC
Crystal, MN STP
Crystal City, MO STL
TX LAR
Crystal Falls, MI MAR
Crystal Lake, IL RCK
Crystal River, FL SP
Crystal Springs, MS JKS
Cuba, MO JC
NM GLP
NY BUF
Cuba City, WI MAD
Cudahy, CA LA
WI MIL
Cuero, TX VIC
Cullman, AL BIR
Cullom, IL PEO
Culpeper, VA ARL
Culver, IN FTW
Culver City, CA LA
Cumberland, KY LEX
MD BAL
RI PRO
WI SUP
Cumming, GA ATL
Cunningham, KS WCH
Cupertino, CA SJ
Curdsville, KY OWN
Currie, MN WIN
Curtis, NE LIN
Curwensville, PA E
Cushing, OK TLS
Custar, OH TOL
Custer, MI GR
SD RC
WI LC

Cut Bank, MT HEL
Cut–Off, LA HT
Cutchogue, NY RVC
Cutler, CA FRS
Cutler Bay, FL MIA
Cuyahoga Falls, OH CLV
Cynthiana, KY COV
Cypress, CA ORG
D'Hanis, TX SAT
D'Iberville, MS BLX
Dade City, FL SP
Dahlgren, IL BEL
Dahlonega, GA ATL
Daingerfield, TX TYL
Dakota Dunes, SD SFS
Dale, IN EVN
Dale City, VA ARL
Dalhart, TX AMA
Dallas, GA ATL
OR P
PA SCR
TX DAL
Dallastown, PA HBG
Dalton, GA ATL
MA SPR
PA SCR
Daly City, CA SFR
Dalzell, IL PEO
Damar, KS SAL
Damascus, MD WDC
Damiansville, IL BEL
Damon, TX GAL
Dana Point, CA ORG
Danbury, CT BGP
CT SAM
CT PSC
CT NTN
TX GAL
Dania, FL MIA
Daniel Island, SC CHR
Danielson, CT NOR
Dannemora, NY OG
Danvers, MA BO
Danville, CA OAK
IL PEO
IN IND
KY LEX
OH COL
PA HBG
VA RIC
Daphne, AL MOB
Darby, PA PH
Dardenne Prairie, MO STL
Darien, CT BGP
IL JOL
Darien Center, NY BUF
Darlington, PA SAM
WI MAD
Darnestown, MD SYM
MD WDC
Dartmouth, MA SAM
Darwin, MN NU
Dauphin, PA HBG
Dauphin Island, AL MOB
Davenport, CA MRY
IA DAV
WA SPK
Davey, NE LIN
David, KY LEX
David City, NE LIN
Davidsonville, MD BAL
Davidsville, PA ALT
Davie, FL MIA
Davis, CA SAC
Davis Park, NY RVC
Davison, MI LAN
Dawson, MN NU
NE LIN
Dawson Springs, KY OWN
Dawsonville, GA ATL
Dayton, KY COV
KY SYM
MN STP
NV RNO
OH CIN
OH OLL
OH PRM
TN KNX
TX BEA
WA SPK
Daytona Beach, FL ORL
Dayville, CT NOR
De Forest, WI MAD
De Funiak Springs, FL PT
De Motte, IN LFT
De Pere, WI GB
De Queen, AR LR
De Ridder, LA LKC
De Smet, SD SFS
De Soto, MO STL
De Witt, MI LAN

DeBary, FL	ORL
DeKalb, IL	RCK
DeLand, FL	ORL
DePue, IL	PEO
DeQuincy, LA	LKC
DeSmet, ID	B
DeWitt, IA	DAV
NY	SY
Deal, NJ	TR
Dearborn, MI	DET
MI	STN
MI	ROM
Dearborn Heights, MI	DET
MI	STN
Decatur, AL	BIR
GA	ATL
IL	SFD
IN	FTW
MI	KAL
TX	FWT
Decherd, TN	NSH
Decorah, IA	DUB
Dedham, IA	SC
MA	BO
Deep River, CT	NOR
Deephaven, MN	STP
Deer Lodge, MT	HEL
Deer Park, NY	RVC
TX	GAL
WA	SPK
Deer River, MN	DUL
Deerbrook, WI	GB
Deerfield, IL	CHI
KS	DOD
MI	LAN
Deerfield Beach, FL	MIA
Defiance, IA	DM
MO	STL
OH	TOL
Del City, OK	OKL
Del Norte, CO	PBL
Del Rio, TX	SAT
Deland, FL	ORL
Delano, CA	FRS
MN	STP
Delanson, NY	ALB
Delavan, IL	PEO
WI	MIL
Delaware, OH	COL
Delaware City, DE	WIL
Delcambre, LA	LAF
Delhi, IA	DUB
NY	ALB
Dell Rapids, SD	SFS
Delmar, NY	ALB
Delphi, IN	LFT
Delphos, OH	TOL
Delran, NJ	TR
Delray Beach, FL	NTN
FL	PMB
Delta, CO	PBL
Delta Junction, AK	FBK
Delton, MI	KAL
Deltona, FL	ORL
Demarest, NJ	NEW
Deming, NM	LSC
Demopolis, AL	BIR
Demotte, IN	LFT
Denham Springs, LA	BR
Denison, IA	SC
TX	DAL
Denmark, WI	GB
Dennison, OH	COL
Dent, MN	SCL
Denton, NE	LIN
TX	FWT
Denver, CO	DEN
CO	STN
CO	HPM
NC	CHL
Denver City, TX	LUB
Denville, NJ	PAT
Depauw, IN	IND
Depew, NY	BUF
Dequincy, LA	LKC
Derby, CT	HRT
KS	WCH
NY	BUF
Derby Line, VT	BUR
Derry, NH	MAN
PA	GBG
Derwood, MD	WDC
Des Allemands, LA	NO
Des Moines, IA	DM
WA	SEA
Des Plaines, IL	CHI
Descanso, CA	SD
Desert Hot Springs, CA	SB
Deshler, OH	TOL
Destin, FL	PT
Destrehan, LA	NO

Detroit, MI	DET
MI	OLL
MI	ROM
MI	STN
Detroit Lakes, MN	CR
Deville, LA	ALX
Devils Lake, ND	FAR
Devine, TX	SAT
Devon, PA	PH
Dewey, OK	TLS
Dexter, ME	PRT
MI	LAN
MO	SPC
NM	LSC
Diamond Bar, CA	LA
Diamondhead, MS	BLX
Diberville, MS	BLX
Diboll, TX	TYL
Dickeyville, WI	MAD
Dickinson, ND	BIS
TX	GAL
Dickson, TN	NSH
Dickson City, PA	SCR
Dieterich, IL	SFD
Dighton, KS	DOD
MA	FR
Dilley, TX	SAT
Dillingham, AK	ANC
Dillon, MT	HEL
SC	CHR
Dilworth, MN	CR
Dime Box, TX	AUS
Dimmitt, TX	AMA
Dimock, SD	SFS
Dinuba, CA	FRS
Dittmer, MO	STL
Divide, CO	COS
Dix Hills, NY	BRK
NY	RVC
Dixon, CA	SAC
IL	RCK
MO	JC
NM	SFE
Dobbs Ferry, NY	NY
Dodge, NE	OM
WI	LC
Dodge Center, MN	WIN
Dodge City, KS	DOD
Dodgeville, WI	MAD
Dolan Springs, AZ	PHX
Dolgeville, NY	ALB
Dona Ana, NM	LSC
Donaldson, IN	FTW
Donaldsonville, LA	BR
Donegal, PA	GBG
Doniphan, MO	SPC
NE	LIN
Donna, TX	BWN
Donora, PA	PBR
PA	PIT
Doral, FL	ARL
FL	MIA
Doraville, GA	ATL
Dorchester, MA	BO
Dorr, MI	KAL
Dos Palos, CA	FRS
Dothan, AL	MOB
Douglas, AZ	TUC
GA	SAV
MA	WOR
MI	KAL
WY	CHY
Douglassville, PA	ALN
Douglaston, NY	BRK
Douglasville, GA	ATL
Dousman, WI	MIL
Dover, DE	WIL
MA	BO
NH	MAN
NH	SAM
NJ	PAT
OH	COL
TN	NSH
Dover Plains, NY	NY
Dowagiac, MI	KAL
Downers Grove, IL	JOL
Downey, CA	LA
Downieville, CA	SAC
Downingtown, PA	PH
Downs, IL	PEO
Doylesburg, PA	HBG
Doylestown, OH	CLV
PA	PH
WI	MAD
Dracut, MA	BO
Drake, ND	FAR
Draper, UT	SLC
Drayton, ND	FAR
Dresden, OH	COL
Drexel Hill, PA	PH
Dripping Springs, TX	AUS

Drummond, MT	HEL
Dryden, MI	DET
Du Bois, PA	E
PA	PBR
Du Quoin, IL	BEL
Dublin, CA	OAK
GA	SAV
OH	COL
Dubois, IL	BEL
IN	EVN
Dubuque, IA	DUB
Dudley, MA	WOR
PA	ALT
Dufur, OR	BAK
Dulac, LA	HT
Dulce, NM	GLP
Duluth, GA	ATL
MN	DUL
MN	SUP
Dumas, AR	LR
TX	AMA
Dumfries, VA	ARL
Dumont, NJ	NEW
Dunbar, PA	GBG
Duncan, OK	OKL
Duncansville, PA	ALT
Duncanville, TX	DAL
Dundas, IL	BEL
Dundee, IL	RCK
Dunedin, FL	SP
Dunellen, NJ	MET
NJ	PSC
Dunkerton, IA	DUB
Dunkirk, IN	LFT
NY	BUF
Dunlap, IA	DM
TN	KNX
Dunmore, PA	PSC
PA	SCR
Dunn, NC	R
Dunnellon, FL	ORL
Dunseith, ND	FAR
Dunsmuir, CA	SAC
Dunwoody, GA	ATL
Dupo, IL	BEL
Dupont, LA	ALX
PA	SCR
Duquesne, PA	PBR
PA	PIT
Durand, IL	RCK
MI	LAN
WI	LC
Durango, CO	PBL
Durant, OK	TLS
Durham, CT	NOR
NC	R
NH	MAN
Durhamville, NY	SY
Duryea, PA	SCR
Dushore, PA	SCR
Duson, LA	LAF
Dutton, MT	HEL
Duvall, WA	SEA
Duxbury, MA	BO
Dwight, IL	PEO
NE	LIN
Dyer, IN	GRY
Dyersburg, TN	MEM
Dyersville, IA	DUB
Dysart, PA	ALT
Eagan, MN	NU
MN	STP
Eagle, ID	B
WI	MIL
Eagle Butte, SD	RC
Eagle Harbor, MI	STN
Eagle Lake, TX	VIC
Eagle Pass, TX	LAR
Eagle River, AK	ANC
WI	SUP
Earlimart, CA	FRS
Earling, IA	DM
Earlington, KY	OWN
Earlville, IA	DUB
IL	PEO
Earth City, MO	STL
East Aurora, NY	BUF
East Berlin, CT	HRT
East Bernard, TX	VIC
East Boston, MA	BO
East Brady, PA	E
PA	GBG
East Bridgewater, MA	BO
East Brookfield, MA	WOR
East Brunswick, NJ	MET
NJ	PSC
East Carbon, UT	SLC
East Chicago, IN	GRY
IN	ROM
East China, MI	DET
East Dubuque, IL	RCK

East Elmhurst, NY	BRK
East Falmouth, MA	FR
East Freetown, MA	FR
East Glendale, NY	BRK
East Grand Forks, MN	CR
East Grand Rapids, MI	GR
East Greenbush, NY	ALB
East Greenwich, RI	PRO
East Hampton, CT	NOR
NY	RVC
East Hanover, NJ	PAT
East Hartford, CT	HRT
East Haven, CT	HRT
East Helena, MT	HEL
East Islip, NY	RVC
East Jordan, MI	GLD
East Lansdowne, PA	PH
East Lansing, MI	LAN
East Liverpool, OH	Y
East Longmeadow, MA	SPR
East Lyme, CT	NOR
East McKeesport, PA	PIT
East Meadow, NY	RVC
East Millinocket, ME	PRT
East Moline, IL	PEO
East Newark, NJ	NEW
East Norriton, PA	PH
East Northport, NY	RVC
East Orange, NJ	NEW
East Palo Alto, CA	SJ
CA	SFR
East Patchogue, NY	RVC
East Peoria, IL	PEO
IL	SFD
IL	RCK
East Providence, RI	PRO
East Rochester, NY	ROC
East Rockaway, NY	RVC
East Rutherford, NJ	NEW
East Saint Louis, IL	BEL
East Sandwich, MA	FR
East Stroudsburg, PA	SCR
East Syracuse, NY	SY
East Taunton, MA	FR
East Tawas, MI	GLD
East Templeton, MA	WOR
East Troy, WI	MIL
East Vandergrift, PA	GBG
East Walpole, MA	BO
East Wenatchee, WA	YAK
East Windsor, CT	HRT
Easthampton, MA	SPR
Eastlake, OH	CLV
Eastman, GA	SAV
WI	LC
Easton, CA	FRS
CT	BGP
KS	KCK
MD	WIL
MO	KC
PA	ALN
PA	SAM
Eastpointe, MI	DET
Eastport, NY	RVC
Eastvale, CA	SB
Eaton, OH	CIN
Eaton Rapids, MI	LAN
Eatontown, NJ	TR
NJ	CAM
Eau Claire, WI	LC
Eau Galle, WI	LC
Ebensburg, PA	ALT
Ebony, VA	RIC
Echo, LA	ALX
Ecorse, MI	DET
Edcouch, TX	BWN
Eddystone, PA	PH
Eddyville, KY	OWN
Eden, NC	CHL
NY	BUF
SD	SFS
TX	SAN
WI	MIL
Eden Prairie, MN	STP
Eden Valley, MN	SCL
Edenton, NC	R
Edgar, WI	LC
Edgard, LA	NO
Edgefield, SC	CHR
Edgeley, ND	FAR
Edgemere, MD	BAL
Edgerton, OH	TOL
WI	MAD
Edgewater, MD	BAL
NJ	NEW
Edgewood, IA	DUB
KY	COV
MD	BAL
Edina, MN	STP
MO	JC
Edinboro, PA	E

Edinburg, TX	BWN
TX	SYM
Edinburgh, IN	IND
Edison, NJ	MET
Edmond, OK	OKL
Edmonds, WA	SEA
Edmonton, KY	L
Edmore, MI	GR
Edna, TX	VIC
Edroy, TX	CC
Edwards, CO	DEN
Edwardsburg, MI	KAL
Edwardsville, IL	SFD
PA	PHU
Effingham, IL	SFD
KS	KCK
Egg Harbor, WI	GB
Egg Harbor Township, NJ	CAM
Eggertsville, NY	BUF
Egypt, OH	CIN
El Cajon, CA	SD
CA	OLD
CA	SPA
CA	OLL
El Campo, TX	VIC
El Centro, CA	SD
El Cerrito, CA	OAK
El Dorado, AR	LR
KS	WCH
El Dorado Hills, CA	SAC
El Dorado Springs, MO	SPC
El Mirage, AZ	PHX
El Monte, CA	LA
El Paso, IL	PEO
TX	ELP
TX	OLL
El Reno, OK	OKL
El Rito, NM	SFE
El Segundo, CA	LA
CA	NTN
El Sobrante, CA	OAK
Elberon, NJ	TR
Elberta, AL	MOB
Elbow Lake, MN	SCL
Elburn, IL	RCK
Elcho, WI	GB
Eldersburg, MD	BAL
Eldon, MO	JC
Eldora, IA	DUB
Eldorado, IL	BEL
TX	SAN
WI	MIL
Eldred, PA	E
Eldridge, IA	DAV
Elgin, IL	RCK
NE	OM
OK	OKL
OR	BAK
TX	AUS
Elizabeth, CO	COS
IL	RCK
MN	SCL
NJ	NEW
NJ	PSC
NJ	PHU
PA	PIT
Elizabeth City, NC	R
Elizabethton, TN	KNX
Elizabethtown, IL	BEL
KY	L
NY	OG
PA	HBG
Elk City, OK	OKL
Elk Grove, CA	SAC
Elk Grove Village, IL	CHI
Elk Mound, WI	LC
Elk Point, SD	SFS
Elk Rapids, MI	GLD
Elk River, MN	SCL
Elkader, IA	DUB
Elkhart, IA	DM
IN	FTW
KS	DOD
Elkhart Lake, WI	MIL
Elkhorn, NE	OM
WI	MIL
Elkins, WV	WH
Elkins Park, PA	PH
Elkland, PA	SCR
Elko, NV	RNO
Elko/New Market, MN	STP
Elkridge, MD	BAL
Elkton, FL	STA
KY	OWN
MD	WIL
VA	RIC
Elkview, WV	WH
Ellenburg Center, NY	OG
Ellendale, ND	FAR
Ellensburg, WA	YAK
Ellenville, NY	NY

Ellicott City, MD	BAL
Ellicottville, NY	BUF
Ellijay, GA	ATL
Ellington, CT	NOR
Ellinwood, KS	DOD
Ellis, KS	SAL
Ellis Grove, IL	BEL
Ellisville, MO	STL
Ellsworth, KS	SAL
ME	PRT
WI	LC
Ellwood City, PA	PIT
Elm Creek, NE	GI
Elm Grove, WI	MIL
Elma, IA	DUB
NY	BUF
WA	SEA
Elmendorf, TX	SAT
Elmer, NJ	CAM
Elmhurst, IL	JOL
NY	BRK
Elmhurst Twp., PA	SCR
Elmira, MI	GLD
NY	ROC
Elmira Heights, NY	STF
Elmont, NY	MCE
NY	RVC
Elmore, AL	MOB
OH	DET
Elmsford, NY	NY
Elmwood, IL	PEO
WI	LC
Elmwood Park, IL	CHI
NJ	NEW
Elon, NC	R
Eloy, AZ	TUC
Elrama, PA	PIT
Elrosa, MN	SCL
Elsa, TX	BWN
Elsberry, MO	STL
Elsmere, KY	COV
Elton, LA	LKC
Eltopia, WA	SPK
Elverson, PA	PH
Elwood, IN	LFT
Ely, MN	DUL
NV	LAV
Elyria, OH	CLV
Elyria Township, OH	CLV
Elysburg, PA	HBG
Elysian, MN	STP
Emerson, NE	OM
NJ	NEW
Emery, SD	SFS
Emeryville, CA	OAK
Emily, MN	DUL
Emlenton, PA	E
Emmaus, PA	ALN
Emmetsburg, IA	SC
Emmett, ID	B
MI	DET
Emmitsburg, MD	BAL
Emmonak, AK	FBK
Emory, TX	TYL
Empire, MI	GLD
Emporia, KS	KCK
VA	RIC
Emporium, PA	E
Encinal, TX	LAR
Encinitas, CA	SD
Encino, CA	LA
Enderlin, ND	FAR
Endicott, NY	SY
Endwell, NY	SY
Enfield, CT	HRT
IL	BEL
NH	MAN
England, AR	LR
Englewood, CO	DEN
FL	VEN
NJ	NEW
OH	CIN
Englewood Cliffs, NJ	NEW
Enid, OK	OKL
Ennis, TX	DAL
Enola, PA	HBG
Enosburg Falls, VT	BUR
Enterprise, AL	MOB
OR	BAK
Enumclaw, WA	SEA
Ephraim, UT	SLC
Ephrata, PA	HBG
WA	YAK
Epping, NH	MAN
Epworth, IA	DUB
Erath, LA	LAF
Erdenheim, PA	PH
Erie, CO	DEN
IL	RCK
KS	WCH
MI	DET

PA	E
PA	PBR
Erlanger, KY	COV
Ernest, PA	PBR
Erwin, TN	KNX
Escanaba, MI	MAR
Escondido, CA	SD
Esmond, ND	FAR
Esopus, NY	NY
Espanola, NM	SFE
Essex, CT	NOR
MD	BAL
Essex Junction, VT	BUR
Essexville, MI	SAG
Estacada, OR	P
Estes Park, CO	DEN
Estherville, IA	SC
Ettrick, WI	LC
Euclid, OH	CLV
OH	PRM
Eudora, KS	KCK
Eufaula, AL	MOB
Eugene, MO	JC
OR	P
Eunice, LA	LAF
Eureka, CA	SR
IL	PEO
KS	WCH
MO	STL
MT	HEL
NV	RNO
SD	SFS
Eureka Springs, AR	LR
Eustis, FL	ORL
Eutaw, AL	BIR
Evangeline, LA	LAF
Evans City, PA	PIT
Evans Mills, NY	OG
Evanston, IL	CHI
IL	MCE
WY	CHY
Evansville, IL	BEL
IN	EVN
WI	MAD
Evart, MI	GR
Eveleth, MN	DUL
Everett, MA	BO
PA	ALT
WA	SEA
Evergreen, CO	DEN
LA	ALX
Evergreen Park, IL	CHI
Everson, PA	GBG
Ewa, HI	HON
Ewa Beach, HI	HON
Ewen, MI	MAR
Ewing, MO	JC
NE	OM
Excelsior, MN	STP
Excelsior Springs, MO	KC
Exeter, CA	FRS
NE	LIN
NH	MAN
PA	SCR
RI	PRO
Export, PA	GBG
Exton, PA	PH
Fabens, TX	ELP
Fair Haven, NJ	TR
VT	BUR
Fair Lawn, NJ	NEW
Fair Oaks, CA	SAC
Fairbank, IA	DUB
Fairbanks, AK	FBK
Fairborn, OH	CIN
Fairbury, IL	PEO
NE	LIN
Fairchance, PA	GBG
Fairdale, KY	L
Fairfax, CA	SFR
MN	NU
OK	TLS
SD	RC
VA	ARL
VT	BUR
Fairfield, CA	SAC
CT	BGP
IA	DAV
IL	BEL
KY	L
MT	HEL
NJ	NEW
OH	CIN
PA	HBG
TX	TYL
VT	BUR
Fairfield Bay, AR	LR
Fairfield Glade, TN	KNX
Fairford, AL	MOB
Fairhaven, MA	FR
Fairhope, AL	MOB

Fairlawn, OH	CLV
OH	OLL
Fairless Hills, PA	PH
Fairmont, MN	WIN
WV	WH
Fairmont City, IL	BEL
Fairmount, ND	FAR
NY	SY
Fairport, NY	ROC
Fairport Harbor, OH	CLV
Fairview, NJ	NEW
PA	E
Fairview Heights, IL	BEL
Fairview Park, OH	CLV
OH	PRM
Faith, SD	RC
Falcon, CO	COS
Falconer, NY	BUF
Falfurrias, TX	CC
Fall Creek, WI	LC
Fall River, MA	FR
MA	STF
MA	SAM
Fallbrook, CA	SD
Fallentimber, PA	ALT
Fallon, NV	RNO
Falls, PA	SCR
Falls Church, VA	ARL
Falls City, NE	LIN
TX	SAT
Falls Creek, PA	E
Fallston, MD	BAL
Falmouth, KY	COV
MA	FR
ME	PRT
Fancy Farm, KY	OWN
Far Rockaway, NY	BRK
Fargo, ND	FAR
Faribault, MN	STP
Farley, IA	DUB
Farmer City, IL	PEO
Farmers Branch, TX	DAL
TX	SYM
Farmersville, IL	SFD
Farmingdale, NJ	TR
NY	RVC
Farmington, CT	HRT
IA	DAV
IL	PEO
ME	PRT
MI	DET
MI	OLN
MN	STP
MO	STL
NH	MAN
NM	GLP
PA	GBG
Farmington Hills, MI	DET
MI	OLD
MI	EST
Farmingville, NY	RVC
Farmville, NC	R
VA	RIC
Farnham, NY	BUF
Farrell, PA	E
Faulkner, MD	WDC
Faulkton, SD	SFS
Fayette, IA	DUB
MO	JC
MS	JKS
OH	TOL
Fayetteville, AR	LR
GA	ATL
IL	BEL
NC	R
NC	SAM
NY	SY
OH	CIN
TN	NSH
TX	AUS
Feasterville, PA	PH
Federal Way, WA	SEA
Feeding Hills, MA	SPR
Fellsmere, FL	PMB
Felton, CA	MRY
Fenelton, PA	PIT
Fennimore, WI	MAD
Fennville, MI	KAL
Fenton, LA	LKC
MI	LAN
MO	STL
Ferdinand, IN	EVN
Fergus Falls, MN	SCL
Ferguson, MO	STL
Fernandina Beach, FL	STA
Ferndale, CA	SR
WA	SEA
Fernley, NV	RNO
Ferriday, LA	ALX
Ferris, TX	DAL
Fertile, MN	CR

Fessenden, ND	FAR
Festus, MO	STL
Fife, WA	SEA
Fillmore, CA	LA
NY	BUF
Fincastle, VA	RIC
Findlay, OH	TOL
Finleyville, PA	PIT
Firebaugh, CA	FRS
Fisher, MN	CR
Fishers, IN	LFT
Fishers Island, NY	NOR
Fishkill, NY	NY
Fiskdale, MA	WOR
Fitchburg, MA	WOR
Flagler Beach, FL	STA
Flagstaff, AZ	PHX
Flanders, NJ	PAT
NJ	PSC
Flandreau, SD	SFS
Flasher, ND	BIS
Flat Rock, MI	DET
Flatonia, TX	AUS
TX	VIC
Fleming Island, FL	STA
Flemingsburg, KY	COV
Flemington, NJ	MET
Flint, MI	LAN
MI	OLL
MI	STN
TX	TYL
Flint Hill, MO	STL
Floodwood, MN	DUL
Flora, IL	BEL
Floral City, FL	SP
Floral Park, NY	BRK
NY	RVC
Florence, AL	BIR
AZ	TUC
CO	PBL
KY	COV
OR	P
SC	CHR
TX	AUS
WI	GB
Floresville, TX	SAT
Florham Park, NJ	PAT
Florida, NY	NY
Florida City, FL	MIA
Florissant, MO	STL
Flossmoor, IL	CHI
Flourtown, PA	PH
Flowery Branch, GA	ATL
Flowood, MS	JKS
Floydada, TX	LUB
Floyds Knobs, IN	IND
Flushing, MI	LAN
MI	PRM
NY	BRK
Foley, AL	MOB
MN	SCL
Follansbee, WV	WH
Folly Beach, SC	CHR
Folsom, CA	SAC
LA	NO
Fond Du Lac, WI	MIL
Fond du Lac, WI	MIL
Fonda, IA	SC
NY	ALB
Fontana, CA	SB
CA	HPM
WI	MIL
Footville, WI	MAD
Force, PA	E
Ford City, PA	GBG
PA	SJP
Fords, NJ	MET
Fordsville, KY	OWN
Fordyce, AR	LR
NE	OM
Foreman, AR	LR
Forest, MS	JKS
Forest City, IA	DUB
NC	CHL
PA	SCR
Forest Grove, OR	P
Forest Hill, MD	BAL
Forest Hills, NY	BRK
Forest Lake, MN	STP
Forest Park, IL	CHI
Forestburgh, NY	NY
Foreston, MN	SCL
Forestport, NY	SY
Forestville, CT	HRT
MD	MCE
MD	WDC
Forked River, NJ	TR
Forks, WA	SEA
Forman, ND	FAR
Forney, TX	DAL
Forrest City, AR	LR
Forsyth, MO	SPC
MT	GF
Fort Ann, NY	ALB
Fort Ashby, WV	WH
Fort Atkinson, WI	MAD
Fort Benton, MT	GF
Fort Bragg, CA	SR
Fort Branch, IN	EVN
Fort Calhoun, NE	OM
Fort Collins, CO	DEN
Fort Covington, NY	OG
Fort Davis, TX	ELP
Fort Defiance, AZ	GLP
Fort Dodge, IA	SC
Fort Edward, NY	ALB
Fort Gratiot, MI	DET
Fort Hancock, TX	ELP
Fort Jennings, OH	TOL
Fort Jones, CA	SAC
Fort Kent, ME	PRT
Fort Lauderdale, FL	MIA
FL	SAM
FL	SYM
Fort Leavenworth, KS	KCK
Fort Lee, NJ	NEW
Fort Loramie, OH	CIN
Fort Lupton, CO	DEN
Fort Madison, IA	DAV
Fort Mc Clellan, AL	BIR
Fort Mill, SC	CHR
Fort Mitchell, AL	MOB
KY	COV
Fort Monroe, VA	RIC
Fort Morgan, CO	DEN
Fort Myers, FL	VEN
Fort Myers Beach, FL	VEN
Fort Oglethorpe, GA	ATL
Fort Payne, AL	BIR
Fort Pierce, FL	PMB
FL	PSC
Fort Pierre, SD	RC
Fort Plain, NY	ALB
Fort Recovery, OH	CIN
Fort Riley, KS	SAL
Fort Scott, KS	WCH
Fort Shaw, MT	GF
Fort Smith, AR	LR
Fort Stockton, TX	SAN
Fort Sumner, NM	SFE
Fort Thomas, KY	COV
Fort Thompson, SD	SFS
Fort Totten, ND	FAR
Fort Walton Beach, FL	PT
Fort Washington, MD	WDC
Fort Wayne, IN	FTW
Fort Worth, TX	FWT
TX	POC
Fort Wright, KY	COV
Fort Yates, ND	BIS
Fortuna, CA	SR
Fortville, IN	IND
Fosston, MN	CR
Foster, RI	PRO
Foster City, CA	SFR
Fostoria, OH	TOL
Fountain City, WI	LC
Fountain Hill, PA	ALN
Fountain Hills, AZ	PHX
Fountain Valley, CA	ORG
Fowler, CA	FRS
IN	LFT
KS	DOD
MI	LAN
Fowlerville, MI	LAN
Fox Chase Manor, PA	PH
PA	PHU
Fox Lake, WI	MIL
Fox Point, WI	MIL
Foxborough, MA	BO
Foxfield, CO	DEN
Foxholm, ND	BIS
Frackville, PA	ALN
PA	PHU
Framingham, MA	BO
MA	SYM
Francis Creek, WI	GB
Frankenmuth, MI	SAG
Frankfort, IL	JOL
IN	LFT
KS	KCK
KY	LEX
MI	GLD
NY	ALB
Franklin, IN	IND
KY	OWN
LA	LAF
MA	BO
MN	NU
NC	CHL
NH	MAN
NJ	PAT
OH	CIN
PA	E
TN	NSH
TX	AUS
VA	RIC
WI	MIL
WV	WH
Franklin Furnace, OH	STU
Franklin Lakes, NJ	NEW
Franklin Park, IL	CHI
Franklin Square, NY	RVC
Franklinton, LA	NO
Franklinville, NY	BUF
Frankston, TX	TYL
Franktown, CO	OKL
Fraser, MI	DET
Frazee, MN	CR
Frazier Park, CA	FRS
Frederic, WI	SUP
Frederick, CO	DEN
MD	BAL
Fredericksburg, TX	SAT
VA	ARL
Fredericktown, MO	SPC
PA	PIT
Fredonia, KS	WCH
NY	BUF
WI	MIL
Free Soil, MI	GR
Freeburg, IL	BEL
MO	JC
Freedom, PA	PIT
WI	GB
Freehold, NJ	TR
Freeland, MI	SAG
PA	PSC
PA	SCR
Freeport, IL	RCK
MN	SCL
NY	RVC
PA	GBG
TX	GAL
Freer, TX	CC
Freeville, NY	ROC
Fremont, CA	OAK
CA	SYM
MI	GR
NE	OM
OH	TOL
French Lick, IN	IND
French Settlement, LA	BR
Frenchburg, KY	LEX
Frenchtown, MT	HEL
Frenchville, ME	PRT
PA	E
Fresh Meadows, NY	BRK
NY	STF
Fresno, CA	FRS
Friday Harbor, WA	SEA
Fridley, MN	STP
Friend, NE	LIN
Friendship, WI	LC
Friendsville, PA	SCR
Friendswood, TX	GAL
Friona, TX	AMA
Frisco, CO	DEN
TX	DAL
TX	FWT
Front Royal, VA	ARL
Frontenac, KS	WCH
MN	STP
MO	STL
Frostburg, MD	BAL
Fruita, CO	PBL
Fruitland, ID	B
Fryburg, PA	E
Frydek, TX	GAL
Fulda, MN	WIN
Fullerton, CA	ORG
NE	OM
Fulshear, TX	GAL
Fulton, IL	RCK
KY	OWN
MD	BAL
MO	JC
NY	SY
Fultonville, NY	ALB
Fuquay–Varina, NC	R
Gadsden, AL	BIR
Gaffney, SC	CHR
Gahanna, OH	COL
Gaines, MI	LAN
Gainesville, FL	STA
GA	ATL
TX	FWT
VA	ARL
Gaithersburg, MD	WDC
Galena, AK	FBK
IL	RCK
MD	WIL
Galena Park, TX	GAL
Gales Ferry, CT	NOR
Galesburg, IL	PEO
Galeton, PA	E
Galion, OH	TOL
Gallatin, MO	KC
TN	NSH
Galliano, LA	HT
Gallipolis, OH	STU
Gallitzin, PA	ALT
Galloway, NJ	CAM
Gallup, NM	GLP
Galt, CA	SAC
Galva, IL	PEO
Galveston, TX	GAL
Gambrills, MD	BAL
Ganado, AZ	GLP
TX	VIC
Garberville, CA	SR
Garciasville, TX	BWN
Garden, MI	MAR
Garden City, KS	DOD
MI	DET
NY	RVC
TX	SAN
Garden Grove, CA	ORG
Garden Plain, KS	WCH
Gardena, CA	LA
Gardendale, AL	BIR
Gardiner, NY	NY
Gardner, KS	KCK
MA	WOR
Gardnerville, NV	RNO
Garfield, NJ	NEW
TR	NM	LSC
Garfield Heights, OH	CLV
Garland, TX	DAL
TX	SYM
Garner, IA	DUB
NC	R
NC	SJP
Garnerville, NY	NY
Garnett, KS	KCK
Garretson, SD	SFS
Garrett, IN	FTW
Garrett Park, MD	WDC
Garrettsville, OH	Y
Garrison, MN	DUL
ND	BIS
NY	NY
Garwood, NJ	NEW
Gary, IN	GRY
Garyville, LA	NO
Gas City, IN	LFT
Gassaway, WV	WH
Gastonia, NC	CHL
Gate City, VA	RIC
Gates Mills, OH	CLV
Gatesville, TX	AUS
Gatlinburg, TN	KNX
Gautier, MS	BLX
Gaylord, MI	GLD
MN	NU
Gays Mills, WI	LC
Geddes, SD	SFS
Genesee Depot, WI	MIL
Geneseo, IL	PEO
ND	FAR
NY	ROC
Geneva, AL	MOB
IL	RCK
IN	FTW
NE	LIN
NY	ROC
OH	Y
Genoa, IL	RCK
NE	OM
OH	TOL
WI	LC
George West, TX	CC
Georgetown, CA	SAC
CT	BGP
DE	WIL
IL	PEO
IN	IND
KY	LEX
MA	BO
MN	CR
OH	CIN
SC	CHR
TX	AUS
Gering, NE	GI
Germantown, IL	BEL
MD	WDC
NY	ALB
OH	CIN
TN	MEM
WI	MIL
Gervais, OR	P
Gettysburg, PA	HBG
SD	SFS
Getzville, NY	BUF

Ghent, MN	NU
Gibbon, MN	NU
Gibbsboro, NJ	CAM
Gibbstown, NJ	CAM
Gibson, LA	HT
Gibson City, IL	JOL
Gibsonburg, OH	TOL
Gibsonia, PA	PBR
PA	PIT
Giddings, TX	AUS
Gig Harbor, WA	SEA
Gilbert, AZ	HPM
AZ	PHX
MN	DUL
Gilberts, IL	RCK
Gilbertville, IA	DUB
MA	WOR
Gillespie, IL	SFD
Gillett, WI	GB
Gillette, WY	CHY
Gilman, IL	JOL
MN	SCL
WI	SUP
Gilmer, TX	TYL
Gilroy, CA	SJ
Girard, IL	SFD
KS	WCH
OH	Y
PA	E
PA	PBR
Gladewater, TX	TYL
Gladstone, MI	MAR
MO	KC
NJ	PAT
Gladwin, MI	SAG
Gladwyne, PA	PH
Glandorf, OH	TOL
Glasgow, KY	L
MO	JC
MT	GF
Glassboro, NJ	CAM
Glassport, PA	PIT
Glastonbury, CT	HRT
CT	STF
Glen Allen, VA	RIC
VA	SAM
Glen Burnie, MD	BAL
Glen Carbon, IL	SFD
Glen Cove, NY	RVC
NY	STF
Glen Dale, WV	WH
Glen Echo, MD	WDC
Glen Ellyn, IL	JOL
Glen Head, NY	RVC
Glen Lyon, PA	SCR
Glen Mills, PA	PH
Glen Rock, NJ	NEW
Glen Rose, TX	FWT
Glen Ullin, ND	BIS
Glenburn, ND	BIS
Glencoe, MN	NU
Glendale, AZ	PHX
CA	LA
CA	OLN
NY	BRK
WI	MIL
Glendale Heights, IL	JOL
Glendive, MT	GF
Glendora, CA	LA
CA	MCE
Glenmora, LA	ALX
Glennallen, AK	ANC
Glenolden, PA	PH
Glenrock, WY	CHY
Glens Falls, NY	ALB
Glenshaw, PA	PIT
Glenside, PA	PH
Glenview, IL	CHI
IL	SYM
Glenville, NY	ALB
WV	WH
Glenwood, AR	LR
IA	DM
IL	CHI
MN	SCL
Glenwood City, WI	SUP
Glenwood Springs, CO	DEN
Glidden, IA	SC
WI	SUP
Globe, AZ	TUC
Gloucester, MA	BO
NJ	CAM
VA	RIC
Glouster, OH	STU
Gloversville, NY	ALB
Gloverville, SC	CHR
Gluckstadt, MS	JKS
Glyndon, MD	BAL
Gobles, MI	KAL
Goddard, KS	WCH
Godfrey, IL	SFD

Goetzville, MI	MAR
Goffstown, NH	MAN
Gold Hill, OR	P
Golden, CO	DEN
Golden Meadow, LA	HT
Golden Valley, MN	STP
Goldendale, WA	YAK
Goldsboro, NC	R
Goldthwaite, TX	AUS
Goleta, CA	LA
Goliad, TX	VIC
Gonic, NH	MAN
Gonzales, CA	MRY
LA	BR
TX	SAT
Goodhue, MN	STP
Gooding, ID	B
Goodland, KS	SAL
Goodman, WI	GB
Goodrich, MI	LAN
Goodyear, AZ	PHX
AZ	TUC
Goose Creek, SC	CHR
Gordon, NE	GI
Gorham, KS	SAL
NH	MAN
Goshen, CT	HRT
IN	FTW
NY	NY
Gould, AR	LR
Gouldsboro, PA	SCR
Gouverneur, NY	OG
Gowanda, NY	BUF
Gower, MO	KC
Graceville, MN	NU
Graford, TX	FWT
Grafton, IL	SFD
MA	WOR
ND	FAR
OH	CLV
WI	MIL
WV	WH
Graham, TX	FWT
Grambling, LA	SHP
Grampian, PA	E
Granada Hills, CA	LA
Granbury, TX	FWT
Granby, CO	DEN
CT	HRT
MA	SPR
Grand Bay, AL	MOB
Grand Blanc, MI	EST
MI	LAN
Grand Canyon, AZ	PHX
Grand Chenier, LA	LKC
Grand Coteau, LA	LAF
Grand Coulee, WA	YAK
Grand Forks, ND	FAR
Grand Haven, MI	GR
Grand Island, NE	GI
NY	BUF
Grand Isle, LA	HT
Grand Junction, CO	PBL
IA	SC
Grand Ledge, MI	LAN
Grand Marais, MI	MAR
MN	DUL
Grand Meadow, MN	WIN
Grand Mound, IA	DAV
Grand Prairie, TX	DAL
TX	FWT
Grand Rapids, MI	GR
MI	STN
MN	DUL
OH	TOL
Grand Rivers, KY	OWN
Grand Ronde, OR	P
Grand Terrace, CA	SB
Grandview, MO	KC
WA	YAK
Grandville, MI	GR
Granger, IA	DM
IN	FTW
TX	AUS
WA	YAK
Grangeville, ID	B
Granite Bay, CA	SAC
Granite City, IL	SFD
Granite Falls, MN	NU
Graniteville, VT	BUR
Grant, NE	LIN
Grants, NM	GLP
Grants Pass, OR	P
Granville, IA	SC
IL	PEO
NY	ALB
OH	COL
Grapevine, TX	FWT
Grass Lake, MI	LAN
Grass Valley, CA	SAC
Gray, LA	NO

LA	PBR
Grayling, MI	GLD
Grayslake, IL	CHI
Grayson, KY	LEX
Great Barrington, MA	SPR
Great Bend, KS	DOD
PA	SCR
Great Falls, MT	GF
VA	ARL
Great Meadows, NJ	MET
NJ	PHU
Great Mills, MD	WDC
Great Neck, NY	RVC
Greeley, CO	DEN
KS	KCK
Green Bay, WI	GB
Green Isle, MN	NU
Green Lake, WI	MAD
Green Pond, NJ	PAT
Green River, WY	CHY
Green Valley, AZ	TUC
Greenacres, FL	PMB
FL	SAM
Greenbelt, MD	WDC
Greenbrae, CA	SFR
Greenbush, MN	CR
Greencastle, IN	IND
PA	HBG
Greendale, WI	MIL
Greene, IA	DUB
NY	SY
Greeneville, TN	KNX
Greenfield, CA	MRY
IA	DM
IL	SFD
IN	IND
MA	SPR
OH	CIN
WI	MIL
Greenfield Center, NY	ALB
Greenlawn, NY	RVC
Greenleaf, WI	GB
Greenport, NY	RVC
Greensboro, GA	ATL
NC	CHL
Greensburg, IN	IND
KS	DOD
PA	GBG
PA	PBR
Greenup, IL	SFD
Greenville, AL	MOB
IL	SFD
IN	IND
ME	PRT
MI	GR
MS	JKS
NC	R
NH	MAN
NY	ALB
OH	CIN
PA	E
RI	PRO
SC	CHR
SC	POC
TX	DAL
WI	GB
Greenwald, MN	SCL
Greenwell Springs, LA	BR
Greenwich, CT	BGP
NY	ALB
Greenwood, IN	IND
MS	JKS
SC	CHR
Greenwood Lake, NY	NY
Greenwood Village, CO	DEN
Greer, SC	CHR
SC	SAM
Gregory, SD	RC
TX	CC
Grenada, MS	JKS
Grenora, ND	BIS
Grenville, SD	SFS
Gresham, OR	P
WI	GB
Gretna, LA	NO
NE	OM
Grey Eagle, MN	SCL
Greybull, WY	CHY
Gridley, CA	SAC
Griffin, GA	ATL
Griffith, IN	GRY
Grinnell, IA	DAV
KS	SAL
Griswold, CT	NOR
IA	DM
Groom, TX	AMA
Grosse Ile, MI	DET
Grosse Pointe, MI	DET
Grosse Pointe Farms, MI	DET
Grosse Pointe Park, MI	DET
Grosse Pointe Woods, MI	DET

Grosse Tete, LA	BR
Groton, CT	NOR
NY	ROC
SD	SFS
Grove, OK	TLS
Grove City, MN	NU
OH	COL
PA	E
Grove Hill, AL	MOB
Groveport, OH	COL
Groves, TX	BEA
Groveton, NH	MAN
Grovetown, GA	SAV
Grulla, TX	BWN
Guadalupe, AZ	PHX
CA	LA
Guerneville, CA	SR
Guernsey, WY	CHY
Gueydan, LA	LAF
Guilderland, NY	ALB
Guilford, CT	HRT
IN	IND
Gulf Breeze, FL	PT
Gulf Shores, AL	MOB
Gulfport, FL	SP
MS	BLX
Gun Barrel City, TX	TYL
Gunnison, CO	PBL
Guntersville, AL	BIR
Gurnee, IL	CHI
Gustine, CA	FRS
Guthrie, KY	OWN
OK	OKL
Guthrie Center, IA	DM
Guttenberg, IA	DUB
Guymon, OK	OKL
Guys Mills, PA	E
Gwinn, MI	MAR
Gwynedd Valley, PA	PH
Hacienda Heights, CA	LA
Hackberry, LA	LKC
Hackensack, MN	DUL
NJ	NEW
Hackettstown, NJ	MET
Haddon Heights, NJ	CAM
Haddonfield, NJ	CAM
Hadley, MA	SPR
Hagaman, NY	ALB
Hagerstown, MD	BAL
Hague, ND	BIS
Hahnville, LA	NO
Haiku, HI	HON
Hailey, ID	B
Haines, AK	JUN
Haines City, FL	ORL
Haines Falls, NY	ALB
Hainesport, NJ	TR
NJ	CAM
Halbur, IA	SC
Haledon, NJ	PAT
Hales Corners, WI	MIL
Halethorpe, MD	BAL
Half Moon Bay, CA	SFR
Halifax, MA	BO
Hallandale Beach, FL	MIA
Hallettsville, TX	VIC
Hallock, MN	CR
Halstead, KS	WCH
Ham Lake, MN	STP
Hamburg, IA	DM
NJ	PAT
NY	BUF
PA	ALN
Hamden, CT	HRT
Hamel, MN	STP
Hamilton, AL	BIR
MA	BO
MO	KC
MT	HEL
NJ	TR
NY	SY
OH	CIN
TX	AUS
Hamilton Square, NJ	TR
Hamlet, IN	GRY
NC	CHL
Hamlin, NY	ROC
Hammond, IN	GRY
IN	NTN
LA	BR
WI	SUP
Hammondsport, NY	ROC
Hammonton, NJ	CAM
Hampden, MA	SPR
Hampshire, IL	RCK
Hampstead, NC	R
NH	MAN
Hampton, IA	DUB
MN	STP
NH	MAN
NJ	MET

VA	RIC
Hampton Bays, NY	RVC
Hamptonville, NC	CHL
Hamtramck, MI	DET
MI	STN
Hana, HI	HON
Hanahan, SC	CHR
Hanceville, AL	BIR
Hancock, MD	BAL
MI	MAR
NY	ALB
Hanford, CA	FRS
Hankinson, ND	FAR
Hannibal, MO	JC
NY	SY
Hanover, IL	RCK
KS	SAL
MA	BO
MD	BAL
NH	MAN
PA	HBG
Hanover Park, IL	CHI
Hanover Township, PA	SCR
Hanson, MA	BO
Hapeville, GA	ATL
Happy, TX	AMA
Harahan, LA	NO
Harbor Beach, MI	SAG
Harbor Springs, MI	GLD
Harborcreek, PA	E
Hardin, IL	SFD
KY	OWN
MT	GF
Hardinsburg, KY	OWN
Hardwick, VT	BUR
Hardyston, NJ	PAT
Harker Heights, TX	AUS
Harlan, IA	DM
KY	LEX
Harlingen, TX	BWN
Harlowton, MT	HEL
Harmony, MN	WIN
Harper, KS	WCH
TX	SAT
Harpers Ferry, IA	DUB
Harrah, OK	OKL
Harriman, NY	NY
TN	KNX
Harrington Park, NJ	NEW
Harrisburg, IL	BEL
PA	HBG
PA	PSC
Harrison, AR	LR
MI	SAG
NJ	NEW
NY	NY
OH	CIN
Harrison City, PA	GBG
Harrison Township, MI	DET
Harrisonburg, VA	RIC
Harrisonville, MO	KC
Harrisville, MI	DET
MI	GLD
NY	OG
RI	PRO
WV	WH
Harrodsburg, KY	LEX
Hart, MI	GR
Hartford, CT	HRT
CT	STF
MI	KAL
SD	SFS
WI	MIL
Hartford City, IN	LFT
Hartington, NE	OM
Hartland, WI	MIL
Hartsdale, NY	NY
Hartshorne, OK	TLS
Hartsville, SC	CHR
Hartwell, GA	ATL
Harvard, IL	RCK
MA	WOR
NE	LIN
Harvey, IL	CHI
LA	NO
ND	FAR
Harvey Cedars, NJ	TR
Harveys Lake, PA	SCR
Harwick, PA	PIT
Harwinton, CT	HRT
Harwood Heights–Norridge, IL	CHI
Hasbrouck Heights, NJ	NEW
Haskell, NJ	PAT
Hastings, MI	KAL
MN	STP
NE	LIN
PA	ALT
Hastings–on–Hudson, NY	NY
Hatboro, PA	PH
Hatch, NM	LSC
Hatfield, MA	SPR

PA	PH
Hatley, WI	LC
Hattiesburg, MS	BLX
Hattieville, AR	LR
Haubstadt, IN	EVN
Hauppauge, NY	RVC
Havana, IL	PEO
Havelock, NC	R
Haverford, PA	PH
Haverhill, MA	BO
Haverstraw, NY	NY
Havertown, PA	PH
Havre, MT	GF
Havre de Grace, MD	BAL
Hawaiian Gardens, CA	LA
Hawarden, IA	SC
Hawesville, KY	OWN
Hawi, HI	HON
Hawk Point, MO	STL
Hawk Run, PA	PBR
Hawley, MN	CR
PA	SCR
Haworth, NJ	NEW
Hawthorne, CA	LA
NJ	PAT
NV	RNO
NY	NY
Hayden, AZ	TUC
Haydenville, MA	SPR
Hayfield, MN	WIN
Hays, KS	SAL
MT	GF
Haysville, KS	WCH
Hayward, CA	OAK
WI	SUP
Hazard, KY	LEX
Hazel Crest, IL	CHI
Hazel Green, WI	MAD
Hazel Park, MI	DET
Hazelton, ND	BIS
Hazelwood, MO	STL
Hazen, ND	BIS
Hazleton, PA	PSC
PA	SCR
Healdsburg, CA	SR
Healdton, OK	OKL
Healy, AK	FBK
Hearne, TX	AUS
Heart Butte, MT	HEL
Heath, OH	COL
Hebbronville, TX	LAR
Heber Springs, AR	LR
Hebron, CT	NOR
IN	GRY
ND	BIS
NE	LIN
Hecker, IL	BEL
Hector, MN	NU
Hedgesville, WV	WH
Helena, AR	LR
MT	HEL
OH	TOL
Helenwood, TN	KNX
Hellertown, PA	ALN
Helmetta, NJ	MET
Helmville, MT	HEL
Helotes, TX	SAT
TX	SYM
Helper, UT	SLC
Hemet, CA	SB
Hemlock, MI	SAG
Hemphill, TX	TYL
Hempstead, NY	RVC
NY	STF
TX	GAL
Henderson, KY	OWN
MN	NU
NC	R
NV	LAV
TX	TYL
Hendersonville, NC	CHL
TN	NSH
Hennepin, IL	PEO
Hennessey, OK	OKL
Henniker, NH	MAN
Henning, MN	SCL
Henrico, VA	RIC
Henrietta, NY	POC
NY	ROC
TX	FWT
Henry, IL	PEO
SD	SFS
Henryetta, OK	TLS
Heppner, OR	BAK
Herculaneum, MO	STL
Hercules, CA	OAK
Hereford, AZ	TUC
TX	AMA
Herington, KS	SAL
Herkimer, NY	ALB
Herman, MN	SCL

Hermann, MO	JC
Herminie, PA	GBG
PA	PBR
Hermiston, OR	BAK
Hermitage, MO	JC
PA	E
PA	PBR
Hermosa Beach, CA	LA
Hernando, MS	JKS
Herndon, VA	ARL
Heron Lake, MN	WIN
Herreid, SD	SFS
Herrin, IL	BEL
Herron, MI	GLD
Herscher, IL	JOL
Hershey, PA	HBG
Hesperia, CA	SB
Hessmer, LA	ALX
Hettinger, ND	BIS
Heuvelton, NY	OG
Hewitt, NJ	PAT
WI	LC
Hewlett, NY	RVC
Hialeah, FL	MIA
Hiawatha, IA	DUB
KS	KCK
Hibbing, MN	DUL
Hickman, KY	OWN
Hickory, NC	CHL
Hickory Hills, IL	CHI
Hicksville, NY	RVC
OH	TOL
Hidalgo, TX	BWN
Higganum, CT	NOR
Higgins Lake, MI	GLD
Higginsville, MO	KC
High Bridge, NJ	MET
High Point, NC	CHL
High Ridge, MO	STL
High Springs, FL	STA
Highland, CA	SB
IL	SFD
IN	GRY
MI	DET
NY	NY
WI	MAD
Highland Beach, FL	PMB
Highland Falls, NY	NY
Highland Heights, KY	COV
OH	CLV
Highland Lakes, NJ	PAT
Highland Mills, NY	NY
Highland Park, IL	CHI
NJ	MET
Highland Springs, VA	RIC
Highlands, TX	GAL
Highlands Ranch, CO	COS
Highmore, SD	SFS
Hightstown, NJ	TR
Highwood, IL	CHI
Hilbert, WI	GB
Hill City, KS	SAL
SD	RC
Hillcrest Heights, MD	WDC
Hilliard, OH	COL
Hillman, MI	GLD
MN	SCL
Hills, IA	DAV
Hillsboro, IL	SFD
MO	STL
ND	FAR
OH	CIN
OR	P
TX	FWT
WI	LC
Hillsborough, NC	R
NH	MAN
NJ	MET
NJ	PHU
Hillsborough Township, NJ	PSC
Hillsdale, MI	LAN
NJ	NEW
Hillside, IL	CHI
NJ	NEW
Hillsville, PA	PIT
Hilltown, PA	PH
Hilmar, CA	FRS
Hilo, HI	HON
Hilton, NY	ROC
Hilton Head Island, SC	CHR
Hinckley, MN	DUL
OH	CLV
Hinesburg, VT	BUR
Hinesville, GA	SAV
Hingham, MA	BO
Hinsdale, IL	JOL
Hinton, WV	WH
Hitchcock, TX	GAL
Ho Ho Kus, NJ	NEW
Hobart, IN	GRY
Hobbs, NM	LSC

Hobe Sound, FL	PMB
Hoboken, NJ	NEW
Hobson, TX	SAT
Hockessin, DE	WIL
Hodge, LA	SHP
Hodgenville, KY	L
Hoffman Estates, IL	CHI
Hogansburg, NY	OG
Hohenwald, TN	NSH
Hoisington, KS	DOD
Holbrook, AZ	GLP
MA	BO
NY	RVC
Holden, MO	KC
Holdenville, OK	TLS
Holdingford, MN	SCL
Holdrege, NE	LIN
Holgate, OH	TOL
Holiday, FL	SP
Holland, MI	GR
NY	BUF
PA	PH
Holland Patent, NY	SY
Hollandale, WI	MAD
Holley, NY	BUF
Hollidaysburg, PA	ALT
Hollis, NY	BRK
NY	SYM
Hollis Hills, NY	BRK
Hollister, CA	MRY
Holliston, MA	BO
Holly, CO	PBL
MI	DET
Holly Lake Ranch, TX	TYL
Holly Springs, MS	JKS
Hollywood, CA	STN
FL	MIA
MD	WDC
Holmdel, NJ	TR
Holmen, WI	LC
Holstein, IA	SC
Holton, KS	KCK
Holts Summit, MO	JC
Holtville, CA	SD
Holy Cross, AK	FBK
IA	DUB
Holyoke, CO	DEN
MA	SPR
Homer, AK	ANC
NY	SY
Homer City, PA	PBR
Homer Glen, IL	JOL
IL	PRM
Homestead, FL	MIA
PA	PIT
Hometown, IL	CHI
Homewood, IL	CHI
IL	JOL
Homosassa, FL	SP
Hondo, TX	SAT
Honeoye, NY	ROC
Honeoye Falls, NY	ROC
Honesdale, PA	SCR
Honey Grove, TX	DAL
Honokaa, HI	HON
Honolulu, HI	HON
Hood River, OR	BAK
Hooksett, NH	MAN
Hoopa, CA	SR
Hooper, NE	OM
Hooper Bay, AK	FBK
Hoopeston, IL	PEO
Hoosick Falls, NY	ALB
Hooversville, PA	ALT
Hopatcong, NJ	PAT
Hope, AR	LR
Hope Mills, NC	R
Hope Valley, RI	PRO
Hopedale, MA	WOR
OH	STU
Hopelawn, NJ	MET
Hopewell, NJ	TR
VA	RIC
Hopewell Junction, NY	NY
Hopkins, MN	STP
Hopkinsville, KY	OWN
Hopkinton, IA	DUB
MA	BO
Horace, ND	FAR
Horicon, WI	MIL
Horizon City, TX	ELP
Hornell, NY	ROC
Horseheads, NY	ROC
Horseshoe Bay, TX	AUS
Horseshoe Bend, AR	LR
Horsham, PA	PH
Horton, KS	KCK
Hortonville, WI	GB
Hoschton, GA	ATL
Hospers, IA	SC
Hot Springs, AR	LR

SD	RC
VA	RIC
Hot Springs National Park, AR	LR
Hot Springs Village, AR	LR
Houck, AZ	GLP
Houghton, IA	DAV
MI	MAR
Houlton, ME	PRT
Houma, LA	HT
Housatonic, MA	SPR
House Springs, MO	STL
Houston, MN	WIN
MO	SPC
TX	GAL
TX	OLL
TX	POC
TX	STN
TX	PBR
Houtzdale, PA	E
Hoven, SD	SFS
Howard, SD	SFS
Howard Beach, NY	BRK
Howard City, MI	GR
Howardstown, KY	L
Howell, MI	LAN
NJ	TR
Howells, NE	OM
Howes, SD	RC
Howland, ME	PRT
Hoxie, KS	SAL
Hubbard, OH	Y
Huber Heights, OH	CIN
Hubertus, WI	MIL
Hudson, FL	SP
MA	BO
MI	LAN
NH	MAN
NY	ALB
NY	STF
OH	CLV
WI	SUP
Hudson Falls, NY	ALB
Huffman, TX	GAL
Hughson, CA	STO
Hugo, OK	TLS
Hugoton, KS	DOD
Hulbert, OK	TLS
Hull, MA	BO
Humble, TX	GAL
Humboldt, IA	SC
SD	SFS
TN	MEM
Humphrey, NE	OM
Hungerford, TX	VIC
Hunlock Creek, PA	SCR
Hunt Valley, MD	BAL
Hunter, NY	STF
Huntersville, NC	CHL
Huntingburg, IN	EVN
Huntingdon, PA	ALT
Huntingdon Valley, PA	PH
PA	SYM
Huntington, IN	FTW
NY	RVC
WV	WH
Huntington Beach, CA	ORG
Huntington Park, CA	LA
Huntington Station, NY	RVC
Huntingtown, MD	WDC
Huntley, IL	RCK
Huntsville, AL	BIR
AR	LR
OH	CIN
TX	GAL
UT	SLC
Hurley, NM	LSC
NY	NY
WI	SUP
Huron, CA	FRS
OH	TOL
SD	SFS
Hurricane, WV	WH
Hurst, TX	FWT
Hurt, VA	RIC
Hurtsboro, AL	MOB
Huslia, AK	FBK
Hutchinson, KS	WCH
MN	NU
Hutto, TX	AUS
Huttonsville, WV	WH
Hyannis, MA	FR
Hyattsville, MD	WDC
Hyde Park, MA	BO
NY	NY
UT	SLC
Hydes, MD	BAL
Iberia, MO	JC
Ida, MI	DET
Ida Grove, IA	SC
Idabel, OK	TLS
Idaho Falls, ID	B

Idaho Springs, CO	DEN
Idalou, TX	LUB
Idyllwild, CA	SB
Ignacio, CO	PBL
Ijamsville, MD	BAL
Ilion, NY	ALB
Imlay City, MI	DET
Immaculata, PA	PH
Immokalee, FL	VEN
Imogene, IA	DM
Imperial, CA	SD
MO	STL
NE	LIN
PA	PIT
Imperial Beach, CA	SD
Inchelium, WA	SPK
Incline Village, NV	RNO
Independence, IA	DUB
KS	WCH
KY	COV
LA	BR
MO	KC
OH	CLV
OH	OLL
OR	P
WI	LC
Indialantic, FL	ORL
Indian Creek, IL	CHI
Indian Head, MD	WDC
Indian Lake, NY	OG
Indian River, MI	GLD
Indian Rocks Beach, FL	SP
Indiana, PA	GBG
Indianapolis, IN	IND
IN	PRM
Indianola, IA	DM
MS	JKS
NE	LIN
Indiantown, FL	PMB
Indio, CA	SB
Inez, TX	VIC
Ingalls, KS	DOD
Ingleside, IL	CHI
TX	CC
Inglewood, CA	LA
Ingram, TX	SAT
Inkster, MI	DET
Interlachen, FL	STA
Interlaken, NY	ROC
International Falls, MN	DUL
Intervale, NH	MAN
Inver Grove Heights, MN	STP
Inverness, FL	SP
IL	CHI
Inwood, NY	RVC
WV	WH
Iola, KS	WCH
Ione, WA	SPK
Ionia, MI	GR
Iota, LA	LAF
Iowa, LA	LKC
Iowa City, IA	DAV
Iowa Falls, IA	DUB
Iowa Park, TX	FWT
Ipswich, MA	BO
SD	SFS
Ira Township, MI	DET
Ireland, IN	EVN
Irene, SD	SFS
Iron Mountain, MI	MAR
Iron River, MI	MAR
WI	SUP
Irondale, AL	BIR
Irons, MI	GR
Ironton, MO	SPC
OH	STU
Ironwood, MI	MAR
Irvine, CA	ORG
CA	POC
KY	LEX
Irving, TX	DAL
TX	PBR
Irvington, KY	OWN
NJ	NEW
NY	NY
Irwin, IL	JOL
PA	GBG
Irwindale, CA	LA
Isanti, MN	SCL
Iselin, NJ	MET
Ishpeming, MI	MAR
Island Park, NY	RVC
Isle La Motte, VT	BUR
Isleta Pueblo, NM	SFE
Isleton, CA	SAC
Islip, NY	RVC
Islip Terrace, NY	RVC
Issaquah, WA	SEA
Italy, TX	DAL
Itasca, IL	JOL
Ithaca, MI	SAG

NY	ROC
Ivanhoe, MN	NU
Ivesdale, IL	PEO
Jabor, Jaluit, MI	MI
Jackson, AL	MOB
CA	SAC
GA	ATL
KY	LEX
MI	LAN
MN	WIN
MO	SPC
MS	JKS
NE	OM
NJ	TR
OH	COL
TN	MEM
WY	CHY
Jackson Heights, NY	BRK
Jacksonville, AL	BIR
AR	LR
FL	OLD
FL	SYM
FL	STA
FL	SAM
IL	SFD
NC	R
NC	POC
TX	TYL
Jacksonville Beach, FL	STA
Jaffrey, NH	MAN
Jal, NM	LSC
Jamaica, NY	BRK
Jamaica Estates, NY	BRK
Jamaica Plain, MA	BO
MA	STF
MA	SAM
Jamesburg, NJ	MET
Jamestown, ND	FAR
NY	BUF
OH	CIN
RI	PRO
TN	KNX
Jamison, PA	PH
Jamul, CA	SD
Janesville, MN	WIN
WI	MAD
Jarrell, TX	AUS
Jasper, AL	BIR
GA	ATL
IN	EVN
TX	BEA
Jay, ME	PRT
Jeanerette, LA	LAF
Jeannette, PA	GBG
PA	SJP
Jefferson, GA	ATL
IA	SC
LA	NO
MA	WOR
NC	CHL
OH	Y
SD	SFS
TX	TYL
WI	MAD
Jefferson City, MO	JC
TN	KNX
Jefferson Hills, PA	PIT
Jeffersonville, IN	IND
NY	NY
Jemez Pueblo, NM	SFE
Jemez Springs, NM	SFE
Jena, LA	ALX
Jenison, MI	GR
Jenkins, KY	LEX
Jenkintown, PA	PH
PA	PHU
Jennings, LA	LKC
Jensen Beach, FL	PMB
Jermyn, PA	SCR
Jerome, ID	B
Jersey City, NJ	NEW
NJ	PSC
NJ	PHU
Jersey Shore, PA	SCR
Jerseyville, IL	SFD
Jessup, PA	PSC
PA	SCR
Jesup, GA	SAV
IA	DUB
Jetmore, KS	DOD
Jewett City, CT	NOR
Jim Falls, WI	LC
Jim Thorpe, PA	ALN
Joanna, SC	CHR
Jobstown, NJ	TR
Joelton, TN	NSH
Johannesburg, MI	GLD
John Day, OR	BAK
Johns Creek, GA	ATL
Johns Island, SC	CHR
Johnsburg, IL	RCK

Johnson City, NY	SY
NY	STF
TN	KNX
Johnsonburg, PA	E
Johnston, IA	DM
RI	PRO
Johnston City, IL	BEL
Johnstown, CO	DEN
NY	ALB
OH	COL
PA	ALT
PA	SJP
PA	PBR
Joliet, IL	JOL
Jolon, CA	MRY
Jonesboro, AR	LR
GA	ATL
Jonesburg, MO	JC
Jonestown, MS	JKS
Jonesville, VA	RIC
Joplin, MO	SPC
Joppa, MD	BAL
Jordan, MN	STP
NY	SY
Jordan Valley, OR	BAK
Jourdanton, TX	SAT
Julesburg, CO	DEN
Julian, CA	SD
Junction, TX	SAN
Junction City, KS	SAL
OR	P
WI	LC
Juneau, AK	JUN
Jupiter, FL	PMB
Justice, IL	CHI
Kahoka, MO	JC
Kahuku, HI	HON
Kahului, HI	HON
Kailua, HI	HON
Kailua–Kona, HI	HON
Kalaheo, HI	HON
Kalamazoo, MI	KAL
Kalaupapa, HI	HON
Kalida, OH	TOL
Kalispell, MT	HEL
Kalkaska, MI	GLD
Kalona, IA	DAV
Kalskag, AK	FBK
Kaltag, AK	FBK
Kamiah, ID	B
Kamuela, HI	HON
Kanab, UT	SLC
Kandiyohi, MN	NU
Kane, PA	E
Kaneohe, HI	HON
Kankakee, IL	JOL
Kannapolis, NC	CHL
Kansas City, KS	KCK
MO	KC
MO	PRM
Kansasville, WI	MIL
Kapaa, HI	HON
Kaplan, LA	LAF
Kapolei, HI	HON
Karnes City, TX	SAT
Kathleen, GA	SAV
Katonah, NY	NY
Katy, TX	GAL
Kaufman, TX	DAL
Kaukauna, WI	GB
Kaunakakai, HI	HON
Kayenta, AZ	GLP
Keams Canyon, AZ	GLP
Keansburg, NJ	TR
Kearney, MO	KC
NE	GI
Kearneysville, WV	WH
Kearns, UT	SLC
Kearny, AZ	TUC
NJ	NEW
Keene, NH	MAN
Keeseville, NY	OG
Keizer, OR	P
Kekaha, HI	HON
Keller, TX	FWT
WA	SPK
Kelliher, MN	CR
Kellnersville, WI	GB
Kellogg, ID	B
Kelly, KS	KCK
Kelso, MO	SPC
WA	SEA
Kemmerer, WY	CHY
Kenai, AK	ANC
Kenansville, NC	R
Kendall, WI	LC
Kendall Park, NJ	MET
Kendallville, IN	FTW
Kenedy, TX	SAT
Kenilworth, NJ	NEW
Kenmare, ND	BIS

Kenmore, NY	BUF
NY	STF
Kennebunk, ME	PRT
Kennebunkport, ME	PRT
Kenner, LA	NO
Kennesaw, GA	ATL
Kennett, MO	SPC
Kennett Square, PA	PH
Kennewick, WA	YAK
Kenosha, WI	MIL
WI	SYM
Kensington, CA	OAK
CT	HRT
MD	WDC
Kent, CT	HRT
MN	SCL
OH	Y
PA	GBG
WA	SEA
Kentfield, CA	SFR
Kentland, IN	LFT
Kenton, OH	COL
Kenyon, MN	STP
Keokuk, IA	DAV
Keota, IA	DAV
Kerens, TX	DAL
Kerhonkson, NY	STF
Kerman, CA	FRS
Kermit, TX	ELP
WV	WH
Kernersville, NC	CHL
Kerrville, TX	SAT
Kersey, PA	E
Keshena, WI	GB
Ketchikan, AK	JUN
Kettering, OH	CIN
Kew Gardens, NY	ROM
Kewanee, IL	PEO
Kewaskum, WI	MIL
Kewaunee, WI	GB
Key Biscayne, FL	MIA
Key Largo, FL	MIA
Key West, FL	MIA
Keyport, NJ	TR
Keyser, WV	WH
Keystone Heights, FL	STA
Kickapoo (Edwards), IL	PEO
Kiel, WI	GB
Kieler, WI	MAD
Kihei, HI	HON
Kilgore, TX	TYL
Killdeer, ND	BIS
Killeen, TX	AUS
Killingworth, CT	NOR
Kilmarnock, VA	ARL
Kiln, MS	BLX
Kimball, MN	SCL
NE	GI
SD	SFS
Kimberling City, MO	SPC
Kimberly, WI	GB
Kimberton, PA	PH
Kincaid, IL	SFD
Kinder, LA	LKC
Kindred, ND	FAR
King City, CA	MRY
King of Prussia, PA	PH
Kingfisher, OK	OKL
Kingman, AZ	PHX
KS	WCH
Kings Park, NY	RVC
Kingsburg, CA	FRS
Kingsford, MI	MAR
Kingsland, TX	AUS
Kingsley, IA	SC
MI	GLD
Kingsport, TN	KNX
Kingston, MA	BO
NY	NY
PA	PSC
PA	SCR
RI	PRO
Kingstree, SC	CHR
Kingsville, MD	BAL
OH	Y
TX	CC
Kingwood, WV	WH
Kinnelon, NJ	PAT
Kinsley, KS	DOD
Kinston, NC	R
Kiowa, KS	DOD
Kirkland, WA	SEA
Kirksville, MO	JC
Kirkwood, MO	STL
NY	SY
Kirtland, OH	CLV
Kissimmee, FL	ORL
Kittanning, PA	GBG
Kittery, ME	PRT
Kitty Hawk, NC	R
Klamath Falls, OR	BAK
Klawock, AK	JUN
Knights Landing, CA	SAC
Knightstown, IN	IND
Knottsville, KY	OWN
Knox, IN	GRY
Knox City, TX	FWT
Knoxville, IA	DAV
TN	KNX
TN	PBR
Kodiak, AK	ANC
Kohler, WI	MIL
Kokomo, IN	LFT
Koloa, HI	HON
Konawa, OK	OKL
Kosciusko, MS	JKS
Kotlik, AK	FBK
Kotzebue, AK	FBK
Kountze, TX	BEA
Kouts, IN	GRY
Koyukuk, AK	FBK
Krakow, WI	GB
Kranzburg, SD	SFS
Krebs, OK	TLS
Krotz Springs, LA	LAF
Kula, HI	HON
Kulpmont, PA	HBG
Kutztown, PA	ALN
Kyle, TX	AUS
L'Anse, MI	MAR
La Canada Flintridge, CA	LA
La Conner, WA	SEA
La Crescent, MN	WIN
La Crescenta, CA	LA
La Crosse, WI	LC
La Feria, TX	BWN
La Follette, TN	KNX
La Grande, OR	BAK
La Grange, IL	CHI
TX	AUS
TX	VIC
La Grange Park, IL	CHI
La Grulla, TX	BWN
La Habra, CA	ORG
La Jolla, CA	SD
La Joya, NM	SFE
TX	BWN
La Junta, CO	PBL
La Luz, NM	LSC
La Marque, TX	GAL
La Mesa, CA	SD
CA	STN
NM	LSC
La Mirada, CA	LA
La Moure, ND	FAR
La Pine, OR	BAK
La Place, LA	NO
La Plata, MD	WDC
La Porte, IN	GRY
TX	GAL
La Pryor, TX	LAR
La Puente, CA	LA
La Quinta, CA	SB
La Salle, IL	PEO
La Valle, WI	MAD
La Verne, CA	LA
La Vernia, TX	SAT
LaBelle, FL	VEN
LaCenter, KY	OWN
LaCoste, TX	SAT
LaCrosse, KS	DOD
LaGrange, GA	ATL
IN	FTW
KY	L
LaGrangeville, NY	NY
LaMoure, ND	FAR
Labadieville, LA	BR
Lac du Flambeau, WI	SUP
Lacey, WA	SEA
Laceyville, PA	SCR
Lackawanna, NY	BUF
NY	STF
Lacombe, LA	NO
Lacon, IL	PEO
Laconia, NH	MAN
Ladera Ranch, CA	ORG
Ladue, MO	STL
Lady Lake, FL	ORL
Ladysmith, VA	RIC
WI	SUP
Lafayette, CA	OAK
CO	DEN
IN	LFT
LA	LAF
MN	NU
NY	SY
TN	NSH
Lafayette Hill, PA	PH
Lafitte, LA	NO
Laflin, PA	SCR
Lago Vista, TX	AUS
Laguna, NM	GLP
Laguna Beach, CA	ORG
Laguna Heights, TX	BWN
Laguna Hills, CA	ROM
Laguna Niguel, CA	ORG
Laguna Woods, CA	ORG
Lagunitas, CA	SFR
Lahaina, HI	HON
Laingsburg, MI	LAN
Lake Almanor, CA	SAC
Lake Ariel, PA	SCR
Lake Arrowhead, CA	SB
Lake Arthur, LA	LKC
Lake Balboa, CA	LA
Lake Charles, LA	LKC
Lake City, FL	STA
IA	SC
MI	GLD
MN	WIN
SC	CHR
Lake Clear, NY	OG
Lake Dallas, TX	FWT
Lake Elmo, MN	STP
Lake Forest, CA	ORG
IL	CHI
Lake Geneva, WI	MIL
Lake George, NY	ALB
Lake Harmony, PA	ALN
Lake Havasu City, AZ	PHX
Lake Hopatcong, NJ	PAT
Lake Jackson, TX	GAL
Lake Katrine, NY	NY
Lake Leelanau, MI	GLD
Lake Linden, MI	MAR
Lake Mills, WI	MAD
Lake Milton, OH	Y
Lake Nebagamon, WI	SUP
Lake Odessa, MI	GR
Lake Orion, MI	DET
Lake Oswego, OR	P
Lake Ozark, MO	JC
Lake Park, MN	CR
Lake Placid, FL	VEN
NY	OG
Lake Providence, LA	SHP
Lake Ridge, VA	ARL
Lake Ronkonkoma, NY	RVC
Lake Saint Louis, MO	STL
Lake St. Croix Beach, MN	STP
Lake Station, IN	GRY
Lake Stevens, WA	SEA
Lake View, NY	BUF
Lake Villa, IL	CHI
Lake Village, AR	LR
IN	LFT
Lake Wales, FL	ORL
Lake Winola, PA	SCR
Lake Worth, FL	PMB
Lake Wylie, SC	CHR
Lake Zurich, IL	CHI
Lakehurst, NJ	TR
Lakeland, FL	ORL
GA	SAV
LA	BR
Lakemont, Altoona, PA	ALT
Lakeport, CA	SR
MI	DET
Lakeside, CA	SD
Lakeview, OR	BAK
Lakeville, CT	HRT
MA	BO
MN	STP
Lakeway, TX	AUS
Lakewood, CA	LA
CO	DEN
CO	OLL
NJ	TR
NY	BUF
OH	CLV
WA	SEA
WI	GB
Lakewood Ranch, FL	VEN
Lakin, KS	DOD
Lakota, ND	FAR
Lamar, CO	PBL
MO	SPC
TX	CC
Lamberton, MN	NU
Lambertville, NJ	MET
Lame Deer, MT	GF
Lamesa, TX	LUB
Lamont, CA	FRS
Lamoure, ND	FAR
Lampasas, TX	AUS
Lanai City, HI	HON
Lanark Village, FL	PT
Lancaster, CA	LA
KY	LEX
MA	WOR
NH	MAN
NY	BUF
NY	STF
OH	COL
PA	HBG
SC	CHR
TX	DAL
WI	MAD
Lancing, TN	KNX
Land O'Lakes, FL	SP
WI	SUP
Lander, WY	CHY
Landisville, NJ	CAM
Landover Hills, MD	WDC
Lanesville, IN	IND
Lanett, AL	BIR
Langdon, ND	FAR
Langhorne, PA	PH
Langley, OK	TLS
WA	SEA
Lanham, MD	WDC
Lansdale, PA	PH
Lansdowne, MD	BAL
PA	PH
Lanse, MI	MAR
Lansford, ND	FAR
PA	ALN
PA	PSC
Lansing, IA	DUB
IL	CHI
KS	KCK
MI	LAN
MI	NTN
NY	ROC
Lantana, FL	PMB
Laona, WI	GB
Lapeer, MI	DET
Laramie, WY	CHY
Larchmont, NY	NY
Larchwood, IA	SC
Laredo, TX	LAR
Largo, FL	SP
MD	WDC
Larimore, ND	FAR
Larkspur, CA	SFR
Larned, KS	DOD
Larose, LA	HT
Las Animas, CO	PBL
Las Cruces, NM	LSC
Las Vegas, NM	SFE
NV	HPM
NV	LAV
NV	OLL
NV	SPA
Lastrup, MN	SCL
Latham, NY	ALB
Lathrop, CA	STO
Laton, CA	FRS
Latrobe, PA	GBG
PA	SJP
PA	PBR
Lauderdale-by-the-Sea, FL	MIA
Laughlin, NV	LAV
Laupahoehoe, HI	HON
Laurel, MD	BAL
MD	WDC
MS	BLX
MT	GF
NE	OM
Laurence Harbor, NJ	MET
Laurens, IA	SC
Laurie, MO	JC
Laurinburg, NC	R
Lavallette, NJ	TR
Laveen, AZ	PHX
Laverock, PA	PH
Lavonia, GA	ATL
Lawrence, KS	KCK
KS	STN
MA	BO
MA	SAM
MA	NTN
NE	LIN
Lawrenceburg, IN	IND
KY	LEX
TN	NSH
Lawrenceville, GA	ATL
IL	BEL
NJ	TR
Lawtell, LA	LAF
Lawton, OK	OKL
Layton, UT	SLC
Le Center, MN	STP
Le Mars, IA	SC
Le Roy, NY	BUF
Le Sueur, MN	STP
LeClaire, IA	DAV
Lead, SD	RC
Leadville, CO	COS
League City, TX	GAL
Leavenworth, KS	KCK
WA	YAK
Leawood, KS	KCK
Lebanon, CT	NOR

IL	BEL
IN	LFT
KY	L
MO	SPC
NH	MAN
OH	CIN
OR	P
PA	HBG
TN	NSH
VA	RIC
Lebanon Junction, KY	L
Lebeau, LA	LAF
Lecanto, FL	SP
Lecompte, LA	ALX
Ledyard, IA	SC
Lee, IL	RCK
MA	SPR
Lee Center, NY	SY
Leechburg, PA	GBG
Leeds, AL	BIR
Lees Summit, MO	KC
Leesburg, FL	ORL
VA	ARL
Leesville, LA	ALX
Leetonia, OH	Y
Lefor, ND	BIS
Lehigh Acres, FL	VEN
Lehighton, PA	ALN
Leicester, MA	WOR
Leigh, NE	OM
Leipsic, OH	TOL
Leisenring, PA	PBR
Leisure City, FL	MIA
Leitchfield, KY	OWN
Leland, MS	JKS
Lemay, MO	STL
Lemhi, ID	B
Lemmon, SD	RC
Lemon Grove, CA	SD
Lemont, IL	CHI
IL	LFT
Lemoore, CA	FRS
Lena, IL	RCK
WI	GB
Lenexa, KS	KCK
Lenni, PA	PH
Lennox, SD	SFS
Lenoir, NC	CHL
Lenoir City, TN	KNX
Lenox, IA	DM
MA	SPR
Lenox Dale, MA	SPR
Leola, SD	SFS
Leominster, MA	WOR
Leon, IA	DM
Leonardtown, MD	WDC
Leonia, NJ	NEW
Leonville, LA	LAF
Leopold, IN	IND
MO	SPC
Leslie, MI	LAN
Levelland, TX	LUB
Levittown, NY	RVC
PA	PH
PA	PSC
Lewes, DE	WIL
Lewis Run, PA	E
Lewisburg, PA	HBG
TN	NSH
Lewisport, KY	OWN
Lewiston, ID	B
ME	PRT
MI	GLD
MN	WIN
NY	BUF
Lewistown, IL	PEO
MT	GF
PA	HBG
Lewisville, TX	FWT
TX	OLL
Lexington, KY	LEX
MA	BO
MA	OLN
MI	SAG
MO	KC
MS	JKS
NC	CHL
NE	GI
OH	TOL
SC	CHR
TN	MEM
TX	AUS
VA	RIC
Lexington Park, MD	WDC
Libby, MT	HEL
Liberal, KS	DOD
Liberty, IL	SFD
IN	IND
KY	L
MO	KC
NY	NY
TN	NSH
TX	BEA
Liberty Township, OH	CIN
Libertytown, MD	BAL
Libertyville, IL	CHI
Lidderdale, IA	SC
Lidgerwood, ND	FAR
Liebenthal, KS	DOD
Lighthouse Point, FL	MIA
Ligonier, IN	FTW
PA	GBG
Liguori, MO	STL
Lihue, HI	HON
Lilburn, GA	ATL
Lillian, AL	MOB
Lilly, PA	ALT
Lima, NY	ROC
OH	TOL
Lime Ridge, WI	MAD
Limerick, ME	PRT
Limon, CO	COS
Lincoln, CA	SAC
IL	PEO
KS	SAL
ME	PRT
NE	LIN
NH	MAN
RI	NTN
RI	PRO
Lincoln City, OR	P
Lincoln Park, MI	DET
NJ	PAT
Lincolnton, NC	CHL
Lincroft, NJ	TR
Lindale, TX	TYL
Linden, CA	STO
NJ	NEW
NJ	PSC
VA	ARL
Lindenhurst, NY	RVC
NY	STF
Lindenwold, NJ	CAM
Lindsay, CA	FRS
NE	OM
TX	FWT
Lindstrom, MN	STP
Linesville, PA	E
Linn, MO	JC
Lino Lakes, MN	STP
Linthicum Heights, MD	BAL
Linton, IN	EVN
ND	BIS
Linwood, MA	WOR
MI	SAG
NJ	CAM
Lisbon, ND	FAR
NY	OG
OH	Y
Lisbon Falls, ME	PRT
Lisle, IL	JOL
Litchfield, CT	HRT
IL	SFD
MN	NU
NH	MAN
OH	CLV
Lithia Springs, GA	ATL
Lithonia, GA	ATL
Lititz, PA	HBG
Little Canada, MN	STP
Little Chute, WI	GB
Little Compton, RI	PRO
Little Egg Harbor Twp, NJ	TR
Little Falls, MN	SCL
NJ	OLN
NJ	PAT
NY	ALB
Little Ferry, NJ	NEW
Little Hocking, OH	STU
Little Meadows, PA	NTN
Little River, KS	WCH
Little Rock, AR	LR
Littlefield, TX	LUB
Littlestown, PA	HBG
Littleton, CO	COS
CO	DEN
MA	BO
NH	MAN
Live Oak, FL	STA
Livermore, CA	OAK
IA	SC
Liverpool, NY	SY
Livingston, AL	BIR
CA	FRS
IL	SFD
MT	GF
NJ	NEW
TX	BEA
Livingston Manor, NY	NY
Livonia, LA	BR
MI	DET
MI	OLL
MI	PRM
MI	MCE
NY	ROC
Llano, TX	AUS
Lock Haven, PA	ALT
Lockeford, CA	STO
Lockhart, TX	AUS
Lockport, IL	JOL
LA	HT
NY	BUF
Locust Valley, NY	STF
Lodge Grass, MT	GF
Lodi, CA	STO
NJ	NEW
WI	MAD
Logan, IA	DM
KS	SAL
OH	COL
WV	WH
Logansport, IN	LFT
Loganville, GA	SYM
Loma Linda, CA	SB
Lombard, IL	JOL
IL	OLL
Lomira, WI	MIL
Lomita, CA	LA
Lompoc, CA	LA
London, KY	LEX
OH	COL
Londonderry, NH	MAN
Lone Pine, CA	FRS
Long Beach, CA	LA
MS	BLX
NY	RVC
Long Branch, NJ	TR
Long Grove, IA	DAV
Long Island City, NY	BRK
NY	STF
Long Lake, MN	STP
WI	GB
Long Prairie, MN	SCL
Long Valley, NJ	PAT
Longboat Key, FL	VEN
Longmeadow, MA	SPR
Longmont, CO	DEN
Longview, TX	TYL
WA	SEA
Longville, MN	DUL
Longwood, FL	ORL
Lonsdale, MN	STP
Loogootee, IN	EVN
Lookout Mountain, GA	ATL
Loomis, CA	SAC
Loose Creek, MO	JC
Lorain, OH	CLV
OH	PRM
OH	SJP
Lordsburg, NM	LSC
Loreauville, LA	LAF
Loretto, KY	L
MN	STP
PA	ALT
TN	NSH
Los Alamitos, CA	ORG
Los Alamos, NM	SFE
Los Altos, CA	SJ
Los Altos Hills, CA	SJ
Los Angeles, CA	LA
CA	OLN
CA	OLL
Los Banos, CA	FRS
Los Fresnos, TX	BWN
Los Gatos, CA	SJ
CA	MRY
CA	HPM
Los Lunas, NM	SFE
Los Nietos, CA	LA
Los Ojos, NM	SFE
Los Osos, CA	MRY
Lost Nation, IA	DAV
IA	DUB
Lott, TX	AUS
Loudonville, NY	ALB
OH	CLV
Louisa, KY	LEX
Louisburg, KS	KCK
NC	R
Louisiana, MO	JC
Louisville, CO	DEN
KY	L
KY	SYM
MS	JKS
OH	Y
Loup City, NE	GI
Loveland, CO	DEN
OH	CIN
Lovell, WY	CHY
Lovelock, NV	RNO
Loves Park, IL	RCK
Lovilia, IA	DAV
Loving, NM	LSC
Lovingston, VA	RIC
Lovington, NM	LSC
Lowell, IN	GRY
MA	BO
MI	GR
OH	STU
VT	BUR
Lowellville, OH	Y
Lower Brule, SD	RC
Lower Burrell, PA	GBG
Lowry, MN	SCL
Lowville, NY	OG
Loyal, WI	LC
Lubbock, TX	LUB
Lucan, MN	NU
Lucerne Valley, CA	SB
Lucinda, PA	E
Luck, WI	SUP
Ludington, MI	GR
Ludlow, KY	COV
MA	SPR
MA	STF
VT	BUR
Luebbering, MO	STL
Lufkin, TX	TYL
Lugoff, SC	CHR
Lukachukai, AZ	GLP
Luling, LA	NO
TX	AUS
Lumberton, MS	BLX
NC	R
NM	GLP
TX	BEA
Lunenburg, MA	WOR
Luray, VA	ARL
Lusk, WY	CHY
Lutherville, MD	BAL
Lutherville Timonium, MD	BAL
Lutz, FL	SP
Luverne, MN	WIN
Luxemburg, IA	DUB
WI	GB
Luzerne, PA	SCR
Lydia, LA	LAF
Lyford, TX	BWN
Lykens, PA	HBG
Lynbrook, NY	RVC
Lynch, NE	OM
Lynchburg, VA	RIC
Lynden, WA	SEA
Lyndhurst, NJ	NEW
OH	CLV
Lyndon Station, WI	LC
Lyndora, PA	PBR
PA	SJP
Lynn, MA	BO
Lynnfield, MA	BO
Lynnwood, WA	SEA
Lynwood, CA	LA
Lyon Mountain, NY	OG
Lyons, IL	CHI
KS	WCH
NE	OM
NY	ROC
WI	MIL
Lytle, TX	SAT
Mableton, GA	ATL
Mabton, WA	YAK
Macclenny, FL	STA
Macdona, TX	SAT
Macedon, NY	ROC
Macedonia, OH	CLV
Machias, ME	PRT
Mackinac Island, MI	MAR
Mackinaw City, MI	GLD
Macomb, IL	PEO
MI	DET
Macon, GA	SAV
MO	JC
Madawaska, ME	PRT
Madeira Beach, FL	SP
Madelia, MN	WIN
Madera, CA	FRS
Madill, OK	OKL
Madison, AL	BIR
CT	HRT
FL	PT
IL	SFD
IL	STN
IN	IND
MN	NU
MS	JKS
NE	OM
NJ	PAT
OH	CLV
SD	SFS
TN	NSH
VA	ARL
WI	MAD
WV	WH
Madison Heights, MI	DET

Madison Lake, MN	STP
MN	WIN
Madisonville, KY	OWN
LA	NO
TN	KNX
TX	TYL
Madras, OR	BAK
Madrid, IA	SC
NE	GI
NY	OG
Magee, MS	JKS
Maggie Valley, NC	CHL
Magna, UT	SLC
Magnolia, AR	LR
DE	WIL
TX	GAL
Magnolia Springs, AL	MOB
Mahanoy City, PA	ALN
PA	PSC
Mahnomen, MN	CR
Mahomet, IL	PEO
Mahopac, NY	NY
Mahtomedi, MN	STP
Mahwah, NJ	NEW
Maine, NY	SY
Makawao, HI	HON
Makoti, ND	BIS
Malakoff, TX	TYL
Malden, MA	BO
Malibu, CA	LA
Malone, NY	OG
WI	MIL
Malta, MT	GF
Malvern, AR	LR
PA	PH
Malverne, NY	RVC
Mamaroneck, NY	NY
Mammoth, AZ	TUC
Mammoth Lakes, CA	STO
Mamou, LA	LAF
Man, WV	WH
Manahawkin, NJ	TR
Manalapan, NJ	TR
NJ	MCE
Manasquan, NJ	TR
Manassas, VA	ARL
VA	PHU
Manawa, WI	GB
Mancelona, MI	GLD
Manchester, CT	HRT
IA	DUB
MA	BO
MD	BAL
MI	LAN
MO	STL
NH	MAN
NH	STF
NH	NTN
TN	NSH
Manchester Center, VT	BUR
Manchester Township, NJ	TR
Manchester by the Sea, MA	BO
Mandan, ND	BIS
Mandaree, ND	BIS
Manderson, SD	RC
Mandeville, LA	NO
Mangum, OK	OKL
Manhasset, NY	RVC
Manhattan, IL	JOL
KS	SAL
Manhattan Beach, CA	LA
Manheim, PA	HBG
Manistee, MI	GLD
Manistique, MI	MAR
Manitou Beach, MI	LAN
Manitowish Waters, WI	SUP
Manitowoc, WI	GB
WI	MIL
Mankato, KS	SAL
MN	WIN
Manley, NE	LIN
Manlius, NY	SY
Manly, IA	DUB
Manning, IA	SC
SC	CHR
Mannington, WV	WH
Manomet, MA	BO
Manor, TX	AUS
TX	SYM
Manorville, NY	RVC
Mansfield, LA	SHP
MA	FR
OH	TOL
PA	SCR
TX	FWT
Manson, IA	SC
Mansura, LA	ALX
Mantador, ND	FAR
Manteca, CA	STO
Manteno, IL	JOL
Mantua, NJ	CAM
OH	Y
Manvel, ND	FAR
TX	GAL
Manville, NJ	MET
RI	PRO
Many, LA	SHP
Maple City, MI	GLD
Maple Glen, PA	PH
Maple Grove, MN	STP
Maple Heights, OH	CLV
Maple Hill, KS	KCK
Maple Lake, MN	STP
Maple Mount, KY	OWN
Maple Park, IL	RCK
Maple Shade, NJ	TR
Mapleton, IA	SC
MN	WIN
Mapleville, RI	PRO
Maplewood, MN	STP
MO	STL
NJ	NEW
Maquoketa, IA	DUB
Marana, AZ	TUC
Marathon, FL	MIA
WI	LC
Marathon City, WI	LC
Marble Falls, TX	AUS
Marblehead, MA	BO
OH	PRM
OH	TOL
Marbury, AL	MOB
Marceline, MO	JC
Marcellus, NY	SY
Marco Island, FL	VEN
Marcus, IA	SC
Marengo, IA	DAV
IL	RCK
Marfa, TX	ELP
Margaretville, NY	ALB
Margate, FL	MCE
FL	MIA
FL	SYM
NJ	CAM
Margate City, NJ	CAM
Maria Stein, OH	CIN
Marianna, AR	LR
FL	PT
Maricopa, AZ	TUC
Marienthal, KS	DOD
Marietta, GA	ATL
NY	SY
OH	STU
Marina, CA	MRY
Marine City, MI	DET
Marine on St. Croix, MN	STP
Marinette, WI	GB
Maringouin, LA	BR
Marion, IA	DUB
IL	BEL
KS	WCH
KY	OWN
MA	FR
OH	COL
VA	RIC
Marionville, MO	SPC
Mariposa, CA	FRS
Marked Tree, AR	LR
Markham, IL	CHI
Marksville, LA	ALX
Marlboro, NJ	TR
NY	NY
Marlborough, CT	HRT
MA	BO
Marlin, TX	AUS
Marlinton, WV	WH
Marlton, NJ	TR
Marmarth, ND	BIS
Marmora, NJ	CAM
Marne, MI	GR
Marquette, MI	MAR
Marrero, LA	NO
Marriottsville, MD	BAL
Mars Hill, NC	CHL
Marseilles, IL	PEO
Marshall, AK	FBK
IL	SFD
MI	KAL
MN	NU
MO	JC
TX	TYL
Marshalltown, IA	DUB
Marshfield, MA	BO
MO	SPC
WI	LC
Mart, TX	AUS
Marthasville, MO	STL
Martin, KY	LEX
OH	TOL
SD	RC
TN	MEM
Martindale, TX	AUS
Martinez, CA	OAK
Martins Creek, PA	ALN
Martins Ferry, OH	STU
Martinsburg, MO	JC
WV	WH
Martinsville, IN	IND
NJ	MET
VA	RIC
Marty, SD	SFS
Mary Esther, FL	PT
Marydel, MD	WIL
Maryknoll, NY	NY
Maryland Heights, MO	STL
Marylhurst, OR	P
Marysville, CA	SAC
KS	KCK
MI	DET
OH	COL
PA	HBG
WA	SEA
Maryville, IL	SFD
MO	KC
Masaryktown, FL	SP
Mascoutah, IL	BEL
Mashpee, MA	FR
Mason, MI	LAN
OH	CIN
TX	AUS
Mason City, IA	DUB
Masontown, PA	GBG
Maspeth, NY	BRK
Massapequa, NY	RVC
Massapequa Park, NY	RVC
Massena, IA	DM
NY	OG
Massillon, OH	Y
Mastic Beach, NY	RVC
Masury, OH	Y
Matamoras, PA	SCR
Matawan, NJ	TR
NJ	MET
NJ	PSC
Mathews, VA	RIC
Mathis, TX	CC
Mattapan, MA	BO
Mattapoisett, MA	FR
Mattawa, WA	YAK
Mattawan, MI	KAL
Matteson, IL	CHI
Mattoon, IL	SFD
Mauldin, SC	CHR
Maumee, OH	TOL
Maurepas, LA	BR
Maurice, LA	LAF
Mauriceville, TX	BEA
Mauston, WI	LC
Maximo, OH	Y
Maybrook, NY	NY
Mayer, AZ	PHX
Mayetta, KS	KCK
Mayfield, KY	OWN
Maynard, MA	BO
Maynardville, TN	KNX
Mays Landing, NJ	CAM
Maysel, WV	WH
Maysville, KY	COV
Mayville, ND	FAR
WI	MIL
Maywood, CA	LA
IL	CHI
IL	SYM
NJ	NEW
Mazomanie, WI	MAD
Mc Intosh, SD	RC
Mc Kean, PA	E
Mc Lean, VA	ARL
Mc Leansboro, IL	BEL
McAdoo, PA	ALN
PA	PHU
PA	PSC
McAfee, NJ	PAT
McAlester, OK	TLS
McAllen, TX	BWN
McCall, ID	B
McCamey, TX	SAN
McComb, MS	JKS
McConnellsburg, PA	ALT
McCook, NE	LIN
McCormick, SC	CHR
McDonald, OH	Y
PA	PIT
McDonough, GA	ATL
McEwen, TN	NSH
McFarland, CA	FRS
WI	MAD
McGehee, AR	LR
McGrath, AK	FBK
McGregor, MN	DUL
TX	AUS
McHenry, IL	RCK
McKees Rocks, PA	PBR
PA	PIT
PA	SJP
McKeesport, PA	PBR
PA	PIT
PA	ROM
PA	SJP
McKenzie Bridge, OR	P
McKinleyville, CA	SR
McKinney, TX	DAL
McLaughlin, SD	RC
McLean, VA	ARL
VA	NTN
VA	WDC
McMechen, WV	WH
McMinnville, OR	P
TN	NSH
McMurray, PA	PIT
McNair, TX	GAL
McPherson, KS	WCH
McRae, GA	SAV
McSherrystown, PA	HBG
Mcnary, AZ	GLP
Mead, CO	DEN
NE	LIN
Meade, KS	DOD
Meadow Lands, PA	PIT
Meadowbrook, PA	PH
Meadville, PA	E
Mecca, CA	SB
Mechanicsburg, OH	CIN
PA	HBG
Mechanicsville, IA	DAV
MD	WDC
VA	RIC
Mechanicville, NY	ALB
Medfield, MA	BO
Medford, MA	BO
MN	WIN
NJ	TR
NY	RVC
OK	OKL
OR	P
WI	SUP
Media, PA	PH
Medical Lake, WA	SPK
Medicine Lodge, KS	DOD
Medina, NY	BUF
OH	CLV
Medway, MA	BO
Meeker, CO	DEN
Megargel, TX	FWT
Meherrin, VA	RIC
Melbourne, FL	ORL
KY	COV
Melbourne Beach, FL	ORL
Melcher, IA	DAV
Mellen, WI	SUP
Mellette, SD	SFS
Melrose, IA	DAV
MA	BO
MA	POC
MN	SCL
WI	LC
Melrose Park, IL	CHI
PA	PHU
Melville, LA	LAF
NY	RVC
Melvindale, MI	DET
Memphis, MI	DET
MO	JC
TN	MEM
TX	AMA
Mena, AR	LR
Menahga, MN	SCL
Menands, NY	ALB
Menard, TX	SAN
Menasha, WI	GB
Mendham, NJ	PAT
Mendocino, CA	SR
Mendon, MI	KAL
NY	ROC
Mendota, CA	FRS
IL	PEO
MN	STP
Mendota Heights, MN	OLL
MN	STP
Menlo Park, CA	SJ
CA	SFR
Menoken, ND	BIS
Menominee, MI	MAR
Menomonee Falls, WI	MIL
Menomonie, WI	LC
Mentor, MN	CR
OH	CLV
Mentor–on–the–Lake, OH	PRM
Mequon, WI	MIL
Meraux, LA	NO
Merced, CA	FRS
Mercedes, TX	BWN
Mercer, PA	E
WI	SUP

Mercer Island, WA	SEA
Merchantville, NJ	CAM
Meredith, NH	MAN
Meriden, CT	HRT
Meridian, ID	B
MS	JKS
Merion Station, PA	PH
Mermentau, LA	LAF
Merrick, NY	RVC
Merrill, IA	SC
OR	BAK
WI	SUP
Merrillville, IN	GRY
IN	PRM
Merrimack, NH	MAN
Merritt Island, FL	ORL
Mesa, AZ	PHX
ID	B
Mesilla, NM	LSC
Mesilla Park, NM	LSC
Mesquite, NV	LAV
TX	DAL
TX	MCE
Metairie, LA	NO
Metamora, IL	PEO
Methuen, MA	BO
MA	NTN
Metropolis, IL	BEL
Metuchen, NJ	MET
Mexia, TX	AUS
Mexico, ME	PRT
MO	JC
NY	SY
Mexico Beach, FL	PT
Meyersdale, PA	ALT
Meyersville, TX	VIC
Miami, AZ	TUC
FL	ARL
FL	PSC
FL	SAM
FL	SJP
FL	NTN
FL	MIA
OK	TLS
Miami Beach, FL	MIA
Miami Gardens, FL	MIA
Miami Lakes, FL	MIA
Miami Shores, FL	MIA
Miamisburg, OH	CIN
Michigan Center, MI	LAN
Michigan City, IN	GRY
Middle Village, NY	BRK
Middlebourne, WV	WH
Middleburg, FL	STA
VA	ARL
Middleburg Heights, OH	CLV
Middleburgh, NY	ALB
Middlebury, CT	HRT
VT	BUR
Middlefield, CT	NOR
Middlesboro, KY	LEX
Middlesex, NJ	MET
Middleton, MA	BO
WI	MAD
Middletown, CA	SR
CT	NOR
DE	WIL
MD	BAL
NJ	TR
NY	NY
NY	STF
OH	CIN
PA	HBG
RI	PRO
Middletown Springs, VT	BUR
Midland, MD	BAL
MI	SAG
PA	PIT
TX	SAN
Midland City, AL	MOB
Midland Park, NJ	NEW
Midlothian, IL	CHI
VA	RIC
Midvale, UT	SLC
Midway City, CA	ORG
Midwest City, OK	OKL
Mifflintown, PA	HBG
Milaca, MN	SCL
Milan, IL	PEO
IN	IND
MI	LAN
MO	JC
NM	GLP
OH	TOL
Milbank, SD	SFS
Miles, TX	SAN
Miles City, MT	GF
Milford, CT	HRT
DE	WIL
IA	SC
MA	WOR

MI	DET
NH	MAN
NJ	MET
OH	CIN
PA	SCR
UT	SLC
Mililani Town, HI	HON
Mill Creek, WA	SEA
Mill Valley, CA	SFR
Milladore, WI	LC
Millbrae, CA	OLL
CA	SFR
Millbrook, NY	NY
Millbury, MA	WOR
Milledgeville, GA	ATL
Millen, GA	SAV
Miller, SD	SFS
Miller City, OH	TOL
Millersburg, OH	COL
PA	HBG
Millersville, MD	BAL
Millington, TN	MEM
Millis, MA	BO
Millstadt, IL	BEL
Millstone Township, NJ	TR
Milltown, NJ	MET
Millville, MA	WOR
NJ	CAM
NJ	PHU
Milmont Park, PA	PH
Milnor, ND	FAR
Milpitas, CA	SJ
CA	SYM
Milroy, MN	NU
Milton, FL	PT
LA	LAF
MA	BO
PA	HBG
VT	BUR
WI	MAD
Milton Freewater, OR	BAK
Milwaukee, WI	MIL
WI	STN
WI	NTN
Milwaukie, OR	P
Mims, FL	ORL
Minden, LA	SHP
NE	LIN
Mineola, NY	RVC
TX	TYL
Mineral, VA	RIC
Mineral Point, WI	MAD
Mineral Ridge, OH	Y
Mineral Wells, TX	FWT
Minersville, PA	ALN
PA	PSC
PA	PHU
Minerva, OH	STU
Minetto, NY	SY
Mingo Junction, OH	PBR
OH	STU
Minneapolis, KS	SAL
MN	OLL
MN	STP
MN	STN
MN	PRM
Minneota, MN	NU
Minnetonka, MN	STP
Minong, WI	SUP
Minooka, IL	JOL
Minot, ND	BIS
Minster, OH	CIN
Minto, ND	FAR
Minturn, CO	DEN
Mio, MI	GLD
Miramar, FL	MIA
Miramar Beach, FL	PT
Mishawaka, IN	FTW
IN	STN
Mishicot, WI	GB
Misquamicut, RI	PRO
Mission, KS	KCK
SD	RC
TX	BWN
Mission Hills, CA	LA
Mission Viejo, CA	ORG
Missoula, MT	HEL
Missouri City, TX	GAL
TX	SYM
Missouri Valley, IA	DM
Mitchell, IN	IND
NE	GI
SD	SFS
Mitchellville, MD	WDC
Moab, UT	SLC
Moberly, MO	JC
Mobile, AL	MOB
AL	POC
Mobridge, SD	SFS
Mocanaqua, PA	SCR
Mocksville, NC	CHL

Modesto, CA	STO
Mogadore, OH	Y
Mohall, ND	BIS
Mohawk, NY	ALB
Mohnton, PA	ALN
Mokane, MO	JC
Mokena, IL	JOL
Molalla, OR	P
Moline, IL	PEO
KS	WCH
Momence, IL	JOL
Monaca, PA	PIT
Monahans, TX	ELP
Moncks Corner, SC	CHR
Mondovi, WI	LC
Monee, IL	JOL
Monessen, PA	GBG
PA	PBR
Moneta, VA	RIC
Monett, MO	SPC
Monkton, MD	BAL
Monmouth, IL	PEO
OR	P
Monmouth Beach, NJ	TR
Monmouth Junction, NJ	MET
Monona, IA	DUB
WI	MAD
Monongah, WV	WH
Monongahela, PA	PIT
Monroe, CT	BGP
GA	ATL
LA	SHP
MI	DET
NC	CHL
NY	NY
OH	CIN
WA	SEA
WI	MAD
Monroe City, MO	JC
Monroe Township, NJ	MET
Monroeville, AL	MOB
IN	FTW
OH	TOL
PA	PBR
PA	PIT
Monrovia, CA	LA
Monsey, NY	NY
Monson, MA	SPR
Mont Belvieu, TX	BEA
Mont Clare, PA	PSC
Montague, MI	GR
NJ	PAT
Montauk, NY	RVC
Montclair, CA	SB
NJ	NEW
Monte Vista, CO	PBL
Montebello, CA	LA
Montegut, LA	HT
Montello, WI	MAD
Monterey, CA	MRY
IN	LFT
Monterey Park, CA	LA
Montevallo, AL	BIR
Montevideo, MN	NU
Montezuma, OH	CIN
Montfort, WI	MAD
Montgomery, AL	MOB
IN	EVN
MN	STP
NY	NY
WV	WH
Montgomery City, MO	JC
Monticello, AR	LR
IA	DUB
IL	PEO
IN	LFT
KY	LEX
MN	STP
NY	NY
UT	SLC
Montoursville, PA	SCR
Montpelier, OH	TOL
VA	RIC
VT	BUR
Montrose, CA	LA
CA	OLN
CO	PBL
IL	SFD
MI	LAN
MO	KC
NY	NY
PA	SCR
SD	SFS
Montvale, NJ	NEW
Montville, NJ	PAT
Monument, CO	COS
Moodus, CT	NOR
Mooers, NY	OG
Mooers Forks, NY	OG
Moon Township, PA	PIT
Moore, OK	OKL

Moore Haven, FL	VEN
Moorefield, WV	WH
Moorestown, NJ	TR
Mooresville, IN	IND
NC	CHL
Mooreton, ND	FAR
Moorhead, MN	CR
Moorpark, CA	LA
Moose Lake, MN	DUL
Moosup, CT	NOR
Mora, MN	SCL
NM	SFE
Moraga, CA	OAK
Moreauville, LA	ALX
Morehead, KY	LEX
Morehead City, NC	R
Morenci, AZ	TUC
Moreno Valley, CA	SB
Morgan, MN	NU
TX	FWT
Morgan City, LA	HT
LA	LAF
Morgan Hill, CA	SJ
Morganfield, KY	OWN
Morganton, NC	CHL
Morgantown, KY	OWN
WV	WH
WV	PBR
Morganza, LA	BR
MD	WDC
Moriarty, NM	SFE
Morning View, KY	COV
Morrice, MI	LAN
Morrilton, AR	LR
Morris, IL	JOL
IN	IND
MN	SCL
NY	ALB
Morris Plains, NJ	PAT
Morrisdale, PA	E
Morrison, IL	RCK
Morrisonville, IL	SFD
NY	OG
Morristown, NJ	PAT
NY	OG
TN	KNX
Morrisville, NY	SY
PA	PH
VT	BUR
Morro Bay, CA	MRY
Morrow, LA	LAF
OH	CIN
Morse, LA	LAF
Morse Bluff, NE	LIN
Morton, IL	PEO
MN	NU
PA	PH
TX	LUB
WA	SEA
Morton Grove, IL	CHI
IL	MCE
IL	SYM
Moscow, ID	B
PA	SCR
Moses Lake, WA	YAK
Mosinee, WI	LC
Moss Beach, CA	SFR
Moss Bluff, LA	LKC
Moss Point, MS	BLX
Mott, ND	BIS
Moulton, AL	BIR
TX	VIC
Moultrie, GA	SAV
Mound, MN	STP
Mound Bayou, MS	JKS
Mound City, IL	BEL
Moundsville, WV	WH
Mount Airy, MD	BAL
Mount Angel, OR	P
Mount Arlington, NJ	PAT
Mount Calvary, WI	MIL
Mount Carmel, IL	BEL
PA	HBG
PA	PHU
Mount Carroll, IL	RCK
Mount Clemens, MI	DET
Mount Dora, FL	ORL
Mount Ephraim, NJ	CAM
Mount Holly, NJ	TR
Mount Hope, KS	WCH
Mount Horeb, WI	MAD
Mount Ida, AR	LR
Mount Jewett, PA	E
Mount Joy, PA	HBG
Mount Laurel, NJ	TR
Mount Morris, MI	LAN
Mount Olive, IL	SFD
NC	R
Mount Pleasant, IA	DAV
MI	SAG
PA	GBG

SC	CHR
TX	TYL
Mount Pocono, PA	SCR
Mount Rainier, MD	WDC
Mount Saint Francis, IN	IND
Mount Shasta, CA	SAC
Mount St. Francis, IN	IND
Mount St. Joseph, OH	CIN
Mount Sterling, IL	SFD
KY	LEX
Mount Union, PA	ALT
Mount Vernon, AL	MOB
IA	DUB
IL	BEL
IN	EVN
KY	LEX
MO	SPC
NY	NY
TX	TYL
WA	SEA
Mount Victoria, MD	WDC
Mount Washington, KY	L
Mountain City, TN	KNX
Mountain Grove, MO	SPC
Mountain Home, AR	LR
ID	B
TX	SAT
Mountain Home A F B, ID	B
Mountain Lakes, NJ	PAT
Mountain Top, PA	SCR
Mountain View, AR	LR
CA	SJ
HI	HON
MO	SPC
Mountain Village, AK	FBK
Mountainair, NM	SFE
Mountainside, NJ	NEW
Mountlake Terrace, WA	SEA
Moville, IA	SC
Moweaqua, IL	SFD
Moxee, WA	YAK
Mt. Airy, NC	CHL
Mt. Kisco, NY	NY
Mt. Lebanon, PA	PIT
Mt. Prospect, IL	CHI
Mt. Vernon, OH	COL
Mt. Zion, IL	SFD
Muenster, TX	FWT
Mukwonago, WI	MIL
Muleshoe, TX	LUB
Mullen, NE	GI
Mullens, WV	WH
Mullica Hill, NJ	CAM
Mulvane, KS	WCH
Muncie, IN	LFT
Muncy, PA	SCR
Munday, TX	FWT
Mundelein, IL	CHI
Munhall, PA	PBR
PA	PIT
Munich, ND	FAR
Munising, MI	MAR
Munjor, KS	SAL
Munnsville, NY	SY
Munster, IN	GRY
IN	STN
IN	PRM
Murdock, MN	NU
Murfreesboro, TN	NSH
Murphy, NC	CHL
Murphy Village, SC	CHR
Murphysboro, IL	BEL
Murray, KY	OWN
UT	OLL
UT	SLC
Murrells Inlet, SC	CHR
Murrieta, CA	SB
Murrysville, PA	GBG
Muscatine, IA	DAV
Muse, PA	PIT
Muskego, WI	MIL
Muskegon, MI	GR
Muskegon Heights, MI	GR
Muskogee, OK	TLS
Mustang, OK	OKL
Myerstown, PA	HBG
Myrtle Beach, SC	CHR
Myrtle Creek, OR	P
Mystic, CT	NOR
Naalehu, HI	HON
Naches, WA	YAK
Nacogdoches, TX	TYL
Nada, TX	VIC
Nadeau, MI	MAR
Nahant, MA	BO
Nampa, ID	B
Nanakuli, HI	HON
Nanticoke, PA	PHU
PA	SCR
Nantucket, MA	FR
Nanty–Glo, PA	ALT
PA	PBR
Nanuet, NY	NY
Napa, CA	SR
Naperville, IL	JOL
Naples, FL	VEN
Napoleon, IN	IND
ND	FAR
OH	TOL
Napoleonville, LA	BR
Naranja, FL	MIA
Narberth, PA	PH
Narragansett, RI	PRO
Narrowsburg, NY	NY
Nashotah, WI	MIL
Nashua, IA	DUB
NH	MAN
Nashville, AR	LR
IL	BEL
IN	IND
KS	WCH
TN	NSH
Nashwauk, MN	DUL
Nassau, NY	ALB
Natchez, LA	ALX
MS	JKS
Natchitoches, LA	ALX
Natick, MA	BO
National City, CA	SD
MI	GLD
Natrona Heights, PA	PIT
Naugatuck, CT	HRT
Nauvoo, IL	PEO
Navajo, NM	GLP
Navarre, FL	PT
OH	Y
Navasota, TX	GAL
Nazareth, KY	L
MI	KAL
PA	ALN
TX	AMA
Nebraska City, NE	LIN
Necedah, WI	LC
Nederland, TX	BEA
Needham, MA	BO
Needles, CA	SB
Needville, TX	GAL
Neenah, WI	GB
Neffs, OH	STU
Negaunee, MI	MAR
Neillsville, WI	LC
Nekoosa, WI	LC
Neligh, NE	OM
Nelsonville, OH	STU
Nenana, AK	FBK
Neodesha, KS	WCH
Neola, IA	DM
Neopit, WI	GB
Neosho, MO	SPC
Neptune, NJ	TR
Nerinx, KY	L
Nesbit, MS	JKS
Nesconset, NY	RVC
Nespelem, WA	SPK
Nesquehoning, PA	ALN
PA	PSC
Ness City, KS	DOD
Netcong, NJ	PAT
Nevada, MO	KC
Nevada City, CA	SAC
Nevis, MN	CR
New Albany, IN	IND
MS	JKS
OH	COL
New Alexandria, PA	GBG
New Almelo, KS	SAL
New Athens, IL	BEL
New Baden, IL	BEL
New Baltimore, MI	DET
MI	MCE
PA	ALT
New Bavaria, OH	TOL
New Bedford, MA	FR
MA	SAM
New Berlin, IL	SFD
NY	SY
WI	MIL
New Bern, NC	R
New Bethlehem, PA	E
New Blaine, AR	LR
New Bloomfield, PA	HBG
New Boston, MI	DET
OH	COL
TX	TYL
New Braunfels, TX	SAT
New Bremen, OH	CIN
New Brighton, MN	STP
PA	PIT
New Britain, CT	HRT
CT	STF
CT	PSC
New Brunswick, NJ	MET
NJ	PSC
New Buffalo, MI	KAL
New Cambria, MO	JC
New Canaan, CT	BGP
New Caney, TX	GAL
New Carlisle, IN	FTW
OH	CIN
New Castle, DE	WIL
IN	IND
PA	PIT
PA	SAM
VA	RIC
New City, NY	NY
New Cumberland, PA	HBG
WV	WH
New Cuyama, CA	LA
New Egypt, NJ	TR
New England, ND	BIS
New Fairfield, CT	BGP
New Franken, WI	GB
New Freedom, PA	HBG
New Hampton, IA	DUB
New Hartford, CT	HRT
NY	SY
New Haven, CT	HRT
CT	STF
IN	FTW
KY	L
MO	STL
New Hill, NC	R
New Holland, PA	HBG
New Holstein, WI	GB
New Hope, KY	L
MN	STP
PA	PH
New Hyde Park, NY	MCE
NY	RVC
New Iberia, LA	LAF
New Ipswich, NH	MAN
New Kensington, PA	GBG
New Lebanon, NY	ALB
New Leipzig, ND	BIS
New Lenox, IL	JOL
New Lexington, OH	COL
New Lisbon, WI	LC
New London, CT	NOR
MN	NU
NH	MAN
OH	TOL
WI	GB
New Lothrop, MI	SAG
New Madrid, MO	SPC
New Market, MN	STP
TN	KNX
New Martinsville, WV	WH
New Melle, MO	STL
New Middletown, OH	Y
New Milford, CT	HRT
NJ	NEW
New Monmouth, NJ	TR
New Munich, MN	SCL
New Munster, WI	MIL
New Orleans, LA	NO
LA	PBR
New Oxford, PA	HBG
New Paltz, NY	NY
New Philadelphia, OH	COL
PA	ALN
New Port Richey, FL	SP
FL	PSC
New Prague, MN	STP
New Providence, NJ	NEW
New Richland, MN	WIN
New Richmond, OH	CIN
WI	SUP
New Riegel, OH	TOL
New Ringgold, PA	ALN
New River, AZ	PHX
New Roads, LA	BR
New Rochelle, NY	NY
NY	MCE
New Rockford, ND	FAR
New Salem, ND	BIS
PA	PBR
New Smyrna Beach, FL	ORL
New Town, ND	BIS
New Trier, MN	STP
New Ulm, MN	NU
TX	VIC
New Vernon, NJ	PAT
New Vienna, IA	DUB
New Washington, OH	TOL
New Waverly, TX	GAL
New Windsor, NY	NY
New York, NY	NY
NY	PRO
NY	STF
NY	PSC
New York Mills, NY	SY
Newark, CA	OAK
DE	WIL
NJ	NEW
NJ	PSC
NJ	PHU
NY	ROC
OH	COL
VT	STF
Newaygo, MI	GR
Newberg, OR	P
Newberry, MI	MAR
SC	CHR
Newburg, MD	WDC
WI	MIL
Newburgh, IN	EVN
NY	NY
Newbury, OH	CLV
Newbury Park, CA	LA
Newburyport, MA	BO
Newcastle, WY	CHY
Newcomb, NY	OG
Newcomerstown, OH	COL
Newfane, NY	BUF
Newfield, NJ	CAM
Newington, CT	HRT
Newman, CA	STO
Newmarket, NH	MAN
Newnan, GA	ATL
Newport, KY	COV
MI	DET
NH	MAN
NY	ALB
OR	P
RI	PRO
TN	KNX
VT	BUR
WA	SPK
Newport Beach, CA	ORG
Newport News, VA	RIC
Newry, PA	ALT
Newtok, AK	FBK
Newton, IA	DAV
IL	BEL
IL	SFD
KS	WCH
MA	BO
MA	OLD
NC	CHL
NJ	PAT
WI	GB
Newton Falls, OH	Y
OH	PBR
Newton Grove, NC	R
Newtown, CT	BGP
PA	PH
Newtown Square, PA	PH
PA	SAM
Nez Perce, ID	B
Niagara, WI	GB
Niagara Falls, NY	BUF
NY	STF
Niagara University, NY	BUF
Niantic, CT	NOR
Niceville, FL	PT
Nicholasville, KY	LEX
Nicholson, PA	SCR
Nicktown, PA	ALT
Nicollet, MN	NU
Nightmute, AK	FBK
Niles, IL	CHI
MI	KAL
OH	Y
Nine Mile Falls, WA	SPK
Nipomo, CA	MRY
Nisswa, MN	DUL
Nitro, WV	WH
Nixa, MO	SPC
Nixon, TX	SAT
Noblesville, IN	LFT
Nogales, AZ	TUC
Nokomis, FL	VEN
IL	SFD
Nome, AK	FBK
Norco, CA	SB
LA	NO
Norcross, GA	ATL
GA	SYM
Norfolk, MA	BO
NE	OM
NY	OG
VA	RIC
Norge, VA	RIC
Normal, IL	PEO
Norman, OK	OKL
OK	OLL
Normandy, MO	STL
Norridge, IL	CHI
Norris, TN	KNX
Norristown, PA	PH
North Adams, MA	SPR
North Andover, MA	BO
North Arlington, NJ	NEW
North Attleboro, MA	FR

North Augusta, SC	CHR
North Aurora, IL	RCK
North Baltimore, OH	TOL
North Bay, NY	SY
North Beach, MD	WDC
North Bend, NE	OM
OH	CIN
OR	P
North Bennington, VT	BUR
North Bergen, NJ	NEW
North Bethesda, MD	WDC
North Branch, MI	DET
MN	STP
North Branford, CT	HRT
North Brookfield, MA	WOR
North Brunswick, NJ	MET
North Caldwell, NJ	NEW
North Canton, OH	Y
North Cape May, NJ	CAM
North Charleston, SC	CHR
North Chesterfield, VA	RIC
North Chili, NY	ROC
North Collins, NY	BUF
North Conway, NH	MAN
North Creek, NY	ALB
North Dartmouth, MA	FR
North Dighton, MA	FR
North East, PA	E
North Easton, MA	FR
North English, IA	DAV
North Falmouth, MA	FR
North Fond du Lac, WI	MIL
North Grafton, MA	WOR
North Grosvenordale, CT	NOR
North Guilford, CT	HRT
North Haledon, NJ	PAT
North Haven, CT	HRT
North Highlands, CA	SAC
North Hills, CA	LA
North Hollywood, CA	LA
CA	NTN
CA	OLD
CA	SPA
CA	MCE
North Huntingdon, PA	GBG
PA	PBR
North Jackson, OH	Y
OH	OLL
North Judson, IN	GRY
North Kingstown, RI	PRO
North Lake, WI	MIL
North Las Vegas, NV	LAV
North Lauderdale, FL	MIA
North Lewisburg, OH	CIN
North Lima, OH	Y
North Little Rock, AR	LR
North Manchester, IN	FTW
North Mankato, MN	NU
North Merrick, NY	RVC
North Miami, FL	MIA
North Miami Beach, FL	MIA
North Muskegon, MI	GR
North Myrtle Beach, SC	CHR
North Olmsted, OH	CLV
North Oxford, MA	WOR
North Palm Beach, FL	PMB
North Plainfield, NJ	MET
North Plains, OR	P
North Platte, NE	GI
NE	LIN
North Pole, AK	FBK
North Port, FL	SJP
FL	VEN
North Providence, RI	PRO
North Reading, MA	BO
North Richland Hills, TX	FWT
North Ridgeville, OH	CLV
North Riverside, IL	CHI
North Royalton, OH	CLV
OH	PRM
North Saint Paul, MN	STP
North Scituate, RI	PRO
North Smithfield, RI	PRO
North Stonington, CT	NOR
North Syracuse, NY	SY
North Tonawanda, NY	BUF
North Troy, VT	BUR
North Vernon, IN	IND
North Wales, PA	PH
North Wildwood, NJ	CAM
North Wilkesboro, NC	CHL
Northampton, MA	SPR
PA	ALN
PA	PHU
Northboro, MA	WOR
Northbridge, MA	WOR
Northbrook, IL	CHI
IL	EST
Northern Cambria, PA	ALT
PA	SJP
PA	PBR
Northfield, IL	CHI
MA	SPR
MN	STP
NJ	CAM
OH	CLV
VT	BUR
Northford, CT	HRT
Northglenn, CO	DEN
Northlake, IL	CHI
IL	NTN
Northport, NY	RVC
WA	SPK
Northridge, CA	LA
Northvale, NJ	NEW
Northville, MI	DET
NY	ALB
Northwood, OH	PRM
Norton, KS	SAL
MA	FR
OH	CLV
VA	RIC
Nortonville, KS	KCK
Norwalk, CA	LA
CT	BGP
CT	SYM
IA	DM
OH	TOL
Norway, ME	PRT
MI	MAR
Norwell, MA	BO
Norwich, CT	NOR
NY	SY
Norwichtown, CT	NOR
Norwood, MA	BO
MN	STP
NJ	NEW
NY	OG
PA	PH
Notre Dame, IN	FTW
Novato, CA	SFR
Novi, MI	DET
Nulato, AK	FBK
Nutley, NJ	NEW
Nyack, NY	NY
Nyssa, OR	BAK
O Fallon, IL	BEL
O'Donnell, TX	LUB
O'Fallon, MO	STL
O'Neill, NE	OM
Oak Brook, IL	JOL
Oak Creek, WI	MIL
Oak Forest, IL	CHI
Oak Grove, KY	OWN
LA	SHP
MN	STP
Oak Harbor, OH	TOL
WA	SEA
Oak Hill, WV	WH
Oak Lawn, IL	CHI
Oak Park, IL	CHI
MI	DET
MI	EST
Oak Park Heights, MN	STP
Oak Ridge, NJ	PAT
TN	KNX
Oak Ridge–Milton, NJ	PAT
Oakbrook Terrace, IL	JOL
IL	OLL
Oakdale, CA	STO
CT	NOR
IL	BEL
LA	LKC
MN	STP
NE	OM
NY	RVC
PA	PIT
Oakes, ND	FAR
Oakfield, NY	BUF
Oakhurst, CA	FRS
Oakland, CA	OAK
MD	BAL
NJ	NEW
Oakland City, IN	EVN
Oakland Gardens, NY	BRK
Oakland Park, FL	MIA
Oakley, CA	OAK
KS	SAL
Oaklyn, NJ	CAM
Oakmont, PA	PIT
Oakridge, OR	P
Oakville, CA	SR
CT	HRT
MO	STL
Oberlin, KS	SAL
LA	LKC
OH	CLV
Obernburg, NY	NY
Ocala, FL	ORL
Occidental, CA	SR
Ocean Beach, NY	RVC
Ocean City, MD	WIL
NJ	CAM
Ocean Grove, NJ	TR
Ocean Springs, MS	BLX
Oceanside, CA	SD
CA	POC
CA	NTN
NY	RVC
Oconee, IL	SFD
Oconomowoc, WI	MIL
Oconto, WI	GB
Oconto Falls, WI	GB
Odebolt, IA	SC
Odem, TX	CC
Odenton, MD	BAL
Odessa, MO	KC
TX	SAN
Oelwein, IA	DUB
Ogallala, NE	GI
Ogden, IA	SC
UT	SLC
Ogdensburg, NJ	PAT
NY	OG
Ogema, MN	CR
Oglala, SD	RC
Oglesby, IL	PEO
Ohio, IL	PEO
Ohkay Owingeh, NM	SFE
Oil City, PA	E
Ojai, CA	LA
Okanogan, WA	SPK
Okarche, OK	OKL
Okawville, IL	BEL
Okeechobee, FL	PMB
Okeene, OK	OKL
Okemos, MI	LAN
Oklahoma City, OK	OKL
OK	SYM
Oklee, MN	CR
Okmulgee, OK	TLS
Olathe, KS	KCK
Old Bethpage, NY	SYM
Old Bridge, NJ	MET
Old Forge, NY	OG
PA	PSC
PA	SCR
Old Hickory, TN	NSH
Old Lyme, CT	NOR
Old Mill Creek, IL	CHI
Old Monroe, MO	STL
Old Orchard Beach, ME	PRT
Old Saybrook, CT	NOR
Old Tappan, NJ	NEW
Old Town, ME	PRT
Old Westbury, NY	RVC
Oldenburg, IN	IND
Olean, NY	BUF
NY	SAM
NY	PSC
Olema, CA	SFR
Olive Branch, MS	JKS
Olive Hill, KY	LEX
Olivia, MN	NU
Olmito, TX	BWN
Olmitz, KS	DOD
Olmsted Falls, OH	CLV
Olney, IL	BEL
MD	WDC
Olpe, KS	KCK
Olton, TX	LUB
Olympia, WA	HPM
WA	ROM
WA	SEA
Olympia Fields, IL	CHI
Olyphant, PA	PHU
PA	SCR
Omaha, NE	OM
NE	STN
Omak, WA	SPK
Omro, WI	GB
Ona, WV	WH
Onaga, KS	KCK
Onalaska, WI	LC
Onamia, MN	SCL
Onawa, IA	SC
Onaway, MI	GLD
Oneida, NY	SY
WI	GB
Onekama, MI	GLD
Oneonta, AL	BIR
NY	ALB
Onida, SD	SFS
Onley, VA	RIC
Onset, MA	FR
Onsted, MI	DET
Ontario, CA	SB
NY	ROC
OR	BAK
Ontonagon, MI	MAR
Opelika, AL	MOB
Opelousas, LA	LAF
Oquossoc, ME	PRT
Oracle, AZ	TUC
Oradell, NJ	NEW
Oran, MO	SPC
Orange, CA	OLL
CA	ORG
CT	HRT
MA	SPR
NJ	NEW
TX	BEA
VA	ARL
Orange Beach, AL	MOB
Orange Cove, CA	FRS
Orange Grove, TX	CC
Orange Park, FL	STA
Orangeburg, NY	NY
SC	CHR
Orangevale, CA	SAC
CA	SPA
Orbisonia, PA	ALT
Orchard Lake, MI	DET
Orchard Park, NY	BUF
Ord, NE	GI
Orefield, PA	ALN
Oregon, IL	RCK
OH	TOL
WI	MAD
Oregon City, OR	P
Oreland, PA	PH
Orem, UT	SLC
Oriental, NC	R
Orinda, CA	OAK
Orion, IL	PEO
Oriska, ND	FAR
Oriskany Falls, NY	SY
Orland, CA	SAC
Orland Hills, IL	CHI
Orland Park, IL	CHI
Orlando, FL	ORL
FL	SAM
FL	SYM
FL	PSC
FL	POC
Orleans, MA	FR
NE	LIN
Ormond Beach, FL	ORL
Orofino, ID	B
Orono, ME	PRT
Oroville, CA	SAC
WA	SPK
Orr, MN	DUL
Orrtanna, PA	HBG
Orrville, AL	MOB
OH	CLV
Ortonville, MI	DET
MN	NU
Orwell, OH	Y
Orwigsburg, PA	ALN
Osage, IA	DUB
Osage City, KS	KCK
Osakis, MN	SCL
Osawatomie, KS	KCK
Osborne, KS	SAL
Osceola, AR	LR
IA	DM
NE	LIN
WI	SUP
Osceola Mills, PA	E
Oscoda, MI	GLD
Osgood, IN	IND
OH	CIN
Oshkosh, WI	GB
Oskaloosa, IA	DAV
Oslo, MN	CR
Osmond, NE	OM
Osprey, FL	VEN
Osseo, MN	STP
Ossineke, MI	GLD
Ossining, NY	NY
Osterville, MA	FR
Oswego, IL	JOL
KS	WCH
NY	SY
Osyka, MS	JKS
Othello, WA	SPK
Otis Orchards, WA	SPK
Otisville, MI	LAN
NY	NY
Oto, IA	SC
Otsego, MI	KAL
Ottawa, IL	PEO
KS	KCK
OH	TOL
Otter River, MA	WOR
Ottoville, OH	TOL
Ottsville, PA	PH
Ottumwa, IA	DAV
Ouray, CO	PBL
Overgaard, AZ	GLP
Overland, MO	STL
Overland Park, KS	KCK
Overton, NV	LAV

Ovid, MI	LAN
NY	ROC
Oviedo, FL	ORL
Owasso, OK	TLS
Owatonna, MN	WIN
Owego, NY	ROC
Owen, WI	LC
Owensboro, KY	OWN
Owensville, MO	JC
OH	CIN
Owings, MD	WDC
Owings Mills, MD	BAL
Owingsville, KY	LEX
Owosso, MI	LAN
Oxford, CT	HRT
IA	DAV
IN	LFT
MA	WOR
MI	DET
MS	JKS
NJ	MET
NY	SY
OH	CIN
PA	PH
Oxnard, CA	LA
CA	ROM
Oxon Hill, MD	WDC
Oyster Bay, NY	RVC
Ozark, AL	MOB
AR	LR
MO	SPC
Ozona, TX	SAN
Ozone, AR	LR
Ozone Park, NY	BRK
NY	STF
Pacific, MO	STL
Pacific Grove, CA	MRY
Pacific Palisades, CA	LA
Pacifica, CA	SFR
Pacoima, CA	LA
Paden City, WV	WH
Paducah, KY	OWN
Page, AZ	GLP
Pagosa Springs, CO	PBL
Pahala, HI	HON
Pahoa, HI	HON
Pahokee, FL	PMB
Pahrump, NV	LAV
Paia, HI	HON
Paincourtville, LA	BR
Painesville, OH	CLV
Painesville Township, OH	CLV
Paintsville, KY	LEX
Pajaro, CA	MRY
Pala, CA	SD
Palacios, TX	VIC
Palatine, IL	CHI
IL	STN
Palatka, FL	STA
Palestine, TX	TYL
Palisades Park, NJ	NEW
Palm Bay, FL	ORL
Palm Beach, FL	PMB
Palm Beach Gardens, FL	PMB
Palm City, FL	PMB
Palm Coast, FL	STA
Palm Desert, CA	SB
Palm Harbor, FL	SP
Palm Springs, CA	SB
FL	PMB
Palmdale, CA	LA
Palmer, AK	ANC
MA	SPR
Palmerton, PA	ALN
PA	PHU
Palmetto, FL	VEN
Palmetto Bay, FL	MIA
Palmview, TX	BWN
Palmyra, MO	JC
NE	LIN
PA	HBG
VA	RIC
WI	MAD
Palo Alto, CA	SJ
Palos Heights, IL	CHI
Palos Hills, IL	CHI
Palos Park, IL	CHI
IL	STN
Pampa, TX	AMA
Pana, IL	SFD
Panama, IA	DM
Panama City, FL	PT
Panama City Beach, FL	PT
Panhandle, TX	AMA
Panna Maria, TX	SAT
Panora, IA	DM
Panorama City, CA	LA
Paola, KS	KCK
Paoli, IN	IND
PA	PH
Paonia, CO	PBL
Papaikou, HI	HON
Papillion, NE	OM
Paradis, LA	NO
Paradise, CA	SAC
MI	MAR
Paradox, NY	ALB
Paragould, AR	LR
Paramount, CA	LA
Paramus, NJ	NEW
Parchment, MI	KAL
Pardeeville, WI	MAD
Paris, AR	LR
IL	SFD
KY	LEX
TN	MEM
TX	TYL
Parisville, MI	SAG
Park, KS	SAL
Park City, UT	SLC
Park Falls, WI	SUP
Park Forest, IL	CHI
IL	JOL
Park Hills, KY	COV
MO	STL
Park Rapids, MN	CR
Park Ridge, IL	CHI
NJ	NEW
Park River, ND	FAR
Parker, AZ	TUC
CO	COS
SD	SFS
Parkers Prairie, MN	SCL
Parkersburg, WV	WH
Parkesburg, PA	PH
Parkland, FL	MIA
Parkman, OH	CLV
Parks, LA	LAF
Parkston, SD	SFS
Parkton, MD	BAL
Parkville, MD	BAL
Parlier, CA	FRS
Parlin, NJ	MET
Parma, OH	CLV
OH	SJP
OH	PRM
Parma Heights, OH	CLV
Parnell, MO	KC
Parrish, FL	VEN
Parshall, ND	BIS
Parsippany, NJ	PAT
Parsons, KS	WCH
Pasadena, CA	LA
MD	BAL
TX	GAL
Pascagoula, MS	BLX
Pasco, WA	SPK
Pascoag, RI	PRO
Paso Robles, CA	MRY
Pass Christian, MS	BLX
Passaic, NJ	PAT
NJ	PHU
NJ	PSC
Patagonia, AZ	TUC
Patchogue, NY	RVC
Paterson, NJ	PAT
NJ	SYM
Patterson, CA	STO
LA	LAF
NY	NY
Pattison, TX	GAL
Patton, PA	ALT
PA	PBR
Paulding, OH	TOL
Paulina, LA	BR
Pavilion, NY	BUF
Paw Paw, MI	KAL
Pawcatuck, CT	NOR
Pawhuska, OK	TLS
Pawleys Island, SC	CHR
Pawling, NY	NY
Pawnee Rock, KS	DOD
Pawtucket, RI	PRO
Paxton, IL	JOL
MA	WOR
Paynesville, MN	SCL
Payneville, KY	L
Payson, AZ	PHX
AZ	POC
AZ	TUC
UT	SLC
Pe Ell, WA	SEA
Peabody, MA	BO
Peachtree City, GA	ATL
Peachtree Corners, GA	ATL
Peapack, NJ	MET
Pearce, AZ	TUC
Pearisburg, VA	RIC
Pearl, MS	JKS
Pearl City, HI	HON
Pearl River, LA	NO
NY	NY
Pearland, TX	GAL
Pearsall, TX	SAT
Pecatonica, IL	RCK
Peckville, PA	SCR
Pecos, NM	SFE
TX	ELP
Peebles, OH	CIN
Peekskill, NY	NY
NY	PSC
Pekin, IL	PEO
Pelham, NH	MAN
NY	NY
Pelham Manor, NY	NY
Pelican Rapids, MN	SCL
Pella, IA	DAV
Pellston, MI	GLD
Pembina, ND	FAR
Pembine, WI	GB
Pembroke, GA	ATL
MA	BO
Pembroke Pines, FL	MIA
Pen Argyl, PA	ALN
Pena Blanca, NM	SFE
Penacook, NH	MAN
Penasco, NM	SFE
Pender, NE	OM
Pendleton, OR	BAK
Penelope, TX	FWT
Penfield, IL	PEO
NY	ROC
Peninsula, OH	CLV
Penitas, TX	BWN
Penn Hills, PA	PIT
Penn Yan, NY	ROC
Penndel, PA	PH
Penngrove, CA	SR
Pennington, NJ	TR
Pennsauken, NJ	CAM
Pennsburg, PA	PH
Pensacola, FL	PT
Peoria, AZ	PHX
IL	OLL
IL	PEO
Peoria Heights, IL	PEO
Peosta, IA	DUB
Peotone, IL	JOL
Pepper Pike, OH	CLV
Pepperell, MA	BO
Pequannock, NJ	PAT
Pequot Lakes, MN	DUL
Peralta, NM	SFE
Perham, MN	SCL
Perkins, MI	MAR
Perris, CA	SB
CA	SPA
Perry, FL	PT
IA	DM
KS	KCK
MO	JC
NY	BUF
OH	CLV
OK	OKL
Perry Hall, MD	BAL
Perryopolis, PA	GBG
PA	PBR
Perrysburg, OH	TOL
Perryton, TX	AMA
Perryville, MD	WIL
MO	STL
Perth Amboy, NJ	MET
NJ	PHU
NJ	PSC
Peru, IL	PEO
IN	LFT
NY	OG
Peshtigo, WI	GB
Petal, MS	BLX
Petaluma, CA	SR
Peterborough, NH	MAN
Petersburg, AK	JUN
IL	SFD
IN	EVN
NE	OM
VA	RIC
WV	WH
Petersham, MA	SAM
MA	WOR
Petoskey, MI	GLD
Pevely, MO	STL
Pewamo, MI	GR
Pewaukee, WI	MIL
Pewee Valley, KY	L
Pflugerville, TX	AUS
Pharr, TX	BWN
Phelan, CA	SB
Phenix City, AL	MOB
Philadelphia, MS	JKS
PA	PH
PA	SYM
PA	SAM
PA	PSC
PA	MCE
PA	PHU
Philip, SD	RC
Philippi, WV	WH
WV	OLL
Philipsburg, PA	ALT
Phillips, WI	SUP
Phillipsburg, KS	SAL
NJ	MET
NJ	PSC
Philo, IL	PEO
Philpot, KY	OWN
Phlox, WI	GB
Phoenicia, NY	NY
Phoenix, AZ	HPM
AZ	NTN
AZ	OLL
AZ	PHX
AZ	SYM
AZ	STN
NY	SY
Phoenixville, PA	PH
PA	PHU
Picayune, MS	BLX
Pickens, SC	CHR
Pickerel, WI	GB
Pickerington, OH	COL
Pico Rivera, CA	LA
Piedmont, CA	OAK
MO	SPC
OK	OKL
SD	RC
Pierce, NE	OM
Pierce City, MO	SPC
Pierceton, IN	FTW
Piermont, NY	NY
Pierre, SD	SFS
Pierre Part, LA	BR
Pierron, IL	SFD
Pierz, MN	SCL
Piffard, NY	ROC
Pigeon Forge, TN	KNX
Pikeville, KY	LEX
Pilot Grove, MO	JC
Pilot Point, TX	FWT
Pilot Rock, OR	BAK
Pilot Station, AK	FBK
Pinckney, MI	LAN
Pinckneyville, IL	BEL
Pinconning, MI	SAG
Pine Bluff, AR	LR
Pine Bluffs, WY	CHY
Pine Bush, NY	NY
Pine City, MN	DUL
NY	ROC
Pine Island, MN	STP
NY	NY
Pine Mountain, GA	SAV
Pine Plains, NY	NY
Pine Prairie, LA	LAF
Pine Ridge, SD	RC
Pinecrest, FL	MIA
Pinedale, WY	CHY
Pinehurst, NC	R
Pinellas Park, FL	SP
Pinetop, AZ	GLP
Pineville, LA	ALX
Pinole, CA	OAK
Pinon, AZ	GLP
Pipestone, MN	WIN
Piqua, OH	CIN
Pirtleville, AZ	TUC
Piscataway, NJ	MET
Pisek, ND	FAR
Pismo Beach, CA	MRY
Pitman, NJ	CAM
Pittsboro, NC	R
Pittsburg, CA	OAK
KS	WCH
TX	TYL
Pittsburgh, PA	PBR
PA	SJP
PA	SYM
PA	PIT
Pittsfield, IL	SFD
MA	SPR
MA	STF
NH	MAN
Pittsford, NY	ROC
VT	BUR
Pittston, PA	PSC
PA	SCR
Pittstown, NJ	MET
Pittsville, WI	LC
Placentia, CA	NTN
CA	ORG
Placerville, CA	SAC
Plain, WI	MAD
Plain City, OH	COL
Plainfield, CT	NOR
IL	JOL

IN	IND
NJ	NEW
WI	GB
Plains, KS	DOD
MT	HEL
PA	SCR
Plainsboro, NJ	MET
Plainview, MN	WIN
NE	OM
NY	RVC
TX	LUB
Plainville, CT	HRT
KS	SAL
MA	BO
Plaistow, NH	MAN
Planada, CA	FRS
Plankinton, SD	SFS
Plano, IL	JOL
TX	DAL
Plant City, FL	SP
FL	SYM
Plantation, FL	MIA
Plantersville, TX	GAL
Plantsville, CT	HRT
Plaquemine, LA	BR
Platte, SD	SFS
Platte Center, NE	OM
Platte City, MO	KC
Plattekill, NY	NY
Platteville, CO	DEN
WI	MAD
Plattsburg, MO	KC
Plattsburgh, NY	OG
Plattsmouth, NE	LIN
Plaucheville, LA	ALX
Playa del Rey, CA	LA
Plaza, ND	BIS
Pleasant City, OH	PBR
Pleasant Grove, AL	BIR
Pleasant Hill, CA	OAK
MO	KC
Pleasant Mount, PA	SCR
Pleasant Prairie, WI	MIL
Pleasant Valley, NY	NY
Pleasanton, CA	OAK
CA	SAC
TX	SAT
Pleasantville, NJ	CAM
NJ	SAM
NY	NY
Plentywood, MT	GF
Plover, WI	LC
WI	SUP
Plum, PA	PIT
Plum City, WI	LC
Plymouth, IN	FTW
MA	BO
MI	DET
MI	LAN
MI	NTN
MN	STP
NC	R
NH	MAN
OH	TOL
PA	PHU
PA	SCR
WI	MIL
Plymouth Meeting, PA	PH
Pocahontas, AR	LR
IA	SC
Pocasset, MA	FR
Pocatello, ID	B
Pocomoke City, MD	WIL
Pocono Pines, PA	SCR
Pocono Summit, PA	PSC
Point Arena, CA	SR
Point Lookout, NY	RVC
Point Pleasant, NJ	TR
WV	WH
Point Pleasant Beach, NJ	TR
Point Richmond, CA	OAK
Pointe A La Hache, LA	NO
Poland, OH	Y
Polo, IL	RCK
Polson, MT	HEL
Pomeroy, OH	STU
WA	SPK
Pomfret, CT	NOR
MD	WDC
Pomona, CA	LA
NJ	CAM
Pompano Beach, FL	MIA
Pompey, NY	SY
Pompton Lakes, NJ	PAT
Pompton Plains, NJ	PAT
Ponca, NE	OM
Ponca City, OK	OKL
Ponchatoula, LA	BR
Ponte Vedra Beach, FL	STA
Pontiac, IL	BEL
IL	PEO

MI	DET
Pontotoc, MS	JKS
Poolesville, MD	WDC
Poplar, MT	GF
Poplar Bluff, MO	SPC
Poquonock, CT	HRT
Porcupine, SD	RC
Port Allen, LA	BR
Port Angeles, WA	SEA
Port Aransas, TX	CC
Port Arthur, TX	BEA
Port Austin, MI	SAG
Port Barre, LA	LAF
Port Carbon, PA	ALN
Port Charlotte, FL	VEN
Port Chester, NY	NY
Port Clinton, OH	TOL
Port Edwards, WI	LC
Port Ewen, NY	NY
Port Gibson, MS	JKS
Port Henry, NY	OG
Port Huron, MI	DET
Port Isabel, TX	BWN
Port Jefferson, NY	RVC
Port Jefferson Station, NY	RVC
Port Jervis, NY	NY
Port Lavaca, TX	VIC
Port Leyden, NY	OG
Port Murray, NJ	MET
Port Neches, TX	BEA
Port Orange, FL	ORL
Port Orchard, WA	SEA
Port Reading, NJ	MET
Port Richey, FL	SP
Port Saint Lucie, FL	PMB
Port Sanilac, MI	SAG
Port St. Joe, FL	PT
Port St. Lucie, FL	PMB
Port Sulphur, LA	NO
Port Tobacco, MD	WDC
Port Townsend, WA	SEA
Port Vue, PA	PIT
Port Washington, NY	RVC
WI	MIL
Port Wentworth, GA	SAV
Portage, IN	GRY
MI	KAL
PA	ALT
PA	PBR
WI	MAD
Portage Des Sioux, MO	STL
Portageville, MO	SPC
Portales, NM	SFE
Porter, TX	GAL
Porterfield, WI	GB
Porterville, CA	FRS
Portland, CT	NOR
IN	LFT
ME	PRT
MI	GR
OR	P
OR	OLL
OR	HPM
OR	BAK
TX	CC
Portola, CA	SAC
Portola Valley, CA	SFR
Portsmouth, IA	DM
NH	MAN
OH	COL
RI	PRO
VA	RIC
Posen, IL	CHI
MI	GLD
Poseyville, IN	EVN
Post, TX	LUB
Post Falls, ID	B
Poteau, OK	TLS
Poteet, TX	SAT
Poth, TX	SAT
Potomac, MD	WDC
Potomac Falls, VA	ARL
Potosi, MO	STL
WI	MAD
Pottstown, PA	PH
PA	PHU
PA	PSC
Pottsville, PA	ALN
Poughkeepsie, NY	NY
Poulsbo, WA	SEA
Poultney, VT	BUR
Poway, CA	SD
Powell, OH	COL
WY	CHY
Powers Lake, ND	BIS
Powhatan, VA	RIC
WV	WH
Poynette, WI	MAD
Prague, NE	LIN
OK	OKL
Prairie Du Chien, WI	LC

Prairie Village, KS	KCK
Prairie du Rocher, IL	BEL
Prairie du Sac, WI	MAD
Prairieville, LA	BR
Pratt, KS	DOD
Prattville, AL	MOB
Prayer Town, TX	AMA
Premont, TX	CC
Prescott, AZ	PHX
MI	GLD
WI	LC
Prescott Valley, AZ	PHX
Presho, SD	RC
Presidio, TX	ELP
Preston, CT	NOR
IA	DUB
Prestonsburg, KY	LEX
Price, UT	SLC
Prichard, AL	MOB
Priest River, ID	B
Primos, PA	PH
Prince Frederick, MD	WDC
Princess Anne, MD	WIL
Princeton, FL	MIA
IL	PEO
IN	EVN
KY	OWN
MA	WOR
MN	SCL
NJ	TR
WI	MAD
WV	WH
Princeton Jct., NJ	TR
Princeville, IL	PEO
Prineville, OR	BAK
Prior Lake, MN	STP
Proctor, MN	DUL
VT	BUR
WV	WH
Progreso, TX	BWN
Prophetstown, IL	RCK
Prospect, CT	HRT
KY	L
PA	PIT
Prospect Heights, IL	CHI
Prospect Park, NJ	PAT
Prosper, TX	FWT
Prosser, WA	YAK
Protivin, IA	DUB
Providence, RI	PRO
Provincetown, MA	FR
Prudenville, MI	GLD
Pryor, MT	GF
OK	TLS
Pueblo, CO	PBL
Pueblo West, CO	PBL
Pueblo of Acoma, NM	GLP
Pulaski, NY	SY
PA	PIT
TN	NSH
WI	GB
Pullman, WA	SPK
Punta Gorda, FL	VEN
Punxsutawney, PA	E
PA	PBR
Purcell, OK	OKL
Purcellville, VA	ARL
Put-In-Bay, OH	TOL
Putnam, CT	BUR
CT	NOR
Putney, VT	BUR
Puyallup, WA	SEA
Pylesville, MD	BAL
Quaker Hill, CT	NOR
Quakertown, PA	PH
Quarryville, PA	HBG
Queen Creek, AZ	PHX
Queens, NY	BRK
Queens Village, NY	BRK
Queensbury, NY	ALB
Questa, NM	SFE
Quincy, CA	SAC
FL	PT
IL	SFD
MA	BO
WA	YAK
Quinlan, TX	DAL
Quinque, VA	RIC
Quinton, VA	RIC
Raceland, LA	HT
Racine, WI	MIL
WI	SYM
Radcliff, KY	L
Radford, VA	RIC
Radnor, PA	PH
PA	OLN
Radom, IL	BEL
Raeford, NC	R
Raeville, NE	OM
Ragley, LA	LKC
Rahway, NJ	MCE

NJ	NEW
NJ	PSC
Rainelle, WV	WH
Rainier, OR	P
Raleigh, NC	R
NC	SJP
NC	SAM
Ralls, TX	LUB
Ralston, NE	OM
Ramah, NM	GLP
Ramey, PA	E
PA	SJP
Ramona, CA	SD
OK	TLS
Ramsey, IL	SFD
MN	STP
NJ	NEW
Rancho Cordova, CA	SAC
Rancho Cucamonga, CA	SB
Rancho Dominguez, CA	LA
Rancho Palos Verdes, CA	LA
Rancho Santa Fe, CA	SD
Rancho Santa Margarita, CA	ORG
Ranchos De Taos, NM	SFE
Rancocas, NJ	TR
Randall, MN	SCL
Randallstown, MD	BAL
Randolph, MA	BO
NE	OM
NJ	PAT
NY	BUF
VT	BUR
Random Lake, WI	MIL
Ranger, TX	FWT
Ransomville, NY	BUF
Rantoul, IL	PEO
Rapid City, SD	RC
Rapid River, MI	MAR
Rapids City, IL	PEO
Raritan, NJ	MET
Ratcliff, AR	LR
Raton, NM	SFE
Ravena, NY	ALB
Ravenna, KY	LEX
MI	GR
NE	GI
OH	Y
Ravenswood, WV	WH
Rawlins, WY	CHY
Ray Township, MI	DET
Raymond, IL	SFD
MS	JKS
WA	SEA
Raymondville, TX	BWN
Raymore, MO	KC
Rayne, LA	LAF
Raynham Center, MA	FR
Raytown, MO	KC
Rayville, LA	SHP
Raywick, KY	L
Raywood, TX	BEA
Reading, MA	BO
OH	CIN
PA	ALN
PA	PHU
Red Bank, NJ	TR
Red Bluff, CA	SAC
Red Bud, IL	BEL
Red Cloud, NE	LIN
Red Hook, NY	NY
Red Lake, MN	CR
Red Lake Falls, MN	CR
Red Lodge, MT	GF
Red Oak, IA	DM
Red Springs, NC	R
Red Wing, MN	STP
Redding, CA	SAC
CT	BGP
Redfield, SD	SFS
Redford, MI	DET
NY	OG
Redford Township, MI	DET
Redgranite, WI	GB
Redlands, CA	SB
Redmond, OR	BAK
WA	SEA
Redondo Beach, CA	LA
Redwood City, CA	SJ
CA	SFR
Redwood Falls, MN	NU
Redwood Valley, CA	STN
Reed, KY	OWN
Reed City, MI	GR
Reedley, CA	FRS
Reedsburg, WI	MAD
Reedsport, OR	P
Reese, MI	SAG
Reeseville, WI	MIL
Refugio, TX	CC
Regent, ND	BIS
Rego Park, NY	BRK

Rehoboth Beach, DE	WIL
Reidsville, NC	CHL
Reinbeck, IA	DUB
Remington, IN	LFT
Remsen, IA	SC
Remus, MI	GR
Renault, IL	BEL
Reno, NV	RNO
Renovo, PA	ALT
Rensselaer, IN	LFT
NY	ALB
Renton, WA	SEA
Renville, MN	NU
Republic, MI	MAR
WA	SPK
Reseda, CA	LA
Reserve, LA	NO
NM	GLP
Reston, VA	ARL
Revere, MA	BO
Revillo, SD	SFS
Reynolds, IN	LFT
ND	FAR
Reynoldsburg, OH	COL
Reynoldsville, PA	E
Rhame, ND	BIS
Rhinebeck, NY	NY
Rhineland, MO	JC
Rhinelander, WI	SUP
Rialto, CA	SB
Rib Lake, WI	SUP
Ribera, NM	SFE
Rice, MN	SCL
Rice Lake, WI	SUP
Riceville, IA	DUB
Rich Fountain, MO	JC
Richardson, TX	DAL
Richardton, ND	BIS
Richboro, PA	PH
Richfield, MN	STP
OH	CLV
Richford, VT	BUR
Richland, IA	DAV
NJ	CAM
NY	SY
WA	YAK
Richland Center, WI	LC
Richmond, CA	OAK
IL	RCK
IN	IND
KY	LEX
MI	DET
MN	SCL
MO	KC
OH	STU
TX	GAL
VA	RIC
VT	BUR
Richmond Heights, MO	STL
Richmond Hill, GA	SAV
NY	BRK
Richwood, TX	GAL
WV	WH
Richwoods, MO	STL
Riderwood, MD	BAL
Ridge, MD	WDC
Ridge Manor, FL	SP
Ridgecrest, CA	FRS
Ridgefield, CT	BGP
NJ	NEW
Ridgefield Park, NJ	NEW
Ridgeland, SC	CHR
Ridgely, MD	WIL
Ridgeway, WI	MAD
Ridgewood, NJ	NEW
NY	BRK
Ridgway, PA	E
Ridley Park, PA	PH
Riegelsville, PA	PH
Rifle, CO	DEN
Ringtown, PA	ALN
Ringwood, NJ	PAT
Rio Bravo, TX	LAR
Rio Grande, OH	STU
Rio Grande City, TX	BWN
Rio Hondo, TX	BWN
Rio Rancho, NM	SFE
Rio Rico, AZ	TUC
Rio Vista, CA	SAC
Ripley, MS	JKS
OH	CIN
Ripon, CA	STO
WI	MIL
Rittman, OH	CLV
Ritzville, WA	SPK
River Edge, NJ	NEW
River Falls, WI	LC
WI	SUP
River Forest, IL	CHI
River Grove, IL	CHI
River Ridge, LA	NO
Riverbank, CA	STO
Riverdale, CA	FRS
GA	ATL
IL	CHI
MD	WDC
NY	NY
Riverdale Park, MD	WDC
Riverhead, NY	RVC
NY	STF
Riverside, CA	SB
CA	OLL
CT	BGP
IA	DAV
IL	CHI
NJ	TR
RI	PRO
Riverton, IL	SFD
NJ	TR
UT	SLC
WY	CHY
Riverview, FL	SP
MI	DET
Riviera, TX	CC
Riviera Beach, FL	PMB
Roanoke, IL	PEO
IN	FTW
VA	RIC
VA	SAM
Roanoke Rapids, NC	R
Roaring Brook Twp., PA	SCR
Roaring Spring, PA	ALT
Robbinsdale, MN	STP
Robertsdale, AL	MOB
Robesonia, PA	ALN
Robinson, IL	SFD
Robinsonville, MS	JKS
Robstown, TX	CC
Rochelle, IL	RCK
Rochelle Park, NJ	NEW
Rochester, IL	SFD
IN	LFT
MI	DET
MN	WIN
NH	MAN
NY	NTN
NY	STF
NY	ROC
PA	PIT
Rochester Hills, MI	DET
Rock Creek, OH	Y
Rock Falls, IL	RCK
Rock Hill, SC	CHR
Rock Island, IL	PEO
Rock Rapids, IA	SC
Rock Springs, WY	CHY
Rock Valley, IA	SC
Rockaway, NJ	PAT
NY	BRK
OR	P
Rockaway Beach, NY	BRK
Rockaway Park, NY	BRK
Rockaway Point, NY	BRK
Rockdale, IL	JOL
TX	AUS
Rockford, IA	DUB
IL	RCK
MI	GR
OH	CIN
WA	SPK
Rockland, MA	BO
WI	LC
Rockledge, FL	ORL
Rocklin, CA	SAC
Rockport, IN	EVN
TX	CC
Rocksprings, TX	SAT
Rockville, CT	NOR
IN	IND
MD	WDC
MN	SCL
VA	RIC
Rockville Centre, NY	RVC
Rockwall, TX	DAL
Rockwell, IA	DUB
Rockwood, MI	DET
Rocky Ford, CO	PBL
Rocky Hill, CT	HRT
Rocky Mount, MO	STL
NC	R
VA	RIC
Rocky Point, NY	RVC
Rocky River, OH	CLV
Rodeo, CA	OAK
Roebling, NJ	TR
NJ	PSC
NJ	ROM
Roeland Park, KS	KCK
Rogers, AR	LR
MN	STP
TX	AUS
Rogers City, MI	GLD
Rogersville, MO	SPC
TN	KNX
Roggen, CO	DEN
Rohnert Park, CA	SR
Rolette, ND	FAR
Rolla, MO	JC
ND	FAR
Rolling Meadows, IL	CHI
Rolling Prairie, IN	GRY
Rollingstone, MN	WIN
Roma, TX	BWN
Rome, GA	ATL
NY	SY
Rome City, IN	FTW
Romeo, MI	DET
Romeoville, IL	JOL
Romney, WV	WH
Romulus, MI	DET
Ronan, MT	HEL
Ronceverte, WV	WH
Ronkonkoma, NY	RVC
Roosevelt, NY	RVC
UT	SLC
Roosevelt Island, NY	NY
Rootstown, OH	Y
Rosamond, CA	FRS
Roscoe, IL	RCK
PA	PIT
Roscommon, MI	GLD
Roseau, MN	CR
Rosebud, SD	RC
Roseburg, OR	P
Rosedale, MS	JKS
NY	BRK
Roseland, NE	LIN
NJ	NEW
Roselle, IL	JOL
NJ	NEW
Roselle Park, NJ	NEW
Rosemead, CA	LA
Rosemont, IL	CHI
PA	PH
Rosemount, MN	STP
Rosenberg, TX	GAL
Rosendale, NY	NY
Roseville, CA	SAC
MI	DET
MN	STP
Rosholt, SD	SFS
Roslindale, MA	BO
Roslyn, NY	RVC
PA	PH
Ross, CA	SFR
Rossford, OH	SJP
OH	TOL
Rossville, KS	KCK
Roswell, GA	ATL
GA	PSC
NM	LSC
Rotan, TX	LUB
Rothschild, WI	LC
Round Lake, IL	CHI
NY	ALB
Round Rock, TX	AUS
Roundup, MT	GF
Rouses Point, NY	OG
Rouseville, PA	E
Rowena, TX	SAN
Rowland Heights, CA	LA
Rowlett, TX	DAL
Roxboro, NC	R
Roxbury, MA	BO
Roy, NM	SFE
Royal, IA	SC
Royal City, WA	YAK
Royal Oak, MI	DET
Royal Palm Beach, FL	PMB
Royalton, MN	SCL
Royersford, PA	PH
Ruby, AK	FBK
Rudolph, WI	LC
Rudyard, MI	MAR
Rugby, ND	FAR
Ruidoso, NM	LSC
Rulo, NE	LIN
Rumford, RI	PRO
Rumson, NJ	TR
Runge, TX	SAT
Runnemede, NJ	CAM
Running Springs, CA	SB
Rupert, ID	B
Rush, NY	ROC
Rush City, MN	STP
Rushford, MN	WIN
Rushville, IL	PEO
IN	IND
Ruskin, FL	SP
Russell, KS	SAL
MA	SPR
Russells Point, OH	CIN
Russellton, PA	PIT
Russellville, AL	BIR
AR	LR
KY	OWN
MO	JC
Russia, OH	CIN
Ruston, LA	SHP
Ruth, MI	SAG
Rutherford, NJ	NEW
Ruthven, IA	SC
Rutland, MA	WOR
VT	BUR
Rutledge, TN	KNX
Rydal, PA	PH
Rye, NY	NY
Rye Beach, NH	MAN
Rye Brook, NY	NY
Sabattus, ME	PRT
Sabetha, KS	KCK
Sabinal, TX	SAT
Sac City, IA	SC
Saco, ME	PRT
Sacramento, CA	HPM
CA	SYM
CA	STN
CA	NTN
CA	SAC
Saddle Brook, NJ	NEW
Saddle River, NJ	NEW
Safety Harbor, FL	SP
Safford, AZ	TUC
Sag Harbor, NY	RVC
Saginaw, MI	SAG
Sahuarita, AZ	TUC
St. Agatha, ME	PRT
St. Albans, ME	PRT
NY	BRK
VT	BUR
WV	WH
St. Amant, LA	BR
St. Ann, MO	STL
St. Anne, IL	JOL
St. Anthony, ID	B
IN	EVN
MN	STP
ND	FAR
St. Augustine, FL	STA
St. Benedict, KS	KCK
LA	NO
OR	P
St. Bernard, LA	NO
St. Bonaventure, NY	BUF
St. Bonifacius, MN	STP
St. Catharine, KY	L
St. Charles, IL	RCK
MI	SAG
MN	WIN
MO	STL
St. Clair, MI	DET
MO	STL
PA	ALN
Saint Clair, PA	ALN
St. Clair Shores, MI	DET
St. Clairsville, OH	STU
St. Cloud, FL	ORL
MN	SCL
Saint Cloud, MN	SCL
St. Columbans, NE	OM
St. Croix, IN	IND
St. David, AZ	TUC
St. Edward, NE	OM
St. Elizabeth, MO	JC
St. Francis, KS	SAL
KY	L
SD	RC
WI	MIL
St. Francisville, LA	BR
St. Gabriel, LA	BR
St. George, UT	SLC
St. Hedwig, TX	SAT
St. Helen, MI	GLD
St. Helena, CA	SR
St. Helena Island, SC	CHR
St. Helens, OR	P
St. Henry, OH	CIN
St. Ignace, MI	MAR
St. Ignatius, MT	HEL
St. Inigoes, MD	WDC
St. James, LA	BR
MN	WIN
MO	JC
NY	RVC
St. John, FL	STA
IN	GRY
KS	DOD
ND	FAR
WA	SPK
St. Johns, AZ	GLP
FL	STA
MI	LAN
St. Johnsbury, VT	BUR
St. Joseph, LA	ALX

MI	KAL
MN	SCL
MO	KC
MO	STN
St. Leo, FL	SP
MN	NU
St. Libory, IL	BEL
NE	GI
St. Louis, MO	MIL
MO	STL
MO	STN
MO	PRM
MO	OLL
MO	WCH
MO	WIN
Saint Louis, MO	STL
St. Louis County, MO	STL
St. Louis Park, MN	STP
St. Maries, ID	B
St. Martin, MN	SCL
OH	CIN
St. Martinville, LA	LAF
St. Mary, MO	STL
St. Mary of the Woods, IN	IND
St. Mary's, MO	BEL
St. Mary's City, MD	WDC
St. Marys, AK	FBK
GA	SAV
IA	DM
KS	KCK
OH	CIN
PA	E
WV	WH
St. Meinrad, IN	IND
St. Michael, AK	FBK
MN	STP
ND	FAR
PA	ALT
St. Michaels, AZ	GLP
St. Nazianz, WI	GB
WI	ROM
St. Paul, KS	WCH
MN	STP
MN	SYM
MO	STL
NE	GI
OR	P
VA	RIC
St. Paul Park, MN	STP
St. Pete Beach, FL	SP
St. Peter, MN	NU
St. Peters, MO	STL
St. Petersburg, FL	SP
Saint Petersburg, FL	SP
St. Petersburg, FL	SJP
FL	PSC
St. Regis Falls, NY	OG
St. Robert, MO	JC
St. Rose, IL	BEL
St. Simons Island, GA	SAV
St. Stephen, MN	SCL
St. Stephens, WY	CHY
St. Theresa, WI	MIL
St. Thomas, MO	JC
St. Xavier, MT	GF
Salado, TX	AUS
Salamanca, NY	BUF
Salem, IL	BEL
IN	IND
MA	BO
MA	STF
MO	SPC
NH	MAN
NY	ALB
OH	Y
OR	P
SD	SFS
VA	RIC
WV	WH
Salida, CO	COS
Salina, KS	SAL
Salinas, CA	MRY
Saline, MI	LAN
Salisbury, MD	WIL
MO	JC
NC	CHL
PA	ALT
Sallisaw, OK	TLS
Salmon, ID	B
Salt Lake City, UT	SLC
Salt Point, NY	NY
Saltaire, NY	RVC
Sammamish, WA	SEA
San Andreas, CA	STO
San Angelo, TX	SAN
San Anselmo, CA	SFR
San Antonio, FL	SP
TX	OLL
TX	SYM
TX	SAT
San Benito, TX	BWN
San Bernardino, CA	SB
CA	NTN
San Bruno, CA	SFR
San Carlos, AZ	TUC
CA	SFR
San Clemente, CA	ORG
San Diego, CA	SD
CA	HPM
TX	CC
San Dimas, CA	LA
San Elizario, TX	ELP
San Fernando, CA	LA
CA	SYM
San Fidel, NM	GLP
San Francisco, CA	SFR
CA	STN
San Gabriel, CA	LA
San Isidro, TX	BWN
San Jacinto, CA	SB
San Jose, CA	SJ
CA	SYM
San Juan, TX	BWN
San Juan Bautista, CA	MRY
San Juan Capistrano, CA	ORG
San Leandro, CA	OAK
San Lorenzo, CA	OAK
San Luis, AZ	TUC
CO	PBL
San Luis Obispo, CA	HPM
CA	MRY
San Manuel, AZ	TUC
San Marcos, CA	SD
TX	AUS
San Marino, CA	LA
San Mateo, CA	SFR
San Miguel, CA	MRY
San Pablo, CA	OAK
San Patricio, NM	LSC
San Pedro, CA	LA
San Rafael, CA	SFR
San Ramon, CA	OAK
San Saba, TX	AUS
San Tan Valley, AZ	TUC
San Ysidro, CA	SD
Sanborn, IA	SC
MN	NU
Sanbornville, NH	MAN
Sand Lake, MI	GR
Sand Springs, OK	TLS
Sanderson, TX	SAN
Sandoval, IL	BEL
Sandpoint, ID	B
Sandstone, MN	DUL
Sandusky, MI	SAG
OH	TOL
Sandwich, IL	RCK
Sandy, OR	P
UT	SLC
Sandy Hook, KY	LEX
Sandyston, NJ	PAT
Sanford, FL	ORL
ME	PRT
MI	SAG
NC	R
Sanger, CA	FRS
Sanibel, FL	VEN
Santa Ana, CA	ORG
CA	SYM
CA	SPA
Santa Barbara, CA	LA
Santa Clara, CA	SJ
CA	STN
NM	LSC
Santa Clarita, CA	LA
Santa Cruz, CA	MRY
NM	SFE
Santa Fe, NM	SFE
Santa Fe Springs, CA	LA
Santa Margarita, CA	MRY
Santa Maria, CA	LA
Santa Monica, CA	LA
Santa Paula, CA	LA
Santa Rosa, CA	SR
NM	SFE
TX	BWN
Santa Rosa Beach, FL	PT
Santa Susana Knolls, CA	LA
Santa Ynez, CA	LA
Santa Ysabel, CA	SD
Santee, CA	SD
SC	CHR
Sapulpa, OK	TLS
Saranac, MI	GR
Saranac Lake, NY	OG
Sarasota, FL	VEN
Saratoga, CA	SJ
NY	ALB
WY	CHY
Saratoga Springs, NY	ALB
Sardinia, NY	BUF
Sarita, TX	CC
Sartell, MN	SCL
Satanta, KS	DOD
Saugerties, NY	NY
Saugus, MA	BO
Sauk Centre, MN	SCL
Sauk City, WI	MAD
Sauk Rapids, MN	SCL
Sauk Village, IL	CHI
Saukville, WI	MIL
Sault Sainte Marie, MI	MAR
Sausalito, CA	SFR
Savage, MN	STP
Savanna, IL	RCK
Savannah, GA	SAV
MO	KC
TN	MEM
Saxon, WI	SUP
Sayre, PA	PHU
PA	SCR
Sayreville, NJ	MET
Sayville, NY	RVC
Scales Mound, IL	RCK
Scammon Bay, AK	FBK
Scappoose, OR	P
Scarborough, ME	PRT
Scarsdale, NY	NY
Scenic, AZ	PHX
Schaller, IA	SC
Schaumburg, IL	CHI
Scheller, IL	BEL
Schenectady, NY	ALB
Schererville, IN	GRY
Schertz, TX	SAT
Schiller Park, IL	CHI
Schnellville, IN	EVN
Schriever, LA	HT
Schroon Lake, NY	OG
Schulenburg, TX	VIC
Schuyler, NE	OM
Schuylerville, NY	ALB
Schuylkill Haven, PA	ALN
Schwenksville, PA	PH
Scio, OR	P
Scituate, MA	BO
Scobey, MT	GF
Scotch Plains, NJ	NEW
Scotia, CA	SR
NY	ALB
Scotland, SD	SFS
Scott, LA	LAF
Scott AFB, IL	BEL
Scott City, KS	DOD
MO	SPC
Scott Twp., PA	SCR
Scottdale, PA	GBG
PA	PBR
Scotts Valley, CA	MRY
Scottsbluff, NE	GI
Scottsboro, AL	BIR
Scottsburg, IN	IND
Scottsdale, AZ	PHX
AZ	SPA
Scottsville, KY	OWN
NY	ROC
VA	RIC
Scranton, AR	LR
PA	NTN
PA	PHU
PA	POC
PA	PSC
PA	SCR
PA	SAM
Sea Cliff, NY	RVC
Sea Girt, NJ	TR
Sea Isle City, NJ	CAM
Seaford, DE	WIL
NY	RVC
Seahurst, WA	SEA
Seal Beach, CA	ORG
Sealy, TX	GAL
Searcy, AR	LR
Seaside, CA	MRY
OR	P
Seaside Heights, NJ	TR
Seaside Park, NJ	TR
Seat Pleasant, MD	WDC
Seattle, WA	HPM
WA	NTN
WA	SEA
WA	STN
Seaview, WA	SEA
Sebastian, FL	PMB
Sebastopol, CA	SR
Seboyeta, NM	GLP
Sebree, KY	OWN
Sebring, FL	VEN
OH	Y
Secane, PA	PH
Secaucus, NJ	NEW
Secretary, MD	WIL
Security, CO	COS
Sedalia, CO	COS
MO	JC
Sedan, KS	WCH
Sedona, AZ	PHX
Sedro Woolley, WA	SEA
Seekonk, MA	FR
Seffner, FL	SP
FL	SYM
Seguin, TX	SAT
Selah, WA	YAK
Selby, SD	SFS
Selden, KS	SAL
NY	RVC
Seligman, AZ	PHX
Selinsgrove, PA	HBG
Sellersburg, IN	IND
Sellersville, PA	PH
Selma, AL	MOB
CA	FRS
TX	SAT
Selmer, TN	MEM
Selz, ND	FAR
Seminole, FL	SP
TX	LUB
Semmes, AL	MOB
Senatobia, MS	JKS
Seneca, IL	PEO
KS	KCK
MO	SPC
SC	CHR
Sentinel Butte, ND	BIS
Sequim, WA	SEA
Sesser, IL	BEL
Setauket, NY	RVC
Severn, MD	BAL
Severna Park, MD	BAL
Seward, AK	ANC
KS	DOD
NE	LIN
PA	GBG
Sewell, NJ	CAM
Sewickley, PA	PIT
Seymour, CT	HRT
IL	PEO
IN	IND
TN	KNX
TX	FWT
WI	GB
Shady Cove, OR	P
Shadyside, OH	STU
Shafer, MN	STP
Shafter, CA	FRS
Shaker Heights, OH	CLV
Shakopee, MN	STP
Shallotte, NC	R
Shallowater, TX	LUB
Shamokin, PA	HBG
PA	PHU
Shamrock, TX	AMA
Shandon, OH	CIN
Shannon, IL	RCK
Sharon, CT	HRT
KS	DOD
MA	BO
PA	E
WI	MIL
Sharpsburg, PA	PIT
Sharpsville, PA	E
Shavano Park, TX	SAT
Shavertown, PA	SCR
Shaw, MS	JKS
Shaw Island, WA	SEA
Shawano, WI	GB
Shawnee, KS	KCK
OK	OKL
Shawnee Mission, KS	KCK
Shawneetown, IL	BEL
Sheboygan, WI	MIL
Sheboygan Falls, WI	MIL
Sheffield, IL	PEO
MA	SPR
OH	CLV
PA	E
PA	PBR
Sheffield Lake, OH	CLV
Shelbina, MO	JC
Shelburne, VT	BUR
VT	SAM
Shelburne Falls, MA	SPR
Shelby, MS	JKS
MT	HEL
NC	CHL
NE	LIN
OH	TOL
Shelby Twp., MI	DET
MI	EST
Shelbyville, IL	SFD
IN	IND
KY	L
TN	NSH
Sheldon, IA	SC

Shell Knob, MO	SPC
Shell Lake, WI	SUP
Shelter Island Heights, NY	RVC
Shelton, CT	BGP
WA	SEA
Shenandoah, IA	DM
PA	ALN
PA	PHU
Shepherd, MI	SAG
Shepherdstown, WV	WH
Shepherdsville, KY	L
Sherburne, NY	SY
Sheridan, AR	LR
CO	DEN
MT	HEL
OR	P
WY	CHY
Sherman, CT	BGP
IL	SFD
TX	DAL
Sherman Oaks, CA	LA
CA	HPM
CA	ROM
Sherrill, NY	SY
Sherwood, AR	LR
OR	P
WI	GB
Shieldsville, MN	STP
Shillington, PA	ALN
Shiloh, IL	BEL
Shiner, TX	VIC
Shinglehouse, PA	E
Shinnston, WV	WH
Shippensburg, PA	HBG
Shiprock, NM	GLP
Shirley, MA	BO
Shoemakersville, PA	ALN
Shohola, PA	SCR
Shoreham, NY	RVC
Shoreline, WA	SEA
Shoreview, MN	STP
Shorewood, IL	JOL
WI	MIL
Short Hills, NJ	NEW
Shoshone, ID	B
Show Low, AZ	GLP
Shreveport, LA	SHP
Shrewsbury, MA	WOR
MO	STL
Shrub Oak, NY	NY
Shullsburg, WI	MAD
Shumway, IL	SFD
Sibley, IA	SC
Sicklerville, NJ	CAM
Sidney, MT	GF
NE	GI
NY	ALB
OH	CIN
Sierra Madre, CA	LA
Sierra Vista, AZ	TUC
Sigel, IL	SFD
Signal Mountain, TN	KNX
Sigourney, IA	DAV
Sikeston, MO	SPC
Siler City, NC	R
Silex, MO	STL
Siloam Springs, AR	LR
Silsbee, TX	BEA
Silver Bay, MN	DUL
Silver City, NM	LSC
Silver Creek, NE	OM
NY	BUF
Silver Lake, MN	NU
Silver Spring, MD	PHU
MD	WDC
Silverado, CA	ORG
Silverthorne, CO	DEN
Silverton, CO	PBL
OR	P
TX	AMA
Simi Valley, CA	LA
CA	OLL
Simmesport, LA	ALX
Simpsonville, SC	CHR
Simsbury, CT	HRT
Sinking Spring, PA	ALN
Sinsinawa, WI	MAD
Sinton, TX	CC
Sioux Center, IA	SC
Sioux City, IA	SC
Sioux Falls, SD	SFS
Sioux Rapids, IA	SC
Siren, WI	SUP
Sisseton, SD	SFS
Sisters, OR	BAK
Sistersville, WV	WH
Sitka, AK	JUN
Skaneateles, NY	SY
Skiatook, OK	TLS
Skidmore, TX	CC
Skillman, NJ	MET
Skokie, IL	CHI
Skowhegan, ME	PRT
Slater, MO	JC
Slatersville, RI	PRO
Slatington, PA	ALN
Slaton, TX	LUB
Slayton, MN	WIN
Sleepy Eye, MN	NU
Sleepy Hollow, NY	NY
NY	SAM
Slickville, PA	GBG
Slidell, LA	NO
Slinger, WI	MIL
Slingerlands, NY	ALB
Slippery Rock, PA	PIT
Sloan, NY	BUF
Sloatsburg, NY	NY
NY	STF
Smethport, PA	E
Smiley, TX	SAT
Smithfield, NC	R
RI	PRO
VA	RIC
Smithton, IL	BEL
Smithtown, NY	RVC
Smithville, MO	KC
TN	NSH
TX	AUS
Smyrna, DE	WIL
GA	ATL
TN	NSH
Sneedville, TN	KNX
Snellville, GA	ATL
Snohomish, WA	SEA
Snoqualmie, WA	SEA
Snowflake, AZ	GLP
Snowmass, CO	DEN
Snyder, NE	OM
NY	BUF
TX	LUB
Sobieski, WI	GB
Socorro, NM	SFE
TX	ELP
Soda Springs, ID	B
Soddy Daisy, TN	KNX
Solana Beach, CA	SD
Soldotna, AK	ANC
Soledad, CA	MRY
Solomon, AZ	TUC
KS	SAL
Solomons, MD	WDC
Solon, IA	DAV
OH	CLV
OH	PRM
OH	SJP
Solon Springs, WI	SUP
Solvang, CA	LA
Solvay, NY	SY
Somers, NY	NY
Somers Point, NJ	CAM
Somerset, KY	LEX
MA	FR
NJ	MET
NJ	PSC
NJ	SYM
NJ	SAM
OH	COL
PA	ALT
TX	SAT
WI	SUP
Somersville, CT	NOR
Somersworth, NH	MAN
Somerton, AZ	TUC
Somerville, MA	BO
NJ	MET
TN	MEM
TX	AUS
Somonauk, IL	RCK
Sonoita, AZ	TUC
Sonoma, CA	SR
Sonora, CA	STO
TX	SAN
Soquel, CA	MRY
Sorrento, LA	BR
Sound Beach, NY	RVC
Sour Lake, TX	BEA
South Abington Township, PA	SCR
South Amboy, NJ	MET
South Amherst, OH	CLV
South Barre, MA	WOR
South Beloit, IL	RCK
South Bend, IN	FTW
South Boston, MA	BO
VA	RIC
South Bound Brook, NJ	MET
South Burlington, VT	BUR
South Charleston, OH	CIN
WV	WH
South Dartmouth, MA	FR
South Deerfield, MA	SPR
MA	STF
South Easton, MA	FR
South El Monte, CA	LA
South Euclid, OH	CLV
South Fork, PA	ALT
South Gate, CA	LA
South Glastonbury, CT	HRT
South Glens Falls, NY	ALB
South Grafton, MA	WOR
South Hadley, MA	SPR
South Haven, MI	KAL
South Heart, ND	BIS
South Hero, VT	BUR
South Hill, VA	RIC
South Holland, IL	CHI
South Houston, TX	GAL
South Huntington, NY	RVC
South Hutchinson, KS	WCH
South Kingstown, RI	PRO
South Lake Tahoe, CA	SAC
South Lyon, MI	DET
South Mantoloking, NJ	TR
South Milwaukee, WI	MIL
South Orange, NJ	NEW
South Ozone Park, NY	BRK
South Park, PA	PIT
South Pasadena, CA	LA
South Pittsburg, TN	KNX
South Plainfield, NJ	MET
South Portland, ME	PRT
South Prince George, VA	RIC
South Richmond Hill, NY	BRK
South Riding, VA	ARL
South River, NJ	MET
South San Francisco, CA	SFR
South Sioux City, NE	OM
South St. Paul, MN	STP
South Wilmington, IL	JOL
South Windsor, CT	HRT
South Yarmouth, MA	FR
Southampton, NY	RVC
PA	PH
Southaven, MS	JKS
Southborough, MA	WOR
Southbridge, MA	WOR
Southbury, CT	HRT
Southern Pines, NC	R
Southfield, MI	DET
MI	SYM
MI	EST
Southgate, KY	COV
MI	DET
Southington, CT	HRT
Southold, NY	RVC
Southport, NC	R
Southwest Ranches, FL	MIA
Southwick, MA	SPR
Spalding, MI	MAR
NE	GI
Sparkill, NY	NY
Sparks, MD	BAL
NV	RNO
Sparta, IL	BEL
MI	GR
NJ	PAT
TN	NSH
WI	LC
Spartanburg, SC	CHR
Spearfish, SD	RC
Spearman, TX	AMA
Spearville, KS	DOD
Speculator, NY	OG
Spencer, IA	SC
IN	IND
MA	WOR
WV	WH
Spencerport, NY	ROC
Spencerville, OH	TOL
Spicer, MN	NU
Spirit Lake, IA	SC
Splendora, TX	GAL
Spokane, WA	SPK
Spokane Valley, WA	HPM
WA	SPK
Spooner, WI	SUP
Spotswood, NJ	MET
Spotsylvania, VA	ARL
Spreckels, CA	MRY
Spring, TX	GAL
Spring Branch, TX	SAT
Spring City, PA	PH
Spring Green, WI	MAD
Spring Grove, IL	RCK
PA	HBG
Spring Hill, FL	SP
TN	NSH
Spring House, PA	PH
Spring Lake, MI	GR
NJ	TR
Spring Mills, PA	ALT
Spring Valley, CA	SD
IL	PEO
MN	WIN
NY	NY
NY	MCE
NY	STF
WI	LC
Springbrook, IA	DUB
NY	BUF
Springdale, AR	LR
PA	PIT
Springer, NM	SFE
Springerville, AZ	GLP
Springfield, CO	PBL
GA	SAV
IL	SFD
KY	L
MA	SAM
MA	SPR
MN	NU
MO	SPC
NE	OM
NJ	NEW
OH	CIN
OR	P
OR	STN
PA	PH
TN	NSH
VA	ARL
VA	WDC
VT	BUR
Springfield Gardens, NY	BRK
Springville, IA	DUB
NY	BUF
Spruce Pine, NC	CHL
Spur, TX	LUB
Stafford, TX	GAL
TX	SYM
TX	MCE
VA	ARL
Stafford Springs, CT	NOR
Stamford, CT	BGP
CT	STF
NY	ALB
TX	LUB
Stanberry, MO	KC
Standish, ME	PRT
MI	SAG
Stanford, CA	SJ
MT	GF
Stanley, ND	BIS
WI	LC
Stanton, CA	ORG
KY	LEX
MI	GR
NE	OM
TN	MEM
TX	SAN
Stanwood, WA	SEA
Staples, MN	SCL
Stapleton, NE	GI
Star City, AR	LR
IN	LFT
Star Lake, NY	OG
Starke, FL	STA
Starkville, MS	JKS
State College, PA	ALT
PA	PBR
Staten Island, NY	NY
NY	STF
Statesboro, GA	SAV
Statesville, NC	CHL
Staunton, IL	SFD
VA	RIC
Stayton, OR	P
Ste. Genevieve, MO	STL
Ste. Marie, IL	SFD
Steamboat Springs, CO	DEN
Stebbins, AK	FBK
Steele, ND	FAR
Steeleville, IL	BEL
Steelton, PA	HBG
Steger, IL	JOL
Steinauer, NE	LIN
Stella Niagara, NY	BUF
Stephan, SD	SFS
Stephen, MN	CR
Stephenson, MI	MAR
Stephenville, TX	FWT
Sterling, CO	DEN
IL	RCK
MA	WOR
VA	ARL
Sterling Heights, MI	DET
MI	PRM
MI	EST
Stetsonville, WI	SUP
Steubenville, OH	STU
Stevens Point, WI	LC
Stevenson, MD	BAL
Stevensville, MT	HEL
Stewart, MN	NU
Stewartsville, NJ	MET

Stewartville, MN	WIN
Stickney, IL	CHI
Still River, MA	WOR
Stillwater, MN	STP
NY	ALB
OK	TLS
Stirling, NJ	PAT
Stockbridge, MA	SPR
WI	GB
Stockdale, TX	SAT
Stockton, CA	STO
IL	RCK
Stone Harbor, NJ	CAM
Stone Lake, WI	SUP
Stone Mountain, GA	ATL
Stoneboro, PA	E
Stoneham, MA	BO
Stoneville, NC	CHL
Stonewall, TX	SAT
Stonewood, WV	WH
Stonington, CT	NOR
IL	SFD
Stony Point, NY	NY
Storm Lake, IA	SC
Storrs, CT	NOR
Stoughton, MA	BO
WI	MAD
Stow, OH	CLV
Stowe, PA	PH
VT	BUR
Strafford, PA	PH
Strandquist, MN	CR
Strasburg, ND	BIS
Stratford, CT	BGP
TX	AMA
WI	LC
Stratton, CO	COS
Strawberry Point, IA	DUB
Streamwood, IL	CHI
Streator, IL	PEO
Streetsboro, OH	Y
Strongsville, OH	CLV
Stroudsburg, PA	SCR
Struthers, OH	Y
Strykersville, NY	BUF
Stuart, FL	PMB
IA	DM
NE	OM
Sturgeon Bay, WI	GB
Sturgis, KY	OWN
MI	KAL
SD	RC
Sturtevant, WI	MIL
Stuttgart, AR	LR
Stuyvesant, NY	ALB
Suamico, WI	GB
Subiaco, AR	LR
Sublette, IL	RCK
Sublimity, OR	P
Succasunna, NJ	PAT
Sudbury, MA	BO
Suffern, NY	NY
Suffield, CT	HRT
Suffolk, VA	RIC
Sugar Creek, MO	KC
MO	PRM
Sugar Grove, IL	RCK
OH	COL
Sugar Land, TX	GAL
Sugar Notch, PA	SCR
Sugarloaf, PA	PSC
Suitland, MD	WDC
Sulligent, AL	BIR
Sullivan, IL	SFD
IN	EVN
MO	STL
WI	MAD
Sullivan's Island, SC	CHR
Sulphur, LA	LKC
Sulphur Springs, TX	TYL
Summerfield, FL	ORL
KS	KCK
Summerhill, PA	ALT
Summersville, WV	WH
Summerton, SC	CHR
Summerville, SC	CHR
Summit, IL	CHI
NJ	NEW
Summit Hill, PA	ALN
Sumner, IA	DUB
WA	SEA
Sumter, SC	CHR
Sun City, AZ	PHX
CA	SB
Sun City Center, FL	SP
Sun City West, AZ	PHX
Sun Lakes, AZ	PHX
Sun Prairie, WI	MAD
Sun Valley, CA	LA
ID	B
NV	RNO

Sunapee, NH	MAN
Sunbury, OH	COL
PA	HBG
Suncook, NH	MAN
Sunfish, KY	OWN
Sunland Park, NM	LSC
Sunman, IN	IND
Sunny Hills, FL	PT
Sunny Isles Beach, FL	MIA
Sunnyside, WA	YAK
Sunnyvale, CA	SJ
Sunrise, FL	MIA
Sunriver, OR	BAK
Sunset Hills, MO	STL
Superior, AZ	TUC
NE	LIN
WI	SUP
Suring, WI	GB
Surprise, AZ	PHX
Susanville, CA	SAC
Susquehanna, PA	SCR
Sussex, NJ	PAT
Sutton, MA	WOR
NE	LIN
Suttons Bay, MI	GLD
Swainsboro, GA	SAV
Swampscott, MA	BO
Swan Lake, MT	HEL
Swansboro, NC	R
Swansea, MA	FR
Swanton, OH	TOL
VT	BUR
Swanville, MN	SCL
Swarthmore, PA	PHU
Swartswood, NJ	PAT
Swartz Creek, MI	LAN
Swedesboro, NJ	CAM
Swedesburg, PA	PH
Sweeny, TX	GAL
Sweet Home, OR	P
TX	VIC
Sweetwater, TX	SAN
Swinomish, WA	SEA
Switzerland, FL	STA
Swormville, NY	BUF
Swoyersville, PA	SCR
Sybertsville, PA	PSC
Sycamore, IL	RCK
OH	TOL
Sykeston, ND	FAR
Sykesville, PA	E
PA	PBR
Sylacauga, AL	BIR
Sylmar, CA	LA
Sylva, NC	CHL
Sylvania, GA	SAV
OH	TOL
Syosset, NY	RVC
Syracuse, IN	FTW
KS	DOD
NE	LIN
NY	SY
NY	STF
Tabb, VA	RIC
Taberg, NY	SY
Tabernacle, NJ	TR
Tabor, SD	SFS
Tacoma, WA	SEA
Taft, CA	FRS
TX	CC
Taftville, CT	NOR
Tahlequah, OK	TLS
Tahoe City, CA	SAC
Takoma Park, MD	WDC
Talcott, WV	WH
Talkeetna, AK	ANC
Talladega, AL	BIR
Tallahassee, FL	PT
Tallassee, AL	MOB
Talleyville, DE	WIL
Tallmadge, OH	CLV
Tallulah, LA	ALX
Tama, IA	DUB
Tamaqua, PA	ALN
Tamarac, FL	MIA
Tamaroa, IL	BEL
Tampa, FL	SP
FL	SAM
Tampico, IL	RCK
Tanana, AK	FBK
Taneytown, MD	BAL
Tannersville, PA	SCR
Taos, NM	SFE
Tappahannock, VA	RIC
Tappan, NY	NY
Tarboro, NC	R
Tarentum, PA	PBR
PA	PIT
Tariffville, CT	HRT
Tarkio, MO	KC
Tarpon Springs, FL	SP

Tarrytown, NY	NY
Tarzana, CA	LA
Taunton, MA	FR
Tavernier, FL	MIA
Tawas City, MI	GLD
Taylor, MI	DET
TX	AUS
Taylor Mill, KY	COV
Taylors, SC	CHR
Taylors Falls, MN	STP
Taylorsville, UT	SLC
Taylorville, IL	SFD
Tazewell, VA	RIC
Tea, SD	SFS
Teaneck, NJ	NEW
Techny, IL	CHI
Tecumseh, MI	LAN
NE	LIN
Tehachapi, CA	FRS
Tekamah, NE	OM
Tekoa, WA	SPK
Tell City, IN	IND
Teller, AK	FBK
Telluride, CO	PBL
Temecula, CA	SB
CA	NTN
Tempe, AZ	PHX
Temperance, MI	DET
Temple, TX	AUS
Temple City, CA	LA
Temple Terrace, FL	SP
Tenafly, NJ	NEW
Tennessee Ridge, TN	NSH
Tequesta, FL	PMB
FL	SAM
Terre Haute, IN	IND
Terrell, TX	DAL
Terrytown, LA	NO
Terryville, CT	HRT
CT	STF
Teutopolis, IL	SFD
Tewksbury, MA	BO
MA	BUR
Texarkana, AR	LR
TX	TYL
Texas City, TX	GAL
Thatcher, AZ	TUC
The Colony, TX	FWT
TX	STN
The Dalles, OR	BAK
The Rock, GA	ATL
The Woodlands, TX	GAL
Theodore, AL	MOB
Theriot, LA	HT
Thermopolis, WY	CHY
Thibodaux, LA	HT
Thief River Falls, MN	CR
Thomas, WV	WH
Thomasboro, IL	PEO
Thomaston, CT	HRT
Thomasville, AL	MOB
GA	SAV
NC	CHL
Thompson, CT	NOR
ND	FAR
OH	CLV
Thompson Falls, MT	HEL
Thomson, GA	ATL
Thoreau, NM	GLP
Thornton, CO	DEN
Thornwood, NY	NY
Thorp, WI	LC
Thousand Oaks, CA	LA
Three Bridges, NJ	MET
Three Forks, MT	HEL
Three Lakes, WI	SUP
Three Oaks, MI	KAL
Three Rivers, CA	FRS
MA	SPR
MI	KAL
TX	CC
Throop, PA	SCR
Tiburon, CA	SFR
Tickfaw, LA	BR
Ticonderoga, NY	OG
Tidioute, PA	E
Tierra Amarilla, NM	SFE
Tiffin, OH	TOL
Tifton, GA	SAV
Tigard, OR	P
Tigerton, WI	GB
Tijeras, NM	SFE
Tilden, NE	OM
Tillamook, OR	P
Tiltonsville, OH	STU
Timber Lake, SD	RC
Timonium, MD	BAL
Tinley Park, IL	CHI
Tintah, MN	SCL
Tioga, ND	BIS
Tipp City, OH	CIN

Tipton, CA	FRS
IA	DAV
IN	LFT
KS	SAL
MO	JC
Tishomingo, OK	OKL
Tiskilwa, IL	PEO
Titusville, FL	ORL
NJ	TR
PA	E
Tiverton, RI	PRO
Tivoli, NY	NY
TX	CC
Toccoa, GA	ATL
Tohatchi, NM	GLP
Tok, AK	FBK
Toksook Bay, AK	FBK
Toledo, OH	SYM
OH	TOL
WA	SEA
Tolland, CT	NOR
Tolleson, AZ	PHX
Tolono, IL	PEO
Tomah, WI	LC
Tomahawk, WI	SUP
Tomales, CA	SFR
Tomball, TX	GAL
Tombstone, AZ	TUC
Tome, NM	SFE
Toms River, NJ	TR
NJ	PSC
NJ	PHU
Tonawanda, NY	BUF
Tonganoxie, KS	KCK
Tonica, IL	PEO
Tonkawa, OK	OKL
Tonopah, AZ	PHX
NV	LAV
Tontitown, AR	LR
Tooele, UT	SLC
Topawa, AZ	TUC
Topeka, KS	KCK
Toppenish, WA	YAK
Topping, VA	RIC
Topsfield, MA	BO
Toronto, OH	PBR
OH	STU
Torrance, CA	LA
Torrington, CT	HRT
CT	SAM
WY	CHY
Totowa, NJ	PAT
Towanda, PA	SCR
Tower, MN	DUL
Town and Country, MO	STL
Towner, ND	FAR
Townsend, MA	BO
MT	HEL
TN	KNX
Towson, MD	BAL
MD	POC
Tracy, CA	STO
MN	NU
Tracyton, WA	SEA
Traer, IA	DUB
Trafford, PA	GBG
Tranquillity, CA	FRS
Trappist, KY	L
Travelers Rest, SC	CHR
Traverse City, MI	GLD
Tremont, PA	ALN
Trempealeau, WI	LC
Trenary, MI	MAR
Trenton, IL	BEL
MI	DET
MO	KC
NE	LIN
NJ	TR
NJ	PHU
NJ	ROM
NJ	PSC
OH	CIN
Tres Pinos, CA	MRY
Trevorton, PA	HBG
Triangle, VA	ARL
Tribes Hill, NY	ALB
Tribune, KS	DOD
Trinidad, CO	PBL
Trinity, FL	SP
TX	TYL
Troy, AL	MOB
IL	SFD
KS	KCK
MI	DET
MI	EST
MI	OLD
MO	STL
NY	ALB
NY	STF
OH	CIN
Truckee, CA	SAC

Trumansburg, NY	ROC
Trumbull, CT	BGP
CT	PSC
Trussville, AL	BIR
Truth or Consequences, NM	LSC
Truxton, NY	SY
Tryon, NC	CHL
Tualatin, OR	P
Tuba City, AZ	GLP
Tubac, AZ	TUC
Tuckahoe, NY	NY
Tuckerton, NJ	TR
Tucson, AZ	HPM
AZ	TUC
AZ	STN
Tucumcari, NM	SFE
Tujunga, CA	LA
CA	OLN
Tukwila, WA	SEA
Tulare, CA	FRS
Tularosa, NM	LSC
Tulelake, CA	SAC
Tulia, TX	AMA
Tullahoma, TN	NSH
Tully, NY	SY
Tulsa, OK	OLL
OK	TLS
Tunkhannock, PA	SCR
Tununak, AK	FBK
Tupelo, MS	JKS
Tupper Lake, NY	OG
Turkey, TX	AMA
Turlock, CA	SPA
CA	STO
Turners Falls, MA	SPR
Turnersville, NJ	CAM
Turtle Creek, PA	PIT
Turton, SD	SFS
Tuscaloosa, AL	BIR
Tuscola, IL	SFD
Tuscumbia, AL	BIR
Tuskegee Institute, AL	MOB
Tustin, CA	ORG
CA	ROM
Tutwiler, MS	JKS
Tuxedo, NY	NY
Twain Harte, CA	STO
Twentynine Palms, CA	SB
Twin Falls, ID	B
Twin Lakes, WI	MIL
Twinsburg, OH	CLV
Twisp, WA	SPK
Two Harbors, MN	DUL
Two Rivers, WI	GB
Tybee Island, GA	SAV
Tyler, MN	NU
TX	TYL
Tyndall, SD	SFS
Tyngsborough, MA	BO
Tyringham, MA	SPR
Tyrone, GA	ATL
PA	ALT
Ubly, MI	SAG
Uhland, TX	AUS
Ukiah, CA	SR
CA	STN
Ulster Park, NY	NY
Ulysses, KS	DOD
NE	LIN
Umbarger, TX	AMA
Unalakleet, AK	FBK
Unalaska, AK	ANC
Uncasville, CT	NOR
Underhill Center, VT	BUR
Underwood, MN	SCL
ND	BIS
Union, KY	COV
MO	STL
NJ	NEW
OR	BAK
SC	CHR
Union City, CA	OAK
CT	HRT
IN	LFT
NJ	NEW
OK	OKL
PA	E
TN	MEM
Union Gap, WA	YAK
Union Grove, WI	MIL
Union Springs, AL	MOB
Uniondale, NY	RVC
Uniontown, KY	OWN
OH	Y
OH	CLV
PA	GBG
PA	SAM
PA	PBR
Unionville, CT	HRT
United, PA	GBG
University City, MO	STL
University Heights, OH	CLV
University Park, PA	ALT
Upland, CA	SB
Upper Arlington, OH	COL
Upper Darby, PA	PH
Upper Marlboro, MD	WDC
Upper Montclair, NJ	NEW
Upper Saddle River, NJ	NEW
Upper Sandusky, OH	TOL
Upper St. Clair, PA	PBR
Upsala, MN	SCL
Upton, MA	WOR
Urbana, IL	PEO
OH	CIN
Urbandale, IA	DM
Utica, IL	PEO
KY	OWN
MI	DET
NY	SY
NY	NTN
NY	STF
NY	SAM
OH	COL
Uvalde, TX	SAT
Uwchlan, PA	PH
Uxbridge, MA	WOR
Vacaville, CA	SAC
Vacherie, LA	BR
Vail, AZ	TUC
Valatie, NY	ALB
Valdez, AK	ANC
Valdosta, GA	SAV
Vale, NC	CHL
OR	BAK
Valentine, NE	GI
Valhalla, NY	NY
Valier, MT	HEL
Valinda, CA	LA
Vallejo, CA	SAC
Valley, NE	OM
Valley Center, CA	SD
KS	WCH
Valley City, ND	FAR
OH	CLV
Valley Lee, MD	WDC
Valley Park, MO	STL
Valley Stream, NY	RVC
Valmeyer, IL	BEL
Valparaiso, IN	GRY
NE	LIN
Valrico, FL	SP
Valyermo, CA	LA
Van Alstyne, TX	DAL
Van Buren, AR	LR
ME	PRT
Van Horn, TX	ELP
Van Horne, IA	DUB
Van Nuys, CA	LA
Van Wert, OH	TOL
Vanceburg, KY	COV
Vancleave, MS	BLX
Vancouver, WA	SEA
Vandalia, IL	SFD
MO	JC
OH	CIN
Vanderbilt, TX	VIC
Vandergrift, PA	GBG
Vanderwagen, NM	GLP
Vashon, WA	SEA
Vassar, MI	SAG
Vaughn, NM	SFE
Vega, TX	AMA
Velva, ND	FAR
Veneta, OR	P
Venice, CA	LA
FL	VEN
Ventnor, NJ	CAM
Ventura, CA	LA
CA	ROM
Verdigre, NE	OM
Vergennes, VT	BUR
Vermilion, OH	TOL
Vermillion, MN	STP
SD	SFS
Vernal, UT	SLC
Verndale, MN	SCL
Vernon, CA	LA
CT	NOR
NY	SY
TX	FWT
Vernonia, OR	P
Vero Beach, FL	PMB
Verona, NJ	NEW
NY	SY
PA	PIT
WI	MAD
Verplanck, NY	NY
Versailles, CT	NOR
KY	LEX
OH	CIN
Veseli, MN	STP
Vestal, NY	SY
Vicksburg, MI	KAL
MS	JKS
Victor, IA	DAV
NY	ROC
Victoria, KS	SAL
MN	STP
TX	VIC
Victorville, CA	SB
Vidalia, GA	SAV
LA	ALX
Vidor, TX	BEA
Vienna, IL	BEL
MO	JC
OH	Y
VA	ARL
WV	WH
Viera, FL	ORL
Villa Hills, KY	COV
Villa Maria, PA	PIT
Villa Park, IL	JOL
Villa Ridge, MO	STL
Villanova, PA	PH
Villanueva, NM	SFE
Ville Platte, LA	LAF
Vina, CA	SAC
Vincennes, IN	EVN
Vine Grove, KY	L
Vineland, NJ	CAM
Vineyard Haven, MA	FR
Vinita, OK	TLS
Vinton, IA	DUB
LA	LKC
Viola, KS	WCH
Violet, LA	NO
Virden, IL	SFD
Virgil, IL	RCK
Virginia, IL	SFD
MN	DUL
Virginia Beach, VA	RIC
Virginia City, NV	RNO
Virginia Dale, CO	DEN
Virginia Gardens, FL	MIA
Viroqua, WI	LC
Visalia, CA	FRS
Vista, CA	SD
Vivian, LA	SHP
Volga, IA	DUB
Volo, IL	CHI
Voluntown, CT	NOR
Von Ormy, TX	SAT
Voorheesville, NY	ALB
Vulcan, MI	MAR
WaKeeney, KS	SAL
Wabash, IN	FTW
Wabasha, MN	WIN
Wabasso, MN	NU
Wabeno, WI	GB
Waco, TX	AUS
Waconia, MN	STP
Waddington, NY	OG
Wadena, MN	SCL
Wading River, NY	RVC
Wadsworth, IL	CHI
OH	CLV
Waggaman, LA	NO
Wagner, SD	SFS
Wagon Mound, NM	SFE
Wagoner, OK	TLS
Wahiawa, HI	HON
Wahkon, MN	SCL
Wahoo, NE	LIN
Wahpeton, ND	FAR
Waialua, HI	HON
Waianae, HI	HON
Waihee, HI	HON
Wailuku, HI	HON
Waimanalo, HI	HON
Waipahu, HI	HON
Waite Park, MN	SCL
Wake Forest, NC	R
Wakefield, MA	BO
MI	MAR
RI	PRO
Wakeman, OH	TOL
Walbridge, OH	TOL
Walden, NY	NY
Waldorf, MD	WDC
Waldport, OR	P
Waldron, AR	LR
Walhalla, ND	FAR
Walker, IA	DUB
MN	DUL
Walkersville, MD	BAL
Walkerton, IN	FTW
IN	GRY
Wall, PA	PBR
SD	RC
TX	SAN
Walla Walla, WA	SPK
Wallace, ID	B
NC	R
NE	LIN
Walled Lake, MI	DET
Wallingford, CT	HRT
PA	PH
VT	BUR
Wallington, NJ	NEW
Wallis, TX	GAL
Walls, MS	JKS
Walnut, CA	LA
IL	PEO
Walnut Creek, CA	OAK
Walnut Grove, CA	SAC
MN	NU
Walnut Ridge, AR	LR
Walnutport, PA	ALN
Walpole, MA	BO
Walsenburg, CO	PBL
Walsh, IL	BEL
Walterboro, SC	CHR
Waltham, MA	BO
Walton, KY	COV
NY	ALB
Wamego, KS	KCK
Wanatah, IN	GRY
Wantagh, NY	RVC
Wapakoneta, OH	CIN
Wapato, WA	YAK
Wapella, IL	PEO
Wappingers Falls, NY	NY
Wapwallopen, PA	SCR
Ward, SC	CHR
Ware, MA	SPR
Wareham, MA	FR
Warminster, PA	PH
Warner, NH	MAN
Warner Robins, GA	SAV
Warren, AR	LR
IL	RCK
MA	WOR
MI	DET
MI	OLL
MI	STN
MI	EST
MI	NTN
MN	CR
NJ	MET
OH	Y
OH	PBR
PA	E
RI	PRO
Warrensburg, MO	KC
NY	ALB
Warrenton, MO	STL
VA	ARL
Warrenville, IL	JOL
Warrington, PA	PH
PA	PHU
Warroad, MN	CR
Warsaw, IL	PEO
IN	FTW
KY	COV
MO	JC
NY	BUF
Warson Woods, MO	STL
Warwick, NY	NY
RI	PRO
Wasco, CA	FRS
OR	BAK
Waseca, MN	WIN
Washburn, ND	BIS
WI	SUP
Washington, DC	PHU
DC	WDC
DC	SAM
DC	POC
GA	ATL
IA	DAV
IL	PEO
IN	EVN
KS	SAL
LA	LAF
MI	DET
MO	STL
NC	R
NJ	MET
NJ	SYM
PA	PIT
TX	AUS
VA	ARL
Washington Court House, OH	COL
Washington Depot, CT	HRT
Washington Township, NJ	NEW
Washingtonville, NY	NY
Wasilla, AK	ANC
Watchung, NJ	MET
Waterbury, CT	HRT
CT	SAM
CT	SYM
VT	BUR
Waterflow, NM	GLP

Waterford, CT	NOR
CT	NTN
MI	DET
NY	ALB
PA	E
WI	MIL
Waterloo, IA	DUB
IL	BEL
IN	FTW
NY	ROC
WI	MAD
Watersmeet, MI	MAR
Watertown, CT	HRT
MA	BO
MN	STP
NY	OG
SD	SFS
WI	MAD
Waterville, ME	PRT
ME	SAM
MN	STP
NY	SY
WA	YAK
Watervliet, MI	KAL
NY	ALB
NY	STF
NY	SAM
Watford City, ND	BIS
Wathena, KS	KCK
Watkins, MN	NU
MN	SCL
Watkins Glen, NY	ROC
Watonga, OK	OKL
Watseka, IL	JOL
Watsonville, CA	MRY
Waubun, MN	CR
Wauchula, FL	VEN
Wauconda, IL	CHI
Waukee, IA	DM
Waukegan, IL	CHI
Waukesha, WI	MIL
Waukon, IA	DUB
Waumandee, WI	LC
Waunakee, WI	MAD
Waupaca, WI	GB
Waupun, WI	MIL
Wauregan, CT	NOR
Wausau, WI	LC
Wausaukee, WI	GB
Wauseon, OH	TOL
Wautoma, WI	GB
Wauwatosa, WI	MIL
Wauzeka, WI	LC
Waveland, MS	BLX
Waverly, IA	DUB
KY	OWN
MN	STP
NE	LIN
OH	COL
Waxahachie, TX	DAL
Waycross, GA	SAV
Wayland, MA	BO
MI	KAL
NY	ROC
Waymart, PA	SCR
Wayne, IL	JOL
MI	DET
NE	OM
NJ	PAT
PA	PH
WV	WH
Waynesboro, GA	SAV
MS	BLX
PA	HBG
VA	RIC
Waynesburg, OH	Y
OH	STU
PA	PIT
Waynesville, NC	CHL
OH	CIN
Wayside, NJ	TR
Wayzata, MN	STP
Weatherford, OK	OKL
TX	FWT
Weatherly, PA	ALN
Weaverville, CA	SAC
Webb City, MO	SPC
Webster, MA	WOR
MN	STP
NY	ROC
SD	SFS
WI	SUP
Webster City, IA	DUB
Webster Groves, MO	STL
Webster Springs, WV	WH
Wedron, IL	PEO
Weed, CA	SAC
Weedsport, NY	ROC
Weehawken, NJ	NEW
Weimar, TX	VIC
Weiner, AR	LR
Weirton, WV	WH
WV	PBR
Weiser, ID	B
Welch, WV	WH
Wellesley, MA	BO
Wellesley Hills, MA	BO
Wellfleet, MA	FR
Wellington, FL	PMB
KS	WCH
OH	CLV
Wellman, IA	DAV
Wells, ME	PRT
MN	WIN
NV	RNO
Wellsboro, PA	SCR
Wellsburg, WV	WH
Wellston, OH	COL
Wellsville, NY	BUF
Wellton, AZ	TUC
Welsh, LA	LKC
Wenatchee, WA	YAK
Wendell, NC	R
Wendover, UT	SLC
Wenona, IL	PEO
Wentzville, MO	STL
Wernersville, PA	ALN
Weslaco, TX	BWN
Wesley, IA	SC
Wesley Hills, NY	NY
NY	SYM
Wessington Springs, SD	SFS
West, TX	AUS
West Allis, WI	MIL
West Babylon, NY	RVC
West Bend, IA	SC
WI	MIL
West Bloomfield, MI	DET
MI	EST
West Boylston, MA	WOR
West Branch, IA	DAV
MI	GLD
West Brandywine, PA	PH
West Bridgewater, MA	BO
West Brookfield, MA	WOR
West Brooklyn, IL	RCK
West Burke, VT	STF
West Burlington, IA	DAV
West Chazy, NY	OG
West Chester, OH	CIN
PA	PH
West Chicago, IL	JOL
West Clarksville, NY	BUF
West Covina, CA	LA
CA	OLL
West Deptford, NJ	CAM
West Des Moines, IA	DM
West Easton, PA	PHU
West End, NJ	TR
West Falls, NY	BUF
West Fargo, ND	FAR
West Frankfort, IL	BEL
West Greenwich, RI	PRO
West Grove, PA	PH
West Harrison, NY	NY
West Hartford, CT	HRT
West Harwich, MA	FR
West Haven, CT	HRT
CT	MCE
UT	SLC
West Hazleton, PA	SCR
West Hempstead, NY	RVC
West Hollywood, CA	LA
FL	MIA
West Hyattsville, MD	WDC
West Islip, NY	RVC
West Jefferson, OH	COL
West Jordan, UT	SLC
West Lafayette, IN	LFT
West Liberty, IA	DAV
KY	LEX
WV	WH
West Long Branch, NJ	TR
West Memphis, AR	LR
West Middlesex, PA	E
West Mifflin, PA	PIT
West Milford, NJ	PAT
West Milton, OH	CIN
West Milwaukee, WI	MIL
West Monroe, LA	SHP
West Mount Vernon, AL	MOB
West New York, NJ	NEW
West Newbury, MA	BO
West Newton, PA	GBG
West Nyack, NY	NY
West Orange, NJ	NEW
West Palm Beach, FL	PMB
West Park, NY	NY
West Paterson, NJ	NTN
West Peoria, IL	PEO
West Pittston, PA	SCR
West Plains, MO	SPC
West Point, IA	DAV
MS	JKS
NE	OM
NY	NY
VA	RIC
West Portsmouth, OH	COL
West Redding, CT	BGP
West River, MD	BAL
West Roxbury, MA	BO
MA	NTN
West Rutland, VT	BUR
West Sacramento, CA	SAC
West Salem, OH	CLV
WI	LC
West Sedona, AZ	PHX
West Seneca, NY	BUF
West Simsbury, CT	HRT
West Springfield, MA	SPR
West St. Paul, MN	STP
West Sunbury, PA	PIT
West Trenton, NJ	TR
West Union, IA	DUB
OH	CIN
West Valley, NY	BUF
West Valley City, UT	SLC
West Warren, MA	WOR
West Warwick, RI	PRO
West Winfield, NY	ALB
West Wyoming, PA	SCR
West Yellowstone, MT	HEL
Westampton, NJ	TR
Westborough, MA	WOR
Westbrook, CT	NOR
ME	PRT
MN	WIN
Westbury, NY	PSC
NY	RVC
Westchester, IL	CHI
Westcliffe, CO	PBL
Westerly, RI	PRO
Western Springs, IL	CHI
Westernport, MD	BAL
Westerville, OH	COL
OH	NTN
Westfield, IN	LFT
MA	SPR
NJ	NEW
NY	BUF
VT	BUR
Westford, MA	BO
Westhampton Beach, NY	RVC
Westlake, LA	LKC
OH	CLV
Westlake Village, CA	LA
Westland, MI	DET
Westminster, CA	ORG
CO	DEN
MA	WOR
MD	BAL
Westmont, IL	JOL
Westmorland, CA	SD
Weston, CT	BGP
FL	MIA
MA	BO
MO	KC
NE	LIN
PA	SCR
VT	BUR
WI	LC
WV	WH
Westphalia, IA	DM
MI	LAN
MO	JC
Westport, CT	BGP
MA	FR
SD	SFS
Westville, IL	PEO
Westville Grove, NJ	CAM
Westwego, LA	NO
Westwood, MA	BO
NJ	NEW
Wethersfield, CT	HRT
Wever, IA	DAV
Wexford, PA	PIT
Weyauwega, WI	GB
Weymouth, MA	BO
Wharton, NJ	PAT
TX	VIC
Wheat Ridge, CO	DEN
Wheatfield, IN	LFT
Wheatland, WY	CHY
Wheaton, IL	GB
IL	RCK
IL	IND
IL	JOL
MD	WDC
MN	SCL
Wheelersburg, OH	COL
Wheeling, IL	CHI
WV	WH
WV	OLL
WV	SJP
Whippany, NJ	PAT
NJ	PHU
Whistler, AL	MOB
White, SD	SFS
White Bear Lake, MN	STP
White Castle, LA	BR
White Deer, TX	AMA
White Hall, IL	SFD
White Haven, PA	SCR
White Lake, MI	DET
SD	SFS
WI	GB
White Mills, KY	L
White Oak, PA	PIT
White Pigeon, MI	KAL
White Pine, MI	MAR
White Plains, NY	NY
NY	PSC
White River, SD	RC
White River Junction, VT	BUR
White Salmon, WA	YAK
White Sulphur Springs, MT	HEL
WV	WH
White Swan, WA	YAK
Whitefish, MT	HEL
Whitefish Bay, WI	MIL
Whitehall, MT	HEL
NY	ALB
PA	ALN
WI	LC
Whitehouse, OH	TOL
TX	TYL
Whitehouse Station, NJ	MET
Whitelaw, WI	GB
Whiteriver, AZ	GLP
Whitesboro, NY	SY
Whitestone, NY	BRK
Whitesville, KY	OWN
Whitethorn, CA	SR
Whiteville, NC	R
Whitewater, WI	MIL
Whiting, IN	GRY
IN	PRM
NJ	TR
Whitinsville, MA	WOR
Whitman, MA	BO
Whitney, PA	GBG
Whitney Point, NY	SY
Whittemore, MI	GLD
Whittier, CA	LA
Wichita, KS	WCH
Wichita Falls, TX	FWT
Wickatunk, NJ	TR
Wickenburg, AZ	PHX
Wickford, RI	PRO
Wickliffe, OH	CLV
Wiggins, MS	BLX
Wilber, NE	LIN
Wilbraham, MA	SPR
Wilbur, WA	SPK
Wilburton, OK	TLS
Wilcox, PA	E
Wilder, KY	COV
Wildomar, CA	SB
Wildwood, FL	ORL
MO	STL
NJ	CAM
Wilkes-Barre, PA	PHU
PA	PSC
PA	SCR
PA	SAM
Willard, OH	TOL
WI	LC
Willcox, AZ	TUC
Williams, AZ	PHX
CA	SAC
IA	DUB
Williams Bay, WI	MIL
Williamsburg, IA	DAV
KY	LEX
PA	ALT
VA	PSC
VA	RIC
Williamson, WV	WH
Williamsport, IN	LFT
MD	BAL
PA	SCR
Williamston, MI	LAN
NC	R
Williamstown, KY	COV
MA	SPR
NJ	CAM
NJ	SYM
PA	HBG
Williamsville, NY	BUF
NY	SAM
Willimantic, CT	NOR
CT	STF
Willingboro, NJ	TR
Willington, CT	NOR

Williston, FL	STA
ND	BIS
VT	BUR
Williston Park, NY	RVC
Willits, CA	SR
Willmar, MN	NU
Willoughby, OH	CLV
Willoughby Hills, OH	CLV
Willow City, ND	FAR
Willow Grove, PA	PH
Willow River, MN	DUL
Willow Springs, IL	CHI
MO	SPC
Willowick, OH	CLV
Willows, CA	SAC
Wills Point, TX	TYL
Willsboro, NY	OG
Wilmerding, PA	PIT
Wilmette, IL	CHI
Wilmington, CA	LA
DE	PHU
DE	WIL
IL	JOL
MA	BO
NC	R
OH	CIN
VT	BUR
Wilmore, PA	ALT
Wilson, KS	SAL
NC	R
Wilsonville, OR	P
Wilton, CT	BGP
CT	SYM
IA	DAV
ND	BIS
ND	STN
Wimberley, TX	AUS
Wimbledon, ND	FAR
Winamac, IN	LFT
Winchendon, MA	WOR
Winchester, CA	SB
KY	LEX
MA	BO
VA	ARL
Winchester Center, CT	HRT
Wind Lake, WI	MIL
Windber, PA	ALT
PA	PBR
Winder, GA	ATL
Windham, CT	NOR
NH	MAN
NY	ALB
Windom, MN	WIN
Windsor, CA	SR
CO	DEN
CT	HRT
ME	PRT
NC	R
NY	SY
VT	BUR
Windsor Locks, CT	HRT
Windthorst, TX	FWT
Winfield, AL	BIR
IL	JOL
KS	WCH
Winlock, WA	SEA
Winn, MI	SAG
Winnebago, NE	OM
Winneconne, WI	GB
Winnemucca, NV	RNO
Winner, SD	RC
Winnetka, CA	LA
IL	CHI
Winnfield, LA	ALX
Winnie, TX	BEA
Winnsboro, LA	ALX
SC	CHR
TX	TYL
Winona, MN	WIN
Winooski, VT	BUR
Winslow, AR	LR
AZ	GLP
ME	PRT
Winsted, CT	HRT
MN	NU
Winston–Salem, NC	CHL
Winter, WI	SUP
Winter Garden, FL	ORL
Winter Haven, FL	ORL
Winter Park, FL	ORL
Winter Springs, FL	ORL
Winterhaven, CA	SD
Winters, CA	SAC
TX	SAN
Winterset, IA	DM
Wintersville, OH	STU
Winthrop, MA	BO
ME	PRT
MN	NU
Wisconsin Dells, WI	MAD
Wisconsin Rapids, WI	LC
WI	SUP
Wishek, ND	FAR
Wisner, NE	OM
Wittenberg, WI	LC
Wixom, MI	DET
Woburn, MA	BO
Wofford Heights, CA	FRS
Wolcott, CT	HRT
NY	ROC
Wolf Point, MT	GF
Wolfeboro, NH	MAN
Wolfforth, TX	LUB
Wonder Lake, IL	RCK
Wood Dale, IL	JOL
Wood Ridge, NJ	NEW
Wood River, IL	SFD
NE	GI
Woodbourne, NY	NY
Woodbridge, CT	HRT
NJ	MET
VA	ARL
Woodburn, OR	P
Woodbury, CT	HRT
MN	STP
NJ	CAM
NY	RVC
Woodbury Heights, NJ	CAM
Woodcliff Lake, NJ	NEW
Woodhaven, MI	DET
NY	BRK
Woodhull, IL	PEO
Woodinville, WA	SEA
Woodlake, CA	FRS
Woodland, CA	SAC
WA	SEA
Woodland Hills, CA	LA
Woodland Park, CO	COS
NJ	PAT
NJ	PSC
Woodlawn, VA	RIC
Woodridge, IL	JOL
Woodruff, WI	SUP
Woodsboro, TX	CC
Woodsfield, OH	STU
Woodside, NY	BRK
Woodstock, GA	ATL
IL	RCK
MD	BAL
NY	NY
VA	ARL
VT	BUR
Woodsville, NH	MAN
Woodville, FL	PT
MS	JKS
TX	BEA
Woodward, OK	OKL
Woodworth, LA	ALX
Woonsocket, RI	PRO
RI	STF
SD	SFS
Wooster, OH	CLV
Worcester, MA	NTN
MA	WOR
MA	SAM
NY	ALB
Worland, WY	CHY
Worthington, IA	DUB
MN	WIN
OH	COL
Wrangell, AK	JUN
Wray, CO	DEN
Wrentham, MA	BO
Wright, KS	DOD
Wrightsville Beach, NC	R
Wrightwood, CA	SB
Wurtsboro, NY	NY
Wyalusing, PA	SCR
Wyandanch, NY	RVC
Wyandotte, MI	DET
Wyckoff, NJ	NEW
Wylie, TX	DAL
Wymore, NE	LIN
Wynantskill, NY	ALB
Wyncote, PA	PH
Wyndmere, ND	FAR
Wyndmoor, PA	PH
Wynne, AR	LR
Wynnewood, PA	PH
PA	OLN
Wynot, NE	OM
Wyoming, IL	PEO
MI	GR
OH	CIN
PA	SCR
Wytheville, VA	RIC
Xenia, OH	CIN
Yakima, WA	YAK
Yakutat, AK	JUN
Yale, MI	DET
Yalesville, CT	HRT
Yamhill, OR	P
Yankton, SD	SFS
Yardley, PA	PH
Yardville, NJ	TR
Yarnell, AZ	PHX
Yatesboro, PA	GBG
Yazoo City, MS	JKS
Yellow Springs, OH	CIN
Yellville, AR	LR
Yelm, WA	SEA
Yerington, NV	RNO
Yoakum, TX	VIC
Yoder, IN	FTW
Yonges Island, SC	CHR
Yonkers, NY	NY
NY	MCE
NY	NTN
NY	SYM
NY	STF
Yorba Linda, CA	ORG
York, NE	LIN
PA	HBG
SC	CHR
York Haven, PA	HBG
Yorktown, TX	VIC
VA	RIC
Yorktown Heights, NY	NY
Yorkville, IL	JOL
Youngstown, NY	BUF
OH	Y
OH	OLL
OH	PBR
OH	SJP
Youngsville, LA	LAF
PA	E
Youngtown, AZ	PHX
Youngwood, PA	GBG
Yountville, CA	SR
Ypsilanti, MI	LAN
Yreka, CA	SAC
Yuba City, CA	SAC
Yucaipa, CA	SB
Yucca Valley, CA	SB
Yukon, OK	OKL
PA	GBG
Yulan, NY	NY
Yuma, AZ	TUC
CO	DEN
Zachary, LA	BR
Zaleski, OH	COL
Zanesville, OH	COL
Zapata, TX	LAR
Zelienople, PA	PIT
Zephyr Cove, NV	RNO
Zephyrhills, FL	SP
Zillah, WA	YAK
Zion–Beach Park, IL	CHI
Zionsville, IN	LFT
Zumbrota, MN	STP
Zuni, NM	GLP
Zwolle, LA	SHP

Diocesan Abbreviations

ARCHDIOCESES AND DIOCESES

(ALB) Albany (New York)
(ALN) Allentown (Pennsylvania)
(ALT) Altoona-Johnstown (Pennsylvania)
(ALX) Alexandria (Louisiana)
(AGN) Agana (Guam)
(AMA) Amarillo (Texas)
(ANC) Anchorage (Alaska)
(ARE) Arecibo (Puerto Rico)
(ARL) Arlington (Virginia)
(ATH) Apostolate to Hungarians
(ATL) Atlanta (Georgia)
(AUS) Austin (Texas)
(B) Boise (Idaho)
(BAK) Baker (Oregon)
(BAL) Baltimore (Maryland)
(BEA) Beaumont (Texas)
(BEL) Belleville (Illinois)
(BGP) Bridgeport (Connecticut)
(BIR) Birmingham (Alabama)
(BIS) Bismarck (North Dakota)
(BLX) Biloxi (Mississippi)
(BO) Boston (Massachusetts)
(BR) Baton Rouge (Louisiana)
(BRK) Brooklyn (New York)
(BUF) Buffalo (New York)
(BUR) Burlington (Vermont)
(BWN) Brownsville (Texas)
(CAM) Camden (New Jersey)
(CC) Corpus Christi (Texas)
(CGS) Caguas (Puerto Rico)
(CHI) Chicago (Illinois)
(CHK) Chalan Kanoa
(CHL) Charlotte (North Carolina)
(CHR) Charleston (South Carolina)
(CHY) Cheyenne (Wyoming)
(CI) Caroline Islands
(CIN) Cincinnati (Ohio)
(CLV) Cleveland (Ohio)
(COL) Columbus (Ohio)
(COS) Colorado Springs (Colorado)
(COV) Covington (Kentucky)
(CR) Crookston (Minnesota)
(DAL) Dallas (Texas)
(DAV) Davenport (Iowa)
(DEN) Denver (Colorado)
(DET) Detroit (Michigan)
(DM) Des Moines (Iowa)
(DOD) Dodge City (Kansas)
(DUB) Dubuque (Iowa)
(DUL) Duluth (Minnesota)
(E) Erie (Pennsylvania)
(ELP) El Paso (Texas)
(EST) Saint Thomas the Apostle, Chaldean (Michigan)
(EVN) Evansville (Indiana)
(FAJ) Fajardo-Humacao (Puerto Rico)
(FAR) Fargo (North Dakota)
(FBK) Fairbanks (Alaska)
(FgM) Foreign Mission Section
(FR) Fall River (Massachusetts)
(FRS) Fresno (California)
(FTW) Fort Wayne-South Bend (Indiana)
(FWT) Fort Worth (Texas)
(GAL) Galveston-Houston (Texas)
(GLD) Gaylord (Michigan)
(GB) Green Bay (Wisconsin)
(GBG) Greensburg (Pennsylvania)
(GF) Great Falls-Billings (Montana)
(GI) Grand Island (Nebraska)
(GLP) Gallup (New Mexico)
(GR) Grand Rapids (Michigan)
(GRY) Gary (Indiana)
(HBG) Harrisburg (Pennsylvania)
(HEL) Helena (Montana)
(HON) Honolulu (Hawaii)
(HPM) Holy Protection of Mary Byzantine (Arizona)
(HRT) Hartford (Connecticut)
(HT) Houma-Thibodaux (Louisiana)
(IND) Indianapolis (Indiana)
(JC) Jefferson City (Missouri)
(JKS) Jackson (Mississippi)
(JOL) Joliet in Illinois
(JUN) Juneau (Alaska)
(KAL) Kalamazoo (Michigan)
(KC) Kansas City-St. Joseph (Missouri)
(KCK) Kansas City in Kansas
(KNX) Knoxville (Tennessee)
(L) Louisville (Kentucky)
(LA) Los Angeles (California)
(LAF) Lafayette (Louisiana)
(LAN) Lansing (Michigan)
(LAR) Laredo (Texas)
(LC) La Crosse (Wisconsin)
(LEX) Lexington (Kentucky)
(LFT) Lafayette in Indiana
(LIN) Lincoln (Nebraska)
(LIT) Apostolate for Lithuanian Catholics (New York)
(LKC) Lake Charles (Louisiana)
(LR) Little Rock (Arkansas)
(LSC) Las Cruces (New Mexico)
(LUB) Lubbock (Texas)
(LAV) Las Vegas (Nevada)
(MAD) Madison (Wisconsin)
(MAN) Manchester (New Hampshire)
(MAR) Marquette (Michigan)
(MCE) St. Mary, Queen of Peace, Syro-Malankara (New York)
(MEM) Memphis (Tennessee)
(MET) Metuchen (New Jersey)
(MGZ) Mayaguez (Puerto Rico)
(MI) Marshall Islands
(MIA) Miami (Florida)
(MIL) Milwaukee (Wisconsin)
(MO) Military Services, U.S.A. (Maryland)
(MOB) Mobile (Alabama)
(MRY) Monterey in California
(NEW) Newark (New Jersey)
(NO) New Orleans (Louisiana)
(NOR) Norwich (Connecticut)
(NSH) Nashville (Tennessee)
(NTN) Newton, Melkite-Greek (Massachusetts)
(NU) New Ulm (Minnesota)
(NY) New York (New York)
(OAK) Oakland (California)
(OG) Ogdensburg (New York)
(OKL) Oklahoma City (Oklahoma)
(OLD) Our Lady of Deliverance-Syriac (New Jersey)
(OLL) Our Lady of Lebanon of Los Angeles (California)
(OLN) Our Lady of Nareg-Armenian (California)
(OM) Omaha (Nebraska)
(ORG) Orange in California
(ORL) Orlando (Florida)
(OWN) Owensboro (Kentucky)
(P) Portland in Oregon
(PAT) Paterson (New Jersey)
(PBL) Pueblo (Colorado)
(PBR) Pittsburgh-Byzantine (Pennsylvania)
(PCE) Ponce (Puerto Rico)
(PEO) Peoria (Illinois)
(PH) Philadelphia (Pennsylvania)
(PHU) Philadelphia-Ukrainian (Pennsylvania)
(PHX) Phoenix (Arizona)
(PIT) Pittsburgh (Pennsylvania)
(PMB) Palm Beach (Florida
(POC) Personal Ordnariate of the Chair of St. Pete (Texas
(POD) Prelature of the Holy Cross and Opus De (New York
(PRM) Parma-Byzantine (Ohio
(PRO) Providence (Rhode Island
(PRT) Portland (Maine
(PSC) Passaic-Byzantine (New Jersey
(PT) Pensacola-Tallahassee (Florida
(R) Raleigh (North Carolina
(RC) Rapid City (South Dakota
(RCK) Rockford (Illinois
(RIC) Richmond (Virginia
(RNO) Reno (Nevada
(ROC) Rochester (New York
(ROM) St. George-Romanian (Ohio
(RVC) Rockville Centre (New York
(SAC) Sacramento (California
(SAG) Saginaw (Michigan
(SAL) Salina (Kansas
(SAM) St. Maron (New York
(SAN) San Angelo (Texas
(SAT) San Antonio (Texas
(SAV) Savannah (Georgia
(SB) San Bernardino (California
(SC) Sioux City (Iowa
(SCL) St. Cloud (Minnesota
(SCR) Scranton (Pennsylvania
(SD) San Diego (California
(SEA) Seattle (Washington
(SFD) Springfield in Illinoi
(SFE) Santa Fe (New Mexico
(SFR) San Francisco (California
(SFS) Sioux Falls (South Dakota
(SHP) Shreveport (Louisiana
(SJ) San Jose in Californi
(SJN) San Juan (Puerto Rico
(SJP) St. Josaphat-Ukrainian(Ohio
(SLC) Salt Lake City (Utah
(SP) St. Petersburg (Florida
(SPA) St. Peter the Apostle, Chaldean (California
(SPC) Springfield-Cape Girardeau (Missouri
(SPK) Spokane (Washington
(SPP) Samoa-Pago Pag
(SPR) Springfield in Massachusett
(SR) Santa Rosa in Californi
(STA) St. Augustine (Florida
(STF) Stamford-Ukrainian (Connecticut
(STL) St. Louis (Missouri
(STN) St. Nicholas-Ukrainian (Illinois
(STO) Stockton (California
(STP) St. Paul and Minneapolis (Minnesota
(STU) Steubenville (Ohio
(STV) St. Thomas in the Virgin Islands
(SUP) Superior (Wisconsin
(SY) Syracuse (New York
(SYM) St. Thomas Syro-Malabar (Illinois
(TLS) Tulsa (Oklahoma
(TOL) Toledo (Ohio
(TR) Trenton (New Jersey
(TUC) Tucson (Arizona
(TYL) Tyler (Texas
(VEN) Venice (Florida
(VIC) Victoria in Texas
(WCH) Wichita (Kansas
(WDC) Washington (District of Columbia
(WH) Wheeling-Charleston (West Virginia
(WIL) Wilmington (Delaware
(WIN) Winona-Rochester (Minnesota
(WOR) Worcester (Massachusetts
(Y) Youngstown (Ohio
(YAK) Yakima (Washington

eximious®
PASCHAL CANDLES
Lilium™
The Lilium™ Paschal Candle – a name taken from the Latin for lily – features a handsome fleur-de-lis cross at the heart of its design. An ancient and regal symbol of the Holy Trinity, the fleur-de-lis reminds us of the glorious divinity of the Father, Son, and Holy Spirit and is exquisitely expressed here in royal blue with accents of gold leaf. Adorning the ornamental bands are bees, a symbol of sacrifice so beautifully celebrated in the Easter Exsultet. Individually hand-crafted, each Lilium™ candle is a truly majestic celebration of the Resurrection of our Lord and the gift of eternal life.
eximious® PASCHAL CANDLES
(EG-'ZIM-E-ES) MEANS DISTINGUISHED, UNPARALLELED, EXTRAORDINARY
Each and every eximious® Paschal candle is made-to-order. eximious® Paschal candle designs are unique and allow the candle decorators' artistic talent to fingerprint each individual candle. No two candles are exactly alike; every candle is an individual work of art.

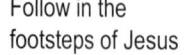

Diocese of Albany

(Dioecesis Albanensis)

Most Reverend

EDWARD B. SCHARFENBERGER

Bishop of Albany; ordained July 2, 1973; appointed Bishop of Albany February 11, 2014; ordained and installed April 10, 2014. *Chancery Office: Pastoral Center, 40 N. Main Ave., Albany, NY 12203.*

Most Reverend

HOWARD J. HUBBARD, D.D.

Bishop Emeritus of Albany; ordained December 18, 1963; appointed February 1, 1977; ordained and installed March 27, 1977; retired February 11, 2014. *Res.: 125 Eagle St., Albany, NY 12202.* Tel: 518-462-3804.

Chancery Office: Pastoral Center, 40 N. Main Ave., Albany, NY 12203. Tel: 518-453-6600; Fax: 518-453-6795.

Web: www.rcda.org

Email: chancery@rcda.org

ESTABLISHED APRIL 23, 1847.

Square Miles 10,419.

(Incorporated by a special act of the Legislature of the State of New York, April 12, 1941, with the title "The Roman Catholic Diocese of Albany, New York").

Comprises the entire Counties of Albany, Columbia, Delaware, Fulton, Green, Montgomery, Otsego, Rensselaer, Saratoga, Schenectady, Schoharie, Warren and Washington and that part of Herkimer and Hamilton Counties, south of the northern line of the townships of Ohio and Russia, as existing in 1872 in the State of New York.

For legal titles of parishes and diocesan institutions, consult the Chancery Office.

STATISTICAL OVERVIEW

Personnel	
Bishop	1
Retired Bishops	1
Priests: Diocesan Active in Diocese	93
Priests: Diocesan Active Outside Diocese	3
Priests: Retired, Sick or Absent	91
Number of Diocesan Priests	187
Religious Priests in Diocese	36
Total Priests in Diocese	223
Extern Priests in Diocese	8
Ordinations:	
Diocesan Priests	1
Transitional Deacons	2
Permanent Deacons	2
Permanent Deacons in Diocese	110
Total Brothers	60
Total Sisters	510
Parishes	
Parishes	126
With Resident Pastor:	
Resident Diocesan Priests	91
Resident Religious Priests	4
Without Resident Pastor:	
Administered by Priests	9
Administered by Deacons	9
Administered by Religious Women	4
Administered by Lay People	9
Missions	15
Professional Ministry Personnel:	
Sisters	16
Lay Ministers	335
Welfare	
Catholic Hospitals	2
Homes for the Aged	6
Total Assisted	900
Residential Care of Children	2
Total Assisted	48
Day Care Centers	1
Total Assisted	39
Specialized Homes	4
Total Assisted	363
Special Centers for Social Services	85
Total Assisted	77,894
Residential Care of Disabled	18
Total Assisted	108
Other Institutions	1
Total Assisted	25
Educational	
Seminaries, Diocesan	1
Students from This Diocese	11
Diocesan Students in Other Seminaries	20
Total Seminarians	31
Colleges and Universities	4
Total Students	9,000
High Schools, Diocesan and Parish	4
Total Students	862
High Schools, Private	3
Total Students	1,144
Elementary Schools, Diocesan and Parish	18
Total Students	3,582
Elementary Schools, Private	1
Total Students	111
Catechesis/Religious Education:	
High School Students	4,000
Elementary Students	9,994
Total Students under Catholic Instruction	28,724
Teachers in the Diocese:	
Priests	6
Lay Teachers	555
Vital Statistics	
Receptions into the Church:	
Infant Baptism Totals	2,378
Minor Baptism Totals	100
Adult Baptism Totals	60
Received into Full Communion	84
First Communions	2,262
Confirmations	2,107
Marriages:	
Catholic	436
Interfaith	158
Total Marriages	594
Deaths	4,122
Total Catholic Population	307,206
Total Population	1,360,500

Former Bishops—His Eminence JOHN CARDINAL MCCLOSKEY, D.D., ord. Jan. 12, 1834; appt. Bishop of Axiere and Coadjutor to the Bishop of New York, Nov. 21, 1843; cons. March 10, 1844; transferred to Albany, May 21, 1847; promoted to New York, May 6, 1864; created Cardinal Priest of the Holy Roman Church, March 15, 1875, under the title Sanctae Mariae supra Minervam; died Oct. 10, 1885; Rt. Rev. JOHN J. CONROY, ord. May 21, 1842; appt. Bishop July 7, 1865; cons. Oct. 15, 1865; resigned Oct. 16, 1877; transferred to the See of Curium, March 22, 1878; died Nov. 20, 1895; Rt. Rev. Msgrs. FRANCIS MCNEIRNY, D.D., ord. Aug. 17, 1854; appt. Bishop of Rhesina and Coadjutor to the Bishop of Albany, Dec. 22, 1871; cons. April 21, 1872; appt. Administrator of the Diocese of Albany, Jan. 18, 1874; Bishop of Albany, by right of succession, Oct. 16, 1877; died Jan. 2, 1894; THOMAS M. A. BURKE, D.D., ord. June 30, 1864; preconized May 18, 1894; cons. July 1, 1894; died Jan 20, 1915; THOMAS F. CUSACK, D.D., ord. May 30, 1885; cons. Titular Bishop of Themiscyra and Auxiliary to the Archbishop of New York, April 25, 1904; transferred to Albany, July 5, 1915; died July 12, 1918; Most Revs. EDMUND F. GIBBONS, D.D., ord. May 27, 1893; appt. Bishop, Feb. 1, 1919; cons. March 25, 1919; resigned Nov. 10, 1954; transferred to See of Verbe; died June 19, 1964; WILLIAM A. SCULLY, D.D., ord. Sept. 20, 1919; appt. Coadjutor Bishop "cum jure successionis," Aug. 21, 1945; cons. Oct. 24, 1945; succeeded to See, Nov. 10, 1954; died Jan. 5, 1969; EDWARD J. MAGINN, D.D., ord. June 10, 1922; appt. Titular Bishop of Curium & Auxiliary Bishop of Albany June 27, 1957; appt. Apostolic Admin. for the Diocese of Albany Jan. 10, 1966; appt. ended March 18, 1969; died Aug. 21, 1984.; EDWIN B. BRODERICK, D.D., ord. May 30, 1942; appt. Titular Bishop of Tizica and Auxiliary of New York, March 8, 1967; cons. April 21, 1967; transferred to Albany, March 19, 1969; resigned June 2, 1976; appt. Exec. Dir. Catholic Relief Services, June 3, 1976; retired Sept. 1985; died July 2, 2006.; HOWARD J. HUBBARD, ord. Dec. 18, 1963; appt. Feb. 1, 1977; ord. and installed March 27, 1977; retired Feb. 11, 2014.

Pastoral Center—Pastoral Center, 40 N. Main Ave., Albany, 12203. Tel: 518-453-6600; Fax: 518-453-6793. Office Hours: Mon.-Fri. 8:30-4:30.

Vicar General—40 N. Main Ave., Albany, 12203-1422. Tel: 518-453-6612. Very Rev. DAVID R. LEFORT, S.T.L., V.G.

Moderator of the Curia—Very Rev. DONALD L. RUTHERFORD, 40 N. Main Ave., Albany, 12203-1422. Tel: 518-453-6612.

Chancellor—40 N. Main Ave., Albany, 12203. Tel: 518-453-6612. MR. GIOVANNI VIRGIGLIO.

Finance Department—40 N. Main Ave., Albany, 12203. Tel: 518-453-6640; Fax: 518-453-8454. MR. JOHN HUTCHINSON, CFO, Email: john.hutchinson@rcda.org; BARBARA MURIN, Comptroller, Email: barbara.murin@rcda.org; LAURETTE AHLEMEYER, Parish Support Specialist, Email: laurette.ahlemeyer@rcda.org; TERRY LANTRY, Internal Auditor, Email: terry.lantry@rcda.org.

Insurance Office—Catholic Mutual Group, 5 Computer Dr. W., Ste. 206, Albany, 12205. Tel: 518-445-6250; Fax: 518-445-6253. JON ROCCO, Claims & Risk Mgr., Email: jrocco@catholicmutual.org; KATHLEEN

WILLIAMS, Asst. Claims & Risk Mgr., Email: kwilliams@catholicmutual.org; CHERYL DYKSTRA, Sec., Email: cdykstra@catholicmutual.org.

Office of Human Resources and Safe Environment—40 N. Main Ave., Albany, 12203-1422.
Tel: 518-453-6635; Fax: 518-453-8446; Email: diocesan.hr@rcda.org. JOYCE C. TARANTINO, Esq., Dir. Human Resources & Safe Environment; BRIAN P. EVERS, Assoc. Dir. Safe Environment; ERINA DACEY, Human Resources Administrative Asst.; JENNIFER GOYETTE, Safe Environment Administrative Asst.; MS. JOAN MINEAU, Benefits Coord.

Pastoral Planning—Deacon FRANK C. BERNING, D.Min., Dir., Tel: 518-453-6679; Email: frank.berning@rcda.org; ANNE BORGHETTI, Administrative Asst., Tel: 518-453-6661; Email: anne.borghetti@rcda.org.

Archivist—AMY BROZIO-ANDREWS, 40 N. Main Ave., Albany, 12203. Tel: 518-453-6669; Email: amy.brozio-andrews@rcda.org.

Office of Canonical Services—40 N. Main Ave., Albany, 12203. Tel: 518-453-6620; Fax: 518-453-6778; Email: tribunal@rcda.org. Office Hours: 8:30-4:30 (By appointment only)

Vicar Judicial—Very Rev. JAMES I. DONLON, J.C.D.

Judges—Very Rev. ANTHONY M. BARRATT, E.V.; Rev. DAVID V. BERBERIAN, J.C.L.; Very Rev. JAMES I. DONLON, J.C.D.; Rev. MATTHEW H. FRISONI, J.C.L.; Mr. J. MICHAEL RITTY, Ph.D., J.C.L.

Defenders of the Marriage Bond in First Instance—Rev. JOSEPH J. KOURY, J.C.D.; Sr. MARILYN VASSALLO, C.S.J., J.C.L.

Promoter of Justice—Sr. MARILYN VASSALLO, C.S.J., J.C.L.

Advocates—Revs. THOMAS KRUPA; JOSEPH O'BRIEN; JOHN L. MOYNA.

Bishop's Delegate for Marriage Dispensations—Very Rev. JAMES I. DONLON, J.C.D.; Rev. MATTHEW H. FRISONI, J.C.L.

Notaries—Mrs. ANNE SCHMIDT; MS. ANNA COLELLO.

Metropolitan Tribunal—Serving as: The Court of First Instance - Archdiocese of New York; The Court of Second Instance - Province of New York/ Archdiocese for Military Services, *1011 First Ave., New York, 10022.*
Tel: 212-371-1000, Ext. 3200; Tel: 646-794-3200; Email: tribunal@archny.org. Very Rev. RICHARD L. WELCH, C.Ss.R., J.C.D., M.R.E., M.Div., Judicial Vicar.

Presbyteral Council—Most Rev. EDWARD B. SCHARFENBERGER, D.D., Pres.; Very Rev. ANTHONY M. BARRATT, E.V., Appointed Member; Rev. WINSTON L. BATH, Elected Member, (Retired); Very Rev. JAMES BELOGI, E.V., Appointed Member; Rev. JOHN J. BRADLEY, Elected Member; Very Revs. JOSEPH G. BUSCH, E.V., Sec.; MICHAEL CAMBI, E.V., Appointed Member; Revs. RICHARD CARLINO, Elected Member; PAUL G. CATENA, Elected Member; THOMAS H. CHEVALIER, Elected Member; JOHN CRONIN, Elected Member; Very Rev. CHRISTOPHER DEGIOVINE, E.V., Elected Member; Rev. L. EDWARD DEIMEKE, E.V., Appointed Member, (Retired); Very Revs. JAMES I. DONLON, J.C.D., Staff; DAVID R. LEFORT, S.T.L., V.G., Staff; Revs. F. RICHARD LESSER, Chair; RANDALL P. PATTERSON, Vice Chair; DANIEL J. QUINN, Appointed Member; Very Revs. MARK G. REAMER, O.F.M., E.V., Appointed Member; DONALD L. RUTHERFORD, Staff; Rev. STEVEN SCARMOZZINO, Elected Member; Very Revs. CHRISTOPHER WELCH, E.V., Appointed Member; THOMAS ZELKER, E.V., Appointed Member.

Diocesan College of Consultors—Rev. WINSTON L. BATH, (Retired); Very Revs. JAMES BELOGI, E.V.; JOSEPH G. BUSCH, E.V.; Rev. PAUL G. CATENA; Very Revs. CHRISTOPHER DEGIOVINE, E.V.; DAVID R. LEFORT, S.T.L., V.G.; Revs. F. RICHARD LESSER; RANDALL P. PATTERSON; Very Rev. MARK G. REAMER, O.F.M., E.V.

Regional Episcopal Vicars—Very Revs. JAMES BELOGI, E.V., Tech Valley Vicariate; JOSEPH G. BUSCH, E.V., Adirondack Vicariate; MICHAEL CAMBI, E.V., Leatherstocking Vicariate; ANTHONY M. BARRATT, E.V., Hudson Valley Vicariate; MARK G. REAMER, O.F.M., E.V., Beverwyck Vicariate; CHRISTOPHER WELCH, E.V., Mohawk Valley Vicariate; THOMAS ZELKER, E.V., Taconic Vicariate.

Diocesan Offices and Directors

Unless otherwise indicated all Diocesan Offices and Directors are located at: *The Pastoral Center, 40 N. Main Ave., Albany, 12203.* Tel: 518-453-6600; Fax: 518-453-6793.

Office of Real Property—Tel: 518-453-6623;
Fax: 518-641-6825. PAUL A. EHMANN, Dir., Email: paul.ehmann@rcda.org; LORI CHERA, Admin., Email: lori.chera@rcda.org.

Apostleship of Prayer—The Pastoral Center, 40 N. Main Ave., Albany, 12203. Tel: 518-453-6643.

Bishop's Appeal—THOMAS PRINDLE, Exec. Dir., Tel: 518-453-6680.

Black Catholic Apostolate of the Diocese of Albany / St. Joan of Arc Parish—Rev. KOFI NTSIFUL-AMISSAH, Admin., 76 Menand Rd., Menands, 12204. Tel: 518-463-0378; Email: sjoa@nycap.rr.com.

Korean Catholic Apostolate of Albany—15 Exchange St., Albany, 12205. Tel: 518-438-1805. Rev. JAEUNG DAMIAN LEE, Chap.

Vietnamese Apostolate—Rev. JOHN T. PROVOST, Pastor. Coordinators: GIANG (JOHNNY) TRAN; KHIET NGUYEN, Sacred Heart Church, 33 Walter St., Albany, 12204.

Emmaus Retreat Ministry to College Age People—Spiritual Directors of Ministry: MAUREEN ATHENS, Co Dir.; MR. CHRIS O'NEILL, Co Dir., Email: chrisrory@me.com.

Catholic Deaf Ministry—MRS. ROSEMARIE TOBIN, Liaison, c/o Catholic Schools Office - Persons with Disabilities, 40 N. Main Ave., Albany, 12203. Tel: 518-453-6602; Email: deaf@rcda.org; Web: www.rcda.org/offices/disabilities-and-deaf-ministry.

Cemeteries—RICHARD TOUCHETTE, Exec. Dir., Catholic Cemeteries of the Roman Catholic Diocese of Albany, New York, 48 Cemetery Ave., Menands, Albany, 12204. Tel: 518-432-4953; Email: rick@adcemeteries.org; Web: www.capitaldistrictcemeteries.org.

Censor Librorum—Pastoral Center, 40 N. Main Ave., Albany, 12203. Tel: 518-453-6600.

Architecture and Building Commission—Rev. RANDALL P. PATTERSON, Chm.; LORI CHERA, Coord., Tel: 518-453-6622; Fax: 518-641-6825; Email: abc@rcda.org; ROSLYN WEBBER, Construction Project Coord.

Communications Office—MARY DETURRIS POUST, Dir., Tel: 518-453-6618; Email: mary.deturrispoust@rcda.org; KATHRYN COSTELLO, Communications Specialist, Tel: 518-453-6618; Email: kathryn.costello@rcda.org.

Office of Parish Services—RENEE MORGIEWICZ, Coord. Parish Svcs., Tel: 518-453-6609.

Cursillo in Christianity—Sr. MONICA MURPHY, C.S.J., Spiritual Dir., 44 Highland Ave., Albany, 12203. Tel: 518-449-9024. Lay Directors: TOM MOLLOY; LINDA MOLLOY, 32 Snowberry Rd., Malta, 12020. Tel: 518-899-9631.

Diocesan Service Committee for Charismatic Renewal—Co Liaisons: DIAN SEAVER, Tel: 518-663-5125; Email: seaverdiane@yahoo.com; JACK ELLSBURY, Email: john_ellsbury@earthlink.net.

Diocesan Stewardship Office—THOMAS PRINDLE, Exec. Dir., Tel: 518-453-6680.

Office of Information Technology—GERALYN A. FOX, Dir., Tel: 518-453-6685; Fax: 518-453-6779.

Catholic Charities of Diocese of Albany, Inc.; St. Vincent's Child Care Society, Inc.—MR. VINCENT W. COLONNO, CEO & Sec. to Bishop for Health & Social Svcs. & Sec. St. Vincent's Child Care Society, Inc., Tel: 518-453-6650; Fax: 518-453-6792; MICHELE KELLY, CFO.

Catholic Charities Agencies and Commissions—THERESA LUX, Dir., Catholic Charities of Columbia & Greene Counties, 431 E. Allen St., Hudson, 12534. Tel: 518-828-8660. 66 William St., Catskill, 12414. Tel: 518-943-1462; DAVID COVEY, Dir. Catholic Charities of Fulton & Montgomery Counties, 55 E. Main St., Ste. 100, Johnstown, 12095-2641. Tel: 518-762-8313. 1 Kimball St., Amsterdam, 12010. Tel: 518-842-4202; MAUREEN PETRIE, Dir., Catholic Charities of Herkimer County, 61 West St., Ilion, 13357. Tel: 315-894-9917; LYNN GLUECKERT, Dir., Catholic Charities of Delaware, Otsego, and Schoharie Counties, 176 Main St., Oneonta, 13820. Tel: 607-432-0061. 489 W. Main St., Cobleskill, 12043. Tel: 518-234-3581; Sr. CHARLA COMMINS, C.S.J., Dir., Catholic Charities of Saratoga, Warren & Washington Counties, 142 Regent St., Saratoga Springs, 12866. Tel: 518-587-5000. 35 Broad St., Glens Falls, 12801. Tel: 518-793-6212; MARLENE HILDENBRANDT, Dir. Catholic Charities Senior & Caregiver Support Svcs., Catholic Charities of Schenectady County, 1462 Erie Blvd., Schenectady, 12305. Tel: 518-372-5667; JENNIFER HYDE, Dir., Roarke Ctr., 107 Fourth St., Troy, 12180. Tel: 518-273-8351. Catholic Charities Tri-County Svcs., 50 Herrick St., Rensselaer, 12144. Tel: 518-512-3577. Sunnyside Child Development Ctr., 9th St. at Ingalls Ave., Troy, 12180. Tel: 518-214-5986; MR. VINCENT W. COLONNO, Dir., Commission on Aging, Dir. Commission on Restorative Justice; Deacon WALTER AYRES, Dir., Commission on Peace & Justice, Tel: 518-453-6650; ANNE MARIE COUSER, Dir., Catholic Charities Community Maternity Svcs., 27 N. Main Ave., Albany, 12203. Tel: 518-482-8836; AARON HOWLAND, Dir., Catholic Charities Disabilities Svcs., 1 Park Pl., Ste. 200, Albany, 12205. Tel: 518-783-1111; SANDRA YOUNG, Dir., Catholic Charities Housing Office, 41 N. Main Ave., Albany, 12203. Tel: 518-459-0183; STEPHANIE LAO, Dir., Catholic Charities AIDS Svcs., Dir. Catholic Charities Care Coord. Svcs.; Sr. BETSY VAN DEUSEN, C.S.J., Dir. Diocesan Jail Ministry, 40 N. Main Ave., Albany, 12203. Tel: 518-453-6650.

United Tenants of Albany—ERIN REALE, Dir., 255 Orange St., Ste. 104, Albany, 12210. Tel: 518-436-8997.

Catholic Campaign for Human Development—Sr. BETSY VAN DEUSEN, C.S.J., Dir., 40 N. Main Ave., Albany, 12203. Tel: 518-453-6650.

Catholic Relief Services—Sr. BETSY VAN DEUSEN, C.S.J., Dir., Catholic Relief Svcs.; DAVID MEYERS, Dir., Immigration Svcs., Catholic Charities of the Diocese of Albany, 40 N. Main Ave., Albany, 12203. Tel: 518-453-6650.

Health and Hospitals Office—MR. VINCENT W. COLONNO, Bishop's Rep., Tel: 518-453-6650.

Catholic Women's Service League—MARCIA MAHONEY, Pres. Moderators: Bros. JOHN MCMANUS, F.S.C.; RICHARD LEO MCALICE, F.S.C., LaSalle School, 391 Western Ave., Albany, 12203. Tel: 518-242-4731.

Ladies of Charity—ANN ROSE, Pres., 40 N. Main Ave., Albany, 12203. Tel: 518-598-9697; Web: localbany.org.

Spiritual Director—Rev. PATRICK J. BUTLER, St. Edward the Confessor, 569 Clifton Park Rd., Clifton Park, 12065. Tel: 518-371-7372.

Society of St. Vincent de Paul—Albany District Presidents' Council of Albany PAUL J. BUEHLER JR., 20 Heather Ln., Delmar, 12054. Tel: 518-937-0411; Email: bopeco518@gmail.com. District of Schenectady: Church of the Immaculate Conception (Glenville): JOSEPH AGLIOI, Pres., Email: miouaglio@aol.com. St. Paul the Apostle: MARTY HULETT, Pres., Email: martiehulett@yahoo.com. District of Albany: St. Thomas the Apostle: PETER MCGINTY, Pres., Email: pncgen3@verizon.net. St. Francis of Assisi: PATRICIA POLAN, Pres., Email: ppolan1@nycap.rr.com. Cathedral of the Immaculate Conception: DENNIS FEENEY, Pres., Email: dfeeny@lawfcm.com. St. Vincent DePaul.

St. Luke's Guild of Catholic Physicians—c/o Chancery, 40 N. Main Ave., Albany, 12203. Tel: 518-453-6612 ; Email: stlukes.guild@rcda.org. Very Rev. DAVID R. LEFORT, S.T.L., V.G., Contact.

Community Health Alliance—MR. VINCENT W. COLONNO, Bishop's Rep., Tel: 518-453-6650.

Consultation Center of the Diocese of Albany—A nonprofit Mental Health Center which provides quality professional psychological counseling services and educational programs in the area of mental health to individuals and groups.

Office—Rev. THOMAS E. KONOPKA, L.C.S.W., Dir.; Sr. MARY FRANCES BECK, S.N.J.M., Admin. Dir.; Rev. ANTHONY J. CHIARAMONTE, Ph.D., Counselor; KATHLEEN STIFFEN, Administrative Asst., 790 Lancaster St., Albany, 12203. Tel: 518-489-4431; Fax: 518-489-5189; Email: consultation.center@rcda.org; Web: consultationcenteralbany.org.

Psychological Counseling—Provides individual therapy, marriage and couples counseling, psychological testing and consultative services to individuals and groups in matters calling for psychological expertise.

Educational Programs—Offers lectures and workshops in the area of mental health and personal growth. The Center also offers specialized workshops and training programs to meet the needs of various groups, especially in ministerial leadership.

Spiritual Direction—Provides a program of individual spiritual direction for any person interested in developing a deeper relationship with God.

Director Pastoral Care Ministry—The Office of Pastoral Care provides support to the work of Parish Pastoral Care Coordinators, Bereavement Ministers, Wakes and Funeral Ministers, Lay Ecclesial Ministers and Volunteer Visitors, providing resources, training and consultation. MS. HARLEY MCDEVITT, Pastoral Center: 40 N. Main Ave., Albany, 12203-1422. Tel: 518-641-6823; Fax: 518-641-6819; Email: harley.mcdevitt@rcda.org.

Diocesan Pastoral Council—ROSLYN WEBBER, Admin., Pastoral Center, 40 N. Main Ave., Albany, 12203-1422. Tel: 518-453-6622; Email: roslyn.webber@rcda.org.

Prevention Services - Catholic Schools Office—
Tel: 518-453-6666; Fax: 518-453-6667. MRS. JACQUELYN CHIERA, Dir. Prevention Svcs.; MRS. MAUREEN BERNSTEIN, Prevention Educator, Pro-

vides prevention education to Catholic schools in the Albany Diocese.

Ecumenical and Interreligious Affairs of the Roman Catholic Diocese of Albany, Commission for—MRS. AUDREY HUGHES; Deacon WALTER AYRES; MRS. LYNN WATERMAN; MARYANN POSTAVA-DAVIGNON, Administrative Asst.; MRS. JOAN LIPSCOMB; MRS. KATHLEEN DUFF; MR. FRANK M. PELL; Rev. DONNA ELIA, Protestant Observer; JAMES KANE, Dir.; DAVID MICKIEWICZ; MR. EDWARD FALTERMAN; MS. ANNE SNYDER; MS. ANNE WASIELEWSKI; MR. DAVID AMICO.

The Evangelist—Diocesan Newspaper, Albany Catholic Press Assoc., Inc. Tel: 518-453-6688; Fax: 518-453-8448; Email: info@evangelist.org.

Holy Name Societies—c/o Rev. Donald Rutherford, Pastoral Center: Moderator of the Curia, 40 N. Main Ave., Albany, 12203. Tel: 518-453-6612.

Office of Vocations Diocese of Albany—Very Rev. ANTHONY F. LIGATO, Vicar Vocations, Vicar/Dir. Priesthood Vocations, Vicar/Dir. Vocations for Rel. Life, Vicar Diaconate Initial Formation; SARAH RAVILLE GUERRA, Admin. Asst. to Vicar for Vocations, Tel: 518-453-6690.

Permanent Deacons Office—Deacons MARK LEONARD, Dir. Office of Diaconate, Tel: 518-453-6678; PAUL KISSELBACK, Dir. Initial Diaconate Formation, Tel: 518-453-6670; Email: paul.kisselback@rcda.org; EDWARD R. SOLOMON, Dir. Diaconal Ongoing Formation, Tel: 518-453-6678; Email: edward.solomon@rcda.org.

The Foundation of the Roman Catholic Diocese of Albany—Most Rev. EDWARD B. SCHARFENBERGER, D.D., Pres.; THOMAS PRINDLE, Exec. Dir.

Office of Prayer & Worship—Very Rev. ANTHONY M. BARRATT, E.V., Dir.; SARAH RAVILLE GUERRA, Administrative Asst., 40 N. Main Ave., Albany, 12203. Tel: 518-453-6645; Fax: 518-453-6793; Email: prayer&worship@rcda.org.

Vicar for Clergy—Very Rev. JAMES A. EBERT, Tel: 518-453-6643.

Priests Placement Committee—Very Rev. JAMES A. EBERT, Chm., Tel: 518-453-6643; Revs. JOHN T. PROVOST; JOHN J. BRADLEY; DAVID V. BERBERIAN, J.C.L.; THOMAS LAWLESS.

Ministers to Retired Priests—Revs. PAUL C. COX, (Retired); GEORGE G. ST. JOHN, (Retired); JOHN D. KIRWIN, (Retired); RICHARD J. LESKOVAR, (Retired); WINSTON L. BATH, (Retired); DOMINIC INGEMIE, (Retired).

Ongoing Formation and Continuing Education—Revs. EDWARD KACERGUIS, Chm.; JAY ATHERTON; Very Rev. ANTHONY M. BARRATT, E.V.; Rev. JOHN CRONIN; Very Rev. MARK G. REAMER, O.F.M., E.V.; Revs. SCOTT VANDERVEER; DOMINIC INGEMIE, (Retired).

Priests Retirement Board—Revs. THOMAS F. BERARDI, Chm., (Retired), Tel: 518-452-1156; DAVID V. BERBERIAN, J.C.L.; JAMES T. FITZMAURICE; ROBERT J. HOHENSTEIN, (Retired); THOMAS MORRETTE; JOHN T. PROVOST; STEVE MATTHEWS; KENNETH DOYLE; JOHN YANAS; Very Rev. JAMES A. EBERT, Ex Officio; MR. JOHN HUTCHINSON, CFO & Ex Officio.

Administrative Advocate for Deacons—Deacon MARK LEONARD, Dir. Office of Diaconate, Tel: 518-453-6678.

Society for the Propagation of the FaithPontifical Mission Societies Society for the Propagation of the Faith Society of St. Peter the Apostle Missionary Childhood Association Missionary Union of Priests & Religious 40 N. Main Ave., Albany, 12203. Tel: 518-453-6675. Rev. MICHAEL A. FARANO, Dir.; MS. PATRICIA STEWART, Sec.; MS. KATHY ZORIAN, Bookkeeper.

Schools: Diocesan School Board—

President—MRS. CAROLYN KELLY.

Office of the Superintendent—Tel: 518-453-6666; Tel: 518-453-6602. MR. GIOVANNI VIRGIGLIO, Supt. Schools, Email: giovanni.virgiglio@rcda.org; DR. CHRISTOPHER BOTT, Assoc. Supt. Schools, Email: christopher.bott@rcda.org (Tues.-Thurs. 8am-4pm); MRS. PATRICIA RICCHIUTI, Exec. Asst. to Supt., Email: patricia.ricchiuti@rcda.org (8am-4pm).

Directors—MRS. JO-ANN GAMELLO, Dir. Financial Oper., Email: joann.gamello@rcda.org; MRS. TERRI MCGRAW, Consultant for Curriculum, Instruction & Assessment, Email: terri.mcgraw@rcda.org; MRS. JACQUELYN CHIERA, Dir. Prevention Svcs., Email: jacquelyn.chiera@rcda.org; MRS. ROSEMARIE TOBIN, Consultant for Persons with Disabilities, Email: rosemarie.tobin@rcda.org (variable schedule); MR. NATE VAN DEUSEN, Dir. Educational Technology & Communications, Email: nathan.vandeusen@rcda.org; MS. KATHLEEN YANAS, Dir. Advancement & Strategic Partnerships; MS. BRIDGET FRAMENT, Personnel Svcs. Coord., Email: bridget.frament@rcda.org.

Support Professionals—MRS. MAUREEN BERNSTEIN, Prevention Educator, Email: maureen.bernstein@rcda.org; MR. SAL CARBONE, Occupational Safety Coord., Tel: 518-853-4001; Email: sjcarbone@rcda.org; MRS. EILEEN KEEGAN, Administrative Asst., Email: eileen.keegan@rcda.org (Mon.-Fri. morning); MR. DANIEL JAROMIN, Accounting Assoc.; MS. CARYN HUBER, Accounting Assoc., Email: caryn.huber@rcda.org.

Scouting—Deacons PETER R. QUINN, Chap., P.O. Box 448, New Lebanon, 12125-0448. Tel: 518-794-0544; WILLIAM H. GAUL JR., Chap. Emeritus, 12 Woodlake Dr., Gansevoort, 12831-1817. Tel: 518-587-4631.

St. Bernard's School of Theology and Ministry—Deacon FRANK C. BERNING, D.Min., Assoc. Dean; ANNE BORGHETTI, Coord. Academic Oper. at Albany, Tel: 518-453-6760; Fax: 518-453-6793; Email: stbernards@rcda.org.

Acting Vicar for Religious—Very Rev. DAVID R. LEFORT, S.T.L., V.G., Tel: 518-453-6612; Email: david.lefort@rcda.org.

Assistance Coordinator—40 N. Main Ave., Albany, 12203. Tel: 518-453-6646; Email: assistance.coordinator@rcda.org. FREDERICK JONES.

Spanish Apostolate—Tel: 518-210-2347. Rev. JORGE A. REYES, O.S.A., Dir., Tel: 518-530-9094; Email: jreyesosa@aol.com.

Catholic Education and Faith Formation Services—Very Rev. ROBERT LONGOBUCCO, E.V., Vicar, Catholic Faith Formation & Educ., Tel: 518-453-6670; Email: robert.longobucco@rcda.org; MR. GIOVANNI VIRGIGLIO, Supt. Schools, Tel: 518-453-6666; Tel: 518-453-6602; Email: giovanni.virgiglio@rcda.org; MR. DAVID AMICO, Dir. Lay Ministry Formation, Tel: 518-453-6670; Email: david.amico@rcda.org; MARY FAY, Assoc. Dir., Marriage Formation & Family Life, Tel: 518-453-6644; Email: mary.fay@rcda.org; CATHERINE REID, Dir. Campus Ministry, Tel: 620-762-6026; Email: creid@albany.edu; DAVID STAGLIANO, Assoc. Dir. Campus Ministry & Youth Ministry, Tel: 518-453-6610; Email: david.stagliano@rcda.org; JOYCE SOLIMINI, Assoc. Dir. Lay Ministry Formation, Sacramental/RCIA Formation and Adult Catechesis, Tel: 518-453-6645; Email: joyce.solimini@rcda.org.

CLERGY, PARISHES, MISSIONS AND PAROCHIAL SCHOOLS

CITY OF ALBANY

(ALBANY COUNTY)

1—CATHEDRAL OF THE IMMACULATE CONCEPTION (1848) Email: CathedraloftheImmaculateConception.Albany@rcda.org. Very Rev. David R. LeFort, S.T.L., V.G.; Rev. John Tallman, Parochial Vicar; Most Rev. Howard James Hubbard, D.D., In Res., (Retired).
Rectory Office—125 Eagle St., 12202.
Tel: 518-463-4447; Fax: 518-514-1441; Email: CICAlban@rcda.org; Web: www.cathedralic.com.
Religious Education Office—Tel: 518-436-7918.
CATHEDRAL SOCIAL SERVICES, Tel: 518-463-2279.
Catechesis Religious Program—Thomas Fowler, D.R.E. Students 42.
Convent—93 Park Ave., 12202. Tel: 518-436-7697. Sisters 4.

2—ALL SAINTS CATHOLIC CHURCH
16 Homestead St., 12203. Tel: 518-482-4497; Fax: 518-482-4719; Email: AllSaintsCatholicChurch.Albany@rcda.org. Mailing Address: 12 Rosemont St., 12203. Rev. Thomas Lawless; Deacons Gary O'Connor; Timothy J. McAuliffe.
School—All Saints Catholic Academy, (Grades N-8), 10 Rosement St., 12203. Tel: 518-438-0066; Fax: 518-438-0066. Ms. Traci Johnson, Prin. Lay Teachers 20; Students 194.
Catechesis Religious Program—Students 109.

3—BLESSED SACRAMENT (1902)
607 Central Ave., 12206. Tel: 518-482-3375; Fax: 518-482-3376; Email: BlessedSacrament.Albany@rcda.org; Web: www.blessedsacramentalbany.org. Revs. Joseph O'Brien; George St. John, (In Res.); Francis O'Connor, (In Res.); Sr. Judith Kapp, R.S.M., Pastoral Assoc.; Rev. Juanito Asprec.
School—Blessed Sacrament School, (Grades PreK-8), 605 Central Ave., 12206. Tel: 518-438-5854; Fax: 518-438-1532; Email: bss@nycap.rr.com. Sr. Patricia Lynch, R.S.M., Prin. Lay Teachers 18; Sisters of Mercy 1; Students 186.
Catechesis Religious Program—Clustered with St. Mary. Students 161.
Shrine—Shrine of Our Lady of the America's, 273 Central Ave., 12206. Tel: 518-465-3685; Fax: 518-462-5487. Rev. Francis O'Connor, Chap.
Sister Maureen Joyce Center—369 Livingston Ave., 12208. Tel: 518-462-9885. 35 Sheridan Ave., 12208. Tel: 518-465-8262. Soup kitchen, food pantry & outreach.

4—ST. CASIMIR, Closed. For inquiries for parish records, please contact Blessed Sacrament.

5—ST. CATHERINE OF SIENA, Merged with St. Theresa of Avila, Albany to form Parish of Mater Christi, Albany. Worship Site.

6—CHURCH OF THE HOLY CROSS, Merged with St. Margaret Mary, Albany to form All Saints Catholic Church, Albany.

7—ST. FRANCIS OF ASSISI PARISH (2010)
391 Delaware Ave., 12209. Tel: 518-434-4028; Fax: 518-434-1097. Revs. Paul Smith, Sacramental Min., (Retired); Sean O'Brien, Sacramental Min.; John Lanese, Sacramental Min., (Retired); David Jones, Sacramental Min., (Retired); Dorothy A. Sokol, Parish Life Dir.
Catechesis Religious Program—Students 44.

8—ST. GEORGE, Closed. For inquiries for Sacramental records, please contact St. Joan of Arc/The Black Apostolate, Menands.

9—HOLY FAMILY PARISH (2005) [JC] Closed. For inquiries for parish records, contact Blessed Sacrament, Albany.

10—ST. JAMES, Merged with St. John-St. Ann to form St. Francis of Assisi Parish.

11—ST. JOHN-ST. ANN, Merged with St. James to form St. Francis of Assisi Parish.

12—ST. JOSEPH, Closed. For inquiries for sacramental records please contact Sacred Heart of Jesus, Albany.

13—ST. MARGARET MARY, Merged with Church of the Holy Cross, Albany to form All Saints Catholic Church, Albany. Worship Site.

14—ST. MARY (1797) Deacon George E. Witko; Revs. Michael Flannery, Parochial Vicar; John T. Provost; Deacon Walter C. Ayres. In Res., Rev. L. Edward Diemke.
Res.: 10 Lodge St., 12207-2196. Tel: 518-462-4254; Fax: 518-462-4255; Email: StMarys.Albany@rcda.org; Web: www.hist-stmarys.org.
Catechesis Religious Program—Clustered with Blessed Sacrament.

15—OUR LADY HELP OF CHRISTIANS, (German), Closed. For inquiries for parish records please see Cathedral of the Immaculate Conception.

16—OUR LADY OF ANGELS, [CEM] Suppressed. For inquiries for parish records please contact Blessed Sacrament, Albany.

17—PARISH OF MATER CHRISTI (2009)
40 Hopewell St., 12208. Tel: 518-489-3204; Fax: 518-482-3721; Email: MaterChristi.Albany@rcda.org; Web: parishes.rcda.org/MaterChristi. Very Rev. James A. Ebert; Rev. John Cronin, Parochial Vicar; Deacon Frank C. Berning, D.Min.
School—Mater Christi School, (Grades PreK-8), 35 Hurst Ave., 12208. Tel: 518-489-3111; Fax: 518-489-5863; Email: ewell@materchristischool.org. Theresa L. Ewell, Prin. Lay Teachers 30; Students 244; Pre-K Students 8.
Catechesis Religious Program—Students 320.

18—ST. PATRICK, Suppressed. For inquiries for parish records please contact Blessed Sacrament, Albany.

19—SACRED HEART OF JESUS
33 Walter St., 12204. Tel: 518-434-0680; Email: sacredheartjesus.albany@rcda.org. Rev. John T. Provost; Deacon Walter C. Ayres, Parish Life Dir.; Sr. Peg Sullivan, Parish Social Ministry Coord.
Catechesis Religious Program—Students 7.

20—ST. TERESA OF AVILA, Merged with St. Catherine of Siena, Albany to form Parish of Mater Christi, Albany.

21—ST. VINCENT DE PAUL, Revs. Leo P. O'Brien, Sacramental Min.; Michael A. Farano, Sacramental Min.; Ms. Elizabeth Simcoe, Parish Life Coord.
Parish Office: 900 Madison Ave., 12208.
Tel: 518-489-5408; Fax: 518-489-5474; Email: secretary@stvincentalbany.org; Web: www.stvincentalbany.org.
Catechesis Religious Program—Students 164.

OUTSIDE THE CITY OF ALBANY

ALTAMONT, ALBANY CO., ST. LUCY/ST. BERNADETTE
113 Grand St., Altamont, 12009. P.O. Box 678, Altamont, 12009. Rev. Paul Smith, Sacramental Min., (Retired); Sisters Patricia Davis, Pastoral Assoc.; Mary Lou Liptak, R.S.M., Parish Life Coord.
Parish House—109 Grand St., Altamont, 12009.
Tel: 518-861-8770; Fax: 518-861-8770; Email: slucys@nycap.rr.com.
Catechesis Religious Program Students 100.

AMSTERDAM, MONTGOMERY CO.

1—ST. CASIMIR, [CEM] (Lithuanian), Closed. For

inquiries for parish records, contact St. Mary's, Amsterdam.

2—St. John the Baptist, [CEM] (Polish), Closed. For inquiries for parish records, contact St. Stanislaus, Amsterdam.

3—St. Joseph, Merged into St. Joseph-St. Michael-Our Lady of Mount Carmel in 1980. All inquiries should be directed to the listed address, 39 St. John St. & 58 Grove St., Amsterdam, NY 12010.

4—St. Joseph-St. Michael-Our Lady of Mount Carmel, [CEM 3] Canonically merged parishes in 1980. Rev. Lawrence J. Decker.
Mailing Address, Office & Res.: 39 St. John St., P.O. Box 699, Amsterdam, 12010. Tel: 518-843-3250; Fax: 518-843-4070; Email: mt.carmel699@albany.twcbc.com.
Catechesis Religious Program—Students 55.

5—St. Mary (1839) [CEM]
Web: stmaryamsterdam.com. Rev. Jeffrey L'Arche, M.S., B.S., S.T.B.; Deacon Michael C. Ryba, Dir., Admin. & Fin.
Res.: 156 E. Main St., Amsterdam, 12010.
Tel: 518-842-4500; Fax: 518-843-1068; Email: StMarys.Amsterdam@rcda.org.
School—St. Mary Institute, (Grades PreK-8), 10 Kopernik Dr., Amsterdam, 12010. Tel: 518-842-4100; Fax: 518-842-0217; Email: dauriom@smik8.org; Web: saintmarysinstitute.com. Maureen Daurio, Prin. Lay Teachers 20; Students 250.
Catechesis Religious Program—Students 250.

6—St. Michael the Archangel, Merged into St. Joseph-St. Michael-Our Lady of Mount Carmel in 1980. All inquiries should be directed to the listed address, 39 St. John St. & 58 Grove St., Amsterdam, NY 12010.

7—Our Lady of Mt. Carmel, (Italian), Merged in 1980 into St. Joseph-St. Michael-Our Lady of Mount Carmel. All inquiries should be directed to the listed address, 39 St. John St. & 58 Grove St., Amsterdam, NY 12010.

8—St. Stanislaus (1894) [CEM] (Polish)
50 Cornell St., Amsterdam, 12010. Tel: 518-842-2771 ; Fax: 518-842-2621; Email: StStanislaus.Amsterdam@rcda.org. Rev. O. Robert De Martinis; Deacon Michael C. Ryba, Dir. Fin. & Admin.
Res.: 73 Reid St., Amsterdam, 12010.
Tel: 518-843-3893.
St. John Paul II Parish Center—46 Cornell St., Amsterdam, 12010. Tel: 518-842-2771; Fax: 518-842-2621.
Catechesis Religious Program—Students 41.

Athens, Greene Co, St. Patrick (1921)
24 North Washington St., Athens, 12015. Rev. L. Edward Deimeke, E.V., (Retired); Mrs. Janine O'Leary.
Res.: 19 N. Franklin St., Athens, 12015.
Tel: 518-945-1656; Fax: 518-947-6362; Email: cspacny@aol.com.
Catechesis Religious Program—Mrs. Anita J. Emery, Faith Formation Ministry Coord., Tel: 518-947-9444. Students 60.

Averill Park, Rensselaer Co., St. Henry (1868) [CEM 2]
39 Old Rte. 66, Averill Park, 12018.
Tel: 518-674-3818; Fax: 518-674-1043; Web: www.sthenrysaverillpark.org. P.O. Box 550, Averill Park, 12018. Rev. Thomas F. Holmes; Deacons Frank S. Lukovits, Samaritan Hospital, Troy; St. Henry's, Averill Park; Robert Pasquarelli, St. Henry's, Averill Park; Rensselaer County Jail Ministry; Master of Ceremonies.
Res.: 17 Crystal Lake Rd., Averill Park, 12018.
Catechesis Religious Program—Students 220.

Ballston Lake, Saratoga Co., Our Lady of Grace (1922) Revs. John Varno, (Retired); Peter D. Russo; Deacon Frank Thomas, M.D., M.T.S., M.A., Our Lady of Grace, Ballston Lake; Chaplain, Union College.
Res.: 73 Midline Rd., Ballston Lake, 12019.
Tel: 518-399-5713; Fax: 518-399-5761; Email: OurLadyofGrace.BallstonLake@rcda.org; Web: www.olgchurchbl.org.
Catechesis Religious Program—Students 163.

Ballston Spa, Saratoga Co., St. Mary, [CEM] Rev. Francis Vivacqua; Deacon Ronald T. Hogan.
Res.: 167 Milton Ave., Ballston Spa, 12020.
Tel: 518-885-7411; Fax: 518-885-6863; Email: stmbspa@nycap.rr.com.
School—St. Mary School, (Grades PreK-5), 40 Thompson St., Ballston Spa, 12020.
Tel: 518-885-7300; Fax: 518-885-7378; Email: office@smsbspa.org; Web: smsbspa.org. Mrs. Lynn Fitzgerald, Prin. Lay Teachers 15; Sisters 1; Students 140.
Catechesis Religious Program—Tel: 518-884-8479; Web: stmarysballstonspa.org. Jake Stomieroski, D.R.E. Students 455.
Mission—St. Mary's of Galway, 2113 East St., Galway, Saratoga Co. 12074. Tel: 518-885-7411; Web: stmarysballstonspa.org.

Berlin, Rensselaer Co., Sacred Heart, Closed. For inquiries for parish records, contact Our Lady of Victory, Troy.

Bolton Landing, Warren Co., Blessed Sacrament, [CEM]
7 Goodman Ave., Bolton Landing, 12814.
Tel: 518-644-3861; Fax: 518-644-3861; Email: BlessedSacrament.BoltonLanding@rcda.org. 12 Goodman Ave., P.O. Box 266, Bolton Landing, 12814. Rev. John O'Kane; Deacon Joseph Tyrrell, Parish Life Dir.
Catechesis Religious Program—Students 32.

Broadalbin, Fulton Co., St. Joseph's Church (1890)
North & N. Main Sts., Broadalbin, 12025. P.O. Box 538, Broadalbin, 12025. Rev. Anastacio Segura.
Parish Office: 7 North St., P.O. Box 538, Broadalbin, 12025-0538. Tel: 518-883-3774; Fax: 518-883-6381; Email: stjosephschurch@yahoo.com.
Catechesis Religious Program—Katy Ryan, Coord. Sacramental Prep. Students 60.

Cairo, Greene Co., Sacred Heart
Email: SacredHeart.Cairo@rcda.org. Rev. Steve Matthews.
Res.: 35 Church St., Cairo, 12413. Tel: 518-622-3319; Email: sacredheartolok@gmail.com; Web: sholk.weebly.com.
Catechesis Religious Program—Barbara Koerner-Fox, D.R.E. Students 113.
Shrine—Our Lady of Knock Shrine, 2052 Rt. 145, East Durham, 12423. Tel: 518-634-7448. P.O. Box 223, East Durham, Greene Co. 12423.

Cambridge, Washington Co., St. Patrick, [CEM] Jeffrey C. Peck, Parish Life Dir.; Very Rev. Thomas Zelker, E.V., Sacramental Min.
Res.: 17 S. Park St., Cambridge, 12816-1248.
Tel: 518-677-2757; Fax: 518-677-2810; Email: StPatricks.Cambridge@rcda.org.
Catechesis Religious Program—Students 29.

Canajoharie, Montgomery Co., St. Peter's and Paul's, [CEM] Merged with St. James, Fort Plain & St. Patrick, St. Johnsville to form Parish of Our Lady of Hope, Fort Plain. Worship Site.

Castleton On Hudson, Rensselaer Co., Sacred Heart (1887) [CEM 2]
Web: www.sacredheartchurchcastletonny.org. Rev. Thomas Krupa; Deacon Thomas Nash.
Res.: 3 Catholic Way, Castleton On Hudson, 12033-1543. Tel: 518-732-2155; Fax: 518-732-4906; Email: SacredHeart.CastletononHudson@rcda.org.
Catechesis Religious Program—Students 215.

Catskill, Greene Co., St. Patrick (1859)
Tel: 518-943-3150; Fax: 518-943-5257; Email: StPatricks.Catskill@rcda.org. Rev. L. Edward Deimeke; Mrs. Janine O'Leary.
Office: 66 William St., Catskill, 1975.
Tel: (518) 943-3150; Fax: (518) 943-5257; Email: cspacny@aol.com.
School—(Grades PreK-8), 80 Woodland Ave., Catskill, 12414. (School closed June 6, 2007.).
Catechesis Religious Program—Mrs. Anita J. Emery, Faith Formation Ministry Coord. Students 60.

Chatham, Columbia Co., St. James
117 Hudson Ave., Chatham, 12037.
Tel: 518-392-4991; Fax: 518-392-9205; Email: StJames.Chatham@rcda.org; Web: www.stjameschatham.org. 129 Hudson Ave., Chatham, 12037. Rev. George Fleming.
Catechesis Religious Program—Students 226.

Cherry Valley, Otsego Co., St. Thomas the Apostle (1903)
1 Church St, Cherry Valley, 13320. Email: StThomas.CherryValley@rcda.org; Web: www.turnpikecatholics.com. Mailing Address: P.O. Box 246, Cherry Valley, 13320. Deacon Richard Brown; Rev. Kenneth Doyle, Sacramental Min.; Mrs. Karen J. Walker, Parish Life Coord.; Deacon Randy Velez, Jail Ministry.
Res.: 24 Maple Ave., Cherry Valley, 13320.
Tel: 607-264-3779; Fax: 607-264-3779; Email: stthomascv@nycap.rr.com; Web: turnpikecatholics.com.
Catechesis Religious Program—Mrs. Karen J. Walker, Faith Formation Coord. Students 15.

Chestertown, Warren Co.

1—St. John the Baptist, Merged with Blessed Sacrament, Hague to form Parish of St. Isaac Jogues, Chestertown. Worship Site.

2—Parish of St. Isaac Jogues 2010
86 Riverside Dr., Chestertown, 12817.
Tel: 518-824-1176. P.O. Box 471, Chestertown, 12817. Rev. John O'Kane.
Res.: 63 Riverside Dr., Chestertown, 12817.
Catechesis Religious Program—Barbara Carlozzi, D.R.E. Students 48.

Claverack, Columbia Co., St. John Vianney, Merged with St. Bridget, Copake Falls to form Parish of Our Lady of Hope, Copake Falls. Worship Site.

Clifton Park, Saratoga Co., St. Edward the Confessor
Fax: 518-371-1206. Rev. Patrick J. Butler; Deacons Walter J. MacKinnon; Richard Dicaprio.
Church: 569 Clifton Park Center Rd., Clifton Park, 12065-4838. Tel: 518-371-7372; Email: stedwards@stedwardsny.org; Web: stedwardsny.org.
Catechesis Religious Program—Students 1,200.

Clinton Heights, Rensselaer Co., St. Mary Church of St. Mary at Clinton Heights
Web: www.stmaryny.org. Deacon Gregory Mansfield; Rev. Thomas E. Konopka, L.M.S.W.; Deacons Al Censullo; Timothy Kosto.
Res.: 163 Columbia Tpke., Rensselaer, 12144-3521.
Tel: 518-449-2232; Fax: 518-449-2234; Email: office@stmaryny.org; Web: www.stmaryny.org.
Catechesis Religious Program—Students 400.

Cobleskill, Schoharie Co., St. Vincent de Paul, [CEM]
Mailing Address: 138 Washington Ave., Cobleskill, 12043. Tel: 518-234-2892; Web: stvincentdepaulcobleskillny.com. Rev. James Donlon, Sacramental Min.; Deacon Gary Surman; Sr. Connie James, S.N.D., Parish Life Coord.; Greg Rys, Campus Min., Suny Cobleskill; Ms. Rachael Rys, Sec.
Catechesis Religious Program—Students 155.

Cohoes, Albany Co.

1—St. Agnes-St. Patrick, Closed. For inquiries for parish records contact Holy Trinity, Cohoes.

2—St. Bernard, Closed. For inquiries for parish records contact Holy Trinity, Cohoes.

3—Holy Trinity, [CEM]
122 Vliet Blvd., Cohoes, 12047-1842.
Tel: 518-237-2373; Email: HolyTrinity.Cohoes@rcda.org; Web: www.holytrinitycohoes.org. Rev. Brian K. Slezak.
See Cohoes Catholic School, Cohoes under Consolidated Elementary Schools located in the Institution section.
Catechesis Religious Program—Students 86.

4—St. Joseph, [CEM] (French), Closed. For inquiries for parish records contact Holy Trinity, Cohoes.

5—St. Marie, Closed. For inquiries for parish records contact Holy Trinity, Cohoes.

6—St. Michael, [CEM]
Ontario St. at Page Ave., Cohoes, 12047.
Tel: 518-357-5151; Web: stmichaelsofcohoes.org. 20 Page Ave., Cohoes, 12047. Rev. Peter Tkocz.
Res.: 36 Page Ave., Cohoes, 12047. Tel: 518-237-5151 .
Catechesis Religious Program—Students 57.

7—St. Rita-Sacred Heart, Closed. For inquiries for parish records, contact Holy Trinity, Cohoes.

Colonie, Albany Co.

1—St. Clare, Rev. Ronald Menty, Sacramental Min.; Nancy A. Volks, Parish Life Dir.
Res.: 1947 Central Ave., Colonie, 12205-4299.
Tel: 518-456-3112; Fax: 518-456-1072; Email: StClares.Colonie@rcda.org.
Catechesis Religious Program—Students 276.

2—Our Lady of Mercy, Merged with St. Francis de Sales, Loudonville to form Christ Our Light Roman Catholic Church, Loudonville.

Cooperstown, Otsego Co., St. Mary, [CEM 2]
Web: www.stmaryscoop.org. Rev. John P. Rosson.
Res.: 31 Elm St., Cooperstown, 13326.
Tel: 607-547-2213; Fax: 607-547-5742; Email: cooperstownpriest@gmail.com; Web: www.stmaryscoop.org.
Catechesis Religious Program—Students 200.

Copake Falls, Columbia Co.

1—St. Bridget, [CEM] Merged with St. John Vianney, Claverack to form Parish of Our Lady of Hope, Copake Falls. Worship Site.

2—Parish of Our Lady of Hope (2009) [CEM 2]
Tel: 518-329-4711; Fax: 518-329-4240. Rev. George Brennan.
Res.: 8074 State Rte. 22, Copake Falls, 12517.
Tel: 518-329-4711; Email: ourladyofhope.copakefalls@rcda.org.
Catechesis Religious Program—Students 34.

Corinth/Lake Luzerne, Saratoga Co.

1—Holy Mother and Child Parish (2009) [CEM 2]
405 Palmer Ave., Corinth, 12822. Tel: 518-654-2113. P.O. Box 470, Lake Luzerne, 12846. Rev. Kenneth J. Swain.
Res.: 323 Lake Ave., P.O. Box 470, Lake Luzerne, 12846. Tel: 518-696-2625.
Catechesis Religious Program—Students 72.

2—Immaculate Conception, [CEM] Merged with Holy Infancy, Lake Luzerne to form Holy Mother and Child Parish, Corinth. Worship Site.

Coxsackie, Greene Co., St. Mary (1854) [CEM]
Mansion St. at Washington Ave., Coxsackie, 12051. Rev. Scott VanDerveer.
Res.: 80 Mansion St., Coxsackie, 12051.
Tel: 518-731-8800; Fax: 518-731-8505.
Catechesis Religious Program—Students 19.

Crescent, Saratoga Co., St. Mary's Church St. Mary's Church, Crescent, Rev. Joseph Cebula; Deacon Andrew Grebe.
Parish Center—86 Church Hill Rd., Waterford, 12188. Tel: 518-371-9632; Fax: 518-371-7235; Email: smcsec@nycap.rr.com; Web: www.stmaryscrescent.com.

Catechesis Religious Program—Students 405.
DELANSON, SCHENECTADY CO., OUR LADY OF FATIMA (1952) Rev. James G. Davis.
Res.: 1735 Alexander Rd., P.O. Box 219, Delanson, 12053-0219. Tel: 518-895-2788; Fax: 518-895-2991; Email: OurLadyofFatima.Delanson@rcda.org.
Catechesis Religious Program—Students 79; Adults (Generations of Faith) 60.
DELHI, DELAWARE CO., ST. PETER
10 Cross St., Delhi, 13753. Tel: 607-746-2503; Fax: 607-746-7651. Mailing Address: 8 Franklin St., Delhi, 13856. Rev. Edward Golding, Admin.; Deacon Dr. Michael Freeman.
Res.: 15 Benton Ave., Walton, 13856.
Catechesis Religious Program—Katherine Gielskie, D.R.E. Students 37.
DELMAR, ALBANY CO., ST. THOMAS THE APOSTLE (1910) Revs. David V. Berberian, J.C.L.; James D. Daley, Pastor Emeritus, (Retired); Richard J. Leskovar, Sacramental Min., (Retired).
Res.: 35 Adams Pl., Delmar, 12054.
Tel: 518-439-4951; Fax: 518-439-0108; Email: office@stthomas-church.org; Web: www.stthomas-church.org.
School—St. Thomas the Apostle School, (Grades PreK-8), 42 Adams Pl., Delmar, 12054.
Tel: 518-439-5573; Fax: 518-478-9773; Email: info@stthomas-school.org; Web: www.stthomas-school.org. Mr. Thomas Kane, Prin. Lay Teachers 16; Students 207.
Catechesis Religious Program—Patricia Staerker. Students 452.
DOLGEVILLE, HERKIMER CO., ST. JOSEPH, [CEM 2] N. Helmer Ave. at W. State St., Dolgeville, 13329. Rev. Terence P. Healy, Sac. Min., (Retired); Deacon James W. Bower, Admin.
Res.: 31 N. Helmer Ave., Dolgeville, 13329.
Tel: 315-429-8338; Email: StJosephs.Dolgeville@rcda.org.
Catechesis Religious Program—Students 34.
EAST GREENBUSH, RENSSELAER CO., HOLY SPIRIT, Rev. Joseph O'Brien; Deacon William Dringus.
Res.: 667 Columbia Tpke., East Greenbush, 12061.
Tel: 518-477-7925; Fax: 518-477-7926; Email: HolySpirit.EastGreenbush@rcda.org; Web: holyspiriteg.weconnect.com.
School—(Grades PreK-8), 54 Highland Dr., East Greenbush, 12061. Tel: 518-477-5739;
Fax: 518-477-5743; Email: hsoffice@hsseg.org. Joseph Slichko, Prin.; Laura Wolderczak, Librarian. Lay Teachers 16; Students 218.
Catechesis Religious Program—Students 335.
EDMESTON, OSWEGO CO., NATIVITY OF B.V.M., Closed. For inquiries for parish records, contact Holy Cross, Morris.
FONDA, MONTGOMERY CO., ST. CECILIA, [CEM]
26 Broadway, Fonda, 12068. Tel: 518-853-4195; Email: StCecilias.Fonda@rcda.org. P.O. Box 837, Fonda, 12068. Very Rev. Christopher Welch, E.V.
Catechesis Religious Program—Students 62.
FORT ANN, WASHINGTON CO., ST. ANN'S ROMAN CATHOLIC CHURCH
85 George St., Fort Ann, 12827. Tel: 518-639-5218; Email: StAnns.FortAnn@rcda.org. P.O. Box 226, Fort Ann, 12827. Rev. Rendell R. Torres.
Catechesis Religious Program— (Combined with Our Lady of Hope, Whitehall) Students 67.
FORT EDWARD, WASHINGTON CO., ST. JOSEPH, [CEM] Rev. Thomas Babiuch; Julie Leonelli, Pastoral Assoc. for Faith Formation.
Res.: 166 Broadway, Fort Edward, 12828.
Tel: 518-747-5117; Fax: 518-747-3444; Email: StJosephs.FortEdward@rcda.org.
Catechesis Religious Program—Students 119.
FORT PLAIN, MONTGOMERY CO.
1—ST. JAMES, Merged with St. Peter's and Paul's, Canajoharie & St. Patrick, St. Johnsville to form Parish of Our Lady of Hope, Fort Plain. Worship Site.
2—PARISH OF OUR LADY OF HOPE (2009) [CEM]
115 Reid St., Fort Plain, 13339.
Office: 119 Reid St., Fort Plain, 13339.
Tel: 518-993-3822; Tel: (518) 993-4025;
Fax: 518-993-3823; Email: ourladyofhope@frontier.com.
Catechesis Religious Program—Michaela Germond, D.R.E. (Intergenerational Program) Students 58.
FRANKFORT, HERKIMER CO.
1—ST. MARY, Merged with SS. Peter & Paul, Frankfort, to form Our Lady Queen of Apostles, Frankfort, Jan. 8, 1995.
2—OUR LADY QUEEN OF APOSTLES (1995) [CEM]
412 Frankfort St., Frankfort, 13340. Web: olqoa.info. 414 Frankfort St., Frankfort, 13340. Rev. Paul G. Catena; Deacon Michael Carbone.
Res.: 109 West St., Ilion, 13357. Tel: 315-894-2360;
Fax: 315-894-2025; Email: OurLadyQueenofApostles.Frankfort@rcda.org.
Catechesis Religious Program—Students 128.
3—SS. PETER & PAUL, Merged with St. Mary, Frankfort, to form Our Lady Queen of Apostles, Frankfort, Jan. 8, 1995.
GERMANTOWN, COLUMBIA CO., RESURRECTION, [CEM] Merged with Church of St. Mary, Hudson to form Parish of the Holy Trinity, Hudson. Worship Site.
GLENS FALLS, WARREN CO.
1—ST. ALPHONSUS, [CEM] Closed. For inquiries for parish records contact St. Mary, Glens Falls.
2—ST. MARY
Web: stmarysglensfalls.org. Revs. Thomas Morrette; Desmond Rossi, Parochial Vicar; Deacon F. David Powers, Tel: 518-792-0989, Ext. 35.
Res.: 62 Warren St., Glens Falls, 12801-4530.
Tel: 518-792-0989; Fax: 518-792-0251; Email: StMarys.GlensFalls@rcda.org; Web: www.stmarysglensfalls.org.
School—St. Mary's / St. Alphonsus Regional School, (Grades PreK-8), 10-12 Church St., Glens Falls, 12801. Tel: 518-792-3178; Fax: 518-792-6056. Timothy Forti, Prin.
Catechesis Religious Program—Students 350.
GLENVILLE, SCHENECTADY CO., IMMACULATE CONCEPTION
Tel: 518-399-9168; Fax: 518-384-3278; Web: www.icglenville.com. Revs. Jerome R. Gingras; J. Thomas Connery, Pastor Emeritus, (Retired); Deacon Michael P. Melanson.
Res.: 400 Saratoga Rd., Glenville, 12302.
Tel: 518-399-9168; Email: icchurch400@gmail.com; Web: www.ic-glenville.com.
Catechesis Religious Program—Students 484.
GLOVERSVILLE, FULTON CO.
1—CHURCH OF THE HOLY SPIRIT (2009)
153 S. Main St., Gloversville, 12078.
Tel: 518-725-3143; Email: HolySpirit.Gloversville@rcda.org. Mailing Address: 149 S. Main St., Gloversville, 12078. Revs. Matthew Wetsel; Donald Czelusniak.
Res.: 205 Glebe St., Johnstown, 12095.
Tel: 518-762-2011; Fax: 518-725-7245.
Catechesis Religious Program—Students 101.
2—ST. MARY, Closed. For inquiries for parish records, contact Church of the Holy Spirit, Gloversville.
3—ST. MARY OF MT. CARMEL, [CEM] Merged Consolidated from Our Lady of Mount Carmel and St. Mary in 1990. Merged with Sacred Heart, Gloversville to form Church of the Holy Spirit, Gloversville. Worship Site.
4—SACRED HEART, Merged with St. Mary of Mt. Carmel, Gloversville to form Church of the Holy Spirit, Gloversville.
GRAFTON, RENSSELAER CO.
1—ST. JOHN FRANCIS REGIS, Closed. For inquiries for parish records, contact Our Lady of Victory, Troy.
2—PARISH OF OUR LADY OF THE SNOW, Closed. For inquiries for parish records, contact Our Lady of Victory, Troy.
GRAND GORGE, DELAWARE CO., ST. PHILIP NERI, Merged with Sacred Heart, Stamford to form Sacred Heart/St. Philip Neri, Stockton.
GRANVILLE, WASHINGTON CO.
1—ST. MARY, Closed. For inquiries for parish records contact St. Mary's Roman Catholic Church Roman Catholic Community of Granville, Granville, NY.
2—ST. MARY'S ROMAN CATHOLIC CHURCH ROMAN CATHOLIC COMMUNITY OF GRANVILLE, Consolidated St. Mary's, All Saints, and Our Lady of Mount Carmel. Rev. Joseph Arockiasamy; Deacon Jon Ramey.
Res.: 23 Bulkley Ave., Granville, 12832.
Tel: 518-642-1262; Email: StMarys.Granville@rcda.org.
Parish Center—All Saints House, 3 Morrison Ave., Granville, 12832.
Catechesis Religious Program—Students 207.
GREEN ISLAND, ALBANY CO., ST. JOSEPH, Merged with St. Brigid's, Immaculate Conception, Our Lady of Mt. Carmel, St. Patrick's & Sacred Heart of Mary, Watervliet to form Immaculate Heart of Mary, Watervliet. Church not closed.
GREENFIELD CENTER, SARATOGA CO., ST. JOSEPH
3159 Rte. 9N, Greenfield Center, 12833. Web: www.stjosephschurchgreenfieldcenter.org. Mailing Address: P.O. Box 547, Greenfield Center, 12833-0568. Rev. Simon Udemgba, Ph.D., Admin.; Deacon John Barone; Margie Carroll, Pastoral Assoc.
Catechesis Religious Program—Margie Carroll, D.R.E. Total Enrollment 51.
Rectory: 3159 Rte. 9N, Greenfield Center, 12833-0568. Tel: 518-893-7680; Web: www.stjosephschurchgreenfieldcenter.org. P.O. Box 547, Greenfield Center, 12833.
Mission—St. Paul, 771 Rte. 29, Rock City Falls, Saratoga Co. 12863. Tel: 518-893-7680; Email: StJosephStPaul@gmail.com. P.O. Box 547, Greenfield Center, 12833.
GREENVILLE, GREENE CO., ST. JOHN THE BAPTIST
4987 Rt. 81, Greenville, 12083. Tel: 518-966-8317;
Fax: 518-966-4652; Email: StJohntheBaptist.Greenville@rcda.org; Web: sjbg.weebly.com. Mailing Address: P.O. Box 340, Greenville, 12083. Connie Parente, Pastoral Assoc.; Rev. Steve Matthews.
Catechesis Religious Program—Students 85.
GREENWICH, WASHINGTON CO., ST. JOSEPH St. Joseph's (1867)
35 Hill St., Greenwich, 12834. Very Rev. Martin J. Fisher, E.V.
Res.: 36 Bleecker St., Greenwich, 12834.
Tel: 518-692-2159; Email: parish@nycap.rr.com.
Catechesis Religious Program—Maryann Kelleher, D.R.E. Students 129.
GUILDERLAND, ALBANY CO., CHRIST THE KING
20 Sumter Ave., 12203. Tel: 518-456-1644; Email: ChristTheKing.Westmere@rcda.org; Web: www.ctkparishny.org. Rev. James Fitzmaurice; Deacons Joseph F. Markham, Deacon Emeritus; Anthony Cortese.
Catechesis Religious Program—Students 225.
HAGAMAN, MONTGOMERY CO., ST. STEPHEN, [CEM]
Web: www.ststephensofhagamanny.org. Rev. O. Robert De Martinis; Deacon Michael C. Ryba, Dir. of Fin. & Admin.
Res.: 51 Pawling St., P.O. Box 81, Hagaman, 12086.
Tel: 518-843-2951; Email: StStephens.Hagaman@rcda.org.
Catechesis Religious Program—Students 72.
HAGUE, WARREN CO., BLESSED SACRAMENT, Merged with St. John the Baptist, Chestertown to form Parish of St. Isaac Jogues, Chestertown. Worship Site-Summer only.
HAINES FALLS, GREENE CO.
1—IMMACULATE CONCEPTION, [CEM] Merged with Sacred Heart, Palenville to form Immaculate Conception, Haines Falls. Worship Site.
2—SACRED HEART-IMMACULATE CONCEPTION CHURCH
N. Lake Rd., Haines Falls, 12436. Mailing Address: P.O. Box 379, Haines Falls, 12436. Rev. Jay Atherton.
Office: 61 N. Lake Rd., Haines Falls, 12436.
Tel: 518-589-5577; Email: SacredHeartICC.HainesFalls@rcda.org.
Catechesis Religious Program—Students 40.
Shrine—Wayside Shrine of the Immaculate Conception, Haines Falls, Greene Co.
HANCOCK, DELAWARE CO., ST. PAUL THE APOSTLE, [CEM 2]
346 W. Main St., Hancock, 13783. Tel: 607-637-2571;
Fax: 607-637-3203; Email: StPaultheApostle.Hancock@rcda.org; Web: stpaulshancock.org. Rev. Daniel J. Quinn.
Catechesis Religious Program—Patricia Brown, D.R.E. Students 36.
HERKIMER, HERKIMER CO.
1—ST. ANTHONY-ST. JOSEPH
229 S. Main St., Herkimer, 13350. Tel: 315-866-2892; Tel: 315-866-6373; Fax: 315-867-6186; Email: StAnthonyStJosephs.Herkimer@rcda.org. 228 S. Main St., Herkimer, 13350. Rev. Quy Vo.
Office: 344 S. Washington St., Herkimer, 13350.
Catechesis Religious Program—Patricia Foss, D.R.E. Students 72.
2—ST. FRANCIS DE SALES, [CEM]
N. Bellinger St. and Bellinger Ave., Herkimer, 13350. Tel: 315-866-4282; Fax: 315-866-9043. 219 N. Bellinger St., Herkimer, 13350. Rev. Mark Cunningham.
Parish Center—219 N. Bellinger St., Herkimer, 13350. Tel: 315-866-4282; Email: StFrancisdeSales.Herkimer@rcda.org.
Res.: 25 Park Pl. S., Herkimer, 13350.
Tel: 315-866-7103.
School—St. Francis de Sales School, (Grades PreK-6), 220 Henry St., Herkimer, 13350.
Tel: 315-866-4831; Email: stfran@twcny.rr.com. Kathleen Coye, Prin. Lay Teachers 7; Sisters of St. Joseph of Carondelet 2; Students 89.
Catechesis Religious Program—Students 265.
Convent—One Park Pl., Herkimer, 13350.
Tel: 315-866-4492.
HOOSICK FALLS, RENSSELAER CO., IMMACULATE CONCEPTION, [CEM] Very Rev. Thomas Zelker, E.V.
Res.: 67 Main St., Hoosick Falls, 12090.
Tel: 518-686-5064; Email: immconcept@aol.com; Web: icchoosickfalls.com.
School—St. Mary Academy, (Grades PreK-8), 4 Parsons Ave., Hoosick Falls, 12090.
Tel: 518-686-4314; Fax: 518-686-5957; Email: principal@smahf.org; Web: smahf.org. Michael Piatek, Prin. Lay Teachers 14; Students 120.
HUDSON FALLS, WASHINGTON CO.
1—IMMACULATE HEART OF MARY, (French), Merged with St. Paul, Hudson Falls. Now called Church of St. Mary's/St. Paul's, Roman Catholic Community of Hudson Falls/Kingsbury.
2—ST. PAUL, (French), Merged with Immaculate Heart of Mary, Hudson Falls. Now called Church of St. Mary's/St. Paul's, Roman Catholic Community of Hudson Falls/Kingsbury.
3—ROMAN CATHOLIC COMMUNITY OF HUDSON FALLS/KINGSBURY, [CEM 2] (Sandy Hill) Rev. Thomas

Babiuch; Mrs. Patty Fitzgerald, Office Mgr. & Sec.; Deacon William F. Bazinet.
Res.: 11 Wall St., Hudson Falls, 12839.
Tel: 518-747-4823; Fax: 518-747-2265; Email: smspsecretary@yahoo.com.
Catechesis Religious Program—Students 187.

HUDSON, COLUMBIA CO.
1—CHURCH OF ST. MARY, Merged Canonically merged with Our Lady of Mount Carmel and Our Lady of Perpetual Help-Sacred Heart in 1991. Merged with Resurrection, Germantown to form Parish of the Holy Trinity, Hudson. Worship Site.
2—OUR LADY OF MT. CARMEL, Merged with Church of St. Mary in 1991. All inquiries should be directed to P.O. Box 323, Hudson, NY 12534. Tel: 518-828-1334.
3—OUR LADY OF PERPETUAL HELP-SACRED HEART, (Polish), Merged with Church of St. Mary in 1991. All inquiries should be directed to P.O. Box 323, Hudson, NY 12534. Tel: 518-828-1334.
4—PARISH OF THE HOLY TRINITY 2009 [CEM]
429 E. Allen St., Hudson, 12534.
Tel: 518-828-1334 (Hudson Office);
Tel: 518-537-6136 (Germantown Office);
Fax: 518-828-2783; Email: HolyTrinity.Hudson@rcda.org; Web: holytrinityhudson.org. P.O. Box 323, Hudson, 12534. Rev. Winston L. Bath, Pastor Emeritus, (Retired); Very Rev. Anthony M. Barratt, E.V.; Deacon Richard Washburn.
Catechesis Religious Program—301 East Allen St., Hudson, 12534. Students 210.
Mission—Nativity, Linlithgo, Columbia Co.

ILION, HERKIMER CO., ANNUNCIATION, [CEM]
50 West St., Ilion, 13357. Fax: 315-894-1550. Rev. Paul G. Catena; Deacon Michael Carbone.
Catechesis Religious Program—Students 11.

JOHNSONVILLE, RENSSELAER CO., ST. MONICA'S CHURCH, Closed. For inquiries for parish records, contact Transfiguration Parish, Troy.

JOHNSTOWN, FULTON CO.
1—ST. ANTHONY, [CEM] (Slovak), Merged with Immaculate Conception, Johnstown and St. Patrick, Johnstown to form Holy Trinity, Johnstown.
2—HOLY TRINITY PARISH, [CEM 2]
E. Clinton St. and Glebe St., Johnstown, 12095. Web: www.holytrinityjohnstown.com. 207 Glebe St., Johnstown, 12095. Rev. Donald Czelusniak. In Res., Rev. Dennis Murphy, (Retired).
Catechesis Religious Program—Students 140.
3—IMMACULATE CONCEPTION, [CEM 3] (Italian), Merged with St. Anthony, Johnstown and St. Patrick, Johnstown to form Holy Trinity, Johnstown.
4—ST. PATRICK, [CEM] Merged with Immaculate Conception, Johnstown and St Anthony, Johnstown to form Holy Trinity Parish, Johnstown.

LAKE GEORGE, WARREN CO., SACRED HEART
Web: www.sacredheartlg.org. Deacon Frank D. Herlihy; Rev. Nellis Tremblay, (Retired); Deacon Ryan McNulty; Very Rev. Joseph G. Busch, E.V
Res.: 50 Mohican St., Lake George, 12845.
Tel: 518-668-2046; Fax: 518-668-4377; Email: kathy.dorman4@gmail.com; Web: www.sacredheartlg.org.
Catechesis Religious Program—Torie Wattendorf, Coord. Faith Formation. Students 166.

LAKE LUZERNE, WARREN CO., HOLY INFANCY, [JC] Merged with Immaculate Conception, Corinth to form Holy Mother and Child Parish, Corinth. Worship Site.

LATHAM, ALBANY CO.
1—ST. AMBROSE (1924)
Web: stambroselatham.com. Rev. Brian Kelly; Deacons Andrew Grebe, Pastoral Assoc.; Helmut Neurohr; Frank Garceau.
Res.: 347 Old Loudon Rd., Latham, 12110.
Tel: 518-785-1351; Fax: 518-785-1951; Email: SaLatham@rcda.org.
School—St. Ambrose School, (Grades PreK-8), Tel: 518-785-6453; Email: principal@stambroselatham.com. Mrs. Terri McGraw, Prin. Lay Teachers 17; Sisters 2; Students 162.
Catechesis Religious Program—Students 287.
2—OUR LADY OF THE ASSUMPTION, Rev. James D. Daley, (Retired); Deacon Paul Kisselback; Rev. Geoffrey D. Burke.
Res.: 498 Watervliet-Shaker Rd., Latham, 12110.
Tel: 518-785-0234; Fax: 518-785-0420; Email: OurLadyoftheAssumption.Latham@rcda.org.
Catechesis Religious Program—Students 370.

LITTLE FALLS, HERKIMER CO.
1—HOLY FAMILY, [CEM]
763 E. Main St., Little Falls, 13365.
Tel: 315-823-3410; Fax: 315-823-2701; Email: HolyFamily.LittleFalls@rcda.org. Rev. Terence P. Healy, In Res., (Retired); Deacon James Bower, Admin.; Mary Puznowski, Music Dir. In Res.
Catechesis Religious Program—Students 152.
2—ST. JOSEPH, Merged with St. Mary and Sacred Heart to form Holy Family Parish, Little Falls.
3—ST. MARY, Merged with St. Joseph and Sacred Heart to form Holy Family Parish, Little Falls.
4—SACRED HEART, (Polish), Merged with St. Joseph and St. Mary to form Holy Family Parish, Little Falls.

LOUDONVILLE, ALBANY CO.
1—CHRIST OUR LIGHT ROMAN CATHOLIC CHURCH
1 Maria Dr., Loudonville, 12211. Tel: 518-459-6635; Email: ChristOurLightChurch.Loudonville@rcda.org; Web: www.christourlightchurch.org. Deacon Richard J. Thiesen, Parish Life Dir.
Catechesis Religious Program—Students 205.
2—ST. FRANCIS DE SALES (1972) Merged with Our Lady of Mercy, Colonie to form Christ Our Light Roman Catholic Church, Loudonville. Worship Site.
3—ST. PIUS X
Mailing Address: 23 Crumitie Rd., Loudonville, 12211. Revs. James J. Walsh; Michael A. Farano, Pastor Emeritus.
School—St. Pius X School, (Grades PreK-8), 79 Upper Loudon Rd., Loudonville, 12211.
Tel: 518-465-4539; Fax: 518-465-4895; Email: principal@nycap.rr.com. Dennis Mullahy, Prin. Students 717.
Catechesis Religious Program—Students 695.

MARGARETVILLE, DELAWARE CO., SACRED HEART
Tel: 845-586-2665. Very Rev. Michael Cambi, E.V.
Res.: 38 Academy St., P.O. Box 909, Margaretville, 12455. Tel: 845-586-2665; Email: shcatholicchurch@icloud.com.
Catechesis Religious Program—Doris Warner, D.R.E. Students 10.
Mission—St. Ann, Andes, Delaware Co.

MECHANICVILLE, SARATOGA CO.
1—ALL SAINTS ON THE HUDSON, [CEM 3]
52 William St., Mechanicville, 12118.
Tel: 518-664-3354; Fax: 518-664-9971; Email: stpeter271@aol.com; Web: allsaintsny.net. Revs. Ronald G. Matulewicz, (Retired); Robert J. Hohenstein, (Retired); Patrick Rice
Legal Name: Roman Catholic Community of All Saints on the Hudson
St. Paul Church—121 N. Main St., Mechanicville, 12118.
St. Peter Church, 895 Hudson Ave., Stillwater, 12170.
Catechesis Religious Program—Students 355.
Mission—St. Isaac Jogues, 716 Rte. 9P, Saratoga Lake, Saratoga Co. 12866. (Summer).
2—ASSUMPTION-ST. PAUL, Merged with St. Peter the Apostle, Stillwater to form Roman Catholic Community of All Saints on the Hudson, Stillwater.

MENANDS, ALBANY CO., ST. JOAN OF ARC, Rev. Kofi Ntsiful Amissah.
Parish Office & Res.: 76 Menand Rd., Menands, 12204. Tel: 518-463-0378; Fax: 518-463-0489; Email: sjoa@nycap.rr.com.
Catechesis Religious Program—

MIDDLEBURGH, SCHOHARIE CO.
1—ST. CATHERINE, Merged with St. Joseph, Schoharie to form Parish of Our Lady of the Valley, Middleburgh. Worship Site.
2—PARISH OF OUR LADY OF THE VALLEY
Main St. at Wells Ave., Middleburgh, 12122.
Tel: 518-702-4385. P.O. Box 311, Middleburgh, 12122. Rev. James G. Davis.
Res.: 111 Wells Ave., Middleburgh, 12122.
Tel: 518-827-3301; Email: OurLadyoftheValley.Middleburgh@rcda.org.
Catechesis Religious Program—Students 32.

MOHAWK, HERKIMER CO., BLESSED SACRAMENT
71 E. Main St., Mohawk, 13407. Sr. Mary Jo Tallman, C.S.J., Parish Life Coord.; Rev. Mark Cunningham, Sacramental Min.
Res.: 54 E. Main St., Mohawk, 13407.
Tel: 315-866-1752; Email: BlessedSacrament.Mohawk@rcda.org.
Catechesis Religious Program—Students 241.

MORRIS, OTSEGO CO., HOLY CROSS (1946)
96 Main St., Morris, 13808-0118. Tel: 607-263-5143. P.O. Box 118, Morris, 13808. Maureen E. Joy, Parish Life Coord.
Catechesis Religious Program—Students 18.

NASSAU, RENSSELAER CO., ST. MARY, [CEM]
26 Church St., Nassau, 12123. Tel: 518-766-2701; Fax: 518-766-7535; Email: StMarys.Nassau@rcda.org; Web: stmarysnassau.org. Mailing Address: P.O. Box 435, Nassau, 12123. Revs. Thomas F. Holmes; John Close, Sacramental Min.
Res.: 26 Church St., Nassau, 12123.
Tel: 518-766-2701; Fax: 518-766-7535; Email: StMarys.Nassau@rcda.org.
Catechesis Religious Program—Students 101.

NEW LEBANON, COLUMBIA CO., IMMACULATE CONCEPTION, [CEM]
732 U.S. Rte. 20, P.O. Box 218, New Lebanon, 12125. Tel: 518-794-7651; Email: immaculateconception.newlebanon@rcda.org. Rev. John Close; Deacon Peter R. Quinn.
Mission—St. Joseph's, Stephentown, Rensselaer Co.

NEWPORT, HERKIMER CO., ST. JOHN THE BAPTIST
7516 N. Main St., Newport, 13416. Rev. Quy Vo.
Res.: 7514 N. Main St., P.O. Box 475, Newport, 13416. Tel: 315-845-8017; Email: StJohntheBaptist.Newport@rcda.org.
Catechesis Religious Program—Students 91.

NORTH CREEK, WARREN CO., ST. JAMES 1884 [CEM]
Mailing Address: P.O. Box 471, Chestertown, 12817. Email: StJames.NorthCreek@rcda.org. 237 Main St., North Creek, 12853. Rev. John O'Kane.
Parish Center: 86 Riverside Dr., P.O. Box 471, Chestertown, 12817. Tel: 518-824-1176;
Tel: 518-251-2518; Fax: 518-953-1688; Email: northernpointscluster@gmail.com; Email: StJames.NorthCreek@rcda.org.
Catechesis Religious Program—Barbara Carlozzi, D.R.E. Students 19.

NORTHVILLE, FULTON CO., ST. FRANCIS OF ASSISI (1922)
501 Bridge St., Northville, 12134. Tel: 518-863-4736; Fax: 518-863-4128; Email: StFrancisofAssisi.Northville@rcda.org. P.O. Box 126, Northville, 12134. Rev. Anastacio Segura.
Catechesis Religious Program—Katy Ryan, Coord. Sacramental Preparation, Tel: 518-863-2262. Students 31.

ONEONTA, OTSEGO CO., ST. MARY (1883) [CEM]
37 Walnut St., Oneonta, 13820. Rev. David Mickiewicz.

PALENVILLE, GREENE CO., SACRED HEART, Merged with Immaculate Conception, Haines Falls to form Sacred Heart-Immaculate Conception, Haines Falls. Worship Site.

PHILMONT, COLUMBIA CO., SACRED HEART, [CEM] Closed. For inquiries for parish records, contact Parish of Our Lady of Hope, Copake Falls.

PITTSTOWN, RENSSELAER CO., ST. GEORGE, Closed. For inquiries for parish records, contact Immaculate Conception, Hoosick Falls.

QUEENSBURY, WARREN CO., OUR LADY OF THE ANNUNCIATION (1970) (Mission of St. Mary, Glens Falls from 1963-1970) Very Rev. Joseph G. Busch, E.V.
Res.: 448 Aviation Rd., Queensbury, 12804.
Tel: 518-793-9677; Fax: 518-793-9678; Email: ola1963@roadrunner.com; Web: www.olaqueensbury.org.
Catechesis Religious Program—Patti Abbott, C.R.E. Students 217.

RAVENA, ALBANY CO., ST. PATRICK, [CEM] Rev. Scott VanDerveer; Deacon Steve Young.
Res.: 21 Main St., Ravena, 12143. Tel: 518-756-3145; Fax: 518-756-8411; Email: StPatricks.Ravena@rcda.org.
Catechesis Religious Program—Students 89.

RENSSELAER, RENSSELAER CO.
1—ST. JOHN THE EVANGELIST, [CEM] Merged with St. Joseph, Rensselaer to form Parish of St. John the Evangelist and St. Joseph's, Rensselaer.
2—ST. JOSEPH (1915) Merged with St. John the Evangelist, Rensselaer to form Parish of St. John the Evangelist and St. Joseph's, Rensselaer.
3—PARISH OF ST. JOHN THE EVANGELIST AND ST. JOSEPH'S (2006) [CEM]
54 Herrick St., Rensselaer, 12144. P.O. Box 256, Rensselaer, 12144. Deacon E. Gregory Mansfield.
Res.: 50 Herrick St., Rensselaer, 12144.
Parish Office: 53 Herrick St., Rensselaer, 12144.
Tel: 518-465-0482; Fax: 518-449-7088; Email: sjesjparish@aol.com; Web: www.churchofstjohnstjoseph.org.
Catechesis Religious Program— Combined program with St. Joseph. Students 112.

RICHFIELD SPRINGS, OTSEGO CO., ST. JOSEPH, [CEM] Merged with St. Joseph, West Winfield to form St. Joseph the Worker, Richfield Springs. Worship Site.

ROUND LAKE, SARATOGA CO., CORPUS CHRISTI (1946)
Mailing Address: 2001 Rte. 9, Round Lake, 12151-1701. Tel: 518-877-8506; Fax: 518-877-5620; Email: CorpusChristi.RoundLake@rcda.org; Web: www.corpuschristichurch.net. Deacon Andrew Haskins; Rev. F. Richard Lesser; Barbara Wallis, Assoc. for Admin./Parish Secretary.
Res.: 23 Pepperbush Pl., Ballston Spa, 12020.
Catechesis Religious Program—Students 231.

ST. JOHNSVILLE, MONTGOMERY CO., ST. PATRICK, Merged with St. James, Fort Plain & St. Peter's & Paul's, Canajoharie to form Parish of Our Lady of Hope, Fort Plain. Worship Site.

SALEM, WASHINGTON CO., HOLY CROSS, [CEM]
247 Main St., Salem, 12865. Email: HolyCross.Salem@rcda.org; Web: battenkillcatholic.org/. Very Rev. Martin J. Fisher, E.V., Sacramental Min.; Jeffrey C. Peck, Parish Life Dir.
Catechesis Religious Program—Students 19.

SARATOGA SPRINGS, SARATOGA CO.
1—ST. CLEMENT, Revs. Edmund Faliskie, Admin.; Robert Harrison, Parochial Vicar; Arthur Tuttle, C.Ss.R., Parochial Vicar; Deacons Larry Willette; William H. Gaul Jr.
Res.: 231 Lake Ave., Saratoga Springs, 12866.
Tel: 518-584-6122; Fax: 518-584-2644; Email: StClements.SaratogaSprings@rcda.org.
School—St. Clement School, Tel: 518-584-7350; Fax: 518-587-2623; Email: stclem@stclementsschool.

org. Mrs. Jane E. Kromm, Prin. Lay Teachers 22; Students 230.
Catechesis Religious Program—Students 603.
Mission—Gansevoort, St. Therese, Tel: 518-587-3180.
2—ST. PETER, [CEM] Rev. Thomas H. Chevalier; Deacons Edward R. Solomon; Brian Levine.
Office: 241 Broadway, Saratoga Springs, 12866.
Tel: 518-584-2375; Fax: 518-584-5471; Email: StPeters.SaratogaSprings@rcda.org; Web: www.stpetersaratoga.com.
Priest Res.: 88 Regent St., Saratoga Springs, 12866. Tel: 518-584-8127.
Catechesis Religious Program—Students 534.
SCHAGHTICOKE, RENSSELAER CO.
1—CHURCH OF THE HOLY TRINITY, [CEM] Merged with Church of St. Bonaventure, Speigletown to form Transfiguration Parish, Troy. For parish records contact Transfiguration Parish, Troy.
2—ST. JOHN THE BAPTIST, Merged with St. Monica, Johnsonville to form Church of the Holy Trinity, Schaghticoke.
SCHENECTADY, SCHENECTADY CO.
1—ST. ANTHONY, (Italian)
Nott St. at Seward Pl., Schenectady, 12305.
Tel: 518-374-4591; Fax: 518-377-5245; Email: StAnthonys.Schenectady@rcda.org; Web: stanthonyschurch.net. 331 Seward Pl., Schenectady, 12305. Rev. Richard A. Carlino; Sr. Maria Rose Querini, M.P.V., Pastoral Assoc.
Catechesis Religious Program—806 Union Ave., Schenectady, 12308. Combined with & held at St. John the Evangelist, 806 Union St., Schenectady. Students 202.
Convent—1834 Van Vranken Ave., Schenectady, 12308. Tel: 518-346-2060.
2—CHURCH OF ST. ADALBERT (1903) [CEM] (Polish)
Crane St. Hill, Schenectady, 12303. 550 Lansing St., Schenectady, 12303-1195. Deacon Joseph M. Cechnicki, Parish Life Coord.
Catechesis Religious Program—Students 32.
3—SS. CYRIL AND METHODIUS, Closed. For inquiries for parish records contact Our Lady of Mount Carmel, Schenectady.
4—ST. GABRIEL THE ARCHANGEL (1956) Very Rev. James Belogi, E.V.; Rev. Leo Market, Pastor Emeritus.
Parish Offices: 3040 Hamburg St., Schenectady, 12303. Tel: 518-355-6600; Fax: 518-982-1035; Email: StGabrieltheArchangel.Rotterdam@rcda.org.
Catechesis Religious Program—Students 163.
5—ST. HELEN, Merged with Our Lady of Fatima, Schenectady to form St. Kateri Tekakwitha, Schenectady.
6—HOLY CROSS, Closed. For inquiries for parish records, contact St. John the Evangelist, Schenectady.
7—IMMACULATE CONCEPTION, Merged with Our Lady of the Assumption to form Our Lady Queen of Peace.
8—ST. JOHN THE BAPTIST, [CEM] Closed. For inquiries for parish records, contact St. John the Evangelist, Schenectady.
9—ST. JOHN THE EVANGELIST
812 Union St., Schenectady, 12308. Rev. Richard A. Carlino.
Res.: 802 Union St., Schenectady, 12308.
Tel: 518-372-4619; Fax: 518-372-0992.
Office: 806 Union St., Schenectady, 12308.
Tel: 518-372-3381; Email: StJohntheEvangelistChurch.Schenectady@rcda.org.
Catechesis Religious Program—Combined with St. Anthony's Students 249.
10—ST. JOSEPH (1862) [CEM 2] (German)
600 State St., Schenectady, 12305. Rev. Dominic P. Isopo.
Res.: 225 Lafayette St., Schenectady, 12305.
Tel: 518-374-4466; Fax: 518-374-4466; Email: saintjoes225@yahoo.com.
Catechesis Religious Program—Students 17.
11—ST. KATERI TEKAKWITHA PARISH (2012)
2216 Rosa Rd., Schenectady, 12309.
Tel: 518-346-6137; Fax: 518-346-5390; Web: www.stkateriparish.org. Very Rev. Robert Longobucco, E.V.; Deacon Donald Thomas Sharrow; Mr. Lawrence Grimmer, Parish Mgr.
Rectory—1805 Union St., Schenectady, 12309.
School—St. Kateri Tekakwitha Parish School, (Grades PreK-5), 1801 Union St., Schenectady, 12309. Tel: 518-382-8225; Fax: 518-382-3522; Email: principal@stkaterischool.org. Tosha Grimmer, Prin. Lay Teachers 22; Students 250.
Catechesis Religious Program—Students 510.
12—ST. LUKE
1235 State St., Schenectady, 12304. Rev. Dominic P. Isopo.
Res.: 1241 State St., Schenectady, 12304.
Tel: 518-346-3405; Fax: 518-346-3406; Email: slrcc7@aol.com; Web: www.stlukesschenectady.org.
Catechesis Religious Program—Students 104.
13—ST. MADELEINE SOPHIE, Very Rev. James Belogi, E.V.; Deacons Earle E. Flatt, (Retired); Gregory J. Zoltowski.
Res.: 3040 Hamburg St., Schenectady, 12303.
Tel: 518-355-0421; Fax: 518-355-0412; Email: pstmade1@nycap.rr.com; Web: www.smsparish.org.
School—St. Madeleine Sophie School, (Grades PreK-5), 3510 Carman Rd., Schenectady, 12303.
Tel: 518-355-3080; Fax: 518-355-3106; Email: ksloan@smsschool.org. Mrs. Kelly Sloan, Prin.; Cathy Aloisi, Librarian. Lay Teachers 26; Students 200.
Catechesis Religious Program—3514 Carman Rd., Schenectady, 12303. Donna Simone, Pastoral Assoc. for Faith Formation. Students 474.
14—ST. MARY, [CEM] (Polish), Closed. For inquiries for parish records, contact St. John the Evangelist, Schenectady.
15—OUR LADY OF FATIMA, Merged with St. Helen, Schenectady to form St. Kateri Tekakwitha, Schenectady.
16—OUR LADY OF MT. CARMEL 1922 (Italian)
Mailing Address: 1255 Pleasant St., Schenectady, 12303-1999. Tel: 518-393-4109; Fax: 518-393-4100; Web: www.mountcarmelschdy.com. Deacon James E. O'Rourke.
Res.: 2777 Albany St., Schenectady, 12304.
Roman Catholic Faith Formation—2777 Albany St., Schenectady, 12304.
Catechesis Religious Program—Students 25.
17—OUR LADY OF THE ASSUMPTION, Closed. For inquiries for parish records contact Our Lady Queen of Peace, Schenectady.
18—OUR LADY QUEEN OF PEACE (2010)
210 Princetown Rd., Schenectady, 12306-1520.
Tel: 518-346-4926; Fax: 518-374-5670; Email: OurLadyQueenofPeace.Rotterdam@rcda.org. Rev. Vincent J. Ciotoli; Deacon Joseph Brennan.
Worship Site: Former Our Lady of the Assumption, Rotterdam.
Catechesis Religious Program—Students 325.
Mission—St. Margaret of Cortona, 1228 Main St., Rotterdam Junction, Schenectady Co. 12150.
19—ST. PAUL THE APOSTLE
2733 Albany St. at Kings Rd., Schenectady, 12304. Deacon James E. O'Rourke.
Res.: 2777 Albany St., Schenectady, 12304.
Tel: 518-377-8886; Fax: 518-377-4371; Email: StPaultheApostle.Schenectady@rcda.org.
School— Closed.
Catechesis Religious Program—Students 176.
20—SACRED HEART-ST. COLUMBA, Merged with St. Joseph, Schenectady. For inquiries for parish records contact St. Joseph.
21—ST. THOMAS THE APOSTLE, Closed. For inquiries for parish records please see Our Lady of Mt. Carmel, Schenectady.
SCHOHARIE, SCHOHARIE CO., ST. JOSEPH, Closed. For inquiries for parish records please contact Our Lady of the Valley, Middleburgh.
SCHUYLERVILLE, SARATOGA CO.
1—NOTRE DAME-VISITATION, [CEM 2] Very Rev. Martin J. Fisher, E.V.
Parish House—18 Pearl St., Schuylerville, 12871.
Tel: 518-695-3391; Email: mfisher21@nycap.rr.com.
Catechesis Religious Program—Tel: 518-695-3318; Fax: 518-695-4854. Marie Ehlinger, D.R.E. Students 122.
2—VISITATION OF THE BLESSED VIRGIN MARY, Closed. For inquiries for parish records contact Notre Dame de Lourdes Parish, Schuylerville.
SCOTIA, SCHENECTADY CO., ST. JOSEPH CHURCH (1939)
231 Second St., Scotia, 12302. Tel: 518-346-2316; Fax: 518-374-3383; Web: www.stjosephschurchscotia.net. Rev. Peter D. Russo; Deacons John P. Crane; Stephen M. Lape.
Parish Center—Office: 45 MacArthur Dr., Scotia, 12302. Tel: 518-346-2316; Email: StJosephs.Scotia@rcda.org.
Catechesis Religious Program—Students 161.
SIDNEY, DELAWARE CO., SACRED HEART (1921) Rev. Bernard Osei Ampong.
Res.: 15 Liberty St., Sidney, 13838.
Tel: 607-563-1591; Fax: 607-563-7066; Email: SacredHeart.Sidney@rcda.org.
Catechesis Religious Program—Students 105.
Missions—St. Ambrose—Unadilla, Otsego Co.. (Closed).
St. Paul, Franklin, Delaware Co.. (Closed).
SOUTH GLENS FALLS, SARATOGA CO., ST. MICHAEL THE ARCHANGEL 1955 Rev. Guy A. Childs.
Res.: 80 Saratoga Ave., South Glens Falls, 12803.
Tel: 518-792-5859; Fax: 518-792-5850; Email: smichael@nycap.rr.com; Web: stmichaelschurchsgf.com.
Catechesis Religious Program—Students 170.
SOUTH KORTRIGHT, DELAWARE CO., CHURCH OF THE MOST PRECIOUS BLOOD OF JESUS, Merged with Sacred Heart, Stamford.
SPEIGLETOWN, RENSSELAER CO., ST. BONAVENTURE, Closed. As of 7/1/2010 Sacramental records are at Transfiguration Parish, Troy.
STAMFORD, DELAWARE CO.
1—SACRED HEART, [CEM]
Web: sacredheartstamford.org. Very Rev. Michael Cambi, E.V.
Office & Rectory: 27 Harper St., Stamford, 12167.
Tel: 607-652-7170; Fax: 607-652-9250; Email: SacredHeart.Stamford@rcda.org.
Catechesis Religious Program— Combined with St. Philip Neri Mission. Students 100.
Mission—St. Philip Neri, Grand Gorge, 12434.
2—SACRED HEART, Merged with St. Philip Neri, Grand Gorge to form Sacred Heart/St. Philip Neri, Stamford.
STILLWATER, SARATOGA CO., ST. PETER THE APOSTLE, [CEM] Merged with Assumption-St. Paul, Mechanicville to form Roman Catholic Community of All Saints on the Hudson, Stillwater.
STOTTVILLE, COLUMBIA CO., HOLY FAMILY, Merged with St. Mary/Nativity, Stuyvesant Falls to form Church of St. Joseph, Stuyvesant. Worship Site.
STUYVESANT, COLUMBIA CO.
1—CHURCH OF ST. JOSEPH
1820 Rte. 9, Stuyvesant, 12173. Tel: 518-799-5411; Fax: 518-799-3144. Revs. Jorge A. Reyes, O.S.A., Hispanic Min.; George Fleming; Daniel J. Quinn.
Worship Site, 2824 Atlantic Ave., Stottville, 12534.
Catechesis Religious Program—Students 48.
2—NATIVITY/ST. MARY'S, Merged with Holy Family, Stottville to form Church of St. Joseph, Stuyvesant. Worship Site.
STUYVESANT FALLS, COLUMBIA CO., ST. MARY/NATIVITY, [CEM] Merged with Holy Family, Stottville to form Church of St. Joseph, Stuyvesant.
SUMMIT, SCHOHARIE CO., ST. ANNA, Closed. For inquiries for parish records, contact St. Vincent de Paul, Cobleskill.
TRIBES HILL, MONTGOMERY CO., SACRED HEART
111 Third Ave., Tribes Hill, 12177. Tel: 518-829-7301 ; Email: SacredHeart.TribesHill@rcda.org. P.O. Box 264, Tribes Hill, 12177. Very Rev. Christopher Welch, E.V.
Catechesis Religious Program—Students 60.
TROY, RENSSELAER CO.
1—ST. ANTHONY OF PADUA, [CEM] Holds records of St. Peter's; St. Patrick's; St. Anthony of Padua (territorial) Churches, Troy. Revs. Richard Donovan; Jorge A. Reyes, O.S.A., Hispanic Apostolate; Deacon Charles Z. Wojton. In Res., Rev. Primo Piscitello.
Res.: 28 State St., Troy, 12180-3916.
Tel: 518-273-8622; Fax: 518-273-2731; Email: StAnthonyofPadua.Troy@rcda.org. Rev. Jorge A. Reyes, O.S.A.
Catechesis Religious Program—Students 18.
2—ST. AUGUSTINE
Fourth Ave. & 115th St., Lansingburgh, 12182. Revs. David J. Kelley, O.S.A.; Michael Stanley, O.S.A., Parochial Vicar; John McAtee, O.S.A., Parochial Vicar; Jorge A. Reyes, O.S.A., Dir. Spanish Apostolate.
Res.: 25 115th St., Troy, 12182. Tel: 518-235-3861; Fax: 518-233-0284; Email: frdkelley@nycap.rr.com.
Catechesis Religious Program—Students 100.
3—ST. FRANCIS DE SALES, Closed. For inquiries for parish records, contact Our Lady of Victory, Troy.
4—HOLY TRINITY, (Polish), Closed. For inquiries for parish records, contact St. Joseph's Church, Troy.
5—ST. JOSEPH, [CEM]
Web: stjosephcatholicchurch-troy.org. Revs. James R. Sidoti, O.Carm.; Lucian W. Beltzner, O.Carm., Parochial Vicar; Sunny Mathew, In Res. Latin Masses: Mon., Wed., Fri., & Sun. at 12pm
Res.: 416 Third St., Troy, 12180. Tel: 518-274-6720; Fax: 518-272-6503; Email: stjoes-carm@nycap.rr.com.
Catechesis Religious Program—Patti Schwartz, D.R.E. Students 40.
6—ST. LAWRENCE, Closed. For inquiries for parish records contact St. Joseph Parish, Troy.
7—ST. MARY, Closed. For inquiries for parish records, contact St. Joseph, Troy.
8—ST. MICHAEL THE ARCHANGEL (1874) Very Rev. Anthony F. Ligato; Rev. James M. Mackey, Sacramental Min., (Retired), Tel: 518-283-6110, Ext. 212; Deacon Robert Sweeney, Dir. Pastoral Care, Tel: 518-283-6110, Ext. 203; Barbara Berger, Pastoral Assoc. Faith Formation & Youth Min., Tel: 518-283-6110; Tel: 518-283-6110, Ext. 204; Theresa Reid, Business Mgr.
Church: 175 Williams Rd., Troy, 12180.
Tel: 518-283-6110; Email: StMichaeltheArchangel.Troy@rcda.org.
Catechesis Religious Program—Students 150.
Missions—Van Rensselaer Manor, County Nursing Home—North Greenbush, Rensselaer Co.
The Springs Nursing Home, Troy, Rensselaer Co.
9—OUR LADY OF VICTORY 1922
Tel: 518-273-7602 (Office). Rev. Randall P. Patterson; Deacons Brian Lewis; Willis R. Wolfe.
Res.: 55 N. Lake Ave., Troy, 12180.
Tel: 518-273-7602; Fax: 518-273-0310; Email: olvparish01@aol.com; Web: www.olv-troy.org.
School—Our Lady of Victory Pre-K Program, 451 Marshland Ct., Troy, 12180. Tel: 518-274-6202;

Fax: 518-271-8680; Email: olvprek@nycap.rr.com. Rev. Tiffany Crownover, Dir. (Pre-K, 3 & 4).
Catechesis Religious Program—Students 210.
Mission—Our Lady of the Snow, 31 Owen Rd., Grafton, Rensselaer Co. 12082. Tel: 518-276-7602.
10—ST. PATRICK, Closed. For inquiries for parish records, contact St. Anthony of Padua, Troy.
11—ST. PAUL THE APOSTLE, Closed. For inquiries for parish records, contact Our Lady of Victory, Troy.
12—ST. PETER, [CEM] Closed. For inquiries for parish records, contact St. Anthony of Padua, Troy.
13—SACRED HEART
Web: sacredhearttroy.com. Revs. John Yanas; James Vaughan, Pastor Emeritus, (Retired); Antonio Morabito, Pastoral Assoc. for Admin.
Res.: 310 Spring Ave., Troy, 12180.
Tel: 518-274-1363; Fax: 518-274-3015; Email: SacredHeart.Troy@rcda.org.
School—Sacred Heart School, (Grades PreK-6), 308 Spring Ave., Troy, 12180. Tel: 518-274-3655;
Fax: 518-274-8270. Susan Kern Merrill, Prin.; Theresa Jarvis, Librarian.
Catechesis Religious Program—Matthew Ingold, D.R.E. Students 105.
14—TRANSFIGURATION PARISH (2010) Formed from merger of Holy Trinity, Schaghticoke and Church of St. Bonaventure, Speigletown.
17 South Main St., Schaghticoke, 12154.
Tel: 518-235-0337; Fax: 518-235-8726; Email: TransfigurationParish.Troy@rcda.org; Web: transfigurationparish.net. 50 Hillview Dr., Troy, 12182. Rev. Dominic Ingemie, (Retired); Deacons Christopher Keough, Parish Life Coord.; Charles Valenti.
Worship Sites—
St. Bonaventure—
Holy Trinity.
Catechesis Religious Program—Students 148.
15—ST. WILLIAMS, Closed. For inquiries for parish records, contact Sacred Heart, Troy.
VALATIE, COLUMBIA CO., ST. JOHN THE BAPTIST, [CEM] Rev. George Fleming.
Res.: 1025 Kinderhook St., Valatie, 12184.
Tel: 518-758-9401; Fax: 518-758-9409; Email: StJohntheBaptist.Valatie@rcda.org; Web: www.stjohnsvalatie.org.
Catechesis Religious Program—Students 470.
VOORHEESVILLE, ALBANY CO., ST. MATTHEW (1962) Very Rev. Christopher DeGiovine, E.V.
Res.: 25 Mountainview St., Voorheesville, 12186-9551. Tel: 518-765-2805; Fax: 518-765-3701; Email: stmatthewsvoorheesville@verizon.net; Web: www.stmatthewsvoorheesville.org.
Catechesis Religious Program—Email: stmatthewsfaithdevelopment@verizon.net. Students 212.
WALTON, DELAWARE CO., ST. JOHN THE BAPTIST
19 Benton Ave., Walton, 13856. Tel: 607-865-7394; Web: www.catholicwalton.com. Mailing Address: 25 Benton Ave., Walton, 13856-0315. Rev. Edward Golding; Deacon Dr. Michael Freeman.
Res.: 15 Benton Ave., Walton, 13856-0315.
Tel: 607-865-4720.
Catechesis Religious Program—Katherine Gielskie, D.R.E. Students 42.
Mission—Holy Family, 14918 State Hwy. 30, Downsville, Delaware Co. 13755.
WARRENSBURG, WARREN CO., ST. CECILIA 1874 [CEM] Email: SCWarren@rcda.org. Rev. Paul C. Cox, Sacramental Min., (Retired); Sr. Linda Hogan, C.S.J., Parish Life Coord.
Res.: 3802 Main St., Warrensburg, 12885-1629.
Tel: 518-623-3021; Email: sister.linda@stceciliaschurch.com; Web: stceciliaschurch.com.
Catechesis Religious Program—Students 34.
WATERFORD, SARATOGA CO.
1—ST. ANNE, Closed. For inquiries for parish records, contact St. Mary of the Assumption, Waterford.
2—ST. MARY OF THE ASSUMPTION, [CEM]
Broad and Sixth Sts., Waterford, 12188. Revs. David J. Kelley, O.S.A.; Michael Stanley, O.S.A., Parochial Vicar; John F. McAfee, O.S.A., Parochial Vicar.
Res.: 119 Broad St., Waterford, 12188-2397.
Tel: 518-237-3131; Fax: 518-237-9625; Email: StMarys.Waterford@rcda.org; Web: stmaryswaterford.org.
School—St. Mary's Catholic School, 12 Sixth St., Waterford, 12188. Tel: 518-237-0652;
Fax: 518-233-0898; Email: principalstmarys@nybiz.rr.com. Mary Rushkoski, Prin. Lay Teachers 20; Students 245.
Catechesis Religious Program—Faith Formation Program is located at St. Mary of the Assumption. Students 152.
WATERVLIET, ALBANY CO.
1—ST. BRIGID, Merged with Immaculate Conception, Our Lady of Mt. Carmel, St. Patrick's and Sacred Heart of Mary, Watervliet & St. Joseph, Green Island, to form Immaculate Heart of Mary, Watervliet. Church not closed.
2—IMMACULATE CONCEPTION, [CEM] (Polish), Merged with St. Brigid's, Our Lady of Mt. Carmel, St. Patrick's, Sacred Heart of Mary, Watervliet & St. Joseph's, Green Island to form Immaculate Heart of Mary, Watervliet. Church not closed.
3—IMMACULATE HEART OF MARY (2005)
Tel: 518-273-6030; Fax: 518-273-3978; Web: rcpw.weebly.com. Very Rev. Donald L. Rutherford, Sacramental Min.; Deacons Alfred R. Manzella, Parish Life Coord.; Mark J. Leonard.
Parish Office: 2416 7th Ave., Watervliet, 12189.
Tel: 518-273-6020; Email: ihm@rcpw.org.
St. Isaac Jogues House of Discernment—695 Fifth Ave., Watervliet, 12189. Tel: 518-687-2107.
Catechesis Religious Program—Students 52.
4—OUR LADY OF MT. CARMEL, (Italian), Merged with St. Brigid's, Immaculate Conception, St. Patrick's, Sacred Heart of Mary, Watervliet & St. Joseph, Green Island to form Immaculate Heart of Mary, Watervliet. Church not closed.
5—ST. PATRICK, Merged with St. Brigid's, Immaculate Conception, Our Lady of Mt. Carmel, Sacred Heart of Mary, Watervliet & St. Joseph's Green Island, to form Immaculate Heart of Mary, Watervliet. Church not closed.
6—SACRED HEART OF MARY, Closed. Consolidated with St. Brigid's, Immaculate Conception, Our Lady of Mt. Carmel, St. Patrick's, Watervliet & St. Joseph's, Green Island to form Immaculate Heart of Mary, Watervliet.
WEST TAGHKANIC, COLUMBIA CO., HOLY CROSS, Merged with Sacred Heart, Philmont, to form St. John Vianney, Claverack, NY 12153-0477. Tel: 518-851-1333. For inquiries for parish records contact Parish of Our Lady of Hope, Copake Falls.
WEST WINFIELD, HERKIMER CO.
1—ST. JOSEPH, [CEM] Merged with St. Joseph, Richfield Springs to form St. Joseph the Worker, Richfield Springs. Worship Site.
2—ST. JOSEPH THE WORKER (2009)
Mailing Address: 303 W. Main St., West Winfield, 13491. Tel: 315-858-1682; Tel: 315-822-3191; Web: parishes.rcda.org/StJosephtheworker. Rev. Silvester Sarihaddulz.
Business Office: 35 Canadarago St., Richfield Springs, 13439.
Res.: 305 W. Main St., West Winfield, 13491-2904.
Tel: 315-822-3191; Fax: 315-858-1682; Email: sntjos9@aol.com.
Catechesis Religious Program—P.O. Box 791, Richfield Springs, 13491. Ruth Rowe, D.R.E.; Cathy Mackin, D.R.E. Students 99.
WHITEHALL, WASHINGTON CO.
1—NOTRE DAME DES VICTOIRES, Merged with Our Lady of Angels, Whitehall to form Our Lady of Hope, Whitehall.
2—OUR LADY OF ANGELS, Merged with Notre Dame des Victoires, Whitehall to form Our Lady of Hope, Whitehall.
3—OUR LADY OF HOPE
9 Wheeler Ave., Whitehall, 12887. Tel: 518-499-1656; Fax: 518-499-2489; Email: OurLadyofHope/StAnns.Washington@rcda.org. Rev. Rendell R. Torres.
Catechesis Religious Program— Combined with Chapel of the Assumption. Students 52.
Mission—Assumption, Huletts Landing.
WINDHAM, GREENE CO., ST. THERESA OF CHILD JESUS, Rev. Jay Atherton; Deacon Peter Sedlmeir.
Res.: 5188 State Rte. 23, Windham, 12496.
Tel: 518-734-3352; Email: sttheresaofthechildjesus.windham@rcda.org.
Catechesis Religious Program—Email: stcjwind@rcda.org. Deacon Peter Sedlmeir. Students 30.
Mission—St. Joseph's Chapel, Ashland, Greene Co.
WORCESTER, OTSEGO CO., ST. JOSEPH, Rev. Juanito Asprec, Interim Priest.
Res.: 201 Main St., P.O. Box 156, Worcester, 12197.
Tel: 607-397-9373; Email: StJosephs.Worcester@rcda.org.
Mission—St. Mary, [CEM] Schenevus, Otsego Co.
WYNANTSKILL, RENSSELAER CO., ST. JUDE THE APOSTLE
43 Brookside Ave., Wynantskill, 12198-0347.
Tel: 518-283-1162; Fax: 518-286-2808; Email: StJudetheApostle.Wynanstkill@rcda.org. Very Rev. Anthony F. Ligato, Admin.; Deacon Warren A. Safford.
Res.: 6 Schuyler Ct., Wynantskill, 12198-0347.
Parish Office: 42 Dana Ave., Wynantskill, 12198-0347.
School—St. Jude the Apostle School, (Grades PreK-6), 35 Dana Ave., Wynantskill, 12198.
Tel: 518-283-0333; Fax: 518-283-0475; Email: principal@sjsalbany.org; Web: www.sjsalbany.org. Miss Carol Larkin, Librarian; Danielle Cox, Prin. Lay Teachers 24; Students 260.
Catechesis Religious Program—Students 252.

Chaplains of Public Institutions

ALBANY. *Albany County Jail*. (Assigned to Deanery Priests).
Albany County Nursing Home.
Albany Medical Center Hospital. Rev. Robert E. DeLeon, C.S.C., Deacon Warren A. (Ed) Dorsch.
Capital District Psychiatric Center. Rev. Thomas Konopka, Sacramental Min., Deacon Charles Hall.
Columbia County Jail. Deacon Warren A. (Ed) Dorsch.
Hudson Park Rehabilitation & Nursing Center.
New York State Department of Corrections and Community Supervision. Alicia Smith-Roberts, Dir. Ministerial, Family, Volunteer Services, Tel: 518-402-1700.
St. Peter's Hospital. Revs. David Dietsche, Chap., Joseph Mali, Chap., Steven Scarmozzino, Chap., John Tallman, Chap.
St. Peter's Nursing & Rehabilitation Center. Sisters Mary Bruce, C.S.J., Patricia Houlihan, R.S.M.
Stratton Veterans' Administration Medical Center. Friar Igor Burdikoff, Revs. Edward Budnick, Joseph Grasso, C.PP.S., Kofi Ntsiful-Amissah, Alfred Siegel, Deacon Gerald Ladouceur.
Teresian House. Rev. Jeffrey L'Arche, M.S., B.S., S.T.B.
COMSTOCK. *Great Meadows Correctional Institution*. Deacon Ryan McNulty, Chap.
COXSACKIE. *Coxsackie Correctional Facility*. Rev. Dennis Tamburello, O.F.M., Sacramental Min., Anne Narciso, Chap.
Greene Correctional Facility. Rev. Dennis Tamburello, O.F.M., Sacramental Min., Deacon Steve Young, Sacramental Min.
GLENS FALLS. *Glens Falls Hospital*. Sr. Donna Irvine, S.S.N.D., Chap.
Hudson Correctional Facility. Rev. Dennis Tamburello, O.F.M., Sacramental Min., Gerald Van Alstine, Chap.
SCHENECTADY. *Ellis Hospital*. Ms. Angela Marczewski, Chap.
TROY. *Samaritan Hospital*. Revs. Camillus Mourice, Martin Wendell, Deacon Frank S. Lukovits, Marge Milanese, Chap.
Seton Health. Rev. George Bouchaaya, M.L.M., Deacon Albert Schrempf, Sr. Patricia Woolheater, C.S.J.
Van Rensselaer Manor. Vacant.
Washington Correctional Facility. Deacon Miguel Fabian, Chap.

Special Assignment:
Most Rev.—
Hubbard, Howard James, D.D., Bishop Emeritus (Retired), (Retired), Pastoral Center, 40 N. Main Ave., 12203
Very Revs.—
Barratt, Anthony M., E.V., Dir. Office of Prayer & Worship, Pastoral Center, 40 N. Main Ave., 12203
Donlon, James I., J.C.D., Judicial Vicar, Diocesan Tribunal, Pastoral Center, 40 N. Main Ave., 12203
Ebert, James A., Vicar for Clergy, Pastoral Center, 40 N. Main Ave., 12203
LeFort, David R., S.T.L., V.G., Vicar Gen., Pastoral Center, 40 N. Main Ave., 12203
Ligato, Anthony, Vicar, Vocations, Pastoral Center, 40 N. Main Ave., 12203
Longobucco, Robert, E.V., Vicar, Catholic Formation & Education, Pastoral Center, 40 N. Main Ave., 12203
Reamer, Mark G., O.F.M., E.V., Guardian Siena College Friary, 515 Loudon Rd., Loudonville, 12211
Rutherford, Donald L., Mod. of the Curia, Pastoral Center, 40 N. Main Ave., 12203
Revs.—
Amissah, Kofi Ntsiful, Dir., Black Catholic Apostolate, 76 Menand Rd., Menands, 12204. Chap., Stratton Veterans Administration Medical Center
Asma, Lawrence F., C.M., Chap. to Daughters of Charity, 96 Menand Rd., 12204
Chepaitis, Peter, O.F.M., Bethany Ministries, 175 Mill Ln., P.O. Box 432, Middleburgh, 12122
DeLeon, Robert E., C.S.C., St. Joseph's Center, 495 Maple Ln., Valatie, 12184
Frisoni, Matthew H., J.C.L., Diocesan Tribunal, 40 N. Main Ave., 12203
Grasso, Joseph, Chap. Stratton Veterans Administration Medical Center, 113 Holland Ave., 12208
Kall, Tony, O.F.M.Conv., Guardian Immaculate Conception Friary, P.O. Box 629, Rensselaer, 12144. Tel: 518-265-0747
Konopka, Thomas E., L.M.S.W., Dir. Consultation Center, 790 Lancaster St., 12203
Lee, Jaeung Damian, Chap. Holy Family Korean Apostolate, 17 Exchange St., 12205

Mali, Joseph, Chap. St. Peter's Hospital, 78 Slingerland St., 12202
Reyes, Jorge A., O.S.A., Chap. Spanish Apostolate, St. Mary's, 119 Broad St., Waterford, 12118
Scarmozzino, Steven, Chap. St. Peter's Hospital, 465 State St., 12203
Tallman, John, Chap., St. Peter's Hospital, 125 Eagle St., 12203
Tyson, Michael, O.F.M., Dir., St. Francis Chapel, Siena Friary, 515 Loudon Rd., Loudonville, 12211.

On Duty Outside the Diocese:
Revs.—
Fragomeni, Richard N., 5401 S. Cornell Ave., Chicago, IL 60615-5698
Hurst, Thomas R., S.S., St. Mary's Seminary & Univ., 5400 Roland Ave., Baltimore, MD 21210.

Military Chaplains:
Rev.—
Hammond, David J., L.T., C.H.C., U.S.N., LT, CHC, USN, USS Bonhomme Richard (LHD 6), Unit 100184, Box 802, FPO, AP 96617.

Leave of Absence:
Revs.—
Celeste, Charles R.
Ryan, Daniel P.
Tressic, David L.
Turner, Bernard R.

Retired Clergy:
Revs.—
Ahern, Bernard J., (Retired), 4418 Poppy Tree Ln., Jacksonville, FL 32258
Allie, Stanley J., (Retired), Sacred Heart Church, 1201 Bogard Rd., Wasilla, AK 99643
Anselment, Joseph E., Emeritus, Landing of Queensbury, (Retired), 27 Woodvale Rd., Queensbury, 12804
Barker, Joseph F., (Retired), Teresian House, 200 Washington Ave. Ext., Rm. 101, 12203
Bath, Winston L., (Retired), Parish of the Holy Trinity, P.O. Box 323, Hudson, 12534
Berardi, Thomas F., (Retired), 105 Sand Pine Ln., 12203
Brucker, George W., (Retired), 25 St. Anthony Ln., Rensselaer, 12144
Cahill, William, (Retired), Beltrone Living Center, 6 Winners Cir., Apt. 229, Colonie, 12205
Cairns, John L., (Retired), 23 Oak Brook Commons, Clifton Park, 12065
Cantwell, Edward F., (Retired), Barnwell Nursing and Rehabilitation, 3230 Church St., Valatie, 12184
Chiaramonte, Anthony, (Retired), 465 State St., 12203
Condon, Liam, (Retired), 709 E. River Dr., Lake Luzerne, 12846
Connery, J. Thomas, (Retired), 396 Saratoga Rd., Glenville, 12302
Cox, Paul C., (Retired), P.O. Box 134, Kattskill Bay, 12844
Curran, Anthony, (Retired), c/o Mrs. Ellen Hanafin, 2330 N. Old Post Rd., Castleton, 12033
Daley, James D., (Retired), 69 Murray Ave., Delmar, 12054
Deimeke, L. Edward, E.V., (Retired), St. Mary's Parish, 10 Lodge St., 12207
DePascale, Daniel F., (Retired), The Palms of Ponte Vedra, 405 Solana Rd., Ste. 221, Ponte Vedra Beach, FL 32082
DeRose, Martin, (Retired), 110 Evelyn Ave., Amsterdam, 12010
Donnelly, Robert, (Retired), 300 Mill Rose Ct., Slingerlands, 12159
Doyle, Kennth, (Retired), Avila, 30 Columbia Cir., Apt. 342, 12203
DuBois, Francis J., (Retired), 43 Sturbridge Way, Brewster, MA 02631
Facci, John, S.A.C., (Retired), 2 Tyron Ave., Apt. 13, Glenville, 12302
Falletta, Joseph, (Retired), P.O. Box 512, Kinderhook, 12106
Farano, Michael A., 4101 Stonegate Dr., Rensselaer, 12144
Forno, Adam, (Retired), 3505 Oaks Way, #312, Pompano Beach, FL 33069
Gaffigan, William J., (Retired), 32 Mill St., P.O. Box 201, Hagaman, 12086
Gelfenbien, Gary Paul, (Retired), St. James Church, 129 Hudson Ave., Chatham, 12037
Gerken, Theodore J., (Retired), 207 S. Main St., P.O. Box 335, Germantown, 12526
Gregory, Kenneth W., (Retired), 17 Riverview Terr., Rensselaer, 12144
Hayes, Thomas J., D.Min., (Retired), 35 Hampton Cir., Mechanicville, 12118
Healy, Terence P., (Retired), St. Joseph's Rectory, 31 N. Helmer Ave., Dolgeville, 13329
Hohenstein, Robert J., (Retired), 7C Kingdom Way, Mechanicville, 12118
Hunter, John J., (Retired), 133 Saratoga Rd., Bld. 104, Apt. 5, Glenville, 12302
Iannotti, Pascal A., (Retired), 204 Linden Ct., Amsterdam, 12010
Ingemie, Dominic, (Retired), 4312 Stonegate Dr., Rensselaer, 12144
Jones, David J., M.M., (Retired), 221 Fifth Ave., Troy, 12180
Jupin, Alan D., (Retired), Beltrone Living Center, 6 Winners Cir., Apt. 545, Latham, 12205
Kane, James J., (Retired), Beltrone Living Center, 6 Winners Cir., Colonie, 12205
Kirwin, John D., (Retired), 94 Lincoln Ave., Saratoga Springs, 12866
Lamanna, Alfred, (Retired), The Prospect Inn, 200 N. Prospect St., Apt. J, Herkimer, 13350
Lanese, John, (Retired), 177 Hollywood Ave., 12209
Leskovar, Richard J., (Retired), Beltrone Living Center, 6 Winners Circle, Apt. 622, Colonie, 12205
Lonergan, James Barry, (Retired), 187 E. Sanford St., Glens Falls, 12801
Mackey, James M., (Retired), 38 Oak Brook Commons, Clifton Park, 12065
Maher, Daniel J., (Retired), 2305 Florence Dr., Latham, 12110
Manerowski, Joseph, (Retired), St. Mary's Church, 62 Warren St., Glens Falls, 12801
Markert, Leo F., (Retired), 133 Saratoga Rd., Bldg. S, Apt. #5, Glenville, 12302
Matulewicz, Ronald G., (Retired), 3 Sevilla Dr., Clifton Park, 12065
McCloskey, Francis G., (Retired), Teresian House, 200 Washington Ave. Ext., 12203
McTavey, Lawrence, V.F., (Retired), c/o Michael O'Brien: 4 Via Maestra Dr., Glenville, 12302
Menty, Ron, (Retired), Avila, 30 Columbia Cir., Apt. 244, 12203
Molyn, John A., (Retired), 12 Willmon Rd., Hudson, 12534
Motta, Anthony, (Retired), Sacred Heart-Immaculate Conception, P.O. Box 379, Haines Falls, 12436
Moyna, John L., (Retired), 207 Greenwich Dr., 12203
Murphy, Dennis, (Retired), Church of the Holy Trinity, 205 Glebe St., Johnstown, 12095
Noone, David E., (Retired), 730 Villagio Pl., Apt. 408, Fayetteville, NC 28303
O'Brien, Leo P., 100 White Pine Dr., 12203
O'Connor, Frank, (Retired), Blessed Sacrament Church, 607 Central Ave., 12203
O'Grady, John F., S.S.D., S.T.D., (Retired), 1000 Quayside Ter., #2104, Miami, FL 33138
O'Neill, James, (Retired), 2 Webster St., 12208
Ophals, Donald J., (Retired), Beltrone Living Center, 6 Winners Circle, Apt. 345, Colonie, 12205
Pape, William H., (Retired), 4303 Stonegate Dr., Rensselaer, 12144
Pereira, Cyril F., (Retired), 2256 Burdett Ave., #2017, Troy, 12180
Polenz, Gordon, (Retired), 13 Sun Air Blvd. E., Haines City, FL 33844
Potvin, Leo F., (Retired), Gabriel House, 73 First St., Ilion, 13357
Powhida, Robert, (Retired), P.O. Box 153, South Glens Falls, 12803
Rebeyro, Lloyd, (Retired), 4 Proctor Ct., Loudonville, 12211. Tel: 518-265-9974
Schiffer, James, (Retired), 1101 Wild Ginger Ln., Fleming Island, FL 32003
Schmitt, Michael T., (Retired), Teresian House, 200 Washington Ave. Ext., Room 129, 12203
Shanley, Owen F., (Retired), 195 Partyka Dr., P.O. Box 914, Broadalbin, 12025
Shaw, Richard D., (Retired), 2 Webster St., 12208
Smith, Paul, (Retired), 37 Parkwood St. E., 12203
Somerville, Alvin, O.F.M.Conv., (Retired), 75 St. Francis Pl., Rensselaer, 12144
St. John, George G., (Retired), Blessed Sacrament Church, 607 Central Ave., 12206
Swierzowski, Stanislaus J., (Retired), 48 Van Derveer St., Amsterdam, 12010
Tartaglia, Paul P., (Retired), 465 State St., 12203. (June-Nov.)
Testa, Richard, (Retired), St. Joseph Residence, Little Sisters of the Poor, 1365 Enfield St., Enfield, CT 06082
Toole, Arthur A., (Retired), 38 Oak Brook Commons, Clifton Park, 12065
Tremblay, Nellis, (Retired), P.O. Box 134, Kattskill Bay, 12844
Urban, Carl, (Retired), 48 Annabelle Pl., Schenectady, 12306
Vail, Thomas, (Retired), 76 Moreland St., Little Falls, 13365
Van Wormer, Giles, O.F.M. Conv., (Retired), Atria Shaker, 345 Northern Blvd., Apt. 239, 12204
Varno, John J., (Retired), Our Lady of Grace Church, 73 Midline Rd., Ballston Lake, 12019
Vaughan, James, (Retired), Sacred Heart Church, 310 Spring Ave., Troy, 12180
Vosko, Richard, (Retired), 4611 Foxwood Dr. S., Clifton Park, 12065
Weider, Gregory S., (Retired), 7 Eastmount Dr., Apt. 216, Slingerlands, 12159
Young, Peter G., (Retired), 40 Eagle St., 12207.

Permanent Deacons:
Ackerson, Dana G., (Retired), (Relocated)
Ayres, Walter, St. Mary's, Albany; Sacred Heart, Albany
Baechel, Kenneth, (Retired), (Relocated)
Barone, John, St. Joseph's, Greenfield Center
Bazinet, William F., St. Joseph's, Fort Edward; R.C. Community of Hudson Falls/Kingsbury, Hudson Falls
Beckman, Martin L., (Retired), St. Vincent de Paul, Albany
Berning, Frank C., D.Min., Diocesan Dir. of Pastoral Planning; Dir. of St. Bernard's, Albany
Bower, James W., Annunciation, Ilion
Boyd, Danny S., (Retired), St. Therese Mission, Gansevoort
Brady, Robert, (Retired)
Brennan, Joseph, Our Lady, Queen of Peace, Schenectady; Deacon Life & Ministry Council
Brett, William, Chap., Our Lady of Mercy Life Center, Guilderland; Daughters of Sarah, Albany
Brown, Richard J., St. Thomas the Apostle, Cherry Valley
Carbone, Michael S., Our Lady Queen of Apostles, Frankfort; Master of Ceremonies
Cechnicki, Joseph M., Church of St. Adalbert, Schenectady; Master of Ceremonies
Christiano, Gerald, (Retired), St. Anthony of Padua & Our Lady of Victory, Troy
Cohen, Andrew J., (Retired)
Cortese, Anthony, Christ the King, Westmere
Crane, John P., St. Joseph's, Scotia; Baptist Retirement Home, Scotia
Cullinane, John F., (Retired)
DeLorenzo, Joseph P., Holy Family, Little Falls
Devine, Patrick, (Retired), (Relocated)
Dicaprio, Richard, St. Edward the Confessor, Clifton Park
Dorsch, Warren A. (Ed), Philmont-Mellenville Food Pantry; Chaplain, Hudson Correctional Facility; Columbia County Sheriff & Jail; Albany Medical Center; Master of Ceremonies
Dringus, William, Holy Spirit, East Greenbush; Master of Ceremonies
Fabian, Miguel, Chap., Shrine Church of Our Lady of the Americas, Albany; Spanish Apostolate; Chaplain, Washington Correctional Facility
Flatt, Earle E., (Retired), St. Madeleine Sophie, Guilderland; Deacon Life & Ministry Council
Dr. Freeman, Michael, St. Peter's, Delhi
Garceau, Frank, St. Ambrose, Latham
Gaul, William H. Jr., (Retired)
Gorman, William, D.Min., Ph.D., (Retired), (Relocated)
Grebe, Andrew, St. Mary's, Crescent
Grigaitis, Jerry, (Retired)
Groesbeck, Lawrence E., Holy Spirit, Gloversville; Holy Trinity, Johnstown
Gutierrez, Moises R., (Retired), (Relocated)
Hall, Charles H. III, Capital District Psychiatric Center, Albany
Haskins, Andrew, Corpus Christi, Round Lake
Henkel, William G., St. Francis de Sales, Herkimer; Faith Formation, Herkimer area; Master of Ceremonies
Herlihy, Frank D., (Retired), Sacred Heart, Lake George
Hogan, Ronald T., St. Mary's, Ballston Spa
Hook, J. Neil, (Retired)
Jones, Dennis A., (Retired), Annunciation, Ilion; Our Lady Queen of Apostles, Frankfort
Kelenski, Eugene, (Retired), (Relocated)
Keough, Christopher, Parish Life Dir., Transfiguration Parish, Troy/ Schaghticoke
Kisselback, Paul, Our Lady of the Assumption, Latham; Dir. of Diaconal Initial Formation; Master of Ceremonies
Kosto, Timothy, St. Mary's, Clinton Heights
Ladouceur, Gerald J., Mater Christi, Albany; Community Hospice, Albany; Master of Ceremonies
Lape, Stephen M., St. Joseph's, Scotia
Leonard, Mark J., Dir., Office of the Diaconate, Immaculate Heart of Mary, Watervliet
Levine, Brian, St. Peter's, Saratoga Springs
Lewis, Brian, Our Lady of Victory, Troy
Lukovits, Frank S., (Retired), Samaritan Hospital, Troy; St. Henry's, Averill Park
MacKinnon, Walter J., (Retired), St. Edward the Confessor, Clifton Park

Manno, Peter, (Retired)
Mansfield, E. Gregory, Parish Life Dir., St. John the Evangelist & St. Joseph, Rensselaer; Master of Ceremonies
Manzella, Alfred R., Deacon Life & Ministry Council; Parish Life Dir, Immaculate Heart of Mary, Watervliet
Markham, Joseph F., (Retired), Christ the King, Albany
Matthews, Gerard F.
McAuliffe, Timothy J., All Saints, Albany
McDonald, Michael F., St. Mary's, Coxsackie; Master of Ceremonies
McNulty, Ryan, Sacred Heart, Lake George; Chaplain, Great Meadow Correctional Facility
Melanson, Michael P., Immaculate Conception, Glenville; Master of Ceremonies
Miles, Gary, St. Clare's, Colonie
Nash, Thomas, Sacred Heart, Castleton
Neurohr, Helmut N., St. Ambrose, Latham
O'Connell, Thomas, (Retired)
O'Connor, Gary, All Saints Catholic Church, Albany; Master of Ceremonies
O'Neill, Charles, (Retired)
O'Rourke, James E., St. Paul's/Mt. Carmel, Schenectady
Pagano, Joseph S., (Retired)
Pasquarelli, Robert, St. Henry's, Averill Park; Rensselaer County Jail Ministry; Master of Ceremonies
Picher, Gary R., Parish Life Dir., St. Joseph, Greenfield Center (Mission: St. Paul's Rock City Falls); Master of Ceremonies
Powers, David, St. Mary's, Glens Falls; Master of Ceremonies
Quinn, Peter R., Immaculate Conception, New Lebanon, Assoc. Dir. Catholic Scouting
Ramey, Jon, St. Mary's, Granville
Riggi, Gary J., Our Lady of the Valley, Middleburgh; Diaconate Formation Faculty; Master of Ceremonies
Roemer, Paul W. Sr., (Retired)
Romand, Joseph A., Christ Son of Justice, Troy
Rucinski, Robert T., (Retired)
Ryba, Michael C., Dir. of Finance and Admin., Amsterdam Parishes; Montgomery County Convalescent Home; Montgomery County Prison; St. Stanislaus, Amsterdam; Master of Ceremonies
Safford, Warren A., St. Jude the Apostle, Wynantskill; Deacon Life & Ministry Council
Sakowicz, Albert J., (Retired)
Schrempf, Albert G., Holy Trinity, Cohoes; Seton Health, Troy
Sedlmeir, Peter, St. Theresa's, Windham
Sharrow, Thomas, St. Kateri Tekakwitha, Schenectady; Deacon Life & Ministry Council
Sheppeck, Michael L., (Retired)
Solar, Richard S., (Retired)
Solomon, Edward R., Dir., Ongoing Formation, St. Peter's Saratoga
South, Owen D., (Retired)
Ste-Marie, Ronald, Sts. Anthony & Joseph, Herkimer
Steiger, Larry, Our Lady of Hope, Fort Plain
Sullivan, Raymond, Ph.D., (Retired), Blessed Sacrament, Albany; Master of Ceremonies
Surman, Gary J., St. Vincent de Paul, Cobleskill; Adjoining Ministries Family Life Office; Master of Ceremonies
Sweeney, Robert, St. Michael the Archangel, Troy
Tapia, Ramon R., St. John the Evangelist/St. Anthony's, Schenectady
Thiesen, Richard J., Parish Life Dir., Christ Our Light, Schenectady
Thomas, Frank, M.D., M.T.S., M.A., Parish Life Director, Our Lady of Grace, Ballston Lake; St. Luke's Guild
Trawinski, Peter J., (Retired)
Turcotte, Arthur W., (Retired), St. Clement's, Saratoga Springs
Tyrrell, Joseph, Parish Life Dir., Blessed Sacrament, Bolton Landing
Valenti, Charles, Transfiguration Parish, Troy
Velez, Randy, St. Thomas the Apostle, Cherry Valley
Washburn, Richard, Holy Trinity, Hudson; Brookwood Secure Center (NYS DFY), Claverack
Willette, Lawrence, St. Clement, Saratoga Springs
Wilson, Gerard R., (Retired)
Witko, George E., (Retired)
Wojton, Charles Z., St. Anthony of Padua, Troy
Wolfe, Willis R., Our Lady of Victory, Troy
Wubbenhorst, Robert H., (Retired), Master of Ceremonies
Young, Steve, Prison Chap., Greene Correctional
Zoltowski, Gregory J., St. Madeleine Sophie/St. Gabriel's, Guilderland.

INSTITUTIONS LOCATED IN DIOCESE

[A] SEMINARIES, RELIGIOUS OR SCHOLASTICATES

CATSKILL. *St. Anthony Friary*, 24 Harrison St., P.O. Box 487, Catskill, 12414-0487. Tel: 518-943-3451; Fax: 518-943-1573; Email: stanthonycatskill@gmail.com. Revs. Regis Gallo, O.F.M.; John Bavaro, O.F.M.; Albin Fusco, O.F.M.; Albert McMahon, O.F.M.; Paul Guido, O.F.M.; Isaac J. Calicchio, O.F.M.; Bro. Joseph La Gressa, O.F.M.; Rev. Joseph Lorenzo, O.F.M., Supr. Order of Friars Minor. Brothers 1; Priests 7.

RENSSELAER. *Conventual Franciscan Friars* Immaculate Conception Province Treasurer, P.O. Box 629, Rensselaer, 12144. Tel: 518-472-1000; Tel: 518-472-1016; Tel: 518-472-1007; Fax: 518-472-1013; Email: provsec1@olaprovince.org; Web: www.olaprovince.org. 75 St. Francis Pl., Rensselaer, 12144-2142. Very Rev. James McCurry, O.F.M.Conv., Min. Prov.; Revs. Henry Madigar, O.F.M.Conv.; Giles Van Wormer, O.F.M.Conv., (Retired); Friar Tony Kall, O.F.M.Conv., Guardian; Bro. Andre Picotte, O.F.M.Conv. Order Friars Minor Conventual. Priests 2.

[B] COLLEGES AND UNIVERSITIES

ALBANY. *St. Bernard's School of Theology and Ministry at Albany*, 40 N. Main Ave., 12203. Tel: 518-453-6760; Fax: 518-453-6793; Email: stbernards@rcda.org; Web: stbernards.edu. Deacon Frank C. Berning, D.Min., Dir. Extension Program of St. Bernard's School of Theology and Ministry, Rochester, NY. Graduate School of Theology & Ministry Studies. Lay Staff 5; Priests 6; Sisters 2.

The College of Saint Rose (Corporate Name) 432 Western Ave., 12203. Tel: 518-454-5111; Tel: 800-657-8556; Fax: 518-337-2345; Email: admit@strose.edu; Web: www.strose.edu. Dr. Carolyn J. Stefanco, Pres.; Craig Tynan, Registrar; Joan Horgan, Dir. Campus Min. Founded by the Sisters of St. Joseph of Carondelet in 1920. Lay Teachers 208; Sisters 2; Students 4,411.

Maria College, 700 New Scotland Ave., 12208. Tel: 518-438-3111; Email: bwales@mariacollege.edu; Web: MariaCollege.edu. Dr. Thomas Gamble, Pres.; Dr. John Kowal, Vice Pres. Academic Affairs; Mrs. Frances Bernard, Dir. of Business Affairs; Beth Wales, Dir. of Mktg. & Communications. Two-Year Career College with a RN Baccalaureate Completion Program (for registered nurses). Lay Teachers 63; Sisters 5; Students 800.

LOUDONVILLE. *Siena College*, 515 Loudon Rd., Loudonville, 12211. Tel: 518-783-2300; Fax: 518-783-4293; Web: www.siena.edu. Dr. Margaret Madden, Vice Pres. Academic Affairs; Paul Stec, Vice Pres. Fin. & Admin.; Ned Jones, Vice Pres. Enrollment Mgmt.; Dr. Maryellen Gilroy, Vice Pres. Student Life; Mark Frost, Vice Pres. Facilities; James A. Serbalik, Registrar; Loretta Ebert, Dir. of Library. Founded in 1937 by the Franciscan Friars, Order of Friars Minor, Province of the Most Holy Name of Jesus. Students 3,255; Full-time Faculty 221; Part-time Faculty 109.

Siena Friary, Franciscan Friars - Holy Name Province, Inc. Very Rev. Mark G. Reamer, O.F.M., E.V., Guardian Siena Friary; Revs. Lawrence Anderson, O.F.M., College Chap.; Julian A. Davies, O.F.M.; Daniel P. Dwyer, O.F.M.; Peter A. Fiore, O.F.M.; Linh Hoang, O.F.M.; Michael Joyce, O.F.M.; F. Gerard Lee, O.F.M., Dir., St. Francis Chapel; Daniel C. Nelson, O.F.M.; Sean O'Brien, O.F.M.; Paul Osborne, O.F.M.; Kenneth Paulli, O.F.M.; Ignatius Smith, O.F.M., Vicar; Dennis Tamburello, O.F.M., Vicar; Michael Tyson, O.F.M.; Bros. Brian C. Belanger, O.F.M.; George Camacho, O.F.M.; F. Edward Coughlin, O.F.M., Pres.; Edgardo Zea, O.F.M.; Dennis Bennett, O.F.M.

[C] HIGH SCHOOLS, DIOCESAN

ALBANY. *Bishop Maginn High School*, 75 Park Ave., 12202. Tel: 518-463-2247; Fax: 518-463-9880; Email: signor@bishopmaginn.org; Web: www.bishopmaginn.org. Mr. Christopher Signor, Prin. Lay Teachers 16; Priests 1; Sisters 1; Students 150.

AMSTERDAM. *Bishop Scully High School*, c/o 40 N. Main Ave., 12203-1422. Tel: 518-842-4100. Closed.

SARATOGA SPRINGS. *Saratoga Central Catholic High School*, (Grades 6-12), 247 Broadway, Saratoga Springs, 12866. Tel: 518-587-7070; Fax: 518-587-0678; Email: lombard@saratogacatholic.org; Web: www.saratogacatholic.org. Mr. L. Stephen Lombard, Prin.; Dennis Ostrowski, Vice Prin. Lay Teachers 22; Students 222.

SCHENECTADY. *Notre Dame-Bishop Gibbons School*, (Grades 6-12), (Coed) 2600 Albany St., Schenectady, 12304. Tel: 518-393-3131; Fax: 518-370-3817; Email: fuscop@nd-bg.org; Web: www.nd-bg.org. Peter Fusco, High School Prin.; Patrick Moran, Asst. Prin. Lay Teachers 24; Students 246.

TROY. *Catholic Central High School*, (Grades 7-12), 625 Seventh Ave., Troy, 12182. Tel: 518-235-7100; Fax: 518-237-1796; Web: www.cchstroy.org. Dr. Christopher Bott, Prin. Lay Teachers 37; Sisters 2; Students 500.

[D] HIGH SCHOOLS, PRIVATE

ALBANY. *Academy of the Holy Names Upper and Middle Schools*, (Grades 6-12), 1075 New Scotland Rd., 12208. Tel: 518-438-7895; Fax: 518-482-4650; Email: mavigliante@ahns.org; Web: www.ahns.org. Ms. Mary Anne Vigliante, Head of School; Mrs. Michele Musto, Div. Head. Lay Teachers 41; Sisters 6; Students 240.

The Christian Brothers' Academy of Albany, (Grades 5-12), 12 Airline Dr., 12205. Tel: 518-452-9809; Fax: 518-452-9804; Web: www.cbaalbany.org. Dr. James Schlegel, Head of School. Brothers of the Christian Schools.JROTC College Prep. Program. Lay Teachers 40; Students 517.

Mercy High, Private School for Girls Closed. c/o 40 N. Main Ave., 12203.

TROY. *LaSalle Institute*, (Grades 6-12), 174 Williams Rd., Troy, 12180. Tel: 518-283-2500; Fax: 518-283-6265; Email: info@lasalleinstitute.org; Web: www.lasalleinstitute.org. Mr. Joseph Raczkowski, Prin.; Steven Sgambelluri, Prin. of Middle School. Brothers of the Christian Schools. Brothers 8; Lay Teachers 35; Sisters 1; Students 410.

[E] ELEMENTARY SCHOOLS, PRIVATE

LOUDONVILLE. *Saint Gregory's School*, (Grades N-8), 121 Old Niskayuna Rd., Loudonville, 12211-1399. Tel: 518-785-6621; Fax: 518-782-1364; Email: abarr@saintgregorysschool.org; Web: www.saintgregorysschool.org. Alan Barr, Prin. An independent Catholic day school for boys staffed by laity (Nursery-8). Girls admitted in Nursery through Kindergarten classes. Lay Teachers 25; Students 130.

[F] CONSOLIDATED ELEMENTARY SCHOOLS

ALBANY. *Cathedral Academy*, 75 Park Ave., 12202. Tel: 518-449-5232. Closed.

COHOES. *Cohoes Catholic School* Closed. One St. Marie's Ln., Cohoes, 12047. Tel: 518-235-5202; Fax: 518-453-6666.

GLEN FALLS. *St. Mary's/St. Alphonsus Regional Catholic School*, (Grades PreK-8), 10-12 Church St., Glens Falls, 12801. Tel: 518-792-3178; Fax: 518-792-6056; Web: www.smsaschool.org. Mrs. Patricia Balmer, Prin.

WATERFORD. *St. Mary's School*, (Grades PreK-8), 12 Sixth St., Waterford, 12188. Tel: 518-237-0652; Fax: 518-233-0898; Email: principalstmarys@nybiz.rr.com; Web: www.smswaterford.org. Mary Rushkoski, Prin. Lay Teachers 17; Students 225.

[G] RESIDENTIAL INSTITUTIONS FOR CHILDREN & ADOLESCENTS

ALBANY. *Saint Anne Institute*, 160 N. Main Ave., 12206. Tel: 518-437-6500; Fax: 518-437-6555; Email: acortese@s-a-i.org; Web: www.stanneinstitute.org. Anthony G. Cortese, CEO & Pres. St. Anne's offers Residential, Educational, and Community-Based Counseling services to youth, adults, and families. We operate a residential facility for girls 12-21, a junior and senior High School for girls 12-21, a preschool for boys and girls ages 3-5, a community-based counseling program for adults, boys, girls, and families; after school programs for boys and girls 13-18; and a Street Outreach Program for boys and girls who are homeless or living on the streets. We have an expertise in working with youth, adults, and families who have been sexually victimized or are struggling with sexual aggressive behaviors. We contract with County Departments of Social Services and School Districts; we take third party payments from insurance companies and we make arrangement on a sliding scale for clients to pay as they receive services. Bed Capacity 60; Tot Asst. Annually 700; Total Staff 256; Residential 60; Community Counseling 200.

St. Catherine's Center for Children, 40 N. Main Ave., 12203. Tel: 518-453-6700; Fax: 518-453-6712; Email: jryan@st-cath.org; Web: www.st-cath.org. Frank Pindiak, Exec. Dir. Residential and day treatment, group homes and foster family programs for children with special needs. Community based prevention programs; Parent aides; Parent

Training; Transitional Program for Homeless Families. Students 50; Tot Asst. Annually 1,700.

LaSalle School, Inc., 391 Western Ave., 12203. Tel: 518-242-4731; Fax: 518-242-4747; Email: information@lasalle-school.org; Web: www.lasalle-school.org. David Wallace, Exec. Dir. Residential and day programs, independent living program, sexual victim/offender program, licensed substance abuse treatment program, and preventative services for boys (ages 12-18) and their families in New York State. Registered New York State Junior and Senior High School and certified School of Special Education. Brothers of the Christian Schools 5; Resident Students 75; Day Students 35; Evening Reporting Center 15; Community Connections 15.

WATERVLIET. *St. Colman's Home*, 11 Haswell Rd., Watervliet, 12189. Tel: 518-273-4911; Fax: 518-273-3312. Sr. S. Joseph Mary, P.B.V.M., Dir. Social Svcs. Sisters of the Presentation of the B.V.M. Children 40.

[H] GENERAL HOSPITALS

ALBANY. *St. Clare's Corporation*, 40 N. Main Ave., 12203-1422. Tel: 518-453-6650; Fax: 518-453-6792. Joseph Profiti, Pres., Email: joseph.pofit@rcda.org.

St. Clare's Holding Company, Inc., 40 N. Main Ave., 12203-1422. Tel: 518-453-6650; Web: www.stclares.org.

St. Peter's Hospital of the City of Albany, 315 S. Manning Blvd., 12208. Tel: 518-525-1550; Fax: 518-525-5596; Email: virginia.golden@sphp.com; Web: www.sphp.com. Virginia L. Golden, CEO. Bed Capacity 442; Tot Asst. Annually 500,000; Total Staff 3,965.

St. Peter's Addiction Recovery Center, 8 Mercycare Ln., Guilderland, 12084. Tel: 518-452-6700; Fax: 518-452-6770; Email: patrick.carrese@sphp.com. Patrick Carrese, Exec. Dir. Bed Capacity 40; Tot Asst. Annually 600; Total Staff 48.

AMSTERDAM. *St. Mary's Healthcare*, 427 Guy Park Ave., Amsterdam, 12010. Tel: 518-842-1900; Fax: 518-842-0107; Email: cortesej@ascension.org; Email: michelle.vangordon@ascension.org. Mr. Victor Giulianelli, FACHE, B.S., M.S., Pres. & CEO. Sponsored by Ascension Health Ministries (Ascension Sponsor, a Public Juridic Person) Bed Capacity 290; Tot Asst. Annually 418,719; Total Staff 1,600.

St. Mary's Hospital Auxiliary, Inc., 427 Guy Park Ave., Amsterdam, 12010. Tel: 518-841-7136; Email: medwidc@smha.org. Colleen Medwid, Contact Person.

The Foundation of St. Mary's at Amsterdam, Inc., 427 Guy Park Ave., Amsterdam, 12010. Tel: 518-841-7478; Fax: 518-841-7182.

RENSSELAER. *The Community Hospice, Inc.*, 295 Valley View Blvd., Rensselaer, 12144. Tel: 518-724-0284; Fax: 518-285-8151; Email: michelle.mazzacco@sphp.com; Web: www.communityhospice.org. Administrative Office: 445 New Karner Rd., 12208. Michelle Mazzacco, Vice Pres. Community Svcs. and Hospice. Bed Capacity 14; Tot Asst. Annually 4,062; Total Staff 269.

TROY. *Seton Health System, Inc.*, 1300 Massachusetts Ave., Troy, 12180. Tel: 518-268-5000; Fax: 518-268-5257; Email: info@setonhealth.org; Web: www.sphp.com. Norman E. Dascher, CEO. Trinity Health

Seton Health System, Inc. Bed Capacity 20; Tot Asst. Annually 337,887; Total Staff 668.

Seton Health at Schuyler Ridge Residential Healthcare, One Abele Blvd., Clifton Park, 12065. Tel: 518-371-1400; Email: m18104@sphp.com; Web: schuylerridge.org. Freddy Makoyi, Dir. Bed Capacity 120; Tot Asst. Annually 336; Total Staff 196.

[I] SERVICES FOR ELDERLY

GERMANTOWN. *The Carmelite System, Inc.*, 646 Woods Rd., Germantown, 12526-5617. Tel: 518-537-7500; Fax: 518-537-7501; Email: xsusansan@carmelitesystem.org; Web: Carmelitesystem.org. Mother M. Mark Louis Anne Randall, O.Carm., Chair.

TROY. *Eddy Licensed Home Care Agency*, 433 River St., Troy, 12180. Tel: 518-274-6200; Fax: 518-274-2908 ; Email: michelle.mazzacco@sphp.com; Web: www.sphp.com. Michelle Mazzacco, Vice Pres. Community Svcs. & Hospice.

[J] NURSING AND AGED HOMES

ALBANY. *McAuley Living Services* Closed 40 N. Main Ave., 12203-1422. Tel: 518-453-6600.

Teresian House (1974) 200 Washington Ave. Ext., 12203. Tel: 518-456-2000; Fax: 518-456-1142; Web: www.teresianhouse.com. Sr. Robert Mullen, O.-Carm., Admin.; Rev. Jeffrey L'Arche, M.S., B.S., S.T.B., Chap.; Sandy Leboeuf, Dir. Pastoral Care. Sponsorship: Roman Catholic Diocese of Albany-Corporate Title: Teresian House Nursing Home Co., Inc.; Served by: Carmelite Sisters for the Aged and Infirm Bed Capacity 300; Respite Beds 2.

Teresian House Foundation.

Villa Mary Immaculate dba St. Peter's Nursing & Rehabilitation Center, 301 Hackett Blvd., 12208. Tel: 518-525-7600; Fax: 518-525-7673; Email: kathleen.jones@sphp.com; Web: www.sphp.com. Kathleen Jones, Exec. Dir. Bed Capacity 160; Tot Asst. Annually 650; Total Staff 250.

AMSTERDAM. *Mt. Loretto Nursing Home* Closed 40 N. Main Ave., 12203-1422. Tel: 518-453-6600. Mr. Brian Chamberlin, Admin.

CASTLETON. *Resurrection Nursing Home* Closed 40 N. Main Ave., 12203. Tel: 518-453-6600; Fax: 518-453-6793.

CATSKILL. *St. Joseph's Villa Senior Living Services*, Pastoral Center, Diocese of Albany, 40 N. Main Ave., 12203-1422.

CLIFTON PARK. *Schuyler Ridge - The Eddy*, One Abele Dr., Clifton Park, 12065. Tel: 518-371-1400; Fax: 518-371-1240; Email: christine.urbano@sphp.com; Web: schuylerridge.org. Christine Urbano, Exec. Dir. Bed Capacity 120; Tot Asst. Annually 220; Total Staff 250.

GERMANTOWN. *Avila Institute of Gerontology, Inc.*, 600 Woods Rd., Germantown, 12526. Tel: 518-537-5000 ; Fax: 518-537-4725; Email: srpeter@avilainstitute.org; Web: www.avilainstitute.org. Sisters M. Jeanne Francis Haley, O.Carm., Pres.; Peter Lillian, O.Carm., Dir. Carmelite Sisters for the Aged and Infirm.(Educational Institute) Provides education and seminars and develops curricula, etc., on aging issues.

GUILDERLAND. *Our Lady of Mercy Life Center*, 2 Mercycare Ln., Guilderland, 12084. Tel: 518-464-8100; Fax: 518-464-8111; Email: sandra.sullivansmith@sphp.com; Web: www.sphp.com. Sandra Sullivan Smith, Exec. Dir. Bed Capacity 160; Tot Asst. Annually 252.

LATHAM. *Our Lady of Hope Residence*, 40 N. Main Ave., 12203.

[K] APARTMENTS FOR ELDERLY

ALBANY. *Bishop Broderick Apartments Housing Development Fund Co., Inc.* dba Bishop Broderick Apts., 50 Prescott St., 12205. Tel: 518-869-7441; Fax: 518-869-0443; Email: bpaul@depaulhousing.com; Web: www.depaulhousing.com. Jill McLellan Phelps, Dir.; Barbara J. Paul, Community Mgr. Affordable housing for seniors and people with physical disabilities.

C.S.C. Housing Development Fund Co., Inc. dba Sanderson Court Senior Apts., 6 Carondelet Dr., Watervliet, 12189. Tel: 518-782-1123; Fax: 518-782-1125; Web: www.depaulhousing.com. Jessica Shellhamer, Dir. Affordable housing for seniors.

Cusack Community Service Corporation, 40 N. Main Ave., 12203. Tel: 518-459-0183; Fax: 518-459-0202; Email: deborah.dammobrien@rcda.org. Deborah Damm O'Brien, Exec. Dir.

DePaul Housing Management Corp., 41 N. Main Ave., 12203. Tel: 518-459-0183; Fax: 518-459-0202; Email: diocesan.housing@rcda.org; Web: www.depaulhousing.com. Ms. Mary Beth Purcell, Exec.; Jill McLellan Phelps, Dir. Affordable Housing Admin. Managing diocesan sponsored housing for persons who are elderly or mobility impaired.

Teresian House Housing Corporation dba Avila, 100 White Pine Dr., 12203. Tel: 518-640-9400; Email: ffoley@avilaretirement.com; Web: www.avilaretirementcommunity.com. Francis X. Foley Jr., CEO. 168 Apartments, 24 Cottages.

St. Vincent Apartments Housing Development Fund Co., Inc., 475 Yates St., 12208. Tel: 518-482-8915; Fax: 518-489-1220; Email: lcaroccia@depaulhousing.com; Web: www.depaulhousing.com. Jill McLellan Phelps, Dir.; Lorraine Caroccia, Community Mgr. Affordable housing for seniors and people with physical disabilities. Total Apartments 59.

CLIFTON PARK. *Halfmoon Housing Development Fund Co., Inc.* dba Bishop Hubbard Senior Apartments, 54 Katherine Dr., Clifton Park, 12065. Tel: 518-383-2705; Fax: 518-383-6350; Web: www.depaulhousing.com. Jill McLellan Phelps, Dir.; Jessica Shellhamer, Mgr. Affordable housing for seniors and people with physical disabilities. Total Apartments 49.

DELHI. *Delhi Housing Development Fund Co., Inc. I and II* dba Delhi Senior Community, 7 Main St., Delhi, 13753. Tel: 607-746-8142; Fax: 607-746-6546; Email: mary.thompson@depaulhousing.com; Web: www.depaulhousing.com. Jill McLellan Phelps, Dir.; Mary Thompson, Mgr. Total Apartments 45.

RENSSELAER. *East Greenbush Housing Development Fund Co., Inc.* dba Branson Manor Senior Apartments, 3 Grandview Dr., Rensselaer, 12144. Tel: 518-283-8280; Fax: 518-283-8292; Email: bweatherwax@depaulhousing.com; Web: www.depaulhousing.com. Jill McLellan Phelps, Dir.; Barbara Weatherwax, Community Mgr. Affordable housing for seniors and people with physical disabilities. Total Apartments 49.

Franciscan Heights Community Service Corp. dba Franciscan Heights Senior Community, 1 St. Anthony Ln., Rensselaer, 12144. Tel: 518-432-3555 ; Fax: 518-432-3553; Web: www.depaulhousing.com. Jill McLellan Phelps, Dir.; Laurie Bender, Mgr. Apartments and Cottages 85.

ROTTERDAM. *Rotterdam Housing Development Fund Co., Inc.* dba Father Leo O'Brien Senior Community, 3151 Marra Ln., Schenectady, 12303. Tel: 518-357-4424; Fax: 518-357-9377; Email: jmills@depaulhousing.com; Web: www.depaulhousing.com. Jill McLellan Phelps, Dir.; Julie Mills, Mgr. Affordable housing for seniors. Total Apartments 49.

SCHENECTADY. *LCS Housing Development Fund Company, Inc.* dba The Lawrence Commons, 2660 Albany St., Schenectady, 12304. Tel: 518-393-2412; Fax: 518-346-2686; Email: jmills@depaulhousing.com; Web: www.depaulhousing.com. Jill McLellan Phelps, Dir.; Julie Mills, Mgr. Affordable housing for people with physical disabilities. Apartments 12.

SLINGERLANDS. *Marie-Rose Manor HDFCI*, 100 Marquis Dr., Slingerlands, 12159. Tel: 518-459-0204; Fax: 518-459-0527; Email: nichole.davis@rcda.org; Web: www.depaulhousing.com. Jill McLellan Phelps, Dir.; Nichole Davis, Mgr. Affordable housing for seniors. Total Apartments 49.

WATERVLIET. *Delatour Housing Development Fund Company, Inc.* dba Carondelet Commons Senior Apartments, 2 Carondelet Dr., Watervliet, 12189. Tel: 518-783-0444; Fax: 518-783-0456; Email: jessica.shellhamer@rcda.org; Web: www.depaulhousing.com. Jill McLellan Phelps, Dir.; Jessica Shellhamer, Sr. Property Mgr. Affordable housing for seniors and people with physical disabilities. Total Apartments 49.

Fontbonne Manor Housing Development Fund Company, Inc. dba Fontbonne Manor Senior Apts., 10 Carondelet Dr., Watervliet, 12189. Tel: 518-782-2780; Fax: 518-782-2778; Web: www.depaulhousing.com. Jill McLellan Phelps, Dir.; Jessica Shellhamer, Mgr. Affordable housing for seniors. Total Apartments 49.

Italian-American Housing Development Fund Co., Inc. dba Cabrini Acers Senior Apts., 4 Carondelet Dr., Watervliet, 12189. Tel: 518-785-0050; Fax: 518-785-0110; Email: jessica.shellhamer@rcda.org; Web: www.depaulhousing.com. Jessica Shellhamer, Sr. Property Mgr. Affordable housing for seniors and people with physical disabilities. Total Apartments 49. Wynantskill

S.J. Housing Development Fund Company, Inc. dba St. Jude's Apartments, 50 Dana Ave., Wynantskill, 12198. Tel: 518-283-5690; Fax: 518-283-5893; Email: bweatherwax@depaulhousing.com; Web: www.depaulhousing.com. Jill McLellan Phelps, Dir.; Barbara Weatherwax, Community Mgr. Affordable housing for seniors and people with physical disabilities. Apartments 49.

[L] MONASTERIES AND RESIDENCES OF PRIESTS AND BROTHERS

ALBANY. *Vincentian Fathers Residence*, 96 Menands Rd., 12204-1499. Tel: 518-462-1811; Email: revlasma@yahoo.com. Rev. Lawrence F. Asma, C.M. Priests 1.

RENSSELAER. *Franciscan Mission House*, 517 Washington Ave., Rensselaer, 12144. Tel: 518-465-0062; Fax: 518-472-1013; Email: fmadirector@gmail.com; Web: www.thefma.org. Rev. Antone Kandrac, O.F.M.Conv.; Bro. Leo Merriman, O.F.M.Conv. Promotion Center for Order's Missions.

Immaculate Conception Friary - Order of Friars Minor Conventual (1872) (Immaculate Conception Province) 75 St. Francis Pl., P.O. Box 629, Rensselaer, 12144. Tel: 518-472-1007; Fax: 518-472-1013; Email: provsec1@olaprovince.org; Web: www.olaprovince.org. Revs. Anthony Kall, O.F.M.Conv., Guardian; Alvin Somerville, O.-F.M.Conv., (Retired); Firmin Finn, O.F.M.Conv., Chap.; Giles Van Wormer, O.F.M. Conv., (Retired); Bro. Andre Picotte, O.F.M.Conv. (Corporate Name: Order Minor Conventuals, Inc.).

VALATIE. *Brothers of Holy Cross of the Eastern Province of the United States of America, Inc.*, 495 Maple Ln., Valatie, 12184. Tel: 512-442-7856, Ext. 303; Email: financemoreau@gmail.com. Mark Knightly, Sec.; Bro. William Zaydak, Pres.

St. Joseph Center Residence for retired Holy Cross Brothers and Priests. 495 Maple Ln., Valatie, 12184. Tel: 518-784-9481; Fax: 518-784-9494; Email: sjcval@gmail.com. Rev. Robert E. DeLeon, C.S.C., Pastoral Care Albany Medical Center & Chap., St. Joseph Center.

[M] CONVENTS AND RESIDENCES FOR SISTERS

ALBANY. *Daughters of Charity of St. Vincent de Paul* Home for the Senior Sisters of the Daughters of Charity of St. Vincent de Paul 96 Menand Rd., 12204-1499. Tel: 518-462-1811; Fax: 518-429-2050; Email: tom.beck@doc.org. Sr. Margaret Tuley, Supr. Sisters 34.

Daughters of Charity of St. Vincent de Paul House, 96 Menand Rd., 12204-1499. Tel: 518-462-5593; Fax: 518-429-2050; Email: tom.beck@doc.org; Web: www.daughtersofcharity.org. Sr. Rose Ann Aguilar, Supr. Sisters 17.

Religious of the Sacred Heart, 128 W. Lawrence St., 12203. Tel: 518-489-8280.

Sisters of Mercy of the Americas - Northeast Community, 634 New Scotland Ave., 12208. Tel: 518-437-3000; Fax: 518-437-3030. Sisters M. Kathleen Pritty, R.S.M., Local Coord.; Mary Ann LoGiudice, R.S.M., Local Coord. Sisters 82.

Sisters of the Holy Names of Jesus and Mary, U.S. - Ontario Province, Regional Center, 360 Whitehall Rd., #122, 12208. Tel: 503-675-7123; Fax: 503-675-7138; Email: vcummings@snjmuson.org; Web: www.snjmusontario.org. Sr. Maureen Delaney, S.N.J.M., Prov., Prov. (Corporate Name: Sisters of the Holy Names of Jesus and Mary of the New York Province, Inc.) Sisters 25.

CASTLETON ON HUDSON. *Provincial House, Juniorate and Novitiate of the Sisters of the Resurrection*, 35 Boltwood Ave., Castleton On Hudson, 12033-1097. Tel: 518-732-2226; Fax: 518-732-2898; Email: crsister@resurrectionsisters.org; Web: www.resurrectionsisters.org. Sisters Dolores Stepien, C.R., Prov. Supr.; Alexandra Jazwinski, C.R.; Dolores Palermo, C.R., Dir. Novices

Sisters of the Resurrection, N.Y., Inc. Sisters 30.

Chaplain's Residence, 34 Boltwood Ave., Castleton On Hudson, 12033.

Retreat and Vacation Home, 325 Madonna Lake Rd., Cropseyville, 12052-1819. Tel: 518-279-1673.

DELMAR. *Mill Hill Sisters Franciscan House* Regional House 703 Derzee Ct., Delmar, 12054. Tel: 518-512-4362; Fax: 518-512-4362; Email: jdever001@nycap.rr.com. Sr. Judith Dever, F.M.S.J., Admin. Sisters 2.

GERMANTOWN. *St. Teresa's Motherhouse*, Avila on the Hudson: 600 Woods Rd., Germantown, 12526-5639. Tel: 518-537-5000; Fax: 518-537-5226; Email: smrc@stmhcs.org; Web: www.carmelitesisters.com. Mother M. Mark Louis Anne Randall, O.Carm., Prioress Gen.; Rev. James Hess, Chap. Carmelite Sisters for the Aged and Infirm. Motherhouse and Novitiate. Sisters 30.

Postulation Office aka Venerable Mary Angeline Teresa McCrory, O.Carm., Germantown. Tel: 518-537-5000; Fax: 518-537-5226. Mother M. Angeline Teresa, O.Carm., Servant of God; Rev. Mario Esposito, O.Carm., Vice Postulator; Andrea Ambrosi, Postulator.

LATHAM. *Sisters of St. Joseph of Carondelet (Albany Province)*, St. Joseph's Provincial House, 385 Watervliet-Shaker Rd., Latham, 12110-4799. Tel: 518-783-3500; Fax: 518-783-3672; Web: www.csjalbany.org. Rev. Geoffrey D. Burke, Chap.; Sisters Mary Anne Heenan, C.S.J., Province Leadership Team-Prov. Dir.; Kathleen Eiffe, C.S.J., Province Leadership Team-Exec. Committee; Jeanne Marie Gocha, C.S.J., Province Leadership Team; Sean Peters, C.S.J., Province Leadership Team; Katherine Arseneau, C.S.J., Province Leadership Team; Eileen McCann, C.S.J., Province Leadership Team-1st. Councilor & Treas. Sisters 288.

WATERVLIET. *St. Colman's Convent*, 11 Haswell Rd., Watervliet, 12189. Tel: 518-273-4911; Fax: 518-273-3312. Mother Mary Carmel, First Councillor Admin. Motherhouse and Novitiate of Sisters of the Presentation of the B.V.M.

[N] HOUSES OF PRAYER AND RETREAT HOUSES

AURIESVILLE. *Shrine of Our Lady of Martyrs*, Rte. 5S, Fultonville, 12072. Tel: 518-630-9922; Email: friendsofauriesville@gmail.com; Web: www.auriesvilleshrine.com. 136 Shrine Rd., Fultonville, 12072. National Shrine of the Jesuit Martyrs of North America.

CHESTERTOWN. *The Priory of St. Benedict, Inc.*, 135 Priory Rd., P.O. Box 336, Chestertown, 12817-0336. Tel: 518-494-3733; Email: office@prioryretreathouse.org; Web: www.prioryretreathouse.org. Dustin Katona, Exec. Dir.

LAKE GEORGE. *St. Mary on the Lake*, 3535 State Route 9L, Lake George, 12845. Tel: 518-668-5594; Email: frankd@paulist.org; Web: www.stmaryslakegeorge.com. Rev. Frank Desiderio, Dir. Summer retreat of the Paulist Fathers.

MIDDLEBURGH. *Bethany Ministries*, 104 Grove St., Apt. 2, P.O. Box 432, Middleburgh, 12212. Tel: 518-827-4699; Email: bethmin@midtel.net; Web: www.bethmin.org. Rev. Peter Chepaitis, O.F.M., Dir.

PARADOX. *Pyramid Life Center* Corporation Name: Albany Catholic Youth Association, Inc. Box 103, Paradox, 12858. 1 Pyramid Rd., Paradox, 12858. Tel: 518-585-7545; Fax: 518-585-7545; Email: monicaplc@aol.com; Web: www.pyramidlife.org. Sr. Monica Murphy, C.S.J., Dir. Summer, fall and winter retreat house, located at Pyramid Lake.

QUEENSBURY. *Wellsprings Outreach*, 230 Robert Gardens N., #5, Queensbury, 12804. Tel: 518-745-1617; Email: laratondafms@yahoo.com; Web: www.wellspringsoutreach.org. Bro. Michael Laratonda, B.A., M.A., Certified Spiritual Dir. & Hospital Chap. Programs in Spirituality (Holistic Retreats & Workshops Chapter Facilitation for Religious Congregations, Spiritual Direction).

SCHENECTADY. *Dominican Retreat and Conference Center*, 1945 Union St., Schenectady, 12309. Tel: 518-393-4169; Fax: 518-393-4525; Email: dslcny@nybiz.rr.com; Web: www.dslcny.org. Sr. Susan M. Zemgulis, O.P., Admin. Residence Facilities for 50; Non-resident Facilities for 90 to 100.

UNADILLA. *Gilead, Inc.* Closed 40 N. Main Ave., 12203.

VALATIE. *St. Joseph Center*, 495 Maple Ln., Valatie, 12184. Tel: 518-784-9481; Fax: 518-784-9494; Email: sjcval@gmail.com; Web: www.stjosephcentervalatie.org. Bro. Mark Knightly, C.S.C., B.A., M.A., M.S.W.

[O] YOUTH TREATMENT FACILITIES

ALBANY. *Hospitality House Therapeutic Community Inc.*, 271 Central Ave., 12206. Tel: 518-434-6468; Fax: 518-434-6302; Web: www.hospitalityhousetc.org. Young Do, Exec. Dir.; Linda Smith, Dir. Opers. A private, not-for-profit, intensive residential treatment program for males, 18 years or older, with a history of drug and/or substance abuse.

ALTAMONT. *Bernard and Caroline Cobb Memorial School*, 11 Haswell Road, Watervliet, 12189. Tel: 518-861-6446; Tel: 518-273-4911; Fax: 518-273-3312.

[P] SHRINES

FONDA. *The National Shrine of Saint Kateri Tekakwitha and Friary*, 3636 State Hwy. 5, P.O. Box 627, Fonda, 12068. Tel: 518-853-3646; Email: nationalkaterishrine@gmail.com; Web: www.katerishrine.com. Rev. Tony Kall, O.F.M.Conv., Chap.; Bill Jacobs, Shrine Dir.

[Q] CAMPUS MINISTRY

ALBANY. *University at Albany, State University of New York* (Albany Collegiate Interfaith Center, Inc.) with offices at The Interfaith Center. 1400 Washington Ave., 12222. Tel: 518-489-8573, Ext. 22; Fax: 518-489-8575; Email: creid@albany.edu. Catherine Reid, Campus Min.

COBLESKILL. *State University of New York College of Agricultural & Technology at Cobleskill*, St. Vincent DePaul Church, 138 Washington Ave., Cobleskill, 12043. Tel: 518-234-2892. Sr. Connie James, S.N.D., Campus Min.

GLENS FALLS. *Adirondack Community College*, c/o 40 N. Main Ave., 12203. Tel: 518-793-9677.

LOUDONVILLE. *Siena College*, Office of the College Chaplain: 515 Loudon Rd., Loudonville, 12211. Tel: 518-783-2332; Fax: 518-783-2549; Email: chaplainsoffice@siena.edu; Web: www.siena.edu. Kate Kaufman-Burns, Dir. of Liturgical Arts; Rev. Larry Anderson, O.F.M., Chap.; Colleen Sheedy, Asst.

ONEONTA. *Newman Clubs - SUNY Oneonta and Hartwick College*, Newman House: 77 Spruce St., Oneonta, 13820. Tel: 518-791-8095. Peter Derway, Campus Min. Corporate Title: Oneonta Newman Catholic Community.

SARATOGA. *Skidmore College*, 815 N. Broadway, Saratoga, 12866. Tel: 518-580-8340; Email: kdiggory@skidmore.edu. Parker Diggory, Dir.

SCHENECTADY. *Catholic Chaplain, Union College*, Reamer Campus Center #203, 807 Union St., Schenectady, 12308-3152. Tel: 518-388-6087; Email: stagliad@union.edu; Web: www.union.edu/studentlife/religious_programs/ catholic. David Stagliano, Campus Min.

TROY. *Hudson Valley Community College*, 80 Vandenburgh Ave., Troy, 12180. Tel: 518-629-7168; Web: www.hvcc.edu. Michelle Thivierge, Campus Min.

The Rensselaer Newman Foundation, 110 Eighth St., Troy, 12180. Tel: 518-276-6518; Fax: 518-274-5945; Email: fred@rpi.edu; Web: www.christsunofjustice.org. Rev. Edward Kacerguis, Chap.

University Parish of Christ Sun of Justice, 2125 Burdett Ave., Troy, 12180. Tel: 518-274-7793; Fax: 518-274-5945. Rev. Edward Kacerguis.

Chapel + Cultural Center, 10 Tom Phelan Pl., Troy, 12180. Tel: 518-274-7793; Fax: 518-274-5945; Email: fred@rpi.edu. Rev. Edward Kacerguis.

Russell Sage College, 65 1st St., Troy, 12180. Tel: 518-244-4507; Email: george2@sage.edu. Michelle Thirvierge, Campus Min.

[R] MISCELLANEOUS LISTINGS

ALBANY. *Assisi in Albany, Inc.*, c/o First Lutheran Church: 646 State St., 2nd Fl., 12203. Tel: 518-391-2675; Fax: 518-472-1013; Email: assisiinalbany@yahoo.com; Web: www.assisiinalbany.com. Rev. Anthony Kall, O.F.M.-Conv.; Pamela Bullock, Dir.

Broderick Community Service Organization, 40 N. Main Ave., 12203-1422. Tel: 518-453-6623. Paul A. Ehmann.

Burke Community Service Corp., Inc., 40 N. Main Ave., 12203. Tel: 518-453-6623; Fax: 518-641-6825; Email: paul.ehmann@rcda.org. Paul A. Ehmann, Contact Person.

Care for Life Foundation, 40 N. Main Ave., 12203-1422. Tel: 518-453-6650. Joseph Profit, Contact Person.

The Cathedral Restoration Corp., 40 N. Main Ave., 12203. Tel: 518-463-4447; Fax: 518-436-5177; Email: ecathedra@nycap.rr.com. Rev. William H. Pape, Sec. & Treas., (Retired).

Crusade for Family Prayer, Inc., Albany Diocesan Pastoral Center, 40 N. Main Ave., 12203. Tel: 800-299-7729; Fax: 508-238-3953. Rev. Wilfred Raymond, C.S.C. Sponsored by Congregation of Holy Cross.

Diocesan AIDS Services, 100 Slingerland St., 12202. Tel: 518-449-3581; Fax: 518-426-3662. Stephanie Lao, Exec. Dir.

Diocesan Investment and Loan Trust, 40 N. Main Ave., 12203-1422. Tel: 518-641-6948; Email: virginia.kunkel@rcda.org. Very Rev. David R. LeFort, S.T.L., V.G., Trustee.

Emmaus House, 45 Trinity Pl., 12202. Tel: 518-482-4966. Fred Boehrer, Co-Dir.; Diana Conroy, Co-Dir. Albany Catholic Worker Community. Bed Capacity 8; Tot Asst. Annually 200; Total Staff 12.

The Family Rosary, Inc., Albany Diocesan Pastoral Center, 40 N. Main Ave., 12203. Tel: 508-238-4095; Fax: 508-238-3953; Email: cslattery@hcfm.org; Web: www.familyrosary.org. Rev. Wilfred Raymond, C.S.C., Pres.; Cindy Slattery, CFO; Laetitia Rhatigan, Contact Person. Sponsored by Congregation of Holy Cross.

Family Theater Ministries, Albany Diocesan Pastoral Center, 40 N. Main Ave., 12203. Tel: 800-299-7729; Fax: 508-238-3953. Rev. Wilfred Raymond, C.S.C. Sponsored by Congregation of Holy Cross.

The Foundation of the Roman Catholic Diocese of Albany, New York, Inc., 40 N. Main Ave., 12203. Tel: 518-453-6657; Fax: 518-453-8440.

St. Francis Chapel St. Francis Chapel (Albany), Franciscan Friars-Holy Name Province, Inc., Wolf Road Shoppers Park: 145A Wolf Rd., 12205. Tel: 518-459-2854; Fax: 518-783-4195; Web: sites.google.com/site/stfrancischapel/. Order of Friars Minor Province of the Most Holy Name of Jesus.

Legal Title: St. Francis Chapel (Albany), Franciscan Friars-Holy Name Province, Inc.

Holy Cross International, Inc., Congregation of Holy Cross International, Inc., c/o Pastoral Center, 40 N. Main Ave., 12203. Tel: 518-463-1177; Email: selgas1967@gmail.com.

Korean Apostolate of the Roman Catholic Diocese of Albany, 15 Exchange St., 12202. Tel: 518-438-1805 . Rev. Jaeung Damian Lee, Chap.

LaSalle Albany, Inc., Christian Brothers Academy, 12 Airline Dr., 12205. Tel: 518-452-9809; Fax: 518-452-9804; Email: schlegel@cbaalbany.org; Web: www.cbaalbany.org. Dr. James Schlegel, Head of School.

McCloskey Community Service Corporation, 41 N. Main Ave., 12203. Tel: 518-459-0183; Fax: 518-459-0202; Email: Diocesan.Housing@rcda.org. Mr. Thomas Coates, Exec.

Mill Hill Sisters Charitable Trust, 703 Derzee Ct., Delmar, 12054. Tel: 518-512-4362; Email: jdever001@nycap.rr.com. Sr. Judith Dever, F.M.S.J., Admin.

New York State Catholic Conference, 465 State St., 12203. Tel: 518-434-6195; Fax: 518-434-9796; Email: info@nyscatholic.org; Web: www.nyscatholic.org. Richard E. Barnes, Exec. Dir.

Noonan Community Service Corporation, c/o Chancery Office, 40 N. Main Ave., 12203-1422. Tel: 518-453-6641; Fax: 518-453-8454. c/o Chancery Office.

St. Peter's Auxiliary, St. Peter's Health Partners, 315 S. Manning Blvd., 12208. Tel: 518-525-1515; Email: jane.norris@sphp.com; Web: www.sphp.com. Jane Norris, Dir.

Seton Health Foundation, Inc., 310 S. Manning Blvd., 12208. Tel: 518-482-4433; Fax: 518-482-4593; Email: peter.semenza@sphp.

com; Web: setonhealth.org. Peter D. Semenza, Vice Pres. Philanthropy.

Sisters of the Holy Names of Jesus & Mary of the New York Province, Inc., 1121 New Scotland Ave., 12208-1198. Tel: 503-675-7125; Fax: 503-675-7138. Mrs. Vicki Cummings, Treas. Continuing Support Charitable Trust to provide for the needs of the Tutwiler Clinic, Tutwiler, Mississippi.

St. Peter's Hospital Foundation, Inc., 310 S. Manning Blvd., 12208. Tel: 518-482-4433; Fax: 518-482-4593; Email: shannon.galuski@sphp.com; Web: www.sphp.com. Shannon Galuski, Exec. Dir.

Support Fund Trust of the Province of St. Thomas of Villanova, c/o 40 N. Main Ave., 12203.

The Community Hospice Foundation, Inc., 295 Valley View Blvd., Rensselaer, 12144. Email: smanny@communityhospice.org; Web: www.communityhospice.org. St. Peter's Health Partners, 315 S. Manning Blvd., 12208. Tel: 518-482-4433. Stephen J. Manny, Exec. Dir.

CASTLETON ON HUDSON. *Cooperative Christian Ministries of Schodack, Inc* aka CCMS The Anchor, 92 S. Main St., Castleton On Hudson, 12033-0092. Tel: 518-732-4120. Formal Name: C.C.M. of Schodack.

GERMANTOWN. *Carmelite Sisters of the Aged and Infirm Continuing Care Trust*, 600 Woods Rd., Germantown, 12526. Tel: 518-537-5000; Email: srvrobert@stmhcs.org. Mother M. Mark Louis Anne Randall, O.Carm., Trustee.

Oneness in Peace Center, Inc., 49 Main St., Germantown, 12526-5328. Tel: 518-537-5678; Email: rccgtown@gmail.com. Sr. Vergilia Jim, O.S.F., Dir., Prog. Presenter & Peace Educator Consultant; Claire Langie.

GLENVILLE. *Albany, New York Chapter of Magnificat, Inc.*, P.O. Box 340, Clifton Park, 12065. 5 Valleywood Dr., Glenville, 12302. Tel: 518-810-1310; Email: albanymagnificat@gmail.com; Web: magnificat-ministry.net/chapters/chapter-states-n/ny-albany/. Diane Bigos, Contact Person.

LATHAM. *The Sister M. Athanasia Gurry Trust Fund of the Sisters of St. Joseph*, 385 Watervliet-Shaker Rd., Latham, 12110-4799. Tel: 518-783-3519; Fax: 518-783-1123; Email: LMB@csjalbany.org. Sisters Eileen McCann, C.S.J., Treas.; Mary Anne Heenan, C.S.J., Pres.

MENANDS. *Catholic Cemeteries of the Roman Catholic Diocese of Albany, New York*, 48 Cemetery Ave., Menands, 12204. Tel: 518-432-4953; Fax: 518-427-8035. Richard Touchette, Exec. Dir.

Medicus Christi, LTD, 16 MacAffer Dr., Menands, 12204-1208. Tel: 518-772-5119; Email: marottaghana@aol.com.

NISKAYUNA. *Villa Fusco Child Day Care (Pre-K)*, 955 Balltown Rd., Niskayuna, 12309. Tel: 518-377-1613; Fax: 518-377-1613; Email: sharmilamathew@77gmail.com. Sharmila Mathew, Supr. Daughters of Charity of the Most Precious Blood. Capacity 16; Clergy 4; Students 16.

NORTH CREEK. *North Country Ministry, Inc.*, Leaven House, 32 Circle Ave., P.O. Box 111, North Creek, 12853. Tel: 518-251-4460 (North Creek); Tel: 518-623-2829 (Warrensburg); Fax: 518-251-5483; Email: ncm32@frontier.com. Bro. James Posluszny, C.S.C., Dir.

RENSSELAER. *Circles of Mercy, Inc.*, 11 Washington St., Ste. A, Rensselaer, 12144. Tel: 518-462-0899; Fax: 518-462-2892; Email: circlesofmercy@nycap.rr.com; Web: www.circlesofmercy.org. Richard S. Zazycki, Exec. Dir.

Franciscans in Collaborative Ministry, Inc., 517 Washington Ave., Rensselaer, 12144. Tel: 518-472-1000; Fax: 518-472-1013. Very Rev. James McCurry, O.F.M.Conv., Minister Prov.

Franciscorps, Inc., 571 Washington Ave., Rensselaer, 12144. Tel: 518-472-1000; Fax: 518-472-1013; Email: francorps@gmail.com; Web: www.olaprovince.org.

Order of Friars Minor Conventual Immaculate Conception Province Charitable Trust (Established 1990) P.O. Box 629, Rensselaer, 12144. Tel: 518-472-1000; Fax: 518-472-1013; Email: treasurer1@olaprovince.org; Web: www.olaprovince.org. Rev. Mitchell Sawicki.

SCHENECTADY. *Christ Child Society of Albany*, 2922 W. Old State Rd., Schenectady, 12303. Tel: 518-356-1058. Jeanette M. May, Pres.

Secular Order of Discalced Carmelites, 104 Midline Rd., Ballston Lake, 12019. Tel: 518-248-4291; Email: secularcarmelit@gmail.com. P.O. Box 408, Schenectady, 12301. Joyce A. Panserella, Pres.

TROY. *Catholic School Administrators' Association of New York State*, P.O. Box 487, Waterford, 12188. Tel: 518-273-1205; Fax: 518-273-1206; Email: csaanys@nycap.rr.com; Web: www.csaanys.org. Carol Geddis, Exec. Dir.

Seton Auxiliary, Inc., 1300 Massachusetts Ave., Troy, 12180. Tel: 518-268-5505; Email: colleen.rouche@sphp.com; Web: sphp.com. Colleen P. Roche, Mgr. Community Educ. & Volunteers.

VALATIE. *Moreau Province Charitable Trust*, 495 Maple Ln., Valatie, 12184. Tel: 203-937-3250; Email: gcscsc@gmail.com. Bro. George Schmitz, Chm.

[S] SUMMER CAMPS

ALBANY. *Camp Scully*, 40 N. Main Ave., 12203. Tel: 518-453-6613; Tel: 518-283-1617 (Synders Lake); Fax: 518-453-6792; Email: campscully@ccalbany.org; Web: campscully.squarespace.com. Summer Address, 24 Camp Scully Way, Wynantskill, 12198. Colin Stewart, Dir. A program of Catholic Charities of the Diocese of Albany; Day & resident camp for children 5-17. Under direction of Catholic Charities of the Diocese of Albany. Financed by local Youth Bureaus, the Albany Catholic Diocese, USDA Summer Program and by contributions. For day camp per week 80.

TROY. *Troy CYO Day Camp*, 237 Fourth St., Box 867, Troy, 12180. Tel: 518-274-2630; Fax: 518-274-2734 ; Email: rpisci2624@aol.com. Raymond R. Piscitelli, Exec. Dir. Sponsored by Troy Youth Organization, Inc. for Boys and Girls, ages 5-12 yrs.

RELIGIOUS INSTITUTES OF MEN REPRESENTED IN THE DIOCESE

For further details refer to the corresponding bracketed number in the Religious Institutes of Men or Women section.

[0140]—*The Augustinians*—O.S.A.
[0330]—*Brothers of the Christian Schools* (New York Prov.)—F.S.C.
[0600]—*Brothers of the Congregation of Holy Cross* (Eastern Prov.)—C.S.C.
[2070]—*Carmelite Fathers*—O.Carm.
[1330]—*Congregation of the Mission* (Eastern Prov.)—C.M.
[0520]—*Franciscan Friars* (Immaculate Conception Prov.)—O.F.M.
[0480]—*Friars Minor Conventual* (Prov. of Immaculate Conception)—O.F.M.Conv.
[0690]—*Jesuit Fathers and Brothers* (New York Prov.)—S.J.
[0720]—*The Missionaries of Our Lady of La Salette* (Prov. of Our Lady of Seven Dolors)—M.S.
[0520]—*Order of Friars Minor* (Most Holy Name Prov.)—O.F.M.
[1070]—*Redemptorist Fathers* (Baltimore Prov.)—C.Ss.R.

RELIGIOUS INSTITUTES OF WOMEN REPRESENTED IN THE DIOCESE

[0330]—*Carmelite Sisters for the Aged and Infirm*—O.Carm.
[2980]—*Congregation of Notre Dame*—C.N.D.
[0760]—*Daughters of Charity of St. Vincent de Paul*—D.C.
[0740]—*Daughters of Charity of the Most Precious Blood*—D.C.P.B.
[1070-05]—*Dominican Sisters of Amityville*—O.P.
[1115]—*Dominican Sisters of Peace*—O.P.
[]—*Holy Union Sisters*—S.U.S.C.
[]—*Mill Hill Franciscan Missionaries of St. Joseph*—F.M.S.J.
[4180]—*Religious Venerini Sisters*—M.P.V.
[2970]—*School Sisters of Notre Dame*—S.S.N.D.
[]—*Sisters of the Good Shepherd*—R.G.S.
[1990]—*Sisters of the Holy Names of Jesus and Mary*—S.N.J.M.
[2575]—*Sisters of Mercy of the Americas* (Albany)—R.S.M.
[2990]—*Sisters of Notre Dame de Namur*—S.N.D.deN.
[3320]—*Sisters of the Presentation of the B.V.M.*—P.B.V.M.
[3480]—*Sisters of the Resurrection*—C.R.
[2160]—*Sister Servants of the Immaculate Heart of Mary* (Pennsylvania)—I.H.M.
[3840]—*Sisters of St. Joseph of Carondelet*—C.S.J.
[4070]—*Society of the Sacred Heart*—R.S.C.J.

DIOCESAN CEMETERIES

ALBANY. *Our Lady of Angels Cemetery*, 1389 Central Ave., 12205. Tel: 518-463-0134; Fax: 518-427-8035; Email: info@rcdacemeteries.org; Web: www.capitaldistrictcemeteries.org. Mailing Address: 48 Cemetery Ave., Menands, 12204. Richard Touchette, Dir.

COHOES. *St. Agnes Cemetery*, 79 St. Agnes Hwy., Cohoes, 12047. Tel: 518-463-0134; Fax: 518-427-8035; Email: info@rcdacemeteries.org; Web: www.capitaldistrictcemeteries.org. Mailing Address: 48 Cemetery Ave., Menands, 12204. Richard Touchette, Dir.

GLENMONT. *Calvary Cemetery*, 481 Rte. 9 W., Glenmont, 12077. Mailing Address: 48 Cemetery Ave., Menands, 12204. Tel: 518-463-0134; Fax: 518-427-8035; Email: info@rcdacemeteries.org; Web: www.capitaldistrictcemeteries.org. Richard Touchette, Dir.

Our Lady Help of Christians Cemetery, 41 Jolley Rd., Glenmont, 12077. Tel: 518-463-0134; Fax: 518-427-8035; Email: info@rcdacemeteries.org; Web: www.capitaldistrictcemeteries.org. Mailing Address: 48 Cemetery Ave., Menands, 12204. Richard Touchette, Dir.

GLENVILLE. *St. Anthony's Cemetery*, 27 Glenridge Rd., Glenville, 12302. Tel: 518-374-5319; Fax: 518-374-1820; Email: info@rcdacemeteries.org; Web: www.capitaldistrictcemeteries.org. Mailing Address: 48 Cemetery Ave., Menands, 12204. Richard Touchette, Dir.

MENANDS. *St. Agnes Cemetery*, 48 Cemetery Ave., Menands, 12204. Tel: 518-463-0134; Fax: 518-427-8035; Email: info@rcdacemeteries.org; Web: www.capitaldistrictcemeteries.org. Richard Touchette, Dir. Niskayuna

Most Holy Redeemer Cemetery, 2501 Troy Rd., Niskayuna, 12309. Tel: 518-374-5319; Fax: 518-374-1820; Email: info@rcdacemeteries.org; Web: www.capitaldistrictcemeteries.org. Mailing Address: 48 Cemetery Ave., Menands, 12204. Richard Touchette, Dir.

ROTTERDAM. *St. Cyril & St. Method Cemetery*, 611 Duanesburg Rd., Rotterdam, 12306. Tel: 518-374-5319; Fax: 518-374-1820; Email: info@rcdacemeteries.org; Web: www.capitaldistrictcemeteries.org. Mailing Address: 48 Cemetery Ave., Menands, 12204. Richard Touchette, Dir.

Holy Cross Cemetery, 1456 Dunnsville Rd., Rotterdam, 12306. Tel: 518-374-1820; Email: info@rcdacemeteries.org; Web: www.capitaldistrictcemeteries.org. Mailing Address: 48 Cemetery Ave., Menands, 12204. Richard Touchette, Dir.

SCHENECTADY. *St. Mary's Cemetery*, 738 McClellan St., Schenectady, 12304. Tel: 518-374-5319; Fax: 518-374-1820; Email: info@rcdacemeteries.org; Web: www.capitaldistrictcemeteries.org. Mailing Address: 48 Cemetery Ave., Menands, 12204. Richard Touchette, Dir.

TROY. *St. Jean Baptiste Cemetery*, 968 Spring Ave. Ext., Troy, 12180. Tel: 518-463-0134; Fax: 518-427-8035; Email: info@rcdacemeteries.org; Web: www.capitaldistrictcemeteries.org. Mailing Address: 48 Cemetery Ave., Menands, 12204. Richard Touchette, Dir.

St. John's Cemetery, 250 Cemetery Ave., Troy, 12180. Tel: 518-463-0134; Fax: 518-427-8035; Email: info@rcdacemeteries.org; Web: www.capitaldistrictcemeteries.org. Mailing Address: 48 Cemetery Ave., Menands, 12204. Richard Touchette, Dir.

St. Mary's Cemetery of Troy, Inc., 79 Brunswick Rd., Troy, 12180. Tel: 518-463-0134; Fax: 518-427-8035 ; Email: info@rcdacemeteries.org; Web: www.capitaldistrictcemeteries.org. Mailing Address: 48 Cemetery Ave., Menands, 12204. Richard Touchette, Dir.

WATERFORD. *St. Joseph's Cemetery*, 40 Middletown Rd., Waterford, 12188. Tel: 518-463-0134; Fax: 518-427-8035; Email: info@rcdacemeteries.org; Web: www.capitaldistrictcemeteries.org. Richard Touchette, Dir.

WATERVLIET. *Immaculate Conception Cemetery*, 29 Delatour Rd., Watervliet, 12189. Tel: 518-463-0134 ; Fax: 518-427-8035; Email: info@rcdacemeteries.org; Web: www.capitaldistrictcemeteries.org. Mailing Address: 48 Cemetery Ave., Menands, 12204. Richard Touchette, Dir.

St. Patrick Cemetery, 150 Troy Rd., Watervliet, 12189. Tel: 518-463-0134; Fax: 518-427-8035; Email: info@rcdacemeteries.org; Web: www.capitaldistrictcemeteries.org. Mailing Address: 48 Cemetery Ave., Menands, 12204. Richard Touchette, Dir.

NECROLOGY

† Dunbar, Francis, (Retired), Died Jul. 16, 2018
† Lefebvre, James, (Retired), Died Mar. 6, 2018
† Schweigardt, Erwin H., (Retired), Died Jul. 16, 2018

Diocese of Alexandria

(Dioecesis Alexandrina in Louisiana)

Most Reverend

GREGORY M. AYMOND

Archbishop of New Orleans and Apostolic Administrator of Alexandria; ordained May 10, 1975; ordained Auxiliary Bishop of New Orleans January 10, 1997; appointed Coadjutor Bishop of Austin June 2, 2000; installed Bishop of Austin August 3, 2000; appointed Archbishop of New Orleans June 12, 2009; Pallium conferred by Pope Benedict XVI at the Vatican June 29, 2009; installed Archbishop of New Orleans August 20, 2009; appointed Apostolic Administrator of Alexandria April 3, 2019.

(VACANT SEE)

Chancery Office: 4400 Coliseum Blvd., P.O. Box 7417, Alexandria, LA 71306. Tel: 318-445-2401 (Receptionist); Tel: 318-445-6424 (Auto Attendant); Fax: 318-448-6121.

Web: www.diocesealex.org

ERECTED AS DIOCESE OF NATCHITOCHES JULY 29, 1853.

Square Miles 11,108.

Transferred to Alexandria August 6, 1910 and became Diocese of Alexandria.

Redesignated Diocese of Alexandria-Shreveport on January 12, 1977; split, forming two Dioceses, the Diocese of Alexandria and the Diocese of Shreveport as of June 16, 1986.

Comprises the Counties (parishes) of Rapides, Avoyelles, Concordia, Catahoula, LaSalle, Grant, Natchitoches, Vernon, Tensas, Caldwell, Winn, Franklin and Madison.

For legal titles of parishes and diocesan institutions, consult the Chancery Office.

STATISTICAL OVERVIEW

Personnel	
Priests: Diocesan Active in Diocese	42
Priests: Diocesan Active Outside Diocese	5
Priests: Retired, Sick or Absent	22
Number of Diocesan Priests	69
Religious Priests in Diocese	5
Total Priests in Diocese	74
Extern Priests in Diocese	15
Ordinations:	
Diocesan Priests	1
Permanent Deacons	9
Permanent Deacons in Diocese	23
Total Brothers	3
Total Sisters	19
Parishes	
Parishes	50
With Resident Pastor:	
Resident Diocesan Priests	36
Resident Religious Priests	6
Without Resident Pastor:	
Administered by Priests	8
Missions	21
Professional Ministry Personnel:	
Brothers	3
Sisters	14
Lay Ministers	52
Welfare	
Catholic Hospitals	1
Total Assisted	235,420
Homes for the Aged	1
Total Assisted	104
Residential Care of Disabled	1
Total Assisted	202
Educational	
Diocesan Students in Other Seminaries	10
Total Seminarians	10
High Schools, Diocesan and Parish	3
Total Students	663
Elementary Schools, Diocesan and Parish	7
Total Students	1,941
Catechesis/Religious Education:	
High School Students	757
Elementary Students	1,773
Total Students under Catholic Instruction	5,144
Teachers in the Diocese:	
Brothers	1
Sisters	10
Lay Teachers	227
Vital Statistics	
Receptions into the Church:	
Infant Baptism Totals	483
Minor Baptism Totals	72
Adult Baptism Totals	76
Received into Full Communion	115
First Communions	574
Confirmations	466
Marriages:	
Catholic	135
Interfaith	43
Total Marriages	178
Deaths	543
Total Catholic Population	35,402
Total Population	389,837

Former Bishops—Rt. Revs. AUGUSTUS M. MARTIN, ord. Sept. 25, 1825; cons. Nov. 30, 1853; died Sept. 29, 1875; FRANCIS XAVIER LERAY, ord. March 19, 1852; cons. Bishop of Natchitoches, April 22, 1877; named Bishop of Janopolis, Coadjutor of New Orleans, and Administrator of Natchitoches, Oct. 23, 1879; promoted to the See of New Orleans, Dec. 1883; died Sept. 23, 1887; ANTHONY DURIER, D.D., ord. Oct. 27, 1856; cons. March 19, 1885; died Feb. 28, 1904; Most Revs. CORNELIUS VAN DE VEN, ord. May 31, 1890; cons. Nov. 30, 1904; made assistant at the Pontifical Throne, Nov. 12, 1929; died May 8, 1932; DANIEL FRANCIS DESMOND, D.D., ord. June 9, 1911; cons. Bishop of Alexandria Jan. 5, 1933; died Sept. 11, 1945; CHARLES P. GRECO, D.D., ord. July 25, 1918; cons. Feb. 25, 1946; retired May 22, 1973; died Jan. 20, 1987; LAWRENCE P. GRAVES, D.D., J.C.L., ord. June 11, 1942; cons. April 25, 1969; installed Bishop of Alexandria, Sept. 18, 1973; retired July 14, 1982; died Jan. 15, 1994; WILLIAM B. FRIEND, ord. Oct. 30, 1979; installed Bishop of Alexandria-Shreveport Jan. 11, 1983; then after Diocese of Alexandria-Shreveport was divided into two dioceses June 16, 1986; installed Bishop of Shreveport July 30, 1986; retired Dec. 20, 2006; died April 2, 2015.; JOHN C. FAVALORA, ord. Dec. 20, 1961; appt. Bishop of Alexandria June 16, 1986; ord. and installed July 29, 1986; installed Bishop of St. Petersburg May 16, 1989; installed Archbishop of Miami Dec. 20, 1994; retired April 20, 2010.; SAM G. JACOBS, ord. June 6, 1964; appt. Bishop of Alexandria July 1, 1989; ord. and installed Aug. 24, 1989; appt. Bishop of Houma-Thibodaux Aug. 1, 2003; installed Oct. 10, 2003; retired Sept. 23, 2013.; RONALD P. HERZOG, ord. June 1, 1968; appt. Bishop of Alexandria Oct. 27, 2004; ord. and installed Jan. 5, 2005; retired Feb. 2, 2017; died April 12, 2019.; DAVID P. TALLEY, ord. June 3, 1989; appt. Titular Bishop of Lambaesis and Auxiliary Bishop of Atlanta Jan. 3, 2013; ord. April 2, 2013; appt. Coadjutor Bishop of Alexandria Sept. 21, 2016; installed Nov. 7, 2016; Succeeded Feb. 2, 2017; appt. Bishop of Memphis March 5, 2019; installed April 2, 2019.

St. Joseph Catholic Center—Diocese of Alexandria, 4400 Coliseum Blvd., Alexandria, 71303-3597. Mailing Address: P.O. Box 7417, Alexandria, 71306-0417. Tel: 318-445-2401 Receptionist; Tel: 318-445-6424 Auto-Attendant; Fax: 318-448-6121; Web: www.diocesealex.org. Office Hours: Mon.-Thurs. 8am-5pm.

All offices as above unless listed otherwise. Send requests for matrimonial dispensations to the Diocesan Tribunal.

Coordinating Staff

Vicar General—Rev. STEPHEN SCOTT CHEMINO, V.G., J.C.L., Tel: 318-445-6424, Ext. 204; Email: frchemino@diocesealex.org.

Chancellor—Rev. CHAD A. PARTAIN, Chancellor & Archivist, Tel: 318-445-6524, Ext. 228; Email: frcpartain@diocesealex.org.

Vice Chancellor—Deacon RICHARD MITCHELL, Tel: 318-445-6524, Ext. 206; Email: dcnrmitchell@diocesealex.org.

Director of Catholic Charities and Special Ministries—(family life and worship) Rev. STEPHEN SCOTT CHEMINO, Tel: 318-445-6424, Ext. 204; Email: frchemino@diocesealex.org.

Superintendent of Catholic Schools—MR. THOMAS ROQUE, Tel: 318-445-6424, Ext. 224; Email: troque@diocesealex.org.

Director of Development and Public Affairs—COLE CHURCHMAN, Tel: 318-445-6424, Ext. 220; Email: cchurchman@diocesealex.org.

Chief Financial Officer—DAVID BROOK, Tel: 318-445-6424, Ext. 214; Email: dbrook@diocesealex.org.

Director of Religious Formation and Training—(Steubenville Conference) VACANT.

Secretary to the Bishop—DEBORAH DEOROSAN, Tel: 318-445-6424, Ext. 201; Fax: 318-767-1230; Email: ddeorosan@diocesealex.org.

Other Diocesan Services

Archivist—Rev. CHAD A. PARTAIN, Tel: 318-445-6524, Ext. 228; Email: frcpartain@diocesealex.org.

Vicar for Clergy—P.O. Box 459, Lecompte, 71346-0459. Tel: 318-776-9480. Revs. ADAM FREDERICK TRAVIS, V.C., Email: fratravis@diocesealex.org; JOHN WILTSE, V.C., Assoc. Dir., Email: frjwiltse@diocesealex.org.

Communications—CARI TERRACINA, Publications, Tel: 318-445-6424, Ext. 255; Email: cari.williams@diocesealex.org; JOAN FERGUSON, Multi-Media, Tel: 318-445-6524, Ext. 264; Email: iferguson@diocesealex.org.

Continuing Education of the Clergy—2262 Hwy. 484, Natchez, 71456. Tel: 318-379-2521. Rev. CHARLES RAY, Email: frcray@parish.diocesealex.org.

Diaconate Program—Deacon RICHARD MITCHELL, Tel: 318-445-6524, Ext. 206; Email: dcnrmitchell@diocesealex.org.

Diocesan Tribunal—(canonical services) PATRICIA THOMAS, Moderator of the Tribunal Chancery, Tel: 318-445-6424, Ext. 263; Fax: 318-767-0872; Email: pthomas@diocesealex.org.

Judges—Revs. PETER A. FAULK, J.C.L., J.V., Tel: 318-445-6424, Ext. 217; Email: frpfaulk@diocesealex.org; D. BRUCE MILLER, J.C.L., Tel: 318-445-6424, Ext. 261; Email: frbmiller@diocesealex.org; STEPHEN SCOTT CHEMINO, V.G., J.C.L., Tel: 318-445-6424, Ext. 204; Email: frchemino@diocesealex.org.

Defender of the Bond and Promoter of Justice—Rev. JAMES A. FERGUSON, J.C.L., Tel: 318-445-6424, Ext. 265; Email: frjferguson@diocesealex.org.

Notary—KATHY COLE, Tel: 318-445-6424, Ext. 262; Email: kcole@diocesealex.org.

Hispanic Ministry—Rev. STEPHEN SCOTT CHEMINO, Mailing Address: P.O. Box 7417, Alexandria, 71306-0417. Tel: 318-445-6424, Ext. 204.

Liturgy Commission—Deacon RICHARD MITCHELL, Tel: 318-445-6424, Ext. 206; Email: dcnrmitchell@diocesealex.org.

Life and Justice—3822 Bayou Rapides Rd., Alexandria, 71303. Tel: 318-445-7141, Ext. 12. Rev. CRAIG SCOTT, V.C., V.F., Email: frcscott@parish.diocesealex.org.

Catholic Medical Association of Central Louisiana—P.O. Box 9, Plaucheville, 71362. Tel: 318-922-3131. Rev. MARTIN L. LAIRD, Email: frmlaird@parish.diocesealex.org.

Maryhill Renewal Center—600 Maryhill Rd., Pineville, 71360. Tel: 318-640-1378. LUTHER "LUKE" WHITE, Facility Mgr., Tel: 318-613-7155; Tel: 318-542-1707; Email: dcnlwhite@diocesealex.org.

Protection of Children—

Program Director—PAM DELRIE, Tel: 318-445-6424, Ext. 213; Email: pdelrie@diocesealex.org.

Victim Assistance Minister—DR. LEE KNEIPP, Clinical Psychologist, Mailing Address: P.O. Box 7417, Alexandria, 71306-0417. Tel: 318-445-6424, Ext. 229.

Administrator and Assessor, Code of Pastoral Conduct—Rev. STEPHEN SCOTT CHEMINO, V.G., J.C.L., Tel: 318-445-6424, Ext. 204; Email: frchemino@diocesealex.org.

Coordinator for Religious—Sr. SANDRA NORSWORTHY, O.L.S.

Vocations and Seminarians—Rev. LOUIS E. SKLAR, Dir., P.O. Box 7417, Alexandria, 71306-0417. Tel: 318-445-6424, Ext. 260; Email: frlsklar@diocesealex.org.

College of Consultors—Rev. STEPHEN SCOTT CHEMINO, V.G., J.C.L.; Rev. Msgr. STEVE J. TESTA, (Retired); Revs. MARTIN L. LAIRD; D. BRUCE MILLER, J.C.L.; CRAIG SCOTT, V.C., V.F.; JOY RETNAZIHAMONI ANTONY, (India); LOUIS E. SKLAR; JAMES A. FERGUSON, J.C.L.; MARC A. NOEL, (Canada); RUSTY P. RABALAIS, V.F.; CHAD A. PARTAIN, Chancellor.

Presbyteral Council—Elected Members: Revs. CHAD A. PARTAIN; MARTIN L. LAIRD; JOSE A. ROBLES-SANCHEZ, (Puerto Rico); WADE DECOSTE, (Canada); BRIAN SEILER. Appointed Members: Revs. DWIGHT DE JESUS, (Philippines); JOSE PALLIPURATH, (India); KENNETH OBIEKWE, (Nigeria). Ex Officio: Revs. STEPHEN SCOTT CHEMINO, V.G., J.C.L.; CRAIG SCOTT, V.C., V.F.; JOHN O'BRIEN, (Canada) V.F.; RUSTY P. RABALAIS, V.F.; JOHN PARDUE, V.F.; D. BRUCE MILLER, J.C.L.; LOUIS E. SKLAR; CHARLES RAY; ADAM FREDERICK TRAVIS, V.C.; JOHN WILTSE, V.C.; Rev. Msgr. STEVE J. TESTA, Vicar, Retired Clergy, (Retired).

Deans—Revs. JOHN O'BRIEN, (Canada) V.F., Natchitoches Deanery; JOHN PARDUE, V.F., Eastern Deanery; CRAIG SCOTT, V.C., V.F., Central Deanery; RUSTY P. RABALAIS, V.F., Avoyelles Deanery.

Diocesan Representatives

Boy Scouts of America—

Region 5 Chaplain—VACANT.

Diocesan, Region 5 & Louisiana Purchase Council Chaplain—Rev. STEPHEN J. BRANDOW, Mailing Address: P.O. Box 39, Tioga, 71477-0039. Tel: 318-473-0010, Ext. 2539.

Catholic Relief Services—VACANT.

Louisiana Interchurch Council—Rev. STEPHEN SCOTT CHEMINO, V.G., J.C.L., Ecumenical Liaison, Tel: 318-445-6424, Ext. 204; Email: frchemino@diocesealex.org.

Holy Childhood Association—Rev. CHAD A. PARTAIN, Dir., Tel: 318-445-6424, Ext. 228.

Propagation of the Faith and Foreign Mission EducationRev. CHAD A. PARTAIN, Dir., Tel: 318-445-6424, Ext. 228.

Catholic Charismatic Renewal of Cenla—DIANE ARDOINE, Tel: 318-419-1547; Email: dianeardoine@yahoo.com.

CLERGY, PARISHES, MISSIONS AND PAROCHIAL SCHOOLS

CITY OF ALEXANDRIA

(RAPIDES PARISH)

1—ST. FRANCIS XAVIER CATHEDRAL (1834) Revs. James A. Ferguson, J.C.L., Rector; William Gearheard, Parochial Vicar; Deacons Richard Mitchell; Luke White.
Res.: 626 Fourth St., 71301-8424. Tel: 318-445-1451; Fax: 318-445-1433; Email: aryder@parish.diocesealex.org; Web: www.sfxcathedral.org.
Catechesis Religious Program—Rev. William Gearheard, D.R.E., Email: fwrgearheard@diocesealex.org; Mary Lou Maples, D.R.E., Tel: 318-443-1562; Email: maplesml@suddenlink.net. Students 27.

2—ST. FRANCES XAVIER CABRINI (1947)
2211 E. Texas Ave., 71301-4207. Revs. Chad A. Partain; Joseph C. Desimone, Parochial Vicar; Deacon Lawrence Feldkamp.
Res.: 2012 Wedgewood Ave., 71301.
Tel: 318-445-4588; Fax: 318-443-7156; Web: www.cabrinichurch.com.
School—(Grades PreK-8), 2215 E. Texas Ave., 71301. Tel: 318-448-3333; Fax: 318-448-3343; Web: www.cabrinischool.com. Sr. Nina Vincent, O.L.S., Prin. Lay Teachers 23; Students 293; Clergy / Religious Teachers 3.
Catechesis Religious Program—Clayton Cobb, D.R.E., Tel: 318-448-3333; Email: ccobb@cabrinischool.com. Students 46.

3—ST. JAMES MEMORIAL (1911) Rev. Michael Craig Scott, V.C., Admin.
714 Winn St., 71301. Tel: 318-487-9512;
Fax: 318-445-9826.
Catechesis Religious Program—Natile Nelson, D.R.E. Students 23.

4—ST. JULIANA (1959) Rev. Jose A. Robles-Sanchez, (Puerto Rico).
Res.: 900 Daspit St., 71302-5343. Tel: 318-445-6700; Fax: 318-445-9826; Web: www.stjulianaccf.org.
Catechesis Religious Program—Angela Lee, D.R.E. Students 29.

5—OUR LADY OF PROMPT SUCCOR (1947) Revs. Daniel P. O'Connor, V.F.; Derek Ducote, Parochial Vicar; Deacon William Aldridge.
Res.: 401 21st St., 71301-6548. Tel: 318-445-3693; Fax: 318-445-8471; Email: parishmanager@olpschurch.org; Web: www.olpschurch.org.
School—Our Lady of Prompt Succor School, (Grades PreK-6), 420 21st St., 71301. Tel: 318-487-1862; Fax: 318-473-9321; Email: olpsoffice@promptsuccor.org; Web: www.promptsuccor.org. Jo Tassin, Prin. Lay Teachers 39; Students 410.
Catechesis Religious Program—Michelle Lemoine, D.R.E., Tel: 318-305-3898; Email: dre@olpschurch.org. Students 221.

6—ST. RITA (1940)
4401 Bayou Rapides Rd., 71303. Tel: 318-445-7120; Web: www.strita.org. Mailing Address: 3822 Bayou Rapides Rd., 71303. Revs. Michael Craig Scott, V.C.; David J. Braquet, Parochial Vicar; Daniel Hart, Parochial Vicar; Peter A. Faulk, J.C.L., J.V., In Res.
Res.: 214 N. 17th St., 71301. Tel: 318-445-7120; Email: strita@strita.org.
Catechesis Religious Program—Sr. Nell Murray, M.S.C., D.R.E., Email: srnell@strita.org. Students 117.

OUTSIDE THE CITY OF ALEXANDRIA

BELLEDEAU, AVOYELLES PARISH, ST. MARTIN OF TOURS (1950) [CEM] Rev. Kurian Zachariah, (India); Deacon Darrell Dubroc.
Res.: 1981 Hwy 114, Hessmer, 71341.
Tel: 318-563-9097; Email: frkzachariah@parish.diocesealex.org.
Catechesis Religious Program—

BORDELONVILLE, AVOYELLES PARISH, ST. PETER (1903) [CEM]
Mailing Address: P.O. Box 31, Bordelonville, 71320. Rev. Shouraiah Ramji, (India).
Res.: 4702 Hwy. 451, Bordelonville, 71320-0031.
Tel: 318-997-2151; Fax: 318-997-2159; Email: stpeter@centurytel.net.
Catechesis Religious Program—Terri Guillory, D.R.E. Students 19.

BOYCE, RAPIDES PARISH, ST. MARGARET (1936) Rev. Silverino Kwebuza, A.J., (Uganda).
Res.: 402 Ryan St., Boyce, 71409. Tel: 318-793-8811; Email: silvakza@rocketmail.com.
Catechesis Religious Program—
Missions—St. Cyril—Hwy. 8, Flatwoods, Rapides Parish 71427. Rev. Dan Cook, Sacramental Min.
St. Margaret Mary, Hwy. 119, Gorum, Natchitoches Parish 71434.

BROUILLETTE, AVOYELLES PARISH, ST. GENEVIEVE (1953) [CEM] Rev. Abraham Palakkattuchira, (India).
Res.: 4052 Hwy. 452, Marksville, 71351-3530.
Tel: 318-253-9237; Fax: 318-253-0703; Email: st.genevievebrou@yahoo.com.
Catechesis Religious Program—Janice Brevelle, D.R.E., Tel: 318-253-4519; Email: djb3bvfd@wildblue.net. Students 33.

BUNKIE, AVOYELLES PARISH, ST. ANTHONY OF PADUA (1904) [CEM]
P.O. Box 719, Bunkie, 71322-0719. Rev. Stephen Scott Chemino, V.G., J.C.L.
Res.: 409 St. John St., Bunkie, 71322-0719.
Tel: 318-346-7274; Fax: 318-346-7475; Email: stanthonyscathol@bellsouth.net; Email: frchemino@diocesealex.org.
School—St. Anthony of Padua School, (Grades PreK-8), 116 S. Knoll St., Bunkie, 71322.
Tel: 318-346-2739; Fax: 318-346-9191; Email: sassecure@bellsouth.net. Aimee Hays, Prin. Lay Teachers 10; Sisters 2; Students 195; Clergy / Religious Teachers 2.
Catechesis Religious Program—Carol Steckler, D.R.E., Tel: 318-346-7274; Email: frchemino@diocesealex.org. Students 37.

CAMPTI, NATCHITOCHES PARISH, NATIVITY OF THE BLESSED VIRGIN MARY (1831) [CEM 3] Rev. George Pookkattu, C.M.I., (India).
Res.: 119 Tally St., Campti, 71411. Tel: 318-476-2116 ; Email: Nativityofbvmcampti@gmail.com.
Missions—St. Joseph—2443 Hwy 1226, Natchitoches, 71457.
Our Lady of the Holy Rosary, 131 Pardee Rd., Campti, 71411.
Catechesis Religious Program—Liz LaBorde, D.R.E., Tel: 318-663-0563; Email: dlaborde3161@gmail.com. Students 12.

CHENEYVILLE, RAPIDES PARISH, ST. JOSEPH (1966) [CEM]
P.O. Box 446, Cheneyville, 71325-0446. Rev. Dwight De Jesus, (Philippines).
Res.: 301 Stanley St., Cheneyville, 71325.
Tel: 318-279-2394; Email: frddejesus@parish.diocesealex.org.

CLOUTIERVILLE, NATCHITOCHES PARISH, ST. JOHN THE BAPTIST (1816) [CEM]
P.O. Box 40, Cloutierville, 71416-0040. Rev. Christian Iheanyichukwu Ogbonna, (Nigeria).
Res.: 423 Hwy. 495, Cloutierville, 71416-0040.
Tel: 318-379-2231; Fax: 318-379-2236; Email: stjohnthebaptist_catholicchurch@yahoo.com.
Catechesis Religious Program—Jannie LaCour, D.R.E., Tel: 318-379-2121; Email: stjohnthebaptist_catholicchurch@yahoo.com. Students 7.
Missions—Holy Rosary—2262 Emmanuel Rd., Emmanuel, Natchitoches Parish 71416. Shirley M. Chevalier.
Holy Family, 17398 Hwy 1, Monet Ferry, Natchitoches Parish 71446.

COLFAX, GRANT PARISH, ST. JOSEPH (1897)
P.O. Box 243, Colfax, 71417. Rev. Silverino Kwebuza, A.J., (Uganda); Deacon Emile Barre III.
Res.: 139 Second St., Colfax, 71417-0243.
Tel: 318-627-3952; Email: silvakza@rocketmail.com.
Mission—St. Patrick, 624 Rowena St., Montgomery, 71454. P.O. Box 158, Montgomery, Grant Parish 71454.
Catechesis Religious Program—Rachel Bruce, D.R.E. Students 16.

COTTONPORT, AVOYELLES PARISH, ST. MARY ASSUMPTION (1889) [CEM 4]
P.O. Box 1123, Cottonport, 71327-1123. Rev. John Wiltse, V.C., Admin.
Res.: 820 Front St., Cottonport, 71327-1123.
Tel: 318-876-3681; Fax: 318-876-3686; Email: cbernard@stmaryscottonport.com; Web: www.stmaryscottonport.com.
School—St. Mary Assumption School, (Grades PreK-8), 850 Front St., Cottonport, 71327-1123.
Tel: 318-876-3651; Email: principal@stmaryscottonport.com. Nathan Laborde, Prin. Lay Teachers 12; Students 245; Clergy / Religious Teachers 1.
Catechesis Religious Program—Students 63.

DEVILLE, RAPIDES PARISH

1—STS. FRANCIS AND ANNE CATHOLIC CHURCH (2010)
Mailing Address: P.O. Box 3147, Pineville, 71361. Rev. Binochan Pallipparambil, (India); Deacon Gregory LeBlanc.
Church: 143 Boone Miller Rd., Deville, 71328-9445.
Tel: 318-767-2078; Email: kmh50@bellsouth.net.
Catechesis Religious Program—Rudy Mitchel, D.R.E. Students 60.

2—ST. JOHN THE BAPTIST (1942) [CEM 2]
P.O. Box 7, Deville, 71328. Rev. Anthony Dharmaraj, M.S.F.S., (India).
Res.: 1024 Hwy. 1207, Deville, 71328-0007.
Tel: 318-466-5587; Email: sheripaulstjohn@gmail.com.
Catechesis Religious Program—Students 100.
Missions—St. Winifred—2644 Hwy 107, Effie, Avoyelles Parish. Sheri Paul, Email: spaul@parish.diocesealex.org.
St. John the Baptist, 334 Community Center Rd., Moncla, Avoyelles Parish 71328.

DUPONT, AVOYELLES PARISH, IMMACULATE CONCEPTION (1945) [CEM]
P.O. Box 385, Dupont, 71329-0385. Rev. George Krosfield, (Philippines) (Retired).
Res.: 5765 Hwy 107 S., Dupont, 71329-0385.
Tel: 318-922-3248.

Catechesis Religious Program—Angela Dixon, D.R.E. Students 41.

ECHO, RAPIDES PARISH, ST. FRANCIS DE SALES (1894) [CEM]
100 Echo St., Echo, 71330. Tel: 318-563-4530; Fax: 318-563-4530. P.O. Box 37, Echo, 71330-0037. Rev. Dwight De Jesus, (Philippines).
Catechesis Religious Program—Inez Herde, D.R.E., Tel: 318-201-4760; Email: lambert_s@bellsouth.net. Students 56.

EVERGREEN, AVOYELLES PARISH, LITTLE FLOWER (1928) [CEM 2]
Mailing Address: P.O. Box 20, Evergreen, 71333-0020. Rev. Bartholomew Ibe, (Nigeria).
Res.: 2912 Main St., Evergreen, 71333-0020.
Tel: 318-346-2840; Fax: 318-346-4989; Email: litflowr@bellsouth.net.
Catechesis Religious Program—Students 11.
Mission—St. Charles, Highway 361, Goudeau, Avoyelles Parish 71333.

FERRIDAY, CONCORDIA PARISH, ST. PATRICK (1952) [JC]
P.O. Box 369, Ferriday, 71334. Rev. John Pardue, V.F.
Res.: 601 Florida Ave., Ferriday, 71334.
Tel: 318-757-3834; Email: stpatrickchurch@bellsouth.net.
Catechesis Religious Program—
Mission—St. Gerard, 303 Willow St., Jonesville, Catahoula Parish 71343. Tel: 318-339-6143.

GLENMORA, RAPIDES PARISH, ST. LOUIS (1941)
P.O. Box 636, Glenmora, 71433. Rev. Kenneth Obiekwe, (Nigeria).
Res.: 826 8th St., Glenmora, 71433-0636.
Tel: 318-748-8324; Fax: 318-748-8324; Email: stlouisglenmora@yahoo.com.
Catechesis Religious Program—6684 Hwy. 112, Elmer, 71424. Students 8.
Missions—St. Peter—[CEM] 6684 Hwy. 112, Elmer, Rapides Parish 71424.
St. Jude, 78 Price Rd., Sieper, Rapides Parish 71472.

HESSMER, AVOYELLES PARISH, ST. ALPHONSUS (1898) [CEM]
3645 Main St., Hessmer, 71341. P.O. Box 66, Hessmer, 71341-0066. Rev. Edwin Rodriguez-Hernandez, (Puerto Rico).
3658 Main St., Hessmer, 71341. Tel: 318-563-4550; Fax: 318-563-8395; Email: fredwinrod@yahoo.com.
Catechesis Religious Program—Tina Laborde, D.R.E. Students 115.

ISLE BREVELLE, NATCHITOCHES PARISH, ST. AUGUSTINE'S (1856) [CEM] Rev. Charles Ray; Deacon Michael L. Young.
Res.: 2262 Hwy. 484, Natchez, 71456-3622.
Tel: 318-379-2521; Fax: 318-379-6085; Email: staugustinechrch@hughes.net.
Catechesis Religious Program—Mrs. Deloris Jones, D.R.E., Tel: 318-471-4764; Email: jdeloris51@yahoo.com. Students 18.
Missions—St. Charles—4078 Louisiana State Hwy. 494, Bermuda, 71456-3622.
St. Anne, 3659 Old River Rd., Natchitoches, 71457.

JENA, LASALLE PARISH, ST. MARY (1949)
1571 N. Second St., Jena, 71342. Tel: 318-992-1019; Email: stmary1@centurytel.net. Rev. Jason E. Gootee.
Catechesis Religious Program—Students 23.
Mission—St. Edward, 2711 Hwy. 8, Pollock, Grant Parish 71432. Fax: 318-992-1019.

LECOMPTE, RAPIDES PARISH, ST. MARTIN (1932)
P.O. Box 459, Lecompte, 71346-0459. Revs. Adam Frederick Travis, V.C.; Peter A. Faulk, J.C.L., J.V., Parochial Vicar; Deacon William Travis.
Res.: 1815 St. Martin St., Lecompte, 71346-0459.
Tel: 318-776-9480; Fax: 318-776-9921; Email: stmartinscatholi@bellsouth.net.
Catechesis Religious Program—Robyn Carrington, D.R.E. Students 81.
Mission—Our Lady of Guadalupe, 10 Butter Cemetery Rd., Forest Hill, 71430.

LEESVILLE, VERNON PARISH, ST. MICHAEL (1946)
604 S. 5th St., Leesville, 71446. Mailing Address: 105 W. South St., Leesville, 71446. Rev. Kenneth J. Michiels; Deacons William Endris; Stephen Gramigna.
Res.: 202 W. Harriet, Leesville, 71446.
Tel: 337-239-2656; Fax: 337-239-2657; Email: stmichaelschurch@bellsouth.net.
Catechesis Religious Program—Tammy Cecil, D.R.E.; Tara Rindahl, D.R.E. Students 142.

MANSURA, AVOYELLES PARISH
1—OUR LADY OF PROMPT SUCCOR (1937)
P.O. Box 67, Mansura, 71350. Rev. Irion St. Romain.
Res.: 1910 Escude St., Mansura, 71350-0067.
Tel: 318-964-2654; Email: fristromain@parish.diocesealex.org.
Catechesis Religious Program—Students 25.
2—ST. PAUL THE APOSTLE (1796) [CEM]
Mailing Address: P.O. Box 130, Mansura, 71350-0130. Rev. Irion St. Romain.
Res.: 1879 Leglise St., Mansura, 71350-0130.
Tel: 318-597-2231; Fax: 318-597-2231; Email: stpaulmansura@yahoo.com.
Catechesis Religious Program—Amie Smith, D.R.E. Students 69.

MARKSVILLE, AVOYELLES PARISH
1—HOLY GHOST CATHOLIC CHURCH (1919) [CEM 2] Rev. Abraham Varghese, (India); Deacon Ted Moulard.
Res.: 121 S. Preston St., Marksville, 71351-3034.
Tel: 318-253-7131; Fax: 318-253-7136; Email: holyghostchur783@bellsouth.net.
Catechesis Religious Program—Francine Darby, D.R.E. Students 50.
Mission—St. Richard, 265 St. Richards Loop Rd., Marksville, Avoyelles Parish 71351.
2—ST. JOSEPH'S (1869) [CEM 2] Revs. Rusty P. Rabalais, V.F.; Dutch Voltz III; Deacon Gary Schupbach.
Res.: 141 S. Washington, Marksville, 71351-3025.
Tel: 318-253-7561 (Office); Email: stjosephofc@kricket.net.
Catechesis Religious Program—Nancy Desselle, D.R.E. Students 109.
3—OUR LADY OF LOURDES (1948) [CEM 4] Rev. Kurian Zachariah, (India); Deacon Darrell Dubroc.
Res.: 1315 Eggbend Rd., Marksville, 71351-4223.
Tel: 318-253-9936; Fax: 318-253-6300; Email: lourdeschurch@bellsouth.net; Web: www.ollsjbchurch.org.
Catechesis Religious Program—Samantha Dupuy, Tel: 318-305-2186; Email: samantha.dupuy2186@gmail.com. Students 105.

MOREAUVILLE, AVOYELLES PARISH
1—OUR LADY OF SORROWS (1944) [CEM]
Mailing Address: P.O. Box 247, Moreauville, 71355-0247. Rev. Jose Pallipurath, (India).
Res.: 524 Main St., Moreauville, 71355-0247.
Tel: 318-985-2968; Email: frjpallipurath@parish.diocesealex.org.
Catechesis Religious Program—
2—SACRED HEART (1860) [CEM] Rev. Jose Pallipurath, (India).
Res.: 9986 Bayou Des Glaises St., Moreauville, 71355-9702. Tel: 318-985-2774; Email: shc_moreauville@yahoo.com; Web: www.shcmoreauville.org.
School—Sacred Heart School, (Grades PreK-8), 9968 Bayou Des Glaises, P.O. Box 179, Moreauville, 71355. Tel: 318-985-2772; Fax: 318-985-2164; Email: sacredheart@kricket.net; Web: www.shsmoreauville.com. Sr. Sandra Norsworthy, O.L.S., Prin.; Rhonia Smith, Librarian. Lay Teachers 33; Sisters of Our Lady of Sorrows 3; Students 385; Clergy / Religious Teachers 3.
Catechesis Religious Program—Monique Mayeux, D.R.E., Tel: 318-985-2288; Andre Spruill, D.R.E., Tel: 318-359-7542; Email: aspruill@avoyellespsb.com. Students 63.

NATCHITOCHES, NATCHITOCHES PARISH
1—ST. ANTHONY OF PADUA (1935) [JC]
P.O. Box 432, Natchitoches, 71458-0432. Revs. John O'Brien, (Canada) V.F.; John K. Brocato, Parochial Vicar; Wade DeCoste, (Canada) Parochial Vicar; Thomas Elmus Paul, In Res.; Deacon Steven Newbury.
Res.: 911 Fifth St., Natchitoches, 71457.
Tel: 318-352-2559; Fax: 318-352-2528; Email: spadua@bellsouth.net.
Catechesis Religious Program—Students 102.
2—HOLY CROSS (1968) Rev. Marc A. Noel, (Canada).
Res.: 129 Second St., Natchitoches, 71457.
Tel: 318-352-2615; Fax: 318-352-2615; Email: holycross129@gmail.com.
Catechesis Religious Program—Janice Herbert, D.R.E., Tel: 318-352-4889; Email: holycross129@gmail.com. Students 25.
3—IMMACULATE CONCEPTION (1728) [CEM] Revs. Blake Paul Deshautelle; Luke LaFleur, Parochial Vicar; Deacon John Whitehead.
Res.: 145 Church St., Natchitoches, 71457.
Tel: 318-352-3422; Fax: 318-352-3822; Email: office@minorbasilica.org; Web: MinorBasilica.org.
School—St. Mary's Catholic School, (Grades PreK-12), 1101 E. Fifth St., Natchitoches, 71458-2070.
Tel: 318-352-8394; Fax: 318-352-5798; Email: dnorman@smstigers.org; Web: smstigers.org. Mrs. Andrea Harrell, Prin.; Krista Sklar, Librarian. Lay Teachers 35; Students 385.
Catechesis Religious Program—Kathleen Hicks, D.R.E., Tel: 318-663-2414; Email: retiredaunt@gmail.com. Students 65.

PINEVILLE, RAPIDES PARISH, SACRED HEART (1933) Revs. D. Bruce Miller, J.C.L.; Walter Ajaero, (Nigeria) Parochial Vicar; Deacon Tommy Robichaux.
Res.: 600 Lakeview, Pineville, 71360-7519.
Tel: 318-445-2497; Fax: 318-443-0808; Email: rgraham@jesusinpineville.com; Web: www.JesusinPineville.com.
Catechesis Religious Program—Melanie Delahoussaye, D.R.E. Students 301.

PLAUCHEVILLE, AVOYELLES PARISH, MATER DOLOROSA (1879) [CEM]
P.O. Box 9, Plaucheville, 71362-0009. Rev. Martin L. Laird.
Res.: 3458 Hwy 107 S., Plaucheville, 71362-0009.
Tel: 318-922-3131; Fax: 318-922-3664; Email: materdolorosa@suddenlink.net; Web: www.materdolorosaplaucheville.com.
School—St. Joseph Elementary School, (Grades PreK-8), Tel: 318-922-3401; Fax: 318-922-3776; Email: adesoto@sjsplaucheville.org; Email: balbritton@sjsplaucheville.org; Web: www.sjsplaucheville.org. Billy Albritton, Prin.
Legal Title: St. Joseph School Lay Teachers 18; Students 153.
High School—St. Joseph High School, Billy Albritton, Prin. Lay Teachers 17; Students 56; Clergy / Religious Teachers 2.
Catechesis Religious Program—Ashley DeSoto, D.R.E., Tel: 318-264-1552; Email: adesoto@sjsplauchevulle.org. Students 39.

POWHATAN, NATCHITOCHES PARISH, ST. FRANCIS OF ASSISI (1952)
179 Hwy. 485, Natchitoches, 71457. Rev. Thomas Elmus Paul.
179 Hwy. 485, Powhatan, 71457. Tel: 318-352-8819.
Catechesis Religious Program—
Mission—St. Anne, [CEM] 4310 Hwy. 485, Robeline, Natchitoches Parish 71457.

REXMERE, AVOYELLES PARISH, ST. MICHAEL (1964) [CEM]
142 Rexmere Ln., Kleinwood, 71320. P.O. Box 31, Bordelonville, 71320-0031. Rev. Shouraiah Ramji, (India).
Res.: 4702 Hwy. 451, Bordelonville, 71320-0031.
Tel: 318-997-2151; Fax: 318-997-2159; Email: stpeter@centurytel.net.
Catechesis Religious Program—

ST. JOSEPH, TENSAS PARISH, ST. JOSEPH (1940) [JC]
P.O. Box 198, St. Joseph, 71366-0198. Rev. Peter Kuligowski, (Poland) V.F.
919 Plank Rd., St. Joseph, 71366-0198.
Tel: 318-766-3565.
Catechesis Religious Program—Michael Vizard, D.R.E. Students 21.
Mission—St. Francis of Assisi, 142 Main St,., Waterproof, Tensas Parish 71375.

SIMMESPORT, AVOYELLES PARISH, CHRIST THE KING (1935) [CEM]
P.O. Box 186, Simmesport, 71369-0186. Rev. Paul Kunnumpuram, M.S.F.S., (India).
Res.: 705 Main St., Simmesport, 71369.
Tel: 318-941-2381; Email: christtheking186@gmail.com.
Catechesis Religious Program—Liz Jeansonne, D.R.E., Tel: 318-305-8182; Email: crazymama416@yahoo.com. Students 26.

TALLULAH, MADISON PARISH, ST. EDWARD (1936)
P.O. Box 1308, Tallulah, 71284-1308. Rev. Ryan P. Humphries, V.F.
Res.: 204 Hwy. 80 E., Tallulah, 71282-1308.
Tel: 318-574-1677; Email: stedwardtallulah@gmail.com.
Catechesis Religious Program—Louise Magoun, D.R.E., Tel: 318-574-0773; Email: lmagoun@bellsouth.net. Students 20.

TIOGA, RAPIDES PARISH, IMMACULATE HEART OF MARY (1971) Rev. Rick Gremillion; Deacon L.G. Deloach.
Res.: 1220 Tioga Rd., Ball, 71405. Tel: 318-640-9446; Fax: 318-640-3864; Email: tara@ihmarychurch.org; Web: www.ihmarychurch.org.
Catechesis Religious Program—Students 104.

VIDALIA, CONCORDIA PARISH, OUR LADY OF LOURDES (1887) [JC]
P.O. Box 460, Vidalia, 71373-0460. Rev. Joseph Xavier Vethamanicham, (India).
Res.: 503 Texas St., Vidalia, 71373.
Tel: 318-336-5450; Fax: 318-336-9770; Email: ollourdes@bellsouth.net.
Catechesis Religious Program—Brigid Martin, D.R.E. Students 5.

WINNFIELD, WINN PARISH, OUR LADY OF LOURDES (1988)
P.O. Box 1412, Winnfield, 71483-1412. Rev. Brian Seiler, Admin.
Res.: 772 Country Club Rd., Winnfield, 71483-1412.
Tel: 318-628-2561; Email: tracymkelley@outlook.com; Email: ollwinnfield@diocesealex.org.
Mission—St. William, 4580 Main St., Olla, La Salle Parish 71465. Tel: 318-495-5356; Fax: 318-495-3579.
Catechesis Religious Program—Laurie Derr, D.R.E., Tel: 318-628-4079; Email: laure.derr@hotmail.com. Students 28.

WINNSBORO, FRANKLIN PARISH, ST. MARY (1945)
P.O. Box 58, Winnsboro, 71295. Rev. Dale Meade.
Res.: 1712 West St., Winnsboro, 71295-3240.
Tel: 318-435-8580; Email: saintmaryscc@bellsouth.net.
Catechesis Religious Program—Cindy Futch, D.R.E. Students 28.

Mission—St. John, 7900 Hwy. 165, Columbia, Caldwell Parish 71295.

WOODWORTH, RAPIDES PARISH, CONGREGATION OF MARY, MOTHER OF JESUS (2008)
9323 Hwy. 165 S., Woodworth, 71485.
Tel: 318-487-9894; Email: mmjwoodworth@suddenlink.com; Web: www.mmjchurch.org. P.O. Box 408, Woodworth, 71485.
Rev. Paul M. LaPalme; Deacon Paul Sunderhaus
Legal Name: Congregation of Mary, Mother of Jesus Roman Catholic Church, Woodworth, Louisiana
Catechesis Religious Program—Brinda Edwards, D.R.E., Tel: 317-250-9997; Email: ccd@mmjchurch.org. Students 43.

Chaplains of Public Institutions

ALEXANDRIA. *Christus St. Frances Cabrini Hospital*, 3330 Masonic Dr., 71301. Tel: 318-487-1122; Email: frjretnazihamoni@diocesealex.org. Rev. Joy Retnazihamoni Antony, (India) Chap.
Rapides Regional Medical Center, 211 4th St., 71301. Tel: 318-769-3000. Rev. William Gearheard.

PINEVILLE. *Central Louisiana State Hospital*, W. Shamrock Ave., P.O. Box 5031, Pineville, 71361. Tel: 318-484-6357; Tel: 318-484-6352. Rev. Stephen J. Brandow.
Veterans Administration Medical Center, Shreveport Hwy., Pineville, 71360. Tel: 318-473-0010. Rev. Stephen J. Brandow, Staff Chap.

On Duty Outside the Diocese:
Rev.—
Vead, Victor P., Federal Correctional Complex, Beaumont, TX.

Absent on Leave:
Revs.—
Catella, Anthony
Deevy, Edward
Imamshah, Harold, (Trinidad and Tobago)
Ishmael, Keith E.
Melcher, Luke A.
Michalchuk, Jack H., (Canada)
Reynolds, Taylor
Sierra-Posada, Pedro J., (Colombia).

Retired:
Rev. Msgrs.—
Hoppe, Ronald C., (Retired)
Testa, Steve J., (Retired)
Timmermans, John, (The Netherlands) (Retired)
Revs.—
Aelavanthara, Antony, V.F., (Retired)
Allen, Terry, (Retired)
Corkery, Daniel, (Ireland) (Retired)
Cunningham, John H., (Retired)
Fey, Thomas J., (Retired)
Foster, James A., (Retired)
Hasieber, Joseph S., (Retired)
Krosfield, George, (Philippines) (Retired)
Lyons, Frederick J., (Retired)
Mathews, James R., (Retired)
Messina, Angelo, (Retired)
Morgan, Charles J., (Retired)
Nayak, Christudas, (India) (Retired)
Ryan, John, (Ireland) (Retired)
Thomas, Jacob, (India) (Retired)
Thompson, August L., (Retired)
Viviano, Nino, (Retired).

Permanent Deacons:
Adkins, Mark
Aldridge, William
Barre, Emile III
Daigrepont, William, (Retired), Avoyelles Prison Ministry
Deloach, L.G.
Dubroc, Darrell
Endris, William
Feldkamp, Lawrence
Gramigna, Stephen
Gremillion, Norman, (Retired)
LeBlanc, Gregory
Marye, Todd J., (Outside the diocese)
McCusker, Patrick, (On Leave)
Mitchell, Richard
Moulard, Ted
Newbury, Steven
Pelto, Clifford, (Retired)
Plaisance, Paul J., (Retired)
Robichaux, Tommy
Schupbach, Gary
Shaidnagle, William, (Outside the diocese)
Sunderhaus, Paul
Travis, William
White, Luther "Luke"
Whitehead, John
Young, Michael L.

INSTITUTIONS LOCATED IN DIOCESE

[A] HIGH SCHOOLS, DIOCESAN

ALEXANDRIA. *Holy Savior Menard Central*, (Grades 7-12), 4603 Coliseum Blvd., 71303. Tel: 318-445-8233 ; Fax: 318-448-8170; Email: dskelly@holysaviormenard.com; Web: www.holysaviormenard.com. Rev. Charles Ray, Pres.; Dwayne Lemoine, Prin.; Monica De Lacerda, Librarian. Junior & High School. Lay Teachers 40; Students 482.

[B] GENERAL HOSPITALS

ALEXANDRIA. *Christus Health Central Louisiana* dba Christus St. Frances Cabrini Hospital, 3330 Masonic Dr., 71301. Tel: 318-448-6701; Fax: 318-448-6754; Email: kim.kelsch@christushealth.org; Web: www.cabrini.org. Christopher Karam, CEO; Patrick Braquet, Dir.; Judy Deshotels, Vice Pres., Mission Integration; Rev. Joy Retnazihamoni Antony, (India) Chap. Bed Capacity 293; Sisters of Charity of the Incarnate Word 1; Tot Asst. Annually 235,420; Total Staff 1,491.
Christus St. Frances Cabrini Hospital Foundation of Alexandria, Inc., 3330 Masonic Dr., 71301. Tel: 318-448-6580; Fax: 318-443-3072; Email: kim.kelsch@christushealth.org; Web: www.christuscabrinifoundation.org. Nancy R. Hellyer, CEO; Walker Ashley, Dir.

[C] PROTECTIVE INSTITUTIONS

ALEXANDRIA. *St. Mary's Residential Training School, Inc.*, 6715 Hwy. 1 N., Boyce, 71409. Tel: 318-445-6443, Ext. 2102; Fax: 318-449-8520; Email: christi.guillot@stmarys-rts.org; Email: pauline.bordelon@stmarys-rts.org; Email: info@stmarys-rts.org; Web: www.stmarysalexandria.org. P.O. Drawer 7768, 71306. Christi Guillot, Admin.; Tony "Bo" Vets, Prog. Dir. Bed Capacity 202; Students 202; Tot Asst. Annually 202; Total Staff 350.
Our Lady of Sorrows Community Homes, 347 Browns Bend Rd., 71303. Tel: 318-487-8897; Fax: 318-487-9987; Email: mavisolsusa@aol.com. Sr. Mavis Champagne, O.L.S., Admin. Congregation of the Sisters of Our Lady of Sorrows of the U.S.A., Inc. Bed Capacity 20; Lay Staff 25; Residents 20; Sisters 3; Tot Asst. Annually 20; Total Staff 25.

[D] HOMES FOR AGED

ALEXANDRIA. *Our Lady's Manor, Inc.*, 402 Monroe St., 71301. Tel: 318-473-2560; Fax: 318-443-2449; Email: ourladysmanor@olpschurch.org. Ms. Christina Brumley, Admin. HUD subsidized apartment complex for the elderly. Apartments 104.

[E] RESIDENCES OF PRIESTS AND BROTHERS

PLAUCHEVILLE. *Brothers of the Holy Eucharist*, P.O. Box 25, Plaucheville, 71362. Tel: 318-922-3630. Bro. Anthony Dugas, F.S.E., Supr. Brothers 3.

[F] CONVENTS AND RESIDENCES FOR SISTERS

ALEXANDRIA. *Congregation of the Marianites of Holy Cross*, St. Rita Convent, 1717 Ashley Ave., 71301. Tel: 318-448-8001; Email: srnell@strita.org. Sr. Nell Murray, M.S.C., D.R.E. Sisters 1.
Sisters of Our Lady of Sorrows, St. Joseph Convent, 440 Browns Bend Rd., 71303. Tel: 318-787-5513; Email: stjoe97@aol.com. Sr. Nina Vincent, O.L.S., Supr. Sisters 6.
Sisters of the Holy Family, 3000 Elliott St., 71301. Tel: 318-483-9480; Email: eholmes@cabrinischool.com. Sr. Gloria Lewis, S.S.F., Local Leader. Sisters 2.

MOREAUVILLE. *Sisters of Our Lady of Sorrows*, Sacred Heart Convent, 9968 Bayou Des Glaises Rd., P.O. Box 179, Moreauville, 71355. Tel: 318-985-2994; Fax: 318-985-2164; Email: sheartc@yahoo.com. Sisters Kalen Sarmiento, Supr.; Sandra Norsworthy, O.L.S., Prin. Sisters 3.

[G] RETREAT HOUSES

PINEVILLE. *Maryhill Renewal Center*, 600 Maryhill Rd., Pineville, 71360. Tel: 318-640-1378; Email: khatcher@diocesealex.org; Web: www.diocesealex.org. David Brook, Contact Person.

[H] CATHOLIC CHARITIES AND SPECIAL MINISTRIES

ALEXANDRIA. *Catholic Charities and Special Ministries*, 4400 Coliseum Blvd., 71303. Tel: 318-445-2401; Fax: 318-448-6121; Email: frchemino@diocesealex.org; Web: www.diocesealex.org. P.O. Box 7417, 71306. Rev. Stephen Scott Chemino, V.G., J.C.L., Dir. Tot Asst. Annually 240.

[I] NEWMAN CENTERS

ALEXANDRIA. *Louisiana State University at Alexandria*, Catholic Student Center, 8100 Hwy. 71-S, 71302-9633. Tel: 318-473-6494; Email: lray@diocesealex.org. Mrs. Lynn Ray, Campus Min.; Rev. Joseph C. Desimone, Chap.

NATCHITOCHES. *Northwestern State University*, Holy Cross Catholic Student Center, 129 Second St., Natchitoches, 71457. Tel: 318-352-2615; Email: holycross129@gmail.com; Web: www.holycross129.org. Rev. Marc A. Noel, (Canada) Chap.

[J] MISCELLANEOUS

ALEXANDRIA. *Catholic Charitable Endowment of Alexandria*, 4400 Coliseum Blvd., 71303. Tel: 318-445-2401; Fax: 318-448-6121; Email: dbrook@diocesealex.org. P.O. Box 7417, 71306-0417. David Brook, Sec.
The Catholic Foundation of North-Central Louisiana, Inc., P.O. Box 12833, 71315. Tel: 318-487-9222; Email: cfnclouisiana@gmail.com. Joseph L. Hebert, Pres.
Manna House, 2655 Lee St., 71303. Tel: 318-445-9053; Email: cenlamannahouse@gmail.com; Web: www.givetomannahouse.com. P.O. Box 6011, 71307. Chris Soprano, Pres.; Jessica Viator, Dir.; Rev. Dan Cook, Chap.
Tekakwitha Conference National Center, 2225 N. Bolton Ave., 71303-4408. Tel: 318-483-3908; Fax: 318-483-3909; Email: tekconf@gmail.com; Web: www.tekconf.org. Mr. Robert Barbry II, Exec.

HESSMER. *Magnificat - Central Louisiana Chapter of the Diocese of Alexandria*, P.O. Box 37, Hessmer, 71341. Tel: 318-563-8213; Email: msgd_@bellsouth.net; Email: dianeardoin@yahoo.com. M. Sue Dauzat, Contact Person.

RELIGIOUS INSTITUTES OF MEN REPRESENTED IN THE DIOCESE

For further details refer to the corresponding bracketed number in the Religious Institutes of Men or Women section.

[]—*Apostles of Jesus (Uganda)*—A.J.
[0620]—*Brothers of the Holy Eucharist*—F.S.E.
[0275]—*Carmelites of Mary Immaculate*—C.M.I.
[0520]—*Franciscan Friars*—O.F.M.
[]—*Missionaries of St. Francis de Sales* (France)—M.S.F.S.

RELIGIOUS INSTITUTES OF WOMEN REPRESENTED IN THE DIOCESE

[2410]—*Congregation of the Marianites of Holy Cross*—M.S.C.
[1950]—*Congregation of the Sisters of the Holy Family*—S.S.F.
[1010]—*Sisters of Divine Providence of San Antonio, Texas*—C.D.P.
[3120]—*Sisters of Our Lady of Sorrows*—O.L.S.
[]—*Sisters of the Living Word*—S.L.W.
[]—*Sisters of the Secular Institute of the Two Hearts*—S.I.T.H.

DIOCESAN CEMETERIES

LECOMPTE. *Lecompte Cemetery*, P.O. Box 7417, 71306-0417. Tel: 318-445-2401, Ext. 215; Email: dbrook@diocesealex.org. David Brook, Contact Person

PINEVILLE. *Maryhill Cemetery for Clergy*, 600 Maryhill Rd., Pineville, 71360. Tel: 318-445-2401, Ext. 202; Email: dmetoyer@diocesealex.org. Rev. Chad A. Partain, Chancellor

NECROLOGY

† Herzog, Ronald P., Bishop Emeritus of Alexandria., Died Apr. 12, 2019
† Allen, Terry Edward, (Retired), Died Dec. 24, 2018
† Roy, Sheldon, Died Jan. 27, 2018

An asterisk (*) denotes an organization that has established tax-exempt status directly with the IRS and is not covered by the USCCB Group Ruling.

Diocese of Allentown

(Dioecesis Alanopolitana)

Most Reverend

ALFRED A. SCHLERT, D.D., J.C.L.

Bishop of Allentown; ordained September 19, 1987; appointed Bishop of Allentown June 27, 2017; ordained and installed August 31, 2017. *Office: 4029 W. Tilghman St., Allentown, PA 18104.*

Chancery Office: 4029 W. Tilghman St., Allentown, PA 18104. Mailing Address: P.O. Box F, Allentown, PA 18105-1538. Tel: 610-437-0755; Fax: 610-433-7822.

Most Reverend

EDWARD P. CULLEN, D.D.

Retired Bishop of Allentown; appointed Auxiliary Bishop of Philadelphia and Titular Bishop of Paria in Preconsilare February 8, 1994; consecrated April 14, 1994; appointed Bishop of Allentown December 16, 1997; installed Third Bishop of Allentown February 9, 1998; retired May 27, 2009. *Office: 4029 W. Tilghman St., Allentown, PA 18104. Mailing Address: P.O. Box F, Allentown, PA 18105.*

ESTABLISHED JANUARY 28, 1961.

Square Miles 2,773.

Comprises the Counties of Berks, Carbon, Lehigh, Northampton and Schuylkill in the State of Pennsylvania.

Legal Title: The Diocese of Allentown, each parish in the diocese, and each regional Catholic elementary school are organized as separate Pennsylvania Charitable Trusts. The formal name of each of those Charitable Trusts does include the phrase "Charitable Trust" and, for the purposes of this listing, it is understood that the phrase is part of their names.

STATISTICAL OVERVIEW

Personnel	
Bishop	1
Retired Bishops	1
Priests: Diocesan Active in Diocese	96
Priests: Diocesan Active Outside Diocese	7
Priests: Retired, Sick or Absent	49
Number of Diocesan Priests	152
Religious Priests in Diocese	43
Total Priests in Diocese	195
Extern Priests in Diocese	2
Ordinations:	
Diocesan Priests	1
Transitional Deacons	3
Permanent Deacons in Diocese	126
Total Brothers	12
Total Sisters	270
Parishes	
Parishes	84
With Resident Pastor:	
Resident Diocesan Priests	70
Resident Religious Priests	1
Without Resident Pastor:	
Administered by Priests	13
Professional Ministry Personnel:	
Brothers	12
Sisters	270
Welfare	
Catholic Hospitals	2
Total Assisted	411,761
Homes for the Aged	13
Total Assisted	1,100
Day Care Centers	1
Total Assisted	37
Specialized Homes	2
Total Assisted	1,252
Special Centers for Social Services	6
Total Assisted	16,193
Educational	
Diocesan Students in Other Seminaries	16
Total Seminarians	16
Colleges and Universities	2
Total Students	5,602
High Schools, Diocesan and Parish	6
Total Students	3,134
Elementary Schools, Diocesan and Parish	31
Total Students	7,047
Non-residential Schools for the Disabled	3
Total Students	119
Catechesis/Religious Education:	
High School Students	32
Elementary Students	9,120
Total Students under Catholic Instruction	25,038
Teachers in the Diocese:	
Sisters	20
Lay Teachers	760
Vital Statistics	
Receptions into the Church:	
Infant Baptism Totals	1,872
Adult Baptism Totals	88
First Communions	1,976
Confirmations	2,126
Marriages:	
Catholic	318
Interfaith	125
Total Marriages	443
Deaths	2,445
Total Catholic Population	252,088
Total Population	1,272,212

Former Bishops—Most Revs. JOSEPH MCSHEA, D.D., appt. Titular Bishop of Mina and Auxiliary Bishop of Philadelphia Feb. 8, 1952; cons. March 19, 1952; appt. Bishop of Allentown Feb. 15, 1961; installed April 11, 1961; retired Feb. 8, 1983; died Nov. 28, 1991; THOMAS J. WELSH, D.D., J.C.D., appt. Titular Bishop of Scattery Island and Auxiliary Bishop of Philadelphia, Feb. 18, 1970; cons. April 2, 1970; appt. First Bishop of Arlington, June 4, 1974; installed Aug. 13, 1974; appt. Bishop of Allentown, Feb. 8, 1983; installed Second Bishop of Allentown, March 21, 1983; retired Dec. 16, 1997; died Feb. 19, 2009; EDWARD PETER CULLEN, D.D., ord. May 19, 1962; appt. Auxiliary Bishop of Philadelphia and Titular Bishop of Paria in Preconsilare Feb. 8, 1994; cons. April 14, 1994; appt. Bishop of Allentown Dec. 16, 1997; installed Third Bishop of Allentown Feb. 9, 1998; retired May 27, 2009.; JOHN O. BARRES, S.T.D., J.C.L., D.D., ord. Oct. 21, 1989; appt. Bishop of Allentown May 27, 2009; installed July 30, 2009; appt. Bishop of Rockville Centre Dec. 9, 2016; installed Jan. 31, 2017.

Vicar General—4029 W. Tilghman St., Allentown, 18105-1538. Mailing Address: P.O. Box F, Allentown, 18105-1538. Tel: 610-437-0755; Fax: 610-433-7822. Rev. Msgr. DAVID L. JAMES, V.G., M.Div., J.C.L.

Chancellor—Rev. EUGENE P. RITZ, M.Div., M.A., J.C.L., 4029 W. Tilghman St., Allentown, 18105-1538. Tel: 610-437-0755; Fax: 610-433-7822. Mailing Address: P.O. Box F, Allentown, 18105-1538.

Assistant in the Diocesan Curia—4029 W. Tilghman St., Allentown, 18105. Tel: 610-437-0755; Fax: 610-433-7822. *Mailing Address: P.O. Box F, Allentown, 18105-1538.* Rev. KEITH A. MATHUR, M.A., M.Div.

Office of Rite of Christian Initiation of Adults (RCIA)—Tel: 610-437-0755; Fax: 610-433-7822; Email: kmathur@allentowndiocese.org. Rev. KEITH A. MATHUR, M.A., M.Div.

Council of Priests/Diocesan Consultors—4029 W. Tilghman St., P.O. Box F, Allentown, 18105. Tel: 610-437-0755; Fax: 610-433-7822.

College of Consultors—Rev. Msgrs. DAVID L. JAMES, V.G., M.Div., J.C.L.; JOSEPH A. DESANTIS, M.Div.; Rev. ANDREW N. GEHRINGER, M.Div., M.A., S.T.B.; Rev. Msgrs. WILLIAM F. GLOSSER, V.F., M.A.; JOHN P. MURPHY; GERALD E. GOBITAS, Th.M.; FRANCIS P. SCHOENAUER, M.Div.; STEPHEN J. RADOCHA, V.F., M.Div.; ROBERT J. WARGO, M.Div.

Ex Officio Member—Rev. Msgr. DAVID L. JAMES, V.G., M.Div., J.C.L.

Secretary for Clergy—Rev. ADAM C. SEDAR, M.Div., M.A.

Elected Members—Revs. DONALD W. CIENIEWICZ, M.Div.; JOHN M. GIBBONS; RONALD J. MINNER, M.Div.; WILLIAM T. CAMPION, M.Div., Th. M; BERNARD J. EZAKI, M.Div., M.A.; MARK R. SEARLES, M.Div., M.A.; KEITH R. LASKOWSKI, M.Div., M.A., S.T.B.; Rev. Msgrs. THOMAS P. KOONS, V.R., J.C.L., M.A., M.Div.; ROBERT J. BISZEK, (Retired).

Appointed Members—Revs. DAVID J. LOEPER; BRIAN M. MILLER; ANDREW N. GEHRINGER, M.Div., M.A., S.T.B.; ANTHONY P. MONGIELLO; EUGENE P. RITZ, M.Div., M.A., J.C.L.; CHRISTOPHER M. ZELONIS, M.Div., M.A.

Finance Council—4029 W. Tilghman St., P.O. Box F, Allentown, 18105-1538. Tel: 610-437-0755; Fax: 610-433-7822. Most Rev. ALFRED A. SCHLERT, J.C.L., Ph.D., S.T.D., 4029 W. Tilghman St., P.O. Box F, Allentown, 18105-1538. Tel: 610-437-0755; Fax: 610-433-7822; MR. DENNIS DOMCHEK; MR. DANIEL C. CONFALONE; Rev. Msgr. DAVID L. JAMES, V.G., M.Div., J.C.L.; MRS. AUDRA J. KAHR; MR. HERMAN L. RIJ; MR. PAUL E. HUCK; MR. ROBERT J. SNYDER; MR. PHILIP J. MASON; MR. DENNIS C. MORTON; THOMAS F. TRAUD, Esq.; MR. MARK E. SMITH, CPA.

Victim Assistance Coordinator—MS. WENDY S. KRISAK, M.A., N.C.C., L.P.C., Tel: 800-791-9209; Fax: 610-435-4367; Email: wkrisak@allentowndiocese.org.

Censor of Books—Rev. Msgr. MICHAEL J. CHABACK.

Diocesan Tribunal—Very Rev. JOHN J. PAUL, M.S.C., V.J., S.T.L., J.C.D., Judicial Vicar, 202 N. 17th St., Allentown, 18104. Tel: 610-434-3200; Fax: 610-433-3104.

Judges—Rev. Msgrs. DAVID J. MORRISON, Judge Emeritus, (Retired); THOMAS P. KOONS, V.R.,

J.C.L., M.A., M.Div.; VICTOR F. FINELLI, J.C.L., Th.M., M.Div.
Promoter of Justice—Rev. EUGENE P. RITZ, M.Div., M.A., J.C.L.
Defenders of the Bond—Rev. Msgr. DAVID L. JAMES, V.G., M.Div., J.C.L.; Rev. DAVID J. KOZAK, J.C.L.
Advocates—Rev. Msgrs. ROBERT J. BISZEK, (Retired); DAVID L. JAMES, V.G., M.Div., J.C.L.; Rev. DANIEL E. KRAVATZ, M.A.; Deacons RICHARD L. BENKOVIC; WILLIAM R. HASSLER.
Notaries—MRS. PATRICIA ECHTERNACH; MRS. KATHLEEN SNYDER.

Vicar for Religious—Rev. Msgr. THOMAS P. KOONS, V.R., J.C.L., M.A., M.Div., 7660 Imperial Way, Ste. 125, Allentown, 18195. Tel: 610-434-3200; Fax: 610-433-3104; Email: tkoons@allentowndiocese.org.

Vicars Forane—Rev. Msgr. JOHN G. CHIZMAR, V.F., M.Div., Carbon Deanery; Very Rev. THOMAS P. BORTZ, V.F., M.Div., S.T.B., Berks County; Rev. Msgrs. DANIEL J. YENUSHOSKY, V.F., Th.M., Lehigh Deanery; STEPHEN J. RADOCHA, V.F., M.Div., Northampton Deanery; WILLIAM F. GLOSSER, V.F., M.A., Schuylkill Deanery.

Human Resources—Mailing Address: P.O. Box F, Allentown, 18105-1538. Tel: 610-871-5200, Ext. 204; Fax: 610-871-5211; Email: jweaver@allentowndiocese.org. MRS. JILL WEAVER, Dir.

Benefits and Payroll Manager—MR. THOMAS O. KERN, Tel: 610-871-5200, Ext. 2109; Fax: 610-871-5211; Email: tkern@allentowndiocese.org.

Office of Hispanic Affairs—2121 Madison Ave., Bethlehem, 18018-4642. Tel: 610-289-8900. MRS. BERNARDA LIRIANO, Dir.

Secretariat for Clergy—Mailing Address: P.O. Box F, Allentown, 18105-1538. Tel: 610-437-0755; Fax: 610-433-7822. Rev. ADAM C. SEDAR, M.Div., M.A., Sec., Email: asedar@allentowndiocese.org.
Priest Personnel Office—Rev. ADAM C. SEDAR, M.Div., M.A., Dir., Mailing Address: P.O. Box F, Allentown, 18105-1538. Tel: 610-437-0755; Fax: 610-433-7822; MRS. CHRISTINA SHUPE, Dir. Priests Svcs., Tel: 484-456-5038; Fax: 610-694-9998.
Office for Vocations Promotion—Rev. MARK R. SEARLES, M.Div., M.A., Dir., Tel: 610-437-4601, Ext. 199; Email: msearles@allentowndiocese.org.
Office of Seminarian Formation—Rev. CHRISTOPHER S. BUTERA, M.Div., M.A., Dir., Tel: 610-437-0755; Email: cbutera@allentowndiocese.org; Web: www.beapriest.com.
Holy Family Villa for Priests—1325 Prospect Ave., Bethlehem, 18018-4916. Tel: 610-694-0395; Fax: 610-694-9990. Rev. E. MICHAEL CAMILLI, M.S.C., S.T.L., M.S.L.S., H.E.L., Spiritual Dir.
Office for Permanent Diaconate Formation—2121 Madison Ave., Bethlehem, 18018-4642. Tel: 610-332-0442; Fax: 610-332-0444; Email: diaconate@allentowndiocese.org. Rev. EUGENE P. RITZ, M.Div., M.A., J.C.L., Dir. Formation.

Secretariat for Catholic Life and Evangelization—MS. MARY FRAN HARTIGAN, M.A., Sec., 2121 Madison Ave., Bethlehem, 18017-4642. Tel: 610-289-8900; Fax: 610-289-7917; Email: mhartigan@allentowndiocese.org.
Office of Marriage and Natural Family Planning—MR. ROBERT J. OLNEY, Email: rolney@allentowndiocese.org.
Office of Youth, Young Adult and Family Ministry—MS. THEA ACLO, Dir., Email: taclo@allentowndiocese.org; MRS. ALEXA SMITH, Asst. Dir., Tel: 610-289-8900; Fax: 610-289-7917; Email: asmith@allentowndiocese.org; MR. DANIEL JONES, Asst. Coord./CYO; FRANCESCA FRIAS, Asst. Coord.
Office of Adult Formation—Director of Faith Formation: MS. MARY FRAN HARTIGAN, M.A., Tel: 610-289-8900; Fax: 610-289-7917; Email: mhartigan@allentowndiocese.org. Assistant Director: MR. RICK DOOLEY.
Office of Pro-Life Activities and Social Concerns—MS. MARY FRAN HARTIGAN, M.A.
Multi-Cultural Affairs—MS. MARY FRAN HARTIGAN, M.A., Tel: 610-289-8900; Fax: 610-289-7917; Email: mhartigan@allentowndiocese.org.
Office of Prison Ministry—Sr. MARTHA ZAMMATORE, O.S.F., Liaison, Tel: 610-289-8900; Email: mzammatore@dioceseofallentown.org.
Office for Ministry with Persons with Disabilities—Sr. JANICE MARIE JOHNSON, R.S.M., Dir., Tel: 610-870-5200, Ext. 2280.
Ecumenical and Interreligious Dialogue—Rev. JOHN A. KRIVAK, M.Div., Th.M., M.Ed., Ed.D., Annunciation B.V.M., 122 Union St., Catasauqua, 18032-1923. Tel: 610-264-0332; Email: jkrivak@allentowndiocese.org.

Secretariat for Temporal Services—MR. MARK E. SMITH, CPA, CFO & Sec., P.O. Box F, Allentown, 18105-1538. Tel: 610-871-5200, Ext. 2205; Fax: 610-871-5211; Email: msmith@allentowndiocese.org.
Accounting Services—JEFFREY K. BUCK, Controller, Tel: 610-871-5200, Ext. 2102; Fax: 610-871-5211; Email: jbuck@allentowndiocese.org; MR. FRANK J. UNGER, CPA, Asst. Controller, Tel: 610-871-5200, Ext. 2239; Fax: 610-871-5211; Email: funger@allentowndiocese.org.
Parish and School Support Services—MRS. LESLIE SHIROCK, Tel: 610-871-5200, Ext. 2228; Fax: 610-871-5211; Email: lshirock@allentowndiocese.org.
Cemeteries—Rev. Msgr. WILLIAM F. BAVER, M.Div., Th.M., C.C.C.E., K.C.H.S., Dir., P.O. Box F, Allentown, 18105-1538. Tel: 610-871-5200, Ext. 2234; Fax: 610-871-5211; Email: wbaver@allentowndiocese.org.
Insurance and Real Estate—MS. KELLY C. BRUCE, A.R.M., Dir., Tel: 610-871-5200, Ext. 2203; Email: kbruce@allentowndiocese.org.
Secretariat for Stewardship and Development—MR. PAUL ACAMPORA, Sec. & Exec. Dir. Bishop's Annual Appeal, P.O. Box F, Allentown, 18105-1538. Tel: 610-871-5200, Ext. 2210; Fax: 610-871-5211.

Secretariat for Catholic Education—MR. JOHN BAKEY, Chancellor, 1425 Mountain Dr. N., Bethlehem, 18015-4722. Email: jbakey@allentowndiocese.org; DR. PHILIP J. FROMUTH, Ph.D., Supt., Tel: 610-866-0581; Email: pfromuth@allentowndiocese.org.
Deputy Superintendent, Secondary Education and Special Education—DR. BROOKE C. TESCHE, Tel: 610-866-0581.
Personnel (Elementary and Secondary)—MS. KIMBERLY A. FETTER, Asst. Supt., Tel: 610-866-0581; Email: kfetter@allentowndiocese.org.
Assistant Superintendent, Government Programs / Instructional Technology—MRS. KATHLEEN BONDI, M.Ed., Tel: 610-866-0581; Email: kbondi@allentowndiocese.org.
Assistant Superintendent Religious Education—MS. ALEXANDRIA M. CIRKO, Tel: 610-866-0581; Email: acirko@allentowndiocese.org.

Secretariat for Youth Protection and Catholic Human Services—Mailing Address: P.O. Box F, Allentown, 18105-1538. Tel: 610-871-5200, Ext. 2204; Email: prusso@allentowndiocese.org. MS. PAMELA J. RUSSO, M.S.W., M.S.
Holy Family Manor—MRS. SUSAN REGALIS, N.H.A., N.H.A., Admin., 1200 Spring St., Bethlehem, 18018. Tel: 610-865-5595; Fax: 610-997-8454; Web: www.hfmanor.org.
Holy Family Personal Care Homes—MRS. KAREN ABRUZZESE, Coord., 1200 Spring St., Bethlehem, 18018. Email: bruzzese@hfmanor.org; Web: www.hfpersonalcare.org.
Diocesan Medical Ethicist—Rev. JOHN A. KRIVAK, M.Div., Th.M., M.Ed., Ed.D., Annunciation B.V.M., 122 Union St., Catasauqua, 18032-1923. Tel: 610-264-0332; Fax: 610-264-5271.

Secretariat for External Affairs—MR. MATTHEW T. KERR, Sec., Mailing Address: P.O. Box F, Allentown, 18105-1538. Tel: 610-871-5200, Ext. 2265; Fax: 610-439-7694; Email: mkerr@allentowndiocese.org.
Office of Communications—MR. MATTHEW T. KERR, Dir., Tel: 610-871-5200, Ext. 2265; Fax: 610-439-7694; Email: mkerr@allentowndiocese.org.
Coordinator of Diocesan Mission Promotion—MR. PAUL G. WIRTH, Tel: 610-871-5200, Ext. 2274; Fax: 610-439-7694; Email: pwirth@allentowndiocese.org.
Digital Media Specialist—Tel: 610-871-5200, Ext. 2214; Fax: 610-439-7694. MS. ELIZABETH BARTOLAI.
Office of Government Affairs—MR. MATTHEW T. KERR, Dir., Tel: 610-871-5200, Ext. 2265; Fax: 610-439-7694; Email: mkerr@allentowndiocese.org.
The A.D. Times—MRS. JILL M. CARAVAN, Editor & Dir., Tel: 610-871-5200, Ext. 2264; Fax: 610-439-7694; Email: adtimes@allentowndiocese.org.

Affiliated Organizations

American Catholic Overseas Aid Fund—Mailing Address: P.O. Box F, Allentown, 18105-1538. Tel: 610-437-0755; Fax: 610-433-7822.

Blue Army of Our Lady of Fatima—Rev. DOMINIC THAO PHAM, M.Div., Spiritual Dir., St. Ann Parish, 415 S. Sixth St., Emmaus, 18049-3703. Tel: 610-695-2426.

Catholic Daughters of the Americas—Deacon KEVIN C. WASIELEWSKI, Diocese Committee Chap.
Ashland - Court St. Joan of Arc #225—VACANT.
Easton - Court Easton #358—VACANT.
Frackville - Court St. James #1029—VACANT.
Jim Thorpe - Court Ryan #911—Rev. JAMES J. WARD, M.Div., Chap.
Shenandoah - Court Annunciation #175—Rev. Msgr. RONALD C. BOCIAN, M.Div., M.Ed., Chap.

Catholic Men of Good News (CMOGN)—
Diocesan Spiritual Director—Rev. RICHARD C. BRENSINGER, M.Div., St. Christopher Catholic Newman Ctr., 15207 Kutztown Rd., Kutztown, 19530-9281. Tel: 610-683-8467.

Charismatic Renewal—St. Anne Rectory, 450 E. Washington Ave., Bethlehem, 18017-5944. Tel: 610-867-5039. Rev. CLIFTON E. BISHOP, Bishop's Liaison.

Courage / Encourage—Rev. RICHARD C. BRENSINGER, M.Div., Dir.; Deacon CHRISTOPHER MAY, Asst. Dir., Tel: 610-683-8467; Email: courage@allentowndiocese.org.

Cursillo Movement—Rev. MARTIN F. KERN, Spiritual Dir., St. Columbkill Rectory, 200 Indian Spring Rd., Boyertown, 19512-2008. Tel: 610-367-2371; Fax: 610-369-0242.

Equestrian Order of the Holy Sepulchre of Jerusalem—Ss. Simon & Jude Rectory: 730 W. Broad St., Bethlehem, 18018-5295. Tel: 610-866-5582; Email: wbaver@allentowndiocese.org. Rev. Msgr. WILLIAM F. BAVER, M.Div., Th.M., C.C.C.E., K.C.H.S., Coord.

Father Walter Ciszek Prayer League, Inc. (The)—Rev. Msgr. RONALD C. BOCIAN, M.Div., M.Ed., Bd. Pres., The Ciszek Center, 18 E. Oak St., Shenandoah, 17976-2356. Tel: 570-462-2270; Fax: 570-462-2274; Email: fwccenter@ciszek.org; Web: www.ciszek.org.

Holy Name Societies—Rev. PAUL L. ROTHERMEL, M.Div., Th.M., M.A., St. Charles Borromeo, 1115 Walnut St., Ashland, 17921-1944. Tel: 570-875-1521.

Lay Fraternities of St. Dominic—
Expectation of the Blessed Mother Chapter 405—
Notre Dame of Bethlehem—1861 Catasauqua Rd., Bethlehem, 18018. MR. JOHN TUCKER, O.P., Pres.
St. Louis deMontfort Chapter 406—
Sacred Heart of Jesus—Burkhardt Bldg., 121 Wabash St., Bath, 18014. MS. SANDRA TUCKER, O.P., Pres.

Legatus—RAY BISHOP, Pres., Email: rbishop@bishopphoto.com; Rev. Msgr. JOHN P. MURPHY, Chap.

Legion of Mary—MR. JOE AKKARA, Pres., 29 Mulligan Dr., Reading, 19606. Tel: 610-301-5139.

Operation Rice Bowl—1040 Flexer Ave., Allentown, 18103-5520. Tel: 610-433-7413; Fax: 610-433-2308. Rev. Msgr. JOHN P. MURPHY, Dir.; MR. EDWARD L. LISZKA, Administrative Asst.

Our Lady's Missionaries of the Eucharist—A Public Association of Christ's Faithful. *640 E. Main St., Birdsboro, 19508-2002.* Email: olme@olme.org; Web: www.olme.org. Sr. JOAN NOREEN, O.L.M.E., Contact Person.

Secular Franciscan Order - St. Francis Fraternity—St. Francis Retreat House, 3918 Chipman Rd., Easton, 18045-3014. Tel: 610-258-3053; Fax: 610-258-2412. NANCY SNYDER, O.F.S., Min., 1296 Hedgerow Dr., Easton, 18040. Tel: 610-252-5230; Email: lmpnurpara@msn.com.

Serra Clubs—
Serra Club of Allentown—Rev. Msgr. DANIEL J. YENUSHOSKY, V.F., Th.M., Chap.; MS. ELIZABETH STEHNACH, Pres., 2444 W. Washington St., Allentown, 18104. Tel: 610-349-4104; Email: elizabeth.stehnach@gmail.com.
Serra Club of Bethlehem—Rev. ANTHONY P. MONGIELLO, Chap.; MS. MARY FUEHRER, Pres., 1949 Kingsley Dr., Bethlehem, 18018. Tel: 610-865-4346; Email: fp3310@aol.com.
Serra Club of Reading—PAUL T. ESSIG, Esq., 3804 Reiff Pl., Reading, 19606. Tel: 610-779-0772; Email: pessig@hvmllaw.com; Rev. EDWARD J. ESSIG, Chap.
Carbon / Schuylkill Serra Club—VACANT, Chap.; DIANE SURAVICZ, Vice Pres. Programs, 1877 Quakake Rd., Weatherly, 18255. Tel: 570-427-8724.

St. Thomas More Society—Mailing Address: c/o The Diocese of Allentown, P.O. Box F, Allentown, 18105. Tel: 610-433-6461; Email: allentownstms@gmail.com; Web: www.stmsallentown.org. MR. MATTHEW J. KLOIBER, Pres.; Rev. Msgr. EDWARD J. COYLE, M.A., Th.M., Chap.

Third Order Secular Carmelites—Mailing Address: Sacred Heart Parish, P.O. Box 6217, Reading, 19610. Tel: 610-372-4010. EILEEN OBROCHTA, Dir.

CLERGY, PARISHES, MISSIONS AND PAROCHIAL SCHOOLS

CITY OF ALLENTOWN

(LEHIGH COUNTY)

1—CATHEDRAL OF ST. CATHARINE OF SIENA (1919) (Indian) Rev. Msgr. Francis P. Schoenauer, M.Div.; Rev. Brendon M. Laroche, Parochial Vicar; Deacons William Hassler; Robert H. Snyder; Ricardo Ceballos. In Res., Rev. Achilles Ayaton.
Res.: 1825 W. Turner St., 18104. Tel: 610-433-6461; Fax: 610-433-5452; Email: secretary@cathedral-church.org; Web: www.cathedral-church.org.
See John Vianney Regional School under Regional Catholic Elementary Schools, Diocesan located in the Institution section.
Catechesis Religious Program—Joy Baron. Students 602.

2—ST. FRANCIS OF ASSISI (1928) Rev. Msgr. Victor F. Finelli, J.C.L., Th.M., M.Div.; Deacons Robert P. Young; Ricardo Reyes.
Business Office—1046 W. Cedar St., 18102-1304.
Tel: 610-433-6102; Fax: 610-434-6972; Email: parishoffice@stfrancisallentown.org; Web: www.stfrancisallentown.org.
See St. John Vianney Regional School under Regional Catholic Elementary Schools, Diocesan located in the Institution section.
Catechesis Religious Program—Tel: 610-435-0364. Students 67.

3—IMMACULATE CONCEPTION (1857) [CEM] (Declared National Shrine of Our Lady of Guadalupe, Mother of the Americas 1974). Revs. John M. Gibbons, Admin.; George R. Winne; Harold F. Dagle, M.A., Pastor Emeritus, (Retired); Deacon Richard L. Benkovic.
Res.: 501 Ridge Ave., 18102. Tel: 610-433-4404; Fax: 610-433-8401; Email: iccallentown@gmail.com.
Schools-See St. Elizabeth Regional School under Regional Catholic Elementary Schools, Diocesan located in the Institution section.
Catechesis Religious Program—Students 25.

4—ST. JOHN THE BAPTIST, [CEM] (Slovak) Rev. Gregory R. Karpyn, B.A., M.A., M.Div., Admin.
Res.: 924 N. Front St., 18102-1912.
Tel: 610-432-0034; Fax: 610-432-2776; Email: stJohnBaptistPa@gmail.com.
See St. Elizabeth Regional School under Regional Catholic Elementary Schools, Diocesan located in the Institution section.

5—OUR LADY HELP OF CHRISTIANS (1927) Rev. Jose G. (Father Johnson) Kochuparambil, Admin.; Deacon Ricardo Reyes.
Res.: 444 N. Jasper St., 18109-2666.
Tel: 610-432-9384; Fax: 610-782-9297; Email: ourladyhlp@aol.com; Web: www.OLHCparish.net.
Catechesis Religious Program—Students 25.
Convent—922 Hanover Ave., 18109-2011.
Tel: 610-433-4915.

6—ST. PAUL (1928) Rev. Michael E. Mullins, M.Div., M.A., S.T.B.; Deacons Gary Granato; Cu T. Than; Jose F. DeCastro; Saul Hernandez. In Res., Rev. Msgr. Robert J. Biszek, (Retired).
Res.: 920 S. Second St., 18103. Tel: 610-797-9733; Fax: 610-797-9537; Email: sprccbulletin@rcn.com; Web: stpaulrc.com.
Church: Second St. & Susquehanna St., 18103.
See John Vianney Regional School under Regional Catholic Elementary Schools, Diocesan located in the Institution section.
Catechesis Religious Program—Students 75.

7—SS. PETER AND PAUL (1912) (Polish)
1065 Fullerton Ave., 18102. Revs. Gregory R. Karpyn, B.A., M.A., M.Div., Admin.; Ladislaus J. Dudek, Pastor Emeritus, (Retired).
Parish Office & Res.: 924 N. Front St., 18102-1912.
Tel: 610-432-0034; Fax: 610-432-2776; Email: sspeterandpaulpa@gmail.com.
See St. Elizabeth Regional School under Regional Catholic Elementary Schools, Diocesan located in the Institution section.
Catechesis Religious Program—Students 4.

8—SACRED HEART OF JESUS (1869) [CEM] Rev. John M. Gibbons; Deacons Roberto Reyes; Julian Corchado; Claudio F. Cruz; Rev. George R. Winne; Deacons C. Miguel Vargas; Jose Santos-Gonzales.
Res.: 336 N. Fourth St., 18102-3008.
Tel: 610-434-5171; Fax: 610-434-2441; Email: shparishsec@gmail.com.
School—Sacred Heart of Jesus School, (Grades PreK-8), 325 N. Fourth St., 18102-3007.
Tel: 610-437-3031; Fax: 610-437-2724; Email: altlsh@ptd.net. James Krupka, Prin. Regional school Lay Teachers 13; Students 227.
Catechesis Religious Program—317 N. 4th St., 18102. Students 206.

9—ST. STEPHEN OF HUNGARY (1915) (Hungarian) Revs. Gregory Pendergraft, F.S.S.P.; Joseph Favole-Mihm.
Res.: 510 W. Union St., 18101-2307.
Tel: 610-439-0111; Fax: 610-439-6048; Email: saintstephenfssp@gmail.com; Web: www.lehighvalleylatinmass.org.
See Sacred Heart School, Allentown under Regional Catholic Elementary Schools, Diocesan located in the Institution section.
Catechesis Religious Program—

10—ST. THOMAS MORE (1966) Rev. Msgr. John P. Murphy; Rev. James M. Harper; Deacons James R. Duncan; James Toolan; Thomas F. Shubella; Christopher C. Kinsella Jr. In Res., Rev. Mark R. Searles, M.Div., M.A.
Res.: 1040 Flexer Ave., 18103-5520.
Tel: 610-433-7413; Fax: 610-433-2308; Email: rectory@stmchurchallentown.org; Web: www.stmchurchallentown.org.
School—St. Thomas More School, Tel: 610-432-0396; Fax: 610-432-1395; Email: altlstm@ptd.com; Web: www.stmschoolpa.com. Ms. Amanda Salovay, Vice Prin., Middle School; Mrs. Michele Ryan, Prin. Primary School (K-4); Sr. Patricia Luss, O.S.F., Vice Prin., Primary School.
Catechesis Religious Program—Kevin Damitz, D.R.E. Students 455.
Convent—992 Flexer Ave., 18103-3664.
Tel: 610-437-9520; Fax: 610-432-9359.

OUTSIDE CITY OF ALLENTOWN

ASHLAND, SCHUYLKILL CO., ST. CHARLES BORROMEO (2015)
Mailing Address: 1115 Walnut St., Ashland, 17921-1844. Tel: 570-875-1521; Fax: 570-875-2635; Email: catholicchurchashland@msn.com. 1104 Walnut St., Ashland, 17921. Rev. Paul L. Rothermel, M.Div., Th. M., M.A.
Worship Site: St. Vincent de Paul, 260 N. 2nd St., Girardville, 17935.
See Trinity Academy at the Father Walter J. Ciszek Education Center, Shenandoah under Regional Catholic Elementary Schools located in the Institution section.
Catechesis Religious Program—Students 92.

BALLY, BERKS CO., MOST BLESSED SACRAMENT (1741) [CEM] Rev. Kevin M. Gualano, Admin.; Deacons Thomas J. Murphy; Michael J. Boyle.
Res.: 610 Pine St., Box C, Bally, 19503-1003.
Tel: 610-845-2460; Fax: 610-845-2660; Email: mbs.car@comcast.net.
See St. Francis Academy, Bally under Regional Catholic Elementary Schools, Diocesan located in the Institution section.
Catechesis Religious Program—Students 115.

BANGOR, NORTHAMPTON CO., OUR LADY OF GOOD COUNSEL (1915) [CEM] Rev. Stephen L. Maco, M.Div., M.Ed.; Deacon Ronald R. Pasquino.
Res.: 436 S. Second St., Bangor, 18013-2514.
Tel: 610-588-5445; Fax: 610-599-6997; Email: ourladystvincent@gmail.com; Web: www.ourladystvincent.com.
See Immaculate Conception School, Pen Argyl under Regional Catholic Elementary Schools, Diocesan located in the Institution section.
Catechesis Religious Program—Students 136.
Mission—St. Vincent de Paul, 720 Delaware Ave., Portland, Northampton Co. 18351.

BARNESVILLE, SCHUYLKILL CO., ST. RICHARD (1950) Revs. Francis J. Baransky; Joseph T. Whalen, M.Div., Pastor Emeritus; Stephen J. Halabura, Pastor Emeritus, (Retired); Deacon John A. Setlock.
Res.: 799 Barnesville Dr., Barnesville, 18214-2616.
Tel: 570-467-2315; Fax: 570-467-2462; Email: strichard@frontiernet.org; Web: www.strichard.org.
Catechesis Religious Program—Students 35.

BATH, NORTHAMPTON CO., SACRED HEART OF JESUS (1920) [CEM]
117 Washington St., Bath, 18014. Rev. Christopher S. Butera, M.Div., M.A., Admin.; Deacons Lewis T. Ferris; Edward J. Saukulak.
Res.: 210 E. Northampton St., Bath, 18014-1625.
Tel: 610-837-7874; Fax: 610-837-4570; Email: msansonetti@sacredheartbath.org; Web: www.sacredheartbath.org.
School—Sacred Heart of Jesus School, (Grades PreK-8), 115 Washington St., Bath, 18014-1524.
Tel: 610-837-6391; Fax: 610-837-2469; Email: office@shschool.us; Web: www.sacred-heart-school.com. Ann Marie Thomas, Prin. Lay Teachers 13; Students 103.
Catechesis Religious Program—Students 122.

BETHLEHEM, LEHIGH CO.

1—ASSUMPTION B.V.M. (1927) Rev. Msgrs. Nevin J. Klinger, M.A., J.C.L.; Robert J. Coll, Pastor Emeritus, (Retired); Deacons Donald W. Elliott; Stewart T. Herman.
Res.: 4101 Old Bethlehem Pike, Bethlehem, 18015-9097. Tel: 610-867-7424; Fax: 610-867-8301; Email: abvm@ptd.net; Web: www.assumptionbethlehem.com.
See St. Michael the Archangel School, Coopersburg under Regional Catholic Elementary Schools, Diocesan located in the Institution section.
Catechesis Religious Program—Christina Bigatel Durback, D.R.E. Students 321.

2—NOTRE DAME OF BETHLEHEM (1954) Rev. Msgr. Thomas D. Baddick, Th.M.; Deacon Dr. William F. Urbine; Revs. Venatius T. Karobo, A.J., Chap.; Daniel E. Kravatz, M.A.; Deacon Richard T. Sewald Jr.
Res.: 1861 Catasauqua Rd., Bethlehem, 18018-1298.
Tel: 610-866-4371; Fax: 610-866-9065; Email: notredamesec@gmail.com; Web: www.ndbethlehemchurch.org.
School—Notre Dame of Bethlehem School, (Grades PreK-8), 1835 Catasauqua Rd., Bethlehem, 18018-1211. Tel: 610-866-2231; Fax: 610-866-4374; Email: altlndb@ptd.net; Web: www.ndbethlehemschool.org. Mrs. Kathy Maziarz, Prin. Lay Teachers 36; Students 431.
Catechesis Religious Program—Students 201.

3—SS. SIMON AND JUDE (1917) Rev. Msgr. William F. Baver, M.Div., Th.M., C.C.C.E., K.C.H.S.; Deacons Reuben H. Hartzell Jr.; Jeffrey R. Trexler, Ph.D.
Res.: 730 W. Broad St., Bethlehem, 18018.
Tel: 610-866-5582; Fax: 610-866-2992; Email: secretary@simonandjudepa.org.
Catechesis Religious Program—Students 26.

BETHLEHEM, NORTHAMPTON CO.

1—ST. ANNE (1929) Revs. Anthony P. Mongiello; Eugene P. Ritz, M.Div., M.A., J.C.L.; Frans J. Berkhout, M.Div., M.Ed.; Deacon Richard G. Scrak Jr.
Res.: 450 E. Washington Ave., Bethlehem, 18017-5944. Tel: 610-867-5039; Fax: 610-882-4094; Email: church@stannebethlehem.org; Web: www.stannechurchbethlehem.org.
School—St. Anne School, (Grades PreK-8), 375 Hickory St., Bethlehem, 18017-5944.
Tel: 610-868-4182; Tel: 610-868-7513 (pre-school); Fax: 610-868-8709; Email: altnsa@ptd.net; Web: www.stannebethlehem.org. Mrs. Karen Bentz, Prin. Students 390.
Catechesis Religious Program—Students 180.

2—HOLY GHOST (1871) [CEM] (German)
417 Carlton Ave., Bethlehem, 18017-1535. Rev. David J. Kozak, J.C.L., Admin.; Stephen T. Gorbos Jr.
Tel: 610-867-9382, Ext. 3; Email: hghostchurch@gmail.com; Web: www.holyghost-church.org.
Catechesis Religious Program—

3—HOLY INFANCY (1861) [CEM] Revs. Andrew N. Gehringer, M.Div., M.A., S.T.B.; Keith A. Mathur, M.A., M.Div., (In Res.); Deacons Rodoberto Matos; Gerardo Berrios; Jose A. Ocampo.
Res.: 312 E. Fourth St., Bethlehem, 18015-1706.
Tel: 610-866-1121; Fax: 610-866-7094; Email: holyinfancybethlehem@gmail.com.
School—Holy Infancy School, (Grades PreK-8), 127 E. 4th St., Bethlehem, 18015-1707.
Tel: 610-868-2621; Fax: 610-868-5402; Email: altnhi@ptd.net. Mrs. Marjorie Manasse, Prin. Students 130.
Catechesis Religious Program—Sr. Luiza Simon, D.R.E. Students 187.

4—INCARNATION OF OUR LORD PARISH (2008) [CEM]
Thomas and Buchanan Sts., Bethlehem, 18015. Rev. David J. Kozak, J.C.L., Admin.; Deacon Stephen T. Gorbos Jr.
Mailing Address & Rectory: 617 Pierce St., Bethlehem, 18015-3498. Tel: 610-866-3391; Fax: 610-866-6490; Email: iparish@ptd.net; Web: incarnationofourlord.com.
Convent—520 Buchanan St., Bethlehem, 18015-3499. Tel: 610-866-0275.
Catechesis Religious Program—417 Carlton Ave., Bethlehem, 18015. Mrs. Lisa Benedek, D.R.E. Students 10.

5—OUR LADY OF PERPETUAL HELP (1963) Rev. Msgr. Edward R. Sacks, M.Ed.; Rev. Abraham Ha, M.Div.; Deacons George C. Kelly Jr.; Donald J. Dupont; Ralph K. Sullivan. In Res., Rev. Msgr. David J. Morrison, (Retired).
Res.: 3219 Santee Rd., Bethlehem, 18020.
Tel: 610-867-8409; Fax: 610-867-4870; Email: olphers@ptd.net.
School—Our Lady of Perpetual Help School, (Grades K-8), 3221 Santee Rd., Bethlehem, 18020.
Tel: 610-868-6570; Fax: 610-868-7941. Danielle Frio, Prin. Lay Teachers 14; Students 240.
Catechesis Religious Program—Carol Salabsky, D.R.E. Students 335.

6—SACRED HEART OF JESUS (1936)
Email: sacredheartrectory1936@gmail.com. Rev. Robert J. George, M.Div.; Deacons Hugh Carlin; Joseph B. Juhasz.
Res.: 1817 First St., Bethlehem, 18020.
Tel: 610-865-5042; Fax: 610-865-1912; Email: sacredheartrectory1936@gmail.com.
Catechesis Religious Program—Students 125.

BOYERTOWN, BERKS CO., ST. COLUMBKILL (1921) Rev.

Martin F. Kern; Deacons Joseph L. Paschall Jr.; James A. Kochu; Joseph Petrauskas.
Res.: 200 Indian Spring Rd., Boyertown, 19512-2008. Tel: 610-367-2371; Fax: 610-369-0242; Email: lisad@stcolumbkill.com; Web: stcolumbkill.org.
See St. Francis Academy, Bally under Regional Catholic Elementary Schools, Diocesan located in the Institution section.
Catechesis Religious Program—Students 422.

CATASAUQUA, LEHIGH CO., ANNUNCIATION B.V.M.-ST. MARY'S (1857) [CEM] (German) Rev. John A. Krivak, M.Div., Th.M., M.Ed., Ed.D.
Res.: 122 Union St., Catasauqua, 18032-1923. Tel: 610-264-0332; Fax: 610-264-5271; Email: kim.stmarys122@gmail.com.
Catechesis Religious Program—Sharon Hontz, D.R.E. Students 64.

CATASAUQUA, NORTHAMPTON CO., ST. JOHN FISHER (2014)
1229 3rd St., Catasauqua, 18032-2716. Tel: 610-264-1972; Fax: 610-264-2105; Email: slchurch@rcn.com; Web: stjohnfisherparish.com. Rev. Eric J. Gruber, M.Div., Admin.; Deacon John C. O'Connell.
Schools-See Good Shepherd Regional School, Northampton under Regional Catholic Elementary Schools located in the Institution section.
Catechesis Religious Program—

COOPERSBURG, LEHIGH CO., ST. JOSEPH (1927) [CEM] Rev. Thomas R. Buckley; Deacon Conrad Paulus.
Res.: 5050 St. Joseph's Rd., Coopersburg, 18036-8920. Tel: 610-965-2877; Fax: 610-965-8317; Email: stjoes@ptd.net; Web: www.stjoescoopersburg.org.
See St. Michael the Archangel School, Coopersburg & Bethlehem under Regional Catholic Elementary Schools, Diocesan located in the Institution section.
Catechesis Religious Program—Students 128.

COPLAY, LEHIGH CO., ST. PETER (1927) [CEM] (Austrian—Hungarian) Rev. Msgr. John J. Martin; Deacons Thomas B. Reimer; Maurice E. Kelly.
Res.: 4 S. Fifth St., Coplay, 18037. Tel: 610-262-2417; Fax: 610-262-2652; Email: Saintpetercoplay@aol.com; Web: www:stpeterchurchcoplay.com.
See Good Shepherd School, Northampton under Regional Catholic Elementary Schools, Diocesan located in the Institution section.
Catechesis Religious Program—Holy Apostles Religious Education Program, (Serving St. Peter, Coplay & Holy Trinity & St. John the Baptist, Whitehall) 3008 S. Ruch St., Whitehall, 18052. Tel: 610-261-0144. Mrs. Barbara Majkowski, C.R.E. Students 90.

DOUGLASSVILLE, BERKS CO., IMMACULATE CONCEPTION (1916) [CEM 2] Rev. Msgr. John B. McCann; Deacons Paul J. Hiryak Jr.; James A. Bardi; Charles A. Giordano. In Res., Rev. Leo S. Stajkowski, (Retired).
Res.: 905 Chestnut St., Douglassville, 19518-9006. Tel: 610-582-2411; Fax: 610-404-2609; Email: secretary@icbvm.org; Web: www.icbvm.org.
School—Immaculate Conception Academy, (Grades K-8), 903 Chestnut St., Douglassville, 19518. Tel: 610-404-8645; Fax: 610-404-4890; Email: christine.foley@icaknights.org; Web: www.icaberks.org. Mrs. Christine Foley, Prin. Lay Teachers 14; Students 238.
Catechesis Religious Program—Students 335.

EASTON, NORTHAMPTON CO.
1—ST. ANTHONY OF PADUA (1909) [CEM] (Italian) Rev. Stanley M. Moczydlowski, M.B.A., M.Div.; Deacons Charles A. DeBellis; Kenneth L. Weiland.
Res.: 900 Washington St., Easton, 18042-4342. Tel: 610-253-7188; Fax: 610-253-6184; Email: stanthonys@rcn.com.
Catechesis Religious Program—Students 97.
2—ST. JANE FRANCES DE CHANTAL (1920) [JC]
Mailing Address: 4049 Hartley Ave., Easton, 18045. Tel: 610-253-3553; Email: info@stjanesofeastonpa.com; Web: www.stjanesofeastonpa.com. Rev. Msgr. Stephen J. Radocha, V.F., M.Div.; Revs. David M. Anthony; Bernard J. Ezaki, M.Div., M.A.; Deacons Robert W. Rodgers; Ranulfo Raymundo; Gene G. Schroth Jr.; Stephen J. Synoracki; Kevin C. Wasielewski; Noreen McDonough, Business Mgr.
Res.: 123 S. Nulton Ave., Easton, 18045-3791.
School—St. Jane Frances de Chantal School, (Grades PreK-8), 1900 Washington Blvd., Easton, 18042-4619. Tel: 610-253-8442; Fax: 610-253-2427; Email: principal@stjaneschool.com. Mrs. Marybeth Okula, Prin. Lay Teachers 27; Students 495.
Catechesis Religious Program—Kevin Kimmel, D.R.E. (Children); Mrs. Kelly DeRaymond, Dir. Adult Rel. Formation. Students 425.
3—OUR LADY OF MERCY PARISH (2008) Rev. Keith R. Laskowski, M.Div., M.A., S.T.B.; Deacons Isidro Gonzalez-Rivera; Henry J. Fleck Jr. In Res., Rev. Elias Munyaneza, A.J.
Office & Rectory: 132 S. Fifth St., Easton, 18042-4418. Tel: 610-252-7381; Email: info@olomercy.com; Web: www.olomercy.com.
Catechesis Religious Program—Mrs. Kelly DeRaymond, D.R.E. Students 65.

EMMAUS, LEHIGH CO., ST. ANN (1931) [CEM] Rev. Msgr. Edward J. Coyle, M.A., Th.M.; Rev. Dominic Thao Pham, M.Div.; Rev. Msgr. Thomas E. Hoban, Pastor Emeritus, (Retired); Deacons Dominick F. Amedeo Jr.; Peter H. Schutzler; Richard A. Fenton.
Res.: 415 S. Sixth St., Emmaus, 18049-3703. Tel: 610-965-2426; Fax: 610-967-1099; Email: churchofstann@rcn.com; Web: www.churchstann.org.
School—St. Ann School, (Grades PreK-8), 435 S. 6th St., Emmaus, 18049. Tel: 610-965-9220; Email: altlsa@ptd.net. Diana Kile, Prin.
Catechesis Religious Program—Students 364.

FOUNTAIN HILL, LEHIGH CO., ST. URSULA (Bethlehem P.O.) (1919) Rev. Robert J. Potts; Deacon David K. Rohner.
Res.: 1300 Broadway, Fountain Hill, 18015-4099. Tel: 610-867-5122; Fax: 610-867-6569; Email: stursulahill@gmail.com.
Catechesis Religious Program—Anne Korves, D.R.E. Students 57.

FRACKVILLE, SCHUYLKILL CO., ST. JOSEPH (1909) [CEM] Mailing Address: 7 S. Broad Mountain Ave., Frackville, 17931-1800. Tel: 570-874-0610; Fax: 570-874-0969; Email: frackvillerc3@verizon.net; Web: www.frackvillecatholic.org. Rev. Brian M. Miller.
Res.: 99 N. Line St., Frackville, 17931-1501.
See Trinity Academy at the Father Walter J. Ciszek Education Center, Shenandoah under Regional Catholic Elementary Schools, Diocesan located in the Institution section.
Catechesis Religious Program—Students 122.

HAMBURG, BERKS CO., ST. MARY (1854) [CEM]
Mailing Address: P.O. Box 189, Reading, 19526-0189. 94 Walnut Rd., Hamburg, 19526. Tel: 610-562-7657; Fax: 610-562-0379; Email: stmaryhamburg@aol.com; Web: www.stmaryhamburg.org. Rev. Donald W. Cieniewicz, M.Div.; Deacons Henry G. Gordon; Thomas B. Drogalis.
Res.: 100 Walnut Rd., Hamburg, 19526.
Catechesis Religious Program—Students 97.
Station—Hamburg State School and Hospital, Hamburg. Tel: 610-562-6063.

HELLERTOWN, NORTHAMPTON CO., ST. THERESA OF THE CHILD JESUS (1925)
Easton Rd. & Leonard St., Hellertown, 18055-1127. Rev. Jerome A. Tauber, M.Div., S.T.B.; Deacon Gerald R. Schmidt.
Res.: 1408 Easton Rd., Hellertown, 18055-1127. Tel: 610-838-7045; Fax: 610-838-0932; Email: sttheresacj@gmail.com; Web: www.sttheresaotcj.org.
School—St. Theresa of the Child Jesus School, (Grades PreK-8), 300 Leonard St., Hellertown, 18055-1199. Tel: 610-838-8161; Fax: 610-838-1915; Email: school@sttheresaotcj.org. Mrs. Diana Tice, Prin. Lay Teachers 15; Students 126.
Catechesis Religious Program—Students 169.
Convent—255 Wilson Ave., Hellertown, 18055-1454. Sr. Marian Bernadette Chuk, I.H.M., Supr.

JIM THORPE, CARBON CO.
1—IMMACULATE CONCEPTION (1848) [CEM]
178 W. Broadway, Jim Thorpe, 18229. Rev. James J. Ward, M.Div.
Res.: 180 W. Broadway, Jim Thorpe, 18229. Tel: 570-325-2791; Fax: 570-325-2427; Email: iccjt@ptd.net; Web: iccjimthorpe.org.
See St. Joseph Regional Academy, Jim Thorpe under Regional Catholic Elementary Schools, Diocesan located in the Institution section.
Catechesis Religious Program—Students 77.
2—ST. JOSEPH (1871) [CEM] Rev. James J. Ward, M.Div.; Deacon John J. Mroz.
Res.: 526 North St., Jim Thorpe, 18229. Tel: 570-325-3731; Fax: 570-325-2523; Email: stjosjt@ptd.net; Web: stjosephchurch-jimthorpe.org.
Schools-See St. Joseph Regional Academy, Jim Thorpe under Regional Catholic Elementary Schools, Diocesan located in the Institution section.
Catechesis Religious Program—Students 63.

KUTZTOWN, BERKS CO., ST. MARY (1919) Rev. Msgr. Walter T. Scheaffer; Deacon James Russo; Sr. Marie Clark, M.S.C., Pastoral Min.
Res.: 14833 Kutztown Rd., Kutztown, 19530. Tel: 610-683-7443; Tel: 610-683-7466 (Church); Fax: 610-683-7625; Email: stmarysktown@ptd.net; Web: www.stmaryskutztown.com.
Catechesis Religious Program—Students 182.

LAKE HARMONY, CARBON CO., ST. PETER THE FISHERMAN (1982)
33 Trinity Cir., Lake Harmony, 18624-0237. Rev. Msgr. John G. Chizmar, V.F., M.Div.
Res.: Lake Dr., Lake Harmony, 18624-0237. Tel: 570-722-2034; Fax: 570-722-1348; Email: stpeter@ptd.net.
Catechesis Religious Program Denise Wettstein, D.R.E. Students 85.

LANSFORD, CARBON CO., ST. KATHARINE DREXEL PARISH (2008) [CEM 3] Merged with St. Joseph, Summit Hill.
See Our Lady of the Angels Academy, Lansford under Regional Catholic Elementary Schools, Diocesan located in the Institution section.

LEHIGHTON, CARBON CO., SS. PETER AND PAUL (1885) [CEM] (German) Rev. William N. Seifert, M.Div.; Deacon Joseph C. Wilhelm Jr.
Res.: 260 N. Third St., Lehighton, 18235-1595. Tel: 610-377-3690; Fax: 610-377-0721; Email: sspp@ptd.net.
Catechesis Religious Program—Deacon Joseph C. Wilhelm Jr., D.R.E. Students 67.

MAHANOY CITY, SCHUYLKILL CO., ST. TERESA OF CALCUTTA PARISH (2008)
600 W. Mahanoy Ave., Mahanoy City, 17948. Rev. Kevin P. Gallagher; Deacon David J. Henninger.
Office: 614 W. Mahanoy Ave., Mahanoy City, 17948-2416. Tel: 570-773-2771; Fax: 570-773-1937; Email: blessedteresa1@verizon.net.
See Trinity Academy, Shenandoah under Regional Catholic Elementary Schools, Diocesan located in the Institution section.
BTOC Education Center—29 S. Catawissa St., Mahanoy City, 17948. Tel: 570-773-2668.
Catechesis Religious Program—Mrs. Lynn Minalda, D.R.E. Students 81.

MARTINS CREEK, NORTHAMPTON CO., ST. ROCCO (1929) Rev. Joseph J. Kweder, M.Div., Admin.; Rev. Msgr. James J. Reichert, Pastor Emeritus, (Retired).
Res.: 6658 School St., Martins Creek, 18063-0010. Tel: 610-258-9059; Fax: 610-258-4780; Email: strocco@enter.net; Web: strocco.org.
See Immaculate Conception School, Pen Argyl under Regional Catholic Elementary Schools, Diocesan located in the Institution section.
Catechesis Religious Program—Students 64.

MCADOO, SCHUYLKILL CO., ALL SAINTS PARISH (2008)
Mailing Address: 35 N. Cleveland St., McAdoo, 18237-1842. Rev. Msgr. William T. Baker, S.T.L.; Deacon James M. Warnagiris.
Worship Site: Our Lady of Lourdes, 318 Plane St., Weatherly, 18255.
Catechesis Religious Program—Ms. Grace Smith, C.R.E. Students 55.

MINERSVILLE, SCHUYLKILL CO.
1—ST. MATTHEW THE EVANGELIST (2008)
135 Spruce St., Minersville, 17954. Rev. Leo J. Maletz, Email: ssk1905@verizon.net; Deacon James P. Henninger.
Parish Center: 120 Oak St., Minersville, 17954. Tel: 570-544-5485.
Rectory—139 Spruce St., Minersville, 17954-1642. Tel: 570-544-2211; Email: ssk1905@verizon.net; Web: www.stmatthewtheevangelistparish.org.
See Assumption BVM Regional School, Pottsville, under Regional Catholic Elementary Schools, Diocesan located in the Institution section.
St. Vincent De Paul Center—400 Church St., Minersville, 17954. Tel: 570-544-6484.
Catechesis Religious Program—301 Heffner St., Minersville, 17954. Students 51.
2—ST. MICHAEL THE ARCHANGEL PARISH (2008)
541 Sunbury St., Minersville, 17954-1016. Rev. Christopher M. Zelonis, M.Div., M.A., Admin., St. Clare of Assisi, Saint Clair.
Rectory—538 Sunbury St., Minersville, 17954-1015. Tel: 570-544-4741; Fax: 570-544-4742; Email: stmichaels@stmichaelarchangelparish.org.
See Assumption BVM, Pottsville, under Regional Catholic Elementary Schools, Diocesan located in the Institution section.
Catechesis Religious Program—Sr. Catherine T. Brennan, S.S.J., D.R.E. Students 131.
Convent—Tel: 570-544-2016; Email: ssjmin@comcast.net.

MOHNTON, BERKS CO., ST. BENEDICT'S (1955) Rev. Philip F. Rodgers.
Res.: 2020 Chestnut Hill Rd., Mohnton, 19540-8243. Tel: 610-856-1006; Fax: 610-856-1035; Email: secretary@churchofsaintbenedict.org.
See La Salle Academy and Early Childhood Center, Shillington under Regional Catholic Elementary Schools, Diocesan located in the Institution section.
Catechesis Religious Program—Students 274.

NAZARETH, NORTHAMPTON CO., HOLY FAMILY (1908) [CEM 2]
410 W. Center St., Nazareth, 18064-1300. Revs. Joseph F. Tobias, M.S.C.; Joseph Kanimea, M.S.C.; Deacons Thomas J. Ely; Michael J. Toolan; Richard Haddon; Rev. Frank Natale.
Res.: 23 Forest Dr., Nazareth, 18064-1300. Tel: 610-759-0870; Fax: 610-746-2026; Email: hfp23@rcn.com; Web: www.holyfamilynazarethpa.com.
School—Holy Family School, (Grades PreK-8), 17 N. Convent Ave., Nazareth, 18064-1324. Tel: 610-759-5642; Fax: 610-759-0386; Email: altnhf@ptd.net; Web: holyfamilynazareth.com. Mrs. Christine Bruce, Prin. Lay Teachers 28; Students 319.

Catechesis Religious Program—Students 456.

NESQUEHONING, CARBON CO., ST. FRANCIS OF ASSISI PARISH (2008) Merged with St. Joseph, Summit Hill. See Our Lady of the Angels Academy, Lansford under Regional Catholic Elementary Schools, Diocesan located in the Institution section.

NEW PHILADELPHIA, SCHUYLKILL CO., HOLY CROSS PARISH (2008) [CEM 3]
101 Valley St., New Philadelphia, 17959-1243. Rev. Ronald J. Minner, M.Div.
Office & Rectory: 99 Valley St., New Philadelphia, 17959-1243. Tel: 570-277-6800; Fax: 570-277-0528; Email: hcchurch99@gmail.com.
See Assumption BVM Elementary School, Pottsville under Regional Catholic Elementary Schools, Diocesan located in the Institution section.
Catechesis Religious Program—Students 63.

NORTHAMPTON, NORTHAMPTON CO.

1—ASSUMPTION OF THE BLESSED VIRGIN MARY (1922) [CEM] (Slovak) Rev. Msgr. Thomas P. Koons, V.R., J.C.L., M.A., M.Div.
Res.: 2174 Lincoln Ave., Northampton, 18067-1257. Tel: 610-262-2559; Fax: 610-262-1613; Email: bvm1922@rcn.com; Web: bvm-northampton.com/.
See Good Shepherd School, Northampton under Regional Catholic Elementary Schools, Diocesan located in the Institution section.
Catechesis Religious Program—Students 121.

2—QUEENSHIP OF MARY PARISH (2008)
Mailing Address: 1308 Newport Ave., Northampton, 18067. Rev. Patrick H. Lamb, M.Div.; Rev. Msgr. John S. Campbell, Pastor Emeritus, (Retired); Deacon Michael W. Doncsecz. In Res., Rev. Msgr. Michael J. Chaback, S.T.D., (Retired).
Rectory—1324 Newport Ave., Northampton, 18067-1442. Tel: 610-262-2227; Email: info@queenshipmary.com; Web: queenshipofmary.weconnect.com.
See Good Shepherd School, Northampton under Regional Catholic Elementary Schools, Diocesan located in the Institution section.
Catechesis Religious Program—Students 141.

OREFIELD, LEHIGH CO., ST. JOSEPH THE WORKER (1948) Rev. Msgr. Robert J. Wargo, M.Div.; Rev. Francis Iroot, A.J., Parochial Vicar; Deacons Bruno Schettini; Anthony L. Brasten; Sherwood C. Readinger.
Res.: 1879 Applewood Dr., Orefield, 18069-9507. Tel: 610-395-2876; Fax: 610-395-2616; Email: rectory@stjw.org; Web: www.stjw.org.
School—St. Joseph the Worker School, (Grades K-8), 1858 Applewood Dr., Orefield, 18069-9535. Tel: 610-395-7221; Fax: 610-395-7904; Email: altlsj@ptd.net; Web: www.stjosephtheworkerschool.org. Joseph Disadore, Prin.; Timothy Kelley, Asst. to Prin. Students 400.
Catechesis Religious Program—Students 530.

PALMERTON, CARBON CO., SACRED HEART (1908) [CEM] Rev. William T. Campion, M.Div., Th. M; Deacon Edward J. Girard.
Res.: 243 Lafayette Ave., Palmerton, 18071-1511. Tel: 610-826-2335; Fax: 610-826-5360; Email: shpmtn@ptd.net; Web: www.shcpalmerton.org.
See St. John Neumann Regional School, Palmerton-Slatington under Regional Catholic Elementary Schools, Diocesan located in the Institution section.
Catechesis Religious Program—Students 99.

PEN ARGYL, NORTHAMPTON CO., ST. ELIZABETH OF HUNGARY (1929) [CEM]
Babbitt and Heller Aves., Pen Argyl, 18072. Rev. Msgr. Vincent P. York; Deacons Francis A. Elchert; Fred W. Wall.
Res.: 300 W. Babbitt Ave., Pen Argyl, 18072-0126. Tel: 610-863-4777; Fax: 610-863-7449; Email: donnam1@rcn.com.
See Immaculate Conception School, Pen Argyl under Regional Catholic Elementary Schools, Diocesan located in the Institution section.
Catechesis Religious Program—Students 141.
Convent—111-115 Lobb Ave., Pen Argyl, 18072. Tel: 610-863-9214.

PORT CARBON, SCHUYLKILL CO., ST. STEPHEN (1847) [CEM]
Mailing Address: 250 E. Hancock St., Saint Clair, 17970. Rev. Msgr. William F. Glosser, V.F., M.A., Admin.
Res.: 218 Valley St., Port Carbon, 17965-1636. Tel: 570-429-0370; Fax: 570-429-0630; Email: saintstephen2@verizon.net; Web: saintstephen2.com.
See Assumption BVM School, Pottsville under Regional Catholic Elementary Schools, Diocesan located in the Institution section.
Catechesis Religious Program—Students 40.

POTTSVILLE, SCHUYLKILL CO.

1—ST. JOHN THE BAPTIST (1841) [CEM 3] (German) Rev. David J. Loeper; Deacon Lawrence J. Lonergan.
Res.: 913 Mahantongo St., Pottsville, 17901-3024. Tel: 570-622-5470; Fax: 570-622-4589; Email: stjbparish@comcast.net.
See Assumption BVM School, Pottsville under Regional Catholic Elementary Schools, Diocesan located in the Institution section.
Catechesis Religious Program—Students 126.

2—ST. PATRICK (1827) [CEM 3]
Fourth and Mahantongo Sts., Pottsville, 17901-3012. Rev. Msgr. Edward J. O'Connor, M.Th., M.S.W., V.F.; Rev. Barnabas Shayo, A.J.; Deacons John E. Quirk; Lawrence J. Lonergan.
Res.: 319 Mahantongo St., Pottsville, 17901-3012. Tel: 570-622-1802; Fax: 570-622-2593; Email: dwalker.stpats@gmail.com; Web: stpatrickpottsville.org.
See Assumption BVM School, Pottsville under Regional Catholic Elementary Schools, Diocesan located in the Institution section.
Catechesis Religious Program—Dale Verchick, D.R.E. Students 87.

READING, BERKS CO.

1—ST. CATHARINE OF SIENA (1925) Rev. Msgr. Edward R. Domin; Deacons Craig A. Fry; Gregory G. Schneider; John J. Stapleton; Rev. John Rother. In Res., Rev. Msgr. James A. Treston, (Retired).
Res.: 2427 Perkiomen Ave., Reading, 19606. Tel: 610-779-4005; Fax: 610-779-0859; Email: stcatharineofsiena@hotmail.com; Web: www.scsreading.org.
Worship Site: St. Mary Church—250 S. 12th St., Reading, 19602.
Church: 4975 Boyertown Pike, Reading, 19606. Tel: 610-779-4090.
School—St. Catharine of Siena School (1925) (Grades PreK-8), 2330 Perkiomen Ave., Reading, 19606-2048. Tel: 610-779-5810; Fax: 610-779-6888; Email: altbscs@ptd.net. Marcella Kraycik, Prin. Lay Teachers 18; Sisters 4; Students 274.
Catechesis Religious Program—Students 360.
Convent—2328 Perkiomen Ave., Reading, 19606. Tel: 610-779-5583.

2—SS. CYRIL AND METHODIUS (1895) (Slovak), Merged with St. Peter the Apostle, Reading.

3—HOLY GUARDIAN ANGELS (1929) Revs. Robert T. Finlan, M.Div., M.A., M.Ed.; E. Michael Camilli, M.S.C., S.T.L., M.S.L.S., H.E.L., Senior Priest; Deacon John B. Gallagher.
Res.: 3121 Kutztown Rd., Reading, 19605-2659. Tel: 610-921-2729; Fax: 610-921-8886; Email: novakangel@comcast.net; Web: www.hgaparish.com.
See Holy Guardian Angels Regional School, Reading under Regional Catholic Elementary Schools, Diocesan located in the Institution section.
Catechesis Religious Program—3125 Kutztown Rd., Reading, 19605. Mr. Andrew Angstadt, C.R.E. Students 173.

4—HOLY ROSARY (1904) (Italian)
Mailing Address: P.O. Box 6726, Reading, 19610. Lakeview Dr. at Cherry St., West Reading, 19610. Rev. Msgr. Joseph A. DeSantis, M.Div.; Rev. John A. Hutta; Deacon Christopher May.
Res.: 740 Cherry St., West Reading, 19611. Tel: 610-373-5579; Fax: 610-372-0130; Email: holyrosarychurch01@comcast.net.
Catechesis Religious Program—Students 37.
Convent—237 Franklin St., Reading, 19602. Tel: 610-375-9072; Fax: 610-375-4895; Email: srdivinezeal@hotmail.com. Sr. Marietta Castellano, F.D.Z., Supr.

5—ST. JOSEPH (1891)
1022 N. Eighth St., Reading, 19604. Rev. Msgr. John J. Grabish; Revs. Joseph S. Ganser; Quyet A. Pham; Deacon Francisco De La Gracia Colon.
Res.: 1018 N. Eighth St., Reading, 19604-2210. Tel: 610-376-2976; Fax: 610-376-2825; Email: sjcparish@comcast.net; Web: www.sjcreading.com.
See Holy Guardian Angels Regional School, Reading under Regional Catholic Elementary Schools, Diocesan located in the Institution section.
Catechesis Religious Program—Students 211.

6—ST. MARGARET (1920) Rev. Angel L. Garcia-Almodovar, M.Div.; Deacons Ramon L. Rolon; Gregory G. Schneider; Bruce S. C. Swist.
Res.: 925 Centre Ave., Reading, 19601-2105. Tel: 610-376-2919; Fax: 610-376-2462; Email: stmargaretchurch@rcchurch.comcastbiz.net; Web: stmargaretsreading.org.
School—St. Margaret School, 235 Spring St., Reading, 19601-2121. Tel: 610-375-1882; Fax: 610-376-2291; Email: stmargaretoffice@comcast.net; Web: www.smsreading.com. Sr. Marian Michele Smith, I.H.M., Prin.
Catechesis Religious Program—Sr. Honoria Smith, I.H.M., D.R.E.
Convent—233 Spring St., Reading, 19601-2121. Tel: 610-372-1302; Email: stmgrtconvent@holmail.com.

7—ST. MARY (1888) [CEM] (Polish), Merged with St. Catharine of Siena, Reading.

8—ST. PAUL (1860) [CEM] (German) Rev. Msgr. John J. Grabish; Revs. Quyet A. Pham; Joseph S. Ganser; Deacon Francisco Najera-Ramirez.
Res.: 151 N. 9th St., Reading, 19601. Tel: 610-372-1531; Fax: 610-372-7478; Email: stpaulsrcchurch@comcast.net.
Catechesis Religious Program—Students 412.

9—ST. PETER THE APOSTLE (1752) [CEM]
322 S. Fifth St., Reading, 19602-2311. Rev. Msgr. Thomas J. Orsulak, M.Div., Th.M.; Deacons Mariano Torres; Leopoldo Alvarado; Howard J. Schultz; Rev. Jared V. Zambelli.
Res.: 322 S. Fifth St., Reading, 19602-2311. Tel: 610-372-9652; Fax: 610-374-3351; Email: stpeterchurch@comcast.net.
Worship Site: SS. Cyril and Methodius, 449 S. 6th St., Reading, 19602.
School—St. Peter the Apostle School, 225 S. Fifth St., Reading, 19602-1816. Tel: 610-374-2447; Fax: 610-374-3415; Email: altbsp@ptd.com; Web: stpeterschoolreading.org. Sr. Anna Musi, I.H.M., Prin. Lay Teachers 13; Students 268.
Catechesis Religious Program—Sr. Margaret Pavluchuk, I.H.M., D.R.E. Students 295.
Convent—218 S. Fifth St., Reading, 19602-1841. Tel: 610-373-6185; Email: speter7@aol.com. Sr. Joanne Ralph, I.H.M., Supr.

RINGTOWN, SCHUYLKILL CO., ST. MARY (1923) [CEM]
Mailing Address: 84 N. Center St., Ringtown, 17967-9731. Tel: 570-889-3850; Fax: 570-889-5005; Email: smsjparishes@gmail.com; Web: www.stmarystjoseph.net. 82 N. Center St., Ringtown, 17967-9731. Rev. Eric N. Tolentino, M.Div., Admin.
Res.: 14 E. Oak St., Sheppton, 18248.
See Trinity Academy at the Father Walter J. Ciszek Education Center, Shenandoah under Regional Catholic Elementary Schools, Diocesan located in the Institution section.
Catechesis Religious Program—

ROBESONIA, BERKS CO., ST. FRANCIS DE SALES (1982)
Mailing Address: 321 N. Church St., Robesonia, 19551. Rev. Edward J. Essig.
Res.: 320 N. Church St., Robesonia, 19551. Tel: 610-693-5851; Fax: 610-693-5852; Email: stfrancisrob82@verizon.net; Web: www.stfrancisroby.org.
Catechesis Religious Program—Alison Snyder, D.R.E. Students 146.

ROSETO, NORTHAMPTON CO., OUR LADY OF MT. CARMEL (1897) [CEM 2] (Italian) Revs. James G. Prior, C.M.; Thomas W. Prior, C.M.
Rectory—560 N. Sixth St., Bangor, 18013. Tel: 610-588-2183; Fax: 610-588-6973; Email: olmcparishroseto@gmail.com.
Catechesis Religious Program—Students 92.

SAINT CLAIR, SCHUYLKILL CO., ST. CLARE OF ASSISI PARISH (2008) Rev. Msgr. William F. Glosser, V.F., M.A.
Rectory—250 E. Hancock St., Saint Clair, 17970. Tel: 570-429-0370 (Office); Fax: 570-429-0630; Email: SCAssisi@ptd.net; Web: stclareassisi.weebly.com.
See Assumption BVM School, Pottsville under Regional Catholic Elementary Schools, Diocesan located in the Institution section.
Catechesis Religious Program—Mr. Thomas Dowd, D.R.E. Students 85.

SCHUYLKILL HAVEN, SCHUYLKILL CO., ST. AMBROSE (1851) [CEM] Rev. Msgr. Edward S. Zemanik, M.Div.; Rev. Michael J. Stone, Pastor Emeritus, (Retired).
Res.: 201 Randel St., Schuylkill Haven, 17972-1495. Tel: 570-385-1031; Email: sambrose1@comcast.net.
School—St. Ambrose School, (Grades PreK-8), 302 Randel St., Schuylkill Haven, 17972-1421. Tel: 570-385-2377; Fax: 570-385-2387; Email: stambroseadmin@comcast.net; Web: www.stambroseproud.com. Carol Boyer, Prin. Students 74.
Catechesis Religious Program—Students 190.

SHENANDOAH, SCHUYLKILL CO., DIVINE MERCY (2014)
224 W. Cherry St., Shenandoah, 17976. Rev. Msgr. Ronald C. Bocian, M.Div., M.Ed.
Mailing Address & Rectory: 108 W. Cherry St., Shenandoah, 17976-2209. Tel: 570-462-1968; Email: info@dmparish.com; Web: www.dmparish.com.
Worship Site: St. Casimir Church, 229 N. Jardin St., Shenandoah, 17976.
See Trinity Academy at the Father Walter J. Ciszek Education Center, Shenandoah under Regional Catholic Elementary Schools located in the Institution section.
Catechesis Religious Program—Students 161.

SHEPPTON, SCHUYLKILL CO., ST. JOSEPH (1894) [CEM] [JC]
Mailing Address: 84 N. Center St., Ringtown, 17967-9731. Tel: 570-889-3850; Fax: 570-889-5005; Email: smsjparishes@gmail.com; Web: www.stmarystjoseph.net. 14 E. Oak St., Sheppton, 17967. Rev. Eric N. Tolentino, M.Div., Admin.
Catechesis Religious Program—Students 11.

SHILLINGTON, BERKS CO., ST. JOHN BAPTIST DE LA SALLE (1948)
Mailing Address: 420 Holland St., Shillington, 19607. Tel: 610-777-1697; Fax: 610-777-4468; Email: st.jbdls@verizon.net; Web: www.

stjohnsfamilyoffaith.com. 42 Kerrick Rd., Shillington, 19607. Rev. Richard H. Clement, M.Div.; Deacon Felix J. Lombardo.
Res.: 400 Holland St., Shillington, 19607.
See La Salle Academy and Early Childhood Center, Shillington under Regional Catholic Elementary Schools, Diocesan located in the Institution section.
Catechesis Religious Program—Bernadette H. Yohn, D.R.E. Students 176.

SINKING SPRING, BERKS CO., ST. IGNATIUS LOYOLA (1965)
St. Albans Dr. & Whitfield Blvd., Sinking Spring, 19608-1028. Very Rev. Thomas P. Bortz, V.F., M.Div., S.T.B.; Revs. Guency Isaac; Stephan A. Isaac; Rev. Msgr. James A. Treston, Pastor Emeritus, (Retired); Deacons Frederick J. Lanciano Jr.; Edward L. Sanders.
Res.: 2810 St. Alban's Dr., Sinking Spring, 19608-1028. Tel: 610-678-3767; Fax: 610-678-4483; Email: ignatiusrect@aol.com; Web: www.stignatiusreading.org.
School—St. Ignatius Loyola School, (Grades PreK-8), 2700 St. Albans Dr., Reading, 19609.
Tel: 610-678-0111; Fax: 610-670-5795; Email: ignatiusrect@aol.com; Web: www.stignatiusvikings.org. Mr. Robert Birmingham, Prin.
Catechesis Religious Program—2710 St. Alban's Dr., Reading, 19609. Students 658.
Convent—2601 St. Alban's Dr., West Lawn, 19609.
Tel: 610-678-2769.

SLATINGTON, LEHIGH CO., ASSUMPTION B.V.M. (1883) [CEM]
649 W. Washington St., Slatington, 148080-1618. Rev. Eric A. Arnout, M.Div., Admin.; Deacon Fredric Bloom.
Res.: 633 W. Washington St., Slatington, 18080-1618. Tel: 610-767-2214; Fax: 610-767-2702; Email: abvm@ptd.net; Web: abvmslat.weconnect.com.
See St. John Neumann Regional School, Palmerton-Slatington under Regional Catholic Elementary Schools, Diocesan located in the Institution section.
Catechesis Religious Program—Monica E. Prudente, D.R.E. Students 103.

SUMMIT HILL, CARBON CO., ST. JOSEPH (1850) [CEM 3]
Mailing Address & Res.: 118 N. Market St., Summit Hill, 18250-1108. Tel: 570-645-2664;
Fax: 570-645-3037; Email: lisassjpv@gmail.com; frhoffasjpv@gmail.com; Web: www.stjscatholicchurch.org. 462 W. Ludlow St., Summit Hill, 18250-1108. Rev. Allen J. Hoffa, M.Div.
Church: 462 W. Ludlow St., Summit Hill, 18250-1108.
Catechesis Religious Program—Deacon Joseph Canno, D.R.E. Twinned with Coaldale/Lansford. Students 77.
Shrine—Diocesan Shrine of St. Therese of Lisieux, 1 E. Garibaldi Ave., Nesquehoning, 18240. Rev. Allen J. Hoffa, M.Div., Admin.

TAMAQUA, SCHUYLKILL CO., ST. JOHN XXIII (2014)
Mailing Address: 307 Pine St., Tamaqua, 18252.
Tel: 570-225-7410; Email: secretary@sj23tamaqua.org; Web: www.sj23tamaqua.org. Rev. John A. Frink, M.Div.
Worship Site: SS. Peter & Paul.
See St. Jerome Regional School, Tamaqua under Regional Catholic Elementary Schools located in the Institution section.
Catechesis Religious Program—Students 180.

TREMONT, SCHUYLKILL CO., MOST BLESSED TRINITY PARISH (2008) Rev. Jason F. Stokes.
Rectory & Mailing Address: 113 Cherry St., Tremont, 17981. Tel: 570-695-3648;
Fax: 570-695-2275; Email: mbtparish2008@hotmail.com; Web: mostblessedtrinity.us.
See Assumption BVM, Pottsville, under Regional Catholic Elementary Schools, Diocesan located in the Institution section.
Catechesis Religious Program—Students 66.

WALNUTPORT, NORTHAMPTON CO., ST. NICHOLAS (1974) [CEM]
4412 Mountain View Dr., Walnutport, 18088-9728. Rev. Msgr. Thomas A. Derzack, M.Div.; Deacon Michael W. Kudla.
Res.: 1152 Oak Rd., Walnutport, 18088-9728.
Tel: 610-767-3107; Fax: 610-760-6241; Email: stnick11@ptd.net; Web: stnicholaswalnutport.parishesonline.com.
See St. John Neumann Regional School, Palmerton-Slatington under Regional Catholic Elementary Schools, Diocesan located in the Institution section.
Catechesis Religious Program—Students 125.

WEATHERLY, CARBON CO., OUR LADY OF LOURDES PARISH (2008) Merged with All Saints, McAdoo.

WEST READING, BERKS CO., SACRED HEART (1917)
Mailing Address: P.O. Box 6217, Reading, 19610-0217. Lakeview Dr. at Cherry St., West Reading, 19610-0217. Tel: 610-372-4010; Fax: 610-372-4926; Email: shpmtn@ptd.net; Web: www.shrcparish.org. Rev. Msgr. Joseph A. DeSantis, M.Div.; Rev. John A. Hutta; Deacon William R. Kase.
Res.: 740 Cherry St., West Reading, 19611.
School—Sacred Heart School, 701 Franklin St., West Reading, 19611-1029. Tel: 610-373-3316;
Fax: 610-375-7299; Email: altbsh@ptd.net; Web: www.sacredheartreading.com. Mrs. Katherine Napolitano, Prin. Lay Teachers 13; Students 130.
Catechesis Religious Program—Students 87.

WHITEHALL, LEHIGH CO.
1—ST. ELIZABETH OF HUNGARY (1941) Rev. John S. Pendzick; Deacon Michael T. Meder.
Res.: 618 Fullerton Ave., Whitehall, 18052-6726.
Tel: 610-266-0695; Fax: 610-266-1548; Email: info@sercc.org; Web: www.sercc.org.
See St. Elizabeth Regional School, Whitehall under Regional Catholic Elementary Schools, Diocesan located in the Institution section.
Catechesis Religious Program—Students 125.

2—HOLY TRINITY (1928)
4456 Main St., Whitehall, 18052-2415. Rev. Msgr. Daniel J. Yenushosky, V.F., Th.M.; Deacons Eugene J. Wyrwa; Michael J. Laroche; Arthur L. Chin-Fatt. In Res., Rev. Msgr. David L. James, V.G., M.Div., J.C.L.
Res.: 4102 S. Church St., Whitehall, 18052-2415.
Tel: 610-262-9315; Email: holytrinityrcc@gmail.com; Web: holytrinitywhitehall.weconnect.com.
See Good Shepherd Catholic School, Northampton under Regional Catholic Elementary Schools, Diocesan located in the Institution section.
Catechesis Religious Program—Holy Apostles Religious Education Program, (Serving St. Peter, Coplay & Holy Trinity & St. John the Baptist, Whitehall) 3008 S. Ruch St., Whitehall, 18052.
Tel: 610-261-0144. Miss Emily Fantauzzo, D.R.E.; Mrs. Barbara Majkowski, Sacramental Coord. Students 152.

3—ST. JOHN THE BAPTIST (1927) [CEM]
Ruch St. & Park Ave., Whitehall, 18052. Rev. Msgrs. Gerald E. Gobitas, Th.M.; Albert J. Byrne, V.F., M.Div., Pastor Emeritus. In Res., Rev. Msgr. Thomas E. Hoban, (Retired).
Res.: 3024 S. Ruch St., Whitehall, 18052.
Tel: 610-262-2260; Email: stjohnsstiles@aol.com.
See Good Shepherd Catholic School, Northampton under Regional Catholic Elementary Schools, Diocesan located in the Institution section.
Catechesis Religious Program—Holy Apostles Religious Education Program, (Serving St. Peter, Coplay & Holy Trinity & St. John the Baptist, Whitehall) 3008 S. Ruch St., Whitehall, 18052.
Tel: 610-261-0144. Mrs. Barbara Majkowski, C.R.E. Students 254.

Chaplains of Public Institutions

ALLENTOWN. *Above & Beyond Mountain View*. (St. Catharine of Siena).
Arden Court. (St. Catharine of Siena).
Cedarbrook Nursing Home. (St. Catharine of Siena).
Country Meadows. (St. Catharine of Siena).
Devon House Personal Care Home. (1930) (St. Thomas More).
Good Shepherd Home and Rehabilitation Hospital. Deacon Cu T. Than(St. Paul).
Lehigh County Prison. (Sacred Heart).
Lehigh Valley Hospital, Allentown Campus, 17th and Chew Sts., 18103. (St. Catharine of Siena).
Lehigh Valley Hospital at Cedar Crest,
Tel: 610-402-8465 Pastoral Care. Rev. Joseph P. Becker, O.S.F.S., M.A., Deacon Anthony L. Brasten(St. Thomas More).
Liberty Manorcare. (St. Catharine of Siena).
Luthercrest. (St. Joseph, Orefield).
ManorCare Nursing Home. (St. Thomas More).
Phoebe Devitt Home. (St. Catharine of Siena).
St. Luke's Hospital, Allentown Campus. (St. Catharine of Siena).
Westminster Village. (Our Lady Help of Christians).

BETHLEHEM. *Atria*. (Notre Dame of Bethlehem).
Lehigh Valley Muhlenberg Medical Center. (Notre Dame of Bethlehem).
Lehigh Valley Muhlenberg Rehab Center. (Notre Dame of Bethlehem).
Lutheran Manor of the Lehigh Valley, Inc.. (Notre Dame of Bethlehem).
Manor Care Nursing and Rehabilitation Centers I and II. (Notre Dame of Bethlehem).
Sterling-Heights Gracious Retirement Living. (Notre Dame of Bethlehem).

COALDALE. *Edgemont Lodge Assisted Living Personal Care Home*. St. Joseph, Summit Hill.
St. Luke's Miners Memorial Medical Center. St. Joseph, Summit Hill.

EASTON. *Abington Manor*. (Our Lady of Mercy).
Easton Home. (Our Lady of Mercy).
Easton Hospital. (Priests of Easton Area).
Easton Nursing Center. (Our Lady of Mercy).
New Eastwood Care & Rehabilitation Center. (St. Jane Frances de Chantal).
Northampton County Prison. (Our Lady of Mercy).
The Gardens for Memory Care at Easton. (Our Lady of Mercy).

FOUNTAIN HILL. *Cedarbrook*. (Lehigh County Home) St. Ursula.
St. Luke's University Health Network. Rev. Frank Berkout.

HAMBURG. *Laurel Nursing Center*. (St. Mary).

LEHIGHTON. *St. Luke's Gnaden Huetten Campus*. (SS. Peter and Paul).
Mahoning Valley Nursing Home. (SS. Peter & Paul).

MACUNGIE. *Lehigh Center Nursing Home and Assisted Living*. (St. Thomas More).

NAZARETH. *Gracedale (Northampton County Home)*. Deacon Michael J. Toolan(Holy Family Nazareth).

NEW TRIPOLI. *Cornerstone Living*. (St. Joseph the Worker, Orefield).

ORWIGSBURG. *Orwigsburg Center*. (St. Ambrose, Schuylkill Haven).
Pinebrook Personal Care Center. (St. Ambrose, Schuylkill Haven).

PALMERTON. *St. Luke's Palmerton Campus*. Rev. William T. Campion, M.Div., Th. M, Chap.(Sacred Heart).

POTTSVILLE. *Luther Ridge*. Rev. Christopher M. Zelonis, M.Div., M.A.
Manor Care. Rev. Christopher M. Zelonis, M.Div., M.A.
Providence Place. Rev. Christopher M. Zelonis, M.Div., M.A.
Schuylkill County Prison. St. Patrick, Pottsville.
Schuylkill Manor. Rev. Christopher M. Zelonis, M.Div., M.A.
Schuylkill Medical Center East, 700 E. Norwegian St., Pottsville, 17901. Rev. Christopher M. Zelonis, M.Div., M.A.
Schuylkill Medical Center South, 420 S. Jackson St., Pottsville, 17901. Rev. Christopher M. Zelonis, M.Div., M.A.
York Terrace Nursing Home. Rev. David J. Loeper.

READING. *Berks County Jail*. (St. Ignatius Loyola, Sinking Spring; St. Peter, Reading - Spanish Speaking Inmates).
Berks-Heim (Berks County Home). (St. Ignatius Loyola, Sinking Spring).

SCHUYLKILL HAVEN. *Rosewood*. (St. Ambrose).

SINKING SPRING. *Columbia Cottage*. (St. Ignatius Loyola).

TREXLERTOWN. *Mosser Nursing Home*. (St. Joseph the Worker, Orefield).

WEATHERLY. *Heritage Hill (Personal Care)*. All Saints, McAdoo.
Weatherwood - Carbon County Nursing Home & Rehabilitation Center. All Saints, McAdoo.

WERNERSVILLE. *Phobe Berks Village*. (St. Ignatius Loyola).

WESCOSVILLE. *Lehigh County Home*. (Cedarbrook) (St. Catharine of Siena, Allentown.).

WEST READING. *Manorcare Health Services*. (Sacred Heart).
Reading Hospital and Medical Center. Deacon William R. Kase(Sacred Heart).
Spruce Manor Nursing and Rehabilitation Center. (Sacred Heart).

WHITEHALL. *Fellowship Manor*. (St. John the Baptist).

WYOMISSING. *County Meadows*. (St. Ignatius Loyola, Sinking Spring).
Highlands at Wyomissing. (Sacred Heart).

On Duty Outside the Diocese:
Rev. Msgr.—
Baker, Andrew R., S.T.D., Rector, Vice Pres., 16300 Old Emmitsburg Rd, Emmitsburg, MD 21727-7797. Tel: 301-447-6122
Revs.—
Connolly, James M.T., 151 Old Buckroe Rd., Apt. 115, Hampton, VA 17959-1235
Gillis, David C., P.O. Box 602, Greentown, 18436
Thomas, James J., 905 N. Allerton Rd., Belleville, IL 62221.

Unassigned:
Rev. Msgr.—
Flanagan, Bernard A., M.Div.
Revs.—
Ardinger, Scott R., M.Div., M.A., S.T.B.
Brennan, Edmund J.
Fanti, Joseph J.
Onyegbule, Cletus S.
Wakefield, Christopher L.

Retired:
Rev. Msgrs.—
Bartkus, Algimantas A., (Retired), 7000 Beach Plaza, #405, St. Pete Beach, FL 33706-2091
Benestad, Thomas J., M.Div., (Retired), 1299 Ocean Blvd. K-2, Boca Raton, FL 33432-7729
Biszek, Robert J., (Retired), 920 S. 2nd St., 18103-3402
Bukaty, Lawrence J., (Retired), P.O. Box F, 18105-1538
Callaghan, Aloysius R., (Retired), 2260 Summit Ave., St. Paul, MN 55105-5050

Campbell, John S., (Retired), 9002 Robin Hood Dr., Kunkletown, 18058
Chaback, Michael J., S.T.D., (Retired), Queenship of Mary Rectory, 1324 Newport Ave., Northampton, 18067-1442
Coll, Robert J., (Retired), 2956 Gilford Way, Naples, FL 34119-7523
Forst, Robert M., (Retired), 1325 Prospect St., Bethlehem, 18018-4916
Handges, William E., (Retired), 215 W. Arch St., Pottsville, 17901-2941
Hoban, Thomas E., (Retired), St. John the Baptist, 3024 Ruch Ave., Whitehall, 18052
Kozel, Robert F., (Retired), 3276 Oakland Square Dr., Bethlehem, 18020-2941
Morrison, David J., (Retired), Our Lady of Perpetual Help Parish Center, 3219 Santee Rd., Bethlehem, 18020-2833
Reichert, James J., (Retired), P.O. Box 765, Effort, 18330-8734
Rigney, Dennis A., (Retired), 580 Yellow Pine Dr., Auburn, 17922
Smith, Joseph P.T., (Retired), 1879 Applewood Dr., Orefield, 18069-9536
Sobiesiak, Joseph R., (Retired), 8963 Joann Dr., Citrus Springs, FL 34434-4970
Treston, James A., (Retired), St. Catherine of Siena Parish Center, 2427 Perkiomen Ave., Reading, 19606-2049

Revs.—
Beers, John Michael, Ph.D., (Retired), P.O. Box 172, Berkeley Springs, WV 25411
Caesar, Floyd Jr., (Retired), 1345 Martin Ct., Apt. 928, Bethlehem, 18108-2583
Connolly, Edward B., M.Div., M.Ed., (Retired), 364 Valley St., New Philadelphia, 17959-1235
Dagle, Harold F., M.A., (Retired), St. Mary, 2 N. 8th St., Lebanon, 17046
Dene, Charles J., (Retired), Divine Mercy Rectory, 129 S. Jardin St., Shenandoah, 17976-2209
Dudek, Ladislaus J., (Retired), UL Wojtarowicz 27A, Tarnow, Poland 33-100
Fromholzer, Francis J., (Retired), P.O. Box F, 18105
Grundowski, Francis M., (Retired), P.O. Box 13553, Reading, 19612-3553
Halabura, Stephen J., (Retired), Holy Family Villa, 1325 Prospect St., Bethlehem, 18018-4916
Hulko, Joseph D., (Retired), Holy Family Villa, 1325 Prospect Ave., Bethlehem, 18018-4916
Jankaitis, Ronald V., (Retired), 103 N. Cherry St., Frackville, 17931-1406
Killian, Wayne E., M.A., M.S., (Retired), Holy Family Villa, 1325 Prospect Ave., Bethlehem, 18018-4916
Linkchorst, William J., (Retired), 503 W. Centre St., Mahanoy City, 17948
Little, John J.L., (Retired), Holy Family Villa, 1325 Prospect Ave., Bethlehem, 18018
Lofton, James J., (Retired), 1755 Oak Ct., Orwigsburg, 17961
McConaghy, Robert J., (Retired), EDSA Guadalupe Viejo, 1200 Makati City, Philippines
Mihalak, James J., (Retired), P.O. Box F, 18105-1538
Palmieri, Luigi, (Retired), Holy Family Villa, 1325 Prospect Ave., Bethlehem, 18018-4916
Paskowicz, Marian, (Retired), 469 Ridge Line Ct., Dayton, OH 45458
Sattler, Frederick F., (Retired), Holy Family Villa, 1325 Prospect Ave., Bethlehem, 18018
Shanfelt, Thomas G., (Retired), 920 North St., Jim Thorpe, 18229-2216
Sheehan, Joseph A., (Retired), Holy Family Villa, 1325 Prospect Ave., Bethlehem, 18018
Stajkowski, Leo S., (Retired), Immaculate Conception B.V.M. Rectory, 905 Chestnut St., Douglassville, 19518-9006
Stone, Michael J., (Retired), P.O. Box 1080, Albrightsville, 18210-1080.

Permanent Deacons:
Alvarado, Leopoldo, St. Peter, Reading
Amedeo, Dominik F. Jr., St. Ann, Emmaus
Bardi, James A., Immaculate Conception BVM, Douglassville
Benkovic, Richard L., Immaculate Conception, Allentown
Berrios, Gerardo, Holy Infancy, Bethlehem
Bloom, Fredric, Assumption B.V.M., Slatington
Bogusky, Joseph H., Annunciation B.V.M., Catasauqua
Boyle, Michael J., Most Blessed Sacrament, Bally
Brasten, Anthony L., St. Joseph the Worker, Orefield
Campanell, Anthony T., (Retired)
Cannon, Joseph T., St. Joseph, Summit Hill
Carlin, Hugh, Sacred Heart, Bethlehem (Miller Heights)
Ceballos, Ricardo, Cathedral of St. Catharine of Siena, Allentown
Centeno, Jesus, (Retired)
Chin-Fatt, Arthur L., Holy Trinity Parish, Whitehall
Close, Richard B., (Retired)
Colon, Francisco De La Gracia, St. Joseph, Reading
Colon, Julio, (Retired)
Corchado, Julian, Sacred Heart of Jesus, Allentown
Coyle, Charles A., (Retired)
Cruz, Claudio F., Sacred Heart of Jesus, Allentown
De Bellis, Charles A., (Retired)
DeCastro, Jose F., St. Paul, Allentown
Doncsecz, Michael W., Queenship of Mary, Northampton
Drogalis, Thomas B., St. Mary, Hamburg
Duncan, James R., St. Thomas More, Allentown
Dupont, Donald J., Our Lady of Perpetual Help, Bethlehem
Elchert, Francis A., St. Elizabeth of Hungary, Pen Argyl
Elliott, Donald W., Assumption B.V.M., Bethlehem
Ely, Thomas J., Holy Family, Nazareth
Fenton, Richard A., St. Ann, Emmaus
Ferris, Lewis T., Sacred Heart, Bath
Fleck, Henry J. Jr., (Retired)
Fry, Craig A., St. Catharine of Siena, Reading
Gallagher, John B., Holy Guardian Angels, Reading
Giordano, Charles A., Immaculate Conception BVM, Douglassville
Girard, Edward J., Sacred Heart, Palmerton
Godiska, Joseph F., (Retired)
Gonzalez-Rivera, Isidro, Office of the Permanent Diaconate; Our Lady of Mercy, Easton
Gorbos, Stephen T. Jr., Holy Ghost/Incarnation of Our Lord, Bethlehem
Gordon, Henry G., St. Mary, Hamburg
Granato, Gary J., St. Paul, Allentown
Haddon, Richard, Holy Family, Nazareth
Hartzell, Reuben H. Jr., SS. Simon and Jude, Bethlehem
Hassler, William R., Cathedral of St. Catharine of Siena, Allentown
Henninger, David J., St. Teresa of Calcutta, Mahanoy City
Henninger, James P., St. Matthew the Evangelist, Minersville
Herman, Stewart T., Assumption BVM, Bethlehem
Hernandez, Saul, St. Paul, Allentown
Hiryak, Paul J. Jr., Immaculate Conception BVM, Douglassville
Juhasz, Joseph B., Sacred Heart, Bethlehem
Kase, William R., Sacred Heart, West Reading
Kelly, George C. Jr., Our Lady of Perpetual Help, Bethlehem
Kelly, Maurice E., St. Peter, Coplay
Kinsella, Christopher C. Jr., St. Thomas Moore, Allentown
Kochu, James A., St. Columbkill, Boyertown
Konopelski, John P., (Retired)
Kudla, Michael W., St. Nicholas, Walnutport
Lanciano, Frederick J. Jr., St. Ignatius Loyola, Sinking Spring
LaPolice, George D., (Retired)
Laroche, Michael J., Holy Trinity, Whitehall
Lombardo, Felix J., St. John the Baptist de la Salle, Shillington
Lonergan, Lawrence J., St. John the Baptist/St. Patrick, Pottsville
Matos, Rodoberto, Holy Infancy, Bethlehem
May, Christopher, Holy Rosary/Sacred Heart, Reading
Meder, Michael T., St. Elizabeth of Hungary, Whitehall
Morales, Edison, (On Duty Outside the Diocese)
Mroz, John J., St. Joseph, Jim Thorpe
Murphy, John W. Jr., (Retired)
Murphy, Thomas J., St. Francis Academy and Most Blessed Sacrament, Bally
Najera-Ramirez, Francisco, St. Paul, Reading
O'Connell, John C., St. John Fisher, Catasauqua
Ocampo, Jose A., Holy Infancy, Bethlehem
Palmeri, Charles V., St. Rocco, Martins Creek
Paschall, Joseph L. Jr., (Retired)
Pasquino, Ronald R., Our Lady of Good Counsel, Bangor
Paulus, Conrad, St. Joseph Parish, Coopersburg
Petrauskas, Joseph, St. Columbkill, Boyertown
Quirk, John E., St. Patrick, Pottsville
Raymundo, Ranulfo, St. Jane Frances de Chantal, Easton
Readinger, Sherwood C., St. Joseph the Worker, Orefield
Reimer, Thomas B., St. Peter, Coplay
Reyes, Ricardo, Our Lady Help of Christians, Allentown
Reyes, Roberto, Sacred Heart of Jesus, Allentown
Rodgers, Robert W., St. Jane Frances de Chantal, Easton
Rodriguez, Angelino D., St. Paul Parish, Allentown
Rodriguez, Nicasio, (Retired)
Rohner, David K., St. Ursula, Fountain Hill
Rolon, Ramon L., St. Margaret, Reading
Russo, James, St. Mary, Kutztown
Sablone, Stephen F., (Retired), (Inactive, Health Issues)
Sanders, Edward L., St. Ignatius Loyola, Sinking Spring
Santos-Gonzalez, Jose M., Sacred Heart of Jesus, Allentown
Saukulak, Edward J., Sacred Heart, Bath
Schettini, Bruno, St. Joseph the Worker, Orefield
Schmidt, Gerald R., Office for Pastoral Planning; St. Theresa of the Child Jesus, Hellertown
Schneider, Gregory G., St. Margaret, Reading
Schroth, Gene G. Jr., St. Jane Frances de Chantal, Easton
Schultz, Howard J., St. Peter the Apostle, Reading
Schutzler, Peter H., Office of the Permanent Diaconate; St. Ann, Emmaus
Scrak, Richard G. Jr., Catholic Charities Ecumenical Kitchen, Allentown; St. Anne, Bethlehem
Setlock, John A., St. Richard, Barnesville
Sewald, Richard T. Jr., Notre Dame of Bethlehem
Shubella, Thomas F., St. Thomas More, Allentown
Snyder, Robert H., Cathedral of St. Catherine of Siena, Allentown
Stapleton, John J., St. Catharine of Siena, Reading
Sullivan, Ralph K., Our Lady of Perpetual Help, Bethlehem
Swist, Bruce S. C., St. Margaret, Reading
Synoracki, Stephen J., St. Jane Frances de Chantal, Easton
Than, Cu T., St. Paul, Allentown
Thoden, Richard M. Jr., (Retired)
Thompson, John F., (Retired)
Toolan, James, St. Thomas More, Allentown
Toolan, Michael J., Gracedale Nursing Home & Holy Family, Nazareth
Torres, Mariano, St. Peter the Apostle, Reading
Trexler, Jeffrey R., Ph.D., SS. Simon & Jude, Bethlehem
Dr. Urbine, William F., Notre Dame of Bethlehem
Vargas, C. Miguel, Sacred Heart of Jesus, Allentown
Visot, Luis R., (Retired)
Wall, Fred W., St. Elizabeth of Hungary, Pen Argyl
Warnagiris, James M., All Saints, McAdoo
Wasielewski, Kevin C., St. Jane Frances de Chantal, Easton
Weiland, Kenneth L., St. Anthony of Padua, Easton
Wilhelm, Joseph C. Jr., SS. Peter & Paul, Lehighton
Wyrwa, Eugene J., (Retired)
Young, Robert P., St. Francis of Assisi, Allentown.

INSTITUTIONS LOCATED IN DIOCESE

[A] COLLEGES AND UNIVERSITIES

CENTER VALLEY. *DeSales University*, 2755 Station Ave., Center Valley, 18034-9568.
Tel: 610-282-1100; Fax: 610-282-1480; Email: admiss@desales.edu; Web: www.DeSales.edu. Revs. Alexander T. Pocetto, O.S.F.S., Ph.D., Senior Vice Pres. (Ret.); Sr. Salesian Scholar, (Retired); Daniel Lannen, O.S.F.S., Chap.; Mr. Thomas Mantoni, Registrar; Mr. Thomas Campbell, Vice Pres. Inst. Advancement; Mr. Robert J. Snyder, Vice Pres., Admin. & Finance; Revs. Douglas C. Burns, O.S.F.S., M.Div., Prof.; Daniel G. Gambet, O.S.F.S., Ph.D., Pres. Emeritus, (Retired); Bro. Daniel P. Wisniewski, O.S.F.S., Ph.D., Provost; Mrs. Linda Zerbe, Dean Students; Mr. Peter Rautzhan, Assoc. VP., Admin. & Planning; Mrs. Mary Birkhead, Dean Enrollment Mgmt.; Mr. Michael Sweetana, Dir. Finance & Treas.; Mrs. Debbie Malone, Dir. Library; Dr. Gerard Joyce, Exec. Vice Pres.; Bro. Joseph G. Schodowski, O.S.F.S., A.A., Ge. Maintenance; Mrs. Magdalene Riggins, Dir. Campus Ministry; Rev. John I. Extejt, O.S.F.S., M.S., M.Div., M.A.T., Instructor Mathematics; Robert Blumenstein; Mary Gotzon, Administrative Asst. to Pres.; Lore McFadden, Dir. Programs-Salesian Center for Faith & Culture; Tom McNamara, Exec. Dir.; Lisa Plummer, Dir. Institutional Research & Analysis; Bro. Harry Schneider, O.S.F.S., Instructional Applications Specialist; Rev. Kevin Nadolski, O.S.F.S., Vice Pres.; Marc Albanese, Vice Pres.; David Gilfoil, Vice Pres.; Rev. James J. Greenfield, O.S.F.S., Pres. DeSales University is a medium-sized, private, four-year Catholic university with a Salesian mission administered by the Oblates of St. Francis

de Sales. Clergy 7; Lay Teachers 368; Students 4,225.

READING. *Alvernia University* (1958) 400 Saint Bernardine St., Reading, 19607. Tel: 610-796-8200; Fax: 610-796-8324; Email: tom.flynn@alvernia.edu; Web: www.alvernia.edu. Thomas F. Flynn, Ph.D., Pres.; Ms. Christine Saadi, Dir., Student Financial Planning; Mr. Douglas Smith, Vice Pres., Fin. & Admin.; Dr. John McCloskey Jr., Vice Pres., Enrollment Mgmt; Ms. Beki Stein, Registrar; Dr. Evelina Panayotova, Dir., Inst. Research; Dr. Joseph Cicala, Vice Pres. Univ. Life; Dr. Shirley Williams, Provost; Mr. Jay Worrall, Dir., Holleran Center for Community Engagement; Mr. Anthony DeMarco, Vice Pres., Advancement; Ms. Julianne Wallace, Dir. Campus Ministry & Chap.; Ms. Rebecca Finn-Kenney, Dean Admissions; Ms. Deidra Hill, Vice Pres., Mktg. & Communications; Sr. Roberta McKelvie, O.S.F., Asst. to Pres., Mission Integration & Educ. Bernardine Sisters of the Third Order of St. Francis.Catholic Franciscan University, coeducational, accredited, offering undergraduate & graduate education in Liberal Arts & Professional Programs & Doctoral Program in Leadership. Lay Teachers 110; Sisters 2; Students 3,525.

[B] HIGH SCHOOLS, DIOCESAN

ALLENTOWN. *Allentown Central Catholic High School, Inc.*, 301 N. Fourth St., 18102-3098.
Tel: 610-437-4601; Fax: 610-437-6760; Email: webmaster@acchs.info; Web: www.acchs.info. Mrs. Diane Young, Vice Prin.; Rev. Mark R. Searles, M.Div., M.A., Chap.; Mr. Randy Rice, Prin. Lay Teachers 55; Priests 1; Students 810.

BETHLEHEM. *Bethlehem Catholic High School, Inc.*, 2133 Madison Ave., Bethlehem, 18017-4699.
Tel: 610-866-0791; Fax: 610-866-4429; Email: altnbchs@ptd.net; Web: www.becahi.org. Mrs. Holly Denofa, Prin.; Mr. Michael Grasso, Dean, Student Life; Rev. Kevin J. Bobbin, M.A., S.T.B., M.Div., Chap.; Holly Magalengo, Dir., Advancement. Founded as two-year commercial high school, 1897.; Founded as four-year comprehensive high school, 1925. Clergy 2; Lay Teachers 40; Priests 1; Students 722.

EASTON. *Notre Dame High School, Inc.*, 3417 Church Rd., Easton, 18045-2999. Tel: 610-868-1431;
Fax: 610-868-6710; Email: altnndhs@ptd.net; Web: www.ndcrusaders.org. Mr. Mario Lucrezi, Prin.; Miss Jaclyn Welsh, Asst. Prin.; Rev. Christopher S. Butera, M.Div., M.A., Chap. Lay Teachers 38; Priests 1; Students 520.

POTTSVILLE. *Nativity B.V.M. High School, Inc.*, One Lawtons Hill, Pottsville, 17901-2795.
Tel: 570-622-8110; Fax: 570-622-0454; Email: nativitybvm@nativitybvm.net; Web: www.nativitybvm.net. Mrs. Lynn Sabol, Prin.; Mrs. Jennifer Daubert, Dir. Devel.; Rev. David J. Loeper, Chap. Lay Teachers 20; Students 201.

READING. *Berks Catholic High School, Inc.*, 955 E. Wyomissing Blvd., Reading, 19611-1799.
Tel: 610-374-8361; Fax: 610-374-4309; Email: tbalistrere@berkscatholic.org. Tony Balistrere, M.Ed., Prin. Lay Teachers 42; Enrollment 815.

TAMAQUA. *Marian High School, Inc.*, 166 Marian Ave., Tamaqua, 18252. Tel: 570-467-3335;
Fax: 570-467-0186; Email: altsmhs@ptd.net; Web: www.mariancatholicshs.org. Rev. Brian M. Miller, Chap.; Jean M. Susko, M.Ed., Prin. Lay Teachers 27; Students 356.

[C] REGIONAL CATHOLIC ELEMENTARY SCHOOLS

ALLENTOWN. *St. John Vianney Regional School*, (Grades PreK-8), 210 N. 18th St., 18104.
Tel: 610-435-8981; Fax: 610-437-7951; Email: drkleintop@stjohnvianneyschool.org; Web: www.stjohnvianneyschool.org. Dr. Emily J. Kleintop, Prin. Lay Teachers 25; Students 333.

Sacred Heart School, (Grades PreK-8), 325 N. Fourth St., 18102-3007. Tel: 610-437-3031;
Fax: 610-437-2724; Email: altlsh@ptd.net; Web: sacredheartrs.org. James Krupka, Prin. Serving Sacred Heart & St. Stephen, Allentown. Lay Teachers 9; Students 232.

BALLY. *St. Francis Academy*, 668 Pine St., Bally, 19503. Tel: 610-845-7364; Fax: 610-845-2223; Email: sfacademy@aol.com; Web: www.sfabally.org. Phillip Repko, Prin. Serving Most Blessed Sacrament, Bally, St. Columbkill, Boyertown, and St. Mary, Kutztown. Lay Teachers 10; Students 160.

BETHLEHEM. *St. Michael the Archangel School*, (Grades PreK-8), Tel: 610-867-8422; Fax: 610-865-2098; Email: cweiss@st-mikes.com; Web: st-mikes.com. Mrs. Colleen Weiss, Prin. Serving Assumption B.V.M., Bethlehem; St. Joseph, Coopersburg (Limeport) Lay Teachers 25; Students 290.

St. Michael the Archangel School, (Grades PreK-4), 5040 St. Joseph's Rd., Coopersburg, 18036.
Tel: 610-965-4441; Fax: 610-965-1030. Mrs. Colleen Weiss, Prin. Lay Teachers 15; Students 160.

Middle School, (Grades 5-8), Main Office. 4121 Old Bethlehem Pike, Bethlehem, 18015.
Tel: 610-867-8422; Fax: 610-865-2098. Mrs. Colleen Weiss, Prin. Lay Teachers 25; Students 290.

JIM THORPE. *St. Joseph Regional Academy*, (Grades K-8), 25 W. 6th St., Jim Thorpe, 18229-2120.
Tel: 570-325-3186; Fax: 570-325-2090; Email: altcsjra@ptd.net; Web: www.sjracademy@ptd.net. B. Christopher Cooper, Prin. Serving St. Joseph, Immaculate Conception, Jim Thorpe, St. Peter the Fisherman, and Lake Harmony. Lay Teachers 8; Students 100.

NORTHAMPTON. *Good Shepherd Catholic School*, (Grades PreK-8), 1300 Newport Ave., Northampton, 18067. Tel: 610-262-9171;
Fax: 610-262-2202; Email: altngs@ptd.net; Web: www.gscatholic.com. John-Paul Crescenzo, Prin. Serving Queenship of Mary, Assumption B.V.M., Northampton; St. John Fisher, Catasauqua; St. Peter, Coplay; St. John the Baptist & Holy Trinity, Whitehall. Lay Teachers 17; Preschool 25; Students 201.

PALMERTON-SLATINGTON. *St. John Neumann Regional School*, (Grades K-8), Palmerton Campus: 259 Lafayette Ave., Palmerton, 18071.
Tel: 610-826-2354; Fax: 610-826-6444; Email: altcsjn@ptd.net; Web: www.sjnrschool.org. Slatington Campus: 641 W. Washington St., Slatington, 18080-1618. Tel: 610-767-2935;
Fax: 610-767-2948. Sr. Virginia Stephanie Bator, S.S.J., M.S., Prin. Serving St. Nicholas, Berlinsville; Sacred Heart, Palmerton; Assumption B.V.M., Slatington. Lay Teachers 8; Sisters 1; Students 81.

PEN ARGYL. *Immaculate Conception School*, (Grades K-6), 290 W. Babbitt Ave., Pen Argyl, 18072.
Tel: 610-863-4816; Fax: 610-863-8158; Email: altnics@ptd.net; Web: www.immaculateconceptionschool.net. Sr. Maria Luz, O.P., Prin. Regional school; Serving St. Elizabeth, Pen Argyl; St. Rocco, Martins Creek. Lay Teachers 4; Sisters 5; Students 153.

POTTSVILLE. *Assumption BVM School*, (Grades K-8), 112 S. Seventh St., Pottsville, 17901-3079.
Tel: 570-622-0106; Tel: 570-622-1765;
Fax: 570-622-4737; Email: altsabvm@ptd.net; Web: www.assumptionbvmschool.net. Mrs. Teresa Keating, Prin. Serving St. Patrick, St. John the Baptist, Pottsville, St. Matthew the Evangelist, St. Michael the Archangel, Minersville & Most Blessed Trinity, Tremont; St. Clare of Assisi; Saint Clair; Holy Cross, New Philadelphia; St. Stephen, Port Carbon. Lay Teachers 12; Students 162.

READING. *Holy Guardian Angels Regional School, Reading*, (Grades PreK-8), 3125 Kutztown Rd., Reading, 19605-2659. Tel: 610-929-4124;
Fax: 610-929-1623; Email: altbhga@ptd.net; Web: www.hgaschool.org. Mrs. Maureen Wallin, Prin.; Ms. Rebecca Kinyo, Technology Coord./STEM Instructor. Serving Holy Guardian Angels and St. Joseph, Reading. Lay Teachers 27; Students 448.

St. Ignatius Loyola School, (Grades PreK-8), 2700 St. Alban's Dr., Reading, 19609-1134.
Tel: 610-678-0111; Fax: 610-670-5795; Email: admin@stignatiusvikings.org; Web: www.stignatiusvikings.org. Mr. Robert Birmingham, Prin. Regional school; Serving St. Ignatius Loyola, Sinking Spring; St. Francis de Sales, Robesonia. Lay Teachers 26; Sisters 1; Students 360.

SHENANDOAH. *Trinity Academy at the Father Walter J. Ciszek Education Center*, (Grades K-8), 233 W. Cherry St., Shenandoah, 17976. Tel: 570-462-3927; Fax: 570-462-4603; Email: altsta@ptd.net; Web: www.trinitymatters.com. Jane Ryan, Librarian; Sr. Margaret McCullough, I.H.M., Prin. Serving Divine Mercy, Shenandoah; St. Joseph, Frackville; St. Charles Borromeo, Ashland; Blessed Teresa of Calcutta, Mahanoy City; St. Mary, Ringtown; St. Joseph, Shepton Lay Teachers 11; Religious 5; Students 142.

SHILLINGTON. *La Salle Academy*, (Grades PreK-8), 440 Holland St., Shillington, 19607-3260.
Tel: 610-777-7392; Fax: 610-777-1280; Email: altblsa@ptd.net; Web: www.lsabear.org. Mr. Stephen W. Mickvlik, M.Ed., Prin. Regional school; Serving St. John Baptist de La Salle, Shillington; St. Benedict, Mohnton; Lay Teachers 16; Students 217.

TAMAQUA. *St. Jerome Regional School* (1919) 50 Meadow Ave., Tamaqua, 18252-4313.
Tel: 570-668-2757; Fax: 570-668-6101; Email: altssj@ptd.net; Web: www.sjrschool.com. Amy Harris-Miskar, Prin. Serving St. John XXIII, Tamaqua, St. Richard, Barnesville, All Saints, McAdoo, St. Joseph, Summit, Hill. Lay Teachers 10; Students 197.

WHITEHALL. *St. Elizabeth Regional School* (1953) 433 Pershing Blvd., Whitehall, 18052.
Tel: 610-264-0143; Fax: 610-264-1563; Email: altlse@ptd.net; Web: www.sercc.org/school. Mrs. Linda M. Schiller, Prin. Serving St. Elizabeth, Whitehall; Annunciation, Catasauqua; St. John the Baptist, SS. Peter & Paul, Immaculate Conception, Allentown Lay Teachers 15; Students 175.

[D] SPECIAL SCHOOLS

ALLENTOWN. *Mercy Special Learning Center, Inc.* (1954) 830 S. Woodward St., 18103-3440.
Tel: 610-797-8242; Fax: 610-797-9092; Email: school@mercyspeciallearning.org; principal@mercyspeciallearning.org; Web: mercyschool.org. Elizabeth L. Grys, Prin. Ages: 3 years to post 21. Lay Teachers 8; Students 75.

EASTON. *The Aquinas Program - Secondary Level Notre Dame High School, Inc.*, 3417 Church St., Easton, 18045-2999. Tel: 610-868-1431; Fax: 610-868-8710; Email: altnndhs@ptd.net. Dr. Brooke C. Tesche, Supvr.; Mr. Mario Lucrezi, Prin. Students 62.

POTTSVILLE. *St. Joseph Center for Special Learning, Inc.*, 2075 W. Norwegian St., Pottsville, 17901-1907. Tel: 570-622-4638; Fax: 570-622-3420; Email: altssjc@ptd.net; Web: www.stjosephctr.com. Mr. Roobhenn Smith, Prin. Special learning program for students 4-21. Also offers an adult habilitation program. Lay Teachers 3; Students 17.

READING. *The Aquinas Program St. Margaret School*, 233 Spring St., Reading, 19601-2121.
Tel: 610-375-1882; Fax: 610-376-2291; Email: altbsmg@ptd.net. Sr. Marian Michele Smith, I.H.M., Prin.; Dr. Brooke C. Tesche, Dir., Tel: 610-866-0581, Ext. 25; Fax: 610-867-8702. Lay Teachers 2; Students 38.

SHILLINGTON. *John Paul II Center for Special Learning, Inc.* (1982) 1092 Welsh Rd., Shillington, 19607-0097. Tel: 610-777-0605; Fax: 610-777-0682; Email: madams@johnpauliicenter.org; Web: www.johnpaulIIcenter.org. Mrs. Mary A. Adams, Prin. Lay Teachers 5; Students 45.

[E] CATHOLIC CHARITIES AND SOCIAL AGENCIES

ALLENTOWN. *Catholic Charities, Inc.*, 900 S. Woodward St., 18103-4179. Tel: 610-435-1541;
Fax: 484-664-7794; Web: www.catholiccharityad.org. Teri Dakuginow, Prog. Admin.; Robert Nicolella, Supvr.
Branch Offices:
(For Lehigh, Northampton, Schuylkill, Carbon & Berks Cos.)

Lehigh-Northampton Counties Branch Office, 900 S. Woodward St., 18103-4179. Tel: 610-435-1541;
Fax: 610-435-4367; Email: rnicolella@allentowndiocese.org. Robert Nicolella, Admin.

Schuylkill Carbon Counties Branch Office, 13 Westwood Center, Pottsville, 17901-1800.
Tel: 570-628-0466; Fax: 570-628-3343; Email: rnicolella@allentowndiocese.org. Robert Nicolella, Admin.

Berks County Branch Office, 234 Grace St., Reading, 19611-1946. Tel: 610-376-7144; Fax: 610-376-7145; Email: rnicolella@allentowndiocese.org. Ms. Diane Bullard, M.S., Sec., Catholic Human Svcs.

[F] GENERAL HOSPITALS

ALLENTOWN. *Sacred Heart Hospital* (1912) 421 Chew St., 18102-3490. Tel: 610-776-4500;
Fax: 610-776-4559; Web: shh.org. Mr. John Nespoli, Pres. & CEO; Rev. John G. Hilferty, Chap. & Dir. Pastoral Care; Sr. Josanne Huber, M.S.C., Chap. Bed Capacity 215; Patients Asst Anual. 170,553; Priests 1; Sisters 1; Skilled Nursing Beds 22; Total Staff 1,118; Lay Chaplain 1.

READING. *Penn State Health Saint Joseph*, 2500 Bernville Rd., P.O. Box 316, Reading, 19603-0316.
Tel: 610-378-2000; Fax: 610-378-2798. John R. Morahan, Pres. & CEO. Opened Aug. 26, 1873. St. Joseph Regional Health Network is acquired by the newly created Penn State Health, and becomes the first hospital in the organization and is now known as Penn State Health St. Joseph. Bassinets 22; Bed Capacity 204; Patients Asst Anual. 267,908; Sisters 4; Total Staff 1,436.

[G] SKILLED NURSING FACILITIES

BETHLEHEM. *Holy Family Manor of Catholic Senior Housing and Health Care Services, Inc.* (1963) Skilled and intermediate nursing care facility for the aged, chronically ill, or invalid. Holy Family Manor: a division of Catholic Senior Housing and Health Care Services, Inc. 1200 Spring St., Bethlehem, 18018. Tel: 610-865-5595;
Fax: 610-997-8454; Email: sregalis@hfmanor.org; Web: www.hfmanor.org. Mrs. Susan Regalis, N.H.A., N.H.A., Admin.; Rev. Venatius T. Karobo, A.J., Chap. Capacity 208; Total Staff 323; Total Assisted 421.

SHOEMAKERSVILLE. *Covenant Home Care, Inc.*, 1223 Pottsville Pike, Shoemakersville, 19555-1719.
Tel: 800-726-8761; Fax: 610-562-0107; Email: jeff.

yockavitch@chihealthathome.com; Web: www.covenanthc.org. Jeff Yockavitch, Dir. Operations.

[H] HOMES AND SERVICES FOR THE ELDERLY AND CONVALESCENT

BETHLEHEM. *Grace Mansion Personal Care Home of Catholic Senior Housing and Health Care Services, Inc.*, 1200 Spring St., Bethlehem, 18018. Tel: 610-865-6748; Fax: 610-997-8444; Email: kabruzzese@hfmanor.org; Web: www.hfpersonalcare.org. Mrs. Karen Abruzzese, Admin. Personal care home for 28 elderly. Total in Residence 28; Total Staff 13.

Holy Family Apartments of Catholic Housing Corporation of Bethlehem, 330-338 13th Ave., Bethlehem, 18018. Tel: 610-866-4603; Fax: 610-866-1622; Email: kohm@cshhcs.org. Karen Ohm, Mgr.; Mr. Randall Wadsworth, Dir. Catholic housing for the elderly. Total Staff 2; Apartments 50.

Trexler Pavilion, Assisted Living Residence of Catholic Senior Housing and Health Care Services, Inc., 1220 Prospect Ave., Bethlehem, 18018. Tel: 610-868-7776; Fax: 610-865-7775; Email: kabruzzese@hfmanor.org; Web: www.hfpersonalcare.org. Mrs. Karen Abruzzese, Dir. Residential Svcs. Personal care/assisted living facility for 23 elderly. Bed Capacity 23; Total Staff 10; Total Assisted 27.

EASTON. *Antonian Towers, Inc.*, 2405 Hillside Ave., Easton, 18042. Tel: 610-258-2033; Fax: 610-258-6541; Email: jkern@cshhcs.org. Mrs. Judith Kern, Mgr. Catholic housing for the elderly. Total in Residence 50; Total Staff 2; Apartments 50.

LAURELDALE. *Queen of Angels Apartments of Catholic Housing Corporation of Northern Berks County*, 22 Rothermel St., Reading, 19605. Tel: 610-921-3115; Fax: 610-921-8576; Email: iolsson@cshhcs.org. Mr. Randall Wadsworth, Dir., Catholic Housing Corporations. Catholic housing for the elderly. Total in Residence 47; Total Staff 2; Apartments 45.

NEW PHILADELPHIA. *Holy Family Apartments of Catholic Housing Corporation of New Philadelphia*, c/o Neumann Apartments, 25 N. Nichols St., St. Clair, 17970. Tel: 570-429-0699; Fax: 570-429-2368; Email: pharris@cshhcs.org. Mr. Randall Wadsworth, Dir., Catholic Housing Corporations. Total Staff 2; Apartments 11.

ORWIGSBURG. *Holy Family Adult Day Care*, 900 W. Market St., Orwigsburg, 17961. Tel: 570-366-2924; Fax: 570-366-2301; Email: lherb@allentowndiocese.org. Mrs. Linda Herb, Dir. Day care for the elderly. Total Staff 6; Clients 27.

POTTSVILLE. *Queen of Peace Apartments of Catholic Housing Corporation of Schuylkill County*, 777 Water St., Pottsville, 17901. Tel: 570-628-4504; Fax: 570-628-4712; Email: dhess@cshhcs.org. Mrs. Diana Hess, Mgr.; Mr. Randall Wadsworth, Dir., Catholic Housing Corporations. Catholic housing for the elderly. Total in Residence 48; Total Staff 2; Apartments 48.

READING. *Sacred Heart Villa - Personal Care Community of the Missionary Sisters of the Most Sacred Heart of Jesus* (2003) 51 Seminary Ave., Reading, 19605. Tel: 610-929-5751; Fax: 610-743-7451; Email: nadams.shv@gmail.com; Web: sacredheartvillapa.org. Mrs. Mary Kusnierz, Admin. Bed Capacity 100; Tot Asst. Annually 90; Total Staff 55; Total Assisted 79.

SAINT CLAIR. *Neumann Apartments of Catholic Housing Corporation of St. Clair*, 25 N. Nichols St., St. Clair, 17970. Tel: 570-429-0699; Fax: 570-429-2368; Email: pharris@cshhcs.org. Ms. Patricia Harris. Catholic housing for the elderly. Total in Residence 24; Total Staff 2; Apartments 24.

[I] HOMES FOR PRIESTS

BETHLEHEM. *Holy Family Villa*, Mailing Address: P.O. Box F, 18018-1538. 1325 Prospect Ave., Bethlehem, 18018-4916. Tel: 610-694-0395; Fax: 610-694-9990; Email: JBuck@AllentownDiocese.org. In Res. Rev. Msgr. Robert M. Forst, (Retired); Revs. Stephen J. Halabura, (Retired); Joseph D. Hulko, (Retired); Wayne E. Killian, M.A., M.S., (Retired); Luigi Palmieri, (Retired); Frederick F. Sattler, (Retired); Joseph A. Sheehan, (Retired); John J.L. Little, (Retired).

[J] MONASTERIES AND RESIDENCES OF PRIESTS AND BROTHERS

BETHLEHEM. *Barnabite Fathers of the Lehigh Valley, Inc., Barnabite Spiritual Center*, 4301 Hecktown Rd., Bethlehem, 18020-9704. Tel: 610-691-8648; Email: BarnabiteSpiritualCenter@gmail.com; Web: www.barnabites.com. Very Rev. Robert B. Kosek, C.R.S.P., Ph.D., Supr., Mod. of Spiritual Center; Rev. Paul M. Marconi, C.R.S.P., Vicar.

CENTER VALLEY. *Oblates of St. Francis de Sales*, Wills Hall, 2755 Station Ave., Center Valley, 18034-9568. Tel: 610-282-3300; Fax: 610-282-3962; Email: willshallosfs@gmail.com; Web: www.desales.edu. Revs. Joseph P. Becker, O.S.F.S., M.A.; Shaju K. Kanjiramparayil, O.S.F.S.; Douglas C. Burns, O.S.F.S., M.Div., Supr.; Daniel G. Gambet, O.S.F.S., Ph.D., (Retired); Bro. Daniel P. Wisniewski, O.S.F.S., Ph.D.; Revs. James J. Greenfield, O.S.F.S.; Alexander T. Pocetto, O.S.F.S., Ph.D., (Retired); John I. Extejt, O.S.F.S., M.S., M.Div., M.A.T.; Bro. Harry G. Schneider, O.S.F.S.; Revs. Kevin Nadolski, O.S.F.S.; Daniel Lannen, O.S.F.S.; Bro. Joseph G. Schodowski, O.S.F.S., A.A. Total in Residence 12.

Sacred Heart Villa, Missionaries of the Sacred Heart, 3300 Station Ave., Center Valley, 18034-9563. Tel: 610-282-1415, Ext. 35; Fax: 610-282-0610; Email: rwkpng03@mscparish.com; Web: www.misacor-usa.org. Revs. E. Michael Camilli, M.S.C., S.T.L., M.S.L.S., H.E.L.; Leon Weisenberger, M.S.C.; Joseph T. Muller, M.S.C.; Thomas Carney, M.S.C.; Bros. George Farkas, M.S.C.; Warren Perreto; Revs. Richard Kennedy, M.S.C., Supr.; Richard Huber, M.S.C.; Very Rev. John J. Paul, M.S.C., V.J., S.T.L., J.C.D.; Bros. Gene Thomas, M.S.C.; Michael Tomcics, M.S.C.; Revs. John Schweikert, M.S.C.; Joseph Gleixner, M.S.C.; Mark McDonald, M.S.C.; Andrew Torma, M.S.C.; Bro. Joseph Tesar, M.S.C. Brothers 8; Priests 5.

EASTON. *St. Francis Friary*, 3908 Chipman Rd., Easton, 18045-3014. Tel: 610-515-0867; Fax: 610-515-0902. Bros. Mark Ligett, O.F.M., Guardian; Edward Skutka, O.F.M.; Rev. Henry Beck, O.F.M., Vicar. Franciscan Province of St. John the Baptist. Brothers 2; Priests 1; Total in Residence 3.

NEW RINGGOLD. *Cistercian Monastery*, St. Mary's Priory, 70 Schuylkill Rd., New Ringgold, 17960-9703. Tel: 570-943-2645; Fax: 570-943-3035. Very Rev. Luke Anderson, O.Cist., Th.M., Ph.D., Prior. Fathers 1.

NORTHAMPTON. **Apostles of Jesus* (1968) 829 Main St., Northampton, 18067-1838. Tel: 610-502-1732; Fax: 610-502-1733; Email: ajregionalusa@gmail.com; Web: www.apostlesofjesusmissionaries.com. Revs. Avitus Siriwa, A.J., Sec.; Augustine L. Idra, A.J., Regl. Supr.; Richard O'Nymawaro, A.J., Mission Dir.; Bruno Dongo, A.J., Financial Sec.

WERNERSVILLE. *Jesuit Community of St. Isaac Jogues (Jesuit Center)* (1930) Mailing Address: P.O. Box 223, Wernersville, 19565-0223. 501 N. Church Rd., Wernersville, 19565-0223. Tel: 610-678-8085; Fax: 610-678-8747; Email: gbursj@gmail.com. Rev. George W. Bur, S.J., Supr.; Ms. Jill Eppie, Treas. Brothers 1; Priests 8; Total Staff 1. In Res. Revs. John P. Barron, S.J.; Lucien F. Longtin, S.J.; Robert D. Wiesenbaugh, S.J.; Edward M. Ifkovits, S.J.; Thomas J. Kuller, S.J.; Thomas P. McDonnell, S.J.; Bro. Christopher Derby, S.J.; Rev. Frank Kaminski, S.J.

[K] CONVENTS AND RESIDENCES OF SISTERS

BETHLEHEM. *St. Joseph Convent*, 2133 Madison Ave., Bethlehem, 18017-4642. Tel: 610-865-4691; Email: ssj2133@aol.com. Sisters 7.

Monocacy Manor (1947) 395 Bridle Path Rd., Bethlehem, 18017. Tel: 610-866-2597; Fax: 610-861-7478; Email: monocacyfranciscans@schoolsistersosf.org; Web: www.schoolsistersosf.org. Sisters Frances Duncan, O.S.F., Prov.; Bonnie Marie Kleinschuster, O.S.F., Supr. School Sisters of the Third Order Regular United States Prov. Sisters 22.

COOPERSBURG. *Carmelite Monastery* (1931) St. Therese of the Child Jesus and St. Mary Magdalen de Pazzi, St. Therese's Valley. 3551 Lanark Rd., Coopersburg, 18036-9324. Tel: 610-797-3721; Fax: 610-797-8510; Email: carmelitemonasterylehighvalley@gmail.com; Web: www.carmelite-nuns.com. Rev. Apostles Jesus, Chap.; Sr. Mary Veronica, Prioress. Carmelite Nuns of the Ancient Observance (Calced) O.Carm. Professed Nuns 6.

EASTON. *Angelic Sisters of St. Paul*, Mother of Divine Providence Convent, 4196 William Penn Hwy., Easton, 18045-5067. Tel: 610-258-7792; Fax: 610-258-7792; Email: angelicsistersofsaintpaul@yahoo.com. Sr. Pasqualina Pascarella, A.S.P., Supr. Sisters 3.

MAHANOY CITY. *Missionaries of Charity*, St. Teresa Convent, 536 W. South St., Mahanoy City, 17948-2422. Tel: 570-773-1420. Sr. M. Josephine, M.C., Supr. Missionaries of Charity. Sisters 5.

PEN ARGYL. *Dominican Daughters of the Immaculate Mother*, 115 Lobb Ave., Pen Argyl, 18072. Tel: 610-863-9214; Fax: 610-863-8158. Sr. Maria Luz, O.P., Supr. Sisters 5.

READING. *The Bernardine Sisters of the Third Order of Saint Francis*, 450 St. Bernardine St., Reading, 19607-1737. Tel: 484-334-6976; Fax: 610-777-3973; Email: RobertaAnn@bfranciscan.org; Web: www.bfranciscan.org. Sr. Marilisa H. da Silva, O.S.F., Congregational Min.

The Bernardine Sisters of the Third Order of Saint Francis, Generalate, (aka Bernardine Franciscan Sisters).

Chevalier House, 43 Seminary Ave., Reading, 19605. Tel: 610-929-8348; Fax: 610-929-0762; Email: jdecembrino@mscreading.org; Web: www.mscreading.org. Sisters 2.

St. Clare Convent, 450 St. Bernardine St., Reading, 19607-1736. Tel: 484-755-5360; Fax: 610-777-3973; Email: skateri@bfranciscan.org; Web: www.bfranciscan.org. Sr. Kateri Peake, O.S.F., Contact Person. Bernardine Franciscan Sisters. Sisters 2.

Hannibal House - Spiritual Center (1887) Daughters of Divine Zeal, F.D.Z., 1526 Hill Rd., Reading, 19602-1410. Tel: 610-375-1738; Tel: 610-375-9072; Fax: 610-375-2188; Email: srdivinezeal@hotmail.com. Sisters 3.

House of Nazareth (Casa Nazaret), 532 Spruce St., Reading, 19602. Tel: 610-378-1947; Email: casa_nazareth@aol.com. Sr. Marta Munoz, Supr. Residence of the Poor Sisters of St. Joseph who work in Spanish Apostolate of Berks County. Sisters 4.

St. Ignatius Loyola Convent, 2601 St. Alban Dr., Reading, 19609-1132. Tel: 610-750-5445. Sr. Rosemarie Bartnicki, O.S.F., Local Min. Sisters 3.

St. Joseph Villa (1967) 464 Bernardine St., Reading, 19607. Tel: 610-777-5556; Fax: 610-777-5545; Email: administrator@saintjosephvilla.com; Web: www.saintjosephvilla.com. Victoria L. Mitchell, Admin.; Rev. Ronald P. Bowman, M.Div., M.A., Chap.; Sr. Mary Joseph Tirpak, O.S.F., Supr. Retirement Home of the Bernardine Sisters of the Third Order of St. Francis. Sisters 60.

MSC Province Center, 2811 Moyers Ln., Reading, 19605. Tel: 610-929-5944; Fax: 610-929-3634; Email: USAMSC@mscreading.org; Web: www.mscreading.org. Sr. Rosemarie Sommers, M.S.C., Province Leader. Provincial offices of Missionary Sisters of the Most Sacred Heart of Jesus. Sisters 4. *Our Lady of the Sacred Heart Convent*, 2811 Moyers Ln., Reading, 19605. Tel: 601-929-5944; Fax: 610-929-3634; Email: mscsisters@aol.com. Sr. Rosemarie Sommers, M.S.C., Prov. Supr. Sisters 4.

Precious Blood Convent (1885) 1094 Welsh Rd., Reading, 19607-9363. Tel: 610-777-1624; Fax: 610-777-3359; Email: cps.shillington@comcast.net; Web: www.preciousbloodsisters.com. Sisters Monica Mary Ncube, C.P.S., Prov. Supr.; Christa-Mary Jones, C.P.S., Local Supr. Residence for Missionary Sisters of the Precious Blood. Sisters 15.

Sacred Heart Convent, 460 St. Bernardine St., Reading, 19607-1737. Tel: 484-334-7000; Fax: 484-334-6808; Email: localminister@bfranciscan.org; Web: www.bfranciscan.org. Sr. Kateri Peake, O.S.F., Admin., Tel: 610-777-7221. Motherhouse; Residence for Bernardine Sisters of Third Order of St. Francis. Professed Sisters 35.

Sacred Heart Villa, 51 Seminary Ave, Reading, 19605-2621. Tel: 610-929-5751; Fax: 610-743-7451; Email: maebigos1423@gmail.com. Sisters Rosemarie Sommers, M.S.C., Prov. Supr.; Mary Anne Bigos, M.S.C., Local Supr. Motherhouse, Retirement Home of Missionary Sisters of the Most Sacred Heart of Jesus.Attended by Chaplain. Professed Sisters 16.

WEATHERLY. *Sisters Apostles of the Descent of the Holy Spirit*, 484 Pump House Rd., Weatherly, 18255. Tel: 570-427-2467; Fax: 570-427-2545; Email: sisters@peacepentecost.org. Sr. Mary Jerome Kim, S.A.H.S., Supr. Sisters 4.

[L] RETREAT HOUSES

BETHLEHEM. *St. Francis Center for Renewal, Inc. (Monocacy Manor)* (1948) 395 Bridle Path Rd., Bethlehem, 18017. Tel: 610-867-8890; Fax: 610-865-1122; Email: stfranciscenter@gmail.com; Web: www.stfrancisctr.org. Sisters M. Anita Kuchera, O.S.F., Asoc. Dir.; M. Marguerite Stewart, O.S.F., Spiritual Dir.; Barbara DeStefano, Assoc. Dir.; Janice Gough, Devel.; Sr. Virginelle Makos, O.S.F., Dir. Weekend Retreats, Twilight Retreats, and Days of Recollection; retreats for men and women, marriage encounter; engaged encounters; parish retreats; workshops; youth groups; weekends; privately directed retreats; private retreats, spiritual direction. Lay Staff 4; Total Staff 12; Professed Sisters 8.

EASTON. *St. Francis Retreat House, Inc.*, 3918 Chipman Rd., Easton, 18045-3014. Tel: 610-258-3053; Fax: 610-258-2412; Email: stfranrh@rcn.com; Web: www.stfrancisretreathouse.org. Bro. Mark Ligett, O.F.M., Admin.; Rev. Henry Beck, O.F.M., Admin.; Sr. Regina Roskosny, O.S.F., Admin. Retreatants 100.

READING. *Mariawald Renewal Center*, 1094 Welsh Rd., Reading, 19607-9363. Tel: 610-777-0135;

Fax: 610-777-3359; Email: mariawaldcenter@gmail.com; Web: www.mariawaldrenewal.com. Sr. Christa-Mary Jones, C.P.S., Coord. Single, & double occupancy. Capacity 38; Units 19.

[M] CENTERS FOR SPIRITUAL GROWTH

READING. *McGlinn Conference and Spirituality Center*, 460 St. Bernardine St., Reading, 19607-1737.
Tel: 484-334-6807; Fax: 484-334-6808; Email: mcglinncc@bfranciscan.org. Sr. Shaun Kathleen Wilson, O.S.F., Dir. The Center is located in the Bernardine Franciscan Motherhouse. Able to provide space for days of reflection and workshops for groups up to 125 persons. Spiritual direction and directed/private retreats available. Chapel and dining facility available. Total Staff 2.

WERNERSVILLE. *Jesuit Center for Spiritual Growth*, Mailing Address: P.O. Box 223, Wernersville, 19565-0223. 501 N. Church Rd., Wernersville, 19565. Tel: 610-678-8085; Fax: 610-670-3650; Email: jescntsec@jesuitcenter.org; Web: www.jesuitcenter.org. Rev. George W. Bur, S.J., Rector; Susan Bowers Baker, Dir. of Spiritual Growth Programs, Staff; Rev. John P. Barron, S.J.; Bro. Christopher Derby, S.J.; Mr. David Gross. Directed retreats, programs in prayer, discernment, psychology and spirituality. Priests 1; Total Staff 7; Total Assisted 10,750.

[N] NEWMAN CENTERS

ALLENTOWN. *Albright College (Reading)*, Mailing Address: St. Christopher Catholic Newman Center, 15207 Kutztown Rd., Kutztown, 19530-9281. Tel: 610-683-8467; Email: catholicchaplain@kutztown.edu. 1621 N. 13th St., Reading, 19612. Rev. Richard C. Brensinger, M.Div., Campus Ministry.

Alvernia College (Reading), Office of Campus Ministry, 400 St. Bernardine St., Reading, 19607.
Tel: 610-796-8300; Fax: 610-796-8324; Email: julianne.wallace@alvernia.edu. Ms. Julianne Wallace, Campus Min.

DeSales University (Center Valley), 2755 Station Ave., Center Valley, 18034-9568.
Tel: 610-282-1100, Ext. 1898; Fax: 610-282-1772; Email: Magdalene.Riggins@desales.edu. Mrs. Magdalene Riggins, Dir.

Kutztown University (Kutztown), St. Christopher Catholic Newman Center, 15207 Kutztown Rd., Kutztown, 19530-9218. Tel: 610-683-8467; Email: catholicchaplain@kutztown.edu; Web: www.saintchristopher-ku.org. Rev. Richard C. Brensinger, M.Div., Campus Ministry.

Lafayette College (Easton), Newman House, 119 McCartney St., Easton, 18042-7647.
Tel: 610-253-5044; Email: bobbink@lafayette.edu. Rev. Kevin J. Bobbin, M.A., S.T.B., M.Div., Chap.

Lehigh University (Bethlehem), Newman Center at Lehigh University, 417 Carlton Ave., Bethlehem, 18015-1583. Tel: 610-758-4148; Fax: 610-758-6392; Email: cbutera@allentowndiocese.org. Rev. Christopher S. Butera, M.Div., M.A., Chap.

Moravian College (Bethlehem), 1200 Main St., Bethlehem, 18018. Tel: 610-289-8900; Email: adoncsecz@allentowndiocese.org. Mailing Address: 2121 Madison Ave., Bethlehem, 18017. Mrs. Alexa Smith, Campus Min.

Muhlenberg College (Allentown), Newman Center, 2339 Liberty St., 18104-5586. Tel: 484-664-3122; Email: frkeving@icloud.com. Rev. Kevin M. Gualano, Chap.

[O] MISCELLANEOUS

ALLENTOWN. *Allentown Catholic Beneficial Association, Inc.*, Mailing Address: P.O. Box 1458, 18105-1458. 1515 Martin Luther King Jr. Dr., 18102-4500. Tel: 610-871-5200; Email: JBuck@AllentownDiocese.org. Peter Sipple, Chm.

Allentown Catholic Capital Campaign Charitable Trust, Mailing Address: P.O. Box F, 18102-4500. 1515 Martin Luther King Jr. Dr., 18102-4500.
Tel: 610-871-5200; Email: JBuck@AllentownDiocese.org. Mr. Paul Acampora, Contact Person.

Allentown Catholic Communications, Inc., Mailing Address: P.O. Box F, 18102-1538. 1515 Martin Luther King Jr. Dr., 18102-4500.
Tel: 610-871-5200, Ext. 264; Fax: 610-439-7694; Email: JBuck@AllentownDiocese.org. Mr. Matthew T. Kerr, Contact Person.

The Allentown Catholic Unitized Investment Fund Charitable Trust, Mailing Address: P.O. Box F, 18102-4500. 1515 Martin Luther King Jr. Dr., 18102-4500. Tel: 610-871-5200, Ext. 2102; Email: JBuck@AllentownDiocese.org. Mr. Mark E. Smith, CPA, Contact Person.

Bishop's Annual Appeal Charitable Trust, Mailing Address: P.O. Box F, 18105-1538. 1515 Martin Luther King Jr. Dr., 18102-4500.
Tel: 610-871-5200, Ext. 2102; Email: JBuck@AllentownDiocese.org. Mr. Paul Acampora, Contact Person.

Catholic Charities of the Diocese of Allentown, Inc., 900 S. Woodward St., 18103-4179.
Tel: 610-435-1541; Fax: 484-664-7784; Web: catholiccharityad.org. Mrs. Julie Scheck, Dir. Advancement; Ms. Diane Bullard, M.S., Sec.; Ms. Susan Mazza, Finance Supvr.

**Catholic Foundation of Eastern Pennsylvania, Inc.*, Mailing Address: P.O. Box 1430, 18105-1430. 1515 Martin Luther King Jr. Dr., 18102-4500.
Tel: 610-871-5200, Ext. 2102; Email: JBuck@AllentownDiocese.org. Mr. Paul E. Huck, Chm.

Clergy Third Age Charitable Trust, Mailing Address: P.O. Box F, 18105-1538. 1515 Martin Luther King Jr. Dr., 18102-4500. Tel: 610-871-5200; Email: JBuck@AllentownDiocese.org. Rev. Adam C. Sedar, M.Div., M.A., Contact Person; Rev. Msgr. Gerald E. Gobitas, Th.M., Contact Person.

Diocesan Cemetery Perpetual Care Charitable Trust, Mailing Address: P.O. Box F, 18105-1538. 1515 Martin Luther King Jr. Dr., 18102-4500.
Tel: 610-871-5200; Email: JBuck@AllentownDiocese.org. Rev. Msgr. William F. Baver, M.Div., Th.M., C.C.C.E., K.C.H.S., Contact Person.

Diocese of Allentown Lay Employees Retirement Plan, Mailing Address: P.O. Box F, 18105-1538. 1515 Martin Luther King Jr. Dr., 18102-4500.
Tel: 610-871-5200, Ext. 2102; Email: JBuck@AllentownDiocese.org. Mr. Herman L. Rij, Trustee.

Retirement Plan for the Ordained Diocesan Priests of the Diocese of Allentown, Mailing Address: P.O. Box F, 18105-1538. 1515 Martin Luther King Jr. Dr., 18102-4500. Tel: 610-871-5200, Ext. 2102; Email: JBuck@AllentownDiocese.org. Rev. Msgr. John G. Chizmar, V.F., M.Div., Trustee.

Supplemental Health Care Benefits Charitable Trust, Lay Employees, Mailing Address: P.O. Box F, 18105-1538. 1515 Martin Luther King Jr. Dr., 18102-4500. Tel: 610-871-5200, Ext. 2102; Email: JBuck@AllentownDiocese.org. Mr. Mark E. Smith, CPA, Contact Person.

BETHLEHEM. *Catholic Senior Housing and Health Care Services, Inc.*, 1200 Spring St., Bethlehem, 18018.
Tel: 610-865-5595; Email: mmelnic@cshhcs.org; Web: www.cshhcs.org. Michael Melnic, CEO.

Eastern Pennsylvania Scholarship Foundation Charitable Trust, 1425 Mountain Dr. N., Bethlehem, 18015-4722.
Tel: 610-866-0581, Ext. 2344; Email: narant@allentowndiocese.org. Mr. John Bakey, Chancellor Catholic Educ.; Nina Arant, Program Mgr,.

Mary's Shelter, Inc., Cay Galgon Center, 714 W. Broad St., Bethlehem, 18018. Tel: 610-867-9546; Fax: 610-419-3255; Email: cgc@marysshelter.org. Mailing Address: Business Office, 736 Upland Ave., Reading, 19607. Cory Lamack, M.S.W., Prog. Dir.

Stephen's Place, Inc., 729 Ridge Ave., Bethlehem, 18015-3621. Tel: 610-861-7677; Fax: 610-861-7677; Email: vlongcope@msn.com; Web: www.stephensplace.com. Sr. Virginia Longcope, M.S.C., Dir. A nonprofit residential community designed to meet the needs of the adult non-violent offender with a history of substance abuse. Bed Capacity 7; Tot Asst. Annually 165; Total Staff 9; Residential Families 15; Community Families 150.

Lay Fraternities of St. Dominic, Expectations of the Blessed Mother Chapter 405, Mailing Address: 121 Nonemaker Rd., Kutztown, 19530. 1861 Catasquqa Rd., Bethlehem, 18018-1298.
Tel: 610-285-2288; Email: jptucker2@verizon.net. Mr. John Tucker, O.P., Pres.

CENTER VALLEY. *Mission Vehicle Association, Inc.*, 3300 Station Ave., Center Valley, 18034-9563.
Tel: 610-737-5440; Email: emcamilli@aol.com. Rev. E. Michael Camilli, M.S.C., S.T.L., M.S.L.S., H.E.L., Contact Person.

EASTON. *Secular Franciscan Fraternity, Secular Franciscan Order, St. Francis Retreat House, Inc.*, St. Francis Retreat House, 3918 Chipman Rd., Easton, 18045-3014. Tel: 610-252-5230; Email: lmpnurpara@msn.com. Nancy Snyder, O.F.S., Min.

EMMAUS. *Blue Army of Our Lady of Fatima*, St. Ann, 415 S. Sixth St., Emmaus, 18049-3703.
Tel: 610-965-2426; Email: churchofstann@rcn.com. Rev. Dominic Thao Pham, M.Div., Spiritual Dir.

ORWIGSBURG. *Holy Family Adult Day Care of Catholic Senior Housing and Health Care Services, Inc.*, 900 W. Market St., Orwigsburg, 17961-1008.
Tel: 570-366-2924; Fax: 570-366-2301; Email: lherb@allentowndiocese.org. Mrs. Linda Herb, Dir.

Seton Manor, Inc., 1000 Seton Dr., Orwigsburg, 17961. Tel: 314-733-8000; Email: jimpicciche@ascension.org; Web: www.ascension.org. Joseph R. Impiccishe, Exec.

POTTSVILLE. *Servants to All, Inc.*, Mailing Address: P.O. Box 1354, Pottsville, 17901-3001. 4 S. Centre St., Pottsville, 17901. Tel: 570-728-2917; Email: servantstoall@comcast.net; Web: servantstoall.org. Albert Nastasi, Founder.

READING. *Bernardine Center (Bernardine Franciscans, Delaware County)*, 450 St. Bernardine St., Reading, 19607-1737. Tel: 484-334-6976;
Fax: 610-777-3973; Email: RobertaAnn@bfranciscan.org; Web: www.bfranciscan.org. Sr. Marilisa H. da Silva, O.S.F., Congregational Min.

Bernardine Franciscan Sisters Congregational Leadership Offices, 450 St. Bernardine St., Reading, 19607-1737. Tel: 484-334-6976;
Fax: 617-777-3973; Email: Robertaann@bfranciscan.org; Web: www.bfranciscan.org. Sr. Marilisa H. da Silva, O.S.F., Supr.

Bernardine Franciscan Sisters Mission and Ministries Charitable Trust, 450 St. Bernardine St., Reading, 19607-1737. Tel: 484-334-6976;
Fax: 610-777-3973; Email: RobertaAnn@bfranciscan.org; Web: www.bfranciscan.org. Sr. Marilisa H. da Silva, O.S.F., Chm.

**Clare of Assisi House*, 325 S. 12th St., Reading, 19602. Tel: 484-869-5483; Email: robin.ball@clareofassisihouse.org; Web: www.clareofassisihouse.org. Robin Ball, Exec. Dir.

Dayspring Homes, Inc., P.O. Box 158, Reading, 19607-0172. 430 Hazel St., Reading, 19611.
Tel: 610-376-5648; Fax: 610-374-9086; Email: dayspringhomes@dayspringhomes.org. Ms. Stacy Grube, C.E.O.; Sr. Francis Bisland, C.P.S.

Mary's Shelter, Inc., Mailing Address: 736 Upland Ave., Reading, 19607. 325 S. 12 St., Reading, 19607. Tel: 610-603-8010; Fax: 610-603-8012; Email: office@marysshelter.org; Web: www.marysshelter.org. Christine Folk, R.N., Exec. Dir.; Danielle Monahan, M.S.W., Asst. Exec. Dir. A residence for pregnant, homeless young women. Bed Capacity 10; Total Staff 10; Community Families 600; Residential Families 45.

SHILLINGTON. **St. Francis Home*, 144 Hillside Dr., Shillington, 19607. Tel: 610-898-4242; Email: information@stfrancishomereading.org; Web: www.stfrancishomereading.org. Nancy Schwartz.

RELIGIOUS INSTITUTES OF MEN REPRESENTED IN THE DIOCESE

For further details refer to the corresponding bracketed number in the Religious Institutes of Men or Women section.

[]—*Apostles of Jesus*—A.J.
[]—*Cistercian Monks of the Strict Observance*—O.Cist.
[0160]—*Clerics Regular of St. Paul* (Barnabite Fathers)—C.R.S.P.
[1330]—*Congregation of the Mission (Vincentian Fathers)* (Eastern Prov.)—C.M.
[0520]—*Franciscan Fathers* (St. John the Baptist Province)—O.F.M.
[0690]—*Jesuit Fathers* (Maryland Prov.)—S.J.
[1110]—*Missionaries of the Sacred Heart* (American Prov.)—M.S.C.
[0920]—*Oblates of St. Francis de Sales*—O.S.F.S.
[]—*Priestly Fraternity of St. Peter*—F.F.S.P.

RELIGIOUS INSTITUTES OF WOMEN REPRESENTED IN THE DIOCESE

[0120]—*Angelic Sisters of St. Paul*—A.S.S.P.
[1810]—*Bernardine Sisters of the Third Order of St. Francis (Bernardine Franciscan Sisters)*—O.S.F.
[0320]—*Carmelite Nuns of the Ancient Observance*—O.Carm.
[1065]—*Dominican Daughters of the Immaculate Mother*—O.P.
[1470]—*Franciscan Sisters of St. Joseph*—F.S.S.J.
[2710]—*Missionaries of Charity*—M.C.
[2800]—*Missionary Sisters of the Most Sacred Heart of Jesus* (American Province)—M.S.C.
[2850]—*Missionary Sisters of the Precious Blood*—C.P.S.
[3250]—*Poor Sisters of St. Joseph*—P.S.S.J.
[1700]—*School Sisters of the Third Order of St. Francis* (United States Prov.)—O.S.F.
[]—*Sisters Apostles of the Descent of the Holy Spirit*—S.A.H.S.
[0660]—*Sisters of Christian Charity*—S.C.C.
[]—*Sisters of Mercy* (Mid-Atlantic Community)—R.S.M.
[]—*Sisters of St. Agnes*—C.S.A.
[]—*Sisters of St. Francis of Philadelphia* (Glen Riddle)—O.S.F.
[3830]—*Sisters of St. Joseph*—S.S.J.
[2170]—*Sisters, Servants of the Immaculate Heart of Mary*—I.H.M.

DIOCESAN CEMETERIES

ALLENTOWN. *Diocesan Cemetery Perpetual Care Trust*, Mailing Address: P.O. Box F, 18105-1538. 547 N. Krocks Rd., 18106-9732. Tel: 610-395-3819;
Fax: 610-366-3713; Email:

JBuck@AllentownDiocese.org. Mr. Larry Hillanbrand, Supt.

BETHLEHEM. *Diocesan Cemetery Perpetual Care Trust*, Mailing Address: P.O. Box F, 18105-1538. 2575 Linden St., Bethlehem, 18017-3842. Tel: 610-866-2372; Fax: 610-866-9277; Email: JBuck@AllentownDiocese.org. Mr. Larry Hillanbrand, Supt.

NECROLOGY

† Hartgen, Dennis T., (Retired), Died Nov. 21, 2018
† Muntone, Anthony D., (Retired), Died May. 30, 2018
† Wassel, Anthony F., (Retired), Died May. 4, 2018
† Ahrensfield, Michael E., Lehighton, PA SS. Peter and Paul, Died Sep. 10, 2018
† Bechtel, James C., (Retired), Died Oct. 21, 2018
† Braudis, Joseph M., (Retired), Died Dec. 7, 2018
† McElduff, Edward W., (Retired), Died Oct. 21, 2018

An asterisk (*) denotes an organization that has established tax-exempt status directly with the IRS and is not covered by the USCCB Group Ruling.

Diocese of Altoona-Johnstown

(Dioecesis Altunensis-Johnstoniensis)

Most Reverend

MARK L. BARTCHAK

Bishop of Altoona-Johnstown; ordained May 15, 1981; appointed Bishop of Altoona-Johnstown January 14, 2011; installed April 19, 2011. *Chancery Office: 927 S. Logan Blvd., Hollidaysburg, PA 16648.*

The Chancery: 927 S. Logan Blvd., Hollidaysburg, PA 16648. Tel: 814-695-5579; Fax: 814-695-8894.

Web: www.dioceseaj.org

Email: tdegol@dioceseaj.org

ESTABLISHED DIOCESE OF ALTOONA, MAY 27, 1901.

Square Miles 6,674.

Redesignated Diocese of Altoona-Johnstown, October 9, 1957.

Comprises the Counties of Bedford, Blair, Cambria, Centre, Clinton, Fulton, Huntingdon and Somerset in the State of Pennsylvania.

For legal titles of parishes and diocesan institutions, consult the Chancery Office.

STATISTICAL OVERVIEW

Personnel	
Bishop	1
Priests: Diocesan Active in Diocese	53
Priests: Diocesan Active Outside Diocese	4
Priests: Retired, Sick or Absent	43
Number of Diocesan Priests	100
Religious Priests in Diocese	76
Total Priests in Diocese	176
Extern Priests in Diocese	1
Ordinations:	
Transitional Deacons	1
Permanent Deacons	1
Permanent Deacons in Diocese	38
Total Brothers	21
Total Sisters	80
Parishes	
Parishes	86
With Resident Pastor:	
Resident Diocesan Priests	64
Resident Religious Priests	18
Without Resident Pastor:	
Administered by Deacons	4
Missions	5
Welfare	
Homes for the Aged	3
Total Assisted	351
Special Centers for Social Services	2
Total Assisted	27,732
Educational	
Diocesan Students in Other Seminaries	5
Total Seminarians	5
Colleges and Universities	2
Total Students	3,175
High Schools, Private	4
Total Students	946
Elementary Schools, Diocesan and Parish	13
Total Students	2,143
Catechesis/Religious Education:	
High School Students	1,996
Elementary Students	4,348
Total Students under Catholic Instruction	12,613
Teachers in the Diocese:	
Priests	1
Brothers	1
Sisters	3
Lay Teachers	311
Vital Statistics	
Receptions into the Church:	
Infant Baptism Totals	709
Minor Baptism Totals	40
Adult Baptism Totals	63
Received into Full Communion	56
First Communions	756
Confirmations	939
Marriages:	
Catholic	197
Interfaith	110
Total Marriages	307
Deaths	1,439
Total Catholic Population	75,061
Total Population	652,410

Former Bishops—Rt. Rev. EUGENE A. GARVEY, D.D., ord. Sept. 22, 1869; cons. Sept. 8, 1901; died Oct. 22, 1920; Most Revs. JOHN JOSEPH MCCORT, D.D., ord. Oct. 14, 1883; cons. Titular Bishop of Azotus and Auxiliary to the Archbishop of Philadelphia, Sept. 17, 1912; appt. Coadjutor cum jure successionis to the Bishop of Altoona, Jan. 27, 1920; appt. Bishop of Altoona, Oct. 22, 1920; appt. Assistant at the Pontifical Throne, Oct. 5, 1933; died April 21, 1936; RICHARD T. GUILFOYLE, D.D., ord. June 2, 1917; appt. Aug. 8, 1936; cons. Nov. 30, 1936; died June 10, 1957; HOWARD J. CARROLL, D.D., ord. April 2, 1927; appt. Dec. 5, 1957; cons. Jan. 2, 1958; died March 21, 1960; J. CARROLL MCCORMICK, D.D., ord. July 10, 1932; cons. April 20, 1947; appt. June 25, 1960; transferred to See of Scranton March 4, 1966; retired Feb. 15, 1983; died Nov. 2, 1996; JAMES J. HOGAN, D.D., ord. Dec. 8, 1937; appt. Titular Bishop of Philomelium and Auxiliary of Trenton, Nov. 27, 1959; cons. Feb. 25, 1960; appt. to the See of Altoona-Johnstown May 23, 1966; retired Oct. 17, 1986; died June 14, 2005; JOSEPH V. ADAMEC, D.D., S.T.L., ord. July 3, 1960; appt. Bishop of Altoona-Johnstown March 17, 1987; ord. and installed May 20, 1987; retired Jan. 14, 2011; died March 20, 2019.

Diocesan Officials

Bishop—Most Rev. MARK LEONARD BARTCHAK, J.C.D., 927 S. Logan Blvd., Hollidaysburg, 16648. Tel: 814-695-5579; Fax: 814-695-8894.

Vicar General—Very Rev. ALAN E. THOMAS, V.G., 927 S. Logan Blvd., Hollidaysburg, 16648. Tel: 814-695-5579; Tel: 814-742-7075 (Res.); Fax: 814-695-8894; Email: athomas@dioceseaj.org.

Judicial Vicar—Very Rev. JOHN D. BYRNES, J.V., J.C.L., 933 S. Logan Blvd., Hollidaysburg, 16648. Tel: 814-693-9485; Tel: 814-472-8551 (Res.); Fax: 814-696-6725; Email: jbyrnes@dioceseaj.org.

Bishop's Vicar for Religious—Very Rev. ANTHONY FRANCIS SPILKA, O.F.M.Conv., St. Francis of Assisi, 120 Barron Ave., Johnstown, 15906. Tel: 814-539-1632; Fax: 814-536-7024.

Chancellor—MRS. TERESA M. STAYER, 927 S. Logan Blvd., Hollidaysburg, 16648. Tel: 814-695-5579; Fax: 814-695-8894; Email: tstayer@dioceseaj.org.

Vicars Forane

Altoona Deanery—Very Rev. LUBOMIR J. STRECOK, V.F., Sacred Heart Rectory, 511 20th St., Altoona, 16602. Tel: 814-943-8553; Fax: 814-943-1556.

Johnstown Deanery—Very Rev. MARK S. BEGLY, V.F., Our Mother of Sorrows Rectory, 407 Tioga St., Johnstown, 15905. Tel: 814-535-7646; Fax: 814-536-7850.

Northern Deanery—Very Rev. JOSEPH W. FLEMING, V.F., St. Catherine of Siena Rectory, 205 W. Market St., Mount Union, 17066. Tel: 814-542-4582.

Prince Gallitzin Deanery—Very Rev. LEONARD E. VOYTEK, V.F., St. Mary Rectory, 1020 Caroline St., Nanty Glo, 15943. Tel: 814-749-9103; Fax: 814-749-5463.

Southern Deanery—Very Rev. ANGELO J. PATTI, V.F., St. Peter Rectory, 433 W. Church St., Somerset, 15501. Tel: 814-443-6574; Fax: 814-445-7766.

Diocesan Offices

Building Commission—VACANT.

Campus Ministry—Rev. Msgr. MICHAEL A. BECKER, Coord., 309 Lotz Ave., Lakemont, Altoona, 16602. Tel: 814-942-5503; Fax: 814-943-8832.

Catholic Charities—MRS. JEAN JOHNSTONE, Exec. Dir., 1300 12th Ave., P.O. Box 1349, Altoona, 16603. Tel: 814-944-9388; Fax: 814-941-2677; Email: jjohnstone@dioceseaj.org.

Altoona Office—1300 Twelfth Ave., P.O. Box 1349, Altoona, 16603. Tel: 814-944-9388; Fax: 814-941-2677; Email: jjohnstone@dioceseaj.org. MRS. JEAN JOHNSTONE, Exec. Dir.

Johnstown Office—321 Main St., Ste. 5G, Johnstown, 15901. Tel: 814-535-6538; Fax: 814-535-2235; Email: jjohnstone@dioceseaj.org.

Bellefonte Office—213 E. Bishop St., P.O. Box 389, Bellefonte, 16823. Tel: 814-353-0502; Fax: 814-353-0515; Email: jjohnstone@dioceseaj.org. *Emergency Homeless Shelter: Martha & Mary House, 899 Bedford St., Johnstown, 15902.* Tel: 814-254-4413; Fax: 814-254-4430; Email: jjohnstone@dioceseaj.org.

Catholic Relief Services & Foreign Mission Outreach—VACANT.

Cemetery Commission—VACANT.

Chancery—MRS. TERESA M. STAYER, Chancellor, 927 S. Logan Blvd., Hollidaysburg, 16648, Tel: 814-695-5579; Fax: 814-695-8894; Email: tstayer@dioceseaj.org.

Children and Youth Protection—927 S. Logan Blvd., Hollidaysburg, 16648. Tel: 814-695-5579; Fax: 814-695-8894; Email: coconnor@dioceseaj.org. MRS. CINDY O'CONNOR, Dir.

Communications—MR. TONY DEGOL, Sec., 925 S. Logan Blvd., Hollidaysburg, 16648. Tel: 814-695-5579; Fax: 814-695-8894; Email: tdegol@dioceseaj.org.

Commission for Life and Justice—5379 Portage St., Lilly, 15938. Tel: 814-886-5551.

Development—925 S. Logan Blvd., P.O. Box 409, Hollidaysburg, 16648. Tel: 814-695-5577; Fax: 814-696-9516; Email: pseasoltz@dioceseaj.org. MRS. PAMELA SEASOLTZ, Dir.

Diocesan Liturgy Committee—Sr. LINDA LAMAGNA, C.C.W., Chm., 925 S. Logan Blvd., Hollidaysburg,

16648. Tel: 814-693-9870; Email: srllamagna@gmail.com.

Dmitri Manor - Priests' Residence - St. Mary's Lane—Rev. Msgr. ROBERT J. SALY, 927 S. Logan Blvd., Hollidaysburg, 16648. Tel: 814-696-4698; Tel: 814-696-4126 (Res.).

Ecumenical Minister—Rev. Msgr. MICHAEL A. BECKER, 309 Lotz Ave., Lakemont, Altoona, 16602. Tel: 814-942-5503; Fax: 814-943-8832.

Education—MS. JO-ANN SEMKO, Dir., Email: jsemko@dioceseaj.org; MRS. PEGGY BECK, Exec. Prog. Asst., 933 S. Logan Blvd., Hollidaysburg, 16648. Tel: 814-693-1401; Fax: 814-696-6725; Email: pbeck@dioceseaj.org.

Director of Facilities—MR. ERNIE ENEDY, 927 S. Logan Blvd., Hollidaysburg, 16648. Tel: 814-695-5579; Fax: 814-695-8894; Email: eenedy@dioceseaj.org.

Family Life Office—5379 Portage St., Lilly, 15938-1091. Tel: 814-886-5551.

Finance—927 S. Logan Blvd., Hollidaysburg, 16648. Tel: 814-695-5579; Fax: 814-695-8894. MR. MATT STEVER, CFO, Email: mstever@dioceseaj.org.

Fulton County Catholic Mission—110 S. Third St., McConnellsburg, 17233. Tel: 717-485-5917; Tel: 717-485-0661; Fax: 717-485-3855.

Holy Childhood—VACANT.

Human Resources—MRS. LYNETTE MCEVOY, PHR, SHRM-CP, Dir., 927 S. Logan Blvd., Hollidaysburg, 16648. Tel: 814-695-5579; Fax: 814-695-8894; Email: lmcevoy@dioceseaj.org.

Technology Services—MR. DAVID EGER, Dir., 927 S. Logan Blvd., Hollidaysburg, 16648. Tel: 814-695-5579; Fax: 814-695-8894; Email: deger@dioceseaj.org.

Technology Services Support Specialist—MR. MARK FETSKO II, Email: mfetsko@dioceseaj.org.

Technology Services Support Technician—MR. GREGORY CLAPPER, Email: gclapper@dioceseaj.org.

Technology Services Coordinator—MRS. ALISON LINK, Email: alink@dioceseaj.org.

Inter-Faith Minister—Very Rev. MARK S. BEGLY, V.F., Our Mother of Sorrows Rectory, 415 Tioga St., Johnstown, 15905. Tel: 814-535-7646; Fax: 814-536-7850.

Liturgy—Rev. Msgr. ROBERT C. MAZUR, 925 S. Logan Blvd., Hollidaysburg, 16648. Tel: 814-693-9870; Fax: 814-696-9516.

Ongoing Formation of the Clergy—927 S. Logan Blvd., Hollidaysburg, 16648. Tel: 814-695-5579; Fax: 814-695-8894.

Parish Life Office—925 S. Logan Blvd., Hollidaysburg, 16648. Tel: 814-693-9605; Fax: 814-696-9516. Rev. Msgr. ROBERT C. MAZUR, Dir.

Adult Enrichment—Deacon MICHAEL L. RUSSO, Ministerial Coord., 925 Park Ave., Johnstown, 15902. Tel: 814-361-2000; Email: michael.russo@atlanticbb.net.

Christian Initiation of Adults—MRS. JEANNE THOMPSON, Ministerial Coord., Tel: 814-693-9605; Fax: 814-696-9516; Email: jthompson@dioceseaj.org.

Lay Ecclesial Ministry—Deacon MICHAEL L. RUSSO, Ministerial Coord., 925 Park Ave., Johnstown, 15902. Tel: 814-361-2000; Email: michael.russo@atlanticbb.net.

Diocesan Contact for Parish Pastoral Councils—Rev. Msgr. ROBERT C. MAZUR, Ministerial Coord., Tel: 814-693-9605; Fax: 814-696-9516.

Stewardship—Rev. Msgr. ROBERT C. MAZUR, Ministerial Coord., Tel: 814-693-9605; Fax: 814-696-9516.

Ministerial Coordinator of Evangelization / Catholics Returning—St. Joseph, 623 E. Third St., Bellwood, 16617. Tel: 814-742-7075; Email: srllamagna@gmail.com. Sr. LINDA LAMAGNA, C.C.W., Ministerial Coord.

Youth Ministry, Religious Education and Sacramental Preparation—MRS. FRANCINE M. SWOPE, Coord., 933 S. Logan Blvd., Hollidaysburg, 16648. Tel: 814-693-1401; Fax: 814-696-6725; Email: fswope@dioceseaj.org.

Office of the Permanent Diaconate—Deacon MICHAEL L. RUSSO, Dir., 925 S. Logan Blvd., Hollidaysburg, 16648. Tel: 814-693-9870; Tel: 814-695-8894; Fax: 814-696-9516; Email: michael.russo@atlanticbb.net.

Presbyteral Council—Very Rev. ANGELO J. PATTI, V.F., Chm., St. Peter, 433 W. Church St., Somerset, 15501. Tel: 814-443-6574; Fax: 814-445-7766; Email: apatti@dioceseaj.org.

Priests' Personnel Board—Very Rev. ALAN E. THOMAS, V.G., 927 S. Logan Blvd., Hollidaysburg, 16648. Tel: 814-695-5579; Fax: 814-695-8894; Email: athomas@dioceseaj.org.

Priests' Retirement Plan—Rev. WALTER J. MOLL JR., St. Patrick Rectory, 609 Park Ave., Johnstown, 15902. Tel: 814-539-2186; Fax: 814-539-2410.

Propagation of the FaithVACANT.

Retreat & Conference Center—Mailing Address: St. John the Baptist Retreat Center, P.O. Box 10, New Baltimore, 15553. Tel: 814-733-2210; Fax: 814-733-2966.

St. Vincent de Paul Society—MR. ANTHONY CONSIGLIO, Exec. Dir., 1215 Seventh Ave., P.O. Box 231, Altoona, 16601. Tel: 814-943-1981; Fax: 814-201-2540; Email: avcdepaul@atlanticbbn.net.

Scouting—Rev. JOSEPH T. ORR, Holy Spirit, 3 E. Walnut St., Lock Haven, 17745. Tel: 570-748-4594; Fax: 570-893-8229.

Temporalities—MR. MATT STEVER, CFO, 927 S. Logan Blvd., Hollidaysburg, 16648. Tel: 814-695-5579; Fax: 814-695-8894; Email: mstever@dioceseaj.org.

Tribunal—Tel: 814-693-9485; Fax: 814-696-6725. Very Rev. JOHN D. BYRNES, J.V., J.C.L., Email: jbyrnes@dioceseaj.org.

Victims' Advocate and Victim Assistance Coordinator—1300 Twelfth Ave., P.O. Box 1349, Altoona, 16603. Tel: 814-944-9388; Fax: 814-941-2677. MRS. JEAN JOHNSTONE, Email: jjohnstone@dioceseaj.org.

Vocation—Rev. MATTHEW A. REESE, Dir., 925 S. Logan Blvd., Hollidaysburg, 16648. Tel: 814-695-5579, Ext. 2681; Fax: 814-696-9516; Email: vocations@dioceseaj.org.

CLERGY, PARISHES, MISSIONS AND PAROCHIAL SCHOOLS

CITY OF ALTOONA

(BLAIR COUNTY)

1—CATHEDRAL OF THE BLESSED SACRAMENT (1851)
One Cathedral Sq., Altoona, 16601-3315.
Tel: 814-944-4603; Fax: 814-942-4337; Email: altcathedral@dioceseaj.org; Web: www.altoonacathedral.org. Rev. Msgr. Robert C. Mazur, Rector; Rev. Dennis M. Kurdziel.
Catechesis Religious Program—Students 120.

2—HOLY ROSARY (1901) Very Rev. Ronald V. Osinski, V.F.
Res.: 416 6th Ave., Altoona, 16602. Tel: 814-942-0364 ; Email: horo@atlanticbb.net.
Catechesis Religious Program—900 N. 4th St., Altoona, 16601. Mrs. Suzanne L. Barry, D.R.E. Students 37.

3—IMMACULATE CONCEPTION (1860) [CEM] (St. Mary's)
1405 Fifth Ave., Altoona, 16602. Tel: 814-942-2416; Email: stmaryaltoona@dioceseaj.org; Web: stmaryschurchaltoona.wixsite.com/saintmarys. Very Rev. Lubomir J. Strecok, V.F., Admin.
See Altoona Central Catholic School, Altoona under Elementary Diocesan Schools located in the Institution section.
Catechesis Religious Program—Debbie Bartley, D.R.E. Students 54.

4—ST. JOHN THE EVANGELIST (1921)
309 Lotz Ave., Lakemont, Altoona, 16602.
Tel: 814-942-5503; Email: stjohnevangelistaltoona@dioceseaj.org; Web: www.stjohsaltoona.org. Rev. Msgr. Michael A. Becker; Deacon Gene P. Neral.
Catechesis Religious Program—Students 95.

5—ST. LEO THE GREAT (1911) Merged with SS. Peter & Paul to form Our Lady of Fatima, Altoona.

6—ST. MARK'S (1890) Very Rev. Ronald V. Osinski, V.F.
Res.: 416 Sixth Ave., Altoona, 16602.
Tel: 814-942-0364; Fax: 814-942-1127; Email: stmarkaltoona@dioceseaj.org; Web: www.churchofsaintmarks.org.
Catechesis Religious Program—Students 53.
Chapel—Valley View Home for the Aged, Tel: 814-944-0845.

7—OUR LADY OF FATIMA (1995) [CEM]
2010 12th Ave., Altoona, 16601. Rev. Msgr. Robert C. Mazur, Parochial Admin.
Res.: Cathedral of the Blessed Sacrament, 1 Cathedral Sq., Altoona, 16601. Tel: 814-942-0371; Email: olfoffio@hotmail.com; Web: www.ourladyoffatimaaltoona.org.
See Altoona Central Catholic School, Altoona under Elementary Diocesan Schools located in the Institution section.
Catechesis Religious Program—1304 13th Ave., Altoona, 16603. Students 6.

8—OUR LADY OF LOURDES (1923) Rev. James M. Dugan.
Res.: 2716 Broad Ave., Altoona, 16601.
Tel: 814-943-6185; Fax: 814-943-1968; Email: jdugan@diocesaj.org.
Catechesis Religious Program—Students 51.

9—OUR LADY OF MT. CARMEL (1905) (Italian) Revs. Frank Scornaienchi, T.O.R.; Carl Vacek, T.O.R. In Res., Rev. Terrence T. Smith, T.O.R.
Res.: 806 11th St., Altoona, 16602. Tel: 814-942-8501 ; Fax: 814-944-2208; Email: olmc806@aol.com; Web: www.mountcarmelaltoona.com.
See Holy Trinity Catholic School, Altoona under Elementary Diocesan Schools located in the Institution section.
Catechesis Religious Program—Karen Snowden, D.R.E. Students 76.
Convent—
Mission—Our Lady of the Assumption (1925) Hileman St. & Adams Ave., Altoona, Blair Co. 16602.

10—SS. PETER AND PAUL (1911) (Polish), Merged with St. Leo the Great to form Our Lady of Fatima, Altoona.

11—ST. ROSE OF LIMA (1924)
5514 Roselawn Ave., Altoona, 16602.
Tel: 814-944-8509; Fax: 814-942-1095; Email: strosealtoona@dioceseaj.org; Email: bsaylor@dioceseaj.org; Web: www.stroselima.com. Rev. Brian R. Saylor; Deacon James L. Woomer Sr. In Res., Rev. Carl A. Spishak, (Retired).
Catechesis Religious Program—Bernice Shoenfelt, D.R.E. Students 131.

12—SACRED HEART (1890)
511 20th St., Altoona, 16602. Tel: 814-943-8553; Fax: 814-943-1556; Email: sacredheartaltoona@dioceseaj.org; Web: www.sacredheartaltoona.org. Very Rev. Lubomir J. Strecok, V.F.
Formation Center—2009 Sixth Ave., Altoona, 16602. Tel: 814-944-3922.
Catechesis Religious Program—Students 123.

13—ST. THERESE OF THE CHILD JESUS (1927) Rev. D. Timothy Grimme, Email: frdtimgrimme@aol.com; Deacon Thomas J. McFee.
Res.: 2301 5th St., Altoona, 16601-3863.
Tel: 814-942-4479; Fax: 814-942-1873; Email: sttheresealtoona@atlanticbb.net.
See Holy Trinity Regional Catholic School, Altoona under Elementary Diocesan Schools located in the Institution section.
Catechesis Religious Program—Mary Beth Schmidhamer, D.R.E. Students 125.

CITY OF JOHNSTOWN

(CAMBRIA COUNTY)

1—ST. JOHN GUALBERT CATHEDRAL (1835) [CEM 2] Very Rev. James F. Crookston, Rector; Rev. Clarence S. Bridges; Deacon John J. Concannon, (Retired); Rev. Sean K. Code, Campus Min.
Res.: 117 Clinton St., P.O. Box 807, Johnstown, 15907. Tel: 814-536-0117; Email: sjgcathedral@outlook.com.
Catechesis Religious Program—124 Maple Ave., Johnstown, 15901. Students 33.

2—ST. ANDREW (1956) Rev. Matthew A. Reese.
Res.: 1621 Ferndale Ave., Johnstown, 15905.
Tel: 814-288-4324.
Catechesis Religious Program—Students 73.

3—ST. ANTHONY'S (1905) (Italian), Merged with SS. Peter & Paul, Johnstown to form St. Clare of Assisi, Johnstown.

4—ST. BARNABAS (1954) (Slovenian), Merged with St. Gregory, Johnstown to form SS. Gregory & Barnabas, Johnstown.

5—ST. BENEDICT'S (1911) Revs. David S. Peles; Peter Crowe, Parochial Vicar.
Res.: 2310 Bedford St., Johnstown, 15904.
Tel: 814-266-9718; Fax: 814-269-4220; Email: SBpastor@atlanticbb.net; Web: www.stbenedictchurch.org.
School—Divine Mercy Catholic Academy East Campus, (Grades PreK-6), 2306 Bedford St., Johnstown, 15904. Tel: 814-266-3837; Fax: 814-266-7718; Email: podratsky.marylo@divinemercy.academy; Web: www.divinemercy.academy. Mrs. Mary Jo Podratsky, Vice Prin. Clergy 16; Lay Teachers 16; Students 147.
Catechesis Religious Program—Students 222.

6—SS. CASIMIR & EMERICH (1997) [CEM 2] (Polish—Hungarian), Closed. For inquiries for parish records please see Resurrection Roman Catholic Church (814-539-5788).

7—ST. CLARE OF ASSISI (2000) [CEM 2] (Italian—Slovak)
110 Maple Ave., Johnstown, 15901.
Tel: 814-535-1133; Email: stclareofassisi@atlanticbb.net. 124 Maple Ave., Johnstown, 15901. Rev. Mathew Misurda.

8—ST. CLEMENT (1956)
114 Lindberg Ave., Johnstown, 15905.
Tel: 814-255-4422; Email: stclementchurch@atlanticbb.net; Web: www.stclementjohnstown.org. Rev. William E. Rosenbaum.
See Divine Mercy Catholic Academy under Education Consolidated Elementary Schools located in the Institution section.

Catechesis Religious Program—Mandy Vigna, D.R.E. Students 82.

9—ST. COLUMBA'S (1888) [CEM] Closed. For inquiries for parish records please see Resurrection Roman Catholic Church (814-539-5788).

10—ST. EMERICH'S (1905) (Hungarian), Merged with St. Casimir's, Johnstown to form SS. Casimir & Emerich, Johnstown.

11—ST. FRANCIS OF ASSISI (1922) [CEM] (Slovak) 120 Barron Ave., Johnstown, 15906. Tel: 814-539-1632; Email: sfassisich@atlanticbbn.net. Very Rev. Anthony Francis Spilka, O.F.M.Conv.
Catechesis Religious Program—Carol Pisula, D.R.E. Students 34.

12—SS. GREGORY & BARNABAS (2001) 120 Boltz St., Johnstown, 15902. Web: www.ssgregbar.org. Rev. Robert L. Ruston.
Catechesis Religious Program—Mary Helen Percinsky, D.R.E. Students 99.

13—ST. GREGORY'S (1919) Merged with St. Barnabas, Johnstown to form SS. Gregory & Barnabas, Johnstown.

14—IMMACULATE CONCEPTION (1859) [CEM] (German), Closed. For inquiries for parish records please see Resurrection Roman Catholic Church (814-539-5788).

15—ST. JOSEPH'S (1852) (German), Merged with Our Lady of Mercy to form St. John Gualbert Cathedral, Johnstown.
See Central Catholic Elementary School, Johnstown under Elementary Diocesan Schools located in the Institution section.

16—ST. MICHAEL'S (1910) (German) Mailing Address: 180 Gilbert St., Johnstown, 15906. Tel: 814-535-6277; Email: stmichaeljtown@dioceseaj.org. Very Rev. Mark S. Begly, V.F., Admin.
Res.: 407 Tioga St., Johnstown, 15905-2347. Tel: 814-535-7646; Fax: 814-536-7850.
Catechesis Religious Program—(Clustered with Our Mother of Sorrows) Students 4.

17—OUR LADY OF MERCY (1921) Merged with St. Joseph to form St. John Gualbert Cathedral, Johnstown.

18—OUR MOTHER OF SORROWS (1920) Very Rev. Mark S. Begly, V.F.; Deacon Scott Q. Little.
Res.: 407 Tioga St., Johnstown, 15905. Tel: 814-535-7646; Fax: 814-536-7850; Email: office@omostoday.com; Web: www.omostoday.com.
Catechesis Religious Program—Mr. John Livingston, D.R.E. Students 137.

19—ST. PATRICK'S (1904) 609 Park Ave., Johnstown, 15902. Tel: 814-539-2186; Email: stpats@floodcity.net. Rev. Walter J. Moll Jr.; Deacon Joseph Dalla Valle.
Catechesis Religious Program—625 Park Ave., Johnstown, 15902. Ms. Margaret Sindleri, D.R.E. Students 22.

20—SS. PETER AND PAUL'S (1918) Merged with St. Anthony, Johnstown to form St. Clare of Assisi, Johnstown.

21—RESURRECTION ROMAN CATHOLIC CHURCH (2009) [CEM] [JC] 408 8th Ave., Johnstown, 15906. Tel: 814-539-5788; Email: resurrectionjtown@dioceseaj.org; Web: resurrectionparishjohnstown.com. Rev. George M. Gulash; Deacon Samuel M. Cammarata.
Church: 324 Chestnut St., Johnstown, 15906.
Catechesis Religious Program—Christine Babik, D.R.E. Students 36.

22—ST. ROCHUS (1900) [CEM] (Croatian), Closed. For inquiries for parish records please see Resurrection Roman Catholic Church (814-539-5788).

23—ST. STEPHEN, FIRST KING OF HUNGARY (1891) [CEM] (Slovak), Closed. For inquiries for parish records please see Resurrection Roman Catholic Church (814-539-5788).

24—ST. THERESE OF THE CHILD JESUS (1929) [CEM] (Slovenian) Rev. Bernard Karmanocky, O.F.M.
Res.: 536 Decker Ave., Johnstown, 15906. Tel: 814-539-7633; Email: sttheresejtown@dioceseaj.org.
Convent—702 Saybrook Pl., Johnstown, 15906.
Mission—St. Anne's (1935) 533 Woodland Ave., Moxham, Cambria Co. 15902.
Catechesis Religious Program—Students 41.

25—VISITATION OF THE B.V.M. (1927) Rev. John J. Slovikovski.
Res.: 1127 McKinley Ave., Johnstown, 15905. Tel: 814-536-6110; Fax: 814-536-3709; Email: visitationjtown@dioceseaj.org; Web: www.visitationchurch.net.
Catechesis Religious Program—Students 40.

OUTSIDE THE CITIES OF ALTOONA AND JOHNSTOWN

ACOSTA, SOMERSET CO., ST. JOHN THE BAPTIST'S (1912) Merged with St. Joseph, Boswell, and St. Stanislaus, Boswell, to form All Saints Church, Boswell.

ASHVILLE, CAMBRIA CO., ST. THOMAS AQUINAS (1889) [CEM] Mailing Address: 692 Glendale Valley Blvd., Fallentimber, 16639. Tel: 814-943-5437; Email: dzupon@dioceseaj.org. 159 Hickory St., P.O. Box 5, Ashville, 16613. Rev. Robert P. Reese.
Catechesis Religious Program—Donna Stoy, D.R.E. Students 45.

BAKERTON, CAMBRIA CO., SACRED HEART (1904) Merged with St. Patrick, Spangler, to form St. Jude, Elmora.

BARNESBORO, CAMBRIA CO.

1—CHRIST THE KING (1993) Merged with St. Stanislaus Kostka, Barnesboro; St. John the Baptist, Northern Cambria; Our Lady of Mt. Carmel, Northern Cambria; Holy Cross, Northern Cambria to form Prince of Peace, Northern Cambria.

2—ST. STANISLAUS KOSTKA (1906) (Polish), Merged with Christ the King, Barnesboro; St. John the Baptist, Northern Cambria; Our Lady of Mt. Carmel, Northern Cambria; Holy Cross, Northern Cambria to form Prince of Peace, Northern Cambria.

BEANS COVE, BEDFORD CO., SEVEN DOLORS B.V.M. (1878) [CEM] Mailing Address: 2174 Beans Cove Rd., Clearville, 15535-7901. Tel: 814-767-9522; Fax: 814-767-8158; Email: mac@sevendolorsBVM.org. Rev. Derek Fairman.
Res.: 161 E. First Ave., Everett, 15537. Tel: 814-652-5854.
Catechesis Religious Program—Shelley Cessna, D.R.E. Students 5.

BEAVERDALE, CAMBRIA CO.

1—ST. AGNES (1909) Merged with St. Joseph, Beaverdale, and Corpus Christi, Dunlo, to form Holy Spirit Church, Beaverdale.

2—HOLY SPIRIT (1995) [CEM 2] Closed. For inquiries for parish records please see St. Michael, St. Michael, PA (814-495-9640).

3—ST. JOSEPH'S (1904) (Slovak), Merged with St. Agnes, Beaverdale, and Corpus Christi, Dunlo, to form Holy Spirit Church, Beaverdale.

BEDFORD, BEDFORD CO., ST. THOMAS (1816) [CEM 2] Rev. Richard B. Tomkosky.
Res.: 215 E. Penn St., Bedford, 15522. Tel: 814-623-5526; Fax: 814-623-1741; Web: www.stthomasbedford.com.
School—St. Thomas School, (Grades PreK-5), 129 W. Penn St., Bedford, 15522. Tel: 814-623-8873; Fax: 814-623-1208; Email: stthomastiger@gmail.com. Amy Higgins, Prin. Lay Teachers 7; Students 53.
Catechesis Religious Program—Students 65.

BELLEFONTE, CENTRE CO., ST. JOHN THE EVANGELIST (1828) [CEM 2] Rev. George I. Jakopac; Deacon Thomas E. Boldin.
Res.: 134 E. Bishop St., Bellefonte, 16823. Tel: 814-355-3134; Fax: 814-355-4820; Email: saintjohnsoff@gmail.com; Web: www.bellefontecatholicchurch.org.
School—St. John the Evangelist School, (Grades PreK-5), 116 E. Bishop St., Bellefonte, 16823. Tel: 814-355-7859; Fax: 814-355-2939; Email: admin@saintjohnsch.net; Web: www.saintjohnsch.net. Kristina Tice, Prin. Lay Teachers 8; Students 130.
Catechesis Religious Program—Mark Leskovansky, D.R.E. Students 232.

BELLWOOD, BLAIR CO., ST. JOSEPH'S (1890) 623 E. Third St., Bellwood, 16617. Tel: 814-742-7075; Email: stjosephbellwood@dioceseaj.org; Web: stjosephbellwood.org. Very Rev. Alan E. Thomas, V.G.; Sr. Linda LaMagna, C.C.W., Pastoral Assoc.
Catechesis Religious Program—Mike Isola, D.R.E. Students 81.

BOSWELL, SOMERSET CO.

1—ALL SAINTS (1995) [CEM 3] Mailing Address: 325 Quemahoning St., Boswell, 15531. Rev. Aron M. Maghsoudi, Admin.; Deacon Jay A. Pyle.
Res.: 205 Woodstown Hwy., Davidsville, 15928. Tel: 814-629-5551; Email: allsaintsboswell@dioceseaj.org.
Catechesis Religious Program—Students 47.

2—ST. STANISLAUS (1901) (Polish), Merged with St. John the Baptist, Acosta to form All Saints Church, Boswell.

CARROLLTOWN, CAMBRIA CO., ST. BENEDICT'S (1846) [CEM 3] Very Rev. Jude W. Brady, O.S.B., V.F.
Res.: 100 Main St., P.O. Box 447, Carrolltown, 15722. Tel: 814-344-6548; Fax: 814-344-8656; Email: sbcjwb@comcast.net; Web: saintbenedictchurch.com.
School—St. Benedict's School, (Grades PreK-8), 119 S. Church St., P.O. Box 596, Carrolltown, 15722. Tel: 814-344-6512; Fax: 814-344-8530; Email: jmaucieri@benedictpride.org. Mr. Jeffery F. Maucieri, Prin. Brothers 1; Clergy 3; Lay Teachers 12; Sisters 2; Students 83.
Catechesis Religious Program—Students 215.

CASSANDRA, CAMBRIA CO., ST. AGNES (1909) Closed. For inquiries for parish records contact the chancery.

CENTRAL CITY, SOMERSET CO.

1—ST. JOHN THE BAPTIST (1917) (Slovak), Merged with Sacred Heart of Jesus, Central City to form Our Lady Queen of Angels, Central City.

2—OUR LADY QUEEN OF ANGELS (1999) [CEM 2] Rev. Aron M. Maghsoudi.
Res.: 738 Sunshine Ave., Central City, 15926-1233. Tel: 814-754-5224; Fax: 814-754-4447; Email: olqoacentralcity@dioceseaj.org; Web: www.ladyqueenofangels.org.
Catechesis Religious Program—Students 44.

3—SACRED HEART OF JESUS (1914) (Polish), Merged with St. John the Baptist, Central City to form Our Lady Queen of Angels, Central City.

CHEST SPRINGS, CAMBRIA CO., ST. MONICA'S (1859) [CEM] Unassigned. Rev. David R. Rizzo, J.C.L.
Res.: 803 St. Augustine Rd., Dysart, 16636. Tel: 814-674-8550.
Church: 3037 Colonel Drake Hwy., Chest Springs, 16624. Tel: 814-674-5613; Email: saintmon.office@verizon.net.
Catechesis Religious Program—Students 88.

CLARENCE, CENTRE CO.

1—ST. MICHAEL'S (1900) [CEM] (Slovak), Merged with St. Mary's, Snow Shoe to form Queen of Archangels, Clarence.

2—QUEEN OF ARCHANGELS (2005) [CEM 2] 102 Church St., Clarence, 16829. Tel: 814-387-6762; Email: queenofarchclarence@dioceseaj.org. Rev. Michael A. Wolfe, Adm.
Catechesis Religious Program—Students 77.
Mission—204 S. 4th St., Snow Shoe, Centre Co. 16874.

COLVER, CAMBRIA CO., HOLY FAMILY (1912) [CEM] (Polish) Rev. Christopher Lemme, T.O.R.
Res.: 562 Fifth St., P.O. Box 543, Colver, 15927. Tel: 814-748-7054; Fax: 814-748-7254; Email: holyfamilycolver@dioceseaj.org.
Catechesis Religious Program—Students 40.

CONEMAUGH, CAMBRIA CO.

1—ASSUMPTION OF B.V.M. (1910) [CEM] Merged with Sacred Heart, Conemaugh to form Church of the Transfiguration, Conemaugh.

2—CHURCH OF THE TRANSFIGURATION (2008) [CEM 2] 340 Second St., Conemaugh, 15909. Tel: 814-535-2250. 220 Oak St., Conemaugh, 15909. Rev. Robert C. Hall.
Catechesis Religious Program—Mrs. Louise Brezovic, D.R.E. Students 26.

3—SACRED HEART (1902) [CEM] Merged with Assumption of B.V.M., Conemaugh to form Church of the Transfiguration, Conemaugh.

COUPON, CAMBRIA CO., ST. JOSEPH'S (1855) [CEM 2] Closed. For inquiries for parish records please see St. Demetrius, Gallitzin (814-886-7941).

CRESSON, CAMBRIA CO.

1—ST. ALOYSIUS (1838) [CEM] 7911 Admiral Peary Hwy., Cresson, 16630. Rev. Leo F. Arnone, Email: frleoarnone@gmail.com.
Res.: 211 Powell Ave., Cresson, 16630.
See All Saints Catholic School under Elementary Diocesan Schools located in the Institution section.
Catechesis Religious Program—Deborah Baker, D.R.E. Students 116.

2—ST. FRANCIS XAVIER (1908) [CEM] 211 Powell Ave., Cresson, 16630. Tel: 814-886-2374; Fax: 814-886-2498; Email: fxparish@dioceseaj.org; Web: www.saintfrancisxaviercresson.org. Rev. Leo F. Arnone.
See All Saints Catholic School under Elementary Diocesan Schools located in the Institution section.
Catechesis Religious Program—Mrs. Tracey Ingold, Dir. Faith Formation. Students 113.

DAVIDSVILLE, SOMERSET CO., ST. ANNE (1911) [CEM 2] Mailing Address: 205 Woodstown Hwy., P.O. Box 500, Davidsville, 15928. Tel: 814-479-2664; Fax: 814-479-7702; Email: sannep@atlanticbb.net. Rev. Peter Crowe, Admin.; Deacon Jay A. Pyle.
Catechesis Religious Program—Students 33.

DUDLEY, HUNTINGDON CO., IMMACULATE CONCEPTION (1856) [CEM] 1416 Dudley Rd., P.O. Box 188, Dudley, 16634. Tel: 814-635-2919; Email: iccdudley@dioceseaj.org; Web: www.iccdudley.com. Rev. Matthew B. Baum, Admin.

DUNCANSVILLE, BLAIR CO., ST. CATHERINE OF SIENA (1963) Mailing Address: 308 Old Rte. 22, P.O. Box 88, Duncansville, 16635. Tel: 814-696-4126; Fax: 814-317-7767; Email: stcatherinesienaduncansville@dioceseaj.org. Rev. Msgr. Robert J. Saly.
Res.: 417 Elm Ln., Duncansville, 16635.
Catechesis Religious Program—Students 54.

DUNLO, CAMBRIA CO., CORPUS CHRISTI (1903) Merged with St. Agnes and St. Joseph, Beaverdale to form Holy Spirit Church, Beaverdale.

EBENSBURG, CAMBRIA CO., HOLY NAME (1816) [CEM] Mailing Address: 500 N. Julian St., Ebensburg, 15931. Tel: 814-472-7244; Fax: 814-472-7249; Email: holynameebg@verizon.net; Web: www.holynameebg.org. Deacon Michael Condor Jr.; Rev. Msgr. David A. Lockard.

School—Holy Name School, (Grades PreK-8), Tel: 814-472-8817; Fax: 814-471-0500; Email: holynameelementary@comcast.net. Mrs. Robin McMullen, Prin. Lay Teachers 21; Students 325.

Catechesis Religious Program—Diane Bopp, D.R.E.; Nancy McCulley, D.R.E. Students 267.

EHRENFELD, CAMBRIA CO., OUR LADY OF MT. CARMEL (1892) Merged with St. James and St. Anthony's, South Fork to form Most Holy Trinity, South Fork.

ELMORA, CAMBRIA CO., ST. JUDE (1995) Closed. For inquiries for parish records contact the chancery.

EMEIGH, CAMBRIA CO., MOST PRECIOUS BLOOD, See separate listing. See Christ the King, Barnesboro.

EVERETT, BEDFORD CO., ST. JOHN THE EVANGELIST (1971)

161 E. First Ave., Everett, 15537. Tel: 814-652-5854; Email: stjohn022@comcast.net; Web: www.stjohneverettpa.org. Rev. Derek Fairman.

Church: 163 E. First Ave., Everett, 15537.

Catechesis Religious Program—Students 24.

FALLENTIMBER, CAMBRIA CO.

1—ST. JOAN OF ARC (1995) Rev. Robert P. Reese.

Res.: 692 Glendale Valley Blvd., Fallentimber, 16639. Tel: 814-943-5437; Email: ssjoanandthomasonpa53@outlook.com.

Catechesis Religious Program—Students 9.

2—ST. MARY MAGDALEN'S (1889) Closed. Merged with St. Richard's Mission, Blandburg to form St. Joan of Arc Church, Fallentimber.

GALLITZIN, CAMBRIA CO.

1—ST. DEMETRIUS (2000) [CEM 2] Rev. Albert H. Ledoux, M.Div., M.A.

Res.: 811 Church St., Gallitzin, 16641.

Tel: 814-408-2371; Fax: 814-408-2372; Email: stdemetriusgallitzin@dioceseaj.org.

Catechesis Religious Program—Students 97.

2—OUR LADY OF CZESTOCHOWA (1903) (Polish), Merged with St. Patrick, Gallitzin to form St. Demetrius, Gallitzin.

3—ST. PATRICK'S (1850) Merged with Our Lady of Czestochowa, Gallitzin to form St. Demetrius, Gallitzin.

HASTINGS, CAMBRIA CO., ST. BERNARD (1890) [CEM 2] Rev. Thaddeus E. Rettger, O.S.B.; Deacons Michael Anna; Christopher S. Conner.

Res.: 148-Apt. 2 Seventh Ave., P.O. Box 497, Hastings, 16646. Tel: 814-247-6558;

Fax: 814-247-8522; Email: stjanine@comcast.net.

Catechesis Religious Program—Mrs. Vickie Conner, D.R.E. Students 112.

Mission—St. Boniface Chapel, 1278 Main St., St. Boniface, Cambria Co. 16675.

HOLLIDAYSBURG, BLAIR CO.

1—ST. MARY'S (1841) [CEM 2]

312 Clark St., 16648. Tel: 814-695-0622;

Fax: 814-696-9609; Email: ecunningham@dioceseaj.org; Web: www.webparish.com/aj/saintmarys. Rev. Anthony J. Legarski; Deacon Charles R. Ahearn.

See Hollidaysburg Consolidated Catholic Elementary, Hollidaysburg under Elementary Diocesan Schools located in the Institution section.

Catechesis Religious Program—Mrs. Connie Curfman, D.R.E. Students 130.

2—ST. MICHAEL'S (1862) [CEM] (German) Rev. Msgr. Stanley B. Carson, V.F.

Res.: 301 Spruce St., 16648. Tel: 814-695-0912;

Fax: 814-693-9820; Email: stmichaelhburg@dioceseaj.org; Web: www.stmichael-hldg-pa.org.

See Hollidaysburg Consolidated Catholic Elementary, Hollidaysburg under Elementary Diocesan Schools located in the Institution section.

Catechesis Religious Program—Susan M. Teske, D.R.E. Students 221.

HOOVERSVILLE, SOMERSET CO., HOLY FAMILY (1911) [CEM] Deacon Joseph W. Visinsky; Rev. Karl Kolodziejski, O.F.M.Conv.

Res.: 321 Sugar St., P.O. Box 187, Hooversville, 15936. Tel: 814-798-2933; Fax: 814-798-8601; Email: holyfamilyhooversville@dioceseaj.org.

Catechesis Religious Program—Students 38.

HUNTINGDON, HUNTINGDON CO., MOST HOLY TRINITY (1826) [CEM]

Mailing Address: 524 Mifflin St., Huntingdon, 16652. Rev. Mark R. Reid.

Res.: 1000 Warm Springs Ave., Huntingdon, 16652.

Tel: 814-643-0160; Email: mhtcc@comcast.net; Web: www.mhtcc.org.

Catechesis Religious Program—Rita Martinez, D.R.E. Students 107.

LILLY, CAMBRIA CO.

1—ST. BRIGID'S (1883) Merged with Our Lady of Mount Carmel, Lilly to form Our Lady of the Alleghenies, Lilly.

2—OUR LADY OF MT. CARMEL (1910) (Polish), Merged with St. Brigid, Lilly to form Our Lady of the Alleghenies, Lilly.

3—OUR LADY OF THE ALLEGHENIES (1995) [CEM 2] Rev. Kevin Queally, T.O.R.; Deacon Samuel F. Albarano Jr.

Res.: 608 Main St., Lilly, 15938. Tel: 814-886-2504; Fax: 814-884-4952; Email: olallegh@comcast.net.

Catechesis Religious Program—Students 85.

LOCK HAVEN, CLINTON CO.

1—ST. AGNES (1873) [CEM] Merged with Immaculate Conception, Lock Haven to form Holy Spirit Church, Lock Haven.

2—HOLY SPIRIT PARISH (2012) [CEM 2] Rev. Joseph T. Orr; Deacons Philip Gibson, Email: anneandohil@aol.com; Calvin J. Young.

Res.: 3 E. Walnut St., Lock Haven, 17745.

Tel: 570-748-4594; Email: mhau@dioceseaj.org; Email: jorr@dioceseaj.org; Web: holyspiritlockhaven.org/.

School—Lock Haven Catholic School, (Grades PreK-8), 311 W. Water St., Lock Haven, 17745.

Tel: 570-748-7252; Fax: 570-748-1939; Email: principal@lhcs.org. Michele Alexander, Prin. Lay Teachers 14; Students 168.

Catechesis Religious Program—Tammy Nesbitt, D.R.E. Students 67.

3—IMMACULATE CONCEPTION (1852) [CEM] Merged with St. Agnes, Lock Haven to form Holy Spirit Church, Lock Haven.

LORETTO, CAMBRIA CO., BASILICA OF ST. MICHAEL THE ARCHANGEL (1799) [CEM] Very Rev. John D. Byrnes, J.C.L.; Deacon Richard T. Golden, Tel: 814-495-9673.

Res.: 321 St. Mary, P.O. Box 10, Loretto, 15940.

Tel: 814-472-8551; Fax: 814-471-4959; Email: basilicasm@dioceseaj.org; Web: www.basilicasm-loretto.org.

School—Basilica of St. Michael the Archangel School, 301 St. Elizabeth St., P.O. Box 67, Loretto, 15940. Tel: 814-472-9117; Fax: 814-472-9117; Email: vkrug@st-michael-school.org. Renee Phister, Prin. Lay Teachers 9; Students 113.

Catechesis Religious Program—Students 115.

MCCONNELLSBURG, FULTON CO., ST. STEPHEN'S (1962) 303 Lincoln Way E., McConnellsburg, 17233.

Tel: 717-485-3723; Fax: 717-485-3855; Web: www.fultoncatholic.com. Rev. Matthew B. Baum, Admin.

MEYERSDALE, SOMERSET CO., SS. PHILIP AND JAMES (1850) [CEM 2] Rev. Stephen Shin, O.F.M.Cap.

Res.: 247 High St., Meyersdale, 15552.

Tel: 814-634-8150; Fax: 814-634-0983.

Catechesis Religious Program—Students 31.

Mission—St. Gregory (1907) Church St., Berlin, Somerset Co. 15530.

MOUNT UNION, HUNTINGDON CO., ST. CATHERINE OF SIENA (1912) [CEM]

Mailing Address: 205 W. Market St., Mount Union, 17066. Rev. Joseph W. Fleming.

Res.: 203 W. Market St., Mount Union, 17066.

Tel: 814-542-4582; Email: stcatherine@comcast.net; Web: www.scosmu.org.

Catechesis Religious Program—Students 33.

MUNDYS CORNER, CAMBRIA CO., ST. JOHN VIANNEY'S (1950) Rev. Andrew R. Draper, T.O.R.; Deacon Thomas M. Buige.

Res.: 3513 William Penn Ave., Johnstown, 15909.

Tel: 814-322-4789; Fax: 814-322-3799; Email: stjohnvianney@atlanticbb.net; Web: www.sjvcc.com.

Catechesis Religious Program—Students 74.

NANTY-GLO, CAMBRIA CO., SAINT MARY'S CHURCH (1902) [CEM] Merged with SS. Timothy & Mark, Twin Rocks Very Rev. Leonard E. Voytek, V.F.; Deacon James J. Janosik.

Res.: 1020 Caroline St., Nanty-Glo, 15943.

Tel: 814-749-9103; Fax: 814-749-5463; Email: stmarynantyglo@dioceseaj.org.

Catechesis Religious Program—Students 105.

NEW BALTIMORE, ST. JOHN THE BAPTIST (1829) [CEM] Revs. Mark Pattock, O.F.M.Cap.; Roman Kozacheson, O.F.M.Cap, (In. Res.); Stephen Shin, O.F.M.Cap., (In Res.).

Res.: 101 Findley St., P.O. Box 10, New Baltimore, 15553. Tel: 814-733-2210; Fax: 814-733-2966; Email: stjohnbaptistnewbaltimore@dioceseaj.org.

Catechesis Religious Program—Students 53.

NEWRY, BLAIR CO., ST. PATRICK (1816) [CEM 2]

P.O. Box 398, Newry, 16665. Rev. Allen P. Zeth, Admin.

Res.: 704 Patrick Ln., Newry, 16665.

Tel: 814-695-3413; Fax: 814-695-1733; Email: stpatricksnewry@yahoo.com; Web: www.saintpatricknewry.org.

School—St. Patrick School, (Grades PreK-8),

Tel: 814-695-3819; Fax: 814-695-5274; Email: dmessner@stpatsnewry.org. Dr. Donna Messner, Prin. Clergy 1; Lay Teachers 10; Sisters 1; Students 61.

Catechesis Religious Program—Students 66.

NICKTOWN, CAMBRIA CO., ST. NICHOLAS (1861) [CEM] Rev. Jeremiah Lange, O.S.B.

Res.: 1169 Alverda Rd., P.O. Box 37, Nicktown, 15762. Tel: 814-948-9614; Fax: 814-948-5232; Email: stnicholasnicktown@dioceseaj.org; Web: www.saintnicholasparish.org.

See Northern Cambria Catholic School, Nicktown under Elementary Schools Diocesan located in the Institution section.

Catechesis Religious Program—Students 114.

NORTHERN CAMBRIA, CAMBRIA CO.

1—HOLY CROSS (1893) Merged with St. Stanislaus Kostka, Barnesboro; Christ the King, Barnesboro; St. John the Baptist, Northern Cambria; Our Lady of Mt. Carmel, Northern Cambria to form Prince of Peace, Northern Cambria.

2—ST. JOHN THE BAPTIST (1896) (Slovak), Merged with St. Stanislaus Kostka, Barnesboro; Christ the King, Barnesboro; Holy Cross, Northern Cambria; Our Lady of Mt. Carmel, Northern Cambria to form Prince of Peace, Northern Cambria.

3—OUR LADY OF MT. CARMEL (1908) (Italian), Merged with St. Stanislaus Kostka, Barnesboro; Christ the King, Barnesboro; Holy Cross, Northern Cambria; St. John the Baptist, Northern Cambria to form Prince of Peace, Northern Cambria.

4—PRINCE OF PEACE (2000) [CEM 5] Rev. Donald W. Dusza; Deacon Gary F. Gill.

Res.: 811 Chestnut Ave., Northern Cambria, 15714.

Tel: 814-948-6842; Fax: 814-948-6585; Email: princepeacenorcambria@dioceseaj.org.

School—Northern Cambria Catholic School, (Grades PreK-8), Tel: 814-948-8900; Fax: 814-948-8720; Email: tburba@northerncambriacatholic.org. Theresa Burba, Prin. See Elementary Diocesan Schools under Institutions Located in the Diocese. Lay Teachers 13; Students 89.

Catechesis Religious Program—Students 118.

ORBISONIA, HUNTINGDON CO., ST. MARY'S (1840) [CEM 2]

Mailing Address: 20896 Croghan Pike, Orbisonia, 17243-9000. Tel: 814-447-3172; Tel: 814-447-9030; Email: stmaryorbisonia@dioceseaj.org. Very Rev. Joseph W. Fleming, V.F.

Res.: St. Catherine of Siena, 203 W. Market St., Mount Union, 17066. Tel: 814-542-4582.

Catechesis Religious Program—Students 8.

PATTON, CAMBRIA CO.

1—ST. GEORGE (1907) (Slovak), Merged with Our Lady of Perpetual Help, Patton and St. Lawrence to form Queen of Peace, Patton.

2—OUR LADY OF PERPETUAL HELP (1892) Merged with St. George, Patton, and St. Lawrence to form Queen of Peace, Patton.

3—QUEEN OF PEACE (1995) [CEM 2] Rev. Ananias Buccicone, O.S.B.

Res.: 907 Sixth Ave., Patton, 16668.

Tel: 814-674-8983; Fax: 814-674-8805; Email: queenofpeacepatton@dioceseaj.org.

Catechesis Religious Program—Students 40.

PENNS VALLEY, CENTRE CO., ST. KATERI TEKAKWITHA (1986) [JC] Rev. George I. Jakopac.

Res.: 3503 Penns Valley Rd., P.O. Box 159, Spring Mills, 16875. Tel: 814-422-8983; Email: blessedkateri@dioceseaj.org.

Catechesis Religious Program—Students 36.

PHILIPSBURG, CENTRE CO., SS. PETER AND PAUL (1868) [CEM] [JC] Rev. John M. Gibbons.

Res.: 400 S. Fourth St., Philipsburg, 16866.

Tel: 814-342-1700; Fax: 814-342-5480; Email: lawasilko@gmail.com.

Catechesis Religious Program—Students 72.

PORTAGE, CAMBRIA CO.

1—ASSUMPTION B.V.M. (1907) (Slovak), Merged with Sacred Heart of Jesus to form Our Lady of the Sacred Heart, Portage.

2—HOLY FAMILY (2015) Rev. Thomas Stabile, T.O.R.

Res.: 509 Caldwell Ave., Portage, 15946.

Tel: 814-736-4279; Fax: 814-736-4764; Email: holyfamilyportage@comcast.net.

Catechesis Religious Program—Students 121.

3—ST. JOHN THE BAPTIST (1923) [CEM] (Hungarian), Merged with Our Lady of the Sacred Heart, Portage.

4—ST. JOSEPH (1898) Merged with Our Lady of the Sacred Heart, Portage to form Holy Family, Portage.

5—OUR LADY OF THE SACRED HEART (1999) [CEM 3] (Polish—Hungarian), Merged with St. Joseph's, Portage to form Holy Family, Portage.

6—SACRED HEART OF JESUS (1909) (Polish), Merged with Assumption of the Blessed Virgin Mary, Portage to form Our Lady of the Sacred Heart, Portage.

RENOVO, CLINTON CO., ST. JOSEPH'S (1869) [CEM 3] Rev. Joseph T. Orr, Admin.

Res.: 925 Huron Ave., Renovo, 17764.

Tel: 570-923-0172; Email: stjosephrenovo@dioceseaj.org.

Catechesis Religious Program—Students 34.

REVLOC, CAMBRIA CO., MOST HOLY REDEEMER (1920) Closed. For inquiries for parish records contact the chancery.

ROARING SPRING, BLAIR CO., ST. THOMAS MORE (1969) Rev. Leo A. Lynch.

Res.: 825 Williams St., Roaring Spring, 16673.

Tel: 814-224-4522; Fax: 814-224-4522; Email: stthomasmoreroaringspring@dioceseaj.org.

Catechesis Religious Program—Students 41.

SALISBURY, SOMERSET CO., ST. MICHAEL'S (1887) [CEM 2] Deacon William R. Underhill, Parochial Admin.;

Revs. Nathan Munsch, O.S.B., Sacramental Min.; Benoit Alloggia, O.S.B., Sacramental Min.
Res.: 1316 St. Paul Rd., P.O. Box 36, Salisbury, 15558-0036. Tel: 814-662-2958; Email: stmichaelwestsalisbury@dioceseaj.org.
Mission—St. Mary's (1906) 215 Warrens Mill Rd., Meyersdale, Somerset Co. 15552. P.O. Box 36, Salisbury, 15558-0036.
Catechesis Religious Program—Students 21.
ST. AUGUSTINE, CAMBRIA CO., ST. AUGUSTINE (1847) [CEM]
803 St. Augustine Rd., Dysart, 16636.
Tel: 814-674-8550; Email: parishoffice.staug.stmon@verizon.net. Rev. David R. Rizzo, J.C.L.
Catechesis Religious Program—Students 95.
ST. BONIFACE, CAMBRIA CO., ST. BONIFACE CHAPEL (1859) Merged to form St. Bernard, Hastings.
ST. LAWRENCE, CAMBRIA CO., ST. LAWRENCE'S (1853) Merged with Our Lady of Perpetual Help and St. George, Patton to form Queen of Peace, Patton.
ST. MICHAEL, CAMBRIA CO., ST. MICHAEL'S (1913) [CEM] Rev. Brian Lee Warchola, Admin.
Res.: 751 Locust St., Box 103, St. Michael, 15951.
Tel: 814-495-9640; Fax: 814-495-9424; Email: saintmichaelsecretaries@yahoo.com; Web: www.saintmichaelchurch.weebly.com.
Catechesis Religious Program—Laurie Sloan, D.R.E. Students 118.
SNOW SHOE, CENTRE CO., ST. MARY'S (1865) [CEM] (Irish), Merged with St. Michael, Clarence to form Queen of Archangels, Clarence.
SOMERSET, SOMERSET CO.
1—ST. PETER IN CHAINS (1995)
Mailing Address: S.C.I.-Somerset, 1590 Walters Mill Rd., Somerset, 15501-0001. Tel: 814-443-8100; Email: dhornick@dioceseaj.org. Very Rev. Daniel J. O'Neill, V.F., Sacramental Min.; Deacon David G. Hornick, Chap.; Revs. Brian Lee Warchola, Sacramental Min.; Stephen Shin, O.F.M.Cap., Sacramental Min.
2—ST. PETER'S (1920) [CEM] Very Rev. Angelo J. Patti, V.F.
Res.: 433 W. Church St., Somerset, 15501.
Tel: 814-443-6574; Fax: 814-445-7766; Email: cwagner@dioceseaj.org.
School—St. Peter's School, (Grades PreK-6),
Tel: 814-445-6662; Email: principal@stpetersparish.com. Mrs. Jill Harris, Prin. Lay Teachers 9; Students 100.
Catechesis Religious Program—Students 144.
SOUTH FORK, CAMBRIA CO.
1—ST. ANTHONY'S (1905) (Polish), Merged with St. James, South Fork and Our Lady of Mt. Carmel, Ehrenfeld to form Most Holy Trinity, South Fork.
2—ST. JAMES (1906) Merged with St. Anthony, South Fork and Our Lady of Mt. Carmel, Ehrenfeld to form Most Holy Trinity, South Fork.
3—MOST HOLY TRINITY (1995) [CEM 2] Rev. Joseph C. Nale.
Res.: 550 Main St., South Fork, 15956.
Tel: 814-495-4419; Fax: 814-495-9104; Email: mostholytrinitysouthfork@dioceseaj.org.
Catechesis Religious Program—Mrs. Betty Rosmus, D.R.E. Students 47.
SPANGLER, CAMBRIA CO., ST. PATRICK'S (1902) Merged with Sacred Heart, Bakerton to form St. Jude, Elmora.
STATE COLLEGE, CENTRE CO.
1—GOOD SHEPHERD (1989)
Mailing Address: 867 Gray's Woods Blvd., Port Matilda, 16870. Rev. Charles M. Amershek Jr., V.F.; Deacons Michael A. Ondik Jr., Tel: 814-237-1857; Jack E. Orlandi, Tel: 814-692-7472.
Res.: 835 Gray's Woods Blvd., Port Matilda, 16870.
Tel: 814-238-2110; Fax: 814-238-3484; Email: gsoffice@goodshepherd-sc.org; Web: www.goodshepherd-sc.org.
Catechesis Religious Program—Students 267.
2—OUR LADY OF VICTORY (1908) Very Rev. Neil R. Dadey, V.F.; Deacon David C. Lapinski; Revs. Jonathan Dickson, Parochial Vicar; Antony Sudherson, H.G.N., Parochial Vicar.
Res.: 820 Westerly Pkwy., State College, 16801.
Tel: 814-237-7832; Fax: 814-237-6709; Email: office@ourladyofvictory.com; Web: ourladyofvictory.com.
Child Care—Preschool, Tel: 814-238-6616. Lay Teachers 12; Students 105.
School—Our Lady of Victory School, (Grades PreK-8), 800 Westerly Pkwy., State College, 16801.
Tel: 814-238-1592; Fax: 814-238-4553; Email: weaklands@olvcs.org; Web: olvcatholicschool.org. Samantha Weakland, Prin. Lay Teachers 25; Students 333.
Catechesis Religious Program—Jim Hoy, D.R.E. Students 376.
SUMMERHILL, CAMBRIA CO., ST. JOHN (1903) [CEM]
538 Main St., P.O. Box 248, Summerhill, 15958.
Tel: 814-495-5241; Fax: 814-495-9522; Email: stjic@comcast.net. Rev. Leon Hont, O.S.B.
Mission—Immaculate Conception (1854) 1640 New Germany Rd., P.O. Box 248, Summerhill, Cambria Co. 15958.
Catechesis Religious Program—Kimberly Gates, Acting C.R.E. Students 134.
TWIN ROCKS, CAMBRIA CO.
1—ST. CHARLES (1917) Merged with Immaculate Conception Mission, Vintondale to form SS. Timothy & Mark Church, Twin Rocks & SS. Timothy & Mark Chapel, Vintondale.
2—SS. TIMOTHY & MARK (1995) [CEM] Merged with St. Mary, Nanty Glo (Tel: 814-749-9103; Fax: 814-749-5463).
TYRONE, BLAIR CO., ST. MATTHEW (1853) [CEM 2] Rev. Jozef Kovacik.
Res.: 1205 Cameron Ave., Tyrone, 16686.
Tel: 814-684-1480; Fax: 814-684-7969; Email: stmatthewtyrone@gmail.com; Web: www.stmatthewtyrone.org. Cemeteries: Oak Grove & St Luke's.
School—St. Matthew School, (Grades PreK-6), 1105 Cameron Ave., Tyrone, 16686. Tel: 814-684-3510; Email: dstpierre@stmatthew-school.org. Mrs. Debbie St. Pierre, Prin. Lay Teachers 8; Students 97.
Catechesis Religious Program—Students 199.
WILLIAMSBURG, BLAIR CO., ST. JOSEPH (1861) [CEM 2]
628 W. First St., Williamsburg, 16693.
Tel: 814-832-2137; Email: stjosephwilliamsburg@dioceseaj.org. Deacons Kevin Nester, Admin.; George Watcher.
Catechesis Religious Program—Students 22.
WILMORE, CAMBRIA CO., ST. BARTHOLOMEW'S (1840) [CEM] [JC]
185 Church Hill Rd., Wilmore, 15962. 550 Main St., South Fork, 15956. Tel: 814-495-4419; Email: stbartwilmore@hotmail.com. Rev. Joseph C. Nale.
Catechesis Religious Program—Diana Frantz, D.R.E. Students 44.
WINDBER, SOMERSET CO.
1—ST. ANTHONY OF PADUA (1908) [CEM] (Italian) Rev. Roderick N. Soha, T.O.R. In Res., Rev. Lawrence L. Lacovic, (Retired).
Res.: 2201 Graham Ave., Windber, 15963.
Tel: 814-467-7292; Fax: 814-467-9182; Email: stanthonyswindber@msn.com; Web: stanthonyswindber.com.
School—Divine Mercy Catholic Academy East Campus, (Grades PreK-6), 2306 Bedford St., Johnstown, 15904. Tel: 814-266-3837; Fax: 814-266-7718; Email: mpodratsky@divinemercy.academy. Thomas Smith, Prin.; Mrs. Mary Jo Podratsky, Vice Prin. Lay Teachers 16; Students 178.
Catechesis Religious Program—Students 81.
2—SS. CYRIL AND METHODIUS (1906) [CEM 2] (Slovak)
Mailing Address: 604 Graham Ave., Windber, 15963. Tel: 814-467-7042; Email: sscyrilmethodius@yahoo.com; Web: www.sscmwindber.com. Deacon Thomas M. Papinchak; Revs. Lawrence L. Lacovic, Senior Priest, (Retired); Roderick N. Soha, T.O.R.
Res.: 2201 Graham Ave., Windber, 15963.
Tel: 814-467-7292.
Catechesis Religious Program—600 Graham Ave., Windber, 15963. Tel: 814-467-9670. Violet Bunk, D.R.E.; Roxanne Newcomer, D.R.E. Students 21.
3—ST. ELIZABETH ANN SETON (2000) [CEM 2]
605 Graham Ave., Windber, 15963.
Tel: 814-467-7191; Fax: 814-467-1621; Email: stelizaseton@comcast.net. Rev. Roderick N. Soha, T.O.R.; Deacon Thaddeus J. Janisko. In Res., Rev. Lawrence L. Lacovic, (Retired).
Catechesis Religious Program—Windber Catechetical Center, P.O. Box 36, Windber, 15963. Students 97.
4—HOLY CHILD JESUS (1921) (Irish), Closed. For inquiries for sacramental records, please contact SS. Cyril & Methodius.
5—ST. JOHN CANTIUS (1898) (Polish), Merged with St. Mary's, Windber to form St. Elizabeth Ann Seton, Windber.
6—ST. MARY'S (1914) (Hungarian), Merged with St. John Cantius, Windber to form St. Elizabeth Ann Seton, Windber.

Chaplains of Public Institutions

ALTOONA. *UMPC Altoona*, 620 Howard Ave., Altoona, 16601. Tel: 841-946-2011. Revs. D. Timothy Grimme, Asst. Chap., Christopher Panagoplos, T.O.R., Chap., Alfred Patterson, O.S.B., Chap., Deacon Michael Anna, Chap.
Veterans Medical Center, 2907 Pleasant Valley Blvd., Altoona, 16602. Tel: 814-943-8164. Rev. Msgr. Bernard A. Przybocki, Chap., (Retired).
JOHNSTOWN. *Conemaugh Health System*.
Main Campus, 1086 Franklin St., Johnstown, 15905. Tel: 814-534-9000. Revs. Sean K. Code, Chap., Peter Crowe, Chap.
Lee Campus, 320 Main St., Johnstown, 15901. Tel: 814-534-9000. Revs. Sean K. Code, Chap., Peter Crowe, Chap.
BELLEFONTE. *State Correctional Institution - Benner Township*, 301 Institution Dr., Bellefonte, 16823. Tel: 814-353-3630, Ext. 3730. Rev. John M. Gibbons, Chap., Tel: 814-353-3630, Ext. 3730, Deacon Jack E. Orlandi, Chap., 102 Centennial Hills Rd., Port Matilda, 16870. Tel: 814-692-7472.
State Correctional Institution - Rockview Our Lady of the Mount, Box A, Bellefonte, 16823.
Tel: 814-355-4874, Ext. 232. Rev. John M. Gibbons, Sacramental Min., Tel: 814-355-3134 (Res.), Deacon Thomas E. Boldin, Catholic Chap. & Admin., 2139 Zion Rd., Bellefonte, 16823. Tel: 814-355-4234.
EBENSBURG. *Ebensburg Center*, 4501 Admiral Peary Hwy., Ebensburg, 15931. Tel: 814-472-7350. Sr. Judith Kenaan, C.S.J., Assoc. Chap.
Laurel Crest Rehabilitation & Special Care Center, 429 Manor Dr., Ebensburg, 15931.
Tel: 814-472-8100, Ext. 3119. Vacant(Vacant).
HUNTINGDON. *State Correctional Institution*, St. Dismas, 1100 Pike St., Huntingdon, 16652.
Tel: 814-643-6520, Ext. 213. Rev. Matthew B. Baum, Sac. Min., Deacon Thomas J. McFee, Chap. & Admin.
LORETTO. *Federal Correctional Institution*, P.O. Box 1000, Loretto, 15940. Tel: 814-472-4140, Ext. 155. Franciscan Friars, TOR, Chaps.
SMITHFIELD. *State Correctional Institution*, 1120 Pike St., Huntingdon, 16652. Tel: 814-643-6520. Rev. James M. Dugan, Chap.
SOMERSET. *State Correctional Institution*, St. Peter in Chains, 1590 Walters Mill Rd., Somerset, 15510.
Tel: 814-443-8100. Revs. Stephen Shin, O.F.M.-Cap., Sacramental Min., Brian Lee Warchola, Sacramental Min., Deacon David G. Hornick, Chap.
State Correctional Institution, Laurel Highlands, 5706 Glades Pike Rd., P.O. Box 631, Somerset, 15501. Tel: 814-445-6501. Revs. Karl Kolodziejski, O.F.M.Conv., Sacramental Min., Aron M. Maghsoudi, Sacramental Min., Deacon David G. Hornick, Chap.
STATE COLLEGE. *Mount Nittany Medical Center*, 1800 E. Park Ave., State College, 16803.
Tel: 814-231-7000. Revs. Jonathan Dickson, Chap., Antony Sudherson, H.G.N., Chap.

Priests Active Outside the Diocese:
Rev.—
Kuligowski, Peter J., V.F., P.O. Box 198, St. Joseph, LA 71366. Tel: 318-766-3565.

Military Chaplains:
Revs.—
Arnone, Leo F., LCDR, CHC, USNR, PSC 831, Box 0014, Fpo, AE 09363
Halka, Frantisek A., HHC 2 Cab, Unit 1571, Box 941, Apo, AP 96271-5711
Ugo, Charles Chidindu, 4277 Larson St., Apt. 65, Olivehurst, CA 95961.

Absent on Leave:
Rev. Msgr.—
Little, Anthony B.
Revs.—
Arseneault, David J.
Bodziak, Charles F.
Cingle, Martin A.
Coveney, James B., M.A., M.Div., (Retired)
Kelly, Robert J., Ph.D.
Maurizio, Joseph D. Jr.
Onyeocha, Chinemere Raphael.

Retired:
Rev. Msgrs.—
Gaus, Arnold L., (Retired), 856 Cambria St., Cresson, 16630. Tel: 814-886-2510
Kline, Roy F., (Retired), 1037 S. Logan Blvd., 16648. Tel: 814-695-5571
Przybocki, Bernard A., (Retired), 7923 Admiral Peary Hwy., Cresson, 16630
Sasway, John R., V.F., (Retired), 484 Carney Rd., Lilly, 15938. Tel: 814-886-4103
Saylor, Philip, (Retired), 310 S. Allen St., State College, 16801
Servinsky, Michael E., V.G., S.T.L., J.C.L., D.Min., (Retired), 2728 S. Ocean Shore Blvd., Flagler Beach, FL 32136
Swope, Timothy J., V.F., (Retired), Dmitri Manor, 150 St. Mary's Ln., Suite 11, 16648
Tomaselli, Samuel J., (Retired), 855 W. Sanner St., Somerset, 15501
Valko, George J., (Retired), 5922 Willow Bridge Loop, Ellenton, FL 34222
Revs.—
Balestino, Francis P., (Retired), P.O. Box 817, Johnstown, 15907
Becker, David R., (Retired), 1101 Flamingo Dr., Apt. 6105, Altoona, 16602. Tel: 814-935-3588
Bendzella, Sylvester J., (Retired), 150 St. Mary's Ln., Ste. 3, 16648

Boslett, Donald E., (Retired), John Paul II Manor, 856 Cambria St., Cresson, 16630
Brezovec, John F., (Retired), John Paul II Manor, 856 Cambria St., Cresson, 16630
Crosser, Raymond G., (Retired), 100 Beckman Dr., 4D, Altoona, 16602
Ellias, John J., (Retired), 118 Mechanic St., Everett, 15537
Gardner, Clement, (Retired), 801 Logandale Dr., Altoona, 16601. Tel: 814-943-2948
Gergel, Stephen J., Lt. USN, (Retired), 116 Lake Manor Dr., Kingsland, GA 31548
Grega, Bernard F., (Retired)
Imgrund, Norman P., (Retired), 2257 Sulphur Run Rd., Jersey Shore, 17740
Knapik, Andrew G., (Retired), P.O. Box 112, Wildwood, 15091
Lacovic, Lawrence L., (Retired), St. Anthony of Padua, 2201 Graham Ave., Windber, 15963. Tel: 814-467-7292
Robine, Paul M., (Retired), 21 Country Club Rd., Cresson, 16630. Tel: 814-866-2573
Roesch, David H., (Retired), Dmitri Manor, 150 St. Mary's Ln., Suite 5, 16648
Spishak, Carl A., (Retired), 5514 Roselawn Ave., Altoona, 16602. Tel: 814-944-8509
Stanko, Andrew C., V.F., (Retired)
White, Bernard L., (Retired), 150 St. Mary's Lane, 16648. Tel: 814-696-4698.

Permanent Deacons:
Ahearn, Charles R., St. Mary, Hollidaysburg
Albarano, Samuel F. Jr., Our Lady of the Alleghenies, Lilly
Anna, Michael, St. Bernard, Hastings; Chap., UPMC
Beavers, Thomas T., St. John the Baptist, New Baltimore
Boldin, Thomas E., Chap., St. John the Evangelist, Bellefonte, Catholic Chap. & Admin.; Our Lady of the Mount-SCI, Rockview
Buige, Thomas M., St. John Vianney, Mundy's Corner
Cammarata, Samuel M., Resurrection, Johnstown
Concannon, John J., St. John Gualbert Cathedral, Johnstown
Condor, Michael Jr., Holy Name, Ebensburg
Conner, Christopher S., St. Bernard, Hastings
Dalla Valle, Joseph, St. Patrick, Johnstown
Gibboney, Donald, Most Holy Trinity, Huntingdon
Gibson, Philip, Holy Spirit, Lock Haven
Gill, Gary F., Prince of Peace, Northern Cambria
Golden, Richard T., Basilica of St. Michael, Loretto
Hornick, David G., St. Michael, St. Michael; Chap. SCI Laurel Highlands, Somerset
Ivanits, Laszlo P., Penn State Catholic Campus Ministry
Janisko, Thaddeus J., St. Elizabeth Ann Seton, Windber
Janosik, James J., St. Mary, Nanty Glo
Kolonich, Ronald A., St. Peter, Somerset
Lapinski, David C., Our Lady of Victory, State College
Little, Scott Q., Our Mother of Sorrows, Johnstown
McFee, Thomas J., St. Therese of the Child Jesus, Altoona; Chap., Smithfield, SCI; Chap. & Admin., St. Dismas, SCI Huntingdon
Neral, Gene P., St. John the Evangelist, Lakemont
Nester, Kevin, Admin., St. Joseph, Williamsburg
Ondik, Michael A. Jr., (Retired), Good Shepherd, State College
Orlandi, Jack E., Good Shepherd, State College; Chap., SCI Benner Township
Papinchak, Thomas M., SS Cyril & Methodius, Windber
Pyle, Jay A., All Saints, Boswell; St. Anne, Davidsville
Roth, John D., St. Catherine of Siena, Mount Union
Russo, Michael L., St. Benedict, Johnstown
Szwarc, John J.
Underhill, William R., Adm., St. Michael, Salisbury/ St. Mary, Pocahontas
Visinsky, Joseph W., (Leave of Absence)
Woomer, James L. Sr., St. Rose of Lima, Altoona
Young, Calvin J., Holy Spirit, Lock Haven
Becker, Bruce L., St. Francis of Assisi, Johnston.

INSTITUTIONS LOCATED IN DIOCESE

[A] COLLEGES AND UNIVERSITIES
(NON-DIOCESAN)

CRESSON.
Mount Aloysius College (1853) 7373 Admiral Peary Hwy., Cresson, 16630. Tel: 814-886-4131; Fax: 814-886-2978; Email: cnelen@mtaloy.edu; Web: www.mtaloy.edu. Dr. John Mills, Pres.; Mr. Frank Crouse, Vice Pres. Enrollment Management; Dr. Jane Grassadonia, Vice Pres. Student Affairs. Sisters of Mercy. Lay Teachers 203; Sisters 3; Students 1,877; Total Staff 157.

LORETTO.
St. Francis University, P.O. Box 600, Loretto, 15940-0600. Tel: 814-472-3001; Fax: 814-472-3003 ; Email: vsoyka@francis.edu; Web: www.francis.edu. Rev. Malachi Van Tassell, T.O.R., Ph.D., Pres.; Dr. Wayne Powel, Provost; Erin McCloskey, Vice Pres. Enrollment Mgmt.; Jeffrey Savino, Vice Pres. Finance & Admin.; Mr. Robert Crusciel, Vice Pres. Advancement; Mr. Randy Frye, Dean Business; Don Miles, Dir. Residence Life; Ms. Sandra Balough, Dean Library Svcs.; Ms. Julie Barris, Dir. Career Devel. & Continuing Educ.; Mr. George Pyo, Dir. Computer Svcs.; Mr. Bobby Anderson, Assoc. Dir. Student Activities; Ms. Renee Bernard, Dir. Advising & Retention, Ctr. Acad. Success; Susan Robinson, Dir. Athletics; Mr. David Wilson, Dir. Counseling; Rev. Joseph Lehman, T.O.R., Dir., Mission Integration; Bro. Gabriel Mary Amato, T.O.R., Coord. Dorothy Day Center; Revs. Joseph Chancler, T.O.R., Adjunct Instructor Math; Christopher Dobson, T.O.R., Dir., Campus Ministry; Bros. Shamus McGrenra, T.O.R., Dir. Intl. Admissions; Richard Gates, T.O.R., Center for Academic Success; Dennis Snyder, T.O.R., Dept., Educ.; Rev. Peter Lyons, T.O.R., Philosophy & Religious Studies. Priests 4; Students 2,353; Lay Professors 140.

[B] HIGH SCHOOLS, PRIVATE

ALTOONA. **Bishop Guilfoyle Catholic High School*, 2400 Pleasant Valley Blvd., Altoona, 16602. Tel: 814-944-4014; Fax: 814-944-8695; Web: www.bishopguilfoyle.org. Mr. Joseph Adams, Pres.; Joan Donnelly, Prin.; Michael Cacciotti, Asst. Prin. & Athletic Dir. Lay Teachers 28; Students 311; Total Staff 44.

JOHNSTOWN. **Bishop McCort Catholic High School*, 25 Osborne St., Johnstown, 15905. Tel: 814-536-8991; Fax: 814-535-4118; Email: tfleming@mccort.org; Web: www.mccort.org. Tom Fleming, Prin., Chief Administrative Officer & Contact Person; Rev. William E. Rosenbaum, Chap.; Stephen Cotchen, Vice Prin. Lay Teachers 42; Priests 1; Students 319.

BOALSBURG. *St. Joseph's Catholic Academy*, (Grades 9-12), 901 Boalsburg Pike, Boalsburg, 16827. Tel: 814-808-6118; Fax: 814-808-6178; Email: jkozak@stjoeacad.org. Ms. Jennifer Mallett, Prin. Clergy 1; Lay Teachers 21; Priests 1; Students 153.

EBENSBURG. **Bishop Carroll Catholic High School*, 728 Ben Franklin Hwy., Ebensburg, 15931. Tel: 814-472-7500; Fax: 814-472-8020; Email: lweber@bishopcarroll.org; Web: bishopcarroll.com. Lorie Ratchford, Prin.; Rev. Joseph C. Nale, Chap. Lay Teachers 21; Priests 1; Religious 1; Students 218.

[C] ELEMENTARY DIOCESAN SCHOOLS

ALTOONA. *Holy Trinity Catholic School – Middle School Campus*, (Grades 5-8), 5519 Sixth Ave., Altoona, 16602. Tel: 814-942-7835; Fax: 814-942-1095; Email: spencer.elaine@holytrinitycatholic.school. Mrs. Elaine Spencer, Prin. Lay Teachers 16; Students 179.

JOHNSTOWN. *Divine Mercy Catholic Academy West Campus*, (Grades PreK-6), Tel: 814-539-5315; Email: batzel.rosemary@divinemercy.academy. Rose Batzel, Vice Prin. Lay Teachers 19; Students 235.

CRESSON. *All Saints Catholic School*, (Grades PreK-8), 220 Powell Ave., Cresson, 16630. Tel: 814-886-7942; Fax: 814-886-7942; Email: allsaints@ascsknights.org; Web: www.ascsknights.org. Kathleen L. Maurer, Prin. Serves the following parishes: St. Francis Xavier; St. Aloysius; Our Lady of the Allegheniess; St. Thomas Aquinas; St. Demetrius; St. Bartholomew; St. Joseph; St. Monica. Lay Teachers 14; Preschool 26; Students 119.

NICKTOWN. *Northern Cambria Catholic School*, 3278 Blue Goose Rd., Nicktown, 15762. Tel: 814-948-8900; Fax: 814-948-8720; Email: nccs@northerncambriacatholic.org; Web: www.daj.k12.pa.us/nccs. P.O. Box 252, Nicktown, 15762-0252. Theresa Burba, Prin. Serves St. Nicholas & Prince of Peace. Lay Teachers 12; Students 99.

[D] HOMES FOR AGED
(NON-DIOCESAN)

HOLLIDAYSBURG.
Garvey Manor (1965) 1037 S. Logan Blvd., 16648. Tel: 814-695-5571; Fax: 814-695-8516; Email: garveymanor@garveymanor.org; Web: www.garveymanor.org. Sr. M. Joachim Anne Ferenchak, O.Carm., Admin. Senior Care Complex: Nursing, Personal Care, Independent Living. Aged Residents 167; Bed Capacity 180; Carmelite Sisters for the Aged and Infirm 5; Tot Asst. Annually 266; Total Staff 289.
St. Leonard's Home, Inc., 601 N. Montgomery St., 16648. Tel: 814-695-9581; Fax: 814-695-2606; Tel: 814-695-2920 (Other); Email: srcindy@juno.com; Web: www.stleonardshome.org. Sr. Cynthia Meyer, C.S.F.N., Pres. CEO
St. Leonard's Home, Inc. Bed Capacity 28; Sisters of the Holy Family of Nazareth 1; Tot Asst. Annually 40; Total Staff 15.

(DIOCESAN)

HOLLIDAYSBURG.
Dmitri Manor Priests' Residence, 150 St. Mary's Ln., 16648. Tel: 814-696-4698. Diocese of Altoona-Johnstown, 927 S. Logan Blvd., 16602. Rev. Msgr. Robert J. Saly. Aged Residents 12; Bed Capacity 12; Staff 1.

[E] MONASTERIES AND RESIDENCES OF PRIESTS AND BROTHERS
(NON-DIOCESAN)

HOLLIDAYSBURG.
St. Bernardine Monastery (1925) 768 Monastery Rd., 16648. Tel: 814-695-3992; Tel: 814-693-0166; Fax: 814-695-1611; Email: webrequests@thefranciscanfriars.org; Web: www.thefranciscanfriars.org. Revs. Robert D'Aversa, Supr.; Anthony Criscitelli; Very Rev. Eugene Kubina, T.O.R., (Retired); Revs. William P. Linhares, T.O.R.; Leonard J. Blostic, T.O.R., (Retired); Kenneth La Pan, T.O.R., (Retired); Patrick Seelman, T.O.R., (Retired); Bro. Tello Truong Vu, T.O.R.; Revs. William Santre, T.O.R., (Retired); Bradley Baldwin, T.O.R.; Adrian Tirpak, T.O.R. Brothers 1; Priests 10. *Franciscan Friars, T.O.R. Development Office and Mass Association*, 788 Monastery Rd., P.O. Box 139, 16648. Tel: 814-695-3802; Fax: 814-695-1611; Email: webrequests@thefranciscanfriars.org; Web: www.thefranciscanfriars.org. Mrs. Kellie Wesner Bettwy, Dir. Fin. & Devel. *Province Econome's Office* (1925) P.O. Box 117, 16648. Tel: 814-696-3321; Fax: 814-695-1611; Email: jen@thefranciscanfriars.org; Web: www.thefranciscanfriars.org. Rev. Anthony Criscitelli, Treas.
St. Joseph Friary, 501 Walnut St., 16648. Tel: 814-695-5802; Email: webrequests@thefranciscanfriars.org.. Rev. Christopher Panagoplos, T.O.R. Priests 1.

LORETTO.
St. Bonaventure Hall, St. Bonaventure Friary, P.O. Box 155, Loretto, 15940-0155. Tel: 814-419-8842; Email: jstandre@franciscanstor.org. Rev. Jonathan St. André, T.O.R., Dir. Novices; Bro. Gabriel Mary Amato, T.O.R., Dir. Postulants. Brothers 2; Postulants 5; Priests 2.
St. Francis Friary at Mount Assisi, 141 St. Francis Dr., P.O. Box 40, Loretto, 15940-0040. Tel: 814-419-8827; Fax: 814-472-8992 (Provincial Office); Email: fjmorman@gmail.com; Web: www.franciscanstor.org. Revs. Terry Adams, T.O.R.; Augustine Belinda, T.O.R.; David Bonarrigo, T.O.R.; Gervase Cain, T.O.R.; Joseph Chancler, T.O.R.; Richard L. Davis, T.O.R., Min. Prov.; Bro. Lawrence Hilferty; Revs. Patrick George, T.O.R., Tel: 814-472-5324, Ext. 302; Robert Hilz, T.O.R.; David Kraeger, T.O.R.; Ivan Lebar, T.O.R.; Joseph Markalonis, T.O.R.; Brian Miller, T.O.R.; David Morrier, T.O.R.; Francis Moyher, T.O.R.; Jonathan St. André, T.O.R., Novices Dir.; Laurence R. Uhlman, T.O.R.; Samuel Vaccarella, T.O.R.; Bros. Gabriel Mary Amato, T.O.R., Dir., Postulants; Edward Bennett, T.O.R.; John Patrick Calvey, T.O.R.; Callistus Gerardi, T.O.R.; Damien Koehler, T.O.R.; Stephen Liebal, T.O.R.; Bernard Nicolosi, T.O.R.; Norman MeNelis, T.O.R.; Michael Tripka, T.O.R.; Revs. Benjamin Medeisos, T.O.R.; James V. Morman, T.O.R., Local Min.; Julio Rivero, T.O.R.; Robert Sisk, T.O.R.; Fidelis Weber. Brothers 10; Postulants 2; Priests 20.

[F] CONVENTS AND RESIDENCES FOR SISTERS
(NON-DIOCESAN)

ALTOONA.
Carmelite Community of the Word-St. John of the Cross Convent, 35 Seneca Ave., Altoona, 16602. Tel: 814-942-5747; Fax: 814-942-8052; Email: srllamagna@gmail.com. Sr. Linda LaMagna, C.C.W., Admin. Carmelite Community of the Word. Sisters 3; Total in Residence 3.

CRESSON.
Sister Servants of the Most Sacred Heart of Jesus (1894) Sacred Heart Province, 866 Cambria St., Cresson, 16630-1713. Tel: 814-886-4223; Fax: 814-886-4735; Email: sscjusaprovince@gmail.com. Mother Klara Slonina, Prov.; Sisters Mary Joseph Calore, Prov. Asst.; Margaret Mary Hill, Vicar. Total in Residence 6; Professed Sisters 26.

John Paul II Manor Personal Care Home, 856 Cambria St., Cresson, 16630. Tel: 814-886-7961; Email: administrator@johnpaul2manor.org; Web: www.johnpaul2manor.org. Sisters Mary Joan Greenburg, Sup.; Mary Andrew Hooper, Admin. Residents 35.

EBENSBURG.

Carmelite Community of the Word (1971) St. Therese Convent, 218 W. Lloyd St., Ebensburg, 15931. Tel: 814-472-9457; Fax: 814-472-5105; Email: ebensburgccw@aol.com. Sr. Judith Karlak, C.C.W., Admin. Total in Residence 3.

Sisters of St. Ann Mother House, 1120 N. Center St., P.O. Box 328, Ebensburg, 15931. Tel: 814-472-9354; Fax: 814-472-9354; Email: sistersann35@gmail.com; Email: anthos1944@gmail.com; Web: www.suoredisantanna.org. Sr. Diana L. Polanco, Supr. Sisters of St. Ann. Total in Residence 5.

GALLITZIN.

Carmelite Community of the Word-Incarnation Center, 394 Bem Rd., Gallitzin, 16641. Tel: 814-886-4098; Fax: 814-886-7115; Email: newsccw@yahoo.com; Web: ccwsisters.org. Sr. Marilyn Welch, C.C.W., Admin. Total in Residence 3.

Little Sisters of Jesus, 347 Tunnel Hill St., Gallitzin, 16641. Tel: 814-886-4679. Sr. MaryJo Byrne, Contact Person. Total in Residence 3.

LORETTO.

Carmel of St. Therese of Lisieux (1927) 2101 Manor Dr., P.O. Box 57, Loretto, 15940-0057. Tel: 814-472-8620; Fax: 814-472-6231; Email: info@lorettocarmel.org; Web: www.lorettocarmel.org. Mother John of the Cross, O.C.D., Prioress. Discalced Carmelite Nuns. Postulants 1; Nuns with Solemn Vows 9.

MCCONNELLSBURG.

Carmelite Community of the Word, Fulton County Mission, 110 S. Third St., McConnellsburg, 17223. Tel: 717-485-5917; Tel: 717-485-0661; Fax: 717-485-3855; Email: mmonahan@dioceseaj.org. Sr. Martha Burbulla, Dir. Total in Residence 2.

PORTAGE.

Sister Servants of the Most Sacred Heart of Jesus, St. Joseph Convent, 1872 Munster Rd., Portage, 15946. Tel: 814-886-4459; Email: sisterjacinta@gmail.com. Mother Jacinta Miryam Hanley, S.S.C.J., Supr. Sisters 7.

[G] CAMPUS MINISTRY

ALTOONA. *Office of Campus Ministry*, Saint John the Evangelist Rectory, 309 Lotz Ave., Altoona, 16602. Tel: 814-942-5503; Fax: 814-943-8832; Email: mbecker253@aol.com. 933 S. Logan Blvd., 16648. Rev. Msgr. Michael A. Becker, Coord.

Juniata College, 1905 More St., Huntington, 16652. Tel: 814-641-3362 (Office); Fax: 814-641-3317; Email: baerl@juniata.edu. Ms. Lisa Baer, Campus Min.; Rev. Matthew B. Baum, Sacramental Min.

Lock Haven University (Lock Haven), Newman Center, 445 W. Main St., Lock Haven, 17745. Tel: 570-748-8592; Fax: 570-748-8592 (Call ahead) ; Email: christopher.klopp@gmail.com. Rev. Joseph Orr, Sacramental Min.; Mr. Christopher Klopp, Campus Min.

Mount Aloysius College (Cresson), 7373 Admiral Peary Hwy., Cresson, 16630. Tel: 814-886-6483; Fax: 814-886-2978; Email: akanich@mtaloy.edu. Mrs. Amy Kanich, Dir.; Rev. Msgr. Michael A. Becker, Sacramental Min.; Ryan Beiswenger, Campus Min.

Penn State University, Altoona, Edith Davis Eve Chapel Room 113, 3000 Ivyside Park, Altoona, 16601. Tel: 814-949-5137; Email: andre.mccarville@gmail.com. Very Rev. Alan E. Thomas, V.G., Sacramental Min.; Andre McCarville, Campus Min.

Penn State University, University Park, 205C Pasquerilla Spiritual Center, University Park, 16802. Tel: 814-865-4281; Fax: 814-865-2972; Email: catholic@psu.edu; Web: www.psu.edu/catholic. Revs. Matthew T. Laffey, O.S.B., Dir. Campus Ministry; David R. Griffin, O.S.B., Campus Min.; Deacon Laszlo P. Ivanits, Campus Min.

St. Francis University (Loretto), P.O. Box 600, Loretto, 15940. Tel: 814-472-3172; Fax: 814-472-2840; Email: cdobson@francis.edu. Rev. Christopher Dobson, T.O.R., Dir. Campus Ministry; Mr. Paul Girardi, Assoc. Campus Min.

University of Pittsburgh at Johnstown, 450 Schoolhouse Rd., Johnstown, 15904. Tel: 814-269-2007; Fax: 814-269-7128; Email: lmccrary@dioceseaj.org. Mrs. LaDonna McCrary, Campus Min.; Rev. George M. Gulash, Chap. & Sacramental Min.

[H] NEWMAN CENTERS
(NON-DIOCESAN)

UNIVERSITY PARK.

Penn State Catholic Community, 205 Pasquerilla Spiritual Center, University Park, 16802. Tel: 814-865-4281; Fax: 814-865-2972; Email: catholic@psu.edu; Web: www.psu.edu/catholic. Revs. Matthew T. Laffey, O.S.B., Dir.; David R. Griffin, O.S.B., Campus Min.; Deacon Laszlo P. Ivanits, Campus Min. Total in Residence 2; Total Staff 6; Catholic Students attending Penn State University 9,500.

[I] MISCELLANEOUS LISTINGS
(DIOCESAN)

HOLLIDAYSBURG.

Diocese of Altoona-Johnstown Mutual-Aid-Plan Trust, 927 S. Logan Blvd., 16648.

(NON-DIOCESAN)

HOLLIDAYSBURG.

Second Century Scholarship Fund (2001) Diocese of Altoona-Johnstown, 927 S. Logan Blvd., 16648. Tel: 814-695-5577; Fax: 814-696-9516; Email: pseasoltz@dioceseaj.org; Web: www.secondcenturyfund.org. Mrs. Pamela Seasoltz, Dir.; Mr. Matthew Stever, Corporate Sec. Student Scholarships 1,625.

LORETTO.

American Parish Youth Center, Inc., P.O. Box 40, Loretto, 15940. Tel: 814-419-8885; Fax: 814-419-8881; Email: framarco@aol.com. P.O. Box 26, Loretto, 15940. Rev. Malachi Van Tassell, T.O.R., Ph.D., Treas. Clergy 2.

Diocese of Altoona-Johnstown, 925 S. Logan Blvd., 16648. Tel: 814-695-5579; Fax: 814-696-9516. Rev. Matthew A. Reese, Dir.

Office of Vocations, Diocese of Altoona-Johnstown, 925 S. Logan Blvd., 16648. Tel: 814-695-5579; Fax: 814-696-9516; Email: vocations@dioceseaj.org. Rev. Matthew A. Reese, Dir.

Office of Ongoing Formation of Clergy, 1127 McKinley Ave., Johnstown, 15905-4323. Tel: 814-536-6110; Fax: 814-536-3709. Very Rev. Angelo J. Patti, V.F.

NEW BALTIMORE.

St. John The Baptist Retreat Center, 101 Findley St., P.O. Box 10, New Baltimore, 15553. Tel: 814-733-2210; Fax: 814-733-2966; Email: momhanknb@yahoo.com. Rev. Mark Pattock, O.F.M.Cap., Dir. Total Staff 5.

RELIGIOUS INSTITUTES OF MEN REPRESENTED IN THE DIOCESE

For further details refer to the corresponding bracketed number in the Religious Institutes of Men or Women section.

[0200]—*Benedictine Monks*—O.S.B.
[0470]—*The Capuchin Friars*—O.F.M.Cap.
[1000]—*Congregation of the Passion*—C.P.
[0480]—*Conventual Franciscans* (St. Anthony of Padua Prov.)—O.F.M.Conv.
[0520]—*Franciscan Friars*—O.F.M.
[0560]—*Third Order Regular of Saint Francis* (Provs. of Sacred Heart, Immaculate Conception)—T.O.R.

RELIGIOUS INSTITUTES OF WOMEN REPRESENTED IN THE DIOCESE

[0100]—*Adorers of the Blood of Christ*—A.S.C.
[0315]—*Carmelite Community of the Word*—C.C.W.
[0330]—*Carmelite Sisters for the Aged and Infirm*—O.Carm.
[3710]—*Congregation of the Sisters of Saint Agnes*—C.S.A.
[0420]—*Discalced Carmelite Nuns*—O.C.D.
[1070-03]—*Dominican Sisters*—O.P.
[1170]—*Felician Sisters*—C.S.S.F.
[2330]—*Little Sisters of Jesus*—L.S.J.
[3630]—*Servants of the Most Sacred Heart of Jesus*—S.S.C.J.
[0570]—*Sisters of Charity of Seton Hill, Greensburg, Pennsylvania*—S.C.
[2575]—*Sisters of Mercy of the Americas* (Dallas Regional Community)—R.S.M.
[1620]—*Sisters of Saint Francis of Millvale, Pennsylvania*—O.S.F.
[3780]—*Sisters of Ss. Cyril and Methodius*—SS.C.M.
[3718]—*Sisters of St. Ann* (Italy)—S.S.A.
[3830]—*Sisters of St. Joseph*—C.S.J.
[1970]—*Sisters of the Holy Family of Nazareth*—C.S.F.N.
[3260]—*Sisters of the Precious Blood (Ohio)*—C.PP.S.
[2160]—*Sisters, Servants of the Immaculate Heart of Mary* (Scranton, PA)—I.H.M.
[4160]—*Vincentian Sisters of Charity*—V.S.C.

NECROLOGY

† Adamec, Joseph V., Bishop Emeritus of Altoona-Johnstown., Died Mar. 20, 2019
† Stein, Timothy P., Altoona, St. Mary, Died Apr. 19, 2018
† Zatalava, James D., (Retired), Died May. 30, 20108

An asterisk (*) denotes an organization that has established tax-exempt status directly with the IRS and is not covered by the USCCB Group Ruling.

Diocese of Amarillo

(Dioecesis Amarillensis)

Most Reverend

PATRICK J. ZUREK, D.D.

Bishop of Amarillo; ordained June 29, 1975; appointed Auxiliary Bishop of San Antonio and Titular Bishop of Tamugadi January 5, 1998; consecrated February 16, 1998; appointed Bishop of Amarillo January 3, 2008; installed Feb. 22, 2008.

Most Reverend

JOHN W. YANTA, D.D.

Retired Bishop of Amarillo; ordained March 17, 1956; appointed Titular Bishop of Naratcata and Auxiliary Bishop of San Antonio October 27, 1994; consecrated December 30, 1994; appointed Bishop of Amarillo January 21, 1997; installed March 17, 1997; retired January 3, 2008.

Diocesan Pastoral Center: 4512 N.E. 24th Ave., Amarillo, TX 79107. Tel: 806-383-2243; Fax: 806-383-8452. *Mailing Address: P.O. Box 5644, Amarillo, TX 79117-5644.*

Web: www.amarillodiocese.org

ERECTED A DIOCESE BY POPE PIUS XI, AUGUST 25, 1926.

Square Miles 25,800.

Comprises that part of the State of Texas known as the Panhandle, and extending thence southward; bounded on the east by Oklahoma, and by the eastern county line of Childress and by the southern lines Childress, Hall, Briscoe, Swisher, Castro and Parmer Counties; the western boundary is the New Mexico state line from the southern line of Parmer County, Texas, northward to the northwestern corner of the Panhandle of Texas. There are 26 counties.

For legal titles of parishes and diocesan institutions, consult the Chancery Office.

STATISTICAL OVERVIEW

Personnel	
Bishop	1
Retired Bishops	1
Priests: Diocesan Active in Diocese	25
Priests: Diocesan Active Outside Diocese	3
Priests: Retired, Sick or Absent	7
Number of Diocesan Priests	35
Religious Priests in Diocese	2
Total Priests in Diocese	37
Extern Priests in Diocese	9
Ordinations:	
Diocesan Priests	1
Transitional Deacons	2
Permanent Deacons in Diocese	48
Total Sisters	96
Parishes	
Parishes	38
With Resident Pastor:	
Resident Diocesan Priests	22
Resident Religious Priests	2
Without Resident Pastor:	
Administered by Priests	14
Missions	11
Professional Ministry Personnel:	
Sisters	11
Lay Ministers	49
Welfare	
Day Care Centers	1
Total Assisted	140
Specialized Homes	3
Total Assisted	284
Special Centers for Social Services	1
Total Assisted	3,000
Other Institutions	1
Educational	
Diocesan Students in Other Seminaries	6
Total Seminarians	6
High Schools, Diocesan and Parish	1
Total Students	100
Elementary Schools, Diocesan and Parish	4
Total Students	595
Catechesis/Religious Education:	
High School Students	1,968
Elementary Students	3,104
Total Students under Catholic Instruction	5,773
Teachers in the Diocese:	
Sisters	3
Lay Teachers	62
Vital Statistics	
Receptions into the Church:	
Infant Baptism Totals	736
Minor Baptism Totals	161
Adult Baptism Totals	14
Received into Full Communion	58
First Communions	1,128
Confirmations	983
Marriages:	
Catholic	125
Interfaith	26
Total Marriages	151
Deaths	335
Total Catholic Population	45,130
Total Population	472,472

Former Bishops—Most Revs. RUDOLPH ALOYSIUS GERKEN, D.D., ord. June 10, 1917; cons. April 26, 1927; installed Bishop of Amarillo, April 28, 1927; elevated to the Metropolitan See of Santa Fe, NM, June 2, 1933; died March 2, 1943; ROBERT E. LUCEY, ord. May 14, 1916; cons. May 1, 1934; installed May 16, 1934; elevated to the Metropolitan See of San Antonio, Jan. 22, 1941; LAURENCE J. FITZSIMON, D.D., ord. May 17, 1921; cons. Oct. 22, 1941; installed Nov. 5, 1941; died July 2, 1958; JOHN L. MORKOVSKY, appt. Auxiliary of Amarillo, Dec. 22, 1955; named Bishop of Amarillo, Aug. 18, 1958; transferred to as Coadjutor Bishop of Galveston-Houston "cum jure successionis," April 16, 1963; LAWRENCE M. DEFALCO, D.D., ord. June 11, 1942; appt. April 16, 1963; cons. May 30, 1963; installed June 13, 1963; retired Aug. 28, 1979; died Sept. 22, 1979; LEROY T. MATTHIESEN, D.D., M.A., LITT.D, ord. March 10, 1946; appt. March 25, 1980; ord. Bishop, May 30, 1980; retired Jan. 21, 1997; died March 22, 2010.; JOHN W. YANTA, D.D., ord. March 17, 1956; appt. Titular Bishop of Naratcata and Auxiliary Bishop of San Antonio Oct. 27, 1994; cons. Dec. 30, 1994; appt. Bishop of Amarillo Jan. 21, 1997; installed March 17, 1997; retired Jan. 3, 2008.

Diocesan Officials

Diocesan Pastoral Center—4512 N.E. 24th Ave., Amarillo, 79107. Tel: 806-383-2243; Fax: 806-383-8452; Web: www.amarillodiocese.org. *Mailing Address: P.O. Box 5644, Amarillo, 79117-5644.*

Vicar General—Very Rev. FRANCISCO PEREZ, J.C.L.

Moderators of the Curia—Very Rev. FRANCISCO PEREZ, J.C.L.; Rev. Msgr. MICHAEL P. COLWELL, J.C.L.

Vicar of Clergy—Rev. JOHN VALDEZ.

Vicars Forane—Revs. TONY NEUSCH, South Deanery; HECTOR MADRIGAL, Central Deanery; FRANCISCO PENEZ, East Deanery; CESAR GOMEZ, North Deanery.

Diocesan Tribunal—

Judicial Vicar—Rev. JOSE RICARDO ZANETTI, J.C.L.

Judges—Rev. Msgr. MICHAEL P. COLWELL, J.C.L.; Very Rev. FRANCISCO PEREZ, J.C.L.; Rev. JOSE RICARDO ZANETTI, J.C.L.

Defenders of the Bond—Rev. LAWRENCE JOHN, J.C.L.; MARTHA LILIANA CARRERO MONTEALEGRE, J.C.D. (Cand.) Rome, Italy; Rev. MIECZYSLAW MITCHELL PRZEPIORA.

Advocates—Revs. JOSE GOMEZ; DAVID CONTRERAS; HAIDER QUINTERO; TONY NEUSCH.

Notaries—MS. CAROL SANFORD; MS. SUSAN GARNER; Deacon ROBERT ARANDA.

Chancellor—Rev. LAWRENCE JOHN, J.C.L.

Archivist—MS. SUSAN GARNER.

Executive Assistant to the Bishop—ROBERT ARANDA.

Diocesan Advisory Councils

Presbyteral Council—Revs. JOSE RICARDO ZANETTI, J.C.L.; ROBERT A. BUSCH, Ph.D.; AROKIARAJ MALAPADY; NICHOLAS J. GERBER. Bishop's Appointee: Ex Officio: Very Rev. FRANCISCO PEREZ, J.C.L., Vicar Gen.; Revs. JOHN VALDEZ, Vicar of Clergy; HECTOR MADRIGAL, Dean; TONY NEUSCH, Dean; CESAR GOMEZ, Dean.

College of Consultors—Rev. JOHN VALDEZ; Rev. Msgr. MICHAEL P. COLWELL, J.C.L.; Rev. JAMES SCHMITMEYER; Very Rev. FRANCISCO PEREZ, J.C.L.

Diocesan Pastoral Council—VACANT.

Priests' Pension Plan Retirement Committee—Rev. ROBERT A. BUSCH, Ph.D., Supt.; Most Rev. PATRICK J. ZUREK, D.D.; Rev. ANTHONY CARL NEUSCH.

Vocation Development Team—Revs. GABRIEL GARCIA, O.F.M., Vocation Dir.; JOHN VALDEZ; JOSE RICARDO ZANETTI, J.C.L.; JAMES SCHMITMEYER.

Deacon Director—Deacon BLAINE WESTLAKE.

Diocesan Departments

Director of Youth—OSCAR GUZMAN.

Office for the Catholic Schools—ANGI SEIDENBERGER, Supt.

Christian Formation Commission—Sr. MARIA ELENA LOPEZ-FERRER, S.S.N.D.

Department of Communications—CHRIST ALBRACHT, Editor "The West Texas Catholic"; MICHAEL NEUBERGER, Graphic Artist Print Shop.

Department of Finances and Ecclesiastical Properties—Fiscal Manager—Deacon PHIL WHITSON, CFO.
Administrative Services—Deacon PHIL WHITSON, Human Resources Mgr. & Employee Benefits; IVY TAYLOR, Risk Mgr., Real Estate Records & Asbestos Mgmt. in Schools.
Office of Development and Stewardship—KIM RICHARD, Dir.
United Catholic Appeal—KIM RICHARD, Dir.
Webmaster / IT Manager—CODY ROSE.

General Auxiliary Pastoral Services

Diocesan Attorney—FREDERICK J. GRIFFIN, 504 S. Polk, Amarillo, 79101.
Promoter of Justice—Rev. Msgr. MICHAEL P. COLWELL, J.C.L.
Victim Assistance Coordinator—Mailing Address: P.O. Box 5644, Amarillo, 79117-5644. Tel: 806-372-7960. SHARON DELGADO.
Charter Review Board—LOUISE ROSS, Chm.; FRANK JONES; DOROTHY GUGGEMOS; CHARLES MESTAS.
Ex Officio—Very Rev. FRANCISCO PEREZ, J.C.L.; Rev. JOHN VALDEZ; Deacon BLAINE WESTLAKE; FREDERICK J. GRIFFIN.
Coalition for Catholic Social Services - CCSS—VACANT.
Catholic Historical Society—MS. SUSAN GARNER, Pres.; ANN WELD, Museum Cur.
Rural Life Director—Rev. JAMES SCHMITMEYER.
Propagation of the FaithRev. MIECZYSLAW MITCHELL PRZEPIORA. Rite of Christian Initiation of Adults Commission: Sr. MARIA ELENA LOPEZ-FERRER, S.S.N.D.

Auxiliary Pastoral Services for Laity

Diocesan Council of Catholic Women—1200 S. Washington, Amarillo, 79102. Rev. Msgr. REX NICHOLL, Mod.; JULIE NEUSCH, Pres.
Director of Prison Ministry—Tel: 806-364-8432. Deacon ANDRES GONZALEZ, Dir.; KENT HOLTING, Coord.
Marriage Encounter—Rev. ROBERTO ROBLEDO.
Engaged Encounter—Director: Deacon BLAINE WESTLAKE. Coordinators: Deacon HENRY WILHELM; LORI WILHELM; MOLLY VILLEGAS, Contact, Tel: 806-383-2243, Ext. 116.
Catholic Student Center at West Texas A & M University—Rev. GRANT SPINHIRENE, Dir., Campus Min.; BETTY ARAGON, Asst. Dir., 2614 Fourth Ave., Canyon, 79015. Tel: 806-655-4345.
Scouting—Deacon ROBERT SMITH.
Serra Club—LEON CHURCH, Pres.
Natural Family Planning Coordinator—DR. FAYE USALA, Tel: 806-379-9224.
Cursillo Movement—Rev. MARCO ANTONIO GONZALEZ, Spiritual Dir. Lay Directors: LUPE GOMEZ, Amarillo; MARISOL CASTANON, Amarillo.
A.C.T.S. Movement—Rev. Msgr. HAROLD L. WALDOW, Chap., (Retired). Co Chaplains: Deacons JACKIE GUNNELS; BOB BIRKENFELD. Retrouvaille: SHELLEY SAMPLE, B.S., F.C.P., Pres., Tel: 806-379-9224.
Family Life Commission—VACANT.
Office for the Permanent Diaconate—Deacon BLAINE WESTLAKE, Coord.
Continuing Education of Clergy—Rev. ROBERT A. BUSCH, Ph.D., Supt.
Priests' Retirement—Deacon PHIL WHITSON.
Neocatechumenite—Tel: 806-202-5812. ANTONIO BARBA; LOURDES BARBA.
Hispanic Ministry—Rev. HECTOR MADRIGAL.
National Catholic Association of Diocesan Directors of Hispanic Ministry (NCADDHM)—Rev. HECTOR MADRIGAL, Pres., St. Joseph, 4122 S. Bonham St., Amarillo, 79110-1113.

CLERGY, PARISHES, MISSIONS AND PAROCHIAL SCHOOLS

CITY OF AMARILLO

(POTTER COUNTY)

1—SACRED HEART CATHEDRAL, Closed. This parish ceased to exist 1/19/75. For inquiries contact the Diocese of Amarillo: P.O. Box 5644, Amarillo, TX 79117-5644. Tel: 806-383-2243.

2—BLESSED SACRAMENT, Rev. Marco Antonio Gonzalez; Deacons Mark Seidlitz; Rene Perez; Bryan L. Lewis.
Res.: 4112 S.E. 25th St., 79103. Tel: 806-374-1132; Fax: 806-372-3631; Email: Blessedsacramentamarillo@gmail.com; Web: www.blessedsacramentchurch.org.
Catechesis Religious Program—Students 245.

3—ST. FRANCIS, Rev. Shane Wieck, Pastoral Assoc.
Res.: 5005 Klinke Rd., 79108-9628.
Tel: 806-335-1872; Email: khruday20@gmail.com; Email: shanewieck@yahoo.com.
Catechesis Religious Program—Students 33.

4—ST. HYACINTH'S, Rev. Jose Ricardo Zanetti, J.C.L.; Deacons Arnold Schwertner; Henry Wilhelm.
Res.: 4500 W. Hills Tr., 79106. Tel: 806-358-1351; Fax: 806-467-1708; Email: sth4500@outlook.com; Web: sthyacinthamarillo.org.
Catechesis Religious Program—Students 60.

5—ST. JOSEPH'S, Rev. Hector Madrigal; Deacon Jose Joaquin Castaneda.
Res.: 4122 Bonham St., 79110. Tel: 806-355-5621; Tel: 806-355-5663; Fax: 806-355-5622; Email: parish.office@stjosephamarillo.com; Web: www.stjosephamarillo.com.
See St. Joseph's School, Amarillo under Elementary Schools, City-Wide located in the Institution section.
Child Care—St. Joseph's Day Care Center, 4108 S. Bonham St., 79110. Tel: 806-353-7043; Email: gail.accdc@yahoo.com. Gail Sainz, Dir. Students 140.
Catechesis Religious Program—Sr. Hilda Rodriguez, D.R.E.; Gail Sainz, D.R.E. Students 232.

6—ST. LAURENCE CHURCH, Revs. Haider Quintero; Anthony Raju Yanamala, Vicar; Shane Wieck; Deacons Alfredo Alarcon; David Duenes; Pablo Morales; Miguel Tovar.
Res.: 2300 N. Spring St., 79107. Tel: 806-383-2261; Fax: 806-383-2266; Email: stlaurencepastor@yahoo.com.
Catechesis Religious Program—Sr. Valentine A. Curry, F.M.I., D.R.E. Students 518.

7—ST. MARTIN DE PORRES MISSION, Rev. Msgr. Rex Nicholl.
Res.: 1507 N. Adams St., 79107. Tel: 806-376-8771; Email: rex.nicholl@yahoo.com.
Catechesis Religious Program—Students 11.

8—ST. MARY'S CATHEDRAL, Rev. Msgr. Michael P. Colwell, J.C.L., Rector; Revs. Grant Spinhirne, Parochial Vicar; John Lawrence, J.C.L., In Res.; Deacons Robert Smith; John Peters; Robert Aranda.
Res.: 1200 Washington St., 79102. Tel: 806-376-7204; Fax: 806-376-7972; Email: friemel@stmarysamarillo.com; Web: www.stmarysamarillo.com.
See St. Mary's School and St. Mary's Montessori Preschool, Amarillo under Elementary Schools, City-Wide located in the Institution section.
Catechesis Religious Program—Students 554.

9—OUR LADY OF GUADALUPE, Rev. Jose Gomez; Deacons Armando Esparza; Andres Gonzalez.
Res.: 1210 S.E. 11th Ave., 79102. Tel: 806-372-1128; Fax: 806-372-2225; Email: guadalupe@nts-online.net.
Catechesis Religious Program—Students 175.

10—OUR LADY OF VIETNAM
2001 N. Grand St., 79107. Rev. Paul Nuyen.
Res.: 3334 N.E. 20th Ave., 79107. Tel: 806-383-8669; Email: maryleocmc@yahoo.com.
Catechesis Religious Program—Students 85.

11—ST. THOMAS THE APOSTLE, Rev. John Valdez; Deacons Blaine Westlake; Phillip Eugene Whitson.
Res.: 4100 S. Coulter Dr., 79109. Tel: 806-358-2461; Fax: 806-358-2529; Email: rwalker@stthomasamarillo.org; Web: www.stthomasamarillo.org.
Catechesis Religious Program—Kerry Acker, D.R.E. Students 441.

OUTSIDE THE CITY OF AMARILLO

BORGER, HUTCHINSON CO., ST. JOHN THE EVANGELIST, Rev. James Schmitmeyer.
Res.: 201 St. John's Rd., Borger, 79007.
Tel: 806-274-7064; Fax: 806-274-3941; Email: stjohntx@gmail.com; Web: saintjohntx.org.
Catechesis Religious Program—Ivonne Manriquez, D.R.E. Students 97.
Mission—St. Ann's, Stinnett, Hutchinson Co.

BOVINA, PARMER CO., ST. ANN'S
3rd St., Box 660, Bovina, 79009. Rev. Gregory Bunyan; Deacon Teodoro Chavez.
Res.: 409 S. 3rd St., Box 660, Bovina, 79009.
Tel: 806-251-1511; Email: padrehenryw1@hotmail.com; Email: normalv@wtrt.net.

CACTUS, MOORE CO., OUR LADY OF GUADALUPE, Rev. Roberto Robledo.
Church: 1501 Center Dr., P.O. Box 118, Cactus, 79013. Tel: 806-966-5984; Email: robertorobledo7@hotmail.com.
Catechesis Religious Program—Students 113.

CANADIAN, HEMPHILL CO., SACRED HEART, Rev. Joji Konkala; Deacon Jose Jesus Gutierrez.
Rectory—721 Main St., Canadian, 79014.
Church: 804 Kingman Ave., P.O. Box 938, Canadian, 79014. Tel: 806-323-6608; Email: reddyjojisun@gmail.com.
Catechesis Religious Program—Students 97.

CANYON, RANDALL CO., ST. ANN'S
Mailing Address: P.O. Box 59, Canyon, 79015. Rev. Robert A. Busch, Ph.D.; Deacons Gabriel Rivas; John David Rausch; Eldon Knox.
Res.: 605 38th St., Canyon, 79015.
Tel: 806-655-3302, Ext. 0; Fax: 806-655-3384; Email: st.anncc@yahoo.com; Web: www.stannsofcanyon.org. Students 171.
Catechesis Religious Program—Adrian Johnson, D.R.E. Students 174.

CHILDRESS, CHILDRESS CO., HOLY ANGELS
P.O. Box 608, Childress, 79201. Rev. Nicholas J. Gerber.
Res.: 308 Ave. B, S.W., Childress, 79201.
Tel: 940-937-3946; Fax: 940-937-0668; Email: pastor@holyangelchildresstx.com; Web: www.holyangelchildresstx.com.
Catechesis Religious Program—P.O. Box 192, Childress, 79201. Elizabeth Oronia, D.R.E. Students 63.

CLARENDON, DONLEY CO., ST. MARY'S
815 McClelland St., P.O. Drawer C, Clarendon, 79226. Tel: 806-874-3910; Email: samraj_1973@yahoo.co.in. Rev. Arokia Raj Samala.
Catechesis Religious Program—Students 26.

DALHART, HARTLEY CO., ST. ANTHONY OF PADUA
411 E. Texas Blvd., Dalhart, 79022.
Tel: 806-244-4128; Email: jlawrence2002@gmail.com. P.O. Box 1029, Dalhart, 79022. Rev. Lawrence John, J.C.L.; Deacon Louis Paul Artho.
Res.: 410 E. 13th, Box 1029, Dalhart, 79022.
School—St. Anthony of Padua School, (Grades K-6), P.O. Box 1329, Dalhart, 79022. Tel: 806-244-4811; Email: batenhorst@mysapcs.net. Mrs. Shay Batenhorst, Principal. Lay Teachers 11; Students 110; Clergy / Religious Teachers 1.
Catechesis Religious Program—Jovita Anzaldua, D.R.E.; Suzanne Foley, C.R.E.; Deacon Michael Anzaldua, Youth Min. Students 272.
Convent—School Sisters of St. Francis 2.
Mission—St. Mary's, Texline, Dallum Co.. Students 272.

DIMMITT, CASTRO CO., IMMACULATE CONCEPTION
1001 W. Halsell St., Dimmitt, 79027.
Tel: 806-647-4219; Tel: 806-647-0105; Email: iccdimmitt@windstream.net; Web: www.iccdimmitt.org. 905 W. Halsell St., Dimmitt, 79027. Rev. Arokiaraj Malapady; Deacons Jose Garcia; John Nino; Richard Martinez, RCIA Coord.
Catechesis Religious Program—Gloria Hernandez, D.R.E. Students 251.
Mission—St. John Nepomucene, 312 7th St., Hart, Castro Co. 79043. Tel: 806-938-2936; Email: saintjohnhart@gmail.com. P.O. Box 288, Hart, 79043. Mary Chavez, Sec.

DUMAS, MOORE CO., SS. PETER AND PAUL
915 S. Maddox, Dumas, 79029. Email: stspeterandpaul@hotmail.com; Web: www.sppdumas.org. P.O. Box 503, Dumas, 79029. Rev. Gabriel Garcia, O.F.M.
Catechesis Religious Program—Ofelia Garbalena, D.R.E. Students 436.
Mission—Christ the King, P.O. Box 681, Sunray, Moore Co. 79086. Deacon Wayne Norrell.

FRIONA, PARMER CO., ST. TERESA OF JESUS, Rev. Gregory Bunyan; Deacon Jose Correa.
Res.: 401 W. 17th, Friona, 79035-9601.
Tel: 806-250-2871; Fax: 806-250-3549; Email: greg_bunyanz@hotmail.com.
Catechesis Religious Program—Students 175.

GROOM, CARSON CO., IMMACULATE HEART OF MARY, [CEM] Rev. Arokia Raj Samala.
Res.: 411 Ware Ave., P.O. Box 130, Groom, 79039.
Tel: 806-248-7584; Email: samraj_1973@yahoo.co.in.
Catechesis Religious Program—Nicole Kuehler, D.R.E. Students 31.

GRUVER, HANSFORD CO., CRISTO REDENTOR
202 E. Hwy. 15, P.O. Box 238, Gruver, 79040.
Tel: 806-659-2166; Tel: 806-644-2166; Email: sacredheartspearmancatholic@gmail.com; Web: www.sacredheartspearman.com. Rev. Anthony Raju Yanamala, Admin.; Deacon Davin Winger.
Mailing Address: P.O. Box 127, Spearman, 79081.
Catechesis Religious Program—Sugueila Garcia, D.R.E. Students 2.

HAPPY, SWISHER CO., HOLY NAME OF JESUS, [CEM]
2610 4th Ave., Umbarger, 79015. Rev. Grant Spinhirne, Admin.
Res.: 317 W. Main, P.O. Box 128, Happy, 79042.
Tel: 806-558-2871; Tel: 806-499-3531; Email: frgrantspinhirne@gmail.com.
Catechesis Religious Program—Students 6.

HEREFORD, DEAF SMITH CO.

1—ST. ANTHONY'S
Tel: 806-364-6150; Fax: 806-364-0969; Email: stanthonyshfd@wtrt.net. Rev. Anthony Carl Neusch.
Business Office—114 Sunset Dr., Hereford, 79045.
Res.: 115 N. 25 Mile Ave., Hereford, 79045.
School—St. Anthony Catholic School, (Grades PreK-6), 120 W. Park Ave., Hereford, 79045.
Tel: 806-364-1952; Email: mrscopeland@stanthonysaints.com; Web: www.

stanthonysaints.com. Anna Copeland, Prin. Lay Teachers 11; Students 110.
Catechesis Religious Program—Aracely Correa, D.R.E. Students 45.

2—SAN JOSE, Revs. Jose Ramon Molina Mora, Parochial Admin.; Nestor Lara, Vicar; Deacons Richard Mendez; Paul Herrera Jr.
Res.: 735 Brevard, Hereford, 79045.
Tel: 806-364-5053; Fax: 806-364-2880; Email: sanjosechurch@gmx.com.
Catechesis Religious Program—Elda Lucio, D.R.E.

MEMPHIS, HALL CO., SACRED HEART
Mailing Address: 213 N. Third St., P.O. Box 239, Memphis, 79245. Tel: 806-259-2178; Email: pastor@sacredheartmemphistx.com; Web: www.sacredheartmemphistx.com. Rev. Nicholas J. Gerber.
Catechesis Religious Program—Students 36.

NAZARETH, CASTRO CO., HOLY FAMILY, Rev. Bhaskar Adusupalli, Admin.; Deacon Bob Birkenfeld.
Res.: 210 St. Joseph, P.O. Box 100, Nazareth, 79063.
Tel: 806-945-2616; Fax: 806-945-2564; Email: holyfamily@hfpn.org; Web: www.hfpn.org.
Catechesis Religious Program—201 St. Joseph St, Nazareth, 79063. Gladys Fortenberry, D.R.E. Students 167.

PAMPA, GRAY CO., ST. VINCENT DE PAUL, Very Rev. Francisco Perez, J.C.L.; Rev. Juan Carlos Barragan, Vicar.
Res.: 810 W. 23rd Ave., Pampa, 79065.
Tel: 806-665-8933; Fax: 806-665-2840.
Catechesis Religious Program—Marian Dawes, D.R.E. Students 326.

PANHANDLE, CARSON CO., ST. THERESA
125 Little Flower Way, P.O. Box 366, Panhandle, 79068. Tel: 806-537-3677; Email: sgarner@dioama.org; Web: www.theresacatholicchurchpanhandletexas.org. Rev. Hrudaya Kondamudi.
Catechesis Religious Program—Students 8.

PERRYTON, OCHILTREE CO., IMMACULATE CONCEPTION
1000 S.W. 15th Ave., Perryton, 79070.
Tel: 806-435-3802; Fax: 806-648-1490; Email: icccptx@gmail.com. Rev. Cesar Gomez; Deacon Sergio Estrada.
Catechesis Religious Program—Sr. Carol Prenger, S.S.N.D., D.R.E. Students 490.
Mission—St. Peter, Booker, Lipscomb Co.. Deacon Felix Tudon.

SHAMROCK, WHEELER CO., ST. PATRICK, Merged with Sacred heart Church, Canadian.
Tel: 806-256-5358; Email: saintpatricksrock14@yahoo.com.
Catechesis Religious Program—Students 16.

SILVERTON, BRISCOE CO., OUR LADY OF LORETTO
303 Pulitzer St., Silverton, 79257. Tel: 806-823-2548; Email: arturomeza59@yahoo.com. Rev. Msgr. Arturo Meza.
Catechesis Religious Program—Students 10.
Mission—St. Juan Diego, P.O. Box 62, Quitaque, 79255.

SPEARMAN, HANSFORD CO., SACRED HEART, Rev. Anthony Raju Yanamala, Admin.; Deacon Davin Winger.
Res.: 901 S. Roland, P.O. Box 127, Spearman, 79081.
Tel: 806-659-2166; Fax: 806-644-2166; Email: sacredheartspearmancatholic@gmail.com; Web: www.sacredheartspearman.com.
Catechesis Religious Program—Olivia Mendoza, D.R.E. Students 33.
Mission—Cristo Redentor, P.O. Box 238, Gruver, Hansford Co. 79040.

STRATFORD, SHERMAN CO., ST. JOSEPH'S
Mailing Address: 515 S. Pearl St., Box 28, Stratford, 79084. Tel: 806-366-5687; Email: robertoRobledo7@hotmail.ocm. Rev. Roberto Robledo.
Catechesis Religious Program—Students 107.
Mission—Our Lady of Guadalupe, Box 28, Cactus, Sherman Co. 79084.

TULIA, SWISHER CO., CHURCH OF THE HOLY SPIRIT
513 S. Austin, P.O. Box 806, Tulia, 79088.
Tel: 806-994-3511; Fax: 806-994-3510; Email: holyspirit_saintpaul@hotmail.com. Rev. David Contreras; Deacon Jackie Gunnels. In Res.
Catechesis Religious Program—200 S.E. 5th St., P.O. Box 806, Tulia, 79088. Mayra Vega, D.R.E. Students 155.
Mission—St. Paul the Apostle, P.O. Box 231, Kress, Swisher Co. 79052. Tel: 806-823-2548.

TURKEY, HALL CO., ELIZABETH ANN SETON, Rev. Msgr. Arturo Meza.
Res.: 902 Alexander Ave., P.O. Box 206, Turkey, 79261. Tel: 806-823-2548; Email: arturomeza59@yahoo.com.
Catechesis Religious Program—

UMBARGER, RANDALL CO., ST. MARY'S, [CEM]
22830 Pondaseta Rd., Umbarger, 79091.
Tel: 806-499-3531; Email: stmarysumb@midplains.coop; Web: stmarysumbarger.com. Rev. Grant Spinhirne, Admin.
Res.: P.O. Box 105, Umbarger, 79091.
Catechesis Religious Program—Students 40.

VEGA, OLDHAM CO., IMMACULATE CONCEPTION
905 S. Main St', Vega, 79092. Tel: 806-286-0149. P.O. Box 250, Vega, 79092. Rev. Mieczyslaw Mitchell Przepiora.
Catechesis Religious Program—Michelle Baca, D.R.E. Students 62.

WELLINGTON, COLLINGSWORTH CO., OUR MOTHER OF MERCY, Rev. Nicholas J. Gerber.
Church: 1108 Floydada, P.O. Box 686, Wellington, 79095. Tel: 806-256-5358; Email: saintpatricksrock14@yahoo.com; Web: ourmotherofmercywellingtontx.com.
Catechesis Religious Program—Jennifer Lopez, D.R.E. Students 38.

WHITE DEER, CARSON CO., SACRED HEART CATHOLIC CHURCH
500 N. Main St., White Deer, 79097.
Tel: 806-883-4781; Email: sacredheartchurchwhitedeer@gmail.com. P.O. Box 427, White Deer, 79097. Rev. Hrudaya Kondamudi.
Catechesis Religious Program—Catherina Stokes, D.R.E. Students 9.

In Residence of the Diocese of Amarillo:
Rev.—
Matthew, Ron, Hartly, Texas.

On Duty Outside the Diocese:
Revs.—
Afunugo, Emmanuel, D.D.
Rosolen, Emil.

Unassigned:
Revs.—
Dreher, Daniel A.
Lindley, Philip
Pavone, Frank
Phan, Phu T., J.C.L.
Raef, Scott.

Retired:
Rev. Msgrs.—
Bixenman, Joseph E., (Retired)
Kuehler, Norbert, (Retired), 4210 N.E. 18th, 79107. Chaplain Franciscan Sisters
Malnar, Matthew, (Retired), Independence, WI
Waldow, Harold L., (Retired), 6707 Club Meadows Dr., 79124
Revs.—
Greka, David, (Retired), Allpena, MI
Sweeney, Edward, (Retired), 2400 E. Willow Creek, 79108.

Permanent Deacons:
Alarcon, Alfredo, St. Laurence Church, Amarillo
Allein, Bill, (Retired)
Anzaldua, Michael, St. Anthony of Padua, Dalhart
Aranda, Robert, St. Mary's Cathedral, Amarillo
Artho, Louis Paul, St. Anthony's Church, Dalhart
Artho, Raymond, Immaculate Conception, Vega
Beauchamp, Joe, (Retired)
Birkenfeld, Bob, Holy Family Church, Nazareth
Brockman, Jerome, (Retired)
Brown, Jim, (Retired)
Castaneda, Jose Joaquin, St. Joseph, Amarillo
Chavez, Teodoro, St. Ann's Church, Bovina
Cloud, Jonny E., (Retired)
Correa, Jose, St. Teresa's Church, Friona
Dorsey, Bill, (Retired)
Duenes, David, St. Laurence Church, Amarillo
Esparza, Armando, Our Lady of Guadalupe, Amarillo
Estrada, Sergio, Immaculate Conception, Perryton
Frausto, Joseph, (Retired), (On Leave of Absence)
Garcia, Jose, Immaculate Conception, Dimmitt
Gonzalez, Andy, Our Lady of Guadalupe, Amarillo
Guerrero, Jesse, (Retired)
Gunnells, Jackie, Church of the Holy Spirit, Tulia
Gutierrez, Jose Jesus, Sacred Heart Church, Canadian
Hein, Ronald, (Inactive)
Herrera, Paul Jr., San Jose, Hereford
Hochstein, Joe, Holy Family, Nazareth
Jimenez, Zeferino, (Retired)
Knox, Beck, (Retired)
Lewis, Bryan L., Blessed Sacrament, Amarillo
Martinez, Richard, Immaculate Conception, Dimmitt
Mason, Wilbur, (Retired)
McVay, Mark, St. Vincent de Paul, Pampa
Mendez, Ricardo, San Jose Church, Hereford
Morales, Pablo, St. Laurence Church, Amarillo
Nino, John, Immaculate Conception, Dimmitt
Norrell, Wayne, Christ the King Church, Sunray
Perez, Jesus Rene, Blessed Sacrament Church, Amarillo
Peters, John, St. Mary's, Amarillo
Pevehouse, Terry, (Retired)
Ramos, Leo, (Retired)
Rausch, John David, St. Ann's Church, Amarillo
Rivas, Gabriel, St. Ann's Church, Canyon
Schwertner, Arnold, St. Hyacinth's, Amarillo
Seidlitz, Mark, Blessed Sacrament Church, Amarillo
Smith, Robert, St. Mary's Church, Amarillo
Tovar, Miguel, St. Laurence Church, Amarillo
Tudon, Felix, St. Peter's, Booker
Valdez, Pete, (Retired)
Westlake, Blaine, St. Thomas Church, Amarillo; Dir. of Diaconate, Safe Environment Office
Whitson, Phillip Eugene, St. Thomas the Apostle, Amarillo; CFO Diocese of Amarillo
Wilhelm, Joseph, St. Hyacinth's, Amarillo
Winger, Davin, Sacred Heart, Spearman.

INSTITUTIONS LOCATED IN DIOCESE

[A] HIGH SCHOOLS, CITY-WIDE

AMARILLO. *Holy Cross Catholic Academy*, (Grades 6-12), (Coed) 4110 S. Bonham, 79110-1113.
Tel: 806-355-9637; Fax: 806-353-9520; Email: hcca@holycrossama.org; Web: www.holycrossama.org. Angela Seidenberger, Head of School. Lay Teachers 19; Priests 1; Sisters 1; Students 100.

[B] ELEMENTARY SCHOOLS, CITY-WIDE

AMARILLO. *St. Joseph's School* aka St. Joseph Catholic Elementary and Montessori Preschool, (Grades PreK-5), 4118 S. Bonham St., 79110.
Tel: 806-359-1604; Fax: 806-359-1605; Email: office@stjosephlearning.com; Email: d.hernandez@stjosephlearning.com; Web: www.stjosephschoolamarillo.com. David Hernandez, Prin.
St. Joseph Catholic Elementary and Montessori Preschool Lay Teachers 12; Sisters 1; Students 155; Clergy / Religious Teachers 1.
St. Mary's Cathedral School, (Grades K-5), 1200 S. Washington St., 79102. Tel: 806-376-9112; Fax: 806-376-4314; Email: aranda@stmarysamarillo.com; Web: www.stmarysamarillo.org. Linda Aranda, Prin.; Amanda McDonald, Librarian; Lora Hoelting, Montessori Dir. Clergy 4; Lay Teachers 20; Sisters 2; Students 205.

[C] HOMES FOR THE AGED

PANHANDLE. *St. Joseph's Home for Retired Priests*, P.O. Box 1444, Panhandle, 79068. Cell: 806-570-0844. Rev. James Hutzler, (Retired).

[D] COALITION OF CATHOLIC SOCIAL SERVICES

AMARILLO. *Catholic Charities of the Texas Panhandle*, 2801 Dunivan Cir., 19109. Tel: 806-376-4571;
Fax: 806-345-7911; Email: jgulde@cctxp.org; Web: www.cctxp.org. Box 15127, 79105-5127. Jeff Gulde, Exec. Dir. Tot Asst. Annually 3,996; Total Staff 53.
Downtown Women's Center, Inc., 409 S. Monroe, 79101. Tel: 806-372-3625; Fax: 806-372-9026; Email: diann@dwcenter.org; Web: www.dwcenter.org. Diann Gilmore, Exec. Dir. Bed Capacity 147; Tot Asst. Annually 284; Total Staff 49.

[E] CATHOLIC CHILDREN'S DEVELOPMENT CENTERS

AMARILLO. *Amarillo Catholic Children's Development Centers*, 4108 Bonham St., P.O. Box 19726, 79110.
Tel: 806-353-7043; Email: sgarner@dioama.org. Gail Saiz, Contact Person. Students 140; Teachers 5; Caregivers 11.
St. Joseph Catholic Elementary and Montessori Preschool, 4118 S. Bonham St, 79110.
Tel: 806-359-1604; Web: www.stjosephschoolamarillo.com. David Hernandez, Prin. Lay Teachers 12; Priests 1; Sisters 1; Students 155.

[F] RETREAT HOUSES

AMARILLO. *Bishop DeFalco Retreat Center*, 2100 N. Spring St., 79107. Tel: 806-383-1811;
Fax: 806-383-6919; Email: general@bdrc.org; Web: www.bdrc.org. Linda Astuto, Exec. Dir.
Bishop DeFalco Retreat Center Foundation, 2100 N. Spring St., 79107. Tel: 806-383-1811; Email: general@bdrc.org; Web: www.bdrc.org. Linda Astuto, Dir.

CHANNING. *Prayer Town Emmanuel Retreat House*, 404 Holy Way, P.O. Box 64, Prayer Town, 79010.
Tel: 806-534-2207; Tel: 806-534-2312;
Fax: 806-534-2223; Web: www.dljc.org. Mother

Juana Teresa Chung, D.L.J.C., Supr. The Disciples of the Lord Jesus Christ. Sisters 40.

[G] CONVENTS AND RESIDENCES FOR SISTERS

AMARILLO. *St. Francis Convent, Novitiate and U.S. Provincial House*, 4301 N.E. 18th St., 79107. Tel: 806-383-5769; Email: stfrancisconvent@outlook.com; Web: franciscansistersofmaryimmaculate.net. Sisters Valentine A. Curry, F.M.I., Vicar; Liliana Salazar, Supr. Franciscan Sisters of Mary Immaculate of the Third Order of St. Francis. Sisters 20.

Madres Clarisas Capuchinas, Capuchin Nuns of St. Clare, 4201 N.E. 18th Ave., 79107. Tel: 806-383-9877; Tel: (806) 383-6771; Email: clarescap@gmail.com. Sr. Maria De La Luz Solorio, Abbess. Convent of the Blessed Sacrament and Our Lady of Guadalupe Sisters 16.

CHANNING. *Disciples of the Lord Jesus Christ*, 404 Holy Way, Prayer Town, 79010. P.O. Box 64, Prayer Town, 79010. Tel: 806-534-2312; Fax: 806-534-2223; Email: dljcsisters@gmail.com; Web: www.dljc.org. Mother Juana Teresa Chung, D.L.J.C., Supr. Gen.; Rev. Mieczyslaw Mitchell Przepiora, Chap. Sisters 40.

PANHANDLE. *Sancta Maria Convent (North American Region and Novitiate)*, 119 Franciscan Way, P.O. Box 906, Panhandle, 79068-0906. Tel: 806-537-3182; Fax: 806-537-5498; Email: schsrs@gmail.com; Web: www.panhandlefranciscans.org. Sr. Mary Michael Husemam, Regl. Supr. School Sisters of the Third Order of St. Francis. Sisters 18.

[H] CAMPUS MINISTRY

CANYON. *Catholic Student Center at West Texas A & M University*, 2610 Fourth Ave., Canyon, 79015. Tel: 806-655-4345; Fax: 806-655-0534; Email: csc@wtcsc.com; Web: www.wtcsc.org. Rev. Grant Spinhirne, Dir.; Betty Aragon, Asst. Dir.

[I] MISCELLANEOUS LISTINGS

AMARILLO. *Amarillo Catholic School System*, 4512 N.E. 24th Ave., 79107. Tel: 806-383-2243, Ext. 110; Fax: 806-383-8452; Email: sgarner@dioama.org. Rev. Robert A. Busch, Ph.D., Supt. of Catholic Schools.

Amarillo Scholarship Endowment and Assistance Fund, 4512 N. E. 24th Ave., 79117-5644. Tel: 806-383-2243; Fax: 806-383-8452. Rev. Robert A. Busch, Ph.D., Supt. of Catholic Schools.

**Catholic Radio of the Texas High Plains*, 4037 S.W. 50th Ave., Ste. 101, 79109. Tel: 806-350-1360; Email: stval@kdjw.org; Web: www.kdjw.org. Dale Artho, Pres.

Engaged Encounter, 9205 Clint Ave., 79119. Tel: 806-383-2243, Ext. 116; Tel: 806-336-5180; Email: AVillegas@dioama.org; Web: amarillodiocese.org. Deacon Henry Wilhelm, Dir.

Holy Family Parish of Nazareth, Texas Endowment Foundation, Diocese of Amarillo, 4512 N. E. 24th Ave., 79107. Tel: 806-383-2243; Fax: 806-383-8452; Email: pwhitson@amarillodiocese.org. Deacon Phil Whitson, CFO; Most Rev. Patrick J. Zurek, D.D., Bd.; Rev. Bhaskar Adusupalli.

Marriage Encounter, 2610 4th Ave., Canyon, 79015. Cell: 806-367-4606; Email: s.c.schwind@gmail.com. Patrick Kratochvil, Ecclesiastical Team; Virginia Kratochvil, Ecclesiastical Team; Rev. Christopher Schwind, Spiritual Advisor.

Monsignor B.A. Erpen Trust Fund (1985) Diocese of Amarillo, 4512 N. E. 24th Ave., 79107. Tel: 806-383-2243; Fax: 806-383-8452; Email: pwhitson@dioama.org. Deacon Phil Whitson, CFO; Most Rev. Patrick J. Zurek, D.D., Trustee; Rev. Msgr. Harold L. Waldow, Trustee, (Retired).

Project Solidarity (1999) Diocese of Amarillo, 4512 N. E. 24th Ave., 79107. Tel: 806-383-2243; Fax: 806-383-8452; Email: mcolwell@amarillodiocese.org. Rev. Christopher Schwind, Chancellor.

Roman Catholic Diocese of Amarillo Deposit and Loan Fund, 4512 N. E. 24th Ave., 79107. Tel: 806-383-2243; Fax: 806-383-8452; Email: pwhitson@amarillodiocese.org. Deacon Phil Whitson, CFO; Most Rev. Patrick J. Zurek, D.D.; Rev. Msgr. Joseph E. Bixenman, (Retired).

Texas Panhandle Catholic Endowment Foundation (1985) 4512 N. E. 24th Ave., 79107. Tel: 806-383-2243; Fax: 806-383-8452; Email: pwhitson@amarillodiocese.org. Most Rev. Patrick J. Zurek, D.D., Trustee; Robert Neslage, Trustee; Ed Wieck, Trustee; Frank Walsh, Trustee; Daniel Martinez, Trustee; Dr. Anh My Do, Trustee.

RELIGIOUS INSTITUTES OF MEN REPRESENTED IN THE DIOCESE

For further details refer to the corresponding bracketed number in the Religious Institutes of Men or Women section.

[]—*Congregation of Mother Coredemptrix*—C.M.C.

[]—*Crusaders of the Holy Spirit*—C.H.S.

RELIGIOUS INSTITUTES OF WOMEN REPRESENTED IN THE DIOCESE

[]—*Congregation of the School Sisters of Notre Dame*—S.S.N.D.

[0965]—*Disciples of the Lord Jesus Christ*—D.L.J.C.

[1500]—*Franciscan Sisters of Mary Immaculate of the Third Order of St. Francis of Assisi*—F.M.I.

[1695]—*School Sisters of the Third Order of St. Francis, (Panhandle, Texas)*—O.S.F.

[]—*St. Clare Capuchin Sisters*—C.P.C.

NECROLOGY

† Stalter, Cal, (Retired), Died Aug. 6, 2018

† Keller, Ken, Nazareth, TX Holy Family, Died Mar. 1, 2018

An asterisk (*) denotes an organization that has established tax-exempt status directly with the IRS and is not covered by the USCCB Group Ruling.

Archdiocese of Anchorage

(Archidioecesis Ancoragiensis)

Most Reverend

ANDREW E. BELLISARIO, C.M.

Apostolic Administrator of Anchorage and Bishop of Juneau; ordained June 16, 1984; appointed Bishop of Juneau July 11, 2017; ordained and installed October 10, 2017; appointed Apostolic Administrator of Anchorage June 7, 2019.

(VACANT SEE)

Chancery Office: 225 Cordova St., Anchorage, AK 99501. Tel: 907-297-7700; Fax: 907-279-3041.

Web: www.archdioceseofanchorage.org

ESTABLISHED FEBRUARY 9, 1966.

Square Miles 138,985.

Comprises the Third Judicial Division of Alaska.

For legal titles of parishes and archdiocesan institutions, consult the Chancery Office.

STATISTICAL OVERVIEW

Personnel	
Retired Archbishops	1
Priests: Diocesan Active in Diocese	12
Priests: Diocesan Active Outside Diocese	1
Priests: Diocesan in Foreign Missions	1
Priests: Retired, Sick or Absent	4
Number of Diocesan Priests	18
Religious Priests in Diocese	12
Total Priests in Diocese	30
Extern Priests in Diocese	9
Ordinations:	
Transitional Deacons	1
Permanent Deacons in Diocese	27
Total Brothers	1
Total Sisters	23
Parishes	
Parishes	23
With Resident Pastor:	
Resident Diocesan Priests	7
Resident Religious Priests	7
Without Resident Pastor:	
Administered by Priests	7
Administered by Deacons	1
Administered by Professed Religious Men	1
Missions	7
Pastoral Centers	1
Professional Ministry Personnel:	
Brothers	1
Sisters	5
Lay Ministers	22
Welfare	
Catholic Hospitals	4
Total Assisted	109,144
Special Centers for Social Services	4
Total Assisted	28,992
Educational	
Diocesan Students in Other Seminaries	2
Total Seminarians	2
High Schools, Diocesan and Parish	1
Total Students	46
High Schools, Private	1
Total Students	31
Elementary Schools, Diocesan and Parish	4
Total Students	298
Elementary Schools, Private	1
Total Students	92
Catechesis/Religious Education:	
High School Students	822
Elementary Students	1,062
Total Students under Catholic Instruction	2,353
Teachers in the Diocese:	
Lay Teachers	46
Vital Statistics	
Receptions into the Church:	
Infant Baptism Totals	359
Minor Baptism Totals	40
Adult Baptism Totals	43
Received into Full Communion	59
First Communions	407
Confirmations	315
Marriages:	
Catholic	66
Interfaith	29
Total Marriages	95
Deaths	119
Total Catholic Population	24,115
Total Population	481,023

Former Archbishops—Most Revs. JOSEPH T. RYAN, D.D., Archbishop of Anchorage; ord. June 3, 1939; cons. March 25, 1966; installed April 14, 1966; transferred to as Coadjutor Military Vicar of U.S. Armed Forces Dec. 13, 1975; appt. First Archbishop of the Archdiocese for the Military Services, U.S.A., March 16, 1985; died Oct. 9, 2000; FRANCIS T. HURLEY, D.D., Archbishop of Anchorage; ord. June 16, 1951; appt. Titular Bishop of Daimlaig and Auxiliary of Juneau, Feb. 4, 1970; cons. March 19, 1970; appt. Bishop of Juneau, July 20, 1971; installed Sept. 8, 1971; appt. Archbishop of Anchorage, May 4, 1976; installed July 8, 1976; retired March 3, 2001; died Jan. 10, 2016.; ROGER L. SCHWIETZ, O.M.I., D.D., (Retired), ord. Dec. 20, 1967; appt. Bishop of Duluth Dec. 12, 1989; cons. and installed Bishop of Duluth Feb. 2, 1990; appt. Coadjutor Archbishop of Anchorage Jan. 18, 2000; Succeeded to the See March 3, 2001; retired Nov. 9, 2016.

Chancellor/Chief of Staff—JOHN T. HARMON, Tel: 907-297-7702.

Vicar General—Very Rev. THOMAS C. LILLY, V.G., Tel: 907-273-1555.

Pastoral Center—

Chancellor/Chief of Staff—JOHN T. HARMON, Tel: 907-297-7702.

Secretary to Archbishop Paul D. Etienne, D.D., S.T.L.—MRS. KIMBERLY BAKIC, Tel: 907-297-7755.

Secretary to Archbishop Emeritus Roger L. Schwietz, O.M.I.—MRS. JESSICA ESTES, Tel: 907-297-7720.

Stewardship/Development Office—Tel: 907-297-7790. VACANT, Dir.; MELISSA HERNANDEZ, Devel. Assoc.

Tribunal—225 Cordova St., Anchorage, 99501-2409. Tel: 907-297-7724.

Judicial Vicar—Rev. PATRICK TRAVERS, J.C.L., J.D.

Judge—Deacon WILLIAM FINNEGAN, J.C.L.

Defender of the Bond—Rev. SCOTT GARRETT, J.C.L.

Notaries—Sr. JOAN OBERLE, C.PP.S.; ANGIE CAGLE, Administrative Asst., Tel: 907-297-7724.

Diocesan Consultors—Very Rev. THOMAS C. LILLY, V.G.; Revs. SCOTT MEDLOCK; SCOTT GARRETT, J.C.L.; VINCENT BLANCO; ARTHUR RORAFF; SHIJO KANJIRATHAMKUNNEL, C.M.

Archdiocesan Offices and Directors

Apostleship of the Sea—Port Chaplain: SALLY BOSTWICK, Anchorage.

Archdiocesan Newspaper—Catholic Anchor JOEL DAVIDSON, Editor, Pastoral Center, 225 Cordova St., Anchorage, 99501. Tel: 907-297-7730.

Magadan Mission—Rev. MICHAEL SHIELDS.

Campaign for Human Development—Deacon JAMES MICK FORNELLI.

Catholic Social Services—3710 E. 20th Ave., Anchorage, 99508. Tel: 907-222-7300; Fax: 907-258-1091. LISA AQUINO, Exec. Dir., Tel: 907-222-7351; SARAH MOURACADE, Communications Mgr.; KJERSTI LANGNES, Deputy Dir., Tel: 907-222-7338.

Board Members—MICHAEL FREDERICKS; CINDY GOUGH; STORMY JARVIS; WALTER WILLIAMS; ELAINE KROLL; GERARD DIEMER; CHRISTIAN MUNTEAN; MARK FINEMAN; JOHN CONWAY; LISA BRUNER; ANCHALA KLEIN; JEFF BAIRD.

Ex Officio—Rev. SCOTT MEDLOCK.

Hispanic Ministry—Sr. MARY PETER DIAZ, D.C.

Korean Ministry—Rev. PETER KIM, 7206 Lake Otis Pkwy., Anchorage, 99507. Tel: 907-333-5307; Fax: 907-333-2888.

Native Ministry—Sr. MARY PETER DIAZ, D.C.

Office of Catechesis & Catholic Schools—BONNIE BEZOUSEK, Dir., Tel: 907-297-7732.

Office of Evangelization & Discipleship—MATTHEW BECK, Dir., Tel: 907-297-7734.

Office of Finance—MS. MONIKA SCOTT, CFO, Tel: 907-297-7723.

Office of Safe Environment—JENNIFER MICHAELSON, Dir., Tel: 907-297-7729.

Permanent Diaconate—Deacon JAMES MICK FORNELLI, Tel: 907-223-1090.

Holy Spirit Center—ALAN MUISE, Dir., 10980 Hillside Dr., Anchorage, 99507. Tel: 907-346-2343, Ext. 205.

Victim Assistance Coordinator—HEIDI CARSON, Tel: 907-297-7786.

Vocations—Rev. ARTHUR RORAFF.

Director of Seminarians—Very Rev. THOMAS C. LILLY, V.G.

CLERGY, PARISHES, MISSIONS AND PAROCHIAL SCHOOLS

CITY OF ANCHORAGE

1—HOLY FAMILY CATHEDRAL (1915) [JC]

Mailing Address: 811 W. 6th Ave., 99501-2093. Tel: 907-276-3455; Fax: 907-258-9785; Email: deacondave@holyfamilycathedral.org; Email: frontdesk@holyfamilycathedral.org; Web: holyfamilycathedral.org. Revs. Steve Maekawa, O.P.; Dominic David Maichrowicz, O.P., Parochial Vicar; Pius Youn, Parochial Vicar; Bro. Columban Hall, In Res.; Deacon David Van Tuyl.

Catechesis Religious Program—Toni Berkenbush, D.R.E. Students 82.

2—ST. ANDREW KIM, (Korean)
7206 Lake Otis Pkwy., 99507. Tel: 907-333-5307; Fax: 907-333-2888. Rev. Peter Kim, 7206 Lake Otis Pkwy., 99507. Tel: 907-333-5307; Fax: 907-333-2888
Legal Name: Corp. of St. Andrew Kim Parish of the Korean Community
Catechesis Religious Program—Students 32.
3—ST. ANTHONY, Rev. Vincent Blanco; John M. White, Admin.; Mrs. Mary Jo Cunniff, Liturgy Dir.
Res.: 825 Klevin St., 99508-2698. Tel: 907-333-5544; Fax: 888-571-0966.
Catechesis Religious Program—Ms. Jill Popoalii, D.R.E. Students 82.
4—ST. BENEDICT, Very Rev. Thomas C. Lilly, V.G.; Rev. Robert Whitney, Parochial Vicar.
Res.: 8110 Jewel Lake Rd., 99502. Tel: 907-243-2195; Fax: 907-243-0088; Email: parishsecretary@stbenedictsak.com; Web: www.stbenedictsak.com.
Catechesis Religious Program—Robert McMorrow II, D.R.E., Tel: 907-273-1552; Email: rmcmorrow@stbenedictsak.com. Students 53.
5—CORP. OF ST. CHRISTOPHER BY THE SEA CHURCH
107 Riverside, P.O. Box 405, Unalaska, 99685.
Tel: 907-581-4022; Email: stchrsea@yahoo.com. Rev. Daniel J. Hebert; Deacon Daniel Winters.
Catechesis Religious Program—Students 27.
6—ST. ELIZABETH ANN SETON (1975)
2901 E. Huffman Rd., 99516. Tel: 907-345-4466; Fax: 907-345-6361; Email: saintelizabeth.alaska@akseas.net; Web: www.akseas.net. Rev. Patrick Brosamer; Armand Dice; Deacons Kurt Adler; Michael Hawker; Dez Martinez.
Tel: 907-334-9633.
Catechesis Religious Program—Students 347.
Mission—Our Lady of the Snows
370 Northface Rd., Girdwood, 99587.
Tel: 907-783-1171; Email: reservations@chapelourladyofthesnows.org; Web: www.chapelourladyofthesnows.org. Maggie Donnelly, Tel: 907-783-1171; Email: akskidogs@gmail.com.
7—HOLY CROSS (1984) Rev. Andrew Lee, K.M.S.
Res.: 2627 Lore Rd., 99507-5722. Tel: 907-349-8388; Fax: 907-344-3388; Email: holycrossak@gmail.com; Web: www.holycrossalaska.net.
Catechesis Religious Program—Students 156.
8—OUR LADY OF GUADALUPE CO CATHEDRAL (1970) Revs. Shijo Kanjirathamkunnel, C.M., Rel. Order Leader; Henry Grodecki; Jesus Gabriel Medina Claro.
Res.: 3900 Wisconsin St., 99517. Tel: 907-248-2000; Email: olg@olgak.org.
Catechesis Religious Program—Students 181.
9—ST. PATRICK (1971) Revs. Scott Medlock; Daniel J. Hebert, Parochial Vicar; Deacons Felix Maguire; James Mick Fornelli.
Res.: 2111 Muldoon Rd., 99504-3612.
Tel: 907-337-1538; Fax: 907-337-5460; Web: www.st.patsak.org.
Catechesis Religious Program—John Barrientes, D.R.E., Tel: 907-337-1538. Students 231.
10—ST. PAUL MIKI, Closed. For inquiries for parish records contact St. Elizabeth Ann Seton Parish, Anchorage.

OUTSIDE THE CITY OF ANCHORAGE

BIG LAKE, MATANUSKA-SUSITNA BOROUGH, OUR LADY OF THE LAKE CHURCH (2007)
P.O. Box 520769, Big Lake, 99652. Tel: 907-892-6492; Fax: 907-892-6497; Email: frmichael@sacredheartwasilla.org. Revs. Joseph McGilloway, Canonical Pastor; Michael Ko, K.M.S.
Catechesis Religious Program—Students 26.
Mission—St. Christopher, P.O. Box 412, Willow, 99688.

CORDOVA, VALDEZ-CORDOVA CO., ST. JOSEPH
P.O. Box 79, Cordova, 99574. Rev. Michael Hak Hyeon Kim.
Res.: 220 Adams Ave., Cordova, 99574.
Tel: 907-424-3637; Email: stjoecor@gci.net.
Catechesis Religious Program—Students 37.

DILLINGHAM, DILLINGHAM CO., HOLY ROSARY, Rev. Scott Garrett, J.C.L.
Res.: 509 Airport Road, P.O. Box 810, Dillingham, 99576. Tel: 907-842-5581; Email: holyrosaryalaska@hotmail.com; Web: www.holyrosaryalaska.org.
Catechesis Religious Program—
Mission—St. Theresa, P.O. Box 269, Naknek, Bristol Bay Borough 99633.

EAGLE RIVER, ANCHORAGE BOROUGH, ST. ANDREW (1968) Rev. Arthur Roraff; Most Rev. Roger L. Schwietz, In Res.; Deacons Jim Lee; Mark Merrill.
Res.: 16300 Domain Ln., Eagle River, 99577.
Tel: 907-694-2170; Fax: 907-694-1385; Email: parishsecretary@aksaintandrews.org; Web: www.aksaintandrews.org.
Catechesis Religious Program—Students 255.

GLENNALLEN, VALDEZ-CORDOVA CO., HOLY FAMILY (1955)
Mailing Address: P.O. Box 126, Glennallen, 99588.
Cell: 907-350-8210; Email: hermon@mtaonline.net. Rev. Scott Medlock, Canonical Pastor; Deacon Jon Hermon, Parish Life Coord.
Catechesis Religious Program—Students 5.

HOMER, KENAI PENINSULA BOROUGH, ST. JOHN THE BAPTIST
255 Ohlson Ln., Homer, 99603. Tel: 907-235-8436; Email: st.john@gcl.net. Revs. Thomas Rush, O.M.I.; Roger Bergkamp, O.M.I.
Res.: 222 W. Redoubt Ave., Soldotna, 99669.
Mission—St. Peter the Apostle, Box 39290, Ninilchik, 99639. Tel: 907-567-3490.
Catechesis Religious Program—Students 19.

KENAI, KENAI PENINSULA BOROUGH, OUR LADY OF THE ANGELS
225 S. Spruce Rd., Kenai, 99611. Tel: 907-283-4555; Email: ladyoftheangels@gmail.com; Web: www.kenaicatholicchurch.org. Revs. Thomas Rush, O.M.I.; Roger Bergkamp, O.M.I.
Res.: 222 W. Redoubt Ave., Soldotna, 99669.
Tel: 907-262-4749.
Catechesis Religious Program—Students 97.

KODIAK, KODIAK ISLAND BOROUGH, ST. MARY'S St. Mary's Catholic Church, Rev. Frank Reitter.
Res.: 2934 Mill Bay Rd., Kodiak, 99615.
Tel: 907-486-5411; Fax: 907-486-2719; Email: saintmary@gci.net.
Catechesis Religious Program—Patilou Peralta, D.R.E., Tel: 907-539-2686; Email: cep_kidz@hotmail.com. Students 87.

PALMER, MATANUSKA-SUSITNA BOROUGH, ST. MICHAEL (1935)
Email: frontdesk@st-mikesparish.org. Most Reverend Paul D. Etienne, D.D., S.T.L.; Rev. Jaime Mencias, Parochial Vicar.
Res.: 432 E. Fireweed Ave., Palmer, 99645.
Tel: 907-745-3229; Email: frontdesk@st-mikesparish.org.
Catechesis Religious Program—Students 129.

SEWARD, KENAI PENINSULA BOROUGH, SACRED HEART (1910)
P.O. Box 770, Seward, 99664. Rev. Scott Medlock, Canonical Pastor; Deacon Walter Corrigan; Rev. Richard Tero, (Retired).
Res.: 409 Fifth Ave., Seward, 99664.
Tel: 907-224-5414; Email: walter.corrigan@gmail.com; Email: sacredheartseward@gmail.com.
Catechesis Religious Program—Students 35.
Mission—St. John Neumann Church, Snug Harbor Road, Cooper Landing, Cooper Landing.
Tel: 907-595-1300. P.O. Box 737, Cooper Landing, 99572.

SOLDOTNA, KENAI PENINSULA BOROUGH, OUR LADY OF PERPETUAL HELP (1961) Rev. Roger Bergkamp, O.M.I.; Deacon Dave Carey; Revs. Ronald Meyer; Thomas Rush, O.M.I.; Marlys Verba, Parish Life Coord.
Res.: 222 W. Redoubt Ave., Soldotna, 99669.
Tel: 907-262-4749; Email: marlys.verba@gmail.com.
Catechesis Religious Program—Tel: 907-262-5542. Students 70.

TALKEETNA, MATANUSKA-SUSITNA BOROUGH, ST. BERNARD (1970)
22036 S. F St., P.O. Box 510, Talkeetna, 99676.
Tel: 907-315-6120; Email: rstein@matnet.com. Renamary Rauchenstein, Parish Dir.; Rev. Joseph McGilloway, Canonical Pastor.
Mission—St. Philip Benizi, P.O. Box 13475, Trapper Creek, 99683.

VALDEZ, VALDEZ-CORDOVA CO., ST. FRANCIS XAVIER (1908) Revs. Scott Medlock, Canonical Pastor; Eric Wiseman; Deacon Daniel Stowe; Michael R. Franklin, Parish Life Dir.
Res.: 341 Pioneer Dr., P.O. Box 908, Valdez, 99686.
Tel: 907-835-4556; Email: stfrnxav@cvalaska.net.
Catechesis Religious Program—Kristina Brown, D.R.E. Students 12.

WASILLA, MATANUSKA-SUSITNA BOROUGH, SACRED HEART, [CEM] Rev. Joseph McGilloway.
Res.: 1201 E. Bogard Rd., Wasilla, 99654-6523.
Tel: 907-376-5087; Email: diane@sacredheartwasilla.org; Email: julie@sacredheartwasilla.org; Email: beverly@sacredheartwasilla.org; Email: shparish@mtaonline.net; Email: frjoseph@sacredheartwasilla.org; Web: www.sacredheartwasilla.org.
Catechesis Religious Program—Julie DeKreon, Email: . Students 185.

On Duty Outside Archdiocese:
Rev.—
Walsh, Leo, S.T.D., Rome, Italy.

Retired:
Revs.—
Abele, Alan Carl, (Retired)
Allie, Stanley, (Retired)
Bugarin, Fred, (Retired)
Desso, Leo C., (Retired)
Tero, Richard, (Retired).

Permanent Deacons:
Adler, Kurt, Anchorage
Allor, Raymond W., (Retired), Albany, OR
Azpilcueta, Gustavo, Anchorage
Cable, Jay, (Retired), Wasilla
Carey, David, Soldotna
Corrigan, Walter, Seward
Ernst, Richard, Pittsburgh
Finnegan, William, J.C.L., Anchorage
Foreman, Dennis, (Retired), Anchorage
Fornelli, James Mick, Anchorage
Frost, William, (Retired), Wasilla
Greene, Theodore, (Retired), Anchorage
Gunnell, Scott, Wasilla
Hawker, Michael, Anchorage
Hermon, Jon, Palmer
Larroque, Robert, (Retired), Portland, OR
Lee, Jim, Eagle River
Leuenberger, Curt, Palmer
Maguire, Felix M., (Retired), Tuscon
Maiman, Leslie T., Ph.D., Texas
Martinez, Dez, Anchorage
Merrill, Mark, Eagle River
Moore, Harry, Palmer
Ruiz, Gabriel, Anchorage
Schutt, David E., (Retired), Wasilla
Stowe, Daniel, (Retired), Valdez
Suley, David John, Maryland
Tunilla, Bill, Anchorage
Van Tuyl, David, Anchorage
Winters, Daniel, Dutch Harbor.

INSTITUTIONS LOCATED IN DIOCESE

[A] GRADE SCHOOLS, HIGH SCHOOLS PAROCHIAL

ANCHORAGE. *St. Elizabeth Ann Seton School*, (Grades 1-6), 2901 E. Huffman Rd., 99516.
Tel: 907-345-3712; Fax: 907-345-2910; Email: kathy@akseas.com; Web: www.akseas.com. Peggy Dennehy, Admin.; Kathy Gustafson, Prin. Lay Teachers & Staff 17; Students 169.
Holy Rosary Academy, (Grades K-12), 1010 W. Fireweed Ln., 99503. Tel: 907-276-5822;
Fax: 907-258-1055; Email: frontoffice@hraak.com; Web: www.hraak.com. Ann Williams, Prin.; Austin Welsh, Vice Prin.; John Fleming, Bd. Liaison; John Woyte, Business Mgr.; Robyn Woyte, Office Mgr. Lay Teachers 21; Students 123; Clergy / Religious Teachers 1.
Lumen Christi High School, (Grades 7-12), 8110 Jewel Lake Rd., Bldg. D., 99502. Tel: 907-245-9231 ; Fax: 907-245-9232; Email: lchs@lumenchristiak.com; Web: www.lumenchristiak.com. Brian Ross, Prin. Lay Teachers 12; Students 72; Clergy / Religious Teachers 2.

KODIAK. *St. Mary's*, (Grades PreK-8), 2932 Mill Bay Rd., Kodiak, 99615. Tel: 907-486-3513;
Fax: 907-486-3117; Email: tschneider@smskodiak.org; Email: arubina@smskodiak.org. Brian Cleary, Co-Prin.; Teri Schneider, Co-Prin., Email: tschneider@smskodiak.org. Lay Teachers 6; Students 80.

WASILLA. *Corp. of Our Lady of the Valley Catholic School, Inc.*, (Grades PreK-8), 1201 E. Bogard Rd., Wasilla, 99654. Tel: 907-376-0883; Email: ksmith@valleycatholicschool.org; Web: www.olvwasilla.com. Joyce Lund, Prin. Lay Teachers 8; Students 77; Staff 10.

[B] GENERAL HOSPITALS

ANCHORAGE. *Providence Alaska Medical Center*, 3200 Providence Dr., 99508. Tel: 907-212-2211;
Fax: 907-212-3041. c/o Providence Health & Svcs. - Alaska, P.O. Box 196501, 99519-6501. Dr. Michael Bernstein, Chief Medical Officer; Robert Honeycutt, Chief Operating Officer; Dr. Richard Mandsager, CEO. Properties, entities, and divisions owned or operated: Providence Health System-Washington; Providence Alaska Medical Center, Anchorage, AK, Providence Extended Care Center, Anchorage, AK, Providence Health System Housing dba Providence Horizon House, Anchorage, AK. Bed Capacity 401; Tot Asst. Annually 96,524; Total Staff 2,609.

KODIAK. *Providence Kodiak Island Medical Center*, 1915 E. Rezanof Dr., Kodiak, 99615.
Tel: 907-486-3281; Fax: 907-481-2336; Email: regina.bishop@providence.org. c/o Providence Health & Svcs. - Alaska, P.O. Box 196501, 99519-

6501. Gina Bishop, Admin. Bed Capacity 47; Tot Asst. Annually 7,780; Total Staff 224.

SEWARD. *Providence Seward Medical & Care Center*, 417 First Ave., Seward, 99664. Tel: 907-224-5205; Fax: 907-224-7248; Web: alaska.providence.org/locations/p/psmcc#llaid=5875. Mr. Donald Hanna, Admin. Bed Capacity 46; Tot Asst. Annually 2,294; Total Staff 134.

VALDEZ. *Providence Valdez Medical Center*, 911 Meals Ave., P.O. Box 550, Valdez, 99686-0550. Tel: 907-835-2249; Fax: 907-835-1980; Email: jeremy.oneil@providence.org. Mr. Jeremy O'Neil, Admin. Bed Capacity 21; Tot Asst. Annually 2,546; Total Staff 94.

[C] NURSING HOMES

ANCHORAGE. *Providence Extended Care*, 920 Compassion Cir., 99503. Tel: 907-212-9200; Fax: 907-212-9193; Email: angela.lewis@providence.org. Angela Lewis, Admin. *Sisters of Providence in Washington*. Bed Capacity 96; Tot Asst. Annually 31; Staff 185.

[D] CATHOLIC SOCIAL SERVICES

ANCHORAGE. *Brother Francis Shelter*, 1021 E. Third Ave., 99501. Tel: 907-277-1731; Email: klangnes@cssalaska.org; Email: ldhaquino@cssalaska.org; Web: www.cssalaska.org. 3710 E. 20th Ave., 99508. Lisa Aquino, Exec.; David Rittenberg, Dir.; Kjersti Langnes, Dir. Overnight shelter for homeless men and women. Bed Capacity 240; Tot Asst. Annually 3,479; Total Staff 17.

Catholic Social Services Center, 3710 E. 20th Ave., 99508. Tel: 907-222-7300; Fax: 907-258-1091; Email: info@cssalaska.org; Web: www.cssalaska.org. Lisa Aquino, Exec. Dir.; Kjersti Langnes, Deputy Dir.; Paul Bly, Finance Dir.; Tricia Teasley, Devel. & Community Rels. Dir.; Brigette Guzy, HR Dir.; Issa Spatrisano, Dir.; Kris Race, Dir.; Chris Kukay, Dir.; Sharese Hughes, Dir.; David Rittenberg, Prog. Dir.; Robin Dempsey, Prog. Dir.; Tami Jo Watson, Prog. Dir. Tot Asst. Annually 22,911; Total Staff 134.

Charlie Elder House, 3015 Yale Dr., 99508. Tel: 907-277-8622; Fax: 907-277-2326; Email: bstepp@cssalaska.org; Email: klangnes@cssalaska.org; Email: iinthaly@cssalaska.org; Email: ldhaquino@cssalaska.org; Web: www.cssalaska.org. 3710 E. 20th Ave., 99508. Lisa Aquino, Exec.; Kjersti Langnes, Dir.; Cheri Race, Dir.; Benita Stepp, Prog. Mgr. Tot Asst. Annually 11; Total Staff 2.

Clare House, 4110 Spenard Rd., 99517. Tel: 907-563-4545; Email: shughes@cssalaska.org; Email: klangnes@cssalaska.org; Email: ldhaquino@cssalaska.org; Web: www.cssalaska.org. 3710 E. 20th Ave., 99508. Lisa Aquino, Exec.; Kjersti Langnes, Dirl; Sharese Hughes, Prog. Dir. Temporary shelter for homeless women and women with children. Tot Asst. Annually 371; Total Staff 12.

[E] CONVENTS AND RESIDENCES FOR SISTERS

ANCHORAGE. *Daughters of Charity*, 3424 E. 15th Ave., 99508. Tel: 907-258-3424; Fax: 907-258-3424; Email: docanchorage@aol.com. Sr. Mary Peter Diaz, D.C., Sr. Servant. Sisters 3.

Sisters of Perpetual Adoration, 2645 E. 72nd Ave., 99507. Tel: 907-344-3330; Fax: 907-522-2945; Email: adoratricesak@gmail.com. Supr. Mother Evelia Alicia Martinez, Supr. Sisters 9.

Sisters of St. Paul de Chartres, 7206 Lake Otis Pkwy., 99507. 3005 W. 34th Ave., Apt. 4, 99517. Tel: 907-258-3273; Fax: 907-333-2888; Email: rl374@naver.com. Sisters Youngson Yoo, Contact Person; Hyeyong Hwang, Contact Person. Sisters 2.

[F] RETREAT HOUSES

ANCHORAGE. *Catholic Retreat House Ministries, Inc.* aka Holy Spirit Center, 10980 Hillside Dr., 99507. Tel: 907-297-7700; Fax: 907-279-3041; Email: hsc@holyspiritcenterak.org; Web: www.holyspiritcenterak.org. Alan Muise, Dir.

[G] MISCELLANEOUS

ANCHORAGE. *Alaska Conference of Catholic Bishops*, 225 Cordova St., 99501. Tel: 907-297-7744; Email: mgore@caa-ak.org. Ms. Mary Gore, Exec. Dir.

Archdiocese of Anchorage Priests Pension Trust, 225 Cordova St., 99501. Tel: 907-297-7723; Fax: 907-279-3041; Email: mscott@caa-ak.org. Ms. Monika Scott, Treas.

**St. Catherine of Siena CUF Chapter, Inc.*, P.O. Box 220106, 99522-0106. Tel: (907) 243-8168; Email: cufanchorage@gmail.com.

Catholic Foundation of Alaska, 225 Cordova St., 99501. Tel: 907-297-7723; Fax: 907-279-3885; Email: mscott@caa-ak.org. John T. Harmon, Chancellor.

Covenant House Alaska, 755 A St., 99501. Tel: 907-272-1255; Fax: 907-272-1466; Email: akear@covenanthouseak.org. PO Box 100620, 99510. Alison Kear, CEO. Comprehensive services for homeless, trafficked, and at-risk youth. Bed Capacity 103; Tot Asst. Annually 2,220; Total Staff 96.

Providence Alaska Foundation, Anchorage, Alaska, c/o Providence Health & Svcs. - Alaska, P.O. Box 196501, 99519-6501. Suzanne Rudolph, Pres. Total Staff 9.

Providence Horizon House, 4140 Folker St., 99508. Tel: 907-212-5340; Fax: 907-212-5360; Email: theresa.gleason@providence.org. c/o Providence Health & Svcs. - Alaska, P.O. Box 196501, 99519-6501. Theresa Gleason, Dir., Email: theresa.gleason@providence.org. Assisted Living Residents 79; Total Staff 68; Units 85.

Providence In-Home Services, 4001 Dale St., Suite 101, 99507. Tel: 907-563-0130; Fax: 907-563-0135; Email: deborah.seidl@providence.org. Deborah Seidl, Prog. Dir. Total Staff 73.

PALMER. *Bishop's Attic II, Inc.*, 840 S. Bailey St., Palmer, 99645. Tel: 907-745-4215; Fax: 907-745-4209; Email: thebishopsattic2@hotmail.com. Jack Williamson, Exec.

RELIGIOUS INSTITUTES OF MEN REPRESENTED IN THE ARCHDIOCESE

For further details refer to the corresponding bracketed number in the Religious Institutes of Men or Women section.

[1330]—*Congregation of the Western Mission*.
[]—*Korean Missionary Society*—K.M.S.
[0910]—*Oblates of Mary Immaculate*—O.M.I.
[0430]—*Order of Preachers-Dominicans* (Oakland Prov.)—O.P.

RELIGIOUS INSTITUTES OF WOMEN REPRESENTED IN THE ARCHDIOCESE

[0760]—*Daughters of Charity of St. Vincent DePaul*—D.C.
[2330]—*Little Sisters of Jesus*—L.S.J.
[3190]—*Nuns of Perpetual Adoration of the Blessed Sacrament* (Mexico)—A.P.
[3980]—*Sisters of St. Paul de Chartres*—S.P.C.
[]—*Sisters of the Eucharistic Heart of Jesus*—E.H.J.
[3270]—*Sisters of the Most Precious Blood* (O'Fallon, MO)—C.PP.S.

An asterisk (*) denotes an organization that has established tax-exempt status directly with the IRS and is not covered by the USCCB Group Ruling.

Diocese of Arlington

(Dioecesis Arlingtonensis)

Most Reverend

MICHAEL F. BURBIDGE, ED.D., D.D.

Bishop of Arlington; ordained May 19, 1984; appointed Auxiliary Bishop of Philadelphia and Titular Bishop of Cluain Iraird June 21, 2002; consecrated September 5, 2002; appointed Fifth Bishop of Raleigh June 8, 2006; installed August 4, 2006; appointed Fourth Bishop of Arlington October 4,2016; installed December 6, 2016. *The Chancery: 200 N. Glebe Rd., Ste. 914, Arlington, VA 22203.*

The Chancery: 200 N. Glebe Rd., Ste. 914, Arlington, VA 22203. Tel: 703-841-2500; Fax: 703-524-5028.

ESTABLISHED AUGUST 13, 1974.

Square Miles 6,541.

Comprises the following 21 Counties in Northern Virginia: Arlington, Clarke, Culpeper, Fairfax, Fauquier, Frederick, King George, Lancaster, Loudoun, Madison, Northumberland, Orange, Page, Prince William, Rappahannock, Richmond, Shenandoah, Spotsylvania, Stafford, Warren and Westmoreland and the 7 independent cities of Alexandria, Fairfax City, Falls Church, Fredericksburg, Manassas, Manassas Park and Winchester.

For legal titles of parishes and diocesan institutions, consult the Chancery Office.

STATISTICAL OVERVIEW

Personnel	
Bishop	1
Retired Bishops	1
Abbots	1
Priests: Diocesan Active in Diocese	138
Priests: Diocesan Active Outside Diocese	15
Priests: Diocesan in Foreign Missions	2
Priests: Retired, Sick or Absent	30
Number of Diocesan Priests	185
Religious Priests in Diocese	51
Total Priests in Diocese	236
Extern Priests in Diocese	26
Ordinations:	
Diocesan Priests	3
Transitional Deacons	5
Permanent Deacons in Diocese	93
Total Brothers	12
Total Sisters	104
Parishes	
Parishes	70
With Resident Pastor:	
Resident Diocesan Priests	61
Resident Religious Priests	9
Missions	6
Professional Ministry Personnel:	
Sisters	25
Lay Ministers	7
Welfare	
Catholic Hospitals	1
Total Assisted	28,989
Health Care Centers	7
Total Assisted	32,283
Day Care Centers	37
Total Assisted	1,844
Specialized Homes	2
Total Assisted	121
Special Centers for Social Services	40
Total Assisted	19,549
Other Institutions	4
Total Assisted	1,350
Educational	
Diocesan Students in Other Seminaries	46
Total Seminarians	46
Colleges and Universities	3
Total Students	4,071
High Schools, Diocesan and Parish	4
Total Students	3,565
High Schools, Private	1
Total Students	363
Elementary Schools, Diocesan and Parish	37
Total Students	11,087
Elementary Schools, Private	2
Total Students	279
Catechesis/Religious Education:	
High School Students	3,183
Elementary Students	28,751
Total Students under Catholic Instruction	51,345
Teachers in the Diocese:	
Priests	7
Brothers	1
Sisters	21
Lay Teachers	1,404
Vital Statistics	
Receptions into the Church:	
Infant Baptism Totals	5,700
Minor Baptism Totals	480
Adult Baptism Totals	354
Received into Full Communion	487
First Communions	6,924
Confirmations	6,473
Marriages:	
Catholic	1,066
Interfaith	227
Total Marriages	1,293
Deaths	1,987
Total Catholic Population	458,211
Total Population	3,298,694

Former Bishops—Most Revs. THOMAS J. WELSH, D.D., J.C.D., appt. Titular Bishop of Scattery Island and Auxiliary Bishop of Philadelphia on Feb. 18, 1970; cons. April 2, 1970; appt. as 1st Bishop of Arlington on June 4, 1974; installed on Aug. 13, 1974; transferred to the See of Allentown, Feb. 8, 1983; resigned Dec. 16, 1997; appt. Diocesan Administrator; retired Feb. 9, 1998; died Feb. 19, 2009.; JOHN R. KEATING, D.D., J.C.D., ord. Dec. 20, 1958; appt. Second Bishop of Arlington on June 7, 1983; cons. and installed on Aug. 4, 1983; died March 22, 1998; PAUL S. LOVERDE, D.D., S.T.L., J.C.L., (Retired), ord. Dec. 18, 1965; appt. Titular Bishop of Ottabia and Auxiliary Bishop of Hartford Feb. 3, 1988; cons. April 12, 1988; appt. Bishop of Ogdensburg Nov. 11, 1993; installed as Eleventh Bishop of Ogdensburg Jan. 17, 1994; appt. Bishop of Arlington Jan. 25, 1999; installed as Third Bishop of Arlington March 25, 1999; retired Oct. 4, 2016.

The Chancery

The Chancery—200 N. Glebe Rd., Ste. 914, Arlington, 22203. Tel: 703-841-2500; Fax: 703-524-5028. Office Hours: Mon.-Fri. 8:30-4:30Address all official business to this office.

Bishop—Most Rev. MICHAEL F. BURBIDGE, Ed.D., D.D., 200 N. Glebe Rd., Ste. 914, Arlington, 22203. Tel: 703-841-2511.

Vicar General and Moderator of the Curia—Very Rev. THOMAS P. FERGUSON, J.C.L., Ph.D., V.G., 200 N. Glebe Rd., Ste. 917, Arlington, 22203. Tel: 703-841-2563; Fax: 703-524-5028.

Chancellor—200 N. Glebe Rd., Ste. 914, Arlington, 22203. Tel: 703-841-2511; Fax: 703-524-5028. Rev. JAMIE R. WORKMAN, J.C.L.

General Counsel—MR. MARK E. HERRMANN, Esq., 200 N. Glebe Rd., Ste. 922, Arlington, 22203. Tel: 703-841-2524; Fax: 703-524-5028.

Episcopal Vicar for Charitable Works—Very Rev. ROBERT C. CILINSKI, 200 N. Glebe Rd., Ste. 250, Arlington, 22203. Tel: 703-841-3830.

Episcopal Vicar for Clergy and Director of the Diaconate Formation Program—Very Rev. PAUL D. SCALIA, 200 N. Glebe Rd., Ste. 901, Arlington, 22203. Tel: 703-841-3809; Fax: 703-841-8472.

Episcopal Vicar for Faith Formation—200 N. Glebe Rd., Ste. 265, Arlington, 22203. Tel: 703-841-8552 ; Fax: 703-524-8670. Very Rev. WILLIAM P. SAUNDERS, Ed.D., V.F.

Diocesan Finance Officer—TIMOTHY R. COTNOIR, CPA, 200 N. Glebe Rd., Ste. 922, Arlington, 22203. Tel: 703-841-2543; Fax: 703-524-5028.

Finance & Accounting Office—ANN DEPUE, CPA, Controller, Tel: 703-841-3813; Fax: 703-524-5028; JOEL GOZA, Asst. Controller, 200 N. Glebe Rd., Ste. 922, Arlington, 22203. Tel: 703-841-3842; Fax: 703-524-5028.

Deans—Revs. JAMES S. BARKETT, V.F.; FRANCIS M. DE ROSA, V.F.; MICHAEL J. DOBBINS, V.F.; Very Revs. ANDREW J. FISHER, V.F.; PATRICK L. POSEY, V.F.; LEE R. ROOS, J.C.L., V.F.; Rev. MICHAEL G. TAYLOR, V.F.

The Tribunal

The Tribunal—200 N. Glebe Rd., Ste. 524, Arlington, 22203. Tel: 703-841-2555; Fax: 703-841-0693.

Judicial Vicar—Very Rev. ROBERT J. RIPPY, J.C.L., J.V., Tel: 703-841-2556; Fax: 703-841-0693.

Adjutant Judicial Vicar—Very Rev. LEE R. ROOS, J.C.L., V.F., Tel: 703-841-2563; Fax: 703-841-0693.

Diocesan Judges—Rev. PAUL F. DELADURANTAYE, S.T.D.; Very Rev. THOMAS P. FERGUSON, J.C.L., Ph.D., V.G.; Revs. PATRICK HOLROYD; MARTIN MCGUILL, J.C.D., (Retired); MS. JOYCE MACDONALD, J.C.L.; MRS. TARA A. MCINTOSH, J.C.L.; Very Revs. ROBERT J. RIPPY, J.C.L., J.V.; LEE R. ROOS, J.C.L., V.F.; Revs. WILLIAM B. SCHARDT, J.C.L.; DAVID A. WHITESTONE, J.C.L.

Defenders of the Bond—Rev. Msgr. ROBERT E. AVELLA; Rev. PAUL A. BERGHOUT; Deacon WILLIAM J. DONOVAN, J.C.L.; Revs. THOMAS J. LEHNING, S.T.L., Ph.D.; DONALD J. PLANTY, J.C.D.; GREGORY S. THOMPSON; JAMIE R. WORKMAN, J.C.L.

Promoter of Justice—Very Rev. LEE R. ROOS, J.C.L., V.F.

Auditor—MRS. JOYCE M. MACDONALD, J.C.L.

Advocates—Revs. EDWARD R. HORKAN; JOEL D. JAFFE; MICHAEL C. ISENBERG; ANTHONY J. KILLIAN.

Notaries—Revs. COLIN P. DAVIS; JOSEPH D. BERGIDA; STEVEN G. OETJEN; DORT A. BIGG; JOSEPH M. RAMPINO; THOMAS B. CAVANAUGH; STEPHEN M. VACCARO; KEITH D. CUMMINGS; CHRISTOPHER P. CHRISTENSEN; JORDAN WILLARD; KEVIN J. DANSEREAU; JEB S. DONELAN; DAVID A. DUFRESNE; RICHARD E. DYER JR.; JOSEPH W. FARRELL; ANDREW W. HAISSIG; CHRISTOPHER H. HAYES; RICHARD A. MISERENDINO; NOAH C. MOREY; WILLIAM B. SCHIERER; ERIC L. SHAFER; J. SCOTT SINA; STEVEN R. WALKER; MS. LILA BLACK; Revs. MICHAEL J. FOLMAR; NICHOLAS J. SCHIERER; CHRISTOPHER F. TIPTON.

Diocesan Offices

Diocesan Offices—Unless otherwise noted, all offices are located at: *200 N. Glebe Rd., Arlington, 22203*.

Accounting Office—LAURA CAYRAMPOMA, Accounting Dir., Ste. 917, Tel: 703-841-2682.

Archives—Ste. 917 Tel: 703-841-2340. SR. RENEE MAREK, F.S.E.

Arlington Catholic Herald, Inc.—MICHAEL F. FLACH, Editor & Gen. Mgr.; ANN AUGHERTON, Mng. Editor, Ste. 615, Tel: 703-841-2590; Fax: 703-524-2782; Web: www.catholicherald.com.

Campus Ministry—Rev. CHRISTOPHER T. VACCARO, Bishop's Liaison, 1614 College Ave., Fredericksburg, 22401. Tel: 540-373-6746.

Catholic Charities of the Diocese of Arlington—Ste. 250 ART BENNETT, Pres. & C.E.O., Tel: 703-841-3895; Fax: 703-841-3840; Web: www.ccda.net.

Car Ministry—Tel: 703-841-3898. MARIA GUADALUPE MAGDALENO.

Pregnancy and Adoption Services—MEAGHAN LANE, M.S.W., Prog. Mgr., 9380 Forestwood Ln., Unit A, Manassas, 20110. Tel: 703-425-0100.

Christ House Transitional Housing—131 S. West St., Alexandria, 22314. Tel: 703-549-8644. JOHN CROFT, Prog. Dir.

Christians Are Networking (CAN) Jobs Ministry—SALLY O'DWYER, M.A., Tel: 703-841-3838.

Emergency Assistance—SHERRI LONGHILL, Prog. Dir., 316 E. Market St., Leesburg, 20176. Tel: 703-443-2481.

Family Services—3251 Old Lee Hwy., Ste. 402, Fairfax, 22030. Tel: 703-425-0109. MS. ANNE DEVINE, Prog. Dir., 1101 Stafford Ave., Fredericksburg, 22401. Tel: 540-371-1124.

Hogar Immigrant Services—

Legal Services—STACY JONES, Prog. Dir., 6301 Little River Tpke., Ste. 700, Alexandria, 22312. Tel: 703-534-9805.

Education Services—JACKELINE CHAVEZ, Prog. Mgr., 8251 Shoppers Sq., Manassas, 20111. Tel: 571-208-1572.

Migration and Refugee Services—BELAYNEH LOPPISSO, Prog. Dir., 8247 Shoppers Sq., Manassas, 20111. Tel: 571-292-2259.

Mobile Response Center—CATHERINE HASSINGER, Prog. Dir., Tel: 703-841-2581.

Mother of Mercy Free Medical Clinic—MS. ALEXANDRA LUEVANO, Dir., 9380 Forestwood Ln., Unit B, Manassas, 20110. Tel: 703-420-8993.

Opioid Crisis Services—ART BENNETT, Tel: 703-841-3895.

Parish Liaison Network—SALLY O'DWYER, M.A., Vice Pres. & Dir. Volunteers, Tel: 703-841-3838.

Prison Ministry—BILL HALL, Coord., Tel: 703-841-3832.

Saint Lucy Food Distribution Program—VINCE CANNAVA, Prog. Dir., 8426-28 Kao Cir., Manassas, 20110. Tel: 703-479-2975.

Saint Margaret of Cortona Transitional Residences—VERONICA ROTH, Prog. Dir., 1423 G St., Unit A, Woodbridge, 22191. Tel: 703-910-4845.

Welcome Home Re-Entry Program—SALLY O'DWYER, M.A., Tel: 703-841-3838.

Senior Services/St. Martin de Porres Senior Center—4650 Taney Ave., Alexandria, 22304. Tel: 703-751-2766. ANNE COYNE, Prog. Mgr.

Catholic Education, Office of Catechetics—Very Rev. WILLIAM P. SAUNDERS, Ed.D., V.F., Ste. 265, Tel: 703-841-2554; Fax: 703-524-8670; MR. SOREN T. JOHNSON, Dir. Evangelization, Ste. 265, Tel: 703-841-2533; MR. JOHN KNUTSEN, Dir., Adult Faith Formation, Ste. 265, Tel: 703-841-3802; MRS. M. PROVIE RYDSTROM, Coord. Pastoral Ministry for the Hearing Impaired, Tel: 703-978-7997 (V-TTD); MS. NANCY EMMANUEL, Dir., Spec. Rel. Educ. (SPRED), Cell: 703-850-7038.

Office of Catholic Schools—DR. JENNIFER BIGELOW, Supt. Schools, Ste. 503, Arlington. Tel: 703-841-2519; Fax: 703-524-8670; Sr. KARL ANN HOMBERG, S.S.J., Asst. Supt. Leadership; RENEE WHITE, Asst. Supt.; DIANE ELLIOTT, M.Ed., Asst. Supt.; LESLIE LIPOVSKI, Asst. Supt.; MATTHEW ZIMMERMANN, School Finance Officer; AMBER DISE, Diocesan School Health Coord.

Office of Charismatic Renewal—TERRY RIGGINS, Liaison, Ste. 620, Tel: 703-224-1474.

Child Protection and Safety—Deacon R. MARQUES SILVA, Dir., Ste. 605, Tel: 703-841-3847.

Communications Office—MR. BILLY ATWELL, Chief Communications Officer, Ste. 906, Tel: 703-841-2592; ANGELA PELLERANO, Dir. Media Rels., Ste. 906, Tel: 703-841-2517; Fax: 703-524-5028; Email: communications@arlingtondiocese.org.

Development Office—ROBERT P. MUELLER, Exec. Dir., Ste. 811. Tel: 703-841-2545; Fax: 703-528-3057.

Information Technology—KIMBERLY T. MURPHY, Dir., Ste. 610, Tel: 703-841-3825; Fax: 703-841-4786.

Planning, Construction and Facilities—Ste. 704. Tel: 703-841-2572; Fax: 703-276-9486. VACANT, Dir.

Ecumenical and Interreligious Affairs Commission—Rev. DONALD J. ROONEY, M.A., M.Div., Chm., Tel: 540-373-6491.

Human Resources—TERESA D'ELIA, Dir., Ste. 205, Tel: 703-841-2522.

Marriage, Family, and Respect Life Office—THERESE BERMPOHL, Exec. Dir., Ste. 523. Tel: 703-841-2550; Fax: 703-807-2032; Email: familylife@arlingtondiocese.org.

Gabriel Project-Pregnancy Assistance Program—SARAH LAPIERRE, Prog. Dir., Ste. 523, Tel: 703-841-3812.

Marriage Preparation & Enrichment—Conferences for the Engaged Tel: 703-841-3807; Email: cfe@arlingtondiocese.org. ALEX WOLFE, Prog. Specialist.

Project Rachel Post-Abortion Outreach—SARAH LAPIERRE, Prog. Dir., Tel: 703-841-2504; Tel: 888-456-4673 (24 hrs.); Email: projectrachel@arlingtondiocese.org.

Respect Life/Pro-Life Activities—MRS. AMY MCINERNY, J.D., Dir., Ste. 523, Tel: 703-841-2550; Email: respectlife@arlingtondiocese.org.

Young Adult Ministry—Tel: 703-841-2549; Email: yam@arlingtondiocese.org. VACANT, Prog. Specialist.

Divine Worship Office—DR. JAMES STARKE, Dir., Ste. 265, Tel: 703-841-2554; DR. RICHARD GIBALA, Diocesan Music Coord., Tel: 703-524-2815.

Diaconal Formation Program—Very Rev. PAUL D. SCALIA, Dir., Ste. 901, Tel: 703-841-3809.

Office of Multicultural Ministries—MRS. CORINNE MONOGUE, Dir., Ste. 820, Tel: 703-841-3888.

Pontifical Mission Societies and Propagation of the FaithVery Rev. PATRICK L. POSEY, V.F., Dir., Tel: 703-532-8815.

Spanish Apostolate—Rev. JOSE EUGENIO HOYOS, Dir.

Risk Management, Office of—MARY STEWART, Dir., Ste. 630, Tel: 703-841-2503; Fax: 703-841-4786.

Victim Assistance Coordinator—FRANK MONCHER, Ph. D., Ste. 605, Tel: 703-841-2530.

Vocations, Office of—Rev. MICHAEL C. ISENBERG, Dir.; Mother MARIA GONZALEZ, P.S.S.J., Coord. Hispanic Women's Vocations.

Youth, Campus, and Young Adult Ministry, Office of—KEVIN BOHLI, Exec. Dir., Ste. 540, Tel: 703-841-2559; Fax: 703-807-2032.

Scouting & Camp Fire, Diocesan Committee on—MARK KRAMER, Chm.; Rev. ANDREW W. HAISSIG, Chap.

Consultative Bodies

Clergy Personnel Board—Very Rev. PAUL D. SCALIA, 200 N. Glebe Rd., Ste. 901, Arlington, 22203. Tel: 703-841-3809; Fax: 703-841-8472.

Diaconal Council—Tel: 703-969-1103. Deacon JAMES C. HEPLER, Chm.

Diocesan Consultors—Very Rev. ROBERT C. CILINSKI; Rev. Msgr. JOHN C. CREGAN, (Retired); Very Rev. ANDREW J. FISHER, V.F.; Rev. RAMEL O. PORTULA, C.I.C.M.; Very Revs. THOMAS P. FERGUSON, J.C.L., Ph.D., V.G.; PAUL D. SCALIA; ROBERT J. RIPPY, J.C.L., J.V.; Revs. JAMIE R. WORKMAN, J.C.L.; MATTHEW H. ZUBERBUELER.

Diocesan Finance Council—Most Rev. MICHAEL F. BURBIDGE, Ed.D., D.D., Chm., Tel: 703-841-2511; TIMOTHY R. COTNOIR, CPA, Diocesan Finance Officer, Tel: 703-841-2543.

Presbyteral Council—Most Rev. MICHAEL F. BURBIDGE, Ed.D., D.D., Pres.; Rev. RAMON A. BAEZ, Recording Sec.

Sisters' Council—Sr. JUDITH GEBELEIN, F.S.E., Pres., Tel: 703-204-0837; ELIZABETH ANN GOLTMAN, I.H.M., Vice Pres., Tel: 703-237-1424.

CLERGY, PARISHES, MISSIONS AND PAROCHIAL SCHOOLS

COUNTY OF ARLINGTON

1—CATHEDRAL OF ST. THOMAS MORE (1938) Very Rev. Robert J. Rippy, J.C.L., J.V., Rector; Revs. Christopher P. Christensen, Parochial Vicar; Michael C. Isenberg, In Res.
Res.: 3901 Cathedral Ln., 22203. Tel: 703-525-1300; Fax: 703-528-5760; Web: www.cathedralstm.org.
School—Cathedral of St. Thomas More School, (Grades PreK-8),
105 N. Thomas St., 22203. Tel: 703-528-6781; Fax: 703-528-5048; Email: stmoffice@stmschool.org; Email: tashworth@stmschool.org; Web: www.stmschool.org. Mrs. Eleanor S. McCormack, Prin. Lay Teachers 31; Students 400.
Catechesis Religious Program—Lynn Jones, D.R.E. Students 289.

2—ST. AGNES (1936) Revs. Frederick H. Edlefsen; Scott Sina, Parochial Vicar; Res. Thomas Nguyen, In Res.; Rev. Cedric M. Wilson, O.S.A., In Res.
Res. & Office: 1910 N. Randolph St., 22207-3046.
Tel: 703-525-1166; Email: parishoffice@saintagnes.org; Web: www.saintagnes.org.
School—St. Agnes School, (Grades PreK-8),
2024 N. Randolph St., 22207-3031. Tel: 703-527-5423; Fax: 703-525-4689; Email: jkuzdzal@saintagnes.org; Web: www.saintagnes.org. Jennifer Kuzdzal, Prin. Clergy 4; Lay Teachers 36; Students 465.
Catechesis Religious Program—
Email: dre@saintagnes.org. Bernadette Michael, D.R.E., Tel: 703-527-1129. Students 374.

3—ST. ANN (1947) Revs. Ramel O. Portula, C.I.C.M.; Leoyd Sanggaria, Parochial Vicar; Deacon William J. Donovan, J.C.L.
Res.: 5300 10th St. N., 22205. Tel: 703-528-6276; Fax: 703-522-4758; Email: aogden@stann.org; Web: www.stannchurch.org.
School—Saint Ann Catholic School, (Grades PreK-8),
980 N. Frederick St., 22205. Tel: 703-525-7599; Fax: 703-525-2687; Email: stann@stann.org; Web: www.stann.org. Ms. Mary E. Therrell, Prin. Lay Teachers 21; Students 213.
Catechesis Religious Program—
Tel: 703-528-6199. Amy Strickland, Email: stannreled@gmail.com. Students 778.

4—ST. CHARLES BORROMEO (1909) Revs. Donald J. Planty, J.C.D.; Richard E. Dyer Jr., Parochial Vicar; Deacon Forrest Wallace.
Res.: 3304 N. Washington Blvd., 22201.
Tel: 703-527-5500; Fax: 703-527-1108; Email: parishoffice@stcharleschurch.org; Web: www.stcharleschurch.org.
School—St. Charles Borromeo School, (Grades PreK-8),
3299 N. Fairfax Dr., 22201. Tel: 703-527-0608; Email: office@stcharlesarlington.org; Web: www.stcharlesarlington.org. Amy Fry, Dir. Lay Teachers 12; Students 172.
Catechesis Religious Program—Francesca Gross, D.R.E.; Jim Schuster, D.R.E. Students 516.

5—HOLY MARTYRS OF VIETNAM CATHOLIC CHURCH (1979) (Vietnamese) Revs. Liem Trung Tran, O.P.; John Son Hoang, O.P., Parochial Vicar; Joseph Tien Minh Vu, O.P., Parochial Vicar; Thomas Luan Pho, O.P., Parochial Vicar. In Res., Revs. Hung Q. Le, O.P.; Khan Duy Pham, O.P.
Res.: 915 S. Wakefield St., 22204. Tel: 703-553-0370; Fax: 703-553-0371; Email: office@cttdva.com; Web: www.cttdva.com.
Catechesis Religious Program—Students 556.
Mission—Our Lady of La Vang Mission
661 Cedar Spring Rd., Centreville, 20121.

6—OUR LADY OF LOURDES (1946) Rev. Msgr. Robert E. Avella; Rev. Joseph R. Kenna, Parochial Vicar.
Res.: 830 23rd St. S., 22202. Tel: 703-684-9261; Fax: 703-684-6342; Email: olol@comcast.net; Web: www.ololcc.net.
Catechesis Religious Program—
Email: dre@ololcc.net. Ms. Laura de la Torre, D.R.E. Students 145.

7—OUR LADY, QUEEN OF PEACE (1945)
2700 19th St S., 22204. Revs. Timothy J. Hickey, C.S.Sp.; Martin Tu Quoc Vu, Parochial Vicar; Deacon Antonio J. Remedios.
Res.: 1901 S. Edgewood St., 22204. Tel: 703-979-5580; Email: office@ourladyqueenofpeace.org; Email: office@olqpva.org; Web: www.olqpva.org.
Catechesis Religious Program—Theresa Palmisano, D.R.E., Email: tpalmisano@olqpva.org. Students 1,116.

OUTSIDE THE COUNTY OF ARLINGTON

ALEXANDRIA, ALEXANDRIA CO.

1—BLESSED SACRAMENT (1946)
1427 W. Braddock Rd., Alexandria, 22302.
Tel: 703-998-6100; Email: ddauray@blessedsacramentcc.org. Revs. John D. Kelly, V.F.; Kevin J. Dansereau, Parochial Vicar; Joseph M. Rampino, Parochial Vicar; Mark Carrier, Parochial Vicar.
Res.: 1407 W. Braddock Rd., Alexandria, 22302.
Tel: 703-998-6100; Fax: 703-671-3219; Email: parish_office@blessedsacramentcc.org; Web: www.blessedsacramentcc.org.
School—Blessed Sacrament School, (Grades PreK-8), 1417 W. Braddock Rd., Alexandria, 22302.
Tel: 703-998-4170; Fax: 703-998-5033; Email: schoolinfo@bssva.org; Web: bssva.org. Mrs. Valerie Garcia, Prin. Clergy 1; Lay Teachers 22; Students 302.
Catechesis Religious Program—Students 357.

2—ST. JOSEPH'S (1915) Rev. Donald M. Fest, S.S.J.; Deacon Albert A. Anderson Jr.
Res.: 711 N. Columbus St., Alexandria, 22314.
Tel: 703-836-3725; Fax: 703-837-9066; Email: stjosephalexva@gmail.com; Web: stjosephva.org.
Catechesis Religious Program—Ms. Princess McEvilley, D.R.E., Tel: 703-863-6306; Email: dstprincess@gmail.com. Students 42.

3—BASILICA OF ST. MARY (1795) [CEM]
313 Duke St., Alexandria, 22314. Web: www.stmaryoldtown.org. Revs. Edward C. Hathaway, Rec-

tor; David A. Dufresne, Parochial Vicar; Andrew W. Haissig, Parochial Vicar; Kevin Barnekow, In Res.; Edward J. Bresnahan, In Res.
Res.: 310 Duke St., Alexandria, 22314.
Tel: 703-836-4100; Fax: 703-549-3605; Email: admin@stmaryoldtown.org; Web: www.saintmaryoldtown.org.
School—St. Mary's School, (Grades PreK-8), 400 Green St., Alexandria, 22314. Tel: 703-549-1646; Fax: 703-519-0840; Email: jcantwell@smsva.org; Web: www.smsva.org. Mrs. Janet Cantwell, Prin. Clergy 5; Lay Teachers 48; Students 710.
Catechesis Religious Program—Students 293.

4—St. Rita (1914) Revs. Daniel N. Gee; Vincent D. Bork, Parochial Vicar; Deacon Stephen J. Dixon.
Res.: 3815 Russell Rd., Alexandria, 22305.
Tel: 703-836-1640; Fax: 703-706-0484; Email: stritaofficedre@gmail.com; Web: www.strita-parish.net.
School—St. Rita School, (Grades PreSchool-8), 3801 Russell Rd., Alexandria, 22305. Tel: 703-548-1888; Fax: 703-229-6548; Email: saintritaschool@me.com; Web: www.saintrita-school.org. Mrs. Mary Pat Schlickenmaier, Prin. Clergy 1; Lay Teachers 22; Sisters of St. Joseph 2; Students 255.
Catechesis Religious Program—Betsy Nunn, D.R.E., Email: stritadre@gmail.com. Students 199.
Convent—Sisters of St. Joseph, 231 W. Glebe Rd., Alexandria, 22305. Tel: 703-683-1929.

Alexandria, Fairfax Co.

1—Good Shepherd (1965) Very Rev. Thomas P. Ferguson, J.C.L., Ph.D., V.G.; Rev. Ramon A. Baez, Parochial Vicar; Deacons Thomas G. White Jr.; Julian Gutierrez; Patrick A. Ouellette; Michael J. O'Neil.
Church & Mailing Address: 8710 Mount Vernon Hwy., Alexandria, 22309. Tel: 703-780-4055; Email: office@gs-cc.org; Web: www.gs-cc.org.
Catechesis Religious Program—Students 1,135.

2—St. Lawrence (Franconia) (1967) Revs. Ronald J. Gripshover Jr.; Daniel S. Spychala, Parochial Vicar; Joseph Ocran, In Res.; Deacon Michael A. Waters.
Res.: 6222 Franconia Rd., Alexandria, 22310.
Tel: 703-971-4378; Fax: 703-971-0331; Email: office@stlawrencealex.org; Web: www.stlawrencealex.org.
Catechesis Religious Program—Students 227.

3—St. Louis (1949) Revs. Keith M. O'Hare; Dort A. Bigg, Parochial Vicar; Paul Dudzinski, Parochial Vicar; Bryan Duggan, In Res.
Res.: 2907 Popkins Ln., Alexandria, 22306.
Tel: 703-765-4421; Fax: 703-765-1750.
School—St. Louis School, (Grades PreSchool-8), 2901 Popkins Ln., Alexandria, 22306.
Tel: 703-768-7732; Fax: 703-768-3836; Email: office@stlouisschool.org; Email: kmcnutt@stlouisschool.org; Web: www.stlouisschool.org. Kathleen McNutt, Prin. Lay Teachers 35; Students 512.
Catechesis Religious Program—Students 369.

4—Queen of Apostles (1963)
4401 Sano St., Alexandria, 22312. Revs. Leopoldo M. Vives, D.C.J.M.; Javier O'Connor, D.C.J.M., Parochial Vicar; Ignacio de Ribera, D.C.J.M., In Res.; Deacon Richard C. Caporiccio.
Res.: 4329 Sano St., Alexandria, 22312.
Tel: 703-354-8711; Fax: 703-354-0766; Email: general@queenofapostles.org; Web: www.queenofapostles.org.
School—Queen of Apostles School, (Grades K-8), 4409 Sano St., Alexandria, 22312. Tel: 703-354-0714; Fax: 703-354-1820; Email: info@queenofapostlesschool.org; Web: www.queenofapostlesschool.org. Jodi Reagan, Prin. Clergy 1; Lay Teachers 17; Students 182.

Annandale, Fairfax Co.

1—St. Ambrose (1966) Very Rev. Andrew J. Fisher, V.F.; Rev. Christopher H. Hayes, Parochial Vicar.
Church & Office Mailing Address: 3901 Woodburn Rd., Annandale, 22003. Tel: 703-280-4400; Email: information@stambroseva.org; Web: www.stambroseva.org.
Res.: 3801 Woodburn Rd., Annandale, 22003.
School—St. Ambrose School, (Grades PreK-8), 3827 Woodburn Rd., Annandale, 22003. Tel: 703-698-7171; Fax: 703-698-7170; Email: arowley@stambroseschool.org; Email: cyaglou@stambroseschool.org; Web: stambroseschool.org. Mrs. Angela Rowley, Prin. Clergy 2; Lay Teachers 19; Students 205.
Catechesis Religious Program—Students 270.

2—Holy Spirit (1964)
8800 Braddock Rd., Annandale, 22003.
Tel: 703-978-8074; Email: parish@holyspiritchurch.us; Web: www.holyspiritchurch.us. Mailing Address: 5121 Woodland Way, Annandale, 22003. Revs. John M. O'Donohue; Peter O. Okola, A.J., Parochial Vicar; Carroll L. Oubre, Parochial Vicar; Deacons Nicholas J. LaDuca Jr.; Thomas L. Grodek.
School—Holy Spirit School, (Grades PreK-8), 8800 Braddock Rd., Annandale, 22003. Tel: 703-978-7117; Fax: 703-978-7438; Email: mashby@holyspiritflames.org; Web: www.holyspiritflames.org. Mrs. Maureen Ashby, Prin. (Extended Day Care available)(Special Education Resource Program available) Lay Teachers 32; Students 441.
Catechesis Religious Program—Email: religious.ed@holyspiritchurch.us. Anson Groves, D.R.E. Students 558.

3—St. Michael (1953) Revs. Alexander R. Drummond; Brian B. McAllister, Parochial Vicar; Stefan P. Starzynski, In Res.; Deacons Roger T. Ostrom; David S. McCaffrey.
Res.: 7401 St. Michael's Ln., Annandale, 22003.
Tel: 703-256-7822; Fax: 703-256-7122; Email: church@stmikes22003.org; Web: www.stmichaelannandale.org.
School—St. Michael School, (Grades K-8), Tel: 703-256-1222; Email: daniel.cinalli@stmikes22003.org. Mr. Daniel Cinalli, Prin.; Richard Webb, Business Mgr. Clergy 11; Lay Teachers 10; Students 222.
Catechesis Religious Program—Mrs. Adina Ordonez, D.R.E. Students 100.
Convent—Sisters of Our Lady of La Salette (SNDS), 7421 St. Michael's Ln., Annandale, 22003.
Tel: 703-865-8767.

Ashburn, Loudoun Co., St. Theresa (1991) Revs. Richard M. Guest; Jordan Willard, Parochial Vicar; Nicholas R. Barnes, Parochial Vicar; Deacon Paul Konold.
Rectory—43367 Icepond Dr., Ashburn, 20147.
Tel: 703-729-2287; Email: office@sainttheresaparish.com; Web: www.sainttheresaparish.com.
Church: 21371 St. Theresa Ln., Ashburn, 20147.
School—St. Theresa School, (Grades K-8), 21370 St. Theresa Ln., Ashburn, 20147. Tel: 703-729-3577; Fax: 703-729-8068; Email: schooloffice@stsashburn.com; Web: www.stsashburn.com. Carol Krichbaum, Prin. Lay Teachers 36; Students 440.
Catechesis Religious Program—Carol Krichbaum, D.R.E.; Larry Bayne, D.R.E., Email: reoffice@sainttheresaparish.com; Paul Dwyer, Youth Ministry. Students 1,873.

Berryville, St. Bridget of Ireland Parish
1024 W. Main St., Berryville, 22611.

Burke, Fairfax Co., Church of the Nativity (W. Springfield) (1973)
Mailing Address: 6400 Nativity Ln., Burke, 22015.
Tel: 703-455-2400; Fax: 703-455-6832; Email: abenson@nativityburke.org; Web: www.nativityburke.org. Very Rev. Robert C. Cilinski; Rev. Stephen Vaccaro, Parochial Vicar; Deacon Richard Kelly.
Res.: 9523 Lyra Ct., Burke, 22015. Tel: 703-913-2306.
School—Church of the Nativity School, (Grades PreK-8), 6398 Nativity Ln., Burke, 22015.
Tel: 703-455-2300; Fax: 703-569-8109; Email: mkelly@nativityschool.org; Web: www.nativityschool.org. Ms. Maria E. Kelly, Prin. Clergy 8; Lay Teachers 18; Students 263.
Catechesis Religious Program—Students 1,525.
Convent—Handmaids of Reparation of the Sacred Heart of Jesus, 6300 Capella Ave., Burke, 22015.
Tel: 703-455-4180.

Chantilly, Fairfax Co.

1—St. Timothy (1969) Revs. David P. Meng; Joseph W. Farrell, Parochial Vicar; William B. Schierer, Parochial Vicar; Deacons David E. Conroy Sr.; James C. Hepler; Gerard-Marie Anthony.
Res.: 13807 Poplar Tree Rd., Chantilly, 20151.
Tel: 703-378-7461; Tel: 703-378-7646; Email: fdebrey@sttimothyparish.org; Web: www.sttimothyparish.org.
School—Saint Timothy School, (Grades K-8), 13809 Poplar Tree Rd., Chantilly, 20151. Tel: 703-378-6932; Fax: 703-378-1273; Email: info@sainttimothyschool.org; Web: www.sainttimothyschool.org. Michael Pryor, Prin. Lay Teachers 37; Sisters 1; Students 717.
Catechesis Religious Program—Students 862.

2—St. Veronica (1999)
3460 Centreville Rd., Chantilly, 20151.
Tel: 703-773-2000; Fax: 703-773-2001; Email: info@stveronica.net; Web: www.stveronica.net. Revs. Dennis W. Kleinmann; Robert J. Wagner, Parochial Vicar; Deacon J. Paul Ochenkowski.
School—St. Veronica School, (Grades PreK-8), 3460B Centreville Rd., Chantilly, 20151.
Tel: 703-773-2020; Fax: 703-991-9103; Email: info@stveronicaschool.org; Web: www.stveronica.net/school. Mrs. Elizabeth Goldman, Prin. Lay Staff 45; (Full-time, paid) 45; Students 386.
Catechesis Religious Program—Email: re@stveronica.net. Rev. Michael C. Isenberg, D.R.E., Email: info@stveronica.net. Students 385.

Clifton, Fairfax Co.

1—St. Andrew the Apostle (1989) Revs. Christopher J. Mould; Joseph D. Bergida, Parochial Vicar; Justin Puthussery, In Res.
School—St. Andrew the Apostle School, (Grades PreK-8), 6720-B Union Mill Rd., Clifton, 20124-1115. Tel: 703-817-1774; Fax: 703-817-1721; Email: office@standrew-clifton.org; Web: www.standrew-clifton.org. Mary Baldwin, Prin. Lay Teachers 30; Students 206.
Catechesis Religious Program—Mrs. Patty Laing, D.R.E., Email: plaing@st-andrew.org. Students 395.

2—St. Clare of Assisi (1981) Rev. Thomas J. Lehning, S.T.L., Ph.D.; Deacon Michael J. Mochel, D.R.E.
Church & Rectory: 12409 Henderson Rd., Clifton, 20124. Tel: 703-266-1310; Tel: 703-266-7293; Fax: 703-266-7011; Email: office@stclareclifton.org; Web: www.stclareclifton.org.
Catechesis Religious Program—Students 53.

Colonial Beach, Westmoreland Co., St. Elizabeth of Hungary (1906) [JC] Revs. Francis M. de Rosa, V.F.; Eric L. Shafer, Parochial Vicar.
Res.: 21 Irving Ave., Colonial Beach, 22443.
Tel: 804-224-7221; Email: office@saintselizabethandanthony.com; Web: www.saintselizabethandanthony.com.
Catechesis Religious Program—Students 121.
Mission—St. Anthony's, [CEM] (King George) 11 Irving Ave., Colonial Beach, Westmoreland Co. 22443.

Culpeper, Culpeper Co., Precious Blood (1880) [CEM] Revs. Kevin B. Walsh; Augustine M. Tran, Parochial Vicar; Deacon Ramon Tirado.
Res.: 114 E. Edmondson St., Culpeper, 22701.
Tel: 540-825-8945; Fax: 540-825-8987; Email: office@preciousbloodcatholicchurch.com; Web: www.preciousbloodcatholicchurch.com.
Catechesis Religious Program—Tel: 540-825-1339; Email: DRE@preciousbloodcatholicchurch.com. Mrs. Kelly Wilton, D.R.E. Students 311.

Dale City, Prince William Co., Holy Family (1970) Revs. Wilson I. Korpi; John T. O'Hara, Parochial Vicar; Luis Quinones, Ph.D., Parochial Vicar; Keith D. Cummings, In Res.; Deacons Vincent Einsmann; Helio A. Gomez; Joseph L. Santiago.
Res.: 14190 Ferndale Rd., Dale City, 22193.
Tel: 703-670-8161; Fax: 703-670-8323; Email: parishoffice@holyfamilydalecity.org; Web: www.holyfamilycatholicchurchdalecity.org.
School—Holy Family School, (Grades PreK-8), Tel: 703-670-3138; Email: principal@holyfamilydalecity.org; Web: www.holyfamilydalecity.org. Mrs. Sarah Chevlin, Prin., Email: principal@hfccdc.com; Judi Peacott, Dir. (PreK). Lay Teachers 21; Students 278.
Catechesis Religious Program—Students 665.

Fairfax, Fairfax Co.

1—St. Mary of Sorrows (1858) [CEM] Revs. James S. Barkett, V.F.; Donald C. Greenhalgh, Pastor Emeritus, (Retired); Francis J. Peffley, Parochial Vicar; Deacons Jeffrey M. Meyers; David M. Maurer.
Mailing & Parish Center Address: 5222 Sideburn Rd., Fairfax, 22032-2640. Tel: 703-978-4141; Fax: 703-978-2568; Email: kathyc@stmaryofsorrows.org; Web: stmaryofsorrows.org.
Historic Church—5612 Ox Rd., Fairfax Station, 22039.
Res.: 11112 Fairfax Station Rd., Fairfax Station, 22039.
Catechesis Religious Program—Aida Willis, D.R.E., Email: aidaw@stmaryofsorrows.org; Madeline Bernero-Ledon, D.R.E. (7-8), Email: maddyl@stmaryofsorrows.org; Mark Stinard, Youth Min., Email: marks@stmaryofsorrows.org. Students 556.

2—St. Paul Chung (1986) (Korean) Rev, Inhyun Andrew Paik; Rev. Myeongjun Bang, Parochial Vicar.
Res.: 4708 Rippling Pond Dr., Fairfax, 22033-5077.
Tel: 703-818-9707; Fax: 703-968-3013; Email: sthasang@gmail.com; Web: www.stpaulchung.org.
Church & Mailing Address: 4712 Rippling Pond Dr., Fairfax, 22033-5077. Tel: 703-968-3010.
Catechesis Religious Program—Students 246.

Fairfax City, Fairfax Co., St. Leo the Great (1957) Revs. David A. Whitestone, J.C.L.; Christopher F. Tipton, Parochial Vicar; William M. Aitcheson, Parochial Vicar; Stephen J. Schultz, In Res.; Deacons Jose J. Lopez; R. Marques Silva.
Res.: 3700 Old Lee Hwy., Fairfax, 22030.
Tel: 703-273-5369; Email: webmaster@stleofairfax.com; Web: www.stleofairfax.com.
School—St. Leo the Great School, (Grades PreK-8), 3704 Old Lee Hwy., Fairfax, 22030.
Tel: 703-273-1211; Fax: 703-273-6913; Email: ddipippa@saintleothegreatschool.org; Email: office@saintleothegreatschool.org; Web: www.saintleothegreatschool.org. Mr. David DiPippa, Prin. Lay Teachers 30; Students 397.
Catechesis Religious Program—Melissa Land. Students 546.
Stations—Fairfax Nursing Home—Fairfax.
Tel: 703-273-7705.

Commonwealth Care Center, Fairfax, 22030. Tel: 703-934-5060.
The Gardens at Fair Oaks, Fairfax, 22030. Tel: 703-278-1001.
Sunrise Assisted Living at George Mason, Fairfax, 22030. Tel: 703-934-5069.

FALLS CHURCH, FAIRFAX CO.

1—ST. ANTHONY (1952) Revs. Matthew H. Zuberbueler; Alan Ventura, Parochial Vicar; Jeb S. Donelan, Parochial Vicar & D.R.E.; Deacon Mario Mendoza. In Res., Revs. Jose Eugenio Hoyos; Anthony Appiah.
Res.: 3305 Glen Carlyn Rd., Falls Church, 22041. Tel: 703-820-7111; Fax: 703-379-9195; Email: office@stanthonyparish.org; Web: www.stanthonyparish.org.
Catechesis Religious Program—Students 494.

2—ST. JAMES (1892) [CEM] Very Rev. Patrick L. Posey, V.F.; Revs. Joseph Q. Vu, Parochial Vicar; Steven G. Oetjen, Parochial Vicar; Deacons James A. Fishenden; Edward C. Gliot. In Res., Revs. Gregory S. Thompson; Ghenghan Mbinkar; Denis Tameh.
Res.: 905 Park Ave., Falls Church, 22046. Tel: 703-532-8815; Fax: 703-533-7644; Email: rectory@stjamescatholic.org; Web: www.stjamescatholic.org.
School—St. James School, (Grades K-8), 830 W. Broad St., Falls Church, 22046. Tel: 703-533-1182, Ext. 100; Fax: 703-532-8316; Email: mainoffice@saintjamesschool.org. Sr. Mary Sue Carwile, I.H.M., Prin. Clergy 1; Lay Teachers 28; Students 450; Sisters (Servants of the Immaculate Heart of Mary) 5.
Catechesis Religious Program—Sr. Regina Rosarii McLallen, I.H.M., D.R.E. Students 463.
Convent—Sisters, Servants of the Immaculate Heart of Mary, 101 N. Spring St., Falls Church, 22046. Tel: 703-532-2388.

3—ST. PHILIP (1962) Revs. Denis M. Donahue; Steven R. Walker, Parochial Vicar; Tarsicio Buitrago, In Res., (Retired); Deacon Vincent Cong T. Nguyen.
Res.: 7500 St. Philip's Ct., Falls Church, 22042. Tel: 703-573-3808; Fax: 703-462-8565; Email: businessmanager@stphilipsparish.com; Web: www.stphilipsparish.com.
Child Care—St. Philip Early Childhood Center, 7506 St. Philip Ct., Falls Church, 22042. Tel: 703-573-4570; Email: info@stphilipecc.org; Web: stphilipecc.org. Ann Stich, Dir. Lay Teachers 10; Students 165.
Convent—Franciscan Sisters of the Eucharist, 7504 St. Philip's Ct., Falls Church, 22042. Tel: 703-204-0837. Sisters 5.
Catechesis Religious Program—Students 339.

FREDERICKSBURG, FREDERICKSBURG CO.

1—SAINT JUDE (2003)
3501 Lee Hill School Rd., Fredericksburg, 22408. Tel: 540-891-7350; Fax: 540-891-1810; Email: parishoffice@stjudechurch.us; Web: www.StJudeChurch.us. Revs. James C. Hudgins; Stephen M. Vaccaro, In Res.; Deacons Robert A. Cronican; Robert A. Lyons.
Catechesis Religious Program—Email: ReligiousEd@StJudeChurch.us. Students 265.

2—ST. MARY OF THE IMMACULATE CONCEPTION (1858) Revs. John P. Mosimann, V.F.; Michael J.R. Kelly, Parochial Vicar; Colin P. Davis, Parochial Vicar; Michael J. Folmar, Parochial Vicar; Deacons Alberto G. Bernaola; Richard P. Delio.
Res.: 1009 Stafford Ave., Fredericksburg, 22401-5418. Tel: 540-373-6491; Fax: 540-371-0251; Email: stmary@stmaryfred.org; Web: www.stmaryfred.org.
School—Holy Cross Academy, (Grades PreK-8), 250 Stafford Lakes Pkwy., Fredericksburg, 22406. Tel: 540-286-1600; Fax: 540-286-1625; Email: holycrossacademy@holycrossweb.com; Web: www.holycrossweb.com. Sr. Susan Louise Eder, O.S.F.S., Prin., Email: principal@holycrossweb.com; Victoria Ellis, Librarian. Clergy 3; Lay Teachers 37; Oblate Sisters of St. Francis de Sales 3; Students 517; Total Staff 52.
Catechesis Religious Program—Aristides Lucas, D.R.E., Email: alucas@stmaryfred.org. Students 1,065.
Convent—Oblate Sisters of St. Francis de Sales, St. Mary Convent, 1316 Royston St., Fredericksburg, 22401. Tel: 540-371-1652; Fax: 540-371-1652.

3—ST. PATRICK (1983) Revs. John A. Ziegler; Jerry A. Wooton, Parochial Vicar; Deacons David E. Conroy; Paul A. D'Antonio; William D. Pivarnik; James M. Stenstrom; Donald L. Perusi.
Church:Tel: 540-785-5299; Fax: 540-785-5692; Email: office@saintpatrickparish.org; Web: www.saintpatrickparish.org.
School—St. Patrick School, (Grades PreK-8), 9151 Ely's Ford Rd., Fredericksburg, 22407. Tel: 540-786-2277; Fax: 540-785-2213; Email: mmassad@saintpatrickschoolva.org; Email: stpatschurch@comcast.net; Web: saintpatrickschool.com. Mr. George Elliott, Prin. Lay Teachers 16; Students 226.
Catechesis Religious Program—Students 159.

FRONT ROYAL, WARREN CO., ST. JOHN THE BAPTIST (1884) Revs. Jerome W. Fasano; Phillip M. Cozzi, Parochial Vicar; Deacon Ralph A. Goldsmith.
Res.: 123 W. Main St., Front Royal, 22630. Tel: 540-635-3780; Fax: 540-635-2683; Email: stjohns@sjtb.org; Web: www.sjtb.org.
Catechesis Religious Program—David Wallace, D.R.E., Email: dwallace@sjtb.org. Students 587.

GAINESVILLE, PRINCE WILLIAM CO., HOLY TRINITY (2001) Revs. Thomas P. Vander Woude; John Edwin Thayer Tewes, Parochial Vicar; Augustine M. Tran, Parochial Vicar; Deacon Scott A. Ross.
Church: 8213 Linton Hall Rd., Gainesville, 20155. Web: www.holytrinityparish.net.
Res.: 13260 McCartney Ct., Bristow, 20136. Tel: 703-753-6700; Fax: 703-753-6286; Email: businessmanager@holytrinityparish.net.
Catechesis Religious Program—Jen Carmichael, D.R.E. Students 1,426.

GORDONSVILLE, ORANGE CO., ST. MARK'S (1972) Merged with St. John's, Orange to form St. Isidore the Farmer, Orange.

GREAT FALLS, FAIRFAX CO., ST. CATHERINE OF SIENA (1979)
Mailing Address: 1020 Springvale Rd., Great Falls, 22066. Tel: 703-759-4350; Fax: 703-759-3753; Email: office@saintcatherineschurch.org; Web: www.saintcatherineschurch.org. Rev. Jerry Porkorsky.
School—Siena Academy, Tel: 703-759-4129; Email: office@sienamontessori.org. Ruth Barwick, Head of School. Lay Teachers 11; Students 96.
Catechesis Religious Program—Kimberly Liuaudais, D.R.E. Students 160.

HERNDON, FAIRFAX CO., ST. JOSEPH (1950) Revs. Thomas G. Bourque, T.O.R.; Alberto Bueno, T.O.R., Parochial Vicar; Vincent Yeager, Parochial Vicar; Patrick Wittle, T.O.R., In Res.
Res.: 750 Peachtree St., Herndon, 20170. Tel: 703-880-4300; Fax: 703-880-4320; Email: mkirby@sjcherndon.org; Web: www.sjcherndon.org.
School—St. Joseph School, (Grades K-8), Tel: 703-880-4350; Email: twesthues@sjcherndon.org; Web: sjschoolva.org. Mrs. Denise Rutledge, Prin. Lay Teachers 30; Students 513.
Catechesis Religious Program—Reyes Ruiz, D.R.E., Email: . Students 656.

KILMARNOCK, LANCASTER CO., ST. FRANCIS DE SALES (1966) [CEM 2] Revs. Michael T. Orlowsky; Andrew J. Heintz, Parochial Vicar.
Res.: 154 E. Church St., Kilmarnock, 22482-0759. Tel: 804-435-1511; Fax: 804-436-9614; Email: stfrancis@va.metrocast.net; Web: www.stfranciskilmarnock.org.
Catechesis Religious Program—Students 50.
Mission—St. Paul, (Hague) 7808 Cople Hwy., Hague, Westmoreland Co. 22469. Tel: 804-472-3090; Fax: 804-472-3092; Email: saintpaulhague@gmail.com.

LAKE RIDGE, PRINCE WILLIAM CO., ST. ELIZABETH ANN SETON (1976)
Mailing Address: 12807 Valleywood Dr., Lake Ridge, 22192. Tel: 703-494-4008; Fax: 703-494-1995; Email: christine.ohearn@seas1.org. Revs. Brian Bashista; Edwin E. Perez, Parochial Vicar; Deacon Robert Warner Jr.
Catechesis Religious Program—Tel: 703-494-3966; Fax: 703-494-8005. Jackie Ezersky, D.R.E. (Grades K-5); Kathy Lord, D.R.E. (Middle School). Students 482.

LEESBURG, LOUDOUN CO., ST. JOHN THE APOSTLE (1926) [CEM]
Mailing Address: 101 Oakcrest Manor Dr., N.E., Leesburg, 20176-2221. Tel: 703-777-1317; Fax: 703-771-9016; Email: church@stjohnleesburg.com; Web: saintjohnleesburg.org. Revs. Kevin J. Larsen; Anthony J. Killian, Parochial Vicar.
Res.: 302 N. King St., N.E., Leesburg, 20176. Tel: 703-777-6477.
Catechesis Religious Program—Edward V. Spinelli, D.R.E. Students 1,305.

LURAY, PAGE CO., OUR LADY OF THE VALLEY (1954)
Mailing Address: 200 Collins Ave., Luray, 22835. Tel: 540-743-4919; Fax: 540-743-2490; Web: ourladyofthevalleyluray.org. Rev. Edward R. Horkan.
Catechesis Religious Program—Carolyn Pandolfo, D.R.E., Tel: 540-742-1107; Email: cmpandolfo@aol.com. Students 18.

MADISON, MADISON CO., OUR LADY OF THE BLUE RIDGE (1977) Rev. James C. Bruse.
Res.: 692 Lonnie Burke Rd., Madison, 22727. Tel: 540-948-4144; Fax: 540-948-3325; Email: olbr@comcast.net; Email: james.bruse@arlingtondiocese.org.
Catechesis Religious Program—Students 48.

MANASSAS, PRINCE WILLIAM CO.

1—ALL SAINTS (1879)
9300 Stonewall Rd., Manassas, 20110. Tel: 703-368-4500; Fax: 703-257-9299; Web: www.allsaintsva.org. Very Rev. Lee R. Roos, J.C.L., V.F.; Revs. Noah C. Morey, Parochial Vicar; Juan Puigbo, Parochial Vicar; Mauricio R. Pineda, Parochial Vicar; Deacons John W. Eberlein; Richard O'Connell, (Retired); Brian R. Majewski; Orlando J. Barros; James R. Van de Voorde.
School—All Saints School, (Grades PreK-8), 9294 Stonewall Rd., Manassas, 20110. Tel: 703-368-4400; Fax: 703-393-2157; Email: office@allsaintsva.org; Web: www.allsaintsvaschool.org. Mr. David E. Conroy Jr., Prin.; Stefanie Horgan, Asst. Prin. Lay Teachers 32; Students 524.
Catechesis Religious Program—Tel: 703-393-2142; Fax: 703-393-2157; Web: www.allsaintsreligiouseducation.org. Samantha Welsh, D.R.E., (Elementary-English), RCIA. Students 1,410.
Mission—St. Gabriel Mission, 9110 Railroad Dr., Ste. 300, Manassas Park, 20111.

2—SACRED HEART (1984) [CEM]
Mailing Address: 12975 Purcell Rd., Manassas, 20112-3217. Tel: 703-590-0030; Email: office@shcva.org; Web: www.shcva.org. Rev. Michael J. Bazan; Deacons Gerald J. Moore; Alfred Caporaletti; Timothy H. Slayter; Mr. Carol Weyel, Business Mgr.; Mrs. Dianne Anderson, Youth Min.; Mr. Anna Schroeder, Music Min.; Mrs. Arden Blair, Sec.
Res.: 6258 Terrapin Dr., Manassas, 20112. Tel: 703-791-5131.

MCLEAN, FAIRFAX CO.

1—ST. JOHN THE BELOVED (1913) Revs. Christopher J. Pollard; John H. Melmer, Parochial Vicar; Janusz Mocarski, In Res.
Res.: 6420 Linway Ter., McLean, 22101. Tel: 703-356-7916; Fax: 703-356-4517; Web: www.StJohnCatholicMcLean.org. Rev. Janusz Mocarski.
School—St. John the Beloved School, (Grades PreSchool-8), 6422 Linway Ter., McLean, 22101. Tel: 703-356-7554; Fax: 703-448-3811; Email: rev.pastors@comcast.net; Web: www.stjohnacademy.org. Michael Busekrus, Headmaster. Clergy 4; Lay Teachers 22; Students 229.
Catechesis Religious Program—Students 269.

2—ST. LUKE (1961) Revs. David L. Martin; Anthony J. Pinizzotto, Parochial Vicar; Jamie R. Workman, J.C.L., In Res.; Dr. Paul Skevington, Liturgy Dir.
Res.: 7001 Georgetown Pike, McLean, 22101. Tel: 703-356-1255; Fax: 703-442-0848; Email: parishoffice@saintlukemclean.org; Web: www.saintlukemclean.org.
School—St. Luke School, (Grades PreK-8), 7005 Georgetown Pike, McLean, 22101. Tel: 703-356-1508; Fax: 703-356-1141; Email: frontoffice@stlukeschool.com; Web: www.stlukeschool.com. Louis M. Silvano, Prin. Lay Teachers 40; Students 207.
Catechesis Religious Program—Tel: 703-356-8419. Joyce Franklin, D.R.E. Students 370.

MIDDLEBURG, LOUDOUN CO., ST. STEPHEN THE MARTYR (1975)
Mailing Address: 23331 Sam Fred Rd., Middleburg, 20117-3221. Tel: 540-687-6433; Fax: 540-687-5170; Web: www.saint-stephen.org. Rev. Christopher D. Murphy.
Res.: 23309 Sam Fred Rd., Middleburg, 20117.
Church: Intersection of Rte. 50 & Sam Fred Rd., Middleburg, 20117.
Catechesis Religious Program—Students 349.
Mission—St. Katharine Drexel, 14535 John Marshall Hwy., Ste. 210, Gainesville, Prince William Co. 20155. Tel: 703-754-8444; Fax: 703-754-7443.

ORANGE, ORANGE CO.

1—ST. ISIDORE THE FARMER (2002) Rev. Terrence R. Staples.
Res.: 14405 St. Isidore Way, Orange, 22960. Tel: 540-672-4933, Ext. 30; Email: admin@saintisidorethefarmer.comm; Web: www.saintisidorethefarmer.com.
Church: 14414 St. Isidore Way, Orange, 22960-2573.
Catechesis Religious Program—
Tel: 540-672-4933, Ext. 3; Email: st.isidore.dre.pa@gmail.com. Students 45.

2—ST. JOHN'S (1946) Merged with St. Mark's, Gordonsville to form St. Isidore the Farmer, Orange.

POTOMAC FALLS, LOUDOUN CO., OUR LADY OF HOPE (2000) Very Rev. William P. Saunders, Ed.D., V.F.; Rev, Nicholas J. Schierer, Parochial Vicar.
Church: 46639 Algonkian Pkwy., Potomac Falls, 20165. Tel: 703-433-6770; Fax: 703-433-6771; Email: hello@ourladyofhope.net; Web: www.ourladyofhope.net.
School—Our Lady of Hope School, (Grades K-8), 46633 Algonkian Pkwy., Potomac Falls, 20165. Tel: 703-433-6760; Fax: 703-433-6761; Email: school@ourladyofhope.net; Web: www.school.ourladyofhope.net. Mary Beth Pittman, Prin. Lay Teachers 14; Students 211.
Catechesis Religious Program—Cathy Barshop, D.R.E. Students 425.

PURCELLVILLE, LOUDOUN CO., ST. FRANCIS DE SALES (1967) Revs. Ronald S. Escalante; Mark Mullaney, Parochial Vicar; Deacon Lawrence V. Hammel.
Res.: 37730 St. Francis Ct., Purcellville, 20132. Tel: 540-338-6440; Fax: 540-338-6431; Email: a.

harrison@saintfrancisparish.org; Web: www.saintfrancisparish.org.
Catechesis Religious Program—Students 810.

RESTON, FAIRFAX CO.

1—ST. JOHN NEUMANN (1979) Revs. Joseph T. Brennan, O.S.F.S.; Robert Mancini, O.S.F.S., Parochial Vicar; Donald J. Heet, O.S.F.S., Parochial Vicar; Richard DeLillio, In Res.; William N. Dougherty, O.S.F.S., In Res.; Deacons John A. Wagner; Dennis A. Holley; Atanacio Sandoval.
Res.: 11900 Lawyers Rd., Reston, 20191-4299.
Tel: 703-860-8510; Fax: 703-860-2136; Email: info@saintjn.org; Web: www.saintjn.org.
Catechesis Religious Program—Mrs. Marcella Abatemarco, D.R.E. Students 1,257.

2—ST. THOMAS A BECKET (1970)
1421 Wiehle Ave., Reston, 20190. Tel: 703-437-7113; Fax: 703-689-3814; Web: www.stbchurch.com. Rev. William B. Schardt, J.C.L.
Res.: 1418 Greenmont Ct., Reston, 20190.
Tel: 703-437-7113.
Catechesis Religious Program—Betsy Coffey, Dir., Middle & High School Faith Formation (6-12); Susan Reilly, Dir., Pre-K-Grade 5 Faith Formation. Students 424.

SOUTH RIDING, LOUDOUN CO., CORPUS CHRISTI (2014)
4130 Amberwood Plaza, Ste. 150, South Riding, 20152. Tel: 703-378-1037; Fax: 703-378-4442; Email: info@corpuschristi.org. Revs. Michael G. Taylor, V.F.; Charles W. Merkle III, Parochial Vicar.
Catechesis Religious Program—Students 626.

SPOTSYLVANIA, SPOTSYLVANIA CO., ST. MATTHEW (1999)
Mailing Address: 8200 Robert E. Lee Dr., Spotsylvania, 22551. Tel: 540-582-5575;
Fax: 540-582-8639; Email: stmatthewsec@comcast.net; Web: www.stmatthewspotsylvania.org. Rev. Paul M. Eversole; Deacons John A. Hubbarth, Business Mgr.; Mike Strain.
Catechesis Religious Program—Students 180.

SPRINGFIELD, FAIRFAX CO.

1—ST. BERNADETTE (1959) Revs. Donald J. Rooney, M.A., M.Div.; Richard A. Miserendino, Parochial Vicar; Deacon John Carlisle.
Church & Res.: 7600 Old Keene Mill Rd., Springfield, 22152-2022. Tel: 703-451-8576; Fax: 703-269-1121; Email: office@stbernpar.org; Web: www.stbernpar.org.
School—St. Bernadette School, (Grades PreSchool-8), 7602 Old Keene Mill Rd., Springfield, 22152-2099.
Tel: 703-451-8696; Fax: 703-269-1116; Email: school@stbernschool.org; Web: www.stbernpar.org. Barbara Dalmut, Prin. Lay Teachers 35; Students 415.
Catechesis Religious Program—Barbara Dalmut, D.R.E.; Martha Drennan, D.R.E., Email: mdrennan@stbernpar.org; Kara Lilly, Youth Ministry, Email: . Students 444.

2—ST. RAYMOND OF PENAFORT (1997) Revs. John C. De Celles; Charles C. Smith, Parochial Vicar.
Parish Office & Res.: 8750 Pohick Rd., Springfield, 22153. Tel: 703-440-0535; Fax: 703-440-0538; Email: straychrch@aol.com; Web: straymonds.org.
Catechesis Religious Program—Mary Salmon, D.R.E. Students 282.

STAFFORD, STAFFORD CO., ST. WILLIAM OF YORK (1971) Revs. Robert J. DeMartino; Lino Rico Rostro, Parochial Vicar; Deacon James J. Benisek.
Res. & Mailing Address: 3130 Jefferson Davis Hwy., Stafford, 22554. Tel: 540-659-1102;
Fax: 540-659-5637; Web: www.swoycc.org.
School—St. William of York School, (Grades PreK-8), Tel: 540-659-5207; Email: dlima@stwillschool.org; Web: www.stwillschool.org. Mr. David Lima, Prin. Lay Teachers 35; Students 225.
Catechesis Religious Program—Students 490.

STERLING, LOUDOUN CO., CHRIST THE REDEEMER (1972) Revs. Joel D. Jaffe; Mark E. Moretti, Parochial Vicar.
Res.: 12494 Cliff Edge Dr., Herndon, 20170.
Tel: 703-430-1686.
Church: 46833 Harry Byrd Hwy., Sterling, 20164.
Tel: 703-430-0811; Email: J.Jaffe@arlingtondiocese.org; Email: Donna.Ata@ctrcc.org; Web: www.ctrcc.org.
Catechesis Religious Program—Mr. Jay Cuasay, D.R.E. High School/Confirmation; Mrs. M. Amelia Silva, D.R.E. Hispanic; S. Hunter Lillis, D.R.E. English K-6. Students 765.

TRIANGLE, PRINCE WILLIAM CO., ST. FRANCIS OF ASSISI (1957) Revs. John F. O'Connor, O.F.M.; John V. Alderson, O.F.M., Parochial Vicar; Ignatius Harding, O.F.M., Parochial Vicar; Deacons Henry Fulmer; Michael Gomes.
Res.: 18726 Kerill Rd., Triangle, 22172.
Tel: 703-221-5697; Web: www.stfrncis.org.
Church: 18825 Fuller Heights Rd., Triangle, 22172.
Tel: 703-221-4044; Email: phillipss.sfas@gmail.com; Email: edk@stfrncis.org.
School—St. Francis of Assisi School, (Grades PreK-8), Tel: 703-221-3868; Email: tricia.barber@verizon.net; Web: www.stfas.org. Dr. Tricia Barber, Prin. Clergy 10; Lay Teachers 27; Students 240.
Catechesis Religious Program—Students 740.

VIENNA, FAIRFAX CO.

1—ST. MARK (1965) [CEM] Rev. Patrick Holroyd; Deacons John P. Allen; Charles Duck.
Res.: 9970 Vale Rd., Vienna, 22181.
Tel: 703-281-9100; Fax: 703-281-0675; Web: www.stmark.org; Email: csheehan@stmark.org.
School—St. Mark School, (Grades PreK-8), 9972 Vale Rd., Vienna, 22181. Tel: 703-281-9103; Email: gostmark@stmark.go. Darcie Girmus, Prin. Clergy 7; Lay Teachers 32; Students 400.
Catechesis Religious Program—Students 670.

2—OUR LADY OF GOOD COUNSEL (1956) Revs. Matthew J. Hillyard, O.S.F.S.; John J. Dolan, O.S.F.S., Parochial Vicar; Patrick J. Kifolo, O.S.F.S., In Res.; William J. Metzger, O.S.F.S., In Res.; Deacons Thomas G. White Jr., Admin.; Christopher G. Moore; Mr. Gerard Hall, Liturgy Dir.; Mr. Derek Rogers, Youth Min.
Office, Res. & Mailing Address: 8601 Wolftrap Rd., Vienna, 22182-5026. Tel: 703-938-2828;
Fax: 703-938-2829; Email: info@olgcva.org; Web: www.olgcva.org.
School—Our Lady of Good Counsel School, (Grades PreK-8), Tel: 703-938-3600; Email: info@olgcschool.org; Web: olgcschool.org. Mrs. Adrianne Jewett, Prin. Lay Teachers 39; Students 395; Clergy / Religious Teachers 1.
Catechesis Religious Program—Amy Winkler, D.R.E. Students 707.

WARRENTON, FAUQUIER CO., ST. JOHN THE EVANGELIST (1874) Revs. James R. Gould; Isaiah Bugaku, A.J., Parochial Vicar; Henry Ernesto Rivera, Parochial Vicar; Deacons Don Libera; Jonathan A. Williams.
Res.: 271 Winchester St., Warrenton, 20186.
Tel: 540-347-4886; Fax: 540-347-1274; Email: info@stjohntheevangelist.org; Web: www.stjohntheevangelist.org.
School—St. John the Evangelist School, (Grades PreK-8), 111 John E. Mann St., Warrenton, 20186.
Tel: 540-347-2458; Fax: 540-349-8007; Email: tmacdonald@sjesva.org; Email: kgay@sjesva.org. Temple MacDonald, Prin. Lay Teachers 24; Students 195.
Catechesis Religious Program—Students 662.

WASHINGTON, RAPPAHANNOCK CO., ST. PETER (2005)
12762 Lee Hwy., Washington, 22747.
Tel: 540-675-3432; Fax: 540-675-1053; Email: stpeterschurch@comcast.net. Rev. Kevin J. Beres; Deacon Robert E. Benyo.
Catechesis Religious Program—Students 43.

WINCHESTER, FREDERICK CO., SACRED HEART OF JESUS (1870) [CEM]
120 Keating Dr., Winchester, 22601-2806. Revs. Bjorn C. Lundberg; Michael R. Duesterhaus, Parochial Vicar; Stephen Holmes, Parochial Vicar; Deacon Mark R. Maines.
Res.: 130 Keating Dr., Winchester, 22601-2806.
Tel: 540-662-5858; Fax: 540-313-4915; Email: office@sacredheartwinchester.org; Web: sacredheartwinchester.org.
School—Sacred Heart of Jesus School, (Grades PreK-8), 110 Keating Dr., Winchester, 22601-2806.
Tel: 540-662-7177; Email: sparks@sacredheartva.org; Web: sacredheartva.org. Mrs. Susan Parks, Prin. Clergy 16; Lay Teachers 18; Students 257.
Catechesis Religious Program—Julia Carty, D.R.E. Students 774.
Mission—St. Bridget of Ireland, Berryville, Clarke Co.

WOODBRIDGE, PRINCE WILLIAM CO., OUR LADY OF ANGELS (1959) Revs. J. Kevin O'Keefe; Zacarias Martinez, Parochial Vicar; Thomas B. Cavanaugh, Parochial Vicar; Alexander Diaz, Parochial Vicar; Deacons Anthony E. Calderon, D.R.E.; Danny E. Johnson, (Retired); Emil P. Myskowski, (Retired).
Res.: 13752 Mary's Way, Woodbridge, 22191.
Tel: 703-494-2444; Tel: 703-494-5015;
Fax: 703-494-0005; Web: www.olacc.org.
Catechesis Religious Program—13750 Mary's Way, Woodbridge, 22191. Tel: 703-494-3696; Email: ACalderon@olacc.org. Students 913.

WOODSTOCK, SHENANDOAH CO., ST. JOHN BOSCO (1888) Revs. Michael J. Dobbins, V.F.; Richard J. Ley, Parochial Vicar; Deacon Steven M. Clifford.
Res.: 315 N. Main St., Woodstock, 22664.
Tel: 540-459-4448; Fax: 540-459-4406; Email: office@sjbwoodstock.org; Web: www.sjbwoodstock.org.
Church: 315 N. Main St., Woodstock, 22664.
Catechesis Religious Program—Sr. Laura Elena Nieves, P.C.I., D.R.E. Students 176.
Mission—Our Lady of the Shenandoah, 240 Fritzel Way, P.O. Box 654, Basye, Shenandoah Co. 22810. Tel: 540-856-2411; Email: office@sjbwoodstock.org.

DIOCESAN MISSION PARISHES

DOMINICAN REPUBLIC

1—SAN FRANCISCO DE ASIS, BANICA
Mailing Address: 200 N. Glebe Rd., Ste. 914, 22203.
Tel: 829-665-3687; Email: frohare@yahoo.com; Web: www.banicamission.com. Revs. Stephen F. McGraw; Jason Weber, Parochial Vicar; Deacon Roberto Alcantara.
Catechesis Religious Program—Sr. Gracia Viel, D.R.E.

2—SAN JOSE, PEDRO SANTANA
Mailing Address: 200 N. Glebe Rd., Ste. 914, 22203. Web: www.banicamission.com. Revs. Stephen F. McGraw; Jason Weber, Parochial Vicar.
Catechesis Religious Program—Sr. Gracia Viel, D.R.E.

On Duty Outside the Diocese:
Revs.—
Albertson, Eric J., CH (Col.)
Burchell, Jason C., CH (LT.)
deLadurantaye, Paul F., S.T.D., 00120 Vatican City State
Dundon, Luke R., CH (LT.), LHD-6, Fpo, AP 96617-1656
Fimian, Kevin J., Virginia Beach
Gross, Lee W., S.T.L., Mount St. Mary Seminary, Emmitsburg, MD
Hanley, Daniel F., Vatican City State 00120
Heisler, John F., M.A., Pontifical College Josephinum, Columbus, OH
Hinkle, James C., CH (LT.)
Magat, Geronimo A., Pontifical Canadian College, Rome, Italy
McGraw, Stephen F., Dominican Republic
Mode, Daniel L., CH (Capt.)
Mullins, Richard A., St. Thomas the Apostle Church, Washington, D.C.
Nassetta, Peter W., Y.A., Campus Min., JMU Campus Ministry, Harrisonburg
Riley, John J., Augustine Institute, Greenwood Village, CO
Terrien, Lawrence B., S.S., Dir. Spiritual Life Progs., Systematic Theology, St. Mary's Seminary & University, 5400 Roland Ave., Baltimore, MD 21210-1994
Weber, Jason, Banica Mission, Dominican Republic
Weston, Michael D., Basilica of the National Shrine of the Immaculate Conception, Washington D.C.

Military Chaplains:
Revs.—
Albertson, Eric J., CH (Col.)
Burchell, Jason C., CH (LT.)
Dundon, Luke R., CH (LT.)
Hinkle, James C., Ch (LT.)
Mode, Daniel L., CH (Capt.).

On Leave of Absence:
Revs.—
Bartlett, Brendan W.
Belli, Bryan W.
Erbacher, William J.
Ettner, Wilhelm J.
Tran, Nhi Dinh
Tucker, James A.

Retired:
Rev. Msgrs.—
Cosby, R. Roy, M.A., V.G., (Retired), Rockville, VA
Cregan, John C., (Retired), Annandale, VA
Hendrick, Frank J., (Retired), Southern Pines, NC
Mahler, Frank E., (Retired), Henrico, VA
Revs.—
Biniek, Joseph P., (Retired), New Orleans, LA
Brooks, Robert C., (Retired), Arlington, VA
Buckner, Christopher M., (Retired), Herndon, VA
Buitrago, Tarsicio, (Retired), Falls Church, VA
Clark, Joseph J., (Retired), Rehoboth Beach, DE
Daly, Jerome R., (Retired), Fort Belvoir, VA
Greenhalgh, Donald C., (Retired), Fairfax, VA
Grinnell, Horace H., (Retired), Annandale, VA
Krempa, Stanley J., V.F., (Retired), Alexandria, VA
Majka, Philip S., (Retired), Annandale, VA
McAfee, Franklyn M., (Retired), Hyattsville, MD
McGuill, Martin, J.C.D., (Retired), Ft. Myer, VA
Mendez, Francisco, (Retired), Annandale, VA
O'Brien, Cornelius, (Retired), County Cork, Ireland
Richardson, M. Paul, (Retired), Annandale, VA
Specht, Terry W., (Retired), Arlington, VA
Trinkle, Clarence M., (Retired), Linden, VA
Trong, John T.B., (Retired), Annandale, VA
Weymes, Gerald, (Retired), Ashburn, VA.

Permanent Deacons:
Allen, John P., St. Mark, Vienna
Anderson, Albert A. Jr., St. Joseph, Alexandria
Anthony, Gerard-Marie, St. Timothy, Chantilly
Barros, Orlando J., All Saints, Manassas
Benisek, James J., St. William of York, Stafford
Benyo, Robert E., St. Peter, Washington
Bernaola, Alberto G., St. Mary, Fredericksburg
Betit, Eugene D., (Leave of Absence)
Braun, Richard L., (Leave of Absence)

Burrell, Richard L., (Retired)
Caporaletti, Alfred, Sacred Heart, Manassas
Clifford, Steven M., St. John Bosco, Woodstock
Conroy, David E. Sr., St. Timothy, Chantilly; St. Patrick, Fredericksburg
Cronican, Richard A., St. Jude, Fredericksburg
D'Antonio, Paul A., St. Patrick, Fredericksburg
Delio, Richard P., St. Mary of the Immaculate Conception, Fredericksburg
Dixon, Stephen J., St. Rita, Alexandria
Donovan, William J., J.C.L., St. Ann, Arlington
Duck, Charles, St. Mark, Vienna
Eberlein, John W., All Saints, Manassas
Einsmann, W. Vincent, Holy Family, Dale City
Fishenden, James A., St. James, Falls Church
Fursman, Thomas M., St. Isidore the Farmer, Orange
George, Paul J., (Leave of Absence)
Gillispie, Robert R., (Leave of Absence)
Gliot, Edward C., St. James, Falls Church
Goldsmith, Ralph A., St. John the Baptist, Front Royal
Gomez, Helio A., Holy Family, Dale City
Gregory, Paul A., St. Matthew, Spotsylvania
Grodek, Thomas L., Holy Spirit, Annandale
Gutierrez, Julain J., Good Shepherd, Alexandria
Hammel, Lawrence V., St. Francis de Sales, Purcellville
Hepler, James C., St. Timothy, Chantilly
Holley, Dennis A., St. John Neumann, Reston
Hubbarth, John A., St. Matthew, Spotsylvania
Kenski, Frank G., (Retired)
Konold, Paul, St. Theresa, Ashburn
LaDuca, Nicholas J. Jr., Holy Spirit, Annandale
Libera, Donald P. Jr., St. John the Evangelist, Warrenton
Ligon, Jack M., (Retired)
Lopez, Jose J., St. Leo the Great, Fairfax
Lyons, Robert A., St. Jude, Fredericksburg
Maines, Mark R., Sacred Heart of Jesus, Winchester
Majewski, Brian R., All Saints, Manassas
Mallon, John B., (Leave of Absence)
Maurer, David M., St. Leo the Great, Fairfax
McCaffrey, David S., St. Michael, Annandale
Mendoza, Mario L., St. Anthony, Falls Church
Meyers, Jeffrey M., St. Mary of Sorrows, Fairfax
Mochel, Michael J., St. Clare of Assisi, Clifton
Moore, Christopher G., Our Lady of Good Counsel, Vienna
Moore, Gerald J., Sacred Heart, Manassas
Myskowski, Emil P., (Retired)
Nguyen, Vincent Cong T., St. Philip, Falls Church
Nickle, Dennis E., (Leave of Absence)
O'Connell, Richard T., (Retired)
O'Neil, Michael J., Good Shepherd, Alexandria
Ochenkowski, J. Paul, St. Veronica, Chantilly
Ostrom, Roger T., (Retired)
Ouellette, Patrick A., Good Shepherd, Alexandria
Pardo, Jose I., (Retired)
Perusi, Donald L., St. Patrick, Fredericksburg
Pham, Kien Minh, (Retired)
Pivarnik, William D., (Retired)
Prien, Richard K., Diocese of Richmond
Ramirez, Eduardo A., (Leave of Absence)
Remedios, Antonio J., Our Lady, Queen of Peace, Arlington
Ross, Scott A., Holy Trinity, Gainesville
Sandoval, Atanacio, St. John Neumann, Reston
Santiago, Joseph L., Holy Family, Dale City
Silva, R. Marques, St. Leo the Great, Fairfax
Singer, Joseph R., (Retired)
Slayter, Timothy H., Sacred Heart, Manassas
Soutuyo, Francisco R., (Leave of Absence)
Stenstrom, James M., St. Patrick, Fredericksburg
Strain, Patrick M., St. Matthew, Spotsylvania
Tirado, Ramon, Precious Blood, Culpeper
Van de Voorde, James R., All Saints, Manassas
Vivaldi, Noel, St. Leo the Great, Fairfax
Wagner, John A., St. John Neumann, Reston
Warner, Robert W. Jr., St. Elizabeth Ann, Seton, Lake Ridge
Waters, Michael A., St. Lawrence, Alexandria
Whelan, Edward F. Jr., St. Matthew, Spotsylvania
White, Thomas G. Jr., Good Shepherd, Alexandria
Williams, Jonathan A., St. John the Evangelist, Warrenton.

INSTITUTIONS LOCATED IN DIOCESE

[A] COLLEGES AND UNIVERSITIES

ARLINGTON. *Marymount University*, 2807 N. Glebe Rd., 22207. Tel: 703-284-1598; Fax: 703-284-1595; Email: mshank@marymount.edu; Email: hphillip@marymount.edu; Web: www.marymount.edu. Dr. Matthew D. Shank, Pres.; Rev. Thomas M. Yehl, Y.A., Chap. Religious of the Sacred Heart of MaryResident and Non-resident coed students. Clergy 1; Sisters 2; Students 3,418; Lay Faculty & Staff 550; Clergy / Religious Teachers 1.

FRONT ROYAL. *Christendom College*, 134 Christendom Dr., Front Royal, 22630. Tel: 540-636-2900; Email: walter@christendom.edu; Web: www.christendom.edu. Rev. Marcus A. Pollard, Chap.; Timothy T. O'Donnell, S.T.D., Pres. Resident and Non-resident students. Lay Teachers 53; Priests 3; Students 504; Clergy / Religious Teachers 2.

[B] GRADUATE SCHOOLS

ARLINGTON. **Divine Mercy University*, (Grades Masters-Doctorate), 2001 Jefferson Davis Hwy., Ste. 511, 22202. Tel: 703-416-1441; Fax: 703-416-8588; Email: communications@divinemercy.edu; Web: www.divinemercy.edu. Rev. Charles Sikorsky, L.C., Pres. Dedicated to the development and promotion of approaches to mental health founded in the Catholic vision of the human person. Master of Science (M.S.) in Clinical Mental Health Counseling and Doctor of Psychology (Psy.D.) degrees in Clinical Psychology. Faculty 35; Priests 4; Students 325; Total Staff 35.

ALEXANDRIA. *Notre Dame Graduate School of Christendom College*, 4407 Sano St., Alexandria, 22312. Web: www.graduate.christendom.edu. Robert Matava, Ph.D., Dean; Maura McMahon, Registrar & Business Officer; Joseph Arias, Dean, Students & Asst. Prof.; Annie Adams, Librarian; Virginia Norris, Admin. Asst. to the Dean. Lay Teachers 12; Priests 8; Total Enrollment 149; Total Staff 4; Clergy / Religious Teachers 5.

[C] HIGH SCHOOLS, DIOCESAN

ARLINGTON. *Bishop Denis J. O'Connell High School*, 6600 Little Falls Rd., 22213. Tel: 703-237-1400; Fax: 703-237-1465; Email: apaulson@bishopoconnell.org; Web: www.bishopoconnell.org. Dr. Joseph E. Vorbach III, Ph. D., Pres.; Carl O. Patton, Prin; Erin O'Malley, Dean, Student Srvcs.; Sr. Catherine Hill, I.H.M., Dean, Academics; Meghan Lonergan, Dean, Mission; Frank Roque, Dean; Rev. Gregory S. Thompson, Chap.; Mrs. Eva Gonsalves, Librarian. Clergy 1; Lay Teachers 151; Priests 1; Sisters 5; Students 1,195; Total Staff 157; Clergy / Religious Teachers 6.

ALEXANDRIA. *Bishop Ireton High School*, 201 Cambridge Rd., Alexandria, 22314. Tel: 703-751-7606; Fax: 703-212-8173; Email: john.lilly@bishopireton.org; Web: www.bishopireton.org. Dr. Thomas Curry, Head, School; Denise Tobin, Prin.; Rev. Edwin Bresnahan, Chap. & Dir. Campus Ministry; Stephen Crooker, Dir. Instruction; Mary Jordan, Asst. Prin. Student Life; Lonnell Battle, Asst. Prin. Academics; Elizabeth Jones, Librarian; Mrs. Gail Georgieff, Registrar; Mrs. Lisa Ring, Business Mgr. Brothers 1; Lay Teachers 65; Nurses 1; Priests 1; Sisters 1; Students 795; Staff 42.

DUMFRIES. *Saint John Paul the Great Catholic High School*, 17700 Dominican Dr., Potomac Shores, 22026. Tel: 703-445-0300; Fax: 703-445-0301; Email: info@jpthegreat.org; Web: www.jpthegreat.org. Sr. Mary Veronica Keller, O.P., Pres.; Shawn McNulty, Prin.; Dr. Adam Bigbee, Vice Prin.; Chris VanderWoude, Dir.; Rev. Keith D. Cummings, Chap.; Ms. Mary Gildersleeve, Contact Person; Mr. Tom Giska, Dir. Guidance; Lisa Fred, Librarian; Laurie Wavering, Registrar; Andrew Hawley, Business Mgr. (Full-time, paid) 57; Priests 1; Sisters 4; Students 743; Clergy / Religious Teachers 3.

FAIRFAX. *Saint Paul VI Catholic High School*, 10675 Fairfax Blvd., Fairfax, 22030. Tel: 703-352-0925; Fax: 703-273-9845; Web: www.paulvi.net. Mrs. Virginia Colwell, Headmaster; Thomas G. Opfer, Prin.; Eileen Hanley, Dir. of Admissions & Asst. Prin.; Rev. Stephen J. Schultz, Chap. Deacons 1; Lay Teachers 91; Priests 1; Students 853; Religious Teachers 1.

[D] ELEMENTARY SCHOOLS, PRIVATE

BRISTOW. *Linton Hall*, (Grades PreK-8), 9535 Linton Hall Rd., Bristow, 20136. Tel: 703-368-3157; Fax: 703-368-3036; Email: lhs@lintonhall.edu; Web: www.lintonhall.edu. Mrs. Elizabeth Poole, Prin. Lay Teachers 24; Benedictine Sisters of Virginia 2; Students 163.

SPRINGFIELD. **Angelus Academy*, (Grades PreK-8), 7644 Dynatech Ct., Springfield, 22153. Tel: 703-924-3996; Fax: 703-924-9683; Email: principal@angelusacademy.org; Web: www.angelusacademy.org. Vivian Zini, Prin. Lay Teachers 24; Students 116.

[E] INTERPAROCHIAL SCHOOLS

CULPEPER. *Epiphany School*, (Grades PreK-8), 1211 E. Grandview Ave., Culpeper, 22701. Tel: 540-825-9017; Fax: 540-825-1733; Email: office@epiphanycatholicschool.org; Web: www.epiphanycatholicschool.org. James F. Oliver, Prin. Sponsoring parishes: Precious Blood, Culpeper; Our Lady of the Blue Ridge, Madison; St. Isidore the Farmer, Orange and St. Peter, Washington, VA. Clergy 3; Lay Teachers 23; Priests 2; Students 134.

WOODBRIDGE. *St. Thomas Aquinas Regional School*, (Grades PreK-8), 13750 Mary's Way, Woodbridge, 22191. Tel: 703-491-4447; Fax: 703-492-8828; Email: office@aquinastars.org; Web: www.aquinastars.org. Sr. Kateri Rose Masters, O.P., Prin. Sponsoring parishes: Our Lady of Angels, Woodbridge; St. Elizabeth Ann Seton, Lake Ridge; and Sacred Heart, Manassas. Lay Teachers 42; Dominican Sisters, Congregation of St. Cecilia 4; Students 440; Total Staff 46; Religious Teachers 4.

[F] DAY CARE AND CHILD LEARNING CENTERS

ALEXANDRIA. *Blessed Sacrament Grade School and Early Childhood Center*, (Grades PreK-8), 1417 W. Braddock Rd., Alexandria, 22302. Tel: 703-998-4170; Fax: 703-998-5033; Email: schoolinfo@blessedsacramentcc.org; Web: www.BlessedSacramentcc.org. Mrs. Valerie Garcia, Prin. Clergy 1; Lay Teachers 35; Students 225; Clergy / Religious Teachers 1.

St. Gabriel's (Children 2-5 years) 4319 Sano St., Alexandria, 22312. Tel: 703-354-0395; Fax: 703-354-0395; Email: stgdaycare@gmail.com. Mother Maria Gonzalez, P.S.S.J., Local Supr. Poor Sisters of St. Joseph (Buenos Aires). Lay Teachers 6; Sisters 4; Students 45.

[G] MONASTERIES AND RESIDENCES OF PRIESTS AND BROTHERS

ARLINGTON. *Missionhurst, C.I.C.M.-Central House and Provincialate*, 4651 N. 25th St., 22207. Tel: 703-528-3800; Fax: 703-528-5355; Email: provincial@missionhurst.org; Email: provsec@missionhurst.org; Email: ustreasurer@missionhurst.org; Web: www.missionhurst.org. Rev. Randy Gonzales, C.I.C.M., Dir., Promotion; Very Rev. Celso Tabalanza, C.C.C.M., Supr.; Revs. Joseph Giordano, C.I.C.M., Rector; Jean-Marie Mvumbi Phongo, Prov. Treas.; Michael Hann, C.I.C.M., Supr.; Joseph Smits, C.I.C.M., (Retired); William Wyndaele, C.I.C.M., (Retired); Pascal Ngboloma Kumanda, C.I.C.M., Non-parochial Ministry; Joseph Dewaele, C.I.C.M., (Retired); Tim Atkin; Andre Kazadi; David Curran, C.I.C.M., (Retired); John Van de Paer, C.I.C.M., (Retired). Congregation of the Immaculate Heart of Mary foreign and home missions.
American I.H.M. Province, Inc.
Immaculate Heart Missions, Inc.
Missionhurst, Inc.

BERRYVILLE. *Community of Cistercians of the Strict Observance, Inc.*, 901 Cool Spring Ln., Berryville, 22611-2700. Tel: 540-955-4383; Tel: 540-955-1425; Fax: 540-955-1356; Email: holycross@hcava.org; Web: www.virginiatrappists.org. Rev. Joseph Wittstock, O.C.S.O., Abbot; Bro. John Atkinson, O.C.S.O.; Revs. Paschal Balkan, O.C.S.O.; Vincent Collins, O.C.S.O.; Maurice Flood, O.C.S.O.; James Orthmann, O.C.S.O., Guestmaster; Bros. Christopher Harmon, O.C.S.O.; Luke Scheuerell, O.C.S.O.; Martin Statz, O.C.S.O.; Joseph Vantu, O.C.S.O.; Efrain Sosa, O.C.S.O., Prior, Novice Master & Vocation Dir. Order of Cistercians of the Strict Observance (Trappist). Priests 6; Residents 11; Community 11; Solemnly Professed Non-priest Monks 5.

[H] CONVENTS AND RESIDENCES FOR SISTERS

ARLINGTON. *Religious of the Sacred Heart of Mary*, Marymount Convent, 2807 N. Glebe Rd., 22207-4299. Tel: 703-908-7526; Fax: 703-284-5992; Email: jamx434@aol.com; Web: www.rshm.org. Sr. Jacqueline Murphy. Sisters 1.

Sisters, Servants of the Immaculate Heart of Mary, Immaculate Heart Convent, 2844 N. Rochester St., 22213. Tel: 703-536-4531; Email: ihmdjo@bishopconnell.org; Web: www.ihmimmaculata.org. Sr. Regina Havens, I.H.M., Supr. Sisters 5.

ALEXANDRIA. *Daughters of St. Paul*, 1025 King St., Alexandria, 22314. Tel: 703-549-3806; Tel: 703-549-1323 (Convent); Email: alexandria@pauline.org; Web: www.pauline.org. Sr. M. Elizabeth Borobia, F.S.P., Local Supr. Sisters 1.

Poor Clare Monastery of Mary, Mother of the Church, 2505 Stonehedge Dr., Alexandria, 22306. Tel: 703-768-4918; Fax: 703-765-2985. Mother Mary Therese, P.C.C., Supr. Observing the Primitive Rule of St. Clare. Postulants 1; Sisters 8; Solemnly Professed 13; Simply (Temporary) Professed 1.

Poor Sisters of St. Joseph, St. Gabriel Convent, 4319 Sano St., Alexandria, 22312. Tel: 703-354-0395; Fax: 703-642-2691; Email: pssjalexandria@gmail.com. Mother Maria Gonzalez, P.S.S.J., Local Supr. Poor Sisters of St. Joseph's Buenos Aires Regional House and Novitiate 8.

BRISTOW. *St. Benedict Monastery / Benedictine Sisters of Virginia*, Benedictine Sisters of Virginia, 9535 Linton Hall Rd., Bristow, 20136-1217. Tel: 571-428-2500; Tel: 703-361-0106; Fax: 703-361-0254; Email: cdwyer@osbva.org; Web: www.osbva.org. Sr. Cecilia Dwyer, O.S.B., Prioress, Tel: 703-368-4848. B.E.A.C.O.N.: Benedictine Educational Assistance Community Outreach to Neighbors, Benedictine Pastoral Center, Linton Hall School, Benedictine Counseling Center. Sisters Resident at Motherhouse 29; Professed Sisters 30.

FAIRFAX. *Adorers of the Holy Cross*, 10917 Marilta Ct., Fairfax, 22030. Tel: 703-591-0862; Fax: 703-591-0862; Email: mtgdlva@yahoo.com. Sr. Theresa Tuyen Thanh Nguyen, M.T.G., Supr. Sisters 6.

Sisters of Our Lady of La Salette (Grenoble, France), 7421 St. Michael's Ln., Annandale, 22003. Tel: 703-865-8767; Email: marijosnds@hotmail.com; Email: sistersoflasalette@yahoo.com; Web: www.soeurs-lasalette.com. Sisters Maria Josephine S. Valenton, S.N.D.S., Admin.; Emelita S. Sobrepena, S.N.D.S., Supr.; Ma. Milagros C. dela Cruz, S.N.D.S., Supr.; Francoise Rasoarivao, Supr.; Leonida Equilos, S.N.D.S., Treas.; Aniliza P. Juan, S.N.D.S.; Kai Ra Nangzing, S.N.D.S.; Rosanne Shemchuk, S.N.D.S.; Zin Thida Htun; Hkawn Htoi Kareng

Legal Name: Sisters of Our Lady of La Salette, Mary Mother of Life, USA Delegation Procure, Corporation. Sisters 10.

FALLS CHURCH. *Franciscan Sisters of the Eucharist*, 7504 St. Philip's Ct., Falls Church, 22042. Tel: 703-204-0837; Fax: 571-419-6214; Email: fallschurch@fsecommunity.org. Sr. Judith Gebelein, F.S.E., Supr. Sisters 5.

LINDEN. *Saint Dominic's Monastery, Dominican Nuns (Contemplative)*, 2636 Monastery Rd., Linden, 22642-5371. Tel: 540-635-3259; Fax: 540-635-5086; Email: monastery@lindenopnuns.org. Sr. Mary Fidelis, O.P., Prioress. Novices 1; Postulants 1; Sisters 6; Solemnly Professed 6; Simply Professed 2.

WOODBRIDGE. *Dominican Sisters Convent* (Congregation of St. Cecilia) 5009 Bobcat Ct., Woodbridge, 22193. Tel: 703-878-7823; Fax: 703-878-7824. Sr. Mary Veronica Keller, O.P., Supr. Sisters 8.

WOODSTOCK. *Pax Christi Institute*, 1769 Quicksburg Rd., Quicksburg, 22847. Tel: 540-740-9108; Fax: 540-740-4236; Email: lauranieves98@yahoo.com. Sr. Guadalupe Therese Licea, P.C.I., Supr. Sisters 2.

[I] RETREAT HOUSES

BERRYVILLE. *Retreat House, Holy Cross Abbey*, 901 Cool Spring Ln., Berryville, 22611-2700. Tel: 540-955-4383; Fax: 540-955-1356; Email: information@hcava.org; Web: www.virginiatrappists.org. Rev. James Orthmann, O.C.S.O., Guest Master.

WHITE POST. *San Damiano Spiritual Life Center*, 125 Old Kitchen Rd., White Post, 22663. Tel: 540-868-9220; Email: SanDamiano@ArlingtonDiocese.org; Web: www.ArlingtonDiocese.org. Deacon Mark R. Maines, Dir.

[J] CAMPUS MINISTRY

ARLINGTON. *Marymount University*, 2807 N. Glebe Rd., 22207. Tel: 703-284-1607; Fax: 703-284-3850; Email: ministry@marymount.edu; Web: www.marymount.edu. Rev. Thomas M. Yehl, Y.A., Chap. & Dir., Email: tmyehl@gmail.com. Campus Ministry.

FAIRFAX. *George Mason University, Catholic Campus Ministry*, 4515 Roberts Rd., Fairfax, 22032. Tel: 703-425-0022; Fax: 703-425-0753; Email: chaplain@gmu.edu; Web: gmuccm.org. Rev. James R. Searby, Chap. & Dir. Campus Ministry; Jennifer Ryan, Campus Min.; Kristen Juda, Campus Min.; John More, Asst. Campus Min.

St. Robert Bellarmine Chapel, George Mason University, 4515 Roberts Rd., Fairfax, 22032. Tel: 703-425-0022; Fax: 703-425-0753; Email: chaplain@gmu.edu; Web: gmuccm.org. Rev. James R. Searby, Chap. Catholic Campus Ministry.

FREDERICKSBURG. *University of Mary Washington*, Catholic Campus Ministry, 1614 College Ave., Fredericksburg, 22401. Tel: 540-373-6746; Email: fathervaccaro@umwccm.org; Web: umwcatholic.org. Rev. Christopher T. Vaccaro, Chap. & Dir.; Katrina Orteyza, Campus Min.; Ms. Sarah Taylor, Campus Min.; Mrs. Kathreja Sarfati, Admin.; David Thielman, Music Min.; Mrs. Carmel Domingue, Bookkeeper.

[K] MISCELLANEOUS

ARLINGTON. *Arlington Diocesan Investment and Loan Corp.*, 200 N. Glebe Rd., Ste. 914, 22203. Tel: 703-841-2500; Fax: 703-524-5028; Email: m.herrmann@arlingtondiocese.org. Very Rev. Thomas P. Ferguson, J.C.L., Ph.D., V.G., Pres.

**Commissioned by Christ*, 200 N. Glebe Rd., Ste. 700, 22203.

Diocese of Arlington Scholarship Foundation, Inc., 200 N. Glebe Rd., Ste. 914, 22203. Tel: 703-841-2500; Fax: 703-524-5028; Email: m.herrmann@arlingtondiocese.org. Very Rev. Thomas P. Ferguson, J.C.L., Ph.D., V.G., Pres.

The Foundation for the Catholic Diocese of Arlington, Inc., 200 N. Glebe Rd., Ste. 914, 22203. Tel: 703-841-2500; Fax: 703-524-5028; Email: m.herrmann@arlingtondiocese.org. Very Rev. Thomas P. Ferguson, J.C.L., Ph.D., V.G., Pres.

Rooted in Faith-Forward in Hope, Inc., 200 N. Glebe Rd., Ste. 914, 22203. Tel: 703-841-2500; Fax: 703-524-5028; Email: m.herrmann@arlingtondiocese.org. Very Rev. Thomas P. Ferguson, J.C.L., Ph.D., V.G., Pres.

The Women's Apostolate to Youth, 7503 Wilderness Way, Fairfax Station, 22039. Tel: 571-225-0044; Tel: 703-569-8750; Email: SMwithHAM@verizon.net; Email: womenofway@gmail.com; Web: womensapostolatetoyouth.blogspot.com. Sally Allman, Dir.

Youth Apostles Institute, An Association of Christian Faithful, 1600 Carlin Ln., McLean, 22101-4100. Tel: 703-556-0914; Fax: 703-556-9455; Email: ya.opsmanager@gmail.com; Web: www.youthapostles.org. Revs. Ramon Dominguez, Y.A.; Michael F. Kuhn, Y.A.; Peter W. Nassetta, Y.A.; David M. Sharland, Y.A.; Thomas M. Yehl, Y.A. Youth Apostles is a community of Consecrated priests, Consecrated laymen, married, and single men who work with other volunteers to inspire young people to live a Christ-like life through parish and college campus ministries. Students 1,000; Clergy / Religious Teachers 11.

ALEXANDRIA. **Pan American Catholic Health Care Network*, 8021 Lynnfield Dr., Alexandria, 22306.

ANNANDALE. **Catholic Athletes For Christ*, 3703 Cameron Mills Rd., Annandale, 22305. Tel: 703-239-3070; Email: info@catholicathletesforchrist.org; Email: ray@catholicathletesforchrist.org; Web: www.catholicathletesforchrist.org. Mr. Ray McKenna, Pres.

DUMFRIES. **St. Luke Foundation for Haiti*, 3999 Great Harvest Ct., Dumfries, 22025. Tel: 703-580-8850; Fax: 703-580-8840; Email: fkrafft1@comcast.net. Frank Krafft, Treas.

FAIRFAX. *Alpha Omega Clinic and Consultation Services*, 3607A Chain Bridge Rd., Fairfax, 22030. Tel: 301-767-1733; Fax: 301-767-1743; Email: alphaomegaclinic@verizon.net; Web: www.aoccs.org. Rev. Frank Formolo.

**Divine Mercy Care*, 4001 Fair Ridge Dr., Ste. 305, Fairfax, 22033-2917. Tel: 703-934-5552; Fax: 703-934-2187; Email: info@divinemercycare.org; Web: www.divinemercycare.org. John T. Bruchalski, M.D., F.A.C.O.G., Board Chm., Email: info@divinemercycare.org; Karen Cassidy, COO.

FRONT ROYAL. **Human Life International*, 4 Family Life Ln., Front Royal, 22630. Tel: 540-635-7884; Email: hli@hli.org; Web: www.hli.org. Rev. Shenan J. Boquet, Pres.

**Seton Home Study School*, 1350 Progress Dr., Front Royal, 22630. Tel: 540-636-9990; Fax: 540-636-1602; Email: info@setonhome.org; Web: www.setonhome.org. Dr. Mary K. Clark, Dir.

MANASSAS. **Cardinal Newman Society*, 10432 Balls Ford Rd,, Ste. 300, Manassas, 20109. Tel: 703-367-0333; Fax: 703-396-8668; Email: operations@cardinalnewmansociety.org. Patrick J. Reilly, Pres.

MCLEAN. **Institute of Catholic Culture*, P.O. Box 10101, Mc Lean, 22102. Tel: 540-635-7155; Email: info@instituteofcatholicculture.org; Web: www.instituteofcatholicculture.org. Rev. Hezekias Carnazzo, Dir.

Secular Institute "Stabat Mater", 2001 Great Falls St., McLean, 22101. Tel: 703-536-3546; Email: aperezalca@cox.net; Web: www.stabatmater.net. Antonio Perez-Alcala, Local Dir.

SPOTSYLVANIA. *St. Francis Catholic Worker (West)*, 9631 Peppertree Rd., Spotsylvania, 22553. Tel: 540-972-3218; Email: stfranciscw@wildblue.net; Web: www.catholicworker.org. Mr. John Mahoney, Vice Pres. Total in Residence 2.

VIENNA. *Mount Tabor Society, Inc.*, 2363 Hunter Mill Rd., Vienna, 22181. Tel: 703-261-6857; Email: provincial@missionhurst.org. Rev. William G. Quigley, C.I.C.M., Rector. A House of Prayer and Christian Community.

RELIGIOUS INSTITUTES OF MEN REPRESENTED IN THE DIOCESE

For further details refer to the corresponding bracketed number in the Religious Institutes of Men or Women section.

[]—*Apostles of Jesus*—A.J.
[0350]—*Cistercians Order of the Strict Observance* (Trappists)—O.C.S.O.
[0650]—*Congregation of the Holy Spirit*—C.S.Sp.
[]—*Disciples of the Hearts of Jesus and Mary*—D.C.J.M.
[0520]—*Franciscan Friars* (Holy Name Prov.)—O.F.M.
[0860]—*Missionhurst Congregation of the Immaculate Heart of Mary*—C.I.C.M.
[0920]—*Oblates of St. Francis de Sales* (Wilmington-Philadelphia Prov.)—O.S.F.S.
[]—*Order of St. Augustine (Augustinians)*—O.S.A.
[0975]—*Society of Our Lady of the Most Holy Trinity*—S.O.L.T.
[0700]—*St. Joseph Society of the Sacred Heart* (Baltimore, MD)—S.S.J.
[0560]—*Third Order Regular of Saint Francis* (Sacred Heart Prov.)—T.O.R.
[]—*Vietnamese Dominican Fathers* (Calgary, Alberta, Canada)—O.P.
[]—*Youth Apostles*—Y.A.

RELIGIOUS INSTITUTES OF WOMEN REPRESENTED IN THE DIOCESE

[4155]—*Adorers of the Holy Cross*—M.T.G.
[0230]—*Benedictine Sisters of Virginia*—O.S.B.
[1920]—*Congregation of the Sisters of the Holy Cross*—C.S.C.
[1070-07]—*Dominican Sisters Congregation of St. Cecilia*—O.P.
[1250]—*Franciscan Sisters of the Eucharist*—F.S.E.
[]—*Franciscan Sisters of the Immaculate Conception of Glasgow, Scotland*—O.S.F.
[1880]—*Handmaidens of Reparation of the Sacred Heart of Jesus*—A.R.
[3060]—*Oblate Sisters of St. Francis de Sales*—O.S.F.S.
[3760]—*Order of St. Clare (Cloistered)*—P.C.C.
[]—*Pax Christi Institute* (Corpus Christi, TX)—P.C.I.
[0950]—*Pious Society of Daughters of St. Paul*—F.S.P.
[3250]—*Poor Sisters of St. Joseph*—P.S.S.J.
[3465]—*Religious of the Sacred Heart of Mary* (Eastern North Amer. Prov.)—R.S.H.M.
[2990]—*Sisters of Notre Dame*—S.N.D.
[]—*Sisters of Our Lady of La Salette* (Grenoble, France)—S.N.D.S.
[3893]—*Sisters of St. Joseph of Chestnut Hill* (Philadelphia)—S.S.J.
[]—*Sisters of the Humility of Mary*—H.M.
[2170]—*Sisters, Servants of the Immaculate Heart of Mary*—I.H.M.

NECROLOGY

† Hamilton, Daniel E., (Retired), Died Dec. 26, 2018
† Pilon, Mark A., (Retired), Died Mar. 19, 2018

An asterisk (*) denotes an organization that has established tax-exempt status directly with the IRS and is not covered by the USCCB Group Ruling.

Archdiocese of Atlanta

(Archidioecesis Atlantensis)

Most Reverend

BERNARD E. SHLESINGER, III

Auxiliary Bishop of Atlanta; ordained June 22, 1996; appointed Auxiliary Bishop of Atlanta and Titular Bishop of Naiera May 15, 2017; ordained July 19, 2017.

(VACANT SEE)

Catholic Center Archdiocese of Atlanta: 2401 Lake Park Dr., S.E., Smyrna, GA 30080-8862. Tel: 404-920-7300; Fax: 404-920-7301.

Web: www.archatl.com

Most Reverend

JOEL M. KONZEN, S.M.

Auxiliary Bishop of Atlanta; ordained May 19, 1979; appointed Auxiliary Bishop of Atlanta, Moderator of the Curia and Titular Bishop of Leavenworth February 5, 2018; ordained April 3, 2018.

ESTABLISHED JULY 2, 1956.

Square Miles 21,445.

Canonically Erected November 8, 1956; created an Archdiocese February 21, 1962.

Comprises the 69 Counties in the northern part of the State of Georgia, north of and including the following counties: Lincoln, McDuffie, Warren, Hancock, Baldwin, Putnam, Jasper, Monroe, Upson, Meriwether and Troup

Patrons of the Archdiocese: I. Our Blessed Lady under the title of the Immaculate Heart of Mary; II. Saint Pius X.

For legal titles of parishes and archdiocesan institutions, consult the Archbishop's office.

STATISTICAL OVERVIEW

Personnel	
Archbishops	1
Auxiliary Bishops	2
Abbots	1
Retired Abbots	1
Priests: Diocesan Active in Diocese	144
Priests: Diocesan Active Outside Diocese	9
Priests: Retired, Sick or Absent	39
Number of Diocesan Priests	192
Religious Priests in Diocese	92
Total Priests in Diocese	284
Extern Priests in Diocese	5
Ordinations:	
Diocesan Priests	5
Transitional Deacons	1
Permanent Deacons	10
Permanent Deacons in Diocese	279
Total Brothers	1
Total Sisters	100
Parishes	
Parishes	91
With Resident Pastor:	
Resident Diocesan Priests	70
Resident Religious Priests	15
Without Resident Pastor:	
Administered by Priests	5
Administered by Deacons	1
Missions	11
New Parishes Created	1
Professional Ministry Personnel:	
Sisters	6
Lay Ministers	322
Welfare	
Catholic Hospitals	3
Total Assisted	257,133
Homes for the Aged	2
Total Assisted	558
Special Centers for Social Services	5
Total Assisted	57,342
Educational	
Diocesan Students in Other Seminaries	52
Total Seminarians	52
Colleges and Universities	2
Total Students	490
High Schools, Diocesan and Parish	3
Total Students	2,341
High Schools, Private	9
Total Students	2,397
Elementary Schools, Diocesan and Parish	15
Total Students	5,474
Elementary Schools, Private	3
Total Students	1,099
Catechesis/Religious Education:	
High School Students	10,990
Elementary Students	29,792
Total Students under Catholic Instruction	52,635
Teachers in the Diocese:	
Priests	17
Sisters	12
Lay Teachers	1,190
Vital Statistics	
Receptions into the Church:	
Infant Baptism Totals	7,133
Minor Baptism Totals	966
Adult Baptism Totals	609
Received into Full Communion	850
First Communions	8,894
Confirmations	6,182
Marriages:	
Catholic	1,120
Interfaith	301
Total Marriages	1,421
Deaths	1,607
Total Catholic Population	1,170,000
Total Population	7,480,000

Former Archbishops—Most Revs. FRANCIS E. HYLAND, D.D., J.C.D., appt. Titular Bishop of Gomphi and Auxiliary Bishop of Savannah-Atlanta, Oct. 15, 1949; cons. Dec. 21, 1949; First Bishop of Atlanta, July 17, 1956; installed on Nov. 8, 1956; resigned and appointed Titular Bishop of Bisica, Oct. 11, 1961; died Jan. 31, 1968; PAUL J. HALLINAN, D.D., appt. Bishop of Charleston, Sept. 9, 1958; cons. Oct. 28, 1958; elevated to the Archiepiscopal dignity, Feb. 21, 1962; installed First Archbishop of Atlanta, March 29, 1962; died March 27, 1968; JOSEPH L. BERNARDIN, D.D., appt. Auxiliary of Atlanta, March 9, 1966; cons. April 26, 1966; appt. Gen. Sec. U.S.C.C., April 5, 1968; died Nov. 14, 1996.; THOMAS A. DONNELLAN, appt. Bishop of Ogdensburg, March 4, 1964; cons. April 9, 1964; appt. to Atlanta, May 29, 1968; installed July 16, 1968; died Oct. 15, 1987; EUGENE A. MARINO, S.S.J., D.D., appt. Auxiliary of Washington, July 15, 1974; appt. Archbishop of Atlanta, March 14, 1988; installed May 5, 1988; resigned July 10, 1990; died Nov. 12, 2000; JAMES P. LYKE, O.F.M., Ph.D., appt. Auxiliary Bishop of Cleveland and Titular Bishop of Fornos Maggiore, June 30, 1979; cons. Aug. 1, 1979; appt. Apostolic Administrator Archdiocese of Atlanta, July 10, 1990; appt. Archbishop of Archdiocese of Atlanta, April 30, 1991; installed June 24, 1991; Palium conferred June 29, 1991; died Dec. 27, 1992; JOHN FRANCIS DONOGHUE, D.D., ord. June 4, 1955; appt. Bishop of Charlotte Nov. 6, 1984; installed second Bishop Dec. 18, 1984; appt. Archbishop of Atlanta June 22, 1993; installed Aug. 18, 1993; retired Dec. 9, 2004; died Nov. 11, 2011.; WILTON D. GREGORY.

Vicars General—Most Rev. JOEL M. KONZEN, S.M., V.G., Auxiliary Bishop of Atlanta, Mod. of the Curia, Email: bishopkonzen@archatl.com; KIRIAL DEROZAS-MILES, Exec. Asst., Tel: 404-920-7319; Fax: 404-920-7316; Email: kmiles@archatl.com; Most Rev. BERNARD E. SHLESINGER III, V.G., Auxiliary Bishop of Atlanta, Email: bishopshlesinger@archatl.com; VERONICA REYES, Exec. Asst., Tel: 404-920-7333; Fax: 404-920-7331; Email: vreyes@archatl.com.

Chancellor—Tel: 404-920-7325; Fax: 404-920-7326. Deacon DENNIS J. DORNER, B.A., Tel: 404-920-7325; Fax: 404-920-7326; Email: ddorner@archatl.com; KATH OWENS, Exec. Asst., Tel: 404-920-7328; Fax: 404-920-7326; Email: kowens@archatl.com; JOY PLACE, Administrative Asst., Tel: 404-920-7307; Fax: 404-920-7326; Email: jplace@archatl.com.

Office of Divine Worship—PATRICIA DEJARNETT, Ph.D., Tel: 404-920-7339; Fax: 404-920-7326; Email: pdejarnett@archatl.com.

Chief Operating Office—DAVID R. SPOTANSKI, COO, Tel: 404-920-7323; Fax: 404-920-7316; Email: dspotanski@archatl.com.

Judicial Vicar—Tel: 404-920-7500; Fax: 404-920-7501; Email: dketter@archatl.com. Rev. DANIEL P. KETTER, J.C.L.

Secretary for Finance—BRADLEY WILSON, CFO, 2401 Lake Park Dr., S.E., Smyrna, 30080-8862. Tel: 404-920-7404; Fax: 404-920-7401; Email: bwilson@archatl.com.

Secretary for Catholic Charities Atlanta—VANESSA RUSSELL, CEO, 2401 Lake Park Dr., S.E., Smyrna, 30080-8862. Tel: 404-920-8862; Fax: 404-920-7726; Email: vrussell@catholiccharitiesatlanta.com.

Secretary for Communications—PAULA GWYNN GRANT, Tel: 404-920-7344; Fax: 404-920-7341; Email: pgrant@archatl.com.

Secretary for Schools—DIANE STARKOVICH, Ph.D., 2401 Lake Park Dr., S.E., Smyrna, 30080-8862. Tel: 404-920-7700; Fax: 404-920-7701; Email: dstarkovich@archatl.com.

Secretary for Office of Formation and Discipleship—2401 Lake Park Dr., S.E., Smyrna, 30080-8862. Tel: 404-920-7624; Fax: 404-920-7621; Email: alichtenwalner@archatl.com. ANDREW W. LICHTENWALNER, Ph.D.

Secretary for Human Resources—CHARLES THIBAUDEAU, 2401 Lake Park Dr., S.E., Smyrna, 30080-8862. Tel: 404-920-7482; Fax: 404-920-7481; Email: cthibaudeau@archatl.com.

Archbishop's Office—2401 Lake Park Dr., S.E., Smyrna, 30080-8862. Tel: 404-920-7300; Fax: 404-920-7301; Web: www.archatl.com. MARDESSA SMITH, Sr. Exec. Asst., Tel: 404-920-7303; Fax: 404-920-7301; Email: mwsmith@archatl.com; LILIANA EMURA, Administrative Asst., Tel: 404-920-7304; Fax: 404-920-7301; Email: lemura@archatl.com.

College of Consultors—Most Revs. JOEL M. KONZEN, S.M., V.G.; BERNARD E. SHLESINGER III, V.G.; Rev. Msgrs. W. JOSEPH CORBETT, V.F.; ALBERT W. JOWDY, M.Div.; FRANCIS G. MCNAMEE; DANIEL STACK; Very Rev. JUDE MICHAEL KRILL, O.F.M.Conv., V.F.; Revs. HENRY ATEM, V.F.; ERIC J. HILL; Very Rev. DANIEL P. KETTER, J.C.L.; Rev. MARK STARR.

Deans—Revs. JOHN T. HOWREN, V.F., Northeast Metro Deanery; PAUL A. FLOOD, V.F., North Metro

Deanery; JOHN KOZIOL, O.F.M.Conv., V.F., South Deanery; PAUL D. WILLIAMS JR., V.F., Northwest Deanery; HENRY ATEM, V.F., Southwest Deanery; PABLO POLOCHE, V.F., Northeast Deanery; ROBERTO ORELLANA, V.F., Southeast Deanery; STEPHEN J. LYNESS, V.F., East Deanery; JOHN WALSH, V.F., Northwest Metro Deanery; Very Rev. VICTOR A. GALIER, M.Div., Th.M., V.F., Central Deanery.

Priest Personnel—2401 Lake Park Dr., S.E., Smyrna, 30080-8862. Most Rev. BERNARD E. SHLESINGER III, V.G., Dir.

Vicars for Clergy—Rev. Msgr. HENRY C. GRACZ, M.Div.; Very Rev. RICHARD B. MORROW, B.A., (Retired); Revs. FAUSTO MARQUEZ; JOHN M. MURPHY; FRANCIS TRAN.

Vicar for Consecrated Life—Sr. MARGARET MCANOY, I.H.M., 2401 Lake Park Dr., S.E., Smyrna, 30080-8862. Tel: 404-920-7652.

Archdiocesan Offices

Archives and Records—2401 Lake Park Dr., S.E., Smyrna, 30080-8862. Tel: 404-920-7690. Deacon DENNIS J. DORNER, B.A., Chancellor, Email: ddorner@archatl.com; ANGELIQUE M. RICHARDSON, C.A., Dir. Archives & Records, Tel: 404-920-7694; Fax: 404-920-7691; Email: arichardson@archatl.com; MELANIE MAXWELL, C.A., C.R.A., Records Mgr./Asst. Archivist, Tel: 404-920-7695; Fax: 404-920-7691; Email: mmaxwell@archatl.com; GEOFFREY HETHERINGTON, Archivist/Records Analyst, Tel: 404-920-7693; Fax: 404-920-7691; Email: ghetherington@gmail.com; CLAIRE GALLOWAY JENKINS, C.A., C.R.M., I.G.P., Project Mgr., Tel: 404-920-7692; Fax: 404-920-7691; Email: cjenkins@archatl.com.

Campus Ministry—2401 Lake Park Dr., S.E., Smyrna, 30080-8862. Tel: 404-920-7620; Fax: 404-920-7621; Web: www.archatl.com. VACANT.

Catholic Charities of Atlanta—2401 Lake Park Dr., S.E., Smyrna, 30080-8862. Tel: 404-920-7725; Fax: 404-920-7726 (Confidential Fax); Web: www.catholiccharitiesatlanta.org. GREG THOMPSON, Bd. Chair, Tel: 678-231-1923; Email: gstomco@gmail.com.

Catholic Housing Initiatives, Inc.—VANESSA RUSSELL, 2401 Lake Park Dr., S.E., Smyrna, 30080. Tel: 404-920-7729; Fax: 404-920-7726.

Catholic Retirement Facilities, Inc.—2973 Butner Rd., S.W., Atlanta, 30331. Tel: 404-346-0745; Fax: 404-346-0747. LARGINE JOHNSON, Mgr.

Catholic Construction Services, Inc.—2401 Lake Park Dr., S.E., Smyrna, 30080-8862. Tel: 404-920-7860; Fax: 404-920-7861. JOHN F. SCHIAVONE, Dir. Real Estate Devel., Tel: 404-920-7873; Fax: 404-920-7861; Email: jschiavone@archatl.com; DONNA L. WORLEY, Administrative Project Mgr., Tel: 404-920-7863; Fax: 404-920-7861; Email: dworley@archatl.com; KELLY GRANT, Administrative Asst., Tel: 404-920-7865; Fax: 404-920-7861; Email: kgrant@archat.com.

Senior Project Managers—RANDY HOOD, Tel: 404-920-7867; Fax: 404-920-7861; Email: rhood@archatl.com; DENNIS W. KELLY, Tel: 404-920-7868; Fax: 404-920-7861; Email: dkelly@archatl.com; CARL TREVATHAN, Tel: 404-920-7866; Fax: 404-920-7861; Email: ctrevathan@archatl.com; CARRINGTON MOULTRIE, Sr. Project Mgr., Tel: 404-920-7864; Fax: 404-920-7861; Email: cmoultrie@archatl.com; KARL KOENIG, Project Mgr., Tel: 404-920-7869; Fax: 404-920-7861; Email: kkoenig@archatl.com.

Catholic Schools—2401 Lake Park Dr., S.E., Smyrna, 30080-8862. Tel: 404-920-7700; Fax: 404-920-7701; Web: www.archatl.com. DIANE STARKOVICH, Ph.D., Supt. & Member of the Secretariat, Tel: 404-920-7700; Fax: 404-920-7701; Email: dstarkovich@archatl.com; CONNIE URBANSKI, Ed. D., Assoc. Supt., Tel: 404-920-7716; Fax: 404-920-7701; Email: curbanski@archatl.com; BRIAN DOOLING, Dir. Mktg. & Enrollment, Tel: 404-920-7714; Fax: 404-920-7701; Email: bdooling@archatl.com; NANCY DILLY, School Psychologist, Tel: 404-920-7713; Fax: 404-920-7701; Email: ndilly@archatl.com; MARY JO NICHOLS, Dir. Parish Pre-Schools, Tel: 404-920-7704; Fax: 404-920-7701; Email: mnichols@archatl.com; DONNA TOMLINSON, Administrative Asst. to School Psychologist, Tel: 404-920-7709; Fax: 404-920-7701; Email: dtomlinson@archatl.com; DEBRA WHEELER, Catholic Schools Program Specialist, Tel: 404-920-7708; Fax: 404-920-7701; Email: dwheeler@archatl.com; BRIANNA RODRIGUEZ RIVERA, Receptionist & Administrative Asst., Tel: 404-920-7702; Fax: 404-920-7701; Email: brrivera@archatl.com.

Chancery Facility Management (CFM)—2401 Lake Park Dr., S.E., Smyrna, 30080. Tel: 404-920-7875; Fax: 404-920-7876. ROB MCKINNON, Dir., Email: rmckinnon@archatl.com; PORTIA RILEY, Office Mgr., Email: priley@archatl.com; ARTHUR GLOVER, Facility Supvr., Email: aglover@archatl.com. Facilities Technicians: DEUNTAE ROBINSON, Email: drobinson@archatl.com; JIM HAVERKOS, Email: jhaverkos@archatl.com; CHRISTOPHER WYNNE, Email: cwynne@archatl.com.

Child and Youth Protection—2401 Lake Park Dr., S.E., Smyrna, 30080-8862. Tel: 404-920-7550; Tel: 888-437-0764 (24-Hour Reporting Hotline); Fax: 404-920-7551; Email: ocyp@archatl.com. MARY SUSAN "SUE" STUBBS, Dir. Victim Assistance, Tel: 404-920-7554; Email: sstubbs@archatl.com; TERRY MOSS, Safe Environment Coord., Tel: 404-920-7489; Email: tmoss@archatl.com; PERLA FREED, Dir. Safe Environment, Tel: 404-920-7553; Email: pfreed@archatl.com; GINA GARCIA, OCYP Prog. Asst., Tel: 404-920-7552; Email: ggarcia@archatl.com.

Communications—2401 Lake Park Dr., S.E., Smyrna, 30080-8862. Tel: 404-920-7340; Fax: 404-920-7341; Web: www.archatl.com. PAULA GWYNN GRANT, Dir. & Member of Secretariat, Tel: 404-920-7344; Fax: 404-920-7341; Email: pgrant@archatl.com; TATIANA VILLA, Media & Communications Specialist, Tel: 404-920-7349; Fax: 404-920-7341; Email: tvilla@archatl.com; ALLEN KINZLY, Multimedia Specialist, Tel: 404-920-7348; Fax: 404-920-7341; Email: akinzly@archatl.com; JONATHON HANTEN, Web Devel., Tel: 404-920-7343; Fax: 404-920-7341; Email: jhanten@archatl.com; DAVID PACE, Creative Dir., Tel: 404-920-7342; Fax: 404-920-7341; Email: dpace@archatl.com; SAMANTHA SMITH, Media & Communications Specialist, Tel: 404-920-7346; Fax: 404-920-7341; Email: ssmith@archatl.com; JOANIE SANTANDER, Administrative Asst., Tel: 404-920-7352; Fax: 404-920-7341; Email: jsantander@archatl.com.

The Georgia Bulletin Newspaper—2401 Lake Park Dr., S.E., Smyrna, 30080-8862. Tel: 404-920-7430 ; Fax: 404-920-7431; Web: www.georgiabulletin.org. NICHOLE GOLDEN, Editor, Tel: 404-920-7436; Email: ngolden@georgiabulletin.org; TOM AISTHORPE, Advertising Mgr., Tel: 404-920-7441; Email: taisthorpe@georgiabulletin.org; TINA LEVITT, Business Mgr., Tel: 404-920-7437; Email: tlevitt@georgiabulletin.org; MICHAEL ALEXANDER, Staff Photographer, Tel: 404-920-7432; Email: malexander@georgiabulletin.org; ANDREW NELSON, Staff Reporter, Tel: 404-920-7433; Email: anelson@georgiabulletin.org; TOM SCHULTE, Graphic Designer, Tel: 404-920-7438; Email: tschulte@georgiabulletin.org.

Office of Life, Dignity and Justice—Deacon DENNIS J. DORNER, B.A., Sr. Dir., Tel: 404-920-7325; Fax: 404-920-7326; Email: ddorner@archatl.com; IMELDA RICHARD, Administrative Asst., Tel: 404-920-7350; Email: irichard@archatl.com.

Respect Life—JOEY MARTINECK, Dir., Tel: 404-920-7362; Fax: 404-920-7361; Email: jmartineck@archatl.com.

Jail and Prison Ministry—Deacon RICHARD P. TOLCHER, Dir., Tel: 404-920-7357; Fax: 404-920-7356; Email: rtolcher@archatl.com.

Justice and Peace—KAT DOYLE, Dir., Tel: 404-920-7897; Email: kdoyle@archatl.com; JAYNA HOFFACKER, Prog. Asst., Tel: 404-920-7898; Email: jhoffacker@archatl.com.

Georgia Catholic Conference—FRANK MULCAHY, Dir., Tel: 404-920-7367; Email: fmulcahy@archatl.com.

Disabilities Ministry—MAGGIE ROUSSEAU, Dir., Tel: 404-920-7682; Fax: 404-920-7341; Email: mrousseau@archatl.com.

Office of Formation and Discipleship—2401 Lake Park Dr., S.E., Smyrna, 30080-8862. Tel: 404-920-7620; Fax: 404-920-7621; Web: www.archatl.com; Email: ofd@archatl.com. ANDREW W. LICHTENWALNER, Ph. D., Dir. & Member of the Secretariat, Tel: 404-920-7624; Fax: 404-920-7621; Email: alichtenwalner@archatl.com; IVONNE S. VREELAND, Oper. Mgr., Tel: 404-920-7623; Tel: 404-920-7623; Fax: 404-920-7621; Email: ivreeland@archatl.com; DESTINY MARQUEZ, Administrative Asst., Tel: 404-920-7622; Fax: 404-920-7621; Email: dmarquez@archatl.com; CATHY MARBURY, Assoc. Dir. Rel. Educ., Tel: 404-920-7625; Fax: 404-920-7621; Email: cmarbury@archatl.com; BENEDICT ESPOSITO, Media Specialist, Tel: 404-920-7634; Fax: 404-920-7621; Email: besposito@archatl.com; VACANT, Assoc. Dir. Youth Min.; PATRICE SPIROU, Assoc. Dir. Evangelization & Catechesis, Tel: 404-920-7630; Fax: 404-920-7621; Email: pspirou@archatl.com; DANIEL WEST, Assoc. Dir. Marriage & Family Min./Pastoral Care Min., Tel: 404-920-7631; Fax: 404-920-7621; Email: dwest@archatl.com; PATRICK J. METTS, L.P.C., Assoc. Dir. Marriage & Family Min./Pastoral Care Min., Tel: 404-920-7643; Fax: 404-920-7621; Email: pmetts@archatl.com; VACANT, Assoc. Dir. Adult & Campus Ministry, Tel: 404-920-7642; Fax: 404-920-7621; WILLIAM L. CLARKE, Assoc. Dir. Professional Devel., Tel: 404-920-7635; Fax: 404-920-7621; Email: wclarke@archatl.com; MONICA OPPERMANN, Assoc. Dir. Evangelization, Tel: 404-920-7632; Fax: 404-920-7621; Email: moppermann@archatl.com.

Retrouvaille—Coordinators: ZACK HAMILTON; HEATHER HAMILTON, 2401 Lake Park Dr., S.E., Smyrna, 30080. Email: retroatlove@gmail.com; Web: www.retrouvailleofatlanta.org. Secretary Couple: BOB BOTTE; KAREN BOTTE, Email: bottekb@aol.com.

Engaged Encounter—Coordinators: YVONNE GREEN; JIM GREEN, 2401 Lake Park Dr., S.E., Smyrna, 30080. Tel: 404-216-9502; Web: www.atlcee.org; KEISHA LANCELIN; COLBY LANCELIN, Email: atlceelc@gmail.com.

LLASU-Llamados a Ser Uno—(Marriage preparation in Spanish).Co-Directors: MIGUEL ZUMARAN; CARMEN SALDANA, Email: carmen.saldana@diazfoods.com; VANGIE ZUMARAN, 2401 Lake Park Dr., S.E., Smyrna, 30080. Tel: 678-327-6388; Email: vzumaran@gmail.com; Web: www.archatl.com; LORENA MENDEZ.

Finance Office—2401 Lake Park Dr., S.E., Smyrna, 30080-8862. Tel: 404-920-7400; Fax: 404-920-7401. BRADLEY WILSON, CFO & Member of the Secretariat, Tel: 404-920-7404; Fax: 404-920-7401; Email: bwilson@archatl.com; MICHAEL WARREN, Controller, Tel: 404-920-7411; Fax: 404-920-7401; Email: mwarren@archatl.com; ELSA RULLAN, Planning Mgr., Tel: 404-920-7403; Fax: 404-920-7401; Email: erullan@archatl.com; PATRICK WARNER, Parish Systems Mgr., Tel: 404-920-7410; Fax: 404-920-7401; Email: pwarner@archatl.com; TANYA MAX, Administrative Asst., Tel: 404-920-7426; Fax: 404-920-7401; Email: tmax@archatl.com; CAMTUYEN PHAM, Accounting Mgr., Tel: 404-920-7402; Fax: 404-920-7401; Email: cpham@archatl.com; MARY ANN BROWN, Accounting Asst., Tel: 404-920-7407; Fax: 404-920-7401; Email: mabrown@archatl.com; YANIRA KOCH, Accounting Asst., Tel: 404-920-7425; Email: ykoch@archatl.com; HOLLY ORSAGH, Audit Mgr., Tel: 404-920-7906; Fax: 404-920-7401; Email: horsagh@archatl.com; JEFFREY DEAN, Payroll Mgr., Tel: 404-920-7418; Email: jdean@archatl.com; ANDY HOECKELE, Cash Receipts Clerk, Tel: 404-920-7419; Email: ahoeckele@archatl.com; NEEMA MOLLEL, Sr. Accountant, Tel: 404-920-7406; Email: nmollel@archatl.com; SUSAN SHIRLEY, Parish Systems Admin., Tel: 404-920-7408; Email: sshirley@archatl.com; PATRICIA BISHOP, Accounting Clerk, Tel: 404-920-7610; Email: pbishop@archatl.com; JACK HUSACK, Shared Accounting Svcs. Mgr., Tel: 404-920-7416; Email: jhusack@archatl.com; NANCY VON HAGEL, S.A.S. Accountant, Tel: 404-920-7420; Email: nvonhagel@archatl.com; MIRAMAR SALAMAH, S.A.S. Accountant, Tel: 404-920-7442; Email: msalamah@archatl.com; TERESA NGUYEN, S.A.S. Accountant, Tel: 404-920-7417; Email: tnguyen4@archatl.com.

Office of Intercultural and Ethnic Diversity—2401 Lake Park Dr., S.E., Smyrna, 30080-8862. Tel: 404-920-7580; Fax: 404-920-7581. JAIRO MARTINEZ, Dir., Tel: 404-920-7583; Fax: 404-920-7581; Email: jmartinez@archatl.com; ASHLEY MORRIS, Assoc. Dir., Tel: 404-920-7586; Fax: 404-920-7581; Email: amorris@archatl.com; CARMEN L. COYA-VAN DUIJN, Asst. Dir. Intercultural Competencies & Communications, Tel: 404-920-7587; Fax: 404-920-7581; Email: ccoya@archatl.com; YOLANDA V. MUNOZ, Asst. Dir. Hispanic & Latino Cultures, Tel: 404-920-7584; Fax: 404-920-7581; Email: ymunoz@archatl.com; GRACIELA (GRACIE) MULERO, Office Mgr., Tel: 404-920-7585; Fax: 404-920-7581; Email: gmulero@archatl.com.

Human Resources—2401 Lake Park Dr., S.E., Smyrna, 30080-8862. Tel: 404-920-7480; Fax: 404-920-7481; Web: www.archatl.com. CHARLES THIBAUDEAU, Dir. & Member of the Secretariat, Tel: 404-920-7482; Fax: 404-920-7481; Email: cthibaudeau@archatl.com; MARQUITA RICHBURG, Human Resources Mgr., Tel: 404-920-7483; Fax: 404-920-7481; Email: mrichburg@archatl.com; PERLA FREED, Dir. Safe Environment, Tel: 404-920-7550; Fax: 404-920-7551; GINA GARCIA, Prog. Asst., Tel: 404-920-7552; Fax: 404-920-7551; Email: ggarcia@archatl.com; LILY GALLAGHER, Benefits Mgr., Tel: 404-920-7485; Fax: 404-920-7481; Email: lgallagher@archatl.com; ROSA MONTANO-PARKER, Senior Benefits Specialist, Tel: 404-920-7486; Fax: 404-920-7481; Email: rmontano-parker@archatl.com; TERRY MOSS, Safe Environment Prog. Coord., Tel: 404-920-7489; Fax: 404-920-7551; ERIN HAWTHORNE, Human Resources Specialist, Tel: 404-920-7488; Fax: 404-920-7481; Email: ehawthorne@archatl.com; GISELLA COTTER, Human Resources Coord., Tel: 404-920-7490; Fax: 404-920-7481; Email: gcotter@archatl.com; EYVONNE MEADORS, Receptionist, Tel: 404-920-

7800; Fax: 404-920-7481; Email: receptionist@archatl.com; SHANNON WIGGINS, HRMS Analyst, Tel: 404-920-7492; Fax: 404-920-7481; Email: swiggins@archatl.com; VANESSA URREA, Human Resources Asst., Tel: 404-920-7495; Fax: 404-920-7481; Email: vurrea@archatl.com; FAY DUHE, Sr. Benefits Specialist, Tel: 404-920-7484; Fax: 404-920-7481; Email: fduhe@archatl.com.

Information Technology—2401 Lake Park Dr., S.E., Smyrna, 30080-8862. Tel: 404-920-7450; Fax: 404-920-7451. *Help Desk:* Tel: 404-920-7450; Email: support@archatl.com. TOM HARDY, Dir. Information Technology, Tel: 404-920-7454; Fax: 404-920-7451; Email: thardy@archatl.com; TOMASZ KASPRZYK, Information Technology Mgr., Tel: 404-920-7455; Fax: 404-920-7451; Email: tkasprzyk@archatl.com; JONATHAN UGOLICK, Information Technology Support Specialist III, Tel: 404-920-7458; Fax: 404-920-7451; Email: jugolick@archatl.com; THOMAS NEMCHIK, Information Technology Support Specialist II, Tel: 404-920-7453; Fax: 404-920-7451; Email: tnemchik@archatl.com; CHAD SIGLER, Consultant, Tier III, Tel: 404-920-7456; Fax: 404-920-7451; Email: csigler@archatl.com.

Metropolitan Tribunal—2401 Lake Park Dr., S.E., Smyrna, 30080-8862. Tel: 404-920-7500; Fax: 404-920-7501; Web: www.archatl.com/offices/tribunal; Email: tribunal@archatl.com. On September 23, 2016, the Supreme Tribunal of the Apostolic Signatura approved the restoration of the Metropolitan Tribunal of Atlanta as the Court of second Instance for the Province of Atlanta.With the same Decree, the Holy See also approved the designation of the Metropolitan Tribunal of Cincinnati as the local appellate tribunal for all judicial cases heard in the first instance by the Metropolitan Tribunal of Atlanta.

Judicial Vicar—Very Rev. DANIEL P. KETTER, J.C.L., Tel: 404-920-7500; Fax: 404920-7501; Email: dketter@archatl.com.

Adjutant Judicial Vicar—Rev. MICHAEL U. ONYEKURU, J.C.D., Email: monyekuru@archatl.com.

Court Administrator—MR. LUIS O. CAPACETTI, J.C.L., Tel: 404-920-7510; Email: lcapacetti@archatl.com.

Senior Office Administrator—CHRISTINE M. DIMARTINO, Tel: 404-920-7509; Email: cdimartino@archatl.com.

Archdiocesan Judges—Rev. Msgr. EDWARD J. DILLON, J.C.D., Email: edillon@archatl.com; Very Rev. PEDRO POLOCHE, J.C.L., V.F., Email: ppoloche@archatl.com; Rev. MICHAEL U. ONYEKURU, J.C.D., Email: monyekuru@archatl.com; FELIX MENENDEZ, J.C.D., S.T.L., Tel: 404-920-7528; Email: fmenendez@archatl.com; MR. LUIS O. CAPACETTI, J.C.L., Tel: 404-920-7510; Email: lcapacetti@archatl.com.

Court Expert—ANN G. HOWE PH.D., Tel: 404-920-7507; Email: ahowe@archatl.com.

Promoter of Justice—Rev. PAUL A. BURKE, J.C.L., Tel: 404-920-7514; Email: pburke@archatl.com.

Defenders of the Bond—MR. ROBERT BROWN, J.C.L., J.D., Sr. Defender of the Bond, Tel: 404-920-7524; Email: rbrown@archatl.com; Rev. ELYN M. MACEK, J.C.L., J.D., Tel: 404-920-7564; Email: emacek@archatl.com; ANNA MARIE CHAMBLEE, J.C.L., Tel: 404-920-7518; Email: amchamblee@archatl.com.

Advocates—JOSEPH TOVAR, Chief Advocate, Tel: 404-920-7503; Email: jtovar@archatl.com; CHARLES JONES, Tel: 404-920-7527; Email: cbjones@archatl.com; Deacons MIGUEL A. ECHEVARRIA, Tel: 404-920-7334; Email: mechevarria@archatl.com; SCOTT PARKER, Tel: 404-920-7516; Email: sparker@archatl.com; Sr. CRYSTAL PAYMENT, Tel: 404-920-7515; Email: spayment@archatl.com.

Notaries—ANGELA PRATT, Senior Notary, Tel: 404-920-7511; Email: apratt@archatl.com; MICHELE CHAMORRO, Instructor/Notary for Informal Cases, Tel: 404-920-7523; Email: mchamorro@archatl.com; PABLO CEPEDA, Tel: 404-920-7525; Email: pcepeda@archatl.com; MRS. THUY HOANG, Tel: 404-920-7519; Email: thoang@archatl.com; ANDREANA HERRERA, Tel: 404-920-7517; Email: aherrera@archatl.com; SANDRA RIVERA, Tel: 404-920-7520; Email: srivera@archatl.com; DALIA BARRIOS, Notary for Informal Cases, Tel: 404-920-7525; Email: dbarrios@archatl.com; LISETTE REYES, Tel: 404-920-7512; Email: lreyes@archatl.com; YOLANDA BERRIOS, Notary for Informal Cases, Tel: 404-920-7505; Email: yberrios@archatl.com; MARIEL VICTORIA-TELLES, Tel: 404-920-7512; Email: mtelles@archatl.com; VY VU, Tel: 404-920-7519; Email: vvu@archatl.com.

Receptionist—CARMEN ALVAREZ, Tel: 404-920-7520; Email: calvarez@archatl.com.

Permanent Diaconate—2401 Lake Park Dr., S.E., Smyrna, 30080-8862. Tel: 404-920-7325; Fax: 404-920-7326. Deacon DENNIS J. DORNER, B.A., Dir. Office of Permanent Diaconate, Tel: 404-920-7325; Fax: 404-920-7326; Email: ddorner@archatl.com; VACANT, Office of Permanent Diaconate & Spiritual Dir.; Deacon JOSE G. ESPINOSA, Assoc. Co-Dir. Formation, Office of Permanent Diaconate, Tel: 404-920-7386; Fax: 404-920-7326; Email: jespinosa@archatl.com; PENNY SIMMONS, Assoc. Co-Dir. Formation, Office of Permanent Diaconate, Tel: 404-920-7385; Fax: 404-920-7326; Email: psimmons@archatl.com; KATH OWENS, Exec. Asst., Tel: 404-920-7328; Fax: 404-920-7326; Email: kowens@archatl.com; JOY PLACE, Administrative Asst., Tel: 404-920-7307; Fax: 404-920-7326; Email: jplace@archatl.com.

Stewardship—2401 Lake Park Dr., S.E., Smyrna, 30080-8862. Tel: 404-920-7600; Fax: 404-920-7601; Web: www.archatl.com; Web: www.appeal.archatl.com. CHRISTOPHER "KIT" PARKER, Exec. Dir., Tel: 404-920-7615; Email: kparker@archatl.com; NANCY H. STOEHR, Annual Appeal Coord., Tel: 404-920-7614; Fax: 404-920-7601; Email: nstoehr@archatl.com; TRACY ZELCZAK, Database Admin., Tel: 404-920-7606; Fax: 404-920-7601; Email: tzelczak@archatl.com; JULIETA SANCHEZ, Admin. Asst., Tel: 404-920-7605; Email: jsanchez@archatl.com.

Office of Planning and Research—2401 Lake Park Dr., S.E., Smyrna, 30080. Tel: 404-920-7850; Fax: 404-920-7851. JENNIFER MILES, Mgr., Tel: 404-920-7852; Email: jmiles@archatl.com.

Vocations—2401 Lake Park Dr., S.E., Smyrna, 30080-8862. Tel: 404-920-7460; Fax: 404-920-7461; Web: www.calledbychrist.com. Rev. TRI JOHN-BOSCO NGUYEN, Dir., Tel: 404-920-7460; Fax: 404-920-7461; Email: tnguyen2@archatl.com; SALLY SCARDASIS, Exec. Asst., Tel: 404-920-7463; Fax: 404-920-7461; Email: sscardasis@archatl.com; PILAR CASTANEDA, Intl. Liaison & Finance Analyst, Tel: 404-920-7464; Fax: 404-920-7461; Email: pcastaneda@archatl.com.

Other Archdiocesan Offices

AACCW—JULIE PARDO, Pres., 826 Serramonte Dr., Marietta, 30068. Email: pardofran@bellsouth.net; Rev. WILLIAM M. WILLIAMS, Spiritual Moderator, Queen of Angels Catholic Church, 1326 Washington Rd., Thomson, 30824. Tel: 706-595-2913; Fax: 706-595-9636; Email: ourladyqofa@comcast.net.

Cursillo—Sr. MARGARET MCANOY, I.H.M., Dir., 2401 Lake Park Dr., S.E., Smyrna, 30080-8862. Tel: 404-920-7652; Email: mmcanoy@archatl.com.

Georgia Catholic Conference—FRANK MULCAHY, 2401 Lake Park Dr., S.E., Smyrna, 30080-8862. Tel: 404-920-7367; Email: fmulcahy@georgiacc.org.

Archdiocese of Atlanta Catholic Committee on Scouting—Deacon THOMAS E. GOTSCHALL, Chap., 525 Indian Mill Ct., Alpharetta, 30022. Tel: 770-490-9436; Email: gotschall@mindspring.com.

Archdiocesan Councils, Boards, Commissions, and Committees

Atlanta Conference of Sisters—Sr. MARGARET MCANOY, I.H.M., 2401 Lake Park Dr., S.E., Smyrna, 30080-8862. Tel: 404-920-7652; Fax: 404-920-7611; Email: mmcanoy@archatl.com.

Compensation Committee—ROCHESTER ANDERSON, Chm.

Audit Committee—JOHN NEE, Chm.

Benefits Committee—ROCHESTER ANDERSON, Chm.

Budget and Operations Committee—VALERIE LANDAU, Chm.

Catholic Charities of the Archdiocese of Atlanta, Inc.—GREG THOMPSON, Chm.; LISA MENENDEZ, Vice Chair; MIKE DOWDLE, Sec.

Council of Priests—Rev. Msgr. DANIEL STACK, Chm., Saint Thomas Aquinas Catholic Church, 535 Rucker Rd., Alpharetta, 30004. Tel: 770-475-4501; Fax: 770-772-0355; Email: dstack@sta.org.

Eucharistic Congress Committee—Deacon DENNIS J. DORNER, B.A., Chancellor & Dir. Office of Permanent Diaconate, Tel: 404-920-7325; Fax: 404-920-7326; Email: ddorner@archatl.com; KATH OWENS, Exec. Asst., Tel: 404-920-7328; Fax: 404-920-7326; Email: kowens@archatl.com.

Finance Council—KIERAN QUINN, Chm.

Investment Committee—MICHAEL MOHR, Chm.

Advisory Board on Sexual Abuse of Minors—Rev. Msgr. EDWARD J. DILLON, J.C.D., Promoter of Justice.

Liturgical Commission—VACANT.

Project Review Committee—HAL BARRY, Chm.

St. George Village—Catholic Community Retirement Center, 11350 Woodstock Rd., Roswell, 30075. MR. MARK A. LOWELL, Exec. Dir.

Board of Directors—Most Rev. BERNARD E. SHLESINGER III, V.G.; THOMAS CUNNANE; CHARLES THIBAUDEAU; DAVID R. SPOTANSKI; BRADLEY WILSON, CFO, Archdiocese of Atlanta; MICHAEL DUKES; Deacon DENNIS J. DORNER, B.A., Sec.; ROBERT FINK.

Council of Deacons—Deacon ROGER A. FRASER, Chm.

Diaconate Formation Advisory Board—Facilitators: Deacon JOSE G. ESPINOSA; PENNY SIMMONS.

Archdiocese of Atlanta Pastoral Council—VACANT, Chm.

Archdiocesan School Advisory Council—AUGUSTO ELIAS, Chm.

CLERGY, PARISHES, MISSIONS AND PAROCHIAL SCHOOLS

CITY OF ATLANTA

(FULTON COUNTY)

1—CATHEDRAL OF CHRIST THE KING (1936) [CEM]
2699 Peachtree Rd., N.E., Atlanta, 30305.
Tel: 404-233-2145; Fax: 404-233-4984; Email: ask@ctking.com; Web: www.cathedralctk.com. Most Rev. Wilton D. Gregory, S.L.D., Archbishop of Atlanta; Rev. Msgr. Francis G. McNamee, Rector; Very Rev. Richard B. Morrow, B.A., Parochial Vicar, (Retired); Revs. Carlos Cifuentes, Parochial Vicar; Peeter Pedroza, C.M.F., Parochial Vicar; Deacons Christopher J. Andronaco; John J. McManus, J.D., J.C.L.; Whitney Robichaux; Gerald Zukauckas. In Res., Rev. Msgr. Richard J. Lopez, (Retired).
See Cathedral of Christ the King Catholic School, Atlanta under Archdiocesan Schools, located in the Institution section.
Catechesis Religious Program—Students 1,161.
Mission—Christ the King Mission, Pastoral Center: 3349 Buford Hwy., N.E., Ste. 28-C, Brookhaven, 30329. Rev. Carlos Cifuentes.

2—ST. ANTHONY OF PADUA (1903) Very Rev. Victor A. Galier, M.Div., Th.M., V.F.; Deacons Leviticus Jelks; William H. Simmons III.
Church: 928 Ralph David Abernathy Blvd., S.W., Atlanta, 30310. Tel: 404-758-8861; Fax: 404-755-6755; Email: dpatrickbates@stanthonyatlanta.org; Web: stanthonyatlanta.org.
Catechesis Religious Program—Students 55.

3—ST. DOMINIC
Mailing Address: 5 Concourse Pkwy., #200, Atlanta, 30328. Rev. Robert B. Gramann.
School—St. Joseph School, (Grades K-5), 5 Concourse Pkwy., #200, Atlanta, 30328.
Tel: 770-828-4045. Mr. Brett Mason, Prin. Lay Teachers 14; Students 318.
Catechesis Religious Program—Students 62.

4—HOLY CROSS (1964)
3773 Chamblee Tucker Rd, Atlanta, 30341. Email: ftanzosch@holycrossatlanta.org. Very Rev. Jude Michael Krill, O.F.M.Conv., V.F.; Revs. Calixto Salvatierra, Parochial Vicar; Thomas Reist, O.F.M.Conv., Parochial Vicar; Deacon Bernardo Buzeta.
Church & Res.: 3175 Hathaway Ct., Atlanta, 30341.
Tel: 770-939-3501; Email: greggwatson1@gmail.com; Web: www.holycrossatlanta.org.
Catechesis Religious Program—Students 1,010.

5—HOLY SPIRIT (1964) Rev. Msgr. Edward J. Dillon, J.C.D.; Rev. Tamiru Atraga, Parochial Vicar; Deacons Stephen G. Demko; Trini Merlo; William F. McCarthy; Allen Underwood; Mark D. Mitchell.
Church: 4465 Northside Dr., N.W., Atlanta, 30327.
Tel: 404-252-4513; Fax: 404-252-1162; Email: jbohling@hsccatl.com; Web: hsccatl.com.
See Holy Spirit Preparatory School, Atlanta, under Independent Schools located in the Institution Section.
Catechesis Religious Program—Students 500.
Mission—Centro Catolico del Espiritu Santo, Pastoral Center: 120 Northwood Dr., Ste. B5-8, Atlanta, Fulton Co. 30342. Tel: 404-303-9927; Fax: 404-303-0620; Email: mmanrique@hsccatl.com. Deacon Jose T. Merlo-Quintero.

6—IMMACULATE HEART OF MARY (1958) Rev. Msgr. Albert W. Jowdy, M.Div.; Rev. Carlos Ortega; Deacons Robert J. Hauert; Erik Wilkinson.
Church: 2855 Briarcliff Rd., N.E., Atlanta, 30329.
Tel: 404-636-1418; Fax: 404-636-4394; Email: rplachta@ihmatlanta.org; Email: ajowdy@ihmatlanta.org; Email: bhauert@ihmatlanta.org; Web: ihmatlanta.org.
See Immaculate Heart of Mary Catholic School, Atlanta & St. Pus X Catholic High School located in the Institution section.

Catechesis Religious Program—Drew Denton, D.R.E. Students 675.

7—MOST BLESSED SACRAMENT (1960) Rev. Desmond Drummer, Admin.; Deacon Frederick Toca.
Church: 2971 Butner Rd., S.W., Atlanta, 30331.
Tel: 404-349-9263; Fax: 404-629-1287; Email: office@mbschurch.com; Web: www.mbschurch.com.
Catechesis Religious Program—Students 53.

8—OUR LADY OF LOURDES CATHOLIC CHURCH (1912) Revs. Jeffery Ott, O.P.; Bruce Schultz, O.P.; Deacons Chester H. Griffin; Lennison Alexander; Kenneth Bell.
Church: 25 Boulevard, N.E., Atlanta, 30312.
Tel: 404-522-6776; Fax: 404-222-0202; Email: Bookkeeper@lourdesatlanta.org; Web: www.lourdesatlanta.org.
Catechesis Religious Program—Mrs. Theresa Bowen, D.R.E. Students 152.

9—OUR LADY OF THE ASSUMPTION (1951) Revs. Edwin L. Keel, S.M., Supr.; James D. Duffy, S.M., M.Div.; Joel R. Grissom, S.M., Parochial Vicar; Deacons Chris Thompson; Terry Biglow; Antonius Anugerah; Edward Patterson; William H. O'Donoghue.
Church: 1350 Hearst Dr., N.E., Brookhaven, 30319.
Tel: 404-261-7181; Fax: 404-364-1913; Web: www.olachurch.org.
See Our Lady of the Assumption Catholic School, Atlanta & Marist School located in the Institution section.
Catechesis Religious Program—Mark Dannenfelser, D.R.E. Students 431.
Chapels—Marist School—3790 Ashford Dunwoody Rd., Atlanta, 30319. Web: www.marist.com.
St. Joseph Hospital, 5665 Peachtree Dunwoody Rd., NE, Atlanta, 30319. Tel: 678-843-4062.

10—ST. PAUL OF THE CROSS (1954) Revs. Jerome McKenna, C.P.; Patrick Dagherty, C.P.; Deacons George Smith; Joseph Goolsby.
Church: 551 Harwell Rd., N.W., Atlanta, 30318.
Tel: 404-696-6704; Fax: 404-696-4735; Email: stpaulofthecrossatl@gmail.com; Web: saintpaulofthecross.org.
Catechesis Religious Program—Students 184.

11—SHRINE OF THE IMMACULATE CONCEPTION (1848) Rev. Msgr. Henry C. Gracz, M.Div.; Rev. Dennis Dorner, Parochial Vicar; Deacons Dominic Saulino Jr.; Bob Klein; Ronald Manning.
Church: 48 Martin Luther King, Jr. Dr., S.W., Atlanta, 30303-3599. Tel: 404-521-1866;
Fax: 404-639-7947; Email: contactus@catholicshrineatlanta.org; Web: www.catholicshrineatlanta.org.
Catechesis Religious Program—Stacey Jones, D.R.E. Students 83.

12—THE BASILICA OF THE SACRED HEART OF JESUS (1880) Rev. Msgr. Edward Thein; Deacons Michael K. Balfour; Marino Gonzalez.
Church: 353 Peachtree St., N.E., Atlanta, 30308.
Tel: 404-522-6800; Fax: 404-524-5440; Email: receptionist@sacredheartatlanta.org; Web: www.sacredheartatlanta.org.
Catechesis Religious Program—Students 300.
Mission—San Felipe de Jesus, 925 Conley Rd., Forest Park, Clayton Co. 30297. Tel: 404-675-0540;
Fax: 404-675-0733; Email: missionsanfelipe@bellsouth.net. Rev. Jacques E. Fabre, C.S., Admin. & Spiritual Dir.

OUTSIDE CITY OF ATLANTA

ACWORTH, COBB CO., ST. CLARE OF ASSISI (2014)
6301 Cedarcrest Rd., Acworth, 30101.
Tel: 770-485-0825; Fax: 770-485-0940; Email: cfigueroa@stclarecc.org; Web: stclarecc.org. Rev. Mark Starr, Admin.; Deacon Thomas J. Ryan.
Catechesis Religious Program—Students 285.

ALPHARETTA, FULTON CO., ST. THOMAS AQUINAS (1972) [CEM] Rev. Msgr. Daniel Stack; Rev. Jaime Rivera, Parochial Vicar; Deacons William W. Keeling; Edmund LaHouse; John Strachan; Kevin F. Tracy; Arthur Lerma; Jesus Nerio; Steven W. Shawcross; Thomas F. McGivney; Bernard J. Casey.
Church: 535 Rucker Rd., Alpharetta, 30004.
Tel: 770-475-4501; Fax: 770-772-0355; Web: www.sta.org.
Catechesis Religious Program—Students 920.

ATHENS, CLARKE CO., ST. JOSEPH (1873)
958 Epps Bridge Pkwy., Athens, 30606.
Tel: 706-548-6332; Fax: 706-354-1783; Email: parishoffice@stjosephathens.com; Web: www.stjosephathens.com. Revs. Paul Moreau, B.A.; Timothy E. Nadolski, Parochial Vicar; Deacons Jim Gaudin; Scott E. Medine.
See St. Joseph's Catholic School, Athens & Monsignor Donovan High School in the Institution section.
Catechesis Religious Program—Lynn Langston, D.R.E. Students 584.
Chapel—Catholic Student Center at The University of Georgia, 1344 S. Lumpkin St., Athens, 30605-1345. Tel: 706-543-2293; Fax: 706-543-2541; Web: www.uga.edu/cc. Revs. Thomas F. Vigliotta, O.F.M., Dir. Campus Ministry; John C. Coughlin, O.F.M., Assoc. Campus Min.

BLAIRSVILLE, UNION CO., ST. FRANCIS OF ASSISI (1966) [CEM] [JC] Rev. Gaurav Manu Shroff; Deacons Lawrence Casey; Paul Dietz; John J. Barone.
Church: 3717 Hwy. 515 E., Blairsville, 30512-3288.
Tel: 706-745-6400; Fax: 706-745-1468; Email: office@stfrancisblairsville.com.
Catechesis Religious Program—Students 85.

BLUE RIDGE, FANNIN CO., ST. ANTHONY St. Anthony Catholic Church (1976) [CEM]
967 E. Main St., P.O. Box 1448, Blue Ridge, 30513.
Tel: 706-632-5970; Fax: 706-632-2120; Email: stanthony@tds.net; Web: www.saintanthonyblueridge.com. Rev. John T. Conway; Deacon John Mason.
Catechesis Religious Program—Students 22.

CALHOUN, GORDON CO., ST. CLEMENT (1958)
Mailing Address: 875 Hwy. 53, S.W., Calhoun, 30701. Tel: 706-629-2345; Fax: 706-625-5219; Email: mdutton@stclementsga.org; Web: www.stclementsga.org. Rev. Feiser Elliott Munoz, Admin.
Catechesis Religious Program—Students 271.

CANTON, CHEROKEE CO., OUR LADY OF LASALETTE (1984)
2941 Sam Nelson Rd., Canton, 30114.
Tel: 770-479-8923 (Office);
Fax: 770-479-6025 (Office); Email: accountingmanager@lasalettecanton.com; Web: lasalettecanton.com. Rev. Victor J. Reyes, M.Div.; Deacons Charles E. Carignan; John Stanley. 3 English Masses, one Spanish
Tel: 770-479-8923; Fax: 770-479-6025; Email: accountingmanager@lasalettecanton.com; Web: lasalettecanton.com.
Catechesis Religious Program—Email: ffeng@lasalettecanton.com; Email: ffesp@lasalettecanton.com; Web: lasalettecanton.com. Jullian Guidry, D.R.E.; Maria Perez, D.R.E. Students 302.

CARROLLTON, CARROLL CO., CHURCH OF OUR LADY OF PERPETUAL HELP (1962) [CEM] Rev. Mario A. Lopez; Leslie Robinson, Admin.; Deacons Jon Gary Atkinson; James C. Harkins.
Church: 210 Old Center Point Rd., Carrollton, 30117.
Tel: 770-832-8977; Fax: 770-832-1666; Email: administrator@olphcc.org; Web: www.olphcc.org.
NEWMAN CENTER UNIVERSITY OF WEST GEORGIA, Email: canolaura2016@gmail.com.
Catechesis Religious Program—Timothy Brodeur, D.R.E. Students 459.

CARTERSVILLE, BARTOW CO., ST. FRANCIS OF ASSISI (1969) [JC] Rev. Juan Anzora; Deacons Miguel A. Echevarria; Thomas Coffey.
Church: 850 Douthit Ferry Rd., Cartersville, 30120.
Tel: 770-382-4549; Fax: 770-382-4506; Email: stfrancis.assisi201@gmail.com; Web: www.stfac.org.
Catechesis Religious Program—Students 711.

CEDARTOWN, POLK CO., ST. BERNADETTE (1941) [JC] Rev. Timothy Gallagher; Deacon Jose M. Orellana.
Church: 100 Evergreen Ln., Cedartown, 30125.
Tel: 770-748-1517; Fax: 770-748-6051; Email: sbccedartown@gmail.com; Web: www.stbernadettecc.org.
Catechesis Religious Program—Laura Hernandez, D.R.E., Spanish; Janet Johnson, D.R.E., English. Students 300.

CLARKESVILLE, HABERSHAM CO., ST. MARK (1964) (Hispanic)
Mailing Address: 5410 Hwy. 197 S., Clarkesville, 30523. Tel: 706-754-4518; Fax: 706-754-9751; Email: office.stmp@gmail.com. Rev. Jose Luis Hernandez-Ayala; Deacons William M. Brown; Richard Marinchak; Gary J. Roche.
Capilla Santo Domingo, 427 Cash St., Cornelia, 30531.
Catechesis Religious Program—Students 325.

CLAYTON, RABUN CO., ST. HELENA CATHOLIC CHURCH (1961)
137 Meadow Stream Ln., Clayton, 30525.
Tel: 706-782-5152; Fax: 706-782-5152; Email: sthelenachurchclayton@windstream.net. P.O. Box 534, Clayton, Rabun Co. 30525. Very Rev. Pedro Poloche, J.C.L., V.F.
Catechesis Religious Program—

CLEVELAND, WHITE CO., ST. PAUL THE APOSTLE (1964)
1243 Hulsey Rd., Cleveland, 30528.
Tel: 706-865-4474; Fax: 706-219-3009; Web: stpaulcleveland.com. Rev. Fabio Alvarez-Posada.
Catechesis Religious Program—Students 125.

CONYERS, ROCKDALE CO., ST. PIUS X (1974) Rev. Juan F. Areiza, V.F.; Deacons Brian Kilkelly; Fred Johns; Stuart A. Mead.
Church: 2621 Hwy. 20, S.E., Conyers, 30013-2424.
Tel: 770-483-3660; Fax: 770-483-7006; Email: churchoffice@spxconyers.com; Web: www.spxconyers.com.
Catechesis Religious Program—Students 411.

COVINGTON, NEWTON CO., ST. AUGUSTINE OF HIPPO (1977) Rev. Roberto Orellana, V.F.
Church: 11524 Hwy. 278 E., Covington, 30014.
Tel: 770-787-1064; Fax: 770-787-0871; Email: office@staugcc.org.
Catechesis Religious Program—Students 207.
Mission—St. James, 562 Vine St., Madison, Morgan Co. 30650. Tel: 706-342-9661; Web: www.sjccmadison.org. Rev. Randall T. Mattox, M.Div.

CUMMING, FORSYTH CO.

1—ST. BRENDAN THE NAVIGATOR (2000)
4633 Shiloh Rd., Cumming, 30040. Tel: 770-205-7969; Fax: 770-205-5040; Email: jgarrett@stbrendansatl.com; Web: www.StBrendansATL.com. Revs. Mathew Van Smoorenburg, L.C.; Patrick Langan, L.C.; Paul Alger, L.C., Parochial Vicar; Deacons Roger A. Fraser; Eduardo J. Rubio; Luis C. Lorza; Rev. Nikola Derpick, (In Res.).
Catechesis Religious Program—Students 1,231.

2—GOOD SHEPHERD (1975) Revs. Diosmar Natad, V.F.; Javier Munoz, Parochial Vicar; Deacons Ralph LaMachia; Donald N. Nadeau; John R. Peterson.
Church: 3740 Holtzclaw Rd., Cumming, 30041.
Tel: 770-887-9861; Fax: 770-887-2241; Web: www.gsrcc.net.
Catechesis Religious Program—Students 683.

DAHLONEGA, LUMPKIN CO., ST. LUKE (1960) Deacons Robert H. Grimaldi; Dennis J. Dorner, B.A.
Church: 91 N. Park St., Dahlonega, 30533.
Tel: 706-864-4779; Email: office@stlukerrc.org; Email: aschmalen@stlukercc.org; Web: www.stlukercc.org.
Catechesis Religious Program—Students 145.
Station—University of North Georgia Catholic Campus Ministry, Email: college@stlukercc.org; Web: www.stlukercc.org/college.

DALLAS, PAULDING CO., ST. VINCENT DE PAUL (2003)
680 W. Memorial Dr., Dallas, 30132.
Tel: 770-443-0566 (Office);
Fax: 770-443-1612 (Office); Email: church@svdpatl.com; Web: saintvincentdepaulchurch.org. Revs. Adrian C.H. Pleus; Omar Loggiodice, In Res.; Deacons James McDermott; Jose Perez.
Catechesis Religious Program—Students 252.

DALTON, WHITFIELD CO., ST. JOSEPH (1941) [JC] Revs. Paul D. Williams Jr., V.F.; Salomon Garcia, Parochial Vicar; Very Rev. Jose Duvan Gonzalez, Parochial Vicar.
Church & Res.: 968 Haig Mill Lake Rd., Dalton, 30720. Tel: 706-278-3107; Fax: 706-278-6902; Email: sjccdalton@gmail.com; Web: www.sjccdalton.com.
Capilla San Juan Diego, 1609 E. Morris St., Dalton, 30720.
Mission—Capella Santo Toribio Romo, 2402 U.S. Hwy. 76, Chatsworth, 30705.
Catechesis Religious Program—Students 1,451.

DAWSONVILLE, DAWSON CO., CHRIST THE REDEEMER CATHOLIC CHURCH (1982) Rev. Brian J. Higgins; Deacon Joseph C. Anzalone.
Church: 991 Kilough Church Rd., Dawsonville, 30534. Tel: 706-265-1361; Email: office@ctrcc.net.
Catechesis Religious Program—Students 85.

DECATUR, DEKALB CO.

1—STS. PETER AND PAUL (1959) [JC] Revs. Bryan D. Small; Carl Jean, Chap.; Deacons Jerry M. Lett; Alfred Mitchell; Augustin Pierre-Louis; James Anderson Jr.; J. Tony King.
Church & Res.: 2560 Tilson Rd., Decatur, 30032.
Tel: 404-241-5862 (Office);
Fax: 404-241-5839 (Office); Email: parishoffice@stspandp.com; Web: www.stspandp.com.
See St. Peter Claver Regional Catholic School, Decatur under Archdiocesan Schools, located in the Institution section.
Catechesis Religious Program—Students 65.

2—ST. THOMAS MORE (1941) Revs. Mark F. Horak, S.J.; Timothy Stephens, Parochial Vicar; Pat Earl, S.J., Parochial Vicar.
Church: 636 W. Ponce de Leon Ave., Decatur, 30030.
Tel: 404-378-4588; Fax: 404-378-0506; Web: www.stmgaparish.org.
See St. Thomas More Catholic School, Decatur under Archdiocesan Schools, located in the Institution section.
Catechesis Religious Program—Students 481.

DORAVILLE, DEKALB CO., KOREAN MARTYRS CATHOLIC CHURCH (1977)
6003 Buford Hwy., N.E., Doraville, 30340.
Tel: 770-455-1380; Fax: 770-455-4262; Email: kmccga.office@gmail.com; Web: www.kmccga.org. Revs. Chae-Uk Johan Lee, S.J.; Ondohk Kang; Man Young Chung.
Catechesis Religious Program—Students 247.
Mission—St. Andrew Kim Korean Catholic Church, 2249 Duluth Hwy., Duluth, 30097. Tel: 770-622-2577; Fax: 678-802-2879; Email: office@sakc.org; Web: www.sakc.org.

DOUGLASVILLE, DOUGLAS CO., ST. THERESA OF THE CHILD JESUS St. Theresa Catholic Church (1985) Revs. Joseph Shaute; Luis E. Alvarez, Parochial Vicar; Deacons Ronald A. St. Michel; Israel D. Melara.
Church: 4401 Prestley Mill Rd., Douglasville, 30135.

Tel: 770-489-7115; Fax: 770-489-4873; Email: admin@sttheresacc.org; Web: www.sainttheresacatholicchurch.org.
Catechesis Religious Program—Theresa Butorac, D.R.E. Students 353.

DULUTH, GWINNETT CO.
1—MISION DEL DIVINO NINO JESUS
4400 Abbotts Bridge Rd., Duluth, 30097.
Tel: 678-417-7912. Revs. Carlos Quintero, Admin.; Roberto Herrera, Parochial Vicar.

2—ST. MONICA (1994)
1700 Buford Hwy., Duluth, 30097. Tel: 678-584-9947; Fax: 678-584-9760; Email: karen.lastufka@saintmonicas.com; Web: www.saintmonicas.com. Revs. John F. Durkin Jr.; Tan Robert Pham, S.J., Parochial Vicar; Deacons Paul Lee Doppel; John Koppenaal; Bob Tipton.
Rectory—3393 Forrestwood Dr., Suwanee, 30024.
Catechesis Religious Program—Students 572.

DUNWOODY, DEKALB CO., ALL SAINTS (1977) Rev. Msgr. Hugh M. Marren; Rev. Daniel Rogaczewski, Parochial Vicar; Deacons William Garrett; Edward Krise; Ricardo D. Medina.
Church: 2443 Mount Vernon Rd., Dunwoody, 30338-3099. Tel: 770-393-3255; Web: www.allsaints.us.
Catechesis Religious Program—Students 330.

ELLIJAY, GILMER CO., GOOD SAMARITAN CATHOLIC CHURCH (1986)
55 Church St., Ellijay, 30540. Tel: 706-636-2772; Fax: 706-636-2776; Email: gsam@etcmail.com; Web: goodsamaritanellijay.com. Rev. Carlos E. Vargas; Deacons Paul Schueth; Greg Orf.

FAYETTEVILLE, FAYETTE CO., ST. GABRIEL (1993) Rev. Richard Anh Vu; Deacon Jerome P. Daly.
Church: 152 Antioch Rd., Fayetteville, 30215-5702.
Tel: 770-461-0492; Fax: 770-461-0374; Email: info@stgabrielga.com; Web: www.stgabrielga.com.
Catechesis Religious Program—Students 280.

FLOWERY BRANCH, HALL CO., PRINCE OF PEACE (1978) Revs. Eric J. Hill; Branson S. Hipp, Parochial Vicar; Deacons William A. Donohue; Nicholas G. Johnson; Michael R. Jones; Paul Krarup; William E. Speed, (Retired); Tom G. Walter; Robert Perri; Rev. Msgr. James A. Schillinger, S.T.L., (In Res.).
Church: 6439 Spout Springs Rd., Flowery Branch, 30542. Tel: 678-960-0040; Fax: 678-960-0078; Email: info@popcatholicchurch.org; Web: www.popfb.org.
Catechesis Religious Program—Students 1,469.

FOREST PARK, CLAYTON CO., SAN FELIPE DE JESUS Misión Católica San Felipe de Jesús
925 Conley Rd., Forest Park, 30297.
Tel: 404-675-0540; Email: missionsanfelipe@bellsouth.net. Revs. Jacques E. Fabre, C.S., Admin.; Victor Córdova González, Parochial Vicar.

FORT OGLETHORPE, CATOOSA CO., ST. GERARD MAJELLA (1952)
3049 LaFayette Rd., Fort Oglethorpe, 30742.
Tel: 706-861-9410; Fax: 706-866-0574; Email: secretary@saintgerardmajella.net; Email: frwise2@gmail.com. Rev. Richard P. Wise, V.F., Pastoral Min./Coord., (Retired).
Catechesis Religious Program—Students 28.

GAINESVILLE, HALL CO.
1—ST. JOHN PAUL II CATHOLIC MISSION
2410 S Smith Rd. S.W., Gainesville, 30504.
Tel: 770-532-6772. Revs. William Canales, Admin.; Hernan Quevedo Rodriguez, Parochial Vicar. Mission of Our Lady of the Americas.

2—ST. MICHAEL (1933)
1440 Pearce Cir., N.E., Gainesville, 30501-2457.
Tel: 770-534-3338; Fax: 770-535-2440; Email: k.lampert@saintmichael.cc; Web: www.saintmichael.cc. Revs. Timothy M. Hepburn; Gerardo Ceballos Gonzalez, Parochial Vicar; Deacons Kenneth W. Lampert, Business Mgr.; William L. Bohn; Michael Kennedy; Gilberto Perez.
Catechesis Religious Program—Students 990.
Mission—St. John Paul II Catholic Mission, 622 Shallowford Rd., N.W., Ste. P, Gainesville, 30604.
Tel: 770-532-6772; Email: info.jp2tc@gmail.com.

GREENSBORO, GREENE CO., CHRIST OUR KING AND SAVIOR (1992) Formerly Christ Our Savior, Eatonton and Christ Our King, Greensboro.
6341 Lake Oconee Pkwy., Greensboro, 30642.
Tel: 706-453-7292; Fax: 706-453-7095; Email: cokas.office@gmail.com; Web: www.cokas.org. Rev. Michael Silloway.
Catechesis Religious Program—Beth Mappes, D.R.E.; Laura Brennan, Youth Min.; John Steadman, Business Mgr.; Lily Vaughn, Sec. Students 248.

GRIFFIN, SPALDING CO., SACRED HEART (1941) Rev. Dennis R. Juan; Deacons Felix Marrero; Kenneth P. Bishop.
Church: 1323 MacArthur Dr., Griffin, 30224.
Tel: 770-227-2378; Email: shpriest@comcast.net; Web: www.sacredheartofgriffin.org.
Catechesis Religious Program—Students 103.

HAPEVILLE, FULTON CO., ST. JOHN THE EVANGELIST (1954) Revs. Michael U. Onyekuru, J.C.D.; Thomas A. Zahuta, Parochial Vicar; Fausto Marquez, Parochial Vicar.
Res.: 3370 Sunset Ave., Hapeville, 30354.
Church: 230 Arnold St., Atlanta, 30354-1530.
Tel: 404-768-5647; Fax: 404-767-6416.
See St. John the Evangelist School, Hapeville under Archdiocesan Schools, located in the Institution section.
Catechesis Religious Program—Students 269.

HARTWELL, HART CO., SACRED HEART OF JESUS (1977) [CEM] [JC] Rev. Rafael Castano Fernandez; Deacons Jerry Korte; Barry S. Phillips.
Church: 1009 Benson St., Hartwell, 30643.
Tel: 706-376-4112; Fax: 706-376-4112; Email: sacredhearthartwell@gmail.com; Web: www.sacredheartofhartwell.com.
Mission—Saint Mary's Catholic Church, 155 Forest Ave., Elberton, 30635.

JACKSON, BUTTS CO., SAINT MARY, MOTHER OF GOD CATHOLIC CHURCH (1960)
359 Old Griffin Rd., Jackson, 30233.
Tel: 770-775-4162; Fax: 770-775-4174; Email: szieg@stmaryjackson.org. Rev. Jose M. Kochuparampil, Admin.
Catechesis Religious Program—Melanie Reed, D.R.E.; Brenda Patterson, D.R.E. Students 58.

JASPER, PICKENS CO., OUR LADY OF THE MOUNTAINS (2004) Very Rev. Charles A. Byrd Jr., V.F.
Church: 1908 Waleska Hwy. 108, Jasper, 30143.
Tel: 706-253-3078; Fax: 706-253-3077; Email: ladyofthemts@ellijay.com; Web: www.olmjasper.com.
Catechesis Religious Program—Linda Hermann, D.R.E. Students 130.

JEFFERSON, JACKSON CO., ST. CATHERINE LABOURE CATHOLIC CHURCH (2011)
180 Elrod Rd., Jefferson, 30549. Tel: 706-367-7220; Email: info@stcatherinelabourega.org. Rev. Vincent P. Sullivan; Deacons Curtis D. Marsh; Pablo Perez.
Catechesis Religious Program—Students 103.

JOHNS CREEK, FULTON CO.
1—ST. BENEDICT (1987) Revs. Paul A. Flood, V.F.; John P. Knight, Parochial Vicar; Joseph Mullakkara, M.S.F.S., Parochial Vicar; Thang M. Pham, Parochial Vicar; Deacons Derek Gant; Gerard G. Kazin; John D. Puetz; Jaime Morgan.
Church: 11045 Parsons Rd., Johns Creek, 30097.
Tel: 770-442-5903; Email: office@stbenedict.net; Web: www.stbenedict.net.
Catechesis Religious Program—Students 840.
Mission—Mision del Divino Nino Jesus, 4400 Abbotts Bridge Rd., Duluth, Gwinnett Co. 30097.
Tel: 678-417-7912. Rev. Carlos Quintero, Admin.

2—ST. BRIGID (1998) [CEM]
3400 Old Alabama Rd., Johns Creek, 30022.
Tel: 678-393-0060; Fax: 678-393-0071; Email: office@saintbrigid.org; Web: www.saintbrigid.org. Revs. Neil J. Herlihy; Peter Ha; William T. Hao, Parochial Vicar; Deacons David L. Briselden; Ron Leidenfrost; Leo Gahafer; Henry R. Hein; Tom Huff.
See Holy Redeemer Catholic School, Alpharetta under Archdiocesan Schools located in the Institution section.
Catechesis Religious Program—Students 1,220.

JONESBORO, CLAYTON CO., ST. PHILIP BENIZI (1965) Revs. John Koziol, O.F.M.Conv., V.F.; Vincent Gluc, O.F.M.Conv., Parochial Vicar; Luis Palacios-Rodriguez, Parochial Vicar; Deacons Peter B. Swan Sr.; Etienne Francisco Rodriguez; Gregory L. Pecore; Matias A. Casal; John Halloran; Nicholas Dragone, Music Min. & Liturgy Dir.; Helen Frazier, Business Mgr.; Lorraine Miller, RCIA Coord.; Mrs. Patricia Turmel, Sec.
Church: 591 Flint River Rd., Jonesboro, 30238-3452.
Tel: 770-478-0178; Fax: 770-471-2079; Email: parishoffice@stphilipbenizi.org; Web: www.stphilipbenizi.org.
Catechesis Religious Program—Lorraine Miller, D.R.E. Students 625.

KENNESAW, COBB CO., ST. CATHERINE OF SIENA (1981) Rev. Neil Dhabliwala; Deacons Jose G. Espinosa; Bradford Young; Stephen Ponichtera.
Church: 1618 Ben King Rd., N.W., Kennesaw, 30144.
Tel: 770-428-7139; Fax: 770-428-0131; Web: stcatherinercc.org.
See St. Catherine of Siena Catholic School, Kennesaw under Archdiocesan Schools, located in the Institution section.
Catechesis Religious Program—Joan Hennes, D.R.E. Students 243.

LAGRANGE, TROUP CO., ST. PETER (1936) Rev. Timothy Gadziala, J.C.L.
Church: 200 LaFayette Pkwy., LaGrange, 30241.
Tel: 706-884-4224; Email: info@stpeterslagrange.net; Web: www.stpeterslagrange.com.
Catechesis Religious Program—Michael Barrett, D.R.E. Students 145.
Mission—St. Elizabeth Seton, 2904 Judson Bulloch Rd., P.O. Box 638, Warm Springs, Meriwether Co. 31830.

LAWRENCEVILLE, GWINNETT CO.
1—ST. LAWRENCE (1974) [CEM] Revs. John T. Howren, V.F.; Mark E. Thomas, Parochial Vicar; Patrick J. Kingery, Parochial Vicar; Deacons Terry D. Millinger; Richard Downey, (Retired); Jose Ortiz-Velasquez; Robert Riddett; Richard Hogan; Peter Ranft; David Schreckenberger.
Church: 319 Grayson Hwy., Lawrenceville, 30046.
Tel: 770-963-8992; Fax: 770-963-1710; Email: info@saintlaw.org; Web: www.saintlaw.org.
Catechesis Religious Program—Students 1,044.

2—ST. MARGUERITE D'YOUVILLE (1994) Revs. Tomy Joseph Puliyanampattayil, M.S.F.S.; Joseph Mendes, M.S.F.S.; Wieslaw Berdowicz, S.Chr., Parochial Vicar; Deacons George D. Angelich; Kapya Ngoy.
Church: 85 Gloster Rd. NW, Lawrenceville, 30044.
Tel: 770-381-7337; Tel: 770-381-8062;
Fax: 770-381-6568; Email: secretary@stmdy.com; Email: finance@stmdy.com; Email: frtomy@stmdy.com; Email: pastor@stmdy.com.
Catechesis Religious Program—Students 113.

LILBURN, GWINNETT CO.
1—ST. JOHN NEUMANN (1977) Revs. Sunny Joseph Punnakuziyil, M.S.F.S.; Abel Guerrero-Oeta; Deacons Greg Ollick; Michael Hayward; Mike Byrne; Manuel Echevarria.
Church: 801 Tom Smith Rd., Lilburn, 30047-2299.
Tel: 770-923-6633; Fax: 770-381-7856; Email: parish@sjnlilburn.com; Web: www.sjnlilburn.com.
Catechesis Religious Program—Students 782.

2—OUR LADY OF THE AMERICAS CATHOLIC MISSION (1989) Revs. Luis Guillermo Cordoba; Carlos Bustamante, Parochial Vicar; Deacon John Martin.
Church: 4603 Lawrenceville Hwy., Lilburn, 30047.
Tel: 770-717-1517; Fax: 770-717-1312; Email: ljaramillo@oloacm.org; Email: rrosenberger@oloacm.org; Web: www.oloacm.org.
Catechesis Religious Program—
Tel: 770-717-1517, Ext. 27. Leonardo Jaramillo-Giraldo, D.R.E. Students 1,725.

3—ST. STEPHEN THE MARTYR (1999) Rev. Brian T. Lorei; Deacons Evelio Garcia-Carreras; Michael K. Mobley Sr.; Richard C. Kaszycki.
Church & Res.: 5373 Wydella Rd., S.W., Lilburn, 30047. Tel: 770-381-7488; Email: secretary@ststephenthemartyr.info; Web: www.ststephenthemartyr.info.
Catechesis Religious Program—Students 90.

LITHIA SPRINGS, DOUGLAS CO., ST. JOHN VIANNEY (1958) Rev. Ignacio Morales; Deacons Francis Przybylek; Felix Rentas.
Church: 1920 Skyview Dr., Lithia Springs, 30122.
Tel: 770-941-2807; Fax: 770-941-5821; Email: parishoffice@sjvpar.net; Web: www.sjvpar.net.
Catechesis Religious Program—Students 402.

LITHONIA, DEKALB CO., CHRIST OUR HOPE (1984)
1786 Wellborn Rd., Lithonia, 30058.
Tel: 770-482-5017; Fax: 770-482-9476; Email: parish@christourhopeatl.org; Web: www.christourhopeatl.org. Rev. John Paul Ezeonyido.
Catechesis Religious Program—Students 73.

LOOKOUT MOUNTAIN, WALKER CO., OUR LADY OF THE MOUNT (1947) [JC] Rev. Thomas Benjamin Shuler.
Church: 1227 Scenic Hwy., Lookout Mountain, 30750. Tel: 706-820-0680; Fax: 706-820-2797; Web: www.olmcc.com. (Memorial Garden For Ashes).
Catechesis Religious Program—Email: mvoges@olmcc.com. Students 41.
Mission—St. Katharine Drexel, 109 New England Rd., P.O. Box 1032, Trenton, Dade Co. 30753-1032.

MABLETON, COBB CO., ST. FRANCIS DE SALES (1999) Revs. Joseph DeGuzman, F.S.S.P.; James Smith, Pastoral Assoc.; Deacon Douglas J. Anderson.
Church: 587 Landers Dr., Mableton, 30126.
Tel: 770-948-6888; Email: officesfds@gmail.com; Web: www.stfrancisdesalesatl.com.
Catechesis Religious Program—Students 83.

MADISON, SAINT JAMES
562 Vine St., Madison, 30650. Tel: 706-342-9661; Email: amitchellstj@gmail.com; Web: sjccmadison.org. Rev. Randall T. Mattox, M.Div.

MARIETTA, COBB CO.
1—ST. ANN (1978) Revs. Raymond G. Cadran, M.S.; Robert Zaw Lwin, M.S., Parochial Vicar; John Gabriel, M.S., Parochial Vicar; Joseph G. Aquino, M.S., In Res.; Deacons Thomas P. Badger; Edmund M. Grabowy; Bobby Allen Jennings; J. Nicholas Morning.
Church: 4905 Roswell Rd., N.E., Marietta, 30062.
Tel: 770-552-6400; Tel: 770-552-6400 (Res.);
Fax: 770-552-6420; Email: jherrel@st-ann.org; Web: www.st-ann.org.
Catechesis Religious Program—Steve Botsford, D.R.E. Students 500.

2—CHURCH OF THE TRANSFIGURATION (1977) Revs. Fernando Molina-Restrepo; Brian McNavish, Parochial Vicar; Fred W. Wendel, Parochial Vicar; Deacons Paul A. Gorski; Peter Harris; Paul Frankli.
Church: 1815 Blackwell Rd., N.E., Marietta, 30066-2911. Tel: 770-977-1442; Email: lrega@transfiguration.com; Web: www.transfiguration.com.

Catechesis Religious Program—Joyce Guris, D.R.E. Students 288.

3—HOLY FAMILY CATHOLIC CHURCH (1973) Revs. Miguel Grave de Peralta; Junot Nelvy, Parochial Vicar; Very Rev. Daniel P. Ketter, J.C.L., In Res.; Rev. Michael Christopher Revak, In Res.; Deacons Al Gallagher; David Barron; Peter Harris.
Church: 3401 Lower Roswell Rd., Marietta, 30068-3974. Tel: 770-973-0038; Fax: 770-578-0475; Web: www.holyfamilycc.org.
Catechesis Religious Program—Cathy Biscan, D.R.E. Students 581.

4—SAINT JOSEPH (1952) Rev. Msgr. John P. Walsh, V.F.; Revs. Bryan J. Kuhr, Parochial Vicar; Guyma Noel, Parochial Vicar; Deacons Thomas Shaver; Bruce Reed; Francis Devereux; Norman K. Keller; Phillip G. Smilski; Kenneth Williams.
Church: 87 Lacy St., N.W., Marietta, 30060.
Tel: 770-422-5633; Fax: 770-422-1148; Email: breed@saintjosephcc.org; Web: www.saintjosephcc.org.
See St. Joseph Catholic School, Marietta under Archdiocesan Schools, located in the Institution section.
Catechesis Religious Program—Students 1,667.

MCDONOUGH, HENRY CO., ST. JAMES THE APOSTLE (1979) Rev. Liam Coyne; Deacon Charles Iner. In Res., Rev. Msgr. Terry W. Young, V.F., (Retired).
Church: 1000 Decatur Rd., Hwy. 155, McDonough, 30252. Tel: 770-957-5441; Fax: 770-957-0383; Email: bstonecipher@stjamesapostle.com; Web: www.stjamesapostle.com.
Catechesis Religious Program—Students 617.

MILLEDGEVILLE, BALDWIN CO., SACRED HEART OF JESUS (1874) Rev. Dung Nguyen, J.C.L.; Deacons Cesar Basilio; John W. Shoemaker, (Retired).
Church: 110 N. Jefferson St., P.O. Box 754, Milledgeville, 31061. Tel: 478-452-2421 (Res.);
Fax: 478-454-1110; Email: sacredheartmga@gmail.com; Web: www.sacredheartmilledgeville.org.
Catechesis Religious Program—Students 57.

MONROE, WALTON CO., ST. ANNA (1951) [JC] Rev. Daniel R. Toof.
Church: 1401 Alcovy St., Monroe, 30655.
Tel: 770-267-7637; Fax: 770-267-0465; Email: blake@st-annas.com; Web: www.st-annas.com.
Catechesis Religious Program—Deborah Farabaugh, D.R.E. Students 41.

NEWNAN, COWETA CO.

1—ST. GEORGE (1952) [JC] Rev. Henry Atem, V.F.; Deacons James R. Bishop; Steve Beers; William H. Heinsch; Edward Buckley. In Res., Rev. Alvaro D. Avendano, (Retired).
Church: 771 Roscoe Rd., Newnan, 30263.
Tel: 770-251-5353; Fax: 770-251-2053; Web: www.stgeorgecatholicchurch.org.
Catechesis Religious Program—Students 300.

2—ST. MARY MAGDALENE (1999)
3 Village Rd., Newnan, 30265-6162.
Tel: 770-253-1888; Fax: 770-253-1290; Email: smmcc@smmcatholic.org; Web: www.smmcatholic.org. Very Rev. Terence Crone, V.F.; Deacons Paul S. Swope Jr.; Donald S. Parker.
Catechesis Religious Program—Students 351.

NORCROSS, GWINNETT CO.

1—HOLY VIETNAMESE MARTYRS CATHOLIC CHURCH (2013) Rev. Tuan Quoc Tran; Tuan Pham; Rev. Cong Tan Nguyen, Parochial Vicar; Deacon Hoa (Joseph) V. Pham.
Church: 4545A Timmers Way, Norcross, 30093.
Tel: 770-921-0077;
Tel: 678-654-2530 (Finance Office);
Tel: 678-357-5661 (Pastor); Email: info@cttdvnatl.org; Web: www.cttdvnatl.org.
Catechesis Religious Program—Sr. Hanh Nguyen, D.R.E. Students 1,023.

2—SAINT PATRICK (1968) Revs. Refugio Onate-Melendez; Cyril Soo-Gil Chae, Parochial Vicar; Bradley A. Starr, Parochial Vicar; Deacon Jose Narvaez.
Church & Res.: 2140 Beaver Ruin Rd., Norcross, 30071. Tel: 770-448-2028; Fax: 678-615-3224; Email: rmelendez@stpatricksga.org; Web: www.stpatricksga.org.
Catechesis Religious Program—Students 798.
Mission—Our Lady of the Americas Catholic Mission, 4603 Lawrenceville Hwy., Lilburn, Gwinnett Co. 30047. Tel: 770-717-1517;
Fax: 770-717-1312.

PEACHTREE CORNERS, GWINNETT CO., MARY OUR QUEEN CATHOLIC CHURCH (1994)
6260 The Corners Pkwy., Peachtree Corners, 30092.
Tel: 770-416-0002; Email: office@maryourqueen.com; Web: www.maryourqueen.com. Rev. Darragh Griffith.
Catechesis Religious Program—Students 192.

PEACHTREE CITY, FAYETTE CO., HOLY TRINITY (1973) (Hispanic) Revs. John Murphy; Pavol Brenkus, Parochial Vicar; Dairo Antonio Rico, Parochial Vicar; Deacons Anthony F. Cuomo; Ben Gross, (Retired); Terry S. Blind; Mark A. Sholander; Richard Schmidt; Mark F. Friedlein.
Church: 101 Walt Banks Rd., Peachtree City, 30269.
Tel: 770-487-7672; Fax: 770-486-9152; Email: HolyTrinity@HolyTrinityPTC.com; Web: www.holytrinityptc.org.
See Our Lady of Mercy Catholic High School, Fairburn under Archdiocesan Schools located in the Institution section.
Catechesis Religious Program—Students 1,059.

RIVERDALE, CLAYTON CO., OUR LADY OF VIETNAM (1989) [JC] (Vietnamese) Revs. Peter Duc Vu; Dominic Tran, Parochial Vicar; Deacons Peter Hung Viet Huynh; Joseph Phu Nguyen.
Church: 91 Valley Hill Rd., Riverdale, 30274.
Tel: 770-472-9963; Fax: 770-472-9392; Email: info@gxdmvn.org; Web: www.giaoxuducmevietnam.org.
Catechesis Religious Program—Students 510.

THE ROCK, UPSON CO., ST. PETER THE ROCK (2005)
3594 Barnesville Hwy., P.O. Box 280, The Rock, 30285. Tel: 706-648-2599; Fax: 706-648-4040; Email: Bluger@stpetertherock.com; Web: www.stpetertherock.com. Rev. Liem Nguyen; Deacon Thomas Kretzmer.
Catechesis Religious Program—Students 70.

ROME, FLOYD CO., ST. MARY (1930) Very Rev. Rafael Carballo, V.F.; Rev. Valery Akoh, Parochial Vicar; Deacons Stuart L. Neslin; James S. Thacker; Joseph C. Eustace.
Res.: 911 N. Broad St., Rome, 30161.
Tel: 706-290-9000; Tel: 706-290-9054;
Fax: 706-295-1717; Web: www.smcrome.org.
Catechesis Religious Program—Joandra Mendoza, D.R.E. Students 476.

ROSWELL, FULTON CO.

1—ST. ANDREW (1981) Revs. Daniel J. Fleming, V.F.; Jorge Carranza; Deacons Jose G. Campos; Thomas E. Gotschall.
Res.: 115 River Lake Ct., Roswell, 30075.
Church: 675 Riverside Rd., Roswell, 30075.
Tel: 770-641-9720; Fax: 770-641-8584; Email: frontdesk@standrewcatholic.org; Web: www.standrewcatholic.org.
Catechesis Religious Program—Students 443.

2—ST. PETER CHANEL (1998)
11330 Woodstock Rd., Roswell, 30075.
Tel: 678-277-9424; Fax: 678-277-9423; Email: ktracy@stpeterchanel.org; Web: www.stpeterchanel.org. Rev. Msgr. Peter J. Rau, V.F.; Revs. Brian J. Bufford, Parochial Vicar; Robert Frederick, Chap.; Deacons William Keen; Martin J. Lampe, (Retired); Michael Bickerstaff; Scott A. Sparks; John Wojcik; David J. Thomasberger; Kevin F. Tracy, Business Mgr.; Joseph F. Crowley; Jane Jackson, Music Min.
Catechesis Religious Program—Rosemary Potts, D.R.E. Students 1,155.

SANDY SPRINGS, SAINT JUDE THE APOSTLE (1960) [CEM] Rev. Msgr. W. Joseph Corbett, V.F.; Rev. Roberto Suarez Barbosa, Parochial Vicar; Deacons Gary E. Schantz; James A. Tramonte; Raymond F. Egan; Mrs. Colleen Tyner, Dir.; Mr. Mike Higgins, Dir.; Mrs. Kathleen Woods, Business Mgr.; Mrs. Kerry Arias, Parish Life Coord.; Mrs. Kathy Cahill, Music Min.; Mrs. Roberta Meadows.
Church: 7171 Glenridge Dr. N.E., Sandy Springs, 30328. Tel: 770-394-3896; Fax: 770-415-3567; Email: rmeadows@judeatl.com; Web: www.judeatl.com.
See St. Jude the Apostle Catholic School, Atlanta under Archdiocesan Schools, located in the Institution section.
Catechesis Religious Program—
Tel: 770-394-3896, Ext. 525; Email: mrobert@judeatl.com. Ms. Martha Robert, D.R.E.; Mrs. Colleen Tyner, Dir. of Opers. Students 561.

SMYRNA, COBB CO.

1—HOLY NAME OF JESUS CHINESE CATHOLIC MISSION
5395 Light Cir., N.W., Norcross, 30071.
Tel: 678-691-3261; Email: info@hnojatl.org; Web: hnojatl.org. Rev. William T. Hao. Chinese Mass.

2—ST. THOMAS THE APOSTLE (1966) Revs. Brian R. Sheridan, M.S., V.F.; Jaime Molina-Juarez, M.N.M., Parochial Vicar; Clemente Mario, Parochial Vicar; Paul G. Rainville, M.S., In Res.; Deacons Michael Garrett; Earl D. Jackson.
Church: 4300 King Springs Rd SE, 30082-4214.
Tel: 770-432-8579; Fax: 770-432-8570; Email: stthomasga@stthomastheapostle.org; Web: stthomastheapostle.org.
Catechesis Religious Program—Tel: 770-432-5329; Email: ssenecal@stthomastheapostle.org. Susan Senecal, D.R.E. Students 1,098.

SNELLVILLE, GWINNETT CO., ST. OLIVER PLUNKETT (1978) Revs. Cyriac Mattathilanickal; Baiju Augustine, Parochial Vicar; Deacons Michael S. Chavez; Rafael Cintron; Jim Skolds; William Jindrich; Randall Ory, Liturgy Dir.
Church & Res.: 3200 Brooks Dr., Snellville, 30078.
Tel: 770-979-2500; Fax: 770-985-6590; Web: www.stolivers.com.
Catechesis Religious Program—Students 1,169.

STONE MOUNTAIN, DEKALB CO., CORPUS CHRISTI (1971) [JC] Revs. Paschal Amagba, C.M.F.; Gregory D. Kenny, C.M.F., Parochial Vicar; Malachy Osunwa, Parochial Vicar; Francesco Iacona, C.M.F., In Res.; Deacon Ken W. Melvin; Marlice Casnave, Business Mgr.
Church: 600 Mountain View Dr., Stone Mountain, 30083. Tel: 770-469-0395; Fax: 770-469-0568; Email: corpuschristicc@mindspring.com; Web: www.corpuschristicc.org.
Catechesis Religious Program—Students 380.

THOMSON, MCDUFFIE CO., QUEEN OF ANGELS (1955) Rev. Stephen J. Lyness, V.F.
Church: 1326 Washington Rd., Thomson, 30824.
Tel: 706-595-2913; Web: www.qofa.us.
Catechesis Religious Program—Students 60.

TOCCOA, STEPHENS CO., ST. MARY (1956) [JC] Rev. Vincent Sullivan; Deacon Gregory Ollick.
Res.: 231 Rothell Rd. Ext., Toccoa, 30577.
Tel: 706-886-2819; Email: stmarystoccoa@gmail.com; Web: www.stmarystoccoaga.com.
Catechesis Religious Program—Jessica Burger, D.R.E. Students 32.

TYRONE, FULTON CO., ST. MATTHEW (1979) Rev. Kevin J. Hargaden, M.Div.; Deacons William Hampton; Jim G. Weeks; Gayle P. Peters; King E. Cooper; Harold Leon Roberts.
Church: 215 Kirkley Rd., Tyrone, 30290-9549.
Tel: 770-964-5804; Email: sikhwan@saintmatthew.us; Web: www.saintmatthew.us.
Catechesis Religious Program—Saul Onate-Perez, D.R.E. Students 227.

WASHINGTON, WILKES CO., ST. JOSEPH (1840) [CEM] [JC2] Rev. Stephen J. Lyness, V.F.
Church: 1015 N. By Pass Hwy. 78 W., Washington, 30673. Tel: 706-678-2110; Web: stjosephscc.com.
Catechesis Religious Program—Students 60.

WINDER, BARROW CO., ST. MATTHEW (1999)
25 Wilkins Rd., S.W., Winder, 30680-1009.
Tel: 770-867-4876; Fax: 770-867-6034; Email: busmgr@saintmatthewcc.org; Web: www.saintmatthewcc.org. Rev. Gilbert Exume; Deacons Luis Londono; Lawrence J. Welsh; Earl D. Buckley; Jaime Agudelo.
Rectory—450 Winston Manor Dr., Winder, 30680.
Catechesis Religious Program—Students 348.

WOODSTOCK, CHEROKEE CO., ST. MICHAEL THE ARCHANGEL (1995) Rev. Larry Niese; Deacons Victor L. Taylor; John Buchholz; Jack Herndon; Jose I. Pupo.
Church & Res.: 490 Arnold Mill Rd., Woodstock, 30188. Tel: 770-516-0009; Fax: 770-516-4664; Email: lniese@saintmichaelcc.org; Email: hcarignan@saintmichaelcc.org; Web: www.saintmichaelcc.org.
Catechesis Religious Program—Elizabeth Bonutti, D.R.E. Students 939.

Chaplains of Public Institutions

ATLANTA. *Atlanta Veterans Administration Hospital*, 1670 Clairmont Rd., Decatur, 30033.
Tel: 404-321-6111.
Cobb County Jail, 1825 County Services Pkwy., Marietta, 30060. Tel: 770-499-4200.
Dobbins Air Force Base, 94 AW/HC, 1311 Patrol Rd., Dobbins Air Force Base, 30069-5003.
Tel: 404-919-4955; Tel: 404-919-4956. Vacant.
Hartsfield Jackson International Airport, Interfaith Airport Chaplaincy, P.O. Box 20801, Atlanta, 30320. Tel: 404-762-1051; Web: www.airportchapel.org; Web: www.archatl.com/ministries-services/airport-chap- laincy-program; Web: www.ATLchapel.org. Revs. Desmond Drummer, Chap., Gregory Goolsby, Chap., William Norvel, S.S.J., Chap., Deacons William (Bill) L. Hampton, Chap., Alfred Mitchell, Chap., Whitney Robichaux, Chap., Peter B. Swan Sr., Chap.
Prison Apostolate. Revs. Adam Z. Ozimek, Chap., William M. Williams, Chap.
U.S. Penitentiary, 601 McDonough Blvd., Atlanta, 30315. Tel: 404-635-5100. Vacant.

JACKSON. *Georgia Diagnostic & Classification Center*, Diagnostic & Classification, 2978 Hwy. 36 W., Jackson, 30233. Tel: 770-504-2000.

Special or Other Archdiocesan Assignment:
Rev. Msgr.—
Schillinger, James A., S.T.L., Full-time Coord., Archdiocesan Ongoing Formation of Priests.

On Duty Outside the Archdiocese:
Revs.—
Anderson, John R., Archdiocese of New York, ArchCare
Ballman, Luke R., S.T.L., USCCB, Washington, D.C.
Briese, Llane B., St. Vincent de Paul Regional Seminary, FL
David, Craig, VA East Syracuse, NY
Jean, Thony Roody, Canada

Sevaraj, Balappa, India.

On Academic Studies:
Revs.—
Azar, Nicholas G., Accademia Alfonsiana
Bremer, Michael K., Mundelein Seminary
Metz, John Michael, Mundelein Seminary.

Military Chaplains:
Rev.—
Caballejo, Yuen Servanez, United States Regular Army, Germany.

On Leave of Absence:
Revs.—
Ha, Hieu Minh
Lopez, Armando Herejon
Luna, Jesus Trujillo
Teran Sanchez, Juan Jose.

On Medical Leave:
Rev.—
Loggiodice, Omar.

Retired:
Rev. Msgrs.—
Bishop, Patrick A., (Retired)
Branch, Edward B., (Retired)
Dora, Peter A., M.Div., (Retired)
Fennessy, James J., (Retired)
Fogarty, Paul, (Retired)
Hoffman, William G., (Retired)
Lopez, Richard J., (Retired)
Van Phuong, Francis Pham, (Retired)
Young, Terry W., V.F., (Retired), Senior Priest in Residence, Saint James the Apostle Catholic Church, 1000 Decatur Rd. (GA Hwy. 155), Mcdonough, 30253-1779
Very Revs.—
McGuinness, David, V.F., (Retired)
Morrow, Richard B., B.A., (Retired), 2699 Peachtree Rd., Atlanta, 30305. Cathedral of Christ the King
Revs.—
Adams, James P., (Retired), Florida
Adamski, John S., (Retired), 41 Finch Tr., Atlanta, 30308
Avendano, Alvaro D., (Retired)
Berny, Paul W., M.A., (Retired)
Curran, Anthony T., (Retired)
Danneker, Edward A.J., (Retired), Holy Cross Catholic Church, 3175 Hathaway Ct., NE, Atlanta, 30341
Dye, David M., (Retired)
Fallon, John C., (Retired)
Foley, Walter W., (Retired), 561 Raindrop Cir., Hartwell, 30643
Harrison, James, (Retired)
Kieran, John C., (Retired), Senior Priest in Residence
Mateus, Norberto, (Retired), c/o Archdiocese of Atlanta, 2401 Lake Park Dr., S.E., 30080-8862
McCormick, Patrick J., (Retired), Saint John Apostle & Evangelist, 95-370 Kuahelani Ave., Mililani, HI 96789
Medlin, Douglas S., (Retired), P.O. Box 224, Sautee Nacoochee, 30571
Meehan, Thomas J., (Retired), P.O. Box 5778, Atlanta, 31107
Richardson, Francis X., (Retired)
Rudd, Thad B., (Retired), 540 Ascension Trail, Cleveland, 30528
Ryan, Tim, (Retired), 1310 Primrose Dr., Roswell, 30076
Sexstone, James H., (Retired), Saint Thomas Aquinas Catholic Church, 535 Rucker Rd., Alpharetta, 30004
Tibbetts, Richard K., (Retired)
Wilber, Stewart A., (Retired)
Williamson, Christopher, (Retired)
Wise, Richard P., V.F., (Retired), 11350 Woodstock Rd., Unit #2121, Roswell, 30075
Yander, Steven L., (Retired).

Permanent Deacons:
Agudelo, Jaime, St. Matthew, Winder
Anderson, Douglas J., (Inactive)
Anderson, James Jr., Sts. Peter and Paul, Decatur
Andronaco, Christopher J., Cathedral of Christ the King, Atlanta
Angelich, George D., (Retired), (Inactive)
Anugerah, Antonius, Our Lady of the Assumption, Atlanta
Anzalone, Joseph C., Christ Redeemer, Dawsonville
Anzalone, Joseph S., (On Duty Outside the Archdiocese)
Atkinson, Jon G., Our Lady of Perpetual Help, Carrollton
Badger, Thomas P., St. Ann, Marietta
Baker, David A., (On Duty Outside of the Archdiocese)
Balfour, Michael K., Sacred Heart, Atlanta
Barker, Joseph J., St. John the Evangelist, Hapeville
Barone, John J., St. Francis of Assisi, Blairsville
Barron, David, Holy Family, Marietta
Basilio, Cesar, Sacred Heart, Milledgeville
Bathea, Val, (On Duty Outside the Archdiocese)
Bedard, Walter T. Sr., (Retired)
Beers, Steven (Steve), St. George's, Newnan
Bevacqua, Bill J., (Retired)
Bickerstaff, Michael, St. Peter Chanel, Roswell
Biglow, Ernest, Our Lady of the Assumption, Atlanta
Bishop, James R., St. George's, Newnan
Bishop, Kenneth P., Sacred Heart, Griffin
Blind, Terry S., Holy Trinity, Peachtree City
Bohn, William L., St. Michael, Gainesville
Borsavage, Charles T., (Retired)
Boyd, William J., Mary Our Queen, Peachtree Corners
Briggs, Michael R., (Leave of Absence)
Briselden, David L., St. Brigid, Johns Creek
Brown, Raymond E., (Retired), (On Duty Outside the Archdiocese)
Brown, William M., St. Mark, Clarkesville
Brunton, Robert, (On Duty Outside of the Archdiocese)
Buckley, Earl D., St. Matthew, Winder
Buckley, Edward, St. George, Newnan
Buzeta, Bernardo, Holy Cross, Atlanta
Byrne, Michael T., Chap., St. Thomas More Society, Inc., Atlanta; St. John Neumann, Lilburn
Campbell, Brian J., (On Duty Outside the Archdiocese)
Campos, Jose G., St. Andrew, Roswell
Carazza, Dennis M., (On Duty Outside the Archdiocese)
Carignan, Charles E., Our Lady of LaSalette, Canton
Carr, Ronald S., (Retired)
Casal, Matias A., St. Philip Benizi, Jonesboro
Casey, Bernard J., St. Thomas Aquinas, Alpharetta
Casey, Lawrence B., St. Francis of Assisi, Blairsville
Chambliss, Leonard P. Jr., (On Duty Outside of the Archdiocese)
Chavez, Michael S., St. Oliver Plunkett, Snellville
Cintron, Rafael, St. Oliver Plunkett, Snellville
Coffey, Thomas, St. Francis of Assisi, Cartersville
Collins, Gerald A., (On Duty Outside the Archdiocese)
Comeau, Ronald A., (Retired)
Connell, Jerry F., (Retired)
Cooper, King E., St. Matthew, Tyrone
Coughlin, Frank F., (Retired)
Crowley, Joseph F., St. Peter Chanel, Roswell
Cuomo, Anthony F., Holy Trinity, Peachtree City
Daly, Jerome P., St. Gabriel, Fayetteville
Demko, Stephen G., Holy Spirit, Atlanta
Devereux, Francis, St. Joseph, Marietta
Dietz, Paul E., St. Francis of Assisi, Blairsville
Donohue, William A., Prince of Peace, Flowery Branch
Doppel, Paul Lee, St. Monica, Duluth
Dorner, Dennis J., B.A., Chancellor, Dir. Permanent Diaconate, St. Luke the Evangelist, Dahlonega
Downey, Richard, St. Lawrence, Lawrenceville
Duffield, John P., St. Anna, Monroe
Easterwood, James M., (Retired), Transfiguration, Marietta
Echevarria, Manuel, St. John Neumann, Lilburn
Echevarria, Miguel A., St. Francis of Assisi, Cartersville
Egan, Raymond F., Chancery, Atlanta; Interfaith Airport Chaplaincy
Espinosa, Jose G., Assoc. Co-Dir. Formation, St. Catherine of Siena, Kennesaw
Eustace, Joseph C., St. Mary's, Rome
Fagan, Robert P., St. Michael, Gainesville
Feliu, Albert L., St. Marguerite D'Youville, Lawrenceville
Figueredo, Alberto, (Inactive)
Ford, Stanley B., (Retired)
Fragale, David A., The Catholic Church of Transfiguration, Marietta
Franklin, Paul H., The Catholic Church of the Transfiguration, Marietta
Fraser, Roger A., St. Brendan, Cumming
Friedlein, Mark F., Holy Trinity, Peachtree City
Gahafer, Leo, St. Brigid, Johns Creek
Gallagher, Alexander S., Holy Family, Marietta
Galvis, Enrique L., (Retired)
Gant, Derek, St. Benedict, Johns Creek
Garcia, Carlos M., (On Duty Outside the Archdiocese)
Garcia-Carreras, Evelio, St. Stephen the Martyr, Lilburn
Garrett, Michael, St. Thomas the Apostle, Smyrna
Garrett, William, All Saints, Dunwoody
Gaudin, James M. Jr., St. Joseph's, Athens
Geroski, Dayle H., (Retired)
Gonzalez, Marino, Sacred Heart, Atlanta
Goolsby, Joseph B., (Retired)
Gorman, Chester, St. Brendan the Navigator, Cumming
Gorski, Paul A., Transfiguration, Marietta
Gotschall, Thomas E., St. Andrew, Roswell
Grabowy, Edmund M., St. Ann's, Marietta
Gregerson, Robert J., (On Duty Outside of Archdiocese)
Griffin, Chester H., Our Lady of Lourdes, Atlanta
Grimaldi, Robert H., St. Luke the Evangelist, Dahlonega
Gross, Benedict, (Retired)
Grubbs, Burgess David, (Retired)
Hampton, William (Bill) L., St. Matthew's, Tyrone
Hanson, David, (On Duty Outside of the Archdiocese)
Harkins, James C., Our Lady of Perpetual Help, Carrollton
Harris, Peter, Church of the Transfiguration, Marietta
Harvey, John M., (On Duty Outside the Archdiocese)
Hauert, Robert J., Immaculate Heart of Mary, Atlanta; Faith Alliance of Metro, Atlanta
Hayward, Jerome, St. John Neumann, Lilburn
Head, Francis D., (On Duty Outside the Archdiocese)
Hein, Henry R., St. Brigid, Johns Creek
Heinsch, William H., St. George, Newnan
Herndon, Jack, St. Michael the Archangel Woodstock
Hettel, Louis A., (Retired)
Hogan, Richard, St. Lawrence, Lawrenceville
Huff, Tom, St. Brigid, Johns Creek
Hunkele, Thomas H., (Retired)
Huynh, Hung Viet (Vic), Our Lady of Vietnam, Riverdale
Jackson, Earl D., St. Thomas the Apostle, Smyrna
Jelks, Leviticus, St. Anthony's, Atlanta
Jennings, Bobby Allen, St. Ann, Marietta
Jimenez, Arturo P., (Retired)
Jindrich, William L., St. Oliver Plunkett, Snellville
Johns, Fred, St. Pius X, Conyers
Johnson, Nicholas, Prince of Peace, Flowery Branch
Jones, Frederick T., (Retired)
Jones, Michael R., Prince of Peace, Flowery Branch
Kaszycki, Richard C., St. Steven the Martyr, Lilburn
Kazin, Gerard G., St. Benedict, Duluth
Keeling, William W., St. Thomas Aquinas, Alpharetta
Keen, William, St. Peter Chanel, Roswell
Keller, Norman K., St. Joseph, Marietta
Kelsey, Donald A., (Retired)
Kennedy, Michael L., St. Michael's, Gainesville
Kepshire, Robert J., Diocese of Savannah
Kilkelly, Brian, St. Pius X, Conyers
King, A.B. III, Diocese of Birmingham
Kirksey, Timothy K., (Retired)
Klein, Bob, Shrine of the Immaculate Conception, Atlanta
Kolodziej, Keith M., St. Ann, Marietta
Koppernaal, John A., St. Monica, Duluth
Korte, Jerry R., (Retired)
Krarup, Paul E., Prince of Peace, Flowery Branch
Kretzmer, Thomas, St. Peter the Rock, The Rock
Krise, Edward, All Saints, Dunwoody
Krupa, Bradford, St. Clement, Calhoun
LaHouse, Edmund J., St. Thomas Aquinas, Alpharetta
LaMachia, Ralph, Good Shepherd, Cumming
Lampe, Martin J., (Retired)
Lampert, Kenneth W., St. Michael, Gainesville
Lange, William G., (Retired)
Lerma, Arthur, St. Thomas Aquinas, Alpharetta
Lett, Jerry M., (Retired)
Londono, Luis, St. Matthew, Winder
Lorza, Luis C., St. Brendan the Navigator, Cumming
Manning, Ronald, Shrine of the Immaculate Conception, Atlanta
Marchildon, Donald W., (Retired)
Marinchak, Richard J., St. Mark's, Clarkesville
Marrero, Felix, Sacred Heart, Griffin
Marsh, Curtis D., St. Mary, Toccoa
Marten, William H., (Leave of Absence)
Martorell, Gerardo G., (Retired)
Mason, John, St. Anthony's, Blue Ridge
McCarthy, Kevin J., (On Duty Outside the Archdiocese)
McCarthy, William F., Holy Spirit, Atlanta
McDermott, James, St. Vincent de Paul, Dallas
McGivney, Thomas F., St. Thomas Aquinas, Alpharetta
McGrane, Thomas J., (On Duty Outside the Archdiocese)
McGuire, John P., St. Francis of Assisi, Blairsville
McHugh, Al C., (Retired)
McKenzie, William, St. Patrick, Norcross

McManus, John J., J.D., J.C.L., Cathedral of Christ the King, Atlanta; Corpus Christi, Stone Mountain
McNabb, Scott J.N., (On Duty Outside the Archdiocese)
Mead, Stuart A., St. Pius X, Conyers
Medina, Ricardo D., All Saints, Dunwoody
Medine, Scott E., St. Joseph, Athens
Melara, Israel D., St. Theresa, Douglasville
Melvin, Ken W., Corpus Christi, Stone Mountain
Merlo-Quintero, Jose T., Centro Catolico at Holy Spirit, Atlanta
Metzger, Thomas J., St. Anna, Monroe
Meuninck, Tilton (T.C.), (Retired)
Mickle, Richard A., (On Duty Outside the Archdiocese)
Miles, Philip, (On Duty Outside the Archdiocese)
Millinger, Terry D., St. Lawrence, Lawrenceville
Mitchell, Alfred, Sts. Peter & Paul, Decatur; Interfaith Chaplaincy Airport
Mitchell, Mark D., Holy Spirit, Atlanta
Mobley, Michael K. Sr., St. Stephen the Martyr, Lilburn
Monahan, William J., (Retired)
Moncrief, Wayland, (On Duty Outside the Archdiocese)
Moore, Dennis, (Retired)
Morning, J. Nicholas, St. Ann, Marietta
Nacey, Wayne, (On Duty Outside the Archdiocese)
Nadeau, Donald N., Good Shepherd, Cumming
Narvaez, Jose A., St. Patrick's, Norcross
Nerio, Jesus, St. Thomas Aquinas, Alpharetta
Neslin, Stuart L., St. Mary, Rome
Ngoy, Kapya, St. Marguerite D'Youville, Lawrenceville
Nguyen, Joseph Phu, Our Lady of Vietnam, Riverdale
O'Donoghue, William H., Our Lady of the Assumption, Atlanta
Ollick, Gregory, St. John Neumann, Lilburn; St. Mary, Toccoa
Orellana, Jose M., St. Bernadette, Cedartown
Ortiz-Velasquez, Jose, St. Lawrence, Lawrenceville
Parker, Donald S., St. Mary Magdalene, Newnan
Patterson, Edward, Our Lady of the Assumption, Atlanta
Payne, William E. Jr., (Retired), Shrine of the Immaculate Conception, Atlanta
Pecore, Gregory L., St. Philip Benizi, Jonesboro
Perez, Gilberto, Saint Michael, Gainesville
Perez, Jose, St. Vincent de Paul, Dallas
Perez, Pablo, St. Catherine of Laboure, Jefferson
Perri, Robert, Prince of Peace, Flowery Branch
Peters, Gayle P., St. Matthew, Tyrone
Peterson, John R., Good Shepherd, Cumming
Pham, Hoa (Joseph) V., Holy Vietnamese Martyrs Mission, Atlanta
Phillips, Barry S., Sacred Heart of Jesus, Hartwell
Pierre-Louis, Augustin, Ss. Peter & Paul, Decatur
Ponichtera, Stephen, St. Catherine of Siena, Kennesaw
Przybylek, Francis, St. John Vianney, Lithia Springs
Publicover, Bruce C., (Retired)
Puetz, John D., St. Benedict, Duluth
Pupo, Jose I., St. Michael the Archangel, Woodstock
Ranft, Peter, St. Lawrence, Lawrenceville
Readdy, Robert G., (Retired)
Reed, William Bruce Jr., St. Joseph, Marietta
Reimer, Cecil R., Holy Cross, Atlanta
Rentas, Felix, St. John Vianney, Lithia Springs
Rhodes, Joseph, St. Pius X, Conyers
Rich, Robert M., (Retired)
Richardson, Raymond L., (Retired), Christ Redeemer, Dawsonville
Riddett, Robert, St. Lawrence, Lawrenceville
Rivera, Prudencio I., (Retired)
Robichaux, Whitney F. Jr., Cathedral of Christ the King, Atlanta; Interfaith Chaplaincy Airport
Roche, Gary J., (On Duty Outside of the Archdiocese)
Rodriguez, Etienne Francisco, St. Philip Benizi, Jonesboro
Ruberte, Joseph, Mary Our Queen, Norcross
Rubio, Eduardo J., St. Brendan the Navigator, Cumming
Ryan, Thomas J., St. Clare, Acworth
Sambrone, Fred J. Jr., (Retired)
Sandusky, Thomas J., (On Duty Outside the Archdiocese)
Santa, Edward A., (Retired)
Saulino, Dominic Jr., Shrine of the Immaculate Conception, Atlanta
Schantz, Gary E., St. Jude the Apostle, Atlanta
Schmidt, Richard, Holy Trinity, Peachtree City
Schreckenberger, David, St. Lawrence, Lawrenceville
Schueth, Paul, Good Samaritan, Ellijay
Shaver, Thomas R., St. Joseph's, Marietta
Shawcross, Steven W., St. Thomas Aquinas, Alpharetta
Shoemaker, John W., (Retired)
Sholander, Mark A., Holy Trinity, Peachtree City; The Interfaith Airport Chaplaincy, Inc., Atlanta; Holy Trinity, Peachtree City
Silvestri, Thomas D., (Retired), Chap., Georgia Diagnostic and Correctional Center, Jackson
Simmons, William H. III, St. Anthony of Padua, Atlanta
Sinanian, Loris, (On Duty Outside the Archdiocese)
Skolds, Jim, St. Oliver Plunkett, Snellville
Smilski, Phillip G., St. Joseph, Marietta
Smith, George, St. Paul of the Cross, Atlanta
Smith, Robert B., (Retired)
Sparks, Scott A., St. Peter Chanel, Roswell
Speed, William (Bill) E., Prince of Peace, Flowery Branch
St. Michel, Ronald A., St. Theresa, Douglasville
Stagg, James A., (Retired)
Stanley, John C., Our Lady of LaSalette, Canton
Stewart, James M., (Retired)
Stone, James E., (Retired)
Strachan, John S., St. Thomas Aquinas, Alpharetta
Suever, Richard M., (Retired)
Sutter, Edward L., (Retired)
Swan, Peter B. Sr., St. Philip Benizi, Jonesboro
Swope, Paul S. Jr., St. Mary Magdalene, Newnan
Taylor, Victor L., St. Michael the Archangel, Woodstock
Thacker, James S., Saint Mary, Rome
Thibodeau, Richard, St. Paul the Apostle, Cleveland
Thomasberger, David J., St. Peter Chanel, Roswell
Thompson, Chris, Our Lady of Assumption, Atlanta
Timme, John W., (Leave of Absence)
Tipton, Robert F., St. Monica, Duluth
Toca, Frederick, Most Blessed Sacrament, Atlanta
Tolcher, Richard P., Prison Ministry; St. John the Evangelist, Hapeville
Tracy, Kevin F., St. Thomas Aquinas, Alpharetta
Tramonte, James A., St. Jude the Apostle, Sandy Springs
Underwood, Froilan (Allen) V., Holy Spirit, Atlanta
Vargas, Hector M., (Leave of Absence)
Walter, Tom G., Prince of Peace, Flowery Branch
Weeks, Jim G., St. Matthew's, Tyrone
Weiss, Dr. James (Jim), Holy Cross, Atlanta
Welsh, Lawrence J., St. Matthew, Winder
Williams, James H., (Retired)
Williams, Kenneth, St. Joseph, Marietta
Wojcik, John, St. Peter Chanel, Roswell
Wolf, James P., St. Brigid, Johns Creek
Woods, Michael, (On Duty Outside the Archdiocese)
Young, Bradford, St. Catherine of Siena, Kennesaw
Zaworski, Thomas E., (Retired)
Zukauckas, Gerald, Cathedral of Christ the King, Atlanta.

INSTITUTIONS LOCATED IN DIOCESE

[A] SEMINARIES, RELIGIOUS OR SCHOLASTICATES

ATLANTA. *Aquinas Center of Theology at Emory University*, The Luce Center, 1531 Dickey Dr., Atlanta, 30322. Tel: 404-727-8860; Email: acamer4@emory.edu; Web: www.aquinas.emory.edu. Craig C. Mullins, Chair; Dr. Phillip Thompson, Dir. Students 7; Total Staff 3.

[B] COLLEGES AND UNIVERSITIES

ATLANTA. *Holy Spirit College, Inc.*, 4465 Northside Dr., N.W., Atlanta, 30327. Tel: 678-904-4959; Fax: 404-252-1162; Email: kschulman@holyspiritcollege.org; Web: www.holyspiritcollege.org. Rev. Msgr. Edward J. Dillon, J.C.D., Chancellor; Gareth N. Genner, Pres.; Kim Schulman, Registrar; Eric Wearne, Provost; Christopher Gustafson, Vice-Provost. Lay Teachers 3; Priests 4; Students 23.

Pontifex University, 4465 Northside Dr., N.W., Atlanta, 30327. Tel: 678-904-4959; Email: dclayton@pontifex.university; Web: www.pontifex.university/. Gareth N. Genner, Pres.; David Clayton, Dean. Lay Teachers 11; Priests 19; Students 467.

[C] ARCHDIOCESAN SCHOOLS, PARISH

ATLANTA. *Christ the King Catholic School* (1937) (Grades K-8), (Co-ed) 46 Peachtree Way N.E., Atlanta, 30305. Tel: 404-233-0383; Fax: 404-266-0704; Web: www.christking.org. Brian C. Newhall, Prin.; Shaun Bland, Vice Prin.; Andree Davila, Librarian. Lay Teachers 45; Students 554.

Immaculate Heart of Mary Catholic School (1958) (Grades K-8), 2855 Briarcliff Rd., N.E., Atlanta, 30329. Tel: 404-636-4488; Fax: 404-636-1853; Email: kdesormeaux@ihmschool.org; Web: www.ihmschool.org. Kellie DesOrmeaux, Prin.; Bob Baldonado, Vice Prin. Lay Teachers 36; Students 502.

St. Jude the Apostle Catholic School (1962) (Grades K-8), 7171 Glenridge Dr., N.E., Atlanta, 30328. Tel: 770-394-2880; Fax: 770-804-9248; Email: pchilds@saintjude.net; Web: saintjude.net. Patty Childs, Prin.; Eleneora Straub, Librarian. Lay Teachers 35; Students 492.

Our Lady of the Assumption Catholic School (1952) (Grades PreK-8), 1320 Hearst Dr., N.E., Atlanta, 30319. Tel: 404-364-1902; Fax: 404-364-1914; Email: office@olaschool.org; Web: olaschool.org. Lisa Cordell, Prin.; Diane Miller-Deasy, Librarian. Lay Teachers 44; Students 526.

St. Pius X Catholic High School (1958) (Coed) 2674 Johnson Rd., N.E., Atlanta, 30345. Tel: 404-636-3023; Fax: 404-633-8387; Email: mfree@spx.org; Web: spx.org. Rev. Reybert Pineda Avellanada, Chap.; Mr. Stephen Spellman, Prin.; John B. Griffith, Dean Academics; Rachel Braham, Dean Students; Edye Simpson, Dean Students; Aaron Parr, Admissions; Robin Tanis, Librarian; Chad Barwick, Pres. Priests 1; Students 1,096; Teachers 96; Total Staff 42.

ATHENS. *St. Joseph Catholic School* (1949) (Grades PreK-8), 958 Epps Bridge Pkwy., Athens, 30606. Tel: 706-543-1621; Fax: 706-543-0149; Email: theresa.napoli@sjsathens.org; Web: sjsathens.org. Theresa Napoli, Prin.; Tina Bortle, Dir., Develop. & Admissions. Lay Teachers 18; Students 144; Clergy / Religious Teachers 2; Staff 8.

DECATUR. *St. Peter Claver Regional Catholic School* (2001) (Grades PreK-8), 2560 Tilson Rd., Decatur, 30032. Tel: 404-241-3063; Fax: 404-241-4382; Email: sgreenwood@spc-school.org; Web: www.spc-school.org. Susanne Greenwood, Prin.; Mrs. Anna Abbott, Admin.; Alejandra Gordon, Business Mgr. Lay Teachers 12; Students 129; Clergy / Religious Teachers 1.

St. Thomas More Catholic School (1950) (Grades K-8), 630 W. Ponce De Leon Ave., Decatur, 30030. Tel: 404-373-8456; Fax: 404-377-8554; Email: stm@stmga.org; Web: www.stmga.org. Mr. Jerry Raymond, Prin.; Yvette McNett, Asst. Prin.; Eileen Maron, Admissions; Ansley Murphey, Devel.; Laura Ayala, Librarian. Lay Teachers 35; Students 481.

FAYETTEVILLE. *Our Lady of Mercy Catholic High School*, 861 Hwy. 279, Fayetteville, 30214. Tel: 770-461-2202; Fax: 770-461-9353; Email: mbeno@mercycatholic.org; Web: www.mercycatholic.org. William Dooley, Prin.; Cynthia Launay-Fallasse, Admissions & Devel.; Mark Beno, Business Mgr. Lay Teachers 30; Priests 1; Total Enrollment 250.

HAPEVILLE. *St. John the Evangelist Catholic School* (1954) (Grades PreK-8), 240 Arnold St., Hapeville, 30354. Tel: 404-767-4312; Fax: 404-767-0359; Email: office@sjecs.net; Web: www.sjecs.org. Karen Vogtner, B.S., M.Ed., Prin. Lay Teachers 21; Sisters 1; Students 303.

JOHN'S CREEK. *Holy Redeemer Catholic School* (1999) (Grades K-8), 3380 Old Alabama Rd., Johns Creek, 30022. Tel: 770-410-4056; Fax: 770-410-1454; Email: info@hrcatholicschool.org; Web: www.hrcatholicschool.org. Lauren Schell, Prin.; Sue Kalinauskas, Asst. Prin.; Jeannie Barden, Librarian; Ms. Brenda Leslie, Controller. Lay Teachers 42; Students 456.

KENNESAW. *St. Catherine of Siena Catholic School* (2002) (Grades K-8), 1618 Ben King Rd., Kennesaw, 30144. Tel: 770-419-8601; Fax: 678-626-0000; Email: smjacinta@scsiena.org; Web: www.scsiena.org. Sr. Mary Jacinta, O.P., Prin.; Rev. Neil Dhabliwala. Lay Teachers 25; Sisters 4; Students 346; Total Staff 18.

LILBURN. *St. John Neumann Regional Catholic School* (1986) (Grades PreK-8), (Regional) 791 Tom Smith Rd., S.W., Lilburn, 30047. Tel: 770-381-0557; Fax: 770-381-0276; Email: jbroom@sjnrcs.org; Web: www.sjnrcs.org. Dr. Julie Broom, Prin.; Mrs. Rosa Garcia, Admin. Lay Teachers 20; Students 278.

MARIETTA. *St. Joseph Catholic School* (1953) (Grades K-8), 81 Lacy St., Marietta, 30060. Tel: 770-428-3328; Fax: 770-424-2960; Email: jbrodell@stjosephschool.org; Web: stjosephschool.org. Patricia Allen, Ph.D., Prin.; Jill Rice, M.Ed., Vice Prin.; Tara Klodnicki, Librarian. Lay Teachers 36; Students 450.

ROME. *St. Mary's Catholic School* (1945) (Grades PreK-8), 401 E. Seventh St., Rome, 30161. Tel: 706-234-4953; Fax: 706-234-3030; Email: mreder@smsrome.org; Web: www.smsrome.org. Melissa Reder, Prin. Lay Teachers 21; Students 223; Clergy / Religious Teachers 3.

ROSWELL. *Blessed Trinity Catholic High School* (2000) 11320 Woodstock Rd., Roswell, 30075. Tel: 678-277-9083; Fax: 678-277-9756; Email: bmarks@btcatholic.org; Web: www.btcatholic.org. Revs. Robert Frederick, Chap.; Augustine Tran, J.C.L.; Brian Marks, Pres.; Cathy Lancaster, Prin.; Susan Dorner, Vice Prin.; Ramon Villacura, Vice Prin.; Ms. Brenda Leslie, Controller. Lay Teachers 76; Priests 2; Total Enrollment 994; Total Staff 115; Clergy / Religious Teachers 2.

Queen of Angels Catholic School Queen of Angels Catholic School (1999) (Grades K-8), 11340 Woodstock Rd., Roswell, 30075. Tel: 770-518-1804; Fax: 770-518-0945; Email: jarthur@qaschool.org; Web: www.qaschool.org. Jamie Arthur, Prin.; Mrs. Danielle Montepare, Prin.; Mrs. Debra Kopec, Business Mgr.; Ms. Brenda Leslie, Controller; Mrs. Sue VanRooyen, Librarian. Lay Teachers 35; Students 489; Total Staff 64; Clergy / Religious Teachers 1.

TYRONE. *Our Lady of Victory Catholic School* (1999) (Grades PreK-8), 211 Kirkley Rd., Tyrone, 30290. Tel: 770-306-9026; Fax: 770-306-0323; Email: gwilkerson@olvpatriots.org; Email: cnardozza@olvpatriots.org; Web: www.olvcatholicschoolk-8.org. Cori Nardozza, Admin.; George Wilkerson, Prin. Lay Teachers 15; Nurses 1; Students 113; Counselor 1; Clergy / Religious Teachers 1; Admin. Facilities Staff 3.

[D] INDEPENDENT SCHOOLS

ATLANTA. *Cristo Rey Atlanta Jesuit High School, Inc.*, 222 Piedmont Ave., N.E., Atlanta, 30308. Tel: 404-637-2800; Email: ivasquez@cristoreyatlanta.org; Web: www.cristoreyatlanta.org. Dom Mazzone, Chm.; Bill Garrett, Pres.; Mrs. Diane Bush, Prin. Lay Teachers 29; Priests 1; Students 519; Clergy / Religious Teachers 6.

**Holy Spirit Preparatory School, Inc.*, (Grades PreK-12), Holy Spirit Preparatory School, Inc., 4449 Northside Dr., Atlanta, 30327. Tel: 678-904-2811 (Office); Fax: 678-904-4984; Email: admissions@holyspiritprep.org; Web: www.holyspiritprep.org. Kyle M. Pietrantonio, M.Ed., Headmaster; Rev. Juan Jose Hernandez, L.C., Chap. Lay Teachers 72; Priests 2; Students 548; Clergy / Religious Teachers 4.

Upper School Campus, (Grades 8-12), 4449 Northside Dr., Atlanta, 30327. Tel: 678-904-2811; Fax: 678-904-4983; Email: admissions@holyspiritprep.org. Jocelyn Sotomayor, M.Ed., Prin., Upper School Campus.

Lower School Campus, (Grades PreK-7), 4820 Long Island Dr., Atlanta, 30342. Tel: 404-255-0900; Fax: 404-255-0914; Email: admissions@holyspiritprep.org; Web: www.holyspiritprep.org. Peter F. Schultz, M.Ed., Prin.; Karyn Vickery, Vice Prin.

Preschool Campus, 4465 Northside Dr., Atlanta, 30327. Tel: 404-252-8008; Fax: 404-903-4983; Email: admissions@holyspiritprep.org; Web: www.holyspiritprep.org. Kristina Wilhelm, Dir.

**Marist School*, (Grades 7-12), 3790 Ashford Dunwoody, N.E., Atlanta, 30319-1899. Tel; 770-457-7201; Fax: 770-457-8402; Email: info@marist.com; Web: www.marist.com. Revs. Francis J. Kissel, S.M.; Ralph F. Olek, S.M., Supr.; David D. Musso, S.M., Chap.; William F. Rowland, S.M., Pres. A Private Catholic School.; College Preparatory Day School conducted by The Marist Fathers and Brothers. Corporate Title: Marist School, Inc. Lay Teachers 101; Priests 5; Students 1,106; Total Staff 222; Lay Faculty 20; Clergy / Religious Teachers 3. In Res. Rev. Thomas E. Ellerman, S.M., S.T.L., (Retired).

ATHENS. **Monsignor Donovan Catholic High School* (2003) 590 Lavender Rd., Athens, 30606. Tel: 706-433-0223; Fax: 706-433-0229; Email: pgessner@mdchs.org; Web: www.mdchs.org. Mr. Paul Gessner, Headmaster. Lay Teachers 23; Students 102; Total Staff 25; Religious Teachers 1; Clergy / Religious Teachers 1.

CUMMING. **Pinecrest Academy, Inc.* (1993) (Grades PreK-12), 955 Peachtree Pkwy., Cumming, 30041. Tel: 770-888-4477; Fax: 770-888-0404; Web: www.pinecrestacademy.org. Revs. William Brock, L.C., Chap.; Daren Weisbrod, L.C., Chap.; Matthew A. Kaderabek, L.C., Chap.; Edward Spurka, Head of School; Mrs. Joan McCabe, VP Fin. & CEO; Ms. Laura Fowler, Media Specialist; Mrs. Denise Cress, Middle School Prin.; Mrs. Madeliene Flanagan, Lower School Prin. Brothers 1; Lay Teachers 90; Priests 4; Students 694; Female Consecrated 4; Religious Teachers 4.

DULUTH. **Notre Dame Academy* (2005) (Grades PreK-12), 4635 River Green Pkwy., Duluth, 30096. Tel: 678-387-9385 (Office); Fax: 678-990-9353; Email: dorr@ndacademy.org; Email: kpizzarelli@ndacademy.org; Web: www.ndacademy.org. Debra Orr, Head of School; Julia Derucki, Prin., Middle School; John Henry Spann, Prin., Upper School; Stacy Stanford, Advancement Dir.; Sharon Colletta, Dir. of Early Years Campus; Elizabeth Boureuf, Dir.; Reilly Campbell, Dir.; Nadia Murray, Dir. Independent, Marist School. Preschool program for children ages 2, 3 & 4 Students 543; Clergy / Religious Teachers 3.

Early Years School, Notre Dame Academy, (Grades PreK-K), 3345 Peachtree Industrial Blvd., Duluth, 30096. Tel: 678-387-9385 (Office); Fax: 678-990-9353; Email: scolletta@ndacademy.org; Web: www.ndacademy.org. Sharon Colletta, Dir. Independent, Marist School. Lay Teachers 56; Students 100; Religious Teachers 1.

[E] GENERAL HOSPITALS

ATHENS. *St. Mary's Health Care System, Inc.* dba St. Mary's Hospital, 1230 Baxter St., Athens, 30606-3791. Tel: 706-389-3273; Fax: 706-389-3271; Email: SLackey@stmarysathens.org; Web: www.stmarysathens.org. David Montez Carter, Pres. Catholic Health Ministries. Bed Capacity 196; Nurses 700; Tot Asst. Annually 150,000; Total Staff 2,600; Other Sister Personnel 1.

St. Mary's Hospital Chapel, Tel: 706-389-3000; Fax: 706-389-3931; Email: ploome@stmarysathens.org; Web: www.stmarysathens.org. Nurses 342; Total Staff 1,421.

FORT OGLETHORPE. *CHI Memorial Hospital - Georgia*, 100 Gross Crescent Cir., Fort Oglethorpe, 30742. Tel: 402-343-4413; Fax: 402-343-4449; Email: angela.noel@alegent.org. Mr. Lawrence Schumacher, C.E.O.; Angela Noel, Dir. Taxation. Bed Capacity 179; Tot Asst. Annually 29,630; Total Staff 188.

GREENSBORO. *Good Samaritan Hospital, Inc.* dba St. Mary's Good Samaritan Hospital, 5401 Lake Oconne Pkwy., Greensboro, 30642. Tel: 706-453-7331; Fax: 706-453-2812; Email: tadcock@stmarysathens.org; Web: stmarysgoodsam.org. Tanya Adcock, Pres. Catholic Health Ministries. Bed Capacity 25; Nurses 55; Tot Asst. Annually 41,830; Total Staff 165.

[F] SPECIAL HOSPITALS

ATLANTA. *Saint Joseph's Mercy Care Services* Mercy Care (1985) 424 Decatur St., Atlanta, 30312-1848. Tel: 678-843-8500; Fax: 678-843-8501; Email: aebberwein@mercyatlanta.org; Email: jwallace@mercyatlanta.org; Web: mercyatlanta.org. Sr. Angela Marie Ebberwein, R.S.M., Vice Pres. Division of Saint Joseph's Health System.

Legal Title: Saint Joseph's Mercy Services, Inc. Sisters 2; Total Staff 235; Total Assisted 57,342.

Our Lady of Perpetual Help Home, 760 Pollard Blvd., S.W., Atlanta, 30315. Tel: 404-688-9515; Email: sistermiriam49@gmail.com; Web: olphhome.org. Sr. Miriam Smith, O.P., Supr.; Rev. Paul A. Burke, Chap. Dominican Sisters of HawthorneNursing Home for Free Care of Cancer Patients.

Servants of Relief for Incurable Cancer Bed Capacity 35; Priests 1; Sisters 16; Tot Asst. Annually 120; Total Staff 35.

ROME. *Mercy Senior Care, Inc.* dba Mercy Care Rome, Inc., P.O. Box 866, Rome, 30162-0866. Tel: 706-291-8496; Fax: 706-295-5953; Email: emolina@mercyrome.org. Sr. Angela Marie Ebberwein, R.S.M., Vice Pres.; Elizabeth Molina, R.N., B.S.N., M.A., Exec. Dir. Total Staff 15; Total Assisted 408.

[G] MONASTERIES AND RESIDENCES OF PRIESTS

ATLANTA. *Augustine House, Dominicans Friars of Atlanta*, 780 Lakeview Ave., N.E., Atlanta, 30308-1845. Tel: 919-793-3325; Email: bbsop@aol.com. Revs. Bruce Schultz, O.P., Parochial Vicar; John Joseph Blase Boll, O.P., Chap., Emory Uni.; Arthur Kirwin, O.P., Supr.; Jeffery Ott, O.P.

Marist Provincial Office, Society of Mary - Atlanta Province, 3790 Ashford-Dunwoody Rd. N.E., Atlanta, 30319. P.O. Box 888263, Atlanta, 30356. Tel: 770-451-1316 (Treas. Office); Fax: 678-550-7650; Email: provincialoffice@marist.com; Email: pfrechette@maristsociety.org; Web: www.societyofmaryusa.org. Rev. Paul Frechette, S.M., Prov. Society of Mary (Marists) (S.M)P.O. Box 81144, Atlanta, 30366-1144. Revs. Paul Frechette, S.M., Prov.; John H. Harhager, S.M., Treas.

CONYERS. *The Monastery of the Holy Spirit*, 2625 Hwy. 212 S.W., Conyers, 30094-4044. Tel: 770-483-8705; Fax: 770-760-0989; Email: info@trappist.net; Email: monastery@trappist.net; Web: www.trappist.net. Revs. Francis Michael Stiteler, O.C.S.O., Abbot Emeritus; Methodius Telnack, O.C.S.O., Cellerar; Gerard Gross, O.C.S.O., Music Min.; John M. O'Brien, O.C.S.O.; Eduardo Rodriguez, O.C.S.O.; Thomas F. Smith, O.C.S.O.; Augustine Myslinski, O.C.S.O., Abbot; James Stephen Behrens, O.C.S.O.; Matt G. Torpey, O.C.S.O.; Bros. Elias Marechal, O.C.S.O., Novice Master; Mark Dohle, O.C.S.O., Prior; Cassian Russell, O.C.S.O., Sub-Prior; Callistus Crichlow, O.C.S.O., Contact Person. Priests 9; Professed Brothers 28.

CUMMING. *Legionaries of Christ, Incorporated*, 8825 Fulham Ct., Cumming, 30041. Tel: 770-828-4950; Email: eramirez@arcol.org. Revs. Daren Weisbrod, L.C., Supr.; Frank Formolo, L.C., Admin.; John O'Connor, L.C., Prov.; Daniel Brandenburg, Prov. Asst.; Michael Brisson, L.C., Sec.; David Daly, L.C., Prov. Asst.; Shawn Aaron, L.C., Prov. Asst.; Matthew Van Smoorenburg, L.C.; Paul Alger, L.C.; Patrick Langan, L.C.; Kevin Baldwin, L.C., Chap.; Matthew A. Kaderabek, L.C., Chap. Total in Residence 12. *Legionaries of Christ*, Spalding Community, 2595 Spalding Dr., Atlanta, 30350. Tel: 914-295-7780; Fax: 770-393-0934; Email: lotero@legionaries.org; Web: www.legionariesofchrist.org. Revs. Brian Hoelzen, L.C., Youth Work; Martin Connor, L.C., RC Local Dir.; Kevin Lixey, L.C., Chap., Regnum Christi Adults, Community Supr.; David Steffy, L.C., Pres. of Pinecrest School; Deacon David Barton, L.C., Youth Work; Revs. Juan Jose Hernandez, L.C., Chap., Holy Spirit Prep School; James Swanson, L.C., Regnam Christi Women Section; Lino Otero, L.C.

DECATUR. *Atlanta Jesuit Community, Inc.*, 624 W. Ponce de Leon Ave., Decatur, 30030. Tel: 617-826-9767; Email: tkenny@jesuits.org. 636 W. Ponce de Leon Ave., Decatur, 30030. Rev. Thomas J. Kenny, S.J., Jesuit Supr.

LOGANVILLE. *The Missionaries of St. Francis de Sales - MSFS USA Vice Province* (1838) 3887 Rosebud Rd., Loganville, 30052-4656. Tel: 470-268-4069; Fax: 470-275-5057; Email: msfsinc2011@hotmail.com; Web: www.fransaliansusa.com. Revs. Joseph Mullakkara, M.S.F.S., Supr.; Joseph Pottemmel, M.S.F.S., Prov. Bursar & Chap.; Tomy Joseph Puliyanampattayil, M.S.F.S., Prov.; Mathew Elayadathamadam, M.S.F.S.; Sunny Punnakuzhiy, M.S.F.S.; Joseph Mendes, M.S.F.S.

Legal Title: Missionaries of St. Francis de Sales, Inc.

Villa Luyet, 3474 Pate Dr., Snellville, 30078-5000. Tel: 770-972-0202; Email: jpottemmel@gmail.com; Fax: 678-336-9118.

[H] CONVENTS AND RESIDENCES OF SISTERS

ATLANTA. *Missionaries of Charity* (1993) 995 St. Charles Ave., N.E., Atlanta, 30306-4211. Tel: 404-892-5111. Sisters M. Jonathan, MC, Regl. Supr.; Drita Maris, MC, Supr. Sisters 6.

BUFORD. *Missionary Sisters of the Sacred Heart "Ad Gentes"* (1949) 6401 New Bethany Rd., Buford, 30518. Tel: 678-482-1530; Fax: 678-482-1530; Email: xeniagonzalez@bellsouth.net. Sisters Inés G. Ramos Tapia, M.A.G., B.A., M.A., Gen. Coord. of M.A.G. Sisters in U.S.A.; Beatriz Taneco Bieira, M.A.G., B.A., L.P., Pastoral Assoc.; Xenia Gonzalez, M.A.G., B.A., M.A., Treas. & Pastoral Assoc.; Veronica F. Ramos, M.A.G., B.A., M.A., Pastoral Assoc.; Esther Ordonez, M.A.G., B.A., Pastoral Assoc.; Maria L. Ramos, M.A.G., Pastoral Assoc.; Pilar Hinojosa, M.A.G., B.A., Pastoral Assoc. To serve the Hispanic Community. Sisters 7.

SNELLVILLE. *Monastery of the Visitation*, 2055 Ridgedale Dr., Snellville, 30078. Tel: 770-972-1060 ; Tel: 770-972-1062; Email: superiormaryfield@gmail.com. Sr. Teresa Maria J. Kulangara, V.H.M., Supr. (Maryfield); Strictly cloistered contemplative Office of First Federation. Vocation retreats for women interested in a religious vocation. Sisters 6.

[I] RETREAT HOUSES

ATLANTA. *Ignatius House*, 6700 Riverside Dr., N.W., Atlanta, 30328-2710. Tel: 404-255-0503; Fax: 404-256-0776; Web: www.ignatiushouse.org. Cathi Spornick, Dir.; Maria Gaeta Cressler, Exec. Dir. Total Staff 16.

CONYERS. *Monastery of the Holy Spirit*, 2625 Hwy. 212, S.W., Conyers, 30094. Tel: 770-760-0959; Fax: 770-760-0989; Email: retreat@trappist.net; Web: www.trappist.net. Revs. Augustine Myslinski, O.C.S.O., Abbot; Francis Michael Stiteler, O.C.S.O., Abbot Emeritus; Bros. Mark Dohle, O.C.S.O., Retreat House Guest Master; Callistus Crichlow, O.C.S.O., Contact Person. Private retreats for men and women.

HOSCHTON. *Sisters of the Cenacle*, 5913 Jackson Trail Rd., Hoschton, 30548. Tel: 706-654-3460; Email: atlantacenacle@gmail.com; Web: www.cenaclesisters.org. Sisters Susan Arcaro, R.C.; Barbara Young, R.C. Congregation of Our Lady of the Retreat in the CenacleRetreat Ministry, Spiritual Development Programs, Spiritual Direction, and Other Forms of Spiritual Ministry. Sisters 2.

[J] CAMPUS MINISTRY CENTERS

ATLANTA. *Campus Ministry*, Archdiocese of Atlanta, 2401 Lake Park Dr., 30080-8862.

Tel: 404-920-7620; Fax: 404-920-7621; Email: ofd@archatl.com. Andrew W. Lichtenwalner, Ph. D., Dir.

Atlanta University Complex-The Catholic Center, 809 Beckwith St., S.W., Atlanta, 30314-3720. Tel: 404-755-9394; Fax: 404-755-3460; Email: lykehouse@lykehouse.org. Rev. Urey P. Mark, S.V.D., Campus Min.

Berry College, 911 N. Broad St., Rome, 30161. Tel: 706-290-9000; Email: cbchurch@smcrome.org. Mr. John Catton, Pres.

Catholic Center Georgia State University, Student Center West, Room 483, P.O. Box 3965, Atlanta, 30302. Tel: 678-794-3200; Email: rudyru777run@yahoo.com; Web: lykehouse.org. Rev. Urey P. Mark, S.V.D.; Rudy Schlosser, Campus Min.

Clark Atlanta, 809 Beckwith Street, SW, Atlanta, 30314. Tel: 404-755-2646; Email: rudyru777run@yahoo.com; Web: www.lykehouse.org. Rev. Urey P. Mark, S.V.D., Campus Min.; Rudy Schlosser, Dir.

Emory University, Agnes Scott College, 1753 N. Decatur Rd., N.E., Atlanta, 30307. Tel: 404-636-7237; Email: emorycatholic@gmail.com; Web: www.emory.edu. Rev. John Joseph Blase Boll, O.P., Chap.; Mr. Michael Zauche, Campus Min.; Ms. Victoria Schwartz, Admin.

Georgia College & State University (Milledgeville), 211 W. Greene St., Milledgeville, 31061. Tel: 478-453-7758; Email: deaconcesar@gmail.com. Deacon Cesar Basilio, Campus Min.

Georgia Gwinnett College, 319 Grayson Hwy., Lawrenceville, 30046. Tel: 770-963-8992; Email: Mhamilton5@ggc.edu. Mr. Matt Hamilton, Pres.

Georgia Tech Catholic Center, 172 4th St. N.W., Atlanta, 30313. Tel: 404-892-6759; Email: info@gtcatholic.org; Web: gtcatholic.org. Rev. Joshua Allen, S.T.L., Chap.; Mr. Patrick Williams, Campus Min.; Patty Schmitt, Dir.; Mrs. Chris Martineck, Admin.

Kennesaw State University, 3487 Campus Loop Rd., N.W., Kennesaw, 30144. Tel: 770-423-9909; Email: info@ccksu.org; Web: www.ccksu.org. Rev. Joseph E. Morris, Chap.; Andrew Knuckles, Pres.; Debra Bonda, Admin.

Morehouse College, 809 Beckwith Street, SW, Atlanta, 30314. Tel: 404-755-2646; Email: umark@archatl.com; Email: rudyru777run@yahoo.com; Web: www.lykehouse.org. Rev. Urey P. Mark, S.V.D., Chap.; Rudy Schlosser, Campus Min.

Oglethorpe University, 2855 Briarcliff Rd. NE, Atlanta, 30329. Tel: 404-261-7181; Email: aodonoghue@olachurch.org; Web: www.oglethorpe.edu. Angela O'Donoghue, Campus Min.

Spellman College, 809 Beckwith Street, SW, Atlanta, 30314. Tel: 404-755-2646; Email: umark@archatl.com; Email: rudyru777run@yahoo.com; Web: lykehouse.org. Rev. Urey P. Mark, S.V.D., Chap.; Rudy Schlosser, Campus Min.

University of Georgia - Catholic Student Center, 1344 S. Lumpkin St., Athens, 30605. Tel: 706-543-2293; Fax: 706-543-2541; Web: www.ccatuga.org. Rev. Francis Critch, O.F.M., Dir.; Mrs. Angie Hall, Dir. (Athens).

University of North Georgia (Dahlonega), St. Luke the Evangelist Church, 91 N. Park St., Dahlonega, 30533. Tel: 706-864-4779; Fax: 706-864-2568; Web: ungcatholic.org. Rev. John M. Matejek; Molly Clavenna, Campus Min.

University of West Georgia, 1601 Maple St., Carrollton, 30118. Tel: 770-832-8977; Email: Pastor@olphcc.org; Web: www.olphcc.org. Rev. Mario A. Lopez; Ms. Molly Gilroy, Pres.

[K] CATHOLIC CONTINUING CARE RETIREMENT CENTER

ROSWELL. *Catholic Continuing Care Retirement Communities Inc.* aka St. George Village, 11350 Woodstock Rd., Roswell, 30075. Tel: 770-645-2340; Email: mlowell@stgeorgevillage.org; Web: www.stgeorgevillage.org. Mr. Mark A. Lowell, Exec. Dir., Tel: 678-987-0404; Bradley Wilson, CEO.

[L] MISCELLANEOUS LISTINGS

ATLANTA. **Atlanta Catholic Radio, Inc.*, P.O. Box 88892, Atlanta, 30356. Email: carol@theQuestAtlanta.com.

The Catholic Charismatic Renewal for the Archdiocese of Atlanta, 1786 Wellborn Rd., Lithonia, 30058. Tel: 770-482-5017; Fax: 770-482-9476; Email: contact@atlccr.org; Web: www.atlccr.org.

**The Catholic Foundation of North Georgia*, 5871 Glenridge Dr., Ste. 300, Atlanta, 30328. Nancy Dinka Coveny, Pres., Email: ncoveny@cfnga.org.

Christ Child Society of Atlanta, Georgia, Inc., P.O. Box 88705, Atlanta, 30356. Tel: 770-956-7380; Cell: 404-312-9656; Email: treasurerchristchildatlanta@gmail.com; Web: www.christchildatlanta.org. Kathryn (Casey) Long, Pres.; Annemarie Boehnlein, Treas. Volunteers 100.

Georgia Patron of the Arts in the Vatican Museums, Inc., 610 Carriage Way N.W., Atlanta, 30327. Tel: 404-550-6646; Email: carolyn.johnson@georgiavaticanpatrons.org. Carolyn Johnson, Contact Person.

Good Shepherd Services of Atlanta, Inc. (1993) (Incorporated as Good Shepherd Corporation) 2426 Shallowford Terr., Chamblee, 30341. Tel: 770-986-8279; Tel: 770-455-9379; Fax: 678-587-5546; Email: christshepherd51@yahoo.com. Sr. Christine Truong, M.S.W., Dir.

Good Shepherd Corporation Atlanta

Main Office, Fax: 770-451-0156; Email: shepherdatlanta@yahoo.com.

Good Shepherd Outreach Center, Fax: 770-451-0156 ; Tel: 770-986-8279; Email: acctg.gssa@gmail.com. Sr. Madeleine Munday, Pres. Sisters 1; Tot Asst. Annually 2,000; Total Staff 8.

Saint Joseph's Health System (1985) 424 Decatur St., Atlanta, 30312. Tel: 678-843-8500; Fax: 678-843-8501; Email: aebberwein@mercyatlanta.org; Email: jwallace@mercyatlanta.org; Web: www.mercyatlanta.org. Tom Andrews, CEO; Sr. Angela Marie Ebberwein, R.S.M., Vice Pres. Holding company sponsored by Catholic Health Ministries Inc. which operates Saint Joseph's Mercy Foundation Inc., Saint Joseph's Mercy Care Services, & Mercy Senior Care (Rome, GA).

MERCY CARE FOUNDATION, 5134 Peachtree Rd., Chamblee, 30341. Tel: 678-843-8670; Email: foundation@mercyatlanta.org. Steve Siler, Pres.

Mercy Care Foundation, Inc. (1981) 5134 Peachtree Rd., Chamblee, 30341. Tel: 678-843-8670; Fax: 678-843-8679; Web: www.mercyatlanta.org. Steve Siler, Pres. Total Staff 8.

Mercy Services Downtown, Inc., 424 Decatur St., Atlanta, 30312. Tel: 678-843-8500; Fax: 678-843-8501. Sr. Angela Marie Ebberwein, R.S.M., Sec. & Vice Pres.

Patrons of the Arts in the Vatican Museums, Inc., 4449 Northside Dr., Atlanta, 30328. Tel: 717-746-8529; Fax: 404-221-1006; Email: ggenner@gmail.com. Gareth N. Genner, Dir. & Sec.

Renovacion Carismatica Catolica Hispana De Atlanta, 490 Arnold Mill Rd., Woodstock, 30188. Tel: 678-213-0685; Fax: 770-516-4664.

The Sanctuary of Culture Foundation, Inc., 5 Concourse Pkwy., Ste. 200, Atlanta, 30328. Tel: 770-828-4000; Web: sanctuaryofculture.org/. Rev/ Laurence Spiteri, CEO; R. Brett Grayson, Sec.

SJHS JOC Holdings, Inc., 424 Decatur St., S.E., Atlanta, 30312. Tel: 678-843-8500; Email: jwallace@mercyatlanta.org; Web: www.mercyatlanta.org. Sr. Angela Marie Ebberwein, R.S.M., Vice Pres.

The Solidarity Association, 5 Concourse Pkwy., Ste. 200, Atlanta, 30328. Tel: 770-828-4000; Web: www.solidarityassociation.com. Frank J. Hanna III, Moderator; R. Brett Grayson, Treasurer.

ATHENS. *St. Mary's Good Samaritan Foundation, Inc.*, 1230 Baxter St., Athens, 30606. Tel: 706-389-3926. Ansley Martin, Dir.

CONYERS. *Magnificat - Joyful Visitation Chapter, Inc.* (1922) 203 Kelvington Way, Peachtree City, 30269. Tel: 770-486-1537; Email: patforest@mindspring.com. Pat Forest, Dir.

COVINGTON. *Society of Our Lady of the Most Holy Trinity*, SOLT Lay Community, 110 Aspen Dr., Covington, 30016-5824. Tel: 770-787-6468; Email: soltgaoffice@ourladylovesyou.org. Rev. James E. Blount, Lay Formation Dir.

CUMMING. *Vocation Action Circle, Inc.*, 2820 Bordeaux Blvd., Cumming, 30041. Tel: 914-703-0874; Email: jmgonzales@vocation.com. Rev. Frank Formolo, L.C., Sec.

DECATUR. **Allegre Point Senior Residences, Inc.*, 3391 Flat Shoals Rd., Decatur, 30034. Tel: 404-241-7224 ; Fax: 877-693-2333; Email: info@mercyhousing.org; Web: www.mercyhousing.org.

HAPEVILLE. **Pregnancy Aid Clinic*, 531 Forest Pkwy., Forest Park, 30297. Email: lregan@pregnancyaidclinic.org. P.O. Box 92, Roswell, 30077. Tel: 404-763-4357; Email: mbrown@pregnancyaidclinic.org; Web: www.pregnancyaidclinic.com. Marla Brown, CEO; Lisa Regan, Contact Person.

LOVONIA. *St. Mary's Sacred Heart Hospital, Inc.* dba St. Mary's Sacred Heart Hospital, 367 Clear Creek Pkwy., Lavonia, 30553. Tel: 706-356-7800; Fax: 706-356-7828; Email: jenglish@stmarysathens.org; Web: www.stmaryssacredheart.org. Mr. Jeff English, Pres. Bed Capacity 56; Nurses 113; Tot Asst. Annually 65,303; Total Staff 320; Inpatients 1,605.

PEACHTREE CORNERS. *Rebuilding Hope Missions, Inc.* (2018) 3945 Holcomb Bridge Rd., Ste. 300, Peachtree Corners, 30092. Cell: 770-714-9484; Email: info@rebuildinghopemissions.com. Mr. Randy Ortiz, Pres.

PEMBROKE. **Mercy Housing Pembroke, Inc.* aka McFadden Place, 80 McFadden Pl., Pembroke, 31321. Tel: 404-873-3887; Fax: 877-693-2333; Email: info@mercyhousing.org; Web: www.mercyhousing.org.

ROSWELL. **Catholics Come Home*, 560 W. Crossville Rd., Ste. 101, Roswell, 30075. Tel: 678-585-7886; Fax: 678-585-7854; Web: www.Catholicscomehome.org. Tom Peterson, Pres.

Home and Family, Incorporated (1996) 30 Mansell Ct., Ste. 103, Roswell, 30076. Tel: 770-828-4950; Email: office@missionnetworkatlanta.org. Rev. Martin Connor, L.C., Pres.

Horizons Institute, Inc., 30 Mansell Ct., Ste. 103, Roswell, 30076. Tel: 770-828-4950. Rev. Frank Formolo, L.C., Authorized Rep.

LCNA Atlanta, Incorporated, 30 Mansell Ct., Ste. 103, Roswell, 30076. Tel: 770-828-4950; Email: eramirez@arcol.org. Rev. Michael Brisson, L.C., Sec.

Legion of Christ, Atlanta, Inc., 30 Mansell Ct., Ste. 103, Roswell, 30076. Tel: 770-828-4950; Email: eramirez@arcol.org. Rev. Michael Brisson, L.C., Sec.

Lux et Vita, Inc., 30 Mansell Ct., Ste. 103, Roswell, 30076. Tel: 678-938-4500; Fax: 678-828-4955; Email: eramirez@arcol.org; Web: www.legionairesofchrist.org. Rev. Frank Formolo, L.C., Asst. Sec.

**Mission Network USA, Inc.*, 30 Mansell Ct., Ste. 103, P.O. Box 1466, Roswell, 30076. Tel: 770-828-4950; Fax: 770-828-4955; Web: www.missionnetwork.com. Rev. Frank Formolo, L.C., Treas.

New Fire Evangelization Inc., 30 Mansell Ct., 103, Roswell, 30076. Tel: 770-828-4950. Rev. Frank Formolo, L.C., Authorized Rep. *Norcross Pastoral Center, Inc.*, 30 Mansell Ct., Ste. 103, Roswell, 30076. Tel: 770-828-4950; Email: fformolo@legionaries.org. Revs. Michael Brisson, L.C., Contact Person; James Swanson, L.C., Retreats, Promotion Work; Martin Connor, L.C.

RC Education Inc., 30 Mansell Ct., Ste. 103, Roswell, 30076. Tel: 770-828-4950; Fax: 770-828-4955; Email: eramirez@arcol.org; Web: www.rceducation.org. Rev. Frank Formolo, L.C., Treas.

**Virtue Media, Inc.*, 560 W. Crossville Rd., Ste. 101, Roswell, 30075. Tel: 770-559-5533; Fax: 678-585-7854; Email: tom@virtuemedia.org. Tom Peterson, Pres.

SMYRNA. *AoA Canon 281.2 Trust* (2018) 2401 Lake Park Dr., S.E., 30080. Tel: 404-920-7404; Email: bwilson@archatl.com. Most Rev. Wilton D. Gregory, S.L.D., Trustee.

AoA Common Trust Fund (2018) 2401 Lake Park Dr., S.E., 30080. Tel: 404-920-7404. Most Rev. Wilton D. Gregory, S.L.D., Trustee.

AoA Deposit and Loan Fund, 2401 Lake Park Dr., S.E., 30080. Tel: 404-920-7404; Email: bwilson@archatl.com. Most Rev. Wilton D. Gregory, S.L.D., Trustee.

AoA Parish Real Estate Trust, 2401 Lake Park Dr., S.E., 30080. Tel: 404-920-7404; Email: bwilson@archatl.com. Most Rev. Wilton D. Gregory, S.L.D., Trustee.

AoA Properties Holding, Inc., 2401 Lake Park Dr. S.E., 30080. Tel: 400-920-7800; Fax: 404-920-7801; Email: bwilson@archatl.com. Most Rev. Wilton D. Gregory, S.L.D., Pres.; John F. Schiavone, Vice Pres.; Bradley Wilson, Treasurer; Deacon Dennis J. Dorner, B.A., Sec.

Archdiocese of Atlanta Priests Payroll Services, 2401 Lake Park Dr., S.E., 30080-8862. Tel: 404-920-7400; Fax: 404-920-7401; Email: bwilson@archatl.com. Bradley Wilson, CEO; Jeffrey Dean, Contact Person.

Catholic Education of North Georgia, Inc., 2401 Lake Park Dr. S.E., 30080. Tel: 404-920-7800; Fax: 404-920-7801; Email: bwilson@archatl.com. Most Rev. Wilton D. Gregory, S.L.D., Pres.; Bradley Wilson, Treas.; Diane Starkovich, Ph.D., CEO; Deacon Dennis J. Dorner, B.A., Sec.

Catholic Retirement Facilities, Inc. St. Joseph Place, 2973 Butner Rd., SW, Atlanta, 30331. Tel: 404-920-7800; Email: mchapman@archatl.com. 2401 Lake Park Dr., SE, 30080. Vanessa Russell, CEO; Melissa Chapman, Treas.

G.R.A.C.E. Scholars, Inc., 2401 Lake Park Dr. S.E., 30080. Tel: 404-920-7900; Fax: 404-920-7901; Email: askgrace@gracescholars.org; Web: www.gracescholars.org. Bradley Wilson, C.E.O.; Melissa Bassett, Exec.

Nuestra Fe Catholic Broadcasting, Inc., 2401 Lake Park Dr., S.E., 30080. Tel: 404-449-0727; Email: jmartinez@archatl.com; Web: www.nuestrafeatlanta.com. Mr. Angel Garcia, Pres.; Jairo Martinez, Vice Pres.; Bradley Wilson, Treas.; Deacon Dennis J. Dorner, B.A., Sec.

The Roman Catholic Archdiocese of Atlanta Group Health Care Plan Trust, 2401 Lake Park Dr., S.E., 30080.

RELIGIOUS INSTITUTES OF MEN REPRESENTED IN THE ARCHDIOCESE

For further details refer to the corresponding bracketed number in the Religious Institutes of Men or Women section.

[0350]—*Cistercians Order of the Strict Observance-Trappists*—O.C.S.O.
[0360]—*Claretian Missionaries* (Eastern Province)—C.M.F.
[]—*Congregation of the Missionaries of Saint Charles Scalabrinians*—C.S.
[1000]—*Congregation of the Passion* (Prov. of St. Paul of the Cross)—C.P.
[0480]—*Conventual Franciscans* (Prov. of St. Anthony of Padua, Baltimore)—O.F.M.Conv.
[0520]—*Franciscan Friars* (Prov. of the Most Holy Name of Jesus)—O.F.M.
[0690]—*Jesuit Fathers and Brothers* (New Orleans Prov.)—S.J.
[0730]—*Legionaries of Christ*—L.C.
[0780]—*Marist Fathers* (San Francisco-Washington Prov.)—S.M.
[0720]—*The Missionaries of Our Lady of La Salette*—M.S.
[]—*Missionaries of St. Francis de Sales* (Annecy, France)—M.S.F.S.
[]—*Order of Friars Preachers Dominicans*—O.P.
[1065]—*The Priestly Fraternity of St. Peter*—F.S.S.P.
[]—*Salesians of St. John Bosco*—S.D.B.
[]—*Society of Christ*—S.Chr.
[]—*Society of Our Lady of the Most Holy Trinity*—S.O.L.T.

RELIGIOUS INSTITUTES OF WOMEN REPRESENTED IN THE ARCHDIOCESE

[3110]—*Congregation of Our Lady of the Retreat in the Cenacle*—R.C.
[]—*Daughters of Mary Mother of Mercy* (Nigeria).
[1070-13]—*Dominican Sisters (Adrian, MI)*—O.P.
[]—*Dominican Sisters of St. Cecilia* (Nashville, TN).
[1070-23]—*Dominican Sisters of St. Rose of Lima (Hawthorne, NY)*—O.P.
[]—*Dominican Sisters of Vietnam*.
[1070-03]—*Dominican Sisters (Sinsinawa, WI)*—O.P.
[]—*Franciscan Sisters of Our Lady of Refuge* (Mexico)—R.F.R.
[1870]—*Handmaids of the Sacred Heart of Jesus (Philadelphia, PA)*—A.C.J.
[2575]—*Institute of the Sisters of Mercy of the Americas* (Belmont, NC)—R.S.M.
[2710]—*Missionaries of Charity*—M.C.
[]—*Missionary Sisters of the Most Sacred Heart* (Reading, PA).
[]—*Missionary Sisters of the Sacred Heart "Ad Gentes"* (Mexico)—M.A.G.
[]—*Sisters of Charity of St. Elizabeth* (Convent Station, NJ).
[]—*Sisters of Jesus of Kkottongnae* (Korea).
[3840]—*Sisters of St. Joseph of Carondelet (St. Louis, MO)*—C.S.J.
[1830]—*The Sisters of the Good Shepherd (Silver Spring, MD)*—R.G.S.
[4190]—*Sisters of the Visitation*—V.H.M.
[]—*Sisters of the Visitation of Holy Mary*.
[2150]—*Sisters, Servants of the Immaculate Heart of Mary (Monroe, MI)*—I.H.M.

ARCHDIOCESAN CEMETERIES

CARROLLTON. *Our Lady of Perpetual Help*, Our Lady of Perpetual Help Church, 210 Old Center Point Rd., Carrollton, 30117. Tel: 404-920-7800. Deacon Raymond F. Egan

SHARON. *Locust Grove*, Archdiocese of Atlanta, 2401 Lake Park Dr., 30080. Tel: 404-920-7800; Email: regan@archatl.com. Deacon Raymond F. Egan, Contact Person

Purification, St. Joseph's Catholic Church, U.S. Hwy. 78, Washington, 30673. Tel: 706-678-2110; Email: regan@archatl.com. Deacon Raymond F. Egan, Contact Person

SPARTA. *Sparta*, Archdiocese of Atlanta, 2401 Lake Park Dr., 30080. Tel: 404-920-7800; Email: regan@archatl.com. Deacon Raymond F. Egan, Contact Person

WASHINGTON. *Saint Patrick's Cemetery*, St. Joseph's, U.S. Hwy. 78, Washington, 30673. Tel: 706-678-2110; Email: regan@archatl.com. Deacon Raymond F. Egan, Contact Person

NECROLOGY

† Churchwell, Stephen T., Metropolitan Tribunal, Archdiocese of Atlanta, Died May. 31, 2018
† McCormick, Daniel J., (Retired), Died Apr. 19, 2018
† Redden, Michael J., (Retired), Died Sep. 25, 2018
† Sherliza, Michael S., Marietta, GA St. Joseph, Died Oct. 22, 2018
† Zivic, Richard A., (Retired), Died Aug. 23, 2018

An asterisk (*) denotes an organization that has established tax-exempt status directly with the IRS and is not covered by the USCCB Group Ruling.

Diocese of Austin

(Dioecesis Austiniensis)

Most Reverend

JOE S. VASQUEZ

Bishop of Austin; ordained June 30, 1984; appointed Titular Bishop of Cova and Auxiliary Bishop of Galveston-Houston November 30, 2001; ordained January 23, 2002; appointed Bishop of Austin January 26, 2010; installed March 8, 2010. *Office: 6225 Hwy. 290 E., Austin, TX 78723.*

Pastoral Center: 6225 E. US 290 Hwy. SVRD EB, Austin, TX 78723. Tel: 512-949-2400; Fax: 512-949-2520.

Web: www.austindiocese.org

Email: info@austindiocese.org

ERECTED 1947.

Square Miles 21,066.

Comprises the Counties of Mills, Hamilton, San Saba, Lampasas, Coryell, McLennan, Limestone, Bell, Falls, Robertson, Mason, Llano, Burnet, Williamson, Milam, Brazos, Blanco, Travis, Bastrop, Lee, Burleson, Washington, Hays, Caldwell and the part of Fayette County north of the Colorado River in the State of Texas.

For legal titles of parishes and diocesan institutions, consult the Chancery Office.

STATISTICAL OVERVIEW

Personnel	
Bishop	1
Priests: Diocesan Active in Diocese	111
Priests: Diocesan Active Outside Diocese	6
Priests: Retired, Sick or Absent	34
Number of Diocesan Priests	151
Religious Priests in Diocese	49
Total Priests in Diocese	200
Extern Priests in Diocese	23
Ordinations:	
Diocesan Priests	3
Transitional Deacons	1
Permanent Deacons in Diocese	234
Total Brothers	36
Total Sisters	77
Parishes	
Parishes	102
With Resident Pastor:	
Resident Diocesan Priests	82
Resident Religious Priests	19
Without Resident Pastor:	
Administered by Priests	1
Missions	21
Pastoral Centers	3
Professional Ministry Personnel:	
Brothers	29
Sisters	32
Lay Ministers	376
Welfare	
Catholic Hospitals	5
Total Assisted	1,669,624
Homes for the Aged	2
Total Assisted	464
Day Care Centers	1
Total Assisted	131
Specialized Homes	2
Total Assisted	213
Special Centers for Social Services	4
Total Assisted	8,316
Educational	
Diocesan Students in Other Seminaries	28
Total Seminarians	28
Colleges and Universities	1
Total Students	4,861
High Schools, Diocesan and Parish	4
Total Students	1,084
High Schools, Private	2
Total Students	465
Elementary Schools, Diocesan and Parish	15
Total Students	4,053
Elementary Schools, Private	1
Total Students	426
Catechesis/Religious Education:	
High School Students	10,222
Elementary Students	24,623
Total Students under Catholic Instruction	45,762
Teachers in the Diocese:	
Priests	6
Brothers	16
Sisters	13
Lay Teachers	1,043
Vital Statistics	
Receptions into the Church:	
Infant Baptism Totals	6,050
Minor Baptism Totals	885
Adult Baptism Totals	342
Received into Full Communion	690
First Communions	7,387
Confirmations	5,440
Marriages:	
Catholic	1,209
Interfaith	308
Total Marriages	1,517
Deaths	1,872
Total Catholic Population	612,388
Total Population	3,315,582

Former Bishops—Most Revs. LOUIS J. REICHER, D.D., ord. Dec. 6, 1918; appt. first Bishop of Austin Nov. 29, 1947; cons. April 14, 1948; died Feb. 23, 1984; VINCENT M. HARRIS, D.D., ord. March 19, 1938; appt. Bishop of Beaumont July 4, 1966; cons. Sept. 28, 1966; transferred to Austin April 21, 1971; succeeded to the See Nov. 16, 1971; retired Feb. 25, 1986; died March 31, 1988; JOHN E. MCCARTHY, D.D., Bishop of Austin; ord. May 26, 1956; appt. Titular Bishop of Pasadena and Auxiliary Bishop of Galveston-Houston, Jan. 23, 1979; cons. March 14, 1979; appt. Bishop of Austin, Dec. 24, 1985; installed Feb. 25, 1986; retired Jan. 2, 2001; died Aug. 18, 2018; GREGORY M. AYMOND, ord. May 10, 1975; appt. Titular Bishop of Acolla and Auxiliary Bishop of New Orleans Nov. 19, 1996; ord. Jan. 10, 1997; appt. Coadjutor Bishop of Austin June 1, 2000; installed Aug. 3, 2000; succeeded to the See of Austin Jan. 2, 2001; appt. Archbishop of New Orleans, June 12, 2009; installed Aug. 20, 2009.

Office of the Vicar General—Most Rev. DANIEL E. GARCIA.

Moderator of the Curia—Most Rev. DANIEL E. GARCIA.

Office of the Chancellor—Deacon RON WALKER, Chancellor; NANCY SANDER, Vice Chancellor.

Pastoral Center—Mailing Address: 6225 E. US 290 Hwy. SVRD EB, Austin, 78723. Tel: 512-949-2400; Fax: 512-949-2524. Office Hours: Mon.-Fri. 8:30 am -5 pm.

Deans—

Austin Central—Very Rev. BASIL AGUZIE, M.S.P.

Austin North—Very Rev. MATTHEW IWUJI, J.U.D.

Austin South—Very Rev. GLYNN (BUD) ROLAND JR.

Bastrop/Lockhart—Very Rev. EDWARD KARASEK.

Brenham/La Grange—Very Rev. NOCK W. RUSSELL.

Bryan/College Station—Very Rev. ALBERT LAFORET JR.

Georgetown/Round Rock—Very Rev. WILLIAM ROBERT STRATEN.

Killeen/Temple—Very Rev. RICHARD O'ROURKE, M.S.C.

Lampasas/Marble Falls—Very Rev. RUBEN PATINO, C.S.P.

San Marcos—Very Rev. DAVID LEIBHAM.

Waco—Very Rev. DANIEL LIU.

College of Consultors—Most Rev. DANIEL E. GARCIA; Very Revs. JUAN CARLOS LOPEZ; DANIEL LIU; Rev. Msgrs. JOHN A. MCCAFFREY; LOUIS PAVLICEK, (Retired); Revs. MELVIN DORNAK; VICTOR MAYORGA, (Colombia); JAMES MISKO; GEORGE JOSEPH.

Finance Council—Most Revs. JOE S. VASQUEZ, Bishop of Austin; DANIEL E. GARCIA, Auxiliary Bishop of Austin; KARL KUYKENDALL; MARY BETH KOENIG; JOSE MONTEMAYOR; PATRICIA OHLENDORF; Rev. Msgr. JOHN A. MCCAFFREY; JULIE BENKOSKI; REID SHARP; DAVE OLANDER; Deacon SWITZER L. DEASON; DON E. COX; PAUL STONE.

Presbyteral Council—Most Revs. JOE S. VASQUEZ; DANIEL E. GARCIA; Rev. Msgr. LOUIS PAVLICEK, (Retired); Revs. BRIAN MCMASTER; MELVIN DORNAK; CHRISTOPHER J. DOWNEY; VICTOR MAYORGA, (Colombia); Very Revs. JUAN CARLOS LOPEZ; BASIL AGUZIE, M.S.P.; DANIEL LIU; TIMOTHY S. NOLT; NOCK W. RUSSELL; Rev. Msgr. THOMAS FRANK, (Retired); Revs. BRION ZARSKY; HECTOR VEGA, I.S.P.; BONIFACE ONJEFU; PIUS T. MATHEW; JAMES MISKO; RAMIRO TARAZONA; PETER WALSH, C.S.C.; RICH ANDRE, C.S.P.; CARLO BENJAMIN MAGNAYE, M.F., M.F.

Secretariats and Secretariat Directors—

Business and Finance—MARY BETH KOENIG, Dir.

Administration—Deacon RON WALKER, Dir.

Formation and Spirituality—ALISON TATE.

Stewardship, Development and Communication—SCOTT WHITAKER, Dir.

Life, Charity and Justice—F. DEKARLOS BLACKMON, Obl.S.B., Dir.

Clergy and Religious—Very Rev. JUAN CARLOS LOPEZ.

Diocesan Offices

Office of Canonical and Tribunal Services—6225 E. US 290 Hwy. SVRD EB, Austin, 78723-1025. Tel: 512-949-2479; Fax: 512-949-2522. Direct all inquiries concerning marriage nullity, dispensation and permissions to this address.

Judicial Vicar—Very Rev. CHRISTOPHER FERRER, J.C.L.

Adjutant Judicial Vicar—Rev. JOZEF MUSIOL, S.D.S., J.C.D.

Diocesan Tribunal Judges—Very Revs. CHRISTOPHER FERRER, J.C.L.; MATTHEW IWUJI, J.U.D.; Rev. JOZEF MUSIOL, S.D.S., J.C.D.; Deacon MICHAEL P. FORBES, J.C.L., M.C.L.; THOMAS HOWARD, J.D.; HARVEY BOLLICH, Ph.D.

Defender of the Bond—NWAZI B. NYIRENDA, J.C.L.

Notaries—HARVEY BOLLICH, Ph.D.; DEBORAH R. PATIN; JANIE CUELLAR; THOMAS HOWARD, J.D.; MARIO MAYO, B.S.; KATHERINE KOENIG; RICHARD MAYO, B.S.; PATRICIA THOMPSON, M.A., M.R.E., M.A.A.C.C.D.; NWAZI B. NYIRENDA, J.C.L.; GLORIA VILLARREAL; FERNANDA JAIMES, B.A.; CELESTE JUAREZ; PAUL MADRID, M.A., J.D.;

JEREMIAH O'FIHELLY, B.A.; MARSHA BENDA, B.A.; BLANCHE GONZALES.

Advocates—Priests, Deacons, Religious, and Parish Associates exercising ministry in the Diocese of Austin.

Advocates for the Respondent in English—Deacon THEODORE BAKER; PATRICIA THOMPSON, M.A., M.R.E., M.A.A.C.C.D.

Regional Advocate for Respondent (English)—Deacon JEROME KLEMENT, Ed.D.

Advocate for the Respondent in Spanish—JANIE CUELLAR; CARMEN CORTES-HARMS, M.A., PHR.

Advocate for the Respondent in Vietnamese—Sr. ANE NGUYEN, C.S.C., B.A.

Field Workshop Facilitator in Spanish—CARMEN CORTES-HARMS, M.A.

Auditor—JEREMIAH O'FIHELLY, B.A.

Auditor / Editor—KATHERINE KOENIG.

Assessors—HARVEY BOLLICH, Ph.D.; THOMAS HOWARD, J.D.; PAUL MADRID, M.A., J.D.; RICHARD MAYO, B.S.; FERNANDA JAIMES, B.A.; ROBERT PINE, M.Sc.

Diocesan Archives and Records—Deacon RON WALKER, Chancellor, 6225 E. US 290 Hwy. SVRD EB, Austin, 78723. Tel: 512-949-2400.

Office of Black Catholics—6225 E. US 290 Hwy. SVRD EB, Austin, 78723. Tel: 512-949-2471; Email: dekarlos-blackmon@austindiocese.org. F. DEKARLOS BLACKMON, Obl.S.B., Dir.

Office of Facilities—PATRICK BAKER, Dir., Mailing Address: 6225 E. US 290 Hwy. SVRD EB, Austin, 78723. Tel: 512-949-2418; Fax: 512-949-2525.

Catholic Campaign for Human Development—F. DEKARLOS BLACKMON, Obl.S.B., Dir., Mailing Address, 6225 E. US 290 Hwy. SVRD EB, Austin, 78723. Tel: 512-949-2471.

Office of Catholic Schools—Mailing Address: 6225 E. US 290 Hwy. SVRD EB, Austin, 78723. Tel: 512-949-2499; Fax: 512-949-2520. MRS. MISTY POE, M.Ed., Supt.

Cedarbrake Catholic Retreat Center—BRIAN EGAN, Dir., Mailing Address: P.O. Box 58, Belton, 76513. Tel: 254-780-2436.

Office of Stewardship and Development—SCOTT WHITAKER, Dir., Mailing Address: 6225 E. US 290 Hwy. SVRD EB, Austin, 78723. Tel: 512-949-2441; Fax: 512-949-2520.

Catholic Spirit Newspaper—SHELLEY METCALF, Editor, Mailing Address: 6225 E. US 290 Hwy. SVRD EB, Austin, 78723. Tel: 512-949-2443; Fax: 512-949-2523; Email: catholic-spirit@austindiocese.org.

Office of Youth, Young Adult and Campus Ministry—6225 E. US 290 Hwy. SVRD EB, Austin, 78723. ALISON TATE, Dir., Tel: 512-949-2465; Cell: 512-924-9815; Email: alison-tate@austindiocese.org; YAZMIN MANI, Coord. Pastoral Juvenil Hispana; JENNIFER KODYSZ, Assoc. Dir., Tel: 512-949-2467; Email: jennifer-kodysz@austindiocese.org.

Cemeteries—PATRICK BAKER, Mailing Address: 6225 E. US 290 Hwy. SVRD EB, Austin, 78723. Tel: 512-949-2418.

Office of Hispanic Ministry—6225 Hwy. 290 E., Austin, 78723. Tel: 512-949-2426. LILY MORALES.

Office of Communications—CHRISTIAN GONZALEZ, Dir., Mailing Address: 6225 E. US 290 Hwy. SVRD EB, Austin, 78723. Tel: 512-949-2456.

Office of Human Resources—ALICIA HUITRON, SHRM-CP, 6225 E. US 290 Hwy. SVRD EB, Austin, 78723. Tel: 512-949-2451; Fax: 512-949-2524.

Office of Priestly Life and Formation—10205 North FM 620, Austin, 78726. Tel: 512-258-1161. Rev. MICHAEL O'CONNOR, (England).

Office of Minister to Priests—Mailing Address: 6225 E. US 290 Hwy. SVRD EB, Austin, 78723. Tel: 512-949-2406. Rev. BRUCE NIELI, C.S.P., Minister to Priests.

Office of Minister to Retired Priests—Deacon MICHAEL AARONSON, Dir., St. John Paul II Res. for Priests, 2550 E. University Ave., #13, Georgetown, 78626. Tel: 512-784-8395.

John Paul II Residence for Priests—Deacon MICHAEL AARONSON, Dir., 2550 E. University Ave., #13, Georgetown, 78626. Tel: 512-784-8395.

Deaf Ministry—VACANT.

Office of Diaconal Ministry—Deacon RON WALKER, Dir., 6225 E. US 290 Hwy. SVRD EB, Austin, 78723. Tel: 512-949-2452.

Office of Diaconate Formation—Associate Directors: Deacons GUADALUPE RODRIGUEZ, Tel: 512-949-2410; Email: guadalupe-rodriguez@austindiocese.org; DANIEL LUPO, 6225 E. US 290 Hwy. SVRD EB, Austin, 78723. Tel: 512-949-2411; Email: dan-lupo@austindiocese.org; FELIPA (PHILIS) ESQUIVEL, Assoc. Dir., Candidates' Wives Formation, Tel: 512-949-2812; Email: philis-esquivel@austindiocese.org.

Office of Finance—MARY BETH KOENIG, CFO, Mailing Address: 6225 E. US 290 Hwy. SVRD EB, Austin, 78723. Tel: 512-949-2400.

Office of Information Technology—JEFF HARDY, Dir., Mailing Address: 6225 E. US 290 Hwy. SVRD EB, Austin, 78723. Tel: 512-949-2400.

Ecumenism and Interfaith Affairs—Rev. CHARLES LARRY COVINGTON, Dir., 4311 Small Dr., Austin, 78731. Tel: 512-451-5121.

Office of Life, Charity and Justice—F. DEKARLOS BLACKMON, Obl.S.B., Dir., 6225 E. US 290 Hwy. SVRD EB, Austin, 78723. Tel: 512-949-2471.

Associate Director Criminal Justice—6225 E. US 290 Hwy. SVRD EB, Austin, 78723. Tel: 512-949-2460. JOHN GILLULY.

Texas Mission Council—Mailing Address: 6225 E. US 290 Hwy. SVRD EB, Austin, 78723. Tel: 512-949-2407. VIANEY HERNANDEZ.

Office of Mission and Mission Education—Mailing Address: 6225 E. US 290 Hwy. SVRD EB, Austin, 78723. Tel: 512-949-2407. VIANEY HERNANDEZ.

Pontifical Mission Societies—Mailing Address: 6225 E. US 290 Hwy. SVRD EB, Austin, 78723. Tel: 512-949-2407. VIANEY HERNANDEZ.

Diocesan Mission Council—Mailing Address: 6225 E. US 290 Hwy. SVRD EB, Austin, 78723. Tel: 512-949-2407. VIANEY HERNANDEZ.

Office of Evangelization & Catechesis—6225 E. US 290 Hwy. SVRD EB, Austin, 78723. Tel: 512-949-2492; Fax: 512-949-2520. CAROLYN MARTINEZ, Coord. Catechesis, Tel: 512-949-2461; GUSTAVO RODRIGUEZ, M.A., Dir. Evangelization & Catechesis, Tel: 512-949-2469; VACANT, Assoc. Dir. Catechesis; JULIANA RUEDA, Coord. Evangelization & Outreach, Tel: 512-949-2422.

Rural Life—VACANT.

Special Collections—Mailing Address: 6225 E. US 290 Hwy. SVRD EB, Austin, 78723. Tel: 512-949-2444; Fax: 512-949-2520. MARGARET KAPPEL.

Office of Vicar for Priests—Very Rev. JUAN CARLOS LOPEZ, 6225 E. US 290 Hwy. SVRD EB, Austin, 78723. Tel: 512-949-2431; Fax: 512-949-2524.

Office for Religious—VACANT.

Office of Ethics and Integrity in Ministry—EMILY HURLIMANN, Assoc. Dir., Mailing Address: 6225 E. US 290 Hwy. SVRD EB, Austin, 78723. Tel: 512-949-2447.

Coordinator of Pastoral Care—Tel: 512-949-2400. ILEANA HINOJOSA.

Office of Vocations—Rev. JONATHAN D. RAIA, Dir., 6225 E. US 290 Hwy. SVRD EB, Austin, 78723. Tel: 512-949-2405; Email: fr-jonathan-raia@austindiocese.org. Vocation Team: Revs. GREGORY DON GERHART, St. Mary Catholic Ctr., 603 Church Ave., College Station, 77840. Tel: 979-846-5717; KEITH KOEHL, St. Mary of the Assumption Catholic Church, 408 Washburn, Taylor, 76574. Tel: 512-365-2175; FRANCISCO RODRIGUEZ III, Our Lady of Guadalupe Catholic Church, 707 S. Sixth St., Temple, 76504. Tel: 254-773-6779; RYAN C. HIGDON, St. Mary Catholic Center, 603 Church Ave., College Station, 77840. Tel: 979-846-5717; Very Revs. DAVID LEIBHAM, Santa Cruz Catholic Church, 1100 Main St., P.O. Box 187, Buda, 78610. Tel: 512-312-2520; JUAN CARLOS LOPEZ, Vicar for Priests, 6225 Hwy. 290 E., Austin, 78723. Tel: 512-949-2431; Most Revs. DANIEL E. GARCIA, 6225 E. US 290 Hwy. SVRD EB, Austin, 78723. Tel: 512-949-2401; JOE S. VASQUEZ, 6225 E. US 290 Hwy. SVRD EB, Austin, 78723. Tel: 512-949-2415.

Office of Legal Services and General Counsel—6225 E. US 290 Hwy. SVRD EB, Austin, 78723. Tel: 512-949-2400. Deacon RON WALKER, Gen. Counsel, Tel: 512-949-2452; NANCY SANDER, Vice Chancellor, Tel: 512-949-2427.

Office of Worship—Mailing Address: 6225 E. US 290 Hwy. SVRD EB, Austin, 78723. Tel: 512-949-2400. DAVID WOOD, Dir., Tel: 512-949-2453.

Cedarbrake Retreat Center—BRIAN EGAN, Dir., Mailing Address: P.O. Box 58, Belton, 76513-0058. Tel: 254-780-2436.

CLERGY, PARISHES, MISSIONS AND PAROCHIAL SCHOOLS

CITY OF AUSTIN

(TRAVIS COUNTY)

1—ST. MARY CATHEDRAL (1852) Very Rev. Timothy S. Nolt, Rector; Rev. Everado Casarez; Deacons Vincent A. Boyle; Guadalupe Rodriguez Jr.
Res.: 203 E. 10th St., 78701. Tel: 512-476-6182; Fax: 512-476-8799; Email: office@smcaustin.org; Web: www.smcaustin.org.
School—Cathedral School of St. Mary, (Grades PreK-8), 910 San Jacinto, 78701. Tel: 512-476-1480; Fax: 512-476-9922; Email: principal@cssmaustin.org; Web: www.smcschoolaustin.org. Robert LeGros, Prin. Lay Teachers 15; Students 195; Clergy / Religious Teachers 5.
Catechesis Religious Program—Email: jdrummond@smcautin.org. Jaeson Drummond, D.R.E. Students 174.

2—ST. ALBERT THE GREAT (1987) [CEM] Very Rev. Matthew Iwuji, J.U.D.; Rev. Alberto Carbajal, Parochial Vicar; Deacons Gary Perkins; David Ochoa; Jose Trujillo.
Res.: 12041 Bittern Hollow, 78758. Tel: 512-837-7825 ; Fax: 512-834-2377; Email: info@saintalbert.org; Web: www.saintalbert.org.
Catechesis Religious Program—David Guilianelli Sr., D.R.E. Students 851.

3—ST. ANDREW KIM TAEGON KOREAN CATHOLIC CHURCH (1984) (Korean) Rev. Francis Chung, Tel: 512-326-3225.
Church: 6523 Emerald Forest, 78745.
Tel: 512-326-3225; Email: kcc.jlee@gmail.com; Web: kcc-austin.org/web.
Catechesis Religious Program—Students 51.

4—ST. AUSTIN (1908) Revs. Charles Kullmann, C.S.P.; Rich Andre, C.S.P.; Richard Sparks, C.S.P.; Deacons William Billy Atkins; Dan Wright. In Res., Revs. Larry Rice, C.S.P., M.Div.; "Jimmy" Yao Hsu, C.S.P., M.Div.; Bro. Robert Clark, F.M.S.
Res.: 2026 Guadalupe St., 78705. Tel: 512-477-9471; Fax: 512-477-9430.
School—St. Austin School, (Grades PreK-8), 1911 San Antonio St., 78705. Tel: 512-477-3751; Fax: 512-477-3079; Web: www.staustinschool.org. Fred Valle, Prin.; Kathy Hymel, Librarian. Lay Teachers 20; Students 211.
Catechesis Religious Program—Students 239.

5—ST. CATHERINE OF SIENA (1979) Revs. Patrick Coakley, M.S.C.; Ray Pothireddy; Deacons Christopher Schroeder; Jesse Casarez; Arthur Cavazos.
Church: 4800 Convict Hill Rd., 78749.
Tel: 512-892-2420; Fax: 512-892-0488.
Res.: 4916 Flaming Oak, 78749.
Rectory—5515 Davis Ln. Unit 71, 78749.
Catechesis Religious Program—Students 650.

6—CHURCH OF THE RESURRECTION, EMMAUS (1963) [CEM] [JC] Revs. Samuel Hose; Rito Davila; Deacons Terry Guilbert; John Hill.
Mailing Address & Res.: 1718 Lohman's Crossing, Lakeway, 78734. Tel: 512-261-8500; Fax: 512-261-8200; Email: emmaus@emmausparish.org; Web: www.emmausparish.org.
Catechesis Religious Program—Bertha Halfmann, D.R.E. Students 931.
Chapel—Queen of Angels Chapel, 20600 Siesta Shores Rd., Spicewood, Travis Co. 78669.

7—CRISTO REY (1950) (Hispanic)
2208 E. 2nd St., 78702. Tel: 512-477-1099 (Office); Fax: 512-480-9604; Email: cristoreycc@craustin.com; Web: austincristorey.org. Revs. Marcelino Pena Tadeo, O.F.M.Conv.; Enrique Hernandez Montoya; Calogero Drago, O.F.M.Conv.
Res.: 2107 E. 2nd St., 78702. Tel: 512-474-6376.
Catechesis Religious Program—2215 E. 2nd St., 78702. Students 793.

8—HOLY CROSS (1936) (African American)
1610 E. 11th St., 78702. Tel: 512-472-3741; Fax: 512-472-3783; Email: holycrossaustin@grandecom.net; Web: www.holycrossaustin.org. Very Rev. Basil Aguzie, M.S.P.
Res.: 1607 E. 11th St., 78702. Tel: 512-322-0603.
Catechesis Religious Program—Students 77.

9—HOLY VIETNAMESE MARTYRS (1990) (Vietnamese) Rev. Le-Minh Pham; Deacon Hoa Mai
Legal Name: Holy Vietnamese Martyrs Catholic Church - Austin, Texas
Res.: 1107 E. Yager Ln., 78753. Tel: 512-834-8483; Fax: 512-821-1155; Email: kimhoanly@gmail.com.
Catechesis Religious Program—Students 638.

10—ST. IGNATIUS MARTYR (1937)
126 W. Oltorf St., 78704. Tel: 512-442-3602; Fax: 512-916-4440; Email: office@st-ignatius.org; Web: st-ignatius.org. 2308 Euclid Ave., 78704. Revs. John Dougherty; Dennis Strach II, C.S.C.; Deacons Ron Walker; Karl Romkema.
School—St. Ignatius Martyr School, (Grades PreK-8), 120 W. Oltorf St., 78704. Tel: 512-442-8547; Fax: 512-442-8685; Email: office@st-ignatius.org; Web: school.st-ignatius.org. Fred Valle, Prin. Aides 3; Lay Teachers 20; Students 240; Religious Teachers 1.
Catechesis Religious Program—Tel: 512-442-8656. Anna Alicia Chavez, D.R.E. Students 625.

11—ST. JOHN NEUMANN (1984)
Mailing Address: 5455 Bee Cave Rd., 78746.

Tel: 512-328-3220; Fax: 512-328-3226; Email: broland@sjnaustin.org; Web: sjnaustin.org. Very Rev. Glynn (Bud) Roland Jr.; Rev. Payden Red Blevins; Deacons Peter DiGiuseppe; Manuel Torres; Michael DeWayne Glenn.
Catechesis Religious Program—Students 707.
12—St. Julia (1957) (Hispanic)
Mailing Address: 3010 Lyons Rd., 78702.
Tel: 512-926-4186; Fax: 512-926-7414; Email: sta.julia1957@gmail.com. Rev. Bradford Hernandez; Deacon Ralph Arevalo Jr.
Res.: 900 Tillery Rd., 78702.
Catechesis Religious Program—Students 227.
13—St. Louis (1952) Revs. James Misko; Douglas Jeffers; Jesse Martinez; Deacons Rob Embry; Javier Maldonado; Luis Villa.
Res.: 7601 Burnet Rd., 78757. Tel: 512-454-0384; Fax: 512-454-2010; Email: evelyn.mcnair@st-louis.org; Web: www.st-louis.org.
School—St. Louis School, (Grades PreK-8), Tel: 512-454-0384, Ext. 242; Fax: 512-454-7252. Cindy Lee, Prin.; Brian Kemp, Librarian. Lay Teachers 19; Students 229.
Catechesis Religious Program—
Tel: 512-454-0384, Ext. 225. Amy Allert, D.R.E., Adult Ministries; Sumayah Abullarade, D.R.E., Hispanic Adult & Family Ministries; Betty Franceschi, D.R.E., Childhood Ministries; Paul Stadelman, D.R.E. Youth Ministry; Marybeth Skinnell, D.R.E. Early Childhood; Coral Migoni-Ryan, D.R.E. Sr. Ministry; Elena Murdock, Youth Min.; Dona LeBlanc, D.R.E.; Margaret English-Knipp, D.R.E.; Jackie Forsyth, D.R.E. Students 693.
14—St. Margaret of Scotland (1984) Closed. For inquiries for parish records contact the chancery.
15—Nuestra Senora De Dolores (1952) (Hispanic) Rev. Juan Pablo Barragan Mendoza, T.O.R., (Mexico) Parochial Admin.
Res.: 1111 Montopolis Dr., 78741. Tel: 512-385-4333; Email: JBarragan2024@hotmail.com.
Catechesis Religious Program—Students 508.
16—Our Lady of Guadalupe (1907) (Hispanic)
1206 E. 9th St., 78702. Tel: 512-478-7955; Email: friarflorencio@olgaustin.org; Email: annette@olgaustin.org; Web: olgaustin.org. Rev. Florencio Rodriguez, T.O.R.; Deacon Mario Renteria.
Rectory—912 Lydia, 78702.
Catechesis Religious Program—Mary Nieves, D.R.E.
17—St. Paul (1989)
Mailing Address: 10000 David Moore Dr., 78748.
Tel: 512-280-4460; Email: bdugas@saintpaulaustin.org. Revs. Gerold Langsch, I.S.P.; Johnson Nellissery, I.S.P., (India); Deacons Salomon Villegas; Michael Marchek. In Res., Revs. Christian Christensen, I.S.P., (Chile); Hector Vega, I.S.P.
Res.: 10120 Aly May, 78748. Tel: 512-280-7230; Fax: 512-236-5274.
Catechesis Religious Program—
Tel: 512-280-4460, Ext. 122; Fax: 512-280-7219. Ana Jackoskie, D.R.E. Students 360.
18—St. Peter the Apostle (1962)
Mailing Address: P.O. Box 17575, 78760-7575. Rev. Christopher Ferrer, M.F., J.V.; Deacon John S. Pickwell, B.A.
Res.: 4600 E. Ben White Blvd., 78741.
Tel: 512-442-0655; Email: stpetersaustin@gmail.com.
Catechesis Religious Program—Tel: 512-442-2769; Email: st.peterapostle.dre@gmail.com. Lupita Bodony, D.R.E. Students 279.
19—Sacred Heart (1958) Revs. Mark Hamlet; Alejandro Caudillo; Deacons Robert Martinez; Willie Cortez.
Res.: 5909 Reicher Dr., 78723. Tel: 512-926-2552; Fax: 512-926-5138; Email: sacredheartatx@gmail.com; Web: www.sacredheartchurchaustin.org.
Catechesis Religious Program—Mary Cortez, D.R.E. Students 1,787.
20—San Francisco Javier (1941) (Hispanic) Rev. Abraham Puentes-Mejia.
Res.: 9110 Hwy. 183 S., 78747. Tel: 512-243-1404; Fax: 512-243-2995; Email: sfcc1@austin.rr.com.
Catechesis Religious Program—Students 432.
Mission—San Juan Diego, 216 Stony Point Dr., Del Valle, Travis Co. 78617. Tel: 512-247-2476.
21—San Jose (1939)
Email: san-jose-office@sanjosechurch.org. Revs. Alberto J. Borruel; Gregory Don Gerhart, Parochial Vicar; Deacons Alfred Benavides; Agapito Lopez.
Catechesis Religious Program—Students 1,020.
22—Santa Barbara Catholic Church -Austin, Texas (1991) (Hispanic)
Mailing Address: 13713 FM 969, 78724.
Tel: 512-276-7718; Email: santa_barbara@craustin.com. Rev. Jorge Hernandez de Luna, O.F.M.Conv.; Fr. Francisco Osnaya Vargas.
Catechesis Religious Program—Students 130.
23—St. Theresa (1968) Revs. Larry Covington; Neville Jansze; Deacons Tony Pynes; George Zacek; Eugene Wohlfarth.
Res.: 4311 Small Dr., 78731. Tel: 512-451-5121; Fax: 512-453-6824; Email: jamie@sttaustin.org; Web: www.sttaustin.org.
Rectory—3907 Walnut Clay, 78731.
Tel: 512-323-6160.
School—St. Theresa School, (Grades PreK-8),
Tel: 512-451-7105; Fax: 512-451-8808. Ann Walters, Pres.; Terri Lindstrom, Librarian. Lay Teachers 40; Students 400.
Catechesis Religious Program—Tel: 512-451-2940. Marie Cehovin, D.R.E. Students 550.
24—St. Thomas More (1978) Revs. Michael O'Connor, (England); Kurtis Wiedenfeld; Deacons Peter A. Schwab, Ph.D.; Thomas Mallinger; Thomas Johnson; Daniel Lupo; Michael T. Gesch; Patrick Thomas O'Beirne; Thomas Suniga.
Office: 10205 N. FM 620, 78726. Tel: 512-258-1161; Fax: 512-258-8812; Email: info@stmaustin.org; Web: www.stmaustin.org.
Catechesis Religious Program—Tel: 512-258-1944; Fax: 512-331-9248; Email: cynthia@stmaustin.org. Cynthia Klaer-Jordan, D.R.E. Students 1,134.
25—St. Thomas More Chapel (1958) Closed. For inquiries for sacramental records please see St Mary's Cathedral, (512-476-6182). Res: 1600 N. Congress, Austin, TX 78701.
26—St. Vincent de Paul (1995)
Mailing Address: 9500 Neenah Ave., 78717.
Tel: 512-255-1389; Tel: 512-249-1549;
Fax: 512-246-2373; Email: josie@svdpparish.org; Web: www.svdpparish.org. Revs. Edward C. Koharchik, M.A., M.S.; Richard Tijerina.
Catechesis Religious Program—Mhel Galaviz, Dir. Elementary; Luc Tran, Middle School & High School Youth Min. Students 608.

OUTSIDE CITY OF AUSTIN

Andice, Williamson Co., Santa Rosa (1937) [CEM]
Mailing Address: 6571 FM 970, Florence, 76527-4473. Tel: 254-793-0273; Fax: 254-793-0149; Email: srdl.business@gmail.com; Web: www.srdl-cc.org. Rev. Larry Stehling.
Catechesis Religious Program—Karen Kurtin, D.R.E. Students 192.
Bastrop, Bastrop Co., Ascension Catholic Church (1864)
Mailing Address: 905 Water St., Bastrop, 78602.
Tel: 512-321-3552; Fax: 512-332-0404; Email: mainoffice@ascen.org; Web: ascensionbastrop.com. Rev. Ramiro Tarazona; Deacons Bill Hobby; Paul Cooke.
Res.: 905 Pecan St., Bastrop, 78602.
Catechesis Religious Program—Deborah Esquivel, D.R.E. Students 525.
Belton, Bell Co., Christ the King (1969) Rev. Jungtack (John) Kim; Deacons Armando Aguirre; William Shoemake; Oscar Valeriano.
Res.: 210 E. 24th Ave., Belton, 76513.
Tel: 254-939-0806; Fax: 254-831-4005; Email: accounting@ctkbelton.org; Email: fr.kim@ctkbelton.org; Web: www.ctkbelton.org.
Catechesis Religious Program—Students 464.
Bertram, Burnet Co., Holy Cross (1941) Attended by Our Mother of Sorrows, Burnet.
520 TX 29, Bertram, 78605. Tel: 512-756-4410;
Fax: 512-852-4730; Email: omoscc@omoscc.com. Mailing Address: 507 Buchanan Dr., Burnet, 78611. Rev. Jose Luis Comparan.
Catechesis Religious Program—Students 25.
Mission—Our Mother of Sorrows, Tel: 512-756-4410; Fax: 512-852-4730.
Blanco, Blanco Co., St. Ferdinand (1940) [CEM] Deacons Jessie Esquivel; Antonio Barbour.
Res.: 25 Main St., Blanco, 78606. Tel: 830-833-5227; Fax: 830-833-9978; Email: admin@stferdinandblanco.org; Web: stferdinandblanco.org.
Catechesis Religious Program—Students 155.
Missions—Good Shepherd—285 US 281, Johnson City, Blanco Co. 78636.
St. Mary's Help of Christians, CR 473, Twin Sisters, Blanco Co. 78606.
Bremond, Robertson Co., St. Mary (1879) [CEM] Revs. Celso A. Yu, M.F.; Richard Dee Du, M.F.
Res.: 715 N. Main St., Bremond, 76629-5173.
Tel: 254-746-7789; Fax: 254-746-7789; Email: justinbremond@yahoo.com; Web: www.catholicbremond.us.
Catechesis Religious Program—P.O. Box 145, Bremond, 76629. Tel: 979-450-6194; Email: lindaantis@yahoo.com. Linda Antis, D.R.E. Students 112.
Brenham, Washington Co., St. Mary of the Immaculate Conception (1870) [CEM] Revs. Ernesto Elizondo; Vincent Romuald, S.R.C., Parochial Vicar; Deacons Samuel Reyes; Steve Medina; Al Prescott.
Office: 701 Church St., Brenham, 77833.
Tel: 979-836-4441; Email: mike@brenhamcatholic.org; Email: elizabeth@brenhamcatholic.org; Web: www.stmarysbrenham.org.
Rectory—608 S. Baylor, Brenham, 77833.
Catechesis Religious Program—Sr. Kathleen Skog, O.S.F., D.R.E. Students 477.
Mission—Sacred Heart, Latium, 77833.
Bryan, Brazos Co.
1—St. Anthony (1896) [JC] (Italian) Rev. Joseph Varickamackal, (India); Deacons Michael G. Beauvais; Andy Perrone; Bill Scarmardo.
Res.: 401 S. Parker, Bryan, 77803. Tel: 979-823-8145; Fax: 979-823-6001; Email: bscamardo@gmail.com.
Catechesis Religious Program—Students 225.
Mission—San Salvador, Bryan, Brazos Co. 77803.
2—St. Joseph (1873) [CEM 2]
Mailing Address: 507 E. 26th St., Bryan, 77803.
Tel: 979-822-2721; Fax: 979-779-3120; Email: frjohn@stjosephbcs.org; Email: hmetzer@stjosephbcs.org; Web: www.stjosephbcs.org. Rev. Msgr. John A. McCaffrey; Rev. Jared Cooke; Deacons Gary Nelson; Patrick Gallagher; Jeffrey Olsenholler.
Res.: 600 E. 26th St., Bryan, 77803.
School—St. Joseph School, (Grades PreK-12), 600 S. Coulter Dr., Bryan, 77803. Tel: 979-822-6641;
Fax: 979-779-2810; Email: jrike@stjosephschoolbcs.org; Web: www.stjosephschoolbcs.org. Mr. Jim Rike, Pres. & Prin. Lay Teachers 40; Students 350; Religious Teachers 12.
Catechesis Religious Program—Tel: 979-823-5568;
Tel: 979-485-9910 Youth Ministry; Email: lstoremski@stjosephbcs.org; Email: matt@ablazeyouth.org. Matt Rice, Youth Min.; Lisa Storemski, D.R.E. Students 517.
3—San Salvador, Attended by Mission of St. Anthony, Bryan
Mailing Address: 401 S. Parker, Bryan, 77803.
Tel: 979-823-8145. Rev. Joseph Varickamackal, (India).
4—Santa Teresa (1940) (Hispanic) Revs. Victor Mayorga, (Colombia); John Boiko; Deacon Fred Molina.
Res.: 1212 Lucky, Bryan, 77803. Tel: 979-822-2932; Fax: 979-822-6957; Email: st.teresa@verizon.net.
Catechesis Religious Program—Martha Gallegos, D.R.E.
Buda, Hays Co., Santa Cruz (1941)
P.O. Box 187, Buda, 78610-0187. Very Rev. David Leibham; Rev. Amado Ramos; Deacons Rodolfo L. Gonzalez; Rey Garza; Benjamin Garcia; John Kerrigan; Robert Johnson, Business Mgr.; Juanita Rodriguez, Parish Sec.
Res.: 1100 Main St., Buda, 78610. Tel: 512-312-2520; Fax: 512-295-2034; Email: Santacruz@austin.rr.com.
School—Santa Cruz School, (Grades PreK-8), 1100 Main St., P.O. Box 160, Buda, 78610.
Tel: 512-312-2137; Fax: 512-312-2143; Email: sflanagan@sccstx.org. Susan Flanagan, Prin. Lay Teachers 28; Sisters 4; Students 305; Religious Teachers 5.
Catechesis Religious Program—Joanna Rubio, D.R.E. Students 1,845.
Burlington, Milam Co., St. Michael (1879) Attended by St. Ann, Rosebud.
85 Church Ave., Burlington, 76519.
Tel: 254-869-2169; Email: stmichaels85@windstream.net. Rev. John Kelley III.
Catechesis Religious Program— See St. Ann, Rosebud. Patsy Moeller, D.R.E.
Burnet, Burnet Co., Our Mother of Sorrows (1941) Rev. Jose Luis Comparan.
Res.: 507 Buchanan Dr., Burnet, 78611-2304.
Tel: 512-756-4410; Fax: 512-852-4730; Email: omoscc@omoscc.com; Web: omoscc.com.
Catechesis Religious Program—Students 135.
Mission—Holy Cross, 520 TX 29 Hwy., Bertram, Burnet Co. 78605. Mariana Mata, Contact Person.
Caldwell, Burleson Co., St. Mary (1895) [CEM] (Hispanic)
Mailing Address: 509 N. Thomas, Caldwell, 77836.
Tel: 979-567-3667; Email: office-manager@stmaryscaldwell.com; Web: www.stmaryscaldwell.com. Rev. Bernard T. Hung; Deacons John Young; Ernesto Valenzuela Sr.
Res.: 500 West OSR, Caldwell, 77836.
Catechesis Religious Program—Students 123.
Mission—Holy Rosary, [CEM] 8610 FM 2774, Caldwell, Burleson Co. 77836. Tel: 979-535-7704.
Calvert, Robertson Co., St. Mary (1876) [CEM] (Hispanic), Closed. See St. Mary's Church, Hearne.
Cameron, Milam Co., St. Monica (1883) [CEM] Rev. Dimitrij Colankin; Deacons Earl Colley; John (Jack) Murphy; Michael Schoppe, Business Mgr.; Gilda Gonzales, Sec. Admin.
Church: 306 S. Nolan Ave., Cameron, 76520.
Tel: 254-697-2107; Fax: 254-697-3334; Email: saintmonicatx@gmail.com.
Catechesis Religious Program—Email: soniaperez2005@att.net. Sonia Eva Vega-Perez, D.R.E. and Youth Minister; Maria Cazares, Elementary Coord.; Sanjuana Cardona, Confirmation and High School Coord. Students 172.
Cedar Park, Williamson Co., St. Margaret Mary (1942)

1101 W. New Hope Dr., Cedar Park, 78613.
Tel: 512-259-3126; Fax: 512-259-9658; Email: adrian@stmargaretmary.com. Revs. Luis Alberto Caseres; Barry Cuba, S.T.B., M.A., M.Div.; Deacons Phillip Roberge; Paul Rodriguez; John (Jack) Murphy; John McCardle; Dave Montoya.
Res.: 12451 R.R. 2243, Leander, 78641.
Catechesis Religious Program—Tel: 512-260-0162; Fax: 512-259-9658. Robin Hambright, D.R.E. Students 751.

CHAPPELL HILL, WASHINGTON CO., ST. STANISLAUS CATHOLIC CHURCH (1889) [CEM] [JC2] (Polish) Rev. Jozef Musiol, S.D.S., J.C.D.
Res.: 9175 FM 1371, Chappell Hill, 77426.
Tel: 979-836-3030; Fax: 979-836-7170.
Catechesis Religious Program—C.C.E. Program only (24 students).

CHINA SPRING, MCLENNAN CO., ST. PHILIP CATHOLIC CHURCH - CHINA SPRING, TEXAS (1996) Attended by Mission of St. Louis, Waco.
Mailing Address: P.O. Box 430, China Spring, 76633. Tel: 254-836-1825; Email: stphilipcs@att.net. Revs. John Guzaldo; Augustine Ariwaodo; Deacon Jerry Opperman.
Catechesis Religious Program—Tel: 254-733-8420; Fax: 254-836-0600. Students 43.

COLLEGE STATION, BRAZOS CO.
1—ST. MARY (1926)
603 Church Ave., College Station, 77840.
Tel: 979-846-5717; Fax: 979-846-4493; Email: info@aggiecatholic.org; Web: www.aggiecatholic.org. Revs. Brian L. McMaster; Augustine Ariwaodo; Gregory Don Gerhart; Deacons David Reed; Glen Milton.
Res.: 600 Church Ave., College Station, 77840.
2—ST. THOMAS AQUINAS CATHOLIC PARISH (1982) Very Rev. Albert Laforet Jr.; Deacons Frank Ashley; Dave Mayes; Ronald Fernandes; Mark Nicholas Olivieri; Pat Moran.
Res.: 2541 Earl Rudder Fwy. S., College Station, 77845. Tel: 979-693-6994 (Office); Fax: 979-260-4502 ; Email: business@stabcs.org; Web: www.stabcs.org.
Catechesis Religious Program—Darren Seibert, D.R.E.; Jeffrey Gore, Dir.; Diana Jetter; Leanne Tirado, Business Mgr. Students 561.

COPPERAS COVE, CORYELL CO., HOLY FAMILY (1963) Rev. Patrick Ebner; Deacons Tim Dorsey; James Hayden; Jim DiSimoni.
Res.: 1001 Georgetown Rd., Copperas Cove, 76522.
Tel: 254-547-3735; Fax: 254-542-7626; Email: kkennedy@hf-cc.org; Web: hf-cc.org.
Catechesis Religious Program—Students 224.

CYCLONE, BELL CO., ST. JOSEPH (1902) [CEM] (Czech—German)
Mailing Address: 20120 FM 485, Burlington, 76519.
Tel: 254-985-2280; Email: cyclone.marak@gmail.com. Rev. George Thirumangalam, C.M.I.
Catechesis Religious Program—Tel: 254-541-7950; Email: svwallace@hotmail.com. Shirley Hoelscher, D.R.E. Students 43.
Mission—Ss. Cyril & Methodius, Burlington.

DIME BOX, LEE CO., ST. JOSEPH (1909) [CEM] Rev. Joy J. Adimakkeel.
Church: 8282 FM 141, Dime Box, 77853.
Tel: 979-884-3100; Fax: 979-884-1100; Email: stjoedb@verizon.net.
Catechesis Religious Program—Tel: 979-542-6161. Ida Schuman, D.R.E. Students 31.
Mission—Holy Family (1990) P.O. Box 541, Lexington, Lee Co. 78947. Tel: 949-773-2500.

DRIPPING SPRINGS, HAYS CO., ST. MARTIN DE PORRES (1974)
26160 Ranch Rd. 12, Dripping Springs, 78620.
Tel: 512-858-5667; Fax: 512-858-1467; Web: stmartindp.org. P.O. Box 1062, Dripping Springs, 78620. Rev. Cesar Charlie Garza; Deacons Edward Rositas, Pastoral Assoc.; Daniel Pearson; Geoffrey Robert Unger; Judy Tixier, Business Mgr.; Kevin Kapchinski, Youth Min.
Tel: 512-858-5667, Ext. 202.
Catechesis Religious Program—Email: deaconed@stmartindp.org. Students 453.

ELGIN, BASTROP CO., SACRED HEART (1908) [JC] (Hispanic)
302 W. 11th St., Elgin, 78621. Tel: 512-281-3536; Fax: 512-281-2527; Email: church@sacredheartofelgin.org; Web: www.sacredheartofelgin.org. Rev. George Joseph; Deacon Larry Dunne.
Res.: 400 W. 11th St., Elgin, 78621.
Tel: 512-281-4478.
Catechesis Religious Program—Nancy Luna, D.R.E. Students 488.

ELK, MCLENNON CO., ST. JOSEPH (1925) [CEM] Attended by St. Martin, Tours.
Mailing Address: 301 St. Martins Church Rd., West, 76691. Tel: 254-822-1145; Fax: 254-822-0171. Rev. Walter Dhanwar, I.M.S.
Res.: 9656 Elk Rd., West, 76691.
Catechesis Religious Program—Leslie Moore, D.R.E. Students 34.

ELLINGER, FAYETTE CO., ST. MARY CATHOLIC CHURCH (1855) [CEM] (Czech), Attended by Mission of St. John Catholic Church, Fayetteville.
815 St. Mary's Church Rd., Ellinger, 78940.
Tel: 979-378-2277; Fax: 979-378-4407; Email: stsjm@stjohnfayetteville.com; Web: www.stmaryellinger.com. Mailing Address: P.O. Box 57, Fayetteville, 78940. Very Rev. Nock W. Russell; Deacon Robert Jasek.
Catechesis Religious Program— Religious education classes combined with St. Johns, Fayetteville 209 E. Bell St., Fayetteville, 78940. Email: lmayorga@stjohnfayetteville.com. Lexxus Mayorga, D.R.E.

FAYETTEVILLE, FAYETTE CO., ST. JOHN THE BAPTIST (1870) [CEM] (Czech)
207 E. Bell St., Fayetteville, 78940.
Tel: 979-378-2277; Fax: 979-378-4407; Email: stsjm@stjohnfayetteville.com; Web: www.stjohnfayetteville.com. Mailing Address: P.O. Box 57, Fayetteville, 78940. Very Rev. Nock W. Russell; Deacon Robert Jasek
St John Catholic Church
Res.: 205 E. Bell St., Fayetteville, 78940.
Tel: 979-378-2003.
Catechesis Religious Program—209 E. Bell St., Fayetteville, 78940. Email: lmayorga@stjohnfayetteville.com. Lexxus Mayorga, D.R.E. Students 106.
Missions—St. Mary—815 St Mary's Church Rd., Ellinger/Hostyn Hill, Fayette Co. 78940. Amy Babin, Contact Person.
St. Martin, 3490 S. Hwy. 237, Round Top, Fayette Co. 78940. Amy Babin, Contact Person.

FRANKLIN, ROBERTSON CO., ST. FRANCIS OF ASSISI (1997)
Tel: 979-828-9025 (Rectory);
Tel: 979-828-1269 (Office); Email: st.francis316@valornet.com. Revs. Celso A. Yu, M.F.; Richard Dee Du, M.F.; Deacon Luis Doriocourt.
Res.: 1371 W. FM 1644, P.O. Box 543, Franklin, 77856. Tel: 979-828-1269; Email: st.francis316@valornet.com; Web: www.stfrancisofassisiparish.org.
Catechesis Religious Program—2963 FM 2446, Franklin, 77856. Mary McNair, D.R.E. Students 97.

FRENSTAT, BURLESON CO., HOLY ROSARY (1888) [CEM 2] (Czech), Attended by St. Mary's, Caldwell Rev. Bernard T. Hung.
Church: 8610 FM 2774, Caldwell, 77836-5574.
Fax: 979-535-7704; Email: office-manager@stmaryscaldwell.com; Web: www.holyrosaryfrenstat.com.
Rectory—500 West O.S.R., Caldwell, 77836.
Tel: 979-567-3667.
Catechesis Religious Program—Margaret Polansky, D.R.E. Students 27.

GATESVILLE, CORYELL CO., OUR LADY OF LOURDES (1946)
Mailing Address: 1108 W. Main St., Gatesville, 76528-1123. Tel: 254-865-6710; Fax: 254-865-6710; Email: ourladygatesville@gmail.com. Rev. Timothy V. Vaverek
Legal Name: Our Lady of Lourdes Catholic Church - Gatesville, Texas
Catechesis Religious Program—Students 80.

GEORGETOWN, WILLIAMSON CO., ST. HELEN (1932) Very Rev. William Robert Straten; Rev. Sang Ky Quan; Deacons Joe Ruiz; Vern Dawson; Michael Aaronson.
Res.: 2700 E. University Ave., Georgetown, 78626-7300. Fax: 512-863-8558.
School—St. Helen School, (Grades PreK-8),
Tel: 512-863-4677; Fax: 512-869-3244. Mary Kay Sims, Interim Prin.; Janice Cervenka, Librarian. Students 152; Teachers 16.
Catechesis Religious Program—Tel: 512-863-8558. Russ Hoyt, Dir. of Evangelization and Catechesis. Students 866.

GIDDINGS, LEE CO., ST. MARGARET (1944) [JC] (German—Hispanic)
485 S. Leon St,, Giddings, 78942. Rev. Uchechukwu Andeh.
Res.: 526 S. Grimes St., Giddings, 78942.
Church: 276 Bellville St., Giddings, 78942.
Tel: 979-542-0217; Email: gpalacios@stmargaretgiddings.org; Web: stmargaretgiddings.org.
Catechesis Religious Program—
Tel: 979-542-0217 (Office);
Tel: 979-716-0051 (RE Dir.). Suzanne Peschke, D.R.E. (Upper & Lower Grades). Students 310.
Mission—St. Mary's in Pin Oak, Smithville.

GOLDTHWAITE, MILLS CO., ST. PETER, MISSION OF ST. MARY, SAN SABA (1885) [JC] Attended by Mission of St. Mary, San Saba.
Mailing Address: 1212 Reynolds St., Goldthwaite, 76844. Tel: 325-648-3732; Email: stpeters@centex.net. P.O. Box 352, Goldthwaite, 76844. Rev. Javier Toscano
Legal Title: St. Peter's Catholic Church, Goldthwaite, Texas, 76844
Res.: St. Mary Catholic Church, 504 W. Wallace, San Saba, 76877. Tel: 325-372-7339.
Catechesis Religious Program—Mrs. Stephany Eoff, D.R.E. Students 2.

GRANGER, WILLIAMSON CO., SS. CYRIL AND METHODIUS (1891) [CEM 2] [JC] (Czech)
Mailing Address: P.O. Box 608, Granger, 76530. Rev. Hilario Guajardo.
Parish Office: 104 N. Brazos, Granger, 76530.
Tel: 512-859-2223; Email: sscmchurch@gmail.com.
Res.: 300 W. Davilla, Granger, 76530.
Tel: 512-859-2224.
Catechesis Religious Program—103 N. Guadalupe, P.O. Box 956, Granger, 76530. Students 160.

HAMILTON, HAMILTON CO., ST. THOMAS CATHOLIC CHURCH - HAMILTON, TEXAS (1965) Attended by Our Lady of Lourdes, Gatesville
843 N. Nicholson Dr., Hamilton, 76531. Email: stthomashamilton@gmail.com. Rev. Timothy V. Vaverek.
Catechesis Religious Program—Students 35.

HARKER HEIGHTS, BELL CO., ST. PAUL CHONG HASANG (1986)
Mailing Address: P.O. Box 2414, Harker Heights, 76548. Very Rev. Richard O'Rourke, M.S.C.; Rev. Joseph (Sae Eul) Kim; Deacons Klaus Adam; Alfred Mojica Ponce.
Res.: 1000 E. FM 2410, Harker Heights, 76548.
Tel: 254-698-4338; Email: spaul@hot.rr.com; Web: stpaulchonghasang.org.
Catechesis Religious Program—Mr. Michael Candelas, D.R.E. Students 306.

HEARNE, ROBERTSON CO., ST. MARY (1872) [CEM] (Italian—Mexican-American) Rev. Ramon Frayna; Deacon Concepcion Louna.
Res.: 402 W. First St., Hearne, 77859.
Tel: 979-279-2233; Email: saintmarys402@aol.com; Web: www.stmaryhearne.org.
Catechesis Religious Program—Madeline Zeig, D.R.E. Students 246.

HORSESHOE BAY, BURNET CO., ST. PAUL THE APOSTLE (1982)
201 Dalton Cir., P.O. Box 8019, Horseshoe Bay, 78657. Tel: 830-598-8342; Email: stpaul@zeecon.com; Web: www.stpaulshorseshoebay.org. Rev. Ruben M. Patino, C.S.P.; Deacon John DeLa Garza.
Res.: 116 Dalton Cir., Horseshoe Bay, 78657.
Catechesis Religious Program—Students 18.

HUTTO, WILLIAMSON CO., ST. PATRICK (2000)
Mailing Address: 2500 Limmer Loop, Hutto, 78634.
Tel: 512-759-3712; Fax: 512-759-3728; Email: info@stpatrickhutto.org; Web: www.stpatrickhutto.org. Rev. Adrian Chishimba.
Catechesis Religious Program—Email: re@stpatrickhutto.org. Nancy Longo, D.R.E. Students 65.

JARRELL, WILLIAMSON CO., HOLY TRINITY CATHOLIC CHURCH - CORN HILL, TEXAS (1889) [CEM] (Czech—German) Rev. Stephen Nesrsta.
Res.: 8626 FM 1105, Jarrell, 76537.
Tel: 512-863-3020; Email: holytrinitycc@yahoo.com; Web: www.holytrinityofcornhill.org.
Catechesis Religious Program—Lucille D'Elia, D.R.E. Students 81.

KILLEEN, BELL CO., ST. JOSEPH (1954) Rev. Christopher J. Downey.
Res.: 2903 E. Rancier Ave., Killeen, 76543.
Tel: 254-634-7878; Fax: 254-634-1508; Email: elva@stjoseph.church.
School—St. Joseph School, (Grades PreK-6), 2901 E. Rancier Ave., Killeen, 76543. Tel: 254-634-7272; Fax: 254-634-1224. Katherine Grooms, Prin.; Mrs. Debbie Istas, Library Mgr. Lay Teachers 7; Students 69.
Catechesis Religious Program—
Tel: 254-634-7878, Ext. 105. Students 530.

KINGSLAND, LLANO CO., ST. CHARLES BORROMEO (1965)
Mailing Address: P.O. Box 1748, Kingsland, 78639. Rev. Uche Evaristus Obikwelu; June Schuh, Admin.
Legal Name: St. Charles Borromeo Catholic Church - Kingsland, Texas
Church & Rectory: 1927 Hwy. 1431, Kingsland, 78639. Tel: 325-388-3742; Email: stcharles@nctv.com.
Catechesis Religious Program—1748 RR 1431, Kingsland, 78639. Richard Collins, D.R.E. Students 50.
Mission—Our Lady of the Lake (Sunrise Beach), 304 Hillview Dr., Horseshoe Bay, Burnet Co. 78657-6043.

KOVAR, BASTROP CO., STS. PETER AND PAUL (1906) (Czech) Now a mission of St. Paul, Smithville. Mailing Address: 204 Mills St., Smithville, TX 78957. Tel: 512-237-2179.

KYLE, HAYS CO., ST. ANTHONY MARIE DE CLARET (1909) (Hispanic) Revs. Miguel Duarte; Jason Bonifazi; Deacons Joe Flores; Richard Duecker, (Retired); Jeff Caderhead.
Office: 801 N. Burleson St., P.O. Box 268, Kyle, 78640. Tel: 512-268-5311 (Church);
Fax: 512-268-0144; Email: admin@samckyle.org.

Rectory—279 Greene, Kyle, 78640. Tel: 512-523-9122 .
Catechesis Religious Program—Students 1,100.

LA GRANGE, FAYETTE CO., SACRED HEART OF JESUS (1886) [JC] Rev. Matthew Kinney; Deacon Mike Meismer.
Res.: 539 E. Pearl, P.O. Box 548, La Grange, 78945. Tel: 979-968-3430; Fax: 979-968-5740; Email: frmkinney@gmail.com.
School—Sacred Heart of Jesus School, (Grades PreK-6), Tel: 979-968-3223; Fax: 979-968-3215.
Catechesis Religious Program—Students 206.

LAGO VISTA, TRAVIS CO., ST. MARY, OUR LADY OF THE LAKE (1970) [CEM]
Mailing Address: 6100 Lohman Ford Rd., Lago Vista, 78645. Tel: 512-267-2644; Email: office@stmaryourlady.org; Web: www.stmaryourlady.org. Rev. Rakshaganathan Selvaraj; Deacon Edward Faulk
Legal Name: St. Mary, Our Lady of the Lake Catholic Church - Lago Vista, Texas
Rectory—20400 Dawn Dr., Lago Vista, 78645. Tel: 512-267-1524.
Catechesis Religious Program—Students 77.

LAMPASAS, TRAVIS CO., ST. MARY OF THE IMMACULATE CONCEPTION (1885) Rev. Paul Hudson.
Church & Mailing Address: 701 N. Key Ave., Lampasas, 76550-0866. Tel: 512-556-5544; Email: smccltx@gmail.com.
Catechesis Religious Program—Students 108.
Mission—Good Shepherd Catholic Church (1927) 411 W. Main St., Lometa, Lampasas Co. 76853.

LATIUM, WASHINGTON CO., SACRED HEART CATHOLIC CHURCH - LATIUM, TEXAS (1872) [CEM] Attended by St. Mary, Brenham.
701 Church St., Brenham, 77833. Tel: 979-836-4441.

LEXINGTON, LEE CO., HOLY FAMILY CATHOLIC CHURCH - LEXINGTON, TEXAS (1990) [JC] Mission of St. Joseph, Dime Box.
Mailing Address: 1027 FM 696 East, P.O. Box 541, Lexington, 78947. Tel: 979-773-2500; Email: holyfamilylex@verizon.net. Rev. Joy J. Adimakkeel.
Res.: 8282 FM 141, Dime Box, 77853. Tel: 979-884-3100.
Catechesis Religious Program—Kristen Bryan, D.R.E. Students 41.

LLANO, LLANO CO., HOLY TRINITY CATHOLIC CHURCH - LLANO, TEXAS (1890)
Mailing Address: 700 Bessemer Ave., P.O. Box 698, Llano, 78643. Tel: 325-247-4481; Fax: 325-248-0691; Email: holytrinityllano@gmail.com. 708 Bessemer, Llano, 78643. Rev. Melvin Dornak.
Catechesis Religious Program—Students 57.
Mission—St. Joseph, 216 Ave. B, Mason, Mason Co. 76856. Tel: 325-347-6932.

LOCKHART, CALDWELL CO., ST. MARY (1887) [CEM 2] Very Rev. Edward Karasek; Deacons Guadalupe Aguilar; William Haywood; Patrick Venglar; Sylvia V. Rodriguez, Business Admin.
Res.: 205 W. Pecan, Lockhart, 78644. Tel: 512-398-4649; Fax: 512-398-2285; Email: secretary.smvl@gmail.com; Web: www.smvl.org.
Catechesis Religious Program—Tel: 512-216-7794; Fax: 512-398-2285. Eva Mendez, D.R.E. Students 467.

LOMETA, LAMPASAS CO., GOOD SHEPHERD (1927) Attended by St. Mary, Lampasas.
Mailing Address: 701 N. Key Ave., Lampasas, 76550-0866. Tel: 512-556-5544; Fax: 512-556-6967; Email: smccltx3@gmail.com; Email: smccltx@gmail.com. Rev. Paul Hudson.
Church: 500 W. Main St., Lometa, 76853.
Catechesis Religious Program—Students 30.

LOTT, FALLS CO., SACRED HEART (1905) [CEM] (Italian—German), Attended by St. Joseph, Marlin.
213 N. 6th St., Lott, 76656. Tel: 254-803-8888; Fax: 254-803-8888; Email: stjosephmarlin@gmail.com. Mailing Address: P.O. Box 371, Marlin, 76661. Rev. Ronald Joseph Feather.
Catechesis Religious Program—Colleen Lawson, R.C.I.A. Coord. Clustered with St. Joseph, Marlin. Students 3.

LULING, CALDWELL CO., ST. JOHN THE EVANGELIST (1879) [CEM]
500 E. Travis St., Luling, 78648. Tel: 830-875-5354; Fax: 830-875-3533; Email: stjohn_luling@att.net; Web: www.stjohnluling.com. Rev. Howard Goertz; Deacon Paul Easterling.
Catechesis Religious Program—Marilyn Williams, D.R.E. Students 226.

MANOR, TRAVIS CO., ST. JOSEPH (1876) [JC] (Hispanic) 1300 Old Hwy. 20, Manor, 78653.
Tel: 512-272-4004 (Rectory); Fax: 512-272-8939; Email: st_joseph_manor@sbcglobal.net. Mailing Address: P.O. Box 389, Manor, 78653. Rev. Gregory McLaughlin; Deacons William Vela; Roy R. Barkley; Pedro Barrera III.
Catechesis Religious Program—Students 236.

MARAK, MILAM CO., SS. CYRIL AND METHODIUS (1903) [CEM] [JC2] (Czech) Attended from St. Joseph's, Cyclone.
Mailing Address: 20120 FM 485, Burlington, 76519. Tel: 254-985-2280; Email: cyclone.marak@gmail.com; Web: marakchurch.org. Rev. George Thirumangalam, C.M.I.
Legal Name: SS. Cyril and Methodius Catholic Church - Marak, Texas
Res. & Church: 6633 FM 2266, Buckholts, 76518.
Catechesis Religious Program—Students 40.

MARBLE FALLS, BURNET CO., ST. JOHN THE EVANGELIST (1961) Rev. Pedro Garcia Ramirez; Deacons Eraclio Solorzano; Paul Lavallee; Edward Holicky; Curt Haffner.
Church: 105 Hwy. 1431 E., Marble Falls, 78654. Tel: 830-693-5134; Fax: 830-798-9574; Email: stjohnmarblefalls@gmail.com; Web: www.stjohnsmarblefalls.org.
Catechesis Religious Program—Amy Corley, D.R.E. Students 354.

MARLIN, FALLS CO., ST. JOSEPH (1872) (Italian—Polish) Rev. Ronald Joseph Feather.
Church: 311 Oaks St., Box 371, Marlin, 76661. Tel: 254-803-8888; Fax: 254-803-8888; Email: stjosephmarlin@gmail.com.
Catechesis Religious Program—Rose Ann Espinoza, D.R.E. Students 152.
Mission—Sacred Heart, [CEM] 213 N. 6th St., Lott, Falls Co. 76656.

MARTINDALE, CALDWELL CO., IMMACULATE HEART OF MARY (1908)
Mailing Address: P.O. Box 117, Martindale, 78655. Rev. Rafael Padilla Valdes; Diana Arroyo, Business Admin.
Church: 312 Lockhart St., Martindale, 78655. Tel: 512-357-6573; Fax: 512-357-4430; Email: office@ihmmartindale.org.
Catechesis Religious Program—Tel: 512-357-9076. Georgina Cruz, D.R.E. Students 250.

MASON, MASON CO., ST. JOSEPH (1873) Attended by Holy Trinity, Llano.
Mailing Address: P.O. Box 972, Mason, 76856. Rev. Melvin Dornak.
Church: 216 Ave. B, Mason, 76856. Tel: 325-347-6932; Email: stjoseph_mason@yahoo.com.
Catechesis Religious Program—Tel: 325-347-4310; Email: gkaderka01@gmail.com. Gladys Kaderka, D.R.E. Students 48.

MCGREGOR, MCLENNAN CO., ST. EUGENE CATHOLIC CHURCH - MCGREGOR, TEXAS (1958) [JC] (Hispanic) Rev. Boniface Onjefu.
Res.: 207 N. Johnson Dr., McGregor, 76657. Tel: 254-840-3174; Fax: 254-840-0174; Email: stemcgregor@yahoo.com; Web: steugenemcgregor.com.
Catechesis Religious Program—Aurelia Montoya, D.R.E. Students 186.
Mission—Our Lady of San Juan, 203 Avenue A, Moody, 76557.

MEXIA, LIMESTONE CO., ST. MARY (1886) [JC] Rev. Justin M. Nguyen; Deacons Daniel Ramirez; Dwight Mahoney; Richard Johnson; Gordon Kenneth Lee.
Res. & Mailing Address: 606 N. Bonham St., Mexia, 76667. Tel: 254-562-3619; Email: stmarysmexia@yahoo.com; Web: stmarysmexia.org.
Catechesis Religious Program—Filomena Contreras, D.R.E.; Gladys Mendoza, D.R.E. Students 313.

MOODY, MCLENNAN CO., OUR LADY OF SAN JUAN (1991) (Hispanic) Mission of St. Eugene, McGregor.
401 2nd St., Moody, 76557. Tel: 254-853-9011; Email: ourladyofsanjuan@yahoo.com; Email: stemcgregor@yahoo.com. Rev. Boniface Onjefu
Legal Name: Our Lady of San Juan Catholic Mission Church - Moody, Texas
Church & Mailing Address: 207 N. Johnson Dr., Mc Gregor, 76657. Tel: 254-840-3174; Fax: 254-840-0174 .
Catechesis Religious Program—Cindy Vega, D.R.E. Students 42.

OLD WASHINGTON-ON-THE-BRAZOS, WASHINGTON CO., BLESSED VIRGIN MARY (1849) (African American), Attended by St. Ann, Somerville.
Mailing Address: 17370 Sweed Rd., P.O. Box 485, Washington, 77880. Tel: 936-878-2910; Tel: 936-870-5579; Email: Elizondo@bvmtx.org. Revs. Ernesto Elizondo; Vincent Romuald, S.R.C.; Deacon Limas Sweed Sr.
Catechesis Religious Program—Students 12.

PFLUGERVILLE, TRAVIS CO., ST. ELIZABETH (1932)
Mailing Address: 1520 N. Railroad Ave., Pflugerville, 78660. Tel: 512-251-9838; Fax: 512-251-9868; Email: info@stelizabethpf.org; Web: www.stelizabethpf.org. Revs. Efrain Villanueva; Jesse Martinez; Deacons Barry Ryan; Emmanuel Nwokocha.
Res.: 1104 Lincoln Sparrow Cove, Pflugerville, 78660.
Catechesis Religious Program—Tressi Breecher, D.R.E. Students 1,546.

PIN OAK, BASTROP CO., ST. MARY (1866) [CEM] (German), Attended by St. Margaret, Giddings.
Mailing Address: c/o St. Margaret Catholic Church, 485 S. Leon St., Giddings, 78942. Rev. Uchechukwu Andeh.
Church: 732 FM 2104, Smithville, 78957. Tel: 979-542-0217 (Office); Fax: 979-542-4186; Email: gpalacios@stmargaretgiddings.org; Web: stmargaretgiddings.org.
Catechesis Religious Program—Suzanne Peschke, D.R.E. Students 2.

ROCKDALE, MILAM CO., ST. JOSEPH (1880)
234 San Gabriel, Rockdale, 76567. Email: stjosephroc@yahoo.com. Rev. Pedro Castillo, (Colombia); Deacon August Coelho.
Rectory—521 E. Davilla St., Rockdale, 76567. Tel: 512-446-2196.
Church: 234 San Gabriel St., Rockdale, 76567. Tel: 512-446-2049; Email: stjosephroc@yahoo.com.
Catechesis Religious Program—Email: beholub@gmail.com. Bonnie Holub, D.R.E. Students 212.

ROCKNE, BASTROP CO., SACRED HEART (1876) [CEM] (German) Rev. Dariusz Ziebowicz, S.D.S.; Deacons Roger Muehr; Alvin Frerich.
Church: 4045 FM 535, Bastrop, 78602. Tel: 512-321-7991; Fax: 512-303-2723; Email: shcrockne@hwtx.com.
Catechesis Religious Program—Bill Kadura, D.R.E. Students 227.
Mission—Assumption of the Blessed Virgin Mary, [CEM] String Prairie, Bastrop Co.. Tel: 830-839-4580 .

ROGERS, BELL CO., ST. MATTHEW (1991)
Mailing Address: P.O. Box 69, Rogers, 76569. Revs. Francisco Rodriguez III, Parochial Admin.; Alirio Fernandez; Gennie Tepera, Contact Person.
Church: 10451 E. Hwy. 190, Rogers, 76569. Tel: 254-642-0312; Email: stmatthewtx@aol.com.
Catechesis Religious Program—Sara Fuchs, D.R.E. Students 45.

ROSEBUD, FALLS CO., ST. ANN, ROSEBUD (1915) [CEM] Rev. John Kelley III.
Church: 511 S. Stallworth St., Rosebud, 76570. Tel: 254-869-2169; Email: stmichaels85@windstream.net.
Catechesis Religious Program—104 Mayer St., Rosebud, 76570. Patsy Moeller, D.R.E. Students 20.
Mission—St. Michael (1879) 85 Church Ave., Burlington, 76519.

ROUND ROCK, WILLIAMSON CO.
1—ST. JOHN VIANNEY (1997)
3201 Sunrise Rd., Round Rock, TX 78665. Tel: 512-218-1183; Fax: 512-218-8272; Email: business@sjvroundrock.org; Web: www.sjvroundrock.org. Rev. Thomas John Reitmeyer, Parochial Admin.; Deacons Gene Saienga; Frank McCormick.
Catechesis Religious Program—Fax: 512-218-8272. Students 407.

2—ST. WILLIAM (1956) Revs. Dean E. Wilhelm; Alirio Fernandez; Henry Cuellar Jr.; Deacons Concepcion Castillo, (Retired); Wilfredo Colon; Richard Kotrola; Michael P. Forbes, J.C.L., M.C.L.; Alejandro Lara; Steven Pent.
Mailing Address & Office: 620 Round Rock W. Dr., Round Rock, 78681-5017. Tel: 512-255-4473; Fax: 512-255-8126; Email: office@saintwilliams.org; Email: business@saintwilliams.org; Email: agonzalez@saintwilliams.org; Web: www.st-william.org.
Rectory—1105 Deer Run, Round Rock, 78681-6436. Tel: 512-358-6063.
Catechesis Religious Program—Students 1,929.

SALADO, BELL CO., ST. STEPHEN (1989)
Mailing Address: P.O. Box 662, Salado, 76571. Rev. Jude Uche, M.S.P.
Rectories—601 FM 2268, Salado, 76571. Tel: 254-947-5582.
1500 Oak Park, Salado, 76571. Tel: 254-239-1814.
Church: 601 FM 2268 (Holland Rd.), P.O. Box 662, Salado, 76751. Tel: 254-947-8037; Fax: 254-947-8091 ; Email: office@sainstephenchurch.org.
Catechesis Religious Program—Laura Snyder, D.R.E. Students 219.

SAN MARCOS, HAYS CO.
1—ST. JOHN THE EVANGELIST (1883) Revs. Victor Mayorga, (Colombia); John Boiku; Deacons Jesse Mojica; Luis Francisco Silguero. In Res., Rev. Brion Zarsky.
Res.: 624 E. Hopkins, San Marcos, 78666. Tel: 512-353-8969; Fax: 512-396-7522.
Catechesis Religious Program—Tel: 512-353-5065. Students 691.
Mission—Guadalupe Chapel, 218 Roosevelt, San Marcos, Hays Co. 78666.

2—OUR LADY OF WISDOM CATHOLIC CHURCH 2013
100 Concho St., San Marcos, 78666. Tel: 512-392-5925; Fax: 512-392-5922; Email: office@txstatecatholic.org; Email: admin@txstatecatholic.org; Web: www.txstatecatholic.org. Rev. Jesse Martinez, Parochial Admin.; Deacon Cristobal Luna; Alejandra Martinez, Business Mgr.

Legal Name: Our Lady of Wisdom Catholic Church - San Marcos, Texas.

SAN SABA, SAN SABA CO., ST. MARY (1967) (Hispanic) Mailing Address: P.O. Box 415, San Saba, 76877. Tel: 325-372-3679; Fax: 325-372-6569; Email: stmarys@centex.net. Rev. Javier Toscano.
Church: 504 W. Wallace, San Saba, 76877. Tel: 830-319-4382.
Catechesis Religious Program—Michael Bohensky, D.R.E. (San Saba). Students 161.

SMITHVILLE, BASTROP CO., ST. PAUL CATHOLIC CHURCH (1896) Rev. Pius T. Mathew; Deacon Bernard Meuth.
Res.: 204 Mills St., Smithville, 78957.
Tel: 512-237-3299; Email: secr.stpaulcc@gmail.com.
Catechesis Religious Program—Tel: 512-237-3299. Maria De Los Angeles Garza, D.R.E. Students 138.
Mission—Sts. Peter and Paul, Kovar, Bastrop Co.

SOMERVILLE, BURLESON CO., ST. ANN (1913) Rev. Ernesto Elizondo.
Church: 333 Thornberry Dr., P.O. Box 99, Somerville, 77879. Tel: 979-596-1966; Fax: 979-596-2857; Email: secretary.stanns@gmail.com; Web: www.saintann-somerville.org.
Catechesis Religious Program—Students 15.
Mission—Blessed Virgin Mary Chapel (1849) [JC] Washington. Tel: 936-878-2910.

STONY POINT, TRAVIS CO., SAN JUAN DIEGO - STONY POINT (1987) (Mexican), Attended by San Francisco Javier, Austin.
Mailing Address: 9110 U.S. Hwy. 183 S., 78747. Rev. Abraham Puentes-Mejia, Parochial Admin.
Church: 216 Stony Point Dr., Del Valle, 78617.
Tel: 512-243-1404; Email: sfcc1@austin.rr.com.
Catechesis Religious Program—Students 35.

STRING PRAIRIE, BASTROP CO., ST. MARY OF THE ASSUMPTION (1876) [CEM] (German), Attended by Sacred Heart, Rockne.
Mailing Address: 4045 FM 535, Bastrop, 78602.
Tel: 512-321-7991; Fax: 512-303-2723; Email: shcrockne@hwtx.com. Rev. Dariusz Ziebowicz, S.D.S.
Catechesis Religious Program—Mrs. Deanna Seidel, D.R.E. Students 70.

SUNRISE BEACH, LLANO CO., OUR LADY OF THE LAKE (1962) Attended by St. Charles Borromeo, Kingsland Business Address: 304 Hillview Dr., Horseshoe Bay, 78657. Tel: 830-598-7327. Rev. Uche Evaristus Obikwelu.
Church: 120 R.R. 2233, Sunrise Beach, 78643.

TAYLOR, WILLIAMSON CO.
1—ST. MARY OF THE ASSUMPTION (1877) [CEM]
301 E. 4th St., Taylor, 76574. Email: churchoffice@stmarystaylor.org; Web: smtaylor.org. Rev. Keith Koehl; Deacons David Pustka; Marc Griffin.
Res.: 408 Washburn St., Taylor, 76574.
School—St. Mary of the Assumption School, (Grades PreK-8), 520 Washburn St., Taylor, 76574.
Tel: 512-352-2313; Email: Principal@StMarysTaylor.org; Web: smcst.org. Heidi Altman, Prin.; Daniel Yezak, Dir. Technology. Lay Teachers 23; Students 174; Religious Teachers 4.
Catechesis Religious Program—Tel: 512-352-2133. Frances Albert, D.R.E. Students 171.
Convent—317 E. 4th St., Taylor, 76574.
Tel: 512-352-2144. Sisters 1.
2—OUR LADY OF GUADALUPE (1914) [CEM] (Hispanic)
110 W. Rio Grande St., Taylor, 76574.
Tel: 512-365-2380; Fax: 512-365-1733; Email: nsdguadalupe@att.net; Email: NSDGREd@att.net; Web: NSDGuadalupe.org. Rev. Jairo Sandoval Pliego; Deacon Alfredo Torres.
Res.: 113 Dickey St., Taylor, 76574.
Catechesis Religious Program—Sisters of St. John Bosco Parish Center, 111 W. Rio Grande St., Taylor, 76574. Students 177.

TEMPLE, BELL CO.
1—ST. LUKE (1969) [CEM] [JC] Revs. John Guzaldo; Vincent Tranh Nguyen, C.Ss.R., Chap.; Deacons Jerome J. Klement; James Madsen.
Res.: 2807 Oakdale, Temple, 76502.
Tel: 254-773-1561; Fax: 254-773-3710; Email: office@slparish.org; Web: www.slparish.org.
Catechesis Religious Program—
Tel: 254-773-8874, Ext. 19; Email: jordanna@slparish.org. Students 376.
2—ST. MARY CATHOLIC CHURCH (1883) [JC]
Parish Office: 1018 S. 7th St., Temple, 76504.
Tel: 254-773-4541; Fax: 254-774-7044; Email: stmaryoffice@stmarytempletx.org. Rev. Steven J. Sauser; Deacon Bonifacio (Barney) Rodriguez; Becky Theisen, Contact Person.
Rectory—1004 S. 7th St., Temple, 76504.
Tel: 254-773-3238.
School—St. Mary Catholic Church School;, (Grades PreK-8), 1019 S. 7th St., Temple, 76504.
Tel: 254-778-8141; Fax: 254-778-1396. Theresa Wyles, Prin.; Bernadette Hickman, Librarian. Lay Teachers 14; Students 204.
Catechesis Religious Program—Email: patricia.stamour@stmarytempletx.org. Patricia St. Amour, Dir. of Faith Formation. Students 155.
3—OUR LADY OF GUADALUPE (1952) (Hispanic) Revs. Francisco Rodriguez III, Parochial Admin.; Alirio Fernandez; Deacons J. Margarito Alvarado; Claudio Sanchez; Joe Vela
Legal Name: Our Lady of Guadalupe Catholic Church - Temple, Texas
Res.: 707 S. 6th St., Temple, 76504.
Tel: 254-773-6779; Fax: 254-773-5469; Email: rchavez@olgtemple.org.
Catechesis Religious Program—Mary Garcia, D.R.E. Students 510.
Mission—St. Mathew's Catholic Church, 14051 US 190, Rogers, 76569. Tel: 254-642-0312; Email: stmatthewtx@aol.com. Gennie Tepera, Contact Person.

TOURS, MCLENNAN CO., ST. MARTIN (1870) [CEM] (German—Czech) Rev. Walter Dhanwar, I.M.S.
Res.: 301 St. Martin's Church Rd., West, 76691-2135.
Tel: 254-822-1145; Email: stmartins.tours@gmail.com.
Catechesis Religious Program—Tel: 254-749-4605; Email: kkmidd@hotmail.com. Kayla Sinkule, D.R.E. Students 120.
Mission—St. Joseph, Elk, McLennon Co. 76691.

UHLAND, HAYS CO., ST. MICHAEL (1924) [CEM] [JC] (Hispanic) Rev. Rafael Padilla Valdes; Deacon W. J. Ham.
Church and Mailing: 80 S. Old Spanish Tr., Uhland, 78640. Tel: 512-398-7475; Email: stmichaelsuhland@austin.rr.com.
Catechesis Religious Program—Carolyn Martinez, D.R.E. Students 70.

WACO, MCLENNAN CO.
1—ST. FRANCIS ON THE BRAZOS (1924) [JC] (Hispanic)
Mailing Address: 315 Jefferson Ave., Waco, 76701. Fr. Jose Eduardo Jazo-Tarin.
Res.: 301 Jefferson Ave., Waco, 76701.
Tel: 254-752-8434; Tel: 254-752-1012;
Tel: 254-752-1159; Fax: 254-752-2415; Email: churchoffice@stfrancistorwaco.org; Web: stfrancistorwaco.org.
Child Care—Nursery & Kindergarten, 612 N. 3rd St., Waco, 76701. Tel: 254-753-5565; Fax: 254-757-0537. Sr. Catherine Vallespir, F.H.M., Prin. Lay Teachers 10; Sisters 4; Students 131.
Catechesis Religious Program—Email: rosie_escobedo@stfrancistorwaco.org. Rosie Lee Escobedo, D.R.E. Students 198.
Convent—
Mission—Santa Rita, Satin, Satin Falls Co.
2—ST. JEROME (1982)
9820 Chapel Rd., Waco, 76712. Tel: 254-666-7722; Fax: 254-666-4848; Email: secretary@stjeromewaco.org; Web: www.stjeromewaco.org. Rev. Rakshaganathan Selvaraj; Deacons Raeford Carter; Greg George; Raymond Jones.
Catechesis Religious Program—Tel: 254-666-6222; Email: religious-education@stjeromewaco.org. Christine Moore, D.R.E. Students 480.
3—ST. JOHN THE BAPTIST (1953) (African American)
Mailing Address: P.O. Box 585, Waco, 76704-0585. Rev. Cyril Ngbede Ejaidu; Sylvia Glynn, Business Admin. & Finance Sec.
Res.: 1312 Dallas St., Waco, 76704-0585.
Tel: 254-753-6742; Email: ejaiducyril@gmail.com.
Catechesis Religious Program—Tel: 254-313-2852; Email: mina_lozano@gmail.com. Jessica Lozano, D.R.E. Students 3.
4—ST. JOSEPH (1950) Rev. Albert Capello Ruiz.
Res.: 1011 Boston St., Waco, 76705.
Tel: 254-799-2531; Fax: 254-799-1015; Email: stjosephwaco@aol.com.
Catechesis Religious Program—Tel: 254-799-6646. Rosemary Berrios, D.R.E. Students 115.
5—ST. LOUIS (1964) Revs. John Guzaldo; Augustine Ariwaodo.
Res.: 2001 N. 25th St., P.O. Box 5040, Waco, 76708.
Tel: 254-754-1221; Fax: 254-754-4019; Email: stlouischurch@waco.twcbc.com; Web: www.stlouiswaco.com.
School—St. Louis School, (Grades PreK-8),
Tel: 254-754-2041; Fax: 254-754-2091. Nisa Lagle, Prin.; Angela Corley, Librarian. Lay Teachers 27; Students 274.
Catechesis Religious Program—Antonia Duran, D.R.E. Students 229.
6—ST. MARY OF THE ASSUMPTION (1870) Rev. Joseph F. Geleney Jr.; Deacons James Fitzpatrick; James Poole.
Church & Mailing Address: 1401 Washington Ave., Waco, 76701. Tel: 254-753-0146; Email: mail@stmarys-waco.org.
Catechesis Religious Program—Jeanne M. Arensman, C.R.E. Students 65.
7—SACRED HEART CATHOLIC CHURCH - WACO, TEXAS (1957) (Spanish) Rev. Carlo Benjamin Magnaye, M.F., M.F.; Deacons Antonio Arocha; Lorenzo Garcia.
Res.: 2621 Bagby Ave., Waco, 76711.
Tel: 254-756-2656; Fax: 254-756-6302; Email: sacredheartwaco@yahoo.com; Web: www.sacredheartwaco.com.
Catechesis Religious Program—2710 Speight Ave., Waco, 76711. Rebecca Salazar, D.R.E. Students 726.

WARRENTON, FAYETTE CO., ST. MARTIN CATHOLIC CHURCH - WARRENTON, TEXAS (1888) [CEM] Historic chapel, mission of St John, Fayetteville.
3490 S. Hwy. 237, Round Top, 78940.
Tel: 979-378-2277; Email: stsjm@stjohnfayetteville.com. Mailing Address: P.O. Box 57, Fayetteville, 78940. Very Rev. Nock W. Russell.

WEST, MCLENNAN CO., ST. MARY'S CHURCH OF THE ASSUMPTION (1892) [CEM] (Czech)
301 S. Harrison, West, 76691. Tel: 254-826-3705; Fax: 254-826-5497; Email: office@assumptionwest.org. Mailing Address: P.O. Box 276, West, 76691. Rev. David Trahan II.
Church: 303 S. Harrison, West, 76691.
School—St. Mary Church of the Assumption School, (Grades PreK-8), Tel: 254-826-5991; Fax: 254-826-7047. Ericka Sammons, Prin. Lay Teachers 11; Students 145.
Catechesis Religious Program—Email: capustejovsky@sbcglobal.net. Jason Janek, D.R.E.; Lori Janek, D.R.E. Students 143.

WESTPHALIA, FALLS CO., CHURCH OF THE VISITATION (1883) [CEM] (German)
144 County Rd. 3000, Lott, 76656-3827.
Tel: 254-584-4983; Fax: 254-584-4983; Email: westphaliaparish@gmail.com; Web: www.churchofthevisitation.org. Rev. Edwin Kaqoo; Deacons Bill Smetana, (Retired); Charlie Wright.
Catechesis Religious Program—Students 103.

WIMBERLEY, HAYS CO., ST. MARY (1956) [CEM] Rev. Daniel E. Garcia; Deacon Jorge Guerrero.
Res. Rectory Office: 6 Palos Verdes, 14711 Ranch Rd. 12, Wimberley, 78676. Tel: 512-847-9181 (Church); Fax: 512-847-5573; Email: office@saintmaryswimberley.com.
Catechesis Religious Program—Tel: 512-847-1662. Minerva Martinez, C.R.E.; Morag Sell, Youth Ministry Coord. Students 134.

Chaplains of Public Institutions

AUSTIN. *St. David's Hospital*. Attended by St. Austin Catholic Church. 2010 Guadalupe, 78705.
Tel: 512-477-9471. Vacant.
School for the Blind. Attended by St. Louis Church. 7601 Burnet Rd., 78757. Tel: 512-454-0384. Vacant.
School for the Deaf, 2309 Euclid St., 78704.
Tel: 512-442-3602. Attended by St. Ignatius Catholic Church.
Seton / Brackenridge Hospital, Tel: 512-324-1480; Tel: 512-324-7106. Rev. Frank Zlotkowski, C.S.C., Chap., Brackenridge Hospital.
State Hospital, 4110 Guadalupe, 78751.
Tel: 512-836-1213. Attended by St. Austin Church, Tel: 512-477-9471.

GATESVILLE. *Texas Department of Criminal Justice*, P.O. Box 665, Gatesville, 76528. Rev. Timothy V. Vaverek.

GIDDINGS. *State School*, Tel: 979-542-0217. Rev. Uchechukwu AndehAttended by St. Margaret, Giddings. Tel: 409-542-3380.

MEXIA. *State School*, 606 N. Bonham, Mexia, 76667.
Tel: 254-562-3619. Rev. Justin M. Nguyen.

TEMPLE. *Baylor Scott & White Healthcare*, 2401 S. 31st St., Temple, 76508. Sr. Delia M. Herrera, Chap.
V.A. Hospital, 1901 S. First St., Temple, 76501.
Tel: 254-778-4811, Ext. 4879. Rev. Leonard Onwumere, Chap.

WACO. *V.A. Hospital*, 4800 Memorial Dr., Waco, 76711.
Tel: 254-752-6581. Rev. Leonard Onwumere, Chap.

Chaplains of the Military:
Revs.—
George, George C., Chap., (Retired), 15519 Luna Ridge, Helotes, 78023
Johnson, Charles W., (LT), C.H.C., U.S.N., Navy
Moss, Don, C.H.C., U.S.N.R., Scott Air Force Base, IL.

On Duty Outside the Diocese:
Rev. Msgr.—
Jenkins, Ron, The Catholic Univ. of America, 620 Michigan Ave., N.E., Washington, DC 20064
Revs.—
Dewitt, Sean Regan, Apostolic Signatura, Villa Strich, Via Della Nocetta 63, 00164 Rome, Italy
Eilers, Brian Joseph, St. Mary's Seminary, 9845 Memorial Dr., Houston, 77024
Strieder, Leon, St. Mary's Seminary, 9845 Memorial Dr., Houston, 77024.

Retired:
Rev. Msgrs.—
Brooks, Bill, (Retired), 3201 Esperanza Crossing, Apt. 502, 78758. Tel: 512-560-4438
Deane, Joseph, (Retired), 2550 E. University Ave., #701, Georgetown, 78626

Frank, Tom, (Retired), 2550 E. University Ave. #1001, Georgetown, 78626
Goertz, Victor, (Retired), 2550 E. University Ave., #202, Georgetown, 78626. Tel: 512-864-0912
Holtman, Elmer, (Retired), 2805 RR 2341, Burnet, 78611. Tel: 512-517-5290
Johnson, Oliver F., (Retired), 7709 Beckett Rd., Rm. 2151, 78749. Tel: 512-796-6112
Nguyen, Joe Van Anh, (Retired), 1309 Sweet Leaf Ln., Pflugerville, 78660
Pavlicek, Louis, (Retired), 1105 Deer Run, Round Rock, 78681. Tel: 512-763-6495
Rozycki, Isidore, (Retired), P.O. Box 147, Axtell, 76624. Tel: 254-715-0913
Urban, Lonnie A., (Retired), 2550 E. University Ave., #301, Georgetown, 78626
Wozniak, Louis, (Retired), 2212 Rifle Bend Dr., Georgetown, 78626. Tel: 512-864-1907
Zientek, Benedict Julian, (Retired), 1700 E Stone St., Brenham, 77834
Zientek, Boleslaus John, (Retired), 2407 Holcombe Blvd., Houston, 77021. Tel: 281-797-5916

Revs.—
Bertini, Angelo, (Retired), 2550 E. University Ave., #1002, Georgetown, 78626
Carr, Walter, (Retired), 2550E. University Ave. #102, Georgetown, 78626. Tel: 512-763-1662
Chalupa, Fred, J.C.L., (Retired), 2550 E. University Ave., #102, Georgetown, 78626. Tel: 512-864-7680
Chamberlain, Thomas G., (Retired), St. John Paul Residences for Priests, 2550 E. University #802, Georgetown, 78626. Tel: 254-913-6193
Clancy, Raphael "Ray", (Retired), 6474 E. Burdett Dr., Prescott Valley, AZ 86314. Tel: 928-237-5255
Connelly, Laurence, (Retired), 7 Tourney Cv., 78738
Dowling, Ray, (Retired), 7230 Wyoming Springs, Rm 110, Round Rock, 78681. Tel: 512-763-9494
Duffy, John, 2026 Guadalupe St., 78705. Tel: 646-736-9172
Evans, James L., (Retired), 6704 Cypress Pt. N., 78746
Ferrer, Gonzalo, (Retired), 160 Biels Loop, Killeen, 76542. Tel: 512-497-2151
Frazer, Edward J., S.S., M.A., S.T.L., (Retired), 12813 Summit Tr., Belton, 76513
Frazer, Joseph, (Retired), P.O. Box 1083, Penney Farms, FL 32079. Tel: 904-284-6016
Garner, Kirby D., (Retired), P.O. Box 370, Bastrop, 78602
George, George C., (Retired), 15519 Luna Ridge, Helotes, 78023. Tel: 210-67-7888
Hanus, Thomas J., (Retired), P.O. Box 141, Lyons, 77863. Tel: 979-596-2197
Heimsoth, Larry, (Retired), 2642 Marlandwood Cir., Temple, 76502. Tel: 254-496-7647
Lee, Sang Yil, (Retired), 867 Riverside Dr., Killeen, 76542. Tel: 254-285-1501
Loftin, Don, (Retired), 2550 E. University Ave. #801, Georgetown, 78626. Tel: 512-591-7372
Martinez, Adam, (Retired), 740 W. Goforth Rd., Buda, 78610. Tel: 512-357-6573
McCabe, Peter, (Retired), 831 Tehuacana Hwy., Mexia, 76667. Tel: 956-212-3473
McCallum, Paul F., (Retired), 2550 E. University Ave., #101, Georgetown, 78626. Tel: 512-864-7814
Mikkelson, Scott, (Retired), 2550 E. University, #702, Georgetown, 78626. Tel: 512-819-9362
Nielson, Ken, (Retired), 751 Sugar Pine St., Oceanside, CA 92058. Tel: 760-214-1946
Niemira, Thomas, (Retired), 908 Queen Elizabeth Dr., McGregor, 76657. Tel: 254-666-0571
Olnhausen, James Robert, (Retired), 114-B Commercial Dr., Bastrop, 78602. Tel: 512-565-9761
Rai, Kevin, (Retired), 905 Duncan Ln., 78705. Tel: 512-499-0901
Robertson, James E., (Retired), 2550 E. University Ave., #402, Georgetown, 78626. Tel: 512-680-9086
Romanski, Gregory A., (Retired), 8017 Raintree Pl., 78759. Tel: 512-751-1377
Van Winkle, Charles, C.S.C., (Retired), 921 St. Edwards Dr., 78704. Tel: 512-382-7324.

Permanent Deacons:
Aaronson, Michael, St. Helen, Georgetown
Abraham, Ellis, (Retired)
Adam, Klaus, St. Paul Chong Hasang, Harker Heights
Aguilar, Guadalupe, (Retired)
Aguirre, Armando, Christ the King, Belton
Alvarado, J. Margarito, Our Lady of Guadalupe, Temple
Arellano, Joe, (Retired)
Arevalo, Ralph Jr., St. Julia, Austin
Arocha, Antonio, Sacred Heart, Waco
Ashley, Frank, St. Thomas Aquinas, College Station
Atkins, William Billy, St. Austin, Austin
Baker, Theodore, (Retired)
Banda, Cruz Jr., (Retired)
Barbour, Antonio, St. Ferdinand, Blanco
Barkley, Roy R., (Retired)
Barrera, Pedro III, St. Joseph, Manor
Beauvais, Michael George, St. Anthony, Bryan.
Beltran, Victor, (Retired)
Benavides, Alfred, (Retired)
Berg, Jim, (Inactive)
Bigelow, Richard A., (Retired)
Boren, David, St. William Catholic Church, Round Rock
Botello, Richard, (Retired)
Boyle, Vincent A., St. Mary's Cathedral, Austin
Cadenhead, Jeff, St. Anthony Marie de Claret Catholic Church, Kyle
Cardon, Dave, St. Mary of the Immaculate Conception Church, Lampasas
Cardona, David, (Serving in another Diocese)
Carter, Raeford, St. Jerome, Waco
Casarez, Jesse, St. Catherine of Siena, Austin
Castillo, Concepcion, (Retired)
Cavazos, Arthur, St. Catherine of Siena, Austin
Coelho, August, St. Joseph, Rockdale
Colley, Earl, St. Monica, Cameron
Colon, Wilfrido, (Retired)
Conrads, Michael, (Retired)
Cooke, Paul, Ascension, Bastrop
Cortez, Willie, Sacred Heart, Austin
Crochet, Larry R., (Retired)
Cuevas, Alfonso, St. Vincent de Paul, Austin
Davis, Roy, (Retired)
Dawson, Vern, St. Helen, Georgetown
De La Garza, John J. Jr., (Retired)
DiGiuseppe, Peter, (Retired)
DiSimoni, Jim, Holy Family Catholic Church, Copperas Cove
Doriocourt, Luis, St. Francis of Assisi, Franklin
Dorsey, Timothy, Holy Family, Copperas Cove
Duecker, Richard, (Retired)
Dufour, Elmore Generes, (Retired)
Dunne, Larry, Sacred Heart, Elgin
Duran, Everardo, (Retired)
Easterling, Paul, St. John the Evangelist, Luling
Egan, Dennis, (Retired)
Embry, Rob, St. Louis, Austin
Endris, Louis, (Retired)
Eskew, Harold Jr., (Retired)
Esquivel, Benito, St. Ferdinand, Blanco; Good Shepherd, Johnson City
Fahlund, Nelson, (Retired)
Faulk, Edward, St. Mary, Our Lady of the Lake, Lago Vista
Fell, Channing, St. John Vianney, Round Rock
Fernandes, Ronald, St. Thomas Aquinas, College Station
Fitzpatrick, James, St. Mary, Church of the Assumption, Waco
Flores, Joe, (Retired)
Forbes, Michael P., J.C.L., M.C.L., St. William Catholic Church, Round Rock
Franklin, John, (Retired)
Frerich, Alvin, Sacred Heart, Rockne
Gallagher, Pat, St. Joseph, Bryan
Garcia, Ben, Santa Cruz, Buda
Garcia, Lorenzo, Sacred Heart, Waco
Garza, Jesse M., (Retired)
Garza, Jessie C., (Retired)
Garza, Juan, (Retired)
Garza, Reyes, Santa Cruz, Buda
George, Gregory, St. Jerome, Waco
George, Robert, (Inactive)
Gesch, Michael T., St. Thomas Moore, Austin
Gessler, Don, M.D., M.B.A., (Retired)
Glenn, Michael DeWayne, St. John Neumann, Austin
Gonzales, Gumisindo, (Retired)
Gonzalez, Rodolfo L., Santa Cruz, Buda
Griffin, Marc, St. Mary, Taylor
Guerrero, Jorge, St. Mary, Wimberley
Guilbert, Terry, Emmaus, Lakeway
Gutierrez, Joe V., (Retired), (Inactive)
Gutierrez, Roberto, St. John the Evangelist Parish, San Marcos
Haffner, Curt, St. John the Evangelist Catholic Church, Marble Falls
Hansen, Clarence, (Inactive)
Hargraves, Wilfred, (Retired)
Hayden, James (Tim), Holy Family, Copperas Cove
Haywood, Daryl, (Retired)
Hill, Brian James, St. Margaret Mary Parish, Cedar Park
Hill, John, Emmaus, Lakeway
Hobby, Bill, (Leave of Absence)
Holicky, Edward F. Jr., St. John, Marble Falls
James, Ray, (Retired)
Jan, Leroy, (Serving in another Diocese)
Januszewski, Bill, (Retired)
Jasek, Frank, (Retired)
Jasek, Robert, (Retired)
Jasso, Carlos, (Retired)
Jimenez, Jose, (Retired)
Johnson, Richard, St. Mary, Mexia
Johnson, Tom, (Retired)
Jones, Fred, St. Elizabeth Ann Seton Catholic Community, Fort Hood
Jones, Ray, St. Jerome, Waco
Kennedy, Pat, (Retired)
Kerrigan, John, Santa Cruz, Buda
Kim, Peter, (Retired)
Klement, Jerry, Ed.D., (Retired)
Kotrola, Richard, St. William, Round Rock
Lara, Alejandro, St. William, Round Rock
Lara, Victor, St. William, Round Rock
Lastovica, Ronnie, Prison Ministry
Lavallee, Paul, St. John, Marble Falls
Lee, Gordon Kenneth, St. Mary Parish, Mexia
Lilliard, George, (Retired)
Long, William (Bill), (Retired)
Lopez, Agapito, San Jose, Austin
Luna, Conception, St. Mary, Hearne
Luna, Cris, Our Lady of Wisdom, San Marcos
Lupo, Daniel, St. Thomas More, Austin
Madsen, James, St. Luke, Temple
Mahoney, Dwight, (Retired)
Mai, Hoa, Holy Vietnamese Martyrs, Austin
Maldonado, Javier, St. Louis King of France, Austin
Mallinger, Thomas, St. Thomas More, Austin
Marchek, Michael, St. Paul, Austin
Martinez, Jesse, (Retired)
Martinez, Roberto, Sacred Heart, Austin
Mayes, Dave, St. Thomas Aquinas, College Station
McCardle, John, St. Margaret Mary Catholic Church, Cedar Park
McCormick, Frank, St. John Vianney, Round Rock
Medina, Aurelio, (Retired)
Medina, Steve, St. Mary, Brenham
Meismer, Mike, Sacred Heart, La Grange
Menchaca, Richard, (Retired)
Mendez, Jose, San Jose, Austin
Meuth, Bernard, St. Paul, Smithville
Milton, Glen, St. Mary Catholic Center, College Station
Mojica, Jessie, St. John the Evangelist, San Marcos
Molina, Fred, Santa Teresa, Bryan
Monroe, Frank, J.D., (Retired)
Montag, Eugene, (Retired)
Montoya, Dave, St. Margaret Mary, Cedar Park
Moore, Paul, Fort Hood
Moore, Ray, (Retired)
Morales, David L., (Retired)
Moran, Elias, (Serving in another diocese)
Moran, Pat, (Serving in another diocese)
Morse, Eugene, (Retired)
Muehr, Roger, Sacred Heart, Rockne
Murphy, John (Jack), St. Monica, Cameron
Murray, Patrick, (Retired)
Nelson, Gary, (Retired)
Nissen, Kevin, St. Peter the Apostle, Austin
Nwokocha, Emmanuel, St. Elizabeth, Pflugerville
O'Beirne, Patrick Thomas, St. Thomas More Parish, Austin
O'Neill, John T., (Retired)
Ochoa, David, St. Albert the Great, Austin
Ojeda, Johnny, (Retired)
Olivieri, Mark Nicholas, St. Thomas Aquinas Parish, College Station
Olsenholler, Jeffrey, St. Joseph Catholic Church, Bryan
Pearson, Daniel, St. Martin de Porres, Dripping Springs
Pent, Steven, St. William, Round Rock
Perrone, Andy, St. Anthony, Bryan
Pickwell, John S., B.A., Pastoral Center, Austin
Pina, Steve, (Inactive)
Ponce, Alfred Mojica, St. Paul Chong Hasang Parish, Harker Heights
Poole, James, (Retired)
Prescott, Allen, (Retired)
Prewitt, Sidney (Butch), (Retired), Pastoral Center
Pustka, David, St. Mary of the Assumption, Taylor
Pynes, Tony, St. Theresa, Austin
Ramirez, Daniel, (Retired)
Ramos, Jose Gomez Sr., St. Joseph Parish, Killeen
Reed, David, St. Mary Catholic Center, College Station
Renteria, Mario, Our Lady of Guadalupe, Austin
Reyes, Samuel, St. Mary, Caldwell
Roberge, Philip R., St. Margaret Mary, Cedar Park
Rodgers, James, (Serving in another diocese)
Rodriguez, Bonifacio, St. Mary, Temple
Rodriguez, Guadalupe Jr., St. Mary Cathedral, Austin
Rodriguez, J. Paul, St. Margaret Mary, Cedar Park
Rohaly, Ernie, (Retired)
Romero, Octabiano, (Inactive)
Rosales, Hector, Dolores, Austin
Rositas, Edward, St. Martin de Porres, Dripping Springs
Ruiz, Joe, St. Helen, Georgetown
Ryan, Barry, St. Elizabeth, Pflugerville
Saienga, Gene, St. John Vianney, Round Rock
Sanchez, Claudio, Our Lady of Guadalupe, Temple
Sanders, Raymond, M.S., M.A., Ed.D., (Retired)
Scarmardo, Bill, St. Anthony, Bryan

Schroeder, Christopher, St. Catherine of Siena, Austin
Schwab, Peter A., Ph.D., (Retired)
Scott, Bill, (Retired)
Sekel, David, (Serving in another Diocese)
Shoemake, William, Christ the King, Belton
Silguero, Luis Francisco, (Retired)
Sims, Donald, St. Ann, Somerville
Sis, Ray, (Retired)
Smetana, Bill, (Retired)
Snigger, Robert J., (Inactive)
Solorzano, Eraclio, St. John, Marble Falls
Sudderth, Thomas Gregory, St. Mary Parish, Wimberely
Suniga, Thomas, St. Thomas More Parish, Austin
Sweed, Limas, Blessed Virgin Mary, Washington
Sykora, Ron, St. Mary, Church of the Assumption, West
Torres, Alfredo, Our Lady of Guadalupe, Taylor
Torres, Manuel, St. John Neumann, Austin
Trujillo, Jose, St. Albert the Great, Austin
Tyboroski, Julian, (Retired)
Unger, Geoffrey Robert, St. Martin de Porres Parish, Dripping Springs
Valenzuela, Ernesto Sr., St. Mary Parish, Caldwell
Valeriano, Oscar, Christ the King, Belton
Van Til, Robert Willem, St. Patrick Parish, Hutto
Vande Vorde, Tim, St. Michael Catholic Church, Uhland
Vargas, Domingo, (Retired)
Vela, Joe, (Retired)
Vela, William, St. Joseph, Manor
Venglar, Patrick, (Retired)
Villa, Luis, St. Louis, Austin
Villarreal, Rodolfo Leandro III, (Serving in another diocese)
Villegas, Salomon, St. Paul, Austin
Vocelka, F. Jay, (Retired)
Walker, Ron, St. Ignatius Martyr, Austin
Washburne, Marc, (Serving in another diocese)
Wearden, Glen E., (Retired)
Wehrer, Robert, (Retired), Sacred Heart, Waco
Weiland, James, Ascension, Bastrop
Wohlfarth, Eugene, Immaculate Heart of Mary, Martindale
Wright, Charlie, Visitation, Westphalia
Wright, Dan, St. Austin, Austin
Young, John, (Retired)
Zacek, George, St. Theresa, Austin.

INSTITUTIONS LOCATED IN DIOCESE

[A] COLLEGES AND UNIVERSITIES

AUSTIN. *St. Edward's University*, 3001 S. Congress Ave., 78704-6489. Tel: 512-448-8400; Fax: 512-448-8492; Email: seu.admit@stedwards.edu; Web: www.stedwards.edu. Rev. Peter Walsh, Campus Min. Established in 1878 by the Congregation of Holy Cross and chartered by the state in 1885. Holy Cross Brothers 16; Priests 2; Sisters 1; Students 4,861; Total Staff 1,017; Lay Professors 484.

Officers: Dr. George E. Martin, Pres.; Sr. Donna M. Jurick, S.N.D., Vice Pres., Academic Affairs; Paige Booth, Vice Pres. Mktg. & Enrollment Mgmt.; Cristina Bordin, Liaison to the Bd. of Trustees & Sustainability Coord.; Christine Campbell, Assoc. Vice Pres., Mktg.; Bill Clabby, Assoc. Vice Pres., Global Initiatives; Doris Constantine, Assoc. Vice Pres., Student Fin. Svcs.; Erin W. Delffs, Assoc. Vice Pres., Fin.; Joe DeMedeiros, Vice Pres., Univ. Advancement; Benjamin R. Hockenhull, Assoc. Vice Pres., Digital Innovation; Cyndy Johnson, Asst. Vice Pres., Business Svcs.; Dr. Lisa Kirkpatrick, Vice Pres., Student Affairs & Title IX Coord.; Kimberly Kvaal, Vice Pres. Fin. Affairs; Tracy Manier, Assoc. Vice Pres. & Dean, Admissions; Molly Minus, Assoc. Vice Pres., Academic Affairs & Dir., McNair Scholars Prog.; Bhuban Pandey, Assoc. Vice Pres., Inst. Effectiveness & Research; Lori West Peterson, Assoc. Vice Pres., Faculty Devel. & Academic Progs.; Michael W. Peterson, Assoc. Vice. Pres., Facilities; Rosemary Samora Rudnicki, Asst. Vice Pres., Human Resources; Justin Sloan, Chief Data Officer & Spec. Asst. to the Pres., Data Strategy; Angela Svoboda, Assoc. Vice Pres., Digital Effectiveness; Nicole Guerrero Trevino, Assoc. Vice Pres., Student Academic Support Svcs.; David Waldron, Vice Pres. Information Technology; Rev. Peter Walsh, C.S.C., Dir., Campus Min.

[B] HIGH SCHOOL, DIOCESAN

AUSTIN. *St. Dominic Savio Catholic High School*, 9300 Neenah Ave., 78717. Tel: 512-388-8846; Fax: 512-388-1335. Dr. Joan Wagner, Ph.D., Pres.; Mr. Morgan Daniels, Prin.; Miss Diane Powell, Librarian. Lay Teachers 30; Sisters 3; Students 381.

San Juan Diego Catholic High School (2002) 800 Herndon Ln., 78704. Tel: 512-804-1935; Fax: 512-804-1937; Email: info@sjdchs.org; Web: sjdchs.org. Pamela S. Jupe, Prin. Lay Teachers 15; Total Enrollment 171; Total Staff 27.

BRYAN. *St. Joseph High School*, 600 S. Coulter, Bryan, 77803. Tel: 979-822-6641; Fax: 979-779-2810; Email: jrike@stjosephschoolbcs.org. Jim Rike, Prin. Lay Teachers 40; Students 350.

WACO. *Reicher Catholic High School* (1954) 2102 N. 23rd St., Waco, 76708. Tel: 254-752-8349; Fax: 254-752-8408; Email: jheiple@reicher.org; Web: www.reicher.org. Mindy Taylor, Prin.; Carolyn Casey, Librarian. Deacons 1; Lay Teachers 25; Sisters 1; Students 183.

[C] HIGH SCHOOL, PRIVATE

AUSTIN. *St. Michael's Catholic Academy* (1984) 3000 Barton Creek Blvd., 78735. Tel: 512-328-2323; Fax: 512-328-2327; Web: www.smca.com. Dawn Nicols, Head of School. Lay Teachers 49; Students 372.

TEMPLE. *Holy Trinity Catholic High School* (1997) 6608 W. Adams Ave., Temple, 76502. Tel: 254-771-0787; Fax: 254-771-2285; Email: admissions@holytrinitychs.org; Web: www.holytrinitychs.org. Mr. Jim Rike, Prin.; Cindy Allen, Librarian; Isabelle Summers, Admin.; Rebecca Brink, Athletic Dir. Lay Teachers 12; Total Enrollment 93; Total Staff 13.

[D] ELEMENTARY SCHOOL, DIOCESAN

AUSTIN. *Holy Family Catholic School* (2000) (Grades PreK-8), 9400 Neenah Ave., 78717. Tel: 512-246-4455; Fax: 512-246-4454; Email: hfcs@holyfamilycs.org; Web: www.holyfamilycs.org. Dr. Joan Wagner, Ph.D., Pres.; Mrs. Kelly Laster, Prin.; Alyson Banda, Librarian. Lay Teachers 26; Sisters 3; Students 543.

[E] ELEMENTARY SCHOOL, PRIVATE

AUSTIN. *St. Gabriel's Catholic School*, (Grades PreK-8), (Legal name: Southwest Austin Catholic School Inc.) 2500 Wimberly Ln., 78735. Tel: 512-327-7755; Fax: 512-327-4334; Web: sgs-austin.org. Dan McKenna, Head, School; James Melone, Head, Middle School; Colleen Lynch, Head, Lower School; Allison Snyder, Librarian. Lay Teachers 57; Total Enrollment 426.

[F] GENERAL HOSPITALS

AUSTIN. *Seton Family of Hospitals*, 1345 Philomena St., 78723. Tel: 512-324-1908; Web: www.seton.net; Email: andy.davis@ascension.org. Mr. William Davis, Pres. d/b/a's: Dell Children's Medical Center, Austin; Dell Seton Medical Center at The University of Texas, Austin; Seton Bertram Healthcare Center, Bertram; Seton Burnet Healthcare Center, Burnet; Seton Edgar B. Davis Hospital, Luling; Seton Highland Lakes Hospital, Burnet; Seton Lampasas Healthcare Center, Lampasas; Seton Lockheart Family Health Center, Lockhart; Seton Marble Falls Healthcare Center, Marble Falls; Seton Medical Center Austin, Austin; Seton Medical Center Hays, Kyle; Seton Medical Center Williamson, Round Rock; Seton Northwest Hospital, Austin; Seton Pflugerville Healthcare Center, Pflugerville; Seton Shoal Creek Hospital, Austin; Seton Smithville Regional Hospital, Smithville; Seton Southwest Hospital, Austin; Seton Topfer Community Health Center, Austin Bed Capacity 1,613; Tot Asst. Annually 877,790; Total Staff 9,456; Staff 8,474.

BRYAN. *Burleson St. Joseph Health Center of Caldwell, Texas*, 2801 Franciscan Dr., Bryan, 77802. Tel: 979-776-2599; Fax: 409-774-4590; Email: bstanford@st-joseph.org; Web: www.st-joseph.org. James Schuessler, Pres. & CEO, St. Joseph Health System; John Hughson, BSJHC Admin. Bed Capacity 25; Tot Asst. Annually 22,930; Total Staff 81.

CHI St. Joseph Health Center, 2801 Franciscan Dr., Bryan, 77802. Tel: 979-776-3777; Fax: 979-774-4590; Email: rnapper@st-joseph.org; Web: www.st-joseph.org. Rick Napper, Pres. and CEO, CHI St. Joseph Health System; Jeb Blair, Bd. Chm. Bed Capacity 247; Patients Asst Anual. 265,403; Sisters of St. Francis of Sylvania, OH 4; Total Staff 1,925.

CHI St. Joseph Services Corp., 2801 Franciscan Dr., Bryan, 77802. Tel: 979-776-3777; Fax: 979-774-4590; Email: rnapper@st-joseph.org; Web: www.st-joseph.org. Rick Napper, CEO, CHI St. Joseph Health System; Jeb Blair, Bd. Chm. Bed Capacity 309; Sisters of St. Francis of Sylvania, OH 4; Tot Asst. Annually 333,328; Total Staff 2,993; LTC Beds 233; LTC Staff 199.

WACO. *Providence Health Services of Waco* (1904) 6901 Medical Pkwy., P.O. Box 2589, Waco, 76712. Tel: 254-751-4000; Fax: 254-751-4769; Email: Philip.Patterson@ascension.org; Web: www.providence.net. Sr. Ellen LaCapria, Chairwoman; Mary Stein, Dir. Providence Health Center-Medical/Surgical/OB/Pediatrics Acute Care; DePaul Center - Psychiatric Care. Bed Capacity 285; Daughters of Charity of St. Vincent de Paul 4; Tot Asst. Annually 170,173; Total Staff 1,691.

[G] MONASTERIES AND RESIDENCES OF PRIESTS AND BROTHERS

AUSTIN. *Congregation of Holy Cross, Moreau Province* (1837) 1101 St. Edward's Dr., 78704-6512. Tel: 512-442-7856; Fax: 512-444-3133; Email: financemoreau@gmail.com; Web: www.holycrossbrothers.org. Bros. Thomas Dziekan, Prov.; Donald Blauvelt, C.S.C., Vicar; Harold Ehlinger, C.S.C., Treas.; Richard Critz, C.S.C., B.A., M.A., Sec. Corporate Title: Congregation of Holy Cross, Moreau Province, Inc. Religious 102. *Brother John Baptist Province Center* (1956) 1101 St. Edward's Dr., 78704-6512. Tel: 512-442-7856; Fax: 512-444-3133; Email: financemoreau@gmail.com; Web: www.holycrossbrothers.org. Bros. William Zaydak, C.S.C., Prov. Supr.; Mark Knightly, C.S.C., B.A., M.S.W., Sec.; David Turmel, C.S.C., Steward; William Nick, C.S.C., Vicar Prov.; Richard Critz, C.S.C., B.A., M.A., Admin. Svcs. Total in Province 103. *Brother Vincent Pieau Residence* (1997) 921 St. Edward Dr., 78704. Tel: 512-493-0121; Fax: 512-493-0158. Bro. Sam Robin, C.S.C., Dir. Brothers 23; Priests 4. *St. Joseph Hall Residence, St. Edward's University*, 3001 S. Congress Ave., 78704-6489. Tel: 512-448-8628; Fax: 512-448-8638; Email: brohar72@msn.com. Bros. Harold Hathaway, Dir.; Howard Metz, C.S.C., Dir. Brothers 13; Priests 3.

Dominican Friars of Austin (1960) 2502 Comburg Castle Way, 78748-5258. Tel: 512-282-3908; Email: chiefop7@gmail.com. Revs. James A. McDonough, O.P., Supr.; Gerardo Guerra-Mayaudon, O.P.; Bro. Angel Mendez, O.P.

Schoenstatt Fathers, 225 Addie Roy Rd., 78746-4124. Tel: 512-301-8762; Email: info@schoenstatt.us; Email: frpatricio@schoenstatt.us; Web: www.schoenstatt-fathers.org/en/. Revs. Patricio Rodriguez, I.S.P., Supr.; Raimundo Costa, I.S.P., Moderator; Christian Christensen, I.S.P.; Gerold Langsch, I.S.P.; Johnson Nellissery, I.S.P.; Hector Vega, I.S.P.

BREMOND. *Clerical Congregation Missionaries of Faith* (1972) 715 N. Main St., Bremond, 76629-5173. Tel: 254-746-7789; Fax: 254-746-7789; Email: yucelski@missionariesoffaith.us; Cell: (979) 224-2373; Web: www.missionariesoffaith.us. Rev. Celso A. Yu, M.F., Supr. Clergy 21.

GEORGETOWN. *Pope John Paul II, Residence for Priests*, 2550 E. University Ave., #13, Georgetown, 78626. Tel: 512-868-3454; Fax: 512-869-0614.

TOURS. *Missionary Society of St. Paul, MSP*, P.O. Box 662, Salado, 76691. Tel: 254-947-8037; Fax: 254-822-0171. Rev. Jude Uche, M.S.P.

[H] CONVENTS AND RESIDENCES FOR SISTERS

AUSTIN. *Congregation of the Sisters of the Holy Cross*, La Casa Convent, 2213 Euclid Ave., 78704. Tel: 512-441-6693; Email: sbrennan@cscsisters.org. Sr. Suzanne Brennan, C.S.C., Treas. *Sisters of the Holy Cross, Inc.* Sisters 2.

Congregation of the Sisters of the Holy Cross, Our Lady of Victory Convent, 2215 Euclid Ave., 78704-5214. Tel: 512-441-2927; Email: sbrennan@cscsisters.org. Sr. Suzanne Brennan, C.S.C., Treas. *Sisters of the Holy Cross, Inc.* Sisters 2.

Daughters of Mary Help of Christians (Salesian Sisters of St. John Bosco), St. Mary Mazzarello Convent, 2109 E. Second St., 78702. Tel: 512-474-2312; Fax: 512-474-2314; Email: itapia@craustin.com. Sisters 4.

Dominican Sisters of Mary, Mother of the Eucharist, 5501 E. State Hwy. 29, Georgetown, 78626. Tel: 512-863-4826.

Franciscan Sisters Daughters of Mercy (Hermanas Franciscanas Hijas de la Misericordia) (1856) House of Formation, 1207 Montopolis Dr., 78741. Tel: 512-385-5090. Sr. Rose Moreno, F.H.M., M.A., Supr. Sisters 3.

St. Francis Convent, 612 N. 3rd St., Waco, 76701. Tel: 254-753-5565. Sisters 4.

Missionary Sisters of the Immaculate Conception of the Mother of God, 4211-B Shoalwood, 78756. Tel: 512-451-2890; Email: jreisch@prodigy.net.

Sinsinawa Dominican Sisters (1848) 6008 Club Terr., 78741. Tel: 512-385-1719. Sisters 3.

Sisters of Charity of the Incarnate Word, 8233

Summer Side Dr., 78759. Tel: 512-451-0272; Tel: 512-231-9512 (Home); Fax: 512-451-0284.

Sisters, Servants of the Immaculate Heart of Mary, 2606 East Side Dr., 78704. Tel: 512-442-5295.

BRENHAM. *Pax Christi Sisters - Pax Christi Institute*, 9300 Hwy. 105, Brenham, 77833. Tel: 979-251-7450; Fax: 979-251-7450.

Sisters of St. Francis of Our Lady of Lourdes (O.S.F.) (1916) 2514 Clare Ct., Apt. A, Bryan, 77802. Tel: 979-777-0578; Fax: 979-836-9383. Sisters 2.

BRYAN. *Sisters of St. Francis of Our Lady of Lourdes*, 2516 Clare Ct., Apt. B, Bryan, 77802. Tel: 979-219-0316; Fax: 409-774-4590; Email: pdunn@st-joseph.org; Web: www.st-joseph.org. Sisters 4.

SOMERVILLE. *Missionary Ecumenical*, P.O. Box 367, Somerville, 77879. Tel: 979-595-1494; Fax: 979-596-1494. Sisters 2.

WACO. *Franciscan Sisters Daughters of Mercy* (Franciscanas Hijas de la Misericordia) 612 N. Third St., Waco, 76701. Tel: 254-753-5565; Email: churchoffice@stfrancistorwaco.org. Sisters 4. 1207 Montopolis Dr., 78741. Sisters 2.

[I] HOMES FOR THE AGED & HANDICAPPED

BRYAN. *St. Joseph Manor* (1999) 2333 Manor Dr., Bryan, 77802. Tel: 979-821-7330; Fax: 979-821-7301; Email: ksims@st-joseph.org. James Schuessler, Pres. & CEO, St. Joseph Health System; Kyle Sims, Admin. Bed Capacity 121; Tot Asst. Annually 352; Total Staff 109.

CALDWELL. *CHI Burleson St. Joseph Manor*, 1022 Presidential Corridor, Hwy. 21E, Caldwell, 77836. Tel: 979-567-0920; Fax: 979-567-4811; Email: jthreadgill@st-joseph.org. Rick Napper, Pres. & CEO, CHI St. Joseph Health System. Bed Capacity 112; Staff 81.

[J] MISSION CENTERS

WACO. *St. Francis Mission Center*, 612 N. Third St., Waco, 76701. Tel: 254-753-5565; Fax: 254-757-0537; Email: barbarajhtexas@hotmail.com. Sisters Jacinta Amengual, F.H.M., Supr.; Maria Izquierdo, F.H.M., Catechetical, Kindergarten & Nursery; Catherine Vallespir, F.H.M., Catechetical, Kindergarten & Nursery. Franciscan Sisters Daughters of Mercy. Sisters 4; Students 131; Total Staff 13.

[K] RENEWAL CENTERS

BELTON. *Cedarbrake Catholic Retreat Center* (1979) 5602 S. Hwy. 317 N., Temple, 76502. Tel: 254-780-2436; Fax: 254-780-2684; Email: cedarbrake@austindiocese.org. Total in Residence 2; Total Staff 12.

[L] NEWMAN APOSTOLATE

AUSTIN. *University Catholic Center*, 2010 University Ave., 78705. Tel: 512-476-7351; Fax: 512-476-7377; Email: catholic@utcatholic.org; Web: www.utcatholic.org. Revs. "Jimmy" Yao Hsu, C.S.P., M.Div., Camp Min.; Larry Rice, C.S.P., M.Div., Dir. Serving the Catholic community at the University of Texas. Total Staff 10.

BRYAN. *Blinn College Catholic Student Union*, Blinn College, 2423 Blinn Blvd., Bldg. E, Bryan, 77802. Tel: 979-209-7634; Fax: 979-209-7430. For Catholic students attending Blinn Jr. College. Staff 1.

WACO. *St. Peter Catholic Student Center at Baylor University*, 1415 S. 9th St., Waco, 76706-0060. Tel: 254-757-0636; Fax: 254-714-0639; Email: office@baylorcatholic.org; Web: www.baylorcatholic.org. P.O. Box 6060, Waco, 76706. Very Rev. Daniel Liu, Dir.; John Smith, Dir. Devel.; Amy Lopez, Center Coord. For Catholic students attending Baylor University, Texas State Technical College, and McLennan Community College.

[M] FOUNDATIONS, ENDOWMENTS & TRUSTS

AUSTIN. *Blue Ladies Minerals, Inc.*, 1201 W. 38th St., 78705-1056. Tel: 512-324-1990; Fax: 512-324-1989; Email: Miguel.Romano@ascension.org. Donna Budak, Exec. Dir.

Catholic Foundation - Diocese of Austin, Mailing Address: 6225 Hwy. 290 E., 78723. Tel: 512-949-2400; Fax: 512-949-2520; Email: scott-whitaker@austindiocese.org; Web: www.catholicfdn.org. Scott Whitaker, Exec.

Diocese of Austin Pension Plan and Trust The Diocese of Austin Pension Plan and Trust 6225 Hwy. 290 E., 78723. Tel: 512-949-2400; Email: krystal-reyes@austindiocese.org. Very Rev. Timothy S. Nolt, Chm,; Rev. Msgr. John A. McCaffrey, Trustee; Revs. Larry Covington, Trustee; Stephen Nesrsta, Trustee; Rev. Msgr. Thomas Frank, (Retired); Rev. Barry Cuba, S.T.B., M.A., M.Div.; Very Rev. Daniel Liu; Rev. James Misko.

Clerical Endowment Fund, 205 W. Pecan, Lockhart, 78644. Tel: 512-398-4649. Very Rev. Edward Karasek.

CMC Foundation of Central Texas dba Dell Children's Medical Center Foundation, 1345 Philomena St., 78723. Tel: 512-324-0170; Fax: 512-324-0798; Email: KKatz@ascension.org; Web: www.dellchildrens.net/support-dell-childrens/. Kristi Katz, Exec. Dir.

Father Bernard C. Goertz Scholarship Trust Fund, Sacred Heart Church, 136 Tucker Ln., Red Rock, 78662. Tel: 512-321-5735.

Fickett Health Legacy, Inc., Mailing Address: 1201 W. 38th St., 78705. Tel: 512-324-1990; Fax: 512-324-7989; Email: Miguel.Romano@ascension.org. Donna Budak, Exec. Dir.

Holy Family Catholic School Foundation (2000) 9400 Neenah Ave., 78717. Tel: 512-246-4455; Fax: 512-246-4454; Email: hfcs@holyfamilycs.org; Web: www.holyfamilycs.org. Dr. Joan Wagner, Ph. D., Pres.

Seton Fund of the Daughters of Charity of St. Vincent de Paul, Inc., 1201 W. 38th St., 78705. Tel: 512-324-1990; Email: DBudak@ascension.org; Web: www.setonfund.org. Mr. Miguel Romano, Pres.

Seton Hays Foundation, 6001 Kyle Pkwy., Kyle, 78640. Tel: 512-504-5061; Fax: 512-268-8710; Email: LsLotz@ascension.org; Web: www.setonhaysfoundation.org. 1345 Philomena Street, 78723. Linda Lotz, Exec. Dir.

St. Joseph's Foundation of Bryan, 2801 Franciscan Dr., Bryan, 77802. Tel: 979-774-4087. Thomas J. Pool, Exec.

St. Joseph's School Memorial Endowment Fund, 507 E. 26th St., Bryan, 77803. Tel: 979-822-2721; Fax: 979-779-3120; Email: frjohn@stjosephbcs.org; Web: www.stjosephschoolbcs.org. Rev. Msgr. John A. McCaffrey.

Twenty-Six Doors, Inc., 1201 W. 38th St., 78705. Tel: 512-324-1990; Fax: 512-324-1989; Email: Miguel.Romano@ascension.org. Attn: Seton Foundations, 1345 Philomena Street, 78723. Donna Budak, Exec. Dir.

BRYAN. *St. Joseph Memorial Endowment Fund*, St. Joseph's, 507 E. 26th, Bryan, 77803. Tel: 979-822-2721; Fax: 979-779-3120; Email: frjohn@stjosephbcs.org; Web: www.stjosephbcs.org. Rev. Msgr. John A. McCaffrey.

ROUND ROCK. *Seton Williamson Foundation*, 201 Seton Pkwy., Round Rock, 78665. Tel: 512-324-4090; Fax: 512-324-4657; Web: www.setonwilliamsonfdn.org; Email: dbudak@ascension.org. Donna Budak, Exec. Dir.

[N] MISCELLANEOUS

AUSTIN. *Catholic Archives of Texas*, 6225 Hwy. 290 E., 78723. Tel: 512-476-6296; Fax: 512-476-3715; Email: marian@txcatholic.org; Email: eric@txcatholic.org; Web: txcatholic.org/catholic-archives-of-texas/. Dr. Marian J. Barber Ph.D., Ph. D., Dir.; Eric J. Hartmann, Archivist. Historical collection of the Church in the Southwest and Texas from 1519.

Catholic Charities of Central Texas, 1625 Rutherford Ln., 78754. Tel: 512-651-6100; Fax: 512-651-6101.

Immigration Legal Services, Tel: 512-651-6125. Sara Ramirez, Dir.

Catholic Family Fraternal of Texas. KJZT, P.O. Box 18896, 78760-8896. Tel: 512-444-9586; Fax: 512-444-6887. Loretta Stahl, Pres. & CEO.

Catholic Southwest, 6225 Hwy. 290 E., 78723. Tel: 512-476-6296; Fax: 512-476-6296; Email: marian@txcatholic.org; Web: txcatholic.org/catholic-southwest/. Dr. Richard Fossey, Editor.

Juan Diego Missionary Society, 4606 E. St. Elmo, 78744. Tel: 512-731-8434; Fax: 512-441-0928; Email: jdms1981@gmail.com. Elias and Christina Limon, Dir.

Juan Diego Work / Study Program, Inc., 800 Herndon Ln., 78704. Tel: 512-804-1935; Fax: 512-804-1937; Web: www.sjdchs.org. Pamela S. Jupe, Prin.

Ladies of Charity of Austin, TX (1890) P.O. Box 9566, 78766. Tel: 512-416-7959; Fax: 512-507-5091. Anna LaFuente, Pres., Tel: 512-388-1989 (Home).

**Mary's Touch*, P.O. Box 341991, 78734. Tel: 512-965-4449; Email: info@marystouch.org; Web: www.marystouch.org. Susana Garza, Exec.; Cheri Lomonte, Founder.

North Central Catholic School Corporation (1996) 9400 Neenah Ave., 78717. Tel: 512-246-4455; Fax: 512-246-4454; Email: hfcs@holyfamilycs.org; Web: www.holyfamilycs.org. Dr. Joan Wagner, Ph. D., Pres.; Mrs. Kelly Laster, Prin.; Mrs. Kelly Laster, Bus. Mgr.

Seton Clinical Enterprise Corporation, 1345 Philomena St., 78723. Tel: 512-324-0000; Email: ClCarsner@ascension.org. Mr. Clayton Carsner, Pres.

Seton Healthcare Family, 1345 Philomena St., 78723. Tel: 512-324-0000; Email: Craig.Cordola@ascension.org. Mr. Craig Cordola, Pres.

Seton Insurance Services Corporation, 1345 Philomena St., 78723. Tel: 512-324-1986; Email: TBruce@ascension.org. Mr. Trent Bruce, Pres.

Society of St. Katharine Drexel, 503 Vale St., 78746. Tel: 512-838-6142. Merlie Morales, Pres., Tel: 512-328-2744.

**Society of St. Vincent de Paul, Diocesan Council of Austin*, P.O. Box 9070, 78766. Tel: 512-251-6995; Fax: 512-919-4715.

Texas Catholic Conference of Bishops, 1600 N. Congress Ave., Suite B, P.O. Box 13285, 78701. Tel: 512-339-9882; Fax: 512-339-8670; Email: info@txcatholic.org; Email: jennifer@txcatholic.org; Web: www.txcatholic.org. P.O. Box 13285, 78711. Lisette Allen, M.A., M.Ed., Supt.; Marian Barber, Dir. Catholic Archives of Texas; Jennifer Carr-Allmon, Exec.

Texas Catholic Historical Society, 6225 Hwy. 290 E., 78723. Tel: 512-476-6296; Fax: 512-476-3715; Email: marian@txcatholic.org; Web: txcatholic.org/archives-2/. Sr. Madeleine Grace, C.V.I., Pres.; Claudia Anderson, Vice Pres.

BASTROP. *Ladies of Charity of Bastrop, TX*, P.O. Box 1060, Bastrop, 78602. Tel: 512-321-9819; Fax: 512-321-1647.

BRYAN. *Council of Catholic Women*, 1315 Barak Ln., Bryan, 77802. Tel: 979-846-0617; Email: judithl@suddenlink.net; Web: www.adccw.com. Dianne Friend, Pres.

BUDA. *St. Mary's Academy Alumnae Association*, 16005 Scenic Oak Tr., Buda, 78610. Tel: 512-312-0836; Email: cbattal44@gmail.com. Catherine Attal, Contact Person.

COLLEGE STATION. *The Apostles of the Interior Life*, 603 Church Ave., College Station, 77840.

JARRELL. *Cursillo*, Our Lady of Guadalupe Cursillo Center, 200 W. FM 487, P.O. Box 65, Jarrell, 76537. Silvia Villarreal, Dir., Spanish, Tel: 512-746-2041 (Office); Tel: 254-541-9287; Robin Spencer, Dir., English, Tel: 512-746-2041; Tel: 254-518-3609.

National Cursillo Movement, Inc., 250 W. FM 487, Jarrell, 76537. Tel: 512-746-2020; Fax: 512-746-2030.

LAGRANGE. *Catholic Union of Texas, The K.J.T.* (1889) P.O. Box 297, La Grange, 78945-0297. Tel: 979-968-5877; Fax: 979-968-5823; Email: president@kjtnet.org; Web: www.kjtnet.org. Christopher L. Urban, Pres. KJT NEWS (official publication).

ROUND ROCK. *Christ Child Society of Texas, Capital Area, Inc.* (2004) P.O. Box 5953, Round Rock, 78683. Email: texascapital@nationalchristchildsoc.org. Sarah Brunet, Pres.; Joan Watkins, Pres.

SALADO. *Catholic Vocation Advocates - Central Texas*, 1417 Elizabeth Cir., Salado, 76571. Tel: 254-328-3708; Email: cbroecker@live.com. C. David Broecker, Pres.

Serra Club - Austin, P.O. Box 156, Salado, 76571. Tel: 512-330-1028; Email: carrie@carrieweikert.com. Carrie Weikert, Contact Person.

WACO. *Ladies of Charity of Waco, TX* (1895) 501 E. Navarro, Mart, 76664. Tel: 254-876-2277; Fax: 254-876-2535; Email: imaginit@juno.com. Jeanne M. Arensman, Pres.; Lorraine Brooks, Financial Sec.

**Providence Foundation, Inc.*, 6901 Medical Pkwy., Waco, 76712. Tel: 254-751-4762; Email: Miguel.Romano@ascension.org. Jana Whitaker, Exec.

Providence Park, Inc. dba St. Elizabeth Place, St. Catherine Center,Providence Village, 300 W. Highway 6, Waco, 76712-7910. Tel: 254-761-8500; Fax: 254-761-8050; Email: molmstea@ascension.org; Email: amanda.sonnier@ascension.org; Web: ascensionliving.org. Ms. Melissa Hall, Admin. Providence Park Inc. is held by Ascension Living, a subsidiary of Ascension Health

Providence Park Inc. DBA St. Elizabeth Place, St. Catherine Center.

RELIGIOUS INSTITUTES OF MEN REPRESENTED IN THE DIOCESE

For further details refer to the corresponding bracketed number in the Religious Institutes of Men or Women section.

[]—*Carmelites of Mary Immaculate* (Province of St. Joseph)—C.M.I.

[0600]—*Congregation of Holy Cross-Brothers* (Moreau Prov.)—C.S.C.

[0610]—*Congregation of Holy Cross-Priests* (Indiana Prov., Notre Dame, IN)—C.S.C.

[0480]—*Conventual Franciscans* (Mexico City)—O.F.M.Conv.

[]—*Indian Missionary Society* (Ranchi Region)—I.M.S.

[]—*Marist Brothers*—F.M.S.

[]—*Missionaries of Faith* (U.S. Region, Bremond, TX)—M.F.

[]—*Missionaries of St. Paul* (Houston, TX)—M.S.P.

[1110]—*Missionaries of the Sacred Heart* (San Antonio, TX)—M.S.C.

[0430]—*Order of Preachers-Dominicans* (New Orleans, LA)—O.P.

[1030]—*Paulist Fathers* (Jamaica Estates, NY)—C.S.P.
[]—*Secular Order of Schoenstatt Priests*—I.S.P.
[]—*Servants of the Risen Christ.*
[]—*Society of Jesus*—S.J.
[1200]—*Society of the Divine Savior* (Polish Province, US, Porth, TX)—S.D.S.
[]—*Society of the Divine Savior*—S.D.S.
[0560]—*Third Order Regular of Saint Francis* (Vice-Province of Santa Maria de Guadalupe, Mexico)—T.O.R.

RELIGIOUS INSTITUTES OF WOMEN REPRESENTED IN THE DIOCESE

[]—*Apostles of the Interior Life*—A.V.I.
[1010]—*Congregation of Divine Providence* (San Antonio, TX)—C.D.P.
[]—*Congregation of the Sisters of Charity of the Incarnate Word* (Houston, TX)—C.C.V.I.
[]—*Daughters of Divine Love*—D.D.L.
[0850]—*Daughters of Mary Help of Christians* (San Antonio, TX)—F.M.A.
[]—*Daughters of Mary Mother of Mercy*—D.M.M.M.
[]—*Disciples of Jesus*—D.J.
[1070-19]—*Dominican Sisters* (Houston, TX)—O.P.
[1070-03]—*Dominican Sisters* (Sinsinawa, WI)—O.P.
[]—*Dominican Sisters of Mary, Mother of the Eucharist*—O.P.
[]—*Ecumenica Missionaries* (Rome, Italy)—M.E.
[]—*Eudist Servants of the Eleventh Hour* (Tijuana, Mexico)—E.S.E.H.
[1235]—*Franciscan Sisters Daughters of Mercy (Franciscanas Hijas de la Misericordia)* (U.S. delegation: Waco, TX)—F.H.M.
[1430]—*Franciscan Sisters of Our Lady of Perpetual Help* (St. Louis, MO)—O.S.F.
[]—*Missionary Servants of Divine Providence*—M.S.D.P.
[2760]—*Missionary Sisters of the Immaculate Conception* (Paterson, NJ)—S.M.I.C.
[]—*Pax Christi Institute*—P.C.I.
[2970]—*School Sisters of Notre Dame* (St. Louis, MO; Dallas, TX)—S.S.N.D.
[]—*Sisters for Christian Community*—S.F.C.C.
[1530]—*Sisters of St. Francis of Our Lady of Lourdes* (Sylvania, OH)—O.S.F.
[1920]—*Sisters of the Holy Cross* (Notre Dame, IN)—C.S.C.
[]—*Sisters of Jesus the Savior*—S.J.S.
[3000]—*Sisters of Notre Dame de Namur - Ohio Province* (Cincinnati, OH)—S.N.D.deN.
[]—*Sisters of Sacred Sciences* (India)—S.S.S.
[]—*Sisters of St. John Bosco* (Taylor, TX)—S.J.B.
[2150]—*Sisters, Servants of the Immaculate Heart of Mary* (Monroe, MI)—I.H.M.

NECROLOGY

† McCarthy, John E., Retired Bishop of Austin, Died Aug. 18, 2018

An asterisk (*) denotes an organization that has established tax-exempt status directly with the IRS and is not covered by the USCCB Group Ruling.

Diocese of Baker

(Dioecesis Bakeriensis)

Most Reverend

LIAM S. CARY

Bishop of Baker; ordained September 5, 1992; appointed Bishop of Baker March 8, 2012; installed May 18, 2012.

ESTABLISHED JUNE 19, 1903.

Square Miles 66,826.

Comprises the Counties of Baker, Crook, Deschutes, Gilliam, Grant, Harney, Hood River, Jefferson, Klamath, Lake, Malheur, Morrow, Sherman, Umatilla, Union, Wallowa, Wasco and Wheeler in the State of Oregon.

For legal titles of parishes and diocesan institutions, consult the Chancery Office.

Diocesan Pastoral Office: 641 S.W. Umatilla Ave., Redmond, OR 97756. Tel: 541-388-4004; Fax: 541-388-2566.

Email: chancellor1@dioceseofbaker.org

STATISTICAL OVERVIEW

Personnel	
Bishop	1
Priests: Diocesan Active in Diocese	20
Priests: Diocesan Active Outside Diocese	1
Priests: Retired, Sick or Absent	13
Number of Diocesan Priests	34
Religious Priests in Diocese	11
Total Priests in Diocese	45
Extern Priests in Diocese	15
Ordinations:	
Transitional Deacons	1
Permanent Deacons in Diocese	9
Total Brothers	2
Total Sisters	9
Parishes	
Parishes	36
With Resident Pastor:	
Resident Diocesan Priests	20
Resident Religious Priests	10
Without Resident Pastor:	
Administered by Priests	6
Missions	23
Closed Parishes	1
Professional Ministry Personnel:	
Brothers	2
Sisters	9
Lay Ministers	25
Welfare	
Catholic Hospitals	4
Total Assisted	1,530,811
Homes for the Aged	5
Special Centers for Social Services	4
Educational	
Diocesan Students in Other Seminaries	3
Total Seminarians	3
Elementary Schools, Diocesan and Parish	4
Total Students	502
Catechesis/Religious Education:	
High School Students	472
Elementary Students	2,580
Total Students under Catholic Instruction	3,557
Teachers in the Diocese:	
Sisters	5
Lay Teachers	48
Vital Statistics	
Receptions into the Church:	
Infant Baptism Totals	664
Minor Baptism Totals	102
Adult Baptism Totals	35
Received into Full Communion	45
First Communions	788
Confirmations	770
Marriages:	
Catholic	121
Interfaith	15
Total Marriages	136
Deaths	278
Total Catholic Population	29,595
Total Population	512,104

Former Bishops—Most Revs. CHARLES J. O'REILLY, D.D., ord. June 29, 1890; appt. June 24, 1903; cons. Bishop of Baker City, Aug. 25, 1903; transferred to the See of Lincoln March 20, 1918; died Feb. 4, 1923; LEO F. FAHEY, D.D., ord. May 29, 1926; appt. Titular Bishop of Ipsus and Coadjutor "cum jure successionis" March 13, 1948; cons. May 26, 1948; died March 31, 1950; JOSEPH F. MCGRATH, D.D., appt. assistant at the Pontifical Throne, Bishop of Baker City; ord. Dec. 21, 1895; appt. Dec. 21, 1918; cons. March 25, 1919; died April 12, 1950; FRANCIS P. LEIPZIG, D.D., ord. April 14, 1920; appt. Bishop of Baker July 18, 1950; cons. Sept. 12, 1950; retired May 4, 1971; died Jan. 17, 1981; THOMAS J. CONNOLLY, D.D., J.C.D., ord. April 8, 1947; appt. May 4, 1971; cons. June 30, 1971; retired Nov. 19, 1999; died April 24, 2015.; ROBERT FRANCIS VASA, D.D., J.C.L., ord. May 22, 1976; appt. Bishop of Baker Nov. 19, 1999; cons. and installed Jan. 26, 2000; appt. Coadjutor Bishop of Santa Rosa in California Jan. 24, 2011; installed March 6, 2011.

Vicar General—Very Rev. RICHARD O. FISCHER.

Judicial Vicar—Very Rev. ANDREW SZYMAKOWSKI.

Chancellor—VACANT.

Diocesan Pastoral Office—641 S.W. Umatilla Ave., Redmond, 97756. Tel: 541-388-4004; Fax: 541-388-2566.

Receptionist—PATTI RAUSCH.

Secretaries—TERRI ISOM; LEAH BICKETT.

Diocesan Tribunal—Tel: 541-388-4004.

Judicial Vicar and Chief Judge—Very Rev. ANDREW SZYMAKOWSKI.

Judge—VACANT.

Defender of the Bond and Promoter of Justice—VACANT.

Tribunal Assistant & Auditor—MARILYN RANSOM.

Coordinator and Notary—MARY WIMER.

Council of Priests—Most Rev. LIAM S. CARY; Very Revs. RICHARD O. FISCHER; ANDREW SZYMAKOWSKI; Revs. JOSE THOMAS MUDAKODIYIL; ROGATIAN URASSA; VICTOR MENA; BAILEY CLEMENS; SHIJU THURUTHIYIL, (India); FRANCIS OBIJEKWU, S.M.M.M., (Nigeria).

Diocesan Consultors—Very Revs. RICHARD O. FISCHER; RONALD E. MAAG; Rev. JOSEPH LEVINE; Very Rev. DANIEL J. MAXWELL.

Deans—Central: Very Rev. TODD UNGER. Eastern: Very Rev. STANISLAUS STRZYZ. Northern: Very Rev. CHARLES NNABUIFE. Southern: Rev. ROGATIAN URASSA. Western: VACANT.

Diocesan Offices and Directors

Board of Education—DENNIS DEMPSEY, Supt.; Very Rev. TODD UNGER; Revs. ROGER FERNANDO; JOSEPH LEVINE; JOSE THOMAS MUDAKODIYIL, Principals of Schools and Representatives from each Parish School Board.

Building Committee—Most Rev. LIAM S. CARY; HOPE BURKE; Very Rev. RICHARD O. FISCHER.

Campus Ministry Apostolate—VACANT.

Catholic Services—VACANT.

Church Property, Administration of—HOPE BURKE.

Diocesan Attorney—MR. GREGORY LYNCH.

Diocesan Development Office—641 S.W. Umatilla Ave., Redmond, 97756. Tel: 541-388-4004. HOPE BURKE.

Diocesan Finance Minister—HOPE BURKE.

Diocesan Financial Board—Most Rev. LIAM S. CARY; HOPE BURKE; GARY THOMPSON; RICHARD GRALL; HAROLD CALDWELL; Very Rev. RICHARD O. FISCHER; TOM MACDONALD.

Diocesan Superintendent of Schools—641 S.W. Umatilla Ave., Redmond, 97756. Tel: 541-388-4004 ; Fax: 541-388-2566. DENNIS DEMPSEY.

Director of Campaign for Human Development—VACANT.

Director of Catholic Hospitals—641 S.W. Umatilla Ave., Redmond, 97756. Very Rev. RICHARD O. FISCHER.

Friends of the Catholic University of America—VACANT.

Health and Retirement Board—Most Rev. LIAM S. CARY; Very Revs. TODD UNGER, Sec. & Treas.; ROBERT GREINER; LUIS M. FLORES-ALVA; Rev. ROGATIAN URASSA; Very Rev. STANISLAUS STRZYZ.

Office of Worship and Spirituality—VACANT.

Natural Family Planning—641 S.W. Umatilla Ave., Redmond, 97756. Tel: 541-388-4004. VACANT.

Director of Youth Ministry—641 S.W. Umatilla Ave., Redmond, 97756. Tel: 541-388-4004. VACANT.

Director of Religious Education—641 S.W. Umatilla Ave., Redmond, 97756. Tel: 541-388-4004. VACANT.

Director of Evangelization and Catechesis—JOSH SCHAAN.

Priests' Continuing Education Committee—VACANT.

R.C.I.A. Office—641 S.W. Umatilla Ave., Redmond, 97756. Tel: 541-388-4004.

Diocesan Scout Director—JANET SCHWARZ, 20980 Via Bonita, Bend, 97702. Tel: 541-388-4004.

Victim Assistance Coordinator—ANGELINA MONTOYA, Tel: 541-388-9271.

Vocation Director—P.O. Box 693, Hood River, 97031. Tel: 541-798-5823; Email: vocations@dioceseofbaker.org. Rev. TOMY CHOWARAN.

CLERGY, PARISHES, MISSIONS AND PAROCHIAL SCHOOLS

BAKER CITY

(COUNTY OF BAKER), CATHEDRAL OF ST. FRANCIS DE SALES St. Francis de Sales Cathedral (1871) [CEM] Rev. Suresh Telagani.

Res.: 2235 First St., Baker City, 97814.

Tel: 541-523-4521; Email: office@sfdsc.org; Web: www.saintfranciscathedral.com.

Catechesis Religious Program—Email: ann.kniesel@sfdsc.org. Ann Kniesel, D.R.E. Students 28.

Missions—St. Therese—135 W Bell St., Halfway, Baker Co. 97834. Tel: 541-742-4488; Email: yvoriggs@pinetel.com. Yvonne Riggs, Contact Person.

St. Anthony, 500 E. St., North Powder, Union Co. 97867. Tel: 541-856-3475; Email: jaro@eoni.com. Jackie Fritz, Contact Person.

OUTSIDE BAKER CITY

ARLINGTON, GILLIAM CO., ST. FRANCIS
Main & Ivy, Arlington, 97812. Tel: 541-384-5271; Email: stjohncondon@gmail.com; Web: stjohncondon.org. P.O. Box 485, Condon, 97823. Very Rev. Robert Greiner.

BEND, DESCHUTES CO., ST. FRANCIS OF ASSISI (1904) Revs. Jose Thomas Mudakodiyil, Email: frjosethomasm@gmail.com; Victor Mena Martinez, Parochial Vicar.

Office—Office: 2450 NE 27th St., Bend, 97701. Tel: 541-382-3631; Fax: 541-385-8879; Email: adminasst@stfrancisbend.org; Web: www.stfrancisbend.org.

School—St. Francis of Assisi School, (Grades PreK-8), Tel: 541-382-4701. Crystal Nunez-Mooney, Prin. Clergy 1; Lay Teachers 18; Students 143; Clergy / Religious Teachers 2.

Catechesis Religious Program—Email: faithformation@stfrancisbend.org. Janet Schwarz, D.R.E. Students 336.

BOARDMAN, MORROW CO., OUR LADY OF GUADALUPE
Mailing Address: 78922 Olson Rd., Boardman, 97818. Tel: 541-481-2024; Email: guadalupeboardman@gmail.com. P.O. Box 1277, Boardman, 97818. Very Rev. Luis M. Flores-Alva.

Catechesis Religious Program—Students 260.

BURNS, HARNEY CO., HOLY FAMILY (1899)
678 N. Egan, Burns, 97720. Tel: 541-573-2613; Email: jmjparish@centurylink.net. Very Rev. Stanislaus Strzyz.
Res.: 685 N. Fairview Ave., Burns, 97720.

Catechesis Religious Program—620 N. Egan St., Burns, 97720. Andrea Nichols, D.R.E. Students 71.

Missions—Our Lady of Loretto—78884 Drewsey Rd., Drewsey, 97904.

St. Thomas, 64302 Main Ave., Crane, Harney Co. 97732.

St. Charles, 5232 Hwy 20, Juntura, Malheur Co. 97911.

CHILOQUIN, KLAMATH CO., OUR LADY OF MT. CARMEL (1926)
P.O. Box 396, Chiloquin, 97624. Rev. Stephen Abraham Manthuruthil, S.D.B.
Res.: 503 W. Chocktoot St., Chiloquin, 97624. Tel: 541-783-2411; Email: catholicrect037@centurytel.net.

Catechesis Religious Program—Danette Hood, D.R.E.

Mission—St. James the Apostle, 61000 Hwy. 140 E., Bly, Klamath Co. 97622.

CONDON, GILLIAM CO., ST. JOHN (1925)
Mailing Address: P.O. Box 485, Condon, 97823. Very Rev. Robert Greiner, Admin.
Res.: 412 W. Walnut St., Condon, 97823.
Tel: 541-384-5271; Email: stjohncondon@gmail.com; Web: stjohncondon.org.

Catechesis Religious Program—Tel: 541-384-5003; Email: threecrossesquilting@gmail.com. Judy Thomsen, D.R.E. Students 12.

Mission—St. Catherine, 675 Washington St., Fossil, 97823.

DUFUR, WASCO CO., ST. ALPHONSUS (1911)
P.O. Box 395, Dufur, 97021. Rev. Fabian Nwokorie, (Nigeria).
Res.: 425 N.E. Second St., Dufur, 97021.
Tel: 541-467-2580; Email: stalphonsuscc@ortelco.net.

Catechesis Religious Program—

Mission—St. Mary, Rev. Fabian Nwokorie, (Nigeria).

ELGIN, UNION CO., ST. MARY (1966)
92 S. 12th, Elgin, 97827. Tel: 541-437-8101; Email: garlitzj@eoni.com. P.O. Box 97, Elgin, 97827. Rev. Saji K. Thomas.

Catechesis Religious Program—Mrs. Nancy Wheeling, D.R.E. Students 14.

ENTERPRISE, WALLOWA CO., ST. KATHERINE'S (1923)
P.O. Box 370, Enterprise, 97828. Rev. Thomas Puduppulliparamban, Admin.
Res.: 301 E. Garfield St., Enterprise, 97828.
Tel: 541-426-4008; Tel: 541-426-3043; Email: stkatherineenterprise@gmail.com; Web: www.stkatherineenterprise.org.

Catechesis Religious Program—Sye Barcik, D.R.E. Students 30.

Mission—St. Pius X, 407 S. Pine St., Wallowa, Wallowa Co. 97885.

HEPPNER, MORROW CO., ST. PATRICK'S (1887)
525 Gale St., Heppner, 97836. P.O. Box 633, Heppner, 97836. Rev. Papa Rao Pasala.

Catechesis Religious Program—Kathy Cutsforth, D.R.E.; Launa Woods, Youth Min. Students 50.

HERMISTON, UMATILLA CO., OUR LADY OF ANGELS (1910) Very Rev. Daniel J. Maxwell; Rev. Eduardo Nebelung, (Argentina); Deacon Jesus Esparaza; Kay Edwards, Administrative Asst.
Res.: 565 Hermiston Ave., Hermiston, 97838.
Tel: 541-567-5812; Fax: 541-564-0933; Email: kay@ourladyofangelscc.org; Email: chuchy@ourladyofangelscc.org; Web: www.ourladyofangelscc.org.

Catechesis Religious Program—Tel: 541-567-3825. Bonifacio Banuelos, D.R.E. Students 315.

HOOD RIVER, HOOD RIVER CO., IMMACULATE CONCEPTION St Mary's Catholic Church (1906) [CEM] Rev. Tomy Chowaran.
Res.: 1501 Belmont Ave., P.O. Box 693, Hood River, 97031. Tel: 541-386-3373; Fax: 541-386-1451; Email: stmaryshroffice@gmail.com.

Catechesis Religious Program—Tel: 541-387-6797; Email: youthmin14@hotmail.com. Patricia Romero, Youth Min. Students 120.

IONE, MORROW CO., ST. WILLIAM
110 Main St., Ione, 97843. Tel: 541-676-9462. P.O. Box 633, Heppner, 97836. Rev. Papa Rao Pasala.

Catechesis Religious Program—Jeri McElligott, D.R.E. Students 41.

JOHN DAY, GRANT CO., SAINT ELIZABETH OF HUNGARY CATHOLIC CHURCH (1939) Rev. Christie Tissera.
Res.: 111 S.W. 2nd Ave., P.O. Box 189, John Day, 97845. Tel: 541-575-1459; Fax: 541-575-5548; Email: saintelizabethcc@centurylink.com.

Catechesis Religious Program—Tel: 541-575-0415.

Mission—St. Anne.

JORDAN VALLEY, MALHEUR CO., ST. BERNARD (1915)
208 Yturri Blvd., Jordan Valley, 97910. Very Rev. Bailey Clemens.
Res.: P.O. Box 186, Jordan Valley, 97910.
Tel: 541-586-2266; Fax: 541-586-2448; Web: www.stbernardsjordanvalley.com.

Catechesis Religious Program—Students 21.

Mission—Holy Family, 3520 Arock Rd., Arock, Malheur Co. 97902.

KLAMATH FALLS, KLAMATH CO.

1—ST. PIUS X (1957) [CEM] Revs. Shiju Thuruthiyil, (India); Ildefonce Mapara, O.S.B., (Tanzania) In Res.
Res.: 4880 Bristol Ave., Klamath Falls, 97603.
Tel: 541-884-4242; Fax: 541-885-8724; Email: office@piusxkf.com; Web: www.piusxkf.com.

Catechesis Religious Program—Tel: 541-882-7593; Fax: 541-882-7593. Mr. Charles Catterall, D.R.E. Students 133.

2—SACRED HEART (1904) Rev. Rogatian Urassa; Mr. Matthew Hoffman, Music Min.; Mrs. Sharla Bishop, Pastoral Assoc.
Res.: 815 High St., Klamath Falls, 97601.
Tel: 541-884-4566; Email: paul@sacredheartkf.org; Email: rsafari@sacredheartkf.org; Email: sharla@sacredheartkf.org; Web: www.sacredheartkf.org.

Catechesis Religious Program—Email: paul@sacredheartkf.org. Paul Chutikorn, D.R.E. Students 86.

LA GRANDE, UNION CO., OUR LADY OF THE VALLEY (1914) (Under the title of the Immaculate Conception) Rev. Saji K. Thomas.

Parish Office—1002 L Ave., La Grande, 97850.
Tel: 541-963-7341; Fax: 541-963-0006; Email: info@olvcatholic.org; Web: www.olvcatholic.org.
Res.: 1101 4th St., La Grande, 97850.

Catechesis Religious Program—Tel: 541-763-7341; Email: avillagomez@olvcatholic.org. Amanda Villagomez, D.R.E. Students 59.

LA PINE, DESCHUTES CO., HOLY REDEEMER (1983) Rev. Paul Antao; Mrs. Heather Meeuwsen, Finance Mgr.; LorriAnn Landles, Youth Group Coord.; Mrs. Donna Pigman, Sec.
Res.: 16137 Burgess Rd., P.O. Box 299, La Pine, 97739. Tel: 541-536-3571; Fax: 541-536-5647; Email: holyrdmr@msn.com.

Catechesis Religious Program—Tel: 541-536-1992; Email: dre@bendbroadband.com. Mary Scarlato, D.R.E. Students 20.

Missions—Our Lady of the Snows—120 Mississippi Dr., Gilchrist, 97737. Mrs. Donna Pigman, Contact Person.

Holy Family, 57255 Fort Rock Rd., Fort Rock, 97735. Mrs. Donna Pigman, Sec.

Holy Trinity, 18143 Cottonwood Rd., Sunriver, 97707. Tel: 541-593-5990.

LAKEVIEW, LAKE CO., ST. PATRICK CATHOLIC CHURCH OF LAKEVIEW, INC. St. Patrick Church (1912)
12 North G St., P.O. Box 29, Lakeview, 97630.
Tel: 541-947-2741; Email: saintpatrick1911@outlook.com; Web: www.stpatricklakeview.com. Rev. Thomas Philip, Admin.
Res.: 163 S. G St., P.O. Box 29, Lakeview, 97630.

Catechesis Religious Program—185 S. G St., P.O. Box 29, Lakeview, 97630. Tel: 541-947-2820; Email: carlaalbertson50@gmail.com. Carla Albertson, D.R.E. Students 10.

Missions—St. Richard Catholic Church of Adel, Inc.—17570 20 Mile Rd., Adel, Lake Co. 97620. Suzanne Steward, Contact Person.

St. Thomas Catholic Church of Plush, 28163 Plush Ave., Plush, Lake Co. 97637. Suzanne Steward, Contact Person.

St. John Catholic Church of Paisley, Inc., 1115 Main St., Paisley, Lake Co. 97636. Suzanne Steward, Contact Person.

MADRAS, JEFFERSON CO., ST. PATRICK (1955) Very Rev. Richard O. Fischer.
Res.: 341 S.W. J St., Madras, 97741.
Tel: 541-475-2936; Fax: 541-475-0539; Email: office@stpatmadras.com.

Catechesis Religious Program—Tel: 541-325-7346; Email: ym@stpatmadras.com. Alma Alonso, D.R.E. Students 235.

Mission—St. Kateri Tekakwitha, 4190 Hwy. 26, Warm Springs, 97761. Very Rev. Richard O. Fischer, Contact Person. (Indian Reservation).

MERRILL, KLAMATH CO., ST. AUGUSTINE (1939)
P.O. Box 340, Merrill, 97633. Rev. Francis Obijekwu, S.M.M.M., (Nigeria)

St. Augustine Catholic Church of Merrill, Inc.
Res.: 905 E. Front St., Merrill, 97633.
Tel: 541-798-5823; Email: staugustine@fireserve.net.

Catechesis Religious Program—Tel: 541-892-3946; Email: chichemama@msn.com. Cynthia R. Cowan-Taylor, D.R.E. Students 110.

Mission—St. Frances Cabrini, 31400 Hwy 70, Bonanza, 97623.

MILTON FREEWATER, UMATILLA CO., ST. FRANCIS OF ASSISI (1940)
925 Vining St., Milton Freewater, 97862.
Tel: 541-938-5436; Fax: 541-938-3536; Email: stfrancismfw@gmail.com. Rev. Charles Chika Nnabuife.

Catechesis Religious Program—Martha Jimenez, D.R.E. Students 167.

NYSSA, MALHEUR CO., ST. BRIDGET OF KILDARE (1951) Rev. Anish Philip.
Res.: 504 Locust Ave., Nyssa, 97913-3235.
Tel: 541-372-3133; Fax: 541-372-5620; Email: st.bridgetofkildare@yahoo.com.

Catechesis Religious Program—Ms. Mary Clark, D.R.E. Students 139.

ONTARIO, MALHEUR CO., BLESSED SACRAMENT (1911) Rev. Roger Fernando.

Office—Office: 829 S.W. Second Ave., Ontario, 97914-2695. Tel: 541-889-8469; Fax: 541-889-8483; Email: ontario.blessedsacrament@gmail.com; Web: www.blessedsacramentontario.org.

School—Saint Peter, (Grades PreK-6), 98 S.W. Ninth St., Ontario, 97914. Tel: 541-889-7363; Fax: 541-889-2852; Email: hernandez@stpetercatholicschool.com; Web: www.stpetercatholicschool.com. Armida Hernandez, Prin. Lay Teachers 5; Religious 1; Students 64; Clergy / Religious Teachers 1.

Catechesis Religious Program—Tel: 541-889-8404. Angelica Corona, D.R.E. Students 270.

PENDLETON, UMATILLA CO.

1—ST. ANDREW'S INDIAN MISSION (1847) [CEM] Rev. Michael J. Fitzpatrick, S.J.
Res.: 48022 St. Andrews Rd., Pendleton, 97801.
Tel: 541-276-6155; Fax: 541-276-0767; Email: standrews676@gmail.com.

Catechesis Religious Program—Tel: 541-276-0767; Email: fernoliver47@gmail.com. Fern Oliver, D.R.E. Students 20.

Mission—Sacred Heart, P.O. Box 665, Athena, 97813.

2—ST. MARY (1902) [CEM] Rev. Kumar Udagandla; Deacon Martin Omar Tores.
Res.: 800 S.E. Court Ave., Pendleton, 97801.
Tel: 541-276-3615; Fax: 541-276-7484; Email: stmary@eoni.com.

Catechesis Religious Program—Tel: 541-276-6163. Shirley Baker, C.R.E. Students 82.

PILOT ROCK, UMATILLA CO., ST. HELEN (1930)
740 S.W. Birch St., Pilot Rock, 97868.
Tel: 541-443-3151; Email: byrneslaura@yahoo.com. P.O. Box V, Pilot Rock, 97868. Rev. Kumar Udagandla.

Catechesis Religious Program—

PRINEVILLE, CROOK CO., ST. JOSEPH (1943) Rev. Joseph T. Kunnelaya.
Res.: 150 E. First, P.O. Box 1315, Prineville, 97754.
Tel: 541-447-6475; Fax: 541-416-9141; Email: stjosephparish@bendbroadband.com; Web: stjosephsparish.org.

Catechesis Religious Program—200 E. First St., P.O. Box 721, Prineville, 97754. Barbara Dalton, D.R.E. Students 60.

REDMOND, DESCHUTES CO., ST. THOMAS (1941) Very Rev. Todd Unger

Legal Title: Saint Thomas Catholic Church of Redmond, Inc
Res.: 1720 N.W. 19th, 97756. Tel: 541-923-3390; Fax: 541-548-6630; Email:

fathertodd@stthomasredmond.com; Web: www.stthomasredmond.com.
School—St. Thomas Academy, (Grades PreSchool-5), 1720 N.W. 19th, 97756. Tel: 541-548-3785; Email: admin@redmondacademy.com; Web: www.redmondacademy.com. Patty Schulte, Prin. Clergy 1; Lay Teachers 8; Students 96; Clergy / Religious Teachers 1.
Catechesis Religious Program—Tel: 541-923-0597; Email: stthomasministry@gmail.com. Noel Roy, D.R.E. & Youth Min. Students 142.

SISTERS, DESCHUTES CO., ST. EDWARD THE MARTYR (1984)
P.O. Box 489, Sisters, 97759-0489. Rev. Joseph Thomas.
Res.: 123 Trinity Way, Sisters, 97759.
Tel: 541-549-0751; Tel: 541-549-9391; Email: stedward@bendbroadband.com.
Catechesis Religious Program—Tania Robolledo, C.R.E. Students 48.

THE DALLES, WASCO CO., ST. PETER (1848) [CEM]
P.O. Box 41, The Dalles, 97058. Rev. Joseph Levine; Ms. Maria Ledezma, Business Mgr.; Mr. Rod Ontiveros, Cemetary Sexton; Mrs. Taunia Canchola, Sec.; Deacon Ireneo Ledezma.
Res.: 1222 W. 10th St., The Dalles, 97058.
Tel: 541-296-2026; Fax: 541-296-5835; Email: staff@stpeterstd.org; Email: parishsecretary@stpeterstd.org; Web: stpeterstd.org.
School—St. Mary's Academy, (Grades PreK-8), 1112 Cherry Heights Rd., The Dalles, 97058.
Tel: 541-296-6004; Fax: 541-296-7858; Email: office@smatd.org; Web: www.smatd.org. Kim Koch, Prin. Lay Teachers 17; Students 199; Clergy / Religious Teachers 1.
Catechesis Religious Program—1222 W 10th St, The Dalles, 97058. Email: dre@stpeterstd.org. Mrs. Jamie Bailey, D.R.E. Students 135.

UNION, UNION CO., SACRED HEART (1905)
340 S. 10th St., P.O. Box 473, Union, 97883.
Tel: 541-562-5486; Email: sacred.heart.cc@gmail.com. Rev. Saji K. Thomas.
Catechesis Religious Program—

VALE, MALHEUR CO., ST. PATRICK (1946)
P.O. Box J, Vale, 97918. Rev. Camillus Fernando, (Sri Lanka).
Res.: 690 A St. W., Vale, 97918. Tel: 541-473-3906; Fax: 541-473-2010; Email: camifatima@yahoo.com.
Catechesis Religious Program—Tel: 541-473-3848. Susan Seals, D.R.E. Students 38.
Mission—St. Joseph.

WASCO, MALHEUR CO., ST. MARY (1954)
P.O. Box 14, Wasco, 97065. Rev. Fabian Nwokorie, (Nigeria).
Res.: 807 Barnett St., Wasco, 97065.
Tel: 541-442-8560; Fax: 541-442-8569; Email: stmarywasco@embarqmail.com.
Catechesis Religious Program—Tel: 541-473-3906. Molly Belshe, D.R.E.; Cindy Brown, Youth Min.
Mission—St. John the Baptist.

Military Services:
Rev.—
Colvin, Andrew, CHC, USN, Naval Base Guam Chapel, PSC 455, Box 159, FPO, AP 96540-1011.

Retired:
Very Rev.—
Maag, Ronald E., P.O. Box 1801, Hood River, 97031
Revs.—
Albrecht, Louis Henry, (Retired), 84-05 Makau St., Waianae, HI 96792-1823. Tel: 541-786-3835
Bower, Lawrence C., (Retired), 215 Woodward Blvd., Summerville, SC 29483. Tel: 843-815-1285
Condon, Gerald W., (Retired), P.O. Box 822, Heppner, 97836
Dreisbach, Charles V., (Retired), 230 Newcastle, Klamath Falls, 97601. Tel: 541-882-6016
Fisher, A. J., (Retired), 1200 W. Dimond #14105, Anchorage, AK 99515
Hickie, Noel, (Retired), 1305 Willagillespie Rd., Eugene, 97401
Homes, Dennis, (Retired), 2300 Central Ave., N., Great Falls, MT 59401. Tel: 406-564-3697
Hopp, Raymond, (Retired), 1800 N. 4th St. #28, Lakeview, 97630
Kiely, Cornelius, (Retired), Co. Cork, Ireland
Reeves, Joseph, (Retired), 2610 SW. 23rd, Apt. 21, 97756. Tel: 503-260-4381.

INSTITUTIONS LOCATED IN DIOCESE

[A] GENERAL HOSPITALS

BAKER CITY. *Saint Alphonsus Medical Center - Baker City, Inc.*, 3325 Pocahontas Rd., Baker City, 97814. Tel: 541-523-6461 (Hospital); Fax: 541-523-8151. Phil Harrop, Pres. Bed Capacity 25; Tot Asst. Annually 49,508; Staff 184.

HOOD RIVER. *Providence Hood River Memorial Hospital*, 810 12th St., Hood River, 97031. Tel: 541-386-3911; Fax: 541-387-6462; Email: mark.thomas@providence.org; Web: www.providence.org. 4400 N.E. Halsey St., Bldg. 2-Ste. 595, Portland, 97213. Jeanie Vieira, R.N., Exec.; Mark Thomas, Dir. Providence St. Joseph Health Bed Capacity 25; Tot Asst. Annually 96,601; Total Staff 550.

ONTARIO. *Saint Alphonsus Medical Center - Ontario, Inc.*, 351 S.W. Ninth St., Ontario, 97914. Tel: 541-881-7000; Fax: 541-881-7184; Web: www.saintalphonsus.org/ontario. Mr. Kenneth Hart, Pres. Bed Capacity 49; Tot Asst. Annually 70,620; Total Staff 467.

PENDLETON. *St. Anthony Hospital*, 2801 St. Anthony Way, Pendleton, 97801. Tel: 541-276-5121; Fax: 541-278-3671; Email: vonnismonton@chiwest.com; Web: www.sahpendleton.org. Harold Geller, Pres. Bed Capacity 25; Sisters of St. Francis of Philadelphia 1; Tot Asst. Annually 1,314,082; Total Staff 366.

[B] MONASTERIES AND RESIDENCES FOR PRIESTS AND BROTHERS

GILCHRIST. *Monastery of Annunciation Hermitage* (1983) 146640 Hwy. 97 N., Gilchrist, 97737. P.O. Box 250, Crescent, 97733-0250. Rev. Arsenius Anachoreta, Hieromonk. Clergy 1; Solemnly Professed 1.

[C] CONVENTS

BEND. *Sisters of Mary of Kakamega*, 2863 N.E. Jill Ave., Bend, 97701. Tel: 541-588-2416; Email: sabinambenge16@gmail.com; Web: www.somkakamega.org. Sr. Sabina Mbenge, Rel. Order Leader. Sisters 400; Professed Sisters 15.

[D] MISCELLANEOUS

BEND. *Baker Diocese Vocations Committee*, 641 S.W. Umatilla Ave., 97756. Tel: 541-388-4004; Email: patti@dioceseofbaker.org. Patti Rausch, Sec.
The Health and Retirement Association of the Diocese of Baker, Oregon, 641 S.W. Umatilla Ave., 97756. Tel: 541-388-4004; Fax: 541-388-2566; Email: fathertodd@stthomasredmond.com. Very Rev. Todd Unger, Plan Admin.
The Legacy of Faith Catholic Community Foundation of Oregon, 641 S.W. Umatilla Ave., 97756. Tel: 541-388-4004; Fax: 541-388-2566. Mark French, Exec.

HOOD RIVER. *Providence Brookside Manor*, 1550 Brookside Dr., Hood River, 97031. Tel: 541-387-6370; Fax: 541-387-8272; Email: jamie.hanshaw@providence.org. Ms. Jamie Henshaw, Exec.
Providence Dethman Manor, 1205 Montello St., Hood River, 97031. Tel: 541-386-8278; Fax: 541-387-8279; Email: shannan.stickler@providence.org. Shannan Stickler, Dir.
Providence Down Manor, 1950 Sterling Pl., Hood River, 97031. Tel: 541-387-8290; Fax: 541-386-2456; Email: jamie.hanshaw@providence.org. Ms. Jamie Henshaw, Dir,.
Providence Hood River Memorial Hospital Foundation, 810 12th St., P.O. Box 149, Hood River, 97031. Tel: 541-387-6342; Fax: 541-387-6462; Email: laurie.kelley@providence.org. Susan Frost, Dir.

KLAMATH FALLS. *St. Maurus Hanga Abbey*, 4880 Bristol Ave., Klamath Falls, 97603. Fax: 541-885-8724; Email: hangawater@gmail.com; Web: hangaabbey.org. Rev. Ildefonce Mapara, O.S.B., (Tanzania) Dir.

SUNRIVER. *Holy Trinity Community Outreach Care and Share*, 18160 Cottonwood Rd., P.M.B. 501, Sunriver, 97707. Tel: 541-593-5990; Email: holyrdmr@msn.com. Ms. Madeline Bednarek, Coord. of Care & Share.

RELIGIOUS INSTITUTES OF MEN REPRESENTED IN THE DIOCESE

For further details refer to the corresponding bracketed number in the Religious Institutes of Men or Women section.

[0690]—*Jesuit Fathers and Brothers* (Oregon Prov.)—S.J.
[]—*St. Maurus Hanga Abbey, O.S.B.*
[]—*Oblates of Sacred Heart*.

RELIGIOUS INSTITUTES OF WOMEN REPRESENTED IN THE DIOCESE

[2470]—*Maryknoll Sisters of St. Dominic*—M.M.
[]—*Salesian Sisters of St. John Bosco*.
[]—*Sisters of Mary of Kakamega*.
[1650]—*Sisters of St. Francis of Philadelphia*—O.S.F.

NECROLOGY

† Jasper, John, (Retired), Died Jan. 9, 2018

An asterisk (*) denotes an organization that has established tax-exempt status directly with the IRS and is not covered by the USCCB Group Ruling.

Archdiocese of Baltimore

(Archidioecesis Baltimorensis)

His Eminence

EDWIN CARDINAL O'BRIEN, S.T.D., D.D.

Grand Master, Equestrian Order of the Holy Sepulcher of Jerusalem, Archbishop Emeritus of Baltimore; ordained May 29, 1965; appointed Auxiliary Bishop of New York February 6, 1996; Episcopal Ordination March 25, 1996; appointed Coadjutor Archbishop for the Military Services April 8, 1997; acceded as Archbishop August 12, 1997; appointed Archbishop of Baltimore July 12, 2007; installed Fifteenth Archbishop of Baltimore October 1, 2007; appointed Grand Master of the Equestrian Order of the Holy Sepulchre of Jerusalem and Archbishop Emeritus of Baltimore August 29, 2011; elevated to College of Cardinals February 18, 2012. *Office: Equestrian Order of the Holy Sepulchre of Jerusalem, 00120.*

Most Reverend

DENIS J. MADDEN

Retired Auxiliary Bishop of Baltimore; ordained April 1, 1967; appointed Auxiliary Bishop of Baltimore and Titular Bishop of Baia May 10, 2005; ordained August 24, 2005; retired December 5, 2016. *320 Cathedral St., Baltimore, MD 21201.* Tel: 410-547-5452.

Most Reverend

WILLIAM E. LORI, S.T.D.

Archbishop of Baltimore; ordained May 14, 1977; appointed Titular Bishop of Bulla and Auxiliary Bishop of Washington April 20, 1995; appointed Bishop of Bridgeport January 23, 2001; installed March 19, 2001; appointed Archbishop of Baltimore March 20, 2012; installed as sixteenth Archbishop of Baltimore May 16, 2012. *320 Cathedral St., Baltimore, MD 21201.* Tel: 410-547-5437.

Chancery Office: 320 Cathedral St., Baltimore, MD 21201. Tel: 410-547-5446; Fax: 410-727-8234.

Web: www.archbalt.org

Email: chancery@archbalt.org

Most Reverend

MARK E. BRENNAN

Auxiliary Bishop of Baltimore; ordained May 15, 1976; appointed Titular Bishop of Rusibisir and Auxiliary Bishop of Baltimore December 5, 2016; installed January 19, 2017. *Office: 320 Cathedral St., Baltimore, MD 21201.*

Most Reverend

ADAM J. PARKER

Auxiliary Bishop of Baltimore; ordained May 27, 2000; appointed Titular Bishop of Tasaccora and Auxiliary Bishop of Baltimore December 5, 2016; installed January 19, 2017. *Office: 320 Cathedral St., Baltimore, MD 21201.*

Square Miles 4,801.

Established a Diocese November 6, 1789; Established an Archdiocese April 8, 1808.

Comprises the City of Baltimore and Allegany, Anne Arundel, Baltimore, Carroll, Frederick, Garrett, Harford, Howard and Washington Counties.

By a Decree of the Sacred Congregation of the Propaganda, July 19, 1858, approved by His Holiness, Pius IX, July 25, 1858, "Prerogative of Place" was conferred on the Archdiocese of Baltimore. By the explicit words of said decree of the Holy See, the Archbishop of Baltimore takes precedence over all Archbishops of the United States (not Cardinals) in Councils, gatherings and meetings of whatever kind of the Hierarchy (in concillis, coetibus et comitiis quibuscumque) regardless of the seniority of other Archbishops in promotion or ordination. Decree signed by Cardinal Barnabo, August 15, 1858.

For legal titles of parishes and archdiocesan institutions, consult the Chancery Office.

STATISTICAL OVERVIEW

Personnel	
Archbishops	1
Auxiliary Bishops	2
Retired Bishops	1
Priests: Diocesan Active in Diocese	133
Priests: Diocesan Active Outside Diocese	10
Priests: Retired, Sick or Absent	61
Number of Diocesan Priests	204
Religious Priests in Diocese	290
Total Priests in Diocese	494
Extern Priests in Diocese	71
Ordinations:	
Diocesan Priests	4
Transitional Deacons	4
Permanent Deacons	1
Permanent Deacons in Diocese	181
Total Brothers	28
Total Sisters	614
Parishes	
Parishes	139
With Resident Pastor:	
Resident Diocesan Priests	81
Resident Religious Priests	26
Without Resident Pastor:	
Administered by Priests	32
Administered by Deacons	1
Missions	7
Closed Parishes	3
Professional Ministry Personnel:	
Brothers	1
Sisters	23
Lay Ministers	276
Welfare	
Catholic Hospitals	5
Total Assisted	1,785,488
Health Care Centers	5
Total Assisted	3,358
Homes for the Aged	24
Total Assisted	6,896
Residential Care of Children	5
Total Assisted	1,125
Day Care Centers	6
Total Assisted	1,280
Specialized Homes	8
Total Assisted	2,231
Special Centers for Social Services	28
Total Assisted	534,126
Residential Care of Disabled	1
Total Assisted	228
Other Institutions	1
Total Assisted	7,852
Educational	
Seminaries, Diocesan	2
Students from This Diocese	39
Students from Other Diocese	276
Diocesan Students in Other Seminaries	6
Total Seminarians	45
Colleges and Universities	4
Total Students	10,706
High Schools, Diocesan and Parish	6
Total Students	2,798
High Schools, Private	13
Total Students	6,382
Elementary Schools, Diocesan and Parish	39
Total Students	13,697
Elementary Schools, Private	7
Total Students	1,295
Non-residential Schools for the Disabled	1
Total Students	130
Catechesis/Religious Education:	
High School Students	4,250
Elementary Students	23,401
Total Students under Catholic Instruction	62,704
Teachers in the Diocese:	
Priests	33
Brothers	34
Sisters	38
Lay Teachers	4,145
Vital Statistics	
Receptions into the Church:	
Infant Baptism Totals	4,969
Adult Baptism Totals	445
Received into Full Communion	593
First Communions	4,859
Confirmations	3,701
Marriages:	
Catholic	892
Interfaith	300
Total Marriages	1,192
Deaths	3,759
Total Catholic Population	501,174
Total Population	3,261,853

Former Archbishops—Most Revs. JOHN CARROLL, D.D., cons. Aug. 15, 1790; Archbishop, April 8, 1808; died Dec. 3, 1815; LEONARD NEALE, D.D., cons. Coadjutor, Dec. 7, 1800; acceded to the See of Baltimore Dec. 3, 1815; died June 18, 1817; AMBROSE MARECHAL, S.S., D.D., cons. Dec. 14, 1817; died Jan. 29, 1828; JAMES WHITFIELD, D.D., cons. May 25, 1828; died Oct. 19, 1834; SAMUEL ECCLESTON, S.S., D.D., cons. Sept. 14, 1834; died April 22, 1851; FRANCIS PATRICK KENRICK, D.D., cons. June 6, 1830; Coadjutor Bishop of Philadelphia; promoted to the See of Baltimore Aug. 19, 1851; died July 8, 1863; MARTIN JOHN SPALDING, D.D., cons. Sept. 10, 1848; Coadjutor Bishop of Louisville; promoted to the See of Baltimore May 6, 1864; died Feb. 7, 1872; JAMES ROOSEVELT BAYLEY, D.D., cons. Oct. 30, 1853; Bishop of Newark; promoted to the See of Baltimore July 30, 1872; died Oct. 3, 1877; His Eminence JAMES CARDINAL GIBBONS, D.D., cons. Vicar Apostolic of North Carolina, Aug. 16, 1868; transferred to See of Richmond, July 30, 1872; promoted to the See of Baltimore, Oct. 3, 1877; created Cardinal Priest of S. Maria in Trastevere, June 7, 1886; died March 24, 1921; Most Revs. MICHAEL J. CURLEY, D.D., cons. Bishop of St. Augustine, June 30, 1914; promoted to the See of Baltimore Aug. 10, 1921; died May 16, 1947; FRANCIS P. KEOUGH, D.D., cons. Bishop of Providence, May 22, 1934; promoted to the See of Baltimore Nov. 29, 1947; died Dec. 8, 1961; His Eminence LAWRENCE CARDINAL SHEHAN, cons. Auxiliary Bishop of Baltimore, Dec. 12, 1945; transferred to Diocese of Bridgeport, Aug. 25, 1953; appt. Coadjutor Archbishop of Baltimore, July 10, 1961; acceded to the See of Baltimore Dec. 8, 1961; created Cardinal Priest of S. Clemente, Feb. 22, 1965; retired March 25, 1974; died Aug. 26, 1984; Most Rev. WILLIAM DONALD BORDERS, D.D., appt. Bishop of Orlando, May 2, 1968; cons. June 14, 1968; promoted to the See of Baltimore March 25, 1974; installed June 26, 1974; retired April 6, 1989; died April 19, 2010.; His Eminence WILLIAM CARDINAL KEELER, ord. July 17, 1955; appt. Titular Bishop of Ulcinium and Auxiliary

Bishop of Harrisburg July 24, 1979; ord. Bishop Sept. 21, 1979; appt. Bishop of Harrisburg Nov. 10, 1983; installed Jan. 4, 1984; appt. Archbishop of Baltimore April 6, 1989; installed as Fourteenth Archbishop of Baltimore May 23, 1989; created Cardinal Priest & appt. Titular Church of Santa Maria degli Angeli Nov. 26, 1994; retired July 12, 2007; died March 23, 2017.; EDWIN F. O'BRIEN, ord. May 29, 1965; appt. Titular Bishop of Tizica and Auxiliary Bishop of New York Feb. 6, 1996; cons. March 25, 1996; appt. Coadjutor April 8, 1997; succeeded as Ordinary to the Military Services Aug. 12, 1997; appt. Archbishop of Baltimore July 12, 2007; installed as fifteenth Archbishop of Baltimore Oct. 1, 2007; appt. Grand Master of the Equestrian Order of the Holy Sepulchre of Jerusalem Aug. 29, 2011; elevated to Cardinal Deacon & appt. Titular Church of St. Sebastian on the Palatine Hill Feb. 18, 2012.

Vicars General—Rev. Msgr. JAMES W. HANNON, Vicar; Most Revs. DENIS J. MADDEN, D.D., V.G.; ADAM J. PARKER, D.D., V.G., Moderator of the Curia.

Office of the Archbishop—Most Rev. WILLIAM E. LORI, S.T.D., Tel: 410-547-5437; Fax: 410-727-8234; Email: archbishop@archbalt.org.

Priest Secretary to the Archbishop—Rev. LOUIS A. BIANCO, Tel: 410-547-5568; Email: lbianco@archbalt.org.

Office of the Cardinal Archbishop Emeritus, Edwin F. O'Brien—Equestrian Order of the Holy Sepulcher of Jerusalem, 00120 Vatican City State, Europe.

Office of the Eastern Vicariate—

Eastern Vicar—Most Rev. MARK E. BRENNAN, D.D., V.G., Tel: 410-547-5527; Email: mark.brennan@archbalt.org.

Pastoral Associate to the Eastern Vicar—MANUEL ALIAGA, M.P.A., Ph.D. Candidate, Tel: 410-547-3148; Email: manuel.aliaga@archbalt.org.

Office of the Western Vicariate—

Western Vicar—Rev. Msgr. JAMES W. HANNON, Tel: 410-547-5302; Email: jhannon@archbalt.org.

Pastoral Associate to the Western Vicar—DR. CHRISTOPHER J. YEUNG, Tel: 410-547-5456; Email: christopher.yeung@archbalt.org.

Office of the Urban Vicariate—

Urban Vicar—Most Rev. DENIS J. MADDEN, D.D., V.G., Tel: 410-547-5452; Email: uvicar@archbalt.org.

Pastoral Associate to the Urban Vicar—JULIE ST. CROIX, Tel: 410-547-5488; Fax: 410-727-5432; Email: julie.stcroix@archbalt.org.

Office of the Vicar General/Moderator of the Curia—Most Rev. ADAM J. PARKER, V.C., Moderator of the Curia, Tel: 410-547-5447; Fax: 410-727-5432; Email: aparker@archbalt.org.

Office of Pastoral Planning—DAPHNE DALY, Dir., Tel: 410-547-5545; Fax: 410-547-5432; Email: daphne.daly@archbalt.org.

Office of the Chancellor—DR. DIANE L. BARR, J.D., J.C.D., Ph.D., Chancellor, Tel: 410-547-5446; Fax: 410-727-8234.

Office of Child and Youth Protection—
Tel: 410-547-5599;
Tel: 866-417-7469 (Victim Assistance Hotline); Email: jburkhardt@archbalt.org. JERRI BURKHARDT, Dir.

Communications Office—SEAN T. CAINE, Dir. & Vice Chancellor, Tel: 410-547-5378; Fax: 410-625-8480; Email: scaine@archbalt.org.

Councils and Committees of the Archdiocese of Baltimore—

Consultors—Rev. Msgr. JAMES W. HANNON, Vicar; Most Rev. DENIS J. MADDEN, D.D., V.G.; Rev. Msgr. JAMES BARKER; Rev. GERARD C. FRANCIK; Rev. Msgr. RICHARD E. CRAMBLITT, V.F.; Rev. EDWARD S. HENDRICKS; Rev. Msgr. JOSEPH L. LUCA; Most Rev. ADAM J. PARKER, D.D., V.G.; Rev. JAMES PROFFITT; Rev. Msgr. RICHARD W. WOY; Rev. DONALD GRZYMSKI, O.F.M.Conv.; Most Rev. MARK E. BRENNAN, D.D., V.G.

Presbyteral Council—Most Rev. WILLIAM E. LORI, S.T.D., Chm.

Ex Officio—Most Revs. DENIS J. MADDEN, D.D., V.G.; ADAM J. PARKER, D.D., V.G.; MARK E. BRENNAN, D.D., V.G.; Rev. Msgr. JAMES W. HANNON, Vicar.

Elected Members—Revs. ERNEST W. CIBELLI; JEFF S. DAUSES; TIMOTHY DORE, O.F.M.Conv.; WILLIAM F. FRANKEN; EDWARD S. HENDRICKS; DONALD A. STERLING, D.Min.; JOHN A. WILLIAMSON; DONALD GRZYMSKI, O.F.M.Conv.; ERIK J. ARNOLD; RICHARD GRAY; JASON WORLEY; BRIAN M. RAFFERTY, S.T.L., (Retired).

Appointed Members—Rev. Msgr. JOSEPH L. LUCA; Revs. JUAN RUBIO; MICHAEL S. TRIPLETT, V.F.; Rev. Msgrs. RICHARD W. WOY; RICHARD B. HILGARTNER JR.; Rev. JAMES D. PROFFITT; Rev. Msgr. RICHARD E. CRAMBLITT, V.F.

Board of Financial Administration—Most Rev. WILLIAM E. LORI, S.T.D., Chm.; BRIAN ROGERS, Vice Chm.; Sr. HELEN AMOS, R.S.M.; JOHN BALCH; DR. DIANE L. BARR, J.D., J.C.D., Ph.D.; Most Rev. MARK E. BRENNAN, D.D., V.G.; Rev. Msgr. PAUL G. COOK, (Retired); BEVERLY A. COOPER; HUGH EVANS; GREG KELLY; DAVID KINKOPF; PATRICK MADDEN; MR. WILLIAM J. MCCARTHY JR.; STEPHEN MEANS; MR. DANIEL PALLACE; Most Rev. ADAM J. PARKER, D.D., V.G.; MS. KATHLEEN K. MAHAR; MS. BONNIE PHIPPS; Rev. Msgr. JAMES W. HANNON; MICHAEL J. RUCK SR.; LEONARD A. STROM; TYLER TATE; Most Rev. DENIS J. MADDEN, D.D., V.G.

Priest Personnel Board Members—Rev. Msgr. LLOYD AIKEN; Revs. FRANK J. BRAUER; JEFFREY S. DAUSES; MICHAEL FOPPIANO; Rev. Msgr. RICHARD B. HILGARTNER; Revs. CHRISTOPHER WHATLEY; CHRISTOPHER P. MOORE, (Retired); T. AUSTIN MURPHY JR.; Rev. Msgrs. KEVIN T. SCHENNING; RICHARD H. TILLMAN, (Retired).

Deacon Personnel Board Members—Deacons SCOTT R. LANCASTER; JAMES L. MANN; PAUL T. MANN; DAVID A. PAGE; MRS. KATHY A. PASSAUER; Deacons HARBEY SANTIAGO; GEORGE SISSON; JAMES R. SULLIVAN; MRS. KATHLEEN SULLIVAN.

Facilities and Real Estate Commission—MR. DANIEL PALLACE, Chm.

Lay Employees Retirement Board—RAYMOND BRUSCA, Chm.

Senior Priests' Retirement Board—Rev. JAMES PROFFITT, Chm.

Metropolitan Tribunal—Tel: 410-547-5533;
Fax: 410-576-6932; Email: tribunal@archbalt.org.

Judicial Vicar—Very Rev. GILBERT J. SEITZ, J.C.L., M.Div.

Adjutant Judicial Vicars—Revs. JOHN B. WARD, J.C.L., J.D.; WILLIAM GRAHAM, O.F.M.Cap., J.C.L., M.A.

Judges—Revs. MICHAEL J. CARRION; CHRISTOPHER P. MOORE, (Retired); Deacon ANTHONY NORCIO, J.C.L.

Defenders of the Bond—Revs. GONZALO CADAVID-RIVERA, J.C.L.; JOSE OPALDA, J.C.L.

Notaries—TERESA EWEN; KELSEY C. LACOUR; SUSAN A. SMITH.

Department of Catholic Schools - Office of the Superintendent—Tel: 410-547-5515. DR. DONNA HARGENS, Exec. Dir. & Supt. Catholic Schools.

Chancellor for Education—JAMES B. SELLINGER, Email: jim.sellinger@archbalt.org.

Department of Development—
Tel: 888-202-5113 (Toll Free); Tel: 410-547-5356; Fax: 410-625-8485; Email: giving@archbalt.org; Web: www.archbalt.org/giving. PATRICK MADDEN, Exec. Dir., Tel: 410-547-5381; Email: pmadden@archbalt.org.

Department of Evangelization - Office of the Executive Director—DR. JOHN ROMANOWSKY, Ph. D., Exec. Dir.

Division of Catechetical and Pastoral Formation—
Tel: 410-547-5470. VACANT.

Office of Hispanic Ministry—LIA R. SALINAS, Dir., Tel: 410-547-5363; Email: lia.salinas@archbalt.org.

Office of Marriage & Family Life—EDWARD P. HERRERA, Dir., Tel: 410-547-5420; Email: edward.herrera@archbalt.org.

Division of Youth and Young Adult Ministry—
Tel: 410-547-5372. CRAIG GOULD, Dir., Tel: 410-547-5371; Email: craig.gould@archbalt.org.

Division of Campus Ministry for Universities and Colleges—SARAH JARZEMBOWSKI, Coord., College Campus & Young Adult Ministries; VACANT, Coppin State Univ.; VACANT, Goucher College/Hood College; VACANT, University of Baltimore; Deacon WARDELL BARKSDALE, Morgan State Univ., Tel: 410-404-7133; Email: w.barksdale@morgan.edu; PAUL GALLAGHER, Campus Min., McDaniel College, Tel: 410-848-4744; Email: pgallagher@sjwest.org; Rev. GODSWILL AGBAGWA, Frostburg State Univ., Tel: 240-284-2079; Email: godswill.agbagwa@archbalt.org; Deacon JAMES M. NUZZO, Stevenson Univ., Tel: 410-984-3292; Email: jnuzzo2010@comcast.net; Revs. MATTHEW T. BUENING, Chap., Towson Univ., Tel: 410-828-0622; Email: mbuening@towson.edu; DOMINIC BUMP, O.P., Chap., Johns Hopkins Univ., Tel: 443-955-1993; HUGH VINCENT, O.P., Johns Hopkins Univ., Tel: 410-235-2294, Ext. 6; Email: hughiebro@yahoo.com; TESSLA BABCOCK, Univ. of Maryland Baltimore County, Tel: 443-938-1931; Email: tesslab1@umbc.edu.

Office of Divine Worship—JULIE GRACE MALES, Dir., Tel: 410-547-5403.

Office of Deaf Ministry—CHRIS M. DUCK, Coord., Tel: 410-547-5419; Email: chris.duck@archbalt.org.

Office of Special Needs Ministry—
Tel: 410-547-5410. VACANT, Dir.

Office of Prison Ministry—Deacon SEIGFRIED PRESBERRY, Dir., Tel: 410-547-5575; Fax: 410-347-7896; Email: spresberry@archbalt.org.

Office of Respect Life—Tel: 410-547-5537; Email: johanna.coughlin@archbalt.org. JOHANNA COUGHLIN, Dir.

Youth Retreat House, Monsignor O'Dwyer—15523 York Rd., P.O. Box 310, Sparks, 21152.
Tel: 410-472-2400; Tel: 410-666-2400;
Fax: 410-472-3281; Email: odwyer@archbalt.org. MICHAEL DOWNES, Dir., Email: michael.downes@archbalt.org.

Department of Management Services - Office of the Executive Director—Tel: 410-547-5322;
Fax: 410-332-8233; Email: mgmtserv@archbalt.org. JOHN M. MATERA, CPA, Exec. Dir. & CFO, Email: jmatera@archbalt.org.

Division of Facilities and Real Estate Management—Tel: 410-547-5366;
Fax: 410-837-2932; Email: facserv@archbalt.org. NOLAN MCCOY, Dir., Tel: 410-547-5335; Tel: 410-547-5335; Email: nmccoy@archbalt.org.

Division of Fiscal Services—Tel: 410-547-5313;
Fax: 410-332-8233; Email: fiscal@archbalt.org. JOHN M. MATERA, CPA, Dir. & Controller, Tel: 410-547-5442; Email: jmatera@archbalt.org.

Division of Information Technology—
Tel: 410-547-5582; Fax: 410-332-8233; Email: it@archbalt.org. MR. MARCUS MADSEN, C.I.O. & Dir., Tel: 410-547-5539; Email: marcus.madsen@archbalt.org.

Employee Benefits, Division of—PETRA R. PHELPS, Dir., Tel: 410-547-5317; Email: pphelps@archbalt.org.

Human Resources, Division of—Web: www.archbalt.org/humanresources. JOSEPH T. SMITH, Exec. Dir. HR, Tel: 410-547-5432; Email: joseph.smith@archbalt.org; VACANT, Div. Dir., Tel: 410-547-5448.

Archives of the Archdiocese of Baltimore—Associated Archives: St. Mary's Seminary & University, 5400 Roland Ave., Baltimore, 21210. Tel: 410-864-4074; Fax: 410-864-3690; Email: archives@stmarys.edu; Web: www.stmarys.edu/archives. DR. TRICIA PYNE, Ph.D., Dir., Tel: 410-864-3691; Email: tpyne@stmarys.edu.

Catholic Campaign For Human Development—Purpose: To promote social justice education and provide technical assistance and funding for self-help groups through the annual pre-Thanksgiving CCHD collection appeal.
Tel: 410-235-5136; Tel: 410-547-5446. Rev. Msgr. WILLIAM F. BURKE, Archdiocesan Dir.

Division of Clergy Personnel—Rev. Msgr. JAMES W. HANNON, Div. Dir., Tel: 410-547-5302; Email: jhannon@archbalt.org.

Office of Pastoral Service for Retired Priests—
Tel: 410-547-5382. Rev. WILLIAM P. FOLEY, Email: wfoley@archbalt.org.

Office of Vocations—Web: www.becomeapriest.org. Rev. STEPHEN P. ROTH, Dir., Tel: 410-547-5426; Email: sroth@archbalt.org.

Office of the Diaconate—Rev. Msgr. JAMES W. HANNON, Dir., Tel: 410-547-5302.

Pastoral Service to Retired Deacons—Deacon MICHAEL P. MCCOY, Tel: 410-547-5382; Email: mmccoy@archbalt.org.

Deacon Formation Program—Rev. MICHAEL S. TRIPLETT, V.F., Email: mtriplett@archbalt.org.

Maryland Catholic Conference—10 Francis St., Annapolis, 21401-1714. Tel: 410-269-1155;
Fax: 410-269-1790; Email: info@mdcathcon.org; Web: www.mdcathcon.org. MRS. MARY ELLEN RUSSELL, Exec. Dir.

Black Catholic Ministries—Tel: 410-625-8472;
Fax: 410-625-8485; Email: aacm@archbalt.org. Sr. GWYNETTE PROCTOR, S.N.D.deN., Dir., Email: aacm@archbalt.org.

Vicar for African-American Catholic Ministries—
Most Rev. DENIS J. MADDEN, D.D., V.G.

Office of Consecrated Life—Tel: 410-547-5584. VACANT.

Office of Hispanic Ministries—Tel: 410-547-5363;
Fax: 410-625-8485; Email: lia.salinas@archbalt.org. LIA R. SALINAS, Dir.

Vicar for Hispanic Ministry—Most Rev. MARK E. BRENNAN, D.D., V.G., Auxiliary Bishop.

Missions Office—VACANT. The Missions Office is responsible for the following programs: Society for the Propagation of the Faith; Society of St. Peter the Apostle; Missionary Childhood Association; Baltimore Haiti Solidarity Project.

Associated Catholic Charities—With delegated authority from the archbishop to manage and direct the service mission of the Church in the archdiocese as present in Catholic Charities and as visible in the divisions, offices, institutions and programs which fall within the aegis of Catholic

Charities. Tel: 410-547-5490; Email: info@cc-md.org; Web: www.cc-md.org. MR. WILLIAM J. MCCARTHY JR., Exec. Dir., For detailed information on specific Catholic Charities and its programs, please refer to the Institution Section.

Cemetery Management—

*Director of Cemeteries—*Rev. PATRICK M. CARRION, B.A., S.T.D., S.T.M., M.A.S.

CLERGY, PARISHES, MISSIONS AND PAROCHIAL SCHOOLS

METROPOLITAN BALTIMORE

(BALTIMORE CITY AND BALTIMORE COUNTY)

1—CATHEDRAL OF MARY OUR QUEEN (1954) [CEM] Rev. Msgr. Richard W. Woy, Rector; Rev. Andrew T. DeFusco; Deacon William W. Senft. In Res., Rev. Msgr. James W. Hannon; Most Rev. Adam J. Parker, D.D., V.G.; Rev. Joseph F. Breighner, (Retired).

Res.: 5200 N. Charles St., 21210-2098.

Tel: 410-464-4000; Fax: 410-464-4060; Email: cathedral@archbalt.org; Web: www.cathedralofmary.org.

School—Cathedral of Mary Our Queen School, (Grades K-8), 111 Amberly Way, 21210-2098. Tel: 410-464-4100; Fax: 410-464-4137; Email: scmoq@cmoq.org; Web: www.schoolofthecathedral.org. Brent Dawson, Asst. Prin.; Michael Wright, Prin.; Rachel Mejibovsky, Asst. Prin. Lay Teachers 30; Students 450.

*Catechesis Religious Program—*Tel: 410-464-4010. Mrs. Sherri Rachuba, D.R.E. Students 210.

OFFICE OF MUSIC MINISTRY, Tel: 410-464-4020. Glenn Osborne, Email: gosborne@cmoq.org.

2—ST. AGNES (Catonsville) (1852) [CEM] Rev. Michael Foppiano; Deacon John Ames; Melissa Bickford, Music Min. In Res., Rev. Joseph M. O'Meara, (Retired).

Res.: 5422 Old Frederick Rd., 21229.

Tel: 410-744-2900; Fax: 410-744-8304; Email: sagnes@archbalt.org; Web: www.stagnescatholicchurch.org.

*Catechesis Religious Program—*Amanda Barrick, D.R.E. & Youth Min. Students 185.

3—ST. AMBROSE (1907) (African American)

Email: bbrown@saintambrose.com; Email: pastor@saintambrose; Web: saintambrose.com. Revs. Paul Zaborowski, O.F.M.Cap.; John McCloskey, Chap.; Deacons Seigfried Presberry; Steven Rubio; Betty Butler, Music Min. In Res., Revs. William Graham, O.F.M.Cap., J.C.L., M.A.; John Petrikovic.

Res.: 4502 Park Heights Ave., 21215.

Tel: 410-367-9918; Fax: 410-542-6056; Email: pastor@saintambrose.com; Web: www.saintambrose.com.

*Catechesis Religious Program—*Sr. Mary Stephen Beauford, O.S.P., D.R.E. Students 50.

OUTREACH CENTER, (St. Vincent de Paul Society) 3445 Park Heights Ave., 21215. Tel: 410-225-0870. Ms. Laura Spada, Dir.

4—ST. ANDREW, Closed. 1974. Parish records available at the Chancery. Tel: 410-547-5446.

5—ST. ANN (1873) (African American) Twinned with St. Wenceslaus, Baltimore. Rev. Timothy Dore, O.F.M.Conv.; Rogelio D'Almeida, Admin. In Res., Rev. Jordan Hite, T.O.R.

Res.: 528 E. 22nd St., 21218. Tel: 410-235-8169; Fax: 410-235-8253; Email: stann528@comcast.net; Web: anchoredinfaith.com.

*Catechesis Religious Program—*Students 35.

6—ST. ANTHONY OF PADUA (1884) Twinned with Most Precious Blood. Revs. Ty S. Hullinger, S.T.B.; Anthony Abiamiri; Deacon Joseph C. Krysiak, Pastoral Assoc.

Res.: 4414 Frankford Ave., 21206. Tel: 410-488-0400; Fax: 410-488-0032; Email: sapmpb@comcast.net; Web: www.sapmpb.org.

*Catechesis Religious Program—*Tel: 410-488-0400; Fax: 410-488-0032. Students 22.

7—ST. ATHANASIUS (1891) Rev. Robert A. DiMattei Jr.; Deacon Michael A. Dodge.

Res.: 4708 Prudence St., 21226. Tel: 410-355-5740; Fax: 410-355-8122; Email: sathana@archbalt.org; Web: www.athanasius.org.

*Catechesis Religious Program—*Tel: 410-355-2540. Mary Beth Barnes, D.R.E. & Pastoral Assoc., Tel: 410-355-2450; Leo Quinn, Youth Min. Students 70.

8—ST. AUGUSTINE (Elkridge) (1844) [CEM] Rev. John A. Williamson; Deacons Thomas J. Yannuzzi; Robert K. Smith.

Res.: 5976 Old Washington Rd., Elkridge, 21075.

Tel: 410-796-1520; Fax: 410-796-8172; Email: staugustine@archbalt.org; Web: www.ccasta.org.

*Catechesis Religious Program—*Tel: 410-796-8150. Michele Poligardo, Admin. Rel. Education; Cathy Carlin, Dir., Faith Min. & Engagement; Vikto Nowack, Dir. Youth Min. & Engagement, Tel: 410-796-2720. Students 455.

9—ST. BARNABAS, Closed. 1931. Parish records available at St. Pius V Church. Tel: 410-523-1930.

10—BASILICA OF THE NATIONAL SHRINE OF THE ASSUMPTION OF THE BLESSED VIRGIN MARY (1806) (Co-Cathedral). Corporate Title: The Trustees of the Catholic Cathedral Church of Baltimore (The Basilica); Basilica of the Assumption Historic Trust, Inc. Established for the Preservation of the Basilica as a National Landmark of American Architecture. Most Rev. Denis J. Madden, D.D., V.G., Interim Dir. & Aux. Bishop; Rev. James E. Boric; Deacons Robert M. Shephard; Sean Keller.

*The Archbishop's Residence—*408 N. Charles St., 21201. Tel: 410-727-3564; Fax: 410-539-0407; Email: basilica@archbalt.org; Web: www.baltimorebasilica.org. In Res., Most Rev. William E. Lori, S.T.D., Archbishop.

11—ST. BENEDICT (1893) Rt. Rev. Paschal A. Morlino, O.S.B.; Mrs. Maggie Barrick.

Res.: 2612 Wilkens Ave., 21223. Tel: 410-947-4988; Fax: 410-947-6009; Email: stbenedictbalto@gmail.com; Web: www.saintbenedict.org.

*Catechesis Religious Program—*Leah Paslick, D.R.E.; David Barber, Youth Min. Students 38.

12—ST. BERNARD, (Korean), Closed. For parish records prior to 1989 contact the chancery office. For parish records past 1989 contact Holy Korean Martyrs, Baltimore.

13—ST. BERNARDINE (1928) (African American) Rev. Msgr. Richard J. Bozzelli; Deacons Wardell Barksdale, Email: barksdalejr@aol.com; Philip W. Harcum, (Retired).

Res.: 3812 Edmondson Ave., 21229.

Tel: 410-362-8664; Email: stbernardine@archbalt.org; Web: www.stbernardinechurch.org.

*Catechesis Religious Program—*618 Mt. Holly St., 21229. Tel: 410-362-8978. Beverly White, Sunday School Dir. Students 122.

14—BLESSED SACRAMENT CHURCH (1911) Rev. Joseph L. Muth Jr.; Deacon Paul D. Shelton.

Res.: 4103 Old York Rd., 21218-1237.

Tel: 410-323-0424; Fax: 410-323-4478; Email: blesssac@aol.com.

*Catechesis Religious Program—*Students 7.

15—ST. BRIGID (1854) Rev. Joseph G. Bochenek, (Retired); Bette Brocato, Pastoral Assoc.

Res.: 901 S. Ellwood Ave., 21224. Tel: 410-563-1717; Fax: 410-563-1776; Email: sbrigid@archbalt.org; Web: www.saintbrigid-canton.com.

*Catechesis Religious Program—*Jo Ellen Shorb, C.R.E., Youth Min. Students 50.

16—ST. CASIMIR (1902) Rev. Dennis Grumsey, O.F.M.Conv.; Bernadette Vece, Pastoral Assoc. & Music Dir. In Res., Rev. Romuald Meogrossi, O.F.M.Conv.

Res.: 2800 O'Donnell St., 21224. Tel: 410-276-1981; Fax: 410-732-7436; Email: st.casimir@verizon.net; Web: www.stcasimir.org.

School—St. Casimir Catholic School, (Grades PreK-8), 1035 S. Kenwood Ave., 21224. Tel: 410-342-2681; Fax: 410-342-5715; Email: school@stcasimirschool.us; Web: www.stcasimirschool.us. Noreen Heffner, Prin. See separate listing.

17—CATHOLIC COMMUNITY AT RELAY (1972)

5025 Cedar Ave., 21227. Tel: 410-247-4033; Email: admin.ccr@comcast.net; Web: www.cc-relay.org. Maria Gamble-Farkas, Admin.; Linda Lombardo, Coord.; Bill Pfeifer, Coord. Total Staff 2.

18—CATHOLIC COMMUNITY OF ASCENSION AND ST. AUGUSTINE ROMAN CATHOLIC CONGREGATION, INC.

5976 Old Washington Rd., Elkridge, 21075.

Tel: 410-242-2292; Tel: 410-796-1520;

Fax: 410-242-0807; Fax: 410-796-8172; Web: ccasta.org. Rev. John A. Williamson.

19—CATHOLIC COMMUNITY OF SOUTH BALTIMORE ROMAN CATHOLIC CONGREGATION, INC. (1858) [CEM] (German)

Tel: 410-752-8498; Email: pcarrion@archbalt.org. Rev. Patrick M. Carrion, B.A., S.T.D., S.T.M., M.A.S.

Res.: 110 E. West St., 21230. Tel: 410-752-8498; Fax: 410-752-2703; Email: pcarrion@archbalt.org; Web: www.southbaltcatholic.org.

Church: 108 E. West St., 21230.

*Catechesis Religious Program—*Students 35.

20—ST. CECILIA (1902) Twinned with Immaculate Conception, Baltimore. Rev. Eugene Sheridan, C.M.; Bro. William Stover, C.M., Pastoral Assoc.

Res.: 3300 Clifton Ave., 21216. Tel: 410-624-3600; Fax: 410-945-0157; Email: office@churchofstcecilia.org; Web: www.churchofstcecilia.org.

*Catechesis Religious Program—*Francis Woodus, D.R.E.; Annette Thomas, RCIA Coord. Students 39.

21—ST. CHARLES BORROMEO (Pikesville) (1848) [CEM] Rev. Msgr. Lloyd Aiken; Revs. Raymond C. Chase; Hamilton Okeke; Deacon Stephen R. Roscher; Chris Welsh, Pastoral Assoc.

Res.: 101 Church Ln., 21208. Tel: 410-486-5400; Fax: 410-486-5421; Email: charlesst@comcast.net; Web: www.ourstcharles.org.

*Catechesis Religious Program—*Alec Danz, Youth Min. & C.R.E. Students 92.

22—CHRIST THE KING (Dundalk) (1957) Closed. For inquiries for parish records please see St. Rita, Baltimore.

23—CHURCH OF THE ANNUNCIATION (1968) Rev. Justin Ratajczak, O.F.M.Conv.; Sr. Susan Engel, M.H.S.H., Pastoral Assoc.; John Holland, Music Min.

Res.: 5212 McCormick Ave., 21206.

Tel: 410-866-4020; Fax: 410-866-2754; Email: cota.parish@verizon.net.

*Catechesis Religious Program—*Tel: 410-866-4706. Mrs. Kathy Brotzman, C.R.E. Students 63.

24—CHURCH OF THE ASCENSION (Halethorpe) (1913) Rev. John A. Williamson; Deacons Thomas J. Yannuzzi; Robert K. Smith; Bonnie Kabara, Music Min.

Res.: 4603 Poplar Ave., Halethorpe, 21227-4029.

Tel: 410-242-2292; Fax: 410-242-6807; Email: ascebalt@archbalt.org; Web: www.ccasta.org.

*Catechesis Religious Program—*Cathy Carlin, C.R.E.; Vikto Nowack, Coord. Youth Ministry. Students 105.

25—CHURCH OF THE IMMACULATE CONCEPTION (Towson) (1883) [CEM] Revs. Joseph F. Barr; Francis Ouma; Deacon James L. Mann Jr. In Res., Rev. Msgr. Richard H. Tillman, (Retired).

Res.: 200 Ware Ave., Towson, 21204.

Tel: 410-427-4700; Fax: 410-427-4795; Email: info@theimmaculate.org; Web: www.theimmaculate.org.

School—Church of the Immaculate Conception School, (Grades PreK-8), 112 Ware Ave., Towson, 21204. Tel: 410-427-4800; Fax: 410-427-4895; Email: cdixon@theimmaculate.org; Web: www.theimmaculate.org/school. Mrs. Madeline Meaney, Prin.

Catechesis Religious Program—School of Religion, Students 140.

26—ST. CLARE (Essex) (1956) Rev. Richard Gray; Deacon Paul Mann, Pastoral Assoc.

Res.: 714 Myrth Ave., 21221-4898. Tel: 410-687-6011 ; Fax: 410-687-3054; Email: sclare@archbalt.org; Web: www.saintclare.moonfruit.com.

*Catechesis Religious Program—*Tel: 410-686-7693; Fax: 410-687-2518. Susan Bangert, D.R.E., Email: sbangert@saintclare.org. Students 140.

27—ST. CLEMENT (Lansdowne) (1891) Deacon Paul A. Gifford, Pastoral Life Dir.; Revs. Thomas R. Malia; Roger Britto Fernandez. Serving the Spanish and English speaking communities of Lansdowne, Baltimore Highlands, Riverview, Lakeland, Westport, and Morrel Park.

Res.: 2700 Washington Ave., 21227.

Tel: 410-242-1025; Fax: 410-242-1227; Web: www.stclement1.org.

*Catechesis Religious Program—*Dan Miller, Youth Min. Students 80.

28—ST. CLEMENT MARY HOFBAUER (Rosedale) (1925) Rev. Vincent Gluc, O.F.M.Conv.; Deacon Francis Zeiler, Email: fzeiler@archbalt.org. In Res., Revs. Bernard Dudek, O.F.M. Conv.; Thomas E. Walsh, O.F.M.Conv.

Res. & Parish Office: 1212 Chesaco Ave., 21237.

Tel: 410-686-6188; Fax: 410-686-6198; Email: parishoffice@stclementmh.org; Web: www.stclementmh.org.

*Catechesis Religious Program—*Tel: 410-391-5028. Students 90.

29—CORPUS CHRISTI (1881) Rev. Martin H. Demek; Deacons Frank Hodges; Fritz Bauerschmidt; Daniel Meyer, Music Min.

Res.: 110 W. Lafayette Ave., 21217.

Tel: 410-523-4161; Fax: 410-669-0349; Email: cchristi@archbalt.org; Web: www.corpuschristibaltimore.org.

*Catechesis Religious Program—*Students 70.

30—ST. DOMINIC (1906)

5310 Harford Rd., 21214. Tel: 410-488-0400, Ext. 107 ; Tel: 410-426-0360; Email: sapmpb@comcast.net; Email: dominicfaith@aol.com. 4414 Frankford Ave., 21206. Rev. Ty S. Hullinger, S.T.B.; Sr. Catherine Manning, S.S.N.D., Pastoral Assoc.

*Catechesis Religious Program—*Tel: 410-426-0360. Students 30.

31—ST. EDWARD (1880) Rev. Honest Munishi, C.S.Sp.; Deacon Carl A. Anderson.

Res.: 901 Poplar Grove St., 21216-4350.

Tel: 410-362-2000; Fax: 410-945-7113; Email: stedwardsparish@verizon.net; Web: www.stedwardchurchmd.org.

*Catechesis Religious Program—*Students 70.

32—ST. ELIZABETH OF HUNGARY (1895) Rev. David Kashen, O.F.M.Conv., Admin.

Mailing & Office Address: 2638 E. Baltimore St., 21224. Tel: 410-675-8260; Fax: 410-675-2530; Email: stliz1@comcast.net; Web: www.stlizbmore.org.

*Catechesis Religious Program—*Students 20.

33—FOURTEEN HOLY MARTYRS, Closed. 1964. Parish

records available at Transfiguration Catholic Community. Tel: 410-685-5044.

34—ST. FRANCIS OF ASSISI (1927)
Tel: 410-235-5136; Email: SFABalt@archbalt.org; Web: www.sfabalt.org. Rev. Msgr. William F. Burke; Rev. Joseph J. Bonadio, P.S.S., M.Rel.Ed., D.Min., S.T.L., Asst. Priest, (Retired); Mrs. Gina Poggioli Gross, Sec.; Mrs. Jean Kelley, Dir. of Music; Dr. Richard Allen, Organist.
Res.: 3615 Harford Rd., 21218. Tel: 410-235-5136; Fax: 410-467-9503; Email: sfabalt@archbalt.org; Web: www.sfabalt.org.
School—St. Francis of Assisi School, (Grades PreK-8), 3617 Harford Rd., 21218. Tel: 410-467-1683; Fax: 410-467-9449; Email: info@sfa-school.org; Web: sfa-school.org. Mr. John D'Adamo, Prin. Lay Teachers 25; Students 260.
Catechesis Religious Program—Lauren Voos, D.R.E.; Ms. Amelia Voos, Youth Min. Students 50.

35—ST. FRANCIS XAVIER (1793) Rev. Xavier Edet, S.S.J., Admin.; Kenyatta Haridison, Music Min., Tel: 410-254-0099.
Res.: 1501 E. Oliver St., 21213. Tel: 410-727-3103; Fax: 410-625-9587; Email: sfxbalt@archbalt.org; Web: www.archbalt.org/parishes/all-parishes/st-francis-xavier-baltimore.
Catechesis Religious Program—Tel: 410-837-0556. Sr. Magdala Marie Gillbert, O.S.P., D.R.E., Tel: 410-837-0636. Students 117.

36—ST. GABRIEL (1997) Formerly St. Lawrence and Our Lady of Perpetual Help, Woodlawn. Rev. Msgr. Thomas L. Phillips, Email: tphillips@archbalt.org.
Parish Office: 6950 Dogwood Rd., 21244-2658.
Tel: 410-298-8888; Fax: 410-944-7409; Email: stgabriel@archbalt.org; Web: www.stgabrielch.org.
See John Paul Regional Catholic School, Inc., Baltimore under Elementary/Middle Schools, Private located in the Institution section.
Catechesis Religious Program—Sr. Sonia Marie Fernandez, Dir. Christian Formation & Pastoral Assoc.

37—ST. GREGORY THE GREAT (1884) (African American) Rev. Jean-Pierre Kapumet Tambwe, C.S.Sp.; Sisters Anthonia Ugwu, O.S.P., Pastoral Assoc.; Cassandra Boykin, Dir.; Gloria Williams, Dir.
Res. & Church: 1542 N. Gilmor St., 21217-2304.
Tel: 410-523-0061; Tel: 410-523-0063;
Fax: 410-669-1385; Email: sggreat@archbalt.org; Web: www.archbalt.org/parishes/all-parishes/st-gregory-the-great.
Catechesis Religious Program—Shirley Hampton, C.R.E. Students 52.

38—HOLY CROSS, Merged with St. Mary Star of the Sea & Our Lady of Good Counsel to form Catholic Community of South Baltimore Roman Catholic Congregation, Inc.

39—HOLY KOREAN MARTYRS (1989) [CEM] (Korean) Revs. Joseph Y. Kim; Hyong Cho.
Res.: 5801 Security Blvd., 21207. Tel: 410-265-8885; Fax: 410-265-1655; Email: kmartyrs@archbalt.org; Web: www.hkmcc.us.
Catechesis Religious Program—Students 165.

40—HOLY ROSARY (1887) [CEM] (Polish) Rev. Ryszard Czerniak, S.Chr. In Res., Rev. Zdzislaw Nawrocki, S.Chr.
Res.: 408 S. Chester St., 21231. Tel: 410-732-3960; Fax: 410-675-4917; Email: holyrosarybalto@comcast.net; Web: www.holyrosarypl.org.
Catechesis Religious Program—Students 35.

41—ST. IGNATIUS CHURCH (1856)
Tel: 410-727-3848; Email: parish@stignatius.net; Web: www.st-ignatius.net. Rev. James A. Casciotti, S.J.; Deacon Paul Webber, Business Mgr.
Church: 740 N. Calvert St., 21202. Tel: 410-727-3848 ; Fax: 410-837-8883; Email: parish@st-ignatius.net; Web: www.st-ignatius.net.
Catechesis Religious Program—Students 30.

42—IMMACULATE CONCEPTION (1850) (African American) Twinned with St. Cecilia, Baltimore. Rev. Eugene Sheridan, C.M.; Bro. William Stover, C.M., Pastoral Assoc. & Dir. Outreach.
Res.: 3300 Clifton Ave., 21216. Tel: 410-624-3600; Fax: 410-945-0157; Email: IConception@archbalt.org.
Catechesis Religious Program—Yvonne Taylor, D.R.E. Students 26.

43—IMMACULATE HEART OF MARY (Baynesville) (1948) Revs. Michael W. Carrion; Stephen D. Gosnell, K.H.S., (Retired); Deacon Jack Martin; Rev. Scott P. Detisch, M.Div., Ph.D. (cand.), Weekend Asst.
Res.: 8501 Loch Raven Blvd., 21286.
Tel: 410-668-7935; Fax: 410-661-6560; Email: ihmparish@immaculateheartofmary.com; Web: www.immaculateheartofmary.com.
School—Immaculate Heart of Mary School, (Grades PreK-8), Tel: 410-668-8466; Fax: 410-668-6171. Anders Alicea, Prin. Lay Teachers 33; Students 505.
Catechesis Religious Program—Tel: 410-661-3820; Fax: 410-661-3838. Tony Magliano, Pastoral Assoc., Faith Formation & Outreach Ministries. Students 138.

44—ST. ISAAC JOGUES (1968) Rev. Stephen P. Roth; Deacons James Westwater, Dir.; Michael R. Baxter, Dir. Faith Formation, Tel: 410-665-2569.
Church Office: 9215 Old Harford Rd., 21234.
Tel: 410-661-4888; Fax: 410-882-1484; Email: sij@sij.org; Web: www.sij.org.
Res.: 9400 Old Harford Rd., 21234.
Catechesis Religious Program—Tel: 410-665-2561; Tel: 410-668-3686 Youth Ministry Office. Students 452.

45—ST. JAMES AND ST. JOHN, Closed. 1986. Parish records available at the Chancery. Tel: 410-547-5446.

46—ST. JEROME (1887) Merged with St. Martin and St. Peter the Apostle, Baltimore to form Transfiguration Roman Catholic Church, Baltimore.

47—ST. JOHN GERMAN CATHOLIC CHURCH, Closed. in 1841. Original records, stored at The Catholic Center, are available to researchers on microfilm at the Maryland State Archives in Annapolis.

48—ST. JOHN THE EVANGELIST, Closed. in 1966. Parish records available at the Chancery. Tel: 410-547-5446.

49—ST. JOSEPH, Closed. in 1962. Parish records available at Holy Cross Rectory. Tel: 410-752-8498.

50—ST. JOSEPH (Fullerton) (1860) [CEM] (German) Revs. Jesse L. Bolger; Joseph T. Langan; Deacons William J. DeAngelis, Pastoral Assoc.; Timothy D. Maloney.
Res.: 8420 Belair Rd., 21236. Tel: 410-256-1630; Fax: 410-529-2990; Email: stjoefullerton@archbalt.org; Web: www.stjoefullerton.org.
School—St. Joseph School, (Grades PreK-8), 8416 Belair Rd., 21236. Tel: 410-256-8026; Fax: 410-529-7234; Email: office@stjoefullerton.org; Web: www.stjoeschool.org. Kenneth Pipkin, Prin. Lay Teachers 25; Students 490.
Catechesis Religious Program—Students 421.

51—ST. JOSEPH PASSIONIST MONASTERY PARISH (1868) Rev. Michael A. Murphy, Admin.
Res.: 251 S. Morley St., 21229. Tel: 410-566-0877; Fax: 410-233-4974; Email: info@sjmp.org; Web: www.sjmp.org.
Catechesis Religious Program—Students 80.

52—ST. JUDE SHRINE (1917) (Italian) Revs. Salvatore C. Furnari, S.A.C., M.Div., Pastoral Dir.; Vensus George, S.A.C., Assoc. Pastoral Dir.
Res.: 308 N. Paca St., P.O. Box 1455, 21203.
Tel: 410-685-6026; Fax: 410-244-5728; Email: info@stjudeshrine.org; Web: stjudeshrine.org.
St. Jude Shrine Corp.—512 W. Saratoga St., 21203. Tel: 410-685-6026; Web: www.stjudeshrine.org.

53—ST. KATHARINE OF SIENNA, Closed. in 1986. Parish records available at St. Wenceslaus Church. Tel: 410-675-7304.

54—ST. LAWRENCE (1962) Merged with The Shrine of Our Lady of Perpetual Help, Baltimore, to form St. Gabriel Parish, Baltimore. Records available at St. Gabriel Parish.

55—ST. LEO THE GREAT (1881) (Italian) Rev. Bernie Carman, S.A.C.; Sr. Mary Catherine Duerr, S.U.S.C., Pastoral Care; Deacon Douglas P. Kendzierski.
Res.: 227 S. Exeter St., 21202-4451.
Tel: 410-675-7275; Fax: 410-675-8292; Email: SLeo@archbalt.org; Web: saintleorcc.com.
Catechesis Religious Program—

56—LITTLE FLOWER, SHRINE OF (1926) Rev. Michael J. Orchik, V.F.
Res.: 3500 Belair Rd., 21213. Tel: 410-483-1700; Fax: 410-488-6482; Email: slflower@archbalt.org; Web: www.shrineofthelittleflower.org.
Catechesis Religious Program—Students 17.

57—ST. LUKE (Edgemere) (1888) Revs. Austin Murphy; Gregory Rapisarda; Deacon Herman S. Wilkins, D.R.E.
Res.: 7517 North Point Rd., Edgemere, 21219-1499.
Tel: 410-477-5200; Fax: 410-477-5996; Email: stlukromcathchur@yahoo.com; Web: www.olhstchurch.com.
School—Our Lady of Hope/St. Luke's School, (Grades PreK-8), Tel: 410-288-2793. Sr. Irene Mary Pryle, S.S.N.D., Prin.
Catechesis Religious Program—Tel: 410-477-5201; Fax: 410-477-2022. Students 91.

58—ST. MARK (Catonsville) (1888)
Email: smcatons@archbalt.org. Rev. Christopher Whatley, Email: cwhatley@archbalt.org; Deacon Seigfried Presberry; Nora C. Reiter, Pastoral Assoc.
Res.: 30 Melvin Ave., Catonsville, 21228.
Tel: 410-744-6560; Fax: 410-747-3182; Email: smcatons@archbalt.org; Web: www.stmarkchurch-catonsville.org.
School—St. Mark School, (Grades PreK-8), 26 Melvin Ave., 21228. Tel: 410-744-6560; Fax: 410-747-3188; Email: info@stmark-school.org; Web: www.stmark-school.org. Stephanie Rattell, Asst. Prin.
Catechesis Religious Program—Students 869.

59—ST. MARTIN (1865) (African American), Merged with St. Jerome and St. Peter the Apostle, Baltimore to form Transfiguration Roman Catholic Church, Baltimore.

60—ST. MARY OF THE ASSUMPTION (1849) [CEM] Revs. Martin S. Nocchi, S.T.B., M.D.; Samuel V. Young; Deacon Miguel Sainz.
Res.: 5502 York Rd., 21212. Tel: 410-435-5900; Fax: 410-435-1287; Email: stmaryotag@archbalt.org; Web: www.saintmarygovans.org.
Catechesis Religious Program—Students 13.

61—ST. MARY, STAR OF THE SEA (1868) Merged with Holy Cross and Our Lady of Good Counsel to form Catholic Community of South Baltimore Roman Catholic Congregation, Inc.

62—ST. MATTHEW (1949) Rev. Joseph L. Muth Jr.
Res.: 5401 Loch Raven Blvd., 21239.
Tel: 410-433-2300; Fax: 410-433-5263; Email: stmattrc@gmail.com; Web: stmatthewbaltimore.org.
See Cardinal Shehan School, Baltimore under Elementary Schools, Regional and Community located in the Institution section.
Catechesis Religious Program—Tel: 410-444-4563; Fax: 410-444-6502. Students 90.
Convent—Notre Dame Mission Volunteers - Americorps, 5405 Loch Raven Blvd., 21239.
Tel: 410-523-6844; Email: natloffice@ndmva.org; Web: www.combonisrs.com.
Immigration Outreach Services Center, Inc.—
Tel: 410-323-8564; Fax: 410-323-8598; Web: www.ioscbaltimore.org.

63—ST. MICHAEL (Broadway) (1852) (Hispanic), Closed. For inquiries for parish records contact the chancery.

64—ST. MICHAEL (Overlea) (1914) Rev. Jose Opalda, J.C.L.; Deacon Henry C. Davis, Pastoral Assoc., Tel: 410-665-1054, Ext. 109.
Res.: 2 Willow Ave., 21206. Tel: 410-665-1054; Fax: 410-665-4024; Email: parish@smoverlea.org; Web: www.smoverlea.org.
School—St. Michael School, (Grades K-8), 10 Willow Ave., 21206. Tel: 410-668-8797; Fax: 410-663-9277; Email: school@stmstc.org; Web: https://stmstc.org/. Mr. Paul Kristoff, Prin., Tel: 410-668-8797, Ext. 122; Dr. Jane C. Towery, Prin. Lay Teachers 16; Students 395.
Catechesis Religious Program—Nikki Lux, D.R.E., Tel: 410-668-8797, Ext. 106. Students 125.

65—ST. MILDRED CHURCH, Closed. in 1967. Parish records available at Our Lady of Hope Rectory. Tel: 410-284-6600.

66—ST. MONICA, Closed. 1959. Parish records available at the Chancery. Tel: 410-547-5446.

67—MOST PRECIOUS BLOOD (1948) Twinned with St. Anthony of Padua, Baltimore.
5010 Bowleys Ln., 21206. Revs. Ty S. Hullinger, S.T.B.; Anthony Abiamiri; Deacon Joseph C. Krysiak, Pastoral Assoc.
Office: 4414 Frankford Ave., 21206.
Tel: 410-488-0400; Fax: 410-488-0032; Email: sapmpb@comcast.net; Web: www.sapmpb.org.
Church: 5010 Bowleys Ln., 21206.
Catechesis Religious Program—Twinned with St. Anthony of Padua, Baltimore.

68—THE NATIONAL SHRINE OF ST. ALPHONSUS LIGUORI (1845) (Lithuanian) Revs. Joel E. Kiefer; William F. Spacek; Deacon Hugh H. Mills Jr., Business Mgr.
Res.: 114 W. Saratoga St., 21201. Tel: 410-685-6090; Fax: 410-244-1670; Email: alphonsus9@verizon.net; Web: www.stalphonsusbalt.org.

69—NEW ALL SAINTS (1912) (African American) Rev. Donald A. Sterling, D.Min.
Res.: 4408 Liberty Heights Ave., 21207.
Tel: 410-542-0445; Fax: 410-542-8852; Email: office@naschurch.org; Web: www.naschurch.org.
Catechesis Religious Program—Rernard Baker, Dir., Youth Ministry; Elizabeth Dorsey; Ingrid McLaughlin, Admin. Rel. Educ. Students 35.

70—OUR LADY OF FATIMA (1951) Revs. Richard K. Poetzel, C.Ss.R.; Arthur Gildea, C.Ss.R.; Bro. DeSales Zimpfer, C.Ss.R., Assoc.; Deacon Alphonse Bankard III.
Res.: 6420 E. Pratt St., 21224. Tel: 410-633-9393; Fax: 410-633-8699; Email: lfatima@archbalt.org.
Catechesis Religious Program—Tel: 410-633-6526. Sr. Rita Dorn, S.S.N.D., D.R.E. Students 47.

71—OUR LADY OF GOOD COUNSEL (1859) Merged with Holy Cross & St. Mary Star of the Sea to form Catholic Community of South Baltimore Roman Catholic Congregation, Inc.

72—OUR LADY OF HOPE (1967) Revs. T. Austin Murphy Jr.; Gregory Rapisarda; Deacon Herman S. Wilkins.
Res.: 1727 Lynch Rd., 21222. Tel: 410-284-6600; Fax: 410-282-9361; Email: lhope@archbalt.org; Web: www.ourladyofhope.church.
School—Our Lady of Hope School, (Grades PreK-8), 8003 N. Boundary Rd., 21222. Tel: 410-288-2793; Fax: 410-288-2850; Email: ipryle@archbalt.org; Web: www.olhsl.com. Sr. Irene Mary Pryle, S.S.N.D., Prin. Lay Teachers 24; School Sisters of Notre Dame 2; Students 311.
Catechesis Religious Program—8003 N. Boundary

Rd., 21222. Tel: 410-282-3120; Fax: 410-282-9361. Students 155.
Convent—8001 N. Boundary Rd., 21222.
Tel: 410-282-3800; Fax: 410-288-2850. School Sisters of Notre Dame.

73—OUR LADY OF LA VANG (2000)
335 Sollers Point Rd., 21222. Tel: 410-282-1496; Fax: 410-282-1497; Email: olol_baltimore@yahoo.com; Web: www.olol-baltimore.net. Rev. Joseph Chuc Tran, M.M., M.M.
Catechesis Religious Program—Anna Trinh Nguyen, D.R.E.

74—OUR LADY OF LOURDES, Closed. 1995. Parish records available at The New All Saints Church. Tel: 410-542-0445.

75—OUR LADY OF MOUNT CARMEL (Middle River) (1887) Rev. Msgr. Robert L. Hartnett; Rev. Patrick E. Besel.
Res.: 1704 Old Eastern Ave., 21221.
Tel: 410-686-4972; Fax: 410-574-8785; Web: www.olmcmd.org.
Catechesis Religious Program—Tel: 410-238-1167; Fax: 410-574-8785. Students 187.

76—OUR LADY OF PERPETUAL HELP (1936) Merged with St. Lawrence, Baltimore, to form St. Gabriel Parish, Baltimore. Records available at St. Gabriel.

77—OUR LADY OF POMPEI (1924) Revs. Luigi Esposito; Giuliano Gargiulo.
Res.: 3600 Claremont St., 21224. Tel: 410-675-7790; Fax: 410-563-9067; Email: pompeich1@verizon.net; Web: www.olpmd.org.
Catechesis Religious Program—Mrs. Dorothy Locco, D.R.E.

78—OUR LADY OF SORROWS, Closed. 1935. Parish records available at Holy Cross Rectory. Tel: 410-752-8498.

79—OUR LADY OF THE ANGELS CATHOLIC COMMUNITY (Catonsville) (1993) Service senior citizens w/in community.
Mailing Address: 711 Maiden Choice Ln., Catonsville, 21228. Tel: 410-247-4779;
Fax: 410-737-8826; Email: langels@archbalt.org. Rev. Leo J. Larrivee, P.S.S., M.A. (Theol.), M.A. (Hist.); Sr. Eileen McKeever, S.S.N.D., Pastoral Assoc.; Deacon Jack Coster.

80—OUR LADY OF VICTORY (Arbutus) (1952) Revs. John C. Rapisarda; Joshua Laws; Deacon William Jauquet.
Res.: 4414 Wilkens Ave., 21229. Tel: 410-242-0131; Fax: 410-242-6963; Email: parish@olvictory.org; Web: www.olvictory.org.
School—Our Lady of Victory School, (Grades PreK-8), 4416 Wilkens Ave., 21229. Tel: 410-242-3688;
Fax: 410-242-8867; Email: wcottrell@olvictory.org; Web: www.olvmd.org. Lois Gorman, Prin. Lay Teachers 24; Students 475.
Catechesis Religious Program—Tel: 410-242-9533; Email: smithgl@mail.olvschool.com. Gloria Smith, D.R.E. Students 57.

81—OUR LADY, QUEEN OF PEACE (1953) (Middle River) Rev. Kevin A. Mueller; Deacon G. Anthony Roberts.
Res.: 10003 Bird River Rd., 21220. Tel: 410-686-3085 ; Fax: 410-687-1916; Email: qpeace@archbalt.org; Web: www.olqpmd.org.
Catechesis Religious Program—
Tel: 410-686-3085, Ext. 120; Fax: 410-687-1916. Kathy Shadrach, C.R.E.; Debbie Boblitz, C.R.E. Students 98.

82—ST. PATRICK, Closed. Now a Mission of Sacred Heart of Jesus, Baltimore.

83—ST. PAUL'S (1888) Closed. Parish records available at St. Francis Xavier. Tel: 410-727-3103.

84—ST. PETER CLAVER (1888) (African American) Very Rev. Ray P. Bomberger, S.S.J.; Rev. Joseph DelVecchio, S.S.J.; Deacon Willard Witherspoon Jr.
Res.: 1546 N. Fremont Ave., 21217.
Tel: 410-669-0512; Fax: 410-383-8227; Email: spclaver@archbalt.org; Web: www.josephite.com/parish/md/spc.
Catechesis Religious Program—Dorothy Kutcherman, C.R.E.; Ernestine Watkins, Youth Min. Students 54.

85—ST. PETER THE APOSTLE (1842) Merged with St. Jerome and St. Martin, Baltimore to form Transfiguration Roman Catholic Church, Baltimore.

86—SS. PHILIP AND JAMES (1897) Rev. David Mott, O.P.; Ron Meyers, Pastoral Assoc.; Revs. Hugh Vincent Dyer, O.P., Pastoral Assoc.; Matthew Erickson, O.P.; Deacon Mark Soloski, Ph.D.
Res.: 2801 N. Charles St., 21218. Tel: 410-235-2294; Fax: 410-243-5262; Email: info@philipandjames.org; Web: www.philipandjames.org.
Catechesis Religious Program—

87—ST. PIUS V (1878) [JC] (African American) Very Rev. Ray P. Bomberger, S.S.J.; Rev. Joseph DelVecchio, S.S.J.; Deacon Willard Witherspoon Jr.
Res.: 1546 N. Fremont Ave., 21217-0550.
Tel: 410-523-1930; Fax: 410-383-8227; Email: stpiusv@verizon.net; Web: www.archbalt.org/parishes/all-parishes/st-pius-v.
Catechesis Religious Program—Mrs. Jean Brent, D.R.E.; Sonja Smith, Youth Min.; Michael Smith, Youth Min. Students 11.

88—ST. PIUS X (1958) Revs. Martin S. Nocchi, S.T.B., M.D.; Samuel V. Young; Deacon Patrick E. Woods.
Parish Office: 6428 York Rd., 21212.
Tel: 410-427-7500; Fax: 410-377-2651; Email: info@stpius10.org; Web: stpius10.org/parish.
School—St. Pius X School, (Grades PreK-8), 6432 York Rd., 21212. Tel: 410-427-7400;
Fax: 410-372-0552; Email: jripley@stpius10school.org; Web: stpius10school.org/contact-us. Jennifer Ripley, Prin. Lay Teachers 29; School Sisters of Notre Dame 3; Students 402.
Catechesis Religious Program—Tel: 410-427-7500. Students 240.

89—ST. RITA (1922) Revs. George Gannon, Tel: 410-284-0388, Ext. 18; Gregory Rapisarda; Deacon George T. Evans; Sr. Michael Marie Hartman, I.H.M., Dir., Tel: 410-284-0388, Ext. 15.
Res.: 2907 Dunleer Rd., 21222. Tel: 410-284-0388; Fax: 410-814-2341; Email: SRita@archbalt.org; Web: www.saintritadundalk.org.
Catechesis Religious Program—Tel: 410-284-7355. Students 85.

90—ST. ROSE OF LIMA (1914)
Mailing Address: 4708 Prudence St., 21226. Rev. Robert A. DiMattei Jr.; Deacon Michael A. Dodge.
Res.: 3803 4th St., 21225. Tel: 410-355-8515;
Fax: 410-355-8122; Email: strose@archbalt.org; Web: starl.org.
Catechesis Religious Program—Mary Beth Barnes, D.R.E. & Pastoral Assoc.; Leo Quinn, Youth Min. Students 43.

91—SACRED HEART OF JESUS-SAGRADO CORAZON DE JESUS (1873)
Tel: 410-263-2396; Fax: 410-263-3027; Web: shjbaltimore.com. Revs. Bruce Lewandowski, C.Ss.R.; Kenneth Gaddy, C.Ss.R.; Leslie Owen; Edmundo Molina; John Kingsbury, In Res.; John Bauer, C.Ss.R., In Res.; Bro. Raphael Rock, C.Ss.R., In Res.; Deacon Edison Morales.
Res.: 600 S. Conkling St., 21224-4203.
Tel: 410-342-4336; Fax: 443-759-9862; Email: shjesus@archbalt.org; Web: www.shjbaltimore.com.
Catechesis Religious Program—Estella Chavez, D.R.E. & RCIA Coord. Students 45.
Mission—St. Patrick (Broadway) (1792) Bank St. & Broadway, 21231. Email: smikepat95@hotmail.com.
ST. JOHN NEUMAN RESIDENCE, St. John Neumann Residence - Stella Maris: 2300 Dulaney Valley Rd., Timonium, 21093. Tel: 410-427-7841; Email: secprovince@redemptorists.net. Revs. John Harrison, C.Ss.R., Admin.; Jack Fiske, C.Ss.R., Asst. Supt.; Most Rev. Ellot Thomas, In Res.; Revs. Carl Hoegerl, In Res.; Andrew Carr, C.Ss.R., In Res.; John Gauci, In Res.; Arthur Wendel, In Res.; Richard K. Poetzel, C.Ss.R., In Res.; Brendan Greany, In Res.; James H. Brennan, S.S., In Res., (Retired); Timothy Keating, In Res.; John Lavin, C.Ss.R., In Res.; Kevin Milton, C.Ss.R., In Res.; Thomas Barrett, In Res.; Thomas G. Sullivan, C.Ss.R., In Res.; Felix Catala Rodos, In Res.; Bros. Stephen Lendvay, In Res.; Thomas Kuhn, In Res. Bed Capacity 11; Tot Asst. Annually 15; Total Staff 12.

92—SACRED HEART OF MARY (1925) [CEM] Revs. George Gannon; Greg Rapisarda; Bro. William Ciganek, C.F.X., Pastoral Assoc.
Res.: 6736 Youngstown Ave., 21222-1097.
Tel: 410-633-2828; Fax: 410-633-0349; Email: shmary@archbalt.org; Web: www.shmparish.org.
Catechesis Religious Program—Michael Demski, Children's Faith Formation. Students 123.

93—SHRINE OF THE SACRED HEART (Mt. Washington) (1867) Rev. William A. Au, Ph.D., Tel: 410-466-6884, Ext. 12.
Res.: 1701 Regent Rd., 21209. Tel: 410-466-6884;
Fax: 410-664-0523; Email: shshrine@archbalt.org; Web: www.theshrine.org.
Catechesis Religious Program—
Tel: 410-466-6884, Ext. 14. Bernetta Palasik, Dir. Faith Formation, Tel: 410-466-6884, Ext. 16; Stephen Cox, Dir. Adult Faith Formation. Students 168.

94—ST. STANISLAUS KOSTKA (1880) (Polish), Closed. For inquiries for parish records please contact St. Casimir, Baltimore. Tel: 410-276-1981; 732-7436 (fax).

95—ST. THOMAS AQUINAS (1867) Rev. Silvester Kim.
Res.: 1008 W. 37th St., 21211. Tel: 410-366-4488; Email: staquina@archbalt.org; Web: thomasaquinasbaltimore.myfreesites.net.
Catechesis Religious Program—Susan Sousa, C.R.E. Students 40.

96—ST. THOMAS MORE (1961) Rev. Msgr. James P. Farmer; Deacon Michael P. McCoy.
Parish Center & Mailing Address: 6806 McClean Blvd., 21234. Tel: 410-444-6500; Fax: 410-444-6502; Email: stmore@archbalt.org; Web: www.churchstmore.net.
See Cardinal Shehan School, Baltimore under Elementary Schools, Regional and Community located in the Institution section.
Catechesis Religious Program—Tel: 410-444-4563. Anna Rosario Trujillo, C.R.E. Students 39.

97—TRANSFIGURATION CATHOLIC COMMUNITY (2004) Rev. Augustine Etemma Inwang, M.S.P., (Nigeria).
Office: 775 W. Hamburg St., 21230.
Tel: 410-685-5044 (Office); Fax: 410-625-2406; Email: marie.pennix@archbalt.org; Web: transfigurationbalt.org.
Catechesis Religious Program—Alan Cramblitt, C.R.E. Students 84.

98—ST. URSULA (Parkville) (1937)
Tel: 410-665-2111; Tel: 410-661-0600; Web: www.stursulaparish.org. Rev. Jason Worley; Deacon Donald R. Cupps.
Res.: 8801 Harford Rd., 21234. Tel: 410-665-2111;
Fax: 410-665-0758; Email: stursula@comcast.net; Web: www.stursulaparish.org.
Catechesis Religious Program—Tel: 410-655-4106;
Tel: 410-665-2111; Email: theresa.calva@archbal.org; Web: www.stursulaparish.org. Laura Wetherington, D.R.E., Tel: 410-665-4106. Students 716.

99—ST. VERONICA (1945) (African American) Rev. Stephen Ositimehin; Deacon Jhan Harris.
Res.: 806 Cherry Hill Rd., 21225. Tel: 410-355-7466;
Fax: 410-355-7741; Email: stveronicas@gmail.com; Web: www.archbalt.org/parishes/all-parishes/st-veronica.
Catechesis Religious Program—Students 108.

100—ST. VINCENT DE PAUL (1840) [CEM] Revs. Raymond Chase; Richard T. Lawrence, Pastor Emeritus, (Retired). In Res., Rev. Charles Canterna.
Res.: 120 N. Front St., 21202-4804.
Tel: 410-962-5078; Fax: 410-953-8427; Email: svdepaul@archbalt.org; Web: stvchurch.org.
Endowment—St. Vincent de Paul Church Historic Trust, Inc., Tel: 410-962-5078.
Jonestown Planning Council, Inc.—
Tel: 410-962-5078.
Child Care—Jonestown Day Care Center, Inc.
Catechesis Religious Program—Students 55.

101—ST. WENCESLAUS (1872) Rev. Timothy Dore, O.F.M.Conv.
Res.: 2111 Ashland Ave., 21205. Tel: 410-675-7304;
Fax: 410-675-5746; Email: swenceslaus@archbalt.org; Web: www.stwen.org.
See Queen of Peace Elementary Cluster, St. James and St. John School, Baltimore under Elementary Schools, Regional and Community located in the Institution section.
Catechesis Religious Program—Students 43.

102—ST. WILLIAM OF YORK (1914) Revs. Michael Foppiano, Admin.; Joseph M. O'Meara, (Retired).
Res.: 600 Cooks Ln., 21229. Tel: 410-566-2140;
Fax: 410-362-5475; Email: swybalt@archbalt.org; Web: www.stwilliamofyorkchurch.org.
Catechesis Religious Program—Tel: 410-566-6152. Peggy Mrozek, D.R.E. (Children); Wayne Hipley, Youth Min. Students 45.

OUTSIDE METROPOLITAN BALTIMORE

ABERDEEN, HARFORD CO., ST. JOAN OF ARC (1920) Rev. William F. Franken; Deacons Daniel Kopczyk; Raymond T. Van Pelt III.
Office: 222 S. Law St., Aberdeen, 21001.
Tel: 410-272-4535; Fax: 410-272-9025; Email: stjoanarc@archbalt.org; Web: www.stjoanarc.org.
Res.: 257 S. Law St., Aberdeen, 21001.
School—St. Joan of Arc School, (Grades PreK-8), 230 S. Law St., Aberdeen, 21001. Tel: 410-272-1387;
Fax: 410-272-1959; Email: school@stjoanarc.org; Web: www.school.stjoanarc.org. Mrs. Virginia Bahr, Prin. Lay Teachers 17; Students 194.
Catechesis Religious Program—Tel: 410-272-6944. Students 152.

ABINGDON, HARFORD CO., ST. FRANCIS DE SALES (1866) [CEM]
Tel: 410-676-5119; Fax: 410-676-7520; Email: sfabing@archbalt.org; Web: www.stfrancisabingdon.org. Revs. John B. Ward, J.C.L., J.D.; Jaime Garcia-Vazquez; Deacon James R. Sullivan.
Res.: 1450 Abingdon Rd., Abingdon, 21009.
Tel: 410-676-5119; Fax: 410-676-7520; Email: sfabing@archbalt.org; Web: www.stfrancisabingdon.org.
Catechesis Religious Program—Tel: 410-676-3354. Students 700.

ANNAPOLIS, ANNE ARUNDEL CO.

1—ST. ANDREW BY THE BAY (Annapolis) (1981) Rev. Jeffrey S. Dauses; Deacons David Tengwall; Anthony Norcio, J.C.L.; William Fleming.
Parish Center—701 College Pkwy., Annapolis, 21409. Tel: 410-974-4366; Fax: 410-974-4339; Email: sabbanna@archbalt.org; Web: www.standrewbythebay.org.
Catechesis Religious Program—Students 609.

2—ST. MARY (1853) [CEM] Revs. John G. Tizio, C.Ss.R.; Robert Wojtek, C.Ss.R.; Andrew Costello, C.Ss.R.; Patrick Flynn, C.Ss.R.; Joseph Krastel, C.Ss.R.; Kevin Milton, C.Ss.R.; David Verghese, C.Ss.R.; Charles Hergenroeder, C.Ss.R.; Miguel Martinez,

C.Ss.R.; Deacon Leroy S. Moore. In Res., Rev. Alphonsus Olive, C.Ss.R.
Res.: 109 Duke of Gloucester St., Annapolis, 21401. Tel: 410-263-2396; Fax: 410-263-3027; Email: stmarys_annapolis@archbalt.org; Web: www.stmarysannapolis.org.
School—St. Mary School, (Grades K-8), 111 Duke of Gloucester St., Annapolis, 21401. Tel: 410-263-2869; Fax: 410-269-6513; Email: websiteinfo@stmarysannapolis.org; Web: www.stmarysannapolis.org/page/es-homepage. Rebecca Zimmerman, Prin. Lay Teachers 47; Sisters 1; Students 823.
High School—St. Mary High School, 113 Duke of Gloucester St., Annapolis, 21401. Tel: 410-263-3294; Fax: 410-269-7843; Web: www.stmarysannapolis.org/page/about/welcome. Mindi Imes, Prin.; Fred Haller, Pres. Lay Teachers 37; School Sisters of Notre Dame 1; Students 500.
Catechesis Religious Program—Tel: 410-990-4779; Fax: 410-263-7381. Students 1,498.
Convent—4 Shipwright St., Annapolis, 21401. Tel: 410-269-0568. School Sisters of Notre Dame 2.
Mission—St. John Neuman, 620 N. Bestgate Rd., Annapolis, Anne Arundel Co. 21401. Tel: 410-266-2497.

BEL AIR, HARFORD CO., ST. MARGARET (1905) Rev. Msgr. Kevin T. Schenning; Revs. Nicodemus Konza; John Cunningham; Mrs. Mary Ellen Bates, Business Mgr.; Deacons Patrick J. Goles; Victor Petrosino; Martin E. Wolf; John Chott; James DeCapite.
Res.: 141 Hickory Ave., Bel Air, 21014. Tel: 410-838-6969; Fax: 410-879-2518; Email: smbelair@archbalt.org; Web: www.stmargaret.org.
School—St. Margaret School, (Grades PreK-8), 205 Hickory Ave., Bel Air, 21014. Tel: 410-879-1113; Email: smsch@archbalt.org; Web: smsch.org. Madeleine Hobik, Prin. Lay Teachers 30; Students 863.
Catechesis Religious Program—Tel: 410-838-4224. Students 1,600.
Mission—St. Mary Magdalen, 1716 Churchville Rd., Bel Air, Harford Co. 21015.

BOONSBORO, WASHINGTON CO., ST. JAMES BOONSBORO (2008)
121 N. Main St., Boonsboro, 21713. Tel: 301-432-2887; Fax: 301-432-4511; Email: businessofficestjames@archbalt.org; Web: www.stjamesmd.org. Rev. John J. Jicha; Deacon Paul A. Nicholas; Erin Breeden, Liturgical Ministry
Legal Name: St. James Boonsboro Roman Catholic Congregation, Inc.
Catechesis Religious Program—Linda Becker, D.R.E.

BRADSHAW, BALTIMORE CO., ST. STEPHEN (1863) [CEM] Revs. Lawrence F. Kolson; Paul Breczinski; Deacon Frank R. Laws.
Res.: 8030 Bradshaw Rd., Bradshaw, 21087. Tel: 410-592-7071; Fax: 410-592-6803; Email: ststephen@archbalt.org; Web: www.ststephenbradshaw.org.
School—St. Stephen School, (Grades PreK-8), 8028 Bradshaw Rd., Bradshaw, 21087. Tel: 410-592-7617; Fax: 410-592-7330; Email: info@ssschool.org; Web: www.ssschool.org. Mrs. Mary M. Patrick, Prin. Lay Teachers 25.
Catechesis Religious Program—Tel: 410-592-8666. Sr. Angela DeFontes, O.S.F., D.R.E. Students 402.

BRUNSWICK, FREDERICK CO., ST. FRANCIS OF ASSISI (1893) [CEM] Rev. Msgr. Robert J. Jaskot, B.S., S.T.L., S.T.B.; Rev. George A. Limmer, Assigned Priest, (Retired); Deacons Wayne Matthews; Chuck McCandless; Faye Williams, Business Mgr.
Res.: 113 First Ave., Brunswick, 21716. Tel: 301-834-9185; Fax: 301-834-4162; Email: stsmparishoffice@verizon.net; Web: www.stfrancis-stmary.org.
Catechesis Religious Program—Edgar D. Haynes, Faith Formation Dir. Students 90.
Mission—St. Mary's, Petersville, Frederick Co. 21758.

BUCKEYSTOWN, FREDERICK CO., ST. JOSEPH-ON-CARROLLTON MANOR (1811) [CEM]
Mailing Address: P.O. Box 33, Buckeystown, 21717. Tel: 301-663-0907; Fax: 301-874-0247; Email: sjbuckey@archbalt.org; Web: www.stjoesbuckeystown.org. Rev. Lawrence K. Frazier, (Retired), Email: pastor@stjosebuckeystown.org; Deacon Gregory Rausch.
Res.: 5843 Manor Woods Rd., Frederick, 21703.
Catechesis Religious Program—
Tel: 301-663-0907, Ext. 12; Fax: 301-874-0247. Ashley Arominski, Youth & Young Adult Ministry. Students 354.

CLARKSVILLE, HOWARD CO., ST. LOUIS (1855) [CEM] Rev. Msgr. Joseph L. Luca; Rev. Peter Literal; Deacons Fred L. Mauser; Scott R. Lancaster; Frank Sarro; Frank Ziegler; Marianne M. Faulstich, Pastoral Assoc.
Res.: 12500 Clarksville Pike, Clarksville, 21029. Tel: 410-531-6040; Fax: 410-531-6191; Email: parishoffice@stlouisparish.org; Web: www.stlouisparish.org.
School—St. Louis School, (Grades PreK-8), Tel: 410-531-6664; Fax: 410-531-6690; Web: www.stlouisparish.org/school. Mrs. Mary Theresa Weiss, Prin., Email: tweiss@stlouisparish.org. Lay Teachers 27; Sisters 1; Students 475.
Catechesis Religious Program—Tel: 410-531-6688; Fax: 410-531-6689; Web: www.stlouisparish.org/reled. Victoria Yozwiak, D.R.E.; Patrick Sprankle, Dir. Youth Ministry. Students 1,330.

COCKEYSVILLE, BALTIMORE CO., ST. JOSEPH (1852) [CEM] Rev. Msgr. Richard B. Hilgartner; Rev. Carlos Osorio; Kati Besole, Pastoral Assoc.; Deacons Edward Sulivan; Donald Awalt; Ann Marie Labin, R.N., Pastoral Assoc.; Dr. John Mojzisek, Mission & Planning.
Res.: 101 Church Ln., Cockeysville, 21030. Tel: 410-683-0600; Fax: 410-628-2956; Email: rhilgartner@sjpmd.org.
School—St. Joseph School, (Grades K-8), 105 Church Ln., Cockeysville, 21030. Tel: 410-683-0600; Fax: 410-628-6814; Email: info@sjpmd.org; Web: school.sjpmd.org. Mrs. Maggie Dates, Prin. Lay Teachers 25; Sisters 2; Students 406.
Catechesis Religious Program—Fax: 410-628-6814. Marie Lybolt, Family & Youth Faith Formation; Ryan Ackerman, Family & Youth Faith Formation; Mrs. Amy Buttarazzi, Family & Youth Faith Formation. Students 442.

COLUMBIA, HOWARD CO., ST. JOHN THE EVANGELIST (1967)
5885 Robert Oliver Pl., Columbia, 21045. Tel: 410-964-1434; Tel: 410- 964-1425; Fax: 410-730-9253; Email: srucker@sjerc.org; Web: www.sjerc.org. Revs. Gerard J. Bowen, Tel: 410-964-1425, Ext. 315; Ferdinand Ezenwachi, Tel: 410-964-1425, Ext. 313; Gene Nickol; Deacon James J. Benjamin, M.D., Tel: 410-730-1543.
Res.: Columbia, 21044.
Interfaith Centers—10431 Twin Rivers Rd., Columbia, 21044. Tel: 410-964-1425; Fax: 410-730-9253; Web: www.sjerc.org. (Wilde Lake).
Catechesis Religious Program—Tel: 410-964-1440. Students 490.

CRESAPTOWN, ALLEGANY CO., ST. AMBROSE (1886) [CEM] Closed. For inquiries for parish records contact the chancery.

CROFTON, ANNE ARUNDEL CO., ST. ELIZABETH ANN SETON (1976) Rev. Paul Sparklin, Tel: 410-721-5770, Ext. 234; Sr. Katherine O'Donnell, R.S.M., Pastoral Assoc., Tel: 410-721-5770, Ext. 233; Deacon Frederick Seibold.
Office: 1800 Seton Dr., Crofton, 21114. Tel: 410-721-5770; Fax: 410-721-5508; Email: seascrof@archbalt.org; Web: www.seaseton.org.
See School of the Incarnation, Inc., Gambrills under Elementary Schools, Regional and Community located in the Institution section.
Catechesis Religious Program—Tel: 410-721-5774. John Russell, Coord. Youth Ministry, Tel: 410-721-5774, Ext. 229. Students 280.

CUMBERLAND, ALLEGANY CO.
1—ST. MARY (1900) [CEM] (Italian), Closed. For inquiries for parish records please see Our Lady of the Mountains.
2—OUR LADY OF THE MOUNTAINS, ROMAN CATHOLIC CONGREGATION, INC. (2011) [CEM] (Irish) Revs. Gregory Chervenak, O.F.M.Cap.; Louis Petruha, O.F.M.Cap., In Res.; Bro. James Watson, O.F.M.Cap., Parochial Vicar; Deacons David A. Conley, (Retired); Loren Mooney, (Retired); Francis L. Werner Jr., (Retired)
Legal Name: Our Lady of the Mountains, Roman Catholic Congregation, Inc.
Res.: 201 N. Centre St., Cumberland, 21502. Tel: 301-777-1750; Fax: 301-777-2669; Email: olmcumberland@archbalt.org; Web: www.olmcumberland.org.
School—Bishop Walsh School, (Grades PreK-12), 700 Bishop Walsh Rd., Cumberland, 21502. Tel: 301-724-5360; Email: jcessna@bishopwalsh.org; Web: bishopwalsh.org. Dr. Raymond Kiddy, Prin.
Catechesis Religious Program—Tel: 301-724-0288. Monica Beck, Coord. Faith Formation. Students 74.
Convent—School Sisters of Notre Dame, 209 N. Centre St., Cumberland, 21502.
3—ST. PATRICK, Merged For inquiries for parish records contact Our Lady of the Mountains, Cumberland.
4—SS. PETER AND PAUL (1848) [CEM] (German), Closed. For inquiries for parish records please see Our Lady of the Mountains, Cumberland.

DAVIDSONVILLE, ANNE ARUNDEL CO., HOLY FAMILY (1929) Rev. Andrew D. Aaron; Deacon Doug Lovejoy.
Res.: 826 W. Central Ave., P.O. Box 130, Davidsonville, 21035-0130. Tel: 410-269-0586; Tel: 301-261-7399; Fax: 410-798-5315; Email: office@hfccmail.org; Web: www.holyfamilychurch.com.
See School of the Incarnation under Elementary Schools, Regional and Community located in the Institution section.
Catechesis Religious Program—Tel: 410-798-5680. Amy Burgess, D.R.E.; Christy Cosgrove, Adult Enrichment Coord., Tel: 410-798-5680, Ext. 34; Michael MacDonald, Youth Min., Tel: 410-798-5680, Ext. 33. Students 576.

EDGEWATER, ANNE ARUNDEL CO., OUR LADY OF PERPETUAL HELP (1976) Rev. Timothy Klunk.
Res.: 515 Loch Haven Rd., Edgewater, 21037. Tel: 443-203-1002; Fax: 410-798-0076; Email: secretary@olph.net; Web: www.olph.net.
See School of the Incarnation, Gambrills under Elementary Schools, Regional and Community in the Institution Section.
Catechesis Religious Program—Patricia Dixon, A.R.E., Tel: 443-203-1002, Ext. 14. Students 125.

EDGEWOOD, HARFORD CO., PRINCE OF PEACE (1977) Revs. Jack Ward; Jamie Garcia.
Office Address—2600 Willoughby Beach Rd., Edgewood, 21040-3412. Tel: 410-679-5912; Fax: 410-676-0326; Email: ppedgewd@archbalt.org; Web: www.orgsites.com/md/peace_edgewood.
Catechesis Religious Program—Sr. Susanne Bunn, M.H.S.H., Dir. Faith Formation. Students 84.

ELLICOTT CITY, HOWARD CO.
1—OUR LADY OF PERPETUAL HELP (1893) [CEM] Rev. Erik J. Arnold; Sr. Lorraine McGraw, O.S.F., Tel: 410-747-4334, Ext. 314; Lisa Sliker, Admin.
Res.: 4795 Ilchester Rd., Ellicott City, 21043-6898. Tel: 410-747-4334; Fax: 410-747-4399; Email: lphelli@archbalt.org; Web: www.olphparish.org.
School—Our Lady of Perpetual Help School, (Grades K-8), 4801 Ilchester Rd., Elliott City, 21043. Tel: 410-744-4251; Fax: 410-788-5210; Email: bmunoz@olphschool.org; Web: olphschool.org. Victor Pellechia, Prin. Lay Teachers 22; Students 230.
Catechesis Religious Program—Tel: 410-747-0131; Fax: 410-788-8905. Mrs. Judy Gruel, D.R.E. Students 561.
2—ST. PAUL (1838) [CEM] Rev. Warren V. Tanghe; Deacons Joseph E. Knepper; George Krause; Patricia Frederick, Pastoral Assoc.
Res.: 3755 St. Paul St., Ellicott City, 21043. Tel: 410-465-1670; Fax: 410-313-8551; Email: stpaulsrc@archbalt.org; Web: www.stpaulec.org.
Catechesis Religious Program—Tel: 410-465-0622. Kenneth DeMoll, Coord. Youth Ministry. Students 237.
3—RESURRECTION (1974) Rev. Msgr. John A. Dietzenbach, V.F., Tel: 410-461-9111, Ext. 202; Rev. Canisius T. Tah; Deacons John Comegna; Frank O'Keefe. In Res., Rev. Edward S. Szymanski, Chap. Howard Co. General Hospital, (Retired).
Office: 3175 Paulskirk Dr., Ellicott City, 21042-2698. Tel: 410-461-9112; Fax: 410-203-9419; Email: aappleby@res-ec.org; Web: www.res-ec.org.
School—Resurrection/St. Paul, (Grades K-8), 3155 Paulskirk Dr., Ellicott City, 21042-2698. Tel: 410-461-9111; Fax: 410-988-5470; Email: jdewey@resstpaul.org; Web: www.resstpaul.org. Karen Murphy, Prin. Lay Teachers 32; Students 452.
Catechesis Religious Program—
Tel: 410-461-9111, Ext. 221. Kate Kleintank, D.R.E., Tel: 410-461-9111, Ext. 222; Martha Bode, Dir. Adult Education, Tel: 410-461-9111, Ext. 204; Kenneth DeMoll, Youth Min., Tel: 410-461-9111, Ext. 206. Students 820.

EMMITSBURG, FREDERICK CO.
1—ST. ANTHONY SHRINE (1805) [CEM] Rev. J. Collin Poston; Deacon John A. Hawkins.
Res. & Office Address: 16150 St. Anthony Rd., Emmitsburg, 21727. Tel: 301-447-2367; Fax: 301-447-3618; Email: saolmc@archbalt.org; Web: www.sasolmc.org.
Catechesis Religious Program—Tel: 301-271-4099; Fax: 301-271-7127. Sr. M. Valenta Rusin, F.S.S.J., D.R.E. & Pastoral Min. Students 36.
2—ST. JOSEPH (1793) [CEM 2] Revs. John J. Holliday, C.M.; Charles F. Krieg, C.M.
Res.: 47 DePaul St., Emmitsburg, 21727. Tel: 301-447-2326; Fax: 301-447-3679; Email: stjosephemmitsburg@comcast.net; Web: www.stjosephemmitsburg.org.
Catechesis Religious Program—Email: rrocal@adelphia.net. Doria Wolfe, C.R.E. Students 110.

FALLSTON, HARFORD CO., ST. MARK (1887) Rev. Gerard C. Francik; Deacons Charles W. Hicks, (Retired); Martin DePorres Perry; Mrs. Charlotte Henderson, Pastoral Assoc.
Res.: 2407 Laurel Brook Rd., Fallston, 21047. Tel: 443-299-6489; Fax: 443-299-6894; Email: stmark@archbalt.org; Web: www.saintmarkfallston.org.
Catechesis Religious Program—Tel: 410-879-1706; Fax: 410-877-3502. Mrs. Bridgit Goedeke, Admin. Faith Formation. Students 554.

FREDERICK, FREDERICK CO.
1—ST. JOHN THE EVANGELIST (1763) [CEM] Revs. J. Kevin Farmer; Charles M. Wible; Deacons John L.

Manley; Daniel C. Roff; Michael J. Currens; Douglas J. Nathan.
Res.: 112 E. Second St., Frederick, 21701.
Tel: 301-662-8288; Fax: 301-698-1832; Email: stjohnfrederick@archbalt.org; Web: www.stjohn-frederick.org.
See St. John Regional Catholic School, Frederick under Elementary Schools, Regional and Community located in the Institution section.
Catechesis Religious Program—Tel: 301-662-6722; Fax: 301-695-7024. Ms. Amy Spessard, D.R.E. Students 387.
2—ST. KATHARINE DREXEL (2000) Rev. Keith W. Boisvert, Email: skdpastor@saintdrexel.org; Deacons Timothy J. Moore Sr.; Jeff Sutterman, Email: skddeacon@saintdrexel.org; Kevin Kulesa; Leah Huber, Pastoral Assoc.; Brian McCrohan, Pastoral Assoc.; Anna Maria Alvarado, Pastoral Assoc.; Kathy Moore, Pastoral Assoc.
Legal Name: St. Katharine Drexel Roman Catholic Congregation, Inc.
8428 Opossumtown Pike, Frederick, 21702.
Tel: 301-360-9581; Fax: 301-360-9582; Email: stkatharinedrexel@saintdrexel.org; Web: www.saintdrexel.org.
Catechesis Religious Program—Alexis Zabsonre, C.R.E. & Outreach to Immigrants. Students 175.
FROSTBURG, ALLEGANY CO.
1—DIVINE MERCY PARISH (2016)
44 E. Main St., Frostburg, 21532. Tel: 301-689-6767; Fax: 301-689-6411; Email: smfrostb@archbalt.org. Revs. Edward S. Hendricks; Eric Gauchat, O.F.M.-Cap., Sacramental Min. & Catholic Health Care Ministry; Deacon Harold Bradley; Edward Jones, Business Mgr.; Alison Lyons, Music Min.
Worship Sites—
St. Ann, 12814 New Germany Rd., Grantsville, 21536.
St. Gabriel, 19110 S. Eutaw St., Barton, 21521.
St. Joseph, 19925 Church St., Midland, 21532.
St. Michael, Frostburg.
St. Peter, Westernport.
Catechesis Religious Program—Joseph Keating, D.R.E.; Kathleen Broadwater, Youth Min.
2—ST. MICHAEL (1852) [CEM] Merged with St. Ann, Grantsville; St. Gabriel, Barton; St. Joseph, Midland & St. Peter, Westernport to form Divine Mercy Parish, Frostburg.
FULTON, HOWARD CO., ST. FRANCIS OF ASSISI (1988) Revs. Dennis P. Diehl, K.H.S., (Retired); Joachim Giermek, O.F.M.Conv.; Deacon Joseph McKenna; Berta Sabrio, Pastoral Assoc., Worship & Faith Formation.
Office: 8300 Old Columbia Rd., Fulton, 20759.
Tel: 410-792-0470; Fax: 410-792-0472; Email: office@instrumentofpeace.org; Web: www.instrumentofpeace.org.
Catechesis Religious Program—Becki Kaman, Dir., Youth & Family Minstries. Students 491.
GAMBRILLS, ANNE ARUNDEL CO., CHURCH OF THE HOLY APOSTLES (2004) Merged with St. Joseph, Odenton to form St. Joseph, Odenton/Church of the Holy Apostles, Odenton.
GLEN BURNIE, ANNE ARUNDEL CO.
1—CHRIST THE KING ROMAN CATHOLIC CONGREGATION, INC.
7436 Baltimore-Annapolis Blvd., Glen Burnie, 20161. Tel: 410-766-5070; Web: ctkgb.org. 126 Dorsey Rd., Glen Burnie, 21061. Rev. C. Lou Martin.
2—CHURCH OF THE GOOD SHEPHERD (1972) Rev. C. Lou Martin.
Res.: 1451 Furnace Ave., Glen Burnie, 21060.
Tel: 410-766-5070; Fax: 410-760-6738; Email: goodshepherd9@comcast.net; Web: ctkgb.org.
See Arthur Slade Regional Catholic School, Glen Burnie under Elementary Schools, Regional and Community located in the Institution section.
Catechesis Religious Program—Students 48.
3—CRUCIFIXION, CHURCH OF THE (1972) Rev. C. Lou Martin.
Rectory—100 Scott Ave., Glen Burnie, 21060.
Tel: 410-766-5070; Email: Crucifix@archbalt.org; Web: ctkgb.org.
Catechesis Religious Program—
4—HOLY TRINITY (1919) Revs. C. Lou Martin; Vincent Arisukwu; Jesus Aguirre Guzman; Deacons Kevin Brown; Allen Green; German E. Flores; Kathy Ferris, Business Mgr.
Res.: 7436 Baltimore-Annapolis Blvd., Glen Burnie, 21061. Tel: 410-766-1214; Web: www.cc-gb.org.
Parish Center—126 Dorsey Rd., Glen Burnie, 21061.
Tel: 410-766-5070; Fax: 410-760-6738; Email: HTrinity@archbalt.org; Web: www.ctkgb.org.
See Monsignor Slade Catholic School, Glen Burnie under Elementary Schools, Regional and Community located in the Institution section.
Catechesis Religious Program—Tel: 410-768-3890; Fax: 410-760-6738. Dan Miller, Youth Faith Formation & High School Sacraments; Joyce Pagan, Youth Min. Students 500.
GLYNDON, BALTIMORE CO., SACRED HEART (1873)
65 Sacred Heart Ln., P.O. Box 3672, Glyndon, 21071-3672. Tel: 410-833-1696; Fax: 410-833-2676; Email: parish@shgparish.org; Web: www.shgparish.org. Rev. Msgr. Lloyd Aiken, Email: laiken@archbalt.org; Revs. Hamilton Okeke; Hilario Avenando, Email: fr.hilario@shgparish.org; Deacons James A. Ryan; James Nuzzo.
School—Sacred Heart School, (Grades PreK-8), 63 Sacred Heart Ln., P.O. Box 3672, Glyndon, 21071-3672. Tel: 410-833-0857; Fax: 410-833-0914; Email: info@shgschool.org; Web: www.shgsc.org. Jeanne Cossentino, Prin. Lay Teachers 39; Sisters 1; Students 775.
Catechesis Religious Program—Tel: 410-833-8515. Sr. Cecilia Cyford, S.S.J., D.R.E. Students 574.
Convent—Sacred Heart, 81 Sacred Heart Ln., P.O. Box 3672, Glyndon, 21071-3677. Tel: 410-526-1327.
GRANTSVILLE, NORTHERN GARRETT CO., ST. ANN (1976) Merged with St. Gabriel, Barton; St. Joseph, Midland; St. Michael, Frostburg & St. Peter, Westernport to form Divine Mercy Parish, Frostburg.
HAGERSTOWN, WASHINGTON CO.
1—ST. ANN (1966) Rev. Msgr. J. Bruce Jarboe; Deacons William Nairn; Gary Fulmer.
Church & Res.: 1525 Oak Hill Ave., Hagerstown, 21742. Tel: 301-733-0410; Fax: 301-733-6218; Email: church@stannchurch.com; Web: www.stannchurch.com.
Catechesis Religious Program—
Tel: 301-733-0410, Ext. 20. Thuy Anh Hoang, Faith Formation Dir. Students 284.
2—ST. JOSEPH (1951) Rev. John J. Jicha.
Res.: 17630 Virginia Ave., Hagerstown, 21740-7829.
Tel: 301-797-9445; Fax: 301-797-2490; Email: stjoe@archbalt.org; Web: www.mystjoseph.org.
Catechesis Religious Program—Tel: 301-790-1610. Linda Becker, C.R.E.; Tim Barr, Youth Min. & Sacramental Preparations Coord. Students 160.
3—ST. MARY (1790)
Tel: 301-739-0390, Ext. 110; Email: church@saintmarysonline.org; Web: www.saintmarysonline.org. Revs. Ernest W. Cibelli; Lawrence P. Adamczyk.
Res.: 224 W. Washington St., Hagerstown, 21740.
Tel: 301-739-0390; Fax: 301-739-7082; Email: church@saintmarysonline.org; Web: www.saintmarysonline.org.
School—St. Mary School, (Grades PreK-8), 218 Washington St., Hagertown, 21740.
Tel: 301-733-1184; Fax: 301-745-4997; Email: kgross@stmarycatholicschool.org; Web: www.stmarycatholicschool.org. Mrs. Patricia McDermott, Prin. Lay Teachers 24; School Sisters of Notre Dame 2; Students 260.
Catechesis Religious Program—Tel: 301-739-0390; Email: jmccarter@saintmarysonline.org. Jan McCarter, D.R.E. Students 166.
HANCOCK, WASHINGTON CO., ST. PETER'S (1834) [CEM] Rev. John J. Lombardi.
Res. & Mailing Address: 16 E. High St., Hancock, 21750. Tel: 301-678-6339; Fax: 301-678-6608; Email: officestpeter@verizon.net.
Mission—St. Patrick's (1860) [CEM] 12517 St. Patrick Rd., S.E., Little Orleans, Allegany Co. 21766.
Catechesis Religious Program—Miss Susan Taylor, A.R.E. Students 85.
HAVRE DE GRACE, HARFORD CO., ST. PATRICK'S (1847) [CEM] Rev. Dale Picarella; Sr. Frances Schiminsky, O.S.F., Pastoral Assoc.; Marge Fair, Admin.; Sandy Krass, Sec.; Edward McKay, Business Mgr.
Res.: 615 Congress Ave., Havre de Grace, 21078.
Tel: 410-939-2525; Fax: 443-502-8490; Email: sphgrace@archbalt.org; Web: stpatrickhdg.org.
Catechesis Religious Program—Tel: 410-939-2544. Annmarie Dirndorfer, Coord. Faith Formation. Students 145.
HICKORY, HARFORD CO., ST. IGNATIUS (1792) [CEM] Rev. Msgr. James Barker; Revs. Stephen Sutton; Isaac K. Mokovo; Deacons Peter J. Calabrese; Lee A. Benson; Jim Longenecker.
Res.: 533 E. Jarrettsville Rd., Forest Hill, 21050-1603. Tel: 410-879-1926; Tel: 410-838-2106;
Fax: 410-879-1352; Email: SIhickor@archbalt.org; Web: www.stignatiushickory.org.
Catechesis Religious Program—Tel: 410-879-9390. Todd Twining, Faith Formation; Nancy Long Elder, Faith Formation; Cetta York, Coord. Family Ministry; Susanna Twining, Dir. Youth Min. Students 1,280.
HUNT VALLEY, BALTIMORE CO., CATHOLIC COMMUNITY OF ST. FRANCIS XAVIER (1988)
13717 Cuba Rd., P.O. Box 407, Hunt Valley, 21030.
Tel: 410-785-0356; Fax: 410-785-1628; Email: sfhunt@archbalt.org; Web: www.ccsfx.org. Rev. Frank J. Brauer; Rev. Msgr. Thomas J. Donellan, Pastor Emeritus; Deacon Donald Murray, Diaconal Ministry, RCIA; Patricia Allshouse, Pastoral Assoc., Email: pallshouse@ccsfx.net.
Catechesis Religious Program—Ms. Joanie Carlson, Coord. Middle School; Ryan Ackerman, Youth Min. Students 445.
HYDES, BALTIMORE CO., ST. JOHN THE EVANGELIST-LONG GREEN VALLEY (1822) [CEM] Rev. Msgr. Richard E. Cramblitt, V.F.
Res.: 13305 Long Green Pike, Hydes, 21082.
Tel: 410-592-6209; Fax: 410-817-4432; Email: sjehydes@sjehydes.org; Web: sjehydes.org.
Catechesis Religious Program—M. Theresa Konitzer, D.R.E.; Mrs. M. Colleen Sisolak, Youth & Young Adult Ministry; Sr. Carol Czyzewski, F.S.S.J., Adult Faith Formation. Students 427.
IJAMSVILLE, FREDERICK CO., ST. IGNATIUS OF LOYOLA (1983) Rev. Michael J. Jendrek, Tel: 301-695-8845, Ext. 206; Deacons Larry Matheny, Pastoral Assoc., Tel: 301-695-8845, Ext. 204; David J. Ebner; James M. Cyr.
Office: 4103 Prices Distillery Rd., Ijamsville, 21754.
Tel: 301-695-8845; Fax: 301-695-0259; Email: SILurban@archbalt.org; Web: www.e-stignatius.org.
See St. John Regional Catholic School, Frederick under Elementary Schools, Regional and Community located in the Institution section.
Catechesis Religious Program—Carol Smith, Dir. Faith Formation, Tel: 301-695-8845, Ext. 210; Chris Sparks, Coord. Youth Ministry. Students 764.
JESSUP, ANNE ARUNDEL CO., ST. LAWRENCE MARTYR (1866) [CEM] Revs. Victor J. Scocco, O.SS.T.; Binoy Akkalayil, O.SS.T.; Deacon John Sedlevicius. In Res., Rev. Thomas J. Burke, O.SS.T., S.T.M., S.T.D., B.A.
Res.: 7669 Clark Rd., Hanover, 21076.
Tel: 410-799-1970; Fax: 410-799-1134; Email: office@saintlawrencemartyr.org; Web: www.saintlawrencemartyr.org.
See Arthur Slade Regional Catholic School, Glen Burnie under Elementary Schools, Regional and Community located in the Institution section.
Catechesis Religious Program—St. Lawrence School of Religion, 2821 Jessup Rd., P.O. Box 1188, Jessup, 20794. Tel: 410-799-7790; Fax: 410-799-7291. Mrs. Valerie Magnuson, D.R.E. Students 76.
JOPPA, HARFORD CO., CHURCH OF THE HOLY SPIRIT (1963) Rev. Joseph C. Simmons.
Res.: 540 Joppa Farm Rd., Joppa, 21085.
Tel: 410-679-2191; Email: hspiritchurch@comcast.net; Web: www.holyspiritjoppa.org.
Catechesis Religious Program—Tel: 410-679-5912. Sr. Susanne Bunn, M.H.S.H., Dir. Faith Formation. Students 99.
LAUREL, ANNE ARUNDEL CO., RESURRECTION OF OUR LORD (1968) Rev. Hector Mateus-Ariza, Admin.; Deacons Lawrence P. Teixeira; Jose L. Gabin; Shaun Guevarra, Pastoral Assoc.
Office Address: 8402 Brock Bridge Rd., Laurel, 20724. Tel: 410-792-7982; Fax: 410-792-8337; Email: rollaure@archbalt.org; Web: www.roollaurel.org.
Res.: 407 Forest Bridge Ct., Laurel, 20724.
Tel: 301-498-7107; Fax: 410-792-8337; Email: rollaure@archbalt.org; Web: www.roollaurel.org.
Catechesis Religious Program—Tel: 301-498-9803. Students 174.
LIBERTYTOWN, FREDERICK CO., ST. PETER THE APOSTLE (1821) [CEM] Rev. Jason Worley; Deacons Jack Martin; Gerald B. Jennings.
Res.: 9201 Green Valley Rd., Libertytown, 21762.
Tel: 301-898-5111 (Office); Fax: 301-898-0465; Email: jworley@stpeter-libertytown.org; Web: www.stpeter-libertytown.org.
Church: 9190 Church St., Union Bridge, 21791.
Catechesis Religious Program—Ms. Carolyn Nolan, C.R.E. (Adults). Students 713.
LINTHICUM HEIGHTS, ANNE ARUNDEL CO., ST. PHILIP NERI (1964) Rev. Michael DeAscanis; Deacons Robert Keeley; Edward Whitesell.
Parish Center—6405 S. Orchard Rd., Linthicum Heights, 21090-2628. Tel: 410-859-0571;
Fax: 410-859-5047; Email: StPhilip@archbalt.org; Web: www.saintphilipnerichurch.org.
School—St. Philip Neri School, (Grades K-8), 6401 Orchard Rd., Linthicum Heights, 21090.
Tel: 410-859-1212; Fax: 410-859-5480; Email: spnschool@archbalt.org; Web: https://www.st.philip-neri.org/. Kate Daley, Prin. Lay Teachers 24; Students 389.
Catechesis Religious Program—
Tel: 410-859-4950, Ext. 224;
Tel: 410-859-0571, Ext. 224 (Rel. Ed. Office). Laura Graham, D.R.E.; Hilary Bateman, Dir. Youth Ministry. Students 310.
LONACONING, ALLEGANY CO., ST. MARY OF THE ANNUNCIATION (1865) [CEM] Closed. For inquiries for parish records contact the chancery.
MANCHESTER, CARROLL CO., ST. BARTHOLOMEW (1864) Rev. Michael J. Roach.
Mailing Address & Parish Center: 3071 Park Ave., Manchester, 21102. Tel: 410-239-8881;
Fax: 410-10404; Email: shirley.mangold@archbalt.org; Web: stbartholomewmanchester.org.
Res.: 2940 Park Ave., P.O. Box 448, Manchester, 21102-0448. Tel: 410-239-8207; Fax: 410-239-3216.

Catechesis Religious Program—Lynn Szymanski, C.R.E.; Linda Sterner, Youth Coord.; Kelly Guest, Youth Coord. Students 466.

MIDDLETOWN, FREDERICK CO., HOLY FAMILY CATHOLIC COMMUNITY (1986) Rev. Msgr. Robert J. Jaskot, B.S., S.T.L., S.T.B.; Deacons George Sisson; George Wunderlich; Wayne Matthews; Chuck McCandless.
Res.: 3240 Old National Pike, Middletown, 21769. Tel: 301-371-3239.
Church & Mailing Address: 7321 Burkittsville Rd., Middletown, 21769. Tel: 301-473-4800;
Fax: 301-371-6810; Email: info@hfccmd.org; Web: www.hfccmd.org.
Catechesis Religious Program—Carolyn Rohr, Dir. Youth Ministry. Students 522.

MIDLAND, ALLEGANY CO., ST. JOSEPH (1891) [CEM] (Irish), Merged with St. Ann, Grantsville; St. Gabriel, Barton; St. Michael, Frostburg & St. Peter, Westernport to form Divine Mercy Parish, Frostburg.

MILLERSVILLE, ANNE ARUNDEL CO., OUR LADY OF THE FIELDS (1965) [CEM]
1070 Cecil Ave. S., Millersville, 21108.
Tel: 410-923-7060; Fax: 410-923-6978. Rev. Msgr. Jay O'Connor; Rev. Ross E. Conklin Jr.
Res.: 1069 S. Cecil Ave., Millersville, 21108.
Tel: 410-987-1551; Fax: 410-987-9723; Email: lfields@archbalt.org; Web: www.ourladyofthefields.org.
See School of the Incarnation, Inc., Gambrills under Elementary Schools, Regional and Community located in the Institution section.
Catechesis Religious Program—Tel: 410-923-2195. Dr. Thomas E. Little, Pastoral Assoc., Evangelization & Faith Formation, Tel: 410-923-7025. Students 1,052.

MOUNT SAVAGE, ALLEGANY CO., ST. PATRICK (1863) [CEM] Closed. For inquiries for parish records contact the chancery.

OAKLAND, GARRETT CO., ST. PETER THE APOSTLE (1852) [CEM] Rev. C. Douglas Kenney.
Res.: 208 S. Fourth St., Oakland, 21550.
Tel: 301-334-2202; Fax: 301-334-9006; Email: spsecretary@archbalt.org; Web: www.garrettstpeter.org.
Catechesis Religious Program—Betty Eaton, D.R.E. Students 67.
Mission—St. Peter at the Lake, 1140 Mosser Rd., Mc Henry, Garrett Co. 21541. Dolores Gloeckl, Lake Center Coord.

ODENTON, ANNE ARUNDEL CO.
1—ST. JOSEPH (1924) Merged with Church of the Holy Apostles, Gambrills to form St. Joseph, Odenton/Church of the Holy Apostles, Odenton.
2—ST. JOSEPH, ODENTON (1924) Rev. James P. Kiesel; Deacons David A. Page; Keith Chase; David Roling.
Mailing Address & Church: 1283 Odenton Rd., Odenton, 21113. Tel: 410-674-9238;
Fax: 410-674-4761; Email: info@stjosephodenton.org; Web: www.stjosephodenton.org.
See School of the Incarnation, Inc., Gambrills under Elementary Schools, Regional and Community located in the Institution section.
Catechesis Religious Program—Pete Ball, D.R.E. Students 236.

PARKTON, BALTIMORE CO., OUR LADY OF GRACE (1974) Rev. Michael S. Triplett, V.F.; Deacon James Prosser.
Res.: 425 Everett Rd., Monkton, 21111.
Fax: 410-329-6830; Email: ehagner@ourladygrace.org; Web: www.ourladygrace.org.
Parish Center—18310 Middletown Rd., Parkton, 21120. Tel: 410-329-6826; Fax: 410-329-6830; Email: ehagner@ourladygrace.org.
Catechesis Religious Program—Students 472.

PASADENA, ANNE ARUNDEL CO.
1—ST. JANE FRANCES DE CHANTAL (Riviera Beach) (1946)
Tel: 410-255-4646; Fax: 410-437-5191. Rev. Msgr. Carl F. Cummings; Deacon Steven C. House; Mrs. Gina Bujanowski, Business Mgr.; Mrs. Tracey Laber, Sec.; Marianne Gregory, Music Min.; Katie Torrey, RCIA Coord.; Claire Horvath, Youth Min.
Res.: 8499 Virginia Ave., Pasadena, 21122-3097.
Tel: 410-255-4646; Fax: 410-437-5191; Email: stjane@archbalt.org; Web: www.stjane.org.
School—St. Jane Frances de Chantal School, (Grades PreK-8), 8513 Saint Jane Dr., Pasadena, 21122. Tel: 410-255-4750; Fax: 410-360-6720; Email: office@stjaneschool.org; Web: www.stjaneschool.org. Elena Simmons, Prin. Lay Teachers 23; Students 574.
Catechesis Religious Program—Tel: 410-437-4727. Katie Torrey, C.R.E.; Claire Horvath, Youth Ministry Coord. Students 361.
2—OUR LADY OF THE CHESAPEAKE (1980) Rev. Brian M. Rafferty, S.T.L., (Retired); Deacon Richard W. Clemens; Rodney Amero; Judy Glinka, Business Mgr.
Church: 8325 Ventnor Rd., Pasadena, 21122.
Tel: 410-255-3677; Fax: 410-437-7527; Email: lchesape@archbalt.org; Web: www.olchesapeake.org.
See Arthur Slade Regional Catholic School, Glen Burnie under Elementary Schools, Regional and Community in the Institution Section.
Catechesis Religious Program—Fax: 410-437-7527. Stacey Beres, D.R.E. & Administrative Asst.; Rodney Romero, Coord. Liturgical Music & Liturgy Planning; Tim Janiszewski, Pastoral Assoc., Youth Ministry & Evangelization. Students 456.

POPLAR SPRINGS, HOWARD CO., ST. MICHAEL (1879) [CEM]
1125 St. Michael's Rd., Mount Airy, 21771-3235. Rev. Michael J. Ruane.
Res.: 1200 St. Michaels Rd., Mount Airy, 21771-3202. Tel: 410-489-4211; Tel: 410-442-2845.
Parish Center—Tel: 410-489-7667;
Fax: 410-442-1486; Email: Parish_Secretary@stmichaelpoplarsprings.org; Web: www.stmichaelspoplarsprings.org.
Catechesis Religious Program—Tel: 410-489-7667; Fax: 410-442-1486. Stacey Ford, D.R.E.; Theodore P. Burkhardt, Youth & Young Adult Ministry. Students 820.

PYLESVILLE, HARFORD CO., ST. MARY (1855) [CEM] Rev. A. Henry Kunkel III; Deacons Gary E. Dumer Jr.; Phillip Seneschal; Barbara Sadler, Business Mgr.; Diana Weidner, Admin.
Res.: 1021 St. Mary's Rd., Pylesville, 21132.
Tel: 410-838-7471; Fax: 410-452-8493; Email: smpylesv@archbalt.org; Web: www.stmaryspylesville.org.
Catechesis Religious Program—Janet Young, Coord. Faith Formation; Rachel Bittner, Youth Min. Students 353.

RANDALLSTOWN, BALTIMORE CO., HOLY FAMILY (1876) [CEM] Rev. Raymond L. Harris Jr.; Dennis W. Kast, Business Mgr., Tel: 410-922-3800. In Res., Rev. Msgr. William A. Collins, (Retired).
Res., Church & Office: 9531 Liberty Rd., Randallstown, 21133. Tel: 410-922-3800;
Fax: 410-922-3804; Email: HFRandal@archbalt.org; Web: www.holyfamilyrandallstown.org.
Catechesis Religious Program—Tel: 410-922-2805. Students 107.

SEVERN, ANNE ARUNDEL CO., ST. BERNADETTE (1972) Deacon W. Fredrick Passauer, Parish Admin.; Susan Yost, Pastoral Assoc., Tel: 410-969-2872.
Res.: 801 Stevenson Rd., Severn, 21144.
Tel: 410-969-2783; Fax: 410-969-2789; Email: StBernadette@archbalt.org; Web: www.stbernadette.org.
See Arthur Slade Regional Catholic School, Glen Burnie under Elementary Schools, Regional and Community located in the Institution section.
Catechesis Religious Program—Tel: 410-969-2786. Pat Radford, C.R.E., Email: pradford@stbernadette.org; Rena Black, Coord. Youth Ministry. Students 225.

SEVERNA PARK, ANNE ARUNDEL CO., ST. JOHN THE EVANGELIST (1927) Revs. James Proffitt; George Asigre; Deacons Ronald Thompson; Nick Pitocco.
Res.: 689 Ritchie Hwy., S.E., Severna Park, 21146.
Tel: 410-647-4884; Fax: 410-544-3047; Email: SJEsever@archbalt.org; Web: www.stjohnsp.org.
School—St. John the Evangelist School, (Grades K-8), 669 Ritchie Hwy., Severna Park, 21146.
Tel: 410-647-2283; Fax: 410-431-5438; Email: cbuckstaff@stjohnsp.org; Web: www.stjohnspschool.org. J. Casey Buckstaff, M.A.T., Prin. Lay Teachers 30; Sisters of St. Joseph, Chestnut Hill 5; Students 460.
Catechesis Religious Program—Tel: 410-647-4892. Students 770.
Convent—679 Ritchie Hwy., Severna Park, 21146. Tel: 410-647-2041. Sisters of St. Joseph 5.

SYKESVILLE, CARROLL CO., ST. JOSEPH (1868) [CEM] Rev. Neville O'Donohue, S.M.; Deacons Michael Dvorak; Vito Piazza Sr., M.A.Th., M.A.Ch.Min.; Karl Bayhi; Lyle Peters, Liturgy & Music Min.
Office: 915 Liberty Rd., Sykesville, 21784.
Tel: 443-920-9191; Fax: 443-920-9192; Email: parishoffice@saintjoseph.cc; Web: www.saintjoseph.cc.
Res.: 6049 Kennard Ct., Eldersburg, 21784.
Tel: 410-795-2722.
Catechesis Religious Program—Tel: 410-920-9102. Nora Rozelle, D.R.E. (First Sacraments); Ann Schwartz, Youth Min. Students 1,295.

TANEYTOWN, CARROLL CO., ST. JOSEPH (1797) [CEM] Rev. John F. Lesnick; Rev. Msgr. Martin E. Feild, Pastor Emeritus; Deacons Darrell W. Smith; Stanley Wise, (Retired).
Res.: 44 Frederick St., Taneytown, 21787.
Tel: 410-756-2500; Fax: 410-756-1260; Email: sjtaney@archbalt.org; Web: www.st-joseph-taneytown.com.
Catechesis Religious Program—Tel: 410-876-8108. Terry A. Smith, A.R.E.; Jim McCarron, RCIA Coord. Students 182.

THURMONT, FREDERICK CO., OUR LADY OF MOUNT CARMEL (1856) [CEM] Rev. J. Collin Poston; Sr. M. Valenta Rusin, F.S.S.J., Pastoral Min. & D.R.E.; Deacon John A. Hawkins.
Office: 16150 St. Anthony Rd., Emmitsburg, 21727.
Tel: 301-447-2367; Fax: 410-271-7127; Email: saolmc@archbalt.org; Web: www.sasolmc.org.
Church: 103 N. Church St., Thurmont, 21788.
Catechesis Religious Program—18 N. Altamont Ave., Thurmont, 21788. Tel: 301-271-4099;
Fax: 301-271-7127. Sr. M. Valenta Rusin, F.S.S.J., Pastoral Min./DRE, Tel: 301-271-4099. Students 94.

TIMONIUM, BALTIMORE CO., CHURCH OF THE NATIVITY (1968) Rev. Michael White; Tom Corcoran, Pastoral Assoc.
20 E. Ridgely Rd., Timonium, 21093.
Tel: 410-252-6080; Fax: 410-252-2657; Email: nlord@archbalt.org; Web: www.churchnativity.com.
Catechesis Religious Program—Students 562.

WALKERSVILLE, FREDERICK CO., ST. TIMOTHY (1980) Rev. Juan Vazquez-Rubio, O.SS.T.; Deacons Jim Barth; Robert Price; Linda Lebo, Music Min., Tel: 301-845-8041.
Church: 8651 Biggs Ford Rd., Walkersville, 21793.
Tel: 301-845-8043; Fax: 301-845-4902; Email: sainttimothy@archbalt.org; Web: www.stimothys.org.
Catechesis Religious Program—Tel: 301-845-8025. Yvette Leith, Dir. Faith Formation; Marissa Alspaugh, Dir. Youth Ministry. Students 275.

WEST RIVER, ANNE ARUNDEL CO., OUR LADY OF SORROWS (1866) [CEM] Rev. Timothy Klunk.
Res.: 101 Owensville Rd., West River, 20778.
Tel: 410-867-2059; Fax: 410-867-8276; Email: ols@archbalt.org; Web: www.olos.us.
Catechesis Religious Program—Tel: 410-867-1941. Mary Catherine Ball, Faith Formation Admin. Students 309.

WESTERNPORT, ALLEGANY CO., ST. PETER (1857) [CEM] Merged with St. Ann, Grantsville; St. Gabriel, Barton; St. Joseph, Midland & St. Michael, Frostburg to form Divine Mercy Parish, Frostburg.

WESTMINSTER, CARROLL CO., ST. JOHN (1853) [CEM] Revs. Mark S. Bialek; Christopher de Leon; Deacons Donald W. Miller; Joseph M. Cinquino; Mark Ripper; Paul G. Cooke. In Res., Rev. Gonzalo Cadavid-Rivera, J.C.L.
Res.: 43 Monroe St., Westminster, 21157.
Tel: 410-848-4744; Tel: 410-876-2248;
Fax: 410-857-1519; Email: sjwest@archbalt.org; Web: www.sjwest.org.
Catechesis Religious Program—Tel: 410-848-8443. Jordan Tippett, D.R.E. Students 968.

WILLIAMSPORT, WASHINGTON CO., ST. AUGUSTINE (1854) Rev. John J. Jicha; Rev. Msgr. Alfred E. Smith, Pastor Emeritus, (Retired); Deacon Paul A. Nicholas.
Res.: 32 E. Potomac St., Williamsport, 21795.
Tel: 301-223-7959; Fax: 301-223-9506; Email: sawilliam@archbalt.org; Web: www.mystaugustinemd.org.
Catechesis Religious Program—Marie Watkins, C.R.E. Students 35.

WOODSTOCK, BALTIMORE CO., ST. ALPHONSUS RODRIGUEZ (1869) [CEM] Rev. Joseph P. Lacey, S.J.; Dee Papania, Pastoral Assoc.
Res.: 10800 Old Court Rd., Woodstock, 21163-1107.
Tel: 410-461-5267; Fax: 410-750-7286; Email: business@stalchurch.org; Web: www.stalchurch.org.
Catechesis Religious Program—Valerie Herrington, Youth Min. Students 246.

Chaplains of Public Institutions

BALTIMORE. *Baltimore City Jail Detention Center - Women*, 401 Eager St., 21202. Tel: 410-209-4216. Sr. Kathy Clatin, Chap.
Carroll County Detention Center. Debbie Loveland, Volunteer Coord., Tel: 410-857-1201.
Franklin Square Hospital Center. Rev. Rey D. LandichoCovered on rotating basis by Our Lady of Mt. Carmel; Our Lady Queen of Peace; St. Stephen Bradshaw; St. Michael the Archangel; St. Clare; St. Leo; Church of the Annunciation.
Greater Baltimore Medical Center, Tel: 410-427-4700 . Immaculate Conception, Towson; St. Leo.
Harbor Hospital. (1959) Tel: 410-685-2255. St. Veronica.
James Lawrence Kernan Hospital, Tel: 410-298-8888 . St. Gabriel, Woodlawn.
Johns Hopkins Bayview Medical Center,
Tel: 410-633-9393. Rev. Patrick E. Besel, Chap. Most Precious Blood; Our Lady of Hope; Our Lady of Pompei; St. Anthony of Padua.
Johns Hopkins Hospital. Rev. Albert Duggan, Chap. St. Brigid; St. Leo.
Maryland General Hospital. St. Ignatius.
Maryland Penitentiary Complex, 954 Forest St., 21202.
Northwest Hospital Center, Tel: 410-922-3800. Holy Family, Randallstown.

Sheppard Pratt Hospital, Tel: 410-427-4700. Immaculate Conception, Towson.
Sinai Hospital of Baltimore. Covered on rotating basis by St. Ambrose; Shrine of the Sacred Heart.
Union Memorial Hospital. SS. Philip & James & St. Thomas Aquinas.
University of Maryland Medical Center. Rev. Samuel Uzoukwu, Chap.St. Mary, Star of the Sea; Holy Cross.
University of Maryland- R. Adams Crowley Shock Trauma.
ANNAPOLIS. *Anne Arundel Medical Center*, Tel: 410-263-3294. St. Mary, Annapolis.
COLUMBIA. *Howard County General Hospital*, Tel: 410-964-1425. St. John the Evangelist, Columbia; St. Francis of Assisi, Fulton; Church of the Resurrection, Ellicott City; Our Lady of Perpetual Help, Ellicott City; St. Alphonsus Rodriguez, Woodstock.
CUMBERLAND. *Western Maryland Health Center*, Tel: 301-777-2990. Our Lady of the Mountains, Cumberland; St. Ann, Hagerstown; St. Peter Westernport; St. Mary, Cumberland.
FREDERICK. *Frederick Memorial Hospital*, Tel: 301-662-8288. St. John the Evangelist, Frederick; St. Timothy, Walkersville.
HAGERSTOWN. *Roxbury Correctional Institution*, Hagerstown, 21740. Tel: 240-420-1601.
HAVRE DE GRACE. *Harford Memorial Hospital*, Tel: 410-939-2525. St. Patrick, Havre de Grace.
GLEN BURNIE. *Baltimore Washington Medical Center*. Covered on rotating basis by Holy Trinity; St. Bernadette (Severn), Our Lady of the Chesapeake; Church of the Crucifixion; St. Bernadette, Severn; St. Jane Frances de Chantal, Pasadena; Church of the Good Shepherd.
JESSUP. *Clifton T. Perkins Hospital*, Jessup, 20794. Tel: 410-724-3076.
Maryland Correctional Institution for Women, Jessup, 20794. Tel: 410-547-5475. Kathy Reid, Volunteer Coord., Tel: 410-795-7838, Ext. 113.
Maryland Correctional Institution-Jessup, Jessup, 20794. Tel: 410-799-0100, Ext. 2836. Vacant, Chap.
Patuxent Institution, Jessup, 20794. Tel: 410-518-9977. Bill Cornelius, Volunteer Coord.
OAKLAND. *Garrett County Memorial Hospital*, Tel: 301-334-2204. St. Peter the Apostle, Oakland.
WESTMINSTER. *Carroll Hospital Center*, Tel: 410-848-4744. St. John, Westminster.

Special Assignment:
Most Revs.—
Lori, William E., S.T.D., Archbishop of Baltimore
Brennan, Mark E., D.D., V.G., Eastern Vicar
Madden, Denis J., D.D., V.G., Urban Vicar
Parker, Adam J., D.D., V.G., Vicar Gen., Catholic Ctr.
Rev. Msgr.—
Hannon, James W., Dir., Clergy Personnel; Western Vicar
Very Rev.—
Seitz, Gilbert J., J.C.L., M.Div., Judicial Vicar, Metropolitan Tribunal
Revs.—
Bianco, Louis A., Sec. to Archbishop
Chase, Raymond C., Pastor, St. Vincent de Paul, Catholic Charities
Foley, William P., Coord., Pastoral Care for Retired & Senior Priests
Johnson, Lawrence M., Stella Maris, Pastoral Care
Lim, Roque G., Chap., Harford County Parishes
Malia, Thomas R., Hospital Chap., Mercy Medical Center
Martin, Raymond, Hospital Chap., Carroll and Howard Counties
Nolan, Brian P., Dir. Campus Ministry, Mount St. Mary's University
Spacek, William F., Hospital Chap., Anne Arundel County Churches.

On Duty Outside the Archdiocese:
Revs.—
Cummings, McLean A., The Vatican, Congregation for Oriental Churches
Lobert, Richard C., Chap. Fr. Gabriel Richard HS, Ann Arbor, MI
Morey, Robert E., Diocese of Charleston.

Military Chaplains:
Revs.—
Cotton, Stephen D., Chap., U.S. Army, Kentucky
Goulet, Daniel R., Battalion Chap., Capt., U.S. Army
Kruse, David B., Chap., Maj., U.S. Air Force
Ochalek, Arkadiusz, Chap., U.S. Army, Basic Officer Leader Course
Wood, Tyson J., Chap., U.S. Army.

Priests Absent:
Rev. Msgr.—
Kinsella, John
Revs.—
Fell, Timothy J.
Kim, Silvester
Mahon, M. Shawn
Marrero, Angel M.

Retired:
Rev. Msgrs.—
Amato, Nicholas P., (Retired), 7320 Woodbine Rd., Airville, PA 17302
Auer, John J., (Retired), St. Stephen's Green AL314, 2525 Pot Spring Rd., Timonium, 21093
Bastress, Arthur, P.A., (Retired), St. Stephen's Green AL335, 2525 Pot Spring Rd., Timonium, 21093
Baumgartner, A. Thomas, (Retired), St. Stephen's AL306, 2525 Pot Spring Rd., Timonium, 21093
Byrnes, Paul A., (Retired), 210 Hazelhurst Ln., Swanton, 21561
Collins, William A., (Retired), 9533 Liberty Rd., Randallstown, 21133
Cook, Paul G., (Retired), Mercy Ridge S735, 2525 Pot Spring Rd., Timonium, 21093
Cramblitt, Richard E., V.F.
Donellen, Thomas J., (Retired), St. Stephens Green AL327, 2525 Pot Spring Rd., Timonium, 21093
Field, Martin E., (Retired), Mercy Ridge S627, 2525 Pot Spring Rd., Timonium, 21093
Kenney, Jeremiah F., Ph.D., (Retired), 12 Bandon Ct., Unit 104, Timonium, 21093
Lizor, Joseph S. Jr., (Retired), Heartlands, 3010 N. Ridge Rd., C-509, Ellicott City, 21043
Meisel, Charles F., (Retired), Stella Maris, 2525 Pot Spring Rd., Timonium, 21093
Moeller, George B., (Retired), Mercy Ridge S728, 2525 Pot Spring Rd., Timonium, 21093
Murphy, Richard J., (Retired), 7431 Willow Rd., #40, Frederick, 21702
Schleupner, G. Michael, V.F., (Retired), P.O. Box 403, Whiteford, 21160-0403
Tewes, Thomas J., (Retired), Mercy Ridge S727, 2525 Pot Spring Rd., Timonium, 21093
Tillman, Richard H., (Retired), Immaculate Conception Church, 200 Ware Ave., Towson, 21204
Revs.—
Abrahams, John J., (Retired), 46 Abrahams Rd., Port Deposit, 21904
Albright, Robert E., (Retired), 7415 Chesapeake Rd., 21220
Bochenek, Joseph G., (Retired), Our Lady of Pompei, 3600 Claremont St., 21224
Breighner, Joseph F., (Retired), Cathedral Rectory, 5300 N. Charles St., 21210
Buttner, Michael T., (Retired), 304 Willrich Cir., J, Forest Hill, 21050-1359
Carney, John J., (Retired), Brightview Assisted Living #316, 8100 Rossville Blvd., 21236
Cieri, Domenic L., (Retired), 13910 Glen High Rd., Baldwin, 21013
Cosgrove, Joseph J., (Retired), Mercy Ridge S718, 2525 Pot Spring Rd., Timonium, 21093
Cunningham, John P., (Retired), 1305 Scottsdael Dr. Unit P, Bel Air, 21015
Diehl, Dennis P., K.H.S., (Retired), Mercy Ridge S5606, 2525 Pot Spring Rd., Timonium, 21093
Dowdy, James H., (Retired), 202 Burkwood Ct., Unit K, Bel Air, 21015
Frazier, Lawrence K., (Retired), 903 McLendon Dr., Frederick, 21702
Gosnell, Stephen D., K.H.S., (Retired), Mercy Ridge S634, 2525 Pot Spring Rd., Timonium, 21093
Hammond, Martin, (Retired), St. Augustine Church, 5976 Old Washington Rd., Elkridge, 21075
Henry, Paul J., (Retired), Mercy Ridge S618, 2525 Pot Spring Rd., Timonium, 21093
Holthaus, Paul G., (Retired), Mercy Ridge S617, 2525 Pot Spring Rd., Timonium, 21093
Karoor, Isaac M., (Retired), 1111 King Arthur Ct., Sykesville, 21784
Lawrence, Richard T., (Retired), 250 S. President St., #910, 21202
Le Fevre, Francis J., 24 Green Bridge Dr., Newark, DE 19713
Limmer, George A., (Retired), 716 Naples Dr., Hagerstown, 21740
Livigni, Salvatore, (Retired), St. Michael the Archangel, 2 Willow Ave., 21206
Logue, Mark J., (Retired), 2057 Ramblewood Rd., Rehoboth Beach, DE 19971
Lupico, Samuel, (Retired), St. Mary's, Govans, 5502 York Rd., 21212
McGovern, Walter J., (Retired), Mercy Ridge S734, 2525 Pot Spring Rd., Timonium, 21093
McLaughlin, Neil R., (Retired), Mercy Ridge S309, 2525 Pot Spring Rd., Timonium, 21093
Mohl, Andrew S., (Retired), 401 E. Lehman St., Lebanon, PA 17046
Moore, Christopher P., (Retired), 8406 Willow Rd., Parkville, 21234
Nickol, G. Eugene, (Retired), Our Lady Queen of Peace, 10003 Bird River Rd., Middle River, 21220
O'Brien, William J. III, (Retired), 323 Mount Royal Ave., Aberdeen, 21001-1946
O'Meara, Joseph M., (Retired), 5422 Old Frederick Rd., 21229
Rafferty, Brian M., S.T.L., (Retired)
Reusing, James M., (Retired), 205 E. Joppa Rd., #2707, Towson, 21286
Roman, Manuel R., (Retired), Heartlands Senior Living, 3004 N. Ridge Rd., H102, Ellicott City, 21043
Ryan, Thomas, (Retired), 4016 Cloverland Dr., Phoenix, 21131
Snouffer, Philip T., (Retired), 8820 Walther Blvd., Apt. 1401, 21234
Szymanski, Edward S., (Retired), Mercy Ridge S733, 2525 Pot Spring Rd., Timonium, 21093
Thomas, Paul K., (Retired), 637 Dover St., 21230
Viola, William L., (Retired), 8935 Carlisle Ave., Nottingham, 21236
Vu Dinh Hoat, Rochus, (Retired), 1900 Grand Ave., Carthage, MO 64836-3500
Warman, William C., (Retired), 167 Mount Bethel Rd., Warren, NJ 07059
Wenderoth, Joseph R., (Retired), Mercy Ridge S309, 2525 Pot Spring Rd., Timonium, 21093
Wilson, Stuart T., (Retired), 5269 N. Spring Pointe, Tucson, AZ 85749
Witthauer, Paul G., (Retired), St. Stephen's Green, Dublin Court, 2525 Pot Spring Rd., Timonium, 21093
Zoubek, Ronald, (Retired), 1 Greenwood Ave., 21206.

Permanent Deacons:
Ames, John, St. Agnes; St. William of York
Anderson, Carl A., St. Edward, Baltimore
Anderson, Scott E., St. Joseph on Carrollton Manor
Antczak, George W., (Retired)
Awalt, Donald, St. Joseph, Cockeysville
Bagley, Kevin, St. Leo the Great
Baker, Robert L., (Inactive)
Bankard, Alphonse C. III, Our Lady of Fatima, Baltimore
Barbernitz, Peter M., Dir. Evangelization, St. John the Evangelist, Columbia
Barksdale, Wardell, St. Bernardine
Barth, Jim, St. Timothy Parish, Walkersville
Bauerschmidt, Frederick C., Corpus Christi
Baxter, Michael R., (Inactive)
Bayhi, Karl, (Retired), St. Joseph, Sykesville
Beales, Thomas W., (Inactive)
Benjamin, James, St. John the Evangelist, Columbia
Benson, Lee A., St. Ignatius, Hickory
Bieberich, Charles, Our Lady of Victory
Bradley, Harold, St. Michael, Frostburg; St. Peter, Westernport; St. Gabriel, Barton; St. Joseph, Midland; St. Mary, Lonaconing; St. Ann, Grantsville
Britton, Clifford L., (Inactive)
Brown, Kevin, Christ the King Church, Glen Burnie
Calabrese, Peter, St. Ignatius, Hickory
Chase, Keith, Our Lady of the Fields
Chesnavage, Albert W., (Retired)
Chott, John, St. Margaret, Bel Air
Ciesla, Paul R., (Retired)
Cinquino, Joseph M., St. John, Westminster
Clemens, Richard W., Our Lady of the Chesapeake
Cohagan, Mark D., Catholic Community of South Baltimore
Comegna, John, Church of the Resurrection, Ellicott City
Conley, David A., (Retired), Our Lady of the Mountains
Connor, Jack, (Retired), St. Andrew by the Bay; Annapolitan Nursing Home
Cordova-Ferrer, Nathaniel D., Our Lady of Perpetual Help
Coster, John E., (Retired)
Cupps, Donald R., St. Ursula Church; Knights of Columbus
Currens, Michael J., St. John the Evangelist, Frederick
Cyr, James M., St. Ignatius of Loyola, Ijamsville
Czajkowski, Philip D., St. John, Westminster
Davis, Henry C., St. Michael the Archangel, Overlea
DeAngelis, William J., St. Joseph, Fullerton
DeCapite, James, St. Margaret, Bel Air
Dodge, Michael A., St. Athanasius & St. Rose of Lima Parish
Dumer, Gary E. Jr., St. Mary's, Pylesville
Dutan, Carlos L., St. Clement I, Lansdowne
Dvorak, Michael A., St. Joseph, Eldersburg
Ebner, David J., St. Ignatius of Loyola, Ijamsville
Evans, George T., (Retired), St. Rita
Fallon, William L., (Inactive)

Fleming, William, St. Andrew by the Bay
Flores, German E., Christ the King Church, Glen Burnie
Fulmer, Gary Lee, St. Ann, Hagerstown
Gabin, Jose L., Resurrection of Our Lord
Gifford, Paul A., St. John the Evangelist, Columbia
Goles, Patrick J., St. Margaret, Bel Air
Greene, Allen R., Christ the King Church, Glen Burnie
Grillo, Anthony, (Retired), Our Lady of the Fields
Gross, Theodore C., (Retired; Inactive)
Harcum, Philip W., (Retired; Inactive)
Harris, Jhan M., St. Veronica
Hawkins, John A., (Inactive)
Hayden, Frank S. III, Catholic Community of Ascension and St. Augustine
Heathcott, Brent L., Our Lady of Sorrows
Hicks, Charles W., (Retired), St. Mark, Fallston
Hiebler, Charles H. Jr., Immaculate Heart of Mary
Hodges, Frank P., (Retired), Corpus Christi Church
Hostutler, Kevin J., St. Louis, Clarksville
House, Steven C., St. Jane de Chantal
Hultquist, Bruce K., St. Margaret, Bel Air
Jauquet, William, Our Lady of Victory
Jennings, Gerald B., St. Peter the Apostle, Libertytown
Justice, Brandon, Chap., Howard Cty. Police; Our Lady's Center, Ellicott City
Keeley, Robert L., (Retired), St. Philip Neri
Keller, Sean P., Basilica of the Assumption of the B.V.M.
Kendzierski, Douglas P., St. Leo the Great
Knepper, Joseph E., St. Paul, Ellicott City
Kopczyk, Daniel R., St. Joan of Arc
Kosla, Albert F., (Retired; Inactive)
Krause, George S. Jr., St. Paul, Ellicott City; Boy Scouts of America
Krysiak, Joseph C., (Retired)
Kulesa, Kevin, St. Katherine Drexel, Frederick; Hagerstown Prison Ministry
Lancaster, Scott R., St. Louis, Clarksville
Latrick, Donald P., (Retired; Inactive)
Laws, Francis R., St. Stephen, Bradshaw
Loepker, Mark S., Our Lady of the Fields
Logenecker, James R., St. Ignatius, Hickory; Upper Chesapeake Medical Center
Lopata, Dean M., (Retired; Inactive), St. John, Severna Park
Lovejoy, C. Douglas, Chap., UMBC; Holy Family, Davidsonville
Ludwikowski, David J., St. Casimir
MacKnew, J. Donald, (Retired), St. Margaret, Bel Air
Maloney, Timothy D., St. Joseph, Fullerton
Manley, John L., St. John the Evangelist, Frederick
Mann, James L. Jr., Oak Crest Retirement Community
Mann, Paul T., St. Clare
Martin, John M., Immaculate Heart of Mary; Genesis Cromwell & Loch Raven Nursing Homes
Martin, John W., St. Peter the Apostle, Libertytown
Mason, James L., St. Peter, Hancock
Matheny, Lawrence G., St. Ignatius of Loyola, Ijamsville; Deacon Formation Team Member
Matthews, Russell, (Retired), St. Francis Xavier, Baltimore; Baltimore Nursing Home
Matthews, Wayne, St. Francis of Assisi, Brunswick; St. Mary, Petersville; Holy Family, Middletown
Mauser, Fred L., St. Louis, Clarksville
McCandless, Charles, St. Francis of Assisi, Brunswick; St. Mary's, Petersville
McCoy, Michael P., St. Thomas More
Miller, Eugene J. Jr., (Inactive)
Mills, Hugh H. Jr., (Retired), St. Clement, Lansdowne; Chap., VA Medical Center
Mooney, Loren, Our Lady of the Mountains, Cumberland
Moore, LeRoy S., St. Mary, Annapolis
Moore, Timothy J. Sr., St. Katherine, Drexel
Morales, Edison, Sacred Heart of Jesus
Murray, J. Donald, St. Francis Xavier, Hunt Valley
Nairn, William P., St. Ann, Hagerstown
Nathan, Douglas J., St. John the Evangelist, Frederick
Nicholas, Paul A., St. Joseph, Hagerstown; St. James, Boonsboro; St. Augustine, Williamsport
Norcio, Anthony F., Ph.D., Asst. Dir., Office of the Diaconate Formation, St. Andrew by the Bay
Novak, Richard D., (Retired), Sacred Heart of Jesus
Nuzzo, James M., Sacred Heart, Glyndon; Campus Ministry, Stevenson Univ.
O'Keefe, Francis, Church of the Resurrection, Ellicott City
Page, David A., (Retired), St. Joseph, Odenton
Passauer, W. Fredrick, Christ the King Church, Glen Burnie
Perry, Martin DePorres, St. Mark, Fallston
Petrosino, Victor R., St. Margaret, Bel Air
Piazza, Vito S., St. Joseph, Sykesville
Piet, Stanley G., (Retired)
Pitocco, Nickolas, St. John the Evangelist, Severna Park
Presberry, Seigfried, Dir., Prison Ministry, St. Mark, Catonsville
Price, Robert, St. Timothy, Walkersville
Prosser, James, Our Lady of Grace Parish, Parkton
Rafter, John J. Jr., (Retired; Inactive)
Rausch, P. Gregory, M.D., St. Joseph-on-Carrollton Manor
Reid, Kevin F., Liaison to the Deacon Personnel Board, Catholic Community of South Baltimore
Ripper, Mark, St. John, Westminster
Roberts, Gerald A., Our Lady Queen of Peace
Rodriguez, Alex, St. Francis de Sales
Roff, Daniel C., (Retired), St. John, Frederick
Roling, David A., St. Joseph, Odenton; Church of the Holy Apostles, Gambrills
Roscher, Stephen R., St. Charles Borromeo, Pikesville
Rose, Alan, (Retired), St. Ursula
Rose, Scott, St. John the Evangelist, Frederick; Esperanza Center
Russell, George A., St. Mary, Annapolis
Ryan, James A., Sacred Heart, Glyndon
Sainz, Miguel E., St. Mary of the Assumption, Govans; Hispanic Apostolate
Santiago, Harbey, St. Michael, Poplar Springs
Sarro, Frank A., St. Louis, Clarksville; Tribunal
Schoennagel, Frederick, (Retired), St. John the Evangelist, Hydes
Schwartz, Patrick C., Chap., Howard County Detention Center
Sedlevicius, John, St. Lawrence the Martyr, Jessup
Seibold, Frederick, St. Elizabeth Ann Seton, Crofton
Seneschal, Phillip, St. Mary of the Assumption, Pylesville
Senft, William W., Cathedral of Mary Our Queen
Shelton, Paul D., Blessed Sacrament, Baltimore
Shephard, Robert M., Basilica and MD State Prison System
Sisson, George, Holy Family, Middletown
Smith, Darrell, St. Joseph, Taneytown
Smith, Robert K., St. Francis of Assisi, Fulton
Soloski, Mark, Ph.D., SS. Philip and James Parish
Stoops, Edward J., (Retired; Inactive)
Sullivan, Edward C., (Retired), St. Joseph, Cockeysville
Sullivan, James R., St. Francis de Sales, Abingdon
Sutterman, Jeffrey M., St. Katharine Drexel, Frederick
Teixeira, Lawrence P., Resurrection of Our Lord, Laurel
Tengwall, David L., St. Andrew by the Bay
Thompson, Ronald, St. John the Evangelist, Severna Park
Tilghman, Timothy, Dir. Devel., Josephite Mother House
Trautwein, Ralph, St. Ignatius, Hickory
Turner, B. Curtis, Prin., St. Frances Academy
Van Pelt, Raymond T. III, St. Joan of Arc
Weber, Paul A., St. Ignatius, Baltimore
Werner, Francis L. Jr., (Retired), Our Lady of the Mountain
Westwater, James, (Retired), St. Isaac Jogues
Whitesell, Edward, St. Philip Neri
Wilkins, Herman S., Our Lady of Perpetual Help, Edgewater
Wise, Stanley, (Retired), St. Joseph, Taneytown
Witherspoon, Willard Jr., St. Peter Claver/St. Pius V
Wolf, Joseph, Our Lady of Mount Carmel, Thurmont; St. Anthony Shrine, Elkridge
Wolf, Martin E., Deacon Formation Team Member, St. Margaret's, Bel Air
Woods, Patrick E., St. Pius X; Prison Ministry, Baltimore City
Yannuzzi, Thomas J., Church of the Ascension, Halethorpe; St. Augustine, Elkridge
Zeiler, Francis, Clergy Liaison, Project Rachel, St. Clement Mary Hofbauer
Ziegler, Frank.

INSTITUTIONS LOCATED IN DIOCESE

[A] SEMINARIES, ARCHDIOCESAN

BALTIMORE. *St. Mary's Seminary and University*, 5400 Roland Ave., 21210-1994. Tel: 410-864-4000; Fax: 410-864-4278; Web: www.stmarys.edu. Most Rev. William E. Lori, S.T.D., Archbishop of Baltimore, Chancellor, Chm. Bd. of Trustees; Rev. Philip J. Brown, P.S.S., J.D., J.C.D., S.T.B., J.C.L., B. Music, Pres. & Rector/Vice Chancellor, Ecclesiastical Faculty; Richard G. Childs, M.B.A., C.P.A., Vice Pres., Finance; Mrs. Elizabeth L. Visconage, B.S., Vice Pres., Advancement & Human Resources; Rev. D. Brent Laytham, Ph.D., M.Div., Dean, St. Mary's Ecumenical Institute; Ms. Paula Thigpen, M.A., M.Div., Univ. Registrar; Thomas Raszewski, M.A., M.L.S., Dir. of the Knott Library; Rev. Edward Griswold, D.Min., S.T.L., Vice Rector & Dir. Pastoral Formation; Rev. Msgr. David I. Fulton, J.C.D., S.T.D., Dir., Continuing Formation Programs, Priests; Arryn Milne, B.S., Dir., Information Svcs.; Revs. James L. McKearney, P.S.S., M.Div., S.T.L., S.T.D., Dir. of Liturgy; Lawrence B. Terrien, P.S.S., Ph.D., S.T.D., S.T.L., Dir., Spiritual Life Programs; Thomas J. Burke, O.SS.T., S.T.M., S.T.D., B.A., Assoc. Prof., Systematic Technology, Dean, School of Theology & Praeses, Ecclesiastical Faculty; Scott P. Detisch, M.Div., Ph.D. (cand.), Assoc. Prof., Systematic Theology; Thomas R. Hurst, P.S.S., S.T.L., Ph.D., Assoc. Prof. Sacred Scripture; Robert F. Leavitt, P.S.S., S.T.D., Prof. Systematic Theology, France-Merrick Univ. Prof., (Retired); Jerome Magat, P.S.S., M.A., M.Div., Asst. Prof., Systematic Theology, France-Merrick University Prof.; Brian K. Carpenter, P.S.S., B.S., M.Div., S.T.L., Asst. Prof., Systematic Theology; Michael J. Gorman, Ph.D., Raymond E. Brown Prof., Biblical & Theological Studies; Peter Paul Seaton, Ph.L., Ph.D., Asst. Prof. Philosophy; Ximena DeBroeck, M.A., Ph.D. Candidate, B.S., Asst. Prof., Sacred Scripture; Very Rev. Thomas R. Ulshafer, P.S.S., S.T.L., Ph.D., Assoc. Prof. of Moral Theology, (Retired); Emily Hicks, English Instructor; Bill Scalia, English Instructor; Manuel Aliaga, M.P.A., Ph.D. Candidate, Adjunct Instructor, Spanish; Deacon George Russell, B.A., M.A., Ph.D., Ph.L., Adjunct Instructor, Philosophy; Rev. Patrick M. Carrion, Adjunct Instructor, Pastoral Theology; Brandon Parlopiano, Ph.D., Adjunct Visiting Asst. Affiliate Prof. of History; Deacon Michael A. Dvorak, Adjunct Instructor, Pastoral Theology; Rev. Martin S. Nocchi, S.T.B., M.D., Adjunct Instructor, Faith Studies; Christopher Dreisbach, M.A., Ph.D., Adjunct Prof. of Systematic & Moral Theology; Patricia LeNoir, M.A., Adjunct Instructor, Faith Studies; Patricia Fosarelli, M.D., D.Min., Adjunct Instructor in Pastoral Theology; Brian D. Berry, Adjunct Prof. of Moral Systematic Theology; Very Rev. Gilbert J. Seitz, J.C.L., M.Div., Adjunct Instructor Canon Law

St. Mary's Seminary and University Deacons 2; Lay Teachers 13; Priests 14; Diocesan Seminarians 56; Diocesan Seminarians on Pastoral Leave 7.

Ecumenical Institute of Theology, Tel: 410-864-4200 ; Fax: 410-864-4205. Thomas Raszewski, M.A., M.L.S., Dir., Knott Library.

EMMITSBURG. *Mount St. Mary's Seminary* (1808) 16300 Old Emmitsburg Rd., Emmitsburg, 21727-7797. Tel: 301-447-5295; Fax: 301-447-5895; Email: seminaryinfo@msmary.edu; Web: www.msmary.edu/seminary.

An integral part of the corporation known as Mount St. Mary's University and Seminary. Lay Teachers 10; Priests 15; Total Enrollment 119; Lay Administrators 3; Support Staff 3; Diocesan Seminarians 115; Religious Seminarians 4.

Administration: Dr. Timothy E. Trainor, Ph.D., Interim Pres.; Rev. Msgrs. Andrew R. Baker, S.T.D., Vice Pres. & Rector; Anthony Frontiero, S.T.D., Dir. of Human Formation; Revs. Lee W. Gross, S.T.L., Dean of Students & Asst. Prof., Liturgy, Systematic Theology & Latin; J. Daniel Mindling, O.F.M.Cap., S.T.D., Academic Dean, Dir. of Intellectual Formation & Prof., Moral Theology; John J. Dietrich, Dir. Spiritual Formation & Dir. Liturgy; Kenneth D. Brighenti, Ph.D., Vice Rector, Dir. of Pastoral Formation; Mr. Charles L. Kuhn, Dir. Library; Mrs. Amelia Y. Tigner, Seminary Registrar; Mrs. Susan L. Nield, Admin. Asst., Rector, Admissions & Archives.

Full Time Faculty: Revs. Thomas J. Lane, S.S.L., S.T.D., Prof., Sacred Scripture; Lawrence J. Donohoo, S.T.D., Ph.D., Assoc. Prof. Systematic Theology; Charles P. Connor, S.T.L., Ph.D., Asst. Prof., Church History; Pietro Rossotti, S.T.D., Asst. Prof., Systematic Theology; Thomas J. Smith, Spiritual Direction & Formation Advising; John P. Trigilio, Ph.D., Spiritual Direction & Formation Advising; Dr. Christopher J. Anadale, Ph.D., Dir., Masters Arts, Philosophical Studies; William A. Bales, Ph.D., Assoc. Prof., Sacred Scripture; John D. Love, S.T.D., Assoc. Prof., Systematic Theology; Owen M. Phelan, Ph.D., Assoc. Prof., Church History; Steven C. Smith, Ph. D., Assoc. Prof., Sacred Scripture; Deborah Wentling, M.A., ESL Coord.; Ms. Julia Parker, M. Mus. Ed., Organist/Dir. Liturgical Music; Mrs. Caroline Purcell, M.A., ESL Instructor; John-Mark L. Miravalle, S.T.D., Dir. of Pre-Theology, Asst. Prof., Moral & Systematic Theology; Rev. Msgr. Michael Heintz, Ph.D., Asst. Prof. of Systematic Theology.

Part Time Faculty: Revs. Michael J. Roach, Adjunct Prof., Church History; Lawrence J. McNeil,

D.Min., Adjunct Prof., Church History; Juan Esposito, J.C.D., Adjunct Prof., Canon Law; Christa Bucklin, Ph.D., Adjunct Prof. Pastoral Spanish.

[B] COLLEGES AND UNIVERSITIES

BALTIMORE. **Loyola University Maryland*, 4501 N. Charles St., 21210. Tel: 410-617-2000; Tel: 800-221-9107; Fax: 410-617-5196; Web: www.loyola.edu. Rev. Brian F. Linnane, S.J., Pres., Email: blinnane@loyola.edu. Lay Teachers 428; Priests 9; Total Enrollment 6,084; Total Staff 1,303.

Loyola Graduate Center-Columbia Campus, 8890 McGaw Rd., Columbia, 21045-5245. Tel: 410-617-7600; Fax: 410-617-7643.

Loyola Graduate Center-Timonium Campus, 2034 Greenspring Dr., Timonium, 21093. Tel: 410-617-1500; Fax: 410-617-1518. Rev. Brian F. Linnane, S.J., Pres.; Amanda Thomas, Dean, Loyola College; Amy R. Wolfson, Vice Pres. Academic Affairs; Kathleen Getz, Dean, Sellinger School of Business & Mgmt.; Dr. Susan Donovan, Exec. Vice Pres., Email: sdonovan@loyola.edu; Randall Gentzler, Vice Pres. Finance & Treas.; Terrence Sawyer, Vice Pres. Advancement, Email: tsawyer@loyola.edu; Marc Camille, Vice Pres. Enrollment Mgmt. & Communications; Sheilah Horton, Vice Pres., Student Devel. & Dean, Students; Revs. Charles Borges, S.J.; Joseph S. Rossi, S.J., Email: jrossi@loyola.edu.

Jesuit Community of Loyola University, Inc., Tel: 410-617-2318; Fax: 410-617-2125. Revs. John D. Savard, S.J.; Charles Borges, S.J.; Timothy B. Brown, S.J.; John J. Conley, S.J.; Frank R. Haig, S.J.; James J. Kelly, S.J.; Brian F. Linnane, S.J.; John P. Murray, S.J.; Thomas E. Roach, S.J.; Joseph S. Rossi, S.J.

Mount St. Agnes College, Tel: 410-617-2271; Fax: 410-617-5413. Sisters of Mercy of the Americas.(Merged with Loyola College.).

Notre Dame of Maryland University, 4701 N. Charles St., 21210. Tel: 410-435-0100; Fax: 410-532-5791; Web: www.ndm.edu. Gino Gemignani, Chm. Bd. of Trustees; Marylou Yam, Pres.; Russ Warren, Interim Vice Pres. Academic Affairs; Heidi Lippmeier Fletcher, Vice Pres. Enrollment Mgmt.; Sharon Bogdan, Registrar; Tanya Easton, Vice Pres. Institutional Advancement; Sr. Eileen O'Dea, Vice Pres. Mission; Barbara Preece, Librarian. School Sisters of Notre Dame. Residents 245; Sisters 12; Students 2,764; Total Staff 198; Lay Professors 120.

EMMITSBURG. *Mount Saint Mary's University* (1808) Emmitsburg, 21727. Tel: 301-447-6122; Fax: 301-447-5860; Email: communications@msmary.edu; Web: www.msmary.edu. Dr. Timothy E. Trainor, Ph.D., Interim Pres.; Mr. Charles L. Kuhn, Dean, Library; Mr. David C. Reeder, Dir. Financial Aid; Dr. David McCarthy, Assoc. Provost; Dr. Jennie Hunter-Cevera, Interim Provost; Mr. Michael Post, Vice Pres., Enrollment Mgmt. & Student Affairs; Mr. Christopher Weber, Registrar; William E. Davies, Vice Pres., Business & Finance; Rev. Msgr. Andrew R. Baker, S.T.D., Vice Pres. & Rector; Revs. Brian P. Nolan, Chap.; James Donohue, C.R.; Mr. Bob Brennan, Vice Pres., Inst. Advancement; Dr. Paula Whetsel-Ribeau, Assoc. Provost, Student Engagement & Success. Lay Teachers 196; Priests 8; Sisters 2; Total Enrollment 2,186.

[C] HIGH SCHOOLS, ARCHDIOCESAN

BALTIMORE. *Archbishop Curley High School* (1961) 3701 Sinclair Ln., 21213. Tel: 410-485-5000; Fax: 410-485-2545; Email: dgrzymski@archbishopcurley.org; Web: www.archbishopcurley.org. Revs. Donald Grzymski, O.F.M.Conv., Pres.; Matthew Foley, O.F.M.Conv., Campus Min. & Guardian; Brian Kohler, Prin. Administered by Order of Friars Minor Conventual, Our Lady of Angels Province (USA). Brothers 1; Lay Teachers 40; Priests 3; Students 563; Total Staff 69.

CUMBERLAND. *Bishop Walsh School* (1966) (Grades PreK-12), 700 Bishop Walsh Rd., Cumberland, 21502. Tel: 301-724-5360; Fax: 301-722-0555; Email: jcessna@bishopwalsh.org; Web: www.bishopwalsh.org. Dr. Ray Kiddy, Prin. School Sisters of Notre Dame. Lay Teachers 37; Sisters 1; Students 312.

ESSEX. *Our Lady of Mount Carmel Catholic School*, (Grades PreK-12), 1706 Old Eastern Ave., Essex, 21221. Tel: 410-686-0859; Fax: 410-686-4916; Email: colszewski@olmemd.org; Web: http://olmcmd.org/. Christopher M. Ashby, Prin.; Christine Olszewski, Prin.; Lawrence Callahan, Pres. Lay Teachers 50.

SEVERN. *Archbishop Spalding High School* (1966) 8080 New Cut Rd., Severn, 21144. Tel: 410-969-9105; Fax: 410-969-1026; Email: info@archbishopspalding.org; Web: www.archbishopspalding.org. Ms. Kathleen K. Mahar, Pres.; Lewis VanWambeke, Prin. Lay Teachers 90; Students 1,228.

[D] HIGH SCHOOLS, PRIVATE

BALTIMORE. *Calvert Hall* (1845) 8102 La Salle Rd., 21286. Tel: 410-825-4266; Fax: 410-825-6826; Email: communications@calverthall.com; Web: www.calverthall.com. Bro. John Kane, F.S.C., Ed. D., Pres.; Mr. Charles Stembler, Prin. Conducted by the Brothers of the Christian Schools (F.S.C.). Brothers 14; Lay Teachers 94; Students 1,190.

The Catholic High School of Baltimore (1939) 2800 Edison Hwy., 21213. Tel: 410-732-6200; Fax: 410-732-7639; Email: tchs@thecatholichighschool.org; Web: www.thecatholichighschool.org. Dr. Barbara Nazelrod, Pres.; Mrs. Sharon Johnston, Prin.; Mrs. Valerie Shinsky, Dean of Students; Gina Batchelder, Dean of Academics. The Sisters of St. Francis of Philadelphia. Lay Teachers 28; Sisters 1; Students 333; Total Staff 57.

Cristo Rey Jesuit High School, 420 S. Chester St., 21231. Tel: 443-573-9881; Fax: 443-573-9897; Web: www.cristoreybalt.org. Dr. William Heiser, Pres.; Walter Reap, Prin.; Leigh Profit, Dir. Finance. Lay Teachers 25; Priests 1; Students 350; Clergy / Religious Teachers 1; Staff 37.

St. Frances Academy (1828) (Coed) 501 E. Chase St., 21202. Tel: 410-539-5794; Fax: 410-685-2650; Email: sfa@sfacademy.org; Web: www.sfacademy.org. Sr. John Francis Schilling, O.S.P., Pres.; Dr. Curtis Turner, Prin.; Mr. Marc Boles, Asst. Prin. Oblate Sisters of Providence. Lay Teachers 13; Sisters 2; Students 142; Friar 1.

Institute of Notre Dame (1847) 901 Aisquith St., 21202. Tel: 410-522-7800; Fax: 410-522-7810; Email: info@indofmd.org; Web: indofmd.org. Dr. David C. Ring Jr., Ed.D., Pres.; Ms. Christine E. Szala, Prin.; Mrs. Diana Franz, Asst. Prin. Academic Affairs, Email: dfranz@indofmd.org; Ms. Helen Bruns, Dean, Students

Institute of Notre Dame, Inc. Lay Teachers 24; Sisters 3; Students 268; Lay Employees 28; Counselors 2.

Loyola Blakefield (1852) (Grades 6-12), P.O. Box 6819, 21285-6819. Tel: 410-823-0601; Fax: 410-825-7756; Email: communications@loyolablakefield.org; Web: www.loyolablakefield.org. John F. Marinacci, Prin.; Mr. Anthony I. Day, Pres. Lay Teachers 95; Priests 3; Students 949.

Mercy High School (1960) 1300 E. Northern Pkwy., 21239-1998. Tel: 410-433-8880; Fax: 410-323-8816; Email: mercy@mercyhighschool.com; Web: www.mercyhighschool.com. Jeanne A. Blakeslee, Prin.; Mary Beth Lennon, Pres. Sisters of Mercy of the Americas. Lay Teachers 49; Sisters 2; Students 287; Total Staff 66.

Mount de Sales Academy (1952) 700 Academy Rd., 21228. Tel: 410-744-8498; Fax: 410-744-5105; Email: mdsa@mountdesales.org; Web: www.mountdesales.org. Sr. Mary Thomas, Prin.; Rose Thompson, Vice Prin.; Theresa Greene, Vice Prin. Lay Teachers 44; Sisters 6; Students 490.

Mt. St. Joseph College High School (1876) 4403 Frederick Ave., 21229. Tel: 410-644-3300; Fax: 410-646-6220; Email: dave@admin.msjnet.edu; Web: www.msjnet.edu. George E. Andrews Jr., Pres.; Mr. David Norton, Prin. Xaverian Brothers. Brothers 1; Lay Teachers 88; Priests 1; Students 884; Total Staff 148.

BEL AIR. *The John Carroll School* (1964) 703 E. Churchville Rd., Bel Air, 21014. Tel: 410-879-2480; Fax: 410-836-8514; Email: jcs@johncarroll.org; Web: www.johncarroll.org. Steve DiBiagio, Pres.; Tom Durkin, Prin.; Zac Ufnar, Campus Min. Employees 110; Lay Teachers 70; Students 672; Total Staff 40.

BUCKEYSTOWN. *Saint John's Catholic Preparatory* (1829) (Coed) 3989 Buckeystown Pike, P.O. Box 909, Buckeystown, 21717. Tel: 301-662-4210; Fax: 301-892-6877; Email: mschultz@saintjohnsprep.org; Web: www.saintjohnsprep.org. Dr. Thomas Powell, Pres.; Mr. Marc Minsker, Prin. Lay Teachers 33; Students 294; Total Staff 58.

HAGERSTOWN. *St. Maria Goretti High School* (1955) (Coed) 1535 Oak Hill Ave., Hagerstown, 21742. Tel: 301-739-4266; Fax: 301-739-4261; Email: info@goretti.org; Web: www.goretti.org. Bridget Bartholomew, Prin.; Matthew Miller, Dean of Students; Holly Katrina, Dir., Admissions; Mr. Christopher Cosentino, Pres.; JoAnn Hevey, Dir., Finance. Administrators 10; Lay Teachers 23; Students 211; Total Staff 39; Support Staff 9.

[E] MIDDLE/HIGH SCHOOLS, PRIVATE

LUTHERVILLE TIMONIUM. *Maryvale Preparatory School* (1945) (Grades 6-12), (Girls) 11300 Falls Rd., Lutherville Timonium, 21093. Tel: 410-252-3366; Fax: 410-308-1497; Email: lanahanj@maryvale.com; Web: www.maryvale.com. Tracey H. Ford, Pres. Lay Teachers 57; Students 415; Total Staff 32.

TOWSON. *Notre Dame Preparatory School* (1873) (Grades 6-12), 815 Hampton Ln., Towson, 21286. Tel: 410-825-0590; Fax: 410-825-0982; Email: admissions@notredameprep.com; Web: www.notredameprep.com. Sisters Patricia McCarron, S.S.N.D., Headmistress; Karen Kane, S.S.N.D., Prin.

Notre Dame Preparatory School, Inc. Lay Teachers 99; Sisters 3; Students 808; Total Staff 152.

[F] ELEMENTARY/MIDDLE SCHOOLS, REGIONAL AND COMMUNITY

BALTIMORE. *Holy Angels Catholic School, Inc.*, 1201 S. Caton Ave., 21227. Tel: 443-602-3200; Fax: 443-602-3210; Email: tmartin@hacschool.org; Web: www.hacschool.org. Kathleen Filippelli, Prin. Lay Teachers 12.

[G] ELEMENTARY SCHOOLS, PRIVATE

BALTIMORE. *Mother Seton Academy*, (Grades 6-8), 2215 Greenmont Ave., 21218-5421. Tel: 410-563-2833; Fax: 410-563-7353; Email: contact@mothersetonacademy.org; Web: www.mothersetonacademy.org. Sr. Margaret (Peggy) Juskelis, S.S.N.D., Pres.; Dr. Gregory Sucre, Prin. Innovative Middle School for Inner City Youth. Brothers 2; Lay Teachers 15; Sisters 6; Students 74.

Sisters Academy of Baltimore, Inc. (2004) (Grades 5-8), 139 First Ave., 21227. Tel: 410-242-1212; Fax: 410-242-5104; Email: ecopple@sistersacademy.org; Web: www.sistersacademy.org. Sr. Delia Dowling, S.S.N.D., Pres., Email: ddowling@sistersacademy.org; Eileen Copple, Prin. Lay Teachers 13; Religious 2; Students 71.

ELLICOTT CITY. *Trinity School* (1941) (Grades PreK-8), 4985 Ilchester Rd., Ellicott City, 21043. Tel: 410-744-1524; Fax: 410-744-3617; Email: kking@trinityschoolmd.org; Web: trinityschoolmd.org. Sr. Catherine Phelps, S.N.D.deN., Prin., Email: cphelps@trinityschoolmd.org. Lay Teachers 31; Sisters of Notre Dame de Namur 1; Students 365.

EMMITSBURG. *Mother Seton School*, (Grades PreK-8), 100 Creamery Rd., Emmitsburg, 21727. Tel: 301-447-3161; Fax: 301-447-3914; Email: office@mothersetonschool.org; Web: www.mothersetonschool.org. Sr. Brenda Manahan, D.C., Prin. Lay Teachers 22; Students 235; Clergy / Religious Teachers 2.

[H] ELEMENTARY SCHOOLS, REGIONAL AND COMMUNITY

BALTIMORE. *St. Agnes Roman Catholic Elementary School*, (Grades PreK-8), 603 St. Agnes Ln., 21229. Tel: 410-747-4070; Fax: 443-636-5455; Email: rcostante@stagnesschool.net; Web: www.stagnesschool.net. Rob Costante, Prin. Lay Teachers 20.

Archbishop Borders School Language Immersion School Partner Language Spanish 3500 Foster Ave., 21224. Tel: 410-276-6534; Fax: 410-276-6915; Email: principal@abbschool.com; Web: abbschool.com. Alicia A. Freeman, Prin. Lay Staff 24; Students 190.

Cardinal Shehan School, (Grades PreK-8), 5407 Loch Raven Blvd., 21239-2996. Tel: 410-433-2775; Fax: 410-323-6131; Email: ljames@cardinalshehanschool.org; Web: cardinalshehanschool.org. Mrs. Fametta Jackson, Prin.; Dr. Darnell Yates, Asst. Prin.; Mrs. Rose Long, Admin. Asst. Serving St. Matthew and St. Thomas More Parishes. Lay Teachers 25; Sisters 1; Students 398.

St. Ignatius Loyola Academy (1993) (Grades 5-8), 300 E. Gittings St., 21230. Tel: 410-539-8268; Fax: 410-539-4821; Email: info@saintignatius.org; Web: www.saintignatius.org. John Ciccone, Pres.; Teresa Scott, Prin. Middle School for boys from low income families. Lay Teachers 19; Students 96.

St. James and St. John School (1847) (Grades PreK-8), 1012 Somerset St., 21202. Tel: 410-342-3222; Fax: 410-732-1323; Email: helpdesk@archbalt.org; Web: ssjjschool.org. Dr. La Uanah King-Cassell, Prin. Lay Teachers 14; Students 227.

St. Ursula Roman Catholic Elementary School, 8900 Harford Rd., 21234-4193. Tel: 410-665-3533; Fax: 410-661-1620; Email: susoffice@stursula.org; Web: www.stursula.org. Deborah Glinowiecki, Prin. Lay Teachers 30.

ELKRIDGE. *St. Augustine School, Inc.*, (Grades PreK-8), 5990 Old Washington Rd., Elkridge, 21075. Tel: 410-796-3040; Fax: 410-579-1165; Email: dball@staug-md.org; Web: www.staug-md.org. Denise Ball, Prin. Lay Teachers 14.

ELLICOTT CITY. *Resurrection St. Paul School, Inc.*, (Grades PreK-8), 3155 Paulskirk Dr., Ellicott City, 21042. Tel: 410-461-9111; Fax: 410-988-5470; Email: kmurphy@resstpaul.org; Web: www.resstpaul.org. Karen Murphy, Prin. Lay Teachers 30; Students 406.

ESSEX. *Our Lady of Mount Carmel Catholic School*, (Grades PreK-12), 1706 Old Eastern Ave., Essex, 21221. Tel: 410-686-4972; Fax: 410-686-4916; Email: olmchsch@archbalt.org; Web: www.olmcmd.org. Rev. Msgr. Larry Callahan, Pres.; Christopher Ashby, Prin., Upper School; Christine Olszewski, Prin., Lower School. Lay Teachers 39; Sisters 1.

FREDERICK. *St. John Regional Catholic School*, (Grades PreK-8), 8414 Opossumtown Pike, Frederick, 21702. Tel: 301-662-6722; Fax: 301-695-7505; Email: koboyle@sjrcs.org; Web: www.sjrcs.org. Mrs. Karen Smith, Prin., Email: ksmith@sjrcs.org; Mr. Will Knotek, Asst. Prin. Lay Teachers 36; Students 550.

GAMBRILLS, ANNE ARUNDEL. *School of the Incarnation, Inc.* (1999) (Grades PreK-8), 2601 Symphony Ln., Gambrills, 21054. Tel: 410-519-2285; Fax: 410-519-2286; Email: lshipley@schooloftheincarnation.org; Web: www.schooloftheincarnation.org. Mrs. Lisa Shipley, Prin.; Laura Minakowski, Asst. Prin. An interparish school of the Archdiocese of Baltimore established 1999. Parishes: Our Lady of the Fields, Millersville; St. Joseph, Odenton; Our Lady of Perpetual Help, Edgewater; Holy Family, Davidsonville and St. Elizabeth Ann Seton, Crofton. Lay Staff 70; Lay Teachers 38; Students 801.

GLEN BURNIE. *Monsignor Slade Catholic School* (1954) (Grades PreK-8), 120 Dorsey Rd., Glen Burnie, 21061. Tel: 410-766-7130; Fax: 410-787-0594; Email: mscs@msladeschool.com; Web: www.msladeschool.com. Alexa A. Cox, Prin. Serving Glen Burnie, Pasadena, Hanover and Severn Parishes. Lay Teachers 36; Students 651.

HYDES. *St. John the Evangelist School (Long Green Valley)*, (Grades PreK-8), 13311 Long Green Pike, Hydes, 21082. Tel: 410-592-9585; Fax: 410-817-4548; Email: mtpetrides@StJohnSchoolLGV.org; Web: stjohnschoollgv.org. Mrs. Christine Blake, Prin. Lay Teachers 22; Students 185; Total Staff 29.

KINGSVILLE. *St. Stephen School* (1863) (Grades PreK-8), 8028 Bradshaw Rd., Kingsville, 21087-1807. Tel: 410-592-7617; Fax: 410-592-7330; Email: info@ssschool.org; Web: www.ssschool.org. Mrs. Mary M. Patrick, Prin. Lay Teachers 21; Students 361; Instructional Aides 8.

LINTHICUM HEIGHTS. *St. Philip Neri School, Inc.*, (Grades PreK-8), 6401 S. Orchard Rd., Linthicum Heights, 21090. Tel: 410-859-1212; Fax: 410-859-5480; Email: info@st.philip-neri.org; Web: www.st.philip-neri.org. Catherine Daley, Prin.; Mrs. Sue Wenzlick, Advancement Dir. Aides 4; Lay Teachers 25.

PARKTON. *Our Lady of Grace Preschool*, (Grades PreK-PreK), 18310 Middletown Rd., Parkton, 21120. Tel: 410-329-6956; Fax: 410-357-5793; Email: slake@ourladygrace.org; Web: olgs.org/. Sally Lake, Dir. Lay Teachers 3; Students 35; Clergy / Religious Teachers 1; Instructional Assistants) 2.

WESTMINSTER. *St. John School (Westminster) Roman Catholic Elementary School*, 45 Monroe St., Westminster, 21157. Tel: 410-848-7455; Fax: 410-848-2822; Email: jtolj@sjwestschool.org; Web: www.sjwestschool.org. Mrs. Jo Marie Tolj, Prin. Lay Teachers 15.

[I] SPECIAL EDUCATION

BALTIMORE. *St. Elizabeth School, Inc.*, (Grades 1-12), 801 Argonne Dr., 21218-1998. Tel: 410-889-5054; Fax: 410-889-2356; Email: jmalin@stelizabeth-school.org; Web: www.stelizabeth-school.org. Mrs. Erin Upton, Prin.; Judy Malin, Admin. Dir.; Mrs. Kristin O'Ferrall, Development Dir.; Mr. Michael Thorne, Exec. Dir. Aides 82; Lay Teachers 23; Students 123; Other Lay Staff 21.

TIMONIUM. *Villa Maria School at Dulaney Valley* (Timonium Campus) 2300 Dulaney Valley Rd., Timonium, 21093. Tel: 667-600-3100; Fax: 410-560-1347; Email: bhines@cc-md.org; Web: www.catholiccharities-md.org/services/villa-maria-school. Brenda Hines, Prin. Non-public special education for children with emotional/multiple disabilities, ages 3-15. Children 75; Lay Teachers 20; Teacher Aides 17.

[J] CHILD CARE CENTERS

BALTIMORE. *Bon Secours Family Support Center*, 26 N. Fulton Ave., 21223. Tel: 410-362-3629; Fax: 410-362-3649; Web: www.bonsecours.org/bshsi. Brenda K. Jones, Svc. Coord., Email: Brenda_Jones@bshsi.com; Lori H. Fagan, Dir.

Bon Secour of Maryland Foundation, Inc. Tot Asst. Annually 350; Total Staff 21.

Good Shepherd Services, 4100 Maple Ave., 21227. Tel: 410-247-2770; Fax: 410-247-3242; Email: info@goodshepherdcenter.org; Web: www.gssmaryland.org. Michele Wyman, R.N., M.S.N., Pres. & CEO; Angela Lingham, Education Dir.; Sr. Mary Carol McClenon, Mission Integration Coord.; Dr. Shawn Mason. Residential psychiatric treatment for adolescent girls and boys with emotional and behavioral problems.

House of the Good Shepherd of the City of Baltimore Capacity 105; Lay Teachers 17; Sisters 10; Students 91; Total Staff 274; Total Assisted 184.

Mount Providence Child Development Center, 701 Gun Rd., 21227. Tel: 410-247-0449; Fax: 410-247-1150; Email: mpcdc@oblatesisters.com; Web: www.mpcdc.com. Sr. Brenda Cherry, O.S.P., Dir. Oblate Sisters of Providence. Lay Teachers 14; Sisters 3; Students 52; Total Staff 18.

TIMONIUM. *Francis X. Gallagher Services*, 2520 Pot Spring Rd., Timonium, 21093. Tel: 410-252-4005; Fax: 410-560-3495; Web: www.cc-md.org/gallagher. Kathy Clemente, Admin. Residential, day habilitation, supported employment, respite care and medical day programs for the people with intellectual disabilities. Total Staff 520; Residential Capacity 264; Day Capacity 230; Total Assisted 468.

[K] GENERAL HOSPITALS

BALTIMORE. *St. Agnes HealthCare, Ascension Health*, 900 Caton Ave., 21229-5299. Tel: 667-234-6000; Fax: 667-234-2109; Email: webmasterBAL@ascension.org; Web: www.stagnes.org. Keith Vander Kolk, Pres. & CEO; Mary Austin, Chief Mission Integration Officer. Ascension Health. Bed Capacity 287; Priests 1; Tot Asst. Annually 102,984; Total Staff 2,918.

St. Agnes Foundation, Inc., Tel: 667-234-3155; Fax: 667-234-3533; Email: Foundation@stagnes.org; Web: www.givesaintagnes.org. Kirstan Cecil, Chief Devel. & Mktg. Officer. (Subsidiary of St. Agnes HealthCare, Inc.).

Bon Secours Baltimore Health Corporation, Inc. (1919) 2000 W. Baltimore St., 21223. Tel: 410-362-3000; Fax: 410-362-3126; Email: inforequest@bshsi.org; Web: www.bonsecoursbaltimore.org. Samuel L. Ross, M.D., M.S., CEO, Email: samuel_ross@bshsi.org; Sr. Anne Lutz, Bd. Pres.; Matt Hemelt, Bd. Chair; Sr. Mary Skopal, S.S.J., Dir. of Pastoral Care, Email: mary_skopal@bshsi.org. Bon Secours Ministry. Bed Capacity 141; Patients Asst Anual. 250,880; Sisters of Bon Secours 5; Total Staff 974.

The following are tax exempt subsidiaries of the Bon Secours Baltimore Health Corporation, Inc.

Bon Secours Hospital Baltimore, Inc. (1920) .

Bon Secours Community Health Works, Inc. (1994) Email: ghughes@mail.mchr.state.md.us.

Bon Secours of Maryland Foundation, Inc. (1991) .

MedStar Good Samaritan Hospital, 5601 Loch Raven Blvd., 21239. Tel: 443-444-8000; Fax: 443-444-4599; Web: www.goodsam-md.org. Bradley Chambers, Pres.; Sharon Bottcher, Vice Pres. Nursing; Rev. Guy Kagere, Dir. Pastoral Care; Deborah Bena, R.N., Health Min. Coord.; John Smyth, Bd. Chm. Adult acute care teaching hospital with a strong tradition of community care and home to more than 200 hospital based physicians. Bed Capacity 316.

Mercy Health Services Inc., 301 St. Paul Pl., 21202. Tel: 410-332-9000; Fax: 410-962-1303; Email: rrice@mdmercy.com; Web: www.mdmercy.com. Thomas Mullen, Pres. & CEO; Rev. Thomas R. Malia, Chap. & Asst. to Mission Pres.; Sr. Carole Rybicki, S.S.F., Chap.; Rev. Augustine Etemma Inwang, M.S.P., (Nigeria); Kathy Ault, Dir. Pastoral Care & Chap.; Donna Dougherty, Chap.; Rev. Paul J. Shaughnessy, S.J., Chap.; Sandy Michocki, Chap.; Mary Tracy, Chap. Institute of the Sisters of Mercy of the Americas.Sisters of Mercy, South Central CommunitySubsidiaries: Mercy Medical Center Inc.; St. Paul Place Specialists, Inc.; Healthcare for the Homeless; Maryland Family Care; Mercy Transitional Care; Stella Maris, Inc.; Cardinal Shehan Center, Inc.; Mercy Health Foundation, Inc.; Mercy Ridge. Bed Capacity 183; Employees 5,039; Patients Asst Anual. 895,756; Sisters 10; Total Staff 4,528.

TOWSON. *University of Maryland St. Joseph Medical Center* (1864) 7601 Osler Dr., Towson, 21204. Tel: 410-337-1000; Fax: 410-337-1024; Email: michael.doiron@umm.edu; Web: www.stjosephtowson.com. Dr. Thomas B. Smyth, M.D., Pres. & CEO; Dr. Michael Doiron, J.C.D., Ph.D., Vice Pres., Mission & Dir. Spiritual. Uni. of Maryland Medical System/Archdiocese of Baltimore. Nurses 776; Patients Asst Anual. 120,136; Total Staff 2,434; Beds 247.

Chaplains: Revs. Joseph Palathingal; Robert Phillips, S.J.; Judith Ann Hvisc, Chap.; Maureen O'Brien, Chap.; Kathy Edelmann, Chap.

[L] NURSING HOMES (SKILLED) AND REHABILITATION CENTERS

BALTIMORE. *Belvedere Green / Woodbourne Woods at Medstar Good Samaritan*, 1651 E. Belvedere Ave., 21239. Tel: 410-433-7255; Fax: 443-444-4599. Bradley Chambers, Pres.

The Neighborhoods at St. Elizabeth, 3320 Benson Ave., 21227-1035. Tel: 410-644-7100; Fax: 410-646-6589; Email: info@catholiccharities-md.org; Web: www.catholiccharities-md.org. Rev. Raymond C. Chase, Chap. Sponsored by Associated Catholic Charities.

St. Elizabeth Rehabilitation and Nursing Center. Bed Capacity 162; Sisters 1; Total Staff 220.

EMMITSBURG. *St. Joseph's Ministries, Inc.*, 331 S. Seton Ave., Emmitsburg, 21727. Tel: 301-447-7000; Fax: 301-447-7015; Email: carla.brown@ascension.org. Carla Brown, Admin. & CEO. Sponsored by Ascension Health. Bed Capacity 113; Total Staff 169.

[M] HOMES FOR AGED

BALTIMORE. *St. Charles Villa*, 603 Maiden Choice Ln., 21228-3697. Tel: 410-747-1211; Fax: 410-747-2460. Revs. Cale J. Crowley, P.S.S., M.Div., Ph.D., Dir., (Retired); Joseph J. Bonadio, P.S.S., M.Rel.Ed., D.Min., S.T.L., (Retired); Gerald L. Brown, P.S.S., M.Div., Ph.D., M.Com., (Retired); Daniel J. Doherty, P.S.S., B.A., M.Div., S.T.L.; John F. Mattingly, P.S.S., M.A., M.S.L.S., S.S.L., (Retired); John E. McMurry, P.S.S., S.T.L., Ph.D., (Retired); Vincent deP. McMurry, P.S.S., M.A., S.T.L., (Retired). Bed Capacity 22; Bed Capacity 22; Priests 8; Total in Residence 8; Total Staff 6.

St. Joseph's Nursing Home (1934) 1222 Tugwell Dr., 21228. Tel: 410-747-0026; Fax: 410-747-0386; Email: st.josephs@stjosephs.net. Sr. Krystyna Mroczek, Admin.

Sisters Servants of Mary Immaculate, Inc. Bed Capacity 44; Residents 44; Sisters 11; Total Staff 60; Total Assisted 80.

St. Martin's Home for Aged, Little Sisters of the Poor, Baltimore Inc., 601 Maiden Choice Ln., 21228. Tel: 410-744-9367; Fax: 410-747-6380; Email: msbaltimore@littlesistersofthepoor.org; Email: colbaltimore@littlesistersofthepoor.org; Web: www.littlesistersofthepoorbaltimore.org. Sr. Joseph Caroline Beutler, Supr.; Rev. Stanley W. DeBoe, O.SS.T., Chap.; Sr. Loraine Maguire, L.S.P., Prov. Aged Residents 65; Sisters 17; Total Staff 136; Intermediate Care Beds 38; Assisted Living 18; Apartments 9; Total Assisted 65.

TIMONIUM. *Stella Maris* (1953) 2300 Dulaney Valley Rd., Timonium, 21093. Tel: 410-252-4500 (office); Fax: 410-560-9675; Email: ljohnso2@stellamaris.org; Web: www.stellamaris.org. Sr. Karen McNally, R.S.M., Chief Admin. Officer; Rev. Lawrence M. Johnson, Dir. of Pastoral Care. The management corporation for all programs of Stella Maris. Long-term care; sub-acute care; home health; rehabilitative services; in-patient and home hospice; skilled home care; personal care; independent living; counseling/bereavement services for adults and children; and Senior day care. All applications for the facilities of Stella Maris are processed directly through the Admissions Office at Stella Maris. Bed Capacity 412; Priests 1; Residents 384; Sisters 7; Lay Personnel 794; Staff 802; Total Assisted 139,752.

[N] SOCIAL SERVICES

BALTIMORE. *Franciscan Center, Inc.* (1968) 101 W. 23rd St., 21218. Tel: 410-467-5340; Fax: 410-467-4569; Email: info@fcbmore.org; Web: www.fcbmore.org. Mary W. Ducey, Exec. Dir. Sisters of St. Francis of Assisi. Total Staff 21; Total Assisted 100,000.

Mount Providence Reading Center, 701 Gun Rd., 21227. Tel: 410-247-0448; Fax: 410-242-4963; Email: sisterconstance@oblatesisters.com; Web: www.oblatesisters.com. Sr. M. Constance Fenwick, O.S.P., Dir. Oblate Sisters of Providence. Students 27; Total Staff 4; Total Assisted 27.

Trinitarian Counseling Services, Inc., 8400 Park Heights Ave., P.O. Box 5719, 21282. Tel: 410-486-5764; Fax: 410-486-0614; Email: treasurer@trinitarians.org. Very Rev. William J. Axe, O.SS.T., Pres. Total Staff 1; Total Assisted 15.

EMMITSBURG. *Seton Center, Inc.*, 26 E. Lincoln Ave., Emmitsburg, 21727. Tel: 301-447-6102; Fax: 301-447-1748; Email: setoncenterinc@doc.org; Web: www.setoncenterinc.org. Sr. Martha Beaudoin, D.C., Admin. Daughters of Charity.Social Service; Outreach; Seton Family Store. Tot Asst. Annually 600; Total Staff 11; Volunteers 105.

PASADENA. *Mary's Center, Inc.* (1990) P.O. Box 1804, Pasadena, 21123-1804. Tel: 410-761-8082; Tel: 301-739-1234 (Hagerstown); Fax: 410-761-0330; Email: info@maryscentermd.org. 7567 Ritchie Hwy., Glen Burnie, 21061. Judith A. Crowninshield, Dir. Pregnancy Support Svcs. Free pregnancy tests; material assistance to women & babies in need. Additional offices in Hagerstown, MD (1200 Dual Hwy.) & Baltimore, MD (740 N. Calvert St.) Tot Asst. Annually 607; Total Staff 40.

[O] ASSOCIATED CATHOLIC CHARITIES

BALTIMORE. *Associated Catholic Charities, Inc. (Catholic Charities)*, 320 Cathedral St., 3rd Floor, 21201-4421. Email: info@catholiccharities-md.org; Web: www.catholiccharities-md.org.

Management Team:

Associated Catholic Charities Inc., 320 Cathedral St., 3rd Floor, 21201-4421. Tel: 410-547-5490; Fax: 410-752-2873. Mr. William J. McCarthy Jr., Exec. Dir.; Mary Anne O'Donnell, Asst. Dir. & Chief Administrative Officer, Tel: 410-547-5495.

Associated Catholic Charities Inc., 228 W. Lexington St., 21201-3443. Tel: 410-261-6787; Fax: 410-889-0203. Amy Collier, Dir. Community Svcs. Div.

Associated Catholic Charities Inc., 1966 Greenspring Dr., St. 200, Timonium, 21093-4164. Tel: 667-600-2231; Fax: 410-561-7741. Scott Becker, CFO.

Associated Catholic Charities Inc., 3320 Benson Ave., 21227-1035. Tel: 667-600-2276; Fax: 410-560-3495. Arnold Eppel, Dir., Sr. Svcs. Division.

Associated Catholic Charities Inc., 1966 Greenspring Dr., Ste. 200, Timonium, 21093-4164. Tel: 667-600-2297; Fax: 410-561-7728. Diane Polk, Chief Human Resources Officer.

Associated Catholic Charities Inc., 2600 Pot Spring Rd., Timonium, 21093-2732. Tel: 410-252-4000, Ext. 1601; Fax: 410-252-3040. Scott Becker; Arnold Eppel; Mike Gross; Kevin Keegan; Mr. William J. McCarthy Jr.; Mary Anne O'Donnell; Diane Polk; Christopher Vaughan.

Associated Catholic Charities Inc., 2300 Dulaney Valley Rd., Timonium, 21093-4164. Tel: 410-252-4700, Ext. 128; Fax: 410-252-3040. Ezra Buchdahl, Admin., St. Vincent's Villa.

Services for Children & Families:

Harford County, Early Head Start, 422 S. Stokes St., Havre De Grace, 21078. Tel: 410-526-1940; Fax: 410-272-6082.

Carroll County, Head Start and Early Head Start and PreK School, 255 Clifton Blvd., Ste. 101, Westminster, 21157-4785. Tel: 410-871-2450; Fax: 410-876-8630.

Center for Family Services - International Adoptions, 2601 N. Howard St., Ste. 200, 21218. Tel: 410-659-4050; Fax: 410-685-2365.

Center for Family Services - Pregnancy, Parenting and Domestic Adoption Svcs., 2601 N. Howard St., Ste. 200, 21218. Tel: 410-659-4050; Fax: 410-685-2365.

Center for Family Services - Therapeutic Alternative Shelter Care (TASC), 2601 N. Howard St., Ste. 200, 21218-4979. Tel: 410-685-2363; Fax: 410-685-2365.

Center for Family Services - Treatment Foster Care, 2601 N. Howard St., Ste. 200, 21218-4979. Tel: 410-685-2363; Fax: 410-685-2365.

Catholic Charities Head Start of Baltimore City, 915 Sterrett St., 21230-2502. Tel: 410-685-1700; Fax: 410-685-2546.

Treatment Foster Care HOPE Program, 2601 N. Howard St., Ste 200, 21218. Tel: 410-685-2363, Ext. 108.

Baltimore City Child and Adolescent Response (Foster/Kinship Care Stabilization Program), 1118 S. Light St., #200, 21230-4152. Tel: 410-727-4800; Fax: 410-727-5853.

St. Vincent's Villa Diagnostic Evaluation and Treatment Program, 2600 Pot Spring Rd., Timonium, 21093-2732. Tel: 410-252-4000; Fax: 410-561-8109.

Villa Maria - Behavioral Health Clinics:

Villa Maria of Anne Arundel Country Behavioral Health Clinic, 1111 Benfield Rd., #104, Millersville, 21108-3003. Tel: 410-729-8494; Fax: 410-451-0701.

Villa Maria at Lansdowne Behavioral Health Clinic, 2700 Washington Ave., Halethorpe, 21227-3115. Tel: 410-368-3984; Fax: 410-536-1290.

Villa Maria of Harford County Behavioral Health Clinic, 1301 Continental Dr., Ste. 101, Abingdon, 21009-2338. Tel: 410-676-4002; Fax: 410-676-7365.

Villa Maria of Carroll County Behavioral Health Clinic, 1129 Business Parkway S., Ste. A, Westminster, 21157. Tel: 410-848-2037; Fax: 410-848-5273.

Villa Maria of Frederick County Behavioral Health Clinic, 111 E. Church St., Frederick, 21701-5403. Tel: 301-694-6654; Tel: 301-898-7900 (Voicemail); Fax: 301-694-8221.

Villa Maria of Washington County Behavioral Health Clinic, 229 N. Potomac St., Hagerstown, 21740-3812. Tel: 301-733-5858; Fax: 301-733-5626.

Villa Maria of Mountain Maryland Behavioral Health Clinic, 300 E. Oldtown Rd., Ste. 1, Cumberland, 21502-3600. Tel: 301-777-8685; Fax: 301-777-8687.

Villa Maria Behavioral Health Clinic at Fallstaff, 6999 Reisterstown Rd., Ste. 4, 21215-1492. Tel: 410-585-0598; Fax: 410-585-0589.

Home-Based Respite Program (Cecil, Harford, Baltimore County & Baltimore City), 2601 N. Howard St., 2nd Fl., 21218-4979. Tel: 410-685-2363; Fax: 410-685-2364.

In-Home Intervention Services, 2601 N. Howard St., 21218-4979. Tel: 410-685-2362; Fax: 410-685-2364.

St. Vincent's Villa Residential Treatment Center, 2600 Pot Spring Rd., Timonium, 21093-2739. Tel: 410-252-4000; Fax: 410-561-8109.

Safe Start, 1301 Continental Dr., Ste. 101, Abingdon, 21009-2338. Tel: 410-676-4002; Fax: 410-676-4002.

Villa Maria - Schools:

Villa Maria School, 2300 Dulaney Valley Rd., Timonium, 21093-2739. Tel: 410-252-6343; Fax: 410-560-1347.

Villa Maria School at St. Vincent's Center Type III Diagnostic Program, 2600 Pot Spring Rd., Timonium, 21093. Tel: 410-252-4000; Fax: 410-453-9712.

School-Based Mental Health Programs Baltimore County, Harford County, Baltimore City, Carroll County, Washington County, Allegany Count, Frederick County, Anne Arundel County, 2600 Pot Spring Rd., Timonium, 21093-2739. Tel: 410-252-4700; Fax: 410-252-3040. Carl Fornoff, Contact Person (Balt. Co. & Anne Arundel Co.); Diane Shannon, Contact Person (Balt. City & Harford Co.); Lisa Serfass, Contact Person (Frederick Co.), Contact Person (Frederick Co.).

Parochial School Consultation Program, 2300 Dulaney Valley Rd., Timonium, 21093. Tel: 410-252-4700; Fax: 410-252-3040.

Lansdowne Therapeutic After School Program, 2700 Washington Ave., 21227-3115. Tel: 410-368-3984; Fax: 410-536-1290.

Towson Therapeutic After School Program, 1220 E. Joppa Rd., Towson, 21286-5810. Tel: 410-705-4790 ; Fax: 410-252-3040.

St. Vincent's Villa Therapeutic Weekend Respite Program, 2600 Pot Spring Rd., Timonium, 21093-2739. Tel: 410-252-4700, Ext. 107; Fax: 410-252-3040.

Family Support Groups and Resource Center, 2600 Pot Spring Rd., Timonium, 21093-2739. Tel: 410-252-4000, Ext. 1663; Fax: 410-252-3040.

Family Systems Navigator, 2600 Pot Spring Rd., Timonium, 21093-2739. Tel: 410-252-4700, Ext. 265; Fax: 410-252-3040.

Villa Maria at Edgewood Middle School, 2311 Willoughby Beach Rd., Edgewood, 21040. Tel: 410-252-6343; Fax: 410-612-1518.

Head Start Mental Health Consultation (Baltimore City, Harford and Carroll Counties), 6999 Reisterstown Rd., 21215-1492. Tel: 410-585-0598; Fax: 410-676-7365.

Timonium Out-Patient Mental Health Clinic, 1220 E. Joppa Rd., Towson, 21286-5810. Tel: 410-705-4790.

White Oak Counseling (White Oak School), 8401 Leefield Rd., Timonium, 21093. Tel: 410-252-4700, Ext. 126; Fax: 410-561-9073.

Baltimore City Regional Expanded School Mental Health/Early Childhood Mental Health Services, 6999 Reisterstown Rd., 21215. Tel: 410-585-0598; Fax: 410-585-0589.

Brief Strategic Family Therapy, 2600 Pot Spring Rd., Lutherville Timonium, 21093-2739. Tel: 410-252-4000.

Carroll County Head Start-Parents as Teachers, 255 Clifton Blvd., Ste. 101, Westminster, 21157-4785. Tel: 410-871-2450.

Kinship Care Family Support Groups, St. Rita Parish Ctr., 2903 Dunleer Rd., Dundalk, 21222-5113. Tel: 410-252-4000, Ext. 1515.

Early Childhood Mental Health Screening, 2600 Pot Spring Rd., Timonium, 21093-2739. Tel: 410-252-4700.

Kinship Care Systems Navigations, 2903 Dunleer Rd., Dundalk, 21222-5113. Tel: 410-252-4000, Ext. 1515.

Making All the Children Healthy (M.A.T.C.H.) Mental Health Assessment, 2601 N. Howard St., Ste. 200, 21218-4979. Tel: 410-659-4050; Fax: 410-685-2364.

Mental Health Counseling for Deaf Clients (Fallstaff Outpatient Mental Health Clinic), 6999 Resiterstown Rd., 21215-1492. Tel: 410-585-0598.

School Based Behavioral Health Services (Allegany, Anne Arundel, Baltimore, Baltimore City, Washington, Frederick and Harford County) 1220 E. Joppa Rd., Towson, 21286-5810. Tel: 410-705-4790; Fax: 410-252-3040.

Therapeutic Mentoring Program, 2600 Pot Spring Rd., Timonium, 21093-2739. Tel: 410-252-4000, Ext. 1637; Fax: 410-561-8109.

Community Services:

Anna's House, 607 N. Tollgate Rd., Bel Air, 21014-0088. Tel: 410-803-2130; Fax: 410-638-1753.

Esperanza Center, 430 S. Broadway, 21231-2409. Tel: 676-600-2900; Fax: 410-675-1451; Email: esperanzainfo@cc-md.org; Web: www.catholiccharities-md.org/services/immigration. Tot Asst. Annually 11,121; Total Staff 40.

**Cherry Hill Town Center (Cherry Hill Town Center, Inc.)*, 634 Cherry Hill Rd., 21225-1229. Tel: 410-354-0167.

Our Daily Bread Employment Center, 725 Fallsway, 21202-4147. Tel: 443-986-9000; Fax: 410-962-8933.

Holden Hall, 761 W. Hamburg St., 21230-2535. Tel: 410-347-9830; Fax: 410-347-9831.

Social Concerns, 228 W. Lexington St., Ste. 220, 21201-3432. Tel: 410-261-6781; Fax: 410-889-0203.

My Sister's Place Women's Center, 17 W. Franklin St., 21201-5005. Tel: 410-727-3523; Fax: 410-727-1611.

My Sister's Place Lodge, 111 W. Mulberry St., 21201-3619. Tel: 410-528-9002; Fax: 410-528-9004.

Christopher Place Employment Academy, 725 Fallsway, 21202-4147. Tel: 443-986-9000; Fax: 410-962-8932.

Parish Social Ministry, 228 W. Lexington St., Ste. 220, 21201-3432. Tel: 410-261-6781; Fax: 410-889-0203.

Project BELIEVE, 725 Fallsway, 21202-4147. Tel: 443-986-6766; Fax: 410-962-8932.

Project FRESH Start (Family Relocation, Empowerment, and Self-Help), 228 W. Lexington St., Ste. 220, 21201-3432. Tel: 410-261-6766; Fax: 410-889-0203.

Project SERVE (Service and Education through Residential Volunteer Experience), 228 W. Lexington St., Ste. 220, 21201-3432. Tel: 410-261-6774; Fax: 410-889-0203.

Alternative Spring Break, 228 W. Lexington St., Ste. 220, 21201-3432. Tel: 410-261-6774; Fax: 410-889-0203.

Employment Services, 725 Fallsway, 21202-4147. Tel: 443-986-9000; Fax: 410-962-8930.

Samaritan Center, 17 W. Franklin St., 21201-5005. Tel: 410-468-4632; Fax: 410-659-0642.

Sarah's House, 2015 20th St., Fort Meade, 20755-1301. Tel: 410-551-7722; Fax: 410-551-7279.

Senior Community Service Employment Program (SCSEP), 228 W. Lexington St., Ste. 220, 21201-3432. Tel: 410-261-6767; Fax: 410-235-5781.

Services for Seniors:

Answers for the Aging, 3300 Benson Ave., 21227-1035. Tel: 410-646-0100; Tel: 888-502-7587; Fax: 410-646-0500.

Caritas House Assisted Living, 3308 Benson Ave., 21227-1035. Tel: 667-600-2660; Fax: 410-646-6565; Email: rrich@cc-md.org.

**Catholic Charities Senior Community at Aberdeen*, 901 Barnett La., Aberdeen, 21001-1748. Tel: 410-273-0435; Fax: 410-273-0439.

Catholic Charities Senior Community at Abingdon, 3001 St. Clair Dr., Abingdon, 21009-3225. Tel: 410-569-3630; Fax: 410-273-0916. Debbie Seigle, Contact Person.

Catholic Charities Senior Community Application/Information Requests, 1966 Greenspring Dr., Ste. 200, Timonium, 21093-4164. Tel: 443-798-3423.

**Catholic Charities Senior Community at Arundel Woods (Glen Burnie Senior Housing, Inc.)*, 403 W. Ordnance Rd., Glen Burnie, 21061-6448. Tel: 410-424-3535; Fax: 410-424-4484.

Catholic Charities Senior Community at Basilica Place (The Catholic Charities Housing, Inc.), 124 W. Franklin Street, 21201-4576. Tel: 410-539-0418 ; Fax: 410-752-6207.

**Catholic Charities Senior Community at Coursey Station (Coursey Station Apartments, Inc.)*, 200 First Ave., Lansdowne, 21227-3031. Tel: 410-242-6167; Fax: 410-242-3459.

Catholic Charities Senior Community at DePaul House (DePaul House, Inc.), 3300 Benson Ave., 21227-1030. Tel: 410-644-8484; Fax: 410-644-1334.

**Catholic Charities Senior Community at Friendship Station (Odenton Senior Housing, Inc.)*, 1212 Odenton Rd., Odenton, 21113-1629. Tel: 410-519-6085; Fax: 410-519-6092.

Catholic Charities Senior Community at Friendship Village, 1212 Odenton Rd., Odenton, 21113-1629. Tel: 410-519-6085; Fax: 410-305-0481.

**Catholic Charities Senior Community at Holy Korean Martyrs (Woodlawn Senior Housing, Inc.)*, 5500 Lexington Rd., Woodlawn, 21207-5600. Tel: 410-944-5959; Fax: 410-944-0555.

Catholic Charities Senior Community at Our Lady of Fatima I & II, 6424 E. Pratt St., 21224-2818. Tel: 410-631-3555; Fax: 410-631-3556; Web: www.cc-md.org.

**Catholic Charities Senior Community at Owings Mills New Town (Owings Mills Senior Community,*

Inc.), 9773 Groffs Mill Dr., Owings Mills, 21117-6005. Tel: 410-902-8222; Fax: 410-902-0250.
**Catholic Charities Senior Community at Reister's Clearing*, 304 Cantata Ct., Reisterstown, 21136-6471. Tel: 410-517-4994; Fax: 410-517-0095.
**Catholic Charities Senior Community at Reister's View*, 306 Cantata Ct., Reisterstown, 21136-6472. Tel: 410-517-4994; Fax: 410-517-4995.
Catholic Charities Senior Community at St. Charles House (St. Charles House, Inc.), 11 Church Ln., Pikesville, 21208-6607. Tel: 410-484-6125.
**Catholic Charities Senior Community at St. Joachim House (St. Joachim House, Inc.)*, 3310 Benson Ave., 21227-1075. Tel: 410-644-8269; Fax: 410-525-9227.
**Catholic Charities Senior Community at St. Luke's Place (St. Luke's Apartments, Inc.)*, 2825 Lodge Farm Rd., Edgemere, 21219-1347. Tel: 410-477-3661; Fax: 410-477-0199.
**Catholic Charities Senior Community at Starner Hill Apartments (Backbone Housing, Inc.)*, 25 N. Pennsylvania Ave., Grantsville, 21536-1390. Tel: 301-895-5842; Fax: 301-895-3762.
**Catholic Charities Senior Community at Trinity House Apartments (Trinity House Apartments, Inc.)*, 409 Virginia Ave., Towson, 21286-5372. Tel: 410-825-5288; Fax: 410-825-5592.
Catholic Charities Senior Housing at St. Mark's, 19 Winters Ln., Catonsville, 21228-4499. Tel: 410-788-0972.
Congregate Housing Services Program, 1966 Greenspring Dr., Timonium, 21093-4164. Tel: 443-798-3423; Fax: 410-561-3056.
Everall Gardens, 6100 Everall Ave., 21206-1946. Tel: 410-444-5850; Fax: 410-444-0190.
GreenHouse Residences at Stadium Place, 1010 E. 33rd St., 21218-3780. Tel: 410-554-9890; Fax: 410-554-9897; Web: www.cc-md.org. Susan Stone, Admin.
Kessler Park, 4230 Hollins Ferry Rd., Lansdowne, 21227-3468. Tel: 410-247-9244; Fax: 410-247-9245.
The Neighborhoods at St. Elizabeth Rehabilitation and Nursing Center (Jenkins Memorial Nursing Home, Inc.), 3320 Benson Ave., 21227-1035. Tel: 410-646-6597; Fax: 410-646-6589.
Pastoral Care at the Jenkins Senior Living Community, 3320 Benson Ave., 21227-1035. Tel: 410-646-6513; Fax: 410-646-6541.
St. Ann Adult Day Services, 3308 Benson Ave., 21227-1001. Tel: 410-646-0320; Fax: 410-644-0320.
Services for Individuals with Intellectual Disabilities:
Francis X. Gallagher Services, 2520 Pot Spring Rd., Timonium, 21093-2730. Tel: 410-252-4005; Fax: 410-560-3495. Programs include vocational, adult medical day & residential services.
The Bethany Community, Inc., Tel: 410-252-4005; Fax: 410-560-3495.
Other Associated Catholic Charities, Inc. Corporations:
661 Corporation, 1966 Greenspring Dr., Ste. 200, Timonium, 21093-4164. Tel: 443-519-2383.
The Children's Fund, Inc., 320 Cathedral St., 21201. Tel: 410-547-5469; Fax: 410-752-2873.
TIMONIUM. *Village Crossroads Senior Housing II, Inc.*, 1966 Greenspring Dr., Ste. 200, Timonium, 21093. Tel: 443-798-3423; Fax: 410-561-3056; Web: www.cc-md.org. Aileen McShea Tinney, Vice Pres.

[P] RETREAT HOUSES FOR MEN, WOMEN AND YOUTH

SPARKS. *Msgr. Clare J. O'Dwyer Retreat House*, 15523 York Rd., P.O. Box 310, Sparks, 21152. Tel: 410-472-2400; Fax: 410-472-3281; Email: odwyer@archbalt.org; Web: www.msgrodwyer.org. Cassandra Palmer, Contact Person. Capacity 90; Retreatants 6,000; Total Staff 11.

[Q] MONASTERIES AND RESIDENCES OF PRIESTS AND BROTHERS

BALTIMORE. *St. Ambrose Friary*, 4502 Park Heights Ave., 21215. Tel: 202-549-6591; Fax: 410-367-9918; Email: pastor@saintambrose.com; Web: saintambrose.com. Revs. Paul Zaborowski, O.F.M.-Cap.; William Graham, O.F.M.Cap., J.C.L., M.A., Adjutant Judicial Vicar; John McCloskey, Chap.; John Petrikovic, O.F.M.Cap., Preaching Min.
Colombiere Jesuit Community St. Claude La Colombiere Jesuit Community. 5704 Roland Ave., 21210-1399. Tel: 410-532-1400; Fax: 410-532-1419. Revs. Harry F. Geib, S.J., Supr., Tel: 443-451-1659; Tel: 443-921-1335 (Office); David G. Allen, S.J., Pastoral Ministry; Walter A. Buckius, S.J.; Vincent deP. Alagia, S.J., Pastoral Ministry; G. Richard Dimler, S.J., Pastoral Ministry; Bernard G. Filmyer, S.J., Pastoral Ministry; James N. Gelson, S.J., Pastoral Ministry; John C. Haughey, S.J., Research & Writing; Joseph J. Hayden, S.J., House Min.; G. Harry Hock, S.J., Pastoral Ministry; Liborio J. LaMartina, S.J., Resident Archivist & Sacristan, Tel: 410-532-1420; John Lange, S.J.; Robert B. Lawton, S.J., Pastoral Ministry; Raymond M. Lelii, S.J., Pastoral Ministry; Dominic W. Maruca, S.J., Pastoral Ministry; James O'Brien, S.J.; Francis M. O'Connor, S.J., Pastoral Ministry; G. Donald Pantle, S.J., Pastoral Ministry; James F. Salmon, S.J., Pastoral Ministry; Timothy J. Stephens, S.J., Province Treas.; Joseph Tylenda, S.J.; Bros. Paul Cawthorne, S.J.; John B. Hollywood, S.J.; Revs. James L. Connor, S.J.; Robert E. Hamm, S.J.; John Mawhinney, S.J.; Richard P. McHugh, S.J.; Kenneth Meehan, S.J.; William J. Watters, S.J.
Congregation of the Holy Spirit, 2846 W. Lafayette Ave., 21216. Tel: 443-835-4008; Fax: 410-945-7113.
Holy Trinity Monastery dba Holy Trinity Fathers, Inc. of Maryland; DBA The Trinitarians, Inc.; AKA Order of the Most Holy Trinity and of the Captives, 8400 Park Heights Ave., 21208. Tel: 410-486-5171; Fax: 410-486-0614; Email: treasurer.provincial@gmail.com; Web: trinitarians.org. P.O. Box 5719, 21282. Very Rev. Albert M. Anuszewski, O.SS.T., Prov.; Most Rev. Jose T. Narlaly, O.SS.T., Min. Gen.; Very Rev. James R. Day, O.SS.T., Pres.; Rev. Kurt J. Klismet, O.SS.T., Treas.; Very Rev. Juan Molina, O.SS.T., Dir.; Revs. James Mark Adame, O.SS.T., Dir. of Vocations; Santhosh George, O.SS.T., Dir. of Mission Advancement; Thomas A. Morris, O.SS.T.; Victor J. Scocco, O.SS.T.; William Sullivan, O.SS.T.; Binoy Akkalayil, O.SS.T.; Daniel Houde, O.SS.T.; Roy Kurian Kalachalil, O.SS.T.; Lijo Abraham Vattukulathil, O.SS.T.; Stanley W. DeBoe, O.SS.T., Chap.; Very Rev. Tom Dymowski, O.SS.T., Chap.; Revs. Charles J. Flood, O.SS.T., Chap.; Damian Anuszewski, O.SS.T., Teacher; Very Rev. William J. Axe, O.SS.T., In Res.; Revs. Ken Borgesen, O.SS.T., In Res.; David Colella, O.SS.T, In Res.; Michael Conway, O.SS.T., In Res.; Gerard Lynch, O.SS.T., In Res.; Joshy Abraham Mappilaparambil, O.SS.T., In Res.; J. Edward Owens, O.SS.T., In Res.; Alfonso Serna, O.SS.T., In Res.; Very Rev. Frank Whatley, O.SS.T., In Res.; Revs. Alberto Rodriguez, O.SS.T., In Res.; Juan Vazquez-Rubio, O.SS.T., In Res.; Bro. Richard Giner, O.SS.T., In Res.; Revs. Thomas J. Burke, O.SS.T., S.T.M., S.T.D., B.A., Assigned Elsewhere; William J. Moorman, O.SS.T., Ph.D., Assigned Elsewhere; Edward Wagner, O.SS.T., Assigned Elsewhere; Philip Cordisco, O.SS.T., Assigned Elsewhere; Ireneusz Ekiert, O.SS.T., Assigned Elsewhere; Raphael Baidoo, O.SS.T., Assigned Elsewhere; Adelson S. Moreira, O.SS.T., Assigned Elsewhere; Lawrence C. Hernandez, O.SS.T., Assigned Elsewhere; Bro. Patrick G. Wildgen, O.SS.T., Assigned Elsewhere
Legal Title: DBA Holy Trinity Fathers, Inc. of Maryland, DBA The Trinitarians, Inc. Priests 32.
Immaculate Heart of Mary Friary, 4220 Erdman Ave., 21213. Tel: 410-485-5511; Fax: 410-485-1090; Email: mjfoley@archbishopcurley.org. Revs. Donald Grzymski, O.F.M.Conv., Vicar; Nicholas Rokitka, O.F.M.Conv., Treas.; Matthew Foley, O.-F.M.Conv., Guardian; Bros. Lawrence LaFlame, O.F.M.Conv.; Emmanuel Wenke. Residence of Franciscan Friars, O.F.M.Conv., conducting Archbishop Curley High School. Brothers 2; Priests 3; Total Staff 5.
Jesuit Community of Loyola University Maryland, Inc., Ignatius House, 4603 Millbrook Rd., 21212-4721. Tel: 410-617-2318; Fax: 410-617-2125; Email: jsavard@loyola.edu. Revs. John D. Savard, S.J., Rector; Charles Borges, S.J.; Timothy B. Brown, S.J.; John J. Conley, S.J.; Michael P. Corcoran, S.J., Science Teacher, Cristo Rey Jesuit H.S.; Vincent G. Conti, S.J., Prov. Socius, Maryland Province; John R. Donahue, S.J., Email: jrdonahue@loyola.edu; Lloyd D. George, S.J.; Frank R. Haig, S.J.; Robert M. Hussey, S.J., Prov., Maryland Province; James J. Kelly, S.J.; Brian F. Linnane, S.J., Pres., Loyola Univ. Maryland; Mr. Dayne Malcolm, S.J., Spanish Teacher, Cristo Rey Jesuit H.S.; Revs. F. Joseph Michini, S.J.; John P. Murray, S.J.; Jordan J. Orbe, S.J.; Robert L. Phillips, S.J.; Thomas E. Roach, S.J.; Joseph S. Rossi, S.J.; T. Howland Sanks, S.J.; Bruce A. Steggert, S.J. Total in Residence 25.
St. Joseph Society of the Sacred Heart House of Central Administration, 911 W. Lake Ave., 21210. Tel: 410-727-3386; Fax: 410-727-1006; Email: josephite1@aol.com; Web: www.josephite.com. Very Revs. Michael L. Thompson, S.S.J., Supr. Gen.; Roderick J. D. Coates, S.S.J., Vicar Gen.; Thomas R. Frank, S.S.J., Consultor Gen.; Nelson A. Moreira, S.S.J., Treas. & Rector. Priests 3.
St. Joseph's Manor, 911 W. Lake Ave., 21210-1022. Tel: 410-323-3829; Fax: 410-435-1853. Very Rev. Paul Oberg, S.S.J., Rector; Revs. Daniel Bastianelli, S.S.J., (Retired); Joseph N. Begay, S.S.J., (Retired); Dermot Brady, S.S.J., (Retired); George Burden, S.S.J., (Retired); Francis Bulter, S.S.J., (Retired); Robert DeGrandis, S.S.J., (Retired); Joseph DelVecchio, S.S.J.; James A. Hayes, S.S.J., (Retired); Howard Johnson, S.S.J., (Retired); James E. McLinden, S.S.J., (Retired); Charles Moffatt, S.S.J., (Retired); Edward J. Mullowney, S.S.J., (Retired); Bro. Charles Douglas, S.S.J., (Retired). Home for retired priest & brothers of St. Joseph's Society of the Sacred Heart. Brothers 1; Priests 17. In Res. Revs. John Filippelli, S.S.J., (Retired); Frank Hull, S.S.J.; Robert Zawacki, S.S.J., (Retired); John O'Hallaran, S.S.J., (Retired).
St. Joseph's Passionist Community, 251 S. Morley St., 21229. Tel: 410-566-0877; Fax: 410-233-4974; Email: info@sjmp.org; Web: www.sjmp.org. Rev. Michael A. Murphy, Pastor. Congregation of the Most Holy Cross and Passion of Our Lord Jesus Christ. Brothers 1; Priests 1.
Pallottine Center for Apostolic Causes, 512 W. Saratoga St., 21201. Tel: 410-685-3063; Fax: 410-234-1459. Rev. Peter T. Sticco, S.A.C., Dir. Promotional Center for St. Jude Shrine.
St. Jude Shrine-Pallottine Missions; Pallottine Center for Apostolic Causes, Inc.
The Redemptorists, 600 S. Conkling St., 21224.
Society of St. Sulpice, Province of the United States, 5408 Roland Ave., 21210-1988. Tel: 410-323-5070; Fax: 410-433-6524; Email: jkemper@sulpicians.org; Web: sulpicians.org. Very Rev. Ronald D. Witherup, P.S.S., S.T.L., S.T.M., Ph.D., Supr. General, 6 rue du Regard, Paris, France 75006; Revs. John C. Kemper, P.S.S., M.Div., M.A., D.Min., Prov.; Phillip J. Brown, P.S.S., J.D., S.T.B., J.C.D., Rector; Gerald D. McBrearity, P.S.S., M.A., S.T.B., D.Min., Rector; Shoba Nyambe, P.S.S., B.D., S.T.L., Rector; Jaime E. Robledo, M.Div., S.T.L., Ph.D. (Cand.), Rector; Hy K. Nguyen, P.S.S., M.Div., M.A., S.T.D., Vice-Rector; Gladstone H. Stevens, P.S.S., S.T.L., Ph.D., Vice-Rector; Renato Lopez, P.S.S., S.S.L., Ph.L., Vice-Rector for Formation; Timothy C. Chikweto, P.S.S., S.T.L., B.D., Vice-Rector; Martin J. Burnham, S.T.B., M.Div., Spiritual Advisor/Care Svcs.; Leonardo J. Gajardo, P.S.S., S.T.L., J.C.L., S.T.B., Liturgy Dir.; Vincent D. Bui, P.S.S., M.A., S.T.B., J.C.L., Liturgy Dir.; Inniah Christy Arockiaraj, P.S.S., D.Min., Ph.L., Ph.D., Dir. Pastoral Formation; Richard M. Gula, P.S.S., S.T.L., S.T.M., Ph.D., Prov. Sec. & Dir. of Personnel; David D. Thayer, P.S.S., S.T.L., Ph.D., S.T.M., M.A., Dir. Intellectual Formation; Dominic Ciriaco, M.A., M.Div., Assoc. Dir. Intellectual Formation; Nam J. Kim, P.S.S., M.A., S.T.L., S.T.D., Formation Advisor/Spiritual Dir.; Anthony J. Pogorelc, P.S.S., M.Div., M.S., Ph.D., S.T.L., Coord. of Human Formation; Melvin C. Blanchette, P.S.S., M.A., Ph.D., Extern Spiritual Advisor, (Retired); Carlos Piedrahita, Formator; Luis Corneli, Formation Advisor; Simon Cheba, Formation Faculty; Shawn Gould, Formation Faculty; Emmanuel M. Ichidi, B.D., Formation Faculty; Kasweka Joseph Chamwaza, B.D., Formation Faculty; Neal Mulyata, Formation Faculty; Eugene H. Mwanza, P.S.S., B.D., M.Th., Formation Faculty; Edward M. Mwepya, B.D., Formation Faculty; Victor S. Shikaputo, P.S.S., S.T.L., S.T.D., B.D., Formation Faculty; Paul A. Maillet, P.S.S., M.M., M.Div., S.T.L., S.T.D., Formation Faculty; Daniel F. Moore, P.S.S., M.A., S.T.L., S.T.D., Formation Faculty; Brian K. Carpenter, P.S.S., B.S., M.Div., S.T.L., Graduate Student; Robert J. Cro, M.Div., M.A., S.T.B., Graduate Student; Peter M. Kwaleyela, B.D., Graduate Student; Geronimo A. Magat, M.Div., M.A., Graduate Student; Victor Mwanamwambwa, P.S.S., B.D., M.S., Graduate Student; Very Rev. Thomas R. Ulshafer, P.S.S., S.T.L., Ph. D., (Retired); Revs. Michael L. Barre, P.S.S., S.T.L., Ph.D., (Retired); James W. Lothamer, P.S.S., S.T.B., M.A., Ph.D., (Retired); Robert F. Leavitt, P.S.S., S.T.D., (Retired); Cornelius Hankomoone, P.S.S., S.T.L., S.T.D., Sabbatical; Thomas R. Hurst, P.S.S., S.T.L., Ph.D., Individual Assignments; Daniel J. Doherty, P.S.S., B.A., M.Div., S.T.L., Individual Assignments; Joseph T. Ky, P.S.S., M.A., Individual Assignments, (Retired); William E. Hartgen Jr., P.S.S., M.A., Individual Assignments, (Retired); John S. Kselman, P.S.S., S.T.L., Ph.D., Individual Assignments, (Retired); James P. Oberle, P.S.S., S.T.B., S.T.L., Ph.D., Individual Assignments, (Retired); Patrick Simutowe, P.S.S., S.T.L., B.D., S.T.D., Individual Assignments; Joseph J. Bonadio, P.S.S., M.Rel.Ed., D.Min., S.T.L., Individual Assignments, (Retired); Edward J. Frazer, P.S.S., M.A., S.T.L., Individual Assignments, (Retired); John F. Mattingly, P.S.S., M.A., M.S.L.S., S.S.L., Individual Assignments, (Retired); Peter W. Gray, P.S.S., M.A., Ph.D., S.T.M., Individual Assignments; John E. McMurry, P.S.S., S.T.L., Ph.D., Individual Assignments, (Retired); Leo J. Larrivee, S.S., Individual Assignments; Gerald L. Brown, P.S.S., M.Div., Ph.D., M.Com., Individual Assignments, (Retired); Frederick J. Cwiekowski, P.S.S., M.A., S.T.D., Individual Assignments, (Retired); Gerald D. Coleman,

P.S.S., M.A., S.T.L., Ph.D., Individual Assignments, (Retired); Louis M. Reitz, P.S.S., S.T.L., M.S.L.S., M.Ed., Individual Assignments, (Retired); Lawrence B. Terrien, P.S.S., Ph.D., S.T.D., S.T.L., Individual Assignments; James E. Myers, P.S.S., M.Div., Individual Assignments; James L. McKearney, P.S.S., M.Div., S.T.L., S.T.D., Individual Assignments; J. Michael Strange, P.S.S., M.A., M.T.S., Individual Assignments, (Retired); Howard P. Bleichner, P.S.S., Dr. Theol., Individual Assignments, (Retired); Richard B. MacDonough, P.S.S., S.T.L., Ph.D., Individual Assignments, (Retired). (Associated Sulpicians of the United States); Represented in the Archdioceses and Dioceses of: Baltimore, Bridgeport, Dallas, Lansing, Los Angeles, Monterey, Oakland, Scranton, San Antonio, San Francisco, San Jose, Springfield-Cape Girardeau, and Washington, DC. Also in Paris, France, Rome, Italy & Ireland.; Missions: Kabwe & Lusaka in Zambia, Central Africa Priests in Society of St. Sulpice 64.

Xaverian Brothers Generalate, 4409 Frederick Ave., 21229. Tel: 410-644-0034; Fax: 410-644-2762; Email: development@xaverianbrothers.org; Web: xaverianbrothers.org. Bros. Edward Driscoll, C.F.X., Rel. Order Leader; John Hamilton, C.F.X., Vicar Gen.; Paul J. Murray, C.F.X., Leadership Team; Lawrence Harvey, C.F.X., Leadership Team; Mrs. Rhonda Tully, M.A., CFO, (Retired); Mr. Shawn Lynch, Business Mgr.; Mr. Benjamin Horgan, Dir. of Formation XBSS; Christopher Irr, Dir. of Communications; Dr. Patrick J. Slattery, Exec. Dir. of Sponsorship. Legal Titles and Schools Sponsored: Xaverian Brothers USA, Inc. (f/k/a The American Central Province of the Xaverian Brothers Inc., The American Northeast Province of the Xaverian Brothers, Inc., and the Working Boys Home, Inc.); St. Mary's-Ryken High School, Inc.; Our Lady of Good Counsel High School, Inc.; St. Xavier High School, Inc.; Xaverian High School, Inc.; Mt. St. Joseph High School, Inc.; Xaverian Brothers Auxiliary; St. Michael's High School Alumni Association; Nazareth Regional High School, Inc.; St. John's Preparatory School, Inc.; St. John's High School, Inc.; Xaverian Brothers High School, Inc.; Malden Catholic High School, Inc.; Xavier High School, Inc.; Isidore Charitable Trust; Lowell Catholic High School, Inc.; St. Bernard School of Montville, Inc. Brothers 192.

CUMBERLAND. *Our Lady of the Mountains Friary*, 300 1/2 E. Oldtown Rd., Cumberland, 21502. Tel: 301-777-7946; Email: gcguardian@aol.com. Revs. Gregory Chervenak, O.F.M.Cap., Guardian, Pastor at Our Lady of the Mountains & Vicar Forane; Eric Gauchat, O.F.M.Cap., Chap., SS. Peter & Paul (Cumberland) & St. Ambrose (Cresaptown).; Louis Petruha, O.F.M.Cap., In Res.; Bros. James Watson, O.F.M.Cap., Parochial Vicar; Walter Robb, Dir.

Province of St. Augustine of the Capuchin Order Brothers 1; Priests 6.

ELDERSBURG. *Society of Mary (Marianists)*, Marianist Community, 6049 Kennard Ct., Eldersburg, 21784. Tel: 410-795-2722; Fax: 410-795-7516. Revs. Neville O'Donahue, S.M., Pastor; David McGuigan, S.M., Dir.; Bros. Jesse O'Neill, S.M.; Justin Quiroz, S.M. Brothers 2; Priests 2.

ELLICOTT CITY. *Franciscan Friars - Our Lady of the Angels Province, Inc.*, 12300 Folly Quarter Rd., Ellicott City, 21042-1419. Tel: 410-531-1400; Fax: 410-531-4881; Email: provsec1@olaprovince.org; Web: www.olaprovince.org. Rev. Richard-Jacob Forcier, O.F.M.Conv., Contact Person.

Friary of St. Joseph Cupertino, 12290 Folly Quarter Rd., Ellicott City, 21042-1425. Tel: 410-531-2800; Fax: 410-531-2801. Conventual Franciscan Friars. Corporate Title: Franciscan Friars Minor Conventuals of MD, Inc.*Shrine of St. Anthony*, Tel: 410-531-2800; Fax: 410-531-2801. Revs. Michael Heine, O.F.M.Conv., Dir., Shrine of St. Anthony & Guardian, St. Joseph Cupertino Friary, Dir. Carrollton Hall; Emmanuel Acquaye, O.F.M.-Conv.; Hilary Brzostowski, O.F.M.Conv.; Thomas Lavin, O.F.M.Conv.; Julio Martinez, O.F.M.Conv.; Dennis Mason, O.F.M.Conv.; Friar Douglas McMillan, O.F.M.Conv.; Revs. Edward Ouma Owino, O.F.M.Conv,; Peter Damian Fehlner, O.F.M.Conv. *Companions of St. Anthony*, 12290 Folly Quarter Rd., Ellicott City, 21042. Tel: 410-531-2800; Fax: 410-531-2801. *Companions Evangelization & Mail Order Office*, Tel: 410-988-9833; Fax: 410-988-9705. Revs. Michael Heine, O.F.M.-Conv., Guardian; Thomas Lavin, O.F.M.Conv.

Order of Friars Minor Conventual, 12300 Folly Quarter Rd., Ellicott City, 21042-1419. Tel: 410-531-1400; Fax: 410-531-4881; Email: provsec1@olaprovince.org; Web: www.olaprovince.org. Very Rev. James McCurry, O.F.M.Conv., Min. Prov.; Revs. Richard-Jacob Forcier, O.F.M.Conv., Province Sec.; Joachin Giermek, O.F.M.Conv.; Robert Twele Esq., O.F.M.Conv., Counselor Catholic Relief Svs.; Michael J. Lasky, O.F.M.Conv., Justice & Peace Coord.; Michael Heine, O.F.M.Conv., Vicar; David Blowey, O.F.M.Conv., Outside the U.S.A.; Vincent Lachendro, O.F.M.Conv., Outside the U.S.A.; Thomas Reist, O.F.M.Conv., Outside the U.S.A.; Martin Breski, O.F.M.Conv., Outside the U.S.A.; Jude Winkler, O.F.M.Conv., Outside the U.S.A.; Stephen King, O.F.M.Conv., Outside the U.S.A.; Nicholas Swiatek, O.F.M.Conv., Outside the U.S.A.; Timothy Kulbicki, O.F.M.Conv., S.T.B., H.E.D., Outside the U.S.A.; Bro. Daniel Geary, O.F.M.Conv., Outside the U.S.A.

Order of Friars Minor Conventual, St. Anthony of Padua Province, U.S.A., Inc.; Franciscan Minor Conventuals of Maryland, Inc. of Ellicott City, MD.; The Franciscan Fathers, Minor Conventuals, of St. Stanislaus Church of Baltimore City, Inc.; Franciscan Friars, St. Anthony of Padua Province, Education Fund, Inc.; Franciscan Friars, St. Anthony of Padua Province, Fund for the Aged and Infirm Friars, Inc.; St. Francis of Assisi Community, Inc., Companions of St. Anthony.

St. Stanislaus Cemetery Inc; AnthonyCorps, Inc.

Fr. Justin Ministry Fund, Inc.

Franciscan Friars-Our Lady of the Angels Province, Inc.

Carrollton Hall, Inc. Total in Residence 208.

EMMITSBURG. *St. Vincent's House*, P.O. Box 376, Emmitsburg, 21727. Tel: 301-447-2326; Fax: 301-447-3579; Email: stjosephemmitsburg@comcast.net; Web: www.emmitsburg.net/stjosephparish. Revs. John J. Holliday, C.M., Pastor, Supr.; Charles F. Krieg, C.M., Parochial Vicar/Asst. Supr.; Francis W. Sacks, C.M., Chap.; Stephen P. Trzecieski, C.M., Chap. Priests 4.

TOWSON. *Jesuit Jamshedpur Mission Society, Inc.*, 8600 La Salle Rd., Ste. 620, Towson, 21286-2014. Tel: 443-921-1311; Fax: 443-921-1313; Email: martreasurer@jesuits.org; Web: www.mdsj.org. Rev. Richard McGowan, Treas.

Jesuit Mission Bureau, Maryland Province Inc., 8600 LaSalle Rd., Ste. 620, Towson, 21286-2014. Tel: 443-921-1311; Fax: 443-921-1313; Email: martreasurer@jesuits.org; Web: www.mdsj.org. Rev. Richard McGowan, Treas.

Jesuit Seminary Guild, Maryland Province, Inc., 8600 La Salle Rd., Ste. 620, Towson, 21286-2014. Tel: 443-921-1311; Fax: 443-921-1313; Email: martreasurer@jesuits.org; Web: www.mdsj.org. Rev. Richard McGowan, Treas.

Maryland Province of the Society of Jesus, 8600 LaSalle Rd., Ste. 620, Towson, 21286-2014. Tel: 443-921-1310; Fax: 443-921-1313; Email: marjesuits@jesuits.org; Web: www.mdsj.org. Revs. Robert M. Hussey, S.J., Provincial; Vincent G. Conti, S.J., Socius; Richard McGowan, Treas.; Liborio J. LaMartina, S.J., Resident Archivist; George Witt, S.J., Asst. for Spirituality Ministries; Philip Florio, Asst. for Vocations; James J. Miracky, S.J., Asst. for Higher Ed; Nick Napolitano, Asst. for Social Ministries; Mrs. Maura Parker, R.N., C.P.H.Q, Asst. for Health Care; Rev. Edward Quinnan, Asst. for Pastoral Ministries; Very Rev. Myles Sheehan, S.J., Asst. for Senior Jesuits; Revs. John Wronski, Asst. for Formation; Eugene J. Barber, S.J., Serving Abroad; Mr. Cesare Campagnoli, S.J., Serving Abroad; Revs. Edgar J. Debany, S.J., Serving Abroad; James M. Desjardins, S.J., Serving Abroad; Brendan Hurley, S.J., Serving Abroad; Michael J. Kuchera, S.J., Serving Abroad; A. Richard Sotelo, S.J., Serving Elsewhere

Corporation of the Roman Catholic Clergymen, Maryland Brothers 10; Novices 4; Priests 218; Religious 249; Scholastics 17.

[R] CONVENTS AND RESIDENCES FOR SISTERS

BALTIMORE. *Carmelite Communities Assoc.*, 1318 Dulaney Valley Rd., 21286-1399. Tel: 410-823-7415; Email: srmarjorie@gmail.com; Web: www.ccacarmels.org. Sr. Bernadette Therese Huang, Pres. Sisters 12.

Carmelite Sisters of Baltimore (1790) 1318 Dulaney Valley Rd., 21286-1399. Tel: 410-823-7415; Fax: 410-823-7418; Email: info@baltimorecarmel.org; Web: www.baltimorecarmel.org. Sr. Judith Long, O.C.D., Prioress. Discalced Carmelite Nuns. Professed Sisters 16.

Chesapeake Province of the Sisters of Notre Dame de Namur, Provincial Offices, 305 Cable St., 21210-2511. Tel: 410-243-1993; Fax: 410-243-2279; Email: susan.young@sndden.org; Web: www.sndden.org. Sisters Barbara Barry, Rel Order Leader; Edie Daly, S.N.D.deN, Rel Order Leader; Barbara Ann English, S.N.D.deN., Rel Order Leader; Mary Farren, S.N.D.deN., Rel Order Leader; Anne Malone, S.N.D.deN., Rel Order Leader; Catherine Waldron, S.N.D.deN., Rel Order Leader

Chesapeake Province of the Sisters of Notre Dame de Namur, Inc. Sisters in Province 44.

Comboni Missionary Sisters, 5401 Loch Raven Blvd., 21239-2902. Tel: 410-323-1469; Fax: 410-323-9632; Web: www.combonisrs.com. Sisters Andre T. Rothschild, C.M.S., Supr.; Ilaria Buonriposi, C.M.S.; Maria Mercedes Castillo Razo, C.M.S.; Olga Estela Sanchez Caro, C.M.S.; Sandra R. Amado, C.M.S.; Weynshet Tadesse Haile, C.M.S. Sisters 5.

Little Sisters of Jesus-Regional Residence, 400 N. Streeper St., 21224-1230. Tel: 410-327-7863; Email: ritalsj@hotmail.com; Web: www.rc.net/org/littlesisters. Sr. Rita Farina, L.S.J., Regl. Supr. Sisters 5.

Little Sisters of the Poor, Baltimore Province, Inc. (1869) 601 Maiden Choice Ln., 21228-3698. Tel: 410-744-9367; Fax: 410-747-0601; Email: mpbaltimore@littlesistersofthepoor.org; Email: cpbaltimore@littlesistersofthepoor.org; Web: www.littlesistersofthepoor.org. Sisters Loraine Maguire, L.S.P., Provincial; Robert Tait, Prov. Asst. Sisters 3.

Maria Health Care Center, Inc., 6401 N. Charles St., 21212. Tel: 410-377-3011; Fax: 410-377-6042; Email: eowen@ssndba.org. Sr. Edward Owen Jr., Admin. Health Center for School Sisters of Notre Dame and other Religious Congregations.

Mission Helper Center, 1001 W. Joppa Rd., 21204-3787. Tel: 410-823-8585; Fax: 410-825-6355; Email: elangmead@missionhelpers.org; Web: www.missionhelpers.org. Sisters Elizabeth Langmead, M.H.S.H., Pres., Vice Pres. & Treas.; Maria Luz Ortiz, M.H.S.H., Vice Pres.; Marilyn Dunphy, M.H.S.H., Treas. Sisters 46; Total Staff 11; Sisters in Diocese 31.

Missionaries of Charity (1950) Gift of Hope Convent, 818 N. Collington Ave., 21205. Tel: 410-732-6056. Sr. Cecil Ann, M.C., Supr. Sisters 4; Tot Asst. Annually 800; Total in Residence 10.

Our Lady of Mt. Providence Convent-Motherhouse, 701 Gun Rd., 21227. Tel: 410-242-8500; Fax: 410-242-4963; Email: srcrescentia@oblatesisters.com. Sisters Mary Alexis Fisher, O.S.P., Supr. Gen.; Mary Lorraine George, O.S.P., Asst. Gen.; Mary Crescentia, Proctor, Sec.; Sharon Young, Treas. Oblate Sisters of Providence.Attended by Capuchin Franciscan Friars and Josephite Fathers. Total Staff 37; Sisters in the Motherhouse 43; Sisters in the Diocese 47; Oblate Sisters 57.

The School Sisters of Notre Dame Atlantic-Midwest Province (1876) 6401 N. Charles St., 21212. Tel: 410-377-7774; Fax: 410-377-5363; Email: ckrohe@amssnd.org; Web: www.ssnd.org. Sr. Charmaine Krohe, S.S.N.D., Prov. Leader; Rev. Roman Kozacheson, O.F.M.Cap, Chap. Sisters 513.

Atlantic-Midwest Province of the School Sisters of Notre Dame, Inc.

SSND Service Corporation.

SSND Care, Inc.

SSND Real Estate Holding Corporation.

SSND Real Estate Trust.

SSND Continuing Care Trust.

SSND Charitable Annuity Trust.

Atlantic-Midwest Province Endowment Trust.

School Sisters of Notre Dame in the City of Baltimore, Inc., 6401 N. Charles St., 21212. Tel: 410-377-7774; Fax: 410-377-5363; Email: ckrohe@amssnd.org; Email: swall@amssnd.org; Web: ssnd.org. Sr. Charmaine Krohe, S.S.N.D., Prov. Sisters 167.

Sisters of the Good Shepherd (1864) 4100 Maple Ave., 21227-4099. Tel: 410-247-2770; Fax: 410-242-5890; Email: sr.mary.carol@gssmaryland.org. Sr. Mary Carol McClenon, R.G.S., Supr. Sisters 13; Total Staff 4.

Sisters of the Good Shepherd-St. Joseph Residence (1864) 4130 Maple Ave., 21227-4007. Tel: 410-247-3898; Fax: 410-242-5890. Sr. Mary Carol McClenon, R.G.S., Local Leader. Infirmary for the Mid-North America Province. Sisters 13; Total Staff 27.

Sisters Servants of Mary Immaculate, Inc., 1220 Tugwell Dr., 21228. Tel: 410-747-1353; Fax: 410-747-0386. Sr. Danuta Zielinska, Prov. Supr. Convent and Novitiate. Sisters 19.

St. Clare of Assisi, Inc. (2003) 3725 Ellerslie Ave., 21218. Tel: 410-235-9277; Fax: 410-243-2569; Email: etcarr@msn.com; Web: www.lakeosfs.org. Sisters Ellen Carr, O.S.F., Admin. Dir.; Jodene Wydeven, O.S.F., Local Coord. Clare of Assisi, Inc. operates Clare Court Convent, a retirement residence for members of The Sisters of St. Francis of Assisi, Inc., formerly Franciscan Sisters of Baltimore. Sisters 8; Total Staff 14.

The Villa (1971) 6806 Bellona Ave., 21212-1299. Tel: 410-377-2450; Fax: 410-377-2501. Melissa McIntosh, Admin. Convent for Retired Sisters of Mercy, Mission Helpers of the Sacred Heart, and other religious.

Mercy Villa Convent, Inc. Sisters 26; Total Staff 43.

CATONSVILLE. *The Home of the All Saints Sisters of the Poor of Baltimore City*, 1501 Hilton Ave., P.O. Box

3127, Catonsville, 21228-0127. Tel: 410-747-4104; Fax: 410-747-3321. Mother Emily Ann Lindsey, Prioress; Sr. Christina Christie, Sub-Prioress. All Saints is a traditional Community desiring to uphold orthodox Christian faith and morality and to support the Apostolic tradition in ministry and practice. We are united by our common commitment to the One Lord Jesus Christ and by the desire to live for Him. We are a diocesan religious community.

St. Gabriel's Retreat House, 1201 Hilton Ave., P.O. Box 3106, Catonsville, 21228-0127. Tel: 410-747-6767; Web: www.allsaintssisters.org. St. Gabriel's is a small retreat house serving men and women, as well as priests and religious seeking quiet and spiritual refreshment. Small groups are also welcome. Retreatants are encouraged to enter into the silence and prayerful spirit of the Priory, attend Mass at the Priory Chapel, and may join the Sisters for the Divine Office. Many individuals throughout the course of a year partake of the homey and relaxed atmosphere which enables their souls to convalesce.

EMMITSBURG. *Daughters of Charity of St. Vincent de Paul, Province of St. Louise-St. Joseph House*, 333 S. Seton Ave., Emmitsburg, 21727. Tel: 301-447-3121; Fax: 301-447-7095; Web: www.daughtersofcharity.org. Sr. Clarisse Correia, Supr. Sisters 65.

LUTHERVILLE. *Emmanuel Monastery* (1971) 2229 W. Joppa Rd., Lutherville, 21093-4601. Tel: 410-821-5792; Fax: 410-296-9560; Email: bensrs@emmanuelosb.org; Email: jmstief@emmanuelosb.org; Web: www.emmanuelosb.org. Sr. Patricia Kirk, O.S.B., Rel Order Leader. Benedictine Sisters of Baltimore. Ministering in Education, Pastoral Ministry, Retreats and Spiritual Direction, Social Services, Justice Ministry, Hospital Ministry. Sisters 14.

MARRIOTTSVILLE. *Sisters of Bon Secours, USA, Leadership Office* (1824) Marriottsville, 21104. Tel: 410-442-1333; Fax: 410-442-1394; Web: www.bonsecours.us. Sr. Rose Marie Jasinski, C.B.S., Pres. Total Staff 60; Retired Sisters in Baltimore 9; Total in Residence in Baltimore 19; Total in Residence in U.S. 27; Retired Sisters in U.S. 11.

STEVENSON. *Maryland Province Center* (1934) 1531 Greenspring Valley Rd., Stevenson, 21153. Tel: 410-486-5599; Fax: 410-486-5466; Email: sndmd@aol.com; Web: www.sndden.org. Sisters Carol Lichtenberg, S.N.D.deN., Prov. Moderator; Kathleen Harmon, S.N.D.deN., Team Member; Linda Soucek, S.N.D.deN., Team Member; Kristin Matthes, S.N.D.deN., Team Member. Additional Projects Sponsored: Maryland Province Center, Stevenson, MD; Villa Julie Residence, Stevenson, MD; Notre Dame Academy, Villanova, PA; Trinity School, Ellicott City, MD; Maryvale Preparatory School, Brooklandville, MD.; Additional Projects Co-Sponsored: The Development Office, a joint project of the Maryland, Chesapeake & Notre Dame Base Communities Provinces; Sisters Academy of Baltimore, co-sponsored by the School Sisters of Notre Dame, The Sisters of Bon Secours, The Sisters of Notre Dame de Namur and The Sisters of Mercy.

Baltimore Province of the Sisters of Notre Dame de Namur, Inc.

Sisters of Notre Dame de Namur, Maryland Province, Charitable Trust

Cemetery Perpetual Trust Total Staff 3; Sisters in Province 61; Sisters in Diocese 35.

Villa Julie Residence, 1531 Greenspring Valley Rd., Stevenson, 21153. Tel: 410-486-6946; Fax: 410-484-6930. Residence for retired Sisters of Notre Dame de Namur Sisters 32.

[S] NEWMAN CENTERS

BALTIMORE. *Division Of Campus Ministry For Universities And Colleges*, Mailing Address: Archdiocese of Baltimore, Dept. of Evangelization, 320 Cathedral St., 21201. Tel: 410-547-5321; Fax: 410-625-8481. 43 Monroe St., Westminster, 21157. Tel: 410-848-8443; Email: pgallagher@sjwest.org. Purpose: To bring the presence of the Church to college and university campuses by offering spiritual, liturgical, social, service and educational experiences to the campus communities of non-Catholic academic institutions within the Archdiocese.

Coppin State University, St. Cecilia Church, 3300 Clifton Ave., 21216. Tel: 410-624-3600.

Frostburg State University, Osborne Newman Center, 130 S. Broadway, Frostburg, 21532. Tel: 301-689-5041; Email: kbroadwater@archbalt.org.

Johns Hopkins University, SS. Philip & James, 2801 N. Charles St., 21218. Tel: 410-235-2294.

McDaniel College, St. John Church, 43 Monroe St., Westminster, 21157. Tel: 410-848-8443; Email: pgallagher@sjwest.org.

Morgan State University, St. Matthew Church, 5401 Loch Raven Blvd., 21239. Tel: 410-433-2300; Email: joemuth@verizon.net.

Stevenson University, Sacred Heart Church, 65 Sacred Heart Ln., P.O. Box 3672, Glyndon, 21071-3672. Tel: 410-833-1696; Email: srjude@shgparish.org.

Towson University, Newman Center, 7909 York Rd., Towson, 21204. Tel: 410-828-0622; Email: tryan@archbalt.org.

University of Maryland, Baltimore County (UMBC), Our Lady of Perpetual Help, Ellicott City, 4795 Ilchester Rd., Ellicott City, 21043. Tel: 410-747-4334; Email: frjohn@umbc.edu.

Goucher College / Hood College / UMAB.

Catholic Universities in the Archdiocese:.

Loyola University, 4501 N. Charles St., 21210. Tel: 410-617-2444; Fax: 410-617-2052.

Mount St. Mary's University, Emmitsburg, 21727. Tel: 301-447-5223; Fax: 301-447-5868; Email: nolan@msmary.edu. Rev. Brian P. Nolan, Chap. & Dir. Campus Ministry.

Notre Dame of Maryland University, 4701 N. Charles St., 21210. Tel: 410-532-5565; Fax: 410-532-5796; Email: mlees@ndm.edu. Melissa Lees, Dir. Campus Ministry.

[T] FOUNDATIONS, FUNDS AND TRUSTS

BALTIMORE. *Archbishop Curley High School Endowment Trust*, 3701 Sinclair Ln., 21213. Tel: 410-485-5000; Fax: 410-485-1090. Rev. Donald Grzymski, O.F.M.Conv.

Bon Secours of Maryland Foundation, Inc. aka Bon Secours Community Works (1919) 26 N. Fulton Ave., 21223. Tel: 410-362-3629; Fax: 410-362-3443; Email: anita_crockett@bshsi.org; Web: bonsecours.com/baltimore/community-commitment/community-works. Samuel L. Ross, M.D., M.S., CEO. Total Staff 37; Total Assisted 9,657.

The following are tax exempt subsidiaries of the Bon Secours of Maryland Foundation, Inc.

Bon Secours Housing, Inc. aka Hollins Terrace (1983).

Bon Secours Housing II, Inc. aka Benet House (1987).

Unity Properties, Inc. (1993).

Bon Secours Baltimore Development, Inc. (2005).

The Catholic Community Foundation of the Archdiocese of Baltimore, Inc., 320 Cathedral St., 21201. Tel: 410-547-5356; Fax: 410-625-8485; Email: catholiccommunityfoundation@archbalt.org; Web: www.ccfmd.org. Patrick Madden, Exec. Dir.

Chancery Office, 320 Cathedral St., 21201. Tel: 410-547-5446; Fax: 410-727-5432; Email: chancery@archbalt.org; Web: www.archbalt.org. Dr. Diane L. Barr, J.D., J.C.D., Ph.D., Chancellor, Tel: 410-547-5446.

Archbishop of Baltimore Annual Appeal Trust / Cardinal's Lenten Appeal, Tel: 410-547-5439; Fax: 410-727-8234.

Archdiocesan Health Plan Trust Fund Agreement, Tel: 410-547-5317; Fax: 410-783-5993.

Archdiocesan General Insurance Program Trust, Tel: 410-547-5317; Fax: 410-783-5993.

Archdiocesan Priests Post-Retirement Benefits Plan Trust Fund, 320 Cathedral St., 21201. Tel: 410-547-5317; Fax: 410-783-5993; Email: pphelps@archbalt.org. Petra R. Phelps, Contact Person.

Cemetery Continuing Care Trust St. Patrick's Havre de Grace, Cemetery Continuing Care Trust; Holy Cross Cemetery Continuing Care Trust; St. Joseph, Fullerton, Cemetery-Continuing Care Trust Agreement; St. Mary of the Assumption, Govans, Cemetery Continuing Care Trust; St. Mary's, Pylesville Cemetery, Continuing Care Trust.

Christian Brothers Community Support Charitable Trust, Tel: 732-380-7926.

Corpus Christi Jenkins Memorial Trust, Inc., Tel: 410-523-4161; Fax: 410-523-5745.

Dart, Inc.

The Dr. Charles J. Foley Sr. and Mildred H. Foley Memorial Endowment Trust, Tel: 410-547-5322; Fax: 410-332-8233. Provides annual support for over 300 programs and agencies of the Archdiocese.

Franciscan Sisters of Baltimore, Inc., Trust, Tel: 410-235-2496; Fax: 410-243-2569.

The Gallagher Family Fund, 320 Cathedral St., 21201. Tel: 410-547-5322; Fax: 410-332-8233.

**G S Housing, Inc.*

John Paul II Regional School, Inc., (Grades PreK-8), Tel: 410-944-0367; Fax: 410-265-5316.

The Marion Burk Knott Scholarship Fund, Educational Trust, Tel: 301-603-9501.

Marianist Charitable Trust, Tel: 410-366-1300; Fax: 410-889-5743.

Maryvale Educational Fund, Inc., Tel: 410-252-3366; Fax: 410-561-1826.

Mercy Primary Care Group, Inc., Tel: 410-332-9000; Fax: 410-962-1303.

The National Black Catholic Congress, Inc., Tel: 410-547-8496; Fax: 410-752-3958; Email: nbcc@nbccongress.org; Web: www.nbccongress.org.

Neumann Early Childhood Center, Inc., Tel: 410-547-5495.

Our Lady of Good Counsel Historic Trust, Inc., Tel: 410-752-0205; Fax: 410-576-0929.

Plan of Self-Insurance Trust, Tel: 410-547-5317; Fax: 410-783-5993.

The Priests Continuing Education and Formation Endowment Trust, Tel: 410-547-5317; Fax: 410-783-5993.

St. Gregory the Great Housing Committee, Inc., Tel: 410-523-0061; Fax: 410-669-1385.

St. Jane Frances Educational Endowment Trust, Tel: 410-255-4750; Fax: 410-350-6720.

St. John Neumann Regional School, Inc., Tel: 301-724-4055; Fax: 301-724-4827.

St. John the Evangelist School Endowment Trust, 689 Ritchie Hwy., Severna Park, 21146. Tel: 410-647-2283.

St. Jude Shrine Corporation, Tel: 410-685-6026; Fax: 410-244-5728.

St. Mark's Parish School Endowment Trust, Tel: 410-747-6613; Fax: 410-747-3188.

St. Peter's Cemetery Restoration Fund, Inc., Tel: 410-547-5300; Fax: 410-332-8233.

St. Pius V Housing Committee, Inc., Tel: 410-523-1930; Fax: 410-523-8164.

St. Vincent De Paul Historic Trust, Inc., Tel: 410-547-5377; Fax: 410-625-8483.

Sacred Heart Community Health Services, Inc., Tel: 301-723-5222.

Sacred Heart Foundation, Inc., Tel: 301-723-5222.

Sacred Heart Hospital of the Sisters of Charity, Inc., Tel: 410-723-5222.

School Sisters of Notre Dame in the City of Baltimore Charitable Trust, Inc., Tel: 410-377-7774; Fax: 410-377-5363.

Sisters of Notre Dame de Namur Charitable Trusts, Tel: 410-255-1577.

Sisters of Notre Dame de Namur, Maryland Province, Charitable Trust, Tel: 410-486-5382; Fax: 410-486-5466.

Women's Auxiliary Board, Tel: 410-547-5356. Funds provide partial tuition for thousands of low income students in designated Baltimore City Catholic Schools.

**St. Elizabeth School Foundation, Inc.*, 801 Argonne Dr., 21218-1998. Tel: 410-889-5054; Fax: 410-889-2356. Gregory E. Paranzino, Pres., Bd. of Directors.

The Immaculate Heart of Mary School Endowment Trust, 8501 Loch Raven Blvd., 21286. Tel: 410-668-8466; Fax: 410-668-6171; Email: dschiavone@immaculateheartofmary.com; Email: aalicea@ihmschoolmd.org; Email: dsperato@ihmschoolmd.org. Rev. Michael W. Carrion.

St. Joseph Manor Foundation, Inc., 911 W. Lake Ave., 21210. Tel: 410-727-3386; Fax: 410-727-1006; Email: josephite1@aol.com; Web: www.josephite.com. Very Rev. Michael L. Thompson, S.S.J., Contact Person.

The Josephite Retirement and Disability Benefits Trusts (2003) 911 W. Lake Ave., 21210. Tel: 410-727-3386; Fax: 410-727-1006; Email: josephite1@aol.com; Web: www.josephite.com. Very Rev. Michael L. Thompson, S.S.J., Supr. Gen.

The Josephite Seminarian Education Trust (2003) 911 W. Lake Ave., 21210. Tel: 410-727-3386; Fax: 410-727-1006; Email: josephite1@aol.com; Web: www.josephite.com. Very Rev. Michael L. Thompson, S.S.J., Supr. Gen.

St. Luke Parish Education Endowment Trust, 7517 N. Point Rd., 21219. Tel: 410-477-5200; Fax: 410-477-5996; Email: stlukedgemere@yahoo.com. Revs. Austin Murphy; Gregory Rapisarda. Purpose: to support the youth of the parish who attend catholic schools. Total Staff 1; Total Assisted 40.

St. Matthew's Parish Endowment Trust, 5401 Loch Raven Blvd., 21239. Tel: 410-433-2300; Email: stmattrc@gmail.com; Fax: 410-433-5263. Rev. Joseph L. Muth Jr., Contact Person.

Mercy Health Foundation, Inc., 301 St. Paul Pl., 21202. Tel: 410-332-9874; Fax: 410-685-7464; Email: amccomiskey@mdmercy.com; Web: mdmercy.com. Thomas R. Mullen, Pres. & CEO.

Partners in Excellence Scholarship Program, 320 Cathedral St., 21201. Tel: 410-625-8452. This Program provides partial tuition assistance to low income families wishing to send their children to a Catholic School in Baltimore City.

The Paul Van Gerwin Religious & Charitable Trust, 4409 Frederick Ave., 21229. Tel: 410-644-0034; Email: rtully@xaverianbrothers.org. Mrs. Rhonda Tully, M.A., Contact Person, (Retired).

The Sacred Heart of Mary Cemetery Continuing Care Trust, 6736 Youngstown Ave., 21222. Tel: 410-633-2828; Fax: 410-633-0349. Rev. George Gannon.

The Seton Keough High School Endowment Trust, 1201 Caton Ave., 21227. Tel: 410-646-4444; Fax: 443-573-0107; Web: www.setonkeough.com.

St. Thomas Aquinas School Foundation Trust, 3710 Roland Ave., 21211. Tel: 410-889-4618; Fax: 410-889-1956; Email: starch@archbalt.org. Larry Glose, Contact Person.

BEL AIR. *John Carroll Foundation of the Roman Catholic Archdiocese of Baltimore*, Archdiocese of Baltimore, 320 Cathedral St., 21201.

ANNAPOLIS. *St. Andrew by the Bay Endowment Trust*, 701 College Pkwy., Annapolis, 21409. Tel: 410-974-4366; Fax: 410-974-4339; Email: sabbanna@archbalt.org; Web: standrewbythebay.org. Rev. Jeffrey S. Dauses.

COCKEYSVILLE. *St. Joseph, Texas Endowment Trust*, 101 Church Ln., Cockeysville, 21030. Tel: 410-683-0600; Fax: 410-628-2956; Email: rhilgartner@archbalt.org. Rev. Msgr. Richard B. Hilgartner, Contact Person; Rev. Carlos Osorio.

CUMBERLAND. *The SS. Peter & Paul Parish Endowment Trust*, c/o Our Lady of the Mountain, 300 E. Oldtown Rd., Ste. 2, Cumberland, 21502. Tel: 301-777-1750; Fax: 301-777-2669; Email: olmcumberland@archbalt.org.

ELKRIDGE. *St. Augustine School, Inc.*, 5990 Old Washington Rd., Elkridge, 21075. Tel: 410-796-3040; Fax: 410-579-1165; Web: www.staug-md.org. Patricia Schratz, Prin.

ELLICOTT CITY. *The St. Paul's Parish Endowment Trust*, 3755 St. Paul St., Ellicott City, 21043. Tel: 410-465-1670; Fax: 410-313-8551; Email: office@stpaulcc.org. Rev. Matthew T. Buening.

GLEN BURNIE. *The Church of the Good Shepherd Parish Endowment Trust*, 1451 Furnace Ave., Glen Burnie, 21060. Tel: 410-766-5070; Fax: 410-760-6738. Parish Center: 126 Dorsey Rd., Glen Burnie, 21061. Revs. C. Lou Martin; Angel A. Marrero.

KINGSVILLE. *St. Stephen School Endowment Trust*, 8028 Bradshaw Rd., Kingsville, 21087-1807. Tel: 410-592-7617; Fax: 410-592-7330.

MARRIOTTSVILLE. *Bon Secours Mercy Health, Inc.*, 1505 Marriottsville Rd., Marriottsville, 21104. Tel: 410-442-3505; Fax: 410-442-3256; Email: Kerri_Hewitt@bshsi.org; Web: www.bshsi.org. Chris Allen, Chair & Bd. of Directors; John Starcher Jr., CEO.

MIDLAND. *St. Joseph Midland Cemetery Continuing Care Trust*, 44 E. Main St., Frostburg, 21532. Rev. Edward S. Hendricks; Edward Jones, Business Mgr.

St. Joseph Midland Parish Endowment Trust, 44 E. Main St., Frostburg, 21532. Tel: 301-689-6767; Fax: 301-689-6411. Rev. Edward S. Hendricks.

PASADENA. *St. Jane Frances Educational Endowment Trust*, 8499 Virginia Ave., Pasadena, 21122. Tel: 410-255-4646; Fax: 410-437-5191; Web: stjane.org.

SYKESVILLE. *St. Joseph Catholic Community Endowment Trust*, 915 Liberty Rd., Sykesville, 21784. Tel: 443-920-9191; Fax: 443-920-9192; Email: parishoffice@saintjoseph.cc; Web: www.saintjoseph.cc. Rev. Neville O'Donohue, S.M., Pastor; Deacons Michael Dvorak; Karl Bayhi; Vito Piazza Sr., M.A.Th., M.A.Ch.Min.

TOWSON. *The Immaculate Conception Elementary School Endowment Trust*, 200 Ware Ave., Towson, 21204. Tel: 410-427-4700; Fax: 410-427-4795; Email: info@theimmaculate.org; Web: www.theimmaculate.org. Rev. Joseph F. Barr.

Maryland Province of the Society of Jesus Aged and Infirm Trust, 8600 LaSalle Rd., Ste. 620, Towson, 21286. Tel: 443-921-1319; Fax: 443-921-1313; Email: martreasurer@jesuits.org. Rev. Richard McGowan, Treas.

Maryland Province of the Society of Jesus Formation Trust, 8600 LaSalle Rd., Ste. 620, Towson, 21286. Tel: 443-921-1319; Fax: 443-921-1313; Email: martreasurer@jesuits.org. Rev. Richard McGowan, Treas.

WESTERNPORT. *St. Peter's, Westernport, School Endowment Trust*, 44 E. Main St., Frostburg, 21532. Tel: 301-689-6767; Fax: 301-689-6411; Email: edward.jones@archbalt.org; Web: www.divinemercymd.org. Rev. Edward S. Hendricks; Edward Jones, Business Mgr.

[U] MISCELLANEOUS

BALTIMORE. *African Conference of Catholic Clergy & Religious in the United States, Inc.*, c/o NBCC, 320 Cathedral St., 21201. Tel: 770-251-5353, Ext. 202; Fax: 770-251-2053; Web: www.acccrus.org. Rev. Henry Atem, Pres.

Saint Agnes Hospital Foundation, Inc., 900 Caton Ave., SAHC Box 123, 21229. Tel: 667-234-3155; Fax: 667-234-3533; Email: kirstan.cecil@ascension.org; Web: www.stagnes.org. Kirstan Cecil, Pres.

Alhambra, International Order of (1904) Supreme Headquarters, 4200 Leeds Ave., 21229. Tel: 410-242-0660; Fax: 410-536-5729; Email: salaam@orderofalhambra.org; Web: www.OrderAlhambra.org. Roger J. Reid, Exec. Dir. Nonprofit organization dedicated to assisting the developmentally disabled.

Baltimore Archdiocesan Holy Name Union (1911) 212 Elinor Ave., 21236. Tel: 410-661-3170. Rev. Michael W. Carrion, Spiritual Dir., 8501 Lock Raven Blvd., Towson, 21286-2313. Tel: 410-668-7935, Ext. 203; Carroll W. Pupa, Pres., 212 Elinor Ave., 21236. Tel: 410-262-7955. Purpose: Promotes reverence for the Sacred Names of God and Jesus Christ, obedience and loyalty to the magisterium of the Catholic Church, personal sanctification, holiness of its members and opposes pornography, blasphemous and obscene speech. Also support youth ministry, corporal and spiritual works of mercy, seminarian grants, vocation recruitment and Catholic high school grants as well as the cause for the canonization of their founder Blessed John of Vercelli.

Basilica of the Assumption Historic Trust, Inc., 409 Cathedral St., 21201. Tel: 410-727-3565; Fax: 410-539-0407; Web: www.baltimorebasilica.org. Bob Brown, Devel. Dir.; Kathy Wandishin, Devel. Exec. Asst.

The Benedictine Society of Baltimore, Inc., 2612 Wilkens Ave., 21223. Tel: 410-947-4988; Email: stbenedictbalto@gmail.com. Rt. Revs. Douglas Nowicki, Pres.; Paschal A. Morlino, O.S.B., Vice Pres. Administrators 1; Volunteers 12.

Bon Secours Baltimore Development, Inc., 26 N. Fulton Ave., 21223. Tel: 410-362-3199; Fax: 410-362-3670; Email: george_kleb@bshsi.org.

Bon Secours Baltimore Health System Foundation, 2000 W Baltimore St, 21223. Tel: 410-362-3090; Fax: 410-362-3578. Julie Mercer, Vice Pres. Philanthropy.

**Cardijn Associates, Inc.* (1994) 4513 Bayonne Ave., 21206. Tel: 410-488-7936; Email: nancyconrad@verizon.net. Ms. Nancy Lee Conrad, Sec.

Caroline Center (1996) 900 Somerset St., 21202. Tel: 410-563-1303; Fax: 410-563-1302; Email: carolinecenter@caroline-center.org; Web: Caroline-Center.org. Lynn Selby, Exec. Employment training education for low income women.

The Caroline Freiss Center, Inc. Tot Asst. Annually 320; Total Staff 36.

Cathedral Library, 5200 N. Charles St., 21210. Tel: 410-464-4041. Laura M. Perry, Dir. Staffed by the Catholic Evidence League.; Maintain a lending library open to anyone in the archdiocese on Monday from 10:00 AM-2:00 PM & Sunday from 9:30 AM-1:00 PM. Total Staff 7.

Catholic Alumni Club of Baltimore (1961) 4132 E. Joppa Rd., Ste. 11, P.O. Box 837, Perry Hall, 21236. Tel: 410-698-3889; Email: info@cacbaltimore.org; Web: www.cacbaltimore.org.

Catholic Evidence League of Baltimore (1922) c/o Cathedral of Mary Our Queen, 5200 N. Charles St., 21210. Tel: 410-464-4000. Mrs. Barbara Melanson, Pres. The object of this association is to increase in its members knowledge of the history, teaching, and laws of the Catholic Church, and to make more effective an application of these teachings to their lives and to the general life of the community. Meeting on First Fridays from October through May at the Cathedral of Mary Our Queen for Rosary, Mass, Luncheon, and Speaker.

Catholic Relief Services - United States Conference of Catholic Bishops, 228 W. Lexington St., 21201. Tel: 410-625-2220; Fax: 410-234-2986; Web: www.crs.org. Dr. Carolyn Y. Woo, Pres. For a more detailed explanation of this organization, please consult the A-pages located in the front of the Directory.

Catholic Relief Services Foundation, Inc., 228 W. Lexington St., 21201. Tel: 410-951-7546; Fax: 443-825-3886. Rev. Robert Twele Esq., O.F.-M.Conv., Sec.

Catholic War Veterans USA, Inc., 9511-P Kingscroft Ter., Perry Hall, 21128. Tel: 410-299-7283; Email: cwvmd@yahoo.com; Web: www.cwvmd.org. Gilbert T. Barker, Dept. Commander; Rev. Coman Timoney, Post Chap.

Christ Child Society of Baltimore, Inc., P.O. Box 584, Riderwood, 21139. Tel: 410-812-0620; Email: info@christchildbaltimore.org. Maureen Flynn, Pres.

Christian Life Community Regional Information Center (1967) 615 Rest Ave., Catonsville, 21228. Tel: 410-465-1312; Email: cazieba@yahoo.com; Web: www.clc-usa.org. Carol A. Zieba, Regional Chm.; Al Yarzebinsky, Treas. CLC is a lay organization that forms and sustains men and women, adults and youth, who commit themselves to the church and its mission in the world and feel the urgent need to unite their human life in all its dimensions with the fullness of their Christian faith and to work for social justice. Members come together in community to share their experience of Ignatian spirituality and mission.

Christlife, Inc. (1995) 600 Cooks Ln., 21229. Tel: 443-388-8910; Email: info@christlife.org; Web: www.christlife.org. Mr. Dave Nodar, Dir.

Cristo Rey Corporate Internship Program, Inc., 420 S. Chester St., 21231. Tel: 410-727-3255; Fax: 443-573-9898. Dr. William Heiser, Pres.; Janet Shock, Dir.; Leigh Profit, Dir. Finance. Staff 5.

Esperanza Center Health Services Inc., 320 Cathedral St., 21201. Tel: 443-825-3450; Fax: 443-573-6100. Mr. William J. McCarthy Jr., Dir.

Food for Thought, Inc., 1625 E. Baltimore, 21231. Tel: 410-563-0081; Fax: 410-327-1345; Email: srmaryannh@aol.com. Sr. Mary Ann Hartnett, S.S.N.D., Dir. Tutorial program for children & adult literacy.

Friends of Ijebu-Ode Diocese, Inc., 7811 Stonebriar Dr., Glen Burnie, 21060. Tel: 410-727-3386; Fax: 443-883-3464; Email: nelsonssj@hotmail.com; Email: frsalbert@yahoo.com. Very Rev. Nelson A. Moreira, S.S.J., Sec.-Treas.; Rev. Albert Adeleke, Vice Pres.

**G S Properties, Inc.*, 5601 Loch Raven Blvd., 21239. Tel: 410-772-6768; Fax: 410-772-6624; Web: www.medstarhealth.org.

Ignatian Volunteer Corps, 112 E. Madison St., Ste. 300, 21202. Tel: 410-752-4686; Fax: 410-752-8480; Email: info@ivcusa.org; Email: ptillman@ivcusa.org; Web: www.ivcusa.org. Ms. Mary C. McGinnity, Exec. Dir.; Rev. James R. Conroy, S.J., Founder; Thomas Ulrich, Dir., Prog. Operations & Regl. Devel.

Inter Parish Loan Fund, Inc., 320 Cathedral St., 21201. Tel: 410-547-5322; Fax: 410-332-8233. William J. Baird III, Sec.

Jesuit Volunteers Jesuit Volunteer Corps, 801 St. Paul St., 21202. Tel: 410-244-1733; Email: info@jesuitvolunteers.org; Web: www.jesuitvolunteers.org. Tom Chabolla, Pres.

Legion of Mary, 313 Streett Cir., Forest Hill, 21050. Tel: 703-408-5779. Dianne Van Pelt, Pres. Baltimore Comitium, governing body for the Legion of Mary in the Baltimore Archdiocese.

Loyola Early Learning Center, Inc., 801 St. Paul St., 21202. Tel: 410-727-3848; Email: parish@st-ignatius.net. Rev. William Watters, S.J., Pres.

Marian House, Inc., 949 Gorsuch Ave., 21218. Tel: 410-467-4121; Fax: 410-467-6709; Email: pmciver@marianhouse.org; Web: www.marianhouse.org. Katie Allston, LCSW-C, Exec. Dir.

Mother Seton House on Paca Street, Inc., 600 N. Paca St., 21201. Tel: 410-728-6464; Fax: 410-669-8140; Web: www.stmaryspacast.org. Deacon Vito Piazza Sr., M.A.Th., M.A.Ch.Min., Dir. The Mother Seton House on Paca Street is part of the St. Mary's Spiritual Center and Historic Site. The federal style house served as home (1808) and school for St. Elizabeth Ann Seton, America's first native-born canonized saint. Also on the site is the Historic Seminary Chapel that served the needs of our nation's first Roman Catholic Seminary (1791). The Historic Site is owned and operated by the Society of St. Sulpice, Province of the US. The site is open Monday-Friday from 12 noon to 3:30 pm and Saturday-Sunday from 1-3 pm. Entrance to the site is free, with off street parking.

The Mount Saint Agnes Theological Center for Women, Inc., 909 Poplar Hill Rd., 21210. Tel: 410-435-7500; Fax: 410-435-9522; Email: wisdom@mountsaintagnes.org; Web: www.mountsaintagnes.org. Sr. Mary Aquin O'Neill, R.S.M., Ph.D., Dir.; Sarah Holby, Administrative Asst. Total Staff 2.

**Murphy Initiative for Justice and Peace*, 1001 W. Joppa Rd., 21204. Tel: 410-823-8585; Email: info@murphyinitiative.org. Jane M. Heil, Co-Dir.

My Sister's Place Women's Center Fund, Inc., 320 Cathedral St., 21201-4421. Tel: 410-547-5490; Email: wmccarth@cc-md.org. Mr. William J. McCarthy Jr., Exec. Dir.

Nigeria-Igbo Catholic Community, P.O. Box 66027, 21239. Tel: 443-857-9991; Email: office@niccchurch.org; Web: www.niccchurch.org. Patrick E. Nwakuba, Chm.; Ignatius Nwankwo, Vice Chm.; Felix Opara, Sec.; Rev. Anthony Abiamiri. Purpose: to provide an environment for all Igbos in the Baltimore Metropolitan area to worship in their native language.

Our Daily Bread Employment Center Fund, Inc., 320 Cathedral St., 21201-4421. Tel: 410-547-5490; Email: wmccarth@cc-md.org. Mr. William J. McCarthy Jr., Exec. Dir.

Pallottine Charitable, Educational and Apostolic Ministry Trust, 512 W. Saratoga St., 21201. Tel: 410-685-3064.

Radio Mass of Baltimore, Inc., St. Ignatius Church, 740 N. Calvert St., 21202. Tel: 410-539-7812; Fax: 410-837-8883; Web: www.radiomass.org. Rev. James A. Casciotti, S.J., Dir.; Mrs. Carolyn Dunne, Admin. Mass is broadcast every Sunday morning from St. Ignatius Church at 9:03 A.M. on WCBM - 680 AM Radio dial and rebroadcast at 6:03 P.M. on WCBM - 680 AM.

Reparation Society of the Immaculate Heart of Mary, Inc. (1946) Fatima House, 7920 Beverly Ave., 21234. Tel: 973-220-6995; Tel: 732-421-4791; Email: smithnursing@gmail.com. Rev. Anthony Mastroeni, S.T.D., J.D., Pres.; Sr. Elias Margand, Admin. Purpose: To promote prayer and penance in reparation to the Immaculate Heart of Mary in accordance with the message of Fatima. Total in Residence 1; Volunteers 2.

Sarah's House Fund, Inc., 320 Cathedral St., 21201-4421. Tel: 410-547-5490; Email: wmccarth@cc-md.org. Mr. William J. McCarthy Jr., Exec. Dir.

Serra Foundation, 320 Cathedral St., 21201. Tel: 410-547-5426; Fax: 410-234-2953; Web: www.bmorevocations.org. Rev. James L. Sorra, Vocations Dir.; John Jordan, Treas., Tel: 410-561-7572.

Society of St. Sulpice Foundation US, Inc., 5408 Roland Ave., 21210. Tel: 410-323-5070; Fax: 410-433-6524; Email: jkemper@sulpicians.org. Rev. John C. Kemper, P.S.S., M.Div., M.A., D.Min., Board Chair.

Stella Maris Seafarers' Center, 320 Cathedral St., 21201. Tel: 443-845-7227; Fax: 410-288-5504; Email: aosbalt@gmail.com; Web: www.aosbalt.org. Rev. Msgr. John L. FitzGerald, Dir.; Andrew Middleton, Dir. Opers. Christian hospitality services in the Catholic tradition with spiritual, temporal, and emotional support for seafarers and their families. Also, transportation to and from ships for their crew members to the local Stella Maris Seafarers' Center and the city.

St. Thomas More Society of Maryland Inc., 1614 E. Churchville Rd., Ste. 104, Bel Air, 21015. Tel: 443-602-3939; Fax: 410-864-8131. Deacon Gary E. Dumer Jr., Pres. The local branch of the St. Thomas More Society.

**The Thomas O'Neill Catholic Health Care Fund, Inc.*, 5601 Lock Raven Blvd., 21239. Tel: 410-772-6768; Fax: 410-772-6624.

Union of Catholic Apostolate USA, Inc., 512 W. Saratoga St., 21201. Tel: 302-956-0039; Fax: 410-244-5728; Email: usncc@sacapostles.org. Rev. Gregory P. Serwa, S.A.C., Pres.

ANNAPOLIS. *Christ Child Society of Annapolis*, P.O. Box 1801, Annapolis, 21404. Tel: 410-271-3392. Patricia Margerum, Pres.

Mid-Atlantic Catholic Schools Consortium, 10 Francis St., Annapolis, 21401. Tel: 410-269-1155; Fax: 410-269-1790; Email: midatlanticcsc@gmail.com. Nanette Mack, Admin.

Perpetual Help Center, 1019 N. 5th St., Philadelphia, PA 19123. Tel: 410-990-1680; Fax: 410-990-1683; Email: kwhaleye@redemptorists.net; Web: www.perpetualhelpcenter.org. PO Box 29308, Philadelphia, PA 19125. Raymond Collins, Rector.

COLUMBIA. *Catholic Single Again Council of Baltimore*, 7547 Rainflower Way, Columbia, 21046. Tel: 410-302-0754; Email: catholicsingleagaincouncil@gmail.com; Web: www.singleagain.itgo.com. Myra Fecteau, Pres.; Jeanne Hoover, Vice Pres.; Mary Ann Leard, Treas.

CROWNSVILLE. **Springhill Center for Family Development*, 1134 Bacon Ridge Rd., Crownsville, 21032. Tel: 410-923-8900. Rev. John Hopkins, L.C., Exec. Dir.; Carrie Osborn, Contact Person. A Catholic organization enriching and strengthening family life in the community; addresses the needs of the modern family through quality programs and counseling services.

DUNKIRK. *Family of the Americas Foundation, Inc.* (1977) P.O. Box 1170, Dunkirk, 20754-1170. Tel: 301-627-3346; Tel: 800-443-3395; Fax: 301-627-0847; Email: familyplanning@yahoo.com; Web: familyplanning.net.

ELLICOTT CITY. *AnthonyCorps, Inc.* (2003) 12300 Folly Quarter Rd., Ellicott City, 21042. Tel: 410-531-1400; Fax: 410-531-4881; Email: treasurer1@olaprovince.org. Rev. Mitchell Sawicki, O.F.M.Conv., Treas.

The Baltimore Catholic League, 4725 Dorsey Hall Dr., Ste. A-610, Ellicott City, 21042. Tel: 410-461-4612; Fax: 410-461-4613. John E. Degele Jr.

Catholic Daughters of the Americas, 3774 Plum Meadows Dr., Ellicott City, 21042. Debbie Lattus, State Regent. Religious, charitable and educational to serve the needs of the Church and community through apostolate, renewal, community and youth. Catholic women 18 years or older in good standing with the Church are eligible for membership.

**Faith Journeys Foundation, Inc.*, P.O. Box 1222, Ellicott City, 21041. Tel: 410-916-9677; Email: fjourneys@aol.com; Web: www.faithjourneys.org. Ms. Lynn A. Cassella-Kapusinski, B.A., M.F.A., M.S., N.C.C., L.G.P.C., Pres. & Founder.

Fr. Justin Ministry Fund, Inc., 12300 Folly Quarter Rd., Ellicott City, 21042. Tel: 410-531-1400; Fax: 410-531-4881; Email: treasurer1@olaprovince.org. Revs. Mitchell Sawicki, O.F.M.Conv.; Richard-Jacob Forcier, O.F.M.Conv.

Franciscan Friars Conventual - Solidarity Fund, Inc., 12300 Folly Quarter Rd., Ellicott City, 21042.

EMMITSBURG. *National Shrine of St. Elizabeth Ann Seton / Seton Heritage Ministries, Inc.*, 339 S. Seton Ave., Emmitsburg, 21727. Tel: 301-447-6606; Fax: 301-447-6061; Email: rob.judge@setonshrine.org; Web: www.setonshrine.org. Robert Judge, Exec. Dir.

OWINGS MILLS. *The Maryland State Council, Knights of Columbus*, Maryland State Council, 10815 Stang Rd., Owings Mills, 21117-4607. Tel: 410-521-6200; Email: kofc-md@verizon.net. Rev. Milton E. Jordan, State Chap.; Stephen J. Adamczyk, State Deputy; Romeo Gauthier, Exec. Sec.

TIMONIUM. *Odenton Senior Housing II, Inc.*, 1966 Greenspring Dr., Ste. 200, Timonium, 21093. Tel: 667-600-2280; Fax: 443-798-3451; Web: www.cc-md.org. Arnold Eppel, Vice Pres.

RELIGIOUS INSTITUTES OF MEN REPRESENTED IN THE ARCHDIOCESE

For further details refer to the corresponding bracketed number in the Religious Institutes of Men or Women section.

[0200]—*Benedictine Monks (Latrobe, PA)*—O.S.B.
[0330]—*Brothers of the Christian Schools* (Baltimore Prov.)—F.S.C.
[0470]—*The Capuchin Friars* (Prov. of St. Augustine)—O.F.M.Cap.
[]—*Franciscan Friars Conventual*—O.F.M.Conv.
[0520]—*Franciscan Friars (Most Holy Name)*—O.F.M.
[]—*Franciscan Third Order Regular*—T.O.R.
[]—*St. Joseph's Society of the Sacred Heart*—S.S.J.
[]—*Josephite Fathers & Brothers*—S.S.J.
[0730]—*Legionaries of Christ*—L.C.
[]—*The Marianists*—S.M.
[0854]—*Missionary Society of St. Paul of Nigeria*—M.S.P.
[]—*Norbertine Fathers* (Immaculate Conception Priory, DE)—O.Praem.
[]—*Pallottines*—S.A.C.
[]—*Passionists*—C.P.
[1070]—*Redemptorist Fathers* (Baltimore Prov.)—C.SS.R.
[1260]—*Society of Christ*—S.Ch.
[]—*Society of Jesus*—S.J.
[]—*Sulpicians*—S.S.
[]—*Trinitarians*—O.SS.T.
[]—*Vincentians*—C.M.
[]—*Xaverian Brothers*—C.F.X.

RELIGIOUS INSTITUTES OF WOMEN REPRESENTED IN THE ARCHDIOCESE

[]—*All Saints Sisters of the Poor*—A.S.S.P.
[0230]—*Benedictine Sisters of Pontifical Jurisdiction* (Baltimore)—O.S.B.
[]—*Carmelites*—O.C.D.
[0690]—*Comboni Missionary Sisters*—C.M.S.
[]—*Congregation of the Sister of Merciful Jesus*—C.S.M.J.
[0760]—*Daughters of Charity of St. Vincent de Paul*—D.C.
[1070-03]—*Dominican Sisters*—O.P.
[1070-13]—*Dominican Sisters*—O.P.
[]—*Dominican Sisters of St. Cecilia.*
[1470]—*Franciscan Sisters of St. Joseph*—F.S.S.J.
[1840]—*Grey Nuns of the Sacred Heart* (Pennsylvania)—G.N.S.H.
[]—*Holy Union Sisters*—S.U.S.C.
[2330]—*Little Sisters of Jesus*—L.S.J.
[2340]—*Little Sisters of the Poor*—L.S.P.
[2470]—*Maryknoll Sisters* (New York)—M.M.
[2720]—*Mission Helpers of the Sacred Heart*—M.H.S.H.
[2710]—*Missionaries of Charity* (New York)—M.C.
[]—*Missionary Servants of the Most Blessed Trinity*—M.S.B.T.
[3040]—*Oblate Sisters of Providence*—O.S.P.
[]—*Oblates of St. Martha.*
[3465]—*Religious of the Sacred Heart of Mary* (New York)—R.S.H.M.
[]—*Religious Sisters of Mercy Sisters of Mercy of the Americas*—R.S.M.
[2970]—*School Sisters of Notre Dame*—S.S.N.D.
[]—*Sisters for Christian Community*—C.F.C.C.
[]—*Sisters of Bon Secours*—C.B.S.
[0640]—*Sisters of Charity* (Halifax)—S.C.
[]—*Sisters of Mercy of the Americas*—R.S.M.
[3000]—*Sisters of Notre Dame de Namur*—S.N.D.deN.
[]—*Sisters of Notre Dame de Namur*—S.N.D.deN.
[]—*Sisters of Notre Dame de Namur* (Ohio Prov.)—S.N.D.deN.
[1705]—*Sisters of St. Francis of Assisi*—O.S.F.
[1650]—*Sisters of St. Francis of Philadelphia*—O.S.F.
[3893]—*Sisters of St. Joseph*—S.S.J.
[]—*Sisters of the Good Shepherd*—R.G.S.
[]—*Sisters of the Good Shepherd - Contemplative.*
[1990]—*Sisters of the Holy Names of Jesus and Mary*—S.N.J.M.
[]—*Sisters of the Humility of Mary* (Villa Maria, PA)—H.M.
[3610]—*Sisters Servants of Mary Immaculate*—S.S.M.I.
[2160]—*Sisters, Servants of the Immaculate Heart of Mary*—I.H.M.
[4120]—*Ursuline Nuns, of the Congregation of Kentucky*—O.S.U.

ARCHDIOCESAN CEMETERIES

BALTIMORE. *New Cathedral Cemetery*, 4300 Old Frederick Rd., 21229. Tel: 410-566-7770; Fax: 410-566-0709

NECROLOGY

† Carey, David M., (Retired), Died Nov. 2, 2018
† Donaghy, Thomas J., Ph.D., (Retired), Died Jan. 4, 2018
† Kelly, John L., (Retired), Died May. 18, 2018
† Moore, John, (Retired), Died Jun. 25, 2018
† Muller, Kennard, (Retired), Died Mar. 20, 2018
† Muller, Myles, (Retired), Died Apr. 3, 2018

An asterisk (*) denotes an organization that has established tax-exempt status directly with the IRS and is not covered by the USCCB Group Ruling.

Diocese of Baton Rouge

(Dioecesis Rubribaculensis)

Most Reverend

MICHAEL G. DUCA, J.C.L.

Bishop of Baton Rouge; ordained April 29, 1978; appointed Bishop of Shreveport April 1, 2008; consecrated and installed May 19, 2008; appointed Sixth Bishop of Baton Rouge June 26, 2018; installed August 24, 2018. *Bishop's Office: P.O. Box 2028, Baton Rouge, LA 70821-2028.* Tel: 225-242-0247; Fax: 225-336-8768; Email: bishop@diobr.org.

Chancery Office: Catholic Life Center, 1800 S. Acadian Thruway, P.O. Box 2028, Baton Rouge, LA 70821-2028. Tel: 225-387-0561; Fax: 225-336-8789.

Web: www.diobr.org

Email: chancery@diobr.org

ESTABLISHED JULY 20, 1961.

Square Miles 5,513.

Comprises the civil parishes (counties) of Ascension, Assumption, East Baton Rouge, West Baton Rouge, Iberville, Pointe Coupee, East Feliciana, West Feliciana, St. Helena, Tangipahoa, Livingston and St. James in the State of Louisiana.

For legal titles of parishes and diocesan institutions, consult the Chancery Office.

STATISTICAL OVERVIEW

Personnel	
Bishop	1
Retired Bishops	1
Priests: Diocesan Active in Diocese	50
Priests: Retired, Sick or Absent	20
Number of Diocesan Priests	70
Religious Priests in Diocese	29
Total Priests in Diocese	99
Extern Priests in Diocese	7
Ordinations:	
Transitional Deacons	1
Permanent Deacons in Diocese	70
Total Brothers	19
Total Sisters	72
Parishes	
Parishes	64
With Resident Pastor:	
Resident Diocesan Priests	40
Resident Religious Priests	10
Without Resident Pastor:	
Administered by Priests	13
Administered by Deacons	1
Professional Ministry Personnel:	
Brothers	4
Sisters	7
Lay Ministers	71
Welfare	
Catholic Hospitals	3
Total Assisted	733,627
Homes for the Aged	6
Total Assisted	821
Specialized Homes	5
Total Assisted	506
Special Centers for Social Services	7
Total Assisted	301,000
Educational	
Diocesan Students in Other Seminaries	18
Seminaries, Religious	1
Total Seminarians	18
Colleges and Universities	1
Total Students	1,400
High Schools, Diocesan and Parish	5
Total Students	3,718
High Schools, Private	2
Total Students	2,243
Elementary Schools, Diocesan and Parish	22
Total Students	11,029
Non-residential Schools for the Disabled	1
Total Students	47
Catechesis/Religious Education:	
High School Students	3,070
Elementary Students	7,392
Total Students under Catholic Instruction	28,917
Teachers in the Diocese:	
Priests	1
Brothers	1
Sisters	7
Lay Teachers	1,251
Vital Statistics	
Receptions into the Church:	
Infant Baptism Totals	1,956
Minor Baptism Totals	114
Adult Baptism Totals	129
Received into Full Communion	209
First Communions	2,120
Confirmations	1,978
Marriages:	
Catholic	414
Interfaith	210
Total Marriages	624
Deaths	1,374
Total Catholic Population	225,703
Total Population	1,001,957

Former Bishops—Most Revs. ROBERT E. TRACY, D.D., LL.D., appt. Titular Bishop of Sergentza and Auxiliary of Lafayette March 18, 1959; cons. May 19, 1959; appt. First Bishop of Baton Rouge Aug. 10, 1961; retired March 21, 1974; died April 4, 1980; JOSEPH V. SULLIVAN, S.T.D., appt. Titular Bishop of Tagamuta and Auxiliary of Kansas City-St. Joseph March 3, 1967; cons. April 3, 1967; appt. Second Bishop of Baton Rouge Aug. 5, 1974; died Sept. 4, 1982; STANLEY JOSEPH OTT, S.T.D., appt. Titular Bishop of Nicives and Auxiliary of New Orleans May 24, 1976; cons. June 29, 1976; appt. Third Bishop of Baton Rouge Jan. 18, 1983; installed March 25, 1983; died Nov. 28, 1992; ALFRED C. HUGHES, S.T.D., ord. Dec. 15, 1957; appt. Auxiliary of Boston and Titular Bishop of Massimiana in Bizacena, July 21, 1981; cons. Sept. 14, 1981; appt. to Baton Rouge Sept. 7, 1993; installed Fourth Bishop of Baton Rouge, Nov. 4, 1993; appt. Coadjutor Archbishop of New Orleans, Feb. 16, 2001; installed May 2, 2001; ROBERT W. MUENCH, D.D., ord. June 18, 1968; appt. Titular Bishop of Mactaris and Auxiliary Bishop of New Orleans May 8, 1990; cons. June 29, 1990; appt. Bishop of Covington Jan. 5, 1996; installed March 19, 1996; appt. Bishop of Baton Rouge Dec. 15, 2001; installed Fifth Bishop of Baton Rouge March 14, 2002; retired June 26, 2018.

Vicar General/Moderator of the Curia—Very Rev. THOMAS C. RANZINO, V.G.

Chancery Office—Catholic Life Center, 1800 S. Acadian Thruway, P.O. Box 2028, Baton Rouge, 70821-2028. Tel: 225-387-0561; Fax: 225-336-8789; Email: chancery@diobr.org. Office Hours: Mon.-Fri. 8:30-4:30.

Chancellor—Very Rev. JU HYUNG (PAUL) YI.

Diocesan Tribunal—Catholic Life Center, 1800 S. Acadian Thruway, P.O. Box 1087, Baton Rouge, 70821-1087. Tel: 225-336-8755; Fax: 225-242-0229; Email: tribunal@diobr.org.

Judicial Vicar—Very Rev. PAUL D. COUNCE, J.C.L., M.C.L.

Promoter of Justice—Very Rev. VINCENT J. DUFRESNE, S.T.L., J.C.L., V.F.

Judges—Revs. JAMIN S. DAVID, J.C.L.; MICHAEL J. MORONEY; FRANK M. UTER.

Defenders of the Bond—Very Revs. VINCENT J. DUFRESNE, S.T.L., J.C.L., V.F.; MATTHEW P. LORRAIN, V.F.; Revs. MATTHEW C. DUPRE; GERARD R. MARTIN.

Notaries—MRS. ANN T. BOLTIN; MRS. V. EILEEN BOURGEOIS; MS. MARY LAYMAN.

College of Consultors—Very Revs. PAUL D. COUNCE, J.C.L., M.C.L.; RANDY M. CUEVAS, S.T.L., V.F.; THOMAS C. RANZINO, V.G.; JU HYUNG (PAUL) YI; Revs. MICHAEL J. SCHATZLE; ROBERT F. STINE, (Retired); MILES D. WALSH, S.T.D.

Vicar for Religious Men and Women—Very Rev. JU HYUNG (PAUL) YI.

Diocesan Corporation (The Roman Catholic Church of the Diocese of Baton Rouge)—Most Rev. MICHAEL G. DUCA, J.C.L., Pres.; Very Revs. THOMAS C. RANZINO, V.G., Vice Pres.; JU HYUNG (PAUL) YI, Sec.; MR. GLENN J. LANDRY JR., Treas.

Diocesan Offices and Directors

Apostolate to the Deaf—VACANT, Dir.

Archives and Records Management—MRS. ANN T. BOLTIN, Mailing Address: P.O. Box 2028, Baton Rouge, 70821-2028. Tel: 225-242-0224; Fax: 225-242-0299; Email: archives@diobr.org.

Black Catholics—Deacon ALFRED P. ADAMS SR., P.O. Box 30, Convent, 70723-0030. Tel: 225-562-3255; Fax: 225-562-3255; Email: bcatholics@diobr.org.

Campus Ministry—LSU Box 25131, Baton Rouge, 70803-5131. Tel: 225-344-8595; Fax: 225-344-1920; Email: amerrick@diobr.org; Web: ctklsu.org. Rev. ANDREW J. MERRICK.

Catholic Charismatic Renewal—MRS. DOTTY LOAR, Lay Dir., Tel: 225-636-2464; Email: loard2@hotmail.com.

Catholic Charities of the Diocese of Baton Rouge, Inc.—MR. DAVID C. AGUILLARD, M.P.A., M.H.A., Exec. Dir., Office, 1900 S. Acadian Thruway, P.O. Box 1668, Baton Rouge, 70821-1668. Tel: 225-336-8770; Fax: 225-336-8745; Email: info@ccdiobr.org; Web: www.ccdiobr.org.

Catholic Social Services—Maternity, Adoption & Behavioral Health Dept. STEPHANIE STERLING, L.C.S.W., 1900 S. Acadian Thruway, P.O. Box 1668, Baton Rouge, 70821-1668. Tel: 225-336-8708; Fax: 225-336-8745; Email: adopt@ccdiobr.org; Web: www.adoptccdiobr.org.

Social and Community Responsibility Department—MS. JENNIFER HILL, Email: jhill@ccdiobr.org.

Cemeteries—Rev. FRANK M. UTER, P.O. Box 1609, Denham Springs, 70727-1609. Tel: 225-665-5359; Fax: 225-665-4422; Email: futer@diobr.org.

Child and Youth Protection Office—MRS. AMY J. CORDON, Dir., Mailing Address: P.O. Box 2028, Baton Rouge, 70821-2028. Tel: 225-242-0202; Fax: 225-242-0233; Email: childprotection@diobr.org.

Clergy Personnel—Rev. FRANK M. UTER, Chm., P.O.

Box 1609, Denham Springs, 70727-1609. Tel: 225-665-5359; Email: futer@diobr.org.

Board Members—Very Revs. THOMAS C. RANZINO, V.G., Ex Officio; JU HYUNG (PAUL) YI; Revs. GERARD R. MARTIN; CAYE A. NELSON III, V.F.; PHILIP F. SPANO.

Ecumenical Affairs—Rev. MICHAEL J. MORONEY, 14040 Greenwell Springs Rd., Greenwell Springs, 70739-3302. Tel: 225-261-4650; Fax: 225-261-5650; Email: ecumenism@diobr.org.

Evangelization and Catechesis Office—MRS. DINA DOW, Dir., P.O. Box 2028, Baton Rouge, 70821-2028. Tel: 225-242-0137; Fax: 225-242-0245; Email: evangelization@diobr.org.

Communications—MRS. KELLY ALEXANDER, Media Liaison, Tel: 225-936-7373; Fax: 225-336-8789; Email: kalexander@diobr.org; MR. STEVE LEE, P.O. Box 2028, Baton Rouge, 70821-2028. Tel: 225-242-0215; Fax: 225-242-0134; Email: television@diobr.org.

Continuing Formation for the Clergy—Very Rev. RANDY M. CUEVAS, S.T.L., V.F., Dir., 2025 Stuart Ave., Baton Rouge, 70808. Tel: 225-343-6657; Fax: 225-344-6847; Email: clergyformation@diobr.org.

Stewardship Office—MRS. TAMMY V. ABSHIRE, C.F.R.E., Dir., Mailing Address: P.O. Box 2028, Baton Rouge, 70821-2028. Tel: 225-336-8790; Fax: 225-336-8710; Email: stewardship@diobr.org.

Finance—Mailing Address: P.O. Box 2028, Baton Rouge, 70821-2028. Tel: 225-387-0561;
Fax: 225-336-8789. MR. GLENN J. LANDRY JR., Fiscal Officer.

Human Resources—MRS. ANITA L. KRAIL, S.P.H.R., Dir., P.O. Box 2028, Baton Rouge, 70821-2028. Tel: 225-387-0561; Fax: 225-336-8789; Email: akrail@diobr.org.

Hispanic Apostolate—6380 Hooper Rd., Baton Rouge, 70806-4702. Email: hapostol@bellsouth.net. MRS. JULIA SCARNATO, Dir.; Rev. ROBERT HALTER, C.Ss.R., Chap.

Newspaper "The Catholic Commentator"—MR. RICHARD MEEK, Exec. Editor & Gen. Mgr., Office, 1800 S. Acadian Thruway, Baton Rouge, 70821-1668. Email: tcc@diobr.org. Mailing Address: P.O. Box 3316, Baton Rouge, 70821-3316. Tel: 225-387-0983; Fax: 225-336-8710.

Marriage and Family Life Department—MR. DARRYL P. DUCOTE, L.C.S.W., Dir., Office: 1800 S. Acadian Thruway, P.O. Box 2028, Baton Rouge, 70821-2028. Tel: 225-336-8770; Fax: 225-336-8745; Email: dducote@diobr.org.

Permanent Diaconate Office—Rev. JAMIN S. DAVID, J.C.L., Dir. Formation, Email: jdavid@diobr.org; Deacon JOHN VERON, Dir. Deacon Life & Ministry, P.O. Box 2028, Baton Rouge, 70821-2028. Tel: 225-387-0561; Email: jveron@diobr.org.

Presbyteral Council—Very Revs. RANDY M. CUEVAS, S.T.L., V.F.; THOMAS C. RANZINO, V.G.; JU HYUNG (PAUL) YI; Revs. HOWARD R. ADKINS, (Retired); J. CARY BANI; MARK B. BEARD; PATRICK J. BROUSSARD JR.; JAMIN S. DAVID, J.C.L.; MATTHEW J. GRAHAM; JOSHUA D. JOHNSON; MICHAEL A. MICELI; MICHAEL J. SCHATZLE; ROBERT F. STINE, (Retired); MILES D. WALSH, S.T.D.

Propagation of the Faith and Association of Holy ChildhoodVACANT, Dir.; MRS. LENNETTE LASSEIGNE, Coord., P.O. Box 2028, Baton Rouge, 70821-2028. Tel: 225-242-0115; Fax: 225-242-0343; Email: missions@diobr.org.

Catholic Schools—DR. MELANIE B. VERGES, Ed.D., Supt.; MR. MICHAEL C. MILLER, Asst. Supt., Mailing Address: P.O. Box 2028, Baton Rouge, 70821-2028. Tel: 225-336-8735; Fax: 225-336-8711; Email: secretary@csobr.org.

Separated and Divorced—VACANT.

Serra Clubs—P.O. Box 2028, Baton Rouge, 70821-2028. Tel: 225-336-8778; Fax: 225-336-8710; Email: vocations@diobr.org. Rev. ANDREW J. MERRICK, Spiritual Advisor.

Society of St. Vincent De Paul—MR. MICHAEL J. ACALDO, CEO, Email: macaldo@svdpbr.com; Rev. GERALD H. BURNS, Spiritual Advisor, (Retired), 7915 Menlo Dr., Baton Rouge, 70808-6781. Tel: 225-252-5814.

Victim Assistance Coordinator—MRS. AMY J. CORDON, Mailing Address: P.O. Box 2028, Baton Rouge, 70821-2028. Tel: 225-242-0202; Fax: 225-242-0233; Email: childprotection@diobr.org.

Vietnamese Apostolate—Rev. TAN VIET NGUYEN, I.C.M., Dir., 2305 Choctaw Dr., Baton Rouge, 70805-7910. Tel: 225-357-4800; Fax: 225-354-0611.

Vocations—Mailing Address: P.O. Box 2028, Baton Rouge, 70821-2028. Tel: 225-336-8778;
Fax: 225-336-8710; Email: vocations@diobr.org. Very Rev. MATTHEW P. LORRAIN, V.F., Dir. Seminarians; Rev. ANDREW J. MERRICK, Dir. Vocations; MRS. LISETTE BORNE, Assoc. Dir.

Worship, Office of—Very Rev. THOMAS C. RANZINO, V.G., Dir., P.O. Box 2028, Baton Rouge, 70821-2028. Tel: 225-387-0561; Fax: 225-336-8789; Email: worship@diobr.org.

CLERGY, PARISHES, MISSIONS AND PAROCHIAL SCHOOLS

CITY OF BATON ROUGE

(EAST BATON ROUGE PARISH)

1—ST. JOSEPH CATHEDRAL (1792) [CEM 2] Very Rev. Paul D. Counce, J.C.L., M.C.L.; Deacon Gary C. Mooney, Pastoral Min./Coord.
Res.: 412 North St., 70802-5496. Tel: 225-387-5928; Fax: 225-387-5929; Email: office@cathedralbr.org; Web: www.cathedralbr.org.
Catechesis Religious Program—Students 20.

2—ST. AGNES (1917) Revs. Charbel Jamhoury, O.L.M.; J. Clifton Hill, C.S.Sp., In Res.
Res.: 749 East Blvd., 70802-6398. Tel: 225-383-4127; Email: saintagnes2@bellsouth.net.
Catechesis Religious Program—Tel: 225-338-1511; Email: saccd@att.net. Donna Davis, C.R.E. Students 70.

3—ST. ALOYSIUS (1955)
Mailing Address: 2025 Stuart Ave., 70808-3998.
Tel: 225-343-6657; Fax: 225-344-6847; Email: emartin@staloysiusparish.com; Web: www.aloysius.org. Very Rev. Randy M. Cuevas, S.T.L., V.F.; Rev. Edwin J. Martin; Deacon P. Chauvin Wilkinson Jr.
School—St. Aloysius School, (Grades PreK-8), 4001 Mimosa St., 70808-3998. Tel: 225-383-3871; Email: ecandilora@aloysius.org; Web: www.aloysius.org. Mrs. Erin Candilora, Prin. Lay Teachers 85; Students 1,200.
Catechesis Religious Program—Mrs. Patricia Greely, D.R.E. Students 193.

4—STS. ANTHONY OF PADUA AND LE VAN PHUNG (1920) Rev. Tan Viet Nguyen, I.C.M.
Res.: 2305 Choctaw Dr., 70805-7910.
Tel: 225-357-4800; Fax: 225-354-0611; Email: veronica.williams.st.anthony@gmail.com; Email: RevTanNguyen16@gmail.com.
Catechesis Religious Program—Email: cuik25@gmail.com. Nguyen Anh Dung, D.R.E. Students 413.

5—ST. CHARLES BORROMEO (1964) Closed. For inquiries for parish records contact St. Gerard Majella, Baton Rouge.

6—CHRIST THE KING (1980)
Mailing Address: LSU Box 25131, 70803-0106. Rev. Andrew J. Merrick; Mrs. Alison Dazzio, Admin.; Mrs. Jennifer Moore, Business Mgr.; Mrs. Carla Rutherford, Sec.
Office: 11 Fraternity Ln., 70803. Tel: 225-344-8595; Email: jmoore@ctklsu.org; Email: amerrick@ctklsu.org; Email: adazzio@cctklsu.org; Email: crutherford@ctklsu.org; Web: www.ctklsu.org.
Catechesis Religious Program—Mrs. Beryl Herbert, D.R.E. Students 13.

7—ST. FRANCIS DE SALES PARISH (1979) Closed. For inquiries for parish records contact the diocesan archives.

8—ST. FRANCIS XAVIER CATHOLIC CHURCH (1918) Rev. Edward Chiffriller, S.S.J.
Res.: 1143 S. 11th St., 70802-4997. Tel: 225-383-3479 ; Email: secretary@sfxc.brcoxmail.com.
School—St. Francis Xavier School, (Grades PreK-8), Tel: 225-387-6639; Fax: 225-383-1215; Email: sfxadmin@sfx.brcoxmail.com; Web: www.sfxbr.org. Ms. Paula Fabre, Prin. Clergy 1; Students 165.
Catechesis Religious Program—Students 71.

9—ST. GEORGE (1908) [CEM] Revs. Martin A. Hernandez, J.C.L., Admin.; Michael J. Schatzle; Very Rev. Paul A. Gros, V.F.; Deacons Stephen Brunet; John Veron.
Office: 7808 St. George Dr., 70809-4699.
Tel: 225-293-2212; Email: info@st-george.org; Web: www.st-george.org.
School—St. George School, (Grades PreK-8), 7880 St. George Dr., 70809-4699. Tel: 225-293-1298;
Fax: 225-293-4886; Email: jack.nelson@sgschoolbr.org; Web: www.st-georgeschool.com. Mr. Jack Nelson, Prin. Lay Teachers 63; Students 1,063.
Catechesis Religious Program—Tel: 225-293-2212; Email: mollyr@st-george.org; Email: karenf@st-george.org. Mrs. Molly Rose, D.R.E.; Mrs. Karen Fawley, D.R.E.; Mr. Blake Bruchhaus, Liturgy Dir.; Mrs. Kristel Neupert, Pastoral Assoc.; Mr. Josh Boudreaux, Youth Min. Students 120.

10—ST. GERARD MAJELLA (1944)
5354 Plank Road, 70805. Revs. Chuong Cao, C.Ss.R.; Robert Halter, C.Ss.R.; Gilbert Enderle, Vicar of Hispanic Min. In Res., Revs. Donald MacKinnon, C.Ss.R.; Donnell Kirchner, (In Res.).
Res.: 3808 Gerard St., 70805-2834. Tel: 225-355-2553 ; Email: admin@stgerardmajellachurch.org.
Catechesis Religious Program—Students 7.

11—IMMACULATE CONCEPTION (1953) Very Rev. Thomas F. Clark, S.J., V.F.
Res.: 1565 Curtis St., 70807-4906. Tel: 225-775-7067; Email: clarktf2002@yahoo.com.
Catechesis Religious Program—Email: g1930@att.net. Students 120.

12—ST. JEAN VIANNEY (1975) Very Rev. Thomas C. Ranzino, V.G.; Deacons Brent Duplessis; Daniel S. Borne; Jeff R. Easley; Ricky Anthony Patterson.
Res.: 16166 S. Harrell's Ferry Rd., 70816-3199.
Tel: 225-753-7950; Email: churchinfo@stjeanvianney.org; Web: www.stjeanvianney.org.
School—St. Jean Vianney School, (Grades K-8), 16266 S. Harrell's Ferry Rd., 70816-3103.
Tel: 225-751-1831; Fax: 225-752-8774; Email: wross@stjeanvianneyschool.org; Web: www.stjeanvianneyschool.org. Wendy Ross, Prin.; Kerry Ferrara, Librarian. Lay Teachers 29; Students 461.
Child Care—Preschool, Tel: 225-752-5356. Mrs. Amie Williams, Dir. Lay Teachers 11; Students 83.
Catechesis Religious Program—Tel: 225-751-2926; Email: dlouviere@stjeanvianney.org. Denise Louviere, D.R.E. Students 0.

13—ST. JUDE THE APOSTLE (1966) Revs. Caye A. Nelson III, V.F.; Ryan Hallford; Deacons James J. Morrissey; Curt P. Reeson. In Res.
Res.: 9150 Highland Rd., 70810-4096.
Tel: 225-766-2431; Email: deaconjames@stjudecatholic.org; Web: stjudecatholic.org.
School—St. Jude the Apostle School, (Grades PreK-8), Tel: 225-769-2344; Email: mgardiner@stjudebr.org. Ms. Tina Schexnaydre, Prin.; Mrs. Terri Legendre, Librarian. Lay Teachers 54; Students 567.
Catechesis Religious Program—Students 21.

14—ST. LOUIS, KING OF FRANCE (1966) Closed. For inquiries for parish records contact St. Thomas More, Baton Rouge.

15—MOST BLESSED SACRAMENT (1979) Rev. Philip F. Spano; Deacons Donald J. Musso; Mark Thomas Berard.
Res. & Mailing Address: 15615 Jefferson Hwy., 70817-6311. Tel: 225-752-6230; Email: churchoffice@mbsparish.org.
School—Most Blessed Sacrament School, (Grades K-8), 8033 Baringer Rd., 70817-6000.
Tel: 225-751-0273; Fax: 225-753-7259; Email: cgioe@mbsbr.org; Web: www.mbsbr.org. Ms. Cheri Gioe, Prin. Lay Teachers 28; Students 519.
Catechesis Religious Program—Tel: 225-751-5867; Fax: 225-751-6738. Mr. David P. Planche, D.R.E. Students 307.

16—OUR LADY OF MERCY (1947) Revs. Cleo J. Milano, S.T.L., V.F.; Nutan S. Minj, I.M.S.; Deacon Richard H. Grant.
Office: 445 Marquette Ave., 70806-4497.
Tel: 225-926-1883; Email: cleo.milano@olomchurch.com; Web: www.olomchurch.com.
Res.: 450 Marquette Ave., 70806-4497.
School—Our Lady of Mercy School, (Grades PreK-8), 400 Marquette Ave., 70806-4498. Tel: 225-924-1054; Fax: 225-923-2201; Email: cporche@olomschool.org; Web: www.olomschool.org. Mr. Chris Porche, Prin.; Mrs. Mari Buzbee, Contact Person. Lay Teachers 55; Students 940.
Catechesis Religious Program—Students 69.

17—ST. PATRICK (1974) Rev. Michael A. Miceli; Deacon J. Peter Walsh.
Res.: 12424 Brogdon Ln., 70816-4801.
Tel: 225-753-5750; Fax: 225-756-9636; Email: info@stpatrickbr.org; Web: www.stpatrickbr.org.
Catechesis Religious Program—Email: scolomb@stpatrickbr.org. Ms. Lisa Trahan, D.R.E. Students 132.

18—ST. PAUL THE APOSTLE (1960)
3912 Gus Young Ave., 70802. Tel: 225-383-2537; Email: stpaulbr@aol.com; Web: stpaulbr.org. Rev. Richard R. Andrus Jr., S.V.D.; Deacon Benjamin J. Dunbar.
Catechesis Religious Program—Mrs. Martha Davis, D.R.E. Students 72.

19—ST. PIUS X (1963) Closed. For inquiries for parish records contact the Diocesan Archives Dept.

20—SACRED HEART OF JESUS (1928) Rev. Miles D. Walsh, S.T.D.; Deacon Clayton A. Hollier, Pastoral Assoc.
Res.: 2250 Main St., 70802-3198. Tel: 225-387-6671; Fax: 225-387-6674; Email: info@sacredheartbtr.com; Web: www.sacredheartbr.org.
School—Sacred Heart of Jesus School, (Grades PreK-8), 2251 Main St., 70802. Tel: 225-383-7481; Fax: 225-383-1810; Email: info@sacredheartbr.com; Web: www.sacredheartbr.com. Mr. C.J. Laird, Prin. Lay Teachers 23; Students 248.

Catechesis Religious Program—Tel: 225-387-6671, Ext. 213; Email: ltomecek@sacredheartbr.org. Mrs. Lori Tomecek, C.R.E. Students 33.

21—ST. THOMAS MORE (1959) Rev. Michael J. Alello; Deacon Joseph Scimeca.
Office: 11441 Goodwood Blvd., 70815-6299.
Tel: 225-275-3940; Email: info@stmchurch.org; Web: stmchurch.org.
School—St. Thomas More School, (Grades K-8), 11400 Sherbrook Dr., 70815. Tel: 225-275-2820; Fax: 225-275-0376; Email: armstrongj@stmbr.org; Web: www.stmbr.org. Dr. Judy Armstrong, Prin. Lay Teachers 68; Students 625.
Child Care—Preschool, 11500 Sherbrook Dr., 70815.
Catechesis Religious Program—Students 49.

OUTSIDE THE CITY OF BATON ROUGE

ALBANY, LIVINGSTON PARISH, ST. MARGARET QUEEN OF SCOTLAND (1910) [CEM]
P.O. Box 100, Albany, 70711-0100. Tel: 225-567-3573 ; Tel: 225-567-2031; Email: stmargaretchurch@bellsouth.net; Web: stmargaretstthomas.com. 30300 Catholic Hall Rd., Hammond, 70403. Rev. Jamin S. David, J.C.L.; Deacons William Corbett; Timothy T. Messenger Sr.
Catechesis Religious Program—Email: lmhanewinkel@gmail.com. Mrs. Lucie Hanewinkel, D.R.E. Students 93.
Chapel—St. Thomas the Apostle Chapel, 32191 Hwy. 22, Springfield, 70462.

AMITE, TANGIPAHOA PARISH, ST. HELENA (1868)
Mailing Address: 122 S. First St., Amite, 70422-2701. Tel: 985-748-9057; Email: donna@sthelenachurch.net; Web: sthelenachurch.net. Revs. Mark B. Beard; Howard R. Adkins, In Res., (Retired).

BAKER, EAST BATON ROUGE PARISH, ST. ISIDORE THE FARMER (1958) Rev. Frank B. Bass; Deacons Micheal J. Joseph; Thomas Dennis Benoit.
Res.: 5657 Thomas Rd., 70811-7356.
Tel: 225-775-8850; Email: rmabilestisidore101@yahoo.com; Web: www.stisidorecommunity.org.
Catechesis Religious Program—Ms. Monice Oliphant, D.R.E. Students 84.

BAYOU PIGEON, IBERVILLE PARISH, ST. JOAN OF ARC (1965) Closed. For inquiries for parish records contact St. Joseph the Worker, Pierre Part.

BELLE ROSE, ASSUMPTION PARISH, ST. JULES (1912) [CEM 2]
7165 Hwy. 1, Belle Rose, 70341-0038. P.O. Box 38, Belle Rose, 70341-0038. Rev. Matthew J. Graham.
Catechesis Religious Program—Students 28.
Chapel—Brusly / St. Martin, St. Martin.

BRUSLY, WEST BATON ROUGE PARISH, ST. JOHN THE BAPTIST (1835)
402 S. Kirkland Dr., Brusly, 70719. Very Rev. Matthew P. Lorrain, V.F.
Res.: P.O. Box 248, Brusly, 70719-0248.
Tel: 225-749-2189; Email: sjbbrusly1835@gmail.com; Web: www.sjb-brusly.com.
Catechesis Religious Program—Email: june@sjbcc.brcoxmail.com. June Hebert, D.R.E. Students 355.

CONVENT, ST. JAMES PARISH, ST. MICHAEL THE ARCHANGEL (1812) [CEM 2]
Mailing Address: P.O. Box 129, Paulina, 70763.
Tel: 225-869-5751; Fax: 225-869-4166; Email: office@rivrdcat.org; Web: www.rivrdcat.org. 6490 LA Hwy. 44, Convent, 70723. Very Rev. Vincent J. Dufresne, S.T.L., J.C.L., V.F.; Rev. Alexander J. Sheldon; Deacons Alfred P. Adams Sr.; Mario P. (Sam) Sammartino.
Catechesis Religious Program—Students 48.

DARROW, ASCENSION PARISH, ST. ANTHONY OF PADUA (1962)
37311 Hwy. 22, Darrow, 70725. Tel: 225-675-8126; Fax: 225-675-6150; Email: stanne@eatel.net; Web: stannestanthony.org. P.O. Box 9, Sorrento, 70778. Rev. Keun-Soo Lee, Ph.D.; Deacon Jerry W. Braud.
Catechesis Religious Program—Tel: 225-675-6528. Combined with St. Anne, Sorrento.

DENHAM SPRINGS, LIVINGSTON PARISH, IMMACULATE CONCEPTION aka Church of the Immaculate Conception and Mission of the Sacred Heart (1960)
865 Hatchell Ln., Denham Springs, 70726.
Tel: 225-665-5359; Email: churchoffice@icc-msh.org; Web: www.icc-msh.org. Mailing Address: P.O. Box 1609, Denham Springs, 70727-1609. Revs. Frank M. Uter; Amal Raj Savarimuthu, I.M.S.; Deacons George J. Hooper; Michael T. Chiappetta; Rudolph W. Stahl.
Catechesis Religious Program—Tel: 225-665-5926. Mrs. Gwen Richard, D.R.E. Students 802.

DONALDSONVILLE, ASCENSION PARISH

1—ASCENSION OF OUR LORD JESUS CHRIST (1772) [CEM] Very Rev. Ju Hyung (Paul) Yi.
Res.: 716 Mississippi St., P.O. Box 508, Donaldsonville, 70346-0508. Tel: 225-473-3176; Fax: 225-473-3256; Email: ascensionofourlord@gmail.com; Web: www.donaldsonvillecatholics.com.
Catechesis Religious Program—Tel: 225-776-4131; Email: susanj777@aim.com. Susan Jumonville, D.R.E. Students 9.

2—ST. CATHERINE OF SIENA (1924) Rev. Charles Atuah; Deacon Edward Joseph Gauthreaux.
Res.: P.O. Box 428, Donaldsonville, 70346-0428.
Tel: 225-473-8350; Email: stcatherinechurch@cox.net.
Catechesis Religious Program—Students 92.

3—ST. FRANCIS OF ASSISI (1884) [CEM] Very Rev. Ju Hyung (Paul) Yi.
Res.: 818 W. Tenth St., Donaldsonville, 70346-9501.
Tel: 225-473-3176; Fax: 225-473-3256; Email: ascensionofourlord@gmail.com; Web: www.donaldsonvillecatholics.com.
Catechesis Religious Program—716 Mississippi St, Donaldsonville, 70346. Tel: 225-776-4131; Email: susanj777@aim.com. Susan Jumonville, D.R.E. Students 4.

FRENCH SETTLEMENT, LIVINGSTON PARISH, ST. JOSEPH (1849) [CEM] Very Rev. Jason P. Palermo, V.F.; Deacons James A. Little; Leon Roy Murphy Jr.
Res.: 15710 Louisiana Hwy. 16, French Settlement, 70733-9802. Tel: 225-698-3110; Email: stjosephfs@eatel.net; Web: stjosephstephen.weconnect.com.
Catechesis Religious Program—Tel: 225-698-6318. Mrs. Barbara Berthelot, D.R.E. Students 174.

GONZALES, ASCENSION PARISH

1—ST. MARK (1973) Rev. Rubin R. Reynolds.
Res.: 42021 Hwy. 621, Gonzales, 70737-9354.
Tel: 225-647-8461; Email: stmark@eatel.net; Web: www.stmarkgonzales.org.
Catechesis Religious Program—Ms. Mary Kruse, D.R.E. Students 563.

2—ST. THERESA OF AVILA (1918) [CEM] Rev. Eric V. Gyan; Deacon Jodi A. Moscona.
Res.: 1022 N. Burnside Ave., Gonzales, 70737-2551.
Tel: 225-647-6588; Email: lgautreau001@eatel.net; Web: www.st-theresa-of-avila.com.
School—St. Theresa Middle School, (Grades 4-8), 212 E. New River St., Gonzales, 70737-2499.
Tel: 225-647-2803; Fax: 225-647-7814; Email: chrismusso@sjp-sta.org. Ms. Chris Musso, Prin. Lay Teachers 25; Students 361.
Catechesis Religious Program—Email: ablair@eatel.net. Mrs. Alice Blair, D.R.E. Students 224.

GRAMERCY, ST. JAMES PARISH, MOST SACRED HEART OF JESUS (1961)
Mailing Address: P.O. Box 129, Paulina, 70763-0129. Very Rev. Vincent J. Dufresne, S.T.L., J.C.L., V.F.; Rev. Alexander J. Sheldon.
Church: 616 E. Main St., Gramercy, 70052.
Catechesis Religious Program—Ms. Harriet Melancon, D.R.E. (Elementary); Mrs. Melissa Laurent, D.R.E. (High School). Students 118.

GREENWELL SPRINGS, EAST BATON ROUGE PARISH, ST. ALPHONSUS LIGUORI (1962) Rev. Michael J. Moroney; Deacons Robert J. Kusch; Ronald James Hebert.
Res.: 14040 Greenwell Springs Rd., Greenwell Springs, 70739-3302. Tel: 225-261-4650; Email: melissa@alphonsus.org; Web: alphonsus.org.
School—St. Alphonsus Liguori School, (Grades PreK-8), 13940 Greenwell Springs Rd., Greenwell Springs, 70739. Tel: 225-261-5299;
Fax: 225-261-2795; Email: cryals@stalphonsusbr.org; Web: www.stalphonsusbr.org. Mrs. Cynthia Ryals, Prin. Lay Teachers 27; Students 464.
Catechesis Religious Program—Email: dre@alphonsus.org. Mrs. Olga Johnson, D.R.E. Students 357.

GROSSE TETE, IBERVILLE PARISH, ST. JOSEPH (1904) [CEM]
76940 Gum St., Grosse Tete, 70740-0008.
Tel: 225-625-2438; Email: office@triparishes.org; Web: www.triparishes.org. Revs. Christopher J. Decker; Amrit Raj, I.M.S.
Catechesis Religious Program—11140 Hwy 77, Maringouin, 70757. Email: pchampagne@triparishes.org. Peggy Champagne, D.R.E. Students 21.

HAMMOND, TANGIPAHOA PARISH, HOLY GHOST (1902)
601 N. Oak St., Hammond, 70401-2529.
Tel: 985-345-3360, Ext. 0; Email: lsmith@hgchurch.org; Web: www.hgchurch.org. Revs. Roberto Merced, O.P.; Cayet N. Mangiaracina, O.P.; Deacon Mauricio Salazar, O.P.
School—Holy Ghost School, (Grades PreK-8), 507 N. Oak St., Hammond, 70401-2598. Tel: 985-345-0977; Fax: 985-542-6545; Email: secretary@hgschool.org; Web: www.hgschool.org. Mrs. Donna Wallette, Prin. Lay Teachers 44; Students 775.
Catechesis Religious Program—Email: tlabbe@hgchurch.org. Mrs. Trisha Labbe, D.R.E. Students 169.

INDEPENDENCE, TANGIPAHOA PARISH, MATER DOLOROSA (1908)
620 3rd St., P.O. Box 349, Independence, 70443-0349. Tel: 985-878-9639; Fax: 985-878-6260; Email: fran@materdolorosa.net; Email: joyce@materdolorosa.net. Rev. Reuben Dykes; Deacons Francis M. Minor; Natale J. Garofalo.
School—Mater Dolorosa School, (Grades PreK-8), 509 Pine Street, P.O. Box 380, Independence, 70443-0380. Tel: 985-878-4295; Fax: 985-878-4888; Email: csantangelo@mdeagles.org. Cheryl Santangelo, Prin. Lay Teachers 13; Students 145.
Catechesis Religious Program—Email: carol@materdolorosa.net. Ms. Carol A. Young, D.R.E. Students 83.
Chapel—Husser, St. Dominic.

LABADIEVILLE, ASSUMPTION PARISH, ST. PHILOMENA (1847) [CEM]
118 Convent St., Labadieville, 70372.
Tel: 985-526-4247; Email: philomena1847@gmail.com. P.O. Box 99, Labadieville, 70372-0099. Rev. Joseph H. Vu. Clustered with Assumption and St. Anne Churches.
Catechesis Religious Program—Students 108.

LAKELAND, POINTE COUPEE PARISH, IMMACULATE CONCEPTION (1859) [CEM 2]
P.O. Box 158, Lakeland, 70752-0158. Rev. C. Todd Lloyd.
Res.: 12369 LA Hwy. 416, Lakeland, 70752-0158.
Tel: 225-627-5124; Email: icclakeland@gmail.com; Web: www.immaculateconceptionlakeland.com.
Catechesis Religious Program—Students 278.

LIVONIA, POINTE COUPEE PARISH, ST. FRANCES XAVIER CABRINI (1955) [CEM]
TriParish Pastoral Center, 11140 Hwy 77, Maringouin, 70755. Revs. Christopher J. Decker; Amrit Raj, I.M.S.
Res.: 3523 Hwy. 78, P.O. Box 128, Livonia, 70755-0128. Tel: 225-637-2438; Fax: 225-625-3513; Email: office@triparishes.org; Web: www.triparishes.org.
Catechesis Religious Program—Email: pchampagne@triparishes.org. Peggy Champagne, D.R.E. Students 161.
Chapel—Fordoche, St. Catherine of Siena, 4324 N. Railroad Ave., Fordoche, 70732. Email: cdecker@triparishes.org.

MARINGOUIN, IBERVILLE PARISH, IMMACULATE HEART OF MARY (1964) [CEM]
Mailing Address: 11140 Hwy. 77, Maringouin, 70757-3504. Revs. Christopher J. Decker; Amrit Raj, I.M.S.
Res.: 76940 Gum St., Grosse Tete, 70740. Email: araj@triparishes.org.
Catechesis Religious Program—Email: pchampagne@triparishes.org. Peggy Champagne, D.R.E. Students 32.

MAUREPAS, LIVINGSTON PARISH, ST. STEPHEN THE MARTYR (1964) Very Rev. Jason P. Palermo, V.F.; Deacons Leon Roy Murphy Jr.; James A. Little.
Res.: 22494 LA Hwy. 22, Maurepas, 70449-3404.
Tel: 225-695-6310; Email: saintstephen@eatel.net; Web: stjosephststephen.weconnect.com.
Catechesis Religious Program—Students 58.

MORGANZA, POINTE COUPEE PARISH, ST. ANN (1872) [CEM 3] Rev. P. Brent Maher.
Res.: 182 Church St., P.O. Box 128, Morganza, 70759-0128. Tel: 225-694-3781; Fax: 225-694-3711; Email: stannmorganza@gmail.com; Web: www.goodsaintann.com.
Catechesis Religious Program—Tel: 225-694-2132. Janice Newton, C.R.E. Students 40.
Chapel—Innis, St. Vincent De Paul.

NAPOLEONVILLE, ASSUMPTION PARISH

1—ST. ANNE (1874) [CEM 2] Rev. Joseph H. Vu.
Res.: P.O. Box 99, Napoleonville, 70390-0090.
Tel: 985-369-6656; Fax: 985-369-9718; Email: stanne02@att.net; Web: www.stassumption.org.
Catechesis Religious Program—Tel: 985-369-2130. Mrs. Kathy Landry, D.R.E. Students 190.

2—ST. BENEDICT THE MOOR (1911) [CEM 2]
5479 Hwy. 1, Napoleonville, 70390-2410.
Tel: 985-513-3470; Email: stbenaug1911@gmail.com; Web: www.stbenaug.com. P.O. Box 220, Napoleonville, 70390. Rev. Eliseus D. Ibeh, M.S.P. Oldest African American Parish in the Diocese of Baton Rouge
Catechesis Religious Program— twinned with St. Augustine. 147 Bertrand St., Napoleonville, 70390. Tel: 985-369-6928; Tel: 985-513-1794; Email: msjerrywms2010@gmail.com; Email: ramairs44@aol.com. 145 Ideal St., Belle Rose, 70341. Mrs. Jerilyn S. Williams, D.R.E.; Ramona Melancon, D.R.E. Students 22.
Chapel—St. Augustine Church, 174 Hwy. 1003, Belle Rose, 70341. Tel: 985-513-3470; Email: stbenaug1911@gmail.com; Web: www.stbenaug.com. Rev. Eliseus D. Ibeh, M.S.P., Contact Person.

NEW ROADS, POINTE COUPEE PARISH

1—ST. AUGUSTINE (1923) Rev. Patrick S. Healy, S.S.J.; Deacon Thomas Robinson.
Res.: 809 New Roads St., P.O. Box 548, New Roads, 70760-0548. Tel: 225-638-7553; Email: sac@josephite.com.
Catechesis Religious Program—Students 45.

2—ST. MARY OF FALSE RIVER (1865) [CEM 2] Rev.

Patrick J. Broussard Jr.; Deacons Thomas M. Robinson; Michael Francis Thompson.
Res.: 348 W. Main St., New Roads, 70760-3587.
Tel: 225-638-9665; Email: tlejeune@stmarysfr.org; Web: www.stmarysfr.org.
Catechesis Religious Program—Tel: 225-324-5007; Email: tcaguillard@hotmail.com. Mr. Tim Aguillard, D.R.E.; Mr. Trudy Aguillard, D.R.E. Students 101.
Chapel—Pointe Coupee, St. Francis, 10364 Pointe Coupee Rd., New Roads, 70760.

PAINCOURTVILLE, ASSUMPTION PARISH, ST. ELIZABETH (1840) [CEM]
119 Hwy. 403, Paincourtville, 70391.
Tel: 225-473-8569; Fax: 225-473-2950; Email: office@sesjchurch.com; Web: www.sesjchurch.com. Mailing Address: P.O. Box 1, Paincourtville, 70391-0001. Rev. Matthew J. Graham.
Catechesis Religious Program—Students 56.

PAULINA, ST. JAMES PARISH, ST. JOSEPH (1900) [CEM]
2130 Rectory St., Paulina, 70763. Tel: 225-869-5751; Tel: 225-869-4166; Email: office@rivrdcat.org; Web: www.rivrdcat.org. Mailing Address: P.O. Box 129, Paulina, 70763-0129. Very Rev. Vincent J. Dufresne, S.T.L., J.C.L., V.F.; Rev. Alexander J. Sheldon.
Catechesis Religious Program—Mrs. Melissa Laurent, D.R.E. (High School); Mrs. Donna Waguespack, D.R.E. (Elementary). Students 363.
Chapel—Lutcher, Our Lady of Prompt Succor.

PIERRE PART, ASSUMPTION PARISH, ST. JOSEPH THE WORKER (1858) [CEM 2]
3304 Hwy. 70 S., Pierre Part, 70339-0190.
Tel: 985-252-6633; Fax: 985-252-8011; Email: office@sjworker.org; Web: www.sjworker.org. P.O. Box 190, Pierre Part, 70339. Rev. Al M. Davidson.
Res.: 1022 Bayou Dr., Pierre Part, 70339-0190.
Tel: 985-252-6008; Email: fral@sjworker.org.
Catechesis Religious Program—Email: janice@sjworker.org. Mrs. Janice D. Pintado, D.R.E. Students 321.

PLAQUEMINE, IBERVILLE PARISH
1—ST. CLEMENT OF ROME (1964) Closed. For inquiries for parish records contact St. John the Evangelist, Plaquemine.
2—ST. JOHN THE EVANGELIST (1850) [CEM] Rev. Gregory J. Daigle; Deacon Alfred J. Ricard.
Office: 57805 Main St., Plaquemine, 70764-2531.
Tel: 225-687-2402; Email: stjohnchurchplaq@sj.brcoxmail.com; Web: www.stjohnchurchplaq.org.
Res.: 57810 Plaquemine St., Plaquemine, 70764-2538.
Catechesis Religious Program—Students 177.

PLATTENVILLE, ASSUMPTION PARISH, ASSUMPTION OF THE BLESSED VIRGIN MARY (1793) [CEM]
5604 Royal St., Napoleonville, 70390-0099.
Tel: 985-369-6656; Fax: 985-369-9718; Email: stanne011@gmail.com. Mailing Address: P.O. Box 99, Napoleonville, 70390-0099. Rev. Joseph H. Vu.
Catechesis Religious Program—Mrs. Kathy Landry, D.R.E. Students 190.

PONCHATOULA, TANGIPAHOA PARISH, ST. JOSEPH (1875) [CEM]
Mailing Address: P.O. Box 368, Ponchatoula, 70454-0368. Tel: 985-386-3749; Fax: 985-386-4188; Email: talbert64@gmail.com; Web: www.stjosephsonline.com. Office: 330 West Pine St., Ponchatoula, 70454-0368. Church: 225 N. 8th St., Ponchatoula, 70454-0368. Rev. Paul A. McDuffie; Deacons Larry Melancon; Michael A. Agnello.
School—St. Joseph School, (Grades PreK-8), 175 N. Eighth St., Ponchatoula, 70454-3306.
Tel: 985-386-6421; Fax: 985-386-0560; Web: sjscrusaders.org. Mrs. Danette Ragusa, Prin. Lay Teachers 28; Students 500.
Catechesis Religious Program—Email: pbacile@sjscursaders.org. Paige Bacile, D.R.E. Students 218.

PORT ALLEN, WEST BATON ROUGE PARISH, HOLY FAMILY (1920)
474 N. Jefferson, P.O. Box 290, Port Allen, 70767-0290. Rev. David E. Allen; Deacon Minos Ponville Jr.
Res.: P.O. Box 290, Port Allen, 70767-0290.
Tel: 225-383-1838; Email: holyfamilycathol@bellsouth.net; Web: holyfamilychurchpa.org.
School—Holy Family School, (Grades PreK-8), 335 N. Jefferson Ave., Port Allen, 70767-2798.
Tel: 225-344-4100; Fax: 225-344-1928; Email: mcomeau@hfspa.com; Web: holyfamilyschool.com. Mr. Michael Comeau, Prin. Clergy 2; Lay Teachers 40; Students 420.
Child Care—Preschool, 415 N. Jefferson Ave., Port Allen, 70767-2727. Tel: 225-343-6541;
Fax: 225-344-4100. Leigh Le Blanc, Dir. Lay Teachers 4; Students 30.
Catechesis Religious Program—Tel: 225-336-4463. Students 72.

PRAIRIEVILLE, ASCENSION PARISH, ST. JOHN THE EVANGELIST (1919) Rev. Gerard R. Martin; Deacons Randy Clement; Claude H. Bourgeois Jr.
Res.: 15208 Hwy. 73, Prairieville, 70769-3507.
Tel: 225-673-8307; Email: stjohnchurch@eatel.net.
Catechesis Religious Program—Tel: 225-673-8402; Email: marlene@eatel.net. Mrs. Marlene Bruce, D.R.E. Students 1,354.

ST. AMANT, ASCENSION PARISH, HOLY ROSARY (1905) [CEM 2] Rev. Joshua D. Johnson; Deacon Eliazar Salinas Jr.
Res.: 44450 Hwy. 429, St. Amant, 70774-4597.
Tel: 225-647-5321; Email: sgautreau@olohr.com.
Catechesis Religious Program—Tel: 225-647-3696. Wendy Enloe, D.R.E. Students 504.
Chapel—Lake, Sacred Heart.

ST. FRANCISVILLE, WEST FELICIANA PARISH, OUR LADY OF MOUNT CARMEL (1874)
11485 Ferdinand St., St. Francisville, 70775. Rev. J. Cary Bani.
Res.: P.O. Box 1249, St. Francisville, 70775-1249.
Tel: 225-635-3630; Fax: 225-635-2344; Email: olmcchurch@bellsouth.net; Web: www.felicianacatholic.org.
Catechesis Religious Program—Email: marygodke@gmail.com. Ms. Mary Godke, D.R.E. Students 126.
Chapels—Jackson, Our Lady of Perpetual Help—3147 Church St., Jackson, 70748. Michelle Carter, Contact Person.
Angola, St. Augustine, Louisiana State Penitentiary, [CEM] Tel: 225-655-4411, Ext. 2028.
Angola, Our Lady of Guadalupe, Louisiana State Penitentiary.

ST. GABRIEL, IBERVILLE PARISH, ST. GABRIEL THE ARCHANGEL (1769) [CEM]
Email: myratircuit@bellsouth.net; Email: stgabrielcatholi@bellsouth.net. Rev. Charles R. Landry; Deacon Thomas E. Labat Sr.
Res.: 1510 Spanish Lakes Ave., St. Gabriel, 70776.
Tel: 225-642-8441; Email: sgablandry@bellsouth.net.
Catechesis Religious Program—Email: myratircuit@bellsouth.net. Myra Tircuit, D.R.E. Students 31.

ST. JAMES, ST. JAMES PARISH, ST. JAMES (1767) [CEM]
6613 Hwy. 18, St. James, 70086-9054.
Tel: 225-265-4210; Tel: 225-265-4225; Email: stjameschurch@canecatholics.com; Email: chymel@canecatholics.com; Web: www.canecatholics.com. Revs. Matthew E. McCaughey; Bradley A. Doyle, Parochial Vicar. Clustered with St.Philip and Our Lady of Peace.
Catechesis Religious Program—Tel: 225-265-4085; Email: saubert@canecatholics.com. Stephanie Aubert, D.R.E. Students 31.

SORRENTO, ASCENSION PARISH, ST. ANNE (1963)
P.O. Box 9, Sorrento, 70778. Rev. Keun-Soo Lee, Ph. D.; Deacon Jerry Braud.
Res.: 7348 Main St., Sorrento, 70778-0009.
Tel: 225-675-8126; Email: stanne@eatel.net; Web: stannestanthony.org.
Catechesis Religious Program—Email: stannepsr@eatel.net. Anne Miller, D.R.E.; Paula Robert, D.R.E. Attended by St. Anthony of Padua, Darrow Students 120.

TICKFAW, TANGIPAHOA PARISH, OUR LADY OF POMPEII PARISH (1973)
14450 Hwy. 442, Tickfaw, 70466. Rev. Michael A. Galea, Sacramental Min.; Deacon Albert Levy III, Parish Life Coord.
Res.: P.O. Box 276, Tickfaw, 70466-0276.
Tel: 985-345-8957; Email: deacon@ourladyofpompeiiparish.com.
Catechesis Religious Program—Sr. Joel Gubler, O.P., D.R.E.

VACHERIE, ST. JAMES PARISH
1—OUR LADY OF PEACE (1864) [CEM]
13281 Hwy. 644, Vacherie, 70090-3102.
Tel: 225-265-3953; Fax: 225-265-2507; Email: jchiasson@canecatholics.com; Email: chymel@canecatholics.com; Web: www.canecatholics.com. Revs. Matthew E. McCaughey; Bradley A. Doyle; Deacon Ricky P. Oubre. Clustered with St. James and St. Philip Parishes.
Catechesis Religious Program—Tel: 225-265-4085; Email: saubert@canecatholics.com. Stephanie Aubert, D.R.E. Students 239.
2—ST. PHILIP (1873) [CEM] Revs. Matthew E. McCaughey; Bradley A. Doyle, Parochial Vicar. Clustered with St. James and Our Lady of Peace.
Res.: 1175 Hwy. 18, Vacherie, 70090-9527.
Tel: 225-265-4085; Fax: 225-265-9348; Email: chymel@canecatholics.com; Email: frmatthewmcc@canecatholics.com; Web: www.canecatholics.com.
Catechesis Religious Program—Email: saubert@canecatholics.com. Stephanie Aubert, D.R.E. Students 54.

WHITE CASTLE, IBERVILLE PARISH, OUR LADY OF PROMPT SUCCOR (1899) [CEM 2]
Mailing Address: P.O. Box 249, White Castle, 70788-0249. Tel: 225-545-3635; Fax: 225-545-8615; Email: olpschurch@cox.net. 32615 Bowie St., White Castle, 70788. Very Rev. Ju Hyung (Paul) Yi, Admin.
Catechesis Religious Program—32625 Bowie St., White Castle, 70788. Tel: 985-519-4123; Email: wchs722003@yahoo.com. Sheila Daigle, D.R.E. Students 43.

ZACHARY, EAST BATON ROUGE PARISH, ST. JOHN THE BAPTIST (1964)
4826 Main St., Zachary, 70791-3935. Rev. M. Jeffery Bayhi.
Res.: 4727 McHugh Dr., Zachary, 70791-3935.
Tel: 225-654-5778; Email: Frontdesk@sjb-ola.org; Web: sjb-ola.org.
Catechesis Religious Program—Tel: 225-654-5885; Fax: 225-654-5294; Email: religioused@sjb-ola.org. Students 319.
Chapel—Clinton, Our Lady of the Assumption.

Chaplains of Public Institutions

BATON ROUGE. *Baton Rouge General Medical Center*, P.O. Box 3611, 70821-3611. Tel: 225-387-7000. Rev. Peter A. Dang, Chap.

ANGOLA. *Louisiana State Penitentiary*, P.O. Box 428, Angola, 70712-0428. Tel: 225-655-4411, Ext. 2028; Tel: 225-655-3243. Mr. Gerald (Jay) Jackson, Lay Chap.St. Augustine & Our Lady of Guadalupe Chapels.

ST. GABRIEL. *Hunt Correctional Institute*, Hunt Correctional Institute, P.O. Box 174, St. Gabriel, 70776-0174. Tel: 225-642-3306; Email: aricard@diobr.org. Deacons Jeff Easley, Alfred J. Ricard, Mr. Jules Tolivar, Chap.
LA Correctional Institute For Women, Mailing Address: P.O. Box 26, St. Gabriel, 70726-0026. Tel: 225-642-5529, Ext. 240. Deacon Timothy T. Messenger Sr., Chap.

Retired:
Revs.—
Adkins, Howard R., (Retired), 122 S. First St., Amite, 70422
Blanchard, Donald V., (Retired), 5323 Blair Ln., Apt. K204, 70809. Tel: 225-571-1028
Brunet, Jules A., (Retired), 604 Country Club Blvd., Thibodaux, 70301. Tel: 985-209-5701
Burns, Gerald H., (Retired), 7915 Menlo Ave., 70808. Tel: 225-388-5391
Camilleri, Joseph M., (Retired), 1974, 2624 Hundred Oaks Ave., 70809-1529
Carville, John, S.T.D., (Retired), 3553 Hyacinth St., 70808-2849. Tel: 225-383-8320
Duhe, Thomas P., (Retired), 2164 Olive St., 70806
Gautreau, Henry W., Ph.D., (Retired), 421-D Longwood Ct., 70806. Tel: 225-346-8873; Tel: 225-346-8873
Koehler, Jon C., (Retired), 12125 Mirkwood Ave., 70810-3190. Tel: 225-939-3633
Laird, Kenneth W., (Retired), 3331 Myrtle Grove, 70810-1232. Tel: 225-625-7656
Marcell, Robert G., (Retired), P.O. Box 172, Morgan City, 70381-0172. Tel: 225-346-8258
Messina, Victor G., (Retired), P.O. Box 496, St. Benedict, 70457. Tel: 225-405-4339
Nutter, Nicholas John III, (Retired), 18809 Wildlife Way Dr., 70817
Palang, Mansueto P., (Retired)
Russo, Anthony J., (Retired), 4145 Pine Park Dr., 70809-2385. Tel: 225-226-8569
Sheehy, Sean O., Ed.D., (Retired), Listowel, Meen, County Kerry Ireland
Stine, Robert F., (Retired), 11392 Palmetto Lake Ave., Denham Springs, 70726
Young, Gerard F., (Retired), P.O. Box 345, Darrow, 70725-0345. Tel: 225-278-2466.

Permanent Deacons:
Adams, Alfred P. Sr., St. Michael the Archangel, Convent; Dir. Black Catholics
Agnello, Michael A., St. Joseph Parish, Ponchatoula
Ard, Donald L., (On Leave)
Bains, Frank E., (Retired)
Benoit, Thomas Dennis, St. Isidore, Baker
Berard, Mark Thomas, Most Blessed Sacrament, Baton Rouge
Berthelot, Willie M., (Retired)
Blair, William B., (Retired)
Borne, Daniel S., St. Jean Vianney, Baton Rouge
Bourgeois, Claude H. Jr., St. John the Evangelist, Prairieville
Braud, Jerry W., St. Anne Church, Sorrento; St. Anthony, Darrow
Brunet, Stephen, St. George, Baton Rouge
Campeaux, Barry G., (Retired), (Archdiocese of New Orleans)
Chiappetta, Michael T., Immaculate Conception, Denham Springs; Chaplain, Nursing Home Ministry
Clement, Randall A., St. John the Evangelist, Prairieville
Collura, Samuel C., (Retired)
Corbett, William, St. Margaret, Albany
Dawson, David L. III, Sacred Heart of Jesus, Baton Rouge

Decker, Guy E., (Retired)
Dunbar, Benjamin J., St. Paul the Apostle, Baton Rouge
Duplantis, Kirk, St. Gabriel
Duplessis, W. Brent, (Retired)
Easley, Jeff R., St. Jean Vianney, Baton Rouge; Chaplain, Hunt Correctional Institute
Ferguson, H. John III, (Retired)
Garofalo, Natale J., Mater Dolorosa; Chaplain, Tangipahoa Parish Prison
Gauthreaux, Edward Joseph, St. Catherine of Siena, Donaldsonville
Gonzales, Steven Carl, St. Mark, Gonzales
Grant, Richard H., Our Lady of Mercy, Baton Rouge
Hebert, Ronald James, St. Alphonsus Church, Greenwell Springs
Hollier, Clayton A., Sacred Heart, Baton Rouge
Hooper, George J., Immaculate Conception, Denham Springs
Joseph, Micheal J., St. Isidore the Farmer, Baker
Jung, John A. Jr., (Retired), Relocated Archdiocese of New Orleans
Kusch, Robert J., St. Alphonsus Liguori, Greenwell Springs
LeGrange, Ronald D., (On Leave)
Levy, Albert III, Our Lady of Pompeii, Tickfaw
Little, James A., St. Joseph Church, French Settlement
Lorenz, Fallon H., (Retired), (Archdiocese of New Orleans)
McDonner, Robert, Immaculate Conception, Lakeland
McGinnis, John Louis Jr., (On Leave)
Melancon, Larry, St. Joseph, Ponchatoula
Messenger, Timothy T. Sr., St. Margaret, Albany; Chaplain, LCIW
Minor, Francis M., Mater Dolorosa, Independence
Mooney, Gary C., St. Joseph Cathedral, Baton Rouge
Morrissey, James J., St. Jude the Apostle Parish, Baton Rouge
Moscona, Jodi A., St. Theresa of Avila, Gonzales
Murphy, Leon Roy Jr., St. Joseph, French Settlement; St. Stephen, Maurepas
Musso, Donald J., Most Blessed Sacrament, Baton Rouge
Navarra, Roger A., (On Leave)
Nola, Angelo S., Our Lady of Mt. Carmel, St. Francisville
Oubre, Ricky P., Our Lady of Peace, Vacherie
Ourso, Stephen Paul, (Retired)
Patterson, Ricky Anthony, St. Jean Vianney, Baton Rouge
Ponville, Minos Jr., Holy Family, Port Allen
Reeson, Curles P., St. Jude The Apostle, Baton Rouge
Ricard, Alfred J., St. John the Evangelist, Plaquemine; Chaplain, Hunt Correctional Institute
Robinson, Thomas H., St. Mary of False River & St. Augustine, New Roads
Salazar, Mauricio, O.P., Holy Ghost, Hammond
Salinas, Eliazar Jr., Holy Rosary, St. Amant
Sammartino, Mario P. (Sam), St. Joseph, St. Michael, Convent; Sacred Heart Church, Gramercy; St. Michael, Paulina
Scimeca, Joseph, St. Thomas More, Baton Rouge
Stahl, Rudolph W., Immaculate Conception, Denham Springs; Jetson Correctional Institute
Thompson, Michael Francis, St. Mary of False River, New Roads
Traylor, John T., (Retired)
Veron, John, St. George, Baton Rouge; Dir. Deacon Life and Ministry
Walsh, J. Peter, St. Patrick, Baton Rouge
Wax, James E., (Retired)
Webre, Milton G., (Retired), (Diocese of Denver)
Wilkinson, P. Chauvin Jr., St. Aloysius, Baton Rouge.

INSTITUTIONS LOCATED IN DIOCESE

[A] COLLEGES AND UNIVERSITIES

BATON ROUGE. *Franciscan Missionaries of Our Lady University*, (Grades Associate-Masters), 5414 Brittany Drive, 70808. Tel: 225-768-1710; Fax: 225-768-0811; Email: kimberly.melancon@franu.edu; Web: www.franu.edu. Dr. Tina Holland, Pres.; Sr. Martha Abshire, Vice Pres.; Bro. Edward Violett, Vice Pres. Clergy 3; Lay Teachers 78; Students 1,418; Clergy / Religious Teachers 3.

[B] DIOCESAN HIGH SCHOOLS, INTERPAROCHIAL

BATON ROUGE. *St. Michael the Archangel Diocesan Regional High School*, 17521 Monitor Ave., 70817. P.O. Box 86110, 70879-6110. Ms. Ellen B. Lee, Prin.; Ms. Amy Donaldson, Librarian. Lay Teachers 41; Students 573.

DONALDSONVILLE. *Ascension Catholic Diocesan Regional School*, (Grades 7-12), 311 St. Vincent St., Donaldsonville, 70346-2697. Tel: 225-473-9227 ; Fax: 225-473-1243; Web: www.acbulldogs.org. Ms. Sandy Pizzolato, Prin. Serving parishes in Donaldsonville, St. James, Belle Rose, Vacherie, White Castle, Darrow, Gonzales, Convent, Paincourtville and Plattenville. Lay Teachers 15; Students 210.

HAMMOND. *St. Thomas Aquinas Regional Catholic High School*, 14520 Voss Dr., Hammond, 70401-9801. Tel: 985-542-7662; Fax: 985-542-4010; Email: pat.sanguinetti@stafalcons.org; Web: www.stafalcons.org. Pat Sanguinetti, Prin. Dominican Sisters, Springfield, IL. Lay Teachers 25; Students 292.

NEW ROADS. *Catholic High School of Pointe Coupee*, (Grades 7-12), 504 Fourth St., New Roads, 70760-3499. Tel: 225-638-9313; Fax: 225-638-6471; Email: highschooloffice@catholicpc.com; Web: www.catholicpc.com. Mrs. Colleen Caillet, Prin. Serving parishes in Lakeland, Livonia, Morganza, New Roads and Maringouin. Lay Teachers 25; Students 300.

PLAQUEMINE. *St. John Interparochial High School*, (Grades 7-12), 24250 Regina St., Plaquemine, 70764-3598. Tel: 225-687-3056; Fax: 225-687-3530; Email: cschlatre@stjohnschool.org; Web: www.stjohnschool.org. Mrs. Cherie Schlatre, Prin. Serving parishes in Plaquemine, Brusly, Port Allen, Grosse Tete, St. Gabriel and White Castle. Lay Teachers 20; Students 140.

[C] HIGH SCHOOLS, PRIVATE

BATON ROUGE. *Catholic High School*, (Grades 8-12), 855 Hearthstone Dr., 70806-5599.
Tel: 225-383-0397; Fax: 225-383-0381; Email: info@catholichigh.org; Web: www.catholichigh.org. Mr. Gerald E. Tullier, Pres.; Mrs. Lisa Harvey, Prin. Boys 1,138; Brothers of the Sacred Heart 2; Lay Teachers 101; Students 1,138; Clergy / Religious Teachers 2.

**St. Joseph's Academy*, St. Joseph's Academy, 3015 Broussard St., 70808-1198. Tel: 225-383-7207; Fax: 225-344-5714; Web: www.sjabr.org. Mrs. Jan Rhorer Breen, Pres.; Stacia Andricain, Prin. Girls 1,105; Lay Teachers 75; Sisters of St. Joseph 3; Students 1,105; Clergy / Religious Teachers 3.

[D] DIOCESAN ELEMENTARY SCHOOLS, INTERPAROCHIAL

DONALDSONVILLE. *Ascension Regional Elementary School*, (Grades PreK-6), 618 Iberville Street, Donaldsonville, 70346-3499.
Tel: 225-473-9227, Ext. 250; Fax: 225-264-6193; Web: ascensioncatholic.org. Ms. Sandy Pizzolato, Prin. Serving parishes in Donaldsonville, St. James, Belle Rose, Vacherie, White Castle, Darrow, Gonzales, Convent, Paulina, Paincourtville, and Plattenville. Lay Teachers 20; Students 264.

Redemptorist St. Gerard Elementary School, (Grades PreK-8), 3655 St. Gerard Ave., 70805-2898.
Tel: 225-355-1437; Fax: 225-355-1879; Email: redemptoristelem@csobr.org; Email: awiles@resbr.org; Web: resbr.org. Aimee Wiles, Prin. Lay Teachers 24; Students 275.

NEW ROADS. *Catholic Elementary School of Pointe Coupee*, (Grades PreK-6), 304 Napoleon St., New Roads, 70760-3527. Tel: 225-638-9313;
Fax: 225-638-9953; Web: www.catholicpc.com. Mr. Jason Chauvin, Prin.; Mrs. Julia Labatut, Librarian. Serving parishes in Lakeland, Livonia, Morganza, New Roads and Maringouin. Lay Teachers 21; Students 409.

PAINCOURTVILLE. *St. Elizabeth Interparochial*, (Grades PreK-8), 6051 Convent St., Paincourtville, 70391-0420. Tel: 985-369-7402; Fax: 985-369-1527; Email: kherpich@sescubs.com; Web: www.sescubs.com. P.O. Drawer M, Paincourtville, 70391. Rev. Matthew J. Graham; Dr. Kathy Herpich, Admin.; Mrs. Lisa Triagle, Teacher. Serving parishes in Belle Rose, Bertrandville, Napoleonville, Paincourtville, Pierre Part, Plattenville and Labadieville. Lay Teachers 16; Students 220; Religious Sisters 2; Clergy / Religious Teachers 1.

PAULINA. *St. Peter Chanel Interparochial School*, (Grades PreK-8), 2590 LA Hwy. 44, Paulina, 70763. Tel: 225-869-5778; Fax: 225-869-8131; Email: ppoche@stpchanel.org; Web: www.stpchanel.org. Mrs. Paula Poche, Prin.; Mrs. Sandi Waguespack, Librarian. Serving parishes in Paulina, Gramercy, Convent, Vacherie, St. James Lutcher and Grand Point. Lay Teachers 21; Students 299.

PLAQUEMINE. *St. John Interparochial Elementary/ Middle School*, (Grades PreK-8), 58645 St. Clement Ave., Plaquemine, 70764-3599.
Tel: 225-687-6616; Fax: 225-687-6984; Email: cschlatre@stjohnschool.org; Web: www.stjohnschool.org. Mrs. Cherie Schlatre, Prin. Serving parishes in Plaquemine, Brusly, Grosse Tete, White Castle, Baton Rouge, St. Gabriel, Maringouin, Bayou Pigeon, and Donaldsonville. Lay Teachers 17; Students 310.

PRAIRIEVILLE. *St. John Primary School* aka East Ascension/East Iberville Regional Catholic School Partnership, (Grades PreK-3), 37407 Duplessis Rd., Prairieville, 70769-4321. Tel: 225-647-2803; Email: kimnaquin@sjp-sta.org. Mrs. Kim Naquin, Prin. Lay Teachers 23; Students 380.

[E] SCHOOL, EXCEPTIONAL CHILDREN

BATON ROUGE. *Special Education Program*, P.O. Box 2028, 70821. Bethany Robicheaux, Dir. Students 135; Teachers and Staff 50.

[F] GENERAL HOSPITALS

BATON ROUGE. *Our Lady of the Lake Hospital, Inc.*, 5000 Hennessy Blvd., 70808-4398.
Tel: 225-765-6565; Fax: 225-766-5645; Email: scott.wester@fmolhs.org; Email: renee.brown@fmolhs.org; Web: www.ololrmc.com. Sr. Barbara Arceneaux, O.S.F., Supr.; Mr. K. Scott Wester, CEO; Revs. Donatus O. Ajoko, (Nigeria); Samuel C. Maranto, C.Ss.R.; Johnson Kuriapilly. Franciscan Missionaries of Our Lady (North American Province). Bed Capacity 736; Patients Asst Anual. 340,866; Sisters 14; Tot Asst. Annually 650,000; Total Staff 7,000.

Tau Center, 8080 Margaret Ann Dr., 70809-3444.
Tel: 225-767-1320; Fax: 225-767-1327; Email: katherine.hillis@fmolhs.org. Bed Capacity 47.

GONZALES. *Our Lady of the Lake Ascension Community Hospital, Inc.* aka St. Elizabeth Hospital, 1125 W. Hwy. 30, Gonzales, 70737-5000. Tel: 225-647-5071; Fax: 225-765-9806; Email: Robert.Burgess@fmolhs.org; Email: Mona.day@fmolhs.org; Web: www.steh.com. Mr. Robert Burgess, Pres. & CEO; Rev. Denis O. Ekwugha, (Nigeria) Priest/Pastoral Care. Bed Capacity 78; Tot Asst. Annually 50,627; Total Staff 430; Cost of Community Benefit Provided 946,978.24.

NAPOLEONVILLE. *Our Lady of the Lake Assumption Community Hospital, Inc.* aka Assumption Community Hospital, 135 Hwy. 402, Napoleonville, 70390-2217. Tel: 985-369-3600; Fax: 985-369-4271; Email: Letonia.Howard@fmolhs.org; Email: Christy.Hockaday@fmolhs.org. Ms. Christy Hockaday, CEO. Fully owned subsidiary of Our Lady of the Lake Regional Medical Center. Bed Capacity 15; Patients Asst Anual. 33,000; Total Staff 50.

[G] HOMES AND SPECIAL CARE FACILITIES

BATON ROUGE. *Elderly HUD Housing of Our Lady of the Lake Hospital, Inc.*, 5000 Hennessy Blvd., 70808-4398. Tel: 225-765-6565; Email: wendy.hellinger@fmolhs.org. Ms. Patricia Hima, Dir.

Chateau Louise, 7565 Bishop Ott Dr., 70806.
Tel: 225-926-5918; Email: karen.allen@fmolhs.org. CW (Neil) Nett, Exec. Dir. Housing for elderly and handicapped persons.

Assisi Village, Inc., 7585 Bishop Ott Dr., 70806-8922. Tel: 225-926-5918; Fax: 225-927-1742; Email: karen.allen@fmolhs.org. Ms. Karen B. Allen, Pres. Housing facilities for elderly persons.

Calais House, Inc., 7545 Bishop Ott Dr., 70806-8900. Tel: 225-927-1889; Fax: 225-927-1742. Housing facilities for elderly persons.

Villa St. Francis, Inc., 7575 Bishop Ott Dr., 70806-8906. Tel: 225-927-0070; Fax: 225-927-1742; Email: evogt@fmolhs.org. Housing facilities for elderly and handicapped persons.

Ollie Steele Burden Manor, Inc., 4250 Essen Ln., 70809-2196. Tel: 225-926-0091; Fax: 225-926-4937; Email: karen.allen@fmolhs.org. Ms. Karen B. Allen, Pres. Our Lady of the Lake Regional Medical Center, Our Lady of the Lake Pastoral Care. Bed Capacity 164; Tot Asst. Annually 300; Total Staff 172.

[H] MONASTERIES AND RESIDENCES OF PRIESTS OR BROTHERS

BATON ROUGE. *Brothers of the Sacred Heart*, 4345 Woodside Dr., 70808. Tel: 225-223-6920. 4600 Elysian Fields Ave., New Orleans, 70122. Bros. Lemoyne Roger, Dir.; Ray Hebert, S.C., 2928 Florida St., 70802. Brothers 16; Ordained 2. 801 Hearthstone Dr., 70806. Tel: 225-663-6783; Email: roperal2141@gmail.com. Bros. Roger Lemoine, S.C., Dir., Residence; James Burns, S.C.; Ramon Daunis, S.C.; Carl Evans, S.C.; Harold Harris, S.C.; Noel Lemmon, S.C.; Malcolm Melcher, S.C. 2928 Florida St., 70802. Email: pomontero@yahoo.com. Bro. Paul Montero, S.C., Contact Person;

Bros. Ronald Hingle, Prov. Asst.; Clifford King, Supr.; Bros. Marcus Turcotte, S.C.; William Cawley, S.C.

St. Gerard Residence, 5354 Plank Rd., 70805. Tel: 225-355-2600; Email: rhalter69@gmail.com. Revs. Robert Halter, C.Ss.R., Supr.; Chuong Cao, C.Ss.R., Pastor; Gilbert Enderle, Chap.; Donnell Kirchner, Chap.; Donal MacKinnon, Chap.; Bro. Clement J. Furno, C.Ss.R., In Res. Brothers 1; Priests 5.

Incarnatio Consecratio Missio (Vietnamese Institute) 2580 Tecumseh St., 70805-7999. Tel: 225-302-7457 ; Fax: 225-358-9198; Email: nvhung@bellsouth.net. Very Rev. Hung Viet Nguyen, I.C.M., (Vietnam) Supr. General; Revs. Martin Thanh Nguyen, I.C.M.; Peter Neuman, I.C.M.

[I] CONVENTS AND RESIDENCES FOR SISTERS

BATON ROUGE. *Congregation of St. Joseph*, 3134 Hundred Oaks Ave., 70808. Tel: 225-332-2999; Fax: 225-379-7930; Web: www.csjoseph.org. Sr. Theresa Pitruzzello, Coord. of Community Life. Sisters of St. Joseph 30.

Maryville Novitiate and Provincial House, Inc., 4200 Essen Ln., 70809-2196. Tel: 225-922-7443; Fax: 225-922-7497; Email: barcenea@fmolhs.org; Web: www.fmolsisters.com. Sr. Barbara Arceneaux, O.S.F., Prov. Sisters 13. *Franciscan Missionaries of Our Lady North American Province Inc.*, 4200 Essen Ln., 70809-2196. Tel: 225-922-7443; Fax: 225-922-7497; Email: barbara.arceneaux@fmolhs.org. Sr. Barbara Arceneaux, O.S.F., Prov. Sisters 14.

Missionaries of Charity, 737 East Blvd., 70802-6399. Tel: 225-383-8367. Sisters M. Jonathan, MC, Regl. Supr.; M. Celian, MC, Supr. Missionaries of Charity. Tot Asst. Annually 500; Total Staff 6.

[J] RETREAT HOUSES

BATON ROUGE. *Bishop Robert E. Tracy Center*, P.O. Box 2028, 70821-2028. Tel: 225-336-8750; Fax: 225-336-8725; Email: tracycenter@diobr.org. 1800 S. Acadian Thruway, 70808. Mr. Craig Michelet, Admin.

CONVENT. *Manresa House of Retreats*, Office: 5858 Louisiana Highway 44, P.O. Box 89, Convent, 70723-0089. Tel: 225-562-3596; Tel: 800-782-9431; Fax: 225-562-3147; Email: manresahr@bellsouth.net; Web: www.manresala.org. Mr. Tim Murphy, Dir.; Revs. Leonard E. Kraus, S.J., Supr.; Michael French, Dir.; Peter J. Callery, S.J., Assoc. Dir.; Richard Buhler, Dir.

PONCHATOULA. *Rosaryville/Spirit Life Center*, 39003 Rosaryville Rd., Ponchatoula, 70454-7001. Tel: 225-294-5039; Fax: 225-294-3510; Email: scallais@oppeace.org; Web: www.rosaryvillela.com. Ms. Suzette Callais, Dir.

Rosaryville Cemetery.

[K] CAMPUS MINISTRY

BATON ROUGE. *Christ the King Parish and Catholic Center*, 11 Fraternity Ln., 70803-0106. Tel: 225-344-8595; Fax: 225-344-1920; Email: adazzio@ctklsu.org; Web: www.ctklsu.org. PO Box 411, 70821-0411. Mrs. Alison Dazzio, Admin.; Rev. Andrew J. Merrick, Pastor; Mrs. Jennifer Moore, Business Mgr.; Mrs. Carla Rutherford, Sec.

Martin Luther King, Jr. Catholic Student Center, St. Joseph Chapel, Southern University, 586 Harding Blvd., 70807-5301. Tel: 225-775-8691; Fax: 225-775-2702; Email: mlkcatholiccenter@gmail.com; Web: www.immaculateconceptionbr.org. Very Rev. Thomas F. Clark, S.J., V.F., Chap. Total Catholic Students 1,000.

HAMMOND. *St. Albert the Great Catholic Student Center*, 409 W. Dakota St., Hammond, 70401-2517. Tel: 985-345-7206; Fax: 985-345-7206; Email: stalbertselu@gmail.com; Web: www.stalbertselu.org. Rev. Michael J. O'Rourke, O.P., Dir. Serving Southeastern Louisiana University. Catholic Students 4,500.

[L] MISCELLANEOUS

BATON ROUGE. *Bishop Stanley J. Ott Shelter Program*, P.O. Box 127, 70821-0127. Tel: 225-383-7343; Fax: 225-383-6623; Tel: 225-383-7837; Email: macaldo@svdpbr.com; Web: svdpbr.org. 220 St. Vincent de Paul Place, 70802. Mr. Michael J. Acaldo, Pres. & CEO

Particular Council of St. Vincent de Paul Guest Nights of Emergency Shelter 30,000.

Catholic Charities of the Diocese of Baton Rouge, Inc., 1900 S. Acadian Thruway, 70808-1688. Tel: 225-336-8770; Fax: 225-336-8745; Email: daguillard@ccdiobr.org; Web: www.ccdiobr.org. Mailing Address: P.O. Box 1668, 70821-1668. Mr. David C. Aguillard, M.P.A., M.H.A., Exec. Dir.

Joseph Homes, Inc.

Child Nutrition Program, 1800 S Acadian Thruway, 70808. Tel: 225-387-6421; Email: cnp@diobr.org; Web: www.cnpbr.org. 3300 Hundred Oaks Ave, 70808. Mrs. Lynda Carville, Dir.

Closer Walk Catholic Communications, 4256 North Blvd., 70879-8279. Tel: 225-615-7085; Fax: 225-615-7086; Email: admin@cwm.brcoxmail.com; Web: www.closerwalkcatholiccommunications.com. P.O. Box 87279, 70879-8279. Rev. M. Jeffery Bayhi, Pres.

Franciscan Missionaries of Our Lady Health System, 4200 Essen Ln., 70809-2196. Tel: 225-923-2701; Fax: 225-926-4846; Web: www.fmolhs.org. Mr. Michael McBride, Pres.

Franciscan Ministry Fund, Inc., 4200 Essen Ln., 70809. Tel: 225-922-7443; Fax: 225-922-7497; Email: peter.guarisco@fmolhs.org. Sr. Barbara Arceneaux, O.S.F., Contact Person.

Haiti Project, Inc., 4200 Essen Ln., 70809-2196. Tel: 225-922-7443; Fax: 225-922-7497; Email: martha.abshire@fmolhs.org. Sr. Barbara Arceneaux, O.S.F., Pres.

Magnificat Diocese of Baton Rouge Chapter, 1646 Great Oak Dr., 70810.

Maternity Adoption & Behavioral Health, 1900 S. Acadian Thruway, 70808. Tel: 225-336-8708; Fax: 225-336-8703; Email: adopt@ccdiobr.org; Web: www.adoptbatonrouge.com. Stephanie Sterling, L.C.S.W., Dir. Bed Capacity 8; Tot Asst. Annually 60; Total Staff 8.

St. Michael's Home (Vietnamese) 2305 Choctaw Dr., 70805-7999. Tel: 225-357-1204; Fax: 225-354-0611; Email: nvhung@bellsouth.net. Very Rev. Hung Viet Nguyen, I.C.M., (Vietnam) Supr. Gen., Tel: 225-302-7457; Fax: 225-358-9198.

**Myriam's House* (Particular Council of St. Vincent de Paul of B.R., LA.) P.O. Box 127, 70821-0127. Tel: 225-383-7343; Tel: 225-383-7837, Ext. 0; Fax: 225-383-6623; Email: macaldo@svdpbr.com; Web: svdpbr.org. 1141 West Chimes Street, 70802. Mr. Michael J. Acaldo, CEO.

Franciscan PACE, Inc., Franciscan Missionaries of Our Lady, 4200 Essen Ln., 70809. Tel: 225-923-2701; Fax: 225-926-4846; Email: karen.allen@fmolhs.org. Ms. Karen B. Allen, Exec. Dir.

**Particular Council of St. Vincent de Paul of Baton Rouge, Louisiana*, P.O. Box 127, 70821-0127. Tel: 225-383-7837; Email: macaldo@svdpbr.org. David Acaldo, CEO.

Redemptorist Fathers of Baton Rouge, Inc., 5354 Plank Rd., 70805. Tel: 225-355-2553; Fax: 225-356-7472; Email: jromero1@redemptorists-denver.org; Web: redemptorists-denver.org. Revs. Chuong Cao, C.Ss.R., Pastor; Robert Halter, C.Ss.R., Chap.; Donald MacKinnon, C.Ss.R., in residence; Samuel C. Maranto, C.SS.R., in residence; Gilbert Enderle, in residence.

**SJA Foundation*, SJA Foundation, 3015 Broussard St., 70808. Tel: 225-383-7207; Email: geraldm@sjabr.org; Email: laplacej@sjabr.org; Web: sjabr.org. Mrs. Jan Rhorer Breen, Exec.

St. Joseph Spirituality Center, 2980 Kleinert Ave., 70806-6800. Tel: 225-383-3349; Email: dianne@stjocenter.org; Web: www.stjocenter.org. Dianne Hanley, Dir. Congregation of St. Joseph Sisters 1.

**The Society of St. Vincent de Paul Foundation*, P.O. Box 127, 70821-0127. Tel: 225-383-7837; Email: macaldo@svdpbr.org. David Acaldo, CEO.

St. Vincent de Paul Baton Rouge Council, P.O. Box 127, 70821-0127.

**St. Vincent DePaul Community Pharmacy, Inc.*, Mailing Address: P.O. Box 127, 70821-0127. Tel: 225-383-7450; Fax: 225-383-4774; Tel: 225-383-7837; Email: macaldo@svdpbr.com; Web: svdpbr.org. 1647 Convention Street, 70802. Mr. Michael J. Acaldo, CEO. Prescriptions Filled 7,278.

St. Vincent DePaul Dining Room, Mailing Address: P.O. Box 127, 70821-0127. Tel: 225-383-7837; Tel: 225-383-7439; Fax: 225-383-6623; Email: macaldo@svdpbr.com; Web: svdpbr.org. 220 St. Vincent de Paul Place, 70802. Mr. Michael J. Acaldo, CEO

Particular Council of St. Vincent de Paul Meals Served 270,000.

St. Vincent DePaul Stores, Mailing Address: P.O. Box 127, 70821-0127. Tel: 225-267-5447; Fax: 225-267-5157; Tel: 225-383-7837, Ext. 0; Email: macaldo@svdpbr.com; Web: svdpbr.org. 1466 North Street, 70802. Mr. Michael J. Acaldo, CEO, Tel: 225-383-7837

Particular Council of St. Vincent de Paul.

[M] FOUNDATIONS, FUNDS AND TRUSTS

BATON ROUGE. *Baton Rouge Chancery Office*, Mailing Address: P.O. Box 2028, 70821-2028. 1800 S. Acadian Thruway, 70808-1698. Tel: 225-387-0561; Fax: 225-336-8789; Email: chancery@diobr.org. Very Revs. Ju Hyung (Paul) Yi, Chancellor; Thomas C. Ranzino, V.G., Vicar.

Ascension Catholic Interparochial School Endowment Fund, 311 St. Vincent Street, Donaldsonville, 70346. Tel: 225-473-9227; Fax: 225-473-9235; Email: sandy.pizzolato@acbulldogs.org. Very Rev. Ju Hyung (Paul) Yi, Pastor.

Bishop Stanley J. Ott Works of Mercy Trust, P.O. Box 2028, 70821-2028. Tel: 225-387-0561; Fax: 225-336-8789. Mr. Glenn J. Landry Jr., Treas.

Diocese of Baton Rouge Clergy Retirement Plan, 1800 S. Acadian Thruway, 70808. Tel: 225-387-0561; Fax: 225-336-8789; Email: glandry@diobr.org. P.O. Box 2028, 70821-2028. Mr. Glenn J. Landry Jr., Treas.

Diocese of Baton Rouge Lay Retirement Plan, 1800 S. Acadian Thruway, 70808. Tel: 225-387-0561; Fax: 225-336-8742. P.O. Box 2028, 70821-2028. Mr. Glenn J. Landry Jr., Treas.

Catholic Foundation of the Diocese of Baton Rouge, 1800 S. Acadian Thruway, 70808. Tel: 225-387-0561; Fax: 225-336-8789. P.O. Box 2028, 70821-2028. Mr. Glenn J. Landry Jr., Treas.

CHS Foundation, 855 Hearthstone Dr., 70806. Tel: 225-389-0978; Fax: 225-389-0983; Email: gtullier@catholichigh.org. Mr. Gerald E. Tullier, Pres.

Nim Pecquet Holy Family School Foundation, 335 North Jefferson Ave, Port Allen, 70767. Tel: 225-344-4100; Fax: 225-344-1928; Email: mcomeau@hfspa.com; Web: holyfamilyschool.com. Mr. Michael Comeau, Prin.; Rev. David E. Allen, Pastor.

Our Lady of Perpetual Help Trust, P.O. Box 1249, 70775. Tel: 225-635-3630; Fax: 225-635-2344; Email: olmcchurch@bellsouth.net. Rev. J. Cary Bani, Pastor.

Our Lady of the Lake Foundation, 5000 Hennessy Blvd., 70808-9907. Tel: 225-765-5000; Fax: 225-765-6480. Christel Slaughter, Pres.

Pamphile and Mabyn Donaldson Trust for St. Thomas More, 11441 Goodwood Blvd., 70815. Tel: 225-275-3940; Email: info@stmchurch.org. Rev. Michael J. Alello, Pastor.

Pointe Coupee Catholic Interparochial School Endowment Fund, 504 4th St., New Roads, 70760-3499. Tel: 225-638-9313; Fax: 225-638-6471; Email: highschooloffice@catholicpc.com.

The Roman Catholic Church of The Diocese of Baton Rouge, Deposit and Loan Fund, Inc., 1800 S. Acadian Thruway, 70808-1698. Tel: 225-387-0561; Fax: 225-336-8789. Mr. Glenn J. Landry Jr., C.F.O.

Sacred Heart School Endowment Fund, 2251 Main St., 70802-3144. Tel: 225-383-7481; Fax: 225-383-1810. Rev. Miles D. Walsh, S.T.D.

St. Aloysius School Endowment Fund, 2025 Stuart Ave, 70808. Tel: 225-383-3871; Fax: 225-383-4500; Email: info@aloysius.org; Web: school.aloysius.org. Very Rev. Randy M. Cuevas, S.T.L., V.F.

St. Joseph Cathedral Cemetery Fund, 412 North Street, 70802. Tel: 225-387-5928; Fax: 225-387-5929; Email: office@cathedralbr.org. Very Rev. Paul D. Counce, J.C.L., M.C.L., Rector.

St. Joseph Cathedral Trust & Bettie Womack Dedicated Cathedral Trust Funds, 412 North Street, 70802. Tel: 225-387-5928; Fax: 225-387-5929; Email: office@cathedralbr.org. Very Rev. Paul D. Counce, J.C.L., M.C.L., Rector.

St. Theresa of Avila Catholic School Educational Foundation, 212 E. New River St., Gonzales, 70737. Tel: 225-647-2803; Fax: 225-647-7814; Email: chrismusso@sjp-sta.org. Ms. Chris Musso, Prin.; Mrs. Kim Naquin, Prin.

St. Thomas More School Endowment Trust, 11400 Sherbrook, 70815. Tel: 225-275-2820; Fax: 225-275-0376; Web: www.stmbr.org. Mr. Brian Moscona, Prin. Students 625; Staff 69.

Veritas Foundation, 14520 Voss Drive, Hammond, 70401. Tel: 985-542-7662; Fax: 985-542-4010; Email: pat.sanguinetti@stafalcons.org. Pat Sanguinetti, Prin.

CONVENT. *Hynes Fund*, Mailing Address: 5858 Louisiana Highway 44, P.O. Box 89, Convent, 70723-0089. Tel: 800-782-9431; Fax: 225-562-3147; Email: manresahr@bellsouth.net. Mr. Tim Murphy, Dir.

The Administrators of the Rev. John W. Hynes, S.J., Manresa Memorial Endowment Fund, Inc.

RELIGIOUS INSTITUTES OF MEN REPRESENTED IN THE DIOCESE

For further details refer to the corresponding bracketed number in the Religious Institutes of Men or Women section.

[1100]—*Brothers of the Sacred Heart* (New Orleans Prov.)—S.C.

[1070]—*Congregation of the Most Holy Redeemer-Redemptorists*—C.Ss.R.

[]—*Incarnatio Consecratio Missio*—I.C.M.

[]—*Indian Missionary Society*—I.M.S.

[0854]—*Missionaries of St. Paul*—M.S.P.
[0430]—*Order of Preachers-Dominicans* (Prov. of St. Martin de Porres)—O.P.
[0690]—*Society of Jesus* (Central & Southern Prov.)—S.J.
[0420]—*Society of the Divine Word* (Southern Prov.)—S.V.D.
[0700]—*St. Joseph's Society of the Sacred Heart-Josephites*—S.S.J.

RELIGIOUS INSTITUTES OF WOMEN REPRESENTED IN THE DIOCESE

[]—*Congregation of Hospitaler Sisters of Mercy*—H.S.M.
[]—*Congregation of the Mother of Carmel*—C.M.C.
[3832]—*Congregation of the Sisters of St. Joseph*—C.S.J.
[]—*Congregation of the Sisters of the Holy Family*—S.S.F.
[]—*Daughters of Mary Mother of the Church*—D.M.
[1115]—*Dominican Sisters of Peace*—O.P.
[1380]—*Franciscan Missionaries of Our Lady*—F.M.O.L.
[]—*Hospitaler Sisters of Mercy*—S.O.M.
[2187]—*Incarnatio Consecratio Missio*—I.C.M.
[2410]—*Marianites of Holy Cross*—M.S.C.
[2590]—*Mercedarian Sisters of the Blessed Sacrament*—H.M.S.S.
[2710]—*Missionaries of Charity*—M.C.
[]—*Sisters of Mercy of Holy Cross*—S.C.S.C.
[]—*Sisters of Notre Dame de Namur*—S.N.D.deN.
[]—*Sisters of St. Joseph of Carondelet* (Albany Province)—C.S.J.

NECROLOGY

† Mascarella, Patrick J., (Retired), Died Jan. 24, 2019
† Vavasseur, Henry C., (Retired), Died Oct. 26, 2018

An asterisk (*) denotes an organization that has established tax-exempt status directly with the IRS and is not covered by the USCCB Group Ruling.

Diocese of Beaumont

(Dioecesis Bellomontensis)

Most Reverend

CURTIS JOHN GUILLORY, S.V.D., D.D.

Bishop of Beaumont; ordained December 16, 1972; appointed Titular Bishop of Stagno and Auxiliary Bishop of Galveston-Houston December 29, 1987; consecrated February 19, 1988; appointed Bishop of Beaumont June 2, 2000; installed July 28, 2000. *Mailing Address: P.O. Box 3948, Beaumont, TX 77704-3948. Office: 710 Archie St., Beaumont, TX 77701-2802.* Tel: 409-924-4310; Fax: 409-838-4511.

Catholic Pastoral Center: 710 Archie St., Beaumont, TX 77701-2802. Mailing Address: P.O. Box 3948, Beaumont, TX 77704-3948. Tel: 409-924-4300; Fax: 409-838-4511.

Web: www.dioceseofbmt.org

Email: chancery@dioceseofbmt.org

ESTABLISHED SEPTEMBER 29, 1966.

Square Miles 7,878.

Comprises the counties of Chambers, Hardin, Jasper, Jefferson, Liberty, Newton, Orange, Polk and Tyler.

For legal titles of parishes and diocesan institutions, consult the Catholic Pastoral Center.

STATISTICAL OVERVIEW

Personnel	
Bishop	1
Priests: Diocesan Active in Diocese	27
Priests: Diocesan Active Outside Diocese	1
Priests: Retired, Sick or Absent	10
Number of Diocesan Priests	38
Religious Priests in Diocese	21
Total Priests in Diocese	59
Extern Priests in Diocese	6
Ordinations:	
Diocesan Priests	1
Transitional Deacons	1
Permanent Deacons in Diocese	46
Total Brothers	2
Total Sisters	18
Parishes	
Parishes	42
With Resident Pastor:	
Resident Diocesan Priests	25
Resident Religious Priests	17
Missions	6
Closed Parishes	2
Welfare	
Catholic Hospitals	3
Total Assisted	351,343
Special Centers for Social Services	1
Total Assisted	5,186
Educational	
Students from This Diocese	2
Diocesan Students in Other Seminaries	3
Total Seminarians	5
High Schools, Diocesan and Parish	1
Total Students	420
Elementary Schools, Diocesan and Parish	4
Total Students	1,028
Catechesis/Religious Education:	
High School Students	1,827
Elementary Students	5,373
Total Students under Catholic Instruction	8,653
Teachers in the Diocese:	
Lay Teachers	121
Vital Statistics	
Receptions into the Church:	
Infant Baptism Totals	944
Adult Baptism Totals	83
First Communions	1,377
Confirmations	934
Marriages:	
Catholic	122
Interfaith	35
Total Marriages	157
Deaths	704
Total Catholic Population	68,597
Total Population	643,798

Former Bishops—Most Revs. VINCENT M. HARRIS, D.D., ord. March 19, 1938; appt. Bishop of Beaumont, July 4, 1966; cons. Sept. 28, 1966; installed as First Bishop of Beaumont, Sept. 29, 1966; appt. Titular Bishop of Rotaria and Coadjutor with right of succession to the Bishop of Austin, TX, April 21, 1971; succeeded to See as Second Bishop of Austin, Nov. 16, 1971; died March 31, 1988; WARREN L. BOUDREAUX, J.C.D., D.D., ord. May 30, 1942; appt. Titular Bishop of Calynda and Auxiliary Bishop of Lafayette, LA, May 19, 1962; cons. July 25, 1962; appt. second Bishop of Beaumont, June 4, 1971; installed Aug. 25, 1971; appt. first Bishop of Houma-Thibodaux, March 2, 1977; installed as first Bishop of Houma-Thibodaux, June 5, 1977; died Oct. 6, 1997; BERNARD J. GANTER, D.D., ord. May 22, 1952; appt. first Bishop of Tulsa, Dec. 19, 1972; cons. and installed, Feb. 7, 1973; appt. third Bishop of Beaumont, Oct. 3, 1977; installed Dec. 13, 1977; died Oct. 9, 1993; JOSEPH A. GALANTE, D.D., J.C.D., ord. May 16, 1964; appt. Titular Bishop of Equilum & Auxiliary Bishop of San Antonio Oct. 13, 1992; cons. Dec. 11, 1992; appt. Bishop of Beaumont, April 5, 1994; installed May 9, 1994; appt. Coadjutor Bishop of Dallas, Nov. 23, 1999; installed Jan. 14, 2000; appt. Bishop of Camden, March 23, 2004; installed April 30, 2004.

Catholic Pastoral Center—710 Archie St., Beaumont, 77701-2802. Tel: 409-924-4300; Fax: 409-838-4511 Office Hours: 8-5. *Mailing Address: P.O. Box 3948, Beaumont, 77704-3948.*

Vicars General and Moderator of the Curia—Mailing Address: P.O. Box 3948, Beaumont, 77704-3948. Tel: 409-924-4303; Fax: 409-838-4511; Email: vicargeneral@dioceseofbmt.org. Rev. Msgr. MICHAEL A. JAMAIL, J.C.D., Ed.D., V.G., Vicar Gen. & Moderator; Very Rev. M. SHANE BAXTER, S.T.L., Pro-V.G.

Office of the Bishop—Most Rev. CURTIS J. GUILLORY, S.V.D., D.D., Email: bishop@dioceseofbmt.org.

Episcopal Vicars—Central Vicariate: Rev. Msgr. WILLIAM MANGER, M.Ed., E.V., Mailing Address: St. Anne, P.O. Box 3429, Beaumont, 77704-3429. Eastern Vicariate: Very Rev. JOSEPH P. DALEO, E.V., Mailing Address: St. Mary Church, 912 W. Cherry Ave., Orange, 77630-5017. Northern Vicariate: Very Rev. RONALD B. FOSHAGE, M.S., E.V., Mailing Address: St. Michael, P.O. Box 239, Jasper, 75951-0239. Southern Vicariate: Very Rev. REJIMON GEORGE, C.M.I., E.V., St. Therese, Little Flower, 6412 Garnet Ave., Port Arthur, 77640-1308. Western Vicariate: Very Rev. JOSEPH KHANH HO, S.T.L., J.C.L., Holy Trinity, P.O. Box 290, Mont Belvieu, 77580-0290.

Diocesan College of Consultors—Rev. Msgr. MICHAEL A. JAMAIL, J.C.D., Ed.D., V.G.; Very Rev. M. SHANE BAXTER, S.T.L., Pro-V.G.; Revs. KEVIN BADEAUX, J.C.L.; CONSTANTINO BARRERA; RODEL FALLER; Very Rev. REJIMON GEORGE, C.M.I., E.V.; Revs. D. STEPHEN MCCRATE; ANDREW R. MOORE, M.Div.; EATHAN OAKES; Very Rev. LUONG QUANG TRAN, J.C.L.

Presbyteral Council—Rev. ANDREW R. MOORE, M.Div.; Rev. Msgr. MICHAEL A. JAMAIL, J.C.D., Ed.D., V.G.; Rev. KEVIN BADEAUX, J.C.L.; Very Rev. REJIMON GEORGE, C.M.I., E.V.; Revs. CONSTANTINO BARRERA; RODEL FALLER; D. STEPHEN MCCRATE; EATHAN OAKES; AUGUSTINE WALL, S.V.D.; Very Revs. LUONG QUANG TRAN, J.C.L.; SHANE BAXTER, S.T.L., Pro-V.G.

Clergy Personnel Board—Mailing Address: P.O. Box 3429, Beaumont, 77704-3429. Rev. MARTIN LESTER NELSON, J.C.L., Chm., (Retired).

Chancellor—Sr. ESTHER DUNEGAN, I.W.B.S., J.C.L., Mailing Address: P.O. Box 3948, Beaumont, 77704-3948. Tel: 409-924-4304; Fax: 409-838-4511; Email: chancellor@dioceseofbmt.org.

Chief Financial Officer—Mailing Address: Diocese of Beaumont, P.O. Box 3948, Beaumont, 77704-3948. Tel: 409-924-4313; Fax: 409-838-4511. SABRINA VROOMAN, CPA.

Diocesan Finance Council—Mailing Address: P.O. Box 3948, Beaumont, 77704-3948. SABRINA VROOMAN, CPA.

Human Resources Director—BEVERLY ESCAMILLA, P.H.R., Mailing Address: Diocese of Beaumont, P.O. Box 3948, Beaumont, 77704-3948. Tel: 409-924-4314; Fax: 409-924-4396; Fax: 409-838-4511.

Diocese of Beaumont Retirement Committee—MR. MIKE EAVES, Chm., Mailing Address: P.O. Box 3948, Beaumont, 77704-3948. Tel: 409-924-4314.

Tribunal—Mailing Address: Catholic Pastoral Center, P.O. Box 3948, Beaumont, 77704-3948. Tel: 409-924-4319; Fax: 409-838-4511.

Judicial Vicar—Very Rev. LUONG QUANG TRAN, J.C.L.

Diocesan Judges—Very Rev. LUONG QUANG TRAN, J.C.L., Judicial Vicar; Rev. Msgr. KENNETH R. GREIG; Rev. STEVEN L. LEGER, S.T.L., J.C.L.; Very Rev. JOSEPH KHANH HO, S.T.L., J.C.L.; Revs. MARTIN LESTER NELSON, J.C.L., (Retired); KEVIN BADEAUX, J.C.L.; ERNIE CARPIO, J.C.L.; Sr. ESTHER DUNEGAN, I.W.B.S., J.C.L.

Promoter of Justice—Rev. Msgr. MICHAEL A. JAMAIL, J.C.D., Ed.D., V.G.

Defenders of Bond—Rev. Msgr. MICHAEL A. JAMAIL, J.C.D., Ed.D., V.G.; MR. ROBERT FLUMMERFELT, J.C.L.; Sr. MARGARET RAMSDEN, J.C.L.

Assessor—Rev. FRANK MAIDA.

Psychologist for the Tribunal—Rev. Msgr. MICHAEL A. JAMAIL, J.C.D., Ed.D., V.G.

Court Expert—MRS. BECKY RICHARDS, M.S.L.P.C.

Secretary-Notary—MARILYN PRICE.

Victim Assistance Coordinator—MRS. BECKY RICHARD, M.S., L.P.C., Mailing Address: 2780 Eastex Freeway, Beaumont, 77703. Tel: 409-924-4400, Ext. 4433; Fax: 409-832-0145; Email: brichard@catholiccharitiesbmt.org.

Diocesan Departments

Apostleship of the Sea—Rev. SINCLAIR OUBRE, J.C.L., Diocesan Dir., 1500 Jefferson Dr., Port Arthur, 77642. Tel: 409-749-0171; Fax: 409-985-5945; Email: aos-beaumont@dioceseofbmt.org.

Office of Evangelization & Catechesis—Mailing Address: P.O. Box 3948, Beaumont, 77704-3948. Tel: 409-924-4323; Fax: 409-838-4511. BRYAN REISING, Dir.

Catholic Schools—MARCIA STEVENS, Supt., Mailing Address: P.O. Box 3948, Beaumont, 77704-3948. Tel: 409-924-4322; Fax: 409-838-4511.

Office of Stewardship & Communications—LETTY LANZA, Dir., P.O. Box 3948, Beaumont, 77704-3948. Tel: 409-924-4302; Fax: 409-838-4511.

East Texas Catholic Newspaper—710 Archie St., Beaumont, 77701-2802. Tel: 409-924-4350; Fax: 409-838-4511. MR. WALKER WOODING, Editor.

Diaconate, Permanent Diaconate—Rev. Msgr. JEREMIAH J. MCGRATH, D.Min., Vicar, Mailing Address: St. Anthony Cathedral Basilica, P.O. Box 3309, Beaumont, 77704-3309. Tel: 409-833-6433; Fax: 409-833-6688; Deacon STEVE OBERNUEFEMANN, Dir., 210 Thornridge, Bridge City, 77611-2355. Tel: 409-626-4029; Fax: 409-838-4511.

Diaconate Formation—Mailing Address: St. Francis of Assisi Church, 4300 Meeks Dr., Orange, 77632-4508. Tel: 409-883-9153; Fax: 409-883-9154. Rev. SINCLAIR OUBRE, J.C.L., Dir.

Multi-Parish Accounting—CATHY FAVRE, Dir., Mailing Address: P.O. Box 3948, Beaumont, 77704-3948. Tel: 409-924-4335.

Propagation of the Faith: Mission CoopLETTY LANZA, Mailing Address: P.O. Box 3948, Beaumont, 77704-3948. Tel: 409-924-4302; Fax: 409-838-4511.

Hispanic Ministry—JESUS ABREGO, Dir., Mailing Address: P.O. Box 3948, Beaumont, 77704-3948. Tel: 409-924-4331; Fax: 409-838-4511.

African American Ministry—LINDA DUHON-LACOUR, Dir., Mailing Address: P.O. Box 3948, Beaumont, 77704-3948. Tel: 409-924-4333; Fax: 409-838-4511.

Worship; Liturgical Commission; Diocesan Choir—ROSALIND SANCHEZ, M.A., Dir., Mailing Address: P.O. Box 3948, Beaumont, 77704-3948. Tel: 409-924-4321; Fax: 409-838-4511.

Principal Master of Episcopal Ceremonies—Deacon DAVID LUTHER, 172 Dale St., Jasper, 75951. Tel: 409-384-1521.

Family Life Ministry—JEROME CABEEN, Dir., Mailing Address: P.O. Box 3948, Beaumont, 77704-3948. Tel: 409-924-4390; Fax: 409-838-4511.

Criminal Justice Ministry—Deacon THOMAS M. EWING JR., Dir., Mailing Address: P.O. Box 3948, Beaumont, 77704-3948. Tel: 409-924-4329; Fax: 409-838-4511.

Director of Seminarians—Rev. CONSTANTINO BARRERA, Mailing Address: P.O. Box 3948, Beaumont, 77704-3948. Tel: 409-924-4361.

Vocations—Rev. CONSTANTINO BARRERA, Mailing Address: P.O. Box 3948, Beaumont, 77704-3948. Tel: 409-924-4361.

Office of Youth Ministry—MELANIE EHRLICH, Dir., Mailing Address: P.O. Box 3948, Beaumont, 77704-3948. Tel: 409-924-4362; Fax: 409-838-4511.

Ecumenical Interreligious Affairs Officer—Rev. Msgr. JEREMIAH J. MCGRATH, D.Min., Mailing Address: St. Anthony Cathedral Basilica, P.O. Box 3309, Beaumont, 77704-3309. Tel: 409-833-6433; Fax: 409-833-6688.

Committees, Boards, Commissions

Diocesan Review Board—Mailing Address: P.O. Box 3948, Beaumont, 77704-3948. MRS. MICHELE SMITH, J.D., Chair.

Diocesan African American Commission—MR. WILLIAM JAMES CARTER, Chm., Mailing Address: P.O. Box 3948, Beaumont, 77704-3948. Tel: 409-924-4325; Fax: 409-838-4511.

Diocesan Building Commission—MR. HAMIL CUPERO JR., Chm., Mailing Address: P.O. Box 3948, Beaumont, 77704. Tel: 409-924-4313.

Catholic Committee on Scouting—Mailing Address: 7001 Kelliwood Dr., Port Arthur, 77642. Tel: 409-727-3064. MR. MIKE SIGUR, Chm.

Catholic Daughters of America—Mailing Address: 1400 15th St., Orange, 77630. Tel: 409-883-4021. JANETTE BOEHME, Pres., Orange Chapter.

Catholic Women, Council of—MELINDA TURTLEDOVE, Pres., Mailing Address: P.O. Box 85, Hampshire, 77622. Tel: 409-828-0277; Rev. MARTIN LESTER NELSON, J.C.L., Moderator, (Retired).

Charismatic Prayer Renewal—Rev. Msgr. WILLIAM MANGER, M.Ed., E.V., Group Liaison, Mailing Address: St. Anne Church, P.O. Box 3429, Beaumont, 77704-3429.

Commission for Continuing Education of Clergy & Religious—Rev. JAMES D. MCCLINTOCK, Mailing Address: St. Mary Church, 9894 Gilbert Rd., Beaumont, 77705-8878. Tel: 409-794-2548; Fax: 409-794-3411.

R.C.I.A. Commission—Mailing Address: P.O. Box 3948, Beaumont, 77704-3948. Tel: 409-924-4323; Fax: 409-838-4511. BRYAN REISING, Chm.

Diocesan School Board—7880 Cobblestone Ct., Beaumont, 77713. Tel: 409-892-1274; Cell: 409-273-1518; Email: noelorl@aol.com. ELISE FULTON-SMITH, Chm.

Vocation Board—Mailing Address: P.O. Box 3429, Beaumont, 77704-3948. Tel: 409-924-4363. Rev. CONSTANTINO BARRERA, Vocations Dir.

CLERGY, PARISHES, MISSIONS AND PAROCHIAL SCHOOLS

CITY OF BEAUMONT

(JEFFERSON COUNTY)

1—ST. ANTHONY CATHEDRAL BASILICA (1879)
700 Jefferson St., 77704-3309. Tel: 409-833-6433; Email: support@stanthonycathedral.org; Web: www.stanthonycathedralbasilica.org. P.O. Box 3309, 77704-3309. Rev. Msgr. Jeremiah J. McGrath, D.Min.; Revs. Joseph Kattakkara, C.M.I., In Res.; Jaison Jacob, C.M.I., In Res.; Deacons Flint Barboza, Pastoral Assoc.; Laurence David.
School—St. Anthony Cathedral Basilica School, (Grades PreK-8), 850 Forsythe, 77701-2890. Tel: 409-832-3486; Fax: 409-838-9051; Email: frunnels@sacbstx.org; Web: www.sacbstx.org. Felicia Runnels, Prin. Lay Teachers 18; Students 190.
Catechesis Religious Program—Email: edu@stanthonycathedral.org. Yazmin Mani, D.R.E. Students 120.

2—ST. ANNE (1937)
2715 Calder Ave., 77704. Tel: 409-832-9963; Fax: 409-832-9964; Email: stannechurch@gtbizclass.com; Web: www.stannebmt.org. P.O. Box 3429, 77704-3429. Rev. Msgr. William Manger, M.Ed., E.V.; Rev. Ernie Carpio, J.C.L., Parochial Vicar; Rev. Msgr. Michael A. Jamail, J.C.D., Ed.D., V.G., In Res.; Deacons Clint Elkins; George Wood; Ben Yett.
School—St. Anne School, (Grades PreK-8), 375 N. 11th St., 77702-1834. Tel: 409-832-5939; Email: akiker@sasbmt.com; Web: www.sasbmt.com. Alison Kiker, Prin.; Anna Wallace, Librarian. (Formerly St. Anne Tri-Parish School) Lay Teachers 42; Students 568.
Catechesis Religious Program—Tel: 409-832-8107; Fax: 409-832-5099; Email: drestanne@gtbizclass.com. Kristine Knowles, D.R.E. Students 131.

3—BLESSED SACRAMENT (1915) [CEM] (African American)
780 Porter St., 77701-7198. Tel: 409-833-6089; Email: bsccatholic@gmail.com; Email: pofoha@dobcentral.org. Rev. Paul Ofoha, M.S.P.
Catechesis Religious Program—Students 16.

4—CRISTO REY (1951) (Hispanic)
767 Ave. A, 77701. Tel: 409-835-7788; Email: lurriza@dobcentral.org. Rev. Luis Urriza, O.S.A.
Catechesis Religious Program—Tel: 409-835-7240. Students 157.

5—ST. JOSEPH (1905) (Italian—Vietnamese)
1115 Orange St., 77701-4392. Tel: 409-835-5662; Email: ltran0101@yahoo.com; Email: kbui@dobcentral.ort. Rev. Khue Si Bui.
Catechesis Religious Program—Students 91.

6—ST. JUDE THADDEUS (1978)
6825 Gladys, 77706-3239. Tel: 409-866-5088; Email: stjude@stjudebmt.org; Web: www.stjudebmt.org. Rev. Thomas E. Phelan, M.S.W.; Deacons Randy Cashiola; Frank Maida; Gordon Cabra, (Retired).
Catechesis Religious Program—Students 427.

7—OUR LADY OF THE ASSUMPTION (1951)
4445 Ave. A, 77705-4998. Tel: 409-835-5343; Fax: 409-835-5344; Email: oloa4445@gt.rr.com; Email: apaulose@dobcentral.org; Web: www.assumptionbmt.org. Rev. Antony Paulose, C.M.I.; Deacon Harry Davis.
Catechesis Religious Program—Students 52.

8—OUR MOTHER OF MERCY (1937) (African American)
3390 Sarah St., 77705-3098. Tel: 409-842-5533; Fax: 409-842-4710; Email: parish@omomcc.org; Email: neffiong@dobcentral.org; Web: www.omomcc.org. Rev. Noel Effiong, M.S.P.
Catechesis Religious Program—Tel: 409-842-0112. Students 98.

9—ST. PIUS X (1954)
5075 Bigner Rd., 77708-5299. Tel: 409-892-3316; Email: stpiusxbmt@yahoo.com. Rev. Augustine Wall, S.V.D.; Deacon Anthony Goudeau.
Catechesis Religious Program—Tel: 409-892-6052. Students 70.

OUTSIDE THE CITY OF BEAUMONT

AMES, LIBERTY CO., OUR MOTHER OF MERCY (1903) [CEM] (African American)
101 Donatto St., Ames, 77575. Email: ourmotherofmercyames@yahoo.com. Mailing Address: P.O. Box 264, Liberty, 77575-0264. Tel: 936-336-3004; Fax: 936-336-5955. Rev. Ayo Emmanuel Efodigbue, M.S.P.
Catechesis Religious Program—Carolyn Victorian, D.R.E. Students 16.

ANAHUAC, CHAMBERS CO., OUR LADY OF LIGHT (1938)
Rev. Stephen McCrate, S.T.L.; Deacon Steve McGaha.
Res.: 2207 S. Main, Anahuac, 77514.
Tel: 409-267-3158; Fax: 409-267-4047; Email: g.bialowas@yahoo.com.
Catechesis Religious Program—Students 178.

BRIDGE CITY, ORANGE CO., ST. HENRY (1948)
475 W. Roundbunch Rd., Bridge City, 77611-0427. Tel: 409-735-2422; Email: office@sthenrybctx.org. Mailing Address: P.O. Box 427, Bridge City, 77611-0427. Rev. Steven L. Leger, S.T.L., J.C.L.; Deacon Steve Obernuefemann.
Catechesis Religious Program—Tel: 409-735-8642. Students 322.

BUNA, JASPER CO., ST. FRANCIS OF ASSISI MISSION (1968-2017) Closed. For inquirers about mission records, contact St. Maurice Church, Mauriceville, TX.

CHEEK, JEFFERSON CO., ST. MARTIN DE PORRES MISSION (1972) (African American)
7467 Boyt Rd., 77705. Tel: 409-794-2548; Fax: 409-794-3411; Email: stmarycc@hotmail.com. Mailing Address: 9894 Gilbert, 77705. Rev. James D. McClintock; Deacons Allan Santos; Mirley Esprit.
Catechesis Religious Program— (with St. Mary, Fannett) Tel: 409-794-1725.

CHINA, JEFFERSON CO., OUR LADY OF SORROWS (1918)
245 W. Hwy. 90, China, 77613. Tel: 409-752-3571; Fax: 409-752-5134; Email: olos1@sbcglobal.net; Web: ourladyofsorrowschina.com. P.O. Box 38, China, 77613-0038. Very Rev. Luong Quang Tran, J.C.L.
Catechesis Religious Program—Students 65.

CLEVELAND, LIBERTY CO., ST. MARY (1950)
702 E. Houston St., Cleveland, 77327.
Tel: 281-592-2985; Email: stmarycleveland01@att.net; Email: valexius@dobcentral.org; Web: www.stmarysclevelandtx.com. P.O. Box 816, Cleveland, 77328-0816. Revs. Vincent Alexius, S.V.D.; Joseph Jessing, S.V.D., Parochial Vicar; Deacons David Mueller; Larry Terrell.
Catechesis Religious Program—Bridgette McMillan, R.C.I.A.; Juan Rodriguez, R.C.I.A.; Ivette Ramirez, St. Mary's K-12 Religious Dept. Students 106.

CORRIGAN, POLK CO., ST. MARTIN DE PORRES MISSION (1971) (Hispanic)
104 Gossett Rd., Corrigan, 75939. Tel: 936-967-8385; Fax: 936-967-4657; Email: viavitela@gmail.com; Email: stjoe@eastex.net. Mailing Address: P.O. Box 930, Livingston, 77351-0930. Rev. Tarsisius Puling, S.V.D.
Catechesis Religious Program—P.O. Box 275, Moscow, 75960-0275. Tel: 936-581-3188. Mrs. Sylvia Vitela, D.R.E. Students 60.

DAYTON, LIBERTY CO., ST. JOSEPH THE WORKER (1945) [CEM]
804 S. Cleveland, Dayton, 77535. Tel: (936) 258-5735 ; Email: officestjoseph@comcast.net; Email: rzawadzki@dobcentral.org. P.O. Box 640, Dayton, 77535-0640. Rev. Richard Zawadzki, S.V.D.
Catechesis Religious Program—Students 316.

EASTGATE, LIBERTY CO., ST. ANNE MISSION (1918)
804 S. Cleveland, Dayton, 77535-0640.
Tel: 936-258-5735; Email: officestjoseph@comcast.net; Email: stjosephdayton@comcast.net; Email: rzawadzki@doibcentral.org. P.O. Box 640, Dayton, 77535-0640. Rev. Richard Zawadzki, S.V.D.

FANNETT, JEFFERSON CO., ST. MARY (1964) Formerly St. Mary, Hamshire (1899). Damaged by Hurricane Harvey 09/2017.
9894 Gilbert Rd., 77705-8878. Tel: 409-794-2548; Email: jmcclintock@dobcentral.org; Email: stmarycc@hotmail.com; Web: www.stmaryandstmartin.com. Rev. James D. McClintock; Deacons Allan Santos; Mirley Esprit.
Catechesis Religious Program—9894 Gilbert Rd., 77705-8878. Tel: 409-794-1725. Debbie Peltier, D.R.E. Students 266.

GROVES, JEFFERSON CO.

1—IMMACULATE CONCEPTION, Merged with St. Peter, Groves to form Immaculate Conception-St. Peter, Groves.

2—IMMACULATE CONCEPTION-ST. PETER (1928)
6250 Washington, Groves, 77619. Tel: 409-962-0255; Email: icc-groves@gtbizclass.com; Email:

jcoon@dobcentral.org. Rev. J.C. Coon; Deacons Willie Posey; Keith Fontenot.
Catechesis Religious Program—Students 57.
3—ST. PETER THE APOSTLE (1972) Merged with Immaculate Conception Church, Groves to form Immaculate Conception-St. Peters Church.
JASPER, JASPER CO., ST. MICHAEL (1952)
2898 U.S. Hwy. 190 W., Jasper, 75951.
Tel: 409-384-2447; Fax: 409-384-2447; Email: stmrectory@gmail.com; Email: rfoshage@dobcentral.org. P.O. Box 239, Jasper, 75951-0239. Very Rev. Ronald B. Foshage, M.S., E.V.; Deacons David Luther; William (Bill) Lawrence; Glen Hebert.
Catechesis Religious Program—Regina Lawrence, D.R.E. Students 200.
Mission—Our Lady of LaSalette.
Station—Toledo Village, Jasper.
LIBERTY, LIBERTY CO., IMMACULATE CONCEPTION (1756) [CEM]
411 Milam, Liberty, 77575-4730. Tel: 936-336-7267; Email: iccliberty@comcast.net; Web: www.icclibertytx.org. Rev. Andy Dinh Vu, S.V.D.
Catechesis Religious Program—Email: iccdre@comcast.net. Patty Lucas, D.R.E. Students 315.
LIVINGSTON, POLK CO., ST. JOSEPH (1970)
2590 U.S. Hwy. 190 W., Livingston, 77351-0930.
Tel: 936-967-8385; Email: tpuling@dobcentral.org; Email: stjoe@eastex.net; Web: stjoseph-livingston-tx.org. P.O. BOX 930, Livingston, 77351. Rev. Tarsisius Puling, S.V.D.; Jeanette Ford, Sec.
Catechesis Religious Program—Tel: 936-646-4685. Rosario Mendez, D.R.E. Students 296.
LUMBERTON, HARDIN CO., INFANT JESUS (1948)
243 S. LHS Dr., Lumberton, 77657. Web: www.infantjesuscclumberton.com. Mailing Address: P.O. Box 8180, Lumberton, 77657-0180.
Tel: 409-755-1734; Email: infantjesus@gt.twcbc.com. Revs. Andrew R. Moore, M.Div.; Duc Duong; Deacons L.D. Keen; Garry LeBlanc; Bruce Grimes.
Catechesis Religious Program—Stacy Keen, D.R.E. Students 240.
MAURICEVILLE, ORANGE CO., ST. MAURICE (1966)
9079 Hwy. 62 N., Orange, 77632. Tel: 409-745-4060; Email: Stmaurice2@aol.com. P.O. Box 940, Mauriceville, 77626-0940. Rev. Delphyn J. Meeks.
Catechesis Religious Program—Students 30.
MONT BELVIEU, CHAMBERS CO., HOLY TRINITY (2003)
Church: 3515 Trinity Dr., Mont Belvieu, 77580-0290. Web: www.htcc-mb.org. Mailing Address: P.O. Box 290, Mont Belvieu, 77580-0290. Tel: 281-576-4990; Email: office@htcc-mb.org. Very Rev. Joseph Khanh Ho, S.T.L., J.C.L.; Deacon Eugene R. LeBlanc.
Catechesis Religious Program—Students 198.
NEDERLAND, JEFFERSON CO., ST. CHARLES BORROMEO (1923)
211 Hardy Ave., Nederland, 77627-7326.
Tel: 409-722-3413; Email: stcharlesnederland@gmail.com; Web: www.stcharlesnederland.org. 130 Hardy Ave., Nederland, 77627-7326. Revs. John Hughes, M.Div.; Eathan Oakes, Parochial Vicar; Deacon Chris Penning, D.O.
Catechesis Religious Program—Tel: 409-722-0421; Fax: 409-722-5848. Students 613.
ORANGE, ORANGE CO.
1—ST. FRANCIS OF ASSISI (1978)
4300 Meeks Dr., Orange, 77632-4508.
Tel: 409-833-9153; Fax: 409-883-9154; Email: soubre@dobcentral.org; Web: stfrancisorangetx.org. Rev. Sinclair Oubre, J.C.L.; Deacons Keith Hebert; Hector Maldonado; Tommy Ewing.
Catechesis Religious Program—Tel: 409-883-8232. Students 202.
2—ST. MARY (1880) [CEM]
912 W. Cherry St., Orange, 77630-5017.
Tel: 409- 883-2883; Email: jdaleo@dobcentral.org; Email: stmary@gtbizclass.com; Web: www.stmaryorange.org. Very Rev. Joseph P. Daleo, E.V.; Deacons Melvin Payne; David Bonneaux.
School—St. Mary School, (Grades PreK-8), 2600 Bob Hall Rd., Orange, 77630-2418. Tel: 409-883-8913; Fax: 409-883-0827; Email: principal@stmaryschooltx.org; Web: www.stmaryschooltx.org. Dr. Cynthia Jackson, Prin. Lay Teachers 18; Students 103.
Catechesis Religious Program—Tel: 409-886-0841; Fax: 409-886-0841; Email: debra@stmaryorange.org. Students 46.
3—ST. THERESE (1924) (African American)
1409 N. Sixth St., Orange, 77630-3927.
Tel: 409-883-3783; Email: sttherese1350@yahoo.com; Web: stthereseorangetx.org. Rev. Donatus Mgbeajuo, M.S.P.; Deacon Julian Richard.
Catechesis Religious Program—Students 9.
ORANGEFIELD, ORANGE CO., ST. HELEN (1938)
8105 FM 1442, Orange, 77630. Tel: 409-735-2200; Email: sthelenorange@gmail.com. Rev. Michael A. Strother, M.Div.
Catechesis Religious Program—Tel: 409-988-9920. Sheila Babin, D.R.E. Students 88.
PORT ARTHUR, JEFFERSON CO.
1—ST. CATHERINE OF SIENA (1954)
3706 Woodrow Dr., Port Arthur, 77642-2320.
Tel: 409-962-5715; Email: afondren@stccpa.com; Email: rfaller@dobcentral.org; Web: www.stccpa.com. Rev. Rodel Faller.
School—St. Catherine of Siena School, (Grades PreK-8), Tel: (409) 962-3011; Email: rfaller@dobcentral.org; Web: stcats.org. Renee Tolin, Prin. Lay Teachers 18; Students 174.
Catechesis Religious Program—Kim Tran, D.R.E. Students 37.
2—ST. JAMES (1929)
3617 Gulfway Dr., Port Arthur, 77642-3675.
Tel: 409-985-8865; Email: stjamespa39@yahoo.com. Rev. David A. Edwards, M.Div.; Deacon John Janise.
Catechesis Religious Program—
3—ST. JOHN (1951) (African American), Merged with Sacred Heart-St. Mary Church to form Sacred Heart Church, Port Arthur.
4—ST. JOSEPH (1951)
4600 Procter St., Port Arthur, 77642-1365.
Tel: 409-982-6409; Email: kbadeaux@dobcentral.org; Email: stjochurch@att.net; Web: www.stjosephportarthur.org. Rev. Kevin Badeaux, J.C.L.; Deacon Luis Javier Magana.
5—ST. MARY (1903) (African American), Merged with Sacred Heart, Port Arthur in 2006 to form Sacred Heart-St. Mary Parish, Port Arthur.
6—OUR LADY OF GUADALUPE (1927) (Hispanic)
3648 S. Sgt. Lucian Adams Dr., Port Arthur, 77642-6403. Tel: 409-962-6777; Fax: 409-963-0669; Email: olgsecretary@outlook.com; Email: olgchurchpa@gmail.com; Web: www.olg-pa.org. Rev. Urbano Saenz-Ramirez, O.S.A.; Tatiana Owens, D.R.E.; Kelly DelaRosa, Youth Min.; Maria Ortiz, Music Min.; Virginia Espinola, Sec.
Catechesis Religious Program—3648 S. Sgt. Lucian Adams Dr., Port Arthur, 77642. Tatiana Owens, D.R.E. Students 480.
7—QUEEN OF VIETNAM (1977) (Vietnamese)
801 Ninth Ave., Port Arthur, 77642-3329.
Tel: 409-983-7676; Fax: 409-982-1212; Email: queenofvnchurch@hotmail.com. Revs. Kha Tran; Tuyen Tran, Parochial Vicar.
Catechesis Religious Program—
Convent—1148 Ninth Ave., Port Arthur, 77642.
Tel: 409-985-5102; Fax: 409-985-5102; Email: queenofvnchurch@hotmail.com. Sr. Immaculata Nguyen, In Res. Dominican Sisters 4.
8—SACRED HEART (1915) (African American), Merged with St. Mary, Port Arthur in 2006 to form Sacred Heart-St. Mary Parish, Port Arthur.
9—SACRED HEART CHURCH (2006)
920 Booker T. Washington Ave., Port Arthur, 77640-4923. Tel: 409-985-5104; Fax: 409-982-0106; Email: sacredheart@gt.rr.com; Web: sacredheartstmarypa.org. Anthony Afangide.
Catechesis Religious Program—Brenda Broussard, D.R.E. Students 41.
10—SACRED HEART-ST. MARY PARISH, Merged with St. John, Port Arthur to form Sacred Heart Church, Port Arthur.
11—ST. THERESE THE LITTLE FLOWER OF JESUS (1928)
6412 Garnet Ave., Port Arthur, 77640-1308.
Tel: 409-736-1536; Email: officelittleflower@gtbizclass.com. Very Rev. Rejimon George, C.M.I., E.V.
Catechesis Religious Program—Email: littleflower_dre@yahoo.com. Tara Morgan, D.R.E. Students 106.
PORT NECHES, JEFFERSON CO., ST. ELIZABETH (1922)
2006 Nall St., Port Neches, 77651-3714.
Tel: 409-727-8874; Email: donna@stepncatholic.org; Web: www.stepncatholic.org. Very Rev. Shane Baxter, S.T.L., Pro-V.G.; Rev. Shiju Augustine, Parochial Vicar; Deacon Ivan Watson.
Catechesis Religious Program—Tel: 409-722-5941. Students 392.
RAYWOOD, LIBERTY CO., SACRED HEART (1952) [CEM] (African American)
3730 FM 160 N., Raywood, 77582. Tel: 936-587-4631; Fax: 936-587-1012; Email: sacredheartchurchraywood@yahoo.com. P.O. Box 429, Raywood, 77582. Rev. Ayo Emmanuel Efodigbue, M.S.P.
Catechesis Religious Program—Students 25.
SABINE PASS, JEFFERSON CO., ST. PAUL MISSION (1955-2009) Closed. For inquiries for parish records contact St. John, Port Arthur.
SAM RAYBURN, JASPER CO., ST. RAYMOND MISSION (1970)
FM 1007 at 225, Sam Rayburn, 75951. Mailing Address: P.O. Box 239, Jasper, 75951-0239.
Tel: 409-384-2447; Email: stmrectory@gmail.com. Very Rev. Ronald B. Foshage, M.S., E.V.; Deacons William (Bill) Lawrence; Glen Hebert; David Luther.
SILSBEE, HARDIN CO., ST. MARK THE EVANGELIST (1940)
905 N. Ninth St., Silsbee, 77656. Tel: 409-385-4498; Email: mevangelist@sbcglobal.net. Revs. Andrew R. Moore, M.Div.; Duc Duong; Deacons L.D. Keen; Garry LeBlanc; Bruce Grimes.
Catechesis Religious Program—Students 82.
SOUR LAKE, HARDIN CO., OUR LADY OF VICTORY (1906)
210 W. Barkley, Sour Lake, 77659. Tel: 409-287-3287; Fax: 409-287-3271; Email: olov1@att.net; Email: rwaggoner@dobcentral.org; Web: olovcatholic.com. P.O. Box 1359, Sour Lake, 77659. Rev. Ross E. Waggoner; Deacon Clay Kuykendall.
Catechesis Religious Program—Students 56.
Mission—Holy Spirit Mission, 470 Monroe, Kountze, 77625-5414.
VIDOR, ORANGE CO., OUR LADY OF LOURDES (1938)
1600 N. Main, Vidor, 77662-3014. Tel: 409-769-2865; Fax: 409-769-2865; Email: ourladyoflourdes@sbcglobal.net; Web: olol.weconnect.com. Rev. Paul Sumler; Deacon Stephen Sellers.
Catechesis Religious Program—Tel: 409-769-6758; Email: dreolol@sbcglobal.net. Michael Strother, D.R.E. Students 87.
WINNIE, CHAMBERS CO., ST. LOUIS (1947)
315 W. Buccaneer Dr., Winnie, 77665-9711.
Tel: 409-296-4200;
Tel: 281-635-1857 (Emergency Only);
Fax: 409-296-9715; Email: slccsec@gmail.com. Rev. Stephen McCrate, S.T.L.; Deacon Steve McGaha; Mrs. Karen Bolmanskie, Sec.
Catechesis Religious Program—Michelle Crone, D.R.E. Students 281.
WOODVILLE, TYLER CO., OUR LADY OF THE PINES (1950)
1601 Pine St., Woodville, 75979. Mailing Address: P.O. Box 2029, Woodville, 75979-2029.
Tel: 409-283-5367; Email: frossi@dobcentral.org; Email: olopcc@sbcglobal.net; Web: www.ourladyofthepinescatholicchurch.com. Rev. Msgr. Frank H. Rossi.
Catechesis Religious Program—Diane Sanderson, D.R.E. Students 63.

Chaplains of Public Institutions

BEAUMONT. *Baptist Hospital*. Revs. Donatus Mgbeajuo, M.S.P., Chap., Paul Ofoha, M.S.P., Chap.
JEFFERSON COUNTY. *Convalescent Home Ministry*. Revs. Jaison Jacob, C.M.I., Chap., Joseph Kattakkara, C.M.I.

Prisons

LIVINGSTON. *Beaumont - Federal Correctional Complex*. Deacon Thomas M. Ewing Jr.
Livingston: Polunsky Unit - Death Row.

On Duty Outside the Diocese:
Rev.—
Arce, Neil A., On Leave.

Retired:
Rev. Msgrs.—
Culotta, Salvador J., (Retired)
Dempsey, James, (Retired)
Greig, Kenneth, (Retired)
Malain, Dan, D.Min., (Retired)
Vanderholt, James, D.Min., (Retired)
Revs.—
Beck, R. Patrick, (Retired)
Conroy, Francis X., (Retired)
Iglesias, Clement, (Retired)
Mudd, Earl, (Retired)
Nelson, Martin Lester, J.C.L., (Retired)
Placette, David D., (Retired).

Permanent Deacons:
Arceneaux, Jude, (Retired)
Barboza, Flint, St. Anthony Cathedral Basilica, Beaumont
Bonneaux, David, St. Mary, Orange
Broussard, Dallas, (Retired)
Cabra, Gordon, (Retired)
Cashiola, Randy, St. Jude Thaddeus, Beaumont
Cockburn, Rudy, (Retired)
David, Laurence, St. Anthony Cathedral Basilica, Beaumont
Davis, Harry, (Retired), Our Lady of the Assumption, Beaumont
Dubois, Harvey, (Retired)
Elkins, Clint, St. Anne, Beaumont
Espirit, Mirley, St. Mary, Fannett; St. Martin de Porres, Cheek
Ewing, Thomas M. Jr., St. Francis of Assisi, Orange; Beaumont Federal Correctional Complex; Dir. Office of Criminal Justice Ministry
Fontenot, Keith, Immaculate Conception St. Peter Church, Groves
Goudeau, Anthony, St. Pius X, Beaumont
Griffin, Marc, (Currently on loan to Diocese of Austin)

Grimes, Bruce, Infant Jesus, Lumberton; St. Mark, Silsbee
Hebert, Glen, St. Michael Church, Jasper TX; Our Lady of LaSalette, Kirbyville; St. Raymond, Sam Rayburn
Hebert, Keith, St. Francis of Assisi, Orange
Istre, Timothy, (Living within the Diocese of Fort Worth)
Jannise, John, St. James, Port Arthur
Keen, L. D., Infant Jesus, Lumberton; St. Mark, Silsbee
Kenny, Hazen, (Retired)
Kuykendall, Clay, Our Lady of Victory, Sour Lake
Lawrence, William (Bill), St. Michael, Jasper; Our Lady of La Salette, Kirbyville; St. Raymond, Sam Rayburn
LeBlanc, E. R., (Retired)
LeBlanc, Garry, Infant Jesus, Lumberton; St. Mark, Silsbee
Luther, David, Prin. Master Episcopal Ceremonies, St. Michael, Jasper; Our Lady of LaSalette, Kirbyville; St. Raymond, Sam Rayburn
Magana, Luis Javier, St. Joseph, Port Arthur
Maida, Frank, St. Jude Thaddeus, Beaumont
Maldonado, Hector, St. Francis of Assisi, Orange
Marion, Mike, Medical Leave
McGaha, Steve, St. Louis Church, Winnie
Mueller, David, St. Mary, Cleveland
Obernuefemann, Steve, St. Henry, Bridge City; Dir. Permanent Diaconate
Payne, Melvin, St. Mary, Orange
Penning, Chris, D.O., St. Charles, Nederland
Posey, Willie, Immaculate Conception St. Peter Church, Groves
Richard, Julian, Medical Leave
Santos, Allan, (Retired), St. Mary, Fannett
Scheurich, Joseph, (Retired)
Sellers, Stephen, Our Lady of Lourdes, Vidor
Terrell, Larry, St. Mary, Cleveland, Prison/Jail Ministry
Watson, Ivan, St. Elizabeth, Port Neches
Wood, George, St. Anne, Beaumont
Yett, Ben, St. Anne Church, Beaumont.

INSTITUTIONS LOCATED IN DIOCESE

[A] HIGH SCHOOLS, DIOCESAN

BEAUMONT. *Monsignor Kelly Catholic High School*, 5950 Kelly Dr., 77707. Tel: 409-866-2351; Fax: 409-866-0917; Email: rbemis@mkchs.com; Email: rbemis@dobcentral.org; Web: www.mkchs.com. Mr. Roger Bemis, Prin.; Rev. Msgr. Dan Malain, D.Min., Chap., (Retired); Nina Felix, Librarian. Lay Teachers 33; Students 450.

[B] GENERAL HOSPITALS

BEAUMONT. *CHRISTUS Southeast Texas Health System - St. Elizabeth* (1962) 2830 Calder Ave., 77726. Tel: 409-236-7171, Ext. 7107; Fax: 409-236-8191; Email: daniel.ford@christushealth.org; Email: deborah.tucker@christushealth.org; Web: www.christushospital.org. P.O. Box 5405, 77726-5405. Mr. Paul Trevino, C.E.O.; Rev. Emmanuel Chikezie, (Nigeria) Chap. Operated by CHRISTUS Southeast Texas. Bed Capacity 437; Patients Asst Anual. 226,827; Tot Asst. Annually 351,343; Total Staff 1,620.

JASPER. *CHRISTUS Southeast Texas Health System - Jasper Memorial*, 1275 Marvin Hancock Dr., Jasper, 75951. Tel: 409-384-5461; Fax: 409-384-1829. Mr. Paul Trevino, C.E.O. Operated by CHRISTUS Southeast Texas - Jasper Memorial. Bed Capacity 59; Patients Asst Anual. 68,086; Tot Asst. Annually 351,343; Total Staff 167.

PORT ARTHUR. *CHRISTUS Southeast Texas Health System - St. Mary* (1930) 3600 Gates Blvd., Port Arthur, 77643. Tel: 409-985-7431, Ext. 5100; Fax: 409-989-1033; Email: daniel.ford@christushealth.org; Email: deborah.tucker@christushealth.org; Web: www.christushospital.org. P.O. Box 3696, 77643. Mr. Paul Trevino, CEO & Pres.; Rev. Leonard Ogbonna, (Nigeria) Chap. Operated by CHRISTUS Southeast Texas Health System Bed Capacity 227; Patients Asst Anual. 56,430; Tot Asst. Annually 351,343; Total Staff 192.

[C] MONASTERIES AND RESIDENCES OF PRIESTS AND BROTHERS

BEAUMONT. *Holy Cross Monastery*, 9920 N. Major Dr., 77713-7618. Tel: 409-899-3554; Fax: 409-899-3558; Email: porter@holycrossmonks.org; Web: www.holycrossmonks.org. Bro. Michael Gallagher, Vice Pres. Benedictine Monks.

[D] NEWMAN CENTERS

BEAUMONT. *Lamar University-Catholic Student Center*, 1010 E. Virginia, 77704. Mailing Address: P.O. Box 3948, 77704-3948. Tel: 409-924-4360; Email: vocationsandcampus@dioceseofbmt.org; Web: www.dioceseofbmt.org. Rev. Constantino Barrera, Dir.

[E] RETREAT CENTERS

BEAUMONT. *Holy Family Retreat Center*, 9920 N. Major Dr., 77713-7618. Tel: 409-899-5617; Email: retreatcenter@dioceseofbmt.org. Rev. Peter C. Funk, Dir.; Bro. Michael Gallagher, Asst. Dir. Destroyed by Hurricane Harvey - Will be rebuilt.

[F] SOCIAL AGENCIES - Catholic Charities of Southeast Texas

BEAUMONT. *Catholic Charities of Southeast Texas*, 2780 Eastex Fwy., 77703-4617. Mrs. Carolyn R. Fernandez, CEO. Tot Asst. Annually 5,186; Total Staff 17.

Counseling Services, 2780 Eastex Fwy., 77703-4617. Tel: 409-924-4410; Fax: 409-832-0145. Randi Fertitta, M.S., L.P.C., L.P.A., Vice Pres. Tot Asst. Annually 103; Total Staff 1.

Elijah's Place (2003) Children's grief support group. 2780 Eastex Fwy., 77703. Tel: 409-924-4433; Fax: 409-832-0145. Mrs. Becky Richard, M.S., L.P.C., Prog. Mgr. Tot Asst. Annually 82; Staff 5.

Hospitality Center, 3959 Gulfway Dr., Port Arthur, 77642. Tel: 888-982-4842; Tel: 404-924-4406; Fax: 409-983-7145; Email: cvara@catholiccharitiesbmt.org; Web: www.catholiccharitiesbmt.org. 2780 Eastex Freeway, 77703. Christina V. Green, Dir. Tot Asst. Annually 2,103; Total Staff 2; Meals Served 44,574.

Immigration Services, 2780 Eastex Fwy., 77703-4617. Tel: 409-924-4413; Fax: 409-832-0145. Alma Garza-Cruz, Dir. Tot Asst. Annually 1,145; Total Staff 4.

Parish Social Ministry, 2780 Eastex Fwy., 77703-4617. Tel: 409-924-4415; Fax: 409-832-0145. Coquese Williams, Dir. Total Staff 1.

Disaster Response, 2780 Eastex Fwy., 77703-4617. Tel: 409-924-4426; Email: crobertson@catholiccharitiesbmt.org; Web: www.catholiccharitiesbmt.org. Christopher Robertson, Prog. Coord., Tel: 409-924-4426; Fax: 409-832-0145. Tot Asst. Annually 1,419; Total Staff 3.

Asset Building Case Management, 2780 Eastex Fwy., 77703-4617. Tel: 409-924-4425; Fax: 409-832-0145; Email: mhopson@catholiccharitiesbmt.org. Madison Hopson, Dir. Tot Asst. Annually 362; Total Staff 2.

[G] FOUNDATIONS, ENDOWMENTS AND TRUSTS

BEAUMONT. *St. Anthony School Foundation, Inc.*, 850 Forsythe, 77701. Tel: 409-832-3486; Fax: 409-813-3337; Email: gdixonpeters@sacbstx.org; Email: rhubbell@sacbstx.org; Web: sacbstx.org. Geneva Dixon-Peters, Admin.; Renee Hubbell, Sec. Volunteers 11.

Catholic Clerical Student Fund, P.O. Box 3948, 77704-3948. Tel: 409-924-4313; Email: svrooman@dioceseofbmt.org. Ms. Renella Primeaux, Coord.

The Catholic Foundation of the Diocese of Beaumont, Inc., P.O. Box 3948, 77704-3948. Tel: 409-924-4313 ; Fax: 409-838-4511; Email: svrooman@dioceseofbmt.org. Sabrina Vrooman, C.P.A., CFO.

CHRISTUS Health Foundation of Southeast Texas, 2830 Calder Ave., 77702. Tel: 409-236-7555; Fax: 409-236-7346; Email: ivy.pate@christushealth.org; Web: www.christussoutheasttexasfoundation.org. Mrs. Ivy Pate, Pres.

Monsignor Kelly Catholic High School Foundation, Inc., 5950 Kelly Dr., 77707. Tel: 409-866-2351; Fax: 409-866-0917; Email: rbemis@mkchs.com; Email: rbemis@dobcentral.org. Donald Jowers, Pres.

ORANGE. *St. Mary School Foundation, Inc.*, 912 Cherry St., Orange, 77630. Tel: 409-883-2883; Fax: 409-883-3547; Email: stmary@gtbizclass.com. Very Rev. Joseph P. Daleo, E.V., Admin.

[H] MISCELLANEOUS

BEAUMONT. *Abiding Place Catholic Charismatic Renewal Center*, 4440 Chaison, 77705. Tel: 409-832-9963; Email: ncl890@aol.com. St. Anne Church, P.O. Box 3429, 77704. Tammy Toups, Dir.

PORT ARTHUR. *Apostleship of the Sea of the United States of America (AOSUSA)* (1976) 1500 Jefferson Dr., Port Arthur, 77642-0646. Tel: 409-985-4545; Fax: 409-985-5945; Email: aosusa@sbcglobal.net; Web: www.aos-usa.org. Capt. George P. McShea Jr., Pres.; Rev. Sinclair Oubre, J.C.L., Trustee; Ms. Doreen M. Badeaux, Sec. Gen.

RELIGIOUS INSTITUTES OF MEN REPRESENTED IN THE DIOCESE

For further details refer to the corresponding bracketed number in the Religious Institutes of Men or Women section.

[0140]—*The Augustinians* (Prov. of Castile, Spain)—O.S.A.
[]—*The Augustinians* (Prov. of Nigeria)—O.S.A.
[]—*Benedictine Monks*—O.S.B.
[0275]—*Carmelites of Mary Immaculate* (Chanda, India)—C.M.I.
[]—*Carmelites of Mary Immaculate* (Andhra Pradesh, India)—C.M.I.
[]—*Congregation of the Mother of the Redeemer* (Missouri)—C.R.M.
[]—*Franciscan Missionaries of Hope*—F.M.H.
[0720]—*The Missionaries of Our Lady of La Salette* (Prov. of Mary Queen)—M.S.
[]—*Missionary Society of St. Paul*—M.S.P.
[0420]—*Society of the Divine Word* (Southern Province of St. Augustine)—S.V.D.

RELIGIOUS INSTITUTES OF WOMEN REPRESENTED IN THE DIOCESE

[]—*Daughters of Mary Mother of Mercy*—D.M.M.M.
[1070-19]—*Dominican Sisters*—O.P.
[]—*Missionary Carmelites of St. Teresa* (Houston)—C.M.S.T.
[]—*Sisters of the Destitute* (India)—S.D.
[2205]—*Sisters of the Incarnate Word and Blessed Sacrament* (Corpus Christi)—I.W.B.S.
[]—*Vietnamese Dominican Sisters* (Houston)—O.P.

DIOCESAN CEMETERIES

BEAUMONT. *Blessed Sacrament Cemetery*, 780 Porter St., 77701. Tel: 409-833-6089; Fax: 409-833-6091. Rev. Paul Ofoha, M.S.P., Pastor

Hebert Catholic Cemetery-Stivers Lane, c/o Diocese of Beaumont, P.O. Box 3948, 77704-3948. Tel: 409-924-4313; Email: svrooman@dioceseofbmt.org. Sabrina Vrooman, CPA, Admin.

AMES. *Our Mother of Mercy Cemetery*, c/o Our Mother of Mercy Church, P.O. Box 264, Liberty, 77575-0264. Tel: 936-336-3004; Fax: 936-336-5955; Email: ourmotherofmercyames@yahoo.com. Rev. Ayo Emmanuel Efodigbue, M.S.P., Pastor

EASTGATE. *St. Anne Cemetery*, c/o St. Joseph, the Worker Church, P.O. Box 640, Dayton, 77535-0640. Tel: 936-258-5735; Email: stjosephdayton@comcast.net. Rev. Richard Zawadzki, S.V.D., Pastor

LIBERTY. *Immaculate Conception Cemetery*, 411 Milam, Liberty, 77575-4730. Tel: 936-336-7267; Fax: 936-336-9740; Email: iccliberty@comcast.net. Rev. Andy Dinh Vu, S.V.D., Pastor

ORANGE. *St. Mary Cemetery*, c/o St. Mary Church, 912 W. Cherry St., Orange, 77630-5017. Tel: 409-883-7390; Fax: 409-883-3547; Email: stmary@gtbizclass.com. Very Rev. Joseph P. Daleo, E.V., Admin.

PORT ARTHUR. *Calvary Cemetery*, Diocese of Beaumont, P.O. Box 3948, 77704-3948. Tel: 409-924-4313; Fax: 409-722-8312; Fax: 409-838-4511; Email: svrooman@dioceseofbmt.org. Sabrina Vrooman, CPA, Admin.

An asterisk (*) denotes an organization that has established tax-exempt status directly with the IRS and is not covered by the USCCB Group Ruling.

Diocese of Belleville

(Dioecesis Bellevillensis)

Most Reverend

EDWARD K. BRAXTON, PH.D., S.T.D.

Bishop of Belleville; ordained May 13, 1970; appointed Auxiliary Bishop of St. Louis and Titular Bishop of Macomades Rusticiana March 28, 1995; ordained May 17, 1995; appointed Bishop of Lake Charles December 12, 2000; installed February 22, 2001; appointed Bishop of Belleville March 15, 2005; installed June 22, 2005. *Mailing Address: The Chancery, 222 S. Third St., Belleville, IL 62220.* Tel: 618-277-8181.

The Chancery: 222 S. Third St., Belleville, IL 62220-1985. Tel: 618-277-8181; Fax: 618-277-0387.

Web: www.diobelle.org

Email: info@diobelle.org

ERECTED JANUARY 7, 1887.

Square Miles 11,678.

Comprises Illinois south of the northern limits of the Counties of St. Clair, Clinton, Marion, Clay, Richland and Lawrence.

For legal titles of parishes and diocesan institutions, consult the Chancery Office.

STATISTICAL OVERVIEW

Personnel	
Bishop	1
Priests: Diocesan Active in Diocese	48
Priests: Retired, Sick or Absent	40
Number of Diocesan Priests	88
Religious Priests in Diocese	33
Total Priests in Diocese	121
Extern Priests in Diocese	13
Ordinations:	
Diocesan Priests	1
Permanent Deacons in Diocese	43
Total Brothers	4
Total Sisters	107
Parishes	
Parishes	106
With Resident Pastor:	
Resident Diocesan Priests	54
Resident Religious Priests	4
Without Resident Pastor:	
Administered by Priests	46
Administered by Deacons	1
Administered by Religious Women	1
Pastoral Centers	1
Closed Parishes	1
Welfare	
Catholic Hospitals	5
Total Assisted	587,811
Homes for the Aged	2
Total Assisted	231
Day Care Centers	1
Total Assisted	40
Educational	
Diocesan Students in Other Seminaries	5
Total Seminarians	5
High Schools, Diocesan and Parish	3
Total Students	946
Elementary Schools, Diocesan and Parish	26
Total Students	4,537
Catechesis/Religious Education:	
High School Students	272
Elementary Students	4,604
Total Students under Catholic Instruction	10,364
Teachers in the Diocese:	
Lay Teachers	436
Vital Statistics	
Receptions into the Church:	
Infant Baptism Totals	902
Minor Baptism Totals	165
Adult Baptism Totals	81
Received into Full Communion	110
First Communions	1,015
Confirmations	1,050
Marriages:	
Catholic	214
Interfaith	111
Total Marriages	325
Deaths	1,001
Total Catholic Population	90,968
Total Population	841,814

Former Bishops—Most Revs. JOHN JANSSEN, D.D., ord. Nov. 19, 1858; cons. April 25, 1888; died July 2, 1913; HENRY J. ALTHOFF, D.D., ord. July 26, 1902; appt. Dec. 4, 1913; cons. Feb. 24, 1914; died July 3, 1947; ALBERT R. ZUROWESTE, D.D., ord. June 8, 1924; appt. Nov. 29, 1947; cons. Jan. 29, 1948; retired Sept. 3, 1976; died March 28, 1987; WILLIAM M. COSGROVE, D.D., ord. Dec. 18, 1943; Auxiliary Bishop of Cleveland June 19, 1968; cons. Sept. 3, 1968; appt. Bishop of Belleville Sept. 3, 1976; installed Oct. 28, 1976; retired May 19, 1981; died Dec. 11, 1992; JOHN N. WURM, S.T.D., Ph.D., ord. April 3, 1954; Auxiliary Bishop of St. Louis June 25, 1976; cons. Aug. 17, 1976; appt. Bishop of Belleville Sept. 19, 1981; installed Nov. 4, 1981; died April 27, 1984; JAMES P. KELEHER, S.T.D., M.Ed., ord. April 12, 1958; appt. Bishop of Belleville Oct. 23, 1984; cons. Dec. 11, 1984; transferred to Kansas City, KS Sept. 8, 1993; WILTON D. GREGORY, S.L.D., ord. May 9, 1973; appt. Auxiliary Bishop of Chicago and Titular Bishop of Oliva Oct. 31, 1983; cons. Dec. 13, 1983; appt. Bishop of Belleville Dec. 29, 1993; installed Feb. 10, 1994; appt. Archbishop of Atlanta Dec. 9, 2004; installed Jan. 17, 2005.

Diocese of Belleville Chancery Office—222 S. Third St., Belleville, 62220-1985. Tel: 618-277-8181; Fax: 618-277-0387.

Diocesan Pastoral Center—2620 Lebanon Ave., Belleville, 62221. Tel: 618-235-9601; Fax: 618-235-7416.

Vicar General—Rev. Msgr. JOHN W. MCEVILLY, V.G.

Moderator of the Curia—Rev. Msgr. JOHN W. MCEVILLY, V.G.

Administrative Assistant to the Vicar General—LINDA M. KREHER.

Chancellor and Office of Canonical Affairs—Deacon DOUGLAS L. BOYER, M.S.C.M.

Administrative Assistant to the Chancellor—LINDA M. KREHER.

Vicars for Priests—Rev. Msgr. JOHN W. MCEVILLY, V.G.

Administrative Assistant to the Bishop—MRS. JUDY HOFFMANN.

Archivist—2620 Lebanon Ave., Belleville, 62221. Tel: 618-722-5057; Fax: 618-277-0387. Sr. MARY FRAN FLYNN, S.S.N.D.

Diocesan Tribunal—Diocesan Pastoral Center, 2620 Lebanon Ave., Belleville, 62221. Tel: 618-212-0050; Fax: 618-722-5030. Address all rogatory commissions to the Judicial Vicar at the Tribunal.

Judicial Vicar—Very Rev. JAMES M. NALL, J.C.L., Tel: 618-722-5025.

Judges—Very Rev. JAMES M. NALL, J.C.L., Tel: 618-722-5025; Rev. Msgr. JAMES E. MARGASON, M.Div., J.C.L.

Promoter Justitiae—Tel: 618-722-5027. Rev. PAUL R. WIENHOFF, J.C.L.

Defensores Vinculi—Tel: 618-722-5027. Very Rev. Msgr. THOMAS D. FLACH, V.F., (Retired); Revs. PAUL R. WIENHOFF, J.C.L.; DENNIS F. VOSS, (Retired).

Advocates—Rev. Msgr. JOHN T. MYLER, S.T.D., V.F.; Deacon ROBERT LANTER.

Notary/Ecclesiastical Notary/Administrative Assistant for Tribunal—MRS. RENEE QUIRIN, Tel: 618-722-5029.

Diocesan Consultors—Rev. Msgr. JOHN W. MCEVILLY, V.G.; Very Revs. JOHN C. IFFERT, V.F.; MARK D. STEC, V.F.; Revs. URBAN OSUJI, C.M.; JAMES E. DEITERS; RONALD J. WEBER; Deacon DOUGLAS L. BOYER, M.S.C.M.; Rev. Msgrs. DANIEL J. JUREK, (Retired); JOHN T. MYLER, S.T.D., V.F.; Rev. STANLEY J. KONIECZNY.

Diocesan Vicars Forane—Rev. Msgr. JOHN T. MYLER, S.T.D., V.F., Metro East Vicariate; Very Revs. MARK D. STEC, V.F., East Vicariate; JOHN C. IFFERT, V.F., North Central Vicariate; STEVEN L. BEATTY, V.F., South Vicariate; EUGENE H. WOJCIK, V.F., West Vicariate.

Diocesan Finance Office—MR. MICHAEL GIBBONS, CFO, Tel: 618-722-5015; MR. DAVID WAELTZ, Comptroller, Chancery Office. Tel: 618-722-5008; Fax: 618-722-5019.

Diocesan Finance Council—Most Rev. EDWARD K. BRAXTON, Bishop of Belleville; MRS. JEANETTE BAX-KURTZ; Rev. Msgr. JOHN W. MCEVILLY, V.G.; MR. MICHAEL GIBBONS, CFO; Deacons LINUS H. KLOSTERMANN; CHARLES A. LITTEKEN; Very Rev. EUGENE H. WOJCIK, V.F.; MR. RAYMOND HEINEN; MR. MICHAEL HOPKINS; Very Rev. JOHN C. IFFERT, V.F.; MR. JOSEPH KOPPEIS; MS. JESSICA BUATTE.

Diocesan Pastoral Council—Most Rev. EDWARD K. BRAXTON, Bishop of Belleville; MR. JERRY DESOTO; MR. DENNIS LAAKE; MS. PHYLLIS MENSING; MR. BRIAN NIERMAN; Sr. DIANE M. TURNER, S.S.N.D.; Rev. VON C. DEEKE; MS. KATHY MULVIN.

Building Commission, Chancery Office—Deacon BILL JOHNSON, Dir. Facilities & Risk Mgmt.

Catholic Campaign for Human Development—222 S. Third St., Belleville, 62220. Tel: 618-235-9601.

Catholic Charities of Southern Illinois—Formerly Catholic Charities *222 S. Third St., Belleville, 62220.* MR. GERARD F. HASENSTAB, Exec. Dir. Catholic Urban Programs, Web: www.catholiccharitiesstl.org.

Chairperson of the Board—LYNN CLAPP.

Catholic Urban Programs—#7 Vieux Carre Dr., East Saint Louis, 62203. Tel: 618-398-5616; Fax: 618-398-9005. *Mailing Address: P.O. Box 3310, East Saint Louis, 62203.* MR. GERARD F. HASENSTAB, Exec. Dir.; VANESSA MARION, Case Mgr.; MS. TONI MOHAMMAD, Asst. Exec. Dir.; TROY HERRING, CFO; RHONDA HERRING, Administrative Asst.

Holy Angels Shelter—MS. PAULYN SNYDER, Social Svc. Coord., 1410 N. 37th St., East St. Louis, 62203. Tel: 618-874-4079; Fax: 618-874-8277.

Griffin Center—Mailing Address: P.O. Box 2185, East Saint Louis, 62202. DR. HENRIETTA YOUNG, Prog. Dir.; ALEXANDRA GRAHAM, Prog. Coord.; Sr. JULIA HUISKAMP, D.C., Business Mgr.

Site Locations under Griffin—

Griffin Center—2630 Lincoln Ave., East St. Louis, 62204. LORETTA SMITH, Site Dir.

Roosevelt Center—1328 N. 44th St., East Saint Louis, 62204. CARLA HARRIELL, Site Dir.

Weather-Owens Center—1400 Missouri Ave., East Saint Louis, 62201. MS. DOLL WILLIAMS, Site Dir.

De Shields-Robinson Center—1235 McCasland, East Saint Louis, 62201. YOLANDA MOODY, Site Dir.

Forest Village—4330 Forest Blvd., East Saint Louis, 62204. SANTOSHA SCOTT, Site Dir.

Neighborhood Law Office—614 N. 7th St., East Saint Louis, 62201. Mailing Address: P.O. Box 3310, East Saint Louis, 62203. Tel: 618-271-7820; Fax: 618-271-7821. SARA SIEGEL.

Catholic Diocese of Belleville Cemetery Association—MR. JOSEPH P. HUBBARD, Tel: 618-394-0126; Tel: 618-397-0181; DEE DEE MURRAY, Contact, Mt. Carmel. Tel: 618-397-0181; Fax: 618-397-0802. Covers: Immaculate Conception, Centreville; Holy Cross, Fairview Heights; St. Philip, East St. Louis, IL.

Child Protection and Victim Assistance—MR. DON SAX, Dir., 222 S. Third, Belleville, 62220. Tel: 618-277-8181.

Child Protection Office—2620 Lebanon Ave., Bldg. 6, Belleville, 62221. MRS. LYNN MUSCARELLO, Coord., Tel: 618-722-5026; Fax: 618-212-0055; Email: lmuscarello@diobelle.org; MARY ELLEN ACHE, Administrative Asst., Tel: 618-722-5055; Email: mache@diobelle.org.

Clergymen's Aid Society—Most Rev. EDWARD K. BRAXTON, Chm.; Rev. EDWARD F. SCHAEFER, Pres.; Rev. Msgrs. JAMES A. BUERSTER, V.F., Treas.; MARVIN C. VOLK, St. James, 405 W. Madison, Millstadt, 62260. Tel: 618-476-3513; Fax: 618-476-7357.

Communications / Media—Rev. Msgr. JOHN T. MYLER, S.T.D., V.F., 200 W. Harrison, Belleville, 62220. Tel: 618-234-1166.

Diocesan Development Office; Catholic Service and Ministry Appeal; Planned Giving; Foundations & Corporations—Chancery: 222 S. Third St., Belleville, 62220. Tel: 618-722-5007; Fax: 618-277-0819. MS. JUDY PHILLIPS, Dir.

Diocesan Liturgical Commission—Rev. Msgr. DAVID M. DARIN, Chm., Tel: 618-233-3500, Ext. 3.

Daystar Community Program—Serving Alexander and Pulaski Counties. Daystar Community Program, *909 Washington Ave., Cairo, 62914.* Tel: 618-734-0178. MS. SHERRY MILLER, Dir., Email: daystarcommunityprogram@gmail.com.

Diaconate, Office of Permanent—Deacon ROBERT LANTER, Coord. of Deacon, Diocesan Pastoral Center, 2620 Lebanon Ave., Belleville, 62221. Tel: 618-722-5042; Very Rev. EUGENE H. WOJCIK, V.F., Dir. Deacon Formation.

Office of Vocation and Deacon Formation—Very Rev. EUGENE H. WOJCIK, V.F., Deacon Formation, Email: genewojcik@hotmail.com; Rev. NICHOLAS G. JUNKER, Dir. Vocations; MRS. PATTI WARNER, Assoc. Dir. Formation, Diocesan Pastoral Center, 2620 Lebanon Ave., Belleville, 62221. Tel: 618-722-5043.

Diocesan Liaison for International Priests & Seminarians—Rev. VON C. DEEKE, 301 N. Main St., P.O. Box 126, Hecker, 62248. Tel: 618-473-2217.

Diocesan Council of Catholic Women—Rev. DENNIS F. VOSS, Diocesan Moderator, (Retired); JOYCE HRABUSICKY, Pres., 604 Branch St., Ellis Grove, 62241. Email: joyceh1@hotmail.com.

Ecumenical and Interreligious Affairs—Rev. ROBERT B. FLANNERY, 303 S. Poplar St., Carbondale, 62901. Tel: 618-457-4556.

Formation of Priests—Rev. JAMES R. DEITERS, Chm., St. Clare Catholic Church, 1411 Cross Rd., Shiloh, 62269. Tel: 618-632-3562.

Faith Formation—2620 Lebanon Ave., Bldg. 6, Belleville, 62221. Tel: 618-722-5037. MR. JAIME GIL NUNEZ, Dir.

Superintendent of Schools—2620 Lebanon Ave., Belleville, 62221. Tel: 618-235-9601; Fax: 618-235-7115; Email: jbirdsong@diobelle.org. MR. JONATHAN SKIP BIRDSONG, Dir. Education.

Diocesan Board of Education—MR. BEN FUEHNE, Pres.

Hispanic Ministry—MS. LUCY BARRAGAN, Coord., Tel: 618-722-5050; MS. ADA JIMENEZ, Family Advocate, Tel: 618-722-5051; Sr. JOAN HORNICK, A.S.C., Communications Coord., 2620 Lebanon Ave., Belleville, 62221. Tel: 618-722-5049.

Holy Childhood Association—Rev. Msgr. JOHN T. MYLER, S.T.D., V.F., 200 W. Harrison St., Belleville, 62220. Tel: 618-234-1166.

Hospitals—Rev. EUGENE J. NEFF, Delegate, Ministry to Sick and Aged, 2620 Lebanon Ave., Belleville, 62221. Tel: 618-235-9991.

Insurance Commission—MR. MICHAEL GIBBONS, Dir.

Facilities and Risk Management—Deacon WILLIAM P. JOHNSON, Dir. and Claims & Risk Mgr., Diocesan Pastoral Center. Tel: 618-233-1090; Email: bjohnson@diobelle.org.

Office of Pastoral Services—Diocesan Pastoral Center, 2620 Lebanon Ave., Belleville, 62221. Tel: 618-235-9601. MRS. SUE HUETT, Dir. Pastoral Svcs., Diocesan Pastoral Center. Tel: 618-722-5038.

Newman Catholic Student Center—MR. TIM TAYLOR, Dir., 715 S. Washington St., Carbondale, 62901. Tel: 618-529-3311; Email: tim@siucnewman.org.

Newman Auxiliary—MS. MARGE MANGAN, Pres., 9741 Stilley's Mill Dr., Marion, 62959. Tel: 618-982-2218.

Newspaper, "The Messenger"—Diocesan Pastoral Center, 2620 Lebanon Ave., Belleville, 62221. Tel: 618-722-5044. MR. CHRISTOPHER ORLET, Editor.

Ondessonk, Camp—Diocese of Belleville, Department of Outdoor Education: MR. DAN KING, Exec. Dir., 3760 Ondessonk Rd., Ozark, 62972. Tel: 618-695-2489; Tel: 877-659-2267 (Toll Free); Fax: 618-695-3593.

Respect Life / Project Rachel Pastoral Center—Diocesan Pastoral Center, 2620 Lebanon Ave., Belleville, 62221. Tel: 618-235-9601; Tel: 888-456-4673 (Project Rachel Hotline).

Propagation of the FaithRev. Msgr. JOHN T. MYLER, S.T.D., V.F., 200 W. Harrison St., Belleville, 62220. Tel: 618-234-1166.

Office of Review Board—Tel: 800-640-3044 (Hotline). MR. DON SAX, Dir.

Office of Youth Ministry—Diocesan Pastoral Center, 2620 Lebanon Ave., Belleville, 62221. Tel: 618-722-5037. MR. JAIME GIL NUNEZ, Dir.; Rev. BERNARD C. GOEDDE JR., Spiritual Moderator.

Our Brothers' Keepers of Southern Illinois—Mailing Address: P.O. Box 398, East Saint Louis, 62202. Tel: 618-482-5570; Fax: 618-482-5574; Email: obkministry2@gmail.com; Web: obkministry.org. MR. LOUIS SLAPSHAK, Email: lslap@mindspring.com.

Rural Life Conference—Rev. ROBERT J. ZWILLING, Dir., Email: godislove333@hotmail.com; MRS. SUE HUETT, Contact, Tel: 618-722-5038; Email: shuett@diobelle.org.

St. Vincent de Paul Society—CHARLIE CULLEN, Pres.; MS. PATRICIA HOGREBE, Exec. Dir., 13 Vieux Carre Dr., Ste. 2, East St. Louis, 62205. Tel: 618-394-0126. Mailing Address: P.O. Box 3415, East Saint Louis, 62203.

Sick and Aged (Ministry)—Rev. EUGENE J. NEFF, Dir., Diocesan Pastoral Center. Tel: 618-235-9991.

Vocation Office—Pastoral Center, 2620 Lebanon Ave., Belleville, 62221. Tel: 618-235-9601, Ext. 1482. MRS. PATTI WARNER, Assoc. Dir. Formation, Tel: 618-722-5043.

CLERGY, PARISHES, MISSIONS AND PAROCHIAL SCHOOLS

CITY OF BELLEVILLE

(ST. CLAIR COUNTY)

1—CATHEDRAL OF ST. PETER (1842) [CEM]
200 W. Harrison St., 62220-2090. Tel: 618-234-1166; Email: cathedralbelle@gmail.com; Web: www.cathedralbelle.org. Rev. Msgr. John T. Myler, S.T.D., V.F., Rector; Rev. Stephen Pautler, Parochial Vicar; Deacons David Fields; Wayne L. Weiler.
School—Notre Dame Academy-Cathedral Campus, (Grades 1-8), 200 S. Second St., 62220. Tel: 618-233-6414; Fax: 618-233-3587; Email: linda.hobbs@notredamebelleville.org; Web: notredamebelleville.com. Linda Hobbs, Prin. Lay Teachers 19; School Sisters of Notre Dame 1; Students 69.
Catechesis Religious Program— (Combined with St. Mary, Belleville.) Email: tmarkus@ssndcp.org. Sr. Theresa Markus, S.S.N.D., D.R.E.; Miss Jane Stock, D.R.E.; Mr. Charles York, Business Mgr. Students 49.

2—ST. AUGUSTINE OF CANTERBURY (1955)
1910 W. Belle St., 62226. Tel: 618-233-3813; Email: ginnyg@stasaints.org; Web: www.stasaints.org. Rev. Msgr. William P. McGhee.
School—Notre Dame Academy - St. Augustine Campus, 1900 W. Belle St., 62220. Fax: 618-234-6414; Email: Linda.hobbs@notredamebelleville.org. 1706 West Main Street, 62220. Linda Hobbs, Prin. Children were moved to Notre Dame Academy - Cathedral Campus.
Catechesis Religious Program—(Combined with St. Mary, Belleville, Cathedral, Belleville, St. Luke's, Belleville and St. Teresa, Belleville) Students 21.

3—BLESSED SACRAMENT (1927)
8707 W. Main St., 62223. Tel: 618-397-2287; Web: bellevillecatholic.com. Rev. Matthew J. Elie; Rev. Msgr. John W. McEvilly, V.G., In Res.; Karen Ferrara, Business Mgr.
Res.: 5923 N. Belt W., 62223. Tel: 618-234-6196; Email: office@bellevillecatholic.com.
School—Blessed Sacrament School, 8809 W. Main St., 62223. Tel: 618-397-1111; Fax: 618-397-8431; Email: blsac@hotmail.com; Web: www.blessedsacramentbelleville.com/. Ms. Claire Hatch, Prin. Lay Teachers 14; Students 186.
Catechesis Religious Program—5303 W. Main St., 62226. Tel: 618-397-2287; Email: kahrens@bjpc.com. Karen Vick, D.R.E. Students 10.

4—CHAPEL OF ST. JOHN CHILDREN'S HOME, [CEM]
Mailing Address: Chancery Office, 222 S. Third St., 62220. Tel: 618-277-8181; Fax: 618-277-0387; Email: jmcevilly@diobelle.org. Rev. Msgr. John W. McEvilly, V.G.

5—ST. HENRY (1925) Rev. Kenneth J. York, J.C.L.
Res.: 5315 W. Main St., 62226. Tel: 618-233-2423; Email: sthenryc@peaknet.net; Web: www.sthenrybelleville.com.
Catechesis Religious Program—Mrs. Kim Ahrens, Dir. Students 78.

6—ST. LUKE (1883)
1201 Lebanon Ave., 62220. Rev. Msgr. David M. Darin, Canonical Pastor; Deacon Robert Lanter; Sr. Grace Marie Mueller, S.S.N.D., Parish Life Coord.
Res.: 301 N. Church St., 62220. Tel: 618-233-3500; Email: ccrawford@stteresabelleville.org; Web: www.stlukebelleville.org.
Catechesis Religious Program—Tel: 618-236-1839. Students 40.

7—ST. MARY (1893) Rev. Christopher Anyanwu.
Res.: 1706 W. Main St., 62226. Tel: 618-233-2391; Email: stmarychurch1893@sbcglobal.net; Web: www.stmarybelleville.org.
See Notre Dame Academy of Belleville - St. Mary Campus.
Catechesis Religious Program—Sr. Theresa Markus, S.S.N.D., D.R.E., Tel: 618-234-1166; Email: tmarkus@ssndcp.org. Twinned with St. Augustine, Belleville. Students 130.

8—OUR LADY QUEEN OF PEACE (1955)
5923 N. Belt West, 62223. Tel: 618-397-2287; Email: qpparish@qofp.com; Email: office@bellevillecatholic.com; Web: bellevillecatholic.com. 8707 W. Main St., 62223. Rev. Matthew J. Elie; Ms. Karen Ferrara, Business Mgr.
School—Our Lady Queen of Peace School, (Grades K-8), 5915 N. Belt W., 62223. Tel: 618-234-1206; Fax: 618-234-6123; Email: qpschool@qofp.com; Web: www.qofp.com. Michelle Tidwell, Prin. Lay Teachers 15; Students 151.
Catechesis Religious Program—5303 Main St., 62226. Email: kahrens@bjpc.com. Karen Vick, D.R.E. Students 6.

9—ST. TERESA OF THE CHILD JESUS (1926) (Little Flower)
1201 Lebanon Ave., 62221. Tel: 618-233-3500; Email: ccrawford@stteresabelleville.org; Web: www.stteresabelleville.com. Rev. Msgr. David M. Darin.
School—St. Teresa of the Child Jesus School, (Grades PreK-8), 1108 Lebanon Ave., 62221. Tel: 618-235-4066; Fax: 618-235-7930; Email: ccrawford@stteresabelleville.org; Web: www.stteresa.pvtk12.il.us. Sandra Jouglard, Prin. Clergy 1; Lay Teachers 20; Students 210.
Catechesis Religious Program—Email: jlohmann.stteresa@gmail.com. Jenifer Lohmann, Diocesan D.R.E. Students 61.

OUTSIDE THE CITY OF BELLEVILLE

ALBERS, CLINTON CO., ST. BERNARD (1908) [CEM]
202 N. Broadway, Albers, 62215. Tel: 618-248-5112; Fax: 618-248-5595; Email: st.bernard@charter.net. P.O. Box 10, Albers, 62215. Rev. Anthony O. Onyango, Admin.; Deacons Glennon J. Netemeyer, Pastoral Assoc.; Kevin T. Templin.
Catechesis Religious Program—Tel: 618-248-5134; Fax: 618-248-5134 (Call First); Email: stdamians@wisperhome.com. Students 129.

ANNA, UNION CO., ST. MARY (1857)
Res.: 402 Freeman, Anna, 62906. Tel: 618-833-5835; Email: stmaryanna@live.com.

Catechesis Religious Program—Tel: 618-833-3131. Students 52.

AVA, JACKSON CO., ST. ELIZABETH (1890) Closed. For inquiries for parish records contact the chancery.

AVISTON, CLINTON CO., ST. FRANCIS OF ASSISI (1865) [CEM] (German) Rev. Daniel L. Friedman; Deacons Stephen AuBuchon, RCIA Coord. - Adult Ed. Dir.; Charles A. Litteken, Youth Min.; Mrs. Carolyn Kampwerth, Business Mgr.
Res.: 251 S. Clinton, Box 93, Aviston, 62216-0093. Tel: 618-228-7219; Email: parish@stfrancisav.org; Web: www.stfrancisav.org.
Catechesis Religious Program—Email: DRE@stfrancisav.ort. Mrs. Milissia Faust, D.R.E. Students 249.

BARTELSO, CLINTON CO., ST. CECILIA (1885) (German) Rev. Msgr. James A. Buerster, V.F.
Res.: 304 S. Washington St., P.O. Box 176, Bartelso, 62218. Tel: 618-765-2162; Email: cechbart@frontier.com.
Catechesis Religious Program—Ms. Betty Budde, C.R.E.; Debra Gerdes, C.R.E. Students 166.

BEAVER PRAIRIE, CLINTON CO., ST. FELICITAS (1883) [CEM]
Mailing Address: 13322 Church Rd., Carlyle, 62231. Tel: 618-594-3040; Fax: 618-594-3040; Email: dmtssnd@wisperhome.com. Revs. Edward F. Schaefer; Lawrence M. Nickels, O.F.M., Sacramental Min.; Sr. Diane M. Turner, S.S.N.D., Pastoral Life Coord.
Catechesis Religious Program—Students 15.

BECKEMEYER, CLINTON CO., ST. ANTHONY (1905) [CEM] Rev. Charles W. Tuttle.
Res.: 451 W. 3rd St., P.O. Box 305, Beckemeyer, 62219. Tel: 618-227-8236; Email: stanthny@papadocs.com.
Catechesis Religious Program—295 N. Clinton St., Breese, 62230. Tel: 618-526-7746. Mrs. Darlene Menietti, Diocesan D.R.E. Combined with All Saints, Breese. Students 22.

BENTON, FRANKLIN CO., ST. JOSEPH (1872) [CEM] Rev. Urban Osuji, C.M.
Res.: 506 W. Main, Benton, 62812. Tel: 618-438-9941; Email: stjoebentonil@gmail.com; Web: www.catholicchurchesofrendlake.com.
Catechesis Religious Program—Robin Giroux, D.R.E. Students 38.

BREESE, CLINTON CO.

1—ST. AUGUSTINE (1912) [CEM] Rev. Charles W. Tuttle.
Res.: 525 S. Third St., Breese, 62230.
Tel: 618-526-4362; Email: augustine306@att.net.
Catechesis Religious Program—295 N. Clinton, Breese, 62230. Tel: 618-526-7746. 493 N. 2nd St., Breese, 62230. Mrs. Darlene Menietti, Diocesan D.R.E. Students 22.

2—ST. DOMINIC (1858) [JC]
493 N. Second St., Breese, 62230. Tel: 618-526-7746; Fax: 618-526-7755; Email: saintdominic@papadocs.com; Web: www.saintdominicbreese.org. Rev. Patrick N. Peter; Deacon Linus H. Klostermann.
Catechesis Religious Program—Email: dmenietti@charter.net. Mrs. Darlene Menietti, D.R.E. Students 214.

BRIDGEPORT, LAWRENCE CO., IMMACULATE CONCEPTION (1856) [CEM] Closed. For inquiries for sacramental records please see St. Lawrence, Lawrenceville.

CAHOKIA, ST. CLAIR CO.

1—ST. CATHERINE LABOURE (1959) Closed. For inquiries for parish records contact the chancery.

2—HOLY FAMILY (1699) [CEM 3]
116 Church St., Cahokia, 62206. Tel: 618-337-4548; Email: holyfamilycahokia@yahoo.com; Web: holyfamily1699.org. Rev. Linus Umoren, C.M., Admin.; Kathy Bellmann, Sec.
Catechesis Religious Program— Joint with Sacred Heart, Dupo Donna Paul, Sec. Students 24.

CAIRO, ALEXANDER CO., ST. PATRICK (1838) [CEM]
312 9th St., Cairo, 62914. Rev. Michael Christopher Mujule, (Uganda); Ms. Mary Helen Wissinger, Sec.
Church: 312 9th St., Cairo, 62914. Tel: 618-734-2061; Email: stpatrick.cairo@gmail.com; Web: stpatrickcairo.com.
Catechesis Religious Program—Ms. Mary Helen Wissinger, D.R.E.

CARBONDALE, JACKSON CO., ST. FRANCIS XAVIER (1900) Rev. Robert B. Flannery.
Res.: 303 S. Poplar St., Carbondale, 62901-2709. Tel: 618-457-4556; Fax: 618-457-7368; Email: sfrancis@clearwave.com; Web: www.stfxcarbondale.org.
Catechesis Religious Program—Ms. Toni Intravaia, D.R.E. Students 48.

CARLYLE, CLINTON CO., ST. MARY (1853) [CEM] (Immaculate Conception)
1171 Jefferson St., Carlyle, 62231. Tel: 618-594-2225; Email: stmaryc@sbcglobal.net; Web: www.carlylecatholicchurch.com. P.O. Box 179, Carlyle, 62231. Rev. George A. Mauck.
Catechesis Religious Program—Tel: 618-594-2284. Ms. Ellen Knolhoff, D.R.E. Students 146.

CARMI, WHITE CO., ST. POLYCARP (GERMAN) (1847) [CEM]
209 Fourth St., Carmi, 62821. Tel: 618-380-2262; Email: wccatholic@gmail.com. Rev. Vincent J. Obi, (Nigeria) Admin.
Catechesis Religious Program—Julie Jackson, D.R.E. Students 28.

CARTERVILLE, WILLIAMSON CO., CHURCH OF THE HOLY SPIRIT (1974)
300 N. Pine St., Carterville, 62918.
Tel: 618-985-2900; Tel: 618-925-5099; Email: holyspiritparish300@gmail.com. Rev. Msgr. Kenneth J. Schaefer, Canonical Pastor; Rev. Richard G. Mohr, Sacramental Min., (Retired); Sr. Phyllis Schenk, D.R.E.
Catechesis Religious Program—300 N. Pine St., Carterville, 62918. Mrs. Jennifer Flath, Contact Person. Students 63.

CASEYVILLE, ST. CLAIR CO., ST. STEPHEN (1893)
901 S. Main St., Caseyville, 62232. Tel: 618-397-0666; Email: office@ststephencaseyville.org; Web: www.ststephencaseyville.org. P.O. Box 458, Caseyville, 62232. Revs. James Nall; Nicholas G. Junker, Sacramental Min.; Jeanne Adamske, Pastoral Assoc.
Catechesis Religious Program—Email: faithform@ststephencaseyville.org. Carrie Rose, D.R.E. Students 100.

CENTRALIA, MARION CO., ST. MARY (1857) [CEM]
424 E. Broadway, Centralia, 62801.
Tel: 618-532-6291; Fax: 618-532-4758; Email: parish@stmarycentralia.org. Rev. Dale A. Maxfield.
Rectory—645 S. Lincoln Blvd., Centralia, 62801.
School—St. Mary School, c/o St. Mary Parish, 424 E. Broadway, Centralia, 62801. Tel: 618-532-3473; Email: principal@stmarycentralia.org. Mr. Jason Swann, Prin. Lay Teachers 5; Students 63.
Catechesis Religious Program—Mrs. Vicki Laquet, C.R.E. Students 45.

CENTREVILLE, ST. CLAIR CO., IMMACULATE CONCEPTION (1858) [CEM] Closed. For inquiries for parish records contact the chancery.

CHESTER, RANDOLPH CO., ST. MARY HELP OF CHRISTIANS (1842) [CEM]
911 Swanwick St., Chester, 62233. Tel: 618-826-2444; Email: stmaryschester@yahoo.com. Very Rev. Eugene H. Wojcik, V.F.
School—St. Mary Help of Christians School, 835 Swanwick St., Chester, 62233. Tel: 618-826-3120; Email: stmarychester@hotmail.com. Mrs. Janelle Robinson, Prin., Email: stmarychester@hotmail.com; Web: www.stmaryschester.com. Lay Teachers 8; Students 74.
Catechesis Religious Program—Tel: 618-826-2526. Mrs. Brenda Congiardo, Contact Person. Students 23.

CHRISTOPHER, FRANKLIN CO., ST. ANDREW (1905) [CEM] Rev. Urban Osuji, C.M.; Deacon Michael A. Rowland, Parochial Admin.
Res.: 412 E. Washington St., Christopher, 62822. Tel: 618-724-4114; Email: standrew@11.net; Email: st.andrewcatholicchurch@yahoo.com; Web: www.catholicchurchesofrendlake.com.
Catechesis Religious Program—Robin Giroux, D.R.E. Students 42.

COBDEN, UNION CO., ST. JOSEPH (1883) [CEM]
101 Centennial St., Cobden, 62920.
Tel: 618-893-2276; Email: fr.uriel.salamanca@gmail.com; Web: www.stjosephcobden.com. P.O. Box 237, Cobden, 62920. Rev. Uriel Salamanca, Admin.; Deacon Patrick Patterson.
Catechesis Religious Program—Tel: 618-893-2368; Email: skinnerstudioscobden@gmail.com. Ms. Jill Skinner, D.R.E. Students 29.

COLUMBIA, MONROE CO., IMMACULATE CONCEPTION OF THE B.V.M. (1846) [CEM]
411 Palmer Rd., Columbia, 62236. Tel: 618-281-5105; Email: khuels@iccmail.org; Web: www.icc-columbia-il.us. Rev. Msgr. Carl E. Scherrer; Rev. Gary Hogan, Sacramental Min.
School—Immaculate Conception of the B.V.M. School, 321 S. Metter, Columbia, 62236.
Tel: 618-281-5353; Fax: 618-281-6044; Email: mkish@htc.net. Mr. Michael Kish, Prin. Lay Teachers 18; Students 314.
Catechesis Religious Program—Mrs. Lizanne Young, Dir. Faith Formation, Tel: 618-281-5105, Ext. 354; Heather Schaefer, IC PSR Dir., Tel: 618-281-5105, Ext. 352. Students 170.

COULTERVILLE, RANDOLPH CO., ST. ANTHONY, Closed. For inquiries for parish records contact the chancery.

DAHLGREN, HAMILTON CO., ST. JOHN NEPOMUCENE (1893) [CEM] (German)
705 W. Main St., Dahlgren, 62828. Tel: 618-648-2490; Email: catholic@hamiltoncom.net; Web: www.hamiltoncountycatholic.org. P.O. Box 220, Dahlgren, 62828. Rev. Slawomir Ptak, (Poland) Admin.; Deacon Archie L. Bowers Jr.
Res.: 709 W. Main St., Mc Leansboro, 62859.

DAMIANSVILLE, CLINTON CO., ST. DAMIAN (1861) [CEM] (German—Hispanic)
One W. Main St., Damiansville, 62215.
Tel: 618-248-5134; Fax: 618-248-5134; Email: stbernard@wisperhome.com. Rev. Anthony O. Onyango, Admin.; Deacons Glennon J. Netemeyer, Pastoral Assoc.; Kevin T. Templin.
Res.: 202 N. Broadway, P.O. Box 10, Albers, 62215-0010.
Catechesis Religious Program—Students 78.

DU QUOIN, PERRY CO., SACRED HEART OF JESUS (1863) [CEM]
100 W. Main St., Du Quoin, 62832. Rev. Joseph Oganda.
Res.: 17 N. Walnut St., Du Quoin, 62832.
Tel: 618-542-3423; Email: sacredheartduquoin@gmail.com.
Catechesis Religious Program—Mary Beth Lane, D.R.E. Students 47.

DUBOIS, WASHINGTON CO., ST. CHARLES BORROMEO (1877) [CEM] Rev. Oliver Nwachukwu, Ph.D., Admin.
Res.: 223 S. 3rd. St., P.O. Box 6, Dubois, 62831.
Tel: 618-787-2781; Email: stcharleschurch@wisperhome.com.
Catechesis Religious Program—Judy Pieszchalski, C.R.E. Students 16.

DUPO, ST. CLAIR CO., SACRED HEART OF JESUS (1914)
100 S. 3rd St., P.O. Box 35, Dupo, 62239.
Tel: 618-286-3224; Email: holyfamilycahokia@yahoo.com. Rev. Linus Umoren, C.M.
Catechesis Religious Program—Students 10.

EAST ST. LOUIS, ST. CLAIR CO.

1—ST. AUGUSTINE OF HIPPO (2006)
408 Rev. Joseph Brown Blvd., East Saint Louis, 62205. Tel: 618-274-0655; Email: staugustineofhippo@sbcglobal.net. Rev. Carroll Mizicko, O.F.M.
Catechesis Religious Program—Mrs. Eleanor Gregory, C.R.E. Students 40.
Chapel—Sister Thea Bowman Chapel, 8313 Church Ln., East Saint Louis, 62203.

2—IMMACULATE CONCEPTION (1895) (Lithuanian)
1509 Baugh Ave., East Saint Louis, 62205.
Tel: 618-274-0655; Email: cmofm1968@yahoo.com. Rev. Carroll Mizicko, O.F.M.

ELDORADO, SALINE CO., ST. MARY (1900) [CEM]
2000 W. Poplar, Harrisburg, 62946. Rev. Abraham O. Adejoh.
Parish Center/Office: 1158 N. 2nd St., Eldorado, 62930. Tel: 618-253-7408; Email: Stmaryhb@frontier.com.
Catechesis Religious Program—Tashina Wood, Dir. Students 65.

ELIZABETHTOWN, HARDIN CO., ST. JOSEPH (1897) [CEM]
IL 146-185 E Rd., Box 140, Elizabethtown, 62931-9711. Tel: 618-253-7408; Email: stmaryhb@frontier.com. 2000 West Poplar, Harrisburg, 62946. Rev. Abraham O. Adejoh.
Catechesis Religious Program—Tel: 618-287-4824. Debbie Soward, D.R.E. Students 14.

ELLIS GROVE, RANDOLPH CO., DIVINE MATERNITY OF THE B.V.M. (1933)
7362 Shawneetown Tr., Ellis Grove, 62241.
Tel: 618-859-3541; Email: stboniface1860@hotmail.com. Rev. Larry A. Lemay.
Catechesis Religious Program—Email: vjbtmb@egyptian.net. Ms. Tammy Bert, Diocesan D.R.E. Students 16.

ENFIELD, WHITE CO., ST. PATRICK (1830) [CEM] (Irish)
1377 County Rd. 25, E., Enfield, 62835. Rev. Vincent J. Obi, (Nigeria) Admin.
St. Polycarp Church, Res. & Office: 209 Fourth St., Carmi, 62821. Tel: 618-380-2262; Email: wccatholic@gmail.com; Web: www.whitecountycatholic.org.
Catechesis Religious Program—Vince Mitchell, D.R.E. Students 9.

EQUALITY, GALLATIN CO., ST. JOSEPH (1873) [CEM] Closed. Parish suppressed. For inquiries for parish records contact St. Kateri, Ridgeway.

EVANSVILLE, RANDOLPH CO., ST. BONIFACE (1860) [CEM]
1007 Olive St., Evansville, 62242. Tel: 618-853-4435; Email: stboniface1860@hotmail.com. Rev. Larry A. Lemay.
Catechesis Religious Program—Students 39.

FAIRFIELD, WAYNE CO., ST. EDWARD (1881) Rev. Charles Anyaoku, Admin.
Res.: 300 N.W. 5th St., Fairfield, 62837.
Tel: 618-847-7931; Fax: 618-842-7393; Email: stedwardcatholicchurch01@frontier.com; Web: stedwardfairfield.com.
Catechesis Religious Program—Ms. Sarah Pickens, C.R.E., C.R.E. Students 23.

FAIRMONT CITY, ST. CLAIR CO., HOLY ROSARY (1922)
2716 N. 42nd St., Fairmont City, 62201.
Tel: 618-274-3486; Email: hrosaryfc@aol.com. Rev. David M. Wilke, Pastor.
Catechesis Religious Program—Students 148.

FAIRVIEW HEIGHTS, ST. CLAIR CO., HOLY TRINITY CATHOLIC CHURCH (1951)
505 Fountains Pkwy., Fairview Heights, 62208.
Tel: 618-628-8825; Email: office@holytrinityil.org; Web: www.holytrinityil.org. Revs. James Nall; Nich-

olas G. Junker; Deacons Arthur Hampton; Tom Powers.
School—Holy Trinity Catholic Church School, 504 Fountains Pkwy., Fairview Heights, 62208.
Tel: 618-628-7395; Fax: 618-628-1570; Email: kfrawley@htcs.org. Kristy Frawley, Prin. Students 190; Teachers 18.
Catechesis Religious Program—Ben Zuber, D.R.E. Students 96.

FAYETTEVILLE, ST. CLAIR CO., ST. PANCRATIUS (1837) [CEM]
2213 N. 2nd St., Fayetteville, 62258.
Tel: 618-677-3319; Email: Saintpancratius@yahoo.com. Revs. Paul R. Wienhoff, J.C.L.; Allen J. Maes, O.M.I., Sacramental Min.
Catechesis Religious Program—Tel: 618-677-2717. Karen Hale, D.R.E. Students 7.

FLORA, CLAY CO., ST. STEPHEN (1854) [CEM] Rev. Charles Anyaoku, Admin.
Res.: 812 N. Main St., Flora, 62839.
Tel: 618-662-6261; Email: dtherdes@bspeedy.com.
Catechesis Religious Program—Tel: 618-662-8121. Students 21.

FREEBURG, ST. CLAIR CO., ST. JOSEPH (1857) [CEM]
6 N. Alton St., Freeburg, 62243. Tel: 618-539-3209; Email: parish@stjosephfreeburg.org; Web: www.stjosephfreeburg.org. P. O. Box 98, Freeburg, 62243. Rev. Mark D. Reyling, V.F.; Deacon Corby Valentine.
School—St. Joseph School, (Grades PreK-8), 2 N. Alton St., Freeburg, 62243. Tel: 618-539-3930; Fax: 618-539-0254; Email: office@stjosephschoolfreeburg.org; Web: www.stjosephschoolfreeburg.org. John Correll, Prin. Lay Teachers 11; Students 115.
Catechesis Religious Program—Cindy Ingold, D.R.E. Students 152.

GERMANTOWN, CLINTON CO., ST. BONIFACE (1837) [CEM]
402 Munster St., Germantown, 62245. P.O. Box 280, Germantown, 62245. Rev. Msgr. James A. Buerster, V.F.
Catechesis Religious Program—Students 210.

GRAND CHAIN, PULASKI CO., ST. CATHERINE (1891) [CEM] Closed. For inquiries for sacramental records please see St. Patrick Church, Cairo.

HARRISBURG, SALINE CO., ST. MARY (1907) [CEM]
2000 W. Poplar St., Harrisburg, 62946. Rev. Abraham O. Adejoh.
Office: 2000 W. Poplar St., Harrisburg, 62946.
Tel: 618-253-7408; Email: stmaryhb@frontier.com.
Catechesis Religious Program—Tel: 618-252-7874. Students 57.

HECKER, MONROE CO., ST. AUGUSTINE OF CANTERBURY (1824) [CEM]
310 N. Main St., Hecker, 62248. Tel: 618-473-2217; Email: staug@htc.net. P.O. Box 126, Hecker, 62248. Rev. Von C. Deeke.
Pastor's Res.: 925 Centerville Ave., 62221.
Church Address: 310 N. Main St., P.O. Box 126, Hecker, 62248. Tel: 618-473-2217; Email: staug@htc.net.

HERRIN, WILLIAMSON CO., OUR LADY OF MOUNT CARMEL (1900) [CEM]
316 W. Monroe St., Herrin, 62948. Tel: 618-942-3114 ; Email: olmc@live.com. Rev. Msgr. Kenneth J. Schaefer.
School—Our Lady of Mount Carmel School, (Grades K-8), 400 W. Monroe St., Herrin, 62948. Lay Teachers 18; Students 277.
Catechesis Religious Program—Students 125.

JOHNSTON CITY, WILLIAMSON CO., ST. PAUL (1904) Merged
1103 Washington Ave., Johnston City, 62951.
Tel: 618-983-5073; Email: stpaulsw47@gmail.com; Web: stjoseph-stpaul.com. Rev. Brian Barker. Partnership with St. Joseph, Marion.
Catechesis Religious Program—Students 18.

KASKASKIA, RANDOLPH CO., IMMACULATE CONCEPTION (1675) [CEM] (French—Native American) (Independent Mission)
Mailing Address: 6450 Klein Ln., St. Mary's, MO 63673. Tel: 618-615-5747; Fax: 618-826-2667; Email: elyons@powrup.net. Ms. Mary Brown, Sec.

KINMUNDY, MARION CO., ST. ELIZABETH ANN SETON (1878)
Mailing Address: 812 W. Main St., Salem, 62881.
Tel: 618-548-0899; Fax: 618-548-0269; Email: sttheresaparish@hotmail.com; Web: www.stelizabethkinmundy.org. Rev. Benjamin J. Stern.
Catechesis Religious Program—N. Madison St., Kinmundy, 62854. Anne Hoover, Diocesan D.R.E. Students 11.

LAWRENCEVILLE, LAWRENCE CO., ST. LAWRENCE (1909) [JC] Rev. Ronald J. Weber, Admin.
Res.: 1006 Collins, Lawrenceville, 62439.
Tel: 618-943-5255; Email: stlawrence@nwcable.net; Web: www.catholiccommunityofstlawrence.com.
Catechesis Religious Program—Students 63.

LEBANON, ST. CLAIR CO., ST. JOSEPH (1862) [CEM]
901 N. Alton St., Lebanon, 62254. Tel: 618-537-2575; Fax: 618-537-0147; Email: lebstjoepa@gmail.com; Email: lebstjoe@sbcglobal.net; Web: www.stjosephlebanon.org. Rev. Msgr. James E. Margason, M.Div., J.C.L.; Deacon George G. Mills Jr.; Deborah Kuth, Pastoral Assoc.
Res.: 205 Rasp St., Shiloh, 62269.
Catechesis Religious Program—Students 17.

LIVELY GROVE, WASHINGTON CO., ST. ANTHONY (1868) [CEM] Rev. Tadeusz Jozef Gegotek.
Church: 6101 St. Anthony Church Rd., Oakdale, 62268. Tel: 618-824-6271.
Catechesis Religious Program—Email: stanthonys@egyptian.net. Students 2.

MADONNAVILLE, MONROE CO., IMMACULATE CONCEPTION (1833) Closed. For inquiries for parish records contact Sts. Peter & Paul Parish, Waterloo.

MARION, WILLIAMSON CO., ST. JOSEPH (1940) Very Rev. Msgr. Thomas D. Flach, V.F., (Retired).
Res.: 600 N. Russell St., Marion, 62959.
Tel: 618-993-3194, Ext. 1; Email: secsjm@frontier.com; Web: www.stjoseph-stpaul.com.
Catechesis Religious Program—Email: cresjm@frontier.com. Angela Lees, D.R.E. Students 91.

MARYDALE, CLINTON CO., ST. TERESA OF AVILA (1919)
18021 Marydale Rd., Carlyle, 62231.
Tel: 618-594-3266; Email: stteresa@tincans.net. Rev. George A. Mauck, Canonical Pastor; Deacons Charles A. Litteken, Admin.; John Hempen.
Catechesis Religious Program— Merged with St. Mary Catholic Church. Students 44.

MASCOUTAH, ST. CLAIR CO., HOLY CHILDHOOD OF JESUS (1857) [CEM]
104 N. Independence St., Mascoutah, 62258.
Tel: 618-566-2958; Email: hcc@holychildhoodchurch.com. Rev. Paul R. Wienhoff, J.C.L.
School—Holy Childhood of Jesus School, 215 N. John St., Mascoutah, 62258. Tel: 618-566-2922; Fax: 618-566-2720; Email: hcs@holychildhoodschool.com; Web: www.holychildhoodschool.com. Claudia Dougherty, Prin. Lay Teachers 11; Students 126.
Catechesis Religious Program—Email: hcc@holychildhoodchurch.com. Wendy Uhl, D.R.E. Students 107.

MCLEANSBORO, HAMILTON CO., ST. CLEMENT (1881) [CEM] (German)
603 E. Market St., Mc Leansboro, 62859.
Tel: 618-648-2490; Email: catholic@hamiltoncom.net; Web: www.hamiltoncountycatholic.org. 7598 Piopolis Rd., McLeansboro, 62859. Rev. Slawomir Ptak, (Poland) Admin.; Deacon Archie L. Bowers Jr.
101 N. Hancock St., Mc Leansboro, 62859.

METROPOLIS, MASSAC CO., ST. ROSE OF LIMA (1872) Rev. Michael Christopher Mujule, (Uganda) Admin.
Res.: 315 E. Third St., Metropolis, 62960-2229.
Tel: 618-524-8202; Email: stroseoflimametropolis@comcast.net; Web: www.strosemetropolis.com.
Catechesis Religious Program—405 E. Third St., Metropolis, 62960. Christy Willmes, C.R.E.

MILLSTADT, ST. CLAIR CO., ST. JAMES (1851) [CEM] Rev. Msgr. Marvin C. Volk; Deacon Ronald Karcher.
Res.: 405 W. Madison St., Millstadt, 62260.
Tel: 618-476-3513; Email: rectory@stjamesmillstadt.com; Web: www.stjamesmillstadt.com.
School—St. James School, 412 W. Washington, Millstadt, 62260. Tel: 618-476-3510; Email: michele.bell@stjamesmillstadt.com; Web: www.stjamesmillstadt.com. Steve Kidd, Prin. Lay Teachers 10; Students 99.
Catechesis Religious Program—Students 74.

MODOC, RANDOLPH CO., ST. LEO (1893) [CEM] Closed. For inquiries for sacramental records please see St. Joseph, Prairie du Rocher.

MOUND CITY, PULASKI CO., CHURCH OF THE IMMACULATE CONCEPTION-ST. MARY (1863) [CEM] Closed. For inquiries for sacramental records please see St. Patrick, Cairo.

MOUNT CARMEL, WABASH CO., ST. MARY (1836) [CEM]
125 W. Fifth St., Mount Carmel, 62863.
Tel: 618-262-5337; Email: smsparish@hotmail.com; Web: www.stmarysparish.net. Rev. Robert J. Zwilling; Deacons Charles Speaks; Stephen Lowe.
School—St. Mary School, (Grades PreK-8), 417 Chestnut St., Mount Carmel, 62863.
Tel: 618-263-3183; Fax: 618-263-3596; Web: www.smsrockets.net. Mrs. Cindy Brogan, Prin. Lay Teachers 15; Students 142.
Catechesis Religious Program—Students 30.

MOUNT VERNON, JEFFERSON CO., ST. MARY THE IMMACULATE CONCEPTION (1871) [CEM]
1550 Main St., Mount Vernon, 62864.
Tel: 618-244-1559; Email: church@stmarymtvernon.org; Web: www.stmarymtvernon.org. Very Rev. John C. Iffert, V.F.
Res.: 204 N. 16th St., Mount Vernon, 62864.
School—St. Mary the Immaculate Conception School, (Grades PreK-8), 1416 Main St., Mount Vernon, 62864. Tel: 618-242-5353; Fax: 618-242-5365; Email: bheinzman@stmarymtvernon.org; Web: www.stmary.school. Mr. Brett Heinzman, Prin. Clergy 1; Lay Teachers 10; Students 150.
Catechesis Religious Program—Email: tfoulks@stmarymtvernon.org. Teresa Foulks, D.R.E. Students 166.

MURPHYSBORO, JACKSON CO., ST. ANDREW (1868) [CEM]
724 Mulberry St., Murphysboro, 62966. Web: 618-687-2012; Email: sec@stamboro.org; Web: www.standrewmboro.church. Rev. Gary P. Gummersheimer.
School—St. Andrew School, 723 Mulberry St., Murphysboro, 62966. Tel: 618-687-2013; Fax: 618-684-4969; Email: trammel@sasmboro.org; Web: saintandrew-school.org. Ms. Jennifer Martin, Prin. Lay Teachers 14; Students 145.
Catechesis Religious Program—Mrs. Jennifer Craig, Catholic Youth Faith Formation. Students 19.

NASHVILLE, WASHINGTON CO., ST. ANN (1874) [CEM] Rev. Andrew J. Knopik.
Office: 695 S. Mill St., Nashville, 62263. Linda Williams, Contact Person.
Res.: 631 S. Mill St., Nashville, 62263.
Tel: 618-327-3232; Email: lwilliams@stannnashville.org.
School—St. Ann School, (Grades K-8), 675 S. Mill St., Nashville, 62263. Tel: 618-327-8741; Fax: 618-327-4904; Email: principal@stannnashville.org. Mr. Pierre Antoine, Prin. Lay Teachers 8; Preschool 11; Students 68.
Catechesis Religious Program—Tel: 618-314-6635; Email: wetslugs@yahoo.com. Stephanie Goedken, D.R.E. Students 65.

NEW ATHENS, ST. CLAIR CO., ST. AGATHA (1870) [CEM] Rev. Mark D. Reyling, V.F.
Res.: 205 S. Market St., New Athens, 62264.
Tel: 618-475-2331; Email: jthomas@stagathaparish.com.
School—St. Agatha School, (Grades K-8), 207 S. Market St., New Athens, 62264. Tel: 618-475-2170; Fax: 618-475-3177; Email: slanham@stagathaparish.com. Sarah Lanham, Prin. Lay Teachers 6; Students 74.
Catechesis Religious Program—Tel: 618-295-2686. Students 16.

NEW BADEN, CLINTON CO., ST. GEORGE (1894) [CEM 2] Rev. Eugene J. Neff; Deacon John C. Fridley.
Res.: 200 N. 3rd St., New Baden, 62265.
Tel: 618-588-4323; Email: saintgcatholicchurch@gmail.com; Web: www.stgeorgefamily.org.
Catechesis Religious Program—Students 143.

O'FALLON, ST. CLAIR CO.
1—ST. CLARE (1867) [CEM] Rev. James E. Deiters; Deacons Dennis W. Vander Ven; John J. Gomez; Stephen Eros, Music Min.; Matt Flynn, RCIA Coord.; Jane Dotson, D.R.E.; Ed Seipp, Business Mgr.; Pat Jurgensmeyer, Facilities Mgr.; Paulo D'Amico, Cemetery Sexton
Legal Title: St. Clare of Assisi Parish
Res.: 205 W. Third, O Fallon, 62269.
School—St. Clare School, (Grades PreK-8), 214 W. 3rd St., O'Fallon, 62269. Tel: 618-632-6327; Fax: 618-632-5587; Email: clarice.mckay@saintclareschool.org; Web: saintclareschool.org. Mrs. Clarice McKay, Prin. Clergy 1; Lay Teachers 28; Students 494.
2—ST. NICHOLAS (1982)
625 St. Nicholas Dr., O Fallon, 62269.
Tel: 618-632-1797; Fax: 618-632-7703; Email: busadmin@stnicholasofallon.org; Web: www.stnicholasofallon.org. Rev. Msgr. William J. Hitpas; Deacon Gary H. Mueller; Ann Daniels, Admin.
Res.: 900 N. Smiley, O Fallon, 62269.
Catechesis Religious Program—Email: anndaniels@stnicholasofallon.org; Email: dre@stnicholasofallon.org; Email: martierheaume@gmail.com. Ms. Barbara Furdek, D.R.E.; Mrs. Martha Rheaume, D.R.E. Students 256.

OKAWVILLE, WASHINGTON CO., ST. BARBARA (1867) [CEM]
P.O. Box 494, Okawville, 62271. Rev. Tadeusz Jozef Gegotek.
Res.: 305 N. Front St., P.O. Box 106, Okawville, 62271. Tel: 618-243-6236; Email: stbarbara.okaw@gmail.com.
Catechesis Religious Program—Tel: 618-243-6236. Beth Anderson, D.R.E.; Pam Swatala, D.R.E. Students 52.

OLNEY, RICHLAND CO., ST. JOSEPH (1857) [CEM]
220 S. Elliot St., Olney, 62450. Tel: 618-392-8181; Email: stjosephchurch_olney@yahoo.com; Web: www.stjosephchurcholney.com. Very Rev. Mark D. Stec, V.F.; Caroline Trimble.
School—St. Joseph School, Tel: 618-395-3081; Email: office@stjoeolney.com. Mrs. Carol Potter, Prin. Lay Teachers 16; Students 259.
Catechesis Religious Program—Email: stjoecre@gmail.com. Kelly Richardson, D.R.E. Students 28.

PADERBORN, ST. CLAIR CO., ST. MICHAEL (1843) [CEM] (German)
4576 Buss Branch Rd., Waterloo, 62298.

Tel: 618-473-2915; Email: stmichaels4@aol.com. Rev. Stanley J. Konieczny.
Catechesis Religious Program—Tel: 618-473-2915. Ms. Jackie Billings, C.R.E. Students 39.

PINCKNEYVILLE, PERRY CO., ST. BRUNO (1872) [CEM] 204 N. Gordon St., Pinckneyville, 62274.
Tel: 618-357-5510; Email: stbrunochurch@yahoo.com. Rev. Augustine Ibezimako, Admin.
School—St. Bruno School, (Grades PreK-8), 210 N. Gordon St., Pinckneyville, 62274. Tel: 618-357-8276; Fax: 618-357-6425; Email: brittany.goldman@stbrunoschool.com. Mrs. Brittany Goldman, Prin. Lay Teachers 10; Students 90.
Catechesis Religious Program—Email: kmrs65@wildblue.net. Ms. Kathy Sprehe, D.R.E. Students 50.

PIOPOLIS, HAMILTON CO., ST. JOHN THE BAPTIST (1841) [CEM]
7598 Piopolis Rd., McLeansboro, 62859.
Tel: 618-648-2490; Email: catholic@hamiltoncom.net; Web: www.hamiltoncountycatholic.org. Rev. Slawomir Ptak, (Poland) Admin.; Deacon Archie L. Bowers Jr.
Catechesis Religious Program—Mrs. Megan Woodrow, D.R.E. Students 67.

POND SETTLEMENT, GALLATIN CO., ST. PATRICK (1842) Closed. Parish suppressed. For inquiries for parish records contact St. Kateri Tekakwitha, Shawneetown.

POSEN, WASHINGTON CO., OUR LADY OF PERPETUAL HELP (1901) [CEM]
19824 Posen Rd., Nashville, 62263-6122.
Tel: 618-327-3556; Email: olph-smm@hughes.net. Rev. Bernard C. Goedde Jr.
Catechesis Religious Program—Students 19.

PRAIRIE DU ROCHER, RANDOLPH CO., ST. JOSEPH (1721) [CEM] Rev. Msgr. Dennis R. Schaefer.
Res.: 802 Middle St., Prairie du Rocher, 62277.
Tel: 618-284-3314; Email: sjospdr@htc.net.
Catechesis Religious Program—Students 55.

RADDLE, JACKSON CO., ST. ANN (1875)
Mailing Address: 724 Mulberry St., Murphysboro, 62966. Rev. Gary P. Gummersheimer.
Church: 101 Raddle Ln., Jacob, 62950.
Catechesis Religious Program—Students 12.

RADOM, WASHINGTON CO., ST. MICHAEL THE ARCHANGEL (1874) [CEM] (Polish) Rev. Oliver Nwachukwu, Ph.D., Admin.
Church & Res.: 52 S. Third St., P.O. Box 128, Radom, 62876. Tel: 618-485-2265; Email: stmichaelsradom@frontier.com.
Catechesis Religious Program—Students 19.

RED BUD, RANDOLPH CO., ST. JOHN THE BAPTIST (1862) [CEM]
515 Locust St., Red Bud, 62278. Tel: 618-282-3222; Fax: 618-282-6867; Email: drschaefer49@hotmail.com; Email: rhondaj@htc.net; Web: www.sjbcatholicredbud.com. Rev. Msgr. Dennis R. Schaefer.
School—St. John the Baptist School, 519 Hazel St., Red Bud, 62278. Tel: 618-282-3215;
Fax: 618-282-6790; Email: sjbhill@hotmail.com; Web: www.sjbcatholicschoolredbud.org. Ms. Kristine Hill, Prin. Lay Teachers 12; Students 84.
Catechesis Religious Program—Students 78.

RENAULT, MONROE CO., OUR LADY OF GOOD COUNSEL (1879) [CEM]
2038 Washington St., P.O. Box 98, Renault, 62279.
Tel: 618-458-7710; Email: olgcrenault@gmail.com. Rev. John Kizhakedan, C.M.I.

RIDGWAY, GALLATIN CO., ST. JOSEPH (1870) [CEM] Closed. Parish suppressed. For inquiries for parish records contact St. Kateri Tekakwitha.

ROYALTON-ZEIGLER, FRANKLIN CO., ST. ALOYSIUS/SACRED HEART (1919) [JC]
212 S. Pecan St., Royalton, 62983. Rev. Eusebius C. Mbidoaka, Ph.D., S.T.D., Admin.
Res.: 703 E. Main, West Frankfort, 62896.
Tel: 618-932-2828; Email: johnthebaptist@mchsi.com.
Catechesis Religious Program—Students 51.

RUMA, RANDOLPH CO., ST. PATRICK (1818) [CEM] Rev. Msgr. Dennis R. Schaefer.
Res.: #1 Pioneer Ln.-Ruma, Red Bud, 62278.
Tel: 618-282-3176; Email: stpats@htc.net.

ST. FRANCISVILLE, LAWRENCE CO., ST. FRANCIS XAVIER (1836) [CEM] (French), Closed. For inquiries for sacramental records please see St. Lawrence, Lawrenceville.

ST. LIBORY, ST. CLAIR CO., ST. LIBORIUS (1838) [CEM] Rev. Paul R. Wienhoff, J.C.L.; Deacon Andrew Lintker.
Res.: 911 Sparta St., P.O. Box 331, St. Libory, 62282.
Tel: 618-768-4921; Email: stlrectory@wishperhome.com.
Catechesis Religious Program—Jeni Sandheinrich. Students 57.

ST. ROSE, CLINTON CO., ST. ROSE (1868) [CEM] Rev. Edward F. Schaefer.
Res.: 18010 St. Rose Rd., St. Rose, 62230-2506.
Tel: 618-526-4118; Email: belpsros@papadocs.com.
Catechesis Religious Program—Marilyn Bruggemann, D.R.E. Students 130.

ST. SEBASTIAN, WABASH CO., ST. SEBASTIAN (1871) [CEM] Rev. Robert J. Zwilling.
Office: 4921 N. 1400 Blvd., Mount Carmel, 62863.
Tel: 618-298-2589; Email: GodisLove333@hotmail.com.
Catechesis Religious Program—Students 62.

SALEM, MARION CO., ST. THERESA OF AVILA (1868) [CEM]
812 W. Main St., Salem, 62881. Tel: 618-548-0899; Email: sttheresaparish@hotmail.com; Web: www.StTheresaSalem.org. Rev. Benjamin J. Stern.
Res.: 719 Markland St., Salem, 62881.
Catechesis Religious Program—Ms. Denise McCormack, C.R.E. Students 32.

SANDOVAL, MARION CO., ST. LAWRENCE (1871) [CEM]
Mailing Address: P.O. Box 278, Sandoval, 62882. Rev. Dale A. Maxfield.
Office: 412 N. Vine St., P.O. Box 278, Sandoval, 62882.
Res.: 645 S. Lincoln, Centralia, 62801.
Church: 311 W. Missouri St., Sandoval, 62882.
Tel: 618-247-3300; Email: stlawrence@frontiernet.net; Web: www.saintlawrencesandoval.org.
Catechesis Religious Program—Students 5.

SCHELLER, JEFFERSON CO., ST. BARBARA (1898)
4281 N. Scheller Ln., Scheller, 62883.
Tel: 618-244-1559; Email: frjohn@stmarymtvernon.org. Very Rev. John C. Iffert, V.F.
Catechesis Religious Program—Students 40.

SESSER, FRANKLIN CO., ST. MARY (1909) Rev. Urban Osuji, C.M.; Deacon Michael A. Rowland, Parochial Admin.
Church: 100 N. Poplar St., P.O. Box 568, Sesser, 62884. Tel: 618-625-5053; Email: stjosephbentonil@gmail.com.
Res.: 101 N. Poplar St., Sesser, 62884.
Catechesis Religious Program—Students 8.

SHAWNEETOWN, GALLATIN CO.
1—ST. KATERI TEKAKWITHA (2012)
211 W. Edwards St., Ridgway, 62979.
Tel: 618-272-7059; Email: gallatincatholic@gmail.com; Web: stkateri.net. P.O. Box 190, Ridgway, 62979. Very Rev. Steven L. Beatty, V.F.
Catechesis Religious Program—Ms. Michele Raper. Students 88.
2—ST. MARY (1842) [CEM] Closed. Parish suppressed. For inquiries for parish records contact St. Kateri Tekakwitha, Shawneetown.

SHILOH, ST. CLAIR CO., CORPUS CHRISTI (1913)
205 Rasp St., Shiloh, 62269. Tel: 618-632-7614; Email: corpuschristi1@sbcglobal.net. Rev. Msgr. James E. Margason, M.Div., J.C.L.; Deacon George G. Mills Jr.
Catechesis Religious Program—Tel: 618-632-7614; Email: ccshilohym@sbcglobal.net. Ms. Sarah Ayran, Diocesan DRE. Students 129.

SMITHTON, ST. CLAIR CO., ST. JOHN THE BAPTIST (1867) [CEM] Rev. Stanley J. Konieczny.
Res.: 10 S. Lincoln St., Smithton, 62285-1614.
Tel: 618-234-2068; Email: skonieczny@stjohnsschool.us; Web: www.stjohnschool.us.
School—St. John the Baptist School, St. John the Baptist School, 10 S. Lincoln St., Smithton, 62285-1614. Tel: 618-233-0581; Email: Principal@stjohnsschool.us. Roy Monti, Prin. Lay Teachers 8; Students 105.
Catechesis Religious Program—Students 90.

SPARTA, RANDOLPH CO., OUR LADY OF LOURDES (1897)
611 W. Broadway St., Sparta, 62286.
Tel: 618-443-2811; Email: ollsparta@yahoo.com. Rev. Vincent Mukasa, Admin.
Catechesis Religious Program—Tel: 618-443-2878. Mrs. Jessica Soderlund, C.R.E. Students 35.

STONEFORT, WILLIAMSON CO., ST. FRANCIS DE SALES (1879)
Mailing Address: 2020 State Rte. 146 E., Vienna, 62995. Tel: 618-658-4501; Email: spccil@frontier.com; Web: www.stpaulvienna.org. 400 Mulberry St., Stonefort, 62987. Rev. Thomas M. Barrett. Students attend Vie.

STRINGTOWN, RICHLAND CO., ST. JOSEPH (1841) [CEM]
6342 N. Stringtown Rd., Olney, 62450.
Tel: 618-754-3676; Fax: 618-988-7099; Email: stjoestringtown@hotmail.com; Web: www.stjosephstringtown.com. Mailing Address: P.O. Box 10, Dundas, 62425. Very Rev. Mark D. Stec, V.F.
Res.: 215 S. Elliot St., Olney, 62450.
Catechesis Religious Program—Tel: 618-754-3049. Ms. Donna Zwilling, C.R.E. Students 32.

TAMAROA, PERRY CO., IMMACULATE CONCEPTION (1904)
533 W. 2nd North St., Tamaroa, 62888.
Tel: 618-496-5867; Tel: 618-542-3423; Email: sacredheartduquoin@gmail.com. Rev. Joseph Oganda.
Catechesis Religious Program—Tel: 618-496-3100. Students 3.

TIPTON, MONROE CO., ST. PATRICK (1850) [CEM]
5675 LL Rd., Waterloo, 62298. Tel: 618-458-6875; Email: stpatrickstipton@gmail.com; Web: www.stpatrickstipton.org. Rev. John Kizhakedan, C.M.I., Admin.; Susan Muszynski, Sec.
Catechesis Religious Program—Students 20.

TODDS MILL, PERRY CO., ST. MARY MAGDALEN (1868) [CEM]
5047 Todds Mill Rd., Pinckneyville, 62274-2235. Rev. Bernard C. Goedde Jr.
Res. & Business Office: 19824 Posen Rd., Nashville, 62263-6122. Tel: 618-327-3556; Email: olph-smm@hughes.net.
Catechesis Religious Program—Students 1.

TRENTON, CLINTON CO., ST. MARY (1858) [CEM] (German) Rev. Joseph C. Rascher.
Res.: 215 W. Kentucky St., Trenton, 62293.
Office: 218 W. Kentucky St., Trenton, 62293.
Tel: 618-224-9335; Email: stmary@stmarytrenton.com; Web: www.stmarytrenton.com.
Catechesis Religious Program—Mrs. Kim Moss, C.R.E. Students 105.

ULLIN, PULASKI CO., OUR LADY OF FATIMA (1949) [CEM] Closed. For inquiries for parish records contact the chancery.

VALMEYER, MONROE CO., SEVEN DOLORS OF THE B.V.M. (1921) Rev. Felix Chukwuma.
Res.: 101 S. Meyer Ave., Valmeyer, 62295.
Tel: 618-935-2247; Email: smoffice@htc.net.
Catechesis Religious Program—Students 18.

VIENNA, JOHNSON CO., ST. PAUL (1895) [JC] Rev. Thomas M. Barrett.
Res.: 2020 State Rte. 146 E., Vienna, 62995.
Tel: 618-658-4501; Email: spccil@frontier.com; Web: www.stpaulvienna.org.
Catechesis Religious Program—Students 18.

WALSH, RANDOLPH CO., ST. PIUS V (1905)
7681 Walsh Rd., Walsh, 62297. Tel: 618-853-4404; Email: stpius@accessus.net. Rev. Vincent Mukasa.
Catechesis Religious Program—Students 7.

WASHINGTON PARK, ST. CLAIR CO., ST. MARTIN OF TOURS, Closed. For inquiries for parish records contact the chancery.

WATERLOO, MONROE CO., SS. PETER AND PAUL (1843) [CEM] Revs. Osang Idagbo, C.M., (Nigeria); Sebastian Ukoh, C.M., (Nigeria); Deacon Thomas J. Helfrich; Ms. Karen Seaborn, Pastoral Assoc.
Res.: 204 W. Mill St., Waterloo, 62298.
Tel: 618-939-6426; Email: pbm@ssppcc.org.
School—SS. Peter and Paul School, 217 W. Third St., Waterloo, 62298. Tel: 618-939-7217;
Fax: 618-939-5994. Lori Matzenbacher, Prin. Lay Teachers 33; Students 263.
Catechesis Religious Program—
Tel: 618-939-6426, Ext. 24; Email: psrnews@ssppcc.org. Angela Atkinson, D.R.E. Students 190.

WENDELIN, CLAY CO., HOLY CROSS (1870) [CEM]
5782 Ingraham Ln., Newton, 62448.
Tel: 618-752-5671; Email: holycrosschurch@frontier.com; Web: www.holycrosswendelin.com. Very Rev. Mark D. Stec, V.F.
Res.: 215 S. Elliott St., Olney, 62450.
Catechesis Religious Program—Maria Rudolphi, C.R.E. Students 135.

WEST FRANKFORT, FRANKLIN CO., ST. JOHN THE BAPTIST (1916) [CEM] Rev. Eusebius C. Mbidoaka, Ph.D., S.T.D., Admin.
Res.: 703 E. Main St., West Frankfort, 62896.
Tel: 618-932-2828; Email: johnthebaptist@mchsi.com; Web: stjohnschurch-wf.org.
School—St. John the Baptist School, St. John the Baptist School, 702 East Poplar, West Frankfort, 62896. Tel: 618-937-2017; Email: stjohns@roe21.org. Mr. Kevin Spiller, Prin. Lay Teachers 6; Students 57.
Catechesis Religious Program—Students 10.

WILLISVILLE, PERRY CO., ST. JOSEPH (1903) [CEM]
Mailing Address: 501 Broadway, P.O. Box 85, Steeleville, 62288. Tel: 618-853-4435;
Fax: 618-853-4435; Email: frlarrylemay@gmail.com. Rev. Larry A. Lemay.
Office: 1007 Olive St., Evansville, 62242.
Catechesis Religious Program—

ZEIGLER, FRANKLIN CO., SACRED HEART, Merged with St. Aloysius, Royalton to form St. Aloysius/Sacred Heart, Royalton-Zeigler.

SACRAMENTAL RECORDS LOCATED IN CHANCERY ARCHIVES:
1—ST. ADALBERT CHURCH, EAST ST. LOUIS.
2—ST. ANTHONY, COULTERVILLE.
3—ST. AUGUSTINE CHURCH, EAST ST. LOUIS.
4—SS. CYRIL AND METHODIUS CHURCH, EAST ST. LOUIS.
5—ST. ELIZABETH CHURCH, EAST ST. LOUIS.
6—ST. HENRY CHURCH, EAST ST. LOUIS.
7—HOLY ANGELS CHURCH, EAST ST. LOUIS.
8—IMMACULATE CONCEPTION, CENTREVILLE.
9—IMMACULATE CONCEPTION, EAST ST. LOUIS.
10—IMMACULATE CONCEPTION, KASKASKIA.
11—ST. JOHN FRANCIS REGIS, EAST ST. LOUIS.
12—ST. JOHN'S ORPHANAGE, BELLEVILLE.
13—ST. JOSEPH CHURCH, WETAUG.
14—ST. JOSEPH, EAST ST. LOUIS.
15—ST. MARTIN OF TOURS, WASHINGTON PARK.

16—ST. MARY CHURCH, EAST ST. LOUIS.
17—OUR LADY OF FATIMA, ULLIN.
18—ST. PATRICK, EAST ST. LOUIS.
19—ST. PHILIP, EAST ST. LOUIS.
20—SACRED HEART CHURCH, EAST ST. LOUIS.
21—ST. CATHERINE LABOURNE, CAHOKIA.
22—ST. THOMAS CHURCH, MILLSTADT.

Chaplains of Correctional Institutions and State Hospitals

CENTRALIA. *Centralia Correctional Center*, P.O. Box 1266, Centralia, 62801.

INA. *Big Muddy River Correctional Center*.
Lawrence Prison, P.O. Box 300, Harrisburg, 62946.

MARION. *Federal Maximum Security Prison*, P.O. Box 2000, Marion, 62959.
Veterans Hospital. Attended from St. Joseph, Marion.

MENARD. *Menard Correctional Center*, P.O. Box 711, Menard, 62259.

PINCKNEYVILLE. *Pinckneyville Correctional Facility*. Attended from St. Mary Church, Anna.

VIENNA. *Shawnee Correctional Center*, Box 400, Vienna, 62995.
Vienna Correctional Center.

Leave of Absence:
Revs.—
Harbaugh, Paul E.
Hechenberger, Gerald R.
Judkins, Brett
Murry, Trevor K.
O'Guinn, Jon
Palas, Sean
Sebescak, Gary
Unverferth, Steven R.
Witte, Steven D.

Retired:
Most Rev.—
Schlarman, Stanley G., D.D., (Retired)
Very Rev. Msgr.—
Flach, Thomas D., V.F., (Retired)
Rev. Msgrs.—
Baumann, Theodore J., (Retired)
Blazine, James A., (Retired)
Haselhorst, Vincent, (Retired)
Jurek, Daniel J., (Retired)
Lawler, Joseph A., V.F., (Retired)
Very Rev.—
Schultz, C. Raymond, V.F., (Retired)
Revs.—
Ancheril, Jose, (Retired)
Blaes, Donald A., (Retired)
Chlopecki, Robert J., (Retired), (On Leave)
Crook, David G., (Retired), (On Leave)
Dougherty, James R., (Retired)
Engelhart, Henry R., (Retired)
Geller, Charles H., (Retired)
Grogan, James Clyde, (Retired)
Hayes, Leo J., (Retired)
Humphrey, Steven, (Retired)
Karban, Roger R., (Retired)
Kreher, Albert E., (Retired), (On Leave)
Long, James T., (Retired)
Mohr, Richard G., (Retired)
Peterson, Louis P., (Retired), (On Leave)
Poole, Steven F., (Retired)
Ratermann, Jerome B., (Retired), (On Leave)
Rowe, William J., (Retired)
Rudolphi, Stephen A., (Retired)
Ruppert, Alan E., (Retired), (On Leave)
Thoonkuzhy, Joseph, (Retired)
Trapp, Joseph L., (Retired)
Van Oss, James R., (Retired)
Voelker, David A., (Retired)
Voelker, James A., (Retired)
Voss, Dennis F., (Retired).

Permanent Deacons:
Andrews, Stephen P.
AuBuchon, Stephen
Bach, Gerald Sr.
Bagby, Richard
Bowers, Archie L. Jr.
Boyer, Douglas L., M.S.C.M., Chancellor
Cerneka, Peter III, (Retired)
Cozzi, Daniel
DeRousse, Timothy J.
DuBois, Omer E., (Retired)
Eischens, Steven M.
Fields, David
Fridley, John
Gillan, Garth, Ph.D., M.S., (Retired)
Gomez, John J.
Hampton, Arthur
Helfrich, Thomas J.
Hempen, John
Hilliard, Kenneth W.
Kabat, Mark F.
Karcher, Ronald
Klostermann, Linus H.
Lanter, Robert
Law, James
Lintker, Andrew, (Retired)
Litteken, Charles A.
Lowe, Stephen
Mills, George G. Jr.
Mote, John H.
Mueller, Gary H.
Munie, George J., (Retired)
Netemeyer, Glennon J.
Olson, Richard H., (Retired)
Patterson, Pat
Powers, Thomas
Riesenberger, Randall L.
Rowland, Michael A.
Sparling, Don
Speaks, Charles
Templin, Kevin T.
Tiberi, Ronald
Valentine, Corby
Vander Ven, Dennis W.
Weiler, Wayne L.

INSTITUTIONS LOCATED IN DIOCESE

[A] HIGH SCHOOLS, DIOCESAN

BELLEVILLE. *Althoff Catholic High School*, 5401 W. Main St., 62226-4796. Tel: 618-235-1100; Fax: 618-235-9535; Web: www.althoff.net. Mr. David L. Harris, M.S., Prin. Lay Teachers 29; Students 341; Clergy / Religious Teachers 3.
Althoff Catholic High School Educational Endowment Trust, 222 S. 3rd St., 62220. Tel: 618-277-8181; Email: enastoff@diobelle.org. Mr. David L. Harris, M.S., Contact Person.

BREESE. *Mater Dei High School*, 900 N. Mater Dei Dr., Breese, 62230. Tel: 618-526-7216; Fax: 618-526-8310; Email: knights@materdeiknights.org; Email: dlitteken@materdeiknights.org; Web: www.materdeiknights.org. Mr. Dennis Litteken, Prin.; Rev. Charles W. Tuttle, Chap.; Deb Foote, Registrar; Beth Grapperhaus, Librarian. Central Catholic High School for Clinton Co. Lay Teachers 35; Priests 1; Students 400; Clergy / Religious Teachers 1.

WATERLOO. *Gibault Catholic High School*, 501 Columbia Ave., Waterloo, 62298. Tel: 618-939-3883; Fax: 618-939-7215; Email: russhart@gibaulthawks.com; Web: www.gibaultonline.com. Mr. Russell Hart, Prin. Lay Teachers 26; Priests 1; Students 211; Teachers 20; Clergy / Religious Teachers 2.

[B] ELEMENTARY SCHOOLS

BREESE. *All Saints Academy*, (Grades PreK-8), 295 N. Clinton St., Breese, 62230. Tel: 618-526-4323; Fax: 618-526-2547; Email: drbooth@asasaints.com; Web: www.asasaints.com. Dr. Robin Booth, Prin.; Ms. Jane Klostermann, Librarian; Ms. Marietta Kuhl, Librarian. Consolidated schools of Saint Augustine, Saint Dominic parishes, Breese, IL, and St. Anthony Parish, Beckemeyer, IL. Lay Teachers 21; Students 292.

EAST SAINT LOUIS. *Sister Thea Bowman Catholic School*, (Grades K-8), 8213 Church Ln., East Saint Louis, 62203. Tel: 618-397-0316; Fax: 618-397-0337; Email: thea_bowman@yahoo.com; Email: nickerson.bowman@gmail.com; Web: www.stbcs.com. Mr. Daniel Nickerson, Admin. Brothers 1; Lay Teachers 16; Sisters 2; Students 130; Clergy / Religious Teachers 2.

FAIRVIEW HEIGHTS. *Holy Trinity Catholic School*, (Grades PreSchool-8), Consolidated schools of St. Stephen Parish, Caseyville, IL 504 Fountains Pkwy., Fairview Heights, 62208. Tel: 618-628-7395; Fax: 618-628-1570; Email: office@holytrinityedu.org; Web: www.holytrinityedu.org. Mr. Michael Oslance, Prin. Lay Teachers 14; Priests 1; Students 231.

[C] DAY CARE CENTERS

BELLEVILLE. *St. Henry Creative Learning Center* (1980) 5303 W. Main St., 62226. Tel: 618-234-6061; Fax: 618-234-6801; Email: st.henryclc1@yahoo.com. Ms. Judy Shovlin, Dir.; Ms. Mary Haas, Co-Dir. Children 40; Lay Teachers 10; Students 32.

[D] GENERAL HOSPITALS

BREESE. *St. Joseph Hospital of the Hospital Sisters of the Third Order of St. Francis* aka St. Joseph's Hospital Breese (1897) 9515 Holy Cross Ln., P. O. Box 99, Breese, 62230. Tel: 618-526-4511; Fax: 618-526-8022; Email: Chris.Klay@hshs.org; Web: www.stjoebreese.com. Mr. Chris Klay, Pres.; Sr. Pam Falter, Pastoral Min./Coord. Hospital Sisters of the Third Order of St. Francis. Bed Capacity 44; Sisters 1; Tot Asst. Annually 102,657; Staff 304.

CENTRALIA. **St. Mary's Hospital*, 400 N. Pleasant Ave., Centralia, 62801. Tel: 618-436-8000; Fax: 618-436-8024; Email: rhonda.edmonson@ssmhealth.com; Web: www.smgsi.com. Mr. Damon Harbison, Pres. Bed Capacity 112; Felician Sisters 3; Tot Asst. Annually 103,986; Staff 765.

MOUNT VERNON. **Good Samaritan Regional Health Center*, 1 Good Samaritan Way, Mount Vernon, 62864. Tel: 618-242-4600; Tel: 618-899-1002; Email: jeanette.young@ssmhealth.com; Web: www.ssmhealthillinois.com. Kerry Swanson, Pres.; Mr. Jeffrey Stewart, Dir. Pastoral Care. Member of SSM Health Care. Bed Capacity 142; Tot Asst. Annually 114,582; Staff 1,288.

MURPHYSBORO. *St. Joseph Memorial Hospital*, 2 S. Hospital Dr., Murphysboro, 62966. Tel: 618-684-3156; Fax: 618-529-0529; Email: susan.odle@sih.net; Web: www.sih.net. Sue Odle, R.N., M.S.N., Admin.; Sr. Rachel Castillo, Spiritual Care Mgr. Adorers of the Blood of ChristA service of Southern Illinois Healthcare. Bed Capacity 25; Sisters 1; Tot Asst. Annually 29,156; Total Staff 237.

O'FALLON. *St. Elizabeth Hospital* (1875) 1 St. Elizabeth's Blvd., O'Fallon, 62269. Tel: 618-234-2120; Fax: 618-222-4650; Email: Amy.Bulpitt@hshs.org; Web: www.steliz.org. Patricia Fischer, CEO. Hospital Sisters of the Third Order of St. FrancisClinically Affiliated with St. Louis University School of Medicine. Bed Capacity 144; Patients Asst Anual. 231,277; Sisters 2; Tot Asst. Annually 237,430; Staff 1,210.

[E] HOMES FOR SENIOR CITIZENS

BELLEVILLE. *Apartment Community of Our Lady of the Snows*, 726 Community Dr., 62223. Tel: 618-394-6400; Fax: 618-398-8788; Email: bprosser@apartmentcommunity.org; Email: srichards@omiusa.org; Web: apartmentcommunity.org. Mrs. Barbara Prosser, Pres.; Revs. Thomas Hayes, O.M.I.; Joe Ferraioli, O.M.I.; Andrew G. Chalkey, O.M.I., In Res.; Donald Dietz, In Res.; Urban Figge, O.M.I., In Res.; John R. Madigan, O.M.I., In Res.; Joseph Menker, O.M.I., In Res.; Terence Fiegel, In Res.; Bros. Victor Capek, O.M.I., In Res.; William Johnson, O.M.I., In Res.; William Lundberg, O.M.I., In Res. Independent Apartments 124; Skilled Care Beds 57; Assisted Living 38; Staff 160.
Charles and Bertha Hincke Residence for Priests and Sense Residence, 2620 Lebanon Ave., 62221. Tel: 618-234-5722; Fax: 618-234-5792; Email: hinckehome@gmail.com. Ms. Joline Beck, Mgr. Owned by Diocese of Belleville. Bed Capacity 21; Guests 12; Staff 11.

[F] MONASTERIES AND RESIDENCES OF PRIESTS AND BROTHERS

BELLEVILLE. *Missionary Oblates of Mary Immaculate - St. Henry's Oblate Residence*, 200 N. 60th St., 62223. Tel: 618-233-2991; Email: sthenryomi@charter.net. Revs. James F. Allen, O.M.I., Supr.; Joseph Ferraioli, O.M.I.; Thomas Hayes, O.M.I.; Michael Hussey, O.M.I.; George Knab, O.M.I.; Elmar Mauer, O.M.I; Eugene V. Prendiville; Thomas J. Singer, O.M.I.; Clarence Zachman, O.M.I.; Bro. Andrew Lawlor, O.M.I.; Revs. Allen J. Maes, O.M.I., In Res.; David Kalert, In Res.; Dale Schlitt, In Res.; Norman Volk, In Res.; Gregory Cholewa, In Res.; Thomas Killeen, In Res. Brothers 1; Priests 14.
Shrine of Our Lady of the Snows, 442 S. DeMazenod Dr., 62223-1023. Tel: 618-397-6700; Fax: 618-397-1210; Email: info@snows.org; Web: www.snows.org. Revs. Juan Gaspar, O.M.I., Supr.; Andrew Knop, Dir.; Elvis Mwamba, Dir. of Pilgrimages; Bro. Thomas Ruhmann, O.M.I.; Rev. Harold Fisher, O.M.I. Missionary Oblates of Mary Immaculate.

EAST SAINT LOUIS. *St. Benedict the Black Friary* (2002) 404 N. 14th St., East Saint Louis, 62201. Tel: 618-482-5570; Fax: 618-482-5574; Email: cnreuter@yahoo.com. Revs. Carroll Mizicko, O.F.M., Pastor St. Augustine of Hippo; John Eaton, O.F.M., Prov. Devel. Dir.; Bro. Thomas Eaton, O.F.M.

[G] CONVENTS AND RESIDENCES FOR SISTERS

BELLEVILLE. *Hospital Sisters of The Third Order of St. Francis* (1844) 1000 Royal Heights Rd., Apt. 58,

62226. Tel: 618-233-1687; Fax: 618-233-1687; Email: sistertk1948@yahoo.com; Web: www.springfieldfranciscans.org.

Poor Clare Monastery of Our Lady of Mercy (1986) 300 N. 60th St., 62223. Tel: 618-235-4407; Fax: 618-235-4426; Email: mbmeyer1860@verizon.net; Web: www.poorclares-belleville.info. Mother Mary Giovanna, P.C.C., Abbess. Sisters 11.

RUMA. *Adorers of the Blood of Christ*, 2 Pioneer Ln., Ruma Center, Red Bud, 62278. Tel: 618-282-3848; Fax: 618-282-3266; Web: www.adorers.org. Sisters Barbara Franklin, Dir.; Barbara Smith, Dir.; Angela J. Schrage, A.S.C., Dir. Sisters 39; Total Membership of the U.S. Region 183.

[H] RETREAT HOUSES

BELLEVILLE. *King's House Retreat and Renewal Center* (1951) 700 N. 66th St., 62223-3949. Tel: 618-397-0584; Fax: 618-397-5123; Email: info@kingsretreatcenter.org; Web: www.kingsretreatcenter.org. Deacon Douglas L. Boyer, Dir.; Revs. Mark Dean, O.M.I.; Salvador Gonzales, O.M.I.

[I] NEWMAN CENTERS

CARBONDALE. *The Newman Catholic Student Center*, 715 S. Washington, Carbondale, 62901. Tel: 618-529-3311; Fax: 618-549-9401; Email: office@siucnewman.org; Web: www.siucnewman.org. Mr. Tim Taylor, Dir.

[J] MISCELLANEOUS LISTINGS

BELLEVILLE. *Ancient Order of Hibernians*, 127 S. Douglas St., 62220. Tel: 618-257-2146; Email: patrickhdc@yahoo.com; Web: www.aohil1.com. Mr. Patrick J. Hickey, Contact Person.

Catholic Committee on Scouting of the Diocese of Belleville, 417 Meadowlark Ln., 62220. Tel: 618-233-4303; Fax: 618-233-4303; Email: rahermann417@gmail.com. Robert Hermann, Chm.

Catholic Community Foundation for the Diocese of Belleville, 222 S. 3rd St., 62220-1985. Tel: 618-277-8181; Email: enastoff@diobelle.org. Rev. Msgr. John W. McEvilly, V.G., Vicar; Mr. Michael Gibbons, Treas.

Catholic Diocese of Belleville General Fund, 222 S. Third St., 62220. Tel: 618-277-8181; Email: enastoff@diobelle.org. Rev. Msgr. John W. McEvilly, V.G., Vicar; Mr. Michael Gibbons, Treas.

Catholic Holy Family Society, Mary Barbara Kurtz, P.O. Box 327, 62222. Tel: 618-233-0286; Fax: 618-277-8259; Email: mbkurtz@chfsociety.org; Web: www.chfsociety.org. Mrs. Sandra Bouchard, C.O.O.

Catholic War Veterans, 3535 State Rte. 159, Freeburg, 62243. Tel: 618-234-3074; Email: rsatc82@att.net. Mailing Address: P.O. Box 325, 62222. Rick Schmidt, Commander.

D & L Fund, NFP, 222 S. Third St., 62220. Tel: 618-277-8181; Fax: 618-722-5019; Email: enastoff@diobelle.org. Rev. Msgr. John W. McEvilly, V.G., Vicar; Mr. Michael Gibbons, Trustee.

Diocese of Belleville The Catholic Service and Ministry Appeal, 222 S. Third St., 62220. Tel: 618-722-5007; Email: enastoff@diobelle.org. Rev. Msgr. John W. McEvilly, V.G., Vicar; Ms. Judy Phillips, Dir.; Mr. Michael Gibbons, Treas.

Engaged Encounter, 2620 Lebanon Ave., 62221. Tel: 618-235-9601; Email: gerry.bach@sbcglobal.net; Web: www.eeofs-il.org. Mr. Jerry Bach, Coord.; Ms. Ann Bach, Coord.

Ministry Formation Fund, NFP, 222 S. Third St., 62220. Tel: 618-277-8181; Fax: 618-277-0819; Email: enastoff@diobelle.org. Rev. Msgr. John W. McEvilly, V.G., Vicar; Mr. Michael Gibbons, Treas.

Missionary Association of Mary Immaculate-Missionary Oblates of Mary Immaculate, 9480 N. De Mazenod Dr., 62223. Tel: 618-398-4848; Fax: 618-398-8788; Email: jmadigan@oblatesusa.org; Web: www.oblatesusa.org. Revs. Andrew Knop, Dir.; John R. Madigan, O.M.I., Chap. Serving the missions of the Missionary Oblates, the National Shrine of Our Lady of the Snows, and the Tekakwitha Indian Missions.

Property & Liability Insurance Fund, NFP, 222 S. Third St., 62220. Tel: 618-277-8181; Fax: 618-722-5019; Email: enastoff@diobelle.org. Rev. Msgr. John W. McEvilly, V.G., Vicar; Mr. Michael Gibbons, Treas.

Secular Franciscan Order of St. Peter Fraternity, 8540 Little Prairie Road, Nashville, 62263. Tel: 618-424-7792; Email: Fransfo@aol.com. Peggy Overmann, Chairperson.

Serra Club of St. Clair County, 1333 Goldfinch Dr., 62223. Tel: 618-473-3513; Email: jtraney@me.com. 1333 Goldfinch Dr., 62223. Tel: 618-632-7541.

TEC (Teens Encounter Christ), 2620 Lebanon Ave., 62221. Cell: 618-722-5037; Web: www.bellevilletec.com. Michelle Biver, Chairperson.

Victorious Missionaries, 442 S. DeMazenod Dr., 62223. Tel: 618-394-6281 (Voice/TDD); Fax: 618-397-1210; Email: truhmann@snows.org; Web: www.vmusa.org. Bro. Thomas Ruhmann, O.M.I., National Dir.; Ms. Bette Meyer, Min. Asst. Spiritual Support Network for people with disabilities, chronic illness, and those who want to share the journey.

World Apostolate of Fatima, The Blue Army, U.S.A., 200 West Harrison Street, 62220-1985. Tel: 618-234-1166; Email: jtm300@aol.com. Rev. Msgr. John T. Myler, S.T.D., V.F., Spiritual Advisor, Tel: 618-234-1166.

CARLYLE. *Carlyle Priest Center*, 17440 Highline Rd., Carlyle, 62231. Tel: 618-277-8181; Email: mgibbons@diobelle.org. 222 S. Third St., 62220. Mr. Michael Gibbons, Business Mgr. Contact the Chancery, Tel: 618-277-8181.

CENTRALIA. **St. Mary's - Good Samaritan, Inc.*, 400 N. Pleasant Ave., Centralia, 62801. Tel: 618-436-8000 ; Email: kerry.swanson@ssmhealth.com; Web: www.smgsi.com. Kerry Swanson, Pres. Co-Sponsored by the Franciscan Sisters of Mary and the Felician Sisters.

St. Mary's Hospital Foundation, 400 N. Pleasant Ave., Centralia, 62801. Tel: 618-899-1047; Fax: 618-899-4808. Mrs. Kim McMillan, Chm.

DU QUOIN. *Catholic Daughters of the Americas*, 7545 Kimmel Rd., Du Quoin, 62832. Tel: 618-542-5230. Elizabeth Wynn, Chm.

EDWARDSVILLE. *Daughters of Isabella*, Precious Blood Circle #718, 522 N. Walnut, Pontiac, 61764. Tel: 815-844-7594. Ms. Amelia Wesselmann, Diocesan Chairperson, 248 W. Elm St., Aviston, 62216. Tel: 618-228-7372.

MOUNT VERNON. *SSM Health Good Samaritan Hospital Foundation*, 1 Good Samaritan Way, Mount Vernon, 62864. Tel: 618-899-1047; Fax: 618-899-4701. Mrs. Marcia Scott, Trustee.

O'FALLON. *Ancient Order of Hibernians (LAOH)*, 530 Scott Troy Rd., O Fallon, 62269. Tel: 618-581-9198.

Worldwide Marriage Encounter, 118 Woodbourne Ct., O Fallon, 62269. Tel: 618-622-8851; Email: joepatkaiser@yahoo.com; Web: www.aweekendofdiscovery.org. Joe Kaiser, Chm.

SCOTT AFB. *Scott Air Force Base*, Scott AFB Chapel, 375 AW/HC, 320 Ward Dr., Bldg. 1620, Scott AFB, 62225-5256. Tel: 618-256-3962; Fax: 618-256-1018; Email: hurley.thurston.ctr@us.af.mil. Hurley Thurston, CTR, USAF, Pastoral Min./ Coord.

INCORPORATED CEMETERIES

BELLEVILLE. *Catholic Diocese of Belleville Cemetery Association* Dee Dee Murray, Contact Person, Tel: 618-397-0181. Covers: Mt. Carmel, Belleville; Immaculate Conception, Centreville; Holy Cross, Fairview Hts; St. Phillips, East St. Louis, IL

Green Mount Catholic Cemetery of the Cathedral Congregation of Belleville, 200 W. Harrison St., 62220. Tel: 618-234-4858; Fax: 618-234-2957; Email: Cathedralbelle@gmail.com. Nancy Lowe, Sec.

BREESE. *St. Dominic Roman Catholic Cemetery of Breese*

FAIRVIEW HEIGHTS. *St. Adalbert Association (An Illinois Religious Corporation)*

O'FALLON. *Mount Calvary Cemetery of St. Clare Roman Catholic Congregation*

VILLA RIDGE. *Calvary Cemetery of St. Patrick Roman Catholic Church of Cairo*

NECROLOGY

† Frerker, John W., (Retired), Died Jun. 17, 2018

† Higuera, Federico, Anna, IL St Mary, Died Sep. 4, 2018

† Koehr, Louis, (Retired), Died Nov. 2, 2018

An asterisk (*) denotes an organization that has established tax-exempt status directly with the IRS and is not covered by the USCCB Group Ruling.

Diocese of Biloxi

(Dioecesis Biloxiiensis)

Most Reverend

LOUIS F. KIHNEMAN

Bishop of Biloxi; ordained November 18, 1977; appointed Bishop of Biloxi December 16, 2016; installed April 28, 2017. *Office: 1790 Popps Ferry Rd., Biloxi, MS 39532-2118.*

Chancery Office: 1790 Popps Ferry Rd., Biloxi, MS 39532-2118. Tel: 228-702-2100; Fax: 228-702-2125.

Most Reverend

ROGER P. MORIN

Retired Bishop of Biloxi; ordained April 15, 1971; appointed Auxiliary Bishop of New Orleans and Titular Bishop of Aulon February 11, 2003; ordained April 22, 2003; appointed Bishop of Biloxi March 2, 2009; installed April 27, 2009; retired December 16, 2016. *Office: 1790 Popps Ferry Rd., Biloxi, MS 39532-2118.*

ESTABLISHED MARCH 1, 1977.

Square Miles 9,653.

Comprises 17 counties in southern Mississippi: Jackson, Harrison, Hancock, George, Stone, Pearl River, Greene, Perry, Forrest, Lamar, Marion, Walthall, Wayne, Jones, Covington, Jefferson Davis and Lawrence.

Legal Title: "Catholic Diocese of Biloxi".
For legal titles of parishes and diocesan institutions, consult the Chancery Office.

STATISTICAL OVERVIEW

Personnel	
Bishop	1
Retired Bishops	1
Priests: Diocesan Active in Diocese	40
Priests: Retired, Sick or Absent	17
Number of Diocesan Priests	57
Religious Priests in Diocese	18
Total Priests in Diocese	75
Extern Priests in Diocese	7
Ordinations:	
Diocesan Priests	2
Transitional Deacons	1
Permanent Deacons in Diocese	41
Total Brothers	10
Total Sisters	23
Parishes	
Parishes	43
With Resident Pastor:	
Resident Diocesan Priests	32
Resident Religious Priests	6
Without Resident Pastor:	
Administered by Priests	5
Missions	8
Professional Ministry Personnel:	
Sisters	4
Lay Ministers	15
Welfare	
Homes for the Aged	8
Total Assisted	689
Special Centers for Social Services	7
Total Assisted	518,417
Other Institutions	1
Total Assisted	3,532
Educational	
Diocesan Students in Other Seminaries	6
Total Seminarians	6
High Schools, Diocesan and Parish	4
Total Students	1,240
High Schools, Private	1
Total Students	380
Elementary Schools, Diocesan and Parish	10
Total Students	2,314
Catechesis/Religious Education:	
High School Students	965
Elementary Students	2,863
Total Students under Catholic Instruction	7,768
Teachers in the Diocese:	
Brothers	5
Sisters	2
Lay Teachers	392
Vital Statistics	
Receptions into the Church:	
Infant Baptism Totals	636
Minor Baptism Totals	118
Adult Baptism Totals	90
Received into Full Communion	139
First Communions	800
Confirmations	747
Marriages:	
Catholic	138
Interfaith	84
Total Marriages	222
Deaths	651
Total Catholic Population	57,543
Total Population	824,910

Former Bishop—Most Revs. JOSEPH LAWSON HOWZE, D.D., ord. May 7, 1959; appt. Titular Bishop of Maxita and Auxiliary of Natchez-Jackson Nov. 8, 1972; ord. Bishop Jan. 28, 1973; appt. Bishop of Biloxi March 1, 1977; installed June 6, 1977; retired May 15, 2001; died Jan. 9, 2019.; THOMAS J. RODI, ord. May 20, 1978; appt. Bishop of Biloxi May 15, 2001; ord. and installed July 2, 2001; appt. Archbishop of Mobile April 2, 2008; installed June 6, 2008.; ROGER P. MORIN, (Retired), ord. April 15, 1971; appt. Auxiliary Bishop of New Orleans and Titular Bishop of Aulon Feb. 11, 2003; ord. April 22, 2003; appt. Bishop of Biloxi March 2, 2009; installed April 27, 2009; retired Dec. 16, 2016.

Office of the Bishop—1790 Popps Ferry Rd., Biloxi, 39532-2118. Tel: 228-702-2111.

Vicar General—Rev. Msgr. T. DOMINICK FULLAM, J.C.L., V.G., 1790 Popps Ferry Rd., Biloxi, 39532-2118. Tel: 228-702-2114.

Moderator of Curia—Rev. Msgr. T. DOMINICK FULLAM, J.C.L., V.G., 1790 Popps Ferry Rd., Biloxi, 39532-2118. Tel: 228-702-2114.

Chancery Office—1790 Popps Ferry Rd., Biloxi, 39532-2118. Tel: 228-702-2100; Fax: 228-702-2125. Office Hours: Mon.-Fri. 8:30-5All offices are at this address unless otherwise noted.

Pastoral Services—Deacon GAYDEN R. HARPER, Tel: 228-702-2107.

Special Delegate for Matrimonial Dispensations—Rev. Msgr. JOHN R. MCGRATH, J.C.L., (Retired), Tel: 228-702-2117.

Chancellor—Sr. REBECCA A. RUTKOWSKI, O.S.F., Tel: 228-702-2136.

Office of Stewardship and Development—Tel: 228-702-2100. MR. DAVID WYRWICH, Dir.

Marriage Tribunal—

Judicial Vicar—Tel: 228-702-2117. Very Rev. CHARLES W. NUTTER, J.C.L., J.V.

Tribunal Judge—Rev. Msgr. JOHN R. MCGRATH, J.C.L., (Retired).

Promoter of Justice—Rev. Msgr. MICHAEL J. THORNTON, J.C.L., (Retired).

Tribunal Judges—Rev. Msgr. JOHN R. MCGRATH, J.C.L., (Retired); Very Rev. CHARLES W. NUTTER, J.C.L., J.V.

Defenders of the Bond—Rev. Msgrs. T. DOMINICK FULLAM, J.C.L., V.G.; JAMES P. MCGOUGH, J.C.D., (Retired); Rev. THOMAS S. CONWAY; Rev. Msgr. MICHAEL J. THORNTON, J.C.L., (Retired).

Pro-Synodal Judge—Rev. Msgr. JAMES P. MCGOUGH, J.C.D., (Retired).

Advocates—Rev. PATRICK J. MOCKLER; Deacon JOHN R. HENDERSON; MR. DAVID WYRWICH; Deacon ROBERTO JIMENEZ.

Secretary and Ecclesiastical Notary (Court of First Instance)—MS. FRANCES T. GESELL.

Auditor—VACANT.

Deans—Very Revs. DENNIS J. CARVER, V.F., East Central Coast Deanery; JOSEPH M. UKO, V.F., Central Coast Deanery; MICHAEL P. O'CONNOR, V.F., West Coast Deanery; VACANT, East Coast Deanery; Very Rev. MARK A. ROPEL, V.F., Northern Deanery.

College of Consultors—Very Rev. DENNIS J. CARVER, V.F.; Rev. Msgrs. T. DOMINICK FULLAM, J.C.L., V.G.; JOHN R. MCGRATH, J.C.L., (Retired); Revs. CUTHBERT R. O'CONNELL; I. ANTHONY ARGUELLES, (Retired); Very Rev. MICHAEL P. O'CONNOR, V.F.; Rev. Msgr. MICHAEL J. THORNTON, J.C.L., (Retired).

Diocesan Attorney—CHRISTIAN STRICKLAND, Mailing Address: 2355 Pass Rd., Biloxi, 39531. Tel: 228-388-7441.

Department of Finance—TAMMY W. DILORENZO, CPA, Dir., Tel: 228-702-2118.

Department of Information Technology—MS. BEVERLY M. BAKER; Technical Support/Database Admin., Tel: 228-702-2175.

Office of Human Resources—Deacon GAYDEN R. HARPER, Tel: 228-702-2107.

Catholic Foundation of the Diocese of Biloxi, Inc.—MR. DAVID WYRWICH, Exec. Dir., Tel: 228-702-2100.

Mission Office—Rev. MICHAEL P. AUSTIN, Tel: 228-452-4686.

Office of Communication—TERRANCE P. DICKSON, Dir., 1790 Popps Ferry Rd., Biloxi, 39532-2118. Tel: 228-702-2126; Fax: 228-702-2128; Email: tdickson@biloxidiocese.org.

Gulf Pine Catholic Newspaper—TERRANCE P. DICKSON, Editor, Tel: 228-702-2126; Tel: 228-702-2127; Fax: 228-702-2128; Email: tdickson@biloxidiocese.org.

Department of Education—KATHERINE LINGENFELDER, Administrative Asst., Tel: 228-702-2130; Tel: 228-702-2100.

Office of Superintendent of Catholic Schools—DR.

RHONDA P. CLARK, Supt., Tel: 228-702-2130; Tel: 228-702-2129.

Resource Center—MR. LEO TRAHAN; HILLARY ROTH.

Office of Special Education—DR. RHONDA P. CLARK, Tel: 228-702-2130.

Office of Religious Education—MR. LEO TRAHAN, Dir., Tel: 228-702-2131.

CDB Religious Education, Inc.—MR. LEO TRAHAN, Contact Person, 1790 Popps Ferry Rd., Biloxi, 39532-2118. Tel: 228-702-2131.

Office of Youth Ministry—RAY LACY, Dir., Tel: 228-702-2142.

Catholic Boy Scouts—Office of Youth Ministry Tel: 228-702-2142.

Campus Ministry—Very Rev. MARK A. ROPEL, V.F., 3117 W. Fourth St., Hattiesburg, 39401. Tel: 601-264-5192.

Priests' Continuing Education and Retreat Programs—Rev. CUTHBERT R. O'CONNELL, 236 S. Beach Blvd., Waveland, 39576.

Ecumenical & Interreligious Affairs—MR. LEO TRAHAN, Contact Person, Tel: 228-702-2131.

Liturgy, Office of—Rev. MICHAEL P. AUSTIN, Dir., 22342 Evangeline Rd., Pass Christian, 39571. Tel: 228-452-4686.

Diocesan Liturgical Commission—Rev. MICHAEL P. AUSTIN, Chm.; MR. JASON GREEN; Rev. DOMINIC PHAM; MS. PAULA SPEARS; Deacon WILLIAM J. VRAZEL; Rev. Msgr. T. DOMINICK FULLAM, J.C.L., V.G.

Catholic Charities—Legal Title: Catholic Charities of South Mississippi *Administrative Office: 1790 Popps Ferry Rd., Biloxi, 39532-2118.* Tel: 228-701-0555. JENNIFER WILLIAMS, L.S.W., Diocesan Dir.

East Coast Deanery Outreach Center—1930 Old Mobile Ave., Pascagoula, 39567. Tel: 228-567-0001. Case Managers: HIEN NGUYEN; Sr. MARIVEL WITRAGO, M.N.J.S.

Disaster Recovery Program—NANCY LOFTUS, L.S.W., 1450 North St., Gulfport, 39507. Tel: 228-701-0555.

Western Deanery Outreach Center—MARY MCLEOD, Case Mgr.; ANNE HALE, Case Mgr., 640 Hwy. 90, Waveland, 39576. Tel: 228-467-2600.

Central and East Central Coast Deanery Outreach Center—RACHEL ALSTON, Case Mgr., 2204 24th Ave., Gulfport, 39507. Tel: 228-864-4221.

Food Bank—JENNIFER KEEGAN, Dir., 333 Cowan Rd., Gulfport, 39501. Tel: 228-822-0836.

Migration and Refugee Center—MAGDA LELEAUX, Dir., 1450 North St., Gulfport, 39507. Tel: 228-374-6554.

Family Life Office—Tel: 228-701-0555.

Catholic Charities Housing Association of Biloxi, Inc.—

Santa Maria Retirement Apartments; Villa Maria Retirement Apartments—Most Rev. LOUIS F. KIHNEMAN III, Pres.; GREG CRAPO, Contact Person, Tel: 228-702-2100.

Samaritan Housing, Inc.—Most Rev. LOUIS F. KIHNEMAN III, Pres.; GREG CRAPO, Contact Person, Tel: 228-702-2100.

Notre Dame de la Mer, Inc.—Most Rev. LOUIS F. KIHNEMAN III, Pres.; GREG CRAPO, Contact Person, Tel: 228-702-2100.

Gabriel Manor, Inc.—Most Rev. LOUIS F. KIHNEMAN III, Pres.; GREG CRAPO, Contact Person, Tel: 228-702-2100.

Caritas Manor, Inc.—Most Rev. LOUIS F. KIHNEMAN III, Pres.; GREG CRAPO, Contact Person, Tel: 228-702-2100.

Carlow Manor—Most Rev. LOUIS F. KIHNEMAN III, Pres.; GREG CRAPO, Contact Person, Tel: 228-702-2100.

Gabriel Manor II, Inc.—Most Rev. LOUIS F. KIHNEMAN III, Pres.; GREG CRAPO, Contact Person, Tel: 228-702-2100.

Apostleship of the Sea—Port of Gulfport: Deacon JOHN R. HENDERSON.

Vietnamese Apostolate—Rev. THANG JOHN PHAM.

Prison Apostolate—Jackson County Jails: Deacon GERALD PICKICH, Tel: 228-702-2107. Harrison County Jails: Deacon GERALD PICKICH, Tel: 228-702-2107. Hancock County Jails: Deacon GERALD PICKICH, Tel: 228-702-2107. South Mississippi Correctional Facility: Rev. IGNACIO JIMENEZ MORALES, Tel: 601-426-3473.

Diocesan Boards and Committees—

Association of Priests (Diocese of Biloxi and Jackson)—Most Revs. LOUIS F. KIHNEMAN III, Bishop of Biloxi & Co Chm.; JOSEPH R. KOPACZ, Bishop of Jackson & Co-Chm.; Revs. PATRICK J. MOCKLER, Pres.; JASON JOHNSTON, Sec., Treas., & Pres.-Elect. Trustees: Rev. THOMAS S. CONWAY; Rev. Msgr. MICHAEL J. THORNTON, J.C.L., (Retired); Revs. LINCOLN DALL; RUSTY VINCENT.

Board for the Formation, Life and Ministry of Permanent Deacons—Very Rev. DENNIS J. CARVER, V.F.; Rev. RYAN M. MCCOY; Very Rev. MICHAEL P. O'CONNOR, V.F.; Deacons DAVID W. ALLEN; GAYDEN R. HARPER, Chm.; ROBERT E. ILLANNE; WILLIAM J. VRAZEL; RONALD ALEXANDER JR.

Building and Real Estate Committee—Rev. MICHAEL P. AUSTIN, Chm.; CHUCK COLLINS; ROBERT STARKS; STEPHEN STOJCICH; BOB MANDAL; TAYLOR GUILD; SALLY JOACHIM; DAVID ALLEN, Esq.; MARION HARDY; MICHAEL COSTELLI; CHRIS CRIGHTON.

Catholic Foundation-Diocese of Biloxi—Most Rev. LOUIS F. KIHNEMAN III, Pres.; Rev. Msgr. T. DOMINICK FULLAM, J.C.L., V.G., Vice Pres.; MR. DAVID WYRWICH, Exec. Dir.; HENRY N. DICK III, Esq.; JOSEPH HUDSON; TED LONGO; VONRETTA J. SINGLETON; ROBERT TUCEI; WILLIAM WARD; TAMMY W. DILORENZO, CPA, Advisor.

Catholic Housing Board—Most Rev. LOUIS F. KIHNEMAN III; GREG CRAPO, Sec.; Rev. Msgr. T. DOMINICK FULLAM, J.C.L., V.G.; TAMMY W. DILORENZO, CPA; Sr. REBECCA A. RUTKOWSKI, O.S.F.; SALVADOR DOMINO; GARY YOUNG; Very Rev. CHARLES W. NUTTER, J.C.L., J.V.; Deacon MICHAEL M. HARRIS; CHERYL THOMPSON; JENNIFER WILLIAMS, L.S.W.; RACHEL ALSTON; Deacon NORBERT LLOYD JR.

Finance Council—Most Rev. LOUIS F. KIHNEMAN III; Rev. Msgrs. JOHN R. MCGRATH, J.C.L., (Retired); T. DOMINICK FULLAM, J.C.L., V.G.; TAMMY W. DILORENZO, CPA; DAVID ALLEN, Esq.; HENRY FOX; M.C. PRINCY HARRISON; WILLIAM KEARNEY; BILLY KNIGHT SR.; JOSEPH P. HUDSON; STEVE MONTAGNET JR.; MR. DAVID WYRWICH.

Insurance Committee—Most Rev. LOUIS F. KIHNEMAN III; Rev. Msgr. T. DOMINICK FULLAM, J.C.L., V.G.; Deacon JOHN E. JENNINGS; DR. RHONDA P. CLARK; GREG CRAPO; CYNTHIA HAHN. Advisor: TAMMY W. DILORENZO, CPA.

Mission Board—Most Rev. LOUIS F. KIHNEMAN III; Rev. MICHAEL P. AUSTIN.

Personnel Board—Rev. Msgr. MICHAEL J. THORNTON, J.C.L., (Retired); Very Revs. DENNIS J. CARVER, V.F.; MICHAEL P. O'CONNOR, V.F.; Rev. Msgr. T. DOMINICK FULLAM, J.C.L., V.G.; Rev. ROBERT P. HIGGINBOTHAM; Rev. Msgr. JOHN R. MCGRATH, J.C.L., (Retired); Rev. SATISH BABURAO ADHAV, (India).

Presbyteral Council—Most Rev. LOUIS F. KIHNEMAN III, Pres.; Very Rev. DENNIS J. CARVER, V.F.; Rev. I. ANTHONY ARGUELLES, (Retired); Rev. Msgrs. T. DOMINICK FULLAM, J.C.L., V.G.; JOHN R. MCGRATH, J.C.L., (Retired); Revs. SERGIO A. BALDERAS, (Mexico); PATRICK J. MOCKLER; RYAN M. MCCOY; HENRY B. MCINERNEY; Very Revs. MARK A. ROPEL, V.F.; MICHAEL P. O'CONNOR, V.F.; Rev. JOSEPH TRUONG Q. TRINH; Very Rev. JOSEPH M. UKO, V.F.; Rev. SATISH BABURAO ADHAV, (India).

Retired Priests' Committee—Most Rev. LOUIS F. KIHNEMAN III; Rev. Msgrs. T. DOMINICK FULLAM, J.C.L., V.G.; JOHN R. MCGRATH, J.C.L., (Retired); JAMES P. MCGOUGH, J.C.D., (Retired); Very Rev. MICHAEL P. O'CONNOR, V.F.; Revs. GEORGE E. MURPHY, (Retired); HENRY B. MCINERNEY.

Diocesan School Advisory Council—DR. RANDY ROTH; DAVE WARE; Rev. MARTIN JOSEPH GILLESPIE; MICHAEL BRUFFEY, Esq.; LINDA HEBERT; Rev. COLTEN SYMMES; KATHY SPRINGER; DR. RHONDA P. CLARK; MRS. ELIZABETH FORTENBERRY; BRIAN SANDERSON.

Consultative Committee for Safe Environment—Rev. KENNETH RAMON-LANDRY; DR. RICHARD SCHMIDT; CAROLYN PERRY; JOHN MICHAEL O'KEEFE; ALICIA TARRANT.

Advisory Board for de l'Epee Deaf Center—GREG CRAPO, Dir.; Most Rev. LOUIS F. KIHNEMAN III; Deacon JOHN R. HENDERSON; CHARLES HEWES; JOSEPH VINCENT; WILLIAM MCCOLLISTER; VICKI MILLER; DORIS MAHALAK; RAYANNE WEISS; Rev. JAMES ROBERTS; DARLENE ROJAS; BEN DILORENZO; DENNIS OLIVER; RONALD COCHRAN, Esq.; KATHLEEN TALLEY; DARLENE DUFFANO; HELEN MARGIOTTA; SUSAN MCCORMICK; DOUG BRADFORD; JAMIE OLSON; MANUEL ROJAS.

Miscellaneous Apostolates—

Campaign for Human Development—JENNIFER WILLIAMS, L.S.W., 1790 Popps Ferry Rd., Biloxi, 39532-2118. Tel: 228-701-0555.

Catholic Relief Services—MR. GREGORY K. CRAPO, B.S., M.B.A, 1790 Popps Ferry Rd., Biloxi, 39532-2118. Tel: 228-897-2280.

Catholic University, Friends of—Rev. Msgr. T. DOMINICK FULLAM, J.C.L., V.G., 1790 Popps Ferry Rd., Biloxi, 39532-2118.

Charismatic Renewal—Rev. GEORGE R. KITCHIN, Dir., St. Mary Parish, 809 De La Pointe Dr., Gautier, 39553.

Cursillo and Retreats—VACANT, 14595 Vidalia Rd., Pass Christian, 39571. Tel: 228-255-7560.

**Deaf and Disabled, Office of the*—Rev. ANTHONY DOAN TRAN, Chap.; MR. GREGORY K. CRAPO, B.S., M.B.A, Dir., 1450 North St., Gulfport, 39507. Tel: 228-897-2280 (Voice); Tel: 228-206-6062 (Video Phone); Fax: 228-897-2462.

Latin American Apostolate—Mission-Saltillo, Mexico, co-sponsored with Diocese of Jackson VACANT, Av. Central 4649, Col. Vista Hermosa, Saltillo, Coah CP, Mexico 25010.

Legion of Mary—Contact: Office of Pastoral Svcs.. Tel: 228-702-2107.

Permanent Diaconate Program—1790 Popps Ferry Rd., Biloxi, 39532. Tel: 228-702-2107. Deacons GAYDEN R. HARPER, Dir.; MELVIN J. LANDRY JR., Assoc. Dir. Formation; KARL KOBERGER, Assoc. Dir. Formation; RALPH TORRELLI, Assoc. Dir. Continuing Educ.; WILLIAM J. VRAZEL, Assoc. Dir. Liturgy and Devel.; GERALD PICKICH, Assoc. Dir. Prison Ministry; ERNEST VANCOURT, Assoc. Dir. Formation; MICHAEL M. HARRIS, Assoc. Dir.; DAVID ALLEN, Esq., Assoc. Dir. Continuing Educ.

Pontifical Association of the Holy Childhood—Rev. MICHAEL P. AUSTIN, Dir., 22342 Evangeline Rd., Pass Christian, 39571. Tel: 228-452-4686.

Propagation of the Faith—Rev. MICHAEL P. AUSTIN, Dir., 22342 Evangeline Rd., Pass Christian, 39571. Tel: 228-452-4686.

Vocations—Revs. ADAM URBANIAK, Dir., 503 Convent Ave., Pascagoula, 39567. Tel: 228-762-1653; COLTEN SYMMES, Asst. Vocation Dir., 870 Howard Ave., Biloxi, 39530. Tel: 228-374-1717.

CDB Seminarian Education, Inc.—Rev. ADAM URBANIAK, Contact Person, 503 Convent Ave., Pascagoula, 39567. Tel: 228-762-1653.

Victim Assistance Coordinator—EMILY CLOUD, Tel: 228-424-7292; Email: ecloud78@gmail.com.

CLERGY, PARISHES, MISSIONS AND PAROCHIAL SCHOOLS

CITY OF BILOXI

(HARRISON COUNTY)

1—CATHEDRAL OF THE NATIVITY OF THE BLESSED VIRGIN MARY (1843) Very Rev. Dennis J. Carver, V.F., Rector; Rev. Colten Symmes.

Res.: 870 Howard Ave., 39530. Tel: 228-374-1717; Email: jhewitt@nativitybvm.org; Web: nativitybvmcathedral.org.

School—Nativity BVM School, (Grades 1-6), 1046 Beach Blvd., 39530. Tel: 228-432-2269; Fax: 228-432-9421; Email: nbvmbiloxi@aol.com; Web: www.nativitybvm.org. Sr. Mary Jo Mike, O.S.F., Prin.; Kelly Pennell, Librarian. Lay Teachers 13; Sisters 1; Students 165.

Catechesis Religious Program— Twinned with Nativity BVM Parish. Students 105.

2—BLESSED FRANCIS XAVIER SEELOS (2005)

356 Lameuse St., 39530. Tel: 228-435-0007; Fax: 228-435-7555; Email: rev_andoh@yahoo.com; Email: BlessedSeelosCC@yahoo.com. Mailing Address: P.O. Box 347, 39533-0347. Rev. Godfrey Andoh; Deacon Melvin J. Landry Jr.

Res.: 724 Bradford St., 39530.

Catechesis Religious Program—Email: bunwalq@yahoo.com. Cheryl Thompson, D.R.E. Students 3.

3—VIETNAMESE MARTYRS CHURCH (2000) [JC] (Vietnamese)

171 Oak St., 39530. Tel: 228-374-1116; Fax: 228-374-9344; Email: vnmartyrsblx@gmail.com. 172 Oak St., 39530. Rev. Thang John Pham.

Catechesis Religious Program—Students 126.

4—ST. LOUIS (1957) Closed. For inquiries for sacramental records, please see Blessed Francis Xavier Seelos, Biloxi.

5—ST. MARY (1967)

8343 Woolmarket Rd., 39532. Tel: 228-392-1999; Fax: 228-392-4552; Cell: 228-731-2747; Email: stmarybiloxi@yahoo.com; Web: www.stmarycc.net. Rev. Msgr. T. Dominick Fullam, J.C.L., V.G.; Deacons Gerald Pickich; Al Stockert.

Catechesis Religious Program—Lucy Peterson, D.R.E.; Matthew Johnson, Youth Min. Students 28.

6—ST. MICHAEL (1917)

177 First St., 39533. Tel: 228-435-5578; Email: stmichaelschurch@cableone.net; Web: stmichaelchurchbilox.com; Web: facebook.com/Stmichaelbiloxi. P.O. Box 523, 39533. Rev. Gregory Barras.

Res.: 310 Lovers Ln., Ocean Springs, 39564.

Catechesis Religious Program—Nativity Sacred Heart Center, 370 Nativity Dr., 39530. Students 14.

7—OUR LADY OF FATIMA (1957)

2090 Pass Rd., 39531. Tel: 228-388-3887;

Tel: 228-388-3891; Fax: 228-388-7069; Email: fatima@cableone.net; Web: www.fatima-biloxi.com. Revs. Henry B. McInerney; Daniel Martinez Patino, Parochial Vicar; Deacons Paul G. Mathern; Ronald Alexander Jr.

School—Our Lady of Fatima School, (Grades PreK-6), 320 Jim Money Rd., 39531. Tel: 228-388-3602; Fax: 228-385-1140; Email: chahn@olfschool.org; Web: www.olfschool.org. Mrs. Cindy Hahn, Prin.; Jacqueline Coale, Librarian. Lay Teachers 18; Students 204.

Catechesis Religious Program—Tel: 228-388-5737; Email: fatimaccd@cableone.net. Students 156.

8—OUR MOTHER OF SORROWS (1914) (African American)
803 Division St., 39530. Tel: 228-435-0007; Fax: 228-435-7555; Email: rev_andoh@yahoo.com; Email: OurMotherofSorrowsCC@yahoo.com. Mailing Address: P.O. Box 347, 39533-0347. Rev. Godfrey Andoh; Deacon Richard Smith.

Catechesis Religious Program—Email: bunwalq@yahoo.com. Cheryl Thompson, D.R.E. Students 4.

9—SACRED HEART (1921)
10446 LeMoyne Blvd., D'Iberville, 39540. Tel: 228-392-4526; Email: sacredheartparish@cableone.net. Rev. Dominic Pham.

School—Sacred Heart School, (Grades 1-6), 10482 Lemoyne Blvd., D'Iberville, 39540. Tel: 228-392-4180 ; Fax: 228-392-4859; Email: rlopez@sacredheartelementary.org; Web: www.sacredheartelementary.org. Richard Lopez, Prin.; Barbara Ziz, Librarian. Lay Teachers 14; Students 99; Librarians 1.

Catechesis Religious Program—
Tel: 228-359-5509 Elementary. Mrs. Sarah Landry, D.R.E., Elementary; Mrs. Christa Hedman, D.R.E., High School. Students 110.

OUTSIDE THE CITY OF BILOXI

BASSFIELD, JEFFERSON DAVIS CO., ST. PETER (1904) [CEM 2] [JC2] (Irish)
4135 Hwy. 42, Bassfield, 39421. Tel: 601-943-6688; Fax: 601-943-8055; Email: stpetersms@windstream.net. P.O. Box 10, Bassfield, 39421. Chinnappa R. Mark, H.G.N., Admin.

Catechesis Religious Program—Linda Bass, D.R.E. Students 57.

Mission—St. Lawrence, P.O. Box 16, Monticello, Lawrence Co. 39654.

BAY ST. LOUIS, HANCOCK CO.

1—OUR LADY OF THE GULF (1847) [CEM] Very Rev. Michael P. O'Connor, V.F.; Deacons Eddie Renz; Mike Harris, Email: michael_m_harris@me.com; Mrs. Kathleen LeBlanc, Pastoral Assoc.; Mrs. Annette Encrapera, Sec.
Res.: 228 S. Beach Blvd., Bay St. Louis, 39520. Tel: 228-467-6509; Email: olgchurch39520@gmail.com.

School—Holy Trinity Catholic Elementary, (Grades 1-6), 301 S. Second St., Bay St. Louis, 39520. Tel: 228-467-5158; Fax: 228-467-9742; Email: mroberts@holytrinitycatholic.net; Email: dlizana@holytrinitycatholic.net; Web: www.holytrinitycatholic.net. Desiree Lizana, Prin.; Mrs. Mary Roberts, Sec. Lay Teachers 20; Students 232.

Catechesis Religious Program—Students 88.

2—ST. ROSE DE LIMA (1924) (African American)
301 S. Necaise Ave., Bay St. Louis, 39520. Tel: 228-467-7347; Tel: 228-467-7357; Fax: 228-467-7740; Email: st.rose_delima@yahoo.com. Rev. Agustinus Seran, S.V.D.

Catechesis Religious Program—Tel: 228-342-5172. Mrs. Joan Thomas, D.R.E. Students 56.

CLERMONT HARBOR, HANCOCK CO., ST. ANN (1915) [CEM]
5858 Lower Bay Rd, Bay St. Louis, 39520. Tel: 228-467-5128; Fax: 228-467-5638; Email: stanncathparish@att.net. Rev. George Manchapilly, C.M.I.

Catechesis Religious Program—Students 30.

Chapels—St. Joseph Chapel—5383 Hwy. 604, Pearlington, 39572.

Holy Infant of Good Health Chapel.

COLUMBIA, MARION CO., HOLY TRINITY (1959)
1429 N. Park Ave., Columbia, 39429. Tel: 601-736-3136; Fax: 601-736-1920; Email: holytrinitycc@gmail.com. Rev. Martin Joseph Gillespie.

Catechesis Religious Program—Jessica Martin, D.R.E. Students 15.

Mission—St. Paul the Apostle, 702 Union Rd., Tylertown, Walthall Co. 39667. Tel: 601-876-6422. P.O. Box 470, Tylertown, 39667.

Catechesis Religious Program—Audrey Rink, D.R.E. (St. Paul Mission). Students 15.

DELISLE, HARRISON CO.

1—MOST HOLY TRINITY PARISH (1869)
Mailing Address: 9062 Kiln DeLisle Rd., Pass Christian, 39571. Tel: 228-255-1294; Fax: 228-255-7479; Web: www.mhtcatholic.org. Rev. Patrick J. Mockler.
Res.: 7625 Fairway Dr., Diamondhead, 39525.

Catechesis Religious Program—Tina Balentine, D.R.E. Students 168.

2—ST. STEPHEN (1874) Closed. For inquiries for parish records see Most Holy Trinity, Pass Christian.

GAUTIER, JACKSON CO., ST. MARY (1968)
809 De La Pointe Rd., Gautier, 39553. Tel: 228-497-2364; Email: stmarygautier@yahoo.com. Rev. George R. Kitchin; Deacon Robert E. Illanne.

Catechesis Religious Program—Kim Duffy, D.R.E. Students 59.

GULFPORT, HARRISON CO.

1—ST. ANN (1939) Rev. Khoa Phi Vo.
Res.: 23529 Hwy. 53, Gulfport, 39503. Tel: 228-832-2560; Email: stanncatholic@bellsouth.net.

Catechesis Religious Program—Tel: 228-831-9452. Robert Earl Lizana, D.R.E. Students 74.

Mission—Our Lady of Chartres, Big Creek Rd., Delmas Dedeaux, Harrison Co. 39503.

2—ST. JAMES (1898) [CEM]
366 Cowan Rd., Gulfport, 39507. Tel: 228-896-6059; Email: dchevalierstjames@gmail.com. Very Rev. Charles W. Nutter, J.C.L., J.V.; Deacon John R. Henderson, Pastoral Assoc.

School—St. James School, (Grades 1-6), 603 West Ave., Gulfport, 39507. Tel: 228-896-6631; Fax: 228-896-6638; Email: jbroadus@stjamesgulfport.com; Web: www.stjamesgulfport.com. Mrs. Jennifer Broadus, Prin.; Connie Favret, Librarian. Lay Teachers 18; Students 294.

Catechesis Religious Program—Rob Russo, D.R.E. Students 119.

3—ST. JOHN THE EVANGELIST (1900)
2414 17th St., Gulfport, 39501. Tel: 228-864-2272; Fax: 228-864-2273; Email: stjohnthee@stjohngulfport.org; Web: stjohngulfport.org. Rev. Ryan M. McCoy.
Res.: 2411 17th St., Gulfport, 39501.

High School—St. Patrick High School, 18300 St. Patrick Rd., 39532-8655. Tel: 228-702-0500; Fax: 228-702-0511; Web: mbuckley@stpatrickhighschool.net; Web: www.stpatrickhighschool.net. Mr. Matthew Buckley, Principal. Lay Teachers 29; Students 400.

Catechesis Religious Program—Email: lhebert@stjohngulfport.org. Linda Hebert, D.R.E. Students 10.

4—ST. JOSEPH CATHOLIC CHURCH (Northwood Hills) (1966)
12290 DePew Rd., Gulfport, 39503. Tel: 228-832-3244; Fax: 228-832-1166; Email: stjosephgulfport@bellsouth.net. Very Rev. Joseph M. Uko, V.F.; Deacon Karl Koberger.

Catechesis Religious Program—Email: jenholl630@hotmail.com. Mrs. Jenny Hollingsworth, D.R.E. Students 113.

5—ST. THERESE (1932) (African American)
3521 19th St., Gulfport, 39501. Tel: 228-863-0624; Email: st_therese_church@yahoo.com. Rev. Joseph Doyle, Admin.; Deacon Gerard Norris.

Catechesis Religious Program—Students 37.

HATTIESBURG, FORREST CO.

1—HOLY ROSARY (1949) (African American) Rev. Kenneth Ramon-Landry.
Res.: 900 Dabbs St., Hattiesburg, 39401. Tel: 601-584-6528; Email: HolyRosary1949@aol.com.

Catechesis Religious Program—

2—SACRED HEART (1900) [CEM]
313 Walnut St., P.O. Box 1027, Hattiesburg, 39401. Tel: 601-583-9404; Email: sacheartchurch@aol.com; Web: www.sacredhearthattiesburg.com. Revs. Kenneth Ramon-Landry; Alwin Samy, Parochial Vicar; Deacons Warren Goff, RCIA Director; Randy Duke.

School—Sacred Heart Elementary School, (Grades 1-6), 608 Southern Ave., Hattiesburg, 39401. Tel: 601-583-8683; Fax: 601-583-8684; Email: vflanagan@shshattiesburg.com; Web: www.shshattiesburg.com. Vicki Flanagan, Prin., Elementary; Karyn Walsh, Librarian. Lay Teachers 53; Students 739; Asst. Teachers 7.

High School—Sacred Heart High School, (Grades 7-12), 510 W. Pine St., Hattiesburg, 39401. Tel: 601-450-5736; Fax: 601-450-5739; Email: eyankay@shhattiesburg.com. Dr. Elizabeth Yankay, Prin.

Catechesis Religious Program—Email: abarquero1@yahoo.com. Mr. Alejandro Barquero, D.R.E. Students 40.

3—ST. THOMAS AQUINAS (1968) (University of Southern Mississippi-Student Parish)
3117 W. Fourth St., Hattiesburg, 39401. Tel: 601-264-5192; Email: church@stthomas-usm.org; Web: www.stthomas-usm.org. Very Rev. Mark A. Ropel, V.F.; rev. David Milton, H.G.N., Parochial Vicar.

Catechesis Religious Program—Tel: 601-270-5789. Renee Licatenhan, D.R.E. Students 150.

KILN, HANCOCK CO., ANNUNCIATION (1869) [CEM] Revs. Robert P. Higginbotham; Richard-Paul LaCorte, (In Res.).
Res.: 5370 Kiln-DeLisle Rd., Kiln, 39556. Tel: 228-255-1800; Fax: 228-255-1894; Email: annunciationkiln@att.net.

Catechesis Religious Program—Ashley Appel, D.R.E. Students 46.

LAUREL, JONES CO., IMMACULATE CONCEPTION (1887) Rev. Ignacio Jimenez-Morales, Admin.; Deacons Richard Hollingsworth; David Hughes Sr.
Res.: 833 W. Sixth St., Laurel, 39440. Tel: 601-426-3473; Email: iccparishsecretary@gmail.com; Web: laurelcatholic.com.

Catechesis Religious Program—Students 161.

LONG BEACH, HARRISON CO., ST. THOMAS THE APOSTLE (1903)
Mailing Address: 720 East Beach Blvd., P.O. Box 1529, Long Beach, 39560. Tel: 228-863-1610; Email: secretary@saintthomaslb.org; Web: www.SaintThomasLB.org. Revs. Cuthbert R. O'Connell; James Michael Smith, Parochial Vicar; Deacon Ernest Vancourt. In Res., Rev. Patrick O'Shaughnessy, (Retired).
Res.: 725 N. Nicholson, P.O. Box 1529, Long Beach, 39560.

School—St. Vincent de Paul Elementary, (Grades 1-6), 4321 Espy Ave., Long Beach, 39560. Tel: 228-222-6000; Fax: 228-222-6003; Email: cchurch@svdpcatholicschool.org; Email: mfairley@svdpcatholicschool.org; Email: pseal@svdpcatholicschool.org; Email: vladner@svdpcatholicschool.org; Web: www.svdpcatholicschool.org. Carol Church, Prin. (Interparochial) Lay Teachers 25; Students 362.

Catechesis Religious Program—Tel: 228-868-3774; Email: religiouseducation@saintthomaslb.org. Sr. Cecilia Nguyen, C.C.S.S., D.R.E.

LUMBERTON, LAMAR CO.

1—OUR LADY OF PERPETUAL HELP (1922) [CEM] Rev. Fintan J. Kilmurray.
Res.: 379 W. Seneca Rd., Lumberton, 39455-7728. Tel: 601-796-3053; Fax: 601-796-3023; Email: fjklum-pop@bellsouth.net.

Catechesis Religious Program—Students 64.

Mission—St. Joseph, 17 Bilbo Hill, P.O. Box 202, Poplarville, Pearl River Co. 39470.

2—ST. FABIAN CATHOLIC PARISH
5266 Old Hwy. 11, Ste. 50-214, Hattiesburg, 39402. Tel: 601-467-5620; Email: church@saintfabian.com; Cell: 601-467-7421; Web: www.saintfabian.com. Rev. Thomas S. Conway.

MOSS POINT, JACKSON CO., ST. JOSEPH (1950)
4114 First St., Moss Point, 39563. Tel: 228-475-0777; Fax: 228-475-3672. P.O. Box 8549, Moss Point, 39562-8549. Rev. Peter Varghese, C.M.I.; Deacons Emery E. Elder; Frank W. Martin.

Catechesis Religious Program—Students 29.

Mission—St. Ann, 21424 Hwy. 613, Moss Point, Jackson Co. 39562. Tel: 228-588-0599; Email: hurleystann@gmail.com. P.O. Box 244, Hurley, 39555. Sheila Knapp, Contact Person.

OCEAN SPRINGS, JACKSON CO.

1—ST. ALPHONSUS (1860)
502 Jackson Ave., Ocean Springs, 39564. Tel: 228-875-5419; Fax: 228-875-5410; Email: stals@cableone.net; Web: www.osstalphonsus.org. Revs. Michael E. Snyder; Tomasz Golab, Parochial Vicar; Deacon James Gunkel.

School—St. Alphonsus School, (Grades 1-6), 504 Jackson Ave., Ocean Springs, 39564. Tel: 228-875-5329; Fax: 228-875-3584; Email: school@stal.org. Dr. Pamala Rogers, Prin. Lay Teachers 13; Students 174.

Catechesis Religious Program—Tel: 228-872-2652; Email: pcronin@cableone.net. Pat Cronin, D.R.E. Students 175.

2—ST. ELIZABETH ANN SETON (1975)
4900 Riley Rd., Ocean Springs, 39564. Tel: 228-875-0654; Fax: 228-875-6852; Email: office@stelseton.com; Web: stelseton.com. Rev. Sergio A. Balderas, (Mexico); Deacons Michael Butler; Martin Finnegan.

Catechesis Religious Program—Mrs. Linda Holtorf, D.R.E. Students 209.

PASCAGOULA, JACKSON CO.

1—OUR LADY OF VICTORIES (1855)
3109 Magnolia St., Pascagoula, 39567. Tel: 228-762-1653; Tel: 228-762-1663; Email: ourladyofvictories@yahoo.com; Web: www.olvpascagoula.com. P.O. Box 368, Pascagoula, 39568. Rev. Adam Urbaniak.

Catechesis Religious Program—Tel: 228-623-4747. Michele Hill, D.R.E. Students 75.

2—ST. PETER THE APOSTLE (1907) [CEM] (African American)
1715 Telephone Rd., Pascagoula, 39568-0876. Tel: 228-762-1759; Email: stpeterparishpascagoula@gmail.com; Web: www.

stpeterparishpascagoula.org. Mailing Address: P.O. Box 876, Pascagoula, 39568. Rev. Joseph Benjamin, S.S.J.
Catechesis Religious Program—Students 42.
3—SACRED HEART (1962)
3702 Quinn Dr., Pascagoula, 39581.
Tel: 228-762-1837; Fax: 228-762-1958; Email: heartline@cableone.net. Mailing Address: P.O. Box 2190, Pascagoula, 39569. Rev. Everardo Mora Torres, Admin.
School—Resurrection School-Elementary, (Grades 1-6), 3704 Quinn Dr., Pascagoula, 39581-2356.
Tel: 228-762-7207; Fax: 228-762-0611; Email: nhamilton@rcseagles.com; Web: www.rcseagles.com. Noah Hamilton, Prin.; Linda Wiggins, Librarian; Bonnie Smith, Librarian. Lay Teachers 25; Students 274.
Catechesis Religious Program—Students 43.
PASS CHRISTIAN, HARRISON CO.
1—HOLY FAMILY PARISH (Pineville) (2005) [CEM]
Mailing Address: 22342 Evangeline Dr., Pass Christian, 39571. Tel: 228-452-4686; Email: holyfamilyparish@cableone.net; Web: holyfamilyparish.cc. Rev. Michael P. Austin; Deacon William J. Vrazel
Legal Title: St. Paul Catholic Church; Our Lady of Lourdes Catholic Church
Res.: 22410 Glad Acres, Pass Christian, 39571.
School—St. Vincent de Paul Elementary, (Grades 1-6), Tel: 228-222-6000; Email: cchurch@svdpcatholicschool.org. Carol Church, Prin. (Interparochial) Lay Teachers 25; Students 362.
Catechesis Religious Program—Linden Williams, D.R.E. (at St. Vincent De Paul) Students 366.
2—OUR MOTHER OF MERCY (1911) [JC] (African American)
216 Saucier Ave., Pass Christian, 39571.
Tel: 228-452-4514; Email: ourmotherofmercy2018@gmail.com. Rev. Michael Vu, S.V.D.
Catechesis Religious Program—Tel: 228-452-4573. Students 77.
3—ST. PAUL, Closed. For inquiries for parish records contact Holy Family, Pass Christian.
4—SACRED HEART (Dedeaux) (1967)
14595 Vidalia Rd., Pass Christian, 39571.
Tel: 228-255-7560; Fax: 288-255-7888; Email: holygroundeagle@aol.com. Rev. Bartosz T. Kunat; Deacon Roberto Jimenez.
Catechesis Religious Program—Students 143.
Station—Cursillo Center, (Dedeaux) Pass Christian. Tel: 228-255-0430.
PEARLINGTON, HANCOCK CO., ST. JOSEPH (1939) [JC] Closed. For inquiries for sacramental records, please see St. Ann, Clermont Harbor.
PICAYUNE, PEARL RIVER CO., ST. CHARLES BORROMEO (1950)
1000 5th Ave., Picayune, 39466. Tel: 601-798-4779; Email: stcharlesinfo@gmail.com; Web: www.scborromeo.org. Revs. Bernard J. Papania Jr.; Marcin Wiktor, Parochial Vicar; Very Rev. John T. Noone, V.F., (Retired); Deacons Brian Klause; Douglas R. McNair.
School—St. Charles Borromeo Catholic Elementary School, (Grades 1-8), 1006 Goodyear Blvd., Picayune, 39466. Tel: 601-799-0860; Fax: 601-798-7574; Email: stcb.principal@stcbcatholicschool.org; Web: www.stcbcatholicschool.org. Dr. Sharon Guepet, Prin. Lay Teachers 15; Students 106.
Catechesis Religious Program—Mrs. Jill Bordelon, D.R.E.; Ms. Marianne Schmidt, Youth Min. Students 176.
PINEVILLE, HARRISON CO., OUR LADY OF LOURDES (Pass Christian) (1973) Closed. Please see Holy Family, Pass Christian.
VANCLEAVE, JACKSON CO., HOLY SPIRIT CATHOLIC CHURCH (1980) Rev. Piotr A. Kmiecik; Deacons John E. Jennings; Norbert Lloyd Jr.
Res.: 6705 Jim Ramsey Rd., Vancleave, 39565.
Tel: 228-283-5252; Fax: 228-283-5255; Email: holyspiritcc@bellsouth.net; Web: holyspiritcc.com.
Catechesis Religious Program—Students 50.
Mission—Christ the King, 10601 Daisy Vestry, Latimer, Jackson Co. 39565.
WAVELAND, HANCOCK CO., ST. CLARE (1919)
236 S. Beach Blvd., Waveland, 39576.
Tel: 228-467-9275; Email: stclarecatholic@yahoo.com. P.O. Box 500, Waveland, 39576. Rev. Jacob Mathew Smith, O.F.M.; Deacon Michael Saxer.
Catechesis Religious Program—Tel: 228-216-4365. Students 41.
WAYNESBORO, WAYNE CO., ST. BERNADETTE (1977) [JC2]
401 Mississippi Dr., Waynesboro, 39367.
Tel: 601-735-9420; Email: iccparishsecretary@gmail.com. Rev. Ignacio Jimenez-Morales, Admin.; Deacons Richard Hollingsworth; David Hughes Sr.
Catechesis Religious Program—Students 18.
Mission—Holy Trinity, 911 Jackson Ave., P.O. Box 896, Leakesville, Perry Co. 39451.
Tel: 601-394-6761.
WHITE CYPRESS, HANCOCK CO., ST. MATTHEW THE APOSTLE (1982) [CEM]
27074 St. Matthews Church Rd., Perkinston, 39373.
Tel: 228-255-7720; Fax: 228-255-7786; Email: stshadhav@gmail.com. Rev. Satish Baburao Adhav, (India); Deacon Richard John Kren.
Catechesis Religious Program—Email: lesleyhavard@live.com. Lesley Havard, D.R.E. Students 102.
WIGGINS, STONE CO., ST. FRANCIS XAVIER (1961) [JC]
1026 Central Ave. E., Wiggins, 39577. Cell: 601-528-1393; Email: stfxstl@gmail.com. Rev. Michael A. Marascalco; Deacon Steven Beckham.
Catechesis Religious Program—Leona O'Neil, D.R.E. Students 97.
Mission—St. Lucy, 125 Scott Rd., Lucedale, George Co. 39452.
Catechesis Religious Program—Patricia Howell, D.R.E.
Station—Perkinston Junior College, Perkinston.

Chaplains of Public Institutions

BILOXI. *Keesler Airforce Base*. Rev. John Reutemann, Chap.
V.A. Center. Revs. Philip Audet, Hospital, Truong Quang Trinh.
COLUMBIA. *Industrial and Training School*. Rev. Martin Joseph Gillespie.
GULFPORT. *Naval Construction Battalion Center*. Rev. Patrick J. Mockler.
HATTIESBURG. *University of Southern Mississippi*. Very Rev. Mark A. Ropel, V.F.
LEAKESVILLE. *South Mississippi Correctional Institution*. Rev. Ignacio Jimenez Morales.

Retired:
Most Rev.—
Morin, Roger P., D.D., (Retired)
Rev. Msgrs.—
McGough, James P., J.C.D., (Retired)
McGrath, John R., J.C.L., (Retired)
Mercier, Joseph, (Retired)
Thornton, Michael J., J.C.L., (Retired)
Revs.—
Arguelles, I. Anthony, (Retired)
Dilettuso, Joseph, (Retired)
Fannon, Noel, (Retired)
Farrell, Bernard P., (Retired)
Izral, John, (Retired)
Kelleher, Michael, (Retired)
Kelly, John J., (Retired)
Lohan, Louis, (Retired)
Lynch, Antone, (Retired)
Murphy, George E., (Retired)
Noone, John T., (Retired)
O'Shaughnessy, Patrick, (Retired)
Phan, Dominic, (Retired)
Tracey, Michael, (Retired)
White, Thomas, (Retired).

Permanent Deacons:
Alexander, Ronald Jr., Our Lady of Fatima, Biloxi
Allen, David W., St. John's, Gulfport
Arellano, Jesus, BVM Cathedral, Biloxi
Beckham, Steven, St. Francis Xavier, Wiggins
Butler, Michael, St. Elizabeth Seton, Ocean Springs
Conason, Rick, St. John, Gulfport
Duke, Randy, Sacred Heart, Hattiesburg
Elder, Emery, St. Joseph, Moss Point
Everard, Robert, (Retired)
Finnegan, Martin, (Retired)
Gilly, Michael, Our Lady of Victories, Pascagoula
Goff, Warren P. Sr., Sacred Heart, Hattiesburg
Gunkel, James, St. Alphonsus, Ocean Springs
Harper, Gayden R., Our Lady of Victories, Pascagoula
Harris, Michael M., Our Lady of the Gulf, Bay St. Louis
Henderson, John R., St. James, Gulfport
Hollingsworth, Richard A., Immaculate Conception, Laurel
Hughes, David O., (Retired)
Illanne, Robert E., St. Mary, Gautier
Jennings, John E., Holy Spirit, Vancleave
Jimenez, Roberto, Sacred Heart, Pass Christian
Klause, Brian, St. Charles Borromeo, Picayune
Koberger, Karl, St. Joseph, Gulfport
Kren, Richard John, St. Matthew, White Cypress
Landry, Melvin J. Jr., Blessed Francis Xavier Seelos, Biloxi
LeBlanc, Tom, (Retired)
Lloyd, Norbert, Christ the King, Latimer
Martin, Frank W., St. Ann Mission, Hurley
Matherne, Paul, Our Lady of Fatima, Biloxi
McNair, Douglas R., St. Charles Borromeo, Picayune
Norris, Gerald, St. Therese Lisieux, Gulfport
Pickich, Gerald, St. Mary, Woolmarket
Ramos, Eduardo, Most Holy Trinity, Pass Christian
Renz, Edward, Our Lady of the Gulf, Bay St. Louis
Roberts, Truett, St. Fabian, Hattiesburg
Saxer, Michael, St. Clare, Waveland
Smith, Richard, Our Mother of Sorrows, Biloxi
Stockert, Al, St. Mary, Biloxi
Torrelli, Ralph, St. Thomas, Hattiesburg
Vancourt, Ernest, St. Thomas the Apostle, Long Beach
Vrazel, William J., Holy Family, Pass Christian.

INSTITUTIONS LOCATED IN DIOCESE

[A] HIGH SCHOOLS, INTERPAROCHIAL

BILOXI. *St. Patrick Catholic High School*, (Grades 7-12), (Coed) 18300 St. Patrick Rd., 39532.
Tel: 228-702-0500; Fax: 228-702-0511; Email: mbuckley@stpatrickhighschool.net; Email: information@stpatrickhighschool.net; Web: www.stpatrickhighschool.net. Matt Buckley, Prin. (Full-time, paid) 16; Lay Teachers 28; Students 418; Clergy / Religious Teachers 1.
BAY ST. LOUIS. *Our Lady Academy*, (Grades 7-12), (Girls) 222 S. Beach Blvd., Bay St. Louis, 39520-4320. Tel: 228-467-7048; Fax: 228-467-1666; Email: marilyn.pigott@ourladyacademy.com; Web: www.ourladyacademy.com. Marilyn Pigott, Prin.; Anna Brannin, Librarian. Lay Teachers 19; Sisters of Mercy 2; Students 250; Clergy / Religious Teachers 2.
PASCAGOULA. *Resurrection Catholic High School*, (Grades 7-12), (Coed) 520 Watts Ave., Pascagoula, 39567. Tel: 228-762-3353; Fax: 228-769-1226; Email: nhamilton@rcseagles.com; Email: bwilliamson@rcseagles.com; Web: www.rcseagles.com. Noah Hamilton, Prin.; Mrs. Bobbie Williamson, Business Mgr. Lay Teachers 49; Students 521; Clergy / Religious Teachers 5.
Resurrection Elementary School, (Grades 1-6), 3704 Quinn Dr., Pascagoula, 39581. Tel: 228-762-7207; Fax: 228-762-0611; Email: nhamilton@rcseagles.com. Noah Hamilton, Prin; Bonnie Smith, Librarian; Mr. Aaron Frederic, Admin. Lay Teachers 31; Students 286.

[B] HIGH SCHOOLS AND ELEMENTARY SCHOOLS, PRIVATE

BAY ST. LOUIS. *Saint Stanislaus College* (1854) (Grades 7-12), 304 S. Beach Blvd., Bay St. Louis, 39520-4301. Tel: 228-467-9057; Fax: 228-466-2972; Email: admissions@ststan.com; Web: www.ststan.com. Bro. Barry Landry, S.C., Pres.; Mr. Gary Blackburn, Prin.; Richard Gleber, Dir. Admissions; Anna Brannin, Librarian. Brothers of the Sacred Heart.Boys boarding and day school, secondary and junior high. Brothers 5; Lay Teachers 28; Students 375; Total Staff 76; Clergy / Religious Teachers 1.
Camp Stanislaus, Tel: 228-467-9057;
Fax: 228-466-2972. Boys' summer program for ages 9-15.

[C] HOUSING FOR THE ELDERLY

BILOXI. *Gabriel Manor*, 2321 Atkinson Rd., 39531.
Tel: 228-388-1013; Fax: 228-388-1176; Email: gabrielmanor@sunstatesmgmt.com. Cheryl Alexander, Mgr. Bed Capacity 72; Total in Residence 73; Total Staff 3.
Gabriel Manor II, Inc.
Santa Maria Retirement Apartments, 1788 Medical Park Dr., 39532. Tel: 228-388-2495;
Fax: 228-388-2405; Email: aaguilar@sunstatesmgmt.com. Andrea Aguilar, Business Mgr. Bed Capacity 209; Tot Asst. Annually 209; Total Staff 7.
BAY ST. LOUIS. *Notre Dame de la Mer Retirement Apartments*, 292 Hwy. 90, Bay St. Louis, 39520.
Tel: 228-467-2885; Fax: 228-466-6300; Email: notredame@sunstatesmgmt.com. Brittany Gray, Business Mgr. Total in Residence 60; Total Staff 2.
GULFPORT. *Carlow Manor*, 15195 Barbara Dr., Gulfport, 39503. Tel: 228-539-0707;
Fax: 228-539-0704; Email: carlowmanor@sunstatesmgmt.com. Rhonda Barton, Mgr. Bed Capacity 40; Tot Asst. Annually 40; Total Staff 2.
OCEAN SPRINGS. *Samaritan House* (1987) 642 Jackson Ave., Ocean Springs, 39564. Tel: 228-875-1087;
Fax: 228-872-9500; Email: samaritanhouse@sunstatesmgmt.com. Ms. Sharon Ballow, Mgr. Tot Asst. Annually 49; Total in Residence 54; Total Staff 2.
Villa Maria Retirement Apartments, 921 Porter Ave.,

Ocean Springs, 39564. Tel: 228-875-8811; Fax: 228-875-8889; Email: villamaria@sunstatesmgmt.com. Jeanne Duplechin, Mgr. Total in Residence 235; Total Staff 16.

PETAL. *Caritas Manor*, 145 W. 10th Ave., Petal, 39465. Tel: 601-545-7744; Fax: 601-545-7740; Email: caritasmanor@sunstatesmgmt.com. Melissa Gatlin, Contact Person. Total in Residence 32; Total Staff 2.

[D] MONASTERIES AND RESIDENCES OF PRIESTS AND BROTHERS

BAY ST. LOUIS. *St. Augustine's Residence* (1920) 199 Seminary Dr., Bay St. Louis, 39520. Tel: 228-467-6414; Fax: 228-466-5618; Email: svdbaysaintlouis@gmail.com. Very Rev. Paul P. Kahan, S.V.D., Provincial Supr.; Revs. James A. Pawlicki, S.V.D., Rector; George Gormley, S.V.D., Treas.; Joseph Dang, Spiritual Advisor; Walter Bracken, S.V.D., Chap. Retreat Center; Joseph Vu Dao, S.V.D.; Bros. Richard Chambers, S.V.D.; Matthew Connors, S.V.D.; James Heeb, S.V.D. Brothers 4; Priests 8.

St. Augustine's Residence, 199 Seminary Dr., Bay St. Louis, 39520. Tel: 228-467-6414; Fax: 228-466-5618; Email: pawlicki@icloud.com. Rev. James A. Pawlicki, S.V.D., Contact Person.

Brothers of the Sacred Heart, 114 Bookter St., Bay St. Louis, 39520. Tel: 228-216-2503; Email: bgcouvillion@gmail.com. Bros. Eduardo Baldioceda, S.C., Mgr.; Raymond Sylve, S.C.; Bernard Couvillion, S.C., Dir.; Francis Fleming, S.C.; Barry Landry, S.C. Total in Residence 5.

Media Production Center "In A Word", 199 Seminary Dr., Bay St. Louis, 39520. Tel: 228-344-3166; Fax: 228-466-5618; Email: inawordsvd@gmail.com; Web: www.inaword.com. Very Rev. James Pawlicki, S.V.D., Dir.

Southern Province of St. Augustine - Provincial Offices, 204 Ruella St., Bay St. Louis, 39520. Tel: 228-467-4322; Fax: 228-466-5618; Email: gggormley864@yahoo.com; Web: www.svdsouth.com. Rev. Michael Somers; Very Rev. Paul P. Kahan, S.V.D., Prov.; Rev. George Gormley, S.V.D., Treas. Society of the Divine Word. Brothers 5; Priests 59; Parishes 34; Mission Stations 10; Elementary Schools 3. *Province Development Office*, 199 Seminary Dr., Bay St. Louis, 39520. Tel: 228-467-3815; Fax: 228-466-5618; Email: gggormley864@yahoo.com. Rev. Thomas Potts, S.V.D., Dir.

[E] CONVENTS AND RESIDENCES FOR SISTERS

BILOXI. *Sisters of Mercy Convent*, 11454 Spring Ln., 39532. Tel: 228-297-9097; Email: klajoie@mercysc.org. Sr. Kim Marie Lajoie, R.S.M., Contact Person. Religious Sisters of Mercy of the Americas 5.

GULFPORT. *Community of Charity and Social Services*, Our Lady of Tapao Convent, 2805 Oakridge Cir., Gulfport, 39507. Tel: 228-243-0784. Sr. Mary Ngoc Nguyen, Contact Person. Sisters 1.

LONG BEACH. *Presentation Sisters*, 18091 Commission Rd., Long Beach, 39560. Tel: 228-864-8418; Fax: 228-864-1627; Email: pres18091@cableone.net; Web: www.pbvmunion.org. Sr. Mary Kealy, P.B.V.M., Contact Person. Union of the Sisters of the Presentation of the Blessed Virgin Mary. Sisters 2.

[F] NEWMAN CENTERS

HATTIESBURG. *University of Southern Mississippi*, St. Thomas Aquinas Catholic Church, 3117 W. Fourth St., Hattiesburg, 39401. Tel: 601-264-5192; Fax: 601-264-0834; Email: church@stthomas-usm.org; Web: www.stthomas-usm.org. Very Rev. Mark A. Ropel, V.F., Chap. Priests 2; Staff 8.

[G] MISCELLANEOUS

BILOXI. *Magnificat - Mississippi Gulf Coast Chapter*, 1501 Popps Ferry Rd., Office, 39532. Tel: 228-392-0697; Fax: 228-396-8487; Email: ylivaccari@earthlink.net. Mrs. Yvette D. Livaccari, Contact Person.

RELIGIOUS INSTITUTES OF MEN REPRESENTED IN THE DIOCESE

For further details refer to the corresponding bracketed number in the Religious Institutes of Men or Women section.

[1100]—*Brothers of the Sacred Heart*—S.C.
[]—*Carmelites of Mary Immaculate*—C.M.I.
[]—*The Cistercian Order of the Strict Observance*—O.C.S.O.
[]—*Franciscan Friars*—O.F.M.
[]—*Heralds of Good News*—H.G.N.
[]—*Redemptorist Fathers*—C.Ss.R.
[0420]—*Society of the Divine Word*—S.V.D.
[0700]—*St. Joseph's Society of the Sacred Heart*—S.S.J.

RELIGIOUS INSTITUTES OF WOMEN REPRESENTED IN THE DIOCESE

[]—*Community of Charity and Social Services*—C.C.S.S.
[]—*Daughters of Our Lady of the Holy Rosary*—F.M.S.R.
[2575]—*Institute of the Sisters of Mercy of the Americas*—R.S.M.
[]—*Missionaries of the Holy Infant Jesus of Good Health*—M.N.J.S.
[3280]—*Presentation of the Blessed Virgin Mary Sisters*—P.B.V.M.
[]—*Sisters for Christian Community*—S.F.C.C.
[]—*Sisters of Mercy* (Ireland)—R.S.M.
[1510]—*Sisters of St. Francis*—O.S.F.

NECROLOGY

† Howze, Joseph Lawson, Bishop Emeritus of Biloxi, Died Jan. 9, 2019

An asterisk (*) denotes an organization that has established tax-exempt status directly with the IRS and is not covered by the USCCB Group Ruling.

Diocese of Birmingham

(Dioecesis Birminghamiensis)

Most Reverend

ROBERT J. BAKER, S.T.D.

Bishop of Birmingham; ordained March 21, 1970; appointed Bishop of Charleston July 12, 1999; ordained and installed September 29, 1999; appointed Bishop of Birmingham August 14, 2007; installed October 2, 2007.

Chancery Office: Catholic Diocese of Birmingham, P.O. Box 12047, Birmingham, AL 35202-2047. Tel: 205-838-8322; Fax: 205-836-1910.

Web: www.bhmdiocese.org

ESTABLISHED JUNE 28, 1969.

Square Miles 28,091.

Comprises the Counties of North Alabama in an irregular line between the Counties (west to east) of Sumter and Choctaw and following the base of the following Counties: Marengo, Perry, Chilton, Coosa, Tallapoosa and Chambers or comprising the Counties of: Bibb, Blount, Calhoun, Chambers, Cherokee, Chilton, Clay, Cleburne, Colbert, Coosa, Cullman, DeKalb, Etowah, Fayette, Franklin, Greene, Hale, Jackson, Jefferson, Lamar, Lauderdale, Lawrence, Limestone, Madison, Marengo, Marion, Marshall, Morgan, Perry, Pickens, Randolph, St. Clair, Shelby, Sumter, Talladega, Tallapoosa, Tuscaloosa, Walker and Winston.

Legal Title: The Catholic Bishop of Birmingham in Alabama, a Corporation Sole.
For legal titles of institutions, consult the Chancery Office

STATISTICAL OVERVIEW

Personnel	
Bishop	1
Abbots	1
Retired Abbots	1
Priests: Diocesan Active in Diocese	54
Priests: Diocesan Active Outside Diocese	4
Priests: Retired, Sick or Absent	15
Number of Diocesan Priests	73
Religious Priests in Diocese	32
Total Priests in Diocese	105
Extern Priests in Diocese	17
Ordinations:	
Diocesan Priests	1
Religious Priests	2
Transitional Deacons	1
Permanent Deacons	24
Permanent Deacons in Diocese	97
Total Brothers	28
Total Sisters	105
Parishes	
Parishes	56
With Resident Pastor:	
Resident Diocesan Priests	36
Resident Religious Priests	20
Without Resident Pastor:	
Administered by Deacons	1
Administered by Lay People	1
Missions	19
Professional Ministry Personnel:	
Sisters	3
Lay Ministers	67
Welfare	
Catholic Hospitals	5
Total Assisted	695,739
Specialized Homes	1
Total Assisted	30
Special Centers for Social Services	11
Total Assisted	28,500
Other Institutions	1
Total Assisted	2
Educational	
Diocesan Students in Other Seminaries	7
Students Religious	3
Total Seminarians	10
High Schools, Diocesan and Parish	4
Total Students	1,160
High Schools, Private	2
Total Students	331
Elementary Schools, Diocesan and Parish	15
Total Students	3,562
Elementary Schools, Private	2
Total Students	224
Catechesis/Religious Education:	
High School Students	1,199
Elementary Students	6,388
Total Students under Catholic Instruction	12,874
Teachers in the Diocese:	
Priests	9
Sisters	8
Lay Teachers	454
Vital Statistics	
Receptions into the Church:	
Infant Baptism Totals	1,939
Minor Baptism Totals	308
Adult Baptism Totals	210
Received into Full Communion	455
First Communions	2,483
Confirmations	1,872
Marriages:	
Catholic	606
Interfaith	162
Total Marriages	768
Deaths	649
Total Catholic Population	104,837
Total Population	3,073,473

Former Bishops—Most Revs. JOSEPH G. VATH, ord. June 7, 1941; appt. Auxiliary Bishop of Mobile-Birmingham March 25, 1966; cons. May 26, 1966; transferred to the Diocese of Birmingham Dec. 9, 1969; died July 14, 1987; RAYMOND J. BOLAND, D.D., ord. June 16, 1957; appt. Bishop of Birmingham Feb. 2, 1988; cons. March 25, 1988; transferred to Kansas City-St. Joseph Sept. 9, 1993; retired May 24, 2005; died Feb. 27, 2014; DAVID E. FOLEY, D.D., ord. May 26, 1956; appt. Titular Bishop of Ottaba and Auxiliary Bishop of Richmond, Virginia May 3, 1986; cons. June 27, 1986; appt. Bishop of Birmingham March 22, 1994; installed May 13, 1994; retired May 10, 2005; died April 17, 2018.

Chancery Office—Mailing Address: P.O. Box 12047, Birmingham, 35202-2047. Web: www.bhmdiocese.org. *Catholic Diocese of Birmingham, 2121 Third Ave. N., Birmingham, 35203.* Tel: 205-838-8322; Fax: 205-836-1910. Address all Diocesan Correspondence to the above P.O. Box unless otherwise indicated. Telephones listed below.

Office of the Bishop—MRS. KRISTIN SESSIONS, Sec., Tel: 205-838-8318; DONNA MEALER, Exec. Asst., Tel: 205-833-0175.

Chancellor—Very Rev. BRYAN W. JERABEK, J.C.L.

Priests'/Presbyteral Council—Most Rev. ROBERT J. BAKER, S.T.D., Pres.; Very Revs. BRYAN W. JERABEK, J.C.L.; JOSEPH G. CULOTTA, V.C., Chair; Rev. JOSE B. CHACKO; Very Revs. JAMES A. HEDDERMAN, Sec.; J. THOMAS ACKERMAN, V.F., Vice Chair; Rev. ROBERT J. SULLIVAN, V.F.; Very Revs. VINCENT E. BRESOWAR, V.F.; VERNON F. HUGULEY, V.F.; MICHAEL J. DEERING, V.G.; MICHAEL MAC MAHON, V.F.; Rev. Msgrs. MARTIN M. MULLER, V.F.; PAUL L. ROHLING; MICHAEL F. SEXTON, V.F., (Retired); Very Revs. BRYAN K. LOWE, Vicar for Finance; WILLIAM P. LUCAS, V.F.

Consultants to the Presbyteral Council—Very Revs. GREGORY T. BITTNER, J.C.L., J.D., Observer; RICHARD A. CHENAULT JR.; MARK T. SPRUILL, O.B.S.B.

Diocesan College of Consultors—Very Rev. BRYAN W. JERABEK, J.C.L.; Most Rev. ROBERT J. BAKER, S.T.D., Chair; Rev. PATRICK P. CULLEN; Very Revs. JOSEPH G. CULOTTA, V.C.; JEREMIAH DEASY, V.F.; MICHAEL J. DEERING, V.G.; WILLIAM P. LUCAS, V.F.; MICHAEL MAC MAHON, V.F.; Rev. Msgr. MARTIN M. MULLER, V.F.; Very Rev. RAYMOND J. REMKE, V.F.; Rev. Msgrs. PAUL L. ROHLING; MICHAEL F. SEXTON, V.F., (Retired).

Diocesan College of Vicars—Very Revs. MICHAEL J. DEERING, V.G.; GREGORY T. BITTNER, J.C.L., J.D., Judicial Vicar; JOSEPH G. CULOTTA, V.C., Vicar for Clergy and Ecumenical & Interfaith Dialogue; RICHARD A. CHENAULT JR., Vicar for Vocations; MARK T. SPRUILL, O.B.S.B., Vicar for Hispanic Ministry; RICHARD E. DONOHOE, S.T.D., Vicar for Catholic Charities; VERNON F. HUGULEY, V.F., West Birmingham Deanery & Vicar for Black Catholic Ministry; BRYAN K. LOWE, Vicar for Finance; J. THOMAS ACKERMAN, V.F., Southwest Deanery; Rev. ROBERT J. SULLIVAN, V.F., East Birmingham Deanery; Very Rev. MICHAEL MAC MAHON, V.F., Northeast Deanery, Tel: 205-991-5488; Tel: 205-881-4781; Rev. Msgr. MARTIN M. MULLER, V.F., Central Birmingham Deanery; Very Revs. VINCENT E. BRESOWAR, V.F., Northwest Deanery; WILLIAM P. LUCAS, V.F., Southeast Deanery.

Diocesan Pastoral Council—Most Rev. ROBERT J. BAKER, S.T.D., Pres., Members include lay representatives of the Diocesan Deaneries, four Vicars for Deaneries, four religious and a staff representative.

Diocesan Finance Council—Most Rev. ROBERT J. BAKER, S.T.D., Pres.; Very Rev. BRYAN K. LOWE, Chm. Members: Very Revs. GREGORY T. BITTNER, J.C.L., J.D.; MICHAEL J. DEERING, V.G.; Rev. ROBERT J. SULLIVAN, V.F.; RAY G. DYER JR., CPA; PAUL J. SHARBEL; JIM FRANKLIN; JOHN KERPER; DAVID SEELEY; JOHN HARDIN. Staff Members: MR. BOB M. SELLERS JR., CFO; DONNA MEALER, Exec. Asst., Plus members of Diocesan Committees: Deposit & Loan, Presbyteral, Consultors, Audit, Investment, Property, Review Board, Notary, and Ecclesiastical Notary.

Tribunal—Please address all rogatory commissions and matrimonial matters to the Office of the Tribunal. Very Rev. GREGORY T. BITTNER, J.C.L., J.D., Judicial Vicar, Tel: 205-838-8307; CYWILLA FABIJANIC, Moderator of Tribunal Chancery & Ecclesiastical Notary; MATTIE SHUMATE, Administrative Asst. & Ecclesiastical Notary; Very Rev. BRYAN W. JERABEK, J.C.L., Judge; Deacon DANIEL J. LAURITA, J.C.L., Defender of the Bond; MARGARET P. CHALMERS, J.C.D., J.D., Judge.

Catholic Social Services & Emergency Services—ALBERT MANZELLA, Exec. Dir., Tel: 205-969-8947; CAROL GRAY, Asst. Exec. Dir., Tel: 205-239-9105.

Catholic Family Services—1515 12th Ave. S., Birmingham, 35205. Tel: 205-324-6561. OSWALDO H. CHAVEZ, Rgnl. Dir.

Catholic Family Services Offices—CATHIE MCDANIEL, Rgnl. Dir., 1010 Church St.,

Huntsville, 35804. Tel: 256-536-0073; DEBBIE BUFFALOE, L.G.S.W., 1111 E. College St., Florence, 35630. Tel: 256-768-1550; Email: cfsdebb@att.net.

Catholic Centers of Concern—Birmingham; Anniston; Gadsden; Huntsville; Eutaw; Tuscaloosa.

Apostolate to the Aged—VACANT.

Engaged Encounter—DAN CATT; TERRY CATT, 2116 Bailey Brook Dr., Birmingham, 35244. Tel: 205-307-8316.

Natural Family Planning—THERESA SHIRLEY, B.S., F.C.P.I., 1538 Shamrock Dr., Gardendale, 35071. Tel: 334-312-0000.

Department of Education—DR. DAVID ANDERS, Ph.D., Dir. Catholic Educ. & Lifelong Formation.

Catholic Schools—JULIE EMORY-JOHNSON, Dir. Pro-Tempore, Tel: 205-838-8303; VACANT, Dir. Curriculum.

Religious Education—DANIEL MCCORMICK, Dir., Tel: 205-776-7128.

Young Adult Ministry—DIANA URBINA, Coord., Tel: 205-776-7179; Email: durbina@bhmdiocese.org.

Apostolate with Persons Having Intellectual and Developmental Disabilities—Rev. PATRICK P. CULLEN, Dir.; Sr. MARY VERNON GENTLE, R.S.M., Assoc. Dir., P.O. Box 10044, Birmingham, 35202-0044. Tel: 205-251-1279; Fax: 205-251-1284; Email: mvgentle@aol.com.

Office of Child and Youth Protection—Deacon FRANK R. SLAPIKAS, Dir., Tel: 205-776-7186.

Victim Assistance Coordinator—ALBERT MANZELLA, Tel: 205-969-8947; Email: amanzella@bhmdiocese.org.

Safe Environment Coordinator—DONALD SCHWARZHOFF, Tel: 205-838-8301.

Campus Ministry—JOHN MARTIGNONI, Dir., Tel: 205-776-7163; Email: jmartignoni@bhmdiocese.org.

Catholic Scouting—DONALD SCHWARZHOFF, Dir., Tel: 205-838-8301.

Toy Bowl Association—Mailing Address: P.O. Box 12047, Birmingham, 35202-2047. Tel: 205-838-8303.

Diocesan School Board—WILLIAM KLUS, Chm., Tel: 256-518-9212.

Finance Office and Administration—Very Rev. BRYAN K. LOWE, Vicar of Finance.

Chief Financial Officer—MR. BOB M. SELLERS JR., Tel: 205-833-0173.

Annual Catholic Charities Appeal—Catholic Relief Services, and National and Special Collections Very Rev. RICHARD E. DONOHOE, S.T.D., Dir., Tel: 205-838-8309.

Human Resources—INA COOLEY, Mgr., Tel: 205-838-8321.

Family Life Ministry—JOHN MARTIGNONI, Dir., Tel: 205-776-7163; Email: jmartignoni@bhmdiocese.org.

Beginning Experience—HELEN BOWERS.

Cursillo Program—MARK BONUCCHI, Lay Dir., Mailing Address: P.O. Box 1308, Cullman, 35055. Email: mmbonucchi@msn.com; Web: www.bhmcursillo.org.

Hispanic Ministries—Very Rev. MARK T. SPRUILL, O.B.S.B., Vicar; MARIA JOSE BONILLA, Dir. Hispanic Youth Ministry & Hispanic Affairs, Tel: 205-776-7181.

Hispanic Social Services—Sr. GABRIELA RAMIREZ, M.G. Sp.S., Dir., 92 Oxmoor Rd., Birmingham, 35209. Tel: 205-987-4771.

Lay Ministries Program—JOHN MARTIGNONI, Dir., Tel: 205-776-7163; Email: jmartignoni@bhmdiocese.org.

Marriage Encounter—STEVE HUFFMAN; JANETTA HUFFMAN, 8015 Craigmont Rd., Huntsville, 35802. Tel: 256-882-2430.

Black Catholic Ministry—JAMES WATTS, Dir.

Pro-Life Activities—Very Rev. ALAN C. MACKEY, Vicar.

Propagation of the Faith and Holy ChildhoodVery Rev. RAYMOND J. REMKE, V.F., Dir.; CHRISTINA WRIGHT, Asst. Dir., Tel: 205-776-7004.

St. John Vianney Vocation Society of Birmingham—BOB EICOU, Pres., Tel: 205-936-9973.

Vocations—Very Rev. RICHARD A. CHENAULT JR., Vicar; MRS. KRISTIN SESSIONS, Administrative Asst., Tel: 205-838-2184.

One Voice—Diocesan weekly MARY ALICE CROCKETT, Mng. Editor, Tel: 205-838-8305; ANN LANZI, Circulation; MARY DILLARD, Photojournalist & Art Dir., The Birmingham Catholic Press, Inc., P.O. Box 10822, Birmingham, 35202. Tel: 205-838-8305; Fax: 205-838-8319.

Catholic Women of the Diocese of Birmingham—SALLY SPRINGROSE, Tel: 205-991-8870; Email: sspringrose@gmail.com.

Priests' Retirement Fund—MR. HENRY SMITH, c/o Priests' Retirement Fund, P.O. Box 10247, Birmingham, 35202-2047. Tel: 205-833-0173.

Office of the New Evangelization and Stewardship—JOHN MARTIGNONI, Dir., Tel: 205-776-7163; Email: jmartignoni@bhmdiocese.org.

CLERGY, PARISHES, MISSIONS AND PAROCHIAL SCHOOLS

CITY OF BIRMINGHAM

(JEFFERSON COUNTY)

1—ST. PAUL'S CATHEDRAL (1871)
Mailing Address: P.O. Box 10044, 35202-0044. Tel: 205-251-1279; Email: krista@stpaulsbhm.org; Web: www.stpaulsbhm.org. Very Rev. Bryan W. Jerabek, J.C.L., Rector & Chancellor, (On Sabbatical); Rev. Joshua Altonji, Parochial Vicar; Deacons Neal Kay; Edward W. Zieverink. In Res., Rev. Patrick P. Cullen.
Res.: 2120 Third Ave. N., 35203.
Catechesis Religious Program—Students 143.
Mission—St. Stephen the Martyr Catholic University Chapel, 1515 12th Ave. S., Jefferson Co. 35205.

2—ST. ANTHONY'S (1900) Closed. For inquiries for parish records contact St. Paul Cathedral, Birmingham.

3—ST. BARNABAS (1908)
P.O. Box 610304, 325261. Rev. Douglas Michael Vu. In Res., Rev. Msgr. Eugene O'Connor, (Retired).
Res.: 7921 First Ave. N., 35206. Tel: 205-833-0334.
School—St. Barnabas School, (Grades K-8), 7901 First Ave. N., 35206. Tel: 205-836-5385; Fax: 205-833-0272; Email: admin@stbcsbhm.org; Web: www.stbcsbhm.org. John Parker, Prin. Lay Teachers 14; Students 143.
Catechesis Religious Program—Brett Burkholder, D.R.E. Students 19.

4—ST. BERNARD'S (Inglenook) (1928) Closed. For inquiries for parish records contact St. Paul Cathedral, Birmingham.

5—BLESSED SACRAMENT (1911) [CEM] Rev. Jim W. Booth.
Res.: 1460 Pearson Ave., S.W., P.O. Box 110006, 35211. Tel: 205-785-9840; Email: church@myblessedsacrament.org; Web: www.myblessedsacrament.org.
Convent—Matt Talbot Mission House, Tel: 205-578-2988; Email: franciscanspjcalabama@gmail.com.

6—ST. FRANCIS XAVIER (1953)
2 Xavier Cir., 35213. Tel: 205-871-5411; Email: saintfrancis@sfxbirmingham.com; Web: SFXBirmingham.com. P.O. Box 130669, 35213. Rev. Robert J. Sullivan, V.F.; Very Revs. Raymond J. Remke, V.F., Parochial Vicar; Gregory T. Bittner, J.C.L., J.D., In Res.; Sisters Sara Burress, O.S.B., Pastoral Assoc.; Janet Marie Flemming, O.S.B., Pastoral Assoc.
School—St. Francis Xavier School, (Grades K-8), Tel: 205-871-1687; Email: office@sfxcatholic.com; Web: www.sfxcatholic.com. Mr. J. Wright, Prin.; Mrs. Vickie Battles, Sec. Lay Teachers 17; Students 200; Staff 6.
Catechesis Religious Program—Shaun Byrne, D.R.E. Students 498.

7—HOLY FAMILY (1938) (African American) Rev. Justin Nelson Alphonse, C.P.; Deacons Gerald Motherway; Jacky M. Rodgers; Peter V. Smith. In Res., Revs. Alex Steinmiller, C.P.; Alphonse Justin Nelson, C.P.
Res.: 1910 19th St., 35218. Tel: 205-780-3440; Email: frnelsoncp@yahoo.com.
School—Holy Family School, (Grades K-8), 1916 19th St. Ensley, 35218. Tel: 205-785-5858; Fax: 205-785-2666; Email: mooresidney45@gmail.com. Sidney Moore, Prin. Lay Teachers 7; Students 70.
Catechesis Religious Program—Trudi Webb Stinson, D.R.E. Students 60.
Mission—St. Mary's (1943) 6101 Dr. Martin Luther King Dr., Fairfield, Jefferson Co. 35064. Rev. Justin Nelson Alphonse, C.P.
Catechesis Religious Program—Wade White, D.R.E. Students 20.

8—HOLY ROSARY (Gate City) (1889)
7414 Georgia Rd., 35212. Tel: 864-616-1770; Email: pastor@holyrosarybirmingham.org; Web: www.holyrosarybirmingham.org. Rev. Jon Chalmers.

9—ST. JOHN BOSCO (1973) Closed. For inquiries for parish records, please contact Holy Rosary, Birmingham.

10—ST. JOSEPH (1921) (Hispanic)
3020 Ave. K (Ensley), 35218. Tel: 205-788-5721; Fax: 205-788-7146; Email: stjosephbham@gmail.com. Rev. Patricio Manosalvas, C.P.
Res.: 1013 30th St., 35218.
Catechesis Religious Program—Olivia Miranda Rogue, D.R.E. Students 142.

11—ST. LUKE HWANG (1995) (Korean)
Cell: 205-223-5460. Rev. Sang Baek Lawrence Lee.
Res.: 759 Valley St., 35226. Tel: 205-881-7890; Email: symeonlee@hotmail.com.

12—ST. MARGARET'S (1986) Closed. For inquiries for parish records contact Blessed Sacrament Parish, Birmingham.

13—ST. MARK THE EVANGELIST (1999)
Mailing Address: P.O. Box 380396, 35238-0396. Tel: 205-980-1810; Fax: 205-980-9208; Email: stmarkrc@bellsouth.net; Web: stmarkrc.org. 7340 Cahaba Valley Rd., 35242. Very Rev. Joseph G. Culotta, V.C.; Sr. Madeline Contorno, O.S.B., Pastoral Assoc.; Deacon Philip F. Boettcher.
Catechesis Religious Program—Email: pfboettcher@att.net. Mary Beth Crumly, D.R.E.; Phil Boettcher, RCIA Coord. Students 244.

14—ST. MARK'S (1904) Closed. For inquiries for parish records contact St. Paul's Cathedral, Birmingham.

15—OUR LADY OF FATIMA (1905) (African American) Rev. Godwin S. Ani, S.S.J.; Deacon Douglas C. Moorer.
Res.: 708 First St. S., 35205. Tel: 205-322-1205; Email: olf@josephite.com.
Catechesis Religious Program—Tel: 205-251-8395. Mrs. Theresa Nalls, D.R.E. Students 36.

16—OUR LADY OF LA VANG PARISH @ ST. JOHN BOSCO CHURCH (2005)
5224 1st Ave. N., 35212. 142 52nd Pl. N., 35212. Tel: 205-253-7674. Rev. Andrew M. Nguyen.

17—OUR LADY OF LOURDES (1959) Rev. George Steinmiller, Admin.; Deacon William F. Brandt.
Res.: 980 Huffman Rd., 35215. Tel: 205-836-2274; Email: ololc@bham.rr.com; Web: www.ollcbham.com.
Catechesis Religious Program—Email: hhwhiz@att.net. Harrison Whisenant Jr., D.R.E. Students 158.

18—OUR LADY OF SORROWS (1887) Rev. Msgr. Martin M. Muller, V.F.; Revs. Balta Raju Reddy Pentareddy, Parochial Vicar; Frankline Fomukong, Parochial Vicar.
Res.: 1730 Oxmoor Rd., 35209. Tel: 205-871-8121; Fax: 205-871-8180; Email: ols@ourladyofsorrows.com.
School—Our Lady of Sorrows School, (Grades K-8), 1720 Oxmoor Rd., 35209. Tel: 205-879-3237; Fax: 205-879-9332; Email: mjdorn@olsschool.com. Mary Jane Dorn, Prin.; Karen Sullivan, Librarian. Lay Teachers 30; Students 484.
Catechesis Religious Program—Tel: 205-871-1431; Fax: 205-871-1487. Suzanne Corso, D.R.E.; Marcy Flemming, D.R.E. Students 386.

19—OUR LADY OF THE VALLEY (1974) Rev. Msgr. Paul L. Rohling; Rev. Liju Paul Parambath; Deacons Bob Martin; Robert G. Long; Dan Whitaker; Ms. Theresa Thienpont, Music Min.
Res.: 5514 Double Oak Ln., 35242. Tel: 205-991-5488 ; Fax: 205-991-5181; Email: olvchurch@olvsch.com; Web: www.olvbirmingham.com.
School—Our Lady of the Valley School, (Grades K-8), 5510 Double Oak Ln., 35242. Tel: 205-991-5963; Fax: 205-991-1251; Email: kzielinski@olvsch.com. Katie Zielinski, Prin.; Jennifer Elliott, Librarian. Lay Teachers 19; Students 285.
Catechesis Religious Program—Tel: 205-991-5489. Mrs. Leslie Smith, D.R.E. Students 323.

20—OUR LADY QUEEN OF THE UNIVERSE (1955) (African American)
961 Center St. N., 35204. Very Rev. Richard E. Donohoe, S.T.D.; Deacon Rufus N. Biggs Sr.
Res.: 949 Center St. N., 35204. Tel: 205-328-7729; Fax: 205-328-7703; Email: olqucatholicchurch@gmail.com.
Catechesis Religious Program—Angela Rembert, C.R.E. Students 22.
Mission—Sacred Heart, 3401 27th Ct. N., Collegeville, Jefferson Co. 35207.

21—ST. PETER THE APOSTLE (1962) [CEM]
2061 Patton Chapel Rd., 35216. Rev. Thomas M. Kelly, F.T.C.L.; Deacons Sam Anzalone; John H. Cooper; Christopher J. Rosko; Jose Vazquez.
Res.: 3429 Sheila Dr., 35216. Tel: 205-822-4480; Email: stpeterapostle@bellsouth.net.
Catechesis Religious Program—
Tel: 205-822-4480, Ext. 24. Marcella Stobert, D.R.E. Students 372.

22—PRINCE OF PEACE (1984) Revs. John Fallon; Joy Thomas Nellissery; Jose Luis Guevara Gomez, (BIR); Henry McDaid, Chap., (Retired); G. Rick DiGiorgio.
Church & Mailing Address: 4600 Preserve Pkwy, Birmingham (Hoover), 35226. Tel: 205-822-9125; Tel: 205-824-7886; Email: church.office@popcatholic.org; Web: www.popcatholic.org.
Res.: 10-A Shades Crest Rd., 35226.
School—Prince of Peace School, (Grades PreK-8), 4650 Preserve Pkwy., 35226. Tel: 205-824-7886; Fax: 205-824-2093; Email: lbertolini@popcatholic.org; Web: popcatholic.org. Kelly Doss, Pres.; Connie Angstadt, Prin. Lay Teachers 41; Students 485.

Catechesis Religious Program—Fax: 205-822-9127; Email: megan.everett@popcatholic.org. Megan Everett, D.R.E. Students 1,429.

23—SACRED HEART (1955) Closed. See Our Lady Queen of the Universe, Birmingham for details.

24—ST. STANISLAUS (1914)
Mailing Address: 904 Indiana St., 35224.
Tel: 205-785-9625; Email: ststans@bellsouth.net. Very Rev. Vernon F. Huguley, V.F.
Catechesis Religious Program—

25—ST. STEPHEN THE MARTYR CATHOLIC UNIVERSITY CHAPEL (1991) Closed. Now a mission of Cathedral of St. Paul, Birmingham.

26—ST. THERESA'S, Closed. For inquiries for parish records contact St. Paul's Cathedral, Birmingham.

OUTSIDE THE CITY OF BIRMINGHAM

ADAMSVILLE, JEFFERSON CO., ST. PATRICK'S (1983) [CEM]
301 Shamrock Tr., Adamsville, 35005.
Tel: 205-798-5326; Email: saintpat@catholicjewel.com; Web: www.saintpatrickcc.com. Very Rev. Vernon F. Huguley, V.F.
Res.: 404 Brian Dr., Adamsville, 35005.
Family Life Center—Tel: 205-798-0372.
Catechesis Religious Program—Students 52.

ALEXANDER CITY, TALLAPOOSA CO., ST. JOHN THE APOSTLE (1948)
454 N. Central Ave., Alexander City, 35010.
Tel: 256-234-3631; Fax: 256-234-3789; Email: stjohnsalexcity@gmail.com. Rev. Rayapu Reddy Thirumalareddy, Admin.
Res.: 63 Parks Ave., Alexander City, 35010.
Catechesis Religious Program—Tel: 256-409-9146; Fax: 256-234-3789. Rev. Peter Reddy, D.R.E. Students 55.
Mission—St. Mark (1994) 460 Country Club Rd., P.O. Box 98, Ashland, Clay Co. 36251.

ANNISTON, CALHOUN CO.

1—ALL SAINTS (1939)
Mailing Address: P.O. Box 4862, Anniston, 36204. Email: bgreen5356@aol.com. 1112 W. 15th St., Anniston, 36201. Tel: 256-237-9230;
Fax: 256-237-9230. B. Dianne Green, Parish Dir.
Catechesis Religious Program—Rose Munford, D.R.E. Students 2.

2—SACRED HEART OF JESUS (1886)
1301 Golden Springs Rd., Anniston, 36207.
Tel: 256-237-3011; Fax: 256-241-2048; Email: church@sacredheartanniston.org. P.O. Box 5010, Anniston, 36205. Rev. Charles Alookaran.
Res.: 1018 Tutwiler Ct., Anniston, 36207.
School—Sacred Heart of Jesus School, (Grades K-12), 16 Morton Rd., Fort McClellan, 36205.
Tel: 256-237-4231; Fax: 256-241-2353; Email: jrussell@shcards.org; Web: www.sacredheartcardinals.org. Jeremiah Russell, Prin. Lay Teachers 26; Students 280.
Catechesis Religious Program—Tel: 256-237-3011. Carla Keith, D.R.E. Students 149.

ASHLAND, CLAY CO., ST. MARK'S, See separate listing. See St. John the Apostle, Alexander City for details.
460 Country Club Rd., Ashland, 36251.
Tel: 256-354-3598; Email: frpeterreddy@gmail.com. P.O. Box 98, Ashland, 36251. Rev. Peter Reddy.

ATHENS, LIMESTONE CO., ST. PAUL'S St. Paul Catholic Church (1959)
1900 Hwy 72 W., Athens, 35611. Tel: 256-232-4191; Email: stpauloffice@gmail.com; Web: stpaulcatholicchurchathens.org. Rev. Tom Velliyedathu; Deacon Charles L. Butler.
Catechesis Religious Program—Email: dre.stpauloffice@gmail.com. Ann-Margaret Chapman, D.R.E. Students 282.

BESSEMER, JEFFERSON CO.

1—ST. ALOYSIUS CHURCH (1886)
Mailing Address: 751 Academy Dr., Bessemer, 35022. Tel: 205-424-2984; Fax: 205-426-5753; Email: staloysius@bellsouth.net. Rev. Gerald Holloway; Stephanie Gerson, Pastoral Assoc.
Res.: 112 Woodland Rd., Bessemer, 35020.
Catechesis Religious Program—Students 30.

2—ST. FRANCIS OF ASSISI (1940) (African American)
2400 Seventh Ave. N., Bessemer, 35020.
Tel: 205-428-4758; Fax: 205-428-4751; Email: stfrancisbessemer@gmail.com. Rev. Paul Asih, M.S.P.
Res.: 2410 7th Ave. N., Bessemer, 35020.
Catechesis Religious Program—Students 22.

CLANTON, CHILTON CO., CHURCH OF THE RESURRECTION
300 First Ave., Clanton, 35045. Tel: 205-755-5498; Email: rescath@gmail.com; Web: rescath.org. Rev. Bruce Bumbarger; Deacon James L. Barrett.
Catechesis Religious Program—Vickie Henriguez, D.R.E. Students 175.

CULLMAN, CULLMAN CO., SACRED HEART (1877) [CEM] (German)
205 Third Ave., S.E., Cullman, 35055. Revs. Patrick Egan, O.S.B.; Fabio Alonso Gomez Palacio, Parochial Vicar; Deacons William Roberson, (Emeritus-Retired); Ramon D. Rodriguez; Kenneth M. Kreps; Peter C. Nassetta; George Schaefers Jr.; Craig R. Smith.
Res.: 217 Second St., S.E., Cullman, 35055.
Tel: 256-734-3730.
School—Sacred Heart School, (Grades K-6), 112 2nd Ave. S.E., Cullman, 35055. Tel: 256-734-4563;
Fax: 256-734-5882; Email: ghughes@shscullman.org. Gregory E. Hughes, Prin.; Robin Skipper, Librarian. Lay Teachers 13; Students 194.
Catechesis Religious Program—Fharis Richter, D.R.E. Students 189.
Mission—St. Boniface, [CEM] .

DECATUR, MORGAN CO.

1—ST. ANN'S (1870) [JC] Closed. For more information please see Annunciation of the Lord, Decatur.

2—ANNUNCIATION OF THE LORD St. Ann Catholic Church (2003) Revs. Charles Merrill; Wyman Vintson, Parochial Vicar; Deacons Dennis Kobs; Patrick W. Lappert; Javier Ramirez; Richard A. Chenault Sr.; Louis J. Sciaroni; Robert M. Catanach
Legal Titles: St. Ann Catholic Church
Res.: 3910 Spring Ave., S.W., Decatur, 35603.
Tel: 256-353-2667; Email: parish@annunlord.com; Web: www.annunlord.com.
School—St. Ann Catholic School, 3910A Spring Ave SW, Decatur, 35603. Tel: 256-353-6543;
Fax: 256-353-0705; Email: secretary@saintanndecatur.org. Ben Leach, Prin. Lay Teachers 10; Students 111.
Catechesis Religious Program—
Tel: 256-353-2667, Ext. 108; Email: religion@saintanndecatur.org. Patrice Lappert, D.R.E. Students 329.

DEMOPOLIS, MARENGO CO., ST. LEO (1936)
P.O. Box 937, Demopolis, 36732. Rev. Lawrence E. Shinnick.
Res.: 307 S. Main Ave., P.O. Box 937, Demopolis, 36732. Tel: 334-289-2767; Email: stleothegreatcatholic@gmail.com.
Catechesis Religious Program—Jennifer Helms, D.R.E. Students 54.
Missions—Our Lady of Lourdes— (1959) 8 Erwin Woods Dr., Greensboro, Hale Co. 37644.
St. Mary (1948) 274 Wilson Ave., Eutaw, Greene Co. 35462. (African American & Latino).

EUTAW, GREENE CO., ST. MARY (1948) (African American—Hispanic), Closed. See St. Leo, Demopolis for details.

FAIRFIELD, JEFFERSON CO., ST. MARY (1943) Closed. See Holy Family, Birmingham for details.

FLORENCE, LAUDERDALE CO.

1—ST. JOSEPH CATHOLIC CHURCH (1898)
121 Plum St., Florence, 35630. Tel: 256-764-3303;
Fax: 256-718-0208; Email: secretary@stjosephflorence.org; Web: www.stjosephflorence.org. 203 Plum St., Florence, 35630. Rev. Roy Runkle; Deacon Gregory J. Beam.
Res.: 302 Plum St., Florence, 35630.
School—St. Joseph Catholic Church School, (Grades K-8), 115 Plum St., Florence, 35630.
Tel: 256-766-1923; Tel: 256-766-1955;
Fax: 256-766-1713; Email: principal@catholichill.com; Web: www.catholichill.com. Kelley Dewberry, Prin. Lay Teachers 19; Students 134.
Catechesis Religious Program—Students 79.

2—ST. MICHAEL (1873) [CEM] Rev. John O'Donnell, O.S.B.; Deacon Stephen J. Kirkpatrick.
Res.: 2751 County Rd. 30, Florence, 35634.
Tel: 256-764-1885; Fax: 256-349-2186; Email: stmichaelcatholic@gmail.com; Web: www.stmichaelscatholic.org.
Catechesis Religious Program—Tel: 706-338-2262; Email: jenhalen@hotlmail.com. Jennifer Halen, D.R.E., (High School). Students 48.

FORT PAYNE, DE KALB CO., OUR LADY OF THE VALLEY (1959)
2910 Gault Ave. N., Fort Payne, 35967.
Tel: 256-845-4774; Email: olvfp@farmerstel.com; Web: www.olvfortpayne.com. Mailing Address: P.O. Box 681446, Fort Payne, 35968. Very Rev. Mark T. Spruill, O.B.S.B.
Rectory—2907 Alabama Ave. N., Fort Payne, 35967.
Catechesis Religious Program—Jenny Roberts, D.R.E.; Maria del Consuelo Palacios, Hispanic Coord. Students 454.

GADSDEN, ETOWAH CO.

1—ST. JAMES (1912) Rev. Jose B. Chacko; Deacons J. Fred Williams; Robert A. McCormick.
Res.: 1321 Monte Vista Dr., Gadsden, 35904.
Church: 622 Chestnut St., Gadsden, 35901.
Tel: 256-546-2975.
School—St. James School, (Grades K-8), 700 Albert Rains Blvd., Gadsden, 35901. Tel: 256-546-0132;
Fax: 256-546-0134; Email: madams@stjamesgadsden.org; Web: www.stjamesgadsden.org. Michele Adams, Prin.; Cynthia Hill, Librarian. Lay Teachers 13; Students 138.
Catechesis Religious Program—Judy Ritter, D.R.E. Students 123.

2—ST. MARTIN DE PORRES, Closed. For inquiries for parish records contact St. James, Gadsden.

GARDENDALE, JEFFERSON CO., ST. ELIZABETH ANN SETON (1976)
Mailing Address: 334 Main St., P.O. Box 1027, Gardendale, 35071. Tel: 205-631-9398;
Fax: 205-631-5781; Email: seascc@yahoo.com; Web: www.seasgardendale.org. Rev. Johnson Tharayil.
Res.: 205 Powell Dr., Gardendale, 35071.
Catechesis Religious Program—Mary McMinn, D.R.E.; Laura Hollis, Youth Dir. Students 101.
Mission—St. Henry, [CEM] 211 5th St., Warrior, Jefferson Co. 35180.

GUNTERSVILLE, MARSHALL CO., ST. WILLIAM (1952)
929 Gunter Ave., Guntersville, 35976.
Tel: 256-582-4245; Email: church.stwilliam@gmail.com; Web: www.stwilliamchurch.com. Rev. Timothy Pfander; Deacon Kenneth D. Hall.
Catechesis Religious Program—Yolanda Nieto, D.R.E. Students 4,500.
Mission—Chapel of the Holy Cross, 1534 Whitesville Rd., Albertville, Marshall Co. 35950.
Tel: 256-891-0550; Email: juan@stwilliamchurch.com. Juan Nunez, Contact Person.

HUNTSVILLE, MADISON CO.

1—GOOD SHEPHERD (1981)
13550 Chaney Thompson Rd. S.E., Huntsville, 35803-2326. Tel: 256-882-1844; Fax: 256-882-1841; Email: goodshep@hiwaay.net; Web: www.goodshephsv.org. Deacon Paul T. Keil.
Catechesis Religious Program—Email: gsreled@hiway.net. Trina Maxwell, D.R.E. Students 260.

2—HOLY SPIRIT (1965) Very Rev. Michael Mac Mahon, V.F.; Revs. Jonathan Paul Howell; Peter Park, Admin.; Deacons Louis J. Citrano; Lee G. Heckman; Antonio Moreno; Lawrence E. Sisterman; Michael P. Sudnik; Robert J. Becher; Matthew J.S. Koh.
Res.: 625 Airport Rd. S.W., Huntsville, 35802.
Tel: 256-881-4781; Email: hschurch@holyspirithsv.com; Web: www.holyspirithsv.com.
School—Holy Spirit School, (Grades PreK-8), 619 Airport Rd., S.W., Huntsville, 35802.
Tel: 256-881-4852; Fax: 256-881-4904; Email: admin@hstigers.org; Web: www.hstigers.org. Vince Aquila, Prin. Lay Teachers 38; Students 369.
Catechesis Religious Program—Tel: 256-881-0345. Mrs. Tracy Finke, D.R.E. Students 572.

3—ST. JOSEPH (1952) [CEM]
2300 Beasley Ave., N.W., Huntsville, 35816.
Tel: 256-534-8459; Email: parish@saintjosephcc.com; Web: www.saintjosephcc.com. Rev. Joseph Lubrano, S.D.S.; Deacon John J. Barisa.
Res.: 1004 Council St., Huntsville, 35816.
School—Holy Family School-Huntsville, (Grades PreK-8), Tel: 256-539-5221; Fax: 256-533-0747. Dr. Libby Parker, Prin. Lay Teachers 22; Students 260.
Catechesis Religious Program—Carmen Amato, D.R.E. Students 120.

4—ST. MARY OF THE VISITATION (1861)
Tel: 256-536-6349; Tel: 256-536-6760;
Fax: 256-536-6349; Email: smvparish@smvparish.com. Deacon James G. Bodine; Rev. William Kelly, S.D.S.; Deacon Louis J. Citrano.
Res.: 222 Jefferson St. N., Huntsville, 35801.
Catechesis Religious Program—220 Lincoln St. NE, Huntsville, 35801. Tel: 256-536-6760; Email: rmatteson@smvparish.com. Rita Matteson, C.R.E. Students 87.

5—OUR LADY, HELP OF CHRISTIANS (2013)
1201 Kingsbury Ave., Huntsville, 35801.
Tel: 256-801-9157; Email: ourladyhoc@icloud.com; Web: ourladyhelpofchristians-al.org. Rev. Alan C. Mackey.
Catechesis Religious Program—Jennifer Mackintosh, D.R.E. Students 74.

6—OUR LADY QUEEN OF THE UNIVERSE (1965)
Mailing Address: 2421 Shady Ln. Dr. NW, Huntsville, 35810. Rev. Davis J. Koottala, Admin.; Deacons James G. Bodine; Lawrence Howell.
Res.: 3701 Grizzard Rd., Huntsville, 35810.
Tel: 256-852-0788; Email: olqu@olqu.org; Web: www.olqu.org.
Catechesis Religious Program—Susan Turner, D.R.E. Students 114.

JACKSONVILLE, CALHOUN CO., ST. CHARLES BORROMEO (1964) Rev. James Handerhan; Deacon A. B. King.
Church: 308 Seventh St., N.E., Jacksonville, 36265.
Tel: 256-435-3238; Email: tricia@stcharlescatholicchurch.com; Web: www.stcharlescatholicchurch.com.
Res.: 400 Seventh St., N.E., Jacksonville, 36265.
Catechesis Religious Program—Peggy Sugar, D.R.E. Students 40.
Mission—St. Joachim, 555 Fagan Rd at Babbling Brook Rd, Piedmont, 36272.

JASPER, WALKER CO., ST. CECILIA (1964)
Mailing Address: 2159 Hwy. 195 N., Jasper, 35503.
Tel: 205-384-4800; Email: secretary@stcecilias.net. Rev. Wayne Herpin, S.J.
Catechesis Religious Program—Students 41.

LANETT, CHAMBERS CO., HOLY FAMILY (1915) [CEM]
705 N. Third Ave., Lanett, 36863-0325.

Tel: 334-644-4405; Email: lanettcatholic@gmail.com; Web: www.holyfamilycatholicchurch.net. Rev. Gali Balaswamy, Admin.
Catechesis Religious Program—Students 42.
Mission—Immaculate Conception, 506 County Rd. 1, Wedowee, 36278. Tel: 256-357-2977; Email: immaculateconceptional@gmail.com.

LEEDS, JEFFERSON CO., ST. THERESA OF THE CHILD JESUS (1951)
P.O. Box 525, Leeds, 35094. Rev. E. Gray Bean; Deacon Silverio Rubio Roman.
Res.: 1390 Ashville Ct., Leeds, 35094.
Tel: 205-352-3741; Email: sttheresaleeds@gmail.com; Web: www.sttheresaleeds.org.
Catechesis Religious Program—Samantha Wadsworth, D.R.E. Students 164.

LIVINGSTON, SUMTER CO., ST. FRANCIS OF ASSISI (1972) Administered by The Catholic Church in West Central Alabama. Mission of St. Leo, Demopolis.
Mailing Address: P. O. Box 937, Demopolis, 36732.
Tel: 334-289-2767; Fax: 334-289-6085; Email: stleothegreatcatholic@gmail.com. 101 Meadow Brook Dr., Livingston, 35470. Rev. Lawrence E. Shinnick.
Church: 525 Hwy. 28 E., Livingston, 35470.
Catechesis Religious Program—Grace Neel, Catechist. Students 1.

MADISON, MADISON CO.
1—ST. JOHN THE BAPTIST (1973) Rev. Bryan T. Lowe; Thomas Nattekkadan, Parochial Vicar; Deacons Kevin M. Brady; Dan Laurita; Darrell Diem; Gregory S. Thompson.
Res.: 1059 Hughes Rd., Madison, 35758.
Tel: 256-722-0130; Email: parishoffice@stjohnbchurch.org; Web: www.stjohnbchurch.org.
School—St. John the Baptist School, (Grades PreK-8), 1057 Hughes Rd., Madison, 35758.
Tel: 256-722-0772; Fax: 256-722-0151; Email: slewis@stjohnb.com. Sherry Lewis, Prin.; Jeanne Crown, Librarian. Lay Teachers 32; Students 466.
Catechesis Religious Program—Tel: 256-325-8580; Fax: 256-722-0303. Kathleen Butler, D.R.E. Students 673.
2—MOST MERCIFUL JESUS CATHOLIC CHURCH
10509 Segers Rd., Madison, 35756.
Tel: 256-325-0695; Web: www.mercyparish.church. Rev. Joy Chalissery; Deacons Jeffrey M. Montgomery; Antolin Padron; Richard E. Tuggle.

MONTEVALLO, SHELBY CO., ST. THOMAS THE APOSTLE (1951)
Tel: 205-663-3936; Fax: 205-663-0657; Email: rdunmyer@stthomascatholic.com; Web: stthomascatholic.com. Rev. Raymond A. Dunmyer; Deacons William P. Alexiou; David M. Hicks.
Res. & Mailing Address: 80 St. Thomas Way, Montevallo, 35115.
Catechesis Religious Program—Pat Shoop, D.R.E. Students 432.

MOULTON, LAWRENCE CO., RESURRECTION CATHOLIC CHAPEL (1993)
Mailing Address: P.O. Box 550, Moulton, 35650.
Tel: 256-476-0134; Email: rchen77@hughes.net; Web: www.moultoncatholic.com. Deacons Richard Chenault Sr., Admin.; Robert M. Catanach.
Res.: 8650 Hwy. 33, Moulton, 35650.
Church: 4826 County Rd. 217, Hillsboro, 35643.
Catechesis Religious Program—Students 7.

ONEONTA, BLOUNT CO., CORPUS CHRISTI (1983)
Fax: 205-625-6008. Rev. James P. Hedderman; Deacons Paul I. Mullen; Paul A. Arena.
Church & Res.: 32015 State Hwy. 75, Oneonta, 35121. Tel: 205-625-6078; Email: corpus@otelco.net; Web: corpuschristioneonta.com.
Catechesis Religious Program—Tel: 256-505-7324; Email: mal77@bellsouth.net. Margaret Savannah, D.R.E. Students 199.

PELL CITY, ST. CLAIR CO., OUR LADY OF THE LAKE (1969)
Mailing Address: 4609 Martin St. S., Cropwell, 35054. Tel: 205-525-5161; Tel: 205-525-4711; Email: parish@ollpellcity.com; Web: ollpellcity.com. Very Rev. William P. Lucas, V.F.; Deacons Terrence L. Rumore; Serge L. Brazzolotto; Lee Robinson.
Res.: 117 Ingram Lane, Cropwell, 35054.
Catechesis Religious Program—Email: sonyalewis285@gmail.com. Sonya Lewis, D.R.E. Students 105.

RUSSELLVILLE, FRANKLIN CO., GOOD SHEPHERD CHURCH (1973) Very Rev. Vincent E. Bresowar, V.F.
Res.: 1706 N. Jackson Ave., P.O. Box 878, Russellville, 35653. Tel: 256-332-4861; Email: goodshepherdcc@bellsouth.net.
Catechesis Religious Program—Students 145.

SCOTTSBORO, JACKSON CO., ST. JUDE (1971)
P.O. Box 971, Scottsboro, 35768. Rev. Thomas F. Woods, Admin.
Res.: 17205 Hwy. 35, Scottsboro, 35768.
Tel: 205-574-6156; Email: sjccbulletin@gmail.com.
Catechesis Religious Program—Carol Miller, Anglo D.R.E.; Rosalie Sarno, Hispanic D.R.E. Students 109.

SYLACAUGA, TALLADEGA CO., ST. JUDE (1947)
P.O. Box 111, Sylacauga, 35150. Rev. Shobahn Singareddy.
Res.: 310 W. Bay St., Sylacauga, 35150.
Tel: 256-245-7741; Email: singareddyshobhan@gmail.com.
Catechesis Religious Program—Students 21.
Mission—Holy Name of Jesus, 415 5th Ave., S.W., Childersburg, Talladega Co. 35044.

TALLADEGA, TALLADEGA CO., ST. FRANCIS OF ASSISI (1951) [CEM] Rev. Shobahn Singareddy.
Res.: 722 East St. S., P.O. Box 1142, Talladega, 35161. Tel: 256-362-5372; Email: stfrassisi@catholicexchange.com.
Catechesis Religious Program—Cindi Greene, D.R.E. Students 10.

TRUSSVILLE, JEFFERSON CO., HOLY INFANT OF PRAGUE (1941) [CEM] Very Rev. Jeremiah Deasy, V.F.; Deacons Ed Pruet; Danny W. McCay.
Res.: 4499 Rock Creek Cir., Trussville, 35173.
Church: 8090 Gadsen Hwy., P.O. Box 43, Trussville, 35173. Tel: 205-655-2541; Email: hiopcc@aol.com; Web: hiopcc.org.
Catechesis Religious Program—Email: hiopccTerry@aol.com. Terry Pruet, D.R.E. Students 230.

TUSCALOOSA, TUSCALOOSA CO.
1—ST. FRANCIS OF ASSISI UNIVERSITY PARISH (1929) Very Revs. J. Thomas Ackerman, V.F.; Richard A. Chenault Jr., Campus Min.; Deacons Lawrence R. Magner Jr.; William J. Remmert.
Res.: 811 5th Ave., Tuscaloosa, 35401.
Tel: 205-758-5672; Email: office@stfrancisuofa.com; Web: www.stfrancisuofa.com.
Mission—St. Robert, 407 2nd St., S.W., Reform, Pickens Co. 35481.
2—HOLY SPIRIT (1961) [CEM] Very Rev. Michael J. Deering, V.G.; Deacons Frank R. Slapikas; J. Adrian Straley.
Res.: 612 James I. Harrison Jr. Pkwy. E., Tuscaloosa, 35405.
Church: 733 James I. Harrison Jr. Pkwy. E., Tuscaloosa, 35405. Tel: 205-553-9733; Email: hsc@hschurch.com; Web: www.hschurch.com.
School—Holy Spirit School, (Grades PreK-6), 711 James I. Harrison Jr. Pkwy. E., Tuscaloosa, 35405.
Tel: 205-553-9630; Fax: 205-553-8880; Email: lcorona@holyspirit-al.com; Web: www.holyspirit-al.com. Felicia Corona, Prin. (Grades PreK-6). Lay Teachers 24; Students 292.
Catechesis Religious Program—Jeanne Doyle, D.R.E. Students 84.
Mission—St. John, c/o Very Rev. Michael Deering at Holy Spirit, 8th & Lurleen Wallace Blvd., Tuscaloosa, Tuscaloosa Co. 35401.

TUSCUMBIA, COLBERT CO., OUR LADY OF THE SHOALS (1869) [CEM] Rev. John Michael Adams.
Res.: 904 E. 3rd St., Tuscumbia, 35674.
Church: 200 E. Commons St. N., Tuscumbia, 35674.
Tel: 256-383-7207; Fax: 256-383-7883; Email: office@ourladyoftheshoals.org; Web: www.ourladyoftheshoals.org.
Catechesis Religious Program—Tena Flanagan, D.R.E. Students 128.

WINFIELD, MARION CO., HOLY SPIRIT (1965)
2710 U.S. Hwy. 43 N., Winfield, 35594.
Tel: 205-487-3616; Fax: 205-487-3616; Email: our3churches@outlook.com. Rev. Anthony J. Weis.
Catechesis Religious Program—Students 30.
Missions—Holy Family—423 19th St., N.W., Fayette, Fayette Co. 35555.
Our Lady of Guadalupe, 485 Layne Hill Dr., Haleyville, Winston Co. 35565.

On Special or Other Diocesan Assignment:
Most Rev.—
Marino, Joseph, Apostolic Nuncio to Bangladesh, U.N. Rd. 2, Baridhana, P.O. Box 6003, Dhaka, Bangladesh 1212
Revs.—
Bazzel, Kevin M., Official of the Congregation of Clergy of the Holy See
Klauck, Michael
McDonald, John G., Carl J. Peter Chair of Homiletics, Pontifical North American College, Rome.

Retired:
Rev. Msgrs.—
O'Connor, Eugene, (Retired)
Sexton, Michael F., V.F., (Retired)
Very Rev.—
Tierney, Patrick J., V.F., (Retired), 10162 151st St., Orland Park, IL 60462
Revs.—
Blazak, Camillus, (Retired), 533 Alexian Way #111, Signal Mountain, TN 37377
Brennan, Matthew, (Retired), 18 Main St., Carnew, County Wicklow Ireland
Fisher, Albert, (Retired)
Keiser, Raymond W., (Retired), 3011 Massey Rd., Apt. E, Vestavia, 35216
McDaid, Henry, (Retired), 10-B Shades Crest Rd., 35226. Tel: 205-989-4060
Murrin, Raymond J., (Retired), 18 Merrion Ct., Ailesbury Rd., Dublin 4, Ireland
Muscolino, Frank J., (Retired), 2600 Arlington Ave., Apt. 52, 35205. Tel: 205-933-5252
O'Donoghue, Patrick, (Retired), Haleyville, St. Anne's Rd., Killarney, County Kerry, Ireland
Thorsen, Henry, (Retired), c/o James Thorsen, 4136 Audiss Rd., Milton, FL 32583.

Permanent Deacons:
Alexiou, William P., St. Thomas the Apostle, Montevallo
Anzalone, J.S., St. Peter the Apostle, Birmingham
Arena, Paul A., (Retired), Corpus Christi, Oneonta
Ash, Donald J., (Retired)
Barisa, John J., St. Joseph Church, Huntsville
Barrett, James L., Resurrection, Clanton
Beam, Gregory J., St. Joseph, Florence
Becher, Robert J., Holy Spirit, Huntsville
Biggs, Rufus N. Sr., Our Lady Queen of the Universe, Birmingham
Bodine, James G., Our Lady Queen of the Universe, Huntsville
Boettcher, Philip F., St. Vincent's Hospital Chapel, Birmingham
Brady, Kevin M., St. John the Baptist, Madison
Brandt, William F., Our Lady of Lourdes, Birmingham
Brazzolotto, Serge L., Our Lady of the Lake, Pell City
Butler, Charles L., St. Paul Church, Athens
Catanach, Robert M., Resurrection Chapel, Moulton
Chenault, Richard A. Sr., Resurrection Chapel, Moulton
Citrano, Louis J., St. Mary's, Huntsville
Clawson, William D., Our Lady of the Shoals, Tuscumbia
Cooper, John H., St. Peter the Apostle, Hoover
Cova, Michael A., St. John the Apostle, Alexander City
Dias, Sam A., Diocese of Charleston
Diem, Darrell, St. John the Baptist, Madison
DiGiorgio, G. Rick, Prince of Peace, Birmingham
Germann, Aloysius A., (Retired)
Hall, Kenneth D., St. William, Guntersville
Hanks, William E. Jr., (Retired), St. Peter the Apostle, Hoover
Heckman, Lee G., Holy Spirit Church, Huntsville
Henderson, Walter J., (Retired)
Hicks, David M., St. Thomas the Apostle, Motevallo
Howell, Lawrence, (Retired)
Kay, G. Neal, Cathedral of St. Paul, Birmingham
Keil, Paul T., Good Shepherd, Huntsville
King, Aquila Butler III, St. Charles Borromeo, Jacksonville
Kirkpatrick, Stephen J., St. Michael Church, Florence
Kobs, Dennis, (Retired)
Koh, Matthew J.S., Holy Spirit Church, Huntsville (Korean Community)
Kreps, Kenneth M., Sacred Heart of Jesus, Cullman
Lappert, Patrick W., Annunciation of the Lord, Decatur
Laremore, Robert, (Retired)
Laurita, Dan, St. John the Baptist, Madison
Long, Robert G., Our Lady of the Valley, Birmingham
Magner, Lawrence R. Jr., St. Francis of Assisi University Church, Tuscaloosa
Martin, Robert A. Jr., Our Lady of the Valley, Birmingham
McCay, Danny W., Holy Infant of Prague, Trussville
McCormick, Robert A., St. James, Gadsden
Mickwee, George, (Retired)
Montgomery, Jeffrey M., Most Merciful Jesus Church, Madison
Moorer, Douglas C., Our Lady of Fatima, Birmingham
Moreno, Antonio, Holy Spirit Church, Huntsville
Motherway, Gerald, Holy Family, Birmingham
Mullen, Paul I., (Retired)
Multeri, James R., Our Lady Queen of the Universe, Huntsville
Nassetta, Peter C., Sacred Heart of Jesus, Cullman
Newman, Jeffrey, St. John the Baptist, Madison
Padron, Antolin, Most Merciful Jesus Church, Madison
Pruet, Ed, Holy Infant of Prague, Trussville
Ramirez, Javier, Annunciation of the Lord, Decatur
Remmert, William J., St. Francis University Parish, Tuscaloosa
Roberson, William, (Retired), Sacred Heart, Cullman
Robinson, E. Lee Sr., Our Lady of the Lake, Pell City

Rodgers, Daniel L., St. Stephen the Martyr Catholic University Chapel; Vidi Acosta College Ministry
Rodgers, Jacky M., St. Mary Church, Fairfield
Rodriguez, Ramon D., Sacred Heart of Jesus, Cullman
Roman, Silverio Rubio, St. Theresa, Leeds
Rosko, Christopher J., St. Peter the Apostle, Birmingham
Rumore, Terrence L., Our Lady of the Lake, Pell City
Schaefers, George M., Sacred Heart of Jesus, Cullman
Sciaroni, Louis J., Annunciation of the Lord, Decatur
Sisterman, Lawrence E., Holy Spirit, Huntsville
Slapikas, Frank R., Holy Spirit, Tuscaloosa
Smith, Craig R., Sacred Heart of Jesus, Cullman
Smith, Peter V., St. Mary Church, Fairfield
Straley, J. Adrian, Holy Spirit, Tuscaloosa
Sudnik, Michael P., Holy Spirit, Huntsville
Thompson, Gregory S., St. John the Baptist, Madison
Tuggle, Richard E., Most Merciful Jesus Church, Madison
Varner, David M., St. Mark the Evangelist, Brimingham
Vaughn, Timothy L., St. Elizabeth Ann Seton, Gardendale
Vazquez, Jose R., St. Peter the Apostle, Birmingham
Whitaker, Dan, Our Lady of the Valley, Birmingham
Williams, J. Fred, St. James, Gadsden
Zieverink, Edward Walter Jr., Cathedral of St. Paul, Birmingham.

INSTITUTIONS LOCATED IN DIOCESE

[A] HIGH SCHOOLS, DIOCESAN

BIRMINGHAM. *John Carroll Catholic High School*, 300 Lakeshore Pkwy., P.O. Box 19907, 35209. Tel: 205-940-2400; Fax: 205-945-7429; Email: principal@jcchs.org; Web: www.jcchs.org. Rev. Robert J. Sullivan, V.F., Pres.; Anthony Montalto, Prin. Lay Teachers 46; Priests 2; Sisters 2; Students 500.

FORT MCCLELLAN. *Sacred Heart Catholic High School*, 16 Morton Rd., Fort McClellan, Anniston, 36205. Tel: 265-237-4231; Fax: 256-237-4231; Email: jrussell@shcards.org. Jeremiah Russell, Prin. Lay Teachers 33; Students 280.

HUNTSVILLE. *Saint John Paul II Catholic High School*, 7301 Old Madison Pike, Huntsville, 35806. Tel: 256-430-1760; Fax: 256-430-1766; Web: www.jp2falcons.org. Rev. Jonathan Paul Howell, Chap.; Dr. Lanny Hollis, Headmaster; Mary Powers, Librarian; Rev. Alan Mackey; Kathy Smith, Librarian. Lay Teachers 46; Priests 1; Students 370.

TUSCALOOSA. *Holy Spirit Catholic High School*, (Grades 7-12), 601 James I. Harrison Jr. Pkwy. E., Tuscaloosa, 35405. Tel: 205-553-5606; Fax: 205-556-7103; Email: sperry@holyspirit-al.com; Web: www.holyspirit-al.com. Scott Perry, Prin.; Natalie Blankenship, Librarian. Lay Teachers 22; Sisters 1; Students 240.

[B] HIGH SCHOOLS, PRIVATE

BIRMINGHAM. *Holy Family Cristo Rey Catholic High School*, 2001 19th St. Ensley, 35218. Tel: 205-787-9937; Fax: 205-787-8530; Email: jchalmers@hfcristorey.org; Web: www.hfcristorey.org. Rev. Jon Chalmers, Pres.; Bethany Knighten, Prin. Lay Teachers 19; Priests 1; Students 210; Clergy / Religious Teachers 3.

CULLMAN. *St. Bernard Preparatory School*, (Grades 7-12), 1600 St. Bernard Dr., SE, Cullman, 35055. Tel: 256-739-6682; Fax: 256-734-2925; Email: sbps@stbernardprep.com; Web: www.stbernardprep.com. Rev. Joel W. Martin, O.S.B., Pres.; Fr. Linus Klucsarits, Headmaster; Bro. Thomas Jones, O.S.B., Librarian. Brothers 2; Lay Teachers 25; Priests 4; Students 185; Clergy / Religious Teachers 3.

[C] ELEMENTARY SCHOOLS, PRIVATE

BIRMINGHAM. *St. Rose Academy*, (Grades K-8), 1401 22nd St. S., 35205. Tel: 205-933-0549; Fax: 205-933-0591; Email: smjuliana@saintroseacademyop.com; Web: www.saintroseacademy.com. Sr. Mary Juliana, Prin. Dominican Sisters of Nashville, TN. Clergy 6; Lay Teachers 13; Sisters 6; Students 210; Clergy / Religious Teachers 6; Staff 10.

[D] GENERAL HOSPITALS

BIRMINGHAM. *Holy Name of Jesus Medical Center, Inc.*, 3102 Colony Park Dr., P.O. Box 430212, 35243. Tel: 256-880-7064; Email: shgmsbtM30@aol.com. Sr. Helen Gaffney, M.S.B.T., Pres. & CEO. Tot Asst. Annually 160; Total Staff 1.

St. Vincent's Health System, 810 St. Vincent's Dr., 35205. Tel: 205-939-7688; Fax: 205-930-2284; Email: debra.turner@ascension.org; Web: www.stvhs.com. Jason Alexander, Pres. Ascension Health Ministries (Ascension Sponsorship), A JP Bed Capacity 881; Nurses 2,103; Tot Asst. Annually 451,232; Total Staff 4,277.

St. Vincent's Birmingham, 810 St. Vincent's Dr., 35205. Tel: 205-939-7000; Fax: 205-930-2157; Email: deborah.gilley@ascension.com; Web: www.stvhs.com. Evan Ray, Pres. Ascension Health Bed Capacity 409; Nurses 1,205; Patients Asst Anual. 206,885; Total Staff 2,284.

St. Vincent's East, 50 Medical Park E. Dr., 35235. Tel: 205-838-3000; Fax: 205-838-3326; Email: Kelly.Smith3@ascension.org; Web: www.stvhs.com. Andrew Gnann, Interim Pres. & COO. Ascension Health Ministries (Ascension Sponsor), A Juridic Person Bed Capacity 362; Nurses 684; Tot Asst. Annually 134,704; Total Staff 1,464.

St. Vincent's Blount, 150 Gilbreath Dr., Oneonta, 35121. Tel: 205-274-3000; Fax: 205-274-3002; Email: Michelle.Brown@stvhs.com; Web: www.stvhs.com. Greg Brown, Admin. Ascension Health Ministries (Ascension Sponsor), A Public Juridic Person Bed Capacity 40; Nurses 64; Tot Asst. Annually 35,127; Total Staff 149.

St. Vincent's St. Clair, 7063 Veterans Pkwy., Pell City, 35125. Tel: 205-814-2429; Fax: 205-814-2145; Email: Joanna.Murphree@stvhs.com; Web: www.stvhs.com. Lisa Nichols, Admin. Ascension Health Ministries (Ascension Sponsorship), A Public Juridic Person Bed Capacity 40; Nurses 79; Tot Asst. Annually 52,760; Total Staff 203.

CLANTON. *St. Vincent's Chilton*, 2030 Lay Dam Rd., Clanton, 35405. Tel: 205-258-4400; Email: kelly.latham@ascension.org; Web: www.stvhs.com. Suzannah Campbell, Admin. Ascension Health Ministries (Ascension Sponsor), A Public Juridic Person Bed Capacity 30; Nurses 71; Tot Asst. Annually 21,756; Total Staff 177.

[E] MONASTERIES AND RESIDENCES OF PRIESTS AND BROTHERS

BIRMINGHAM. *Franciscan Missionaries of the Eternal Word, A Public Clerical Association of the Christian Faithful*, 5821 Old Leeds Rd., Irondale, 35210. Tel: 205-271-2937; Fax: 205-271-2949; Email: Fr_Anthony@ewtn.com; Web: www.franciscanmissionaries.com. Revs. Anthony Mary Stelten, M.F.V.A., Community Vicar; Joseph M. Wolfe, M.F.V.A.; Mark Mary Cristina, M.V.F.A., Community Servant; Miguel Marie Soeherman, M.F.V.A., First Councilor; Dominic Mary Garner, M.F.V.A., Second Councilor; Patrick Mary Russell, M.F.V.A.; Leonard Mary Revilla, M.F.V.A.; John Paul Mary Zeller, M.F.V.A.; Paschal Mary Yohe, M.F.V.A.; Bros. Bernard Haire, Treas.; Leo Lehmann, Third Councilor; John Therese Pratka, Member; Rev. Matthew Mary Bartow, Member. Professed 13; Total in Residence 13.

St. John Vianney Residence for Priests, 2724 Hanover Cir. S., 35205. Tel: 205-933-8078; Email: dmealer@bhmdiocese.org. Most Rev. Robert J. Baker, S.T.D., Ordinary.

CULLMAN. *St. Bernard Abbey* (Corporate Title: Benedictine Society of Alabama, Inc.) 1600 St. Bernard Dr., S.E., Cullman, 35055. Tel: 256-734-8291; Fax: 256-734-3885; Email: abcletus@stbernardprep.com; Web: www.stbernardabbey.com. Rt. Revs. Cletus D. Meagher, O.S.B., Abbot; Victor J. Clark, O.S.B., Retired Abbot, (Retired); Revs. Edward P. Markley, O.S.B.; Marcus J. Voss, O.S.B.; Very Rev. Kevin D. McGrath, O.S.B.; Revs. Joel W. Martin, O.S.B.; Howard R. Moussier, O.S.B., (Retired); John O'Donnell, O.S.B.; Patrick Egan, O.S.B.; Bede Marcy, O.S.B.; Francis M. Reque, O.S.B.; Bernard Denson, O.S.B. Brothers 18; Total Priests of Abbey 12.

[F] CONVENTS AND RESIDENCES OF SISTERS

CULLMAN. *Sacred Heart Monastery*, 916 Convent Rd., Cullman, 35055. Tel: 256-734-4622; Tel: 256-734-3835; Fax: 256-255-0048; Email: tonetteosb@shmon.org; Web: www.shmon.org. Sr. Tonette Sperando, O.S.B., Prioress. Benedictine Sisters. Professed Sisters 35.

HANCEVILLE. *Our Lady of the Angels Monastery in Hanceville Alabama*, 3222 County Rd. 548, Hanceville, 35077. Tel: 256-352-6267; Fax: 205-795-5724; Email: secretary@olamnuns.com; Web: www.olamshrine.com. Mother Dolores Marie, P.C.P.A.; Sr. Mary Michael, Vicar. Poor Clare Nuns of Perpetual Adoration. Sisters 12.

IRONDALE. *Sister Servants of the Eternal Word*, 3721 Belmont Rd., Irondale, 35210. Tel: 205-956-6760; Fax: 205-951-0386; Email: info@sisterservants.org. Sr. Louise Marie Flanigan, Supr.
Sister Servants of the Eternal Word, Inc. Sisters 20.

[G] SHRINES

HANCEVILLE. *Shrine of the Most Blessed Sacrament*, 3224 County Rd. 548, Hanceville, 35077. Tel: 256-352-6267; Email: pilgrimages@olamshrine.com; Web: www.olamshrine.com. Rev. Paschal Mary Yohe, M.F.V.A., Admin.

[H] DIOCESAN SOCIAL SERVICE

BIRMINGHAM. *Catholic Center of Concern* (Div. of Catholic Charities) 712 Fourth Ct. W., 35204. Tel: 205-786-4388; Fax: 205-786-6321. Sr. Zelia M. Cordeiro, M.C. Consolata Missionary Sisters. Tot Asst. Annually 1,989; Total Staff 7; Volunteer Hours 6,000; Total Assisted 7,000.

Catholic Family Services, 1515 12th Ave., S., 35205. Tel: 205-324-6561; Fax: 205-323-0475; Email: sbowen@cfsbhm.org; Web: www.cfsbhm.org. Mr. Scott Bowen, Dir. Total Staff 6; Total Assisted 1,095.

ANNISTON. *All Saints Interfaith Center of Concern*, 1513 Noble St., Anniston, 36201. Tel: 256-236-7793; Fax: 256-238-7776; Email: mroberts@centerofconcernanniston.org. Kimberly Johnson, L.P.C. Total Staff 3; Total Assisted 14,000.

EUTAW. *Guadalupan Multicultural Services*, 331 Boligee St., P.O. Box 538, Eutaw, 35462. Tel: 205-372-3497; Fax: 205-372-3497; Email: mtobon@guadalupeusa.org. Tot Asst. Annually 10,000; Total Staff 2; Total Assisted 9,030.

FLORENCE. *Catholic Family Services*, 1111 E. College St., Florence, 35630. Tel: 256-768-1550; Email: cfsdebb@att.net. Debbie Buffaloe, L.G.S.W., Social Worker. Total Staff 1; Total Assisted 342.

GADSDEN. *St. Martin de Porres Catholic Center of Concern*, 612 Chestnut St., Gadsden, 35901. Tel: 256-546-0028; Fax: 256-547-1730; Email: lbean@bhmdiocese.org. Lee Bean, Dir. Total Staff 3; Total Assisted 15,601.

HUNTSVILLE. *Catholic Center of Concern*, 1010 Church St., N.W., P.O. Box 745, Huntsville, 35804. Tel: 256-536-0041; Fax: 256-534-3141; Email: kermit@cfshsv.com. Kermit Elliott, Dir. Total Staff 1; Total Assisted 6,050.

Catholic Family Services, 1010 Church St., N.W., P.O. Box 745, Huntsville, 35804. Tel: 256-536-0073; Fax: 256-534-3141; Email: cathie@cfshsv.com; Web: www.cfsbhm.org. Cathie McDaniel, Dir. Tot Asst. Annually 261; Total Staff 3; Total Families Served 261.

TUSCALOOSA. *Catholic Center of Concern*, 608 James I. Harrison, Jr. Pkwy., Tuscaloosa, 35405. Tel: 205-759-1268; Email: mblathamcss@comcast.net. Misty Moon, Dir. Total Staff 6; Total Assisted 1,029.

[I] CAMPUS MINISTRY

BIRMINGHAM. *St. Stephen the Martyr Catholic University Chapel* St. Stephen the Martyr Catholic University Chapel, 1515 12th Ave. S., 35205. Tel: 205-933-2500; Fax: 205-323-0475; Web: stephenthemartyr.com. Rev. Joshua Altonji, Chap.; Deacon Daniel L. Rodgers, Campus Min. Serves: University of Alabama at Birmingham, Samford University, Birmingham-Southern College. Students 100; Total Staff 2.

FLORENCE. *University of North Alabama*, 1111 E. College St., Florence, 35630. Tel: 256-764-3303; Fax: 256-718-0208; Email: secretary@stjosephflorence.org. Rev. Roy Runkle.

HUNTSVILLE. *Campus Ministry - University of Alabama in Huntsville*, c/o St. Joseph, 2300 Beasley Ave., Huntsville, 35805. Tel: 256-534-8459; Fax: 256-534-8450. Rev. Joseph Lubrano, S.D.S., Contact Person.

JACKSONVILLE. *Jacksonville State University*, 308 Seventh St., N.E., Jacksonville, 36265. Tel: 256-435-3238; Fax: 256-435-4942; Email: tricia@stcharlescatholicchurch.com. Rev. James Handerhan. Total Staff 2; Total in Program 15.

MONTEVALLO. *University of Montevallo Catholic Campus Ministry*, St. Thomas the Apostle Catholic Campus Ministry, 80 St. Thomas Way, Montevallo, 35115. Tel: 205-663-3936; Fax: 205-663-0657; Email: rdunmyer@stthomascatholic.com. Rev. Raymond A. Dunmyer.

TALLADEGA. *Talladega College Catholic Campus Ministry*, St. Francis of Assisi, 722 East Street South, P.O. Box 1142, Talladega, 35160. Tel: 256-362-5372; Email: stfrassisi@catholicexchange.com. Rev. Shobahn Singareddy.

TUSCALOOSA. *Campus Ministry Office - University of*

Alabama, St. Francis University Parish, 811 Fifth Ave., Tuscaloosa, 35401. Tel: 205-758-5672; Fax: 205-758-5673; Email: frrick@stfrancisuofa.com; Web: stfrancisuofa.com. Very Rev. Richard A. Chenault Jr., Campus Min. Total in Residence 1; Total Staff 1.

[J] MISCELLANEOUS LISTINGS

BIRMINGHAM. *St. Barnabas Catholic Education Foundation*, 7921 First Ave. N., 35206. Tel: 205-833-0334; Web: www.barnabascatholic.com. Rev. Douglas Michael Vu; Mr. Bob M. Sellers Jr., CEO.

Birmingham Catholic Center of Concern Fund, 712 4th Ct. W., 35204. Tel: 205-786-4388; Email: zmcordeiro@bhmdiocese.org. Sr. Zelia M. Cordeiro, M.C., Dir.

Blessed Sacrament Catholic Church Endowment Fund, 1460 Pearson Ave., S.W., 35211. Tel: 205-785-9840; Email: church@myblessedsacrament.org. Rev. Jim W. Booth.

Bruno Family's Catholic Diocesan Trust, 2121 3rd Avenue North, P.O. Box 12047, 35203. Tel: 205-838-8322; Fax: 205-836-1910; Email: dmealer@bhmdiocese.org; Web: www.bhmdiocese.org. Mr. Bob M. Sellers Jr., CEO; Donna Mealer, Exec.

Catholic Housing of Birmingham, Inc., 2121 3rd Avenue North, P.O. Box 12047, 35203. Tel: 205-838-8322; Fax: 205-836-1910; Email: dmealer@bhmdiocese.org. Bruce Hoagland, Pres.

Clergy Supplemental Retirement Fund, 2121 Third Ave. N., 35203. Tel: 205-838-8322; Email: mshumate@bhmdiocese.org. Mr. Bob M. Sellers Jr., CEO.

Congregation of the Passion: Holy Family Community, Inc. (House of Religious Men) 1910 19th St., Ensley, 35218. Tel: 205-780-3440; Fax: 205-780-5272. Revs. Alphonse Justin Nelson, C.P., Local Supr.; Alex Steinmiller, C.P.; Patricio Montsalvas Rizzo, C.P. Corporation for Holy Family Church, and Holy Family Middle School, Birmingham, St. Mary's Church, Fairfield, and St. Joseph Church, Birmingham.

Contemplative Outreach Birmingham, 3416 River Tree Ln., 35223. Tel: 205-970-1892; Email: calli.meredith@gmail.com; Web: centeringprayeralabama.wordpress.com. Louise Meredith, Coord.; Diana Tschache, Area Contact Person.

Faith In Education Catholic Schools Fund, 2121 Third Ave. N, 35203. Tel: 205-838-8322; Email: jejohnson@bhmdiocese.org. Julie Emory-Johnson, Dir.

St. Francis Xavier Catholic School Education Foundation, 2 Xavier Cir., 35213. Tel: 205-871-1687; Fax: 205-871-1674; Email: nwright@saintfrancisxavierschool.com; Email: saintfrancis@sfxbirmingham.com; Web: www.sfxbirmingham.com. Mr. Bob M. Sellers Jr., Contact Person; Rev. Robert J. Sullivan, V.F., Pastor. Adult Baptisms (18 & older) 7; Infant Baptisms (up to age 7) 156; Interfaith Marriages 7; Catholic Marriages 17; First Communions 147; Received into Full Communion 11; Deaths 28; Registered Parishioner Households 1,298.

Grace Lay Ministry Fund, 2121 Third Ave. N., 35203. Tel: 205-838-8322; Email: bsellers@bhmdiocese.org. Mr. Bob M. Sellers Jr., CFO.

Grace Liturgical Fund Anna C. Grace Liturgical Fund, 2121 Third Ave. N., 35203. Tel: 205-838-8322; Email: bsellers@bhmdiocese.org. Mr. Bob M. Sellers Jr., CFO.

Holy Family Educational Foundation, 1910 19th St., 35218. Tel: 205-780-3440; Fax: 205-782-5272; Email: lmlang@bellsouth.net; Web: www.passionist.org. Melva Langford, Bd. Chair.

Holy Name of Jesus Hospital Trust (Health and Medical Services) c/o Regions Bank, P.O. Box 1688, 35202. Tel: 205-264-5232; Email: katie.nelson@regions.com. Mr. Bob M. Sellers Jr., CFO Diocese of Birmingham; Katie Nelson, Trustee. Total Assisted 500.

Jack Miller Education Foundation, 300 Lakeshore Pkwy., 35209. Tel: 205-940-2400; Email: bsellers@bhmdiocese.org. Rev. Robert J. Sullivan, V.F., Pres.

John Carroll Catholic High School Educational Foundation, Inc., 300 Lakeshore Pkwy., 35209. Tel: 205-940-2400; Fax: 205-945-7429; Email: bsellers@bhmdiocese.org; Web: www.jcchs.org. Rev. Robert J. Sullivan, V.F., Pres.

John Carroll Catholic High School Endowed Choir Fund, 300 Lakeshore Pkwy., 35209. Tel: 205-940-2400; Email: bsellers@bhmdiocese.org. Rev. Robert J. Sullivan, V.F., Pres.

John Carroll Catholic High School Endowment Scholarship Fund, 300 Lakeshore Pkwy., 35209. Tel: 205-940-2400; Email: bsellers@bhmdiocese.org. Rev. Robert J. Sullivan, V.F., Prin.

St. John Vianney Memorial Fund, 2121 Third Ave. N., 35203. Tel: 205-838-8322, Ext. 309; Email: bsellers@bhmdiocese.org. Mr. Bob M. Sellers Jr., CEO/CFO.

Ladies of Charity of Central Alabama, 2843 Shook Hill Cir., 35223. Tel: 205-601-3973; Email: cssauer@aol.com. Ms. Carol Sauer, Contact Person.

Lee Fisher Memorial Award, 300 Lakeshore Pkwy., 35209. Tel: 205-940-2400; Email: bsellers@bhmdiocese.org. Rev. Robert J. Sullivan, V.F., Prin.

Loraine Cerfolio Memorial Award, 2121 Third Ave. N., 35203. Tel: 205-838-8322; Email: bsellers@bhmdiocese.org. Mr. Bob M. Sellers Jr., CFO.

Magnificat: Mary, Woman of Faith Chapter, 2121 3rd Avenue North, P.O. Box 660136, 35266-0136. Tel: 205-979-7645; Email: carolinamaenza@gmail.com; Web: www.magnificat-birminghamal.org. Virginia Springer, Coord.

The Mary O'Poole Endowment Fund, 2121 Third Ave. N., 35203. Tel: 205-838-8322; Email: bsellers@bhmdiocese.org. Mr. Bob M. Sellers Jr., CFO.

Mattie Palmore Scholarship Fund, 2121 Third Ave. N., 35203. Tel: 205-838-8322; Email: bsellers@bhmdiocese.org. Mr. Bob M. Sellers Jr., CFO.

The Monaghan Fund, 2121 Third Ave. N., 35203. Tel: 205-838-8322; Email: bsellers@bhmdiocese.org. Mr. Bob M. Sellers Jr., C.F.O.

One Voice Endowment Fund, 2121 Third Ave. N., 35203. Tel: 205-838-8305; Fax: 205-838-8319. Sally Crockett, Dir.; Mary Dillard, Photojournalist & Art Dir.

Our Lady of Sorrows Educational School Foundation, 1730 Oxmoor Rd., 35209. Tel: 205-871-8121; Fax: 205-871-8180; Email: ols@ourladyofsorrows.com. Rev. Msgr. Martin M. Muller, V.F.

Our Lady of the Valley Educational Foundation, 5514 Double Oak Ln., 35242. Tel: 205-991-5488; Fax: 205-991-5181; Email: olvchurch@olvsch.com. Rev. Msgr. Paul L. Rohling, Pastor.

St. Peter Child Development Center Fund, 2061 Patton Chapel Rd., 35216. Tel: 205-822-4480; Email: stpeterapostle@bellsouth.net. Rev. Thomas M. Kelly, F.T.C.L., Pastor.

St. Peter's Endowment Foundation, 2061 Patton Chapel Rd., 35216. Tel: 205-822-4480; Email: stpeterapostle@bellsouth.net. Rev. Thomas M. Kelly, F.T.C.L. Total Staff 35; Total Assisted 149.

Schultz Inner City Catholic School Fund, 2121 Third Ave. N., 35203. Tel: 205-838-8322; Email: bsellers@bhmdiocese.org. Mr. Bob M. Sellers Jr., CFO.

St. Thomas More Society of Metro Birmingham, 2011 4th Ave. N., 35203. Tel: 205-639-5300; Email: jwhitaker@wmslawfirm.com. G. Rick DiGiorgio, Chm.; John Whitaker, Pres.

Thomas Scott Messina Memorial Endowment, 300 Lakeshore Pkwy., 35209. Tel: 205-940-2400; Email: bsellers@bhmdiocese.org. Rev. Robert J. Sullivan, V.F., Pres.; Mr. Bob M. Sellers Jr., CFO Diocese of Birmingham.

Tuxedo Junction Catholic Community, Inc., 1910 19th St., Ensley, 35218. Tel: 205-780-3440; Email: kennethblckldg@aol.com. Rev. Robert Crossmyer, C.P., Pastoral Assoc.

Villa Maria I, 500 82nd St. S., 35206. Tel: 205-836-7839; Fax: 205-836-0664; Email: villamariamgr@spm.net. Judy Murphree, Mgr. Total in Residence 63; Total Staff 7.

Villa Maria II, 500 82nd St. S., 35206. Tel: 205-836-7839; Email: villamariamgr@spm.net. Elizabeth Johns, Mgr.

St. Vincent's Foundation, One Medical Park East Dr., 35235. Tel: 205-838-6151; Email: Wayne.Carmello-Harper@ascension.org; Web: www.stvfoundation.org. Wayne Carmello-Harper, Contact Person.

BESSEMER. **Avila Foundation*, 1062 Grand Oaks Dr., Bessemer, 35022. Tel: 818-646-7729; Email: dburke@ewtn.com. Mr. Dan Burke, Pres.

CULLMAN. *Benedictine Sisters Retreat Center*, 916 Convent Rd., Cullman, 35055-2019. Tel: 256-734-8302; Fax: 256-255-0048; Email: retreats@shmon.org; Web: www.shmon.org. Sr. Elisabeth Meadows, O.S.B., Dir. Bed Capacity 73; Total Staff 7.

St. Bernard Abbey Foundation, 1600 St. Bernard Dr., S.E., Cullman, 35055. Tel: 256-734-8291; Fax: 256-734-3885; Email: abcletus@stbernardprep.com; Web: www.stbernardabbey.com. Rt. Rev. Cletus Meagher, O.S.B., Chm.

St. Bernard Preparatory School Educational Foundation, 1600 St. Bernard Dr., S.E., Cullman, 35055. Tel: 256-739-6682; Fax: 256-734-2925; Email: abcletus@stbernardprep.com; Web: www.stbernardprep.com. Rt. Rev. Cletus Meagher, O.S.B., Chm.

Natalie Collier Memorial Scholarship Fund, 205 3rd Ave., S. E., Cullman, 35055. Tel: 256-734-3730; Fax: 256-734-3476; Email: price@sacredheartchurchcullman.org. Rev. Patrick Egan, O.S.B., Pastor.

Sacred Heart Monastery of Cullman, Alabama Foundation, 916 Convent Rd., Cullman, 35055-2019. Tel: 256-734-4622; Tel: 256-734-3835; Fax: 256-255-0048; Email: development@shmon.org; Web: www.shmon.org. Sr. Tonette Sperando, O.S.B., Pres.

Friends of Sacred Heart School Endowment Foundation, 205 3rd Ave., S. E., Cullman, 35055. Tel: 256-734-3730; Fax: 256-734-3476; Email: price@sacredheartchurchcullman.org. Rev. Patrick Egan, O.S.B., Pastor.

DECATUR. *St. Ann's Educational Foundation*, 3910 Spring Ave., S.W., Decatur, 35603. Tel: 256-353-2667; Fax: 256-353-8994; Email: parish@annunlord.com. Mr. Bob M. Sellers Jr., CEO.

FLORENCE. *St. Joseph School Foundation, Florence*, 115 Plum St., Florence, 35630. Tel: 256-766-1923; Email: ceckleck@aol.com; Email: info@stjosephschoolfoundation.org. Mr. Bob M. Sellers Jr., Contact Person.

Society of St. Vincent de Paul, St. Joseph Conference, 659 S. Poplar St., Florence, 35630-6818. Tel: 256-718-0901; Fax: 256-718-0901; Email: stvincent2007@bellsouth.net. Roberta Bergner, Treas.

GADSDEN. *St. James Educational Foundation*, 622 Chestnut Street, Gadsden, 35904. Tel: 256-546-2975. Rev. Jose B. Chacko, Pastor. Total Staff 22.

HUNTSVILLE. *Father Francis Jordan Scholarship Fund*, 2300 Beasley Ave., N.W., Huntsville, 35816. Tel: 256-539-5221; Email: lparker@hfscatholic.com. Billy Roy, Prin.

Holy Spirit Regional School Foundation, 625 Airport Rd., Huntsville, 35802. Tel: 256-881-4852; Fax: 256-881-4904; Email: foundation89@comcast.net; Web: www.hstigers.org. Lee Dumbacher, Admin.

Society of St. Vincent de Paul, District Council of Huntsville, 625 Airport Rd., Huntsville, 35802. Tel: 256-883-0157; Email: hsvsvdp@knology.net. John Wolfsberger, Pres., District Council of Huntsville; Deacon Sam A. Dias, Spiritual Advisor; Patricia Schuessler, Treas.

St. Vincent de Paul Thrift Store, 2140 Jonathan Dr., Huntsville, 35810-3453. Tel: 256-851-8881; Email: dmealer@bhmdiocese.org. Patricia Schuessler, Mgr.

IRONDALE. *Casa Maria Retreat House*, 3721 Belmont Rd., Irondale, 35210. Tel: 205-956-6760; Fax: 205-951-0386; Email: retreats@sisterservants.com. Sr. Louise Marie Flanigan, Dir.

**Eternal Word Television Network, Inc.* (EWTN Global Catholic Network) 5817 Old Leeds Rd., Irondale, 35210. Tel: 205-271-2900; Fax: 205-271-2920; Email: chairman@ewtn.com; Web: www.ewtn.com. Michael P. Warsaw, Chm. Bd. & CEO.

MONTEVALLO. *St. Thomas Education Foundation*, 80 St. Thomas Way, Montevallo, 35115. Tel: 205-663-3936; Email: rdunmyer@stthomascatholic.com. Mr. Bob M. Sellers Jr., Contact Person.

PLEASANT GROVE. **Bible Christian Society*, 544 Park Road, P.O. Box 424, Pleasant Grove, 35127-1613. Tel: 205-744-1856; Email: admin@biblechristiansociety.com; Web: www.biblechristiansociety.com. John Martignoni, Pres.

Queen of Heaven Radio, Inc., 544 Park Road, P.O. Box 483, Pleasant Grove, 35127-1613. Tel: 205-744-4456; Fax: 205-744-4457; Email: info@queenofheavenradio.com. John Martignoni, Pres.

TUSCALOOSA. *The Harrison Family Endowment Trust for the Benefit of Holy Spirit School*, 711 James I. Harrison Jr. Pkwy. E., Tuscaloosa, 35405. Tel: 205-553-9630; Fax: 205-553-8880; Email: sperry@holyspirital.com. Very Rev. Michael J. Deering, V.G.

Holy Spirit School of Tuscaloosa Endowment Foundation, 733 James I. Harrison, Jr. Pkwy. E, Tuscaloosa, 35405. Tel: 205-553-9733; Email: hsc@hschurch.com; Web: www.hschurch.com. Rev. Michael Deering; Mr. Bob M. Sellers Jr., CFO Diocese of Birmingham.

RELIGIOUS INSTITUTES OF MEN REPRESENTED IN THE DIOCESE

For further details refer to the corresponding bracketed number in the Religious Institutes of Men or Women section.

[0200]—*Benedictine Monks*—O.S.B.

[1000]—*Congregation of the Passion*—C.P.
[]—*Franciscan Missionaries of the Eternal Word*—M.F.V.A.
[]—*Incarnatio Consecratio Missio*—(I.C.M.).
[1120]—*Missionaries of the Sacred Hearts of Jesus and Mary*—M.SS.CC.
[1200]—*Society of the Divine Savior*—S.D.S.
[0700]—*St. Joseph's Society of the Sacred Heart* (Baltimore, MD)—S.S.J.

RELIGIOUS INSTITUTES OF WOMEN REPRESENTED IN THE DIOCESE

[0230]—*Benedictine Sisters of Pontifical Jurisdiction*—O.S.B.
[0260]—*Blessed Sacrament Sisters*—S.B.S.
[0720]—*Consolata Missionary Sisters*—M.C.
[0760]—*Daughters of Charity of St. Vincent de Paul*—D.C.
[0820]—*Daughters of the Holy Spirit*—D.H.S.
[1070-03]—*Dominican Sisters* (Adrian, MI)—O.P.
[1070-07]—*Dominican Sisters* (Nashville, TN)—O.P.
[2720]—*Mission Helpers of the Sacred Heart*—M.H.S.H.
[1845]—*Missionaries Guadalupanas of the Holy Spirit*—M.G.Sp.S.
[2790]—*Missionary Servants of the Most Blessed Trinity*—M.S.B.T.
[3210]—*Poor Clares of Perpetual Adoration*—P.C.P.A.
[]—*Sister Servants of the Eternal Word*—S.S.E.W.
[2575]—*Sisters of Mercy of the Americas*—R.S.M.
[1650]—*Sisters of St. Francis of Philadelphia*—O.S.F.
[3840]—*Sisters of St. Joseph of Carondelet*—C.S.J.
[1030]—*Sisters of the Divine Savior*—S.D.S.
[3320]—*Sisters of the Presentation of the B.V.M.*—P.B.V.M.

NECROLOGY

† Underwood, Joseph, (Retired), Died Oct. 30, 2018

An asterisk (*) denotes an organization that has established tax-exempt status directly with the IRS and is not covered by the USCCB Group Ruling.

Diocese of Bismarck

(Dioecesis Bismarckiensis)

Most Reverend

DAVID D. KAGAN, D.D., P.A., J.C.L.

Bishop of Bismarck; ordained June 14, 1975; named Prelate of Honor November 14, 1994; Protonotary Apostolic May 21, 2011; appointed Bishop of Bismarck October 19, 2011; installed November 30, 2011.

Chancery Office: P.O. Box 1575, Bismarck, ND 58502-1575. Tel: 701-223-1347; Fax: 701-223-3693. . *Center for Pastoral Ministry Office, P.O. Box 1137, ND 58502-1137.* Tel: 701-222-3035; Fax: 701-222-0269.

Web: www.bismarckdiocese.com

Most Reverend

PAUL A. ZIPFEL, D.D.

Bishop Emeritus of Bismarck; ordained March 18, 1961; appointed Titular Bishop of Walla Walla and Auxiliary Bishop of St. Louis May 16, 1989; consecrated June 29, 1989; appointed Bishop of Bismarck December 31, 1996; installed February 20, 1997; retired October 19, 2011. *P.O. Box 1137, Bismarck, ND 58502-1137.*

ESTABLISHED DECEMBER 31, 1909.

Square Miles 34,268.

Comprises the Counties of Adams, Billings, Bowman, Burke, Burleigh, Divide, Dunn, Emmons, Golden Valley, Grant, Hettinger, McKenzie, McLean, Mercer, Morton, Mountrail, Oliver, Renville, Sioux, Slope, Stark, Ward and Williams in the State of North Dakota.

For legal titles of parishes and diocesan institutions, consult the Chancery Office.

STATISTICAL OVERVIEW

Personnel	
Bishop	1
Retired Bishops	1
Abbots	1
Priests: Diocesan Active in Diocese	52
Priests: Diocesan Active Outside Diocese	4
Priests: Diocesan in Foreign Missions	1
Priests: Retired, Sick or Absent	9
Number of Diocesan Priests	66
Religious Priests in Diocese	13
Total Priests in Diocese	79
Extern Priests in Diocese	7
Ordinations:	
Diocesan Priests	2
Transitional Deacons	2
Permanent Deacons	5
Permanent Deacons in Diocese	81
Total Brothers	19
Total Sisters	77
Parishes	
Parishes	97
With Resident Pastor:	
Resident Diocesan Priests	41
Resident Religious Priests	2
Without Resident Pastor:	
Administered by Priests	53
Administered by Deacons	1
Professional Ministry Personnel:	
Brothers	1
Sisters	9
Lay Ministers	42
Welfare	
Catholic Hospitals	4
Total Assisted	457,000
Homes for the Aged	8
Total Assisted	845
Other Institutions	1
Total Assisted	100
Educational	
Diocesan Students in Other Seminaries	26
Total Seminarians	26
Colleges and Universities	1
Total Students	3,806
High Schools, Diocesan and Parish	3
Total Students	581
Elementary Schools, Diocesan and Parish	10
Total Students	2,203
Catechesis/Religious Education:	
High School Students	867
Elementary Students	4,537
Total Students under Catholic Instruction	12,020
Teachers in the Diocese:	
Priests	5
Sisters	7
Lay Teachers	245
Vital Statistics	
Receptions into the Church:	
Infant Baptism Totals	907
Minor Baptism Totals	47
Adult Baptism Totals	36
Received into Full Communion	106
First Communions	943
Confirmations	703
Marriages:	
Catholic	189
Interfaith	71
Total Marriages	260
Deaths	716
Total Catholic Population	60,722
Total Population	334,100

Former Bishops—Most Revs. VINCENT DE PAUL WEHRLE, O.S.B., D.D., appt. Bishop of Bismarck, April 9, 1910; cons. May 19, 1910; retired Dec. 11, 1939; named Titular Bishop of Teos by Pope Pius XII; died Nov. 2, 1941; VINCENT J. RYAN, D.D., L.L.D., appt. March 19, 1940; cons. May 28, 1940; died Nov. 10, 1951; LAMBERT A. HOCH, D.D., L.L.D., appt. Jan. 23, 1952; cons. March 25, 1952; transferred to Diocese of Sioux Falls, Dec. 5, 1956; died June 27, 1990; HILARY B. HACKER, D.D., appt. Bishop, Dec. 29, 1956; retired June 28, 1982; died Nov. 6, 1990; JOHN F. KINNEY, D.D., J.C.D., appt. June 28, 1982; Episcopal Ord. Jan. 25, 1977; installed Aug. 23, 1982; transferred to Diocese of St. Cloud, July 6, 1995; PAUL A. ZIPFEL, D.D., (Retired), ord. March 18, 1961; appt. Titular Bishop of Walla Walla and Auxiliary Bishop of St. Louis May 16, 1989; cons. June 29, 1989; appt. Bishop of Bismarck Dec. 31, 1996; installed Feb. 20, 1997; retired Oct. 19, 2011.

Moderator of the Curia—Rev. Msgr. GENE E. LINDEMANN, J.C.L.

Vicar General—Rev. Msgr. GENE E. LINDEMANN, J.C.L.

Center for Pastoral Ministry—520 N. Washingtin St., P.O. Box 1137, Bismarck, 58502. Tel: 701-222-3035 ; Fax: 701-222-0269.

Chancellor—MR. DALE EBERLE.

Office of Canonical Services (Marriage Tribunal)—520 N. Washington St., P.O. Box 1137, Bismarck, 58502-1137. Tel: 701-222-3035. Marriage papers should be directed to Bishop David D. Kagan, P.O. Box 1575, Bismarck, ND 58502-1575.

Judicial Vicar—Rev. CHRISTOPHER J. KADRMAS, J.C.L.

Defensor Vinculi—Rev. DAVID L. ZIMMER, J.C.L.; Rev. Msgr. GENE E. LINDEMANN, J.C.L.; MATTHEW ORZOLEK; DR. RAPHAEL FRACKIEWICZ, J.C.D.

Promoter of Justice—Rev. DAVID L. ZIMMER, J.C.L.

Pro-Synodal Judges—Revs. BRUCE D. KREBS; CHRISTOPHER J. KADRMAS, J.C.L.

Associate Judges—Revs. KEITH N. STREIFEL; DAVID RICHTER; SHANNON G. LUCHT; LATON LOHMAN, J.C.L.

Auditor—AMANDA JENSEN.

Ecclesiastical Notary—SANDRA BREINER.

Presbyteral Council—Rev. Msgr. GENE E. LINDEMANN, J.C.L., Chm., Ex Officio; Revs. BRIAN P. GROSS; KEITH N. STREIFEL, Treas.; TODD KREITINGER; MARVIN J. KLEMMER, (Retired); GARY BENZ; STEPHEN FOLORUNSO; PAUL D. BECKER; ADAM J. MAUS; JARED M. JOHNSON; Rt. Rev. DANIEL MALONEY, O.S.B., M.A.

Diocesan Corporate Board—Most Rev. DAVID D. KAGAN, D.D., P.A., J.C.L., Pres.; Rev. Msgr. GENE E. LINDEMANN, J.C.L., Vice Pres.; Rev. DANIEL J. BERG; MR. DALE EBERLE, Sec.; Rev. Msgr. JAMES B. BRAATEN, Treas.

Diocesan Finance Council—Most Rev. DAVID D. KAGAN, D.D., P.A., J.C.L., Pres.; Rev. Msgrs. GENE E. LINDEMANN, J.C.L., Chm.; JAMES B. BRAATEN; Rev. DANIEL J. BERG; TIM CONLIN; GREG VETTER; MICHAEL T. SCHMITZ. Ex Officio: LAURA J. HUBER; MR. DALE EBERLE; MR. RONALD SCHATZ; MR. KEVIN DVORAK.

The Parish Expansion Fund of the Diocese of Bismarck—Most Rev. DAVID D. KAGAN, D.D., P.A., J.C.L., Pres.; Rev. Msgr. GENE E. LINDEMANN, J.C.L., Vice Pres.; MR. DALE EBERLE, Sec.; LAURA J. HUBER, Treas.; PETE JAHNER; Deacon JAMES WOSEPKA; MOLLY BARNES; BELINDA VOLLMER; ROBERT MONGEON.

Diocesan Offices and Directors

Archives—MR. DALE EBERLE, Tel: 701-204-7216.

Boy Scouts—

National Catholic Committee on Scouting—Deacon HARVEY HANEL, 1918 Grandview Ln., Bismarck, 58503-0849.

Catholic Campaign For Human Development—MR. RONALD SCHATZ, Dir., Center for Pastoral Ministry Office. Tel: 701-204-7202.

Catholic Charities North Dakota—DIANNE NECHIPORENKO, Exec. Dir., 5201 Bishops Blvd.,

Ste. B, Fargo, 58104-7605. Tel: 701-235-4457. 600 S. 2nd St., Ste. 202, Bismarck, 58504. 216 S. Broadway, Ste. 103, Minot, 58701-3852. Tel: 701-852-2854.

Catholic Relief Services—MR. RONALD SCHATZ, Dir., Center for Pastoral Ministry Office. Tel: 701-204-7202.

Office of Vocations—Rev. JOSHUA K. WALTZ, Dir., Tel: 701-204-7197.

Vicar for Presbyters—Rev. Msgr. JAMES B. BRAATEN, 1905 S. 3rd St., Bismarck, 58504-7118. Tel: 701-223-3606.

Office of Divine Worship—Rev. NICK L. SCHNEIDER, S.L.L., S.L.D., Dir., c/o Christ the King, 505 10th Ave., N.W., Mandan, 58554. Tel: 701-663-8842.

Continuing Education for Clergy—Rev. Msgr. PATRICK A. SCHUMACHER, S.T.L., 525 3rd St. E., Dickinson, 58601-4504. Tel: 701-225-3972.

Newspaper—Dakota Catholic Action SONIA MULLALLY, Editor, Center for Pastoral Ministry Office. Tel: 701-204-7190.

North Dakota Catholic Conference—CHRISTOPHER DODSON, 103 S. 3rd St., Ste. 10, Bismarck, 58501-3800. Tel: 701-223-2519; Fax: 701-223-6075; Web: www.ndcatholic.org.

Permanent Diaconate Office—
Episcopal Vicar for Deacons—VACANT.
Director of Deacons—DAVID FLECK, Tel: 701-204-7210 Center for Pastoral Ministry.

Priests' Benefit Association—Most Rev. DAVID D. KAGAN, D.D., P.A., J.C.L., Pres.; Revs. TERRY WIPF, Chm.; SHANE CAMPBELL, Vice Chair; SHANNON G. LUCHT, Sec.; DANIEL J. BERG, Treas.; LAURA J. HUBER, Agent of Record; Rev. CASIMIR S. PALUCK, (Retired); Rev. Msgr. JAMES B. BRAATEN.

Priests' Personnel Board—Rev. DAVID RICHTER, Chm.; Rev. Msgr. PATRICK A. SCHUMACHER, S.T.L.; Revs. AUSTIN A. VETTER; WILLIAM A. RUELLE; JOSHUA K. WALTZ; Most Rev. DAVID D. KAGAN, D.D., P.A., J.C.L., Ex Officio; Rev. Msgrs. JAMES B. BRAATEN, Ex Officio; GENE E. LINDEMANN, J.C.L., Ex Officio.

Propagation of the FaithMR. RONALD SCHATZ, Center for Pastoral Ministry Office. Tel: 701-204-7202.

Communications Office—SONIA MULLALLY, Dir., Center for Pastoral Ministry Office. Tel: 701-204-7190.

Catechesis and Youth—CARRIE DAVIS, Center for Pastoral Ministry, Tel: 701-204-7208.

Bishop's Delegate for Catholic Education—Rev. JUSTIN P. WALTZ, c/o Church of St. Leo, 218 1st St., S.E., Minot, 58701-3920. Tel: 701-838-1026.

Catholic Foundation for the People of the Diocese of Bismarck—MATTHEW STEVENSON, Planned Giving Specialist, Tel: 701-204-7216.

Internal Auditor—Tel: 701-425-0794. Deacon BRENT NASLUND.

Stewardship and Resource Development Office—MR. RONALD SCHATZ, Dir., Center for Pastoral Ministry Office. Tel: 701-204-7202.

Search Program—DEAN JOHS, Center for Pastoral Ministry, Email: .

Victim Assistance Coordinator—MR. DALE EBERLE, Tel: 701-204-7216; Email: deberle@bismarckdiocese.com.

Finance Officer—LAURA J. HUBER, Tel: 701-204-7196.

Family Ministry—TARA BROOKE, Dir., Center for Pastoral Ministry Office. Tel: 701-204-7209.

Respect Life—MARY HUBER, Coord., Email: mhuber@bismarckdiocese.com.

CLERGY, PARISHES, MISSIONS AND PAROCHIAL SCHOOLS

CITY OF BISMARCK

(BURLEIGH COUNTY)

1—CATHEDRAL OF THE HOLY SPIRIT (1945) [JC]
Mailing Address: 519 Raymond St., 58501.
Tel: 701-223-1033; Fax: 701-223-1438; Email: dtrnka@cathedralparish.com; Web: www.cathedralparish.com. Revs. Austin A. Vetter, Rector; Dominic Bouck, Parochial Vicar; John Paul Gardner; Deacons Richard Fettig; Tony Ternes; Ralph von Ruden; Randal Schmidt; Brent Naslund.
Res.: 308 West Ave. B, 58501.
Catechesis Religious Program—Tel: 701-223-5484; Email: dmartinek@cathedralparish.com. Deb Martinek, D.R.E. Students 252.

2—SAINT ANNE (1957) [JC]
1321 Braman Ave., 58501. Tel: 701-223-1549; Fax: 701-250-9214; Email: mkorczak@stannesbismarck.org; Web: www.stannesbismarck.org. Revs. Wayne V. Sattler; Thomas Grafsgaard, Parochial Vicar; Deacons John Bachmeier; Wayne Jundt; Joe Krupinsky; Jerry Volk; Melanie Korczak, Business & Finance Mgr.
Catechesis Religious Program—Email: hkeller@stannesbismarck.org. Holly Keller, D.R.E. Students 228.

3—ASCENSION (1974) [JC] Rev. Msgr. James B. Braaten; Deacons Tony J. Finneman; Doyle F. Schulz; John Paul Martin.
Res.: 1905 S. Third St., 58504-7118.
Tel: 701-223-3606; Fax: 701-223-5783; Email: ascension@midconetwork.com; Web: ascensionbismarck.org.
Catechesis Religious Program—Email: jmattson@ascensionbismarck.org. Jessica Mattson, D.R.E. Students 306.

4—CHURCH OF CORPUS CHRISTI (1964) [JC]
1919 N. Second St., 58501. Tel: 701-255-4600; Fax: 701-255-4616; Email: info@corpuschristibismarck.com; Web: www.corpuschristibismarck.com. Revs. Paul D. Becker; Terry Wipf, Parochial Vicar; Raphael Obotama, Parochial Vicar; Deacons Lonnie Grabowska; Michael Fix; Rex McDowell.
Catechesis Religious Program—Email: Mariah.Conner@corpuschristibismarck.com. Mariah Conner, Asst. D.R.E. Students 655.

5—ST. MARY (1877) [JC]
806 E. Broadway, 58501. Tel: 701-223-5562; Fax: 701-530-0864; Email: smpf@stmarysparishfamily.net; Web: stmarysbismarck.org. Revs. Jared M. Johnson; Christy Pathiala; Deacons Daniel Brooke; Terry Glatt, Outreach & Grief Ministry; Harvey Hanel; Michael Marback, Cemetery Mgr.; Diane Grotewold, Music Min.; Diane Huck, Pastoral Assoc.; Mary Vandal, Sec.; Olivia Richter, Business Mgr.
Catechesis Religious Program—Sheila Gilbertson, Diocesan D.R.E. Students 212.

OUTSIDE THE CITY OF BISMARCK

ALEXANDER, MCKENZIE CO., OUR LADY OF CONSOLATION (1907) Served from Watford City.
3341 137th Ave. N.W., Watford City, 58854.
Tel: 701-842-3791; Email: wcepiphany@gmail.com; Web: www.wcepiphany.com. c/o Epiphany, P.O. Box 670, Watford City, 58854-0670. Rev. Brian P. Gross.
Catechesis Religious Program— (Linked with Epiphany Parish) Tel: 701-842-3505. Amy Campbell, D.R.E.
Mission—Our Lady of Consolation, P.O. Box 976, Watford City, 58854. Tel: 701-842-3503.

ALMONT, MORTON CO., ST. MARY, QUEEN OF PEACE (1907) Served from New Salem.
302 Margaret St., Almont, 58520. c/o St. Pius V, P.O. Box C, New Salem, 58563-0429. Tel: 701-843-7061; Email: stpiusv@westriv.com. Rev. John G. Guthrie.
Catechesis Religious Program—Mrs. Tammy Kunkel, Diocesan D.R.E.

ALPHA, GOLDEN VALLEY CO., MOST HOLY REDEEMER (1919) Closed. For inquiries for parish records contact the chancery.

AMIDON, SLOPE CO., SS. PETER & PAUL (1918) Closed. For inquiries for parish records contact the chancery.

BEACH, GOLDEN VALLEY CO., ST. JOHN THE BAPTIST (1909) [CEM]
162 2nd Ave. S.E., P.O. Box 337, Beach, 58621-0337. Tel: 701-872-4153; Email: stjohn@midstate.net. Rev. Daniel J. Berg; Bro. Samuel Larson, S.D.S.; Deacon James Wosepka.
Catechesis Religious Program—Tel: 701-872-2500; Email: dre@triparishnd.org. Mrs. Lori Holkup, Diocesan D.R.E. Students 57.

BELFIELD, STARK CO., ST. BERNARD (1910) [CEM]
402 3rd Ave. N.E., Belfield, 58622. Tel: 701-575-4295 ; Fax: 701-575-8457; Email: stbernardbelfield@ndsupernet.com; Web: saintbernardbelfield.com. Rev. William A. Ruelle; Deacon Loren Kordonowy.
Res.: P.O. Box 38, Belfield, 58622.
Catechesis Religious Program—Email: wendykordonowy@gmail.com. Wendy Kordonowy, D.R.E. (High School). Students 80.

BENTLEY, HETTINGER CO., SACRED HEART (1920) Closed. For inquiries for parish records contact the chancery.

BERTHOLD, WARD CO., ST. ANN (1903) Served from Stanley.
c/o Queen of the Most Holy Rosary, 217 Dewey St. N.W., P.O. Box 159, Stanley, 58784-0159.
Tel: 701-628-2323; Fax: 701-628-3406; Email: holyrosary@midstatetel.com. Rev. Jason R. Signalness.
Catechesis Religious Program—Tel: 701-628-3405. Rhonda Hanson, D.R.E. Students 29.

BEULAH, MERCER CO.

1—ST. BENEDICT (1911) Closed. For inquiries for parish records contact the chancery.

2—ST. JOSEPH (1915) [CEM] (German—Russian)
115 3rd St., N.E., Beulah, 58523. Mailing Address: P.O. Box 146, Beulah, 58523. Tel: 701-873-5397; Email: stjbeulah@midconetwork.com; Web: www.saints2b.org. Rev. Kenneth Phillips, Email: priest4ever@yahoo.com; Deacon Daniel Wallach.
Res.: 508 1st Ave., N.E., Beulah, 58523.
Tel: 701-595-0291; Email: fr.phillips@midconetwork.com.
Catechesis Religious Program—Email: stjk-12@midconetwork.com. Darlene Mellmer, D.R.E. Students 115.

BLAISDELL, MOUNTRAIL CO., ST. MARGARET (1912) Closed. For inquiries for parish records contact the chancery.

BOWBELLS, BURKE CO., ST. JOSEPH (BOWBELLS) (1905) (German—Scandinavian) Served from Kenmare
102 3rd St. N.W., Bowbells, 58721. Tel: 701-385-4311 ; Email: stagnes@restel.net. P.O. Box 488, Kenmare, 58746-0488. Rev. Joseph Chipson, (India).
Res.: 409 E. Division, P.O. Box 488, Kenmare, 58746. Tel: 701-385-4311; Fax: 701-385-4321; Email: stagnes@restel.net.
Catechesis Religious Program—Email: beckystroklund@gmail.com. Rebecca Stroklund, D.R.E. Combined with St. Agnes, Kenmare Students 3.

BOWMAN, BOWMAN CO., ST. CHARLES (1910)
202 First Ave. S.W., Bowman, 58623.
Tel: 701-523-5292; Email: stcharles2@ndsupernet.com. Rev. Paul Eberle.
Catechesis Religious Program—Email: stcharles3@ndsupernet.com. Tobiann Andrews, D.R.E. (Grades K-6); Barbi Narum, D.R.E. (Grades 7-12). Students 112.

BRADDOCK, EMMONS CO., ST. KATHERINE (1908) Served from Linton.
200 1st Ave. N., Linton, 58552-7311. c/o St. Anthony, 613 N. Broadway, Linton, 58552-7311.
Tel: 701-254-4588; Fax: 701-254-4655; Email: stanthony@bektel.com. Rev. /David L. Zimmer, J.C.L.; Deacon Kenneth Wolbaum.
Catechesis Religious Program—Email: stacatholic/stanthony@bektel.com. Denice Kautz, D.R.E. (Combined with St. Paul) Students 11.

BRISBANE, GRANT CO., HOLY INFANT JESUS (1911) Closed. For inquiries for parish records contact the chancery.

BURLINGTON, WARD CO., ST. FRANCIS OF ASSISI (1889) Closed. For inquiries for parish records contact the chancery.

BUTTE, MCLEAN CO., HOLY GHOST (1939) Closed. For inquiries for parish records contact the chancery.

CANNON BALL, SIOUX CO., ST. ELIZABETH (1897) Served from Fort Yates.
c/o St. Peter, P.O. Box 394, Fort Yates, 58538-0394.
Tel: 701-854-3473; Email: sbms1@hotmail.com; Web: www.catholicindianmission.com. Revs. John Paul Gardner; Biju Antony, I.M.S., (India).

CARSON, GRANT CO., ST. THERESA THE CHILD JESUS (1920) [JC]
204 2nd Ave., N.E., Carson, 58529. Email: stlwrnce@westriv.com; Web: www.catholic3nd.com. Rev. Dennis R. Schafer.
Res.: 421 Court St., Flasher, 58535-7216.
Catechesis Religious Program—Ann Hertz, D.R.E. Students 51.

CARTWRIGHT, MCKENZIE CO., ST. JOSEPH (1913) Closed. For inquiries for parish records contact the chancery.

CENTER, OLIVER CO., ST. MARTIN OF TOURS (1914) [CEM 3] [JC]
322 2nd St. E., P.O. Box 2766, Center, 58530-2766.
Tel: 701-794-3601; Email: stmartin@westriv.com. Rev. John G. Guthrie.
Catechesis Religious Program—Email: joleschm@westriv.com. Joletta Schmidt, D.R.E. Students 26.

COLUMBUS, BURKE CO., ST. MICHAEL (1905) Closed. For inquiries for parish records contact the chancery.

CROSBY, DIVIDE CO., ST. PATRICK (1912) [CEM 4] [JC2] Rev. William P. Cosgrove, Parochial Admin., (Retired).
Res.: 205 1st. St., N.W., P.O. Box 89, Crosby, 58730.
Tel: 701-965-6537; Email: stpatscr@nccray.com.
Catechesis Religious Program—Tel: 701-965-6674. Ms. Vicki Haggin, D.R.E. Students 11.

CROWN BUTTE, MORTON CO., ST. VINCENT (1896)
Rural Mandan, Mandan, 58554. c/o Deacon Steve Brannan, 2119 S. 3rd St., 58504. Cell: 701-202-0111; Cell: 701-202-0111; Email: stevebrannan49@gmail.com. Deacon Steve M. Brannan.
Catechesis Religious Program—Tel: 701-425-6302. Mary McHugh, D.R.E. Students 21.

DE LACS, WARD CO., ST. VINCENT DE PAUL (1912) Closed. For inquiries for parish records contact the chancery.

DICKINSON, STARK CO.

1—ST. JOSEPH (1902) (German—Russian) Revs. Keith N. Streifel; Patrick Ojedeji, Parochial Vicar; Deacons Dallas Carlson; Al Schwindt.
Res.: 240 E. Broadway, Dickinson, 58601.
Tel: 701-483-2223; Fax: 701-483-0648; Email:

stjoseph@goesp.com; Email: stjoseph@ndsupernet.com.
Catechesis Religious Program—Ann Morel, D.R.E. Students 123.
2—ST. PATRICK (1885)
229 Third Ave. W., Dickinson, 58601.
Tel: 701-483-6700; Email: stpatrick@ndsupernet.com. Rev. Todd Kreitinger; Deacons Ron Keller; Ryan Nelson.
Catechesis Religious Program—Tel: 701-483-7168; Email: jess@ndsupernet.com. Jessica Emter, D.R.E. Students 97.
3—QUEEN OF PEACE CHURCH (1973)
725 12th St. W., Dickinson, 58601-3516.
Tel: 701-483-2134; Email: queenofpeace@ndsupernet.com. Rev. Msgr. Thomas J. Richter; Deacon Leonard Krebs.
Catechesis Religious Program—Email: danakostelecky@thequeenofpeace.com. Dana Kostelecky, D.R.E. Students 112.
4—ST. WENCESLAUS (1912) (Bohemian)
525 Third St. E., Dickinson, 58601.
Tel: 701-225-3972; Fax: 701-225-4146; Email: stwenc@ndsupernet.com; Web: www.stwenceslausnd.com. 505 3rd St. E., Dickinson, 58601-4504. Rev. Msgr. Patrick A. Schumacher, S.T.L.; Revs. Jordan Dosch, Parochial Vicar; Kregg W. Hochhalter, In Res.; Deacons Robert Stockert; Robert Zent; Sarah Bengtson, Pastoral Asst.; Nancy Woehl, Business Mgr.
See Dickinson Catholic School, Dickinson under High Schools Interparochial and Parish located in the Institution section.
Catechesis Religious Program—Nicole Berger, Rel. Educ. Coord. Students 105.
DODGE, DUNN CO.
1—ST. MARTIN (1908) Closed. For inquiries for parish records contact the chancery.
2—PRECIOUS BLOOD (1920) Closed. For inquiries for parish records contact the chancery.
DONNYBROOK, WARD CO., ST. ANTHONY (1902) Closed. For inquiries for parish records contact the chancery.
DOUGLAS, WARD CO., HOLY CROSS (1908) Closed. For inquiries for parish records contact the chancery.
DRISCOLL, BURLEIGH CO., ST. ANTHONY (1906) Closed. For inquiries for parish records contact the chancery.
EMMONS, EMMONS CO.
1—ST. BERNARD (1884) Closed. For inquiries for parish records contact the chancery.
2—ST. JOSEPH (1918) Closed. For inquiries for parish records contact the chancery.
ENDRES, MCLEAN CO., ST. ADOLPH (1906) Closed. For inquiries for parish records contact the chancery.
EPPING, WILLIAMS CO., ST. MARY (1915) Closed. For inquiries for parish records contact the chancery.
FALLON, MORTON CO., SS. PETER & PAUL (1907) Closed. For inquiries for parish records contact the chancery.
FAYETTE, DUNN CO., ST. EDWARD (1914) Closed. For inquiries for parish records contact the chancery.
FLASHER, MORTON CO., ST. LAWRENCE (1912) [CEM]
421 Court St., Flasher, 58535-7216.
Tel: 701-597-3228; Email: stlwrnce@westriv.com. Rev. Dennis R. Schafer, Email: drs758@gmail.com.
Catechesis Religious Program—Noel Wax, D.R.E. Students 32.
FORT RICE, MORTON CO., IMMACULATE CONCEPTION (1908) Closed. For inquiries for parish records contact the chancery.
FORT YATES, SIOUX CO., ST. PETER - CATHOLIC INDIAN MISSION (1878) [CEM] (Native American) (Standing Rock Indian Reservation)
201 Church St., Fort Yates, 58538. Tel: 701-854-3473 ; Fax: 701-854-3474; Email: sbms1@hotmail.com. Revs. John Paul Gardner; Biju Antony, I.M.S., (India); Bro. George Maufort, S.D.S.
Res.: P.O. Box 394, Fort Yates, 58538.
School—St. Bernard Mission School, (Grades K-6), Tel: 701-854-7413; Email: bantony@bismarckdiocese.com; Web: www.catholicindianmission.com. Rev. Biju Antony, I.M.S., (India) Supt. Clergy 2; Lay Teachers 2; Students 36.
Catechesis Religious Program—Students 7.
FORTUNA, DIVIDE CO., ST. BERNARD (1918) Closed. For inquiries for parish records contact the chancery.
FOXHOLM, WARD CO., ST. MARY (1887) [CEM] [JC]
17901 128th Ave., N.W., Foxholm, 58718-9643. Revs. Justin P. Waltz; Doug S. Krebs, Parochial Vicar.
Catechesis Religious Program—3535 74th St. N.W., Foxholm, 58718. Tel: 701-784-5815; Email: sarah.stleos@midconetwork.com. Char Ulberg, D.R.E. Students 55.
GARRISON, MCLEAN CO., ST. NICHOLAS (1905) [CEM]
235 Second St., N.E., P.O. Box 870, Garrison, 58540.
Tel: 701-463-2327; Email: joan@stnicholaschurchgarrison.com. Rev. Basil Atwell, O.S.B.
Catechesis Religious Program—235 Second St., N.E., P.O. Box 870, Garrison, 58540. Tel: 701-337-2272. Stephanie Trautman, D.R.E. Students 35.
GAYLORD, STARK CO., OUR LADY OF LOURDES (1910) Closed. For inquiries for parish records contact the chancery.
GLADSTONE, STARK CO., ST. THOMAS (1903) Served from Richardton.
351 Cliff St., Gladstone, 58630. c/o St. Mary, 332 2nd St. N., Richardton, 58652-7141. Tel: 701-974-3569; Fax: 701-974-3317; Email: marych@ndsupernet.com. Rev. Thomas Wordekemper, O.S.B.
Catechesis Religious Program—Jessi Olson, D.R.E.
GLEN ULLIN, MORTON CO.
1—ST. JOSEPH (1918) Served from Glen Ullin.
c/o Sacred Heart, P.O. Box 609, Glen Ullin, 58631-0609. Tel: 701-348-3527; Email: sacredheart@westriv.com; Web: www.sacredheartchurchglenullin.org. Rev. Jeffrey A. Zwack.
Catechesis Religious Program—Twinned with Sacred Heart, Glen Ullin. Students 4.
2—SACRED HEART OF JESUS (1883) [CEM 2] (German—Russian)
203 E. Ash Ave., Box 609, Glen Ullin, 58631-0609.
Tel: 701-348-3527; Email: sacredheart@westriv.com; Web: www.sacredheartchurchglenullin.org. Rev. Jeffrey A. Zwack; Deacon Lance Gartner.
Res.: Box 609, Glen Ullin, 58631-0609.
Tel: 701-348-3518; Email: jzwack@westriv.com.
Catechesis Religious Program—Mrs. Lisa Staiger, Coord., Email: reled@westriv.com; Linda Gartner, Coord. Students 51.
GLENBURN, RENVILLE CO., ST. PHILOMENA (1948) [CEM] (German—Scandinavian)
310 3rd Ave. N., Glenburn, 58740. 218 1st St. S.E., Minot, 58701-3920. Tel: 701-838-1026;
Fax: 701-852-4683; Email: church.stleos@midconetwork.com; Web: www.stleosminot.com. Revs. Justin P. Waltz; Doug S. Krebs, Parochial Vicar.
Catechesis Religious Program—Tel: 701-362-7986. Kelly Zelinski, D.R.E. Enrolled at St. Mary's Foxholm Students 14.
GOLVA, GOLDEN VALLEY CO., ST. MARY'S GOLVA (1906) [CEM] Served from Beach.
405 Gass St., Golva, 58632. c/o St. John the Baptist, P.O. Box 337, Beach, 58621-0337. Tel: 701-872-4153; Fax: 701-872-4377; Email: stjohn@midstate.net; Web: www.triparishnd.org. Rev. Daniel J. Berg.
Catechesis Religious Program—Tel: 701-872-2500; Email: mhauck44@yahoo.com. Mrs. Lori Holkup, D.R.E. High School twinned with St. John, Beach. Students 44.
GRASSNA, EMMONS CO., HOLY TRINITY (1900) Closed. For inquiries for parish records contact the chancery.
GRASSY BUTTE, MCKENZIE CO., ST. PETER CANSIUS (1927) Closed. For inquiries for parish records contact the chancery.
GRENORA, WILLIAMS CO., ST. BONIFACE (1912) [CEM 2] [JC] Served from Williston
300 East St., Williston, 58801. Tel: 701-694-6731; Fax: 701-572-4203; Email: parishsecretary@stjparish.com; Web: www.stjparish.com. Mailing Address: c/o St. Joseph, P.O. Box K, Williston, 58802-1115. Revs. Russell P. Kovash; Joseph A. Evinger; Ray Urbi, Business Mgr.
Res.: 524 1st Ave. W., Williston, 58801.
Tel: 701-572-0236.
Catechesis Religious Program—Tel: 701-572-6731; Email: dre@stjparish.com. Cate Binde, D.R.E. Students 19.
HAGUE, EMMONS CO.
1—ST. ALOYSIUS (1899) Closed. For inquiries for parish records contact the chancery.
2—ST. MARY (1890) [CEM 2] (German—Russian)
210 S 4th St., Hague, 58542. P.O. Box 322, Strasburg, 58573. Tel: 701-336-7172; Email: stspeterandpaul@bektel.com; Web: www.emmonscatholics.org. Rev. Shannon G. Lucht, Admin.
Church: P.O. Box 156, Hague, 58542.
Tel: 701-336-7456.
Catechesis Religious Program—Kathy Nagel, D.R.E. Students 21.
HALEY, BOWMAN CO., ST. STANISLAUS (1908) Closed. For inquiries for parish records contact the chancery.
HALLIDAY, DUNN CO., ST. PAUL (1952) [CEM] [JC] Served from Killdeer
152 3rd Ave. N.W., Halliday, 58636.
Tel: 701-764-5357; Email: stjosephs@ndsupernet.com. P.O. Box 299, Killdeer, 58640. Rev. Darnis Selvanayakam, M.S.F.X., (India).
Catechesis Religious Program—
HANKS, WILLIAMS CO., OUR LADY OF GOOD COUNSEL (1918) Closed. For inquiries for parish records contact the chancery.
HAYMARSH, MORTON CO., ST. CLEMENT (ORATORY) (1887) Served from Hebron.
c/o St. Ann, P.O. Box 12, Hebron, 58638-0012.
Tel: 701-222-3035; Email: bnaslund@bismarckdiocese.com. c/o Deacon Brent Naslund, P.O. Box 1137, 58502-1137. Deacon Brent Naslund, Admin.
Catechesis Religious Program—Twinned with St. Ann's.
HAYNES, ADAMS CO., ST. PETER (1908) Closed. For inquiries for parish records contact the chancery.
HAZELTON, EMMONS CO., ST. PAUL (1905)
372 Harold St., Hazelton, 58544. Rev. David L. Zimmer, J.C.L.; Deacon Kenneth Wolbaum.
Res.: 613 N. Broadway St., Linton, 58552.
Tel: 701-254-4588; Fax: 701-254-4655; Email: stanthony@bektel.com; Web: stanthonylinton.com.
Catechesis Religious Program—Tel: 701-321-3274. Combined with St. Katherine Students 15.
HAZEN, MERCER CO., ST. MARTIN (1914) [CEM] (German—Russian)
Mailing Address: 101 3rd Ave., S.W., P.O. Box 387, Hazen, 58545. Tel: 701-748-2121; Fax: 701-748-6184; Email: stmhazen@westriv.com; Web: www.saints2b.org. Rev. Kenneth Phillips.
Res.: 508 1st. Ave. N.E., P.O. Box 146, Beulah, 58523. Tel: 701-595-0291.
Catechesis Religious Program—Email: stmreled@westriv.com. Michelle Reinhardt, D.R.E. Students 107.
HEBRON, MORTON CO., ST. ANN (1906) [CEM 3] (German)
204 Park St. S., Box 12, Hebron, 58638-0012.
Tel: 701-878-4658; Email: stanns@westriv.com; Web: www.stannshebron.com. Rev. Jeffrey A. Zwack.
Catechesis Religious Program—Diane Wanner, D.R.E. Students 47.
HETTINGER, ADAMS CO., HOLY TRINITY (1916) [CEM] [JC] (German)
405 3rd St. N., Hettinger, 58639. Tel: 701-567-2772. Rev. Charles A. Zins; Deacon Mike Mellmer.
Catechesis Religious Program—Email: joy.laufer@yahoo.com. Joy Laufer, D.R.E. Students 47.
HIRSCHVILLE, STARK CO., ST. PHILIP (1908) Closed. For inquiries for parish records contact the chancery.
HUFF, MORTON CO., ST. MARTIN (1911) [CEM] Served from Mandan.
Mailing Address: c/o Spirit of Life, 801 1st St. S.E., Mandan, 58554-4470. Tel: 701-663-1660; Email: office@myspiritoflife.com; Web: www.myspiritoflife.com. Rev. Msgr. Chad Gion; Rev. Christopher J. Kadrmas, J.C.L.
Church: 5463 Huff St., Huff, 58554.
Catechesis Religious Program—Students 7.
KENMARE, WARD CO., ST. AGNES (1901) [CEM] (Scandinavian—German)
409 E. Division, P.O. Box 488, Kenmare, 58746-0488. Tel: 701-385-4311; Email: stagnes@restel.net. Rev. Joseph Chipson, (India) Parochial Admin.
Catechesis Religious Program—Rebecca Stroklund, D.R.E. Students 33.
KENNEDY, BOWMAN CO., ST. HELENA (1912) Closed. For inquiries for parish records contact the chancery.
KILLDEER, DUNN CO., ST. JOSEPH (1917) [CEM] [JC2]
152 3rd Ave., N.W., P.O. Box 299, Killdeer, 58640-0299. Tel: 701-764-5357; Email: stjosephs@ndsupernet.com. Rev. Darnis Selvanayakam, M.S.F.X., (India); Deacon Dan Tuhy.
Catechesis Religious Program—Jo Ann Lindemann, D.R.E. Students 71.
LANSFORD, BOTTINEAU CO., ST. JOHN'S CHURCH OF LANSFORD (1949) [CEM] Served from Mohall.
680 3rd Ave., Lansford, 58750. Mailing Address: c/o St. Jerome, P.O. Box 457, Mohall, 58761-0457.
Tel: 701-756-6601; Fax: 701-756-6901; Email: amaus@bismarckdiocese.com; Web: mlscatholic.com. Rev. Adam J. Maus.
Catechesis Religious Program—Students 4.
LEFOR, STARK CO., ST. ELIZABETH (1898) [CEM] Served from New England
5043 100D Ave., S.W., Lefor, 58641. P.O. Box 573, New England, 58647-0573. Tel: 701-579-4312;
Fax: 701-579-4874; Email: stmarysne@ndsupernet.com; Web: stmaryschurchnewengland.com. Rev. Gary Benz.
Catechesis Religious Program—Tel: 701-479-4312. Anne Wolf, D.R.E. Attend St. Mary's program.
LIGNITE, BURKE CO., ST. MARY (1920) Closed. For inquiries for parish records contact the chancery.
LINTON, EMMONS CO.
1—ST. ANTHONY (1909) [CEM]
613 N. Broadway, Linton, 58552-7311.
Tel: 701-254-4588; Email: stanthony@bektel.com. Rev. David L. Zimmer, J.C.L.; Susan Schumacher, Business Mgr.
Catechesis Religious Program—Tel: 701-400-4939. Denice Kautz, D.R.E. Students 101.
2—ST. MICHAEL (1915) Served from Strasburg.
2317 79th St. S.E., Linton, 58552. c/o SS. Peter & Paul, P.O. Box 322, Strasburg, 58573-0322.
Tel: 701-336-7172; Email: stspeterandpaul@bektel.com. Rev. Benny D. Putharayil, (India) Parochaial Admin.
Catechesis Religious Program—2183 76th St., S.E., Linton, 58552. Tel: 701-754-2254. Danielle Weigel, D.R.E. Students 18.
MAKOTI, WARD CO., ST. ELIZABETH (1948) Served from Parshall.

4th Ave. & Edwards St., Makoti, 58756. c/o St. Bridget, P.O. Box 519, Parshall, 58770-0519.
Tel: 701-862-3484; Email: saintbridget@restel.com. Rev. Teji John Thanippilly, (India).
Catechesis Religious Program—Email: Bobbi.Shegrud@k12.nd.us. Bobbi Shegrud, D.R.E. Students 5.

MANDAN, MORTON CO.

1—CHRIST THE KING (1957) [CEM]
505-10th Ave., N.W., Mandan, 58554-2552.
Tel: 701-663-8842; Email: katrina.kuntz@christthekingmandan.org; Web: ctkmandan.com. Rev. Nick L. Schneider, S.L.L., S.L.D.; Deacons Dennis Rohr; Bob Nutsch.
School—Christ the King School, (Grades 1-5), Tel: 701-663-6200; Email: derrick.nagel@ctkmandan.com; Web: www.ctkmandan.com. Derrick Nagel, Prin. Lay Teachers 17; Students 91.

2—ST. JOSEPH (1879) [CEM]
108 Third St., N.E., Mandan, 58554.
Tel: 701-663-9562; Email: bkincaid@stjosephmandan.com. Revs. Shane Campbell; Jarad Wolf, Parochial Vicar; Deacons Randall Frohlich; Robert Wingenbach.
School—St. Joseph School, (Grades 1-5), 410 Collins Ave., Mandan, 58554. Tel: 701-663-9563; Fax: 701-663-0183; Email: valerie.vogel@k12.nd.us; Web: www.stjosephmandan.com. Valerie Vogel, Prin.; Josephine Greff, Librarian. Lay Teachers 12; Students 102.
Catechesis Religious Program—Email: lfriesz@stjosephmandan.com. Laurie Friesz, D.R.E. Students 219.

3—SPIRIT OF LIFE (1978)
801 1st St., S.E., Mandan, 58554-4470.
Tel: 701-663-1660; Fax: 701-667-2021; Email: cheryl@myspiritoflife.com; Web: myspiritoflife.com. Rev. Msgr. Chad Gion; Rev. Christopher J. Kadrmas, J.C.L.; Deacon Gary Mizeur; Cheryl Hansen, Finance/Business Admin.
Catechesis Religious Program—Email: karen@myspiritoflife.com. Karen Eggers, D.R.E. Students 184.

MANDAREE, DUNN CO., ST. ANTHONY, [CEM] (Native American) Served from New Town
P.O. Box 760, New Town, 58763-0760.
Tel: 701-627-4423; Email: bobbi.shegrud@k12.nd.us. Rev. Roger A. Synek.
Res.: Fr. Berthold Reservation, 9385 BIA Rte. 12, Mandaree, 58757-9269. Email: stanthony@restel.com.
Catechesis Religious Program—Bobbi Shegrud, Contact Person. Students 33.

MARMARTH, SLOPE CO., ST. MARY (1915) Served from Bowman.
30 5th St. S.W., Marmarth, 58643. c/o St. Charles, 202 1st Ave., S.W., Bowman, 58623-4216.
Tel: 701-523-5292; Fax: 701-523-5415; Email: stcharles@ndsupernet.com. Rev. Paul Eberle.
Catechesis Religious Program—Tel: 701-523-5202. Students 6.

MAX, MCLEAN CO., IMMACULATE CONCEPTION (1908) Served from Garrison.
401 Jacobson Ave., Max, 58759. Tel: 701-463-2327; Email: joan@stnicholaschurchgarrison.com; Web: stnicholaschurchgarrison.com. c/o St. Nicholas, P.O. Box 870, Garrison, 58540-0870. Rev. Basil Atwell, O.S.B.
Catechesis Religious Program—Peggy Bingham, D.R.E. Students 20.

MEDORA, BILLINGS CO., ST. MARY (MEDORA) (1886) [CEM] Served from Beach.
305 4th St., Medora, 58645. c/o St. John the Baptist, P.O. Box 337, Beach, 58621-0337. Tel: 701-872-4153; Fax: 701-872-4377; Email: stjohn@midstate.net; Web: www.triparishnd.org. Rev. Daniel J. Berg.
Catechesis Religious Program—Walt Losinski, D.R.E. (Grades 7-12); Shelly Hauck, D.R.E. (Grades 1-6). Twinned with St. John the Baptist, Beach. Students 1.

MENOKEN, BURLEIGH CO., ST. HILDEGARD (1947) [JC]
17200 Hwy. 10, Menoken, 58558-9604.
Tel: 701-673-3177; Email: sthildegard@bektel.com. Rev. Frank Schuster.
Catechesis Religious Program—Denise Richter, D.R.E. Students 46.

MINER, GRANT CO., MARY IMMACULATE (1912) Closed. For inquiries for parish records contact the chancery.

MINOT, WARD CO.

1—ST. JOHN THE APOSTLE (1961)
Mailing Address: 2600 Central Ave. W., Minot, 58701. Tel: 701-839-7076; Fax: 701-839-2553; Email: stjohnchurch@srt.com; Web: www.stjohnminot.com. Rev. David A. Richter; Deacon Charles Kramer.
Res.: 109-25th St. N.W., Minot, 58703-2862.
Catechesis Religious Program—Email: drestjohn@srt.com. Monica Perry, D.R.E. Students 167.

2—ST. LEO (1886) [CEM] (German)
Mailing Address: 218 1st St. S.E., Minot, 58701.
Tel: 701-838-1026; Fax: 701-852-4683; Email: church.stleos@midconetwork.com; Web: www.stleosminot.com. Revs. Justin P. Waltz; Doug S. Krebs, Parochial Vicar; Jadyn E. Nelson, In Res.; Deacon Lloyd E. Krueger.
Res.: 305 1st. St., S.E., Minot, 58701.
Catechesis Religious Program—Email: beverlt.stleos@midconetwork.com. Beverly Brintnell, D.R.E. Students 100.

3—OUR LADY OF GRACE (1959)
Mailing Address: 707 16th Ave., S.W., Minot, 58701.
Tel: 701-839-6834; Fax: 701-837-1080; Email: admin@olgminot.org; Web: olgminot.weconnect.com. Rev. Bruce D. Krebs; Deacon Steven F. Streitz.
Res.: 715 16th Ave., S.W., Minot, 58701.
Tel: 701-852-3002.
Catechesis Religious Program—Email: education1@olgminot.org. Tanya Watterud, D.R.E., (Grades K-9). Students 282.

4—ST. THERESE THE LITTLE FLOWER (1954) [JC]
919 8th St. N.W., Minot, 58703. 800 University Ave. W., Minot, 58703-2250. Tel: 701-838-1520; Email: littleflowerparish@srt.com; Web: littleflowerminot.com. Rev. Frederick R. Harvey; Deacons Hans G. Gayzur; Tom Magnuson; Linda Aleshire, Business Mgr.
Catechesis Religious Program— (Combined with St. Leo's Parish CCD Program) Tel: 701-838-3638. Students 25.

MOHALL, RENVILLE CO., ST. JEROME (1906) [CEM] [JC]
303 E. Main St., P.O. Box 457, Mohall, 58761-0457.
Tel: 701-756-6601; Fax: 701-756-6901; Email: amaus@bismarckdiocese.com; Web: mlscatholic.com. Rev. Adam J. Maus.
Catechesis Religious Program—Tel: 701-756-6943. Jodi Johnson, D.R.E. Students 30.

MORTON, MORTON CO., SS. PETER & PAUL (1904) Closed. For inquiries for parish records contact the chancery.

MOTT, HETTINGER CO., ST. VINCENT DE PAUL (1907) [CEM]
408 Iowa Ave., Mott, 58646. Tel: 701-824-2651; Email: stvincent@ndsupernet.com; Web: www.stvincentcatholicchurch.com. Rev. Stephen Folorunso; Deacons David M. Crane; Ben Auch.
Catechesis Religious Program—Sherran Meyer, D.R.E. Students 63.

NEW ENGLAND, HETTINGER CO., ST. MARY (1910) [CEM] Rev. Gary Benz; Deacon Victor F. Dvorak.
Rectory—10 - 5th & McKenzie, New England, 58647.
Tel: 701-300-7051.
Parish Office: 437 Main St., P.O. Box 369, New England, 58647. Tel: 701-579-4312;
Fax: 701-579-4874; Email: stmarysne@ndsupernet.com.
Catechesis Religious Program—P.O. Box 573, New England, 58647-0573. Anne Wolf, D.R.E. Students 74.

NEW HRADEC, DUNN CO., SS. PETER AND PAUL (1898) [CEM] Served from Belfield.
101 Lafayette Ave., New Hradec, 58601.
Tel: 701-575-4295; Fax: 701-575-8457; Email: stbernardbelfield@ndsupernet.com. c/o St. Bernard, P.O. Box 38, Belfield, 58622-0038. Rev. William A. Ruelle.

NEW LEIPZIG, GRANT CO., ST. JOHN THE BAPTIST (1911) Served from Mott.
2nd Ave. E., New Leipzig, 58562. Tel: 701-824-2651; Email: stvincentsmott@gmail.com. 408 Iowa Ave., Mott, 58562. Rev. Stephen Folorunso.
Catechesis Religious Program—Mrs. Sherran Mayer, Diocesan D.R.E.

NEW SALEM, MORTON CO., ST. PIUS V (1912) [CEM]
Mailing Address: 202 N. 3rd. St., P.O. Box C, New Salem, 58563-0429. Tel: 701-843-7061; Email: stpiusv@westriv.com. Rev. John G. Guthrie.
Catechesis Religious Program—Ms. Carrie Maier, D.R.E. Students 92.

NEW TOWN, MOUNTRAIL CO., ST. ANTHONY (1954) [CEM 4] [JC] (Native American)
206 Main St., New Town, 58763. Tel: 701-759-3412; Email: StAnthonyMandaree@gmail.com. Rev. Roger A. Synek, Email: stbridget@restel.net; Deacons Daniel Barone; Jim Baker.
Catechesis Religious Program—Bobbi Shegrud, Contact Person. Students 13.

NOONAN, DIVIDE CO., ST. LUKE (1914) Served from Crosby.
300 Main St., Noonan, 58765. c/o St. Patrick, P.O. Box 89, Crosby, 58730-0089. Tel: 701-965-6537; Email: stpatscr@nccray.com. Rev. William P. Cosgrove, Parochial Admin., (Retired).
Catechesis Religious Program—Students 5.

ODENSE, MORTON CO., ST. JOHN (1905) Closed. For inquiries for parish records contact the chancery.

PARSHALL, MOUNTRAIL CO., ST. BRIDGET (1917) [CEM 4] [JC3] (German—Norwegian)
12 First Ave., N.E., P.O. Box 519, Parshall, 58770-0519. Tel: 701-862-3484; Email: saintbridget@restel.com. Rev. Teji John Thanippilly, (India) Parochial Admin.
Catechesis Religious Program—Bobbi Shegrud, D.R.E. Students 15.

PLAZA, MOUNTRAIL CO., SACRED HEART (1910) Served from Parshall.
4th Ave. & Reserve St., Plaza, 58771.
Tel: 701-862-3484; Email: saintbridget@restel.com. c/o St. Bridget, P.O. Box 519, Parshall, 58770-0519. Rev. Teji John Thanippilly, (India).
Catechesis Religious Program—Bobbi Shegrud, Contact Person.

PORCUPINE, SIOUX CO., ST. JAMES (1897) Served from Fort Yates.
c/o St. Peter, P.O. Box 394, Fort Yates, 58538-0394.
Tel: 701-854-3473; Email: sbms1@hotmail.com; Web: www.catholicindianmission.com. Revs. John Paul Gardner; Biju Antony, I.M.S., (India); Bro. George Maufort, S.D.S.

PORTAL, BURKE CO., ST. JOHN THE BAPTIST (1900) Served from Crosby.
21 Dakota Ave., Portal, 58772. Tel: 701-965-6537; Fax: 701-965-6537; Email: stpatscr@nccray.com. c/o St. Patrick, P.O. Box 89, Crosby, 58730-0089. Rev. William P. Cosgrove, Parochial Admin., (Retired).
Catechesis Religious Program—Tel: 701-933-2869. Mary Hawbaker, D.R.E.

POWERS LAKE, BURKE CO., ST. JAMES (1910) [CEM] Served from Tioga.
400 Main St., Powers Lake, 58773. P.O. Box 667, Tioga, 58852-0667. Tel: 701-664-2445; Email: cnelson@bismarckdiocese.com. Rev. Corey M. Nelson.
Catechesis Religious Program—Tel: 701-464-5012. Katy Cvancara, D.R.E. Students 32.

RALEIGH, GRANT CO., ST. GERTRUDE (1913) [CEM]
Mailing Address: 421 Court St., Flasher, 58535-7216. Tel: 701-547-3228; Fax: 701-597-3228; Email: stlwrnce@westriv.com; Web: catholic3nd.com. Rev. Dennis R. Schafer.
Church: 7785 St. Gertrude Ave., Raleigh, 58564.
Catechesis Religious Program—Rosalia Fergel, D.R.E. Students 1.

RAY, WILLIAMS CO., ST. MICHAEL (1903) Served from Tioga.
216 West St., Ray, 58849. c/o St. Thomas the Apostle, P.O. Box 667, Tioga, 58852-0667. Tel: 701-664-2445; Email: jlnorgaard@gmail.com; Web: www.stthomastioga.com. Rev. Corey M. Nelson.
Catechesis Religious Program—Tel: 701-568-2252. Bernadette Purdue, D.R.E. Students 10.

REEDER, ADAMS CO., SACRED HEART (1908) Served from Hettinger.
402 E. 3rd Ave., Reeder, 58649. Tel: 701-567-2772; Email: holytrinity@ndsupernet.com; Web: www.parishesofswnd.com. c/o Holy Trinity, 405 3rd St. N., Hettinger, 58639-7125. Rev. Charles A. Zins.
Catechesis Religious Program—Apryl Pierce, D.R.E. Twinned with Sacred Heart, Scranton. (Reeder & Scranton are combined) Students 9.

REGENT, HETTINGER CO., ST. HENRY (1913) [JC] Served from Mott
150 W. Fifth St., P.O. Box 155, Regent, 58650-0155. Rev. Stephen Folorunso.
Catechesis Religious Program—Mrs. Sherran Mayer, Diocesan D.R.E. Twinned with St. Vincent's, Mott. Students 19.

RHAME, BOWMAN CO., ST. MEL (1914) Served from Bowman.
305 1st Ave. W., Rhame, 58651. c/o St. Charles, 202 1st Ave., S.W., Bowman, 58623-4216.
Tel: 701-523-5292; Email: stcharles@ndsupernet.com. Rev. Paul Eberle.
Catechesis Religious Program—Theresa Fischer, D.R.E. Students 31.

RICHARDTON, STARK CO., ST. MARY (1895) [CEM]
332 2nd St. N., Richardton, 58652-7141.
Tel: 701-974-3315; Fax: 701-974-3317; Email: marych@ndsupernet.com; Web: www.marychurch.org. Rev. Thomas Wordekemper, O.S.B.; Deacon Robert Bohn.
Catechesis Religious Program—Tel: 701-974-3569. Jessi Olson, D.R.E. Students 50.

RIVERDALE, MCLEAN CO., ST. JOHN (1947) Closed. For inquiries for parish records contact the chancery.

ROSENTHAL, EMMONS CO., SACRED HEART (1907) Closed. For inquiries for parish records contact the chancery.

ROSS, MOUNTRAIL CO., ST. FRANCIS (1911) Closed. For inquiries for parish records contact the chancery.

RYDER, WARD CO., ST. CHARLES (1907) Closed. For inquiries for parish records contact the chancery.

ST. ANTHONY, MORTON CO., ST. ANTHONY (1894) Served from Mandan.
2362 County Rd. #136, St. Anthony, 58554.
Tel: 701-663-1660; Fax: 701-667-2021; Email: office@myspiritoflife.com; Web: www.myspiritoflife.com. c/o Spirit of Life, 801 1st St. S.E., Mandan, 58554-4470. Rev. Msgr. Chad Gion; Rev. Christopher J. Kadrmas, J.C.L.; Cheryl Hansen, Business Mgr.
Catechesis Religious Program—Karen Eggers, D.R.E. Students 14.

SCRANTON, BOWMAN CO., SACRED HEART (1928) Served

from Hettinger.
408 Main St., Scranton, 58653. Tel: 701-567-2772; Email: holytrinity@ndsupernet.com; Web: www.parishesofswnd.com. c/o Holy Trinity, 405 3rd St. N., Hettinger, 58639-7125. Rev. Charles A. Zins.
Catechesis Religious Program—Apryl Pierce, C.C.D. Coord. (Elementary); Larry Tibor, D.R.E. (High School); Deacon Mike Mellmer, D.R.E. (Confirmation). (Scranton & Reeder are combined) Students 19.

SELFRIDGE, SIOUX CO., ST. PHILOMENA (1919) [CEM] (German—Russian) Served from Fort Yates
P.O. Box 394, Fort Yates, 58538-0394.
Tel: 701-854-3473; Email: lilliancoyle45@gmail.com. Revs. John Paul Gardner; Biju Antony, I.M.S., (India); Bro. George Maufort, S.D.S.
Catechesis Religious Program—

SENTINEL BUTTE, GOLDEN VALLEY CO., ST. MICHAEL (1891) Closed. For inquiries for parish records contact the chancery.

SHEFFIELD, STARK CO., ST. PIUS (1912) Closed. For inquiries for parish records contact the chancery.

SHERWOOD, RENVILLE CO., ST. JAMES (1911) Served from Mohall.
220 4th Ave. E., Sherwood, 58782. c/o St. Jerome, P.O. Box 457, Mohall, 58761-0457. Tel: 701-756-6601 ; Fax: 701-756-6901; Email: amaus@bismarckdiocese.com; Web: mlscatholic.com. Rev. Adam J. Maus.
Catechesis Religious Program—Students 19.

SHIELDS, MORTON CO., ST. GABRIEL (1912) Closed. For inquiries for parish records contact the chancery.

SOLEN, SIOUX CO., SACRED HEART (1913) Served from Ft. Yates.
c/o St. Peter, P.O. Box 394, Fort Yates, 58538-0394.
Tel: 701-854-3473; Email: sbms1@hotmail.com. Revs. John Paul Gardner; Biju Antony, I.M.S., (India).

SOUTH HEART, STARK CO., ST. MARY (1923) [CEM]
207 4th St. S.W., P.O. Box 189, South Heart, 58655.
Tel: 701-677-5886; Email: stmarysh@ndsupernet.com. Rev. William A. Ruelle.
Catechesis Religious Program—Tel: 701-575-4295. Mrs. Rhonda Steffan, Diocesan D.R.E. Co-op with St. Bernard's, Belfield.

STANLEY, MOUNTRAIL CO., QUEEN OF THE MOST HOLY ROSARY (1908) [JC]
Mailing Address: 426 2nd St., S.E., P.O. Box 159, Stanley, 58784-0159. Tel: 701-628-3405;
Fax: 701-628-3406; Email: holyrosary@midstatetel.com; Web: www.holyrosarystanley.com. Rev. Jason R. Signalness.
Res.: 419 1st St., S.E., P.O. Box 159, Stanley, 58784. Tel: 701-628-2323.
Catechesis Religious Program—Elonda Davidson, D.R.E. Students 96.

STARK, STARK CO., ST. STEPHEN (1900) [CEM] Served from Richardton.
c/o St. Mary, 332 2nd St. N., Richardton, 58652-7141. Tel: 701-974-3569; Email: marych@ndsupernet.com. Rev. Thomas Wordekemper, O.S.B.
Catechesis Religious Program—Jessi Olson, D.R.E. Students 16.

STRASBURG, EMMONS CO., STS. PETER AND PAUL (1889) [CEM] (German—Russian)
505 N. 2nd St., Strasburg, 58573-0322.
Tel: 701-336-7172; Email: stspeterandpaul@bektel.com. Rev. Benny D. Putharayil, (India) Parochial Administrator.
Res.: P.O. Box 322, Strasburg, 58573-0322.
Catechesis Religious Program—Tel: 701-336-4607. Kathleen Kramer Nagel, D.R.E. Students 45.

TAYLOR, STARK CO., ST. PETER (1883) Closed. For inquiries for parish records contact the chancery.

TIOGA, WILLIAMS CO., ST. THOMAS (1914) [JC]
213 N. Gilbertson St., P.O. Box 667, Tioga, 58852-0667. Tel: 701-664-2445; Fax: 701-664-3533; Email: jlnorgaard@gmail.com; Web: www.stthomastioga.com. Rev. Corey M. Nelson.
Catechesis Religious Program—Tel: 701-664-3830. Becky Longie, D.R.E. Students 45.

TOLLEY, WARD CO., SS. PETER & PAUL (1906) Closed. For inquiries for parish records contact the chancery.

TRENTON, WILLIAMS CO., ST. JOHN THE BAPTIST (1890) Served from Williston.
205 2nd St., Trenton, 58801. c/o St. Joseph, P.O. Box K, Williston, 58802-1115. Tel: 701-572-6731;
Fax: 701-572-4203; Email: parishsecretary@stjparish.com; Web: www.sjparish.com. Revs. Russell P. Kovash; Joseph A. Evinger, Parochial Vicar.
Catechesis Religious Program—Email: dre@stjparish.com. Cate Campbell, D.R.E. Students 19.

TURTLE LAKE, MCLEAN CO., ST. CATHERINE (1913) Served from Underwood.
401 Main St., Turtle Lake, 58575. Tel: 701-442-5229; Fax: 701-442-5259; Email: stcatherines@westriv.com; Web: www.centralmcleansaints.com. c/o St. Bonaventure, 503 Grant Ave., Underwood, 58576. Rev. Patrick M. Cunningham.
Catechesis Religious Program—Tel: 701-448-9289. Tammy Sannes, D.R.E. (CCD Program with St. Bonaventure, Underwood) Students 8.

TWIN BUTTES, DUNN CO., ST. JOSEPH (1951) [CEM] Served from Killdeer.
c/o St. Joseph, P.O. Box 299, Killdeer, 58640-0299.
Tel: 701-764-5357; Fax: 701-764-6246; Email: stjosephs@ndsupernet.com; Web: www.stjosephs-killdeer.org. Rev. Darnis Selvanayakam, M.S.F.X., (India).
Catechesis Religious Program—Lori Pemberton Fredericks, D.R.E. Students 51.

UNDERWOOD, MCLEAN CO., ST. BONAVENTURE (1913) [CEM]
505 Grant Ave., Underwood, 58576.
Tel: 701-442-5229; Fax: 701-442-5259; Email: stbonaventureschurch@westriv.com. Rev. Patrick M. Cunningham, Email: stbonaventureschurch@westriv.com.
Res.: 503 Grant Ave., Underwood, 58576-4334.
Catechesis Religious Program—Tammy Sannes, D.R.E. Students 38.

WASHBURN, MCLEAN CO., ST. EDWIN'S CHURCH (1903) Served from Underwood.
906 Northgate Rd., Washburn, 58577. c/o St. Bonaventure, 503 Grant Ave., Underwood, 58576-0240. Tel: 701-442-5229 (St. Bonaventure);
Tel: 701-462-3340; Email: stedwins@westriv.com. Rev. Patrick M. Cunningham.
Catechesis Religious Program—Email: stbonaventureschurch@westriv.com. Rev. Patrick M. Cunningham, D.R.E.; Tammy Sannes, D.R.E. Students 39.

WATFORD CITY, MCKENZIE CO., EPIPHANY (1915)
112 6th Ave., N.E., P.O. Box 670, Watford City, 58854. Tel: 701-842-3505; Email: wcepiphany@gmail.com; Web: www.wcepiphany.com. Rev. Brian P. Gross.
Catechesis Religious Program—Tel: 701-842-3505. Amy Campbell, D.R.E. Students 123.

WHITE EARTH, MOUNTRAIL CO., ST. FRANCIS OF ASSISI (1894) Closed. For inquiries for parish records contact the chancery.

WHITE SHIELD, MCLEAN CO., SACRED HEART (1953) Served from Garrison.
c/o St. Nicholas, P.O. Box 870, Garrison, 58540-0870.
Tel: 701-463-2327; Email: office@stnicholaschurchgarrison.com; Web: www.stnicholaschurchgarrison.com. Rev. Basil Atwell, O.S.B.
Catechesis Religious Program—

WILDROSE, DIVIDE CO., SACRED HEART OF JESUS (1916) Closed. For inquiries for parish records contact the chancery.

WILLA, STARK CO., ST. PLACIDUS (1903) Closed. For inquiries for parish records contact the chancery.

WILLISTON, WILLIAMS CO., ST. JOSEPH (1901) [JC]
Mailing Address: 106 6th St. W., P.O. Box K, Williston, 58802-1115. Tel: 701-572-6731;
Fax: 701-572-4203; Email: parishsecretary@stjparish.com; Web: stjparish.com. Revs. Russell P. Kovash; Joseph A. Evinger, Parochial Vicar; Deacons James A. Haga; Gerald E. Martin.
Res.: 524 First Ave. W., Williston, 58801.
Tel: 701-572-0236; Email: stjosephwillston@gmail.com.
School—St. Joseph School, (Grades PreK-6), 124 6th St. W., Williston, 58801. Tel: 701-572-6384; Email: julie.quamme@k12.nd.su. Julie Quamme, Prin.; Elizabeth Darr, Librarian. Lay Teachers 13; Students 192.
Catechesis Religious Program—Email: dre@stjparish.com. Cate Campbell, D.R.E. Students 142.

WILTON, MCLEAN CO., SACRED HEART (1906) [JC]
212 4th St. N., P.O. Box 128, Wilton, 58579-0128.
Tel: 701-734-8131; Email: sacredht@bektel.com. Rev. Msgr. Gene E. Lindemann, J.C.L.
Catechesis Religious Program—Emily Hutzenbiler, D.R.E. Students 40.

WING, BURLEIGH CO., ST. IGNATIUS (1914) Closed. For inquiries for parish records contact the chancery.

Chaplains of Public Institutions

BISMARCK. *North Dakota State Penitentiary*, 58504. Tel: 701-328-6357. Jim Fritz.

On Duty Outside the Diocese:
Revs.—
Brown, Phillip J., S.S., Pres. & Rector, St. Mary's Seminary & Univ., 5400 Roland Ave., Baltimore, MD 21210
Deichert, Joseph, 12 S. Montana St., Arlington, VA 22204-1062
Ehli, Joshua, Congregation for the Evangelization of Peoples, Rome
Morman, David G., Missionary, Kisii, Kenya, East Africa.

Retired:
Revs.—
Cervinski, Paul, (Retired), 1020 N. 26th St., #3, 58501-3186
Cosgrove, William P., (Retired), P.O. Box 435, Patagonia, AZ 85624-0435
Eckroth, Leonard A., (Retired), P.O. Box 54, Hague, 58542-0054
Heidt, Charles A., (Retired), 4199 13th St., N.W., Lot #28, Garrison, 58540-9423
Kautzman, Jerome G., (Retired), 1020 N. 26th St., Apt. 7, 58501-3186
Klemmer, Marvin, (Retired), 1020 N. 26th St. #8, 58501-3186
O'Leary, John P., (Retired), 1020 N. 26th St., Apt. 1, 58501-3186
Paluck, Casimir S., (Retired), 1020 N. 26th St. #5, 58501-3186
Pfeifer, John M., (Retired), 504 Russell Dr., Apt. 68, Ripon, WI 54971-1058
Schneider, Henry W., (Retired), 1900 28th St., S.W., Minot, 58701-8135.

Permanent Deacons:
Auch, Ben, St. Vincent de Paul, Mott
Bachmeier, John, Saint Anne, Bismarck
Baker, Jim, St. Anthony, New Town
Barone, Daniel, St. Anthony, New Town
Bohn, Robert, St. Mary, Richardton
Brannan, Steve M., St. Vincent de Paul, Crown Butte
Brooke, Dan, St. Mary, Bismarck
Carlson, Dallas, St. Joseph, Dickinson
Clancy, Lynn, (Retired)
Crane, David M., St. Vincent de Paul, Mott
Dangel, Robert A., (Unassigned)
Dean, Dennis L., St. John, Lansford
Due, Keith, St. Hildegard, Menoken
Dvorak, Victor F., St. Mary, New England
Fettig, Richard H., (Retired)
Finneman, Tony, Ascension, Bismarck
Fischer, Leonard, St. Charles, Bowman
Fix, Michael, Corpus Christi, Bismarck
Frohlich, Randall, St. Joseph, Mandan
Gartner, Lance, Sacred Heart, Glen Ullin
Gayzur, Hans, St. Theresa the Little Flower, Minot
Gion, Donald J., (Retired)
Glatt, Terry, St. Mary, Bismarck
Grabar, Ray A., (Retired)
Grabowska, Lonnie, Corpus Christi, Bismarck
Haga, James A., St. Joseph, Williston
Hanel, Harvey, St. Mary, Bismarck
Helbing, Douglas, (Retired)
Hogan, Ronald, (Unassigned)
Jilek, Raymond, (Retired)
Johnson, Ed J. Sr., (Retired)
Jundt, Wayne M., Saint Anne, Bismarck
Keller, Ronald, St. Patrick, Dickinson
Klein, Kenneth M., St. Mary, Bismarck
Kordonowy, Leonard J., (Retired)
Kordonowy, Loren, St. Bernard, Belfield
Kramer, Charles L., St. John the Apostle, Minot
Krebs, Leonard, Queen of Peace, Dickinson
Krueger, Lloyd E., St. Leo, Minot
Krupinsky, Joseph M., Saint Anne, Bismarck
Magnuson, Tom, St. Theresa the Little Flower, Minot
Marback, Michael, St. Mary, Bismarck
Martin, Gerald, St. Joseph, Williston
Martin, John Paul, Ascension, Bismarck
Mathern, Joseph J., (Retired)
Mattson, Joseph M., (Retired)
Mays, Stephen B., (Retired)
McDowall, Rexford R., (Retired)
Melarvie, Joel D., (Retired)
Mellmer, Mike, Holy Trinity, Hettinger
Mizeur, Gary, Spirit of Life, Mandan
Morman, Eugene F., (Retired)
Naslund, Brent, Cathedral of the Holy Spirit, Bismarck
Nelson, Ryan, St. Patrick, Dickinson
Nistler, Donald R., (Retired)
Nutsch, Bob, Christ the King, Mandan
Olson, Robert C., (Retired)
Ringwall, Kris, (Unassigned)
Rohr, Dennis, Christ the King, Mandan
Rustand, Gerald T., (Unassigned)
Schmidt, Randal, Cathedral of the Holy Spirit, Bismarck
Schmit, Kenneth, St. Charles, Bowman
Schneider, Ervin H., (Retired)
Schulz, Doyle, Ascension, Bismarck
Schwindt, Alvin W., St. Joseph, Dickinson
Stockert, Robert, St. Wenceslaus, Dickinson
Streitz, Steven F., Our Lady of Grace, Minot
Ternes, Anthony, Cathedral of the Holy Spirit, Bismarck
Tharaldsen, John, (Retired)
Tuhy, Dan, St. Joseph, Killdeer
Volk, Jerry, Saint Anne, Bismarck

Von Ruden, Ralph, Cathedral of the Holy Spirit, Bismarck
Wallach, Daniel, St. Joseph, Beulah
Wingenbach, Robert, St. Joseph, Mandan
Woiwode, Mike, Unassigned
Wolbaum, Kenneth J., St. Katherine, Braddock
Wolf, Wilfred P., (Retired)
Wosepka, James, St. John the Baptist, Beach
Zent, Robert, St. Wenceslaus, Dickinson.

INSTITUTIONS LOCATED IN DIOCESE

[A] SEMINARIES, RELIGIOUS OR SCHOLASTICATES

RICHARDTON. *Assumption Abbey* (1893) P.O. Box A, Richardton, 58652. Tel: 701-974-3315; Fax: 701-974-3317; Email: monks@assumptionabbey.com; Web: www.assumptionabbey.com. 418 3rd Ave. W., Richardton, 58652. Rev. Valerian Odermann, O.S.B., Ph.D., Chap.; Ven. Bro. Michael Taffe, O.S.B., Ph.D., Prior & Librarian; Revs. Claude Seeberger, O.S.B., M.A., (Retired); Damian Dietlein, O.S.B., S.T.L., Hospital Chap., (Retired); Denis Fournier, O.S.B., Ph.D., Archivist; Terrence Kardong, O.S.B., M.A., S.T.L., Editor; Victor Feser, O.S.B., Ph.D., (Retired); Odo Muggli, O.S.B., Business Mgr.; Rt. Rev. Daniel Maloney, O.S.B., M.A., Chap. & Teacher; Revs. Philip Vanderlin, O.S.B., Pastor; Julian Nix, O.S.B., Pastor; Hugo L. Blotsky, O.S.B., M.A., Assoc. Rev.; Boniface Muggli, O.S.B., Chap., Email: boniface@assumptionabbey.com; Gonzalo Blanco, O.S.B., Subprior (Overseas); Thomas Wordekemper, O.S.B., Pastor; Nicolas Cano, O.S.B., M.A., Headmaster (On Leave); Anthony Baker, O.S.B., Public Rels.; James Kilzer, O.S.B., Asst. Business Mgr.; Basil Atwell, O.S.B., Pastor; Manuel Cely, O.S.B., M.A., Prior (Overseas), (Retired); Benedict Fischer, O.S.B., M.A., Graduate Student; Bro. Alban Petesch, O.S.B., Dir., Formation. Brothers 23; Priests 21; Monks 46.

[B] COLLEGES AND UNIVERSITIES

BISMARCK. *University of Mary* (1959) 7500 University Dr., 58504-9652. Tel: 701-255-7500;
Fax: 701-255-7687; Email: sjzander@umary.edu; Web: www.umary.edu. Rev. Msgr. James P. Shea, Ph.L., Pres.; Dr. Diane Fladeland, Vice Pres. Academic Affairs, Email: dflade@umary.edu; Rev. Anthony Baker, O.S.B., Email: atbaker@umary.edu; David P. Gray, Dir. Library Svcs.; Rev. Robert P. Shea, Univ. Chap. Clergy 1; Lay Teachers 139; Priests 1; Sisters 3; Students 3,396; Clergy / Religious Teachers 1.

[C] HIGH SCHOOLS, INTERPAROCHIAL AND PARISH

BISMARCK. *Light of Christ Catholic Schools of Excellence*, (Grades PreK-12), 1025 N. 2nd St., 58501.
Tel: 701-751-4883 Contact Person, Mike Weisbeck; Email: gvetter@lightofchristschools.org; Web: www.lightofchristschools.org. Gerald Vetter, Pres.; Reed Ruggles, Prin. (St. Mary's Central High School); Michael Bichler, Prin.; Cori Hilzendeger, Prin. (St. Anne Elementary); Matt Strinden, Prin. (Cathedral Elementary); Tony Fladeland, Prin. (St. Mary's Grade School). Lay Teachers 92; Preschool 150; Priests 2; K-12 Students 1,129; Clergy / Religious Teachers 2.

DICKINSON. *Dickinson Catholic Schools* aka Trinity Catholic Schools, (Grades PreK-12), P.O. Box 1177, Dickinson, 58602-1177. Tel: 701-483-6092;
Fax: 701-483-1450; Email: dcsbusinessoffice@gmail.com; Web: www.trinitycatholicschools.com. 810 Empire Rd., Dickinson, 58601. Mr. Steve Glasser, Pres.; Rev. Kregg W. Hochhalter, Dean (Trinity High School); Rachel Ebach, Librarian (Trinity High School); Mrs. Jolyn Tessier, Prin. (Trinity Elementary School West & East); Sr. Rosemarie Dvorak, Librarian (Trinity Elementary School West); Darcy Dahmus, Librarian. Lay Teachers 42; Priests 2; Sisters 2; Students 547; K-12 Students 472; Pre-K Students 75; Clergy / Religious Teachers 1.

Trinity High School (1961) (Grades 7-12), 810 Empire Rd., Dickinson, 58601. Tel: 701-483-6081; Fax: 701-483-1450; Email: dcsbusinessoffice@gmail.com; Web: www.trinityhighschool.com. Mr. Steve Glasser, Pres.; Revs. Kregg W. Hochhalter, Dean; Jordan Dosch, Chap.; Rachel Ebach, Librarian. Lay Teachers 21; Priests 2; Sisters 1; Students 201; Total Staff 22; Clergy / Religious Teachers 1.

MINOT. *Bishop Ryan Catholic School* (1958) (Grades PreK-12), 316 11th Ave., N.W., Minot, 58703-2260. Tel: 701-838-3355; Fax: 701-837-8914; Email: president@brhs.com; Web: www.bishopryan.com. Rev. Jadyn E. Nelson, Pres.; Tanya Steckler, Prin. Grades K-5; Chase Lee, Prin. Grades 6-12; Rev. Doug S. Krebs, Chap.; Barbra Johnson, Librarian, Email: bjohnson@brhs.com. Lay Teachers 38; Preschool 97; Priests 2; Students 332; Clergy/Religious Teachers 2.

[D] GENERAL HOSPITALS

BISMARCK. *St. Alexius Medical Center* (1885) P.O. Box 5510, 58506. 900 East Broadway, 58506-5510.
Tel: 701-530-7000; Fax: 701-530-7284; Email: rjlahren@primecare.org; Web: www.st.alexius.org. Kurt Schley, Admin. & CEO; Sr. Mariah Dietz, O.S.B., Vice Pres. Sisters of St. Benedict. Bed Capacity 287; Priests 1; Sisters 4; Tot Asst. Annually 246,000; Total Staff 1,893.

DICKINSON. *St. Joseph's Hospital and Health Center*, 2500 Fairway St., Dickinson, 58601.
Tel: 701-456-4271; Fax: 701-456-4800; Email: reedreyman@catholichealth.net; Web: chistalexiushealth.org. Reed E. Reyman, Pres. Bed Capacity 25; Nurses 138; Tot Asst. Annually 53,256; Total Staff 273.

GARRISON. *Garrison Memorial Hospital* aka CHI St. Alexius Health Garrison, 407 3rd Ave., S.E., Garrison, 58540-7235. Tel: 701-463-2275;
Fax: 701-463-6422; Email: tgraeber@primecare.org; Web: CHIStAlexiusHealth.org. Tod Graeber, Admin.
Legal Title: Garrison Memorial Hospital Bed Capacity 50; Nurses 46; Sisters of St. Benedict (Bismarck) 1; Tot Asst. Annually 15,000; Total Staff 148.

WILLISTON. *Mercy Medical Center - Affiliate of Catholic Health Initiatives*, 1301 15th Ave. W., Williston, 58801. Tel: 701-774-7400; Fax: 701-774-7479; Email: teriknight@catholichealth.net; Web: www.mercy-williston.org. Dan Bjerknes, Vice Pres. Bed Capacity 25; Tot Asst. Annually 143,287; Total Staff 401.

Mercy Medical Foundation, 1301 15th Ave. W., Williston, 58801. Tel: 701-774-7466;
Fax: 701-774-7479; Email: teriknight@catholichealth.net; Web: www.mercy-williston.org. Dan Bjerknes, Vice Pres. Bed Capacity 25; Tot Asst. Annually 143,287; Total Staff 401.

[E] SPECIAL CARE FACILITIES

BISMARCK. **St. Vincent's, A Prospera Community* (1943) 1021 N. 26 St., 58501-3199.
Tel: 701-323-1999; Fax: 701-323-1989; Email: kgreff4@good-sam.com. Kirk Greff, Admin.
*Part of *Sanford-Good Samaritan Community Health Services, LLC, 4800 W. 57th St., Sioux Falls, SD 57108.* Bed Capacity 101; Sisters of St. Benedict 1; Tot Asst. Annually 200; Total Staff 190.

DICKINSON. *Benedictine Living Communities, Inc.* dba St. Benedicts Health Center, 851 Fourth Ave. E., Dickinson, 58601. Tel: 701-456-7242;
Fax: 701-456-7250; Email: Jon.frantsvog@bhshealth.org; Web: www.saint-benedicts.org. Jon Frantsvog, Admin. Operated by Benedictine Living Communities, Inc. Bed Capacity 140; Tot Asst. Annually 350; Total Staff 250.

Benedictine Living Communities, Inc. dba Benedict Court (2003) 830 2nd Ave. E., Dickinson, 58601.
Tel: 701-456-7242; Fax: 701-456-7250; Email: Jon.frantsvog@bhshealth.org; Web: www.benedict-court.org. Jon Frantsvog, Admin. & Contact Person. Bed Capacity 26; Tot Asst. Annually 100; Total Staff 30.

GARRISON. *Benedictine Living Communities, Inc.* dba Benedictine Living Center of Garrison (1969) 609 4th Ave., N.E., Garrison, 58540. Tel: 701-463-2226; Fax: 701-463-2650; Email: scott.foss@bhshealth.org. Scott Foss, Admin. Operated by Benedictine Health System Long Term Care, Inc. Bed Capacity 52; Tot Asst. Annually 70; Total Staff 75; Assisted-Living Capacity 18.

[F] PROTECTIVE INSTITUTIONS

SENTINEL BUTTE. *Home On The Range* (1950) 16351 I-94, Sentinel Butte, 58654-9500. Tel: 701-872-3745; Fax: 701-872-3748; Email: melr@hotrnd.com; Web: www.hotrnd.com. Dr. Melodie Rose, M.S.W., PsyD., Exec. Dir.; Rev. Daniel J. Berg, Chap. Bed Capacity 40; Tot Asst. Annually 103; Total Staff 96.

[G] HOMES FOR AGED

BISMARCK. *Benedictine Living Communities - Bismarck, Inc.* dba St. Gabriel's Community, 4580 Coleman St., 58503. Tel: 701-751-4224;
Fax: 701-751-4225; Email: steven.przybilla@bhshealth.org; Web: www.stgabrielscommunity.org. Steven Przybilla, Admin. Skilled Nursing Beds 72; Transitional Care Beds 24.

Emmaus Place, 1020 N. 26th St., 58501.
Tel: 701-222-3035; Email: glindemann@bismarckdiocese.com. PO Box 1137, 58502-1137. Revs. Al Bitz, (Retired); Jerome G. Kautzman, (Retired); Marvin J. Klemmer, (Retired); John P. O'Leary, (Retired); Casimir S. Paluck, (Retired); Paul Cervinski, (Retired). Priests retirement home. Bed Capacity 8; Tot Asst. Annually 6; Total in Residence 6; Total Staff 3.

**Marillac Manor, A Prospera Community* (1977) 1016 N. 28th St., 58501. Tel: 701-323-1871;
Fax: 701-323-1875; Email: agreer@good-sam.com; Web: www.good-sam.com/locations/marillac-manor. Angela Greer, Dir.; Kirk Greff, Admin.
*Part of *Sanford-Good Samaritan Community Health Services, LLC, 4800 W. 57th St., Sioux Falls, SD 57108.* Total in Residence 85; Total Staff 5; Retirement Apartments 77.

[H] CONVENTS AND RESIDENCES FOR SISTERS

BISMARCK. *Annunciation Monastery* (1947) 7520 University Dr., 58504-9653. Tel: 701-255-1520;
Fax: 701-255-1440; Email: sm_lardy@hotmail.com; Web: www.annunciationmonastery.org. Sr. Nicole Kunze, O.S.B.; Rt. Rev. Daniel Maloney, O.S.B., M.A., Resident Chap. Motherhouse and Novitiate of the Benedictine Sisters of the Annunciation, B.M.V. Sisters 40.

HAGUE. *Carmel of the Holy Face of Jesus*, 2051 91st St., S.E., Hague, 58542. Tel: 701-336-7907; Email: theholyface@gmail.com; Web: www.carmeloftheholyface.com. Mother Mary Baptist of the Virgin of Carmel, O.C.D. Sisters 3.

RICHARDTON. *Sacred Heart Monastery*, 8969 Hwy. 10, P.O. Box 364, Richardton, 58652.
Tel: 701-974-2121; Fax: 701-974-2124; Email: prioress@sacredheartmonastery.com; Web: www.sacredheartmonastery.com. Sr. Paula Larson, Prioress & Pres. Motherhouse and Novitiate of the Sisters of the Order of St. Benedict. Professed Sisters 17.

[I] MISCELLANEOUS

BISMARCK. *Bismarck Guild*, 2520 Domino Dr., 58503-0825. 4907 S. Bay Dr., Mandan, 58554.
Tel: 701-220-2625; Email: Louise.Murphy@MiddakotaClinic.com. Rev. Msgr. Thomas J. Richter, Chap.

The St. Mary's Central High School Endowment for Operations and Tuition Aid for Students at SMCHS, 1025 N. 2nd St., 58501.
Tel: 701-354-7062; Fax: 701-223-8629; Email: mweisbeck@lightofchristschools.org. Gerald Vetter, Pres.

DICKINSON. *Subiaco Manor* (1990) 2441 10th Ave. W. #10, Dickinson, 58601. Tel: 701-483-2350; Email: subiacomgr@ndsupernet.com. Sr. Carol Axtmann, O.S.B., Resident Mgr. Sponsored by the Benedictine Sisters of Sacred Heart Monastery in Richardton. Total in Residence 10; Total Staff 1.

MANDAN. *The Educational Foundation of Christ the King Parish*, 505 10th Ave., N.W., Mandan, 58554-2552. Tel: 701-663-8842; Email: katrina.kuntz@ctkmandan.com; Web: www.ctkmandan.com. Rev. Nick L. Schneider, S.L.L., S.L.D.

World Apostolate of Fatima, 802 Division St. N.E., Mandan, 58554. Tel: 701-400-0233; Email: doughelbing@gmail.com. Deacon Douglas Helbing, Pres.

RICHARDTON. *Benedictine Sponsorship Board*, 8969 Hwy. 10, P.O. Box 364, Richardton, 58652-0364.
Tel: 701-974-2121; Fax: 701-974-2124; Email: spaula@sacredheartmonastery.com; Web: www.sacredheartmonastery.com. Sr. Paula Larson, Pres. & Contact Person.

PIA Tegler Benedictine Foundation, 8969 Hwy. 10, P.O. Box 364, Richardton, 58652-0364.
Tel: 701-974-2121; Fax: 701-974-2124; Email: busoffice@sacredheartmonastery.com; Web: www.sacredheartmonastery.com. Sisters Marie Hunkler, O.S.B., Pres.; Anna Rose Ruhland, O.S.B., Vice Pres.; Jill West, Sec.

Sacred Heart Benedictine Foundation, 8969 Hwy. 10, P.O. Box 364, Richardton, 58652-0364.
Tel: 701-974-2121; Fax: 701-974-2124; Email: busoffice@sacredheartmonastery.com; Web: www.sacredheartmonastery.com. Sr. Paula Larson, Pres.

Sacred Heart Mission, 418 3rd Ave. W., Richardton, 58652-7100. Tel: 701-974-3315; Fax: 701-974-3317; Email: odo@assumptionabbey.com. Rev. Odo Muggli, O.S.B., Sec. & Treas.

RELIGIOUS INSTITUTES OF MEN REPRESENTED IN THE DIOCESE

For further details refer to the corresponding bracketed number in the Religious Institutes of Men or Women section.

[0200]—*Benedictine Monks* (Richardton, ND)—O.S.B.
[]—*Indian Missionary Society* (Varanasi, U.P., India)—I.M.S.
[1200]—*Society of the Divine Savior* (Milwaukee, WI)—S.D.S.

RELIGIOUS INSTITUTES OF WOMEN REPRESENTED IN THE DIOCESE

[0230]—*Benedictine Sisters of Pontifical Jurisdiction* (Bismarck; Richardton, ND)—O.S.B.
[]—*Congregation of Teresian Carmelites* (Fort Yates, Mandan, ND)—C.T.C.
[]—*The Daughters of Immaculate Mary of Guadalupe* (Williston, ND).
[0420]—*Discalced Carmelite Nuns* (Hague, ND)—O.C.D.
[2970]—*School Sisters of Notre Dame* (Central Pacific Prov.)—S.S.N.D.
[2450]—*Sisters of Mary of the Presentation* (Bismark and Mandan, ND)—S.M.P.

NECROLOGY

† Zastoupil, Steve, (Retired), Died Jul. 2, 2018

An asterisk (*) denotes an organization that has established tax-exempt status directly with the IRS and is not covered by the USCCB Group Ruling.

Diocese of Boise

(Dioecesis Xylopolitana)

Most Reverend

PETER F. CHRISTENSEN

Bishop of Boise; ordained May 25, 1985; appointed Bishop of Superior June 28, 2007; consecrated September 14, 2007; installed September 23, 2007; appointed Bishop of Boise November 4, 2014; installed December 17, 2014. *Chancery Office, 1501 Federal Way, Boise, ID 83705.*

Chancery Office: 1501 Federal Way, Ste. 400, Boise, ID 83705. Tel: 208-342-1311; Fax: 208-342-0224.

Email: clawrence@rcdb.org

ESTABLISHED AS A VICARIATE-APOSTOLIC MARCH 3, 1868.

Square Miles 83,557.

Erected a Diocese by His Holiness Pope Leo XIII, August 26, 1893

Comprises the State of Idaho, with a Total Population of 1,634,464

Legal Title: "Roman Catholic Diocese of Boise". For legal titles of parishes and diocesan institutions, consult the Chancery Office.

STATISTICAL OVERVIEW

Personnel	
Bishop	1
Priests: Diocesan Active in Diocese	40
Priests: Diocesan Active Outside Diocese	2
Priests: Retired, Sick or Absent	24
Number of Diocesan Priests	66
Religious Priests in Diocese	20
Total Priests in Diocese	86
Extern Priests in Diocese	5
Ordinations:	
Diocesan Priests	2
Transitional Deacons	1
Permanent Deacons in Diocese	94
Total Brothers	4
Total Sisters	53
Parishes	
Parishes	50
With Resident Pastor:	
Resident Diocesan Priests	42
Resident Religious Priests	2
Without Resident Pastor:	
Administered by Priests	5

Missions	27
Pastoral Centers	23
Professional Ministry Personnel:	
Sisters	41
Lay Ministers	64
Welfare	
Catholic Hospitals	4
Total Assisted	655,606
Day Care Centers	4
Total Assisted	190
Special Centers for Social Services	19
Total Assisted	450,000
Educational	
Diocesan Students in Other Seminaries	5
Total Seminarians	5
High Schools, Diocesan and Parish	1
Total Students	842
High Schools, Private	1
Total Students	62
Elementary Schools, Diocesan and Parish	14
Total Students	2,836

Catechesis/Religious Education:	
High School Students	1,613
Elementary Students	4,608
Total Students under Catholic Instruction	9,966
Teachers in the Diocese:	
Lay Teachers	237
Vital Statistics	
Receptions into the Church:	
Infant Baptism Totals	1,777
Minor Baptism Totals	187
Adult Baptism Totals	177
Received into Full Communion	252
First Communions	2,149
Confirmations	1,606
Marriages:	
Catholic	420
Interfaith	89
Total Marriages	509
Deaths	904
Total Catholic Population	196,963
Total Population	1,754,208

Former Bishops—Rt. Revs. LOUIS LOOTENS, D.D., ord. June 14, 1851; appt. first Vicar-Apostolic of Idaho, March 3, 1868; cons. Bishop of Castabala, Aug. 9, 1868; resigned July 16, 1876; died Jan. 13, 1898; ALPHONSE JOSEPH GLORIEUX, D.D., ord. Aug. 17, 1867; appt. second Vicar-Apostolic of Idaho, Feb. 27, 1885; cons. Titular Bishop of Apolonia, April 19, 1885; appt. first Bishop of the Diocese of Boise, Aug. 26, 1893; died Aug. 25, 1917; DANIEL MARY GORMAN, D.D., LL.D., ord. June 24, 1892; cons. May 1, 1918; died June 9, 1927; Most Revs. EDWARD JOSEPH KELLY, D.D., ord. June 2, 1917; cons. March 6, 1928; died April 21, 1956; JAMES J. BYRNE, D.D., S.T.D., ord. June 3, 1933; appt. Titular Bishop of Etenna and Auxiliary of St. Paul, July 2, 1947; cons. July 2, 1947; transferred to Boise June 16, 1956; appt. Archbishop of Dubuque, March 19, 1962; retired Aug. 23, 1983; died Aug. 2, 1996; SYLVESTER WILLIAM TREINEN, D.D., ord. June 11, 1946; appt. May 19, 1962; cons. July 25, 1962; retired Aug. 17, 1988; died Sept. 30, 1996; TOD D. BROWN, D.D., ord. May 1, 1963; appt. Dec. 27, 1988; ord. and installed April 3, 1989; appt. Bishop of Orange, June 30, 1998; MICHAEL P. DRISCOLL, ord. May 1, 1965; appt. Titular Bishop of Massita and Auxiliary Bishop of Orange Dec. 19, 1989; cons. March 6, 1990; appt. Bishop of Boise Jan. 19, 1999; installed March 18, 1999; retired Nov. 4, 2014; died Oct. 24, 2017.

Executive Administrative Assistant to Bishop/Vicar General—MARISELA BACA.

Vicar General—Rev. Msgr. JOSEPH A. DA SILVA.

Chancery Office—1501 Federal Way, Ste. 400, Boise, 83705. Tel: 208-342-1311; Fax: 208-342-0224.

Director of Diocesan Projects—MR. CHRISTIAN WELP, Email: cwelp@rcdb.org.

Chancellor—MR. MARK L. RAPER, J.C.L., M.C.L., 1501 S. Federal Way, Ste. 400, Boise, 83705. Email: mraper@rcdb.org.

Office of Hispanic Ministries—VACANT.

Notaries—MR. MARK L. RAPER, J.C.L., M.C.L.; MS. JAN NORIYUKI.

Diocesan Tribunal—1501 Federal, Ste. 400, Boise, 83705. Tel: 208-344-1344; Fax: 208-342-0224. (Direct all correspondence here.)

Director—MR. MARK L. RAPER, J.C.L., M.C.L.

Judicial Vicar—Very Rev. JOSEPH F. MCDONALD III, J.C.L., V.F.

Adjutant Judicial Vicar—Very Rev. GERALD FUNKE, J.C.L., V.U.

Promoter of Justice—MR. MARK L. RAPER, J.C.L., M.C.L.

Notaries—Rev. Msgr. DENNIS WASSMUTH, (Retired); MR. MARK L. RAPER, J.C.L., M.C.L.; COLLEEN CUNNINGHAM; TRACEY KOWALEWSKI; MS. CAROLINE CARTHY-WICKHAM.

Judges—Very Rev. GERALD FUNKE, J.C.L., V.U.; MR. MARK L. RAPER, J.C.L., M.C.L.; Rev. FRANCISCO H. GODINEZ, J.C.L.

Defenders of the Bond—Rev. Msgr. ANDREW SCHUMACHER, (Retired); MR. MARK L. RAPER, J.C.L., M.C.L.

College of Consultors—Very Rev. HENRY CARMONA, J.C.L., V.F.; Rev. CAMILO GARCIA, V.F.; Very Revs. GERALD FUNKE, J.C.L., V.U.; TIMOTHY M. RITCHEY, V.F.; Revs. MARIUSZ MAJEWSKI; ELADIO VIEYRA; Very Rev. MICHAEL A. ST. MARIE, V.F.; Rev. Msgr. JOSEPH A. DA SILVA; Very Rev. JULIO VICENTE, V.F.

Deans—Very Revs. TIMOTHY M. RITCHEY, V.F., Northern Deanery; HENRY CARMONA, J.C.L., V.F., Eastern Deanery; Rev. CAMILO GARCIA, V.F., Western Deanery; Very Revs. GERALD J. FUNKE, V.U., West Central Deanery; PAUL H. WANDER, V.F., North Central Deanery; JULIO VICENTE, V.F., Southern Deanery.

Presbyteral Council—(Vacant) Very Revs. JULIO VICENTE, V.F.; PAUL H. WANDER, V.F.; MICHAEL A. ST. MARIE, V.F.; GERALD FUNKE, J.C.L., V.U.; HENRY CARMONA, J.C.L., V.F.; TIMOTHY M. RITCHEY, V.F.; Revs. CAMILO GARCIA, V.F.; ENRIQUE TERRIQUEZ, V.F., (Retired); MARIUSZ MAJEWSKI; ELADIO VIEYRA; Rev. Msgr. JOSEPH A. DA SILVA.

Priest Personnel Commission—Revs. DAT VU; ROBERT P. COOK; CAMILO GARCIA, V.F.; FRANCISCO GOODINEZ, J.C.L.; MARIUSZ MAJEWSKI; Very Revs. JULIO VICENTE, V.F.; BRADLEY NEELY, V.F.; Rev. Msgr. JOSEPH A. DA SILVA, Ex Officio.

Finance Council—Most Rev. PETER F. CHRISTENSEN, D.D.; Rev. Msgr. JOSEPH A. DA SILVA, Ex Officio; TOM ZABALA; Rev. ROBERT P. COOK; SANDRA DALTON; LARRY HELLHAKE; STANLEY WELSH; ALAN WINKLE; SUSAN COPPLE; MARTIN KNOELK; MR. CHRISTIAN WELP; MR. CHARLES LAWRENCE, Finance Officer.

Building Commission—NICK GUHO; TOM ZABALA; MARK GIER; JAMES MESPLAY; JOHN IRVINE; MATT MAHONEY; CHRIS JONES; RHONDA JALBERT; TOM MANNSCHRECK; MR. CHARLES LAWRENCE, Ex Officio; DAVID LAMARQUE.

Priest Retirement Committee—Rev. Msgr. JOSEPH A. DA SILVA, Ex Officio; Very Revs. PAUL H. WANDER, V.F.; TIMOTHY M. RITCHEY, V.F.; Rev. JOHN R. WORSTER; Rev. Msgr. DENNIS WASSMUTH, (Retired).

Diocesan Offices and Directors

Apostleship of Prayer—VACANT.

Bureau of Information—Idaho Catholic Register, 1501 Federal Way, Ste. 400, Boise, 83705.

Catholic Campaign for Human Development—MR. MARK L. RAPER, J.C.L., M.C.L., 1501 Federal Way, Ste. 400, Boise, 83705-5925.

Catholic Charities of Idaho, Inc.—DOUGLAS ALLES, Exec. Dir.; Most Rev. PETER F. CHRISTENSEN, D.D.

Catholic Communications Center—1501 Federal Way, Ste. 400, Boise, 53705. Deacon EUGENE FADNESS, Dir.

Catholic Relief Services—MR. MARK L. RAPER, J.C.L., M.C.L., 1501 Federal Way, Ste. 400, Boise, 83705.

Catholic Scouts—Rev. ROGER LACHANCE, M.A., Chap., St. Pius X, 625 E. Haycraft, Coeur d'Alene, 83815. Tel: 208-765-5108; DAVID L. DAVIS, Chm., 142 N. 9th St., Pocatello, 83201. Tel: 208-238-5037.

Catholic Daughters of the Americas—Rev. MARIUSZ MAJEWSKI, State Chap., Email: fathermariusz@gmail.com; LOUISE BLUHM, State Regent, Email: lrbluhm1998@roadrunner.com.

Catholic Schools—1501 Federal Way, Ste. 400, Boise, 83705. Dr. SARAH QUILICI, Supt.

Catholic Hospitals—1501 Federal Way, Ste. 400, Boise, 83705. Deacon ROBERT BARROS-BAILEY.

Catholic Liturgical Commission—1501 Federal Way, Boise, 83705. Tel: 208-342-1311. LETITIA THORNTON, Chm., Email: tthornton@rcdb.org; JAKE INECK; MR. LARRY HARRISON.

Censor Librorum—Rev. Msgr. ANDREW SCHUMACHER, (Retired), Tel: 208-746-3362.

Charismatic Renewal—Rev. CARLOS ROSERO PATINO.

Children, Youth and Adult Protection Director—MR. MARK L. RAPER, J.C.L., M.C.L., Tel: 208-350-7560.

Director of Office of Worship—LETITIA THORNTON.

Director of the Permanent Diaconate—Deacon ROBERT BARROS-BAILEY, 1501 S. Federal Way, Ste. #400, Boise, 83705. Tel: 208-342-1311.

Priest Retirement Plan—Direct Inquiries to the Chancery, *1501 Federal Way, Ste. 400, Boise, 83705.*

Cursillo Movement—HOANG TAN, Northern Cursillo Service Admin.; STEVEN MURRAY, Region XII Lay Dir., Email: smurray7880@gmail.com; Rev. JOSE T. RAMIREZ, Spiritual Dir. (Spanish), St. Edward the Confessor, 931 Eastland Dr. N., Twin Falls, 83301.

Development/Stewardship Office—1501 Federal Way, Ste. 400, Boise, 83705. Tel: 208-342-1311; Fax: 208-342-1571. MR. CHARLES LAWRENCE.

Diocesan Ecumenical & Interreligious Officer—Rev. ANTONIO EGUIGUREN, O.F.M.

Director of Youth and Young Adult Evangelization—Deacon SALVADOR CARRANZA, Email: scarranza@rcdb.org; CATHY WHEATON, Admin. Asst., 1501 Federal Way, Boise, 83705. Tel: 208-342-1311.

Director of Religious Education and Catechetical Leadership—JACKIE HOPPER, Email: jhopper@rcdb.org.

Finance Officer—MR. CHARLES LAWRENCE.

Human Resources—MR. CHARLES LAWRENCE.

Idaho Council of Catholic Women—ROSE GLASS, Pres.; Rev. ELADIO VIEYRA, Moderator.

Idaho Catholic Foundation—Most Rev. PETER F. CHRISTENSEN, D.D., Pres.

Knights of Columbus—Very Rev. BENJAMIN R. UHLENKOTT, V.U., State Chap.; MICHAEL TOWNSEND; SHANE GEHRING, State Deputy.

Campus Ministry—1501 Federal Way, Ste. 400, Boise, 83705. Tel: 208-342-1311. Deacon SALVADOR CARRANZA, Coord. Campus Min.

Newspaper—Idaho Catholic Register Most Rev. PETER F. CHRISTENSEN, D.D., Publisher; Deacon EUGENE FADNESS, Editor; ANN BIXBY, Advertising/Business/Circulation.

Respect Life/Prison Ministry Coordinator—Deacon ROBERT BARROS-BAILEY.

Propagation of the FaithMR. MARK L. RAPER, J.C.L., M.C.L., 1501 Federal Way, Ste. 400, Boise, 83705.

St. Vincent de Paul Society—Deacon RICHARD BONNEY II, Spiritual Dir.

National Board Member—JOHN DAHL.

Vocations—Rev. CALEB VOGEL, Dir. Recruitment; Very Rev. GERALD FUNKE, J.C.L., V.U., Dir. Seminarians; MR. CHARLES LAWRENCE, Admin. Coord.; Rev. JOSE T. RAMIREZ, Dir. Hispanic Vocations; MS. CHERI MCCORMACK, Admin. Asst., 1501 S. Federal Way, Ste. 400, Boise, 83705. Tel: 208-342-1311.

CLERGY, PARISHES, MISSIONS AND PAROCHIAL SCHOOLS

CITY OF BOISE

(ADA COUNTY)

1—CATHEDRAL OF ST. JOHN THE EVANGELIST (1906)
707 N. 8th St., 83702. Email: danielg@boisecathedral.org. 807 N. 8th St., 83702. Very Rev. Gerald J. Funke, V.U., Rector; Rev. Antonio Eguiguren, O.F.M., Parochial Vicar; Deacons Tom Dominick; William Burns; Thomas Manschreck; Derrick O'Neill.
Res.: 804 N. 9th St., 83702. Tel: 208-342-3511; Fax: 208-342-1564; Email: frjerry@boisecathedral.org; Web: www.boisecathedral.org.
School—St. Joseph's School, (Grades K-8), 825 W. Fort St., 83702. Tel: 208-342-4909; Fax: 208-342-0997; Email: quilicit@stjoes.com; Web: www.stjoes.com. Tony Quilici, Prin. Lay Teachers 25; Students 405.
Catechesis Religious Program—Email: teresaw@boisecathedral.org. Teresa Wittry, D.R.E. Students 173.

2—ST. MARK'S (1970)
7960 W. Northview, 83704. Tel: 208-375-6651; Fax: 208-375-3211; Email: buhlenkott@stmarksboise.org; Web: www.stmarksboise.org. Very Rev. Benjamin R. Uhlenkott, V.U.; Rev. Reginald Nwauzor, Parochial Vicar; Deacons James Ineck; Clyde Brinegar; Terry Nelson; Jim Pasker; Joseph Rodriguez; Mike Lowe.
School—St. Mark's School, (Grades PreK-8), 7503 W. Northview, 83704. Tel: 208-375-6654; Fax: 208-375-9471; Email: dgordon@stmarksboise.org; Web: www.stmarksboise.com. Donna Gordon, Prin.; Dorothy Sammortino, Librarian. Lay Teachers 20; Students 250.
Catechesis Religious Program—Catechesis of the Good Shepherd, Email: gmortensen@stmarksboise.org. Ginger Mortensen, D.R.E. Students 200.

3—ST. MARY'S (1937) Revs. John R. Worster; Jesus Camacho, Parochial Vicar; Deacons Francis Hess; John Carpenter; Eugene Fadness; Jose Ayala; Imanol Betikoetxea; Monica Pittman, Business Mgr.
Res.: 2612 W. State St., 83702. Tel: 208-344-2597; Fax: 208-344-9337; Email: mpittman@stmarysboise.org; Web: www.stmarysboise.org.
School—St. Mary's School, (Grades K-8), 2620 W. State St., 83702. Tel: 208-342-7476; Fax: 208-345-5154; Email: eldavis@stmarys-boise.org. Tammy Emerich, Prin.; Elaine Davis, Sec. Lay Teachers 11; Students 169.
Catechesis Religious Program—Meg Lawless, D.R.E. Students 298.

4—OUR LADY OF THE ROSARY (1947) Rev. Bruno Segatta, (Retired); Deacons Louis Aaron, Admn.; Mike Servatius; Gary Anderson; Peter Cuppage; Mackensey Chester.
Res.: 1500 E. Wright, 83706. Tel: 208-343-9041; Fax: 208-343-2644; Email: olrboise@olrboise.org; Web: www.olrboise.org.
Catechesis Religious Program—Sarah Taylor, D.R.E. Students 265.
Chapels—Idaho City, St. Joseph's—
Boise, St. Paul's Student Center, Revs. John Bentz, S.J., Chap. & Campus Min.; Radmar Jao, S.J., Co-Chap. & Campus Min.

5—ST. PAUL'S, Closed. See Our Lady of the Rosary, Boise for details.

6—RISEN CHRIST CATHOLIC COMMUNITY (1992) [CEM] Rev. Msgr. Joseph A. da Silva; Deacons Don Blythe, Pastoral Assoc.; Ted Vermaas.
Res.: 11511 W. Lake Hazel Rd., 83709.
Tel: 208-362-6584; Fax: 208-362-9545; Email: office@risenchristboise.org; Web: www.risenchristboise.org.
Catechesis Religious Program—
Tel: 208-362-6584, Ext. 410; Email: ganderson@risenchristboise.org. Deacon Gary Anderson, C.R.E. (Elementary) & Youth Min. Coord. Students 81.

7—SACRED HEART (1952)
Mailing Address: 811 S. Latah St., 83705-0127.
Tel: 208-344-8311; Fax: 208-343-1876; Email: lgraefe@sacredheartboise.org; Web: www.sacredheartboise.org. Rev. Robert P. Cook; Deacons Rick Bonney; Jude Gary; Michael Eisenbeiss, Email: meisen@me.com; Daniel Vawser; Brian Flowers.
School—Sacred Heart School, (Grades PreK-8), 3901 Cassia St., 83705. Tel: 208-344-9738; Fax: 208-343-1939; Email: bcarpenter@sacredheartboise.org; Web: www.sacredheartboise.org. Brock Carpenter, Prin.; Jane Collins, Librarian. Lay Teachers 10; Students 205.
Catechesis Religious Program—Email: dfischer@sacredheartboise.org. Deborah Fischer, D.R.E. (K-6). Students 112.

OUTSIDE THE CITY OF BOISE

ABERDEEN, BINGHAM CO., BLESSED SACRAMENT, Merged with St. Mary, American Falls to form Presentation of the Lord, Aberdeen.

AMERICAN FALLS, POWER CO.

1—ST. MARY, Merged with Blessed Sacrament, Aberdeen to form Presentation of the Lord, Aberdeen.

2—PRESENTATION OF THE LORD
376 Roosevelt St., American Falls, 83211. Email: im4jcru@gmail.com; Web: www.presentationofthelord.org. P.O. Box 117, American Falls, 83211. Tel: 208-220-0868; Fax: 208-226-1125. Rev. Eladio Vieyra, Admin.
Catechesis Religious Program—Victoria Rodriguez, D.R.E. Students 227.
Chapels—Pingree, St. John—
St. Mary, 376 Roosevelt, American Falls, 83211. Tel: 208-226-5217.
Aberdeen, Blessed Sacrament, 667 S. 4th W., Aberdeen, 83210.

ARCO, BUTTE CO., ST. ANN'S, Closed. See St. Charles, Salmon for details.

BLACKFOOT, BINGHAM CO., ST. BERNARD'S
583 W. Sexton St., Blackfoot, 83221. Rev. Jose de Jesus Gonzalez; Deacon Jeff Powers.
Res.: 584 W. Sexton St., Blackfoot, 83221.
Tel: 208-785-1935; Fax: 208-785-7382; Email: st.bernards.office@gmail.com; Web: www.stbernards.us.
Catechesis Religious Program—Students 208.
Chapel—Blessed Kateri Tekakwitha, Sheepskin Rd., Fort Hall, 83203.

BONNERS FERRY, BOUNDARY CO., ST. ANN'S (1800) Rev. Carlos Perez.
Res.: 6712 El Paso, Bonners Ferry, 83805.
Tel: 208-267-2852; Fax: 208-267-8222; Email: st-anns@peoplepc.com; Web: stannsbonnersferry.org.
Catechesis Religious Program—Students 29.

BUHL, TWIN FALLS CO., IMMACULATE CONCEPTION
P.O. Box 626, Buhl, 83316. Rev. Jorge E. Garcia; Deacons James McCaughey; John Plank.
Res.: 1701 Poplar, P.O. Box 626, Buhl, 83316.
Tel: 208-543-5136 (Office); Fax: 208-543-5714; Email: immconchurch@qwestoffice.net; Web: www.icbuhl.org.
1631 Poplar, Buhl, 83316.
Catechesis Religious Program—Cell: edelia.e.miramontes@eaglemail.csi.edu. Edelia Miramontes, D.R.E. Students 33.
Station—Hagerman, St. Catherine's, Hagerman. Tel: 208-837-6592.

BURLEY, CASSIA CO., ST. THERESE LITTLE FLOWER (1938)
1601 Oakley Ave., Burley, 83318. Tel: 208-678-5453; Fax: 208-678-5479; Email: litflowerch@pmt.org; Web: www.sttheresebuley.com. Rev. Mark Uhlenkott, Admin.; Brenda Sanchez, Business Mgr.
Church: 1601 Oakley Ave., Burley, 83318.
Catechesis Religious Program—Email: masfut421@gmail.com. Melissa Santana, D.R.E. Students 410.

CALDWELL, CANYON CO.

1—ST. MARY'S, Merged to form Our Lady of the Valley, Caldwell.

2—OUR LADY OF THE VALLEY, Very Rev. Michael A. St. Marie, V.F.; Deacons Humberto Almeida; Kerry Harris; Pat Kearns; Martin Knoelk, Business Mgr.
Office: 1122 W. Linden St., Caldwell, 83605.
Tel: 208-459-3653; Fax: 208-454-8789; Email: churchoffice@olvcaldwell.org; Web: www.olvcaldwell.net.
Catechesis Religious Program—Email: tbeltran@olvcaldwell.org. Thania Beltran, Dir. Child Min. Students 470.

CHUBBUCK, BANNOCK CO., ST. PAUL'S, Merged with St. Anthony's, Pocatello and St. Joseph, Pocatello to form Holy Spirit Catholic Community, Pocatello.

COEUR D'ALENE, KOOTENAI CO.

1—ST. JOAN OF ARC
773 N. 11th St., Coeur d'Alene, 83814.
Tel: 208-660-6036; Email: kford@stjoanarc.com; Web: www.stjoanarc.com; Web: www.stjoanarc.com. Revs. Dennis M. Gordon, F.S.S.P.; Michael Flick, Pastoral Assoc.; Andrew Rapoport, Pastoral Assoc.; Joseph Terra, Chap. Traditional Latin Mass Parish.

2—ST. PIUS X (1962)
625 E. Haycraft, Coeur d'Alene, 83815.
Tel: 208-765-5108; Email: info@stpiuscda.org. Very Rev. Francisco Q. Flores, V.F.; Deacons Eric Shaber; Chris Stewart, Pastoral Assoc.
Catechesis Religious Program—Deacon Gary McSwain, D.R.E. Students 160.

3—ST. THOMAS THE APOSTLE (1890)
919 E. Indiana Ave., Coeur d'Alene, 83814.
Tel: 208-664-9259; Email: stthomasapostle@roadrunner.com. Rev. Mariusz Majewski.
St. Thomas Parish Center—406 N. 10th St., Coeur d'Alene, 83814. Tel: 208-664-4327.

COTTONWOOD, IDAHO CO., ST. MARY'S (1890) [CEM]
Mailing Address: 503 Garrett St., P.O. Box 425, Cottonwood, 83522-0425. Tel: 208-962-3214; Fax: 208-962-5477; Email: smrectory@triparishchurches.com. Very Rev. Paul H. Wander, V.F.
Church: 508 Church St., Cottonwood, 83522-0425.
Catechesis Religious Program—Tel: 208-962-7098; Email: stmarys_dre@yahoo.com. Heather Uhlenkott, D.R.E. (Children). Students 205.
Chapel—Keuterville, Holy Cross.

COUNCIL, ADAMS CO., ST. JUDE STATION, Closed. See St. Agnes, Weiser for details.

DESMET, BENEWAH CO., SACRED HEART (1842)
127 Byrnes Ave., DeSmet, 83824. Rev. Robert Erickson, S.J.; Deacon Nick Vietri.
Res.: Box 306, DeSmet, 83824. Tel: 208-274-5871; Fax: 208-274-3015; Email: rbterickson@outlook.com.
Catechesis Religious Program—Students 104.
Stations—Plummer, Our Lady of Perpetual Help—1173 East St., Plummer, 83851.
Worley, St. Michael's, W. 9284 I St., Worley, 83876.

EAGLE, ADA CO., ST. MATTHEW, Merged with Holy Spirit, Meridian to form Holy Apostles, Meridian.

EMMETT, GEM CO., SACRED HEART, Rev. Oscar Jaramillo, V.F.; Deacons Alan Shaber; Chris Roeper.
Res.: 211 E. First Street, P.O. Box 63, Emmett, 83617. Tel: 208-365-4320; Fax: 208-365-0754; Email: shc@qwestoffice.net; Web: www.sacredheartemmett.com.
Catechesis Religious Program—Students 159.
Station—Garden Valley, St. Jude, 1056 Banks Lowman Rd., Garden Valley, 83622.

FERDINAND, IDAHO CO., ASSUMPTION (1900)
P.O. Box 425, Cottonwood, 83522-0425.
Tel: 208-962-3214; Fax: 208-962-5477; Email: smrectory@triparishchurches.com; Web: www.triparishchurches.com. 460 Maple St., Ferdinand, 83526. Very Rev. Paul H. Wander, V.F.
Catechesis Religious Program—503 Garrett St., Cottonwood, 83522. Email: pffpdre@gmail.com. Heather Uhlenkott, D.R.E. (Children). Twinned with St. Mary's, Cottonwood.

FRUITLAND, PAYETTE CO., CORPUS CHRISTI CATHOLIC CHURCH (1999)
Mailing Address: 900 N.W. 7th St., Fruitland, 83619. Rev. Camilo Garcia, V.F.; Deacon Tom Turpin.
Res.: 1104 Partridge St., Fruitland, 83619.
Tel: 208-452-5778; Fax: 208-452-6778; Email: corpusxt@aol.com; Web: www.cccatholic.org.
Catechesis Religious Program—Alejandra Molina, D.R.E. Students 130.

GARDEN VALLEY, BOISE CO., ST. JUDE'S, Closed. See Sacred Heart, Emmett for details.

GENESEE, LATAH CO., ST. MARY STATION, See St. Mary's, Moscow for details.
Mailing Address: P.O. Box 9106, Moscow, 83843. Very Rev. Joseph F. McDonald III, J.C.L., V.F.
Res.: 138 N. Jackson, Genesee, 83832.
Tel: 208-882-4813; Email: office@stmarysparishmoscow.org; Web: www.stmarysparishmoscow.org.
Catechesis Religious Program—Kristy Mayer, D.R.E.; Marnie Zenner, D.R.E. (Included with St. Mary's Genesee) Students 35.

GLENNS FERRY, ELMORE CO., OUR LADY OF LIMERICK STATION (1892)
Mailing Address: P.O. Box 310, Mountain Home, 83647. Tel: 208-587-3046. 415 S. Commercial St., Glenns Ferry, 83623. Rev. German Osorio. Bilingual Mass.
Res.: 21 W. Arthur St., Box 216, Glenns Ferry, 83623. Fax: 208-587-5114; Email: fr.osoriog@gmail.com; Web: www.olgcid.org.
Catechesis Religious Program—Students 18.

GOODING, GOODING CO., ST. ELIZABETH'S
Mailing Address: Box 147, Gooding, 83330-0147. 1515 California St., Gooding, 83330. Rev. Jose T. Ramirez; Deacon Javier Leija.
Res.: 326 16th Ave. E., Gooding, 83330.
Tel: 208-934-5634; Fax: 208-934-4910; Email: stelizabethgooding@yahoo.com; Web: www.stelizabethgooding.com.
Catechesis Religious Program—Jaime Novis, D.R.E. (English). Students 34.
Station—Wendell, St. Anthony's, 585 2nd Ave. E., P.O. Box 811, Wendell, 83355.

GRANDVIEW, OWYHEE CO., ST. HENRY CHAPEL
Box 310, Mountain Home, 83647. Tel: 208-587-3046; Fax: 208-587-5114; Web: www.olgcid.org. 510 Idaho St., Grand View, 83624. Rev. German Osorio.
Catechesis Religious Program—Students 8.

GRANGEVILLE, IDAHO CO., SS. PETER AND PAUL (1892)
Rev. John Gathungu, Admin.
Office & Mailing Address: 625 Lake St., Grangeville, 83530. Tel: 208-983-0403; Fax: 208-983-0115; Email: office@stspeterandpaulparish.org; Web: www.stspeterandpaulparish.org.
Res.: 622 S.W. 1st St., Grangeville, 83530.
Tel: 208-983-0403; Fax: 208-983-0115.
Church: 318 South B St., Grangeville, 83530.
School—SS. Peter and Paul School, (Grades PreK-8), 330 S. B St., Grangeville, 83530. Tel: 208-983-2182; Email: lmcdaniel@myspps.org; Web: www.myspps.org. Leslie McDaniel, Prin. Lay Teachers 7; Students 88.
Catechesis Religious Program—Email: uhlenkott@gmail.com. Linda Uhlenkott, D.R.E. Students 49.
Station—Nez Perce, Holy Trinity, P.O Box 65, Nez Perce, 83543. Tel: 208-937-2300. RE Program 23.
Chapel—White Bird, Sacred Heart, See Sts. Peter & Paul, Grangeville for details.

GREENCREEK, IDAHO CO., ST. ANTHONY'S (1900) [CEM]
1070 Greencreek Rd., Greencreek, 83533.
Tel: 208-962-3214; Fax: 208-962-5477; Email: smrectory@triparishchurches.com; Web: www.triparishchurches.com. Very Rev. Paul H. Wander, V.F.
Res.: P.O. Box 425, Cottonwood, 83522.
Catechesis Religious Program— (Included in St. Mary's) 503 Garrett St., Cottonwood, 83522. Email: pffpdre@gmail.com. Heather Uhlenkott, D.R.E. (Children).

HAGERMAN, GOODING CO., ST. CATHERINE'S, Closed. See Immaculate Conception, Buhl for details.

HAILEY, BLAINE CO., ST. CHARLES BORROMEO (1881)
313 1st. Ave. S., Hailey, 83333. Tel: 208-788-3024; Email: stcharleshailey@gmail.com. P.O. Box 789, Hailey, 83333. Rev. Justin Brady; Deacon Luis Ruiz.
Catechesis Religious Program—315 First Ave. S., Hailey, 83333. Tel: 208-788-4742. Students 51.
Chapel—Fairfield, Immaculate Conception.

HOMEDALE, OWYHEE CO., ST. HUBERT, Merged with St. Mary's, Caldwell and Sacred Hearts of Jesus and Mary, Parma to form Our Lady of the Valley, Caldwell.

HORSESHOE BEND, BOISE CO., OUR LADY QUEEN OF ANGELS CHAPEL, Closed. See Holy Apostle, Meridian for details.

IDAHO CITY, BOISE CO., ST. JOSEPH'S CHAPEL, See separate listing.
504 Randolph Ave., Melba, 83641. Tel: 208-466-7031. 1515 8th St. S., Nampa, 83651. Rev. Caleb Vogel.

IDAHO FALLS, BONNEVILLE CO.
1—CHRIST THE KING, Merged with Holy Rosary, Idaho Falls to form Blessed John Paul II Parish, Idaho Falls.
2—HOLY ROSARY, Merged with Christ the King, Idaho Falls to form Blessed John Paul II Parish, Idaho Falls.
3—ST. JOHN PAUL II PARISH
145 E. 9th St., Idaho Falls, 83404. Tel: 208-522-4366; Email: jpii@cableone.net; Web: ifcatholics.net. Very Rev. Raul R. Covarrubias, V.F.; Rev. Carlos Rosero, Parochial Vicar; Deacons Alvaro Ponce; Wence Rodriquez; Chris Reilly; Tom Middleton; Jason Batalden; John Salisbury, Business Mgr.
School—Holy Rosary Bi-Parish Catholic School, (Grades PreSchool-6), 161 9th St., Idaho Falls, 83404. Tel: 208-522-7781; Fax: 208-522-7782; Email: hrsoffice@cableone.net; Web: www.holyrosaryschoolif.org. Carina VanPelt, Prin. Lay Teachers 8; Students 160.
Catechesis Religious Program—Email: johnpaulre@cableone.net. Jodi Bright, D.R.E. Students 175.
Stations—Roberts, St. Anthony's—Roberts.
Mud Lake, St. Ann's, Mud Lake.

JEROME, JEROME CO., ST. JEROME'S (1909) Rev. Adrian Vazquez; Deacon John Baumbach.
Res.: 216 2nd Ave. E., Box 169, Jerome, 83338.
Tel: 208-324-8794; Fax: 208-324-4141; Email: stjerome@cableone.net; Email: officemanager@stjeromeid.org; Web: www.stjeromeidaho.org.
Catechesis Religious Program—Generations of Faith, Email: stjeromecoordinator@gmail.com. Liliana Maciel, D.R.E. Students 239.

KAMIAH, LEWIS CO., ST. CATHERINE OF SIENA (1964) Rev. Sipho Mathabela, Admin.
Res.: 407 7th St., Box 685, Kamiah, 83536-0685.
Tel: 208-935-2130; Fax: 208-476-5121; Email: saintcatherinesparish@hotmail.com; Web: www.saintcatherines.weebly.com.
Catechesis Religious Program—Jeanie Stettler, D.R.E. Students 35.

KELLOGG, SHOSHONE CO., ST. RITA'S
27 Kellogg Ave., Kellogg, 83837-2626.
Tel: 208-784-7361. Very Rev. Timothy M. Ritchey, V.F., Priest Mod.; Rev. Jerome Montez, O.S.B., Sacramental Min.

KEUTERVILLE, IDAHO CO., HOLY CROSS, Merged with St. Mary's, Cottonwood.

LEWISTON, NEZ PERCE CO.
1—ALL SAINTS CATHOLIC PARISH
3330 14th St., Lewiston, 83501. Revs. Bradley Neely; Nathan Dail, Parochial Vicar; Deacons George Ivory; Christopher Davies.
Res.: 1318 19th St., Lewiston, 83501.
Tel: 208-743-1012 (Church); Fax: 208-746-7134; Email: questions@allsaintslewiston.org; Web: www.allsaintslewiston.org.
Res.: 3727 17th St., Lewiston, 83501.
School—All Saints Catholic School, (Grades PreK-6), 3326 14th St., Lewiston, 83501. Tel: 208-743-4411; Fax: 208-743-9563; Email: dhammrich@ascs-pk6.org; Email: allsaints@ascs-pk6.org; Web: www.ascs-pk6.org. Denise Hammrich, Prin. Lay Teachers 7; Students 167.
Catechesis Religious Program—Students 110.
2—ALL SAINTS CATHOLIC CHURCH - OUR LADY OF LOURDES CHURCH, Merged with All Saints Catholic Church - St. Stanislaus Church & All Saints Catholic Chuch - St. James Church, Lewiston to form All Saints Catholic Church, Lewiston.
3—ALL SAINTS CATHOLIC CHURCH - ST. STANISLAUS CHURCH, Merged with All Saints Catholic Church - Our Lady of Lourdes Church, Lewiston & All Saints Catholic Church - St. James Catholic Church to form All Saints Catholic Church, Lewiston.
4—ALL SAINTS CATHOLIC CHURCH - ST. JAMES CHURCH (1970) Merged with All Saints Catholic Church - Our Lady of Lourdes Church, Lewiston & All Saints Catholic Church - St. Stanislaus Church, Lewiston to form All Saints Catholic Church, Lewiston.

MCCALL, VALLEY CO., OUR LADY OF THE LAKE (1916)
Rev. Steven Rukavina.
Res.: 501 Cross Rd., Box 821, McCall, 83638.
Tel: 208-634-5474; Fax: 208-634-5475; Email: info@ollidaho.org; Web: www.ollidaho.org.
Catechesis Religious Program—Debbie McCoy, D.R.E. Students 26.
Station—St. Katharine Drexel, Cascade.
Chapel—Riggins, St. Jerome's.

MERIDIAN, ADA CO.
1—HOLY APOSTLES (1998) [CEM]
6300 N. Meridian Rd., Meridian, 83646.
Tel: 208-888-1182; Email: llawrence@holyapostles.net; Web: www.holyapostlesmeridian.net. P.O. Box 708, Meridian, 83680. Revs. Len MacMillan; John Legerski, Parochial Vicar; Deacons Robert Barros-Bailey; Thomas Blazek; Malherbe Desert; Ralph Flager; John Lee; Gerald D. Pera; Charles Rasmussen; Bernard Rekiere; David Shackley; Ed Spano; Patty Blazek, Pastoral Assoc.; Midge Lee, Pastoral Assoc.; Sarah Clayton, Dir. of Comm.; Jake Ineck, Music Min.; Monique Kilroy, Parish Nurse; Lisa Lawrence, Bookkeeper; Mary Ossenkop, Registrar; Mary Wax, RCIA Coord.
School—St. Ignatius Catholic School, (Grades PreK-8), 6180 N. Meridian Rd., Meridian, 83646.
Tel: 208-888-4759; Email: akane@stignatiusmeridian.org; Web: www.stignatiusmeridian.org. Andi Kane, Prin.; Mandi Ganetti, Librarian. Lay Teachers 24; Students 454.
Holy Apostles Columbarium— (2008) .
Catechesis Religious Program—Email: bhutson@holyapostles.net. Blanca Hutson, Co-D.R.E.; Theresa Malouf, Co-D.R.E.; Rusty Bang, Youth Min. Students 781.
2—HOLY SPIRIT, Merged Sacramental records are at Holy Apostles, Meridian.

MOSCOW, LATAH CO.
1—ST. AUGUSTINE'S, (Catholic Center) Rev. Chase R. Hasenoehrl; Deacons Verne Geidl; Dennis Thomas.
Res.: 628 Deakin Ave., P.O. Box 3457, Moscow, 83843. Tel: 208-882-4613; Fax: 208-882-1756; Email: vandalcatholic@outlook.com; Web: www.vandalcatholics.com.
Station—Potlatch, St. Mary's, 725 Spruce St., P.O. Box 3457, Potlatch, 83855.
2—ST. MARY'S (1882)
618 E. First St., Moscow, 83843. Tel: 208-882-4813. P.O. Box 9106, Moscow, 83843. Very Rev. Joseph F. McDonald III, J.C.L., V.F.; Deacon George Canney.
School—St. Mary's School, (Grades K-8), 412 N. Monroe, Moscow, 83843. Tel: 208-882-2121; Email: jbeller@stmarysmoscow.com; Email: office@stmarysmoscow.com; Web: www.stmarysmoscow.com. Dr. Jennifer Beller, Ph.D., Prin. Lay Teachers 10; Students 86.
Catechesis Religious Program—Students 63.
Station—Genesee, St. Mary's, Genessee.

MOUNTAIN HOME, ELMORE CO., OUR LADY OF GOOD COUNSEL
342 E. Jackson St., Mountain Home, 83647.
Tel: 208-587-3046; Email: psalinas@olgcid.org. P.O. Box 310, Mountain Home, 83647. Rev. German Osorio.
Church: 115 N. 4th St. E., Box 310, Mountain Home, 83647. Fax: 208-587-5114; Web: www.olgcid.org.
Res.: 875 E. 13th North St., Mountain Home, 83647.
Catechesis Religious Program—Lisa Knox, D.R.E. Students 90.
Chapel—Bruneau, St. Bridget, 28672 Hyde St., Bruneau, 83604.
Station—Glenns Ferry, Our Lady of Limerick, 415 S. Commercial, Glenn's Ferry, 83623.
Chapel—Grand View, St. Henry's, 510 Idaho St., P.O. Box 310, Grand View, 83624.

NAMPA, CANYON CO.
1—OUR LADY OF GUADALUPE CHAPEL, Closed. See St. Paul's, Nampa for details.
2—ST. PAUL'S (1898) [CEM]
510 W. Roosevelt Ave., Nampa, 83686.
Tel: 208-466-7031; Fax: 208-467-7203; Email: cvogel@stpaulsnampa.org; Web: www.nampacatholic.church. Mailing Address: 1515 8th St., S., Nampa, 83651. Revs. Caleb Vogel; John Kucera, Parochial Vicar; Deacons Michael Collins; Jose Luis Granados; Morrie Berriochoa, Business Mgr.

School—St. Paul's School, (Grades PreSchool-8), 1515 8th St. South, Nampa, 83651.
Tel: 208-467-3601; Fax: 208-467-6485; Email: scoulter@stpaulsnampa.org; Web: www.stpaulsidaho.org. Scott Coulter, Prin.; Cheryl Brasil, Librarian. Lay Teachers 14; Students 160.
Catechesis Religious Program—Email: mlinan@stpaulsnampa.org. Marisela Linan, D.R.E. Students 337.
Station—Melba, St. Joseph.
Chapels—Silver City, Our Lady of Tears—
Oreana, Our Lady Queen of Heaven.

NEW PLYMOUTH, PAYETTE CO., ST. ALOYSIUS, Merged to form Corpus Christi Catholic Community, Fruitland.

NEZPERCE, LEWIS CO., HOLY TRINITY, See SS. Peter and Paul, Grangeville for details.
P.O. Box 65, Nezperce, 83543. Rev. John Gathungu, Admin.
Res.: 506 Willow St., Nez Perce, 83543.
Tel: 208-937-1095; Email: pastor@stspeterandpaulparish.org; Web: www.stspeterandpaulparish.org.
Catechesis Religious Program— (Combined with SS. Peter and Paul, Grangeville.) Students 21.

OREANA, OWYHEE CO., QUEEN OF HEAVEN CHAPEL, See separate listing. See St. Paul's, Nampa for details.
8102 Oreana Loop Rd., Nampa, 83650.
Tel: 208-466-7031. 1515 8th St. S., Nampa, 83651. Rev. Caleb Vogel.

OROFINO, CLEARWATER CO., ST. THERESA OF THE LITTLE FLOWER (1926) Rev. Sipho Mathabela, Admin.
Res.: 446 Brown Ave., Box 1169, Orofino, 83544.
Tel: 208-476-5121; Fax: 208-476-0792; Email: st.theresa@frontier.com; Web: www.st-theresacatholicchurch.org.
Catechesis Religious Program—Students 21.
Chapel—Pierce, Our Lady of Woodland.

PARMA, CANYON CO., SACRED HEARTS OF JESUS AND MARY, Merged with St. Mary's, Caldwell and St. Hubert's, Homedale to form Our Lady of the Valley, Caldwell.

PAYETTE, PAYETTE CO., HOLY FAMILY, Merged with St. Aloysius, New Plymouth to form Corpus Christi, Fruitland.

POCATELLO, BANNOCK CO.
1—ST. ANTHONY'S, Merged with St. Joseph, Pocatello and St. Paul, Chubbuck to form Holy Spirit Catholic Community, Pocatello.
2—HOLY SPIRIT CATHOLIC COMMUNITY (2003)
524 N. 7th Ave., Pocatello, 83201. Tel: 208-232-1196; Fax: 208-234-1624; Email: holyspirit@hscc.org;
Tel: www.hscc.org. Very Rev. Henry Carmona, J.C.L., V.F.; Deacon Scott Pearhill.
School—Holy Spirit Catholic Community School, (Grades PreK-8), 540 N. 7th Ave., Pocatello, 83201.
Tel: 208-232-5763; Fax: 208-234-1624; Email: corgiatna@hscsidaho.org; Email: hennessypo@hscsidaho.org; Web: www.holyspiritcs.com. Nancy Corgiat, Prin.; Sarah Clarkson, Librarian. Clergy 2; Lay Teachers 16; Students 174.
Catechesis Religious Program—Students 95.
St. John's Catholic Student Center—920 E. Lovejoy St., I.S.U., Box 8129, Pocatello, 83209-0001.
Tel: 208-233-0880; Fax: 208-233-5745.
Chapels—Pocatello, St. Anthony of Padua Chapel—504 N. 7th Ave., Pocatello, 83201.
Pocatello, St. Joseph Chapel, 439 N. Hayes St., Pocatello, 83204.
3—ST. JOSEPH'S, Merged with St. Anthony, Pocatello and St. Paul, Chubbuck to form Holy Spirit Catholic Community, Pocatello.

POST FALLS, KOOTENAI CO., ST. GEORGE'S (1917)
2004 N. Lucas St., Post Falls, 83854.
Tel: 208-773-4715, Ext. 20; Email: pfstgeorge@frontier.com. Very Rev. Timothy M. Ritchey, V.F.; Rev. Constance Swai, Parochial Vicar; Deacons Michael J. Pentony; Jorge Gonzalez; Erik Schirmer; Rosemary McDougall, Parish Nurse.
Res.: P.O. Box 10, Post Falls, 83877.
Tel: 208-773-4715; Fax: 208-777-1549; Email: fathertimritchey@gmail.com; Web: www.stgeorgesidaho.com.
Catechesis Religious Program—Tina Laguna, D.R.E. Students 107.
Chapels—Rathdrum, St. Stanislaus—
Spirit Lake, St. Joseph.

POTLATCH, LATAH CO., ST. MARY'S STATION, See separate listing. See Contact Info for St. Mary's Parish, Moscow.

PRIEST RIVER, BONNER CO., ST. CATHERINE'S
P.O. Box 445, Priest River, 83856. Email: stcatherineparish445@gmail.com. Rev. G. Peter Fernando, Admin.
Res.: 403 Summit Blvd., Priest River, 83856.
Tel: 208-448-2127; Email: petefdo@hotmail.com.
Catechesis Religious Program—Students 1.
Station—St. Blanche, 27832 Hwy. 57, Priest Lake, 83856.

RATHDRUM, KOOTENAI CO., ST. STANISLAUS CHAPEL, Closed. See St. George, Post Falls for details.

RUPERT, MINIDOKA CO., ST. NICHOLAS (1908)
802 F St., Rupert, 83350-0115.
Tel: 208-436-3781, Ext. 101; Email: stnich@pmt.org; Web: stnicholascc.com. P.O. Box 115, Rupert, 83350. Rev. Francisco H. Godinez, J.C.L.; Deacons Jaime Alamillo; Paul Henscheid.
School—St. Nicholas School, (Grades PreSchool-6), 806 F. St., P.O. Box 26, Rupert, 83350.
Tel: 208-436-6320; Fax: 208-436-9158; Email: principal1@stnicholasrupert.org; Web: www.stnicholasrupert.org. Wes Ramaley, Prin.; Page Eberhardt, Librarian. Lay Teachers 13; Students 141.
Catechesis Religious Program—Jasmyn Rogge, D.R.E. Students 177.

ST. ANTHONY, FREMONT CO., MARY IMMACULATE
328 W. 1st N., St. Anthony, 83445. Tel: 208-624-7459 ; Fax: 208-624-7479; Email: idahocatholic@yahoo.com; Web: www.uppervalleycatholic.com. P.O. Box 527, St. Anthony, 83445. Rev. Javier Corral Pina.
Catechesis Religious Program—Bernice Ojeda, D.R.E.; Janeth Rodriguez, D.R.E. (St. Patrick's). Students 96.
Stations—Rexburg, St. Patrick's—38 S. 3rd St. W., Rexburg, 83440.
Driggs, Good Shepherd, 2559 S. Hwy. 33, Driggs, 83422. Michelle Schroeder, D.R.E.; Judy Lou Davis, D.R.E.
Chapel—Island Park, Chapel of the Pines, 4100 S. Big Springs Loop Rd., Island Park, 83429.

SAINT MARIES, BENEWAH CO., ST. MARY IMMACULATE (1912) Very Rev. Timothy M. Ritchey, V.F., Priest Mod.; Rev. Jerome Montez, O.S.B., Sacramental Min.; Deacon Floyd Turner.
Res.: 921 W. Jefferson Ave., P.O. Box 335, St. Maries, 83861. Tel: 208-245-2977; Fax: 208-245-3143 ; Email: fathertimritchey@gmail.com; Web: www.stmariescatholic.com.
Catechesis Religious Program—Students 9.
Station—Harrison, Our Lady of Perpetual Help, 100 Frederick Ave., Harrison, 83833. Tel: 208-539-4130.

SALMON, LEMHI CO., ST. CHARLES aka St. Charles Borromeo (1908)
505 Hope Ave., Salmon, 83467. Tel: 208-756-2432; Email: stcharles@custertel.net; Email: stcharlesfinancial@custertel.net; Web: www.catholicsalmon.com. P.O. Box 550, Salmon, 83467. Rev. Dat Vu; Deacon Dennis Rotondo.
Catechesis Religious Program—Faith Ryan, D.R.E. (Elementary). Students 23.
Stations—Arco, St. Ann—342 Lost River Ave., Arco, 83213. Web: www.charlessalmon.com. P.O. Box 1181, Salmon, 83467.
Challis, St. Louise, 1285 Pleasant Ave., Challis, 83226. Web: www.catholicsalmon.com. P.O. Box 572, Challis, 83226.
Catechesis Religious Program—Students 11.
Mackay, St. Barbara, 505 Park St., Mackay, 83251.
Chapel—Leadore, St. Joseph, 3rd St. & Galena, Salmon, 83467. Tel: 208-756-2432.
Catechesis Religious Program—Students 5.

SANDPOINT, BONNER CO., ST. JOSEPH'S (1907)
601 S. Lincoln Ave., Sandpoint, 83864-0279.
Tel: 208-263-3720; Fax: 208-265-4974; Email: cathy@st-joseph-church.net; Web: st-joseph-church.net. P.O. Box 279, Sandpoint, 83864. Rev. Dennis C. Day, V.F.
Chapel—Clark Fork, Sacred Heart.

SHOSHONE, LINCOLN CO., ST. PETER'S
215 W. B St., Shoshone, 83352. Tel: 208-934-5634. P.O. Box 336, Shoshone, 83352. Rev. Jose T. Ramirez; Deacon Javier Leija.
Catechesis Religious Program—Jaime Novis, D.R.E. Included with St. Elizabeth's, Gooding. Students 30.

SODA SPRINGS, CARIBOU CO., GOOD SHEPHERD CATHOLIC COMMUNITY (1910)
99 W. Center St., Soda Springs, 83276.
Tel: 208-547-3200; Email: GoodShepherdIdaho@gmail.com. Rev. Marcos Sanchez; Deacon David McCarthy.
Catechesis Religious Program—Students 64.
Chapels—Montpelier, Blessed Sacrament—270 N. 8th St., Montpelier, 83254.
Soda Springs, St. Mary's.
Preston, St. Peter's, 302 E. Oneida St., Preston, 83263.
Lava Hot Springs, Our Lady of Lourdes, 132 S. First St. W., Lava Hot Springs, 83246.
St. Paul's, 233 Samaria Ln., Malad, 83252.

SUN VALLEY, BLAINE CO., OUR LADY OF THE SNOWS (1970)
206 E. Sun Valley Rd., Sun Valley, 83353. P.O. Box 1650, Sun Valley, 83353. Rev. Justin Brady.
Res.: 213 Mariposa Rd., Sun Valley, 83340.
Tel: 208-622-3432; Fax: 208-622-4348; Email: parishofficeOLS@gmail.com; Web: www.svcatholic.org.
Catechesis Religious Program—Martha Deffe, D.R.E. Students 59.

TWIN FALLS, TWIN FALLS CO.
1—ST. EDWARD THE CONFESSOR (1920) Very Rev. Julio Vicente, V.F.; Rev. Joseph Lustig, Parochial Vicar; Deacon John Hurley; Rhonda Eldredge, Business Mgr.
Res.: 212 7th Ave. E., Twin Falls, 83301-6321.
Tel: 208-733-3907; Fax: 208-733-3935; Email: mstmarie@cableone.net; Web: www.stedschurch.org.
School—St. Edward the Confessor School, (Grades K-5), 139 Sixth Ave. E., Twin Falls, 83301-6316.
Tel: 208-734-3872; Fax: 208-734-1214; Email: hildangela@sainteddie.org; Web: www.sainteddie.org. Angela Hild, Prin.; Adriana Saldana, Librarian. Lay Teachers 9; Students 135.
Catechesis Religious Program—
Tel: 208-733-3907, Ext. 108; Email: rosasj@cableone.net. Juana Rosas, D.R.E.; Lisa Gifford, Youth Min. Students 320.
OUR LADY OF GUADALUPE, Merged with St. Edward's, Twin Falls to form St. Edward The Confessor, Twin Falls.
2—ST. EDWARD'S, Merged with Our Lady of Guadalupe, Twin Falls to form St. Edward The Confessor, Twin Falls.

WALLACE, SHOSHONE CO., ST. ALPHONSUS, Very Rev. Timothy M. Ritchey, V.F., Priest Mod.; Rev. Jerome Montez, O.S.B., Sacramental Min.
Res.: 214 Pine St., Wallace, 83873. Tel: 208-752-3551 ; Fax: 208-784-7361; Email: fathertimritchey@gmail.com.
Catechesis Religious Program—
Chapel—Mullan, St. Michael's, 3rd & Park St., Mullan, 83846. Tel: 208-539-4130.

WEISER, WASHINGTON CO., ST. AGNES (1878)
P.O. Box 87, Weiser, 83672. Rev. Gabriel Morales, Admin.; Deacon Ignacio Cornejo.
Res.: 214 E. Liberty, Weiser, 83672.
Tel: 208-549-0088; Fax: 208-549-1080; Email: stagnes@catholicweiser.org; Web: www.catholicweiser.org.
Catechesis Religious Program—Tel: 208-550-9600; Email: vmvanness@gmail.com. Vickie VanNess, D.R.E. Students 106.
Stations—Cambridge, Holy Rosary—P.O. Box 335, Cambridge, 83610-0335. Tel: 208-257-3559.
Council, St. Jude the Apostle, 2054 Hwy. 95 N., Council, 83612. Tel: 208-253-6470.

WENDELL, GOODING CO., ST. ANTHONY'S, See separate listing. See St. Elizabeth's, Gooding for details.
585 2nd Ave. E., Wendell, 83355. Tel: 208-934-5634; Email: stelizabethgooding@yahoo.com. P.O. Box 811, Wendell, 83355. Rev. Jose T. Ramirez; Deacon Javier Leija.

Chaplains of Public Institutions

BOISE. *St. Luke's Rehabilitation*, 204 Fort Pl., 83702.
Tel: 208-350-7504; Email: rbarrosbailey@rcdb.org. Attended by St. John's Cathedral, 775 N. 8th St., Boise, ID 83702. Tel: 208-342-3511.
St. Luke's Medical Center, 190 E. Bannock, 83712.
Tel: 208-342-1311; Email: rbarrosbailey@rcdb.org. Attended by St. John Cathedral, 775 N. 8th St., Boise, ID, 83702. Tel: 208-342-3511.
VA Hospital, 5th St. & Fort St., 83401. Email: rbarrosbailey@rcdb.org. VacantAttended by St. John's Cathedral, 775 N. 8th St., Boise, ID, 83702. Tel: 208-342-3511.

COEUR D'ARLENE. *St. Joan of Arc Chapel*, 773 N. 11th St., Coeur d'Alene, 83814. Tel: 208-660-6036; Email: pastor@stjoanarc.com. Rev. Dennis M. Gordon, F.S.S.P.

COTTONWOOD. *Monastery of St. Gertrude*, HC 3 Box 121, Cottonwood, 83522-9408. Tel: 208-962-3224; Fax: 208-962-5031; Email: monastery@stgertrudes.org; Web: www.stgertrudes.org. Rev. Meinrad Schallberger, O.S.B. Nuns 37.

On Duty Outside the Diocese:
Rev.—
Restrepo, Jairo, J.C.L.

On Sabbatical:
Rev.—
Wekerle, Ronald, V.G.

Retired:
Rev. Msgrs.—
Morgan, John W., (Retired)
Schumacher, Andrew, (Retired)
Wassmuth, Dennis, (Retired)
Very Rev.—
Blankinship, Calvin L. Jr., V.F., (Retired)
Revs.—
Camargo, Carlos E., (Retired)
Caulfield, Sean, (Retired)
Dennis, Patrick, (Retired)
Faucher, W. Thomas, J.C.L., (Retired)
Fernandez, Marcellus, (Retired)
Fraser, Donald D., (Retired)
Garatea, Juan M., (Retired), (In Spain)
Haldane, Richard S., V.F., (Retired)

Keller, Thomas, (Retired)
Kish, Leslie P., V.F., (Retired)
Koelsch, John, (Retired)
LaChance, Roger, (Retired)
Loucks, Thomas J., (Retired)
Medina, Mauricio, (Retired)
Muha, Joseph, (Retired)
Riffle, David, (Retired)
Schmidt, Joseph F., (Retired)
Segatta, Bruno, (Retired)
Taylor, William, (Retired)
Terriquez, Enrique, V.F., (Retired).

Permanent Deacons:
Aaron, Louis, Our Lady of the Rosary, Boise
Alamillo, Jaime, St. Nicholas, Rupert
Almeida, Humberto, Our Lady of the Valley, Caldwell
Anderson, Gary, Our Lady of the Rosary, Boise
Aslett, Devon H., (Retired)
Ayala, Jose, St. Mary's, Boise
Barros-Bailey, Robert, Holy Apostles, Meridian
Batalden, Jason, St. John Paul II, Idaho Falls
Baumbach, John, (Retired)
Betikoetxea, Imanol, St. Mary's, Boise
Blazek, Thomas, Holy Apostles, Meridian
Blythe, Don, Risen Christ, Boise
Bonney, Richard II, Sacred Heart, Boise
Booth, William, (Retired)
Bowen, James E., (Retired)
Brinegar, Clyde, St. Mark's, Boise
Burns, William, St. John's, Boise
Canney, George, (Retired)
Carpenter, John, St. Mary's, Boise
Chester, Mackensey, St. Paul Student Center, Boise
Collins, Michael, (Retired)
Cornejo, Ignacio, St. Agnes, Weiser
Daigh, Raymond, (Outside the Diocese)
Davies, Christopher, All Saints, Lewiston
Desert, Malherbe, Holy Apostles, Meridian
Dessert, Michael, (Retired)
Dominick, Thomas, St. John's Cathedral, Boise
Eisenbeiss, Michael, (Retired)
Ellis, Kenneth, (Outside the Diocese)
Fadness, Eugene, St. Mary's, Boise
Flager, Ralph, Holy Apostles, Meridian
Flowers, Brian, Sacred Heart, Boise
Gary, Jude, (Retired)
Geidl, Verne, St. Augustine's, Moscow
Germain, Stephen, (Retired)
Gonzalez, Jorge, (Retired)
Granados, Jose Luis, St. Paul's, Nampa
Harris, C. J., (Retired)
Harris, Kerry, Our Lady of the Valley, Caldwell
Henscheid, Paul, (Retired)
Herrett, James, (Retired), St. Edward's, Twin Falls
Hess, Francis, (Retired)
Hiner, Kenneth, (Retired)
Hurley, John, (Retired)
Kearns, Patrick, Our Lady of the Valley, Caldwell
Kelly, James, (Retired)
Lee, John, Holy Apostles, Meridian
Leija, Javier, St. Elizabeth's, Gooding; St. Peter's, Shoshone
Lowe, Michael, St. Mark's, Boise
McCarthy, David, Good Shepherd, Soda Springs
McCaughey, James, Immaculate Conception, Buhl; St. Catherines, Hagerman
McKinley, John D. Jr., (Retired)
McSwain, Gary, (Retired)
Murphy, Pierce, (Outside the Diocese)
Nelson, Terry, St. Mark's, Boise
Nicholas, Joseph, (Outside the Diocese)
O'Neill, Derrick, St. John's, Boise
Pasker, Jim, St. Mark's, Boise
Pearhill, Scott, Holy Spirit Catholic Community, Pocatello
Pelowitz, Jack, (Retired)
Pentony, Michael J., St. George's, Post Falls
Pera, Gerald D., (Retired)
Petzak, William, (Retired)
Pierce, Ralph, (Retired)
Ponce, Alvaro, St. John Paul II, Idaho Falls
Powers, Jeff, St. Bernard's, Blackfoot
Rasmussen, Charles, (Retired)
Reilly, Christopher, St. John Paul II, Idaho Falls
Rekiere, Bernard, (Retired)
Rodriguez, Wence, (Retired)
Rodriquez, Joseph, St. Marks's, Boise
Roeper, Chris, Sacred Heart, Emmett
Rotondo, Dennis, St. Louise, Challis
Ruiz, Luis, St. Charles, Hailey
Rust, Robert, (Outside the Diocese)
Salazar, Harley, (Outside the Diocese)
Schirmer, Erik, St. George's, Post Falls
Schmidt, Fred, (Retired)
Servatius, Michael, Our Lady of the Rosary, Boise
Shaber, Alan, Sacred Heart, Emmett
Shaber, Eric, St. Pius X, Coeur d'Alene
Shackley, David, Holy Apostles, Meridian
Sokolowski, Don, (Retired)
Solbrig, Charles W., (Retired)
Souza, Edward, (Outside the Diocese)
Tamayo, Juan, (Retired)
Thomas, Dennis, St. Augustine's, Moscow
Turner, Floyd, St. Mary Immaculate, St. Maries
Turpin, Tom, Corpus Christi, Fruitland
Vawser, Daniel, Sacred Heart, Boise
Vermaas, Ted, Risen Christ, Boise
Vietri, Nick, (Retired).

INSTITUTIONS LOCATED IN DIOCESE

[A] HIGH SCHOOLS, INTER-PAROCHIAL

BOISE. *Bishop Kelly High School*, 7009 Franklin Rd., 83709-0922. Tel: 208-375-6010; Fax: 208-375-3626; Email: mcaldwell@bk.org; Web: www.bk.org. Richard Raimondi, Pres.; Mike Caldwell, Prin.; Stephany Herrera, Vice Prin.; Cheryl Hutchinson, Vice Prin.; Kit Parker, Librarian. Lay Teachers 58; Students 842.

COEUR D'ALENE. *Holy Family Catholic School of Coeur d'Alene*, (Grades PreSchool-8), 3005 W. Kathleen Ave., Coeur d'Alene, 83815. Tel: 208-765-4327; Fax: 208-664-2903; Email: barkoosh@hfcs.net; Email: info@hfcs.net; Web: www.hfcs-cda.org. Bridgit Arkoosh, Prin.; Beth Franz, Librarian. Lay Teachers 13; Students 224.

[B] GENERAL HOSPITALS

BOISE. *Saint Alphonsus Health System, Inc.*, 1055 N. Curtis Rd., 83706. Tel: 208-367-2000; Fax: 208-367-3966; Web: www.saintalphonsus.org. Odette Bolano, Pres. Total Staff 372.

Saint Alphonsus Regional Medical Center, Inc. (1894) Saint Alphonsus Health System, 1055 N. Curtis Rd., 83706-1370. Tel: 208-367-2121; Email: odette.bolano@saintalphonsus.org; Web: www.saintalphonsus.org. Odette Bolano, Pres.
Saint Alphonsus Diversified Care, Inc.
Saint Alphonsus Regional Medical Center, Inc.
Saint Alphonsus Building Company, Inc.
Saint Alphonsus Health System, Inc. Bed Capacity 387; Sisters of the Holy Cross 2; Tot Asst. Annually 510,000; Total Staff 2,300.

COTTONWOOD. *St. Mary's Hospital*, 701 Lewiston St., P.O. Box 137, Cottonwood, 83522. Tel: 208-962-3251; Fax: 208-962-3251; Email: barbara.bielenberg@smh-cvhc.org. Lenne Bonner, Pres.; Sr. Barbara A. Bielenberg, O.S.B., Dir., Mission Svc.; Matthew Forge, CAO; Rev. Meinrad Schallberger, O.S.B., Chap. Sponsored by Sisters of St. Benedict, Duluth, MN through Essentia Health. Bed Capacity 25; Sisters 1; Tot Asst. Annually 22,606; Total Staff 243.

NAMPA. *Saint Alphonsus Medical Center - Nampa Inc.*, 4300 E. Flamingo Ave., Nampa, 83686. Tel: 208-205-0055; Fax: 208-205-0048. Travis Leach, Pres. Bed Capacity 109; Tot Asst. Annually 123,000; Total Staff 789.

[C] MONASTERIES AND RESIDENCES OF PRIESTS AND BROTHERS

JEROME. *Monastery of the Ascension*, 541 E. 100 S., Jerome, 83338. Tel: 208-324-2377, Ext. 256; Email: monbusoffice@gmail.com; Email: boniface@idahomonks.org; Web: www.idahomonks.org. Revs. Boniface Lautz, O.S.B., Prior; Andrew Baumgartner, O.S.B., Subprior; Meinrad Schallberger, O.S.B.; Hugh Feiss, O.S.B.; Ezekiel Lotz, O.S.B.; Jerome Montez, O.S.B.; Rt. Rev. Kenneth C. Hein, O.S.B., (Retired); Bros. Sylvester Sonnen, O.S.B.; Selby Coffman, O.S.B.; Tobiah Urrutia, O.S.B.; John Ugolik. The Benedictine Monks of Idaho, Inc.
Legal Title: The Benedictine Monks of Idaho, Inc.

LEMHI. *Hermitage of St. Joseph*, P.O. Box 37, Lemhi, 83465. Tel: 208-350-7504; Email: cwickham@rcdb.org. Bro. Henry Soto, Treas. Hermits of Mt. Carmel.

[D] CONVENTS AND RESIDENCES OF SISTERS

COTTONWOOD. *Monastery of St. Gertrude, Motherhouse and Novitiate*, 465 Keuterville Rd., Cottonwood, 83522-5183. Rev. Meinrad Schallberger, O.S.B., Chap.; Sisters Mary Forman, O.S.B., Prioress; Mary Marge Goeckner, O.S.B., Asst. Prioress. Sisters of St. Benedict 37.

MESA. *Marymount Hermitage, Inc., Hermit Sisters of Mary*, 2150 Hermitage Ln., Mesa, 83643-5005. Tel: 208-256-4354 (Message Only); Email: marymount@ctcweb.net; Web: www.marymount-hermitage.org. Sr. Mary Beverly Greger, H.S.M., Supr. Sisters 1.

POST FALLS. *Carmel of Jesus, Mary and Joseph*, 18772 W. Riverview Dr., Post Falls, 83854. Tel: 208-660-2603.

[E] RETREAT HOUSES

BOISE. *Nazareth* aka Nazareth Retreat Center, 4450 N. Five Mile Rd., 83713-2709. Tel: 208-375-2932; Fax: 208-376-5787; Web: www.nazarethretreatcenter.org. Sr. Susie Johnston, Dir.

COTTONWOOD. *Spirit Center*, 465 Keuterville Rd., Cottonwood, 83522-5183. Tel: 208-962-2000; Email: spiritcenter@stgertrudes.org; Web: www.stgertrudes.org. Krista Green, Dir.

[F] CAMPUS MINISTRY

BOISE. *Boise State University, St. Paul's Catholic Center*, 1915 University Dr., 83706. Tel: 208-343-2128; Fax: 208-367-1110; Email: frtom@broncocatholic.org; Email: operations@broncocatholic.org; Web: www.broncocatholic.org. Revs. Tom Lankenau, Chap.; Radmar Jao, S.J., Co-Chap. & Campus Minister.

CALDWELL. *The College of Idaho*, c/o Our Lady of The Valley, 1122 W. Linden St., Caldwell, 83605. Tel: 208-459-3653; Fax: 208-454-8789; Email: fr.rob@me.com. Cindi Duft, Catholic Ministry Coord.

COEUR D'ALENE. *North Idaho College*, St. Pius X, 625 Haycraft Ave., Coeur d'Alene, 83815. Tel: 208-765-5108; Fax: 208-664-5325; Email: triple.eff@gmail.com. Very Rev. Francisco Q. Flores, V.F.

LEWISTON. *Lewis Clark State College*, All Saints Catholic Community, 3330 14th St., Lewiston, 83501. Tel: 208-743-1012; Fax: 208-746-7134; Email: frneely@allsaintslewiston.org. Rev. Bradley Neely.

MOSCOW. *St. Augustine Catholic Center*, 628 Deakin Ave., Box 3457, Moscow, 83843-1911. Tel: 208-882-4613; Email: stauggies@gmail.com; Email: director@vandalcatholics.com; Web: vandalcatholics.org. Rev. Chase R. Hasenoehrl. (Serving University of Idaho).

POCATELLO. *Idaho State University, St. John's Catholic Student Center* aka Bengal Catholics, 917 E. Lovejoy St., Pocatello, 83201. Tel: 208-233-0880; Email: director@bengalcatholics.com; Web: www.bengalcatholics.com. 921 S. 8th St., Box 8129, Pocatello, 83209. David O'Neill, Campus Min.

TWIN FALLS. *College of Southern Idaho*, 630 Falls Ave., Twin Falls, 83301-6321. Tel: 208-733-3907; Fax: 208-733-3935. 212 7th Ave. E., Twin Falls, 83301-6321. Very Rev. Michael A. St. Marie, V.F.; Rev. Joseph Lustig, Parochial Vicar. Attended by St. Edward the Confessor, Twin Falls.

[G] MISCELLANEOUS

BOISE. *Catholic Charities of Idaho, Inc.*, 7255 W. Franklin Rd., 83709. Tel: 208-345-6031; Fax: 208-345-5674; Email: dalles@ccidaho.org; Web: www.ccidaho.org. P.O. Box 190123, 83719. Douglas Alles, Exec. Dir.; Most Rev. Peter F. Christensen, D.D., Pres. Bd. of Dirs.; Sarah Dunn, Controller. Tot Asst. Annually 3,829; Total Staff 18.

Risen in Christ Prison Re-Entry Conference, 3217 W. Overland Rd., 83705. Tel: 208-331-8409; Email: john.dahl@svdpid.org; Web: www.svdpid.org. 7960 W. Northview St., 83704. Mike Gallagher, Pres.

**Society of St. Vincent de Paul - Southwest Idaho District Council*, 3217 W. Overland Rd., 83705. Tel: 208-344-5403; Email: john.dahl@svdpid.org; Web: svdpid.org. John Dahl, Pres.; Ralph May, Exec.; Diana Tetreault, Business Mgr.

**St. Vincent de Paul Society, St. John's Conference*, 775 N. 8th St., 83702. Tel: 208-331-2208; Email: john.dahl@svdpid.org; Web: www.svdpid.org. Kathy Dahl, Pres.

**St. Vincent de Paul Society, St. Mark's Conference*, 7960 Northview, 83704. Mary Kaineg, Pres.

**St. Vincent de Paul Society, Our Lady of the Rosary Conference*, 1500 E. Wright St., 83706-5358. Tel: 208-331-2208; Email: john.dahl@svdpid.org; Web: www.svdpid.org. 3217 W. Overland Rd., 83705. Brian Krueger, Pres.

**St. Vincent de Paul Society, Risen Christ Conference*, 11511 Lake Hazel Rd., 83709. Tel: 208-344-5403; Email: john.dahl@svdpid.org; Web: www.svdpid.org. Vicki Laidlaw, Pres.; Cathy Yoder, Pres. Total Assisted 375.

**St. Vincent de Paul Society, Sacred Heart Conference*, 811 S. Latah St., 83705. Tel: 208-331-8409; Email: john.dahl@svdpid.org; Web: www.svdpid.org. Sue Robinson, Pres.

**St. Vincent de Paul Society, Thrift Stores*, 6464 W. State St., 83703. Tel: 208-853-4921; Fax: 208-853-4935; Email: john.dahl@svdpid.org; Web: www.svdpid.org. Ralph May, Exec.; Vicky Rowell, Dir.

**Society of St. Vincent de Paul, Holy Apostles Conference*, 6300A N Meridian Rd., Meridian,

83646. Tel: 208-888-1182; Email: john.dahl@svdpid.org; Email: ralph.may@svdpid.org; Web: www.svdpid.org. Cathy Hagdone, Pres.

**Society of St. Vincent de Paul, Our Lady of Good Counsel Conference*, 342 E. Jackson St., Mountain Home, 83647. Tel: 208-331-2208; Email: john.dahl@svdpid.org; Web: www.svdpid.org. Elisa Knox, Pres.

**Society of St. Vincent de Paul, Our Lady of Guadalupe Conference*, 1515 8th St., S., Nampa, 83651. Tel: 208-466-3400; Email: john.dahl@svdpid.org; Web: www.svdpid.org. Maureen Coon, Pres.

**Society of St. Vincent de Paul, Our Lady of the Valley Conference*, 1122 W. Linden St., Caldwell, 83605. Tel: 208-331-8409; Email: john.dahl@svdpid.org; Web: www.svdpid.org. Marilyn Evans, Pres.

COEUR D'ALENE. **St. Vincent de Paul Salvage Bureau, St. Thomas Conference*, 201 E. Harrison Ave., Coeur d'Alene, 83814. Tel: 208-664-3095; Fax: 208-664-1772; Email: jeff@stvincentdepaulcda.org. Mike Kennedy, Pres.; Jeff Conroy, Exec. Dir.

EAGLE. *Mercy Properties II, Inc.*, 540 N. Eagle Rd., Eagle, 83616. Tel: 303-830-3300; Fax: 303-830-3301; Email: jrosenblum@mercyhousing.org. Joe Rosenblum, Sec.

LEWISTON. **Lewis and Clark District Council of St. Vincent de Paul*, 818 11th St., Lewiston, 83501. Tel: 208-798-9574; Email: theresa@mcwessels.org. Theresa Wessels, Pres., Tel: 208-746-7860.

SJRMC, 415 6th St., P.O. Box 816, Lewiston, 83501-0816. Tel: 314-733-8000; Email: jimpicciche@ascension.org; Web: www.ascension.org. 11775 Borman Dr., 2nd Fl., St. Louis, MO 63146. Mr. Joseph Impicciche, Exec.

MOUNTAIN HOME AIR FORCE BASE. *St. Mary's A.F.B.* (Archdiocese for the Military Services) 366 FW/HC, 420 Gunfighter Ave., Mountain Home A F B, 83648. Tel: 208-828-6987; Fax: 208-828-4570; Email: kelly.gray.3.ctr@us.af.mil; Web: www.libertychapelcatholic.weebly.com. Rev. Mario Rosario.

RELIGIOUS INSTITUTES OF MEN REPRESENTED IN THE DIOCESE

For further details refer to the corresponding bracketed number in the Religious Institutes of Men or Women section.

[]—*Apostolic Life Community of Priests*—A.L.C.P.
[0200]—*Benedictine Monks*—O.S.B.
[]—*Hermits of Mt. Carmel*—H.M.C.
[0690]—*Jesuit Fathers* (Oregon Prov.)—S.J.
[]—*Order of Friar Minor Franciscans*—O.F.M.
[1065]—*Priestly Fraternity of St. Peter*—F.S.S.P.

RELIGIOUS INSTITUTES OF WOMEN REPRESENTED IN THE DIOCESE

[0230]—*Benedictine Sisters of Pontifical Jurisdiction*—O.S.B.
[]—*Carmel of Jesus, Mary and Joseph.*
[1920]—*Congregation of the Sisters of the Holy Cross*—C.S.C.
[]—*Hermit Sisters of Mary*—H.S.M.
[1250]—*Institute of the Franciscan Sisters of the Eucharist*—F.S.E.
[2575]—*Institute of the Sisters of Mercy of the Americas*—R.S.M.
[3830]—*Sisters of St. Joseph*—C.S.J.
[1990]—*Sisters of the Holy Names of Jesus and Mary*—S.N.J.M.
[]—*Society of Sisters of the Church*—S.S.C.
[4110]—*Ursuline Nuns* (Western Prov.)—O.S.U.

An asterisk (*) denotes an organization that has established tax-exempt status directly with the IRS and is not covered by the USCCB Group Ruling.

Archdiocese of Boston

(Archidioecesis Bostoniensis)

His Eminence

SEÁN PATRICK CARDINAL O'MALLEY, O.F.M.-CAP.

Archbishop of Boston; ordained priest August 29, 1970; ordained Coadjutor Bishop of St. Thomas in the Virgin Islands August 2, 1984; succeeded to the See, October 16, 1985; Named sixth Bishop of Fall River June 16, 1992; installed August 10, 1992; Named fourth Bishop of Palm Beach September 3, 2002; installed October 19, 2002; Named ninth Bishop and sixth Metropolitan Archbishop of Boston July 1, 2003; installed July 30, 2003; Named Cardinal Priest with the title of Santa Maria della Vittoria, in the consistory of March 24, 2006. *Office: 66 Brooks Dr., Braintree, MA 02184-3839.* Tel: 617-782-2544; Fax: 617-779-3820. *Res.: Cathedral of the Holy Cross, 75 Union Park St., Boston, MA 02118.* Tel: 617-542-5682; Fax: 617-542-5926.

Chancery Office: 66 Brooks Dr., Braintree, MA 02184-3839. Tel: 617-254-0100; Fax: 617-779-4571.

Web: www.bostoncatholic.org

Most Reverend

ROBERT FRANCIS HENNESSEY

Titular Bishop of Tigias, Auxiliary Bishop of Boston, Vicar General and Regional Bishop-Merrimack; ordained priest May 20, 1978; ordained Bishop December 12, 2006. *Office & Res.: 110 Lincoln Ave., Haverhill, MA 01830-6739.* Tel: 978-399-0000; Email: merrimackregion@rcab.org.

Most Reverend

PETER JOHN UGLIETTO

Titular Bishop of Thubursicum, Auxiliary Bishop of Boston, Vicar General and Moderator of the Curia; ordained priest May 21, 1977; ordained Bishop September 14, 2011. *Office: 66 Brooks Dr., Braintree, MA 02184-3839.* Tel: 617-746-5619; Fax: 617-779-5920; Email: vicar_general@rcab.org. *Res.: Saint Patrick Rectory, 9 Pomeworth St., Stoneham, MA 02180-2025.* Tel: 781-438-0960; Fax: 781-438-6809.

Most Reverend

ROBERT PHILIP REED

Titular Bishop of Sufar, Auxiliary Bishop of Boston, Vicar General and Regional Bishop-West; ordained priest July 6, 1985; ordained Bishop August 24, 2016. *Office: 34 Chestnut St., Watertown, MA 02471-9196.* Tel: 508-647-0296; Fax: 617-923-3490; Email: westregion@rcab.org. *Res.: Good Shepherd Rectory, 124 Cochituate Rd., Wayland, MA 01778.* Tel: 508-650-3545; Fax: 508-655-6948.

Most Reverend

MARK O'CONNELL

Titular Bishop of Gigthi, Auxiliary Bishop of Boston, Vicar General and Regional Bishop-North; ordained priest June 16, 1990; ordained Bishop August 24, 2016. *Office: 63 Winter St., North Reading, MA 01864-2282. Res.: Saint Theresa of Lisieux Rectory, 63 Winter St., North Reading, MA 01864-2282.*

Most Reverend

FRANCIS XAVIER IRWIN

Titular Bishop of Ubaza and Vicar General; ordained priest February 2, 1960; ordained Bishop September 17, 1996; retired October 15, 2009. *Res. 36 Kelley Way, Dennis, MA 02660-2736.* Tel: 508-385-6139.

Most Reverend

EMILIO SIMEON ALLUE, S.D.B.

Titular Bishop of Croe and Vicar General; ordained priest December 22, 1966; ordained Bishop September 17, 1996; retired June 30, 2010. *Res.: Saint Theresa of Avila Rectory, 10 Saint Theresa Ave., Boston, MA 02132.* Tel: 617-325-1300; Fax: 617-325-0380.

Most Reverend

ARTHUR LEO KENNEDY

Titular Bishop of Timidana, Vicar General; ordained priest December 17, 1966; ordained Bishop September 14, 2011; retired June 30, 2017. *Office: 66 Brooks Dr., Braintree, MA 02184-3839.* Tel: 617-746-5747. *Office: 25 Avery St., Dedham, MA 02026-2829.* Tel: 781-326-0550; Fax: 781-326-1809. *Res.: St. Mary Rectory, 420 High St., Dedham, MA 02026-2829.* Tel: 781-326-0550; Fax: 781-326-1809.

Most Reverend

JOHN ANTHONY DOOHER

Titular Bishop of Theveste, Vicar General; ordained priest May 21, 1969; ordained Bishop December 12, 2006; retired June 30, 2018. *Office: 236 Pleasant St., Weymouth, MA 02190-2599.* Tel: 781-337-4413; Fax: 781-337-3625; Email: southregion@rcab.org. *Res.: Saint Jerome Rectory, 632 Bridge St., Weymouth, MA 02191-1845.* Tel: 781-335-2038; Fax: 781-340-7165.

Square Miles 2,465.

Created a Diocese April 8, 1808; Made Metropolitan Archdiocese February 12, 1875.

Comprises the Counties of Essex, Middlesex, Norfolk, Suffolk and Plymouth (the towns of Marion, Mattapoisett and Wareham excepted) in the Commonwealth of Massachusetts.

For legal titles of parishes and archdiocesan agencies and institutions, consult the Chancery Office.

STATISTICAL OVERVIEW

Personnel	
Cardinals	1
Auxiliary Bishops	4
Retired Bishops	4
Abbots	1
Retired Abbots	1
Priests: Diocesan Active in Diocese	295
Priests: Diocesan Active Outside Diocese	28
Priests: Retired, Sick or Absent	260
Number of Diocesan Priests	583
Religious Priests in Diocese	378
Total Priests in Diocese	961
Extern Priests in Diocese	54
Ordinations:	
Diocesan Priests	7
Permanent Deacons	6
Permanent Deacons in Diocese	274
Total Brothers	99
Total Sisters	1,413
Parishes	
Parishes	284
With Resident Pastor:	
Resident Diocesan Priests	275
Resident Religious Priests	13
New Parishes Created	12
Professional Ministry Personnel:	
Sisters	8
Lay Ministers	61
Welfare	
Health Care Centers	3
Total Assisted	7,511
Homes for the Aged	16
Total Assisted	2,832
Residential Care of Children	1
Total Assisted	921
Day Care Centers	11
Total Assisted	1,110
Specialized Homes	21
Total Assisted	1,722
Special Centers for Social Services	43
Total Assisted	206,000
Other Institutions	3
Total Assisted	35,410
Educational	
Seminaries, Diocesan	3
Students from This Diocese	45
Students from Other Diocese	108
Diocesan Students in Other Seminaries	6
Seminaries, Religious	1
Students Religious	70
Total Seminarians	121
Colleges and Universities	4
Total Students	23,264
High Schools, Diocesan and Parish	1
Total Students	522
High Schools, Private	27
Total Students	14,091
Elementary Schools, Diocesan and Parish	68
Total Students	17,476
Elementary Schools, Private	9
Total Students	1,535
Non-residential Schools for the Disabled	2
Total Students	138
Catechesis/Religious Education:	
High School Students	28,606
Elementary Students	79,395
Total Students under Catholic Instruction	165,148
Teachers in the Diocese:	
Scholastics	2
Brothers	6
Sisters	12
Lay Teachers	400
Vital Statistics	
Receptions into the Church:	
Infant Baptism Totals	12,637
Minor Baptism Totals	1,601
Adult Baptism Totals	302
Received into Full Communion	325
First Communions	13,849
Confirmations	12,614
Marriages:	
Catholic	2,063
Interfaith	496
Total Marriages	2,559
Deaths	14,544
Total Catholic Population	1,932,653
Total Population	4,156,703

Former Bishops—His Eminence JOHN LEFEVRE CARDINAL DE CHEVERUS, ord. Dec. 18, 1790; appt. first Bishop of Boston, April 8, 1808; ord. Bishop Nov. 1, 1810; Apostolic Administrator of New York, NY (1810-1815); transferred to Montauban, May 3, 1823; appt. Archbishop of Bordeaux Oct. 2, 1826; named Cardinal, Feb. 1, 1836 (died before receiving red hat and titular church); died July 19, 1836; Most Revs. BENEDICT J. FENWICK, S.J., ord. June 11, 1808; appt. second Bishop of Boston, May 10, 1825; ord. Bishop Nov. 1, 1825; died Aug. 11, 1846; JOHN BERNARD FITZPATRICK, ord. June 13, 1840; appt. Titular Bishop of Callipolis and Coadjutor of Boston, Nov. 21, 1843; ord. Bishop March 24, 1844; Succeeded as third Bishop of

Boston, Aug. 11, 1846; died Feb. 13, 1866; JOHN JOSEPH WILLIAMS, D.D., ord. May 17, 1845; appt. Titular Bishop of Tripolis and Coadjutor of Boston, Jan. 8, 1866; ord. fourth Bishop of Boston, March 11, 1866; named first Archbishop of Boston, Feb. 12, 1875; died Aug. 30, 1907; His Eminence WILLIAM HENRY CARDINAL O'CONNELL, ord. June 7, 1884; appt. third Bishop of Portland, Maine, Feb. 8, 1901; ord. Bishop May 19, 1901; appt. Titular Archbishop of Constantia and Coadjutor with right of succession to the Archbishop of Boston, Feb. 8, 1906; appt. fifth Bishop and second Archbishop of Boston, April 30, 1907; named Cardinal, Nov. 27, 1911, Titular Church, San Clemente; died April 22, 1944; RICHARD JAMES CARDINAL CUSHING, ord. May 26, 1921; appt. Titular Bishop of Mela and Auxiliary of Boston, June 10, 1939; ord. Bishop June 29, 1939; appt. sixth Bishop and third Archbishop of Boston, Sept. 25, 1944; named Cardinal December 15, 1958, Titular Church, Santa Susanna; died Nov. 2, 1970; HUMBERTO SOUSA CARDINAL MEDEIROS, ord. June 15, 1946; appt. second Bishop of Brownsville, Texas April 14, 1966; ord. Bishop June 9, 1966; named seventh Bishop and fourth Archbishop of Boston, Sept. 8, 1970; installed Oct. 7, 1970; named Cardinal March 5, 1973, Titular Church, Santa Susanna; died Sept. 17, 1983; BERNARD FRANCIS CARDINAL LAW, ord. priest May 21, 1961; appt. fourth Bishop of Springfield-Cape Girardeau Oct. 22, 1973; ord. Bishop of Springfield-Cape Girardeau Dec. 5, 1973; appt. eighth Bishop and fifth Archbishop of Boston Jan. 11, 1984; installed March 23, 1984; named Cardinal Priest May 25, 1985; Titular Church, Santa Susanna; resigned Dec. 13, 2002; named Archpriest of the Patriarchal Basilica of St. Mary Major, Rome, Italy, May 27, 2004; resigned Nov. 4, 2011; died Dec. 20, 2017.

Vicars General—Most Revs. EMILIO S. ALLUE, S.D.B.; JOHN A. DOOHER; ROBERT F. HENNESSEY; FRANCIS XAVIER IRWIN; ARTHUR L. KENNEDY; PETER J. UGLIETTO; ROBERT P. REED; MARK O'CONNELL.

Regional Bishops and Vicars—

Central - Regional Vicar—Very Rev. JAMES A. FLAVIN, V.E., 841 E. Broadway, Boston, 02127-2302. Tel: 617-269-4001; Fax: 617-269-4006; Email: centralregion@rcab.org. Vicariate I: Very Rev. GEORGE P. EVANS, V.F., A.B., M.Div., S.T.L., S.T.D., Pastor, Holy Name, West Roxbury, Tel: 617-325-4865; Fax: 617-325-5571. Vicariate II: Very Rev. LINH T. NGUYEN, V.F., Pastor, Saint Ambrose and Pastor, Saint Mark, Dorchester, Tel: 617-265-5302; Fax: 617-265-0886. Vicariate III: Very Rev. JAMES J. RONAN, V.F., Pastor, Saint Mary-Saint Catherine of Siena, Charlestown, Tel: 617-242-4664; Fax: 617-242-0016. Vicariate IV: Very Rev. RICHARD W. FITZGERALD, V.F., Admin., Saint Columbkille, Brighton, Tel: 617-547-5593; Fax: 617-547-1505.

Merrimack - Regional Bishop—Most Rev. ROBERT F. HENNESSEY, 110 Lincoln Ave., Haverhill, 01830-6739. Tel: 978-399-0000; Email: merrimackregion@rcab.org. Vicariate I: Very Rev. SHAWN W. ALLEN, V.F., Pastor, Saint Andrew; Pastor, Saint Mary; Pastor, Saint Theresa of Lisieux, Billerica, Tel: 978-663-8816; Fax: 978-663-0577. Vicariate II: Very Rev. SEAN M. MAHER, V.F., Admin., Saint Francis of Assisi, Dracut, Tel: 978-452-6611; Fax: 978-452-0772. Vicariate III: Very Rev. CHRISTOPHER J. CASEY, V.F., Pastor, Our Lady of Good Counsel, Methuen, Tel: 978-686-3984; Fax: 978-686-8300. Vicariate IV: Very Rev. JOHN W. DELANEY, V.F., Pastor, Sacred Hearts, Haverhill, Tel: 978-373-1281; Fax: 978-374-3043.

North - Regional Bishop—Most Rev. MARK O'CONNELL, 63 Winter St., North Reading, 01864-2282. Tel: 978-531-1013; Fax: 978-531-5312; Email: northregion@rcab.org. Vicariate I: Very Rev. PAUL E. RITT, V.F., A.B., M.Div., S.T.L., S.T.D., Pastor, Our Lady of the Assumption and Pastor, Saint Maria Goretti, Lynnfield, Tel: 781-598-4313; Fax: 781-598-0055. Vicariate II: Very Rev. BRIAN L. FLYNN, V.F., Pastor, Saint Mary and Pastor, Sacred Heart, Lynn, Tel: 781-598-4907; Fax: 781-599-2088. Vicariate III: Very Rev. STEPHEN B. ROCK, V.F., Pastor, Saint Agnes and Admin., Saint Athanasius, Reading, Tel: 781-944-0490; Fax: 781-944-4403. Vicariate IV: Very Rev. JOHN F. MULLOY, V.F., Parochial Vicar, Saint Joseph, Malden, Tel: 781-324-0402; Fax: 781-324-1790.

South - Regional Vicar—Very Rev. BRIAN M. FLATLEY, 236 Pleasant St., Weymouth, 02190-2599. Tel: 781-337-4413; Fax: 781-337-3625; Email: southregion@rcab.org. Vicariate I: Very Rev. PAUL T. CLIFFORD, V.F., Pastor, Saint Francis of Assisi and Pastor, Saint Clare, Braintree, Tel: 781-843-1332; Fax: 781-848-0976. Vicariate II: Very Rev. KENNETH V. CANNON, S.X., V.F., Pastor, Saint Mary of the Nativity, Scituate, Tel: 781-545-3335; Fax: 781-544-3678. Vicariate III: Very Rev. WILLIAM D. DEVINE, V.F., Pastor, Saint Thomas Aquinas, Bridgewater, Tel: 508-697-9528; Fax: 508-279-1859. Vicariate IV: Very Rev. ROBERT J. DEEHAN, V.F., Pastor, Holy Family, Duxbury, Tel: 781-934-5055; Tel: 781-934-5796.

West - Regional Bishop—Most Rev. ROBERT P. REED, 34 Chestnut St., Watertown, 02471-9196. Tel: 508-647-0296; Fax: 617-923-3490; Email: westregion@rcab.org. Vicariate I: Very Rev. FRANK J. SILVA, V.F., Pastor, Saint Margaret of Antioch and Admin., Saint Malachy, Burlington, Tel: 781-272-3111; Fax: 781-272-9204. Vicariate II: Very Rev. ADRIAN A. MILIK, V.F., Parochial Vicar, Sacred Heart and Our Lady Help of Christians, Newton, Tel: 617-527-7560; Fax: 617-527-1338. Vicariate III: Very Rev. MICHAEL W. MACEWEN, V.F., Pastor, Saint Linus and Pastor, Saint Patrick, Natick, Tel: 508-653-1093; Fax: 508-650-2922. Vicariate IV: Very Rev. MATTHEW J. WESTCOTT, V.F., Pastor, Saint Mary, Foxborough, Tel: 508-543-7726; Fax: 508-543-7728.

Vicar General and Moderator of the Curia—Most Rev. PETER J. UGLIETTO, 66 Brooks Dr., Braintree, 02184-3839. Tel: 617-746-5619; Fax: 617-746-5920; Email: vicar_general@rcab.org.

Special Assistant to the Vicar General and Assistant Vicar for Administration—Very Rev. WILLIAM P. JOY, 66 Brooks Dr., Braintree, 02184-3839. Tel: 617-746-5618; Fax: 617-746-5920.

Assistant to the Vicar General and Moderator of the Curia for Canonical Affairs—Bro. JAMES M. PETERSON, O.F.M.Cap., 66 Brooks Dr., Braintree, 02184-3839. Tel: 617-746-5650; Fax: 617-746-5920.

Archives—MR. THOMAS LESTER, Archivist, 66 Brooks Dr., Braintree, 02184-3839. Tel: 617-746-5797; Fax: 617-746-4561.

Pontifical Mission Societies—

Pontifical Association of the Holy Childhood—

Pontifical Society for the Propagation of the Faith—

Pontifical Society of Saint Peter the Apostle—Rev. Msgr. WILLIAM P. FAY, Dir., 66 Brooks Dr., Braintree, 02184-3839. Tel: 617-779-3865; Email: officestaff@propfaithatboston.org.

Metropolitan Tribunal

Ecclesiastical Court of the Archdiocese of Boston—66 Brooks Dr., Braintree, 02184-3839. Tel: 617-746-5900; Fax: 617-779-4566.

Judicial Vicar—Rev. JONATHAN DEFELICE, O.S.B.

Archdiocesan Judges—Tribunal Court: Rev. Msgr. MICHAEL S. FOSTER; Rev. WILLIAM C. PALLADINO; Sr. MARGARET L. SULLIVAN, C.S.J.; MS. MARIA GALINDEZ-BIANCO. Associate: Rev. JOSEPH M. HENNESSEY.

Court Advocates/Petitioners—Rev. WLODZIMIERZ SOBOLEWSKI, C.R.; Ms. JULIANNE SHANKLIN.

Court Advocate/Respondent—Rev. PETER G. GORI, O.S.A.

Defenders of the Bond—Revs. JAMES G. BURKE; WILLIAM C. PALLADINO; AIDAN J. WALSH, (Retired).

Promoter of Justice—Revs. RODNEY J. COPP; MARK A. MAHONEY; WILLIAM C. PALLADINO.

Notary—VACANT.

Staff—MS. ELLEN OBSHATKIN; MS. MARISA NOE.

Canonical Affairs Committee—Most Rev. MARK O'CONNELL, Chm.; Revs. JAMES G. BURKE; RODNEY J. COPP; PETER G. GORI, O.S.A.; JAMES J. LAUGHLIN, A.B., M.Div., J.C.L.; WILLIAM C. PALLADINO; WALTER J. WOODS; Sr. MARGARET L. SULLIVAN, C.S.J.

Presbyteral Council—(2014-2019) His Eminence SEAN CARDINAL O'MALLEY, O.F.M.Cap.

Moderator—Rev. KEVIN J. DEELEY.

Ex Officio Members—Most Revs. EMILIO S. ALLUE, S.D.B.; JOHN A. DOOHER; ROBERT F. HENNESSEY; ARTHUR L. KENNEDY; MARK O'CONNELL; ROBERT P. REED; PETER J. UGLIETTO.

Elected Members—

Central Region—Revs. MARIO GUARINO; ANTHONY M. CUSACK; Very Rev. KEVIN J. O'LEARY, V.F.; Rev. BRIAN J. MCHUGH.

Merrimack Region—Revs. RICHARD F. CLANCY; MICHAEL B. MEDAS, M.S.W.

North Region—Revs. KARLO J. HOCURSCAK; CHARLES R. STANLEY; DARIN V. COLARUSSO.

South Region—Revs. LOUIS R. PALMIERI; MARK G. DERRANE; JOSEPH K. RAEKE, V.F.; KWANG H. LEE.

West Region—Revs. WALTER J. WOODS; JAMES M. DIPERRI, M.A., M.Div., J.C.L.; JOSEPH F. MOZER JR., J.C.L.

Senior Priests—Revs. JOHN E. FARRELL, V.F., (Retired); FRANCIS J. CLOHERTY, V.F., (Retired).

Religious Members—Revs. THOMAS CONWAY, O.F.M.; LEONARD COPELAND, O.C.D.; ROBERT L. KEANE, S.J.; JOSEPH MATTEUCIG, S.X.; MICHAEL B. MCGARRY, C.S.P., M.Div., M.A. Theology; Rt. Rev. THOMAS O'CONNOR, O.S.B.; Revs. TUAN NGOC PHAM, O.M.I.; CARLOS E. URBINA, O.S.A.

Appointed Members—Rev. Msgr. GEORGE F. CARLSON, (Retired); Very Revs. JAMES A. FLAVIN, V.E.; WILLIAM P. JOY; BRYAN K. PARRISH; Rev. ROBERT M. BLANEY, V.F.; Very Rev. JOHN J. CONNOLLY, V.F.; Revs. MICHAEL C. HARRINGTON; PHILIP E. MCGAUGH; Very Rev. GERARD PETRINGA, V.E.; Revs. GUY F. SCIACCA; PAUL R. SOPER.

College of Consultors—His Eminence SEAN CARDINAL O'MALLEY, O.F.M.Cap.

Members—Most Revs. JOHN A. DOOHER; ROBERT F. HENNESSEY; ARTHUR L. KENNEDY; MARK O'CONNELL; ROBERT P. REED; PETER J. UGLIETTO; Very Revs. JAMES A. FLAVIN, V.E.; KEVIN J. O'LEARY, V.F.; BRYAN K. PARRISH, V.F.; Revs. JOHN E. FARRELL, V.F., (Retired); JAMES J. LAUGHLIN, A.B., M.Div., J.C.L.

Finance Council—President: His Eminence SEAN CARDINAL O'MALLEY, O.F.M.Cap.; MR. JOHN H. MCCARTHY, Vice Chair; MR. PAUL HANLEY; MS. KIMBERLEY Y. JONES; MR. PETER S. LYNCH; MR. ROBERT M. MAHONEY; MR. GEORGE E. MASSARO; MR. SEAN P. MCGRATH; MR. ROBERT J. MORRISSEY; MR. KEVIN C. PHELAN; MS. MARY L. RYAN; MR. PAUL W. SANDMAN; MR. JOHN E. STRAUB; Most Rev. PETER J. UGLIETTO. Life Members: MR. JOHN A. KANEB; MR. WILLIAM F. MCCALL; MR. JOHN A. MCNEICE JR.; JAMES F. MOONEY.

Archdiocesan Pastoral Council—President: His Eminence SEAN CARDINAL O'MALLEY, O.F.M.Cap.; Rt. Rev. JOHN J. AHERN, V.F.; Rev. GERALD A. SOUZA; Deacons PAUL COUGHLIN; TIMOTHY F. DONOHUE; JOSEPH E. DORLUS; MICHAEL C. JOENS; LOUIS J. PIAZZA; Bro. JOHN KACHINSKY, F.M.S.; Sisters TERESA STEPHEN PEREIRA, O.Carm; MARGARET L. SULLIVAN, C.S.J.; MS. CHRISTINE BRANDT; MS. STEPHANIE BRONNER; MS. PAULA CALLAHAN; MS. JANE MACDONALD; CYNTHIA ROBINSON MARKEY; MS. DENISE MIEDICO; MS. DIANNE M. MILLS; MS. SUSAN MURPHY; MS. KATHLEEN NUGENT; MS. MARINA OLIVEIRA; MS. TRACY PALEN; MS. MICHELLE PARKS; MS. MARIE PHILOMENE PEAN; MS. MARYANN SADOWSKI; DIANNE I. SARAULT; MS. MICHAELLE SYLVESTRE; MR. ROBERT ARMANO; MR. GEORGE BARATTA; MR. JOHN BETTINELLI; MR. PETER BUCK; MR. ROBERT DILANDO; MR. SEAN DOHERTY; MR. ERIK ELDRACHER; MR. ANTHONY ESPOSITO; MR. MICHAEL GALLAGHER; MR. RICHARD GILL; MR. CASEY GRANT; MR. EDWARD KELLY; MR. JASON LAMPRON; MR. JOHN LOZADA; MR. KENNETH J. MCCARTHY; MR. MICHAEL MCCONNELL; MR. MICHAEL MCSHANE; MR. DAVID MELO; MR. PAUL MURPHY; MR. JOSE RAMIREZ; MR. PETER REGAN; MR. JOSEPH P. SULLIVAN; MR. CHARLES VERNON.

Administration and Financial Services—MR. JOHN E. STRAUB, Sec. & Chancellor, 66 Brooks Dr., Braintree, 02184-3839. Tel: 617-746-5670; Tel: 617-746-5656; Fax: 617-779-4571; Email: j_straub@rcab.org.

General Counsel—MR. F. BEIRNE LOVELY JR., Esq., 66 Brooks Dr., Braintree, 02184. Tel: 617-746-5672; Tel: 617-746-5672; Fax: 617-746-5686; Email: beirne_lovely@rcab.org.

Cemeteries—MR. ROBERT VISCONTI, Dir., 175 Broadway, Malden, 02148-6097. Tel: 781-322-6300; Fax: 781-322-3801; Email: rvisconti@rcab.org; Web: ccemetery.org.

Finance and Technology—MS. MAUREEN DONNELLY-CREEDON, Dir., 66 Brooks Dr., Braintree, 02184-3839. Tel: 617-746-5878; Fax: 617-779-4564.

Human Resources—MR. JAMES DIFRANCESCO, Dir., 66 Brooks Dr., Braintree, 02184-3839. Tel: 617-746-5829; Fax: 617-779-4571; Email: jim_difrancesco@rcab.org.

Risk Management—MR. JOSEPH F. MCENNESS, Dir., 66 Brooks Dr., Braintree, 02184-3839. Tel: 617-746-5740; Fax: 617-779-4510; Email: jmcenness@rcab.org.

Parish Services—MS. DENISE MCKINNON-BIERNAT, 66 Brooks Dr., Braintree, 02184-3839. Tel: 617-746-5685; Fax: 617-746-5938; Email: d_mbiernat@rcab.org.

Planning Office for Urban Affairs—MS. LISA ALBERGHINI, Dir., 84 State St., Boston, 02109. Tel: 617-350-8885; Fax: 617-350-8889; Email: lba@poua.org.

Health Benefit Trust, Life and Long-Term Disability Insurance Trust, Transition Assistance—His Eminence SEAN P. CARDINAL O'MALLEY, O.F.M.Cap.; Most Rev. PETER J. UGLIETTO; MR. JOHN E. STRAUB; Rev. ROBERT T. KICKHAM; Very

Rev. BRYAN K. PARRISH; MR. WEIYEN JONAS; MR. DAVID WOONTON.

Archdiocese of Boston Pension Plan—His Eminence SEAN P. O'MALLEY, O.F.M.Cap.; Most Rev. PETER J. UGLIETTO; MR. JOHN E. STRAUB; Rev. ROBERT T. KICKHAM; Very Rev. BRYAN K. PARRISH; MR. PAUL W. SANDMAN; MR. DAVID WOONTON; MR. MICHAEL RYAN; MR. JOHN GIORDANO. Plan Administrator: MS. CAROL GUSTAVSON.

Attorney for the Trust—Wilmer Cutler, Pickering Hale and Dorr. Consultants: October Three Compensation and Benefit Strategies for the pension plans and Mercer for the health plan.

Massachusetts Catholic Self Insurance Group, Inc.—Board of Directors: MR. JOHN E. STRAUB, Pres.; MRS. MAUREEN CREEDON, Treas.; Rev. JAMES M. DIPERRI, M.A., M.Div., J.C.L., Clerk; MR. WILLIAM LABROAD; MR. JOHN M. RILEY; MR. NEIL BUCKLEY; MS. LORI A. FERRANTE. Counsel: MR. TIMOTHY M. MCCRYSTAL, Esq. Administrator: MR. JOSEPH F. MCENNESS. Consultants: MR. JOHN DAWSON; MS. ANN CONWAY.

Investment Advisory Committee—Members: MR. ROBERT J. MORRISSEY; Deacon CHARLES I. CLOUGH; MR. GERALD R. CURTIS; MR. JAMES J. MAHONEY; MR. THOMAS M. O'NEIL; MR. THOMAS C. STAKEM; MS. MICHELLE A. KNIGHT.

Audit Committee—Members: MR. GEORGE E. MASSARO, Chm.; Rev. JOSEPH K. RAEKE, V.F.; MR. PAUL HANLEY; MR. JOHN H. MCCARTHY; MS. MARY L. RYAN; MS. KIMBERLEY Y. JONES; MR. JOHN REDMOND.

Pastoral Building Committee—MR. JOHN E. STRAUB; Very Rev. BRYAN K. PARRISH, V.F.; Revs. PAUL R. SOPER; STEPHEN J. MADDEN; Very Rev. SHAWN W. ALLEN, V.F.

Delegate for Religious—Sr. MARIAN BATHO, C.S.J., Sec., 66 Brooks Dr., Braintree, 02184-3839. Tel: 617-746-5637; Fax: 617-779-4510; Email: sr_marian_batho@rcab.org.

Black Catholic Choir—MR. MEYER CHAMBERS, Tel: 617-448-4578.

African-American Ministry of Cultural Diversity—Tel: 617-746-5794. MS. LORNA DESROSES, Tel: 617-746-5810.

Cape Verdean—MR. ANTONIO PINA, Tel: 508-540-1534; MR. JOHN BARROS, Tel: 617-308-3221.

Congolese—Office of Outreach & Cultural Diversity. Tel: 617-746-5794.

Eritrean—Rev. ABAYNEH GEBREMICHAEL, Tel: 508-583-1121.

Ethiopian—Rev. ABAYNEH GEBREMICHAEL, Tel: 508-583-1121.

Ghanaian—MR. PATRICK SOSSOU, Tel: 617-323-6458.

Haitian—Rev. GUSTAV MIRACLE, Tel: 617-298-0080.

Kenyan—MR. DAN KUREMA, Tel: 978-985-3685.

Nigerian—Rev. JUDE THADDEUS OSUNKWO, (Nigeria) Tel: 617-445-8915.

Ugandan—MR. LENNIE KAFEERO, Tel: 617-548-9678.

Boston Catholic Directory—Rev. ROBERT M. O'GRADY, 66 Brooks Dr., Braintree, 02184-3839. Tel: 617-779-3790; Fax: 617-779-4560; Email: rmogrady@pilotcatholicnews.com.

Campus Ministry—66 Brooks Dr., Braintree, 02184-3839. Tel: 617-746-5856; Fax: 617-782-0213. Rev. ERIC F. CADIN, M.Div., S.T.L.

Boston—

Boston University—Rev. DAVID J. BARNES, M.Div., 211 Bay State Rd., Boston, 02215. Tel: 617-353-3632; Fax: 617-358-2049; Email: frbarnes@bu.edu; Web: bu.edu/catholic/.

Emerson College—MS. KRISTELLE ANGELLI, M.A., Campus Min., 120 Boylston St., Boston, 02116. Tel: 617-783-3924; Email: volservice@aol.com; Web: emerson.edu/student-life/supportservices/spirit ual-life/spiritual-lifeleadership/.

Emmanuel College—Rev. JOHN P. SPENCER, S.J., Campus Min., 400 The Fenway, Boston, 02115. Tel: 617-735-9780; Fax: 617-735-9877; Web: emmanuel.edu/student_life/campus_ministry.html.

Northeastern University—Bro. SAMUEL GUNN, B.H., Campus Min., 68 Saint Stephen St., Boston, 02115. Tel: 617-373-8964; Email: brosam@neu.edu; Web: nucatholics.neu.edu.

Babson Park—

Babson College—VACANT, Campus Min., Galvin Family Chapel, Babson Park, 02457-0310. Tel: 781-239-5623; Web: babson.edu.

Bridgewater—

Bridgewater State University—MS. MARLENE DELEON, Campus Min., 122 Park Ave., Bridgewater, 02324. Tel: 508-531-1346; Email: marlene.deleon@bridgew.edu; Web: bridgew.edu.

Cambridge—

Harvard University—Rev. MICHAEL E. DREA, Campus Min., 20 Arrow St., Cambridge, 02138. Tel: 617-868-6585; Email: mdrea@stpaulparish.org; Web: harvardcatholicchaplaincy.org.

Massachusetts Institute of Technology—Rev. RICHARD F. CLANCY, Campus Min., 40 Massachusetts Ave., Cambridge, 02139-4312. Tel: 617-253-2981; Fax: 617-253-3260; Email: frclancy@mit.edu.

Newton—

Boston College—Rev. ANTHONY PENNA, Dir., McElroy 233, Chestnut Hill, 02467-3805. Tel: 617-552-3475; Fax: 617-552-3473; Email: ministry@bc.edu; Web: bc.edu.

Boston—

Laboure College—Rev. JOHN J. STAGNARO, Campus Min., 2120 Dorchester Ave., Dorchester, 02124-5698. Tel: 617-296-8300; Fax: 617-296-7947; Email: jstagnaro@labourecollege.org; Web: labourecollege.org.

University of Massachusetts-Boston—Rev. PAUL D. HELFRICH, B.H., J.D., S.T.B., M.A., Campus Min., Harbor Campus, Dorchester, 02125-3393. Tel: 617-287-5839; Fax: 617-287-5815; Email: frpaul@brohope.edu; Web: umb.edu.

Framingham—

Framingham State University—MS. HAI OK HWANG, M.Div., Campus Min., 100 State St., Framingham, 01701-9101. Tel: 508-626-4610; Fax: 508-626-4939; Email: hhwang@frc.mass.edu; Web: frc.mass.edu.

Lowell—

University of Massachusetts-Lowell—MS. BERNADINE KENSINGER, Campus Min., Mailing Address: Box 360, Lowell, 01853-0360. Tel: 978-934-5032; Email: bernadine_kensinger@uml.edu; Web: uml.edu.

Medford—

Tufts University—MS. LYNN COOPER, Campus Min., Three The Green, Medford, 02155-5300. Tel: 781-391-7272; Fax: 617-571-5269; Email: lynn.cooper@tufts.edu; Web: tufts.edu.

Milton—

Curry College—Rev. GERARD R. MCKEON, S.J., Spiritual Life Coord., Curry College, Milton, 02186. Tel: 617-333-2289; Fax: 617-333-2014; Email: gmckeonsj@bchigh.edu; Web: curry.edu.

North Andover—

Merrimack College—Rev. KEITH HOLLIS, O.S.A., Campus Min., Grace J. Palmisano Center, North Andover, 01845. Tel: 978-837-5450; Fax: 978-837-5004; Email: hollisk@merrimack.edu; Web: merrimack.edu.

Salem—

Salem State University—MS. JOAN MCCANN, Interfaith Office, 352 Lafayette St., Salem, 01970. Tel: 978-542-6074; Email: jmccann@salemstate.edu.

Waltham—

Bentley University—VACANT, Campus Min., 175 Forest St., Waltham, 02452-4705. Tel: 781-891-2754; Fax: 781-891-2839; Web: bentley.edu.

Brandeis University—Rev. WALTER H. CUENIN, Campus Min., (Retired), Mail Stop 205, Waltham, 02454-9110. Tel: 781-736-3574; Fax: 781-736-3577; Email: whcuenin@hotmail.com.

Wellesley—

Wellesley College—Sr. NANCY CORCORAN, C.S.J., Campus Min., 106 Central St., Wellesley, 02481. Tel: 781-283-2688; Email: ncorcora@wellesley.edu; Web: wellesley.edu.

Weston—

Regis College—Sr. ELIZABETH CONWAY, C.S.J., Campus Min., 235 Wellesley St., Weston, 02493-1571. Tel: 781-768-7063; Fax: 781-768-8339; Web: regiscollege.edu.

Catholic Charitable Bureau of the Archdiocese of Boston, Inc.—MS. DEBORAH KINCADE RAMBO, L.I.C.S.W., Pres., 51 Sleeper St., Boston, 02110. Tel: 617-482-5440; Fax: 617-451-0337; Email: info@ccab.org; Web: www.ccab.org.

Community Service Centers and Divisions—Greater Boston Catholic Charities; Haitian Multi-Service Center; Laboure Center; Merrimack Valley Catholic Charities; Catholic Charities North; Catholic Charities South; Child Care Division; Refugee and Immigration Services Division.

Catholic Charities Senior Management—Rev. PHILLIP B. EARLEY, Gen. Counsel; MS. JENNIFER MENDELSOHN, CFO; MR. LARRY MAYES, Vice Pres. for Programs; MR. KENNETH P. BINDER, Vice Pres. Devel.; MS. KATHRINE HASTINGS, Dir. Devel.; MS. CAROL REILLY, Dir. Human Resources; MR. DAVID I. WALSH, Chief Information Officer; MR. BARRY VERONESI, Controller; MR. DANIEL DORMER, Dir. Real Estate; MS. MARY ANN ANTHONY, Dir. Child Care Div.; MS. VIRGINIA A. DOOCY, M.A., Dir. CC North & Merrimack; MS. MARJEAN A. PERHOT, Dir. Refugee & Immigration Svcs.; MR. DAVID L. PHILLIPS, Dir. CC South; Sr. MARYADELE ROBINSON, D.C., Dir. Laboure Ctr.; MS. VIVIAN SOPER, L.I.C.S.W., Dir. CC Greater Boston.

Greater Boston Catholic Charities—MS. BETH CHAMBERS, M.S.W., Dir. Community Svcs., Services: Basic Needs Emergency Services, Sunset Point Camp, Youth Empowerment, Family Stabilization, Foster Grandparents, Friendly Visitor and Elderly Outreach, Healthy Families, Housing and Transitional Living, Adoption Search., 185 Columbia Rd., Dorchester, 02121. Tel: 617-506-6600; Fax: 617-282-3483.

Greater Boston Catholic Charities at Somerville—270 Washington St., Somerville, 02143. Tel: 617-625-1920; Fax: 617-629-2246.

Teen Center at Saint Peter's—278 Bowdoin St., Dorchester, 02122. Tel: 617-282-3614; Fax: 617-282-3483.

Sunset Point Camp—2 10th St., Hull, 02045. Tel: 781-925-0710; Fax: 781-925-3840.

Saint Ambrose Family Shelter—Tel: 617-288-7675; Fax: 617-288-7037.

Brigid's Crossing—Tel: 978-454-0081; Fax: 978-454-0210.

Robert McBride House—Tel: 617-236-8319; Fax: 617-236-8219.

Seton Manor—Tel: 617-277-7133; Fax: 617-227-7288 .

Genesis II—Tel: 617-332-9905; Fax: 617-964-4354.

Nazareth Residence for Mothers and Children—Tel: 617-541-0100; Fax: 617-541-8781.

St. Patrick's Shelter for Homeless Women—Tel: 617-628-3015; Fax: 617-629-2246.

Laboure Center—Sr. MARYADELE ROBINSON, D.C., Dir., 275 W. Broadway, South Boston, 02127. Tel: 617-268-9670; Fax: 617-268-3088. Services: Basic Needs Emergency Services, T.E.A.M., Youth Tutoring Youth, Family Intervention, Visiting Nurse Services; Pre/Post Adoption Search, Nurse Assistant/Home Health Aide Training.

Metro Boston—

El Centro del Cardenal—MS. DEBORAH KINCADE RAMBO, Interim Dir.; MR. ROBERT HIBBARD, Dir. Adult Educ.; MR. EDWARD CASTRO, Dir. Youth Educ.; MS. BETH CHAMBERS, M.S.W., Dir. Community Svcs., Services: Basic Needs Emergency Services, Adult Basic Education, English for Employment, English for Speakers of Other Languages, Career Pathways, Alternative High School (Diploma), Pa'lante (English and Spanish GED), Parenting Support., 76 Union Park St., Boston, 02118. Tel: 617-542-9292; Fax: 617-542-6912.

Haitian Multi-Service Center—VACANT, Dir., Services: Basic Needs Emergency Services, Outpatient Counseling, Sante Manman se Sante Petite, Elder Services, Adult Education ESOL Classes, Health and Human Services Management Certificate Program; Haitian Earthquake Relief., 185 Columbia Rd., Dorchester, 02121. Tel: 617-506-6600; Fax: 617-474-1009.

Merrimack Valley Catholic Charities—MS. VIRGINIA DOOCEY, Dir., Services: Basic Needs Emergency Services, Outpatient Counseling, Education Center, Mommy and Me Program, Healthy Families, Grandparents as Parents, Parent Aide Program., 354 Merrimack St., Bldg. 1, Rm. 305, Lawrence, 01843. Tel: 978-685-5930; Fax: 978-685-0329. Merrimack Valley Catholic Charities at Lawrence, 50 Cross St., Lawrence, 01841. Tel: 978-685-5930; Fax: 978-685-0329.

Merrimack Valley Catholic Charities at Lowell—70 Lawrence St., Lowell, 01852. Tel: 978-452-1421; Fax: 978-454-9968.

Open Hand Food Pantry—16 Ashland St., Haverhill, 01830. Tel: 978-372-2828.

Food Pantry of Merrimack Valley—174 Central St., Lowell, 01852. Tel: 978-454-9946.

Lowell Food Pantry—70 Lawrence St., Lowell, 01852. Tel: 978-454-9946.

Haverhill Area Healthy Families—191 Merrimack St., Haverhill, 01830. Tel: 978-521-6265.

Merrimack Valley Young Parents Program—45 Merrimack St., Ste. 225, Lowell, 01852. Tel: 978-459-2387; Fax: 978-459-2801.

Catholic Charities North—MS. VIRGINIA A. DOOCY, M.A., Dir., Services: Basic Needs Emergency Services, Mental Health Counseling, Education and Parenting Skills Center, The Asian Center, Office Works, Companions to the Aging, Fathers Support, Young Parents, Parent Aide, Healthy Families, Boyz for Peace.

Catholic Charities North at Lynn—55 Lynn Shore Dr., Lynn, 01902. Tel: 781-593-2312; Fax: 781-581-3270.

Catholic Charities North at Salem—280 Washington St., Salem, 01970. Tel: 978-740-6923; Fax: 978-745-1863.

Catholic Charities North at Gloucester—60 Prospect St., Gloucester, 01930. Tel: 978-283-3055.

Healthy Families North Shore—55 Lynn Shore Dr.,

Lynn, 01902. Tel: 781-593-4515; Fax: 781-593-4615.

Asian Center—55 Lynn Shore Dr., Lynn, 01905. Tel: 781-593-2312.

Catholic Charities South—MS. BETH CHAMBERS, M.S.W., Dir., Services - Basic Needs Emergency Services, Nursing Assistant Training, ESOL, Parent Support Program, Elder Outreach, PALS., 169 Court St., Brockton, 02301. Tel: 508-587-0815; Fax: 508-580-0837.

Nursing Assistant Home Health Aide Training Program—250 Thatcher St., Mater Dei Bldg., Brockton, 02302. Tel: 508-587-0815; Fax: 508-580-0837.

Thrifty Pilgrim Thrift Shop—36 Cordage Park Cir., Plymouth, 02360. Tel: 508-746-6133.

Refugee and Immigration Services—MS. MARJEAN A. PERHOT, Dir., Services: Refugee Resettlement, Refugee Employment Services, Community Interpreter Services, Immigration Legal Services., 275 W. Broadway, South Boston, 02210. Tel: 617-464-8100; Fax: 617-464-8151.

Catholic Charities West—MS. BETH CHAMBERS, M.S.W., Dir. Community Svcs., Services: Basic Needs Emergency Services., 126 Main St., Rm. 6, Milford, 01757. Tel: 508-478-9632.

Behavioral Health - Family Counseling & Guidance Center—MS. DEBORAH KINCADE RAMBO, Interim Dir.

Brockton Clinic—686 N. Main St., Brockton, MA 01923. Tel: 508-587-0815; Fax: 508-586-9446.

Driver Alcohol Education—686 N. Main St., Brockton, 01923. Tel: 508-587-0815.

Danvers Clinic—152 Sylvan St., Danvers, 01923. Tel: 978-774-6820; Fax: 978-777-4242.

Refugee Resettlement—275 W. Broadway, South Boston, 02210. Tel: 617-451-7979.

Refugee Employment Services—275 W. Broadway, South Boston, 02210. Tel: 617-451-7979.

Community Interpreter Services—275 W. Broadway, South Boston, 02210. Tel: 617-451-7979; Fax: 617-629-5768; Email: cis_request@ccab.org.

Immigration Legal Services—275 W. Broadway, South Boston, 02210. Tel: 617-451-7979.

Child Care—MS. MARY ANN ANTHONY, Dir., Child Care Division Office: c/o Nazareth, 19 Saint Joseph St., Jamaica Plain, 02130. Tel: 617-524-9595; Fax: 617-832-7448.

Child Care Sites—

Lynn Child Care—MS. JANET MACDOUGALL, Dir. Child Care Svcs.; MS. BEVERLY PRIFTI, Family Child Care Dir.; MS. JUDY COMER, Asst. Dir., 37 N. Federal St., Lynn, 01905. Tel: 781-598-2759; Fax: 781-581-9740.

Peabody Child Care—MR. CHARLES JOHNSON, Dir. Child Care Svcs.; MS. BEVERLY PRIFTI, Family Child Care Dir.; MS. NADINE LADA, Preschool Prog. Dir.; MR. RALPH LAMONDA, School-Age Prog. Dir., 13 Pulaski St., Peabody, 01960. Tel: 978-532-6860; Fax: 978-531-7429.

Cambridge/Somerville/Malden—MR. RICHARD MURPHY, Dir. Child Care Svcs.; MS. SHARON RICHARDSON-O'CONNELL, Family Child Care Dir., 187 Central St., Somerville, 02145. Tel: 617-623-8555; Fax: 617-623-5014.

North Cambridge Children's Center—MS. CINDY GREEN, Dir. Child Care Svcs., 21C Walden Square Rd., Cambridge, 02140. Tel: 617-876-0503; Fax: 617-497-6464.

Malden Early Education & Learning Program—MS. DIANA MAKHLOUF, Prog. Dir., 77 Salem St., Malden, 02148. Tel: 781-397-1556; Fax: 781-322-4309.

Malden High Teen Parent Child Care—MS. DIANA MAKHLOUF, Dir. Child Care Svcs.; MS. GINNY COHAN, Asst. Dir., 77 Salem St., Malden, 02148. Tel: 781-397-6055; Fax: 781-322-1559.

Laboure Child Care Center—MS. PEGGY KELLY, Dir. Child Care Svcs.; MS. KIM MURRAY, Asst. Dir., 275 W. Broadway, Boston, 02127. Tel: 617-464-8500; Fax: 617-269-1386.

Yawkey Konbit-Kreyol Center for Early Education & Care—SR. ESTHER GARCIA, S.A., Dir. Child Care Svcs., 185 Columbia Rd., Dorchester, 02121. Tel: 617-506-6900.

Nazareth Child Care Center—MS. PAMELA J. PENTON, Dir. Child Care Svcs., 19 Saint Joseph St., Jamaica Plain, 02130. Tel: 617-522-4040; Fax: 617-983-0406.

Caritas Saint Mary Women and Children's Center—MS. JUDITH BECKLER, Pres., 90 Cushing Ave., Boston, 02125. Tel: 617-436-8600; Fax: 617-288-8961; Email: contact@stmaryscenterma.org; Web: www.stmaryscenter.org.

Education—MS. KATHY MEARS, Supt. Schools, Catholic School Office, 66 Brooks Dr., Braintree, 02184-3839. Tel: 617-779-3601; Tel: 617-779-3610; Fax: 617-746-5702.

Catholic School Office—MS. KATHY MEARS, Sec. Educ. & Supt. Schools, Catholic School Office, 66 Brooks Dr., Braintree, 02184-3839. Tel: 617-779-3601; Tel: 617-779-3610; Fax: 617-746-5702.

Associate Superintendent of Mission Effectiveness and Leadership—MR. DANIEL ROY, Email: roy_d@rcab.org.

Data Associate—MS. REBECCA MONGEAU, Email: becky_mongeau@rcab.org.

Director of Academics—DR. ANDREW MILLER, Email: miller_a@rcab.org.

Director of Enrollment Management—SR. BARBARA GUTIERREZ, Email: smith_je@rcab.org.

Director of Government Grants and Programs—MS. MARY GOSLIN, Email: goslin_m@rcab.org.

Director of Research & Data—MS. ANNIE SMITH, Email: smith_a@rcab.org.

Director of School Finance—MS. MARTHA HULTZMAN, Email: martha_hultzman@rcab.org.

Director of School Improvement Planning—MS. JAIME GAUDET, Email: gaudet_j@rcab.org.

Enrollment Associate—MS. MARIANA FONTOURA, Email: fontoura_m@rcab.org.

Manager of School Communications—MS. MEGHAN STELLMAN, Email: mstellman@rcab.org.

Operations Associate—ALEXIS PARRY, Email: alexis_parry@rcab.org.

Senior Financial Analyst—MS. JENNIFER SMITH, Email: jennifer_smith@rcab.org.

Catholic Media—Most Rev. ROBERT P. REED, Sec., 66 Brooks Dr., Braintree, 02184-3839. Web: bostoncatholic.org/catholicmedia.aspx; MR. RICK MOSLEY, Dir. Finance, 34 Chestnut St., Watertown, 02471-9196. Tel: 617-923-0220; Fax: 617-923-3490; Email: rmosley@catholictv.org.

Pilot Bulletins—MR. PAUL BLANCHETTE, Dir., Tel: 617-779-3771; Fax: 617-224-0866; Email: pblanchette@pilotbulletins.net; Web: pilotbulletins.net.

Boston Catholic Directory—Tel: 617-779-3790; Fax: 617-779-4560; Email: rmogrady@pilotcatholicnews.com; Email: directory@pilotcatholicnews.com; Web: bostoncatholicdirectory.com.

Pilot Media Group—MR. ANTONIO M. ENRIQUE, Pres., Tel: 617-779-3781; Fax: 617-779-4562; Email: aenrique@pilotcatholicnews.com; Web: pilotcatholicnews.com; VACANT, Producer, Tel: 617-779-3794; Fax: 617-300-8687; Email: rheil@rcab.org; Web: thegoodcatholiclife.com; Most Rev. ROBERT P. REED, 34 Chestnut St., Watertown, 02471-9196. Tel: 617-923-0220; Fax: 617-923-3490; Email: reed@catholictv.org; MR. LARRY RICARDO, Advertising Mgr., Tel: 617-779-3788; Fax: 617-779-4560; Email: lricardo@pilotcatholicnews.com; Web: pilotcatholicnews.com; MS. MARILYN COLLINS, Business & Circulation Coord., Tel: 617-779-3789; Fax: 617-779-4560; Email: mcollins@pilotcatholicnews.com.

Pilot New Media—MR. DOMENICO BETTINELLI, Creative Dir., Tel: 617-779-3754; Fax: 617-300-8687; Email: dbett@pilotnewmedia.com; Web: pilotnewmedia.com; MR. GEORGE MARTELL, Producer, Tel: 617-779-3753; Fax: 617-300-8687; Email: gmartell@pilotnewmedia.com; Web: pilotnewmedia.com; MS. ANASTACIA MORABITO, Webmaster, Tel: 617-779-3756; Fax: 617-779-4560; Email: amorabito@rcab.org; Web: bostoncatholic.org.

Pilot Printing—MR. MIKE STRONG, Dir., Tel: 617-779-3774; Fax: 617-224-0866; Email: mstrong@pilotbulletins.net; Web: pilotprinting.net; MS. ROSE LENTO, Business Mgr., Tel: 617-779-3773; Fax: 617-224-0866; Email: rlento@pilotbulletins.net; Web: pilotprinting.net.

Radio Apostolate—VACANT, Tel: 617-779-3751; Fax: 617-300-8687; Web: thegoodcatholiclife.com.

The Pilot—MR. ANTONIO M. ENRIQUE, Editor, Tel: 617-779-3781; Fax: 617-779-4562; Email: aenrique@pilotcatholicnews.com; Web: pilotcatholicnews.com; MR. GREGORY L. TRACY, Mng. Editor, Tel: 617-779-3782; Fax: 617-779-4562; Email: gtracy@pilotcatholicnews.com; Web: pilotcatholicnews.com.

CatholicTV Network—Most Rev. ROBERT P. REED, Pres., Email: reed@catholictv.org; MR. JAY FADDEN, Exec. Vice Pres. & Gen. Mgr., 34 Chestnut St., Watertown, 02471-9196. Tel: 617-923-0220; Fax: 617-923-3490; Email: jfadden@catholictv.org; Web: catholictv.com.

Archdiocesan Cemeteries—

The Catholic Cemetery Association of the Archdiocese of Boston, Inc.—MR. ROBERT VISCONTI, Exec. Dir., 100 Cummings Ctr., Ste. 421F, Beverly, 01915. Tel: 781-322-6300 (Office); Fax: 978-969-0493; Web: ccemetery.org.

Archdiocesan Cemeteries—These cemeteries are owned and managed by The Catholic Cemetery Association of the Archdiocese of Boston, Inc.

Boston—Saint Francis de Sales, 313 Bunker Hill St., Boston, 02129-1826. Pastoral Region Central.

Andover—Sacred Heart, Corbett Rd., Andover, 01810. Pastoral Region Merrimack.

Arlington—Saint Paul, 30 Broadway, Arlington, 02179-5523. Pastoral Region North.

Beverly—Saint Mary, 106 Brimbal Ave., Beverly, 01915-1936. Pastoral Region North.

Cambridge—North Cambridge Catholic, 244 Rindge Ave., Cambridge, 02140-2526. Pastoral Region Central.

Framingham—Saint George, 177 Cherry St., Framingham, 01706. Pastoral Region West.

Gloucester—Calvary, 151 Eastern Ave., Gloucester, 01930; Pastoral Region North. Oak Hill, 55 Poplar St., Gloucester, 01930; Pastoral Region North.

Haverhill—Saint James, 360 Primrose St., Haverhill, 01830-3198; Pastoral Region Merrimack. Saint Joseph, 892 Hilldale Ave., Haverhill, 01830; Pastoral Region Merrimack. St. Patrick, 395 N. Broadway, Haverhill, 01830; Pastoral Region Merrimack.

Lynn—Saint Jean, 134 Broadway, Lynn, 01904-1868; Pastoral Region North. Saint Joseph, 134 Broadway, Lynn, 01904-1868; Pastoral Region North. Saint Mary, 190 Lynnfield St., Lynn, 01904; Pastoral Region North.

Malden—Holy Cross, 175 Broadway, Malden, 02148-6097; Pastoral Region North. Saint Mary, 304 Fellsway E., Malden, 02148; Pastoral Region North.

Marblehead—Star of the Sea, 140 Lafayette St., Marblehead, 01947. Pastoral Region North.

Marlborough—Immaculate Conception, Beach St., Marlborough, 01752; Pastoral Region West. Saint Mary, Beach St., Marlborough, 01752; Pastoral Region West.

Salem—Saint Mary, 226 North St., Salem, 01970-1645. Pastoral Region North.

Stoneham—Saint Patrick, 120 Elm St., Stoneham, 02180. Pastoral Region North.

Waltham—Calvary, 250 High St., Waltham, 02154-5914. Pastoral Region West.

Watertown—Catholic Mount Auburn, 64 Cottage St., Watertown, 02472-1516; Pastoral Region West. Saint Patrick, Belmont St., Watertown, 02472; Pastoral Region West.

Winchester—Calvary, 686 Washington St., Winchester, 01890. Pastoral Region North.

Parish Cemeteries—These cemeteries are owned and managed by the respective parishes.

Boston—Saint Augustine, 225 Dorchester Ave., Boston, 02127. Tel: 617-268-1230. Parish: Saint Monica and Saint Augustine Parish. Region: Central.

Abington—Saint Patrick, 455 Plymouth St., Abington, 02351. Tel: 781-982-8974. Parish: Saint Bridget Parish. Region: South.

Amesbury—Saint Joseph, 6 Allen's Court, Amesbury, 01913. Tel: 978-388-0330. Parish: Holy Family Parish. Region: Merrimack.

Avon—Saint Michael, 87 N. Main St., Avon, 02322. Tel: 508-586-7210. Parish: Saint Michael Parish. Region: South.

Ayer—Saint Mary, 31 Shirley St., Ayer, 01432. Tel: 978-772-2414. Parish: Saint Mary Parish. Region: Merrimack.

Bridgewater—Saint Thomas Aquinas, 103 Center St., Bridgewater, 02324. Tel: 508-697-9528. Parish: Saint Thomas Aquinas Parish. Region: South.

Brockton—Calvary, 331 Main St., Brockton, 02301; Parish: Saint Patrick Parish. Region: South. Tel: 508-586-4840. *Saint Patrick, 331 Main St., Brockton, 02301; Parish: Saint Patrick Parish. Region: South*. Tel: 508-586-4840.

Canton—Saint Mary, 700 Washington St., Canton, 02021. Tel: 781-828-0090. *Parish: Saint John the Evangelist Parish. Region: South.*

Concord—Saint Bernard, 70 Monument Square, Concord, 01742. Tel: 978-369-7442. *Parish: Holy Family Parish. Region: West.*

Danvers—Annunciation and Saint Mary, 24 Conant St., Danvers, 01935. Tel: 978-774-0340 Parish: Saint Mary of the Annunciation Parish. Region: North.

Dedham—Saint Mary, 420 High St., Dedham, 02026. Tel: 781-326-0550. *Parish: Saint Mary Parish. Region: West.*

Foxborough—Saint Mary, 58 Carpenter St., Foxborough, 02035. Tel: 508-543-7726. *Parish: Saint Mary Parish. Region: West.*

Framingham—Saint Stephen, 221 Concord St., Framingham, 01702. Tel: 508-875-4788 Parish: Saint Stephen

Parish. Region: West. *Saint Tarcisius, Winthrop St., Framingham, 01702.*
Tel: 508-875-8623 Parish: Saint Tarcisius Parish. Region: West.

Franklin—Saint Mary, Beaver St., Franklin, 02038. Tel: 508-528-6826. *Parish: Saint Mary Parish. Region: West.*

Hingham—Saint Paul, 147 North St., Hingham, 02043. Tel: 781-749-0587. *Parish: Saint Paul Parish. Region: South.*

Holliston—Saint Mary, Washington St., Holliston, 01746. Tel: 508-429-4427. *Parish: Saint Mary Parish. Region: West.*

Hopkinton—Saint John the Evangelist, 20 Church St., Hopkinton, 01748.
Tel: 508-435-3313. *Parish: Saint John the Evangelist Parish. Region: West.*

Kingston—Saint Joseph, Elm St., Kingston, 02364. Tel: 781-585-6679. *Parish: Saint Joseph Parish. Region: South.*

Lawrence—Saint Mary, 29 Barker St., Lawrence, 01841. Tel: 978-682-8181. Parish: Saint Mary of the Assumption. Region: Merrimack.

Lowell—Holy Trinity, 140 Boston Rd., Lowell, 01852.
Tel: 978-452-2564 Parish: Holy Trinity Parish. Region: Merrimack. *Saint Mary, 384 Stevens St., Lowell, 01851.*
Tel: 978-458-8464 Parish: Saint Margaret Parish. Region: Merrimack. *Saint Patrick, 384 Stevens St., Lowell, 01851.*
Tel: 978-458-8464 Parish: Saint Margaret Parish. Region: Merrimack.

Maynard—Saint Bridget, One Percival St., Maynard, 01754. Tel: 978-897-2171. Parish: Saint Bridget Parish. Region: West.

Middleborough—Saint Mary, Wood St., Middleboro, 02346. Tel: 508-947-0444. Parish: Sacred Heart Parish. Region: South.

Needham—Saint Mary, 270 Elliot St., Newton, 02462. Tel: 781-235-1841. Parish: Mary Immaculate of Lourdes Parish. Region: West.

Newburyport—Saint Mary, Green St., Newburyport, 01950. Tel: 978-462-2724. Parish: Immaculate Conception Parish. Region: Merrimack.

North Andover—Holy Sepulchre, 114 S. Broadway, Lawrence, 01843.
Tel: 978-683-9416. Parish: Saint Patrick Parish. Region: Merrimack.

Pepperell—Saint Joseph, Jersey St., Pepperell, 01463. Tel: 978-433-9725. Parish: St. Joseph. Region: Merrimack.

Plymouth—Saint Joseph, 86 Court St., Plymouth, 02360. Tel: 508-746-0663. Parish: Saint Peter Parish. Region: South.

Quincy—Saint Mary, 95 Crescent St., Quincy, 02169. Tel: 617-773-0120. Parish: Saint Mary Parish. Region: South.

Randolph—Saint Mary, 211 N. Main St., Randolph, 02368. Tel: 781-961-9323. Parish: Saint Mary Parish. Region: South.

Rockland—Holy Family, 403 Union St., Rockland, 02370. Tel: 781-878-2306. Parish: Holy Family Parish. Region: South.

Shirley—Saint Anthony of Padua, 12 Phoenix St., Shirley, 01464. Tel: 978-425-4588. Parish: Saint Anthony of Padua Parish. Region: Merrimack.

Stoughton—Holy Sepulchre, Central St., Stoughton, 02072. Tel: 781-344-2073. Parish: Immaculate Conception Parish. Region: South.

Walpole—Saint Francis, Diamond St., Walpole, 02081. Tel: 508-668-4700. Parish: Blessed Sacrament Parish. Region: West.

Wayland—Saint Zepherin, 99 Main St., Wayland, 01778. Tel: 508-653-8013. Parish: Good Shepherd Parish. Region: West.

Westford—Saint Catherine of Alexandria, 107 N. Main St., Westford, 01886. Tel: 978-692-6353. Parish: Saint Catherine of Alexandria Parish. Region: Merrimack.

Weymouth—Saint Francis Xavier, 234 Pleasant St., Weymouth, 02190. Tel: 781-337-3144. Parish: Saint Francis Xavier Parish. Region: South.

Whitman—Saint James, School St., Whitman, 02382. Tel: 781-447-4421. Parish: Holy Ghost Parish. Region: South.

*Private Cemeteries—*These cemeteries are owned and managed by the respective corporations.

Boston—Mount Benedict Cemetery, 409 Corey St., West Roxbury, 02132.
Tel: 617-323-8389 Owner: Boston Catholic Cemetery Association. *Mount Calvary Cemetery, 366 Cummins Hwy., Roslindale, 02131.*
Tel: 617-325-0883 Owner: Boston Catholic Cemetery Association. *New Calvary Cemetery, 800 Harvard St., Mattapan, 02126.*
Tel: 617-296-2339 Owner: Boston Catholic Cemetery Association. *Saint Joseph Cemetery, 990 Lagrange St., West Roxbury, 02132.*
Tel: 617-327-1010 Owner: Holyhood Cemetery Association. *Saint Mary Cemetery, Bernard St., Dorchester, 02124.*
Tel: 617-325-6830 Owner: Boston Catholic Cemetery Association. *Saint Michael Cemetery, 500 Canterbury St., Forest Hills, 02131.*
Tel: 617-524-1036 Owner: Saint Michael Cemetery Association.

Brookline—Holyhood Cemetery, Heath St., Brookline, 02467. Tel: 617-327-1010. Owner: Holyhood Cemetery Association.

Chelmsford—Saint Joseph Cemetery, 96 Riverneck Rd., Chelmsford, 01824-2941. Tel: 978-458-4851. Owner: Saint Joseph Cemetery, Inc.

*Charismatic Renewal—*MR. ALVARO SOARES, Dir. & Liaison, 30 Pond St., Waltham, 02451-4514. Tel: 781-333-5308; Email: staff@crsboston.org; Email: director@crsboston.org.

*Chrism—*CELIA SIROIS, B.A., M.A., Coord., 236 Pleasant St., Weymouth, 02190-2507. Fax: 781-337-3225.

*Clergy Services Group—*Very Rev. BRYAN K. PARRISH, V.F., 66 Brooks Dr., Braintree, 02184-3839. Tel: 617-746-5928; Fax: 617-779-4576.

*Clergy Personnel—*Rev. ROBERT M. BLANEY, V.F., Dir., Tel: 617-746-5866; Fax: 617-746-5614; Email: frrobert_blaney@rcab.org; Deacon PATRICK E. GUERRINI, Asst. Dir., Tel: 617-746-5658; Fax: 617-746-5498; Email: deacon_patrick_guerrini@rcab.org.

*Pastoral Care of Clergy—*VACANT.

*Pastoral Care of Priests & Clergy Fund—*Very Rev. BRYAN K. PARRISH, V.F., Tel: 617-746-5928; Fax: 617-779-4576.

*Priests' Recovery Program—*Very Rev. BRIAN M. CLARY, V.F., Dir., 5 Linden Pl., Brookline, 02445-7311. Tel: 617-473-0444; Fax: 617-734-3001; Email: frbrian2002@yahoo.com.

Senior Priests—60 William Cardinal O'Connell Way, Boston, 02114-2729. Tel: 617-723-3976; Fax: 617-523-0092.

*Clergy Personnel Board—*Ex Officio: Rev. ROBERT M. BLANEY, V.F., Chm. & Member; Most Rev. PETER J. UGLIETTO, Member; Very Rev. KEVIN M. SEPE, Member. Archbishop's Designee: Rev. Msgr. DENNIS F. SHEEHAN, (Retired), (2012-2016). Block: Rev. ARNOLD F. COLLETTI, Block I (-1965), (Retired), (2013-2017); Very Revs. JOHN F. MULLOY, V.F., Block II (1966-1971), (2012-2016); GEORGE P. EVANS, V.F., A.B., M.Div., S.T.L., S.T.D., Block III (1972-1979), (2012-2016); Revs. THOMAS F. NESTOR, A.B., M.Div., Ph.D., Block IV (1980-1989), (2013-2017); JAMES M. MAHONEY, M.Div., Block V (1990-1999), (2011-2015); WILLIAM P. LOHAN, Block VI (2000-), (2013-2017). Region: Very Revs. RICHARD W. FITZGERALD, V.F., Central, (2013-2017); JOHN W. DELANEY, V.F., Merrimack, (2013-2017); STEPHEN B. ROCK, V.F., North, (2013-2017); JASON M. MAKOS, V.F., South, (2013-2017); FRANK J. SILVA, V.F., West, (2013-2017).

*Communications and Public Affairs—*MR. TERRENCE C. DONILON, Sec., 66 Brooks Dr., Braintree, 02184-3839. Tel: 617-746-5775; Fax: 617-779-4572; Email: tdonilon@rcab.org.

*Cor Unum Meal Center—*MS. DIANE JARVIS, Dir., 191 Salem St., Lawrence, 01843-1427. Tel: 978-688-8900; Fax: 978-681-5808; Email: corunummealcenter@comcast.net; Web: www.corunummealcenter.org.

*Courage—*Rev. DEREK J. BOREK, Spiritual Dir., 127 Lake St., Brighton, 02135. Tel: 617-779-4302; Fax: 617-789-2336; Email: courageboston@gmail.com.

Cursillo—66 Brooks Dr., Braintree, 02184-3839.
Tel: 617-779-3640; Fax: 617-779-4570. Rev. JOHN E. SASSANI, A.B., M.Div., Spiritual Dir., Email: jsassani@ourladys.com; MS. MARYANN MCLAUGHLIN, B.A., M.A., Lay Dir., Email: maryann_mclaughlin@rcab.org.

*Ecumenical and Interreligious Affairs—*Most Rev. ARTHUR L. KENNEDY, 66 Brooks Dr., Braintree, 02184-3839. Tel: 617-746-5749; Fax: 617-779-4572.

*EnCourage—*VACANT.

*Secretariat for Evangelization and Discipleship—*Most Rev. ARTHUR L. KENNEDY, Episcopal Vicar for the New Evangelization, 66 Brooks Dr., Braintree, 02184. Email: mostreverendarthur_kennedy@rcab.org; Rev. PAUL R. SOPER, Sec. Evangelization & Discipleship, Tel: 617-746-5853; Email: psoper@rcab.org; Web: bostoncatholic.org/evangelizationanddiscipleship/; MR. MICHAEL LAVIGNE, Asst. Sec. Evangelization & Discipleship, Tel: 617-746-5748; Email: mlavigne@rcab.org.

Office of Divine Worship—66 Brooks Dr., Braintree, 02184-3839. Tel: 617-779-3640; Fax: 617-779-4570. Rev. JONATHAN M. GASPAR, Dir., Tel: 617-746-5880; Email: jgaspar@rcab.org.

*Office of Lifelong Faith Formation and Parish Support—*MR. MICHAEL LAVIGNE, Dir., Tel: 617-746-5748; Email: mlavigne@rcab.org; Web: bostoncatholic.org/lffps.aspx; MRS. EMILY ELLIOTT, Oper. Assoc., Tel: 617-746-5756; Email: eelliott@rcab.org; MR. PATRICK KRISAK, Dir., Training & Support, Tel: 617-746-5753; Email: pkrisak@rcab.org; MRS. AMBER EZEANI, Evangelization Consultant, Tel: 617-746-5755; Email: aezeani@rcab.org; MR. THOMAS LYMAN, Evangelization Consultant, Tel: 617-746-5759; Email: tlyman@rcab.org; MR. CRAIG DYKE, Dir., Family Life, Tel: 617-746-5801; Email: cdyke@rcab.org; MRS. MARY FINNIGAN, Coord., NFP, Tel: 617-746-5803; Email: mfinnigan@rcab.org; Rev. MATTHEW M. WILLIAMS, Dir., Faith Formaiton, Tel: 617-746-5752; Email: fathermatt_williams@rcab.org; MS. KATHRYN BOYLE, Coord., Faith Formation of Children, Tel: 617-746-5758; Email: kboyle@rcab.org; MR. MICHAEL DRAHOS, Coord., Faith Formation of Youth & Young Adults, Tel: 617-746-5751; Email: mdrahos@rcab.org; MRS. SUSAN J. KAY, B.A., M.Ed., Coord., Faith Formation of Adults, Tel: 617-746-5861; Email: skay@rcab.org; MRS. KATHLEEN STEBBINS, Coord., Faith Formation of Youth & Young Adults, Tel: 617-746-5811; Email: kstebbins@rcab.org.

*Office of Outreach and Cultural Diversity—*Rev. MICHAEL C. HARRINGTON, Dir., 66 Brooks Dr., Braintree, 02184-3839. Tel: 617-746-5939; Email: mharrington@rcab.org.

*Office of Pastoral Planning—*Rev. PAUL R. SOPER, Dir., 66 Brooks Dr., Boston, 02135-3193. Tel: 617-746-5865; Fax: 617-746-5614; Email: paul_soper@rcab.org.

Office of Spiritual Life—66 Brooks Dr., Braintree, 02184-3839. Tel: 617-779-3640;
Fax: 617-779-4570. MS. MARYANN MCLAUGHLIN, B.A., M.A., Dir., Tel: 617-746-3640; Email: mmclaugh@rcab.org; Sr. ANNE D'ARCY, C.S.J., Assoc. Dir. Spiritual Life, Tel: 617-779-3648; Fax: 617-779-4570; Fax: 617-779-4570; Email: sdarcy@rcab.org; Revs. DANIEL O'CONNELL, Assoc. Dir. Spiritual Life, Tel: 617-779-3643; Fax: 617-779-4570; Email: roconnell@rcab.org; JOHN E. SASSANI, A.B., M.Div., Assoc. Dir. Spiritual Life, Tel: 617-527-7560, Ext. 215; Fax: 617-779-4570; Email: jsassani@ourladys.com; MS. PATRICIA DEBIASE, Administrative Asst., Tel: 617-779-3645; Fax: 617-779-4570; Email: patricia_debiase@rcab.org; MS. ANN GENNARO, Project Coord., Tel: 617-746-5746; Email: agennaro@rcab.org; MS. DANIELLE OLSEN, Creative Design Specialist, Tel: dolsen@rcab.org.

*Why Catholic?—*MS. MARYANN MCLAUGHLIN, B.A., M.A., Archdiocesan Coord., Tel: 617-779-3640; Fax: 617-779-4570; Email: mmclaugh@rcab.org; MS. ANN M. CUSSEN, Oper. Asst., Tel: 617-779-3644; Fax: 617-779-4570; Email: ann_cussen@rcab.org.

*Airport Chaplaincy—*Rev. RICHARD A. UFTRING, Chap., Logan International Airport, Boston, 02128. Tel: 617-567-2800; Email: fatherrichard@massport.com.

*Office of Black Catholics—*MS. LORNA DESROSES, 66 Brooks Dr., Braintree, 02184-3839. Tel: 617-746-5810; Fax: 617-746-5614; Email: ldesroses@rcab.org; MS. GAIL MATTULINA, Tel: 617-746-5814; Email: gmattulina@rcab.org.

Office of the Deaf Apostolate—66 Brooks Dr., Braintree, 02184-3839. Tel: 617-746-5815; Fax: 617-779-4570; Web: www.deafcatholic.org.

*Director—*Rev. SHAWN P. CAREY, Tel: 781-267-7109 (Work); Tel: 866-572-8386 (Video Phone); Email: frshawn@deafcatholic.org.

*Interpreter Coordinator / Staff Interpreter—*MS. JENNA KISH, Email: jenna_kish@rcab.org.

*Coordinator of the Deaf Senior Wellness Program—*MS. ELIZABETH WHITTACKER, Tel: 617-746-5817 (Work); Email: elizabeth_whittacker@rcab.org. Mass in American Sign Language and Deaf Senior Wellness Program take place at Sacred Heart Parish, 1317 Centre St., Newton, MA 02459. Tel: 617-969-2248.

American Sign—

Danvers—New England Home for the Deaf. Tel: 978-774-0445.

Middleborough—Sacred Heart. Tel: 508-947-0444.

Newton—Sacred Heart. Tel: 617-969-2248.

*Outreach and Cultural Diversity—*Rev. MICHAEL C. HARRINGTON, Dir., 66 Brooks Dr., Braintree, 02184-3839. Tel: 617-746-5794; Fax: 617-746-5614; Email: michael_harrington@rcab.org; Web: catholicculturaldiversity.com; MR. ROBERT KAVANAUGH, Office Coord., Tel: 617-746-5791; Email: robert_kavanaugh@rcab.org; MS. LORNA DESROSES, Dir. Office of Black Catholics, Tel: 617-

746-5810; Email: ldesroses@rcab.org; NATALIA MIGIOLI SOARES, Project Coord./Oper. Assoc., Tel: 617-746-5793; Email: natalia_soares@rcab.org; MS. GAIL MATTULINA, Oper. Asst. for the Office of Black Catholics, Tel: 617-746-5814; Email: gail_mattulina@rcab.org; Rev. SHAWN P. CAREY, Dir. Deaf Apostolate, Tel: 781-267-7109; Email: frshawn@deafcatholic.org; MS. JENNA KISH, Interpreter Coord./Staff Interpreter, Tel: 617-746-5815; Email: jenna.kish@deafcatholic.org; MS. ELIZABETH WHITTAKER, Sr. Deaf Wellness Prog. Coord., Tel: 617-746-5817; Email: elizabeth_whittaker@rcab.org; MS. KAREN MURRAY, Dir. Office for Disabilities, Tel: 617-746-5679; Email: kmurray@rcab.org; Rev. RICHARD A. UFTRING, Airport & Seaport Chap., Logan International Airport, Boston, 02128. Tel: 617-567-2800; Email: fatherrichard@massport.com; Web: bostoncatholic.org/loganairportchaplain.aspx.

Black Catholic Choir—MR. MEYER CHAMBERS, Tel: 617-448-4578.

Brazilian—Office for Cultural Diversity. Tel: 617-746-5794.

Cambodian—Deacon AN ROS, Tel: 978-459-0561.

Chinese—MS. MEE CHAN, Tel: 617-542-8498.

Filipino—MS. GRACITA TENG CHIEFE, Tel: 781-963-1740.

French—Office of Cultural Diversity. Tel: 617-746-5810.

German—Office of Cultural Diversity. Tel: 617-746-5794.

Hmong—Office of Cultural Diversity. Tel: 617-746-5794.

Indian—Office of Cultural Diversity. Tel: 617-746-5794.

Japanese—Office of Cultural Diversity. Tel: 617-746-5794.

Korean—Rev. DOMINIC K. JUNG, C.PP.S., Tel: 617-244-9685.

Lithuanian—Very Rev. STEPHEN P. ZUKAS, V.F., Tel: 617-268-0353.

Polish—Office of Cultural Diversity. Tel: 617-746-5794.

Portuguese—Very Rev. WALTER A. CARREIRO, V.F., Tel: 617-547-5593.

Vietnamese—Very Rev. LINH T. NGUYEN, V.F., Tel: 781-963-1327.

Hispanic Apostolate—Rev. FRANCISCO J. ANZOATEGUI PEIRO; MR. FERNANDO FERNANDEZ-ARELLANO, Coord. Programs, 66 Brooks Dr., Braintree, 02184-3839. Tel: 617-746-5816; Fax: 617-779-4570; Email: fernando_fernandez@rcab.org.

Hispanic Ministry Sites—

Boston—Cathedral of the Holy Cross. Tel: 617-542-5682. *Saint Anthony Shrine.* Tel: 617-542-6440. *Saint Francis Chapel.* Tel: 617-437-7117. *Saint Columbkille.* Tel: 617-782-5774. *Holy Family.* Tel: 617-445-9553. *Saint Mark.* Tel: 617-825-2852. *Saint Christopher.* Tel: 617-436-7273. *Madonna Queen Shrine.* Tel: 617-569-2100. *Most Holy Redeemer.* Tel: 617-567-3227. *Our Lady of the Assumption.* Tel: 617-567-1223. *Our Lady of Lourdes.* Tel: 617-524-0434. *Saint Thomas Aquinas.* Tel: 617-524-0240. *Sacred Heart.* Tel: 617-325-3322. *Our Lady of Perpetual Help-Mission Church.* Tel: 617-445-1524. *Saint Mary of the Angels.* Tel: 617-445-2600. *Saint Patrick.* Tel: 617-445-7645. *Saint Monica and Saint Augustine.* Tel: 617-268-1230. *Saint Mary-Saint Catherine of Siena.* Tel: 617-242-4664.

Brockton—Saint Patrick. Tel: 508-586-4840.

Cambridge—Saint Mary of the Annunciation. Tel: 617-547-0120.

Chelsea—Saint Rose of Lima. Tel: 617-889-2774.

Everett—Saint Anthony of Padua. Tel: 617-387-0310. *Immaculate Conception.* Tel: 617-389-5660.

Framingham—Saint Stephen. Tel: 508-875-4788.

Haverhill—Saint James. Tel: 978-372-8537.

Lawrence—Corpus Christi. Tel: 978-685-1711. *Saint Mary of the Assumption.* Tel: 978-685-1111. *Saint Patrick.* Tel: 978-683-9416.

Lowell—Saint Patrick. Tel: 978-459-0561.

Lynn—Saint Joseph. Tel: 781-599-7040.

Marlborough—Immaculate Conception. Tel: 508-485-0016.

Newton—Saint Ignatius Loyola Church. Tel: 617-552-6100.

Peabody—Saint John the Baptist. Tel: 978-531-0002.

Revere—Immaculate Conception. Tel: 781-289-0735.

Salem—Immaculate Conception. Tel: 978-745-6303.

Somerville—Saint Benedict. Tel: 617-625-0029.

Waltham—Saint Mary. Tel: 781-891-1730.

Woburn—Saint Charles Borromeo. Tel: 781-933-0300.

Liturgies in Other Languages—

American Sign—

Danvers—New England Home for the Deaf. Tel: 978-774-0445.

Middleborough—Sacred Heart. Tel: 508-947-0444.

Newton—Sacred Heart. Tel: 617-969-2248.

Amharic—

Boston—Cathedral of the Holy Cross. Tel: 617-542-5682.

Chinese—

Boston—Saint James the Greater. Tel: 617-542-8498.

Congolese French—

Lynn—Saint Mary. Tel: 781-598-4907.

Haitian Creole—

Brockton—Christ the King. Tel: 508-586-1575.

Cambridge—Saint John the Evangelist. Tel: 617-547-4880.

Chelsea—Our Lady of Grace. Tel: 617-884-0030.

Boston—Saint Matthew. Tel: 617-436-3590.

Everett—Immaculate Conception. Tel: 617-389-5660.

Lynn—Saint Mary. Tel: 781-598-4907.

Boston—Saint Angela Merici. Tel: 617-298-0080.

Somerville—Saint Ann. Tel: 617-625-1904.

Waltham—Saint Charles Borromeo. Tel: 781-893-0330.

Igbo (Nigerian)—

Boston—Saint Katherine Drexel. Tel: 617-445-8915.

Italian—

Boston—Saint Leonard of Port Maurice. Tel: 617-523-2110.

Cambridge—Saint Francis of Assisi. Tel: 617-876-6754.

Boston—Sacred Heart. Tel: 617-567-5776.

Everett—Saint Anthony of Padua. Tel: 617-387-0310.

Lawrence—Corpus Christi. Tel: 978-685-1711.

Khmer (Cambodian)—

Lowell—Saint Patrick. Tel: 978-459-0561.

Kiswahili (Kenyan)—

Lowell—Saint Michael. Tel: 617-846-7400.

Quincy—Sacred Heart. Tel: 978-459-0713.

Winthrop—Saint John the Evangelist. Tel: 617-328-8666.

Korean—

Newton—Saint Antoine Daveluy. Tel: 617-244-0608.

Lithuanian—

Lawrence—Corpus Christi. Tel: 978-685-1711.

South Boston—Saint Peter. Tel: 617-268-0353.

Polish—

Chelsea—Saint Stanislaus. Tel: 617-889-0261.

Lowell—Holy Trinity. Tel: 978-452-2564.

Salem—Saint John the Baptist. Tel: 978-744-1278.

Boston—Our Lady of Czestochowa. Tel: 617-268-4355.

Portuguese (Brazilian)—

Boston—Saint Anthony of Padua. Tel: 617-782-0775.

Cambridge—Saint Anthony of Padua. Tel: 617-547-5593.

Boston—Madonna Queen Shrine. Tel: 617-569-2100.

Everett—Saint Anthony of Padua. Tel: 617-387-0310.

Framingham—Saint Tarcisius. Tel: 508-875-8623.

Gloucester—Holy Family. Tel: 978-281-4820.

Hudson—Saint Michael. Tel: 978-562-2552.

Lowell—Holy Family. Tel: 978-453-2134.

Marlborough—Immaculate Conception. Tel: 508-485-0016.

Maynard—Saint Bridget. Tel: 978-897-2171.

Plymouth—Saint Mary. Tel: 508-746-0426. *Holy Family.* Tel: 781-878-0160.

Rockland—Holy Family. Tel: 781-878-0160.

Salem—Saint Thomas the Apostle. Tel: 978-531-0224.

Somerville—Saint Anthony of Padua. Tel: 617-625-4530.

Stoughton—Immaculate Conception. Tel: 781-344-2073.

Woburn—Saint Charles Borromeo. Tel: 781-933-0300.

Portuguese (Cape Verdean)—

Brockton—Saint Edith Stein. Tel: 508-586-6491.

Boston—Saint Peter. Tel: 617-265-1132. *Saint Patrick.* Tel: 617-445-7645.

Scituate—Saint Mary of the Nativity. Tel: 781-545-3335.

Portuguese (European)—

Cambridge—Saint Anthony of Padua. Tel: 617-547-5593.

Framingham—Saint Tarcisius. Tel: 508-875-8623.

Gloucester—Our Lady of Good Voyage. Tel: 978-283-1490.

Hudson—Saint Michael. Tel: 978-562-2552.

Lawrence—Corpus Christi. Tel: 978-685-1711.

Lowell—Saint Anthony of Padua. Tel: 978-452-1506.

Peabody—Our Lady of Fatima. Tel: 978-532-0272.

Stoughton—Immaculate Conception. Tel: 781-344-2073.

Spanish—

Boston—Cathedral of the Holy Cross. Tel: 617-542-5682. *Saint Anthony Shrine.* Tel: 617-542-6440. *Saint Francis Chapel.* Tel: 617-437-7117. *Saint Columbkille.* Tel: 617-782-5774. *Sacred Heart.* Tel: 617-325-3519. *Our Lady of Perpetual Help.* Tel: 617-445-1524. *Saint Mary of the Angels.* Tel: 617-445-1524. *Saint Patrick.* Tel: 617-445-7645. *Saint Mary-Saint Catherine of Siena.* Tel: 617-242-1750. *Holy Family.* Tel: 617-445-9553. *Saint Ambrose.* Tel: 617-265-5302. *Saint Christopher.* Tel: 617-436-7273. *Boston Madonna Queen Shrine.* Tel: 617-569-2100. *Most Holy Redeemer.* Tel: 617-567-3227. *Our Lady of the Assumption.* Tel: 617-567-1223. *Our Lady of Lourdes.* Tel: 617-524-0434. *Saint Thomas Aquinas.* Tel: 617-524-0240. *Saint Monica and Saint Augustine.* Tel: 617-269-6760.

Brockton—Saint Patrick. Tel: 508-586-4840.

Cambridge—Saint Mary of the Annunciation. Tel: 617-547-0120.

Chelsea—Saint Rose of Lima. Tel: 617-889-2774.

Everett—Saint Anthony of Padua. Tel: 617-387-0310. *Immaculate Conception.* Tel: 617-389-5660.

Framingham—Saint Stephen. Tel: 508-875-4788.

Haverhill—Saint James. Tel: 978-372-8537.

Lawrence—Corpus Christi. Tel: 978-685-1711. *Saint Mary of the Assumption.* Tel: 978-685-1111. *Saint Patrick.* Tel: 978-683-9416.

Lowell—Saint Patrick. Tel: 978-459-0561.

Lynn—Saint Joseph. Tel: 781-599-7040.

Marlborough—Immaculate Conception. Tel: 508-485-0016.

Newton—Saint Ignatius Loyola. Tel: 617-552-6100.

Peabody—Saint John the Baptist. Tel: 978-531-0002.

Revere—Immaculate Conception. Tel: 781-289-0735.

Salem—Immaculate Conception. Tel: 978-745-6303.

Somerville—Saint Benedict. Tel: 617-625-0029.

Waltham—Saint Mary. Tel: 781-891-1730.

Woburn—Saint Charles Borromeo. Tel: 781-933-0300.

Tagalog—

Malden—Saint Joseph. Tel: 781-324-0402.

Quincy—Saint John the Baptist. Tel: 617-773-1021.

Boston—Holy Name. Tel: 617-325-4865.

Tigrinya—

Boston—Cathedral of the Holy Cross. Tel: 617-542-5682.

Vietnamese—

Chelsea—Saint Rose of Lima. Tel: 617-889-2774.

Dorchester—Saint Ambrose. Tel: 617-265-5302.

Boston—Sacred Heart. Tel: 617-567-5776.

Haverhill—Saint James. Tel: 978-372-8537.

Lawrence—Saint Patrick. Tel: 978-683-9416.

Lowell—Saint Patrick. Tel: 978-459-0561.

Malden—Sacred Heart. Tel: 781-324-0728.

Randolph—Saint Bernadette. Tel: 781-963-1327.

Seaport Chaplaincy—Rev. RICHARD A. UFTRING, Chap., Logan International Airport, Boston, 02128. Tel: 617-567-2800; Email: fatherrichard@massport.com.

Social Services and Health Care—Rev. J. BRYAN HEHIR, 66 Brooks Dr., Braintree, 02184-3839. Tel: 617-746-5733; Fax: 617-783-4564; Email: reverend_bryan_hehir@rcab.org. *As of November 5, 2010, TAS-CC, Inc. (formerly Caritas Christi) and its affiliated health care entities sold substantially all of their assets used in the operation of a health care system to Steward Healthcare System LLC ("Steward"). As a result, although the assets were transferred to Steward, almost all of the corporate entities remained directly or indirectly under the control of Corporation Sole or the Archbishop. Each of the asterisked entities were formerly Caritas Christi entities. Each of the asterisked entities is separately incorporated and none of them are consolidated with Corporation Sole for financial reporting purposes.; *TAS-CCHF, Inc; *TAS-CCL, Inc.; *TASCC, Inc.; *TAS-CCDSS, Inc.; *TASCCH, Inc.; *TAS-CCMG, Inc.; *TASCCNS, Inc.; *TAS-CCPN, Inc.; *TASCCSS, Inc.; *TAS-CECL, Inc.; *TASCGSMC, Inc.; *TAS-CGSMPC, Inc.; *TAS-CGSOHS, Inc.; *TAS-CGSROC, Inc.; *TAS-CHC, Inc.; *TAS-CHFH, Inc.; *TAS-CHFHF, Inc.; *TAS-CNEI, Inc.; *TAS-CNH, Inc.; *TAS-CSEHF, Inc.; *TAS-CSEMCB, Inc.; *TAS-CSERC, Inc.; *TAS-CSH, Inc.; *TAS-CSJGH, Inc.; *TAS-CSJNCC, Inc.; *TAS-CVRHS, Inc.; *TAS-CVRMSC, Inc.;

*TAS-CVRSS, Inc.; *TAS-CVRV, Inc.; *TAS-FRMCS, Inc.; *TAS-HCE, Inc.; *TAS-SAHC, Inc.; *TAS-SAHCMS, Inc.; *TAS-SAHCS, Inc.; *TAS-SAJCS, Inc.

Holy Name Societies—MR. ROBERT QUAGAN, 35 Cass St., Boston, 02132-4411. Tel: 617-325-5905; Email: rquagan@comcast.net.

Hospital Chaplain Ministry—Deacon JAMES F. GREER, Dir., 66 Brooks Dr., Braintree, 02184-3839. Tel: 617-746-5843; Fax: 617-746-5754.

Boston—

Arbour Hospital—49 Robinwood Ave., Boston, 02130. Tel: 617-522-4400. Pastoral Care: Our Lady of Lourdes, Jamaica Plain.

Beth Israel Deaconess Medical Center—330 Brookline Ave., Boston, 02215. Tel: 617-667-4205. Pastoral Care: TBA.

Boston Medical Center - Harrison Avenue Campus—818 Harrison Ave., Boston, 02118. Tel: 617-414-7560. Pastoral Care: TBA.

Boston Medical Center - Newton Street Campus—One Medical Center Pl., Boston, 02118-2393. Tel: 617-638-6851. Pastoral Care: TBA.

Brigham and Women's Hospital—75 Francis St., Boston, 02115-6195. Tel: 617-732-7480; Fax: 617-232-2746. Pastoral Care: Sr. KATHLEEN GALLIVAN, S.N.D.

Steward Carney Hospital—2100 Dorchester St., Boston, 02124-5666. Tel: 617-296-4000; Fax: 617-296-9513. Pastoral Care: TBA.

Steward Saint Elizabeth Medical Center—736 Cambridge St., Boston, 02135-2997. Tel: 617-789-3228; Fax: 617-789-2281. Pastoral Care: MS. MAUREEN HIGGINS.

Children's Hospital—300 Longwood Ave., Boston, 02115. Tel: 617-355-4775. Pastoral Care: MS. SHANNON FANNING.

Dana Farber Cancer Institute—44 Binney St., Boston, 02115. Tel: 617-632-3000.

Faulkner Hospital—1153 Centre St., Boston, 02130. Tel: 617-983-7000, Ext. 1556. Pastoral Care: TBA.

Franciscan Children's Hospital—30 Warren St., Boston, 02135. Tel: 617-779-1645. Pastoral Care: STEPHEN MURPHY, M.D.N.

Hebrew Rehabilitation Center—1200 Centre St., Boston, 02131. Tel: 617-361-5249. Pastoral Care: Sacred Heart, Roslindale and Holy Name, West Roxbury.

Jewish Memorial Hospital—59 Townsend St., Boston, 02119. Tel: 617-989-8315. Pastoral Care: Saint Patrick and Saint Mary of the Angels, Roxbury.

Kindred Hospital Boston—1515 Commonwealth Ave., Brighton, 02135. Tel: 617-254-1100. Pastoral Care: Saint Columbkille, Brighton.

Lemuel Shattuck Hospital—170 Morton St., Boston, 02130. Tel: 617-522-8110. Pastoral Care: Our Lady of Lourdes, Jamaica Plain.

Massachusetts General Hospital—55 Fruit St., Boston, 02114. Tel: 617-724-3226; Fax: 617-726-2220. (Pastoral Care: TBA).

New England Baptist Hospital—91 Parker Hill Ave., Boston, 02120. Tel: 617-754-5160. Pastoral Care: Rev. ANDREW ALBERT, S.M.

Shriners Burns Institute—51 Blossom St., Boston, 02114. Tel: 617-722-3000. Pastoral Care: Saint Joseph and Saint Leonard of Port Maurice, Boston.

Spaulding Rehabilitation Hospital—125 Nashua St., Boston, 02114-1198. Tel: 617-572-2780; Fax: 617-573-2419. Pastoral Care: MS. JOAN HORGAN.

Tufts Medical Center—750 Washington St., Boston, 02111. Tel: 617-636-5896. Pastoral Care: Revs. JAMES M. SHAUGHNESSY, S.J.; JANUSZ CHMIELECKI, O.F.M.Conv.

Veterans Administration Health Care System - West Roxbury—1400 VRW Pkwy., Boston, 02132. Tel: 617-323-7700. Pastoral Care: Revs. CLAUDIUS NOWINSKI, M.S.; JOHN J. NICHOLS, (Retired).

Veterans Administration Health Care System - Jamaica Plain—150 S. Huntington Ave., Boston, 02130. Tel: 857-364-5065. Pastoral Care: Rev. PHILIP SALOIS, M.S.

Ayer—

Nashoba Valley Medical Center—200 Groton St., Ayer, 01432. Tel: 978-772-2414. Pastoral Care: St. Mary, Ayer.

Bedford—

Veterans Administration Health Care System - Bedford—200 Spring Rd., Bedford, 01730. Tel: 781-687-2384. Pastoral Care: Rev. SEBASTIAN A. UGOCHUKWU.

Belmont—

McLean Hospital—115 Mill St., Belmont, 02178. Tel: 617-855-2000. Pastoral Care: Saint Luke, Belmont and local parishes.

Beverly—

Beverly Hospital—75 Herrick St., Beverly, 01915. Tel: 978-922-3000, Ext. 2790. Pastoral Care: TBA.

Braintree—

Health South Braintree Hospital—250 Pond St., Braintree, 02184. Tel: 781-348-2500. Pastoral Care: Saint Francis of Assisi.

Northeast Specialty Hospital—2001 Washington St., Braintree, 02185. Tel: 781-952-2254. Pastoral Care: Saint Clare, Braintree.

Brockton—

Brockton Hospital—680 Centre St., Brockton, 02302. Tel: 508-941-7000, Ext. 2550. Pastoral Care: Sr. BARBARA HARRINGTON, O.P.

Steward Good Samaritan Medical Center—235 N. Pearl St., Brockton, 02301. Tel: 508-427-2376. Pastoral Care: MR. GERALD PACIELLO.

McLean Hospital Brockton—940 Belmont St., Brockton, 02402. Tel: 508-894-8420. Pastoral Care: Our Lady of Lourdes, Brockton.

Veterans Administration Health Care System - Brockton—930 Belmont St., Brockton, 02402. Tel: 508-583-4500. Pastoral Care: VACANT.

Brookline—

Bournewood Health System—300 South St., Brookline, 02146. Tel: 617-469-0300. Pastoral Care: Saint Mary of the Assumption, Brookline.

Burlington—

Lahey Clinic—41 Mall Rd., Burlington, 01805. Tel: 781-744-8800. Pastoral Care: MR. WILLIAM W. HOUGHTON; MS. LORRAINE BARRETT.

Cambridge—

Cambridge Hospital—1493 Cambridge St., Cambridge, 02139. Tel: 617-665-1000. Pastoral Care: Local Cambridge Parishes.

Mount Auburn Hospital—330 Mt. Auburn St., Cambridge, 02238. Tel: 617-499-5206. Pastoral Care: MS. MARY HARRISON.

Spaulding Hospital—1575 Cambridge St., Cambridge, 02138-4398. Tel: 617-758-5495. Pastoral Care: MR. BRUCE AGUILAR.

Canton—

Massachusetts Hospital School—Randolph St., Canton, 02121. Tel: 781-828-2440. Pastoral Care: Saint Gerard Mejella, Canton.

Chelsea—

Quigley Memorial Hospital—91 Crest St., Chelsea, 02150. Tel: 617-887-7146. Pastoral Care: Rev. PATRICK F. HEALY, O.M.I.

Concord—

Emerson Hospital—Rte. 2 ORNAC, Box 9120, Concord, 01742-9120. Tel: 978-287-3015. Pastoral Care: MR. TIMOTHY DUFF, S.T.M.

Everett—

Whidden Memorial Hospital—103 Garland St., Everett, 02149. Tel: 617-381-7202. Pastoral Care: Sr. THERESA CARLOW, S.N.D.

Framingham—

Metro West Medical Center - Framingham Campus—115 Lincoln St., Framingham, 01701-9167. Tel: 508-383-1007. Pastoral Care: Sr. BLANCHE LAROSE, S.C.

Gloucester—

Addison Gilbert Hospital—298 Washington St., Gloucester, 01930. Tel: 978-283-4000. Pastoral Care: Holy Family and Our Lady of Good Voyage, Gloucester.

Haverhill—

Merrimack Valley Hospital—140 Lincoln Ave., Haverhill, 01830. Tel: 978-374-2000. Pastoral Care: Saint John the Baptist, Haverhill and local parishes.

Whittier Rehabilitation Hospital—76 Summer St., Haverhill, 01830. Tel: 978-372-8000. Pastoral Care: Saint James, Haverhill.

Lawrence—

Lawrence General Hospital—One General St., Lawrence, 01842. Tel: 978-683-4000. Pastoral Care: MR. CRAIG B. GIBSON.

Lowell—

Lowell General Hospital—295 Varnum Ave., Lowell, 01854. Tel: 978-937-6418. Pastoral Care: MS. CAROL GAGNE.

Saints Memorial Medical Center—One Hospital Dr., Lowell, 01852. Tel: 978-458-1411; Fax: 978-934-8526. Pastoral Care: MS. CAROL GAGNE.

Lynn—

Northshore Medical Center - Lynn—500 Lynnfield St., Lynn, 01904. Tel: 781-477-3955. Pastoral Care: Rev. PAUL G. FLAMMIA.

Marlborough—

Marlborough Hospital—155 Union St., Marlborough, 01752. Tel: 508-958-3536. Pastoral Care: Immaculate Conception, Marlborough and local parishes.

Medford—

Lawrence Memorial Hospital—170 Governor's Ave., Medford, 02155. Tel: 781-306-6665. Pastoral Care: Deacon ROBERT F. BREEN.

Melrose—

Melrose Wakefield Hospital—585 Lebanon St., Melrose, 02176. Tel: 781-979-3011. Pastoral Care: .

Methuen—

Steward Holy Family Medical Center—70 East St., Methuen, 01844. Tel: 978-687-0156. Pastoral Care: Sr. CLAUDIA BLANCHETTE, S.N.D.

Milton—

Milton Hospital—92 Highland St., Milton, 02186. Tel: 617-696-4600, Ext. 1801. Pastoral Care: DR. VIRGINIA ALLEN.

Natick—

Metro West Medical Center - Natick Campus—67 Union St., Natick, 01760. Tel: 508-650-7331. Pastoral Care: Saint Patrick, Natick and local parishes.

Needham—

Beth Israel Deaconess Hospital - Needham—148 Chestnut St., Needham, 02192. Tel: 781-453-3000. Pastoral Care: Needham Parishes.

Newburyport—

Anna Jacques Hospital—25 Highland Ave., Newburyport, 01950. Tel: 978-463-1000. Pastoral Care: Immaculate Conception, Newburyport and local parishes.

Newton—

Newton Wellesley Hospital—2014 Washington St., Newton, 02462. Tel: 617-243-6634. Pastoral Care: TBA.

Norwood—

Steward Norwood Hospital—800 Washington St., Norwood, 02062. Tel: 781-278-6045. Pastoral Care: MS. JOANNE CURRY.

Peabody—

Kindred Hospital Northshore—15 King St., Peabody, 01960. Tel: 978-531-2900. Pastoral Care: Saint John the Baptist, Peabody.

Plymouth—

Jordan Hospital—275 Sandwich St., Plymouth, 02360. Tel: 508-830-2626. Pastoral Care: MS. PATRICIA FEELEY.

Salem—

Northshore Medical Center Salem—57 Highland Ave., Salem, 01970. Tel: 978-741-1215, Ext. 7698. Pastoral Care: MS. JANE KORINS.

Somerville—

Somerville Hospital—230 Highland Ave., Somerville, 02143. Tel: 617-666-4400. Pastoral Care: Saint Catherine of Genoa, Somerville and local parishes.

Stoughton—

New England Sinai Hospital—150 York St., Stoughton, 02072. Tel: 617-344-0600; Fax: 617-297-1302. Pastoral Care: Sr. ELLEN REILLY, S.N.D.

Tewksbury—

Tewksbury Hospital—365 East St., Tewksbury, 01876. Tel: 978-851-7321, Ext. 2889. Pastoral Care: VACANT.

Westwood—

Westwood Lodge Hospital—45 Clapboardtree St., Westwood, 02090. Tel: 781-762-7764. Pastoral Care: Saint Margaret Mary, Westwood.

Weymouth—

South Shore Hospital—55 Fogg Rd., Weymouth, 02190. Tel: 781-340-8589. Pastoral Care: Deacon MARTIN W. HENRY.

Winchester—

Winchester Hospital—41 Highland Ave., Winchester, 01890. Tel: 781-756-2295. Pastoral Care: DR. MARY BETH MORAN.

Woburn—

Health South - New England Rehabilitation Hospital—Two Rehabilitation Way, Woburn, 01801. Tel: 781-935-5050. Pastoral Care: Saint Barbara, Woburn.

Wrentham—

Wrentham Development Center—131 Emerald St., Wrentham, 02093. Tel: 508-384-3114; Fax: 617-779-1119; Email: jvischetti@fhfc.org; Web: fhfc.org. Pastoral Care: Saint Mary, Wrentham.

Institutional Advancement—MS. KATHLEEN F. DRISCOLL, Sec. Advancement Institutional Advancement, RCAB, 66 Brooks Dr., Braintree, 02184-3839. Tel: 617-779-3740; Fax: 617-779-3721; Email: kdriscoll@rcab.org; Web: bostoncatholicappeal.org/ways_give; MS. LYNN MORRIS, Exec. Asst. & Graphic Designer, Tel: 617-779-3742; Fax: 617-779-3721; Email: lmorris@rcab.org; MS. MARY DOORLEY, Vice Pres. Devel., Tel: 617-779-3744; Fax: 617-779-3721; Email: mdoorley@rcab.org; MR. DAMIEN DEVASTO, Chief Leadership Giving Officer, Tel: 617-779-3703; Fax: 617-779-3721; Email: ddevasto@rcab.org; MS. JACQUELINE MILLER, Catholic Appeal Mgr., Tel: 617-746-5774; Fax: 617-779-3721; Email: jmiller@rcab.org; MR. ARTHUR BOYLE,

Devel. Officer, Tel: 617-779-3746; Fax: 617-779-3721; Email: aboyle@rcab.org.

Boston Catholic Development Services—MS. JOANNE BROWN, Gift Processing, Tel: 617-779-3714; Fax: 617-779-3721; Email: jbrown@rcab.org; MS. SANDRA DOWD, Dir. Oper. & Finance, Tel: 617-779-3745; Fax: 617-779-3721; Email: sdowd@rcab.org; MS. KATE DOYLE, Special Projects Mgr., Tel: 617-779-3709; Fax: 617-779-3721; Email: kdoyle@rcab.org; MS. ARLENE DUBROWSKI, Stewardship & Donor Rels. Mgr., Tel: 617-779-3706; Fax: 617-779-3721; Email: adubrowski@rcab.org; MS. MICHELLE HUNTLEY, Communications Assoc., Tel: 617-779-3718; Fax: 617-779-3721; Email: mhuntley@rcab.org; MS. COURTNEY RILEY, Gift Processor, Tel: 617-779-3717; Fax: 617-779-3721; Email: criley@rcab.org; MS. COURTNEY WAHLE, Mktg. Mgr., Tel: 617-779-3713; Fax: 617-779-3721; Email: cwhale@rcab.org; MR. JAMES WILLSON, Devel. Systems Mgr., Tel: 617-779-3724; Email: james_willson@rcab.org.

Catholic Community Fund - Board of Trustees—

Officers—His Eminence SEAN P. O'MALLEY, O.F.M.Cap., Chm., Archbishop of Boston; MS. KATHLEEN F. DRISCOLL, Pres., Sec. Institutional Advancement; MR. JOHN E. STRAUB, Treas., CFO & Chancellor, Archdiocese of Boston; MR. F. BEIRNE LOVELY JR., Esq.; MR. FRANCIS O'CONNOR, Esq., Asst. Trustees: MS. SHEILA C. CAVANAUGH, Corp. Communications Consultant, Belmont; Most Rev. ROBERT PETER DEELEY, V.F., J.C.D.; Rev. RICHARD M. ERIKSON, V.G., Ph.D.; MR. KEVIN P. MARTIN, CPA.

Jewish Relations—Very Rev. DAVID C. MICHAEL, V.F., Dir., 4750 Washington St., Boston, 02132. Tel: 617-323-4410; Fax: 617-323-0423.

Labor Guild—MS. ALLYSON EVERY, Exec. Dir., 85 Commercial St., Weymouth, 02188. Tel: 781-340-7887; Fax: 781-340-5885; Email: laborguild@aol.com; Web: www.laborguild.com.

L'Arche Irenicon, Inc.—MR. SWANNA CHAMPLIN, Exec. Dir., Mailing Address: Box 1177, Haverhill, 01831. Tel: 978-374-6928; Fax: 978-373-9097; Email: office@larcheirenicon.org.

League of Catholic Women—MS. MARY SULLIVAN, Pres., 39 Washington Park Rd., Braintree, 02184. Tel: 781-843-6616.

Legion of Mary—MR. JAMES KJELLANDER, Pres., 75 Union Park St., Boston, 02118-2141. Tel: 617-542-5682; Fax: 617-542-5926.

Life Resources—Residential and Community Services to Adolescents. MS. LYNNE MARIE BIELECKI, Pres., 100 River St., Braintree, 02184-2021. Tel: 781-849-7751; Fax: 781-849-7754; Email: lbielecki@liferesourcesinc.org; Web: www.liferesourcesinc.org.

The Listening Place—Rev. ALFONSE FERREIRA, O.F.M., Dir., 36 Michigan Ave., Lynn, 01902-1934. Tel: 781-592-7396; Fax: 781-595-6724.

Maria Droste Services—Sr. LORRAINE BERNIER, R.G.S., Admin., 1354 Hancock St., Quincy, 02169. Tel: 617-471-5686; Fax: 617-471-6622; Email: mariadroste@verizon.net.

Marian Devotions—VACANT.

Marriage Ministry—Tel: 617-746-5801; Fax: 617-783-5614; Email: kari_colella@rcab.org.

Massachusetts Catholic Conference—MR. JAMES F. DRISCOLL, Exec. Dir., 66 Brooks Dr., Braintree, 02184-3839. Tel: 617-746-5630; Fax: 617-746-5702; Email: jdriscoll@macatholic.org.

New Evangelization of Youth and Young Adults—Rev. MATTHEW M. WILLIAMS, Dir., 66 Brooks Dr., Braintree, 02184-3839. Tel: 617-746-5752; Fax: 617-779-4572; Email: fr.matt@rcab.org.

Notre Dame Education Center—Sr. JOYCE KHOURY, S.N.D., Dir., 200 Old Colony Ave., Boston, 02127. Tel: 617-268-1912; Fax: 617-464-7924; Email: ndecboston@aol.com.

Notre Dame Mission Center—Sr. RUTH DUFFY, S.N.D., Dir., 30 Jeffreys Neck Rd., Ipswich, 01938. Tel: 978-682-6441; Fax: 978-356-3552; Email: ndcimps@aol.com; Web: sndden.org.

Notre Dame Education Center—Sr. EILEEN T. BURNS, S.N.D., Exec. Dir., 354 Merrimack St., Ste. 210, Lawrence, 01843. Tel: 978-682-6441; Fax: 978-974-8940.

Parish Life and Leadership—Very Rev. BRYAN K. PARRISH, V.F., Sec. & Episcopal Vicar, 66 Brooks Dr., Braintree, 02184-3839. Tel: 617-746-5834; Fax: 617-779-4576.

Pastoral Centers—

Saint Anthony of Padua Social Action—43 Holton St., Allston, 02134. Tel: 617-783-2121.

Centro Bom Samaritano—Good Samaritan Center, 116 Concord St., Ste. 3, Framingham, 01702. Tel: 508-628-3721; Fax: 508-875-6358; Email: centrobomsamaritano@hotmail.com.

Centro Comunitario Scalabrini—Sr. ELISETE TERESIHNA SIGNOR, M.S.C.S., 63 Oakes St., Everett, 02149. Tel: 617-387-0822.

Chinese Pastoral Center—Sr. MADELINE GALLAGHER, M.H.S.H., 78 Tyler St., Boston, 02111-1831. Tel: 617-482-2949; Fax: 617-482-2949.

Irish Pastoral Center—KATHLEEN ROHAN, Admin.; Rev. JOHN M. MCCARTHY, (Ireland) Chap., 15 Rita Rd., Dorchester, 02124. Tel: 617-265-5300; Fax: 617-265-5313; Email: ipcboston@yahoo.com.

Other Pastoral Centers—

Our Lady's Guild House—MS. CONNIE PAGAN, Admin., 20 Charlesgate W., Boston, 02215-2703. Tel: 617-536-3000; Fax: 617-536-8508.

Salesian Boys and Girls Club—Rev. JOHN NAZZARO, S.D.B., 150 Byron St., Boston, 02128. Tel: 617-667-6626; Fax: 617-567-0418.

Don Guanella Center—Sr. CHARLEEN BADIOLA, D.S.M.P., 37 Nichols St., Chelsea, 02150-1225. Tel: 617-889-0179.

Pauline Books and Media—Sr. MARY MARTHA MOSS, F.S.P., Dir., 885 Providence Hwy., Dedham, 02026. Tel: 781-326-5385; Fax: 781-461-1013; Email: dedham@paulinemedia.com; Web: pauline.org.

Pauline Center for Media Studies—Sr. MARY SOPHIE STEWART, F.S.P., Dir., 50 Saint Paul's Ave., Boston, 02130-3491. Tel: 617-522-8911; Fax: 617-522-4081; Web: pauline.org.

Pilgrimages—Rev. MICHAEL E. DREA, Coord., 29 Mount Auburn St., Cambridge, 02138. Tel: 617-491-8400; Fax: 617-354-7092.

The Pilot—MR. ANTONIO M. ENRIQUE, Editor, 66 Brooks Dr., Braintree, 02184-3839. Tel: 617-779-3781; Fax: 617-779-4562; Email: aenrique@thebostonpilot.com; Web: pilotcatholicnews.com.

Pregnancy Help—Supporting women in crisis pregnancies. MS. MARY B. GIRARD, R.N., Dir., 77 Warren St., Ste. 251, Brighton Marine Mental Health Center; Steward Saint Elizabeth Medical Center, Boston, MA 02135, Tel: 888-771-3914 (Toll Free In State); Tel: 617-782-5151; Fax: 617-782-1662.

Metro-West—5 Wilson St., Natick, 01760. Tel: 508-651-0753; Fax: 508-651-0754; Email: help@pregnancyhelpboston.org; Web: pregnancyhelpboston.org.

Prison Ministry—Deacon JAMES F. GREER, Dir., 66 Brooks Dr., Braintree, 02184-3839. Tel: 978-746-5842; Fax: 617-742-5754; Email: jgreer@rcab.org.

State Facilities—

Bay State Correctional Facility—VACANT, Chap., 28 Clark St., Norfolk, 02056. Tel: 508-668-1687.

Bridgewater State Hospital—MS. PEG NEWMAN, Coord., 20 Administration Rd., Bridgewater, 02324. Tel: 508-279-4500.

Longwood Treatment Center—MS. PEG NEWMAN, Coord., Two Administration Rd., Bridgewater, 02324. Tel: 508-279-3500.

Massachusetts Correctional Institution - Cedar Junction—VACANT, Chap., Tel: 508-660-8000.

Massachusetts Correctional Institution - Concord—Rev. MICHAEL DIOCHI, Chap., 965 Elm St., Concord, 01742. Tel: 978-405-6100.

Massachusetts Correctional Institution - Framingham—Sr. MAUREEN CLARK, C.S.J., Coord., Mailing Address: Box 9007, Framingham, 01701-9007. Tel: 508-532-5100.

Massachusetts Correctional Institution - Norfolk—Sr. ANNE MARIE RAFTERY, M.F.I.C., Chap., 2 Clark St., Norfolk, 02056. Tel: 508-660-5900.

Massachusetts Correctional Institution - Plymouth—Mailing Address: P.O. Box 207, Carver, 02355-0207. Tel: 508-295-2647.

Massachusetts Correctional Institution - Shirley—Deacon ARTHUR F. ROGERS JR., Coord., Mailing Address: Box 1218, Shirley, 01464-1218. Tel: 978-425-4341.

Massachusetts Treatment Center—30 Administration Rd., Bridgewater, 02324. Tel: 508-279-8100.

Northeast Correctional Center—MS. HERMINA HYACINTHE, Chap., Barretts Mill Rd., Concord, 01742. Tel: 978-369-4120.

Old Colony Correction Center—Deacon ANTHONY J. CONSTANTINO, Coord., One Administration Rd., Bridgewater, 02324. Tel: 508-879-6000.

Pondville Correctional Center—Sr. ANNE MARIE RAFTERY, M.F.I.C., Chap., Mailing Address: Box 146, Norfolk, 02056-0146. Tel: 508-660-3924.

Shattuck Hospital Correctional Unit—180 Morton St., Boston, 02130. Tel: 617-522-7585.

South Middlesex Correctional Center—Sr. MAUREEN CLARK, C.S.J., Coord., 135 Western Ave., Framingham, 01701-0850. Tel: 508-879-1241.

County Facilities—

Essex County Correctional Facility—MR. PAUL SHOAF-KOZAK, 20 Manning Ave., Middleton, 01949. Tel: 978-750-1900.

Middlesex County - House of Correction—Rev. RICHARD A. DESHAIES, S.J., Chap.; Deacon ROBERT F. BREEN, 269 Treble Cove Rd., Billerica, 01821. Tel: 978-667-1711.

Suffolk County Jail—Deacon JERRY RYAN, Chap., 200 Nashua St., Boston, 02118. Tel: 617-635-1100.

Norfolk County Correctional Facility—Rev. THOMAS F. BOUTON, Chap., 200 West St., Dedham, 02026. Tel: 781-329-3705.

Plymouth County Correctional Center—VACANT, 20 Long Pond Rd., Plymouth, 02360. Tel: 508-830-6200.

Suffolk County - House of Correction—Bro. ALAN BEVINS, S.J., Chap., 20 Brandston St., Boston, 02118. Tel: 617-635-1000.

Youth Facilities—

Metro Youth Service Center—Rev. JOSEPH J. BAGGETTA, Chap., 425 Harvard St., Boston, 02124-2737. Tel: 617-727-6603.

Private Associations of Christ's Faithful—

Foyer of Charity—74 Hollett St., Scituate, 02066. Tel: 781-545-1080; Fax: 240-332-5826; Email: fb@foyerofcharity.org; Web: foyerofcharity.org. VACANT, Dir.

Marian Community—154 Summer St., Medway, 02053-0639. Tel: 508-533-5377; Fax: 508-533-2877; Web: mariancommunity.org. VACANT, Dir.

Professional Standards and Oversight—MR. MARK DUNDERDALE, 66 Brooks Dr., Braintree, 02184-3839. Tel: 617-782-2544; Fax: 617-779-3820.

Delegate for Investigations—MR. JAY CROWLEY, Delegate, 66 Brooks Dr., Braintree, 02184-3839. Tel: 617-746-5639; Fax: 617-746-5696.

Pastoral Support and Outreach—MS. VIVIAN SOPER, L.I.C.S.W., Dir., 66 Brooks Dr., Braintree, 02184-3839. Tel: 866-244-9603 (Toll Free); Tel: 781-794-2581 (Local); Fax: 781-794-2584; Email: vivian_soper@rcab.org.

Background Screening—MS. LISA CUTULLE, Dir., 66 Brooks Dr., Braintree, 02184-3839. Tel: 617-746-5840; Fax: 617-779-4565.

Public Association of Christ's Faithful—

Association of Saint Francis De Sales—MS. CATHERINE CULLEN, Area Dir., 10 Wright Ln., Duxbury, 02332. Tel: 781-934-7228; Email: kateycullen@msn.com; Web: desalesassociation.org.

Brotherhood of Hope—Bro. J. RAHL BUNSA, Gen. Supr., 194 Summer St., Somerville, 02143-2525. Tel: 617-623-9592; Fax: 617-625-1837; Email: info@brotherhoodofhope.org; Web: brotherhoodofhope.org.

Franciscans of the Primitive Observance—VACANT, 3 Magazine St., Roxbury, 02119-2705.

Radio—Most Rev. ROBERT P. REED, Dir., Mailing Address: 34 Chestnut St., Box 9196, Watertown, 02471-9196. Tel: 617-923-0220.

Regina Cleri—MR. STEPHEN J. GUST, Dir., 60 William Cardinal O'Connell Way, Boston, 02114-2729. Tel: 617-523-1861; Fax: 617-720-0585; Email: sgust@reginacleri.org.

Respect Life Education Office—MS. COLLEEN DONOHUE, Asst. Dir., 66 Brooks Dr., Braintree, 02184-3839. Tel: 617-746-5684; Fax: 617-747-5702; Email: respectlifeed@rcab.org; Web: respectlifeeducation.com.

Society of Saint James the Apostle—Rev. DAVID M. COSTELLO, (Ireland) Dir., 24 Clark St., Boston, 02109-1127. Tel: 617-742-4715; Fax: 617-723-7389.

Society of Saint Vincent de Paul—MR. EDWARD J. RESNICK, Exec. Dir.; MR. ROBERT V. TRAVERS JR., Pres., 18 Canton St., Stoughton, 02072. Tel: 781-344-3100; Fax: 617-341-4560; Email: execdir@svdpboston.com; Web: svdpboston.com.

Secular Institutes—

Oblate Missionaries of Mary Immaculate—MS. PAULINE LABBE, Dir., 9 Bayberry Dr., Atkinson, NH 03811. Tel: 603-362-9960; Email: pjlabbe1@juno.com.

Caritas Christi—MS. ANNE M. RYAN, Sec., 537 Winter St., Framingham, 01702-5632. Tel: 508-875-7990; Email: aryan1211@aol.com; Web: ccinfo.org.

Secular Augustinians—Rev. GARY N. MCCLOSKEY, O.S.A., 205 Hampshire St., Lawrence, 01841. Tel: 978-685-1111; Fax: 978-686-5555.

Secular Carmelites—MS. LORETTA L. GALLAGHER, O.D.C.S., 36 Virginia Ln., Newburyport, 01950. Tel: 978-462-1057; Email: lorluceri@yahoo.com.

Lay Dominicans—MR. RAYMOND A. DIBONA, O.P., Dir., 45 Trafford St., Quincy, 02169. Tel: 617-472-4446; Email: kmcaldwell@verizon.net.

Secular Franciscans—MS. JACQUELYN D. WALSH, Regl. Min., 102 Everett Cir., Stoughton, 02072-

5101. Tel: 781-344-7719; Email: jackiesfo@juno.com.

Social Services—

Catholic Relief Services—Rev. J. BRYAN HEHIR, 66 Brooks Dr., Braintree, 02184-3839. Tel: 617-746-5733; Fax: 617-779-4571; Email: bryan-hehir@harvard.edu.

Labor Guild—MS. ALLYSON EVERY, Exec. Dir., 85 Commercial St., Weymouth, 02188. Tel: 781-340-7887; Fax: 781-340-5885; Email: laborguild@aol.com; Web: www.laborguild.com.

Life Resources—Residential and Community Services to Adolescents MS. LYNNE MARIE BIELECKI, Pres., 100 River St., Braintree, 02184-2021. Tel: 781-849-7751; Fax: 781-849-7754; Email: lbielecki@liferesourcesinc.org; Web: www.liferesourcesinc.org.

L'Arche Irenicon, Inc.—MR. SWANNA CHAMPLIN, Exec. Dir., Mailing Address: Box 1177, Haverhill, 01831. Tel: 978-374-6928; Fax: 978-373-9097; Email: office@larcheirenicon.org.

Pregnancy Help—Supporting women in crisis pregnancies. MS. MARY B. GIRARD, R.N., Dir., Brighton Marine Health Center, 77 Warren St., Bldg. #2, Boston, 02135. Tel: 888-771-3914 (Toll Free In State); Tel: 617-782-5151; Fax: 617-782-1662.

Metro-West—5 Wilson St., Natick, 01760. Tel: 508-651-0753; Fax: 508-651-0754; Email: help@pregnancyhelpboston.org; Web: pregnancyhelpboston.org.

Project Rachel—Post-Abortion Reconciliation and Healing. MRS. MARIANNE P. LUTHIN, Dir., 5 Wilson St., Natick, 01760. Tel: 508-651-3100; Fax: 508-651-0754; Email: help@projectrachelboston.com; Web: projectrachelboston.com.

Pro-Life Office—MRS. MARIANNE P. LUTHIN, Dir., 5 Wilson St., Natick, 01760. Tel: 508-651-1900; Fax: 508-651-0754; Email: prolifeoffice@rcab.org; Web: bostoncatholic.org/prolifeoffice.aspx.

Respect Life Education Office—MS. COLLEEN DONOHUE, Asst. Dir., 66 Brooks Dr., Braintree, 02184-3839. Tel: 617-746-5684; Fax: 617-747-5702; Email: respectlifeed@rcab.org; Web: respectlifeeducation.com.

Saint Ann's Home, Inc.—MR. DENIS GRANDBOIS, Pres. & CEO, 100-A Haverhill St., Methuen, 01844. Tel: 978-685-5276; Fax: 978-688-4932; Email: dgrandbois@st.annshome.org; Web: st.annshome.org.

Related Services—

Cor Unum Meal Center—MS. DIANE JARVIS, Dir., 191 Salem St., Lawrence, 01843-1427. Tel: 978-688-8900; Fax: 978-681-5808; Email: corunummealcenter@comcast.net; Web: www.corunummealcenter.org.

The Listening Place—Counseling and Spiritual Services. Rev. ALFONSE FERREIRA, O.F.M., Dir., 36 Michigan Ave., Lynn, 01902-1934. Tel: 781-592-7396; Fax: 781-595-6724.

Maria Droste Services—Sr. LORRAINE BERNIER, R.G.S., Admin. & Interim Dir., 1354 Hancock St., Rm. 203, Quincy, 02169. Tel: 617-471-5686; Fax: 617-471-6622; Email: mariadroste@verizon.net.

Project Hope—Little Sisters of the Assumption Family Health Services, Inc. Sr. MARGARET LEONARD, L.S.A., Exec. Dir., 550 Dudley St., Roxbury, 02119. Tel: 617-442-1880; Fax: 617-238-0473; Email: mleonard@prohope.org.

Specialized Catholic Organizations—

Ancient Order of Hibernians - Ladies Auxiliary—VACANT, Chap., 18 Beach Rd., Salisbury, 01953-1436. Tel: 978-465-3334; Fax: 978-465-5524; Email: starsea@seacoast.com; Web: laoh.massboard.org.

Ancient Order of Hibernians—MR. RICHARD J. THOMPSON, Pres., 7 Derby Rd., Watertown, 02472. Tel: 617-924-9765; Email: rthomp521@comcast.net; Web: massaoh.org.

Archdiocesan Union of Holy Name Societies—MR. ROBERT QUAGAN, 35 Cass St., Boston, 02132-4411. Tel: 617-325-5905; Email: rquagan@comcast.net.

Casa Monte Cassino—11 Tileston St., Boston, 02113. Tel: 617-227-1613; Fax: 617-227-1613; Email: casamontecassino@earthlink.net; Web: casamontecassino.org.

Catholic Alumni Club—MR. THOMAS LITRENTA, Pres., 40 Nowell Rd., Melrose, 02176-1242. Tel: 617-261-9600; Email: cachubbub@yahoo.com; Web: caci.org.

Catholic Association of Foresters—MR. JOHN F. ANDERSON, Treas., 132 Forbes Rd., Braintree, 02184-2693. Tel: 781-848-8221; Fax: 781-848-0311; Email: john@catholicforesters.org; Web: catholicforesters.org.

Catholic Daughters of the Americas—MS. JUDITH SHOOTER, Regent, 2 Lester Rd., Danvers, 01923. Tel: 978-774-4158; Email: johbbes1@aol.com; Web: mastatecourt.org.

Catholic Lawyers Guild—PAUL J. MCNAMARA, Esq., Pres., One Lewis Wharf, Boston, 02110. Tel: 617-722-8100.

Daughters of Isabella—MS. THERESA LEWIS, Regent, 72 Seabreeze Dr., South Dartmouth, 02748. Tel: 508-993-5085.

Equestrian Order of the Holy Sepulchre of Jerusalem—MR. JOHN J. MONAHAN, Lieutenant, 340 Main St., Worcester, 01608. Tel: 508-752-3311; Fax: 508-752-3531; Email: eohsjne@aol.com.

Guild of the Infant Savior—MS. SHARON DEEHAN, Pres., 162 Pineridge Rd., North Andover, 01845. Tel: 978-683-9846; Email: sdeehan@comcast.net.

Knights of Columbus—470 Washington St., Norwood, 02062-0194. Tel: 781-551-0628; Fax: 781-551-0490; Email: mastatekofc@verizon.net; Web: massachusettsstatekofc.org.

Knights of Peter Claver—MR. MEYER CHAMBERS, Grand Knight, 32 Courtney Rd., Boston, 02132-1044. Tel: 617-552-1298; Fax: 617-552-3044; Email: meyer.chambers.1@bc.edu; Web: kofpc.org.

League of Catholic Women—MS. MARY SULLIVAN, Pres., 39 Washington Park Rd., Braintree, 02184. Tel: 781-843-6616.

Legion of Mary—MR. JAMES KJELLANDER, Pres., 75 Union Park St., Boston, 02118-2141. Tel: 617-542-5682; Fax: 617-542-5926.

Magnificat Joy of Boston—MS. LOUISE SCIPIONE, Coord., 42 Packard Rd., Stoughton, 02072. Tel: 781-344-6616.

Maria Droste Services—Sr. LORRAINE BERNIER, R.G.S., Admin., 1354 Hancock St., Quincy, 02169. Tel: 617-471-5686; Fax: 617-471-6622; Email: mariadroste@verizon.net.

Nocturnal Adoration Society—MR. GEORGE J. HALLETT, Pres., 45 Courtland Cir., Milton, 02186-4303. Tel: 617-698-6321; Email: geojoshal@aol.com.

Pax Christi USA—Rev. WILLIAM T. KREMMELL, Advisor, (Retired), 27 Bainbridge Rd., Reading, 01867-1810. Tel: 781-944-0330; Fax: 781-944-1266; Email: pax_2_you@yahoo.com.

Pieta—MS. BARBARA WATERS, Coord., 66 Enoch Pond Rd., Wrentham, 02093-1391. Tel: 508-384-6663; Email: hanknann@verizon.net.

Pro Maria Committee—MS. IRENE TREMBLAY, Dir., 112 Norris Rd., Tyngsborough, 01879. Tel: 978-649-1813; Email: irene_tremblay@hotmail.com.

Pro Parvulis—MS. BEVERLY C. BAKER, Treas., 286 Turtle Pond Pkwy., Boston, 02136-1224.

Serra Boston—MR. BRIAN GALLAGHER; MS. LORETTA GALLAGHER, 36 Virginia Ln., Newburyport, 01950. Tel: 978-462-1057; Email: information@serraboston.org; Web: serraboston.org.

Seton Club—MS. JOSEPH WELLER, Pres., 14 Summer St., Saugus, 01906-2139. Tel: 781-233-2497; Fax: 781-231-5569.

Simon of Cyrene Society—Sr. MARGARET YOUNGCLAUS, S.N.D., Dir., Mailing Address: Box 54, Boston, 02127-0054. Tel: 617-268-8393; Email: sndbol@aol.com; Web: simonofcyrene.com.

Society of Saint Vincent de Paul—MR. EDWARD J. RESNICK, Controller, 18 Canton St., Stoughton, 02072. Tel: 781-344-3100; Fax: 617-341-4560; Email: execdir@svdpboston.com; Web: svdpboston.com.

The Gathering Place—Sr. PATRICIA BRENNAN, R.G.S., Dir., 3 Common St., Waltham, 02451-4401. Tel: 781-647-0012; Fax: 781-647-0055; Email: gather1997@aol.com.

The Listening Place—Rev. ALFONSE FERREIRA, O.F.M., Dir., 36 Michigan Ave., Lynn, 01902-1934. Tel: 781-592-7396; Fax: 781-595-6724.

Women Affirming Life—MS. FRANCES X. HOGAN, Pres., Mailing Address: Box 35532, Boston, 02135-0532. Tel: 617-254-2277; Fax: 617-254-2299.

World Apostolate of Fatima—MS. LYNN KENN, Pres., Mailing Address: Box 308, East Bridgewater, 02333-0308. Tel: 508-378-7431; Email: elk314@comcast.net.

Special Needs—

Braintree Cardinal Cushing Centers, Inc.—MR. RON SHEPHERD, Prin., 85 Washington St., Braintree, 02184. Tel: 781-848-6250; Fax: 781-848-0640; Web: www.coletta.org/cardinal/braintree/braintree.htm; Email: rshepherd@cushingcenters.org.

Hanover Cardinal Cushing Centers, Inc.—MS. ROBERTA PULASKI, Dir. Educ., 405 Washington St., Hanover, 02339. Tel: 781-826-6371; Fax: 781-826-1559; Web: www.coletta.org/cardinal/hanoverprogs/hanover.htm; Email: rpulaski@coletta.org.

Vocations—Revs. DANIEL F. HENNESSEY, Dir., 66 Brooks Dr., Braintree, 02184-3839. Tel: 617-746-5949; Fax: 617-779-4570; Email: dhennessey@rcab.org; CARLOS D. SUAREZ, Assoc. Dir., Tel: 617-746-5987; Fax: 617-779-4570; Email: csuarez@rcab.org.

CLERGY, PARISHES, MISSIONS AND PAROCHIAL SCHOOLS

BOSTON

(SUFFOLK COUNTY)

1—CATHEDRAL OF THE HOLY CROSS (1788)
1400 Washington St., Boston, 02118-2141. Very Rev. Kevin J. O'Leary, V.F., Admin.; Rev. Pablo Gomis, Parochial Vicar; Deacons Ricardo M. Mesa; Luciano Herrera. In Res., His Eminence Sean P. O'Malley, O.-F.M.Cap.; Revs. Robert T. Kickham; Jonathan M. Gaspar.
Res.: 75 Union Park St., Boston, 02118-2141.
Tel: 617-542-5682; Fax: 617-542-5926; Email: cathedral2@rcab.org; Web: www.holycrossboston.com.
See Cathedral High School under High Schools, Archdiocesan in the Institution section.
Catechesis Religious Program—
Convent—Mission Helpers of Sacred Heart, 286 Shuwmut Ave., Boston, Suffolk Co. 02118.
Tel: 617-542-1143.

2—ST. ADALBERT (1913) (Polish), Closed. Parish records for all closed, merged & suppressed parishes are located at the Office of the Archives, 66 Brooks Dr., Braintree, MA 02184-3839. Tel: 617-746-5795.

3—ALL SAINTS (1894) Closed. Parish records for all closed, merged & suppressed parishes are located at the Office of the Archives, 66 Brooks Dr., Braintree, MA 02184-3839. Tel: 617-746-5795.

4—ST. AMBROSE (1914)
246 Adams St., Boston, 02122. Tel: 617-265-5302; Fax: 617-265-0886; Email: stambroseparish@comcast.net. Very Rev. Linh T. Nguyen, V.F.; Revs. Anthony M. Cusack, Parochial Vicar; Eric Velasquez. In Res., Revs. Richard C. Conway, (Retired); Thomas F. Bouton; Jacques A. McGuffie.

5—ST. ANDREW (1918) Closed. Parish records for all closed, merged & suppressed parishes are located at the Office of the Archives, 66 Brooks Dr., Braintree, MA 02184-3839. Tel: 617-746-5795.

6—ST. ANGELA MERICI (1907)
1548 Blue Hill Ave., Boston, 02126.
Tel: 617-298-0080; Fax: 617-298-2388; Email: stangelamattapan@gmail.com; Web: www.agmcatholic.org. Revs. Vincent E. Daily; Jean Gustave Miracle, (Haiti) Parochial Vicar; Thomas Rossi, Parochial Vicar; Deacon Joseph E. Dorlus.
School—Saint John Paul II Academy - Mattapan Square Campus, 120 Babson St., Dorchester, 02126.
Tel: 617-265-0019; Fax: 617-296-1659; Email: louann.melino@popejp2catholicacademy.org; Web: www.popejp2catholicacademy.org. Ms. Kathleen Aldridge, Prin.

7—ST. ANN (1889) Revs. Michael E. Drea; Patrick J. Fiorillo, Parochial Vicar.
Res.: 243 Neponset Ave., Dorchester, 02122-3239.
Tel: 617-825-6180; Email: sasbcollaborative@gmail.com; Web: www.saintannneponset.com.
Convent—241 Neponset Ave., Dorchester, 02122.
Tel: 617-288-1202.
Catechesis Religious Program—15 Rita Rd., Dorchester, 02124. Mr. Andrew Genovese, D.R.E. Students 400.

8—ST. ANN (1945) Closed. Parish records for all closed, merged & suppressed parishes are located at the Office of the Archives, 66 Brooks Dr., Braintree, MA 02184-3839. Tel: 617-746-5795.

9—ST. ANNE (1919)
90 W. Milton St., Boston, 02136. Tel: 857-342-9500; Fax: 617-361-6690; Email: achavez@bluehillscollaborative.org; Web: bluehillscollaborative.org. Revs. Ronald D. Coyne; Charles Madi-Okin, Parochial Vicar.
Convent—85 W. Milton St., Readville, 02136.
Tel: 617-361-8224.

10—ST. ANTHONY OF PADUA (1896) Revs. Francis M. Glynn; Francisco C. Martins Silva, (Brazil) Parochial Vicar.
Res.: 43 Holton St., Allston, 02134-1397.
Tel: 617-782-0775; Fax: 617-782-2008; Email: glynnfrank@hotmail.com; Web: www.saintanthonyallston.org.

11—ST. AUGUSTINE (1868) Closed. Parish records for all closed, merged & suppressed parishes are located at the Office of the Archives, 66 Brooks Dr., Braintree, MA 02184-3839. Tel: 617-746-5795.

12—BLESSED SACRAMENT (1891) Closed. Parish records

for all closed, merged & suppressed parishes are located at the Office of the Archives, 66 Brooks Dr., Braintree, MA 02184-3839. Tel: 617-746-5795.

13—ST. BRENDAN (1929)
589 Gallivan Blvd., Boston, 02124-5321.
Tel: 617-436-0310; Fax: 617-436-1386; Email: saintbrendanparish02124@gmail.com; Web: SaintBrendanParish.org. Revs. Michael E. Drea; Patrick J. Fiorillo, Parochial Vicar.
School—St. Brendan School, 29 Rita Rd., Dorchester, 02124-5321. Tel: 617-282-3388; Fax: 617-822-9152; Email: office@stbrendanschool.org; Web: www.stbrendanschool.org. Ms. Maura Burke, Prin. Lay Teachers 12; Students 209.
Catechesis Religious Program—Tel: 617-825-8622. Jean Curley, D.R.E.

14—ST. BRIGID OF KILDARE (1908) Very Rev. Robert E. Casey, V.F.; Thomas M. Olson, Parochial Vicar.
Res.: 841 E. Broadway, Boston, 02127-2302.
Tel: 617-268-2122; Fax: 617-268-2666; Email: stbrigidboston@gmail.com; Web: www.gateofheavenstbrigid.org.
School—South Boston Catholic Academy, (Grades PreK-6), 866 E. Broadway, South Boston, 02127.
Tel: 617-268-2326; Fax: 617-268-7269; Email: office@sbcatholicacademy.org; Web: www.sbcatholicacademy.org. Ms. Nancy Carr, Prin. Lay Teachers 24; Students 354; Religious Teachers 1.
Catechesis Religious Program—James Fowkes, D.R.E.
Convent—100 N St., South Boston, 02127.

15—ST. CATHERINE OF SIENA (1887) Closed. Parish records for all closed, merged & suppressed parishes are located at the Office of the Archives, 66 Brooks Dr., Braintree, MA 02184-3839. Tel: 617-746-5795.

16—ST. CECILIA (1888) Closed.
18 Belvidere St., Boston, 02115-3132.
Tel: 617-536-4548; Fax: 617-536-1781; Email: info@stceciliaboston.org; Web: www.stceciliaboston.org. Rev. John J. Unni.

17—ST. CHRISTOPHER (1956) Rev. George A. Carrigg, Admin.
Res.: 263 Mt. Vernon St., Boston, 02125-3182.
Tel: 617-436-7273; Fax: 617-265-2704; Email: gacstchris@aol.com.

18—ST. COLUMBKILLE (1871) Very Rev. Richard W. Fitzgerald, V.F., Admin.; Revs. Succes Jeanty Jean-Pierre, (Mexico) Parochial Vicar; Christopher W. Bae, Parochial Vicar.
Res.: 321 Market St., Boston, 02135-2126.
Tel: 617-782-5774; Fax: 617-782-7283; Email: office@brightoncatholic.org; Web: www.brightoncatholic.org.
School—St. Columbkille School, 25 Arlington St., Brighton, 02135-2199. Tel: 617-254-3110; Fax: 617-254-3161; Email: info@stcps.org; Web: www.stcps.org. Mr. William Gartside, Prin. Lay Teachers 10; Sisters 4; Students 200.
Catechesis Religious Program—Mr. Christopher Carmody, D.R.E.

19—CONGREGATION OF SAINT ATHANASIUS, Rev. Richard S. Bradford, Admin.
Res.: 767 W. Roxbury Pkwy., Boston, 02132-2121.
Tel: 617-325-5232; Web: www.locutor.net.

20—ST. FRANCIS DE SALES (1859)
313 Bunker Hill St., Boston, 02129-1826.
Tel: 617-242-0147; Fax: 617-242-3026; Email: StFran303@aol.com; Web: www.stfrancisdesalescharlestown.com. Rev. Daniel J. Mahoney.

21—ST. FRANCIS DE SALES-ST. PHILIP (1867) Closed. Parish records for all closed, merged & suppressed parishes are located at the Office of the Archives, 66 Brooks Dr., Braintree, MA 02184-3839. Tel: 617-746-5795.

22—ST. GABRIEL (1934) Closed. St. Gabriel, Brighton was suppressed. This parish's records are located at St. Columbkille, Boston.

23—GATE OF HEAVEN (1862)
615 E. 4th St., Boston, 02127-2302.
Tel: 617-268-3344; Fax: 617-268-2666; Email: gateofheavenboston@gmail.com; Web: www.gateofheavenstbrigid.org. Very Rev. Robert E. Casey, V.F.; Thomas M. Olson, Parochial Vicar.
School—South Boston Catholic Academy, (Grades PreK-6), 866 E. Broadway, South Boston, 02127.
Tel: 617-268-2326; Fax: 617-268-7269; Email: office@sbcatholicacademy.org; Web: www.sbcatholicacademy.org. Ms. Nancy Carr, Prin. Lay Teachers 24; Students 354; Religious Teachers 1.
Catechesis Religious Program—James Fowkes, D.R.E.

24—ST. GREGORY (1863)
2215 Dorchester Ave., Boston, 02124-5607.
Tel: 617-298-2460; Fax: 617-298-9232; Email: stgregoryparish@gmail.com; Web: www.agmcatholic.org. Revs. Vincent E. Daily, S.T.D., S.T.L.; Jean Gustave Miracle, (Haiti) Parochial Vicar; Thomas Rossi, Parochial Vicar; Deacon Joseph E. Dorlus.
School—St. Gregory School, 2214 Dorchester Ave., Dorchester, 02124. Tel: 617-296-1210. Margaret Donovan, Prin. Lay Teachers 18; Students 225.
Catechesis Religious Program—Elizabeth Labbe, D.R.E.

25—HOLY FAMILY (1995)
Mailing Address: 24 Hartford St., Boston, 02122.
Tel: 617-445-9553; Email: stpeterparishdorchester@gmail.com; Web: dorchestercatholic.org. Rev. John A. Currie; Very Rev. John J. Connelly Jr., Parochial Vicar, (Retired); Deacon Paul F. Carroll.
Catechesis Religious Program—336 Saratoga St., East Boston, 02128. Tel: 617-567-6509; Fax: 617-567-2561.

26—HOLY NAME (1927) Very Rev. George P. Evans, V.F., A.B., M.Div., S.T.L., S.T.D.; Revs. Stanley Rousseau, (Haiti) Parochial Vicar; Baldemar Garza; Deacon Timothy F. Donohue.
Res.: 1689 Centre St., Boston, 02132-1292.
Tel: 617-325-4865; Fax: 617-325-5571; Email: contact.hnp@holynameparish.com; Web: www.holynameparish.com.
School—Holy Name School, 535 W. Roxbury Pkwy., West Roxbury, 02132-1292. Tel: 617-325-9338; Fax: 617-325-7885; Email: lynne.workman@holynameparish.com; Web: holynameparishschool.org. Mrs. Linda Workman, Prin. Lay Teachers 40; Sisters 2; Students 572.
Convent—525 W. Roxbury Pkwy., West Roxbury, 02132. Tel: 617-325-5089.

27—HOLY TRINITY (1844) (German), Closed. Parish records for all closed, merged & suppressed parishes are located at the Office of the Archives, 66 Brooks Dr., Braintree, MA 02184-3839. Tel: 617-746-5795.

28—ST. JAMES THE GREATER (1854)
125 Harrison Ave., Boston, 02111. Tel: 617-542-8498; Fax: 617-542-2708; Email: info@bcccstjames.org; Web: www.bcccstjames.org. Very Rev. Kevin J. O'Leary, V.F., Admin.; Rev. Joseph Zhang, A.A., Parochial Vicar; Deacon Francis Sung.
Catechesis Religious Program—Susan Ho, D.R.E.; Teresa Yuen, D.R.E.

29—ST. JOHN CHRYSOSTOM (1952)
4750 Washington St., Boston, 02132.
Tel: 617-323-4410; Fax: 617-323-0423; Email: melanie.rutledge@stjohnchrysostom02132.org; Web: www.stjohnchrysostom02132.org. Rev. John R. Carroll, Admin.

30—ST. JOHN THE BAPTIST (1921) Closed. St. John the Baptist, East Boston was suppressed. This parish's records are located at Sacred Heart, Boston.

31—ST. JOHN-ST. HUGH (1901) Closed. Parish records for all closed, merged & suppressed parishes are located at the Office of the Archives, 66 Brooks Dr., Braintree, MA 02184-3839. Tel: 617-746-5795.

32—ST. JOSEPH (1845) Closed. St. Joseph, Roxbury was suppressed. This parish's records are located at St. Patrick, Boston.

33—ST. JOSEPH (1862) Closed. Parish records for all closed, merged & suppressed parishes are located at the Office of the Archives, 66 Brooks Dr., Braintree, MA 02184-3839. Tel: 617-746-5795.

34—ST. JOSEPH (1938) Closed. Parish records for all closed, merged & suppressed parishes are located at the Office of the Archives, 66 Brooks Dr., Braintree, MA 02184-3839. Tel: 617-746-5795.

35—ST. JOSEPH (1862)
68 William Cardinal O'Connell Way, Boston, 02114-2709. Tel: 617-523-4342; Fax: 617-523-8459; Email: office@stjosephboston.com; Web: www.stjosephboston.com. Rev. Joseph M. White, Admin.
Catechesis Religious Program—Denise Tompkins, D.R.E.

36—ST. JOSEPH-ST. LAZARUS (1892) Rev. Miroslaw Kowalczyk, F.D.P.
Res.: 59 Ashley St., Boston, 02128. Tel: 617-569-0406 ; Fax: 617-569-8212; Email: orioneparish@gmail.com.
Catechesis Religious Program—Maria Zolla, D.R.E.

37—ST. KATHARINE DREXEL (2005)
517 Blue Hill Ave., Boston, 02120. Tel: 617-445-8915; Fax: 617-445-1652. Revs. Oscar J. Pratt, Admin.; Donatus I. Ezenneka, (Nigeria) Parochial Vicar.

38—ST. KEVIN (1945) Closed. Parish records for all closed, merged & suppressed parishes are located at the Office of the Archives, 66 Brooks Dr., Braintree, MA 02184-3839. Tel: 617-746-5795.

39—ST. LAZARUS (1892) Closed. St. Lazarus, East Boston was suppressed. This parish's records are located at St. Joseph-St. Lazarus, Boston.

40—ST. LEO (1902) Closed. Parish records for all closed, merged & suppressed parishes are located at the Office of the Archives, 66 Brooks Dr., Braintree, MA 02184-3839. Tel: 617-746-5795.

41—ST. LEONARD OF PORT MAURICE (1873) Revs. Antonio Nardoianni, O.F.M./I.C.; Claude Scrima, O.F.M./I.C., Parochial Vicar.
Res.: 320 Hanover St., Boston, 02113-1913.
Tel: 617-523-2110; Fax: 617-367-0456; Email: admin@saintleonardchurchboston.org; Web: www.saintleonardchurchboston.org.
School—St. John, 9 Moon St., Boston, 02113.
Tel: 617-227-3143; Fax: 617-227-2188; Email: eharvey@sjsne.com; Web: www.sjsne.com. Ms. Karen McLaughlin, Prin.

42—ST. MARGARET (1893) Closed. Parish records for all closed, merged & suppressed parishes are located at the Office of the Archives, 66 Brooks Dr., Braintree, MA 02184-3839. Tel: 617-746-5795.

43—ST. MARK (1905)
1725 Dorchester Ave., Boston, 02124.
Tel: 617-825-2852; Fax: 617-825-0514; Email: judy.stmarks@comcast.net; Web: stmark-stambrose.org. Very Rev. Linh T. Nguyen, V.F.; Rev. Anthony M. Cusack, Parochial Vicar; Deacon Marcio O. Fonseca.

44—ST. MARY, Closed. St. Mary, North End was suppressed. This parish's records are located at St. Leonard of Port Maurice, Boston.

45—ST. MARY (1828) Closed. Parish records for all closed, merged & suppressed parishes are located at the Office of the Archives, 66 Brooks Dr., Braintree, MA 02184-3839. Tel: 617-746-5795.

46—ST. MARY - ST. CATHERINE OF SIENA (2006)
St. Mary, 55 Warren St., Boston, 02129.
Tel: 617-242-4664; Fax: 617-242-0016; Email: info@stmarystcatherine.org; Web: www.stmarystcatherine.org. Very Rev. James J. Ronan, V.F.; Deacon Daniel R. Burns.

47—ST. MARY OF THE ANGELS (1904)
Mailing Address: 97 South St., Jamaica Plain, 02130. Rev. Carlos F. Flor; Deacons Jesus M. Ortiz; Jose Perez-Rodriguez.
Res.: 377 Walnut Ave., Boston, 02130.
Tel: 617-524-0240; Fax: 617-524-1840; Email: stthsaq@comcast.net; Web: catholicjproxbury.com.
Catechesis Religious Program—Tel: 617-524-0913.

48—ST. MARY, STAR OF THE SEA (1864) Closed. Parish records for all closed, merged & suppressed parishes are located at the Office of the Archives, 66 Brooks Dr., Braintree, MA 02184-3839. Tel: 617-746-5795.

49—ST. MATTHEW (1900) Revs. Vincent E. Daily; Jean Gustave Miracle, (Haiti) Parochial Vicar; Thomas Rossi, Parochial Vicar; Deacon Joseph E. Dorlus.
Res.: 33 Stanton St., Boston, 02124-3716.
Tel: 617-436-3590; Fax: 617-287-2741; Email: presbytery@stmatthewdorchester.org.
Catechesis Religious Program—Josette Rameau, D.R.E.

50—ST. MONICA (1907) Closed. Parish records for all closed, merged & suppressed parishes are located at the Office of the Archives, 66 Brooks Dr., Braintree, MA 02184-3839. Tel: 617-746-5795.

51—ST. MONICA-ST. AUGUSTINE (1907) [CEM]
331 Old Colony Ave., Boston, 02127.
Tel: 617-268-8100; Fax: 617-268-2666; Email: questions@sbscatholic.org; Web: www.sbscatholic.org. Very Rev. James A. Flavin, V.E.; Revs. Gabino Oliva Macias, (Mexico) Parochial Vicar; Gerald A. Souza, Parochial Vicar; Deacons Paul M. Kline; Alejandro Iraola.

52—MOST HOLY REDEEMER (1844)
72 Maverick St., Boston, 02128-1924.
Tel: 617-567-3227; Fax: 617-569-6950. Revs. Thomas S. Domurat; Joel Americo Santos, Parochial Vicar; Deacons Pedro LaTorre; Francis W. McHugh. Member Central Catholic School of East Boston.
See East Boston Central Catholic School under Sacred Heart, East Boston.
Catechesis Religious Program—Angelina Monge, D.R.E.

53—MOST PRECIOUS BLOOD (1880)
25 Maple St., Boston, 02136-2755. Tel: 617-364-9500; Fax: 617-364-2590; Email: achavez@bluehillscollaborative.org; Web: bluehillscollaborative.org. Revs. Ronald D. Coyne; Charles Madi-Okin, Parochial Vicar.
Catechesis Religious Program—Joseph Shaughnessy, D.R.E.

54—OUR LADY OF CZESTOCHOWA (1893) (Polish) Revs. Jerzy Zebrowski, O.F.M.Conv.; Jozef Brzozowski, O.F.M.Conv., Parochial Vicar.
Res.: 655 Dorchester Ave., South Boston, 02127.
Tel: 617-268-4355; Fax: 617-268-4599; Email: parish@ourladyofczestochowa.com; Web: www.ourladyofczestochowa.com.
Convent—666 Dorchester Ave., Boston, 02127.

55—OUR LADY OF KAZAN, Closed. Parish records for all closed, merged & suppressed parishes are located at the Office of the Archives, 66 Brooks Dr., Braintree, MA 02184-3839. Tel: 617-746-5795.

56—OUR LADY OF LOURDES (1908)
14 Montebello Rd., Boston, 02130. Tel: 617-524-0240; Fax: 617-524-1840; Email: stthsaq@comcast.net; Web: catholicjproxbury.com. Rev. Carlos F. Flor; Deacons Jesus M. Ortiz; Jose Perez-Rodriguez.
Catechesis Religious Program—Lourdes Ortiz, D.R.E.

57—OUR LADY OF MT. CARMEL (1905) (Italian), Closed. Parish records for all closed, merged & suppressed parishes are located at the Office of the Archives, 66 Brooks Dr., Braintree, MA 02184-3839. Tel: 617-746-5795.

58—OUR LADY OF OSTROBRAMA, Closed. Parish records for all closed, merged & suppressed parishes are located at the Office of the Archives, 66 Brooks Dr., Braintree, MA 02184-3839. Tel: 617-746-5795.

59—OUR LADY OF PERPETUAL HELP (1868) Revs. Joseph Tizio, C.Ss.R.; Pierre Desruisseaux, C.Ss.R., Admin.; Philip Dabney, C.Ss.R., Parochial Vicar.
Res.: 1545 Tremont St., Boston, 02120-2909.
Tel: 617-445-2600; Fax: 617-445-1857; Email: info@bostonsbasilica.com.
School—Our Lady of Perpetual Help School, (Grades Day Care-6), 94 St. Alphonsus St., Roxbury, 02120.
Tel: 617-442-2660; Fax: 617-442-3775; Email: adutson@missiongrammar.org; Web: www.missiongrammar.org. Aliece Dutson, Prin. Lay Teachers 20; Students 200.
Catechesis Religious Program—Alyson Perry, D.R.E.

60—OUR LADY OF POMPEII, Closed. Parish records for all closed, merged & suppressed parishes are located at the Office of the Archives, 66 Brooks Dr., Braintree, MA 02184-3839. Tel: 617-746-5795.

61—OUR LADY OF THE ASSUMPTION (1869) Rev. Ignatius Mushauko, (Zambia) Admin. Member East Boston Central Catholic School Consortium.
Res.: 404 Sumner St., East Boston, 02128.
Tel: 617-567-1223; Email: olaboston@gmail.com; Web: www.olaeastboston.com.

62—OUR LADY OF THE PRESENTATION (1909) Closed. Parish records for all closed, merged & suppressed parishes are located at the Office of the Archives, 66 Brooks Dr., Braintree, MA 02184-3839. Tel: 617-746-5795.

63—OUR LADY OF THE ROSARY, Closed. Parish records for all closed, merged & suppressed parishes are located at the Office of the Archives, 66 Brooks Dr., Braintree, MA 02184-3839. Tel: 617-746-5795.

64—OUR LADY OF VICTORIES (1880) (French), Closed. Parish records for all closed, merged & suppressed parishes are located at the Office of the Archives, 66 Brooks Dr., Braintree, MA 02184-3839. Tel: 617-746-5795.

65—ST. PATRICK (1836)
400 Dudley St., Boston, 02119-2706.
Tel: 617-445-7645; Fax: 617-445-6166; Email: stpatrickrox@comcast.net; Web: www.saintpatricksroxbury.com. Rt. Rev. John J. Ahern, V.F.; Rev. Bernardino V. Lima, O.F.M.Cap., Parochial Vicar; Deacon Jorge A. Patino.
School—St. Patrick School, 131 Mt. Pleasant Ave., Roxbury, 02119. Tel: 617-427-3881;
Fax: 617-427-4529; Email: mlanata@stpatsroxbury.org; Web: www.saintpatsroxbury.org. Ms. Mary Lanata, Prin. Lay Teachers 17; Sisters 4; Students 251; Religious Brother 1.

66—ST. PAUL (1907) Closed. Parish records for all closed, merged & suppressed parishes are located at the Office of the Archives, 66 Brooks Dr., Braintree, MA 02184-3839. Tel: 617-746-5795.

67—ST. PETER (1872)
311 Bowdoin St., Boston, 02125. Tel: 617-265-1132;
Fax: 617-265-0463; Email: stpeterparishdorchester@gmail.com; Web: www.dorchestercatholic.org. Rev. John A. Currie; Very Rev. John J. Connolly, V.F., Parochial Vicar; Deacon Paul F. Carroll.

68—ST. PETER (1904) (Lithuanian)
75 Flaherty Way, Boston, 02127-2006.
Tel: 617-268-8100; Fax: 617-268-2585; Email: questions@sbscatholic.org. Very Rev. James A. Flavin, V.E.; Revs. Gerald A. Souza, Admin.; Gabino Oliva Macias, (Mexico) Parochial Vicar; Deacons Paul M. Kline; Alejandro Iraola.

69—SS. PETER AND PAUL (1844) Closed. Parish records for all closed, merged & suppressed parishes are located at the Office of the Archives, 66 Brooks Dr., Braintree, MA 02184-3839. Tel: 617-746-5795.

70—ST. PHILIP, Closed. Parish records for all closed, merged & suppressed parishes are located at the Office of the Archives, 66 Brooks Dr., Braintree, MA 02184-3839. Tel: 617-746-5795.

71—ST. RICHARD, Closed. Parish records for all closed, merged & suppressed parishes are located at the Office of the Archives, 66 Brooks Dr., Braintree, MA 02184-3839. Tel: 617-746-5795.

72—SACRED HEART (1873)
45 Brooks St., Boston, 02128-3063.
Tel: 617-567-5776; Fax: 617-567-3042; Email: sacredhearteb@gmail.com; Web: www.SacredHeartEB.or. Rev. Eric M. Bennett, B.S., M.S.P.T., S.T.B., S.T.L., Admin.
School—East Boston Central Catholic School Consortium, 69 London St., East Boston, 02128.
Tel: 617-567-7456; Fax: 617-567-9559; Email: admin@ebccs.org; Web: www.ebccs.org. Robert Casaletto, Prin. Lay Teachers 12; Sisters 1; Students 229.
Catechesis Religious Program— See Holy Family, Boston Tel: 617-567-6509. Sharon A. Rozzi, D.R.E.

73—SACRED HEART (1888) (Italian), Closed. Sacred Heart, North End was suppressed. This parish's records are located at St. Leonard of Port Maurice, Boston.

74—SACRED HEART (1893) Rev. Msgr. Francis H. Kelley, V.F.; Rev. Mario Guarino, Parochial Vicar; Ms. Kathy Sherrod, Pastoral Assoc. In Res., Revs. Eugene P. Sullivan, (Retired); Elias A. Ojomah, (Nigeria).
Res.: 169 Cummins Hwy., Roslindale, 02131-3739.
Tel: 617-325-3322; Fax: 617-325-2145; Email: sacredheartparish@sh-roslindale.org; Web: www.sh-roslindale.org.
School—Sacred Heart School, 1035 Canterbury St., Roslindale, 02131. Tel: 617-323-2500;
Fax: 617-325-7151. Ms. Monica Haldiman, Prin. Lay Teachers 15; Sisters 2; Students 464.
Catechesis Religious Program—Caroline Quiles, D.R.E.

75—ST. STEPHEN (1862)
24 Clark St., Boston, 02109-9923. Tel: 617-523-1230;
Fax: 617-723-7389; Email: info@socstjames.com. Rev. David M. Costello, (Ireland) Admin. In Res., Rev. Patrick J. Universal.

76—ST. STEPHEN, Closed. Parish records for all closed, merged & suppressed parishes are located at the Office of the Archives, 66 Brooks Dr., Braintree, MA 02184-3839. Tel: 617-746-5795.

77—SAINT TERESA OF CALCUTTA (2004)
800 Columbia Rd., Boston, 02125. Tel: 617-436-2190;
Fax: 617-282-5428; Email: bmtdorchester@gmail.com; Web: www.dorchestercatholic.org. Rev. John A. Currie, Admin.; Very Rev. John J. Connolly, V.F., Parochial Vicar; Deacon Paul F. Carroll.

78—ST. THERESA OF AVILA (1895)
2078 Centre St., Boston, 02132-3416.
Tel: 617-325-1300; Fax: 617-325-0380; Web: www.sttheresaparishboston.com. Rev. Msgr. William M. Helmick; Rev. Richard S. Bradford, Parochial Vicar. In Res., Most Rev. Emilio S. Allue, S.D.B.; Rev. Peter P. Nolan, C.S.Sp.
School—St. Theresa of Avila School, 40 St. Theresa Ave., West Roxbury, 02132. Tel: 617-323-1050;
Fax: 617-323-8118; Email: news@sttheresaschoolboston.com; Web: www.sttheresaschoolboston.com. Ms. Jean Leahy, Prin. Lay Teachers 20; Sisters 2; Students 589.
Catechesis Religious Program—Ann Barden, D.R.E.; Diane Flynn, D.R.E.; Ms. Jennifer McKiernan, D.R.E.
Convent—20 Pine Lodge Rd., West Roxbury, 02132. Tel: 617-325-9171.

79—ST. THOMAS AQUINAS (1869) Revs. Carlos F. Flor; Andrea Povero, Parochial Vicar; Deacons Jesus M. Ortiz; Jose Perez-Rodriguez. Collaborative of Parishes of Jamaica Plain & Roxbury
Res.: 97 South St., Boston, 02130. Tel: 617-524-0240;
Fax: 617-524-1840; Email: stthosaq@comcast.net; Web: www.catholicjproxbury.com.
Catechesis Religious Program—Ms. Nancy Thompson, D.R.E.

80—ST. VINCENT DE PAUL (1872)
E & W. 3rd St., Boston, 02127. Tel: 617-268-8100;
Fax: 617-268-1277; Email: stvincentsouthboston@gmail.com. Very Rev. James A. Flavin, V.E.; Revs. Gerald A. Souza, Parochial Vicar; Gabino Oliva Macias, (Mexico) Parochial Vicar; Deacons Paul M. Kline; Alejandro Iraola.

81—ST. WILLIAM (1909) Closed. Parish records for all closed, merged & suppressed parishes are located at the Office of the Archives, 66 Brooks Dr., Braintree, MA 02184-3839. Tel: 617-746-5795.

OUTSIDE THE CITY OF BOSTON

ABINGTON, PLYMOUTH CO.

1—ST. BRIDGET (1863) [JC] Revs. James M. Mahoney, M.Div.; Thomas J. Stanton, Parochial Vicar; Deacons James V. McLaughlin; Joseph T. Nickley. In Res.
Res.: 455 Plymouth St., Abington, 02351-1889.
Tel: 781-878-0900; Fax: 781-878-6566; Email: sbparishsecretary@comcast.net; Web: www.loccc.org.
School—St. Bridget School, Tel: 617-878-8482;
Fax: 781-871-4471; Email: sbsoffice@aol.com; Web: www.stbridgetschool.us. Mr. Matthew Collins, Prin. Lay Teachers 11; Students 249.
Catechesis Religious Program—Tel: 781-878-5950. Anne Fennell, D.R.E.

2—ST. NICHOLAS (1964) Closed. Parish records for all closed, merged & suppressed parishes are located at the Office of the Archives, 66 Brooks Dr., Braintree, MA 02184-3839. Tel: 617-746-5795.

ACTON, MIDDLESEX CO., ST. ELIZABETH OF HUNGARY (1945) Rev. Jeffrey S. Archer.
Res.: 89 Arlington St., Acton, 01720-2503.
Tel: 978-263-4305; Fax: 978-263-9014; Email: office@seoh.org; Web: www.seoh.org.

AMESBURY, ESSEX CO.

1—HOLY FAMILY (1998) [CEM]
2 School St., Amesbury, 01913. Tel: 978-388-0330;
Fax: 978-388-8840; Email: administrativeassistant@livingwatercatholic.org; Web: livingwatercatholic.org. Revs. Scott A. Euvrard; Christopher W. Wallace.
Catechesis Religious Program—Tel: 978-388-3477. Doreen A. Keller, D.R.E.

2—ST. JOSEPH, Closed. Parish records for all closed, merged & suppressed parishes are located at the Office of the Archives, 66 Brooks Dr., Braintree, MA 02184-3839. Tel: 617-746-5795.

3—SACRED HEART, Closed. Parish records for all closed, merged & suppressed parishes are located at the Office of the Archives, 66 Brooks Dr., Braintree, MA 02184-3839. Tel: 617-746-5795.

ANDOVER, ESSEX CO.

1—ST. AUGUSTINE (1866) [CEM] Revs. Peter G. Gori, O.S.A.; Arthur D. Johnson, O.S.A., Parochial Vicar; Deacons Louis J. Piazza; Michael F. Curren; Sr. Madonna Kling, C.D.P., Pastoral Assoc.
Res.: 43 Essex St., Andover, 01810-3748.
Tel: 978-475-0050; Fax: 978-475-3078; Email: info@staugustineparish.org; Web: www.staugustineparish.org.
School—St. Augustine School, 26 Central St., Andover, 01810. Tel: 978-475-2414;
Fax: 978-470-1327; Email: akendall@staugustineschoolandover.org; Web: www.staugustineandover.org. Ms. Paula O'Dea, Prin. Lay Teachers 28; Sisters 1; Students 493.
Catechesis Religious Program—Bridget Rao, D.R.E.
Mission—St. Joseph's (1881) 20 High Vale Ln., Ballardville, 01810.
Convent—Sisters of Notre Dame, 47 Essex St., Andover, Essex Co. 01810. Tel: 978-475-0087.

2—ST. ROBERT BELLARMINE (1961) Rev. Richard T. Conway, V.F.
Res.: 198 Haggetts Pond Rd., Andover, 01810-4218.
Tel: 978-683-8922; Fax: 978-689-8878; Email: rtconway@comcast.net; Web: www.saintroberts.net.
Catechesis Religious Program—Amanda Roberts, D.R.E.

ARLINGTON, MIDDLESEX CO.

1—SAINT AGNES (1872) Very Rev. Brian M. Flatley; Rev. John J. Graham, Parochial Vicar.
Res.: 51 Medford St., Arlington, 02474-3197.
Tel: 781-648-0220; Fax: 781-643-7883; Email: parish@saintagnes.net; Web: www.saintagnes.net.
School—St. Agnes School, 39 Medford St., Arlington, 02474. Tel: 781-643-9031; Fax: 781-643-2834; Email: rpenta@saintagnesschool.us; Web: www.saintagnesschool.com. Mr. Robert Penta, Prin. Lay Teachers 20; Religious 3; Students 400.
High School—Arlington Catholic High School, 16 Medford St., Arlington, 02474. Tel: 781-646-7770;
Fax: 781-648-8345; Email: sbiagioni@achs.net; Web: www.achs.net. Mr. Stephen J. Biagioni, Prin. Lay Teachers 40; Religious 10; Students 800.
Catechesis Religious Program—Tel: 781-646-5579. Ms. Joyce Patriacca, D.R.E.

2—ST. CAMILLUS (1950) Rev. James E. O'Leary. In Res., Rev. Robert M. O'Grady.
Res.: 1175 Concord Tpke., Arlington, 02476-7262.
Tel: 781-643-3132; Fax: 781-643-8228; Email: stcamillus@verizon.net.
Catechesis Religious Program—Catherine Robinson, D.R.E.; John Flahery, D.R.E.

3—ST. JAMES THE APOSTLE (1914) Closed. Parish records for all closed, merged & suppressed parishes are located at the Office of the Archives, 66 Brooks Dr., Braintree, MA 02184-3839. Tel: 617-746-5795.

4—ST. JEROME (1934) Closed. St. Jerome, Arlington was suppressed. This parish's records are located at St. Agnes, Arlington.

ASHLAND, MIDDLESEX CO., ST. CECILIA (1885)
55 Esty St., Ashland, 01721-2126. Tel: 508-881-1107;
Fax: 508-881-8606; Email: business@saintceciliaparish.org; Web: www.saintceciliaparish.org. Rev. Richard P. Cornell; Holly Archer, Business Mgr.
Catechesis Religious Program—Tel: 508-881-6107. Janet Wilkinson, D.R.E.; Jason Giombetti, D.R.E.

AVON, NORFOLK CO., ST. MICHAEL (1908) [CEM] Revs. Thomas C. Boudreau; John E. Kelly, Parochial Vicar; Deacon Stephen M. Buttrick.
Res.: 87 N. Main St., Avon, 02322-1286.
Tel: 508-586-7210; Fax: 508-586-7211; Email: stmichaelsavon@comcast.net; Web: stmichaelavon.org.
Catechesis Religious Program—Elaine Flanagan, D.R.E. Students 89.

AYER, MIDDLESEX CO., ST. MARY (1858) [CEM]
31 Shirley St., Ayer, 01432. Tel: 978-772-2414;
Fax: 978-772-0727; Email: office.mgr@nvcc-ma.org; Web: www.nvcc-ma.org. Rev. Edmond M. Derosier.
Catechesis Religious Program—Tel: 978-772-7474; Email: faithformation@nvcc-ma.org.

BEDFORD, MIDDLESEX CO., ST. MICHAEL (1931) Rev. Msgr. William F. Cuddy, Admin.
Res.: 90 Concord Rd., Bedford, 01730.
Tel: 781-275-6318; Fax: 781-271-9879; Email: parishoffice@bedfordcatholic.org; Web: www.bedfordcatholic.org.
Catechesis Religious Program—Tel: 781-275-6324; Fax: 781-271-0133. Patricia Marks, D.R.E.

BELLINGHAM, NORFOLK CO.

1—ASSUMPTION (1927) Closed. Parish records for all closed, merged & suppressed parishes are located at the Office of the Archives, 66 Brooks Dr., Braintree, MA 02184-3839. Tel: 617-746-5795.

2—ST. BLAISE (1962) Rev. Albert M. Faretra; Deacon Richard J. Brennan.
Res. & Office: 1158 S. Main St., Bellingham, 02019-1597. Tel: 508-966-1258; Fax: 508-966-0310; Email: fatherfaretra@saintblaise.org; Web: www.saintblaise.org.
Catechesis Religious Program—Cheryl Langevin, D.R.E.

3—ST. BRENDAN (1945) Rev. David J. Mullen; Deacon David R. Ghioni.
Res.: 384 Hartford Ave., Bellingham, 02019-1217.
Tel: 508-966-9802; Fax: 508-966-4404; Email: frmullen.saintbrendan@verizon.net; Web: www.saintbrendansparish.org.
Catechesis Religious Program—Gladys Griffin, D.R.E.

BELMONT, MIDDLESEX CO.

1—ST. JOSEPH (1900)
130 Common St., Belmont, 02478-2418.
Tel: 617-484-0279; Fax: 617-484-7831; Email: info@newroadscatholic.org; Web: www.newroadscatholic.org. Rev. Thomas A. Mahoney.
Catechesis Religious Program—Tel: 617-484-1770. Ann Marie Mahoney, C.R.E.

2—ST. LUKE (1919) Revs. Thomas A. Mahoney; John J. Healy, Parochial Vicar.
Res.: 132 Lexington St., Belmont, 02478-1239.
Tel: 617-484-1996; Fax: 617-484-7831; Email: mangelini@newroadscatholic.org; Web: www.newroadscatholic.org.
Catechesis Religious Program—Tel: 617-484-9357. Robert Flaherty, D.R.E.

3—OUR LADY OF MERCY (1926) Closed. Parish records for all closed, merged & suppressed parishes are located at the Office of the Archives, 66 Brooks Dr., Braintree, MA 02184-3839. Tel: 617-746-5795.

BEVERLY, ESSEX CO.

1—ST. ALPHONSUS (1917) Closed. Parish records for all closed, merged & suppressed parishes are located at the Office of the Archives, 66 Brooks Dr., Braintree, MA 02184-3839. Tel: 617-746-5795.

2—ST. JOHN THE EVANGELIST (1955)
111 New Balch St., Beverly, 01915. Rev. Karlo J. Hocurscak; Deacon Michael C. Joens.
Res.: 552 Cabot St., Beverly, 01915.
Tel: 978-922-5542; Fax: 978-921-4563; Email: office@beverlycatholic.com; Web: www.beverlycatholic.com.
School—The Saints Academy, (Grades PreK-8), Tel: 978-922-0048; Fax: 978-927-6694; Email: info@saintsacademy.org; Web: saintsacademy.org. Daniel Bouchard, Prin. Lay Teachers 27; Students 235.
Catechesis Religious Program—Jean Sword, D.R.E. (Elem. School); Jude Odimone Milan, D.R.E. (High School).

3—ST. MARGARET (1905) Rev. Karlo J. Hocurscak; Deacon Michael C. Joens.
Res.: 672 Hale St., Beverly, 01915-2119.
Tel: 978-927-0069; Fax: 978-927-9359; Email: casstmargbf@comcast.net; Web: beverlycatholic.com.
Catechesis Religious Program—Miss Mary Murray, M.S.Ed., D.R.E.

4—ST. MARY STAR OF THE SEA (1870) Rev. Karlo J. Hocurscak; Deacon Michael C. Joens.
Res.: 253 Cabot St., Beverly, 01915-4597.
Tel: 978-922-0113; Fax: 978-922-8501; Email: stmarystar@parishmail.com; Web: www.beverlycatholic.com.
School—St. Mary Star of the Sea School, 13 Chapman St., Beverly, 01915. Tel: 978-927-3259; Fax: 978-927-7170. Sr. Catherine Fleming, S.N.D., Prin.
Catechesis Religious Program—Christine O'Brien, D.R.E.
Convent—St. Mary, 15 Chapman St., Beverly, 01915-4597.

BILLERICA, MIDDLESEX CO.

1—ST. ANDREW (1868) Very Rev. Shawn W. Allen, V.F.; Revs. Ronald L. St. Pierre, Parochial Vicar; Hal N. Obayashi, Parochial Vicar; Deacons Allan R. Shanahan; Phillip T. DiBello.
Res.: 45 Talbot Ave., Billerica, 01862-1414.
Tel: 978-663-3624; Fax: 978-670-1433; Web: www.billericacatholic.org.
Catechesis Religious Program—Tel: 978-667-9024. Ann Marie Huff, D.R.E.

2—ST. MARY (1937) Very Rev. Shawn W. Allen, V.F.; Revs. Ronald L. St. Pierre, Parochial Vicar; Hal N. Obayashi, Parochial Vicar; Deacons Allan R. Shanahan; Phillip T. DiBello.
Res.: 796 Boston Rd., Billerica, 01821.
Tel: 978-663-2215; Fax: 978-663-0127; Email: st.marybillerica@gmail.com; Web: www.billericacatholic.org.
Catechesis Religious Program—Roberta Breen, D.R.E.; James J. Spinale, D.R.E.

3—ST. THERESA OF LISIEUX (1945)
466 Boston Rd., Billerica, 01821-2504.
Tel: 978-663-8816; Fax: 978-663-0577; Email: sttheresaofficemanager@gmail.com; Web: www.billericacatholic.org. Very Rev. Shawn W. Allen, V.F.; Revs. Ronald L. St. Pierre, Parochial Vicar; Hal N. Obayashi, Parochial Vicar; Deacons Phillip T. DiBello; Allan R. Shanahan. Collaborative with St. Mary and St. Andrew
Catechesis Religious Program—Stephanie Tuzzolo, D.R.E.; Lorraine Ronan, D.R.E.; Theresa Grejdus, D.R.E.; Carol Roncari, D.R.E.

BRAINTREE, NORFOLK CO.

1—ST. CLARE (1959)
856 Washington St., 02184-8299. Very Rev. Paul T. Clifford, V.F.; Rev. Donald R. Delay, Parochial Vicar; Deacon Joseph E. MacDonald.
Res.: 1244 Liberty St., 02184-8299.
Tel: 781-848-7480; Fax: 781-356-8380; Email: stclare1@verizon.net; Web: www.stclarebraintree.org.
Catechesis Religious Program—Tel: 781-848-7481. Gilbert Capone, D.R.E.

2—ST. FRANCIS OF ASSISI (1903) Very Rev. Paul T. Clifford, V.F.; Rev. Donald R. Delay, Parochial Vicar; Deacon Joseph E. MacDonald.
Res.: 856 Washington St., 02184-6464.
Tel: 781-843-1332; Fax: 781-848-0976; Email: parish@sfab.org; Web: www.sfab.org.
School—St. Francis of Assisi School, 850 Washington St., 02184. Tel: 781-848-0842; Fax: 781-356-5309; Email: vdebenedictis@sfab.org; Web: www.sfab.org/indexstfrancis.htm. Mr. Brian Cote, Prin.
Catechesis Religious Program—Margaret L. Donaher, D.R.E.

3—ST. THOMAS MORE (1938)
7 Hawthorn Rd., 02184-1402. Tel: 781-843-1980; Email: secretary@shstm.org; Web: www.shstm.org. Rev. Sean M. Connor.
Catechesis Religious Program—Tel: 781-843-2142. Anne Vail, D.R.E.; Jerry Hubbard, D.R.E.

BRIDGEWATER, PLYMOUTH CO., ST. THOMAS AQUINAS (1848) [CEM] Very Rev. William D. Devine, V.F.; Rev. Jason R. Giombetti, Parochial Vicar; Senior Deacon Gerald P. Ryan.
Res.: 103 Center St., Bridgewater, 02324-1397.
Tel: 508-697-9528; Fax: 508-279-1859; Email: stthomasaquinas@comcast.net; Web: www.stthomasaquinas.com.
Catechesis Religious Program—Tel: 508-697-3652; Fax: 508-697-8907. Ms. Francine Bell, D.R.E.

BROCKTON, PLYMOUTH CO.

1—ST. CASIMIR (1898) (Lithuanian), Closed. Parish records for all closed, merged & suppressed parishes are located at the Office of the Archives, 66 Brooks Dr., Braintree, MA 02184-3839. Tel: 617-746-5795.

2—CHRIST THE KING (2004)
54 Lyman St., Brockton, 02302-2461.
Tel: 508-586-1575; Email: secretary@ctkp.org; Web: brocktoncatholic.org. Revs. Joseph K. Raeke, V.F.; Garcia Breneville, (Haiti) Parochial Vicar; Sr. Alice M. Arsenault, S.U.S.C., Pastoral Assoc.; Deacons Philip H. LaFond; Christopher Z. Connelly.
Res.: 71 E. Main St., Brockton, 02302-2461.
Tel: 508-586-6491; Email: contact@brocktoncatholic.org.
Catechesis Religious Program—Judy A. Sullivan, D.R.E.; Mr. Joseph Sanon, D.R.E.
Convent—45 Erie Ave., Brockton, 02302.
Tel: 508-559-7642.

3—ST. COLMAN OF CLOYNE (2004) Closed. Parish records for all closed, merged & suppressed parishes are located at the Office of the Archives, 66 Brooks Dr., Braintree, MA 02184-3839. Tel: 617-746-5795.

4—ST. EDITH STEIN (2003) Revs. Joseph K. Raeke, V.F.; Garcia Breneville, (Haiti) Parochial Vicar; Irineu Costa Correia, (Cape Verde) Parochial Vicar; Deacons Christopher Z. Connelly; Philip H. LaFond; Sr. Eugenia (Sr. Djai) DaSilva, F.I.C., Pastoral Assoc.
Res.: 71 E. Main St., Brockton, 02301-2461.
Tel: 508-586-6491; Fax: 508-587-1796; Email: stedithstein@gmail.com; Web: www.brocktoncatholic.org.
Catechesis Religious Program—Tel: 508-588-7032. Mary Ann Yezukevich, D.R.E.

5—ST. EDWARD (1897) Closed. Parish records for all closed, merged & suppressed parishes are located at the Office of the Archives, 66 Brooks Dr., Braintree, MA 02184-3839. Tel: 617-746-5795.

6—ST. MARGARET (1902) Closed. Parish records for all closed, merged & suppressed parishes are located at the Office of the Archives, 66 Brooks Dr., Braintree, MA 02184-3839. Tel: 617-746-5795.

7—OUR LADY OF LOURDES (1931)
433 West St., Brockton, 02301. Revs. Joseph K. Raeke, V.F.; Irineu Costa Correia, (Cape Verde) Parochial Vicar; Garcia Breneville, (Haiti) Parochial Vicar; Deacons Christopher Z. Connelly; Philip H. LaFond.
Res.: 71 E. Main St., Brockton, 02301-2461.
Tel: 508-586-4715; Fax: 508-584-6257; Email: our.lourdes@comcast.net; Web: brocktoncatholic.org.

8—OUR LADY OF OSTROBRAMA (1914) Closed. Parish records for all closed, merged & suppressed parishes are located at the Office of the Archives, 66 Brooks Dr., Braintree, MA 02184-3839. Tel: 617-746-5795.

9—ST. PATRICK (1856) Revs. Francesco Palombi, (Italy) Admin.; Benito S. Moreno.
Res.: 335 Main St., Brockton, 02301-5396.
Tel: 508-586-4840; Fax: 508-941-0639; Email: stpatrickbrockton@yahoo.com; Web: www.st-pat.com.

10—SACRED HEART (1891) Closed. Parish records for all closed, merged & suppressed parishes are located at the Office of the Archives, 66 Brooks Dr., Braintree, MA 02184-3839. Tel: 617-746-5795.

BROOKLINE, NORFOLK CO.

1—ST. AIDAN (1911) Closed. Parish records for all closed, merged & suppressed parishes are located at the Office of the Archives, 66 Brooks Dr., Braintree, MA 02184-3839. Tel: 617-746-5795.

2—INFANT JESUS (1938) Closed. Parish records for all closed, merged & suppressed parishes are located at the Office of the Archives, 66 Brooks Dr., Braintree, MA 02184-3839. Tel: 617-746-5795.

3—INFANT JESUS-ST. LAWRENCE (Chestnut Hill) (1999) Closed. Parish records for all closed, merged & suppressed parishes are located at the Office of the Archives, 66 Brooks Dr., Braintree, MA 02184-3839. Tel: 617-746-5795.

4—ST. LAWRENCE (1898) Closed. Parish records for all closed, merged & suppressed parishes are located at the Office of the Archives, 66 Brooks Dr., Braintree, MA 02184-3839. Tel: 617-746-5795.

5—ST. MARY OF THE ASSUMPTION (1852)
3 Linden Pl., Brookline, 02445-7311.
Tel: 617-734-0444; Fax: 617-734-3001; Web: www.stmarybrookline.com. Very Rev. Brian M. Clary, V.F.; Deacon Brian K. Kean.
School—St. Mary of the Assumption School, 67 Harvard St., Brookline, 02445. Tel: 617-566-7184; Fax: 617-731-4078; Email: info@Stmarys-Brookline.org; Web: www.stmarys-brookline.org. Dr. Theresa Kirk, Prin.
Catechesis Religious Program—Julianne J. Shanklis, M.Ed., D.R.E.

BURLINGTON, MIDDLESEX CO.

1—ST. MALACHY (1964) Rev. John M. Capuci.
Res.: 99 Bedford St., Burlington, 01803.
Tel: 781-272-5111; Fax: 781-270-9407; Email: office@saint-malachy.org; Web: www.saint-malachy.org.
Catechesis Religious Program—Donald P. Nealon, D.R.E.; Susan Hurton, D.R.E.; Ms. Anna Molettieri, D.R.E.

2—ST. MARGARET OF ANTIOCH (1945)
109 Winn St., Burlington, 01803. Tel: 781-272-3111; Fax: 781-272-9204; Email: stmargaretparish2@verizon.net; Web: www.stmargaretburlington.org. Very Rev. Frank J. Silva, V.F.; Rev. Jiwon Yoon, Parochial Vicar; Deacon Richard F. Bilotta.
Catechesis Religious Program—Tel: 781-935-7373. Mary Murgo, D.R.E.

CAMBRIDGE, MIDDLESEX CO.

1—ST. ANTHONY OF PADUA (1902) (Portuguese) Very Rev. Walter A. Carreiro, V.F.; Rev. Luiz Fernando Franca Lopes, Parochial Vicar; Deacon Paulo C. Torrens.
Res.: 400 Cardinal Medeiros Ave., Cambridge, 02141-1411. Tel: 617-547-5593; Fax: 617-547-1505; Email: info@saintanthonyparish.com; Web: www.saintanthonyparish.com/.
Catechesis Religious Program—Mariazinha Sousa, D.R.E.

2—BLESSED SACRAMENT (1905) Closed. Parish records for all closed, merged & suppressed parishes are located at the Office of the Archives, 66 Brooks Dr., Braintree, MA 02184-3839. Tel: 617-746-5795.

3—ST. FRANCIS OF ASSISI (1917) (Italian)
325 Cambridge St., Cambridge, 02141.
Tel: 617-547-5593; Fax: 617-547-1505; Email: saintfranciscambridge@gmail.com. Very Rev. Walter A. Carreiro, V.F., Admin.; Deacon Paulo C. Torrens.
Res.: 400 Cardinal Medeiros Ave., Cambridge, 02141.

4—ST. HEDWIG (1907) Closed. Parish records for all closed, merged & suppressed parishes are located at the Office of the Archives, 66 Brooks Dr., Braintree, MA 02184-3839. Tel: 617-746-5795.

5—IMMACULATE CONCEPTION (1910) (Lithuanian), Closed. Parish records for all closed, merged & suppressed parishes are located at the Office of the Archives, 66 Brooks Dr., Braintree, MA 02184-3839. Tel: 617-746-5795.

6—IMMACULATE CONCEPTION (1926) Closed. Parish records for all closed, merged & suppressed parishes are located at the Office of the Archives, 66 Brooks Dr., Braintree, MA 02184-3839. Tel: 617-746-5795.

7—ST. JOHN THE EVANGELIST (1893)
2270 Massachusetts Ave., Cambridge, 02140-1837.

Tel: 617-547-4880; Fax: 617-441-8028; Email: info@stjohncambridge.org; Web: www.stjohncambridge.org. Revs. Charles E. Collins; Frantz J. Gilles, O.F.M.Cap., Parochial Vicar.
Catechesis Religious Program—Maureen Megnia, D.R.E.

8—ST. MARY OF THE ANNUNCIATION (1867)
135 Norfolk St., Cambridge, 02139.
Tel: 617-547-0120; Fax: 617-547-0120; Email: saintmarycambridge@gmail.com; Web: www.stmaryoftheannunciation.com. Rev. Michael C. Harrington; Deacon Stanley A. Straub.
Catechesis Religious Program—Tel: 617-547-0145. Maria Bermudez, D.R.E.

9—OUR LADY OF PITY (1892) Closed. Parish records for all closed, merged & suppressed parishes are located at the Office of the Archives, 66 Brooks Dr., Braintree, MA 02184-3839. Tel: 617-746-5795.

10—ST. PATRICK (1908) Closed. Parish records for all closed, merged & suppressed parishes are located at the Office of the Archives, 66 Brooks Dr., Braintree, MA 02184-3839. Tel: 617-746-5795.

11—ST. PAUL (1875)
Bow & Arrow Sts., Cambridge, 02138-6097.
Tel: 617-491-8400; Fax: 617-354-7092; Email: info@stpaulparish.org; Web: www.stpaulparish.org. Revs. William T. Kelly, S.T.D., S.T.L.; Mark W. Murphy, Parochial Vicar.
School—St. Paul's Choir School, Tel: 617-868-8658; Email: wmcivor@choirschool.net; Web: www.bostonboychoir.org. Mr. William McIvor, Headmaster.
Catechesis Religious Program—Ms. Patty Lee, D.R.E.

12—ST. PETER (1848) Rev. Leonard F. O'Malley; Deacons Thomas L. O'Donnell; John Czajkowski.
Res.: 100 Concord Ave., Cambridge, 02138-2297.
Tel: 617-547-4235; Fax: 617-547-1525; Email: office@saintpetercambridge.org; Web: www.saintpetercambridge.org.
School—St. Peter School, 96 Concord Ave., Cambridge, 02138. Tel: 617-547-0101;
Fax: 617-441-8911; Email: bernadetteleahy@gmail.com; Web: www.saint-peter-school.org. Mr. Brian Delaney, Prin. Lay Teachers 7; Sisters 5; Students 201.
Catechesis Religious Program—Kathryn Smith, D.R.E.

13—SACRED HEART (1842)
47 Sixth St., Cambridge, 02141-1594.
Tel: 617-547-0399; Fax: 617-441-8648; Email: sacredheartofj@msn.com. Rev. Joseph L. Curran, Admin.

CANTON, NORFOLK CO.

1—ST. GERARD MAJELLA (1960) Rev. Rodney J. Copp; Deacon Daniel C. Nelson.
Res.: 1860 Washington St., Canton, 02021.
Tel: 781-828-3420; Fax: 781-828-2520; Email: welcome@saintgerard.org; Web: www.saintgerard.org.
Catechesis Religious Program—Eleanor George, D.R.E.

2—ST. JOHN THE EVANGELIST (1861) Rev. Thomas S. Rafferty.
Res.: 700 Washington St., Canton, 02021-3036.
Tel: 781-828-0090; Fax: 781-828-2480; Email: bmckenney@stjohncanton.org; Web: www.stjohncanton.org.
School—St. John the Evangelist School, (Grades PreK-8), 696 Washington St., Canton, 02021-3036.
Tel: 781-828-2130; Fax: 781-828-7563; Email: chris.flieger@sjscanton.org; Web: www.sjscanton.org. Dr. Chris Flieger, Prin. Lay Teachers 25; Students 213.
Catechesis Religious Program—Tel: 781-828-5130. Mrs. Lorraine M. Wright, D.R.E.

CARLISLE, MIDDLESEX CO., ST. IRENE (1960)
181 East St., Carlisle, 01741-1104. Tel: 978-369-3940 ; Fax: 978-287-1440; Email: stirene@comcast.net; Web: www.stirenes.org. Revs. Thomas P. Donohoe; Romain Rurangirwa, (Rwanda) Parochial Vicar; Deacon Dean C. Bulpett.
Catechesis Religious Program—Georgia Winfrey, D.R.E.

CARVER, PLYMOUTH CO., OUR LADY OF LOURDES (1950) Rev. Anthony J. Medairos; Deacon Paul D. Coughlin.
Parish Office: 130 Main St., Carver, 02330-0068.
Tel: 508-866-4000; Fax: 508-866-5588; Email: ololcarver@comcast.net; Web: www.ourladyoflourdescarver.weconnect.com.
Catechesis Religious Program—Tel: 508-866-9211. Linda Cedrone, D.R.E.

CHELMSFORD, MIDDLESEX CO.

1—ST. JOHN THE EVANGELIST (1893) Revs. Brian E. Mahoney; Thomas B. Corcoran, Parochial Vicar; Laurence M. Tocci, Parochial Vicar.
Res.: 115 Middlesex St., Chelmsford, 01863-2030.
Tel: 978-251-8571; Fax: 978-293-0303; Email: churches@chelmsfordcatholic.org; Web: www.saintjohnchelmsford.org.
Catechesis Religious Program—Tel: 978-251-4310. Ms. Debra Anderson, D.R.E.

2—ST. MARY (1931) Revs. Brian E. Mahoney; Thomas B. Corcoran, Parochial Vicar; Laurence M. Tocci, Parochial Vicar; Deacon Francis X. Burke.
Res.: 25 North Rd., Chelmsford, 01824-2767.
Tel: 978-256-2374; Email: rae@chelmsfordcatholic.org; Web: www.saint-mary.org.
Catechesis Religious Program—Ms. Heather Hannaway, D.R.E.

CHELSEA, SUFFOLK CO.

1—OUR LADY OF GRACE (1913)
194 Nichols St., Chelsea, 02150-1225.
Tel: 617-884-0030; Fax: 617-884-0957; Email: ologparish@comcast.net; Web: www.ologp.net. Very Rev. James J. Barry, V.F.
Catechesis Religious Program—Fax: 617-884-2482. Sr. Kathy Stark, D.R.E.

2—OUR LADY OF THE ASSUMPTION (1907) Closed. Parish records for all closed, merged & suppressed parishes are located at the Office of the Archives, 66 Brooks Dr., Braintree, MA 02184-3839. Tel: 617-746-5795.

3—ST. ROSE OF LIMA (1849) Revs. Hilario S. Sanez, (Poland) Admin.; Joseph M. Xuan Thanh-Cahn, C.M.C., Parochial Vicar; Reynaldo Jose Escobar Altamirano, (Switzerland) Parochial Vicar; Deacons Luis F. Rivera; Alejandro Iraola.
Res.: 601 Broadway, Chelsea, 02150-2998.
Tel: 617-889-2774; Fax: 617-889-2854; Email: strosechelsea@hotmail.com.
School—St. Rose of Lima School, 580 Broadway, Chelsea, 02150-2998. Tel: 617-884-2626;
Fax: 617-889-2345; Email: maryannebabs@hotmail.com; Web: www.strosechelsea.com. Ms. Michele Butler, Prin. Lay Teachers 10; Sisters 8; Students 423.
Catechesis Religious Program—Marie Horgan, D.R.E. (English); Sor Ynocencia, D.R.E. (Spanish); Danha Nguyen, D.R.E. (Vietnamese).

4—ST. STANISLAUS (1905) (Polish)
171 Chestnut St., Chelsea, 02150. Tel: 617-889-0261; Fax: 617-466-2107; Email: stanislaus61@comcast.net. Rev. Andrew T. Grelak.

COHASSET, NORFOLK CO., ST. ANTHONY OF PADUA (1886)
2 Summer St., Cohasset, 02025. Tel: 781-383-0219; Fax: 781-383-9948; Email: saintanthonycoh@gmail.com; Web: www.saintanthonycohasset.org. Rev. John R. Mulvehill.
Catechesis Religious Program—Tel: 781-383-0630. Virginia Macleod, D.R.E.

CONCORD, MIDDLESEX CO.

1—ST. BERNARD (1863) Closed. Parish records for all closed, merged & suppressed parishes are located at the Office of the Archives, 66 Brooks Dr., Braintree, MA 02184-3839. Tel: 617-746-5795.

2—HOLY FAMILY (2004)
12 Monument Sq., Concord, 01742.
Tel: 978-369-7442; Fax: 978-371-0853; Email: office@holyfamilyconcord.org; Web: www.holyfamilyconcord.org. Rev. Austin H. Fleming; Deacons Charles I. Clough; Gregory J. Burch.
Catechesis Religious Program—Sandra Meuller, D.R.E.; Helen Cushman, D.R.E.

3—OUR LADY HELP OF CHRISTIANS (1907) Closed. Parish records for all closed, merged & suppressed parishes are located at the Office of the Archives, 66 Brooks Dr., Braintree, MA 02184-3839. Tel: 617-746-5795.

DANVERS, ESSEX CO.

1—ST. MARY OF THE ANNUNCIATION (1871) [CEM] Rev. Michael J. Doyle; Deacons John Koza; Brian Shea.
Res.: 24 Conant St., Danvers, 01923-2968.
Tel: 978-774-0340; Fax: 978-774-9407; Email: stmarydanvers@comcast.net; Web: www.stmarydanvers.org.
School—St. Mary of the Annunciation School, 14 Otis St., Danvers, 01923. Tel: 978-774-0307;
Fax: 978-750-4852; Email: mkelley@stmaryschooldanvers.org; Web: www.stmaryschooldanvers.org. Mr. Sean Reardon, Prin.
Catechesis Religious Program—Tel: 978-774-8605. John J. Dillon, D.R.E.; Judy DiGennaro, D.R.E.

2—ST. RICHARD OF CHICHESTER (1963) Revs. Bruce G. Flannagan; Stephen M. Healy, Parochial Vicar.
Res.: 90 Forest St., Danvers, 01923-1806.
Tel: 978-774-7575; Fax: 978-774-9543; Email: strichcarddanvers@gmail.com; Web: www.strichcarddanvers.org.
School—St. Mary of the Annunciation School, 14 Otis St., Danvers, 01923-1806. Tel: 978-774-0307;
Fax: 978-750-4852; Email: mkelley@stmaryschooldanvers.org; Web: www.stmaryschooldanvers.org. Mr. Sean Reardon, Prin.
Catechesis Religious Program—Doreen Verda, D.R.E.

DEDHAM, NORFOLK CO.

1—ST. MARY (1866) [CEM]
430 High St., Dedham, 02026-2892. Revs. Wayne L. Belschner, A.B., M.Div., S.T.L., Admin.; Mark D. Storey, Parochial Vicar; Senior Deacon Louis W. Sheedy; Deacon Kelley B. McCormick. In Res., Most Rev. Arthur L. Kennedy; Revs. Michael C. Harrington; Eric F. Cadin, M.Div., S.T.L.
Catechesis Religious Program—Tel: 781-329-5488. Sr. Anne Michael Hannigan, S.N.D., D.R.E.

2—ST. SUSANNA (1960) Rev. Stephen S. Josoma.
Res.: 262 Needham St., Dedham, 02026-7009.
Tel: 781-329-9575; Fax: 781-329-5966; Email: saintsusanna@hotmail.com; Web: www.saintsusanna.org.
Catechesis Religious Program—Nancy Leoncini, D.R.E.

DOVER, NORFOLK CO., MOST PRECIOUS BLOOD (1959)
30 Centre St., Dover, 02030-0812. Tel: 508-785-0305; Fax: 508-785-0432; Email: mpb.dover@verizon.net; Web: www.mpb-stp.org. Rev. John J. Grimes, S.T.M., Ph.D.
Catechesis Religious Program—
Tel: 508-785-9909 (Grades 6-12); Tel: 508-785-1217. Ann Carroll, D.R.E. (Grades 1-5); Regina O'Connor, D.R.E. (Grades 6-12).

DRACUT, MIDDLESEX CO.

1—ST. FRANCIS OF ASSISI (1963)
P.O. Box 609, Dracut, 01826-0609. Very Rev. Sean M. Maher, V.F., Admin.; Deacons John C. Hunt; Michael P. Tompkins.
Parish Office: 115 Wheeler Rd., Dracut, 01826-4254.
Tel: 978-452-6611; Fax: 978-452-0772; Email: info@saintfrancis.net; Web: www.saintfrancis.net.
Catechesis Religious Program—Tel: 978-453-4460. Judy Riopelle, D.R.E. Students 307.

2—STE. MARGUERITE D'YOUVILLE (2001) Revs. Richard F. Clancy; Michael J. Harkins, Parochial Vicar; Tinh Van Nguyen, Parochial Vicar; Deacon Everett F. Penney.
Res.: 1340 Lakeview Ave., Dracut, 01826-3499.
Tel: 978-957-0322; Fax: 978-957-5266; Email: smsrbusmgr@gmail.com; Web: www.stemargueritedracut.org.
School—St. Louis de France, 77 Boisvert St., Lowell, 01850. Tel: 978-458-7594; Fax: 978-454-9289; Email: drltrouville@saintlouisschool.org; Web: www.saintlouisschool.org. Dr. Linda Trouville, Prin.
Convent—85 Boisvert St., Lowell, 01850.
Tel: 978-454-5742.

3—ST. MARY OF THE ASSUMPTION (1909) Closed. Parish records for all closed, merged & suppressed parishes are located at the Office of the Archives, 66 Brooks Dr., Braintree, MA 02184-3839. Tel: 617-746-5795.

4—ST. THERESE (1927) Closed. Parish records for all closed, merged & suppressed parishes are located at the Office of the Archives, 66 Brooks Dr., Braintree, MA 02184-3839. Tel: 617-746-5795.

DUXBURY, PLYMOUTH CO., HOLY FAMILY (1945) Rev. J. Thomas Gignac, Parochial Vicar; Very Rev. Robert J. Deehan, V.F.
Church: 601 Tremont St., Duxbury, 02332-4450.
Tel: 781-934-5055; Fax: 781-934-5796; Email: office@holyfamilyduxbury.org; Web: www.holyfamilyduxbury.org.
Catechesis Religious Program—Tel: 781-934-6839. Mrs. Catherine Kelleher, D.R.E.

EAST BRIDGEWATER, PLYMOUTH CO., ST. JOHN THE EVANGELIST (1903) Revs. Paul L. Ring, Admin.; Michael K. Harvey, Parochial Vicar; Deacon Joseph J. Hopgood.
Res.: 210 Central St., East Bridgewater, 02333-1998.
Tel: 508-378-4207; Fax: 508-586-3876; Email: stjohnebridge@comcast.net; Web: www.stjohneb.org.
Catechesis Religious Program—Tel: 508-378-1521. Mrs. Nancy Smith, D.R.E. (Pre-K-K); Richard Grasso, D.R.E. (Gr. 1); Pam LeBlanc, D.R.E. (Gr. 2); Carolyn Sullivan, D.R.E. (Gr. 8-11).

EVERETT, MIDDLESEX CO.

1—ST. ANTHONY OF PADUA (1927) (Italian)
46 Oakes St., Everett, 02149. Tel: 617-387-0310;
Fax: 617-387-1229; Email: stanthony38everett@gmail.com. Rev. Jariro Arial Merchan, C.S., Parochial Vicar.
School—St. Anthony of Padua School, 54 Oakes St., Everett, 02149. Tel: 617-389-2448;
Fax: 617-389-3769; Email: stanthonyeverett@comcast.net; Web: www.saseverett.com. Ms. Maria Giggie, Prin. Lay Teachers 8; Sisters 2; Students 213.
Catechesis Religious Program—Doris DiTullio, D.R.E. (Gr. 1-6 English), Tel: 617-387-4806; Maria Sentance, D.R.E. (Gr. 7-10 English); Maybell Montano, D.R.E. (Spanish).

2—IMMACULATE CONCEPTION (1885)
487 Broadway, Everett, 02149-3603.
Tel: 617-389-5660; Fax: 617-389-2456; Email: xavieriii@aol.com; Web: www.iceverett.com. Revs. Gerald J. Osterman; Donatus I. Ezenneka, (Nigeria) Parochial Vicar.
Catechesis Religious Program—Janine Keller, D.R.E. (Gr. 3-5), Tel: 617-710-4963; Richard Randazzo, D.R.E. (Gr. 6-10), Tel: 617-387-7009; Fran Foley, D.R.E. (Gr. 1 & 2).

3—ST. JOSEPH (1912) Closed. Parish records for all closed, merged & suppressed parishes are located at the Office of the Archives, 66 Brooks Dr., Braintree, MA 02184-3839. Tel: 617-746-5795.

4—ST. THERESE (1927) Closed. Parish records for all closed, merged & suppressed parishes are located at the Office of the Archives, 66 Brooks Dr., Braintree, MA 02184-3839. Tel: 617-746-5795.

FOXBOROUGH, NORFOLK CO., ST. MARY (1859)
58 Carpenter St., Foxborough, 02035.
Tel: 508-543-7726; Fax: 508-543-7728; Email: st.mary@foxboro.comcastbiz.net; Web: www.stmarysfoxboro.org. Very Rev. Matthew J. Westcott, V.F., Admin.
Catechesis Religious Program—Tel: 508-543-4577. Geraldine Saegh, D.R.E.; Catherine Briggs, D.R.E.; Elaine L'Etoile, D.R.E.

FRAMINGHAM, MIDDLESEX CO.

1—ST. BRIDGET (1878)
830 Worcester Rd., Framingham, 01702-2902.
Tel: 508-875-5959; Fax: 508-875-1270; Email: strahan@stbridgetparish.org; Web: www.stbridgetparish.org. Rev. Msgr. Francis V. Strahan, V.F.
School—St. Bridget School, 832 Worcester Rd., Framingham, 01702. Tel: 508-875-0181;
Fax: 508-875-9552; Email: cchaves@saintbridgetschool.info; Web: www.saintbridgetschool.info. Ms. Cathleen R. Chaves, Prin. Lay Teachers 19; Students 344.
Catechesis Religious Program—Gail Barbato, D.R.E. (Gr. K-5); Marguerite Tibbert, D.R.E. (Gr. 6-10).

2—ST. GEORGE (1847) Rev. John M. Rowan.
Res.: 74 School St., Framingham, 01701.
Tel: 508-877-5130; Fax: 508-877-3080; Web: www.churchofstgeorge.org.
Catechesis Religious Program—Paula Dolliver, D.R.E.; Leslee Willitts, D.R.E.

3—ST. JEREMIAH (1958) Closed. Parish records for all closed, merged & suppressed parishes are located at the Office of the Archives, 66 Brooks Dr., Braintree, MA 02184-3839. Tel: 617-746-5795.

4—ST. STEPHEN (1883) [CEM] Revs. Francisco J. Anzoategui Peiro, Admin.; Gabino Oliva Macias, (Mexico) Parochial Vicar; Peter F. DeFazio, Parochial Vicar; Deacons Pedro L. Torres; Alfredo Nieves.
Res.: 221 Concord St., Framingham, 01702.
Tel: 508-875-4788; Fax: 508-875-2577; Email: ststephenchurch1@verizon.net; Web: www.ststephenparish.org.
Catechesis Religious Program—James J. Drummey, D.R.E.; Maria Nieves, D.R.E. Students 300.

5—ST. TARCISIUS (1907) [CEM] (Italian)
562 Waverly St., Framingham, 01702-6925.
Tel: 508-875-8623; Fax: 508-875-6358; Email: sttarcisiuspar.bm@gmail.com; Web: www.sttarcisiusparish.org. Rev. Volmar Scaravelli, C.S.; Senior Deacon Manoel B. DeSousa, (Brazil); Deacon Clayton Moreira.
Catechesis Religious Program—Marie Jutkiewicz, D.R.E.

FRANKLIN, NORFOLK CO., ST. MARY (1877) [CEM] Revs. Brian F. Manning; John L. Sullivan, S.S.L., Parochial Vicar; Ms. Nan Rafter, Pastoral Assoc., Pastoral Assoc.; Deacon Guy C. Saint Sauveur.
Res.: One Church Sq., Franklin, 02038-1896.
Tel: 508-528-0020; Tel: 508-528-1450;
Fax: 508-528-1641; Fax: 508-528-0043; Email: parishpublishing@stmarysfranklin.org; Web: www.stmarysfranklin.org.
Catechesis Religious Program—Isabel Coyne, D.R.E.; Karen Ackles, D.R.E.

GEORGETOWN, ESSEX CO., ST. MARY (2006) Very Rev. Richard T. Burton, V.F.; Deacon Paul A. Dow.
Res.: 94 Andover St., Georgetown, 01833-0396.
Tel: 978-352-2024; Fax: 978-352-2308; Email: rectory@stmarysgr.com; Web: saintmaryparish.org.
Catechesis Religious Program—Tel: 978-352-6540. Mary Williams, D.R.E.

GLOUCESTER, ESSEX CO.

1—ST. ANN (1855) Closed. Parish records for all closed, merged & suppressed parishes are located at the Office of the Archives, 66 Brooks Dr., Braintree, MA 02184-3839. Tel: 617-746-5795.

2—HOLY FAMILY (2005)
St. Ann, 74 Pleasant St., Gloucester, 01930.
Tel: 978-281-4820; Fax: 978-281-4964; Email: office@ccgronline.com; Web: www.ccgronline.com. Rev. James M. Achadinha; Senior Deacon Daniel A. Dunn; Deacon Raymond C. Wellbank.
Catechesis Religious Program—Dawn Alves, D.R.E.; Ms. Kathleen McCabe, D.R.E.

3—OUR LADY OF GOOD VOYAGE (1889) (Portuguese)
144 Prospect St., Gloucester, 01930-3714.
Tel: 978-283-1490; Fax: 978-283-0787; Email: office@ccgronline.com; Web: www.ccgronline.com. Rev. James M. Achadinha; Deacon Raymond C. Wellbank; Senior Deacon Daniel A. Dunn.
Catechesis Religious Program—Tel: 978-283-8597. Sisters Mitrina, C.S.J., D.R.E.; Sebastian, C.S.J., D.R.E.

4—ST. PETER (1928) Closed. Parish records for all closed, merged & suppressed parishes are located at the Office of the Archives, 66 Brooks Dr., Braintree, MA 02184-3839. Tel: 617-746-5795.

5—SACRED HEART (1946) Closed. Parish records for all closed, merged & suppressed parishes are located at the Office of the Archives, 66 Brooks Dr., Braintree, MA 02184-3839. Tel: 617-746-5795.

GROTON, MIDDLESEX CO.

1—ST. JAMES (1945) Closed. Parish records for all closed, merged & suppressed parishes are located at the Office of the Archives, 66 Brooks Dr., Braintree, MA 02184-3839. Tel: 617-746-5795.

2—SACRED HEART, Closed. Parish records for all closed, merged & suppressed parishes are located at the Office of the Archives, 66 Brooks Dr., Braintree, MA 02184-3839. Tel: 617-746-5795.

3—SACRED HEART-ST. JAMES (2003) Merged Parish records for all closed, merged & suppressed parishes are located at the Office of the Archives, 66 Brooks Dr., Braintree, MA 02184-3839. Tel: 617-746-5795.

GROVELAND, ESSEX CO., ST. PATRICK (1946) Closed. Parish records for all closed, merged & suppressed parishes are located at the Office of the Archives, 66 Brooks Dr., Braintree, MA 02184-3839. Tel: 617-746-5795.

HALIFAX, PLYMOUTH CO., OUR LADY OF THE LAKE (1945) Very Rev. Michael A. Hobson, V.F., Admin.; Rev. Kwang H. Lee, Parochial Vicar; Deacons Kevin J. Winn; Timothy A. Booker.
Res.: 580 Monponsett St., Halifax, 02338-1331.
Tel: 781-293-7971; Fax: 781-293-7969; Email: ollc350@aol.com; Web: www.ourladyofthelakehalifax.org.
Catechesis Religious Program—Tel: 781-294-4571. Patsy Gillespie, D.R.E.; Carolyn Sullivan, D.R.E.

HAMILTON, ESSEX CO., ST. PAUL (1922) Rev. J. Michael Lawlor.
Res.: 50 Union St., Hamilton, 01982.
Tel: 978-468-2337; Fax: 978-468-6538; Email: stpaulsparish@verizon.net; Web: www.churchofsaintpaul.net.
Catechesis Religious Program—Tel: 978-468-3617. Jeanne Abbott, D.R.E.

HANOVER, PLYMOUTH CO., ST. MARY OF THE SACRED HEART (1907) Rev. Christopher J. Hickey; Deacons John P. Murray; Roger F. Vierra.
Res.: 392 Hanover St., Hanover, 02339.
Tel: 781-826-4303; Fax: 781-826-5203; Email: info@holymothers.com; Web: www.holymothers.com.
Catechesis Religious Program—Tel: 781-826-2351; Fax: 781-829-9271. Kathy Gallo, D.R.E.

HANSON, PLYMOUTH CO., ST. JOSEPH THE WORKER (1956) Very Rev. Michael A. Hobson, V.F., Admin.; Rev. Kwang H. Lee, Parochial Vicar; Deacons Timothy A. Booker; Kevin J. Winn.
Res.: One Maquan St., Hanson, 02341-1714.
Tel: 781-293-3581; Fax: 781-294-1052; Email: j.worker@comcast.net; Web: www.stjosephtheworker.org.
Catechesis Religious Program—Robin Muise, D.R.E.; Kevin Mossman, D.R.E.; Mary Lewek, D.R.E.

HAVERHILL, ESSEX CO.

1—ALL SAINTS (1998) Rev. Timothy E. Kearney.
Res.: 120 Bellevue Ave., Haverhill, 01832-4798.
Tel: 978-372-7721; Fax: 978-372-2085; Email: aspsec@verizon.net; Web: www.facebook.com/allsaintshaverhill.
School—St. Joseph, 56 Oak Ter., Haverhill, 01832.
Tel: 978-521-4256; Fax: 978-521-2613; Email: sjshavcarolsimone@comcast.net; Web: www.sjshav.com. Ms. Carol J. Simone, Prin.
Catechesis Religious Program—Tel: 978-373-5473. Maureen Cartier, D.R.E.
Child Care—St. Joseph's Early Childhood Ed. Center, 100 Bellevue Ave., Haverhill, 01832.
Tel: 978-372-0111.

2—ST. GEORGE (1961) Closed. Parish records for all closed, merged & suppressed parishes are located at the Office of the Archives, 66 Brooks Dr., Braintree, MA 02184-3839. Tel: 617-746-5795.

3—ST. JAMES (1859)
185 Winter St., Haverhill, 01830-4920.
Tel: 978-372-8537; Fax: 978-373-1505; Email: stjamesrcc@hotmail.com; Web: www.stjamesandjohnhaverhill.org. Very Rev. Robert L. Connors, V.F., Admin.; Deacons Jose N. Agudelo; Nicholas Cruz.
Catechesis Religious Program—Larry N. Webster, D.R.E.

4—ST. JOHN THE BAPTIST (1955) Very Rev. Robert L. Connors, V.F., Admin.; Deacon Nicholas Cruz. In Res., Most Rev. Robert F. Hennessey.
Res.: 114 Lincoln Ave., Haverhill, 01830.
Tel: 978-372-8537; Fax: 978-373-1505; Email: stjamesrcc@hotmail.com; Web: www.stjamesandjohnhaverhill.org.

5—ST. JOSEPH (1876) Closed. Parish records for all closed, merged & suppressed parishes are located at the Office of the Archives, 66 Brooks Dr., Braintree, MA 02184-3839. Tel: 617-746-5795.

6—ST. MICHAEL (1910) Closed. Parish records for all closed, merged & suppressed parishes are located at the Office of the Archives, 66 Brooks Dr., Braintree, MA 02184-3839. Tel: 617-746-5795.

7—ST. RITA (1932) Closed. Parish records for all closed, merged & suppressed parishes are located at the Office of the Archives, 66 Brooks Dr., Braintree, MA 02184-3839. Tel: 617-746-5795.

8—SACRED HEARTS (2007)
165 S. Main St., Haverhill, 01835. Tel: 978-373-1281;
Fax: 978-374-3043; Email: hroche@sacredheartsparish.com; Web: www.sacredheartsparish.com. Very Rev. John W. Delaney, V.F.; Rev. Benjamin T. LeTran, Parochial Vicar; Deacon Eric T. Peabody.
School—St. Bridget School, 31 S. Chestnut St., Haverhill, 01835. Tel: 978-372-5451;
Fax: 978-372-1110; Email: jridgely@sacredheartsbradford.org; Web: www.sacredheartsbradford.org. Ms. Kathleen Blain, Prin. Lay Teachers 9; Sisters 1; Students 247.
Catechesis Religious Program—Bridget Lacefield, D.R.E.

HINGHAM, PLYMOUTH CO.

1—ST. PAUL (1871) [CEM] Revs. Thomas F. Nestor, A.B., M.Div., Ph.D.; Sinisa Ubiparipovic, Parochial Vicar; Michael J. McNamara, Parochial Vicar; Deacon Joseph P. Harrington; Elizabeth Reardon, Pastoral Assoc.; Ms. Susan Troy, Pastoral Min.; Linda Resca, Business Mgr.; Salvatore Bartolotti, Music Min.
Res.: 147 North St., Hingham, 02043-1820.
Tel: 781-749-0587; Fax: 781-749-8053; Email: office@stpaulhingham.net; Web: www.hinghamcatholic.org.
School—St. Paul School, (Grades PreK-8), 18 Fearing Rd., Hingham, 02043. Tel: 781-749-2407; Email: lfasano@spshingham.org; Web: www.stpaulschoolhingham.com. Ms. Lisa Fasano, Prin. Lay Teachers 11; Students 175.
Catechesis Religious Program—Tel: 781-749-5568. Sr. Tania Santander Atauchi, C.D.P., D.R.E.; Mickayla Hagar, Youth Min.

2—RESURRECTION OF OUR LORD AND SAVIOR JESUS CHRIST (1957) Revs. Thomas F. Nestor, A.B., M.Div., Ph.D.; Sinisa Ubiparipovic, Parochial Vicar; Michael J. McNamara, Parochial Vicar; Paul R. Soper, (In Res.); Elizabeth Reardon, Pastoral Assoc.; Adam Trudel, Music Min.
Res.: 1057 Main St., Hingham, 02043-3995.
Tel: 781-749-3577; Fax: 781-740-0689; Email: office@resurrrectionhingham.org; Web: www.hinghamcatholic.org.
Catechesis Religious Program—Terri Dasco, Faith Formation; Mickayla Hagar, Youth Min.

HOLBROOK, NORFOLK CO., ST. JOSEPH (1887) Revs. Thomas C. Boudreau; John E. Kelly, Parochial Vicar; Deacon Stephen M. Buttrick.
Res.: 153 S. Franklin St., Holbrook, 02343.
Tel: 781-767-0605; Fax: 781-767-5225; Email: office@stjosephholbrook.org; Web: www.stjosephholbrook.org.
School—St. Joseph School, 143 S. Franklin St., Holbrook, 02343. Tel: 781-767-1544;
Fax: 781-767-3975; Email: clough.sjs@comcast.net; Web: www.stjosephholbrook.com. Ms. Gretchen Hawley, Prin. Lay Teachers 14; Sisters 2; Students 290.
Catechesis Religious Program—Tel: 781-767-0536. Ms. Maura Burke, D.R.E.

HOLLISTON, MIDDLESEX CO., ST. MARY (1870) [CEM]
708 Washington St., Holliston, 01746.
Tel: 508-429-4427; Fax: 508-429-3324; Email: St.marys2@verizon.net; Web: www.stmarysholliston.com. Rev. Mark J. Coiro; Deacon John D. Barry.
Catechesis Religious Program—Tel: 508-429-6076. Andrea DeMayo, D.R.E.

HOPKINTON, MIDDLESEX CO., ST. JOHN THE EVANGELIST (1866) [CEM] Rev. Richard E. Cannon; Deacon Anthony C. Sicuso.
Res.: 20 Church St., Hopkinton, 01748-1836.
Tel: 508-435-3313; Fax: 508-435-5651; Email: stjohnshopkinton@verizon.net; Web: www.stjohnshopkinton.com.
Catechesis Religious Program—
Tel: 508-435-3313, Ext. 208. Carol Zani, D.R.E.; Ken Lysik, D.R.E.; Elaine Mitsock, D.R.E.

HUDSON, MIDDLESEX CO.

1—CHRIST THE KING (1927) Closed. Parish records for all closed, merged & suppressed parishes are located at the Office of the Archives, 66 Brooks Dr., Braintree, MA 02184-3839. Tel: 617-746-5795.

2—ST. MICHAEL (1870) [CEM]
23 Manning St., Hudson, 01749-2315.
Tel: 978-562-2552; Fax: 978-568-1761; Email: parish@stmikes.org; Web: www.stmikes.org. Rev. Ronald G. Calhoun.
Catechesis Religious Program—Tel: 978-562-7174. Ms. Karen Levelle, D.R.E.

HULL, PLYMOUTH CO., ST. MARY OF THE ASSUMPTION (1938)
204 Samoset Ave., Hull, 02045-0565.

Tel: 781-925-0680; Fax: 781-925-0685; Email: info@stmaryhull.com; Web: stmaryhull.com. Rev. Mark G. Derrane, Admin.; Deacon James C. Theriault.
Catechesis Religious Program—Lisa H. Scarry, D.R.E.

IPSWICH, ESSEX CO.

1—ST. JOSEPH (1889) Closed. Parish records for all closed, merged & suppressed parishes are located at the Office of the Archives, 66 Brooks Dr., Braintree, MA 02184-3839. Tel: 617-746-5795.

2—OUR LADY OF HOPE (1997) Rev. Thomas E. Keyes.
Res.: One Pineswamp Rd., Ipswich, 01938-2922.
Tel: 978-356-3944; Fax: 978-356-9592; Email: rectory@ipswichcatholics.org; Web: www.ipswichcatholics.org.
Catechesis Religious Program—Tel: 978-356-2522. Nancy Salah, D.R.E.

3—SACRED HEART (1908) Closed. Parish records for all closed, merged & suppressed parishes are located at the Office of the Archives, 66 Brooks Dr., Braintree, MA 02184-3839. Tel: 617-746-5795.

4—ST. STANISLAUS (1910) Closed. Parish records for all closed, merged & suppressed parishes are located at the Office of the Archives, 66 Brooks Dr., Braintree, MA 02184-3839. Tel: 617-746-5795.

KINGSTON, PLYMOUTH CO., ST. JOSEPH (1908) [CEM]
270 Main St., Kingston, 02364-1922.
Tel: 781-585-6679; Fax: 781-645-1337; Email: office@stjosephkingston.com; Web: www.stjosephkingston.com. Rev. Walter F. Keymont, Admin.
Catechesis Religious Program—Tel: 781-585-6372. Margaret M. Hall, D.R.E.; Ms. Ann M. Cussen, D.R.E.

LAKEVILLE, PLYMOUTH CO., SAINTS MARTHA AND MARY (1958) Revs. John E. Sheridan; Jude Thaddeus Osunkwo, (Nigeria) Parochial Vicar; Deacons George M. Gabriel; Charles H. Bower.
Res.: 354 Bedford St., Lakeville, 02347-2107.
Tel: 508-947-2107; Fax: 508-947-4333; Web: www.cranberrycatholic.org.
Catechesis Religious Program—Sr. Rachel Labonville, C.S.C., D.R.E.

LAWRENCE, ESSEX CO.

1—ST. ANNE, Closed. Parish records for all closed, merged & suppressed parishes are located at the Office of the Archives, 66 Brooks Dr., Braintree, MA 02184-3839. Tel: 617-746-5795.

2—ASSUMPTION OF THE BLESSED VIRGIN, Closed. Parish records for all closed, merged & suppressed parishes are located at the Office of the Archives, 66 Brooks Dr., Braintree, MA 02184-3839. Tel: 617-746-5795.

3—ASUNCION DE LA VIRGEN MARIA (1993) (Hispanic), Closed. Parish records for all closed, merged & suppressed parishes are located at the Office of the Archives, 66 Brooks Dr., Braintree, MA 02184-3839. Tel: 617-746-5795.

4—ST. AUGUSTINE (1935) Closed. Parish records for all closed, merged & suppressed parishes are located at the Office of the Archives, 66 Brooks Dr., Braintree, MA 02184-3839. Tel: 617-746-5795.

5—CORPUS CHRISTI (2004) Rev. Francis X. Mawn.
Res.: 35 Essex St., Lawrence, 01840-1709.
Tel: 978-685-1711; Fax: 978-691-5927; Email: fxmawn@corpuschristilawrence.org; Web: www.corpuschristilawrence.org.
Catechesis Religious Program—Mary Crow, D.R.E.

6—ST. FRANCIS (1903) Closed. Parish records for all closed, merged & suppressed parishes are located at the Office of the Archives, 66 Brooks Dr., Braintree, MA 02184-3839. Tel: 617-746-5795.

7—HOLY ROSARY (1904) Closed. Parish records for all closed, merged & suppressed parishes are located at the Office of the Archives, 66 Brooks Dr., Braintree, MA 02184-3839. Tel: 617-746-5795.

8—HOLY TRINITY (1905) Closed. Parish records for all closed, merged & suppressed parishes are located at the Office of the Archives, 66 Brooks Dr., Braintree, MA 02184-3839. Tel: 617-746-5795.

9—IMMACULATE CONCEPTION, Closed. Parish records for all closed, merged & suppressed parishes are located at the Office of the Archives, 66 Brooks Dr., Braintree, MA 02184-3839. Tel: 617-746-5795.

10—ST. LAURENCE O'TOOLE, Closed. Parish records for all closed, merged & suppressed parishes are located at the Office of the Archives, 66 Brooks Dr., Braintree, MA 02184-3839. Tel: 617-746-5795.

11—ST. MARY, Closed. Parish records for all closed, merged & suppressed parishes are located at the Office of the Archives, 66 Brooks Dr., Braintree, MA 02184-3839. Tel: 617-746-5795.

12—ST. MARY OF THE ASSUMPTION (2004) Revs. Carlos E. Urbina, O.S.A.; John F. Dello Russo, O.S.A., Parochial Vicar; Aquilino D. Gonzalea, O.S.A., Parochial Vicar; Deacons Jesus Castillo; Alvaro Arsenio Frias.
Res.: 300 Haverhill St., Lawrence, 01840.
Tel: 978-685-1111; Fax: 978-686-5555; Email: stmaryoftheassumptionparish@comcast.net; Web: www.stmaryassumption-lawrence.org.
Catechesis Religious Program—Felix Duran, D.R.E.

13—ST. MARY-IMMACULATE CONCEPTION, Closed. Parish records for all closed, merged & suppressed parishes are located at the Office of the Archives, 66 Brooks Dr., Braintree, MA 02184-3839. Tel: 617-746-5795.

14—ST. PATRICK (1872) [CEM]
114 S. Broadway, Lawrence, 01843-1427. Revs. Paul B. O'Brien; Alonso Macias Zakoda, Parochial Vicar; Deacon George C. Escotto.
Catechesis Religious Program—Ms. Diane Jarvis, D.R.E.

15—SS. PETER AND PAUL (1907) Closed. Parish records for all closed, merged & suppressed parishes are located at the Office of the Archives, 66 Brooks Dr., Braintree, MA 02184-3839. Tel: 617-746-5795.

16—SACRED HEART (1905) Closed. Parish records for all closed, merged & suppressed parishes are located at the Office of the Archives, 66 Brooks Dr., Braintree, MA 02184-3839. Tel: 617-746-5795.

LEXINGTON, MIDDLESEX CO.

1—ST. BRIGID (1848)
1981 Massachusetts Ave., Lexington, 02421-4812.
Tel: 781-862-0335; Fax: 781-862-1409; Email: shepherd@lexingtoncatholic.org; Web: www.lexingtoncatholic.org. Rev. Msgr. Paul V. Garrity, V.F.; Rev. John S. Chen, (China) Parochial Vicar.
Catechesis Religious Program—George Begin, D.R.E. (Gr. 1-8), Tel: 781-862-8724; Megan Chenaille, D.R.E. (Gr. 9-12).

2—SACRED HEART (1931)
16 Follen Rd., Lexington, 02421-4812.
Tel: 781-862-4646; Fax: 781-862-1409; Email: shepherd@lexingtoncatholic.org; Web: www.lexingtoncatholic.org. Rev. Msgr. Paul V. Garrity, V.F.; Rev. John S. Chen, (China) Parochial Vicar.
Catechesis Religious Program—
Tel: 781-861-8385, Ext. 19. George Begin, D.R.E.

LINCOLN, MIDDLESEX CO., ST. JOSEPH (1946) Closed. Parish records for all closed, merged & suppressed parishes are located at the Office of the Archives, 66 Brooks Dr., Braintree, MA 02184-3839. Tel: 617-746-5795.

LITTLETON, MIDDLESEX CO., ST. ANNE (1945) Revs. Peter F. Quinn; Joseph M. Rossi, Parochial Vicar; Deacon William A. Dwyer.
Res.: 75 King St., Littleton, 01460-1528.
Tel: 978-486-4100; Fax: 978-952-6303; Email: staoffice@lwcatholic.org; Web: www.littletoncatholic.org.
Catechesis Religious Program—Jacquelyn Butterfield, D.R.E.; Michelle Hatch, D.R.E.

LOWELL, MIDDLESEX CO.

1—ST. ANTHONY OF PADUA (1901) (Portuguese) Revs. Nicholas A. Sannella; Kenneth Healey, S.M., Parochial Vicar; Deacons Stephen M. Papik; Carlos A. DeSousa.
Res.: 893 Central St., Lowell, 01852-3407.
Tel: 978-452-1506; Fax: 978-458-9662; Email: stanthonylowell@aol.com; Web: www.stanthonylowell.org.

2—HOLY FAMILY (2003)
75 Chamberlain St., Lowell, 01852-5006.
Tel: 978-453-2134; Fax: 978-453-0933; Email: holyfamilylowell@yahoo.com. Rev. Nicholas A. Sannella; Deacon Alvaro J. Soares.
Catechesis Religious Program—Richard Ouellette, D.R.E.

3—HOLY TRINITY (1904) [CEM] (Polish)
350 High St., Lowell, 01852-2760. Tel: 978-452-2564; Web: www.holytrinitylowell.org. Revs. Nicholas A. Sannella; Kenneth Healey, S.M., Parochial Vicar; Deacon Stephen M. Papik.
Catechesis Religious Program—Robert Mullin, D.R.E.

4—IMMACULATE CONCEPTION (1869)
144 E. Merrimack St., Lowell, 01852.
Tel: 978-458-1474; Fax: 978-446-0790; Email: iclowell@yahoo.com; Web: www.iclowell.org. Revs. Nicholas A. Sannella; Kenneth Healey, S.M., Parochial Vicar; Deacon Stephen M. Papik.
School—Immaculate Conception School, 218 E. Merrimack St., Lowell, 01852. Tel: 978-454-5339; Fax: 978-454-6593; Email: icslowell@hotmail.com; Web: www.icslowell.com. Ms. Catherine Fiorino, Prin. Lay Teachers 8; Sisters 1; Students 175.
Catechesis Religious Program—Katherine Gendron, D.R.E.; Susan Hurton, D.R.E.

5—ST. JEAN BAPTISTE, Closed. Parish records for all closed, merged & suppressed parishes are located at the Office of the Archives, 66 Brooks Dr., Braintree, MA 02184-3839. Tel: 617-746-5795.

6—SAINT JEANNE D'ARC (1922) Closed. Parish records for all closed, merged & suppressed parishes are located at the Office of the Archives, 66 Brooks Dr., Braintree, MA 02184-3839. Tel: 617-746-5795.

7—ST. JOSEPH (1908) Closed. St. Joseph, Lowell was suppressed. This parish's records are located at Immaculate Conception, Lowell.

8—ST. LOUIS DE FRANCE (1904) Closed. Parish records for all closed, merged & suppressed parishes are located at the Office of the Archives, 66 Brooks Dr., Braintree, MA 02184-3839. Tel: 617-746-5795.

9—ST. MARGARET OF SCOTLAND (1910) [CEM]
384 Stevens St., Lowell, 01851. Tel: 978-454-5143; Fax: 978-458-8472; Email: dmcandrews@stmargaretlowell.org; Web: www.stmargaretlowell.org. Rev. Raymond P. Benoit, Admin.
School—St. Margaret of Scotland School, 486 Stevens St., Lowell, 01851. Tel: 978-453-8491; Fax: 978-453-1358. Sr. Lori Fleming, S.N.D., Prin. Lay Teachers 19; Sisters 1; Students 382.
Catechesis Religious Program—Tel: 978-459-4481. Paula Nalavich, D.R.E.; Pamela Quinn, D.R.E.

10—ST. MARIE (1931) Closed. Parish records for all closed, merged & suppressed parishes are located at the Office of the Archives, 66 Brooks Dr., Braintree, MA 02184-3839. Tel: 617-746-5795.

11—ST. MICHAEL (1883)
543 Bridge St., Lowell, 01850-2098.
Tel: 978-459-0713; Fax: 978-453-1123; Email: saintmichaels@comcast.net; Web: www.saint-michael.com. Revs. Guy F. Sciacca, Admin.; Robert J. Carr, Parochial Vicar; Samuel K. Mathenge, (Kenya) Parochial Vicar.
School—St. Michael School, 21 Sixth St., Lowell, 01850. Tel: 978-453-9511; Fax: 978-454-4104; Email: sms@saint-michael.com; Web: www.saint-michael.com/school.html. Ms. Mary Frances Chisholm, Prin. Lay Teachers 26; Students 392.
Catechesis Religious Program—Tel: 978-458-1617. Nicole Walsh, D.R.E.; Jean Haumann, D.R.E.

12—NOTRE DAME DE LOURDES (1908) Closed. Parish records for all closed, merged & suppressed parishes are located at the Office of the Archives, 66 Brooks Dr., Braintree, MA 02184-3839. Tel: 617-746-5795.

13—NUESTRA SENORA DEL CARMEN (1990) Closed. Parish records for all closed, merged & suppressed parishes are located at the Office of the Archives, 66 Brooks Dr., Braintree, MA 02184-3839. Tel: 617-746-5795.

14—ST. PATRICK (1831) Revs. Michael O'Hara, O.M.I., Admin.; Daniel Crahen, O.M.I., Parochial Vicar, (Retired); Tuan Ngoc Pham, O.M.I., Parochial Vicar; Deacons Peter An Ros; Jorge A. Patino.
Res.: 282 Suffolk St., Lowell, 01854-4297.
Tel: 978-459-0561; Fax: 978-446-0266; Email: stpatricklowell@comcast.net; Web: www.stpatricklowell.org.
Catechesis Religious Program—Sr. Luzelana Vera, M.S.S., D.R.E.

15—ST. PETER (1841) Closed. Parish records for all closed, merged & suppressed parishes are located at the Office of the Archives, 66 Brooks Dr., Braintree, MA 02184-3839. Tel: 617-746-5795.

16—ST. RITA (1910) Revs. Richard F. Clancy; Michael J. Harkins, Parochial Vicar; Tinh Van Nguyen, Parochial Vicar.
Res.: 158 Mammoth Rd., Lowell, 01854-2619.
Tel: 978-452-4812; Fax: 978-957-5266; Email: smsrbusmgr@gmail.com; Web: www.stritalowell.org.
School—Sainte Jeanne d'Arc, 68 Dracut St., Lowell, 01854. Tel: 978-453-4114; Fax: 978-454-8304; Email: Prescille_Malo@sjdarc.org; Web: www.sjdarc.org. Sr. Prescille Malo, S.C.O., Prin.
Catechesis Religious Program—Gail Irish, D.R.E.

17—SACRED HEART (1884) Closed. Parish records for all closed, merged & suppressed parishes are located at the Office of the Archives, 66 Brooks Dr., Braintree, MA 02184-3839. Tel: 617-746-5795.

LYNN, ESSEX CO.

1—ST. FRANCIS OF ASSISI, Closed. Parish records for all closed, merged & suppressed parishes are located at the Office of the Archives, 66 Brooks Dr., Braintree, MA 02184-3839. Tel: 617-746-5795.

2—HOLY FAMILY (1922) (Italian)
21 Bessom St., Lynn, 01902. Tel: 781-599-7200; Fax: 781-595-7270. Revs. Robert A. Poitras; Godfrey Musabe, Parochial Vicar.
Catechesis Religious Program—Tel: 781-596-2390. Catherine M. Raymond, D.R.E.

3—ST. JOHN THE BAPTIST (1886) Closed. Parish records for all closed, merged & suppressed parishes are located at the Office of the Archives, 66 Brooks Dr., Braintree, MA 02184-3839. Tel: 617-746-5795.

4—ST. JOSEPH (1874)
115 Union St., Lynn, 01902-2905. Tel: 781-599-7040; Email: office@saintjosephlynn.org; Web: www.saintjosephlynn.org. Mailing Address: 29 Green St., Lynn, 01902. Revs. Israel J. Rodriguez, Admin.; Wellington Oliveira, Parochial Vicar; Ignacio D. Berrio, (Colombia) (In Res.).
Convent—43 Green St., Lynn, 01902.
Tel: 781-581-7848. Sisters of St. Joseph 2.

5—ST. MARY (1862) Very Rev. Brian L. Flynn, V.F.; Rev. Huan D. Ngo, Parochial Vicar; Deacons Richard P. Field Jr.; William M. Jackson.
Res.: 8 S. Common St., Lynn, 01902-4489.
Tel: 781-598-4907; Fax: 781-599-2088; Email:

admin@lynncatholic.org; Web: www.lynncatholic.org.
High School—St. Mary High School, 35 Tremont St., Lynn, 01902. Tel: 781-595-7885; Fax: 781-595-4471; Email: cdimaiti@smhlynn.org; Web: www.smhlynn.org. Ms. Grace Cotter Regan, Head of School. Lay Teachers 30; Students 650.
6—ST. MICHAEL (1906) (Polish), Closed. Parish records for all closed, merged & suppressed parishes are located at the Office of the Archives, 66 Brooks Dr., Braintree, MA 02184-3839. Tel: 617-746-5795.
7—ST. PATRICK (1906) Closed. Parish records for all closed, merged & suppressed parishes are located at the Office of the Archives, 66 Brooks Dr., Braintree, MA 02184-3839. Tel: 617-746-5795.
8—ST. PIUS FIFTH (1912) Revs. Robert A. Poitras; Godfrey Musabe, Parochial Vicar; Deacon James T. Hinkle.
Res.: 215 Maple St., Lynn, 01904-2799.
Tel: 781-595-7487; Fax: 781-595-7270; Email: admin@stpiuslynn.org; Web: www.stpiuslynn.org.
School—St. Pius Fifth School, 28 Bowler St., Lynn, 01904. Tel: 781-593-8292; Fax: 781-593-6973; Email: qualityeducation@stpiusvschool.org; Web: www.stpiusvschool.org. Mr. Paul Maestranzi, Prin. Lay Teachers 25; Sisters 3; Students 511.
Catechesis Religious Program—Tel: 781-581-3503. Deborah E. Bartlett, D.R.E.
9—SACRED HEART (1894)
579 Boston St., Lynn, 01905-2160. Tel: 781-593-8047; Fax: 781-599-2088; Email: admin@lynncatholic.org; Web: www.lynncatholic.org. Very Rev. Brian L. Flynn, V.F.; Rev. Huan D. Ngo, Parochial Vicar; Deacons Richard P. Field Jr.; William M. Jackson.
School—Sacred Heart School, 581 Boston St., Lynn, 01905-2160. Tel: 781-592-7581; Fax: 781-595-9948; Email: sacredheartschool@mail.com; Web: www.sacredheartschoollynn.org. Ms. Joanne Eagan, Prin. Lay Teachers 8; Sisters 1; Students 261.
Catechesis Religious Program—Tel: 781-592-1963.

LYNNFIELD, ESSEX CO.
1—ST. MARIA GORETTI (1960) Very Rev. Paul E. Ritt, V.F., A.B., M.Div., S.T.L., S.T.D.; Rev. Anthony V. Luongo, Parochial Vicar; Deacons Thomas L. O'Shea; Edward P. Elibero.
Res.: 112 Chestnut St., Lynnfield, 01940-2405.
Tel: 781-334-2367; Fax: 781-598-0055; Email: jsano@ola-smg.org; Web: www.lynnfieldcatholic.org.
Catechesis Religious Program—Hazel Kochocki, D.R.E.
2—OUR LADY OF THE ASSUMPTION (1937)
758 Salem St., Lynnfield, 01940-2405.
Tel: 781-598-4313; Fax: 781-598-0055; Email: jsano@ola-smg.org; Web: www.lynnfieldcatholic.org. Very Rev. Paul E. Ritt, V.F., A.B., M.Div., S.T.L., S.T.D.; Rev. Anthony V. Luongo, Parochial Vicar; Deacons Thomas L. O'Shea; Edward P. Elibero.
School—Our Lady of the Assumption School, 40 Grove St., Lynnfield, 01940. Tel: 781-599-4422; Fax: 781-599-9280; Email: jgrocki@olalynnfieldschool.com; Web: www.olalynnfieldschool.com. Mr. James J. Grocki Jr., Prin. Lay Teachers 16; Sisters 2; Students 457.
Catechesis Religious Program—Judith Dixon, D.R.E.

MALDEN, MIDDLESEX CO.
1—IMMACULATE CONCEPTION (1854)
600 Pleasant St., Malden, 02148-5313.
Tel: 781-324-4941; Fax: 781-397-8571; Email: info@icmalden.com; Web: icmalden.org/. Revs. Albert L. Capone, Admin.; Francis E. Sullivan, Parochial Vicar.
Catechesis Religious Program—Tel: 781-324-5518. Sr. Margo Shea, C.S.J., D.R.E.
2—ST. JOSEPH (1902)
770 Salem St., Malden, 02148. Tel: 781-324-0402; Fax: 781-324-1790; Email: stjosephs2@comcast.net; Web: www.stjosephparishmalden.com. Rev. William J. Minigan; Very Rev. John F. Mulloy, V.F., Parochial Vicar.
Catechesis Religious Program—Tel: 781-324-2444. David Wilcox, D.R.E.
3—ST. PETER (1972) Closed. Parish records for all closed, merged & suppressed parishes are located at the Office of the Archives, 66 Brooks Dr., Braintree, MA 02184-3839. Tel: 617-746-5795.
4—SACRED HEARTS (1890)
315 Main St., Malden, 02148-7414.
Tel: 781-324-0728; Fax: 781-324-2714; Email: receptionist@sacredheartsparish.org; Web: www.sacredheartsparish.org. Rev. Mark J. DeAngelis, Admin.; Deacons Franklin A. Majia; T. Van Nguyen.
School—Cheverus Catholic School, (Grades PreSchool-8), 30 Irving St., Malden, 02148.
Tel: 781-324-6584; Fax: 781-324-3322; Email: thomas.arria@cheveruschool.com; Web: www.cheverusschool.com. Mr. Thomas P. Arria Jr., Prin. Lay Teachers 22; Students 360.
Catechesis Religious Program—Susan Evans, D.R.E.

MANCHESTER BY THE SEA, ESSEX CO.
1—ST. JOHN THE BAPTIST (1931)
52 Main St., Essex, 01944. Tel: 978-526-1263; Fax: 978-526-4335; Email: shsjparishes@comcast.net; Web: www.mecatholic.org/. Rev. Paul G. Flammia, Admin.
Catechesis Religious Program—Valerie Shippen, D.R.E.
2—SACRED HEART (1905) Rev. Paul G. Flammia, Admin.
Res.: 62 School St., Manchester by the Sea, 01944-1342. Tel: 978-526-1263; Fax: 978-526-4335; Email: shsjparishes@comcast.net; Web: www.mecatholic.com.
Catechesis Religious Program—Valerie Shippen, D.R.E.

MARBLEHEAD, ESSEX CO., OUR LADY, STAR OF THE SEA (1859) Rev. Michael L. Steele; Deacon John E. Whipple.
Res.: 85 Atlantic Ave., Marblehead, 01945.
Tel: 781-631-0086; Fax: 781-631-5668; Email: sosrectory@verizon.net; Web: www.staroftheseamarblehead.org.
Catechesis Religious Program—Tel: 781-631-8340. Jude Odimone-Milan, D.R.E. (Gr. 1-4); Helen Haas, D.R.E. (Gr. 5-8).

MARLBOROUGH, MIDDLESEX CO.
1—ST. ANN (1921) Closed. Parish records for all closed, merged & suppressed parishes are located at the Office of the Archives, 66 Brooks Dr., Braintree, MA 02184-3839. Tel: 617-746-5795.
2—IMMACULATE CONCEPTION (1854)
11 Prospect St., Marlborough, 01752.
Tel: 508-485-0016; Fax: 508-480-9644; Email: parish@icmarlboro.org; Web: www.icmarlboro.com. Revs. Marc J. Bishop, Admin.; Andrea Filippucci, Parochial Vicar; Deacons Charles R. Rossignol; Elcio Ferreira dos Santos.
School—Immaculate Conception School, 25 Washington Ct., Marlborough, 01752.
Tel: 508-460-3401; Fax: 508-460-6003; Email: icmmmccook@ICschool.net; Web: www.icschool.net. Ms. Martha McCook, Prin. Lay Teachers 14; Students 257.
Catechesis Religious Program—Tel: 508-481-7535. Ms. Jennifer McKiernan, D.R.E.
Mission—St. Ann.
3—ST. MARY (1870) Closed. Parish records for all closed, merged & suppressed parishes are located at the Office of the Archives, 66 Brooks Dr., Braintree, MA 02184-3839. Tel: 617-746-5795.
4—ST. MATTHIAS (1963) Rev. Francis P. O'Brien; Deacons Douglas P. Peltak; Paul G. Coletti.
Res.: 409 Hemenway St., Marlborough, 01752-6710.
Tel: 508-460-9255; Fax: 508-480-8801; Email: admin@stmattpar.org; Web: www.stmattpar.org.
Catechesis Religious Program—Karen McNamara, D.R.E.

MARSHFIELD, PLYMOUTH CO.
1—ST. ANN BY THE SEA (1945)
587 Ocean St., Marshfield, 02050. Tel: 781-834-4953; Email: office@stanns.net; Web: www.stanns.net. Rev. John F. Carmichael.
Catechesis Religious Program—Tel: 781-834-8223. Martha McLaughlin, D.R.E.
2—ST. CHRISTINE (1945) Rev. Thomas J. Walsh.
Res.: 1295 Main St., Marshfield, 02050-2029.
Tel: 781-834-6003; Fax: 781-834-4263; Email: stchristinespsh@aol.com; Web: saintchristines.org.
Catechesis Religious Program—Tel: 781-837-0088. Jean Godin, D.R.E.
Mission—St. Theresa's, Marshfield, Plymouth Co.
3—OUR LADY OF THE ASSUMPTION (1949) Rev. Paul J. Aveni, Admin.; Deacon John A. Hulme.
Res.: 40 Canal St., Marshfield, 02050.
Tel: 781-834-6252; Email: info@olamarshfield.org; Web: www.olamarshfield.org.
Catechesis Religious Program—Tel: 781-837-3662; Fax: 781-834-5694. Mary Forrester, D.R.E.

MAYNARD, MIDDLESEX CO.
1—ST. BRIDGET (1881) [CEM] Rev. John P. Prusaitis; Deacon John W. Pepi.
Res.: One Percival St., Maynard, 01754-1699.
Tel: 978-897-2171; Fax: 978-897-5358; Email: stbr.sec1@verizon.net; Web: www.saintbridgetmaynard.com.
Catechesis Religious Program—Tel: 978-897-4612. Joan Ferguson, D.R.E.
2—ST. CASIMIR (1912) Closed. Parish records for all closed, merged & suppressed parishes are located at the Office of the Archives, 66 Brooks Dr., Braintree, MA 02184-3839. Tel: 617-746-5795.

MEDFIELD, NORFOLK CO., ST. EDWARD THE CONFESSOR (1892) Very Rev. John P. Culloty, V.F.; Rev. Gregory G. Vozzo, Parochial Vicar; Deacon Frederick B. Horgan.
Res.: 133 Spring St., Medfield, 02052-2513.
Tel: 508-359-2633; Fax: 508-359-1846; Email: mail@stedward-ma.org; Web: www.steward-ma.org.
Catechesis Religious Program—Tel: 508-359-5853. Terry Ferraris, D.R.E.

MEDFORD, MIDDLESEX CO.
1—ST. CLEMENT (1912) Revs. Stefano Colombo, F.S.C.B., Admin.; Paolo Cumin, F.S.C.B., Parochial Vicar.
Res.: 71 Warner St., Medford, 02155.
Tel: 781-396-3922; Fax: 781-396-2506; Email: secretarystclement@outlook.com; Web: www.saintclementcatholicparish.org.
School—St. Clement School, (Grades K-12), 579 Boston Ave., Medford, 02155. Tel: 781-393-5600; Fax: 781-393-5600; Email: rchevrier@saintclementhigh.org; Web: www.saintclementschool.org. Robert G. Chevrier, Prin. Lay Teachers 17; Sisters of St. Joseph 2; Students 240.
Catechesis Religious Program—Tel: 781-396-3322. Carla Garofalo, D.R.E.
2—ST. FRANCIS OF ASSISI (1921)
114 High St., Medford, 02155. Very Rev. Paul V. Sullivan, V.F.; Rev. Peter H. Shen, (China) Parochial Vicar.
Res.: 441 Fellsway W., Medford, 02155.
Tel: 781-396-0423; Email: medfordcatholic@gmail.com; Web: www. medfordcollaborative.org.
Catechesis Religious Program—Tel: 781-395-4042; Fax: 781-306-0044. Margaret Aranyosi, D.R.E.
3—ST. JAMES (1919) Closed. Parish records for all closed, merged & suppressed parishes are located at the Office of the Archives, 66 Brooks Dr., Braintree, MA 02184-3839. Tel: 617-746-5795.
4—ST. JOSEPH (1883)
114 High St., Medford, 02155. Tel: 781-396-0423; Fax: 781-391-2919; Email: medfordcatholic@gmail.com; Web: www.medfordcollaborative.org. Very Rev. Paul V. Sullivan, V.F.; Rev. Peter H. Shen, (China) Parochial Vicar.
School—St. Joseph School, 132 High St., Medford, 02155. Tel: 781-396-3636; Fax: 781-396-5670; Email: stjosephschool@lycos.com; Web: www.stjosephschoolmedford.com. Mr. James Deveney, Prin. Lay Teachers 14; Sisters 5; Students 342.
Catechesis Religious Program—Tel: 781-395-1784. Phyllis Patten, D.R.E.
Convent—2520 Mystic Valley Pkwy., Medford, 02155. Tel: 781-396-5670.
5—ST. RAPHAEL (1905)
512 High St., Medford, 02155. Tel: 781-488-5444; Fax: 781-483-3375; Web: www.saintraphaelparish.org. Rev. Paul F. Coughlin, Parochial Vicar; Deacon Mark E. Rumley.
School—St. Raphael School, 516 High St., Medford, 02155. Tel: 781-483-3373; Fax: 781-483-3097; Email: mbedrosian@straphaelparishschool.org; Web: www.straphaelparishschool.org. Mr. Mark C. Bedrosian, Prin. Lay Teachers 19; Students 399.
Catechesis Religious Program—Tel: 781-483-1139. Dr. Ginny McCabe, D.R.E.
6—SACRED HEART (1937) Closed. Sacred Heart, Medford was suppressed. This parish's records are located at St. Clement, Somerville.

MEDWAY, NORFOLK CO., ST. JOSEPH (1885)
151 Village St., Medway, 02053. Tel: 508-533-6500; Fax: 508-533-1236. Rev. Msgr. Timothy J. Moran, V.F.; Rev. George E. Fitzsimmons, Parochial Vicar.
Catechesis Religious Program—145 Holliston St., Medway, 02053-1954. Tel: 508-533-7771; Fax: 508-533-0604. Sharon Moore, D.R.E.

MELROSE, MIDDLESEX CO.
1—INCARNATION OF OUR LORD AND SAVIOR JESUS CHRIST (1958)
429 Upham St., Melrose, 02176. Tel: 781-662-8844; Fax: 781-662-9340; Email: i.rectory@comcast.net; Web: www.incarnationmelrose.org. Rev. Stephen J. Madden, Admin.
Catechesis Religious Program—Linda Swett, D.R.E.
2—ST. MARY OF THE ANNUNCIATION (1894)
Herbert St., Melrose, 02176-3827. Tel: 781-665-0152; Fax: 781-665-2750; Web: www.stmarysmelrose.org. Very Rev. Kevin G. Toomey, V.F., Admin.
School—St. Mary of the Annunciation School, 4 Myrtle St., Melrose, 02176. Tel: 781-665-5037; Fax: 781-665-7321; Email: cinboyle@comcast.net; Web: www.stmaryschoolmelrose.org. Ms. Cynthia Boyle, Prin. Lay Teachers 27; Students 405.
Catechesis Religious Program—9 Herbert St., Melrose, 02176. Tel: 781-665-3707. Ms. Sheila Hurley, D.R.E.

MERRIMAC, ESSEX CO., NATIVITY (1891) Closed. Parish records for all closed, merged & suppressed parishes are located at the Office of the Archives, 66 Brooks Dr., Braintree, MA 02184-3839. Tel: 617-746-5795.

METHUEN, ESSEX CO.
1—ST. LUCY (1958)
254 Merrimack St., Methuen, 01844.
Tel: 978-686-3311; Email: methuencatholic@gmail.com; Web: www.methuencatholic.org. Rev. William P. Lohan.
Catechesis Religious Program—Tel: 978-794-0383. Kevin Fitzgerald, D.R.E.
2—ST. MONICA (1917)
212 Lawrence St., Methuen, 01844-3852.
Tel: 978-683-1193; Email: methuencatholic@gmail.

com; Web: www.methuencatholic.org. Rev. William P. Lohan; Deacon John B. Pierce.
School—St. Monica School, Tel: 978-686-1801; Fax: 978-686-3582; Email: saintmonicaoffice@verizon.net; Web: www.methuencatholic.org. Sr. Suzanne Fondini, M.F.I.C., Prin. Lay Teachers 12; Sisters 4; Students 522.
Catechesis Religious Program—Tel: 978-686-9573; Fax: 978-738-8898. Claire Tebeau, D.R.E. (Gr. K-5); Laurene Costello, D.R.E. (Gr. 6-8); Wendy Adams, D.R.E. (Gr. 9-10).
Convent—Tel: 978-682-2448.
3—OUR LADY OF GOOD COUNSEL (2000) Very Rev. Christopher J. Casey, V.F.; Deacon Steven J. Murphy.
Res.: 22 Plymouth St., Methuen, 01844-4299.
Tel: 978-686-3984; Fax: 978-686-8300; Email: olgcparish@comcast.net; Web: www.olgcparish.com.
Catechesis Religious Program—Tel: 978-686-3985. Mark Friedrich, D.R.E.; Mark Houle, D.R.E.
4—OUR LADY OF MOUNT CARMEL (1937) Closed. Our Lady of Mount Carmel, Methuen was suppressed. This parish's records are located at St. Monica, Methuen.
5—ST. THERESA (1936) Closed. Parish records for all closed, merged & suppressed parishes are located at the Office of the Archives, 66 Brooks Dr., Braintree, MA 02184-3839. Tel: 617-746-5795.
MIDDLEBOROUGH, PLYMOUTH CO., SACRED HEART (1885)
340 Centre St., Middleborough, 02346.
Tel: 508-947-0444; Fax: 508-947-4333; Email: hollyclark@cranberrycatholic.org; Web: www.cranberrycatholic.org. Revs. John E. Sheridan; Jude Thaddeus Osunkwo, (Nigeria) Parochial Vicar; Deacons George M. Gabriel; Charles H. Bower.
Catechesis Religious Program—M. Judith West, D.R.E., Tel: 508-947-2050; Michelle Sylvie, D.R.E., Tel: 508-923-1151; Lori Handerhan, D.R.E.
MIDDLETON, ESSEX CO., ST. AGNES (1945) Rev. Michael B. Medas, M.S.W.
Res.: 22 Boston St., Middleton, 01949-2199.
Tel: 978-774-1958; Fax: 978-774-1964; Email: djones@thechristinitiative.org; Web: www.thechristinitiative.org.
Catechesis Religious Program—Tel: 978-777-3404. Sr. Mildred Rothwell, O.S.F., D.R.E.
MILLIS, NORFOLK CO., ST. THOMAS THE APOSTLE (1937)
82 Exchange St., Millis, 02054-1273.
Tel: 508-376-2621; Fax: 508-376-4308; Email: saintthomasapostle@verizon.net; Web: www.stthomastheapostlemillis.org. Rev. Linus Mendis, (Sri Lanka) Admin.
Catechesis Religious Program—Helen Boucher, D.R.E.; Annmarie Fontecchio, D.R.E.
MILTON, NORFOLK CO.
1—ST. AGATHA (1922) Very Revs. William B. Palardy, Ph.D.; Jason M. Makos, V.F., Parochial Vicar; Deacon Daniel F. Sullivan.
Res.: 432 Adams St., Milton, 02186-4399.
Tel: 617-698-2439; Fax: 617-698-1517; Email: rectory@stagathaparish.org; Web: www.stagathaparish.org.
School—St. Agatha School, 440 Adams St., Milton, 02186. Tel: 617-696-3548; Fax: 617-696-6288; Email: msimmons@stagathaparish.org; Web: www.stagathaparish.org/school/. Ms. Maureen C. Simmons, Prin. Lay Teachers 15; Sisters 2; Students 377.
Catechesis Religious Program—Sr. Susan Czaplick, S.S.N.D., D.R.E.
2—ST. ELIZABETH (1946) Very Rev. Stephen P. Zukas, V.F.
Res.: 350 Reedsdale Rd., Milton, 02186-3999.
Tel: 617-696-6688; Fax: 617-698-4864; Email: office@stelizabethmilton.org; Web: www.stelizabethmilton.org.
Catechesis Religious Program—Tel: 617-698-5763. Sr. Mary K. Walsh, C.S.T., D.R.E.
3—ST. MARY OF THE HILLS (1931) Rev. Arthur J. Wright; Deacon Kevin P. Martin.
Res.: 29 St. Mary's Rd., Milton, 02186-2024.
Tel: 617-696-0120; Fax: 617-696-7044; Email: office@smhmilton.org; Web: www.smhmilton.org.
School—St. Mary of the Hills School, 250 Brook Rd., Milton, 02186. Tel: 617-698-2464; Fax: 617-696-9346 ; Email: mcarberry@smhschool.org; Web: www.saintmaryofthehills.org. Ms. Mary Carberry, Prin. Lay Teachers 14; Sisters 2; Students 307.
Catechesis Religious Program—Tel: 617-696-6117. Madeline Feldmann, D.R.E.
4—ST. PIUS TENTH (1954)
101 Wolcott Rd., Milton, 02136. Tel: 857-342-9500; Fax: 617-364-2590; Email: achavez@bluehillscollaborative.org; Web: bluehillscollaborative.org. Revs. Ronald D. Coyne; Charles Madi-Okin, Parochial Vicar.
Catechesis Religious Program—Sheila Farley, D.R.E.
NAHANT, ESSEX CO., ST. THOMAS AQUINAS (1902) Rev. James T. Kelly, Admin.
Res.: 248 Nahant Rd., Nahant, 01908-1340.
Tel: 781-581-0023; Fax: 781-598-8860; Email: nahantrectory@comcast.net; Web: stjohnsswampscott.org.
Catechesis Religious Program—Tel: 781-595-7942. Kathy Marini, D.R.E.
NATICK, MIDDLESEX CO.
1—ST. LINUS (1950) Very Rev. Michael W. MacEwen, V.F.; Rev. Jeffrey S. Archer, Parochial Vicar.
Res.: 119 Hartford St., Natick, 01760.
Tel: 508-653-1093; Fax: 508-650-2922; Email: natickcatholics@gmail.com; Web: natickcatholic.org.
Catechesis Religious Program—Tel: 508-653-6005. Cynthia Giardina, D.R.E.; Laura McLarnon, D.R.E.
2—ST. PATRICK (1858)
46 E. Central St., Natick, 01760. Tel: 508-653-1093; Fax: 508-650-2922; Email: natickcatholics@gmail.com; Web: natickcatholic.org. Very Rev. Michael W. MacEwen, V.F.; Rev. Jeffrey S. Archer, Parochial Vicar.
Catechesis Religious Program—Lisa Correia, D.R.E.
3—SACRED HEART (1891) Closed. Parish records for all closed, merged & suppressed parishes are located at the Office of the Archives, 66 Brooks Dr., Braintree, MA 02184-3839. Tel: 617-746-5795.
NEEDHAM, NORFOLK CO.
1—ST. BARTHOLOMEW (1952) Rev. Derek J. Borek, Admin.
Res.: 1180 Greendale Ave., Needham, 02492-4706.
Tel: 781-444-3434; Fax: 781-449-7550; Email: stbartholomew@comcast.net; Web: www.stbartholomew-needham.org.
Catechesis Religious Program—Tel: 781-444-4343. Melisa Hughes, D.R.E.
2—ST. JOSEPH (1917)
1360 Highland Ave., Needham, 02492-2694.
Tel: 781-444-0245; Fax: 781-444-7713; Web: www.saintjosephparihneedham.com. Very Rev. David C. Michael, V.F.; Rev. Peter L. Stamm, Parochial Vicar.
Schools—Saint Joseph—Elementary School 90 Pickering St., Needham, 02492. Tel: 781-444-4459; Fax: 978-444-0822; Email: pkelly@saintjoes.com; Web: www.saintjoes.com/elementary.cfm. Ms. Charlotte Kelly, Prin. Lay Teachers 34; Students 440.
Monsignor James J. Haddad Middle School, 110 May St., Needham, 02492. Tel: 781-449-0133; Fax: 781-449-8096; Email: jbelliveau@saintjoes.com; Web: www.saintjoes.com. James J. MacDonald.
NEWBURYPORT, ESSEX CO.
1—IMMACULATE CONCEPTION (1848) Revs. Timothy A. Harrison; George E. Morin, Parochial Vicar.
Res.: 42 Green St., Newburyport, 01950-2502.
Tel: 978-462-2724; Fax: 978-234-7399; Email: info@newburyportcatholic.org; Web: www.hriccatholic.org.
School—Immaculate Conception, One Washington St., Newburyport, 01950. Tel: 978-465-7780; Fax: 978-234-7331; Email: reardon@newburyportcatholic.org; Web: www.ICSNewburyport.com. Ms. Mary Reardon, Prin. Lay Teachers 7; Sisters 2; Students 198.
Mission—St. James, Plum Island.
2—ST. LOUIS DE GONZAGUE (1902) (French), Closed. St. Louis de Gonzague, Newburyport was suppressed. This parish's records are located at Immaculate Conception, Newburyport.
NEWTON, MIDDLESEX CO.
1—SAINT ANTOINE DAVELUY (2013) (Korean)
41 Ash St., Newton, 02466. Tel: 617-558-2711; Fax: 617-224-0188; Email: office.kccb@gmail.com; Web: www.stdaveluychurch.org. Rev. Dominic K. Jung, C.PP.S., Admin.; Deacon Cheonil Kim.
2—ST. BERNARD (1876) Closed. Parish records for all closed, merged & suppressed parishes are located at the Office of the Archives, 66 Brooks Dr., Braintree, MA 02184-3839. Tel: 617-746-5795.
3—CORPUS CHRISTI (1922) Closed. Corpus Christi, Newton was suppressed. This parish's records are located at Corpus Christi-St. Bernard, Newton.
4—CORPUS CHRISTI - ST. BERNARD (2006)
Mailing Address: 1523 Washington St., Newton, 02465. Tel: 617-244-0608; Fax: 617-969-1025; Email: info@ccsbparish.org; Web: www.ccsbparish.org. Rev. Daniel C. O'Connell.
Catechesis Religious Program—Maureen Connell, D.R.E.
5—ST. IGNATIUS LOYOLA (1926) Rev. Joseph S. Costantino, S.J.
Res.: 28 Commonwealth Ave., Newton, 02467-3849.
Tel: 617-552-6100; Fax: 617-552-6101; Email: ignatius@bc.edu; Web: www.bc.edu/st-ignatius.
Catechesis Religious Program—Melisa Melnyk, D.R.E.
6—ST. JOHN THE EVANGELIST (1911) Closed. St. John the Evangelist, Newton was suppressed. This parish's records are located at Our Lady Help of Christians, Newton.
7—MARY IMMACULATE OF LOURDES (1870) Very Rev. Charles J. Higgins, V.F.
Res.: 270 Elliot St., Newton, 02464.
Tel: 617-244-0558; Fax: 617-965-4815; Email: info@maryimmaculateoflourdes.org; Web: www.maryimmaculateoflourdes.org.
Catechesis Religious Program—Jean Johnson, D.R.E.
8—OUR LADY HELP OF CHRISTIANS (1878) Rev. John E. Sassani, A.B., M.Div.; Very Rev. Daniel J. Riley, V.F., Admin.; Deacon William B. Koffel.
Res.: 573 Washington St., Newton, 02458-1494.
Tel: 617-527-7560; Fax: 617-527-1338; Email: ourladys@sholnewton.org; Web: www.sholnewton.org.
Catechesis Religious Program—Ms. Rosemary Seibold, D.R.E.; Kara O'Malley, D.R.E. Students 363.
9—ST. PHILIP NERI (1934) Closed. Parish records for all closed, merged & suppressed parishes are located at the Office of the Archives, 66 Brooks Dr., Braintree, MA 02184-3839. Tel: 617-746-5795.
10—SACRED HEART (1890)
1317 Centre St., Newton, 02459-2466.
Tel: 617-969-2248; Fax: 617-965-7515; Email: sacredheart@sholnewton.org; Web: www.sholnewton.org. Rev. John E. Sassani, A.B., M.Div.; Very Rev. Daniel J. Riley, V.F., Admin.; Deacon William B. Koffel.
Catechesis Religious Program—Michelle Solomon, D.R.E.
NORFOLK, NORFOLK CO., ST. JUDE (1949) Very Rev. John P. Culloty, V.F.; Rev. Gregory G. Vozzo, Parochial Vicar; Deacon David R. Ghioni.
Res.: 86 Main St., Norfolk, 02056. Tel: 508-528-0170; Fax: 508-528-1860; Email: stjudenorfolk@comcast.net; Web: www.stjudenorfolk.org.
Catechesis Religious Program—Tel: 508-528-1470. Terry Ferraris, D.R.E.
NORTH ANDOVER, ESSEX CO., ST. MICHAEL (1900) Revs. Kevin J. Deeley; Christopher L. Lowe, Parochial Vicar; Robert Sahayaraj, O.C.D., Parochial Vicar; Deacon Vincent J. Gatto.
Res.: 196 Main St., North Andover, 01845-2598.
Tel: 978-686-4050; Fax: 978-686-5408; Email: st-michael@comcast.net; Web: www.saint-michael.org.
School—St. Michael School, 80 Maple Ave., North Andover, 01845. Tel: 978-686-1862; Fax: 978-688-5144; Web: www.saintmichael.com. Mrs. Susan Gosselin, Prin. Lay Teachers 21; Sisters 1; Students 525.
Catechesis Religious Program—Tel: 978-682-9484. Maryann Marinelli, D.R.E.; Ms. Mary Alice Rock, D.R.E.
NORTH READING, MIDDLESEX CO., ST. THERESA OF LISIEUX (1945) Most Rev. Mark O'Connell; Rev. Thomas J. Reilly, Parochial Vicar; Deacons Tam V. Tran; Alfred O. Balestracci.
Res.: 63 Winter St., North Reading, 01864-2282.
Tel: 978-664-3412; Email: info@sttheresanreading.org; Web: www.sttheresanreading.org.
Catechesis Religious Program—Tel: 978-664-2962. Paula L. Colpitts, D.R.E.; Nancy Cirone, D.R.E.
NORWELL, PLYMOUTH CO., ST. HELEN MOTHER OF THE EMPEROR CONSTANTINE (1950)
383 Washington St., Norwell, 02339.
Tel: 781-826-4303; Fax: 781-826-5203; Email: info@holymothers.com; Web: www.holymothers.com. Rev. Christopher J. Hickey; Deacons John P. Murray; Roger F. Vierra.
Catechesis Religious Program—Mary Nedder, D.R.E.; Kathleen Mogayzel, C.R.E.
NORWOOD, NORFOLK CO.
1—ST. CATHERINE OF SIENA (1890)
549 Washington St., Norwood, 02062-0547.
Tel: 781-762-6080; Fax: 781-255-9312; Email: parish@stcatherinenorwood.org; Web: www.stcatherinenorwood.org. Revs. Stephen S. Donohoe, M.Div., Admin.; Jean P. Aubin, Parochial Vicar; Thomas G. Sullivan, C.Ss.R., Parochial Vicar.
School—St. Catherine of Siena School, 249 Nahatan St., Norwood, 02062. Tel: 781-769-5354; Fax: 781-769-7905; Email: mrusso@scsnorwood.com; Web: www.scsnorwood.com. Mrs. Mary Russo, Prin. Lay Teachers 40; Sisters 1; Students 472.
Catechesis Religious Program—Frank Connell, D.R.E., Tel: 781-254-5087; Marybeth McDonough, D.R.E. Students 759.
2—ST. GEORGE (1912) Closed. St. George, Norwood was suppressed. This parish's records are located at St. Catherine of Siena, Norwood.
3—ST. PETER (1918) Closed. Parish records for all closed, merged & suppressed parishes are located at the Office of the Archives, 66 Brooks Dr., Braintree, MA 02184-3839. Tel: 617-746-5795.
4—ST. TIMOTHY (1963) Very Rev. Gerard Petringa, V.E.
Res.: 650 Nichols St., Norwood, 02062-1099.
Tel: 781-769-2522; Fax: 781-769-9362; Email: sttim@sttim.net; Web: www.sttim.net.
Catechesis Religious Program—Tel: 781-762-4868. Mary Ellen Herx, D.R.E. Students 569.
PEABODY, ESSEX CO.
1—ST. ADELAIDE (1962)
708 Lowell St., Peabody, 01960-3427.
Tel: 978-535-1985; Fax: 978-535-4845; Email:

saintadelaide@verizon.net; Web: www.saintadelaide.com. Revs. Raymond Van De Moortell, Team Ministry; David C. Lewis, Team Ministry.
Catechesis Religious Program—712 Lowell St., Peabody, 01960. Tel: 978-535-5376. Angela Federico, D.R.E.
2—ST. ANN (1937)
140 Lynn St., Peabody, 01960-6432.
Tel: 978-531-1480; Fax: 978 532-3546; Email: pastor@saintannpeabody.com; Web: www.catholic-church.org/st-ann-peabody. Rev. Charles R. Stanley; Deacon Richard W. Cordeau.
Catechesis Religious Program—Tel: 978-531-5791. Ellen Fitzgerald, D.R.E.
3—ST. JOHN THE BAPTIST (1871) Very Rev. John E. MacInnis, V.F.; Revs. Paul G. McManus, Parochial Vicar; Steven Clemence, Parochial Vicar; Senior Deacon Leo A. Martin; Deacon Charles A. Hall.
Res.: 17 Chestnut St., Peabody, 01960-5429.
Tel: 978-531-0002; Fax: 978-531-5199; Email: stjpeabody@parishmail.com; Web: www.stjohnspeabody.com.
School—St. John the Baptist School, 19 Chestnut St., Peabody, 01960-5429. Tel: 978-531-0444;
Fax: 978-531-3569; Email: principla@stjohns-peabody.com. Ms. Maureen J. Kelleher, Prin. Lay Teachers 20; Sisters 2; Students 510.
Catechesis Religious Program—Tel: 978-532-1586. Karen E. Hinton, D.R.E.
4—ST. JOSEPH (1927) Closed. St. Joseph, Peabody was suppressed. This parish's records are located at Archives, Boston.
5—OUR LADY OF FATIMA (1975) (Portuguese)
50 Walsh Ave., Peabody, 01960-1999.
Tel: 978-532-0272; Fax: 978-977-2991; Email: ourladyoffatima@verizon.net; Web: www.ourladyoffatimapeabody.org. Rev. Christopher Gomes.
Catechesis Religious Program—Ms. Frances Taylor, D.R.E.
6—ST. THOMAS THE APOSTLE (1927)
26 North St., Salem, 01960. Tel: 978-531-0224;
Fax: 978-531-6517; Email: stthomas344P@comcast.net; Web: www.stthomaspeabody.org. Very Rev. John E. MacInnis, V.F.; Rev. Steven Clemence, Parochial Vicar; Deacons Charles A. Hall; Carlos S. Valentin.
Catechesis Religious Program—Nancy O'Brine, D.R.E.
PEMBROKE, PLYMOUTH CO., ST. THECLA (1964) Rev. Joseph S. McCarthy, (Retired); Deacons Howard C. League; John A. Sullivan.
Res.: 145 Washington St., Pembroke, 02359.
Tel: 781-826-9786; Fax: 781-826-3484; Email: sttheclaparish@msn.com; Web: www.sttheclapembroke.org.
Catechesis Religious Program—Tel: 781-826-8042. Mary K. Doller, D.R.E.
PEPPERELL, MIDDLESEX CO.
1—ST. JOSEPH (1870) Merged with Sacred Heart-St. James in Groton to form Our Lady of Grace, Pepperell.
2—OUR LADY OF GRACE (2009)
28 Tarbell St., Pepperell, 01463. Tel: 978-433-5737;
Fax: 978-433-9566; Email: parishoffice@ourladyofgracema.org; Web: www.ourladyofgracema.org. Revs. Jeremy P. St. Martin, Admin.; Jason W. Worthley, Parochial Vicar; Deacon Michael J. Markham; Debra Lackey, Business Mgr.
Catechesis Religious Program—Robert Daly, D.R.E.
PLAINVILLE, NORFOLK CO., ST. MARTHA (1953)
227 South St., Plainville, 02762. Tel: 508-699-8543;
Fax: 508-699-6677; Email: stmarthaoffice@pwc.church; Web: www.saintmarthaschurch.org. Revs. Joseph F. Mozer Jr., J.C.L.; William T. Schmidt; Deacons Kenneth W. Oles; Joseph R. Flocco.
Catechesis Religious Program—Sharon Guerin, D.R.E.
PLYMOUTH, PLYMOUTH CO.
1—ST. BONAVENTURE (1950)
801 State Rd., Plymouth, 02360. Tel: 508-224-3636;
Fax: 508-224-5889; Email: stbonoffice1@verizon.net; Web: www.stbonaventureplymouth.org. Rev. Kenneth C. Overbeck.
Catechesis Religious Program—Rachel Patnaude, D.R.E.
Mission—St. Catherine's Chapel, 95 White Horse Rd., White Horse Beach, 02381.
2—SAINT KATERI TEKAKWITHA (1982) Rev. William G. Williams, Admin.; Deacon James F. Greer.
Res.: 126 S. Meadow Rd., Plymouth, 02360.
Tel: 508-747-1568; Fax: 508-747-0616; Email: office@saintkateriplymouth.com; Web: www.saintkateriplymouth.org.
Catechesis Religious Program—Tel: 508-747-1568. Joyce Hokanson, D.R.E.
3—ST. MARY (1915) Rev. Joseph T. MacCarthy.
Res.: 313 Court St., Plymouth, 02360-4336.
Tel: 508-746-0426; Fax: 508-747-5886; Email: jevans@stmarysplymouth.org; Web: www.stmarysplymouth.org.
Catechesis Religious Program—Kathleen Liolios, D.R.E.
4—ST. PETER (1876)
86 Court St., Plymouth, 02360. Tel: 508-746-0663;
Fax: 508-747-1071; Email: stpeterparish@comcast.net; Web: www.stpetersplymouth.com. Revs. William G. Williams; Michael Rora; Deacon Richard J. Cussen.
Catechesis Religious Program—Tel: 508-746-8268. Elizabeth Adey, D.R.E.
QUINCY, NORFOLK CO.
1—ST. ANN (1922) Revs. Louis R. Palmieri; Joseph J. D'Onofrio, Parochial Vicar; Raymond P. Kiley, Parochial Vicar.
Res.: 757 Hancock St., Quincy, 02170.
Tel: 617-479-5400; Fax: 617-479-0955; Email: stann@qcc14.org; Web: www.qcc14.org.
Catechesis Religious Program—One St. Ann Rd., Quincy, 02170. Tel: 617-479-2385. Nancy White, D.R.E.; Joseph DelRosso, D.R.E.
2—ST. BONIFACE (1956) Closed. Parish records for all closed, merged & suppressed parishes are located at the Office of the Archives, 66 Brooks Dr., Braintree, MA 02184-3839. Tel: 617-746-5795.
3—ST. ELIZABETH ANN SETON (2001) Closed. St. Elizabeth Ann Seton, Quincy was suppressed. This parish's records are located at Holy Trinity, Quincy.
4—HOLY TRINITY (2005) Rev. Martin G. Dzengeleski; Deacon William F. Maloney. Comprised of: Our Lady of Good Counsel & Most Blessed Sacrament.
Rectory—227 Sea St., Quincy, 02169.
Tel: 617-479-9200; Email: HTPreled@gmail.com; Email: holytrinityquincyma@gmail.com; Web: holytrinityquincy.com.
Catechesis Religious Program—Denise Gleason, D.R.E.
5—ST. JOHN THE BAPTIST (1863)
44 School St., Quincy, 02169-6602. Tel: 617-773-1021; Fax: 617-773-5608; Email: stjohns@stjohnsquincy.org; Web: www.stjohnsquincy.org. Rev. Robert J. Cullen, Admin.; Deacons Paul A. Lewis; William R. Proulx.
School—Quincy Catholic Academy, 370 Hancock St., Quincy, 02171. Tel: 617-328-3830; Fax: 617-328-6438; Email: khunter@shsquincy.org; Web: www.quincycatholicacademy.org. Ms. Cathy Cameron, Prin.
Catechesis Religious Program—Ms. Joanne Curry, D.R.E.
6—ST. JOSEPH (1917)
550 Washington St., Quincy, 02169-7216.
Tel: 617-472-6321; Fax: 617-471-8849; Email: stjoesquincy@comcast.net; Web: www.stjosephsquincy.org. Rev. Stephen M. Boyle; Deacon Leo J. Donoghue.
Catechesis Religious Program—550 Washington St., Quincy, 02169-7216. Ellen Curran, D.R.E.
7—ST. MARY (1840)
95 Crescent St., Quincy, 02169-4040.
Tel: 617-773-0120; Fax: 617-479-0955; Web: www.qcc14.org. Revs. Louis R. Palmieri; Joseph J. D'Onofrio, Parochial Vicar; Raymond P. Kiley, Parochial Vicar.
Catechesis Religious Program—Tel: 617-773-0515. Ellen March, D.R.E.; Margaret L. Donaher, D.R.E.
8—MOST BLESSED SACRAMENT (1915) Closed. Most Blessed Sacrament, Quincy was suppressed. This parish's records are located at Holy Trinity, Quincy.
9—OUR LADY OF GOOD COUNSEL (1938) Closed. Parish records for all closed, merged & suppressed parishes are located at the Office of the Archives, 66 Brooks Dr., Braintree, MA 02184-3839. Tel: 617-746-5795.
10—SACRED HEART (1903) Revs. Louis R. Palmieri; Joseph J. D'Onofrio, Parochial Vicar; Raymond P. Kiley, Parochial Vicar; Joseph Kim; Deacon Van-Vuong Nguyen.
Res.: 386 Hancock St., Quincy, 02171-2414.
Tel: 617-328-8666; Fax: 617-773-2522; Email: sacredheart@qcc14.org; Web: qcc14.org.
Catechesis Religious Program—Marjory O'Day, D.R.E.
11—STAR OF THE SEA (1945) Closed. Parish records for all closed, merged & suppressed parishes are located at the Office of the Archives, 66 Brooks Dr., Braintree, MA 02184-3839. Tel: 617-746-5795.
RANDOLPH, NORFOLK CO.
1—ST. BERNADETTE (1937)
1031 N. Main St., Randolph, 02368.
Tel: 781-963-1327; Fax: 781-963-0198; Email: inquiries@saintbernadette.us; Web: www.stbernadette.us/. Rev. Anthony V. Le, Admin.; Deacon Thomas P. Burke.
Catechesis Religious Program—Laura Donovan, D.R.E.; Sandy Messia, D.R.E.; Jen Rajani, D.R.E.
2—ST. MARY (1851) Revs. Philip E. McGaugh, Admin.; Ishmael Ixon Chateau, Parochial Vicar; Deacon Jonathan A. Mosely.
Res.: 211 N. Main St., Randolph, 02368.
Tel: 781-963-4141; Fax: 781-963-0884; Email: stmary@stmaryrandolph.org; Web: www.stmaryrandolph.org.
Catechesis Religious Program—Tel: 781-961-5009. Ms. Patricia O'Connor, D.R.E.
READING, MIDDLESEX CO.
1—ST. AGNES (1904) Very Rev. Stephen B. Rock, V.F.; Revs. Edward T. Malone, Parochial Vicar; Lambert K. Nieme; Deacon William K. Reidy.
Res.: 186 Woburn St., Reading, 01867-3599.
Tel: 781-944-0490; Email: stagnes@stagnesreading.org; Web: www.stagnesreading.org.
Catechesis Religious Program—Tel: 781-944-4552;
Fax: 781-944-4403. Eileen A. McGrath, D.R.E.
2—ST. ATHANASIUS (1961) Revs. Darin V. Colarusso; Patrick S. Armano, Parochial Vicar; Deacons Neil J. Sumner; Matthew Baltier.
Rectory—300 Haverhill St., Reading, 01867-1810.
Tel: 781-944-0330; Fax: 781-944-1266; Email: stathanasius@parishmail.com; Web: www.stathanasiusreading.org.
Catechesis Religious Program—Jennifer Campagna, Dir. Faith Formation.
REVERE, SUFFOLK CO.
1—ST. ANTHONY OF PADUA (2001) Revs. George J. Butera; Maria Antony H. Washington, (India) Parochial Vicar; Karunaya Xavier Arulraj, Parochial Vicar; Deacon Joseph A. Belmonte.
Res.: 250 Revere St., Revere, 02151-4618.
Tel: 781-289-1234; Fax: 781-289-6394.
Catechesis Religious Program—Mary Belliveau, D.R.E.
2—IMMACULATE CONCEPTION (1888)
133 Beach St., Revere, 02151. Tel: 781-289-0735;
Fax: 781-286-1124; Email: icrevere@comcast.net; Web: www.icrevere.com. Revs. Jorge Daniel Lazo Pujada, (Italy) Admin.; Felipe de Jesus Gonzalez, Parochial Vicar.
School—Immaculate Conception School, 127 Winthrop Ave., Revere, 02151. Tel: 781-284-0519;
Fax: 781-284-3805; Email: jfelice@icrevere.org. Lay Teachers 10; Sisters 1; Students 269.
Catechesis Religious Program—Tel: 781-289-8126.
3—ST. JOHN VIANNEY (1950) Closed. St. John Vianney, Revere was suppressed. This parish's records are located at St. Anthony of Padua Revere.
4—ST. MARY OF THE ASSUMPTION (1947) Very Rev. James J. Barry, V.F.
Res.: 670 Washington Ave., Revere, 02151.
Tel: 781-284-5252; Fax: 781-284-5801; Email: stmaryrevere@verizon.net; Web: www.stmaryrevere.org.
Catechesis Religious Program—Irene Hunt, D.R.E.
5—OUR LADY OF LOURDES (1905) Closed. Parish records for all closed, merged & suppressed parishes are located at the Office of the Archives, 66 Brooks Dr., Braintree, MA 02184-3839. Tel: 617-746-5795.
6—ST. THERESA (1937) Closed. Parish records for all closed, merged & suppressed parishes are located at the Office of the Archives, 66 Brooks Dr., Braintree, MA 02184-3839. Tel: 617-746-5795.
ROCHESTER, PLYMOUTH CO., ST. ROSE OF LIMA (1980) Closed. St. Rose of Lima, Rochester was suppressed. This parish's records are located at Sacred Heart, Middleborough.
ROCKLAND, PLYMOUTH CO., HOLY FAMILY (1882) [CEM] Revs. James F. Hickey; James O'Driscoll, Parochial Vicar; Valdir Mesquita Ferreira Lima, (Brazil) Parochial Vicar.
Res.: 403 Union St., Rockland, 02370-1799.
Tel: 781-878-0160; Fax: 781-871-6389; Web: www.holyfamilyrockland.org.
School—Holy Family School, 6 Del Prete Ave., Rockland, 02370. Tel: 781-878-1154;
Fax: 781-982-2485; Email: jcahalane@hfsrockland.org; Web: www.hfsrockland.org. Joan Cahalane, Prin. Lay Teachers 14; Religious 3; Students 315.
Catechesis Religious Program—Tel: 781-871-1244. Helen Ulich, D.R.E.
ROCKPORT, ESSEX CO., ST. JOACHIM (1849) Closed. Parish records for all closed, merged & suppressed parishes are located at the Office of the Archives, 66 Brooks Dr., Braintree, MA 02184-3839. Tel: 617-746-5795.
ROWLEY, ESSEX CO., ST. MARY (1945) Closed. St. Mary, Rowley was suppressed. This parish's records are located at St. Mary, Georgetown.
SALEM, ESSEX CO.
1—ST. ANNE (1901) (French)
292 Jefferson Ave., Salem, 01970-2895.
Tel: 978-744-1930; Email: stannesalem@aol.com; Web: www.stannesalem.org. Rev. John G. Kiley, Admin.; Deacon Alfred Sarno.
Catechesis Religious Program—Tel: 978-745-8915. Karen Moran, D.R.E.
2—IMMACULATE CONCEPTION (1826) Very Rev. Daniel J. Riley, V.F.; Revs. Paul G. McManus, Parochial Vicar; Francis E. Sullivan, Parochial Vicar; Deacons Pablo Morel; Jesus M. Pena; Ms. Margo Morin, Pastoral Assoc. In Res., Rev. Lawrence J. Rondeau, (Retired).
Res.: 30 Union St., Salem, 01970-3709.
Tel: 978-745-6303; Fax: 978-744-4382; Email:

icsalem@parishmail.com; Web: www.salemcatholiccommunity.org.
Catechesis Religious Program—
3—ST. JAMES (1850) Very Rev. Daniel J. Riley, V.F.; Revs. Francis E. Sullivan, Parochial Vicar; Gregory G. Vozzo, Parochial Vicar; Deacon Jesus M. Pena; Senior Deacon Norman P. LaPointe; Ms. Margo Morin, Pastoral Assoc. In Res., Rev. Lawrence J. Rondeau, (Retired).
Res.: 30 Union St., Salem, 01970-3709.
Tel: 978-744-1278; Email: rasci@salemcatholiccommunity.org; Web: www.salemcatholiccommunity.org.
Catechesis Religious Program—Tel: 978-744-2230. Diane Santos, D.R.E.
4—ST. JOHN THE BAPTIST (1903) (Polish) Very Rev. Daniel J. Riley, V.F.; Revs. Francis E. Sullivan, Parochial Vicar; Gregory G. Vozzo, Parochial Vicar; Deacon Jesus M. Pena.
Res.: 28 St. Peter St., Salem, 01970.
Tel: 978-744-1278; Fax: 978-744-2093; Email: stjohnthebaptistsalem@verizon.net; Web: www.salemcatholiccommunity.org.
Catechesis Religious Program—Teresa Prochorska, D.R.E.
5—ST. JOSEPH (1873) Closed. Parish records for all closed, merged & suppressed parishes are located at the Office of the Archives, 66 Brooks Dr., Braintree, MA 02184-3839. Tel: 617-746-5795.
6—ST. MARY (1918) Closed. Parish records for all closed, merged & suppressed parishes are located at the Office of the Archives, 66 Brooks Dr., Braintree, MA 02184-3839. Tel: 617-746-5795.
7—MARY, QUEEN OF THE APOSTLES PARISH
15 Hawthorne Blvd., Salem, 01970.
Tel: 978-745-9060; Email: info@salemcatholiccommunity.org; Web: www.salemcatholiccommunity.org. Rev. Robert W. Murray, M.Div.; Senior Deacon Norman P. LaPointe; Deacon Jesus M. Pena.
SALISBURY, ESSEX CO., STAR OF THE SEA (1947)
18 Beach Rd., Salisbury, 01913. Tel: 978-465-3334; Fax: 978-388-8840; Email: administrativeassistant@livingwatercatholic.org; Web: livingwatercatholic.org. Revs. Scott A. Euvrard; Christopher W. Wallace, Parochial Vicar.
SAUGUS, ESSEX CO.
1—BLESSED SACRAMENT (1917)
16 Summer St., Saugus, 01906-2139.
Tel: 781-233-2497; Fax: 781-231-5569; Email: operations@sauguscatholics.org; Web: sauguscatholics.org. Revs. Timothy J. Kelleher; Michael J. Farrell, Parochial Vicar; Senior Deacon Francis M. Gaffney.
Catechesis Religious Program—Tel: 781-231-3699. Donna G. Zinna, D.R.E.
2—ST. MARGARET (1949) Revs. Timothy J. Kelleher; Michael J. Farrell, Parochial Vicar; Senior Deacon Francis M. Gaffney.
Res.: 431 Lincoln Ave., Saugus, 01906-3917.
Tel: 781-233-1040; Email: operations@sauguscatholics.org; Web: sauguscatholics.org.
Catechesis Religious Program—Carol Nadeau, D.R.E.
SCITUATE, PLYMOUTH CO.
1—ST. FRANCES XAVIER CABRINI (1960) Closed. St. Frances Xavier Cabrini, Scituate was suppressed. This parish's records are located at St. Mary of the Nativity, Scituate.
2—ST. MARY OF THE NATIVITY (1921) Very Rev. Kenneth V. Cannon, S.X., V.F.; Deacon Martin W. Henry.
Res.: One Kent St., Scituate, 02066-4215.
Tel: 781-545-3335; Fax: 781-544-3678; Email: Akeefe@stmaryscituate.org; Web: www.stmaryscituate.org.
Catechesis Religious Program—Rosemary Lonborg, D.R.E. (Grades K-5); Ms. Jane Kuklis, D.R.E. (Grades 6-10).
SHARON, NORFOLK CO., OUR LADY OF SORROWS (1906) Rev. Francis J. Daly.
Res.: 59 Cottage St., Sharon, 02067-2132.
Tel: 781-784-2265; Email: parish@olossharon.org; Web: www.olossharon.org.
Catechesis Religious Program—Tel: 781-784-5091. Tami C. Ellis, D.R.E.
SHERBORN, MIDDLESEX CO., ST. THERESA OF LISIEUX (1945)
35 S. Main St., Sherborn, 02030. Tel: 508-653-6253; Fax: 508-651-1318; Email: fr.grimes@st-theresa-sherborn.org; Web: www.mpb-stp.org. Rev. John J. Grimes, S.T.M., Ph.D.
Catechesis Religious Program—Regina O'Connor, D.R.E.
SHIRLEY, MIDDLESEX CO., ST. ANTHONY OF PADUA (1905) [CEM]
14 Phoenix St., P.O. Box 595, Shirley, 01464.
Tel: 978-425-4588; Fax: 978-425-2033; Email: business.mgr@nvcc-ma.org; Web: www.nvcc-ma.org. Rev. Edmond M. Derosier.
Catechesis Religious Program—Tel: 978-425-0980. Donna Vaira, D.R.E.
SOMERVILLE, MIDDLESEX CO.
1—ST. ANN (1881)
399 Medford St., Somerville, 02143.
Tel: 617-625-1904; Fax: 617-625-7043; Email: parish@stannsomerville.org; Web: www.stannsomerville.org. Revs. Brian J. McHugh; Richard G. Curran, Parochial Vicar; David P. Callahan, Parochial Vicar; Deacon Joseph Breyere Guerrier.
2—ST. ANTHONY OF PADUA (1915) (Italian) Rev. Ademir Guerini, C.S., Admin.; Deacon Pedro P. Rodrigues.
Res.: 12 Properzi Way, Somerville, 02143-3226.
Tel: 617-625-4530; Fax: 617-625-2457; Email: stanthonysomer@aol.com.
Catechesis Religious Program—
3—ST. BENEDICT (1911)
21 Hathorn St., Somerville, 02145-3235.
Tel: 617-625-0029; Email: stbenedictsomerville@gmail.com; Web: www.stbenedictsomerville.com. Rev. Carlos A. Lopez, (Puerto Rico) Admin.; Deacon Jose B. Torres.
Catechesis Religious Program—Tel: 617-825-4333. Daisy Gomez, D.R.E.
4—ST. CATHERINE OF GENOA (1891)
185 Summer St., Somerville, 02143-2501.
Tel: 617-666-2087; Fax: 617-666-5470; Email: parishsec@stcgenoa.com; Web: www.stcatherinesomerville.com. Revs. Brian J. McHugh; Richard G. Curran, Parochial Vicar; David P. Callahan, Parochial Vicar; Deacon Joseph Breyere Guerrier.
School—St. Catherine of Genoa School, 192 Summer St., Somerville, 02143-2501. Tel: 617-666-9116; Fax: 617-623-9161; Email: mburns@stcatherinesomerville.org. Ms. Marian Burns, Prin. Lay Teachers 9; Sisters 2; Students 225.
Catechesis Religious Program—
5—ST. JOSEPH (1869)
262 Washington St., Somerville, 02143-3313.
Tel: 617-666-4140; Fax: 617-628-0557; Email: stjoe1869@verizon.net; Web: www.somervillecatholic.org. Revs. Brian J. McHugh; Richard G. Curran, Parochial Vicar; David P. Callahan, Parochial Vicar; Deacon Joseph Breyere Guerrier.
Catechesis Religious Program—John J. Piantedosi, D.R.E.
6—ST. POLYCARP (1927) Closed. Parish records for all closed, merged & suppressed parishes are located at the Office of the Archives, 66 Brooks Dr., Braintree, MA 02184-3839. Tel: 617-746-5795.
STONEHAM, MIDDLESEX CO., ST. PATRICK (1868)
71 Central St., Stoneham, 02180. Tel: 781-438-0960; Fax: 781-435-0075; Email: stpatstone@aol.com; Web: www.stpatrickstoneham.org/. Revs. Mario J. Orrigo, Admin.; Frank D. Campo, Parochial Vicar; Deacons Francis B. Dello Russo; Joseph Cooley. In Res., Most Rev. Peter J. Uglietto.
School—St. Patrick School, 20 Pleasant St., Stoneham, 02180. Tel: 781-438-2593; Fax: 781-438-2543; Email: arthurswanson@yahoo.com; Web: www.stpatrickschoolstoneham.org/index.html. Mr. Arthur Swanson, Prin. Lay Teachers 10; Students 223.
Catechesis Religious Program—Tel: 781-438-1093. Marie Kopf, D.R.E.
STOUGHTON, NORFOLK CO.
1—IMMACULATE CONCEPTION (1872)
179 School St., Stoughton, 02072-2204.
Tel: 781-344-2073; Fax: 781-344-2979; Email: info@stoughtoncatholic.org; Web: stoughtoncatholic.org. Revs. Joseph M. Mazzone; Jose E. Marques, (Brazil) Parochial Vicar; William P. Sexton, Parochial Vicar.
Catechesis Religious Program—Tel: 781-341-0611. Alice Bachant, D.R.E.
2—ST. JAMES (1962) Revs. Joseph M. Mazzone; Jose E. Marques, (Brazil) Parochial Vicar; William P. Sexton, Parochial Vicar.
Res.: 560 Page St., Stoughton, 02072.
Tel: 781-344-9121; Fax: 781-341-9323; Email: info@stoughtoncatholic.org; Web: stoughtoncatholic.org.
Catechesis Religious Program—Tel: 781-297-7582. Mrs. Mary Ann Caldwell, D.R.E.
3—OUR LADY OF THE ROSARY (1958) Closed. Parish records for all closed, merged & suppressed parishes are located at the Office of the Archives, 66 Brooks Dr., Braintree, MA 02184-3839. Tel: 617-746-5795.
STOW, MIDDLESEX CO., ST. ISIDORE (1961)
429 Great Rd., Stow, 01720-2503. Tel: 978-897-2710; Fax: 978-461-0577; Email: info@stisidorestow.org; Web: www.stisidorestow.org. Revs. Walter J. Woods; Paul S. Sughrue, Parochial Vicar; Deacon Charles A. Cornell.
Catechesis Religious Program—Tel: 978-897-9790. Nancy Dome, D.R.E.
SUDBURY, MIDDLESEX CO.
1—ST. ANSELM (1963) Closed. Parish records for all closed, merged & suppressed parishes are located at the Office of the Archives, 66 Brooks Dr., Braintree, MA 02184-3839. Tel: 617-746-5795.
2—OUR LADY OF FATIMA (1955) Rev. Richard M. Erikson; Deacon John D. Nicholson.
Res.: 160 Concord Rd., Sudbury, 01776-2353.
Tel: 978-443-2798; Fax: 978-443-6264; Email: psecretary@fatimasudbury.org; Web: www.fatimasudbury.org.
Catechesis Religious Program—Tel: 978-443-9166. Ms. Susan Murphy, D.R.E.
SWAMPSCOTT, ESSEX CO., ST. JOHN THE EVANGELIST (1905)
178 Humphrey St., Swampscott, 01907-2512.
Tel: 781-593-2544; Fax: 781-593-3616; Email: stjohnsswampscott@gmail.com; Web: www.stjohnsswampscott.org. Rev. James T. Kelly, Admin.; Deacon Andrew J. Acampora.
Catechesis Religious Program—Tel: 781-599-4711. Mr. A. Joseph Hunt, D.R.E.
TEWKSBURY, MIDDLESEX CO., ST. WILLIAM (1935) Very Rev. Andrew Knop, O.M.I., V.F.; Rev. Dwight Hoeberechts, O.M.I., Parochial Vicar; Deacons Gerard J. Hardy; Thomas M. Walsh.
Res.: 1351 Main St., Tewksbury, 01876-2039.
Tel: 978-851-7331; Fax: 978-858-0544; Email: stwilliams.office@gmail.com; Web: www.stwilliamparish.org.
Catechesis Religious Program—Deborah M. Albano, D.R.E.
TOPSFIELD, ESSEX CO., ST. ROSE OF LIMA (1945)
12 Park St., Topsfield, 01983-0458.
Tel: 978-774-1958; Fax: 978-887-8201; Email: djones@thechristinitiative.org; Web: thechristinitiative.org/. Rev. Michael B. Medas, M.S.W.
Catechesis Religious Program—Tel: 978-882-0882. Mary I. Connor, D.R.E.; Kathleen A. Yanchus, D.R.E.
TOWNSEND, MIDDLESEX CO., ST. JOHN THE EVANGELIST (1945) Revs. Jeremy P. St. Martin; Jason W. Worthley, Parochial Vicar.
Res.: One School St., Townsend, 01469-0533.
Tel: 978-597-2291; Fax: 978-597-3401; Email: townsendcatholic.org@gmail.com; Web: townsendcatholic.org.
Catechesis Religious Program—Tel: 978-597-2183. Kathleen Twombly, D.R.E.
TYNGSBOROUGH, MIDDLESEX CO., ST. MARY MAGDALEN (1959)
95 Lakeview Ave., Tyngsborough, 01879.
Tel: 978-649-7315; Fax: 978-957-5266; Email: saintmarymagdalen@verizon.net; Web: www.stmarymagdalenparish.com. Revs. Richard F. Clancy; Michael J. Harkins, Parochial Vicar; Tinh Van Nguyen, Parochial Vicar; Deacon David A. Brooks.
Catechesis Religious Program—Cathy Kennedy, D.R.E.
WAKEFIELD, MIDDLESEX CO.
1—ST. FLORENCE (1947)
47 Butler Ave., Wakefield, 01880-5199.
Tel: 781-245-2711; Fax: 781-245-4512; Email: stflorence@verizon.net; Web: www.stflorence.org. Rev. Vincent J. Gianni.
Catechesis Religious Program—Deanna Kerns, D.R.E.
2—ST. JOSEPH (1854) Rev. Ronald A. Barker; Maureen Miller, Business Mgr.; Anne Grant, Music Dir.
Res.: 173 Albion St., Wakefield, 01880-3224.
Tel: 781-245-5770; Fax: 781-246-2423; Email: office@stjosephwakefield.org; Web: www.stjosephwakefield.org.
School—St. Joseph School, 15 Gould St., Wakefield, 01880-2700. Tel: 781-245-2081; Fax: 781-245-0517; Email: aflynn@stjosephschoolwakefield.org; Web: www.stjosephschoolwakefield.org. Dr. Joseph M. Sullivan, Prin.; Alayne Flynn, Business Mgr. Lay Teachers 27; Students 200.
Catechesis Religious Program—Tel: 781-245-1930. Diane Murphy, D.R.E.; Carissa Thekaekara, Youth Min.
3—MOST BLESSED SACRAMENT (1931)
1155 Main St., Wakefield, 01880-4222. Tel: ; Fax: 781-245-7981; Email: mbsparish1@aol.com; Web: www.mbsparishwakefield.com. Rev. William D. Coughlin.
Catechesis Religious Program—Tel: 781-245-4669; Tel: 781-245-3414. Christine Carlson, D.R.E.; Laurine Kohler, D.R.E.
WALPOLE, NORFOLK CO.
1—BLESSED SACRAMENT (1874)
10 Diamond St., Walpole, 02081. Tel: 508-668-4700; Web: www.matt13catholic.org. Revs. George C. Hines; Joseph M. O'Keefe, S.J., Parochial Vicar; Deacons Reynold G. Spadoni; Alan J. Doty.
School—Blessed Sacrament School, 808 East St., Walpole, 02081. Tel: 508-668-2336; Fax: 508-668-7944; Email: jspillman@blessedsacrament.org; Web: school.blessedsacrament.org. Mr. James Spillman, Prin. Lay Teachers 30; Students 440.

Catechesis Religious Program—Convent—Tel: 508-668-6693.
2—ST. MARY (1931) Revs. George C. Hines; Jean P. Aubin, Parochial Vicar; John J. Healy, Parochial Vicar; Deacons Alan J. Doty; Reynold G. Spadoni.
Res.: 176 Washington St., East Walpole, 02032-0131. Tel: 508-668-4974; Fax: 508-668-3083; Email: office@stmarywalpole.com; Web: matt13catholic.org.
Catechesis Religious Program—Tel: 508-668-6853. Thomas Connor, D.R.E.; Judith Connor, D.R.E.
WALTHAM, MIDDLESEX CO.
1—ST. CHARLES BORROMEO (1909)
51 Hall St., Waltham, 02451-4599. Tel: 781-893-0330 ; Fax: 781-209-0555; Email: stcharleswaltham@yahoo.com. Rev. Michael L. Nolan, Admin.
Catechesis Religious Program—Tel: 781-893-1438. Carol A. Gill, D.R.E.
2—ST. JOSEPH (1894) Closed. Parish records for all closed, merged & suppressed parishes are located at the Office of the Archives, 66 Brooks Dr., Braintree, MA 02184-3839. Tel: 617-746-5795.
3—ST. JUDE (1949) Rev. William T. Leonard.
Res.: 147-R Main St., Waltham, 02453-6622. Tel: 781-893-3100; Fax: 781-893-2424; Email: stjude1@comcast.net; Web: www.rc.net/boston/st-jude.
School—St. Jude School, 175 Main St., Waltham, 02453-6622. Tel: 781-899-3644; Fax: 781-899-3644; Email: saintjudewaltham@comcast.net; Web: www.saintjudewaltham.com. Sr. Katherine Martin Caughey, S.N.D., Prin. Lay Teachers 8; Sisters 2; Students 199.
Catechesis Religious Program—Tel: 781-891-5718. Barbara A. Keville, D.R.E.
4—ST. MARY (1839)
145 School St., Waltham, 02451-4599. Tel: 781-891-1730; Fax: 781-209-0555; Email: stmarywaltham@gmail.com; Web: www.stmarywaltham.org. Rev. Michael L. Nolan; Deacon Eduardo R. Mora.
Catechesis Religious Program—Tel: 781-893-0917. Marjorie Harris, D.R.E.
5—OUR LADY, COMFORTER OF THE AFFLICTED (1930)
920R Trapelo Rd., Waltham, 02452. Tel: 781-894-3481; Email: olcaparish@gmail.com; Web: www.olca.org. Rev. James M. DiPerri, M.A., M.Div., J.C.L.
School—Our Lady's Academy, 920 Trapelo Rd., Waltham, 02452-4841. Tel: 781-899-0353; Fax: 781-891-8734; Email: principal@ourladysacademy.org; Web: www.ourladysacademy.org. Ms. Chandra Minor, Prin. Lay Teachers 8; Students 180.
6—SACRED HEART (1922) (Italian)
100 Newton St., Waltham, 02453. Tel: 781-899-0469; Fax: 781-899-0081; Email: Sacredheart311@aol.com; Web: sacredheart311.com. Rev. Dennis J. Wheatley, O.F.M.
Catechesis Religious Program—Tel: 781-893-8461. Bernadette Scalese, D.R.E.
WATERTOWN, MIDDLESEX CO.
1—ST. PATRICK (1847)
212 Main St., Watertown, 02472. Tel: 617-926-9680; Fax: 617-926-3715; Email: parishoffice@stpatswatertown.org; Web: www.stpatswatertown.org. Very Rev. Kevin M. Sepe; Rev. Matthew J. Conley, Parochial Vicar; Deacon John H. Beagan.
Catechesis Religious Program—Tel: 617-926-3441; Fax: 617-926-3715. Sandy Clancy, D.R.E.
2—SACRED HEART (1893) Very Rev. Kevin M. Sepe; Rev. Matthew J. Conley, Parochial Vicar.
Res.: 770 Mt. Auburn St., Watertown, 02472-1567. Tel: 617-924-9110; Fax: 617-926-3341; Email: parishsacredheart@yahoo.com.
Catechesis Religious Program—Judy Gilreath, D.R.E.
3—ST. THERESA OF THE CHILD JESUS (1927) Closed. Parish records for all closed, merged & suppressed parishes are located at the Office of the Archives, 66 Brooks Dr., Braintree, MA 02184-3839. Tel: 617-746-5795.
WAYLAND, MIDDLESEX CO.
1—ST. ANN (1945) Rev. James J. Laughlin, A.B., M.Div., J.C.L.; Sr. Roberta Rzeznik, S.N.D., Pastoral Assoc.
Res.: 124 Cochituate Rd., Wayland, 01778-2610. Tel: 508-358-2985; Fax: 508-358-3415; Email: parish@saintann.org; Web: www.saintann.org.
Catechesis Religious Program—Jane Asber, D.R.E., Tel: 508-358-2985, Ext. 13.
2—GOOD SHEPHERD PARISH (2011)
St. Ann, 134 Cochituate Rd., Wayland, 01776. Tel: 508-650-3545; Fax: 508-655-6948; Email: parish@goodshepherdwayland.org; Web: www.goodshepherdwayland.org. Rev. David M. O'Leary, Admin.; Deacon Geoffrey W. Higgins.
3—ST. ZEPHERIN (1889) Rev. James J. Laughlin, A.B., M.Div., J.C.L.; Sr. Roberta Reznik, S.N.D., Pastoral Assoc.
Res.: 124 Cochituate Rd., Wayland, 01778-2610. Tel: 508-653-8013; Fax: 508-655-6948; Email: stzepherin@comcast.net; Web: www.stzepherin.org.
Catechesis Religious Program—Sr. Frances Thomas, D.R.E.
WELLESLEY, NORFOLK CO.
1—ST. JAMES THE GREAT (1947) Closed. St. James the Great, Wellesley was suppressed. This parish's records are located at St. Paul, Wellesley.
2—ST. JOHN THE EVANGELIST (1890)
9 Glen Rd., Wellesley, 02481-1600. Tel: 781-235-0045 ; Fax: 781-235-6990; Email: stjohnwellesley@stjohnwellesley.org; Web: saintjohnwellesley.org/. Revs. James J. Laughlin, A.B., M.Div., J.C.L.; Robert J. Blaney, Parochial Vicar.
School—St. John the Evangelist School, 9 Ledyard St., Wellesley, 02481. Tel: 781-235-0300; Fax: 781-207-5379; Email: mdibbert@saintjohnschool.net; Web: www.saintjohnschool.net. Michael Dibbert, Prin. Lay Teachers 5; Sisters 2; Students 187.
Catechesis Religious Program—Tel: 781-235-5337. Linda Messore, D.R.E.; Jane Leonard, D.R.E.; Christine Tierney, D.R.E.
3—ST. PAUL (1922)
500 Washington St., Wellesley, 02482-5907. Tel: 781-235-1060; Fax: 781-235-4620; Email: office@stpaulwellesley.com; Web: www.stpaulwellesley.com. Revs. James J. Laughlin, A.B., M.Div., J.C.L.; Robert J. Blaney, Parochial Vicar.
School—St. Paul School, 10 Atwood St., Wellesley, 02482. Tel: 781-235-1510; Fax: 781-235-4620. Ms. Allison Hoff, Prin. Lay Teachers 7; Sisters 1; Students 184.
Catechesis Religious Program—Tel: 781-235-5012. Kathleen Curley, D.R.E.
WEST BRIDGEWATER, PLYMOUTH CO., ST. ANN (1938)
95 N. Main St., West Bridgewater, 02379-0427. Tel: 508-586-4880; Fax: 508-586-3876; Email: stanns@comcast.net; Web: www.stannswb.com. Revs. Paul L. Ring; Michael K. Harvey, Parochial Vicar.
Catechesis Religious Program—Maria Lallemand, D.R.E.
WEST NEWBURY, ESSEX CO.
1—ST. ANN (1945) Closed. Parish records for all closed, merged & suppressed parishes are located at the Office of the Archives, 66 Brooks Dr., Braintree, MA 02184-3839. Tel: 617-746-5795.
2—HOLY REDEEMER (2006)
Nativity, 4 Green St., Merrimac, 01985. Tel: 978-346-8604; Fax: 978-346-9970; Email: holyredeemer@verizon.net; Web: www.hriccatholic.org. Revs. Timothy A. Harrison; George E. Morin, Parochial Vicar.
Catechesis Religious Program—Doreen O'Leary, D.R.E.
WESTFORD, MIDDLESEX CO., ST. CATHERINE OF ALEXANDRIA (1922) [CEM] Revs. Peter F. Quinn; Joseph M. Rossi, Parochial Vicar; Deacon William A. Dwyer.
Res.: 107 N. Main St., Westford, 01886. Tel: 978-692-6353; Fax: 978-392-0644; Email: office@lwcatholic.org; Web: www.stcatherineparish.org.
Catechesis Religious Program—Ms. Diahne Goodwin, D.R.E.
WESTON, MIDDLESEX CO., ST. JULIA (1919) Rev. Mark A. Mahoney; Deacon Rafeal Brown.
Res.: 374 Boston Post Rd., Weston, 02493-1581. Tel: 781-899-2611; Fax: 781-899-8046; Email: stjulia@stjulia.org; Web: stjulia.org.
Catechesis Religious Program—Sr. Marie LaBollita, S.C., S.C., D.R.E.
Mission—St. Joseph, 142 Lincoln Rd., Lincoln, Middlesex Co. 01773.
WESTWOOD, NORFOLK CO.
1—ST. DENIS (1949) Rev. James G. Burke.
Res.: 157 Washington St., Westwood, 02090-1336. Tel: 781-326-5858; Fax: 781-326-1232; Web: www.stdeniswestwood.com.
Catechesis Religious Program—Mary Campion, D.R.E.; Kathleen A. Burton, D.R.E.
2—ST. MARGARET MARY (1931) Rev. Stephen J. Linehan.
Res.: 845 High St., Westwood, 02090-0386. Tel: 781-326-1071; Fax: 781-329-1879; Email: info@saintmmparish.org; Web: www.saintmmparish.org.
Catechesis Religious Program—Karlene Duffy, D.R.E.
WEYMOUTH, NORFOLK CO.
1—ST. ALBERT THE GREAT (1950)
1130 Washington St., Weymouth, 02184. Tel: 781-337-2171; Fax: 781-331-4192; Email: atgweymouth@gmail.com; Web: www.atgweymouth.org. Mailing Address: 234 Pleasant St., South Weymouth, 02190. Very Rev. Charles J. Higgins, V.F., Admin.; Deacon Joseph A. Canova.
2—ST. FRANCIS XAVIER (1859) [CEM] Very Rev. Charles J. Higgins, V.F., Admin.; Rev. Peter J. Casey, Parochial Vicar; Deacon Joseph A. Canova.
Res.: 234 Pleasant St., Weymouth, 02184. Tel: 781-337-2171; Fax: 781-337-2171; Email: Sfxprsh@gmail.com; Web: www.stfrancisxavier.org.
School—St. Francis Xavier School, Tel: 781-335-6868 ; Email: rmurphy@sfxschoolwey.org; Web: www.saintfrancisxavierschool.org. Mr. Robert Murphy, Prin. Lay Teachers 18; Religious 1; Students 471.
Catechesis Religious Program—Marjorie Kearney, D.R.E.; Barbara Spink, D.R.E.
3—IMMACULATE CONCEPTION (1871)
720 Broad St., Weymouth, 02189. Tel: 781-337-0380; Email: icoffice@catholicweymouth.org; Web: www.catholicweymouth.org. Most Rev. John A. Dooher; Revs. Huy H. Nguyen, Parochial Vicar; John J. Ronaghan, Admin.; Deacon Francis J. Corbett.
Catechesis Religious Program—Tel: 781-337-3024. Ruthann Sinibaldi, D.R.E., Tel: 781-335-3902.
4—ST. JEROME (1928) Most Rev. John A. Dooher; Revs. John J. Ronaghan, Admin.; Huy H. Nguyen, Parochial Vicar; Deacon Timothy J. Maher.
Res.: 632 Bridge St., Weymouth, 02191. Tel: 781-335-2038; Email: sjoffice@catholicweymouth.org; Web: www.catholicweymouth.org.
School—St. Jerome School, 598 Bridge St., Weymouth, 02191. Tel: 781-335-1235; Fax: 781-340-0256; Email: kpuleo@stjeromeschoolweymouth.org; Web: www.stjeromeschoolweymouth.org. Ms. Kathleen Puleo, Prin. Lay Teachers 9; Sisters 1; Students 234.
Catechesis Religious Program—Tel: 781-335-2786. Sr. Barbara Joyce, C.S.J., D.R.E.
5—SACRED HEART (1871)
77 Washington St., Weymouth, 02184. Tel: 781-337-6333; Fax: 781-337-9192; Email: secretary@shstm.org; Web: www.shstm.org. Mailing Address: 55 Commercial St., Weymouth, 02188. Rev. Sean M. Connor.
School—Sacred Heart School, 75 Commercial St., Weymouth, 02188-2604. Tel: 781-335-6010; Fax: 781-331-7936; Email: cbeza@sacredheartschoolweymouth.org; Web: www.sacredheartschoolweymouth.org. Mr. Christopher J. Beza, Prin. Lay Teachers 7; Sisters 2; Students 165.
Catechesis Religious Program—Jean Duke, D.R.E.; Susan McLeod, D.R.E.
WHITMAN, PLYMOUTH CO., HOLY GHOST (1897)
School St., Whitman, 02382. Tel: 781-447-4421; Fax: 781-447-1375; Email: sbparishsecretary@comcast.net; Web: www.loccc.org. Revs. James M. Mahoney, M.Div.; Thomas J. Stanton, Parochial Vicar; Deacons Joseph T. Nickley; James V. McLaughlin.
Catechesis Religious Program—Tel: 781-447-3135. Ann Lawrence, D.R.E.
WILMINGTON, MIDDLESEX CO.
1—ST. DOROTHY (1954)
Mailing Address: 120 Main St., Wilmington, 01887-3519. Tel: 978-658-3550; Fax: 978-658-2008; Web: wilmingtoncatholic.com. Revs. Phillip B. Earley; Augustin A. Anda Gomez, Parochial Vicar; Deacon Joseph M. Fagan Jr.
Catechesis Religious Program—Mary E. Medeiros, D.R.E.
2—ST. THOMAS OF VILLANOVA (1919) Revs. Phillip B. Earley; Augustin A. Anda Gomez, Parochial Vicar; Deacon Joseph M. Fagan Jr.
Res.: 126 Middlesex Ave., Wilmington, 01887-2723. Tel: 978-658-4665; Fax: 978-658-2008; Web: www.wilmingtoncatholic.com.
Catechesis Religious Program—Marilyn Mandosa, D.R.E.
WINCHESTER, MIDDLESEX CO.
1—ST. EULALIA (1966)
50 Ridge St., Winchester, 01890-3633. Tel: 781-729-8220; Fax: 781-729-0919; Web: sainteulalia.org. Rev. James W. Savage.
Catechesis Religious Program—Barbara Penkala, D.R.E.; Donna DiFonzo, D.R.E.
2—IMMACULATE CONCEPTION (1931) Closed. Parish records for all closed, merged & suppressed parishes are located at the Office of the Archives, 66 Brooks Dr., Braintree, MA 02184-3839. Tel: 617-746-5795.
3—ST. MARY (1876) Very Rev. Michael J. Bova Conti, V.F., Admin.
Res.: 158 Washington St., Winchester, 01890. Tel: 781-729-0055; Fax: 781-721-6542; Email: stmarywinchester@comcast.net; Web: www.stmary-winchester.org.
School—St. Mary School, 162 Washington St., Winchester, 01890-2173. Tel: 781-729-5515; Fax: 781-729-1352; Email: emoreilly@comcast.net; Web: www.stmaryswinchester.org. Mr. Michael McCabe, Prin. Lay Teachers 20; Students 198.
Catechesis Religious Program—Tel: 781-729-1965.
WINTHROP, SUFFOLK CO.
1—HOLY ROSARY (1953) Rev. Thomas A. DiLorenzo, Admin.
Church: 1015 Shirley St., Winthrop, 02152-2535.

Tel: 617-846-1210; Fax: 617-539-4402; Email: holyrosaryrectory@comcast.net; Web: www.holyrosaryparish.net.
Catechesis Religious Program—Deborah Tewksbury, D.R.E.

2—ST. JOHN THE EVANGELIST (1907) Rev. Charles E. Bourke; Deacon Vincent J. Leo.
Res.: 320 Winthrop St., Winthrop, 02152-3127.
Tel: 617-846-7400; Fax: 617-539-0627; Web: www.stjohnswinthrop.org.
Catechesis Religious Program—Tel: 617-846-3100. Geraldine Butters, D.R.E.

WOBURN, MIDDLESEX CO.

1—ST. ANTHONY OF PADUA (1945)
851 Main St., Woburn, 01801-1855.
Tel: 781-933-1323; Fax: 781-937-3233; Email: st_anthony_parish@verizon.net. Rev. Richard J. Shmaruk.
Catechesis Religious Program—Sandra Strong, D.R.E.

2—ST. BARBARA (1954) Rev. Thomas J. Powers, Admin.; Deacons Edward S. Giordano; William E. Kerns.
Res.: 138 Cambridge Rd., Woburn, 01801-4772.
Tel: 781-933-4130; Email: stbarbara@woburncatholic.org; Web: www.stbarbaraparish.org.
Catechesis Religious Program—Tel: 781-935-0529. Barbara Jeannotte, D.R.E.

3—ST. CHARLES BORROMEO (1862) Revs. Timothy J. Shea; Daniel P. McCoy, Parochial Vicar; Deacons Philip P. Hardcastle; Edin Velasquez.
Res.: 280 Main St., Woburn, 01801.
Tel: 781-933-0300; Fax: 781-932-7581; Email: admin@sccwoburn.com; Web: www.sccwoburn.com/.
School—St. Charles Borromeo School, 8 Myrtle St., Woburn, 01801. Tel: 781-935-4635;
Fax: 781-935-3121; Email: cblanchette@scswoburn.com; Web: www.saintcharleswoburn.com. Ms. Cara Blanchette, Prin. Lay Teachers 25; Students 350.
Catechesis Religious Program—Cliff Garvey, D.R.E.

4—ST. JOSEPH (1906) Closed. Parish records for all closed, merged & suppressed parishes are located at the Office of the Archives, 66 Brooks Dr., Braintree, MA 02184-3839. Tel: 617-746-5795. Rev. Harold E. LeBlanc, (Retired).

WRENTHAM, NORFOLK CO., ST. MARY (1928)
140 South St., Wrentham, 02093-0326.
Tel: 508-384-3373; Fax: 508-384-5747; Email: stmaryoffice@pwc.church; Web: www.pwc.church. Revs. Joseph F. Mozer Jr., J.C.L.; William T. Schmidt, Parochial Vicar; George G. Hogan, Parochial Vicar, (Retired); Deacons Kenneth W. Oles; Joseph R. Flocco.
Catechesis Religious Program—Tel: 508-384-7922. Roberta Oles, D.R.E.

Priests of the Archdiocese with Other Assignments: The contact information for the following clergy of the Archdiocese of Boston is available from: Clergy Personnel Office, 66 Brooks Dr., Braintree, MA 02184-3839. Tel: 617-746-5866; Fax: 617-746-5614.

Most. Rev.—
Russell, Paul F.

Rev. Msgrs.—
Abruzzese, John A.
McInerny, Paul B.
Oliver, Robert W., B.H., S.T.D., J.C.D.
Parfienczyk, Stanislaw

Very Revs.—
Bova Conti, Michael J., V.F.
Burton, Richard T., V.F.

Revs.—
Ajemian, David J.
Atraga, Tamiru F.
Beauregard, Andrew M., F.P.O.
Best, Russell W.
Butler, Timothy A.
Conole, Robert J.
Davison, Andreas R.
Driscoll, Joseph J.
Farrell, Michael J.
Foley, Thomas S.
Foster, Joseph R.
Galvin, John P., D.Th.
Giroux, Peter F., F.P.O.
Gunter, David W.
Healy, Stephen M.
Helfrich, Paul D., B.H., J.D., S.T.B., M.A.
Hines, George C.
Hurley, Paul K.
Hurley, Sean Patrick, F.P.O.
Jacques, Roger N.
Kelly, Francis J., F.P.O.
Kennedy, William M.
Leblanc, Stephen R.
Lohan, William P.
Malloy, Stephen J.
Marcham, David S.
McCarthy, Sean M.
McGrade, Kevin M.
McNulty, Martin J.
Medio, Joseph Paul, F.P.O.
Merdinger, Philip E., B.H., A.B., M.A., S.T.B.
Monagle, Robert J.
Moran, Terence J., V.F.
Nguyen, Joseph Diem
Picardi, John M.
Pucciarelli, George W.
Randone, Michael C.
Raux, Redmond P.
Sheehan, Michael Francis, F.P.O.
Staley-Joyce, Kevin M.
Storey, Mark D.
Sullivan, Robert E.
White, David P.
Yanju, Henry M.

Senior Priests: For contact information please call or write: Clergy Personnel Office, 66 Brooks Dr., Braintree, MA 02184-3839. Tel: 617-746-5866; Fax: 617-746-5614.

Rev. Msgrs.—
Bourque, Charles J., V.F., (Retired), 700 Washington St., Canton, 02021-3036
Brady, Roger J., (Retired), 81 Hartwell Rd., Bedford, 01730-2408
Carlson, George F., (Retired)
Conley, Peter V., V.F., (Retired)
Contons, Albert J., (Retired), P.O. Box 1025, Humarock, 02047-1025
Coyle, Arthur M., (Retired)
Lind, Joseph G., (Retired), 502 Washington St., Wellesley, 02482-5907
Martocchio, Peter T., (Retired), 632 Bridge St., Weymouth, 02191-1845
McDonough, John P., (Retired), One Pond St., Apt. 4H, Winthrop, 02152-1080
McGann, Francis J., (Retired), 1382 Highland Ave., Needham, 02492-2614
McGrath, Laurence W., M.Div., M.A., M.S., (Retired), 34 Bunerk Hill Rd., Auburn, NH 03032-3528
McRae, Cornelius M., (Retired), P.O. Box 264, Manomet, 02345-0264
Murphy, Frederick J., (Retired), 24 Conant St., Danvers, 01923-2988
Ryan, Paul T., (Retired), 547 Washington St., Norwood, 02062-0547
Sheehan, Dennis F., (Retired)

Very Revs.—
Connelly, John J. Jr., (Retired)
Gariboldi, Ronald J., V.F., (Retired), 6 Driftwood Way, Rockport, 01966

Revs.—
Arsenault, Joseph G., (Retired), 455 Plymouth St., Abington, 02351
Bailey, Paul F., (Retired), 313 Court St., Plymouth, 02360-4336
Barry, Garrett J., (Retired), 66 Brooks Dr., 02184-3839
Bertelli, Ameilio James, (Retired), 4 Payson St., Lexington, 02421-7924
Berube, Paul W., (Retired), 42 Green St., Newburyport, 01950-2647
Bilicky, Louis S., (Retired), 24 Rickey Dr., Maynard, 01754-1052
Blackwood, Wallace E., (Retired)
Blute, Robert H., (Retired), 60 William Cardinal O'Connell Way, Boston, 02114-2729
Bourgault, Ronald L., (Retired), 100 Salisbury Rd., Franklin, NH 03235-2501
Braley, James E.
Broderick, James M., (Retired), 42 Green St., Newburyport, 01950-2647
Browne, Robert M., (Retired), 2 Park Ln., Gloucester, 01930-3924
Buckley, Thomas W., (Retired), 198 Centre St., Abington, 02351-2208
Butler, Allan L. W., (Retired), 27 Vaughan Ave., Whitman, 02382-1307
Butler, James P., (Retired), 11 Courtney St. (#8), Fall River, 02720-6740
Butler, Robert J., (Retired), 432 Adams St., Milton, 02186-4399
Carroll, Edward G., (Retired), 60 William Cardinal O'Connell Way, Boston, 02114-2709
Carroll, William R., (Retired), 27 Sears Ave., Melrose, 02176
Casey, Richard L.
Clifford, Donald P., (Retired), 125 Lakeview Blvd., Plymouth, 02360
Cloherty, Francis J., V.F., (Retired)
Colletti, Arnold F., (Retired)
Connor, Martin P., S.T.L., (Retired), 392 Hanover St., Hanover, 02339
Conroy, Francis M., (Retired), 1529 Washington St., Newton, 02465
Conway, Richard C., (Retired)
Cormier, Leo G., (Retired), 90 Flower Ln., Dracut, 01826-4650
Cormier, Roger C., (Retired), 45 S. Meadow Village, Unit 5, Carver, 02330-1802
Crowley, Daniel J., (Retired), 340 Center St., Middleboro, 02346-2102
Crowley, Richard P., (Retired), 6 Deep Woods Dr., Mattapoisett, 02739
Cuenin, Walter H., (Retired)
Cunney, Henry M., (Retired), 1008 Paradise Rd., Unit 1B, Swampscott, 01907-1303
Curran, Paul E., (Retired), 60 William Cardinal O'Connell Way, Boston, 02114-2729
Daily, Vincent E., (Retired), 1573 Cambridge St., Cambridge, 02138-4370
Daley, Francis E., (Retired), 52 Warr Ave., Wareham, 02571
Darcy, James F., (Retired), 60 William Cardinal O'Connell Way, Boston, 02114-2729
Desmond, Hubert E., (Retired), 51 Broad Reach, Apt. M56A, Weymouth, 02191-2266
Desrosiers, Philip J., (Retired), P.O. Box 8149, Lynn, 01904-0149
DeVeer, Richard S.
Doherty, Henry F., (Retired), 12 Sachem Village Rd., P.O. Box 31, West Dennis, 02670-0031
Doherty, Robert J., (Retired), 13991 Amarilis Ct., Fort Pierce, FL 34951-4201
Donahue, Richard T., (Retired), P.O. Box 371, West Harwich, 02671
Donovan, John L., (Retired), 60 William Cardinal O'Connell Way, Boston, 02114-2729
Dorgan, Gerard L., (Retired), 22 Buttonwood Ln., Peabody, 01960
Doyle, John L., (Retired), 83 Long Ave., Framingham, 01702-5735
Driscoll, Arthur J., (Retired), 57 Sylvan St., Unit 7A, Danvers, 01923-2747
DuFour, Louis C., (Retired), P.O. Box 731, Seabrook, NH 03874-0731
Emerson, George F., (Retired), 650 Nichols St., Norwood, 02062-1099
English, William J., (Retired)
Fagan, Joseph K., M.Div., (Retired), 60 William Cardinal O'Connell Way, Boston, 02114-2729
Farrell, John E., V.F., (Retired), 100 Merrimack Ave., Unit 157, Dracut, 01826
Ferraro, Michael M., (Retired)
Flynn, Arthur C., (Retired), 45 Folly Pond Rd., Apt. 24, Beverly, 01915-5384
Flynn, George R., (Retired), Apartado 18-0825, Lima, Peru
Foley, Thomas C., (Retired), 757 Hancock St., Quincy, 02170-2722
Fraser, Gerald C., (Retired), 60 William Cardinal O'Connell Way, Boston, 02114-2709
Gallagher, Edward L., (Retired), 10036 Connell Rd., San Diego, CA 92131-1430
Gallagher, John E., (Retired), P.O. Box 465, Farmington, ME 04938-0465
Gaudet, Joseph A., (Retired), 39 Revere St., Everett, 02149-3524
Gillespie, Jerome F., (Retired)
Gomes, Ronald A., (Retired)
Guarino, R. Michael, (Retired), 5238 Wellfleet Dr., S., Sarasota, FL 34241
Hickey, Daniel J., (Retired)
Kaufman, Harry J., (Retired)
Keane, John F., (Retired), 7 Bay Rd., P.O. Box 372, West Yarmouth, 02673-5803
Kelley, Arnold E., (Retired), 120 Bellevue Ave., Haverhill, 01832
Kelly, Thomas P., (Retired)
Kennedy, Robert R., (Retired), 26 Breed St., Boston, 02128-2627
King, Philip J., (Retired), 1573 Cambridge St., Cambridge, 02138-4370
Kirke, Eugene K., (Retired), 24 Clark St., Boston, 02109-1127
Koen, Stephen A., (Retired), 3 Indian Mound Ln., Falmouth, 02540
Kremmell, William T., (Retired)
Labrie, Robert G., (Retired)
Lawson, Harold F., (Retired), 60 William Cardinal O'Connell Way, Boston, 02114-2729
LeBlanc, Harold E., (Retired), 66 Brooks Dr., 02184-3839
Lizio, John R., (Retired), 933 Central St., Framingham, 01701-4872
MacDonald, Paul V., (Retired), 90 Oakmere St., Boston, 02132-5531
Magni, Daniel M., (Retired)
Martel, Leo E., (Retired), 32 Kings Dr., Raymond, NH 03077-2682
McCabe, Edward D., (Retired)
McCarthy, James J., (Retired)
McCarthy, Jeremiah J., (Retired), 24 Clark St., Boston, 02109-1103
McDermott, Joseph P., (Retired)
McDonagh, Edward C., (Retired), 5705 Crooked Stick Way, Sparks, NV 89436
McElroy, John W., (Retired), 6 Lakeview Ln., Palm Coast, FL 32137-1490

McGowan, Frederick R., (Retired), 2C Greenleaf Park, Merrimac, 01860-1833
McLaughlin, John E., (Retired), 14 Bradford Rd., Weston, 02493
McLaughlin, Patrick J., (Retired), 432 Adams St., Milton, 02186-4399
McLaughlin, Richard P., (Retired), 14 Boston Ave., Somerville, 02144-2302
McLaughlin, William H., (Retired)
McPartland, Paul G., (Retired), 50 Monument Ave., Boston, 02129-3324
McQuade, Richard E., (Retired), 10 Buttonwood Ln., Scituate, 02066-1107
Mellone, Vincent P., (Retired)
Mendicoa, John M., (Retired), 66 Brooks Dr., 02184-3839
Milling, Robert T., (Retired)
Moran, James F., (Retired), 6101 Edsall Rd., Unit 202, Alexandria, VA 22304
Moran, Richard S., (Retired), 23 Spruce St., Malden, 02148-4416
Morris, John S., (Retired), 505 Mill St., #269, Worcester, 01602-2482
Mottau, Robert S., (Retired), 20 Devens St., Apt. 404, Boston, 02129-3725
Murray, John A., (Retired), 53 George St., Watertown, 02472-3343
Nee, Robert E., (Retired)
Nichols, Henry P., (Retired)
Nichols, John J., (Retired), Capella South 1104, Goat Island, Newport, RI 02840-1582
Noonan, Mark L., Ph.D., (Retired), 78 Bucks Creek Rd., Chatham, 02633
O'Brien, John W., V.F., (Retired)
O'Connor, Maurice J., (Retired), 750 Whittenton St., Unit 723, Taunton, 02780-1353
O'Meara, Gerard J., (Retired), 24 Clark St., Boston, 02109-1127
O'Sullivan, Raymond S., (Retired), 24 Clark St., Boston, 02109-1103
Oates, Thomas F., (Retired), 24 Clark St., Boston, 02109-1103
Owens, Leroy E., (Retired)
Pearsall, William T., (Retired), 60 William Cardinal O'Connell Way, Boston, 02114-2729
Phinn, Paul A., (Retired), 265 Walker St., Box 331, Falmouth, 02541-0331
Poirier, Vincent J., (Retired), 206 Linden Ponds Way, OW614, Hingham, 02043-3767
Powers, Thomas F., V.F., (Retired)
Pratt, Lawrence E., (Retired), 112 Old Wharf Rd, E-3, Dennis Port, 02639-2230
Quinn, Kenneth, (Retired)
Rafferty, James F., V.F., (Retired), 1130 Washington St., Weymouth, 02189-1932
Regan, Michael J., (Retired), 60 William Cardinal O'Connell Way, Boston, 02114-2729
Riley, James H., (Retired), 66 Emerald Dr., Lynn, 01904-1255
Robinson, Joseph P., (Retired), 90 Concord Rd., Bedford, 01730-1539
Rondeau, Lawrence J., (Retired), 161 Federal St., Salem, 01970-3297
Rouse, C. Paul, (Retired), P.O. Box 347, Boston, 02127-0003
Ruggeri, Joseph A., (Retired), 224 Grosbeak Ln., Naples, FL 34114-3013
Sallese, Albert J., (Retired), 1158 Main St., Bellingham, 02019-1597
Salmon, William F., (Retired)
Santerre, Richard R., (Retired), 1573 Cambridge St., Cambridge, 02138-4370
Schatzel, John E., (Retired), P.O. Box 601, Bryantville, 02327-0601
Serena, Edward T., (Retired), 40 South Meadow Village, Unit 6, Carver, 02330-1802
Sheehan, Mark S., (Retired)
Smyth, Joseph P., (Retired), 46 Laurel Ct., Nashua, NH 03062-4461
Soucy, Robert P., (Retired), 112 Old Wharf Rd., E-3, Dennis Port, 02639-2230
Stankard, Albert H.
Sullivan, E. Paul, (Retired), 822 Orleans Rd., Harwich, 02645-3037
Sullivan, Eugene P., (Retired)
Sullivan, Lawrence F., (Retired), 102 Brooksby Village Dr., Unit 317, Peabody, 01960-1460
Tackney, John P., (Retired)
Thomas, Robert W., (Retired), 3115 Corrib Dr., Tallahassee, FL 32309-3307
Tighe, Leonard J., (Retired), 12 Paulman Cir., West Roxbury, 02132
Tully, Eugene D., (Retired), 66 Brooks Dr., 02184-3839
Tynan, Desmond A., (Retired)
Vartzelis, George D., (Retired), 1573 Cambridge St., Cambridge, 02138-4370
Verrill, O. Wendell, V.F., (Retired), 91 Wompatuck Rd., Hingham, 02043-1175
Walsh, Aidan J., (Retired)
Wasnewski, Richard P., (Retired), 46 Village St., Medway, 02053-1048
Wyndham, Thomas F., (Retired), 9 Settlers Ter., Box 801, Eastham, 02642-0801.

Senior Vicars:
Rev.—
Kelly, John E.

Unassigned: For contact information please call or write: Clergy Personnel Office, 66 Brooks Dr., Braintree, MA 02184-3839. Tel: 617-746-5866; Fax: 617-746-5614.
Rev. Msgrs.—
Coyle, Arthur M., (Retired)
Parfienczyk, Stanislaw
Revs.—
Foster, Joseph R.
Moran, Terence J., V.F.
Randone, Michael C.

Permanent Deacons: For contact information please call or write: Office of Diaconal Life & Ministry, 66 Brooks Dr., Braintree, MA 02184-3839. Tel: 617-746-5649.
Acampora, Andrew J.
Agudelo, Jose N.
Alence, Robert W.
Alexander, John F.
An Ros, Peter
Anthony, Thomas A.
Baltier, Matthew
Balzarini, Robert
Barry, John D.
Beagan, John H.
Beatrice, Lee A.
Belmonte, Joseph A.
Bilotta, Richard F.
Biron, Donald R.
Bloom, Laurence J.
Booker, Timothy A.
Borkush, George J.
Brady, Robert F.
Breadmore, Paul
Breen, Robert F.
Brennan, Richard J.
Brent, John A.
Bresnahan, John M.
Brooks, David A.
Brown, Rafael
Bulpett, Dean C.
Burch, Gregory J.
Burke, Francis X.
Burke, Thomas P.
Burkly, John J.
Burns, Daniel R.
Buttrick, Stephen M.
Camacho, Teodoro
Canova, Joseph A.
Carey, John J.
Carroll, Paul F.
Caruso, Philip
Castillo, Jesus
Cavanaugh, Michael J.
Clough, Charles I.
Coletti, Paul G.
Connelly, Christopher Z.
Constantino, Anthony J.
Cooley, Joseph
Corbett, Francis J.
Cordeau, Richard W.
Cornell, Charles A.
Coughlin, Paul D.
Cruz, Nicholas
Curren, Michael F.
Cussen, Richard J.
Czajkowski, John
Delio, Richard P.
Dello Russo, Francis B.
DeSousa, Carlos A.
DiBello, Phillip T.
Donoghue, Leo J.
Donohue, Timothy F.
Dorlus, Joseph E.
Doty, Alan J.
Doucette, Raymond E.
Dow, Paul A.
Dwyer, William A.
Elibero, Edward P.
Escotto, George C.
Fagan, Joseph M. Jr.
Fajardo, Jose
Fernandez, Osvaldo A.
Ferraro, Charles A.
Ferrazzi, Charles J.
Ferreira dos Santos, Elcio
Field, Richard P. Jr.
Fitzgerald, Brendan A.
Flocco, Joseph R.
Fonseca, Marcio O.
Frias, Alvaro Arsenio
Gabriel, George M.
Gatto, Vincent J.
Ghioni, David R.
Giangiordano, David
Giordano, Edward S.
Greer, James F.
Grimley, Edward J.
Guerrier, Joseph Breyere
Guerrini, Patrick E.
Hall, Charles A.
Hanafin, Charles
Hanson, Herbert C.
Hardcastle, Philip P.
Hardy, Gerard J.
Harrington, Joseph P.
Henry, Martin W.
Herrera, Luciano
Hickey, Michael C.
Hidalgo, Nelson J.
Higgins, Geoffrey W.
Hinkle, James T.
Hoaglund, Robert I.
Holderried, Joseph E.
Hopgood, Joseph J.
Horgan, Frederick B.
Horne, Robert P.
Hulme, John A.
Hunt, John C.
Hwang, Augustine J.
Iacono, Paul
Iraola, Alejandro
Jackson, William M.
Joens, Michael C.
Jones, Jonathan F.
Joy, Richard T.
Kane, William F.
Kean, Brian K.
Kearney, James T.
Keefe, Arthur J.
Kelley, Charles
Kerns, William E.
Kim, Cheonil
King, Clifford D.
Kline, Paul M.
Kobrenski, John
Koffel, William B.
Koza, John
L'Italien, George G.
LaFond, Philip H.
Landry, Charles
LaTorre, Pedro
Laws, Brian H.
League, Howard C.
LeDuc, Roland
Leo, Vincent J.
MacDonald, Joseph E.
Maher, Timothy J.
Maloney, William F.
Manzi, James A.
Markham, Michael J.
Martin, Kevin P.
Martinez, Orlando
McCormick, Kelley B.
McHugh, Francis W.
McLaughlin, James V.
Mejia, Franklin A.
Menendez, Silvo J.
Mesa, Ricardo M.
Montes, Eddy M.
Mora, Eduardo R.
Moreira, Cleyton
Morel, Pablo
Morey, Russell W.
Mosely, Jonathan
Mott, Michael M.
Murphy, Steven J.
Murray, John P.
Naveo, Jose D.
Nelson, Daniel C.
Newton, Philip J.
Nguyen, Hon H.
Nguyen, T. Van
Nguyen, Van-Vuong
Nicholson, John D.
Nickley, Joseph T. Jr.
Nieves, Alfredo
O'Donnell, Thomas L.
O'Shea, Thomas L.
Oles, Kenneth W.
Ortiz, Jesus M.
Papik, Stephen M.
Patino, Jorge A.
Peabody, Eric T.
Peltak, Douglas P.
Pena, Jesus M.
Penney, Everett F.
Pepi, John W.
Perez-Rodriguez, Jose
Piazza, Louis J.
Pierce, John B.

Proulx, William R.
Radford, Richard F.
Ramrath, Joseph R.
Reidy, William K.
Rivera, Luis F.
Rivero, Victor R.
Rizzuto, Anthony P.
Robinson, Edwin J.
Rodrigues, Pedro P.
Rogers, Arthur F. Jr.
Rooney, Paul S.
Rosario, Manuel A.
Rossignol, Charles R.
Rumley, Mark E.
Russell, Robert
Ryan, Kenneth N.
Saint Sauveur, Guy C.
Shanahan, Allan R.
Shea, Brian
Sicuso, Anthony C.
Smith, Thomas A.
Soares, Alvaro J.
Spadoni, Reynold G.
Specht, Paul V.
Straub, Stanley A.
Sullivan, Daniel F.
Sullivan, John A.
Sumner, Neil J.
Sung, Francis
Theriault, James C.
Thompson, James
Tompkins, Michael P.
Torrens, Paulo C.
Torres, Jose B.
Torres, Pedro L.
Tran, Tam V.
Tremblay, Francis R.
Turner, J. Robert
Vandi, Dennis
Vargus, Julio C.
Velasquez, Edin
Vierra, Roger F.
Vitale, Paul D.
Walsh, Thomas M.
Webb, Charles P.
Webster, Donald W.
Wheeler, Raymond A.
Whipple, John E.
Winn, Kevin J.
Ynfante, Cristino
Balestracci, Alfred O.
Bankowski, Paul F.
Bower, Charles H.
Boyle, John F.
Breinlinger, Martin E.
Capomaccio, John J.
Chisholm, Finley H.
Cloonan, Paul M.
Connor, John P.
Creutz, Edward F.
DeSousa, Manoel B., (Brazil)
Dunn, Daniel A.
Dzuris, Robert W.
Fenton, Jack H.
Gaffney, Francis M.
Gagne, Ronald D.
Gagnon, Raymond A.
Gardyna, Henry A.
Gaudreau, Robert J.
Geneus, Alfred J.
Guerin, Bertrand H.
Hanlon, Thomas H.
Hardin, Howard P.
Hardy, John W.
Iwanowicz, Michael A.
Jennette, John F.
LaPointe, Norman P.
Leavitt, James P.
Lloyd, Barry V.
MacKinnon, William J.
Marchant, Thomas W.
Markey, Paul G.
Martin, Leo A.
McHugh, John W.
Menz, John R.
Messina, Joseph M.
Miles, Walter J.
Moschetto, Samuel J.
Murphy, Alfred L.
Nagle, William V.
Patrick, Alexander J.
Perea, Antonio M.
Quiles, Francisco M.
Quiles, Jesus M.
Ryan, Gerald P.
Sanchez, Tomas E.
Santosuosso, Alfred E.
Sheedy, Louis W.
Spiri, Guy J.
Stenstrom, Eugene V.
Sullivan, Charles E.
Talbot, William N.
Valeri, Frank A.
Welch, Henry M.
Wise, John W.

INSTITUTIONS LOCATED IN DIOCESE

[A] SEMINARIES, ARCHDIOCESAN

BOSTON. *St. John Seminary* (1884) 127 Lake St., Brighton, 02135. Tel: 617-254-2610;
Fax: 617-787-2336; Email: contact@sjs.edu; Web: www.sjs.edu. Rev. Msgr. James P. Moroney, B.A., S.T.L., S.T.B., Rector. Lay Teachers 9; Priests 23; Students 142; Total Enrollment 142.

School of Theology Rev. Msgr. James P. Moroney, B.A., S.T.L., S.T.B., Rector.

Full-time Faculty: Revs. Joseph Briody, Prof.; Romanus Cessario, O.P., B.A., Theological Advisor to the Rector & Prof.; James J. Conn, S.J., Prof.; Dr. Janet Hunt, Dir., Music & Prof.; Rev. Msgr. John R. McLaughlin, Dir. Spiritual Formation; Rev. Dennis McManus, Prof.; Rev. Msgr. Cornelius M. McRae, Assoc. Spiritual Dir., (Retired); Prof. Paul Metilly, Interim Dir. Academic Formation; Rev. Msgr. Marc Caron, Dir. Sacred Liturgy; Revs. Christopher K. O'Connor, A.B., M.Div., Ph.L., S.T.L., Vice Rector & Prof.; David A. Pignato, Dir., Pre-Theology & Prof.; Edward M. Riley, B.S., M.Div., Dir., Pastoral Formation & Dean, Men; Stephen E. Salocks, Prof.; Joseph F. Scorzello, Spiritual Dir. & Prof.; Raymond Van De Moortell, Dir. Human Formation, Librarian & Prof..; Michael MacInnis, O.F.M./I.C., Dir. Spiritual Formation; Ryan Connors, Moral Theology.

Adjunct Faculty: Dr. Angelica Avcikurt, Prof.; Dr. Philip Crotty, Prof.; Mrs. Maureen DeBernardi, Registrar; Dr. Stephen Fahrig, O.M.V., B.S., S.T.L., S.T.D., Prof.; Mr. Richard Flaherty, Dir., Finances & Operation; Revs. John J. Grimes, S.T.M., Ph.D., Prof.; Peter W. Grover, O.M.V., B.A., S.T.B., S.T.M., Prof.; Rev. Msgr. Robert Johnson, Prof.; Rev. Mark A. Mahoney, Prof.; Dr. Leonard Maluf, Prof.; Rev. Mark W. Murphy, Prof.; Dr. Ann Orlando, Prof.; Dr. Richard A. Spinello, Prof.; Revs. Michael Seewald; Anthony Ward, S.M.; Raymond Van De Moortell, Librarian.

The Theological Institute for the New Evangelization, St. John Seminary, 66 Brooks Dr., 02184. Tel: 617-779-4104; Fax: 617-746-5459; Email: aldona.lingertat@sjs.edu; Web: www.sjs.edu. Rev. Christopher K. O'Connor, A.B., M.Div., Ph.L., S.T.L., Pres. & Dir. Certificate Program; Dr. Aldona Lingertat, B.A., M.A., Ph.D., Vice Pres., Admin. & Dir. Master of Arts in Ministry Prog.; Rev. Msgr. James P. Moroney, B.A., S.T.L., S.T.B.; Dr. Stephen Fahrig, O.M.V., B.S., S.T.L., S.T.D., Dir. Master of Theological Studies, Special Asst. Pres. & Assoc. Dean. Lay Teachers 9; Priests 12; Students 113; Total Enrollment 145.

TI Faculty: Revs. Christopher K. O'Connor, A.B., M.Div., Ph.L., S.T.L., Pres. & Dir. Certificate Program; Wayne L. Belschner, A.B., M.Div., S.T.L., Prof.; Very Rev. George P. Evans, V.F., A.B., M.Div., S.T.L., S.T.D., Prof.; Dr. Angela Franks, B.A., M.A., Ph.D., Dir. Master of Theological Studies Prog. & Prof.; Mrs. Susan J. Kay, B.A., M.Ed., Prof.; Rev. James J. Laughlin, A.B., M.Div., J.C.L., Prof.; Dr. Aldona Lingertat, B.A., M.A., Ph.D., Vice Pres. Admin. & Dir. Master of Arts in Ministry Prog.; Rev. Brian E. Mahoney, Prof.; Ms. MaryAnn McLaughlin, B.A., M.A., Prof. Spiritual Formation; Rev. Thomas F. Nestor, A.B., M.Div., Ph.D., Prof.; Mr. Ken Meltz, A.B., M.A., Liturgical Consultant; Rev. Edward M. Riley, B.S., M.Div., Dir. Field Education; Very Rev. Paul E. Ritt, V.F., A.B., M.Div., S.T.L., S.T.D., Prof.; Revs. Eric F. Cadin, M.Div., S.T.L., Prof.; John E. Sassani, A.B., M.Div., Spiritual Formation; Eric M. Bennett, B.S., M.S.P.T., S.T.B., S.T.L., Prof.; Ms. Jane Devlin, B.A., J.D., J.C.L., Prof.; Celia Sirois, B.A., M.A., Prof.; Dr. Monika Verploegen, B.A., M.A., Ph.D., Formation; Stephen Fahrig, B.S., S.T.L., S.T.D., Dir. Master of Theological Studies, Special Asst. Pres. & Assoc. Dean.

WESTON. *Pope Saint John XXIII National Seminary* (1964) 558 South Ave., Weston, 02493.
Tel: 781-899-5500; Fax: 781-899-9057; Email: seminary@psjs.edu; Web: www.psjs.edu. Very Rev. Brian R. Kiely, V.E., Rector & Pres.; Rev. Msgr. James Mongelluzzo, M.A., S.T.L., S.T.D.; Revs. Michael A. Alfano, M.Div.; Paul D. Helfrich, B.H., J.D., S.T.B., M.A.; Paul E. Miceli, M.Div., D.Min.; William F. Murphy, M.Div., M.Ch.Sp.; Mark S. Yavarone, O.M.V., M.Div., M.A., Ph.D.; Dr. John J. Clabeaux, M.A., Ph.D.; Dr. Anthony W. Keaty, B.A., M.A., M.Div., Ph.D., Academic Dean; Dr. John F. Millard, M.A., Ph.D.; Barbara Mullen-Neem, Librarian. A Major National Seminary open to men over thirty studying for the diocesan and religious priesthood. Lay Teachers 3; Priests 9; Students 62.

[B] SEMINARIES, RELIGIOUS OR SCHOLASTICATES

BOSTON. *Oblate Provincialate*, 2 Ipswich St., Boston, 02215-3607. Tel: 617-536-4141; Fax: 617-536-7016; Email: omv.office@verizon.net; Web: www.omvusa.org. Revs. James Walther, O.M.V., Prov.; Thomas Cannon, O.M.V., Treas. St. Ignatius Province of the Oblates of the Virgin Mary, Inc.

Priests of the Province on Special Assignment:.

Philippines: Revs. Lino Estadilla, O.M.V.; Gerardo Joaquin, O.M.V.; Nnamdi Moneme, O.M.V.; Gregory Short, O.M.V.

Our Lady of Grace Seminary, 1105 Boylston St., Boston, 02215-3604. Tel: 617-266-5999;
Fax: 617-247-7576; Email: tcarzon@omvusa.org; Web: www.omvusa.org. Revs. Thomas Carzon, O.M.V., S.T.L., Rector; Peter W. Grover, O.M.V., B.A., S.T.B., S.T.M., Supr.; Shawn Monahan, O.M.V., Novice Master; John Luong, Dir. St. Ignatius Province of the Oblates of the Virgin Mary, Inc. Lay Teachers 2; Priests 4; Students 9; Religious Teachers 2.

BROOKLINE. *Redemptoris Mater Archdiocesan Missionary Seminary*, 774 Boylston St., Chestnut Hill, 02467-2501. Tel: 617-879-9813;
Tel: 617-879-9814; Fax: 617-879-0170. Revs. Antonio F. Medeiros, Pres.; Roderick A. Crispo, O.F.M., Spiritual Care Svcs.; Lukasz M. Wisniewski, Vice Pres.; George L. Szal, S.M., Spiritual Care Svcs. Clergy 4; Students 23.

FRAMINGHAM. *Sylva Maria* (1952) 567 Salem End Rd., Framingham, 01702-5599. Tel: 508-879-6711; Email: sonskevin@gmail.com; Web: www.sonsofmary.com.ph. Rev. Robert Rivard, F.M.S.I., Office Councilor; Bro. Kevin Courtney, F.M.S.I., Coord. House and Novitiate of the Sons of Mary, Health of the Sick. Brothers 4; Priests 3.

Personnel: Revs. John Coss, F.M.S.I.; John Wallace, F.M.S.I.

NEWTON. *The Ecclesiastical Faculty at Boston College* (known as The Ecclesiastical Faculty, an academic department within the Boston College School of Theology and Ministry) 140 Commonwealth Ave., Newton, 02467. Tel: 617-552-6501;
Fax: 617-552-0811; Email: stm@bc.edu; Web: www.bc.edu/stm. Revs. William P. Leahy, S.J., Ph.D., Pres.; Mark S. Massa, S.J., Dean; Esther Griswold, Librarian. Lay Teachers 20; Priests 11; Sisters 1; Students 400.

[C] COLLEGES AND UNIVERSITIES

BOSTON. *Emmanuel College*, 400 The Fenway, Boston, 02115. Tel: 617-735-9715; Fax: 617-735-9877; Email: president@emmanuel.edu; Web: www.emmanuel.edu. Sr. Janet Eisner, S.N.D., Ph.D., Pres. Emmanuel College; Rev. John P. Spencer, S.J., Vice Pres. Mission & Ministry. Lay Teachers 94; Priests 1; Sisters 1; Students 1,860.

NEWTON. **Boston College* (1863) (Coed) Chestnut Hill, 02467. Tel: 617-552-8000; Web: www.bc.edu. Rev. William P. Leahy, S.J., Ph.D., Pres.; David Quigley, Ph.D., Provost; Thomas Wall, Univ. Librarian. Lay Teachers 753; Priests 29; Sisters 4; Students 14,170.

Morrissey College of Arts and Sciences (1863)
Tel: 617-552-2393; Fax: 617-552-1383. Rev. Gregory Kaischeur, S.J., Dean. Students 5,995.

Graduate School of the Morrissey College of Arts and Sciences (1925) Tel: 617-552-3268;
Fax: 617-552-3700. Rev. Gregory Kalscheur, S.J., Dean. Students 815.

School of Law (1929) Tel: 617-552-4340;
Fax: 617-552-2851. Vincent Rougeau, J.D., Dean. Students 368.

Woods College of Advancing Studies (1929)
Tel: 617-552-3900; Fax: 617-552-3199. Rev. James P. Burns, I.V.D., Dean. Students 551.

Graduate School of Social Work (1936)
Tel: 617-552-4020; Fax: 617-552-2374. Gautam Yadama, Ph.D., Dean. Students 533.

Carroll School of Management (1938)
Tel: 617-552-8420; Fax: 617-552-2593. Andrew C. Boynton, Ph.D., Dean. Students 2,171.

Carroll Graduate School of Management (1957)
Tel: 617-552-8420; Fax: 617-552-2593. Andrew C. Boynton, Ph.D., Dean. Students 541.

Connell School of Nursing (1947) Tel: 617-552-4250;
Fax: 617-552-0745. Susan Gennaro, D.S.N., Dean. Students 615.

Lynch School of Education (1952) Tel: 617-552-4200; Fax: 617-552-0812. Stanton Wortham, Ph.D., Dean. Students 614.

Connell Graduate School of Nursing (1994)

Tel: 617-552-4250; Fax: 617-552-0745. Susan Gennaro, D.S.N., Dean. Students 221.

Lynch Graduate School of Education (1994)
Tel: 617-552-4200; Fax: 617-552-0812. Stanton Wortham, Ph.D., Dean.

The School of Theology and Ministry (2008)
Tel: 617-552-6501; Fax: 617-552-0811. Rev. Thomas D. Stegman, S.J., Dean; Esther Griswold, Librarian. Students 272.

NORTH ANDOVER. *Merrimack College*, 315 Turnpike St., North Andover, 01845-5800. Tel: 978-837-5000 ; Fax: 978-837-5222; Web: www.merrimack.edu. Christopher F. Hopey, Ph.D., Pres.; Carol Glod, Ph. D., Provost; Sara Brazda, Vice Pres., Devel. & Alumni Affairs; Jeffrey Doggett, Executive Vice Pres. & Chief of Staff; Allison Gill, Dean of Students; Rev. Keith Hollis, O.S.A., Dir., Campus Ministry. Lay Teachers 180; Priests 5; Graduate Students 500; Full-Time Undergraduate Students 3,200.

Our Mother of Good Counsel Monastery (1947)
Tel: 978-837-5213; Fax: 978-837-5269. In Res. Revs. Edward J. Enright, O.S.A., Prof. Religious & Theological Studies; Raymond F. Dlugos, O.S.A., Vice Pres. Mission & Student Affairs & Prior St. Ambrose Friary; Richard Piatt, O.S.A., Dir. Rogers Center for the Arts; Stephen Curry, Asst. Dean, School of Educ. & Public Policy & Treas. St. Ambrose Friary.

WESTON. *Regis College* (1927) 235 Wellesley St., Weston, 02493-1571. Tel: 781-768-7000; Fax: 781-768-8339; Email: admission@regiscollege.edu; Web: www.regiscollege.edu. Dr. Antoinette Hays, Ph.D., R.N., Pres.; Mr. Daniel P. Leahy, Dir. Center for Ministry & Service; Jane Peck, Librarian Dir. Lay Teachers 261; Sisters of St. Joseph 4; Students 2,069.

[D] HIGH SCHOOLS, PRIVATE

BOSTON. *Boston College High School*, 150 Morrissey Blvd., Boston, 02125. Tel: 617-436-3900; Fax: 617-929-9459; Email: bconleysj@bchigh.edu; Web: www.bchigh.edu/. Rev. Brian J. Conley, S.J., Supr.; Ms. Grace Cotter Regan, Pres.; Mr. Stephen Hughes, Prin.; Revs. Joseph T. Bennett, S.J., Tel: 617-929-9482; Jon D. Fuller, S.J.; Joseph J. Bruce, S.J.; Francis J. Moy, S.J.; J. Allan Loftus, S.J.; James W. O'Neil, S.J., Tel: 617-929-9452; John A. Predmone, S.J.; Martin G. Shaughnessy, S.J.; Bro. Donald J. Murray, S.J., Tel: 617-436-3900. Lay Teachers 146; Priests 2; Sisters 1; Students 1,582.

Cathedral High School, Inc., 74 Union Park St., Boston, 02118. Tel: 617-542-2325; Fax: 617-542-1745; Email: admissions@cathedralhighschool.net; Web: www.cathedralhighschool.net. Dr. Oscar Santos, Headmaster. Lay Teachers 27; Sisters 3; Students 335; Staff 17.

Catholic Memorial School, (Grades 7-12), (Boys) 235 Baker St., Boston, 02132-4395. Web: www.catholicmemorial.org. Dr. Peter F. Folan, Pres.; Thomas Beatty, Prin. Congregation of Christian Brothers. Boys 698; Brothers 3; Lay Teachers 56.

Cristo Rey Boston High School Corporate Work Study Program, Inc., 100 Savin Hill Ave., Boston, 02125. Tel: 617-825-2580; Fax: 617-825-2613; Email: jthielman@cristoreyboston.org. Jeff Thielman, Contact Person.

Cristo Rey Boston High School, Inc., 100 Savin Hill Ave., Boston, 02125. Tel: 617-825-2580; Fax: 617-825-2613; Email: jmacdonald@cristoreyboston.org. James J. MacDonald, Pres. & Contact Person; Beth Degnan, Prin. Lay Teachers 20; Students 375.

Saint Joseph Preparatory High School, 617 Cambridge St., Boston, 02134-2460. Tel: 617-254-8383 (School Office); Tel: 617-783-4747 (Guidance Office); Fax: 617-254-0240; Email: thomas.nunan@saintjosephprep.org; Web: www.saintjosephprep.org. Thomas Nunan, Head of School; Linda Walkins, Librarian. Sponsored by Sisters of St. Joseph of Boston. Boys 100; Girls 185; Lay Teachers 25; Sisters 5.

BRAINTREE. *Archbishop Williams High School, Inc.* (1949) 80 Independence Ave., 02184. Tel: 781-843-3636; Fax: 781-843-3782; Email: mvolonnino@awhs.org; Web: www.awhs.org. Dr. Michael Volonnino, Prin.; Dennis M. Duggan Jr., Esq., Pres.; Joanna Sands, Librarian. Sisters 1; Students 589; Teachers 67.

BROCKTON. *Cardinal Spellman High School, Inc.* (1958) 738 Court St., Brockton, 02302. Tel: 508-583-6875; Fax: 508-580-1977; Email: cshs@spellman.com; Web: www.spellman.com. Daniel J. Hodes, M.A., Pres.; Dorothy Lynch, Prin.; Diane McDonough, Librarian. Brothers 1; Lay Teachers 520; Students 600.

CAMBRIDGE. *Matignon High School, Inc.*, 1 Matignon Rd., Cambridge, 02140. Tel: 617-876-1212; Fax: 617-661-3905; Web: www.matignon-hs.org. Thomas F. Galligani, Headmaster; Joseph DiSarcina, Prin.; Patricia D'Angelo, Vice Prin. College Preparatory. Lay Staff 50; Religious 1; Students 445.

DANVERS. *St. John's Preparatory School* (1907) (Grades 6-12), 72 Spring St., Danvers, 01923. Tel: 978-774-1050; Fax: 978-774-5069; Email: ehardiman@stjohnsprep.org; Web: www.stjohnsprep.org. Edward Hardiman, Ph.D., Headmaster; Keith Crowley, Ph.D., Prin. Day Students. (Boys) Boys 1,492; Brothers 4; Lay Teachers 173.

DEDHAM. *Ursuline Academy* (1946) (Grades 7-12), 85 Lowder St., Dedham, 02026-4299. Tel: 781-326-6161; Fax: 781-326-4898; Email: klevesque@ursulineacademy.net; Web: www.ursulineacademy.net. Mrs. Rosann Whiting, Pres.; Mrs. Kate Levesque, Prin.; Rose O'Koren, Librarian. Sponsored by Ursuline Sisters of the Central Province, St. Louis, MO.College Preparatory School for Girls. Girls 432; Lay Teachers 39; Total Staff 73.

EVERETT. *Pope John XXIII High School, Inc.* (1966) 888 Broadway, Everett, 02149. Tel: 617-389-0240; Fax: 617-389-2201; Email: info@popejohnhs.org; Web: www.popejohnhs.org. Kathleen Donovan, Pres.; Mary Ann DiMarco, Prin.; Maria Touet, Librarian. Lay Teachers 19; Sisters 1; Students 250; Staff 12.

FRAMINGHAM. *Marian High School, Inc.*, 273 Union Ave., Framingham, 01702. Tel: 508-875-7646; Fax: 508-875-0838; Email: mbaril@marianhigh.org; Email: jermilio@marianhigh.org; Web: www.marianhigh.org. Mr. John J. Ermilio, Pres. & Prin. Lay Teachers 22; Sisters 2; Students 225.

HINGHAM. *Notre Dame Academy* (1853) 1073 Main St., Hingham, 02043. Tel: 781-749-5930; Fax: 781-749-8366; Email: president@ndahingham.com; Web: www.ndahingham.com. Annemarie Kenneally, Pres. Clergy 1; Lay Teachers 51; Sisters 2; (Girls) 550.

KINGSTON. *Sacred Heart School System, Inc.*, (Grades 7-12), 399 Bishops Hwy., Kingston, 02364-2098. Tel: 781-585-7511; Fax: 781-585-1249; Email: admissions@sacredheartkingston.com; Web: www.sacredheartkingston.com. Sr. Myra Rodgers, C.D.P., Pres.; Ed Spadoni, CFO; Tracey Merrill; Dr. Michael Gill, Ed.D., Prin.; Mr. Shaun Morgan, Vice Prin. for Academics; Ms. Ann Taylor, Dir. Admissions; Dave Ellis, Dir., Communs. & Mktg.; Mrs. Susan Gallitano, Dir., Guidance. Lay Teachers 29; Students 339.

LAWRENCE. *Central Catholic High School of Lawrence, Inc.*, 300 Hampshire St., Lawrence, 01841. Tel: 978-682-0260; Fax: 978-685-2707; Email: dkeller@centralcatholic.net; Web: www.centralcatholic.net. Bro. Thomas P. Long, F.M.S., Pres.; Doreen A. Keller, Prin.; Kristina Keleher, Librarian. Conducted by the Marist Brothers of the Schools. Lay Teachers 79; Religious 2; Students 1,340.

Notre Dame Cristo Rey High School (2004) (Co-Ed) 303 Haverhill St., Lawrence, 01840. Tel: 978-689-8222; Fax: 978-689-8728. Sr. Maryalyce Gilfeather, S.N.D.deN., Ph.D., Pres.; Anthony Zavagnin, Prin. Clergy 2; Lay Teachers 23; Priests 1; Students 278.

LOWELL. *Lowell Catholic High School, Inc.*, 530 Stevens St., Lowell, 01851. Tel: 978-452-1794; Email: ed2000@tiac.net. Mr. Edward J. Quinn, Prin. Lay Teachers 18; Sisters 2; Students 280.

MALDEN. *Malden Catholic High School*, 99 Crystal St., Malden, 02148. Tel: 781-322-3098; Fax: 781-397-0573; Email: tyrrelle@maldencatholic.org; Web: www.maldencatholic.org. Edward C. Tyrrell, Headmaster; Bro. Thomas Puccio, C.F.X., Prin.; Karen Davidson-Heller, Librarian. Xaverian Brothers. Boys 575; Brothers 3; Lay Teachers 45.

METHUEN. *Presentation of Mary Academy* (1958) 209 Lawrence St., Methuen, 01844. Tel: 978-682-9391; Fax: 978-975-3595; Email: rmredman@pmamethuen.org; Web: www.pmamethuen.org. Rose Maria Redman, Head of School. Sisters of the Presentation of Mary. Clergy 1; Lay Teachers 26; Sisters 2; Students 184.

MILTON. *Fontbonne Academy* (1954) 930 Brook Rd., Milton, 02186. Tel: 617-696-3241; Fax: 617-696-7688; Web: www.fontbonneacademy.org. Mary Ellen Barnes, Prin.; Florence Lathrop, Librarian. Lay Teachers 35; Sisters of St. Joseph 5; Students 300.

NEEDHAM. *St. Sebastian's School, Inc.*, (Grades 7-12), 1191 Greendale Ave., Needham, 02492. Tel: 781-449-5200; Fax: 781-449-5630; Email: jack_doherty@stsebs.org; Web: www.stsebs.org. Mr. William L. Burke III, Headmaster; Revs. John F. Arens; John U. Paris. Boys 378; Lay Teachers 59; Priests 2.

NEWTON. *Country Day School of the Sacred Heart*, (Grades 5-12), 785 Centre St., Newton, 02158. Tel: 617-244-4246; Fax: 617-965-5313; Email: alazure@newtoncountryday.org; Web: www.newtoncountryday.org. Sr. Barbara Rogers, R.S.C.J., Prin.

Boston Academy of the Sacred Heart Girls 380; Lay Teachers 70; Students 380; Religious of the Sacred Heart 1.

Mount Alvernia High School, (Grades 7-12), 790 Centre St., Newton, 02458. Tel: 617-964-4766 (Convent); Tel: 617-969-2260 (School); Fax: 617-969-4246; Email: MAHSinfo@mountalverniahs.org; Web: mountalverniahs.org. Eileen McLaughlin, Head of School; Kathleen Colin, Asst. Head of School; Erin DiGuardia, Devel. Advancement & Alumnae Rels.; Meredith O'Brien, Library Svcs. Missionary Franciscan Sisters of the Immaculate Conception. Girls 190; Lay Teachers 20; Sisters 2; Total Staff 36.

PEABODY. *Bishop Fenwick High School, Inc.* (1959) 99 Margin St., Peabody, 01960. Tel: 978-587-8300; Fax: 978-587-8309; Email: btz@fenwick.org; Web: www.fenwick.org. Bro. Thomas Zoppo, F.S.C., Prin., Chief Admin. & Contact Person; Diane Smith, Librarian. Lay Teachers 40; Sisters 2; Students 575.

READING. *Austin Preparatory School*, (Grades 6-12), 101 Willow St., Reading, 01867. Tel: 781-944-4900; Fax: 781-944-7530; Email: jhickey@austinprep.org; Web: www.austinprep.org. James Hickey, Ph.D., Headmaster; Rev. Patrick S. Armano, Chap. Administrators 8; Clergy 1; Lay Teachers 71; Students 745.

TYNGSBOROUGH. *Academy of Notre Dame* (1854) Tyngsborough, 01879. Tel: 978-649-7611; Fax: 978-649-2909; Web: www.ndatyngsboro.org. Sr. Patricia Conner, S.N.D., Prin.; Kathy Arsneault, Librarian. Faculty 27; Girls 174; Lay Teachers 26; Religious 1; Sisters of Notre Dame de Namur 1.

WESTWOOD. *Xaverian Brothers High School* (1963) 800 Clapboardtree St., Westwood, 02090. Tel: 781-326-6392; Fax: 781-320-0458; Email: admin@xbhs.com; Web: www.xbhs.com. Dr. Jacob Conca, Prin.; Domenic Lalli, Prin. Xaverian Brothers. Boys 975; Brothers 3; Lay Teachers 77.

[E] ELEMENTARY SCHOOLS, ARCHDIOCESAN

DANVERS. *St. Mary of the Annunciation School*, 14 Otis St., Danvers, 01923. Tel: 978-774-0307; Fax: 978-750-4852; Email: sburrill@smadanvers.org; Web: www.smadanvers.org. Sharon Burrill, Prin. Lay Teachers 16; Students 157.

[F] MONTESSORI SCHOOLS

NEWTON. *Walnut Park Montessori School*, 47 Walnut Park, Newton, 02458. Tel: 617-969-9208; Fax: 617-969-6408; Email: office@walnutparkmontessori.org; Web: www.walnutparkmontessori.org. Nancy Fish, Head of School; Sr. Alice Mary Brady, C.S.J., Librarian. Lay Teachers 14; Religious 4; Students 148.

[G] ELEMENTARY SCHOOLS, PRIVATE

BOSTON. *St. Columbkille School, Inc.*, (Grades PreK-8), 25 Arlington St., Boston, 02135. Tel: 617-254-3110; Fax: 617-254-3161; Email: advancement@stcps.org; Web: www.stcps.org. Mr. William Gartside, Head of School; Alanna O'Grady, Media Specialist. Lay Teachers 32; Students 399.

Saint John Paul II Catholic Academy Inc., 2200 Dorchester Ave., Boston, 02124. Tel: 617-265-0019; Fax: 617-298-2926; Email: kbrandley@sjp2ca.org. Kate Brandley, Dir. Lay Teachers 86; Students 1,076.

Columbia Campus, 790 Columbia Rd., Dorchester, 02125. Tel: 617-265-0019. Claire Barton Sheridan, Prin. Students 360.

Lower Mills Campus, 2214 Dorchester Ave., Dorchester, 02124. Tel: 617-265-0019. Lisa Warshafsky, Prin. Students 275.

Neponset Campus, 239 Neponset Ave., Dorchester, 02122. Tel: 617-265-0019. Kate Brandley, Prin. Students 415.

Mother Caroline Academy (1993) 515 Blue Hill Ave., Dorchester, 02121. Tel: 617-427-1177; Fax: 617-427-7788; Email: info@mcaec.org; Web: www.mcaec.org. Annmarie Quezada, Headmaster

Mother Caroline Academy for Girls, Inc. Clergy 2; Lay Teachers 8; Students 71.

Nativity Preparatory School, (Grades 4-8), 39 Lamartine St., Jamaica Plain, 02130. Tel: 857-728-0031; Fax: 857-728-0037; Email: kmullins@nativityboston.org; Web: www.nativityboston.org. Kyle Mullins, Prin. A Jesuit Middle School.

Nativity Boston, Inc. Lay Teachers 15; Priests 1; (Boys) 73.

BRAINTREE. *Cardinal Cushing Centers*, 85 Washington St., 02184. Tel: 617-848-6250; Fax: 617-848-0640; Email: POmeara@cushingcenters.org; Web: www.Coletta.org. Peter O'Meara, Pres. Day School for multiple handicapped, developmentally delayed children, ages 4-22 years.

St. Coletta's and Cardinal Cushing Schools of MA, Inc. Lay Teachers 7; Students 24.

BROCKTON. *Trinity Catholic Academy, Inc.*, Upper Campus: 37 Erie Ave., Brockton, 02302. Tel: 508-583-6237; Fax: 508-583-6260; Email: dmoran@tcabrockton.org; Web: tcabrockton.org. Lower Campus: 631 N. Main St., Brockton, 02301. Michael A. Green, Ed.D., Regl. Dir.; Ms. Kristin Blanchette, Prin. Lower Campus; Jane Clifford, Librarian Lower Campus; Theresa Ballard, Librarian Upper Campus. Students 337; Unique 36.

GROTON. *Country Day School of the Holy Union* (1949) 14 Main St., Groton, 01450. Tel: 978-448-5646; Fax: 978-448-2392; Email: cdsgroton@yahoo.com; Web: www.cdsgroton.org. Sr. Yvette Ladurantaye, S.U.S.C., Prin. Lay Teachers 21; Holy Union Sisters 1; Students 230.

HANOVER. *Cardinal Cushing Centers, Inc.*, (Grades 1-12), 400 Washington St., Hanover, 02339. Tel: 781-826-6371; Fax: 781-826-1559; Email: POmeara@cushingcenters.org; Email: cbernardi@cushingcenters.org. Peter O'Meara, Pres. Lay Teachers 22; Students 114.

KINGSTON. *Sacred Heart School System, Inc.*, (Grades PreSchool-6), (Day School) 329 Bishops Hwy., Kingston, 02364. Tel: 781-585-2114; Fax: 781-585-6993; Email: admissions@sacredheartkingston.com; Web: www.sacredheartkingston.com. Sr. Myra Rodgers, C.D.P., Pres.; Kim Stoloski, Ed.D., Prin. (Preschool - 6); Sisters Lydia Steele, C.D.P., Vice Prin.-Operations; Angela Provost, C.D.P., Early Childhood Dir.; Ms. Ann Taylor, Admissions Dir.; Tracey Merrill, Dir. Lay Teachers 28; Students 399.

LAWRENCE. *Blessed Stephen Bellesini, O.S.A. Academy, Inc.* (2002) (Grades 5-8), 94 Bradford St., Lawrence, 01840-1003. Tel: 978-989-0004; Fax: 978-989-9404; Email: office@bellesiniacademy.org; Web: www.bellesiniacademy.org. Ms. Julie DiFilippo, Head of School. Lay Teachers 10; Students 116.

Lawrence Catholic Academy of Lawrence, Massachusetts, Inc., 101 Parker St., Lawrence, 01843. Tel: 978-683-5822; Fax: 978-683-1165; Email: jhernandez@lawrencecatholicacademy.org. Mr. Jorge Hernandez, Prin. Clergy 1; Lay Teachers 27; Students 405.

LOWELL. *Ste. Jeanne d'Arc*, 68 Dracut St., Lowell, 01854. Tel: 978-453-4114; Fax: 978-454-8304; Email: pmalo@sjdarc.org. Sr. Prescille Malo, Prin. Sisters 2; Students 282; Full-time 23.

MARLBOROUGH. *Our Lady Thrift Shop* (1973) 197 Pleasant St., Marlborough, 01752. Tel: 508-485-0740; Email: ssch@tiac.net. Sr. Ida M. Devoe, S.S.Ch., Officer of the Board. Religious 5.

NEWTON. *Jackson School Elementary*, (Grades K-6), 200 Jackson Rd., Newton, 02458-1428. Tel: 617-969-1537; Fax: 617-244-8596; Email: info@jacksonschool.org; Web: www.jacksonschool.org. Mrs. Susan G. Niden, Prin. Clergy 1; Lay Teachers 20; Students 150.

Jackson Walnut Park Educational Collaborative, Inc., (Grades PreSchool-6), 47 Walnut Park St., Newton, 02458. Tel: 617-686-0105; Tel: 617-969-9208; Fax: 617-969-6908; Email: victoria.londergan@cojboston.org; Web: www.jacksonschool.org. Victoria N. Londergan, Pres.; Mrs. Susan G. Niden, Prin. (Elementary); Stephanie Marcucci, Prin.; Sr. Diane Neumyer, C.S.J., Librarian. Clergy 2; Lay Teachers (Jackson) 25; Lay Teachers (Walnut Park) 150.

Mount Alvernia Academy, 20 Manet Rd., Newton, 02467. Tel: 617-527-7540; Fax: 617-527-7995; Email: bplunkett@maa.school; Web: www.maa.school. Barbara M. Plunkett, Prin. Lay Teachers 30; Students 296.

QUINCY. *Quincy Catholic Academy of Quincy, Massachusetts, Inc.*, 370 Hancock St., Quincy, 02171. Tel: 617-328-3830; Email: cathy.cameron@quincycatholicacademy.org. Ms. Cathy Cameron, Prin. Lay Teachers 30; Students 328.

TYNGSBOROUGH. *Academy of Notre Dame at Tyngsboro*, 180 Middlesex Rd., Tyngsborough, 01879. Tel: 978-649-7611; Fax: 978-649-2909; Email: jobrien@ndatyngsboro.org; Web: www.ndatyngsboro.org. John O'Brien, Pres. Lay Teachers 35; Sisters of Notre Dame de Namur 1; Students 430.

[H] SPECIAL SCHOOLS

METHUEN. *St. Ann's Home Special Needs School*, 100 A. Haverhill St., Methuen, 01844. Tel: 978-682-5276; Fax: 978-688-4932; Email: dgrandbois@st.annshome.org; Web: www.st.annshome.org. Mr. Denis Grandbois, Exec. Dir. Ungraded special needs school for emotionally disturbed and behaviorally disordered children. Administrators 11; Bed Capacity 159; Lay Teachers 38; Total Staff 300; Psychotherapists 20; Counselors 120; Residential Students 135; Day Students 68; Staff 23.

PEABODY. *Holy Childhood Nursery & Kindergarten* (1854) 5 Wheatland St., Peabody, 01960. Tel: 978-531-4733; Fax: 978-531-2468; Email: carmelite@verizon.net; Web: www.carmelitepreschool.com. Sr. Kathleen A. Bettencourt, I.N.S.C., Coord. & Co-Dir. Lay Teachers 5; Sisters 4; Students 80.

[I] CATHOLIC CHARITIES

BOSTON. *Catholic Charitable Bureau of the Archdiocese of Boston, Inc.* (1903) 51 Sleeper St., Boston, 02210. Tel: 617-482-5440; Fax: 617-451-0337; Email: info@ccab.org; Web: www.ccab.org. Ms. Deborah Kincade Rambo, L.I.C.S.W., Pres. Social Service Agency Total Clients Served (Across Eastern Massachusetts) 200,000.

El Centro Del Cardenal/Catholic Charities, 76 Union Park St., Boston, 02118. Tel: 617-542-9292; Fax: 617-542-6912. Ms. Elisabeth Zweig-Snippe, Contact Person.

Yawky Center for Early Ed & Care Catholic Charities, 185 Columbia Rd., Boston, 02121. Tel: 617-506-6930; Fax: 617-929-0453; Email: esther_garcia@ccab.org; Web: www.ccab.org. Sr. Esther Garcia, S.A., Dir. Community Based Agency of the Catholic Charitable Bureau of the Archdiocese of Boston, Inc.; Day Care. Franciscan Sisters of the Atonement 2.

[J] SOCIETY OF ST. VINCENT DE PAUL

STOUGHTON. *Society of St. Vincent DePaul, Central Office*, 18 Canton St., Stoughton, 02072. Tel: 781-344-3100; Fax: 781-341-4560; Email: ejresnick@svdpboston.org; Web: svdpboston.org. Mr. Edward J. Resnick, Exec. Dir.

[K] CHILD CARE AGENCIES

BOSTON. *Nazareth Child Care Center*, 19 St. Joseph St., Jamaica Plain, 02130. Tel: 617-522-4040; Fax: 617-983-0460; Email: pam-penton@ccab.org. Ms. Pamela J. Penton, Dir.
Catholic Charities dba Nazareth Child Care Center Capacity 83; Total Staff 18.

Nazareth Residence for Mothers and Children, 91 Regent St., Boston, 02119. Tel: 617-541-0100; Fax: 617-541-8781; Email: nazareth_residence@ccab.org. Sr. Mary Farren, R.G.S., Program Dir. Home for homeless mothers and children who are HIV positive. Capacity 9; Total in Residence 22; Total Staff 14; Total Families Assisted Annually 20.

METHUEN. *St. Ann's Home, Inc.*, 100A Haverhill St., Methuen, 01844. Tel: 978-682-5276; Fax: 978-688-4932; Email: dgrandbois@st.annshome.org; Web: www.st.annshome.org. Mr. Denis Grandbois, CEO; Marybeth Gilmore, Business Mgr. Bed Capacity 178; Children 200; Students 80; Total in Residence 145; Total Staff 360.

Residential Treatment Center, Tel: 978-692-5276; Fax: 978-688-4932. Children 165.

[L] GUIDANCE CENTERS

BOSTON. *St. Mary's Center for Women and Children* (1993) 90 Cushing Ave., Boston, 02125. Tel: 617-436-8600; Fax: 617-288-8961; Email: dhoutmeyers@stmaryscenterma.org; Web: www.stmaryscenterma.org. Ms. Deirdre Houtmeyers, Pres. Provides residential, education and training programs for women and children who are homeless or living in poverty. Total Staff 100; Clients Assisted Annually 600.

Salesian Boys & Girls Club (Central Unit) 150 Byron St., Boston, 02128. Tel: 617-567-6626; Fax: 617-568-3851; Email: sbgclub@juno.com; Web: www.salesianclub.com. Salesians of St. John Bosco. Total Staff 29; Total Assisted 3,250.

Orient Heights Unit, 150 Bryon St., Boston, 02128. Tel: 617-567-6626. Rev. John Nazzaro, S.D.B., Exec. Dir., Club Admin. & Rector. Salesian Staff: Rev. James Horan, S.D.B.; Bro. Bernard Dube, S.D.B.

[M] INFORMATION - CONFERENCE CENTERS

BOSTON. *Paulist Center*, 5 Park St., Boston, 02108. Tel: 617-742-4460; Fax: 617-720-5756; Email: imfo@paulistcenter.org; Web: www.paulistcenter.org. Revs. Michael B. McGarry, C.S.P., M.Div., M.A. Theology, Dir.; Charles Cunniff, C.S.P., Pastoral Assoc.; Susan Rutkowski, M.Div., Pastoral Min., Family Rel. Educ. & Social Justice; Patricia Simpson, M.Div., Pastoral Admin.; Peter Ghiloni, Pastoral Min., Liturgy & Music; Kristin Hauser, Pastoral Min., Young Adults
Missionary Society of St. Paul the Apostle in MA.

BROCKTON. *Chapel of Our Savior-Catholic Pastoral and Information Center* (1961) 475 Westgate Dr., Brockton, 02301-1819. Tel: 508-583-8357; Fax: 508-586-5510; Email: Jerrydigiralamo@gmail.com. Bro. Thomas Banacki, S.A., Dir./Guardian; Revs. Gerald DiGiralamo, S.A.; John F. Keane, (Retired); Bros. Louis Marek, S.A., Admin.; Savio McNeice, S.A.; Rev. Damian MacPherson, S.A., Chap. Brothers 3; Priests 2.

[N] SPECIAL HOSPITALS

BOSTON. *Franciscan Hospital for Children*, 30 Warren St., Brighton, 02135. Tel: 617-254-3800; Fax: 617-779-1119; Email: fch@fhfc.org; Web: www.fhfc.org. Mr. Paul Della Rocco, Pres. & CEO. General Pediatrics, Rehabilitation, Special Education, Mental Health Services & Home Care. Bed Capacity 100; Total Staff 650; Number Under Care 59,000; Day Program 90.

[O] SOCIAL SERVICES

BOSTON. *Chinese Catholic Pastoral Center*, 78 Tyler St., Boston, 02111-1831. Tel: 617-482-2949; Fax: 617-482-2949.

Little Sisters of the Assumption, Family Health Service, Inc. (1981) (Project Hope) 550 Dudley St., Boston, 02119. Tel: 617-442-1880; Fax: 617-238-0473; Email: mleonard@prohope.org; Web: www.prohope.org. Project Hope is a multi-service agency at the forefront of efforts in Boston to move families beyond homelessness and poverty. It provides low-income women with children with access to education, jobs, housing and emergency child care services; fosters their personal transformation; and works for broader systems change. Sisters 2; Total Staff 54; Total Assisted 1,000.

LAWRENCE. **M.I. Adult Day Health Center, Inc.*, 189 Maple St., Lawrence, 01841. Tel: 978-682-6321; Fax: 978-975-0050; Email: gerard_foley@mihcs.com; Web: www.mihcs.com. Covenant Health, Inc., 100 Ames Pond Dr., Ste. 102, Tewksbury, 01876. Gerard Foley, Pres. & CEO. Sponsored by Covenant Health Inc., Tewksbury, MA.Adult day health care for senior citizens; also, bilingual/bicultural (Spanish) adult day health care. Total Staff 25.

**M.I. Transportation, Inc.*, 189 Maple St., Lawrence, 01841. Tel: 978-682-7575; Fax: 978-691-5374; Email: gerard_foley@mihcs.com; Web: www.mihcs.com. Covenant Health, Inc., 100 Ames Pond Dr., Ste. 102, Tewksbury, 01876. Sponsored by Covenant Health, Inc., Tewksbury, MA. Total Staff 6.

[P] HOMES FOR AGED-RESIDENTS & NURSING

BOSTON. *Don Orione Nursing Home*, 111 Orient Ave., East Boston, 02128-1006. Tel: 617-569-2100; Fax: 617-561-1138; Email: rgovoni@donorionehome.org. Revs. Miroslaw Kowalczyk, F.D.P.; Gino Marchesani, F.D.P., Chap. Guests 110; Total Staff 230; Sons of Divine Providence (Don Orione Fathers) 5; Total Assisted 185.

Marian Manor (1954) 130 Dorchester St., South Boston, 02127. Tel: 617-268-3333; Fax: 617-268-4589; Email: mbrown@marianmanor.org; Email: srstephen@marianmanor.org; Web: www.marianmanor.org. Sr. Stephen Pereira, Admin. Guests 201; Priests 1; Carmelite Sisters for the Aged and Infirm 10; Total Staff 350.

BROCKTON. *St. Joseph Manor Health Care Inc.* (1965) 215 Thatcher St., Brockton, 02302. Tel: 508-583-5834; Fax: 508-583-8551; Email: jkeane@sjmbrockton.org; Web: www.sjmbrockton.org. Covenant Health, Inc., 100 Ames Pond Dr., Ste. 102, Tewksbury, 01876. Tel: 978-654-6363; Fax: 978-851-0828. James Keane, CEO & Admin. Sponsored by Covenant Health Inc., Tewksbury, MA. Residents 118; Total Staff 221.

Mater Dei Adult Day Health Center, Tel: 508-583-8313; Fax: 508-588-7384. Total Staff 18; Total Assisted Per Day 60.

CAMBRIDGE. *Sancta Maria Nursing Facility* (1948) 799 Concord Ave., Cambridge, 02138. Tel: 617-868-2200; Fax: 617-864-2801. Sr. Mary Banach, D.M., Pastoral Min. Daughters of Mary of the Immaculate Conception.An affiliate of Covenant Health, Inc., Tewksbury, MA. Bed Capacity 141; Residents 132; Sisters 2; Total Staff 217.

**Youville House, Inc.*, 1573 Cambridge St., Cambridge, 02138-4398. Tel: 617-491-1234; Fax: 617-491-8838; Email: info@youvilleassistedliving.org; Web: www.youvilleassistedliving.org. Nicole Breslih, CEO. Sponsored by Covenant Health, Inc., Tewksbury, MA.Youville House is an assisted living residence. Total Apartments 95; Total in Residence 92; Total Staff 80; Residents Assisted Annually 95.

FRAMINGHAM. *Carmel Terrace* (1995) 933 Central St., Framingham, 01701. Tel: 508-788-8000; Fax: 508-626-1603; Web: www.carmelterrace.org. Carmelite Sisters for the Aged and Infirm 3; Total Staff 58; Apartments for Assisted Living of the Elderly 69; Total Assisted 76.

St. Patrick Manor, Inc., 863 Central St., Framingham, 01701. Tel: 508-879-8000; Fax: 508-626-1604; Web: www.stpatricksmanor.

org. Sr. Maureen McDonough, O.Carm., Admin. Bed Capacity 303; Carmelite Sisters for the Aged and Infirm 30; Tot Asst. Annually 650; Total Staff 460.

IPSWICH. *St. Julie Billiart Residential Care Center, Inc.* (2002) 30 Jeffreys Neck Rd., Ipswich, 01938. Tel: 978-356-4381; Fax: 978-356-1380; Email: anna.bussing@sndden.org. Anna Bussing, Admin. Bed Capacity 54; Tot Asst. Annually 60; Total Staff 44.

LAWRENCE. *M.I. Residential Community II, Inc.*, 191 Maple St., Lawrence, 01841. Tel: 978-685-6321; Fax: 978-975-0050; Email: gerard_foley@mihcs.com; Web: www.mihcs.com. Gerard Foley, Pres. & CEO. Sponsored by Covenant Health, Inc., Tewksbury, MA.Independent & assisted living for elderly and handicapped. Total in Residence 120; Total Staff 35; Units 106.

M.I. Residential Community III, Inc., 193 Maple St., Lawrence, 01841. Tel: 978-682-7575; Fax: 978-691-5374; Email: gerard_foley@mihcs.com; Web: www.mihcs.com. Gerard Foley, Pres. & CEO. Sponsored by Covenant Health, Inc., Tewksbury, MA.Independent living for elderly.

M.I. Residential Community, Inc., 189 Maple St., Lawrence, 01841. Tel: 978-685-6321; Fax: 978-975-0050; Email: gerard_foley@mihcs.com; Web: www.mihcs.com. Covenant Health, Inc., 100 Ames Pond Dr., Ste. 102, Tewksbury, 01876. Gerard Foley, Pres. & CEO. Sponsored by Covenant Health, Inc., Tewksbury, MA.Marguerite's House Assisted Living Facility. Total in Residence 121; Total Staff 35; Units 106.

Mary Immaculate Nursing Restorative Center, 172 Lawrence St., Lawrence, 01841. Tel: 978-685-6321; Fax: 978-975-0050; Email: gerard_foley@mihcs.com; Web: www.mihcs.com. Covenant Health, Inc., 100 Ames Pond Dr., Ste. 102, Tewksbury, 01876. Tel: 978-654-6363; Fax: 978-851-0828. Gerard Foley, Pres. & CEO. Sponsored by Covenant Health, Inc., Tewksbury, MA.Multi-level Skilled Nursing Facility; Unit of Mary Immaculate Health Care Services. Residents 231; Total Staff 270.

M.I. Management, Inc., 172 Lawrence St., Lawrence, 01841. Tel: 978-685-6321; Fax: 978-975-0050; Email: gerard_foley@mihcs.com; Web: www.mihcs.com. Gerard Foley, Pres. & CEO. Sponsored by Covenant Health, Inc., Tewksbury, MA.Management company for all Mary Immaculate Facilities.

LEXINGTON. *Youville Place, Inc.* (1997) 10 Pelham Rd., Lexington, 02421-8408. Tel: 781-861-3535; Fax: 781-862-4289; Email: nicolebreslin@youvillehouse.org; Web: youvilleassistedliving.org. Covenant Health, Inc., 100 Ames Pond Dr., Ste. 102, Tewksbury, 01876. Ms. Joanne R. Scianna, COO. Sponsored by Covenant Health, Inc., Tewksbury, MA.Assisted Living Residence.

LOWELL. *D'Youville Life and Wellness Community, Inc.*, 981 Varnum Ave., Lowell, 01854. Tel: 978-569-1000; Fax: 978-453-3561; Email: nprendergast@dyouville.org; Web: www.dyouville.org. Ms. Naomi M. Prendergast, CEO. Sisters of Charity of Ottawa (Grey Nuns of the Cross). Bed Capacity 241; Residents 364; Sisters 5; Tot Asst. Annually 1,500; Total Staff 550.

MARLBOROUGH. *Marie Esther Health Center, Inc.* (1993) 720 Boston Post Rd. E., Marlborough, 01752. Tel: 508-485-3791; Tel: 508-460-1951; Fax: 508-229-2294; Email: ecaron@sistersofsaintanne.org. Total Staff 58; Total Assisted 72.

SOMERVILLE. *Jeanne Jugan Pavilion*, 190 Highland Ave., Somerville, 02143. Tel: 617-776-4420; Fax: 617-625-6720; Email: smmothersuperior@littlesistersofthepoor.org; Web: www.littlesistersofthepoorboston.org. Mother Maureen Weiss, L.S.P., Pres. Residents 29; Total Staff 1; Apartments for the Elderly 27.

Jeanne Jugan Residence, 186 Highland Ave., Somerville, 02143. Tel: 617-776-4420; Fax: 617-623-0707; Email: smmothersuperior@littlesistersofthepoor.org; Web: www.littlesistersofthepoorboston.org. Mother Maureen Weiss, L.S.P., Pres. Residents 111; Little Sisters of the Poor 6; Total Staff 110; Senior Citizen Total in Residence 84.

WALTHAM. *CHS of Waltham* dba Maristhill Nursing and Rehabilitation Center (1969) 66 Newton St., Waltham, 02453-6063. Tel: 781-893-0240; Fax: 781-894-6330; Email: cfenn@maristhill.org; Web: www.maristhill.org. Ms. Carolyn Fenn, Pres. & CEO. Sponsored by Covenant Health, Inc., Tewksbury, MA.

WELLESLEY. *Elizabeth Seton Residence, Inc.*, 125 Oakland St., Wellesley, 02481. Tel: 781-237-2161; Fax: 781-431-2589; Email: lferrante@schalifax.org; Web: www.elizabethseton.org. Ms. Lori A. Ferrante, Admin. Sisters of Charity of St. Vincent de Paul, Halifax, Nova Scotia, Canada.84 Bed Skilled Nursing & Rehab Facility. Medicare-Medicaid Certified. An affiliate of Covenant Health, Inc. Bed Capacity 84; Total Staff 115.

[Q] PERSONAL PRELATURES

CAMBRIDGE. *Prelature of the Holy Cross and Opus Dei*, 25 Follen St., Cambridge, 02138. Tel: 617-354-3204 ; Fax: 617-868-0349; Web: www.opusdei.org. Rev. David J. Cavanagh.

[R] MONASTERIES AND RESIDENCES OF PRIESTS AND BROTHERS

BOSTON. *Augustinians of the Assumption, Inc.* (1989) 330 Market St., Boston, 02135. Tel: 617-783-0400; Fax: 617-783-8030; Email: info@assumption.US; Web: www.assumption.us. Very Rev. Dennis Gallagher, A.A., Prov.; Revs. Alex Apawan Castro, A.A., Treas.; Richard Lamoureux, A.A., Sec.; Gerard Messier, A.A.; Peter Precourt, A.A. Brothers 15; Novices 2; Priests 39; Seminarians 7. *Assumption Guild*, 330 Market St., Brighton, 02135. Tel: 617-783-0495; Fax: 617-783-8030; Email: info@assumption.US; Web: masscardsaa.com. Very Rev. Dennis Gallagher, A.A., Prov. Staff 1.

Serving Abroad: Bro. Ryan Carlsen, A.A.; Rev. Gary Perron, A.A., Parroquia Emperatriz de America, Mercaderes 99, 03900 Mexico D.F., Mexico. Tel: 525-593-2002; Fax: 525-651-2000.

Brotherhood of Hope (1980) 785 Parker St., Boston, 02120. Tel: 617-652-7263; Email: bohinfo@brohope.net; Web: www.brotherhoodofhope.org. Brothers 5; Priests 3; Total in Residence 6; Brothers Elsewhere 13.

Carmelite Monastery (1942) 166 Foster St., Boston, 02135-3902. Tel: 617-787-5056; Fax: 617-783-1396; Email: mdevelisocd@gmail.com. Revs. Paul Fohlin, O.C.D., Subprior; Leonard Copeland, O.C.D., Treas.; Mark-Joseph DeVelis, O.C.D., Prior; Terrence Dougherty, O.C.D.; Anthony Haglof, O.C.D.; Bro. Augustine Wharf, O.C.D.; Rev. David Joseph Centner, O.C.D. Discalced Carmelite Friars. Brothers 1; Priests 6; Total in Residence 7.

St. Christopher Friary, 18 N. Bennet St., Boston, 02113. Tel: 617-742-4190; Fax: 617-742-1676. Bro. Robert Artman, O.F.M., Health Care Dir. & Guardian; Most Rev. Maurice Muldoon, O.F.M.; Revs. Giles Barreda, O.F.M.; Robert J. Caprio, O.F.M.; Norbert DeAmato, O.F.M., (Retired); Roland Petinge, O.F.M., (Retired); Aubert Marie Picardi, O.F.M.; Bros. Charles Trebino, O.F.M.; James T. Welch, O.F.M.; Rev. Richard Donovan, O.F.M. Brothers 3; Priests 8.

St. Francis of Assisi Friary (2008) (The Province of St. Mary of the Capuchin Order, White Plains, NY) 46 Brookside Ave., Jamaica Plain, 02130-2370. Tel: 617-522-6469; Web: www.capuchin.org. Bro. Celestino M. Arias, O.F.M.Cap., M.S.W.; Rev. Patrick Glavin, O.F.M.Cap., (Retired). Student Friars 2.

Franciscans of Primitive Observance, Our Lady of Guadalupe Friary: 3 Magazine St., Boston, 02119. Tel: 617-445-7645; Email: stpatrickrox@comcast.net. Revs. Andrew M. Beauregard, F.P.O., Supr.; Peter F. Giroux, F.P.O., Guardian; Sean Patrick Hurley, F.P.O., Postulant Dir.; Joseph Paul Medio, F.P.O., Novice Master; Michael Francis Sheehan, F.P.O., Vocation Dir.; Bros. Pio Anthony Butti, F.P.O., (Leave of Absence); Francis Godkin, F.P.O.; Felix Mary Waldron, F.P.O., Guardian; James Magdalen Wartman, F.P.O.; Juan Diego Aguilera, F.P.O.; Junipero Antonio, F.P.O.; John Joseph Conard, F.P.O.; Daniel Guillen, F.P.O.; Solanus Rodriguez, F.P.O. Brothers 9; Priests 5; Solemnly Professed 8; Total in Community 14.

Loyola House, 300 Newbury St., Boston, 02115-2801. Tel: 617-755-1625; Email: jshaughnessy@Jesuits.org; Web: Jesuitseast.org. Revs. James M. Shaughnessy, S.J., Supr.; Richard A. Deshaies, S.J., Admin.; Charles B. Connolly, S.J.; John P. Spencer, S.J.; Peter W. Gyves. The Society of Jesus. Priests 5.

Marist Fathers Lourdes Residence, 698 Beacon St., Boston, 02215. Tel: 617-262-2271; Fax: 617-536-1694; Email: denise.damico@aol.com. Revs. George Szal, S.M., Dir.; Andrew Albert, S.M.; Francis Grispino, S.M.; Albert DiIanni, S.M., Ph. D.; Gerard Demers, S.M. Priests 5.

Missionary Society of St. Paul the Apostle in Massachusetts aka The Paulist Fathers, 5 Park St., Boston, 02108. Tel: 617-742-4460; Fax: 617-720-5756; Email: info@paulistcenter.org; Web: www.paulistcenter.org. Rev. Broderick M. Walsh, C.S.P., M.Div., Supr.; Dr. Thomas Ryan, M.A., Dir. Paulist Office for Ecumenical and Interfaith Relations; Revs. Michael B. McGarry, C.S.P., M.Div., M.A. Theology, Dir. Paulist Center; Charles Cunniff, C.S.P.; John Geaney, C.S.P., (Retired); Charles A. Martin, C.S.P.; Robert S. Rivers, C.S.P., S.T.L.

Saint Peter Faber Jesuit Community, Ignatius Loyola Center, 188 Foster St., Boston, 02135-4620. Tel: 617-779-4200; Fax: 617-779-4205; Email: assist.offmgr@faberjc.org. Rev. Richard H. Roos, S.J. Priests 26; Scholastics 41. *Miguel Pro House*, 192-B Foster St., Brighton, 02135-4620. Tel: 617-779-4287; Fax: 617-779-4205. Revs. Richard H. Roos, S.J., Min., Faber Jesuit Community; Vincent Strand, S.J., Student, Boston College School of Theology & Ministry; Jean-Christian Ndoki Ndimba, S.J., Student, Boston College School of Theology & Ministry. *Alberto Hurtado House*, 194 Foster St., Brighton, 02135-4620. Tel: 617-779-4285; Fax: 617-779-4205. Revs. Francis Alvarez, S.J., Student, Boston College; James G. Gartland, S.J., Rector, Faber Jesuit Community; Jason Mujcin Sanchez, Student, Boston College of Theology & Ministry; Kenneth J. Hughes, S.J., Spiritual Dir.; Antuan Ilgit, S.J., Student, Boston College School of Theology & Ministry; Gregory Tan, S.J., Student, Boston College School of Theology & Ministry; Ladislas Nsengiyumua, S.J., Student, Boston College of Theology & Ministry. *Daniel Harrington House I*, 26 Lane Park, Brighton, 02135. Rev. Myles N. Sheehan, S.J., Prov. Asst. Senior Jesuits. *Daniel Harrington House II*, 34 Lane Park, Brighton, 02135. Revs. Francisco Mota, S.J., Student of Theology & Ministry; Raul Saiz Rodriguez, Student Boston College School of Theology & Ministry. *Walter Ciszek House*, 190-A Foster St., Brighton, 02135-4620. Tel: 617-779-4286; Fax: 617-779-4205. Revs. Andre Brouillette, S.J., Faculty, Boston College School of Theology & Ministry; Thomas D. Stegman, S.J., Faculty, Boston College School of Theology & Ministry. *Isaac Jogues House*, 196-A Foster St., Brighton, 02135-4620. Tel: 617-779-4288; Fax: 617-779-4205. Revs. Mario Inzulza, S.J., Student, Boston College School of Theology & Ministry; Michael Simone, S.J., Faculty, Boston College School of Theology & Ministry; Alexander Wainain, S.J., Student, Boston College of Theology & Ministry; Abdon Rwandekwe, S.J., Student, Boston College School of Theology & Ministry; Christopher Ryan, S.J., Student, Boston College School of Theology & Ministry. *Noel Chabanel House*, 196-B Foster St., Brighton, 02135-4620. Tel: 617-779-4269; Fax: 617-779-4205. Revs. Richard J. Clifford, S.J., Visiting Prof., Old Testament, Boston College School of Theology & Ministry; Wojciech Moranski, Student, Boston College School of Theology & Ministry; Gustavo Morello, S.J., (Argentina) Prof. Sociology, Boston College; Ignatius Fominyen Musi, S.J., Student, Boston College School of Theology & Ministry. *Francis Xavier House*, 190-B Foster St., Brighton, 02135-4620. Tel: 617-779-4219; Fax: 617-779-4205. Revs. Brian Dunkle, S.J., Faculty, Boston College School of Theology & Ministry; Ignace Rakotondramiadanirina, S.J., Student, Boston College; Jose Celio dos Santos, S.J., Student, Boston College School of Theology & Ministry; Colleen Dinladzer Nsame, Student, Boston College School of Theology & Ministry; Tan Thanh Tran, S.J., Student, Boston College School of Theology & Ministry. *Edmund Campion House*, 192-A Foster St., Brighton, 02135-4620. Tel: 617-779-4239; Fax: 617-779-4205. Revs. John Baldovin, S.J., Faculty, Boston College School of Theology & Ministry; Javier Diaz Diaz, S.J., Student, Boston College School of Theology & Ministry; Mbuyi Benoit Kulaya, S.J., Student, Boston College School of Theology & Ministry.

Priests of the Assumption, Inc., 330 Market St., Brighton, 02135. Tel: 617-783-0400; Fax: 617-783-8030; Email: info@assumption.us; Web: www.assumption.us. Very Rev. Dennis Gallagher, A.A., Pres.; Revs. Peter Precourt, A.A., Vice Pres.; Alex Apawan Castro, A.A., Treas.; Richard Lamoureux, A.A., Sec. Tot in Congregation 934.

The Salesian Community (1945) 150 Byron St., Boston, 02128. Tel: 617-569-6551; Tel: 617-567-6626; Fax: 617-568-3851; Email: salesians@comcast.net; Web: www.salesiansociety.org. Rev. John Nazzaro, S.D.B., Exec. Dir. Total Assisted 2,800.

San Lorenzo Friary (2002) (The Province of St. Mary of the Capuchin Order, White Plains, New York) 15 Montebello Rd., Boston, 02130-2352. Tel: 617-983-1919; Email: lake.herman@capuchin.org; Web: www.capuchin.org. Rev. John Tokaz, Supr.; Bros. Lake Hermzn, O.F.M.Cap., Vicar & Dir., Formation; Joseph Anderson, O.F.M.Cap.; Paul Fesefeldt, O.F.M.Cap.; Scott Leet, O.F.M.-Cap.; Arnold Lezcano, O.F.M.Cap.; Victor Russak, O.F.M.Cap.; Francisco Serrano. Friars 8; Student Friars 6.

The Society of Jesus of New England-Provincial Offices (1926) 319 Concord Rd., Weston, 02493. Tel: 617-607-2800; Fax: 617-607-2888; Email: unesocius@jesuits.org; Web: www.jesuitseast.org. Revs. Myles N. Sheehan, S.J., Asst. Elderly Jesuits for Mar & Une, Faber Jesuit Community; Joseph A. Appleyard, S.J., Faculty & Staff Formation B.C., Weston-Campion Center; Robert J. Daly,

S.J., Prof. Emeritus Theology, Boston College; Michael G. Boughton, S.J., Asst. for Formation for MAR & UNE, Archdiocese of New York; Charles B. Connolly, S.J., Dir. Donor Relations, Loyola House; Charles A. Frederico, S.J., Vocation Dir. MAR & UNE, Archdiocese of New York; Michael D. Linden, S.J., Supr. Jordan & Iraq, Amman, Jordan; Edward J. Quinnan, S.J., Asst. for Pastoral Ministries for UNE, Archdiocese of New York; James M. Shaughnessy, S.J., Supr. Loyola House, Loyola House; Dennis J. Yesalonia, S.J., Pastor, Archdiocese of New York.

The Society of St. James the Apostle, Inc., 24 Clark St., Boston, 02109. Tel: 617-742-4715; Fax: 617-723-7389; Email: director2012@socstjames.com; Web: socstjames.com. Rev. David M. Costello, (Ireland) Dir. Founded by His Eminence Richard Cardinal Cushing, in 1958 to recruit Diocesan Priest volunteers for South America. See American Foreign Missions section for Diocesan Priests serving in Latin America.

The Order of Friars Minor Province of the Most Holy Name, 100 Arch St., Boston, 02110-1102. Tel: 646-473-0265; Email: hnp@hnp.org; Web: www.hnp.org. Revs. Kevin Mullen, O.F.M., Pres.; Lawrence Hayes, O.F.M., Vice Pres.; Dennis M. Wilson, O.F.M., Treas.; Michael J. Harlan, O.F.M., Sec.

Franciscan Friars-Holy Name Province (MA).

BROCKTON. *Chapel of Our Savior* (1961) 475 Westgate Dr., Brockton, 02301-1819. Tel: 508-583-8357; Fax: 508-586-5510. Bro. Thomas Banacki, S.A., Dir. & Guardian; Revs. Gerald DiGiralamo, S.A.; John F. Keane, (Retired); Bros. Savio McNeice, S.A.; Louis Marek, S.A. Franciscan Friars of the Atonement. Brothers 3; Priests 2.

COHASSET. *Bellarmine House*, 150 Howard Gleason Rd., Cohasset, 02025. Tel: 781-383-0723; Fax: 781-383-3164. Rev. Donald A. MacMillan, S.J., Admin. (Summer Res. for Jesuits of New England Prov.).

DEDHAM. *Society of African Missions* Society of African Missions, Inc. 337 Common St., P.O. Box 47, Dedham, 02026-4030. Tel: 781-326-3288; Tel: 781-326-4670; Fax: 781-326-7627; Email: dedhamhouse@smafathers.org; Web: www.smafathers.org. Revs. Brendan Darcy, S.M.A., Supr.; Richard Angolio, S.M.A. Priests 2.

DUXBURY. *Society of the Divine Word*, 121 Parks St., P.O. Box M, Duxbury, 02331-0614. Tel: 781-585-2460; Fax: 781-585-3770; Email: miramarma@aol.com; Web: www.miramarretreat.org. Revs. Thomas Umbras, S.V.D., Dir., Rector; Joseph Connolly, S.V.D.; Thomas Griffith, S.V.D.; Robert Mallonee, S.V.D.; Donald Skerry, S.V.D.; Bro. Donald Champagne, S.V.D. Brothers 1; Priests 5; Total Staff 18.

HINGHAM. *Glastonbury Abbey* (1954) 16 Hull St., Hingham, 02043. Tel: 781-749-2155; Fax: 781-749-6236; Email: office@glastonburyabbey.org; Web: www.glastonburyabbey.org. Revs. Thomas J. O'Connor, Abbot; Nicholas J. Morcone, O.S.B.; Timothy J. Joyce; Andrew M. Quillen; Gerald T. Leibenguth, O.S.B.; Bros. David K. Coakley, O.S.B., Music Dir.; James Crowley, O.S.B.; Albrecht Nyce, O.S.B.; Daniel F. Walters, O.S.B., Conference Center Dir. Benedictine Monks.Benedictine Monastery. Brothers 4; Priests 5; Retreat House Capacity 32; Conference Center Capacity 180.

HOLLISTON. *Xaverian Missionaries*, 101 Summer St., Holliston, 01746. Tel: 508-429-2144; Fax: 508-429-4793; Email: holliston@xaverianmissionaries.org; Web: www.xaverianmissionaries.org. Revs. Rocco N. Puopolo, S.X., Rector; Tony B. Lalli, S.X.; Adolph J. Menendez, S.X.; Francis Signorelli, S.X.; Carl S. Chudy, S.X.

St. Francis Xavier Foreign Mission Society, Inc. Priests 5.

LAWRENCE. *Marist Brothers*, 26 Leeds Ter., Lawrence, 01843. Tel: 978-686-7411. Bros. Jerry Dowsky, F.M.S.; James Halliday, F.M.S.; John Kachinsky, F.M.S. Brothers 3.

Marist Brothers Residence, 12 Sheridan St., Lawrence, 01841. Tel: 978-682-1163. Bros. Rene D. Roy, F.M.S., Dir.; William Lambert, F.M.S.; Ernest Beland, F.M.S.; Richard Carey, F.M.S.; Kenneth V. Hogan, F.M.S. Brothers 5.

LOWELL. *Missionary Oblates of Mary Immaculate*, 27 Kirk St., Lowell, 01852-1004. Tel: 978-937-9594; Fax: 978-458-3603; Email: andregarinresidence@yahoo.com. Bro. Charles Gilbert, O.M.I., Dir.; Revs. Roger Couture, O.M.I, (Retired); Donald G. Lozier, O.M.I.; Michael O'Hara, O.M.I.; Jerry Orsino, O.M.I. *Andre Garin Retirement Residence*, Lowell. Tel: 978-937-9594; Fax: 978-458-3603; Email: andregarinresidence@yahoo.com. Bro. Charles Gilbert, O.M.I., Dir., Tel: 978-441-1245; Revs. Roger Couture, O.M.I, (Retired); Jerry Orsino, O.M.I.; Donald G. Lozier, O.M.I.

Missionary Oblates of Mary Immaculate (1847) Northeast Area Office, 60 Wyman St., Lowell, 01852-2841. Tel: 978-458-9912; Fax: 978-458-7274; Email: epicard@omiusa.org; Web: www.omiusa.org. Rev. Tuan Ngoc Pham, O.M.I., Dir.; Bro. Richard Cote, O.M.I., Dir.; Revs. George Brown, O.M.I.; Norman Comtois, O.M.I.; Wilfred Harvey, O.M.I.; William Sheehan, O.M.I.; Louis J. Villarreal, O.M.I. Brothers 1; Priests 6. *St. Eugene House (Residence)* (1995) 285 Andover St., Lowell, 01852-1438. Tel: 978-441-0649; Email: epicard@omiusa.org. Revs. Tuan Ngoc Pham, O.M.I., Dir. Northeast Area Vocation; Charles Breault, O.M.I., Dir.; Bro. Richard Cote, O.M.I., Dir.; Revs. William Sheehan, O.M.I., Preacher/Spiritual Direction; Henri Delisle, O.M.I., Reduced Active Ministry. *Oblate Foreign Mission Office, Northeast*, 60 Wyman St., Lowell, 01852-2841. Tel: 978-458-4380; Fax: 978-458-7274; Email: ofm@omiusa.org. Bro. Richard Cote, O.M.I., Dir.

Oblate Vocation Office, Northeast Area, 60 Wyman St., Lowell, 01852-2841. Tel: 978-458-9912; Fax: 978-458-7274; Email: tpham@omiusa.org. Rev. Tuan Ngoc Pham, O.M.I., Dir.

LYNN. *Franciscan Community (Province of Immaculate Conception)*, 38 Michigan Ave., Lynn, 01902. Tel: 617-592-7396; Fax: 781-595-6724. Rev. Alfonse Ferreira, O.F.M., Procurator & Guardian. *The Listening Place (Counseling Center)*, 36 Michigan Ave., Lynn, 01902. Tel: 781-592-7396; Fax: 781-593-8805. Rev. Alfonse Ferreira, O.F.M., Dir.

MEDFORD. *Priestly Fraternity of the Missionaries of St. Charles Borromeo, Inc.*, 71 Warner St., Medford, 02155. Tel: 781-864-3427 (Rev. Colombo); Email: p.cumin@sancarlo.org; Web: www.fraternityofsaintcharles.org. Revs. Stefano Colombo, F.S.C.B., Contact Person; Luca Brancolini, F.S.C.B.; Paolo Cumin, F.S.C.B. *House of Washington DC*, 7600 Carter Ct., Bethesda, MD 20817. Revs. Antonio Lopez, F.S.C.B.; Jose Medina, F.S.C.B.; Paolo Prosperi, F.S.C.B.; Pietro Rossotti, F.S.C.B.; Roberto Amoruso, F.S.C.B.; Ettore Ferrario, F.S.C.B. *House of Denver*, Nativity of Our Lord Parish, 900 W. Midway Blvd., Broomfield, CO 80020-2048. Tel: 303-469-5171. Revs. Michael Carvill, F.S.C.B.; Accursio Ciaccio, F.S.C.B.; Gabriele Azzalin, F.S.C.B.

MILTON. *Oblate Residence (St. Joseph House)*, 65 Fr. Carney Dr., Milton, 02186-4206. Tel: 617-698-6785; Fax: 617-698-7621; Web: www.omvusa.org. Revs. Dennis Brown, O.M.V.; John Ferrara, O.M.V.; Robert Lowrey, O.M.V.; Craig McMahon, O.M.V.; David Nicgorski, O.M.V.; David Yankauskas, O.M.V.; Bro. Joseph O'Connor, O.M.V. Congregation of the Oblates of the Virgin Mary. Brothers 1; Priests 6.

NEWTON. *The Jesuit Community at Boston College* (1863) 140 Commonwealth Ave., St. Mary's Hall, Newton, 02467. Tel: 617-552-8111; Fax: 617-552-2380; Email: longbott@bc.edu; Web: www.bc.edu/sites/jesuit.html. Very Rev. John J. Cecero, S.J., Prov.; Revs. Robert L. Keane, S.J., Rector; Francis R. Herrmann, S.J.; Mark S. Massa, S.J.; Gregory Kalscheur, S.J., Dean College of Arts & Sciences & Graduate School; Casey C. Beaumier, S.J.; James W. Bernauer, S.J.; Richard Blake, S.J.; John Butler, S.J.; Sammy Chong, S.J.; James J. Conn, S.J.; Robert J. Daly, S.J.; Michael F. Davidson, S.J.; Jean Baptiste Diatta, S.J.; Harvey D. Egan, S.J.; Frederick Enman, S.J.; Robert Farrell, S.J.; Peter M. Folan, S.J.; Charles R. Gallagher, S.J.; Juan Garcia-Huidobro, S.J.; Kenneth Himes, O.F.M., (Brooklyn, NY); Ryan Duns, S.J.; Jiang Joseph, S.J.; James Keenan, S.J.; William P. Leahy, S.J., Ph.D., Pres.; Donald A. MacMillan, S.J.; Arthur R. Madigan, S.J.; Paul McNellis, S.J.; Gustavo Morello, S.J., (Argentina); Cyril Opeil, S.J.; John Paris, S.J.; Claude Pavur, S.J.; Oliver P. Rafferty, S.J.; Richard Ross, S.J.; Gregory C. Sharkey, S.J.; Ronald K. Tacelli, S.J.; Marcel Uwineza, S.J., (Rwanda); Andrea Vicini, S.J.; Joseph S. Costantino, S.J.; Gerald F. Finnegan, S.J.; Joseph Weiss, S.J.; Benoit Mbuyi Kulaya, S.J.; John C. Monahan, S.J., Campus Min.; Juan Rivera; John R. Siberski, S.J., Campus Min.; Paul Kalenzi; Brett McLaughlin; Cesr Muziotti; Jude Odiaka; Kevin Quinn; Abdon Rwandekwe, S.J.; Reginald Tiesaah; Quang Tran.

TEWKSBURY. *Oblate World/Missionary Association of Mary Immaculate*, 486 Chandler St., Tewksbury, 01876-0680. Tel: 978-858-0434; Fax: 978-858-3661; Email: oblateworld@omires.com. Very Rev. John F. Hanley, O.M.I., V.F., Dir.

WALTHAM. *Stigmatine Fathers & Brothers Provincial House*, 554 Lexington St., Waltham, 02452. Tel: 718-209-3100; Fax: 781-894-9785; Email: rsw7713@aol.com; Web: www.stigmatines.com. Very Rev. Robert S. White, C.S.S., M.Div., S.T.L., Prov. Total Staff 4.

WESTON. *Campion Health & Wellness, Inc.*, 319 Concord Rd., Weston, 02493-1398. Tel: 781-788-6800; Fax: 781-647-5108; Email: wsmith@campioncenter.org. Revs. Walter J. Smith, S.J., Supr.; David O. Travers, S.J.; Gerard McLaughlin, S.J.; J. Donald Monan, S.J.; Eugene O'Brien, S.J.; Joseph A. Appleyard, S.J.; John Donohue, S.J.; Frederic A. Maples, S.J.; Clarence J. Burby, S.J.; Joseph F. Burke, S.J.; Walter J. Conlan, S.J.; Charles B. Connolly, S.J.; Lawrence E. Corcoran, S.J.; William Joseph Eagan, S.J.; John W. Elder, S.J.; William J. Elliott, S.J.; Michael A. Fahey, S.J.; Michael F. Ford, S.J.; James A. Gillon, S.J.; George A. Gallarelli, S.J.; David H. Gill, S.J.; Paul P. Gilmartin, S.J.; Robert M. Hanlon, S.J.; G. Simon Harak, S.J.; Edward F. Howard, S.J.; James M. Keegan, S.J.; Philip S. Kiley, S.J.; Daniel J. Lusch, S.J.; Robert G. McMillan, S.J.; John J. Mandile, S.J.; James R. Mattaliano, S.J.; Francis J. Moy, S.J.; William L. Mulligan, S.J.; James C. O'Brien, S.J.; Ernest F. Passero, S.J.; Walter R. Pelletier, S.J.; James F.X. Pratt, S.J.; Frank J. Parker, S.J.; Anthony R. Picariello, S.J.; Robert F. Regan, S.J.; John P. Reboli, S.J.; Lawrence D. Ryan, S.J.; Francis J. Ryan, S.J.; Patrick J. Ryan, S.J.; Stephen J. Sanford, S.J.; Thomas J. Sheehan, S.J.; James W. Skehan, S.J.; Simon E. Smith, S.J.; Francis A. Sullivan, S.J.; Richard J. Stanley, S.J.; James F. Walsh, S.J.; John Joseph Walsh, S.J.; James A. Woods, S.J.; Bros. Theodore C. Bender, S.J.; James Thomas Dennehy; Calvin A. Clarke, S.J.; John J. McLane, S.J.; James J. Moran, S.J.; Edward L. Niziolek, S.J. Managed by Covenant Health, Inc. Brothers 3; Priests 41; Total in Community 44.

Campion Center, Inc., 319 Concord Rd., Weston, 02493. Tel: 781-788-6800; Fax: 781-894-5864; Email: wsmith@campioncenter.org; Web: www.campioncenter.org. Revs. Walter J. Smith, S.J., Supr.; James R. Mattaliano, S.J., Dir., Renewal Ctr.; William A. Barry, S.J.; Stephen J. Bonian, S.J.; I. Michael Bellafiore, S.J.; Paul E. Carrier, S.J.; Terrence W. Curry, S.J.; Joseph P. Duffy, S.J.; James J. Fleming, S.J., Ph.D.; Richard P. Guerrera; Gary M. Gurtler, S.J.; Charles J. Healey, S.J., S.T.L., S.T.D.; John W. Howard, S.J.; Paul C. Kenney, S.J.; Joseph V. Owens, S.J.; William C. Russell, S.J.; James F. Talbot, S.J.; Alfred O. Winshman, S.J.; George P. Winchester, S.J.; John E. Surette, S.J.

Campion Residence & Renewal Center, Inc. Priests 21.

[S] CONVENTS AND RESIDENCES FOR SISTERS

BOSTON. *Carmelite Monastery of Boston* (1890) Cloistered. Discalced Carmelite Nuns - O.C.D. 61 Mt. Pleasant Ave., Boston, 02119. Tel: 617-442-1411; Fax: 617-442-0203; Email: carmelitesofboston@gmail.com; Web: www.carmelitesofboston.org. Sr. Mary Teresa Wisniewsk, O.C.D., Prioress. Sisters 9.

The Congregation of the Sisters of Our Lady of Mercy, 241 Neponset Ave., Boston, 02122. Tel: 617-288-1202; Fax: 617-288-1177; Email: mercy@sisterfaustina.org; Web: www.sisterfaustina.org. Professed Sisters 4.

Daughters of St. Paul Inc. (1915) 50 St. Paul's Ave., Boston, 02130-3491. Tel: 617-522-8911; Fax: 617-524-8648; Email: usaprov@paulinemedia.com; Web: www.pauline.org.

Daughters of St. Paul, Inc. Novitiate, Provincialate Headquarters, and Publishing House for U.S. Novices 3; Prov. Community 7; Perpetually Professed Sisters 66; Junior Professed 1.

Pauline Book & Media Center (1988) 885 Providence Hwy., Dedham, 02026. Tel: 781-326-5385; Fax: 781-461-1013.

Franciscan Missionaries of Mary (1990) 284 Foster St., Boston, 02135. Tel: 617-787-1505; Fax: 617-787-1982; Email: nkloanfmm@yahoo.com. Sr. Noreen Murray, F.M.M., Prov. (1990) 3305 Wallace Ave., Bronx, NY 10467-6599. Tel: 718-547-4693; Fax: 718-547-4607.

Franciscan Missionary Sisters for Africa (1957) (USA Headquarters and only house.) 172 Foster St., Brighton, 02135. Tel: 617-254-4343; Email: marymfisher9@gmail.com; Web: www.fmsa.net. Sr. Mary Fisher, F.M.S.A., USA Rep. Serving in Uganda, Kenya, Zambia, Zimbabwe, Sudan and South Africa. Completely a Missionary congregation. Sisters 6.

Franciscan Monastery of St. Clare, The aka Poor Clare Nuns (1906) 920 Centre St., Boston, 02130. Tel: 617-524-1760; Fax: 617-983-5205; Email: bostonpoorclares@yahoo.com; Web: www.poorclarenunsboston.org. Sr. Mary Veronica McGuff, O,S,C,, Abbess. Franciscan Poor Clare Nuns.Solemn Vows. Cloistered Solemnly Professed 14; Extern Sisters 1; Professed Sisters 10.

Franciscan Sisters of the Atonement, 651 Adams St., Boston, 02122. Tel: 617-378-1723.

Little Sisters of the Assumption Convent (1947) 65 Magnolia St., Boston, 02125. Tel: 617-442-9411; Email: mleonard@prohope.org; Web: www.littlesisters.org.

Little Sisters of the Assumption.

Missionary Sisters of St. Columban, 73 Mapleton St., Boston, 02135. Tel: 617-782-5683; Fax: 617-789-3569; Email: columbansbrighton@verizon.net; Web: columbansistersusa.com/columbansisters.org. Sr. Virginia Mozo, S.S.C., U.S. Area Coord.

Missionary Sisters of Saint Columban Professed Sisters 7.

Motherhouse of the Sisters of St. Joseph of Boston (1873) 637 Cambridge St., Boston, 02135.
Tel: 617-783-9090; Fax: 617-783-8246; Email: bostoncsj@csjboston.org; Web: www.csjboston.org. Sr. Rosemary Brennan, C.S.J., Pres. Admin. Offices - 637 Cambridge St. Total in Residence 66.

Sister Disciples of the Divine Master (1924) Convent and Eucharistic Center, 43 West St., Boston, 02111. Tel: 482-682-0978; Tel: 482-423-2629;
Fax: 482-682-3779; Email: sddmboston@aol.com; Web: www.pddm.us. Sr. M. Josephine Fallon, Supr. Sisters 12.

Sisters of Notre Dame de Namur, 351 Broadway, Everett, 02149-3425. Tel: 617-387-2500;
Fax: 617-387-1303; Email: edie.daly@sndden.org. Sisters Barbara Barry, S.N.D.deN., Prov.; Edie Daly, S.N.D.deN., Prov.; Barbara English, S.N.D.-deN., Prov.; Mary M. Farren, S.N.D.deN., Prov.; Anne Malone, S.N.D.deN., Prov.; Catherine Waldron, S.N.D.deN., Prov.

Boston Province of The Sisters of Notre Dame de Namur, Inc. Sisters 137; Total in Community 420.

Sisters of the Eucharistic Heart of Jesus, E.H.J. Sisters/Sisters of the Eucharistic Heart of Jesus, 59 Richmere Rd., Mattapan, 02126.
Tel: 617-296-0167; Cell: 617-767-9097;
Fax: 617-296-0167; Email: ehjsistersboston1@verizon.net; Email: conyewuche@yahoo.com; Web: www.ehjsrsboston.org.

Sisters of the Good Shepherd, 35 Tyndale St., Boston, 02131. Tel: 617-469-2492; Fax: 617-469-9857; Email: smhrgs@verizon.net. Sisters 3.

ANDOVER. *Monastery of St. Clare*, 445 River Rd., Andover, 01810-4213. Tel: 978-683-7599;
Fax: 978-683-6085; Email: tmlacroix@comcast.net. Sr. Therese Marie Lacroix, O.S.C., Abbess. Poor Clare Nuns. Novices 1; Postulants 1; Cloistered Solemnly Professed 6; Extern Perpetually Professed 1.

BROCKTON. *Our Lady of Sorrows Convent*, 261 Thatcher St., Brockton, 02302-3997.
Tel: 508-588-5070; Fax: 508-580-6770; Email: smjv@cjcbrockton.org; Web: www.cjcbrockton.org. Sr. Mary Valliere, C.J.C., Gen. Supr. Poor Sisters of Jesus Crucified and the Sorrowful Mother. Sisters 11.

CAMBRIDGE. *Sancta Maria Convent*, 799 Concord Ave., Cambridge, 02138.
Tel: 617-868-2200, Ext. 2950 (Convent);
Tel: 617-868-2200, Ext. 2100 (Office);
Fax: 617-864-2801.

CHELSEA. *Don Guanella Center, Inc., Daughters of St. Mary of Providence* (1982) 37 Nichols St., Chelsea, 02150. Tel: 617-889-0179; Fax: 617-889-3363; Email: dgcenter.chelsea2@verizon.net; Web: www.donguanellacenter.com. Sr. Charleen Badiola, D.S.M.P., Dir. Emergency residential & respite for developmentally disabled women (ages 18 & older). Families 70; Sisters 2; Total Staff 12.

DANVERS. *Discalced Carmelite Monastery* (1958) 15 Mt. Carmel Rd., Danvers, 01923-3796.
Tel: 978-774-3008; Fax: 978-774-7409; Email: contact@danverscarmel.com. Sr. Michael of Christ the King, O.C.D., Prioress. Total in Residence 12.

DEDHAM. *Ursuline Convent, Inc.*, 65 Lowder St., Dedham, 02026-4205. Tel: 781-326-3158;
Fax: 781-326-4428; Email: nestabeaudoin@verizon.net. Sr. Mercedes Videira, O.S.U., Prioress. Sisters 6.

Ursuline Provincialate (1947) 65 Lowder St., Dedham, 02026-4200. Tel: 781-326-3158. Sr. Angela Krippendorf, O.S.U., Prov. Ursulines of the Roman Union, Northeastern Province 24.

FRAMINGHAM. *Religious of Christian Education, Inc.*, 933 Central St., Framingham, 01701.
Tel: 508-309-7747. Sr. Martha Brigham, R.C.E., Contact Person.

IPSWICH. *Sisters of Notre Dame de Namur* (1804) 30 Jeffreys Neck Rd., Ipswich, 01938-1308.
Tel: 978-380-1372; Fax: 978-356-9759; Email: mary.farren@sndden.org; Web: www.sndden.org. Sisters Barbara Barry, S.N.D.deN., Prov.; Edie Daly, S.N.D.deN., Prov.; Barbara English, S.N.D.-deN., Prov.; Mary M. Farren, S.N.D.deN., Religious Order Leader; Anne Malone, S.N.D.deN., Prov.; Catherine Waldron, S.N.D.deN., Prov.

Notre Dame Training School Sisters 53.

Sisters of Notre Dame de Namur Generalate Office, 30 Jeffrey's Neck Rd., Ipswich, 01938.
Tel: 978-356-2159; Fax: 978-356-1034; Email: connell@sndden.org; Web: www.sndden.org. Sr. Lorraine Connell, S.N.D.deN., Gen. Treas.

Casa Generalizia di Suore di Nostra Signora di Namur, Via Raffaello Sardiello, 20, Rome, Italy 00165. Tel: 39-06-6641-8704;
Fax: 39-06-6641-8709. Sr. Teresita Weind, S.N.D.-deN., Gen. Moderator. (Generalate).

The Sisters of Notre Dame de Namur Generalate, 30 Jeffrey's Neck Rd., Ipswich, 01938.
Tel: 978-356-2159; Fax: 978-356-1034; Email: lorraine.connell@sndden.org; Web: www.sndden.org. Sr. Lorraine Connell, S.N.D.deN., Treas. Professed Sisters 735.

Sisters of Notre Dame de Namur United States East-West Province, Inc., 30 Jeffreys Neck Rd., Ipswich, 01938. Tel: 978-380-1372; Email: mary.farren@sndden.org. Sisters Barbara Barry, S.N.D.-deN., Prov.; Edie Daly, S.N.D.deN., Prov.; Barbara English, S.N.D.deN., Prov.; Mary M. Farren, S.N.-D.deN., Prov.; Anne Malone, S.N.D.deN., Prov.; Catherine Waldron, S.N.D.deN., Prov. Sisters 420.

KINGSTON. *Congregation of the Sisters of Divine Providence* (1851) Providence House, 363 Bishops Hwy., Kingston, 02364. Tel: 781-585-7707;
Fax: 781-422-5236; Email: mbisbey@cdpsisters.org. Sisters Michele Bisbey, Dir.; Juliana Frisoli, Area Asst. Sisters 24.

LEXINGTON. *Congregation of Armenian Catholic Sisters of Immaculate Conception, Inc.*, 6 Eliot Rd., Lexington, 02421. Tel: 781-863-5962;
Fax: 781-862-8479. Sisters 4.

Grey Nuns Area Offices, 10 Pelham Rd., Ste. 1000, Lexington, 02421-8499. Tel: 781-674-7401;
Fax: 781-861-9641; Email: srjeannepoor@verizon.net; Web: www.sgm.qc.ca. Sr. Jeanne Poor, S.G.M., Prov. Headquarters (U.S.A. Area) of the Sisters of Charity of Montreal. "Grey Nuns". Sisters 17. *General Administration*, 138 Rue Saint-Pierre, Montreal, QC Canada H2Y 2L7. Tel: 514-842-9411; Fax: 514-842-7855. Sr. Jeanne Poor, S.G.M., Area Coord. Sisters 1.

LOWELL. *St. Joseph Provincial House*, 559 Fletcher St., Lowell, 01854-3434. Tel: 978-458-4472;
Fax: 978-441-1452; Email: prleblanc2@comcast.net; Web: www.soeursdelachariteottawa.com. Sr. Pauline Leblanc, S.C.O., Prov. Supr. Sisters of Charity of Ottawa (Grey Nuns of the Cross); D'Youville Senior Care Center, Lowell. Sisters 15.

MARLBOROUGH. *Sisters of St. Anne, Provincialate* (1850) 720 Boston Post Rd. E., Marlborough, 01752. Tel: 508-485-3791; Fax: 508-481-4939; Email: sydargy@hotmail.com; Web: sistersofstanne.org. Sr. Yvette Dargy, S.S.A., Prov. Headquarters of American Province. Sisters 80.

Community of the Sisters of Saint Anne, Tel: 508-485-3791; Fax: 508-481-4939. *St. Anne Convent*, 720 Boston Post Rd. E., Marlborough, 01752. Tel: 508-485-3791; Fax: 508-481-4939. Sisters 44.

Sisters of St. Chretienne (1807) 197 Pleasant St., Marlborough, 01752-1169. Tel: 508-485-0740;
Fax: 508-481-0663; Email: chretienne@verizon.net; Web: www.sistersofstchretienne.org. Sr. Lisette Michaud, S.S.Ch., Local Coord. House of Retirement. Sisters 24.

Sisters of St. Chretienne, 207 Pleasant St., Marlboro, 01752-1169. Tel: 508-485-0740;
Fax: 508-481-0663.

Sisters of the Good Shepherd, 406 Hemenway St., Marlborough, 01752. Tel: 508-485-8610;
Fax: 508-460-6372. Sr. Elish McPartland, R.G.S., Contact Person & Pastoral Care. Sisters 13.

METHUEN. *Sisters of the Presentation of Mary*, 209 Lawrence St., Methuen, 01844. Tel: 978-687-1369;
Fax: 978-975-1998; Email: pmprov.us@gmail.com; Email: pmtreasurer209@gmail.com; Web: www.presentationofmary-usa.org. Sr. Helene Cote, P.M., Prov. Presentation of Mary Academy, Methuen, MA. Sisters 39.

MILTON. *Holy Union Sisters* (1826) Province Office, 444 Centre St., P.O. Box 410, Milton, 02186-0006.
Tel: 617-696-8765; Fax: 617-696-8571; Web: www.holyunionsisters.org. Sisters Patricia Heath, S.U.S.C., Province Leadership Team; Yvette Ladurantaye, S.U.S.C., Province Leadership Team; Mary Lou Sullivan, S.U.S.C., Province Leadership Team.

NEWTON. *Immaculate Conception Provincialate* (1873) 790 Centre St., Newton, 02458-2530.
Tel: 617-527-1004; Fax: 617-527-2528; Email: mfic@mficusa.org; Web: www.mficusa.org. Missionary Franciscan Sisters of the Immaculate Conception. Total in Residence 3; Total Staff 3.

Mt. Alvernia Convent (1873) 790 Centre St., Newton, 02458-2530. Tel: 617-969-4766; Fax: 617-527-2528; Email: mtalverniaconvent@comcast.net; Web: www.mficusa.org. Sisters 20; Staff 3.

SOMERVILLE. *Medical Missionaries of Mary, Inc.* (1937) 179 Highland Ave., Somerville, 02143-1515.
Tel: 617-666-3223; Fax: 617-666-1877; Email: mmmsomerville@comcast.net; Web: www.mmmworldwide.org. Sr. Therese McDonough, Contact Person. Medical Missionaries of Mary Motherhouse, Beechgrove, Drogheda, Ireland. Professed Sisters 14.

WALTHAM. *Marist Missionary Sisters*,
Tel: 781-893-0149; Fax: 781-899-6838; Email: admin@maristsmsm.org; Web: www.maristmissionarysmsm.org. Sisters Mary Jane Kenney, Prov.; Helen Muller, Prov. Asst.; Joyce Edelmann, Sec.

Missionary Sisters of the Society of Mary, Inc., S.M.S.M. Sisters 91. *Provincial Offices*, 349 Grove St., Waltham, 02453-6018. Tel: 781-893-0149;
Fax: 781-899-6838; Email: admin@maristsmsm.org; Web: www.maristmissionarysmsm.org. Sisters Mary Jane Kenney, Prov.; Helen Muller, Prov. Asst.; Joyce Edelmann, Sec. Sisters 91. *Residence for Senior Sisters*, 62 Newton St., Waltham, 02453-6058. Tel: 781-893-3960; Email: admin@maristsmsm.org. Sisters 20.

Marillac Residence, 125 Oakland St., Wellesley, 02481-5338. Sisters 20.

Bethany Health Care Centre, 97 Bethany Rd., Framingham, 01702-7296. Tel: 508-872-6750. Sisters 4.

Maristhill Nursing Home, 66 Newton St., Waltham, 02453-6058. Sisters 2.

Other Local Communities:21 Beech St., Belmont, 02478-1299. Tel: 617-489-3587. Sisters 8. 4 Craig St., Framingham, 01701-7664. Tel: 508-877-7371. Sisters 3. 357 Grove St., Waltham, 02453-6018.
Tel: 781-899-3839. Sisters 4.

Sisters of the Good Shepherd, 83-85 Lake St., Waltham, 02451. Tel: 781-891-7688;
Fax: 617-471-6622; Email: elishmcpar@verizon.net; Email: stacey@mariadrostecounseling.com. Sr. Elish McPartland, R.G.S., Contact Person.

WATERTOWN. *Rosary Manor*, One Rosary Dr., Watertown, 02472. Tel: 617-924-1717;
Fax: 617-924-8118; Email: hmccarthy435@gmail.com. Sr. Helen McCarthy, O.P., Coord. Total in Residence 15.

WELLESLEY. *Marillac Residence, Inc.*, 125 Oakland St., Wellesley, 02481-5338. Tel: 781-997-1110;
Fax: 781-997-1147; Email: jbreen@schalifax.org; Web: www.schalifax.ca. Sr. Judith Breen, S.C., Admin. Sisters of Charity, Halifax, Nova Scotia, Canada Sisters 77.

Mount St. Vincent Retirement Community, 125 Oakland St., Wellesley, 02481-5338.
Tel: 781-997-1165; Email: pangevine@schalifax.org; Web: www.schalifax.com. Patricia Angevine, Coord., Care & Community Life. Sisters of Charity (Halifax). Sisters 66.

Sisters of Charity (Halifax) (1849) (Boston Office) Elizabeth Seton Convent, 50 Elm Ave., Wollaston, 02170. Tel: 781-997-1356; Fax: 781-997-1358; Email: mruzzo@schalifax.ca; Web: www.schalifax.ca. Sisters Maryanne Ruzzo, S.C., Congregational Councilor; Kati Hamm, Congregational Councillor & Sec.

Sisters of Charity (Halifax) Corporate Mission, Inc., 125 Oakland St., Wellesley, 02481.
Tel: 781-997-1357; Fax: 781-997-1358; Email: bostreasurer@schalifax.org; Web: www.schalifax.ca. Sr. Joan O'Keefe, S.C., Congregational Leader. Sisters 110.

Sisters of Charity Supporting Corporation (1977) 125 Oakland St., Wellesley, 02481-5338.
Tel: 781-997-1126; Email: mafoster@schalifax.org. Sr. Joan O'Keefe, S.C., Congregational Leader. Sisters 259.

WRENTHAM. *St. Chretienne Regional Offices* (1807) 297 Arnold St., Wrentham, 02093-1798.
Tel: 508-384-8066; Fax: 508-507-3634; Email: ssch@tiac.net; Web: sistersofstchretienne.org. Sr. Suzanne Beaudion, Admin. Sisters of St. Chretienne. Sisters 2; Total in Residence 2.

Mount St. Mary's Abbey (1949) 300 Arnold St., Wrentham, 02093. Tel: 508-528-1282;
Fax: 508-528-5360; Email: sisters@msmabbey.org; Web: www.msmabbey.org. Mother Maureen McCabe, O.C.S.O., Abbess. The Cistercian Nuns of the Strict Observance (Trappistines).

The Cistercians of the Strict Observance in Massachusetts, Inc. Total in Residence 39; Professed Sisters 43.

[T] RETREAT HOUSES

COHASSET. *St. Joseph Retreat Center*, 339 Jerusalem Rd., Cohasset, 02025. Tel: 781-383-6024;
Tel: 781-383-6029; Email: retreat.center@csjboston.org; Web: www.csjretreatcenter.org. Sr. Joan M. McCarthy, C.S.J., Dir. Sisters of St. Joseph 2.

DUXBURY. *Miramar Retreat Center*, 121 Parks St., P.O.

Box M, Duxbury, 02331-0614. Tel: 781-585-2460; Fax: 781-585-3770; Email: miramarma@aol.com; Web: www.miramarretreat.org. Rev. Thomas Umbras, S.V.D., Dir., Rector. Total in Residence 7; Total Staff 18.

GLOUCESTER. *Eastern Point Retreat House*, Gonzaga, 37 Niles Pond Rd., Gloucester, 01930.
Tel: 978-283-0013; Fax: 978-282-1989; Email: office@easternpoint.org; Web: www.easternpoint.org. Revs. James P. Carr, S.J., Dir.; Joseph McHugh, S.J.; Richard J. Stanley, S.J.; Paul M. Sullivan, S.J.; Sr. Madeline Tiberii, S.S.J. Priests 4; Sisters 1; Total Staff 5.

SCITUATE. *Foyer of Charity* (1977) 74 Hollett St., Scituate, 02066. Tel: 781-545-1080; Email: mbradley@foyerofcharity.com; Web: www.foyerofcharity.com. Rev. Matthew Bradley, Dir. Total in Residence 2; Total Staff 6.

WALTHAM. *Espousal Retreat House and Conference Center*, 554 Lexington St., Waltham, 02452.
Tel: 781-209-3120; Fax: 781-893-0291; Email: espousaladmin@gmail.com; Web: www.espousal.org. Rev. Jean Kambou, C.S.S., Admin. Stigmatine Fathers and Brothers.Weekend and Weekly Retreats, Days-Evenings of Recollection. Total Staff 10.

WESTON. *Campion Center Conference & Renewal* (1975) 319 Concord Rd., Weston, 02493-1398.
Tel: 781-419-1337; Email: acopponi@campioncenter.org; Web: www.campioncenter.org. Rev. James J. Fleming, S.J., Ph.D., Dir. Total in Residence 2; Total Staff 2.

[U] RETIREMENT RESIDENCES FOR PRIESTS AND BROTHERS

BOSTON. *Saint Anthony Residence*, 100 Arch St., Boston, 02110-1102. Tel: 646-473-0265; Email: hnp@hnp.org. Rev. Kevin Mullen, O.F.M., Pres. (For Retired Franciscan Friars.) Brothers 4; Priests 11; Total in Residence 15; Retired 14.

Regina Cleri Residence, 60 William Cardinal O'Connell Way, Boston, 02114. Tel: 617-523-1861; Fax: 617-720-0585; Email: sgust@reginacleri.org. Mr. Stephen J. Gust, Dir. Affiliated with Covenant Health, Inc.Residence for Retired Archdiocesan Priests. Priests 57; Sisters 3.

TEWKSBURY. *Immaculate Heart of Mary Residence*, 486 Chandler St., Tewksbury, 01876-2899.
Tel: 978-851-7258; Fax: 978-851-0952; Email: darthur@omires.com. Very Rev. John F. Hanley, O.M.I., V.F., Supr.; Revs. Francis Demers, O.M.I., Second Councilor; Charles Beausoleil, O.M.I.; Richard Bolduc, O.M.I.; Lucien Bouchard, O.M.I., (Retired); Gilmond C. Boucher, O.M.I.; Raymond Crowe, O.M.I.; Adhemar Deveau, O.M.I.; Gerald Flater, O.M.I.; James Flavin, O.M.I.; William Hallahan, O.M.I., (Retired); Patrick F. Healy, O.M.I.; Charles Heon, O.M.I.; Andre Houle, O.M.I.; Robert Levesque, O.M.I.; Richard McAlear, O.M.I.; William McSweeney, O.M.I.; John Morin, O.M.I.; John St. Cyr, O.M.I.; Raymond Steen, O.M.I.; Bros. Augustin Cote, O.M.I., (Retired); Paul Daly, O.M.I.; James H. Lucas, O.M.I.; Revs. Myles Cyr, O.M.I., (Retired); Roger Cyr; Roger Landry, O.M.I.; James Pillar, O.M.I.; Harry Winter, O.M.I. Bed Capacity 35; Brothers 3; Priests 25; Tot Asst. Annually 35; Total Staff 49.

WALTHAM. *Stigmatine Fathers and Brothers*, St. Joseph's Hall, 554 Lexington St., Waltham, 02452.
Tel: 781-209-3100; Email: franthonycorigliano@gmail.com; Web: www.stigmatines.com. Revs. Paul D. Burns, C.S.S.; David F. Gallagher, C.S.S., (Retired); Jean Kambou, C.S.S.; Bro. Antonio Banda Lopez. Priests 3; Professed 1.

[V] RESIDENCES FOR MEN AND WOMEN

BOSTON. *St. Helena House*, 89 Union Park St., Boston, 02118. Tel: 617-426-2922; Fax: 617-542-3460. James A. Smith, Property Mgr. Seniors, low income & disabled persons. Residents 99.

Our Lady's Guild House - Residence for Women, 20 Charlesgate W., Boston, 02215. Tel: 617-536-3000; Fax: 617-536-8508. Constance Pagan, Admin. Residents 133.

[W] PUBLIC ORATORIES AND CHAPELS

BOSTON. *St. Anthony Shrine*, 100 Arch St., Boston, 02110-1100. Tel: 617-542-6440; Fax: 617-542-4225; Email: admin@hnp.org; Web: www.stanthonyshrine.org. Revs. Thomas Conway, O.F.M., Exec. Dir.; Frank Sevola, Guardian; Bro. John Maganzini, O.F.M., Spiritual Dir.; Revs. Brian Cullinane, O.F.M.; Richard C. Flaherty, O.F.M.; Hugh Hines, O.F.M.; Michael Johnson, O.F.M., Vicar; Jacques LaPointe, O.F.M.; Emeric Meier, O.F.M.; Damian Park, O.F.M.; Gene Pistacchio, O.F.M.; Joe Quinn, O.F.M.; Raymond C. Selker II, O.F.M.; Ronald Stark, O.F.M.; Bros. Paul Bourque, O.F.M.; Christopher Coccia, O.F.M., Deacon; Gregory Day, O.F.M.; Thomas Donovan, O.F.M.; Richard James, O.F.M.; John Jaskowiak, O.F.M.; Anthony LoGalbo, O.F.M., Vicar; Kevin McGoff, O.F.M.; Daniel Murray, O.F.M.; Paul O'Keeffe; Sebastian Tobin, O.F.M. Brothers 11; Priests 15.

Chapel of Our Lady of Lourdes, 698 Beacon St., Boston, 02215. Tel: 617-536-2761;
Fax: 617-536-1694; Email: denise.damico@aol.com. Rev. George L. Szal, S.M., Dir. Marist Fathers. Priests 5.

Marist Fathers Residence, Boston.
Tel: 617-262-2271; Fax: 617-536-1694. Revs. Albert DiIanni, S.M., Ph.D.; Francis Grispino, S.M.

Chapel of the Holy Spirit aka The Paulist Center, 5 Park St., Boston, 02108-4802. Tel: 617-742-4460; Fax: 617-720-5756; Email: info@paulistcenter.org; Web: www.paulistcenter.org. Revs. Michael B. McGarry, C.S.P., M.Div., M.A. Theology, Dir.; Broderick M. Walsh, C.S.P., M.Div., Assoc. Dir.; Charles Cunniff, C.S.P., Pastoral Assoc.; Susan Rutkowski, M.Div., Pastoral Min., Family Religious Educ. & Social Ministry.; Patricia Simpson, M.Div., Pastoral Admin.; Peter Ghiloni, Pastoral Min., Liturgy & Music; Kristin Hauser, Pastoral Min., Young Adults. Paulist Fathers, Missionary Society of St. Paul the Apostle in MA, The Paulist Center.

St. Clement Archdiocesan Eucharistic Shrine, 1105 Boylston St., Boston, 02215-3604.
Tel: 617-266-5999; Fax: 617-247-7576; Email: petergrover@juno.com; Web: www.stclementshrine.org. Revs. Peter W. Grover, O.M.V., B.A., S.T.B., S.T.M., Admin.; Thomas Carzon, O.M.V., S.T.L.; Gregory Staab, O.M.V.; Mark S. Yavarone, O.M.V., M.Div., M.A., Ph.D.; John Luong; James Walther, O.M.V., Prov.; Shawn Monahan, O.M.V. St. Ignatius Province of the Oblates of the Virgin Mary. Priests 7.

St. Francis Chapel, 800 Boylston St., #1001, Boston, 02199-8001. Tel: 617-437-7117; Fax: 617-437-8420; Email: director@stfrancischapel.org; Web: www.stfrancischapel.org. Revs. John L. Wykes, O.M.V., Dir.; Peter P. Gojuk, O.M.V.; Robert Lowrey, O.M.V. St. Ignatius Province of the Oblates of the Virgin Mary. Priests 4.

Madonna Queen of the Universe (1987) 150 Orient Ave., Boston, 02128-1006. Tel: 617-569-8792;
Fax: 617-569-8701; Email: madonna_orione@hotmail.com. Revs. Marcelo Boschi, F.D.P., Supr. & Rector; Miguel Alvamir Goncalves, Vice-Rector. Don Orione Fathers.

Our Lady of the Airways Chapel, First Floor, Tower Bldg., Logan International Airport, Boston, 02128.
Tel: 617-567-2800; Email: fatherrichard@massport.com. Rev. Richard A. Uftring.

BROCKTON. *Chapel of Our Saviour*, 475 Westgate Dr., Brockton, 02301-1819. Tel: 508-583-8357;
Fax: 508-586-5510; Web: chapelofoursaviorbrockton.org. Revs. Gerald DiGiralamo, S.A.; John Keane, S.A.; Bros. Thomas Banacki, S.A.; Savio McNeice, S.A.; Louis Marek, S.A. Brothers 3; Priests 2.

HOLLISTON. *Our Lady of Fatima Shrine* (1969) 101 Summer St., Holliston, 01746-5857.
Tel: 508-429-2144; Fax: 508-429-4793; Email: holliston@xaverianmissionaries.org; Web: www.xaverianmissionaries.org. Revs. Rocco N. Puopolo, S.X., Rector; Francis Signorelli, S.X.; Carl S. Chudy, S.X.; Anthony Lalli, S.X.; Adolph J. Menendez, S.X. Xaverian Missionaries. Priests 6.

LOWELL. *St. Joseph the Worker Shrine*, 37 Lee St., Lowell, 01852-1103. Tel: 978-458-6346;
Fax: 978-441-0963; Email: info@stjosephshrine.org; Web: www.stjosephshrine.org. Revs. Terrence E. O'Connell, O.M.I., Dir.; Roger Couture, O.M.I, Parochial Vicar, (Retired); Jerry Orsino, O.M.I., Parochial Vicar; Eugene Tremblay, O.M.I., Parochial Vicar; Stephen Conserva, O.M.I.

Andre Garin Residence, 27 Kirk St., Lowell, 01852-1103. Tel: 978-937-9594; Fax: 978-458-3603; Email: andregarinresidence@yahoo.com. Revs. Terrence E. O'Connell, O.M.I., Dir.; Eugene Tremblay, O.M.I.

PEABODY. *St. Theresa Carmelite Chapel* (1960) North Shore Mall, 4 Wheatland St., Peabody, 01960.
Tel: 978-531-6145; Fax: 978-531-1359; Email: hjones@carmelnet.org; Web: www.carmelitechapel.com. Rev. Kavungal Davy, C.M.I., Admin. Priests 3.

[X] CAMPUS MINISTRY

BOSTON. *The Catholic Center at Boston University*, 211 Bay State Rd., Boston, 02215. Tel: 617-353-3632;
Fax: 617-358-2049; Email: catholic@bu.edu; Web: www.bu.edu/CATHOLIC. Rev. Clifton M. Thuma, Chap.; Bros. Patrick Reilly, B.H.; Samuel Gunn, B.H.; Parker Jordan, B.H., Assoc. Campus Min.; Sr. Olga Yaqob.

Emmanuel College Campus Ministry (1919) 400 The Fenway, Boston, 02115. Tel: 617-735-9703; Web: emmanuel.edu. Sr. Margaret Cummins, S.N.D.

University of Massachusetts at Boston Campus Ministry, Tel: 617-287-5839; Email: paul.helfrich@umb.edu.
Harbor Campus, Dorchester, 02125.
Tel: 617-287-5839; Email: paul.helfrich@umb.edu.

BRIDGEWATER. *Bridgewater State College Catholic Center*, 122 Park Ave., Bridgewater, 02325.
Tel: 508-531-1346; Fax: 508-531-6188; Email: mnolan@bridgew.edu; Web: www.bridgew.edu/depts/cathcntr/. Rev. Michael L. Nolan, Campus Min.

CAMBRIDGE. *Harvard Catholic Center*, 29 Mount Auburn St., Cambridge, 02138. Tel: 617-491-8400;
Fax: 617-354-7092; Email: frkellystpaulparish@gmail.com; Email: gsalzmann@gmail.com; Email: harvardpriest@gmail.com; Web: www.harvardcatholic.org. Revs. George S. Salzmann, O.S.F.S., Chap.; Mark W. Murphy, Chap.; William T. Kelly, Chap.; Mr. Thomas Hogan, Dir.; Douglas Zack, Dir.

Massachusetts Institute of Technology Catholic Community, 40 Massachusetts Ave., W-11, Cambridge, 02139. Tel: 617-253-2981;
Fax: 617-253-3260; Email: catholic@mit.edu; Web: www.web.mit.edu/tcc/. Rev. Daniel P. Moloney. Total Staff 2.

FRAMINGHAM. *Framingham State College Campus Ministry*, 100 State St., Framingham, 01701.
Tel: 508-626-4610; Fax: 508-626-4939; Email: kangeli@framingham.edu. Ms. Kristelle Angelli, M.A., Chap.

LOWELL. *UMass, Lowell Catholic Campus Ministry*, University Crossing 380, 220 Pawtucket St., Lowell, 01854. Tel: 978-934-5032; Email: Catholic_Center@uml.edu; Email: bernadine_kensinger@uml.edu; Web: www.umlcatholic.org; Web: www.uml.edu/student-services/campus-ministry. Ms. Bernadine Kensinger, Campus Min. & Dir. Catholic Campus Ministry. Total Staff 1.

MEDFORD. *Tufts Interfaith Center Tufts University Catholic Chaplaincy*, 58 Winthrop St., Medford, 02155-5300. Tel: 617-627-3427; Email: lynn.cooper@tufts.edu; Web: www.tufts.edu/chaplaincy. Ms. Lynn Cooper, Catholic Chap. Tot Asst. Annually 2,800; Total Staff 1.

NEWTON. *Boston College Campus Ministry*, 140 Commonwealth Ave., Chestnut Hill, 02467.
Tel: 617-552-3475; Fax: 617-552-3044; Email: ministry@bc.edu; Web: www.bc.edu/ministry. Total in Residence 6; Total Staff 14.
McElroy 233, Chestnut Hill, 02467.
Tel: 617-552-3475; Fax: 617-552-3044; Email: ministry@bc.edu; Web: www.bc.edu/ministry.

NORTH ANDOVER. *Merrimack College Campus Ministry Center*, 315 Turnpike St., North Andover, 01845.
Tel: 978-837-5450; Fax: 978-837-5004. Rev. Keith Hollis, O.S.A., Dir.; Jeffrey Wallace; Cara Annese, Campus Min.; Dr. Hugh Hinton, D.M.A., Coord. of Liturgical Music & Dir. Campus Music Activities. Priests 1; Total Staff 5; Total Assisted 2,000.

SALEM. *Salem State College, Catholic Campus Ministry*, 352 Lafayette St., Salem, 01970.
Tel: 978-542-6074; Fax: 978-744-2757; Email: gmckeon@salemstate.edu. Rev. Gerard R. McKeon, S.J.

WALTHAM. *Bentley University Spiritual Life Center* (1917) 175 Forest St., Waltham, 02452-4705.
Tel: 781-891-2435; Fax: 781-891-2839; Email: mdilorenzo@bentley.edu; Web: www.bentley.edu. Maria DiLorenzo, B.A., M.A., Dir. Spiritual Life Center, Catholic Advisor.

Brandeis University Catholic Chaplaincy, Mail stop 205, P.O. Box 549110, Waltham, 02454-9110.
Tel: 781-736-3574; Fax: 781-736-3577; Email: cuenin@brandeis.edu. Rev. Walter H. Cuenin, (Retired).

WELLESLEY. *Babson College Campus Ministry*, 9 Glen Rd., Wellesley, 02181. Sr. Frances Sheehey, O.S.F., Campus Coord.

Wellesley College - Office of Religious and Spiritual Life, Wellesley, 02481. Tel: 781-283-2688;
Fax: 781-283-3676; Email: ncorcora@wellesley.edu.

WESTON. *Regis College Office of Campus Ministry*, 235 Wellesley St., Weston, 02493. Tel: 781-768-7027;
Tel: 781-768-7028; Tel: 781-768-7029;
Fax: 781-768-8339; Email: ministry@regiscollege.edu; Web: www.regiscollege.edu. Sr. Elizabeth Conway, C.S.J., Dir. of Spiritual Life; Rev. Paul E. Kilroy, Chap.

[Y] FOUNDATIONS, FUNDS & TRUSTS

BOSTON. *Chancery Office*, 66 Brooks Dr., 02184-3839.
Tel: 617-254-0100; Fax: 617-783-4564; Web: www.rcab.org. Also see Miscellaneous Section for additional listings.

The Cardinal Medeiros Trust, Tel: 617-254-0100.

Cardinal Cushing General Hospital Foundation, Brockton.

The Carney Hospital Foundation, Inc., 2100 Dorchester Ave., Boston, 02124. Tel: 617-296-1788 . J. Barry Driscoll, Pres.; Paul J. Kingston, Vice Pres.; Daniel J. McDevitt, Sec.; William F. Henderson, Exec. Dir. (Formerly The New Caritas Christi Hospital, Inc.).

The Catholic Cemetery Association Perpetual Care Trust, 66 Brooks Dr., 02184-3839.

**Catholic Schools Foundation, Inc.*, Tel: 617-254-0100; Fax: 617-783-6366. (Formerly St. Anthony's Scholarship Fund, Inc.).

Clergy Benefit Trust, Tel: 617-254-0100; Fax: 617-783-2947.

Clergy Fund Society, Tel: 617-254-0100; Fax: 617-783-2947.

Clergy Medical-Hospitalization Trust, Tel: 617-254-0100; Fax: 617-783-2947.

Archdiocese of Boston Clergy Retirement/Disability Trust, Tel: 617-254-0100; Fax: 617-783-2947.

Family Counseling Endowment Fund, Inc., 141 Tremont St., Boston, 02111. Tel: 617-482-4355.

Marist Capital Trust Fund, c/o Financial Admin., The Missionary Sisters of the Society of Mary, Inc., Sisters of the Society of Mary, Inc., 349 Grove St., Waltham, 02154. Tel: 617-893-0149; Email: admin@maristsmsm.org. Sisters Shirley Foust, Admin.; Phyllis Doucet, Trustee.

Metropolitan Boston Dialysis Center, Inc., 736 Cambridge St., Brighton, 02135.

Mission Promotion, c/o Mission Promoter, 349 Grove St., Waltham, 02453. Tel: 781-893-0149; Email: admin@maristsmsm.org. Sisters Mary Jane Kenney, Prov.; Helen Muller, Prov. Asst.; Joyce Edelmann, Sec. Missionary Sisters of the Society of Mary.

Roman Catholic Archdiocese of Boston Health Benefit Trust, Tel: 617-746-5680; Fax: 617-783-4564. Mr. James M. Walsh, Admin.

Roman Catholic Archdiocese of Boston Insurance Trust, Tel: 617-746-5640; Fax: 617-783-4564. Mr. James M. Walsh, Admin. Benefit Office.

Roman Catholic Archdiocese of Boston Pension Trust, Tel: 617-746-5640; Fax: 617-746-4564. Mr. James M. Walsh, Admin. Benefit Office.

Roman Catholic Archdiocese of Boston Long Term Disability Trust, Tel: 617-746-5640; Fax: 617-783-4564. Mr. James M. Walsh, Admin.

Roman Catholic Archdiocese of Boston Common Investment Fund, Tel: 617-746-5680; Fax: 617-783-4564.

Roman Catholic Archdiocese of Boston Fixed Income Investment Fund, Tel: 617-746-5680; Fax: 617-783-4564.

St. Charles Borromeo Educational Foundation, Inc.

Sacred Heart Trust Fund, c/o Society of Jesus, Trustee, 761 Harrison Ave., Boston, 02118. Tel: 617-536-5604. Bro. H. Francis Cluff, S.J.

St. Elizabeth's Hospital Foundation, Inc., 159 Washington St., Brighton, 02135.

Caritas Holy Family Hospital Foundation, Inc.

The Catholic Community Fund of the Archdiocese of Boston, Inc., 66 Brooks Dr., 02184-3839. Tel: 617-746-5621; Fax: 617-783-6366; Email: lisa_lipsett@rcab.org. Patricia Kelleher Bartram, Pres.

Benefit Trust for Non-Incardinated Priests, Tel: 617-254-0100; Fax: 617-783-2947.

Benefit Trust for Non-Incardinated Priest Duly Assigned for Service in the Archdiocese of Boston.

St. Mary's High School Foundation, Inc., 35 Tremont St., Lynn, 01902. Tel: 781-595-7885; Fax: 781-595-4471. Ms. Grace Cotter Regan, Contact Person.

Clergy Assistance Trust, 66 Brooks Dr., 02184-3839. Tel: 617-746-5615; Fax: 617-783-2947.

Massachusetts Catholic Self-Insurance Group, Inc., 66 Brooks Dr., 02184-3839. Tel: 617-746-5740; Fax: 517-746-5421; Email: Joseph_McEnness@rcab.org. Mr. Joseph F. McEnness, Admin.; Mr. Timothy M. McCrystal, Esq., Counsel.

Board of Directors: Very Rev. Charles J. Higgins, V.F., Clerk; James P. McDonough, Pres.; Mr. John E. Straub, Treas.; Mr. John M. Riley; Mr. Joseph P. Welch; Mr. William LaBroad; Mr. Neil Buckley.

Senior Religious Trust Fund of Marist Fathers of Boston, 13 Isabella St., Boston, 02116. Tel: 617-426-4448; Email: denise.damico@aol.com. Rev. Walter L. Gaudreau, S.M., Supr.

IPSWICH. *Blin Charitable Trust* (1995) 30 Jeffrey's Neck Rd., Ipswich, 01938. Tel: 978-380-1372; Fax: 978-356-9759; Email: mary.farren@sndden.org; Web: www.sndden.org. Sr. Mary M. Farren, S.-N.D.deN., Contact Person. Sisters of Notre Dame de Namur.

LOWELL. *D'Youville Senior Care Foundation, Inc.*, 981 Varnum Ave., Lowell, 01854. Tel: 978-453-3561; Fax: 978-569-1070; Email: nprendergast@dyouville.org; Web: www.dyouville.org. Ms. Naomi M. Prendergast, CEO.

Saints Memorial Medical Center Foundation, P.O. Box 367, Lowell, 01853-0367. Tel: 978-934-8334; Fax: 978-934-8479; Email: fund.kec@tmmc.org; Web: www.saints-memorial.org. Thom Clark, Pres. & CEO; Kevin E. Coughlin, Vice Pres.; D. Harold Sullivan, Chm.

METHUEN. *Caritas Holy Family Hospital Foundation, Inc.*, 70 East St., Methuen, 01844-4597. Tel: 978-687-0151; Fax: 978-688-7689; Email: nmallen@cchcs.org; Web: www.holyfamilyhosp.org. Mrs. Noreen V. Mallen, Exec. Dir.

NEEDHAM. *St. Joseph Parish School Fund, Inc., Needham*, 1382 Highland Ave., Needham, 02492. Tel: 781-444-0245; Fax: 781-444-7713. John Brennan, Treas.

[Z] MISCELLANEOUS

BOSTON. *Boston Inter-Community Ministries, Inc.*, 637 Cambridge St., Boston, 02135. Tel: 617-746-2026; Email: maureen.doherty@csjboston.org. Sr. Maureen Doherty, C.S.J., Contact Person.

The Catholic Lawyers Guild of the Archdiocese of Boston, Inc., One Lewis Wharf, Boston, 02110. Tel: 617-722-8175; Fax: 617-723-1180. Hon. Joseph R. Nolan, Pres.

Corporation for the Sponsored Ministries of the Sisters of St. Joseph of Boston (2000) 637 Cambridge St., Boston, 02135-2800. Tel: 617-746-2190; Fax: 617-746-2194; Email: suzanne.kearney@csjboston.org; Web: www.csjsponsorship.org. Suzanne M. Kearney, Exec. Dir., Email: suzanne.kearney@csjboston.org.

Daughters of St. Paul Defined Pension Plan & Trust, 50 St. Paul's Ave., Jamaica Plain, 02130. Tel: 617-522-8911; Fax: 617-524-8648; Email: mmoran@paulinemedia.com. Sr. Margaret Moran, Treas.

Equestrian Order of the Holy Sepulchre of Jerusalem (1099)

Northeastern Lieutenancy, c/o Rev. Jonathan Gaspar, Pastoral Ctr., 66 Brooks Dr., 02184-3839.

**KOLBE Association, Inc.*, 66 Brooks Dr., 02184-3839. Tel: 617-746-5425; Email: rev.michael.medas@sjs.edu. His Eminence Sean Cardinal O'Malley, O.F.M.Cap., Episcopal Moderator; Rev. Michael B. Medas, M.S.W., Exec. Dir.

Lanteri Charitable Trust, 1105 Boylston St., Boston, 02215-3660. Tel: 617-536-4141; Fax: 617-536-7016; Email: wbrownomv@aol.com. Rev. James Walther, O.M.V., Pres.; David Y. Williams, Trustee; Rev. William M. Brown, O.M.V., Trustee.

League of Catholic Women of the Archdiocese of Boston, St. Mary of the Sacred Heart, 392 Hanover St., Hanover, 02339. Tel: 781-826-4303. Mrs. John F. O'Donoghue Jr., Pres.; Rev. Martin P. Connor, S.T.L., Spiritual Dir., (Retired).

The Literacy Connection (1987) 637 Cambridge St., Brighton, 02135. Tel: 617-746-2100; Fax: 617-783-8246; Email: patricia.andrews@csjboston.org. Sr. Patricia Andrews, C.S.J., Dir.

Lourdes Bureau, 698 Beacon St., Boston, 02215. Tel: 617-536-2761; Fax: 617-536-1694; Email: denise.damico@aol.com. Rev. George L. Szal, S.M., Dir. Marist Fathers.Official Representatives in America for the Shrine of Lourdes, France.

Medaille Corporation, 637 Cambridge St., Boston, 02135. Tel: 617-783-9090; Fax: 617-783-8246; Email: bostoncsj@csjboston.org; Web: www.csjboston.org. Sisters Rosemary Brennan, C.S.J., Pres.; Leila Hogan, C.S.J., Treas.

Most Holy Name of Jesus Federation of Poor Clare Monasteries in the Eastern Region of the United States (1959) Monastery of Saint Clare, 920 Centre St., Boston, 02130. Tel: 617-524-1760; Fax: 617-983-5205; Email: bostonpoorclares@yahoo.com. Sr. Clare Frances McAvoy, O.S.C., Contact Person. Solemn Vows 127; Simple Professed 10.

PACE - Parents Alliance for Catholic Education, 14 Beacon St., Ste. 506, Boston, 02108. Tel: 617-723-9890; Fax: 617-723-9892; Email: fkalisz@paceorg.net; Web: www.paceorg.net. Frederick M. Kalisz Jr., Exec. Dir.

PONTIFICAL MISSION SOCIETIES IN THE ARCHDIOCESE OF BOSTON The Society for the Propagation of the Faith, The Missionary Childhood Association, The Society of Saint Peter Apostle & The Missionary Union of Priests and Religious Mailing Address & Office: Pastoral Center, 66 Brooks Dr., 02184-3839. Tel: 617-542-1776; Fax: 617-542-1778; Email: info@propfaithboston.org; Web: www.propfaithboston.org. Rev. Msgr. William P. Fay, Dir.; Maureen Crowley Heil, Dir., Programs & Devel. Total Staff 7.

Sancta Maria House, Inc. (1972) 11 Waltham St., Boston, 02118-2162. Tel: 617-423-4366.

St. Vincent Pallotti Center for Apostolic Development of Boston, Inc., 66 Brooks Dr., 02184-3839. Tel: 617-783-3924; Email: VolService@aol.com; Web: www.pallotticenterboston.org.

Vox Clara Committee, Inc., 127 Lake St., Boston, 02135. Tel: 617-254-2610; Email: tempio@aol.com. Rev. Msgr. James P. Moroney, B.A., S.T.L., S.T.B., Dir.

**Women Affirming Life, Inc.*, P.O. Box 35532, Boston, 02135. Tel: 617-254-2277; Fax: 617-254-2299; Email: mail@affirmlife.com; Web: www.affirmlife.com. Frances X. Hogan, Pres.

ARLINGTON. *Fidelity House*, 25 Medford St., Arlington, 02474-3105. Tel: 781-648-2005; Fax: 781-648-4604; Email: Fidelityhouse@rcn.com; Web: www.fidelityhouse.org. Edward F. Woods, Dir. Purpose: A community center sponsored by the Saint Agnes Parish providing quality services primarily for youth development with flexible and diverse services for people of all ages.

BEVERLY. *The Catholic Cemetery Association of the Archdiocese of Boston, Inc.*, 100 Cummings Ctr., Ste. 421F, Beverly, 01915. Tel: 781-322-6300; Fax: 978-969-2929; Email: cemetery_contactus@rcab.org; Web: www.ccemetery.org. Robert Visconti, Exec. Dir; David W. Smith, Sec.

BRAINTREE. *Archdiocesan Central High Schools, Inc.*, 66 Brooks Dr., 02184-3839. Tel: 617-779-3601; Fax: 617-746-5702. His Eminence Sean Cardinal O'Malley, O.F.M.Cap.; Kathleen Mears, Supt. Tot Asst. Annually 34,056; Total Staff 4,641.

The Catholic Health Foundation of Greater Boston, Inc., 66 Brooks Dr., 02184. Tel: 617-746-5693; Email: lisa_lipsett@rcab.org. Patricia Kelleher Bartram, Pres.

Fides Insurance Group, Inc., c/o Office of Risk Management, Roman Catholic Archdiocese of Boston, 66 Brooks Dr., 02184.

The Fund for Catholic Schools, Inc dba Campaign for Catholic Schools, 66 Brooks Dr., 02184. Tel: 617-262-5600; Fax: 617-779-3721; Email: campaignforcatholicschools@rcab.org; Web: campaignforcatholicschools.org. Mary Flynn Myers, Pres.; James Walsh, Exec.

CAMBRIDGE. **The Youville House, Inc.*, 1575 Cambridge St., Cambridge, 02138-4398. Tel: 617-876-4344; Email: leaheyd@youville.org; Web: www.youville.org. Mr. T. Richard Quigley, Pres. & CEO; Ms. Marsha V. Whelan, Vice Pres. Mission Integration; Revs. William L. Mulligan, S.J., Chap.; Jennifer Casstevens, Chap.; Ms. Patricia Kennedy, Dir. of Pastoral Care Svcs. & Chap.; Elizabeth Walsh, Chap. Member of Youville Lifecare, Inc. Priests 1; Sisters of Charity (Grey Nuns) 3; Assisted Living Units 95.

CHESTNUT HILL. *Domus Jerusalem, Inc.*, 774 Boylston St., Chestnut Hill, 02467.

EVERETT. *Notre Dame Mission Volunteer Corporation*, 351 Broadway, Everett, 02149. Tel: 978-682-4392; Fax: 617-387-1303; Email: maureen.obrien@sndden.org; Web: www.sndden.org. Sisters Barbara English, S.N.D.deN., Pres.; Maura Browne, S.N.D.deN., Treas.; Maureen O'Brien, S.-N.D.deN., Contact Person.

FRAMINGHAM. *Bethany Health Care Center, Inc.*, 97 Bethany Rd., Framingham, 01702-7237. Tel: 508-872-6750; Fax: 508-875-5425; Email: jacquelyn.mccarthy@csjboston.org; Web: www.bethanyhealthcare.org. Sr. Jacquelyn McCarthy, C.S.J., CEO & Admin. Congregation of Sisters of St. Joseph of Boston. An affiliate of Covenant Health, Inc., Tewksbury.Skilled Nursing Facility and Residential Living Bed Capacity 169.

Bethany Home Care, Inc., 97 Bethany Rd., Framingham, 01702.

**Bethany Hill Place, Inc.*, 89 Bethany Rd., Framingham, 01702. Tel: 508-875-1117; Fax: 508-875-2288; Email: tappert@bethanyhillschool.org. Sponsored by the Sisters of St. Joseph of Boston.41 units of educational housing for low-income people with a variety of needs.

IPSWICH. *Cuvilly Arts and Earth Center, Inc.* (1983) 10 Jeffrey Neck Rd., Ipswich, 01938. Tel: 978-356-4288; Email: cuvilly@verizon.net; Web: cuvilly.org. Sr. Patricia Rolinger, S.N.D.deN., M.A., Exec. Dir. Total Staff 12; Total Assisted 100.

LAWRENCE. *Notre Dame Education Center-Lawrence* (1992) (Adult Literacy) 354 Merrimack St., Ste. 210, Lawrence, 01843. Tel: 978-682-6441; Fax: 978-974-9840; Email: executivedirector@ndeclawrence.com. Sr. Eileen T. Burns, S.N.D., Exec. Dir. Sisters of Notre Dame de Namur.ESOL, Citizenship, Computer, Spanish, Nursing Assistant/HHA Program, High School Equivalency. Sisters 7; Total Staff 19; Adults 109.

Notre Dame High School Corporate Internship Program, Inc. (2004) 303 Haverhill St., Lawrence, 01840. Tel: 978-689-8222; Fax: 978-689-1967. Sr. Maryalyce Gilfeather, S.N.D.deN., Ph.D., Pres.

LOWELL. *Saints Medical Center Inc.*, Saints Medical Center, One Hospital Dr., Lowell, 01852.

Tel: 978-458-1411; Email: sguimond@saintsmedicalcenter.com; Web: www.saintsmedicalcenter.com. Mr. Stephen Guimond, CEO.

METHUEN. *Caritas Holy Family Hospital Men's Guild* (1950) 70 East St., Methuen, 01844-4597.
Tel: 978-687-0156, Ext. 2362; Fax: 978-688-7689; Web: www.holyfamilyhosp.org. Lester Schindel, Pres. & CEO.

Caritas Valley Regional Health System, Inc. (1945) 70 East St., Methuen, 01844-4597.
Tel: 978-687-0151; Fax: 978-688-7689; Web: www.holyfamilyhosp.org.

Caritas Holy Family Hospital, Inc. (1984)
Tel: 978-687-0151; Fax: 978-688-7689.

Caritas Holy Family Hospital Auxiliary (1947)
Tel: 978-687-0156, Ext. 2301; Fax: 978-688-7689.

Caritas Holy Family Hospital Men's Guild (1950)
Tel: 978-687-0156, Ext. 2362; Fax: 978-688-7689.

Caritas Holy Family Hospital Foundation, Inc. (1987) Tel: 978-687-0156, Ext. 2104;
Fax: 978-688-7689.

Caritas Valley Regional Support Services, Inc. (1984) Tel: 978-687-0151; Fax: 978-688-7689.

Caritas Valley Regional Medical Services Corporation (1995) 70 East St., Methuen, 01844.
Tel: 978-687-0151; Fax: 978-682-9908.

Caritas Valley Regional Ventures, Inc.

Greater Lawrence Mental Health Center, Inc.

MILTON. *The Guild of St. Luke of the Archdiocese of Boston, Inc.*, 26 Houston Ave., Milton, 02186.

NEEDHAM. *St. Sebastian's School Fund, Inc.*, 1191 Greendale Ave., Needham, 02492.
Tel: 781-449-5200; Email: jack_doherty@stsebs.org. John J. Doherty, Contact Person & Business Mgr.

NEWTON. *Catholic Purchasing Services, Inc.* (1985) 580 Washington St., Newton, 02458. Tel: 617-965-4343 ; Fax: 617-965-5430; Email: jmorrissey@catholicpurchasing.org; Web: catholicpurchasing.org. Mr. Joseph V. Morrissey, Pres.

QUINCY. *The Good Shepherd: Maria Droste Services*, 1354 Hancock St., Ste. 209, Quincy, 02169.
Tel: 617-471-5686; Fax: 617-471-6622; Email: mariadroste@verizon.net. Sr. Lorraine Bernier, R.G.S.
Madonna Hall Total Staff 5; Volunteers 12; Total Assisted 290.

ROXBURY. *Franciscan Sisters of the Immaculate Conception, Inc.*, 1 Magazine St., Roxbury, 02118.
Tel: 617-445-6178.

SCITUATE. *Mass Times Trust* dba Masstimes.org, 91 Surfside Rd., Scituate, 02066. Mr. Robert A. Hummel, Trustee.

TEWKSBURY. *Covenant Health, Inc.*, 100 Ames Pond, Ste. 102, Tewksbury, 01876. Tel: 978-654-6363; Fax: 978-851-0828; Email: info@covenanthealth.net; Web: www.covenanthealth.net. David R. Lincoln, Pres. & CEO; John Ahle, CFO. Sponsored organizations: Massachusetts: St. Joseph Manor Health Care, Brockton; Youville House Assisted Living Residence, Cambridge; M.I. Adult Day Health Center, Inc., Lawrence; M.I. Management, Lawrence; M.I. Residential Community, Inc., Lawrence; M.I. Residential Community II, Inc., Lawrence; M.I. Residential Community III, Inc., Lawrence, M.I. Transportation, Lawrence; Mary Immaculate Nursing/Restorative Center, Lawrence; Youville Place Assisted Living Residence, Lexington; Youville Hospital and Rehabilitation Center, Tewksbury; Youville Lifecare, Inc., Tewksbury; CHS of Waltham, dba Maristhill Nursing and Rehabilitation Center, Waltham; CHS of Worcester, dba St. Mary's Health Care Center, Worcester. Maine: Alternative Health Services, Bangor; St. Joseph Ambulatory Care, Inc., Bangor; St. Joseph Healthcare Foundation, Bangor; St. Joseph Hospital, Bangor; St. Andre Healthcare Facility, Biddeford; Community Clinical Services, Lewiston; St. Mary's Health System, Lewiston; St. Mary's Regional Medical Center, Lewiston; St. Mary's Residences, Lewiston; Neighborhood Housing Initiative, Lewiston; St. Mary's d'Youville Pavilion, Lewiston. New Hampshire: Souhegan Home and Hospice Care, Inc., Nashua; St. Joseph Hospital DH Family Medicine, Nashua; St. Joseph Hospital of Nashua, NH, Nashua. Pennsylvania: St. Mary's Villa Nursing Home, Elmhurst Township; St. Mary's Villa Personal Care Residence, Elmhurst Township. Rhode Island: Mount St. Rita, Cumberland. Vermont: Fanny Allen Corp., Colchester; Fanny Allen Holdings, Inc., Colchester.; Affiliate organizations: Massachusetts: Sancta Maria Nursing Facility, Cambridge; Bethany Health Care Center, Framingham; Regina Cleri, Boston; Elizabeth Seton Residence, Wellesley; Marillac Residences, Wellesley; Notre Dame du Lac, Worcester; Notre Dame Long Term Care Center, Worcester; Fall River Jewish Home.

**Youville Hospital & Rehabilitation Center, Inc.*, 1575 Cambridge St., Cambridge, 02138-4398.
Tel: 617-876-4344; Fax: 617-547-5501; Email: leaheyd@youville.org; Web: www.youville.org. Covenant Health Systems, Tewksbury, MA. Bed Capacity 180; Patients Asst Anual. 2,340; Priests 1; Total Staff 650.

**Youville Lifecare, Inc.* (1895) Covenant Health, Inc., 100 Ames Pond Dr., Ste 102, Tewksbury, 01876. John Ahle, CFO. Sponsored by Covenant Health, Inc.

WALTHAM. **Marist Missionary Sisters Senior Religious Trust*, 349 Grove St., Waltham, 02453.
Tel: 781-893-0149; Fax: 781-899-6838; Email: admin@maristsmsm.org; Web: www.maristmissionarysmsm.org. Sisters Shirley Foust, Admin.; Phyllis Doucet, Trustee.

RELIGIOUS INSTITUTES OF MEN REPRESENTED IN THE ARCHDIOCESE

For further details refer to the corresponding bracketed number in the Religious Institutes of Men or Women section.

[0130]—*Assumptionists*—A.A.
[1040]—*The Augustinians* (Villanova, PA)—O.S.A.
[0200]—*Benedictine Monks*—O.S.B.
[1350]—*Brothers of St. Francis Xavier*—C.F.X.
[0470]—*The Capuchin Friars* (Prov. of Mary)—O.F.M.Cap.
[0310]—*Congregation of Christian Brothers* (Eastern Prov.)—C.F.C.
[1210]—*Congregation of the Missionaries of St. Charles*—C.S.
[0260]—*Discalced Carmelite Friars*—O.C.D.
[0520]—*Franciscan Friars* (Holy Name, Immaculate Conception Provs.)—O.F.M.
[0530]—*Franciscan Friars of the Atonement*—S.A.
[0690]—*Jesuit Fathers and Brother* (Northeast USA Prov.)—S.J.
[0770]—*The Marist Brothers* (Poughkeepsie, NY)—F.M.S.
[0780]—*Marist Fathers* (Boston Prov.)—S.M.
[0800]—*Maryknoll*—M.M.
[0720]—*The Missionaries of Our Lady of La Salette* (Eastern Prov.)—M.S.
[0910]—*Oblates of Mary Immaculate* (Eastern, St. John the Baptist Provs.)—O.M.I.
[0430]—*Order of Preachers-Dominicans* (Prov. of St. Joseph)—O.P.
[1030]—*Paulist Fathers*—C.S.P.
[1070]—*Redemptorist Fathers* (Baltimore Prov.)—C.SS.R.
[1190]—*Salesians of Don Bosco* (Prov. of St. Philip)—S.D.B.
[0110]—*Society of African Missions*—S.M.A.
[0420]—*Society of Divine Word* (Sacred Heart Prov.)—S.V.D.
[0370]—*Society of St. Columban* (American Region)—S.S.C.
[0410]—*Sons of Divine Providence*—F.D.P.
[1270]—*Sons of Mary Missionary Society*—F.M.S.I.
[1280]—*Stigmatine Fathers and Brothers* (Rome, Italy)—C.S.S.
[1360]—*Xaverian Missionary Fathers*—S.X.

RELIGIOUS INSTITUTES OF WOMEN REPRESENTED IN THE ARCHDIOCESE

[0330]—*Carmelite Sisters for the Aged and Infirm*—O.Carm.
[0670]—*Cistercian Nuns of the Strict Observance*—O.C.S.O.
[0420]—*Discalced Carmelite Nuns*—O.C.D.
[1115]—*Dominican Sisters of Peace*—O.P.
[1370]—*Franciscan Missionaries of Mary*—F.M.M.
[1320]—*Franciscan Missionary Sisters for Africa* (Co. Louth, Ireland)—F.M.S.A.
[1180]—*Franciscan Sisters of Allegany, New York*—O.S.F.
[1840]—*Grey Nuns of the Sacred Heart*—G.N.S.H.
[2070]—*Holy Union Sisters*—S.U.S.C.
[0410]—*Institute of the Sisters of Our Lady of Mt. Carmel*—I.N.S.C.
[2310]—*Little Sisters of the Assumption*—L.S.A.
[2340]—*Little Sisters of the Poor*—L.S.P.
[2420]—*Marist Missionary Sisters-Missionary Sisters of the Society of Mary*—S.M.S.M.
[2480]—*Medical Missionaries of Mary*—M.M.M.
[1360]—*Missionary Franciscan Sisters of the Immaculate Conception*—O.S.F.
[2790]—*Missionary Servants of the Most Blessed Trinity*—M.S.B.T.
[3760]—*Order of St. Clare*—O.S.C.
[0950]—*Pious Society Daughters of St. Paul*—F.S.P.
[3240]—*Poor Sisters of Jesus Crucified and the Sorrowful Mother*—C.J.C.
[3410]—*Religious of Christian Education*—R.C.E.
[2070]—*Religious of the Holy Union of the Sacred Hearts*—S.U.S.C.
[2970]—*School Sisters of Notre Dame*—S.S.N.D.
[0980]—*Sisters Disciples of the Divine Master*—P.D.D.M.
[0490]—*Sisters of Charity of Montreal-Grey Nuns*—S.G.M.
[0500]—*Sisters of Charity of Nazareth*—S.C.N.
[0560]—*Sisters of Charity of Quebec-Grey Nuns*—S.C.Q.
[0590]—*Sisters of Charity of Saint Elizabeth, Convent Station*—S.C.
[0640]—*Sisters of Charity of St. Vincent de Paul, Halifax*—S.C.
[0540]—*Sisters of Charity, At Ottawa-Grey Nuns of the Cross*—S.C.O.
[0990]—*Sisters of Divine Providence*—C.D.P.
[2580]—*Sisters of Mercy of the Union in the United States of America*—R.S.M.
[3000]—*Sisters of Notre Dame de Namur*—S.N.D.deN.
[3360]—*Sisters of Providence of Saint Mary-Of-The-Woods, Indiana*—S.P.
[3830]—*Sisters of Saint Joseph, Springfield*—S.S.J.
[3720]—*Sisters of St. Anne*—S.S.A.
[3750]—*Sisters of St. Chretienne*—S.S.Ch.
[3830]—*Sisters of St. Joseph*—C.S.J.
[0150]—*Sisters of the Assumption B.V.*—S.A.S.V.
[1830]—*Sisters of the Good Shepherd*—R.G.S.
[3310]—*Sisters of the Presentation of Mary*—P.M.
[1490]—*Sisters of the Third Franciscan Order*—O.S.F.
[1705]—*Sisters of the Third Order of St. Francis of Assisi*—O.S.F.
[4060]—*Society of the Holy Child Jesus*—S.H.C.J.
[4070]—*Society of the Sacred Heart*—R.S.C.J.
[4110]—*Ursuline Nuns* (Eastern Prov.)—O.S.U.

ARCHDIOCESAN CEMETERIES

ARLINGTON. *St. Paul*
BEVERLY. *St. Mary*
CAMBRIDGE. *North Cambridge Catholic*
CHARLESTOWN. *St. Francis de Sales*
HAVERHILL. *St. James, St. Joseph & St. Patrick*
LOWELL. *St. Patrick*
LYNN. *St. Mary, St. Joseph & St. Jean Baptiste*
MALDEN. *Holy Cross & St. Mary*
MARBLEHEAD. *Star of the Sea*
SALEM. *St. Mary*
SAXONVILLE. *St. George*
STONEHAM. *St. Patrick*
WALTHAM. *Calvary*
WATERTOWN. *Mount Auburn & St. Patrick*
WOBURN. *Calvary*

PRIVATE CATHOLIC CEMETERIES

CHELMSFORD. *St. Joseph Cemetery, Inc.*, 96 Riverneck Rd., Chelmsford, 01824-2942. Tel: 978-458-4851; Fax: 978-441-3958; Email: clare.cemetery@gmail.com; Web: stjc1894.com. Rev. Charles Breault, O.M.I., Dir. & Contact Person; Clare Taddeo, Asst. Dir. & Contact Person

NECROLOGY

† Edyvean, Walter James, Retired Auxiliary Bishop of Boston, Died Feb. 2, 2019
† Giggi, John Robert, (Retired), Died Aug. 7, 2018
† Borges, Laurence J., (Retired), Died Mar. 10, 2018
† Condon, Edwin A., (Retired), Died May. 1, 2018
† Craig, Richard J., (Retired), Died Oct. 27, 2018
† DeAdder, James W., (Retired), Died Jul. 23, 2018
† Dever, Dennis A., (Retired), Died Mar. 20, 2018
† Fitzpatrick, John P., (Retired), Died Dec. 20, 2018
† Guerrette, William J., (Retired), Died Feb. 28, 2018
† Hickey, Gerald J., (Retired), Died Oct. 17, 2018
† Kane, Joseph M., (Retired), Died Dec. 9, 2018
† Kelly, Patrick J., (Retired), Died Dec. 6, 2018
† Lynch, Leo X., (Retired), Died Feb. 28, 2018
† McGowan, James J., (Retired), Died Aug. 31, 2018
† McNeil, John R., (Retired), Died Dec. 31, 2018
† Meskell, David B., (Retired), Died Feb. 18, 2018
† O'Donnell, John F., (Retired), Died Mar. 21, 2018
† Shea, John J., (Retired), Died Apr. 4, 2018

Diocese of Bridgeport

(Dioecesis Bridgeportensis)

Most Reverend

FRANK J. CAGGIANO

Bishop of Bridgeport; ordained May 16, 1987; appointed Titular Bishop of Inis Cathaig June 6, 2006; episcopal ordination August 22, 2006; appointed Bishop of Bridgeport July 31, 2013; installed Sept. 19, 2013.

Chancery: The Catholic Center, 238 Jewett Ave., Bridgeport, CT 06606-2892. Tel: 203-416-1400; Fax: 203-371-8323.

Web: www.bridgeportdiocese.org

ESTABLISHED AUGUST 6, 1953.

Square Miles 633.

Corporate Title: The Bridgeport Roman Catholic Diocesan Corporation.

Comprises all of Fairfield County in the State of Connecticut.

For legal titles of parishes and diocesan institutions, consult the Chancery at The Catholic Center.

STATISTICAL OVERVIEW

Personnel	
Bishop	1
Priests: Diocesan Active in Diocese	121
Priests: Diocesan Active Outside Diocese	9
Priests: Retired, Sick or Absent	73
Number of Diocesan Priests	203
Religious Priests in Diocese	27
Total Priests in Diocese	230
Extern Priests in Diocese	23
Ordinations:	
Diocesan Priests	1
Transitional Deacons	3
Permanent Deacons	3
Permanent Deacons in Diocese	114
Total Brothers	1
Total Sisters	262
Parishes	
Parishes	82
With Resident Pastor:	
Resident Diocesan Priests	79
Resident Religious Priests	3
Without Resident Pastor:	
Administered by Lay People	1
Welfare	
Catholic Hospitals	1
Total Assisted	72,254
Homes for the Aged	4
Total Assisted	473
Day Care Centers	1
Total Assisted	225
Specialized Homes	1
Total Assisted	20
Special Centers for Social Services	7
Total Assisted	10,949
Other Institutions	15
Total Assisted	16,000
Educational	
Seminaries, Diocesan	2
Students from This Diocese	11
Diocesan Students in Other Seminaries	10
Total Seminarians	21
Colleges and Universities	2
Total Students	12,858
High Schools, Diocesan and Parish	5
Total Students	2,404
High Schools, Private	2
Total Students	1,120
Elementary Schools, Diocesan and Parish	23
Total Students	5,498
Elementary Schools, Private	2
Total Students	402
Non-residential Schools for the Disabled	2
Total Students	73
Catechesis/Religious Education:	
High School Students	2,038
Elementary Students	21,186
Total Students under Catholic Instruction	45,600
Teachers in the Diocese:	
Priests	6
Sisters	11
Lay Teachers	532
Vital Statistics	
Receptions into the Church:	
Infant Baptism Totals	2,798
Minor Baptism Totals	200
Adult Baptism Totals	114
Received into Full Communion	299
First Communions	4,052
Confirmations	4,321
Marriages:	
Catholic	513
Interfaith	81
Total Marriages	594
Deaths	2,815
Total Catholic Population	438,000
Total Population	949,921

Former Bishops—His Eminence LAWRENCE J. CARDINAL SHEHAN, D.D., ord. Dec. 23, 1922; cons. Dec. 12, 1945 as Auxiliary Bishop of Baltimore; installed as first Bishop of Bridgeport, Dec. 1, 1953; transferred to Archdiocese of Baltimore, July 10, 1961; created Cardinal, Feb. 22, 1965; died Aug. 26, 1984; Most Revs. WALTER W. CURTIS, S.T.D., ord. Dec. 8, 1937; appt. Auxiliary Bishop of Newark and Titular Bishop of Bisica in Tunis; cons. Sept. 24, 1957; appt. Bishop of Bridgeport, Sept. 23, 1961; installed Nov. 20, 1961; retired June 28, 1988; died Oct. 18, 1997; EDWARD M. EGAN, J.C.D., ord. Dec. 15, 1957; appt. Titular Bishop of Allegheny and Auxiliary Bishop of New York, April 1, 1985; cons. May 22, 1985; appt. Bishop of Bridgeport, Nov. 8, 1988; installed Dec. 14, 1988; appt. Archbishop of New York, May 11, 2000; installed June 19, 2000; created Cardinal Feb. 21, 2001; retired Feb. 23, 2009; died March 5, 2015.; WILLIAM E. LORI, ord. May 14, 1977; appt. Titular Bishop of Bulla and Auxiliary of Washington April 20, 1995; appt. Bishop of Bridgeport Jan. 23, 2001; installed March 19, 2001; appt. Archbishop of Baltimore March 20, 2012.

Unless otherwise indicated, all Diocesan Offices, including the Chancery and the Tribunal, are located in the Catholic Center, 238 Jewett Ave., Bridgeport, CT 06006-2892. Tel: 203-416-1400; Fax: 203-371-8323. Office Hours: Mon.-Fri. 8:30-4:30.

Vicar General and Moderator of the Curia—Rev. Msgr. THOMAS W. POWERS, S.T.L., Tel: 203-416-1646.

Chancellor—Rev. ROBERT M. KINNALLY, Tel: 203-416-1636.

Judicial Vicar—Rev. ARTHUR C. MOLLENHAUER, J.C.L.

Vicar for Canonical Affairs Related to Clergy—Rev. WILLIAM M. QUINLAN, J.C.L.

Episcopal Delegate for Administration—Deacon PATRICK TOOLE.

Episcopal Vicar for African Americans—Rev. REGINALD D. NORMAN.

Episcopal Vicar for Brazilians—Rev. LEONEL S. MEDEIROS.

Episcopal Vicar for Development—Rev. MICHAEL K. JONES, S.T.D.

Episcopal Vicar for Ecumenical and Interreligious Affairs—Rev. SAMUEL V. SCOTT.

Vicar for Evangelization—Rev. PETER J. TOWSLEY.

Episcopal Vicar for Haitians—Rev. GERARD-FRANTZ DESRUISSEAUX, J.C.L.

Episcopal Vicar for Hispanics—Rev. GUSTAVO A. FALLA.

Episcopal Vicar for Vietnamese Catholics—Rev. AUGUSTINE NGUYEN.

Episcopal Vicar for Senior Priests—Rev. Msgr. WILLIAM J. SCHEYD, P.A., (Retired).

Episcopal Delegate for Religious—Sr. NANCY STRILLACCI, A.S.C.J.

Chief Financial Officer—MR. MICHAEL HANLON.

Office of the Bishop

Office of the Bishop—MRS. DEBRA CHARLES, Exec. Asst. to Bishop, Tel: 203-416-1352; Email: dcharles@diobpt.org.

Vicar General

Vicar General and Moderator of the Curia—Rev. Msgr. THOMAS W. POWERS, S.T.L., Tel: 203-416-1646; MS. ELIZABETH M. AUDA, Exec. Asst. to Vicar Gen., Tel: 203-416-1636; Email: eauda@diobpt.org.

Office of the Chancellor

Chancellor—238 Jewett Ave., Bridgeport, 06606. Rev. ROBERT M. KINNALLY, Tel: 203-416-1635; Email: frkinnally@diobpt.org; MS. ELIZABETH M. AUDA, Exec. Asst. to Chancellor, Tel: 203-416-1636; Email: eauda@diobpt.org.

Archives—Deacon WILLIAM J. BISSENDEN, Archivist, Tel: 203-416-1354; Email: wbissenden@diobpt.org.

The Tribunal

Tribunal—Tel: 203-416-1652.

Judicial Vicar—Rev. ARTHUR C. MOLLENHAUER, J.C.L.

Judges—Revs. ARTHUR C. MOLLENHAUER, J.C.L.; WILLIAM M. QUINLAN, J.C.L.; EILEEN MAGDALEN ROSS, J.C.L.

Defender of the Bond/Promoter of Justice—Rev. WILLIAM M. QUINLAN, J.C.L.; MR. GEORGE NCHUMBONGA.

Ecclesiastical Notary—MS. ANTONIA M. PEREZ.

Consultative Groups

College of Consultors—Most Rev. FRANK J. CAGGIANO, Presider; Revs. THOMAS W. POWERS, Vicar Gen. & Moderator of the Curia; WILLIAM J. SCHEYD, P.A., (Retired); ANDREW G. VARGA; LAURENCE R. BRONKIEWICZ, S.T.D.; Revs. JUAN GABRIEL ACOSTA-QUEVEDO; BRIAN P. GANNON, S.T.D.; IAN JEREMIAH; REGINALD D. NORMAN.

Finance Council—Most Rev. FRANK J. CAGGIANO, Presider; Rev. Msgr. THOMAS W. POWERS, Vicar Gen. & Moderator of the Curia; MR. MICHAEL HANLON; Deacons PATRICK TOOLE; WILLIAM A. KONIERS; MRS. ANNE O. MCCRORY; MR. WILLIAM H. BESGEN; MR. MICHAEL F. HOBEN; MS. CAROL JAMES; MS. PATRICIA ANNE LIND; MR. MICHAEL O'ROURKE; MR. ARTHUR RHATIGAN; MR. JOSEPH D.

ROXE; MR. JAMES WOODS; MR. BRIAN YOUNG; MR. MICHAEL ZAMPARDI; MS. TERESA VASSILIOU; MR. ANDREW SCHULZ; MR. ROBERT SALANDRA.

Council of Deans—Most Rev. FRANK J. CAGGIANO, Presider; Rev. Msgr. THOMAS W. POWERS, Vicar Gen. & Moderator of the Curia; Revs. MICHAEL P. NOVAJOSKY, Deanery A: Queen of Peace; MICHAEL K. JONES, S.T.D., Deanery B: Mystical Rose; BRIAN P. GANNON, S.T.D., Deanery C: Queen of Martyrs; NICHOLAS A. CIRILLO, Deanery D: Our Lady, Queen of Confessors; Rev. Msgr. LAURENCE R. BRONKIEWICZ, S.T.D., Deanery E: Seat of Wisdom; Rev. PETER A. CIPRIANI, Deanery F: Queen Assumed into Heaven; Rev. Msgrs. WALTER C. ORLOWSKI, Deanery G: Mother of Divine Grace; KEVIN T. ROYAL, S.T.L., Deanery H: Cause of Our Joy; Rev. BOSE RAJA SELVARAJ, Deanery I: Mary, Mother of the Church; MR. PATRICK C. TURNER.

Presbyteral Council—Most Rev. FRANK J. CAGGIANO, Presider; Rev. Msgr. THOMAS W. POWERS, Vicar Gen. & Moderator of the Curia; Revs. ROBERT M. KINNALLY, Chancellor; ARTHUR C. MOLLENHAUER, J.C.L., Judicial Vicar; Rev. Msgrs. LAURENCE R. BRONKIEWICZ, S.T.D.; WALTER C. ORLOWSKI; KEVIN T. ROYAL, S.T.L.; WILLIAM J. SCHEYD, P.A., (Retired); Revs. PAUL N. CHECK, S.T.L.; MARCO PACCIANA; BRIAN P. GANNON, S.T.D.; NICHOLAS A. CIRILLO; GUSTAVO A. FALLA; REGINALD D. NORMAN; GERARD-FRANTZ DESRUISSEAUX, J.C.L.; LEONEL S. MEDEIROS; AUGUSTINE NGUYEN; GERALD R. BLASZCZAK, S.J.; WILLIAM M. QUINLAN, J.C.L.; COREY V. PICCININO; MICHAEL P. NOVAJOSKY; MICHAEL K. JONES, S.T.D.; BOSE RAJA SELVARAJ; PETER A. CIPRIANI.

Diaconal Council—Deacons TIMOTHY BOLTON; PATRICK TOOLE; DONALD P. FOUST; FRANK J. MASSO; JOHN DITARANTO; DONALD J. NAIMAN; GERALD H. LAMBERT; DANIEL IANNIELLO; WILLIAM A. SANTULLI; ERNEST JEFFERS; RENATO L. BERZOLLA.

Council of Religious—Sisters NANCY STRILLACCI, A.S.C.J.; PATRICIA ELLS, C.N.D.; MARILYN HAMMILL, C.N.D.; MARY VAN VU, L.H.C.; MELANIE HANNIGAN, O.P.; CAROL ANN NAWRACAJ, O.S.F.; MARILYN MULDOON, O.S.U.; GESUINA GENCARELLI, P.O.S.C.; AMANDA CARRIER, R.S.M.; DANIELLA O'SULLIVAN, S.S.N.D.; MAUREEN FRANCIS FLEMING, S.S.N.D.; MARY JOHN VIANNEY ZULLO, S.S.N.D.; BERNADETTE THERESE SWAN, S.V.; Revs. CHARLES H. ALLEN, S.J.; LOURDURAJ PITCHAI, O. Praem; TOMI THOMAS, I.M.S.

Vocation Advisory & Admission Board—Rev. Msgr. KEVIN T. ROYAL, S.T.L.; Revs. JOHN CONNAUGHTON; REGINALD D. NORMAN; JOSEPH A. MARCELLO; SAMUEL S. KACHUBA; SAMUEL V. SCOTT; JEFFREY W. COUTURE; AUGUSTINE NGUYEN; JOHN JAIRO PEREZ.

Diaconal Vocation Advisory and Admission Board—Most Rev. FRANK J. CAGGIANO, Presider; Deacons GERALD H. LAMBERT; DONALD J. NAIMAN; TIMOTHY BOLTON; JOHN DITARANTO; JOHN W. MAHON; WILLIAM MIRANDA.

Diocesan Liturgical Commission—Most Rev. FRANK J. CAGGIANO, Presider; Rev. Msgrs. THOMAS W. POWERS, S.T.L., Vicar Gen. & Moderator of the Curia; ALAN F. DETSCHER; Revs. PETER F. LENOX; JOSEPH A. MARCELLO; MICHAEL P. NOVAJOSKY; BRIAN P. GANNON, S.T.D.; Deacon JOHN DITARANTO; MR. MAC COONEY; MR. PATRICK DONOVAN; MS. ROSE TALBOT-BABEY; JACQUELINE HERBERT; DR. JUNE-ANN GREELEY; MS. MAUREEN CONSIDINE; DR. JOAN KELLY; MS. DIANE SCOTT; MS. PATRICIA HELLER; MS. CAROL PINARD.

Sacred Arts Committee—Rev. Msgrs. THOMAS W. POWERS, S.T.L.; KEVIN T. ROYAL, S.T.L.; ROBERT E. WEISS; Revs. JOSEPH A. MARCELLO; PETER F. LENOX; PAUL N. CHECK, S.T.L.; GREGG D. MECCA; MICHAEL L. DUNN; MRS. ANNE O. MCCRORY; MR. ANDREW SCHULZ.

Building Commission—MRS. ANNE O. MCCRORY; MRS. CHARLENE PAL; MR. ANDREW SCHULZ; Rev. PETER F. LENOX; MR. JOSEPH G. BURTON; MR. MICHAEL HANLON; MRS. SUSAN LOPICCOLO; MR. PAUL BUTKUS; MR. RICHARD RAPICE; MR. MARTIN TRISTINE; MR. PATRICK C. TURNER.

Diocesan Censor Librorum—Rev. Msgr. CHRISTOPHER J. WALSH, Ph.D., S.T.D.

Education

Bridgeport Diocesan Schools Corporation—Tel: 203-416-1375; Fax: 203-372-1961.

Catholic Schools—DR. STEVEN CHEESEMAN, Supt. Catholic Schools, Tel: 203-416-1380; Email: scheeseman@diobpt.org; MRS. PATRICIA BELL, Exec. Admin. Asst., Tel: 203-416-1375; Email: pbell@diobpt.org; Sr. MARILYN MULDOON, O.S.U., Asst. Supt., Tel: 203-416-1617; Email: srmuldoon@diobpt.org; STACIE L. STUEBER, Assoc. Supt., Tel: 203-416-1397; Email: sstueber@diobpt.org; AMY GRIFFIN, Dir. Community Engagement, Tel: 203-416-1408; Email: agriffin@diobpt.org; KATHRYN CIOFFI, Dir. Educational Technology & Innovation, Tel: 203-416-1669; Email: kcioffi@diobpt.org; MR. NOAH LANGER, Asst. to Supt., Tel: 203-416-1347; Email: noah.langer@diobpt.org.

Ministerial Leadership and Vicar for Clergy

Vicar for Clergy—MRS. PATRICIA NOVAJOSKY, Admin. Asst., Office of Clergy & Religious, Tel: 203-416-1453; Email: pnovajosky@diobpt.org.

Diocesan Director of Vocations & Director of Seminarian Formation—894 Newfield Ave., Stamford, 06905. Tel: 203-322-5331; Fax: 203-461-9876. Rev. JOHN CONNAUGHTON, Email: frconnaughton@diobpt.org; MRS. AMANDA DAY, Asst. to Dir. of Vocations, Email: aday@diobpt.org.

Diaconate Office—Tel: 203-416-1323.

Coordinator of Diaconate Formation and the Diaconate Office—Deacon GERALD H. LAMBERT; MRS. MICHELLE ROWE, Admin. Asst., Office of the Diaconate, Tel: 203-416-1323; Email: michelle.rowe@diobpt.org.

Coordinator of Diaconate Vocations—Deacon TIMOTHY BOLTON.

Coordinator of Diaconate Continuing Formation—Deacon JOHN DITARANTO.

Delegate for Religious/Prison Ministry—Sr. NANCY STRILLACCI, A.S.C.J., Tel: 203-416-1511; Email: srstrillacci@diobpt.org.

St. John Fisher Seminary—894 Newfield Ave., Stamford, 06905. Tel: 203-322-5331; Fax: 203-461-9876. Revs. DAVID C. LEOPOLD, Spiritual Dir., Email: frleopold@diobpt.org; PAUL N. CHECK, S.T.L., Rector, Email: frcheck@diopt.org; MRS. JENNIFER INGALLINERA, Asst. to Rector, Email: jingallinera@diobpt.org.

Redemptoris Mater Seminary—37 Schuyler Ave., Stamford, 06902. Tel: 203-588-1784; Fax: 203-588-1785. Revs. GIANDOMENICO FLORA, Spiritual Dir.; MARCO PACCIANA, Rector, Email: frpacciana@diobpt.org.

Catherine Dennis Keefe Queen of the Clergy Residence—274 Strawberry Hill Ave., Stamford, 06904. Tel: 203-358-9906; Fax: 203-358-9524. MS. VICKEY HICKEY, Admin.

Pastoral Ministry and Social Concerns

The Leadership Institute—The Catholic Center, 238 Jewett Ave., Bridgeport, 06606-2892. MR. PATRICK DONOVAN, Exec. Dir., Tel: 203-416-1657; Email: pdonovan@diobpt.org.

Office of Faith Formation—MS. ROSE TALBOT-BABEY, Coord. Relg. Educ., Tel: 203-416-1648; Email: rtalbotbabey@diobpt.org; MS. DEIRDRA KEARNEY, Office Admin., Tel: 203-416-1670; Email: dkearney@diobpt.org; VACANT, Coord., Youth & Young Adults; VACANT, Marriage Preparation & Coord. Adult Formation, Tel: 203-416-1670; Fax: 203-373-1418; MS. EMMA RYDER, Prog. Coord., The Face of Prayer, Tel: 203-416-1623; Email: eryder@diobpt.org; MS. MAUREEN CIARDIELLO, Coord. Project Rachel/Respect Life, Tel: 203-416-1445; Email: mciardiello@diobpt.org; MRS. MARY BOZZUTI HIGGINS, Dir., Diocesan Youth Choir, Email: mhiggins@diobpt.org; Rev. ANDREW A. VILL, Coord. Catholic Scouts, Tel: 203-324-1553, Ext. 130; Email: frvill@diobpt.org.

Office for Strategic and Pastoral Planning—MR. PATRICK C. TURNER, Dir. Strategic Planning, Tel: 203-416-1633; Email: pturner@diobpt.org.

Pontifical Missions Office/Propagation of the Faith of the Diocese of Bridgeport—Rev. MICHAEL A. BOCCACCIO, Dir., (Retired), Tel: 203-416-1447; Email: frboccaccio@diobpt.org; MRS. ELAINE BISSENDEN, Assoc. Dir., Tel: 203-416-1448; Email: ebissenden@diobpt.org.

Ministry for People With Developmental Disabilities—St. Catherine Center for Special Needs, Inc., 760 Tahmore Dr., Fairfield, 06825. Tel: 203-540-5381, Ext. 2010. HELEN BURLAND, Exec. Dir.

Ministry for Deaf and Hearing Impaired—Rev. NICHOLAS S. PAVIA, Tel: 203-377-4863; Email: frpavia@diobpt.org.

Vicar for Evangelization—Rev. PETER J. TOWSLEY, Tel: 203-748-9029; Email: frtowsley@diobpt.org.

Catholic Charities of Fairfield County, Inc.—Catholic Center, 238 Jewett Ave., Bridgeport, 06606-2892. MR. ALBERT BARBER, Pres., Tel: 203-416-1307; Fax: 203-372-5045; Email: abarber@ccfc-ct.org; MR. MICHAEL TINTRUP, LCSW, C.O.O., Tel: 203-416-1305; Email: mtintrup@ccfc-ct.org; MRS. MARY BETH PETERSEN, Human Resources, Tel: 203-416-1339; Email: mpetersen@ccfc-ct.org.

Office of Safe Environment/Victim Assistance—MRS. ERIN NEIL, Dir., Tel: 203-416-1406; Email: eneil@diobpt.org; MS. ASTRID ALVAREZ, Virtus Training & Development Specialist, Tel: 203-416-1407; Email: aalvarez@diobpt.org.

Haitian-American Catholic Center—93 Hope St., Stamford, 06906. Tel: 203-406-0343; Fax: 203-406-0347. Rev. GERARD-FRANTZ DESRUISSEAUX, J.C.L., Dir.

Connecticut Catholic Conference—134 Farmington Ave., Hartford, 06105. Tel: 203-524-7882. MR. MICHAEL C. CULHANE.

Finance and Management

Office of Finance—MR. MICHAEL HANLON, C.F.O., Tel: 203-416-1390; Email: mhanlon@diobpt.org; MRS. ARLENE PERRICONE, Controller; MS. SUZANNE THIBODEAU, Admin. Asst. to C.F.O., Tel: 203-416-1615; Email: sthibodeau@diobpt.org.

Episcopal Delegate for Administration—Deacon PATRICK TOOLE, Tel: 203-416-1674; Email: dntoole@diobpt.org; MS. ELIZABETH M. AUDA, Exec. Asst., Tel: 203-416-1636; Email: eauda@diobpt.org.

Real Estate and Facilities Management—MR. ANDREW SCHULZ, Dir., Tel: 203-416-1512; Email: aschulz@diobpt.org; MR. RICHARD RAPICE, Project Mgr., Tel: 203-416-1647; Email: rrapice@diobpt.org.

Office of Human Resources—MRS. TRACY CASEY, Chief Human Resources Officer, Tel: 203-416-1419; Email: tracy.casey@diobpt.org; MS. MARTHA VASSAR, Human Resources Asst. Admin., Tel: 203-416-1402; Email: msvassar@diobpt.org.

Insurance Office—MR. JOSEPH G. BURTON, Mgr. Claims & Risk, Catholic Mutual Group, 238 Jewett Ave., Bridgeport, 06606. Tel: 203-416-1310; Fax: 203-371-6139; Email: jburton@catholicmutual.org.

Cemeteries—238 Jewett Ave., Bridgeport, 06606-2892. Tel: 203-416-1492; Fax: 203-374-7588. MR. FRANK SPODNICK, Dir. Catholic Cemeteries.

Legal

Legal Office—MRS. ANNE O. MCCRORY, Chief Legal & Real Estate Officer, Tel: 203-416-1360; Email: amccrory@diobpt.org; MRS. DEBRA TIETJEN, Exec. Asst./Paralegal, Tel: 203-416-1385; Email: dtietjen@diobpt.org; MRS. CHARLENE PAL, Attorney, Tel: 203-416-1393; Email: cpal@diobpt.org.

Diocesan Legal Services—MR. R. SCOTT BEACH, Esq., Day Pitney, LLP, One Canterbury Green, Stamford, 06901.

Notaries—MS. SUZANNE THIBODEAU; MRS. DEBRA TIETJEN; MR. JOHN T. GROSSO.

Ecclesiastical Notary—MS. ANTONIA M. PEREZ.

Catholic Lawyers—Rev. Msgr. J. JAMES CUNEO, J.C.D., Spiritual Moderator, (Retired); LEOPOLD DEFUSCO, Esq., Coord., St. Thomas More Society of Fairfield County, 238 Jewett Ave., Bridgeport, 06606-2892. Tel: 203-374-2590.

Office of Development

Episcopal Vicar for Development—Rev. MICHAEL K. JONES, S.T.D.

Office of Development—238 Jewett Ave., Bridgeport, 06606. MRS. PATRICIA R. HANSEN, Dir. Devel. Oper., Tel: 203-416-1342; Email: phansen@diobpt.org; MRS. PAMELA RITTMAN, Dir. Devel. & Annual Catholic Appeal, Tel: 203-416-1479; Email: prittman@diobpt.org; MS. JOAN TROMBETTA, Devel. Assoc., Tel: 203-416-1475; Email: jtrombetta@diobpt.org; MS. ROSA RODRIGUEZ, Devel. Assoc., Tel: 203-416-1312; Email: rosa.rodriguez@diobpt.org.

Communications

Communications—238 Jewett Ave., Bridgeport, 06606. Web: www.bridgeportdiocese.com. MR. BRIAN D. WALLACE, Dir. & Diocesan Spokesperson, Tel: 203-416-1464; Fax: 203-374-2044; Email: bdwallace@diobpt.org; MR. JOHN T. GROSSO, Dir. Social Media, Tel: 203-416-1643; Email: jgrosso@diobpt.org.

Official Newspaper—"The Fairfield County Catholic", (Monthly) Most Rev. FRANK J. CAGGIANO, Publisher; MR. BRIAN D. WALLACE, Exec. Editor, Tel: 203-416-1464; Fax: 203-374-2044; Email: fcc@diobpt.org.

CLERGY, PARISHES, MISSIONS AND PAROCHIAL SCHOOLS

CITY OF BRIDGEPORT
(FAIRFIELD COUNTY)

1—ST. AUGUSTINE CATHEDRAL (1842) Merged with St. Patrick Church, Bridgeport to form The Cathedral Parish, Bridgeport.

2—THE CATHEDRAL PARISH (2012)
170 Thompson St., 06604. Tel: 203-368-6777; Fax: 203-335-0107; Web: www.thecathedralparish.org. Rev. Michael P. Novajosky.
Catechesis Religious Program—Karen Ballone, Coord. Rel. Educ. Students 231.

3—ST. AMBROSE (1928) Closed. For inquiries for parish records please see Blessed Sacrament Parish.

4—ST. ANDREW (1961)
435 Anton St., 06606. Tel: 203-374-6171; Email: standrewchurch@optimum.net. Revs. Eugene R. Szantyr; Hyginus Ndubueze Agu; Rev. Msgr. Matthew Bernelli, In Res., (Retired).
See St. Andrew, Bridgeport under Elementary Schools located in the Institution section.
Catechesis Religious Program—Tel: 203-374-8118. Susan Baldwin, D.R.E. Students 192.

5—ST. ANN (1922)
481 Brewster St., 06605. Tel: 203-368-1607; Fax: 203-336-4233; Email: office@stannblackrock.com; Web: www.stannblackrock.com. Rev. Elio Sosa, I.V.E.
See St. Ann, Bridgeport under Elementary Schools located in the Institution section.
Catechesis Religious Program—Email: reled@stannblackrock.com. Ms. Diane Scott, D.R.E. Students 140.

6—ST. ANTHONY OF PADUA, Merged with St. Peter, Bridgeport. See separate listing.

7—BLESSED SACRAMENT (1917)
275 Union Ave., 06607. Tel: 203-333-1202; Email: blessedsacramentrc@sbcglobal.net. Rev. Joseph J. Karcsinski; Deacon Ricardo Martinez.
Catechesis Religious Program—Karen Soares-Robinson, D.R.E. Students 35.

8—ST. CHARLES BORROMEO (1902)
391 Ogden St., 06608. Tel: 203-333-2147; Fax: 203-330-8316; Email: info@scbct.org; Web: www.scbct.org. Rev. Msgr. Christopher J. Walsh, Ph.D., S.T.D.
Catechesis Religious Program—Tel: 203-333-3557. Mercedes Rojas, D.R.E. Students 183.

9—SS. CYRIL AND METHODIUS (1907) (Slovak)
79 Church St., 06608. Tel: 203-333-7003; Email: stscyrilandmethodius@institute-christ-king.org; Web: www.institute-christ-king.org/bridgeport. Rev. Andrew Todd.

10—ST. GEORGE (1907) (Lithuanian)
443 Park Ave., 06604. Tel: 203-335-1797; Email: st-george.church@sbcglobal.net. Rev. Msgr. Thomas W. Powers, S.T.L.
Catechesis Religious Program—Tel: 203-330-8409; Email: c-damaris@sersdoras.org; Web: www.ss/musa.org. Sr. Maria Ininatin, S.S.V.M., D.R.E. Students 217.

11—HOLY ROSARY (1903) (Italian), Closed. For inquiries for parish records contact the chancery.

12—ST. JOHN NEPOMUCENE, Closed. For inquiries for parish records contact Holy Name of Jesus, Stratford.

13—ST. JOSEPH'S, Closed. May 23, 1988. For inquiries for parish records contact The Cathedral Parish, Bridgeport.

14—ST. MARY (1857)
25 Sherman St., 06608. Tel: 203-334-8811; Email: stmarychurchbpt@optonline.net; Web: www.stmarychurchbridgeport.org. Revs. Rolando Torres; Jaime Marin, Vicar; Deacon Reynaldo Olavarria.
Catechesis Religious Program—187 Sherman St, Stratford, 06615. Tel: 203-375-4567; Email: lucycord@optonline.net. Luz Cordero, D.R.E. Students 188.

15—ST. MICHAEL THE ARCHANGEL (1899) [CEM] (Polish)
310 Pulaski St., 06608. Tel: 203-334-1822; Email: franciscansbridgeport@gmail.com; Web: www.stmichaelbridgeport.com. Rev. Norbert M. Siwinski, O.F.M.Conv.
Catechesis Religious Program—Students 125.

16—OUR LADY OF FATIMA (1962) (Portuguese)
429 Huntington Rd., 06608. Tel: 203-333-7575. Rev. Joseph De Brito Alves, (Portugal); Deacon Gabriel A. Pereira.
Catechesis Religious Program—Tel: 203-929-1085. Students 122.

17—OUR LADY OF GOOD COUNSEL (1955) [CEM] Closed. For inquiries for parish records contact St. Andrew Parish.

18—ST. PATRICK CHURCH (1889) Merged with St. Augustine Cathedral, Bridgeport to form The Cathedral Parish, Bridgeport.

19—ST. PETER (1900) [CEM] (Spanish)
695 Colorado Ave., 06605. Tel: 203-366-5611; Fax: 203-335-1924. Rev. Jhon Gomez; Deacon Luis Torres.
Catechesis Religious Program—Tel: 203-334-5681; Fax: 203-333-1590. Sr. Anna Rodriguez, M.S.S., D.R.E. Students 210.

20—ST. RAPHAEL (1925) (Italian), Closed. For inquiries for parish records contact the chancery.

OUTSIDE THE CITY OF BRIDGEPORT

BETHEL, FAIRFIELD CO., ST. MARY (1882) [CEM]
26 Dodgingtown Rd., Bethel, 06801.
Tel: 203-744-5777; Email: stmaryoffice@comcast.net; Web: stmarybethel.org. Revs. Corey V. Piccinino; Robert L. Wolfe, Parochial Vicar; Philip Lahn Phan, Parochial Vicar; Deacon John DeRobin.
See St. Mary, Bethel under Elementary Schools located in the Institution section.
Convent—Tel: 203-743-6985.

BROOKFIELD, FAIRFIELD CO.

1—ST. JOSEPH (1941)
Mailing Address: 163 Whisconier Rd., Brookfield, 06804. Tel: 203-775-1035; Fax: 203-775-1684; Email: parishsec@stjosephbrookfield.com; Web: www.stjosephbrookfield.com. Revs. George F. O'Neill; Karol J. Ksiazek; Deacons William J. Shaughnessy; Peter J. Kuhn; Jeffrey Font.
Res.: 159 Whisconier Rd., Brookfield, 06804.
See St. Joseph, Brookfield under Elementary Schools located in the Institution section.
Catechesis Religious Program—Students 425.

2—ST. MARGUERITE BOURGEOYS (1982) [CEM]
138 Candlewood Lake Rd., Brookfield, 06804.
Tel: 203-775-5117; Email: jpiccorelli@stmarguerite.org; Web: www.stmarguerite.org. Rev. Shawn W. Cutler; Deacon Anthony J. Detje.

DANBURY, FAIRFIELD CO.

1—ST. GREGORY THE GREAT (1960)
85 Great Plain Rd., Danbury, 06811.
Tel: 203-797-0222. Rev. Michael L. Dunn; Deacons Robert Blankschen; William D. Murphy; Daniel N. Myott.
See St. Gregory the Great, Danbury under Elementary Schools located in the Institution section.
Catechesis Religious Program—Tel: 203-743-5168. Mrs. Mary Ann Hauser, D.R.E. Students 221.

2—IMMACULATE HEART OF MARY (1980) [CEM] (Portuguese)
149 Deer Hill Ave., Danbury, 06811.
Tel: 203-797-1821; Fax: 203-743-9146; Email: heartofmary@sbcglobal.net. Rev. Jose Brito Martins; Deacon Jose Rodrigues Cabral.
Catechesis Religious Program—Helena Andrade, D.R.E. Students 96.

3—ST. JOSEPH (1905)
8 Robinson Ave., Danbury, 06810-5517.
Tel: 203-748-8177; Email: recstjoseph@yahoo.com. Revs. Samuel V. Scott; Raymond M. Scherba, Parochial Vicar; David W. Franklin, Parochial Vicar; Deacons Donald J. Naiman; Louis Howe; Richard P. Kovacs.
See St. Joseph, Danbury under Elementary Schools located in the Institution section.
Catechesis Religious Program—Tel: 203-778-1920. Mrs. Lynn Smierciak, D.R.E. Students 340.

4—OUR LADY OF GUADALUPE (1985) [CEM] (Spanish)
29 Golden Hill Rd., Danbury, 06811-4629.
Tel: 203-743-1021; Email: guadalupedanbury@gmail.com; Web: www.iglesiaguadalupect.com. Revs. John Jairo Perez; Edicson Orozco, Parochial Vicar; Deacon Rafael Regus.
Catechesis Religious Program—Tel: 203-616-5600; Email: abreuesmeralda@gmail.com. Esmeralda Abreu, D.R.E. Students 513.

5—ST. PETER (1851) [CEM]
104 Main St., Danbury, 06810. Tel: 203-743-2707; Email: office@stpeterdanb.org; Web: www.stpeterdanb.org. Revs. Gregg D. Mecca; Leonel S. Medeiros, Parochial Vicar; Paul F. Merry, In Res.; Jeffrey W. Couture, In Res.; David J. Riley, In Res., (Retired).
See St. Peter School, Danbury under Elementary Schools, Diocesan located in the Institution section.
Catechesis Religious Program—Tel: 203-743-1048; Email: stpeterfuture@stpeterdanb.org. Barbara Siano, D.R.E. Students 730.

6—SACRED HEART OF JESUS (1925)
46 Stone St., Danbury, 06810. Tel: 203-748-9029; Email: office@sacredheartdanbury.org; Web: www.sacredhrtchurch.org. Revs. Peter J. Towsley; Amobi Atuegbu, In Res.
Catechesis Religious Program—Tel: 203-743-0689; Email: danieltome.sacredheart@gmail.com. Dan Tome, D.R.E. Students 53.

DARIEN, FAIRFIELD CO.

1—ST. JOHN (1895) [CEM]
1986 Post Rd., Darien, 06820. Tel: 203-655-1145; Email: stjohnb@optonline.net; Web: stjohndarien.com. Revs. Francis T. Hoffmann; Christopher J. Perrella, Parochial Vicar.
Catechesis Religious Program—Tel: 203-655-8020; Email: religiousedsj@optonline.net. John Cunningham, D.R.E.; Lisa Ioli, D.R.E. (Preschool. Dir.). Students 585.

2—ST. THOMAS MORE (1966)
384 Middlesex Rd., Darien, 06820. Tel: 203-655-3303; Fax: 203-655-6478; Email: office@stmdarienct.org; Web: www.stmdarienct.org. Revs. Paul G. Murphy; John Connaughton.
Res. & Parish Office: 374 Middlesex Rd., Darien, 06820.
Catechesis Religious Program—Tel: 203-655-3077; Fax: 203-655-8901; Email: re@stmdarienct.org. Mary Ellen O'Connor, D.R.E.; Michael Brelsford, Youth Min.; Maria Oliveira, Dir. Preschool. Students 897.

EASTON, FAIRFIELD CO., NOTRE DAME (1956) [CEM]
640 Morehouse Rd., Easton, 06612.
Tel: 203-268-5838; Email: churchladies@optonline.net; Web: www.notredameofeaston.com. Rev. Michael P. Lyons; Deacon Gerald F. Sabol.
Catechesis Religious Program—Tel: 203-261-5596; Email: ndore@optonlin.net. Patricia Steccato, D.R.E. Students 287.

FAIRFIELD, FAIRFIELD CO.

1—ST. ANTHONY OF PADUA (1927)
149 S. Pine Creek Rd., Fairfield, 06824.
Tel: 203-259-0358; Email: stanthonyffld@aol.com. Eleanor W. Sauers, Ph.D., Parish Life Coord.
Catechesis Religious Program—Eleanor W. Sauers, Ph.D., D.R.E. Students 300.

2—ST. EMERY (1932) (Hungarian) (United with St. Stephen's of Bridgeport 1897-1971)
838 King's Hwy. E., Fairfield, 06825-5418.
Tel: 203-334-0312; Email: stemery@optimum.net; Web: www.stemerys.com. Rev. Milan Dimic; Deacon Rudolph P. Trankovich.

3—HOLY CROSS (1913) (Slovenian)
750 Tahmore Dr., Fairfield, 06825-2519.
Tel: 203-372-4594; Fax: 203-372-4668; Email: holy_cross_church@sbcglobal.net; Web: www.holycrosschurchfairfield.com. Rev. Alfred F. Pecaric, S.T.L.
Catechesis Religious Program—Dorothy Fejes, D.R.E. Students 29.

4—HOLY FAMILY (1938)
700 Old Stratfield Rd., Fairfield, 06825.
Tel: 203-336-1835; Email: holychurch@sbcglobal.net; Web: www.holyfamilyrc.com. Rev. Norman J. Guilbert; Deacons John T. Moranski; Joseph DeBiase; Joseph Gagne.
Catechesis Religious Program—70 Laurel St., Fairfield, 06825. Tel: 203-579-4540. Mary Jane Perry, D.R.E. Students 89.

5—OUR LADY OF THE ASSUMPTION (1922) [CEM]
545 Stratfield Rd., Fairfield, 06825.
Tel: 203-333-9065; Email: assumptionfairfield@gmail.com; Web: www.olaffld.org. Revs. Peter A. Cipriani; Michael Flynn, Parochial Vicar; Deacons Kevin Moore; Raymond J. Chervenak.
Catechesis Religious Program—605 Stratfield Rd., Fairfield, 06825. Tel: 203-367-1108; Email: Our.Lady.Assumption@snet.net. Frank Macari, D.R.E. Students 415.
Parish Center—591 Stratfield Rd., Fairfield, 06825.

6—ST. PIUS X (1955) [CEM]
834 Brookside Dr., Fairfield, 06824.
Tel: 203-255-6134; Fax: 203-255-5232; Email: secretary@st-pius.org; Web: www.st-pius.org. Revs. Samuel S. Kachuba; Timothy Iannacone, Parochial Vicar; Kathleen Donnelly, Pastoral Assoc.; Michael Lantowski, Music Min.; Kim Leon, Business Mgr.
Catechesis Religious Program—Email: ppena@st-pius.org; Web: www.st-pius.org/sacramental-prep. Theresa Dawes, Admin.; Kara Clegg, First Communion Coord.; Shari Garcia, Confirmation Coord. & Middle School Youth Min.; Paola Pena, Youth Min. Students 321.

7—ST. THOMAS AQUINAS (1876) [CEM]
1719 Post Rd., Fairfield, 06824. Tel: 203-255-1097; Email: stthoaq@aol.com; Web: stthomasfairfield.com. Revs. Victor T. Martin; Lawrence A. Larson; Roger F. McDonough, In Res., (Retired); Zbigniew Zielinski, J.C.D., In Res.; Mary Jane Edwards, Pastoral Assoc.
See St. Thomas Aquinas, Fairfield under Elementary Schools located in the Institution section.
Catechesis Religious Program—Tel: 203-255-1984; Email: stthoaqccd@aol.com. Jacqueline Herbert, D.R.E. Students 500.

GEORGETOWN, FAIRFIELD CO., SACRED HEART (1881)
30 Church St., Georgetown, 06829.
Tel: 203-544-8345; Email: sacredheartgtn@optonline.net; Web: www.sacredheartgeorgetownct.org. Mailing Address: P.O. Box 388, Georgetown, 06829-0388. Revs. David C. Leopold; John J. Inserra.
Catechesis Religious Program—Tel: 203-544-8423; Email: sacredheart.rel.edu@sbcglobal.net. Students 19.

GREENWICH, FAIRFIELD CO.

1—ST. AGNES (1963)
247 Stanwich Rd., Greenwich, 06830.
Tel: 203-869-5396; Fax: 203-625-0596; Email: stagnesgreenwich@aol.com; Web: www.stagnesrec.org. Rev. James A. McDevitt; Deacon John M. Linsenmeyer.
Catechesis Religious Program—Kathryn Glaser, Pastoral Assoc.; Sindy Aristizabul, Sec. Students 50.

2—ST. MARY (1874) [CEM]
178 Greenwich Ave., Greenwich, 06830.
Tel: 203-869-9393; Email: stmarygrn@gmail.com;

Web: stmarygreenwich.org. Revs. Cyprian P. LaPastina; Rolando Arias Galvis, Parochial Vicar.
Catechesis Religious Program—Tel: 203-869-9250; Email: saintmre@gmail.com. Charlene Prisinzano, D.R.E. Students 177.
3—ST. MICHAEL THE ARCHANGEL (1963) [CEM]
469 North St., Greenwich, 06830. Tel: 203-869-5421; Email: stmichaelsttim@optonline.net. Revs. Ian Jeremiah; Richard D. Murphy.
Catechesis Religious Program—Email: reledstmmichael@gmail.com. Loren Procaccini, D.R.E. Students 487.
Mission—St. Timothy's, 1034 North St., Greenwich, Fairfield Co. 06831.
4—ST. PAUL (1902) [CEM]
84 Sherwood Ave., Greenwich, 06831.
Tel: 203-531-8741; Email: office@stpaulgreenwich.org; Web: www.stpaulgreenwich.org. Rev. Leszek P. Szymaszek.
Catechesis Religious Program—Tel: 203-531-4265. Rosie Pennella, D.R.E. Students 397.
5—ST. ROCH (1928) [JC]
10 St. Roch Ave., Greenwich, 06830.
Tel: 203-869-4176; Email: stroch@optimum.net. Revs. Carl McIntosh; Marcelo R. Lopresti, I.V.E.
Catechesis Religious Program—Students 55.
6—SACRED HEART (1890) [CEM]
Mailing Address: 95A Henry St., Greenwich, 06830.
Tel: 203-531-8730; Fax: 203-531-8794; Email: sacredheartgrn@optonline.net; Web: sacredheartgreenwich.org. Rev. Bose Raja Selvaraj.
Res.: 38 Gold St., Greenwich, 06830.
Catechesis Religious Program—Email: reledsh@optimum.net. Students 176.
MONROE, FAIRFIELD CO., ST. JUDE (1973)
707 Monroe Tpke., Monroe, 06468. Tel: 203-261-6404 ; Email: parish.office@stjuderc.com; Web: www.stjuderc.com. Revs. Henry J. Hoffman; James K. Bates; Deacons David Flynn; John Tuccio; William A. Koniers.
Catechesis Religious Program—Tel: 203-261-6788; Email: religious.education@stjuderc.com. Students 740.
NEW CANAAN, FAIRFIELD CO., ST. ALOYSIUS (1896)
40 Maple St., New Canaan, 06840. Tel: 203-966-0020 ; Email: admin@starcc.com; Web: www.starcc.com. Revs. Robert M. Kinnally; Jose Ignacio A. Ortigas, Parochial Vicar; Deacons William A. Santulli; Stephen W. Pond.
Res.: 39 Maple St., New Canaan, 06840.
See St. Aloysius, New Canaan under Elementary Schools located in the Institution section.
Catechesis Religious Program—Tel: 203-652-1105; Email: marieccd@starcc.com. Mrs. Marie Pascale-Vandall, D.R.E. Students 1,100.
NEW FAIRFIELD, FAIRFIELD CO., ST. EDWARD THE CONFESSOR (1954)
21 Brush Hill Rd., New Fairfield, 06812.
Tel: 203-746-2200; Email: parishoffice@saintedwardchurch.org; Web: saintedwardchurch.org. Revs. Nicholas A. Cirillo; Harry Prieto; Deacon Patrick Shevlin.
Catechesis Religious Program—Tel: 203-746-4270; Email: klaregina@saintedwardchurch.org. Kathryn LaRegina, D.R.E. Students 900.
NEWTOWN, FAIRFIELD CO., ST. ROSE OF LIMA (1859) [CEM]
46 Church Hill Rd., Newtown, 06470.
Tel: 203-426-1014; Email: parishsecretary@strosechurch.com. Rev. Msgr. Robert E. Weiss; Revs. Krzysztof Kuczynski; Alphonse Arokiom; Deacons Richard Scinto; Norman Roos; Daniel O'Connor.
See St. Rose of Lima, Newtown under Elementary Schools located in the Institution section.
Catechesis Religious Program—38 Church Hill Rd., Newtown, 06470. Tel: 203-770-6848; Email: dre@strosechurch.com. Pam Arsenault, Dir., Parish Ed. Students 1,023.
NORWALK, FAIRFIELD CO.
1—ST. JEROME (1960) [CEM]
23 Half Mile Rd., Norwalk, 06851. Tel: 203-847-5649; Email: office@stjeromenorwalk.org; Web: www.stjeromenorwalk.org. Revs. David W. Blanchfield; Rojin Karickal, Parochial Vicar.
Catechesis Religious Program—Tel: 203-846-2111; Email: reachstjerome@optonline.net. Katherine Coyne, D.R.E. Students 320.
2—ST. JOSEPH (South Norwalk) (1895)
85 S. Main St., Norwalk, 06854. Tel: 203-838-4171; Email: stjosono@aol.com. Revs. Peter F. Lenox, Admin.; Jhon Gomez; Otoniel Lizcano, Parochial Vicar; Gerard-Frantz Desruisseaux, J.C.L., In Res.
Catechesis Religious Program—Tel: 203-866-1225; Email: Ariverastjosono@aol.com. Angela Rivera, C.R.E. Students 255.
Convent—14 Chestnut St., Norwalk, 06854.
3—ST. LADISLAUS (1907) [CEM] (Hungarian)
25 Cliff St., Norwalk, 06854. Tel: 203-866-1867;
Fax: 203-866-7830; Email: fracosta@diobpt.org. Rev. Juan Gabriel Acosta-Quevedo.
Catechesis Religious Program—Tel: 203-644-8334; Email: dforcier@optonline.net. Mrs. Donna Forcier, D.R.E. Students 169.
4—ST. MARY (1848) [CEM]
669 West Ave., Norwalk, 06850. Tel: 203-866-5546; Email: frringley@diobpt.org. Rev. Frederick John Ringley Jr.; Deacon Stephan A. Genovese.
Catechesis Religious Program—Tel: 203-866-7429; Fax: 203-866-0127.
5—ST. MATTHEW (1957)
216 Scribner Ave., Norwalk, 06854.
Tel: 203-838-3788, Ext. 101; Email: stmattparish@hotmail.com; Web: www.stmatthewnorwalk.org. Rev. Msgr. Walter C. Orlowski; Revs. Sunil Pereira, I.M.S., Parochial Vicar; Tomi Thomas, I.M.S., Parochial Vicar.
Catechesis Religious Program—
Tel: 203-838-3788, Ext. 107; Email: stmattreled@gmail.com. Erma Moore, D.R.E.; Corinne Murphy, Youth Min.; Elizabeth Reid, Youth Min. Students 401.
6—ST. PHILIP (1964)
One Fr. Conlon Pl., Norwalk, 06851.
Tel: 203-847-4549; Fax: 203-847-4148; Email: info@stphilipnorwalk.org; Web: www.stphilipnorwalk.org. Rev. Sudhir D'Souza; Sr. Mary Ann McPartland, C.N.D., Pastoral Assoc.; Deacons Paul J. Reilly; John W. Mahon.
Catechesis Religious Program—Tel: 203-847-4286; Email: faithformation@stphilipnorwalk.org. Mrs. Dora Deandrade, Dir. Faith Formation. Students 158.
7—ST. THOMAS THE APOSTLE (1935)
203 East Ave., Norwalk, 06855. Tel: 203-866-3141; Fax: 203-866-1189; Email: stthomasnorwalk@optonline.net; Web: stthomasnorwalk.com. Revs. Miroslaw Stachurski; Ralph Segura, Parochial Vicar; Paul Sankar, In Res.
Malta House—5 Prowitt St., Norwalk, 06855.
Tel: 203-857-0088; Fax: 203-857-0018.
Catechesis Religious Program—208 East Ave., Norwalk, 06855. Tel: 203-866-1189; Email: stthomasnorwalkreled@gmail.com. Michelle O'Mara, D.R.E. Students 275.
REDDING, FAIRFIELD CO., ST. PATRICK (1879) (Irish)
169 Black Rock Tpke., Redding, 06896.
Tel: 203-938-2253; Email: stpatrickchurch@optimum.net; Web: www.stpatredding.org. Mailing Address: P.O. Box 119, Redding, 06876. Rev. Joseph Cervero; Deacon William C. Timmel.
Catechesis Religious Program—Tel: 203-664-1387; Email: stpatreddingccd@optimum.net. Jeanine Herman, C.R.E. Students 225.
RIDGEFIELD, FAIRFIELD CO.
1—ST. ELIZABETH SETON (1976)
520 Ridgebury Rd., Ridgefield, 06877.
Tel: 203-438-7292; Email: stsetonparish@comcast.net; Web: sesparish.org. Revs. Joseph A. Prince; Justin Raj, I.M.S., Parochial Vicar; Deacon Francis Foyt.
Catechesis Religious Program—Tel: 203-438-9707. Gigi Pekala, C.R.E.; Marie Trebing, C.R.E. Students 328.
2—ST. MARY (1882) [CEM]
55 Catoonah St., Ridgefield, 06877.
Tel: 203-438-6538; Email: jbrown@smcr.org; Web: smcr.org. Rev. Msgr. Laurence R. Bronkiewicz, S.T.D., Pastor; Rev. Sean R. Kulacz, Parochial Vicar; Deacons Robert A. Salvestrini; Gerald H. Lambert.
School—St. Mary School, 183 Highridge Ave., Ridgefield, 06877. Ms. Anna O'Rourke, Prin. See separate listing under Elementary Schools in the Institution Section. Lay Teachers 27; Students 252.
Catechesis Religious Program—Tel: 203-438-7335; Email: ppostiglione@smcr.org. Patricia Postiglione, D.R.E. Students 1,050.
RIVERSIDE, FAIRFIELD CO., ST. CATHERINE OF SIENA (1913)
4 Riverside Ave., Riverside, 06878. Tel: 203-637-6331 ; Email: rectory@stcath.org; Web: www.stcath.org. Revs. William F. Platt; Mark D'Silva, Parochial Vicar; Rev. Msgr. Alan F. Detscher, Pastor Emeritus; Deacons Renato Berzolla; Robert Henrey; Vincent J. Heidenreich; Eduardo Rodrigues; Louis Howe, Assoc. D.R.E. & Youth Min.
Catechesis Religious Program—6 Riverside Ave., Riverside, 06878. Email: j.pataky@stcath.org. Janis Pataky, D.R.E. Students 754.
SHELTON, FAIRFIELD CO.
1—ST. JOSEPH (1906)
50 Fairmont Pl., Shelton, 06484. Tel: 203-924-8611; Fax: 203-924-9446; Email: stjoseph.rectory@sbcglobal.net; Web: www.sjcshelton.org. Rev. Michael Doguli; Deacons Bradford Smythe; William Miranda.
Catechesis Religious Program—Tel: 203-924-9677; Email: stjosephre@sbcglobal.net. Joshua St. Onge, D.R.E. Students 420.
2—ST. LAWRENCE (1955) [CEM]
505 Shelton Ave., Shelton, 06484. Tel: 203-929-5355; Email: stlawrpar1@aol.com. Revs. Michael K. Jones, S.T.D.; Greg J. Markey; Deacons Frank J. Masso; Anthony Cassaneto.
Catechesis Religious Program—Tel: 203-929-5355; Email: stwannabe@aol.com. Mrs. Karen O'Keefe, C.R.E. Students 77.
3—ST. MARGARET MARY (1963) [CEM]
50 Donovan Ln., Shelton, 06484. Tel: 203-924-4929; Fax: 203-924-1849; Email: stmamar380@yahoo.com; Web: stmmshelton.org. Rev. Ciprian Bejan.
Catechesis Religious Program—Tel: 203-924-2679. Mrs. Jessica Welsch, D.R.E. Students 132.
SHERMAN, FAIRFIELD CO., HOLY TRINITY (1985) [CEM]
15 Rte. 37 Center, P.O. Box 97, Sherman, 06784.
Tel: 860-354-1414; Email: parishoffice@htrccsherman.org. Rev. Richard J. Gemza.
Catechesis Religious Program—Tel: 860-355-1483. Mrs. Michele Curnan, D.R.E. Students 190.
STAMFORD, FAIRFIELD CO.
1—THE BASILICA OF SAINT JOHN THE EVANGELIST (1854)
279 Atlantic St., Stamford, 06901. Tel: 203-324-1553; Email: stjc@optonline.net; Web: stjohnsstamford.com. Rev. Msgr. Stephen M. Di Giovanni, H.E.D.; Revs. Andrew A. Vill, Parochial Vicar; Albert D. Audette, In Res., (Retired).
Catechesis Religious Program—Email: religiouseed@saintjohnsstamford.com. Students 179.
2—ST. BENEDICT (1930) (Slovak), Merged with Our Lady of Montserrat, Stamford to form Saint Benedict - Our Lady of Montserrat, Stamford.
3—SAINT BENEDICT - OUR LADY OF MONTSERRAT (2000) [CEM]
Mailing Address: 1 St. Benedict Cir., Stamford, 06902. Tel: 203-327-7250; Tel: 203-323-7379; Fax: 203-327-7251; Email: myparish@optonline.net. Revs. Gustavo A. Falla; Jose Montoya, (Colombia) Parochial Vicar; Jose Abelardo Vasquez, Parochial Vicar; Abelardo Vasquez, D.R.E.
Catechesis Religious Program—Tel: 203-348-5196; Email: frvasquez@diobpt.org. Students 157.
4—ST. BRIDGET OF IRELAND (1963)
278 Strawberry Hill Ave., Stamford, 06902.
Tel: 203-324-2910; Email: bridgetct@aol.com; Web: www.stbridgetofireland.org. Rev. Edward J. McAuley Jr.
Catechesis Religious Program—Tel: 203-357-8157; Email: stbridgetre@aol.cpm. Mrs. Magdalene Jeffers, D.R.E. Students 76.
5—ST. CECILIA (1926) [CEM]
1184 Newfield Ave., Stamford, 06905-1496.
Tel: 203-322-1562; Email: stceciliastmfrd@optimum.net; Web: stceciliastamford.org. Rev. William M. Quinlan, J.C.L., Admin.; Susan Scanlon Hicks, Liturgy Dir., Music Ministries.
Catechesis Religious Program—Tel: 203-329-8783; Email: faithformation@stceciliastamford.org. Tracey Miller, D.R.E. Students 223.
6—ST. CLEMENT OF ROME (1928)
535 Fairfield Ave., Stamford, 06902.
Tel: 203-348-4206; Email: stclement@optonline.net. Rev. Carlos Rodriques.
Catechesis Religious Program—Tel: 203-348-1233; Email: stclementre@optonline.net. Mrs. Louise Cronin, D.R.E. Students 55.
7—ST. GABRIEL (1963)
914 Newfield Ave., Stamford, 06905.
Tel: 203-322-7426; Fax: 203-968-6266; Email: Gabe914@optonline.net; Web: saintgabrielchurch.org. Revs. William M. Quinlan, J.C.L.; Mariusz Olbrys, Parochial Vicar; Deacons Larry Buzzeo; Jose Viola; Mrs. Gina DeVito, Sec.
Catechesis Religious Program—Tel: 203-329-1978; Email: saintgabrielccd@gmail.com. Maryanne Didelot, D.R.E. Students 141.
8—HOLY NAME OF JESUS (1903) (Polish)
325 Washington Blvd., Stamford, 06902.
Tel: 203-323-4967; Email: info@holynamestamford.org; Web: www.holynamestamgord.org. Revs. Pawel M. Hrebenko; Tomasz Przybyl.
Res.: 4 Pulaski St., Stamford, 06902.
Catechesis Religious Program—Tel: 203-323-4546. Daria Opolski, D.R.E. Students 210.
9—CHURCH OF THE HOLY SPIRIT (1962) [CEM]
403 Scofieldtown Rd., Stamford, 06903-4009.
Tel: 203-322-3722; Email: holyspiritparish@aol.com. Rev. Msgr. Kevin T. Royal, S.T.L.; Revs. Joseph Gill, Res. Priest; John J. Cullen, Ret. Priest.
See Holy Spirit, Stamford under Elementary Schools located in the Institution section.
10—ST. LEO (1960) [CEM]
24 Roxbury Rd., Stamford, 06902. Tel: 203-322-1669; Tel: 203-329-8884; Fax: 203-461-9761. Rev. James D. Grosso.
Catechesis Religious Program—Tel: 203-348-0052; Fax: 203-357-9639. Mrs. Eileen Towne, D.R.E. Students 492.
11—ST. MARY (1907) [CEM]
566 Elm St., Stamford, 06902. Tel: 203-324-7321; Email: stmarystamford@yahoo.com. Revs. Gustavo A. Falla; Jose Montoya, (Colombia) Parochial Vicar;

Marcelo R. Lopresti, I.V.E., Parochial Vicar; James C. Vattakunnel, V.C., Chap., Stamford Hospital.
Catechesis Religious Program—Email: frvasquez@diobpt.org. Rev. Jose Abelardo Vasquez, D.R.E. Students 171.

12—ST. MAURICE (1935) [CEM]
358 Glenbrook Rd., Stamford, 06906-2198.
Tel: 203-324-3434; Email: parishoffice@smcglenbrook.org; Web: www.smglenbrook.org. Rev. Alfred A. Riendeau Jr.
Catechesis Religious Program—
Tel: 203-324-3434, Ext. 707; Email: skluun@smcglenbrook.org. Ms. Sandra Kluun, C.R.E. Students 116.

13—OUR LADY OF MONTSERRAT (1984) (Spanish), Merged with St. Benedict, Stamford to form Saint Benedict - Our Lady of Montserrat, Stamford.

14—OUR LADY STAR OF THE SEA (1964)
1200 Shippan Ave., Stamford, 06902.
Tel: 203-324-4634; Web: ourladystaroftheseastamford.org. Rev. Peter K. Smolik.
Catechesis Religious Program—1170 Shippan Ave., Stamford, 06902. Email: olssdre@yahoo.com. Dee Fumega, C.R.E. Students 121.
Convent—1216 Shippan Ave., Stamford, 06902.

15—SACRED HEART (1920) [CEM] (Italian)
37 Schuyler Ave., Stamford, 06902.
Tel: 203-324-9544; Email: sacredparish@optonline.net; Web: sacredparish@optonline.net. Revs. Alfonso Picone; Martin P. deMayo.
Catechesis Religious Program—Tel: 203-348-3185. Camille Vitti, D.R.E. Students 129.

STRATFORD, FAIRFIELD CO.

1—HOLY NAME OF JESUS (1923) (Slovak)
1950 Barnum Ave., Stratford, 06614.
Tel: 203-375-5815; Fax: 203-375-5954; Email: hnj1950@sbcglobal.net; Web: www.hnojchurch.org. Rev. Albert G. Pinciaro.
Catechesis Religious Program—Tel: 203-378-7407. Sr. Madonna Figura, S.S.C.M., D.R.E. Students 190.
Convent—Parish Center, 2 Mary Ave., Stratford, 06614. Tel: 203-375-5815, Ext. 200.

2—ST. JAMES (1886)
2110 Main St., Stratford, 06615. Tel: 203-375-5887; Fax: 203-378-1562; Email: mkelly.stjamesparish@gmail.com; Web: www.stjamesstratford.com. Revs. Arthur C. Mollenhauer, J.C.L.; Rogerio Silva Perri, Parochial Vicar; Deacons John Piatak; Joseph Koletar.

3—ST. MARK (1960)
500 Wigwam Ln., Stratford, 06614.
Tel: 203-377-0444; Fax: 203-386-8071; Email: paulam500@sbcglobal.net. Revs. Birendra Soreng, (India); Russell Augustine, Parochial Vicar; Deacons T. Emmet Murray; F. Paul Kurmay; Andrew Dzujna.
Catechesis Religious Program—Tel: 203-377-3158; Email: prnettleton@yahoo.com. Mrs. Patricia Nettleton, D.R.E. Students 280.

4—OUR LADY OF GRACE PARISH (1954) [CEM]
497 Second Hill Ln., Stratford, 06614-2595.
Tel: 203-377-0928; Email: parishoffice@olgstratford.com; Web: www.olgstratford.com. Rev. Msgr. Martin P. Ryan, D.Min.; Rev. Udayakumar Xavariapit-Chai, Parochial Vicar; Deacon Robert W. McLaughlin.
Parish Center—345 Second Hill Ln., Stratford, 06614-2595.
Catechesis Religious Program—Tel: 203-375-6133; Email: denisebartelsen@olgstratford.com. Mrs. Denise L. Bartelson, C.R.E. (Pre School Dir.). Students 177.

5—OUR LADY OF PEACE (1948)
651 Stratford Rd., Stratford, 06615.
Tel: 203-377-4863; Email: ourlady@sbcglobal.net. Mailing Address: 10 Ivy St., Stratford, 06615. Rev. Nicholas S. Pavia; Deacon Thomas Fekete.
Res.: 230 Park Blvd., Stratford, 06615.
Catechesis Religious Program—Tel: 203-378-3053. Rev. Nicholas S. Pavia. Students 111.

TRUMBULL, FAIRFIELD CO.

1—ST. CATHERINE OF SIENA (1955) [CEM]
220 Shelton Rd., Trumbull, 06611. Tel: 203-377-3133 ; Email: office@stcatherinetrumbull.com; Web: www.stcathtrumbull.com. Rev. Joseph A. Marcello; Deacon Patrick Toole.
See St. Catherine of Siena, Trumbull under Elementary Schools located in the Institution section.
Catechesis Religious Program—Email: louisestewart@stcatherinetrumbull.com. Louise Stewart, D.R.E. Students 600.

2—CHRIST THE KING (1962) [CEM]
4700 Madison Ave., Trumbull, 06611.
Tel: 203-268-8695; Tel: 203-261-2583; Email: ctkparish@aol.com; Web: christthekingtrumbull.org. Rev. Terrence P. Walsh; Deacon Donald W. Brunetto.
Catechesis Religious Program—Email: ctkfaithformation@att.net. Eileen Wilkins, D.R.E. Students 180.

3—ST. STEPHEN (1953)
6948 Main St., Trumbull, 06611-1340.
Tel: 203-268-6217; Email: ststephenrectory@yahoo.com. Rev. Christopher J. Samele; Deacons Donald J. Ross; John DiTaranto.
Catechesis Religious Program—Tel: 203-268-6860; Email: ststephenfaithformation@gmail.com. Janet Wrabel, D.R.E. Students 425.

4—ST. THERESA (1934) [CEM]
5301 Main St., Trumbull, 06611. Tel: 203-261-3676; Fax: 203-268-8723; Email: parish@sttheresatrumbull.org; Web: www.sttheresatrumbull.org. Revs. Brian P. Gannon, S.T.D.; Flavian Bejan, Parochial Vicar.
See St. Theresa, Trumbull under Elementary Schools located in the Institution section.
Catechesis Religious Program—19 Rosemond Ter., Trumbull, 06611. Tel: 203-261-4706; Email: cre@sttheresatrumbull.org. Joanne Durkin, D.R.E. Students 618.

WESTON, FAIRFIELD CO., ST. FRANCIS OF ASSISI (1955)
35 Norfield Rd., Weston, 06883. Tel: 203-227-1341; Fax: 203-226-1154; Web: www.stfrancisweston.org. Rev. Jeffrey W. Couture.
Res.: 24 Roxbury Rd, Stamford, 06902.
Catechesis Religious Program—Tel: 203-227-8353; Email: bdemattio@stfrancisweston.org. Students 300.

WESTPORT, FAIRFIELD CO.

1—CHURCH OF THE ASSUMPTION (1876) [CEM]
98 Riverside Ave., Westport, 06880.
Tel: 203-227-5161; Fax: 203-226-5448; Email: jbarro@assumption-westport.org; Web: www.assumption-westport.org. Rev. Cyrus Bartolome.
Catechesis Religious Program—Tel: 203-226-5448; Email: cathy.romano@parishmail.com. Cathy Romano, D.R.E. Students 603.

2—ST. LUKE (1957)
49 North Turkey Hill Rd., Westport, 06880.
Tel: 203-227-7245, Ext. 10;
Tel: 203-222-0478, Ext. 25 (Outreach Ministries); Fax: 203-226-8063; Email: stluke@optonline.net; Web: saintlukewestport.org. Mailing Address: 84 Long Lots Rd., Westport, 06880. Rev. Msgr. Andrew G. Varga; Rev. Udayakumar Xavariapitchai, Parochial Vicar; Sr. Maureen Francis Fleming, S.S.N.D., Coord. Pastoral Outreach Activities; Deacons Brian J. Kelly, Ph.D.; Lance C. Fredricks.
Catechesis Religious Program—
Tel: 203-226-0729, Ext. 11 (Religious Formation);
Tel: 203-222-0205 (Youth Ministry); Email: stlukereo@optonline.net. Jacqueline Frusciante, D.R.E.; Ms. Deb Toner, Youth Min. Students 318.

WILTON, FAIRFIELD CO., OUR LADY OF FATIMA (1953)
229 Danbury Rd., Wilton, 06897. Tel: 203-762-3928; Fax: 203-834-1261; Email: secretary@olfwilton.org; Web: www.olfwilton.org. Revs. Reginald D. Norman; Damian Pielesz; Deacon Anthony Conti.
See Our Lady of Fatima, Wilton under Elementary Schools located in the Institution section.
Catechesis Religious Program—225 Danbury Rd., Wilton, 06897. Tel: 203-762-9080; Email: olfreled@gmail.com. Mrs. Kathleen Rooney, D.R.E. Students 936.

Chaplains of Public Institutions

BRIDGEPORT. *Bridgeport Hospital*, 267 Grant St., 06610. Tel: 203-384-3311. Revs. Augustine Okoroafor, Chap., Churchill Penn, Asst. Chap.
Saint Vincent's Medical Center, 2800 Main St., 06606. Tel: 203-576-6000, Ext. 247. Revs. Hyginus Ndubueze Agu, Chap., Albert Forlano, Chap., Joseph J. Schad, S.J., Chap.

DANBURY. *Danbury Hospital*, 24 Hospital Ave., Danbury, 06810. Tel: 203-797-7912. Revs. Jean-Rony Philippe, Chap., Raymond M. Scherba, Asst. Chap.

GREENWICH. *Greenwich Hospital*, 5 Perryridge Rd., Greenwich, 06830. Tel: 203-863-3000. Rev. Christopher Johnson, O.C.D., Staff Chap.

NORWALK. *Norwalk Hospital*, 34 Maple St., Norwalk, 06850. Tel: 203-852-2000. Revs. Paul Raj Sankaralingam, Chap., Marcel St. Jean, Asst. Chap.

STAMFORD. *Stamford Hospital*, 1 Hospital Plaza, Stamford, 06902. Tel: 203-276-1000. Very Rev. Matthew R. Mauriello, Asst. Chap., Rev. James C. Vattakunnel, V.C., Chap.

On Duty Outside the Diocese:
Rev. Msgrs.—
McGrath, Frank C., Ave Maria School of Law, Naples FL 34119
Millea, William V., Via della Nocetta 63, 00164, Rome, Italy
Revs.—
Boyd, Robert J., 32 W. Franklin Ave., Pequannock, NJ 07440
Daigle, David, CHC, USN, LTJG Chap, Ch01, USS Iwo Jima (LHD-7), Fpo, AE 09574-1664
Devore, Daniel B., 9 Arbor Club Dr., Ponte Vedra, FL 32082
Guglielmi, Donald A., S.T.D., Saint Joseph Seminary, 201 Seminary Ave., Yonkers, NY 10704
Julien, Jean Ridly, Columbia University Medical Center, New York 10032
Talar, Charles J.T., St. Mary's Seminary, 9845 Memorial Dr., Houston, TX 77024.

Leave of Absence:
Revs.—
Henderson, Roy
Lynch, Peter J.
Walter, Andrew M.

Retired:
Rev. Msgrs.—
Bernelli, Matthew, (Retired)
Cullen, J. Peter, P.A., (Retired)
Cuneo, J. James, J.C.D., (Retired)
Doyle, Jerald A., J.C.D., Ph.D., (Retired)
Gintoli, Blase M., (Retired)
Grieco, Nicholas V., (Retired)
Pekar, Joseph W., (Retired)
Potter, Joseph D., (Retired)
Sabia, John B., (Retired)
Scheyd, William J., P.A., (Retired)
Shea, Richard J., (Retired)
Surwilo, Edward R., (Retired)
Villamide, Aniceto, (Retired)
Wallin, Kevin W., (Retired)
Watts, Roger J., (Retired)
Revs.—
Arrando, Angelo S., (Retired)
Audette, Albert D., (Retired)
Babeu, Gill C., (Retired)
Bachman, Michael J., (Retired)
Balint, Stephen J., (Retired)
Barachini, Nello, (Retired)
Boccaccio, Michael A., (Retired)
Brady, Philip W., (Retired)
Breen, James E., (Retired)
Carew, Lawrence F., (Retired)
Carey, William F., (Retired)
Carey, William G., (Retired)
Cipolla, Richard G., (Retired)
Colohan, Edward A., (Retired)
Connolly, Mark, (Retired)
Crofut, Robert J., (Retired)
D'Souza, Gilbert P., (Retired)
DeLuca, Stephen J., (Retired)
Fernandez, Jose A., (Retired)
Gay, James A., (Retired)
Giuliani, John B., (Retired)
Gleeson, Stephen J., (Retired)
Igoe, Martin S., (Retired)
Keefe, Bernard A., (Retired)
Kennelly, Daniel, (Retired)
Knurek, Dennis A., (Retired)
Lincon, Joseph B., (Retired)
Long, John Paul, (Retired)
Lynch, Thomas F., (Retired)
Maty, Robert J., (Retired)
McDonough, Roger F., (Retired)
Montanaro, Guido G., (Retired)
Mooney, Patrick, (Retired)
Palacino, Joseph F., (Retired)
Palmer, Michael C., (Retired)
Parampath, Joseph K., J.C.D., (Retired)
Petrucci, Raymond K., (Retired)
Pikulski, John F., Ph.D., (Retired)
Post, Robert J., Ph.D., (Retired)
Punnakunnel, John, (India) (Retired)
Riley, David J., (Retired)
Saba, Joseph J., (Retired)
Sankoorikal, George S., (Retired)
Smolko, John F., (Retired)
Thorne, Thomas P., (Retired)
Tracy, David W., (Retired)
Tufaro, Douglas, (Retired)
Turlick, Donald A., (Retired)
Uzzilio, Robert A., (Retired)
Verrilli, William F., J.C.L., (Retired)
Watts, Albert W., (Retired)
Winn, Frank A., (Retired).

Permanent Deacons:
Africot, Alix, (Retired)
Berger, Rob, (Outside of Diocese)
Bernal, Guillermo, St. Charles Borromeo Parish, Bridgeport
Berzolla, Renato L., (Retired)
Bissenden, William J., (Retired)
Blankschen, Robert, (Retired)
Blier, Roland, (Retired)
Bolton, Timothy, Vincent Hospital, Bridgeport
Brown, James A., (Retired)
Brunetto, Donald W., (Retired)
Buchholz, John, (Outside of Diocese)
Buzzeo, Michael L., (Retired)
Cabral, Jose R., (Retired)

Calabrese, Robert P., (Outside of Diocese)
Caraluzzi, Anthony, (Outside of Diocese)
Carpenter, Gary E., (Outside of Diocese)
Casiano, Jorge, The Cathedral Parish
Cassaneto, Anthony P., St. Lawrence Parish, Shelton
Chervenak, Raymond J., Our Lady of Assumption Parish, Fairfield
Chiappetta, Frank, (Retired)
Conti, Anthony, Our Lady of Fatima Parish, Wilton
Curran, Thomas F., Fairfield University, Fairfield
DeBiase, Joseph, Holy Family Parish, Fairfield
DeRobin, John, St. Mary Parish, Bethel
Detje, Anthony, (Retired)
DiTaranto, John, St. Stephen Parish, Trumbull
Dwyer, Robert, (Outside of Diocese)
Dzujna, Andrew W., St. Mark Parish, Stratford
Esterheld, John, (Outside of Diocese)
Fekete, Thomas, Our Lady of Peace Parish, Stratford
Fenton, Richard A., (Outside of Diocese)
Flynn, David, St. Jude Parish, Monroe
Font, Jeffrey, Immaculate High School, Danbury
Foust, Donald P., St. Margret's Shrine, Bridgeport
Foyt, Francis, (Retired)
Fredricks, Lance C., (Retired)
Gagne, Joseph, (Retired)
Garcia, Santos, Cathedral Parish, Bridgeport
Genovese, Stephan A., St. Mary Parish, Norwalk
Grant, Terence J., (Outside of Diocese)
Heidenreich, Vincent J., St. Catherine, Riverside
Hein, Henry R., (Outside of Diocese)
Henrey, Robert, (Outside of Diocese)
Herman, Paul, (Outside of Diocese)
Howe, Louis, St. Joseph Parish, Danbury
Ianniello, Daniel, (Retired)
Jeffers, Ernest, St. Bridget of Ireland Parish, Stamford
Jennings, Paul J., (Outside of Diocese)
Kelly, Brian J., Ph.D., (Retired)
Kingsley, Jeffrey J., St. Margaret Mary Alacoque Parish, Shelton
Koletar, Joseph, St. James Parish, Stratford
Koniers, William A., Cathedral Parish, Bridgeport
Kovacs, Richard P., St. Gregory the Great Parish, Danbury
Kuhn, Peter J., St. Joseph Parish, Brookfield
Kurmay, Paul F., St. Mark Parish, Stratford
Lambert, Gerald H., St. Theresa Parish, Trumbull
Landry, Ronald, Our Lady of Fatima Parish, Wilton
Linsenmeyer, John M., (Retired)
Mack, Thomas, (Outside of Diocese)
Mahon, John W., St. Philip Parish, Norwalk
Martinez, Ricardo, Blessed Sacrament Parish, Bridgeport
Masaryk, Thomas, St. Margaret Shrine, Bridgeport
Masso, Frank J., (Retired)
McLaughlin, Robert W., Our Lady of Grace Parish, Stratford
McMancus, Thomas J., St. Francis of Assisi Parish, Weston
Miranda, William, St. Joseph Parish, Shelton
Moore, Kevin, Our Lady of Assumption Parish, Fairfield
Moranski, John J., Holy Family Parish, Fairfield
Morris, Robert, (Outside of Diocese)
Murphy, William D., (Retired)
Murray, Emmet, (Retired)
Myott, Daniel N., (Retired)
Naiman, Donald J., St. Joseph Parish, Danbury
Newton, Philip J., (Outside of Diocese)
O'Connor, Daniel, St. Rose of Lima Parish, Newtown
Olavarria, Reynaldo, St. Mary Parish, Bridgeport
Oles, Michael, (Outside of Diocese)
Pereira, Gabriel, Our Lady of Fatima Parish, Bridgeport
Piatak, John, St. James Parish, Stratford
Pierre-Louis, Augustin, (Outside of Diocese)
Pilkington, Paul B., (Retired)
Pond, Stephen W., St. Aloysius Parish, New Canaan
Regus, Rafael, Our Lady of Guadalupe Parish, Danbury
Reilly, Paul, (Retired)
Rigg, Russell T., (Retired)
Rivera, David, St. Charles Borromeo Parish, Bridgeport
Rivera, Ramon, (Outside of Diocese)
Rodrigues, Eduardo, St. Catherine of Siena Parish, Riverside
Rodriguez, Miguel, (Outside of Diocese)
Roos, Norman, St. Rose of Lima Parish, Newtown
Ross, Donald J., St. Stephen Parish, Trumbull
Ruge, Kenneth J., St. Andrew Parish, Bridgeport
Sabol, Gerald, Notre Dame Parish, Easton
Salvestrini, Robert A., (Retired)
Santulli, William A., St. Aloysius Parish, New Canaan
Saranich, Michael, Holy Name of Jesus Parish, Stratford
Scinto, Richard, St. Rose of Lima Parish, Newtown
Shaughnessy, William J., (Retired)
Shevlin, Patrick, St. Edward the Confessor Parish, New Fairfield
Shine, Mark T., (Outside of Diocese)
Smythe, Bradford, St. Joseph Parish, Shelton
Sochacki, David M., St. Margaret Mary Alacoque, Shelton
Stenberg, Richard, (Outside of Diocese)
Tavarez, Fabio, St. Charles Borromeo Parish, Bridgeport
Timmel, William C., St. Patrick Parish, Redding
Toole, Patrick, Catherine of Siena Parish, Trumbull
Torres, Luis, St. Peter Parish, Bridgeport
Trankovich, Rudolph P., (Retired)
Tuccio, John, St. Jude Parish, Monroe
Tugman, John H., (Outside of Diocese)
Vaughn, David J., (Retired)
Vincent, Gauthier, Our Lady Star of the Sea Parish, Stamford
Viola, Jose, St. Gabriel Parish, Stamford
Volpe, James, (Medical Leave).

INSTITUTIONS LOCATED IN DIOCESE

[A] SEMINARIES, DIOCESAN

STAMFORD. *Redemptorist Mater Diocesan Missionary Seminary Diocese of Bridgeport Inc.*, 21 Schuyler Ave., Stamford, 06902.

St. John Fisher Seminary Inc. (1989) 894 Newfield Ave., Stamford, 06905. Tel: 203-322-5331; Fax: 203-461-9876; Email: frcheck@diobpt.org; Web: bridgeportvocations.org. Rev. Msgr. Christopher J. Walsh, Ph.D., S.T.D., Academic Dean; Rev. Paul N. Check, S.T.L., Rector; Rev. Msgr. Thomas W. Powers, S.T.L., Res. Clergy 7; Lay Staff 2; Lay Teachers 5; Priests 2; Students 8.

[B] COLLEGES AND UNIVERSITIES

FAIRFIELD. **Fairfield University* (Coed) 1073 N. Benson Rd., Fairfield, 06824. Tel: 203-254-4000, Ext. 2217; Fax: 203-254-4221; Web: www.fairfield.edu. Mark Nemac, Ph.D., Pres. Lay Teachers 246; Priests 5; Students 5,000; Jesuits 5; Non-Faculty Personnel 525.

**Sacred Heart University*, 5151 Park Ave., Fairfield, 06825-1000. Tel: 203-371-7901; Fax: 203-365-7652; Web: www.sacredheart.edu. John Petillo, Pres. Coeducational and Comprehensive University. Courses offered year round, day & evening. Lay Teachers 560; Priests 2; Students 7,781; Adjunct Priests as Professors 9.

St. Vincent's College, 2800 Main St., 06606. Tel: 203-576-5578; Fax: 203-576-5893. Students 801.

[C] HIGH SCHOOLS, DIOCESAN

BRIDGEPORT. *Kolbe-Cathedral Catholic High School, Inc.* (1963) 33 Calhoun Pl., 06604. Tel: 203-335-2554; Fax: 203-335-2556; Email: cougars@kolbecaths.org; Web: www.kolbecaths.org. Mr. Henry Rondon, Prin. Clergy / Religious Teachers 1; Lay Teachers 25; Students 309.

DANBURY. *Immaculate High School, Inc.* (1962) 73 Southern Blvd., Danbury, 06810. Tel: 203-744-1510; Fax: 203-744-1275; Email: info@immaculatehs.org; Web: immaculatehs.org. Mary R. Maloney, Pres.; Patrick Higgens, Prin. Clergy / Religious Teachers 1; Lay Teachers 65; Students 483.

FAIRFIELD. *Notre Dame Catholic High School, Inc.*, 220 Jefferson St., Fairfield, 06825. Tel: 203-372-6521; Fax: 203-374-4167; Email: ccipriano@notredame.org; Web: www.notredame.org. Mr. Christopher Cipriano, Prin. Lay Teachers 56; Students 491.

STAMFORD. *Trinity Catholic High School, Inc.* (Formerly Stamford Catholic High School) 926 Newfield Ave., Stamford, 06905. Tel: 203-322-3401 ; Fax: 203-322-5330; Email: info@trinitycatholic.org; Web: www.trinitycatholic.org. Ms. Patricia Brady, Headmaster; Scott Smith, Prin.; Rev. Joseph Gill, Chap. Records for Central Catholic High School, Norwich, and St. Mary's High School, Greenwich, located at Trinity. Clergy / Religious Teachers 1; Lay Teachers 37; Students 300.

TRUMBULL. *St. Joseph's High School, Inc.* (1962) 2320 Huntington Tpke., Trumbull, 06611. Tel: 203-378-9378; Fax: 203-378-7306; Email: jkeane@sjcadets.org; Web: www.sjcadets.org. William J. Fitzgerald, Ph.D., M.Div., M.Ed., Pres.; James R. Keane, M.Div., M.Ed., Ph.D., Prin. Clergy / Religious Teachers 1; Lay Teachers 71; Students 821.

[D] SPECIAL SCHOOLS, DIOCESAN

FAIRFIELD. *St. Catherine Academy*, (Grades K-12), 760 Tahmore Dr., Fairfield, 06825. Tel: 203-540-5381; Fax: 203-540-5383; Email: hburland@diobpt.org; Web: www.stcatherineacademy.org. Helen Burland, Exec. Dir.; Mr. Eric Spencer, Prin. Special Needs School. Lay Teachers 3; Sisters 2; Students 17.

[E] HIGH SCHOOLS, PRIVATE

FAIRFIELD. *Fairfield College Preparatory School* (1942) 1073 N. Benson Rd., Fairfield, 06824. Tel: 203-254-4200; Fax: 203-254-4108; Email: rperrotta@fairfieldprep.org; Web: www.fairfieldprep.org. Dr. Robert A. Perrotta, Ed.D., J.D., Prin.; Rev. John J. Hanwell, S.J., Pres. Fairfield Prep. Society of Jesus of New England.A preparatory day school for boys, established in 1942. Lay Teachers 52; Priests 1; Students 804; Total Staff 89.

[F] ELEMENTARY SCHOOLS, DIOCESAN

BRIDGEPORT. *Bridgeport Diocesan Schools Corporation*, 238 Jewett Ave., 06606. Tel: 203-416-1380.

BETHEL. *St. Mary School Bethel LLC*, 24 Dodgingtown Rd., Bethel, 06801-2241. Tel: 203-744-2922; Fax: 203-798-8803; Email: gviceroy@StMaryBethelCT.org; Web: www.stmarybethel.org. Gregory Viceroy, Prin. Lay Teachers 19; Students 192.

DANBURY. *St. Gregory the Great School LLC*, (Grades K-8), 85 Great Plain Rd., Danbury, 06811. Tel: 203-748-1217; Fax: 203-748-0414; Email: info@sgtgs.org; Web: saintgregoryschool.org. Suzanne Curra, Prin. Lay Teachers 25; Students 220.

St. Joseph School Danbury LLC, (Grades PreK-8), 370 Main St., Danbury, 06810. Tel: 203-748-6615; Fax: 203-748-6508; Email: sjsoffice@sjsdanbury.org; Web: www.sjsdanbury.org. Mrs. Kathryn Petrone, Prin. Clergy / Religious Teachers 1; Lay Teachers 18; Students 239.

Saint Peter School LLC, (Grades N-8), 98 Main St., Danbury, 06810. Tel: 203-748-2895; Email: info@spsdanbury.org; Web: www.stpeterschooldanbury.org. Mrs. Mary Lou Torre, Prin. Lay Teachers 22; Students 259.

FAIRFIELD. *Assumption Catholic School LLC*, (Grades PreK-8), 605 Stratfield Rd., Fairfield, 06825. Tel: 203-334-6271; Fax: 203-382-0399; Email: office@oloaffld.org; Email: principal@oloaffld.org; Web: www.assumptionfairfield.org. Mr. Steve Santoli, Prin. Lay Teachers 18; Students 179.

St. Thomas Aquinas School LLC, (Grades PreK-8), 1719 Post Rd., Fairfield, 06824. Tel: 203-255-0556; Fax: 203-255-0596; Email: info@stasonline.net; Web: www.stasonline.net. Ms. Jo Mathieson, Prin. Lay Teachers 28; Students 326.

NEW CANAAN. *St. Aloysius School LLC*, (Grades K-8), 33 South Ave., New Canaan, 06840. Tel: 203-966-0786; Email: jalfone@sasncct.org; Web: sasncct.org. Dr. John R. Alfone, Prin. Clergy / Religious Teachers 3; Lay Teachers 15; Students 143.

NEWTOWN. *St. Rose of Lima School LLC*, (Grades PreK-8), 40 Church Hill Rd., Newtown, 06470. Tel: 203-426-5102; Fax: 203-426-5374; Email: bgjoka@diobpt.org; Web: www.stroseschool.com. Mr. Bardhyl Gjoka, Prin. Clergy / Religious Teachers 1; Lay Teachers 23; Students 256.

NORWALK. *All Saints Catholic School LLC*, (Grades PreK-8), 139 W. Rocks Rd., Norwalk, 06851. Tel: 203-847-3881; Fax: 203-847-8055; Web: www.allsaintsnorwalk.com. Mrs. Linda Dunn, Prin. Lay Teachers 47; Sisters 1; Students 437.

RIDGEFIELD. *St. Mary School Ridgefield LLC*, (Grades K-8), 183 High Ridge Ave., Ridgefield, 06877. Tel: 203-438-7288; Web: www.smsridgefield.org. Ms. Anna O'Rourke, Prin. Lay Teachers 42; Students 226.

STRATFORD. *St. James School LLC*, (Grades PreK-8), 50 Harvey Pl., Stratford, 06615. Tel: 203-375-5994; Fax: 203-380-0749; Email: jack.lynch@sjssct.org; Web: www.stjamesstratford.org. Jack Lynch, Prin. Lay Teachers 26; Students 257.

St. Mark School LLC, (Grades PreK-8), 500 Wigwam Ln., Stratford, 06614. Tel: 203-375-4291; Fax: 203-375-4833; Email: contactus@stmarkschool.org; Web: www.stmarkschool.org. Mr. Scott Clough, Prin. Lay Teachers 17; Students 193.

TRUMBULL. *St. Catherine of Siena School LLC*, (Grades PreK-8), 190 Shelton Rd., Trumbull, 06611. Tel: 203-375-1947; Fax: 203-378-3935; Email: info@scsstrumbull.org; Web: www.stcatherinesienatrumbull.org. Eunice Giaquinto, Prin. Lay Teachers 18; Students 259.

St. Theresa School LLC, (Grades PreK-8), 55 Rosemond Ter., Trumbull, 06611. Tel: 203-268-3236; Fax: 203-268-7966; Email: info@stesonline.org; Web: www.stesonline.org. Mr.

Salvatore Vittoria, Prin. Lay Teachers 20; Students 238.

WILTON. *Our Lady of Fatima School LLC*, (Grades PreK-8), 225 Danbury Rd., Wilton, 06897. Tel: 203-762-8100; Fax: 203-834-0614; Email: ssteele@olfcatholic.org; Web: fatimaschoolwilton.org. Mr. Stanley Steele, Prin. Lay Teachers 16; Students 128.

[G] ACADEMIES, DIOCESAN

BRIDGEPORT. *Catholic Academy of Bridgeport, Inc.*, The Catholic Center, 238 Jewett Ave., 06606. Tel: 203-416-1370; Fax: 203-372-0020; Web: www.cathedralcluster.org.

St. Andrew Academy, (Grades PreK-8), The Catholic Center, 395 Anton St, 06606. Tel: 203-373-1552; Email: lwilson@diobpt.org; Web: standrew.catholicacademybridgeport.org. Lori Wilson, Prin. Lay Teachers 25; Students 244.

St. Ann Academy, (Grades PreK-8), 521 Brewster St., 06605-3409. Tel: 203-334-5856; Fax: 203-333-8263; Email: pgriffin@catholicacademybridgeport.org. Mrs. Patricia Griffin, Prin. Lay Teachers 15; Students 228.

St. Augustine Academy, (Grades 4-8), 63 Pequonnock St., 06604. Tel: 203-366-6500; Fax: 203-362-2934; Email: dboccanfuso@catholicacademybridgeport.org. Deborah Boccanfuso, Prin. Clergy / Religious Teachers 1; Lay Teachers 16; Students 205.

St. Raphael Academy, (Grades PreK-3), 324 Frank St., 06604. Tel: 203-333-6818; Fax: 203-336-9205; Email: choffner@catholicacademybridgeport.org; Web: straphael.catholicacademybridgeport.org. Sr. Christine Hoffner, Prin. Clergy / Religious Teachers 2; Lay Teachers 18; Students 201.

BROOKFIELD. *St. Joseph Catholic Academy of Brookfield, Inc.*, (Grades PreK-8), 5 Obtuse Hill Rd., Brookfield, 06804. Tel: 203-775-2774; Fax: 203-775-5810; Email: pfallon@sjsbrookfield.org; Web: www.sjsbrookfield.org. Mary R. Maloney, Head of School; Mrs. Pamela Fallon, Dir. Lay Teachers 10; Students 103.

GREENWICH. *Greenwich Catholic School, Inc.*, 471 North St., Greenwich, 06830. Tel: 203-869-4000; Fax: 203-869-3405; Email: pkopas@diobpt.org; Web: www.gcsct.org. Mrs. Pat Kopas, Prin. Lay Teachers 36; Students 402.

SHELTON. *Holy Trinity Catholic Academy, Inc.*, (Grades PreK-8), 503 Shelton Ave., Shelton, 06484. Tel: 203-929-4422; Email: llanni@holytrinitycatholicacademy.org; Web: www.holytrinitycatholicacademy.org. Mrs. Lisa Lanni, Prin. Lay Teachers 14; Students 179.

STAMFORD. *The Catholic Academy of Stamford, Inc.*, 948 Newfield Ave., Stamford, 06905. Tel: 203-322-6505; Tel: 203-322-7383; Web: www.catholicacademystamford.org/. Deacon Joseph Gill, Chap. Lay Teachers 42; Students 379.

[H] ELEMENTARY SCHOOLS, PRIVATE

GREENWICH. *Sacred Heart Greenwich*, (Grades PreK-12), Day School for Girls with Coed Early Childhood Education Program 1177 King St., Greenwich, 06831. Tel: 203-531-6500; Fax: 203-531-5206; Email: admissionsoffice@cshct.org; Web: www.cshgreenwich.org. Pamela Juan Hayes, Headmaster; Mr. David Olson, Admin.; Christine D'Alessandro, Admin.; Mrs. Jennifer Bensen, Admin.

Legal Name: Convent of the Sacred Heart Clergy / Religious Teachers 9; Lay Teachers 123; Students 701.

[I] CATHOLIC CHARITIES

BRIDGEPORT. *Catholic Charities*, Catholic Center, 238 Jewett Ave., 06606-2892. Tel: 203-416-1307; Fax: 203-372-5045; Email: abarber@ccfc-ct.org; Web: www.ccfc-ct.org. Mr. Albert Barber, Pres.

Family Directions, 238 Jewett Ave., 06606-2892. Tel: 203-416-1336; Fax: 203-372-5045; Email: azajac@ccfc-ct.org. Amy Zajac, Dir. Family Directions. Adoptions and Home Studies. Tot Asst. Annually 100; Total Staff 1.

Catholic Charities, Danbury, 405 Main St., Ste. 503, Danbury, 06810. Tel: 203-743-4412; Fax: 203-744-3500; Email: csilliman@ccfc-ct.org. Mr. Richard Madwid, Dir. Tot Asst. Annually 2,500; Total Staff 9.

Ways to Work Family Loan Program, 405 Main St., Ste. 503, Danbury, 06810. Tel: 203-743-4412; Fax: 203-744-3500; Email: csilliman@ccfc-ct.org. Silliman Carolyn, Dir. Total Assisted 35.

Catholic Charities, Norwalk, 120 East Ave., Norwalk, 06851. Tel: 203-750-9711; Fax: 203-750-9651; Email: rmadwid@ccfc-ct.org. Mr. Richard Maswid, Dir. Tot Asst. Annually 1,000; Total Staff 5.

Catholic Campaign for Human Development, 238 Jewett Ave., 06606. Tel: 203-416-1307; Email: mtintrup@ccfc-ct.org. Mr. Albert Barber, CEO. Tot Asst. Annually 1,500; Total Staff 1.

Room to Grow School Readiness, 208 East Ave., Norwalk, 06850. Tel: 203-855-0637; Fax: 203-831-8200; Email: nowens@ccfc-ct.org. Nancy Owens, Dir. Clergy 36; Students 128.

Houses of Hospitality:.

New Covenant Center, 174 Richmond Hill Ave, Stamford, 06904. Tel: 203-964-8228; Fax: 203-375-0314; Email: jgutman@ccfc-ct.org. John Gutman, Dir. Total Assisted 2,500.

Thomas Merton Center, 43 Madison Ave., 06604. Tel: 203-367-9036; Fax: 203-367-8828; Email: bjenkins@ccfc-ct.org. Brian Jenkins, Dir. Tot Asst. Annually 6,500; Total Staff 6.

Eat Smart Marketplace Pantry, 43 Madison Ave., 06604. Tel: 203-394-6881; Email: bjenkins@ccfc-ct.org. Brian Jenkins, Director. Tot Asst. Annually 8,500; Total Staff 2.

NEW HEIGHTS, 66 West St., Danbury, 06810. Tel: 203-794-0819; Fax: 203-731-3260. Heather Ely, Dir. Tot Asst. Annually 225; Total Staff 6.

Case Management Program, 24 Grassy Plain St., Bethel, 06801. Tel: 203-748-0848; Fax: 203-796-0046; Email: scole@ccfc-ct.org; Web: www.ccfc-ct.org. Sandy Cole, Vice Pres. Tot Asst. Annually 475; Total Staff 7.

Homeless Outreach Team, 24 Grassy Plain St., Bethel, 06801. Tel: 203-748-0848; Fax: 203-796-0046; Email: mconderino@ccfc-ct.org; Web: www.ccfc-ct.org. Michelle Conderino, Dir. Tot Asst. Annually 275; Total Staff 6.

Senior Nutrition Program, 30 Myano Ln., Ste. 12, Stamford, 06902. Tel: 203-324-6175; Fax: 203-323-1108; Email: mneuberger@ccfc-ct.org. Maureen Neuberger. Tot Asst. Annually 425; Total Staff 9.

Housing Services, 238 Jewett Ave., 06606-2892. Tel: 203-416-1317; Email: dlsmith@ccfc-ct.org. Deborah L. Smith, Dir. Tot Asst. Annually 225; Total Staff 9.

Immigration Services, Catholic Center, 238 Jewett Ave., 06606. Tel: 203-416-1313; Email: aarevalo@ccfc-ct.org. Michael Tintrup, Admin. Tot Asst. Annually 450; Total Staff 3.

[J] DAY NURSERIES

BRIDGEPORT. *Daughters of Charity of the Most Precious Blood Day Nursery* (1908) 1490 North Ave., 06604. Tel: 203-334-7000; Fax: 203-334-7000; Email: daughtersofcharity@yahoo.com. Sr. Rosamma Joseph, Dir. Clergy 1; Sisters 2; Students 9.

STAMFORD. *Our Lady of Grace Preschool & Kindergarten*, 635 Glenbrook Rd., Stamford, 06906. Tel: 203-348-5531; Fax: 203-324-9638; Email: sgesuina@aol.com. Sr. Gesuina Gencarelli, P.O.S.C., Supr. Little Workers of the Sacred Hearts. Clergy 11; Students 125.

[K] GENERAL HOSPITALS

BRIDGEPORT. *St. Vincent's Development Corporation*, 2800 Main St., 06606. Tel: 475-210-5455; Fax: 475-210-5345; Email: kathy.beck@ascension.org; Web: www.stvincents.org. Mrs. Dawn Rudolph, Pres.

St. Vincent's Health Services Corporation, 2800 Main St., 06606. Tel: 475-210-5455; Fax: 475-210-5345; Email: kathy.beck@ascension.org; Web: www.stvincents.org. Mrs. Dawn Rudolph, Pres. Bed Capacity 473; Tot Asst. Annually 230,000; Total Staff 3,000.

St. Vincent's Medical Center, 2800 Main St., 06606. Tel: 203-576-6000; Fax: 475-210-5345; Email: kathy.beck@ascension.org; Web: www.stvincents.org. Mrs. Dawn Rudolph, Pres.; Chris Givens, CFO; Mr. William Hoey, A.C.S.W, L.C.S.W., Vice Pres., Chief Mission Integration Officer. Ascension Health St. Louis, MI Bed Capacity 473; Tot Asst. Annually 206,000; Total Staff 2,350.

St. Vincent's Special Needs Center, Inc., 95 Merritt Blvd., Trumbull, 06611. Tel: 203-375-6400; Fax: 203-380-1190; Web: www.stvincentsspecialneed.org. Dianne Auger, Admin.; Carmine Adimando, Chm. Tot Asst. Annually 1,783; Staff 284.

St. Vincent's Behavioral Health Services, 47 Long Lots Rd., Westport, 06880. Tel: 203-227-1251; Fax: 203-227-8616; Web: www.hallbrooke.org. Andre Newfield, D.O., Chairperson. Bed Capacity 76; Tot Asst. Annually 20,670; Total Staff 300.

St. Vincent's Medical Center Foundation, 2800 Main St., 06606. Tel: 203-576-5451; Fax: 203-576-5880; Email: dianne.auger@stvincents.org; Web: give.stvincents.org. Alfred Pavlis, Chm.; Dianne Auger, Pres. & CEO. Bed Capacity 400; Tot Asst. Annually 110,000; Total Staff 1,700.

[L] HOMES FOR AGED

BETHEL. *Augustana Homes Inc./Augustana Homes Bethel Congregate*, 101 Simeon Rd., Bethel, 06801. Tel: 203-790-9744; Fax: 203-748-8274. Lori Ricci, Regl. Vice Pres. (Winn Residential); Janet Haywood, Contact Person. Total Staff 5; Total Assisted 44.

TRUMBULL. *Carmel Ridge*, 6454 Main St., Trumbull, 06611. Tel: 203-261-2229; Fax: 203-261-2841. Lori Ricci, Regl. Vice Pres. (Winn Residential).

Teresian Towers, 6454 Main St., Trumbull, 06611. Tel: 203-261-2229; Fax: 203-261-2841. Lori Ricci, Regl. Vice Pres. (Winn Residential).

[M] CONVALESCENT HOMES

NORWALK. *Notre Dame Convalescent Home, Inc.* (1952) 76 W. Rocks Rd., Norwalk, 06851. Tel: 203-847-5893; Fax: 203-849-1959. Mother Alain Michel, S.S.T.V., Supr.; Mr. Dana Paul, Admin. Sisters of St. Thomas of Villanova. Patients Asst Anual. 60; Sisters 3; Total Staff 85.

[N] RESIDENCES OF PRIESTS AND BROTHERS

BRIDGEPORT. *Instituto Verbo Encarnado*, St. George Parish, 443 Park Ave., 06604-5493. Tel: 203-335-1797; Fax: 203-334-6359; Email: st_george_church@sbcglobal.net.

FAIRFIELD. *The Fairfield Jesuit Community-Fairfield University*, 1073 N. Benson Rd., Fairfield, 06824-5195. Tel: 203-256-1650; Fax: 203-255-5947; Email: cfabbri@fairfield.edu; Web: www.faculty.fairfield.edu/jesuit. Revs. Kevin Spinale, Prof.; Charles H. Allen, S.J.; Joseph J. Schad, S.J., Chap.; Gerhard H. Bowering, S.J., (Germany); Robert J. Braunreuther, S.J.; Michael J. Doody, S.J.; Thomas J. Fitzpatrick, S.J.; Francis T. Hannafey, S.J.; Walter R. Pelletier, S.J., (Retired); Mark P. Scalese, S.J., M.F.A.; Thomas M. Simisky, S.J.; Bret J. Stockdale, S.J.; Bro. Jonathan Stott, S.J.; Revs. Michael F. Tunney, S.J., Rector; Denis G. Donoghue, S.J.; Gerald R. Blaszcak, S.J.

STAMFORD. *The Catherine Dennis Keefe Queen of the Clergy Retired Priests' Residence*, 274 Strawberry Hill Ave., Stamford, 06902. Tel: 203-358-9906; Fax: 203-358-9524; Email: vhickey@diobpt.org. William J. Scheyd, P.A., Vicar; Rev. Msgrs. J. Peter Cullen, P.A., (Retired); Louis A. DeProfio, Died Aug. 15, 2018; Nicholas V. Grieco, (Retired); Thaddeus F. Malanowski; Roger J. Watts, (Retired), 1418 Windward Rd., Milford, 06460; Rev. Canon Albert W. Watts, J.C.L.; Revs. James E. Breen, (Retired); Edward A. Colohan, (Retired); Michael C. Palmer, (Retired); Robert J. Post, Ph.D., (Retired); John F. Smolko, (Retired), 9808 Dale Dr., Upper Marlboro, MD 20772; Rev. Msgr. Jerald A. Doyle, J.C.D., Ph.D., (Retired); Rev. John Paul Long, (Retired).

[O] CONVENTS AND RESIDENCES FOR SISTERS

BRIDGEPORT. *Convent of Mary Immaculate, Missionary Sisters of the Blessed Sacrament and Mary Immaculate.* Prov. Headquarters. 1111 Wordin Ave., 06605. Tel: 203-334-5681; Fax: 203-604-0866; Email: januariab@gmail.com. Sr. Januaria Beleno, Prior. Assisting the Apostolate to Spanish-Speaking People. Sisters 4.

Daughters of Charity of the Most Precious Blood Convent, 1482 North Ave., 06604. Tel: 203-334-7000; Fax: 203-334-7000; Web: www.dcmpb.org. Sr. Sheeba Thomas, Supr. Sisters 2.

Institute Servants of the Lord and the Virgin of Matara (1988) 153 Linden Ave., 06604-5730. Tel: 203-330-8409; Fax: 203-334-6359; Email: c.damaris@servidoras.org; Web: www.servidoras.org. Sr. Maria in Inatzin Moreno, S.S.V.M., Supr. Sisters 6.

Lovers of the Holy Cross of Govap Bridgeport, 50 Pequonnock St., 06604. Tel: 203-331-1745; Email: maryvanvu.mtg@gmail.com. Sr. Mary Van Vu, L.H.C., Supr. Sisters 5.

Missionaries of Charity, 599 Beechwood Ave., 06604. Tel: 203-336-5626. Sr. M. Regis Devasia, M.C., Contact Person.

**Religious Institute Company of the Savior USA Inc.*, 820 Clinton Ave., 06604.

Sisters of the Company of the Savior, 820 Clinton Ave., 06604. Tel: 203-368-1875; Fax: 203-368-1875; Email: bridgeport@ciasalvador.org; Web: www.ciasalvador.org. Mother Araceli Fernandez, Supr. Spanish-Speaking Apostolate.

MONROE. *Dominican Sisters of Our Lady of the Springs of Bridgeport*, 124 Bug Hill Rd., Monroe, 06468. Tel: 203-880-4455; Fax: 203-880-4455. Sr. Mary Elizabeth Donoghue, O.P., Prioress. Total in Community 20.

Sisters of the Holy Family of Nazareth, C.S.F.N. (1875) 1430 Monroe Tpke., Monroe, 06468. Tel: 203-268-6540; Fax: 203-261-0866; Email: sistersudol1960@gmail.com; Web: www.nazarethcsfn.org. Rev. James J. Cole, Chap. Professed 15; Sisters 15.

NORWALK. *Regional House of Sisters of St. Thomas of Villanova* (1948) 76 W. Rocks Rd., Norwalk, 06851. Tel: 203-847-2885; Email: sstv_usa@sbcglobal.net; Web: www.saintthomasofvillanova.com. Mother

Alain Michel, S.S.T.V., Supr. Gen. Notre Dame Convalescent Homes, Inc. Professed 3.

STAMFORD. *The Bernardine Sisters of the Third Order of St. Francis of Stamford, CT, Inc.* dba Bernardine Franciscan Sisters, Heart of Mary Convent, 163 Sky Meadow Dr., Stamford, 06903-3414. Tel: 203-322-5920; Fax: 203-322-0228. Sisters Deborah Ann Surgot, O.S.F., In Res., Tel: 203-322-8721; Joanne Helen Grejdus, O.S.F., In Res.; Carol Ann Nawracaj, O.S.F., In Res. Sisters 3.

Villa Maria Education Center, Inc. dba Villa Maria School, 161 Sky Meadow Dr., Stamford, 06903. Tel: 203-322-5886; Fax: 203-322-0228; Web: www.villamariaedu.org. Diane McManus, Head of School; Eileen Cassidy, Admin.; Stephanie Myint, Librarian. School for children with learning disabilities (Grades K-9). Administrators 2; Boys 42; Faculty 21; Girls 19; (Full-time, paid) 13; Sisters 1; Students 61; Staff 15.

Franciscan Sisters of the Immaculate Heart of Mary, 1216 Shippan Ave., Stamford, 06902-7425. Tel: 203-569-0310; Email: fihmstamford@yahoo.com. Sr. Balakumari Tiromala Reddy, F.I.H.M., Supr.

Our Lady of Grace Convent, 635 Glenbrook Rd., Stamford, 06906. Tel: 203-348-5531; Fax: 203-324-9638; Email: sgesuina@aol.com; Web: littleworkerposc@aol.com. Sr. Gesuina Gencarelli, P.O.S.C., Supr. Motherhouse and Novitiate of Little Workers of Sacred Hearts.

Sisters of Life, Villa Maria Guadalupe, 159 Skymeadow Dr., Stamford, 06903. Tel: 203-329-1492; Fax: 203-329-1495; Email: vmg@sistersoflife.org. Sr. Bernadette Therese Swan, S.V. Sisters 10.

Villa Divino Amore Convent, Little Workers of the Sacred Hearts of Jesus & Mary, 117 Hope St., Stamford, 06906. Tel: 203-324-2449; Fax: 203-504-8670; Email: sisterenrica@aol.com. Sr. Enrica Capalbo, P.O.S.C., Supr.

WILTON. *Lourdes Health Care Center, Inc.* (1973) 345 Belden Hill Rd., Wilton, 06897-3898. Tel: 203-762-3318; Fax: 203-762-2144; Email: adm@lourdeswilton.org. Sr. Jani Forni, S.S.N.D., Prov. Councilor; Rev. Thomas Elliot, C.S.C., Resident Chap. Sisters 20.

Provincial House, Congregation De Notre Dame, Blessed Sacrament Province, Inc., 30 Highfield Rd., Wilton, 06897. Tel: 203-762-4300; Fax: 203-762-4319; Email: rhager@cnd-m.org; Email: pells@cnd-m.org. Sr. Mary Anne Powers, Prov. Sisters 111.

School Sisters of Notre Dame (1833) 345 Belden Hill Rd., Wilton, 06897. Tel: 203-762-3318; Fax: 203-761-9228; Email: ckrohe@amssnd.org; Web: www.ssnd.org. Sr. Charmaine Krohe, S.S.N.D., Prov.; Rev. Thomas Elliott, C.S.C., Priest, Tel: 203-762-3318. Priests 1; Professed 99.

[P] FOUNDATIONS, TRUSTS AND FUNDS

BRIDGEPORT. *Foundations in Charity Inc.* (2018) 238 Jewett Ave., 06606. Mr. Alfred Barber, Contact Person.

Foundations in Faith Inc. (Formerly Faith in the Future Fund, Inc.) 238 Jewett Ave., 06606.

Inner-City Foundation For Charity & Education (1991) 238 Jewett Ave., 06606-2892. Tel: 203-416-1363; Fax: 203-372-0364; Email: innercity.foundation@snet.net; Web: www.innercityfoundation.org.

We Stand With Christ Inc., 238 Jewett Ave., 06606. Web: www.westandwithchrist.org. Mrs. Patricia R. Hansen, Contact Person.

[Q] GUEST HOUSES

DARIEN. *Convent of St. Birgitta*, 4 Rukenhage Rd., Darien, 06820. Tel: 203-655-1068; Fax: 203-655-3496; Email: conventsb@optonline.net; Web: www.birgittines-us.com. Mother Lilly Sebastian, Contact Person. Sisters 6.

[R] RETREAT HOUSES

BRIDGEPORT. *Queen of Saints, The Catholic Center*, 238 Jewett Ave., 06606. Tel: 203-416-1403. Retreat Facility.

The Urban Center of St. Charles Parish, 1279 E. Main St., 06608. Tel: 203-333-2147; Fax: 203-330-8316.

St. Charles Outreach Program, Tel: 203-333-2147; Fax: 203-330-8316. Rev. Edicson Orozco, Admin.

DANBURY. *Seton Neumann Religious Education Center (Retreat Center)*, 71 Southern Blvd., Danbury, 06810. Tel: 203-748-1187.

DARIEN. *Convent of St. Birgitta*, 4 Runkenhage Rd., Darien, 06820. Tel: 203-655-1068; Fax: 203-655-3496; Email: conventsb@optonline.net; Web: www.birgittines-us.com. Sr. M. Eunice Kulangrathottyil, O.SS.S., Supr.

MONROE. *Marian Heights Convent*, 1428 Monroe Tpke., Monroe, 06468. Tel: 203-268-6540; Fax: 203-261-0866; Web: www.nazarethcsfn.org. Sisters of the Holy Family of Nazareth.

STAMFORD. *Villa Maria Guadalupe, Sisters of Life*, 159 Sky Meadow Dr., Stamford, 06903. Tel: 203-329-1492; Fax: 203-329-1495; Email: retreatregistrations@sistersoflife.org; Web: sistersoflife.org. Sr. Bernadette Therese Swan, S.V., Supr. Owned by Knights of Columbus, operated by Sisters of Life Bed Capacity 60; Sisters of Life 10.

[S] CAMPUS MINISTRY

DANBURY. *Newman Center at Western CT State University*, 7 Eighth Ave., Danbury, 06810. Tel: 203-744-5846; Email: mhossan@wcsu.edu. Rev. Jeffrey W. Couture.

FAIRFIELD. *Fairfield University* (Fairfield) 1073 N. Benson Rd., Fairfield, 06824-5195. Tel: 203-254-4190; Fax: 203-254-4221. Amy Boczer, Dir. Inst. Research; Rev. George E. Collins, S.J.; Mrs. Carolyn M. Rusiackas, Assoc. Univ. Chap.; Wylie J. Smith, Campus Min., Service; Rev. Bret J. Stockdale, S.J., Campus Min.; Jocelyn Collen, Campus Min., Immersions & Pilgrimages; Gregory Vigliotta, Campus Min., Retreats.

[T] SHRINES

BRIDGEPORT. *Shrine of Saint Margaret*, 2523 Park Ave., 06604. Tel: 203-333-9627; Fax: 203-333-9723; Email: saintmargaretshrine@gmail.com. Deacon Donald P. Foust, Admin. of Finances, Facilities and Functions; Rev. Giandomenico Flora, Rector.

[U] MISCELLANEOUS LISTINGS

BRIDGEPORT. *St. Ambrose Corporation*, 238 Jewett Ave., 06606.

Cardinal Shehan Center, Inc., 1494 Main St., 06604. Tel: 203-336-4468; Fax: 203-368-0901; Email: tjo@shehancenter.org; Web: shehancenter.org. Mr. Terry O'Connor, Exec. Dir.

Caroline House, Inc., 574 Stillman St., 06608. Tel: 203-334-0640; Fax: 203-334-0248; Email: thecarolinehouse@snet.org; Web: thecarolinehouse.org. Lucy Freeman, M.S., Exec. Dir.; Christine Matthews Paine, Devel. Dir.

Saint Charles Brazilian Children, 238 Jewett Ave., 06606. Tel: 203-405-1385; Email: josephbi@charter.net. Rev. Thomas P. Thorne, Contact Person, (Retired).

The Diocesan Cemetery Care Fund, Inc., 238 Jewett Ave., 06606. Tel: 203-416-1491; Fax: 203-374-7588.

Holy Rosary, LLC, 238 Jewett Ave., 06606.

**McGivney Community Center, Inc.*, Mailing Address: P.O. Box 5220, 06610-0220. Tel: 203-333-2789; Fax: 203-334-1933; Email: toconnor@mcgivney.org; Web: www.mcgivney.org. Mr. Terry O'Connor, Exec. Dir.

St. Raphael, LLC, 238 Jewett Ave., 06606.

DANBURY. *Magnificat Bridgeport Diocese CT, Inc.* (2003) 6 W. Pine Dr., Danbury, 06811-4316. Tel: 203-744-1856; Email: magnificatbpt@sbcglobal.net; Web: www.triumphantheart.org. Frances Hood, Coord. (Triumphant Heart of Mary Immaculate).

FAIRFIELD. *St. Catherine Center for Special Needs Inc.*, 760 Tahmore Dr., Fairfield, 06825. Tel: 203-540-5381; Fax: 203-540-5383; Email: hburland@diobpt.org; Web: www.stcatherinecenter.org. Helen Burland, Dir.

GREENWICH. *Clemons Productions, Inc.* (1981) (In association with That's The Spirit Productions, Inc.) P.O. Box 7466, Greenwich, 06836. Tel: 203-316-9394; Fax: 203-316-9396; Email: clemons10@aol.com; Web: www.spirituality.org. Rev. Mark Connolly, Pres., (Retired), Tel: 203-316-9394.

Spirituality For Today (1995) Tel: 203-316-9394; Fax: 203-316-9396.

Radio Program: Thoughts for the Week (1993) Tel: 203-316-9394; Fax: 203-316-9396; Web: www.spirituality.org.

**Walking with Purpose, Inc.*, 15 E. Putnam Ave., Greenwich, 06830. Tel: 844-492-5597; Email: support@walkingwithpurpose.com; Web: www.walkingwithpurpose.com.

NORWALK. *Courage International, Inc.*, 8 Leonard St., Norwalk, 06850. Tel: 203-803-1564; Fax: 203-930-2284; Email: office@couragerc.org; Web: www.couragerc.org. Rev. Philip G. Bochanski, Exec. Dir.

Malta House, Inc., 5 Prowitt St., Norwalk, 06855-1203. Tel: 203-857-0088; Fax: 203-857-0018; Email: lfreeman@maltahouse.org.

RIVERSIDE. *The Mother Teresa of Calcutta Center*, P.O. Box 455, Riverside, 06878. Tel: 203-637-7578; Email: tleogallagher@aol.com.

STAMFORD. **The Christopher Mueller Foundation for Polyphony & Chant*, c/o St. Mary Church, 566 Elm St., Stamford, 06902.

St. Camillus Health Center, 494 Elm St., Stamford, 06902. Tel: 203-325-0200; Fax: 203-353-0550; Web: www.stcamillushealth.org. Very Rev. Matthew R. Mauriello, Chap. Total Staff 4.

Haitian American Catholic Center (2000) 93 Hope St., Stamford, 06906. Tel: 203-406-0343; Fax: 203-406-0347. Rev. Jean-Rony Philippe.

**Hard as Nails Ministries, Inc.*, 894 Newfield Ave., Stamford, 06905.

RELIGIOUS INSTITUTES OF MEN REPRESENTED IN THE DIOCESE

For further details refer to the corresponding bracketed number in the Religious Institutes of Men or Women section.

[]—*Indian Missionary Society*—I.M.S.
[]—*Institute of Christ the King Sovereign Priest*—I.C.R.S.S.
[]—*Instituto Verbo Encarnado*—I.V.E.
[0900]—*Order of Canons Regular of Premontre (Norbertines)*—O.Praem.
[]—*Order of Carmelites, Discalced*—O.C.D.
[]—*Order of Friars Minor Conventual*—O.F.M.,Conv.
[0610]—*Priests of the Congregation of Holy Cross* (Prov. of Our Lady of Holy Cross)—C.S.C.
[0420]—*Society of Divine Word*—S.V.D.
[0690]—*Society of Jesus (Jesuits)* (New England Prov.)—S.J.
[]—*Vincentian Congregation*—V.C.

RELIGIOUS INSTITUTES OF WOMEN REPRESENTED IN THE DIOCESE

[0130]—*Apostles of the Sacred Heart of Jesus*—A.S.C.J.
[1810]—*Bernardine Sisters of the Third Order of St. Francis*—O.S.F.
[]—*The Community of the Mother of God of Tenderness*—C.M.G.T.
[0710]—*Company of the Saviour*—C.S.
[4030]—*Congregation of Sisters of St. Thomas of Villanova*—S.S.T.V.
[0740]—*Daughters of Charity of the Most Precious Blood*—D.C.P.B.
[]—*Dominican Sisters of Hope* (Newburgh, NY)—O.P.
[1125]—*Dominican Sisters of Our Lady of the Springs of Bridgeport*—O.P.
[]—*Franciscan Sisters of the Immaculate Heart of Mary*—F.I.H.M.
[2575]—*Institute of the Sisters of Mercy of the Americas*—R.S.M.
[2345]—*Little Workers of the Sacred Hearts of Jesus & Mary*—P.O.S.C.
[]—*Lovers of the Holy Cross of Go Vap*—L.H.C.
[]—*Missionaries of Charity*—M.C.
[]—*Missionary Sisters of the Blessed Sacrament and Mary Immaculate*—M.S.S.M.I.
[0280]—*Order of the Most Holy Savior of St. Bridget (Brigittines)*—O.SS.S.
[2970]—*School Sisters of Notre Dame*—S.S.N.D.
[]—*Sisters of Life*—S.V.
[3000]—*Sisters of Notre Dame de Namur*—S.N.D.deN.
[]—*Sisters of St. Joseph of Chambery*—C.S.J.
[2980]—*Sisters of the Congregation De Notre Dame*—C.N.D.
[1970]—*Sisters of the Holy Family of Nazareth*—C.S.F.N.
[4070]—*Society of the Sacred Heart*—R.S.C.J.
[4110]—*Ursuline Nuns (Roman Union)*—O.S.U.

DIOCESAN CEMETERIES

DANBURY. *St. Peter's*, 71 Lake Ave. Ext., Danbury, 06810. Tel: 203-743-9626; Email: fspodnick@diobpt.org. Mr. Frank Spodnick, Exec.

DARIEN. *St. John's*, 25 Camp Ave., Darien, 06820. Tel: 203-322-0455; Fax: 203-595-9243; Email: fspodnick@diobpt.org. Mr. Frank Spodnick, Exec.

Queen of Peace, 124 Rock Rimmon Road, Stamford, 06903. Mr. Frank Spodnick, Exec.

GREENWICH. *St. Mary's*, 399 North St., Greenwich, 06830. Tel: 203-869-7026; Email: fspodnick@diobpt.org. Mr. Frank Spodnick, Exec.

Putnam, 35 Parsonage Rd., Greenwich, 06830. Tel: 203-869-4828; Fax: 203-869-9246; Email: fspodnick@diobpt.org. 399 North Avenue, Greenwich, 06830. Mr. Frank Spodnick, Exec.

NEWTOWN. *Resurrection*, c/o Gate of Heaven Cemetery, 1056 Daniels Farm Rd., Trumbull, 06611. Tel: 203-268-5574; Fax: 203-268-2203; Email: fspodnick@diobpt.org. 208 S Main Street, Newtown, 06470. Mr. Frank Spodnick, Exec.

NORWALK. *Assumption Green Farms*, Greens Farms Road, Westport, 06880. Mr. Frank Spodnick, Exec.

St. John's & St. Mary's, 223 Richards Ave., Norwalk, 06850. Tel: 203-838-4271; Email: fspodnick@diobpt.org. Mr. Frank Spodnick, Exec.

STRATFORD. *St. Michael's*, 2205 Stratford Ave., Stratford, 06615. Tel: 203-378-0404; Fax: 203-378-0313; Email: fspodnick@diobpt.org. Mr. Frank Spodnick, Exec.

TRUMBULL. *Gate of Heaven*, 1056 Daniels Farms Rd., Trumbull, 06611. Tel: 203-268-5574; Fax: 203-268-2203; Email: fspodnick@diobpt.org. Mr. Frank Spodnick, Exec.

NECROLOGY

† DeProfio, Louis A., (Retired), Died Aug. 15, 2018
† Driscoll, Thomas J., (Retired), Died Dec. 20, 2018
† Esposito, Ernest T., (Retired), Died Jan. 15, 2019
† Green, Thomas J., (On Duty Outside the Diocese), Died Apr. 28, 2018
† Hossan, John B., (Retired), Died May. 6, 2018
† Sanders, John C., (Retired), Died Jan. 6, 2019
† D'Amico, Carducci S., (Retired), Died Nov. 23, 2018
† Donovan, William, (Retired), Died Jun. 27, 2018
† Sangiovanni, William F., (Retired), Died Feb. 4, 2019

An asterisk (*) denotes an organization that has established tax-exempt status directly with the IRS and is not covered by the USCCB Group Ruling.

Diocese of Brooklyn

(Dioecesis Bruklyniensis)

Most Reverend

RAYMOND F. CHAPPETTO, D.D., V.G., V.E.

Auxiliary Bishop of Brooklyn; ordained May 29, 1971; appointed Auxiliary Bishop of Brooklyn and Titular Bishop of Citium May 2, 2012; episcopal ordination July 11, 2012; appointed Vicar General September 19, 2013. *Mailing Address & Office: 310 Prospect Park W., NY 11215.*

Most Reverend

PAUL R. SANCHEZ, D.D.

Auxiliary Bishop of Brooklyn; ordained December 17, 1971; appointed Auxiliary Bishop of Brooklyn and Titular Bishop of Coeliana May 2, 2012; episcopal ordination July 11, 2012. *Mailing Address: Our Lady Queen of Martyrs, 110-06 Queens Blvd., Forest Hills, NY 11375.*

Most Reverend

OCTAVIO CISNEROS, D.D., V.E.

Auxiliary Bishop of Brooklyn; ordained May 29, 1971; appointed Titular Bishop of Eanach Duin June 6, 2006; episcopal ordination August 22, 2006. *Mailing Address: Holy Child Jesus, 111-11 86th Ave., Richmond Hill, NY 11418-1613.*

Most Reverend

WITOLD MROZIEWSKI, D.D.

Auxiliary Bishop of Brooklyn; ordained June 29, 1991; appointed Auxiliary Bishop of Brooklyn and Titular Bishop of Walla Walla May 19, 2015; installed July 20, 2015. *Office: 310 Prospect Park W., Brooklyn, NY 11215. Res.: Holy Cross, 61-21 56 Rd., Maspeth, NY 11378.*

Most Reverend

NICHOLAS DIMARZIO, PH.D., D.D.

Seventh Bishop of Brooklyn; ordained May 30, 1970; appointed Titular Bishop of Mauriana and Auxiliary Bishop of Newark September 10, 1996; consecrated October 31, 1996; appointed Bishop of Camden June 18, 1999; installed July 22, 1999; appointed Bishop of Brooklyn August 1, 2003; installed October 3, 2003. *Office: 310 Prospect Park W., Brooklyn, NY 11215.*

Chancery Office: 310 Prospect Park W., Brooklyn, NY 11215. Tel: 718-399-5990; Fax: 718-399-5934.

Email: curia@diobrook.org

Most Reverend

JAMES MASSA, D.D., V.E.

Auxiliary Bishop of Brooklyn; ordained October 25, 1986; appointed Auxiliary Bishop of Brooklyn and Titular Bishop of Bardstown May 19, 2015; installed July 20, 2015. *Office: 310 Prospect Park W., Brooklyn, NY 11215.*

Most Reverend

NEIL E. TIEDEMANN, C.P.

Auxiliary Bishop of Brooklyn; ordained May 16, 1975; appointed Bishop of Mandeville, Jamaica May 20, 2008; installed August 6, 2008; appointed Titular Bishop of Cova and Auxiliary Bishop of Brooklyn April 29, 2016. *Office: St. Mathias, 310 Prospect Park W., Brooklyn, NY 11215.*

Most Reverend

GUY SANSARICQ, D.D., V.E.

Retired Auxiliary Bishop of Brooklyn; ordained June 29, 1960; appointed Titular Bishop of Glenndalocha June 6, 2006; episcopal ordination August 22, 2006; retired October 6, 2010. *Mailing Address: St. Matthew, 1123 Eastern Pkwy., Brooklyn, NY 11213-4801.*

ESTABLISHED JULY 29, 1853.

Square Miles 179.

Comprises Kings and Queens Counties in the State of New York.

Legal Title: The Roman Catholic Diocese of Brooklyn, New York.
For legal titles of parishes and diocesan institutions, consult the Chancery Office.

STATISTICAL OVERVIEW

Personnel	
Bishop	1
Auxiliary Bishops	6
Retired Bishops	1
Priests: Diocesan Active in Diocese	256
Priests: Diocesan Active Outside Diocese	21
Priests: Retired, Sick or Absent	186
Number of Diocesan Priests	463
Religious Priests in Diocese	174
Total Priests in Diocese	637
Extern Priests in Diocese	82
Ordinations:	
Diocesan Priests	4
Transitional Deacons	4
Permanent Deacons in Diocese	216
Total Brothers	81
Total Sisters	637
Parishes	
Parishes	185
With Resident Pastor:	
Resident Diocesan Priests	151
Resident Religious Priests	21
Without Resident Pastor:	
Administered by Priests	13
Missions	1
Closed Parishes	1
Professional Ministry Personnel:	
Brothers	38
Sisters	17
Lay Ministers	572
Welfare	
Health Care Centers	27
Total Assisted	20,317
Homes for the Aged	29
Total Assisted	2,939
Residential Care of Children	24
Total Assisted	786
Day Care Centers	15
Total Assisted	2,549
Specialized Homes	574
Total Assisted	1,319
Special Centers for Social Services	50
Total Assisted	187,204
Residential Care of Disabled	176
Total Assisted	1,960
Other Institutions	35
Total Assisted	17,443
Educational	
Seminaries, Diocesan	1
Students from This Diocese	13
Students from Other Diocese	32
Diocesan Students in Other Seminaries	31
Total Seminarians	44
Colleges and Universities	3
Total Students	25,298
High Schools, Diocesan and Parish	2
Total Students	771
High Schools, Private	16
Total Students	11,040
Elementary Schools, Diocesan and Parish	80
Total Students	22,797
Elementary Schools, Private	2
Total Students	203
Catechesis/Religious Education:	
High School Students	2,896
Elementary Students	35,011
Total Students under Catholic Instruction	98,060
Teachers in the Diocese:	
Priests	4
Sisters	15
Lay Teachers	1,711
Vital Statistics	
Receptions into the Church:	
Infant Baptism Totals	11,921
Minor Baptism Totals	820
Adult Baptism Totals	627
Received into Full Communion	341
First Communions	10,613
Confirmations	8,965
Marriages:	
Catholic	1,624
Interfaith	227
Total Marriages	1,851
Deaths	7,019
Total Catholic Population	1,500,000
Total Population	5,007,353

Former Bishops—Rt. Revs. JOHN LOUGHLIN, D.D., First Bishop of Brooklyn; ord. Oct. 18, 1840; cons. Oct. 30, 1853; died Dec. 28, 1891; CHARLES E. MCDONNELL, D.D., Second Bishop of Brooklyn; ord. May 19, 1878; cons. April 25, 1892; died Aug. 8, 1921; Most Revs. THOMAS E. MOLLOY, D.D., Third Bishop of Brooklyn; ord. Sept. 19, 1908; cons. Second Auxiliary Bishop of Brooklyn, Oct. 3, 1920; appt. Bishop of Brooklyn, Nov. 21, 1921; installed Feb. 15, 1922; died Nov. 26, 1956; BRYAN J. MCENTEGART, D.D., LL.D., Fourth Bishop of Brooklyn; ord. Sept. 8, 1917; appt. Bishop of Ogdensburg, June 5, 1943; cons. Aug. 3, 1943; appt. Rector of the Catholic University of America, Washington, DC, June 26, 1953; appt. Titular Bishop of Aradi, Aug. 19, 1953; appt. Bishop of Brooklyn, April 16, 1957; installed June 13, 1957; retired and appt. Titular Archbishop of Gabii, July 17, 1968; died Sept. 30, 1968; FRANCIS J. MUGAVERO, D.D., Fifth Bishop of Brooklyn; ord. May 18, 1940; Bishop of Brooklyn; appt. July 15, 1968; cons. Sept. 12, 1968; installed Sept. 12, 1968; retired Feb. 20, 1990; died July 12, 1991; THOMAS V. DAILY, D.D., ord. Jan. 10, 1952; appt. Auxiliary to the Archbishop of Boston and Titular Bishop of Bladia Dec. 31, 1974; cons. Feb. 11, 1975; appt. First Bishop of Palm Beach July 17, 1984; appt. Sixth Bishop of Brooklyn Feb. 20, 1990; took possession April 16, 1990; installed April 18, 1990; retired Aug. 1, 2003; died May 15, 2017.

Central Offices—310 Prospect Park W., Brooklyn, 11215. Tel: 718-399-5900. Office Hours: Mon.-Fri. 8:30-5.

Vicar General—Most Rev. RAYMOND F. CHAPPETTO, D.D., V.G., V.E., 310 Prospect Park W., Brooklyn, 11215. Tel: 718-399-5995; Fax: 718-399-5965.

Moderator of the Curia—Most Rev. JAMES MASSA, D.D.

Auxiliary Bishops of Brooklyn—Most Revs. RAYMOND F. CHAPPETTO, D.D., V.G., V.E., 310 Prospect Park W., Brooklyn, 11215. Tel: 718-399-5995; Fax: 718-399-5965; OCTAVIO CISNEROS, D.D., 7200 Douglaston Pkwy., Douglaston, 11362. Tel: 718-281-9677; JAMES MASSA, D.D., 310 Prospect Park W., Brooklyn, 11215. Tel: 718-399-5995; WITOLD MROZIEWSKI, D.D., J.C.D., 61-21 56th Rd., Maspeth, 11378. Tel: 718-894-1387; NEIL E. TIEDEMANN, C.P., D.D., 58-15 Catalpa Ave., Ridgewood, 11385. Tel: 718-821-6447.

Retired Auxiliary Bishops of Brooklyn—Most Rev. GUY SANSARICQ, D.D., (Retired), 224 Brooklyn Ave., Brooklyn, 11213. Tel: 718-773-3806.

Regional Bishop of Queens—Most Rev. PAUL R. SANCHEZ, D.D., Our Lady Queen of Martyrs Church, 110-06 Queens Blvd., Forest Hills, 11375.

Regional Bishop of Brooklyn—Most Rev. JAMES MASSA, D.D., 310 Prospect Park W., Brooklyn, 11215.

Episcopal Vicars-Territorial—Brooklyn: Rev. Msgr. JOSEPH R. GRIMALDI, J.C.L., 310 Prospect Park W., Brooklyn, 11215. Queens: Very Rev. THOMAS G. PETTEI, 310 Prospect Park W., Brooklyn, 11215. Tel: 718-399-5959.

Vicar for West Indian, Caribbean, and American Black Catholics—Most Rev. NEIL E. TIEDEMANN, C.P., D.D.

Vicar for Canonical Affairs—Rev. Msgr. ANTHONY HERNANDEZ, J.C.L., 310 Prospect Park W., Brooklyn, 11215. Tel: 718-399-5990.

Associate Vicar for Canonical Affairs—Very Rev. ROBERT V. MUCCI, J.C.L., 310 Prospect Park W., Brooklyn, 11215.

Secretariat for Financial Administration/Economy—Rev. Msgr. MICHAEL J. REID, Vicar, 310 Prospect Park W., Brooklyn, 11215. Tel: 718-965-7300, Ext. 1552.

Secretariat for Communications—Rev. Msgr. KIERAN E. HARRINGTON, V.E., Vicar, 1712 10th Ave., Brooklyn, 11215. Tel: 718-499-6461.

Secretariat for Development—Rev. Msgr. JAMIE J. GIGANTIELLO, Vicar, 310 Prospect Park W., Brooklyn, 11215. Tel: 718-965-7300.

Secretariat for Human and Information Resources—VACANT, 310 Prospect Park W., Brooklyn, 11215. Tel: 718-965-7362.

Human Resources Office—310 Prospect Park W., Brooklyn, 11215. Tel: 718-965-7300; Fax: 718-965-7363.

Spiritual Director of the Cathedral Preparatory Seminary—VACANT, Spiritual Dir., 56-25 92nd St., Elmhurst, 11373.

Vicar for Clergy, Consecrated Life and Apostolic Organizations—Most Rev. RAYMOND F. CHAPPETTO, D.D., V.G., V.E., 310 Prospect Park W., Brooklyn, 11215. Tel: 718-399-5995; Fax: 718-399-5965.

Special Assistant to Vicar for Clergy—Rev. EDWARD P. DORAN, Ph.D., (Retired), St. Stanislaus Kostka R.C. Church, 57-15 61st St., Maspeth, 11378. Tel: 718-326-2185.

Vicar for Higher Education—Most Rev. JAMES MASSA, D.D., 310 Prospect Park W., Brooklyn, 11215. Tel: 718-965-7300.

Vicar for Hispanic Concerns—Most Rev. OCTAVIO CISNEROS, D.D., 7200 Douglaston Pkwy., Douglaston, 11362. Tel: 718-281-9677.

Vicar for Human Services—Rev. Msgr. ALFRED P. LOPINTO, V.E., 191 Joralemon St., Brooklyn, 11201.

Associate Vicar for Human Services—Very Rev. PATRICK J. KEATING, 191 Joralemon St., Brooklyn, 11201. Tel: 718-722-6011.

Vicar for Migrant and Ethnic Apostolates—Rev. Msgr. RONALD T. MARINO, V.E., 1258 65th St., Brooklyn, 11219. Tel: 718-236-3000.

Vicar for Ecumenical and Interreligious Affairs—Rev. Msgr. GUY A. MASSIE, Sacred Heart of Jesus and Mary and St. Stephen, 108 Carroll St., Brooklyn, 11231.

Associate Vicar for Ecumenical and Interreligious Affairs—Rev. MICHAEL J. LYNCH, Our Lady of the Cenacle, 136-06 87 Ave., Richmond Hill, 11418. Tel: 718-291-2540.

Finance Officer—MR. JOHN J. BORGIA, CPA, M.B.A., CFO & Treas., 310 Prospect Park W., Brooklyn, 11215. Tel: 718-965-7300; MR. MARTIN J. MCMANUS, CPA, Comptroller, Tel: 718-965-7300, Ext. 1401; Fax: 718-965-7371.

Parish Services Corp.—Rev. Msgr. DAVID L. CASSATO, M.Div., M.S.Ed., Pres.; MR. JOHN J. BORGIA, CPA, M.B.A., Vice Pres.; Rev. Msgr. PETER V. KAIN, Bd. of Dir., (Retired); MR. MARTIN J. MCMANUS, CPA, Treas.; BRIAN T. COSGROVE, Exec. Dir., 310 Prospect Park W., Brooklyn, 11215. Tel: 718-965-7300; Fax: 718-965-7382.

Peter Turner Insurance Co.—100 Bank St., Ste. 500, Burlington, VT 05401. MR. JOHN J. BORGIA, CPA, M.B.A., Exec. Vice Pres.; MR. MARTIN J. MCMANUS, CPA, Treas.; BRIAN T. COSGROVE, Sec. Board of Directors: Rev. Msgrs. DAVID L. CASSATO, M.Div., M.S.Ed.; PETER V. KAIN, (Retired); MR. JOHN G. DOLAN; MS. SUZANNE B. HOLOHAN; MR. SEAN KANE, Esq.; MR. RICHARD CEA; MR. DONALD T. DECARLO, Esq.

Rocklyn Asset Corp.—MS. COLEEN A. CERIELLO, Exec. Dir., 243 Prospect Park W., Brooklyn, 11215. Tel: 718-965-7352; Fax: 718-965-7316; MR. ROBERT DADONA, Dir. Capital Projects, Tel: 718-965-7300, Ext. 1101; Fax: 718-965-7316.

Chancery Office—310 Prospect Park W., Brooklyn, 11215. Tel: 718-399-5990; Fax: 718-399-5934.

Chancellor—Rev. Msgr. ANTHONY HERNANDEZ, J.C.L.

Vice Chancellors—Very Rev. ROBERT V. MUCCI, J.C.L.; Rev. PETER J. PURPURA, J.C.L.; JASMINE SALAZAR, L.M.S.W.

Diocesan Archivist—JOSEPH W. COEN, C.A., 310 Prospect Park W., Brooklyn, 11215. Tel: 718-965-7300, Ext. 1001.

Censors of Books—Rev. Msgrs. PETER I. VACCARI, S.T.L.; JOHN J. STRYNKOWSKI; Rev. MICHAEL J. S. BRUNO.

Assistant to the Bishop—Deacon JAIME VARELA, Tel: 718-399-5970; Fax: 718-399-5975.

Tribunal—7200 Douglaston Pkwy., Douglaston, 11362. Tel: 718-229-8131; Fax: 718-631-1339.

Officialis-Judicial Vicar—Rev. Msgr. STEVEN J. AGUGGIA, J.C.L.

Vice Officiales-Associate Judicial Vicars—Rev. Msgr. JONAS ACHACOSO, J.C.D.; Rev. FRANCIS KWAME ASAGBA, J.C.L.

Diocesan Judges—Rev. DARIUSZ PIOTR BLICHARZ, J.C.D.; Rev. Msgrs. OTTO L. GARCIA, J.C.D.; ANDREW J. VACCARI, J.C.L.; Sr. BERNADETTE M. IZZO, O.P.

Defenders of the Marriage Bond—Rev. Msgr. JOSEPH C. MULQUEEN, J.C.L., (Retired); Rev. WILLIAM M. HOPPE, J.C.L.; Most Rev. WITOLD MROZIEWSKI, D.D., J.C.D.; Rev. ALOYSIUS ENEMALI, J.C.D.

Promoters of Justice—Rev. WILLIAM M. HOPPE, J.C.L.; Most Rev. WITOLD MROZIEWSKI, D.D., J.C.D.

Attorneys and Counselors at Canon Law—Rev. Msgrs. STEVEN J. AGUGGIA, J.C.L.; JONAS ACHACOSO, J.C.D.; OTTO L. GARCIA, J.C.D.; ANDREW J. VACCARI, J.C.L.; JOSEPH C. MULQUEEN, J.C.L., (Retired); Rev. FRANCIS KWAME ASAGBA, J.C.L.; Most Rev. WITOLD MROZIEWSKI, D.D., J.C.D.; Revs. DARIUSZ PIOTR BLICHARZ, J.C.D.; WILLIAM M. HOPPE, J.C.L.; MANUEL DE JESUS RODRIGUEZ.

Auditor—VACANT.

Religious, Episcopal Delegate for—Sr. MARYANN SETON LOPICCOLO, S.C., 310 Prospect Park W., Brooklyn, 11215. Tel: 718-399-5951.

Cemeteries—ELAINE NICODEMO, Dir. & COO; Rev. Msgr. MICHAEL J. REID, CEO/Spiritual Moderator.

Education, Offices—(See Institutions located in the Diocese for details).

Mediation and Arbitration, Board of—Rev. Msgr. STEVEN J. AGUGGIA, J.C.L., Exec. Sec., Mailing Address: 7200 Douglaston Pkwy., Douglaston, 11362.

Office of Priestly Life & Ministry—Cathedral Preparatory School and Seminary, 56-25 92nd St., Elmhurst, 11373. Tel: 718-760-4978; Email: jfonti@diobrook.org. Very Rev. JOSEPH G. FONTI, S.T.L., Dir.

Ministerial Development Program—Very Rev. JOSEPH G. FONTI, S.T.L., Tel: 718-760-4978.

Newspaper "The Tablet"—1712 10th Ave., Brooklyn, 11215. Tel: 718-499-9705. JORGE DOMINGUEZ, Editor.

Office for Clergy Personnel—Deacon JULIO C. BARRENECHE, 310 Prospect Park W., Brooklyn, 11215. Tel: 718-399-5941; Fax: 718-399-5940.

Assignment Board—Most Revs. NICHOLAS DIMARZIO, Ph.D., D.D.; RAYMOND F. CHAPPETTO, D.D., V.G., V.E., (Facilitator); Rev. Msgrs. MICHAEL J. REID; ANTHONY HERNANDEZ, J.C.L.; JOSEPH R. GRIMALDI, J.C.L.; Very Rev. THOMAS G. PETTEI; Deacon JULIO C. BARRENECHE; Rev. RAFAEL J. PEREZ; Very Rev. KEVIN J. SWEENEY.

Mission Office—310 Prospect Park W., Brooklyn, 11215. Tel: 718-965-7300. VACANT.

Vicar for Communications—Rev. Msgr. KIERAN E. HARRINGTON, V.E., Dir., 1712 10th Ave., Brooklyn, 11215. Tel: 718-499-6461.

Retirement Board (Priests)—Most Rev. RAYMOND F. CHAPPETTO, D.D., V.G., V.E., Chair, 310 Prospect Park W., Brooklyn, 11215.

Victim Assistance Coordinator, Office of—JASMINE SALAZAR, L.M.S.W., 310 Prospect Park W., Brooklyn, 11215. Tel: 718-623-5236.

Safe Environment, Office of—310 Prospect Park W., Brooklyn, 11215. Tel: 718-281-9672; Fax: 718-281-9673. MARYELLEN QUINN, Coord.

Vocations, Office of—7200 Douglaston Pkwy., Douglaston, 11362. Tel: 718-827-2454. Rev. SEAN M. SUCKIEL, M.A., M.Div.

Consultative Bodies

Presbyteral Council—Most Revs. NICHOLAS DIMARZIO, Ph.D., D.D.; JAMES MASSA, D.D.; NEIL E. TIEDEMANN, C.P., D.D.; OCTAVIO CISNEROS, D.D.; WITOLD MROZIEWSKI, D.D., J.C.D.; GUY SANSARICQ, D.D., (Retired); RAYMOND F. CHAPPETTO, D.D., V.G., V.E.; PAUL R. SANCHEZ, D.D.; Rev. Msgrs. ANTHONY HERNANDEZ, J.C.L.; JOSEPH R. GRIMALDI, J.C.L.; Revs. THOMAS W. AHERN; CARLOS A. AGUDELO; LIJU AUGUSTINE, C.M.I.; FRANCIS A. COLAMARIA; JOHN GRIBOWICH; JOSEPH M. HOFFMAN; Very Rev. THOMAS G. PETTEI; Revs. GERARD J. SAUER; FRANK L. SCHWARZ; Rev. Msgr. ANDREW J. VACCARI, J.C.L., Exec. Sec.; Revs. FREDERICK CINTRON; JEAN YVON PIERRE; Rev. Msgr. JOHN J. STRYNKOWSKI, (Retired); Rev. ROBERT J. WHELAN.

Diocesan Budget Committee—Rev. Msgr. MICHAEL J. REID; MR. JOHN J. BORGIA, CPA, M.B.A.; MR. MARTIN J. MCMANUS, CPA.

Diocesan College of Consultors—Most Rev. NICHOLAS DIMARZIO, Ph.D., D.D.; Rev. FRANCIS A. BLACK; Most Rev. RAYMOND F. CHAPPETTO, D.D., V.G., V.E.; Rev. JOSEPH T. HOLCOMB; Rev. Msgr. ANTHONY HERNANDEZ, J.C.L.; Most Rev. WITOLD MROZIEWSKI, D.D., J.C.D.; Rev. Msgr. KEVIN B. NOONE, V.E.; Revs. GERARD J. SAUER; PATRICK J. WEST; Most Rev. JAMES MASSA, D.D.; Rev. Msgr. MICHAEL J. REID, Exec. Sec.; MS. COLEEN A. CERIELLO.

Diocesan Finance Council—Rev. Msgr. MICHAEL J. REID; MR. ROBERT COUGHLAN; MR. JOSEPH E. GEOGHAN; MR. PETER LABBAT; MR. JAMES J. MINOGUE; Rev. Msgr. SEAN G. OGLE; Justice JOSEPH P. SULLIVAN; Most Revs. NICHOLAS DIMARZIO, Ph.D., D.D.; RAYMOND F. CHAPPETTO, D.D., V.G., V.E.; Rev. Msgrs. JAMIE J. GIGANTIELLO; KIERAN E. HARRINGTON, V.E.; ALFRED P. LOPINTO, V.E.; Very Rev. ROBERT V. MUCCI, J.C.L.; MS. MAUREEN BATEMAN; MS. COLEEN A. CERIELLO; MR. DONALD T. DECARLO, Esq.; MR. NICK RANIERI; Rev. Msgr. ANTHONY HERNANDEZ, J.C.L., Ex Officio; MR. JOHN J. BORGIA, CPA, M.B.A., Ex Officio; MR. MARTIN J. MCMANUS, CPA, Ex Officio.

Diocesan Diaconal Council—Most Revs. NICHOLAS DIMARZIO, Ph.D., D.D., Chair; RAYMOND F. CHAPPETTO, D.D., V.G., V.E.; Deacons JOHN SUCICH, Co Chm.; CHRISTOPHER A. WAGNER; GUILLERMO GOMEZ; ALBERT SALDANA; JEAN BAPTISTE BOURSIQUOT; CARLOS CULAJAY; JULIO C. BARRENECHE; ARTHUR CUTTER; STANLEY J. GALAZIN; JOHN WARREN, Co Chm.; JORGE A. GONZALEZ; FRANK J. D'ACCORDO; KEVIN F. HUGHES.

Diocesan Pastoral Council—Most Rev. NICHOLAS DIMARZIO, Ph.D., D.D., Pres.

Commissions and Offices for Pastoral Services

Alcoholism Committee—Rev. Msgr. THOMAS M. HAGGERTY, (Retired).

Art and Architecture Commission—Very Rev. JOHN J. O'CONNOR, S.L.L., Exec. Sec.; Revs. ROBERT J. ARMATO, Chm.; HILAIRE BELIZAIRE; MR. GREGORY JACK; Rev. ALONZO Q. COX; Sr. SHEILA BROWN, R.S.M.; MRS. REGINA MORENO; Deacon FRANCIS G. MATEO, Office: Immaculate Conception Center, 7200 Douglaston Pkwy., Douglaston, 11362. Tel: 718-281-9612; Fax: 718-281-9613; Email: liturgy@diobrook.org.

Catholic Charities—Rev. Msgr. ALFRED P. LOPINTO, V.E., Exec. Vice Pres., 191 Joralemon St., Brooklyn, 11201. Tel: 718-722-6000. (See Institutions located in the Diocese for details).

Catholic Migration and Refugee Office—(See Institutions located in the Diocese for details)

Catholic Migration Services, Inc.—Very Rev. PATRICK J. KEATING, CEO, Tel: 718-236-3000.

Chaplains and Uniformed Services, Official—Police Department: Rev. ROBERT J. ROMANO, M.Div., Asst. Chief Chap.; Rev. Msgr. DAVID L. CASSATO, M.Div., M.S.Ed., Deputy Chief Chap. Fire Department: Rev. Msgr. JOHN E. DELENDICK; Rev. JOSEPH M. HOFFMAN. Sanitation Department: Rev. MICHAEL C. GRIBBON. BMT Holy Name Society: VACANT.

Diocesan Liturgy Office—Very Rev. JOHN J. O'CONNOR, S.L.L., Dir., 7200 Douglaston Pkwy., Douglaston, 11362-1997. Tel: 718-281-9612; Fax: 718-281-9613; Email: liturgy@diobrook.org.

Diocesan Real Estate Board and Building Commission—Rev. Msgr. JOHN E. DELENDICK; Rev. WILLIAM F. KRLIS, Chair, (Retired); MS. COLEEN A. CERIELLO; COLLEEN LEFFERTS; Very Rev. ROBERT B. ADAMO; Rev. THOMAS W. AHERN.

Diocesan Food Service—MR. JAMES AUSTIN, Dir., 7200 Douglaston Pkwy., Douglaston, 11362. Tel: 718-229-8001, Ext. 531; Tel: 718-229-8001, Ext. 530.

Diaconate Formation Office—Deacon JORGE A. GONZALEZ, Dir., 310 Prospect Park W., Brooklyn, 11215.

Ecumenical and Interreligious Affairs, Diocesan Commission for—Rev. Msgr. GUY A. MASSIE, Exec. Sec.

Committee for Eastern Orthodox-Catholic

Relations—Rev. Msgr. STEVEN J. AGUGGIA, J.C.L., Chm.

Committee for Catholic-Protestant Relations—Rev. Msgr. JOHN J. STRYNKOWSKI.

Committee for Catholic-Jewish Relations—Rev. Msgr. GUY A. MASSIE.

Catholic Muslim Dialogue—Rev. Msgr. GUY A. MASSIE, Chm.

Catholic Hindu / Buddhist Dialogue—VACANT.

Home School Association—VACANT.

Liturgical Commission—Deacons PHILIP FRANCO, Ph. D.; STANLEY J. GALAZIN; MRS. ROSA GOMEZ; MS. JESSICA TRANZILLO-SMITH; Rev. JOSEPH R. GIBINO, Ph.D.; Deacons GUILLERMO GOMEZ; JORGE A. GONZALEZ; MRS. ANGELA M. LEWIS; Sr. JULIE UPTON, R.S.M.; Very Rev. JOHN J. O'CONNOR, S.L.L., Exec. Sec.; Sr. MARY ANN AMBROSE, C.S.J.; Rev. CARLOS C. VELASQUEZ; Rev. Msgr. SEAN G. OGLE.

Office of Music Ministry—Immaculate Conception Center, 7200 Douglaston Pkwy., Douglaston, 11362. Tel: 718-281-9612; Fax: 718-281-9613.

Music Commission—Very Rev. JOHN O'CONNOR, Exec. Sec.; MR. EMMANUEL BOLOGNA, Chair; MS. JESSICA TRANZILLO-SMITH, Co Chair, Immaculate Conception Center, 7200 Douglaston Pkwy., Douglaston, 11362. Tel: 718-281-9612; Fax: 718-281-9613; Email: liturgy@diobrook.org; STEVEN R. GIUSTO; MICHAEL MARTINKA; STEVEN VAUGHAN; KAREN CAPONITI; CHRISTOPHER H. VATH; STEVEN FRANK; MICHAEL KAMINSKI; STEVEN PETERSON; IVONNE ROJAS; RICH LOUIS-PIERRE; MR. MICHAEL FONTANA; LISA ALLONGO; SCOTT BATTAGLIA.

Pilgrimage Office—Rev. GERARD J. SAUER, Dir., 26-15 154th St., Flushing, 11354. Tel: 718-965-7313; Email: pilgrimages@rcdob.org.

Prison Ministries Office—(See listing under Catholic Charities).

School of Evangelization—MR. THEODORE J. MUSCO, Exec. Dir., Diocese of Brooklyn: 310 Prospect Park W., Brooklyn, 11215. Tel: 718-281-9544; Fax: 718-788-4877; Email: tmusco@diobrook.org.

Pastoral Institute—310 Prospect Park W., Brooklyn, 11215. Tel: 718-965-7300, Ext. 5559. VACANT, Dir.

Coordinator Children's Faith Formation and the Catechumenate—310 Prospect Park W., Brooklyn, 11215. Tel: 718-965-7300, Ext. 2440. JOANN ROA, Email: jroa@diobrook.org.

Coordinator of Adolescent and Young Adult Faith Formation—PAUL MORISI, 310 Prospect Park W., Brooklyn, 11215. Tel: 718-965-7300, Ext. 5556; Email: pmorisi@diobrook.org.

Director of Adult Faith Formation—MR. THEODORE J. MUSCO, 310 Prospect Park W., Brooklyn, 11215. Tel: 718-965-7300, Ext. 5417; Email: tmusco@diobrook.org.

Director of Catholic School Faith Formation and Catechist Formation—MR. THEODORE J. MUSCO, 310 Prospect Park W., Brooklyn, 11215. Tel: 718-281-9544; Email: tmusco@diobrook.org.

Coordinator of RCIA—310 Prospect Park W., Brooklyn, 11215. Tel: 718-965-7300, Ext. 2440. JOANN ROA, Email: jroa@diobrook.org.

Coordinator of Marriage, Family and Respect Life—MR. CHRISTIAN S. RADA, 310 Prospect Park W., Brooklyn, 11215. Tel: 718-965-7300, Ext. 5541; Email: crada@diobrook.org.

CYO (Catholic Youth Organization)—Immaculate Conception Center, 7200 Douglaston Pkwy., Douglaston, 11362. Tel: 718-281-9548. ROBERT CALDERA, Dir.

Apostolic Organizations

Charismatic Groups, Catholic—

Charismatic Renewal (English-speaking) of the Diocese of Brooklyn—JOSEPHINE CACHIA, Dir.; JOSEPHINE MCNALLY, Sec., 240 Jay St., Brooklyn, 11201. Tel: 718-260-9111; Fax: 718-260-9121.

Renouveau Charismatique of the Diocese of Brooklyn—(serving the Haitian Charismatics of the Diocese) Rev. Msgr. JOSEPH P. MALAGRECA, Dir., 2530 Church Ave., Brooklyn, 11226. Tel: 718-469-5900; Fax: 718-469-5901.

Renovacion Carismatica of the Diocese of Brooklyn—(serving the Hispanic Charismatics of the Diocese) Rev. Msgr. JOSEPH P. MALAGRECA, Dir., 2530 Church Ave., Brooklyn, 11226. Tel: 718-469-5900; Fax: 718-469-5901.

Confraternity of the Guard of Honor and Confraternity of the Holy Hour—VACANT.

Confraternity of the Precious Blood—5300 Fort Hamilton Pkwy., Brooklyn, 11219.
Tel: 718-436-1120. Rev. THOMAS DOYLE, Exec. Dir.

Courage Ministry—Rev. Msgr. THOMAS G. CASERTA, M.A., M.Div., D.Min.

Guilds—

Accountant Guild—Rev. Msgr. MICHAEL J. REID, Moderator.

Catholic Cemetery Guild—Rev. Msgr. MICHAEL J. REID, Moderator.

Lawyer—Rev. Msgr. STEVEN J. AGUGGIA, J.C.L., Chap., Catholic Lawyers Guild for Queens Cty.; Very Rev. PATRICK J. KEATING, Chap., Catholic Lawyers Guild for Kings Cty.

Physicians—VACANT.

Teachers—VACANT, Dir.

Holy Name Society—VACANT.

Marriage Encounter—Coordinators: JOHN TORIO; TONI TORIO, Tel: 718-746-8979.

National Council of Catholic Women—MARIBETH STEWART, Pres.

Legion of Mary—Rev. RODNEV LAPOMMERAY, Spiritual Dir.; VACANT, Korean Curia, Flushing Curia; VACANT, Bay Ridge Curia, 82-00 35th Ave., Jackson Heights, 11372. Tel: 718-429-2333.

Nocturnal Adoration Society—Rev. JOHN MADURI.

St. John's Priests Relief Society—Rev. EDWARD M. KACHURKA, Pres.

Apostleship of Prayer—VACANT.

CLERGY, PARISHES, MISSIONS AND PAROCHIAL SCHOOLS

CITY OF NEW YORK

BOROUGH OF BROOKLYN

1—ST. AGATHA'S (1912)
702 48th St., 11220. Tel: 718-436-1080; Email: stagatha@aol.com. Revs. Vincentius T. Do; Juan Pichardo, Parochial Vicar; Sheng Jiao Lin, C.M., Parochial Vicar; Deacon Emilio S. Arteaga.
School—St. Agatha's School, 736 48th St., 11220.
Tel: 718-435-3137; Fax: 718-437-7505. Ms. Alice Rios, Prin. Lay Teachers 12; Students 160.
Please see St. Agatha Catholic Academy in the Institutions Listed in the Diocese section.
Catechesis Religious Program—Gizeth Vecchio, D.R.E. Students 311.

2—ST. AGNES (1878) Merged with Saint Peter-Paul-Our Lady of Pilar, Brooklyn to form Saint Paul and Saint Agnes, Brooklyn. For inquiries and parish records see Saint Paul and Saint Agnes.

3—ALL SAINTS (1867) (Spanish), Merged with Our Lady of Montserrat-St. Ambrose, Brooklyn to form All Saints, Brooklyn. For inquiries and parish records see All Saints.

4—ALL SAINTS (2008)
115 Throop Ave., 11206-4415. Tel: 718-388-1951;
Fax: 718-388-7712; Email: allsaints11206@gmail.com; Web: www.allsaints-brooklyn.org. Revs. Vincenzo Cardilicchia; Romulo Marin, Parochial Vicar; Deacon Carlos A. Martinez.
Worship Site: Our Lady of Montserrat Chapel, 134 Vernon Ave., 11206-4415.
Catechesis Religious Program—Tel: 718-388-5050. Awilda Martinez, D.R.E. (All Saints). Students 232.

5—ST. ALPHONSUS, Merged 1976. For inquiries and parish records see St. Anthony-St. Alphonsus.

6—ST. AMBROSE, Merged 1978. For inquiries and parish records see Our Lady of Monserrate-St. Ambrose.

7—ST. ANDREW THE APOSTLE (1971)
6713 Ridge Blvd., 11220. Tel: 718-680-1010; Email: standrewrc@gmail.com. Rev. Gregory A. Stankus; Deacon Gregory Dixon.
Catechesis Religious Program—Tel: 718-836-4679;
Fax: 718-680-3160. Ann Smyth, D.R.E. Students 226.

8—ST. ANN-ST. GEORGE (1860) Closed. For inquiries for parish records contact the chancery.

9—ANNUNCIATION OF THE BLESSED VIRGIN MARY (1863) (Lithuanian)
Mailing Address: 275 N. Eighth St., 11211.
Tel: 718-384-0223; Fax: 718-384-5838; Email: olmcn8th@yahoo.com; Web: www.olmcchurchbk.com. Rev. Msgr. Jamie J. Gigantiello; Rev. Tomasz Adamczyk, Parochial Vicar.
Church: 259 N. 5th St., 11211.
Catechesis Religious Program—

10—ST. ANSELM (1922)
356 82nd St., 11209. Tel: 718-238-2900; Email: revmaloney@aol.com. Rev. Msgr. John W. Maloney, V.E.; Revs. Frederick Cintron, Parochial Vicar; Martin R. Kull, Parochial Vicar, (Retired); Anthony Alimnonu, Parochial Vicar; Stephen A. Saffron, Parochial Vicar; Bro. Robert E. Duffy, O.S.F., RCIA Coord.; Rev. Msgr. Michael J. Phillips, In Res., (Retired); Deacon Thomas Davis.
School—St. Anselm School, 357 83rd St., 11209.
Tel: 718-745-7643; Fax: 718-745-0086. Mrs. Linda Addonisio, Prin. Lay Teachers 17; Students 273.
Please see St. Anselm Catholic Academy under the Institutions Located in the Diocese section.
Catechesis Religious Program—Tel: 718-745-0077. Sr. Regina Corde, O.P., Pastoral Assoc., Tel: 718-836-0708; Bro. Robert E. Duffy, O.S.F., RCIA Coord. Students 90.
Missionary Cenacle—351 83rd St., 11209.
Tel: 718-836-0957. Missionary Servants of the Most Blessed Trinity 2.

11—ST. ANTHONY-ST. ALPHONSUS (1856)
862 Manhattan Ave., 11222. Tel: 718-383-3339; Email: Ant862@aol.com. Revs. Kavungal Davy, C.M.I.; Antony Vadakara, C.M.I., Parochial Vicar.
Worship Site: Holy Family, 21 Nassau Ave., 11222.
Catechesis Religious Program—Tel: 718-383-6935. Eugenia Calderon, D.R.E. Students 99.

12—ASSUMPTION OF THE BLESSED VIRGIN MARY (1842) (Lithuanian)
64 Middagh St., 11201. Tel: 718-625-1161;
Fax: 718-625-7223; Email: rectory@assumptionparishbrooklyn.org; Web: assumptionparishbrooklyn.org. Revs. Joel M. Warden, C.O., Admin.; Michael J. Callaghan, C.M., Ph. D., B.A., M.Div., M.A.T., Parochial Vicar; Anthony Andreassi, C.O.; Very Rev. Dennis M. Corrado, C.O., In Res.; Rev. Mark J. Lane, C.O., In Res.; Bros. Mark Paul Amatrucola, C.O., In Res.; James Simon, C.O., In Res.
Catechesis Religious Program—Students 30.

13—ST. ATHANASIUS (1913)
2154 61st St., 11204. Tel: 718-236-0124; Email: StAthanasiusNY@hotmail.com. Rev. Msgr. David L. Cassato, M.Div., M.S.Ed.; Revs. Ronald M. D'Antonio, Parochial Vicar; Gabriel Toro-Rivas, Parochial Vicar; Alessandro G. Linardi, Parochial Vicar; Deacons Dante Colandrea; William V. Kelly; Jaime Cobham; Mr. Alvoro Chavarriaga, Pastoral Assoc.
Please see St. Athanasius Catholic Academy under Consolidated Elementary Schools in the Institutions Located in the Diocese section.
Catechesis Religious Program—Tel: 718-331-8811;
Fax: 718-331-2582. Mrs. Nicoletta Milo, D.R.E. Students 745.
Convent—2201 62nd St., 11204. Tel: 718-236-2680.
Chapel—St. Augustine Yu Chin-gil Chapel, 2115 61st St., 11204. Tel: 718-729-0132;
Fax: 718-729-0132.

14—ST. AUGUSTINE (1870)
116 Sixth Ave., 11217. Tel: 718-783-3132; Email: staugustinerc@verizon.net. Revs. Thomas W. Ahern; Thomas F. Brosnan, Parochial Vicar; Rev. Msgr. Robert M. Harris, M.S.W., M.Phil., M.A., In Res., (Retired); Rev. Agnelo Pinto, In Res.; Deacon Dean Dobbins.
Catechesis Religious Program—Students 30.

15—ST. BARBARA (1893)
138 Bleecker St., 11221. Tel: 718-458-3660; Email: 101022@diobrook.org. Rev. Joseph M. Hoffman; Deacon Concepcion Cepin.
Catechesis Religious Program—139 Menaham St., 11221. Tel: 718-453-1406. Ms. Angie Lee Vasquez, D.R.E. Students 465.

16—ST. BENEDICT'S, Closed. For inquiries for parish records contact the chancery.

17—ST. BERNADETTE (1935)
8201 13th Ave., 11228. Tel: 718-837-3400; Email: aquin79@aol.com. Rev. Msgr. Thomas G. Caserta, M.A., M.Div., D.Min.; Rev. Kamil Bober, Parochial Vicar; Deacons Anthony P. Martucci; Frank DeMichele.
Please see St. Bernadette Catholic Academy under Consolidated Elementary Schools in the Institutions Located in the Diocese section.
Catechesis Religious Program—Tel: 718-232-7733. Students 82.

18—ST. BERNARD, Closed. For inquiries for parish records contact the chancery.

19—ST. BERNARD OF CLAIRVAUX (1961)
2055 E. 69th St., 11234. Tel: 718-763-5533; Email: sbchurchbrooklyn@aol.com. Rev. Msgr. Joseph R. Grimaldi, J.C.L.; Rev. Michael G. Tedone, Parochial Vicar; Deacon Frank J. D'Accordo.
Please see St. Bernard Catholic Academy under Consolidated Elementary Schools in the Institutions Located in the Diocese section.
Catechesis Religious Program—Tel: 718-444-4674;
Fax: 718-241-7258. Mrs. Mary Casatelli, D.R.E. Students 192.

20—ST. BLAISE, Merged with St. Francis of Assisi in 1980. For inquiries and parish records see St. Francis of Assisi-St. Blaise.

21—BLESSED SACRAMENT (1891)
198 Euclid Ave., 11208. Tel: 718-827-1200;
Fax: 718-827-2422; Email: receptionbsbk@gmail.com. Revs. Luis Laverde; Jose A. Henriquez, Parochial Vicar.
Please see Blessed Sacrament Catholic Academy under Consolidated Elementary Schools in the Institutions Located in the Diocese section.
Catechesis Religious Program—Tel: 718-277-3231;
Fax: 718-277-3231. Students 654.

22—ST. BONIFACE (1854)
109 Willoughby St., 11201. Tel: 718-875-2096; Email: 101034@diobrook.org. Revs. Joel M. Warden, C.O.; Anthony Andreassi, C.O., Parochial Vicar; Christopher Smith, Business Mgr.
Catechesis Religious Program—Dr. Christina Matone, D.R.E. Students 175.
23—ST. BRENDAN (1907)
1525 E. 12th St., 11230. Tel: 718-339-2828; Email: stbrendanbklyn@aol.com. Rev. Peter D. Gillen; Rev. Msgr. Rocco D. Villani, (Retired).
Catechesis Religious Program—Tel: 718-377-6932; Fax: 718-377-6374. Students 127.
Convent—1526 E. 13th St., 11230. Tel: 718-998-2032.
24—ST. BRIGID (1887)
409 Linden St., 11237. Tel: 718-821-1690; Email: stbrigidinfo@gmail.com. Rev. Jorge Ortiz-Garay, Admin.; Rev. Msgr. James J. Kelly, (Retired); Rev. Joseph F. Dutan, Parochial Vicar.
School—St. Brigid School, 438 Grove St. E., 11237. Tel: 718-821-1477; Fax: 718-821-1079. Lay Teachers 15; Students 203.
Please see St. Brigid Catholic Academy under Consolidated Elementary Schools (Regional) in the Institution section.
Catechesis Religious Program—Tel: 718-821-6401. Jacqueline Perez, D.R.E. Students 1,069.
25—ST. CASIMIR, (Polish), Merged with Our Lady of Czestochowa in 1980. For inquiries and parish records see Our Lady of Czestochowa-St. Casimir.
26—ST. CATHARINE OF ALEXANDRIA (1902)
1119 41st St., 11218. Tel: 718-436-5917; Email: aklocek@diobrook.org. Revs. Andrzej Klocek, (Poland) Admin.; Frederick Cintron; Rev. Msgr. Paul Kodjo, Parochial Vicar; Rev. Tomasz Szczepanczyk, Parochial Vicar; Deacon Gustavo Medina.
Catechesis Religious Program—Tel: 718-436-2471. Mrs. Grace Olavarria, D.R.E. Students 298.
27—THE CATHEDRAL-BASILICA OF ST. JAMES (Jay St. at Tillary) (1822)
250 Cathedral Pl., 11201. Tel: 718-852-4002; Email: fatherpurpura@gmail.com. Rev. Peter J. Purpura, J.C.L.; Deacon Ronald Rizzuto, Pastoral Assoc.
Office: 240 Jay St., 11201. Fax: 718-852-9452; Email: secretary@brooklyncathedral.net; Web: www.brooklyncathedral.net.
28—ST. CATHERINE OF GENOA (1911)
520 Linden Blvd., 11203. Tel: 718-282-7162; Email: stcatherineofgenoa@hotmail.com. Revs. Raphael Kukana, Admin.; Ansemus Mawusi, Parochial Vicar.
Catechesis Religious Program—Tel: 718-469-7505. Marie Rose Terlonge, D.R.E.
29—ST. CECILIA (1871) Merged with St. Nicholas, Brooklyn & St. Francis of Paola, Brooklyn to form Divine Mercy Roman Catholic Church, Brooklyn. For inquiries and parish records see Divine Mercy.
30—ST. CHARLES BORROMEO (1849)
21 Sidney Pl., 11201. Tel: 718-625-1177; Email: rectory@stcharlesbklyn.org. Rev. William Smith; Rev. Msgr. Alfred P. LoPinto, V.E., In Res.; Rev. John Gribowich, In Res.
Catechesis Religious Program—Maureen Pond, D.R.E. Students 78.
31—ST. COLUMBA (1967)
2245 Kimball St., 11234. Tel: 718-338-6265; Email: StColumbaC@aol.com. Rev. Timothy J. Lambert; Deacons Lawrence Coyle; Fred Ritchie.
Catechesis Religious Program—Tel: 718-253-8840. Deacon Frederick V. Ritchie, D.R.E. Students 145.
32—ST. COLUMBKILLE, Closed. Parochial records are located at SS. Cyril and Methodius. Became a mission in 1939.
33—SS. CYRIL AND METHODIUS (1917) (Polish)
150 Dupont St., 11222. Tel: 718-389-4424; Email: parish@cyrilandmethodius.org. Revs. Eugeniusz Kotlinski, C.M.; Slawek Szucki, C.M.; Joseph Wisniewski, C.M.
Catechesis Religious Program—Tel: 718-349-7732.
34—DIVINE MERCY ROMAN CATHOLIC CHURCH (2011)
219 Conselyea St., 11211. Tel: 718-387-0256; Fax: 718-384-0068; Email: fathertom@dmbk.org. Revs. Thomas F. Vassalotti; Rafael J. Perez, Parochial Vicar; Paul Anel, Parochial Vicar; Alexandre Morard, Parochial Vicar; Deacon Carlos Valderrama.
Res.: 84 Herbert St., 11222. Tel: 718-389-0010; Fax: 718-389-5090; Email: divinemercyparish_brooklyn@hotmail.com; Web: divinemercy-brooklyn.org.
Res.: 26 Olive St., 11211. Tel: 718-388-1420; Fax: 718-388-9516; Email: stnicholasrcc@msn.com.
Catechesis Religious Program—1-15 Monitor St., 11222. Tel: 718-389-2546. Amilia Castro, D.R.E. Students 73.
Convent—312 De Voe St., 11211.
35—ST. DOMINIC (1972)
2001 Bay Ridge Pkwy., 11204. Tel: 718-259-4636; Email: saintdominicrectoryoffice@gmail.com. Rev. Msgr. David L. Cassato, M.Div., M.S.Ed., Admin.; Revs. Ronald M. D'Antonio, Admin.; Martin Restrepo, Parochial Vicar; Deacon Anthony Mammoliti.
Catechesis Religious Program—Tel: 718-621-0422. Mrs. Roseanne Bourke, D.R.E. Students 260.
36—ST. EDMUND (1922)
2460 Ocean Ave., 11229-3509. Tel: 718-743-0102; Email: stedmund@aol.com. Revs. David J. Dettmer; Edward Brophy, Pastor Emeritus; Michael J. S. Bruno, In Res.; Deacon Ronald Rizzuto.
School—St. Edmund School, 1902 Ave. T, 11229. Tel: 718-648-9229; Email: saintedmundelem@gmail.com. Ms. Mariann Solano, Prin. Lay Teachers 16; Students 222.
High School—Denis Maloney Institute/St. Edmund Preparatory High School, 2474 Ocean Ave., 11229. Tel: 718-743-6100; Fax: 718-743-5243; Email: jlorenzetti@stedmundprep.org; Web: www.stedmundprep.org. Mr. John Lorenzetti, Prin.; Allison McGinnis, Asst. Prin., Academics; Kevin Raphael, Asst. Prin., Students; Johanna Motta, Librarian. Deacons 2; Lay Teachers 55; Students 750.
Catechesis Religious Program—Tel: 718-743-8107; Fax: 718-891-7834. Mrs. Debra Perillo, D.R.E. Students 58.
37—ST. EDWARD, Merged with St. Michael Archangel in 1942. St. Michael Archangel-St. Edward merged with Sacred Heart in 2008 to form Mary of Nazareth, Brooklyn. For inquiries and parish records see Mary of Nazareth.
38—ST. EPHREM (1921)
929 Bay Ridge Pkwy., 11228. Tel: 718-833-1010; Email: 101053@diobrook.org. Rev. Robert B. Adamo; Rev. Msgrs. Peter V. Kain, (Retired); Theophilus Joseph, Parochial Vicar, (Retired); Rev. Anthony S. Chanan, Parochial Vicar; Deacons Anthony Stucchio; Kevin McLaughlin.
School—St. Ephrem School, 7415 Ft. Hamilton Pkwy., 11228. Tel: 718-833-1440; Fax: 718-745-5301; Email: stephremschool@aol.com; Web: stephremsch.org. Annamarie Bartone, Prin. Lay Teachers 16; Servants of the Immaculate Heart of Mary 2; Students 258.
Catechesis Religious Program—Tel: 718-745-7486; Fax: 718-745-2302; Email: stephremreled@verizon.net. Eileen McGuire, D.R.E. Students 164.
Convent—935 Bay Ridge Pkwy., 11228. Tel: 718-833-1555.
39—EPIPHANY (1905) Merged with SS. Peter and Paul, Brooklyn. For inquiries and parish records see SS. Peter and Paul, Brooklyn.
40—ST. FINBAR (1880)
138 Bay 20th St., 11214. Tel: 718-236-3312; Email: frgelfant@stfinbarbrooklyn.org. Revs. Michael L. Gelfant; Faustino Cordero, In Res., (Retired); Deacons John E. Hull, In Res.; Anthony Favale; Hector S. Blanco.
Catechesis Religious Program—Tel: 718-837-3935. Jennifer Uzzi-Silverio, D.R.E. Students 302.
Convent—131 Bay 19 St., 11214. Tel: 718-259-4439.
41—ST. FORTUNATA (1934)
2609 Linden Blvd., 11208. Tel: 718-647-2632; Email: stfortunatachurch@netzero.net. Revs. Jose F. Herrera; Adriano H. Restrepo, In Res.; Deacons Osborn Miranda; Okafor C. Uzoigwe; Rafael Cabrera.
Catechesis Religious Program—Sisters Norieta Tusi, D.R.E.; Niurka Burgos, RCIA Coord. Students 124.
42—FOURTEEN HOLY MARTYRS, Merged with St. Martin of Tours in 1976. For inquiries and parish records see St. Martin of Tours-Our Lady of Lourdes.
43—ST. FRANCES CABRINI (1963)
1562 86th. St., 11228. Tel: 718-236-9165; Email: sfcabrini1963@gmail.com. Revs. Gaetano J. Sbordone; Clement Okoro, (Nigeria) Parochial Vicar; Deacon Frank A. Morano.
Please see St. Frances Cabrini Catholic Academy, Brooklyn under Consolidated Elementary Schools in the Institutions Located in the Diocese section.
Catechesis Religious Program—21 Bay 11th St., 11228. Tel: 718-232-4228. Students 90.
44—ST. FRANCES CABRINI CHAPEL, Closed. For inquiries for parish records please see Sacred Heart of Jesus and Mary and St. Stephen.
45—ST. FRANCES DE CHANTAL (1891)
1273 58th St., 11219. Tel: 718-436-6407; Email: stfrancesrectory@gmail.com. Revs. Andrzej Kurowski, S.A.C.; Anthony Zemula, S.A.C., Parochial Vicar; Lukasz Dutkiewicz, Parochial Vicar.
Catechesis Religious Program—Students 209.
46—ST. FRANCIS IN THE FIELDS, Closed. For inquiries for parish records contact the chancery.
47—ST. FRANCIS OF ASSISI-ST. BLAISE (1898)
319 Maple St., 11225. Tel: 718-756-2015; Email: sfastb@optonline.net. Rev. Msgr. Paul W. Jervis; Revs. Gerald Dumont, Parochial Vicar; Jean-Pierre Ruiz, S.T.D.; Deacon Wilner Pierre-Louis.
Please see St. Francis of Assisi Catholic Academy under Consolidated Elementary Schools (Regional) in the Institution section.
Catechesis Religious Program—335 Maple St., 11225. Tel: 718-778-1302. Ms. Myrmonde Dorismonde, D.R.E. Students 95.
48—ST. FRANCIS OF PAOLA (1918) (Italian), Merged with St. Nicholas, Brooklyn & St. Cecilia, Brooklyn to form Divine Mercy Roman Catholic Church, Brooklyn. For inquiries and parish records see Divine Mercy.
49—ST. FRANCIS XAVIER (1886)
225 Sixth Ave., 11215. Tel: 718-638-1880; Email: FRANXRC@gmail.com. Rev. William J. Rueger; Sr. Helene Conway, C.S.J., Pastoral Assoc.
Please see St. Francis Xavier Catholic Academy under Consolidated Elementary Schools in the Institutions Located in the Diocese section.
Catechesis Religious Program—Tel: 718-857-2903; Email: hacreled@aol.com. Sr. Helene Conway, C.S.J., D.R.E. Students 145.
50—ST. GABRIEL THE ARCHANGEL (1901) Merged with Saint John Cantius, Brooklyn to form Mary, Mother of the Church, Brooklyn. For inquiries and parish records see Mary, Mother of the Church.
51—ST. GEORGE, Closed. For inquiries for parish records contact the chancery.
52—GOOD SHEPHERD (1927)
1950 Batchelder St., 11229. Tel: 718-998-2800; Fax: 718-382-5428; Email: gsrcc@aol.com. Revs. Thomas Doyle; Mark Simmons, Parochial Vicar; Paul Ifeadi, Parochial Vicar; James E. Devlin, (Retired); Deacon Christopher A. Wagner.
Please see Good Shepherd Catholic Academy under Consolidated Elementary Schools in the Institutions Located in the Diocese section.
Catechesis Religious Program—Tel: 718-375-0899. Elvira Anselmo, D.R.E. Students 408.
53—ST. GREGORY THE GREAT (1905) Merged with St. Matthew, Brooklyn.
54—GUARDIAN ANGEL (1885)
2978 Ocean Pkwy., 11235. Tel: 718-266-1561; Email: Guardianangelc2978@gmail.com. Revs. Francisco J. Walker; Sergiy Emanuel, Parochial Vicar; Deacon Manuel Zelaya.
Catechesis Religious Program—Olga Ortiz, D.R.E. Students 211.
55—HOLY CROSS (1848)
2530 Church Ave., 11226. Tel: 718-469-5900; Email: msgrjoe@aol.com. Rev. Msgr. Joseph P. Malagreca; Rev. Bony Monastere, Parochial Vicar.
Catechesis Religious Program—Tel: 718-941-5066. Catherine Hayes, D.R.E. Students 112.
56—HOLY FAMILY (1880) Merged with St. Thomas Aquinas to form Holy Family-St. Thomas Aquinas. For inquiries and parish records see Holy Family-St. Thomas Aquinas.
57—HOLY FAMILY (1880)
9719 Flatlands Ave., 11236. Tel: 718-257-4423; Email: HfamilyR@aol.com; Web: HolyFamilyCanarsie.org. Very Rev. Edward R. P. Kane; Revs. John J. Amann, Parochial Vicar, (Retired); Robert Pierre-Louis, Parochial Vicar; Michael J. McGee, Parochial Vicar; Yvon H. Aurelien, Parochial Vicar.
Catechesis Religious Program—Tel: 718-257-8016; Fax: 718-272-2279. Brendan Egonu, D.R.E. Students 156.
58—HOLY FAMILY (1905) (Slovak), Merged with St. Anthony-St. Alphonsus. For inquiries and parish records see St. Anthony-St. Alphonsus.
59—HOLY FAMILY-SAINT THOMAS AQUINAS (2008)
249 Ninth St., 11215. Tel: 718-768-9471; Email: mmatthias@diobrook.org. Rev. Mark A. Matthias, Admin.; Most Rev. James Massa, D.D.; Revs. Jesus Cuadros, (Retired); Expedit S. Serunjogi, Part-Time; Francis Fayez, In Res.; Deacon John A. Flannery.
Worship Site: Holy Family Church, 205 14th St., 11215.
Catechesis Religious Program—Sr. Doryne M. Bermoy, F.L.P., D.R.E. Students 171.
60—HOLY INNOCENTS (1910)
279 E. 17th St., 11226. Tel: 718-469-9500; Email: holyinnocentsrcbklyn@yahoo.com. Revs. Pascal Louis; Lazaro Nunez-Renteria, Parochial Vicar; Gerald Dumont, Parochial Vicar; Pedro S. Guerrero, Parochial Vicar.
Catechesis Religious Program—Nancy Gerard, D.R.E. Students 251.
61—HOLY NAME (1878)
245 Prospect Park W., 11215. Tel: 718-768-3071; Email: lawrencedryan@gmail.com. Rev. Lawrence D. Ryan; Rev. Msgr. Michael J. Curran, Part-Time; Revs. Patrick G. Burns, In Res.; Austin Emeh, In Res.; Deacon Abel Torres.
Please see St. Joseph the Worker Catholic Academy under Consolidated Elementary Schools in the Institutions Located in the Diocese section.
Catechesis Religious Program—241 Prospect Park W., 11215. Tel: 718-768-7629; Fax: 718-768-3007. Mrs. Kathryn Sisto, D.R.E. Students 115.
62—HOLY ROSARY (1889) (African American), Merged with Our Lady of Victory & St. Peter Claver, Brooklyn to form Saint Martin de Porres, Brooklyn. For inquiries and parish records see Saint Martin de Porres.
63—HOLY SPIRIT

1712 45th St., 11204. Tel: 718-436-5565; Email: 101084@diobrook.org. Revs. Jose E. Lopez, Admin.; Jon O. Ukaegbu, Parochial Vicar.
Catechesis Religious Program—Mrs. Martha Castro, D.R.E. Students 158.
Convent—1679 47th St., 11204.

64—ST. IGNATIUS (1908) Merged with St. Francis of Assisi-St. Blaise. For inquiries and parish records see St. Francis of Assisi-St. Blaise.

65—IMMACULATE CONCEPTION OF THE BLESSED VIRGIN MARY (1853) Merged with Holy Trinity Parish to form Most Holy Trinity-St. Mary, Brooklyn. For inquiries and parish records, see Most Holy Trinity - St. Mary, Brooklyn.

66—IMMACULATE HEART OF MARY (1893)
2805 Ft. Hamilton Pkwy., 11218. Tel: 718-871-1310; Email: FrGill@ihmbrooklyn.org. Revs. Ilyas Gill, O.F.M., (Pakistan); John P. Cush, B.A., S.T.L., In Res.; Francis Obu-Mends, In Res.; Sr. Mary Ann Ambrose, C.S.J., Pastoral Assoc.; Deacons James D. Noble; John Cantirino; Antonio J. Gonzalez.
Please see St. Joseph the Worker Catholic Academy under Consolidated Elementary Schools (Regional) located in the Institution section.
Catechesis Religious Program—Tel: 718-854-7326. Students 193.

67—ST. JEROME (1901)
2900 Newkirk Ave., 11226. Tel: 718-462-0223; Email: stjeromechurch@hotmail.com. Revs. Jean Yvon Pierre, Admin.; Saint Martin Estiverne, Parochial Vicar; Deacon Paul Norman.
Catechesis Religious Program—Deacon Paul Norman, D.R.E. Students 140.
Convent—455 E. 29th St., 11226. Tel: 718-856-3323.

68—ST. JOHN CANTIUS (1902) Merged with Saint Gabriel the Archangel, Brooklyn to form Mary, Mother of the Church, Brooklyn (2007). For inquiries and parish records see Mary, Mother of the Church.

69—ST. JOHN THE BAPTIST (1868)
333 Hart St., 11206. Tel: 718-455-6864; Email: 101253@diobrook.org. Rev. Astor Rodriguez, C.M., B.S.; Most Rev. Alfonso Cabezas, C.M., In Res.
Worship Site: Our Lady of Good Counsel, 915 Putnam Ave., 11221.
Catechesis Religious Program—Eugenia Ortiz, D.R.E. Students 98.

70—ST. JOHN THE EVANGELIST (1849) Merged with St. Rocco, Brooklyn to form Saint John the Evangelist-Saint Rocco Roman Catholic Church, Brooklyn. For inquiries and parish records see Saint John the Evangelist-Saint Rocco Roman Catholic Church.

71—SAINT JOHN THE EVANGELIST-SAINT ROCCO (2011)
250 21st St., 11215. Tel: 718-768-3751; Email: johnevangelist@verizon.net. Revs. Kenneth J. Grande; Angel Medrano-Matos, Parochial Vicar
Legal Name: Saint John the Evangelist-Saint Rocco Roman Catholic Church
Worship Site: St. Rocco, 216 27th St., 11232.
Tel: 718-768-9798; Fax: 718-768-7742; Email: strcchurch@aol.com; Web: www.saintroccochurch.com.
Catechesis Religious Program—Karen Salinas, D.R.E.

72—ST. JOHN'S CHAPEL, Closed. For inquiries for parish records please see Queen of all Saints Church.

73—ST. JOSEPH (1850)
856 Pacific St., 11238. Tel: 718-638-1071; Email: info@stjosephs-brooklyn.org. Rev. Msgr. Kieran E. Harrington, V.E.; Rev. Charles P. Keeney, Parochial Vicar; Deacons Manuel H. Quintana; Fausto Duran, (Dominican Republic).
Catechesis Religious Program—Students 106.

74—ST. JOSEPH PATRON OF THE UNIVERSAL CHURCH (1921) (Scalabrini Fathers)
185 Suydam St., 11221. Tel: 718-386-0175; Email: st.josephpatronchurch@gmail.com. Revs. Sergio Dall'Agnes; Teofilo Ramirez Moreno, Parochial Vicar; Hoang V. Nguyen, Parochial Vicar.
Catechesis Religious Program—Wanda Marty, D.R.E. Students 458.

75—ST. JUDE SHRINE CHURCH (1961)
1677 Canarsie Rd., 11236. Tel: 718-763-6300; Email: Uncjed@optimum.net. Rev. Msgr. John E. Delendick; Rev. Dominic N. Pepran.
Please see Our Lady of Trust School-St. Jude Campus, Brooklyn under Consolidated Elementary Schools (Regional) located in the Institution section.
Catechesis Religious Program—Tel: 718-241-4030. Ms. Helen Teifer, D.R.E. Students 128.

76—ST. LAURENCE (1964)
1020 Van Siclen Ave., 11207. Tel: 718-649-0545; Email: St.Laurence1020@gmail.com. Very Rev. Edward R. P. Kane, Admin.; Deacon Jean J. Rameau.
Catechesis Religious Program—Email: judinawilson@att.net. Lori Ramos Johnson, D.R.E. Students 47.

77—ST. LEONARD OF PORT MAURICE, Closed. Records at St. Joseph, Patron of the Universal Church.

78—ST. LOUIS, Closed. Became a Mission of St. Lucy in 1939. Parochial records are at St. Lucy-St. Patrick's, 285 Willoughby Ave., 11205. Tel: 718-622-8748; Fax: 718-622-6330.

79—ST. LUCY-ST. PATRICK (1843) Merged with Mary of Nazareth. For inquiries and parish records see Mary of Nazareth.

80—ST. MALACHY (1854) Merged with Saint Michael the Archangel, Brooklyn to form St. Michael-Saint Malachy, Brooklyn. For inquiries and parish records see St. Michael-Saint Malachy.

81—ST. MARGARET MARY (1920)
215 Exeter St., 11235-3725. Tel: 718-891-3100; Fax: 718-891-9677; Email: 101120@diobrook.org. Very Rev. Robert V. Mucci, J.C.L., Admin.

82—ST. MARK (1861)
2609 E. 19th St., 11235. Tel: 718-891-3100; Email: stmarkbrooklyn@gmail.com. Very Rev. Robert V. Mucci, J.C.L.; Revs. Joseph M. Zwosta; Sergiy Emanuel; Michael Panicali; Joseph P. Quigley, (Retired); Deacon Paul P. Morin.
Church: Ocean Ave. & Ave. Z, 11235.
Please see St. Mark Catholic Academy under Consolidated Elementary Schools in the Institutions Located in the Diocese section.
Catechesis Religious Program—Tel: 718-769-6311. Joann Pino, D.R.E. Students 83.

83—SAINT MARTIN DE PORRES (2007)
Tel: 718-574-5772; Email: info@smdpp.org. Revs. Alonzo Q. Cox; Daniel O. Kingsley, Parochial Vicar; Deacon Balfour A. Thompson.
Worship Sites:—
Our Lady of Victory—583 Throop Ave., 11216.
Holy Rosary, 172 Bainbridge St., 11233.
St. Peter Claver, 29 Peter Claver Pl., 11238.
Catechesis Religious Program—Tel: 718-574-5772; Fax: 718-919-2265. Students 35.
Convents—Missionaries of Charity—262 Macon St., 11216.
Daughters of Divine Love.

84—ST. MARTIN OF TOURS-OUR LADY OF LOURDES (1872; 1906)
1288 Hancock St., 11221. Tel: 718-443-8484; Email: JRuiz@diobrook.org. Revs. Juan Ruiz; Lazaro Nunez-Renteria, Parochial Vicar; Pedro N. Ossa, Sr. Active, (Retired); Francis Mann, In Res.; Deacon Alberto Cruz.
Catechesis Religious Program—Held at St. Elizabeth Seton School (751 Knickerbocker Ave., Brooklyn, NY 11221). Students 460.
Chapel—Our Lady of Lourdes Chapel, 89 Furman Ave., 11207.

85—ST. MARY MOTHER OF JESUS (1889)
2326 84th St., 11214. Tel: 718-372-4000; Email: smmj2326@optimum.net. Rev. Msgr. Andrew J. Vaccari, J.C.L.; Rev. Joseph A. Gancila, Parochial Vicar; Deacon Bryan Amore.
Please see St. Mary Mother of Jesus-St. Frances Cabrini Academy, Brooklyn under Consolidated Elementary Schools (Regional) located in the Institution section.
Catechesis Religious Program—Tel: 718-449-8263; Fax: 718-265-6209. Mrs. Maria Beyra, M.A., D.R.E. Students 234.

86—MARY, MOTHER OF THE CHURCH (2007)
749 Linwood St., 11208. Tel: 718-257-0612; Email: marymotherofthechurch749@yahoo.com. Revs. Jose Augustin Opellana; Miguel Zavala, Parochial Vicar; Deacon Rafael Marte.
Worship Site: St. John Cantius, 479 New Jersey Ave., 11207. Tel: 718-342-2679; Fax: 718-342-4878; Email: jcantius@aol.com.
Catechesis Religious Program—666 Essex St., 11208. Tel: 718-649-0450; Fax: 718-649-0450. Angelus Crowell, D.R.E. Students 210.

87—MARY OF NAZARETH (2008)
Tel: 718-625-5115; Email: 101264@diobrook.org. Rev. Robert P. Vitaglione.
Worship Sites:—
Sacred Heart—41 Adelphi St., 11205.
St. Michael the Archangel & St. Edward, 108 St. Edward's St., 11205.
St. Lucy-St. Patrick, 285 Willoughby Ave., 11205.
Catechesis Religious Program—Students 122.

88—ST. MARY OF THE ANGELS, (Lithuanian), Closed. For inquiries for parish records contact the chancery.

89—MARY QUEEN OF HEAVEN (1927)
1395 E. 56th St., 11234. Tel: 718-763-2330; Email: mqhchurch@aol.com. Revs. Thomas F. Leach; Ikenna Okagbue, Parochial Vicar; Deacon Jean Baptiste Boursiquot.
Please see Mary Queen of Heaven Catholic Academy under Consolidated Elementary Schools in the Institutions Located in the Diocese section.
Catechesis Religious Program—Tel: 718-763-2590. Mrs. Mary Casatelli, D.R.E. Students 80.
Convent—Sisters of St. Dominic, 1304 E. 57th St., 11234. Tel: 718-891-7451.

90—ST. MARY STAR OF THE SEA (1851)
467 Court St., 11231. Tel: 718-625-2270; Email: smss1851@aol.com. Rev. Francis T. Shannon.
Catechesis Religious Program—Students 16.

91—ST. MATTHEW (1886)
1123 Eastern Pkwy., 11213. Tel: 718-774-6747; Email: fblack@diobrook.org. Revs. Francis A. Black; Jean-Augustin Francois, Parochial Vicar; Juan D. Luxama; Apollinaris Anyomi, Part Time; Most Rev. Guy Sansaricq, In Res., (Retired); Deacons Mickey Cutter, Business Mgr.; Roy N. George; Nickie Colon.
Worship Sites:—
Our Lady of Charity—1669 Dean St., 11213.
St. Gregory the Great, 224 Brooklyn Ave., 11213.
Please see St. Gregory the Great Catholic Academy under Consolidated Elementary Schools in the Institutions Located in the Diocese section.
Catechesis Religious Program—1351 Lincoln Pl., 11213. Steven J. Horka, D.R.E. Students 260.

92—ST. MICHAEL (1860) Merged with Saint Malachy, Brooklyn to form St. Michael-Saint Malachy, Brooklyn. For inquiries and parish records see St. Michael-Saint Malachy.

93—ST. MICHAEL ARCHANGEL AND ST. EDWARD THE CONFESSOR (1891) Merged with Sacred Heart to form Mary of Nazareth, Brooklyn. For inquiries and parish records see Mary of Nazareth.

94—ST. MICHAEL - SAINT MALACHY (2007)
284 Warwick St., 11207. Tel: 718-647-1818; Email: bpbuckley@yahoo.com. Revs. Brendan Buckley, Admin.; Gerard Mulvey, O.F.M.Cap., Parochial Vicar; Deacon Carlos Garcia.
Res.: 226 Jerome St., 11207. Tel: 718-647-1818.
Catechesis Religious Program—Sr. Maria Madre de las Americas, D.R.E. Students 135.
Convent—129 Van Siclen Ave., 11207.
Tel: 718-647-2751.

95—ST. MICHAEL (1870)
352 42nd St., 11232. Tel: 718-768-6065; Email: ksweeney@diobrook.org. Very Rev. Kevin J. Sweeney; Rev. Gesson Agenis, Parochial Vicar; Rev. Msgr. Thomas J. Healy, In Res., (Retired).
Catechesis Religious Program—Ines Cordero, D.R.E. Students 489.

96—MOST HOLY TRINITY - SAINT MARY (1841)
138 Montrose Ave., 11206. Tel: 718-384-0215; Email: mhtbrooklyn@yahoo.com. Revs. Pedro de Oliveira, O.F.M.Conv.; Mietek F. Wilk, O.F.M.Conv.; Russell Governale, O.F.M.Conv., In Res.; Deacon Nicholas Spano, O.F.M.Conv., In Res.
Catechesis Religious Program—Tel: 718-486-6276. Sr. Carol Wood, F.M.S.A., D.R.E. Students 5.

97—MOST PRECIOUS BLOOD (1927)
70 Bay 47th St., 11214. Tel: 718-372-8022; Email: mpb11214@aol.com. Revs. John Maduri; Israel Perez, Parochial Vicar; Joseph Han, Parochial Vicar.
Catechesis Religious Program—Rosemarie Paccione, D.R.E. Students 95.

98—NATIVITY OF OUR BLESSED LORD, Merged with St. Peter Claver in 1973. St. Peter Claver merged in 2007 to form St. Martin de Porres. For inquiries and parish records see St. Martin de Porres.

99—ST. NICHOLAS (1865) Merged with St. Francis of Paola, Brooklyn & St. Cecilia, Brooklyn to form Divine Mercy Roman Catholic Church, Brooklyn. For inquiries and parish records see Divine Mercy.

100—OUR LADY HELP OF CHRISTIANS (1927)
1315 E. 28th St., 11210. Tel: 718-338-5242; Email: olhcbrooklyn@gmail.com. Revs. Ralph J. Caputo; Josh Hugo, Parochial Vicar.
Please see Midwood Catholic Academy, Brooklyn under Consolidated Elementary Schools (Regional) in the Institution section.
Catechesis Religious Program—Tel: 718-377-6932. Students 22.

101—OUR LADY OF ANGELS (1891)
7320 Fourth Ave., 11209. Tel: 718-836-7200; Email: ola.bayridge@verizon.net. Rev. Msgr. Kevin B. Noone, V.E.; Revs. Richard M. Lewkiewicz, Parochial Vicar, (Retired); Jason N. Espinal, Parochial Vicar; Kenneth J. Calder, (Retired); Deacons Ed Gaine; Charles R. Hurley.
Catechesis Religious Program—Tel: 718-748-6553. Students 260.

102—OUR LADY OF CHARITY (1903) (African American), Merged with St. Matthew, Brooklyn. For inquiries and parish records see St. Matthew, Brooklyn.

103—OUR LADY OF CONSOLATION (1909) (Polish)
184 Metropolitan Ave., 11211. Tel: 718-388-1942; Email: olc11249@gmail.com. Revs. Wieslaw P. Strzadala; Andrzej Wasko, S.D.S., Parochial Vicar.
Catechesis Religious Program—Students 129.

104—OUR LADY OF CZESTOCHOWA-ST. CASIMIR (1896) (Polish)
183 25th St., 11232. Tel: 718-768-5724; Email: olcpny@gmail.com. Revs. Janusz Dymek; Cezariusz W. Jastrzebski, Parochial Vicar.
Catechesis Religious Program—Students 139.

105—OUR LADY OF GOOD COUNSEL (1886) Merged with St. John the Baptist, Brooklyn. For inquiries and parish records see St. John the Baptist, Brooklyn.

106—OUR LADY OF GRACE (1935) (Italian)
430 Avenue W, 11223. Tel: 718-627-2020; Email: ourladyofgrace7@gmail. Revs. Vincent G. Chirichella; Lukasz Lech, Parochial Vicar; Deacon Philip J. Siani.

Please see Our Lady of Grace Catholic Academy under Consolidated Elementary Schools in the Institutions Located in the Diocese section.
Catechesis Religious Program—Tel: 718-375-0404. Phyllis Niwinski, D.R.E. Students 117.

107—OUR LADY OF GUADALUPE (1906) (Italian—Spanish)
7201 Fifteenth Ave., 11228. Tel: 718-236-8300; Email: 101154@diobrook.org. Rev. Msgr. Robert J. Romano; Revs. Anthony F. Raso, Parochial Vicar; Andrew Kofi Soley, Parochial Vicar.
Please see Our Lady of Guadalupe Catholic Academy under Consolidated Elementary Schools in the Institutions Located in the Diocese section.
Catechesis Religious Program—Tel: 718-331-4003. Students 158.

108—OUR LADY OF LORETO (1894) Merged with Our Lady of the Presentation. For records contact the chancery office.

109—OUR LADY OF LOURDES (1872) Merged with St. Martin of Tours, Brooklyn. For inquiries and parish records see St. Martin of Tours-Our Lady of Lourdes, Brooklyn.

110—OUR LADY OF MERCY (1961) Merged with Our Lady of the Presentation-Our Lady of Loreto, Brooklyn to form Our Lady of the Presentation-Our Lady of Mercy Roman Catholic Church, Brooklyn. For inquiries and parish records see Our Lady of the Presentation-Our Lady of Mercy Roman Catholic Church.

111—OUR LADY OF MERCY, Closed. in 1908. Second church at Schermerhorn & Bond closed. For inquiries for parish records contact the chancery.

112—OUR LADY OF MIRACLES (1936)
757 E. 86th St., 11236. Tel: 718-257-2400; Email: ourladyofmiraclesbk@gmail.com. Revs. Jean Delva; Hugues Berrette, Parochial Vicar.
Please see Our Lady of Trust School at Our Lady of Miracles Campus, Brooklyn under Consolidated Elementary Schools (Regional) located in the Institution section.
Catechesis Religious Program—Tel: 718-649-1006. Sr. Doryne M. Bermoy, F.L.P., D.R.E. Students 106.

113—OUR LADY OF MONSERRATE-ST. AMBROSE (1954) Merged with All Saints, Brooklyn. For inquiries and parish records see All Saints.

114—OUR LADY OF MOUNT CARMEL SHRINE CHURCH (1887) (Italian)
275 N. Eighth St., 11211. Tel: 718-384-0223; Email: olmcn8th@yahoo.com. Rev. Msgr. Jamie J. Gigantiello; Rev. Tomasz Adamczyk, Parochial Vicar; Deacon Philip Franco.
School—The Mount Carmel Early Childhood Center, 10 Withers St., 11211. Tel: 718-782-1110; Fax: 718-782-3344.
Catechesis Religious Program—Rosemarie Walsh, D.R.E. Students 137.

115—OUR LADY OF PEACE (1899) (Italian)
522 Carroll St., 11215. Tel: 718-624-5122; Email: oruiz@diobrook.org. Revs. Orlando Ruiz; Brian Jordan, O.S.F., In Res.; Bro. Courtland Campbell, In Res.
Catechesis Religious Program—Lillian Flores, D.R.E. Students 154.
Convent—Hermanas Franciscanas de la Immaculada, 209 First St., 11215. Tel: 718-624-6720 ; Fax: 718-625-7657.

116—OUR LADY OF PERPETUAL HELP BASILICA (1893)
526-59th St., 11220. Tel: 718-492-9200; Fax: 718-439-8528; Email: JWGilmourCSSR@gmail.com; Web: www.olphbkny.org. Revs. Francis Mulvaney, Supr.; James Gilmour, C.Ss.R.; Peter Cao, C.Ss.R., (Vietnam); Kangqiang Lu; John McKenna; John Murray; Ruskin Piedra, C.Ss.R.; Norman S. Bennett, C.Ss.R.; Robert Cheesman, C.Ss.R., In Res.; Joseph Freund, In Res.; Deacon Jesus Soto.
Please see Our Lady of Perpetual Help Catholic Academy Brooklyn under Consolidated Elementary Schools in the Institutions Located in the Diocese section.
Catechesis Religious Program—Tel: 718-439-4795. Maritza Mejia, D.R.E. Students 621.
Immigration Services—Juan Neumann Center, 545 60th St., 11220. Tel: 718-439-8160; Fax: 718-439-8685.

117—OUR LADY OF REFUGE (1911)
2020 Foster Ave., 11210. Tel: 718-434-2090; Email: olrefuge@aol.com. Revs. Michael A. Perry, Pastor Emeritus, (Retired); Saint Charles Borno; Rony Mendes, Parochial Vicar; Lamartine Petit, Parochial Vicar; Jack Fagan, Parochial Vicar; Pedro S. Guerrero, Parochial Vicar; Isaie Jean Louis; Ihor Melnyk.
Catechesis Religious Program—Jennifer Baptiste, D.R.E. Students 302.

118—OUR LADY OF SOLACE (1900)
2866 W. 17th St., 11224. Tel: 718-266-1612; Email: olsshiju@olsbrooklyn.com. Revs. Shiju Chittattukara, S.D.V.; Lorenzo Gomez; Michael Onyekwere.
Catechesis Religious Program—Email: rec@olsbrooklyn.com. Maria Garces, D.R.E.

119—OUR LADY OF SORROWS, Merged with St. Leonard in 1942. For inquiries and parish records see St. Joseph Patron of the Universal Church.

120—OUR LADY OF THE PRESENTATION-OUR LADY OF MERCY (2011)
1677 St. Marks Ave., 11233. Tel: 718-345-2604; Email: olmchurch@verizon.net. Rev. Edward J. Mason; Deacons Jaime Varela; Victorino P. Elijio
Legal Name: Our Lady of the Presentation-Our Lady of Mercy Roman Catholic Church
Additional Worship Site: Our Lady of Mercy, 680 Mother Gaston Blvd., 11212.
Catechesis Religious Program—Nancy Prunes, D.R.E.; Doris Tejada Acham, D.R.E. Students 177.

121—OUR LADY OF THE PRESENTATION-OUR LADY OF LORETO (1887) (African American—Hispanic), Merged with Our Lady of Mercy, Brooklyn to form Our Lady of the Presentation-Our Lady of Mercy Roman Catholic Church, Brooklyn. For inquiries and parish records see Our Lady of the Presentation-Our Lady of Mercy Roman Catholic Church.

122—OUR LADY OF THE ROSARY OF POMPEII (1900) (Hispanic)
225 Seigel St., 11206. Tel: 718-497-0614; Email: ourladyofpompeiibrooklyn@gmail.com. Rev. Vincenzo Cardilicchia, Admin.
Catechesis Religious Program—Students 22.

123—OUR LADY OF VICTORY (1868) Merged with Holy Rosary & St. Peter Claver, Brooklyn to form Saint Martin de Porres, Brooklyn. For inquiries and parish records see Saint Martin de Porres.

124—ST. PATRICK (1849)
9511 Fourth Ave., 11209. Tel: 718-238-2600; Email: parish@stpatrickbayridge.org. Rev. Msgr. Michael J. Hardiman; Revs. Richard Bretone, Parochial Vicar; Gregory M. V. McIlhenney, Parochial Vicar; Peter Poonoly, Parochial Vicar; Thomas Shepanzyk, In Res.; Sr. Jeanne Elaine Matullo, O.P., Pastoral Assoc.
Worship Site: Blessed Sacrament Chapel, 418 95th St., 11209.
Please see St. Patrick Catholic Academy under Consolidated Elementary Schools in the Institutions Located in the Diocese section.
Catechesis Religious Program—Gary M. Arkin, D.R.E. Students 265.

125—ST. PATRICK'S, Merged with St. Lucy's in 1974. St. Lucy-St. Patrick merged with Mary of Nazareth in 2011. For inquiries and parish records see Mary of Nazareth.

126—SAINT PAUL AND SAINT AGNES ROMAN CATHOLIC CHURCH (2007)
433 Sackett St., 11231. Rev. Msgr. Joseph A. Nugent, Admin.; Revs. William Ndi; Peter Mahoney, In Res., (Retired); Deacon Leroy P. Branch.
St. Agnes—433 Sackett St., 11231.
St. Paul—234 Congress St., 11201.
Catechesis Religious Program—William Gorman, D.R.E. Students 50.

127—SS. PETER AND PAUL (1843)
71 S. Third St., 11211. Tel: 718-388-9576; Email: saintspeterandpaul@gmail.com. Revs. Fulgencio Gutierrez; Juan Rosario, Parochial Vicar.
Church: 82 S. 2nd St., 11211.
Worship Site: Epiphany, Church: 96 S. 9th St., 11211.
Catechesis Religious Program—Tel: 718-387-1041. Sr. Maria Bendita Diez, D.R.E. Students 118.

128—ST. PETER CLAVER (1921) Merged with Our Lady of Victory & Holy Rosary, Brooklyn to form Saint Martin de Porres, Brooklyn. For inquiries and parish records see Saint Martin de Porres.

129—ST. PETER-ST. PAUL-OUR LADY OF PILAR (1836) Merged with Saint Agnes, Brooklyn to form Saint Paul and Saint Agnes, Brooklyn. For inquiries and parish records see Saint Paul and Saint Agnes.

130—QUEEN OF ALL SAINTS (1879)
300 Vanderbilt Ave., 11205. Tel: 718-638-7625; Email: qasrccoffice@gmail.com. Rev. Joseph A. Ceriello.
Please see Queen of All Saints Catholic Academy under Consolidated Elementary Schools in the Institutions Located in the Diocese section.
Catechesis Religious Program—Elizabeth Guevara, D.R.E. Students 120.

131—REGINA PACIS VOTIVE SHRINE (1951) For personnel see St. Rosalia.
1230 65th St., 11219. Tel: 718-236-0909; Fax: 718-236-5357; Email: rosalia1230@aol.com.

132—RESURRECTION (1924)
2331 Gerritsen Ave., 11229. Tel: 718-743-7234; Email: 101200@diobrook.org. Revs. William A. With; Michael C. Gribbon, Parochial Vicar.
Catechesis Religious Program—2335 Gerritsen Ave., 11229. Tel: 718-891-0888. Mrs. Angela Parente, D.R.E. Students 228.

133—RESURRECTION CATHOLIC COPTIC CHAPEL (1985)
Mailing Address: 352 42nd St., 11232.
Tel: 718-965-0422; Fax: 718-768-3336. Rev. Msgr. Youssef Bochra Nasri, (Coptic Catholic Patriarchate).
Church: 328 14th St., 11215. Tel: 718-499-6946.

134—ST. RITA (1913) (Spanish)
275 Shepherd Ave., 11208. Tel: 718-647-4910; Email: Parishstrita@brooklyn.com. Rev. William Chacon, (Costa Rica); Deacons Andres de la Rosa; Ricardo Reyes.
Catechesis Religious Program—Mrs. Annemarie Ronacher, D.R.E. Students 220.

135—ST. ROCCO (1902) Merged with St. John the Evangelist, Brooklyn to form Saint John the Evangelist-Saint Rocco Roman Catholic Church, Brooklyn. For inquiries and parish records see Saint John the Evangelist-Saint Rocco Roman Catholic Church.

136—ST. ROSALIA-REGINA PACIS (1904)
1230 65th St., 11219. Tel: 718-236-0909; Email: reginarectory@aol.com. Rev. Msgr. Ronald T. Marino, V.E.; Revs. Marco Brioschi, Parochial Vicar; Nicholas Apollonio; Deacon John J. Dolan; Sr. Clara Wang, Pastoral Assoc.
Regina Center, Inc.—1258 65th St., 11219. Tel: 718-232-4340.
Catechesis Religious Program—
Tel: 718-236-0909, Ext. 40. Jackie Tepedino, D.R.E. Students 218.
Mission—Regina Pacis Votive Shrine, Kings Co.

137—ST. ROSE OF LIMA (1870)
269 Parkville Ave., 11230. Tel: 718-434-8040; Email: ltrocha@yahoo.com. Revs. Lukasz Trocha; Jon O. Ukaegbu, Parochial Vicar; Sr. Maureen Sullivan, C.S.J., Pastoral Assoc. & D.R.E.
Catechesis Religious Program—Students 131.
Convent—Sisters of St. Joseph, 250 Newkirk Ave., 11230. Tel: 718-859-5722.

138—SACRED HEART (1871) Merged with St. Michael Archangel and St. Edward the Confessor to form Mary of Nazareth, Brooklyn. For inquiries and parish records see Mary of Nazareth.

139—SACRED HEART CHAPEL (1996) Closed. For inquiries for parish records contact the Chancery.

140—SACRED HEART MISSION (1942) Closed. For inquiries for parish records contact the Chancery.

141—SACRED HEARTS OF JESUS AND MARY AND ST. STEPHEN (1866) (Italian)
108 Carroll St., 11231. Tel: 718-596-7750; Email: MGM099@gmail.com. Rev. Msgr. Guy A. Massie; Rev. Richard J. Long, M.Div., M.B.A.; Mr. John Heyer II, Pastoral Assoc.
Church: Summit & Hicks Sts., 11231.
Catechesis Religious Program—Tel: 718-596-0880. Mrs. Nancy Arkin, D.R.E. Students 177.

142—ST. SAVIOUR (1905)
611 Eighth Ave., 11215. Tel: 718-768-4055; Email: stsaviourchurch@aol.com. Revs. Frank W. Spacek; Kevin P. Cavalluzzi, Parochial Vicar; Daniel S. Murphy.
Please see St. Saviour's Catholic Academy under Consolidated Elementary Schools (Regional) in the Institution section.
High School—St. Saviour High School, 588 Sixth St., 11215. Tel: 718-768-4406; Fax: 718-369-2688; Email: mckeown.p@stsaviour.org. Sr. Valeria Belanger, S.S.N.D., Prin. Students 173.
Catechesis Religious Program—Tel: 718-768-4055; Fax: 718-768-4872. Patricia M. Rutter, D.R.E. Students 156.
Convent—590 6th St., 11215.

143—SS. SIMON AND JUDE (1897)
185 Van Sicklen St., 11223. Tel: 718-375-9600; Email: rectoryssj@optonline.net. Revs. John Maduri, Admin.; Sijo Muthanattu George, Parochial Vicar; Deacon Andrew T. Mastrangelo.
Catechesis Religious Program—294 Avenue T, 11223. Tel: 718-372-0733; Email: rel.ed@stsimonandjude.org. Sara Nespoli, D.R.E. Students 159.

144—ST. STANISLAUS KOSTKA (1896) (Polish)
607 Humboldt St., 11222. Tel: 718-388-0170; Email: skc11222@aol.com. Revs. Marek W. Sobczak, C.M.; Grezegorz Markulak, Parochial Vicar; Pawel Zych, Parochial Vicar; Joseph Szpilski, C.M., In Res.
Catechesis Religious Program—Tel: 718-388-0170. Krzysztof Gospodarzec, D.R.E. Students 292.

145—ST. STANISLAUS MARTYR, Merged with Holy Family (14th St.) in 1979. For inquiries and records see Holy Family-St. Thomas Aquinas.

146—ST. STEPHEN, Merged with Sacred Hearts in 1941. For inquiries and parish records see Sacred Hearts-St. Stephen Church, Carroll St.

147—ST. SYLVESTER (1923)
416 Grant Ave., 11208. Tel: 718-647-1995; Email: StSylvester416@gmail.com. Revs. Jose F. Herrera, Admin.; Hector Restrepo, Parochial Vicar; Deacons Jose L. Oviedo; Rafael Cabrera.
Catechesis Religious Program—Carmen Perez, D.R.E. Students 125.

148—ST. TERESA OF AVILA (1874)
563 Sterling Pl., 11238. Tel: 718-622-6500; Email: 101223@diobrook.org. Rev. Msgr. Kieran E. Harrington, V.E.; Revs. Charles P. Keeney, Parochial Vicar; Pascal Louis, Parochial Vicar; Lazaro Nunez-Renteria, Parochial Vicar.

Catechesis Religious Program—Guerlyne Bernard, D.R.E. Students 65.
149—St. Therese of Lisieux (1926) (The Little Flower)
1281 Troy Ave., 11203. Tel: 718-451-1500; Email: sttheresels@gmail.com. Revs. Rony Mendes, Admin.; Michel Pierre-Louis, Parochial Vicar.
Catechesis Religious Program—Tel: 718-451-1671; Fax: 718-451-1671. Frances McCormick, D.R.E.
150—St. Thomas Aquinas (1884) Merged with Holy Family to become Holy Family-St. Thomas Aquinas. For inquiries and parish records see Holy Family-St. Thomas Aquinas.
151—St. Thomas Aquinas (1885)
1550 Hendrickson St., 11234. Tel: 718-253-4404; Email: stainfo@stthomasaquinasbrooklyn.com. Revs. Dwayne D. Davis; Clifford Ekueme, Parochial Vicar; Kieran Udeze, Parochial Vicar.
Catechesis Religious Program—
Tel: 718-253-4404, Ext. 31; Fax: 718-338-7757. Robert Ruggiero, D.R.E. Students 109.
152—Transfiguration (1874)
263 Marcy Ave., 11211. Tel: 718-388-8773; Email: 101231@diobrook.org. Rev. Msgr. Anthony Hernandez, J.C.L.; Rev. Jeramias Castillo Liranzo, Parochial Vicar; Deacon Israel Rosario.
Catechesis Religious Program—Ms. Haling Perdomo-Mihalek, D.R.E.; Sr. Peggy Walsh, R.C.I.A. Coord. Students 135.
Southside Mission for Social Services, 280 Marcy Ave., 11211. Tel: 718-388-3784. John Mulhern, Dir.
153—St. Vincent de Paul, Closed. For inquiries for parish records contact the chancery.
154—St. Vincent Ferrer (1923)
1603 Brooklyn Ave., 11210-3495. Tel: 718-859-9009; Email: info@saintvincentferrer.org. Rev. Antonious Peter Gopaul.
Church: E. 37th St. & Glenwood Rd., 11210.
Catechesis Religious Program—Students 81.
155—Visitation of the Blessed Virgin Mary (1854)
98 Richards St., 11231. Tel: 718-624-1572; Email: padreclaudioa@hotmail.com. Revs. Claudio Antecini; Johannes S.A.G. Siegert, Parochial Vicar; Eamon G. Murray; Bro. Davide Cannatella; Sr. Frauke Tinat, Pastoral Assoc.
Catechesis Religious Program—Sylvia Dobles, D.R.E. Students 48.

*BOROUGH AND COUNTY OF QUEENS
1—St. Adalbert (1892) (Polish)
52-29 83rd St., Elmhurst, 11373. Tel: 718-639-0212; Email: 101001@diobrook.org. Revs. Miroslaw Podymniak, O.F.M.Conv., (Poland); Stanislaw Czerwonka, Parochial Vicar; Rapael Zwolenkiewicz; Herman Czaster, O.F.M.Conv., In Res.; Deacon Thomas J. Page.
Please see Saint Adalbert Catholic Academy under Consolidated Elementary Schools in Institutions Located in the Diocese section.
Catechesis Religious Program—
Tel: 718-565-8227. Mary Anne Page, D.R.E. Students 134.
Office for Pastoral Care of the Sick—
2—St. Aloysius (1892)
382 Onderdonk Ave., Ridgewood, 11385.
Tel: 718-821-0231; Email: gpsac@nyc.rr.com. Revs. George Poltorak, S.A.C.; Zbigniew Zieba, Parochial Vicar.
Catechesis Religious Program—
Tel: 718-417-6327. Students 406.
Pastoral Care Office—
Tel: 718-963-7689.
3—American Martyrs (1948)
79-43 Bell Blvd., Oakland Gardens, 11364.
Tel: 718-464-4582; Fax: 718-464-5488; Email: americanmartyrs@aol.com; Web: americanmartyrsqueens.org. Rev. Frank L. Schwarz; Deacon Stanley J. Galazin.
Catechesis Religious Program—
Tel: 718-464-6411. Theresa Asche, D.R.E. Students 159.
4—St. Anastasia (1915)
45-14 245th St., Douglaston, 11362.
Tel: 718-631-4454; Email: info@stanastasia.info. Rev. Msgr. Anthony F. Sherman; Rev. Mark C. Bristol, Parochial Vicar; Rev. Msgr. George J. Ryan, In Res., (Retired); Rev. Anthony M. Rucando, In Res., (Retired); Deacon Vincent A. Lino.
Catechesis Religious Program—
Tel: 718-225-5191. Janine Kramer, D.R.E. Students 164.
5—St. Andrew Avellino (1914)
35-60 158th St., Flushing, 11358. Tel: 718-359-0417; Email: revjholcomb@standrewavellinorcchurch.org. Revs. Joseph T. Holcomb; Ambiorix Osorio, Parochial Vicar; Rev. Msgr. Michael J. Brennan, V.E., (Retired).
Please see St. Andrew Avellino Catholic Academy under Consolidated Schools Elementary in the Institutions Located in the Diocese section.
Catechesis Religious Program—
Tel: 718-445-7012. Mrs. Maria Tortorella, D.R.E.; Sr. Aileen Halleran, S.C., RCIA Coord. Students 281.
6—St. Ann (1927) Merged with Mary's Nativity, Flushing to form Mary's Nativity-Saint Ann. For inquiries and parish records see Mary's Nativity-Saint Ann.
7—St. Anthony of Padua (1937) Merged with St. Teresa of Avila, South Ozone Park to form St. Teresa of Avila-St. Anthony of Padua, South Ozone Park. For inquiries and parish records see St. Teresa of Avila-St. Anthony of Padua.
8—Ascension (1945)
86-13 55th Ave., Elmhurst, 11373. Tel: 718-335-2626 ; Fax: 718-335-4181; Email: ascensionrcchurch@gmail.com. Revs. Jovito B. Carongay Jr.; Kyrian C. Echekwu, Parochial Vicar.
Catechesis Religious Program—Maria Gallo, D.R.E. Students 153.
9—St. Bartholomew (1906)
43-22 Ithaca St., Elmhurst, 11373. Tel: 718-424-5400 ; Email: stbartselmhurst@gmail.com. Revs. Richard J. Beuther; John J. Gildea, Parochial Vicar, (Retired).
Please see St. Bartholomew Catholic Academy under Consolidated Elementary Schools in the Institutions Located in the Diocese section.
Catechesis Religious Program—
44-15 Judge St., Elmhurst, 11373. Tel: 718-898-0096. Sr. Lucy Mendez, D.R.E. Students 1,047.
10—St. Benedict Joseph Labre (1892) (Spanish)
94-40 118th St., South Richmond Hill, 11419.
Tel: 718-849-4048; Email: tbenedictjoseph@gmail.com. Revs. Philip J. Pizzo, (Retired); John Tino, Parochial Vicar.
Catechesis Religious Program—
Tel: 718-849-0246. Mrs. Stephanie Zinser, D.R.E.; Teresa Gomez, R.C.I.A Coord. Students 112.
11—St. Benedict, the Moor (1932) (African American), Merged with St. Bonaventure to form St. Bonaventure-St. Benedict the Moor RC Church. For inquiries and parish records see St. Bonaventure-St. Benedict the Moor RC Church.
12—Blessed Sacrament (1929)
34-43 93rd St., Jackson Heights, 11372.
Tel: 718-639-3888; Fax: 718-478-5536; Email: blessacjh@aol.com; Web: www.blessedsacramentjacksonheightsny.com. Revs. Carlos Quijano, S.J.; Romel Penafiel, Parochial Vicar; Richard Hoare, In Res., (Retired); James Rodriguez, M.A., M.Div., In Res.
Catechesis Religious Program—
93-15 35th Ave., Jackson Heights, 11372.
Tel: 718-639-6159. Sisters Lizbeth Pimentel, P.C.M., D.R.E.; Maria Amador, P.C.M., D.R.E. Students 989.
Convent—
93-11 35th Ave., Jackson Heights, 11372.
Tel: 718-639-1545.
13—Blessed Trinity Roman Catholic Church (2008)
204-25 Rockaway Point Blvd., Rockaway Point, 11697. Tel: 718-634-6357; Fax: 718-634-6222; Email: blessedtrin@aol.com; Web: www.btparish.org. Revs. Peter J. Rayder; Reynolds Basilious, O.C.D.; Deacons Richard G. Lee; James F. Ruoff; Rev. Msgrs. John J. Bracken, (Retired); Ronald Newland; Joseph P. Nagle, In Res.
Additional Worship Sites:—
St. Thomas More-St. Edmund—
Church: 204-25 Rockaway Point Blvd., Rockaway Point, 11697.
St. Genevieve
Church: 6 Beach 178th St., Rockaway Point, 11697.
Catechesis Religious Program—Suzanne O'Connor, D.R.E. Students 224.
14—Blessed Virgin Mary, Help of Christians (1854)
70-31 48th Ave., Woodside, 11377. Tel: 718-672-4848 ; Fax: 718-457-4055; Email: bvmwoodside11377@aol.com; Web: stmarysofwinfield.com. Revs. Christopher M. O'Connor; Uririoghene Melchizedek Okrokoto, Parochial Vicar; Francis Rosario, Parochial Vicar; Deacon Leopoldo Montes.
Catechesis Religious Program—
Tel: 718-672-4784. Patricia Wise, D.R.E. Students 388.
15—St. Bonaventure (1932) Merged with St. Benedict, the Moor to form St. Bonaventure-St. Benedict the Moor RC Church. For inquiries and parish records see St. Bonaventure-St. Benedict the Moor RC Church.
16—St. Bonaventure-St. Benedict the Moor RC Church (2008)
171-17 110th Ave., Jamaica, 11434.
Tel: 718-526-4018; Email: xdxn94c@hotmail.com. Rev. Thaddeus Abraham, (India); Deacon Pascual Olivas.
Res.: 114-58 170th St., Jamaica, 11434.
Tel: 718-526-0040; Fax: 718-526-4825; Email: sst.bonaventure_benedictthemoor@yahoo.com.
Catechesis Religious Program—Mrs. Angela M. Lewis, D.R.E. Students 65.
17—Saint Camillus-Saint Virgilius (2008)
99-15 Rockaway Beach Blvd., Rockaway Beach, 11694. Tel: 718-634-8229; Email: camillusrc@aol.com. Rev. Richard J. Ahlemeyer; Very Rev. Thomas Basquel, C.S.Sp., Parochial Vicar; Revs. Charles Oppong; John Wtulich, In Res., (Retired).
St. Virgilius Church
210 Noel Rd., Broad Channel, 11693.
Tel: 718-634-5680; Fax: 718-424-1538.
Please see Saint Camillus Catholic Academy under Consolidated Elementary Schools in the Institutions Located in the Diocese section.
Catechesis Religious Program—
Tel: 718-634-8229 (St. Camillus);
Tel: 718-634-6237 (St. Virgilius). Sr. Mary Ann Kollmer, O.P., D.R.E. Students 193.
18—St. Catherine of Sienna (1920) Merged with St. Pascal Baylon, to form Our Lady of Light Roman Catholic Church. For inquiries and parish records see Our Lady of Light Roman Catholic Church.
19—Christ the King (1933)
145-39 Farmers Blvd., Springfield Gardens, 11434.
Tel: 718-528-6010; Fax: 718-949-3255; Email: christthekingsg@aol.com; Web: christthekingsg.org. Revs. Gordon P. Kusi, (Ghana); Mark T. Cregan; Deacon Lamont A. Blake.
Catechesis Religious Program—
Tel: 718-528-6010; Email: mdoylectk@verizon.net. Mary Doyle, D.R.E. Students 89.
20—St. Clare (1924)
137-35 Brookville Blvd., Rosedale, 11422.
Tel: 718-341-1018; Email: stclareqns@aol.com. Revs. Andrew L. Struzzieri, D.Min.; Anthony F. Rosado, Parochial Vicar; Deacons Richard L. Hurst; Christopher E. Barber.
Please see Saint Clare Catholic Academy Catholic Academy under Consolidated Elementary Schools in the Institutions Located in the Diocese section.
Catechesis Religious Program—
Tel: 718-527-6153. Lorena DeFilippis, D.R.E. Students 51.
21—St. Clement Pope (1908)
141-11 123rd Ave., South Ozone Park, 11436.
Tel: 718-529-0273; Email: st.clementpope@gmail.com. Revs. Anthony Tagbo Nzegwu, (Nigeria) Admin.; Michael Onyekwere; Ignatius Okoroji, S.D.V., Parochial Vicar; Deacon Nathaniel J. Smith.
Catechesis Religious Program—
120-09 141st St., Jamaica, 11436. Tel: 718-641-1915; Fax: 718-738-0588. Eugene C. Ikafor, D.R.E. Students 36.
22—Corpus Christi (1937)
31-30 61st St., Woodside, 11377. Tel: 718-278-8114; Fax: 718-278-3619; Email: ccparish@ccwoodsideny.org. Revs. Patrick J. West; James A. Hughes, Parochial Vicar; John O'Neill, Part-time; Deacon Juan J. Zhagnay.
Catechesis Religious Program—
Email: dre@ccwoodsideny.org. Augusto F. Lucero, D.R.E. Students 190.
23—St. Elizabeth (1873)
94-20 85th St., Ozone Park, 11416-1237.
Tel: 718-296-4900; Email: stelizabeth94office@gmail.com. Revs. Robert F. Barclay; Jude Zimoha, Parochial Vicar; Jose Avila, Parochial Vicar; Stanley Shinkut, Part Time; Wojciech Waligorski, Part Time.
Catechesis Religious Program—Students 128.
24—St. Fidelis (1856) (Irish—German)
123-06 14th Ave., College Point, 11356.
Tel: 718-445-6164; Email: stfidelischurch01@gmail.com. Rev. Msgr. Denis M. Herron; Revs. Joseph Vu, Parochial Vicar; Killick Pierrilus, Parochial Vicar; Deacons John Reichert; Daniel P. Donnelly.
Catechesis Religious Program—
Tel: 718-539-1249. Anna Klidas, D.R.E. & Dir. School Devel. Students 238.
St. Fidelis Mother and Child Residence
Tel: 718-353-4749.
25—St. Francis de Sales (1906)
129-16 Rockaway Beach Blvd., Belle Harbor, 11694.
Tel: 718-634-6464; Email: 101061@diobrook.org. Revs. William F. Sweeney; James K. Cunningham; Rev. Jose Marie Legaspi; Deacons Vincent M. LaGamba; Armand D'Accordo.
Please see St. Francis de Sales Catholic Academy under Consolidated Elementary Schools in the Institutions Located in the Diocese section.
Catechesis Religious Program—
Tel: 718-945-6911. Mrs. Virginia Clark, D.R.E. Students 346.
26—St. Francis of Assisi (1930)
21-17 45 St., Astoria, 11105. Tel: 718-728-7801; Email: rjmpastor@sfaacademy.org. Rev. Msgr. Ralph J. Maresca; Rev. Francis Kwame Asagba, J.C.L., Parochial Vicar; Deacons John Sucich; Savior Hili; Nicolino Scarlatto.
Catechesis Religious Program—
Tel: 718-278-0259. Mr. Richard Pipchinski, D.R.E. Students 108.
27—St. Gabriel (1923)
26-26 98th St., East Elmhurst, 11369.
Tel: 718-639-0474; Email: stgabriel26@verizon.net.

Revs. Gioacchino Basile; Robert J. Sadlack, Parochial Vicar.
Catechesis Religious Program—Students 291.
28—ST. GENEVIEVE, (German—Irish), Merged with St. Thomas More-St. Edmund to form Blessed Trinity Roman Catholic Church, Rockaway Point, NY. For inquiries and parish records see Blessed Trinity Roman Catholic Church.
29—ST. GERARD MAJELLA (1907)
188-16 91st Ave., Hollis, 11423-2520.
Tel: 718-468-6565; Email: saintgerardm@gmail.com. Revs. Josephjude C. Gannon; Joseph Tharackal; Dawit T. Moroda; Aloysius Enemali, J.C.D.; Deacon Laurence O. McMaster.
Catechesis Religious Program—
Tel: 718-468-1166, Ext. 22. Carmen Macchio, R.C.I.A. Coord. Students 143.
30—ST. GERTRUDE (1911) Merged with St. Mary Star of the Sea to form St. Mary Star of the Sea and St. Gertrude. Parish records at St. Mary Star of the Sea and St. Gertrude.
31—ST. GREGORY THE GREAT (1936)
242-20 88th Ave., Bellerose, 11426.
Tel: 718-347-3707; Email: stgregoffice@aol.com. Rev. Msgr. Edward A. Ryan; Revs. Johnson Nedungadan, C.M., (India); Szymon A. Galazyn, Parochial Vicar; Deacons Arthur Cutter; Robert Zeuner.
Please see St. Gregory the Great Catholic Academy under Consolidated Elementary Schools (Regional) located in the Institution section.
Catechesis Religious Program—
Tel: 718-347-0525. Regina Joyce, D.R.E. Students 153.
Convent—
88-19 Cross Island Pkwy., Bellerose, 11426. 242-11 88th Rd., Bellerose, 11426.
32—ST. HELEN (1960)
157-10 83rd St., Howard Beach, 11414.
Tel: 718-738-1616; Email: sthelenhbny@aol.com. Revs. Francis A. Colamaria; Lukasz Kubiak, Parochial Vicar; Rev. Msgr. Joseph C. Pfeiffer, In Res., (Retired); Deacons Andrew T. Mastrangelo; Richard E. Elrose.
Please see St. Helen Catholic Academy under Consolidated Elementary Schools in the Institutions Located in the Diocese section.
Catechesis Religious Program—
Tel: 718-835-6216. Ms. Sandra Pepitone, D.R.E. Students 383.
33—HOLY CHILD JESUS (1910)
111-11 86th Ave., Richmond Hill, 11418.
Tel: 718-847-1860; Fax: 718-847-2696; Email: hcjchurch@aol.com. Most Rev. Octavio Cisneros, D.D.; Revs. Christopher R. Heanue, Admin.; Francisco J. Ares, In Res.; Deacons Dean Tully; Raul S. Elias; Jeremiah W. Schwarz.
Please see Holy Child Jesus Catholic Academy under Consolidated Elementary Schools in the Institutions Located in the Diocese section.
Catechesis Religious Program—
Tel: 718-805-5771. Students 387.
34—HOLY CROSS (1913) (Polish)
61-21 56th Rd., Maspeth, 11378-2498.
Tel: 718-894-1387; Fax: 718-416-9245; Email: hc6121@aol.com. Rev. Andrzej Salwowski, Admin.; Most Rev. Witold Mroziewski, D.D., J.C.D.; Rev. Daniel K. Rajski, Parochial Vicar.
Catechesis Religious Program—Mrs. Jolanta Neubauer, D.R.E. Students 354.
35—HOLY FAMILY (1940)
175-20 74th Ave., Flushing, 11366-1529.
Tel: 718-969-2448; Email: holyfamilyflushing@gmail.com. Revs. Casper J. Furnari; Anacleto Asebias, Parochial Vicar; Ralph Edel; Deacon Eugene J. Cassidy.
Please see Holy Family Catholic Academy under Consolidated Elementary Schools in the Institutions Located in the Diocese section.
Catechesis Religious Program—
Tel: 718-591-6438. Barbara Makolin, D.R.E. Students 96.
Convent—
175-11 75 Ave., Flushing, 11366.
36—HOLY TRINITY (1965)
14-51 143rd St., Whitestone, 11357.
Tel: 718-746-7730; Email: holytrinityrcchurch@verizon.net. Revs. Joseph R. Gibino, Ph.D.; Vincent M. Daly, (Retired); Deacon Len Sclafani.
Please see Holy Trinity Catholic Academy under Consolidated Elementary Schools in the Institutions Located in the Diocese section.
Catechesis Religious Program—
Email: holytrinityfaithformation@verizon.net. Donna Marie Spoto, D.R.E. Students 238.
37—IMMACULATE CONCEPTION (1924)
86-45 Edgerton Blvd., Jamaica, 11432.
Tel: 718-739-0880; Email: TBrislin@cpprov.org. Revs. William Murphy, C.P.; Theophane Cooney, C.P., Parochial Vicar; Christopher Cleary, C.P., Parochial Vicar; Deacon Daniel R. Rodriguez.
Please see Immaculate Conception Catholic Academy under Consolidated Elementary Schools in the Institutions Located in the Diocese section.
Catechesis Religious Program—
86-16 Midland Pkwy., Jamaica, 11432.
Tel: 718-291-3080. Mrs. Ivonne Rodriguez, RCIA Coord. Students 260.
38—IMMACULATE CONCEPTION (1924)
21-47 29th St., Astoria, 11105. Tel: 718-728-1613; Email: pastor@immacastoria.org; Web: www.immacastoria.org. Rev. Msgr. Fernando A. Ferrarese; Revs. Liju Augustine, C.M.I., Parochial Vicar; William A. McLaughlin, Parochial Vicar; Rev. Msgrs. Charles P. Boccio, Senior Active Priest, (Retired); Vincent F. Fullam, In Res., (Retired); Deacons Elkin D. Tamayo; Francisco J. Hernandez.
Please see Immaculate Conception Catholic Academy in Astoria under Consolidated Elementary Schools (Regional) in the Institution section.
Catechesis Religious Program—
Tel: 718-956-4494. Marylyn Crum, D.R.E. Students 268.
Convent—
21-60 31st St., Long Island City, 11105.
Fax: 718-959-9229.
39—INCARNATION (1927)
89-43 Francis Lewis Blvd., Queens Village, 11427.
Tel: 718-465-8534; Email: 101095@diobrook.org. Very Rev. John J. O'Connor, S.L.L.; Rev. Christopher J. Bethge, Parochial Vicar; Deacons Francois Innocent; Franklin Munoz; Clemenceau Pierre-Antoine; Robinson Despeignes; Luis R. Lopez.
Please see Incarnation Catholic Academy under Consolidated Elementary Schools in the Institutions Located in the Diocese section.
Catechesis Religious Program—Sr. Joan Klimski, O.P., D.R.E. Students 159.
40—SS. JOACHIM AND ANNE (1896)
218-26 105 Ave., Queens Village, 11429.
Tel: 718-465-0124; Email: huguesberrette@yahoo.com. Revs. Hugues Berrette, Admin.; Jean-Francois Nixon, Parochial Vicar; Deacons Emmanuel Coty; Nery R. Escobar.
School—SS. Joachim and Anne School
218-19 105th Ave., Queens Village, 11429.
Tel: 718-465-2230; Fax: 718-468-5698. Linda Freebes, Prin. Lay Teachers 25; Sisters of Notre Dame de Namur 1; Students 490.
Catechesis Religious Program—Peggy Kerolle, D.R.E. Students 163.
41—ST. JOAN OF ARC (1920)
82-00 35th Ave., Jackson Heights, 11372.
Tel: 718-429-2333; Email: joanofarcqueens@aol.com. Rev. Msgr. Otto L. Garcia, J.C.D.; Revs. William K. Aguzey, Parochial Vicar; Johnson Chanassery, O.C.D., Parochial Vicar; Alexander Pinacue, Parochial Vicar; Stephen Valdazo, In Res., (Retired); Sr. Maryann McHugh, C.S.J., Pastoral Assoc.; Deacons Jaime A. Pinzon; Paulo A. Salazar.
School—St. Joan of Arc School
35-27 82nd St., Jackson Heights, 11372.
Tel: 718-639-9020; Fax: 718-639-5428; Email: sjaschool@juno.com; Web: www.sjaschoolny.com. John Fruner, Prin. Lay Teachers 25; Religious 1; Students 485.
Catechesis Religious Program—
Tel: 718-478-5593; Fax: 718-651-8485; Email: sjareled@netzero.com. Noemi Fitzgerald, D.R.E. Students 479.
42—ST. JOHN VIANNEY (1967)
140-10 34th Ave., Flushing, 11354.
Tel: 718-762-7920; Email: stjv@msn.com. Revs. Antonius Ho, C.S.J.B., (Taiwan); Victor Cao, C.S.J.B., Parochial Vicar; Tiancang Zheng, Parochial Vicar; Edward Zhang, C.S.J.B., In Res.; Sr. Monica Gan, C.S.T., Pastoral Assoc.; Deacons Howard H. Fu; Daniel A. Garcia; Stanley Tam.
Catechesis Religious Program—
Tel: 718-961-5092. Shin Hawy Chang, D.R.E. Students 224.
43—ST. JOSAPHAT (1910) (Polish)
34-32 210th St., Bayside, 11361. Tel: 718-229-1663; Email: stjosaphats@aol.com. Revs. Stephen A. Saffron, Admin.; Martin R. Kull, Sr. Active, (Retired); James J. Meszaros, In Res., (Retired).
Catechesis Religious Program—Students 24.
44—ST. JOSEPH (1904) (Polish)
108-43 Sutphin Blvd., Jamaica, 11435-5445.
Tel: 718-739-4781; Email: stjjamaica@gmail.com. Rev. Krystian J. Piasta, O.F.M.
Catechesis Religious Program—Nancy Baer, D.R.E. Students 61.
45—ST. JOSEPH (1877)
43-19 30th Ave., Astoria, 11103. Tel: 718-278-1611; Email: rectory@stjosephlic.org. Revs. Vincent F. Miceli; Cesar Pena, Parochial Vicar; William C. Farrugia, In Res., (Retired); Randy Rentner, In Res.
Please see St. Joseph Catholic Academy under Consolidated Elementary Schools (Regional) located in the Institution section.
Catechesis Religious Program—
Tel: 718-545-7338; Email: sjreled@gmail.com. Loretta Rosas, D.R.E. Students 348.
46—ST. KEVIN (1926)
45-21 194 St., Flushing, 11358. Tel: 718-357-8888; Email: stkevin194@gmail.com. Most Rev. Raymond F. Chappetto, D.D., V.G., V.E.; Rev. Robert Mema, Parochial Vicar; Rev. Msgrs. D. Joseph Finnerty, (Retired); Steven J. Aguggia, J.C.L., In Res.; Deacon Julio C. Barreneche.
Please see St. Kevin Catholic Academy under Consolidated Elementary Schools in the Institutions Located in the Diocese section.
Catechesis Religious Program—
Tel: 718-357-5317. Agnes Rus, D.R.E. Students 119.
47—ST. LEO (1903) (Hispanic—Italian)
104-05 49th Ave., Corona, 11368. Tel: 718-592-7569; Email: saintleo@earthlink.net. Revs. William M. Hoppe, J.C.L.; Diego Villegas, Parochial Vicar; Jose B. Diaz, Parochial Vicar; Johnson Chanassery, O.C.D., Parochial Vicar; Deacon Rodrigo A. Mendez.
Please see St. Leo Catholic Academy under Consolidated Elementary Schools in the Institutions Located in the Diocese section.
Catechesis Religious Program—
Tel: 718-699-8565. Mr. Conrado Hernandez, D.R.E. Students 319.
Mission—Our Lady of Mount Carmel
Corona. 103-56 52nd Ave., Corona, Queens Co. 11368. Tel: 718-592-7569.
48—ST. LUKE (1870)
16-34 Clintonville St., Whitestone, 11357. Rev. Msgr. John C. Tosi; Revs. Peter J. Penton, Parochial Vicar; Paul Y. Kim, Parochial Vicar.
School—St. Luke School
16-01 150th Pl., Whitestone, 11357.
Tel: 718-746-3833; Fax: 718-747-2101. Mrs. Barbara Reiter, Prin. Lay Teachers 32; Students 575.
Catechesis Religious Program—
Tel: 718-746-3409. Sr. Katherine Burke, C.S.J., D.R.E. Students 383.
49—ST. MARGARET (1860)
66-05 79th Pl., Middle Village, 11379.
Tel: 718-326-1911; Email: stmargaretmv@gmail.com. Rev. Robert J. Armato; Rev. Msgr. Robert J. Thelen, S.T.L., KCHS, Parochial Vicar; Revs. Joseph F. Wilson, Parochial Vicar; Michael S. Udoh; Sr. Bridget M. Olwell, O.S.U., Pastoral Assoc.
Please see Saint Margaret Catholic Academy under Consolidated Elementary Schools in the Institutions Located in the Diocese section.
Catechesis Religious Program—
Tel: 718-381-4048. Dolores Voyer, D.R.E. Students 383.
50—ST. MARGARET MARY (1961) Merged with Our Lady of Mount Carmel in 2007. For inquiries and parish records see Our Lady of Mount Carmel, Astoria.
51—ST. MARY (1868)
10-08 49th Ave., Long Island City, 11101.
Tel: 718-786-0705; Email: stmarylic@yahoo.com. Rev. Ralph E. Barile, (Retired); Rev. Msgr. Joseph C. Mulqueen, J.C.L., Sr. Active, (Retired).
Catechesis Religious Program—Students 132.
52—ST. MARY GATE OF HEAVEN (1904)
101-25 104th St., Ozone Park, 11416.
Tel: 718-847-5957; Email: pa381@rcdob.org. Revs. Carlos C. Velasquez; Baltazar Alonzo, Parochial Vicar; Deacons Richard Gilligan; Timothy McBride; Ramon Cruz.
Please see St. Mary Gate of Heaven Catholic Academy under Consolidated Elementary Schools in the Institutions Located in the Diocese section.
Catechesis Religious Program—
Tel: 718-849-9329. Ann Farrell, D.R.E. Students 261.
53—ST. MARY MAGDALENE (1913)
218-12 136th Ave., Springfield Gardens, 11413.
Tel: 718-949-4311; Email: 101126@diobrook.org. Revs. Gordon P. Kusi, (Ghana) Admin.; Cosmas Nzeabalu, Parochial Vicar; Deacons Lee C. Williams; Ernest F. Hart; Sr. Maryellen Kane, C.S.J., Pastoral Assoc.
Catechesis Religious Program—Students 78.
54—ST. MARY STAR OF THE SEA (1857) Merged with St. Gertrude to form St. Mary Star of the Sea and St. Gertrude. For inquiries and parish records see St. Mary Star of the Sea and St. Gertrude.
55—ST. MARY STAR OF THE SEA AND ST. GERTRUDE (2008)
1920 New Haven Ave., Far Rockaway, 11691. Email: 101268@diobrook.org. Revs. Francis T. Shannon; David P. Bertolotti, In Res.; Charles H. White, In Res., (Retired); Deacons Rene Hernandez; Adalberto Montero; Michael C. Moss.
Worship Site: St. Gertrude
Church: 336 Beach 38th St., Far Rockaway, 11691.
Catechesis Religious Program—Students 262.
56—MARY'S NATIVITY (1926) Merged with St. Ann, Flushing to form Mary's Nativity-St. Ann. For inquiries and parish records see Mary's Nativity-St. Ann.
57—MARY'S NATIVITY-SAINT ANN ROMAN CATHOLIC

CHURCH (2012)
46-02 Parsons Blvd., Flushing, 11355.
Tel: 718-359-5996; Email: 101278@diobrook.org; Web: www.marynatstann.org. Revs. Edward M. Kachurka; Louis J. DeGaetano, Parochial Vicar; Jed Sumampong, C.P., Parochial Vicar; Enel Almeus, C.S.Sp.; George A. Pfundstein, Sr. Active, (Retired); Rev. Msgr. Edward J. Bottino, Sr. Active, (Retired); Deacon Elias Yepes.
Worship Site: St. Ann—
142-30 58th Ave., Flushing, 11355-5314.
Tel: 718-886-3890; Fax: 718-358-4964.
Church & Convent: Jasmine Ave. & Parsons Blvd., Flushing, 11355.
Catechesis Religious Program—
142-25 58th Rd., Flushing, 11355. Tel: 718-359-5961; Email: marynatstannoff@aol.com. Mr. Christian S. Rada, D.R.E. Students 73.

58—ST. MATTHIAS (1908)
58-15 Catalpa Ave., Ridgewood, 11385.
Tel: 718-821-6447; Email: 101132@diobrook.org. Most Rev. Neil E. Tiedemann, C.P., D.D.; Revs. Dariusz Piotr Blicharz, J.C.D., Admin.; Sebastian T. Andro, Parochial Vicar; Deacons John E. Sands; Oscar R. Perez.
Please see St. Matthias Catholic Academy under Consolidated Elementary Schools in the Institutions Located in the Diocese section.
Catechesis Religious Program—
Tel: 718-386-1077; Fax: 718-821-6876. Students 276.

59—ST. MEL (1941)
26-15 154th St., Flushing, 11354. Tel: 718-886-0201; Email: 101133@diobrook.org. Revs. Gerard J. Sauer; Jun Hee Lee, Parochial Vicar; Italo Barozzi, (Retired); Deacon Joseph A. Freda.
Please see St. Mel Catholic Academy under Consolidated Elementary Schools in the Institutions Located in the Diocese section.
Catechesis Religious Program—
Tel: 718-461-9840; Fax: 718-886-0882. Ms. Paula Migliore, D.R.E. Students 172.

60—ST. MICHAEL (1833)
136-76 41st Ave., Flushing, 11355. Tel: 718-961-0295 ; Email: stmichael1833@aol.com. Revs. John E. Vesey; Jaime Hernandez, Parochial Vicar; Lianjiang Peter Bai, Parochial Vicar; Rev. Msgr. Edward V. Wetterer, (Retired); Sr. Jane A. Scanlon, C.N.D., M.Div., Pastoral Assoc.
School—St. Michael School
136-58 41st Ave., Flushing, 11355. Tel: 718-961-0246 ; Email: rogonesms@aol.com. Mrs. Maureen Rogone, Prin. Lay Teachers 10; Religious 2; Students 201.
Catechesis Religious Program—
138-25 Barclay Ave., Flushing, 11355.
Tel: 718-961-0312. Students 344.

61—ST. MONICA, (Jamaica), Closed. For inquiries for parish records contact the chancery.

62—MOST PRECIOUS BLOOD (1922)
32-23 36th St., Long Island City, 11106.
Tel: 718-278-3337; Email: mpb1922@yahoo.com. Revs. William F. Krlis, (Retired); Vedran Kirincic, Parochial Vicar; Grzegorz Dziedzic, Parochial Vicar; Jean G. Laguerre, (Haiti) In Res.; Deacon Hector Rodriguez.
School—Most Precious Blood School
32-52 37th St., Long Island City, 11103.
Tel: 718-278-4081; Fax: 718-278-3089. Barbara DeMaio, Prin. Lay Teachers 22; Students 318.
Catechesis Religious Program—
Tel: 718-721-9850. Mrs. Cecelia Uriguen, D.R.E. Students 229.
Convent—
32-16 36th St., Long Island City, 11106.
Tel: 718-278-4706.

63—NATIVITY OF THE BLESSED VIRGIN MARY (1925) Merged with St. Stanislaus Bishop & Martyr, Ozone Park to form Nativity of the Blessed Virgin Mary-St. Stanislaus Bishop & Martyr Roman Catholic Church, Ozone Park. For inquiries and parish records see Nativity of the Blessed Virgin Mary-St. Stanislaus Bishop & Martyr Roman Catholic Church.

64—NATIVITY OF THE BLESSED VIRGIN MARY-SAINT STANISLAUS (2011)
101-41 91st St., Ozone Park, 11416.
Tel: 718-845-3691; Email: nativitystistans@verizon.net. Revs. Paul C. Palmiotto; Angelo B. Pezzullo, (Retired); Jean Farda Tanisma, Parochial Vicar; Ryszard Koper, (Poland) Parochial Vicar; Deacon Edward J. Guster Jr.
Legal Name: Nativity of the Blessed Virgin Mary-Saint Stanislaus Bishop and Martyr Roman Catholic Church
Worship Site: St. Stanislaus, Bishop & Martyr
88-10 102nd Ave., Ozone Park, 11416.
Catechesis Religious Program—
101-41 91st St., Ozone Park, 11416.
Tel: 718-845-1524. Elizabeth Perretta, D.R.E. Students 200.

65—ST. NICHOLAS OF TOLENTINE (1916)
150-75 Goethals Ave., Jamaica, 11432.
Tel: 718-969-3226; Email: jfs777@aol.com. Revs. John Francis; John Gribowich, Parochial Vicar; Thomas Joseph, Parochial Vicar; Lucon Rigaud, Parochial Vicar; Anthony F. Rosado, Parochial Vicar; Benjamin Madu, In Res.; Abraham P. Mathew, In Res., (Retired); Deacons Joseph Catanello; Thomas E. Jorge.
Please see St. Nicholas of Tolentine Catholic Academy under Consolidated Elementary Schools in the Institutions Located in the Diocese section.
Catechesis Religious Program—
150-85 Goethals Ave., Jamaica, 11432.
Tel: 718-591-6536. Monica Gonzalez, D.R.E. Students 220.

66—OUR LADY OF CHINA CHAPEL (1978) Attended by St. John Vianney, Flushing Revs. Antonius Ho, C.S.J.B., (Taiwan); Dehua Zhang, C.S.J.B.
Office: 54-09 92nd St., Elmhurst, 11373.
Tel: 718-699-1929; Email: olcny@msn.com; Web: olc.faithweb.com.
School—Ming Yuan Chinese School
54-17 90th St., Elmhurst, 11373. Tel: 718-271-3944; Email: brotherli2000@yahoo.com. Bro. Peter Li, C.S.J.B., Prin. Lay Teachers 10; Students 350; Religious Teachers 10.
Catechesis Religious Program—
Tel: 718-961-5092; Fax: 718-460-8032.

67—OUR LADY OF FATIMA (1948)
25-02 80th St., Jackson Heights, 11370.
Tel: 718-899-2801; Email: olfatima11370@msn.com. 25-38 80th St., Jackson Heights, 11370. Revs. Darrell Da Costa; Ricardo Perez, Parochial Vicar; Gabriel A. Ahiarakwem, In Res.; James Fedigan, In Res.; Patrick J. Frawley, In Res.; Deacons Marco Lopez; Fabio Parra.
School—Our Lady of Fatima School
25-38 80th St., Jackson Heights, 11370.
Tel: 718-429-7031; Fax: 718-899-2811. Mrs. Cassie Zelic, Prin. Lay Teachers 28; Students 536.
Catechesis Religious Program—
25-56 80th St., Jackson Heights, 11370.
Tel: 718-457-3457. Sr. Patricia Reills, D.R.E. Students 226.
Convent—
25-56 80th St., Jackson Heights, 11370.
Tel: 718-747-3457.

68—OUR LADY OF GRACE (1924)
100-05 159th Ave., Howard Beach, 11414.
Tel: 718-843-6218; Email: olghowardbeach@nyc.rr.com. Revs. Marc E. Swartvagher, S.T.L., Ph.D.; Chidi Benedict; James J. Krische, In Res.; Deacon Alexander Breviario.
Catechesis Religious Program—
Tel: 718-835-2165; Fax: 718-835-4524. Matthew Zinser, D.R.E. Students 331.

69—OUR LADY OF HOPE (1960)
61-27 71st St., Middle Village, 11379.
Tel: 718-429-5438; Fax: 718-429-2764; Email: olhrectory1@yahoo.com; Email: macarrano@juno.com; Web: www.ourladyofhopeparish.org. Revs. Michael A. Carrano; Noel Daduya, Parochial Vicar; Cezariusz W. Jastrzebski, Parochial Vicar; Deacons Robert F. Lavanco; Paul Norman.
Please see Our Lady of Hope Catholic Academy under Consolidated Elementary Schools in the Institutions Located in the Diocese section.
Catechesis Religious Program—
Tel: 718-335-8394; Email: ajcdon23@aol.com. Karen Colletti, D.R.E. Students 330.

70—OUR LADY OF LIGHT ROMAN CATHOLIC CHURCH (2008)
Tel: 718-528-1220; Email: 101269@diobrook.org. Revs. Jeffry T. Dillon; Michael O. Ugbor, Parochial Vicar; Deacons Albert Saldana; Luis C. Taylor; Freddy Torres.
Res.: 118-22 Riverton St., St. Albans, 11412.
Tel: 718-528-1220; Fax: 718-528-7907; Email: info@ourladyoflightparish.com; Web: www.ourladyoflightparish.com.
Rectory—
Tel: 718-468-3511; Fax: 718-479-2303.
Additional Worship Sites:—
St. Catherine of Sienna—
Church: 118-22 Riverton St., St. Albans, 11412.
St. Pascal Baylon
Church: 112-43 198th St., St. Albans, 11412.
*Catechesis Religious Program—*Sr. Mary Jane Rolston, O.P., D.R.E. Students 63.

71—OUR LADY OF LOURDES (1924)
92-96 220th St., Queens Village, 11428.
Tel: 718-479-5111; Email: 101160@diobrook.org. Revs. Patrick H. Longalong; Anthony Gonzalez, Parochial Vicar; Rev. Msgrs. Robert J. Pawson, In Res., (Retired); John F. Casey, In Res., (Retired); Rev. Robert Ambalathingal, In Res., (Retired); Deacons Ricardo Moreno; Walter C. Zimmermann.
Please see Our Lady of Lourdes Catholic Academy under Consolidated Elementary Schools in the Institutions Located in the Diocese section.
Catechesis Religious Program—
Tel: 718-740-4090. Joanne Russo, D.R.E. Students 244.

72—OUR LADY OF MERCY (1930)
70-01 Kessel St., Forest Hills, 11375.
Tel: 718-268-6143; Email: office@mercyhills.org. Rev. Msgr. John A. McGuirl; Rev. Grzegorz Stasiak, (Poland) Parochial Vicar; Deacons Edward Smolinski; Dean Dobbins.
Please see Our Lady of Mercy Catholic Academy under Consolidated Elementary Schools in the Institutions Located in the Diocese section.
Catechesis Religious Program—
70-20 Juno St., Forest Hills, 11375.
Tel: 718-261-6285; Web: www.olmreligioused.com. Susan Karcher, D.R.E. Students 135.

73—OUR LADY OF MOUNT CARMEL (1841)
23-25 Newtown Ave., Long Island City, 11102.
Tel: 718-278-1834; Email: church@mountcarmelastoria.org. Rev. Msgr. Sean G. Ogle; Revs. Josephtan Pham, Parochial Vicar, (Retired); Peter Nguyen, C.S.J.B., Parochial Vicar; Wladyslaw Z. Kubrak, Parochial Vicar; Michael J. McHugh, Parochial Vicar.
Additional Worship Site:—
St. Margaret Mary
Church: 9-18 27th Ave., Long Island City, 11102.
Catechesis Religious Program—
Fax: 718-278-0998. Students 353.

74—OUR LADY OF PERPETUAL HELP (1923)
111-50 115th St., South Ozone Park, 11420.
Tel: 718-843-1212; Email: olphchurchqns@hotmail.com. Rev. Thomas W. Ahern; Deacon Jorge L. Alvarado.
Please see Our Lady of Perpetual Help Catholic Academy (South Ozone Park) under Consolidated Elementary Schools in the Institutions Located in the Diocese section.
Catechesis Religious Program—
Tel: 718-641-6165. Angel Rivera, D.R.E. Students 117.

75—OUR LADY OF SORROWS (1876)
104-11 37th Ave., Corona, 11368. Tel: 718-424-7554; Email: rectory@olschurch-corona.org. Revs. Raymond Roden; Angel Medrano-Matos; Deacons Daniel Diaz; Jose F. Tineo.
Please see Our Lady of Sorrows Catholic Academy under Consolidated Elementary Schools in the Institutions Located in the Diocese section.
Catechesis Religious Program—
Tel: 718-651-5682; Email: olsccd@aol.com. Aurora De La Cruz, D.R.E. Students 1,705.

76—OUR LADY OF THE ANGELUS (1938)
63-63 98th St., Rego Park, 11374. Tel: 718-897-4444; Email: frjohn6363@gmail.com. Revs. John Mendonca; Jose Munoz, Parochial Vicar; Robert Mirsel, S.V.D., In Res.; Deacon Edwin Cancel.
Please see Our Lady of the Angelus Catholic Academy under Consolidated Elementary Schools in the Institutions Located in the Diocese section.
Catechesis Religious Program—
Tel: 718-896-4388. Sr. Gladys Smith, D.R.E. Students 169.

77—OUR LADY OF THE BLESSED SACRAMENT (1930)
34-24 203rd St., Bayside, 11361. Tel: 718-229-5929; Email: frbob@olbs-queens.org. Revs. Robert J. Whelan; Bryan D. Patterson, Parochial Vicar; Brian Carney, In Res.; Deacons Ernesto A. Avallone; William Molloy.
Please see Our Lady of the Blessed Sacrament Catholic Academy under Consolidated Elementary Schools in the Institutions Located in the Diocese section.
Catechesis Religious Program—
Tel: 718-225-6179. Sr. Carla Lorenz, P.B.V.M., D.R.E. Students 153.

78—OUR LADY OF THE CENACLE (1922)
136-06 87th Ave., Richmond Hill, 11418.
Tel: 718-291-2540; Email: olcqueens@gmail.com. Revs. Michael Lynch, S.T.L.; Robert P. Morales, (Retired); Andre F. Saint Preux, S.D.B., In Res.; Pablo Sans, In Res., (Retired); Deacons Eduardo Sencion; Jose Mauricio Rosales.
*Catechesis Religious Program—*Lourdes A. Rodriguez, D.R.E.; Mrs. Marie J. Mondesir, D.R.E. Students 184.

79—OUR LADY OF THE MIRACULOUS MEDAL (1917)
62-81 60th Pl., Ridgewood, 11385. Tel: 718-366-3360; Email: OLMM11385@aol.com. Revs. Anthony J. Sansone; Jaroslaw Szeraszewicz, Parochial Vicar; Johny C. Thomas, Parochial Vicar; Deacon James E. Maloney.
Please see Notre Dame Catholic Academy, Ridgewood under Consolidated Elementary Schools (Regional) located in the Institution section.
Catechesis Religious Program—
Tel: 718-456-3275. Mary Macchiaroli, D.R.E. Students 190.

80—OUR LADY OF THE SKIES CHAPEL (1955) Rev. Krystian J. Piasta, O.F.M., Admin.
Chapel—
JFK International Airport, Terminal 4, Jamaica,

11430. Tel: 718-656-5348; Fax: 718-656-8162; Email: jfkchapel@gmail.com; Web: www.jfkchapel.org.

81—OUR LADY OF THE SNOWS (1948)
258-15 80th Ave., Floral Park, 11004.
Tel: 718-347-6070; Email: church@olsnows.org. Revs. Kevin F. McBrien, S.T.L.; Awoke Alemu Adulo; Raynald B. Nacino, (Philippines) Parochial Vicar; Jeremy A.J. Canna, Parochial Vicar; Deacons Henry J. Smith; Matthew Oellinger; Steven Borheck; John Warren; Kevin F. Hughes; Mrs. Regina Moreno, Pastoral Assoc.
Please see Our Lady of the Snows Catholic Academy under Consolidated Elementary Schools in the Institutions Located in the Diocese section.
Catechesis Religious Program—
Tel: 718-347-3511; Email: rel.ed@olsnows.org. Mrs. Regina Moreno, D.R.E. Students 254.

82—OUR LADY QUEEN OF MARTYRS (1917)
110-06 Queens Blvd., Forest Hills, 11375.
Tel: 718-268-6251; Email: rectoryolqm@aol.com. Most Rev. Paul R. Sanchez, D.D.; Rev. Francis J. Passenant, Admin.; Rev. Msgr. Joseph L. Cunningham, S.T.L., Sr. Active, (Retired); Rev. Antonin Kocurek, Parochial Vicar; Deacons Gregory Kandra; Thomas E. Jorge; Mr. Dennis Portelli, Pastoral Assoc.
Please see Our Lady Queens of Martyrs Catholic Academy under Consolidated Elementary Schools in the Institutions Located in the Diocese section.
Catechesis Religious Program—
Tel: 718-263-0907; Email: olqmreled@verizon.net. Students 200.

83—ST. PANCRAS (1904)
72-22 68th St., Glendale, 11385. Tel: 718-821-2323; Email: 101180@diobrook.org. Revs. Francis J. Hughes; Wladyslaw Z. Kubrak, Parochial Vicar; Daniel K. Rajski, Parochial Vicar.
School—St. Pancras School
68-20 Myrtle Ave., Glendale, 11385.
Tel: 718-821-6721; Fax: 718-418-8991. Mr. Philip Ciani, Prin. Lay Teachers 13; Students 127.
Catechesis Religious Program—
Tel: 718-479-0590. Juan Perez, D.R.E. Students 176.
Convent—
72-25 68th St., Glendale, 11385.

84—ST. PASCAL BAYLON (1930) (African American), Merged with St. Catherine of Sienna to form Our Lady of Light Roman Catholic Church. For inquiries and parish records see Our Lady of Light Roman Catholic Church.

85—ST. PATRICK (1869)
39-38 29th St., Long Island City, 11101.
Tel: 718-729-6060; Email: stpatlic@yahoo.com. Revs. Robert M. Powers; Charles F. Gilley, I.V.Dei., In Res.; Deacon Carlos A. Trochez.
Catechesis Religious Program—
Tel: 718-706-0565; Fax: 718-706-0565. Mrs. Rosa Gomez, D.R.E. Students 1.

86—ST. PAUL CHONG HA-SANG ROMAN CATHOLIC CHAPEL (2006) (Korean)
32-15 Parsons Blvd., Flushing, 11354.
Tel: 718-321-7676; Email: Fr.AndrewKim@gmail.com. Revs. Andrew M. Kim; Heebong Nam, Parochial Vicar; Chulhee Simon Kim, Parochial Vicar; Joseph R. Veneroso, M.M., D.R.E.; Sr. Franka Han.
Catechesis Religious Program—Students 240.
Convent—Olivetan Benedictine Sisters
32-15 Parsons Blvd., Flushing, 11354.

87—ST. PAUL THE APOSTLE (1964)
98-16 55 Ave., Corona, 11368. Tel: 718-271-1100; Email: stpaulcorona@verizon.net. Rev. Carlos A. Agudelo, Admin.; Deacon Fernando Orozco.
Catechesis Religious Program—Students 329.

88—ST. PIUS V (1908)
106-12 Liverpool St., Jamaica, 11435.
Tel: 718-739-3731; Email: stpiusvqueens@gmail.com. Rev. Felix Sanchez, Admin.; Deacon Alfredo Castellanos.
Catechesis Religious Program—Marthe Helmany, D.R.E. Students 84.

89—ST. PIUS X (1960)
148-10 249th St., Rosedale, 11422. Tel: 718-525-9099 ; Email: stpiusxrestore@aol.com. Rev. Jean-Miguel Auguste.
Catechesis Religious Program—Marilyne Jean, D.R.E. Students 40.

90—PRESENTATION OF THE BLESSED VIRGIN MARY (1886)
88-19 Parsons Blvd., Jamaica, 11432.
Tel: 718-739-0241; Email: pbvmsec@msn.com. Revs. Manuel de Jesus Rodriguez; Pedro S. Guerrero, Parochial Vicar; Victor M. Bolanos, Parochial Vicar; Deacons John Solarte; Joseph H. Dass.
Providence House III—
159-23 89th Ave., Jamaica, 11432. Tel: 718-739-1348 .
Youth Ministry Office—
88-13 Parsons Blvd., Jamaica, 11432.
Tel: 718-739-2003; Fax: 718-526-8153.
Catechesis Religious Program—Ms. Beverley Madar, D.R.E. Students 372.

91—QUEEN OF ANGELS (1953)
44-04 Skillman Ave., Long Island City, 11104.
Tel: 718-392-0011; Email: Pastor@queenofangelssnyc.org. Very Rev. Brian P. Dowd; Rev. Msgr. Jonas Achacoso, J.C.D., Parochial Vicar; Very Rev. Thomas G. Pettei, In Res.; Mr. Juan Rodriguez, Pastoral Assoc.
Catechesis Religious Program—
Tel: 718-937-5174. Students 179.

92—QUEEN OF PEACE (1939)
141-36 77th Ave., Flushing, 11367.
Tel: 718-380-5031; Email: queenofpeacerectory@outlook.com. Rev. James L. Tighe; Deacons Jose M. Fernandez; Gregory Bizzoco.
Catechesis Religious Program—Gregory J. Bizzoco Jr., D.R.E. Students 105.
Convent—
Tel: 718-380-4293.

93—ST. RAPHAEL (1868)
35-20 Greenpoint Ave., Long Island City, 11101.
Tel: 718-729-8957; Email: straphaelrectory@yahoo.com. Revs. Jerome T. Jecewicz; Kuno Kim, Parochial Vicar.
Catechesis Religious Program—Sr. Christine Scherer, D.W., D.R.E. Students 90.

94—RESURRECTION-ASCENSION (1926)
61-11 85th St., Rego Park, 11374. Tel: 718-424-5212; Email: rachsch@aol.com. Rev. Salvatore J. Amato.
Please see Resurrection Ascension Catholic Academy under Consolidated Elementary Schools in the Institutions Located in the Diocese section.
Catechesis Religious Program—
Tel: 718-533-7898. Ms. Joyce Mennona, D.R.E. Students 95.

95—ST. RITA (1900)
36-25 11th St., Long Island City, 11106.
Tel: 718-361-1884; Email: jcsnyc2@hotmail.com. Rev. Jose Carlos Da Silva; Deacon Fernando E. Luces.
Catechesis Religious Program—
Tel: 718-361-1884; Fax: 718-786-4573. Helen Foster, D.R.E. Students 135.

96—ST. ROBERT BELLARMINE (1939)
56-15 213th St., Bayside, 11364. Tel: 718-229-6465; Email: SRB@NYC.RR.COM. Revs. Gabriel Lee; Godofredo Felicitas, (Philippines) Parochial Vicar; Pilkoo Hwang, Parochial Vicar; Rev. Msgr. Martin T. Geraghty, (Retired); Deacon Michael J. Brainerd.
Please see Divine Wisdom Catholic Academy under Consolidated Elementary Schools in the Institutions Located in the Diocese section.
Catechesis Religious Program—
Tel: 718-225-3181. Lisa Sampson, D.R.E. Students 228.

97—ST. ROSE OF LIMA (1886)
130 Beach 84th St., Rockaway Beach, 11693.
Tel: 718-634-7394; Email: saintrosepastor@gmail.com. Revs. James A. Kuroly, Admin.; Slawomir Sobiech, Parochial Vicar; Robert W. Czok, (Retired); Deacon Juan M. Carattini.
Please see St. Rose of Lima Catholic Academy under Consolidated Elementary Schools in the Institutions Located in the Diocese section.
Catechesis Religious Program—
Tel: 718-945-4850; Email: job616@aol.com. Students 146.

98—SACRED HEART
115-58 222nd St., Cambria Heights, 11411.
Tel: 718-528-0577; Email: Rectory@sacredheartny.com. Revs. Hilaire Belizaire; Franklin Ezeorah, Parochial Vicar; Deacons Paul Dorsinville; Francois G. Cajoux.
Please see Sacred Heart Catholic Academy under Consolidated Elementary Schools in the Institutions Located in the Diocese section.
Catechesis Religious Program—Sr. Vilma Orejola, F.L.P., RCIA Coord. Students 79.

99—SACRED HEART (1931)
83-17 78th Ave., East Glendale, 11385.
Tel: 718-821-6434; Email: sacredheartglendale@verizon.net. Revs. Fred Marano; Marcin L. Chilczuk, Parochial Vicar; John J. Fullum, (Retired); Deacon Peter Stamm.
Please see Sacred Heart Catholic Academy of Glendale under Consolidated Elementary Schools in the Institutions Located in the Diocese section.
Catechesis Religious Program—
Tel: 718-386-5616. Mrs. Laura Ciraolo, D.R.E. Students 364.

100—SACRED HEART OF JESUS (1878)
215-35 38th Ave., Bayside, 11361. Tel: 718-428-2200; Email: pastorsacredheartbayside@gmail.com. Rev. Msgr. Thomas C. Machalski Jr., M.S.Ed., J.C.L.; Sr. Kathleen Masterson, R.S.M., Pastoral Assoc.; Deacon John F. DeBiase.
Please see Sacred Heart Catholic Academy of Bayside under Consolidated Elementary Schools in the Institutions Located in the Diocese section.
Catechesis Religious Program—
Tel: 718-631-1307. Mrs. Georgette Lyons, D.R.E. Students 201.

101—ST. SEBASTIAN (1894)
39-63 57th St., Woodside, 11377. Tel: 718-429-4442; Email: Kabels@saintsebastianwoodside.org. Revs. Kevin P. Abels, B.A., M.Div.; Rodnev Lapommeray, Parochial Vicar; Joey Francisco, Parochial Vicar; Henry Torres, Parochial Vicar; Deacon Stephen Damato.
Please see St. Sebastian Catholic Academy under Consolidated Elementary Schools in the Institutions Located in the Diocese section.
Catechesis Religious Program—
39-66 58th St., Woodside, 11377. Tel: 718-899-3341. Ms. Sonia Casanova, D.R.E. Students 404.

102—ST. STANISLAUS BISHOP AND MARTYR (1923) (Polish), Merged with Nativity of the Blessed Virgin Mary, Ozone Park to form Nativity of the Blessed Virgin Mary-St. Stanislaus Bishop & Martyr Roman Catholic Church, Ozone Park. For inquiries and parish records see Nativity of the Blessed Virgin Mary-St. Stanislaus Bishop & Martyr Roman Catholic Church.

103—ST. STANISLAUS KOSTKA (1872)
57-15 61st St., Maspeth, 11378-2713.
Tel: 718-326-2185; Email: StStanislausKostka@CatholicWeb.com. Rev. Msgr. Joseph P. Calise; Rev. Joseph Palackal, C.M.I., (India) Parochial Vicar; Deacon David J. Ciorciari.
School—St. Stanislaus Kostka School
61-17 Grand Ave., Maspeth, 11378.
Tel: 718-326-1585; Fax: 718-326-1745; Web: www.ststansschool.org. Sr. Rose Torma, C.S.J., Prin. Lay Teachers 18; Students 216.
Catechesis Religious Program—Students 108.

104—ST. TERESA (1928)
50-20 45th St., Woodside, 11377. Tel: 718-784-2123; Email: 101224@diobrook.org. Rev. Msgr. Steven A. Ferrari, V.E.; Rev. Gary H. Sommermeyer, (Retired); Deacons Martin Soraire; Roberto Abundo; Norberto Saldana, Pastoral Assoc.
Catechesis Religious Program—
Tel: 718-937-4819. Sr. Mary Jane Kelly, O.P., D.R.E. Students 244.

105—ST. TERESA OF AVILA (1929) Merged with St. Anthony of Padua, Flushing to form Saint Teresa of Avila-Saint Anthony of Padua. For inquiries and parish records see Saint Teresa of Avila-Saint Anthony of Padua.

106—SAINT TERESA OF AVILA-SAINT ANTHONY OF PADUA (2012)
109-26 130th St., South Ozone Park, 11420.
Tel: 718-529-3587; Email: 101279@diobrook.org. Revs. Richard W. Conlon; Schned Bruno, Parochial Vicar; Deacons Patrick M. Flanagan; Ruben G. Siavichay.
Res.: 133-25 128th St., South Ozone Park, 11420-3303. Tel: 718-843-7410; Tel: 718-843-3356; Fax: 718-659-1478.
Worship Site: St. Anthony of Padua
127-17 135th Ave, South Ozone Park, 11421.
School—Saint Teresa of Avila-Saint Anthony of Padua School.
Catechesis Religious Program—
Tel: 718-641-5710. Mr. Mark Kruse, D.R.E. Students 82.

107—ST. THOMAS APOSTLE (1910)
87-19 88th Ave., Woodhaven, 11421.
Tel: 718-847-1353; Email: stthomasapostlewdhvn@verizon.net. Rev. Frank C. Tumino; Rev. Msgr. Edward V. Wetterer, (Retired); Deacon Jose A. Contreras.
Please see St. Thomas the Apostle Catholic Academy under Consolidated Elementary Schools in the Institutions Located in the Diocese section.
Catechesis Religious Program—
Tel: 718-441-8409. Sr. Helene Jakubowski, R.S.M., D.R.E. Students 240.

108—ST. THOMAS MORE-ST. EDMUND (1937) Merged with St. Genevieve to form Blessed Trinity Roman Catholic Church, Rockaway Point, NY. For inquiries and parish records see Blessed Trinity Roman Catholic Church.

109—TRANSFIGURATION (1908) (Lithuanian)
64-14 Clinton Ave., Maspeth, 11378.
Tel: 718-326-2236; Email: Transfiguration@CatholicWeb.com. Rev. Msgr. Joseph P. Calise; Revs. Vytautas Volertas, Parochial Vicar; Edward P. Doran, Ph.D., (Retired); Deacons William Oggeri; Arthur J. Griffin; Edward F. O'Connell.
Catechesis Religious Program—Students 73.

110—ST. VIRGILIUS (1914) Merged with St. Camillus in 2008 to form St. Camillus-St. Virgilius. For inquiries and parish records see St. Camillus-St. Virgilius.

Chaplains of Public Institutions

BROOKLYN. *Bernard Fineson Development Center*. Vacant.
Beth Israel Medical Center/Kings Hwy.. Rev. Kieran Udeze.
Brookdale Hospital Medical Center. Angela DiPaola.
Brooklyn Development Center. Vacant.

The Brooklyn Hospital. Rev. Francis Obu-Mends, C.S.Sp., Sarah Spieldenner.
Coney Island Hospital. Rev. Lorenzo Gomez, S.D.V.
SUNY Downstate Medical Center. Rev. Isaïe Jean-Louis, CSSp, (Haiti).
Kings County Hospital Center. Rev. Souvenir Jean Paul, S.M.
Kingsboro Psychiatric Center. Rev. Joseph Tharackal.
Lutheran Medical Center. Rev. Augustine Emeh, (Nigeria).
Maimonides Medical Center of Brooklyn. Rev. Francis Obu-Mends, C.S.Sp.
Methodist Hospital. Revs. Augustine Emeh, (Nigeria), Isaïe Jean-Louis, CSSp, (Haiti).
Metropolitan Detention Center.
NY Community Hospital of Brooklyn. Rev. Kieran Udeze.
Veterans Affairs Healthcare System. Vacant.
Woodhull Medical & Mental Health Center. Rev. Joseph Tharakal.
Wyckoff Heights Hospital. Rev. Francisco J. Ares.
QUEENS. *Creedmoor Psychiatric Center*. Rev. Paul Chenot, C.P.
Elmhurst General Hospital. Rev. Gabriel A. Ahiarakwem.
Flushing Hospital and Medical Center. Revs. Bryan J. Carney, Chap., Anthony Nwachukwu.
Jamaica Hospital - Trump Pavilion. Revs. Andre F. Saint Preux, S.D.B., Joseph Tharackal.
St. John's Episcopal Hospital. Rev. Dawit T. Moroda.
Long Island Jewish Hospital. Revs. Robert Ambalathingal, (Retired), Michael O. Ugbor.
The Mount Sinai Hospital of Queens. Rev. Jean Gerard LaGuerre.
New York Presbyterian/Queens. Revs. Enel Almeus, C.S.Sp., Anthony Nwachukwu.
Northwell Health Forest Hills Hospital, Forest Hills, NY. Rev. Radu Titonea.
NYC Health & Hospitals/Queens-Pastoral Care Office. Sr. Julie Hauser.
Veterans Affairs Extended Care Center, St. Albans, NY. Revs. Edward Conway, OFM, Cap., Richard F. Mattox, OFM, Cap.

Military Chaplains:
Revs.—
Hirten, Timothy J., P.O. Box 141, Bellmore, 11710
Krische, James J., TAAC-S HQ Chaplain, APO AE, 09355
Thevenin, Donelson, U.S. Navy, 670 White Oak Crossing, Swansboro, NC 28584.

Released from Diocesan Assignment:
Rev. Msgrs.—
Buonanno, Vito A., Basilica of the National Shrine of the Immaculate Conception, 400 Michigan Ave. N.E., Washington, DC 20017
Curran, Michael J., St. Joseph Seminary, 201 Seminary Ave., Yonkers, 10704
Maksymowicz, John H., Apostolic Nunciature, 3339 Massachusetts Ave., N.W., Washington, DC 20008
Marchese, Richard E., Apostolic Nunciature, 3339 Massachusetts Ave., N.W., Washington, DC 20008
Pham, Cuong M., Pontifical Council for Legislative Texts, Piazza Pio XII, 10, Rome, Italy 00193
Sarno, Robert J., Congregation for the Causes of Saints, Piazza Pio XII, 10, Vatican City State 00120. (Europe)
Vaccari, Peter I., S.T.L., 201 Seminary Ave., Yonkers, 10704
Wielunski, Gregory C., The Tribunal, Archdiocese of Miami, 9401 Biscayne Blvd., Miami Shores, FL 33138
Revs.—
Bruno, Michael J. S., 201 Seminary Ave., Yonkers, 10704
Caccavale, Charles, St. Joseph Seminary, 201 Seminary Ave., Yonkers, 10704
Cush, John P., B.A., S.T.L., Via del Gianicolo, 14, Rome, Italy 00187
Flores, Raymond
Frawley, Patrick J., Fidelis Care, 95-25 Queens Blvd., Rego Park, 11374
Himes, Michael J., Dept. of Theology, Boston College, Chestnut Hill, MA 02167-3806
Lauder, Robert E., Bishop Mugavero Residence, 7200 Douglaston Pkwy., Douglaston, 11362
Penta, Leo J., Catholic University of Applied Sciences, Kopenicker Allee 39-57, Berlin, Germany
Pierre-Louis, Robert, 454 René-Lévesque Blvd. W., Montreal, PQ Canada H2Z 1A7
Ruiz, Jean-Pierre, S.T.D., SS. Joachim & Anne, 218-26 105th Ave., Queens Village, 11429
Stewart, Edward R.
Zuk, Richard P., P.O. Box 848, Trilby, FL 33593.

Graduate Studies:
Revs.—
Colalella, Nicholas M.
Dorelus, Patrick
Giulietti, Stephen M.
Lee, Jun Hee
Rodriguez, James, M.A., M.Div.
Rodriguez, Manuel de Jesus
Zwosta, Joseph M.

On Leave/Unassigned:
Revs.—
Bain, Andre M.
Brown, Charles L.
Buchanan, Caleb A.
Burgos, Adnel T.
Chilczuk, Marcin L.
Gilbert, Thomas R.
Greene, Michael M.
Herrera, Felix W.
Klein, Dennis D.
Lazar, John E.
Miller, John C.
Miller, Joseph A.
Pattugalan, Giancarlo T.
Perez, Jose
Piro, Gerald J.
Reynolds, James J.
Strzelecki, Dariusz
Suh, Daniel Sang-Bong
Thomas, Marcial
Tobon, John J.
Wulinski, Stanley F.

Retired:
Most Rev.—
Sansaricq, Guy, (Retired), 224 Brooklyn Ave., 11213
Rev. Msgrs.—
Bednartz, August C., (Retired), Bishop Mugavero Residence, 7200 Douglaston Pkwy., Douglaston, 11362
Boccio, Charles P., (Retired), 336 N. Birch Rd., #7A, Fort Lauderdale, FL 33304
Bottino, Edward J., (Retired), Mary's Nativity, 46-02 Parsons Blvd., Flushing, 11355
Bracken, John J., (Retired), 6 Beach 178th St., Breezy Point, 11697
Brennan, Michael J., V.E., (Retired), 35-60 158th St., Flushing, 11358
Cantley, Michael J., (Retired), Bishop Mugavero Residence, 7200 Douglaston Pkwy., Douglaston, 11362
Casey, John F., (Retired), 92-96 220th St., Queens Village, 11428
Cordero, Faustino, (Retired), 138 Bay 20th St., 11214
Darbouze, Rollin, (Retired), 18338 Winter Garden Ave., Port Charlotte, FL 33948
Deas, George T., (Retired), Bishop Mugavero Residence, 7200 Douglaston Pkwy., Douglaston, 11362
Ecker, Robert J., (Retired), 300 Second St., Coronado, CA 92118
Finnerty, D. Joseph, (Retired), 45-21 194 St., Flushing, 11358
Flood, William J., (Retired), Bishop Mugavero Residence, 7200 Douglaston Pkwy., Douglaston, 11362
Foley, Matthew F., (Retired), 91 Hudson Road, Bellerose Village, 11001
Fullam, Vincent F., (Retired), Immaculate Conception, 21-47 29 St., Astoria, 11105
Geraghty, Martin T., (Retired), 56-213th St., Bayside, 11364
Harris, Robert M., M.S.W., M.Phil., M.A., (Retired), P.O. Box 623, Smithtown, 11787
Healy, Thomas J., (Retired), 352 42nd St., 11232
Hinch, Lawrence E., (Retired), 2211 Emmons Ave., 11235
Kain, Peter V., (Retired), 929 Bay Ridge Pkwy., 11228
Keane, Vincent A., (Retired), 7200 Douglaston Pkwy., Douglaston, 11362
Kelly, James J., (Retired), 409 Linden St., 11237
Kelly, Raymond J., S.T.L., (Retired), Bishop Mugavero Residence, 7200 Douglaston Pkwy., Douglaston, 11362
Keppler, John F., (Retired), Bishop Mugavero Residence, 7200 Douglaston Pkwy., Douglaston, 11362
Kutner, Raymond W., J.C.D., (Retired), 605 Oaks Dr., Pompano Beach, FL 33069
Mulkerin, Terrence J., (Retired), 7200 Douglaston Pkwy., Douglaston, 11362
Mulqueen, Joseph C., J.C.L., (Retired), St. Mary, 10-08 49 Ave., Long Island City, 11101
O'Brien, John H., (Retired), 88-19 Parsons Blvd., Jamaica, 11432
Pawson, Robert J., (Retired), 92-96 220th St., Queens Village, 11428
Pfeiffer, Joseph C., (Retired), 157-10 83rd St., Howard Beach, 11414
Phillips, Michael J., (Retired), St. Anselm, 356 82nd St., 11209
Powis, John J., (Retired), 444 E. 20th St., 2C, New York, 10009
Reilly, Philip J., (Retired), Monastery of the Precious Blood, 5400 Fort Hamilton Pkwy., 11219
Ryan, George J., (Retired), 45-14 245th St., Douglaston, 11362
Spengler, James F., (Retired), 7200 Douglaston Pkwy., Douglaston, 11362
Strynkowski, John J., (Retired), 55 Croyden St., Malverne, 11565
Villani, Rocco D., (Retired), St. Brendan, 1525 East 12th St., 11230
Wetterer, Edward V., (Retired), 87-19 88th Ave., Woodhaven, 11421
Revs.—
Amann, John J., (Retired), 9719 Flatlands Ave., 11236
Badia, Leonard F., Ph.D., (Retired), 1717 Homewood Blvd., #213, Delray Beach, FL 33445
Barile, Ralph E., (Retired), 17 Bellew Ave., Eastchester, 10709-3101
Barozzi, Italo, (Retired), 26-15 154th St., Flushing, 11354
Bellantonio, Albert, (Retired), P.O. Box 382, Tannersville, PA 18372
Berran, Donald M., (Retired), 111-50 115 St., South Ozone Park, 11420
Blauvelt, Robert, (Retired), 110-30 221 St., Queens Village, 11429
Boyd, James A., (Retired), 7462 Hanford Pl., San Diego, CA 92111
Bradley, James P., (Retired), 957 NASA Pkwy., #245, Houston, TX 77058-3039
Brady, Edmund P., (Retired), Our Lady of Mount Carmel, 23-25 Newtown Ave., Astoria, 11102
Brophy, Edward G., M.Div., (Retired), 2460 Ocean Pkwy., 11229
Byrne, Hugh A., (Retired), Bishop Mugavero Residence, 7200 Douglaston Pkwy., Douglaston, 11362
Calder, Kenneth J., (Retired), Our Lady of Angels, 7320 Fourth Ave., 11209
Cassar, Edward A., (Retired), 430 Ave. W, 11223
Cestaro, Joseph A., (Retired), 1345 46th St., #4, 11219
Costello, Coleman J., (Retired), Bishop Mugavero Residence, 7200 Douglaston Pkwy., Douglaston, 11362
Cowan, George R., (Retired), Bishop Mugavero Residence, 7200 Douglaston Pkwy., Douglaston, 11362
Coyle, Eugene P., (Retired), 7200 Douglaston Pkwy., Douglaston, 11362
Cuadros, Jesus, (Retired), 249 9th St., 11215
Cunningham, Joseph L., (Retired), 110-06 Queens Blvd., Forest Hills, 11375
Cutrone, Dominick F., (Retired), Our Lady of Grace, 430 Ave. W., 11223
Czok, Robert W., (Retired), St. Rose of Lima, 130 Beach 84 St., Rockaway Beach, 11693
D'Albro, Thomas G., (Retired), 68 Widmer Rd., Wappingers Falls, 12590
Daly, Vincent M., (Retired), 14-51 143rd St., Whitestone, 11357
Denzer, Joseph W., (Retired), Bishop Mugavero Residence, 7200 Douglaston Pkwy., Douglaston, 11362
Devine, James T., (Retired), Bishop Mugavero Residence, 7200 Douglaston Pkwy., Douglaston, 11362
Devlin, James E., (Retired), 1950 Batchelder St., 11229
Diamond, Matthew J., (Retired), 62 Watkins Dr., Sandy Hook, CT 06482
Diffley, Patrick J., (Retired), 7200 Douglaston Pkwy., Douglaston, 11362
Doody, Cyril F., (Retired), 27 Parkway Dr., Sag Harbor, 11963
Doran, Edward P., Ph.D., (Retired), 51-15 61st St., Maspeth, 11378
Estrada, Sabino, (Retired), 39-76 57th St., #3D, Woodside, 11377
Farrugia, William C., (Retired), 20-51 26th St., Astoria, 11105
Finley, James F., (Retired), 195 Falmouth Rd., #8C, Mashpee, MA 02649
Fraser, James F., (Retired), 7200 Douglaston Pkwy., Douglaston, 11362
Fullum, John J., (Retired), 83-17 78th Ave., Glendale, 11385
Garkowski, John J., (Retired), 111-50 115th St., South Ozone Park, 11420
Gildea, John J., (Retired), 43-22 Ithaca St., Elmhurst, 11373

Grzelak, Thaddeus A., (Retired), 4662 Brisa Dr., Palmdale, CA 93551
Haggerty, Thomas M., (Retired), 7600 Shore Front Pkwy., Apt. 12W, Far Rockaway, 11692
Hand, Kenneth J., (Retired), Bishop Mugavero Residence, 7200 Douglaston Pkwy., Douglaston, 11362
Harrington, John P., (Retired), 39-38 29th St., Long Island City, 11101
Hoare, Richard, (Retired), 34-43 93rd St., Jackson Heights, 11372
Iantosca, August J., (Retired), 7200 Douglaston Pkwy., Douglaston, 11362
Keohane, Daniel G., (Retired), Bishop Mugavero Residence, 7200 Douglaston Pkwy., Douglaston, 11362
Kirby, Martin F., M.A., (Retired), 31-30 74th St., East Elmhurst, 11370
Krlis, William F., (Retired), 32-23 36th St., Long Island City, 11106
Kull, Martin R., (Retired), 356 82nd St., 11209
Labita, Francis J., (Retired), Bishop Mugavero Residence, 7200 Douglaston Pkwy., Douglaston, 11362
Leone, James M., (Retired), P.O. Box 426, Mastic Beach, 11951
Lewkiewicz, Richard M., (Retired), 7320 4th Ave., 11209
Lynch, Stephen P., (Retired), 41 Adelphi St., 11205
Mahoney, Peter, (Retired), 433 Sackett St., 11231
Maloney, John P., (Retired), 15 Mineola Ct., Hampton Bays, 11946
Mathew, Abraham P., (Retired), 150-75 Goethals Ave., Jamaica, 11432
Matonti, Charles J., (Retired), St. Columba, 2245 Kimball St., 11234
Maynard, Lewis H., (Retired), 115-50 115th St., South Ozone Park, 11420
Meszaros, James J., (Retired), St. Josaphat, 34-32 210th St., Bayside, 11361
Morales, Robert P., (Retired), 136-06 87th Ave., Richmond Hill, 11418
Murphy, Daniel S., (Retired), 611 8th Ave., 11215
Muthukattil, Thomas, (Retired), 19 Picture Ln., Hicksville, 11801
Nadine, Jerome E., (Retired)
Newell, John J., (Retired), 94 Rose Ave., Floral Park, 11001
Nolan, Joseph M., (Retired), 7200 Douglaston Pkwy., Douglaston, 11362
Ossa, Pedro N., (Retired), St. Martin of Tours, 1288 Hancock St., 11221
Perry, Michael A., (Retired), 2020 Foster Ave., 11210
Pezzullo, Angelo B., (Retired), Nativity of the Blessed Virgin Mary, 101-41 91st St., Ozone Park, 11416
Pfundstein, George A., (Retired), St. Ann, 142-30 58th Ave., Flushing, 11355
Pham, Josephtan, (Retired), 23-25 Newtown Ave., Astoria, 11102
Pizzo, Philip J., (Retired), 94-40 118th St., Richmond Hill, 11419
Quigley, Joseph P., (Retired), St. Mark, 2609 E. 19th St., 11235
Rizzo, Matteo J., (Retired), 3211 Lake Pine Way, Unit A1, Tarpon Springs, FL 34688
Rucando, Anthony M., (Retired), 45-14 245th St., Douglaston, 11362
Sabatos, Daniel C., (Retired), 9 Lenroc Dr., White Plains, 10607
Salerno, Emilio J., (Retired), 118 Lake Emerald Dr. #104, Oakland Park, FL 33309
Sans, Pablo, (Retired), 136-06 87th Ave., Richmond Hill, 11416
Schmidt, Raymond F., (Retired), 7200 Douglaston Pkwy., Douglaston, 11362
Smith, Edward J., (Retired), 241-16 Rushmore Ave., Douglaston, 11362
Smith, LeRoy J., (Retired), 1300 S. A1A, Apt. 221, Jupiter, FL 33477
Sommermeyer, Gary H., (Retired), P.O. Box 765, Southbury, CT 06488
Sweeney, James H., (Retired), 7200 Douglaston Pkwy., Douglaston, 11362
Tivenan, John J., (Retired), 6128 Hadley Commons Dr., Riverview, FL 33578
Valdazo, Stephen, (Retired), 82-00 35th Ave., Jackson Heights, 11372
Varano, Andrew R., (Retired), 219 Conselyea St., 11211
Vella, Joseph, (Retired), 15 Church St., Zebbug, Gozo, ZBB1509, Malta
Walker, Gerard T., (Retired), 8 N. William St., East Patchogue, 11772
Wei, Luke, (Retired), 2886 Fernley Dr. E., West Palm Beach, FL 33415
White, Charles H., (Retired), St. Mary Star of the Sea, 1920 New Haven Ave., Far Rockaway, 11691
Wtulich, John, (Retired), 99-15 Rockaway Blvd., Rockaway Beach, 11694
Zaccagnigno, Raffaele, (Retired), Via Federico Paolini 115, Scala D. int. 11, 00122 Ostia Lido, Rome, Italy.

Permanent Deacons:
Abundo, Roberto S., St. Teresa, Woodside
Agnant, Ronald Y., Holy Innocents, Brooklyn
Alayu, Perlito B., Diocese of Orlando
Alick, Alejandro, (Inactive)
Almendarez, Felipe, Diocese of Brownsville, Texas
Alvarado, Jorge L., Our Lady of Perpetual Help, South Ozone Park
Alvarez, Felipe J., (Retired)
Alvia, Humberto R., Diocese of Venice
Amore, Bryan J., St. Mary Mother of Jesus, Brooklyn
Aris, Anthony J., (Inactive)
Arteaga, Emilio S., St. Agatha, Brooklyn
Asencio, Enrique, (Inactive)
Avallone, Ernesto A., Our Lady of the Blessed Sacrament, Bayside
Barber, Christopher E., St. Clare, Rosedale
Barreneche, Julio C., St. Kevin, Flushing; Sec. Clergy Personnel
Beaubrun, Berthal, (Retired)
Bichotte, Joseph, (Retired)
Bisagni, Domenico, (Inactive)
Bizzoco, Gregory Jr., Queen of Peace, Kew Gardens
Blake, Lamont A., Christ the King, Springfield Gardens
Blanco, Hector S., Our Lady of Perpetual Help, Brooklyn and St. Finbar, Brooklyn
Bobadilla, Antonio, Archdiocese of Miami, FL
Borheck, Steven J., Our Lady of the Snows, N. Floral Park
Boursiquot, Jean B., (Retired)
Brainerd, Michael J., St. Robert Bellarmine, Bayside
Branch, Leroy P., St. Paul & St. Agnes, Brooklyn
Breviario, Alexander, Our Lady of Grace, Howard Beach
Bugay, Josefino Y., (Inactive)
Cabrera, Rafael, St. Fortunata and St. Sylvester, Brooklyn
Caceres, Ycelso, (Inactive)
Cajoux, Francois G., Sacred Heart Cambria Hts.
Calvo, Juan, (Retired)
Cancel, Edwin, Our Lady of the Angelus, Rego Park
Cantirino, John, Immaculate Heart of Mary, Brooklyn
Carattini, Juan M., St. Rose of Lima, Rockaway Beach
Casares, Gabriel, (Inactive)
Cassidy, Eugene J., Holy Family, Flushing
Castellanos, Alfredo, St. Pius V, Jamaica
Castillo, Jorge E., Holy Child Jesus, Richmond Hill
Catanello, Joseph V., St. Nicholas of Tolentine, Jamaica
Cederroth, Charles J., Diocese of Trenton
Cepin, Concepcion, St. Barbara, Brooklyn
Chery, Eric, (Inactive)
Chin, Paul M., St. Paul Chong Ha-Sang Chapel, Flushing
Ciccaroni, Andrew, Diocese of Rockville Centre, NY
Cline, Patrick, (Inactive)
Cobham, Jaime A., St. Athanasius, Brooklyn
Coffey, John P., (Retired)
Colandrea, Dante, St. Athanasius, Brooklyn
Colon, Nickie, St. Matthew, Brooklyn
Colon, Rafael, (Inactive)
Contreras, Jose A., St. Thomas the Apostle, Woodhaven
Contreras, William de Jesus, Diocese of Orlando
Cosgrove, Robert J., (Retired)
Coty, Emmanuel, SS. Joachim & Anne, Queens Village
Coyle, Lawrence E., St. Columba, Brooklyn
Cruz, Alberto, St. Martin of Tours, Brooklyn
Cruz, Rafael, (Inactive)
Cruz, Ramon, St. Mary Gate of Heaven, Ozone Park
Cuccia, Arthur, (Retired)
Culajay, Carlos H., St. Jerome, Brooklyn
Cullen, William B., (On Leave)
Cutter, Arthur, St. Gregory the Great, Bellerose
D'Accordo, Armand C., St. Francis de Sales, Belle Harbor
D'Accordo, Frank J., Saint Bernard, Brooklyn
Da Costa, Dennis A., (Retired)
Damato, Stephen T., St. Sebastian, Woodside
Daniel, Gordon V., (Inactive)
Dass, Joseph H., Presentation of the Blessed Virgin Mary, Jamaica
Davis, Thomas G., St. Anselm, Brooklyn
de la Rosa, Andres, (Retired)
DeBiase, John F., Sacred Hearts of Jesus, Bayside
DeCola, Joseph P., Diocese of Palm Beach, FL
DeMichele, Frank, St. Bernadette, Brooklyn
DeMuro, Salvatore P., (Inactive)
Denzler, Joseph C., Diocese of Charlotte, NC
Deschler, Bernard M., (Retired), Archdiocese of New York
Despeignes, Robinson, Incarnation, Queens Village
Devaney, Thomas J., Archdiocese of Washington, D.C.
Diaz, Daniel, Our Lady of Sorrows, Corona
Diaz, Rafael, (Retired)
Dixon, Gregory D., St. Andrew the Apostle, Brooklyn
Dobbins, Dean, Our Lady of Mercy, Forest Hills
Dolan, John J., St. Rosalia-Regina Pacis, Brooklyn
Donnelly, Daniel P., St. Fidelis, College Point
Dorsinville, Paul C., Sacred Heart, Cambria Heights
Duncan, Isaac, (Retired)
Duran, Fausto, (Dominican Republic) (Retired)
Duran, Juan R., Archdiocese of Saint Paul and Minneapolis, MN
Elias, Raul S., Holy Child Jesus, Richmond Hill
Elijio, Victorino P., Our Lady of Presentation - Our Lady of Mercy
Elrose, Richard E., St. Helen, Howard Beach
Escobar, Nery R., SS. Joachim & Anne, Queens Village
Espinal, Luis J., (Inactive)
Favale, Anthony, St. Finbar, Brooklyn
Ferguson, Randolf, Diocese of Kingston, Jamaica
Fernandez, Jose M., Queen of Peace, Kew Gardens Hills
Fernandez, Justo I., (Inactive)
Flanagan, Patrick M., St. Teresa of Avila-St. Anthony of Padua, South Ozone Park
Flannery, John A., (Retired)
Franco, Philip, Our Lady of Mount Carmel, Brooklyn
Freda, Joseph A., St. Mel, Flushing
Fu, Howard H., St. John Vianney, Flushing
Fugelsang, Louis, (Inactive)
Gaine, Edward S., Our Lady of Angels, Brooklyn
Galazin, Stanley J., American Martyrs, Bayside, Dir. Immaculate Conception Center, Douglaston
Gannon, John J., (Inactive)
Garcia, Carlos, Dir. Jesus of Nazareth Retreat Center, Brooklyn
Garcia, Daniel A., St. John Vianney, Flushing
Garcia, Jimmy, Diocese of Fort Worth, Texas
George, Roy N., (Retired)
Germain, Moliere, (Retired), (Diocese of Hinche, Haiti)
Giglio, John P. Jr., (Inactive)
Gilligan, Richard J., St. Mary Gate of Heaven, Ozone Park
Gomez, Guillermo D., St. Gerard Majella, Hollis
Gonzalez, Antonio J., Immaculate Heart of Mary, Brooklyn
Gonzalez, Jorge A., Dir. Diaconate Formation Office, Brooklyn; St. Michael-St. Malachy, Brooklyn
Gonzalez, Louis A., (Retired)
Gonzalez, Rafael, Diocese of Orlando
Griffin, Arthur J., (Retired)
Guastella, Louis, (Retired)
Guster, Edward J. Jr., Nativity of the Blessed Virgin Mary, Ozone Park
Hart, Ernest F., St. Mary Magdalene, Springfield Gardens
Hernandez, Francisco J., Immaculate Conception, Astoria
Hernandez, Rafael, Diocese of Orlando
Hernandez, Rene, St. Mary Star of the Sea and St. Gertrude, Far Rockaway
Hernandez, Wilfredo, (Retired)
Hili, Saviour, (Retired)
Hughes, Kevin F., Our Lady of the Snows, Floral Park
Hull, John E., (Retired)
Hurley, Charles R., Our Lady of Angels, Brooklyn
Hurst, Richard L., St. Clare, Rosedale
Im, Sokwon, St. Paul Chong Ha-Sang, Flushing
Innocent, Francois, (Retired)
Jolicoeur, Luc, (Inactive)
Jorge, Thomas E., St. Nicholas of Tolentine, Jamaica
Kandra, Gregory, Our Lady Queen of Martyrs, Forest Hills
Kelly, William V., St. Athanasius, Brooklyn
Kennedy, James F., Diocese of St. Petersburg
Killian, John F., (Retired), Diocese of Phoenix, AZ
Lacy, James J., (Retired), Camden, NJ
LaGamba, Vincent M., St. Francis De Sales, Belle Harbor
LaGreca, John J., Diocese of Metuchen, NJ
Lavanco, Robert F., Our Lady of Hope, Middle Village
Lee, Richard G., (Retired)
Lima, Ramon, (Retired)
Lino, Vincent A., St. Anastasia, Douglaston
Lizama, Jose A., St. Bartholomew, Elmhurst
Lonergan, Robert P., St. Josaphat, Bayside
Lopez, Hipolito, (Inactive)
Lopez, Hiram, (Inactive)

Lopez, Marco V., Our Lady of Fatima, Jackson Heights
Luces, Fernando E., St. Rita, Long Island City
Magana, Daniel, St. Batholomew, Elmhurst
Malone, William F., Diocese of Trenton
Maloney, James E., Our Lady of The Miraculous Medal, Ridgewood
Mammoliti, Anthony, (Diocese of Trenton, NJ), St. Dominic, Brooklyn
Marcel, Magloire, (Inactive)
Marchello, Andrew A., (Retired)
Marte, Rafael, Mary Mother of the Church, Brooklyn
Martinez, Carlos A., All Saints, Brooklyn
Martinez, German, (Retired)
Martinez, Manuel I., (Retired)
Martucci, Anthony P., St. Bernadette, Brooklyn
Mastrangelo, Andrew T., St. Helen, Howard Beach
Mateo, Francis G., (On Leave)
Mazza, Nicholas, (Inactive)
McBride, Timothy, St. Mary Gate of Heaven, Ozone Park
McGuire, Joseph P., (Inactive)
McLaughlin, Kevin, St. Ephrem, Brooklyn
McMaster, Laurence O., St. Gerard Majella, Hollis
Medina, Gustavo, St. Catharine of Alexandria, Brooklyn
Mejia, Felix, St. Rita, Brooklyn
Mejia, Rafael A., Diocese of Orlando
Mendez, Rodrigo A., St. Leo, Corona
Mendez, Ruben C., Our Lady of Mount Carmel, Astoria
Miller, Leon F., Diocese of San Jose, CA
Miranda, Osborne, (Retired)
Molloy, William, Our Lady of the Blessed Sacrament, Bayside
Montero, Adalberto, St. Mary Star of Sea & St. Gertrude, Far Rockaway
Montes, Leopoldo R, Blessed Virgin Mary Help of Christians, Woodside
Morales, Julio A., Diocese of Orlando
Morano, Frank A., St. Frances Cabrini, Brooklyn
Moreno, Ricardo, Our Lady of Lourdes, Queens Village
Morin, Paul P., St. Mark, Brooklyn
Moss, Michael C., St. Mary Star of the Sea, Far Rockaway
Mulroy, Martin B., Diocese of Metuchen, NJ
Munoz, Franklin G., Incarnation, Queens Village
Murillo, Julio C., Diocese of Rockville Centre
Murphy, John J., (Retired)
Noble, James D., Immaculate Heart of Mary, Brooklyn
Norman, Paul, Our Lady of Hope, Middle Village
O'Connell, Edward F., St. Stanislaus Kostka, Maspeth and Transfiguration, Maspeth
Occhiuto, Joseph J., (Inactive)
Oellinger, Matthew J., Our Lady of the Snows, North Floral Park
Oggeri, William, (Retired)
Olivas, Pascual B., St. Bonaventure, Jamaica
Orozco, Fernando, St. Paul the Apostle, Corona
Ortiz, Sergio, (Inactive)
Oviedo, Jose L., (Retired)
Page, Thomas J., St. Adalbert, Elmhurst
Panico, Louis J., Blessed Sacrament, Brooklyn
Park, Julio K., (Retired)
Parra, Fabio, Our Lady of Fatima, Jackson Heights
Pascal, Orlando, Georgia
Pavlyshin, Peter, Diocese of Venice
Perez, Oscar R., St. Matthias, Ridgewood
Perez, Richard, (Retired)
Piaubert, Joseph C., Holy Innocents, Brooklyn
Pichardo, Carlos R., Blessed Sacrament, Brooklyn
Pierre-Antoine, Clemenceau, Incarnation, Queens Village
Pierre-Louis, Wilner, St. Francis of Assisi and St. Blaise, Brooklyn
Pinzon, Jaime A., (On Leave)
Pizzimenti, Bruno, (Retired)
Quintana, Manuel H., St. Joseph Co-Cathedral, Brooklyn
Rameau, Jean J., Holy Family, Brooklyn and St. Laurence, Brooklyn
Ramirez, Manuel, (Inactive)
Ramos, James, Archdiocese of NY
Ramos, Jose A., Diocese of Orlando
Reichert, John P., (Retired)
Reyes, Ricardo, Our Lady of the Presentation - Our Lady of Mercy, Brooklyn
Ritchie, Frederick V., St. Columba, Brooklyn
Rizzo, Giovanni A., (Retired)
Rizzuto, Ronald, St. Edmund, Brooklyn
Roberts, Lionel V., (Retired)
Rodriguez, Daniel R., Immaculate Conception, Jamaica
Rodriguez, Hector E., Most Precious Blood, Long Island City
Rodriguez, Manuel L., Diocese of Orlando, FL
Roman, Luis A., (Inactive)
Romano, Gustavo, (Diocese of Puerto Plata, Dom. Rep.) St. Joseph Patron of the Universal Church, Brooklyn
Ronacher, Ronald M., Archdiocese of Newark, NJ
Rosales, Jose Mauricio, Our Lady of the Cenacle, Richmond Hill
Rosario, Israel, (Retired)
Ruiz, Raul, (Retired)
Ruoff, James F., Blessed Trinity, Rockaway Point
Ryan, Kevin F., (Retired)
Saez, Michael A., Holy Name of Jesus, Brooklyn
Salazar, Paulo A., St. Joan of Arc, Jackson Heights
Saldana, Albert, Our Lady of Light, St. Albans
Sampson, Harold S., Archdiocese of San Antonio, TX
Sands, John E., (Retired), St. Matthias, Ridgewood
Santana, Perfecto, (On Leave)
Scarlatto, Nicolino, St. Francis of Assisi, Astoria
Schwarz, Jeremiah W., Holy Child Jesus, Richmond Hill
Sclafani, Leonard A., (Retired)
Sehn, Frank, (Inactive)
Sencion, Eduardo, (Retired)
Siani, Philip J., Our Lady of Grace, Brooklyn
Siavichay, Ruben G., St. Teresa of Avila-St. Anthony of Padua, S. Ozone Park
Simon, Mauclair, St. Jude, Brooklyn
Sinisi, Henry C., (Inactive)
Smith, Nathaniel J., St. Clement Pope, South Ozone Park
Smith, Ramon, (Retired)
Smolinski, Edward A., (Retired)
Solarte, John, Presentation of the Blessed Virgin Mary, Jamaica
Soraire, Martin D., St. Teresa, Woodside
Soto, Jesus, (Retired)
Stamm, Peter, Sacred Heart, Glendale
Stucchio, Anthony, St. Ephrem, Brooklyn
Sucich, John R., St. Francis of Assisi, Long Island City
Tam, Stanley, St. John Vianney, Flushing
Tamayo, Elkin D., Immaculate Conception, Astoria
Taylor, Luis C., (Retired)
Thompson, Balfour A., (On Leave)
Tineo, Jose F., Our Lady of Sorrows, Corona
Tokarcsik, George M., (Inactive)
Torres, Abel, (Retired)
Torres, Freddy, Our Lady of Light, St. Albans
Toussaint, Antoine, (Inactive)
Trochez, Carlos A., St. Patrick, Brooklyn
Troy, Michael J., (Retired)
Tully, Dean T., Holy Child Jesus, Richmond Hill
Uzoigwe, Okafor C., (Retired)
Valderama, Carlos, (Retired)
Van Wassenhove, Raymond J., (Inactive)
Varela, Jaime, (Assistant to the Bishop), Our Lady of the Presentation - Our Lady of Mercy, Brooklyn
Vargas, Juan R., Diocese of Orlando
Vega, Rogelio, St. Sebastian, Woodside
Vicinanza, Michael W., Diocese of Rockville Centre, NY
Wagner, Christopher A., St. Bernard, Brooklyn
Warner, Lester, (Retired)
Warren, John, Our Lady of the Snows, Floral Park
Williams, Lee C., (Retired)
Williamsen, William, (Retired)
Wohlfarth, Eugene R., Diocese of Austin, TX
Yepes, Elias H., (Retired)
Zelaya, Manuel, Guardian Angel, Brooklyn
Zeuner, Robert J., St. Gregory the Great, Bellerose
Zhagnay, Juan J., Corpus Christi, Woodside
Zimmermann, Walter C., (Retired).

INSTITUTIONS LOCATED IN DIOCESE

[A] PASTORAL CENTERS

DOUGLASTON. *Immaculate Conception Center* (1968) 7200 Douglaston Pkwy., Douglaston, 11362-1997. Tel: 718-281-9526; Fax: 718-229-2658; Email: sgalazin@diobrook.org. Deacon Stanley J. Galazin, Dir.; Mr. Howard Maresca, Mgr. Building Svcs.

[B] SEMINARIES, DIOCESAN

DOUGLASTON. *Cathedral Seminary House of Formation*, 7200 Douglaston Pkwy., Douglaston, 11362. Tel: 718-631-4600; Fax: 718-281-9536; Email: ssanto@diobrook.org. Revs. George Sears, Rector; John J. Costello, S.T.L., Vice Rector; James W. King, Dir. of Spiritual Formation; Conrad Osterhout, Spiritual Dir.; Bro. Owen Sadlier, Formation Adviser and Professor; Susan Santo, Admin.; Robert Palumbo, Ph.D., Staff Psychologist. Priests 4; Seminarians 45; Students 45.

ELMHURST. *Cathedral Preparatory School and Seminary*, 56-25 92nd St., Elmhurst, 11373. Tel: 718-592-6800; Fax: 718-592-5574; Email: jfonti@cathedralprep.org. Very Rev. Joseph G. Fonti, S.T.L., Rector & Pres. Lay Teachers 10; Priests 3; Seminarians 158; Students 158; Clergy / Religious Teachers 4.

[C] COLLEGES AND UNIVERSITIES

BROOKLYN. **St. Francis College*, 180 Remsen St., 11201. Tel: 718-522-2300; Fax: 718-237-8964; Email: president@sfc.edu; Web: www.sfc.edu. Mr. Miguel Martinez-Saenz, Pres.; Ms. Mona Wasserman, Librarian. Brothers 4; Lay Teachers 320; Priests 2; Sisters 2; Students 2,413; Total Staff 590.

**St. Joseph's College*, 245 Clinton Ave., 11205. Tel: 718-940-5300; Fax: 718-636-7245; Email: alist@sjcny.edu; Email: adomenech@sjcny.org; Web: www.sjcny.edu. Mr. Donald Boomgaarden, Pres. Under supervision of Board of Trustees. Administrators 3; Lay Teachers 57; Students 1,202; Total Staff 60.

Branch Campus, 155 W. Roe Blvd., Patchogue, 11772. Tel: 631-687-5100; Fax: 631-654-1782; Email: alist@sjcny.edu; Email: adomenech@sjcny.edu; Web: www.sjcny.edu. Mr. Donald Boomgaarden, Pres.; Mr. Rory Shaffer-Walsh, Vice Pres. Institute Advancement; John Roth, M.B.A., CFO; Michelle Papajohn, M.B.A., CIO; Ms. Wendy Turgeon, Interim Exec. Dean; Mr. Michael Hanophy, Interim Exec. Dean; Elizabeth Pollicino Murphy, Ed.D., Exec. Dir. of Libraries. Administrators 2; Faculty 6; Lay Teachers 97; Students 4,115.

QUEENS. *St. John's University* (1870) 8000 Utopia Pkwy., Queens, 11439. Tel: 718-990-6161; Fax: 718-990-5723; Email: admission@stjohns.edu; Web: www.stjohns.edu. Dr. Conrado M. Gempesaw, Ph.D., Pres.; Rev. Bernard M. Tracey, C.M., Exec. Vice Pres., Mission; Dr. Kathryn T. Hutchinson, Vice Pres. Student Affairs; Mr. Christian Vaupel, Vice Pres. for Advancement & Univ. Relations; Sharon Hewitt Watkins, Vice Pres. Business Affairs, CFO & Treas.; Joseph E. Oliva Esq., Vice Pres. for Admin., Sec. & Gen. Counsel; Dr. Simon Geir Moller, Ph.D., Interim Provost & Vice Pres. Academic Affairs; Jorge L. Rodriguez, Vice Provost & Chief Enrollment Officer; Dr. James O'Keefe, Ph.D., Vice Provost for Staten Island Campus; Ms. Nada Llewellyn, Assoc. Vice Pres. of HR, Chief Diversity Officer, & Deputy Gen. Counsel; Dr. Valeda Dent, Ph.D., Dean; Dr. Russell J. DiGate, Ph.D., Dean; Dr. Jeffrey Fagen, Dean; Dr. Katia Passerini, Ph.D., Dean; Dr. Norean R. Sharpe, Dean; Michael A. Simons, J.D., Dean; Ms. Yvonne Pratt-Johnson, Interim Dean; Mr. Mike Cragg, Dir. of Athletics. Sponsored by the Vincentian Priests and Brothers Eastern Province of the Congregation of the Mission. Lay Teachers 663; Priests 7; Students 21,683; Total Enrollment (Undergrad. and Graduate of Queens, Manhattan and Staten Island Campuses, and Rome) 21,683; Queens Campus Enrollment 19,007; Clergy / Religious Teachers 7.

Bread & Life Soup Kitchen.

[D] CAMPUS MINISTRY

BROOKLYN. *Campus Ministers and Ministry Centers*, 310 Prospect Park W., 11215. Tel: 718-965-7300, Ext. 5224; Fax: 347-750-1607; Email: mcuria@diobrook.org. Most Rev. James Massa, D.D., Vicar Higher Educ.; Revs. Richard E. Long, Tel: 718-434-1900. Brooklyn College; Paul A. Wood, Tel: 718-793-3130. Queens College; Richard Bretone, Pratt Institute of Technology; Brian Jordan, O.S.F., Tel: 718-489-5345. St. Francis College; Anthony F. Rosado, Queensborough Community College; Ms. Victoria Santangelo, St. Johns University; Sr. Susan Wilcox, C.S.J., St. Joseph X College; Revs. Kevin P. Cavalluzzi, Tel: 718-522-2105. NY Technical College; Michael G. Tedone, Tel: 718-423-0002. Queensborough Community College; Kingsborough Community College; Grzegorz Dziedzic, Campus Min. Legal Titles & Corporations: Newman Apostolate, Inc.

Legal Titles & Corporations: Newman Apostolate, Inc.

[E] CATHOLIC EDUCATION OFFICES

BROOKLYN. *Office of Faith Formation*, 310 Prospect Park W., 11230. Tel: 718-281-9544; Email: tmusco@diobrook.org; Web: www.dioceseofbrooklyn.org. Mr. Theodore J. Musco, Exec. Dir., School of Evangelization & Dir., Office of Faith Formation, Tel: 718-281-9545; Clendy J. Calderon, Admin. Asst. Office of Faith Formation; Nelsa I. Elias, Facilitator, Participants, Faculty & Curriculum, School of Evangelization; Christine Georgi, Registrar School of Evangelization; Krzysztof Gospodarzec, Liaison to the Polish Community, Office of the Faith Formation; Martha Hernandez, Admin. Asst. School of Evangelization; Rev. James

Kuroly, Chap. Youth and Young Ministry; Joann Roa, Coord. RCIA & Catechetical Initiatives, 310 Prospect Park W., 11215. Tel: 718-965-7300, Ext. 2440; Email: jroa@diobrook.org; Paul Morisi, Coord. Adolescent & Young Adult Faith Formation, Office of the Faith Formation; Mr. Christian S. Rada, Coord. Marriage, Family Life, & Respect Life Ministry, Office of the Faith Formation, Tel: 718-281-9543; Gerald Tortorella, Dir. Pastoral Institute; Elizabeth Urgate, Admin. Asst. Pastoral Institute.

Office of the Superintendent of Schools, 310 Prospect Park W., 11215. Tel: 718-965-7300; Email: tchadztko@diobrook.org; Web: www.dioceseofbrooklyn.org/catholic-ed. Thomas Chadzutko, Ed.D., Supt., Tel: 718-965-7300, Ext. 5419; Fax: 718-788-4535; Bro. Ralph Darmento, F.S.C., Deputy Supt., Tel: 718-965-7300, Ext. 5426; Mrs. Janet E. Heed, District Supt.; Mr. Michael A. LaForgia, District Supt.; Roxanna De Pena-Elder, District Supt.; Michael Greiner, Coord., Educational Technology & Data, Tel: 718-965-7300, Ext. 5557; Joan McMaster, Assoc. Supt. for Prin. & Teacher Personnel, Tel: 718-965-7300, Ext. 2224; Barbara McArdle, Asst. Supt., Catholic Identity & Prin. Faith Formation, Tel: 718-965-7300, Ext. 5427; Diane Phelan, Assoc. Supt., Evaluation of Programs and Students, Tel: 713-965-7300, Ext. 5424; Maria Viesta, Asst. Supt., Academy Governance, Tel: 718-965-7300, Ext. 5424; Elizabeth Frangella, Ed.D., Assoc. Supt., Curriculum, Tel: 718-965-7300, Ext. 2218; Joanne Dreiss, Asst. Supt.; Yinet Liriano, Exec. Asst. to Supt.; Briana Podlovits, Mktg. Specialist; Kelly Gonzalez, Admin. Asst. Brothers 18; Sisters 88; Total Enrollment 24,913.

Diocese of Brooklyn Education Offices

Legal Titles & Corporations: Department of Education, Diocese of Brooklyn; Henry M. Hald High School Association; Saint John's Preparatory School, Brooklyn.

MIDDLE VILLAGE. *Catholic Youth Organization*, 66-25 79th Pl., Middle Village, 11379. Tel: 718-281-9549; Fax: 718-281-9557.

[F] HIGH SCHOOLS, DIOCESAN

BROOKLYN. *Bishop Loughlin Memorial High School* (Coed) 357 Clermont Ave., 11238. Tel: 718-857-2700; Fax: 718-398-4227; Email: dcronin@blmhs.org; Email: dwernersbach@blmhs.org; Web: www.loughlin.org. Bro. Dennis Cronin, F.S.C., Pres.; Edward A. Bolan, Prin.; Cecilia Gottsegen, Asst. Prin. for Academics; Nicole Freeman, Dean; Luis Montes, Dean. Brothers of the Christian Schools 3; Lay Teachers 42; Students 650.

[G] HIGH SCHOOLS, PRIVATE

BROOKLYN. *Bishop Kearney High School* (Girls) 2202 60th St., 11204-2599. Tel: 718-236-6363; Fax: 718-236-7784; Email: eguglielmo@kearneyhs.org; Web: www.bishopkearneyhs.org. Margaret Minson, Head of School; Dr. Ralph Protano, Asst. Head of School. Lay Teachers 23; Sisters 4; Students 248.

Cristo Rey Brooklyn High School, 710 E. 37th St., 11203. Tel: 718-455-3555; Fax: 718-455-3556; Email: jinfortunio@cristoreybrooklyn.org; Email: jdugan@cristoreybrooklyn.org; Email: bhenson@cristoreybrooklyn.org; Web: www.cristoreybrooklyn.org. Robert Catell, Bd. Chm.; William Henson, Pres.; Joseph Dugan, Prin.; John Infortunio, Dir. Opers. & Dean, Students; Luis Posada, Dir. Admissions; Eleanor Winn, Dir.; Joseph Acciarito, Dir. Lay Teachers 21; Students 320; Total Staff 54; Enrollment 320; Clergy / Religious Teachers 2; Staff 31.

Fontbonne Hall Academy (Girls) 9901 Shore Rd., 11209. Tel: 718-748-2244; Fax: 718-745-3841; Email: spicijaric@fontbonne.org; Web: www.fontbonne.org. Maryann Spicijaric, Prin.; Lauriann Wierzbowski, Asst. Prin.; Gloria A. Musto, Dir. Alumnae Rels.; Victoria Adamo, Dir. Admissions; Mr. Joseph Geraci, Dir. of Development. Lay Teachers 37; Sisters of St. Joseph (Brentwood Community) 1; Students 420.

St. Joseph (Girls) 80 Willoughby St., 11201-5265. Tel: 718-624-3618; Fax: 718-624-2792; Email: admin@sjhsbridge.org; Email: clatham@SJHSbridge.org; Web: www.sjhsbridge.org. Caroline Latham, Prin.; Miss Madeline Rivera, Librarian. Lay Teachers 27; Sisters of St. Joseph (Brentwood Community) 5; Students 233.

Nazareth Regional High School (Coed) 475 E. 57th St., 11203. Tel: 718-763-1100, Ext. 223; Fax: 347-527-9154; Email: pquiles@nazarethrhs.org; Web: www.nazarethrhs.org. Providencia Quiles, Prin. Lay Teachers 21; Students 364.

Xaverian (Co-ed) 7100 Shore Rd., 11209. Tel: 718-836-7100; Fax: 718-836-7114; Email: ralesi@xaverian.org; Email: plouisa@xaverian.org; Web: www.xaverian.org. Mr. Robert Alesi, Pres.; Deacon Kevin McCormack, Prin.; Mr. Michael Wilson, Asst. Prin. Discipline & Opers.; Eileen Long Chelales, Dir. of Advancement; Mark Spelman, Dir. of Admissions; Maria Pacheco, Asst. Prin. Student Support; Mr. Daniel Sharib, Asst. Prin. Academics. Deacons 2; Lay Teachers 110; Priests 1; Priests 2; Students 1,400; Xaverian Brothers 1.

ASTORIA. *St. John's Preparatory School* (1870) (Coed) 21-21 Crescent St., Astoria, 11105-3398. Tel: 718-721-7200; Fax: 718-545-9385; Email: whiggins@stjohnsprepschool.org; Web: www.stjohnsprepschool.org. Mr. William A. Higgins, B.A., M.A., M.S., Prin.; Rev. Liju Augustine, Chap.; Valerie Bove, Librarian. Full-time, paid 16; Lay Teachers 32; Priests 2; Sisters 1; Students 585; Religious Teachers 1.

BRIARWOOD. *Archbishop Molloy High School* (Coed) 83-53 Manton St., Briarwood, 11435. Tel: 718-441-2100; Fax: 718-849-8251; Email: president@molloyhs.org; Web: www.molloyhs.org. Richard A. Karsten, Pres.; Darius Penikas, Prin. Brothers 8; Lay Teachers 98; Students 1,510.

COLLEGE POINT. *St. Agnes Academic High School* (Girls) 13-20 124 St., College Point, 11356-1814. Tel: 718-353-6276; Fax: 718-353-6068; Email: snicoletti@stagneshs.org; Email: denise.fetonte@stagneshs.org; Web: stagneshs.org. Susan Nicoletti, Prin.; Mrs. Anne Kelly, Asst. Prin.; Ms. Kathleen Gaughan, Asst. Prin.; Catherine O'Sullivan, Librarian. Lay Teachers 19; Sisters 3; Students 300.

EAST ELMHURST. *Monsignor McClancy Memorial High School* (1956) (Coed) 71-06 31st Ave., East Elmhurst, 11370. Tel: 718-898-3800; Fax: 718-898-3929; Email: docjoerocco@gmail.com; Email: JCastrataro@msgrmcclancy.info; Web: www.msgrmcclancy.org. Bro. Joseph Rocco, S.C., Ed.D., Pres.; Jim Castrataro, Prin.; Mrs. Nicole Alexis-Kane, Librarian. Brothers 12; Lay Teachers 38; Students 647.

FLUSHING. *Holy Cross High School* (1955) (Co-ed) 26-20 Francis Lewis Blvd., Flushing, 11358. Tel: 718-886-7250; Fax: 718-886-7257; Email: info@holycrosshs.org; Web: www.holycrosshs.org. Michael Truesdell, Pres.; Edward Burns, Prin.; Mr. Denis Venturino, Fin. Dir. Lay Teachers 41; Students 565; Holy Cross Fathers 1.

FRESH MEADOWS. *St. Francis Preparatory School*, (Grades 9-12), (Coed) 6100 Francis Lewis Blvd., Fresh Meadows, 11365. Tel: 718-423-8810; Fax: 718-224-2108; Email: 21stcentury@sfponline.org; Web: www.sfponline.org. Bro. Leonard Conway, O.S.F., Pres.; Mr. Patrick McLaughlin, Prin.; Rev. Ralph Edel, Chap. Franciscan Brothers 4; Lay Teachers 142; Priests 1; Sisters 2; Students 2,500; Personnel 41; Clergy / Religious Teachers 7.

JAMAICA ESTATES. *The Mary Louis Academy (College Preparatory)* (Girls) 176-21 Wexford Ter., Jamaica Estates, 11432. Tel: 718-297-2120; Fax: 718-739-0037; Email: marylouisacademy@aol.com; Web: www.tmla.org. Mrs. Ann O'Hagan-Cordes, Prin.; Mrs. Marie Whelan, Librarian. Lay Teachers 67; Sisters of St. Joseph (Brentwood Community) 16; Students 800.

MIDDLE VILLAGE. *Christ the King High School* (Coed) 68-02 Metropolitan Ave., Middle Village, 11379. Tel: 718-366-7400; Fax: 718-366-1165; Web: www.ctkny.org. Ms. Geri Martinez, Prin.; Michael W. Michel, Pres.; Mr. Steven Giusto, Asst. Prin./Dir. of Admissions; Carolann Timpone, Asst. Prin.; Veronica Arbitello, Asst. Prin.; Rev. Frank W. Spacek, School Chap.; Sr. Elizabeth Graham, C.S.J., Campus Min. Lay Teachers 37; Sisters 1; Students 650.

[H] HIGH SCHOOLS, PAROCHIAL

BROOKLYN. *Denis Maloney Institute / St. Edmund Preparatory High School* (Coed) 2474 Ocean Ave., 11229. Tel: 718-743-6100; Fax: 718-743-5243; Email: amcginnis@stedmundprep.org; Web: www.stedmundprep.org. Allison McGinnis, Prin.; Peggy McEvoy, Prin.; Kevin Raphael, Asst. Prin.; Suzanne Lemmon, Librarian. Deacons 2; Lay Teachers 50; Sisters 1; Students 550.

St. Saviour High School (Girls) 588 6th St., 11215. Tel: 718-768-4406; Fax: 718-369-2688; Email: mckeown.p@stsaviour.org; Email: bernstein.m@stsaviour.org; Email: dibenedetto.t@stsaviour.org; Web: www.stsaviour.org. Dr. Paula McKeown, Prin.; Sr. Anne Lally, C.S.J., Campus Min.; Mrs. Margaret Bernstein, Asst. Prin.; Christine Bove, Dir. Devel. (Full-time, paid) 5; Lay Teachers 22; Sisters 2; Students 173.

[I] SPECIAL SCHOOLS

BROOKLYN. *Catherine Laboure Special Education Program*, 744 E. 87th St., 11236. Tel: 718-449-1857 ; Fax: 718-449-0212; Email: catherinelaboure1965@gmail.com; Web: www.laboureschool.org. Ms. Mary Nafash, Prin. Program for mentally challenged students and learning disabled students ages 5-21. Students 41; Lay Teachers and Staff 20.

St. Francis de Sales School for the Deaf in Brooklyn (1960) (Grades PreK-8), 260 Eastern Pkwy., 11225. Tel: 718-636-4573; Fax: 718-636-4577; Email: school@sfdesales.org; Web: www.sfdesales.org. Jennifer White, Bus. Mgr.; Maria Bartolillo, Dir. Infant through Elementary Grades (8th Grade). Lay Teachers 14; Students 70; Religious Teachers 22.

St. Francis de Sales School for the Deaf Development Fund, 260 Eastern Pkwy., 11225. Tel: 718-636-4573; Fax: 718-636-4577; Email: school@sfdesales.org. Maria Bartolillo, Dir.; Jennifer White, Business Mgr.

The Ryken Educational Center, 7100 Shore Rd., 11209. Tel: 718-759-5758; Fax: 718-759-5744; Email: wslow@xaverian.org. William Slow, Dir.

SPRINGFIELD GARDENS. *Martin de Porres School for Exceptional Children, Inc.*, 140 Beach 112th St., Rockaway Park, 11694. Tel: 718-525-5550; Fax: 516-502-2841; Email: edana@mdp.org; Web: www.mdp.org. Mr. Edward Dana, Exec. Dir.; Mr. Joseph Trainor, M.S.W., Asst. Exec. Dir. Specialized day elementary & high school and group residence for emotionally challenged youth ages 6-21. Administrators 5; Classroom Aides 24; Brothers 2; Capacity 480; Sisters 2; Total Staff 227; Asst. Teachers 40; Residential Care Workers 24; Counselors 38; Support Personnel 24; Clergy/Religious Teachers 67.

Additional Sites:

Martin de Porres Elementary School, 621 Elmont Rd., Bldg. A, Elmont, 11003. Tel: 516-616-0671; Fax: 516-616-0674. John Galassi, Prin.

Casa de Casalle Residence, 101-25 104th St., Ozone Park, 11416. Tel: 718-850-0191; Fax: 718-850-0192 . Lennox Bailey, Residence Prog. Dir. Day & residential school for emotionally challenged youth.

[J] CONSOLIDATED ELEMENTARY SCHOOLS (REGIONAL)

BROOKLYN. *Saint Anselm Catholic Academy*, 365 83rd St., 11209. Tel: 718-745-7643; Fax: 718-745-0086; Email: kflanagan@sacany.org. Mr. Kevin Flanagan, Prin. Lay Teachers 21; Students 327.

St. Athanasius Catholic Academy, (Grades N-8), 6120 Bay Pkwy., 11204. Tel: 718-236-4791; Fax: 718-621-1423; Email: dcompetello@diobrook.org. Mrs. Diane Competello, Prin. Lay Teachers 19; Students 374.

St. Bernadette Catholic Academy, (Grades PreK-8), 1313 83rd St., 11228. Tel: 718-236-1560; Fax: 718-236-3364; Web: www.stbernbk.org. Sr. Joan DiRienzo, M.P.F., Prin. Lay Teachers 23; Students 391; Sisters (Religious Teachers Filippini) 4.

St. Bernard Catholic Academy, (Grades PreK-8), 2030 E. 69th St., 11234. Tel: 718-241-6040; Web: www.stbernardcatholicacademy.org. Kathleen Buscemi, Prin. Lay Teachers 17; Students 336.

Blessed Sacrament Catholic Academy, (Grades PreK-8), 187 Euclid Ave., 11208. Tel: 718-235-4863; Fax: 718-235-1132; Email: maryloucelmer@yahoo.com. Marylou Celmer, Prin. Lay Teachers 14; Students 282.

St. Brigid Catholic Academy, (Grades PreK-8), 438 Grove St., 11237. Tel: 718-821-1477; Fax: 718-821-1079; Email: sgonzalez@stbrigidca-brooklyn.org. Ms. Maria Soria, Prin. Lay Teachers 13; Students 192; Teachers 14; Enrollment 207; Enrollment 192.

**Brooklyn Jesuit Prep* (2003) (Grades 5-8), 560 Sterling Pl., 11238. Tel: 718-638-5884; Fax: 718-638-5284; Web: www.brooklynjesuit.org. Ms. Patricia Gauvey, Pres.; Gregory Arte, Prin. Lay Teachers 14; Students 92; Clergy / Religious Teachers 3.

Saint Catherine of Genoa-Saint Therese of Lisieux Catholic Academy, (Grades PreK-8), 4410 Ave. D, 11203. Tel: 718-629-9330; Fax: 718-629-6854; Email: office@scgstl.org. Jeannette Boursiquot-Charles, Prin. Administrators 2; Lay Teachers 16; Students 253; Religious Teachers 15.

St. Frances Cabrini Catholic Academy, 181 Suydam St., 11221. Tel: 718-386-9277; Fax: 718-386-9064; Email: principal@sfc-ca.net; Email: info@sfc-ca.net. Ms. Allison Murphy, Prin. Lay Teachers 13; Students 224.

St. Francis of Assisi Catholic Academy, 400 Lincoln Rd., 11225. Tel: 718-778-3700; Fax: 718-778-7877; Email: finances@sfabrooklyn.org. Ms. Diana Soto, Prin.; Sr. Barbara Yander, Admin. Asst. Lay Teachers 15; Sisters 1; Students 320.

Saint Francis Xavier Catholic Academy, 763 President St., 11215. Tel: 718-857-2559; Fax: 718-857-5391; Email: sfxparkslope@gmail.com; Web: www.sfxca-parkslope.org. Mrs. Dorothy Taylor, Prin. Lay Teachers 15; Students 185.

Good Shepherd Catholic Academy, (Grades PreK-8), 1943 Brown St., 11229. Tel: 718-339-2745; Fax: 718-645-4513; Email: jobrien@gscabk.org;

Web: www.goodshepherdbklyn.org. John O'Brien, Prin. Lay Teachers 17; Students 304.

St. Gregory the Great Catholic Academy, 2520 Church Ave., 11226. Tel: 718-774-3330; Tel: 718-282-2770; Fax: 718-774-3332; Email: sgg991@yahoo.com. Mr. Rudolph Cyrus-Charles, Prin.; Ms. Arlene Stewart, Librarian & Computer Tech. Lay Teachers 19; Students 252.

Holy Angels Catholic Academy, (Grades PreK-8), 337 74th St., 11209. Tel: 718-238-5045; Fax: 718-748-9775; Email: holyangelsoffice@aol.com; Web: www.holyangelsbayridge.org. Mrs. Rosemarie McGoldrick, Prin. Lay Teachers 15; Students 184.

St. Joseph the Worker Catholic Academy, (Grades PreK-8), 241 Prospect Park W., 11215. Tel: 718-768-7629; Fax: 718-768-3007; Email: jgallina@sjwca.org; Web: www.sjwca.org. Mrs. Jennifer Gallina, Prin.; Mrs. Louise Witthohn, Sec. Lay Teachers 15; Students 220.

St. Mark Catholic Academy, (Grades PreK-8), 2602 E. 19th St., 11235. Tel: 718-332-9604; Fax: 718-332-6024; Email: cdonnelly@smsonthebay.com; Email: cdonnelly@diobrook.org; Web: www.smcaonthebay.org. Mrs. Caroline Donnelly, Prin.
Legal Title: St. Mark School Lay Teachers 16; Students 300.

Mary Queen of Heaven Catholic Academy, (Grades PreK-8), Mary Queen of Heaven Catholic Academy: 1326 East 57 St., 11234. Tel: 718-763-2360; Fax: 718-763-7540; Email: mqhsec@optonline.net. 1326 E. 57th St., 11234. Ms. Mary Bellone, Prin. Lay Teachers 13; Students 166; Clergy / Religious Teachers 2.

Midwood Catholic Academy, (Grades PreK-8), 1501 Hendrickson St., 11234. Tel: 718-377-1800; Fax: 718-377-6374; Email: mca1340@yahoo.com; Web: www.midwoodcatholicacademy.org. Mrs. Elena Heimbach, Prin. Lay Teachers 12; Students 236.

Our Lady of Grace Catholic Academy, (Grades K-8), 385 Ave. W, 11223. Tel: 718-375-2081; Fax: 718-376-7685; Email: principal@olgbk.org. Mrs. Kelly Wolf, Prin. Lay Teachers 13; Students 178; Clergy / Religious Teachers 3.

Our Lady of Guadalupe Catholic Academy, (Grades PreK-8), 1514 72nd St., 11228. Tel: 718-236-5587; Fax: 718-236-5587; Email: info@olgacademy.net; Web: olgacademy.net. Muriel Wilkinson, Prin. Lay Teachers 14; Students 160; Religious Teachers 3.

Our Lady of Perpetual Help Catholic Academy, 5902 6th Ave., 11220. Tel: 718-439-8067; Fax: 718-439-8081; Email: mtyndall@olphcab.org. Ms. Margaret Tyndall, Prin. Lay Teachers 16; Students 229; Clergy / Religious Teachers 11.

Our Lady of Trust Catholic Academy, 1696 Canarsie Rd., 11236. Tel: 718-241-6633; Email: oltcasocialmedia@gmail.com. Arlene Barcia, Prin., Email: abarcia9719@optimum.net. Lay Teachers 16; Students 230.

Queen of All Saints Catholic Academy, (Grades K-8), 300 Vanderbilt Ave., 11205. Tel: 718-857-3114; Fax: 718-857-0632; Email: m.pizzi@sfx-qas.org. Ms. Manuela Adsuar-Pizzi, Prin. Lay Teachers 12; Students 122.

Queen of the Rosary Catholic Academy, 11 Catherine St., 11211. Tel: 718-388-7992; Fax: 718-388-7543; Email: queenoftherosaryacademy@gmail.com. Mr. James Daino, Prin. Lay Teachers 13; Students 178; Religious Teachers 15.

Saint Patrick Catholic Academy, (Grades PreK-8), 401 97th St., 11209. Tel: 718-833-0124; Fax: 718-238-6480; Email: administration@stpatrickca.org; Web: www.stpatrickca.org. Lay Teachers 17; Students 190.

Saint Peter Catholic Academy, 8401 23rd Ave., 11214. Tel: 718-372-0025; Fax: 718-265-6498; Email: dalfeo@stpeteracademy-brooklyn.org. Ms. Danielle Alfeo, Prin. Lay Teachers 18; Students 275.

Salve Regina Catholic Academy, (Grades PreK-8), 237 Jerome St., 11207. Tel: 718-277-9000; Tel: 718-277-6766; Fax: 718-348-0513; Email: mdonato@srca.org; Web: www.srca.org. Ms. Michelle Donato, Prin. Administrators 1; Aides 10; Lay Teachers 15; Students 344.

St. Saviour Catholic Academy, 701 Eighth Ave., 11215. Tel: 718-768-8000; Fax: 718-768-0373; Email: swalsh@sscaparkslope.org. Susan McCabe-Walsh, Prin. Lay Teachers 30; Students 366.

St. Stanislaus Kostka Catholic Academy, (Grades PreK-8), 12 Newell St., 11222. Tel: 718-383-1970; Fax: 718-383-1711; Email: ccieloszczyk@ststansacademy.org; Web: www.ststansacademy.org. Ms. Christina Cieloszczyk, Prin. Lay Teachers 17; Students 206.

Visitation Academy, (Grades PreK-8), 8902 Ridge Blvd., 11209. Tel: 718-680-9452; Fax: 718-680-4441; Web: www.visitationacademy.net. Mother Susan Marie Kasprzak, V.H.M., B.A., Supr. & Pres.; Mrs. Jean Bernieri, Prin. Girls 130; Lay Teachers 20; Sisters of the Visitation 3; Students 150; Religious Teachers 5; Clergy / Religious Teachers 2.

ASTORIA. *St. Francis of Assisi School*, 21-18 46th St., Astoria, 11105. Tel: 718-726-9405; Fax: 718-721-2577. Ms. Anne Stefano, Prin. Lay Teachers 22; Students 325.

Immaculate Conception Catholic Academy in Astoria, (Grades PreK-8), 21-63 29th St., Astoria, 11105. Tel: 718-728-1969; Fax: 718-728-3374; Email: principal@iccaastoria.org; Web: www.iccaastoria.org. Eileen Harnischfeger, Prin.
Legal Title: Immaculate Conception Catholic Academy in Astoria. Lay Teachers 20; Students 265.

BAYSIDE. *Our Lady of the Blessed Sacrament Catholic Academy*, 34-45 202nd St., Bayside, 11361. Tel: 718-229-4434; Fax: 718-229-5820; Email: jkane@olbsacademy.org. Joan Kane, Prin. Lay Teachers 21; Students 347.

Sacred Heart Catholic Academy of Bayside, (Grades PreK-8), 216-01 38th Ave., Bayside, 11361. Tel: 718-631-4804; Fax: 718-631-5738; Email: info@sacredheartbayside.org; Web: www.sacredheartbayside.org. Mary-Anne Cooke, Prin.
Legal Titles: Sacred Heart School Lay Teachers 28; Students 325.

BELLE HARBOR. *St. Francis De Sales Catholic Academy*, 219 Beach 129th St., Belle Harbor, 11694. Tel: 718-634-2775; Fax: 718-634-6673; Email: admin@stfrancisschoolbh.net. Lay Teachers 29; Students 545.

CAMBRIA HEIGHTS. *Sacred Heart Catholic Academy*, 115-50 221st St., Cambria Heights, 11411. Tel: 718-527-0123; Fax: 718-527-1204; Email: sacredheartch@gmail.com. Mrs. Yvonne-Therese Russell Smith, Prin.; Mrs. A. Kiffin-Santiago, Librarian. Lay Teachers 15; Students 282.

CORONA. *St. Leo Catholic Academy*, (Grades PreK-8), 104-19 49th Ave., Corona, 11368. Tel: 718-592-7050; Fax: 718-592-0787; Email: office@stleocatholicacademy.org; Web: www.stleocatholicacademy.org. Jennifer Hernandez, Prin.
Legal Title: St. Leo School Lay Teachers 20; Students 348.

Our Lady of Sorrows Catholic Academy (Co-ed) 35-34 105th St., Corona, 11368. Tel: 718-426-5517; Fax: 718-651-5585; Email: board@olscorona.org; Web: www.olscorona.org. Dr. Cristina Cruz, Prin. Lay Teachers 15; Students 262.

DOUGLASTON. *Divine Wisdom Catholic Academy*, (Grades PreK-8), 45-11 245th St., Douglaston, 11362. Tel: 718-631-3153; Fax: 718-631-3945; Email: mbonici@dwcaonline.org; Email: lkeppel@dwcaonline.org; Web: dwcaonline.org. Mrs. Miriam Bonici, Prin.; Mrs. Linda Keppel, Admin.; Mrs. Sylvia Roccia, Admin. Lay Teachers 35; Students 465.

ELMHURST. *Saint Adalbert Catholic Academy*, (Grades PreK-8), 52-17 83rd St., Elmhurst, 11373. Tel: 718-424-2376; Fax: 718-898-7852; Email: tmorris@diobrook.org; Web: www.saintadalbertca.org. Mr. Thomas Morris, Prin. Lay Teachers 21; Sisters 1; Students 333; Religious Teachers 1; Clergy / Religious Teachers 1.

St. Bartholomew Catholic Academy, 44-15 Judge St., Elmhurst, 11373. Tel: 718-446-7575; Email: sbca11373@gmail.com. Mrs. Denise Gonzalez, Prin. Lay Teachers 12; Students 171.

FLORAL PARK. *Our Lady of the Snows Catholic Academy*, (Grades N-8), 79-33 258th St., Floral Park, 11004. Tel: 718-343-1346; Fax: 718-343-7303; Email: Office@olscafp.org; Web: olscafp.org. Mr. Joseph Venticinque, Prin. Nursery (3 yr old) Program through 8th Grade Lay Teachers 28; Students 495.

FLUSHING. *St. Andrew Avellino Catholic Academy*, 35-50 158th St., Flushing, 11358. Tel: 718-359-7887; Fax: 718-359-2295; Email: saintandrewavellino@hotmail.com; Web: standrewavellinoca.com. Debora A. Hanna, Prin. Lay Teachers 19; Students 252.

Holy Family Catholic Academy, 74-15 175th St., Flushing, 11366. Tel: 718-969-2124; Fax: 718-380-2183. Mary Scheer, Prin. Lay Teachers 15; Students 201.

Saint Kevin Catholic Academy, (Grades PreK-8), 45-50 195th St., Flushing, 11358. Tel: 718-357-2110; Fax: 718-357-2519; Email: stkevinschool@yahoo.com; Web: stkevinca.org. Thomas R. Piro, Prin. Lay Teachers 24; Religious 1; Students 304; Clergy / Religious Teachers 2.

Saint Mel Catholic Academy, 154-24 26th Ave., Flushing, 11354. Tel: 718-539-8211; Fax: 718-539-6563; Email: eschneider@stmelsacademy.org; Web: www.stmelsacademy.org. Erin Schneider, Prin.; Daniela Volpe, Vice Prin. Lay Teachers 18; Students 285; Clergy / Religious Teachers 1.

Most Holy Redeemer Catholic Academy, (Grades K-8), 136-58 41st Ave., Flushing, 11355. Tel: 718-961-0284; Tel: 718-961-0246; Fax: 718-961-2013; Web: www.stmichaelsca.org. Mrs. Maureen Rogone, Prin. Lay Teachers 26; Religious 1; Students 303; Clergy / Religious Teachers 2.

FOREST HILLS. *Our Lady of Mercy Catholic Academy*, 70-25 Kessel St., Forest Hills, 11375. Tel: 718-793-2086; Fax: 718-897-2144; Email: principal@mercyhills.org. Ann Quinlivan, Librarian. Lay Teachers 22; Students 296.

Our Lady Queen of Martyrs Catholic Academy, 72-55 Austin St., Forest Hills, 11375. Tel: 718-263-2622; Fax: 718-263-0063; Email: info@olqmca.org; Web: www.olqmca.com. Mrs. Ann Zuschlag, Prin. Lay Teachers 20; Students 321.

GLENDALE. *Sacred Heart Catholic Academy of Glendale*, (Grades PreK-8), 84-05 78th Ave., Glendale, 11385. Tel: 718-456-6636; Fax: 718-456-0286; Email: sacredheartg@aol.com; Web: sacredheartglendale.org. Ms. Joanne Gangi, Prin. Lay Teachers 21; Students 297.

HOWARD BEACH. *Ave Maria Catholic Academy*, (Grades N-8), 158-20 101st St., Howard Beach, 11414. Tel: 718-848-7440; Email: mmcmanus@olgcahb.org; Web: www.olgcahb.org. Marybeth McManus, Prin. Lay Teachers 18; Students 229.

St. Helen Catholic Academy, 83-09 157th Ave., Howard Beach, 11414. Tel: 718-835-4155; Fax: 718-848-8722; Email: info@sthelencatholicacademy.org. Mr. Frederick Tudda, Prin. Lay Teachers 18; Students 305.

JAMAICA. *Immaculate Conception Catholic Academy*, (Grades PreK-8), 179-14 Dalny Rd., Jamaica, 11432. Tel: 718-739-5933; Fax: 718-523-7436; Email: dbreen@iccajamaica. Ms. Dorothea Breen, Prin. Lay Teachers 23; Students 405.

St. Nicholas of Tolentine Catholic Academy, (Grades PreK-8), 80-22 Parsons Blvd., Jamaica, 11432. Tel: 718-380-1900; Fax: 718-591-6977; Email: office@sntschoolny.org; Web: sntschoolny.org. Robert J. Lowenberg, M.A., Prin. Lay Teachers 25; Students 370.

LONG ISLAND CITY. *St. Joseph Catholic Academy*, 2846 44th St., Long Island City, 11103. Tel: 718-728-0724; Fax: 718-728-6142; Email: info@sjcalic.org. Mr. Luke Nawrocki, Prin.; Ms. Margaret Stewart, Librarian. Lay Teachers 21; Students 476.

MIDDLE VILLAGE. *Saint Margaret Catholic Academy*, (Grades PreK-8), 66-10 80th St., Middle Village, 11379. Tel: 718-326-0922; Email: stmargprincipal@gmail.com. Ms. Victoria Richardson, Prin. Lay Teachers 26; Sisters of St. Dominic 1; Students 325.

Our Lady of Hope Catholic Academy, (Grades PreK-8), 61-21 71st St., Middle Village, 11379. Tel: 718-458-3535; Fax: 718-458-9031; Email: olhoff@olhca.org; Email: olhprin@olhca.org; Web: www.olhca.org. Mr. Giuseppe F. Campailla, Prin. Lay Teachers 31; Students 500.

OZONE PARK. *Divine Mercy Catholic Academy*, 101-60 92nd St., Ozone Park, 11416. Tel: 718-845-3074, Ext. 3; Fax: 718-845-5068; Email: m.lods@dmcacademy.com; Web: www.dmcacademy.com. Sr. Francis Marie Wystepek, C.S.F.N., Prin.; Mr. Joseph Christiano, Chm. Bd. Elementary Campus N-8. Aides 4; Full time, paid 3; Lay Teachers 13; Lay Teachers 16; Sisters 1; Students 244.

St. Elizabeth Catholic Academy, (Grades PreK-8), 9401 85th St., Ozone Park, 11416. Tel: 718-641-6990; Fax: 718-323-5010; Email: info@stelizabethca.org. Ms. Jeanne Shannon, Prin. Full-time lay teachers 15; Students 388.

St. Mary Gate of Heaven Catholic Academy, (Grades PreK-8), 104-06 101st Ave., Ozone Park, 11416. Tel: 718-846-0689; Fax: 718-846-1059; Email: pheide@smgh.org; Web: www.smgh.org. Mr. Philip Heide, Prin. Lay Teachers 24; Religious 1; Students 250; Religious Teachers 15; Clergy / Religious Teachers 15.

QUEENS VILLAGE. *Incarnation Catholic Academy*, 89-15 Francis Lewis Blvd., Queens Village, 11427. Tel: 718-465-5066; Fax: 718-464-4128; Email: principal@incrcc.org. Mrs. Satti Marchan, Prin. Lay Teachers 14; Students 248.

REGO PARK. *Our Lady of the Angelus Catholic Academy*, (Grades N-8), 98-05 63rd Dr., Rego Park, 11374. Tel: 718-896-7220; Fax: 718-896-5723; Email: olarcschool@aol.com. Mr. Giuseppe F. Campailla, Prin. Lay Teachers 14; Students 161.

Resurrection Ascension Catholic Academy, (Grades PreK-8), 85-25 61st Rd., Rego Park, 11374. Tel: 718-426-4963; Fax: 718-426-0940; Email: raschool443@aol.com. Joann Heppt, Prin. Lay Teachers 23; Students 342.

RICHMOND HILL. *Holy Child Jesus Catholic Academy*, (Grades PreK-8), 111-02 86th Ave., Richmond Hill, 11418. Tel: 718-849-3988; Fax: 718-850-2842; Email: pwinters@hcjcany.org; Web: www.hcjcany.

org. Ms. Patricia Winters, Prin. Lay Teachers 20; Students 270.

RIDGEWOOD. *St. Matthias Catholic Academy*, (Grades PreK-8), 58-25 Catalpa Ave., Ridgewood, 11385. Tel: 718-381-8003; Fax: 718-381-5319; Email: principal@stmatthiaschool.org; Web: www.stmatthiasca.org. Barbara Wehnes, Prin. Lay Teachers 19; Students 328.

Notre Dame Catholic Academy of Ridgewood, (Grades N-8), 62-22 61st St., Ridgewood, 11385. Tel: 718-821-2221; Fax: 718-821-1058; Web: www.notredame-ca.org. Jennifer DiLorenzo, Prin. Lay Teachers 16; Students 305.

ROCKAWAY BEACH. *Saint Camillus Catholic Academy*, (Grades PreK-8), 185 Beach 99th St., Rockaway, 11694. Tel: 718-634-5260; Fax: 718-634-8253; Email: rcorso@stcamillusca.org; Web: www.stcamillusca.org. Mr. Raffaele Corso, Prin. Lay Teachers 11; Students 146.

Saint Rose of Lima Catholic Academy, (Grades PreK-8), 154 Beach 84th St., Rockaway Beach, 11693. Tel: 718-474-7079; Fax: 718-634-0524; Email: stroseacademyrb@gmail.com; Web: stroseoflimacatholicacademy.org. Theresa S. Andersen, Prin.; Kimberly Wilson, Admin. Lay Teachers 22; Students 369; Clergy / Religious Teachers 1.

ROSEDALE. *Saint Clare Catholic Academy*, 137-25 Brookville Blvd., Rosedale, 11422. Tel: 718-528-7174; Fax: 718-528-4389; Email: stclareschool@nyc.rr.com; Email: scca@stclarecatholicacademy.org; Web: stclarecatholicacademy.org. Mary Rafferty-Basile, Prin. Lay Teachers 20; Students 281.

SOUTH OZONE PARK. *Our Lady of Perpetual Help Catholic Academy*, 111-10 115th St., South Ozone Park, 11420. Tel: 718-843-4184; Fax: 718-843-6838 ; Email: fdeluca@dobmail.org. 111-50 115th St., South Ozone Park, 11420. Mrs. Frances DeLuca, Prin. Lay Teachers 25; Students 403.

WHITESTONE. *Holy Trinity Catholic Academy*, (Grades PreK-8), 14-45 143rd St., Whitestone, 11357. Tel: 718-746-1479; Fax: 718-746-4793; Email: bkavanagh@htcawhitestone.org. Barbara Kavanagh, Prin. Lay Teachers 15; Students 187.

WOODHAVEN. *St. Thomas the Apostle Catholic Academy*, 8749 87th St., Woodhaven, 11421. Tel: 718-847-3904; Fax: 718-847-3513; Email: preggio@diobrook.org. Dr. Phyllis Reggio, Prin. Lay Teachers 18; Students 290; Clergy / Religious Teachers 1.

WOODSIDE. *St. Sebastian Catholic Academy*, 39-76 58th St., Woodside, 11377. Tel: 718-429-1982; Fax: 718-446-7225; Email: staff@stsebastianacademy.org; Web: www.stsebastianacademy.org. Mrs. JoAnn Dolan, Prin.; Mrs. Michelle Picarello, Admin. Lay Teachers 26; Students 466.

[K] CATHOLIC CHARITIES

BROOKLYN. *Catholic Charities, Diocese of Brooklyn*, Central Office, 191 Joralemon St., 11201. Tel: 718-722-6086; Fax: 718-722-6096; Email: jeanne.diulio@ccbq.org; Web: www.ccbq.org. Most Rev. Nicholas A. DiMarzio, Ph.D., D.D., Bishop of Brooklyn; Rev. Msgr. Alfred P. LoPinto, V.E., Pres., CEO & Episcopal Vicar for Human Svcs.; Very Rev. Patrick J. Keating, Deputy CEO; Alan Wolinetz, CFO/Chief Admin. Officer; Emmie Glynn Ryan, Esq., Gen. Counsel & Chief Compliance Officer; Ms. Gladys Rodriguez, C.S.W., Sr. Vice Pres. & Chief Prog. Officer; Patricia Bowles, Sr. Vice Pres./ Chief Prog. Officer & Chief Privacy Officer; Jim Norcott, M.S.W., M.P.A., Sr. Vice Pres. Planning and Evaluation; Richard Slizeski, Vice Pres. Mission; George Stathoudakis, Sr. Vice Pres. Real Estate Asset Mgmt.; Lucy Garrido-Moto, Sr. Vice Pres. Communications; Jean Potvin, Sr. Vice Pres. Giving; Jacqueline Gibbons, Sr. Vice Pres. Human Resources; Patrick Mahon, Chief Information Officer; Christine D'Ottavio, Controller; Alla Eleon, M.B.A., Controller; Delroy Davey, Dir. Budgeting; Michael Cortez, Dir. Shared Svcs.; Stanley Celius, Vice Pres. Progress of Peoples Mgmt. Corp.; Tim McManus, Vice Pres. Catholic Charities Progress of Peoples Devel. Corp. Tot Asst. Annually 66,000; Total Staff 1,504.

Office of Mission, 191 Joralemon St., 7th Fl., 11201. Tel: 718-722-6115; Fax: 718-722-6233; Email: info@ccbq.org. Richard Slizeski, Sr. Vice Pres., Mission.

Advocate for Persons with Disabilities Services, 191 Joralemon St., 7th Fl., 11201. Tel: 718-722-6232; Fax: 718-722-6233; Email: info@ccbq.org. Richard Slizeski, Vice Pres.

Bereavement Services, 191 Joralemon St., 7th Fl., 11201. Tel: 718-722-6503; Email: info@ccbq.org. Richard Slizeski, Vice Pres.

Community Service, 191 Joralemon St., 7th Fl., 11201. Tel: 718-722-6000. Richard Slizeski, Vice Pres.

Vincentian Outreach, 191 Joralemon St., 11201. Tel: 917-960-1232; Email: info@ccbq.org. Richard Slizeski, Vice Pres.

Office of Planning & Evaluation Jim Norcott, M.S.W., M.P.A., Sr. Vice Pres.; Rev. Peter Mahoney, Assoc. Dir., (Retired); Patrick Callaghan, Community Integration Dir., 191 Joralemon St., 11201. Tel: 718-722-6001; Sheldon Peters, Community Integration Dir.; Josefa Castro, Community Integration Dir., 23-40 Astoria Blvd., Astoria, 11102. Tel: 718-726-9790; Fax: 718-728-8817; Debbie Hampson, Community Programming, 23-40 Astoria Blvd., Astoria, 11102. Tel: 718-726-9790; Fax: 718-728-8817.

Comprehensive Human Services:.

Catholic Charities Neighborhood Services, Inc., 191 Joralemon St., 11201. Tel: 718-722-6000; Fax: 718-722-6096; Email: info@ccbq.org; Web: www.ccbq.org. Very Rev. Patrick J. Keating, Deputy CEO; Rev. Msgr. Alfred P. LoPinto, V.E., Exec. Vice Pres. & CEO; Ms. Gladys Rodriguez, C.S.W., Sr. Vice Pres. & Chief Prog. Officer, Family & Community Svcs.; Patricia Bowles, Sr. Vice Pres. & Chief Prog. Officer, Integrated Health & Wellness; Margaret Kelleher, Chm. of Bd. Total Staff 1,290.

CCNS - Family & Community Services:.

CCNS - Senior Services, Tel: 718-722-6095. Samira Alieva, Vice Pres.

The Bay Senior Center, 3643 Nostrand Ave., 11229. Tel: 718-648-2053; Fax: 718-648-7213; Email: info@ccbq.org. Gladys Rodriguez, Senior Vice Pres. & Chief Prog. Officer.

Bayside Senior Center and Bayside Senior Center Transportation Program, 221-15 Horace Harding Expwy., Bayside, 11364. Tel: 718-225-1144; Fax: 718-229-7320; Email: info@ccbq.org; Web: www.ccbq.orq. Gladys Rodriguez, Senior Vice Pres./Chief Program Officer.

Benson Ridge Senior Services Assistance Center 6823 5th Ave., 11220. Tel: 718-680-3530; Fax: 718-680-3654; Email: info@ccbq.org. Gladys Rodriguez, Senior Vice Pres./Chief Program Officer.

Catherine Sheridan Senior Center, 35-24 83rd St., Jackson Heights, 11372. Tel: 718-458-4600; Fax: 718-458-5665; Email: infor@ccbq.org. Gladys Rodriguez, Senior Vice Pres./Chief Program Officer.

CCNS Depression & Substance Abuse Screening & Assistance Program, 168-04 119th Ave., St. Albans, 11412. Tel: 718-358-3541; Fax: 718-961-4712; Email: info@ccbq.org. Gladys Rodriguez, Senior Vice Pres. & Chief Program Officer.

CCNS NE Queens Home Delivered Meals Program, 221-15 Horace Harding Expwy, Bayside, Queens, 11364. Tel: 718-357-4903; Fax: 718-357-5731; Email: info@ccbq.org. Gladys Rodriguez, Senior Vice Pres. & Chief Program Officer. Program is located at the Bayside Senior center temporarily.

CCNS SW Queens Home Delivered Meals Program, 103-02 101st Ave., Ozone Park, 11416. Tel: 718-847-2168; Fax: 718-704-1499; Email: info@ccbq.org. Gladys Rodriguez, Senior Vice Pres. & Chief Program Officer.

CCNS Western Queens Home Delivered Meal Program, 89-18 Astoria Blvd., East Elmhurst, 11369. Tel: 718-806-1080; Fax: 718-806-1074; Email: info@ccbq.org. Gladys Rodriguez, Senior Vice Pres. & Chief Program Officer.

CCNS Social Adult Day Alzheimer's Program, 190-04 119th Ave., St. Albans, 11412. Tel: 718-358-3541; Fax: 718-961-4712; Email: info@ccbq.org. Gladys Rodriguez, Senior Vice Pres. & Chief Program Officer.

Della Monica-Steinway Senior Center, 23-56 Broadway, Astoria, 11106. Tel: 718-626-1500; Fax: 718-278-4432; Email: info@ccbq.org. Gladys Rodriguez, Senior Vice Pres. & Chief Program Officer.

Glenwood Senior Center, 5701 Ave. H, 11234. Tel: 718-241-7711; Fax: 718-241-1936; Email: info@ccbq.org. Gladys Rodriguez, Senior Vice Pres. & Chief Program Officer.

Hillcrest Senior Center, 221-15 Horace Harding Expwy., Bayside, Queens, 11364. Gladys Rodriguez, Senior Vice Pres. & Chief Program Officer. Due to the loss of the lease, planned relocation and the major construction at the new site, center is considered not operational. Seniors are distributed to other centers. Mainly to the Bayside Senior center.

Howard Beach Senior Center, 155-55 Cross Bay Blvd., Howard Beach, 11414. Tel: 718-738-8100; Fax: 718-738-6684; Email: info@ccbq.org. Gladys Rodriguez, Senior Vice Pres. & Chief Program Officer.

The Lodge Senior Center, 7711 18th Ave., 11214. Tel: 718-621-1081; Fax: 718-621-1407; Email: info@ccbq.org. Gladys Rodriguez, Senior Vice Pres. & Chief Prog. Officer.

Narrows Senior Center, 933 54th St., 11219. Tel: 718-232-3211; Fax: 718-232-0512; Email: info@ccbq.org. Ms. Gladys Rodriguez, C.S.W., Senior Vice Pres. & Chief Prog. Officer.

Northside Senior Center, 179 N. 6th St., 11211. Tel: 718-387-2316; Fax: 718-387-3235; Email: info@ccbq.org. Gladys Rodriguez, Senior Vice Pres. & Chief Prog. Officer.

Ozone Park Senior Center, 103-02 101st Ave., Ozone Park, 11416. Tel: 718-847-2100; Fax: 718-847-2166; Email: info@ccbq.org. Gladys Rodriguez, Senior Vice Pres. & Chief Prog. Officer.

Pete McGuinness Senior Center, 715 Leonard St., 11222. Tel: 718-383-1940; Fax: 718-383-1960; Email: info@ccbq.org. Gladys Rodriguez, Senior Vice Pres. & Chief Prog. Officer.

Riverway Senior Center, 230 Riverdale Ave., 11212. Tel: 718-942-5345; Fax: 718-942-5342; Email: info@ccbq.org. Gladys Rodriguez, Senior Vice Pres. & Chief Program Officer.

St. Charles Jubilee Senior Center, 55 Pierrepont St., 11201. Tel: 718-855-0326; Fax: 718-852-5415 ; Email: info@ccbq.org. Gladys Rodriguez, Senior Vice Pres. & Chief Program Officer.

St. Louis Senior Center, 230 Kingston Ave., 11213. Tel: 718-771-7945; Fax: 718-467-2524; Email: info@ccbq.org. Gladys Rodriguez, Senior Vice Pres. & Chief Program Officer.

Seaside Senior Center, 320 Beach 94th St., Rockaway, 11693. Tel: 347-926-4119; Email: info@ccbq.org. Gladys Rodriguez, Senior Vice Pres. & Chief Prog. Officer.

Sheepshead Bay Supportive Services (NORC), 3677 Nostrand Ave. #3-A, 11229. Tel: 718-769-3579; Fax: 718-769-4155; Email: info@ccbq.org. Gladys Rodriguez, Senior Vice Pres. & Chief Prog. Officer.

South Brooklyn Alzheimer's Adult Care Program, 5701 Ave. H, 11234. Tel: 718-241-7711; Tel: 718-241-1936; Email: info@ccbq.org. Gladys Rodriguez, Senior Vice Pres. & Chief Prog. Officer.

Southwest Queens Senior Services, 183-16 Jamaica Ave., 2nd Fl., Jamaica, 11423. Tel: 718-217-0126 ; Fax: 718-217-0495; Email: info@ccbq.org. Gladys Rodriguez, Senior Vice Pres. & Chief Prog. Officer.

Woodhaven-Richmond Hill Senior Center, 89-02 91st St., Woodhaven, 11421. Tel: 718-847-9200; Fax: 718-805-9496; Email: info@ccbq.org. Gladys Rodriguez, Senior Vice Pres. & Chief Prog. Officer.

CCNS - Early Childhood Services

Caritas Training Center, 38-11 27th St., Long Island City, 11101. Tel: 718-937-7640; Fax: 718-392-7928; Email: info@ccbq.org. Ms. Gladys Rodriguez, C.S.W., Senior Vice Pres./ Chief Program Officer.

Colin Newell Early Childhood Development Center, 161-06 89th Ave., Jamaica, 11432. Tel: 718-523-1888; Email: info@ccbq.org. Gladys Rodriguez, Senior Vice Pres. & Chief Program Officer.

Parkside Early Childhood Development Center, 525 Parkside Ave., 11226. Tel: 929-210-9200; Fax: 929-210-9250; Email: info@ccbq.org. Gladys Rodriguez, Senior Vice Pres. & Chief Program Officer.

Queensbridge Early Childhood Development Center, 38-11 27th St., Long Island City, 11101. Tel: 718-937-7640; Fax: 718-392-7928; Email: info@ccbq.org. Gladys Rodriguez, Senior Vice Pres. & Chief Program Officer. Students 154.

Queensbridge Family Child Care, 38-11 27th St., Long Island City, 11101. Tel: 718-786-7523; Fax: 718-786-7309; Email: info@ccbq.org. Gladys Rodriguez, Senior Vice Pres. & Chief Prog. Officer. Students 119.

St. Malachy Early Childhood Development Center, 220 Hendricks St., 11207. Tel: 718-647-0966; Fax: 718-647-1042; Email: info@ccbq.org. Gladys Rodriguez, Senior Vice Pres. & Chief Program Officer. Students 147.

St. Margaret Mary Early Childhood Development Center, 9-16 27th Ave., Long Island City, 11102. Tel: 718-721-8065; Tel: 718-721-8211; Fax: 718-721-7454.

Sunset Park Early Childhood Development Center, 5902 6th Ave., 11220. Tel: 718-768-1012; Tel: 718-768-1607; Fax: 718-768-1607; Email: info@ccbq.org. Gladys Rodriguez, Senior Vice Pres./Chief Program Officer.

Therese Cervini Annex Early Child Development Center, 35-33 104th St., Corona, 11368. Tel: 718-478-2274; Tel: 718-478-2784; Fax: 718-478-3993; Email: info@ccbq.org. Gladys

Rodriguez, Senior Vice Pres. &. Chief Program Officer.
Therese Cervini Family Child Care, 35-33 104th St., Corona, 11368. Tel: 718-334-0806;
Tel: 718-334-0807; Fax: 718-334-0809; Email: info@ccbq.org.
Thomas A. DeStefano Early Childhood Development Center, 300 Vernon Ave., 11206.
Tel: 718-443-2900; Fax: 718-443-2905; Email: info@ccbq.org. Gladys Rodriguez, Senior Vice Pres. & Chief Program Officer.
Vincent J. Caristo Family Child Care, 525 Parkside Ave., 11226. Tel: 718-788-3035;
Tel: 718-788-3036; Fax: 347-750-8367; Email: info@ccbq.org. Gladys Rodriguez, Senior Vice Pres. & Chief Program Officer.
CCNS - Integrated Health and Wellness Martin Sussman, Vice Pres.; Desiree M. Arduini, Vice Pres.; Ellen Wagman, Assoc. Dir.
Integrated Health and Wellness:.
Cribbin House, 218-20 104th Ave., Queens Village, 11429. Tel: 718-776-4190; Fax: 718-464-4849.
104-22 48th Ave., Corona, 11368.
Tel: 718-699-7800; Fax: 718-699-3773.
305 Garfield Pl., 11215. Tel: 718-622-2100;
Fax: 718-622-3850.
225 Brooklyn Ave., 11213. Tel: 718-953-4444;
Fax: 718-953-0622.
132-14 90th St., Ozone Park, 11417.
Tel: 718-848-1970; Fax: 718-323-7349.
Home & Community Based Services aka HCBS-BHS Family Support Svcs.; Medicaid Svc. Coordination; Community Habilitation. 2307 Utica Ave., 2nd Floor, 11234. Tel: 718-377-7757; Email: info@ccbq.org. Patricia Bowles, Senior Vice Pres. & Chief Program Officer.
Helen Owen Carey Residence, 174 Java St., 11222.
Tel: 718-383-2451; Fax: 718-383-1488.
240 McKinley Ave., 11208. Tel: 718-647-7070;
Fax: 718-647-6833.
156 Midwood St., 11225. Tel: 718-282-8045;
Fax: 718-469-2874.
36-40 37th St., Long Island City, 11101.
Tel: 718-215-2183; Fax: 718-215-2172.
90-37 189th St., Hollis, 11423. Tel: 718-464-4090;
Tel: 718-464-0962 (TTY); Fax: 718-468-8919.
145-16 Farmers Blvd., Springfield Gardens, 11434. Tel: 718-712-9054; Fax: 718-723-2877.
4301 8th Ave., 11232. Tel: 718-437-4285;
Fax: 347-505-2556.
2440 Fulton St., 2nd Fl., 11233. Tel: 718-408-5180;
Fax: 718-408-5181.
3730 Shore Pkwy., 11235. Tel: 718-769-8836;
Fax: 718-368-0418.
Supportive Living Apartments, 1615 8th Ave., 11226. Tel: 718-499-3010; Fax: 718-499-2389.
Integrated Health and Wellness - Housing:.
Brooklyn Community Living Program, 195 Bay 19th St., 11214. Tel: 718-253-1366;
Fax: 718-253-5890; Email: info@ccbq.org. Patricia Bowles, Senior Vice Pres./Chief Program Officer.
Brooklyn Supported Housing Programs I (HCRA, BSHIV, & BSHV), 195 Bay 19th St., 11214.
Tel: 718-253-1366; Fax: 718-253-5890; Email: info@ccbq.org. Patricia Bowles, Senior Vice Pres./Chief Program Officer.
Casa Betsaida - Congregate and Apartment Programs, 267 Hewes St., 11211.
Tel: 718-218-7890; Fax: 718-218-8264; Email: info@ccbq.org. Patricia Bowles, Senior Vice Pres./Chief Program Officer.
Central Brooklyn Supported Housing, 195 Bay 19th Street, 11234. Tel: 718-253-1366;
Fax: 718-253-5890; Email: info@ccbq.org. Patricia Bowles, Senior Vice Pres. & Chief Program Officer.
Circle of Hope I & II, 195 Bay 19th St., 2nd Fl., 11214. Tel: 718-338-4716; Fax: 718-338-5383; Email: info@ccbq.org. Patricia Bowles, Senior Vice Pres. & Chief Program Officer.
Queens Community Living Program, 35-24 83rd St., Jackson Heights, 11372. Tel: 718-639-0700;
Fax: 718-639-7684; Email: info@ccbq.org. Patricia Bowles, Senior Vice Pres. & Chief Program Officer.
Queens Supported Housing Programs (I, II, III & IV), 35-24 83rd St., Jackson Heights, 11372.
Tel: 718-639-0700; Email: info@ccbq.org. Patricia Bowles, Senior Vice Pres. & Chief Program Officer.
Supported SRO at Caring Communities - Most Holy Trinity SRO, 157 Graham Ave., 11206.
Tel: 718-963-3956; Email: info@ccbq.org. Patricia Bowles, Senior Vice Pres. & Chief Prog. Officer.
Supported SRO at Caring Communities - Our Lady of Good Counsel SRO, 800-826 Madison St., 11221. Tel: 718-452-3600; Email: info@ccbq.org. Patricia Bowles, Senior Vice Pres./Chief Program Officer.
Supported SRO at Caring Communities - St. Joseph's SRO, 683 Dean St., 11238.
Tel: 718-857-2266; Email: info@ccbq.org. Patricia Bowles, Senior Vice Pres. & Chief Prog. Officer.
Supported SRO at Mercy Gardens, 249 Classon Ave., 11205. Tel: 718-399-8141;
Fax: 718-399-3208; Email: info@ccbq.org. Patricia Bowles, Senior Vice Pres. & Chief Program Officer.
Integrated Health and Wellness - Clinic, Recovery & Rehabilitative Services:.
Behavioral Health Care Coordination Queens HH, 91-14 Merrick Blvd., Fl. 6, Jamaica, 11432.
Tel: 718-408-7178; Email: info@ccbq.org. Patricia Bowles, Senior Vice Pres./Chief Program Officer.
Bohan-Denton Flatlands Guidance Center, 2037 Utica Ave., 11234. Tel: 718-377-5755;
Fax: 718-377-0752; Email: info@ccbq.org. Patricia Bowles, Senior Vice Pres./Chief Program Officer.
Call Center, 191 Joralemon St., 7th Fl., 11201.
Tel: 718-722-6001; Email: info@ccbq.org. Patricia Bowles, Senior Vice Pres./Chief Program Officer.
Catholic Charities Behavioral Health Center - Corona Clinic, 94-14 37th Ave., Jackson Heights, 11372. Tel: 718-779-1600; Email: info@ccbq.org. Patricia Bowles, Senior Vice Pres./Chief Program Officer.
Catholic Charities Behavioral Health Center - Jamaica Clinic, 161-10 Jamaica Ave., 2nd Fl., Jamaica, 11432. Tel: 718-704-5488;
Fax: 718-704-5485; Email: info@ccbq.org. Patricia Bowles, Senior Vice Pres./Chief Program Officer.
Catholic Charities Behavioral Health Center - PROS, 91-14 37th Ave., Jackson Heights, 11372.
Tel: 718-779-1831; Fax: 347-612-4150; Email: info@ccbq.org. Patricia Bowles, Senior Vice Pres./Chief Program Officer.
Catholic Charities Behavioral Health Center - Rockaway Clinic, 18-47 Mott Ave., Far Rockaway, 11691. Tel: 718-337-6800;
Fax: 347-246-9620; Email: info@ccbq.org. Patricia Bowles, Senior Vice Pres./Chief Program Officer.
Catholic Charities Behavioral Health Center - Rockaway PROS, 18-47 Mott Ave., Far Rockaway, 11691. Tel: 718-337-6850; Email: info@ccbq.org. Patricia Bowles, Senior Vice Pres./Chief Program Officer.
Flatbush Addiction Treatment Center, 1463 Flatbush Ave., 2nd Fl., 11210. Tel: 718-951-9009 ; Fax: 718-951-9719; Email: info@ccbq.org. Patricia Bowles, Senior Vice Pres. & Chief Program Officer.
Glendale Mental Health Clinic, 67-29 Myrtle Ave., 2nd Fl., Glendale, 11385. Tel: 718-456-7001;
Fax: 718-456-9470; Email: info@ccbq.org. Patricia Bowles, Senior Vice Pres. & Chief Program Officer.
Jamaica Community Living, 91-14 Merrick Blvd., Jamaica, 11432. Tel: 718-262-8109; Email: info@ccbq.org. Patricia Bowles, Senior Vice Pres. & Chief Program Officer.
The Open Door Club, 2037 Utica Ave., 2nd Fl., 11234. Tel: 718-377-7757; Fax: 718-758-9497; Email: info@ccbq.org. Patricia Bowles, Senior Vice Pres. & Chief Program Officer.
Peer Advocacy, 2037 Utica Ave., 2nd Fl., 11234.
Tel: 718-377-7757; Fax: 718-758-9497; Email: info@ccbq.org. Patricia Bowles, Senior Vice Pres. & Chief Program Officer.
World of Work - Brooklyn, 2037 Utica Ave., 2nd Fl., 11234. Tel: 718-758-9497; Email: info@ccbq.org. Patricia Bowles, Senior Vice Pres. & Chief Program Officer.
Integrated Health and Wellness - Care Coordination & Case Management:.
Behavioral Health Care Coordination - HH, 25 Chapel St., Ste. 901, 11201. Tel: 718-398-0153;
Fax: 718-623-2531; Email: info@ccbq.org. Patricia Bowles, Senior Vice Pres./Chief Program Officer.
Behavioral Health Care Coordination - DOHMH, 25 Chapel St., Ste. 901, 11201.
Tel: 718-398-0153; Fax: 718-623-2531; Email: info@ccbq.org. Patricia Bowles, Senior Vice Pres/ Chief Program Officer.
Central Access: Behavioral Integration Team (CABIT), 191 Joralemon St., 7th Fl., 11201.
Tel: 718-722-6066. Patricia Bowles, Senior Vice Pres. & Chief Program Officer.
Integrated Health Care for Older Adults, 18-47 Mott Ave., 2nd Fl., Far Rockaway, 11691.
Tel: 718-408-6268; Email: info@ccbq.org. Patricia Bowles, Senior Vice Pres. & Chief Program Officer. Program is on hiatus pending contract with a medical inc.
Justice for Juveniles, 191 Joralemon St., 11201.
Tel: 718-408-6268; Email: info@ccbq.org. Patricia Bowles, Senior Vice Pres. & Chief Program Officer.
Mobile Outreach Team, 67-29 Myrtle Ave., 2nd Fl., Glendale, 11385. Tel: 718-456-7001;
Fax: 718-456-9470; Email: info@ccbq.org. Patricia Bowles, Senior Vice Pres. & Chief Program Officer.
Our Lady Queen of Angels Human Service Center, 336 73rd St., 11209. Tel: 718-680-6344;
Fax: 718-680-0331.
Walk In Center, 191 Joralemon St., 1st Fl., 11201.
Tel: 718-722-6002; Email: info@ccbq.org. Patricia Bowles, Senior Vice Pres. & Chief Program Officer.
CCNS - Family Stabilization Services Mary Hurson, Vice Pres.
Brownsville Family Support Center, 1165 Rockaway Ave., 11236. Tel: 718-385-2043;
Fax: 718-385-2179; Email: info@ccbq.org. Ms. Gladys Rodriguez, C.S.W., Senior Vice Pres./ Chief Program Officer.
Brownsville Family Treatment & Rehabilitation, 1165 Rockaway Ave., 11236. Tel: 718-385-2043;
Fax: 718-385-2179; Email: info@ccbq.org. Ms. Gladys Rodriguez, C.S.W., Senior Vice Pres./ Chief Program Officer.
Canarsie Homebase, 3060 Fulton St., 11208.
Tel: 929-234-3036; Fax: 929-234-3035; Email: info@ccbq.org. Ms. Gladys Rodriguez, C.S.W., Admin. Tot Asst. Annually 1,960; Total Staff 38.
CCNS Homebase Mott Avenue Annex, 1847 Mott Ave., 1st Fl., Far Rockaway, 11691.
Tel: 718-647-1000; Fax: 718-327-1429; Email: info@ccbq.org. Gladys Rodriguez, Senior Vice Pres. & Chief Program Officer. Tot Asst. Annually 3,080; Staff 58.
CCNS Immigrant Services ESOL-Civics, 9-18 27th Ave., Astoria, 11102. Tel: 718-726-9790;
Fax: 718-728-8817. Gladys Rodriguez, Senior Vice Pres. & Chief Program Officer. Tot Asst. Annually 54; Total Staff 5.
CCNS Immigrant Services ESOL-Civics, 191 Joralemon St., 2nd Fl., 11201. Tel: 718-722-6009 ; Fax: 718-722-6073. Gladys Rodriguez, Senior Vice Pres. & Chief Program Officer. Tot Asst. Annually 108; Total Staff 4.
COMPASS @ PS 50, 143-26 101st Ave., Jamaica, 11435. Tel: 347-228-7802; Fax: 718-526-7261. Gladys Rodriguez, Senior Vice Pres. & Chief Program Officer. Tot Asst. Annually 457; Total Staff 40.
COMPASS @ PS 106, 1328 Putnam Ave., 11221.
Tel: 718-628-1905, Ext. 1055; Fax: 718-574-1054 . Gladys Rodriguez, Senior Vice Pres. & Chief Program Officer. Tot Asst. Annually 583; Total Staff 34.
East New York Family Support Center, 3060 Fulton St., 11208. Tel: 929-234-3032;
Fax: 929-234-3035; Email: info@ccbq.org. Gladys Rodriguez, Senior Vice Pres. & Chief Program Officer.
Eviction Prevention for Vulnerable Adults (EPVA)/MRT, 191 Joralemon St., 2nd Fl., 11201. Tel: 718-722-6071; Fax: 718-722-6073; Email: info@ccbq.org. Gladys Rodriguez, Senior Vice Pres. & Chief Program Officer. Tot Asst. Annually 500; Total Staff 2.
Far Rockaway Family Treatment & Rehabilitation, 1847 Mott Ave., 1st Fl., Far Rockaway, 11691. Tel: 718-327-3471;
Fax: 718-327-3474; Email: info@ccbq.org. Ms. Gladys Rodriguez, C.S.W., Sr. Vice Pres. & Chief Program Officer.
Healthy Families Bushwick @ PS 106, 1328 Putnam Ave., 11221. Tel: 718-628-1905;
Fax: 718-574-1054. Gladys Rodriguez, Senior Vice Pres. & Chief Program Officer. Tot Asst. Annually 87; Total Staff 2.
Homebase Homelessness Prevention I, 161-10 Jamaica Ave., 5th Fl., Jamaica, 11432.
Tel: 718-674-1000; Fax: 718-674-1008; Email: info@ccbq.org. Gladys Rodriguez, Senior Vice Pres. & Chief Program Officer. Tot Asst. Annually 516,138; Total Staff 59.
Homebase Homelessness Prevention II, 3060 Fulton St., 11208. Tel: 929-234-3036;
Fax: 929-234-3035; Email: info@ccbq.org. Gladys Rodriguez, Senior Vice Pres. & Chief Program Officer. Tot Asst. Annually 1,960; Total Staff 38.
Jamaica Family & Youth Center - General Preventive, 161-10 Jamaica Ave., Fl. 4, Jamaica, 11432. Tel: 718-526-5151; Fax: 718-526-6776; Email: info@ccbq.org. Gladys Rodriguez, Senior Vice Pres. & Chief Program Officer.
Jamaica Family Treatment & Rehabilitation, 161-10 Jamaica Ave., Fl. 4, Jamaica, 11432.
Tel: 718-526-5151; Fax: 718-526-6776; Email: info@ccbq.org. Gladys Rodriguez, Senior Vice Pres. & Chief Program Officer.

Jamaica WIC Program, 161-10 Jamaica Ave., 3rd Fl., Ste. 306, Jamaica, 11432. Tel: 718-657-2580; Fax: 718-657-2590; Email: info@ccbq.org. Gladys Rodriguez, Senior Vice Pres. & Chief Program Officer.

NYCALI/Adult Literacy Initiative, 9-18 27th Avenue, Astoria, 11102. Tel: 718-726-9790. Gladys Rodriguez, Senior Vice Pres. & Chief Program Officer. Tot Asst. Annually 329; Total Staff 8.

Refugee Resettlement Program, 191 Joralemon St., 2nd Fl., 11201. Tel: 718-722-6009; Fax: 718-722-6073; Email: allmina. berisha@ccbq.org. Gladys Rodriguez, Senior Vice Pres. & Chief Program Officer. Tot Asst. Annually 10; Total Staff 1.

Summer Youth Employment (SYEP), 191 Joralemon St., 2nd Fl., 11201. Tel: 718-722-6216 ; Fax: 718-722-6031. Gladys Rodriguez, Senior Vice Pres. & Chief Program Officer. Tot Asst. Annually 1,115; Total Staff 26.

Woodside WIC Programs, 42-71 65th Pl., Woodside, 11377. Tel: 718-715-7001; Fax: 718-943-7013; Email: info@ccbq.org. Gladys Rodriguez, Senior Vice Pres. & Chief Program Officer.

Work, Learn and Grow Employment Program, 191 Joralemon St., 11201. Tel: 718-722-6216; Fax: 718-722-6073. Ms. Gladys Rodriguez, C.S.W., Senior Vice Pres. & Chief Program Officer. Tot Asst. Annually 150; Total Staff 6.

Young Adult Internship Program (YAIP) @ Queens North Community Center, 9-18 27th Ave., Astoria, 11102. Tel: 718-726-9790; Fax: 718-728-8817. Gladys Rodriguez, Senior Vice Pres. & Chief Program Officer. Tot Asst. Annually 105; Total Staff 5.

Housing Development and Management Services Catholic Charities

Catholic Charities Progress of Peoples Development Corporation, 191 Joralemon St., 11201. Tel: 718-722-6000; Email: info@ccbq.org; Web: www.ccbq.org. Rev. Msgr. Alfred P. LoPinto, V.E., CEO; Tim McManus, Vice Pres.; Emmie Glynn Ryan, Esq., Exec. Sec. Total Staff 4.

Progress of Peoples Management Corporation, 191 Joralemon St., 11201. Tel: 718-722-6000; Email: info@ccbq.org. Stanley Celius, Vice Pres.; Emmie Glynn Ryan, Esq., Exec. Sec.; Rev. Msgr. Alfred P. LoPinto, V.E., CEO. Total Staff 153.

Housing Corporations:.

55 Pierrepont Housing Development Corporation, 191 Joralemon St., 11201. Tel: 718-722-6000; Fax: 718-722-6096; Email: info@ccbq.org; Web: www.ccbq.org. Stanley Celius, Vice Pres.

55 Pierrepont Housing Development Fund Corporation, 191 Joralemon St., 11201. Tel: (718) 722-6000; Email: info@ccbq.org; Web: www.ccbq.org. Stanley Celius, Vice Pres.

72 Lewis Avenue Apartments Housing Development Fund Corporation, 191 Joralemon St., 11201. Tel: 718-722-6000; Fax: 718-722-6096; Email: info@ccbq.org; Web: www.ccbq.org. 80 Lewis Avenue, 11206. Stanley Celius, Vice Pres.

101-105 South Eighth Street Apartments Housing Development Fund Corporation, 191 Joralemon St., 11201. Tel: 718-722-6000; Fax: 718-722-6096; Email: jeanne.diulio@ccbq.org; Web: www.ccbq. org. Stanley Celius, Vice Pres.

161-01 89th Avenue Corp., 191 Joralemon St., 11201. Tel: 718-722-6000; Fax: 718-722-6096; Email: info@ccbq.org; Web: www.ccbq.org. Emmie Glynn Ryan, Esq., Sec.

176 South Eighth Street Apartments Housing Development Fund Corporation, 191 Joralemon St., 11201. Tel: 718-722-6000; Fax: 718-722-6096; Email: info@ccbq.org; Web: www.ccbq.org. Stanley Celius, Vice Pres.

Bellerose Senior Housing Development Fund Corp., Inc., 191 Joralemon St., 11201. Tel: 718-722-6000; Fax: 718-722-6096; Email: info@ccbq.org; Web: www.ccbq.org. 238-11 Hillside Avenue, Bellerose, 11426. Stanley Celius, Vice Pres.

Bethlehem Community HDFC Inc., 191 Joralemon St., 11201. Tel: 718-722-6000; Fax: 718-722-6096; Email: info@ccbq.org; Web: www.ccbq.org. Stanley Celius, Vice Pres.

Bishop Boardman Senior HDFC, 191 Joralemon St., 11201. Tel: 718-722-6000; Fax: 718-722-6096; Email: info@ccbq.org; Web: www.ccbq.org. Stanley Celius, Vice Pres.

Bishop Francis J. Mugavero Senior HDFC, 191 Joralemon St., 11201. Tel: 718-722-6000; Fax: 718-722-6096; Email: info@ccbq.org; Web: www.ccbq.org. Stanley Celius, Vice Pres.

Caring Communities Associates HDFC, Inc., 191 Joralemon St., 11201. Tel: 718-722-6000; Email: info@ccbq.org. Stanley Celius, Vice Pres.

Casa Betsaida HDFC, 191 Joralemon St., 11201. Tel: 718-722-6000; Email: info@ccbq.org. Stanley Celius, Vice Pres.

Casa Betsaida Housing Development Fund Corp., 191 Joralemon St., 11201. Tel: 718-722-6000; Email: info@ccbq.org. Stanley Celius, Vice Pres.

Catherine Sheridan HDFC, Inc., 191 Joralemon St., 11201. Tel: 718-722-6000; Fax: 718-722-6096; Email: info@ccbq.org; Web: www.ccbq.org. Stanley Celius, Vice. Pres.

The David Minkin Residence Housing Development Fund Corporation, Inc., 191 Joralemon St., 11201. Tel: 718-722-6000; Fax: 718-722-6096; Email: info@ccbq.org. 5313 9th Ave., 11220. Stanley Celius, Vice Pres.

Emmaus of the Diocese of Brooklyn, Inc., 191 Joralemon St., 11201. Tel: 718-722-6000; Fax: 718-722-6096; Email: info@ccbq.org. Emmie Glynn Ryan, Esq., Sec.

Families Together HDFC, Inc., 191 Joralemon St., 11201. Tel: 718-722-6000; Fax: 718-722-6096; Email: info@ccbq.org. Stanley Celius, Vice Pres.

Holy Spirit Senior Housing Development Fund Corporation, 191 Joralemon St., 11201. Tel: 718-722-6000; Fax: 718-722-6096; Email: info@ccbq.org; Web: www.ccbq.org. Stanley Celius, Vice Pres.

Howard Beach Housing Development Fund Corporation, 191 Jorolemon St., 11201. Tel: 718-722-6000; Fax: 718-722-6096; Email: info@ccbq.org. Stanley Celius, Vice Pres.

Mary Immaculate HDFC, Inc., 191 Joralemon St., 11201. Tel: 718-722-6000; Fax: 718-722-6096; Email: info@ccbq.org. Emmie Glynn Ryan, Esq., Sec.

Mary Immaculate, Inc., 191 Joralemon St., 11201. Tel: 718-722-6000; Fax: 718-722-6096; Email: info@ccbq.org. Emmie Glynn Ryan, Esq., Sec.

Mary Star of the Sea Senior HFDC, 191 Joralemon St., 11201. Tel: 718-722-6000; Email: info@ccbq. org. Stanley Celius, Vice Pres.

Mount Carmel Senior HDFC, 191 Joralemon St., 11201. Stanley Celius, Vice Pres.

Msgr. Edward T. Burke Senior Housing Development Fund Corporation, 191 Joralemon St., 11201. Tel: 718-722-6000; Fax: 718-722-6096; Email: info@ccbq.org. 720 East 8th Street, 11230. Stanley Celius, Vice Pres.

Msgr. John P. O'Brien Senior Housing Development Fund Corporation, 4112 Fort Hamilton Pkwy., 11220. Tel: 718-722-6000; Fax: 718-722-6096; Email: info@ccbq.org. 191 Joralemon St., 11201. Stanley Celius, Vice Pres.

Msgr. Joseph F. Stedman Residence Housing Development Fund Corporation, 930 53rd Street, 11219. Tel: 718-722-6000; Fax: 718-722-6096; Email: info@ccbq.org. 191 Joralemon St., 11201. Stanley Celius, Vice Pres.

Msgr. Thomas Campbell Senior Housing Development Corporation, 191 Joralemon St., 11201. Tel: 718-722-6000; Fax: 718-722-6096; Email: info@ccbq.org. 25-63 22nd Street, Long Island City, 11102. Stanley Celius, Vice Pres.

O.L. Loreto Family Housing Development Fund Corporation, 191 Joralemon St., 11201. Tel: 718-722-6000; Fax: 718-722-6096; Email: info@ccbq.org. Stanley Celius, Vice Pres.

Our Lady of Fatima Apartments Housing Development Fund Corporation, Inc., 191 Joralemon St., 11201. Tel: 718-722-6000; Fax: 718-722-6096; Email: info@ccbq.org. 78-01 30th Avenue, East Elmhurst, 11370. Stanley Celius, Vice Pres.

Pierrepont HDFC, 191 Joralemon St., 11201. Tel: 718-722-6000; Fax: 718-722-6096; Email: info@ccbq.org. Stanley Celius, Vice Pres.

Pierrepont House for the Elderly, Inc., 191 Joralemon St., 11201. Tel: 718-722-6000; Fax: 718-722-6096; Email: info@ccbq.org. Stanley Celius, Vice Pres.

Pope John Paul II Senior Housing Development Fund Corporation, 191 Joralemon St., 11201. Tel: 718-722-6000; Fax: 718-722-6096; Email: info@ccbq.org. 255 Ovington Ave., 11220. Stanley Celius, Vice Pres.

Queens Rehab Corp., 191 Joralemon St., 11201. Tel: 718-722-6000; Fax: 718-722-6096; Email: info@ccbq.org. Emmie Glynn Ryan, Esq., Sec.

St. Brendan Senior Housing Development Fund Corporation, 191 Joralemon St., 11201. Tel: 718-722-6000; Fax: 718-722-6096; Email: info@ccbq.org. 1215 Ave. O, 11230. Stanley Celius, Vice Pres.

Sr. Lucian Senior HDFC, 415 Bleecker St., 11237. Tel: 718-722-6000; Email: info@ccbq.org. 191 Joralemon St., 11201. Stanley Celius, Vice Pres.

St. Lucy/St. Patrick Housing Development Fund Corporation, 191 Joralemon St., 11201. Tel: 718-722-6000; Fax: 718-722-6096; Email: info@ccbq.org. 918 Kent Ave., 11205. Stanley Celius, Vice Pres.

St. Paul the Apostle Senior Housing Development Fund Corporation, 191 Joralemon St., 11201. Tel: 718-722-6000; Fax: 718-722-6096; Email: info@ccbq.org. 55-06 99th St., Corona, 11368. Stanley Celius, Vice Pres.

St. Pius V Senior Housing Development Fund Corporation, 191 Joralemon St., 11201. 105-20 Liverpool Street, Jamaica, 11435. Tel: 718-722-6000; Fax: 718-722-6096; Email: info@ccbq.org. Stanley Celius, Vice Pres.

St. Teresa of Avila Senior HDFC, 191 Joralemon St., 11201. Tel: 718-722-6000; Email: info@ccbq.org. 549-555 St. Johns Pl., 11238. Stanley Celius, Vice Pres.

Sunset Park Housing Development Fund Corporation, Inc., 191 Joralemon St., 11201. Tel: 718-722-6000; Fax: 718-722-6096; Email: info@ccbq.org. 4301 8th Ave., 11232. Stanley Celius, Vice Pres.

Anthonian Hall, Inc., 191 Joralemon St., 11201. Tel: 718-722-6000; Fax: 718-722-6096; Email: info@ccbq.org; Web: www.ccbq.org. Emmie Glynn Ryan, Esq., Sec.

Affiliated Agencies:.

Catholic Guild for the Blind, Inc., 191 Joralemon St., 11201. Tel: 718-722-6000; Fax: 718-722-6096; Email: info@ccbq.org. Emmie Glynn Ryan, Esq., Sec.

Catholic Migration Services, Inc., 191 Joralemon St., 4th Fl., 11201. Tel: 718-236-3000; Fax: 718-256-9707; Email: pkeating@catholicmigration.org; Web: www. catholicmigration.org. Very Rev. Patrick J. Keating, CEO. Tot Asst. Annually 7,000; Total Staff 38.

Pierrepont Charitable Fund, Inc., 191 Joralemon St., 11201. Tel: 718-722-6000; Fax: 718-722-6096; Email: jeanne.diulio@ccbq.org; Web: ccbq.org. Emmie Glynn Ryan, Esq., Sec.

Mary's Hall, Inc., 191 Joralemon St., 11201. Tel: 718-722-6000; Fax: 718-722-6096; Email: info@ccbq.org. Emmie Glynn Ryan, Esq., Sec.

Saints Joachim and Anne Nursing and Rehabilitation Center, 2720 Surf Ave., 11224. Tel: 718-714-4800; Fax: 718-714-0874; Email: info@ccbq.org. Lisa Schiano-Denis, Exec. Dir.; Richard Abrahamsen, Controller. Bed Capacity 200; Tot Asst. Annually 488; Total Staff 277.

Child Welfare Programs, 191 Joralemon St., 11201. Tel: 718-722-6091; Fax: 718-722-6096.

[L] CATHOLIC MIGRATION AND REFUGEE OFFICES

BROOKLYN. *Catholic Migration Services, Inc.*, 191 Joralemon St., 4th Fl., 11201. Tel: 718-236-3000; Fax: 718-256-9707; Email: pkeating@catholicmigration.org; Web: www. catholicmigration.org. Very Rev. Patrick J. Keating, CEO; David Colodny Esq., Dir. Legal Svcs. Total Staff 1.

Queens Office, 47-01 Queens Blvd., Ste. 203, Sunnyside, 11104. Tel: 347-472-3500; Fax: 347-472-3501; Email: pkeating@catholicmigration.org; Web: www. catholicmigration.org. Very Rev. Patrick J. Keating, CEO; David Colodny Esq., Dir. Legal Svcs.

Catholic Migration & Refugee Office (1971) 191 Joralemon St., 4th Fl., 11201. Tel: 718-236-3000; Fax: 718-256-9707; Email: pkeating@catholicmigration.org; Web: www. catholicmigration.org. Very Rev. Patrick J. Keating, CEO. Apostolate Coordinators.

African American Ministry, Tel: 718-574-5772; Fax: 718-919-2265. Rev. Alonzo Q. Cox, Coord., African-American Ministry.

Arabic Speaking Ministry (2003) Tel: 718-768-9471. Rev. Francis Abaskhron, Coord., Arabic Speaking Ministry.

Brazilian Ministry, Tel: 718-361-1884; Fax: 718-786-4573. Rev. Jose Carlos Da Silva, Coord., Brazilian Ministry.

Chinese Ministry-Queens, Tel: 718-961-0714; Fax: 718-460-8032. Rev. Antonius Ho, C.S.J.B., (Taiwan) Coord., Chinese Ministry-Queens.

Chinese Ministry-Brooklyn, Tel: 718-436-1080; Fax: 718-436-8870. Rev. Vincentius T. Do, Coord., Chinese Ministry-Brooklyn, Tel: 718-236-0909; Fax: 718-236-5357.

Czech/Slovak Ministry, Tel: 718-268-6251; Fax: 718-793-2584. Rev. Antonin Kocurek, Coord., Czech/Slovak Ministry.

Croatian Ministry, Tel: 718-278-3337; Fax: 718-278-4354. Rev. Vedran Kirincic, Coord., Croatian Ministry.

Filipino Ministry, Tel: 718-634-6464; Fax: 718-634-0716. Rev. Patrick H. Longalong, Coord., Filipino Ministry.

Ghanaian Ministry, Tel: 718-282-7162; Fax: 718-282-5568. Rev. Charles Akoto Oduro, (Ghana) Coord., Ghanaian Ministry.

Haitian Ministry, Tel: 718-622-6500; Fax: 718-622-2234. Rev. Saint Charles Borno, Coord., Haitian Ministry.

Indian Latin Rite Ministry, Tel: 718-479-5111;

Fax: 718-479-0826. Rev. Robert Ambalathingal, Coord., Indian Latin Rite Ministry, (Retired).
Indonesian Ministry, Tel: 718-897-4444; Fax: 718-897-1453. Rev. Robert Mirsel, S.V.D., Coord., Indonesian Ministry.
Irish Ministry, Tel: 718-392-0011; Tel: 718-392-0012 ; Tel: 718-472-2625; Fax: 718-457-4055. Very Rev. Brian P. Dowd, Coord., Irish Ministry.
Italian Ministry, Tel: 718-236-0124; Fax: 718-236-4960. Rev. Msgr. David L. Cassato, M.Div., M.S.Ed., Coord., Italian Ministry.
Korean Ministry, Tel: 718-229-6465; Fax: 718-229-8126. Rev. Sun Joong Kwon, Coord., Korean Ministry.
Lithuanian Ministry, Tel: 718-326-2236; Fax: 718-326-2249. Rev. Vytautas Volertas, Coord., Lithuanian Ministry.
Mexican Ministry, Tel: 718-821-1690; Fax: 718-386-4302. Rev. Jorge Ortiz-Garay, Coord., Mexican Ministry.
Nigerian Ministry, Tel: 718-949-4311; Fax: 718-528-7208. Rev. Cosmas Nzeabalu, Coord., Nigerian Ministry.
Pakistani Ministry, Tel: 718-871-1310; Fax: 718-633-1866. Rev. Ilyas Gill, O.F.M., (Pakistan) Coord., Pakistani Ministry.
Polish Ministry, Tel: 718-268-6143; Fax: 718-544-3764. Rev. Grzegorz Stasiak, (Poland) Coord., Polish Ministry.
Russian Speaking/Ukrainian Ministry, Tel: 718-891-3100; Fax: 718-891-9677. Rev. Sergiy Emanuel, Coord., Russian/Ukrainian Ministry.
Vietnamese Ministry, Tel: 718-278-1834; Fax: 718-278-0998. Rev. Peter H. Nguyen, Coord., Vietnamese Ministry.
West Indian Ministry, Tel: 718-774-6747; Fax: 718-953-4895. Rev. Francis A. Black, Coord., West Indian Ministry.
Resources, Inc.
Catholic Immigrant Ministries of Brooklyn and Queens, 191 Joralemon St., 11201. Tel: (718) 236-3000; Email: pkeating@catholicmigration.org. Very Rev. Patrick J. Keating, CEO. Tot Asst. Annually 3,000; Total Staff 29.

[M] FOUNDATIONS, FUNDS & TRUSTS

BROOKLYN. *Catholic Foundation for Brooklyn & Queens* (1998) 243 Prospect Park W., 11215. Tel: 718-965-7375; Fax: 888-415-6328; Email: info@cfbq.org; Web: www.catholicfoundationbq.org.
Compostela Fund of the Roman Catholic Diocese of Brooklyn (2002) 310 Prospect Park W., 11215. Tel: 718-965-7300; Fax: 718-965-7311; Email: mreid@diobrook.org. Rev. Msgr. Michael J. Reid, Vicar for Fin. Admin.
St. Elizabeth Ann Seton Charitable Trust, 310 Prospect Park West, 11215. Tel: 718-965-7300; Fax: 718-965-7371; Email: mreid@diobrook.org. Rev. Msgr. Michael J. Reid, Vicar.
Franciscan Brothers Charitable Trust (1999) 135 Remsen St., 11201. Tel: 718-858-8217; Fax: 718-858-8306; Email: generalate@gmail.com; Web: www.francisanbrothers.org. Richard T. Arkwright, Trustee; Robert Schaefer, Trustee; Michael Henning, Trustee.
Franciscan Sisters of the Poor Charitable Trust, 133 Remsen St., 11201. Tel: 718-643-1945; Fax: 718-643-9710; Email: sfp@franciscansisters.org; Web: www.franciscansisters.org. Sr. Licia Mazzia, S.F.P., Congregation Min.
Good Shepherd Charitable Trust, 310 Prospect Park W., 11215. Tel: 718-965-7300; Email: mreid@diobrook.org. Rev. Msgr. Michael J. Reid, Vicar.
St. John Vianney Fund Charitable Trust, 310 Prospect Park West, 11215. Tel: 718-965-7300; Email: mreid@diobrook.org. Rev. Msgr. Michael J. Reid, Vicar.
Mercy Home Foundation, 273 Willoughby Ave., 11205. Tel: 718-832-1075; Fax: 718-832-7612. Sr. Linda Esposito, Contact Person.
Parish Assistance Charitable Trust Fund, 310 Prospect Park W., 11215. Tel: 718-965-7300; Fax: 718-965-7371; Email: mreid@diobrook.org. Rev. Msgr. Michael J. Reid, Vicar.
Saint Vincent DePaul Charitable Trust, 310 Prospect Park W., 11215. Tel: 718-965-7300; Fax: 718-965-7371; Email: mreid@diobrook.org. Rev. Msgr. Michael J. Reid, Vicar.
The Roman Catholic Diocese of Brooklyn, New York Group Medical Insurance Trust, 310 Prospect Park W., 11215. Tel: (718) 965-7300; Email: mreid@diobrook.org. Rev. Msgr. Michael J. Reid, Vicar.
BAYSIDE. *Ozanam Geriatric Foundation* (1997) 42-41 201 St., Bayside, 11361. Tel: 718-971-2020; Fax: 718-971-2025; Email: jcraymond@ozanamhall.org; Web: www.ozanamhall.org.
BRIARWOOD. *Archbishop Molloy High School Charitable Trust*, 85-53 Manton St., Briarwood, 11435. Tel: 718-441-2100; Fax: 718-849-8251; Email: dpenikas@molloyhs.org. Darius Penikas, Prin.
JAMAICA ESTATES. *The Paulist Foundation, Inc.*, 86-11 Midland Pkwy., Jamaica Estates, 11432. Tel: 212-757-8072; Fax: 212-757-8527; Email: admingenoffice@paulist.org. 415 W. 59 St., New York, 10019. Rev. Charles A. Martin, C.S.P., Sec., (Retired).
Paulist Mission Trust, 86-11 Midland Pkwy., Jamaica Estates, 11432. Tel: 212-757-8072; Fax: 212-757-8527; Email: admingenoffice@paulist.org. 415 W. 59 St., New York, 10019. Rev. John J. Foley, C.S.P., Trustee.

[N] SOCIAL SERVICE AGENCIES

BROOKLYN. *Care at Home for the Diocese of Brooklyn, Inc.*, 168 Seventh St., 11215. Tel: 718-832-0550; Email: info@cahny.com. Broughan Gorey, Pres. Tot Asst. Annually 250; Total Staff 190.
Casa Betsaida-Home for people with AIDS, 267 Hewes St., 11211. Tel: 718-218-7890; Fax: 347-457-5768; Email: jose.morales@ccbq.org. Rev. Msgr. Anthony Hernandez, J.C.L., Chm. Bd. Bed Capacity 27; Total Staff 13; Total Assisted 52.
Family Home Care Services of Brooklyn and Queens, Inc., 168th Seventh Ave., 11215. Tel: 718-832-0550 ; Email: info@fhcsny.com. Broughan Gorey, Pres. Tot Asst. Annually 1,000; Total Staff 1,285.
St. Francis Home for Young Men, 132 Eagle St., 11222. Tel: 718-349-1157; Email: info@stfrancishousebriiklyn.com; Web: www.sfhbrooklyn.com. Mr. Joseph Campo, Exec. Dir. Residents 7.
Little Flower Children and Family Services of New York, 191 Joralemon St., 11201-4326. Tel: 718-526-9150; Fax: 718-526-9421; Email: info@lfchild.org; Web: www.LittleFlowerNY.org. Sr. Ellen Zak, Supr.; Corinne Hammons, Exec. Dir.; Kevin Kundmueller, CFO. Foster Care, Post Adoption Services, Services for Developmentally Disabled Adults; Residential Treatment Center; Teen Mothers & Infants in Foster Homes, Bridges to Health, Medicaid Service, Health Home Services, Counseling for Employees of Client Organization. Students 1,655.
Mercy Home for Children (1865) 273 Willoughby Ave., 11205. Tel: 718-832-1075; Fax: 718-832-7612; Email: info@mercyhomeny.org; Web: www.mercyhomeny.org. Janice Aris, Exec. Dir. Under the sponsorship of the Sisters of Mercy. Mercy Home for Children operates Four Intermediate Care Facilities and nine Individual Residential Alternatives for adolescents & adults who are developmentally disabled throughout Brooklyn, Queens and Nassau County. Mercy Home also provides Day habilitation, site base and in home respite services. Mercy Home Creative Arts programs provides an array of therapeutic services to enhance the life experiences for adults and children with Intellectual and Developmental Disabilities. Bed Capacity 109; Residents 109; Sisters 5; Tot Asst. Annually 319; Total Staff 290; Saturday Programs 65; In Home Respite 8; Saturday Creative Arts Center 65.
MercyFirst, 6301 12th Ave., 11219. Tel: 718-232-1500; Fax: 718-232-0331; Web: www.mercyfirst.org. Gerard McCaffery, Pres. & CEO. Residential services provided in campus and group home settings, including diagnostic/group emergency foster care, non-secure detention, hard to place (JD and clinically intensive), abuse treatment and prevention, mother/child, and OMH programs.; Family Foster Care/Adoption, After School, Youth Development Services & Prevention Services programs provide services in Queens and Brooklyn. Bed Capacity 178; Total Staff 524; Children in Care 2,413.
Residential Programs:.
McAuley Residence for Mother and Child (Agency Operated Boarding Home) Tel: 718-469-0360; Fax: 718-940-0406.
Virginia Group Residence for Mother and Child, Tel: 718-369-3812; Fax: 718-369-5891.
Preventive Programs:.
Montague Center, 186 Montague St., 11201. Tel: 718-522-0504; Fax: 718-522-9028.
Gerard C. Durr Center, 333 Ave., 11223. Tel: 718-375-7444; Fax: 718-375-2444.
Rockaway Center, 230 Beach 102 St., Ste. 1-A, Rockaway Park, 11694. Tel: 718-318-6167; Fax: 718-634-6691.
Providence House, Inc. (1979) Administrative Office, 703 Lexington Ave., 11221. Tel: 718-455-0197; Fax: 718-455-0692; Web: www.providencehouse.org. Ms. Danielle Minelli Pagnotta, Exec. Bed Capacity 192; Tot Asst. Annually 450; Total Staff 75.
Providence House 2 (1982) 388 Prospect Ave., 11215. Tel: 718-369-9140; Fax: 718-369-9158; Email: info@providencehouse.org; Web: www.providencehouse.org. Ms. Danielle Minelli Pagnotta, Dir. Tot Asst. Annually 42; Total Staff 4.
Providence House 3 (1983) 159-23 89th Ave., Jamaica, 11432. Tel: 718-739-1348; Fax: 718-526-6315; Email: info@providencehouse.org; Web: www.providencehouse.org. 703 Lexington Ave., 11221. Ms. Danielle Minelli Pagnotta, Dir. Tot Asst. Annually 81; Total Staff 4.
Providence House 4 (1986) 89 Sickles Ave., New Rochelle, 10801. Tel: 914-632-4177; Fax: 914-235-5766; Email: info@providencehouse.org; Web: www.providencehouse.org. 703 Lexington Ave., 11221. Ms. Danielle Minelli Pagnotta, Dir. Tot Asst. Annually 135; Total Staff 5.
Providence House 5 (1986) 396 Lincoln Rd., 11225. Tel: 718-778-1310; Fax: 718-493-5932; Email: info@providencehouse.org; Web: www.providencehouse.org. 703 Lexington Ave., 11221. Ms. Danielle Minelli Pagnotta, Dir. Tot Asst. Annually 20; Total Staff 5.
Providence House 7, 701 Lexington Ave., 11221. Tel: 718-574-6847; Fax: 718-455-0457; Email: info@providencehouse.org; Web: www.providencehouse.org. Ms. Danielle Minelli Pagnotta, Dir.
D'Addario Residence, 275 Kosciuszko St., 11221. Tel: 929-210-9355; Fax: 347-713-0011; Email: info@providencehouse.org; Web: www.providencehouse.org. 703 Lexington Ave., 11221. Ms. Danielle Minelli Pagnotta, Dir. Tot Asst. Annually 63; Total Staff 9.
Bishop Joseph M. Sullivan Residence, 329 Lincoln Rd., 11225. Tel: 929-210-8480; Fax: 929-210-8483; Email: info@providencehouse.org; Web: www.providencehouse.org. 703 Lexington Ave., 11221. Ms. Danielle Minelli Pagnotta, Dir. Tot Asst. Annually 26; Total Staff 5.
St. Vincent's Services, Inc. dba HeartShare St. Vincent's Services (1869) (Formerly St. Vincent's Home for Boys and St. Vincent's Hall, Inc.) 66 Boerum Pl., 11201. Tel: 718-522-3700; Fax: 718-422-2310; Web: www.nsvsnyc.org. Dawn Saffayeh, M.P.A., B.S., Exec. Dir. Services include: Family Foster Boarding Homes & Adoption, Preventive Programs, Specialized Preventive Program for Medically Fragile Children, Primary Care Medical Clinic for children and adolescents, Group Home Services, Children's Community Residences, Supported Housing Programs, NYS Licensed Alcohol and Substance Abuse Outpatient Treatment Program for youth and adults, NYS Licensed Outpatient Mental Health Clinics for children, adolescents and adults, Youth Development Program and Youth After School & Community Programs. Employees 460.
Office Program Centers:.
Executive Offices, 66 Boerum Pl., 5th Fl., 11201. Tel: 718-522-3700; Fax: 718-875-8536.
Article 31 Mental Health Clinic & Article 32 Chemical Dependency Clinic (Queens), 89-31 161st St., Jamaica, 11432. Tel: 718-981-7861.
Article 31 Mental Health Clinic & Article 32 Chemical Dependency Clinic (Staten Island), 56 Bay St., Staten Island, 10301. Tel: 718-981-7861.
GLEN COVE. *SCO Family of Services*, 1 Alexander Pl., Glen Cove, 11542. Tel: 516-671-1253; Tel: 718-895-2555; Fax: 516-671-2899; Email: dodell@sco.org; Web: www.sco.org. Douglas O'Dell, Exec. Dir.; Madeline Martinez, Spec. Asst. to the Exec. Dir. SCO helps vulnerable New Yorkers build a strong foundation for the future. We get young children off to a good start, launch youth into adulthood, stabilize and strengthen families, and unlock potential for children and adults with special needs. SCO provides vital human services throughout New York City and Long Island through more than 80 programs at 110 locations. Services: Early Childhood: Home Visiting, Developmental Playgroups, Early Care & Education; Education and Youth Development: Transfer High Schools, Residential Schools, Day Schools, After School, Summer Programs, School Day Enrichment, Drop-In Center, Non-Secure Placement; Family Support: Child Welfare Preventive, Food Pantries, Single Stop, Adult Education & Employment; Foster Care: Therapeutic Foster Care, Residential Treatment Centers, Agency Operated Boarding Homes; Shelter and Homelessness: Adult & Family Shelters, Youth Shelters, Supportive Housing, Permanent Housing; Special Needs and Behavioral Health: Opportunities at Home, Residential, Clinical Support, Community Support People Served Annually 60,000.
ROCKAWAY PARK. *St. John's Residence for Boys, Inc.*, 150 Beach 110th St., Rockaway Park, 11694. Tel: 718-945-2800, Ext. 1310; Fax: 718-945-4662; Email: poul.jensen@dfa.state.ny.us. Poul Jensen, M.S., Interim Exec. Dir. Residential care for adolescent boys. Non-Secure Detention/Residential

Treatment Center/Non-secure Placement. Residents 57.

Madonna Heights Services, 151 Burr Ln., P.O. Box 8020, Dix Hills, 11746. Tel: 516-643-8800; Fax: 516-491-4440.

[O] RESIDENCES FOR THE AGED

BROOKLYN. *SS. Joachim & Anne Residence, Inc.* dba Saints Joachim + Anne Nursing and Rehabilitation Center, 2720 Surf Ave., 11224. Tel: 718-714-4800; Fax: 718-266-1743. Lisa Schiano-Denis, Exec. Dir. Bed Capacity 200; Tot Asst. Annually 467; Total Staff 276.

BAYSIDE. *Ozanam Hall of Queens Nursing Home, Inc.* (1971) 42-41 201st St., Bayside, 11361. Tel: 718-423-2000; Fax: 718-224-7598; Email: jcraymond@ozanamhall.org; Web: www.ozanamhall.org. Sr. M. Joseph Catherine Raymond, O.Carm., CEO. Carmelite Sisters for the Aged and Infirm and the Diocese of Brooklyn. Bed Capacity 432; Residents 432; Sisters 15; Tot Asst. Annually 1,125; Total Staff 595.

QUEENS VILLAGE. *The Home for the Aged of the Little Sisters of the Poor* dba Queen of Peace Residence (1869) 110-30 221st St., Queens Village, 11429. Tel: 718-464-1800; Fax: 718-464-1786. Mother Superior Celine Therese Vadukkoot, L.S.P. Sisters 17; Total Staff 97; Nursing Beds 53; Independent Living 28.

[P] SETTLEMENT ASSOCIATIONS

GLENDALE. *Catholic Kolping Society of Brooklyn*, 65-04 Myrtle Ave., Glendale, 11385. Tel: 718-456-7727; Tel: (917) 862-0637; Email: kolpingbrooklyn@gmail.com; Email: mrwilliamangelo@aol.com; Email: bill.conte@foxnews.com; Web: www.kolping.org/brooklyn. William A. Conte, Pres.; Patricia Gerage, Fin. Sec.; Jessica Meyer, Vice Pres.

Catholic Kolping Society (Katholischer Gesellen Verein) of Brooklyn, Inc.

[Q] EVANGELIZATION AND RENEWAL CENTERS

BROOKLYN. *Jesus of Nazareth Diocesan Retreat Center*, 475 E. 57th St., 4th Fl., 11203. Tel: 347-710-0010; Fax: 347-710-0014. Deacon Carlos Garcia, Dir.

JAMAICA. *Bishop Molloy Retreat House* (1924) 86-45 Edgerton Blvd., Jamaica, 11432. Tel: 718-739-1229; Fax: 718-739-3421; Email: bmrhpromotions@cpprov.org; Web: www.bishopmolloy.org. Revs. John Michael Lee, C.P., Retreat Dir.; Michael Greene, C.P., Assoc. Passionist Fathers. Administrators 1.

[R] MONASTERIES AND RESIDENCES OF PRIESTS AND BROTHERS

BROOKLYN. *Brothers of the Christian Schools*, 1214-1216 Beverley Rd., 11218. Tel: 718-857-4311; Fax: 718-857-7576. Bros. John Bassett, F.S.C.; Peter Bonventre, F.S.C.; David Carroll, F.S.C., Dir.; Gerard Conforti, F.S.C., Treas.; Ralph Darmento, F.S.C.; Robert Wickman, F.S.C. Brothers 6.

Carmelites of Mary Immaculate, Inc., 862 Manhattan Ave., 11222. Tel: 718-383-3339; Fax: 718-383-5968; Email: cmiusa@hotmail.com; Web: www.cmiusa.org. Revs. Kavungal Davy, C.M.I., Delegate Supr.; Antony Vadakara, C.M.I., Parochial Vicar.

St. Francis Monastery-Generalate Offices of Franciscan Brothers, 135 Remsen St., 11201-4212. Tel: 718-858-8217; Fax: 718-858-8306; Email: generalate@gmail.com; Web: www.franciscanbrothers.org. Bros. Christopher Thurneau, O.S.F., B.A., J.D., Supr. Gen.; Damian Novello, O.S.F., 1st Councilor; Joshua Di Mauro, O.S.F., 2nd Councilor; David Migliorino, O.S.F., 3rd Councilor; Edward Wesley, O.S.F., 4th Councilor; Philip Herte, Treas. Brothers 59.

St. Michael Friary, 282 Warwick St., 11207. Tel: 718-827-6990; Fax: 718-827-5789; Email: buckleybp@gmail.com. Rev. Gerard Mulvey, O.F.M.Cap., Chap.; Bro. Terrence Taffee, O.F.M.Cap., Vicar. Brothers 2; Priests 3.

Oratory of Saint Philip Neri, Congregation Pontifical Rite (1988) 109 Willoughby St., 11201. Tel: 718-875-2096; Fax: 718-875-4678; Email: creekhaven4952@gmail.com; Web: Brooklynoratory.org. Very Rev. Dennis M. Corrado, C.O., Provost; Revs. Mark J. Lane, C.O.; Joel M. Warden, C.O., Vicar; Anthony Andreassi, C.O., Sec.; Michael J. Callaghan, C.O.; Bros. James Simon, C.O.; Mark Paul Amatrucola, C.O. Brothers 2; Priests 5.

Our Lady of Good Counsel (1868) 915 Putnam Ave., 11221. Tel: 718-455-6864; Fax: 718-452-3738. Revs. Emmet J. Nolan, C.M.; Joseph V. Cummins, C.M. In Res. Most Rev. Alfonso Cabezas Aristizabal, C.M., 915 Putnam Ave., 11221.

Redemptorist Fathers of New York, Inc.-Baltimore Province (1969) 7509 Shore Rd., 11209. Tel: 718-833-1900; Fax: 718-630-5666; Email: secprovince@redemptorists.net; Web: www.redemptorists.net. Very Rev. Paul J. Borowski, C.Ss.R., M.Div., Prov. Supr.; Revs. Matthew T. Allman, C.Ss.R., Prov. Asst.; Francis Gargani, C.Ss.R., Supr.; Henry E. Sattler, C.Ss.R., Sec./Treas.; Gerard J. Knapp, C.Ss.R., M.B.A., S.T.L., Vicar. Provincial Residence for Redemptorist Fathers and Brothers Priests 5.

ASTORIA. *Our Lady of China Chapel*, 54-09 92nd St., Elmhurst, 11373. Tel: 718-699-1929; Fax: 718-460-8032; Email: olcny@msn.com; Web: olc.faithweb.com. Revs. Antonius Ho, C.S.J.B., (Taiwan) Dir.; Dehua Zhang, C.S.J.B., Assoc.

DOUGLASTON. *Bishop Mugavero Residence*, 7200 Douglaston Pkwy., Douglaston, 11362. Tel: 718-229-8001, Ext. 411; Fax: 718-428-3070; Email: moellinger@rcdob.org. Deacon Matthew Oellinger, Coord., Office of Sr. Priests. In Res. Rev. Msgrs. August C. Bednartz, (Retired); Michael J. Cantley, (Retired); George T. Deas, (Retired); Conrad R. Dietz, (Retired); Lawrence E. Hinch, (Retired), Sunrise Assisted Living, 2211 Emmons Ave., 11235; Vincent A. Keane, (Retired); Raymond J. Kelly, S.T.L., (Retired); John F. Keppler, (Retired); Terrence J. Mulkerin, (Retired); James F. Spengler, (Retired); Revs. Robert Blauvelt, (Retired), Queen of Peace Residence, 110-30 221st St., Queens Village, 11424; Hugh A. Byrne, (Retired); Coleman J. Costello, (Retired); George R. Cowan, (Retired); Eugene P. Coyle, (Retired); Joseph W. Denzer, (Retired); James T. Devine, (Retired); James Diffley; James F. Fraser, (Retired); Daniel G. Keohane, (Retired); Francis J. Labita, (Retired); Joseph M. Nolan, (Retired); James J. Reynolds; Raymond F. Schmidt, (Retired); Romano A. Zanon.

ELMHURST. *Congregation of St. John the Baptist of China*, 54-17 90th St., Elmhurst, 11373. Tel: 718-271-3944; Email: brotherli2000@yahoo.com. Rev. Antonius Ho, C.S.J.B., (Taiwan) Regl. Supr.; Bro. Peter Li, C.S.J.B., Prov.; Revs. Dehua Zhang, C.S.J.B.; Victor Cao, C.S.J.B.; Thomas Sung, C.S.J.B., (Taiwan) (Retired). Brothers 1; Priests 5.

JAMAICA. *Immaculate Conception Monastery* (1936) 86-45 Edgerton Blvd., Jamaica, 11432. Tel: 718-739-6502; Fax: 718-739-7770; Email: tbrislin@cpprov.org; Web: www.passionists.us. Very Rev. Thomas P. Brislin, Rector; Revs. James O'Shea, C.P., Prov.; Michael Greene, C.P., Dir.; John Michael Lee, C.P., Dir.; William Murphy, C.P.; Theophane Cooney, C.P.; John Douglas, C.P.; Evans Barasa Fwamba, C.P., Chap.; Gilbert Otieno Omolo, C.P., Chap.; Paul Chenot, C.P., Chap.; Jerome Bracken, C.P., Prof.; Bonaventure Moccia, C.P., Sec.; Rogie Castellano, C.P., Vocation Team/Student; Ferdinand Mbuta, Preacher/Student; Joseph F. Jones, C.Ss.R., In Res.; Paul Vaeth, In Res.; Bros. James Bernard Johnson, C.P., In Res.; Michael Stomber, In Res.; Revs. James Barry, C.P.; Alberto Cabrera, C.P.; Christopher Cleary, C.P.; Neil Davin, C.P., (Retired); James Gillette; Victor Hoagland, C.P.; Miroslaw Lesiecki, C.P.; Dominic Papa, C.P., (Retired); Kenan Peters, C.P.; John Powers, C.P.; Vincent Segotta, C.P.; Jed Sumampong, C.P.; Theodore Walsh, C.P.; Vincent Youngberg, C.P.; Bros. Robert McKenna, C.P.; August Parlavechio, C.P.; Angelo Sena, C.P.; Rev. Salvatore Riccardi, C.P. Brothers 5; Priests 29.

Passionist Benefactor's Society, Tel: 718-739-9337; Fax: 718-739-7770; Email: pgrace@cpprov.org; Web: www.passionists.us.

Reverend John B. Murray, C.M. House (1958) St. John's University, 8000 Utopia Pkwy., Jamaica, 11439. Tel: 718-990-6161; Fax: 718-990-5724; Email: flanagap@stjohns.edu. Revs. Bernard M. Tracey, C.M., Exec.; Peter J. Albano, C.M., Ph.D., Visiting Prof., Philosophy; Guillermo Campuzano, C.M., NGO Rep. to the United Nations; James F. Dorr, C.M., Gen. Ministry; Tri Minh Duong, C.M., B.A., M.Div., M.A., Campus Min.; Patrick S. Flanagan, C.M., B.S., M.Div., Ph.D., Supr. & Asst. Prof. Theology & Rel. Studies; John Gouldrick, Campus Min.; Patrick J. Griffin, C.M., B.S., M.Div., Th.M, M.A., Ph.D., Exec. Dir., Vincentian Center for Church & Society; Donald J. Harrington, C.M., B.A., M.Div., Th. M.; John Holliday, Campus Min.; John Maher, C.M., Vocation Dir.; Richard Rock, Campus Min., St. John's University; Michael D. Whalen, C.M., B.A., M.Div., Th.M., M.A., S.T.L., S.T.D., Asst. Supr./Treas.; Dominic Vu, C.M., In Res.; Subhashisa Mandal, In Res.; Christopher Amojo, In Res.; Bro. Martial Fotso, In Res.

OZONE PARK. *Montfort Missionaries Provincialate (Missionaries of the Company of Mary)* (1705) 101-18 104th St., Ozone Park, 11416. Tel: 718-849-5885; Email: montfort.secretariat@gmail.com; Web: montfortusa.org. Rev. Zakarias Beong, S.M.M.; Very Rev. Matthew J. Considine, S.M.M.; Revs. Donald LaSalle, S.M.M., Ozone Park, NY; Alonzo Lazo, S.M.M.; Harry Flores Morales, S.M.M.; Richard Schebera, S.M.M.

Missionaries of the Company of Mary; Montfort Missionaries; Montfort Publications; Montfort Spiritual Association Priests 8.

QUEENS VILLAGE. *DePaul Residence*, 80-14 217th St., Queens Village, 11427. Tel: 718-766-7344; Fax: 718-468-2903. Revs. Michael J. Cummins, C.M.; Richard J. Devine, C.M.; Joseph P. Foley, C.M.

ROCKAWAY PARK. *Franciscan Missionary Brothers of North America New York*, 99-07 Rockaway Beach Blvd., Rockaway Park, 11694. Tel: 718-634-6476; Fax: 718-701-1915; Email: sffriaryny@gmail.com. Bro. Jose Valliara, C.M.S.F., Supr. Gen.

Holy Ghost Fathers of Ireland, 99-15 Rockaway Beach Blvd., Rockaway Park, 11694. Tel: 718-634-8229; Fax: 718-634-8193; Email: tbasquel@aol.com; Web: www.irishspiritans.ie. Very Rev. Thomas Basquel, C.S.Sp., Asst. Sec.; Revs. Diarmuid Casey, C.S.Sp., Treas.; Joseph Glynn, C.S.Sp., Prov. Delegate; Brendan Hally, C.S.Sp., Sec.; Noel P. O'Meara, C.S.Sp.

SPRINGFIELD GARDENS. *Martin De Porres Brothers Community*, 136-01 219th St., Springfield Gardens, 11413. Tel: 347-882-8761; Fax: 718-527-0606; Fax: 800-472-0716; Email: rrbfsc@nyc.rr.com; Email: rrbfsc@mdpgh.org; Web: mdpgh.org. Bros. Raymond R. Blixt, F.S.C., M.A., Prof.; Philip Rofrano, F.S.C., L.C.S.W.; Kevin Finn, F.S.C., M.A., Dir. of Community. Brothers 4. In Res. Bro. Peter Iorlano, F.S.C., M.A.

[S] CONVENTS AND RESIDENCES FOR SISTERS

BROOKLYN. *The Congregation of the Daughters of Mary, Brooklyn*, 332 E. 32nd St., 11226. Tel: 718-856-3323; Fax: 718-703-0980. Sr. Juvenia Joseph, Supr. of House.

Discalced Carmelite Nuns (2004) 361 Highland Blvd., 11207. Tel: 718-235-0422; Fax: 718-235-0542. Mother Ana Maria, O.C.D., Prioress. Sisters 7.

Franciscan Sisters of the Poor, Congregational Office, 133 Remsen St., 11201. Tel: 718-643-1945; Fax: 718-643-9710; Email: sfp@franciscansisters.org; Web: www.franciscansisters.org. Sr. Licia Mazzia, S.F.P., Congregation Min.

Hermanas Franciscanas De La Inmaculada Concepcion, 209 1st St., 11215. Tel: 718-624-6720.

Missionaries of Charity, Contemplative / Our Lady of Lourdes Convent (1982) 34 Aberdeen St., 11207. Tel: 718-443-2868. Sisters M. Joy Zanin, M.C.; M. John Soulis, M.C.; Margaret Mary Arias, M.C.; Marie Bernadette Marva Parker, M.C.; M. Faustina Soumas, M.C.; M. Bernadette Viola, M.C.; M. Teresa Kassab, M.C.; Mary Ann Tang Wing, M.C.; Maria Guadalupe Ramirez Villamizar, M.C.; Mary Judith Sanchez Lopez, M.C. Sisters 10.

The Sisters Adorers of the Precious Blood, 5400 Fort Hamilton Pkwy., 11219-4037. Tel: 718-438-6371; Fax: 718-438-6381. Rev. Msgr. Philip J. Reilly, Chap., (Retired). Sisters 3.

Confraternity of the Precious Blood, 5300 Ft. Hamilton Ave., 11219-4035. Tel: 718-436-1120; Fax: 718-854-6058. Rev. Thomas V. Doyle. Staff 3.

Sisters of Mercy of the Americas, Mid-Atlantic Community (1855) 273 Willoughby Ave., 11205-1487. Tel: 718-622-5750; Web: www.mercymidatlantic.org. Sr. Patricia Vetrano, R.S.M., Pres. Sisters 1,007.

Sisters of the Good Shepherd, 348 Ninth St., 11215. Tel: 718-499-9212; Email: cnolan8345@aol.com. Clare Nolan, Member. Sisters 2.

Provincial Office, 25-30 21st Ave., Astoria, 11105. Tel: 718-278-1155; Fax: 718-278-1158. Sr. Maureen McGowan, R.G.S., Prov. Officer.

Sisters of the Visitation of Brooklyn, NY (1855) 8902 Ridge Blvd., 11209. Tel: 718-745-5151; Fax: 718-745-3680; Email: vamonastery@aol.com; Web: www.brooklynvisitationmonastery.org. Mother Susan Marie Kasprzak, V.H.M., B.A., Supr. Sisters 13; Professed Sisters 13.

ASTORIA. *Provincialate of the Sisters of the Good Shepherd* (1834) (Province of New York/Toronto) 25-30 21st Ave., Astoria, 11105. Tel: 718-278-1155; Email: office@nygoodshepherd.org. Nancy Perez, Admin.; Sr. Maureen McGowan, R.G.S., Prov.

Sisters of the Good Shepherd, Province of New York / Toronto Sisters 2.

Sisters of the Good Shepherd, 61-03 56th Ave., Maspeth, 11378. Tel: 718-418-0280; Email: karen.keegan@nygoodshepherd.org; Email: office@nygoodshepherd.org. Karen Keegan, Contact Person. Sisters 4.

FLUSHING. *The Congregation of the Sisters of Jesus the Savior*, 35 50 158th St., Flushing, 11358. Tel: 718-581-6636. Sisters Mary Fidelis Ezemaduka, S.J.S., Member; Maria Gemma Njeze, S.J.S., Regl. Coord. & Asst. Community Coord.; Christi-

ana Nwachukwu, S.J.S., Regl. & Community Bursar; Janesteve Udo, S.J.S., Community Coord.
Congregation of Sisters of St. Joseph of St. Marc, St. Andrew Avellino, 35-60 158th St., Flushing, 11358. Tel: 425-301-3414; Email: sjsmny11@yahoo.com. Sr. Roseena Cheruvathoor, Supr.
Sisters of St. Joseph of St- Marc Sisters 4.
GLENDALE. *Convent of the Sisters of Mary Reparatrix*, 7225 68th St., Glendale, 11385. Tel: 718-456-4242; Tel: 718-386-1107 (Altar Bread Department); Fax: 718-386-2254; Email: smrnyc@smr.org; Web: www.smr.org. Sr. Pat Mullen, S.M.R., Local Leader. Sisters 2.
JAMAICA. *Ursuline Sisters of Tildonk*, 81-15 Utopia Pkwy., Jamaica, 11432-1308. Tel: 718-591-0681; Fax: 718-969-4275; Email: jcallahan@tildonkursuline.org; Email: mazzara@tildonkursuline.org; Web: www.tildonkursuline.org. Sr. Joanne Callahan, O.S.U.
QUEENS VILLAGE. *St. Ann's Novitiate, Little Sisters of the Poor* (1902) 110-39 Springfield Blvd., P.O. Box 280356, Queens Village, 11428. Tel: 718-464-4920; Fax: 718-479-3126; Email: nvmothersuperior@littlesistersofthepoor.org; Web: www.littlesistersofthepoor.org. Sr. Mary Richard, L.S.P., Supr. & Mistress of Novices. Novices 4; Postulants 1; Sisters 6.
Little Sisters of the Poor aka Province of Brooklyn, Provincial Residence, 110-30 221st St., Queens Village, 11429. Tel: 718-464-1800; Fax: 347-626-2181; Email: provincialbklyn@littlesistersofthepoor.org; Web: www.littlesistersofthepoor.org. Sr. Alice Marie Jones, L.S.P., Prov. Sisters 92.
ROCKAWAY PARK. *Stella Maris Convent, Sisters of St. Joseph*, 140 Beach 112th St., Rockaway Park, 11694-2497. Tel: 718-634-1886; Fax: 718-945-0638.
SOUTH OZONE PARK. *Daughters of Mary Mother of Mercy*, 109-26 130th St., South Ozone Park, 11420. Tel: 718-843-1364; Tel: 646-578-9102. Sr. Bernadette DeLourdes, Regional Supr.

[T] SECULAR INSTITUTES

FLUSHING. *The Institute of the Apostolic Oblates/Pro Sanctity* (1950) 45-30 195th St., Flushing, 11358. Tel: 718-649-0324; Email: apostolicoblates@verizon.net; Web: www.prosanctity.org. Agnes Rus, Local Mod.
JACKSON HEIGHTS. *Asociacion Misioneros Contemplativos Laicos* (Lay Association of Contemplative Missionaries) 3543 84th St., Apt. 308, Jackson Heights, 11372. Tel: 718-592-5458. Antonio Alvarez, Representative; Ana Luisa Ortega, Treas.

[U] MISCELLANEOUS LISTINGS

BROOKLYN. *Aid to the Church in Need, Inc.*, 725 Leonard St., 3rd Fl., 11222-0384. Tel: 718-609-0939; Fax: 718-609-0938; Email: info@churchinneed.org; Web: www.churchinneed.org. Mr. Edward Clancy, Sec.
The Cathedral Club of Brooklyn, P.O. Box 315, 11209-0315. Tel: 718-809-2440; Fax: 646-720-1183; Web: www.cathedralclubbrooklyn.org. James B. McHugh, Bd. Member.
**Catholic Federation of Social Service Agencies of Brooklyn and Queens*, 191 Joralemon St., 11201. Tel: 718-722-6000; Email: info@ccbq.org. William R. Guarinello, M.S., Pres.
**Federation of Oases of Koinonia John the Baptist*, 205 14th St., 11215. Email: segnykjb@hotmail.com; Web: www.visitationbvm-brooklyn.org. 98 Richards St., 11231. Rev. Claudio Antecini.
Ferrini Welfare League, 101-41 91 St., Ozone Park, 11416. Tel: 718-845-0539; Fax: 718-845-8978.
Flowers With Care, Diocese of Brooklyn, Inc., 191 Joralemon St., 11201. Tel: 718-722-6000; Fax: 718-722-6096.
The Franciscan Federation, Third Order Regular of the Sisters and Brothers of the United States, 135 Remsen St., 11201. Tel: 718-858-8819; Email: franfedoffice@franfed.org; Web: www.franfed.org. Bro. Damian Novello, O.S.F., Co-Exec. Dir.; Sr. Carol Woods, S.F.M.A., Co-Exec. Dir.
Franciscan Sisters of the Poor Communities, Inc., 133 Remsen St., 11201. Tel: 718-643-1945; Fax: 718-643-9710. Congregation sponsors: Franciscan Ministries, Inc.
Heart's Home USA, 26 Olive St., 11211. Tel: 718-522-2121; Email: office.heartshomeusa@gmail.com; Web: www.heartshomeusa.org. Ms. Cecile Fourmeaux, Pres.
**HeartShare Human Services of New York, Roman Catholic Diocese of Brooklyn*, 12 MetroTech Center, 29th Fl., 11201. Tel: 718-422-4200; Fax: 718-522-4506; Email: William.Guarinello@Heartshare.org. William R. Guarinello, M.S., C.E.O.
St. John's Bread & Life Program, Inc., 795 Lexington Ave., 11221. Tel: 718-443-2240; Tel: 718-574-0058; Fax: 718-455-7796. Mr. Anthony Butler, Exec. Dir. (Soup Kitchen, Employment Counseling, HIV/AIDS Support Group/Food Pantry, Counseling, Referrals, Advocacy, Project ID, Immigration & Free Tax Prep).
Mercy Medical Mission (Sisters of Mercy Mid-Atlantic Community), 273 Willoughby Ave., 11205. Fax: 718-398-7866.
National Center of the Haitian Apostolate, 332 E. 32nd St., 11226. Tel: 718-856-3323; Fax: 718-703-0980; Web: snaa.org. Most Rev. Guy Sansaricq, Founder & Dir. Emeritus, Haitian Apostolate, (Retired); Rev. Jean Yvon Pierre, Exec. Dir.; Sr. Juvenia Joseph, Office Dir.
Rocklyn Asset Corporation, 243 Prospect Park W., 11215.
Rocklyn Ecclesiastical Corporation, 243 Prospect Park W., 11215.
The Roman Catholic Pontifical Lay Association Memores Domini, 218 76th St., 11209. Tel: 718-833-3992; Email: asala218@gmail.com. Angela Sala, Treas.
Men's House (1993) 218 76 St., 11209. Tel: 718-833-3992; Email: chris.vath@gmail.com. Christopher H. Vath, Head of the House.
Women's House (1993) 10 Kraft Ave., Bronxville, 10708. Tel: 914-395-0019; Email: paolafracmessa@yahoo.com. Paola Fracmessa, Head of the House.
Rosary For Life, Inc., 3309 Ave. P, 11234-3411. Tel: 718-377-6920; Fax: 718-377-6973.
The Ryken Educational Center, 7100 Shore Rd., 11209. Tel: 718-759-5758; Fax: 718-759-5744; Email: wslow@xaverian.org. William Slow, Dean.
Society of the Immaculate Conception of Brooklyn, 310 Prospect Park W., 11215. Tel: 718-965-7326; Fax: 718-965-7325; Email: jnagle@diobrook.org. Rev. Msgr. Joseph P. Nagle, Exec. Dir. (Missionary Society).
ASTORIA. *Good Shepherd Volunteers*, 25-30 21st Ave., Astoria, 11105. Tel: 718-943-7489; Fax: 718-408-2332; Email: GSV@gsvolunteers.org; Web: www.goodshepherdvolunteers.org. Diane Conroy, Dir.
HandCrafting Justice, Inc. (1997) 25-30 21st Ave., Astoria, 11105. Tel: 718-278-1155; Email: mmcgowanrgs@gmail.com; Web: www.handcraftingjustice.org. Sr. Maureen McGowan, R.G.S., Prog. Dir.
FLUSHING. *Pro Sanctity Movement* (1947) 45-30 195th St., Flushing, 11358. Tel: 718-649-0324; Email: prosanctitynewyork@verizon.net; Web: www.nyprosanctity.org. Angela DiPaola, Dir. Pro Sanctity East; Rev. Msgr. Steven J. Aguggia, J.C.L., Spiritual Advisor.
FOREST HILLS. *The Benoit Trust*, 70-20 Juno St., Forest Hills, 11375. Tel: 718-480-1306; Email: brdano@hotmail.com. Bros. Richard Carey, F.M.S., Trustee; Benedict Lo Balbo, F.M.S., Trustee; Hank Sammon, F.M.S., Trustee; Mr. Dennis Hammer, Trustee. Congregation of the Marist Brothers.
The Gregoire Trust, 70-20 Juno St., Forest Hills, 11375. Tel: 718-480-1608; Email: maristbrothersus@aol.com. Bros. Benedict LoBalbo, F.M.S., Trustee; Hank Sammon, F.M.S., Trustee; Mr. Dennis Hammer, Trustee; Bro. Richard Carey, F.M.S., Trustee.
Lewiston Mission Trust, 70-20 Juno St., Forest Hills, 11375. Bros. Edward J. O'Neill, F.M.S., Trustee; Benedict Lo Balbo, F.M.S., Trustee & Contact Person; Yvon Bedard, F.M.S., Trustee.
Marist Brothers of the Schools, Inc., Champagnat Residence, 70-20 Juno St., Forest Hills, 11375. Tel: 718-480-1306; Email: maristbrothersus@aol.com; Web: www.maristbr.com. Bro. Patrick McNamara, Prov. Brothers 130.
HOLLIS HILLS. *Glencara, Inc.* (1996) 86-05 218th St., Hollis Hills, 11427. Tel: 718-454-9804; Fax: 718-454-9804; Email: seanfoley@verizon.net. Sisters Louise Cullen, R.S.M., Bd. of Dir.; Sean Foley, R.S.M., Exec. Dir.; Patricia A. Hartigan Esq., R.S.M., Dir.; Michael G. Leavy, Vice Pres.; Kathleen O'Malley, Treas.; Eileen Trainor, R.S.M., Pres.; Regina Williams, R.S.M., Sec.
JACKSON HEIGHTS. **Eternal Flame of Hope Ministries, Inc.*, c/o Rev. Richard J. Bretone, 74-18 Ditmars Blvd., Jackson Heights, 11370. Tel: 718-274-4919; Tel: 718-636-3584. Rev. Richard J. Bretone, Spiritual Dir.
Preachers of Christ and Mary, 93-11 35th Ave., Jackson Heights, 11372. Tel: 718-205-5494. Sr. Maria Amador, P.C.M., Gen. Supr.
LONG ISLAND CITY. *Hour Children* (1995) 36-11 12th St., Long Island City, 11106. Tel: 718-433-4724; Email: sistertesa@hourchildren.org; Web: www.hourchildren.org. Sr. Teresa Fitzgerald, C.S.J., Exec. Dir. Bed Capacity 85; Total Assisted Annually (Includes work inside prisons) 9,000; Total Staff 70; Families Capacity 85; Volunteers 250.
World Compassion Link, P.O. Box 4279, Long Island City, 11104-9808. Tel: 718-672-4848; Email: omearanoel@gmail.com; Email: tbasquez@aol.com; Web: worldcompassionlink.org. Very Rev. Thomas Basquel, C.S.Sp., Pres. & Treas.; Rev. Noel P. O'Meara, C.S.Sp., Vice Pres.
MIDDLE VILLAGE. *National Italian Apostolate Conference* (1968) 7200 Douglaston Pkwy, Douglaston, 11362. Tel: 718-649-0324; Email: saguggia@gmail.com. Rev. Msgr. Steven J. Aguggia, J.C.L., Exec. Dir.
REGO PARK. *Lifeway Network, Inc.*, 85-10 61st Rd., Rego Park, 11374. Tel: 718-779-8075; Fax: 718-651-5645.
RIDGEWOOD. *Friends of RADIO MARIA, Inc.* (1992) 70-05 Fresh Pond Rd., Ridgewood, 11385. Tel: 718-417-0550; Fax: 718-417-5188; Email: info.nyi@radiomaria.us; Web: nyi.radiomaria.us. Rev. Walter Tonelotto, C.S., Dir.
ROCKAWAY PARK. *Franciscan Missionary Brothers of North America, NY* (1901) 99-07 Rockaway Beach Blvd., Rockaway Park, 11694. Tel: 718-634-6476; Fax: 718-634-5833; Email: sffriary@gmail.com. Bro. Joseph Karimalayil, C.M.S.F., Ph.D., Pres. & Supr. Gen.
WOODHAVEN. *School Sisters of Notre Dame Educational Center*, 87-04 88th Ave., Woodhaven, 11421. Tel: 718-738-0588; Fax: 718-322-5515; Email: ssndec@aol.com; Web: ssndecwomens.com. Sr. Catherine Feeney, S.S.N.D., Exec. Dir. Tot Asst. Annually 110; Staff 8.

RELIGIOUS INSTITUTES OF MEN REPRESENTED IN THE DIOCESE

For further details refer to the corresponding bracketed number in the Religious Institutes of Men or Women section.

[0330]—*Brothers of the Christian Schools*—F.S.C.
[1100]—*Brothers of the Sacred Heart*—S.C.
[0470]—*The Capuchin Friars* (Prov. of St. Mary)—O.F.M.Cap.
[0275]—*Carmelites of Mary Immaculate*—C.M.I.
[]—*Congregation of St. John the Baptist of China, Inc.*—C.S.J.B.
[1330]—*Congregation of the Mission - Philadelphia (Vincentians)*—C.M.
[1330]—*Congregation of the Mission (Vincentian Fathers)*—C.M.
[1210]—*Congregation of the Missionaries of St. Charles*—C.S.
[]—*Congregation of the Missionary Brothers of St. Francis of Assisi*—C.M.S.F.
[1000]—*Congregation of the Passion* (Prov. of St. Paul of the Cross)—C.P.
[0480]—*Conventual Franciscans* (Polish Prov.)—O.F.M.Conv.
[0490]—*Franciscan Brothers of Brooklyn*—O.S.F.
[]—*Franciscan Province of Immaculate Conception*—O.F.M.
[0685]—*Institute of the Incarnate Word*—I.V.E.
[0690]—*Jesuit Fathers and Brothers* (New York Prov.)—S.J.
[]—*Korean Missionary Society*—K.M.S.
[0770]—*The Marist Brothers*—F.M.S.
[1330]—*New England Province of the Congregation of the Mission (Polish))*—C.M.
[0950]—*Oratorians* (Brooklyn)—C.O.
[0990]—*Pallottine*—S.A.C.
[]—*Pallottine* (Polish Prov.)—S.A.C.
[1070]—*The Redemptorists*—C.SS.R.
[0690]—*Society of Jesus*—S.J.
[0990]—*Society of the Catholic Apostolate*—S.A.C.
[1200]—*Society of the Divine Savior*—S.D.S.
[]—*Vocationist Fathers*—S.D.V.
[1350]—*Xaverian Brothers U.S.A., Inc.*—C.F.X.

RELIGIOUS INSTITUTES OF WOMEN REPRESENTED IN THE DIOCESE

[]—*Association of Religious Sisters of the Needy (Nigeria)*—A.R.S.N.
[0330]—*Carmelite Sisters of the Aged and Infirm*—O.Carm.
[2980]—*Congregation of Notre Dame*—C.N.D.
[2950]—*Congregation of Notre Dame de Sion*—N.D.S.
[]—*Congregation of Olivetan Benedictine Sisters* (Korea)—O.S.B.
[2230]—*Congregation of the Infant Jesus*—C.I.J.
[3832]—*Congregation of the Sisters of St. Joseph*—C.S.J.
[0760]—*Daughters of Charity of St. Vincent de Paul*—D.C.
[]—*Daughters of Divine Love*—D.D.L.
[]—*Daughters of Mary*—F.de.M.
[]—*Daughters of Mary Mother of Mercy*—D.M.M.M.
[]—*Daughters of Sacred Passion (Nigeria)*—D.S.P.
[0960]—*Daughters of Wisdom*—D.W.
[0420]—*Discalced Carmelite Nuns*—O.C.D.
[1070-11]—*Dominican Congregation of Our Lady of the Rosary (Sparkill Dominicans)*—O.P.
[1070-05]—*Dominican Sisters* (Amityville, NY)—O.P.
[1115]—*Dominican Sisters of Peace*—O.P.
[]—*Franciscan Missionary Sisters of Assisi*—S.F.M.A.
[]—*Franciscan Sisters of Our Lady of the Poor*—F.L.P.
[]—*Franciscan Sisters of the Immaculate (Honduras)*—H.F.I.
[1440]—*Franciscan Sisters of the Poor*—S.F.P.

[]—*Handmaids of the Divine Redeemer* (Ghana)—H.D.R.
[]—*Handmaids of the Holy Child Jesus* (Nigeria)—H.H.C.J.
[]—*Hermanas Predicadoras de Cristo y Maria* (Columbia)—P.C.M.
[2070]—*Holy Union Sisters*—S.U.S.C.
[]—*Idente Missionaries*—M.Id.
[]—*Little Sisters of St. Therese of the Child Jesus (China)*—C.S.T.
[2340]—*Little Sisters of the Poor*—L.S.P.
[]—*Lovers of the Holy Cross (Vietnam)*—L.H.C.
[2710]—*Missionaries of Charity*—M.C.
[2710]—*Missionaries of Charity (Contemplative)*—M.C.
[]—*Missionary Congregation Sisters Servants of the Holy Spirit*—S.Sp.S.
[]—*Missionary Sisters of the Immaculate Conception (China)*—S.M.I.C.
[]—*Missionary Sisters of the Precious Blood* (Canada)—C.P.S.
[]—*Olivetan Benedictine Sisters of Busan*—O.S.B.
[4190]—*Order of Visitation*—V.H.M.
[]—*Parish Visitors of the Mary Immaculate*—P.V.M.I.
[]—*Religious of Christian Doctrine*—R.C.D.
[3430]—*Religious Teachers Filippini*—M.P.F.
[2970]—*School Sisters of Notre Dame*—S.S.N.D.
[]—*Servants of the Lord and the Virgin of Matara* (Argentina)—S.S.V.M.
[0110]—*Sisters Adorers of the Most Precious Blood*—A.P.B.
[0640]—*Sisters of Charity of St. Vincent de Paul, Halifax*—S.C.
[]—*Sisters of Jesus the Savior* (Nigeria)—S.J.S.
[]—*Sisters of Mary Immaculate* (Kenya)—S.M.I.
[]—*Sisters of Mary Mother of the Church (Nigeria)*—S.M.M.C.
[2575]—*Sisters of Mercy of the Americas* (Mid-Atlantic Community)—R.S.M.
[2990]—*Sisters of Notre Dame*—S.N.D.
[3000]—*Sisters of Notre Dame de Namur*—S.N.D.deN.
[]—*Sisters of Our Lady of Perpetual Help*—S.O.L.P.H.
[3820]—*Sisters of St. John the Baptist*—C.S.J.B.
[3830-05]—*Sisters of St. Joseph*—C.S.J.
[]—*Sisters of St. Joseph of Kenya*—S.S.J.
[]—*Sisters of St. Joseph of St. Marc (France)*—S.J.S.M.
[1830]—*Sisters of the Good Shepherd*—R.G.S.
[1970]—*Sisters of the Holy Family of Nazareth* (Immaculate Heart of Mary Prov.)—C.S.F.N.
[]—*Sisters of the Immaculate Heart of Mary* Kongmoon, China—I.H.M.
[]—*Sisters of the Korean Martyrs*—S.B.K.M.
[3320]—*Sisters of the Presentation of the B.V.M.* (Newburgh)—P.B.V.M.
[]—*Sisters of the Sacred Heart of Jesus*—S.S.H.J.
[2160]—*Sisters, Servants of the Immaculate Heart of Mary*—I.H.M.
[2460]—*Society of Mary Reparatrix*—S.M.R.
[]—*Trinitarian Missionary Sisters*—T.M.S.
[]—*University Sisters of the Assumption*—U.S.A.
[4130]—*Ursuline Sisters of the Congregation of Tildonk, Belgium*—O.S.U.
[4190]—*Visitation Nuns*—V.H.M.

CATHOLIC CEMETERIES

MIDDLE VILLAGE. *Saint John's Cemetery* Operating: St. Johns's Cemetery (Middle Village); Holy Cross Cemetery (Brooklyn); Mount St. Mary Cemetery (Flushing); St. Charles/Resurrection Cemetery (Farmingdale) 80-01 Metropolitan Ave., Middle Village, 11379. Tel: 718-894-4888;
Fax: 718-326-2033; Web: www.ccbklyn.org. Stephen Comando, Exec. Dir.

PARISH CEMETERIES

BROOKLYN. *Trinity*, Tel: 718-894-4888. Most Holy Trinity Parish, Brooklyn.
AMITYVILLE. *Most Holy Trinity*
Most Holy Trinity Parish, Brooklyn.
ROCKAWAY. *St. Mary Star of the Sea Cemetery*, 1920 New Haven Ave., Far Rockaway, 11691.
Tel: 718-894-4888 (Office); Fax: 718-326-4105; Email: MReid@diobrook.org. Rev. Msgr. Michael J. Reid, Vicar

NECROLOGY

† Valero, Rene A., Retired Auxiliary Bishop of Brooklyn., Died Mar. 10, 2019
† Burns, John A., (Retired), Died Jan. 8, 2018
† Dietz, Conrad R., (Retired), Died Sep. 27, 2017
† Feldhaus, Eugene A., (Retired), Died Aug. 21, 2018
† Mahoney, John E., (Retired), Died Feb. 19, 2018
† Rodgers, William J., (Retired), Died Jan. 21, 2018
† White, Leo J., (Retired), Died Jul. 31, 2018
† Charlot, Lucien, (Retired), Died Oct. 7, 2017
† Fernando, Joachim, (Retired), Died Oct. 22, 2017
† Gurrieri, John A., (Retired), Died Sep. 10, 2017
† McGovern, Eugene F., (Retired), Died Nov. 19, 2017
† Noguera, Dagoberto, (Retired), Died Mar. 10, 2018
† Robinson, Robert M., Brooklyn, NY St. Francis-St. Blaise, Died Mar. 13, 2018
† Smith, William A., (Retired), Died Jan. 5, 2018
† Suran, Joaquin, (Retired), Died Dec. 4, 2017

An asterisk (*) denotes an organization that has established tax-exempt status directly with the IRS and is not covered by the USCCB Group Ruling.

Diocese of Brownsville

(Dioecesis Brownsvillensis)

Most Reverend

DANIEL E. FLORES, S.T.D.

Bishop of Brownsville; ordained January 30, 1988; appointed Auxiliary Bishop of Detroit and Titular Bishop of Cozyla October 28, 2006; consecrated November 29, 2006; appointed Bishop of Brownsville December 9, 2009; installed February 2, 2010. *Mailing Address: P.O. Box 2279, Brownsville, TX 78522-2279.*

Most Reverend

RAYMUNDO J. PEÑA, D.D.

Bishop Emeritus of Brownsville; ordained May 25, 1957; appointed Titular Bishop of Trisipa and Auxiliary of San Antonio October 16, 1976; consecrated December 13, 1976; appointed Bishop of El Paso April 29, 1980; installed June 18, 1980; appointed Bishop of Brownsville May 23, 1995; installed August 6, 1995; retired December 9, 2009. *Mailing Address: 700 N. Virgen de San Juan Blvd., San Juan, TX 78589.*

Most Reverend

MARIO A. AVILES, C.O.

Auxiliary Bishop of Brownsville; ordained July 21, 1998; appointed Auxiliary Bishop of Brownsville and Titular Bishop of Cataquas December 4, 2017; installed February 22, 2018. *Mailing Address: 700 N. Virgen de San Juan Blvd., San Juan, TX 78589.*

Established July 10, 1965.

Square Miles 4,296.

Comprises the four Counties of Cameron, Hidalgo, Starr and Willacy in the State of Texas.

For legal titles of parishes and diocesan institutions, consult the Chancery.

Chancery: 1910 University Blvd., P.O. Box 2279, Brownsville, TX 78522-2279. Tel: 956-542-2501; Fax: 956-542-6751.

Web: www.cdob.org

Email: cdob@cdob.org

STATISTICAL OVERVIEW

Personnel	
Bishop	1
Auxiliary Bishops	1
Retired Bishops	1
Priests: Diocesan Active in Diocese	69
Priests: Diocesan Active Outside Diocese	5
Priests: Retired, Sick or Absent	14
Number of Diocesan Priests	88
Religious Priests in Diocese	25
Total Priests in Diocese	113
Extern Priests in Diocese	6
Ordinations:	
Diocesan Priests	1
Permanent Deacons	43
Permanent Deacons in Diocese	117
Total Brothers	11
Total Sisters	63
Parishes	
Parishes	72
With Resident Pastor:	
Resident Diocesan Priests	57
Resident Religious Priests	12
Without Resident Pastor:	
Administered by Priests	2
Completely Vacant	1
Missions	44
Pastoral Centers	2
Professional Ministry Personnel:	
Brothers	1
Sisters	2
Lay Ministers	47
Welfare	
Homes for the Aged	2
Total Assisted	410
Day Care Centers	3
Total Assisted	52
Special Centers for Social Services	6
Total Assisted	157,123
Other Institutions	4
Total Assisted	3,490
Educational	
Diocesan Students in Other Seminaries	16
Total Seminarians	16
High Schools, Private	3
Total Students	562
Elementary Schools, Diocesan and Parish	7
Total Students	1,319
Elementary Schools, Private	3
Total Students	405
Catechesis/Religious Education:	
High School Students	6,869
Elementary Students	19,536
Total Students under Catholic Instruction	28,707
Teachers in the Diocese:	
Priests	4
Brothers	1
Sisters	4
Lay Teachers	203
Vital Statistics	
Receptions into the Church:	
Infant Baptism Totals	5,774
Minor Baptism Totals	700
Adult Baptism Totals	191
Received into Full Communion	245
First Communions	6,060
Confirmations	4,118
Marriages:	
Catholic	951
Interfaith	85
Total Marriages	1,036
Deaths	2,959
Total Catholic Population	1,164,860
Total Population	1,370,424

Former Prelates—Rt. Revs. Dominic Manucy, Titular Bishop of Delma and Vicar Apostolic of Brownsville; cons. Dec. 8, 1874; transferred to Mobile, March 9, 1884; reappointed to Vicariate Apostolic of Brownsville, Feb. 1, 1885; died Dec. 4, 1885; Peter Verdaguer, Titular Bishop of Aulon and Vicar Apostolic of Brownsville; cons. Nov. 9, 1890; died Oct. 26, 1911; Claude Jaillet, O.P., Administrator of Vicariate Apostolic of Brownsville, 1911-1913.

Former Bishops—Most Rev. Adolph Marx, D.D., J.C.D., first Bishop of Brownsville, ord. May 2, 1940; appt. Titular Bishop of Citrus and Auxiliary Bishop of Corpus Christi, July 6, 1956; cons. Oct. 9, 1956; appt. first Bishop of Brownsville, July 19, 1965; installed Sept. 2, 1965; died in Cologne, Germany Nov. 1, 1965; His Eminence Humberto Cardinal Medeiros, D.D., second Bishop of Brownsville, appt. April 14, 1966; cons. June 9, 1966; installed Bishop of Brownsville, June 29, 1966; appt. Archbishop of Boston, Sept. 8, 1970; installed Archbishop of Boston, Oct. 7, 1970; created Cardinal, March 5, 1973; died Sept. 17, 1983; Most Revs. John J. Fitzpatrick, D.D., third Bishop of Brownsville, ord. Dec. 13, 1942; appt. Auxiliary Bishop of Miami, June 24, 1968; cons. Aug. 28, 1968; appt. Bishop of Brownsville, April 27, 1971; installed May 27, 1971; retired Nov. 30, 1991; died July 15, 2006; Enrique San Pedro, S.J., S.T.D., S.S.L., fourth Bishop of Brownsville, ord. March 18, 1957; appt. Auxiliary Bishop of Galveston-Houston April 1, 1986; cons. June 29, 1986; appt. Coadjutor Bishop of Brownsville, Aug. 13, 1991; installed Sept. 26, 1991; succeeded to the See, Nov. 30, 1991; died July 17, 1994; Raymundo J. Pena, D.D., fifth Bishop of Brownsville, (Retired), ord. May 25, 1957; appt. Titular Bishop of Trisipa and Auxiliary of San Antonio Oct. 16, 1976; cons. Dec. 13, 1976; appt. Bishop of El Paso April 29, 1980; installed June 18, 1980; appt. Bishop of Brownsville May 23, 1995; installed Aug. 6, 1995; retired Dec. 9, 2009.

Office of the Bishop—Most Rev. Daniel E. Flores, S.T.D., 1910 University Blvd., P.O. Box 2279, Brownsville, 78522-2279. Tel: 956-550-1510; Tel: 956-550-1530; Fax: 956-550-1565; Email: bishopflores@cdob.org.

Office of the Auxiliary Bishop—700 N. Virgen de San Juan Blvd., San Juan, 78589. Tel: 956-784-5010; Fax: 956-290-9196; Email: bishopaviles@cdob.org. Most Rev. Mario A. Aviles, C.O.

Vicar General—700 N. Virgen de San Juan Blvd., San Juan, 78589. Tel: 956-784-5010; Fax: 956-290-9196; Email: bishopaviles@cdob.org. Most Rev. Mario A. Aviles, C.O.

Deans / Deaneries—Brownsville Deanery: Rev. Michael J. Amesse, O.M.I., Tel: 956-546-3178. Harlingen Deanery: Rev. Robert Charlton, SS.CC., Tel: 956-423-6341. McAllen-Edinburg Deanery: Rev. Msgr. Gustavo Barrera, Tel: 956-686-0251. Mission Deanery: Rev. Isaac Emeka Erondu, Tel: 956-585-2701. Pharr Deanery: Rev. Jose Encarnacion Losoya, C.O., Tel: 956-781-2489. Rio Grande City Deanery: Rev. Thomas W. Sepulveda, C.S.B., Tel: 956-487-2317. San Benito Deanery: Rev. Marco Antonio Reynoso, Tel: 956-399-2022. Weslaco Deanery: Rev. Jean Olivier M. Sambu, Tel: 956-565-1141.

Stewardship & Development Office—Ms. Rosie C. Rodriguez, Dir., 700 N. Virgen de San Juan Blvd., San Juan, 78589. Tel: 956-787-8571; Fax: 956-784-5044; Email: rrodriguez@cdob.org.

Judicial Department and Diocesan Tribunal—700 N. Virgen de San Juan Blvd., San Juan, 78589. Tel: 956-784-5070; Fax: 956-784-5087. Very Rev. A. Oliver Angel, J.C.L., Judicial Vicar, Email:

oangel@cdob.org; MS. ANNITA GONZALEZ, Ecclesiastical Notary & Advocate Facilitator, Email: agonzalez@cdob.org; MRS. NOEMI GOMEZ, Sec., Email: ngomez@cdob.org.

Presiding Judge—Very Rev. A. OLIVER ANGEL, J.C.L.

Promoter of Justice—Rev. Msgrs. GUSTAVO BARRERA; LUIS JAVIER GARCIA, J.C.L.

Procurators and Advocates—MRS. JENEATTE SWANSON, Coord., Email: jswanson@cdob.org.

Court Expert—Sr. NORMA PIMENTEL, M.J., L.P.C.

Associate Judges—Revs. LUIS FERNANDO SANCHEZ, J.C.L.; JOSE RENE ANGEL, J.C.L.; THOMAS G. KULLECK; Rev. Msgr. LUIS JAVIER GARCIA, J.C.L., Judge-Special Cases.

Defenders of the Bond—Rev. Msgrs. GUSTAVO BARRERA, First Instance, Email: gbarrera@cdob.org; LUIS JAVIER GARCIA, J.C.L., First Instance, Email: lgarcia@cdob.org.

Office of the Chancellor—1910 University Blvd., P.O. Box 2279, Brownsville, 78522-2279. Tel: 956-542-2501; Fax: 956-542-6751. Revs. ANDRES EVERARDO GUTIERREZ, Chancellor, Email: agutierrez@cdob.org; LEONEL RODRIGUEZ, Vice Chancellor, Email: lrodriguez@cdob.org; THOMAS G. KULLECK, Historical Archivist, Email: tkulleck@cdob.org.

Episcopal Vicars—Revs. ALFONSO M. GUEVARA, Apostolic Movements & Pastoral Initiatives, Email: aguevara@cdob.org; JUAN PABLO DAVALOS, Pastoral Affairs, Email: jpdavalos@cdob.org; LUIS FERNANDO SANCHEZ, J.C.L., Canonical Affairs, Email: lsanchez@cdob.org.

Moderator of the Curia/Brownsville/San Juan—Most Rev. MARIO A. AVILES, C.O., Moderator of the Curia, 700 N. Virgen de San Juan Blvd., San Juan, 78589. Tel: 956-784-5010; Revs. ANDRES EVERARDO GUTIERREZ, Asst. Moderator of the Curia, 1910 University Blvd., P.O. Box 2279, Brownsville, 78522-2279. Tel: 956-542-2501; Fax: 956-542-6751; Email: agutierrez@cdob.org; LUIS FERNANDO SANCHEZ, J.C.L., Asst. Moderator of the Curia, 700 N. Virgen de San Juan Blvd., San Juan, 78589. Tel: 956-787-8571; Email: lsanchez@cdob.org.

Office for Pastoral Planning—Deacon LUIS ZUNIGA, Dir., Tel: 956-542-2501, Ext. 356; Tel: 956-784-5059; Fax: 956-784-5086; Email: lzuniga@cdob.org.

Diocesan Relations—700 N. Virgen de San Juan Blvd., San Juan, 78589. Tel: 956-781-5323; Fax: 956-784-5082. MRS. BRENDA NETTLES RIOJAS, Dir., Email: bnrpr@cdob.org.

Fiscal Office—1910 University Blvd., P.O. Box 2279, Brownsville, 78522-2279. Tel: 956-542-2501, Ext. 336; Fax: 956-550-1563. *San Juan, 78589.* Tel: 956-787-8571, Ext. 424. MR. JACK GRAHAM, Comptroller, Email: jgraham@cdob.org.

Information Technology—1910 University Blvd., P.O. Box 2279, Brownsville, 78522-2279. Tel: 956-542-2501, Ext. 340; Fax: 956-542-6751. *700 N. Virgen de San Juan Blvd., San Juan, 78589.* Tel: 956-784-5004; Fax: 956-784-5097. MR. ALBERTO ZAVALA, Dir., Tel: 956-550-1540; Email: azavala@cdob.org.

Human Resources Office—1910 University Blvd., P.O. Box 2279, Brownsville, 78522-2279. Tel: 956-542-2501, Ext. 345; Fax: 956-550-1561. MRS. GENOVEVA TREVINO, Dir., Email: gtrevino@cdob.org.

Insurance and Priest Pensions—1910 University Blvd., P.O. Box 2279, Brownsville, 78522-2279. Tel: 956-542-2501, Ext. 349; Fax: 956-550-1586. MARIA C. HERNANDEZ, Insurance Admin., Email: mhernandez@cdob.org.

Building & Property Office—700 N. Virgen de San Juan Blvd., San Juan, 78589. Tel: 956-781-5323; Fax: 956-784-5082. MR. JAVIER SOLIS, Dir., Email: jsolis@cdob.org.

Vicar for Priests—Rev. Msgr. HEBERTO M. DIAZ JR., 1910 University Blvd., P.O. Box 2279, Brownsville, 78522-2279. Tel: 956-542-2501; Fax: 956-542-5751; Email: hdiaz@cdob.org; Rev. JUAN PABLO DAVALOS, Moderator for Recently Ordained Priests.

Office of Permanent Deacons—Rev. FERNANDO GONZALEZ, Dir., 700 N. Virgen de San Juan Blvd., San Juan, 78589. Tel: 956-784-5060; Fax: 956-784-5081.

Vicar for Religious—Rev. THOMAS LUCZAK, O.F.M., Sacred Heart Parish, P.O. Box 370, McAllen, 78505-0370. Tel: 956-686-7711; Fax: 956-686-2028; Sr. NORMA PIMENTEL, M.J., L.P.C., Asst., Tel: 956-702-4088; Fax: 956-782-0418.

Vocations and Seminarian's Office—Revs. JUAN MANUEL SALAZAR, Dir., 700 N. Virgen de San Juan Blvd., San Juan, 78589. Tel: 956-784-5060; Fax: 956-784-5078; Email: jmsalazar@cdob.org; LUIS ROBERTO TINAJERO, Asst. Dir., St. Benedict, P.O. Box 1780, San Benito, 78586. Tel: 956-626-1260; Fax: 956-626-1265; Email: ltinajero@cdob.org.

Campaign for Human Development—Sr. NORMA PIMENTEL, M.J., L.P.C., Diocesan Coord., Mailing Address: P.O. Box 1306, San Juan, 78589. Tel: 956-702-4088; Fax: 956-782-0418.

Catholic Relief Services—700 N. Virgen de San Juan Blvd., San Juan, 78589. Tel: 956-784-5046; Fax: 956-784-5096. MS. OFELIA DE LOS SANTOS, Diocesan Coord., Email: odelossantos@cdob.org.

Immigration Counseling Services—700 N. Virgen de San Juan Blvd., San Juan, 78589. Tel: 956-784-5057; Fax: 956-784-5096. MS. OFELIA DE LOS SANTOS, Dir., Email: odelossantos@cdob.org; SANTA ACUNA, Accredited Rep., Email: sacuna@cdob.org.

Division for Education and Formation—

Media Resource-Library—Sr. MAUREEN CROSBY, S.S.D., Dir., Tel: 956-784-5041; Fax: 956-784-5081; Email: mcrosby@cdob.org.

San Juan Diego Lay Ministry Institute—700 N. Virgen de San Juan Blvd., San Juan, 78589. Deacon LUIS ZUNIGA, Dir., Tel: 956-784-5059; Fax: 956-784-5086; Email: lzuniga@cdob.org.

Catholic Schools Office—700 N. Virgen de San Juan Blvd., San Juan, 78589-3042. Tel: 956-787-8571; Fax: 956-784-5081. Sisters CYNTHIA A. MELLO, S.S.D., Supt., Email: cmello@cdob.org; COLLEEN MATARESE, S.S.D., Dir. Special Progs.

Family Life Office—700 N. Virgen de San Juan Blvd., San Juan, 78589-3042. Tel: 956-784-5012; Fax: 956-784-5081. MRS. LYDIA PESINA, Dir., Email: lpesina@cdob.org; MRS. BLANCA SAENZ, Assoc. Dir., Email: bsaenz@cdob.org; MRS. LINA ZULUAGA, Assoc. Dir., Email: lzuluaga@cdob.org.

Office of Catechesis—700 N. Virgen de San Juan Blvd., San Juan, 78589-3030. Tel: 956-784-5013; Fax: 956-322-4240. MR. LUIS ESPINOZA, Dir., Email: lespinoza@cdob.org.

Office of Liturgy and Worship—700 N. Virgen de San Juan Blvd., San Juan, 78589. Tel: 956-784-5013; Fax: 956-322-4240. MR. LUIS ESPINOZA, Dir., Email: lespinoza@cdob.org.

Office of Youth Ministry—GIOVANNI ADA, Dir., 700 N. Virgen de San Juan Blvd., San Juan, 78589-3042. Tel: 956-781-5323; Fax: 956-784-5081; Email: gada@cdob.org.

Division for Health Care Ministries—700 N. Virgen de San Juan Blvd., San Juan, 78589. Tel: 956-784-5018; Fax: 956-784-5033. MRS. YOLANDA CARRILLO, M.B.A., BCC, Diocesan Dir.

Pro-Life Office—Email: prolife@cdob.org. Rev. DERLIS R. GARCIA, 216 W. 1st St., San Juan, 78589. Tel: 956-783-1196; Email: dgarcia@cdob.org.

Diocesan Attorney—MR. DAVID GARZA, 680 E. St. Charles St., Brownsville, 78520. Tel: 956-541-4914; Fax: 956-542-7403.

Presbyteral Council—Members: Most Rev. DANIEL E. FLORES, S.T.D.; Revs. JOSE RENE ANGEL, J.C.L.; EDUARDO ORTEGA; JOAQUIN ZERMENO; ALEJANDRO F. FLORES; LAWRENCE J. KLEIN; AGLAYDE RAFAEL VEGA; FELIX A. CAZARES; JOSE E. LOSOYA, C.O.; MANOJ KUMAR NAYAK, SS.CC.; JUAN PABLO DAVALOS; LUIS ROBERTO TINAJERO. Ex Officio Members: Most Rev. MARIO A. AVILES, C.O.; Rev. Msgr. HEBERTO M. DIAZ JR.; Revs. ALFONSO M. GUEVARA; ANDRES EVERARDO GUTIERREZ.

Catholic Foundation of the Rio Grande Valley Board—Most Rev. DANIEL E. FLORES, S.T.D.; MR. ALONZO BELTRAN; Rev. Msgr. HEBERTO M. DIAZ JR.; MR. JACK GRAHAM; MS. DELIA CHAVEZ; MR. RICK FLORES.

College of Consultors—Most Revs. DANIEL E. FLORES, S.T.D.; MARIO A. AVILES, C.O.; Revs. JORGE A. GOMEZ; JUAN PABLO DAVALOS; Rev. Msgrs. HEBERTO M. DIAZ JR.; GUSTAVO BARRERA; Revs. ALFONSO M. GUEVARA; AGLAYDE RAFAEL VEGA; FERNANDO GONZALEZ.

Diocesan Finance Council—Most Revs. DANIEL E. FLORES, S.T.D.; MARIO A. AVILES, C.O.; MR. JACK GRAHAM; MR. RUBEN BOSQUEZ; DR. CHARLES ELLARD; MR. HUGH EMERSON; MS. EDNA MARTINEZ; Rev. Msgrs. HEBERTO M. DIAZ JR.; GUSTAVO BARRERA.

Priests' Assignment Board—Most Rev. DANIEL E. FLORES, S.T.D.; Rev. JUAN PABLO DAVALOS, Bishop's Liaison; VACANT, Brownsville Deanery; Revs. RODOLFO FRANCO, Harlingen Deanery; GREGORY T. LABUS, McAllen-Edinburg Deanery; VACANT, Mission Deanery; Revs. JUAN MANUEL SALAZAR, Pharr Deanery; JOAQUIN ZERMENO, Rio Grande City Deanery; MARIO A. CASTRO, San Benito Deanery; VACANT, Weslaco Deanery.

Safety Awareness Program—MR. WALTER LUKASZEK, L.M.S.W., I.P.R., Victim Asst. Coord., Tel: 956-784-5066; Cell: 956-457-0010; Email: wlukaszek@cdob.org; Email: walukaszek@gmail.com.

CLERGY, PARISHES, MISSIONS AND PAROCHIAL SCHOOLS

CITY OF BROWNSVILLE

(CAMERON COUNTY)

1—IMMACULATE CONCEPTION CATHEDRAL (1849)
1218 E. Jefferson St., 78520. Revs. Michael J. Amesse, O.M.I., Rector; Jose R. Torres, O.M.I., Parochial Vicar; Raju Antonisamy, O.M.I., In Res.; Deacon Roberto Cano.
Catechesis Religious Program—Students 153.
Missions—St. Thomas—155 E. Jefferson St., Cameron Co. 78520.
Sacred Heart, 602 E. Elizabeth St., Cameron Co. 78520.

2—CHRIST THE KING (1953)
2255 Southmost Rd., 78521. Tel: 956-546-1982; Fax: 956-546-7120; Email: christ-the-king@cdob.org. Revs. Salvador Ramirez; Ricardo Chavez, Parochial Vicar; Deacon Jose Angel Bernal.
Catechesis Religious Program—Email: pclckbrw@cdob.org. Bro. Moises Lopez, D.R.E. Students 246.
Mission—San Juan Diego de Guadalupe, 4180 S. Browne, Cameron Co. 78521.

3—CHURCH OF THE GOOD SHEPHERD (1968)
2645 Tulipan St., 78521. Tel: 956-542-5142; Fax: 956-542-5278; Email: good-shepherd@cdob.org. Rev. Aglayde Rafael Vega; Deacons Sergio Garcia; Alvino C. Olvera.
Catechesis Religious Program—Mr. Juan Carlos Perez, D.R.E. Students 474.

4—ST. EUGENE DE MAZENOD (1996)
5409 Austin Rd., 78521. Tel: 956-831-9923; Fax: 956-831-3110; Email: st-eugene-demazenod@cdob.org. Rev. Kevin A. Collins, O.M.I.; Deacons Francisco Garza; Jesus G. Hernandez; Roman Ramos.
Catechesis Religious Program—Ms. Eva Guerra, C.R.E. (Grades 1-5); Ms. Belinda Rodriguez, C.R.E. (Grades 6-12). Students 246.

5—HOLY FAMILY (1966)
Mailing Address: 2405 E. Tyler, 78520. Tel: 956-546-6975; Email: holy-family-brw@cdob.org. 2308 E. Tyler, 78520. Rev. Joshua A. Carlos; Deacons Julio Ibarra; Josue Ramirez; Miguel A. Ramirez.
Catechesis Religious Program—Tel: 956-574-9873. Mrs. Amparo Martinez, C.R.E. Students 282.

6—ST. JOSEPH (1953)
555 W. St. Francis St., 78520. Tel: 956-542-2709; Fax: 956-542-2275; Email: saint-joseph-brw@cdob.org. Revs. Oscar O. Siordia; Eusebio Martinez, In Res.; Deacon Mario Rodriguez.
Catechesis Religious Program—Students 242.

7—ST. LUKE (1974)
2800 Rockwell Dr., 78521. Tel: 956-541-1480; Fax: 956-542-8043; Email: saint-luke@cdob.org; Web: www.stlukecc.org. Rev. Fernando Gonzalez; Deacons Cruz Carlos; Javier A. Garcia.
School—St. Luke School, (Grades PreK-8), 2850 Price Rd., 78521. Tel: 956-544-7982; Fax: 956-544-4874; Email: aserrato@cdobcs.org; Web: www.stlukecs.com. Mrs. Anne Marie Serrato, Prin. Lay Teachers 11; Students 94.
Catechesis Religious Program—Tel: 956-541-0184; Email: cce@stlukecc.org. Mrs. Helen Vargas, D.R.E. Students 366.

8—MARY, MOTHER OF THE CHURCH (1967)
1914 Barnard Rd., 78520-8247. Tel: 956-546-3800; Fax: 956-546-1589; Email: saint-mary-brw@cdob.org. Rev. Msgr. Heberto M. Diaz Jr.; Rev. Emmanuel Kwofie, Parochial Vicar; Deacons John P. Kinch; Juan Pablo Navarro; Luis Zuniga.
Schools—Little Saints Learning Center—(2 yr. olds) Tel: 956-546-1805; Fax: 956-546-0787; Email: agomez@cdobcs.org. Mrs. Ana E. Gomez, Prin. Lay Teachers 2; Students 31.
St. Mary Catholic School, (Grades PreK-6), 1300 E. Los Ebanos Blvd., 78520. Tel: 956-546-1805; Fax: 956-546-0787; Email: agomez@cdobcs.org. Mrs. Ana E. Gomez, Prin.; Ms. Judy Faulk, Vice. Prin.; Mrs. Denise Salazar, Library Mgr. Lay Teachers 24; Students 385.
Catechesis Religious Program—Students 277.

9—OUR LADY OF GOOD COUNSEL (1966)
1055 Military Hwy., 78520. Tel: 956-541-8341; Fax: 956-548-0229; Email: lady-of-good-counsel@cdob.org. Rev. Rene Gaytan; Deacon Guadalupe Garcia.
Catechesis Religious Program—Rosario Figueroa, D.R.E. Students 259.

10—OUR LADY OF GUADALUPE (1928)

Mailing Address: P.O. Box 4900, 78523.
Tel: 956-542-4823; Fax: 956-542-5944; Email: olg-brownsville@cdob.org. 1200 E. Lincoln St., 78521. Rev. Francisco Acosta; Deacon Bruno Cedillo.
Catechesis Religious Program—Tel: 956-542-3619. Sr. Arminda Rangel, M.J., D.R.E. Students 195.

11—The Parish of the Lord of Divine Mercy (2005)
650 E. Alton Gloor Blvd., 78526. Tel: 956-544-2112; Email: thelordofdivinemercy@cdob.org; Web: www.lordofdivinemercybrownsville.com. Rev. Juan Pablo Davalos; Deacon Noe Longoria.
Catechesis Religious Program—Email: PCL-LDMBrw@cdob.org. Cristina M. Rodriguez, D.R.E. Students 365.

12—San Felipe de Jesus (1996)
2218 Carlos Ave., 78526-8093. Tel: 956-982-2007; Fax: 956-541-4177; Email: san-felipe-de-jesus@cdob.org. 2215 Rancho Viejo Ave., 78526-8093. Rev. Anthony O'Connor, S.M.
Res.: 2511 Dennis, 78526.
Catechesis Religious Program—Email: PCL-SFJBrw@cdob.org. Mrs. Lourdes Gomez, C.R.E. Students 302.

OUTSIDE THE CITY OF BROWNSVILLE

Alamo, Hidalgo Co., Resurrection (1926) (Formerly St. Joseph/Our Lady of Fatima)
312 N. 9th St., Alamo, 78516. Tel: 956-787-2963; Fax: 956-787-6788; Email: resurrection@cdob.org. Rev. Jose Rene Angel, J.C.L.
Catechesis Religious Program—Ms. Isabel Forquer, C.R.E.; Ms. Janie Mercado, C.R.E. Students 459.

Alton, Hidalgo Co., San Martin de Porres (1967)
621 W. Main Ave., Alton, 78573. Tel: 956-585-8001; Fax: 956-585-0715; Email: smdpalton@cdob.org; Web: sanmartindeporresalton.org. Mailing Address: 106 S. Alton Blvd., P.M.B. 9023, Alton, 78573. Rev. Arturo Castillo; Deacons Antonio M. Arteaga; Armandin Villarreal; Rodrigo Garza Jr.
Catechesis Religious Program—Maria Belen Fuentes, D.R.E. Students 730.
Mission—Capilla Santa Cecilia, 15905 Cantu Rd, Edinburg, 78541.

Donna, Hidalgo Co., St. Joseph (1928)
306 S. D Salinas Blvd., Donna, 78537.
Tel: 956-464-3331; Fax: 956-464-6808; Email: stjoseph-donna@cdob.org; Email: marocha122@gmail.com; Web: stjosephdonna.com. Revs. Robert DeLong, M.S.F., Parish Admin.; Franciscus Asisi Eka Yuantoro, M.S.F., Parochial Vicar; Deacons Hugo De la Cruz; Felipe Almendarez.
Catechesis Religious Program—Tel: 956-464-3472; Email: PCL-SJDonna@cdob.org. Mrs. Liza G. Tobias, D.R.E. Students 690.
Mission—Christ the King, 1/2 Mile S. FM 493, Donna, Hidalgo Co. 78537.

Edcouch, Hidalgo Co., St. Theresa of the Infant Jesus (1948)
200 P. Salazar, P.O. Box 307, Edcouch, 78538.
Tel: 956-262-1347; Fax: 956-262-1348; Email: infant-jesus@cdob.org. Rev. Eduardo Gomez; Deacon Florencio Treviño.
Catechesis Religious Program—Mrs. Susana Espircueta, C.R.E. Students 291.
Mission—Our Lady of Guadalupe, 200 N. Laurel, La Villa, Hidalgo Co. 78562.

Edinburg, Hidalgo Co.

1—Holy Family (1967)
1302 E. Champion, Edinburg, 78539-4864.
Tel: 956-383-5472; Fax: 956-383-5034; Email: holy-family-edinburg@cdob.org. Revs. Thomas Luczak, O.F.M.; Terrence Gorski, O.F.M., Parochial Vicar; Deacon Ruben Lopez.
Catechesis Religious Program—Ms. Susie de la Garza, D.R.E. Students 466.

2—St. Joseph (1948)
114 W. Fay St., Edinburg, 78539. Tel: 956-383-3728; Fax: 956-383-8630; Email: info@stjosephedinburg.org; Email: ccortez@stjosephedinburg.org; Web: stjosephedinburg.org. Rev. Gregory T. Labus; Deacon Silvestre J. Garcia.
School—St. Joseph School, (Grades PreK-8), Preschool & Day Care Center: Little Lamb Learning Center. 119 W. Fay St., Edinburg, 78539.
Tel: 956-383-3957; Fax: 956-318-0681; Email: akarpinski@cdobcs.org; Web: stjoseph-edinburg.org. Mrs. Angelina Karpinski, Prin.; Genie Smith, Librarian. Lay Teachers 14; Students 122.
Catechesis Religious Program—Email: rsauceda@stjosephedinburg.org. Mrs. Rosalinda Sauceda, D.R.E. Students 318.

3—Sacred Heart (1927)
215 N. 16th Ave., Edinburg, 78541.
Tel: 956-383-3253; Fax: 956-383-7311; Email: sacredheartedg@sbcglobal.net. Revs. Manoj Kumar Nayak, SS.CC.; Christopher Santagelò, SS.CC., Parochial Vicar; Richard L. Lifrak, SS.CC., Parochial Vicar; Deacons Jose Peralez III; Raul Rangel.
Catechesis Religious Program—Ms. Susan Mercado, D.R.E. Students 987.
Mission—Capilla de San Jose, 4101 Flores St., Edinburg, Hidalgo Co. 78541. Tel: 956-386-1235; Email: teresadejesus@sacredheartedinburg.org.

El Ranchito, Cameron Co., St. Ignatius of Loyola Parish (1967)
24380 W. U.S. Hwy. 281, San Benito, 78586.
Tel: 956-399-2022; Fax: 956-399-1213; Email: saint-ignatius@cdob.org. Rev. Marco Antonio Reynoso, Parish Admin.; Deacons Arturo Escobedo; Juan Carlos Jasso.
Catechesis Religious Program—Ms. Maria Valdez, D.R.E. Students 370.
Missions—Our Lady of Lourdes—22091 Farmer Ave., San Benito, Cameron Co. 78586. (La Paloma).
Sacred Heart of Jesus, 1419 W. U.S. Hwy. 281, Los Indios, Cameron Co. 78586.

Elsa, Hidalgo Co., Sacred Heart (1948)
1100 N. Broadway, P.O. Box 6, Elsa, 78543.
Tel: 956-262-1406; Fax: 956-262-4265; Email: sacred-heart-elsa@cdob.org. Rev. Cesar Uriel Partida; Deacons David C. Carreon; Gerardo J. Rosa.
Catechesis Religious Program—Adanayri Caamano, D.R.E. Students 56.
Missions—Christ the King—8254 Valdez Rd., Monte Alto, Hidalgo Co. 78538.
Holy Cross Catechetical Center, 434 Mile 15 N, Edcouch, 78596.

Escobares, Starr Co., Sacred Heart (1967)
4987 Old Escobares Hwy 83, P.O Box 1180, Roma, 78584. Tel: 956-849-1741; Fax: 956-847-1502; Email: sacredheartchurch37@gmail.com. Rev. Jerzy Majka, Admin.; Deacons Rosvel Pruneda; Rodolfo C. Salinas; Miguel Villarreal.
Catechesis Religious Program—Mr. Rolando Munoz, D.R.E. Students 297.
Missions—Santa Rosa de Lima—4195 Old Hwy. 83 (La Rosita), Rio Grande City, Starr Co. 78582.
Our Lady of Guadalupe, 1155 N. FM 649 (13 Miles N. of Roma), El Sauz, Starr Co. 78582.

Harlingen, Cameron Co.

1—St. Anthony (1940)
1015 E. Van Buren Ave., Harlingen, 78550.
Tel: 956-428-6111; Fax: 956-428-4276; Email: stanthonychurch2@aol.com. 209 S. 10th, Harlingen, 78550. Revs. Lawrence J. Klein; Ernesto Magallon, In Res.; Deacon Paulo Escobar.
School—St. Anthony School, (Grades PreK-6), 1015 E. Harrison St., Harlingen, 78550. Tel: 956-423-2486 ; Fax: 956-412-0084; Email: kstapleton@cdobcs.org. Mrs. Kathy Stapleton, Prin.; Janie Lozano, Librarian. Lay Teachers 8; Students 110; Clergy / Religious Teachers 1.
Catechesis Religious Program—Mrs. Mary Kyser, D.R.E. Students 630.

2—Immaculate Heart of Mary (1927)
412 S. C St., Harlingen, 78550. Tel: 956-423-0855; Fax: 956-421-1071; Email: ihom@cdob.org. Rev. Msgr. Luis Javier Garcia, J.C.L.; Rev. George A. Gonzalez, In Res.
Catechesis Religious Program—Students 59.

3—Our Lady of the Assumption (1958)
1313 W. Buchanan St., Harlingen, 78550.
Tel: 956-423-4670; Fax: 956-423-5970; Email: ola-harlingen@cdob.org. Rev. Ruben Delgado.
Catechesis Religious Program—Mary Martinez, D.R.E. Students 616.
Mission—San Felipe, 1706 Rangerville Rd., Harlingen, Cameron Co. 78550. Email: ola-harlingen@cdob.org. Rev. Ruben Delgado; Deacon Michael L. Seymour.

4—Queen of Peace (1967)
1509 New Combes Hwy., Harlingen, 78550.
Tel: 956-423-6341; Fax: 956-423-2864; Email: queen-of-peace@cdob.org; Web: qphrl.org. Revs. Robert Charlton, SS.CC.; Brian Guerrini, SS.CC., Parochial Vicar; Deacons Jose G. Aguilera; Benigno Palacios; Juan R. Zamora.
Catechesis Religious Program—Dora Schoonover, D.R.E. Students 233.

Hidalgo, Hidalgo Co., Sacred Heart (1967)
208 E. Camelia Ave., Hidalgo, 78557.
Tel: 956-843-2463; Fax: 956-843-2187; Email: sacredhearthid@cdob.org. P.O. Box 579, Hidalgo, 78557. Rev. Juan Manuel Salazar.
Catechesis Religious Program—Mrs. Elisa Garza, D.R.E. Students 305.

La Feria, Cameron Co., St. Francis Xavier aka Annual (1930)
500 S. Canal St., P.O. Box 116, La Feria, 78559.
Tel: 956-797-2666; Fax: 956-797-3387; Email: st-francis-xavier@cdob.org. Rev. Rodolfo Franco; Deacons Jose G. Gonzalez; Salvador G. Saldivar.
Catechesis Religious Program—Ms. Melissa Mendoza, C.R.E. Students 315.

La Grulla, Starr Co., Holy Family (1967)
W. 107 Private Lazaro Solis St., P.O. Box 67, La Grulla, 78548. Tel: 956-487-3365; Fax: 956-487-4727; Email: holy-family-grulla@cdob.org. Rev. Juan Rogelio Gutierrez, Admin.; Deacon Benito Saenz Jr.
Catechesis Religious Program—Ms. Emedlia Rios, C.R.E.; Mrs. Lilian Maldonado, C.R.E. Students 168.
Missions—Cristo Rey—N. FM 2360 & Eugenio St., La Victoria, Starr Co. 78582.
Our Lady of the Peace, 6689 FM1430, La Casita, Starr Co. 78582.

La Joya, Hidalgo Co., Our Lady, Queen of Angels (1960)
916 S. Leo Ave., La Joya, 78560. Tel: 956-585-5223; Fax: 956-585-4878; Email: olqangels@cdob.org. Rev. Leonel Rodriguez.
Catechesis Religious Program—Email: pcl-olqalajoya@cdob.org. Rosie Gonzalez, D.R.E. Students 228.
Missions—San Jose—41838 Old Military Rd., Havana, Hidalgo Co. 78560.
St. Mary Magdalene, 7100 W. Military Rd. (Abram-Perezville), Mission, Hidalgo Co. 78572. 916 S. Leo Ave., La Joya, 78560.
St. Anthony, 1102 S. Main St., Penitas, Hidalgo Co. 78576.

Los Fresnos, Cameron Co., St. Cecilia (1964)
606 W. Ocean Blvd., Los Fresnos, 78566.
Tel: 956-233-5619; Tel: 956-233-5565; Email: saint-cecilia@cdob.org. Rev. Msgr. Pedro Briseno.
Catechesis Religious Program—Mrs. Yerenia Lizama, D.R.E. Students 273.

Lyford, Willacy Co., Prince of Peace (1967)
8413 Park Ave., P.O. Box 460, Lyford, 78569.
Tel: 956-347-3580; Fax: 956-347-3649; Email: prince-of-peace@cdob.org. Rev. Gabriel I. Ezeh.
Catechesis Religious Program—Students 166.
Missions—Santa Monica—FM 1018 & 1420, Santa Monica, Willacy Co.
St. Martin, 345 N. Martin Cavazos Dr., Sebastian, Willacy Co. 78594.

McAllen, Hidalgo Co.

1—Holy Spirit (1981)
2201 Martin Ave., McAllen, 78504.
Tel: 956-631-5295; Fax: 956-631-5460; Email: hspmcallen@yahoo.com. Rev. Msgr. Louis L. Brum; Rev. Daniel Herve Oyama, (In Res.); Deacons Henry N. Camacopa; Gabriel N. Hernandez; David Espinoza; Reynaldo I. Flores; Crawford A. Higgins; Richard A. Longoria; Luis A. Treviño.
Catechesis Religious Program—Kathy Gamez, D.R.E. Students 1,165.

2—St. Joseph the Worker (1967) Rev. Edouard Atangana, Ph.D., S.T.L.; Deacon Alejandro Gamboa.
Catechesis Religious Program—Tel: 956-686-6871; Email: PCL-SJWMcallen@cdob.org. Norma Salinas, D.R.E. Students 152.

3—Saint Juan Diego Cuauhtlatoatzin (2002)
3413 Helena Ave., McAllen, 78503.
Tel: 956-682-5155; Email: sjdmcallen@cdob.org; Web: sjdmcallen.com. 3408 Idela Ave., McAllen, 78503. Rev. Alejandro F. Flores; Deacons Felix Felix; Jose Javier Garcia; Jose G. Vargas.
Catechesis Religious Program—Monica Rios, D.R.E. Students 202.

4—Our Lady of Perpetual Help (1967)
2209 Kendlewood Ave., McAllen, 78501.
Tel: 956-682-4238; Fax: 956-682-0289; Email: OLPH-McAllen@cdob.org. Revs. Martin de la Cruz; Artemio Jacob, Parochial Vicar; Paul Roman, In Res.; Deacons Rodolfo Sepulveda Jr.; Santos Chapa.
Catechesis Religious Program—Cynthia Gonzalez, D.R.E. Students 490.

5—Our Lady of Sorrows (1941)
1108 W. Hackberry St., McAllen, 78501-4304.
Tel: 956-686-0251; Fax: 956-686-0322; Email: ols@cdob.org. Rev. Msgr. Gustavo Barrera; Revs. Felix A. Cazares, Parochial Vicar; Mishael J. Koday, In Res.; Deacons Juan Gonzalez; Raymond L. Thomas Jr.
School—Our Lady of Sorrows School, (Grades PreK-8), 1100 Gumwood, McAllen, 78501.
Tel: 956-686-3651; Fax: 956-686-1996; Email: ldeleon@cdobcs.org. Mrs. Luisa DeLeon, Prin.; Hugo De La Rosa, Vice Prin.; Ms. Pilar Tijerina, Library Mgr. Lay Teachers 62; Students 449; Clergy / Religious Teachers 1.
Catechesis Religious Program—Margareth Couto, D.R.E.; Irma Cirlos, D.R.E. Students 903.

6—Sacred Heart (1917)
306 S. 15th St., P.O. Box 370, McAllen, 78505-0370.
Tel: 956-686-7711; Fax: 956-686-2028; Email: sacred-heart-mcallen@cdob.org. Revs. Thomas Luczak, O.F.M.; Terrence Gorski, O.F.M.; Deacon Carlos C. Aguilar.
Catechesis Religious Program—Ms. Sandra Kent, D.R.E. Students 276.

McCook, Hidalgo Co., Immaculate Conception (1950)
28212 FM 2058, Edinburg, 78541. Tel: 956-842-3663; Email: jzermeno@cdob.org. Rev. Joaquin Zermeno.
Catechesis Religious Program—CRP, Students 33.
Mission—St. Anne, San Manuel. P.O. Box 134, Linn, 78563.

Mercedes, Hidalgo Co.

1—Our Lady of Mercy (1909)
322 S. Vermont Ave., P.O. Box 805, Mercedes, 78570.
Tel: 956-565-1141; Fax: 956-565-1640; Email:

olm@cdob.org; Web: olmmercedes.org. Rev. Jean Olivier M. Sambu; Deacon Roberto Cantu.
Catechesis Religious Program—Miss Diana Enriquez, D.R.E. Students 249.
2—SACRED HEART CHURCH (1969)
920 Anacuitas, Mercedes, 78570. Tel: 956-565-0271; Fax: 956-565-0272; Email: sacred-heart-mercedes@cdob.org; Web: www.sacredheartmercedes.org. Rev. Eduardo Ortega; Deacons Gilberto Guardiola Jr.; Jose A. Torres.
Res.: 600 N. Washington, Mercedes, 78570.
Catechesis Religious Program—Miss Fabiola Garcia, C.R.E. Students 448.
MISSION, HIDALGO CO.
1—OUR LADY OF GUADALUPE (1899) [CEM]
620 Dunlap St., P.O. Box 1047, Mission, 78572-1047. Tel: 956-585-2623; Fax: 956-584-5856; Email: olgparish@sbcglobal.net. Revs. Roy Lee Snipes, O.M.I.; Richard Philion, O.M.I., Parochial Vicar; Deacon Guillermo F. Bill Castaneda Jr.
Catechesis Religious Program—Sr. Maria Guadalupe Cortes, M.C.P., D.R.E. Students 754.
Chapel—La Lomita.
2—OUR LADY OF ST. JOHN OF THE FIELDS (1967)
1052 Washington St., Mission, 78572. Tel: 956-585-2325; Fax: 956-585-7270; Email: stjohnofthefields@sbcglobal.net. Rev. Francisco Castillo; Deacons Daniel Zamora; Brigido Gonzalez.
Catechesis Religious Program—Ms. Brigida Reyna, C.R.E. Students 393.
3—OUR LADY OF THE HOLY ROSARY (1968)
923 Matamoros St., P.O. Box 1439, Mission, 78572. Tel: 956-581-2193; Fax: 956-581-1906; Email: secretary-olhrmission@cdob.org; Email: olhrmission@gmail.com; Email: admin-olhrmission@cdob.org. Rev. Genaro Henriquez; Deacons Francisco R. Flores; Israel Sagredo; Francisco C. Rugama.
Catechesis Religious Program—Ms. Lilia Rubio, C.R.E. Students 372.
4—ST. PAUL (1915)
1119 Francisco Ave., Mission, 78572. Tel: 956-585-2701; Fax: 956-581-4801; Email: saintpaulchurch@aol.com. Rev. Isaac Emeka Erondu; Deacon Robert Ledesma.
Catechesis Religious Program—Ms. Rosa Jaques, D.R.E. Students 222.
5—SAN CRISTOBAL MAGALLANES & COMPANIONS (2004)
Mailing Address: 4501 Santa Engracia, Mission, 78572. Tel: 956-580-4551; Fax: 956-580-4550; Email: sancristobalm@att.net. Rev. Ignacio Tapia; Deacon Reynaldo Q. Merino.
Catechesis Religious Program—Diana Rodriguez, D.R.E. Students 292.
Missions—Our Lady of Fatima—6634 El Camino Real, Mission, Hidalgo Co. 78572.
Our Lady of Lourdes, 2 1/2 Miles S. Conway, Mission, Hidalgo Co. 78572.
OLMITO, CAMERON CO., OUR HEAVENLY FATHER PARISH (2013)
9178 Tomas Cortez Jr. St., Olmito, 78575. Tel: 956-350-5190; Fax: 844-317-8919; Email: ohfchurch@yahoo.com. P.O. Box 249, Olmito, 78575. Rev. Juan Pablo Robles, Parish Admin.; Deacon Augusto Chapa Jr.
Catechesis Religious Program—Email: pcl-ohfolmito@cdob.org. Enited Garcia, D.R.E. Students 128.
PENITAS, HIDALGO CO., SAINT ANNE (2013)
17109 Coconut Palm Dr., Penitas, 78576. Tel: 956-583-9888; Fax: 956-583-0889; Email: saintanne9813@gmail.com; Web: www.saintannecatholicchurch.org. Revs. Michael Montoya, M.J.; Manuel Gacad, M.J., Parochial Vicar; Deacons Albert Chapa; Jorge I. Hinojosa; Sisters Ann Hayden, Parish Outreach Coord.; Patricia Edmiston, Parish Outreach Coord.
Catechesis Religious Program—Mr. Jorge Hinojosa, D.R.E. Students 237.
Missions—Nuestra Senora de Guadalupe—465 E. Expwy. 83, Sullivan City, Hidalgo Co. 78595. Tel: 956-790-0242.
St. Michael the Archangel, Corner of Rene Lopez St. & Casimiro Ortega St., Los Ebanos, Hidalgo Co. 78565.
St. Juan Diego, 7 Mile Line & Western Ave., Mission, Hidalgo Co. 78572.
PHARR, HIDALGO CO.
1—ST. ANNE, MOTHER OF MARY (1973)
801 E. Juarez, Pharr, 78577. Tel: 956-787-8122; Fax: 956-787-8272; Email: stannepharr@cdob.org.
Res.: 309 N. Fir St., Pharr, 78577.
Catechesis Religious Program—Mr. Isidro Villa, D.R.E. Students 233.
2—ST. FRANCES XAVIER CABRINI (1999)
8001 S. Cage Blvd., Pharr, 78577. Tel: 956-787-3554; Fax: 956-283-1354; Email: st-frances-cabrini@cdob.org. Rev. Miguel Angel Ortega; Deacon Pedro F. Sanchez.
Catechesis Religious Program—Mrs. Blanca Sanchez, C.R.E. Students 619.
3—ST. JUDE THADDEUS (1951)
505 S. Ironwood, Pharr, 78577-1630. Tel: 956-781-2489; Fax: 956-783-4614; Email: admin@stjudethaddeus.net. P.O. Box 1688, Pharr, 78577. Rev. Jose E. Losoya, C.O.; Very Rev. Leo Francis Daniels, C.O., Parochial Vicar; Rev. Jose Juan Ortiz, C.O., Parochial Vicar.
Schools—Oratory Academy of St. Philip Neri—(Grades PreK-8), 1407 W. Moore Rd., Pharr, 78577. Tel: 956-781-3056; Fax: 956-787-1516. Very Rev. Leo Francis Daniels, C.O., Gen. Dir.; Mrs. Izkra Diaz, Prin.; Revs. Jose E. Losoya, C.O., Asst. Prin.; Jose Juan Ortiz, C.O., Rector & Librarian. Lay Teachers 10; Students 219.
Oratory - Athenaeum for University Preparation, (Grades 9-12), 1407 W. Moore Rd., Pharr, 78577. Tel: 956-781-3056; Fax: 956-787-1516. Very Rev. Leo Francis Daniels, C.O., Gen. Dir.; Revs. Jose Encarnacion Losoya, C.O., Vice Prin.; Jose Juan Ortiz, C.O., Rector & Librarian; Mrs. Izkra Diaz, Prin. Lay Teachers 7; Students 82.
Catechesis Religious Program—Mrs. Sochil J. Duran, D.R.E. Students 390.
4—ST. MARGARET MARY (1927)
122 W. Hawk Ave., Pharr, 78577. Tel: 956-787-8563; Fax: 956-702-4509; Email: saint-margaret-mary@cdob.org. Rev. Raymond Nwachukwu.
Catechesis Religious Program—Students 224.
PORT ISABEL, CAMERON CO., OUR LADY STAR OF THE SEA (1927)
705 S. Longoria St., Port Isabel, 78578. Tel: 956-943-1297; Tel: 956-943-1422; Email: olss@cdob.org. Revs. Jesus Guadalupe Garza; Michael Gnanaraj, Parochial Vicar.
Catechesis Religious Program—Mrs. Rosa Gonzalez, D.R.E. Students 452.
Mission—Laguna Heights Chapel, 131 Garfield St., Laguna Heights, Cameron Co. 78578.
PROGRESO, HIDALGO CO., HOLY SPIRIT (1969)
210 Watts Ave., Progreso, 78579. Tel: 956-565-6856; Fax: 956-565-3462; Email: sanespiritupro@yahoo.com. P.O. Box 216, Progreso, 78579. Rev. Amador Garza, Admin.
Catechesis Religious Program—Ms. Eva Flores, D.R.E. Students 172.
Missions—St. Margaret Ann—Military Hwy. 281, Santa Maria, Cameron Co. 78592.
Cristo Rey, Military Hwy. 281, Bluetown, Cameron Co. 78586.
RAYMONDVILLE, WILLACY CO.
1—ST. ANTHONY (1907)
464 S. First St., Raymondville, 78580. Tel: 956-690-4078; Email: st-anthony-raymondville@cdob.org. Rev. Juan Victor Heredia.
2—OUR LADY OF GUADALUPE (1927)
693 N. Third St., Raymondville, 78580. Tel: 956-689-2408; Fax: 956-689-1687; Email: olg-raymondville@cdob.org. Rev. George Kerketta; Deacon Juan Francisco Gonzales.
Catechesis Religious Program—Maria Gonzalez, D.R.E. Students 187.
Missions—St. Patrick—1 Mile S. of 186 on Hwy. 1015, Lasara, Willacy Co. 78561.
St. Anne, Mother of Mary, 1st St. & Paloma St., San Perlita, Hidalgo Co. 78590.
RIO GRANDE CITY, STARR CO.
1—IMMACULATE CONCEPTION (1880) [CEM]
101 E. Third St., Rio Grande City, 78582. Tel: 956-487-2317; Fax: 956-488-8133; Email: novimex@hotmail.com. P.O. Box 1, Rio Grande City, 78582. Revs. Thomas W. Sepulveda, C.S.B.; Oscar Ortega, Parochial Vicar; Oscar Ortega-Mancha, Parochial Vicar; Deacon Romeo Garcia Jr.
School—Immaculate Conception School, (Grades PreK-8), 305 N. Britton Ave., Rio Grande City, 78582. Tel: 956-487-2558; Fax: 956-487-6478; Email: molivarez@icsrio.org. Ms. Maria Elena Olivarez, Prin.; Ms. Donis Garza, Librarian. Lay Teachers 13; Religious 1; Students 178; Clergy / Religious Teachers 1.
Catechesis Religious Program—Araceli Barrientos, C.C.E. Coord. Students 360.
Mission—Sacred Heart, 169 W. Old Hwy. 83, Rio Grande City, Starr Co. 78582.
2—ST. PAUL THE APOSTLE (2009)
5752 E. Hwy 83, Rio Grande City, 78582. Tel: 956-488-8349; Fax: 956-488-8085; Email: san-pablo-rgc@cdob.org. Mailing Address: P.O. Box 269, Garciasville, 78547. Rev. Jesus E. Paredes.
Catechesis Religious Program—Students 73.
RIO HONDO, CAMERON CO., ST. HELEN (1943)
228 Huisache, Rio Hondo, 78583. Tel: 956-748-2327; Fax: 956-748-0089; Email: saint-helen@cdob.org. P.O. Box 451, Rio Hondo, 78583. Rev. Andres Everardo Gutierrez, Parish Admin.; Deacon Catarino Villanueva III.
Catechesis Religious Program—Virginia Salinas, C.R.E. Students 179.
Mission—St. Vincent de Paul, 2513 E. Brown Tract Rd., Lozano, Cameron Co. 78568.
ROMA, STARR CO., OUR LADY OF REFUGE (1853)
4 St. Eugene de Mazenod Ave., P.O. Box 156, Roma, 78584. Tel: 956-849-1455; Fax: 956-849-3498; Email: romachurch@gmail.com. Rev. Paul Wilhelm, O.M.I., Admin.; Deacons Amando Pena Jr.; Jose Humberto Rios.
Catechesis Religious Program—Mrs. Maria Teresa Garcia, D.R.E. Students 473.
Missions—Holy Trinity—4 Miles S. FM 2098, Falcon Heights, Starr Co. 78545. Tel: 956-437-9238.
St. Joseph, Iglesia St., Salineno, Starr Co. 78585. Tel: 956-353-8397.
Holy Family, 202 S. Francesca Ave., Los Saenz, Starr Co. 78584. Tel: 956-849-1127.
Lamb of God, Church St., Fronton, Starr Co. 78584. Tel: 956-849-2199.
SAN BENITO, CAMERON CO.
1—ST. BENEDICT (1912)
351 S. Bowie, P.O. Box 1780, San Benito, 78586. Tel: 956-626-1260; Fax: 956-626-1290; Email: stbenedict@cdob.org. Rev. Luis Roberto Tinajero; Deacon Manuel Sanchez.
Catechesis Religious Program—Gilbert De La Fuente, D.R.E. Students 468.
2—OUR LADY, QUEEN OF THE UNIVERSE (1960)
121 Garrison Dr., San Benito, 78586. Tel: 956-399-2865; Fax: 956-399-2045; Email: ourladyqueenchurch@cdob.org. 1425 N. Sam Houston, San Benito, 78586. Rev. Mario Castro; Deacon Michael Myers.
Catechesis Religious Program—Email: pcl2-olqusanbenito@cdob.org. Mary Arredondo, D.R.E. Students 286.
Mission—St. Joseph, 1001 W. Hwy. 77, San Benito, Cameron Co. 78586.
3—ST. THERESA (1954)
1300 Combes St., San Benito, 78586. Tel: 956-399-3247; Fax: 956-276-0142; Email: sttheresasb@yahoo.com. Rev. Jose M. Villalon Jr.
Catechesis Religious Program—Ms. Isabel Jauregui, C.R.E. Students 371.
SAN CARLOS, HIDALGO CO., ST. JOSEPH THE WORKER (1970)
8310 Highland Ave., Edinburg, 78542. Tel: 956-383-5880; Fax: 956-383-0420; Email: sjwsancarlos@cdob.org. Rev. Jose Garza.
Catechesis Religious Program—Students 679.
Missions—St. Theresa—205 Jefferson Ave., Edinburg, Hidalgo Co. 78542.
St. Frances Xavier Cabrini - Hargill, 2966 Couch Ave, Hargill, 78549.
SAN ISIDRO, STARR CO., ST. ISIDORE (1964)
5160 FM 1017, San Isidro, 78588. Tel: 956-481-3392; Fax: 956-481-3869; Email: sanisidro@cdob.org. P.O. Box 60, San Isidro, 78588. Rev. Joaquin Zermeno, Admin.
Catechesis Religious Program—Students 44.
SAN JUAN, HIDALGO CO.
1—BASILICA OF OUR LADY OF SAN JUAN DEL VALLE
400 N. Virgen de San Juan Blvd., San Juan, 78589. Tel: 956-787-0033; Fax: 956-787-2908; Email: jgomez@cdob.org; Web: www.olsjbasilica.org. P.O. Box 747, San Juan, 78589. Revs. Jorge A. Gomez, Rector; Ariel Angel, Pastoral Assoc.; Samuel Arizpe, Pastoral Assoc.; Deacons Julio Castilleja; Jose Jesus Galvan
Legal Name: Basilica of Our Lady of San Juan del Valle-National Shrine.
2—ST. JOHN THE BAPTIST (1949)
Mailing Address: 216 W. First St., San Juan, 78589. Tel: 956-783-1196; Fax: 956-702-7447; Email: SJBSanJuan@cdob.org; Web: sjtbchurch.myplaceofworship.org. Revs. Alfonso M. Guevara; Derlis R. Garcia, Parochial Vicar; Deacons Agapito L. Cantu; Eduardo Reyna.
Catechesis Religious Program—Tel: 956-783-1068; Email: normagccd@yahoo.com. Ms. Norma Guzman, D.R.E. Students 1,181.
Mission—Immaculate Conception, 901 Church St., San Juan, 78589.
SAN PEDRO, CAMERON CO., SAN PEDRO QUASI PARISH (2017)
7602 Old Military Rd., 78520. Tel: 956-542-2596; Email: san-pedro@cdob.org. P.O. Box 1658, Olmito, 78575. Fax: 956-546-8080. Rev. Joel R. Flores, Admin.
Catechesis Religious Program—CRP, Students 111.
SANTA ROSA, CAMERON CO., ST. MARY (1967) [CEM]
101 San Antonio Ave., P.O. Box 365, Santa Rosa, 78593. Tel: 956-636-1211; Fax: 956-636-2941; Email: st-mary-santa-rosa@cdob.org. Rev. Thomas L. Pincelli; Deacon Gerardo Aguilar.
Catechesis Religious Program—Ms. Latanya Flores, C.R.E. Students 114.
WESLACO, HIDALGO CO.
1—ST. JOAN OF ARC (1929)
109 S. Illinois Ave., Weslaco, 78596. Tel: 956-968-3670; Fax: 956-968-1872; Email: saint-joan-of-arc@cdob.org. Rev. Francisco J. Solis; Deacon Jesus E. Aguayo.
Catechesis Religious Program—Ms. Nellie Vento, C.R.E. Students 504.

2—ST. PIUS X (1955)
600 S. Oklahoma Ave., Weslaco, 78596.
Tel: 956-968-7471; Fax: 956-969-3040; Email: saintpius-x@cdob.org. Rev. Arturo Avalos Cardenas, Parochial Vicar; Deacons Juan Carlos Ortiz Jr.; Sergio Gonzalez.
Catechesis Religious Program—Email: sanjuanabetancourtspx@gmail.com. Irma Rodriguez, D.R.E. Students 777.

3—SAN MARTIN DE PORRES (1967)
901 N. Texas Blvd., Weslaco, 78596.
Tel: 956-968-2691; Fax: 956-968-1473; Email: sanmartin-weslaco@cdob.org. Revs. Esteban Hernandez; Ernest Ukwueze, Parochial Vicar; Deacons Alberto J. Aldana; Leon Diaz; Lorenzo Soto; Juan M. Delgado; Jose G. Garza; Oscar Garcia.
School—San Martin de Porres School, (Grades PreK-5), Preschool & Day Care Center: Little Lions Learning Center. 905 N. Texas Blvd., Weslaco, 78596. Tel: 956-973-8642; Fax: 956-973-0522; Email: rortega@cdobcs.org. Ms. Reyna Ortega, M.Ed., Prin.; Mr. Timothy J. Martinez, Library Mgr. PreK-3-5 Lay Teachers 5; Students 75.
Catechesis Religious Program—Ms. Maria Luisa Villanueva, C.R.E. Students 1,082.
Missions—St. Jude Chapel—Mile 13 1/2 North and Mile 4 West, Weslaco, Hidalgo Co.
Nuestra Senora de Guadalupe, 1909 Corpus Christi Dr. (Expressway Heights), Weslaco, Hidalgo Co. 78599.

Chaplains of Public Institutions.

Health Ministry

BROWNSVILLE. *Valley Baptist Health Systems-Brownsville*, 1040 W. Jefferson St., 78520.
Tel: 956-698-4452. Rev. Eusebio Martinez, Deacon Noe Longoria.
Valley Regional Medical Center, 100 Alton Gloor Blvd., Unit #100A, 78526. Tel: 956-350-7124. Rev. Eusebio Martinez, Sr. Esther F. Rodriguez, O.P., Email: esther.rodriguez@hcahealthcare.com.

EDINBURG. *Doctor's Hospital at Renaissance*, 5501 S. McColl Rd., Edinburg, 78539. Tel: 956-661-7100. Revs. Samuel Arizpe, Daniel Herve Oyama, Mrs. Maria Teresa Chapa, Mr. Jerry Garcia, Lead Chap., Mrs. Bertha G. Garza, Chap. Liaison, Ms. Lorena Tapia Reyes, Mrs. Melida Salinas, Sr. Mary Lucy Ugo, D.D.L.
Edinburg Children's Hospital, 1102 W. Trenton Rd., Edinburg, 78539. Tel: 956-388-6800. Rev. Samuel Arizpe, Mrs. Leticia Garcia.
Edinburg Regional Hospital, 1102 W. Trenton Rd., Edinburg, 78539. Tel: 956-388-6634. Rev. Samuel Arizpe, Mrs. Leticia Garcia.

HARLINGEN. *Harlingen Medical Center*, 5501 S. Expwy. 77, Harlingen, 78550. Tel: 956-365-1844. Rev. Ernesto Magallon, Deacon Jesus H. Reyes.
Valley Baptist Health Systems-Harlingen, 2101 Pease St., Harlingen, 78550. Tel: 956-389-1194. Rev. Ernesto Magallon, Edward Matthew.

MCALLEN. *McAllen Heart Hospital*, 1900 S. "D" St., McAllen, 78503. Tel: 956-994-2107. Rev. Paul Roman, Ms. Velia Flores, Mr. Ruben Wong.
McAllen Medical Hospital, 301 W. Expwy. 83, McAllen, 78503. Tel: 956-632-4388. Rev. Paul Roman, Ms. Velia Flores, Mr. Ruben Wong.
Rio Grande Regional Hospital, 101 E. Ridge Rd., McAllen, 78503. Tel: 956-632-6616. Rev. Paul Roman, Ms. Guadalupe A. Campos.

WESLACO. *Knapp Medical Center*, Tel: 956-968-8567. Rev. Ricardo Chavez, Mrs. Alma Lucila De La Vega.

Jail Ministry

SAN JUAN. *Prison & Jail Ministry*, 700 N. Virgen de San Juan Blvd., San Juan, 78589.
Tel: 956-784-5046. Rev. George A. Gonzalez, Chap., Ms. Ofelia de los Santos, Dir., Victor Villegas, Coord.

On Assignment Outside the Diocese:
Revs.—
Carolan, Craig G., Annunciation of the Lord Parish, P.O. Box 335, Port Austin, MI 48467-0355. Tel:
Lopez, Lionel, Belen Jesuit Preparatory School, 500 S.W. 127th Ave., Miami, FL 33184. Tel: 305-223-8600
Mestas, Leonard J., 22020 Vivienda Ave., Grand Terrace, CA 92313-4432. Tel:
Razo, Manuel Alfredo, S.T.L., St. Mary's Seminary, 9845 Memorial Dr., Houston, 77024-3498
Seitz, Patrick K., Holy Family Church, 152 Florencia Ave., San Antonio, 78228.

On Leave:
Revs.—
Figueroa, Honecimo
Garcia, Jose Luis
Zuniga, Carlos.

Retired:
Rev. Msgrs.—
DaVola, F. Robert, (Retired), St. Paul, 1119 Francisco Ave., Mission, 78572
Doherty, Patrick J., (Retired), St. John Vianney, P.O. Box 747, San Juan, 78589
Nicolau, Juan, Ph.D., S.T.L., (Retired), P.O. Box 4501, McAllen, 78502
Revs.—
Cabanas, R. Jamie, (Retired), St. John Vianney, P.O. Box 747, San Juan, 78589
Chavarria, Horacio, (Retired)
DaCosta, Lee, (Retired), St. John Vianney, P.O. Box 747, San Juan, 78589
Escobedo, Armando, (Retired), 615 Palo Blanco St., Mission, 78572
Frank, Gerald W., (Retired), St. John Vianney, P.O. Box 747, San Juan, 78589
Kuczmanski, Gregory M., (Retired), 2105 S. Cynthia St., D120, McAllen, 78503
Luna, Ignacio, (Retired), P.O. Box 335, La Villa, 78562
Villa, Eduardo, (Retired), P.O. Box 628, Pharr, 78577.

Retired-Religious:
Revs.—
MacDonald, Richard, S.C.J., (Retired), 509 E. Filmore Ave., Harlingen, 78550
Penderghest, William T., SS.CC., (Retired), P.O. Box 532604, Harlingen, 78553.

Permanent Deacons:
Aguayo, Jesus E., St. Joan of Arc, Weslaco
Aguilar, Carlos C., Sacred Heart, McAllen
Aguilar, Gerardo, St. Mary, Santa Rosa
Aguilera, Jose G., Queen of Peace, Harlingen
Aldana, Alberto J., San Martin De Porres, Weslaco
Almendarez, Felipe, St. Joseph, Donna
Arteaga, Antonio M., San Martin de Porres, Alton
Bernal, Jose Angel, Christ the King, Brownsville
Camacopa, Henry N., Holy Spirit, McAllen
Cano, Roberto, Immaculate Conception Cathedral, Brownsville
Cantu, Agapito L., St. John the Baptist, San Juan
Cantu, Roberto, Our Lady of Mercy, Mercedes
Carlos, Cruz, St. Luke, Brownsville
Carreon, David C., Sacred Heart, Elsa
Castaneda, Guillermo F. Bill Jr., Our Lady of Guadalupe, Mission
Castilleja, Julio, Basilica of Our Lady of San Juan del Valle-National Shrine, San Juan
Castro, Jose R., (Retired)
Cedillo, Bruno, Our Lady of Guadalupe, Brownsville
Chapa, Alberto X., (Retired)
Chapa, Augusto Jr., Our Heavenly Father, Olmito
Chapa, Santos, Our Lady of Perpetual Help, McAllen
Crixell, Alfred V., (Retired)
De la Cruz, Hugo, St. Joseph, Donna
Delgado, Juan M., San Martin de Porres, Weslaco
Diaz, Inocencio, (Awaiting Assignment)
Diaz, Leon, San Martin de Porres, Weslaco
Escobar, Paulo, St. Anthony, Harlingen
Escobedo, Arturo, St. Ignatius of Loyola Parish, El Ranchito
Espinoza, David, Holy Spirit, McAllen
Felix, Felix, San Juan Diego, McAllen
Flores, Alejandro, (Retired)
Flores, Benito, (Retired)
Flores, Francisco R., Our Lady of the Holy Rosary, Mission
Flores, Reynaldo I., Holy Spirit, McAllen
Galvan, Jose Jesus, Basilica of Our Lady of San Juan del Valle-National Shrine, San Juan
Gamboa, Alejandro, St. Joseph the Worker, McAllen
Garcia, Guadalupe, Our Lady of Good Counsel, Brownsville
Garcia, Javier A., St. Luke, Brownsville
Garcia, Jose Javier, San Juan Diego, McAllen
Garcia, Oscar, San Martin de Porres, Weslaco
Garcia, Romeo Jr., Immaculate Conception, Rio Grande City
Garcia, Sergio, Good Shepherd, Brownsville
Garcia, Silvestre J., St. Joseph, Edinburg
Garza, Francisco, St. Eugene de Mazenod, Brownsville
Garza, Jose G., San Martin de Porres, Weslaco
Garza, Rodrigo Jr., San Martin de Porres, Alton
Gonzales, Juan F., Our Lady of Guadalupe, Raymondville
Gonzalez, Brigido, Our Lady of St. John of the Fields, Mission
Gonzalez, Jose G., St. Francis Xavier, La Feria
Gonzalez, Juan, Our Lady of Sorrows, McAllen
Gonzalez, Sergio, St. Pius X, Weslaco
Guardiola, Gilberto Jr., Sacred Heart, Mercedes
Guerra, Jose A., (Retired)
Hernandez, Gabriel N., Holy Spirit, McAllen
Hernandez, Jesus G., St. Eugene de Mazenod, Brownsville
Higgins, Crawford A., Holy Spirit, McAllen
Hinojosa, Jorge I., Saint Anne, Peñitas
Ibarra, Genaro, (Retired)
Ibarra, Julio, Holy Family, Brownsville
Jacques, Martin Jr., (Retired)
Jasso, Juan Carlos, St. Ignatius of Loyola Parish, El Ranchito
Kinch, John P., Mary, Mother of the Church, Brownsville
Leal, Ramon G., (Retired)
Ledesma, Robert, St. Paul, Mission
Longoria, Noe, Parish of the Lord of Divine Mercy, Brownsville
Longoria, Richard A., Holy Spirit, McAllen
Lopez, Gilberto, (Retired)
Lopez, Ruben, Holy Family, Edinburg
Merino, Reynaldo Q., San Cristobal Magallanes, Mission
Myers, Michael, Our Lady Queen of the Universe, San Benito
Navarro, Juan Pablo, Mary, Mother of the Church, Brownsville
Oden, Louis, (Retired)
Olvera, Alvino C., Good Shepherd, Brownsville
Ortiz, Juan Carlos Jr., St. Pius X, Weslaco
Palacios, Benigno, Queen of Peace, Harlingen
Pena, Amando Jr., Our Lady of Refuge, Roma
Peralez, Jose III, Sacred Heart, Edinburg
Perez, Gilberto, (Retired)
Perez, Hector, (Retired)
Pruneda, Rosvel, Sacred Heart, Escobares
Ramirez, Josue, Holy Family, Brownsville
Ramirez, Miguel A., Holy Family, Brownsville
Ramos, Roman, St. Eugene de Mazenod, Brownsville
Rangel, Raul, Sacred Heart, Edinburg
Reyes, Jesus H., St. Theresa, San Benito
Reyna, Eduardo, St. John the Baptist, San Juan
Rios, Jose Humberto, Our Lady of Refuge, Roma
Rodriguez, Arturo, (Retired)
Rodriguez, Graciano A., (Awaiting Assignment)
Rodriguez, Mario S., St. Joseph, Brownsville
Rojas, Salvador Sr., (Retired)
Rosa, Gerardo J., Sacred Heart, Elsa
Rugama, Francisco C., Our Lady of Holy Rosary, Mission
Saenz, Benito Jr., Holy Family, Grulla
Sagredo, Israel, Our Lady of the Holy Rosary, Mission
Saldivar, Salvador G., (Retired)
Salinas, Rodolfo C., Sacred Heart, Escobares
Sanchez, Manuel, St. Benedict, San Benito
Sanchez, Pedro F., St. Frances Xavier Cabrini, Pharr
Sepulveda, Rodolfo Jr., Our Lady of Perpetual Help, McAllen
Solis, Heriberto, (Retired)
Soto, Lorenzo, San Martin de Porres, Weslaco
Terrazas, George, (Retired)
Thomas, Raymond L. Jr., Our Lady of Sorrow, McAllen
Torres, Jose A., Sacred Heart, Mercedes
Trevino, Felipe, (Retired)
Treviño, Florencio, St. Theresa of the Infant Jesus, Edcouch
Treviño, Luis A., Holy Spirit, McAllen
Valenzuela, Juan, (Retired)
Vargas, Jose G., St. Juan Diego, McAllen
Villalon, Rene Sr., (Retired)
Villanueva, Catarino III, St. Helen, Rio Hondo
Villarreal, Armandin, San Martin de Porres, Alton
Villarreal, Miguel, Sacred Heart, Escobares
Zamora, Daniel, Our Lady of St. John of the Fields, Mission
Zamora, Juan R., Queen of Peace, Harlingen
Zuniga, Luis, Mary, Mother of the Church, Brownsville.

INSTITUTIONS LOCATED IN DIOCESE

[A] HIGH SCHOOLS

BROWNSVILLE. *Saint Joseph Academy*, (Grades 7-12), 101 St. Joseph Dr., 78520. Tel: 956-542-3581; Fax: 956-542-4748; Email: president@sja.us; Web: www.sja.us. Mr. Michael Motyl, Pres.; Mrs. Melissa Valdez, Prin.; Pamela Quantz, Librarian. Marist Brothers, United States Lay Teachers 33; Students 420; Clergy / Religious Teachers 2.

MISSION. *San Juan Diego Catholic Regional High*

School dba Juan Diego Academy, Mailing Address: P.O. Box 3888, Mission, 78573. Tel: 956-583-2752; Fax: 956-583-3782; Email: glugaresi@juandiegoacademy.org; Web: www.juandiegoacademy.org. 5208 S. FM 494, Mission, 78572. Mr. Gerald Lugaresi, Prin. Lay Teachers 7; Students 86.

PHARR. *Oratory Athenaeum for University Preparation*, (Grades PreK-8), 1407 W. Moore Rd., Pharr, 78577. Tel: 956-781-3056; Fax: 956-787-1516; Email: idiaz@oratoryschools.org; Web: www.oratoryschools.org. Very Rev. Leo Francis Daniels, C.O., Headmaster; Mrs. Izkra Diaz, Prin.; Revs. Jose E. Losoya, C.O., Vice Prin.; Jose Juan Ortiz, C.O., Rector & Librarian. Lay Teachers 7; Students 82.

[B] JUNIOR AND ELEMENTARY SCHOOLS

BROWNSVILLE. *Guadalupe Regional Middle School*, (Grades 6-8), 1214 E. Lincoln St., 78521. Tel: 956-504-5568; Fax: 956-504-9393; Email: mmotyl@guadalupeprep.org; Email: vmiller@guadalupeprep.org; Web: www.guadalupeprep.org. Mr. Michael Motyl, Pres.; Dr. Virginia Miller, Prin.

Legal Title: Guadalupe Educational Center, Inc Lay Teachers 4; Students 67; Clergy / Religious Teachers 1.

Incarnate Word Academy, (Grades PreK-8), (Convent Academy of the Incarnate Word) 244 Resaca Blvd., 78520-7436. Tel: 956-546-4486; Fax: 956-504-3960; Email: edwardcamarillo@iw-academy.org; Web: www.iw-academy.org. Mr. Edward Camarillo, Pres.; Mr. Michael Camarillo, Prin.; Sr. Irma Gonzalez, I.W.B.S., Contact Person; Mrs. Eva Cuellar, Librarian. Sisters of the Incarnate Word and Blessed Sacrament. Lay Teachers 14; Students 148; Clergy / Religious Teachers 1.

St. Luke School, (Grades PreK-8), 2850 E. Price Rd., 78521. Tel: 956-544-7982; Fax: 956-544-4874; Email: stlukecs@cdobcs.org; Web: www.stlukecs.com. Mrs. Anne Marie Serrato, Prin.; Ms. Patty Garza, Library Mgr. Lay Teachers 12; Students 94.

St. Mary Catholic School, (Grades PreK-6), 1300 Los Ebanos Blvd., 78520. Tel: 956-546-1805; Fax: 956-546-0787; Email: agomez@cdobcs.org; Web: stmarys-cs.org. Mrs. Ana E. Gomez, Prin.; Ms. Judy Faulk, Asst. Prin.; Mrs. Denise Salazar, Library Mgr. Lay Teachers 22; Students 354.

EDINBURG. *St. Joseph School*, (Grades PreK-8), 119 W. Fay, Edinburg, 78539. Tel: 956-383-3957; Fax: 956-318-0681; Email: akarpinski@cdodcs.org; Web: www.st-joseph-catholic-school.com. Mrs. Angelina Karpinski, Prin.; Genie Smith, Librarian. Lay Teachers 12; Students 116.

HARLINGEN. *St. Anthony School*, (Grades PreK-6), 1015 E. Harrison, Harlingen, 78550. Tel: 956-423-2486; Fax: 956-412-0084; Email: mjuarez@cdobcs.org; Web: www.saintanthonyeagles.com. Mrs. Kathy Stapleton, Prin.; Janie Lozano, Librarian. Lay Teachers 8; Students 110; Clergy / Religious Teachers 1.

MCALLEN. *Our Lady of Sorrows School*, (Grades PreK-8), 1100 Gumwood, McAllen, 78501. Tel: 956-686-3651; Fax: 956-686-1996; Email: ldeleon@cdobcs.org; Web: www.olsschool.org. Mrs. Luisa De Leon, Prin.; Pilar Tijerina, Library Mgr.; Hugo De La Rosa, Asst. Prin. Lay Teachers 62; Students 449; Clergy / Religious Teachers 1.

PHARR. *Oratory Academy of St. Philip Neri*, (Grades PreK-8), 1407 W. Moore Rd., Pharr, 78577. Tel: 956-781-3056; Fax: 956-787-1516; Email: idiaz@oratoryschools.org; Web: www.oratoryschools.org. Very Rev. Leo Francis Daniels, C.O., Gen. Dir.; Mrs. Izkra Diaz, Prin.; Revs. Jose E. Losoya, C.O., Vice Prin.; Jose Juan Ortiz, C.O., Rector & Librarian. Lay Teachers 10; Students 219; Clergy / Religious Teachers 1.

RIO GRANDE CITY. *Immaculate Conception School*, (Grades PreK-8), 305 N. Britton Ave., Rio Grande City, 78582. Tel: 956-487-2558; Fax: 956-487-6478; Email: molivarez@icsrio.org; Web: www.icsrio.org. Ms. Maria Elena Olivarez, Prin.; Ms. Donis Garza, Librarian. Lay Teachers 13; Students 178; Clergy / Religious Teachers 1.

WESLACO. *San Martin de Porres School*, (Grades PreK-5), 905 N. Texas Blvd., Weslaco, 78596. Tel: 956-973-8642; Fax: 956-973-0522; Email: rortega@cdobcs.org; Web: www.sanmartindpschool.org. Ms. Reyna Ortega, M.Ed., Prin.; Mr. Timothy J. Martinez, Library Mgr. Lay Teachers 4; Students 58.

[C] DAY CARE CENTERS

BROWNSVILLE. *Little Saints Learning Center*, 1300 Los Ebanos Blvd., 78520. Tel: 956-546-1805; Fax: 956-546-0787; Email: agomez@cdobcs.org. Mrs. Ana E. Gomez, Prin. Lay Teachers 2; Students 31.

EDINBURG. *Little Lambs Learning Center*, 119 W. Fay St., Edinburg, 78539. Tel: 956-383-3957; Fax: 956-318-0681. Mrs. Angelina Karpinski, Prin. Lay Teachers 1; Students 6.

WESLACO. *Little Lions Learning Center*, 905 N. Texas Blvd., Weslaco, 78596. Tel: 956-973-8642; Fax: 956-973-0522; Email: rortega@cdobcs.org. Ms. Reyna Ortega, M.Ed., Prin. Lay Teachers 6; Students 17.

[D] CATHOLIC CHARITIES OF THE RIO GRANDE VALLEY

BROWNSVILLE. *Catholic Charities of the Rio Grande Valley Brownsville Office*, 955 W. Price Rd., 78520. Tel: 956-541-0220; Fax: 956-544-7580; Email: egarcia@cdob.org; Web: www.catholiccharitiesrgv.org. P.O. Box 1306, San Juan, 78589. Sr. Norma Pimentel, M.J., L.P.C., Exec. Tot Asst. Annually 48,531; Total Staff 6.

SAN JUAN. *Catholic Charities of the Rio Grande Valley San Juan Main Office*, 700 N. Virgen de San Juan Blvd., San Juan, 78589. Tel: 956-702-4088; Fax: 956-782-0418; Email: egarcia@cdob.org; Web: www.catholiccharitiesrgv.org. Mailing Address: P.O. Box 1306, San Juan, 78589. Sr. Norma Pimentel, M.J., L.P.C., Exec. Dir.; Most Revs. Mario A. Aviles, C.O., Exec. Board; Daniel E. Flores, S.T.D., Exec. Board; Rev. Msgr. Heberto M. Diaz Jr., Exec. Board; Dora Brown, Exec. Board; Silvia Castillo, Exec. Board; Terri Dreftke, Exec. Board; Ashley Feasley, Exec. Board; Herminia Forshage, Exec. Board; Lorena Saenz Gonzalez, Exec. Board; Victor Vasquez, Exec. Board

Catholic Charities of the Rio Grande Valley Tot Asst. Annually 95,912; Total Staff 21.

[E] HOMES FOR THE AGED

SAN JUAN. *San Juan Nursing Home, Inc.*, 300 N. Nebraska Ave., San Juan, 78589. Tel: 956-787-1771; Fax: 956-787-8091; Email: efernandez@sjnhrgv.org; Web: sjnhrgv.org. Most Rev. Daniel E. Flores, S.T.D., Exec. Bd.; Rev. Alfonso M. Guevara, Bishop's Liaison; Eloisa Fernandez, Admin.; Rachel Arcuate, Bd. Member; Mr. Leon De Leon, Bd. Member; Alma R. Garza, Bd. Member; Mr. Javier Garza, Bd. Member; Trino Medina, R.Ph., Bd. Member; Mr. Jaime J. Munoz, Bd. Member. Bed Capacity 201.

[F] RESIDENCES FOR PRIESTS AND BROTHERS

BROWNSVILLE. *Edmund Rice Christian Brothers North America Congregation of Christian Brothers*, Congregation of Christian Brothers, 1200 E. Lincoln St., Apt. B, 78521. Tel: 956-986-0614; Fax: 956-504-9393. Bros. Arthur Williams; Ross Wielatz; Patrick D. McCormack, C.F.C.

The Marist Brothers, 32995 Henderson Rd., Los Fresnos, 78566. Tel: 845-380-8347; Email: mikebill@hotmail.com. Bros. Michael Williams, F.M.S., Dir.; Paul U. Phillipp; Albert Phillipp, F.M.S.; Francis Garza, F.M.S.; Summer Herrick. Brothers 5.

PHARR. *Pharr Oratory of St. Philip Neri of Pontifical Right*, 11317 S. Jackson Road, Pharr, 78577. Tel: 956-843-8217; Email: jlosoya@pharroratory.com. P.O. Box 1698, Pharr, 78577. Very Rev. Leo Francis Daniels, C.O., Provost; Revs. Jose E. Losoya, C.O., Vicar; Jose Juan Ortiz, C.O., Sec.; Bro. Sebastian Caballero.

[G] CONVENTS AND RESIDENCES FOR SISTERS

BROWNSVILLE. *Dominican Sisters of Charity of the Presentation*, 934 W. St. Charles St., 78520. Tel: 956-542-7225; Email: srmarinac@yahoo.com. Sr. Marina Carrascal, Contact Person. Sisters 3.

Missionaries of Jesus, 1501 W. Adams, 78520. Tel: 956-455-1480; Email: npimentel@cdob.org; Web: www.missionariesofjesus.org. Sr. Ninfa Garza, Treas. Sisters 2.

Sisters of the Incarnate Word and Blessed Sacrament, 200 Resaca Blvd., 78520-7436. Tel: 956-546-1685; Email: smigonzalez@iwbscc.org. Sr. Irma Gonzalez, I.W.B.S., Contact Person. Sisters 5.

ALAMO. **Saint Joseph and Saint Rita Monastery of the Capuchin Poor Clare Nuns*, 725 E. Bowie Ave., Alamo, 78516. Tel: 956-781-1044; Email: sclaresalamotx@gmail.com; Web: capuchinnunsalamotx.org. Mailing Address: P.O. Box 1099, Alamo, 78516. Luz Leyva, Contact Person. Sisters 4.

PENITAS. *Missionary Sisters of the Immaculate Heart of Mary*, P.O. Box 1017, Peñitas, 78576. Tel: 956-585-5488; Fax: 956-519-9123; Email: fatima.santiago6@gmail.com. Sr. Fatima Santiago, Contact Person. Sisters 3.

Proyecto Desarrollo Humano Ministry, Tel: 956-580-9726; Fax: 956-519-9123.

PROGRESO. *Institute of the Sisters of St. Dorothy S.S.D.*, 219 W. Palm, Progreso, 78579. Tel: 956-565-9430; Email: cmello@cdob.org. P.O. Box 147, Progreso, 78579. Sr. Cynthia A. Mello, S.S.D., Supr. Sisters 4.

RIO GRANDE CITY. *Benedictine Sisters of the Good Shepherd*, 705 Monastery Ln., Rio Grande City, 78582. Tel: 956-486-2680; Email: sanbenito@granderiver.net. Rev. Thomas Luczak, O.F.M., Spiritual Advisor/ Care Svcs. Sisters 3.

SAN JUAN. *Missionaries of Jesus*, 700 N. Oblate Dr., San Juan, 78589. Tel: 956-455-1484; Email: npimentel@cdob.org; Web: www.missionariesofjesus.org. Sr. Norma Pimentel, M.J., L.P.C., Supr. Sisters 1.

[H] RETREAT HOUSES

SAN JUAN. *St. Eugene de Mazenod Christian Renewal Center*, 400 N. Virgin de San Juan Blvd., San Juan, 78589. Tel: 956-787-0033; Fax: 956-787-2908 ; Email: msalazar@oljsbasilica.org. P.O. Box 747, San Juan, 78589. Ms. Melissa Salazar, Dir.

[I] BASILICA

SAN JUAN. *The Basilica of Our Lady of San Juan del Valle-National Shrine*, 400 N. Virgen de San Juan Blvd., San Juan, 78589. Tel: 956-787-0033; Fax: 956-787-2908; Email: info@olsjbasilica.org. Revs. Jorge A. Gomez, Rector; Ariel O. Angel, J.C.L., Asst. to Rector; Deacons Julio Castilleja; Jose Jesus Galvan.

Religious Gift Shop Genaro Villanueva, Dir.

[J] CAMPUS MINISTRY

EDINBURG. *Campus & Young Adult Ministry*, Catholic Diocese of Brownsville, 700 N. Virgen de San Juan Blvd., San Juan, 78589. Tel: 956-784-5045; Fax: 956-784-5081; Email: cyam@cdob.org; Web: www.cdob.org/youngadults. Raul Cabrera, Dir.; Nadia Chapa, Pastoral Assoc.; Rev. Thomas W. Sepulveda, C.S.B., Chap.; Melinda Garza-Lopez, Pastoral Assoc.

Campus Ministry

Newman Center- Edinburg, 1615 W. Kuhn St., Edinburg, 78541. Tel: 956-383-0133; Email: cyam@cdob.org; Web: www.cdob.org/newmanedinburg. Revs. Richard L. Lifrak, SS.CC., Chap.; Manoj Kumar Nayak, SS.CC., Chap.; Christopher Santangelo, Chap.; Thomas W. Sepulveda, C.S.B., Chap.; Cassandra Robles-Moncivais, Campus Min.; Annie Ortiz, Asst. Campus Min.

Newman Center- Brownsville, 1910 University Blvd., 78520. Tel: 956-541-9697; Email: cyam@cdob.org; Web: www.cdob.org/newmanbrownsville. P.O. Box 2279, 78522-2279. Karla Rodriguez, Campus Min.; Rev. Joel R. Flores, Chap.; Angelica Corona, Asst. Campus Min.

[K] MISCELLANEOUS

BROWNSVILLE. **Bishop Enrique San Pedro Ozanam Center, Inc.*, 656 N. Minnesota Ave., 78521. Tel: 956-831-6331; Fax: 956-831-8577; Email: victor@ozanamcenter.org. Victor Maldonado, Dir. Tot Asst. Annually 1,106.

Catholic Foundation of the Rio Grande Valley, 1910 University Blvd., 78520-4998. Tel: 956-542-2501; Fax: 956-542-6751; Email: hdiaz@cdob.org. Rev. Msgr. Heberto M. Diaz Jr., Vice Chm. & Contact Person.

The Guadalupe Regional Middle School Endowment, 1214 Lincoln St., 78521. Tel: 956-504-5568; Fax: 956-504-9393; Email: mmotyl@guadalupeprep.org. Mr. Michael Motyl, Pres.; Sr. Mary Ann Korcynski, Trustee; Apolonio Borrego, Trustee.

The St. Joseph Academy Endowment, 101 Saint Joseph Dr., 78520-7308. Tel: 956-542-3581; Fax: 956-542-8199; Email: president@sja.us. Mr. Michael Motyl, Pres.; Mr. Patricio Sampayo, Chm.; Bro. Daniel O'Riordan, F.M.S., Trustee; Mr. Carlos Garza, Trustee; John Ford Cowen Jr., Trustee; Dr. Jude Benavides, Trustee.

**Proyecto Juan Diego, Inc.*, 2216 Eduardo Ave., 78526. Tel: 956-542-2334; Fax: 956-542-5055; Email: phylispeters@gmail.com. Mailing Address: P.O. Box 8038, 78526. Sr. Phylis Peters, D.C., Exec. Dir. Tot Asst. Annually 9,818.

Texas Historical Preservation Foundation, 1910 University Blvd., 78522-2279. Tel: 956-542-2501; Fax: 956-550-1563; Email: jgraham@cdob.org. P.O. Box 2279, 78522-2279. Mr. Jack Graham, Contact Person.

Villa Maria Language Institute, 224 Resaca Blvd., 78520-7436. Tel: 956-546-7196; Fax: 956-546-1731; Email: smigonzalez@iwbscc.org; Web: www.villamarialg.com. Sr. Irma Gonzalez, I.W.B.S., Campus Dir.; Fidencio Balli, Business Mgr.

ALAMO. *ARISE-South Tower*, 212 W. San Bernardino, Alamo, 78516. Tel: 956-783-8517; Fax: 956-783-5498; Email: arisesouthtower@gmail.com; Email: arisergv@gmail.com. Ms. Eva Soto, Pres. Tot Asst. Annually 1,050.

ARISE Support Center, 1417 S. Tower Rd., Alamo,

78516. Tel: 956-783-6959; Fax: 956-783-0274; Email: arisergv@gmail.com; Web: www.arisesotex.org. P.O. Box 778, Alamo, 78516. Mrs. Lourdes Flores, Pres.

ARISE Support Center Tot Asst. Annually 560.

EDINBURG. *ARISE-Muniz*, 3917 Jam Sq., Edinburg, 78542. Tel: 956-782-4041; Fax: 956-782-6430; Email: arisemuniz@gmail.com. Ms. Emilia Vega, Pres. Tot Asst. Annually 1,025.

**Shalom Media USA Inc.*, 211 E. Wisconsin Rd., Edinburg, 78539. Tel: 215-366-3031; Web: www.ShalomMedia.org. Santo Thomas, CEO.

HARLINGEN. **RGV Educational Broadcasting, Inc.*, 1701 Tennessee Ave., Harlingen, 78550. Tel: 956-421-4111; Email: cmaley@88fm.org; Web: 88fm.org. Mr. Chris Maley, Interim Gen. Dir.; Mr. Mario Munoz, News Dir.

LOS FRESNOS. *Movimiento Familiar Cristiano: Federacion Brownsville*, 65 Vista del Golf, 78526. Tel: 956-221-1180; Email: Aantoniomtz@hotmail.com; Tel: 956-551-4874; Email: cchayomtz@hotmail.com; Web: www.mfc-fe.org. Antonio Martinez, Pres.; Rosario Martinez, Pres.

MCALLEN. *Comfort House Services, Inc.*, 617 Dallas Ave., McAllen, 78501. Tel: 956-687-7367; Fax: 956-630-6423; Email: comforthouse.dperez@gmail.com. David Perez, Exec. Dir.; Rev. Msgr. Juan Nicolau, Ph.D., S.T.L., Chap., (Retired). Palliative Care to the Terminally Ill. Tot Asst. Annually 209.

Movimiento Familiar Cristiano Federacion Edinburg, 5405 Astro Dr., Mission, 78574. Tel: 956-569-2190; Tel: 956-569-2190; Email: vicmor71@hotmail.com. Veronica Morales, Pres.; Deacon Antonio M. Arteaga, C.F.P., C.T.F.A., Spiritual Dir.

Natural Family Planning, 1510 N. 10th St., Ste. C, McAllen, 78501. Tel: 956-534-4895; Email: Lydia.mendez@cdob.org; Web: simplenatural.org. Lydia Mendez, Dir.

MERCEDES. *La Merced Charitable Trust*, 413 S. Virginia, Mercedes, 78570. Tel: 956-565-2622; Fax: 956-565-4185; Email: rmedrano@cdob.org. 1910 University Blvd., 78520. Most Reverend Daniel E. Flores, S.T.D., Exec. Board; Mr. Jose Luis Gonzalez, Chm.; Mr. Robert A. Calvillo, Vice Chm.; Mr. Roberto Medrano, Dir.; Most Rev. Mario A. Aviles, C.O., Trustee; Rev. Eduardo Ortega, Trustee; Ms. Linda V. Alaniz, Trustee; Mr. Ricardo Garcia, Trustee.

MISSION. *El Rosario Charitable Trust*, 119 Retama, Mission, 78572. Tel: 956-585-5051; Fax: 956-585-9938; Email: rmedrano@cdob.org. Most Rev. Daniel E. Flores, S.T.D., Exec. Board; Mr. Jose Luis Gonzalez, Chm.; Mr. Robert A. Calvillo, Vice Chm.; Mr. Roberto Medrano, Dir.; Rev. Eduardo Ortega, Trustee; Ms. Linda V. Alaniz, Trustee; Mr. Ricardo Garcia, Trustee.

PHARR. *ARISE-Las Milpas*, 125 E. Denny Dr., Pharr, 78577. Tel: 956-783-9293; Fax: 956-783-2099; Email: ariselasmilpas@gmail.com; Web: www.arisesotex.org. Petra Hernandez, Pres. Tot Asst. Annually 855.

Marriage Encounter, Inc., 700 Charlotte Ave., Pharr, 78577. Tel: 956-455-7530; Tel: 956-571-6521; Email: ogserrato@hotmail.com. Mr. Oscar Serrato, Coord.; Mrs. Monica Serrato, Coord.

SAN BENITO. **La Posada Providencia*, 30094 Marydale Rd., San Benito, 78586. Tel: 956-399-3826; Fax: 956-399-2898; Email: zitacdp@lppshelter.org; Web: www.lppshelter.org. Andi Atkinson, Exec. Dir.; Sr. Zita Telkamp, C.D.P., Prog. Dir. A non-profit emergency shelter for indigent immigrants and asylum seekers. They reside in the shelter as they wait for their legal cases to adjudicate before U.S. Immigration Court. Tot Asst. Annually 779.

SAN JUAN. *Catholic Engaged Encounter*, 700 N. Virgen de San Juan Blvd., San Juan, 78589. Tel: 956-784-5012; Fax: 956-784-5081; Email: lpesina@cdob.org. 1304 W. Russel Rd, Edinburg, 78539. Tel: 956-457-9851. Mrs. Lydia Pesina, Dir.; Roel Zamora, Lead Coord. Couple; Estela Zamora, Lead Coord. Couple.

WESLACO. *Movimiento Familiar Cristiano: Federacion Weslaco (Weslaco/Donna/Mercedes)*, 4415 N. Victoria Rd., Donna, 78599. Tel: 956-463-8052; Tel: 956-463-8053; Email: roblesandassoc@gmail.com. P.O. Box 476, Weslaco, 78599. Rev. Robert DeLong, M.S.F., Spiritual Assessor; Alma Robles, Pres.; Reynaldo Robles, Pres.

RELIGIOUS INSTITUTES OF MEN REPRESENTED IN THE DIOCESE

For further details refer to the corresponding bracketed number in the Religious Institutes of Men or Women section.

[0170]—*Basilian Fathers*—C.S.B.
[0310]—*Congregation of Christian Brothers*—C.F.C.
[0630]—*Congregation of the Missionaries of the Holy Family*—M.S.F.
[1130]—*Congregation of the Priests of the Sacred Heart*—S.C.J.
[1140]—*Congregation of the Sacred Hearts of Jesus and Mary*—SS.CC.
[0520]—*Franciscan Friars* (Assumption BVM Prov.)—O.F.M.
[0770]—*The Marist Brothers*—F.M.S.
[0780]—*Marist Fathers*—S.M.
[0852]—*Missionaries of Jesus Inc.*—M.J.
[]—*Missionary Servants of the Cross*—M.S.C.
[0910]—*Oblates of Mary Immaculate*—O.M.I.
[0950]—*Oratorians* (The Oratory of Pharr)—C.O.

RELIGIOUS INSTITUTES OF WOMEN REPRESENTED IN THE DIOCESE

[]—*Benedictine Sisters of the Good Shepherd* (Rio Grande City, TX)—O.S.B.
[]—*Capuchin Poor Clares*—O.S.C.Cap.
[0760]—*Daughters of Charity of St. Vincent de Paul* (St. Louise Prov.)—D.C.
[0793]—*Daughters of Divine Love*—D.D.L.
[0885]—*Daughters of Mary Mother of Mercy*—D.M.M.M.
[1100]—*Dominican Sisters of Charity of the Presentation of the Blessed Virgin*—O.P.
[]—*Dominican Sisters of St. Thomas Aquinas in Mexico*—O.P.
[1310]—*Franciscan Sisters of Little Falls, Minnesota*—O.S.F.
[3790]—*Institute of the Sisters of St. Dorothy*—S.S.D.
[]—*Misioneras Catequistas de los Pobres*—M.C.P.
[1150]—*Misioneras Eucaristicas Franciscanas* (Mexico)—M.E.F.
[]—*Missionaries of Jesus*—M.J.
[2690]—*Missionary Catechists of Divine Providence*—M.C.D.P.
[]—*Missionary Sisters of Mary Immaculate*—M.S.M.I.
[2750]—*Missionary Sisters of the Immaculate Heart of Mary*—I.C.M.
[2970]—*School Sisters of Notre Dame* (Central Pacific Prov.)—S.S.N.D.
[0440]—*Sisters of Charity of Cincinnati, Ohio*—S.C.
[0990]—*Sisters of Divine Providence* (Marie de la Roche Prov.)—C.D.P.
[2575]—*Sisters of Mercy of the Americas* (South Central Community, West Mid-West Community & Mid-Atlantic Community)—R.S.M.
[3718]—*Sisters of St. Ann*—S.S.A.
[1705]—*The Sisters of St. Francis of Assisi*—O.S.F.
[2050]—*Sisters of the Holy Spirit and Mary Immaculate*—S.H.Sp.
[2205]—*Sisters of the Incarnate Word and Blessed Sacrament*—I.W.B.S.

NECROLOGY

† Azcoiti, Vicente, (Retired), Died Dec. 15, 2018

An asterisk (*) denotes an organization that has established tax-exempt status directly with the IRS and is not covered by the USCCB Group Ruling.

Diocese of Buffalo

(Dioecesis Buffalensis)

Most Reverend

RICHARD J. MALONE, TH.D., S.T.L.

Bishop of Buffalo; ordained May 20, 1972; appointed Auxiliary Bishop of Boston and Titular Bishop of Aptuca January 27, 2000; consecrated March 1, 2000; appointed Bishop of Portland, ME February 10, 2004; installed March 31, 2004; appointed Bishop of Buffalo May 29, 2012; installed August 10, 2012. *Chancery Office: 795 Main St., Buffalo, NY 14203-1215.*

Chancery Office: 795 Main St., Buffalo, NY 14203. Tel: 716-847-5500; Fax: 716-847-5557.

Web: www.buffalodiocese.org

Email: dob@buffalodiocese.org

Most Reverend

EDWARD U. KMIEC, D.D., S.T.L.

Bishop Emeritus of Buffalo; ordained December 20, 1961; appointed Titular Bishop of Simidicca and Auxiliary Bishop of Trenton August 26, 1982; consecrated November 3, 1982; appointed Bishop of Nashville October 13, 1992; installed December 3, 1992; appointed Bishop of Buffalo August 12, 2004; installed October 28, 2004; retired May 29, 2012. *Res.: 50 Franklin St., Buffalo, NY 14202.*

Most Reverend

EDWARD M. GROSZ, D.D., V.G.

Auxiliary Bishop of Buffalo; ordained May 29, 1971; appointed November 22, 1989; consecrated February 2, 1990. *Res.: St. Stanislaus Parish, 123 Townsend St., Buffalo, NY 14212-1299.*

ESTABLISHED APRIL 23, 1847

Square Miles 6,357.

Incorporated under the laws of the State of New York October 30th, 1897. Re-incorporated by special act passed April 5, 1951, Chapter 568 of the laws of 1951.

Corporate Title: The Diocese of Buffalo, N.Y.

Comprises the Counties of Erie, Niagara, Genesee, Orleans, Chautauqua, Wyoming, Cattaraugus and Allegany in the State of New York.

For legal titles of parishes and diocesan institutions, consult the Chancery Office.

STATISTICAL OVERVIEW

Personnel	
Bishop	1
Auxiliary Bishops	1
Retired Bishops	1
Priests: Diocesan Active in Diocese	143
Priests: Diocesan Active Outside Diocese	2
Priests: Retired, Sick or Absent	135
Number of Diocesan Priests	280
Religious Priests in Diocese	84
Total Priests in Diocese	364
Extern Priests in Diocese	26
Ordinations:	
Diocesan Priests	4
Transitional Deacons	7
Permanent Deacons	8
Permanent Deacons in Diocese	145
Total Brothers	25
Total Sisters	638
Parishes	
Parishes	161
With Resident Pastor:	
Resident Diocesan Priests	120
Resident Religious Priests	10
Without Resident Pastor:	
Administered by Priests	27
Administered by Deacons	1
Administered by Religious Women	1
Administered by Lay People	2
Missions	2
Pastoral Centers	2
Professional Ministry Personnel:	
Sisters	15
Lay Ministers	100
Welfare	
Catholic Hospitals	4
Total Assisted	981,223
Health Care Centers	2
Total Assisted	2,158
Homes for the Aged	6
Total Assisted	3,127
Day Care Centers	2
Total Assisted	115
Specialized Homes	3
Total Assisted	1,678
Special Centers for Social Services	8
Total Assisted	332,383
Residential Care of Disabled	2
Total Assisted	215
Other Institutions	1
Total Assisted	15,500
Educational	
Seminaries, Diocesan	1
Students from This Diocese	29
Students from Other Diocese	12
Diocesan Students in Other Seminaries	1
Seminaries, Religious	1
Total Seminarians	30
Colleges and Universities	7
Total Students	15,527
High Schools, Private	13
Total Students	4,386
Elementary Schools, Diocesan and Parish	34
Total Students	8,196
Elementary Schools, Private	4
Total Students	648
Non-residential Schools for the Disabled	2
Total Students	1,893
Catechesis/Religious Education:	
High School Students	4,425
Elementary Students	14,812
Total Students under Catholic Instruction	49,917
Teachers in the Diocese:	
Priests	29
Brothers	11
Sisters	34
Lay Teachers	2,330
Vital Statistics	
Receptions into the Church:	
Infant Baptism Totals	2,821
Minor Baptism Totals	156
Adult Baptism Totals	106
Received into Full Communion	161
First Communions	2,791
Confirmations	3,151
Marriages:	
Catholic	773
Interfaith	260
Total Marriages	1,033
Deaths	5,485
Total Catholic Population	571,000
Total Population	1,529,576

Former Bishops—Rt. Revs. JOHN TIMON, C.M., D.D., ord. Sept. 23, 1826; cons. Oct. 17, 1847; died April 16, 1867; STEPHEN V. RYAN, C.M., D.D., ord. June 24, 1849; cons. Nov. 8, 1868; died April 10, 1896; JAMES EDWARD QUIGLEY, D.D., ord. April 13, 1879; cons. Bishop of Buffalo, Feb. 24, 1897; promoted to the Archdiocese of Chicago, Feb. 19, 1903; died July 10, 1915; CHARLES HENRY COLTON, D.D., ord. June 10, 1876; cons. Aug. 24, 1903; died May 9, 1915; His Eminence DENNIS CARDINAL DOUGHERTY, D.D., ord. May 31, 1890; cons. Bishop of Nueva Segovia, June 14, 1903; transferred to the Diocese of Jaro, April 19, 1908; transferred to the Diocese of Buffalo, Dec. 6, 1915; promoted to Archdiocese of Philadelphia, May 1, 1918; created Cardinal, March 7, 1921; died May 31, 1951; Most Revs. WILLIAM TURNER, D.D., ord. Aug. 13, 1893; cons. March 30, 1919; died July 10, 1936; JOHN A. DUFFY, D.D., ord. June 13, 1908; cons. Bishop of Syracuse, June 29, 1933; transferred to the Diocese of Buffalo, April 14, 1937; died Sept. 27, 1944; His Eminence JOHN CARDINAL O'HARA, C.S.C., ord. Sept. 9, 1916; appt. Military Delegate of the Armed Forces and Titular Bishop of Mylasa, Dec. 11, 1939; cons. Jan. 15, 1940; transferred to Buffalo, March 10, 1945; installed May 8, 1945; promoted to the Archdiocese of Philadelphia, Nov. 23, 1951; created Cardinal, Dec. 15, 1958; died Aug. 28, 1960; Most Revs. JOSEPH A. BURKE, D.D., ord. Aug. 3, 1912; cons. Titular Bishop of Vita and Auxiliary, June 29, 1943; promoted to the See, Feb. 9, 1952; died Oct. 16, 1962; JAMES A. MCNULTY, D.D., ord. July 12, 1925; cons. Oct. 7, 1947; Titular Bishop of Methone and Auxiliary Bishop of Newark, NJ; appt. Bishop of Paterson, NJ April 9, 1953; transferred to Buffalo, Feb. 12, 1963; died Sept. 4, 1972; EDWARD D. HEAD, D.D., ord. Jan. 27, 1945; appt. Titular Bishop of Ardstratha and Auxiliary of New York, Jan. 27, 1970; cons. March 19, 1970; appt. Bishop of Buffalo, Jan. 17, 1973; installed March 19, 1973; retired April 18, 1995; died March 29, 2005; HENRY J. MANSELL, D.D., ord. Dec. 19, 1962; appt. Titular Bishop of Marazane and Auxiliary of New York Nov. 24, 1992; ord. Jan. 6, 1993; appt. Bishop of Buffalo April 18, 1995; installed June 12, 1995; promoted to Archbishop of Hartford Oct. 20, 2003; EDWARD U. KMIEC, ord. Dec. 20, 1961; appt. Titular Bishop of Simidicca and Auxiliary Bishop of Trenton Aug. 26, 1982; cons. Nov. 3, 1982; appt. Bishop of Nashville Oct. 13, 1992; installed Dec. 3, 1992; appt. Bishop of Buffalo Aug. 12, 2004; installed Oct. 28, 2004; retired May 29, 2012.

Vicars General—Most Rev. EDWARD M. GROSZ, D.D., V.G.; Rev. PETER J. KARALUS, V.G.

Chancery Office—795 Main St., Buffalo, 14203. Tel: 716-847-5500; Fax: 716-847-5557; Email: dob@buffalodiocese.org. Office Hours: Mon.-Fri. 9-4:30.

Moderator of the Curia—Rev. PETER J. KARALUS, V.G.

Chancellor—Sr. REGINA MURPHY, S.S.M.N.

Secretary to Diocesan Bishop and Vice Chancellor—Rev. RYSZARD S. BIERNAT.

Diocesan Tribunal—795 Main St., Buffalo, 14203. Tel: 716-847-8769; Fax: 716-847-8772; Email: tribunal@buffalodiocese.org. Send all rogatory commissions to the Tribunal.

Judicial Vicar—Rev. Msgr. SALVATORE MANGANELLO, J.C.L., S.T.L.

Defenders of the Bond—Revs. EDWARD R. CZARNECKI, (Retired); FRANCIS X. MAZUR; GREGORY M. FAULHABER, S.T.D.; ROBERT W. ZILLIOX, J.C.L.; Rev. Msgr. DAVID S. SLUBECKY, J.C.L., S.T.L., (Retired).

Advocates—Deacon DANIEL E. BRICK ESQ.; Revs. RICHARD S. DIGIULIO, (Retired); ELIE G. KAIROUZ, J.C.L. (S.A.M.).

Promoter of Justice—Rev. Msgr. W. JEROME SULLIVAN, J.C.D., (Retired).

Judges—Rev. Msgrs. VINCENT J. BECKER, (Retired); SALVATORE MANGANELLO, J.C.L., S.T.L.; PAUL A. LITWIN, J.C.L.; Revs. HENRY A. ORSZULAK, (Retired); ROBERT W. ZILLIOX, J.C.L.

Notaries—LUCILLE BUCZEK; BETTY WEBB.

Consultors, College of—Most Rev. EDWARD M. GROSZ, D.D., V.G.; Rev. Msgrs. DAVID G. LIPUMA; W. JEROME SULLIVAN, J.C.D., (Retired); ROBERT E. ZAPFEL, S.T.D.; Revs. PETER J. KARALUS, V.G.; JAMES C. CROGLIO, L.C.S.W.; DENNIS J. MANCUSO; JOHN M. STAAK, O.M.I., S.T.D.; MICHAEL G. UEBLER; BRYAN J. ZIELENIESKI.

Presbyteral Council—Most Revs. RICHARD J. MALONE, Th.D., S.T.L.; EDWARD M. GROSZ, D.D., V.G.; Revs. JAMES W. HARTWELL; PETER J. KARALUS, V.G.; ANDREW R. LAURICELLA; Rev. Msgr. DAVID G. LIPUMA; Revs. DENNIS J. MANCUSO; MARK J. NOONAN; ROBERT J. ORLOWSKI; JOSEPH D. PORPIGLIA; TODD M. REMICK; JOSEPH S. ROGLIANO; JOHN M. STAAK, O.M.I., S.T.D.; MICHAEL G. UEBLER; Rev. Msgrs. FRANCIS G. WELDGEN, (Retired); ROBERT E. ZAPFEL, S.T.D.; Rev. BRYAN J. ZIELENIESKI; Rev. Msgr. W. JEROME SULLIVAN, J.C.D., (Retired); Revs. EUGENE P. ULRICH; DANIEL J. FAWLS; JAMES R. BASTIAN; THOMAS R. SLON, S.J.; ROSS CHAMBERLAND, O.F.M., M.T.S.; XAVIER SEUBERT, O.F.M., S.T.D.

Finance Council—Most Revs. RICHARD J. MALONE, Th. D., S.T.L.; EDWARD M. GROSZ, D.D., V.G.; MR. JAMES J. BEARDI; Rev. WALTER P. GRABOWSKI; MR. CHARLES A. MENDOLERA, Ex Officio; Rev. Msgr. DAVID S. SLUBECKY, J.C.L., S.T.L., (Retired); MR. STEVEN D. TIMMEL, Ex Officio; MR. JOSEPH F. KAPSIAK; MR. DAVID ROGERS; MS. KAREN L. HOWARD; MR. JAY MCWATTERS, CPA; Revs. ADOLPH M. KOWALCZYK; LOUIS S. KLEIN; PETER J. KARALUS, V.G., Chm.

Vicariates—

Vicars Forane—Revs. JOSEPH S. ROGLIANO, Northwest-Central Buffalo; BRYAN J. ZIELENIESKI, Southeast Buffalo; Rev. Msgr. ROBERT E. ZAPFEL, S.T.D., Northern Erie; Rev. EUGENE P. ULRICH, Eastern Erie; Rev. Msgr. PAUL J.E. BURKARD, Southern Erie; Revs. SEAN E. DIMARIA, Allegany; MITCH BYECK, Tri-County; JAMES VACCO, O.F.M., M.A., Southern Cattaraugus; DARRELL G. DUFFY, Chautauqua; JAMES W. HARTWELL, Genesee-Wyoming; ROBERT S. HUGHSON, Western Niagara; RICHARD A. CSIZMAR, Eastern Niagara-Orleans.

The Diocese of Buffalo, N.Y.—A corporation under the laws of the State of New York. Most Revs. RICHARD J. MALONE, Th.D., S.T.L., Pres.; EDWARD M. GROSZ, D.D., V.G., Vice Pres.; Rev. PETER J. KARALUS, V.G., Vice Pres.; Sr. REGINA MURPHY, S.S.M.N., Sec.

Diocesan Offices and Directors

All offices are located at: 795 Main St., Buffalo, NY 14203. Tel: 716-847-8700; Fax: 716-847-5557 (Unless otherwise noted).

Apostleship of Prayer—Rev. RICHARD M. POBLOCKI, Dir., 20 Peoria Ave., Cheektowaga, 14206.

Apostleship of the Sea—Rev. JOSEPH D. PORPIGLIA, Dir., 26 Erie Ave., Gowanda, 14070.

Archives—Sr. JEAN THOMPSON, O.S.F., Tel: 716-847-5567; Email: archives1@buffalodiocese.org.

Bishop's Committee for Christian Home and Family—MRS. NANCY SCHERR, Moderator, Tel: 716-847-2210.

Boy Scouts—Rev. LEON J. BIERNAT, Chap., Tel: 716-688-5678; MR. JAMES S. SMYCZYNSKI, Committee Chm.; Deacon DANIEL U. GOLINSKI, Vocations & Training Chm.

Buildings and Properties—MICHAEL J. SULLIVAN, Dir., Tel: 716-847-8750; Fax: 716-847-8756.

Camp Turner—JOHN MANN, Steward, 9150 Asp Rd. #3, Salamanca, 14779. Tel: 716-354-4555; Fax: 716-354-2055; Email: campturner@gmail.com.

Catholic Charities—MR. TIMOTHY SEMBER, Chief Devel. Officer; DENNIS C. WALCZYK, CEO, 741 Delaware Ave., Buffalo, 14209. Tel: 716-218-1400; Fax: 716-856-2005.

Catholic Charities Appeal—Office: 741 Delaware Ave., Buffalo, 14209. Tel: 716-218-1400. MR. TIMOTHY SEMBER, Chief Devel. Officer.

Catholic Medical Association—Rev. RICHARD E. ZAJAC, Moderator, 2157 Main St., Buffalo, 14214. Tel: 716-862-1224.

Catholic Relief Services—741 Delaware Ave., Buffalo, 14209. Tel: 716-856-4494.

Chautauqua Catholic Community, Chautauqua Institution—Rev. TODD M. REMICK, Spiritual Dir. & Diocesan Liaison.

Council of Catholic Men—Rev. PAUL P. SABO, Moderator, (Retired).

Cemeteries—CARMEN A. COLAO, Dir., Mt. Olivet Cemetery, 4000 Elmwood Ave., Kenmore, 14217. Tel: 716-873-6500; Fax: 716-873-3247.

Censors–Board of Diocesan Censors of Books and Vigilance for the Faith—Rev. Msgrs. THOMAS E. CRANE, (Retired); ROBERT E. ZAPFEL, S.T.D.; Rev. PETER J. DRILLING, Th.D., (Retired).

Charismatic Renewal Program—Rev. RICHARD S. DIGIULIO, Dir., (Retired).

Diocesan Social Worker—ANTHONY SZAKACS.

Priest Personnel Board—Rev. MICHAEL G. UEBLER, Coord., Tel: 716-847-5537; Rev. Msgrs. JAMES G. KELLY, (Retired); THOMAS F. MALONEY, (Retired); Revs. JOSEPH S. ROGLIANO; GREGORY M. FAULHABER, S.T.D.; SEAN E. DIMARIA.

Pastoral Administrator Board—Most Rev. EDWARD M. GROSZ, D.D., V.G., Coord.; Rev. Msgr. VINCENT J. BECKER, (Retired); Deacon TIMOTHY CRISWELL; Sr. REGINA MURPHY, S.S.M.N.; MR. DENNIS G. MAHANEY; Sr. BARBARA RITER, S.S.M.N.; Rev. MICHAEL G. UEBLER.

Communications—Tel: 716-847-8717. KATHY B. SPANGLER.

Diocesan Directory—GREGG PRINCE, Tel: 716-847-8719.

Public Relations—KRISTINA M. CONNELL, Tel: 716-847-8749; KATHY B. SPANGLER, Tel: 716-847-8717.

Radio Ministry—GREGG PRINCE, Tel: 716-847-8744.

Computer Services (Diocesan)—Tel: 716-847-5500. PAUL MATEJA, Dir.

Continuing Education for Clergy—Rev. ANDREW R. LAURICELLA.

Cursillo Movement—Deacon MICHAEL D. QUINN, Spiritual Dir., Tel: 716-515-8725; MR. DONALD APPENHEIMER, Lay Dir.

Deaf Ministry—Rev. CONRAD P. STACHOWIAK, Chap., 130 Como Park Blvd., South Cheektowaga, 14227.

Advancement Office—RICHARD C. SUCHAN, Exec. Dir., The Foundation of the Roman Catholic Diocese of Buffalo and Diocesan Advancement, Tel: 716-847-8370.

Due Process—Rev. Msgr. SALVATORE MANGANELLO, J.C.L., S.T.L., Chm., Catholic Center, Tel: 716-847-8769; Fax: 716-847-8772.

Ecumenism—Rev. FRANCIS X. MAZUR, Diocesan Liaison.

Catholic Education—MICHAEL C. LAFEVER, Ed.D., Supt. Catholic Schools, Tel: 716-847-5520; MS. ERICA AIKIN, Asst. Supt., Curriculum, Instruction & Assessment; MR. CHRISTIAN RISO, Asst. Supt. Govt. Svcs. & Special Projects, Tel: 716-847-5511.

Eucharistic Adoration—Deacon MICHAEL P. MCKEATING, Tel: 716-847-5548.

Family Life—MRS. NANCY SCHERR, Dir., Tel: 716-847-2210; Fax: 716-847-2206.

Finance Office—MR. STEVEN D. TIMMEL, Tel: 716-847-5500; Fax: 716-847-5557.

Guild for the Blind, Inc.—Office: 741 Delaware Ave., Buffalo, 14209. Tel: 716-218-1400, Ext. 205.

Bishop's Representative for Health Care—Rev. Msgr. ROBERT E. ZAPFEL, S.T.D., Tel: 716-835-8905.

Office of Cultural Diversity—MRS. MILAGROS RAMOS, Dir., Tel: 716-847-2217; Fax: 716-847-2206.

Holy Name Society—Rev. PAUL P. SABO, Moderator, (Retired); RAYMOND ZIENTARA, Exec. Dir. Diocesan Union of Holy Name Societies, Tel: 716-847-2202.

Hospital Chaplains—Rev. RICHARD H. AUGUSTYN, Dir. Hospital Ministry, 100 High St., Buffalo, 14203. Tel: 716-859-5600.

Human Resources—COLLEEN O'CONNELL JANCEVSKI, Dir., Tel: 716-847-8376.

Insurance Services—JOHN SCHOLL, Dir., Tel: 716-847-8394; Fax: 716-847-5538.

Internal Audit—Tel: 716-847-5500; Email: audit@buffalodiocese.org. STEVEN L. HALTER, Chief Audit Exec.

Legion of Mary—Rev. MICHAEL H. BURZYNSKI, Ph.D., Spiritual Dir., Tel: 716-892-5746.

Liaison for Retired Priests—Rev. CHARLES E. SLISZ, Tel: 716-440-5090.

Lifelong Faith Formation and the Catechumenate—MRS. MARY BETH COATES, M.S., MAPM, Diocesan Dir. Lifelong Faith Formation, Tel: 716-847-5510; Email: mcoates@buffalodiocese.org; MS. MAUREEN POULIN, Assoc. Dir., Tel: 716-847-5514.

Liturgical Commission—Rev. CZESLAW M. KRYSA, D.S.L.

Commission for the Promotion of New Evangelization—MR. DENNIS G. MAHANEY, Tel: 716-847-8393.

Newspaper—Western New York Catholic PATRICK MCPARTLAND, Mng. Editor, Tel: 716-847-8743; Fax: 716-847-8722.

Evangelization and Parish Life—MR. DENNIS G. MAHANEY, Dir., Tel: 716-847-8393; Fax: 716-847-2206; Email: parish-life@buffalodiocese.org.

Pastoral Council—JOSEPH CONTI, Exec. Chm.

Care for Creation Commission—Sr. SHARON MARIE GOODREMOTE, F.S.S.J., Chairperson, 5229 S. Park Ave., Hamburg, 14075.

Permanent Diaconate—Deacon TIMOTHY E. CHRISWELL, Dir., Christ the King Seminary, 711 Knox Rd., P.O. Box 607, East Aurora, 14052. Tel: 716-652-4308.

Priests, Vicar for—Rev. JAMES C. CROGLIO, L.C.S.W., 16 Columbus St., Cheektowaga, 14227. Tel: 716-894-2743.

Professional Responsibility Office—STEVEN L. HALTER, Dir., Tel: 716-847-5554.

Pro-Life Activities—CHERYL M. CALIRE, Dir., Tel: 716-847-2205; Fax: 716-847-2206; Email: pro-lifeoffice@buffalodiocese.org.

Propagation of the FaithRev. JUSTUS NDYAMUKAMA, (Tanzania) Tel: 716-847-8773.

Public Policy Committee—KEVIN A. KEENAN, Chm.

Purchasing (Diocesan)—SHELLEY PACILLO, Tel: 716-847-8711; Fax: 716-847-8702; Email: dpd@buffalodiocese.org.

Research and Planning—Sr. REGINA MURPHY, S.S.M.N., Tel: 716-847-5539; Fax: 716-847-5557; Email: rmurphy@buffalodiocese.org.

Safe Environment—DONALD R. BLOWEY JR., Prog. Dir., Tel: 716-847-5532; Fax: 716-847-5593.

Worship, Office Of—Rev. CZESLAW M. KRYSA, D.S.L., Dir., Tel: 716-847-5545; Fax: 716-847-2206; ALAN D. LUKAS, M.Mus., Dir. Music, Mailing Address: Christ the King Seminary, P.O. Box 607, East Aurora, 14052-0607. Tel: 716-652-6565; Fax: 716-652-8903.

Vicar for Religious—Sr. JEAN THOMPSON, O.S.F., Vicar, Tel: 716-847-5529.

Victim Assistance Coordinator—MS. JACQUELINE JOY, Tel: 716-895-3010; Email: jacqueline.joy@ccwny.org.

Vocations—Rev. ANDREW R. LAURICELLA, Dir., Tel: 716-847-5535; Fax: 716-847-2206; Email: vocations@buffalodiocese.org.

Youth and Young Adult Ministry—KATHRYN M. GOLLER, Dir., Tel: 716-847-8789; Fax: 716-847-8797; Email: youth@buffalodiocese.org.

CLERGY, PARISHES, MISSIONS AND PAROCHIAL SCHOOLS

CITY OF BUFFALO

(ERIE COUNTY)

1—ST. JOSEPH CATHEDRAL (1851) Rev. Charles E. Slisz, Rector. In Res., Most Rev. Edward U. Kmiec, D.D., S.T.L., Bishop Emeritus.

Res.: 50 Franklin St., 14202. Tel: 716-854-5855; Email: cslisz2@buffalodioce.org.

See Catholic Academy of West Buffalo, Buffalo under Regional and Consolidated Elementary Schools located in the Institution section.

2—ALL SAINTS (1911) Rev. Angelo M. Chimera.

Res.: 127 Chadduck Ave., 14207-1531.

Tel: 716-875-8183; Email: jlallsaints77@yahoo.com.

Catechesis Religious Program—Email: NBVM@aol.com. Mary Beth Lalka, D.R.E.

3—ST. ANTHONY OF PADUA (1891) (Italian)

160 Court St., 14202. Tel: 716-854-2563; Web: www.

stanthonyofpadua-buffalo.org. Rev. Michael P. Zuffoletto, Admin., (Retired).
See Catholic Academy of West Buffalo, Buffalo under Regional and Consolidated Elementary Schools located in the Institution section.

4—ASSUMPTION (1888) [CEM] Rev. Richard Jedrzejewski. In Res.
Res.: 435 Amherst St., 14207. Tel: 716-875-7626; Email: assumption14207@gmail.com.
See Our Lady of Black Rock Regional School, Buffalo under Regional and Consolidated Elementary Schools located in the Institution section.
Catechesis Religious Program—Mary Lou Wyrobek, D.R.E. Students 48.

5—ST. BERNARD (1906) (Linked with Our Lady of Czestochowa, Cheektowaga) Rev. Marcin Porada, Admin.
Office: 414 S. Ogden, 14206. Tel: 716-822-8856; Email: stbernardsch@gmail.com.
Catechesis Religious Program—St. Bernard Parish Hall, 1988 Clinton St., 14206.

6—BLESSED SACRAMENT (1887) Revs. Paul R. Bossi; Peter J. Karalus, V.G., In Res.
Res.: 1035 Delaware Ave., 14209-1605.
Tel: 716-884-0053; Email: frpaulb@blessedsacrament.org.
See Catholic Academy of West Buffalo, Buffalo under Regional and Consolidated Elementary Schools located in the Institution section.
Catechesis Religious Program—Maureen Meyers, D.R.E.

7—BLESSED TRINITY (1906)
317 Leroy Ave., 14214. Tel: 716-833-0301; Email: blessedtrinitychurch@gmail.com; Web: blessedtrinitybuffalo.org. Rev. Victor Ibhawa, (Nigeria) Temp. Admin.

8—ST. CASIMIR CHURCH (1890) (Polish) Rev. Czeslaw M. Krysa, D.S.L., Rector.
Res.: 160 Cable St., 14206. Tel: 716-824-9589; Email: ckrysa@buffalodiocese.org.
Catechesis Religious Program—1833 Clinton St., 14206.

9—SS. COLUMBA-BRIGID (1888) (Responsible for St. Ann Church site, Broadway & Emslie Sts., Buffalo) 75 Hickory St., 14204. Tel: 716-852-3331; Email: sscolumbabrigid@gmail.com; Web: www.columba-brigid.org. Rev. William J. Weiksnar, O.F.M., M.Div., Ph.D.

10—CORONATION OF THE BLESSED VIRGIN MARY (1950) (Vietnamese)
348 Dewitt St., 14213. Tel: 716-882-2650; Email: pethai2003@yahoo.com. Rev. Peter Hai Nguyen, (Vietnam). In Res., Rev. Andrew Tu Minh Nguyen, (Retired).
See Our Lady of Black Rock, Buffalo under Regional and Consolidated Elementary Schools located in the Institution section.
Catechesis Religious Program—Tel: 716-882-6360.

11—CORPUS CHRISTI (1898) (Polish)
199 Clark St., 14212-1407. Tel: 716-896-1050; Fax: 716-896-1595; Email: office@corpuschristibuffalo.org; Web: www.corpuschristibuffalo.org. Revs. Michael Czyzewski, O.S.P.P.E., Admin.; Tomasz Welk, O.S.P.P.E., In Res.

12—HOLY ANGELS (1852) (Linked with Holy Cross & Our Lady of Hope)
348 Porter Ave., 14201. Tel: 716-885-3767. Revs. John M. Staak, O.M.I., S.T.D., Supr.; Gregory Gallagher; Francisco Gomez; Humphrey Milimo, O.M.I., Parochial Vicar; Deacon Alejandro D. Manunta; Revs. Stephen Vasek, O.M.I., In Res.; Alejandro Roque, In Res.; James Loiacono, O.M.I., In Res.
See Catholic Academy of West Buffalo, Buffalo under Regional and Consolidated Elementary Schools located in the Institution section.
Catechesis Religious Program—Ana Castellano, C.R.E.

13—HOLY CROSS (1914) (Linked with Holy Angels & Our Lady of Hope)
345 Seventh St., 14201. Tel: 716-847-6930; Email: rectory@holycrossbuffalo.com. Revs. Gregory Gallagher; Francisco Gomez; Humphrey Milimo, O.M.I., Parochial Vicar; Deacons Miguel Santos; Jorge L. Silva.
See Catholic Academy of West Buffalo, Buffalo under Regional and Consolidated Elementary Schools located in the Institution section.
Catechesis Religious Program—Jodi Miller, C.R.E.

14—HOLY SPIRIT (1910) (Linked with St. Margaret) Rev. Joseph D. Wolf; Sr. Katherine Marie Bogner, S.S.M.N., Pastoral Assoc.
Parish Center: 85 Dakota Ave., 14216.
Res.: 91 Dakota Ave., 14216. Tel: 716-875-8102; Email: holyspirit.northbuffalo@verizon.net.
Catechesis Religious Program—Miss Karen Adamski, D.R.E.

15—ST. JOHN KANTY (1892) [CEM] (Polish)
101 Swinburne St., 14212. Tel: 716-893-0412; Email: stjohnkantybflo@gmail.com. Rev. Michael H. Burzynski, Ph.D., Admin.
St. Adalbert—(Additional church site) 212 Stanislaus St., 14212.
Catechesis Religious Program—Barbara Myskiewicz, D.R.E.

16—ST. JOSEPH-UNIVERSITY (1850) Revs. Jacob C. Ledwon; Gregory P. Jakubowicz, O.F.M., J.D., Campus Min.; Sr. Jeremy Midura, C.S.S.F., Pastoral Assoc.; Deacon Paul C. Emerson; Patricia Bubar Spear, Pastoral Assoc.; Mr. Paul O. Stage, Campus Min.; Lynn Cercone, Business Mgr.
Res.: 3269 Main St., 14214. Tel: 716-833-0298; Email: ledwon@buffalo.edu; Web: www.stjosephbuffalo.com.
School—St. Joseph-University School, (Grades PreK-8), 3275 Main St., 14214. Tel: 716-835-7395; Fax: 716-833-6550; Email: school@stjosephbuffalo.org; Web: www.stjosephbuffalo.org. Mr. Mark Mattle, Dir. Educ.; M. Anne Wojick, Asst. Prin.; Brenda Gojevic, Librarian. Lay Teachers 16; Students 179.
Catechesis Religious Program—
Tel: 716-833-0298, Ext. 310; Fax: 716-833-7339. Diane M. Brennan, Dir. Faith Formation.

17—ST. KATHARINE DREXEL (2007) Rev. James M. Monaco.
Res.: 118 Schiller St., 14206. Tel: 716-895-6813; Email: skdbuffalo118@gmail.com.
Catechesis Religious Program—

18—ST. LAWRENCE (1929) (Linked with St. Martin de Porres) Rev. Christopher Okoli, (Nigeria); Deacon Paul F. Weisenburger.
Res.: 1520 E. Delavan Ave., 14215. Tel: 716-892-2471 ; Email: stlawrencebuffalo@gmail.com.
Catechesis Religious Program—Patricia Dyer, D.R.E.

19—ST. LOUIS (1829) Rev. Msgr. Salvatore Manganello, J.C.L., S.T.L.
Res.: 35 Edward St., 14202. Tel: 716-852-6044; Email: stlouischurch@verizon.net; Web: www.stlouisrcchurch.org.
See Catholic Academy of West Buffalo, Buffalo under Regional and Consolidated Elementary Schools located in the Institution section.
Catechesis Religious Program—Ashlee Campbell, Dir., Faith Formation.

20—ST. MARGARET (1916) (Linked with Holy Spirit) Rev. Joseph D. Wolf; Sr. Karen Marie Voltz, G.N.S.H., Pastoral Assoc.
Office: 1395 Hertel Ave., 14216. Tel: 716-876-5318; Email: stmargaretparish@aol.com; Web: www.stmargaret-parish.com.
Res.: 91 Dakota Ave., 14216.
Catechesis Religious Program—Tel: 716-875-9478. Miss Karen Adamski, D.R.E.

21—ST. MARK (1908) Rev. Joseph S. Rogliano. (Linked with St. Rose of Lima)
Res.: 401 Woodward Ave., 14214. Tel: 716-836-1600; Fax: saintmks@roadrunner.com.
School—St. Mark School, (Grades K-8), 399 Woodward Avenue, 14214. Tel: 716-836-1191; Email: rclemens@saintmarkschool.com. Mr. Robert Clemens, Prin. Lay Teachers 30; Students 410.
Catechesis Religious Program—Joanne Yakovac, D.R.E.

22—ST. MARTIN DE PORRES (1993) (African American) (Linked with St. Lawrence & Nativity of the Blessed Virgin Mary, Harris Hill) Rev. Peter Ekanem, Admin.; Deacon Ronald Walker.
Office: 555 Northampton St., 14208.
Tel: 716-883-7729; Email: stmartindeporresbuffalo@gmail.com.
Catechesis Religious Program—

23—ST. MARTIN OF TOURS (1926) (Linked with St. Thomas Aquinas) Rev. William J. Quinlivan; Deacon John H. Burke.
Res.: 1140 Abbott Rd., 14220. Tel: 716-823-7077; Email: info@stmartinbuffalo.com.
See South Buffalo Catholic School, Buffalo under Regional and Consolidated Elementary Schools located in the Institution section.
Catechesis Religious Program— Joint program with St. Thomas Aquinas.

24—ST. MICHAEL (1851) Revs. Benjamin Fiore, S.J.; James J. Bowes, S.J.; Joseph J. Kamiensky, S.J.; George H. Belgarde, S.J.; Frederick G. Betti, S.J.; James L. Dugan, S.J.; Richard J. Zanoni, S.J.
Res.: 651 Washington St., 14203. Tel: 716-854-6726; Fax: 716-854-4616; Email: stmichaelchurchbuffalo@gmail.com.
See Catholic Academy of West Buffalo, Buffalo under Regional and Consolidated Elementary Schools located in the Institution section.

25—OUR LADY OF CHARITY (2010) Parish with two sites: St. Ambrose and Holy Family Rev. Bryan J. Zielenieski; Deacons Timothy J. Maloney, Sacramental Min.; Stephen R. Schumer, Sacramental Min.; Sr. Pauline Petruzzella, R.S.M., Visitor to the Sick
Our Lady of Charity Parish
Office, Res. & St. Ambrose Church: 65 Ridgewood Rd., 14220. Tel: 716-822-5962; Fax: 716-822-0966; Email: office@olcp.org; Web: ourladyofcharityparish.com.
Holy Family Church: 1901 S. Park Ave., 14220.
See South Buffalo Catholic School under Regional & Consolidated Elementary schools located in the Institutions section.
Catechesis Religious Program—Karen Kelchlin, C.R.E.; Kathy Mulqueen, C.R.E.; Maureen Brown, C.R.E. Students 327.

26—OUR LADY OF HOPE (2008) (Linked with Holy Angels & Holy Cross) Revs. Gregory Gallagher; Francisco Gomez; Humphrey Milimo, O.M.I.; Ronald Thaler, Pastoral Assoc.
Res.: 18 Greenwood Pl., 14213. Tel: 716-885-2469; Email: ourladyofhopebflo@aol.com.
Church: Lafayette Ave. & Grant St., 14213.
See Catholic Academy of West Buffalo, Buffalo under Regional and Consolidated Elementary Schools located in the Institution section.
Catechesis Religious Program—Sr. Susan Bowles, S.S.M.N., D.R.E. & Outreach Coord.

27—OUR LADY OF PERPETUAL HELP (1897) Rev. Donald J. Lutz.
Res.: 115 O'Connell Ave., 14204. Tel: 716-852-2671.
Catechesis Religious Program—

28—ST. ROSE OF LIMA (1925) Rev. Joseph S. Rogliano. (Linked with St. Mark)In Res., Revs. Francis X. Mazur; Andrew R. Lauricella.
Res.: 401 Woodward Ave., 14214.
Church: 500 Parker Ave., 14216. Tel: 716-834-6688; Email: rose@saintrosebuffalo.org.
Catechesis Religious Program—Tel: 716-833-4100. Mrs. Mary Frances Mc Crorey, D.R.E.

29—ST. STANISLAUS (1873) [CEM] (Polish) Rev. Tomasz Welk, O.S.P.P.E.
Office: 123 Townsend St., 14212. Tel: 716-854-5511; Email: ststanbm@roadrunner.com.
Res.: 199 Clark St., 14212.
Catechesis Religious Program—

30—ST. TERESA (1897)
1974 Seneca St., 14210. Tel: 716-822-0608; Fax: 716-826-3795; Email: teresa14210@yahoo.com; Email: st.teresa.bookkeeper@gmail.com; Web: stteresabuffalo.com. Rev. James B. Cunningham; Deacon Robert A. Dobmeier.
See South Buffalo Catholic School, Buffalo under Regional and Consolidated Elementary Schools located in the Institution section.
Catechesis Religious Program—Tel: 716-822-1702. Cheryl McNerney, D.R.E.

31—ST. THOMAS AQUINAS (1920) (Linked with St. Martin of Tours) Rev. William J. Quinlivan; Deacon John H. Burke.
Res.: 450 Abbott Rd., 14220-1796. Tel: 716-822-1250; Fax: 716-822-2594.
See South Buffalo Catholic School, Buffalo under Regional and Consolidated Elementary Schools located in the Institution section.
Catechesis Religious Program—

OUTSIDE THE CITY OF BUFFALO

AKRON, ERIE CO., ST. TERESA OF AVILA (1859) [CEM] Rev. David D Baker; Deacon Ronald Adamczak.
Res.: 5771 Buell St., P.O. Box 168, Akron, 14001.
Tel: 716-542-9103; Fax: 716-542-2444; Email: stteresasofakron@verizon.net; Web: www.stteresasofakron.com.
Catechesis Religious Program—5773 Buell St., Akron, 14001. Tel: 716-542-9717; Email: ruthwarejko@aol.com. Sr. Mary Ruth Warejko, C.S.S.F., D.R.E. Students 110.

ALBION, ORLEANS CO., HOLY FAMILY (2008) [CEM]
106 S. Main St., Albion, 14411. Tel: 585-589-4243; Email: holyfamilyalbion@rochester.rr.com; Web: www.holyfamilyalbion.com. Rev. Richard A. Csizmar; Deacon James L. Collichio.
Catechesis Religious Program—Tel: 585-589-5236. Miss Nancy J. Sedita, D.R.E.

ALDEN, ERIE CO., ST. JOHN THE BAPTIST (1850) [CEM]
2021 Sandridge Rd., Alden, 14004. Tel: 716-937-6959 ; Fax: 716-937-0075; Email: churchlady@rochester.rr.com; Web: www.stjohnalden.com. Rev. Msgr. Vincent J. Becker, Priest Mod., (Retired); Rev. James A. Walter, Sacramental Min., (Retired); Deborah Brown, Pastoral Admin.; Deacons Marc R. Leaderstorf; Peter J. Donnelly.
School—St. John the Baptist School, (Grades PreK-8), 2028 Sandridge Rd., Alden, 14004.
Tel: 716-937-9483; Fax: 716-937-9794; Email: school.office@stjohnsalden.com; Web: www.stjohnsalden.com. Mrs. Jonna Johnson, Prin.; Janyce Phelps, Librarian. Lay Teachers 18; Students 132.
Catechesis Religious Program—Delphine Leaderstorf, C.R.E. Students 254.

ALLEGANY, CATTARAUGUS CO., ST. BONAVENTURE (1854) Rev. James Vacco, O.F.M., M.A.
Res.: 95 E. Main St., Allegany, 14706.
Tel: 716-373-1330; Email: StBonasChurch@yahoo.com; Web: stbonas.weconnect.com.
See Southern Tier Catholic, Olean under Regional and Consolidated Elementary Schools located in the Institution section.
Catechesis Religious Program—Email:

sbreligiousedyahoo.com. Holly Keenan, D.R.E. Students 185.

ALFRED/ALMOND, ALLEGANY CO., SS. BRENDAN AND JUDE (1992) (Linked with Immaculate Conception, Wellsville, Blessed Sacrament, Andover, St. Mary, Bolivar, and Holy Family of Jesus, Mary & Joseph, Belmont) Rev. Robert Agbo, Parochial Vicar; Deacons David H. Harvey; Joseph A. Pasquella, Pastoral Assoc.; Mr. Chris Yarnal, Campus Min.

St. Brendan Oratory & Res.: 11 S. Main St., Box G, Almond, 14804.

Catechesis Religious Program—Email: kater@iccwlsv.com. Kevin Bartell, D.R.E. Students 13.

Chapel—St. Jude, Parish Office: Lower College Dr., Alfred, 14802. Tel: 585-593-4834; Fax: 607-587-9431; Email: kater@iccwlsv.com.

AMHERST, ERIE CO.

1—ST. GREGORY THE GREAT (1958)

200 St. Gregory Ct., Williamsville, 14221. Revs. Leon J. Biernat; Thomas M. Mahoney; Paul Cygan, Parochial Vicar; Deacons Michael G. Bochiechio; Paul F. Walter Jr.

Res.: 260 St. Gregory Ct., Williamsville, 14221-2635. Tel: 716-688-5678; Email: lbiernat@stgregs.org; Email: tcalandra@stgregs.org.

School—St. Gregory the Great School, (Grades PreK-8), 250 St. Gregory Ct., Williamsville, 14221. Tel: 716-688-5323; Fax: 716-688-6629; Email: jgajewski@stgregs.org. Mrs. Patricia Freund, Prin. Lay Teachers 45; Students 619.

Catechesis Religious Program—Tel: 716-688-5760; Fax: 716-639-8251. Mrs. Joan Rischmiller, D.R.E.

2—ST. LEO THE GREAT (1953) Rev. Msgr. Robert E. Zapfel, S.T.D.; David Ehrke, Business Mgr.

Res.: 885 Sweet Home Rd., Amherst, 14226. Tel: 716-835-8905; Email: office@stleothegreatamherst.com.

Catechesis Religious Program—Email: mruszala@stleothegreatamherst.com. Michael Ruszala, D.R.E. Students 126.

ANDOVER, ALLEGANY CO., BLESSED SACRAMENT (1855) [CEM] (Linked with SS. Brendan & Jude Parish, Alfred/Almond, Immaculate Conception, Wellsville, Holy Family of Jesus, Mary and Joseph, Belmont, and St. Mary, Bolivar)

1 Church St., Andover, 14806. Tel: 585-593-4834; Email: kater@iccwlsv.com. 17 Maple Ave., Wellsville, 14895. Rev. Robert Agbo, Parochial Vicar; Deacons Joseph A. Pasquella; David H. Harvey.

ANGOLA, ERIE CO., MOST PRECIOUS BLOOD (1871) [CEM] Rev. John S. Kwiecien.

Res.: 22 Prospect St., Angola, 14006. Tel: 716-549-0420; Email: rectory14006@gmail.com.

Catechesis Religious Program—

ARCADE, WYOMING CO., ST. MARY (2007) [CEM] Parish with two sites: St. Mary, Arcade; St. Mary, East Arcade. Rev. Joseph A. Gullo.

Office & Res.: 417 Main St., Arcade, 14009-1195. Tel: 585-492-5330; Email: stmaryarcad@gmail.comerc.

See St. Aloysius Regional School, Springville under Regional and Consolidated Elementary Schools located in the Institution section.

Catechesis Religious Program—

ATHOL SPRINGS, ERIE CO., ST. FRANCIS OF ASSISI (1929) S-4263 St. Francis Dr., Hamburg, 14075. Tel: 716-627-2710; Fax: 716-627-5263; Email: sfaoffice@verizon.net; Web: www.stfrancischurch.us. Rev. Ross M. Syracuse, O.F.M.Conv.

Catechesis Religious Program—Tel: 716-627-3357; Email: sfareled@gmail.com. Jean Hymes, C.R.E. Students 100.

ATTICA, WYOMING CO., SS. JOACHIM & ANNE (2008) [CEM] (Parish with two sites: Attica & Varysburg) Rev. George Devanapalle, (India).

Res.: 50 East Ave., Attica, 14011. Tel: 585-591-1228; Email: stjoachimand.anneparish@verizon.net.

Varysburg Site: 2311 Attica Rd., Rte. 98S, Varysburg, 14167.

Catechesis Religious Program—72 E. Ave., Attica, 14011. Tel: 585-591-8611; Email: ssja.reled@gmail.com. Scott Beck, C.R.E. (Attica).

BARKER, NIAGARA CO., OUR LADY OF THE LAKE (2009) [CEM] Parish with two sites: Barker; Lyndonville.

1726 Quaker Rd., Barker, 14012. Tel: 716-795-3331; Email: ourladyofthelakeparish@gmail.com. Rev. Bernard U. Nowak.

Catechesis Religious Program—Tel: 585-590-1791. Mary Joan Heinsler, D.R.E. Students 108.

BATAVIA, GENESEE CO.

1—ASCENSION (2008) [CEM]

19 Sumner St., Batavia, 14020. Rev. David R. Glassmire.

Res.: 15 Sumner St., Batavia, 14020-3634. Tel: 585-343-1796; Fax: 585-343-0919; Email: office@ascensionrcc.com; Email: pastor@ascensionrcc.com; Web: www.ascensionrcc.weconnect.com.

Catechesis Religious Program— (Joint program with Resurrection, Batavia).

2—RESURRECTION (2008) [CEM] Revs. Ivan R. Trujillo; Robert E. Waters, Sr. Parochial Vicar; James L. Fugle; Deacons C. Thomas Casey; Henry E. Moscicki.

Res.: 303 E. Main St., Batavia, 14020. Tel: 585-343-5800; Email: jmotz1230@yahoo.com.

St. Mary's Site: 18 Elliott St., Batavia, 14020.

Catechesis Religious Program—Deacon Henry E. Moscicki, D.R.E.

BELFAST, ALLEGANY CO., ST. PATRICK (1859) [CEM] (Linked with St. Patrick, Fillmore, and Our Lady of the Angels, Cuba)

Mailing Address: c/o Tri-Parish Office, P.O. Box 198, Fillmore, 14735-0198. Rev. Dennis J. Mancuso

St. Patrick's Roman Catholic Church Society of Belfast, New York

Res.: 50 South St., Cuba, 14727.

Church: 7 Merton Ave, Belfast, 14711. Tel: 585-567-2282; Email: frdmancuso@gmail.com; Web: stpatsbelfastfillmore.org.

Catechesis Religious Program—Tel: 585-808-3099; Email: louieshingler@yahoo.com. Ms. Lou Ann Shingler, D.R.E. Students 75.

ST. MARK (1948) 9103 School St., Rushford, 14777. Email: frdmancuso@gmail.org.

BELMONT, ALLEGANY CO., HOLY FAMILY OF JESUS, MARY & JOSEPH (1861) (Linked with St. Mary, Bolivar, Blessed Sacrament in Andover, SS Brendan & Jude in Alfred-Almond and Immaculate Conception in Wellsville)

5 Milton St., Belmont, 14813. Tel: 585-593-4834; Email: kater@iccwlsv.com. 17 Maple Ave., Wellsville, 14895. Rev. Robert Agbo, Parochial Vicar; Deacons David H. Harvey; Joseph A. Pasquella, Pastoral Assoc.

Catechesis Religious Program—Email: newark_ics@msn.com. Mrs. Mary Ann Newark, D.R.E. Students 25.

ST. JOSEPH (1844) Cottage Bridge Rd., Scio, Allegany Co. 14880.

BEMUS POINT, CHAUTAUQUA CO., ST. MARY OF LOURDES (2008) (Parish with two sites: Bemus Point & Mayville) Rev. Todd M. Remick.

Bemus Point Site: 41 Main St., P.O. Box 500, Bemus Point, 14712. Tel: 716-386-2400; Email: office@stmaryoflourdesrcparish.org.

Mayville Site: 24 E. Chautauqua St., Mayville, 14757.

Catechesis Religious Program—Terri Franczak, C.R.E.; Dayle Loutzenhiser, C.R.E.; Kathleen T. Nicastro, Youth Min. (Confirmation/High School).

BERGEN, GENESEE CO., ST. BRIGID (1861) [CEM] (Linked with Our Lady of Mercy, LeRoy) Sacramental records at 44 Lake St., LeRoy

44 Lake St., LeRoy, 14482. Rev. Matthew H. Phelan, O.de.M.

Church: 18 Gibson St., Bergen, 14416. Tel: 585-494-1110; Email: bookkeeper@ourladyofmercyleroy.org.

Catechesis Religious Program—Tel: 585-768-6543; Email: youthminister@ourladyofmercyleroy.org. Rev. James Chia, O.de.M., D.R.E. Students 10.

BLASDELL, ERIE CO., OUR MOTHER OF GOOD COUNSEL (1905) Rev. Robert J. Orlowski; Deacon Michael T. Dulak.

Res.: 3688 S. Park Ave., Blasdell, 14219. Tel: 716-822-2630; Email: omgcrectory@aol.com.

Catechesis Religious Program—Rachael Tremblay, D.R.E.

BOLIVAR, ALLEGANY CO., ST. MARY (1903) [CEM] (Linked with Holy Family of Jesus, Mary & Joseph, Belmont, SS Brendan & Jude in Alfred Almond, Blessed Sacrament in Andover and Immaculate Conception in Wellsville.)

111 Wellsville St., Bolivar, 14715. Tel: 585-593-4834; Email: kater@iccwlsv.com. 17 Maple Ave., Wellsville, 14895. Rev. Robert Agbo, Parochial Vicar; Deacons David H. Harvey; Joseph A. Pasquella, Pastoral Assoc.

Catechesis Religious Program—

BOSTON, ERIE CO., ST. JOHN THE BAPTIST (1869) [CEM] Rev. Piotr Napierkowski, Admin.

Res.: 6895 Boston Cross Rd., Boston, 14025-9601. Tel: 716-941-3549; Email: rectory@stjohnrcchurch.org.

Catechesis Religious Program—Tel: 716-941-6363; Email: reled@stjohnrcchurch.org. William Fleming, D.R.E. Students 191.

ST. MARY, 8175 E. Eden Rd., East Eden, Erie Co. 14057.

BOWMANSVILLE, ERIE CO., SACRED HEART (1920) [CEM] Rev. Robert W. Zilliox, J.C.L.; Deacon Wilson Johnson.

Res.: 5337 Genesee St., Bowmansville, 14026-1098. Tel: 716-683-2375; Email: sheartshrine@aol.com.

Catechesis Religious Program—Tel: 585-894-0154.

CANASERAGA, ALLEGANY CO., ST. MARY (1855) [CEM] Mailing Address: P.O. Box 189, Canaseraga, 14822. Tel: 607-545-8601; Email: arectory@rochester.rr.com. 6 North St., Canaseraga, 14822. Rev. John J. Cullen.

Catechesis Religious Program—Krystal Sarvis, C.R.E.; Robert Brushafer, C.R.E.; Fran Button, C.R.E.

CATTARAUGUS, CATTARAUGUS CO., ST. MARY (1863) (Linked with St. Joseph, Gowanda) Rev. Joseph D. Porpiglia; Cheryl Wilder, Parish Coord.

Res.: 36 Washington St., Cattaraugus, 14719. Tel: 716-257-9351; Email: stmarys@stjoesgowanda.com.

Catechesis Religious Program—

CHEEKTOWAGA, ERIE CO.

1—ST. ALOYSIUS GONZAGA (1940) Rev. Msgr. Peter J. Popadick.

Res.: 157 Cleveland Dr., Cheektowaga, 14215. Tel: 716-833-1715; Email: stalschurch@aol.com.

Catechesis Religious Program—Tel: 716-836-9657.

Convent—130 Highview Rd., Cheektowaga, 14215.

2—INFANT OF PRAGUE (1946) Rev. Raymond G. Corbin; Deacon Brian C. Walkowiak, Parochial Vicar; Sr. M. Antonita Sikorski, C.S.S.F., Pastoral Assoc.

Res.: 921 Cleveland Dr., Cheektowaga, 14225. Tel: 716-634-3660; Email: Infantofpragueparish@gmail.com.

Catechesis Religious Program—

3—ST. JOHN GUALBERT (1917) (Polish)

83 Gualbert Ave., Cheektowaga, 14211. Tel: 716-892-5746; Email: sjgc@roadrunner.com. Revs. Michael H. Burzynski, Ph.D.; Paul Ladda, (Tanzania) Parochial Vicar. In Res., Rev. Patrick Gardocki, O.F.M., (Poland).

4—ST. JOSEPHAT (1906) (Polish) Rev. Richard M. Poblocki.

Res.: 20 Peoria Ave., Cheektowaga, 14206. Tel: 716-893-1086; Email: sjrectory@roadrunner.com.

Catechesis Religious Program—

5—OUR LADY HELP OF CHRISTIANS (1890) [CEM] (National Historic Site); Tridentine Latin Mass Rev. Jeffrey L. Nowak.

Res.: 4125 Union Rd., Cheektowaga, 14225. Tel: 716-634-3420; Email: r33aj@aol.com.

See Mary Queen of Angels School, Cheektowaga under Regional and Consolidated Elementary Schools located in the Institution section.

Catechesis Religious Program—Tel: 716-632-3532; Fax: 716-632-4298. Denise Seeley, D.R.E.

6—OUR LADY OF CZESTOCHOWA (1922) (Polish) (Linked with St. Bernard, Buffalo) Rev. Marcin Porada, Admin.

Res.: 23 Willowlawn Pkwy., 14206. Tel: 716-822-5590; Email: olccktg@gmail.com.

Catechesis Religious Program—Tel: 716-826-3497.

7—ST. PHILIP THE APOSTLE (1967) Rev. David J. Borowiak; Deacon Walter N. Fudala.

Res.: 950 Losson Rd., Cheektowaga, 14227. Tel: 716-668-8370; Email: loaves@roadrunner.com.

Catechesis Religious Program—Tel: 716-668-3344. Ronald Szczerbiak, D.R.E.; Judy Kogut, D.R.E.

8—QUEEN OF MARTYRS (1946) Rev. Louis S. Klein. In Res., Rev. Christopher Okoli, (Nigeria).

Res.: 180 George Urban Blvd., Cheektowaga, 14225-3095. Tel: 716-892-1746.

See Mary Queen of Angels School, Cheektowaga under Regional and Consolidated Elementary Schools located in the Institution section.

Catechesis Religious Program—Tel: 716-895-2162. Michael Sacilowski, D.R.E.

9—RESURRECTION (1944) Rev. Michael K. Brown.

Res.: 130 Como Park Blvd., Cheektowaga, 14227. Tel: 716-683-3712; Fax: 716-685-4487; Email: rescheek@yahoo.com.

Catechesis Religious Program—

CLARENCE, ERIE CO., OUR LADY OF PEACE (1922) Rev. Thomas D. Doyle; Deacon Arthur T. Sullivan Jr.

Res.: 10950 Main St., Clarence, 14031. Tel: 716-759-8554; Fax: 716-759-8537; Email: olpclarence@roadrunner.com; Web: www.olpclarence.org.

Catechesis Religious Program—

CORFU, GENESEE CO., ST. MAXIMILIAN KOLBE PARISH (2009) [CEM] Parish with two sites: Corfu; East Pembroke. Rev. Daniel J. Serbicki.

Office & Res.: 18 W. Main St., P.O. Box 278, Corfu, 14036. Tel: 585-599-4833; Email: stmaxkolbe09@yahoo.com.

East Pembroke Site: 3656 Church St., East Pembroke, 14056.

Catechesis Religious Program—

CUBA, ALLEGANY CO., OUR LADY OF THE ANGELS (1850) [CEM] (Linked with St. Patrick, Belfast & St. Patrick, Fillmore)

c/o Tri-Parish Office, P.O. Box 198, Fillmore, 14735. Tel: 585-567-2282; Email: frdmancuso@gmail.com; Web: stpatsbelfastfillmore.org. 48 South St., Cuba, 14727. Rev. Dennis J. Mancuso

Our Lady of the Angels Roman Catholic Church Society of Cuba, New York

Res.: 50 South St., Cuba, 14727. Tel: 585-567-2282; Email: frdmancuso@gmail.com; Web: olacuba.org.

See Southern Tier Catholic, Olean under Regional

and Consolidated Elementary Schools located in the Institution section.
Catechesis Religious Program—Tel: 585-968-2233; Email: ssmouse@roadrunner.com. Ms. Susan Scott, D.R.E. Students 31.

DARIEN CENTER, GENESEE CO., IMMACULATE HEART OF MARY (2008) [CEM] (Parish with two sites: Darien Center & Bennington Center) Rev. Joseph A. Fiore.
Office: 10675 Allegany Rd., Darien Center, 14040-9701. Tel: 585-547-3547; Email: mblack@rochester.rr.com.
Bennington Center Site: 1230 Clinton St., Attica, 14011.

DEPEW, ERIE CO.

1—BLESSED MOTHER TERESA OF CALCUTTA (1897/2009) [CEM] Rev. Lawrence P. Damian; Deacon John H. Hendricks.
Res.: 496 Terrace Blvd., Depew, 14043.
Tel: 716-683-2746; Email: FRLPD@yahoo.com.
Catechesis Religious Program—Koreen Scalfaro, C.R.E.
Convent—Felician Nuns, 55 Westfield Ave., Depew, 14043.

2—ST. MARTHA (2011)
10 French Rd., Depew, 14043-2129.
Tel: 716-684-6342; Fax: 716-684-1853; Email: info@stmarthadepew.org; Web: www.stmarthadepew.org. Rev. Bartholomew W. Lipiec; Deacon James J. Trzaska.
School—Our Lady of the Blessed Sacrament, (Grades PreK-8), 20 French Rd., Depew, 14043.
Tel: 716-685-2544; Fax: 716-685-9103; Email: dszczepanski@school.olbsdepew.org; Web: www.school.olbsdepew.org. Mrs. Deborah Szczepanski, Prin. Lay Teachers 18; Students 154.
Catechesis Religious Program—Tel: 716-685-2546. Sr. Catherine Taberski, S.S.M.N., D.R.E. Students 153.

DUNKIRK, CHAUTAUQUA CO.

1—BLESSED MARY ANGELA PARISH (2008) [CEM] (Polish) Parish with two sites. Rev. Jan Trela, (Poland); Sr. M. Rachel Mikolajczak, C.S.S.F., Pastoral Assoc. & D.R.E.
Mailing Address: St. Hyacinth Site, 295 Lake Shore Dr. E., Dunkirk, 14048.
Office: St. Hedwig Site, 324 Townsend St., Dunkirk, 14048-3131. Tel: 716-366-2307; Email: office@blessedmaryangeladunkirkny.org.
See Northern Chautauqua Catholic School, Dunkirk under Regional & Consolidated Elementary Schools located in the Institutions section.
Catechesis Religious Program—St. Hyacinth Site: 296 Lake Shore Dr. E., Dunkirk, 14048.

2—ST. ELIZABETH ANN SETON (1975) [CEM] Rev. Dennis G. Riter. In Res., Rev. Walter Werbicki, (Canada).
Res.: 328 Washington Ave., Dunkirk, 14048.
Tel: 716-366-1750; Email: stelizannseton@netsync.net; Web: www.seasdunkirkny.org.
See Northern Chautauqua Catholic School, Dunkirk under Regional and Consolidated Elementary Schools located in the Institution section.
Catechesis Religious Program—Tel: 716-366-2827; Email: seasred@outlook.com. Natalie S. Hoebener, D.R.E. Students 61.

3—HOLY TRINITY (1908) [CEM]
1032 Central Ave., Dunkirk, 14048.
Tel: 716-366-2306; Email: allarewelcome@holytrinitydunkirk.com; Web: holytrinitydunkirk.com. Rev. Daniel P. Walsh.
See Northern Chautauqua Catholic School, Dunkirk under Regional and Consolidated Elementary Schools located in the Institution section.
Catechesis Religious Program—Tel: 716-366-0499; Email: religioused@holytrinitydunkirk.com. Susan Galley, D.R.E.

EAST AURORA, ERIE CO., IMMACULATE CONCEPTION (1901) Rev. Robert W. Wardenski.
Res.: 520 Oakwood Ave., East Aurora, 14052.
Tel: 716-652-6400; Email: immaculateconceptionea@verizon.net.
School—Immaculate Conception School, (Grades K-8), 510 Oakwood Ave., East Aurora, 14052.
Tel: 716-652-5855; Fax: 716-805-0192; Email: es39@buffalodiocese.org. Mr. Scott Kapperman, Prin.; Mrs. Suzanne Gerard, Librarian. Lay Teachers 18; Students 221.
Catechesis Religious Program—Tel: 716-655-0067. Sr. Judith Beiswanger, O.S.F., D.R.E.

EDEN, ERIE CO., IMMACULATE CONCEPTION (1908) [CEM] Rev. Dawid T. Krzeszowski, (Poland) Admin. (Linked with Holy Spirit, North Collins)
Res.: 8791 S. Main St., Eden, 14057.
Tel: 716-992-3933; Fax: 716-992-2201; Email: icceden@gmail.com; Web: www.icceden.org.
Catechesis Religious Program—Email: religiousedicc@gmail.com. Ellen Henning, D.R.E. Students 137.

EGGERTSVILLE, ERIE CO., ST. BENEDICT (1920) Rev. Robert M. Mock. In Res.
Res.: 1317 Eggert Rd., Eggertsville, 14226.
Tel: 716-834-1041; Fax: 716-835-5949; Email: Rectory@Saintbenedicts.com; Web: www.saintbenedicts.com.
School—St. Benedict School, (Grades PreK-8), 3980 Main St., Amherst, 14226. Tel: 716-835-2518; Fax: 716-834-4932; Email: lwojtaszczyk@saintbenedicts.com; Web: www.stbenschool.org. Laurie Wojtaszczyk, Prin.; Judy Eberle, Librarian. Lay Teachers 26; Students 292.
Catechesis Religious Program—Tel: 716-836-6444. Mr. Christopher Hanley, D.R.E.

ELLICOTTVILLE, CATTARAUGUS CO., HOLY NAME OF MARY (1850) [CEM] Revs. Ronald B. Mierzwa; Timothy J. Koester, Admin.
Res.: 22 Jefferson St., P.O. Box 543, Ellicottville, 14731. Tel: 716-699-2592; Email: hnameofmary@roadrunner.com.
Catechesis Religious Program—
ST. PACIFICUS, Chapel Hill Rd., Humphrey, Cattaraugus Co. 14778.

ELMA, ERIE CO.

1—CHURCH OF THE ANNUNCIATION (1905) [CEM]
7580 Clinton St., Elma, 14059. Tel: 716-683-5254; Email: parishoffice.annunciation@gmail.com. Rev. Eugene P. Ulrich; Deacons Joseph P. Mercurio; James J. Jaworski, Pastoral Assoc. for Admin.; Dennis W. Kapsiak; Deborah A. Keenan, Pastoral Assoc. for Ministry.
Catechesis Religious Program—Tel: 716-683-5515. Melissa Weisenburg, Dir., Faith Formation; Sarah Saltarelli, Coord. Youth Ministry.

2—ST. GABRIEL (1925)
5271 Clinton St., Elma, 14059-7617.
Tel: 716-668-4017; Email: stgabriel@stgabeschurch.com; Web: www.stgabeschurch.com. Revs. Walter P. Grabowski; Michael K. Brown, Parochial Vicar.
Catechesis Religious Program—Patricia Palumbo, D.R.E. Students 1,084.

FALCONER, CHAUTAUQUA CO., OUR LADY OF LORETO (1912) (Linked with St. Patrick, Randolph) Rev. Joseph P. Janaczek.
Res.: 309 W. Everett St., Falconer, 14733.
Tel: 716-665-4253; Email: rectoryoll@gmail.com.
Catechesis Religious Program—Tel: 716-665-3764; Email: releddir@gmail.com. Marilyn Wozneak, D.R.E.

FARNHAM, ERIE CO., ST. ANTHONY'S (1904) [CEM]
Mailing Address: P.O. Box A-9, Farnham, 14061. 417 Commercial St., Farnham, 14061. Rev. James W. Fliss.
Res.: 421 Commercial St., Farnham, 14061.
Tel: 716-549-1159; Fax: 716-549-7742; Email: stanthonyfarnham@aol.com; Web: www.stanthonysfarnham.org.
Catechesis Religious Program—Tel: 716-549-2867; Fax: 716-549-7742. Theresa L. White, D.R.E.

FILLMORE, ALLEGANY CO., ST. PATRICK (1881) [CEM] (Linked with St. Patrick, Belfast and Our Lady of the Angels, Cuba)
Tel: 585-567-2282; Email: frdmancuso@gmail.com; Web: stpatsbelfastfillmore.org. Rev. Dennis J. Mancuso
St. Patrick's roman Catholic Church Society of Fillmore, New York
Office: c/o Tri-Parish Office, P.O. Box 198, Fillmore, 14735-0198.
Res.: 50 South St., Cuba, 14727.
Catechesis Religious Program—Tel: 716-713-3204; Email: jaustin@fillmorecsd.org. Mrs. Jennifer Austin, D.R.E.

FRANKLINVILLE, CATTARAUGUS CO., ST. PHILOMENA (1906) [JC] Revs. F. Patrick Melfi, M.Div.; Romulo Montero, Parochial Vicar; David E. Tourville, Parochial Vicar.
Res.: 26 N. Plymouth Ave., Franklinville, 14737.
Tel: 716-676-3629; Email: saintphilomena14737@yahoo.com.
Catechesis Religious Program—

FREDONIA, CHAUTAUQUA CO.

1—ST. ANTHONY (1905) (Linked with St. Joseph, Fredonia) Rev. Joseph Walter.
Office: 66 Cushing St., Fredonia, 14063-1959.
Res.: 42 Orchard St., Fredonia, 14063.
Tel: 716-679-4050; Fax: 716-679-4096.
See Northern Chautauqua Catholic School, Dunkirk under Regional and Consolidated Elementary Schools located in the Institution section.
Catechesis Religious Program—Joanne Catalano, C.R.E.

2—ST. JOSEPH (1899) (Linked with St. Anthony, Fredonia) Rev. Joseph Walter; Deacons Michael C. Lemieux; Matthew A. Hens.
Office: 145 E. Main St., Fredonia, 14063.
Tel: 716-679-4116; Email: stjosephfredonia@yahoo.com.
See Northern Chautauqua Catholic School, Dunkirk under Regional and Consolidated Elementary Schools located in the Institution section.
Catechesis Religious Program— (Intergenerational - 70 households) Tel: 716-672-2647; Email: jbradley@stjosephfredonia.org.

FRENCH CREEK, CHAUTAUQUA CO., CHRIST OUR HOPE (2008) [CEM] (Parish with two sites: French Creek & Sherman)
1762 French Creek Mina Rd., Clymer, 14724-9660.
Tel: 716-355-8891; Email: christourhopeparish@gmail.com. Rev. Mark O. Itua, (Nigeria) Temp. Admin.; Deacon David Armstrong.
Sherman Site: 119 Miller St., Sherman, 14781.
Catechesis Religious Program—

GETZVILLE, ERIE CO., ST. PIUS X (1958)
1700 N. French Rd., Getzville, 14068-1427.
Tel: 716-688-9143; Email: office@stpiusxgetzville.org; Email: office@stpiusxgetzville.org. Rev. Jay W. McGinnis.
Catechesis Religious Program—Tel: 716-688-5417; Email: pam@stpiusxgetzville.org. Pam Rankin, D.R.E. Students 297.

GOWANDA, ERIE CO., ST. JOSEPH (1898) [CEM] (Linked with St. Mary, Cattaraugus) Rev. Joseph D. Porpiglia.
Res.: 26 Erie Ave., Gowanda, 14070.
Tel: 716-532-5100; Email: rectory@stjoesgowanda.com.
Catechesis Religious Program—Email: reled@stjoesgowanda.com. Wilma Parry, D.R.E. Students 59.

GRAND ISLAND, ERIE CO., ST. STEPHEN (1862) [CEM] Revs. Paul M. Nogaro; Martin Gallagher, Parochial Vicar; Deacon Frank S. Kedzielawa. In Res., Rev. Samuel J. Venne.
Res.: 2100 Baseline Rd., Grand Island, 14072.
Tel: 716-773-7647; Email: ststephenswny@ststephensgi.com; Web: www.ststephenswny.com.
School—St. Stephen School, (Grades PreK-8), 2080 Baseline Rd., Grand Island, 14072.
Tel: 716-773-4347; Fax: 716-773-1438; Email: school@ststephensgi.org; Web: www.ststephensgi.org. Mr. Scott Gruenauer, Prin. Lay Teachers 17; Students 200.
Catechesis Religious Program—Tel: 716-773-2002. Angela Diebold, D.R.E.

HAMBURG, ERIE CO.

1—ST. MARY OF THE LAKE (1948)
4737 Lake Shore Rd., Hamburg, 14075.
Tel: 716-627-3123; Email: rectory@smolparish.org; Web: www.smolparish.org. Rev. Edward F. Jost, Admin.; Deacon William J. Walkowiak; Sr. Paula Zelazo, F.S.S.J., Pastoral Assoc.
Catechesis Religious Program—Tel: 716-627-7150. Mrs. Kristine Hider, D.R.E. Students 213.

2—SS. PETER AND PAUL (1844) [CEM] Revs. Arthur E. Mattulke; Cole T. Webster, Parochial Vicar; Patrick T. O'Keefe, Parochial Vicar; Deacons Carlton M. Koester; Robert T. Ciezki; John J. Wlos.
Res.: 66 E. Main St., Hamburg, 14075.
Tel: 716-649-2765; Email: ldoyka@sspphamburg.org.
School—SS. Peter and Paul School, (Grades PreK-8), 68 E. Main St., Hamburg, 14075. Tel: 716-649-7030; Fax: 716-312-9313; Email: principal@sspphamburg.org. Sr. Marilyn Ann Dudek, C.S.S.F., Prin.; Mrs. Diane Liptak, Asst. Prin.; Anne Marie Maggio, Librarian. Clergy Religious Teachers 1; Lay Teachers 22; Students 221.
Catechesis Religious Program—
Tel: 716-649-0231, Ext. 1. Sarah Sutcliff, D.R.E.; Jacob Druzbik, Youth Min. Students 399.

HARRIS HILL, ERIE CO., NATIVITY OF THE BLESSED VIRGIN MARY (1954) (Linked with St. Lawrence & St. Martin de Porres, Buffalo)
4375 Harris Hill Rd., Williamsville, 14221.
Tel: 716-632-8838; Email: karen@nativityharrishill.org. 8500 Main St., Harris Hill, 14221. Revs. Ronald P. Sajdak; Daniel E. Ogbeifun, Parochial Vicar; Deacons Thomas F. Friedman; Carmelo Gaudioso; Amy Vossen Vukelic, Pastoral Assoc.; Ms. Meghan Rogers, Pastoral Associate.
School—Nativity of the Blessed Virgin Mary School, (Grades PreK-8), 8550 Main St., Williamsville, 14221. Tel: 716-633-7441; Fax: 716-626-1637; Email: office@nativityofmaryschool.org; Web: www.nativityofmaryschool.com. Joseph Roaldi, Prin. Lay Teachers 23; Students 239.
Catechesis Religious Program—8550 Main St., Williamsville, 14221. John Wilde, D.R.E.; Lydia Zielinski, Youth Min.; Debbie Daigler, RCIA Coord. Students 641.

HOLLAND, ERIE CO., ST. JOSEPH (1890) [CEM 2] Rev. Benjamin Mariasoosai, (India) Admin.; Deacon Mark D. Kehl.
Res.: 46 N. Main St., Holland, 14080-9509.
Tel: 716-537-9434; Email: stjholland@roadrunner.com.
Catechesis Religious Program—Tel: 716-655-2841; Fax: 716-537-9988. Cathy Levesque, D.R.E.

HOLLEY, ORLEANS CO., ST. MARY (1866) [CEM] Linked with St. Mark, Kendall. Rev. John J. Arogyasami, I.M.S., Admin.
Res.: 13 S. Main St., Holley, 14470-1107.
Tel: 585-638-6718; Email: stmarystmarkbulletin@gmail.com.

Catechesis Religious Program—Dorothy Covell, C.R.E.

JAMESTOWN, CHAUTAUQUA CO.

1—HOLY APOSTLES (2008) [CEM 2] (Parish with two sites) Rev. Dennis W. Mende; Deacon Samuel Pellerito.
Res.: 508 Cherry St., Jamestown, 14701.
Tel: 716-664-5703; Email: sspp@netsync.net.
St. John Site: 270 Newton Ave., Jamestown, 14701.
Catechesis Religious Program—Tel: 716-484-8958; Email: dwoleen@gmail.com. Dianne Woleen, D.R.E. Students 119.

2—ST. JAMES (1910) [CEM] Rev. Darrell G. Duffy; Deacon Michael Lennon.
Res.: 27 Allen St., Jamestown, 14701.
Tel: 716-487-0125; Email: stjamesparish@wny.twcbc.com.
Catechesis Religious Program—Tel: 716-664-4237; Email: faithform@windstream.net. Lisa Snyder, C.R.E.
OUR LADY OF VICTORY, 6 Institute St., Frewsburg, 14738.

KENDALL, ORLEANS CO., ST. MARK (1978) Attended by St. Mary, Holley.
16789 Kenmore Road, Kendall, 14476. Rev. John J. Arogyasami, I.M.S., Admin.
Office & Res.: 13 S. Main St., Holley, 14470-1107.
Tel: 585-638-6718; Email: stmarystmarkbulletin@gmail.com.
Catechesis Religious Program—Tel: 585-659-8631. Dorothy Covell, C.R.E.

KENMORE, ERIE CO.

1—ST. ANDREW (1944) Rev. Matthew J. Zirnheld; Deacon Michael J. Ficorilli. In Res., Rev. Joseph T. Nguyen, (Vietnam).
Res.: 1525 Sheridan Dr., Kenmore, 14217.
Tel: 716-873-6716; Email: bulletinstandrew@gmail.com.
School—St. Andrew School, (Grades PreK-8), 1545 Sheridan Dr., Kenmore, 14217. Tel: 716-877-0422; Fax: 716-877-3973; Email: colleen.politowski@standrewscds.net; Web: www.standrewscds.net. Mrs. Colleen Politowski, Prin. Lay Teachers 25; Students 206.
Catechesis Religious Program—Tel: 716-877-3034. Maryanne Snyder, D.R.E.
Mission—St. Andrew Kim, 9 O'Hara Rd., Tonawanda, Erie Co. 14150.

2—ST. JOHN THE BAPTIST (1836) [CEM] Rev. Michael J. Parker; Deacon James R. Waggoner.
Res.: 1085 Englewood Ave., Kenmore, 14223-1982.
Tel: 716-873-1122; Tel: 716-877-6401; Email: saintjohnsrec@gmail.com; Web: stjohnkenmore.org.
School—St. John the Baptist School, (Grades PreK-8), Tel: 716-877-6401; Web: www.stjohnskenmore.com. Rev. Michael J. Parker, Pastor. Lay Teachers 40; Students 370.
Catechesis Religious Program—Students 46.

3—ST. PAUL (1897) Rev. Joseph E. Vatter; Deacon Richard Parker.
Res.: 33 Victoria Blvd., Kenmore, 14217.
Tel: 716-875-2730; Email: jvatter@stpaulchurchken.org.
Catechesis Religious Program—Tel: 716-873-9429.

LACKAWANNA, ERIE CO.

1—ST. ANTHONY (1917) Rev. Msgr. Paul J.E. Burkard, Admin.; Rev. Henry A. Orszulak, Sacramental Min., (Retired).
Res.: 306 Ingham Ave., Lackawanna, 14218-2511.
Tel: 716-823-0782; Email: pastanthony@verizon.net.
Catechesis Religious Program—Tel: 716-827-8384.

2—OUR LADY OF BISTRICA (1917) (Croatian) Rev. Christopher Coric, O.F.M.Conv., (Croatia).
Res.: 1619 Abbott Rd., Lackawanna, 14218.
Tel: 716-822-0818; Email: rectoryourladyofbistrica@gmail.com.
Catechesis Religious Program—

3—OUR LADY OF VICTORY NATIONAL SHRINE (1854) Rev. Msgr. Paul J.E. Burkard; Rev. Romulus Rosolowski, O.F.M.Conv.
Res.: 767 Ridge Rd., Lackawanna, 14218.
Tel: 716-828-9444; Fax: 716-828-9429; Email: info@ourladyofvictory.org; Web: www.ourladyofvictory.org.
School—Our Lady of Victory National Shrine School, (Grades PreK-8), Tel: 716-828-9434; Email: ckraus@ourladyofvictory.org; Web: www.olvschool.org. Mrs. Carolyn Kraus, Prin. Lay Teachers 18; Sisters 1; Students 187.
Catechesis Religious Program—Tel: 716-828-9437; Email: info@ourladyofvictory.org. Carmel Zomeri, D.R.E.

4—QUEEN OF ANGELS (2008) (Polish) Rev. John F. Kasprzak.
Res.: 144 Warsaw St., Lackawanna, 14218.
Tel: 716-826-0880; Email: qfa144@verizon.net.

LAKE VIEW, ERIE CO., SAINT JOHN PAUL II (1922/2011) 2052 Lake View Rd., Lake View, 14085.
Tel: 716-627-2910; Email: parish@JP2Parish.org; Web: www.jp2parish.org. Revs. Sean E. DiMaria; Michael LaMarca, Parochial Vicar; Carol Mullins, Pastoral Assoc.; Deacons Neal M. Linnan; Dennis P. Conroy.
See Southtowns Catholic School, Lakeview under Regional and Consolidated Elementary Schools located in the Institution section.
Catechesis Religious Program—Tel: 716-627-9397. Mrs. Barbara Manley, D.R.E.

LAKEWOOD, CHAUTAUQUA CO., SACRED HEART (1912) [JC] (Parish with two sites: Lakewood & Panama) Rev. Piotr F. Zaczynski; Deacon Daniel Tyler.
Res.: 380 E. Fairmount Ave., Lakewood, 14750-2197.
Tel: 716-763-2815; Email: sacredheartlkwd@yahoo.com.
Panama Site: Our Lady of the Snows Church: Panama, 14767.
Catechesis Religious Program—Dineen Muniz, D.R.E.

LANCASTER, ERIE CO.

1—ST. MARY OF THE ASSUMPTION (1850) [CEM] Rev. Paul W. Steller, M.A.; Deacons David R. Jerome; John A. Owczarczak.
Res.: 1 St. Mary's Hill, Lancaster, 14086-2094.
Tel: 716-683-6445, Ext. 24; Email: dianez@stmarysonthehill.org; Web: www.stmarysonthehill.com.
School—St. Mary of the Assumption School, (Grades PreK-8), Tel: 716-683-2112, Ext. 121; Email: kwitowskik@smeschool.com; Web: www.smeschool.com. Kim Kwitowski, Prin.; Nancy Anne Jezuit, Dir., Student Affairs. Lay Teachers 16; Students 255.
Catechesis Religious Program—2 St. Mary's Hill, Lancaster, 14086.

2—OUR LADY OF POMPEII (1909/2008)
158 Laverack Ave., Lancaster, 14086.
Tel: 716-683-6522; Email: ladyofpompeii@yahoo.com; Web: www.olpparish.com. Rev. David I. Richards, Admin.; Sr. M. Joyce Frances King, C.S.S.F., Pastoral Assoc.; Deacons Gregory L. Feary, M.A.T., Temp. Pastoral Admin.; John P. Gaulin; David C. Rotterman.
Catechesis Religious Program—Tel: 716-684-4664. Mrs. Diane Liptak, C.R.E. Students 355.

LANGFORD, ERIE CO., EPIPHANY OF OUR LORD (1851/2006) [CEM]
10893 Sisson Hwy. (Langford), North Collins, 14111.
Tel: 716-337-2686; Email: epiphanyparish@gmail.com; Web: www.epiphanyofourlordrc.com. Rev. Mitch Byeck; Deacon Roy P. Dibb.
See St. Aloysius Regional School, Springville under Regional and Consolidated Elementary Schools located in the Institution section.
Catechesis Religious Program—

LEROY, GENESEE CO., OUR LADY OF MERCY (2008) [CEM] (Linked with St. Brigid Parish, Bergen) Rev. Matthew H. Phelan, O.de.M; Deacon David C. Ehrhart; Bro. Martin J. Jarocinski, In Res.
Res.: 44 Lake St., Le Roy, 14482. Tel: 585-768-6543; Email: frdonovan@ourladyofmercyleroy.org; Web: www.ourladyofmercyleroy.org.
Catechesis Religious Program—Email: religiousedi@ourladyofmercyleroy.org.

LEWISTON, NIAGARA CO., ST. PETER (1851) (Parish with two sites: Lewiston and Youngstown)
620 Center St., Lewiston, 14092. Tel: 716-754-4118; Fax: 716-754-4141; Email: pastor@stpeterlewiston.org; Web: www.stpeterlewiston.org. Rev. Msgr. David G. LiPuma.
Worship Site: St. Bernard Church, 218 Hinman St., Youngstown, 14174.
School—St. Peter School, (Grades PreK-8), 140 N. 6th St., Lewiston, 14092. Tel: 716-754-4470; Fax: 716-754-0167; Email: mingham@stpeterrc.org; Web: www.stpeterrc.org. Mrs. Maureen Ingham, Prin. Lay Teachers 20; Students 207.
Catechesis Religious Program—Tel: 716-754-2812; Email: redirector@stpeterlewiston.org. Dianne Wysocki, D.R.E. Students 210.

LOCKPORT, NIAGARA CO.

1—ALL SAINTS (2008) [CEM] Revs. Walter J. Szczesny, M.Div.; Gerald L. Bartko, O.S.F.S.; Sr. Rene Ruberto, S.S.M.N., Pastoral Assoc.
Office: 76 Church St., Lockport, 14094.
Tel: 716-433-3707; Email: office@allsaintslockport.org; Web: www.allsaintslockport.org.
See DeSales Catholic School, Lockport under Regional and Consolidated Elementary Schools located in the Institution section.
Catechesis Religious Program—391 Market St., Lockport, 14094. Tel: 716-433-5792; Email: faithformation@allsaintslockport.org. Molly McClenathan, C.R.E., Grades 1-8. Students 128.
ST. JOSEPH, 391 Market St., Lockport, 14094.

2—ST. JOHN THE BAPTIST (1834) Revs. James A. Waite; Joseph C. Dumphrey, O.S.F.S.
Res.: 168 Chestnut St., Lockport, 14094.
Tel: 716-433-8118; Email: frwaite@stjohnslockport.org.
See DeSales Catholic School, Lockport under Regional and Consolidated Elementary Schools located in the Institution section.
Catechesis Religious Program—Tel: 716-478-3565. Cheryl Lewandowski, C.R.E.

MEDINA, ORLEANS CO., HOLY TRINITY (2008) [CEM] (Parish with two sites: Medina & Middleport) Rev. Daniel J. Fawls.
Res.: 211 Eagle St., Medina, 14103.
Tel: 585-798-0112; Email: holytrinitymedina@hotmail.com.
Middleport Site: 21 Vernon St., Middleport, 14105.
Catechesis Religious Program—Tel: 585-798-5399. Barbara Daluisio, D.R.E.

NEWFANE, NIAGARA CO., ST. BRENDAN ON THE LAKE (2008) [CEM] (Parish with two sites: Newfane & Wilson) Rev. Joseph W. Dudzik; Deacon David H. Harvey.
Res.: 3455 Ewings Rd., Box 87, Newfane, 14108-0087. Tel: 716-778-9822; Email: office@stbrendanonthelake.org.
Wilson Site: 359 Lake St., Wilson, 14172.
Catechesis Religious Program—Ms. Mary Palmer, C.R.E.
ST. CHARLES BORROMEO, 5972 Main St., Olcott, 14126.

NIAGARA FALLS, NIAGARA CO.

1—DIVINE MERCY (2008) (Linked with St. Mary of the Cataract, Niagara Falls)
2437 Niagara St., Niagara Falls, 14303.
Tel: 716-284-6641; Email: dmoffice@divinemercynf.org; Web: www.divinemercynf.org. 335 24th St., Niagara Falls, 14303. Rev. Jacek P. Mazur; Deacon David P. Slish.

2—HOLY FAMILY OF JESUS, MARY AND JOSEPH (2008) [CEM] (Italian) (Parish with two Sites) Rev. Duane R. Klizek. In Res., Revs. John L. Graden, O.S.F.S.; Stewart M. Lindsay, O.S.F.S.; Bro. John Ventresca, O.S.F.S.
Office: St. Joseph Site, 1413 Pine Ave., Niagara Falls, 14301. Tel: 716-282-1379; Web: www.holyfamilyrcchurch.org.
Res.: Our Lady of Mt. Carmel Site, 2486 Grand Ave., Niagara Falls, 14301.
Catechesis Religious Program— (Our Lady of Mt. Carmel Site) Mrs. Rae Pullo, D.R.E.

3—ST. JOHN DE LA SALLE (1907) Rev. Slawomir Siok, S.A.C.
Office & Res.: 8477 Buffalo Ave., Niagara Falls, 14304. Tel: 716-283-2238; Email: stjohndelasalle@juno.com.
Catechesis Religious Program—Tel: 716-283-5140.

4—ST. MARY OF THE CATARACT (1847) (Linked with Divine Mercy, Niagara Falls)
259 Fourth St., Niagara Falls, 14303.
Tel: 716-282-0059; Email: stmarysniagara@gmail.com; Web: www.stmarysnf.net. Rev. Jacek P. Mazur.

5—ST. RAPHAEL (2008) Rev. Ivan Skenderovic.
Res.: 3840 Macklem Ave., Niagara Falls, 14305.
Tel: 716-282-5583; Fax: 716-282-0453; Email: st.raphaelrcparish@gmail.com.
Catechesis Religious Program—1018 College Ave., Niagara Falls, 14305. Tel: 716-282-2944; Email: srpreledmg@gmail.com. Maria Gleason, C.R.E. Students 70.

6—ST. VINCENT DE PAUL (2008) (Parish with two sites) Revs. Robert S. Hughson; Gerald Skrzynski, Parochial Vicar; Deacon David M. Augustyniak.
Res.: 1040 Cayuga Dr., Niagara Falls, 14304.
Tel: 716-553-1637; Email: r.s.hughson@roadrunner.com; Email: carepc@roadrunner.com; Web: svdparish.org.
Worship Sites—
Prince of Peace—1055 N. Military Rd., Niagara Falls, 14304. Tel: 716-283-2715.
St. Leo, 2748 Military Rd., Niagara Falls, 14304. Tel: 716-283-5010, Ext. 200.
Catechesis Religious Program—(St. Leo Site) Tel: 716-297-5010; Fax: 716-297-4648. Sr. Joanne Suranni, C.S.S.F., D.R.E.

NORTH COLLINS, ERIE CO., HOLY SPIRIT (1951) [CEM 2] Rev. John J. Arogyasami, I.M.S., Admin. (Linked with Immaculate Conception, Eden)
Office: 2017 Halley Rd., North Collins, 14111.
Tel: 716-337-3701; Email: hschurch@roadrunner.com.
Catechesis Religious Program—Marge Awald, D.R.E.

NORTH TONAWANDA, NIAGARA CO.

1—ST. JUDE THE APOSTLE (2007) Rev. James W. Kirkpatrick Jr.; Deacons Daniel E. Brick Esq.; Gary C. Terrana
St. Jude the Apostle Roman Catholic Parish of North Tonawanda, New York
Office: 800 Niagara Falls Blvd., North Tonawanda, 14120. Tel: 716-694-0540; Email: stjudetheapostle@roadrunner.com; Web: www.stjudetheapostleparish.org.
Catechesis Religious Program—Email: stjudesfaith@gmail.com. Lynda Mostowy, D.R.E. Students 272.

2—OUR LADY OF CZESTOCHOWA (1903) (Polish) Rev. Gary J. Szczepankiewicz; Deacon John E. Steiner Jr., Pastoral Assoc.
Ministry Center & Mailing Address: 57 Center Ave.,

North Tonawanda, 14120. Tel: 716-693-3822; Email: olcoffice@nt-olc.org.
Res.: 64 Center Ave., North Tonawanda, 14120.
Catechesis Religious Program—Tel: 716-694-3644; Fax: 716-693-1302; Email: kkokanvich@nt-olc.org. Kathryn Kokanovich, D.R.E.

OAKFIELD, GENESEE CO., ST. PADRE PIO (2009) [CEM] Rev. Thaddeus Nicholas Bocianowski; Deacon Paul C. Kulczyk.
Res.: 56 Maple Ave., Oakfield, 14125.
Tel: 585-948-5344; Email: office@padrepiony.org.
Elba Site: 65 S. Main St., Elba, 14058-0185.
Catechesis Religious Program—

OLEAN, CATTARAUGUS CO.
1—ST. JOHN (1896)
931 N. Union St., Olean, 14760. Tel: 716-372-5313; Email: office@sjteolean.org; Web: www.sjteolean.org. 933 N. Union St., Olean, 14760. Revs. F. Patrick Melfi, M.Div.; Romulo Montero, Parochial Vicar; David E. Tourville, Parochial Vicar.
See Southern Tier Catholic, Olean under Regional and Consolidated Elementary Schools located in the Institution section.
Catechesis Religious Program—Tel: 716-372-6633; Fax: 716-795-3919.
2—BASILICA OF ST. MARY OF THE ANGELS (1876)
119 W. Henley St., Olean, 14760. Revs. F. Patrick Melfi, M.Div.; David E. Tourville, Parochial Vicar; Romulo Montero, Parochial Vicar.
Res.: 202 S. Union St., Olean, 14760.
Tel: 716-372-4841; Email: bonnie@smaolean.org; Web: www.smaolean.org.
See Southern Tier Catholic, Olean under Regional and Consolidated Elementary Schools located in the Institution section.
Catechesis Religious Program—Email: naomi@smaolean.org; Email: sregina@smaolean.org; Email: ryen@smaolean.org. Sr. Regina G. Aman, C.R.E.; Naomi Butler, D.R.E.; Ryan Butler, D.R.E. Students 15.
ORATORY OF THE SACRED HEART, 43 Maple Ave., Portville, 14770.

ORCHARD PARK, ERIE CO.
1—ST. BERNADETTE (1957) Rev. Paul D. Seil; Deacon Edward R. Howard.
Res.: 5930 S. Abbott Rd., Orchard Park, 14127-4516.
Tel: 716-649-3090; Email: office@saintbopny.org.
School—Early Childhood Academy, St. Bernadette Parish, 5890 S. Abbott Rd., Orchard Park, 14127.
Tel: 716-649-3369, Ext. 123; Email: office@saintbopny.org. Scherus Rydzewski, Dir.
Catechesis Religious Program—Tel: 716-648-1720; Email: faithformation@saintbophy.org. Mrs. Sharon Urbaniak, D.R.E.
2—ST. JOHN VIANNEY (1958) Revs. Mark J. Noonan; Lukasz Kopala, Pastoral Vicar; Deacon Donald C. Weigel Jr.
Res.: 2950 Southwestern Blvd., Orchard Park, 14127. Tel: 716-674-9133; Fax: 716-674-9134; Email: parishoffice@sjvop.org; Web: saintjohnvianney.com.
School—St. John Vianney School, (Grades PreK-8), Tel: 716-674-9232; Fax: 716-674-9248; Email: sjvschool@sjvop.org; Web: www.sjvop.org. Mr. Glenn Olejniczak, Prin. Lay Teachers 18; Students 225.
Catechesis Religious Program—Tel: 716-674-9145; Email: jgolinski@sjvop.org. Jennifer Golinski, D.R.E. Students 665.
3—NATIVITY OF OUR LORD (1908) [CEM]
43 Argyle Pl., Orchard Park, 14127. Rev. James D. Ciupek; Deacon Samuel G. Puleo.
Res.: 26 Thorn Ave., Orchard Park, 14127.
Tel: 716-662-9339; Email: tredinger@nativityschool.net; Email: jdciupek@nativityschool.net; Web: www.nativityofourlordop.com.
School—Nativity of Our Lord School, (Grades PreK-8), 4414 S. Buffalo St., Orchard Park, 14127.
Tel: 716-662-7572; Email: cgardon@nativityschool.net. Christopher Gardon, Prin.; Mrs. Nancy McNulty, Librarian. Clergy 2; Lay Teachers 19; Students 218.
Catechesis Religious Program—Tel: 716-662-2169. Mary Barone, D.R.E.
4—OUR LADY OF THE SACRED HEART (1920) Rev. Adolph M. Kowalczyk; Deacon Mark J. Hooper.
Res.: 3148 Abbott Rd., Orchard Park, 14127.
Tel: 716-824-2935; Email: rectory@olshop.org.
Catechesis Religious Program—Tel: 716-824-8209. Lynn Lipczynski, C.R.E.

PAVILION, GENESEE CO., MARY IMMACULATE (1865/2010) [CEM] Rev. Innocent Diala, (Nigeria) Admin.; Deacon Walter T. Szczesny. (Merged parish with two sites: Pavilion and East Bethany)
Office: 5865 Ellicott St., East Bethany, 14054.
Tel: 585-584-7031; Email: michurch@rochester.rr.com.
Res.: 11095 Saint Mary St., P.O. Box 442, Pavilion, 14525.
Catechesis Religious Program—

PENDLETON, NIAGARA CO., GOOD SHEPHERD (1847/2009) [CEM] Parish with two sites: Pendleton; Clarence. Rev. Daniel A. Young; Deacon Robert Bauer.
Office & Res.: 5442 Tonawanda Creek Rd., North Tonawanda, 14120-9699. Tel: 716-625-8594; Email: good.shepherd5442@gmail.com.
Clarence Center Site: St. Augustine Campus, 8700 Goodrich Rd., Clarence Center, 14032.
Catechesis Religious Program—Tel: 716-625-8817. Michael Denz, D.R.E.

PERRY, WYOMING CO., ST. ISIDORE (2008) [CEM] (Parish with two sites: Perry & Silver Springs) Rev. Richard W. Blazejewski; Deacon Daniel J. McGuire.
Res. & Office: 8 Park St., Perry, 14530.
Tel: 585-237-2625; Email: jomay53@netscape.net.
Church: 71 Leicester St., Perry, 14530.
Silver Springs Site: 23 Church St., Silver Springs, 14550.
Catechesis Religious Program—

RANDOLPH, CATTARAUGUS CO., ST. PATRICK (1853) [CEM] (Linked with Our Lady of Loreto, Falconer) Mailing Address: 189 Main St., Randolph, 14772. Rev. Joseph P. Janaczek.
Res.: 309 W. Everett St., Falconer, 14733.
St. Patrick Church: 189 Main St., Randolph, 14772.
Tel: 716-358-2991; Email: stpatricksrcc@windstream.net.
Catechesis Religious Program—

RANSOMVILLE, NIAGARA CO., IMMACULATE CONCEPTION (1891) Rev. James R. Bastian; Deacon Paul S. Stankiewicz.
Office: 4671 Townline Rd., Rte. 429, Ransomville, 14131-9740. Tel: 716-731-4822; Fax: 716-731-4911.
Res.: 4720 Plank Rd., Lockport, 14094.
Catechesis Religious Program—Tel: 716-731-5387. Mrs. Judith A. Kirkpatrick, Dir., Faith Formation.

SALAMANCA, CATTARAUGUS CO., OUR LADY OF PEACE (2007) Rev. Mariusz Sierhart, Admin.; Deacon Michael L. Anderson.
Res.: 80 Pimlico Ave., Salamanca, 14779.
Tel: 716-945-4966; Email: pnap2016@gmail.com.
Catechesis Religious Program—

SANBORN, NIAGARA CO., HOLY FAMILY (1953) (Tuscarora Native Americans)
Mailing Address: P.O. Box 167, Youngstown, 14174-0167. Tel: 716-523-9114; Cell: 716-754-9130; Email: Pmccrsp@fatimashrine.com. 5180 Chew Rd., Sanborn, 14132. Rev. Peter M. Calabrese, C.R.S.P.
Res.: 1023 Swan Rd., P.O. Box 167, Youngstown, 14174-0167.
Catechesis Religious Program—

SARDINIA, ERIE CO., ST. JUDE (1953) Rev. Alfons M. Osiander, Th.D.
Res.: 12820 Genesee Rd., P.O. Box 267, Sardinia, 14134-0267. Tel: 716-496-7535; Email: AOsiander@cks.edu.
See St. Aloysius Regional School, Springville under Regional and Consolidated Elementary Schools located in the Institution section.
Catechesis Religious Program—Tel: 716-496-5419.

SILVER CREEK, CHAUTAUQUA CO., OUR LADY OF MT. CARMEL (1882/2008) [CEM] (Parish with two sites: Silver Creek & Forestville) Rev. Daniel F. Fiebelkorn.
Res.: 165 Central Ave., Silver Creek, 14136.
Tel: 716-934-2233; Email: olomc@roadrunner.com.
Forestville Site: 11 Center St., Forestville, 14062.
See Northern Chautauqua Catholic School, Dunkirk under Regional and Consolidated Elementary Schools located in the Institution section.
Catechesis Religious Program—Tel: 716-934-4891.

SLOAN, ERIE CO., ST. ANDREW (1915) Revs. James B. Cunningham, Priest Mod.; James C. O'Connor, Sacramental Min., (Retired); Deacon David E. Clabeaux, Pastoral Admin.
Res.: 34 Francis Ave., Sloan, 14212.
Tel: 716-892-0425; Email: saintandrewsloan@roadrunner.com.
Catechesis Religious Program—Timothy Reddinger, D.R.E.

SNYDER, ERIE CO., CHRIST THE KING (1926)
30 Lamarck Dr., Snyder, 14226. Tel: 716-839-1430; Fax: 716-839-1433; Email: mschaefer@ctksnyder.com; Web: www.ctksnyder.org. Rev. Msgr. Paul A. Litwin, J.C.L.
School—Christ the King School, (Grades PreK-8), 2 Lamarck Dr., Snyder, 14226. Tel: 716-839-0473; Fax: 716-568-8198. Samuel T. Zalacca, Prin. Lay Teachers 22; Students 198.
Catechesis Religious Program—Tel: 716-839-0946.

SPRINGBROOK, ERIE CO., ST. VINCENT (1850) [CEM] Rev. Karl E. Loeb
St. Vincent de Paul Roman Catholic Church
Res.: 6441 Seneca St., P.O. Box 290, Springbrook, 14140. Tel: 716-652-3972; Email: svdparish@gmail.com.
Catechesis Religious Program—Tel: 716-652-7242; Fax: 716-655-3048; Email: stvincentccd@gmail.com. Lisa Benzer, D.R.E.; Ellen Snyder, Youth Min.

SPRINGVILLE, ERIE CO., ST. ALOYSIUS (1853) [CEM] (Linked with St. John the Baptist, West Valley)
190 Franklin St., Springville, 14141-1199.
Tel: 716-592-2701; Email: staloy@roadrunner.com. Rev. Lawrence F. Cobel; Deacon Jeffrey D. Forster.
See St. Aloysius Regional School, Springville under Regional and Consolidated Elementary Schools located in the Institution section.
Catechesis Religious Program—Tel: 716-592-4869; Fax: 716-592-4869.
Convent—Sisters of St. Francis, 71 W. Main St., Springville, 14141.

STRYKERSVILLE, WYOMING CO., ST. JOHN NEUMANN (2008) [CEM] (Parish with two sites: Strykersville & Sheldon) Rev. Johnson Machado, (India) Temporary Admin.
Res.: 3854 Main St., P.O. Box 9, Strykersville, 14145-0009. Tel: 585-457-3222; Email: stjohnneumannparish@gmail.com.
Sheldon Site: 991 Centerline Rd., Strykersville, 14145-9553.
Catechesis Religious Program—
ST. PATRICK, 1468 Main St., Java Center, 14082.

SWORMVILLE, ERIE CO., ST. MARY (1849) [CEM] Revs. Robert W. Zilliox, J.C.L.; Andrew Kosminski, S.A.C.; Deacons Paul Snyder; Gary M. Hoover; Richard R. Stachura Jr.
Res.: 6919 Transit Rd., Box 460, Swormville, 14051.
Tel: 716-688-9380; Email: rectory@stmaryswormville.org; Web: www.stmaryswormville.org.
School—St. Mary School, (Grades PreK-8),
Tel: 716-689-8424; Email: principal@stmaryschoolswormville.org. Mrs. MaryJo Aiken, Prin. Lay Teachers 24; Sisters of the Third Order of St. Francis 1; Students 219.
Catechesis Religious Program—Tel: 716-688-0599; Fax: 716-639-8891; Email: familyfaith@stmaryswormville.org.

TONAWANDA, ERIE CO.
1—ST. AMELIA (1953) Revs. Sebastian C. Pierro; Peter Sanrandreu, Parochial Vicar; Deacons Kenneth R. Monaco; Robert G. Warner. In Res., Rev. Donald L. Measer, (Retired).
Res.: 210 St. Amelia Dr., Tonawanda, 14150.
Tel: 716-836-0011; Fax: 716-832-5439; Email: spierro@stamelia.com; Web: www.stamelia.com.
School—St. Amelia School, (Grades PreK-8), 2999 Eggert Rd., Tonawanda, 14150. Tel: 716-836-2230; Fax: 716-832-9700; Email: office@stameliaschool.org; Web: www.stameliaschool.org. James Mule, Prin. Clergy 3; Lay Teachers 53; Students 643.
Catechesis Religious Program—2999 Eggert Rd., Tonawanda, 14150. Tel: 716-833-8647; Email: stameliareled@yahoo.com. Elaine Volker, C.R.E. Students 343.
2—ST. ANDREW KIM (1993) Mission for Korean Catholics.
Mailing Address: 9 O'Hara Rd., Tonawanda, 14150.
Tel: 716-693-1600; Email: inyongpark521@gmail.com; Web: www.bukoca.org. Rev. Inyong Park, Admin.
Catechesis Religious Program—
3—BLESSED SACRAMENT (1929)
263 Claremont Ave., Tonawanda, 14223.
Tel: 716-834-4282; Fax: 716-834-9573; Email: bsacramentchurch@roadrunner.com; Web: bsacramentchurch.com/. Rev. Matt Mieczyslaw Nycz; Sr. M. Lucette Kinecki, C.S.S.F., Pastoral Assoc. In Res., Rev. Msgr. Leo F. McCarthy, (Retired).
Catechesis Religious Program—Tel: 716-832-6161. Josephine Palumbo, D.R.E.
4—ST. CHRISTOPHER (1928) Rev. Steven A. Jekielek; Deacons Francis A. Zwack; David P. McDermott; Thomas R. Healey.
Church & Parish Office: 2660 Niagara Falls Blvd., Tonawanda, 14150-1499. Tel: 716-692-2660; Email: rectory@saintchris.org.
Outreach Center: St. Edmund Campus, 530 Ellicott Creek Rd., Tonawanda, 14150.
School—St. Christopher School, (Grades PreK-8), Tel: 716-693-5604; Email: school@saintchris.org. Cynthia Bryk, Prin. Lay Teachers 30; Students 427.
Catechesis Religious Program—Tel: 716-694-4310; Email: reled@saintchris.org. Marie Sajda, D.R.E.
5—ST. FRANCIS OF ASSISI (1852) [CEM] Rev. Michael G. Uebler; Deacon Paul H. Bork.
Res.: 73 Adam St., Tonawanda, 14150.
Tel: 716-693-1150; Email: parsih@stfrancistonawanda.org; Web: www.stfrancistonawanda.org.
Catechesis Religious Program—144 Broad St., Tonawanda, 14150. Tel: 716-694-5342; Email: FaithFormation@stfrancistonawanda.org. Sue Ann Saltarelli, D.R.E.
6—ST. TIMOTHY (1960) Rev. Dennis F. Fronckowiak.
Res.: 565 E. Park Dr., Tonawanda, 14150.
Tel: 716-875-9430; Email: sttimothyrcchurc@aol.com; Email: office@sttimsparish.org.
Catechesis Religious Program—Email: dre@sttimsparish.org. Jean Marie Doyle, D.R.E. Students 89.

WARSAW, WYOMING CO., ST. MICHAEL (1858) [CEM]

Rev. James W. Hartwell; Deacons John J. Kelly; Edward M. Birmingham.
Res.: 171 N. Main St., Warsaw, 14569.
Tel: 585-786-2400; Email: stmikwar@rochester.rr.com.
Catechesis Religious Program—

WELLSVILLE, ALLEGANY CO., IMMACULATE CONCEPTION (1850) [CEM] Linked to St. Mary (Bolivar); Blessed Sacrament (Andover); SS Brendan & Jude (Alfred-Almond) & Holy Family of Jesus, Mary & Joseph (Belmont)
6 Maple Ave., Wellsville, 14895. 17 Maple Ave., Wellsville, 14895. Tel: 585-593-4834;
Fax: 585-593-7167; Email: kater@iccwlsv.com; Web: www.icc-ics.com. Rev. Robert Agbo, Parochial Vicar; Deacons David H. Harvey; Joseph A. Pasquella, Pastoral Assoc.
See Immaculate Conception School of Allegany County, Wellsville under Regional and Consolidated Schools located in the Institution section.

WEST FALLS, ERIE CO., ST. GEORGE (Jewettville) (1942/2008)
74 Old Glenwood Rd., West Falls, 14170-9704.
Tel: 716-652-3153; Fax: 716-687-1336; Email: stgeorge.wf@gmail.com; Web: www.stgeorgercchurch.org. Rev. Robert W. Wardenski, Mod.; Rev. Msgr. James E. Wall, Sacramental Min., (Retired); Sr. Lori High, S.S.M.N., Pastoral Admin.

WEST SENECA, ERIE CO.
1—FOURTEEN HOLY HELPERS (1864) [CEM]
1345 Indian Church Rd., West Seneca, 14224.
Tel: 716-674-2374; Email: rectory@14hh.org; Web: www.14hh.org. Rev. David A. Bellittiere; Deacon Thomas E. Scherr.
Catechesis Religious Program—Tel: 716-674-2180. Sharon Voigt, D.R.E.

2—SAINT JOHN XXIII (2008) Rev. John E. Stanton Jr.
Office: 1 Arcade St., West Seneca, 14224.
Tel: 716-823-1090; Email: frjohnstanton@gmail.com.

3—QUEEN OF HEAVEN (1955) Revs. Gregory M. Faulhaber, S.T.D.; Luke Uebler II, Parochial Vicar; Deacons John M. Ruh; Michael J. Dalessandro; Kevin Capanyola, Music Min.
Res.: 4220 Seneca St., West Seneca, 14224.
Tel: 716-674-3468; Email: rectory@qofhchurch.org.
School—Queen of Heaven School, (Grades PreK-8), 839 Mill Rd., West Seneca, 14224. Tel: 716-674-5206; Fax: 716-674-2793; Email: mdamico@qofhschool.org. Mary Damico, Prin.; Karen Gray, Librarian. Lay Teachers 28; Students 332.
Catechesis Religious Program—Tel: 716-675-3714; Email: barbara@qofhchurch.org. Barbara Maloney, D.R.E.; Christopher Wilson, Youth Min.; Jennifer Frost, Youth Min. Students 625.

WEST VALLEY, CATTARAUGUS CO., ST. JOHN THE BAPTIST (1904) [CEM] (Linked with St. Aloysius, Springville) Rev. Lawrence F. Cobel.
Res.: 5381 Depot St., P.O. Box 315, West Valley, 14171-0315. Tel: 716-942-3259; Email: staloy@roadrunner.com.
See St. Aloysius Regional School, Springville under Regional and Consolidated Elementary Schools located in the Institution section.
Catechesis Religious Program—Tel: 716-942-6874. Elaine Ahles, D.R.E.

WESTFIELD, CHAUTAUQUA CO., ST. DOMINIC (2008) [CEM 2] (Parish with two sites: Westfield & Brocton) Rev. Romeo Hontiveros, (Philippines). In Res., Rev. Sean Duggan, O.S.B. (Brocton).
Office & Westfield Site: 15 Union St., Westfield, 14787-1494. Tel: 716-326-2816; Fax: 716-232-4242; Email: stdominic@fairpoint.net; Email: rh4517@gmail.com; Web: www.stdominicrcc.org.
Brocton Site: 12 Central Ave., Brocton, 14716-0675.
Tel: 716-230-4245; Email: sean.duggan@fredonia.edu.
Catechesis Religious Program—Tel: 716-792-4431; Email: diannagiambra@gmail.com. Diana Giambra, D.R.E.

WILLIAMSVILLE, ERIE CO., SS. PETER AND PAUL (1836) [CEM 2] 5480 Main St., Williamsville, 14221. Judith Monaco, Business Mgr.; Rev. Jerome E. Kopec; Deacon Charles D. Esposito; Mr. Robert Grinewich, Pastoral Assoc.
Office: 17 Grove St., Williamsville, 14221. Tel: 716-632-2559; Email: mainofficesspp@roadrunner.com; Web: ssppchurch. com.
School—SS. Peter and Paul School, (Grades PreK-8), 5480 Main St., 14221. Tel: 716-632-6146;
F ax: 716-626-0971; Email: dlester@ssppschool.com; Web: ssppschool.com. Mrs. Deborah Lester, Prin.; Melissa Lindner, Librarian. Lay Teachers 22; Students 170.
Catechesis Religious Program—Tel: 716-632-2678; Email: rspencer@ssppchurch.com. Roberta Spencer, D.R.E.

Chaplains of Public Institutions

Please see pages 1773A and 1773B for listings.

INSTITUTIONS LOCATED IN DIOCESE

[A] SEMINARIES

EAST AURORA. *Christ the King Seminary* (1857) Graduate School of Theology, 711 Knox Rd., P.O. Box 607, East Aurora, 14052. Tel: 716-652-8900; Fax: 716-652-8903; Email: academicoffice@cks.edu; Web: www.cks.edu. Rev. John M. Staak, O.M.I., S.T.D., Interim Pres.-Rector; Mr. Michael Sherry, M.S., M.Div., Dean; Julie Galey, M.S.Ed., Registrar; Rev. Robert A. Wozniak, M.Div., Vice Rector and Dir. of Priestly Formation. Roman Catholic school of theology located in western New York owned and operated by the Diocese of Buffalo. Candidates for ministerial priesthood in the Roman Catholic Church are admitted to the seminary's Program of Priestly Formation under the sponsorship of a bishop. Those preparing for professional Church ministry or ordained ministry in non-Catholic Christian traditions are encouraged to enroll in one of three graduate degree programs offered by the seminary through its Program for Lay Formation. Degree programs offered at the seminary include: Master of Arts in Theology, Master of Arts in Pastoral Ministry, and Master of Divinity. Clergy 12; Students 76.

[B] SEMINARIES, RELIGIOUS

LEWISTON. *St. Anthony M. Zaccaria Seminary*, The Barnabite Fathers of Lewiston, NY, Inc., 981 Swann Rd., Youngstown, 14174-0167.
Tel: 716-754-7448; Fax: 716-754-9130; Email: BarnabitesUSA@fatimashrine.com; Email: pmccrsp@fatimashrine.com; Web: www.fatimashrine.com. P.O. Box 167, Youngstown, 14174-0167. Revs. Peter M. Calabrese, C.R.S.P., Treas.; Julio M. Ciavaglia, C.R.S.P., Supr.; Richard M. Delzingaro, C.R.S.P., Chancellor; Joseph M. Gariolo, C.R.S.P. Priests 4; Religious Teachers 4; Total Staff 5.

[C] COLLEGES AND UNIVERSITIES

BUFFALO. *Canisius College* (1870) 2001 Main St., 14208-1098. Tel: 716-888-2100; Tel: 716-888-2420; Email: montarol@canisius.edu; Email: hayes28@canisius.edu; Web: www.canisius.edu. Mr. John J. Hurley, Pres. Lay Teachers 191; Priests 3; Sisters 1; Total Enrollment 3,734.

**D'Youville College* (1908) 320 Porter Ave., 14201.
Tel: 716-829-8000; Fax: 716-829-7780; Email: Brayjd@dyc.edu; Web: www.dyc.edu. William Mariani, Ph.D., Interim Pres.; Rev. Patrick T. O'Keefe, Dir. Campus Ministry; Rand Bellavia, Librarian. Grey Nuns of the Sacred Heart. Lay Teachers 325; Sisters 2; Students 2,967; Total Staff 592.

Trocaire College (1958) Main Campus, 360 Choate Ave., 14220. Tel: 716-826-1200; Fax: 716-828-6109; Tel: 716-827-4300; Fax: 716-634-6139; Email: deebb@trocaire.edu; Web: www.trocaire.edu. Bassam M. Deeb, Ph.D., Pres.; Richard T. Linn, Ph.D., Senior Vice Pres.; Elise Torre, M.L.S., Librarian. A private career-oriented Catholic College established by the Sisters of Mercy in 1958. Lay Teachers 161; Sisters 3; Students 1,352; Total Staff 115.

Villa Maria College of Buffalo (1960) 240 Pine Ridge Rd., 14225-3999. Tel: 716-896-0700;
Tel: 716-961-1805; Fax: 716-896-0705; Email: karpinskim@villa.edu; Web: www.villa.edu. Matthew Giordano, Ph.D., Interim Pres.; Lucy Bungo, Librarian. Lay Teachers 97; Sisters 9; Students 591; Total Staff 170.

HAMBURG. *Hilbert College* (1957) 5200 S. Park Ave., Hamburg, 14075. Tel: 716-649-7900;
Fax: 716-558-6380; Email: mbrophy@hilbert.edu; Web: www.hilbert.edu/. Michael Brophy, Pres. Lay Teachers 110; Students 1,000.

LEWISTON. *Niagara University* (1856) 5795 Lewiston Rd., Niagara University, 14109. Tel: 716-286-8350; Fax: 716-286-8355; Email: president@niagara.edu; Web: www.niagara.edu. Rev. James J. Maher, C.M., Pres.; Dr. Timothy Ireland, Vice Pres.; Debra A. Colley, Ph.D., Exec. Vice Pres.; Mary E. Borgognoni, Sr. Vice Pres. Operations & Finance. Lay Teachers 164; Priests 8; Religious Teachers 3; Students 3,949.

ST. BONAVENTURE. *St. Bonaventure University* (1858) 3261 W. State Rd., St. Bonaventure, 14778.
Tel: 716-375-2000; Fax: 716-375-2055; Email: sstangle@sbu.edu; Web: www.sbu.edu. Dr. Dennis R. DePerro, Pres. Franciscan Friars, Province of the Holy Name, Order of Friars Minor.School of Arts and Sciences, School of Educ., School of Business, School of Journalism & Mass Communication; School of Franciscan Studies and the Franciscan Institute; Graduate Studies. Brothers 3; Lay Teachers 132; Priests 10; Sisters 2; Students 2,011.
Administration: Andrew Roth, Ph.D., Interim Pres.; Joseph E. Zimer, Ph.D., Vice Pres. Academic Affairs & Provost; Rev. David Couturier, O.F.M.Cap., D.Min., Ph.D., Dir. Mission Integration.

[D] HIGH SCHOOLS, PRIVATE

BUFFALO. *Bishop Timon-St. Jude High School* (1946) 601 McKinley Pkwy., 14220. Tel: 716-826-3610; Fax: 716-824-5833; Email: newton@bishoptmon.com; Web: www.bishoptimon.com. James P. Newton, Prin. Owned and operated by Bishop Timon Board of Trustees. Lay Teachers 23; Religious Teachers 1; Students 180.

Canisius High School (1870) 1180 Delaware Ave., 14209. Tel: 716-882-0466; Fax: 716-883-1870; Email: gaglione@canisiushigh.org; Web: www.canisiushigh.org. Revs. David S. Ciancimino, S.J., Pres.; Michael P. Corcoran, S.J., Campus Min.; Richard J. Zanoni, S.J., Asst. to Pres. Society of Jesus. Lay Teachers 65; Priests 4; Religious Teachers 3; Students 762.

St. Joseph's Collegiate Institute (1861) 845 Kenmore Ave., 14223-3195. Tel: 716-874-4024;
Fax: 716-874-4956; Email: cfulco@sjci.com; Web: www.sjci.com. Christopher Fulco, Pres.; James Spillman, Prin.; Rev. James C. Croglio, L.C.S.W., Chap. of School and Brothers' Community. Brothers of the Christian Schools. (De La Salle Christian Brothers). Brothers 5; Deacons 1; Lay Teachers 49; Priests 1; Religious Teachers 4; Students 657.

Mt. Mercy Academy (1904) 88 Red Jacket Pkwy., 14220. Tel: 716-825-8796; Fax: 716-825-0976; Email: mstaszak@mtmercy.org; Web: www.mtmercy.org. Ms. Margaret Cronin, Pres.; Mrs. Margaret Staszak, Prin.; Peggy Letina, Librarian. Sisters of Mercy. Students 250; Total Staff 51.

Nardin Academy High School (1857) 135 Cleveland Ave., 14222. Tel: 716-881-6262; Fax: 716-881-0086; Email: aforgette@nardin.org; Web: www.nardin.org. Mrs. Marsha Sullivan, Pres.; Adrienne Forgette, Prin. Girls 430; Lay Teachers 44; Religious Teachers 4.

AMHERST. *Buffalo Academy of the Sacred Heart*, 3860 Main St., Amherst, 14226. Tel: 716-834-2101;
Fax: 716-834-2944; Email: Info@sacredheartacademy.org; Web: www.sacredheartacademy.org. Jennifer Demert, Headmistress; Lynn Biniskiewicz, Librarian. Sisters of St. Francis of Penance and Christian Charity. Lay Teachers 54; Sisters 1; Students 540; Total Staff 86.

BATAVIA. *Notre Dame High School of Batavia*, 73 Union St., Batavia, 14020. Tel: 585-343-2783;
Fax: 585-343-7323; Email: ndhs@ndhsbatavia.com; Web: www.ndhsbatavia.com. Mr. Wade Bianco, Prin.; Mr. Mike Rapone, Asst. Prin. & Athletic Dir.; Miss Jennifer Kleparek, Librarian. Owned and operated by Notre Dame Board of Trustees. Lay Teachers 17; Students 144.

HAMBURG. *St. Francis High School* (1927) 4129 Lake Shore Rd., Hamburg, 14075. Tel: 716-627-1200;
Fax: 716-627-4610; Email: frmichaels@stfrancishigh.org; Web: stfrancishigh.org. Rev. Michael Sajda, O.F.M.Conv., Pres.; Mr. Thomas Braunscheidel, Prin. Franciscan Friars Conventual of Our Lady of the Angels Province. Brothers 1; Lay Teachers 38; Priests 3; Religious Teachers 3; Students 479.

Immaculata Academy (Closed) Franciscan Sisters of St. Joseph. Franciscan Sisters of St. Joseph, 5229 S. Park Ave., Hamburg, 14075. Tel: 716-649-1205; Email: ahudzina@fssj.org. Sr. Ann Marie Hudzina, F.S.S.J., Gen. Min.

KENMORE. *Mount St. Mary Academy* (1927) 3756 Delaware Ave., Kenmore, 14217. Tel: 716-877-1358 ; Fax: 716-877-0548; Email: kspillman@msmacademy.org; Web: msmacademy.org. Katherine Spillman, Prin.; Jennifer Santomauro, Librarian. Owned and operated by the Mt. St. Mary Academy Board of Trustees. Girls 310; Lay Teachers 35; Sisters 1.

LANCASTER. *St. Mary's High School*, 142 Laverack Ave., Lancaster, 14086. Tel: 716-683-4824;
Fax: 716-683-4996; Email: lancer@smhlancers.org; Web: www.smhlancers.org. Kevin Kelleher, Head, School; Keith Junik, Dean, Academic Affairs. Owned and operated by St. Mary's Board of Trustees. Lay Teachers 31; Religious Teachers 1; Students 410.

OLEAN. *Archbishop Walsh High School*, 208 N. 24th St., Olean, 14760-1985. Tel: 716-372-8122;
Fax: 716-372-6707; Email: Cristy.Ferry@walshstcs.org; Web: www.stcswalsh.org. Thomas J. Manko, Pres. & Prin.; Rev. David E. Tourville, Admin. Owned and operated by Archbishop Walsh Board of Trustees. Lay Teachers 6; Students 53; Total Staff 11.

TONAWANDA. *Cardinal O'Hara High School*, 39 O'Hara

Rd., Tonawanda, 14150. Tel: 716-695-2600, Ext. 0; Fax: 716-692-8697; Email: mholzerland@cardinalohara.org; Web: www.cardinalohara.com. Mrs. Mary Holzerland, Prin.; Mrs. Jill Monaco, Asst. Prin. Owned and operated by Cardinal O'Hara Board of Trustees. Lay Teachers 31; Priests 1; Religious Teachers 1; Students 279.

[E] ELEMENTARY SCHOOLS, PRIVATE

BUFFALO. *Nardin Academy* (1857) 135 Cleveland Ave., 14222. Tel: 716-881-6262; Fax: 716-881-4190; Email: msullivan@nardin.org; Web: www.nardin.org. Mrs. Marsha Sullivan, Pres.; Callie Georger, Prin.; Christopher Pitek, Prin.; Kristin Whitlock, Montessori Prin. (Montessori-Grade 8) Lay Teachers 59; Elementary & Montessori 420.

The NativityMiguel Middle School of Buffalo, (Grades 5-8), St. Augustine Campus: 21 Davison Ave., 14215. Tel: 716-852-6854; Tel: 716-836-5188; Fax: 716-852-8410; Fax: 716-836-5189; Email: info@nativitymiguelbuffalo.org; Web: nativitymiguelbuffalo.org. Nancy M. Langer, Pres.; Rev. Edward J. Durkin, S.J., Prin. Lay Teachers 11; Priests 1; Sisters 2; Students 80; Total Staff 22.

LEWISTON. *Sacred Heart Villa School*, (Grades PreK-5), 5269 Lewiston Rd., Lewiston, 14092. Tel: 716-284-8273; Tel: 716-285-9257 (school); Fax: 716-284-8273; Email: shivillaschool@gmail.com; Web: www.shvilla.org. Sisters Grace Dike, S.C.G.R., Supr.; Elizabeth Domin, S.C.G.R., Prin. Lay Teachers 1; Religious Teachers 8; Students 37.

STELLA NIAGARA. *Stella Niagara Education Park*, (Grades PreK-8), 4421 Lower River Rd., Stella Niagara, 14144. Tel: 716-754-4314; Fax: 716-754-2964; Email: snepoffice@stella-niagara.com. Sr. Margaret Sullivan, O.S.F., Prin. Sisters of St. Francis of Penance and Christian Charity Clergy 1; Lay Teachers 22; Sisters 2; Students 151.

[F] ELEMENTARY SCHOOLS, SPECIAL

DEPEW. *Cantalician Center for Learning, Inc.* (1955) (Grades PreK-12), 2049 George Urban Blvd., Depew, 14043. Tel: 716-901-8700; Fax: 716-901-8800; Email: ahirtzel@cantalician.org; Web: www.cantalician.org. Anne Spisiak, Exec. Dir.; Mark Bleasy, Prin.; Julie Davis, Prin.; Jason Petko, Dir. Educ. Integrated services to children & adults with developmental disabilities. Services include: Daycare, Preschool and School Age services, Early Childhood Community Services, Day Habilitation Services, Employment Services and Contract Sales through its division, Diversified Labor Solutions. Sisters 1; Students 450; Total Staff 470.

[G] REGIONAL AND CONSOLIDATED ELEMENTARY SCHOOLS

BUFFALO. *Catholic Academy of West Buffalo*, (Grades PreK-8), 1069 Delaware Ave., 14209-1605. Tel: 716-885-6111; Fax: 716-885-6452; Email: gglenn@cawb.org; Web: cawb.org. Sr. Gail Glenn, S.S.J., Prin.; Christine Traum, Librarian; Rev. Paul R. Bossi, Canonical Admin. Lay Teachers 17; Sisters 2; Students 191; Total Staff 24.

Our Lady of Black Rock, (Grades PreK-8), 16 Peter St., 14207. Tel: 716-873-7497; Fax: 716-447-9926; Web: www.olbrschool.org. Mrs. Martha J. Eadie, Prin.; Rev. Richard Jedrzejewski, Canonical Admin. Lay Teachers 19; Religious Teachers 1; Students 200; Total Staff 30.

South Buffalo Catholic School aka Notre Dame Academy, (Grades PreK-8), 1125 Abbott Rd., 14220. Tel: 716-824-0726; Fax: 716-825-7685; Email: tdangelo@notredamebuffalo.org; Web: www.notredamebuffalo.org. Mrs. Tristan D'Angelo, Prin.; Rev. Bryan J. Zielenieski, Admin. Lay Teachers 34; Students 498.

BATAVIA. *St. Joseph Regional School*, (Grades PreK-8), 2 Summit St., Batavia, 14020. Tel: 585-343-8911; Fax: 585-343-8911; Email: kgreen@sjsbatavia.org. Rev. Ivan R. Trujillo, Canonical Admin.; Mrs. Karen Green, Prin. Students 221.

DUNKIRK. *Northern Chautauqua Catholic School* (1989) (Grades PreK-8), 336 Washington Ave., Dunkirk, 14048. Tel: 716-366-0630; Fax: 716-366-5101; Email: ncc_office@nccschool.us; Web: www.nccschool.us. Rev. Daniel P. Walsh, Canonical Admin.; Andy Ludwig, Prin.; Mary Jane Starks, Business Mgr. Lay Teachers 16; Religious Teachers 1; Students 105.

LAKE VIEW. *Southtowns Catholic*, (Grades PreK-8), 2052 Lakeview Rd., Lake View, 14085. Tel: 716-627-5011; Fax: 716-627-5335; Email: mbandelian@southtownscatholic.org; Web: www.southtownscatholic.org. Marc Bandelian, Prin. Clergy 2; Lay Teachers 20; Students 169; Total Staff 25.

LOCKPORT. *DeSales Catholic School*, (Grades PreK-8), 6914 Chestnut School, Lockport, 14094. Tel: 716-433-6422; Fax: 716-434-4002; Email: rahillk@desalescatholicschool.org; Web: www.desalescatholicschool.org. Rev. Walter J. Szczesny, M.Div., Canonical Admin.; Karen Rahill, Prin. (Regional) Lay Teachers 30; Students 307; Total Staff 45.

NIAGARA FALLS. *Catholic Academy of Niagara Falls*, (Grades PreK-8), 1055 N. Military Rd., Niagara Falls, 14304. Tel: 716-283-1455; Fax: 716-283-1355 ; Email: CatholicAcademyNF@gmail.com; Web: Catholicacademyofniagarafalls.com. Rev. Robert S. Hughson, Canonical Admin.; Mrs. Jeannine M. Fortunate, Prin. Lay Teachers 18; Students 200.

OLEAN. *Southern Tier Catholic School*, 208 N. 24th St., Olean, 14760. Tel: 716-372-8122; Fax: 716-372-6707; Email: Cristy.Ferry@walshstcs.org; Web: www.stcswalsh.org. Thomas J. Manko, Pres. & Prin.; Rev. David E. Tourville, Canonical Admin. (Montessori - Grade 8) Clergy 2; Lay Teachers 14; Students 142; Total Staff 18.

SPRINGVILLE. *St. Aloysius Regional School*, (Grades K-8), 186 Franklin St., Springville, 14141-1112. Tel: 716-592-7002; Fax: 716-592-4032; Email: starsoffice@staloysiusregional.com; Web: www.staloysiusregional.com. Mary Beth Webster, Prin.; Deacon Jeffrey D. Forster, Canonical Admin. Lay Teachers 15; Students 84.

WELLSVILLE. *Immaculate Conception School of Allegany County*, (Grades PreK-8), 24 Maple Ave., Wellsville, 14895. Tel: 585-593-5840; Fax: 585-593-5846; Email: icsprincipal24@yahoo.com; Web: www.icc-ics.org. Nora A. Burdick, Prin.; Cyndi Stanton, Librarian; Rev. Sean E. DiMaria, Canonical Admin. Lay Teachers 16; Religious Teachers 1; Students 143.

[H] CATHOLIC CHARITIES

BUFFALO. *The Catholic Charities of the Diocese of Buffalo* (1923) 741 Delaware Ave., 14209. Tel: 716-218-1400; Fax: 716-856-2005; Fax: 716-362-6143. Dennis C. Walczyk, CEO; Mr. Timothy Sember, Chief Devel. Officer. Serving the eight counties of Western New York. Tot Asst. Annually 152,919; Total Staff 489.

Appeal Administration and Publicity Offices Sr. Mary McCarrick, O.S.F., Diocesan Dir.

Agency Administration Sr. Mary McCarrick, O.S.F., Diocesan Dir.; Dennis C. Walczyk, CEO.

The Msgr. Carr Institute, 76 W. Humboldt Pkwy., 14214. Tel: 716-218-1400; Fax: 716-895-1033; Email: mary.mccarrick@wnycc.org. 741 Delaware Avenue, 14209. Sr. Mary McCarrick, O.S.F., Diocesan Dir.; Brian T. O'Herron, M.Ed., M.B.A., Dept. Dir. See separate listing in the Miscellaneous section.

[I] ORPHANAGES AND INFANT HOMES

BUFFALO. *German Roman Catholic Orphan Home*, 795 Main St., 14203. Email: rmurphy@buffalodiocese.org. Inactive.

[J] PROTECTIVE INSTITUTES

BUFFALO. *St. Adalbert's Response to Love Center, Inc.* dba Response to Love Center, 130 Kosciuszko St., 14212. Tel: 716-894-7030; Fax: 716-891-5474; Email: rtlcoffice@gmail.com; Web: www.responsetolovecenter.org. Sr. Mary Johnice Rzadkiewicz, C.S.S.F., Dir. Tot Asst. Annually 9,000.

The Franciscan Center, Inc., 1910 Seneca St., 14210-1842. Rev. Joseph Bayne, O.F.M.Conv., Exec. Dir. (Closed).

LACKAWANNA. **Baker Victory Services* (1851) 790 Ridge Rd., Lackawanna, 14218. Tel: 716-828-9500; Tel: 888-287-1160; Email: info@bakervictoryservices.org; Web: www.bakervictoryservices.org. Rev. Msgr. Paul J.E. Burkard, Pres. of Board; Terese M. Scofidio, CEO. Bakery Victory Services assists children, adults and families through a variety of programs, including daycare, preschool, and school age education; outpatient adolescent mental health; foster care; residential and support programs for individuals with intellectual disabilities and young people who have emotional and behavioral diagnoses; and a full service dental clinic open to the public. Bed Capacity 158; Tot Asst. Annually 24,765; Total Staff 931.

[K] GENERAL HOSPITALS

BUFFALO. *Catholic Health System, Inc.* (1998) 144 Genesee St., 6th Fl. W., 14203. Tel: 716-862-2400; Fax: 716-862-2468; Email: webmaster@WNYCHS.org; Web: www.chsbuffalo.org. Mark A. Sullivan, Pres. Total Staff 9,037.

McAuley-Seton Home Care (1988) 144 Genesee St., 2nd Fl., 14203. Tel: 716-685-4870; Fax: 716-651-9613; Email: jmarkiew@chsbuffalo.org. c/o Catholic Health Systems, 144 Genesee St., 6th Fl. W, 14203. Joyce Markiewicz, Pres. & CEO. Tot Asst. Annually 15,042; Total Staff 344; Mercy Home Care 1,859.

Mercy Hospital (1904) 565 Abbott Rd., 14220. Tel: 716-862-2410; Fax: 716-862-2468; Email: cjurlaub@chsbuffalo.org. 144 Genesee St., 6th Floor West, 14203. Mr. C. J. Urlaub, Pres. & CEO; Eddie Bratko, COO; Shari McDonald, Vice Pres., Patient Care Svcs.; John Kalinowski, Vice Pres. Mission Integration. Sponsored by the Catholic Health System, Inc. Bed Capacity 387; Tot Asst. Annually 103,773; Total Staff 2,600; Total Outpatient Visits 260,159; Total Admissions 19,951.

Sisters Hospital Foundation, Inc., 2157 Main St, 14214. Tel: 716-862-1990; Fax: 716-835-8643; Email: asnyder@chsbuffalo.org; Web: www.chsbuffalo.org/fch/sisters. c/o Catholic Health System, 144 Genesee St., 6th Fl. W., 14203. Anne E. Snyder, Exec. Dir.

Sisters of Charity Hospital of Buffalo, NY (1849) Main Street Campus: 2157 Main St., 14214. Tel: 716-862-1000; Fax: 716-862-1899; Email: mborysza@chsbuffalo.org; Web: www.chsbuffalo.org. c/o Catholic Health Systems, 144 Genesee St., Legal Services, 6th Floor West, 14203. Martin Boryszak, Pres. & CEO; John Sperrazza, COO; Mary Dillon, Vice Pres. Patient Care Svcs.; Paula Moscato, Vice Pres. Mission Integration. Sponsored by the Catholic Health System, Inc. Bed Capacity 378; Tot Asst. Annually 787,714; Total Staff 2,242; Admissions 14,671; Outpatient Visits 354,061.

St. Joseph Campus, 2605 Harlem Rd., 14225. Tel: 716-891-2400; Fax: 716-891-2616; Email: pearnold@chsbuffalo.org. 144 Genesee St., 14203. Peter U. Bergmann, Pres.

KENMORE. *Kenmore Mercy Foundation Inc.* (1980) 2950 Elmwood Ave., Kenmore, 14217. Tel: 716-447-6204 ; Fax: 716-447-6052; Email: sjandzin@chsbuffalo.org; Web: www.chsbuffalo.org/FCH/KenmoreMercy. c/o Catholic Health Systems, 144 Genesee St., 6th Fl. W., 14203. Susan Jandzinski, Exec. Dir.

Kenmore Mercy Hospital, 2950 Elmwood Ave., Kenmore, 14217. Tel: 716-447-6100; Fax: 716-447-6090; Email: wludwig@chsbuffalo.org. c/o Catholic Health Systems, 144 Genesee St., 6th Fl. W., 14203. Walter Ludwig, Pres.; William Vaughan, Vice Pres. Mission Integration; Cheryl Hayes, Vice Pres. Patient Care Svcs. Sponsored by the Catholic Health System, Inc. Bed Capacity 184; Tot Asst. Annually 47,266; Total Staff 938; Outpatient Visits 108,091; Admissions 8,044.

LEWISTON. *Mount St. Mary's Hospital of Niagara Falls*, 5300 Military Rd., Lewiston, 14092-1997. Tel: 716-297-4800; Email: gary.tucker@chsbuffalo.org; Web: www.chsbuffalo.org. Gary Tucker, Pres. & CEO; Rev. Stewart M. Lindsay, O.S.F.S., Chap.; Bernadette Franjoine, Vice Pres. Mission Integration; Jessica Visser, Vice Pres. Patient Care Svcs.; Sisters Linda Lewandowski, O.S.F., Chap.; Judith Terrameo, O.S.F., Chap. Catholic Health System, Inc. Bed Capacity 114; Tot Asst. Annually 42,470; Total Staff 736; Outpatient visits 152,844; Admissions 4,831.

[L] HEALTH CARE FACILITIES

BUFFALO. *St. Francis of Buffalo, Inc.* Formerly known as St. Francis Hospital. 144 Genesee St., Legal Services, 6th Floor West, 14203. Tel: 716-821-4469; Email: jmarkiew@chsbuffalo.org. Joyce Markiewicz, Interim Pres. & CEO.

NORTH TONAWANDA. *Niagara Homemaker Services, Inc.* dba Mercy Home Care of Western New York, 3571 Niagara Falls Blvd., North Tonawanda, 14120. Tel: 716-668-3511; Email: jamarkiew@chsbuffalo.org. c/o Catholic Health Systems, 144 Genesee St, 6th Fl. W., 14203. Joyce Markiewicz, Pres. & CEO. Patients Asst Anual. 1,712; Staff 144.

[M] HOMES FOR AGED

CLARENCE. *Brothers of Mercy Housing Co., Inc.* aka Brothers of Mercy Senior Apartment Complex, 10500 Bergtold Rd., Clarence, 14031. Tel: 716-759-2122; Fax: 716-759-8030; Email: baty@brothersofmercy.org; Web: www.brothersofmercy.org. Mary Baty, Admin. Affordable, Independent Senior Housing Total in Residence 100; Total Staff 4; Apartments 100.

Brothers of Mercy Nursing & Rehabilitation Center, 10570 Bergtold Rd., Clarence, 14031. Tel: 716-759-6985; Fax: 716-759-6223; Email: peter@brothersofmercy.org; Web: www.brothersofmercy.org. Mr. Peter Eimer, CEO; Rev. Eugene S. Slomba, Chap., (Retired). Bed Capacity 240; Tot Asst. Annually 950; Staff 500. In Res. Bro. Fidelis Verrall, F.M.M.

Brothers of Mercy Sacred Heart Home, Inc., 4520 Ransom Rd., Clarence, 14031. Tel: 716-759-2644; Fax: 716-759-6433; Email: marion@brothersofmercy.org; Web: www.

brothersofmercy.org. Mr. Peter Eimer, CEO; Marion Hummell, Admin.; Rev. Eugene S. Slomba, Chap., (Retired). Tot Asst. Annually 106; Total Staff 50.

DUNKIRK. *St. Vincent's Home for the Aged* (Closed).

KENMORE. *McAuley Residence*, 1503 Military Rd., Kenmore, 14217. Tel: 716-447-6600; Fax: 716-447-6620; Email: dclabeaux@chsbuffalo.org. c/o Catholic Health System, 144 Genesee St., 6th Fl. W., 14203. Dawn Clabeaux, Admin. Residential Health Care Facility; Sponsored by the Catholic Health System, Inc. Bed Capacity 160; Total Staff 240; Total Assisted 1,335.

LANCASTER. *St. Elizabeth's Home* (1958) (Closed) c/o Catholic Health System, 144 Genesee St., 6th Fl. W., 14203.

LEWISTON. *Our Lady of Peace, Inc.* dba Our Lady of Peace Nursing Care Residence, 5285 Lewiston Rd., Lewiston, 14092. Tel: 716-298-2900; Fax: 716-298-2800; Email: tdillsworth@ascension.org; Web: www.ascensionliving.org/. Teresa Dillsworth, Exec. Dir.; Carmen Granto, Bd. Chairperson; Rev. Duane R. Klizek, Chap. Bed Capacity 250; Tot Asst. Annually 675; Total Staff 350.

ORCHARD PARK. *Father Baker Manor* (1994) 6400 Powers Rd., Orchard Park, 14127. Tel: 716-667-0001; Fax: 716-667-0028; Email: mwheeler@chsbuffalo.org; Web: www.chsbuffalo.org. c/o Catholic Health System, 144 Genesee St., 6th Fl. W., 14203. Mark Wheeler, Admin. Nursing facility sponsored by the Catholic Health System, Inc. Bed Capacity 160; Total Staff 290; Total Assisted 750.

SILVER CREEK. *St. Columbans on the Lake, Home for the Aged* (1970) 2546 Lake Rd., Silver Creek, 14136. Tel: 716-934-4515; Fax: 716-934-3919; Email: ccolleary@stcolumbanshome.org; Web: www.stcolumbanshome.org. Sr. Corona Colleary, S.S.C., Admin.; Rev. William Schmitt, Chap. Bed Capacity 50; Tot Asst. Annually 150; Total Staff 35; Columban Sisters 13. In Res. Revs. Peter J. Cronin, S.S.C., (Retired); Vincent McCarthy, S.S.C., (Retired); Thomas M. Walsh, S.S.C., (Retired).

WILLIAMSVILLE. *St. Francis of Williamsville* (Closed) c/o Catholic Health System, 144 Genesee St., 6th Fl. W., 14203.
St. Francis of Williamsville.

[N] MONASTERIES AND RESIDENCES OF PRIESTS AND BROTHERS

BUFFALO. *Bishop's Residence*, 127 Wilson St., 14212. Tel: 716-883-7707; Fax: 716-883-7702; Email: rbiernat@buffalodiocese.org. Most Rev. Richard J. Malone, Th.D., S.T.L.; Rev. Ryszard S. Biernat, Bishop's Sec. & Vice Chancellor.

Canisius Jesuit Community Inc., 2001 Main St., Loyola Hall, 14208. Tel: 716-883-7000; Fax: 716-886-6506; Email: tslon@jesuits.org; Web: www.canisius.edu. Revs. Thomas R. Slon, S.J., Rector; Michael P. Corcoran, S.J.; Adelmo Dunghe; David S. Ciancimino, S.J.; Edward J. Durkin, S.J.; Daniel P. Jamros, S.J.; Patrick J. Lynch, S.J.
The Canisius Jesuit Community, Inc.

ATHOL SPRINGS. *St. Francis of Assisi Friary* (1927) 4129 Lake Shore Rd., Athol Springs, 14010-0185. Tel: 716-627-5762; Fax: 716-627-4610; Email: frmichaels@stfrancishigh.org; Web: www.stfrancishigh.org. Revs. Michael Sajda, O.F.M.-Conv., Guardian & Pres.; Francis Lombardo, O.F.-M.Conv., (Retired); Mark David Skura, O.F.M.Conv.; Bros. James Doyle, O.F.M., O.F.M.-Conv.; Brian Newbigging, O.F.M.Conv.; Nicholas Romeo, O.F.M.Conv. Faculty Residence for St. Francis High School Brothers 3; Priests 4; Total in Residence 7.

St. Maximilian Kolbe Friary, 4263 St. Francis Dr., Hamburg, 14075. Tel: 716-627-2710; Fax: 716-627-5263; Email: fr.ross@verizon.net. P.O. Box 182, Athol Springs, 14010. Revs. Ross M. Syracuse, O.F.M.Conv., Guardian; Joseph Bayne, O.F.M.Conv.; Romulus Rosolowski, O.F.M.Conv. Priests 2; Total in Residence 2. *Fr. Justin Senior Friars Residence*, 4190 St. Francis Dr., Hamburg, 14075. Tel: 716-627-5203; Email: fr.ross@verizon.net. Revs. Ross M. Syracuse, O.F.M.Conv., Dir.; Marcel Sokalski, O.F.M.Conv.; Bro. Kenneth Lucas, O.F.M.Conv.; Revs. Michael Taylor, O.F.M.-Conv.; Charles Jagodzinski, O.F.M.Conv. Brothers 1; Priests 4; Total in Residence 5.

CLARENCE. *Brothers of Mercy of Mary Help of Christians, Inc.*, 4520 Ransom Rd., Clarence, 14031. Tel: 716-759-7205; Fax: 716-759-7243; Email: Kenneth@brothersofmercy.org. Bro. Kenneth Thomas, F.M.M.A, Convent Supr.; Rev. Eugene S. Slomba, (Retired); Bro. Edward Lewis, F.M.M.A.
Brothers of Mercy Mary Help of Christians, Inc.

DEPEW. *Msgr. Conniff Residence*, 68 Cowing St., Depew, 14043. Tel: 716-393-3595; Fax: 716-393-3597; Email: eluterek@buffalodiocese.org. Rev. Msgrs. Frederick D. Leising, (Retired); John W. Madsen, (Retired); W. Jerome Sullivan, J.C.D., (Retired); Revs. Robert G. Beiter, (Retired); Richard S. DiGiulio, (Retired); Louis S. Dolinic, (Retired); James J. Kasinski, (Retired); Walter L. Matuszak, (Retired); John J. Mitka, (Retired); John J. Sardina, (Retired); Rev. Msgr. David S. Slubecky, J.C.L., S.T.L., (Retired); Rev. Emil P. Swiatek, (Retired).

LACKAWANNA. *Bishop Head Residence* (2002) 10 Rosary Ave., Lackawanna, 14218. Tel: 716-824-4644; Fax: 716-824-4844; Email: tbornholdt@buffalodiocese.org. Theresa Bornholdt, Admin.; Rev. Msgrs. James F. Campbell, (Retired); Leon M. Neu, (Retired); Kevin T. O'Neill, (Retired); Joseph J. Sicari, (Retired); William O. Wangler, (Retired); Revs. David G. Griffin, (Retired); James M. Augustyn, (Retired); Peter J. Drilling, Th.D., (Retired); Joseph G. Fifagrowicz, (Retired); Mark M. Friel, (Retired); L. Antonio Rodriguez, (Retired); Robert A. Stolinski, (Retired); Harry F. Szczesniak, (Retired); Charles J. Zadora, (Retired).

LEROY. *Our Lady of Mercy Friary*, 44 Lake St., Le Roy, 14482-9701. Tel: 585-768-6543; Fax: 585-768-7093; Email: frphelan@ourladyofmercyleroy.org; Web: www.orderofmercy.org. Revs. Matthew H. Phelan, O.de.M; Kenneth Breen, O.de.M.; Bro. Martin Jarowsinski, O.de.M. Total in Community: Professed Religious 3.

NIAGARA UNIVERSITY. *Vincentian Community at Niagara University*, Vincentian Residence, PO Box 2209, Niagara University, 14109-2209. Tel: 716-286-8110; Fax: 716-286-8766; Email: kcreagh@niagara.edu. Revs. James J. Maher, C.M., Univ. Pres.; William M. Allegretto, C.M.; Itoko Jean Robert Bonenge, C.M.; Kevin G. Creagh, C.M., Ed.D., Supr.; John Doai Kim Dang; Joseph G. Hubbert, C.M.; Joseph L. Levesque, C.M.; Vincent J. O'Malley, C.M.; Bro. Martin J. Schneider, C.M. Total in Residence 9.

NORTH TONAWANDA. *Society of the Catholic Apostolate*, Infant Jesus Delegature, 3452 Niagara Falls Blvd., P.O. Box 563, North Tonawanda, 14120-0563. Tel: 716-694-4313; Email: posiewala@verizon.net. Revs. John Posiewala, S.A.C., Supr. & Prov. Delegate; Severyn J. Koszyk, S.A.C.

ST. BONAVENTURE. *St. Bonaventure Friary* (1856) 1 Friary Circle, St. Bonaventure, 14778. Tel: 716-375-2423; Fax: 716-375-2424; Email: dblake@sbu.edu; Web: www.sbu.edu. Revs. David D. Blake, O.F.M., Ph.D., Guardian; Michael D. Calabria, O.F.M., M.A., Ph.D.; Ross Chamberland, O.F.M., M.T.S.; Francis Di Spigno, O.F.M., M.Div., Guardian; Kyle Haden, O.F.M., Ph.D.; David Couturier, O.F.M.Cap., D.Min., Ph.D.; Dominic V. Monti, O.F.M., Ph.D., Vicar; Peter Schneible, O.F.M., Ph.D.; James Vacco, O.F.M., M.A. Fathers 9.

TONAWANDA. *Maryknoll House; Maryknoll Fathers & Brothers*, 73 Adam St., Tonawanda, 14150. Tel: 716-213-0000; Fax: 716-213-0000; Email: pbork@maryknoll.org; Web: www.maryknollsociety.org. Deacon Paul Bork, Dir. Total Staff 2.

O'Hara Residence (1995) 69 O'Hara Rd., Tonawanda, 14150-6227. Tel: 716-743-0037; Fax: 716-743-8772; Email: kdaigler-santana@buffalodiocese.org. Rev. Msgrs. Francis Braun, (Retired); Angelo M. Caligiuri, (Retired); Rev. James F. Hassett, Res., (Retired); Rev. Msgrs. James N. Connelly, (Retired); Thomas E. Crane, (Retired); James G. Kelly, (Retired); Dino J. Lorenzetti, (Retired); J. Thomas Moran, (Retired); John M. Ryan, (Retired); Richard L. Wetter, (Retired). Total in Residence 9; Total Staff 3.

[O] CONVENTS AND RESIDENCES FOR SISTERS

BUFFALO. *Discalced Carmelite Monastery of St. Teresa of the Child Jesus* (1920) 75 Carmel Rd., 14214. Tel: 716-837-6499; Fax: 716-835-0385; Email: carmelofbuffalo74@gmail.com. Mother Teresa of Jesus, O.C.D., Prioress. Postulants 2; Cloistered Professed Sisters 10; Extern Professed Sisters 2.

Holy Name Province - Provincial Motherhouse, 4421 Lower River Rd., Stella Niagara, 14144-1001. Tel: 716-754-4312; Fax: 716-754-7657; Email: ewyss@stellaosf.org; Web: www.stellaosf.org. Sr. Edith Wyss, O.S.F., Prov. Sisters 101.

Sisters of St. Francis of Holy Name Province, Inc., 4421 Lower River Rd., Stella Niagara, 14144-1001. Tel: 716-754-4312; Fax: 716-754-7657; Email: ewyss@stellaosf.org. Sr. Edith Wyss, O.S.F., Prov. Min.

Center of Renewal, Inc., 4421 Lower River Rd., Stella Niagara, 14144. Tel: 716-754-7376; Fax: 716-754-1223; Email: centerofrenewal@stellaosf.org; Web: www.center-of-renewal.org. Sr. Edith Wyss, O.S.F., Prov. Min.

Francis Center, 335 24th St., Niagara Falls, 14303. Tel: 716-284-2050; Fax: 716-282-3783; Email: bneumeister14301@yahoo.com. Sr. Edith Wyss, O.S.F., Prov. Min.

Stella Niagara Education Park, Inc., 4421 Lower River Rd., Stella Niagara, 14144. Tel: 716-754-4314; Fax: 716-754-2964; Email: snepoffice@stella-niagara.com; Web: www.stella-niagara.org. Sr. Edith Wyss, O.S.F., Prov. Min.

The Stella Niagara Education Park Endowment Foundation, 4421 Lower River Rd., Stella Niagara, 14144. Tel: 716-754-4314; Fax: 716-754-2964; Email: snepoffice@yahoo.com; Web: www.stellaniagara.org. Sr. Edith Wyss, O.S.F., Prov. Min.

The Sisters of St. Francis Retirement Fund, 4421 Lower River Rd., Stella Niagara, 14144. Tel: 716-876-3426; Fax: 716-754-7657; Email: bernbeck@gmail.com. Sr. Edith Wyss, O.S.F., Prov. Min.

The Providence Fund, 4421 Lower River Rd., Stella Niagara, 14144. Tel: 716-754-4312; Fax: 716-754-7657; Email: mauraosf@yahoo.com. Sr. Edith Wyss, O.S.F., Prov. Min.

Buffalo Academy of the Sacred Heart, Inc., 3860 Main St., 14226-3398. Tel: 716-834-2101; Fax: 716-834-2944; Email: ewyss@stellaosf.org; Web: www.sacredheartacademy.org. 4421 Lower River Road, Stella Niagara, 14144. Sr. Edith Wyss, O.S.F., Prov. Min.

Immaculate Heart of Mary Convent (1900) 600 Doat St., 14211. Tel: 716-892-4141; Fax: 716-892-4177; Email: sconniet@feliciansisters.org; Web: www.feliciansistersna.org. Sisters Paul Marie Baczkowski, C.S.S.F., Local Min.; Mary Christopher Moore, C.S.S.F., Provincial Min. Felician Sisters 102.

Monastery of Our Lady of the Rosary (1905) 335 Doat St., 14211-2149. Tel: 716-892-0066; Fax: 716-897-1566; Email: bursar@opnuns.org; Web: opnuns.org. Mother Mary Dominic, Prioress; Rev. Thomas B. Confer, O.P., Chap.
Dominican Nuns of the Perpetual Rosary, Buffalo, NY Sisters 2; Professed Nuns 15.

Sisters of Mercy of the Americas-New York, Pennsylvania, Pacific West Community, Inc., 625 Abbott Rd., 14220. Tel: 716-826-5051; Fax: 716-826-1518; Email: nhoff@mercynyppaw.org; Web: www.mercynyppaw.org. Sr. Nancy Hoff, R.S.M., Rel. Order Leader. Sisters 74; Vowed Members 74; Associates 87.

Mercy Center, Residence for Sisters: 625 Abbott Rd., 14220. Tel: 716-825-5531; Fax: 716-826-1518; Email: dswanson@mercynyppaw.org. Sr. Nancy Hoff, R.S.M., Rel. Order Leader.

Sisters of Social Service of Buffalo (1923) 296 Summit Ave., 14214-1936. Tel: 716-834-0197; Fax: 716-834-6168; Email: almasy.maria@gmail.com; Web: www.sistersofsocialservicebuffalo.org. Sr. Maria Almasy, S.S.S., Delegate. Sisters 10.

Sisters of St. Mary of Namur (1819) St. Mary Center St. Mary Center, 241 Lafayette Ave., 14213-1453. Tel: 716-884-8221; Email: ssmneasternprovince@gmail.com; Web: www.ssmn.us. Sisters Judith Carroll, S.S.M.N., Regl. Supr.; Katherine Marie Bogner, S.S.M.N., Regl. Councillor; Mary Eileen Quinn, Regl. Councillor. Provincial House of the Sisters of St. Mary of Namur. Professed Sisters 64.

St. Mary Center, Community Coordinator, 245 Lafayette Ave., 14213. Tel: 716-885-6252; Fax: 716-381-8428. Sr. Susan Bowles, S.S.M.N., Contact Person; Anne DeVuyst, Contact Person. Sisters 24.

Sisters of St. Mary, 160 Lovering Ave., 14216. Tel: 716-873-9002. Sisters 4.

Sisters of St. Mary, 3100 Elmwood Ave., Kenmore, 14217. Tel: 716-873-8011.

Sisters of St. Mary, 104 Garden St., Lockport, 14094. Tel: 716-433-3966.

Sisters of St. Mary, 2484 River Rd., Niagara Falls, 14304. Tel: 716-884-8221; Email: ssmnprov@verizon.net. 241 Lafayette Avenue, 14213.

ALLEGANY. *Franciscan Sisters of Allegany, New York, Inc.* (1859) 115 E. Main St., Allegany, 14706. Tel: 716-373-0200; Fax: 716-372-5774; Email: fsa@fsallegany.org; Email: congsecretary@fsa.org; Web: www.alleganyfranciscans.org. Sisters Margaret Mary Kimmins, O.S.F., Congregational Min.; Margaret Magee, O.S.F., Asst. Congregational Min. Sisters 68.

St. Elizabeth Motherhouse (1859) 115 E. Main St., Allegany, 14706. Tel: 716-373-0200; Fax: 716-372-5774; Email: mllafferty@fsallegany.org; Web: www.alleganyfranciscans.org. Sisters Margaret Mary Kimmins, O.S.F., Congregational Min. & Pres.; Mary Lou Lafferty, O.S.F., Local Min. Bed Capacity 90; Sisters 74; Tot Asst. Annually 40; Total Staff 80.

CLARENCE. *Congregation of the Sisters of St. Joseph Generalate*, Administrative Offices, 4975 Strickler Rd., Ste. A, Clarence, 14031. Tel: 716-759-6454; Email: mkloss@buffalossj.org; Web: www.

buffalossj.org. Sr. Jean Marie Zirnheld, S.S.J., Pres. Professed Sisters 57.

Sisters of St. Joseph, Clarence Residence, 4975 Strickler Rd., Clarence, 14031. Tel: 716-759-6893; Fax: 716-759-0931; Email: mkloss@buffalossj.org. Sisters Marie Kerwin, S.S.J., Community Life Team; Theresa Moore, S.S.J., Community Life Team. Total in Residence 27.

HAMBURG. *Immaculate Conception Convent*, Franciscan Sisters of St. Joseph, 5229 S. Park Ave., Hamburg, 14075. Tel: 716-649-1205; Fax: 716-202-4940; Email: adminassist@fssj.org; Web: www.franciscansistersofsaintjoseph.org. Sr. Marcia Ann Fiutko, F.S.S.J., Supr. Motherhouse of the Franciscan Sisters of St. Joseph Sisters 51; Sisters in Residence 42; Sisters in Diocese 45.

LEWISTON. *Sisters of the Sacred Heart of Jesus of Ragusa (SCGR)*, 5269 Lewiston Rd., Lewiston, 14092. Tel: 716-284-8273; Fax: 716-284-8273; Email: sacredhrtv@yahoo.com. Sr. Grace, SCGR, Supr. Sisters at Sacred Heart Villa School & Convent 11.

SILVER CREEK. *Missionary Sisters of St. Columban, St. Columban's on the Lake* (1924) 2546 Lake Rd., Silver Creek, 14136. Tel: 716-934-4515; Fax: 716-934-3919; Email: sscarea@gmail.com; Web: www.columbansisters.org. Sr. Corona Colleary, S.S.C., U.S.A. Area Leader. Sisters 140; Professed Sisters 13.

[P] RETREAT HOUSES

WEST CLARKSVILLE. *Mount Irenaeus, Franciscan Mountain Retreat & Holy Peace Friary* (1982) Mount Irenaeus, P.O. Box 100, West Clarksville, 14786. Tel: 585-973-2470; Fax: 585-973-2400; Email: mmarc@sbu.edu; Web: www.mountainonline.org. Rev. Daniel P. Riley, O.F.M., M.A., Pres. & Guardian; Bro. Joseph A. Kotula, O.F.M., Ph.D., Vicar; Rev. Louis M. McCormick, O.F.M., D.Min.; Bro. Kevin Kriso, O.F.M, D.Min., Guardian. Order of Friars Minor Holy Name Province. Total in Residence 4.

[Q] CAMPUS MINISTRY AND NEWMAN CENTERS

BUFFALO. *Canisius College, Campus Ministry Office*, Canisius College Campus Ministry OM 207, 2001 Main St., 14208. Tel: 716-888-2420; Fax: 716-888-3144; Email: campmin@canisius.edu; Web: www.canisius.edu/faith-and-service/campus-ministry. Mr. Michael F. Hayes, Dir. Campus Ministry; Ms. Kaitlyn Buehlmann, Campus Min.; Deacon Gary P. Andelora.

D'Youville College, 320 Porter Ave., 14201. Tel: 716-829-7672; Email: campusministry@dyc.edu. Rev. Janice Mahle, Dir.

State University of New York at Buffalo (Main St. South Campus), St. Joseph University Parish, 3269 Main St., 14214. Tel: 716-833-0298; Fax: 716-833-7339; Email: ledwon@buffalo.edu; Web: www.ubcatholic.org. Rev. Jacob C. Ledwon, Dir.; Mr. Paul O. Stage, Campus Min.; Rev. Gregory P. Jakubowicz, O.F.M., J.D., Campus Min.

SUNY Buffalo State Newman Center, 1219 Elmwood Ave., 14222. Tel: 716-882-1080; Fax: 716-882-6914; Email: newmancenter@buffalostate.edu; Web: newmancenter.wix.com/buffalostate. Rev. Patrick J. Zengierski, Ph.D., Dir.; Austin Reinhart, Campus Min.

Trocaire College, 360 Choate Ave., 14220. Tel: 716-826-1200; Email: tucci@trocaire.edu. Robert Shearn, Dir. Misson Svc. & Campus Ministry.

Villa Maria College, 240 Pine Ridge Rd., 14225. Tel: 716-961-1813; Email: mullinj@villa.edu; Web: www.villa.edu. Joan Mullin, Dir.

ALFRED. *Alfred University and Alfred State College Campus Ministry*, Lower College Dr., P.O. Box 1154, Alfred, 14802. Tel: 607-587-9411; Fax: 607-587-9431; Email: stjude.alfred@gmail.com. Mr. Chris Yarnal, Dir. Campus Ministry.

Niagara University, Campus Ministry, P.O. Box 2016, Niagara University, 14109. Tel: 716-286-8400; Fax: 716-286-8477; Email: ministry@niagara.edu; Web: www.niagara.edu/ministry. Kristina Daloia, Dir. Campus Min.; Revs. Kevin G. Creagh, C.M., Ed.D., Vice Pres., Uni. Mission and Ministry; Vincent J. O'Malley, C.M., Univ. Chap.; William M. Allegretto, C.M., Pastoral Care; John Doai Kim Dang, C.M., Sacramental Care; Ashley Gruhalla, Campus Min.

AMHERST. *State University of New York at Buffalo (North Campus) Newman Center*, 495 Skinnersville Rd., Amherst, 14228. Tel: 716-636-7495; Fax: 716-568-0692; Email: prspat@buffalo.edu; Web: www.newman.buffalo.edu. Rev. Msgr. J. Patrick Keleher, Dir.; Steven Gruhalla, Campus Min.; Kelly Zaky, Campus Min.; Rachel Colegrove, D.R.E.

HAMBURG. *Hilbert College, Campus Ministry Office*, 5200 S. Park Ave., Hamburg, 14075. Tel: 716-649-7900; Fax: 716-649-0702; Email: jpapia@hilbert.edu. Jeffrey Papia, M.T.S., Dir. Mission Integration & Campus Ministry.

ST. BONAVENTURE. *St. Bonaventure University*, 3261 West State Street, P.O. Box AR, St. Bonaventure, 14778. Tel: 716-375-2662; Fax: 716-375-2618; Email: dmooney@sbu.edu. Rev. Francis Di Spigno, O.F.M., M.Div., Exec. Dir., Univ. Ministries; Amanda Naujoks, Campus Min.; Revs. Louis M. McCormick, O.F.M., D.Min.; Ross Chamberland, O.F.M., M.T.S.; Daniel P. Riley, O.F.M., M.A.; Bros. Joseph A. Kotula, O.F.M., Ph.D.; Kevin Kriso, O.F.M, D.Min.

[R] CAMPS AND COMMUNITY CENTERS

SALAMANCA. *Camp Turner*, Office: 9150 Allegany State Park Route 3, P.O. Box 264, Salamanca, 14779. Tel: 716-354-4555; Fax: 716-354-2055; Email: campturner@gmail.com; Web: www.campturner.com. John Mann, Dir. Resident Camp and Conference Center operated by the Catholic Diocese of Buffalo Clergy 50; Students 500.

[S] MISCELLANEOUS

BUFFALO. *Catholic Health System Infusion Pharmacy, Inc.* dba Catholic Health Infusion Pharmacy, 6350 Transit Rd., Depew, 14043. Tel: 716-685-4870; Fax: 716-685-3868; Email: noemail@aol.com. 144 Genesee St., Legal Services, 6th Floor West, 14203. Joyce Markiewicz, Pres. & CEO. A Catholic Health System organization. Patients Asst Anual. 1,208; Staff 32.

Catholic Union Store (1899) 795 Main St., 14203. Tel: 716-847-8715; Fax: 716-847-8702; Email: cus@buffalodiocese.org. James Murphy, Contact Person.

St. Clare Apartments Housing Development Fund Company, Inc. Low income housing for the elderly age 62 and over. c/o Delta Development of Western New York, 525 Washington St., 14203. Tel: 716-847-1635; Fax: 716-856-7201; Email: deborah.photiadis@ccwny.org; Web: www.deltadevelopmentwny.com. Deborah Photiadis, Exec. Residents 39; Staff 2.

Delta Development of Western New York, Inc., c/o Delta Development of WNY, Inc., 525 Washington St., 14203. Tel: 716-847-1635; Fax: 716-856-7201; Email: dphotiadis@deltadevelopment.com. Margaret M. Gillig, Exec. Dir. Staff 6.

50-60 Kosciuszko Street Housing Development Fund Company, Inc. Special Purpose Housing for the chronically mentally ill. c/o Delta Development of WNY, Inc., 525 Washington St., 14203. Tel: 716-847-1635; Fax: 716-856-7201; Email: deborah.photiadis@ccwny.org; Web: www.deltadevelopmentwny.com. Margaret M. Gillig, Exec. Dir. Residents 5; Staff 2.

The Foundation of the Roman Catholic Diocese of Buffalo, NY, Inc., 795 Main St., 14203-1250. Tel: 716-847-8369; Fax: 716-847-5589; Email: devoffice@buffalodiocese.org; Web: www.FRCDB.org. Richard C. Suchan, Exec. Dir.

Immaculate Heart of Mary Home for Children, Inc. (1896) (Closed) 600 Doat St., 14211. Tel: 716-892-4141; Fax: 716-892-4177; Web: www.feliciansna.org.

St. Joseph Investment Fund, Inc., 795 Main St., 14203. Tel: 716-847-5500; Email: pkaralus@buffalodiocese.org. Rev. Peter J. Karalus, V.G., Pres.

Kolping Catholic Young Men's Association of Buffalo, NY dba Kolping Society of Buffalo, 1145 Cleveland Dr., 14225. Tel: 716-632-7360. Willi Evelt, Pres.

La Casa De Los Tainos Housing Development Fund Company, Inc., c/o Delta Development of WNY, Inc., 525 Washington St., 14203. Tel: 716-847-1635 ; Fax: 716-856-7201; Email: deborah.photiadis@ccwhy.org; Web: www.deltadevelopmentwny.com. Margaret M. Gillig, Exec. Dir. Low income housing for the elderly age 62 & over. Residents 49; Staff 2.

Ladies of Charity of Buffalo, Inc., 1122 Broadway, 14212. Tel: 716-895-4001; Email: eileen.nowak@ccwny.org. Mrs. Eileen Nowak, Dir. A ministry of service to the needy in the spirit of St. Vincent de Paul and St. Louise de Marillac, and affiliated with Catholic Charities.

Monsignor Adamski Village Housing Development Fund Company, Inc., 795 Main St., 14203. Tel: 716-847-5571; Fax: 716-847-5557; Email: stimmel@buffalodiocese.org. Mr. Steven D. Timmel, Treas.

Monsignor Adamski Village, Inc., 795 Main St., 14203. Tel: 716-847-5571; Fax: 716-847-5557; Email: stimmel@buffalodiocese.org. Mr. Steven D. Timmel, Contact Person. Facility for elderly and handicapped persons of low income.

The Monsignor Carr Institute, 76 W. Humboldt Pkwy., 14214. Tel: 716-835-9745; Fax: 716-835-6785; Email: mark.barry@wnycc.org; Web: www.ccwny.org. Mark Barry, Dir. Licensed outpatient mental health and substance abuse treatment, community outreach team, senior advocacy and socialization, marriage counseling, school-based drug prevention, adult psychosocial club, abstinence until marriage education. Also licensed outpatient mental health children's clinics serving seriously emotionally disturbed children and providing collateral services for families. Total Assisted 12,515.

Monsignor Kirby Apartments Housing Development Fund Company, Inc., c/o Delta Development of WNY, Inc., 525 Washington St., 14203. Tel: 716-847-1635; Fax: 716-856-7201; Email: deborah.photiadis@ccwny.org; Web: www.deltadevelopmentwny.com. Margaret M. Gillig, Exec. Dir. Low income housing for the elderly age 62 and over. No-smoke facility. Total in Residence 39; Total Staff 2.

Mount St. Mary's Housing Development Fund Company, Inc., c/o Delta Development of WNY, Inc., 525 Washington St., 14203. Tel: 716-847-1635 ; Fax: 716-856-7201; Email: deborah.photiadis@ccwny.org; Web: www.deltadevelopmentwny.com. Margaret M. Gillig, Exec. Dir. Total in Residence 39; Staff 2.

Nazareth Nursing Home (Closed) 144 Genesee St., 6th Floor West, 14203. Joyce Markiewicz, Pres. & CEO.

NyPPaW Fides, Inc., 625 Abbott Rd., 14220. Tel: 716-826-5051; Fax: 716-826-1518; Email: jfrikker@sistersofmercy.org. Sr. Judith Frikker, Chm.

158 Chenango Street Housing Development Fund Company, Inc. dba St. John Bosco Apartments, c/o Delta Development of WNY, Inc., 525 Washington St., 14203. Tel: 716-847-1635; Fax: 716-856-7201; Email: deborah.photiadis@ccwny.org; Web: www.deltadevelopmentwny.com. Deborah Photiadis, Exec. Low income housing for the elderly age 62 and over. Residents 12; Staff 2.

Our Lady of Victory Community Housing Development Organization, Inc., c/o Catholic Health System, 144 Genesee St., Legal Services, 6th Floor West, 14203. Tel: 716-821-4469; Email: lcamara@chsbuffalo.org. Joyce Markiewicz, Pres.

Our Lady of Victory Renaissance Corporation, c/o Catholic Health System, 144 Genesee St., 6th Fl. W., Legal Services, 14203. Tel: 716-821-4469; Email: jmarkiew@chsbuffalo.org. Joyce Markiewicz, Pres.

Our Mother of Good Counsel Housing Development Fund Co., Inc., c/o Delta Development of WNY, Inc., 525 Washington St., 14203. Tel: 716-847-1635 ; Fax: 716-856-7201; Email: deborah.photiadis@ccwny.com; Web: www.deltadevelopmentwny.com. Deborah Photiadis, Exec. Housing for mobility impaired & elderly (62 & up) of low income. Total in Residence 39; Total Staff 2.

St. Rita's Home, Inc. (1940) (Closed) 600 Doat St., 14211. Tel: 716-892-4141; Fax: 716-892-4177; Web: www.feliciansna.org.

Salesian Studios, 152 Plymouth Ave., 14201-1214. Tel: 716-886-6597; Email: tribits@yahoo.com. Rev. Thomas Ribits, O.S.F.S., Dir.

Santa Maria Towers Housing Development Fund Company, Inc., c/o Delta Development of WNY, Inc., 525 Washington St., 14203. Tel: 716-847-1635 ; Fax: 716-856-7201; Email: deborah.photiadis@ccwny.org; Web: www.deltadevelopmentwny.com. Deborah Photiadis, Exec. Housing for mobility impaired & elderly age 62 and older of low income. Total in Residence 114; Staff 5.

Timon Towers Housing Development Fund Company, Inc., c/o Delta Development of WNY, Inc., 525 Washington St., 14203. Tel: 716-847-1635 ; Fax: 716-856-7201; Email: deborah.photiadis@ccwny.org; Web: deltadevelopmentwny.com. Deborah Photiadis, Exec. Low income housing for the mobility impaired and elderly. No smoke policy. Total in Residence 124; Total Staff 5.

St. Timothy's Park Villa Housing Development Fund Company, Inc., c/o Delta Development of WNY, Inc., 525 Washington St., 14203. Tel: 716-847-1635 ; Fax: 716-856-7201; Email: deborah.photiadis@ccwny.org; Web: www.deltadevelopmentwny.com. Deborah Photiadis, Exec. Low income housing for the elderly age 62 and over. No smoke policy. Total in Residence 49; Total Staff 2.

Victorious Missionaries, 795 Main St., 14203. Tel: 716-657-1784; Email: papadeak@verizon.net. 20 Mayfield Drive, West Seneca, 14224. Miss Carol A. Buchla, Pres. & Natl. Representative; Deacon Dennis W. Kapsiak, Spiritual Advisor. A spiritual and social movement for the disabled and chronically ill.

Wheatfield Housing Development Fund Company, Inc., c/o Delta Development of WNY, Inc., 525 Washington St., 14203. Tel: 716-847-1635; Fax: 716-856-7201; Email: deborah.

photiadis@ccwny.org; Web: www.deltadevelopmentwny.com. Margaret M. Gillig, Exec. Dir. Low income housing for the elderly age 62 and over. No smoke policy. Apartments 49; Staff 2.

ALLEGANY. *Canticle Farm, Inc.*, 115 E. Main St., Allegany, 14706. Tel: 716-373-0200, Ext. 3358; Fax: 716-373-3554; Email: office@canticlefarm.org; Email: sistermelissa@canticlefarm.org; Web: www.canticlefarm.org. Shauna Keesler, Chm.; Sr. Melissa Scholl, Pres.

Dr. Lyle F. Renodin Foundation, Inc., 115 E. Main St., Allegany, 14706. Tel: 716-373-0200; Fax: 716-373-9324; Email: LWhitford@FSAllegany.org; Web: www.RenodinFoundation.org. Mary Jo Black, Chm.; Laura Whitford, Pres.

Franciscan Ministries Corporation.

St. Elizabeth Mission Society, Inc. (1947) 115 E. Main St., P.O. Box 86, Allegany, 14706. Tel: 716-373-1130; Fax: 716-373-9324; Email: StElizMission@FSAllegany.org; Email: LWhitford@FSAllegany.org; Web: www.franciscanhope.org. Sarah Bray, Chm.; Laura Whitford, Pres. Employees 3.

ATHOL SPRINGS. *Fr. Justin Rosary Hour*, 4190 St. Francis Dr., P.O. Box 442, Athol Springs, 14010. Tel: 716-627-3861; Fax: 716-926-8501; Email: rosaryhour@yahoo.com; Web: www.rosaryhour.com. Jerry Kornowicz, Office Mgr. A prayer and catechetical program in Polish and English aired over various radio stations and internet, conducted by Our Lady of Angels Province of the Order of Friars Minor Conventual. Lay Staff 4; Priests 1; Total Staff 5.

CHEEKTOWAGA. *Diocesan Counseling Center for Clergy & Religious* dba Diocesan Counseling Center for Church Ministers, 16 Columbus St., Cheektowaga, 14227. Tel: 716-894-2743; Fax: 716-896-6394; Email: james.croglio@ccwny.org. Rev. James C. Croglio, L.C.S.W., Dir. An organization affiliated with Catholic Charities.

DBA Diocesan Counseling Center for Church Ministers.

CLARENCE. *Brothers of Mercy of Montabaur Apartment Complex Inc.*, 4530 Ransom Rd., Clarence, 14031. Tel: 716-407-5100; Email: Valerie@brothersofmercy.org. Ms. Valerie Kane, Admin. Units 111.

Brothers of Mercy Management Company, Inc., 4520 Ransom Rd., Clarence, 14031. Tel: 716-759-6985, Ext. 448; Email: Widmer@brothersofmercy.org. Bro. Kenneth Thomas, F.M.M.A, Pres.; Mr. Peter Eimer, CEO.

KENMORE. *Catholic Cemeteries of the Roman Catholic Diocese of Buffalo, Inc.*, 4000 Elmwood Ave., Kenmore, 14217. Tel: 716-873-6500; Fax: 716-873-3247; Email: cathcemsbflo@buffalodiocese.org; Web: www.buffalocatholiccemeteries.org. Carmen A. Colao, Dir. Cemeteries: Assumption, Grand Island; Gate of Heaven, Lewiston; Holy Cross, Lackawanna; Holy Sepulchre, Cheektowaga; Mount Olivet, Kenmore; Queen of Heaven, Lockport.

K M H Homes, INC., c/o Catholic Health System, 144 Genesee St., 6th Fl. W., Legal Services, 14203. Tel: 716-821-4469; Email: lcamara@chsbuffalo.org. Walter Ludwig, CEO. A holding company of the Catholic Health System.

LACKAWANNA. *Our Lady of Victory Homes of Charity (d/b/a "Father Baker's")* (1851) 780 Ridge Rd., Lackawanna, 14218. Tel: 716-828-9648; Fax: 716-828-9643; Email: dkersten@homesofcharity.org; Web: www.homesofcharity.org. David Kersten, CEO. (Formerly Association of Our Lady of Victory); Formerly included the following Institutions: St. Joseph Orphanage and St. John's Protectory.

Our Lady of Victory Homes of Charity

Society for the Protection of Destitute Roman Catholic Children at Buffalo, NY.

Our Lady of Victory Institutions, Inc., 780 Ridge Rd., Lackawanna, 14218. Tel: 716-828-9640; Email: pburkard@ourladyofvictory.org. Rev. Msgr. Paul J.E. Burkard, Chm. & Pres.

LEWISTON. *Basilica of the National Shrine of Our Lady of Fatima, Inc* aka Fatima Shrine; Our Lady of Fatima Shrine, 1023 Swann Rd., Youngstown, 14174-0167. Tel: 716-754-7489; Fax: 716-754-9130; Email: office@fatimashrine.com; Web: www.fatimashrine.com. P.O. Box 167, Youngstown, 14174. Revs. Julio M. Ciavaglia, C.R.S.P., Rector & Shrine Dir.; Peter M. Calabrese, C.R.S.P., Assoc. Dir. & Treas.; Richard M. Delzingaro, C.R.S.P. Priests 3; Total Staff 21.

NIAGARA UNIVERSITY. *Our Lady of Angels Association* (1918) P.O. Box 1918, Niagara University, 14109-1918. Tel: 716-754-0035; Fax: 716-754-0137; Email: novena@niagara.edu; Web: www.ourladyofangels.net. LuAnn Mastrolembo, Dir. of Devel. Development Office for the Congregation of the Mission, Eastern Province. Total Staff 5.

NORTH TONAWANDA. *Shrine of the Infant Jesus*, 3452 Niagara Falls Blvd., P.O. Box 563, North Tonawanda, 14120-0563. Tel: 716-694-4313; Email: posiewala@verizon.net. Rev. John Posiewala, S.A.C., Dir. Administered by the Pallottine Fathers.

STELLA NIAGARA. *DeSales Resources and Ministries, Inc.* dba Embraced by God (1980) 4421 Lower River Rd., Stella Niagara, 14144-1001. Tel: 716-754-4948; Tel: 800-782-2270; Fax: 716-754-4948; Email: resources@embracedbygod.org; Web: www.embracedbygod.org. Rev. John L. Graden, O.S.F.S., Dir.; Joanne Kinney, Admin.; Shelly Yamonaco, Business Mgr.

DBA Embraced by God Total Staff 3.

[T] CLOSED AND MERGED PARISHES

BUFFALO. *St. Adalbert* (1886) Merged with St. John Kanty Parish and became a second site for use of St. John Kanty. Records at St. John Kanty.

St. Agatha (1921) Closed in merger to form Our Lady of Charity Parish. Records at Our Lady of Charity.

St. Agnes (1883) Closed in merger to form St. Katharine Drexel Parish. Records at St. Katharine Drexel Parish.

St. Ambrose (1930) Name changed when merged with St. Agatha and Holy Family Parishes to form Our Lady of Charity Parish. Records at Our Lady of Charity.

St. Ann Merged into SS. Columba-Brigid Parish. Used temporarily as a second site but closed in 2013. Records at SS. Columba-Brigid.

Annunciation Name changed when merged with Nativity and Our Lady of Loretto Parishes to form Our Lady of Hope Parish at the Annunciation site. Records at Our Lady of Hope.

St. Bartholomew Closed in merger with Blessed Trinity Parish. Records at the Catholic Center, 795 Main St., Buffalo, NY 14203. Tel: 716-847-5567.

St. Benedict the Moor Closed in merger to form St. Martin de Porres Parish. Records at the Catholic Center, 795 Main St. Buffalo, NY 14203. Tel: 716-847-5567.

St. Boniface Closed in merger to form St. Martin de Porres Parish. Records at the Catholic Center, 795 Main St. Buffalo, NY 14203. Tel: 716-847-5567.

St. Brigid

Closed in merger with St. Columba Parish to form SS. Columba-Brigid Parish. Records at SS. Columba-Brigid Parish.

St. Clare (2007) Closed in merger with St. Teresa Parish. Records at St. Teresa Parish.

St. Elizabeth of Hungary (1906) Closed in merger with Assumption Parish. Records at Assumption Parish.

St. Florian (1917) Closed in a merger with All Saints Parish. Records at All Saints Parish.

St. Francis of Assisi Name changed when merged with St. Agnes and Visitation of the B.V.M. parishes to form St. Katharine Drexel Parish at the St. Francis of Assisi site. Records at St. Katharine Drexel Parish.

St. Francis Xavier (1849) Closed in a merger with Assumption Parish. Records at Assumption Parish.

St. Gerard (1902) Closed in merger with Blessed Trinity Parish. Records at Blessed Trinity Parish.

Holy Apostles SS. Peter and Paul (1909) Closed in merger to form St. Clare Parish. Records at St. Teresa Parish.

Holy Family (1902) Merged with St. Agatha and St. Ambrose Parishes to form Our Lady of Charity Parish using both the St. Ambrose and Holy Family sites. Records at Our Lady of Charity.

Holy Name of Jesus Closed. Merged into St. John Gualbert Parish. Records at St. John Gualbert Parish.

Immaculate Conception (1849) Closed when merged into Holy Cross Parish. Records at Holy Cross Parish.

Immaculate Heart of Mary (1946) Closed in merger with St. Aloysius Gonzaga Parish, Cheektowaga. Records at St. Aloysius Gonzaga.

St. James (1916) Closed in merger with Blessed Trinity Parish. Records at Blessed Trinity Parish.

St. Joachim Closed. Records at the Catholic Center, 795 Main St. Buffalo, NY 14203. Tel: 716-847-5567.

St. John the Baptist (1867) Closed. Records at Assumption Parish.

St. John the Evangelist (1906) Closed in merger with St. Teresa Parish. Records at St. Teresa.

St. Luke Closed. Records at the Catholic Center, 795 Main St. Buffalo NY 14203. Tel: 716-847-5567.

St. Mary of Sorrows (1872) Closed & merged into SS Columba-Brigid Parish. Records at SS. Columba-Brigid Parish.

St. Matthew Closed in a merger to form St. Martin de Porres Parish. Records at the Catholic Center, 795 Main St. Buffalo, NY 14203. Tel: 716-847-5567.

St. Monica Closed. Records at the Catholic Center, 795 Main St. Buffalo, NY 14203. Tel: 716-847-5567.

The Nativity of the Blessed Virgin (1898) Closed in merger with Annunciation and Our Lady of Loretto parishes to form Our Lady of Hope Parish. Records at Our Lady of Hope.

Our Lady of Loretto (1940) Closed in merger with Annunciation and Nativity parishes to form Our Lady of Hope Parish. Records at Our Lady of Hope.

Our Lady of Lourdes Closed in merger to form St. Martin de Porres Parish. Records at the Catholic Center, 795 Main St. Buffalo, NY 14203. Tel: 716-847-5567.

Precious Blood (1899) Closed in merger to form St. Clare Parish. Records at St. Teresa Parish.

Queen of Peace (1920) Closed. Merged into St. John Gualbert Parish. Records at St. John Gualbert Parish.

Queen of the Most Holy Rosary Closed. Records at the Catholic Center 795 Main St. Buffalo, NY 14203. Tel: 716-847-5567.

SS. Rita & Patrick (1854) Closed in merger to form St. Clare Parish. Records at St. Teresa Parish.

St. Stephen Name changed when merged with SS. Rita and Patrick, Holy Apostles SS. Peter & Paul, St. Valentine and Precious Blood Parishes to form St. Clare Parish at the St. Stephen site. Site closed in 2016. Records at St. Teresa Parish.

Transfiguration Closed. Records at the Catholic Center, 795 Main St. Buffalo, NY 14203. Tel: 716-847-5567.

St. Valentine (1920) Closed in merger to form St. Clare Parish. Records at St. Teresa Parish.

St. Vincent de Paul Closed. Merged into Blessed Trinity Parish. Records at the Catholic Center, 795 Main St. Buffalo, NY 14203. Tel: 716-847-5567.

The Visitation of the B.V.M. (1898) Closed in merger to form St. Katharine Drexel Parish. Records at St. Katharine Drexel Parish.

ALBION. *St. Joseph* Name changed when merged with St. Mary Assumption to form Holy Family Parish. Records at Holy Family.

St. Mary Assumption (1891) Closed after merging with St. Joseph Parish to form Holy Family Parish at the St. Joseph site. Records at Holy Family.

ANGELICA. *Sacred Heart* (1848) Closed in merger to form Holy Family of Jesus, Mary & Joseph Parish in Belmont. Records at Holy Family of Jesus, Mary & Joseph Parish.

ARCADE. *SS. Peter & Paul* Name changed when merged with St. Mary, East Arcade and Blessed Sacrament, Delevan to form St. Mary Parish in Arcade and using both the Arcade and East Arcade sites. Records at St. Mary Parish, Arcade.

ATTICA. *St. Vincent de Paul* Name changed when merged with St. Joseph Parish in Varysburg to form SS. Joachim & Anne Parish using both the Attica and Varysburg sites. Parish records at SS. Joachim and Anne Parish in Attica.

BARKER. *St. Patrick* (1865) Name changed with merged with St. Joseph Parish, Lyndonville, to form Our Lady of the Lake Parish. Both the Barker and Lyndonville sites are used. Records at Our Lady of the Lake, Barker.

BATAVIA. *St. Anthony* (1908) Merged with Sacred Heart Parish to form Ascension Parish. Site is closed. Records at Ascension Parish.

St. Joseph Name changed when merged with St. Mary to form Resurrection Parish using both sites. Records at Resurrection Parish.

St. Mary (1906) Merged with St. Joseph to form Resurrection Parish using both sites. Records at Resurrection Parish.

Sacred Heart Named changed when merged with St. Anthony Parish to form Ascension Parish. Records at Ascension Parish.

BELMONT. *St. Mary* Named changed when merged with St. Joseph, Scio and Sacred Heart, Angelica to form Holy Family of Jesus, Mary & Joseph at the Belmont site. Records at Holy Family of Jesus, Mary & Joseph.

BEMUS POINT. *Our Lady of Lourdes* Name changed when merged with St. Mary, Mayville to form St. Mary of Lourdes Parish using both sites. Records at St. Mary of Lourdes, Bemus Point.

BENNINGTON CENTER. *Sacred Heart of Jesus* (1872) Merged with Our Lady of Good Counsel, Darien Center to form Immaculate Heart of Mary Parish using both sites. Records at Immaculate Heart of Mary, Bennington Center.

BLISS. *St. Joseph* (1907) Closed in merger to form St. Isidore Parish, Perry & Silver Springs. Records at St. Isidore Parish, Perry.

BRANT. *Our Lady of Mt. Carmel* (1906) Closed in merger with St. Anthony, Farnham. Records at St. Anthony, Farnham.

BROCTON. *St. Patrick* (1922) Merged with St. James Major, Westfield and St. Thomas More, Ripley to form St. Dominic Parish using the Westfield and Brocton sites. Records at St. Dominic, Brocton.

CASSADAGA. *Immaculate Conception* Merged with St. Anthony, Fredonia using both sites until 2014 when Immaculate Conception was closed. Records at St. Anthony, Fredonia.

CHEEKTOWAGA. *Most Holy Redeemer* (1913) Closed in merger with St. Lawrence Parish, Buffalo. Records at St. Lawrence Parish.

Mother of Divine Grace (1946) Closed in merger with Infant of Prague, Cheektowaga. Records at Infant of Prague.

CHERRY CREEK. *St. Elizabeth* Closed. Records at St. Joseph, Gowanda.

CLARENCE CENTER. *St. Augustine* (1949) Merged with Good Shepherd, Pendleton, using both sites. Records at Good Shepherd, Pendleton.

COLDEN. *Our Lady of the Sacred Heart* (1912) Closed in merger with St. George Parish, West Falls. Records at St. George, West Falls.

COLLINS CENTER. *St. Frances Cabrini* (1955) Closed in merger to form Epiphany of Our Lord Parish, Langford. Records at Epiphany of Our Lord Parish.

CORFU. *St. Francis of Assisi* (1898) Name changed when merged with Holy Name of Mary, East Pembroke, to form St. Maximilian Kolbe Parish, using both sites. Records at St. Maximilian Kolbe, Corfu.

CRITTENDEN. *St. Patrick* (1857) Closed in merger with St. Francis of Assisi, Corfu. Records at St. Maximilian Kolbe, Corfu.

DARIEN CENTER. *Our Lady of Good Counsel* (1911) Name changed when merged with Sacred Heart of Jesus, Bennington Center to become Immaculate Heart of Mary using both sites. Records at Immaculate Heart of Mary, Darien Center.

DAYTON. *St. Paul of the Cross* Closed. Records at St. Joseph Parish, Gowanda.

DELEVAN. *Blessed Sacrament* (1947) Closed in merger to form St. Mary Parish, Arcade. Records at St. Mary Parish, Arcade.

DEPEW. *Our Lady of the Blessed Sacrament* (1965) Name changed when merged with St. Barnabas to form St. Martha Parish located at Our Lady of the Blessed Sacrament site. Records at St. Martha Parish.

St. Augustine (1909) Closed in merger with St. James, Depew, to become Blessed Mother Teresa of Calcutta Parish. Records at Blessed Mother Teresa of Calcutta, Depew.

St. Barnabas (1960) Closed in merger to form St. Martha Parish, Depew. Records at St. Martha Parish.

St. James (1897) Name changed when merged with St. Augustine, Depew to form Blessed Mother Teresa of Calcutta, Depew located at the St. James site. Records at Blessed Mother Teresa of Calcutta, Depew.

SS. Peter and Paul (1896) Closed in merger with Our Lady of Pompeii, Lancaster. Records at Our Lady of Pompeii, Lancaster.

DUNKIRK. *St. Hedwig* (1902) Merged with St. Hyacinth Parish to form Blessed Mary Angela Parish, but using both sites. Records at Blessed Mary Angela Parish, St. Hyacinth site.

St. Hyacinth (1875) Name changed when merged with St. Hedwig to form Blessed Mary Angela Parish, but using both sites. Records at Blessed Mary Angela Parish, St. Hyacinth site.

EAST ARCADE. *St. Mary's* (1846) Merged with SS. Peter & Paul, Arcade to form St. Mary Parish, Arcade using both sites. Records at St. Mary, Arcade.

EAST BENNINGTON. *Our Lady Help of Christians* Closed in merger with Darien Center. Records at Immaculate Heart of Mary, Bennington Center.

EAST BETHANY. *Immaculate Conception* (1954) Merged with St. Mary, Pavilion, to form Mary Immaculate Parish using both sites. Records at Mary Immaculate, East Bethany.

EAST EDEN. *St. Mary* (1835) Merged with St. John the Baptist Parish, Boston. St. Mary Church became an oratory of St. John the Baptist. Records at St. John the Baptist.

EAST OTTO. *St. Isidore* Closed in merger with St. Mary Cattaraugus. Records at St. Mary Cattaraugus.

EAST PEMBROKE. *Holy Name of Mary* (1868) Merged with St. Francis of Assisi, Corfu, to form St. Maximilian Kolbe Parish, using both sites. Records at Oakfield site.

EDEN. *St. Mary of the Immaculate Conception* (1858) Closed in merger to form Epiphany of Our Lord Parish, Langford. Records at Epiphany of Our Lord.

ELBA. *Our Lady of Fatima* (1947) Merged with St. Cecilia, Oakfield, to form St. Padre Pio Parish using both sites. Records at St. Padre Pio, Oakfield.

FORESTVILLE. *St. Rose of Lima* (1850) Merged with Our Lady of Mt. Carmel, Silver Creek. Both sites are used. Records at Our Lady of Mt. Carmel, Forestville site.

FRENCH CREEK. *St. Matthias* Name changed when merged with St. Isaac Jogues, Sherman to form Christ Our Hope Parish using both sites. Records at the French Creek site.

FREWSBURG. *Our Lady of Victory* (1950) Merged into St. James Parish, Jamestown. The church became an oratory of St. James Parish. Records at St. James, Jamestown.

FRIENDSHIP. *Sacred Heart* Closed when merged into Our Lady of the Angels, Cuba. Records at Our Lady of the Angels, Cuba.

GASPORT. *St. Mary* (1968) Closed in merger with St. John Parish in Lockport. Records at St. John Parish.

HINSDALE. *St. Helen* (1947) Closed in merger with St. John Parish in Olean. Records at St. John Parish, Olean.

HULBERTON. *St. Rocco* Closed. Records at St. Mary, Holley.

HUMPHREY. *St. Pacificus* (1855) Merged with Holy Name of Mary, Ellicottville, and became an oratory. Records at Holy Name of Mary, Ellicottville.

JAMESTOWN. *St. John* Merged with SS. Peter & Paul to form Holy Apostles Parish using both sites. Records at Holy Apostles, SS. Peter & Paul site.

SS. Peter & Paul Name changed when merged with St. John to form Holy Apostles Parish. Records at Holy Apostles, SS. Peter & Paul site.

JAVA CENTER. *St. Patrick* (1838) Merged with parishes in Sheldon, Strykersville & North Java to form St. John Neumann Parish. St. Patrick church was an oratory of St. John Neumann until its closure in 2017. Records at St. John Neumann, Strykersville.

KNAPP CREEK. *Sacred Heart, Mission of St. Bonaventure Parish Allegany* Closed. Records at St. Mary of the Angels, Olean.

LACKAWANNA. *Assumption* (1918) Closed. Records at the Catholic Center, 795 Main St. Buffalo, NY 14203. Tel: 716-847-5567.

St. Barbara (1903) Closed in merger to form Queen of Angels Parish. Records at Queen of Angels.

St. Hyacinth (1910) Closed in merger to form Queen of Angels Parish. Records at Queen of Angels.

St. Michael the Archangel Name changed when merged with St. Barbara, St. Hyacinth & Our Lady of Grace (Woodlawn) parishes to form Queen of Angels Parish at St. Michael's site. Records at Queen of Angels.

Queen of All Saints (1949) Closed in merger with St. Anthony Parish. Records at St. Anthony, Lackawanna.

LAKE VIEW. *Our Lady of Perpetual Help* (1922) Name changed when merged with St. Vincent, North Evans, to form St. John Paul II Parish at the Lake View site. Records at St. John Paul II.

LANGFORD. *St. Martin* Name changed when merged with parishes in New Oregon and Collins Center to form Epiphany of Our Lord Parish at the Langford site. Records at Epiphany of Our Lord.

LE ROY. *St. Joseph* (1907) Merged with St. Peter Parish & St. Anthony, Lime Rock to form Our Lady of Mercy Parish. St. Joseph Church was an oratory of Our Lady of Mercy until its closure in 2017. Records at Our Lady of Mercy.

St. Peter Name changed when merged with St. Joseph, LeRoy & St. Anthony in Lime Rock to form Our Lady of Mercy Parish at St. Peter's site. Records at Our Lady of Mercy.

LIME ROCK. *St. Anthony* (1907) Closed when merged with St. Joseph & St. Peter parishes in LeRoy to form Our Lady of Mercy Parish. Records at Our Lady of Mercy.

LIMESTONE. *St. Patrick* (1875) Closed in merger with Our Lady of Peace Parish, Salamanca. Records at Our Lady of Peace.

LITTLE VALLEY. *St. Mary* (1874) Closed in merger with St. Mary, Cattaraugus. Records at St. Mary, Cattaraugus.

LOCKPORT. *St. Anthony* (1928) Closed in merger to form All Saints Parish, Lockport. Records at All Saints, Lockport.

St. Joseph (1912) Merged with St. Anthony & St. Patrick parishes to form All Saints Parish and became an oratory of All Saints. Records at All Saints.

St. Mary (1859) Merged with All Saints Parish, Lockport, at the All Saints Site. St. Mary Church is currently being leased. Records at All Saints.

St. Patrick Name changed when merged with St. Anthony & St. Joseph parishes to form All Saints Parish at the St. Patrick site. Records at All Saints.

LYNDONVILLE. *St. Joseph* (1962) Merged with St. Patrick, Barker, to form Our Lady of the Lake Parish, using both the Barker and Lyndonville sites. Records at Our Lady of the Lake, Barker.

MACHIAS. *Holy Family* (1948) Closed in merger with St. Philomena, Franklinville. Records at St. Philomena Franklinville.

MAYVILLE. *St. Mary* (1925) Merged with Our Lady of Lourdes, Bemus Point to form St. Mary of Lourdes Parish using both sites. Records at St. Mary of Lourdes, Mayville.

MEDINA. *St. Mary* Name changed when merged with Sacred Heart, Medina & St. Stephen, Middleport to form Holy Trinity Parish using the St. Mary & St. Stephen sites. Records at Holy Trinity, Medina.

Sacred Heart (1910) Closed when merged with St. Mary, Medina & St. Stephen, Middleport to become Holy Trinity Parish. Records at Holy Trinity, Medina.

MIDDLEPORT. *St. Stephen* (1854) Merged with St. Mary & Sacred Heart, Medina to form Holy Trinity Parish using the St. Mary & St. Stephen sites. Records at Holy Trinity, Medina.

NEWFANE. *St. Bridget* Name changed when merged with Our Lady of the Rosary, Wilson & St. Charles Borromeo, Olcott to form St. Brendan on the Lake Parish using the Newfane and Wilson sites. Records at St. Brendan on the Lake, Newfane.

NIAGARA FALLS. *Prince of Peace* Name changed when merged with St. Leo Parish to form St. Vincent de Paul Parish using both sites. Records at St. Vincent de Paul.

St. Charles Borromeo (1970) Closed in merger with St. John de LaSalle Parish. Records at St. John de LaSalle.

St. George (1915) Closed in merger to form Divine Mercy Parish. Records at Divine Mercy.

Holy Trinity (1902) Closed in merger to form Divine Mercy Parish. Records at Divine Mercy.

St. Joseph Name changed when merged with Our Lady of Mt. Carmel to form Holy Family of Jesus, Mary & Joseph Parish using both sites. Records at Holy Family of Jesus, Mary & Joseph, St. Joseph site.

St. Leo (1957) Merged with Prince of Peace to form St. Vincent de Paul Parish using both sites. Records at St. Vincent de Paul.

Our Lady of Lebanon (1914) Closed in merger to form Divine Mercy Parish. Records at Divine Mercy.

Our Lady of Mount Carmel (1949) Merged with St. Joseph Parish to form Holy Family of Jesus, Mary & Joseph Parish using both sites. Records at Holy Family of Jesus, Mary & Joseph, St. Joseph site.

Our Lady of the Rosary (1906) Closed in merger to form Divine Mercy Parish. Records at Divine Mercy.

Sacred Heart (1854) Closed when merged with St. Teresa Parish to form St. Raphael Parish. Records at St. Raphael.

St. Stanislaus Kostka Name changed when merged with four other parishes to form Divine Mercy Parish at the St. Stanislaus site. Records at Divine Mercy.

St. Teresa of the Infant Jesus Name changed when merged with Sacred Heart Parish to form St. Raphael Parish at the St. Teresa site. Records at St. Raphael.

NORTH EVANS. *St. Vincent* (1914) Closed in merger with Our Lady of Perpetual Help, Lakeview, to form St. John Paul II Parish at the Lakeview site. Records at St. John Paul II.

NORTH JAVA. *St. Nicholas* (1890) Closed in merger to form St. John Neumann Parish. Records at St. John Neumann, Strykersville.

NORTH TONAWANDA. *St. Albert the Great* Name changed when merged with Ascension Parish to form St. Jude the Apostle Parish. Records at St. Jude the Apostle.

Ascension (1887) Closed in merger to form St. Jude the Apostle Parish. Records at St. Jude the Apostle.

St. Joseph (1947) Closed in merger with Our Lady of Czestochowa Parish. Records at Our Lady of Czestochowa.

OAKFIELD. *St. Cecilia* (1906) Name changed when merged with Our Lady of Fatima, Elba, to form St. Padre Pio Parish. Both sites used. Records at St. Padre Pio, Oakfield.

OLCOTT. *St. Charles Borromeo* (1912) Merged with parishes in Wilson & Newfane to form St. Brendan on the Lake Parish. Summer oratory of St. Brendan on the Lake. Records at St. Brendan on the Lake, Newfane.

OLEAN. *Transfiguration* (1902) Merged with St. Helen, Hinsdale, and St. John, Olean, at St. John's site. Church sold to the Maronite Rite Catholics. Records at St. John, Olean.

PANAMA. *Our Lady of the Snows* (1946) Merged into Sacred Heart Parish, Lakewood but Panama site is still used. Records at Sacred Heart, Lakewood.

PAVILION. *St. Mary* (1865) Name changed when merged with Immaculate Conception, East Bethany to form Mary Immaculate, East Bethany. Both sites are used. Records at Mary Immaculate, East Bethany.

PERRY. *St. Joseph* Name changed when merged with St. Stanislaus, Perry, St. Mary, Silver Springs & St. Joseph, Bliss to form St. Isidore Parish using the St. Joseph, Perry & St. Mary, Silver Springs sites. Records at St. Isidore, Perry.

St. Stanislaus Kostka (1910) Closed in merger to form St. Isidore Parish. Records at St. Isidore, Perry.

PERRYSBURG. *St. Joan of Arc* (1950) Closed in merger with St. Joseph, Gowanda. Records at St. Joseph, Gowanda.

PORTAGEVILLE. *Assumption B.V.M.* (1849) Closed in merger with St. Mary, Silver Springs. Records at St. Isidore, Perry.

PORTVILLE. *Sacred Heart* (1909) Merged with St. Mary of the Angels, Olean and became an oratory. Records at St. Mary of the Angels, Olean.

RIPLEY. *St. Thomas More* (1941) Closed in merger to form St. Dominic Parish, Westfield. Records at St. Dominic, Westfield.

RUSHFORD. *St. Mark* (1948) Merged into St. Patrick Parish in Belfast and became a summer oratory of St. Patrick Parish. Records at St. Patrick, Belfast.

SALAMANCA. *Holy Cross* Name changed when merged with St. Patrick to form Our Lady of Peace Parish at the Holy Cross site. Records at Our Lady of Peace.

St. Patrick (1868) Closed in merger with Holy Cross to form Our Lady of Peace Parish. Records at Our Lady of Peace.

SCIO. *St. Joseph* (1844) Merged with two other parishes to form Holy Family of Jesus, Mary & Joseph Parish, Belmont. Oratory of Holy Family of Jesus, Mary & Joseph, Belmont. Records at Holy Family of Jesus, Mary & Joseph, Belmont.

SHELDON. *St. Cecilia* (1848) Merged with parishes in Strykersville, North Java & Java Center to form St. John Neumann Parish using the Sheldon & Strykersville sites. Records at St. John Neumann, Strykersville.

SHERIDAN. *St. John Bosco* (1949) Closed in merger with Our Lady of Mt. Carmel, Silver Creek. Records at Our Lady of Mt. Carmel.

SHERMAN. *St. Isaac Jogues* (1947) Merged with St. Matthias, French Creek to form Christ Our Hope Parish using both sites. Records at Christ Our Hope, French Creek.

SILVER SPRINGS. *St. Mary* (1892) Merged with parishes in Perry & Bliss to form St. Isidore Parish using both the Perry & Silver Springs sites. Records at St. Isidore, Perry.

SINCLAIRVILLE. *St. John the Evangelist* (1940) Closed in merger with Immaculate Conception, Cassadaga. Records at St. Anthony Parish, Fredonia.

SOUTH BYRON. *St. Michael* (1892) Closed in merger with St. Brigid, Bergen. Records at Our Lady of Mercy, LeRoy.

SOUTH DAYTON. *St. John Fisher* (1946) Closed in merger with St. Joseph Parish, Gowanda. Records at St. Joseph, Gowanda.

STRYKERSVILLE. *St. Mary, Queen of the Rosary* Name changed when merged with parishes in Sheldon, North Java & Java Center to form St. John Neumann Parish using the Sheldon & Strykersville sites. Records at St. John Neumann, Strykersville.

TONAWANDA. *St. Edmund* (1965) Closed as a worship site in merger with St. Christopher Parish, Tonawanda. Site used for outreach ministry. Records at St. Christopher Parish.

VANDALIA. *St. John the Baptist* (1900) Merged with St. Bonaventure Parish, Allegany & became an oratory of St. Bonaventure. The oratory closed in 2011. Records at St. Bonaventure, Allegany.

VARYSBURG. *St. Joseph* (1910) Merged with St. Vincent de Paul, Attica to form SS. Joachim & Anne Parish using both the Attica & Varysburg sites. Parish records at SS. Joachim & Anne Parish, Attica.

WEST SENECA. *St. Bonaventure* (1918) Closed in merger with St. William to form St. John XXIII Parish. Records at St. John XXIII Parish, West Seneca.

St. Catherine of Siena (1967) Closed in merger with Queen of Heaven Parish, West Seneca. Records at Queen of Heaven.

St. William Name changed when merged with St. Bonaventure Parish to form St. John XXIII Parish at St. William's site. Records at St. John XXIII Parish, West Seneca.

WESTFIELD. *St. James Major* Name changed when merged with churches in Brocton & Ripley to form St. Dominic Parish, Westfield. Records at St. Dominic, Westfield.

WHEATVILLE. *St. Patrick* (1882) Merged into St. Cecilia, Oakfield and became an oratory of St. Cecilia. The oratory closed in 2012. Records at St. Cecilia.

WHITESVILLE. *St. John of the Cross* (1949) Closed in merger with Immaculate Conception, Wellsville. Records at Immaculate Conception.

WILSON. *Our Lady of the Rosary* (1920) Merged with St. Brigid, Newfane & St. Charles Borromeo, Olcott to form St. Brendan on the Lake Parish using the Newfane & Wilson sites. Records at St. Brendan on the Lake, Newfane.

WOODLAWN. *Our Lady of Grace* (1940) Closed in merger to form Queen of Angels Parish, Lackawanna. Records at Queen of Angels.

YOUNGSTOWN. *St. Bernard* (1846) Merged into St. Peter, Lewiston, to form a single parish but using both church sites. Records at St. Peter, Lewiston.

RELIGIOUS INSTITUTES OF MEN REPRESENTED IN THE DIOCESE

For further details refer to the corresponding bracketed number in the Religious Institutes of Men or Women section.

[0200]—*Benedictine Monks*—O.S.B.
[0810]—*Brothers of Mercy*—F.M.M.A.
[0470]—*Capuchin Franciscan Friars*—O.F.M.Cap.
[0160]—*Clerics Regular of St. Paul*—C.R.S.P.
[1330]—*Congregation of the Mission* (Eastern Prov.)—C.M.
[]—*Conventual Franciscan Friars* (Zagreb, Croatia)—O.F.M.Conv.
[0480]—*Conventual Franciscans* (Our Lady of the Angels Province, USA)—O.F.M.Conv.
[0330]—*De Lasalle Brothers of the Christian Schools* (District of Eastern N. America.)—F.S.C.
[0450]—*Eudist Fathers* (Quebec)—C.J.M.
[0520]—*Franciscan Friars* (Holy Name Prov.)—O.F.M.
[]—*Franciscan Friars* (Krakow, Poland)—O.F.M.
[0690]—*Jesuit Fathers and Brothers* (U.S.A. N.E. Prov.)—S.J.
[0800]—*Maryknoll* (Buffalo)—M.M.
[0910]—*Oblates of Mary Immaculate* (U.S. Prov.)—O.M.I.
[0920]—*Oblates of St. Francis De Sales*—O.S.F.S.
[0970]—*Order of Our Lady of Mercy* (Le Roy)—O.deM.
[0430]—*Order of Preachers-Dominicans* (Prov. of St. Albert and Prov. of St. Joseph)—O.P.
[1010]—*Pauline Fathers*—O.S.P.P.E.
[0370]—*Society of St. Columban*—S.S.C.
[0990]—*Society of the Catholic Apostolate* (Christ the King Prov.)—S.A.C.

RELIGIOUS INSTITUTES OF WOMEN REPRESENTED IN THE DIOCESE

[]—*Congregation of Dominican Sisters of Lang Song* (Vietnam).
[0760]—*Daughters of Charity of St. Vincent de Paul*—D.C.
[]—*Daughters of Mary Mother of Mercy*—D.M.M.M.
[]—*Daughters of Our Lady of the Holy Rosary* (Vietnam)—F.M.S.R.
[0420]—*Discalced Carmelite Nuns*—O.C.D.
[1050]—*Dominican Contemplative Sisters*—O.P.
[1170]—*Felician Sisters*—C.S.S.F.
[1180]—*Franciscan Sisters of Allegany, New York*—O.S.F.
[]—*Franciscan Sisters of St. Joseph* (Kenya)—F.S.J.
[1470]—*Franciscan Sisters of St. Joseph*—F.S.S.J.
[1280]—*Franciscan Sisters of the Immaculate Conception*—O.S.F.
[1840]—*Grey Nuns of the Sacred Heart*—G.N.S.H.
[2575]—*Institute of the Sisters of Mercy of the Americas*—R.S.M.
[2830]—*Missionary Sisters of Our Lady of Mercy*—M.O.M.
[2880]—*Missionary Sisters of St. Columban*—S.S.C.
[3040]—*Oblate Sisters of Providence*—O.S.P.
[]—*Order of Missionaries of Charity of Vinh Diocese* (Vietnam).
[]—*Servants of Mary the Queen* (Zimbabwe)—A.M.R.
[3000]—*Sisters of Notre Dame de Namur* (Ohio Prov.)—S.N.D.deN.
[3950]—*Sisters of Saint Mary of Namur*—S.S.M.N.
[4090]—*Sisters of Social Service*—S.S.S.
[1630]—*Sisters of St. Francis of Penance and Christian Charity*—O.S.F.
[1805]—*Sisters of St. Francis of the Neumann Communities*—O.S.F.
[3830-06]—*Sisters of St. Joseph* (Buffalo, NY)—S.S.J.
[3830-14]—*Sisters of St. Joseph* (Rochester, NY)—S.S.J.
[]—*Sisters of the Sacred Heart of Jesus of Ragusa*—S.C.G.R.

NECROLOGY

† Skupien, Francis M., (Retired), Died Sep. 12, 2018
† Wendzikowski, Mecislaus S., (Retired), Died Jul. 3, 2018
† Dudek, Stanislaw, (Retired), Died Jun. 24, 2018
† Jesionowski, Richard A., (Retired), Died Oct. 27, 2018
† Kuhlmann, John L., (Retired), Died Dec. 21, 2018
† Moss, Robert D., (Retired), Died Mar. 29, 2018

Diocese of Burlington

(Dioecesis Burlingtonensis)

Most Reverend

CHRISTOPHER JAMES COYNE

Bishop of Burlington; ordained June 7, 1986; appointed Auxiliary Bishop of the Archdiocese of Indianapolis January 14, 2011; ordained and installed as Auxiliary Bishop of Indianapolis March 2, 2011; appointed Apostolic Administrator of Indianapolis September 21, 2011; resigned Apostolic Administrator December 3, 2012; appointed Bishop of Burlington December 22, 2014; installed January 29, 2015.

Chancery Office: 55 Joy Dr., South Burlington, VT 05403. Tel: 802-658-6110; Fax: 802-658-0436.

Web: www.vermontcatholic.org

ESTABLISHED JULY 29, 1853.

Square Miles 9,135.

Comprises the State of Vermont.

For legal titles of parishes and diocesan institutions, consult the Chancery Office.

STATISTICAL OVERVIEW

Personnel	
Bishop	1
Priests: Diocesan Active in Diocese	40
Priests: Diocesan Active Outside Diocese	2
Priests: Retired, Sick or Absent	28
Number of Diocesan Priests	70
Religious Priests in Diocese	35
Total Priests in Diocese	105
Extern Priests in Diocese	10
Ordinations:	
Diocesan Priests	1
Religious Priests	3
Transitional Deacons	2
Permanent Deacons in Diocese	39
Total Brothers	16
Total Sisters	90
Parishes	
Parishes	69
With Resident Pastor:	
Resident Diocesan Priests	37
Resident Religious Priests	13
Without Resident Pastor:	
Administered by Priests	19
Missions	24
Pastoral Centers	1
New Parishes Created	3
Closed Parishes	2
Professional Ministry Personnel:	
Lay Ministers	52
Welfare	
Homes for the Aged	4
Total Assisted	230
Special Centers for Social Services	2
Total Assisted	4,500
Educational	
Diocesan Students in Other Seminaries	10
Total Seminarians	10
Colleges and Universities	2
Total Students	2,500
High Schools, Diocesan and Parish	3
Total Students	500
Elementary Schools, Diocesan and Parish	8
Total Students	1,083
Elementary Schools, Private	2
Total Students	398
Catechesis/Religious Education:	
High School Students	700
Elementary Students	2,100
Total Students under Catholic Instruction	7,291
Teachers in the Diocese:	
Priests	6
Sisters	1
Lay Teachers	333
Vital Statistics	
Receptions into the Church:	
Infant Baptism Totals	460
Minor Baptism Totals	59
Received into Full Communion	55
First Communions	536
Confirmations	525
Marriages:	
Catholic	140
Interfaith	54
Total Marriages	194
Deaths	1,228
Total Catholic Population	116,000
Total Population	626,000

Former Bishops—Rt. Revs. LOUIS DE GOESBRIAND, D.D., ord. July 13, 1840; cons. Oct. 30, 1853; died Nov. 3, 1899; JOHN S. MICHAUD, D.D., ord. June 7, 1873; cons. Coadjutor Bishop with right of succession June 29, 1892; succeeded to Nov. 3, 1899; died Dec. 22, 1908; Most Revs. JOSEPH J. RICE, D.D., ord. Sept. 29, 1894; cons. April 14, 1910; died April 1, 1938; MATTHEW F. BRADY, D.D., ord. June 10, 1916; cons. Oct. 26, 1938; transferred to Manchester, NH, Nov. 11, 1944; died Sept. 20, 1959; EDWARD F. RYAN, D.D., ord. Aug. 10, 1905; cons. Jan. 3, 1945; died Nov. 3, 1956; ROBERT F. JOYCE, D.D., ord. May 26, 1923; cons. Auxiliary Bishop Oct. 28, 1954; installed Diocesan Bishop Feb. 26, 1957; retired Jan. 24, 1972; died Sept. 2, 1990; JOHN A. MARSHALL, D.D., ord. Dec. 19, 1953; cons. and installed Jan. 25, 1972; transferred to Springfield, MA, Dec. 27, 1991; died July 3, 1994; KENNETH A. ANGELL, D.D., ord. May 26, 1956; appt. Auxiliary Bishop of Providence Aug. 9, 1974; cons. Oct. 7, 1974; transferred to Bishop of Burlington Oct. 6, 1992; installed Nov. 9, 1992; retired Nov. 9, 2005; died Oct. 4, 2016.; SALVATORE R. MATANO, D.D., S.T.L., J.C.D., ord. Dec. 17, 1971; appt. Coadjutor Bishop of Burlington March 3, 2005; ord. April 19, 2005; succeeded Nov. 9, 2005; appt. Bishop of Rochester Nov. 6, 2013; installed Jan. 3, 2014.

Chancery Office—55 Joy Dr., South Burlington, 05403. Tel: 802-658-6110; Fax: 802-658-0436. Office Hours: Mon.-Fri. 9-12 & 1-5.

Vicar General and Moderator of the Curia—Rev. Msgr. JOHN J. MCDERMOTT, J.C.L., V.G.

Vicar for Clergy—Rev. Msgr. PETER A. ROUTHIER.

Finance Office—MR. MARTIN A. HOAK, Diocesan Finance Officer & Chancellor, 55 Joy Dr., South Burlington, 05403. Tel: 802-658-6110; Fax: 802-658-6113.

Office of the Tribunal—55 Joy Dr., South Burlington, 05403. Tel: 802-658-6110; Fax: 802-658-0436.

Judicial Vicar—Rev. LUKE P. AUSTIN, J.D., J.C.L.

Case Director—MRS. SUSAN WING.

Judges—Revs. DANIEL J. JORDAN, J.C.L.; JOHN MAHONEY JR., J.C.L.; LUKE P. AUSTIN, J.D., J.C.L.

Promoter of Justice—Rev. Msgr. JOHN J. MCDERMOTT, J.C.L.

Defenders of the Bond—Revs. ROGER L. CHARBONNEAU; JOHN G. FELTZ; THOMAS V. MATTISON, J.C.L.; Rev. Msgr. JOHN J. MCDERMOTT, J.C.L.

Advocate—Rev. Msgr. PETER A. ROUTHIER.

Notaries—Revs. ROGER L. CHARBONNEAU; JOHN G. FELTZ; MRS. SUSAN WING.

Diocesan Administrative Board—Rev. Msgrs. JOHN J. MCDERMOTT, J.C.L.; PETER A. ROUTHIER; MRS. RITA M. RIVERS; MR. ROBERT A. ROY; MR. SCOTT BEAUDIN; Mr. MICHAEL TOMCZAK; MR. JAMES BRZOSKA; MR. MARTIN A. HOAK, Finance Officer & D.A.B. Consultant.

Diocesan Consultors—Rev. Msgrs. JOHN J. MCDERMOTT, J.C.L.; PETER A. ROUTHIER; Revs. JULIAN I. ASUCAN; DWIGHT H. BAKER; DAVID G. CRAY, S.S.E.; WILLIAM R. BEAUDIN; YVON J. ROYER.

Deans—Rev. Msgrs. RICHARD G. LAVALLEY; BERNARD W. BOURGEOIS, M.A., M.Div.; Revs. PETER P. O'LEARY; YVON J. ROYER; JUSTIN J. BAKER; THOMAS V. MATTISON, J.C.L.; MAURICE J. ROY; PATRICK J. FORMAN; TIMOTHY P. NAPLES.

Canon 1742 Panel of Pastors—Revs. WILLIAM R. BEAUDIN; CHARLES R. DANIELSON; Rev. Msgr. MICHAEL W. DEFORGE; Revs. BERNARD E. GAUDREAU; JEROME MERCURE; MAURICE J. ROY; YVON J. ROYER.

Diocesan Offices and Directors

Development Office—55 Joy Dr., South Burlington, 05403. Tel: 802-658-6110. MRS. ELLEN KANE, Exec. Dir.

The Blue Army (World Apostolate of Fatima)—Rev. JULIAN I. ASUCAN.

Catholic Committee on Scouting—NORBERT VOGEL, Treas., 205 Biscayne Heights, Colchester, 05446. Tel: 802-862-1756; Email: norb_vogl@hotmail.com; DAVID ELY, Chm., 175 Elmwood Ave., Burlington, 05401. Tel: 802-862-5109.

Building Commission—Chancery Office: 55 Joy Dr., South Burlington, 05403. Tel: 802-658-6110.

Vermont Catholic Charities, Inc.—MS. MARY BETH PINARD, Exec. Dir., Central Office, 55 Joy Dr., South Burlington, 05403. Tel: 802-658-6110; Fax: 802-860-0451. Rutland Office, 24 Center St., Rutland, 05701. Tel: 802-773-3379; Fax: 802-773-7550.

Catholic Campaign for Human Development—55 Joy Dr., South Burlington, 05403. Tel: 802-658-6110; Fax: 802-860-0451.

Catholic Daughters of The Americas—Rev. PATRICK J. FORMAN, Chap., 160 Hinesburg Rd., South Burlington, 05403.

Catholic Relief Services—55 Joy Dr., South Burlington, 05403. Tel: 802-658-6110; Fax: 802-860-0451.

Catholic Golden Age—VACANT.

Censor Librorum—Revs. RICHARD L. VANDERWEEL, S.S.E.; LANCE W. HARLOW, 55 Joy Dr., South Burlington, 05403. Tel: 802-658-6110.

Charismatic Renewal—Rev. LANCE W. HARLOW, Mailing Address: Immaculate Heart of Mary Parish, P.O. Box 1047, Williston, 05495. Tel: 802-878-4513; Deacon DANIEL PUDVAH, 12 Edgewood Ave., Barre, 05641. Tel: 802-479-9407.

Superintendent of Catholic Schools—Office of Catholic Schools: 55 Joy Dr., South Burlington, 05403.

Tel: 802-658-6110. MRS. LISA LAMONDIE-GRENVILLE.

Diocesan Archives—Rev. Msgr. JOHN J. MCDERMOTT, J.C.L.; KATHLEEN MESSIER, Asst. Archivist, 55 Joy Dr., South Burlington, 05403. Tel: 802-658-6110.

Media Relations—MRS. ELLEN KANE, 55 Joy Dr., South Burlington, 05403. Tel: 802-658-6110.

Daughters of Isabella—Rev. YVON J. ROYER, Chap., 85 S. Maple St., Vergennes, 05491-0324. Tel: 802-877-2367.

Diocesan Director of Catholic Cemeteries—MR. ROBERT E. BROWN, 55 Joy Dr., South Burlington, 05403. Tel: 802-658-6110.

Diocesan Finance Council—Ex Officio Member: Rev. Msgr. JOHN J. MCDERMOTT, J.C.L. Board Members: Rev. Msgr. PETER A. ROUTHIER; MAYNARD MCLAUGHLIN; Rev. BRIAN J. CUMMINGS, S.S.E.; MR. J. PAUL GIULIANI, Esq.; MR. MICHAEL HENRY. Consultant: MR. MARTIN A. HOAK, Finance Officer.

Diocesan Director of Facilities and Insurance—MR. PETER WELLS, 55 Joy Dr., South Burlington, 05403. Tel: 802-658-6110.

Diocesan Director of Human Resources—55 Joy Dr., South Burlington, 05403. Tel: 802-658-6110. MRS. MARY FOSTER.

Ecumenical Commission—Rev. Msgr. PETER A. ROUTHIER; Rev. THOMAS V. MATTISON, J.C.L.

Liturgical Commission—55 Joy Dr., South Burlington, 05403. Tel: 802-658-6110. Mr. JOSHUA PERRY.

House of Discernment—Rev. DWIGHT H. BAKER, The Catholic Center at UVM, 390 S. Prospect St., Redstone Campus, Burlington, 05401. Tel: 802-862-8403; Fax: 802-865-9480.

Knights of Columbus—Holy Trinity Parish, 85 St. Paul Ln., Barton, 05822. Rev. TIMOTHY P. NAPLES.

Marriage Encounter, Vermont—JOHN FORCIER; DIANE FORCIER, 15 Mariner Heights, Colchester, 05446. Tel: 802-657-3083.

Office of Continuing Education for Clergy—Rev. Msgr. PETER A. ROUTHIER, Mailing Address: St. Augustine Parish, 16 Barre St., Montpelier, 05602. Tel: 802-223-5285.

Office of Safe Environment Programs—MR. WILLIAM MCSALIS, Mgr. Programs.

The Review Board—Rev. Msgr. JOHN J. MCDERMOTT, J.C.L.; GEORGE ASHLINE, Ph.D.; THERESE M. CORSONES, J.D., Chm.; MINDY PARISI, R.N.; DALE D. STAFFORD, M.D.; MARY FRAN STAFFORD; Rev. CHRISTOPHER MICALE. Ex Officio/Consultant: MR. WILLIAM MCSALIS.

Victim's Assistance Coordinator—MS. SHEILA CONROY.

National Shrine of the Immaculate Conception, Washington—VACANT.

Office of Youth and Young Adult Ministry—MR. WILLIAM GAVIN, Dir., 55 Joy Dr., South Burlington, 05403. Tel: 802-658-6110.

Office of Catechesis and Evangelization—Deacon PHIL LAWSON, Dir., 55 Joy Dr., South Burlington, 05403. Tel: 802-658-6110.

Office of Diocesan Pastoral Planning—Rev. Msgr. JOHN J. MCDERMOTT, J.C.L., Dir., 55 Joy Dr., South Burlington, 05403. Tel: 802-658-6110.

Office of Permanent Diaconate Ministry—Deacon PETER GUMMERE, 55 Joy Dr., South Burlington, 05403. Tel: 802-658-6110.

Magazine—Vermont Catholic *Office: 55 Joy Dr., South Burlington, 05403*. Tel: 802-658-6110; Fax: 802-658-3866.

Priests' Benefit Fund—55 Joy Dr., South Burlington, 05403. Tel: 802-658-6110. Rev. WILLIAM R. BEAUDIN, Chm.

Prison Ministry—Deacon GERALD SCILLA, 55 Joy Dr., South Burlington, 05403. Tel: 802-658-6110.

Propagation of the FaithRev. ROGER L. CHARBONNEAU, Chancery Office: 55 Joy Dr., South Burlington, 05403. Tel: 802-658-6110.

Vermont Catholic Community Foundation—55 Joy Dr., South Burlington, 05403.
Tel: 802-658-6110, Ext. 1226; Email: ekane@vermontcatholic.org. MRS. ELLEN KANE, Dir.

Vermont Cursillo—Rev. DWIGHT H. BAKER, Spiritual Dir., 109 South St., Waterbury, 05676.

Vocations and Seminarians—Rev. JON-DANIEL SCHNOBRICH, Dir., 55 Joy Dr., South Burlington, 05403. Tel: 802-658-6110.

CLERGY, PARISHES, MISSIONS AND PAROCHIAL SCHOOLS

CITY OF BURLINGTON

(CHITTENDEN COUNTY)

1—CATHEDRAL OF THE IMMACULATE CONCEPTION (1830) Closed. For inquiries for parish records contact the chancery.

2—THE CATHEDRAL OF ST. JOSEPH (1850) [CEM]
113 Elmwood Ave., Burlington, 05401.
Tel: 802-658-4333; Email: sjvt@comcast.net; Web: www.catholiccathedralsofburlington. 29 Allen St., Burlington, 05401. Rev. Lance W. Harlow, Rector.
Catechesis Religious Program—Tel: 802-658-4333. Mrs. Dorothy Barewicz, D.R.E. Students 38.

3—CHRIST THE KING-ST. ANTHONY (2007) Parish includes Christ the King, Burlington & St. Anthony, Burlington.
Mailing Address: 305 Flynn Ave., Burlington, 05401.
Tel: 802-862-5784; Web: www.christandanthony.com. Rev. Msgr. John J. McDermott, J.C.L., V.G.; Rev. Joseph Sanderson.
Catechesis Religious Program—Email: mcade@vermontcatholic.org. Meghan Cade, D.R.E. Students 54.

4—ST. MARK'S (1940)
1251 North Ave., Burlington, 05408.
Tel: 802-864-7686; Fax: 802-651-9391; Email: stmarksvt@gmail.com; Web: www.stmarksvt.com. Revs. Dallas T. St. Peter, Admin.; Brian J. O'Donnell, In Res.; Timothy Sullivan, In Res.; Deacon Timothy Gibbo.
Catechesis Religious Program—Simeon Lewis, Youth Min. Students 42.

OUTSIDE THE CITY OF BURLINGTON

ALBURGH, GRAND ISLE CO.

1—OUR LADY OF THE LAKE
501 Rte. 2, South Hero, 05486. Rev. Rogelio Organiza, Admin.
Missions—St. Joseph—Main St., Isle La Motte, Grand Isle Co.
St. Joseph, Rte 2, Grand Isle, Grand Isle Co.

2—ST. AMADEUS (1886) [CEM 2] Merged with St. Rose of Lima to form Our Lady of the Lake.

BARRE, WASHINGTON CO., ST. MONICA (1892)
79 Summer St., Barre, 05641. Tel: 802-479-3253; Email: stmonicarec@aol.com. Revs. Peter P. O'Leary; Avelino Vale, Parochial Vicar; Deacons David Bisson; Daniel Pudvah.
School—St. Monica - St. Michael School, (Grades PreSchool-8), Brenda Buzzell, Prin.; Louise Keane, Librarian.
Catechesis Religious Program—Tel: 802-476-4020. Teresa Hawes, D.R.E. Students 75.

BARTON, ORLEANS CO., MOST HOLY TRINITY (2003) [CEM 4] Parish includes St. Paul, Barton, St. Theresa, Orleans & St. John Vianney, Irasburg.
85 St. Paul Ln., Barton, 05822. Tel: 802-525-3711; Email: TrinityParish@ymail.com; Web: www.mostholytrinityparishvt.com. Rev. Timothy P. Naples.
School—St. Paul School, (Grades PreK-8), Most Holy Trinity Parish, 54 Eastern Ave., Barton, 05822. Mrs. Joanne Beloin, Prin. Lay Teachers 13; Students 51; Clergy / Religious Teachers 2.
Catechesis Religious Program—Mrs. Theresa McAvinney, Family Formation Dir. Students 21.

BELLOWS FALLS, WINDHAM CO., ST. CHARLES (1871) [CEM]
31 Cherry Hill St., Bellows Falls, 05101.
Tel: 802-463-3128; Fax: 802-463-8179; Email: stcharlesrectory@comcast.net; Web: www.stcharleschurchvt.org. Rev. Maria Lazar, H.G.N., Admin.
Catechesis Religious Program—Julie Sines, D.R.E. Students 16.

BENNINGTON, BENNINGTON CO., SACRED HEART ST. FRANCIS DE SALES (1995)
238 Main St., Bennington, 05201. Tel: 802-442-3141; Fax: 802-442-3142; Email: benncath@comcast.net; Web: www.sacredheartsaintfrancis.com. Revs. Robert A. Wiseman, C.S.C.; Hugh Cleary, C.S.C., Parochial Vicar.
School—The School of Sacred Heart St. Francis de Sales, (Grades PreK-8), 307 School St., Bennington, 05201. Tel: 802-442-2446; Fax: 802-442-3584; Email: estesdb@comcast.net. Mr. David B. Estes, Prin.; Marcia Hendery, Librarian; Kathy Murphy, Librarian. Lay Teachers 10; Students 155.

BETHEL, WINDSOR CO., OUR LADY OF THE VALLEY PARISH (2010) Parish includes: St. Anthony, Bethel & St. Elizabeth, Rochester.
221 Church St., Bethel, 05032. Tel: 802-234-9916; Email: info@ourladyvalley.comcastbiz.net. P.O. Box 221, Bethel, 05032. Rev. Andrzej Bednarowicz, Admin.
Res.: 237 Church St., Bethel, 05032.
Catechesis Religious Program—Elijah LaChance, D.R.E. Students 7.

BRADFORD, ORANGE CO., OUR LADY OF PERPETUAL HELP (1945)
113 Upper Plain, Bradford, 05033. Tel: 802-222-5268; Email: olph14@gmail.com; Web: uppervalleyparishes.org. Rev. Rod Oliver Saligan, Admin.
Catechesis Religious Program—Students 46.
Missions—St. Francis of Assisi—Norwich, Windsor Co.
St. Eugene, Wells River, Orange Co.
Our Lady of Light, South Strafford, Orange Co.

BRANDON, RUTLAND CO., OUR LADY OF GOOD HELP (ST. MARY) (1867) [CEM 2]
38 Carver St., Brandon, 05733. Tel: 802-247-6351; Email: olghcc@comcast.net. Rev. Maurice Moreau.
Catechesis Religious Program—Students 32.
Mission—St. Agnes, Leicester, Addison Co.

BRATTLEBORO, WINDHAM CO., ST. MICHAEL (1855) [CEM]
47 Walnut St., Brattleboro, 05301. Tel: 802-257-5101; Email: parish@stmichaelvt.com; Web: stmichaelvt.com. Rev. Justin J. Baker.
School—St. Michael School, (Grades PreK-12), Email: lindsayoneil@smsvt.info; Web: saintmichaelschoolvt.org. Mrs. Elaine Beam, Prin.
Catechesis Religious Program—Students 28.

BRISTOL, ADDISON CO., ST. AMBROSE (1893) [CEM]
11 School St., Bristol, 05443. Tel: 802-453-2488; Email: stambros@comcast.net. Rev. Yvon J. Royer.
Catechesis Religious Program—Students 29.

CAMBRIDGE, LAMOILLE CO., ST. MARY (1914)
312 N. Main St., Cambridge, 05444.
Tel: 802-644-5073; Fax: 802-644-2546; Email: stmarys@pshift.com; Web: stmarysvt.com. P.O. Box 129, Cambridge, 05444. Rev. Christopher Micale, Admin.
Catechesis Religious Program—Students 18.

CASTLETON, RUTLAND CO., ST. JOHN THE BAPTIST (1899)
P.O. Box 128, Castleton, 05735. Tel: 802-468-5706;
Tel: 802-265-3135; Email: mdstjohn@yahoo.com. Revs. Antony Pittappilly, S.D.V.; Vincent Odoemenam, S.D.V.
Res.: 45 North Rd., Castleton, 05735.
Catechesis Religious Program—Tel: 802-468-2155. Luis Bauzo, D.R.E. Students 15.

CHARLOTTE, CHITTENDEN CO., OUR LADY OF MOUNT CARMEL (1858) [CEM]
2894 Spear St., Charlotte, 05445. Tel: 802-425-2253; Email: carmel@gmavt.net; Web: www.olmcvt.org. P.O. Box 158, Charlotte, 05445. Rev. David G. Cray, S.S.E.
Catechesis Religious Program—Marie Cookson, D.R.E. Students 73.

CHESTER, WINDSOR CO., ST. JOSEPH (1946)
10 Pleasant St., Springfield, 05156.
Tel: 802-885-3400; Email: stmarys@vermontel.net. Rev. James E. Zuccaro.
Res.: 96 S. Main St., P.O. Box 1129, Chester, 05143.
Catechesis Religious Program—Students 16.
Station—St. Joseph Chapel, Londonderry.

COLCHESTER, CHITTENDEN CO.

1—HOLY CROSS (1950) [CEM]
416 Church Rd., Colchester, 05446.
Tel: 802-863-3002; Email: parishoffice@holycrossvt.org. Rev. William R. Beaudin.
Catechesis Religious Program—Dorine Boucher, D.R.E. Students 59.

2—OUR LADY OF GRACE (1959)
800 Main St., Colchester, 05446. Tel: 802-878-5987; Email: ologvtparish@comcast.net. Rev. William R. Beaudin.
Catechesis Religious Program—Veronica Hershberger, Pastoral Min./Coord. Students 81.

ENOSBURG FALLS, FRANKLIN CO., ST. JOHN THE BAPTIST (1874) [CEM]
222 Missisquoi St., Enosburg Falls, 05450.
Tel: 802-933-4464; Fax: 802-933-3164; Email: stjohnvt@comcast.net; Web: stjohnbaptistvt.com. P.O. Box 563, Enosburg Falls, 05450. Revs. Stanley Deresienski, S.S.E., Admin.; Soosai Raj, H.G.N., Parochial Vicar.
Catechesis Religious Program—Tel: 802-524-9606. Laurie Oliver, D.R.E. Students 57.

ESSEX CENTER, CHITTENDEN CO., ST. PIUS X (1957)
20 Jericho Rd., Essex Junction, 05452-2707.
Tel: 802-878-5997; Email: saintpiusx@comcast.net; Web: saintpiusx.net. Rev. Charles H. Ranges, S.S.E.; Deacon Gerald Scilla.
Catechesis Religious Program—Tel: 802-878-1182. Andrew Coulter, D.R.E. Students 154.

ESSEX JUNCTION, CHITTENDEN CO., HOLY FAMILY-ST. LAWRENCE (2006) [CEM] Parish includes Holy Family, Essex Junction & St. Lawrence, Essex Junction.
4 Prospect St., Essex Junction, 05452.
Tel: 802-878-5331; Email: holyfamily2@comcast.net; Web: hfslvt.org. 20 Jericho Rd., Essex Junction, 05452. Rev. Charles H. Ranges, S.S.E.
Catechesis Religious Program—158 West Ave., Essex

Junction, 05452. Tel: 802-878-5331, Ext. 202; Email: john.mcmahon@hfslvt.org. Mr. John McMahon, D.R.E. Students 232.

FAIRFAX, FRANKLIN CO., ST. LUKE (1943) [CEM]
17 Huntville Rd., Fairfax, 05454-0007.
Tel: 802-849-6205; Email: stluke17@myfairpoint.net. P.O. Box 7, Fairfax, 05454-0007. Rev. Henry P. Furman; Deacons Stephen J. Ratte; Dennis Moore.
Catechesis Religious Program—Students 70.
Mission—Ascension, Georgia, Franklin Co.

FAIRFIELD, FRANKLIN CO., ST. PATRICK (1858) [CEM]
116 Church Rd., Fairfield, 05455. Tel: 802-827-3203; Email: stpats@myfairpoint.net. P.O. Box 18, Fairfield, 05455. Rev. William P. Giroux.
Catechesis Religious Program—Students 69.
Mission—St. Anthony-St. George, East Fairfield, Franklin Co.

FAIR HAVEN, RUTLAND CO., OUR LADY OF SEVEN DOLORS (1866) [CEM]
10 Washington St., Fair Haven, 05743.
Tel: 802-265-3135; Tel: 802-468-5706. P.O. Box 128, Castleton, 05735. Revs. Vincent Odoemenam, S.D.V.; Antony Pittappilly, S.D.V.
Catechesis Religious Program—Tel: 802-265-8045. Rose Marie Doran, D.R.E. Students 34.
Missions—St. Matthew of Avalon—West Castleton, Rutland Co.
St. Frances Cabrini, West Pawlet, Rutland Co. 05775.

GRANITEVILLE, WASHINGTON CO., ST. SYLVESTER (1895) [CEM]
217 Church Hill Rd., Graniteville, 05654.
Tel: 802-476-3913; Email: stsylvester@myfairpoint.net. Revs. Peter P. O'Leary; Romanus Igweonu.
Catechesis Religious Program—Mrs. Kathleen Grange, D.R.E. Students 24.
Mission—St. Cecilia & St. Frances Cabrini, East Barre, Washington Co.

HARDWICK, CALEDONIA CO., MARY QUEEN OF ALL SAINTS PARISH (1902) [CEM 2] Parish includes St. Norbert, Hardwick; St. Michael, Greensboro Bend & Our Lady of Fatima, Craftsbury.
193 S. Main St., Hardwick, 05843. Tel: 802-472-5544 ; Email: mary_queenofallsaints@comcast.net. P.O. Box 496, Hardwick, 05843. Rev. Msgr. Peter A. Routhier, Admin.
Catechesis Religious Program—Gabrielle Hopkins, D.R.E. Students 12.

HINESBURG, CHITTENDEN CO., ST. JUDE THE APOSTLE (1946)
10759 Rte. 116, Hinesburg, 05461-0069.
Tel: 802-482-2290; Email: StJude@gmavt.com. P.O. Box 69, Hinesburg, 05461-0069. Rev. David G. Cray, S.S.E.
Catechesis Religious Program—Marie Cookson, D.R.E. Students 80.

LUDLOW, WINDSOR CO., ANNUNCIATION OF THE BLESSED VIRGIN MARY (1885)
7 Depot St., Ludlow, 05149. Tel: 802-228-3451; Email: abvludlow@comcast.net. Rev. Thomas L. Mosher.
Catechesis Religious Program—Eileen Dunseith, D.R.E. Students 11.
Mission—Holy Name of Mary, Proctorsville, Windsor Co.

MANCHESTER CENTER, BENNINGTON CO., CHRIST OUR SAVIOR PARISH (1896)
398 Bonnet St., Manchester Center, 05255.
Tel: 802-362-1380, Ext. 1; Email: christosparish@comcast.net; Web: christoursaviorvt.com. Rev. Thomas V. Mattison, J.C.L.
Catechesis Religious Program—Students 83.

MIDDLEBURY, ADDISON CO., ASSUMPTION OF THE BLESSED VIRGIN MARY (1855) [CEM]
326 College St., Middlebury, 05753.
Tel: 802-388-2943; Email: stmarys11@comcast.net; Web: www.churchoftheassumptionvt.org. 73 Weybridge St., Middlebury, 05753. Rev. Luke P. Austin, J.D., J.C.L.
Catechesis Religious Program—Students 125.
Mission—St. Bernadette/St. Genevieve, Shoreham, Addison Co.

MIDDLETOWN SPRINGS, RUTLAND CO., ST. ANNE (1963)
11 Pleasant View Rd., Middletown Springs, 05757.
Tel: 802-287-5703; Email: straphaelparish@myfairpoint.net. 21 E. Main St., Poultney, 05764. Rev. Louduraja Simeone, H.G.N.
Catechesis Religious Program— (Combined with St. Raphael's, Poultney).

MILTON, CHITTENDEN CO., ST. ANN (1866) [CEM]
41 Main St., Milton, 05468. Tel: 802-893-2487;
Tel: 802-893-3897; Fax: 802-893-3701; Email: stannmilt@comcast.net; Email: stann.reled@comcast.net; Web: stannmilton.com. P.O. Box 1, Milton, 05468. Rev. John G. Feltz; Deacon Paul Garrow.
Catechesis Religious Program—Students 103.

MONTPELIER, WASHINGTON CO., ST. AUGUSTINE (1850) [CEM]
16 Barre St., Montpelier, 05602. Tel: 802-223-5285; Email: saintaugustineoffice@comcast.net. Rev. Julian I. Asucan; Deacons Regis E. Cummings; Gesualdo Schneider.
Catechesis Religious Program—Students 47.
Mission—North American Martyrs (1963) Marshfield, Washington Co.

MORRISVILLE, LAMOILLE CO., MOST HOLY NAME OF JESUS PARISH (2008) [CEM]
301 Brooklyn St., Morrisville, 05661.
Tel: 802-888-3318; Email: holysaints@comcast.net. Rev. Francis R. Prive; Deacon Thomas F. Cooney. Parish includes Holy Cross, Morrisville, St. Gabriel, St. Teresa, Hyde Park & St. John the Apostle, Johnson.
Catechesis Religious Program—Mary Elfer, D.R.E. Students 44.

NEWPORT, ORLEANS CO., MATER DEI
191 Clermont Ter., Newport, 05855.
Tel: 802-334-5066; Email: office@materdeivermont.com. Revs. Rijo Johnson; Thomas Kuttikkatt; Denniskingsley Nwagwu, S.D.V.
Child Care—St. Edward's Pre-School,
Tel: 802-873-4570; Fax: 802-334-8877. Theresa Forbes, Dir. Lay Teachers 10; Students 20.
Catechesis Religious Program—Ann Gonyaw, Youth Min. & D.R.E. Students 134.

NORTH BENNINGTON, BENNINGTON CO., ST. JOHN THE BAPTIST (1885) [CEM]
3-5 Houghton St., North Bennington, 05257.
Tel: 802-447-7504. P.O. Box 219, North Bennington, 05257-0219. Revs. Robert A. Wiseman, C.S.C.; Hugh Cleary, C.S.C., Parochial Vicar; Deacon David O'Brien.
Catechesis Religious Program—Luisa B. Millington, D.R.E. Students 43.

NORTH TROY, ORLEANS CO., ST. VINCENT DE PAUL (1939) [CEM]
18 N. Pleasant St., North Troy, 05859.
Tel: 802-744-4066; Tel: 802-988-2608; Email: SacredVincentIgnatiusVermont@gmail.com. P.O. Box 109, Troy, 05868. Rev. Timothy P. Naples.

NORTHFIELD, WASHINGTON CO., ST. JOHN THE EVANGELIST (1865) [CEM]
206 Vine St., Northfield, 05663. Tel: 802-485-8313; Email: stjohned2@gmail.com; Web: www.sjsevt.org. Rev. James C. Dodson.
Catechesis Religious Program—Students 41.
Mission—St. Edward, Williamstown, Orange Co.

ORWELL, ADDISON CO., ST. PAUL (1886) [CEM]
73 Church Rd., Orwell, 05760. Tel: 802-468-5706; Email: mdstjohn@yahoo.com. Revs. Antony Pittappilly, S.D.V.; Vincent Odoemenam, S.D.V.
Catechesis Religious Program—Tel: 802-948-2408. Students 15.

PITTSFORD, RUTLAND CO., ST. ALPHONSUS LIGUORI (1893) [CEM]
2918 U.S. Rte. 7, Pittsford, 05763-9499.
Tel: 802-483-2301; Email: stalphonsus5@myfairpoint.net. Rev. Maurice Moreau.
Catechesis Religious Program—Sarah Carrara. Students 36.

POULTNEY, RUTLAND CO., ST. RAPHAEL (1884) [CEM]
21 E. Main St., Poultney, 05764-1107.
Tel: 802-287-5703; Email: straphaelparish@myfairpoint.net. Rev. Lourduraja Simeone, H.G.N.
Catechesis Religious Program—Students 25.

PROCTOR, RUTLAND CO., ST. DOMINIC (1888) [CEM]
45 South St., Proctor, 05765. 28 Church St., West Rutland, 05777. Rev. Avelino Vale, Admin.
Catechesis Religious Program—Laura Knowles, D.R.E. Students 24.

PUTNEY, WINDHAM CO., OUR LADY OF MERCY (1931)
52 Old Depot Rd., Putney, 05346. Tel: 802-387-5861; Email: olmercy@myfairpoint.net; Web: ourladyofmercyandthewestrivermissions.com. P.O. Box 246, Putney, 05346. Revs. Frederick E. McLachlan, S.S.E.; Francis X. McMahon, S.S.E., Pastor Emeritus, (Retired); Deacons Jerome Driscoll; Richard Anderberg.
Catechesis Religious Program—Students 13.
Missions—St. Edmund of Canterbury—Saxtons River, Windham Co.
Chapel of the Snows, Stratton Mountain, Windham Co.
Our Lady of the Valley, Townshend, Windham Co.

RANDOLPH, ORANGE CO., OUR LADY OF THE ANGELS (2008)
P.O. Box 428, Randolph, 05060. Tel: 802-728-5251; Email: parish@ourladyvt.org. Rev. John M. Milanese.
Res.: 43 Hebard Hill Rd., P.O. Box 428, Randolph, 05060.
Catechesis Religious Program—Students 4.

READSBORO, BENNINGTON CO., ST. JOACHIM (1895)
342 Tunnel St., Readsboro, 05350. Tel: 802-464-7329 ; Email: olfwil@gmail.com; Web: ourladyoffatimavt.org. P.O. Box 188, Wilmington, 05363. Rev. Ilayaraja Amaladass, H.G.N., Admin.
Catechesis Religious Program—Students 6.
Mission—St. John Bosco, Stamford, Bennington Co.

RICHFORD, FRANKLIN CO., ALL SAINTS aka All Saints Parish Charitable Trust (1899) [CEM]
152 Main St., Richford, 05476. Tel: 802-848-7741; Email: info@allsaintsrichford.org; Web: www.allsaintsrichford.org. Revs. Stanley Deresienski, S.S.E.; Soosai Raj, H.G.N., Parochial Vicar; Deacon Clifford Chagnon.
Catechesis Religious Program—Kelly Lagasse, D.R.E. Students 25.
Missions—Our Lady of Lourdes—East Berkshire, Franklin Co.
St. Isidore, Montgomery Center, Franklin Co.

RICHMOND, CHITTENDEN CO., OUR LADY OF THE HOLY ROSARY (1860) [CEM 2]
64 W. Main St., Richmond, 05477. Tel: 802-434-2521; Email: olhr@gmavt.net; Web: olhr-richmond.org. P.O. Box 243, Richmond, 05477. Rev. Daniel J. Jordan, J.C.L.
Catechesis Religious Program—Jill Danilich, D.R.E. Students 49.

RUTLAND, RUTLAND CO.
1—CHRIST THE KING (1907)
66 S. Main St., Rutland, 05701. Tel: 802-773-6820; Email: rwcatholic@gmail.com; Web: www.rwcatholic.org. Rev. Msgr. Bernard W. Bourgeois, M.A., M.Div.; Rev. Matthew Rensch.
Catechesis Religious Program—Email: scarpenter@cksrutland.org. Ms. Sandra Carpenter, D.R.E. Students 131.

2—IMMACULATE HEART OF MARY (1869) [CEM]
18 Lincoln Ave., Rutland, 05701. Tel: 802-773-6820; Email: rwcatholic@gmail.com; Web: www.rwcatholic.org. Christ the King: 66 S. Main St., Rutland, 05701. Rev. Msgr. Bernard W. Bourgeois, M.A., M.Div.; Rev. Matthew Rensch.

3—ST. PETER (1855) [CEM]
134 Convent Ave., Rutland, 05701. Tel: 802-775-1994 ; Email: stpeterrutland@comcast.net. Rev. Thomas R. Houle, O.F.M.Cap.
Catechesis Religious Program—

ST. ALBANS, FRANKLIN CO.
1—HOLY ANGELS (1872) [CEM]
246 Lake St., St. Albans, 05478. Tel: 802-524-2585; Email: holyangelstalbans@msn.com; Web: www.holyangelsvt.org. Revs. Maurice J. Roy; Joseph Ikegbunam; Deacons Duane Langlois; Gabriel Liegy.
Catechesis Religious Program—Students 217.

2—IMMACULATE CONCEPTION (1847) [CEM]
45 Fairfield St., St. Albans, 05478. Tel: 802-524-2585 ; Email: holyangelstalbans@msn.com. 246 Lake St., St. Albans, 05478. Revs. Maurice J. Roy, Admin.; Joseph Ikegbunam, Assoc. Pastor; Deacon Gabriel Gagne.
Catechesis Religious Program—Tel: 802-524-9416. Margaret Rensch, C.R.E. (PreK-8). Students 88.

SAINT JOHNSBURY, CALEDONIA CO., CORPUS CHRISTI PARISH
49 Winter St., St. Johnsbury, 05819.
Tel: 802-748-8129; Email: stjchurch@charter.net; Web: nekcatholic.com. Revs. Karl A. Hahr; Curtis Miller; Deacons Peter Gummere, 55 Joy Dr., 05403. Tel: 802-658-6110; David Baker.
Catechesis Religious Program—506 Summer St., St. Johnsbury, 05819. Tel: 802-748-9256 (PreK-8); Email: stjohnsk8edu@gmail.com. Diane Bailey, D.R.E. (K-8); Kathy Sevigny, D.R.E. (K-8); Eydie Arembury, D.R.E. Students 85.

SHELBURNE, CHITTENDEN CO., ST. CATHERINE OF SIENA (1906) [CEM]
72 Church St., Shelburne, 05482. Tel: 802-985-2373; Email: shelburnecatholic@comcast.net; Web: www.shelburnecatholic.org. P.O. Box 70, Shelburne, 05482. Rev. Msgr. Michael W. DeForge.
Catechesis Religious Program—Marie Cookson, D.R.E. Students 90.

SHELDON SPRINGS, FRANKLIN CO., ST. ANTHONY (1906) [CEM 2]
102 Shawville Rd., Sheldon Springs, 05483.
Tel: 802-933-4464; Fax: 802-933-3164; Email: stjohnvt@comcast.net; Web: stjohnbaptistvt.com. P.O. Box 563, Enosburg Falls, 05450. Revs. Stanley Deresienski, S.S.E., Admin.; Soosai Raj, H.G.N., Parochial Vicar.
Mission—St. Mary, [CEM] (seasonal) 145 Square Rd., Franklin, Franklin Co. 05457. Rev. Stanley Deresienski, S.S.E., Admin.

SOUTH BURLINGTON, CHITTENDEN CO., ST. JOHN VIANNEY (1940)
160 Hinesburg Rd., 05403. Tel: 802-864-4166; Email: sjvianneysbvt@aol.com. Revs. Patrick J. Forman; Steven R. Marchand; Deacons Joseph Lane; Anthony Previti; William Glinka.
Catechesis Religious Program—
Tel: 802-864-4166, Ext. 204. Chelsea Fournier, D.R.E. & Confirmation Coord. Students 131.

SOUTH HERO, GRAND ISLE CO., ST. ROSE OF LIMA (1895) Merged with St. Amadeus, Alburgh to form Our Lady of the Lake.

SPRINGFIELD, WINDSOR CO., MATERNITY OF THE BLESSED VIRGIN MARY (1900) [CEM]
10 Pleasant St., Springfield, 05156.

Tel: 802-885-3400; Email: stmarys@vermontel.net. Rev. Peter Y. Williams.
Res.: 40 Summer St., Springfield, 05156.
Catechesis Religious Program—Eileen Kendall, C.R.E. Students 30.

STOWE, LAMOILLE CO., BLESSED SACRAMENT (1954)
728 Mountain Rd., P.O. Box 27, Stowe, 05672.
Tel: 802-253-7536; Email: bscstowe@myfairpoint.net; Web: catholicchurch-stowe.net. Rev. Msgr. Peter A. Routhier.
Catechesis Religious Program—
Tel: 802-253-7536, Ext. 13. Victoria Colyer, D.R.E. Students 39.

SWANTON, FRANKLIN CO., NATIVITY OF THE BLESSED VIRGIN MARY-ST. LOUIS (2008) [CEM] Parish includes Nativity of the Blessed Virgin Mary, Swanton & St. Louis, Highgate Center.
65 Canada St., Swanton, 05488. Tel: 802-868-4262; Fax: 802-868-9202; Email: nativitybvm-stlouis@comcast.net; Web: nativitystlouis.com. Rev. James E. Zuccaro.
Catechesis Religious Program—Jennifer Ploof, D.R.E. Students 90.

TROY, ORLEANS CO., SACRED HEART OF JESUS (1931) [CEM]
130 S. Pleasent St., Troy, 05868. Tel: 802-744-4066. P.O. Box 109, Troy, 05868. Rev. Timothy P. Naples.
Res.: 18 N. Pleasant St., North Troy, 05859.
Tel: 802-988-2608; Tel: 802-525-3711.
Catechesis Religious Program—Mrs. Theresa McAvinney, D.R.E. Students 26.
Mission—St. Ignatius Loyola, 151 Hazen Notch Rd., Lowell, Orleans Co. 05847.

UNDERHILL CENTER, CHITTENDEN CO., ST. THOMAS (1856) [CEM 3]
6 Green St., Underhill Center, 05490-0003.
Tel: 802-899-4632; Tel: 802-899-4770;
Fax: 802-899-5120; Email: office@stthomasvt.com. P.O. Box 3, Underhill Center, 05490-0003. Rev. Christopher Micale; Deacon Peter Brooks.
Catechesis Religious Program—Tel: 802-899-4770. Laura Lynch Wells, Coord. Students 46.

VERGENNES, ADDISON CO., ST. PETER (1881) [CEM]
85 S. Maple St., Vergennes, 05491-0924.
Tel: 802-877-2367; Email: st.peter.vt@comcast.net; Web: www.stpetersvt.com. P.O. Box 324, Vergennes, 05491. Rev. Yvon J. Royer.
Catechesis Religious Program—Tel: 802-468-7277. Emma Goff, D.R.E. Students 45.

WALLINGFORD, RUTLAND CO., ST. PATRICK (1910) [CEM]
218 N. Main St., Wallingford, 05773.
Tel: 802-773-6820; Email: rwcatholic@gmail.com; Web: www.rwcatholic.org. Christ the King: 66 S. Main St., Rutland, 05701. Rev. Msgr. Bernard W. Bourgeois, M.A., M.Div.; Rev. Matthew Rensch.

WATERBURY, WASHINGTON CO., ST. ANDREW (1869) [CEM]
109 S. Main St., Waterbury, 05676.
Tel: 802-244-7734; Email: rccoffice@gmavt.net. Rev. Jerome Mercure.
Catechesis Religious Program—Amanda Badeau, C.R.E. Students 74.
Missions—Our Lady of the Snows—Waitsfield, Washington Co.
St. Patrick, Moretown, Washington Co.

WEST RUTLAND, RUTLAND CO.
1—ST. BRIDGET (1857) [CEM 2]
28 Church St., West Rutland, 05777.
Tel: 802-438-2490; Email: wrchurches@comcast.net. Rev. Romanus Igweonu, Admin.
Catechesis Religious Program—Students 46.
2—ST. STANISLAUS KOSTKA (1904) [CEM] (Polish)
28 Church St., West Rutland, 05777.
Tel: 802-438-2490; Email: wrchurches@comcast.net. Rev. Romanus Igweonu.
Res.: 23 Barnes St., West Rutland, 05777.

WHITE RIVER JUNCTION, WINDSOR CO., ST. ANTHONY (1869) [CEM 2]
15 Church St., White River Junction, 05001.
Tel: 802-295-2225; Email: administrator@saintanthonychurch.comcastbiz.net; Web: www.stanthonysvt.org. Rev. Charles R. Danielson; Deacon John P. Guarino, Admin.
Religious Education Center—53 Church St., White River Junction, 05001.
Catechesis Religious Program—Julie Hamilton, D.R.E. Students 25.

WILLISTON, CHITTENDEN CO., IMMACULATE HEART OF MARY (1951)
7417 Williston Rd., Williston, 05495.
Tel: 802-878-4513. P.O. Box 1047, Williston, 05495. Rev. Daniel J. Jordan, J.C.L.
Catechesis Religious Program—Students 119.

WILMINGTON, WINDHAM CO., OUR LADY OF FATIMA (1959)
96 E. Main St., Wilmington, 05363.
Tel: 802-464-7329; Email: olfwil@gmail.com; Web: www.ourladyoffatimavt.org. P.O. Box 188, Wilmington, 05363. Rev. Ilayaraja Amaladass, H.G.N., Admin.
Catechesis Religious Program—Students 21.

WINDSOR, WINDSOR CO., ST. FRANCIS OF ASSISI (1886) [CEM]
30 Union St., Windsor, 05089. Tel: 802-674-2157; Email: adminstfrancis@comcast.net. P.O. Box 46, Windsor, 05089. Rev. Charles R. Danielson.
Catechesis Religious Program—Tel: 802-674-4483. Christine Porter, D.R.E. Students 13.

WINOOSKI, CHITTENDEN CO.
1—ST. FRANCIS XAVIER (1868) [CEM]
3 St. Peter St., Winooski, 05404. Tel: 802-655-2290; Email: stfxwin@sover.net. Rev. Msgr. Richard G. Lavalley; Rev. Scott A. Gratton, Parochial Vicar.
Our Lady of Providence Residence, Res.:
Tel: 802-655-2395; Fax: 802-655-3888.
School—St. Francis Xavier School, (Grades PreK-8), 5 St. Peter St., Winooski, 05404. Mr. Eric Becker, Prin.; Mrs. Eileen Barendse, Vice Prin.; Mrs. Kathleen Finn, Librarian. Lay Teachers 17; Students 193.
Catechesis Religious Program—Cell: 802-503-8241. Students 94.
St. Vincent de Paul Center—Tel: 802-655-3006.
Child Care—Extension Program, Tel: 802-655-4660.
2—ST. STEPHEN (1882) [CEM]
115 Barlow St., Winooski, 05404. Tel: 802-655-0318; Email: saintstephenparish@comcast.net. Very Rev. Stephen W. Hornat, S.S.E.
Catechesis Religious Program— (at St. Francis Xavier School) Jeffrey Badillo, D.R.E.

WOODSTOCK, WINDSOR CO., OUR LADY OF THE SNOWS (1894)
7 South St., Woodstock, 05091-0397.
Tel: 802-457-2322; Email: ourladyofthesnows@comcast.net. P.O. Box 397, Woodstock, 05091-0397. Rev. Michael E. Augustinowitz.
Catechesis Religious Program—Sheila Halnon, Rel. Educ. Coord. Students 26.
Mission—Our Lady of the Mountains, Killington, Rutland, Co.

Chaplains of Public Institutions

BURLINGTON. *University of Vermont Medical Center*, Burlington, 05401. Tel: 802-656-2770. Revs. Fidelis Agughara, John T. Crabb, S.J., Richard Eneji, C.S. Sp., Timothy Sullivan.

WATERBURY. *State Hospital*. Rev. Jerome Mercure.

WHITE RIVER JUNCTION. *Veterans Administration Hospital*. Rev. Anthony Madu.

On Duty Outside the Diocese:
Rev.—
Dowd, Barry G., 8300 Vineland Ave., Orlando, FL 32821.

Retired:
Rev. Msgrs.—
Mayo, Reid C., (Retired), 265 Morrison Rd., Barre, 05641. Tel: 802-476-2360
Rivard, Roland J., (Retired), 50 Winding Brook Dr., 05403. Tel: 802-862-0847
Revs.—
Baltz, Albert G., (Retired), 125 Kennedy Dr., #35, 05403. Tel: 802-238-6785
Davignon, Charles P., (Retired), 62 Davingnon Ln., Brownington, 05860
Haskin, Jay C., M.Ch.A., (Retired), 86 Westview Heights Dr., #5-2, Stowe, 05672. Tel: 802-373-4219
Laroche, Leonidas B., (Retired), 718 Maquam Shore Rd., Swanton, 05488. Tel: 802-524-7014
Lively, Joseph A., (Retired), 257 Peacham Pond Rd., Marshfield, 05658. Tel: 802-426-3847
Ravey, Donald J., (Retired), 152 Allen Rd., #234, 05403. Tel: 802-497-1687
Romano, Joseph E., (Retired), 320 Richmond Hill Rd., Cheshire, MA 01225. Tel: 413-743-0817
Rooney, Kevin E., (Retired), 332 Ledgemere Point Rd., Hubbardton, 05735. Tel: 802-273-2448
Roy, Donald J., (Retired), Spanish Lake Mobile Home Park, 1102 Captiva St., Nokomis, FL 34275
Shea, James M., (Retired), 792 Capri Isles Blvd., Venice, FL 34292. Tel: 941-416-2455
Tinney, Richard W., (Retired), Rutland, 05701.

Permanent Deacons:
Anderberg, Richard, Our Lady of the Valley, Townshend
Baker, David, Corpus Christi, St. Johnsbury
Bisson, David, St. Monica, Barre
Blicharz, John, Bellows Falls
Brooks, Peter T., St. Thomas, Underhill Center
Brown, William J. III, (On Duty Outside the Diocese)
Chagnon, Clifford, All Saints, Richford
Cooney, Thomas F., Holy Cross, Morrisville
Cummings, Regis E., St. Augustine, Montpelier
Driscoll, Jerome, Chapel of the Snows, Stratton Mountain
Gagne, Gabriel, St. Mary; St. Albans
Garrow, Paul, St. Ann, Milton
Gibbo, Timothy, St. Mark, Burlington
Glinka, William, St. John Vianney, South Burlington
Guarino, John P., St. Anthony, White River Junction
Gummere, Peter, Corpus Christi, St. Johnsbury
Hawk, Ivan O. III, (On Duty Outside the Diocese)
Keough, Christopher, (On Duty Outside the Diocese)
Lane, Joseph W. Sr., St. John Vianney, South Burlington
Langlois, Duane, Holy Angels, St. Albans
Liegey, Gabriel M. Jr., (Retired)
Mello, Paul, (On Duty Outside the Diocese)
Meyers, Vincent, St. Raphael, Poultney
Moore, Dennis, Ascension, Georgia
Moran, Robert J., (Retired)
O'Brien, David, St. John the Baptist, North Bennington
Previti, Anthony, St. John Vianney, South Burlington
Pudvah, Daniel, St. Monica, Barre
Ramey, Jon, (Retired)
Ratte, Stephen J., St. Luke, Fairfax
Rock, James E., (Retired)
Schneider, Gesualdo, St. Augustine, Montpelier
Scilla, Gerald, St. Pius X, Essex Center.

INSTITUTIONS LOCATED IN DIOCESE

[A] COLLEGES AND UNIVERSITIES

COLCHESTER. *St. Michael's College*, One Winooski Park, Colchester, 05439. Tel: 802-654-2000;
Tel: 802-654-2476; Fax: 802-654-2780; Email: bcummings@smcvt.edu; Web: www.smcvt.edu. Lorraine Sterritt, Pres.; Mary-Kate McKenna, Chm. of the Bd.; Ms. Tara Arcury, Asst. to Pres.; Ms. Dawn M. Ellinwood, Vice Pres. Student Affairs; Mr. Patrick Gallivan, Vice Pres. Govt. & Community Affairs; Rev. Brian J. Cummings, S.S.E., Dir. Campus Ministry; Sarah M. Kelly, Vice Pres. Enrollment & Mktg.; David Barrowclough, Registrar; Jerome P. Monachino, Music Min.; Revs. Lino Oropeza, S.S.E., Campus Min.; Raymond J. Doherty, S.S.E., Campus Min.; David J. Theroux, S.S.E., Dir.; Marcel R. Rainville, S.S.E., Campus Min.; Michael Carter, Prof.; John K. Payne, Dir. Library & Information Svcs. Clergy 2; Lay Teachers 126; Priests 6; Students 2,000; Clergy / Religious Teachers 2.

RUTLAND. **College of St. Joseph in Vermont*, 71 Clement Rd., Rutland, 05701-3899.
Tel: 802-773-5900; Fax: 802-776-5258; Email: richard.lloyd@csj.edu; Web: www.csj.edu. Dr. Richard B. Lloyd, Pres.; Doreen McCullough, Librarian. Lay Teachers 13; Students 267.

[B] CENTRAL HIGH SCHOOLS, DIOCESAN AND PAROCHIAL

RUTLAND. *Mount St. Joseph Academy - Rutland Catholic Schools*, 127 Convent Ave., Rutland, 05701. Tel: 802-775-0151; Fax: 802-775-0424; Email: principal@msjvermont.org; Web: www.msjvermont.org. Mrs. Sarah Fortier, Prin.; Jessica Andette, Librarian. Sisters of St. Joseph. Lay Teachers 17; Priests 1; Students 70.

SOUTH BURLINGTON. *Rice Memorial High School*, 99 Proctor Ave., 05403. Tel: 802-862-6521;
Fax: 802-864-9931; Email: lorenz@rmhsvt.org; Web: www.rmhsvt.org. Sr. Laura Della Santa, R.S.M., Prin.; Lloyd Hulburd, Assoc. Prin. for Academics; Ann Kenney, Librarian. Lay Teachers 30; Students 430; Clergy / Religious Teachers 2.

[C] ELEMENTARY SCHOOLS, PAROCHIAL

BURLINGTON. *Christ The King*, (Grades PreSchool-8), 136 Locust St., Burlington, 05401.
Tel: 802-862-6696; Fax: 802-658-6553; Email: frontoffice@cksvt.org; Web: www.cksvt.org. Mrs. Angela Pohlen, Prin.; Aida Cadrecha, Librarian. Lay Teachers 20; Students 225.

Mater Christi School, (Grades PreSchool-8), 50 Mansfield Ave., Burlington, 05401. Tel: 802-658-3992; Fax: 802-863-1196; Email: afontana@mcschool.org; Web: www.mcschool.org. Mr. Patrick Lofton, Head of School/Prin.; Monica Lyman, Librarian. Lay Teachers 30; Sisters 1; Students 258.

BARRE. *St. Monica - St. Michael School*, (Grades PreSchool-8), St. Monica Parish, 79 Summer St., Barre, 05641. Tel: 802-476-5015; Fax: 802-476-0861; Email: bbuzzell@stmonica-stmichael.org; Web: www.stmonica-stmichael.org. Brenda Buzzell, Prin. Lay Teachers 8; Students 100.

BARTON. *St. Paul's Catholic School*, (Grades PreK-8), 54 Eastern Ave., Barton, 05822. Tel: 802-525-6578; Fax: 802-525-3869; Email: jbeloin@stpaulscatholicschool.com; Web: stpaulscatholicschool.org. Mrs. Joanne Beloin, Prin. Lay Teachers 12; Priests 1; Students 65; Teaching Principal 1.

BENNINGTON. *The School of Sacred Heart St. Francis de Sales*, (Grades PreK-8), 307 School St., Bennington, 05201. Tel: 802-442-2446; Fax: 802-442-2344; Email: estesdb@comcast.net; Web: www.sacredheartbennington.org. Mr. David B. Estes, Prin.; Marcia Hendery, Librarian; Kathy Murphy, Librarian. Lay Teachers 7; Students 155.

BRATTLEBORO. *St. Michael School*, (Grades PreK-12), 48 Walnut St., Brattleboro, 05301. Tel: 802-254-6320; Fax: 802-254-5229; Email: elainebeam@smsvt.info; Web: www.smsvt.org. Mrs. Elaine Beam, Prin. Lay Teachers 11; Students 120.

MORRISVILLE. *Bishop John A. Marshall School*, (Grades PreK-8), 680 Laporte Rd., Morrisville, 05661. Tel: 802-888-4758; Fax: 802-888-3137; Email: cwilson@bjams.org; Web: www.bjams.org. Mrs. Carrie Wilson, Prin.; Mrs. Jennifer Nordenson, Prin. Lay Teachers 19; Students 140.

RUTLAND. *Christ the King*, (Grades PreK-8), 60 S. Main St., Rutland, 05701. Tel: 802-773-0500; Fax: 802-773-0554; Email: shackett@cksrutland.org; Web: www.cksrutland.org. Lila Millard, Prin.; Mrs. Margaret Barbagallo, Librarian. Lay Teachers 18; Students 148.

SAINT JOHNSBURY. *Good Shepherd School*, (Grades PreK-8), 121 Maple St., St. Johnsbury, 05819. Tel: 802-751-8223; Fax: 802-751-8111; Email: lcartularo@goodshepherdschoolvt.org. Mrs. Lynn Cartularo, Prin.; Mrs. Karen Haskins, Librarian. Lay Teachers 11; Students 99.

WINOOSKI. *St. Francis Xavier*, (Grades PreK-8), 5 St. Peter St., Winooski, 05404. Tel: 802-655-2600; Fax: 802-655-3096; Email: jgaudette@sfxut.org; Web: www.sfxut.org. Mr. Eric Becker, Prin.; Eileen Barendes, Prin.; Mrs. Kathleen Finn, Librarian. Lay Teachers 18; Students 171.

[D] HOMES FOR AGED

BURLINGTON. *St. Joseph Residential Care Home*, 243 N. Prospect St., Burlington, 05401. Tel: 802-864-0264; Fax: 802-864-5640; Email: mbelanger@vermontcatholic.org. Ms. Mary Beth Pinard, Dir.; Ms. Mary Belanger. Managed by Vermont Catholic Charities. Guests 40.

DERBY LINE. *Michaud Manor Residential Care Home*, 47 Herrick Rd., Derby Line, 05830. Tel: 802-873-3152; Fax: 802-873-9206; Email: asteinberg@vermontcatholic.org; Web: www.vermontcatholic.org. Ms. Mary Beth Pinard, Dir.; Ms. Anne Steinberg, Admin. Managed by Vermont Catholic Charities. Guests 29.

RUTLAND. *St. Joseph/Kervick Residence*, 131 Convent Ave., Rutland, 05701. Tel: 802-775-5133; Fax: 802-747-0167; Email: jschmelzanbach@vermontcatholic.org. Jeanne Schmelzanbach, Admin.; Ms. Mary Beth Pinard, Dir.; Rev. John W. Hamilton, Resident Chap., (Retired). Managed by Vermont Catholic Charities. Guests 51.

Loretto/Kervick Home, 59 Meadow St., Rutland, 05701. Tel: 802-773-8840; Fax: 802-773-9638; Email: JSchmelzenbach@vermontcatholic.org. Jeanne Schmelzanbach, Admin.; Ms. Mary Beth Pinard, Dir.; Rev. James E. Lawrence, Chap. Managed by Vermont Catholic Charities. Guests 55.

[E] MONASTERIES AND RESIDENCES OF PRIESTS AND BROTHERS

ARLINGTON. *Carthusian Foundation in America, Inc., Charterhouse of the Transfiguration*, 1084 Ave Maria Way, Arlington, 05250. Tel: 802-362-2550; Fax: 802-362-3584; Email: carthusians_in_america@chartreuse.info; Web: transfiguration.chartreux.org. Revs. Johan de Bruijn, O.Cart., (Holland) Librarian; Philip Dahl, O.Cart., (Norway) Sacristan; Lorenzo Maria Tolentino de la Rosa Jr., O.Cart., (Philippines) Prior; Mary Joseph Kim, O.Cart., (Korea, South) Novice Master. Carthusian Foundation, Association Fraternelle Romande. Novices 1; Postulants 2; Aspirant 1; Choir Monks: Simple Professed 1; Converse Brothers: Simple Professed 1; Choir Monks: Solemn Professed 4; Converse Brothers: Solemn Professed 4; Perpetual Donates 1. *Equinox Foundation, LLC*, Equinox foundation llc, 1A Saint Bruno Dr., Arlington, 05250. Tel: 802-362-1115; Fax: 802-362-3346; Email: info@equinoxmountain.com; Web: www.equinoxmountain.com. Mr. Frank Dyer, Business Mgr.

COLCHESTER. *Society of St. Edmund* (Edmundite Generalate) 270 Winooski Park, Colchester, 05439. Tel: 802-654-3400; Fax: 802-654-3409; Email: generalate@aol.com; Web: www.sse.org. Very Rev. Stephen W. Hornat, S.S.E., Supr. Gen.; Revs. Edward J. Dubriske, S.S.E., (Venezuela); Philippe Simonnet, S.S.E., (France). Central Offices, Society of Saint Edmund.*Society of St. Edmund*, 1 Winooski Park, P.O. Box 272, Colchester, 05439. Tel: 802-654-2350; Fax: 802-654-3409; Email: dtheroux@smcvt.edu. Revs. David J. Theroux, S.S.E., Supr.; Richard N. Berube, S.S.E., Treas. Gen. & Dir. Seminarians; Paul E. Couture, S.S.E.; Brian J. Cummings, S.S.E.; Raymond J. Doherty, S.S.E.; Joseph M. McLaughlin, S.S.E.; Marcel R. Rainville, S.S.E.; John T. Scully, S.S.E.; Richard L. Vanderweel, S.S.E.; Bro. Thomas Berube, S.S.E.; Michael Carter; Revs. Stanley Deresienski, S.S.E.; Lino Oropeza, S.S.E. (Edmundite Community at St. Michael's College).

WESTON. *The Benedictine Foundation of the State of Vermont, Inc.*, Weston Priory, 58 Priory Hill Rd., Weston, 05161-6400. Tel: 802-824-5409; Fax: 802-824-3573; Email: brothers@westonpriory.org; Web: www.westonpriory.org. Very Rev. Richard Iaquinto, O.S.B., Prior; Revs. Peter Claude Anctil, O.S.B.; Robert J. Kiernan, O.S.B.; Mark Ronald Nicolosi, O.S.B.; John Hammond, O.S.B. Brothers 7; Priests 5.

[F] CONVENTS AND RESIDENCES OF SISTERS

BURLINGTON. *Sisters of Mercy of the Americas-Northeast Community*, 100 Mansfield Ave., Burlington, 05401. Tel: 802-863-6835; Fax: 802-863-1486; Email: lmacdonald@mercyne.org. Sr. Lucille MacDonald, R.S.M., Local Coord. Sisters 44.

LOWELL. *The Carmelite Nuns of Vermont, Inc.*, St. Joseph's Carmelite Monastery, 386 Stephenson Rd., Lowell, 05847. Tel: 802-744-2346; Email: sdlgocd@gmail.com; Web: carmelitesofvermont.com. Sr. Diane Gauthier, O.C.D., Vicaress. Sisters 5.

WESTFIELD. *Monastery of the Immaculate Heart of Mary*, 4103 VT Rte. 100, P.O. Box 110, Westfield, 05874. Tel: 802-744-6525; Fax: 802-744-6236; Email: monastery@ihmwestfield.com; Web: www.ihmwestfield.com. Sisters Maria Magdalen Grumm, O.S.B., Prioress; Benedict McLaughlin, Subprioress; Rev. Dom Lawrence Brown, O.S.B., Resident Chap., Monk of Clear Creek, OK. Benedictine Cloistered Nuns, Congregation of Solesmes. Postulants 1; Sisters 16; Professed Nuns 13; Novice 2.

WINOOSKI. *Missionary Sisters of Our Lady of Africa (M.S.O.L.A.)*, 47 W. Spring St., Winooski, 05404. Tel: 802-655-2395; Email: arlenegates@yahoo.com. Sr. Arlene Gates, Contact Person. Sisters 5.

Religious Hospitallers of St. Joseph (1636) 47 W. Spring St., Winooski, 05404-1319. Tel: 802-655-2395; Tel: 802-654-1004 Other; Email: rdufault2@gmail.com. Rose-Marie Dufault, R.H.S.J., Supr. Sisters 1.

Sisters of Providence, 47 W. Spring St., Winooski, 05404. Tel: 802-655-2395; Fax: 802-861-2968; Email: olopr@aol.com. Sr. Carmen Proulx, S.P., Coord. Sisters 9.

[G] NEWMAN CENTERS

BURLINGTON. *University of Vermont-The Catholic Center at UVM*, 390 S. Prospect St., Redstone Campus, Burlington, 05401. Tel: 802-862-8403; Fax: 802-865-9480; Email: catholiccenteruvm@gmail.com; Web: www.uvmcatholic.com. Rev. Dwight H. Baker, Dir. In Res.

Castleton State College, Our Lady of Seven Dolors Rectory, 10 Washington St., Fair Haven, 05743. Tel: 802-468-5706; Email: mdstjohn@yahoo.com. Rev. Antony Pittappilly, S.D.V., Chap.

Goddard College (Plainfield), Attended by St. Augustine, 16 Barre St., Montpelier, 05602. Tel: 802-223-5285; Fax: 802-223-3621; Email: saintaugustineoffice@comcast.net. Rev. Michael E. Augustinowitz.

Green Mountain College, St. Raphael Rectory, Main St., Poultney, 05764. Tel: 802-287-5703; Email: rajalurduraj@gmail.com. Rev. Louduraja Simeone, H.G.N.

Johnson State College (Johnson), P.O. Box 339, Morrisville, 05661. Tel: 802-888-3318; Fax: 802-888-6177; Email: holysaints@comcast.net. Rev. Francis R. Prive. Attended by Holy Cross, Morrisville.

Lyndon State College, 49 Winter St., St. Johnsbury, 05819. Tel: 802-748-8129; Email: stjchurch@charter.net. Rev. Curtis Miller, Chap.

Middlebury College, St. Mary Rectory, 326 College St., Middlebury, 05753. Tel: 802-388-2943; Fax: 802-388-6023; Email: stmarys11@comcast.net. Rev. Luke P. Austin, J.D., J.C.L.

Norwich Newman Apostolate, Norwich University, Northfield, 05663. Tel: 802-485-8313; Email: stjohned@trans-video.net. 206 Vine St., Northfield, 05663. Rev. Msgr. Michael W. DeForge, Chap.; Rev. James C. Dodson.

Vermont Technical College, Our Lady of the Angels Parish, Randolph, 05060. Tel: 802-728-3227; Fax: 802-728-3570; Email: chancery@vermontcatholic.org. Rev. John M. Milanese, Chap.

[H] MISCELLANEOUS

BURLINGTON. *Mercy Connections, Inc.*, 255 S. Champlain St., Ste. 8, Burlington, 05401. Tel: 802-846-7062; Fax: 802-846-7237; Email: dfleming@mercyconnections.org; Web: www.mercyconnections.org. Dolly Fleming, Exec. Dir.

BRATTLEBORO. *Neringa, Inc.*, 600 Liberty Hwy., Putnam, CT 06260. Tel: 978-582-5592; Email: info@neringa.org; Web: www.neringa.org. 147 Neringa Rd., Brattleboro, 05301. Dana Vainauskiene, Asst. Exec. Dir.

COLCHESTER. *Fanny Allen Corporation*, c/o Covenant Health, 100 Ames Pond Rd., Ste. 2, Tewksbury, MA 01876. Tel: 978-654-6363; Email: joseph_oconnell@covenanthealth.net. Joseph O'Connell, Controller. Sponsored by Covenant Health Systems, Tewksbury, MA. Fanny Allen Corporation operates a Community Fund that supports charitable organizations serving the poor, the sick and the most vulnerable.

Fanny Allen Holdings, Inc., c/o Covenant Health, 100 Ames Pond Rd., Ste. 2, Tewksbury, MA 01876. Tel: 978-654-6363; Fax: 978-851-0828; Email: josephoconnell@covenanthealth.net. Mrs. Ellen Kane, Pres. Sponsored by Covenant Health Systems, Tewksbury, MA. Fanny Allen Holdings, Inc. oversees property that it owns in Colchester, Vermont, leases to Fletcher Allen Health Care for use as a hospital and promotes its Catholic identity.

ISLE LA MOTTE. *St. Anne's Shrine*, 92 Saint Anne's Rd., P.O. Box 280, Isle La Motte, 05463. Tel: 802-928-3362; Fax: 802-928-3305; Email: fstanne@pshift.com; Web: www.saintannesshrine.org. Rev. Brian J. Cummings, S.S.E., Spiritual Dir. Conducted by Fathers of Society of St. Edmund; Open May 15-Oct. 15.

RANDOLPH. *Prelature of the Holy Cross and Opus Dei*, Wynnview Center, R.D. 1, Sunset Hill, Randolph, 05060. Tel: 802-728-5414; Fax: 802-728-3334; Email: info@opusdei.org; Web: www.opusdei.org.

RELIGIOUS INSTITUTES OF MEN REPRESENTED IN THE DIOCESE

For further details refer to the corresponding bracketed number in the Religious Institutes of Men or Women section.

[0200]—*Benedictine Monks*—O.S.B.
[]—*Capuchin Friars of North America*—O.F.M., Cap.
[0585]—*Heralds of Good News*—H.G.N.
[0280]—*Order of Carthusians*—O.Cart.
[0610]—*Priests of the Congregation of Holy Cross* (Eastern Prov.)—C.S.C.
[1340]—*Society of Divine Vocations (The Vocationists)*—S.D.V.
[]—*Society of Jesus*—S.J.
[0440]—*Society of Saint Edmund*—S.S.E.

RELIGIOUS INSTITUTES OF WOMEN REPRESENTED IN THE DIOCESE

[0170]—*Benedictine Cloistered Nuns of the Congregation of Solesmes*—O.S.B.
[0820]—*Daughters of the Holy Spirit*—D.H.S.
[0420]—*Discalced Carmelite Nuns*—O.C.D.
[1190]—*Franciscan Sisters of the Atonement*—S.A.
[2820]—*Missionary Sisters of Our Lady of Africa*—M.S.O.L.A.
[3440]—*Religious Hospitallers of Saint Joseph*—R.H.S.J.
[2575]—*Sisters of Mercy*—R.S.M.
[3000]—*Sisters of Notre Dame de Namur*—S.N.D.deN.
[3350]—*Sisters of Providence*—S.P.
[]—*Sisters of St. Joseph Society, Inc.*—S.S.J.

DIOCESAN CEMETERIES

SOUTH BURLINGTON. *Resurrection Park Cemetery*, 55 Joy Dr., 05403. Tel: (802) 860-0450; Email: RBrown@vermontcatholic.org. Mr. Robert E. Brown, Diocesan Dir., Catholic Cemeteries

NECROLOGY

† Searles, Wendell H., (Retired), Died Oct. 20, 2018

† Morgan, William P., (Retired), Died May. 25, 2018

† Ward, Donal, (Retired), Died Feb. 20, 2018

An asterisk (*) denotes an organization that has established tax-exempt status directly with the IRS and is not covered by the USCCB Group Ruling.

Diocese of Camden

(Dioecesis Camdensis)

Most Reverend

DENNIS J. SULLIVAN

Bishop of Camden; ordained May 29, 1971; appointed Titular Bishop of Enera and Auxiliary Bishop of New York June 28, 2004; consecrated September 21, 2004; appointed Bishop of Camden January 8, 2013; installed February 12, 2013.

Most Reverend

JOSEPH A. GALANTE, D.D., J.C.D.

Retired Bishop of Camden; ordained May 16, 1964; appointed Titular Bishop of Equilum and Auxiliary Bishop of San Antonio October 13, 1992; consecrated December 11, 1992; appointed Bishop of Beaumont April 5, 1994; installed Bishop of Beaumont May 9, 1994; appointed Coadjutor Bishop of Dallas November 23, 1999; installed January 14, 2000; appointed Bishop of Camden March 23, 2004; installed April 30, 2004; retired January 8, 2013.

IN THE BREAKING OF THE BREAD

Chancery Office: *Camden Diocesan Center, 631 Market St., P.O. Box 708, Camden, NJ 08101.* Tel: 856-756-7900; Fax: 856-963-2655.

ESTABLISHED DECEMBER 9, 1937.

Square Miles 2,691.

Legal Corporate Title: "The Diocese of Camden, New Jersey."

Comprises six Counties in the State of New Jersey–viz., Atlantic, Camden, Cape May, Cumberland, Gloucester and Salem.

For legal titles of parishes and diocesan institutions, consult the Chancery Office.

STATISTICAL OVERVIEW

Personnel	
Bishop	1
Retired Bishops	1
Priests: Diocesan Active in Diocese	103
Priests: Diocesan Active Outside Diocese	7
Priests: Diocesan in Foreign Missions	1
Priests: Retired, Sick or Absent	93
Number of Diocesan Priests	204
Religious Priests in Diocese	27
Total Priests in Diocese	231
Extern Priests in Diocese	15
Ordinations:	
Diocesan Priests	1
Transitional Deacons	2
Permanent Deacons in Diocese	139
Total Brothers	10
Total Sisters	220
Parishes	
Parishes	62
With Resident Pastor:	
Resident Diocesan Priests	58
Resident Religious Priests	3
Without Resident Pastor:	
Administered by Priests	1
Missions	4
Closed Parishes	3
Professional Ministry Personnel:	
Brothers	10
Sisters	53
Lay Ministers	82
Welfare	
Health Care Centers	3
Total Assisted	1,429
Homes for the Aged	1
Total Assisted	55
Day Care Centers	4
Total Assisted	525
Specialized Homes	1
Total Assisted	250
Special Centers for Social Services	9
Total Assisted	33,000
Residential Care of Disabled	1
Total Assisted	55
Other Institutions	3
Total Assisted	115,600
Educational	
Diocesan Students in Other Seminaries	18
Total Seminarians	18
High Schools, Diocesan and Parish	6
Total Students	3,121
High Schools, Private	3
Total Students	1,398
Elementary Schools, Diocesan and Parish	28
Total Students	7,601
Non-residential Schools for the Disabled	1
Total Students	1,353
Catechesis/Religious Education:	
Elementary Students	20,312
Total Students under Catholic Instruction	33,803
Teachers in the Diocese:	
Priests	11
Brothers	3
Sisters	19
Lay Teachers	852
Vital Statistics	
Receptions into the Church:	
Infant Baptism Totals	3,787
Adult Baptism Totals	174
Received into Full Communion	217
First Communions	4,310
Confirmations	3,658
Marriages:	
Catholic	662
Interfaith	200
Total Marriages	862
Deaths	3,538
Total Catholic Population	495,843
Total Population	1,396,740

Former Bishops—Most Revs. BARTHOLOMEW J. EUSTACE, S.T.D., First Bishop of Camden; consecrated March 25, 1938; died Dec. 11, 1956; JUSTIN J. MCCARTHY, S.T.D., LL.D., Second Bishop of Camden; cons. June 17, 1954; appt. to Camden, Jan. 27, 1957; died Dec. 26, 1959; CELESTINE J. DAMIANO, D.D., Third Bishop of Camden; cons. Feb. 11, 1953; transferred to Camden, Jan. 24, 1960, with the personal title of Archbishop; died Oct. 2, 1967; GEORGE H. GUILFOYLE, D.D., J.D., ord. March 25, 1944; appt. Titular Bishop of Marazanae and Auxiliary Bishop of New York, Oct. 17, 1964; cons. Nov. 30, 1964; appt. Fourth Bishop of Camden, Jan. 2, 1968; installed March 4, 1968; retired May 22, 1989; died June 11, 1991; JAMES T. MCHUGH, S.T.D., ord. May 25, 1957; appt. Titular Bishop of Morosbisdo and Auxiliary Bishop of Newark, Nov. 20, 1987; cons. Jan. 25 1988; appt. Fifth Bishop of Camden, May 13, 1989; installed June 20, 1989; appt. Coadjutor Bishop of Rockville Centre, Dec. 7, 1998; installed Third Diocesan Bishop, Jan. 4, 2000; died Dec. 10, 2000; NICHOLAS A. DIMARZIO, Ph.D., D.D., ord. May 30, 1970; appt. Titular Bishop of Mauriana and Auxiliary Bishop of Newark, Sept. 10, 1996; cons. Oct. 31, 1996; appt. Sixth Bishop of Camden June 8, 1999; installed July 22, 1999; appt. Bishop of Brooklyn, Aug. 1, 2003; installed Oct. 3, 2003; JOSEPH A. GALANTE, D.D., J.C.D., (Retired), ord. May 16, 1964; appt. Titular Bishop of Equilum and Auxiliary Bishop of San Antonio Oct. 13, 1992; cons. Dec. 11, 1992; appt. Bishop of Beaumont April 5, 1994; installed Bishop of Beaumont May 9, 1994; appt. Coadjutor Bishop of Dallas Nov. 23, 1999; installed Jan. 14, 2000; appt. Bishop of Camden March 23, 2004; installed April 30, 2004; retired Jan. 8, 2013.

Diocesan Offices

Camden Diocesan Center—631 Market St., Camden, 08102. Tel: 856-756-7900; Fax: 856-963-2655. Some offices are listed at separate locations.

The Diocese of Camden—A corporation under the laws of the State of New Jersey.

Officers—Most Rev. DENNIS JOSEPH SULLIVAN, D.D.; Revs. ROBERT E. HUGHES, V.G., Vice Pres.; JAMES L. BARTOLOMA, J.C.L., Sec.

Diocesan Bishop—Most Rev. DENNIS JOSEPH SULLIVAN, D.D., 631 Market St., Camden, 08102. Tel: 856-583-2808; Fax: 856-963-5777.

Bishop Emeritus—Most Rev. JOSEPH ANTHONY GALANTE, D.D., J.C.D., 631 Market St., Camden, 08102. Tel: 856-583-2808; Fax: 856-963-5777; Email: jgalante@camdendiocese.org.

Secretary to the Bishop—631 Market St., Camden, 08102. Tel: 856-583-2864; Fax: 856-338-0376; Email: michael.romano@camdendiocese.org. Rev. MICHAEL M. ROMANO.

Vicar General/Moderator of the Curia—Rev. ROBERT E. HUGHES, V.G., 631 Market St., Camden, 08102. Tel: 856-583-2803; Fax: 856-338-0376; Email: robert.hughes@camdendiocese.org.

Vicar General—Rev. Msgr. JOHN H. BURTON, V.G., 1655 Magnolia Rd., Vineland, 08360. Tel: 856-691-9077; Fax: 856-692-3305.

Chancellor—Rev. JAMES L. BARTOLOMA, J.C.L., 631 Market St., Camden, 08102. Tel: 856-583-2811; Fax: 856-338-0376.

Vice Chancellors—Rev. Msgrs. JOSEPH W. POKUSA, P.A., J.C.D., (Retired), Tel: 856-583-6162; Fax: 856-756-0113; Email: joseph.pokusa@camdendiocese.org; DOMINIC J. BOTTINO, J.C.L., Tel: 856-583-6162; Fax: 856-756-0113; Email: dominic.bottino@camdendiocese.org; Rev. ROBERT L. SINATRA, J.C.L., Tel: 856-583-6162; Fax: 856-756-0113; Email: robert.sinatra@camdendiocese.org; Deacons MICHAEL J. CARTER, Tel: 856-583-2813; Fax: 856-966-5957; Email: mcarter@camdendiocese.org; FELIX T. MIRANDA, 631 Market St., Camden, 08102. Tel: 856-583-6162; Fax: 856-756-0113; Email: felix.miranda@camdendiocese.org.

Judicial Vicar—Rev. DAVID J. KLEIN, J.C.L., 631

Market St., Camden, 08102. Tel: 856-583-6162; Fax: 856-756-0113.

Vicar for Clergy—631 Market St., Camden, 08101. Tel: 856-583-2854; Fax: 856-966-5957. Rev. NICHOLAS DUDO.

Censor Librorum—Rev. JASON T. ROCKS, S.T.L.

Delegate for Men Religious—Bro. THOMAS OSORIO, O.H., Saint John of God Monastery, 1145 Delsea Dr., Westville Grove, 08093. Tel: 856-848-4700, Ext. 1163; Fax: 856-848-2154.

Delegate for Temporalities and Diocesan Finance Officer—631 Market St., Camden, 08102. Tel: 856-583-2828; Fax: 856-963-2655. LAURA J. MONTGOMERY, CPA.

Delegate for Women Religious—Sr. MARY J. GARRITY, I.H.M., 631 Market St., Camden, 08102. Tel: 856-583-2841; Fax: 856-338-0826.

Delegate for Inter-Parochial Affairs—Rev. Msgr. WILLIAM A. HODGE, V.F., 426 Monmouth St., Gloucester, 08030. Tel: 856-456-0052; Fax: 856-456-1837.

Delegate for Hispanic Ministry—MR. ANDRES ARANGO, 631 Market St., Camden, 08102. Tel: 856-583-6181; Fax: 856-583-6185.

Vicars Forane—

Deanery 1 - West Camden County—Rev. WALTER A. NORRIS, Esq., V.F.

Deanery 2 - East Camden County—Rev. Msgr. LOUIS A. MARUCCI, D.Min., V.F.

Deanery 3 - Gloucester & Salem Counties—Rev. RAYMOND P. GORMLEY, V.F.

Deanery 4 - Atlantic County—Rev. JOHN J. VIGNONE, V.G., V.F.

Deanery 5 - Cape May and Cumberland Counties—Rev. Msgr. JOHN H. BURTON, V.G.

Diocesan Tribunal

Diocesan Tribunal—15 N. 7th St., Camden, 08102. Tel: 856-583-6162; Fax: 856-756-0113.

Judicial Vicar—Rev. DAVID J. KLEIN, J.C.L., Tel: 856-583-6162.

Adjutant Judicial Vicar—Rev. ROBERT L. SINATRA, J.C.L.

Judges—Rev. Msgrs. DOMINIC J. BOTTINO, J.C.L.; PETER M. JOYCE, J.C.L.; Revs. JAMES L. BARTOLOMA, J.C.L.; DAVID J. KLEIN, J.C.L.; ROBERT L. SINATRA, J.C.L.; DR. CHRISTINA M. HIP-FLORES, M.P.P., J.C.D.; DR. LAURA L. MORRISON, J.D., J.C.D., Ph.D.

Defender of the Bond—Rev. Msgr. JOSEPH W. POKUSA, P.A., J.C.D., (Retired).

Promoter of Justice—Rev. Msgr. PETER M. JOYCE, J.C.L.

Marriage Dispensations and Permissions—Deacons MICHAEL J. CARTER; FELIX MIRANDA, Tel: 856-583-6160.

Court Expert—MR. ROD J. HERRERA, L.C.S.W.

Ecclesiastical Notary—MS. DIANE E. GABLE, Tel: 856-583-6151.

Councils—

Presbyteral Council—Most Rev. DENNIS JOSEPH SULLIVAN, D.D., Presider.

Appointed Members—Revs. PERRY A. CHERUBINI; THOMAS A. NEWTON; JOSEPH A. PERREAULT; JOSEPH T. SZOLACK.

Elected Members—

Representatives by Ordination Seniority—Rev. Msgr. PETER M. JOYCE, J.C.L.; Revs. JON P. THOMAS; MICHAEL J. MATVEENKO.

Representative of Religious Priests—Rev. FRANCIS W. DANELLA, O.S.F.S.

Representative for Retired Priests—Rev. JAMES J. DURKIN, (Retired).

Deanery Representatives—Revs. ANTHONY J. MANUPPELLA; JOSEPH A. CAPELLA; DAVID A. GROVER; JOSEPH D. WALLACE; EDWARD F. NAMIOTKA.

International Priests Representatives—Revs. WILSON KIDANGAN PAULOSE; SANJAI DEVIS, V.C.

Ex Officio Members—Rev. Msgr. JOHN H. BURTON, V.G.; Revs. ROBERT E. HUGHES, V.G.; JAMES L. BARTOLOMA, J.C.L.; NICHOLAS DUDO.

Priests Personnel and Policy Board—Ex Officio Members: Rev. Msgr. JOHN H. BURTON, V.G.; Most Rev. DENNIS JOSEPH SULLIVAN, D.D.; Revs. ROBERT E. HUGHES, V.G.; JAMES L. BARTOLOMA, J.C.L.; NICHOLAS DUDO; THOMAS A. NEWTON. Elected Members: Revs. ALLAIN B. CAPARAS; RAYMOND P. GORMLEY, V.F.; Rev. Msgr. JOSEPH W. POKUSA, P.A., J.C.D., (Retired); Revs. DAVID RIVERA; GEORGE C. SEITER; JOSEPH T. SZOLACK.

Continuing Education & Spiritual Formation of Priests (CESF)—Revs. COSME R. DE LA PENA; JOHN J. FISHER, O.S.F.S.; WILLIAM J. KELLY; EDWARD F. NAMIOTKA; EDWARD M. KENNEDY, Chm.; GEORGE C. SEITER; MICHAEL AUGUST DE LEON, A.M.; JOHN A. ROSSI. Ex Officio Members: Most Rev. DENNIS JOSEPH SULLIVAN, D.D.; Rev. Msgr. JOHN H. BURTON, V.G.; Revs. ROBERT E. HUGHES, V.G.; JAMES L. BARTOLOMA, J.C.L.; NICHOLAS DUDO; THOMAS A. NEWTON.

Advanced Studies for Priests—Tel: 856-583-2854. Rev. NICHOLAS DUDO, Vicar.

Liaison with Retired Priests—Rev. Msgr. WILLIAM P. BRENNAN, V.F., (Retired).

Advocate for Priests' Health and Wellness—Rev. THOMAS A. NEWTON.

Health Advocate for Retired Priests—Sr. ROSEMARIE KOLMER, O.S.F., Tel: 856-751-2010; Fax: 856-751-2368.

Canon 1742 Panel—Revs. MARK CAVAGNARO; NICHOLAS DUDO; RAYMOND GORMLEY; DAVID A. GROVER; WALTER NORRIS.

Delegate for Men Religious—Bro. THOMAS OSORIO, O.H., St. John of God Monastery, 1145 Delsea Dr., Westville Grove, 08093. Tel: 856-227-1436, Ext. 21.

Permanent Diaconate—Deacon MICHAEL J. CARTER, Dir. Formation, Tel: 856-583-2813.

Deacon Council—

Ex Officio Members—Deacons MICHAEL J. CARTER; JAMES M. HOGAN.

Appointed Members—Deacons ANTHONY CIOE, Chm.; JOSEPH A. KAIN SR.; J. PETER TRAUM; DAVID MURNANE; JOSEPH F. SEAMAN.

Office of Vocations—Tel: 856-583-2864; Fax: 856-338-0376. Rev. MICHAEL M. ROMANO, Dir. Seminarians.

Vocation Advisory Board—Revs. THOMAS J. BARCELLONA; EDWARD F. HEINTZELMAN; ROBERT E. HUGHES, V.G.; MRS. JOANNE KELLY; MRS. LAURA MIRENDA; Revs. DAVID RIVERA; JOSEPH T. SZOLACK; MRS. CLARE MCNAMEE; DR. ANDREW SAVICKY, Ph. D.; Deacon THOMAS F. O'BRIEN, Ph.D., Ed.D.; Rev. MICHAEL M. ROMANO.

Amicus—Rev. Msgr. JOHN T. FREY, Chap., (Retired), Tel: 856-547-0564.

Diocesan Historian—N.J. Catholic Historical Commission Rev. JOSEPH D. WALLACE.

College of Consultors—Members: Revs. JOSEPH P. CAPELLA; PERRY A. CHERUBINI; ROBERT E. HUGHES, V.G.; ANTHONY J. MANUPPELLA; THOMAS A. NEWTON; JOSEPH A. PERREAULT; JOSEPH T. SZOLACK; THOMAS J. BARCELLONA.

Diocesan Finance Council—Rev. JOSEPH E. PERRAULT; Rev. Msgr. ROGER E. MCGRATH, Ph.D.; Deacon JOHN WERNER; JOHN FINLEY; THOMAS GRANITE; LAURA J. MONTGOMERY, CPA; MR. LAWRENCE J. READER; MS. ANGELA KELLY; PATRICK MCGRORY; ED RADETICH; MS. MEG WORTHINGTON; MR. JOSEPH DIFILIPPO; JOHN CALLAGHAN; EDWARD MERENDA.

Ex Officio Members—Most Rev. DENNIS JOSEPH SULLIVAN, D.D.; Rev. ROBERT E. HUGHES, V.G.; LAURA J. MONTGOMERY, CPA.

Information Technology Services—JOSEPH D. TORRIERI JR., Dir., Tel: 856-583-2888.

Office of Propagation of the Faith and Diocesan Missions—Rev. GEORGE C. SEITER, Dir., Tel: 856-583-2835; Fax: 856-966-5957.

Office of Development—JAMES J. LANAHAN, Dir., Tel: 856-583-6134; Fax: 856-338-0766.

House of Charity-Bishop's Annual Appeal— Tel: 856-583-6195. VACANT, Assoc. Dir. Devel.

Planned Giving—JAMES J. LANAHAN, Tel: 856-583-6134.

Office of Stewardship—Deacon RUSSELL DAVIS, Dir., Tel: 856-583-6102.

South Jersey Scholarship Fund—JAMES J. LANAHAN, Tel: 856-583-6134.

Communications and Community Relations—

Office of Communications—MICHAEL J. WALSH, Dir., Tel: 856-583-6143; Email: michael.walsh@camdendiocese.org; MARIA D'ANTONIO, Communications Coord., Tel: 856-583-6154; Email: mdantonio@camdendiocese.org; MARY MCCUSKER, Mktg. & Communications Coord., Tel: 856-342-8846; JOHN KALITZ, Digital Media Mgr., Tel: 856-583-6193.

Diocesan Newspaper—The Catholic Star Herald *Mailing Address: 15 N. 7th St., Camden, 08102.* Tel: 856-583-6142; Fax: 856-756-7938. MICHAEL J. WALSH, Assoc. Publisher, Tel: 856-583-6143; CARL D. PETERS, Mng. Editor, Tel: 856-583-6147; CYNTHIA E. SOPER, Business Mgr., Tel: 856-583-6142; PAUL J. WORTHINGTON, Advertising Mgr., Tel: 856-583-6166; NEAL CULLEN, Advertising Sales Dir., Tel: 856-524-1034.

Administrative & Financial Services

Diocesan Finance Officer & Bishop's Delegate for Temporalities—LAURA J. MONTGOMERY, CPA, Tel: 856-583-2828.

Diocesan Self-Insurance Plan (DSIP) & Pension Funds—LAURA J. MONTGOMERY, CPA, Tel: 856-583-2828.

Diocesan Liability Insurance Program— Tel: 856-583-2871. BEVLYN DONOHUE.

Financial Services—Tel: 856-583-2822; Fax: 856-963-2655. VACANT.

Comptroller—LISA M. CILIBERTO, CPA, Comptroller, Tel: 856-583-2827; KEVIN DRUM, Asst. Comptroller, Tel: 856-583-2823.

Temporal Services

Temporal Services—MR. LAWRENCE J. READER, Exec. Dir., Tel: 856-583-2821.

Diocesan Engineer—DANIEL G. BOCHANSKI, P.E., Tel: 856-583-2959.

Cemeteries—MARIANNE LINKA, Dir., Tel: 856-583-2820. (For directory of cemeteries, see "Institutions").

Facilities Management—JOSEPH MARTIN, Maintenance, Tel: 856-583-2870; Cell: 609-314-7437.

Real Estate—KENNETH MCILVAINE, Consultant, Tel: 856-579-3040.

Human Resources—NELSON REMETZ, Dir., Tel: 856-583-2868; CANDY NEWHOUSE, Health Insurance, Tel: 856-583-2872.

Office of Pastoral Planning—Rev. JAMES L. BARTOLOMA, J.C.L., Dir., Tel: 856-583-2811; LISA WATSON, Asst. Dir. Pastoral Planning, Tel: 856-583-2843.

Office of Child and Youth Protection—MR. ROD J. HERRERA, L.C.S.W., Dir., Tel: 856-583-6114; Fax: 856-583-1045.

Victim Assistance Coordinator—BARBARA ANN GONDEK, L.C.S.W., Tel: 800-964-6588.

Catholic Schools—

Superintendent of Schools—MARY P. BOYLE, M.Ed., Tel: 856-583-6103; Fax: 856-756-0225.

Assistant Superintendent of Schools—Sr. ROSE DIFLURI, I.H.M., Tel: 856-583-6110.

Curriculum & Assessment—WILLIAM A. WATSON, Ed. D., Dir., Tel: 856-583-6106.

Latino Enrollment Program—MARIANELA NUNEZ, Field Consultant.

School Business & Enrollment—ROSEMARY SCHAMP, Tel: 856-583-6175.

Marketing and Communication—MARY BETH PEABODY, Mgr., Tel: 856-583-6107.

Pastoral Services

Delegate for Hispanic Ministry—MR. ANDRES ARANGO, Tel: 856-583-6181; Fax: 856-583-6185.

Evangelization—MR. ANDRES ARANGO, Dir., Tel: 856-583-6181; Fax: 856-583-6185.

Lay Ministry Formation—MARY LOU HUGHES, Tel: 856-583-2903; Fax: 856-338-0826.

Black Catholic Ministries & Cultural Diversity— Tel: 856-583-2907; Fax: 856-338-0826. VACANT.

Diocesan Gospel Choir—TONYA DORSEY, Coord., Tel: 609-502-7414.

Racial Justice Commission—Tel: 856-583-2907. VACANT.

Faith and Family Life Formation—Co Directors: Sr. KATHLEEN BURTON, S.S.J., Tel: 856-583-6131; MARY LOU HUGHES, Tel: 856-583-6132; Fax: 856-583-6186.

Youth, Young Adult & Campus Ministries—GREGORY A. COOGAN, Dir., Tel: 856-583-2908; Fax: 856-338-0826.

Scouting—JOSEPH BRENNAN, Tel: 856-428-2645; Web: www.snjcatholicscouting.org.

Campus Ministries—

Rutgers University—Rev. KRZYSZTOF WTOREK, Tel: 856-963-1285; Email: camdencm@camdendiocese.org.

Rowan University—St. Bridget Univ. Parish/ Newman Ctr., 1 Redmond Ave., Glassboro, 08028. Tel: 856-881-2554; Fax: 856-881-4183; Web: www.rowan.ccm.com. Rev. MICHAEL J. FIELD, D.Min., Pastor; IVANS SOARES, Coord. Campus Ministry.

Stockton University—Mailing Address: Catholic Campus Ministry Ctr., 235 S. Pomona Rd., P.O. Box 1003, Pomona, 08240. Tel: 609-707-1067; Fax: 609-804-9135; Web: www.ccmstockton.com. ALISON FILION, Dir.

Worship and Christian Initiation—STEPHEN F. OBARSKI, Dir., Tel: 856-583-2865; Fax: 856-338-0826; DAMARIS THILLET, Assoc. Dir., Tel: 856-583-2810; Fax: 856-338-0826.

Liturgical Art and Architectural Commission—Rev. Msgr. JOHN H. BURTON, V.G., Chm., Tel: 856-691-9077; Rev. ROBERT E. HUGHES, V.G., Tel: 856-228-1616; STEPHEN F. OBARSKI, Tel: 856-583-2865.

Diocesan Home and Parish Healthcare Services

Vitality Catholic Healthcare Services—Deacon GERARD J. JABLONOWSKI, Exec. Dir., 631 Market St., Camden, 08102. Tel: 856-583-9196; Fax: 856-225-0096; Email: gerard.jablonowski@camdendiocese.org.

Vitality Health Ministries—
Care Coordination and Consultation Health Resource Call Center—MIMI SCHAIBLE, R.N., M.S.N., M.B.A., Dir., Tel: 856-583-6149; Fax: 856-225-0096; Email: mimi.schaible@camdendiocese.org.
Hospital Chaplaincy—Rev. SANJAI DEVIS, V.C., Dir., 631 Market St., Camden, 08102. Tel: 856-583-6130; Fax: 856-225-0096; Email: sanjai.devis@camdendiocese.org.
Ministry with the Deaf and Persons with Disabilities—Rev. HUGH J. BRADLEY, Co Dir., Tel: 856-583-6111; Fax: 856-225-0096; Email: hugh.bradley@camdendiocese.org; KATE SLOSAR, Co Dir., Tel: 856-283-3962 (Video Phone); Fax: 856-225-0096; Email: kate.slosar@camdendiocese.org.
Office & Worship Site—Saint Teresa of Calcutta, 15 Virginia Ave., Westmont, 08108. Tel: 856-942-1000 (Video Phone); Fax: 856-833-6043.
Parish Based Senior Services—631 Market St., Camden, 08102. Tel: 856-583-6121; Fax: 856-225-0096. ANNE MARIE PIRILLO, Mgr.
Parish Nursing—MARY ANNE SERRA, Dir., 15 N. Seventh St., Camden, 08102. Tel: 856-583-6120; Fax: 856-225-0096; Email: maryann.serra@camdendiocese.org.
Stephen Ministry—Rev. SANJAI DEVIS, V.C., Dir., 631 Market St., Camden, 08102. Tel: 856-583-6130; Fax: 856-225-0096; Email: sanjai.devis@camdendiocese.org.
Charismatic Renewal—Rev. RENE CANALES, Diocesan Moderator, Tel: 856-229-1571; Email: charismaticrenewal@camdendiocese.org.
Hispanic Charismatic Renewal—KATHIA ARANGO, Diocesan Coord., Tel: 954-439-8692.
English Cursillo—Deacon JOSEPH A. GAROSSO, Spiritual Advisor, Tel: 609-805-2211.
Hispanic Cursillo—Deacon ROBERTO P. RODRIGUEZ, Tel: 856-692-6003.
Ecumenical and Inter-Religious Affairs—Coordinators: Rev. JOSEPH D. WALLACE, Tel: 609-522-2709; PATRICIA SANDROW.

CLERGY, PARISHES, MISSIONS AND PAROCHIAL SCHOOLS

CITY OF CAMDEN

(CAMDEN COUNTY)

1—CATHEDRAL OF THE IMMACULATE CONCEPTION (2010) Revs. John J. Fisher, O.S.F.S., Rector; Michael J. McCue, O.S.F.S., Parochial Vicar; Krzysztof Wtorek; Deacons Felix Tito Miranda; Jose Rene Zayas
*Legal Name: The Parish of the Cathedral of the Immaculate Conception, Camden, N.J.*In Res., Bro. Michael O'Neill McGrath, O.S.F.S.
Rectory—642 Market St., 08102-1183.
Tel: 856-964-1580; Fax: 856-757-0438; Email: smackey@camdendiocese.org; Web: www.oblates.org/dsw.
Churches—
Cathedral of the Immaculate Conception, Camden—
Holy Name, Camden.
Our Lady of Mount Carmel and Fatima, Camden, 832 S. 4th St., 08103.
School—Holy Name School, 5th & Vine Sts., 08102. Tel: 856-365-7930; Fax: 856-365-8041. Mrs. Patricia Quinter, Prin.
DeSales Service Works—Tel: 215-582-1666.

2—ST. ANTHONY OF PADUA (1945) (Hispanic), Closed.
Legal Name: St. Anthony of Padua Roman Catholic Church, Camden, N.J.
School—St. Anthony of Padua School, (Grades K-8), 2824 River Ave., 8105. Tel: 856-966-6791;
Fax: 856-966-1616. Dr. Mary Burke, Ed.D., Prin. Lay Teachers 14; Students 180.

3—ST. BARTHOLOMEW'S R.C. CHURCH, CAMDEN, N.J. (1940) (African American), Merged with the Church of St. Joan of Arc, Camden to form St. Josephine Bakhita Parish, Camden.

4—THE CHURCH OF ST. JOAN OF ARC, CAMDEN, N.J. (1920) Merged with St. Bartholomew's R.C. Church, Camden to form St. Josephine Bakhita Parish, Camden.

5—THE CHURCH OF SACRED HEART (1885) Records for St. George kept at Sacred Heart, Camden. Records for Sts. Peter and Paul kept at the Cathedral of the Immaculate Conception, Camden. Records for St. John the Baptist kept at St. Joseph Pro-Cathedral, Camden. Rev. Msgr. Michael J. Doyle; Revs. Gerard C. Marable; Armando Rodriguez Montoya, Parochial Vicar.
Res.: 1739 Ferry Ave., 08104. Tel: 856-966-6700;
Fax: 856-756-0102.
School—The Church of Sacred Heart School, (Grades K-8), Fourth & Jaspers Sts., 08104.
Tel: 856-963-1341; Fax: 856-963-3551. Miss Janet Williams, Prin. Lay Teachers 13; Students 220.
Catechesis Religious Program—Students 32.

6—THE CHURCH OF THE HOLY NAME, CAMDEN, N.J. (1913) (Hispanic), Merged with The Church of the Immaculate Conception, Camden & Our Lady of Mount Carmel/Church of Our Lady of Fatima, Camden to form The Parish of the Cathedral of the Immaculate Conception, Camden.

7—THE CHURCH OF THE IMMACULATE CONCEPTION, CAMDEN, N.J. (1864) [CEM] Merged with The Church of the Holy Name, Camden & Our Lady of Mount Carmel/Church of Our Lady of Fatima, Camden to form The Parish of the Cathedral of the Immaculate Conception, Camden.

8—ST. JOSEPH (1893) (Pro-Cathedral) Revs. Jaime E. Hostios; Fabian Quentero Orozco, Parochial Vicar; Jerold Mariastanislaus; Deacon Omar M. Aguilar; Patrick Cashio, Dir., Romero Ctr.
Legal Name: St. Joseph Catholic Church, East Camden, N.J. (Pro-Cathedral)
Res.: 2907 Federal St., 08105. Tel: 856-964-2776;
Fax: 856-964-0044; Email: mail@sjprocathedral.org; Web: www.sjprocathedral.org. In Res., Rev. Jerold Mariastanislaus.
School—St. Joseph School, (Grades K-8),
Tel: 856-964-4336; Fax: 856-964-1080. Mrs. Frances Montgomery, Prin. Lay Teachers 18; Students 251.
Child Care—St. Joseph Child Development Center, Inc., 17 Church St., 08105. Marie Klein, Dir. Children 90.
Catechesis Religious Program—
Tel: 856-964-2776, Ext. 501. Jocelyn Villa, C.R.E. Students 253.

9—ST. JOSEPHINE BAKHITA PARISH, CAMDEN, N.J. (2010) Closed.
Churches—
St. Bartholomew, Camden—Tel: 856-962-8642;
Fax: 856-962-7123.
St. Joan of Arc, Camden, 3107 Alabama Rd., 08104-3198.

10—ST. JOSEPH'S CATHOLIC CHURCH, CAMDEN, N.J. (1892) [CEM] (Polish), Closed.

11—OUR LADY OF MOUNT CARMEL, CAMDEN, N.J./ CHURCH OF OUR LADY OF FATIMA, CAMDEN, N.J., (Hispanic—Italian), Merged with The Church of the Immaculate Conception, Camden & The Church of the Holy Name, Camden to form The Parish of the Cathedral of the Immaculate Conception, Camden.

OUTSIDE THE CITY OF CAMDEN

ABSECON, ATLANTIC CO., CHURCH OF SAINT ELIZABETH ANN SETON, ABSECON, N.J. (1975) Revs. Perry A. Cherubini; Robert Ngageno, Parochial Vicar.
Res.: 591 New Jersey Ave., Absecon, 08201.
Tel: 609-641-1480; Fax: 609-641-7396.
See Assumption Regional School, Galloway under Regional Schools, Elementary located in the Institution section.
Catechesis Religious Program—Tel: 609-641-7043;
Fax: 609-641-5709. Students 290.
Mission—St. Andrew Kim Korean Catholic Mission, Inc., 702 S. New Rd., Absecon, 08201. Rev. John Seo, Chap.

ATCO, CAMDEN CO.

1—CHRIST THE REDEEMER PARISH, ATCO, N.J., Rev. Christopher M. Mann; Deacon Aaron G. Smith.
Rectory—318 Carl Hasselman Dr., Atco, 08004-1997.
Tel: 856-767-0719; Email: secretary@ctratco.com; Web: www.ctratco.com; Web: www.christtheredeemer.us.
Churches—
Assumption, Atco—
St. Anthony, Waterford.
Sacred Heart, Cedar Brook.
Catechesis Religious Program—Tel: 856-767-3414. David Regn, C.R.E. Students 350.

2—THE CHURCH OF THE ASSUMPTION, ATCO, N.J. (1947) Merged with Parish of Blessed John the Twenty-Third, Blue Anchor; St. Lucy Church, Blue Anchor; Sacred Heart Church, Cedar Brook; and St. Anthony's Church, Waterford to form Christ the Redeemer Parish, Atco.

ATLANTIC CITY, ATLANTIC CO.

1—CHURCH OF ST. NICHOLAS, ATLANTIC CITY, N.J. (1855) Merged with Our Lady Star of the Sea Church, Atlantic City; St. Michael Church, Atlantic City & St. Monica Church, Atlantic City to form The Parish of Saint Monica, Atlantic City. All sacramental records are located at The Parish of Saint Monica, Atlantic City.

2—THE CHURCH OF THE HOLY SPIRIT, ATLANTIC CITY, N.J. (1908) Closed. For sacramental records see the Parish of St. Monica, Atlantic City.

3—ST. MICHAEL'S CHURCH, ATLANTIC CITY, N.J. (1904) (Italian), Merged with Our Lady Star of the Sea Church, Atlantic City; St. Monica Church, Atlantic City & St. Nicholas of Tolentine Church, Atlantic City to form The Parish of Saint Monica, Atlantic City. All sacramental records are located at The Parish of Saint Monica, Atlantic City.

4—ST. MONICA'S CATHOLIC CHURCH, ATLANTIC CITY, N.J. (1925) Merged with Our Lady Star of the Sea Church, Atlantic City; St. Michael Church, Atlantic City & St. Nicholas of Tolentine Church, Atlantic City to form The Parish of Saint Monica, Atlantic City. All sacramental records are located at The Parish of Saint Monica, Atlantic City.

5—OUR LADY, STAR OF THE SEA, ATLANTIC CITY, N.J. (1894) Merged with St. Michael Church, Atlantic City; St. Monica Church, Atlantic City & St. Nicholas of Tolentine Church, Atlantic City to form The Parish of Saint Monica, Atlantic City. All sacramental records are located at The Parish of Saint Monica, Atlantic City.

6—THE PARISH OF SAINT MONICA, Revs. Jon P. Thomas; Fernando R. Carmona, Parochial Vicar; Thanh Q. Pham, Parochial Vicar. In Res., Rev. Robert B. Matysik.
Rectory—2651 Atlantic Ave., Atlantic City, 08401-6489. Tel: 609-345-1878; Fax: 609-348-0248; Email: olss2651@aol.com; Web: www.olssparish.com.
Churches—
Our Lady Star of the Sea—
St. Michael.
St. Monica.
St. Nicholas.
School—The Parish of Saint Monica School, (Grades PreK-8), 15 N. California Ave., Atlantic City, 08401.
Tel: 609-345-0648; Fax: 609-344-6735. Susan J. Tarrant, Prin. Lay Teachers 11; Sisters 3; Students 153.
Catechesis Religious Program—Tel: 609-340-0116. Students 315.
Convent—Sisters of Mercy, 25 N. California Ave., Atlantic City, 08401.

AUDUBON, CAMDEN CO., CHURCH OF THE HOLY MATERNITY, AUDUBON, NJ (1957) Merged with Church of the Sacred Heart, Mount Ephraim to form Emmaus Catholic Community, Mount Ephraim. For inquiries for sacramental records please see St. Rose of Lima, Haddon Heights.

AVALON, CAPE MAY CO.

1—ST. BRENDAN THE NAVIGATOR PARISH, AVALON, N.J. (2010) Rev. Mark R. Cavagnaro, V.F.
Rectory—5012 Dune Dr., Avalon, 08202-1333.
Tel: 609-967-3746; Email: stbrendannav@comcast.net.
Churches—
Maris Stella, Avalon—
St. Paul, Stone Harbor.
Catechesis Religious Program—Tel: 609-967-3017; Email: Faithformationdirector@stbrendanavalon.org. Sr. Joanne Wallace, IHM, D.R.E. Students 27.

2—THE CHURCH OF MARIS STELLA, AVALON, N.J. (1961) Merged with St. Paul's Church, Stone Harbor to form St. Brendan the Navigator, Avalon.

BARRINGTON, CAMDEN CO., CHURCH OF ST. FRANCIS DE SALES, BARRINGTON, N.J. (1955) Merged with The Church of Mary, Mother of the Church, Bellmawr & St. Gregory's Church, Magnolia to form Parish of Saint Rita, Bellmawr.

BELLMAWR, CAMDEN CO.

1—THE CHURCH OF MARY, MOTHER OF THE CHURCH, BELLMAWR, N.J. (1965) Merged with Church of St. Francis de Sales, Barrington & St. Gregory's Church, Magnolia to form Parish of Saint Rita, Bellmawr.

2—THE CHURCH OF THE ANNUNCIATION BVM, BELLMAWR, N.J. (1951) Closed. For inquiries for parish records please see St. Joachim Parish, Bellmawr, NJ.

3—ST. JOACHIM PARISH, BELLMAWR, N.J. (2011) Rev. Piotr Szamocki; Deacon Gerard V. DeMuro.
Worship Sites—
Annunciation, Bellmawr—
Mary, Mother of the Church, Bellmawr.
Saint Anne, Westville.
Rectory—601 Browning Rd., Bellmawr, 08031-0155.
Tel: 856-931-6307; Fax: 856-931-0166; Email: annun.church@comcast.net.
Catechesis Religious Program—Tel: 856-931-8590. Suzanne Fronzek, D.R.E. Students 217.
Convent—424 E. Browning Rd., Bellmawr, 08031. Daughters of Our Lady of the Sacred Heart.

4—PARISH OF SAINT RITA, BELLMAWR, N.J. (2010) Closed. (Parish formed 5-19-2010 from the merger of Mary, Mother of the Church Parish, Bellmawr; St. Francis de Sales Parish, Barrington, and St. Greogory Parish, Magnolia. Parish closed 6-30-2014. Sacramental records for St. Rita Parish and Mary, Mother of the Church Parish are located at St. Joachim Parish, Bellmawr. Sacramental records for St. Francis de Sales Parish and St. Gregory Parish are located at St. Rose of Lima Parish, Haddon Heights.).

BERLIN, CAMDEN CO.

1—CHURCH OF OUR LADY OF MOUNT CARMEL, BERLIN, N.J. (1903) [CEM] Merged with St. Edward's R.C. Church, Pine Hill to form Saint Simon Stock Parish, Berlin.

2—SAINT SIMON STOCK PARISH, BERLIN, N.J. (2009) [CEM] Revs. James O. Dabrowski; Alfred Mungujakisa, Parochial Vicar; Deacons John D. Rich Jr.; Robert M. Iulucci.

Worship Site: O.L. Mt. Carmel, Berlin.

Parish Office: 178 W. White Horse Pike, Berlin, 08009-2023. Tel: 856-767-2563; Fax: 856-767-8791; Email: stsimonstockoffice@gmail.com; Web: www.stsimonstock.net.

Rectory—1 Maple Ave., Berlin, 08009.

See Our Lady of Mt. Carmel, Berlin under Regional Schools, Elementary located in the Institution section.

Catechesis Religious Program—Tel: 856-767-1537. Students 292.

BLACKWOOD, CAMDEN CO.

1—ST. AGNES' CHURCH, BLACKWOOD TERRACE, N.J. (1946) Merged with The R.C. Church of St. Jude, Blackwood to form Our Lady of Hope Parish, Blackwood.

2—OUR LADY OF HOPE PARISH, BLACKWOOD, N.J. (2010) Revs. Joseph T. Szolack; Edward M. Kennedy, Parochial Vicar; John A. DelDuca, (Retired), (Retired); Rene Canales; Deacons Robert P. Foley; Fernando S. Encarnado.

Rectory—701 Little Gloucester Rd., Blackwood, 08012-3311. Tel: 856-228-4331; Tel: 856-228-3171; Fax: 856-227-0743; Email: admin@ourladyofhopenj.org; Web: www.ourladyofhopenj.org.

Churches—

St. Agnes, Blackwood—

St. Jude, Blackwood.

See Our Lady of Hope Regional School, Blackwood under Regional Schools, Elementary located in the Institution section.

Catechesis Religious Program—Mary Jo Dwyer, D.R.E. Students 463.

3—THE R.C. CHURCH OF ST. JUDE, GLOUCESTER TOWNSHIP, N.J. (1961) Merged with St. Agnes' Church, Blackwood to form Our Lady of Hope Parish, Blackwood.

BLUE ANCHOR, CAMDEN CO., PARISH OF BLESSED JOHN THE TWENTY-THIRD, BLUE ANCHOR, N.J. (1925) [CEM] (Italian), Merged with The Church of the Assumption, Atco; St. Lucy Church, Blue Anchor; Sacred Heart Church, Cedar Brook; & St. Anthony's Church, Waterford to form Christ the Redeemer Parish, Atco.

BRIDGETON, CUMBERLAND CO.

1—THE CHURCH OF ST. TERESA AVILA, BRIDGETON, N.J. (1961) Merged with The Church of the Immaculate Conception, Bridgeton; Saint Michael's Roman Catholic Church, Cedarville; St. Mary's Church, Rosenhayn; & St. Anthony's Church, Port Norris to form The Parish of the Holy Cross, Bridgeton.

2—THE CHURCH OF THE IMMACULATE CONCEPTION, BRIDGETON, N.J. (1874) [CEM] Merged with The Church of St. Teresa Avila, Bridgeton; Saint Michael's Roman Catholic Church, Cedarville; St. Mary's Church, Rosenhayn; & St. Anthony's Church, Port Norris to form The Parish of the Holy Cross, Bridgeton.

3—THE PARISH OF THE HOLY CROSS, BRIDGETON, N.J. (2010) Revs. Matthew Weber; David Rivera; Daniel A. DiNardo, In Res. (Retired), (Retired); Deacons Christopher D. Nichols; Donald W. Rogozenski.

Rectory—46 Central Ave., Bridgeton, 08302-2305. Tel: 856-455-2323; Fax: 856-455-7291.

Churches—

St. Anthony, Port Norris—

Immaculate Conception, Bridgeton.

St. Mary, Rosenhayn.

St. Michael, Cedarville.

St. Teresa Avila, Bridgeton.

Catechesis Religious Program—Students 553.

Convent—64 North St., Bridgeton, 08302. Missionary Daughters of the Most Pure Virgin Mary.

Stations—NJ State Medium Security Prison, Bayside Prison—Rte. 47, Leesburg, 08327.

South Woods State Prison, 215 S. Burlington Rd., Bridgeton, 08302.

BRIGANTINE, ATLANTIC CO., ST. THOMAS' CATHOLIC CHURCH, BRIGANTINE, N.J. (1958) Revs. Edward J. Maher; Jose Thomas; Deacon Leonard W. Long.

Res.: 331 8th St. S., Brigantine, 08203.

Tel: 609-266-2123; Fax: 609-266-6416; Email: office@stthomasbrigantine.org; Web: www.stthomasbrigantine.org.

Catechesis Religious Program—Deacon Leonard W. Long, D.R.E. Students 225.

BROOKLAWN, CAMDEN CO., ST. MAURICE'S CHURCH, BROOKLAWN, N.J. (1955) Closed. For inquiries for parish records please see St. Joachim Parish, Bellmawr, N.J.

BUENA BOROUGH, ATLANTIC CO., QUEEN OF ANGELS PARISH, BUENA BOROUGH, N.J. (2001) [CEM] Merged with St. Rose of Lima Church, Newfield & St. Mary Church, Malaga to form Our Lady of the Blessed Sacrament Church, Newfield.

CAPE MAY COURT HOUSE, CAPE MAY CO., OUR LADY OF THE ANGELS (1956) Revs. John A. O'Leary; Cosme R. de la Pena

Legal Name: The Church of Our Lady of the Angels, Cape May Court House, N.J.

Res.: 35 E. Mechanic St., Cape May Court House, 08210. Tel: 609-465-5432; Fax: 609-465-7647; Email: sandy@ourladyoftheangels.net; Web: www.ourladyoftheangels.net.

Parish Center: 35 Mechanic St., Cape May Court House, 08210.

See Bishop McHugh Regional School, Cape May Court House under Regional Schools, Elementary located in the Institution section.

Catechesis Religious Program—Mrs. Joanne Kelly, C.R.E. Students 186.

CAPE MAY, CAPE MAY CO., THE CHURCH OF OUR LADY STAR OF THE SEA, CAPE MAY (1878) [CEM] Revs. Francis W. Danella, O.S.F.S.; David J. Devlin, O.S.F.S.; Ignatius Mathias, O.S.F.S.; Deacon Michael J. Kolakowski.

Res.: 520 Lafayette St., Cape May, 08204.

Tel: 609-884-5311; Fax: 609-542-9702; Web: www.ladystarofthesea.org.

See Cape Trinity Catholic School, N. Wildwood under Regional Schools, Elementary located in the Institution section.

Catechesis Religious Program—Tel: 609-884-5312. Students 36.

Convent—516 Lafayette St., Cape May, 08204. Sisters of St. Joseph of Chestnut Hill.

Chapel—Cape May Point, St. Agnes, (Summer).

CARNEYS POINT, SALEM CO.

1—THE CHURCH OF CORPUS CHRISTI, CARNEYS POINT, N.J. (1966) Merged with Church of the Queen of the Apostles, Pennsville; St. James' Church, Penns Grove; & St. Mary's Catholic Church, Salem to form Saint Gabriel the Archangel Parish, Carneys Point.

2—SAINT GABRIEL THE ARCHANGEL (2010) [CEM] Revs. Charles J. Colozzi; Robert J. D'Imperio; Deacon Robert M. Fanelli

*Legal Name: Saint Gabriel the Archangel Parish, Carneys Point, N.J.*In Res., Rev. Gustavo Agudelo.

Rectory—369 Georgetown Rd., Carney's Point, 08069-2598. Tel: 856-299-3833; Fax: 856-299-3887.

Churches—

Corpus Christi, Carneys Point—

St. James, Pennsgrove.

St. Mary, Salem.

Queen of the Apostles, Pennsville.

Catechesis Religious Program—350 Georgetown Rd., Carney's Point, 08069.

CEDARVILLE, CUMBERLAND CO., ST. MICHAEL'S ROMAN CATHOLIC CHURCH (1942) Merged with The Church of St. Teresa Avila, Bridgeton; The Church of the Immaculate Conception, Bridgeton; St. Mary's Church, Rosenhayn; & St. Anthony's Church, Port Norris to form The Parish of the Holy Cross, Bridgeton.

CHERRY HILL, CAMDEN CO.

1—CHRIST OUR LIGHT (2009) Revs. Thomas A. Newton; Thomas R. Kiely; Jay Ramos, Parochial Vicar; Deacon Joseph F. Seaman

*Legal Name: The Catholic Community of Christ Our Light, Cherry Hill, N.J.*In Res., Rev. Terry M. Odien, (Retired).

Rectory—402 Kings Hwy. N., Cherry Hill, 08034-1091. Tel: 856-667-2440; Fax: 856-482-0332.

Church: Saint Peter Celestine, Cherry Hill.

School—Resurrection Catholic School, (Grades PreK-8), Tel: 856-667-3034; Fax: 856-667-9160. Mrs. Molly Webb, Prin.; Noel Becker, Librarian. Students 350.

Catechesis Religious Program—Students 450.

Convent—Sisters of St. Joseph.

2—THE CHURCH OF ST. PETER CELESTINE, CHERRY HILL, N.J. (1961) Merged with Church of the Queen of Heaven, Cherry Hill to form The Catholic Community of Christ Our Light, Cherry Hill.

3—THE CHURCH OF ST. PIUS X, CHERRY HILL, N.J. (1961) Merged with The Church of the Holy Rosary, Cherry Hill to form Holy Eucharist Parish, Cherry Hill.

4—THE CHURCH OF THE HOLY ROSARY, CHERRY HILL, N.J. (1958) Merged with The Church of St. Pius X, Cherry Hill to form Holy Eucharist Parish, Cherry Hill.

5—CHURCH OF THE QUEEN OF HEAVEN, CHERRY HILL, N.J. (1955) Merged with The Church of St. Peter Celestine, Cherry Hill to form The Catholic Community of Christ Our Light, Cherry Hill.

6—HOLY EUCHARIST PARISH, CHERRY HILL, N.J. (2009) Revs. George C. Seiter; Michael J. Coffey, Senior Priest; Francis Oranefo; Deacons Anthony D. Malatesta; Robert W. Hamilton.

Res.: 344 Kresson Rd., Cherry Hill, 08034.

Tel: 856-429-1330; Fax: 856-429-8679; Email: parishoffice@holyeucharistcherryhill.org.

Churches—

Holy Rosary, Cherry Hill—Cherry Hill, 08034.

St. Pius X, Cherry Hill, Cherry Hill, 08003.

See Christ the King Regional School, Haddonfield under Regional Schools, Elementary located in the Institution section.

Catechesis Religious Program—Tel: 856-428-9207. Students 402.

7—ST. MARY'S R.C. CHURCH, DELAWARE TOWNSHIP, N.J. (1961)

2001 Springdale Rd., Cherry Hill, 08003.

Tel: 856-424-1454; Email: stmarycherryhill@gmail.com; Web: www.stmarycherryhill.org. Rev. Paul A. Olszewski; Rev. Msgr. Dominic J. Bottino, J.C.L., (In Res.); Rev. James H. King, (In Res.).

Catechesis Religious Program—Tel: 856-424-2679. Students 261.

Mission—Korean Catholic Mission, Rev. Sungheum (John) Kim, Admin.

8—ST. THOMAS MORE (1968) Rev. Phillip M. Johnson

Legal Name: The Church of St. Thomas More, Cherry Hill, New Jersey

Res.: 1439 Springdale Rd., Cherry Hill, 08003.

Tel: 856-424-3212; Fax: 856-424-2411; Email: sthomasmore@comcast.net; Web: www.stthomasmorenj.org.

Catechesis Religious Program—Students 171.

CLAYTON, GLOUCESTER CO., ST. CATHERINE'S ROMAN CATHOLIC CHURCH, CLAYTON, N.J. (1943) Merged with R.C. Church of the Nativity, Franklinville to form Parish of St. Michael the Archangel, Franklinville.

COLLINGS LAKES, ATLANTIC CO., OUR LADY OF THE LAKES (1976) Rev. Michael J. Goyette

Legal Name: Church of Our Lady of the Lakes, Collings Lakes, N.J.

Res.: 19 Malaga Rd., Collings Lakes, 08094.

Tel: 609-561-8313; Email: ourladyofthelakesparish@comcast.net.

Catechesis Religious Program—Students 33.

COLLINGSWOOD, CAMDEN CO.

1—ST. TERESA OF CALCUTTA PARISH (2010) Rev. John D. Bohrer, Admin.; Deacon Leo M. Howitz

Legal Name: Saint Teresa of Calcutta Parish, Collingswood, N.J.

Rectory—809 Park Ave., Collingswood, 08108-3147. Tel: 856-858-0298; Fax: 856-858-2796; Email: cvenafra@stteresaofcalcuttanj.org; Web: www.stteresaofcalcuttanj.org.

Churches—

Holy Saviour, Westmont—

St. John, Collingswood.

School—Good Shepherd Regional School, (Grades PreK-8), 100 Lees Ave., Collingswood, 08108.

Tel: 856-858-1562; Fax: 856-858-2943. Mr. Donald W. Garecht, Prin. Lay Teachers 14; Students 189.

Catechesis Religious Program—Email: plipperini@stteresaofcalcuttanj.org. Patricia Lipperini, Ph.D., D.R.E. Students 417.

2—ST. JOHN'S CATHOLIC CHURCH, COLLINGSWOOD, N.J. (1919) Merged with The Church of the Holy Saviour, Westmont to form Blessed Teresa of Calcutta Parish, Collingswood.

3—MOST PRECIOUS BLOOD PARISH, COLLINGSWOOD, N.J. (2011) Rev. Joseph An Nguyen; Deacon Kim T. Nguyen. In Res., Rev. Mike Steve Ezeatu.

Res.: 445 White Horse Pike, West Collingswood, 08107. Tel: 856-854-0364; Fax: 856-869-5129.

Catechesis Religious Program—Students 241.

DELAIR, CAMDEN CO., ST. VERONICA'S R.C. CHURCH, TOWNSHIP OF PENNSAUKEN, NEW JERSEY (1961) Merged with St. Cecilia Church, Pennsauken & St. Veronica R.C. Church, Delair to form Mary, Queen of All Saints, Pennsauken.

DEPTFORD, GLOUCESTER CO., THE CHURCH OF ST. JOHN VIANNEY, GLOUCESTER COUNTY, N.J. (1971) Merged with St. Margaret's Church, Woodbury Heights to form Infant Jesus Parish, Woodbury Heights.

EGG HARBOR CITY, ATLANTIC CO., ST. NICHOLAS' CHURCH, EGG HARBOR CITY (1864) Merged with The Church of the Assumption, Galloway to form Our Lady of Perpetual Help, Galloway.

EGG HARBOR TOWNSHIP, ATLANTIC CO., SAINT KATHARINE DREXEL (2000)

6077 W. Jersey Ave., Egg Harbor Township, 08234.

Tel: 609-645-7313; Fax: 609-645-9680; Email: office@skd-parish.org; Web: www.skd-parish.org. Rev. John J. Vignone, V.G., V.F.

Legal Name: The Church of Saint Katharine Drexel, McKee City, New Jersey

Catechesis Religious Program—Students 522.

ELMER, SALEM CO., ST. ANN'S CATHOLIC CHURCH, ELMER, N.J. (1961) Merged with Church of the Holy Name of Jesus, Mullica Hill & St. Joseph's Catholic Church, Woodstown to form Catholic Community of the Holy Spirit, Mullica Hill.

FRANKLINVILLE, GLOUCESTER CO.

1—ST. MICHAEL THE ARCHANGEL (2010) Rev. Lawrence E. Polansky

Legal Name: Parish of St. Michael the Archangel, Franklinville, N.J.

Rectory—49 W. North St., Clayton, 08312.

Tel: 856-881-9155; Fax: 856-881-9166; Web: www.parishofstmichaelthearchangel.com.

Churches—

St. Catherine of Siena, Clayton—
Nativity, Franklinville, Delsea Dr., Franklinville, 08322.
School—St. Michael the Archangel School, (Grades PreK-8), 51 W. North St., Clayton, 08312.
Tel: 856-881-0067; Fax: 856-881-4064; Email: office@smrsonline.com. Miss Janice Bruni, Prin. Lay Teachers 15; Students 214.
Catechesis Religious Program—Gina Wheeler, D.R.E. Students 251.
2—R.C. CHURCH OF THE NATIVITY, FRANKLINVILLE, N.J. (1961) Merged with St. Catherine's Roman Catholic Church, Clayton to form Parish of St. Michael the Archangel, Franklinville.
GALLOWAY, ATLANTIC CO.
1—THE CHURCH OF THE ASSUMPTION (1938) Merged with St. Nicholas' Church, Egg Harbor City to form Our Lady of Perpetual Help, Galloway.
2—OUR LADY OF PERPETUAL HELP (2012) [CEM] Revs. Thomas J. Barcellona; Vincent Orum, A.J., Parochial Vicar; Deacons Francis A. Cerullo; Michael H. Guerrieri.
Rectory—146 S. Pitney Rd., Galloway, 08205.
Tel: 609-652-0008; Fax: 609-652-0883.
Churches—
The Church of the Assumption, Galloway—
St. Nicholas' Church, Egg Harbor City.
School—Assumption Regional Catholic School,
Tel: 608-652-7134; Fax: 609-652-2544. Mrs. Mary Ellen Schurtz, Prin.
Catechesis Religious Program—
Tel: 609-652-0008, Ext. 208; Fax: 609-652-0883. Nancy Riddell, D.R.E. Students 448.
GIBBSBORO, CAMDEN CO., ST. ANDREW THE APOSTLE (1963) Rev. Msgr. Louis A. Marucci, D.Min., V.F.; Rev. Michael August De Leon, A.M.; Rev. Msgr. John Frey, In Res. (Retired); Deacon William M. Slaven
Legal Name: St. Andrew the Apostle R.C. Church, Gibbsboro, N.J.
Res.: 27 Kresson-Gibbsboro Rd., Gibbsboro, 08026.
Tel: 856-784-3878; Fax: 856-435-7508; Email: office@churchofsaintandrews.org; Web: www.churchofstandrews.org.
See Our Lady of Mt. Carmel, Berlin under Regional Schools, Elementary located in the Institution section.
Catechesis Religious Program—Tel: 856-783-0550. Students 631.
GIBBSTOWN, GLOUCESTER CO.
1—ST. CLARE OF ASSISI PARISH, GIBBSTOWN, N.J. (2010) Revs. David A. Grover; Grace Manano, Parochial Vicar; John Franco Cardenas, Parochial Vicar; Deacons Joseph A. Garozzo; Kevin P. Hannon. Office & Mailing Address: 140 Broad St., Swedesboro, 08085. Tel: 856-467-0037;
Fax: 856-467-0038; Email: info@stclarenj.org; Web: stclarenj.org.
Rectory—313 Memorial Ave., Gibbstown, 08027-1317. Tel: 856-423-0007.
See Guardian Angels Regional School, Gibbstown under Regional Schools, Elementary located in the Institution section.
Catechesis Religious Program—1225 Kings Hwy., Swedesboro, 08085. Tel: 856-467-5426; Email: faithformation@stclarenj.org. Verna Mullen, D.R.E. Students 761.
Convent—320 Memorial Ave., Gibbstown, 08027. Sr. Maria DiRosa, Contact Person. Sisters 3.
2—ST. MICHAEL'S CHURCH, GIBBSTOWN, N.J. (1940) Merged with St. Joseph's Church, Swedesborough & St. John's Church, Paulsboro to form St. Clare of Assisi Parish, Gibbstown.
GLASSBORO, GLOUCESTER CO.
1—ST. BRIDGET'S CATHOLIC CHURCH, GLASSBORO, N.J. (1887) [CEM] (Hispanic) (University Parish)
202 Ellis St., Glassboro, 08028. Rev. Michael J. Field, D.Min.; Deacons Kevin C. Heil; Samuel Soto; Aaron G. Smith.
Res.: 125 Church St., Glassboro, 08028.
Tel: 856-881-2753; Email: parishoffice@stbridgetup.org.
See School under Parish of St. Michael the Archangel, Franklinville.
Catechesis Religious Program—Students 110.
Convent—212 Ellis St., Glassboro, 08028. Franciscan Missionary Sisters of the Immaculate Heart of Mary.
2—THE CHURCH OF OUR LADY OF LOURDES, GLASSBORO, N.J. (1966) Merged with Our Lady Queen of Peace R.C. Church, Pitman, N.J. to form Mary, Mother of Mercy Parish, Glassboro, N.J.
3—MARY, MOTHER OF MERCY PARISH, GLASSBORO, N.J. (2011) Rev. William J. Kelly; Deacons Nicholas Mortelliti; John J. Luko Jr.; Meryl Cerana, Pastoral Assoc. & Bus. Admin. In Res., Rev. Msgr. James R. Tracy, Ph.D., V.F., (Retired); Rev. Joseph J. Adamson, (Retired).
Worship Sites—
Our Lady of Lourdes, Glassboro—500 Greentree Rd., Glassboro, 08028.
Our Lady Queen of Peace, Pitman.
Res.: 161 Pitman Ave., Pitman, 08071.
Tel: 856-881-0909; Fax: 856-881-5457; Web: www.mary-mom.com.
Catechesis Religious Program—Shannon Cassidy, D.R.E.
GLOUCESTER, CAMDEN CO., ST. MARY'S CHURCH, GLOUCESTER (1848) [CEM] Rev. Msgr. William A. Hodge, V.F.; Rev. Kevin J. Mohan; Deacons David W. Murnane; Joseph G. Rafferty Sr. In Res., Rev. Kevin J. Mohan.
Res.: 426 Monmouth St., Gloucester, 08030.
Tel: 856-456-0052; Fax: 856-456-1837; Email: stmaryrectory@comcast.net; Web: www.stmarysgloucester.org.
Catechesis Religious Program—Students 141.
HADDON HEIGHTS, CAMDEN CO., CHURCH OF ST. ROSE, HADDON HEIGHTS, N.J. (1896) Revs. E. Joseph Byerley; Alfred Mungujakisa; Peter M. Idler; Deacons Douglas R. Crawford; James H. Rocks. In Res., Rev. John M. Stabeno, In Res.
Res.: 300 Kings Hwy., Haddon Heights, 08035-1397.
Tel: 856-547-0564; Fax: 856-547-7311; Email: pastor@strosenj.com; Web: www.strosenj.com.
School—Church of St. Rose School, (Grades K-8),
Tel: 856-546-6166; Fax: 856-546-6601; Email: principal@strosenj.com. William Stonis, Prin.; Marguerite Crowell, Librarian. Lay Teachers 18; Students 330.
Catechesis Religious Program—
Tel: 856-546-0564, Ext. 103. Students 308.
HADDON TOWNSHIP, CAMDEN CO.
1—THE CHURCH OF ST. VINCENT PALLOTTI, HADDON TOWNSHIP, N.J. (1963) Merged with St. Aloysius, Oaklyn to form St. Joseph the Worker Parish, Haddon Township, N.J.
2—ST. JOSEPH THE WORKER (2011) Revs. Walter A. Norris, Esq., V.F.; Frederick G. Link, (Retired); John A. Rossi; Deacon Craig A. Bickel
*Legal Name: St. Joseph the Worker Parish, Haddon Township, N.J.*In Res., Rev. John A. Rossi.
Worship Sites—
St. Vincent Pallotti, Haddon Township—
St. Aloysius, Oaklyn.
Parish Office: 901 Hopkins Rd. Ste A, Haddonfield, 08033-3099. Tel: 856-858-1313; Fax: 856-869-9010; Web: www.stjosephtheworker.net.
Catechesis Religious Program—Tel: 856-240-7813; Fax: 856-869-0910. Anita D'Imperio, D.R.E. Students 289.
HADDONFIELD, CAMDEN CO., CHURCH OF CHRIST THE KING, HADDONFIELD, N.J. (1927) Revs. James T. Dever, O.S.F.S.; Joseph A. DiMauro, O.S.F.S.; Deacon Peter J. Powell, (Retired). In Res., Rev. David J. Klein, J.C.L.
Res.: 200 Windsor Ave., Haddonfield, 08033.
Tel: 856-429-1600; Fax: 856-429-2734; Web: ctkhaddonfield.org.
See Christ the King Regional School, Haddonfield under Regional Schools, Elementary located in the Institution section.
Catechesis Religious Program—Students 616.
HAMMONTON, ATLANTIC CO.
1—ST. ANTHONY OF PADUA ROMAN CATHOLIC CHURCH, HAMMONTON, N.J. (1964) Merged with St. Joseph's Church, Hammonton & St. Martin de Porres Roman Catholic Church, Hammonton to form Saint Mary of Mount Carmel Parish, Hammonton.
2—ST. JOSEPH'S CHURCH, HAMMONTON, N.J. (1886) [CEM] Merged with St. Anthony of Padua Roman Catholic Church, Hammonton & St. Martin de Porres Roman Catholic Church, Hammonton to form Saint Mary of Mount Carmel Parish, Hammonton.
3—ST. MARTIN DE PORRES ROMAN CATHOLIC CHURCH, HAMMONTON, N.J. (1962) Merged with St. Anthony of Padua Roman Catholic Church, Hammonton & St. Joseph's Church, Hammonton to form Saint Mary of Mount Carmel Parish, Hammonton.
4—SAINT MARY OF MOUNT CARMEL PARISH, HAMMONTON, N.J. (2010) [CEM] Revs. Peter M. Saporito; David Rivera, Parochial Vicar; Deacons George R. VanLeer; Frank Guaracini Jr. In Res., Rev. Allain B. Caparas.
Rectory—226 French St., Hammonton, 08037.
Tel: 609-704-5945; Fax: 609-704-5249; Email: parishoffice@smmcp.net; Web: www.smmcp.net.
Church: 220 Third St., Hammonton, 08037.
Churches—
St. Anthony, Hammonton—
St. Joseph, Hammonton.
St. Martin de Porres, Hammonton.
See St. Joseph Regional Elementary School, Hammonton under Regional Schools, Elementary located in the Institution Section.
Catechesis Religious Program—Tel: 607-704-2400; Email: rel.ed@comcast.net. Lori Scott Divetta, D.R.E. Students 621.
Convent—219 N. 3rd St., Hammonton, 08037.
LINDENWOLD, CAMDEN CO.
1—CHURCH OF ST. LAWRENCE, LAUREL SPRINGS, N.J. (1896) Merged with The R.C. Church of St. Luke, Stratford & Our Lady of Grace, R.C. Church, Somerdale to form Our Lady of Guadalupe, Lindenwold.
2—OUR LADY OF GUADALUPE PARISH, LINDENWOLD, N.J. (2009) Deacon Nicholas Mortelliti; Revs. Vincent G. Guest; Adam Cichoski, Parochial Vicar; Deacon John A. Contino. In Res., Rev. James L. Bartoloma, J.C.L.
Rectory—100 South Ave., Lindenwold, 08021-1696.
Tel: 856-627-2222; Fax: 856-627-8210. Churches.
St. Lawrence, Lindenwold—
St. Luke, Stratford.
School—John Paul II Regional School, 55 Warwick Rd., Stratford, 08084. Tel: 856-783-3088;
Fax: 856-783-9302. Mrs. Helen Persing, Prin.
Catechesis Religious Program—Students 445.
LINWOOD, ATLANTIC CO., THE CHURCH OF OUR LADY OF SORROWS, LINWOOD, N.J. (1965) Rev. Paul D. Harte, V.F.; Deacon Joseph W. Lonegan.
Res.: 724 Maple, Linwood, 08221. Tel: 609-927-1154; Fax: 609-927-0398; Email: ourladyofsorrowslinwoodnj@verizon.net; Web: www.ourladyofsorrows.us/.
Catechesis Religious Program—Tel: 609-927-0121. Melissa Stuchel, D.R.E. Students 396.
LONGPORT, ATLANTIC CO., CHURCH OF THE EPIPHANY, LONGPORT, N.J. (1954) Merged with Church of the Blessed Sacrament, Margate & St. James Catholic Church, Ventnor to form Holy Trinity Parish, Margate.
MAGNOLIA, CAMDEN CO., ST. GREGORY'S CHURCH, MAGNOLIA, N.J. (1955) Merged with Church of St. Francis de Sales, Barrington & The Church of Mary, Mother of the Church, Bellmawr to form Parish of Saint Rita, Bellmawr.
MALAGA, GLOUCESTER CO., ST. MARY'S ROMAN CATHOLIC CHURCH OF MALAGA, N.J. (1961) Merged with St. Rose of Lima, Newfield, Queen of Angels, Buena Borough to form Our Lady of the Blessed Sacrament, Newfield.
MANTUA, GLOUCESTER CO., R.C. CHURCH OF THE INCARNATION (1956) Revs. Raymond P. Gormley, V.F.; John E. Bruni; Deacons Thomas F. O'Brien, Ph. D., Ed.D.; Joseph Lopes; J. Peter Traum
Legal Name: R.C. Church of the Incarnation, Township of Mantua, New Jersey
Res.: 240 Main St., Mantua, 08051.
Tel: 856-468-1314; Fax: 856-468-4886.
See St. Margaret School, Woodbury Heights under Regional Schools, Elementary located in the Institution section.
Catechesis Religious Program—Tel: 856-468-7566. Students 1,200.
MARGATE, ATLANTIC CO., HOLY TRINITY PARISH, MARGATE, N.J. (2010) Revs. Joseph R. Ferrara, Email: frjoeferrara@comcast.net; Pawel Kryszkiewicz; Deacon Paul R. Bubeck Jr.
Rectory—11 N. Kenyon Ave., Margate City, 08402-1593. Tel: 609-822-7105; Fax: 609-822-3817.
Churches—
Blessed Sacrament, Margate—
Epiphany, Longport.
St. James, Ventnor.
Catechesis Religious Program—Cathy Bubeck, M.A., D.R.E. Students 149.
Convent—St. Joseph Convent, 14 N. Jerome Ave., Margate City, 08402.
MARMORA, CAPE MAY CO.
1—CHURCH OF THE RESURRECTION, MARMORA, N.J. (1975) Merged with St. Casimir's R.C. Church, Woodbine, N.J. & St. Elizabeth's Church, Goshen to form The Parish of St. Maximilian Kolbe, Marmora, N.J.
2—THE PARISH OF ST. MAXIMILIAN KOLBE, MARMORA, N.J. (2011) Rev. Msgr. Peter M. Joyce, J.C.L. In Res., Rev. Jose Ainikkal, C.M.I.
Res.: 200 W. Tuckahoe Rd., Marmora, 08223.
Tel: 609-390-0664; Fax: 609-390-8717.
Catechesis Religious Program—Students 380.
MAYS LANDING, ATLANTIC CO.
1—CHURCH OF ST. VINCENT DE PAUL, MAYS LANDING, N.J. (1906) [CEM] Merged with St. Bernard Mission, Dorothy to form St. Vincent de Paul Parish, Mays Landing.
2—ST. VINCENT DE PAUL PARISH, MAYS LANDING, N.J. (1907) Revs. Edward F. Heintzelman; James H. King; Deacon Richard S. Maxwell. In Res., Rev. James H. King.
Rectory—5021 Harding Hwy., Mays Landing, 08330-1707. Tel: 609-625-2124; Fax: 609-625-8718; Web: www.vincentdepaul.org/index.ofm.
Churches—
St. Bernard, Dorothy—
St. Vincent de Paul, Mays Landing.
School—St. Vincent de Paul Parish, Mays Landing, N.J. School, (Grades PreK-8), 5809 Main St., Mays Landing, 08330. Tel: 609-625-1565;
Fax: 609-625-4703. Miss Linda Pirolli, Prin.
Catechesis Religious Program—Students 218.
MERCHANTVILLE, CAMDEN CO., ST. PETER'S CATHOLIC CHURCH, MERCHANTVILLE, N.J. (1903) Revs. Timothy E. Byerley; Francis Kim, Parochial Vicar; Shajii

Muttathottil, Parochial Vicar; Deacon Michael F. Scott.
Res.: 43 W. Maple Ave., Merchantville, 08109.
Tel: 856-663-1373; Fax: 856-488-0647; Web: www.saintpetermerchantville.com.
School—St. Peter's School, Tel: 856-665-5789; Fax: 856-665-4943; Web: www.stpeterschool.org. Joseph Saffioti, Prin. PreK3-8 Lay Teachers 24; Students 312.
Catechesis Religious Program—Tel: 856-663-4490. Flora Hand, D.R.E. Students 183.

MILLVILLE, CUMBERLAND CO.

1—THE CHURCH OF ST. JOHN BOSCO, MILLVILLE, N.J. (1966) Merged with The Church of St. Mary Magdalen, Millville to form The Parish of All Saints, Millville.

2—THE CHURCH OF SAINT MARY MAGDALEN, MILLVILLE (1864) [CEM] Merged with The Church of St. John Bosco, Millville to form The Parish of All Saints, Millville.

3—THE PARISH OF ALL SAINTS, MILLVILLE, N.J. (2010) [CEM] Rev. Peter M. Idler; Deacons Hipolito Lagares; Severno S. Nasuti Jr.; Russell O. Davis. In Res., Rev. Peter M. Idler.
Rectory—621 Dock St., Millville, 08332-2939.
Tel: 856-825-0021; Fax: 856-825-4338.
Churches—
St. John Bosco, Millville—
Saint Mary Magdalen, Millville.
Catechesis Religious Program—Tel: 609-617-5461. Lisa Caso, D.R.E. Students 162.

MOUNT EPHRAIM, CAMDEN CO.

1—CHURCH OF THE SACRED HEART, MT. EPHRAIM, N.J. (1939) Merged with Church of the Holy Maternity, Audubon to form Emmaus Catholic Community, Mount Ephraim. For inquiries for sacramental records please see St. Rose of Lima, Haddon Heights.

2—EMMAUS CATHOLIC COMMUNITY, MT. EPHRAIM, N.J. (2010) Closed. For inquiries for sacramental records please see St. Rose of Lima, Haddon Heights.

MULLICA HILL, GLOUCESTER CO.

1—CHURCH OF THE HOLY NAME OF JESUS, MULLICA HILL, N.J. (1901) [CEM] Merged with St. Ann's Catholic Church, Elmer & St. Joseph's Catholic Church, Woodstown to form Catholic Community of the Holy Spirit, Mullica Hill.

2—HOLY SPIRIT (2010) [CEM 2]
Parish Office: 17 Earlington Ave., Mullica Hill, 08062-9418. Tel: 856-478-2294; Fax: 856-478-4120; Email: anowicki@holyspiritweb.org; Web: www.holyspiritweb.org. Revs. Anthony R. DiBardino, V.F.; Joseph C. Pham, Email: fr.joseph@holyspiritweb.org; Deacons Robert M. Fanelli; Joseph H. Webb
Legal Name: Catholic Community of the Holy Spirit, Mullica Hill, N.J.
Rectory—51 Broad St., Woodstown, 08098.
Churches—
St. Ann, Elmer—
Holy Name of Jesus, Mullica Hill.
St. Joseph, Woodstown.
Catechesis Religious Program—Email: smongiovi@holyspiritweb.org. Sherry Ann Mongiovi, D.R.E. Students 16.

NATIONAL PARK, GLOUCESTER CO., ST. MATTHEW'S CATHOLIC CHURCH, NATIONAL PARK, N.J. (1915) Merged with Church of the Most Holy Redeemer, Westville Grove & St. Patrick's Church, Woodbury to form Holy Angels Parish, Woodbury. For inquiries for parish records contact Catholic Community of the Holy Spirit, Mullica Hill.

NEWFIELD, GLOUCESTER CO.

1—OUR LADY OF THE BLESSED SACRAMENT, NEWFIELD, N.J. (2011) Rev. Ariel Hernandez; Deacons Kevin L. Laughlin; Anthony M. Jadick. In Res., Rev. Msgr. Victor S. Muro, (Retired), (Retired).
Rectory—104 Catawba Ave., Newfield, 08344-9512.
Tel: 856-213-6259; Fax: 856-213-6279.
Worship Sites—
Saint Rose of Lima, Newfield—
St. Mary, Malaga.
Our Lady of Victories, Landisville.
Saint Michael, Minotola.
Catechesis Religious Program—Students 200.
Convent—Villa Rossello, 1009 Main Rd., Newfield, 08344.
Chapel—St. Barbara Chapel, 2334 E. Oak Rd., Vineland, 08361.
Shrine—St. Padre Pio Shrine, 401 N. Harding Hwy., Box 203, Landisville, 08326.

2—ST. ROSE'S CATHOLIC CHURCH (1922) Merged with Queen of Angels, Buena Borough & St. Mary, Malaga to form Our Lady of the Blessed Sacrament, Newfield.

NORTH CAPE MAY, CAPE MAY CO.

1—THE CHURCH OF ST. JOHN OF GOD, NORTH CAPE MAY, N.J. (1966) Merged with St. Raymond's Catholic Church, Villas to form The Parish of Saint John Neumann, North Cape May.

2—SAINT JOHN NEUMAN (2010) Rev. Ernest R. Soprano
*Legal Name: The Parish of Saint John Neumann, North Cape May, N.J.*In Res., Rev. Robert J. Fritz, (Retired).
Rectory—680 Town Bank Rd., North Cape May, 08204-4413. Tel: 609-884-1656; Fax: 609-898-0673.
Churches—
St. John of God, North Cape May—
St. Raymond, Villas.
Catechesis Religious Program—Tel: 609-886-7640. Sr. Kathleen Nuckols, I.H.M., D.R.E. Students 162.
Convent—25 E. Ocean Ave., Villas, 08251.

NORTHFIELD, ATLANTIC CO.

1—THE CHURCH OF ST. BERNADETTE, NORTHFIELD, N.J. (1966) Merged with St. Peter's Catholic Church, Pleasantville to form St. Gianna Beretta Molla Parish, Northfield.

2—ST. GIANNA BERETTA MOLLA PARISH, NORTHFIELD, N.J. (2010) Revs. Anthony J. Manuppella; Christopher M. Markellos, Parochial Vicar; John Seo, Parochial Vicar. In Res., Rev. Anthony I. Cataudo, O.P., (Retired), (Retired).
Rectory—1421 New Rd., Northfield, 08225-1103.
Tel: 609-646-5611; Fax: 609-484-8345; Email: stgianna@comcast.net.
Church: St. Bernadette, Northfield.
Catechesis Religious Program—Tel: 609-484-0249. Millie DiCicco, D.R.E. Students 243.

OAKLYN, CAMDEN CO., ST. ALOYSIUS CATHOLIC CHURCH, OAKLYN, N.J. (1935) Merged with St. Vincent Pallotti, Haddon Township to form St. Joseph the Worker Parish, Haddon Township, N.J.

OCEAN CITY, CAPE MAY CO.

1—ST. AUGUSTINE'S CATHOLIC CHURCH, OCEAN CITY, N.J. (1894) Merged with The Church of Our Lady of Good Counsel, Ocean City, N.J. and The Church of St. Frances Cabrini, Ocean City, N.J. to form Saint Damien Parish, Ocean City, N.J.

2—THE CHURCH OF ST. FRANCES CABRINI, OCEAN CITY, N.J. (1966) Merged with St. Augustine's Catholic Church, Ocean City, N.J. and The Church of Our Lady of Good Counsel, Ocean City, N.J. to form Saint Damien Parish, Ocean City, N.J.

3—THE CHURCH OF OUR LADY OF GOOD COUNSEL, OCEAN CITY, N.J. (1961) Merged with St. Augustine's Catholic Church, Ocean City, N.J. and The Church of St. Frances Cabrini, Ocean City, N.J. to form Saint Damien Parish, Ocean City, N.J.

4—SAINT DAMIEN PARISH, OCEAN CITY, N.J. (2011)
1310 Ocean Ave., Ocean City, 08226-3295.
Tel: 609-399-0648; Fax: 609-399-0063. Revs. Michael P. Rush; Allen B. Lovell; Alvaro Diaz; Deacons Mark J. Gallagher; Joseph P. Orlando.
Worship Sites—
Saint Augustine, Ocean City—13th St & Wesley Ave., Ocean City, 08226.
Our Lady of Good Counsel, Ocean City, 40th St. & Asbury Ave., Ocean City, 08226.
St. Frances Cabrini, Ocean City, 2nd St. & Atlantic Ave., Ocean City, 08226.
Catechesis Religious Program—Tel: 609-399-2643. Sr. Joelle Thren, S.C.C., D.R.E. Students 240.

PAULSBORO, GLOUCESTER CO., ST. JOHN'S CHURCH, PAULSBORO, N.J. (1904) Merged with St. Michael's Church, Gibbstown & St. Joseph's Church, Swedesborough to form St. Clare of Assisi Parish, Gibbstown.

PENNS GROVE, SALEM CO., ST. JAMES' CHURCH, PENNSGROVE, N.J. (1901) Merged with The Church of Corpus Christi, Carneys Point; Church of the Queen of the Apostles, Pennsville; & St. Mary's Catholic Church, Salem to form Saint Gabriel the Archangel Parish, Carneys Point.

PENNSAUKEN, CAMDEN CO.

1—ST. CECILIA'S CHURCH, NORTH MERCHANTVILLE, N.J. (1939) Merged with St. Veronica's R.C. Church, Delair, to form Mary, Queen of All Saints, Pennsauken.

2—MARY, QUEEN OF ALL SAINTS, PENNSAUKEN, N.J. (2009) Rev. Edward M. Friel; Rev. Msgr. Michael T. Mannion, S.T.L., (Retired); Rev. Joseph P. Capella, S.A.C.
Rectory—4824 Camden Ave., Pennsauken, 08110-1921. Tel: 856-662-2723; Email: maryqueenofallsaints@comcast.net; Web: www.maryqueenofallsaints.org. Churches.
Saint Cecilia, Pennsauken—
Saint Veronica, Delair.
Child Care—Little Angels Child Care Center, 48th St. & Camden Ave., Pennsauken, 08110.
School—St. Cecilia School, (Grades K-8), 4851 Camden Ave., Pennsauken, 08110.
Tel: 856-662-0149; Fax: 856-662-7460; Email: stceciliaschool@yahoo.com. Sr. Alicia Perna, S.S.J., Prin.; Mrs. Denise Carpenter, Librarian. Lay Teachers 15; Students 196.
Catechesis Religious Program—Monica Smith, D.R.E. Students 90.

3—ST. STEPHEN'S (1952) Rev. Daniel M. Rocco
Legal Name: St. Stephen's R.C. Church, Pennsauken Township, N.J.
Res.: 6306 Browning Rd., Pennsauken, 08109.
Tel: 856-662-9339; Email: ecclesia@comcast.net; Web: www.ststephenspennsauken.com.
Catechesis Religious Program—Students 37.

PENNSVILLE, SALEM CO., CHURCH OF THE QUEEN OF THE APOSTLES, PENNSVILLE, N.J. (1955) Merged with The Church of Corpus Christi, Carneys Point; St. James' Church, Penns Grove; & St. Mary's Catholic Church, Salem to form Saint Gabriel the Archangel Parish, Carneys Point.

PINE HILL, CAMDEN CO., ST. EDWARD'S R.C. CHURCH, PINE HILL, NEW JERSEY (1953) Merged with Church of Our Lady of Mount Carmel, Berlin to form Saint Simon Stock Parish, Berlin.

PITMAN, GLOUCESTER CO., OUR LADY QUEEN OF PEACE R.C. CHURCH, PITMAN N.J. (1940) Merged with The Church of Our Lady of Lourdes, Glassboro, N.J. to form Mary, Mother of Mercy Parish, Glassboro, N.J.

PLEASANTVILLE, ATLANTIC CO., ST. PETER'S CATHOLIC CHURCH, PLEASANTVILLE, N.J. (1896) Merged with The Church of St. Bernadette, Northfield to form St. Gianna Beretta Molla Parish, Northfield.

ROSENHAYN, CUMBERLAND CO., ST. MARY'S CHURCH, ROSENHAYN, N.J. (1914) [CEM] Merged with The Church of St. Teresa Avila, Bridgeton; The Church of the Immaculate Conception, Bridgeton; Saint Michael's Roman Catholic Church, Cedarville; & St. Anthony's Church, Port Norris to form The Parish of the Holy Cross, Bridgeton.

RUNNEMEDE, CAMDEN CO.

1—CHURCH OF ST. MARIA GORETTI, RUNNEMEDE, N.J. (1965) Merged with Church of St. Teresa of the Infant Jesus, Runnemede to form Holy Child Parish, Runnemede.

2—CHURCH OF ST. TERESA OF THE INFANT JESUS, RUNNEMEDE, N.J. (1927) Merged with Church of St. Maria Goretti, Runnemede to form Holy Child Parish, Runnemede.

3—HOLY CHILD PARISH, RUNNEMEDE, N.J. (2010)
Parish Office: 13 E. Evesham Rd., Runnemede, 08078-1700. Tel: 856-939-1681; Fax: 856-939-3878; Email: holychildparish@comcast.com. Revs. Joseph F. Ganiel; Antony Savari Muthu; Rev. Msgr. Joseph W. Pokusa, P.A., J.C.D., (Retired); Deacon Leonard P. Carlucci.
Churches—
St. Maria Goretti, Runnemede—
St. Teresa, Runnemede.
See St. Teresa School, Runnemede under Regional Schools, Elementary located in the Institution section.
Catechesis Religious Program—Students 235.
Convent—18 Ardmore Ave., Runnemede, 08078. Sisters, Servants of the Immaculate Heart of Mary.

SALEM, SALEM CO., ST. MARY'S CATHOLIC CHURCH, SALEM (1848) [CEM] Merged with The Church of Corpus Christi, Carneys Point; Church of the Queen of the Apostles, Pennsville; & St. James' Church, Penns Grove to form Saint Gabriel the Archangel Parish, Carneys Point.

SEA ISLE CITY, CAPE MAY CO., ST. JOSEPH'S CATHOLIC CHURCH, SEA ISLE CITY, N.J. (1884) Rev. Joseph A. Perreault; Deacon Joseph A. Murphy.
Res.: 126-44th St., Sea Isle City, 08243.
Tel: 609-263-8696; Fax: 609-263-7884; Email: info@stjosephsic.org; Web: www.stjosephsic.org.
See Bishop McHugh Regional School, Cape May Court House under Regional Schools, Elementary located in the Institution Section.
Catechesis Religious Program—Tel: 609-263-2087. Students 90.

SEWELL, GLOUCESTER CO., CHURCH OF THE HOLY FAMILY, WASHINGTON TOWNSHIP (1974) Revs. John P. Picinic; Alfred Onyutha; Deacons Gerald Jablonowski; Joseph A. Kain Sr.
Res.: 226 Hurffville Rd., Sewell, 08080.
Tel: 856-228-1616; Fax: 856-228-6332; Email: office@churchoftheholyfamily.org; Web: www.churchoftheholyfamily.org.
See Our Lady of Hope Regional School, Blackwood under Regional Schools, Elementary located in the Institution section.
Catechesis Religious Program—Tel: 856-228-2215; Fax: 856-401-1817. Students 4,772.

SICKLERVILLE, CAMDEN CO.

1—ST. CHARLES BORROMEO (1965) Revs. Michael J. Matveenko; Sanjai Devis, V.C.; Deacons Frank J. Campisi; Lawrence S. Farmer, Business Mgr.; Mrs. Mary Ann Exler, Pastoral Assoc.
Legal Name: The Church of St. Charles Borromeo, Washington Township, N.J.
Res.: 176 Stagecoach Rd., Sicklerville, 08081.
Tel: 856-629-0411; Fax: 856-629-9109; Email: secretary@saint-charles-borromeo.org; Web: www.saint-charles-borromeo.org.
See Our Lady of Hope Regional School, Blackwood under Regional Schools, Elementary located in the Institution section.
Catechesis Religious Program—Tel: 856-404-9248. Students 1,380.

2—CHURCH OF ST. JOHN NEUMANN, SICKLERVILLE, N.J. (1977) Merged with St. Mary's Church,

Williamstown to form Our Lady of Peace Parish, Williamstown.

SOMERDALE, CAMDEN CO., OUR LADY OF GRACE, R.C. CHURCH, SOMERDALE, NEW JERSEY (1954) Merged with Church of St. Lawrence, Lindenwold & The R.C. Church of St. Luke, Stratford to form Our Lady of Guadalupe Parish, Lindenwold.

SOMERS POINT, ATLANTIC CO., ST. JOSEPH'S CHURCH, SOMERS POINT, N.J. (1946) Rev. Jaromir Michalak; Deacons Robert G. Oliver; Steven T. Theis.
Res.: 606 Shore Rd., Somers Point, 08244.
Tel: 609-927-3568; Fax: 609-653-8707.
School—St. Joseph Regional School, (Grades PreK-8), Tel: 609-927-2228; Fax: 609-927-7834. Mr. Ted Pugliese, Prin.; Mrs. Jan Hutton, Librarian. Regionalized with Our Lady of Sorrows Parish, Linwood; Saint Damien, Ocean City. Lay Teachers 24; Sisters 1; Students 474.
Catechesis Religious Program—Tel: 609-927-3302. Students 330.
Convent—Sisters of St. Joseph of Chestnut Hill, 580 Shore Rd., Somers Point, 08244.

STONE HARBOR, CAPE MAY CO., ST. PAUL'S CHURCH, STONE HARBOR, N.J. (1911) Merged with The Church of Maris Stella, Avalon to form St. Brendan the Navigator Parish, Avalon.

STRATFORD, CAMDEN CO., THE R.C. CHURCH OF ST. LUKE, STRATFORD, N.J. (1961) Merged with Church of St. Lawrence, Lindenwold & Our Lady of Grace, R.C. Church, Somerdale to form Our Lady of Guadalupe, Lindenwold.

SWEDESBORO, GLOUCESTER CO., ST. JOSEPH'S CHURCH, SWEDESBOROUGH (1854) [CEM 2] Merged with St. Michael's Church, Gibbstown & St. John's Church, Paulsboro to form St. Clare of Assisi Parish, Gibbstown.

TURNERSVILLE, CAMDEN CO., SAINTS PETER AND PAUL (1973) Rev. Msgr. Roger E. McGrath, Ph.D.; Rev. Tomy O. Thomas; Deacon Anthony Cioe
Legal Name: The Church of Saints Peter and Paul, Washington Township, Gloucester County, N.J.
Res.: 362 Ganttown Rd., P.O. Box 1022, Turnersville, 08012. Tel: 856-589-3366; Fax: 856-256-1964; Email: sspp.fin@verizon.net; Web: www.churchofstspeterandpaul.org.
See Our Lady of Hope Regional School, Blackwood under Regional Schools, Elementary located in the Institution section.
Catechesis Religious Program—Students 400.

VENTNOR, ATLANTIC CO., ST. JAMES CATHOLIC CHURCH, VENTNOR, N.J. (1922) Merged with Church of the Epiphany, Longport & Church of the Blessed Sacrament, Margate to form Holy Trinity Parish, Margate.

VILLAS, CAPE MAY CO., ST. RAYMOND'S CATHOLIC CHURCH, WILDWOOD VILLAS, N.J. (1937) Merged with The Church of St. John of God, North Cape May to form The Parish of Saint John Neumann, North Cape May.

VINELAND, CUMBERLAND CO.

1—THE CATHOLIC CHURCH OF THE SACRED HEART, VINELAND, N.J. (1874) (Italian), Merged with The Church of Saint Isidore the Farmer, Vineland, N.J. to form Christ the Good Shepherd Parish, Vineland, N.J.

2—CHRIST THE GOOD SHEPHERD PARISH, VINELAND, N.J. (2011) [CEM] Rev. Msgr. John H. Burton, V.G.; Revs. Wilson Kidangan Paulose, Parochial Vicar (In Res.); Edward R. Kolla, Parochial Vicar; Deacons Robert A. Andreacchio; William J. DeLiberis.
Rectory—1655 Magnolia Rd., Vineland, 08361-6598. Tel: 856-691-9077; Fax: 856-692-3305.
Churches—
The Church of Saint Isidore the Farmer, Vineland—
The Catholic Church of the Sacred Heart, Vineland.
School—Bishop Schad Regional School, 922 E. Landis Ave., Vineland, 08360. Tel: 856-691-4490; Fax: 856-691-5579. Sr. Rosa Maria Ojeda, M.D.P.V.-M., Prin.
Catechesis Religious Program—Tel: 856-563-0482. Joanne Koehler, C.R.E.; Felicita Navarro, Dir. Lifelong Faith Formation. Students 160.

3—THE CHURCH OF ST. FRANCIS OF ASSISI, VINELAND, N.J. (1961) Merged with The Parish of the Immaculate Heart of Mary, La Parroquia Del Inmaculado Corazon De Maria, Vineland to form Divine Mercy, Vineland.

4—THE CHURCH OF SAINT ISIDORE THE FARMER, VINELAND, N.J. (1962) Merged with The Catholic Church of the Sacred Heart, Vineland, N.J. to form Christ the Good Shepherd Parish, Vineland, N.J.

5—DIVINE MERCY, VINELAND, N.J. (2009) Rev. Joel Arciga Camarillo; Deacons Thomas S. Moleski; Roberto P. Rodriguez.
Rectory—23 W. Chestnut Ave., Vineland, 08360-5303. Tel: 856-691-9181; Fax: 856-794-9029.
Churches—
St. Francis of Assisi, Vineland—
Immaculate Heart of Mary, Vineland.
Catechesis Religious Program—
Tel: 856-691-9181, Ext. 13. Students 306.
Convent—Daughters of Mercy, Tel: 856-691-8129.
Pope John Paul II Retreat Center—Tel: 856-691-2299 ; Fax: 856-691-5522.

6—ST. MARY'S (1887) [CEM] Merged with Our Lady of Pompeii, Vineland to form St. Padre Pio Parish, Vineland.

7—OUR LADY OF POMPEII (1909) Merged with St. Mary's, Vineland to form St. Padre Pio Parish, Vineland.

8—ST. PADRE PIO PARISH, VINELAND, N.J. (2003) [CEM] Revs. Robert L. Sinatra, J.C.L.; Sungtteum (John) Kim, Parochial Vicar; Deacon Robert Sampson.
Rectory—4680 Dante Ave., Vineland, 08361-6810. Tel: 856-691-7526; Fax: 856-692-2686.
Church: St. Mary, 736 S. Union Rd., Vineland, 08360.
Church: Our Lady of Pompeii, 4680 Dante Ave., Vineland, 08361.
School—St. Mary School, (Grades PreK-8), 735 Union Rd., Vineland, 08360. Tel: 856-692-8537; Fax: 856-692-5034; Email: mainoffice@smrschool.org; Web: www.smrschool.org. Steven Hogan, Prin.; Raymond Yansick, Librarian. Lay Teachers 20; Students 284.
Convent—741 W. Union Rd., Vineland, 08360.

9—THE PARISH OF THE IMMACULATE HEART OF MARY, LA PARROQUIA DEL INMACULADO CORAZON DE MARIA, VINELAND, NEW JERSEY, Merged with The Church of St. Francis of Assisi, Vineland to form Divine Mercy, Vineland.

WATERFORD, CAMDEN CO., ST. ANTHONY'S CHURCH, WATERFORD, N.J. (1966) Merged with The Church of the Assumption, Atco; Parish of Blessed John the Twenty-Third, Blue Anchor; St. Lucy Church, Blue Anchor; & Sacred Heart Church, Cedarbrook to form Christ the Redeemer Parish, Atco.

WEST COLLINGSWOOD, CAMDEN CO., CHURCH OF THE TRANSFIGURATION, WEST COLLINGSWOOD, N.J. (1950) Merged with The Immaculate Heart of Mary, Woodlynne, N.J. to become Most Precious Blood Parish, Collingswood, N.J.

WESTMONT, CAMDEN CO., THE CHURCH OF THE HOLY SAVIOUR, WESTMONT, N.J. (1928) Merged with St. John's Catholic Church, Collingswood to form Blessed Teresa of Calcutta Parish, Collingswood.

WESTVILLE GROVE, GLOUCESTER CO., CHURCH OF THE MOST HOLY REDEEMER, WESTVILLE GROVE, N.J. (1958) Merged with St. Matthew's Catholic Church, National Park & St. Patrick's Church, Woodbury to form Holy Angels Parish, Woodbury.

WESTVILLE, GLOUCESTER CO.; ST. ANNE'S CHURCH, WESTVILLE, N.J. (1921) Closed. For inquiries for parish records please see St. Joachim Parish, Bellmawr, N.J.

WILDWOOD CREST, CAPE MAY CO., THE CHURCH OF THE ASSUMPTION B.V.M., WILDWOOD CREST, N.J. (1961) Merged with St. Ann's Church, Wildwood to form Notre Dame de la Mer Parish, Wildwood.

WILDWOOD, CAPE MAY CO.

1—ST. ANN'S CHURCH, WILDWOOD, N.J. (1895) Merged with The Church of the Assumption of the B.V.M., Wildwood Crest to form Notre Dame de la Mer Parish, Wildwood.

2—NOTRE DAME DE LA MER PARISH, WILDWOOD, N.J. (2010) Revs. Joseph D. Wallace; Yvans Jazon, Parochial Vicar; Steven V. Pinzon, Parochial Vicar.
Office: 1500 Central Ave., Ste. 100, North Wildwood, 08260-4943. Tel: 609-522-2709, Ext. 210;
Fax: 609-522-9375; Email: mvey@notredamedelamer.org; Web: www.NotreDamedelaMer.org.
Churches—
Assumption of the Blessed Virgin Mary, Wildwood Crest—
St. Ann, Wildwood.
School—Cape Trinity Regional School, (Grades PreK-8), 1500 Central Ave. Ste. 300, North Wildwood, 08260. Tel: 609-522-2704;
Fax: 609-522-5329. Sr. Sheila Murphy, S.S.J., Prin.; Mrs. Jennifer Flud, Librarian. Lay Teachers 17; Sisters 1; Students 239.
Catechesis Religious Program—Email: cmiller@notredamedelamer.org. Mrs. Carolyn Miller, D.R.E. Students 246.
Convent—2900 Pacific Ave., Wildwood, 08260.

WILLIAMSTOWN, GLOUCESTER CO.

1—ST. MARY'S CHURCH, WILLIAMSTOWN, N.J. (1906) [CEM] Merged with Church of St. John Neumann, Sicklerville to form Our Lady of Peace Parish, Williamstown.

2—OUR LADY OF PEACE PARISH, MONROE TOWNSHIP, N.J. (2009)
32 Carroll Ave., Williamstown, 08094-1713.
Tel: 856-629-6142; Email: olopp@olopp.org; Web: olopp.org. Revs. Cadmus D. Mazzarella; Christopher T. Bakey; Deacons John Kacy; Michael McDonaugh; Albert A. LaMonaca Jr.; James J. Hallman.
Rectory—640 S. Main St., Williamstown, 08094.
Church: Saint Mary, Williamstown.
School—Our Lady of Peace Parish, Monroe Township, N.J. School, (Grades K-8), 32A Carroll Ave., Williamstown, 08094. Tel: 856-629-6190;
Fax: 856-728-1437. Mrs. Patricia Mancuso, Prin. Lay Teachers 28; Students 530.
Catechesis Religious Program—Tel: 856-629-0614. Students 625.

WOODBINE, CAPE MAY CO., ST. CASIMIR'S R.C. CHURCH, WOODBINE, N.J. (1939) [CEM] Merged with Church of the Resurrection, Marmora, N.J. & St. Elizabeth's, Goshen to form The Parish of St. Maximilian Kolbe, Marmora, N.J.

WOODBURY HEIGHTS, GLOUCESTER CO.

1—INFANT JESUS PARISH, WOODBURY HEIGHTS, N.J. (2010) Revs. Joseph Luong Pham; Steven J. Rapposelli; Deacon Frank Dunleavy.
Rectory—334 Beech Ave., Woodbury Heights, 08097-1317. Tel: 856-848-0047; Fax: 856-384-8123; Email: theinfantJesusparish@comcast.net; Web: theinfantJesusparish.org.
Churches—
St. John Vianney, Deptford—2901 Good Intent Rd., Deptford, 08096.
St. Margaret, Woodbury Heights, 845 3rd St., Woodbury Heights, 08097.
See St. Margaret Regional School, Woodbury Heights under Regional Schools, Elementary located in the Institution Section.
Catechesis Religious Program—Students 326.
Convent—745 Third St., Woodbury Heights, 08097.
Tel: 856-848-6049; Fax: 856-845-2405. Sr. Dianna Higgins, F.M.I.J., Supr.

2—ST. MARGARET'S CHURCH, WOODBURY HEIGHTS, N.J. (1961) Merged with The Church of St. John Vianney, Deptford to form Infant Jesus Parish, Woodbury Heights.

WOODBURY, GLOUCESTER CO.

1—HOLY ANGELS PARISH, WOODBURY, N.J. (2010) Rev. Msgr. Joseph V. DiMauro, V.F., (Retired); Rev. Hugh J. Bradley; Deacons Vincent Latini; Philip E. Giordano. In Res., Revs. Thomas S. Capperella, (Retired); Ernest E. Amadi.
Rectory—64 Cooper St., Woodbury, 08096-4618.
Tel: 856-845-0123; Fax: 856-845-7409; Email: mail@holyangels.org; Web: www.holyangelsnj.org.
Churches—
St. Matthew, National Park—
Most Holy Redeemer, Westville.
St. Patrick, Woodbury.
School—Holy Trinity Regional School, (Grades PreSchool-8), 1215 Delsea Dr., Westville Grove, 08093. Tel: 856-848-6826; Fax: 856-251-0344. Elsie Tedeski, Prin. Lay Teachers 16; Students 174.
Catechesis Religious Program—Family Faith Formation: 211 Cooper St., Woodbury, 08096. Students 461.

2—ST. PATRICK'S CHURCH, WOODBURY (1877) Merged with Church of the Most Holy Redeemer, Westville Grove & St. Matthew's Catholic Church, National Park to form Holy Angels Parish, Woodbury.

WOODLYNNE, CAMDEN CO., THE IMMACULATE HEART OF MARY, WOODLYNNE, N.J. (1949) (Vietnamese), Merged with Church of the Transfiguration, West Collingswood, N.J. to form Most Precious Blood Parish, Collingswood, N.J.

WOODSTOWN, SALEM CO., ST. JOSEPH'S CATHOLIC CHURCH, WOODSTOWN, N.J. (1895) [CEM] Merged with Church of the Holy Name of Jesus, Mullica Hill & St. Ann's Catholic Church, Elmer to form Catholic Community of the Holy Spirit, Mullica Hill.

Chaplains of Public Institutions

ANCORA. *New Jersey State Psychiatric Hospital*, 301 Spring Garden Rd., Hammonton, 08037.
Tel: 609-561-1700. Rev. Thomas S. Donio, V.F., Chap.

BRIDGETON. *South Woods State Prison*, 215 S. Burlington Rd., Bridgeton, 08302.
Tel: 856-459-7000. Deacon Vincent A. Okoro, Chap.

DELMONT. *Southern State Correctional Facility*, Delmont, 08377. Tel: 856-785-1300, Ext. 6389. Vacant.

FAIRTON. *Federal Correctional Institution*, P.O. Box 280, Fairton, 08320. Tel: 856-227-1436. Rev. Peter M. Idler.

LEESBURG. *Bayside State Medium Security Prison*, Leesburg, 08327. Tel: 856-785-0040.
Chaplaincy, Parish of the Holy Cross.

VINELAND. *Vineland State School*.
Chaplaincy, Christ the Good Shepherd, Vineland, 08361. Tel: 856-691-9077.

WOODBINE. *State Colony*, Woodbine, 08290.
Chaplaincy, St. Maximilian Kolbe Church, Marmora, 08223. Tel: 609-390-0664.

Hospital Chaplaincies

CAMDEN. *Cooper Medical Center*, Tel: 856-583-6600. Rev. Jerold Mariastanislaus, Chap., Sr. M. Mieczyslawa Koczera, L.S.I.C., Assoc. Chap., William J. Wisely, Assoc. Chap.

Our Lady of Lourdes Medical Center, Tel: 856-757-3500. Revs. Mike Steve Ezeatu, Joseph Monahan, T.O.R., Dir. Pastoral Care, Francis Oranefo.

ATLANTIC CITY. *AtlantiCare Regional Medical Center City Division*, Tel: 609-345-4000. Rev. Robert T. Matysik, Chap., Natalie Contento, Chap., Sr. Margaret (Peg) M. Convoy, S.S.J.

BERLIN. *Virtua Health and Rehabilitation Center*, 100 Townsend Ave., Berlin, 08009. Tel: 856-322-3000. Rev. Glenn R. Hartman, Chap., Honora Marie Burke, Assoc. Chap.

BLACKWOOD. *Elmwood Hills Healthcare Center*, 425 Woodbury Turnersville Rd., Blackwood, 08012. Tel: 856-583-6600. Rev. Glenn R. Hartman, Chap., Honora Marie Burke, Chap.

CAPE MAY COURT HOUSE. *Cape Regional Medical Center*, 2 Stone Harbor Blvd., Cape May Court House, 08210. Tel: 609-463-2000. Rev. Cosme R. de la Pena, Chap.

CHERRY HILL. *Jefferson University Hospitals*, Tel: 856-488-6500. Rev. Msgr. Dominic J. Bottino, J.C.L., Chap., Deacon John Rich, Assoc. Chap.

ELMER. *Inspira Medical Center*, Tel: 856-363-1000. Rev. Wilson Kidangan Paulose, Chap., Deacon Arnaldo A. Santos, Assoc. Chap.

POMONA. *AtlantiCare Regional Medical Center Mainland Division*, Tel: 609-652-1000. Rev. Robert T. Matysik, Chap., Deacon Francis A. Cerullo, Assoc. Chap., Sr. Margaret (Peg) M. Convoy, S.S.J., Assoc. Chap.

Bacharach Institute for Rehabilitation, 61 Jimmie Leeds Rd., Pomona, 08240. Tel: 609-652-7000. Rev. Robert T. Matysik, Chap., Deacon Francis A. Cerullo, Assoc. Chap., Sr. Mary Francis Kyle, S.S.J., Chap.

SALEM. *Memorial Hospital of Salem County*, Tel: 856-935-1000. Rev. Wilson Kidangan Paulose, Chap., Deacon Arnaldo A. Santos, Assoc. Chap.

SOMERS POINT. *Shore Medical Center*, Tel: 609-653-3500. Rev. John Perdue, M.SS.CC., Chap.

STRATFORD. *Jefferson Health at Stratford*, Tel: 856-346-6000. Rev. Msgr. Dominic J. Bottino, J.C.L., Chap., Deacon John D. Rich Jr., Assoc. Chap.

VINELAND. *Inspira Medical Center*, Tel: 856-641-1000. Rev. Wilson Kidangan Paulose, Chap., Deacon Arnaldo A. Santos, Assoc. Chap.

VOORHEES. *Virtua Voorhees Hospital*, Tel: 856-247-3000. Rev. Glenn R. Hartman, Chap., Honora Marie Burke, Assoc. Chap.

WASHINGTON TOWNSHIP. *Jefferson Washington Township Hospital*, Tel: 856-582-2500. Rev. Ernest E. Amadi, Chap., Nancy DiSeveria, Assoc. Chap.

WOODBURY. *Inspira Medical Center*, Tel: 856-845-0100. Rev. Ernest E. Amadi, Chap., Nancy DiSeveria, Assoc. Chap.

On Duty Outside the Diocese:

Rev. Msgr.—

Daiber, Sean J., Central Mailing Address, Paroquia de Sao Jose Rua 90 N. 40, Setor Sul, Caiza Postal 716, 74,000 Goiania Goias, Brazil. Brazilian Missions

Revs.—

Hubbs, Timothy L., Chap. (Major), 900 Army-Navy Dr., Apt. 1531, Arlington, VA 22202

Kiely, Thomas R.

Kocik, Francis W., St. Patrick, Pincourt, Ile Perrot, Province of Quebec, Canada. 191 Hawley St., Binghamton, NY 13901

Markellos, Christopher M.

McLaughlin, Peter A., NAS Pensacola, 250 Chambers Ave., Bldg. 634, Pensacola, FL 32508-5217. Tel: 850-452-2025

Murphy, Ronan B., Pope John Paul II House of Discernment, 341 Highland Blvd., Brooklyn, NY 11207

Nwoga, Laserian, 1850 Potts Ferry Rd., Apt. D-422, Biloxi, MS 39532

Orsi, Michael P., 6280 Bellerive Ave., Apt. 204, Naples, FL 34119

Rocks, Jason T., S.T.L.

Retired:

Most Rev.—

Galante, Joseph A., D.D., J.C.D., (Retired), 631 Market St., 08102

Rev. Msgrs.—

Brennan, William P., V.F., (Retired), Sacred Heart Residence, 200 St. Mary's Dr., Cherry Hill, 08003

Casey, John H., (Retired), 104 Wood Ln., Sparta, TN 38583

Clarke, John A., (Retired), 2 Delmar Ave., Brigantine, 08203

Coyne, Michael J., (Retired), Ocean Club, 3101 Boardwalk, TWR. 2 #909, Atlantic City, 08401. Tel: 609-345-2475

Curran, James J., (Retired), Carriage House, 568 N. Evergreen Ave., Apt. 5-B, Woodbury, 08096

DiMauro, Joseph V., V.F., (Retired), 504 New York Ave., Wildwood, 08260

Fitzsimmons, Thomas B., (Retired), P.O. Box 116, Sea Isle City, 08243. Tel: 609-522-2709

Flynn, Thomas M., (Retired), Sacred Heart Residence, 200 St. Mary's Dr., Cherry Hill, 08003. Tel: 856-751-8109

Frey, John T., (Retired), St. Andrew the Apostle, 27 Kresson-Gibbsboro Rd., Gibbsboro, 08026

Gallagher, John Gerald, (Retired), St. Mary's Villa, 220 St. Mary's Dr., Cherry Hill, 08003. Tel: 904-823-0975

Graham, William P., V.F., (Retired), 414 Erie Ave., Carney's Point, 08069. Tel: 856-299-0411

Jordan, Harry J., (Retired), 200 St. Mary's Dr., Cherry Hill, 08003. Tel: 856-874-1959

Mannion, Martin J., (Retired), 11 45th Cove, Brigantine, 08203

Mannion, Michael T., S.T.L., (Retired), Mary, Queen of All Saints, 4824 Camden Ave., Pennsauken, 08110

Martin, Andrew E., (Retired), Nazareth House, 300 Cuthbert Blvd., Cherry Hill, 08002. Tel: 609-513-1709

McDermott, Robert T., V.G., (Retired), Diocese of Camden, 631 Market St., 08102

McIntyre, Thomas J., (Retired), 14 Ealey Ct., Glassboro, 08028

Morgan, Thomas J., (Retired), 306 Arbegast Dr., Brigantine, 08203. Tel: 609-760-9247

Muro, Victor S., (Retired), O.L. of the Blessed Sacrament, 104 Catawba Ave, Newfield, 08344

O'Leary, Cornelius P., (Retired), 25098 Jaclyn Ave., Moreno Valley, CA 92557-5703. Tel: 909-242-6939. 25098 Jaclyn Ave., Moreno Valley, CA 92387

O'Mearain, Ciaran P., (Retired), Dublin, Ireland

Pokusa, Joseph W., P.A., J.C.D., (Retired), Holy Child, 13 E. Evesham Rd., Runnemede, 08078

Quinn, William, (Retired), 307 99th St., Stone Harbor, 08247. Tel: 609-675-6519

Rock, Russell L., (Retired), 200 St. Mary's Dr., Cherry Hill, 08003

Ryan, Timothy A., (Retired), 220 St. Mary's Dr., Cherry Hill, 08003

Scott, Leonard G., (Retired), 604 Cabot Ct., Deptford, 08096. Tel: 856-428-7191

Tracy, James R., Ph.D., V.F., (Retired), 500 Green Tree Rd., Glassboro, 08028. Tel: 856-881-0909

Revs.—

Adamson, Joseph J., (Retired), 161 Pitman Ave., Pitman, 08071

Amabile, Patsy L., (Retired), P.O. Box 1230, Palm City, FL 34991

Annino, Sebastian V., (Retired), Sacred Heart Residence for Priests, 200 St. Mary's Dr., Cherry Hill, 08003

Bajkowski, Dennis W., (Retired), 20 Maple Grove St., Tunkhannock, PA 18657

Battisti, Lewis A., V.F., (Retired), Garden Lake Park #128, 1402 S. Rte. #9, Cape May Court House, 08210

Betz, James, CH(LTC), (Retired), St. Brendan the Navigator, 5012 Dune Dr., Avalon, 08102

Bleiler, William James, (Retired), Sacred Heart Residence, 200 St. Mary's Dr., Cherry Hill, 08003

Bolcar, Andrew J., (Retired), St. Mary's Center, 210 St. Mary's Dr., Cherry Hill, 08003-2517

Brady, Patrick J., (Retired), P.O. Box 2505, Ventnor, 08406

Cairone, A. Robert, (Retired), Sacred Heart Residence, 200 St. Mary's Dr., Cherry Hill, 08003

Capperella, Thomas S., (Retired), St. Mary's Villa, 220 St. Mary's Dr., Cherry Hill, 08003

Carlone, Carmen A., V.F., (Retired), 130 Southampton Dr., Galloway, 08205

Dante, Neal F., (Retired), 5001 Pleasant Mill Rd., Hammonton, 08037. Tel: 609-965-0464

Del Duca, John A., (Retired), 701 Little Gloucester Rd., Blackwood, 08012

DiNardo, Daniel A., (Retired), 1643 S. 17th St., Philadelphia, PA 19145

Durkin, James J., (Retired), 250 St. Mary's Dr., Cherry Hill, 08003

Fasciglione, Massimo S., (Retired), Sacred Heart North, 250 St. Mary's Dr., Cherry Hill, 08003

Fleming, John M., (Retired), Sacred Heart Residence, 200 St. Mary's Dr., Cherry Hill, 08003

Forbes, Richard L., (Retired), Sacred Heart Residence, 200 St. Mary's Dr., Cherry Hill, 08003. Tel: 609-425-8653

Fritz, Robert J., (Retired), St. John Neumann, 680 Town Bank Rd., North Cape May, 08204

Gannon, Bernard J., (Retired), Sacred Heart North, 250 St. Mary's Dr., Cherry Hill, 08003. Tel: 856-874-1915

Gomes, Robert M., (Retired), 1023 McTavish Way, Palm Harbor, FL 34684

Gramigna, Francis J., (Retired), 6015 Black Horse Pike, #51, Egg Harbor Twp., 08046. Tel: 609-871-3890

Gregorio, Robert J., S.T.D., (Retired), 631 Market St., 08102

Hadyka, Richard J., (Retired), 5 Williams Way, Seaville, 08230

Hallahan, Kenneth P., (Retired), 2861 Tuckahoe Rd., 08104

Harshaw, Albert E., (Retired), St. Mary's Villa, 220 St. Mary's Dr., Cherry Hill, 08003

Hewett, Alfred J., (Retired), St. Rose of Lima, 300 Kings Hwy., Haddon Heights, 08035-1397. Tel: 609-547-0564

Jones, J. Overton, (Retired), Sacred Heart Residence, 200 St. Mary's Dr., Cherry Hill, 08003

Jurkowski, Joseph V., (Retired), St. Mary's Villa, 220 St. Mary's Dr., Cherry Hill, 08003

Killeen, John C., (Retired), Sacred Heart Residence, 200 St. Mary's Dr., Cherry Hill, 08003

Kolton, Stanislaus J., (Retired), 117 Brown Ave., Spring Lake, 07762-1017. Tel: 908-449-6364

Kunzman, Richard T., (Retired), 1401 N St., #2041, Washington, DC 20005

Lambert, Cornelius F., (Retired), St. Mary's Center, 210 St. Mary's Dr., Cherry Hill, 08003. Tel: 609-967-3345

LaVerde, Calogero N., (Retired), St. Mary's Villa, 220 St. Mary's Dr., Cherry Hill, 08003

Link, Frederick G., (Retired), St. Joseph the Worker, 901 Hopkins Rd., Suite A, Haddonfield, 08033

Lipinski, Edward J., (Retired), St. Mary's Villa, 220 St. Mary's Dr., Cherry Hill, 08003

Longo, Robert, O.F.M.Cap., (Retired), 115 Weiss, Gibbstown, 08027. Tel: 856-848-2422

Lyons, Edward D., (Retired), Sacred Heart Residence, 200 St. Mary's Dr., Cherry Hill, 08003

Meaney, Brendan J., (Retired), Sacred Heart North, 250 St. Mary's Dr., Cherry Hill, 08003

Messina, Joseph, (Retired), 1209 Burrough's Mill Cir., Cherry Hill, 08002. Tel: 856-342-4104

Minniti, Anthony L., (Retired), 208A Hillcrest Ave., Collingswood, 08108

Minniti, David V., (Retired), 208 A Hillside Ave., Collingswood, 08108. Tel: 856-663-1373

Moore, William F., (Retired), 8-A Florida Ct., Whiting, 08759

Muhlbaier, Howard E., (Retired), Villa at St. Mary's, 220 St. Mary's Dr., Cherry Hill, 08003

O'Neill, Brian E., (Retired), 200 St. Mary's Dr., Cherry Hill, 08003. Tel: 609-980-6095

Odien, Terry M., (Retired), P.O. Box 4161, Cherry Hill, 08034

Patrizio, Anthony, (Retired), 120 Royal St. George Ct., Mays Landing, 08330. Tel: 609-383-8235

Pierce, William M., (Retired), 118 S. 21st St., Apt. 1113, Philadelphia, PA 19103

Rosinski, Edward B., (Retired), 39 Central Ave., Audubon, 08106

Rush, Joseph P., (Retired), St. Mary's Villa, 220 St. Mary's Dr., Cherry Hill, 08003

Ryan, William F., (Retired), Sacred Heart Residence, 200 St. Mary's Dr., Cherry Hill, 08003

Smith, Robert V., (Retired), 200 St. Mary's Dr., Cherry Hill, 08003. Tel: 856-751-1951

Sobolewski, Edward F., (Retired), 408 War Branch Rd., Smithfield, PA 15478

Tovar, Ireneo Lopez, (Retired), 121 Country Club Dr., Tower II, Apt. 403, Lake Placid, FL 33852

Tumosa, John Joseph, (Retired), 1905 3rd St., Philadelphia, PA 19148. Tel: 215-465-2620

Wade, Edward C., (Retired), Queen of Peace, 3011 Telephone Rd., Houston, TX 77023

Wagenhoffer, Josef A., (Retired), 1604 Bay Dr., West Atlantic City, 08232. Tel: 609-504-1305

Weber, Robert P., Ph.D., (Retired), 824 Stokes Ave., Collingswood, 08108. Tel: 856-513-5085.

Permanent Deacons:

Achee, C. J., (Retired)

Aguilar, Omar M.

Andreacchio, Robert A., (Retired)

Becker, Joseph F., (Retired)

Beebe, Joseph F., (Retired)

Berstecher, John L.

Bickel, Craig A.

Bortnowski, Michael G.

Bubeck, Paul R. Jr., (Retired)

Buccilli, Joseph C.

Campisi, Frank J.

Carlucci, Leonard P.

Carter, Michael J.

Cerullo, Francis A.

Cioe, Anthony

Colanero, John D., (Retired)

Contino, John A.
Correa, Luis E., (Retired)
Crawford, Douglas R., (Retired)
Crosson, Francis W., (Retired)
D'Ariano, Michael A.
Danze, Nicholas A., (Retired)
Davidson, Peter R.
Davis, Russell O., (Retired)
Del Rossi, George C., (Retired)
DeLiberis, William J.
DeMuro, Gerard V., (Retired)
Dunleavy, Frank
Encarnado, Fernando S.
Engel, Francis J., (Retired)
Fanelli, Robert M.
Fargnoli, Thomas W.
Farmer, Lawrence S.
Foley, Robert P.
Gallimore, John R., (Retired)
Ganci, Joseph A., (Retired)
Garozzo, Joseph A.
Garufi, Agatino A., (Retired)
Giordano, Philip E.
Girard, Charles J., (Retired)
Guaracini, Frank Jr.
Guerrieri, Michael H., (Retired)
Hafner, Thomas J., (Retired)
Hallman, James J.
Hamilton, Robert W.
Hannon, Kevin P.
Hanrahan, Matthew J., (Retired)
Harkins, Michael J., (Retired)
Heil, Kevin C.
Hogan, James N., (Retired)
Howitz, Leo M.
Iannuzzi, William P., (Retired)
Iulucci, Robert M.
Jablonowski, Gerard J.
Jadick, Anthony M.
Jennings, Thomas E.
Johnson, William G., (Retired)
Kacy, John J.
Kain, Joseph A. Sr.
Kearney, J. Brian, (Retired)
Kenney, Robert M., (Retired)
Kiley, James W., (Retired)
Kolakowski, Michael J.
Lagares, Hipolito
LaMonaca, Albert A. Jr.
Latini, Vincent
Laughlin, Kevin L.
Lauth, William, (Retired)
Lee, Paul K., (Retired)
Liss, George R., (Retired)
Lonergan, Joseph W.
Long, Leonard W.
Lopes, Joseph S.
Loungo, Joseph W., (Retired)
Ludovich, Nicholas P., (Retired)
Luko, John J. Jr.
Malatesta, Anthony D.
Maxwell, Richard S.
McAleer, Charles L. Sr.
McBlain, W. Leo, (Retired)
McDonaugh, Michael L.
Miranda, Felix Tito, (Retired)
Moleski, Thomas S.
Mortelliti, Nicholas V.
Murnane, David W.
Murphy, Joseph A.
Nastasi, Santo A., (Retired)
Nasuti, Samuel S. Jr.
Nguyen, Kim T.
Nichols, Christopher D.
Norquist, William V., (Retired)
O'Brien, Thomas F., Ph.D., Ed.D.
O'Clisham, Liam C., (Retired)
Okoro, Vincent A.
Oliver, Robert G.
Perella, Joseph A., (Retired)
Peters, William L., (Retired)
Peterson, George J., (Retired)
Porowicz, Alfred T., (Retired)
Powell, Peter J.
Quiles, Bernardino S., (Retired)
Rafferty, Joseph G. Sr.
Ramos Vega, Angel R., (Retired)
Rich, John D. Jr.
Riviello, Albert J., (Retired)
Rocks, James H.
Rodriguez, Roberto P.
Rogozenski, Donald W.
Rumaker, William J., (Retired)
Sampson, Richard T.
Santos, Arnaldo A.
Scarpa, Robert F.
Scott, Michael F.
Seaman, Joseph F.
Slaven, William M.
Smith, Aaron G.
Smith, James O.
Soto, Samuel
Tavarez, Ismael P., (Retired)
Traum, J. Peter
Van Leer, George R.
Velez, Aladino, (Retired)
Watts, William L., (Retired)
Webb, Joseph H.
Welsh, Michael L., (Retired)
Werner, John F., (Retired)
Wigglesworth, Richard J., (Retired)
Zayas, Jose Rene.

INSTITUTIONS LOCATED IN DIOCESE

[A] HIGH SCHOOLS, DIOCESAN

ABSECON. *Holy Spirit High School, Absecon, N.J.*, 500 S. New Rd., Absecon, 08201. Tel: 609-646-3000; Fax: 609-646-1770; Email: holyspirithighschool@yahoo.com; Web: www.holyspirithighschool.com. Rev. Perry A. Cherubini, Pres.; Miss Susan W. Dennen, Prin.; Mrs. Joann Malecki, Librarian. Lay Teachers 33; Priests 2; Students 397.

CHERRY HILL. *Camden Catholic High School, Cherry Hill, N.J.* (1887) 300 Cuthbert Rd., Cherry Hill, 08002. Tel: 856-663-2247; Fax: 856-661-0632; Email: anne.buroojy@camdencatholic.org; Web: www.camdencatholic.org. Mrs. Mary Whipkey, Pres.; Mrs. Heather Crisci, Prin.; Lindsey Murphy, Librarian. Lay Teachers 42; Priests 1; Students 745; Staff 7.

HADDONFIELD. *Paul VI High School, Haddon Township, N.J.* (1966) 901 Hopkins Rd., Ste. B, Haddonfield, 08033. Tel: 856-858-4900; Fax: 856-858-6832; Email: principal@pvihs.org; Web: pvihs.org. Mr. Michael Chambers, Pres.; Sr. Marianne McCann, M.P.F., Prin.; Rev. John A. Rossi; Mrs. Michelle Anastasia, Librarian. Lay Teachers 70; Priests 1; Students 1,054; Religious Teachers Filippini 2; Franciscan Missionary Sisters 1.

HAMMONTON. *St. Joseph High School Hammonton, NJ, Inc.*, 328 Vine St., Hammonton, 08037. Tel: 609-561-8700; Fax: 609-561-8701; Email: rdefinis@stjoek12.org; Web: stjoek12.org. Rev. Allain B. Caparas, Prin. & Pres. Lay Teachers 26; Religious 3; Students 280.

[B] HIGH SCHOOLS, PAROCHIAL

GLOUCESTER. *Gloucester Catholic High School, Inc.*, (Grades 7-12), 333 Ridgeway St., Gloucester, 08030. Tel: 856-456-4400; Fax: 856-456-0506; Email: info@gchsrams.org; Web: www.gchsrams.org. Mr. Edward F. Beckett, Prin.; Mr. John T. Colman, Head, School Emeritus; Katharine Coghlan, Public Rels. Deacons 1; Lay Teachers 39; Priests 1; Sisters 1; Students 515; Junior High 47.

NORTH WILDWOOD. *Wildwood Catholic High School*, 1500 Central Ave., #200, North Wildwood, 08260. Tel: 609-522-7257; Fax: 609-522-2453; Email: j.cray@wildwoodcatholic.org; Web: wildwoodcatholic.org. Rev. Joseph D. Wallace, Pres.; Joseph Cray, Prin.; Mr. Sal Zuccarello, Guidance; Mrs. Julie Roche, Contact Person. Lay Teachers 16; Students 167.

[C] HIGH SCHOOLS, PRIVATE

NEWFIELD. *Our Lady of Mercy Academy* (1962) 1001 Main Rd., Newfield, 08344. Tel: 856-697-2008; Fax: 856-697-2887; Email: mrs.kinkade@olmanj.org; Web: www.olmanj.org. Brooke A. Coyle, Prin.; Mary Jane Kinkade, Dir. Mktg. & Devel. Daughters of Our Lady of Mercy. Lay Teachers 21; Sisters 3; Students 150.

PENNSAUKEN. *Bishop Eustace Prep School* (1954) 5552 Rte. 70, Pennsauken, 08109-4798. Tel: 856-662-2160, Ext. 651; Fax: 856-662-0802; Email: brotherjim@eustace.org; Web: www.eustace.org. Bro. James Beamesderfer, S.A.C., Supr. of Rel. Community, Head of Mission, Novice Master; Mr. Philip Gianfortune, Headmaster; Mr. Angelo Milicia, Admin.; Denise Avellino, Librarian; Revs. Robert Nolan, S.A.C., Chap.; Mical Wokciak, S.A.C., Chap.; Sean Paul Phillips, S.A.C., (In Res.). Society of the Catholic Apostolate, Province of the Immaculate Conception. Brothers 1; Lay Teachers 45; Priests 2; Students 525.

RICHLAND. *St. Augustine Preparatory School*, 611 Cedar Ave., Richland, 08350-0279. Tel: 856-697-2600; Fax: 856-697-8389; Email: fr.reilly@hermits.com; Web: www.hermits.com. Rev. Donald F. Reilly, O.S.A., Pres.; Bro. David Graber, M.SS.CC.; Rev. Patrick B. McStravog, O.S.A., Asst. Pres. Mission & Ministry; Bro. Robert Thornton, O.S.A.; Rev. Francis X. Devlin, O.S.A., Prior, Augustinian Community; Kevin Burke, Dean of Academics; Revs. Dennis J. Harten, In Res.; Joseph F. Girone, O.S.A., Falculty. Order of St. Augustine, Province of St. Thomas of Villanova. Brothers 2; Lay Teachers 62; Priests 5; Students 680.

[D] REGIONAL SCHOOLS, ELEMENTARY

BERLIN. *Our Lady of Mt. Carmel Regional School*, (Grades PreK-8), One Cedar Ave., Berlin, 08009. Tel: 856-767-1751; Fax: 856-767-1293; Email: olm@hotmail.com; Web: www.olmc-school.org. Alice Malloy, Prin. Serving St. Simon Stock, Berlin; St. Andrew, Gibbsboro; Mater Ecclesiae, Bellmawr. Lay Teachers 18; Students 220.

BLACKWOOD. *Our Lady of Hope Regional School*, (Grades PreK-8), 420 S. Black Horse Pike, Blackwood, 08012. Tel: 856-227-4442; Fax: 856-227-7115; Email: administration@olohschool.org; Web: www.ourladyofhopecatholicschool.org. Sr. Paula Marie Randow, O.S.F., Prin.; Mr. John T. Cafagna, Asst. Prin.; Mrs. Margie Rocco, Librarian. Serving Our Lady of Hope, Blackwood; SS. Peter & Paul, St. Charles Borromeo, & Holy Family, Washington Township. Lay Teachers 26; Preschool 37; Sisters of St. Francis of Philadelphia 1; Students 406.

CAPE MAY COURT HOUSE. *The Bishop James T. McHugh Regional School, Inc.*, (Grades PreK-8), 2221 Rte. 9 N, Cape May Court House, 08210. Tel: 609-624-1900; Fax: 609-624-9696. Thomas McGuire, Prin.; Sr. Thomas Marie Rakus, Librarian. Lay Teachers 16; Sisters 2; Students 204.

COLLINGSWOOD. *Good Shepherd Regional School*, (Grades PreK-8), 100 Lees Ave., Collingswood, 08108. Tel: 856-858-1562; Fax: 856-858-2943; Email: rbonnette@goodshepherdcollingswood.org; Web: www.goodshepherdcollingswood.org. Raymond A. Bonnette III, Prin. Serving Saint Teresa of Calcutta Parish, Collingswood; Most Precious Blood Parish, W. Collingswood; St. Joseph the Worker Parish, Haddon Township; St. Mary, Gloucester City. Lay Teachers 14; Preschool 35; Students 120.

GALLOWAY. *Assumption Regional School*, (Grades PreK-8), 146 S. Pitney Rd., Galloway, 08205. Tel: 609-652-7134; Fax: 609-652-2544; Email: mschurtz@arcsgalloway.org; Web: www.arcsgalloway.org. Mrs. Mary Ellen Schurtz, Prin.; Rose Faiss, Librarian. Serving St. Elizabeth Ann Seton, Absecon; Our Lady of Perpetual Help, Galloway; St. Thomas, Brigantine. Lay Teachers 28; Students 391.

GIBBSTOWN. *Guardian Angels Regional School*, (Grades PreK-8), Tel: 856-423-9440; Fax: 856-423-9441. Sr. Jerilyn Einstein, F.M.I.J., Prin. Lay Teachers 11; Sisters 3; Students 236.

Gibbstown Campus, (Grades PreK-3), 150 S. School St., Gibbstown, 08027. Tel: 856-423-9440; Fax: 856-423-9441; Email: gars@comcast.net. Sr. Jerilyn Einstein, F.M.I.J., Prin.

Paulsboro Campus, (Grades 4-8), 717 Beacon Ave., Paulsboro, 08066. Tel: 856-423-9401; Fax: 856-423-9403. Sr. Jerilyn Einstein, F.M.I.J., Prin.

HADDONFIELD. *Christ the King Regional School*, (Grades PreK-8), 164 Hopkins Ave., Haddonfield, 08033. Tel: 856-429-2084; Fax: 856-429-4959; Web: www.ckrs.org. Mrs. Anne Hartman, Prin.; Suzanne Urbach, Librarian. Serving Christ the King, Haddonfield; Holy Eucharist, Cherry Hill. Lay Teachers 23; Students 338.

HAMMONTON. *St. Joseph Regional Elementary School*, (Grades PreK-8), 133 N. 3rd St., Hammonton, 08037. Tel: 609-704-2400; Fax: 609-561-4940; Email: info@stjosephprek8.org; Web: www.stjosephprek8.org. Sr. Betty Jean Takacs, M.P.F., Prin. Serving St. Mary of Mt. Carmel, Hammonton. Lay Teachers 17; Preschool 29; Students 127.

RUNNEMEDE. *St. Teresa Regional School*, (Grades PreK-8), 27 E. Evesham Rd., Runnemede, 08078. Tel: 856-939-0333; Fax: 856-939-1204; Email: sscanlon@stteresaschool.org; Web: www.stteresaschool.org. Sr. Nancy Kindelan, I.H.M., Prin.; Linda Price, Librarian. Serving Open Enrollment Lay Teachers 16; Sisters Servants of the Immaculate Heart of Mary 2; Students 190.

Convent, 18 Ardmore Rd., Runnemede, 08078. Tel: 856-939-5508.

VINELAND. *Bishop Schad Regional School*, (Grades PreK-8), 922 E. Landis Ave., Vineland, 08360. Tel: 856-691-4490; Fax: 856-691-5579; Email: mainofc@bsrschool.org; Web: www.bsrschool.us. Sr. Rosa Maria Ojeda, M.D.P.V.M., Prin. Serving Christ the Good Shepherd; Divine Mercy; Holy Cross. Lay Teachers 13; Students 155; Personnel 3.

St. Mary's Regional School, (Grades PreK-8), 735 Union Rd., Vineland, 08360. Tel: 856-692-8537; Fax: 856-692-5034; Email: mainoffice@smrschool.org; Web: www.smrschool.org. Steven P. Hogan,

Prin. Serving St. Padre Pio, East Vineland; All Saints, Millville; Our Lady of the Blessed Sacrament, Newfield. Lay Teachers 22; Students 284.

WOODBURY HEIGHTS. *St. Margaret Regional School* (1963) 773 Third St., Woodbury Heights, 08097-1304. Tel: 856-845-5200; Email: azuccarelli@stmargaret-rs.org; Web: www.stmargarets-rs.org. Sr. Michele DeGregorio, F.M.I.J., Prin. Serving Infant Jesus, Woodbury Heights; Incarnation, Mantua. Lay Teachers 23; Sisters 2; Students 500.

[E] SCHOOLS FOR SPECIAL CHILDREN

WESTVILLE GROVE. *Archbishop Damiano School/St. John of God Community Services* (1965) 1145 Delsea Dr., Westville Grove, 08093.
Tel: 856-848-4700; Fax: 856-848-3965; Email: tosorio@sjogcs.org; Web: www.sjogcs.org. Bro. Thomas Osorio, O.H., Exec. Dir. Brothers 3; Lay Teachers 35; Students 1,000; Total Staff 320.

[F] CATHOLIC FOUNDATIONS

CAMDEN. *Diocese of Camden Trusts, Inc.* (2001) 631 Market St., 08102. Martin F. McKernan Jr., Esq., Contact Person. Lay Staff 1; Priests 2.

Francis, Elizabeth and Edward Roger Welsh Scholarship Trust, 631 Market St., 08102.
Tel: 856-583-2835; Fax: 856-963-2655.

The Frank J. and Rosina W. Suttill Catholic Foundation, 631 Market St., 08102.
Tel: 856-583-2806.

The Sharkey Family Charitable Trust, 631 Market St., 08102. Tel: 856-583-2802.

The Tuition Assistance Fund, Inc., 631 Market St., 08102. Tel: 856-583-6125; Fax: 856-338-0766; Email: jlanahan@camdendiocese.org. James J. Lanahan, Sec.

[G] GENERAL HOSPITALS

CAMDEN. *Our Lady of Lourdes Health Care Services, Inc.*, 1600 Haddon Ave., 08103. Tel: 856-757-3500; Fax: 856-580-6336; Email: hensleyp@lourdesnet.org; Web: www.lourdesnet.org. Reginald Blaber, Pres. Bed Capacity 519; Patients Asst Anual. 288,721; Total Staff 3,859.

Our Lady of Lourdes Medical Center (Formerly Our Lady of Lourdes Hospital)(Parent Corporation: Our Lady of Lourdes Health Care Services, Inc.) 1600 Haddon Ave., 08103. Tel: 856-757-3500; Fax: 856-635-2400; Email: hensleyp@lourdesnet.org. Reginald Blaber, Pres. Franciscan Sisters of Allegany. Bed Capacity 350; Tot Asst. Annually 166,591; Total Staff 1,718.

Our Lady of Lourdes Health Foundation, Inc., 1600 Haddon Ave., 08103. Tel: 856-580-6451;
Fax: 856-580-6450; Email: cilar@lourdesnet.org; Web: www.lourdesnet.org/donating-to-lourdes/. Rev. Joseph Monahan, T.O.R., Chap.

Lourdes Cardiovascular Foundation, Inc., 1600 Haddon Ave., 08103. Tel: 856-482-4950;
Fax: 856-482-4960.

Osborn Family Health Center Inc., 1600 Haddon Ave., 08103. Tel: 856-757-3700; Fax: 856-365-7972.

Our Lady of Lourdes School of Nursing, 1600 Haddon Ave., 08103. Tel: 856-757-3730;
Fax: 856-757-3758; Email: hensleyp@lourdesnet.org; Web: www.lourdesnursingschool.org. Reginald Blaber, Pres.

Our Lady of Lourdes Medical Center Auxiliary, 1600 Haddon Ave., 08103. Tel: 856-705-1373;
Fax: 856-705-1370.

Lourdes Ancillary Services, Inc., 1600 Haddon Ave., 08103. Tel: 856-757-3500; Fax: 856-635-2400; Email: hensleyp@lourdesnet.org. Reginald Blaber, Pres.

Lourdes Cardiology Services, Inc., 1600 Haddon Ave., 08103. Tel: 856-757-3500. Reginald Blaber, Pres.

Life at Lourdes, Inc., 2475 McClelland Boulevard, Pennsauken, 08109. Tel: 856-675-3355;
Fax: 856-675-3687. Marge Sullivan, OSF, Exec. Parent Corp: Our Lady of Lourdes Health Care Services, Inc.

[H] NURSING HOMES

PLEASANTVILLE. *Villa Raffaella*, 917 S. Main St., Pleasantville, 08232. Tel: 609-645-9300;
Fax: 609-645-9600; Email: villaraffaella@msn.com; Web: www.villaraffaella.org. Sr. Elizabeth Rani Gnanapragasam, H.S.M., Admin. Senior Assisted Living Community, Hospitaler Sisters of Mercy. Bed Capacity 55.

[I] HOME CARE

EGG HARBOR TOWNSHIP. *Holy Redeemer Home Care*, 6550 Delilah Rd., Ste. 501, Egg Harbor Township, 08234. Tel: 609-761-0300; Tel: 800-788-3029;
Fax: 609-761-0294. A subsidiary of Holy Redeemer Health System, Inc.

Holy Redeemer Home Care, 1801 Rte. 9 N., Cape May Court House, 08210. Tel: 609-465-2082;
Tel: 800-745-4693; Fax: 609-463-6121; Web: www.holyredeemer.com. Terry Giannetti, Exec. Vice Pres. Sponsor: Sisters of the Holy Redeemer, C.S.R.A subsidiary of the Holy Redeemer, C.S.R.; A Medicare Certified Home Health Agency serving patients in their own homes. A Medicare Certified Hospice Program providing services for terminally ill patients and their families.

Atlantic County Office, 6550 Delilah Rd., Ste. 501, Egg Harbor Township, 08234. Tel: 609-761-0300;
Tel: 800-788-3029; Fax: 609-761-0294.

[J] HOUSING

CAMDEN. *The Diocesan Housing Services Corporation of The Diocese of Camden, Incorporated*, 1845 Haddon Ave., 08103. Tel: 856-342-4125;
Fax: 856-342-4172; Email: Katherine.boyer@camdendiocese.org. Mr. James CAM, Exec.; Katherine Boyer, Dir.

CAPE MAY. *Victorian Towers, Inc.* (1973) 608 Washington St., Cape May, 08204.
Tel: 609-884-5883; Fax: 609-884-5625.

CHERRY HILL. *Benedict's Place, Inc.*, 206 St. Mary's Dr., Cherry Hill, 08003. Tel: 856-874-0183;
Fax: 856-874-0176.

Marian Residence, 1000 Cropwell Rd., Cherry Hill, 08003. Tel: 856-424-1131; Tel: 856-424-1962;
Fax: 856-424-5333. Little Sister Servants of the Immaculate Conception Bed Capacity 5; Total in Residence 2; Total Staff 1.

Village Apartments of Cherry Hill, NJ, Inc., 350 Mt. Carmel Ct., Cherry Hill, 08003. Tel: 856-424-7913;
Fax: 856-424-9211; Email: villageapartments@camdendiocese.org. Total in Residence 148; Total Staff 8.

HAINESPORT. *Domicilium Corporation (Davenport Village)*, 301 Davenport Ave., Hainesport, 08036.
Tel: 609-702-0138; Fax: 609-702-5817.

NORTH CAPE MAY. *Haven House at St. John of God, Inc.*, 676 Townbank Rd., North Cape May, 08204.
Tel: 609-884-4548; Fax: 609-884-4316.

PENNSAUKEN. *Stonegate at St. Stephen, Inc.*, 5101 Stonegate Dr., Ste. 100, Pennsauken, 08109.
Tel: 856-486-7877; Fax: 856-486-1771. Curtis H. Johnson Jr., Sec. & Contact Person.

PLEASANTVILLE. *Village at St. Peter's Inc.*, 25 W. Black Horse Pike, Pleasantville, 08232.
Tel: 609-382-4181; Fax: 609-382-4184.

WEST DEPTFORD. *Shepherd's Farm Senior Housing, Inc.*, 981 Grove Rd., West Deptford, 08086.
Tel: 856-848-4913; Fax: 856-848-4927.

[K] CHILD CARE CENTERS

CAMDEN. *St. Joseph Child Development Center, Inc.*, 17 Church St., 08105. Tel: 856-963-9202;
Fax: 856-963-8940; Email: stjosephcdc@yahoo.com. Margaret Klein, Dir.; Jim Steinitz, Admin. Children 90; Staff 20.

CHERRY HILL. *Blessed Edmund Early Childhood Education Center* (1996) 1000 Cropwell Rd., Cherry Hill, 08003. Tel: 856-424-3063;
Fax: 856-424-3064; Email: blessededmund@verizon.net. Sr. M. Elizabeth Potuczko, Prin. Children 100; Clergy 11; Lay Teachers 4; Sisters 7.

[L] MONASTERIES AND RESIDENCES OF PRIESTS AND BROTHERS

CHERRY HILL. *Sacred Heart Residence for Priests, Inc.*, 200 St. Mary's Dr., Cherry Hill, 08003.
Tel: 856-751-2010; Fax: 856-489-8999. Sr. Rosemarie Kolmer, O.S.F., Coord. *Sacred Heart North*, 250 St. Mary's Dr., Cherry Hill, 08003.
Tel: 856-424-1741; Fax: 856-424-2896. Sr. Rosemarie Kolmer, O.S.F., Coord.

LINWOOD. *Villa Pieta. Missionaries of the Sacred Hearts of Jesus & Mary*, 2249 Shore Rd., P.O. Box 189, Linwood, 08221. Tel: 609-927-5600;
Fax: 609-927-5262; Email: mssccusa@aol.com; Web: missionofsacredhearts.org. Revs. John Perdue, M.SS.CC., Vice Rector; Frederick Clement, M.SS.CC., Rector; Damian Anumba, Priest; Bro. David Graber, M.SS.CC.

MARGATE. *Franciscan Friary* Holy Name Province. 118 S. Mansfield Ave., Margate, 08402-2516. Email: margate1@comcast.net. Total Staff 2.

OCEAN CITY. *Augustinian Friars*, St. Rita of Cascia Cottage, 823 5th St., Ocean City, 08226.
Tel: 609-398-1299. Rev. Joseph S. Mostardi, O.S.A., Guestmaster, Tel: 610-574-3544.

Ocean Rest Summer School and Retreat House, 3041 Central Ave., Ocean City, 08226. Tel: 609-840-6045. Mailing Address: 444-A Rte. 35 S., Eatontown, 07724. Tel: 732-380-7926; Fax: 732-380-7937; Email: juliano@fscdena.org. Bro. Joseph Juliano, F.S.C., Dir. Brothers of Christian Schools Summer School and Retreat House.

PLEASANTVILLE. *Villa Raffaella*, 917 S. Main St., Pleasantville, 08232. Tel: 609-645-9300;
Fax: 609-645-9600. In Res.

WESTVILLE GROVE. *Hospitaller Order of St. John of God* (1965) 1145 Delsea Dr., Westville Grove, 08093. Tel: 856-848-4700, Ext. 1142;
Fax: 856-848-7305; Email: tosorio@sjogcs.org; Web: www.sjog-na.org. Bro. Thomas Osorio, O.H., Prior. Brothers 4.

[M] CONVENTS AND RESIDENCES FOR SISTERS

ATLANTIC CITY. *St. John's Retreat House*, 128 S. Dover Ave., Atlantic City, 08401. Tel: 609-317-4399;
Fax: 609-317-4399. Sr. Maria Silvia Giraldo, Supvr. Little Servant Sisters of the Immaculate Conception. Sisters 2.

CHERRY HILL. *Franciscan Missionary Sisters of the Infant Jesus, Inc.*, U.S. Delegation and Novitiate: 1215 Kresson Rd., Cherry Hill, 08003.
Tel: 856-428-8834; Fax: 856-428-5599; Email: fmijusdel@yahoo.com. Sr. Jerilyn Einstein, F.M.I.J., Delegate Supr. Sisters 12.

Little Servant Sisters of the Immaculate Conception (1942) Provincialate and Novitiate. 1000 Cropwell Rd., Cherry Hill, 08003. Tel: 856-424-1962;
Fax: 856-424-5333; Email: s.dorotab@gmail.com; Web: www.lsic.us. Rev. Zbigniew Majcher, S.D.B., Chap.; Mother Dorota Baranowska, L.S.I.C., Prov. Sisters 68; Professed Sisters 67.

ELMER. *The Sisters of Mary Immaculate of Nyeri, Inc.*, 400 State St., Elmer, 08318. Tel: 856-358-4030; Email: smisep1999@yahoo.com. Sr. Anne Mugo, S.M.I., Delegate Supr. & Contact Person.

NEWFIELD. *Villa Rossello* Provincial House and Novitiate of Daughters of Our Lady of Mercy. 1009 Main Rd., Newfield, 08344. Tel: 856-697-2983;
Fax: 856-697-8595; Email: dmnewfield@yahoo.com. Sr. M. Ambrogina, D.M., Prov. Sisters 12.

PLEASANTVILLE. *Hospitaler Sisters of Mercy Novitiate*, 915 S. Main St., Pleasantville, 08232.
Tel: 609-645-9300; Fax: 609-645-9600; Email: villaraffaella@msn.com. Sr. Sherly Autenico, S.O.M., Supr. Sisters 12.

Hospitaler Sisters of Mercy Convent, 909 S. Main St., Pleasantville, 08232. Tel: 609-677-1407;
Fax: 609-645-9600; Email: hospitaler@comcast.net. Sisters 17.

SEA ISLE CITY. *The Sisters of St. Francis of Philadelphia*, 55th & Landis Ave., Sea Isle City, 08243. Tel: 610-558-7676; Fax: 610-558-6122; Email: roconnor@osfphila.org; Web: www.osfphila.org.

STONE HARBOR. *Villa Maria by the Sea* (1937) 11101 First Ave., Stone Harbor, 08247. Tel: 609-368-3621; Tel: 609-368-5290; Fax: 609-368-0315. Summer retreat house for Sisters Servants of the Immaculate Heart of Mary. (Immaculata, PA).

VENTNOR. *The Benedictine Sisters of Elizabeth, NJ*, 114 S. Troy Ave., Ventnor, 08406. Tel: 609-823-9843.

Holy Family, Seaside Convent, 497 Western Hwy., Blauvelt, NY 10913. Tel: 845-359-5600;
Fax: 845-359-5773; Email: mconnolly@opblauvelt.org. 110 S. Dorset Ave., Ventnor, 08406.
Tel: 609-822-5127. Sr. Michaela Connolly, Prioress. Sisters of St. Dominic (Blauvelt, NY). Sisters 115.

[N] RETREAT HOUSES

CAPE MAY POINT. *Marianist Family Retreat Center*, 417 Yale Ave., Box 488, Cape May Point, 08212-0488. Tel: 609-884-3829; Fax: 609-884-0545; Email: mfrc@capemaymarianists.org; Web: www.capemaymarianists.org. Mr. Anthony Fucci, Center Dir.; Bros. Albert Koch, S.M., (Retired); Edward Unferdorfer, S.M., (Retired); Stan Zubek, S.M., Prog. Staff; Rev. Timothy Dwyer, S.M., Chap.

VINELAND. *Pope John Paul II Retreat Center*, 414 S. 8th St., Vineland, 08360. Tel: 856-691-2299;
Fax: 856-691-5522; Email: sccpjIIrc@aol.com. Margarita Moran, Dir.

[O] APOSTOLIC CENTERS

CAMDEN. *Padre Pio Shrine, Buena Borough, N.J., Inc.*, 401 N. Harding Hwy., Box 203, Landisville, 08326-0203.

BERLIN. *Mater Ecclesiae Mission*, 261 Cross Keys Rd., Berlin, 08009-9431. Tel: 856-753-3408;
Fax: 856-753-2671; Email: rector@materecclesiae.org; Web: www.materecclesiae.org. Revs. Robert C. Pasley, Rector; Glenn R. Hartman.

HADDON HEIGHTS. **Collegium Center for Faith and Culture*, 301 White Horse Pike, Haddon Heights, 08035. Tel: 856-534-0400; Email: brenda@thecollegiumcenter.org. Rev. Timothy E. Byerley, Dir.; Brenda Quinn, Dir., Opers.

[P] FAMILY SERVICES AND COMMUNITY CENTERS OF CATHOLIC CHARITIES

CAMDEN. *Catholic Charities, Diocese of Camden, Inc.* Administrative Office 1845 Haddon Ave., 08103.
Tel: 856-342-4100; Fax: 856-342-4180; Email: kevin.hickey@camdendiocese.org; Web: www.catholiccharitiescamden.org. Kevin H. Hickey,

Exec. Dir., Catholic Charities. Tot Asst. Annually 32,000; Total Staff 100.

Catholic Charities - Camden County, 1845 Haddon Ave., 08103. Tel: 856-342-4100; Fax: 856-342-4180 ; Email: kevin.hickey@camdendiocese.org; Web: catholiccharitiescamden.org. Kevin H. Hickey, Exec. Tot Asst. Annually 32,000; Total Staff 100.

Catholic Charities - Atlantic County, 9 N. Georgia Ave., Atlantic City, 08401. Tel: 609-345-3448; Fax: 609-345-7180.

Catholic Charities - Cape May County, Village Shoppes, 1304 Rte. 47 S., Rio Grande, 08242. Tel: 609-886-2662; Fax: 609-886-3583.

Catholic Charities - Cumberland County, 810 Montrose St., Vineland, 08360. Tel: 856-691-1841; Fax: 856-692-6575.

Catholic Charities - Salem County, 114 State St., Penns Grove, 08069. Tel: 856-299-1296; Fax: 856-299-4010.

Catholic Charities - Gloucester County, 1200 N. Delsea Dr., Ste. One, Westville, 08093. Tel: 856-845-9200; Fax: 856-845-8905; Email: kevin.hickey@camdendiocese.org; Web: catholiccharitiescamden.org. Kevin H. Hickey, Exec. Tot Asst. Annually 32,000; Total Staff 100.

Counseling Center - Cumberland, 810 Montrose St., Vineland, 08360. Tel: 856-691-6084; Fax: 856-691-6179.

Counseling Center - Cape May, Village Shoppes, 1304 Rte. 47 S., Rio Grande, 08242. Tel: 609-886-2662; Fax: 609-886-3583.

Counseling Center - Camden, 1845 Haddon Ave., 08103. Tel: 866-682-2166; Fax: 856-342-4180; Email: sylvia.loumeau@camdendiocese.org; Web: catholiccharitiescamden.org. Sylvia Loumeau, L.C.S.W., Dir. Tot Asst. Annually 200; Total Staff 4.

Guadalupe Family Services Inc., 509 State St., 08102. Tel: 856-365-8081; Fax: 856-365-8247. Sr. Helen Cole, S.S.J., L.C.S.W., Dir.

[Q] CAMPUS MINISTRIES

CAMDEN. *Rutgers University*, c/o 642 Market St., 08102. Tel: 856-963-1285; Email: camdencm@camdendiocese.org. Rev. Krzysztof Wtorek, Chap.

GLASSBORO. *Rowan University*, St. Bridget University Parish/Newman Center, 1 Redmond Ave., Glassboro, 08028. Tel: 856-881-2554; Fax: 856-881-4183; Email: ninacamaioni@gmail.com; Web: www.rowanccm.com. Christina Camaioni, Coord.

POMONA. *Richard Stockton University* (1969) 235 Pomona Rd., Pomona, 08240. Tel: 609-707-1067; Fax: 609-804-9135; Web: www.ccmstockton.com. Lois Dark, Dir.; Rev. James H. King, Chap.

[R] LEGAL SERVICES

CAMDEN. **Camden Center for Law and Social Justice, Inc.* (1994) 509 State St., 08102. Tel: 856-583-2950; Fax: 856-583-2955; Email: jdecristofaro@cclsj.org; Email: info@cclsj.org. Jeffrey S. DeCristofaro, Esq., Dir. Total Staff 6; Clients Assisted Annually 4,000.

Camden Center for Law and Social Justice, Inc. Immigration Services & Legal Assistance to the Poor, 126 N. Broadway, 08103. Tel: 856-583-2950; Fax: 856-583-2955.

[S] MISCELLANEOUS

CAMDEN. *Catholic Business Networrk of South Jersey, Inc.*, 631 Market St., 08102.

Catholic Partnership Schools, Camden, N.J., Inc., 808 Market St., 08102. Tel: 856-338-0966; Fax: 856-338-0965. Sr. Karen Dietrich, S.S.J., Ph. D., Exec. Dir.

DeSales Service Works Inc., 642 Market St., 08102. Tel: 215-582-1666; Email: mccue1959@gmail.com. Rev. Michael J. McCue, O.S.F.S., Dir.

Diocese of Camden Healthcare Foundation, Inc., 631 Market St., 08102.

CAPE MAY. *Soul Mates for Jesus, Inc.*, 1027 Virginia Ave., Cape May, 08204. Tel: 609-884-7176.

NORTH CAPE MAY. *Christ Child Society, Cape May County Chapter*, 680 Town Bank Road, P.O. Box 882, North Cape May, 08204. Tel: 609-602-7682; Email: ccscapemay@gmail.com; Web: christchildcmc.com. Marilyn Kobik, Contact Person.

RELIGIOUS INSTITUTES OF MEN REPRESENTED IN THE DIOCESE

For further details refer to the corresponding bracketed number in the Religious Institutes of Men or Women section.

[0140]—*The Augustinians* (Province of St. Thomas of Villanova, Villanova, PA)—O.S.A.
[0275]—*Carmelites of Mary Immaculate*—C.M.I.
[0260]—*Discalced Carmelite Friars*—O.C.D.
[]—*Disciples of Mary*—A.M.
[]—*Franciscan Fathers, Third Order Regular.*
[0520]—*Franciscan Friars* (Prov. of the Most Holy Name of Jesus)—O.F.M.
[0670]—*Hospitaller Brothers of St. John of God*—O.H.
[1120]—*Missionaries of the Sacred Hearts of Jesus and Mary*—M.SS.CC.
[0920]—*Oblates of St. Francis De Sales* (Wilmington-Philadelphia)—O.S.F.S.
[0430]—*Order of Preachers-Dominicans* (St. Joseph Prov., New York)—O.P.
[1190]—*Salesians of St. John Bosco*—S.D.B.
[0760]—*Society of Mary*—S.M.
[0990]—*Society of the Catholic Apostolate*—S.A.C.
[0420]—*Society of the Divine Word*—S.V.D.
[]—*Vincentian Congregation* (India)—V.C.

RELIGIOUS INSTITUTES OF WOMEN REPRESENTED IN THE DIOCESE

[]—*Daughter of the Heart of Mary.*
[0890]—*Daughters of Our Lady of Mercy*—D.M.
[0900]—*Daughters of Our Lady of the Sacred Heart*—F.D.N.S.C.
[]—*Dominican Sisters of Amityville, N.Y.*
[1105]—*Dominican Sisters of Hope*—O.P.
[]—*Franciscan Missionaries Sisters of the Immaculate Heart of Mary*—F.M.I.H.M.
[1365]—*Franciscan Missionary Sisters of the Infant Jesus*—F.M.I.J.
[1180]—*Franciscan Sisters of Allegany, New York*—O.S.F.
[]—*Franciscan Sisters of the Renewal*—C.F.R.
[]—*Hospitaler Sisters of Mercy* (Pleasantville, NJ)—S.O.M.
[2300]—*Little Servant Sisters of the Immaculate Conception*—L.S.I.C.
[2490]—*Medical Mission Sisters*—M.M.S.
[2717]—*Missionary Daughters of the Most Pure Virgin Mary*—M.D.P.V.M.
[]—*Missionary Servants of the Most Blessed Trinity*—M.B.S.T.
[]—*Missioneras de Maria Formadora.*
[2575]—*Religious Sisters of Mercy of the Americas* (Mid-Atlantic Community)—R.S.M.
[3430]—*Religious Teachers Filippini* (Morristown, NJ)—M.P.F.
[0600]—*Sisters of Charity of St. Joan of Antida*—S.C.S.J.A.
[0660]—*Sisters of Christian Charity*—S.C.C.
[]—*Sisters of Mary Immaculate of Nyeri, Kenya*—S.M.I.
[1490]—*Sisters of Saint Francis of the Neumann Communities.*
[3893]—*Sisters of Saint Joseph of Chestnut Hill, Philadelphia*—S.S.J.
[1650]—*Sisters of St. Francis of Philadelphia*—O.S.F.
[3890]—*Sisters of St. Joseph of Peace*—C.S.J.P.
[2170]—*Sisters, Servants of the Immaculate Heart of Mary* (Immaculata)—I.H.M.
[2160]—*Sisters, Servants of the Immaculate Heart of Mary* (Scranton)—I.H.M.

CEMETERIES

Camden Diocesan Center, 631 Market St., 08102. Marianne Linka, Dir., Tel: 856-583-2820.

ATLANTIC COUNTY

DOROTHY.
St. Bernard Cemetery, Tel: 609-625-2123. (Holy Cross Cemetery, Rte. 40, Mays Landing)

HAMMONTON.
Holy Sepulchre Cemetery, Tel: 609-704-5945. (St. Mary of Mt. Carmel)

LANDISVILLE.
Our Lady of Victories Cemetery, Tel: 856-691-1290 (Call Sacred Heart Cemetery)

MAYS LANDING.
Holy Cross Cemetery & Mausoleum, Rte. 40, Mays Landing, 08330. Tel: 609-625-2123

PLEASANT MILLS.
Our Lady of the Assumption Cemetery
Closed, (Call Holy Cross Cemetery, Mays Landing, 609-625-2123)

CAMDEN COUNTY

BELLMAWR.
St. Mary's Cemetery & Mausoleum, Tel: 856-931-1570

BERLIN.
Gate of Heaven Cemetery, Tel: 856-767-3354

CEDARBROOK.
Sacred Heart Cemetery, Tel: 856-767-0719. (Christ the Redeemer, Atco)

CHEWS LANDING.
St. Joseph's Cemetery and Mausoleum (St. Joseph, Camden) Tel: 856-228-7588

CHERRY HILL.
Calvary Cemetery & Mausoleum, Tel: 856-663-3345

CAPE MAY COUNTY

CLERMONT.
Resurrection Cemetery, Tel: 609-624-1284

COLD SPRINGS.
St. Mary's Cemetery & Mausoleum, Tel: 609-624-1284

GOSHEN.
St. Elizabeth's Cemetery, Tel: 609-624-1284

WOODBINE.
St. Casimir's Cemetery, Tel: 609-624-1284

CUMBERLAND COUNTY

BRIDGETON.
St. Mary's Cemetery, Tel: 856-455-2323. (Holy Cross)

EAST VINELAND.
St. Mary's Cemetery, Tel: 856-691-7526. (Padre Pio)
Our Lady of Pompeii Cemetery, Tel: 856-691-7526. (Padre Pio)

MILLVILLE.
Holy Cross Cemetery, Tel: 856-825-0021. (All Saints, Millville)

ROSENHAYN.
St. Mary's Cemetery, Tel: 856-455-2323. (Holy Cross, Bridgeton)

VINELAND.
Sacred Heart Cemetery & Mausoleum, Tel: 856-691-1290

GLOUCESTER COUNTY

GLASSBORO.
St. Bridget's Cemetery, Tel: 856-881-2753. (St. Bridget Church)

MULLICA HILL.
Holy Name Cemetery, Tel: 856-478-2294. (Catholic Community of the Holy Spirit)

NEWFIELD.
All Saints Cemetery and Mausoleum, Tel: 856-697-1098

SWEDESBORO.
St. Joseph's Cemetery, Tel: 856-767-3354

WILLIAMSTOWN.
St. Mary's Cemetery, Tel: 856-767-3354

SALEM COUNTY

SALEM.
St. Mary's Cemetery, Tel: 856-299-3833. (St. Gabriel Church, Carneys Point)

WOODSTOWN.
St. Joseph's Cemetery, Tel: 856-478-2294. (Catholic Community of the Holy Spirit, Mullica Hill)

An asterisk (*) denotes an organization that has established tax-exempt status directly with the IRS and is not covered by the USCCB Group Ruling.

Diocese of Charleston

(Dioecesis Carolopolitana)

Most Reverend

ROBERT E. GUGLIELMONE

Bishop of Charleston; ordained April 8, 1978; appointed Bishop of Charleston January 24, 2009; consecrated and installed March 25, 2009. *Office: 901 Orange Grove Rd., Charleston, SC 29407.*

Chancery Office: 901 Orange Grove Rd., Charleston, SC 29407. Tel: 843-261-0420; Fax: 843-804-9408.

Web: sccatholic.org

Email: jamie@charlestondiocese.org

ESTABLISHED JULY 11, 1820.

Square Miles 31,189.

Comprises the State of South Carolina.

For legal titles of parishes and diocesan institutions, consult the Chancery Office.

STATISTICAL OVERVIEW

Personnel	
Bishop	1
Retired Abbots	1
Priests: Diocesan Active in Diocese	67
Priests: Diocesan Active Outside Diocese	3
Priests: Retired, Sick or Absent	19
Number of Diocesan Priests	89
Religious Priests in Diocese	43
Total Priests in Diocese	132
Extern Priests in Diocese	33
Ordinations:	
Diocesan Priests	1
Religious Priests	2
Transitional Deacons	2
Permanent Deacons in Diocese	131
Total Brothers	14
Total Sisters	82
Parishes	
Parishes	94
With Resident Pastor:	
Resident Diocesan Priests	29
Resident Religious Priests	10
Without Resident Pastor:	
Administered by Priests	54
Administered by Professed Religious Men	1
Missions	20
Closed Parishes	1
Professional Ministry Personnel:	
Brothers	4
Sisters	20
Lay Ministers	251
Welfare	
Catholic Hospitals	2
Total Assisted	471,265
Homes for the Aged	1
Total Assisted	25
Special Centers for Social Services	11
Total Assisted	48,852
Educational	
Diocesan Students in Other Seminaries	20
Total Seminarians	20
High Schools, Diocesan and Parish	6
Total Students	1,606
High Schools, Private	1
Total Students	661
Elementary Schools, Diocesan and Parish	28
Total Students	4,775
Catechesis/Religious Education:	
High School Students	2,618
Elementary Students	13,367
Total Students under Catholic Instruction	23,047
Teachers in the Diocese:	
Sisters	6
Lay Teachers	659
Vital Statistics	
Receptions into the Church:	
Infant Baptism Totals	2,670
Minor Baptism Totals	403
Adult Baptism Totals	203
Received into Full Communion	344
First Communions	3,269
Confirmations	2,478
Marriages:	
Catholic	511
Interfaith	170
Total Marriages	681
Deaths	1,314
Total Catholic Population	196,736
Total Population	5,024,369

Former Bishops—Rt. Revs. JOHN ENGLAND, D.D., ord. Oct. 11, 1808; first Bishop; cons. Sept. 21, 1820; died April 11, 1842; WILLIAM CLANCY, D.D., ord. May 24, 1823; cons. Dec. 21, 1834, Coadjutor; made Vicar-Apostolic of British Guiana, April 12, 1837; died June 19, 1847; IGNATIUS A. REYNOLDS, D.D., ord. Oct. 24, 1823; second Bishop; cons. March 19, 1844; died March 6, 1855; PATRICK N. LYNCH, D.D., ord. April 5, 1840; third Bishop; cons. March 14, 1858; died Feb. 26, 1882; HENRY P. NORTHROP, D.D., ord. June 25, 1865; fourth Bishop; cons. Titular-Bishop of Rosalia and Vicar-Apostolic of North Carolina, Jan. 8, 1882; transferred to Charleston, by brief dated Jan. 27, 1883; died June 7, 1916; WILLIAM T. RUSSELL, D.D., ord. June 21, 1889; fifth Bishop; cons. March 15, 1917; died March 18, 1927; Most Revs. EMMET M. WALSH, D.D., ord. Jan. 15, 1916; sixth Bishop; cons. Sept. 8, 1927; transferred to Youngstown, Ohio, as Coadjutor Bishop, Sept. 8, 1949; died March 16, 1968; JOHN J. RUSSELL, D.D., ord. July 8, 1923; seventh Bishop; cons. March 14, 1950; transferred to Bishop of Richmond, July 10, 1958; died March 17, 1993; PAUL J. HALLINAN, D.D., ord. Feb. 20, 1937; eighth Bishop; cons. Oct. 28, 1958; transferred to Archbishop of Atlanta, Feb. 21, 1962; died March 27, 1968; FRANCIS F. REH, S.T.L., J.C.D., ord. Dec. 8, 1935; ninth Bishop; cons. June 29, 1962; appt. Titular Bishop of Macriana in Mauretania and Rector of North American College, Rome, Italy, Sept. 5, 1964; transferred to Saginaw, Dec. 18, 1968; installed Feb. 26, 1969; retired April 29, 1980; died Nov. 14, 1994; ERNEST L. UNTERKOEFLER, D.D., J.C.D., S.T.L., tenth Bishop; ord. May 18, 1944; appt. Titular Bishop of Latopolis and Auxiliary Bishop of Richmond, Dec. 13, 1961; cons. Feb. 22, 1962; appt. Bishop of Charleston, Dec. 12, 1964; resigned Feb. 22, 1990; died Jan. 4, 1993; DAVID B. THOMPSON, D.D., J.C.L., eleventh Bishop; ord. May 27, 1950; appt. Coadjutor Bishop of Charleston April 22, 1989; ord. May 24, 1989; succeeded to Bishop of Charleston Feb. 22, 1990; retired July 13, 1999; died Nov. 24, 2013; ROBERT J. BAKER, twelfth Bishop; ord. March 21, 1970; appt. Bishop of Charleston July 13, 1999; cons. Sept. 29, 1999; appt. Bishop of Birmingham Aug. 14, 2007; installed Oct. 2, 2007.

Academy of Life—KATHY SCHMUGGE, Vice Chm.; MICHAEL F. ACQUILANO; MAROLYN BARIL, N.P.; WAYNE FREI, M.D.; ERIC NORTON, M.D.; JOHN QUINN, M.D.; JENNIFER RISINGER, M.D., OB GYN, FCMCI; CHRISTOPHER TOLLEFSEN, Ph.D.

Accounting and Finance Committee—TERENCE J. CONWAY, Chm.; CARL P. BORICK; ROBIN ELY CARROLL; LARRY EARL; JACK GALLAGHER; KELSEY SHOOTER, Recorder.

African-American Catholics—(See Ethnic Ministries, Office of).

Archives & Records Management, Office of—BRIAN P. FAHEY, M.L.I.S., Archivist, Tel: 843-410-1720; Email: bfahey@charlestondiocese.org; MELISSA J. MABRY, M.L.I.S., Assoc. Archivist, Tel: 843-410-1765; Email: mmabry@charlestondiocese.org; CHARLES WUJCIK, Archives Asst., Tel: 843-974-5555; Email: cwujcik@charlestondiocese.org.

Bishop, Office of the—JOAN SMITH, Administrative Asst., Tel: 843-225-7349; Fax: 843-804-9463; Email: jsmith@charlestondiocese.org.

Bishop's Residence—DONALD GLOVER, Mgr. Bishop's Residence & Chef, Tel: 843-327-1212; Email: dglover@charlestondiocese.org; ANALILIA TOVAR, Housekeeper, Email: atovar@charlestondiocese.org.

Building & Renovation Advisory Committee—Rev. Msgr. RICHARD D. HARRIS, V.G., Chm.; Rev. BRYAN P. BABICK, SL.L.; JOHN L. BARKER; TERRI BRISSON; JOSEPH DEPALMA; LYDIA DOYLE; LAWRENCE FLOOD; ELAINE H. FOWLER; DONNIE JAMESON; ROSS KUYKENDALL; PATRICIA MACKIN; STEPHANIE MCLELLAN; ERIC H. MEISTER; MICHEAL OLIVER; DAVID PFROMMER; WILLIAM ROBERTS.

Campaign for Human Development—(See Social Ministry, Office of).

Campus Ministry—(See Education and Faith Formation, Dept. of).

Carter-May Home/St. Joseph Residence—JANINE BAUDER, Admin., 1660 Ingram Rd., Charleston, 29407. Tel: 843-556-8314 (Main); Tel: 843-402-5460 (Office); Fax: 843-556-6879; Email: janine@charlestondiocese.org; Sisters LEENA JOSEPH, S.O.M.; MARIE THERESE RASOARIVAO, S.O.M.; MARY PARACKAL, S.O.M.

Catechetical Advisors, Diocesan Board of—MAUREEN ARNEMAN, Myrtle Beach Deanery Rep.; PAULETTE FLENCH, Myrtle Beach Deanery Rep.; MICHAEL MARTOCCHIO, Ph.D.; CINDY ROTH, Greenville Deanery Rep.; MARY L. SMITH, Charleston Deanery Rep.; DONNA TOMASINI, Columbia Deanery Rep.; NANCY COMPTON, Beaufort Deanery; SHARON WILLI, Charleston Deanery Rep.; ELENA ZIEGLER, Columbia Deanery Rep.

Catholic Women, Council of—Tel: 803-730-0083; Email: scccw.correspondence@gmail.com; Web: www.scccw.org. CHRIS SEGARS, Pres.; Very Rev. FABIO REFOSCO, C.O., V.F., Spiritual Advisor.

Cemeteries—KARMIN MEADE, Dir., Email: kmeade@charlestondiocese.org; PAMELA

PAQUETTE, Administrative Asst., Holy Cross Cemetery. Tel: 843-795-2111; Fax: 843-576-4925; Email: ppaquette@charlestondiocese.org.

Ceremonies, Diocesan Master of—Rev. BRYAN P. BABICK, SL.L., Tel: 843-588-2336; Email: frbabick@charlestondiocese.org.

Chancellor, Office of the—Sr. SANDRA MAKOWSKI, S.S.M.N., J.C.L., Chancellor, Tel: 843-225-7493; Email: smakowski@charlestondiocese.org; CINDY BRYAN, Administrative Asst., Tel: 843-225-7657; Email: cbryan@charlestondiocese.org.

Charismatic Renewal and Prayer Groups—Rev. DANIEL R. PAPINEAU, Diocesan Liaison; MARY WIKLACZ, Chairperson, Tel: 803-309-2480; Email: mdwiklacz@gmail.com; Email: join-us@screnewal.org; Web: www.screnewal.org.

College of Consultors—Rev. Msgrs. RICHARD D. HARRIS, V.G.; D. ANTHONY DROZE, V.G.; RONALD R. CELLINI, V.F.; Very Rev. EDWARD W. FITZGERALD, V.F., J.C.L.; Very Rev. Canon GARY S. LINSKY, V.F.; Very Revs. C. THOMAS MILES, M.C.L., J.C.L.; JAY SCOTT NEWMAN, V.F., J.C.L.; FABIO REFOSCO, C.O., V.F.; GREGORY B. WILSON, V.F.; Rev. DENNIS B. WILLEY.

Continuing Education for Priests—Rev. Msgr. EDWARD D. LOFTON, 11001 Dorchester Rd., Summerville, 29485. Tel: 843-875-5002; Fax: 843-875-4884.

Counseling Services—MARA CALDERON, Ph.D., Licensed Clinical Psychologist, Tel: 843-402-9115, Ext. 17. Services in English and Spanish.

Courage South Carolina Chapters—Rev. JOHN M. ZIMMERMAN, Chap., Web: couragerc.org.

Curia—Most Rev. ROBERT E. GUGLIELMONE; Rev. Msgrs. RICHARD D. HARRIS, V.G.; D. ANTHONY DROZE, V.G., Moderator; RONALD R. CELLINI, V.F., Sec. for Clergy; Very Rev. C. THOMAS MILES, M.C.L., J.C.L., Judicial Vicar; Sisters SANDRA MAKOWSKI, S.S.M.N., J.C.L., Chancellor, Sec. for Curia; PAMELA SMITH, SS.C.M., Ph.D., Sec. for Educ.; JOHN L. BARKER, CFO, Sec. for Admin.; LYDIA DOYLE, Sec. for Planning & Oper.; ELAINE H. FOWLER, Sec. Real Estate; ELIZABETH ISCH, Sec. Human Resources; DR. GUSTAVO VALDEZ, M.T.S., D.Min., Sec. Hispanic Ministry.

Cursillo Movement—ANDREA MARCELLA, Lay Dir., 1206 Shoreland Dr., Sumter, 29154. Tel: 803-840-3892; Email: sccathcursillold@gmail.com; Deacons ROBERT JONES, Spiritual Advisor, Tel: 843-424-7674; Email: rjones174@sc.rr.com; JOHN DEWOLFE, Spiritual Advisor for Men, Tel: 843-785-2895; Email: deacon@holyfamilyhhi.org.

Deans—

Aiken Deanery—Very Rev. GREGORY B. WILSON, V.F., Tel: 803-649-4777; Email: gwilson@charlestondiocese.org.

Beaufort Deanery—Rev. Msgr. RONALD R. CELLINI, V.F., Tel: 843-261-0540; Email: rcellini@charlestondiocese.org.

Charleston Deanery—Very Rev. JOSEPH V. ROMANOSKI, V.F., Tel: 843-556-0801; Email: jromanoski@charlestondiocese.org.

Columbia Deanery—Very Rev. Canon GARY S. LINSKY, V.F., Tel: 803-779-0036; Email: glinsky@charlestondiocese.org.

Greenville Deanery—Very Rev. JAY SCOTT NEWMAN, V.F., J.C.L., Tel: 864-271-8422; Fax: 864-370-9880; Email: jsnewman@charlestondiocese.org.

Myrtle Beach Deanery—Very Rev. EDWARD W. FITZGERALD, V.F., J.C.L., Tel: 843-651-3737; Email: efitzgerald@charlestondiocese.org.

Rock Hill Deanery—Very Rev. FABIO REFOSCO, C.O., V.F., Tel: 803-329-2662; Email: frefosco@charlestondiocese.org.

Diaconate Board—Deacon ANDRE J.P. GUILLET, Chm. & Ex Officio; Rev. Msgr. RONALD R. CELLINI, V.F., Vice Pres. & Ex Officio; Rev. ROBERT A. SPENCER, C.H.C., C.D.R., U.S.N.; Deacons ROBERT A. PIERCE; GERARD THIBODEAUX; THOMAS WHALEN; Sr. PAMELA SMITH, SS.C.M., Ph.D.; MRS. DONNA PIERCE; MRS. LISA THIBODEAUX; MRS. DOROTHY WHALEN.

Diaconate, Office of—Deacon ANDRE J.P. GUILLET, Dir., Tel: 843-261-0536; Cell: 843-323-2384; Email: aguillet@charlestondiocese.org; CRISTENE DIESSO, Coord., Tel: 843-261-0538; Email: cdiesso@charlestondiocese.org.

Divine Worship & Sacraments, Vicar for—Rev. BRYAN P. BABICK, SL.L., Vicar, Tel: 843-588-2336; Email: frbabick@charlestondiocese.org.

Ecumenical & Interreligious Affairs—Rev. C. ALEXANDER MCDONALD, S.T.L., Vicar, Mailing Address: P.O. Box 2704, Irmo, 29063. Email: ecumenical@charlestondiocese.org; MELISSA WALKER, Administrative Asst., Tel: 803-345-7407; Email: mwalker@charlestondiocese.org.

Education and Faith Formation, Department of—Sisters PAMELA SMITH, SS.C.M., Ph.D., Sec. Education & Faith Formation, Tel: 843-261-0495; Email: psmith@charlestondiocese.org; KATHY ADAMSKI, O.S.F., M.A., M.S., Mgr. Pastoral Formation, Tel: 843-261-0498; Email: kadamski@charlestondiocese.org.

Campus Ministry—JAMES GROVE, Dir. Catholic Campus Ministry, Tel: 704-405-5043; Email: jgrove@charlestondiocese.org.

Catechesis & Christian Initiation for Parishes and Schools—MICHAEL MARTOCCHIO, Ph.D., Dir., Tel: 843-261-0503; Email: mmartocchio@charlestondiocese.org; CATHY ROCHE, Administrative Asst., Tel: 843-261-0504; Email: cathy@charlestondiocese.org.

Catholic Schools Office—SANDRA LEATHERWOOD, Supt., Tel: 843-261-0493; Email: sandra@charlestondiocese.org; JACQUALINE KASPROWSKI, Assoc. Dir. Secondary Education, Tel: 803-673-3517; Email: jkasprowski@charlestondiocese.org; KIMBERLY HOPKINS, Coord., Tel: 843-261-0496; Email: khopkins@charlestondiocese.org.

Youth & Young Adult Ministry—JERRY WHITE, Dir., Tel: 843-261-0442; Fax: 843-804-9408; Email: jwhite@charlestondiocese.org; LEXIE SEGREST, Assoc. Dir. Young Adult Ministry, Tel: 843-261-0445; Email: lsegrest@charlestondiocese.org; JESSICA JENKINS, Assoc. Dir. Youth Ministry, Tel: 843-261-0673; Email: jjenkins@charlestondiocese.org; MARY CORDER, Coord., Tel: 843-261-0443; Email: mcorder@charlestondiocese.org.

Ethnic Ministries, Office of—REBECCA MCNAMARA, Administrative Asst., Tel: 864-331-2627; Email: rmcnamara@charlestondiocese.org; MS. KATHLEEN MERRITT, Dir., 204 Douthit St., A1, Greenville, 29601. Tel: 864-331-2633; Fax: 864-331-2631; Email: kmerritt@charlestondiocese.org; MICHAEL TRAN, Asst. Dir., Tel: 864-704-6559; Email: mtran@charlestondiocese.org; Sr. ROBERTA FULTON, S.S.M.N., Asst. Dir. Black Catholic Evangelization, 1662 Ingram Rd., Charleston, 29407. Tel: 864-704-6559; Email: rfulton@charlestondiocese.org.

Vicar for Black Catholics—Rev. MICHAEL C. OKERE, (Nigeria) 2229 Hampton St., Columbia, 29204. Tel: 803-254-6862; Email: mokere@charlestondiocese.org.

Vietnamese Ministry—Rev. DAVID Q. PHAN, O.F.M., Tel: 864-233-7717; Email: dphan@charlestondiocese.org.

Family Life, Office of—Rev. DAVID NERBUN, Vicar Family Life, St. Michael the Archangel Parish, 542 Cypress Ave., Murrells Inlet, 29576. Tel: 843-651-3737; Email: dnerbun@charlestondiocese.org; Web: sccatholic.org/family-life; KATHY SCHMUGGE, Dir., 2764 Pleasant Rd. #10630, Fort Mill, 29708. Tel: 803-547-5063; Email: kschmugge@charlestondiocese.org; Email: familylife@charlestondiocese.org; CHRISTY BROWN, Coord. Project Rachel, 7840 Lamington Dr., Indian Land, 29707. Tel: 803-554-6088; Email: cbrown@charlestondiocese.org; KELLI BALL, NFP Coord., Mailing Address: Diocese of Charleston, NFP Coord., P.O. Box 2, Lexington, 29071. Tel: 803-807-0158; Email: kball@charlestondiocese.org; CAROLE KING, O.F.S., Administrative Asst., Mailing Address: 2645 Ramblewood Rd., Aiken, 29803. Tel: 803-645-3972; Email: carole.king@charlestondiocese.org; MICHELLE LAW, Coord., Marriage & Family Life, Mailing Address: 113 Delchester Dr., Elgin, 29045. Tel: 260-341-7848; Email: mlaw@charlestondiocese.org; NANCY MCGRATH, R.N., B.S., CFCP, CFCE, Mailing Address: 603 Rosebud Ln., Greer, 29650. Cell: 864-270-3655; Email: nmcgrath@charlestondiocese.org.

Finance Council—TIMOTHY CARROLL; SCOTT CRACRAFT; TERENCE J. CONWAY; SHEILA DURANTE; JOSEPH J. KEENAN; JEFFREY REHLING; GUSTAVO SUAREZ, Esq.; PERRY KEITH WARING; KELSEY SHOOTER, Recorder.

Finance, Office of—JOHN L. BARKER, CFO, Tel: 843-261-0470; Email: jbarker@charlestondiocese.org; KELSEY SHOOTER, Exec. Administrative Asst. to CFO, Tel: 843-261-0468; Email: kshooter@charlestondiocese.org.

Financial Services—TERRI BRISSON, Dir. Financial Svcs., Tel: 843-261-0471; Email: tbrisson@charlestondiocese.org; DAVID AMATANGELO, Parish Financial Svcs. Supvr., Tel: 843-261-0483; Email: damatangelo@charlestondiocese.org; JOYCE KIERNAN, Financial Analyst II, Tel: 843-261-0484; Email: jkiernan@charlestondiocese.org; GABRIELA MINER, Accounting Supvr., Tel: 843-261-0474; Email: gminer@charlestondiocese.org; CAMDEN BATTE, Financial Reporting Supvr., Tel: 843-261-0475; Email: cbatte@charlestondiocese.org; LIZ MYSZKA, Staff Accountant, Tel: 843-261-0476; Email: lmyszka@charlestondiocese.org; BRANDON PROSSER, Sr. Accountant, Tel: 843-261-0478; Email: bprosser@charlestondiocese.org; RANDY WARNER, Sr. Accountant, Tel: 843-261-0486; Email: rwarner@charlestondiocese.org; ROBERT HICKS, Staff Accountant, Tel: 843-261-0510; Email: rhicks@charlestondiocese.org; JASON HORNE, Staff Accountant, Tel: 843-261-0481; Email: jhorne@charlestondiocese.org; MITCHELL MCDANIEL, Staff Accountant, Tel: 843-261-0482; Email: mmcdaniel@charlestondiocese.org; ALICE WILLIAMS, Staff Accountant, Tel: 843-261-0480; Email: awilliams@charlestondiocese.org.

General Counsel and Real Estate, Office of—ELAINE H. FOWLER, Gen. Counsel & Dir. Real Estate, Tel: 843-261-0523; Email: efowler@charlestondiocese.org; AMY S. AVILES, Administrative Asst., Tel: 843-261-0524; Email: aaviles@charlestondiocese.org.

Hermits, Director of—Rev. MICHAEL J. OENBRINK, Tel: 843-681-6350; Fax: 843-689-5502; Email: moenbrink@charlestondiocese.org.

Hispanic Ministry, Office of—Rev. TEOFILO TRUJILLO, S.T.L., Vicar, 2252 Woodruff Rd., Simpsonville, 29681. Tel: 864-288-4884; Email: ttrujillo@charlestondiocese.org; DR. GUSTAVO VALDEZ, M.T.S., D.Min., Dir., 1427 Pickens St., Columbia, 29201. Tel: 816-316-0182; Email: gvaldez@charlestondiocese.org; MARIELA LANDAVERDE, Administrative Asst., Tel: 803-602-0397; Email: mlandaverde@charlestondiocese.org; ESTELA LANDAVERDE, Hispanic Youth Ministry Coord., Tel: 571-723-7793; Email: elandaverde@charlestondiocese.org; VICTOR YSISOLA, Hispanic Radio Coord., Tel: 803-726-7770, ext. 67; Cell: 843-696-9846; Email: vysisola@charlestondiocese.org; REINALDO MENDOZA, Hispanic Adult Faith Formation Coord., Tel: 843-480-2095; Email: rmendoza@charlestondiocese.org.

Human Resources, Office of—ELIZABETH ISCH, Dir. Human Resources, Tel: 843-261-0422; Email: eisch@charlestondiocese.org; MATT CAMPBELL, Human Resources Supvr., Tel: 843-261-0427; Email: mcampbell@charlestondiocese.org; SHELBY VINCENT, Human Resources Generalist, Tel: 843-261-0428; Email: svincent@charlestondiocese.org; CLOYD GAFFNEY, Human Resources Generalist, Tel: 843-261-0425; Email: cgaffney@charlestondiocese.org; BERNADET BEST, Human Resources Asst., Tel: 843-261-0421; Email: bbest@charlestondiocese.org.

Child & Youth Protection—BONNIE SIGERS, Safe Environment Mgr., Tel: 843-261-0430; Fax: 843-804-9433; Email: bonnie@charlestondiocese.org; ROSE BUDNEY, Administrative Asst., Tel: 843-261-0431; Email: rbudney@charlestondiocese.org; ANDREA WHIPPLE, Administrative Asst., Tel: 843-261-0432; Email: awhipple@charlestondiocese.org; LOUISA STOREN, L.I.S.W., Victim Assistance Coord., 757 Johnnie Dodds Blvd., Ste. 100, Mount Pleasant, 29464. Tel: 843-856-0748; Tel: 800-921-8122 (Toll Free); Fax: 800-923-8122 (Toll Free).

Information Technology, Office of—ADAM DYSON, Unified Network Group, Tel: 843-261-0521; Email: adyson@unginc.com; ALEX HORTMAN, Tel: 843-261-0520; Email: ahortman@unginc.com.

Insurance—ERIC H. MEISTER, Risk/Claims Mgr., Catholic Mutual Group, 901 Orange Grove Rd., Charleston, 29407. Tel: 843-261-0472; Email: emeister@catholicmutual.org; ELIZABETH TARDITI, Svc. Office Asst., Catholic Mutual Group, 901 Orange Grove Rd., Charleston, 29407. Tel: 843-261-0473; Fax: 843-804-9408; Email: etarditi@catholicmutual.org.

Investment Committee—SCOTT CRACRAFT, Chm.; JOHN L. BARKER, CFO; GEORGIA FRENCH; DANIEL WALLICK; M. DUSTIN WILDER; KELSEY SHOOTER, Recorder.

Marian Programs—Rev. STANLEY SMOLENSKI, S.P.M.A., Dir., 300 Ashton Ave., Kingstree, 29556. Tel: 843-355-3527; Email: olcshrine@gmail.com; Web: www.ourladyofsouthcarolina.net.

Media Relations, Office of—MARIA A. ASELAGE, Dir., Tel: 843-513-7605; Email: maria@charlestondiocese.org.

Missionary Childhood Association—Rev. Msgr. EDWARD D. LOFTON, Dir.; HELENA MONIZ, Assoc. Dir., Mailing Address: St. Theresa, The Little Flower, 11001 Dorchester Rd., Summerville, 29485. Tel: 843-875-5002; Fax: 843-875-4884; Email: propagation@sttheresachurch.com; Web: propfaithcharlestonsc.com.

Multimedia, Office Of—DEIRDRE C. MAYS, Dir., Tel: 843-261-0508; Fax: 843-804-9462; Email: mays@charlestondiocese.org; CAROLINE LINDSEY, Graphic Designer, Tel: 843-261-0517; Email: clindsey@charlestondiocese.org; KEITH JACOBS, Web Devel., Tel: 843-455-3924; Email: kjacobs@charlestondiocese.org; JUANITA

BUSTAMANTE, Video Ministry Producer, Tel: 843-261-0512; Email: jbustamante@charlestondiocese.org; KELLY HARGETT, Multimedia Coord., Tel: 843-261-0516; Email: khargett@charlestondiocese.org.

Newspaper—The Catholic Miscellany
Tel: 843-261-0522; Fax: 843-804-9462; Web: www.themiscellany.org. DEIRDRE C. MAYS, Editor, Tel: 843-261-0508; Email: editor@charlestondiocese.org; CHRISTINA LEE KNAUSS, Staff Writer, Tel: 803-391-6486; Email: cknauss@charlestondiocese.org; AMY WISE TAYLOR, Staff Writer, Tel: 843-261-0514; Email: ataylor@charlestondiocese.org; CAROLINE LINDSEY, Graphic Designer, Tel: 843-261-0517; Email: clindsey@charlestondiocese.org; KELLY HARGETT, Circulation & Advertising Mgr., Tel: 843-261-0516; Email: khargett@charlestondiocese.org.

Official Catholic Directory Committee—MICHAEL F. ACQUILANO; JOHN L. BARKER; LYDIA DOYLE; ELAINE H. FOWLER.

Planning and Operations, Office of—LYDIA DOYLE, Dir., Tel: 843-261-0526; Email: ldoyle@charlestondiocese.org; JAMIE K. ZBYROWSKI, Planning & Operations Supvr., Tel: 843-261-0527; Email: jamie@charlestondiocese.org; MICHEAL OLIVER, Facilities Mgr., Tel: 843-261-0525; Email: moliver@charlestondiocese.org; STEPHANIE MCLELLAN, Bldg. & Renovation Specialist, Tel: 843-261-0528; Email: smclellan@charlestondiocese.org; WADE MCDANIEL, Maintenance, Tel: 843-697-0197; Email: wade@charlestondiocese.org; DAVID PFROMMER, Project Mgr., Tel: 803-753-5817; Email: dpfrommer@charlestondiocese.org; EDDIE WOODS, Supvr. Maintenance & Mechanical Technician, Tel: 843-518-0115; Email: eddie@charlestondiocese.org.

Presbyteral Council—
Deans—Rev. Msgr. RONALD R. CELLINI, V.F.; Very Rev. EDWARD W. FITZGERALD, V.F., J.C.L.; Very Rev. Canon GARY S. LINSKY, V.F.; Very Revs. JAY SCOTT NEWMAN, V.F., J.C.L.; FABIO REFOSCO, C.O., V.F.; JOSEPH V. ROMANOSKI, V.F.; GREGORY B. WILSON, V.F.
Deanery Representatives—Revs. RONALD J. FARRELL; AGUSTIN L. GUZMAN, C.O.; HENRY N. KULAH, (Ghana); C. ALEXANDER MCDONALD, S.T.L.; TIMOTHY D. TEBALT; TEOFILO TRUJILLO, S.T.L.
At Large Representatives—Rev. Msgr. CHESTER M. MOCZYDLOWSKI, D.Min.; Rev. PETER E. SOUSA, C.Ss.R.
Ex-Officio Members—Rev. Msgrs. RICHARD D. HARRIS, V.G., Moderator; D. ANTHONY DROZE, V.G.; Very Rev. C. THOMAS MILES, M.C.L., J.C.L.
Recorders—KATHRYN DANNELLY; DANIEL WAGNER, Ph.D.

Priest Personnel Board—Rev. Msgr. RONALD R. CELLINI, V.F., Chm.; Most Rev. ROBERT E. GUGLIELMONE; Rev. Msgrs. RICHARD D. HARRIS, V.G.; D. ANTHONY DROZE, V.G.; Very Rev. EDWARD W. FITZGERALD, V.F., J.C.L.; Very Rev. Canon GARY S. LINSKY, V.F.; Very Revs. JAY SCOTT NEWMAN, V.F., J.C.L.; FABIO REFOSCO, C.O., V.F.; JOSEPH V. ROMANOSKI, V.F.; GREGORY B. WILSON, V.F.; Rev. TEOFILO TRUJILLO, S.T.L.; Deacon LAWRENCE ROBERTS, Recorder/Sec.

Priest Retirement Committee—JOHN L. BARKER, Chm.; Rev. Msgrs. RICHARD D. HARRIS, V.G.; D. ANTHONY DROZE, V.G.; EDWARD D. LOFTON; Revs. ROGER JAMES MORGAN; MICHAEL J. OENBRINK, V.F.; SCOTT CRACRAFT; JOSEPH J. KEENAN; Deacon LAWRENCE ROBERTS, Member at Large; KELSEY SHOOTER.

Priests, Vicar for—Rev. Msgr. RONALD R. CELLINI, V.F., Vicar, Tel: 843-261-0540; Fax: 843-804-9408; Email: rcellini@charlestondiocese.org; Deacon LAWRENCE ROBERTS, Priest Personnel Coord., Tel: 843-261-0542; Fax: 843-804-9408; Email: lroberts@charlestondiocese.org.

Prison Ministry, Vicar for—Rev. ROBERT F. HIGGINS, c/o Transfiguration Parish, 9720 Wilson Blvd., Blythewood, 29016. Email: rhiggins@charlestondiocese.org; Sr. CHRISTINA MURPHY, S.N.D.deN., Coord. Prison Ministry, Mailing Address: Our Lady of the Hills, 120 Marydale Lane, Columbia, 29210. Tel: 803-772-7400, Ext. 2; Email: cmurphy@charlestondiocese.org.

Propagation of the FaithRev. Msgr. EDWARD D. LOFTON, Dir.; HELENA MONIZ, Assoc. Dir., Mailing Address: 11001 Dorchester Rd., Summerville, 29485. Tel: 843-875-5002; Fax: 843-875-4884; Email: propagation@sttheresachurch.com; Web: propfaithcharlestonsc.com.

Real Estate Committee—JOHN L. BARKER; COLLEEN CARDUCCI; LYDIA DOYLE; ELAINE H. FOWLER; TOMMY HARTNETT; JOSEPH J. KEENAN; MICHAEL ROBINSON; AMY S. AVILES, Recorder.

Religious, Vicar for—Mailing Address: 901 Orange Grove Rd., Charleston, 29407. Tel: 843-225-7493; Email: smakowski@charlestondiocese.org. Sr. SANDRA MAKOWSKI, S.S.M.N., J.C.L.

Retired Priests, Vicar for—Rev. S. THOMAS KINGSLEY, Vicar, Mailing Address: Church of the Nativity, 1061 Folly Rd., Charleston, 29412. Tel: 843-795-3821; Email: skingsley@charlestondiocese.org.

School Marketing & Finance Committee—TIMOTHY CARROLL, Co Chair; JEFFREY REHLING, Co Chair; JOHN L. BARKER; JACQUALINE KASPROWSKI; SANDRA LEATHERWOOD; KELSEY SHOOTER, Recorder.

Scouting, Diocese of Charleston Catholic Committee on—GEORGE FALLER, Chm., 107 Townes Rd., Columbia, 29210. Tel: 803-414-7181; Email: gfaller56@gmail.com; Web: docccs.org; Rev. S. MATTHEW GRAY, Chap., c/o St. Joseph Parish, 3512 Devine St., Columbia, 29205. Tel: 803-254-7646; Email: frgray@stjosephcolumbia.org.

Seminary Admissions Board—Rev. MARK S. GOOD, Chm.; Most Rev. ROBERT E. GUGLIELMONE; Rev. Msgrs. RICHARD D. HARRIS, V.G.; D. ANTHONY DROZE, V.G.; RONALD R. CELLINI, V.F.; Rev. TEOFILO TRUJILLO, S.T.L.; Deacon STEPHEN PLATTE, M.D.; Sr. MARIE CECILIA LAIRD, O.P.; MARY ANN FEY, L.P.C.; KEVIN MARONEY, Esq.; MARGUERITE (PEGGY) WERTZ; VALERIE ANNE GORE, Recorder.

Sites & Boundaries Committee—Rev. Msgr. RICHARD D. HARRIS, V.G.; JOHN L. BARKER, Email: jbarker@charlestondiocese.org; LYDIA DOYLE, Email: ldoyle@charlestondiocese.org.

Social Ministry, Office of—Tel: 843-225-7938; Fax: 843-804-9467. Deacon GABRIEL CUERVO, Interim Sec. Social Ministries & Exec. Dir. Catholic Charities, Email: gcuervo@charlestondiocese.org; MOLLIE KAY, Administrative Asst., Email: mkay@charlestondiocese.org.

South Carolina Catholic Conference—MICHAEL F. ACQUILANO, Dir., Tel: 843-261-0535; Email: macquilano@charlestondiocese.org.

Stewardship & Mission Advancement, Office of—CARRIE MUMMERT, Dir. Stewardship & Mission Advancement, Tel: 843-261-0435; Email: cmummert@charlestondiocese.org; AMANDA KEPSHIRE, Assoc. Dir. Stewardship & Mission Advancement, Tel: 843-261-0518; Email: akepshire@charlestondiocese.org; RUTHIE MAJOR, Office Coord., Tel: 843-261-0438; Email: rmajor@charlestondiocese.org; ANNE DURNEY, Sr. Devel. Asst., Tel: 843-261-0437; Email: adurney@charlestondiocese.org; MICHAEL F. ACQUILANO, Assoc. Dir. Catholic School Devel., Tel: 843-261-0535; Email: macquilano@charlestondiocese.org; LAUREN TURBEVILLE, Bicentennial Campaign Admin. Asst., Tel: 854-222-3994; Email: lturbeville@charlestondiocese.org.

Tribunal, Office of the—901 Orange Grove Rd., Charleston, 29407. Tel: 843-261-0450. All petitions for declarations of invalidity, and other questions related to divorced persons should be sent to the Office of Tribunal. All other prenuptial matters, requests for dispensations, and permissions should be sent to the Office for Matrimonial Concerns and Dispensations, 901 Orange Grove Rd., Charleston, SC 29407. Tel: 843-225-7657.
Judicial Vicar—Very Rev. C. THOMAS MILES, M.C.L., J.C.L.
Moderator of the Tribunal—VALERIE MAXINEAU, J.C.L.
Tribunal Judges—Rev. Msgr. CHARLES H. ROWLAND, P.A., J.C.L.; Very Rev. C. THOMAS MILES, M.C.L., J.C.L.; Rev. H. GREGORY WEST, J.C.L.; Sr. SANDRA MAKOWSKI, S.S.M.N., J.C.L.; VALERIE MAXINEAU, J.C.L.; MARY E. MCKENZIE.
Defender of the Bond—Very Rev. EDWARD W. FITZGERALD, V.F., J.C.L.
Promoter of Justice—Very Rev. EDWARD W. FITZGERALD, V.F., J.C.L.
Procurators/Advocates & Case Analysts—Rev. BRYAN P. BABICK, SL.L.; Deacon THOMAS BARANOSKI; JACKELINE CALLE; MEG WALTER; GREG ALLEN; CHRISTOPHER ARNOLD; WILLIAM GLOVER; THERESA M. PULLIAM.
Consulting Psychological Expert—LEE HARNETT, Ed. S., L.P.C.
Ecclesiastical Notary/Archival Records Technician—CHARLES WUJCIK.
Ecclesiastical Notary—REBECCA POWERS.

Vicar General, Office of the—Rev. Msgrs. RICHARD D. HARRIS, V.G., Tel: 843-261-0436; D. ANTHONY DROZE, V.G., Tel: 843-225-8345; Email: vicargeneral@charlestondiocese.org; KATHRYN DANNELLY, Exec. Asst. to Vicar Gen., 3512 Devine St., Columbia, 29205. Tel: 803-540-1920; Email: kdannelly@charlestondiocese.org.

Victim Assistance Coordinator—LOUISA STOREN, L.I.S.W., L.M.F.T., 757 Johnnie Dodds Blvd., Ste. 100, Mount Pleasant, 29464. Tel: 843-856-0748; Tel: 800-921-8122 (Toll Free); Fax: 843-856-0753; Fax: 800-923-8122 (Toll Free).

Vocations, Office of—Rev. MARK S. GOOD, Vicar, Tel: 843-261-0533; Email: frmark@charlestondiocese.org; DAN LORD, Promotions Mgr., Tel: 843-216-0039; Email: dlord@charlestondiocese.org; VALERIE ANNE GORE, Coord. Vocations, Tel: 843-261-0532; Cell: 803-543-1835; Email: vgore@charlestondiocese.org.

Youth Ministry—(See Education and Faith Formation, Dept. of).

CLERGY, PARISHES, MISSIONS AND PAROCHIAL SCHOOLS

GREATER CHARLESTON

(CHARLESTON COUNTY)

1—CATHEDRAL OF ST. JOHN THE BAPTIST (1821)
120 Broad St., 29401. Tel: 843-724-8395; Email: sstewart@charlestondiocese.org; Web: www.charlestoncathedral.com. 105 Queen St, 29401. Rev. Msgr. Steven L. Brovey, V.F., Rector; Deacons Thomas Baranoski; James Letendre; Charles Olimpio.
School-See Charleston Catholic School under Sacred Heart, Charleston.
Catechesis Religious Program—Students 120.

2—ST. BENEDICT (1999)
950 Darrell Creek Tr., Mount Pleasant, 29466. Tel: 843-216-0039; Fax: 843-971-6789; Email: office@stbenedictparish.org; Email: ajohnston@charlestondiocese.org; Web: www.stbenedictparish.org. Rev. Mark S. Good, Admin.
Catechesis Religious Program—Students 370.

3—BLESSED SACRAMENT (1944)
5 St. Teresa Dr., 29407. Tel: 843-556-0801; Fax: 843-556-2851; Email: lroberson@charlestondiocese.org; Web: www.blsac.org. Very Rev. Joseph V. Romanoski, V.F., Tel: 843-556-0801; Rev. Jose Gabriel Cruz Rodriguez, Parochial Vicar; Deacons Kurt Herbst; James R. Moore; Jerry White; Sr. Colie Stokes, Dir., Adult Formation.
School—Blessed Sacrament School, (Grades PreK-8), 7 St. Teresa Dr., 29407. Tel: 843-766-2128; Fax: 843-766-2154; Email: katharine.murphy@charlestondiocese.org; Web: www.scbss.org. Katharine Murphy, Prin.; Bonnie Perry, Librarian. Lay Teachers 23; Students 239.
Catechesis Religious Program—Students 199.

4—CHRIST OUR KING (1971)
1149 Russell Dr., Mount Pleasant, 29464. Tel: 843-884-5587; Fax: 843-884-7086; Email: dfisher@charlestondiocese.org; Web: www.christourking.org. Revs. Robert A. Spencer, C.H.C., C.D.R., U.S.N.; Patrick O. Eyinla, Parochial Vicar; Deacons Robert Boackle; Kevin Campbell; Donna Lareau, Dir., Adult Formation.
School—Christ Our King Stella Maris School, (Grades PreK-8), 1183 Russell Dr., Mount Pleasant, 29464. Tel: 843-884-4721; Fax: 843-971-7850; Email: frontoffice@coksm.org; Web: www.coksm.org. John Byrnes, Pres.; Susan Splendido, Prin. Lay Teachers 69; Students 579.
Catechesis Religious Program—Students 183.

5—CHRIST THE DIVINE TEACHER (1968) Closed. For inquiries regarding parish records, please contact Sacred Heart Parish, Charleston.

6—CHURCH OF THE NATIVITY (1959)
1061 Folly Rd., 29412. Tel: 843-795-3821; Fax: 843-795-2714; Email: vvazquez@charlestondiocese.org; Web: nativitycharleston.org. Rev. S. Thomas Kingsley.
School—Nativity School, (Grades PreK-8), 1125 Pittsford Cir., 29412. Tel: 843-795-3975; Fax: 843-795-7575; Email: pdukes@charlestondiocese.org; Web: www.nativity-school.com. Ms. Patricia Dukes, Prin.; Paula Hart, Librarian. Lay Teachers 16; Students 109.
Catechesis Religious Program—Mary L. Smith, D.R.E. Students 126.

7—ST. CLARE OF ASSISI (2014)
Mailing Address: 225 Seven Farms Dr., Ste. 107, Daniel Island, 29492. Tel: 843-471-2121; Email: info@clare.church; Email: check@charlestondiocese.org; Web: clare.church. Rev. H. Gregory West, J.C.L.
Catechesis Religious Program—Email: sarah@clare.church. Sarah Viancourt, D.R.E. Students 189.

8—DIVINE REDEEMER (1956)
1106 Fort Dr., Hanahan, 29410-2053. Tel: 843-553-0340; Fax: 843-553-0346; Email: msabback@charlestondiocese.org; Web: www.

divineredeemerchurch.org. Rev. Msgr. Thomas X. Hofmann, J.C.L.; Deacons Andre J.P. Guillet; Gabriel Cuervo.
School—Divine Redeemer Catholic School, (Grades PreK-8), 1104 Fort Dr., Hanahan, 29410-2053. Tel: 843-553-1521; Fax: 843-553-7109; Email: secretary@divineredeemerschool.com; Web: www.divineredeemerschool.com. Dr. Paulette Walker, Prin.; Karen Provost, Librarian. Lay Teachers 10; Students 149.
Catechesis Religious Program—Students 173.
9—HOLY SPIRIT (1938) [CEM]
3871 Betsy Kerrison Pkwy., Johns Island, 29455. Tel: 843-768-0357; Fax: 843-793-2958; Email: kcoder@charlestondiocese.org; Email: ssergi@holyspiritsc.org; Web: www.holyspiritsc.org. Rev. Msgr. Charles H. Rowland, P.A., J.C.L.; Rev. Jose Hugo Ruiz-Marentes, O.F.M., Parochial Vicar; Deacons Mario Cardenas; Joseph Stocker.
Catechesis Religious Program—Students 91.
10—ST. JOHN (1929)
3921 St. John's Ave., North Charleston, 29405-7158. Tel: 843-744-6201; Fax: 843-744-2792; Email: churchoffice@saintjohncatholicsc.org; Email: ebergeron@charlestondiocese.org; Web: www.saintjohncatholicsc.org. Very Rev. Joseph V. Romanoski, V.F., Canonical Pastor; Bros. Edward E. Bergeron, C.F.C., Parish Life Facilitator; Damien Ryan, C.F.C., Pastoral Assoc.; Spencer A. Tafuri, C.F.C., Pastoral Assoc.
School—St. John Catholic School, (Grades PreK-8), Tel: 843-744-3901; Fax: 843-744-3689; Email: schooloffice@saintjohncatholicsc.org; Email: kdurand@charlestondiocese.org; Web: saintjohncatholicsc.org/schoolsite/index.php. Bro. F. Damian Ryan, C.F.C., Pres.; Karen Durand, Prin. Brothers 1; Lay Teachers 8; Students 51.
Catechesis Religious Program—Students 15.
11—ST. JOSEPH (1966)
1695 Wallenberg Blvd., 29407. Tel: 843-556-4611; Fax: 843-556-4612; Email: info@saintjosephchas.com; Email: cpucino@charlestondiocese.org; Web: www.saintjosephchas.com.
Catechesis Religious Program—Email: rita@saintjosephchas.com. Rita Schoene, D.R.E. Students 75.
12—ST. JOSEPH, Closed. For inquiries regarding parish records, please contact St. Joseph Parish, Charleston.
13—ST. MARY OF THE ANNUNCIATION (1789) [CEM]
89 Hasell St., 29401. Tel: 843-722-7696; Fax: 843-577-5036; Email: office@sma.church; Fax: rachterhof@charlestondiocese.org; Web: sma.church. 95 Hasell St., 29401. Revs. H. Gregory West, J.C.L.; Patrick Allen, Parochial Vicar; Deacon Paul M. Rosenblum.
School-See Charleston Catholic School under Sacred Heart, Charleston.
Catechesis Religious Program—Students 41.
14—OUR LADY OF MERCY (1928) Closed. For inquiries regarding parish records, please contact St. Patrick, Charleston.
15—ST. PATRICK (1837) [CEM]
134 St. Phillip St., 29403. Tel: 843-723-6066; Fax: 843-853-8114; Email: bbuford@charlestondiocese.org; Web: www.stpatrickcharleston.org. Mailing Address: P.O. Box 20726, 29413. Rev. Henry N. Kulah, (Ghana).
School-See Charleston Catholic School under Sacred Heart, Charleston.
Catechesis Religious Program—Students 47.
16—ST. PETER, Closed. For inquiries regarding parish records, please contact St. Patrick, Charleston.
17—SACRED HEART (1920)
888 King St., 29403-4139. Tel: 843-722-7018; Email: info@sacredheartcharleston.org; Email: jpayne@charlestondiocese.org; Web: www.sacredheartcharleston.org. Very Rev. C. Thomas Miles, M.C.L., J.C.L.
School—Charleston Catholic School, (Grades PreK-8), 888-A King St., 29403. Tel: 843-577-4495; Fax: 843-577-6916; Email: charlestoncatholic@charlestoncatholic.org; Email: fmckay@charlestondiocese.org; Web: www.charlestoncatholic.com. Fred S. McKay Jr., Prin.; Very Rev. C. Thomas Miles, M.C.L., J.C.L., Chap. Lay Teachers 17; Religious 2; Students 187.
Catechesis Religious Program—Email: angel.shc.dre@gmail.com. Angela M. Prince, D.R.E. Students 23.
18—STELLA MARIS (1845)
1204 Middle St., Sullivan's Island, 29482. Tel: 843-883-3108; Fax: 843-883-3160; Email: jvaughan@charlestondiocese.org; Web: stellamarischurch.org. Mailing Address: P.O. Box 280, Sullivan's Island, 29482. Rev. Msgr. Lawrence B. McInerny, J.C.L.; Rev. John Antonydas Gaspar, Parochial Vicar; Deacon Jason Vaughan, Pastoral Assoc.
School-See Christ Our King Stella Maris School under Christ Our King, Mt. Pleasant.
Catechesis Religious Program—Tel: 843-883-3044. Students 176.
19—ST. THOMAS THE APOSTLE (1966)
6650 Dorchester Rd., North Charleston, 29418. Tel: 843-552-2223; Fax: 843-552-6329; Email: secretary@stthomasparish.net; Email: dkabaitan@charlestondiocese.org; Web: www.stthomascatholicchurch.org. Rev. Arnulfo Jara Galvez, C.M., Admin.; Deacon Joseph Donovan.
School-See Summerville Catholic School under Regional Schools.
Catechesis Religious Program—Students 130.

OUTSIDE OF THE CITY OF CHARLESTON

ABBEVILLE, ABBEVILLE CO., SACRED HEART (1885)
206 N. Main St., Abbeville, 29620. Tel: 864-366-5150; Email: gmayer@charlestondiocese.org; Web: sacredheartabbeville.com. Mailing Address: P.O. Box 812, Abbeville, 29620. Rev. David Michael, Admin.
AIKEN, AIKEN CO.
1—ST. GERARD (1943)
640 Edrie St., N.E., Aiken, 29801. Tel: 803-649-3203; Email: stgerardscatholi@atlanticbbn.net; Email: msolenberger@charlestondiocese.org; Web: stgerardaiken.org. Rev. Emmanuel Andinam, Ph.D., Admin.; Deacon Joseph Dennis.
Catechesis Religious Program—Students 8.
2—ST. MARY HELP OF CHRISTIANS (1853) [CEM]
203 Park Ave., S.E., Aiken, 29801. Tel: 803-649-4777 ; Fax: 888-552-1016; Email: parishoffice@stmarys-aiken.org; Email: pwray@charlestondiocese.org; Web: www.stmarys-aiken.org. Mailing Address: P.O. Box 438, Aiken, 29802. Very Rev. Gregory B. Wilson, V.F.; Rev. Raymond Flores, Parochial Vicar; Deacons Robert A. Pierce; Stephen Platte, M.D.
School—St. Mary Help of Christians Catholic School, (Grades K-8), 118 York St. S.E., Aiken, 29801. Tel: 803-649-2071; Fax: 803-643-0092; Email: cgreen@charlestondiocese.org; Web: www.stmaryschoolaiken.com. Charlene Krushinsky, Prin. Lay Teachers 25; Students 208.
Catechesis Religious Program—Students 258.
ANDERSON, ANDERSON CO.
1—ST. JOSEPH (1868)
1200 Cornelia Rd., Anderson, 29621. Tel: 864-225-5341; Fax: 864-225-6432; Email: info@sjccs.net; Email: DThompson@charlestondiocese.org; Web: www.sjccs.net. Mailing Address: 1303 McLees Rd., Anderson, 29621. Revs. Philip S. Gillespie; David A. Runnion, J.D., (In Res.), (Retired); Deacons Salvatore Cancello; James L. West.
School—St. Joseph Catholic School, (Grades K-8), Tel: 864-760-1619; Email: school.info@sjccs.net; Email: hgiuliani@charlestondiocese.org; Web: www.sjccs.net/73. Mrs. Haymee Giuliani, Prin. Lay Teachers 13; Students 90.
Catechesis Religious Program—Students 54.
2—ST. MARY OF THE ANGELS (1943)
1821 White St., Anderson, 29624. Tel: 864-226-8621; Fax: 864-226-2536; Email: office@sma43.org; Email: jczmyr@charlestondiocese.org; Web: www.sma43.org. Revs. Michael Patrick Jones, O.F.M.; Christopher Dunn, O.F.M., Parochial Vicar; Sr. Mary Frances Cannon, O.S.F., Pastoral Assoc.
Catechesis Religious Program—Tel: 864-226-3881. Students 102.
BARNWELL, BARNWELL CO., ST. ANDREW (1831)
110 Madison St., Barnwell, 29812. Tel: 803-534-8177 ; Email: holytrinityogb@gmail.com; Email: btobon@charlestondiocese.org; Web: www.holytrinitysc.org. Mailing Address: c/o Holy Trinity Parish, 2202 Riverbank Dr., Orangeburg, 29118. Revs. Wilbroad Mwape, Admin.; Gustavo Corredor, S.T.L., Parochial Vicar.
Catechesis Religious Program—Students 16.
BATESBURG-LEESVILLE, LEXINGTON CO., ST. JOHN OF THE CROSS (1959)
320 W. Columbia Ave., Batesburg-Leesville, 29006. Tel: 803-532-1208; Email: sjc@charlestondiocese.org. P.O. Box 2279, Batesburg-Leesville, 29070. Rev. Jose Rodolfo Lache-Avila, (Colombia) S.T.L., Admin.
Catechesis Religious Program—Students 225.
BEAUFORT, BEAUFORT CO., ST. PETER (1846) [CEM]
70 Lady's Island Dr., Beaufort, 29907. Tel: 843-522-9555; Fax: 843-522-0667; Email: mcarrera@stpeters-church.org; Web: www.stpetersbeaufort.org. Revs. Andrew Trapp; Christopher Beyuo, Parochial Vicar; Luis E. Serrano Carrero, C.H.S., Sacramental Responsibilities; Deacons Michael A. Beeler; Eugene Kelenski; William LaCombe; Rev. Robert Galinac, O.F.M.
School—St. Peter Catholic School, (Grades PreK-6), Tel: 843-522-2163; Fax: 843-522-6513; Email: stpetersschool@stpeters-church.org; Email: afeltner@charlestondiocese.org; Web: www.saintpeters.school. Ann Feltner, Prin. Lay Teachers 18; Students 104.
Catechesis Religious Program—Students 181.
BLUFFTON, BEAUFORT CO., ST. GREGORY THE GREAT (1960) [CEM]
31 Saint Gregory Dr., Bluffton, 29909. Tel: 843-815-3100; Fax: 843-815-3150; Email: sgreiner@charlestondiocese.org; Email: mwilliams@charlestondiocese.org; Web: www.sgg.cc. Rev. Msgr. Ronald R. Cellini, V.F.; Revs. Luis E. Serrano Carrero, C.H.S., Parochial Vicar; Derrick Sneyd, Parochial Vicar; Norbert C. Mendonca; Deacons Dennis Burkett, Marriage & Annulment Coord.; John Crapanzano; James Graham; John McCabe, (Retired); Barry O'Brien; Gregory W. Sams, Renewal Min.; Michael Smigelski; Sr. Margarita del Carmen Morales Galdamez, D.J.B.P., Hispanic Min.
School—St. Gregory the Great Catholic School, (Grades PreK-6), Tel: 843-815-9988; Fax: 843-815-6137; Email: ctrott@charlestondiocese.org; Web: www.sggcs.org. Mr. Christopher A. Trott, Prin. Clergy 1; Lay Teachers 17; Sisters 1; Students 190.
Catechesis Religious Program—Students 563.
Chapel—St. Andrew, 220 Pinckney Colony Rd., Bluffton, 29909.
BLYTHEWOOD, RICHLAND CO., TRANSFIGURATION (1998)
306 N. Pines Rd., Blythewood, 29016. Tel: 803-735-0512; Fax: 803-735-1742; Email: office@transfigurationsc.org; Email: vshealy@charlestondiocese.org; Web: www.transfigurationsc.org. Mailing Address: 9720 Wilson Blvd., Blythewood, 29016. Rev. Msgr. James L. LeBlanc; Deacon John Tempesco.
Catechesis Religious Program—Email: dre@transfigurationsc.org. Jim Shubnell, D.R.E. Students 55.
CAMDEN, KERSHAW CO., OUR LADY OF PERPETUAL HELP (1914)
1709 Lyttleton St., Camden, 29020. Tel: 803-432-6131; Fax: 803-432-3440; Email: nromaniello@charlestondiocese.org; Email: OLPH@ourlady-camden.org; Web: ourlady-camden.org. Rev. John M. Zimmerman.
Catechesis Religious Program—Tel: 803-432-8808. Students 127.
CHAPIN, LEXINGTON CO., OUR LADY OF THE LAKE (1989) [CEM]
195 Amicks Ferry Rd., Chapin, 29036. Tel: 803-345-3962; Fax: 803-345-8933; Email: parish.life@ollchapin.org; Email: donnie.jameson@charlestondiocese.org; Web: www.ollchapin.org. Mailing Address: P.O. Box 549, Chapin, 29036. Rev. Dennis B. Willey, Email: pastor@bellsouth.net; Deacons Malcolm Skipper; John Stetar; Gregory Weigold; James Atkinson, (Retired).
Catechesis Religious Program—Students 265.
CHERAW, CHESTERFIELD CO., ST. PETER (1842) [CEM]
602 Market St., Cheraw, 29520. Tel: 843-537-7351; Email: saintpeterscatholic@gmail.com. Sylvere Baloza, C.I.C.M., Admin.; Deacon Gustavo Salazar.
CHESTER, CHESTER CO., ST. JOSEPH (1854)
110 West End, Chester, 29706. Tel: 803-377-4695; Fax: 803-581-7848; Email: stjcoordinator@gmail.com; Email: jrodgers@charlestondiocese.org. Mailing Address: P.O. Box 869, Chester, 29706. Rev. Joseph Francis Pearce, C.O., Admin.
Catechesis Religious Program—
CLEMSON, PICKENS CO., ST. ANDREW (1935)
209 Sloan St., Clemson, 29633. Tel: 864-654-1757; Fax: 864-654-2950; Email: saclemson@charlestondiocese.org; Web: saclemson.org. Mailing Address: P.O. Box 112, Clemson, 29633. Revs. Daniel McLellan, O.F.M.; Robert J. Menard, O.F.M., Dir., Campus Min.; Deacon Richard Campana.
Catechesis Religious Program—Students 152.
COLUMBIA, LEXINGTON CO., OUR LADY OF THE HILLS (1972)
120 Marydale Ln., Columbia, 29210. Tel: 803-772-7400; Fax: 803-798-8030; Email: oloh@charlestondiocese.org; Web: www.ourladyofthehillssc.org. Revs. Peter E. Sousa, C.Ss.R.; Gustavo Corredor, S.T.L., Parochial Vicar; John Murray, C.Ss.R., Parochial Vicar; Deacons Stephen Burdick; Mark Gray; Dennis N. Jones; Charles R. DiRusso, (Retired); Sr. Christina Murphy, S.N.D.-deN., Pastoral Assoc.; Rev. Rodney Olive, C.Ss.R., In Res.
Catechesis Religious Program—Students 440.
COLUMBIA, RICHLAND CO.
1—GOOD SHEPHERD (1984) Merged For inquiries regarding parish records, please contact the Minor Basilica of St. Peter, Columbia.
2—ST. JOHN NEUMANN (1977)
100 Polo Rd., Columbia, 29223. Tel: 803-788-0811; Fax: 803-788-1501; Email: goshesky@sjnchurch.com; Email: sgoodman@sjnchurch.com; Web: www.stjohnneumannsc.com. Mailing Address: 721 Polo Rd., Columbia, 29223. Revs. C. Alexander McDonald, S.T.L.; Robert F. Higgins, Parochial Vicar; Deacon Gerard Thibodeaux.
School—St. John Neumann Catholic School, (Grades PreK-6), 721 Polo Rd., Columbia, 29223. Tel: 803-788-1367; Fax: 803-788-7330; Email:

rpoles@charlestondiocese.org; Web: www.sjncatholic.com. Ronald Poles, Prin.; Ms. Karen Zimmerman, Librarian. Lay Teachers 28; Students 285.
Catechesis Religious Program—Mrs. Cherie Smith, D.R.E. Students 361.

3—ST. JOSEPH (1948)
3600 Devine St., Columbia, 29205. Tel: 803-254-7646 ; Fax: 803-799-7607; Email: mindy@stjosephcolumbia.org; Web: www.stjosephcolumbia.org. Mailing Address: 3512 Devine St., Columbia, 29205. S. Matthew Gray, Pastoral Admin.; Rev. Msgr. Richard D. Harris, V.G.; Mary Cecile Swanton, C.S.J.B., Dir., Spiritual Devel.
School—St. Joseph Catholic School, (Grades PreK-6), 3700 Devine St., Columbia, 29205.
Tel: 803-254-6736; Fax: 803-540-1913; Email: info@stjosdevine.com; Email: dyarnall@charlestondiocese.org; Web: www.stjosdevine.com. Donavan Yarnall, Prin.; Shauna Kinsey, Librarian. Lay Teachers 24; Religious Teachers 1; Students 263.
Catechesis Religious Program—Tel: 803-540-1906. Students 162.

4—SAINT MARTIN DE PORRES (1935)
2229 Hampton St., Columbia, 29204.
Tel: 803-254-6862; Fax: 803-799-4720; Email: stmartincolumbia@charlestondiocese.org; Web: www.stmartincolumbia.org. Rev. Michael C. Okere, (Nigeria) Admin.; Deacon Leland Cave.
School—St. Martin de Porres Catholic School, (Grades PreK-6), 2225 Hampton St., Columbia, 29204. Tel: 803-254-5477; Fax: 803-254-7335; Email: dgilliard@charlestondiocese.org; Web: www.saintmartindeporres.net. Delores Cilliard, Prin.; Doris Arvelo, Librarian. Lay Teachers 12; Sisters 1; Students 41.
Catechesis Religious Program—Students 60.

5—MINOR BASILICA OF ST. PETER (1821) [CEM]
1529 Assembly St., Columbia, 29201.
Tel: 803-779-0036; Fax: 803-799-2438; Email: stpeters@visitstpeters.org; Email: rcarroll@charlestondiocese.org; Web: www.visitstpeters.org. Mailing Address: P.O. Box 1896, Columbia, 29202. Very Rev. Canon Gary S. Linsky, V.F., Rector; Rev. Andrew Fryml, Parochial Vicar; Deacons Ronald J. Anderson; David Thompson; Michael Younginer.
School—St. Peter's Catholic School, (Grades PreK-6), 1035 Hampton St., Columbia, 29201.
Tel: 803-252-8285; Fax: 803-254-4736; Email: awall@charlestondiocese.org; Web: stpeterscatholicschool.org. Aubrey Wall, Prin. Lay Teachers 20; Students 118.
Catechesis Religious Program—Email: donna@visitstpeters.org. Donna Tomasini, D.R.E. Students 256.

6—ST. THOMAS MORE (1953)
1610 Greene St., Columbia, 29201. Tel: 803-799-5870 ; Fax: 803-765-0800; Email: pam@stthomasmoreusc.org; Email: pamela.scott@charlestondiocese.org; Web: stthomasmoreusc.org. Rev. Marcin Zahuta, (Poland); Deacon Stephen Brown.
Catechesis Religious Program—Students 37.

CONWAY, HORRY CO., ST. JAMES THE YOUNGER (1945)
1071 Academy Dr., Conway, 29526.
Tel: 843-347-5168; Fax: 843-347-1212; Email: stjames@stjamesconway.org; Email: stjames@charlestondiocese.org; Web: stjamesconway.org. Revs. Oscar Borda Borda Rojas, (Colombia) S.A., Admin.; Timothy Akanle Akanson, Parochial Vicar; Deacon Jeffrey P. Mevissen.
Catechesis Religious Program—Tel: 843-347-5168; Email: pflench@stjamesconway.org. Paulette Flench, D.R.E. Students 295.

DILLON, DILLON CO., ST. LOUIS (1943)
610 Highway 301 N., Dillon, 29536.
Tel: 843-774-0255; Email: mbineenmukad@charlestondiocese.org; Email: bookkeeper.stlouisdillon@gmail.com; Web: www.sites.google.com/site/stlouisdillon. Rev. Michel Bineen Mukad, Admin.
Catechesis Religious Program—Email: kitsyhunt@bellsouth.net. Mrs. Catherine W. Hunt, D.R.E. Students 56.

EDGEFIELD, EDGEFIELD CO., ST. MARY OF THE IMMACULATE CONCEPTION (1856) [CEM]
302 Jeter St., Edgefield, 29824. Tel: 803-637-6248; Email: rgarcia@charlestondiocese.org; Email: stmarysc@bellsouth.net; Web: www.stmarysedgefield.org. Rev. Filip P. Wodecki, Admin.; Deacon Larry Deschaine.
Catechesis Religious Program—Students 13.

FLORENCE, FLORENCE CO.
1—ST. ANNE (1940) [JC]
113 S. Kemp St., Florence, 29506. Tel: 843-661-5012; Fax: 843-673-2680; Email: BLewis@charlestondiocese.org; Web: stannecatholicparish.com. Rev. Noel Tria, (Philippines); Deacons James H. Johnson, (Retired); Robert C. Gerald Jr.; Robert L. Cox III.
Catechesis Religious Program—Students 45.

2—ST. ANTHONY (1872)
2536 W. Hoffmeyer Rd., Florence, 29501.
Tel: 843-662-5674; Fax: 843-662-4800; Email: afoyle@charlestondiocese.org; Web: www.saintanthony.com. Mailing Address: P.O. Box 5327, Florence, 29502. Rev. Robert E. Morey, J.D.; Deacons Reginald A.T. Armstrong; Bruce Fortnum; Michael Woodall.
School—St. Anthony Catholic School, (Grades PreK-8), Tel: 843-662-1910; Fax: 843-662-5335; Email: thamner@charlestondiocese.org; Web: www.saintanthonycatholic.com. Tracy Hamner, Prin. Lay Teachers 18; Students 113.
Catechesis Religious Program—Students 143.

FOLLY BEACH, CHARLESTON CO., OUR LADY OF GOOD COUNSEL (1950)
56 Center St., Folly Beach, 29439. Tel: 843-588-2336; Fax: 843-588-3478; Email: ndeneane@charlestondiocese.org; Web: www.olgc-follybeach.org. Mailing Address: P.O. Box 1257, Folly Beach, 29439. Rev. Bryan P. Babick, SL.L., Admin.
Catechesis Religious Program—Students 31.

FORT MILL, YORK CO., ST. PHILIP NERI (1993) [CEM]
292 Munn Rd., Fort Mill, 29715. Tel: 803-548-7282; Fax: 803-547-2999; Email: administrativeassistant@saintphilipneri.org; Email: mmontes@charlestondiocese.org; Web: www.saintphilipneri.org. Rev. John P. Giuliani, C.O.; Deacons David Bartholomew; Jon Dwyer; George Johnston; Steven Rhodes.
Catechesis Religious Program—Students 1,013.

GAFFNEY, CHEROKEE CO., SACRED HEART (1955)
407 Grace St., Gaffney, 29340. Tel: 864-489-9453; Fax: 864-489-9150; Email: btorres@charlestondiocese.org. Mailing Address: 205 Sams St., Gaffney, 29340. Rev. Michael F. McCafferty; Deacon Fred Knowles.
Catechesis Religious Program—Students 190.

GEORGETOWN, GEORGETOWN CO.
1—ST. CYPRIAN (1950) Merged For inquiries regarding parish records, please contact St. Mary, Our Lady of Ransom, Georgetown.

2—ST. MARY, OUR LADY OF RANSOM (1899) [JC]
317 Broad St., Georgetown, 29440. Tel: 843-546-7416 ; Fax: 843-546-7003; Email: stmarygeorgetown@charlestondiocese.org; Web: www.stmaryourladyofransom.org. Rev. Richard C. Wilson, Admin.; Deacon Michael Brescia.
Catechesis Religious Program—Students 86.

GLOVERVILLE, AIKEN CO., OUR LADY OF THE VALLEY (1954)
2429 Augusta Rd., Gloverville, 29828.
Tel: 803-593-2241; Email: bthouin@charlestondiocese.org; Web: ourladyofthevalleyparish.org. Mailing Address: P.O. Box 419, Gloverville, 29828. Rev. Filip P. Wodecki, Admin.
Catechesis Religious Program—Students 16.

GOOSE CREEK, BERKELEY CO., IMMACULATE CONCEPTION (1976)
510 St. James Ave., Goose Creek, 29445.
Tel: 843-572-1270; Fax: 843-572-3128; Email: cfaretra@charlestondiocese.org; Web: www.icgc510.org. Revs. Noly Berjuega, C.R.M.; Binil Jose Attappattu, C.R.M., Parochial Vicar; Robson Weber, Parochial Vicar; Deacons Jose Mayen; Daniel McNerny; John Murphy; Lawrence Roberts; Rev. Frank Palmieri, C.R.M., In Res.
School-See Summerville Catholic School under Regional Schools.
Catechesis Religious Program—Students 476.

GREENVILLE, GREENVILLE CO.
1—ST. ANTHONY OF PADUA (1939)
307 Gower St., Greenville, 29611. Tel: 864-233-7717; Fax: 864-233-2852; Email: stanthonysparish@gmail.com; Web: www.newstanthony.com. Revs. Patrick Tuttle, O.F.M.; David Q. Phan, O.F.M., Parochial Vicar; John W. McDowell, O.F.M., Parochial Vicar; Deacons Phil Allen; Dexter Gourdin; Steven Olson; W. James Williams II; Winston C. Wright, (Retired).
School—St. Anthony of Padua Catholic School, (Grades PreK-6), 311 Gower St., Greenville, 29611. Tel: 864-271-0167; Fax: 864-271-2936; Email: mary.martin@charlestondiocese.org; Web: stanthonygreenvillesc.org. Mary Martin, Prin. Lay Teachers 15; Sisters of St. Francis of Neumann Centers 1; Students 138.
Catechesis Religious Program—Students 109.

2—ST. MARY (1852)
111 Hampton Ave., Greenville, 29601.
Tel: 864-271-8422; Fax: 864-370-9880; Email: churchoffice@stmarysgvl.org; Email: pperkins@charlestondiocese.org; Web: www.stmarysgvl.org. Very Rev. Jay Scott Newman, V.F., J.C.L.; Revs. Francisco Cruz Velosa, (Colombia) Parochial Vicar; Jose Orlando Cheverria Jimenez, (Colombia) Parochial Vicar; Deacons Nestor Acosta; Diego Ferro; Alex Garvey; John Heuser; Joseph Sanfilippo Jr.; George Tierney; Thomas Whalen.
School—St. Mary's Catholic School, (Grades PreK-8), 101 Hampton Ave., Greenville, 29601.
Tel: 864-271-3870; Fax: 864-271-0159; Email: school.office@stmarysgvl.org; Web: stmarysgvl.org/theschool. Steven Zimmerman, Prin.; Linda Hilley, Librarian. Lay Teachers 22; Dominicans 3; Students 268.
Catechesis Religious Program—Tel: 864-679-4110; Email: joann.miller@stmarysgvl.org. Joann Miller, D.R.E. Students 313.

3—OUR LADY OF THE ROSARY (1952)
3710 Augusta Rd., Greenville, 29605.
Tel: 864-422-1648; Fax: 864-277-5969; Email: ejones@charlestondiocese.org; Web: www.olrgreenville.com. Rev. Dwight Longenecker; Deacons Richard Ballard, Pastoral Assoc.; Michael Bannio; Edward Case; Ronald Meyer, (Retired); Raymond Perham, (Retired).
School—Our Lady of the Rosary Catholic School, (Grades PreK-8), 2 James Dr., Greenville, 29605.
Tel: 864-277-5350; Fax: 864-277-7745; Email: info@olrschool.net; Email: tcurtin@charlestondiocese.org; Web: olrschool.net. Thomas Curtain, Prin.; Robin Calamia, Librarian. Lay Teachers 22; Students 150.
Catechesis Religious Program—Students 176.

GREENWOOD, GREENWOOD CO., OUR LADY OF LOURDES (1920)
915 Mathis Rd., Greenwood, 29646.
Tel: 864-223-8410; Fax: 864-223-7555; Email: wlordemann@charlestondiocese.org; Web: www.olol.org. Revs. Timothy D. Tebalt; Jose Orlando Cheverria Jimenez, (Colombia) Sacramental Responsibilities; Deacon Joseph P. Biviano.
Catechesis Religious Program—Email: tomrel@embarqmail.com. Students 221.

GREER, GREENVILLE CO.
1—BLESSED TRINITY (1974)
901 River Rd., Greer, 29651. Tel: 864-879-4225;
Tel: 864-655-5140; Fax: 864-879-4261; Email: jlawrence@charlestondiocese.org; Web: www.blessedtrinitysc.org. Rev. Jaime A. Gonzalez, Admin.; Deacon Gary Walczak, (Retired).
Catechesis Religious Program—Students 167.

2—OUR LADY OF LA VANG
Mailing Address: 2020 Gibbs Shoals Rd., Greer, 29650. Tel: 864-395-0202; Email: dphan@charlestondiocese.org. Rev. David Q. Phan, O.F.M., Admin.

HARTSVILLE, DARLINGTON CO.
1—ST. JOSEPH, Closed. For inquiries regarding parish records, please contact St. Mary the Virgin Mother, Hartsville.

2—ST. MARY THE VIRGIN MOTHER (1941)
363 N. 5th St., Hartsville, 29550. Tel: 843-332-7773; Fax: 843-332-2812; Email: stmary2@ymail.com; Email: dkavanagh@charlestondiocese.org; Web: www.stmaryhartsville.org. Rev. Daniel R. Papineau, Admin.
Catechesis Religious Program—Students 57.

HILTON HEAD ISLAND, BEAUFORT CO.
1—ST. FRANCIS BY THE SEA (1984) [CEM]
45 Beach City Rd., Hilton Head Island, 29926.
Tel: 843-681-6350; Fax: 843-689-5502; Email: office@stfrancishhi.org; Email: cduren@charlestondiocese.org; Web: www.stfrancishhi.org. Revs. Michael J. Oenbrink, V.F.; James M. Crowley, Parochial Vicar; Rodolfo Gonzalez, Parochial Vicar; Deacons Galo Barreto, Hispanic Min.; Gerard Hand; Joseph J. Nazarro, (Retired); Patrick Sheehan; Vernon Dobelmann; Sr. Kathleen Kane, S.S.M.N., Pastoral Assoc.
School—St. Francis Catholic School, (Grades PreK-8), Tel: 843-681-6501; Fax: 843-689-3725; Email: bpope@charlestondiocese.org; Web: www.sfcshhi.com. Brian Pope, Prin. Lay Teachers 10; Students 213.
Catechesis Religious Program—
Tel: 843-681-6350, Ext. 248. Students 229.
St. Francis Thrift Shop—6 Southwood Park Dr., Hilton Head Island, 29926. Tel: 843-689-6563. Hal Wieland, Dir.

2—HOLY FAMILY (1966)
24 Pope Ave., Hilton Head Island, 29928.
Tel: 843-785-2895; Email: rdewolfe@charlestondiocese.org; Web: www.holyfamilyhhi.org. Revs. Ronald J. Farrell; Rodolfo Gonzalez, Parochial Vicar; Deacon John DeWolfe.
Catechesis Religious Program—Email: education@holyfamily.hhi.org. Students 264.

JOANNA, LAURENS CO., ST. BONIFACE (1949)
401 N. Main St., Joanna, 29351. Tel: 864-697-6745; Email: stbonifacejoanna@charlestondiocese.org. Rev. Orlando Serrano Ardila, Admin.
Catechesis Religious Program—Students 17.

KINGSTREE, WILLIAMSBURG CO., ST. ANN (1947)
107 Hirsch St., Kingstree, 29556. Tel: 843-355-5234; Fax: 843-353-1354; Email: ftaylor@charlestondiocese.org. Mailing Address: P.O. Box 529, Kingstree, 29556. Rev. Arturo O. Dalupang, Admin.; Deacon Harold Jackson.
Catechesis Religious Program—Students 4.
Convent—908 Thorne Ave., Kingstree, 29556.

Tel: 843-354-9415; Email: stann@ftc-i.net. Sr. Susanne Dziedzic, C.S.S.F., Contact Person. Felician Sisters 3.

LAKE CITY, FLORENCE CO., ST. PHILIP THE APOSTLE (1952) [JC]
120 Westover St., Lake City, 29560.
Tel: 843-394-8343; Email: stphiliplakecity@gmail.com; Email: rthomy@charlestondiocese.org. Mailing Address: P.O. Box 399, Lake City, 29560. Rev. Arturo O. Dalupang, Admin.; Deacon Asuncion Valadez.
Catechesis Religious Program—Students 22.

LAKE WYLIE, YORK CO., ALL SAINTS PARISH
530 Hwy. 274, Lake Wylie, 29710. Tel: 803-831-9095; Email: falley@charlestondiocese.org; Web: allsaintslakewylie.com. Rev. Agustin Guzman, C.O.; Deacons Andrew Fatovic; John Hall; Bro. John F. Kummer, C.O., Pastoral Asst.
Catechesis Religious Program—Students 248.

LANCASTER, LANCASTER CO.
1—ST. CATHERINE OF SIENA (1948)
720 W. Meeting St., Lancaster, 29720.
Tel: 803-283-3362; Email: stcatherineofsiena@charlestondiocese.org; Web: www.stcatherinecatholic.org. Rev. Francis J. Gillespie, S.J., Admin.; Janet Sciulli, Business Mgr.
Catechesis Religious Program—Mary Atkinson, D.R.E. Students 118.

2—OUR LADY OF GRACE
7095 Waxhaw Hwy., Lancaster, 29720.
Tel: 802-283-4969; Fax: 803-283-4970; Email: cbates@charlestondiocese.org; Web: www.gracewepray.org. Rev. Jeffrey F. Kirby, S.T.L.; Deacons Robert Donofrio; Richard Olson.
Catechesis Religious Program—Students 114.

LEXINGTON, LEXINGTON CO., CORPUS CHRISTI (1977)
2350 Augusta Hwy., Lexington, 29072.
Tel: 803-359-4391; Fax: 803-359-8885; Email: gprestia@charlestondiocese.org; Web: www.corpuschristisc.org. Rev. Raymond J. Carlo; Deacons Jack L. Crocker, D.D.S., (Retired); Coleman T. Parks; Richard Gundlach, (Retired), (Retired); Carl Johnson.
Catechesis Religious Program—Students 265.

MANNING, CLARENDON CO., ST. MARY, OUR LADY OF HOPE (2002)
2529 Raccoon Rd., Manning, 29102.
Tel: 803-485-2925; Fax: 803-488-0177; Email: stmaryourladyofhope@charlestondiocese.org; Web: myoloh.org. Rev. Maximino E. Tria Jr., Admin.; Deacon Charles Michael Walsh, (Retired).
Catechesis Religious Program—Students 40.

MCCORMICK, MCCORMICK CO., GOOD SHEPHERD (1964)
1401 Greenwood Hwy., McCormick, 29835.
Tel: 864-852-4722; Fax: 864-852-4723; Email: chahs@charlestondiocese.org; Web: goodshepherdmccormick.com. Mailing Address: P.O. Box 1468, McCormick, 29835. Rev. David Michael, Admin.

MONCKS CORNER, BERKELEY CO., ST. PHILIP BENIZI (1965)
1404 Old Hwy. 52 S., Moncks Corner, 29461.
Tel: 843-761-3777; Fax: 843-761-3780; Email: kgotz@charlestondiocese.org. Rev. Allam Marreddy, (India); Deacon Jerome P. Remkiewicz.
School-See Summerville Catholic School under Regional Schools.
Catechesis Religious Program—Students 74.

MURPHY VILLAGE, EDGEFIELD CO., ST. EDWARD (1964)
1370 Edgefield Rd., Murphy Village, 29860.
Tel: 803-279-1837; Fax: 803-279-9655; Email: tcarroll@charlestondiocese.org. Mailing Address: P.O. Box 6340, North Augusta, 29861. Rev. Cherian Thalakulam, C.M.I., (India).
Catechesis Religious Program—Students 136.

MURRELLS INLET, HORRY CO., ST. MICHAEL (1975)
542 Cypress Ave., Murrells Inlet, 29576.
Tel: 843-651-3737; Fax: 843-651-6316; Email: virginiay@saintmichaelsc.net; Web: www.saintmichaelsc.net. Very Rev. Edward W. Fitzgerald, V.F., J.C.L.; Rev. Jesuprathap Narichetti, (India) Parochial Vicar; Deacons Manny Acosta; Robert T. Davis; Donald C. Efken; Charles Fiore, (Retired); Robert Starr; Andrew Thomas, Pastoral Assoc.; Rev. David Nerbun, In Res.
School—St. Michael Catholic School, (Grades PreK-8), Tel: 843-651-6795; Fax: 843-651-6803; Email: lmartin@saintmichaelsc.org; Email: lmartin@charlestondiocese.org; Web: saintmichaelsc.com. Lionel Martin, Prin. Lay Teachers 18; Students 93.
Catechesis Religious Program—Students 340.

MYRTLE BEACH, HORRY CO., ST. ANDREW (1946)
37th Ave. N. & Hwy. 17 (Kings Hwy.), Myrtle Beach, 29577. Tel: 843-448-5930; Fax: 843-448-3947; Email: standrewmb@charlestondiocese.org; Web: standrewcatholicchurch.org. Mailing Address: 3501 N. Kings Hwy., Ste. 102, Myrtle Beach, 29577. Revs. Roger James Morgan, Parochial Admin.; Jose Quilcate, Parochial Vicar; Deacons Robert Barlow; George Ferland; Robert Jones; Robert Sprouse; Tony Russo.
School—St. Andrew Catholic School, (Grades K-8), 3601 N. Kings Hwy., Myrtle Beach, 29577.
Tel: 843-448-6062; Fax: 843-626-8644; Email: dwilfong@charlestondiocese.org; Web: www.standrewschoolmb.org. Debbie Wilfong, Prin.; Cheryl Sedota, Librarian. Lay Teachers 16; Students 189.
Catechesis Religious Program—Email: standrewreligiouseducation@aol.com. Jennifer Diaz, D.R.E. Students 235.

NEWBERRY, NEWBERRY CO., ST. MARK (1956) [JC]
928 Boundary St., Newberry, 29108.
Tel: 803-276-6446; Email: StMarkNewberry@charlestondiocese.org; Email: frserrano@charlestondiocese.org; Web: www.stmarkcathchurch.org. Rev. Orlando Serrano Ardila, Admin.; Deacons Gerald Loignon Jr.; Al De Lachica.
Catechesis Religious Program—Students 131.

NORTH AUGUSTA, AIKEN CO., OUR LADY OF PEACE (1948)
139 Way of Peace, North Augusta, 29841.
Tel: 803-279-0315; Fax: 815-301-8003; Email: kwahl@charlestondiocese.org; Web: olpchurchna.org. Rev. James Renaurd West, Admin.; Deacons Bob Hookness; Ruben Zamudio.
School—Our Lady of Peace School, (Grades PreK-8), Tel: 803-279-8396, Ext. 100; Fax: 815-301-6770; Email: shickey@charlestondiocese.org; Web: olpschool.us. Stephen Hickey, Prin.; Rev. James Renaurd West, Admin. Clergy 1; Lay Teachers 13; Students 120.
Catechesis Religious Program—Students 183.

NORTH MYRTLE BEACH, HORRY CO., OUR LADY STAR OF THE SEA (1964)
1100 Eighth Ave. N., North Myrtle Beach, 29582.
Tel: 843-249-2356; Fax: 843-249-8514; Email: olss@sc.rr.com; Email: lbritzke@charlestondiocese.org; Web: olssnmb.com. Revs. Raymond Leonard, Admin.; Patrick Balogun, Parochial Vicar; Cirilo Bailon Martinez, Parochial Vicar; Deacons Peter Casamento; Richard Flenke; Andrew Stoshak; Robert Tyson; Sr. Eugenia Mayela Ortega, H.C.J.S., Pastoral Assoc.
School—Holy Trinity Catholic School, (Grades PreK-8), 1760 Living Stones Ln., Longs, 29568.
Tel: 843-390-4108; Fax: 843-390-4097; Email: htcs@sccoast.net; Email: kluzzo@charlestondiocese.org; Web: www.htcatholicschoolmyrtlebeach.com. Karen Luzzo, Prin. Lay Teachers 15; Students 86.
Catechesis Religious Program—Students 155.

ORANGEBURG, ORANGEBURG CO.
1—CHRIST THE KING, Closed. For inquiries regarding parish records please contact Holy Trinity, Orangeburg.

2—HOLY TRINITY (1917)
2202 Riverbank Dr., Orangeburg, 29118.
Tel: 803-534-8177; Email: btobon@charlestondiocese.org; Web: www.holytrinitysc.org. Revs. Wilbroad Mwape, Admin.; Gustavo Corredor, S.T.L., Parochial Vicar; Deacon Gary Janelle.
Catechesis Religious Program—Students 164.

PAWLEYS ISLAND, GEORGETOWN CO., PRECIOUS BLOOD OF CHRIST (1986) [CEM]
1633 Waverly Rd., Pawleys Island, 29585.
Tel: 843-237-3428; Fax: 843-237-2293; Email: coordinator@pbocchurch.com; Email: esullivan@charlestondiocese.org; Web: www.pbocchurch.com. Rev. Paul D. MacNeil; Deacon Stephen Olenchok.
Catechesis Religious Program—Students 149.

PICKENS, PICKENS CO., HOLY CROSS (1965)
558 Hampton Ave., Pickens, 29671.
Tel: 864-878-0574; Email: avillano@charlestondiocese.org; Web: holycrossstluke.org. Rev. James N. Dubrouillet; James Villano.
Catechesis Religious Program—Students 9.

RIDGELAND, JASPER CO., ST. ANTHONY (1963)
10128 S. Jacob Smart Blvd., Ridgeland, 29936.
Tel: 843-726-3606; Fax: 843-726-2110; Email: stanthonyridgeland@charlestondiocese.org; Web: stanthonyridgeland.org. Mailing Address: P.O. Box 548, Ridgeland, 29936. Rev. Norbert C. Mendonca, Admin.
Catechesis Religious Program—Students 56.

ROCK HILL, YORK CO.
1—ST. ANNE (1919)
1694 Bird St., Rock Hill, 29730. Tel: 803-329-2662; Fax: 803-329-2190; Email: john.hall@charlestondiocese.org; Web: www.saintanne.com. Very Rev. Fabio Refosco, C.O., V.F.; Deacons Oliver R. Moore; James P. Hyland.
School—St. Anne Catholic School, (Grades PreK-12), 1698 Bird St., Rock Hill, 29730. Tel: 803-324-4814; Fax: 803-324-0189; Email: sriginos@charlestondiocese.org; Web: www.stanneschool.com. Very Rev. Fabio Refosco, C.O., V.F., Headmaster; Shaileen Riginos, Prin.; Amanda Gilstorf, Librarian. Lay Teachers 45; Priests 2; Students 350.
Catechesis Religious Program—Students 392.

2—ST. MARY (1946)
902 Crawford Rd., Rock Hill, 29730.
Tel: 803-329-1008; Email: stmaryrh@charlestondiocese.org; Web: stmarysrh.org. Rev. Joseph Francis Pearce, C.O.; Deacons Terrence Chisolm; Walter W. Hollis.
Catechesis Religious Program—Students 37.

SANTEE, ORANGEBURG CO., ST. ANN (2004)
2205 State Park Rd., Santee, 29142.
Tel: 803-854-5075; Fax: 803-485-8592; Email: stannsanteefinance@charlestondiocese.org; Web: www.stannsantee.org. Mailing Address: P.O. Box 250, Santee, 29142. Rev. Maximino E. Tria Jr., Admin.; Deacon Robert C. Kronyak.
Catechesis Religious Program—Students 10.

SENECA, OCONEE CO., ST. PAUL THE APOSTLE (1994)
170 Bountyland Rd., Seneca, 29672.
Tel: 864-882-8551; Email: jfife@charlestondiocese.org; Email: jf@saintpaulseneca.org; Web: www.saintpaulseneca.org. Rev. William S. Hearne; Deacons Jerry Schiffer; Randy Sexton.
Catechesis Religious Program—Kim Baker, D.R.E. Students 290.

SIMPSONVILLE, GREENVILLE CO.
1—ST. ELIZABETH ANN SETON (1972)
8 Gillin Dr., Simpsonville, 29680. Tel: 864-263-3445; Fax: 864-263-3428; Email: office@seas-church.org; Email: sstrickland@charlestondiocese.org; Web: www.seas-church.org. Mailing Address: P.O. Box 672, Mauldin, 29662-0672. Rev. Patrick E. Cooper; Deacon William Hudson.
Catechesis Religious Program—Students 53.

2—ST. MARY MAGDALENE (1989)
2252 Woodruff Rd., Simpsonville, 29681.
Tel: 864-288-4884; Fax: 864-297-5804; Email: dcnbert@smmcc.org; Email: nchavez@charlestondiocese.org; Web: www.smmcc.org. Rev. Teofilo Trujillo, S.T.L.; Raynald Nacino, Parochial Vicar; Rev. Rhett B. Williams, Parochial Vicar; Deacons Norberto Chavez, Dir., Business Admin. & Operations; Joseph Ciavardini; Ivan O. Hawk; Roger Schonewald. In Res., Rev. Robert Falabella, C.H.S.
Catechesis Religious Program—
Tel: 864-288-4884, Ext. 205. Students 1,105.

SPARTANBURG, SPARTANBURG CO.
1—JESUS, OUR RISEN SAVIOR (1978)
2575 Reidville Rd., Spartanburg, 29301.
Tel: 864-576-1164; Fax: 864-576-0860; Email: ccorson@charlestondiocese.org; Web: www.jorscc.org. Revs. Edgardo O. Enverga, C.R.M.; Ryan Dela Pena, C.R.M., Parochial Vicar; Jaime A. Gonzalez, Hispanic Min.; Sebastian Thomas, C.R.M., Parochial Vicar; Deacons Peter Curcio, (Retired); Robert M. Sturm, (Retired).
Catechesis Religious Program—Beth Gross, D.R.E. Students 467.

2—ST. JOSEPH, Closed. For inquiries regarding parish records please contact St. Paul the Apostle, Spartanburg.

3—ST. PAUL THE APOSTLE (1881)
290 E. Main St., Spartanburg, 29302.
Tel: 864-582-0674; Fax: 864-582-0716; Email: RGilliam@CharlestonDiocese.org; Web: www.stpaultheapostlespartanburg.org. Mailing Address: 161 N. Dean St., Spartanburg, 29302. Rev. David R. Whitman; Deacon Robert L. Mahaffey Jr.
School—St. Paul the Apostle Catholic School, (Grades PreK-8), 152 Alabama St., Spartanburg, 29302. Tel: 864-582-6645; Fax: 864-582-1225; Email: sptbgpaul@stpaulschoolsc.com; Email: planthier@charlestondiocese.org; Web: stpaulschoolsc.com. Patricia Lanthier, Prin.; Mary Lee, Librarian. Lay Teachers 17; Students 75.
Catechesis Religious Program—Students 260.

SUMMERVILLE, DORCHESTER CO.
1—ST. JOHN THE BELOVED (1898)
28 Sumter Ave., Summerville, 29483.
Tel: 843-873-0631; Web: www.sjbsummerville.org; Fax: 843-873-1431; Email: office@sjbsummerville.org; Email: dmahoney@charlestondiocese.org. Rev. Msgr. Chester M. Moczydlowski, D.Min.; Rev. Jacob P. Joseph, C.M.I., Sr. Priest & Parochial Vicar; Deacons Paul Antor; Harvey Becker; James Walter; Sister Carol Gnau, S.S.N.D., Pastoral Assoc.
See Summerville Catholic School under Regional Schools.
Catechesis Religious Program—Students 322.

2—ST. THERESA THE LITTLE FLOWER (1984)
11001 Dorchester Ave., Summerville, 29485.
Tel: 843-875-5002; Fax: 843-875-4884; Email: office@sttheresachurch.com; Email: STLF@charlestondiocese.org; Web: StTheresaChurch.com. Rev. Msgr. Edward D. Lofton; Rev. Artur Przywara, Parochial Vicar; Deacons Michael Regan; Thomas Wolter; Eugene Phillips, (Retired).
School-See Summerville Catholic School under Regional Schools.
Catechesis Religious Program—Students 203.

SUMTER, SUMTER CO.
1—ST. ANNE AND ST. JUDE (1911) [CEM] (Formerly St.

Anne)
216 E. Liberty St., Sumter, 29150. Tel: 803-773-3524 ; Fax: 803-778-1644; Email: frgio@sasjrcc.org; Email: tpaturzo@charlestondiocese.org; Web: www.sasjrcc.org. Revs. Giovannie B. Nunez, C.R.M.; Rufino C. Madridehos, C.R.M., Parochial Vicar.
School—St. Anne and St. Jude Catholic School, (Grades K-12), 11 S. Magnolia St., Sumter, 29150. Tel: 803-775-3632; Fax: 803-938-9074; Email: kdoyle@charlestondiocese.org; Web: www.sasjcs.com. Kristi Doyle, Prin. Lay Teachers 15; Students 97.
Catechesis Religious Program—Students 150.
2—ST. ANNE AND ST. JUDE (1939) (Formerly St. Jude)
611 W. Oakland Ave., Sumter, 29151. Mailing Address: 216 E. Liberty St., Sumter, 29150. Fax: 803-778-1644; Email: tpaturzo@charlestondiocese.org; Web: www.sasjrcc.org. Revs. Giovannie B. Nunez, C.R.M., Admin.; Rufino C. Madridehos, C.R.M., Parochial Vicar; Deacon Lawrence Corum.

TAYLORS, GREENVILLE CO., PRINCE OF PEACE (1975)
1209 Brushy Creek Rd., Taylors, 29687.
Tel: 864-268-4352; Fax: 864-322-2239; Email: parishoffice@princeofpeacetaylors.org; Email: mrauch@charlestondiocese.org; Web: www.princeofpeacetaylors.net. Revs. Christopher Smith; Richard B. Tomlinson, Parochial Vicar; Deacon Robert Smith.
School—Prince of Peace Catholic School, (Grades PreK-8), Tel: 864-331-2145; Fax: 864-751-5190; Email: tammy.lopez@popcatholicschool.org; Email: tlopez@charlestondiocese.org; Web: www.popcatholicschool.org. Marianne Tully, Interim Prin. Lay Teachers 24; Students 149.
Catechesis Religious Program—Tel: 864-331-3919. Students 210.

UNION, UNION CO., ST. AUGUSTINE (1967)
103 E. South St., Union, 29379. Tel: 864-427-7240; Email: btorres@charlestondiocese.org. Mailing Address: c/o Sacred Heart, 205 Sams St., Gaffney, 29340. Rev. Michael F. McCafferty; Deacon William Bower.
Catechesis Religious Program—Students 1.

WALTERBORO, COLLETON CO.
1—ST. ANTHONY (1917) [CEM]
925 S. Jefferies Blvd., Walterboro, 29488.
Tel: 843-549-5230; Fax: 843-549-9176; Email: mmccollum@charlestondiocese.org. Rev. Anthony Benjamine, (India).
Catechesis Religious Program—Students 42.
2—ST. JOSEPH, Closed. For inquiries regarding parish records please contact St. Anthony, Walterboro.

WARD, SALUDA CO., ST. WILLIAM (1895) [CEM]
1199 Ridge Spring Hwy., Ward, 29166.
Tel: 864-445-7215; Fax: 864-445-1150; Email: jlache-avila@charlestondiocese.org; Web: stwilliamsward.org. Rev. Jose Rodolfo Lache-Avila, (Colombia) S.T.L., Admin.
Catechesis Religious Program—Students 50.

WINNSBORO, FAIRFIELD CO., ST. THERESA (1968)
162 Hwy. 321 Bypass N., Winnsboro, 29180.
Tel: 803-635-2541; Email: ann.smith@charlestondiocese.org; Web: sttheresasc.org. Mailing Address: P.O. Box 1004, Winnsboro, 29180. Rev. Msgr. James L. LeBlanc.

YONGES ISLAND, CHARLESTON CO., ST. MARY (1911)
4255 State Hwy. 165, Yonges Island, 29449.
Tel: 843-889-8549; Fax: 843-564-1748; Email: stmarys165@charlestondiocese.org; Web: stmarysyongesisland.org. Rev. Robert J. Sayer.
Catechesis Religious Program—Students 10.

YORK, YORK CO., DIVINE SAVIOUR (1938)
232 Herndon Ave., York, 29745. Tel: 803-684-3431; Email: tlebanno@charlestondiocese.org. Mailing Address: P.O. Box 341, York, 29745. Rev. Adilso Coelho, C.O.; Deacons Henry Bernal; James Ball.
Catechesis Religious Program—Students 94.

MISSIONS

ALLENDALE
ST. MARY MISSION
3457 Bluff Rd., Allendale, 29810. Tel: 803-534-8177; Email: btobon@charlestondiocese.org; Web: holytrinitysc.org/. c/o Holy Trinity Catholic Church, 2202 Riverbank Dr., Orangeburg, 29118. Revs. Wilbroad Mwape, Admin.; Gustavo Corredor, S.T.L., Parochial Vicar; Clemencia Tobon, Contact Person.
*Catechesis Religious Program*Students 13.

BENNETTSVILLE
ST. DENIS
100 Tyson Ave., Bennettsville, 29512.
Tel: 843-537-7351; Email: dmichael@charlestondiocese.org. c/o St. Peter, 602 Market St., Cheraw, 29520. Sylvere Baloza, C.I.C.M., Admin.

BONNEAU
OUR LADY OF PEACE
224 Murray's Ferry Rd., Bonneau, 29431.
Tel: 843-761-3777; Fax: 843-761-3780; Email: kgotz@charlestondiocese.org; Web: www.spbcc.org. c/o St. Philip Benizi, 1404 Old Hwy. 52 S., Moncks Corner, 29461. Rev. Allam Marreddy, (India); Deacon Jerome P. Remkiewicz.
Catechesis Religious Program.

DARLINGTON
ST. JOSEPH THE WORKER
1308 N. Main St., Darlington, 29532.
Tel: 843-332-7773; Fax: 843-332-2812; Email: dkavanagh@charlestondiocese.org; Web: www.stmaryhartsville.org. c/o St. Mary, the Virgin Mother, 363 N. 5th St., Darlington, 29550. Rev. Daniel R. Papineau, Admin.

EASLEY
ST. LUKE MISSION
4408 Hwy. 86, Easley, 29642. Tel: 864-855-9039; Email: ekyle@charlestondiocese.org; Web: holycrossstluke.org. Rev. James N. Dubrouillet.
*Catechesis Religious Program*Students 95.

EDISTO ISLAND
STS. FREDERICK & STEPHEN MISSION
554 Hwy. 174, Edisto Island, 29438.
Tel: 843-869-0124; Email: edistocatholic@charlestondiocese.org; Web: www.edistocatholic.com. P.O. Box 602, Edisto Island, 29438. Rev. Robert J. Sayer; Deacon Charles LaRosa Jr.
Catechesis Religious Program.

GREAT FALLS
ST. MICHAEL MISSION
310 Chester Ave., Great Falls, 29055.
Tel: 803-283-3362; Email: stmichaelmission@charlestondiocese.org; Web: stcatherinecatholic.org/. c/o St. Catherine, 720 W Meeting St., Lancaster, 29720. Rev. Francis J. Gillespie, S.J., Admin.; Janet Sciulli, Business Mgr.

GREENVILLE
SAN SEBASTIAN MISSION
2300 Old Buncombe Rd., Greenville, 29609.
Tel: 864-400-8034; Email: nacosta@charlestondicoese.org. Very Rev. Jay Scott Newman, V.F., J.C.L.; Deacon Nestor Acosta, Dir., Admin.; Rev. Jose Orlando Cheverria Jimenez, (Colombia) Sacramental Responsibilities.
*Catechesis Religious Program*Students 292.

HAMPTON
ST. MARY MISSION
703 5th St. E., Hampton, 29924. Tel: 803-943-4019; Email: stanthonyridgeland@charlestondiocese.org. Rev. Norbert C. Mendonca, Admin.
Catechesis Religious Program.

HARDEEVILLE
ST. ANTHONY MISSION
1 Charles St., Hardeeville, 29927. Tel: 843-784-2943; Fax: 843-784-5338; Email: stanthonyhardeeville@charlestondiocese.org. Deacons Brian Laws; Albert Schito.
*Catechesis Religious Program*Students 51.

JOHNSONVILLE
ST. PATRICK MISSION
110 Church St., Johnsonville, 29555.
Tel: 843-394-8343; Email: rthomy@charlestondiocese.org. c/o St. Philip, the Apostle, P.O. Box 399, Lake City, 29560. Rev. Arturo O. Dalupang, Admin.; Reveley Thomy, Contact Person.

LAURENS
HOLY SPIRIT MISSION (1963)
1040 W. Main St., Laurens, 29360. Tel: 864-984-2880 ; Fax: 864-984-5028; Email: hslaurens@charlestondiocese.org. Mailing Address: P.O. Box 864, Laurens, 29360. Rev. Orlando Serrano Ardila, Admin.; David Waterman, Contact Person.
*Catechesis Religious Program*Students 48.

LORIS
CHURCH OF THE RESURRECTION (1975)
204 Heritage Rd., Loris, 29569. Tel: 843-756-6168; Fax: 843-756-4197; Email: jorourke@charlestondiocese.org. Revs. Raymond Leonard, Admin.; Patrick Balogun, Parochial Vicar; Cirilo Bailon Martinez, Parochial Vicar; Sr. Eugenia Mayela Ortega, H.C.J.S., Pastoral Assoc.; Deacon James Collins, (Retired), (Retired); Jean ORourke, Contact Person.
*Catechesis Religious Program*Students 81.

MARION
CHURCH OF THE INFANT JESUS
4534 N. Hwy 501 Business, Marion, 29571.
Tel: 843-423-1823; Fax: 843-423-1823; Email: bookkeeper.missioninfantjesus@charlestondiocese.org; Web: www.sites.google.com/site/ijmcharleston. Mailing Address: P.O. Box 520, Marion, 29571. Rev. Michel Bineen Mukad, Admin.; Deacon Donald DeNitto.
*Catechesis Religious Program*Students 1.

PAGELAND
ST. ERNEST, [CEM]
510 Evans Mill Rd., Pageland, 29728.
Tel: 843-537-7351; Email: dmichael@charlestondiocese.org. c/o St. Peter, 602 Market St., Cheraw, 29520. Sylvere Baloza, C.I.C.M., Admin.
Catechesis Religious Program.

ST. HELENA ISLAND
HOLY CROSS MISSION
83 Seaside Rd., Saint Helena Island, 29920.
Tel: 843-838-2195; Email: data@stpetersbeaufort.org; Web: www.stpeters-church.org. c/o St. Peter, 70 Ladys Island Dr., Beaufort, 29907. Revs. Andrew Trapp; Christopher Beyuo, Parochial Vicar; Luis E. Serrano Carrero, C.H.S.

SPRINGFIELD
ST. THERESA MISSION
155 Railroad Ave., Springfield, 29146. Web: holytrinitysc.org/. Revs. Wilbroad Mwape, Admin.; Gustavo Corredor, S.T.L., Parochial Vicar; Clemencia Tobon, Contact Person.
*Catechesis Religious Program*Students 3.

SUMMERTON
ST. MARY MISSION (1914)
12 N. Cantey St., Summerton, 29148.
Tel: 803-485-2925; Fax: 803-488-0117; Email: erossoni@charlestondiocese.org. Rev. Maximino E. Tria Jr., Admin.; Deacon Charles Michael Walsh, (Retired).

WALHALLA
ST. FRANCIS OF ASSISI
103 W. Mauldin St., Walhalla, 29691.
Tel: 864-882-8551; Email: jfife@charlestondiocese.org; Web: www.saintpaulseneca.org. c/o St. Paul the Apostle, 170 Bountyland Rd., Seneca, 29672. Rev. William S. Hearne; Deacons Jerry Schiffer; Randy Sexton.

WALTERBORO
ST. JAMES THE GREATER, [CEM]
3087 Ritter Rd., Walterboro, 29488.
Tel: 843-549-5230; Fax: 843-549-9176; Email: mmccollum@charlestondiocese.org. c/o St. Anthony, 925 S. Jefferies Blvd., Walterboro, 29488. Rev. Anthony Benjamine, (India).
*Catechesis Religious Program*Students 2.

Chaplains of Public Institutions.

Hospitals

CHARLESTON. *Medical University of South Carolina,* P.O. Box 250332, 29425. 171 Ashley Ave., 29425. Tel: 843-792-1414. Rev. JohnBosco Ikemeh, O.P., Chap.
Ralph A. Johnson VA Medical Center, 109 Bee St., 29401. Tel: 888-878-6884.
COLUMBIA. *Providence Health,* 2435 Forest Dr., Columbia, 29204. Tel: 803-256-5300. Rev. Bernard Kyara, A.J., Chap.
GREENVILLE. *St. Francis Downtown,* 1 St. Francis Dr., Greenville, 29601. Tel: 864-255-1000; Web: stfrancishealth.org. Sr. Dorothy Brogan, C.B.S.

Ports

CHARLESTON. *Port of Charleston,* 1662 Ingram Rd., 29407. Tel: 843-973-8758; Email: prosenblum@charlestondiocese.org. Deacon Paul M. Rosenblum, Pastoral Min.

Military Chaplains:
Revs.—
Wodecki, Jeremi C., U.S. Army
Yebra, Bernardino S., (Philippines) CH (Captain), U.S. Army.

Retired:
Most Rev.—
Galeone, Victor, (Retired)
Rev. Msgrs.—
Carter, James A., P.A., (Retired)
Gorski, J. Donald, (Retired)
Lathem, E. Christopher, (Retired), 185 Greenstoke Loop, Tryon, NC 28782
Lehocky, Leigh A., (Retired), 185 Greenstoke Loop, Tryon, NC 28782
Revs.—
Abbott, Donald S., (Retired)
Boyle, Michael, (Retired)
Brenninkmeijer, Paul A., O.S.B., (England) (Retired)
Clarke, Peter, S.T.D., (Retired), 35 Murphy St., North Augusta, 29860
Dux, John, CDR, CHC, USN, (Retired), 311 Ayers Cir., Summerville, 29485
Gahan, Timothy M., (Retired)
Hepner, Ernest, S.T.D., (Retired)
Jackson, Richard W., (Retired)
LaBrecque, Frederick, S.T.L., (Retired)
Ladkau, William D., (Retired)
Morrison, Thomas F., (Retired)
Stenson, Patrick J., M.S.C., (Retired)
Ward, Jerome A., (Retired)
Watters, Timothy J., (Retired).

Permanent Deacons:

Acosta, Manny, St. Michael, Murrells Inlet
Acosta, Nestor, St. Mary, Greenville
Allen, Phil, St. Anthony of Padua, Greenville
Amato, Michael, (Serving Outside the Diocese)
Anderson, Ronald J., St. Peter, Columbia; Asst. Dir. Diaconate
Antor, Paul, St. John the Beloved, Summerville
Armstrong, Reginald, St. Anthony, Florence; Asst. Dir. Diaconate
Arnold, Mark, (Serving Outside the Diocese)
Atkinson, Jim, (Retired)
Ball, James, Divine Saviour, York
Ballard, Richard, Our Lady of the Rosary, Greenville
Bannio, Michael, Our Lady of the Rosary, Greenville
Baranoski, Thomas, Cathedral of St. John the Baptist, Charleston
Barlow, Robert, St. Andrew, Myrtle Beach
Barreto, Galo, St. Francis by the Sea, Hilton Head Island
Bartholomew, David, St. Philip Neri, Fort Mill
Becker, Harvey, St. John the Beloved, Summerville
Beeler, Michael A., St. Peter, Beaufort
Bernal, Henry, Divine Savior, York
Biviano, Joseph P., Our Lady of Lourdes, Greenwood
Boackle, Robert, Christ Our King, Mt. Pleasant
Bower, William, (Retired)
Breeden, John, St. Patrick, Charleston
Brown, Stephen, St. Thomas More, Columbia
Burdick, Steve, Our Lady of the Hills, Columbia
Burkett, Dennis, St. Gregory the Great, Bluffton
Campana, Richard, St. Andrew, Clemson
Campbell, Kevin, Christ Our King, Mt. Pleasant
Cancello, Salvatore, St. Joseph, Anderson
Cardenas, Mario, Holy Spirit, Johns Island
Casamento, Peter, Our Lady Star of the Sea, North Myrtle Beach
Case, Edward, Our Lady of the Rosary, Greenville
Cassandra, Anthony J., (Retired)
Cave, Leland, St. Martin de Porres, Columbia
Chavez, Norberto, St. Mary Magdalene, Simpsonville
Chisolm, Terrence, St. Mary, Rock Hill
Ciavardini, Joseph, St. Mary Magdalene, Simpsonville
Collins, James, (Retired), (Retired)
Cooper, Charles, (Retired)
Corum, Lawrence, (Retired)
Cox, Robert L. III, St. Ann, Florence
Crapanzano, John, St. Gregory the Great, Bluffton
Crocker, Jack L., D.D.S., (Retired)
Cuervo, Gabriel, Divine Redeemer, Hanahan; Asst. Dir. Diaconate
Curcio, Peter A., (Retired), (Retired)
D'Angelo, V. Richard, (Retired)
Davis, Robert T., St. Michael the Archangel, Murrells Inlet
Davis, Thomas E., (Serving Outside the Diocese)
De Lachica, Al, St. Mark, Newberry
De Nitto, Donald, Church of the Infant Jesus, Marion
Dennis, Joseph, St. Gerard, Aiken
Deschaine, Larry, St. Mary of the Immaculate Conception, Edgefield
DeWolfe, John, Holy Family, Hilton Head Island
DiRusso, Charles R., (Retired)
Dobelmann, Vernon, St. Francis by the Sea, Hilton Head Island
Donofrio, Robert, Our Lady of Grace, Lancaster
Donovan, Joseph, St. Thomas the Apostle, N. Charleston
Dudek, Glenn, (Serving Outside the Diocese)
Dwyer, Jon E., St. Philip Neri, Fort Mill
Easterling, Charles M., (Retired)
Efken, Donald C., (Retired)
Egendoerfer, Eugene, (Retired)
Fatovic, Andrew, All Saints, Lake Wylie
Ferland, George, St. Andrew, Myrtle Beach
Ferro, Diego, St. Mary, Greenville
Fiore, Charles, (Retired)
Flenke, Richard, (Retired)
Fortnum, Bruce, St. Anthony, Florence
Frye, Stephen, St. Anne & St. Jude, Sumter
Garvey, Alexander, St. Mary, Greenville
Gerald, Robert C. Jr., St. Ann, Florence
Gourdin, Dexter, St. Anthony of Padua, Greenville
Graham, James, St. Gregory the Great, Bluffton
Graham, Shane, (Retired)
Gray, Mark, Our Lady of the Hills, Columbia
Guillet, Andre J.P., (Retired), Dir., Office of Diaconate
Gundlach, Richard, (Retired), (Retired)
Hall, John, All Saints, Lake Wylie
Hand, Gerald, St. Francis by the Sea, Hilton Head Island
Hawk, Ivan O., St. Mary Magdalene, Simpsonville
Herbst, Kurt, Blessed Sacrament, Charleston
Heuser, John, St. Mary, Greenville
Hollis, Walter W., St. Mary, Rock Hill
Hookness, Robert, Our Lady of Peace, North Augusta
Houle, Matthew, (Serving Outside the Diocese)
Hudson, William, St. Elizabeth Ann Seton, Mauldin
Hyland, James P., St. Anne, Rock Hill
Jackson, Harold I., St. Ann, Kingstree
Janelle, Gary, Holy Trinity, Orangeburg
Johnson, Carl, St. Martin de Porres, Columbia
Johnson, James H., (Retired)
Johnston, George, St. Philip Neri, Fort Mill
Jones, Dennis N., Our Lady of the Hills, Columbia
Jones, Robert, St. Andrew, Myrtle Beach
Karandisevsky, John F., (Retired)
Kelenski, Eugene, St. Peter, Beaufort
Knowles, Fred, Sacred Heart, Gaffney
Kronyak, Robert C., (Retired)
La Rosa, P. Charles Jr., Sts. Frederick & Stephen Mission, Edisto Island
LaCombe, William, St. Peter, Beaufort
Larkin, John S., (Retired)
Laws, Brian, St. Anthony, Hardeeville
Letendre, James, Cathedral of St. John the Baptist
Loignon, Gerald Jr., St. Mark, Newberry
Mahaffey, Robert L. Jr., St. Paul the Apostle, Spartanburg
Mahefky, Paul, (Serving Outside the Diocese)
Mayen, Jose, Immaculate Conception, Goose Creek
McCabe, John, (Retired)
McNerny, Daniel, Immaculate Conception, Goose Creek
Mevissen, Jeffrey P., St. James, Conway
Meyer, Ronald, (Retired)
Moore, James R., Blessed Sacrament, Charleston
Moore, Ray, St. Anne, Rock Hill
Murphy, John, Immaculate Conception, Goose Creek
Murtaugh, Richard J. Jr., (Retired), (Retired)
Nazzaro, Joseph J., (Retired)
O'Brien, Barry, St. Gregory the Great, Bluffton
Olenchok, Stephen, Precious Blood of Christ, Pawley's Island
Olimpio, Charles, Cathedral of St. John the Baptist, Charleston
Olson, Richard, (Retired)
Olson, Steven, St. Anthony of Padua, Greenville
Osbourne, R. Michael, (Serving Outside the Diocese)
Parks, Coleman T., Corpus Christi, Lexington
Pecko, Harry, (Retired)
Peitler, Edward, (Serving Outside the Diocese)
Perham, Raymond, (Retired)
Phillips, Eugene, (Retired)
Pierce, Robert A., St. Mary Help of Christians, Aiken
Platte, Stephen, M.D., St. Mary Help of Christians, Aiken
Regan, Michael, St. Theresa the Little Flower, Summerville
Remkiewicz, Jerome P., (Retired), (Retired)
Rhodes, Steven, St. Philip Neri, Fort Mill
Roberts, Lawrence, Immaculate Conception, Goose Creek
Roseborough, Donald, (Serving Outside the Diocese)
Rosenblum, Paul M., St. Mary of the Annunciation, Charleston
Russo, Tony, St. Andrew, Myrtle Beach
Salazar, Gustavo, St. Peter, Cheraw
Sams, Gregory W., St. Gregory the Great, Bluffton
Sandlin, J. Wescoat, (Retired)
Sanfilippo, Joseph Jr., St. Mary, Greenville
Schiffer, Jerry, St. Paul the Apostle, Seneca
Schito, Albert, St. Anthony, Hardeeville
Schonewald, Roger, St. Mary Magdalene, Simpsonville
Sexton, Randy, St. Paul the Apostle, Seneca
Sheehan, Patrick, St. Francis by the Sea, Hilton Head Island
Skipper, Malcolm, Our Lady of the Lake, Chapin
Smigelski, Michael, St. Gregory the Great, Bluffton
Smith, Robert, Prince of Peace, Taylors
Sprouse, Robert, St. Andrew, Myrtle Beach
Starr, Robert, St. Michael the Archangel, Murrells Inlet
Stetar, John, Our Lady of the Lake, Chapin
Stocker, Joseph, Holy Spirit, John's Island
Stoshak, Andrew, Our Lady, Star of the Sea, North Myrtle Beach
Sturm, Robert M., (Retired)
Tempesco, John, Transfiguration, Blythewood
Thibodeaux, Stick, St. John Neumann, Columbia
Thomas, Andrew, St. Michael the Archangel, Murrells Inlet
Thompson, David, St. Peter, Columbia
Tierney, George, St. Mary, Greenville
Tyson, Robert, (Retired)
Valadez, Asuncion, St. Philip the Apostle, Lake City
Vaughan, Jason, Stella Maris, Sullivan's Island
Villano, John, Holy Cross, Pickens
Walczak, Gary, (Retired)
Walsh, Charles Michael, (Retired)
Walter, James, St. John the Beloved, Summerville
Weigold, Gregory, Our Lady of the Lake, Chapin
West, Larry, (Retired)
Whalen, Thomas, St. Mary, Greenville
White, Jerry, Blessed Sacrament, Charleston
Williams, W. James II, St. Anthony of Padua, Greenville
Wolter, Thomas, St. Theresa the Little Flower, Summerville
Woodall, Michael, St. Anthony, Florence
Wright, Winston C., (Retired)
Younginer, Michael, St. Peter, Columbia
Zamudio, Ruben, Our Lady of Peace, North Augusta.

INSTITUTIONS LOCATED IN DIOCESE

[A] REGIONAL SCHOOLS

SUMMERVILLE. *Summerville Catholic School*, (Grades PreK-8), 226 Black Oak Blvd., Summerville, 29485. Tel: 843-873-9310; Fax: 843-873-5709; Email: jtisdale@charlestondiocese.org; Web: summervillecatholic.org. Charlie Tisdale, Prin. Lay Teachers 16; Sisters 1; Students 168.

[B] HIGH SCHOOLS, DIOCESAN

CHARLESTON. *Bishop England High School*, (Grades 9-12), 363 Seven Farms Dr., 29492.
Tel: 843-849-9599; Fax: 843-849-7849; Email: pfinneran@charlestondiocese.org; Web: www.behs.com. Patrick Finneran, Prin.; Michelle Bing, Librarian; Rev. Bryan P. Babick, SL.L., Chap.; Edson Moya, Campus Min. Lay Teachers 54; Priests 1; Students 684; Total Staff 82.

COLUMBIA. *Cardinal Newman School*, (Grades 7-12), 2945 Alpine Rd., Columbia, 29223.
Tel: 803-782-2814; Fax: 803-782-9314; Email: jkasprowski@charlestondiocese.org; Web: www.cnhs.org. Jacqualine Kasprowski, Prin.; Rev. Andrew Fryml, Chap.; Kathleen Cole, Librarian. Lay Teachers 53; Priests 1; Sisters 1; Students 585.

MYRTLE BEACH. *St. Elizabeth Ann Seton Catholic High School*, 1300 Carolina Forest Blvd., Myrtle Beach, 29579. Tel: 843-903-1400; Fax: 843-903-1402; Email: thanes@charlestondiocese.org; Web: www.setonhighschoolsc.org. Rev. Paul D. MacNeil, Chap.; Ted Hanes, Prin. Lay Teachers 10; Students 31.

RIDGELAND. *John Paul II Catholic School*, (Grades 7-12), 4211 N. Okatie Hwy., Ridgeland, 29936.
Tel: 843-645-3838; Fax: 843-645-3839; Email: wdupre@charlestondiocese.org; Web: www.johnpaul2school.org. Walter Dupre, Prin.; Heather Rembold, Asst. Prin.; Kevin Wald, Dean, Students; Rev. Andrew Trapp, Chap.; Joanne Kearney, Admin. Asst. Deacons 1; Lay Teachers 26; Priests 1; Students 211.

[C] HIGH SCHOOLS, PRIVATE

GREENVILLE. **St. Joseph's Catholic School* (1993) (Grades 6-12), 100 St. Joseph's Dr., Greenville, 29607. Tel: 864-234-9009; Fax: 864-234-5516; Email: kkiser@sjcatholicschool.org; Web: www.sjcatholicschool.org. Keith F. Kiser, Headmaster; Rod McClendon, Librarian. Lay Teachers 82; Priests 1; Students 661.

[D] GENERAL HOSPITALS

CHARLESTON. **Bon Secours St. Francis Xavier Hospital* (1882) 2095 Henry Tecklenburg Dr., 29414.
Tel: 843-402-1001; Fax: 843-402-1769; Email: bonnie.paterniti@rsfh.com; Web: www.rsfh.com. Mr. M. Jackson, CEO; Mark Dickson, Vice Pres., Mission. Sponsored by Bon Secours Ministries. Bed Capacity 204; Tot Asst. Annually 164,107; Total Staff 1,015.

GREENVILLE. *Bon Secours St. Francis Health System, Inc.*, One St. Francis Dr., Greenville, 29601.
Tel: 864-255-1000; Fax: 864-255-1137; Email: irene_holcombe@bshsi.org; Web: www.stfrancishealth.org. R. Craig McCoy, CEO.

St. Francis Hospital, Inc., One St. Francis Dr., Greenville, 29601. Tel: 864-255-1000; Fax: 864-255-1137; Email: irene_holcombe@bshsi.org. R. Craig McCoy, CEO; Deacon Alexander Garvey, Senior V.P. Mission. Bed Capacity 338; Sisters of Bon Secours 4; Tot Asst. Annually 307,158; Total Staff 3,679.

[E] HOMES FOR AGED

CHARLESTON. *Carter-May Home Assisted Living & St. Joseph Residence for Retired Priests*, 1660 Ingram Rd., 29407. Tel: 843-556-8314; Fax: 843-556-6879;

Email: janine@charlestondiocese.org. Mrs. Janine N. Bauder, Admin.; Sisters Leena Joseph, S.O.M., Facility Nurse; Marie Therese Rasoarivao, S.O.M., Medical Tech; Mary Parackal, S.O.M., Medical Tech. Bed Capacity 25; Tot Asst. Annually 25; Total Staff 27.

[F] MONASTERIES AND RESIDENCES OF PRIESTS AND BROTHERS

MONCKS CORNER. *Mepkin Abbey* (1949) (Trappist Monks) Order of Cistercians of the Strict Observance 1098 Mepkin Abbey Rd., Moncks Corner, 29461-4796. Tel: 843-761-8509; Fax: 843-761-6719; Email: frjoetedesco@gmail.com; Web: www.mepkinabbey.org. Rt. Rev. Stanislaus Gumula, O.C.S.O., Former Abbot; Revs. Kevin V. Walsh, O.C.S.O, Prior, Novice Dir., & Vocation Dir.; Guerric Frederick A. Heckel, O.C.S.O., Guestmaster; Richard G. McGuire, O.C.S.O., (Ecuador); Gerard-Jonas Palmares, O.C.S.O., Simple Professed; Joseph Tedesco, O.C.S.O., Superior ad Nutum; Columba Caffrey, Novice; Bros. John Corrigan, O.C.S.O., Cellarer; Juan Fahrner, O.C.S.O., Simple Professed; Paul Gosselin, O.C.S.O.; Francis Ikejiuba, O.C.S.O.; Stephen Petronek, O.C.S.O.; Vincent Rohaley, O.C.S.O.; Mary Joseph Szwedo, O.C.S.O.; Justin Meyers, O.C.S.O., Postulant. Novices 1; Priests 7; Solemn Professed Monks 13; Formation: Simple Professed 1; Total in Community 15.

ROCK HILL. *Oratory of St. Philip Neri, Congregation of the Oratory of Pontifical Rite*, 434 Charlotte Ave., Rock Hill, 29730. Tel: 803-327-2097; Fax: 803-327-6264; Email: rhoratory@comporium.net; Web: www.rockhilloratory.net. P.O. Box 11586, Rock Hill, 29731-1586. Revs. John P. Giuliani, C.O.; Adilso Coelho, C.O.; Agustin Guzman, C.O.; Edward P. McDevitt, C.O., Deputy; Joseph Francis Pearce, C.O., Secretary; Very Rev. Fabio Refosco, C.O., V.F., Provost; Bros. Joseph Guyon, C.O., Vicar; John F. Kummer, C.O., Deputy; Johnni do Bonfim Silva, Seminarian. Brothers 2; Priests 6; Seminarians 2.

[G] CONVENTS AND RESIDENCES FOR SISTERS

CHARLESTON. *Daughters of St. Paul Convent*, 243 King St., 29401. Tel: 843-577-0175; Fax: 843-577-9833; Email: charleston@paulinemedia.com; Web: www.pauline.org. Sisters Margaret Charles Kerry, F.S.P, Supr.; Mary Thecla Paolini, F.S.P.; Lupe Hernandez; Jennifer Hyatt. Sisters 4.

Sisters of Charity of Our Lady of Mercy (1829) 424 Ft. Johnson Rd., 29412. Tel: 843-795-6083; Email: went1050@aol.com; Web: sistersofcharityolm.org. P.O. Box 12410, 29422. Sr. Mary Joseph Ritter, O.L.M., Gen. Supr., Tel: 843-795-2866

Sisters of Charity of Our Lady of Mercy, Inc. Sisters 13.

TRAVELERS REST. *Monastery of St. Clare*, 37 McCauley Rd., Travelers Rest, 29690. Tel: 864-834-8015; Fax: 864-834-5402; Email: info@poorclaresc.com; Web: www.poorclaresc.com. Sr. Carolyn Forgette, O.S.C., Abbess. Franciscan Poor Clare Nuns.

Franciscan Monastery of St. Clare Postulants 2; Sisters 11.

[H] CATHOLIC CHARITIES

CHARLESTON. *Catholic Charities of South Carolina*, 901 Orange Grove Rd., 29407. Tel: 843-531-5542; Email: mkay@charlestondiocese.org; Web: www.charitiessc.org. Tot Asst. Annually 48,852; Total Staff 53.

Coastal Regional Office, 1662 Ingram Rd., 29407. Tel: 843-531-5535; Fax: 843-531-9460; Email: rkaroly@charlestondiocese.org. 901 Orange Grove Rd., 29407. Robyn Karoly, L.M.S.W., Regl. Coord.; Deacon Gabriel Cuervo, Dir. Programs. Tot Asst. Annually 4,757; Total Staff 4.

Columbia Regional Office, 1427 Pickens St., Columbia, 29201. Tel: 855-377-1357, Ext. 3; Fax: 803-771-4787; Email: randerson@charlestondiocese.org. Deacon Ronald J. Anderson, Regl. Coord. Tot Asst. Annually 4,978; Total Staff 1.

Pee Dee Regional Office, 2294 Technology Blvd., Conway, 29526. Tel: 843-438-3108; Fax: 843-347-2722; Email: kkaminski@charlestondiocese.org. Kelly Kaminski, Regl. Coord.; Audra Naramore, Disaster Case Mgr. Tot Asst. Annually 16,028; Total Staff 6.

Piedmont Regional Office, 2300 Old Buncombe Rd., Greenville, 29609. Tel: 864-242-2233, Ext. 2628; Fax: 864-242-1387; Email: krogozenski@charlestondiocese.org. Karl Rogozenski, Regl. Coord. Tot Asst. Annually 5,656; Total Staff 3.

Georgetown Outreach Services Office, 1905 Front St., Georgetown, 29440. Tel: 843-531-5535, Ext. 52; Email: kkaminski@charlestondiocese.org. Kelly Kaminski, Dir., Disaster Svcs.

Gloverville Regional Office, c/o Our Lady of the Valley Catholic Center, 2443 Augusta Rd., Gloverville, 29828. Tel: 803-593-2623; Email: joely@charlestondiocese.org. Joely Leguizamon, Admin. Tot Asst. Annually 8,387; Total Staff 1.

The Mercy Mission Thrift Shop, 19869 Whyte Hardee Blvd., Hardeeville, 29926. Tel: 843-208-2275; Email: mkay@charlestondiocese.org. Tot Asst. Annually 7,503.

Immigration Services - Charleston Office, 590 Lone Tree Dr., Ste. 102, Mount Pleasant, 29464. Tel: 843-388-0089; Fax: 843-856-4515; Email: eguerrero@charlestondiocese.org. Emily Guerrero, Assoc. Dir. Immigration Svcs.; Lauren Comar, J.D., Immigration Attorney; Alyson Runco Beinert, J.D., Immigration Attorney; Andrea Penafiel, BIA Accredited Representative. Tot Asst. Annually 1,543; Total Staff 5.

Immigration Services - Hilton Head Office, 1000 Main St., Ste. 200D, Hilton Head Island, 29926. Tel: 855-377-1357, Ext. 8; Fax: 843-785-2201; Email: mchoy@charlestondiocese.org. Mily Choy, BIA Accredited Representative. Total Staff 2.

Immigration Services - Greenville Office, 204 Douthit St., Ste. A1, Greenville, 29601. Tel: 800-705-8748, Ext. 3; Fax: 864-331-2634; Email: vgarcia@charlestondiocese.org. Vanessa Garcia, Immigration Attorney. Total Staff 2.

Immigration Services - Berea Office, 2300 Old Buncombe Rd., Greenville, 29609. Tel: 800-705-8748, Ext. 6; Fax: 864-331-2634; Email: bsuarez@charlestondiocese.org. Blenda Suarez, Immigration Specialist I. Total Staff 2.

[I] CAMPUS MINISTRIES

CHARLESTON. *Catholic Campus Ministry at the College of Charleston and Medical University of South Carolina*, c/o St. Patrick Parish, 134 Philip St., 29403. Tel: 843-937-5993; Email: cofcatholics@aol.com; Web: cofcatholics.org. P.O. Box 20726, 29413. James Grove, Campus Ministry Dir.

The Citadel, Catholic Campus Ministry, 171 Moultrie St., 29409. Tel: 843-953-7693; Email: jshane@citadel.edu; Web: citadel.edu/catholic. M.S.C. 58, 29409-0058. Joshua R. Shane, M.A., Dir. Campus Ministry; Rev. Msgr. D. Anthony Droze, V.G., Chap.

CLEMSON. *Clemson University, Southern Wesleyan University, and TriCounty Technical College*, Mailing Address: 200 Edgewood Ave., Clemson, 29631. Tel: 864-654-7804; Email: csa@clemson.edu; Web: www.clemsoncatholic.org. Rev. Robert J. Menard, O.F.M., Dir., Campus Min.; Darien Clark, Assoc. Campus Min.

Catholic Campus Ministry for Clemson University; St. Andrew Catholic Student Association.

CLINTON. *Presbyterian College*, 203 S. Adair St., Clinton, 29325. Tel: 864-833-8490; Email: jtkoenig@presby.edu. Rev. Orlando Serrano Ardila, Chap.; Jason Koenig, Advisor.

COLUMBIA. *Allen University and Benedict College*, c/o St. Martin de Porres Parish, 2229 Hampton St., Columbia, 29204. Tel: 803-254-6862; Email: lgharrison@me.com. L. Harrison, Advisor.

Columbia College, c/o St. Patrick Parish, 134 Philip St., 29403. Tel: 843-937-5993; Email: cofcatholics@aol.com. P.O. Box 20726, 29413. James Grove, Dir.

University of South Carolina, Newman Club, St. Thomas More, 1610 Greene St., Columbia, 29201. Tel: 803-799-5870; Email: mzahuta@charlestondiocese.org; Web: stthomasmoreusc.org. Rev. Marcin Zahuta, (Poland) Chap.

CONWAY. *Coastal Carolina University*, Lackey Chapel, 105 University Blvd., Conway, 29526. Tel: 843-290-4106; Email: coastalcatholics@gmail.com; Web: coastalcatholics.org/. c/o St. Michael Catholic Church, 542 Cypress Ave., Murrells Inlet, 29576. Rev. David Nerbun, Chap.

FLORENCE. *Francis Marion University*, 4822 E. Palmetto St., Florence, 29506. Tel: 843-661-1453; Tel: 843-661-1842; Email: rsmith@frmarion.edu; Email: yheyward@frmarion.edu. Dr. Seth Smith, Faculty Advisor; Yulaundra Heyward, Advisor.

GREENVILLE. *Furman University Campus Ministry*, c/o St. Anthony of Padua, 307 Gower Street, Greenville, 29611. Tel: 864-294-2318; Email: frtuttle@charlestondiocese.org; Email: brian.goess@furman.edu. Rev. Patrick Tuttle, O.F.M., Chap.; Dr. Brian Goess, Faculty Advisor.

GREENWOOD. *Lander University Catholic Ministry*, 101 Marble Ct., Greenwood, 29649. Tel: 864-388-8182; Email: abenoit@lander.edu. 320 Stanley Ave., Greenwood, 29649. Rev. Timothy D. Tebalt, Chap.; Andy Benoit, Faculty Advisor.

ORANGEBURG. *South Carolina State University, Claflin University, and Orangeburg Calhoun Technical College*, 516 Stabler Farm Rd., St. Matthews, 29135. Tel: 803-655-5137; Email: gljanelle@gmail.com. Deacon Gary Janelle, Advisor.

ROCK HILL. *Winthrop University*, c/o The Oratory, P.O. Box 11586, Rock Hill, 29731. Tel: 980-729-6360; Email: aguzman@charlestondiocese.org; Email: winthropenewman@yahoo.com. Rev. Agustin Guzman, C.O., Chap.; Courtney Hull, Assoc. Campus Min.

SPARTANBURG. *Converse College*, 580 E. Main St., Spartanburg, 29302. Tel: 864-596-9078; Email: mildred.roche@converse.edu. Prof. Mildred Roche, Faculty Advisor.

Spartanburg Regional Campus Ministry, 544 D N. Church St., Spartanburg, 29303. Tel: 908-451-5684; Email: spartanburgccm@gmail.com. Rev. Ryan Dela Pena, C.R.M., Chap.; Gregory Welch, Regl. Campus Min.

University of South Carolina - Upstate, Catholic Student Association, 800 University Way, Spartanburg, 29303. Tel: 864-503-5886; Email: malexander@uscupstate.edu. Myles Alexander, Advisor.

Wofford College, c/o Office of Government, 429 N. Church St., Spartanburg, 29303. Tel: 864-597-4588; Email: alvisjd@wofford.edu. David Alvis, Advisor.

[J] MISCELLANEOUS

CHARLESTON. *The Barry Charitable Trust*, 424 Ft. Johnson Rd., 29412. Tel: 843-795-2866; Fax: 843-795-6083; Email: went1050@aol.com. P.O. Box 12410, 29422. Sr. Carol Wentworth, Trustee; Bro. Peter Campbell, C.F.X., Trustee; Mr. Dennis F. Atwood, K.S.G., Trustee; Sr. Hertha Longo, C.S.A., Trustee; Richard Malia, Trustee.

Catholic Community Foundation of South Carolina (2017) 901 Orange Grove Rd., 29407. Tel: 843-261-0470; Email: jbarker@charlestondiocese.org. John L. Barker, Treas.

Pauline Books & Media, 243 King St., 29401. Tel: 843-577-0175; Fax: 843-577-9833; Email: charleston@paulinemedia.com; Web: www.pauline.org. Sisters Jennifer Hyatt, Supr.; Lupe Hernandez; Margaret Charles Kerry, F.S.P; Mary Thecla Paolini, F.S.P. Daughters of St. Paul.

SACS Enterprises, LLC, 901 Orange Grove Rd., 29407. Tel: 843-261-0470; Email: jbarker@charlestondiocese.org. John L. Barker, Contact Person.

St. Thomas Aquinas Scholarship Funding Organization, 901 Orange Grove Rd., 29407. Tel: 843-261-0470; Email: jbarker@charlestondiocese.org. John L. Barker, Contact Person.

COLUMBIA. **Family Honor, Inc.* (1987) 1226 Pickens St., Ste. 101, Columbia, 29201. Tel: 803-929-0858; Email: famhonor@aol.com; Web: www.familyhonor.org. Mailing Address: P.O. Box 1414, Columbia, 29202. Brenda Cerkez, Exec. Dir.; Rev. Philip S. Gillespie, Chap.

Healthy Learners, 2749 Laurel St., Columbia, 29204. Tel: 803-454-0350; Fax: 803-454-0354; Web: www.healthylearners.com. Thomas Keith, Dir.

Sisters of Charity Foundation of South Carolina, 2711 Middleburg Dr., Ste. 115, Columbia, 29204-2413. Tel: 803-254-0230; Fax: 803-748-0444; Email: scfsc@sistersofcharitysc.com; Web: www.sistersofcharitysc.com. Thomas Keith, Pres.

GREENVILLE. *Bon Secours St. Francis Health System Foundation, Inc.*, 1 St. Francis Dr., Greenville, 29601. Tel: 864-255-1040; Fax: 864-679-8879; Email: Erik_Whaley@bshsi.org; Email: Karri_Westmoreland@bshsi.org; Email: Debra_Richardson@bshsi.org; Web: www.stfrancisfoundation.com. Erik Whaley, C.F.R.E., Vice Pres.

GREER. **Catholic Radio Association*, 2 Beeco Rd,, Greer, 29650. Tel: 864-438-4801; Email: office@catholicradioassociation.org; Web: www.catholicradioassociation.org. P.O. Box 172051, Spartanburg, 29301. Elizabeth Brennan, Pres.; Patrick Ryan, Chm.

JOHNS ISLAND. *Our Lady of Mercy Community Outreach Services, Inc.* (1989) 1684 Brownswood Rd., Johns Island, 29455. Tel: 843-559-4109; Fax: 843-559-8819; Email: info@olmoutreach.org; Web: olmoutreach.org. Mailing Address: P.O. Box 607, Johns Island, 29457. Mrs. Ericka Plater, Exec. Dir. Sponsored by Sisters of Charity of Our Lady of Mercy. Tot Asst. Annually 6,000; Total Staff 23.

KINGSTREE. *Felician Center, Inc.*, 908 Thorne Ave., Kingstree, 29556. Tel: 843-354-9415; Email: stann@ftc-i.net; Web: www.feliciancentersc.org. Sisters M. Johnna Ciezobka, C.S.S.F., Pres.; Susanne Dziedzic, C.S.S.F., Dir.; Carol Piskor, C.S.S.F., Outreach Coord.

Shrine of Our Lady of South Carolina-Our Lady of Joyful Hope, 330 E. Main St., Kingstree, 29556. Tel: 843-355-3527; Email: olscshrine@gmail.com; Web: www.ourladyofsouthcarolina.net. Mailing Address: 300 Ashton Ave., Kingstree, 29556. Rev.

Stanley Smolenski, S.P.M.A., Office of the Shrine Dir. Administered by the Diocese of Charleston.

LAKE WYLIE. *Magnificat-Greenville, SC Chapter*, 304 Heathwood Ln., Simpsonville, 29681. Cell: 864-967-7463; Email: magnificatgreenvillesc@gmail.com. Lucille Irving, Coord.

LUGOFF. **Children of Mary Religion Camp*, P.O. Box 598, Lugoff, 29078. Tel: 704-853-9534; Email: childrenofmarycamp@gmail.com; Web: childrenofmarycamp.com. Dominique May, Pres.

SIMPSONVILLE. **Society of St. Vincent de Paul*, 700 Farming Creek Dr., Simpsonville, 29680. Tel: 864-979-8429; Email: bergassoc@aol.com. Tom Berg, Diocesan Council Pres.; Kip Kautzky, Piedmont District Pres.; James Hart, Midlands District Pres.; Ben Pogue, Coastal District Pres.

ST. HELENA ISLAND. *St. Francis Center*, 85 Mattis Dr., St. Helena Island, 29920. Tel: 843-838-3924; Fax: 843-888-2152; Email: franctr@islc.net. Mailing Address: P.O. Box 682, St. Helena Island, 29920. Sisters Canice Adams, SS.C.M., Dir.; Marcine Klocko, SS.C.M., Dir. Sisters of Saints Cyril and Methodius, Danville, PA Sisters 2.

RELIGIOUS INSTITUTES OF MEN REPRESENTED IN THE DIOCESE

For further details refer to the corresponding bracketed number in the Religious Institutes of Men or Women section.

[0100]—*Adorno Fathers*—C.R.M.
[]—*Apostles of Jesus*—A.J.
[0200]—*Benedictines* (Conception Abbey)—O.S.B.
[1350]—*Brothers of St. Francis Xavier*—C.F.X.
[0275]—*Carmelites of Mary Immaculate* (St. Joseph Province)—C.M.I.
[0350]—*Cistercians Order of the Strict Observance-Trappist* (Mempkin Abbey)—O.C.S.O.
[0310]—*Congregation of Christian Brothers*—C.F.C.
[1330]—*Congregation of the Mission* (Province of Columbia)—C.M.
[]—*Crusaders of the Holy Spirit* (Province of Argentina)—C.H.S.
[0520]—*Franciscan Friars* (Holy Name Province)—O.F.M.
[0690]—*Jesuit Fathers and Brothers*—S.J.
[0860]—*Missionhurst Congregation of the Immaculate Heart of Mary*—C.I.C.M.
[1110]—*Missionaries of the Sacred Heart* (U.S. Section of the Irish Province)—M.S.C.
[0430]—*Order of Preachers* (St. Joseph the worker, Nigeria, and Ghana)—O.P.
[0950]—*Oratorians* (The Oratory of Rock Hill)—C.O.
[1070]—*Redemptorist Fathers* (Richmond Vice Prov.)—C.SS.R.

RELIGIOUS INSTITUTES OF WOMEN REPRESENTED IN THE DIOCESE

[0270]—*Congregation of Bon Secours*—C.B.S.
[0760]—*Daughters of Charity of St. Vincent de Paul*—D.C.
[0960]—*Daughters of Wisdom* (American Prov.)—D.W.
[]—*Disciples of Jesus of the Good Shepherd* (Mexico)—D.J.B.P.
[1070-13]—*Dominican Sisters* (Adrian, MI)—O.P.
[1070-07]—*Dominican Sisters* (Nashville, TN)—O.P.
[1170]—*Felician Sisters*—C.S.S.F.
[]—*Hospitaler Sisters of Mercy*—S.O.M.
[3760]—*Order of St. Clare*—O.S.C.
[0950]—*Pious Daughters of St. Paul*—F.S.P.
[2970]—*School Sisters of Notre Dame*—S.S.N.D.
[0500]—*Sisters of Charity of Nazareth*—S.C.N.
[0510]—*Sisters of Charity of Our Lady of Mercy*—O.L.M.
[0580]—*Sisters of Charity of St. Augustine*—C.S.A.
[3000]—*Sisters of Notre Dame* (Baltimore, MD)—S.N.D.deN.
[2990]—*Sisters of Notre Dame* (Toledo, OH)—S.N.D.
[3820]—*Sisters of St. John the Baptist*—C.S.J.B.
[3950]—*Sisters of Saint Mary of Namur*—S.S.M.N.
[3780]—*Sisters of Saints Cyril and Methodius*—SS.C.M.
[1570]—*Sisters of St. Francis of the Holy Family* (Dubuque, IA)—O.S.F.
[1805]—*Sisters of St. Francis of the Neumann Communities*—O.S.F.
[2110]—*Sisters of the Humility of Mary*—H.M.
[]—*Sisters of the Sacred Heart of Jesus* (Mexico)—H.C.J.S.

DIOCESAN CEMETERIES

CHARLESTON. *Holy Cross*, 604 Ft. Johnson Rd., 29412. Tel: 843-795-2111; Fax: 843-576-4925; Email: kmeade@charlestondiocese.org. Karmin Meade, Dir.

St. John Cemetery, 200 Coming St., 29402. Tel: 843-795-2111; Email: kmeade@charlestondiocese.org. Mailing Address: c/o Holy Cross Cemetery, 604 Ft. Johnson Rd., 29412. Karmin Meade, Dir.

St. Lawrence Cemetery, 60 Huguenin Ave., 29403. Tel: 843-795-2111; Email: kmeade@charlestondiocese.org. Mailing Address: c/o Holy Cross Cemetery, 604 Fort Johnson Rd., 29412. Karmin Meade, Dir.

N. CHARLESTON. *St. Peter Cemetery*, 2726 Spruill Ave., North Charleston, 29405. Tel: 843-795-2111; Email: kmeade@charlestondiocese.org. Mailing Address: c/o Holy Cross Cemetery, 604 Ft. Johnson Rd., 29412. Karmin Meade, Dir.

An asterisk (*) denotes an organization that has established tax-exempt status directly with the IRS and is not covered by the USCCB Group Ruling.

Diocese of Charlotte

(Dioecesis Carolinana)

Most Reverend

PETER J. JUGIS, J.C.D.

Bishop of Charlotte; ordained June 12, 1983; appointed Bishop of Charlotte August 1, 2003; episcopal ordination October 24, 2003.

CARITAS CHRISTI URGET NOS

Chancery: P.O. Box 36776, Charlotte, NC 28236. Tel: 704-370-6299; Fax: 704-370-3379.

Web: charlottediocese.org

Email: chancery@charlottediocese.org

ERECTED NOVEMBER 12, 1971

Square Miles 20,470.

Comprises the Counties of Alexander, Alleghany, Anson, Ashe, Avery, Buncombe, Burke, Cabarrus, Caldwell, Catawba, Cherokee, Clay, Cleveland, Davidson, Davie, Forsyth, Gaston, Graham, Guilford, Haywood, Henderson, Iredell, Jackson, Lincoln, Macon, Madison, McDowell, Mecklenburg, Mitchell, Montgomery, Polk, Randolph, Richmond, Rockingham, Rowan, Rutherford, Stanley, Stokes, Surry, Swain, Transylvania, Union, Watauga, Wilkes, Yadkin and Yancey in the State of North Carolina.

For legal titles of parishes and diocesan institutions, consult the Chancery.

STATISTICAL OVERVIEW

Personnel	
Bishop	1
Abbots	1
Priests: Diocesan Active in Diocese	98
Priests: Diocesan Active Outside Diocese	5
Priests: Retired, Sick or Absent	25
Number of Diocesan Priests	128
Religious Priests in Diocese	30
Total Priests in Diocese	158
Extern Priests in Diocese	17
Ordinations:	
Transitional Deacons	3
Permanent Deacons	15
Permanent Deacons in Diocese	133
Total Brothers	10
Total Sisters	128
Parishes	
Parishes	73
With Resident Pastor:	
Resident Diocesan Priests	65
Resident Religious Priests	8
Missions	19
Pastoral Centers	2
Professional Ministry Personnel:	
Sisters	7
Lay Ministers	250
Welfare	
Health Care Centers	2
Total Assisted	54,600
Homes for the Aged	3
Total Assisted	316
Specialized Homes	4
Total Assisted	600
Special Centers for Social Services	3
Total Assisted	21,379
Residential Care of Disabled	2
Total Assisted	175
Educational	
Seminaries, Diocesan	1
Diocesan Students in Other Seminaries	36
Total Seminarians	36
Colleges and Universities	1
Total Students	1,549
High Schools, Diocesan and Parish	3
Total Students	1,869
Elementary Schools, Diocesan and Parish	16
Total Students	5,119
Catechesis/Religious Education:	
High School Students	3,615
Elementary Students	20,708
Total Students under Catholic Instruction	32,896
Teachers in the Diocese:	
Priests	7
Brothers	2
Sisters	3
Lay Teachers	643
Vital Statistics	
Receptions into the Church:	
Infant Baptism Totals	4,843
Minor Baptism Totals	553
Adult Baptism Totals	356
Received into Full Communion	724
First Communions	5,476
Confirmations	4,590
Marriages:	
Catholic	724
Interfaith	195
Total Marriages	919
Deaths	1,112
Total Catholic Population	285,655
Total Population	5,281,925

Former Bishops—Most Revs. MICHAEL J. BEGLEY, D.D., ord. May 26, 1934; appt. Nov. 30, 1971; cons. first Bishop of Charlotte Jan. 12, 1972; retired 1984; died Feb. 9, 2002; JOHN F. DONOGHUE, D.D., ord. June 4, 1955; appt. Nov. 6, 1984; installed Dec. 18, 1984; appt. Archbishop of Atlanta June 22, 1993; cons. Aug. 19, 1993; died Nov. 11, 2011; WILLIAM G. CURLIN, D.D., ord. May 25, 1957; appt. Auxiliary Bishop of Washington Nov. 2, 1988; cons. Dec. 20, 1988; appt. Bishop of Charlotte, Feb. 22, 1994; installed April 13, 1994; retired Sept. 10, 2002; died Dec. 23, 2017.

Chancery—P.O. Box 36776, Charlotte, 28236. Tel: 704-370-6299; Fax: 704-370-3379.

Vicar General, Chancellor, and Moderator of the Curia—Mailing Address: P.O. Box 36776, Charlotte, 28236. Very Rev. PATRICK J. WINSLOW, J.C.L., V.G.

Vice Chancellor—Rev. Msgr. ANTHONY J. MARCACCIO, V.F., 2210 N. Elm St., Greensboro, 27408.

Presbyteral Council—Rev. Msgrs. RICHARD BELLOW; ANTHONY J. MARCACCIO, V.F.; Very Revs. ROGER K. ARNSPARGER, V.E.; JOHN J. ECKERT, V.F.; FIDEL C. MELO, V.H.; JOHN T. PUTNAM, J.C.L., J.V.; PETER J. SHAW, V.F.; Revs. DAVID G. BROWN, O.S.B.; FRANCIS T. CANCRO; CARL DEL GIUDICE; JULIO C. DOMINGUEZ; PAUL GARY; CHRISTOPHER M. GOBER; PATRICK T. HOARE; STEPHEN M. HOYT; ALVARO A. RIQUELME, C.Ss.R.; BENJAMIN A. ROBERTS; FRANK J. SEABO; JAMES SHEA, S.J.; JAMES A. STUHRENBERG; JOSHUA A. VOITUS, V.F.; Very Rev. PATRICK J. WINSLOW, J.C.L., V.G.

Chief Financial Officer—WILLIAM G. WELDON, CPA, 1123 S. Church St., Charlotte, 28203. Tel: 704-370-3313.

Controller—MASON T. BEAUMONT, CPA, 1123 S. Church St., Charlotte, 28203. Tel: 704-370-3312.

Diocesan Attorney—JOE DODGE ESQ., 1123 S. Church St., Charlotte, 28203. Tel: 704-370-3346; Email: jfdodge@charlottediocese.org.

Diocesan Properties and Risk Management—ANTHONY J. MORLANDO, Dir., 1123 S. Church St., Charlotte, 28203. Tel: 704-370-3311.

Human Resources and Employee Benefits—TERRI WILHELM, 1123 S. Church St., Charlotte, 28203. Tel: 704-370-3338.

Judicial Vicar—Very Rev. JOHN T. PUTNAM, J.C.L., J.V.

Diocesan Tribunal—1123 S. Church St., Charlotte, 28203. Tel: 704-370-3293. LISA D. SARVIS, Head Tribunal; JOY BARNES, S.I.M., Advocate; DEBBIE M. WRIGHT, Processor; JACINTA LEWIS, Sec. & Notary.

Education—Very Rev. ROGER K. ARNSPARGER, V.E., Vicar Education, 1123 S. Church St., Charlotte, 28203. Tel: 704-370-3210; Fax: 704-370-3291.

Diocesan Consultors—Rev. Msgr. ANTHONY J. MARCACCIO, V.F.; Very Revs. JOHN T. PUTNAM, J.C.L., J.V.; ROGER K. ARNSPARGER, V.E.; WILBUR N. THOMAS, V.F.; Rev. JULIO C. DOMINGUEZ; Very Rev. PATRICK J. WINSLOW, J.C.L., V.G.

Diocesan Offices and Directors

Airport Ministry Program—Deacons PATRICK J. DEVINE; GEORGE A. SZALONY, 1123 S. Church St., Charlotte, 28203. Tel: 704-370-3344; Fax: 704-370-3378.

Archives—VACANT, Dir.; Deacon MATTHEW HANES, Asst. Archivist, 1123 S. Church St., Charlotte, 28203. Tel: 704-370-3215; Fax: 704-370-3378.

Boy Scouts—Deacon MARTIN RICART III, 6031 Roseway Ct., Harrisburg, 28075. Tel: 704-453-1125.

Campus Ministry—MS. MARY WRIGHT, Dir., 1123 S. Church St., Charlotte, 28203. Tel: 704-370-3212; Fax: 704-370-3378.

Communications—DAVID HAINS, Dir., 1123 S. Church St., Charlotte, 28203. Tel: 704-370-3336; Fax: 704-370-3382.

Evangelization & Lay Ministry—DR. FRANK VILLARONGA, Dir., 1123 S. Church St., Charlotte, 28203. Tel: 704-370-3274; Fax: 704-370-3291.

Office of Faith Formation—1123 S. Church St., Charlotte, 28203. Tel: 704-370-3246; Fax: 704-370-3378. Very Rev. ROGER K. ARNSPARGER, V.E., Vicar Education & Dir.; CHRIS BEAL, Prog. Dir.

Youth Ministry—PAUL KOTLOWSKI, 1123 S. Church St., Charlotte, 28203. Tel: 704-370-3211.

Development—1123 S. Church St., Charlotte, 28203. Tel: 704-370-3301; Tel: 704-370-3302; Fax: 704-370-3378. JAMES K. KELLEY, Dir.; BARBARA DE MASE, Assoc. Dir.

Foundation of the Roman Catholic Diocese of Charlotte, Inc., The—JAMES KELLEY, Exec. Dir., 1123 S. Church St., Charlotte, 28203. Tel: 704-370-3301.

Hispanic Ministry—Very Rev. FIDEL C. MELO, V.H., Vicar Hispanic Ministry, 1123 S. Church St., Charlotte, 28203. Tel: 704-370-3269; Fax: 704-370-3291; Rev. JULIO C. DOMINGUEZ, Hispanic Ministry Coord., Smoky Mountain Vicariate; Deacons DARIO OSPINA GARCIA, Hispanic Ministry Coord., Hickory Vicariate; ENEDINO S. AQUINO, Hispanic Ministry Coord., Greenboro Vicariate.

Hmong Ministry—1123 S. Church St., Charlotte, 28203. Tel: 828-584-6012. VACANT.

Human Resources—TERRI WILHELM, Dir., 1123 S. Church St., Charlotte, 28203. Tel: 704-370-3338; Tel: 704-370-3339; Fax: 704-370-3378.

Korean Catholic Cultural Center—Revs. CHONGHYUK PARK, 7109 Robinson Church Rd., Charlotte, 28215. Tel: 704-531-8417; Fax: 704-531-1843; JUNG WOOK LEE, 2516 Glen Meadow Dr., Greensboro, 27455. Tel: 336-282-8663.

African-American Ministry—VACANT, Dir., 1123 S. Church St., Charlotte, 28203. Tel: 704-370-3267; Fax: 704-370-3378.

Media Resource Center—WILLIAM S. GRIFFITH, 1123 S. Church St., Charlotte, 28203. Tel: 704-370-3241; Email: wsgriffith@charlottediocese.org.

Cathedral Publishing Corporation—Mailing Address: P.O. Box 37267, Charlotte, 28237. Tel: 704-370-6299. *1123 S. Church St., Charlotte, 28203.* Tel: 704-370-3336.

Newspaper: "Catholic News Herald"—PATRICIA L. GUILFOYLE, Editor, Mailing Address: P.O. Box 37267, Charlotte, 28237. Tel: 704-370-3333; Tel: 704-370-3334; Fax: 704-370-3382.

Permanent Diaconate—Deacons JOHN MARTINO, Dir.; SCOTT D. GILFILLAN, Dir. Diaconate Formation; EDWARD A. KONARSKI, Asst. Dir. Diaconate Formation, 1123 S. Church St., Charlotte, 28203. Tel: 704-370-6299; Fax: 704-370-3379.

Planning and Research—GEORGE K. COBB, OblSB, Dir., 1123 S. Church St., Charlotte, 28203. Tel: 704-370-3328; Fax: 704-370-3378.

Propagation of the FaithRev. J. PATRICK CAHILL, 1123 S. Church St., Charlotte, 28203. Tel: 704-370-6299; Fax: 704-370-3378.

School—JANICE RITTER, Ed.D., Supt., 1123 S. Church St., Charlotte, 28203. Tel: 704-370-3271; Fax: 704-370-3291.

Mecklenburg Area Catholic Schools—1123 S. Church St., Charlotte, 28203. Tel: 704-370-3270; Fax: 704-370-3291.

Prison Ministry—Contact Permanent Diaconate Office: *1123 S. Church St., Charlotte, 28203.* Tel: 704-370-3344; Fax: 704-370-3378.

Catholic Charities—GERARD A. CARTER, Ph.D., Exec. Dir., 1123 S. Church St., Charlotte, 28203. Tel: 704-370-3228.

Campaign for Human Development—JOSEPH PURELLO, Prog. Dir., 1123 S. Church St., Charlotte, 28203. Tel: 704-370-3283; Fax: 704-370-3277.

Social Concerns and Advocacy—JOSEPH PURELLO, Dir., 1123 S. Church St., Charlotte, 28203. Tel: 704-370-3225; Fax: 704-370-3277.

Victim Assistance Coordinator—DAVID W. HAROLD, A.C.S.W, Tel: 336-714-3202; Email: dwharold@charlottediocese.org.

Vocations—1123 S. Church St., Charlotte, 28203. Revs. CHRISTOPHER M. GOBER, Dir.; JASON K. BARONE, Promoter of Vocations.

Worship—Very Rev. CHRISTOPHER A. ROUX, Rector, St. Patrick Cathedral, 1621 Dilworth Rd., E., Charlotte, 28203. Tel: 704-334-2283; Fax: 704-377-6403.

CLERGY, PARISHES, MISSIONS AND PAROCHIAL SCHOOLS

CITY OF CHARLOTTE

(MECKLENBURG COUNTY)

1—ST. PATRICK CATHEDRAL (1939)
1621 Dilworth Rd., E., 28203. Tel: 704-334-2283; Fax: 704-377-6403; Email: info@stpatricks.org; Email: StPatrickCharlotte@charlottediocese.org; Web: www.stpatricks.org. Very Rev. Christopher A. Roux, Rector; Rev. Christopher A. Bond, Parochial Vicar; Deacons Paul Bruck; Brian P. McNulty; Carlos A. Medina Sr.
Catechesis Religious Program—
Tel: 704-334-2283, Ext. 413. Mrs. Emily Clary, D.R.E.; Mrs. Jessica Martin, D.R.E. Students 90.

2—ST. ANN (1955)
3635 Park Rd., 28209. Tel: 704-523-4641; Fax: 704-527-8671; Email: stanncharlotte@charlottediocese.org; Web: www.stanncharlotte.org. Very Rev. Timothy S. Reid, V.F.; Deacons Thomas D. Sanctis; Peter Tonon.
Catechesis Religious Program—Tel: 704-527-0122; Fax: 704-527-8671. Sr. Mary Elizabeth Askew, D.R.E. Students 136.

3—ST. GABRIEL (1957)
3016 Providence Rd., 28211. Tel: 704-364-5431; Fax: 704-362-5049; Email: jdreyer@stgabrielchurch.org; Email: StGabrielCharlotte@charlottediocese.org; Web: stgabrielchurch.org. Revs. Francis J. O'Rourke, (Retired); Gabriel Carvajal-Salazar; Deacons Mark Diener; Michael F. Goad; Mark J. King; Lawrence P. O'Toole; Bernard Wenning Jr., (Retired).
Res.: 2940 Brookridge Ln., 28211.
Catechesis Religious Program—Tel: 704-366-2738. Susan Krasniewski, D.R.E., Tel: 704-362-5047, Ext. 271; Lisa Gilkey, Asst. Dir. Faith Formation; Denise Gruender, Youth Min. Students 1,291.

4—ST. JOHN NEUMANN (1977)
8451 Idlewild Rd., 28227. Tel: 704-536-6520; Fax: 704-837-8243; Email: office@4sjnc.org; Email: StJohnNeumannCharlotte@charlottediocese.org; Web: www.4sjnc.org. Rev. John F. Starczewski, V.F.; Deacons Joseph C. Denzler; James Gorman.
Catechesis Religious Program—Tel: 704-535-4197. Katie Knogfel, D.R.E.; Meg Vangoethem, D.R.E.; Ms. Megan Stasko, Youth Min. Students 631.

5—ST. JOSEPH CHURCH
4929 Sandy Porter Rd., 28273. Tel: 704-504-0907; Fax: 877-349-1928; Email: stjosephcharlotte@charlottediocese.org; Email: giaoxuthanhgiusecharlotte@gmail.com; Web: www.giaoxuthanhgiuse.net. Rev. Tri Vinh Truong; Sr. Veronica Phuong, Admin. Asst.; Deacon Quang Nguyen.
Catechesis Religious Program—Nhat Uyen Nguyen, D.R.E.; June Vu, D.R.E.; Bang Duong, Youth Min. Students 298.

6—ST. LUKE (1987)
13700 Lawyers Rd., 28227. Tel: 704-545-1224; Email: saintlukechurchminthill@gmail.com; Email: StLukeMintHill@charlottediocese.org; Web: www.stlukechurch.net. Rev. Paul Gary; Deacons Jeffrey S. Evers; Rafael J. Torres.
Rectory—13773 Thompson Rd., 28227.
Tel: 704-246-7151.
Catechesis Religious Program—Tel: 704-545-0065. Amy Ankenbruck, D.R.E.; Ms. Katy De'Ath, Youth Min. Students 515.

7—ST. MATTHEW (1986)
8015 Ballantyne Commons Pkwy., 28277.
Tel: 704-543-7677; Fax: 704-542-7244; Email: office@stmatthewcatholic.org; Email: StMatthewCharlotte@charlottediocese.org; Web: stmatthewcatholic.org. P. O. Box 49349, 28277-0077. Revs. Patrick T. Hoare; Binoy P. Davis, Parochial Vicar; Peter Ascik, Parochial Vicar; Deacons Daren S. Bitter; William G. Griffin; James Hamrlik; Paul H. Herman; Gary J. Schrieber; Jack G. Staub.
Catechesis Religious Program—Tel: 704-541-8362. Ms. Diane Kiradjieff, D.R.E.; Mr. Michael Burck, D.R.E.; Mr. Daniel Torres, Youth Min. Students 4,270.

8—OUR LADY OF CONSOLATION (1955)
2301 Statesville Ave., 28206-1400. Tel: 704-375-4339; Fax: 704-375-8039; Email: olccharlotte@charlottediocese.org; Web: www.ourladyofconsolation.org. Mailing Address: 1235 Badger Ct., 28206. Rev. Basile Sede; Deacon Curtiss Todd.
Catechesis Religious Program—Students 59.
Mission—St. Helen, 1624 Spencer Mountain Rd., Gastonia, 28054. Email: StHelenSpencerMnt@charlottediocese.org; Web: charlottediocese.org/parishes/st-helen/. Deacon Guy Piche.
Catechesis Religious Program—Barbara Gardin, D.R.E. Students 20.

9—OUR LADY OF GUADALUPE CHURCH 2002
6212 Tuckaseegee Rd., 28214. Tel: 704-391-3732; Email: nsguadalupe@bellsouth.net; Email: olgcharlotte@charlottediocese.org; Web: www.parroquiansguadalupe.com. Revs. Vincent H. Finnerty, C.M.; Gregory Gay, Parochial Vicar; Gloria Sierra, Sec.
Catechesis Religious Program—Ms. Maria Rodriguez, D.R.E.; Juan Cajero, Youth Min. Students 980.

10—OUR LADY OF THE ASSUMPTION (1949)
4207 Shamrock Dr., 28215. Tel: 704-535-9965; Fax: 704-535-3621; Email: ourlady11@bellsouth.net; Email: OLACHarlotte@charlottediocese.org; Web: www.ourladyoftheassumptioncharlotte.org. Rev. Philip J. Scarcella, Ph.D., J.C.D.; Deacons Kevin Williams, Youth Min.; Peter Duca, Music Min.; Luis Flores; David S. Reiser, D.R.E.
Catechesis Religious Program—Tel: 704-535-3310. Deacon Kevin Williams. Students 472.

11—ST. PETER (1851)
507 S. Tryon St., 28202. Tel: 704-332-2901; Fax: 704-358-0050; Email: StPeterCharlotte@charlottediocese.org; Email: office@stpeterscatholic.org; Web: www.stpetercatholic.org. Revs. James Shea, S.J.; John Michalowski, S.J., Parochial Vicar; Jim Bowler, Pastoral Min.; Deacons James E. Bozik; Clarke Cochran.
Catechesis Religious Program—Ms. Cathy Chiappetta, D.R.E. Students 301.

12—ST. THOMAS AQUINAS (1978)
1400 Suther Rd., 28213. Tel: 704-549-1607; Fax: 704-549-1614; Email: StThomasCharlotte@charlottediocese.org; Email: church@stacharlotte.com; Web: www.stacharlotte.com. Very Rev. Patrick J. Winslow, J.C.L., V.G.; Rev. Matthew Bean, Parochial Vicar; Deacons Joseph A. Diaz; Martin Ricart III; Paul Sparrow; James H. Witulski.
Res.: 9230 Sandburg Ave., 28213.
Catechesis Religious Program—Tel: 704-549-5160; Fax: 704-503-5060. Sisters Zeny Mofad, O.P., D.R.E.; Edeva Jover, Youth Min. Students 471.
Convent—1216 Ogden Pl., 28213. Tel: 704-503-4934.

13—ST. VINCENT DE PAUL (1965)
6828 Old Reid Rd., 28210. Tel: 704-554-7088; Fax: 704-554-0490; Email: StVincentCharlotte@charlottediocese.org; Web: stvincentdepaulchurch.com. Revs. Joshua A. Voitus, V.F.; Santiago A. Mariani; Deacons John Kopfle; Ruben A. Tamayo, Youth Min.
Catechesis Religious Program—Tel: 704-554-1622. Mr. Riley Provost, D.R.E. Students 698.

OUTSIDE THE CITY OF CHARLOTTE

ALBEMARLE, STANLY CO., OUR LADY OF THE ANNUNCIATION (1934)
416 N. Second St., Albemarle, 28001.
Tel: 704-982-2910; Fax: 704-982-0881; Email: OLAAlbemarle@charlottediocese.org; Email: church@annunciationalbemarle.com; Web: www.annunciationcatholicchurch.ws. Very Rev. Peter L. Fitzgibbons, V.F.
Catechesis Religious Program—Tel: 704-982-1048. Michelle Pantore, D.R.E.; Adam Storms, Youth Min. Students 93.

ANDREWS, CHEROKEE CO., HOLY REDEEMER (1962)
214 Aquone Rd., Andrews, 28901-9776.
Tel: 828-321-4463; Email: HolyRedeemerAndrews@charlottediocese.org; Email: GDByers@charlottediocese.org; Web: charlottediocese.org/parishes/holy-redeemer/. Rev. George D. Byers, C.P.M.
Mission—Prince of Peace, Tel: 828-689-3719; Web: charlottediocese.org/parishes/prince-of-peace/.
Catechesis Religious Program—Irene Weber, D.R.E. Students 37.

ARDEN, BUNCOMBE CO., ST. BARNABAS (1964)
109 Crescent Hill Dr., Arden, 28704.
Tel: 828-684-6098; Fax: 828-684-6152; Email: stbarnabasarden@charlottediocese.org; Web: www.saintbarnabasarden.org. Mailing Address: P.O. Box 39, Arden, 28704. Rev. Adrian Porras; Deacons Rudolph J. Triana, Contact Person; Frank Moyer; Michael L. Stout.
Res.: 311 Roxbury Ct., Arden, 28704.
Catechesis Religious Program—Miss Sheryl Peyton, D.R.E.; Simeon Willis, Youth Min. Students 276.

ASHEBORO, RANDOLPH CO., ST. JOSEPH (1948)
512 W. Wainman Ave., Asheboro, 27203-5342.
Tel: 336-629-0221; Email: stjoe@triad.rr.com; Email: stjosephasheboro@charlottediocese.org; Web: www.stjoenc.org. Rev. Philip Kollithanath.
Res.: 308 S. Park St., Asheboro, 27203.
Tel: 336-687-7003.
Catechesis Religious Program—Ms. Agnes Lyon, D.R.E.; Mr. Manuela Torres, D.R.E. Students 215.

ASHEVILLE, BUNCOMBE CO.

1—BASILICA OF ST. LAWRENCE (1869)
97 Haywood St., Asheville, 28801. Tel: 828-252-6042; Fax: 828-254-0414; Email: basileia@bellsouth.net; Email: StLawrenceAsheville@charlottediocese.org; Web: saintlawrencebasilica.org. P.O. Box 1850, Asheville, 28802. Very Rev. Roger K. Arnsparger, V.E.; Rev. David R. McCanless, Parochial Vicar; Deacon Philip B. Miles; LuWinn Rutherford, Pastoral Assoc.; Andrew Davis, Music Min.
Catechesis Religious Program—Tel: 828-252-8816; Fax: 828-254-0414. Mrs. Elizabeth Girton, D.R.E. Students 410.

2—ST. EUGENE (1957)
72 Culvern St., Asheville, 28804. Tel: 828-254-5193; Email: churcheugene@steugene.org; Email: StEugeneAsheville@charlottediocese.org; Web: www.steugene.org. Rev. J. Patrick Cahill; Deacon Michael Zboyovski Sr.
Catechesis Religious Program—Tracy Jedd, D.R.E.; Ms. Andrea Robles-Leon, Youth Min. Students 280.

BELMONT, GASTON CO., QUEEN OF THE APOSTLES (1965)
503 N. Main St., Belmont, 28012. Tel: 704-825-9600; Email: pastor@queenoftheapostles.org; Web: www.queenoftheapostles.org. Rev. Francis T. Cancro; Deacons John Panzica; William H. Wilson; Jeanne LaFrancis, Pastoral Assoc.; Chrissy Glisson, Music Dir.
Res.: 2121 Ferncliff Ln., Belmont, 28012.
Tel: 704-825-9907.
Catechesis Religious Program—

Tel: 704-825-9600, Ext. 26. Kelly Munsee, D.R.E. Students 282.

BISCOE-CANDOR, MONTGOMERY CO., OUR LADY OF THE AMERICAS
298 Farmers Market Rd., Biscoe, 27209.
Tel: 910-974-3051; Fax: 910-974-4156; Email: ourlady298@embarqmail.com; Email: olabiscoe@charlottediocese.org; Web: ourladycandor.org. Mailing Address: P.O. Box 519, Candor, 27229. Rev. Ricardo Sanchez; Eduardo Sanchez, Accountant; Maria Galarza-Duarte, Sec.; Penny McGrath, Music Dir.
Catechesis Religious Program—Jorge Chavez, D.R.E.; Mary Hindbaugh, D.R.E.; Charles Hindbaugh, D.R.E. Students 371.

BOONE, WATAUGA CO., ST. ELIZABETH (1954)
Mailing Address: 259 Pilgrims Way, Boone, 28607.
Tel: 828-264-8338; Fax: 828-262-3721; Email: StElizabethBoone@charlottediocese.org; Web: www.stehc.org. Rev. Matthew P. Codd; Deacon Michael Leahy.
Catechesis Religious Program—Ellisa Hayes, D.R.E. Students 142.
Mission—Church of the Epiphany, 163 Galax Ln., Blowing Rock, 28607. Tel: 828-264-8338;
Fax: 828-262-3721; Email: mpcodd@charlottediocese.org.

BOONVILLE, YADKINVILLE CO., DIVINE REDEEMER (DIVINO REDENTOR) (2004)
209 Lon Ave., Boonville, 27011. Tel: 336-367-7067;
Fax: 336-367-7954; Email: DivineRedeemerBoonville@charlottediocese.org; Web: divineredeemercc.org. P.O. Box 370, Boonville, 27011. Rev. Jose Enrique Gonzalez-Gaytan; Deacon Michael Langsdorf.
Catechesis Religious Program—Victor Gonzalez, D.R.E.; Mrs. Sergio Lopez, Youth Min. Students 429.

BREVARD, TRANSYLVANIA CO., SACRED HEART (1949)
150 Brian Berg Ln., Brevard, 28712.
Tel: 828-883-9572; Fax: 828-883-9581; Email: shcc@sacredheartnc.org; Email: SacredHeartBrevard@charlottediocese.org; Web: sacredheartcatholicchurchbrevardnc.org. Rev. Shawn O'Neal; Deacon Patrick Crosby.
Catechesis Religious Program—Patricia Poche, D.R.E.; Ms. Jenni Pogue, Youth Min. Students 95.
Mission—St. Jude, 3011 U.S. Hwy. 64 E., Sapphire, 28774. Tel: 828-743-5717; Fax: 828-743-5157; Email: stjudesapphirevalley@charlottediocese.org; Web: charlottediocese.org/parishes/st-jude/. Rev. Casmir Maduakor, Parochial Admin.
Catechesis Religious Program—Mrs. Marianne Vines, D.R.E. Students 11.

BRYSON CITY, SWAIN CO., ST. JOSEPH (1941)
316 Main St., Bryson City, 28713. Tel: 828-488-6766; Email: stjosephbrysoncity@charlottediocese.org; Email: stjosephsbrysoncity@gmail.com; Web: www.stjosephbryson.org. Mailing Address: P.O. Box 727, Bryson City, 28713. Very Rev. Peter J. Shaw, V.F.; Deacon William S. Shaw.
Rectory—Rectory: 234 Arlington Ave., Bryson City, 28713.
Catechesis Religious Program—Kathy Posey, D.R.E.; Barbara Hart, Youth Min. Students 6.
Mission—Our Lady of Guadalupe, 82 Lambert Branch Rd., Cherokee, Swain Co. 28719.
Tel: 828-497-9755.

CANDLER, BUNCOMBE CO., ST. JOAN OF ARC (1928)
768 Ashbury Rd., Candler, 28715. Tel: 828-670-0051;
Fax: 828-670-0052; Email: stjoanofarc@charlottediocese.org; Email: stjoanofarc3640@bellsouth.net; Web: www.stjoanofarccandler.org. Rev. Dean Cesa; Deacon Sigfrido A. Della Valle.
Catechesis Religious Program—Tim Kelley, D.R.E. Students 133.

CLEMMONS, FORSYTH CO., HOLY FAMILY (1980)
4820 Kinnamon Rd., Winston-Salem, 27103.
Tel: 336-778-0600; Fax: 336-766-2918; Email: holyfamilyclemmons@charlottediocese.org; Email: vicki@holyfamilyclemmons.com; Web: holyfamilyclemmons.com. P.O. Box 130, Clemmons, 27012. Very Rev. Michael J. Buttner, V.F.; Rev. Peter Nouck; Deacons Steffen Fohn; John Harrison.
Res.: 2890 Knobb Hill Dr., Clemmons, 27012.
Tel: 336-608-4368.
Catechesis Religious Program—
Tel: 336-766-0600, Ext. 214. Ms. Jennifer Barlow, Youth Min. Students 623.

CONCORD, CABARRUS CO., ST. JAMES (1869)
139 Manor Ave., S.W., Concord, 28025.
Tel: 704-720-0600; Fax: 704-720-0610; Email: bonniew@saintjamescatholic.org; Email: stjamesconcord@charlottediocese.org; Web: www.saintjamescatholic.org. Revs. Jerome L. Chavarria, C.Ss.R.; Charles Donovan, C.Ss.R.; Fabio De Jesus Marin Morales, C.Ss.R.
Res.: 137 Manor Ave. S.W., Concord, 28025.
Tel: 704-720-0608.
Catechesis Religious Program—Kelli Olszewski, D.R.E.; Mr. Michael Quinn, Youth Min. Students 603.

DENVER, LINCOLN CO., HOLY SPIRIT (1988)
537 N. Hwy. 16, Denver, 28037-9235.
Tel: 704-483-6448; Fax: 704-483-6898; Email: HolySpiritDenver@charlottediocese.org; Web: www.holyspiritnc.org. Rev. Carmen Malacari; Deacons Webster James; Matthew Reilly Jr.
Res.: 6789 Hawks Nest Ln., Stanley, 28164-0123.
Tel: 704-820-0153.
Catechesis Religious Program—Mr. Jaymes Summers de Moreno, D.R.E.; Ms. Nicole Waer, Youth Min. Students 268.

EDEN, ROCKINGHAM CO., ST. JOSEPH OF THE HILLS (1938)
316 Boone Rd., Eden, 27288. Tel: 336-623-2661; Email: stjosephofthehills.eden@yahoo.com; Email: StJosephEden@charlottediocese.org; Web: charlottediocese.org/parishes/st-joseph-of-the-hills/. Rev. Pragasam Mariasoosai; Deacon Gerald Potkay.
Catechesis Religious Program—Tel: 336-573-8997. Ms. Mary Ann Ligon, D.R.E. Students 77.

FOREST CITY, RUTHERFORD CO., IMMACULATE CONCEPTION (1950)
1024 W. Main St., Forest City, 28043.
Tel: 828-245-4017; Fax: 828-247-8808; Email: sgdate@charlottediocese.org; Email: ImmConcepForestCity@charlottediocese.org. Very Rev. Herbert Burke, V.F.; Deacons Andrew Cilone; David Faunce.
Catechesis Religious Program—Students 171.

FRANKLIN, MACON CO., ST. FRANCIS OF ASSISI (1953)
299 Maple St., Franklin, 28734. Tel: 828-524-2289; Fax: 828-369-0809; Email: stfrancis299@gmail.com; Email: StFrancisFranklin@charlottediocese.org; Web: www.stfrancisassisifranklin.org. Rev. Tien H. Duong; Deacon David Ramsey.
Catechesis Religious Program—Tel: 828-369-8131. Ms. Denise Cook, D.R.E. Students 147.
Mission—Our Lady of the Mountains, 315 N. 5th St., Highlands, 28741. Tel: 828-526-2418; Email: olmountainshighlands@charlottediocese.org; Web: charlottediocese.org/parishes/our-lady-of-the-mountains/. Rev. Casmir Maduakor, Admin.; Ms. Susan Coram, Sec.
Catechesis Religious Program—Mrs. Marianne Vines, D.R.E. Students 9.

GASTONIA, GASTON CO., ST. MICHAEL (1903)
708 St. Michael's Ln., Gastonia, 28052.
Tel: 704-867-6212; Fax: 704-867-6379; Email: StMichaelGastonia@charlottediocese.org; Web: stmichaelsgastonia.org. Revs. Lucas C. Rossi; James A. Ebright, In Res.; Deacons Timothy Mueller; John P. Weisenhorn.
Res.: 1038 Sherwood Ave., Gastonia, 28052.
School—St. Michael School, (Grades PreK-8),
Tel: 704-865-4382; Fax: 704-864-5108; Web: www.smsgastonia.com. Sheila Levesque, Prin. Lay Teachers 15; Students 150.
Catechesis Religious Program—
Tel: 704-867-6212, Ext. 114. Ms. Mireya Rico, D.R.E.; Ms. Theresa Webster, D.R.E. Students 343.

GREENSBORO, GUILFORD CO.
1—ST. BENEDICT (1901)
109 W. Smith St., Greensboro, 27401.
Tel: 336-272-0303; Email: stbenedictgreensboro@charlottediocese.org; Web: stbenedictgreensboro.net. Rev. James Duc H. Duong.
Catechesis Religious Program—Lynne McGrath, D.R.E. & Youth Min. Students 62.

2—ST. MARY (1928)
1414 Gorrell St., Greensboro, 27401.
Tel: 336-272-8650; Fax: 336-272-3594; Email: StMaryGreensboro@charlottediocese.org; Email: stmarysrccgbo@gmail.com; Web: stmarysgreensboro.org. Revs. William Allegretto; Thomas Sendlein, Parochial Vicar; Linh Nguyen, Parochial Vicar; Deacons Pierre M. K'Briuh; Vincent Shaw Jr.; Emmanuel O. Ukattah.
Church: 812 Duke St., Greensboro, 27401.
Catechesis Religious Program—Genevieve Weech, D.R.E. Students 442.

3—OUR LADY OF GRACE (1952) (Ethel Clay Price Memorial)
2203 W. Market St., Greensboro, 27403.
Tel: 336-274-6520; Fax: 336-274-7326; Email: olggreensboro@charlottediocese.org; Email: olgchurch@olgchurch.org; Web: www.olgchurch.org. Revs. Paul Buchanan; W. Christian Cook, Parochial Vicar; Deacons Carlos Mejias; Timothy Rohan; Jim Toner; Jack Yarbrough.
School—Our Lady of Grace School, (Grades K-8),
Tel: 336-275-1522; Fax: 336-279-8824; Email: olgsch@olgsch.org; Web: www.olgsch.org. Lay Teachers 30; Students 236.
Catechesis Religious Program—Rachel Yarbrough, D.R.E.; Amanda Mast, Youth Min. Students 504.

4—ST. PAUL THE APOSTLE (1974)
2741 Horsepen Creek Rd., Greensboro, 27410.
Tel: 336-294-4696; Email: StPaulGreensboro@charlottediocese.org; Web: www.stpaulcc.org. Rev. Joseph W. Mack; Deacons Gordon L. Forester; Larry Lisk; Michael J. Martini.
Church: 2715 Horse Pen Creek Rd., Greensboro, 27410.
Catechesis Religious Program—Jeannine Martin, D.R.E.; Susan Rabold, Youth Min. Students 317.

5—ST. PIUS THE TENTH (1960)
2210 N. Elm St., Greensboro, 27408.
Tel: 336-272-4681; Fax: 336-272-4681; Email: SPXmail@stpiusxnc.org; Email: StPiusGreensboro@charlottediocese.org; Web: www.stpiusxnc.com. Mailing Address: P.O. Box 13588, Greensboro, 27415-3588. Rev. Msgr. Anthony J. Marcaccio, V.F.; Deacons Philip Cooper; Robert E. Morris; Mrs. Patricia Spivey, Pastoral Assoc.
Res.: 2326 N. Elm St., Greensboro, 27408.
Tel: 336-271-3068.
School—St. Pius the Tenth School, (Grades K-8), 2200 N. Elm St., Greensboro, 27408.
Tel: 336-273-9865; Fax: 336-273-0199; Web: www.spxschool.com. Ann Flynt, Prin., Asst. Prin.; Christopher Kloesz, Asst. Prin.; Christina Foley, Librarian. Lay Teachers 32; Students 451.
Catechesis Religious Program—Mrs. Wendy Barber, D.R.E.; Mrs. Linday Kohl, D.R.E.; Ms. Isabel Streed, Youth Min. Students 387.

HAMLET, RICHMOND CO., ST. JAMES (1910)
1018 West Hamlet Ave., Hamlet, 28345.
Tel: 910-582-0207; Fax: 910-582-7121; Email: stjameshamlet@charlottediocese.org; Web: charlottediocese.org/parishes/st-james/. Mailing Address: P.O. Box 1208, Hamlet, 28345-1208. Rev. Jean-Pierre Swamunu Lhoposo; Deacon Patrick Crosby.
Catechesis Religious Program—Email: stjameshamlet@charlottediocese.org. Cecilia Wilson, D.R.E.; Ms. Christina Dietrich, Youth Min. Students 22.
Mission—Sacred Heart, 205 Rutherford St., Wadesboro, Anson Co. 28710. Email: SacredHeartWadesboro@charlottediocese.org; Web: charlottediocese.org/parishes/sacred-heart/.

HENDERSONVILLE, HENDERSON CO., IMMACULATE CONCEPTION (1912)
208 7th Ave., W., Hendersonville, 28791-3602. Revs. Martin A. Schratz, O.F.M.Cap.; Robert Perez, O.F.M.Cap.; Praveen K. Turaka, O.F.M.Cap.; Deacon Mark D. Nash.
Res.: 914 Thornton Pl., Hendersonville, 28791-3609.
Tel: 828-692-8987.
School—Immaculata, (Grades PreK-8), 711 Buncombe St., Hendersonville, 28791-3609.
Tel: 828-693-3277; Fax: 828-696-3677. Meredith Canning, Prin. Lay Teachers 18; Students 147.
Catechesis Religious Program—Tel: 828-697-7420. Claudia Yepez, D.R.E.; Emily Sevier, Youth Min. Students 369.

HICKORY, CATAWBA CO., ST. ALOYSIUS (1913)
921 2nd St. N.E., Hickory, 28601. Tel: 828-327-2341;
Fax: 828-327-3376; Email: staloysiushickory@charlottediocese.org; Email: info@staloysiushickory.org; Web: www.staloysiushickory.org. Rev. Lawrence M. LoMonaco, V.F.; Deacons Ronald R. Caplette; C. William Schreiber.
Res.: 862 First St., Hickory, 28601.
Catechesis Religious Program—Monica Ebelhack, D.R.E. Students 712.

HIGH POINT, GUILFORD CO.
1—CHRIST THE KING (1940)
1505 E. Martin Luther King, Jr. Dr., High Point, 27260-5455. Tel: 336-883-0244; Fax: 336-884-0244; Email: ChristKingHighPoint@charlottediocese.org; Web: www.christthekinghp.org. Rev. Joseph Long Dinh.
Res.: 1601 E. Martin Luther King, Jr. Dr., High Point, 27260-5455.
Catechesis Religious Program—Ms. Pat Sanchez, D.R.E.; Austine Nwokolo, Youth Min. Students 84.

2—IMMACULATE HEART OF MARY (1947)
Mailing Address: 4145 Johnson St., High Point, 27265. Tel: 336-869-7739; Fax: 336-869-1059; Email: information@ihmchurch.org; Email: ihmhighpoint@CharlotteDiocese.org; Web: www.ihmchurch.org. Revs. Thomas P. Norris, O.S.F.S.; Casmir Maduakor; Deacons Walter Haarsgaard; Francis Skinner.
Res.: 3821 Oak Forest Dr., High Point, 27265.
Tel: 336-886-4847.
School—Immaculate Heart of Mary School, (Grades K-8), Tel: 336-887-2613; Fax: 336-884-1849; Web: www.ihm-school.com. Greg Roberts, Prin. Lay Teachers 14; Students 211.
Catechesis Religious Program—Tel: 336-884-5352. Students 508.

HUNTERSVILLE, MECKLENBURG CO., ST. MARK (1997)
14740 Stumptown Rd., Huntersville, 28078.
Tel: 704-948-0231; Fax: 704-948-8018; Email: StMarkHuntersville@charlottediocese.org; Web: www.stmarknc.org. Very Rev. John T. Putnam, J.C.L., J.V.; Revs. Brian Becker, Parochial Vicar;

Noah C. Carter, Parochial Vicar; Deacons Richard McCarron; Thomas E. McGahey; Robert T. Murphy; Louis A. Pais; Ronald D. Sherwood.
Catechesis Religious Program—Tel: 704-948-1306. Ms. Theresa Benson, D.R.E. Students 1,349.

JEFFERSON, ASHE CO., ST. FRANCIS OF ASSISI (1962)
Mailing Address: P.O. Box 1, Jefferson, 28640.
Tel: 336-246-9151; Fax: 336-246-3141; Email: stfrancisjefferson@charlottediocese.org; Web: stfrancisofassisi-jefferson.org. Rev. James A. Stuhrenberg; Deacon Lee T. Levenson.
Res.: 320 Main St., Jefferson, 28640.
Church: 167 St. Francis Pl., Jefferson, 28640.
Catechesis Religious Program—Patrick Hession, D.R.E. Adult Programs; Celia Cabrera, D.R.E. Grades 1-8; Ramiro Palacios, Youth Min. Students 43.
Mission—St. Frances of Rome, 29 Highland Dr., Sparta, 28675. Tel: 336-372-8846; Web: charlottediocese.org/parishes/st-frances-of-rome/. Mailing Address: P.O. Box 367, Sparta, 28675.
Catechesis Religious Program—Laura Wood, D.R.E. Students 53.

KANNAPOLIS, CABARRUS CO., ST. JOSEPH CHURCH
108 Saint Joseph St., Kannapolis, 28083.
Tel: 704-932-4607; Fax: 704-932-0566; Email: stjosephchurch@ctc.net; Email: StJosephKannapolis@charlottediocese.org; Web: www.saintjosephcatholic.org. Rev. Alvaro A. Riquelme, C.Ss.R.; Deacon Bernardino Velez; Christine DePascale, Business Mgr.
Rectory—137 Manor Ave., Concord, 28026.
Tel: 704-720-0608.
Catechesis Religious Program—Kelly Whitley, D.R.E. Students 197.

KERNERSVILLE, FORSYTH CO., HOLY CROSS (1973) [CEM]
616 S. Cherry St., Kernersville, 27284.
Tel: 336-996-5109; Fax: 336-996-5669; Email: holycrossbernadette@outlook.com; Email: HolyCrossKernersville@charlottediocese.org; Web: www.holycrossnc.com. Rev. Paul Dechant, O.S.F.S.; Deacon Timothy Ritchey.
Child Care—Child Developmental Center,
Tel: 336-996-5144; Fax: 336-996-5115. Cathie Reel, Dir.
Catechesis Religious Program—Marie Kinney, D.R.E.; Denys Davis, Youth Min. Students 479.

LENOIR, CALDWELL CO., ST. FRANCIS OF ASSISI (1936)
328-B Woodsway Ln., N.W., Lenoir, 28645-4356.
Tel: 828-754-5281; Fax: 828-754-5281; Email: StFrancisLenior@charlottediocese.org; Email: stfrancislenoir@charter.net; Web: www.stfrancislenoir.com. Rev. Stephen M. Hoyt; Deacon A. Stephen Pickett.
Res.: 326 Woodsway Ln., N.W., Lenoir, 28645.
Tel: 828-572-2732.
Catechesis Religious Program—Joy Stone, D.R.E.; Sheyla Diaz, Youth Min. Students 152.

LEXINGTON, DAVIDSON CO., OUR LADY OF THE ROSARY (1944)
619 S. Main St., Lexington, 27292-3238.
Tel: 336-248-2463; Fax: 336-238-3241; Email: OLRosaryLexington@charlottediocese.org; Email: parish@olr-nc.org; Web: olr-nc.org. Rev. Ambrose Akinwande, M.S.P.
Catechesis Religious Program—Ms. Diane Hughes, D.R.E.; Sr. Katherine Francis French, S.P., D.R.E. Students 300.

LINCOLNTON, LINCOLN CO., ST. DOROTHY (1944)
148 St. Dorothy Ln., Lincolnton, 28092-9801.
Tel: 704-735-5575; Fax: 704-735-3113; Email: stdorothyLincolnton@charlottediocese.org; Email: office@stdorothys.com; Web: www.stdorothys.com. Rev. David P. Miller.
Res.: 601 N. Grove St., Lincolnton, 28092-9801.
Catechesis Religious Program—Margaret Barrett, D.R.E.; Francis Salmon, Youth Min. Students 210.

MAGGIE VALLEY, HAYWOOD CO., ST. MARGARET OF SCOTLAND (1968)
37 Murphy Dr., Maggie Valley, 28751-1359.
Tel: 828-926-0106; Email: StMargaretMaggieValley@charlottediocese.org; Email: stmargaretmv@bellsouth.net; Web: www.stmargaretofscotlandmv.org. P.O. Box 1359, Maggie Valley, 28751. Rev. Richard R. Benonis, (Retired); Deacon Miles Merwin.
Catechesis Religious Program—Nicki Conroy, D.R.E. Students 37.

MARS HILL, MADISON CO., ST. ANDREW THE APOSTLE (1985)
149 Brook St., Mars Hill, 28754. Tel: 828-689-3719; Email: standrew@mhu.edu; Email: standrewmarshill@charlottediocese.org; Web: standrew-sacredheart.org. Mailing Address: P.O. Box 1406, Mars Hill, 28754-1406. Rev. Frederick H. Werth.
Catechesis Religious Program—Fax: 828-689-3719. Ann Stowe, D.R.E. Students 15.
Mission—Sacred Heart, 20 Summit St., Burnsville, Yancey Co. 28714. Email: standrew@mhu.edu.
Catechesis Religious Program—(Grades K-12), Students 36.

MOCKSVILLE, DAVIE CO., ST. FRANCIS OF ASSISI (1958)
862 Yadkinville Rd., Mocksville, 27028.
Tel: 336-751-2973; Fax: 336-751-9929; Email: office@stfrancismocksville.com; Web: www.stfrancismocksville.com. Rev. Eric Kowalski; Deacon John O. Zimmerle; Sisters Teresa Susana Dandison, R.S.M., Hispanic Min. Coord.; Martha Elizabeth Hoyle, R.S.M., Music Min.; Mr. David Taylor, Business Mgr.
Catechesis Religious Program—Renee Hoke, D.R.E.; Ms. Paula Varona, Youth Min. Students 128.

MONROE, UNION CO., OUR LADY OF LOURDES (1945)
725 Deese St., Monroe, 28112. Tel: 704-289-2773; Fax: 704-283-7210; Email: OLLourdesMonroe@charlottediocese.org; Web: charlottediocese.org/parishes/our-lady-of-lourdes/. Revs. Benjamin A. Roberts; A. Cory Catron; Deacons Guillermo Anzola; Roland R. Geoffroy, (Retired); Sidney Huff; William D. Powers, D.R.E.
Catechesis Religious Program—Ms. Kathleen Prevost, Youth Min. Students 665.

MOORESVILLE, IREDELL CO., ST. THERESE (1946)
217 Brawley School Rd., Mooresville, 28117.
Tel: 704-664-3992; Tel: 704-664-7762; Email: office@sainttherese.net; Email: StThereseMooresville@charlottediocese.org; Web: www.sainttherese.net. Revs. Mark S. Lawlor; Paul McNulty, Parochial Vicar; Paul Asoh, Parochial Vicar; Deacons Myles Decker; Joseph R. Santen; John E. Sims.
Catechesis Religious Program—Tel: 704-664-7762; Fax: 704-664-2045. Carmen Sanjuan, Dir., Faith Formation; David Conklin, Asst. Dir., Faith Formation. Students 959.

MORGANTON, BURKE CO., ST. CHARLES BORROMEO (1947)
728 W. Union St., Morganton, 28655.
Tel: 828-437-3108; Fax: 828-437-6262; Email: scbchurch417@gmail.com; Web: StCharlesMorganton@charlottediocese.org; Web: www.saintcharlesborromeo.org. Very Rev. Kenneth L. Whittington, V.F.; Deacons Edward A. Konarski; John Martino; Miguel P. Sebastian.
Catechesis Religious Program—Ms. Gail Watson, D.R.E. Students 190.
Mission—Our Lady of the Angels, Fax: 828-559-0678; Email: OLAMarion@charlottediocese.org; Email: olotachurch@gmail.com; Web: charlottediocese.org/parishes/our-lady-of-the-angels/. Rev. Carl E. Kaltreider.
Catechesis Religious Program—Marilyn Allison, D.R.E.; Phyllis Ryan, D.R.E. Students 129.

MOUNT AIRY, SURRY CO., HOLY ANGELS (1921)
1208 N. Main St., Mt. Airy, 27030-3640.
Tel: 336-786-8147; Fax: 336-786-8296; Email: HolyAngelsMountAiry@charlottediocese.org; Web: www.mountairycatholicsha.com. Rev. Lawrence W. Heiney; Deacon Wayne J. Nacey.
Catechesis Religious Program—Mrs. Stella Neal, D.R.E.; Ms. Lisa Goodin, Youth Min. Students 190.

MURPHY, CHEROKEE CO., ST. WILLIAM (1952)
765 Andrews Rd., Murphy, 28906. Tel: 828-837-2000; Fax: 828-835-9889; Email: StWilliamMurphy@charlottediocese.org; Email: stwilli@frontier.com; Web: st-william.net. Mailing Address: P.O. Box 546, Murphy, 28906. Rev. H. Alejandro Ayala; Deacon Carl Hubbel.
Catechesis Religious Program—Charlene Davidson, D.R.E.; Mark March, D.R.E. Students 13.
Mission—Immaculate Heart of Mary, 1433 U.S. Hwy. 64 W., Hayesville, 28904. Email: ihmhayesville@charlottediocese.org; Email: willi@frontier.com; Web: www.charlottediocese.org/parishes/st-william/immaculate-heart-of-mary-2.
Catechesis Religious Program—Charlene Davidson, D.R.E. & Youth Min. Students 36.

NEWTON, CATAWBA CO., ST. JOSEPH (1978)
720 W. 13th St., Newton, 28658-3899.
Tel: 828-464-9207; Fax: 828-464-9880; Email: stjoseph78@bellsouth.net; Email: stjosephnewton@charlottediocese.org; Web: www.stjosephrcc.org. Rev. James M. Collins; Deacon Scott D. Gilfillan.
Holy Family Parish Center—Tel: 828-465-2878.
Catechesis Religious Program—Mr. Gustavo Rojo, D.R.E.; Kara Thorpe, D.R.E. Students 188.

NORTH WILKESBORO, WILKES CO., ST. JOHN BAPTIST DE LASALLE (1952)
275 C.C. Wright School Rd., North Wilkesboro, 28659. Tel: 336-838-5562; Email: StJohnNWilkesboro@charlottediocese.org; Web: charlottediocese.org/parishes/st-john-baptiste-de-lasalle. Very Rev. John D. Hanic, V.F.; Deacon Harold Markle, (Retired); Sr. Janice McQuade, S.S.J., Pastoral Assoc.
Catechesis Religious Program—Tel: 336-670-2792. Mary Sorel, D.R.E. Students 265.
Mission—St. Stephen, 101 Hawthorne Rd., Elkin, Surry Co. 28621. Tel: 336-835-3007; Email: connect@ststephennc.org; Email: ststephenelkin@charlottediocese.org.
Catechesis Religious Program—Students 39.

REIDSVILLE, ROCKINGHAM CO., HOLY INFANT (1961)
1042 Freeway Dr., Reidsville, 27320.
Tel: 336-342-1448; Email: holyinfant.reidsville@gmail.com; Email: HolyInfantReidsville@charlottediocese.org; Web: holyinfantreidsville.org. Mailing Address: P.O. Box 1197, Reidsville, 27323-1197. Rev. Frank J. Seabo.
Catechesis Religious Program—Susan McHugh, Youth Min. Students 129.

SALISBURY, ROWAN CO., SACRED HEART (1882)
375 Lumen Christi Ln., Salisbury, 28147.
Tel: 704-633-0591; Fax: 704-647-0126; Email: sburges@shcatholic.org; Email: SacredHeartSalisbury@charlottediocese.org; Web: www.salisburycatholic.org. Very Rev. John J. Eckert, V.F.; Deacon James Mazur.
Res.: 1721 Colony Rd., Salisbury, 28144.
School—Sacred Heart School, (Grades K-8), 385 Lumen Christi Ln., Salisbury, 28147.
Tel: 704-633-2841; Fax: 704-633-6033; Web: www.salisburycatholicschool.org. Francisco J. Cardelle, Prin.; Lynn Frank, Librarian. Lay Teachers 26; Religious 2; Students 213.
Catechesis Religious Program—Michael Becker, D.R.E.

SHELBY, CLEVELAND CO., ST. MARY'S aka St. Mary Help of Christians (1935)
818 McGowan Rd., Shelby, 28150. Tel: 704-487-7697; Email: stmaryshelby@charlottediocese.org; Web: www.saintmaryshelby.org. Rev. Michael T. Kottar; Deacon James P. Trombley.
Catechesis Religious Program—Maureen Westlund, Faith Formation Coord. Students 177.
Mission—Christ the King, 710 Stone St., Kings Mountain, Cleveland Co. 28086. Cell: 704-487-0187.

SPRUCE PINE, MITCHELL CO., ST. LUCIEN (1940)
695 Summit Ave., Spruce Pine, 28777-0688.
Tel: 828-765-2224; Fax: 704-765-2238; Email: stluciensprucepine@charlottediocese.org; Web: charlottediocese.org/parishes/st-lucien. Mailing Address: P.O. Box 688, Spruce Pine, 28777-0688. Rev. Christopher M. Gober.
Mission—St. Bernadette, 2085 State Hwy. 105, Linville, Avery Co. 28646. Tel: 828-898-6900; Fax: 828-898-6900; Email: stbernadettelinville@charlottediocese.org; Web: www.stbernadettelinville.org. Mailing Address: P.O. Box 1252, Linville, 28646. Deacon David Waugh; Ms. Amy Williams, Sec.
Catechesis Religious Program—Ms. Olga Aguayo, D.R.E. (St. Lucien); Will Havron, D.R.E. (St. Bernadette). Students 64.

STATESVILLE, IREDELL CO., ST. PHILIP THE APOSTLE (1898)
Mailing Address: P.O. Box 882, Statesville, 28687-0882. Tel: 704-872-2579; Fax: 704-872-2579; Email: stphilipapostle@bellsouth.net; Web: StPhillipStatesville@charlottediocese.org. Rev. Thomas Kessler; Deacon Charles Brantley.
Church: 525 Camden Dr., Statesville, 28677.
Catechesis Religious Program—Mary Brown, D.R.E.; Ms. Anita Lund, Youth Min. Students 158.
Mission—Holy Trinity, 1039 NC Hwy. 90 W., Taylorsville, Alexander Co. 28681. Tel: 828-632-8009 ; Fax: 828-632-8009; Email: holytrinitytaylorsville@charlottediocese.org; Web: charlottediocese.org/parishes/holy-trinity/. Revs. James M. Byer; Jose Cardenas-Bonilla, Parochial Admin.
Catechesis Religious Program—Paula Matheson, D.R.E. Students 65.

SWANNANOA, BUNCOMBE CO., ST. MARGARET MARY (1936)
102 Andrews Pl., Swannanoa, 28778.
Tel: 828-686-8833; Fax: 828-686-8832; Email: stmmc@charter.net; Email: StMargaretSwannanoa@charlottediocese.org; Web: saintmargaretmarycatholic.org/home.aspx. Rev. Matthew Leonard; Deacons Ralph R. Eckoff; Dan Hoffert.
Res.: 67 Beech Glen Dr., Black Mountain, 28711.
Tel: 828-686-5300.
Catechesis Religious Program—Bea Madden, D.R.E. Students 75.

SYLVA, JACKSON CO., ST. MARY (1955)
22 Bartlett St, Sylva, 28779. Tel: 828-586-9496; Email: StMarySylva@charlottediocese.org; Email: stmarysylva@frontier.com; Web: stmarymotherofgod.com. Rev. Casey A. Coleman; Deacon Matthew Newsome.
Res.: 141 Dillsboro Rd., Sylva, 28779.
Tel: 828-631-0576.
Catechesis Religious Program—Mrs. Lucia Castillo, D.R.E. Students 63.

THOMASVILLE, DAVIDSON CO., OUR LADY OF THE HIGHWAYS (1953)
943 Ball Park Rd., Thomasville, 27360.
Tel: 336-475-2667; Fax: 336-476-3337; Email:

OLHighwaysThomasville@charlottediocese.org; Email: olhsecretary@gmail.com; Web: www.ourladyofthehighwayscatholicchurch.com. Rev. James M. Turner, O.S.F.S.; Deacons Wayne Adams, (Retired); Martin Sheehan.

Catechesis Religious Program—Kathy Laskis, Dir. Faith Formation. Students 335.

TRYON, POLK CO., ST. JOHN THE BAPTIST (1911)
180 Laurel Ave., Tryon, 28782. Tel: 828-895-9574; Email: stjohnchurch@windstream.net; Web: www.stjohntryon.com. Rev. Jason M. Christian; Deacon John J. Riehl.

Catechesis Religious Program—Tel: 828-859-5932. Theresa Finch, D.R.E. Students 70.

WAYNESVILLE, HAYWOOD CO., ST. JOHN THE EVANGELIST (1926)
234 Church St., Waynesville, 28786.
Tel: 828-456-6707; Email: stjohnwaynesville@gmail.com; Email: StJohnWaynesville@charlottediocese.org; Web: stjohnwaynesville.org. Rev. Richard Sutter, Parochial Admin.

Catechesis Religious Program—Mrs. Ana Quintero, D.R.E.; Ms. Rocio Quintero, Youth Min. Students 62.

Mission—Immaculate Conception, 42 Newfound Rd., Canton, Haywood Co. 28716. Email: ImmconcepCanton@charlottediocese.org. Deacon Richard G. Voegele.

WINSTON-SALEM, FORSYTH CO.

1—ST. BENEDICT THE MOOR (1940)
1625 E. Twelfth St., Winston-Salem, 27101.
Tel: 336-725-9200; Fax: 336-397-0898; Email: StBenedictWinstonSalem@charlottediocese.org; Email: sbcchmsd@gmail.com; Web: saintbenedictthemoor.org/. Rev. Henry Tutuwan.

Mission—Good Shepherd, Church: 105 Good Shepherd Dr., King, 27021. Tel: 336-725-9200; Fax: 336-722-4264; Email: goodshepherdking@charlottediocese.org; Web: www.goodshepherdking.org. c/o St. Benedict the Moor Catholic Church, 108 E. 12th St., Winston Salem, 27101. Deacon David Boissey Sr.

Catechesis Religious Program—Ms. Syveria Hauser, D.R.E. Students 261.

2—ST. LEO THE GREAT (1891)
335 Springdale Ave., Winston-Salem, 27104.
Tel: 336-724-0561; Fax: 336-724-7036; Email: mbyoung@stleocatholic.org; Email: StLeoWinstonSalem@charlottediocese.org; Web: www.stleocatholic.org. Revs. Brian J. Cook; Felix Nkafu; Deacons Ralph D'Agostino; Robert DeSautels.
Res.: 334 Springdale Ave., Winston-Salem, 27104.

School—St. Leo the Great School, (Grades PreK-8), 333 Springdale Ave., Winston-Salem, 27104.
Tel: 336-748-8252; Fax: 336-748-9005. Mrs. Georgette Schraeder, Prin. Lay Teachers 17; Religious 1; Students 237.

Catechesis Religious Program—Tel: 336-724-0561. Lauren Gardner, D.R.E.; Ms. Bethany Fischer, Youth Min. Students 343.

Convent—1975 Georgia Ave., Winston-Salem, 27104. Tel: 336-723-3639.

3—OUR LADY OF MERCY (1954)
1730 Link Rd., Winston-Salem, 27103.
Tel: 336-722-7001; Fax: 336-722-0465; Email: mercy@triad.rr.com; Email: olmWinstonSalem@charlottediocese.org; Web: www.ourladyofmercync.org. Revs. Carl S. Zdancewicz, O.F.M.Conv.; Joseph Barry Angelini, O.F.M.Conv.; Deacons Joseph Schumacher; Ramon Ediberto Tejada; Sr. Kathleen Ganiel, O.S.F., Pastoral Assoc.
Friary: 1147 Lockland Ave., Winston-Salem, 27103. Tel: 336-724-6806.

School—Our Lady of Mercy School, (Grades K-8), Tel: 336-722-7204; Fax: 336-725-2294; Email: admin@ourladyofmercyschool.org; Web: www.ourladyofmercyschool.org. Sr. Geri Rogers, S.S.J., Prin.; Jean Degnan, Asst. Prin. Lay Teachers 12; Religious 1; Students 201.

Catechesis Religious Program—
Tel: 336-722-7001, Ext. 26. Sr. Kathleen Ganiel, O.S.F., D.R.E.; Mr. Jose Blanco, Youth Min. Students 501.

Convent—2141 New Castle Dr., Winston-Salem, 27103. Tel: 336-774-3956.

Mission—Our Lady of Fatima, 211 W. 3rd St., Winston-Salem, Forsyth Co. 27101.
Tel: 336-723-8238; Fax: 336-722-0465; Email: olfwinstonsalem@charlottediocese.org.

On Duty Outside the Diocese:
Very Rev.—
Houseknecht, Eric, V.F., (Diocese of Phoenix)
Revs.—
Allen, John, Pontifical College Josephinum
Brzoska, David
Choquet, Alexei R.
Osorio, Louis S.
Wilderotter, Paul C.

Military Chaplains:
Very Rev.—
Fitzgibbons, Peter L., V.F., U.S. Army.

Unassigned:
Revs.—
Pagel, John M.
Tarasi, Carlo D.

Absent On Leave:
Revs.—
Davis, Christopher J.
DeAguilar, Arturo
Hanic, Johnathan
Klepacki, Michael S., (Retired)
Kuhn, Dennis R.
Schneider, John
Tice, Cecil
Williamson, Thomas.

Absent on Medical Leave:
Rev.—
Williams, W. Ray.

Retired:
Rev. Msgrs.—
Bellow, Richard, (Retired)
McSweeney, John J., (Retired), 10309 Paschall Rd., 28278
Showfety, Joseph, (Retired), 7-A Fountain Manor Dr., Taylor Village, 107 Penny Rd., High Point, 27260
Very Revs.—
Kloster, George M., (Retired), P.O. Box 1626, Murphy, 28906
Thomas, Wilbur N., V.F., P.O. Box 18253, Asheville, 28814
Revs.—
Ayathupadam, Joseph, (Retired), P.O. Box 1745, Fort Mill, SC 29716
Cahill, James, (Retired), P.O. Box 1856, Sylva, 28779-1856
Clements, Thomas P., (Retired), 107 Penny Rd., #1012, High Point, 27260
Conway, Robert R., (Retired), 3100 Ashley Town Ctr., Apt. 436, Charleston, SC 29414
DelGiudice, Carl, (Retired), 1647 Settlers Way, Ocean Isle Beach, 28469
Ferris, Robert M., (Retired), 3017 Beaconwood Dr., Greensboro, 27408
Fohn, Kurt M., (Retired), 110 Miss Emery Ln., Lexington, 27295
Hanson, Richard N., (Retired), 1123 S. Church St., 28203
Hawker, James, (Retired), 133 Cmdr. Shea Blvd., Unit 807, Quincy, MA 02171
Hoover, Conrad, (Retired), 1300 Reece Rd., Apt. 505, 28209
Hoover, John P., (Retired), 100 Madora St., Mount Holly, 28120
Latsko, Andrew, (Retired), 227 Isabella Rd., Elverson, PA 19520
Le, Tan Van, (Retired), 1123 S. Church St., 28203
Meehan, Gabriel, (Retired), 805 Foxwood Ct. S.W., Lenoir, 28645
Mulligan, Joseph V., (Retired), 1123 S. Church St., 28203
Sheridan, Edward J., (Retired), 6860 Greedy Hwy., Hickory, 28602
Solari, James K., (Retired), 109 Penny Rd., 219E, High Point, 27260.

Permanent Deacons:
Adams, Wayne, (Retired), (Retired), Our Lady of the Highways, Thomasville
Anzola, Guillermo, Our Lady of Lourdes, Monroe
Aquino, Enedino S., Triad Region; Hispanic Ministry
Atkinson, James, (Living Outside the Diocese)
Barone, John, (Retired), (Inactive)
Bitter, Daren S., St. Matthew, Charlotte
Boissey, David Sr., Good Shepherd, King
Bozik, James E., St. Peter, Charlotte
Brantley, Charles, (Retired), St. Philip the Apostle, Statesville
Bruck, Paul, St. Patrick Cathedral, Charlotte
Caplette, Ronald R., (Retired), St. Aloysius, Hickory
Cilone, Andrew, (Retired), Immaculate Conception, Forest City
Cochan, Clark, St. Peter, Charlotte
Cooper, Philip, St. Pius X, Greensboro
Crosby, Patrick, (Retired), Sacred Heart, Brevard
D'Agostino, Ralph, St. Leo the Great, Winston-Salem
Decker, Myles, St. Therese, Mooresville
Della Valle, Sigfrido A., St. Joan of Arc, Candler
Denzler, John N., St. John Neumann, Charlotte
DeSautels, Charles, St. Leo, Winston-Salem
Devine, Patrick J., Charlotte-Douglas Airport Ministry
Diaz, Joseph A., St. Thomas Aquinas, Charlotte
Diener, Mark, St. Gabriel, Charlotte
Duca, Peter, Our Lady of the Assumption, Charlotte
Eckoff, Ralph R., (Retired), St. Margaret Mary, Swannanoa
Evers, Jeffrey S., St. Luke, Mint Hill
Faunce, David, Immaculate Conception, Forest City
Flores, Louis, Our Lady of the Assumption, Charlotte
Fohn, Stephen, Our Lady of the Assumption, Charlotte
Forester, Gordon L., (Retired), St. Paul the Apostle, Greensboro
Garcia Ospina, Dario, Hispanic Ministry, Hickory Region
Geoffroy, Roland R., (Retired), Our Lady of Lourdes, Monroe
Gilfillan, Scott D., St. Joseph, Newton
Goad, Michael F., St. Gabriel, Charlotte
Gorman, James, St. John Neumann, Charlotte
Griffin, William G., St. Matthew, Charlotte
Haarsgaard, Walter, Immaculate Heart of Mary, High Point
Hamrlik, James, St. Matthew, Charlotte
Harrison, John, Holy Family, Clemmons
Haslett, Bruce H., (Retired), (Living Outside of Diocese)
Herman, Paul, (Retired), St. Matthew, Charlotte
Hoffert, Daniel J., St. Margaret Mary, Swannanoa
Hubbell, Carl, (Retired), St. William, Murphy
Huff, Sidney, (Retired), Our Lady of Lourdes, Monroe
Johnson, James R., (Retired), (Living Outside the Diocese)
K'Briuh, Pierre M., (Retired), St. Mary, Greensboro
Kak, Thomas J., (Retired), (Inactive)
Killian, Philip Jr., (Living Outside the Diocese)
King, David E., Maryfield, Pennybyrn; Maryfield Pennybyrn, High Point
King, Mark J., St. Gabriel, Charlotte
Kingsley, Arthur J., (Retired)
Konarski, Edward A., St. Charles Borromeo, Morganton
Kopfle, John, St. Vincent de Paul, Charlotte
Langsdorf, Michael, Divine Redeemer, Boonville
Leahy, Michael, St. Elizabeth, Boone
Levenson, Lee T., St. Francis of Assisi, Jefferson
Liotard, Paul, (Retired), (Inactive)
Lisk, Larry, St. Paul the Apostle, Greensboro
Lyerly, R. Alexander, (Retired), (Inactive)
Mack, Joseph H. Jr., (Retired), (Living Outside Diocese)
Marini, Anthony, (Retired), (Living Outside the Diocese)
Markle, Harold, (Retired), St. John Baptist de la Salle, North Wilkesboro
Martini, Michael J., St. Paul the Apostle, Greensboro
Martino, John, St. Charles Borromeo, Morganton
Mazur, James, Sacred Heart, Salisbury
McCarron, Richard, St. Mark, Huntersville
McGahey, Thomas E., St. Mark, Huntersville
McNabb, Scott, (Unassigned)
McNulty, Brian P., St. Patrick, Charlotte
Medina, Carlos A. Sr., St. Patrick, Charlotte
Mejias, Marcos, Our Lady of Grace, Greensboro
Merwin, Miles, St Margaret of Scotland, Maggie Valley
Miles, Philip B., St. Lawrence, Asheville
Morris, Robert E., St. Pius the Tenth, Greensboro
Moyer, Frank, St. Barnabas, Arden
Murphy, Robert T., St. Mark, Huntersville
Nacey, Wayne J., Holy Angels, Mount Airey
Nash, Mark D., Immaculate Conception, Hendersonville
Newsome, Matthew, St. Mary, Sylva
Nguyen, Quang, St. Joseph, Charlotte
O'Toole, Lawrence P., (Retired), St. Gabriel, Charlotte
Pais, Louis, St. Mark, Huntersville
Panzica, John, Queen of the Apostles, Belmont
Piche, Guy, (Retired), St. Helen, Spencer Mountain
Pickett, A. Stephen, St. Francis, Lenoir
Potkay, Gerald, (Retired), St. Joseph of the Hills, Eden
Powers, William D., Our Lady of Lourdes, Monroe
Ramsey, David, St. Francis of Assisi, Franklin
Reilly, Matthew Jr., Holy Spirit, Denver
Reiser, David S., Our Lady of the Assumption, Charlotte
Ricart, Martin III, St. Thomas Aquinas, Charlotte
Riehl, John J., St. John the Baptist, Tryon
Ritchey, Timothy, Holy Cross, Kernersville
Rohan, Timothy, (Retired), Our Lady of Grace, Greensboro
Sanctis, Thomas D., St. Ann, Charlotte
Santen, Joseph R., St. Therese, Mooresville
Schreiber, C. William, St. Aloysius, Hickory
Schrieber, Gary J., St. Matthew, Charlotte
Schumacher, Joseph N., (Retired), Our Lady of Mercy, Winston-Salem

Sebastian, Miguel P., St. Charles Borromeo, Morganton
Shaw, Vincent H. Jr., St. Mary, Greensboro
Shaw, William S., St. Joseph, Bryson City
Sheehan, Martin, Our Lady of the Highways, Thomasville
Sherwood, Ronald D., (Retired), St. Mark, Huntersville
Sims, John E., St. Therese, Mooresville
Skinner, Francis, Immaculate Heart of Mary, High Point
Sparrow, Paul, St. Thomas Aquinas, Charlotte
Staub, Jack G., St. Matthew, Charlotte
Steinkamp, Ronald F., St. Pius Tenth, Greensboro
Stout, Michael L., St. Barnabas, Arden
Szalony, George A., (Retired), Charlotte-Douglas Airport Ministry
Tamayo, Ruben A., St. Vincent de Paul, Charlotte
Tejada, Ramon Ediberto, Our Lady of Mercy, Winston-Salem
Todd, Curtiss, (Retired)
Toner, Jim, Our Lady of Grace, Greensboro
Tonon, Peter, St. Ann, Charlotte
Torres, Rafael J., St. Luke, Charlotte
Triana, Rudolph J., (Retired), St. Barnabas, Arden
Trombley, James P., St. Mary, Shelby
Ukattah, Emmanuel O., St. Mary, Greensboro
Vargas, Jose, Immaculate Heart of Mary, High Point
Velez, Bernardino, St. Jpseph, Kannapolis
Voegele, Richard G., (Retired), Immaculate Conception, Canton
Waugh, Donald, St. Bernadette, Linville
Webster, James, Holy Spirit, Denver
Weisenhorn, John P., (Retired), St. Michael, Gastonia
Wenning, Bernard W. Jr., (Retired), St. Gabriel, Charlotte
Williams, Kevin, Our Lady of the Assumption, Charlotte
Wilson, William H., Queen of the Apostles, Belmont
Witulski, James H., St. Thomas Aquinas, Charlotte
Yarbrough, Jack, Our Lady of Grace, Greensboro
Zboyovski, Michael J. Sr., St. Eugene, Asheville
Zimmerle, John O., (Retired), St. Francis of Assisi, Mocksville.

INSTITUTIONS LOCATED IN DIOCESE

[A] COLLEGES AND UNIVERSITIES

BELMONT. **Belmont Abbey College*, 100 Belmont-Mount Holly Rd., Belmont, 28012-1802. Tel: 704-461-6700; Fax: 704-461-6748; Email: ritalewis@bac.edu; Web: belmontabbeycollege.edu. William Thierfelder, Ed.D., Pres.; Allan Mark, Chief Fin. Officer; Donald Beagle, Dir. Library; Rt. Rev. Placid D. Solari, O.S.B., Chancellor; Margot Rhoads, Registrar; David Williams. (Coed) Liberal Arts Senior College. Clergy 2; Lay Teachers 160; Sisters 1; Students 1,549.

The Ecumenical Institute of Wake Forest University and Belmont Abbey College, 100 Belmont-Mt. Holly Road, Belmont, 28012. Tel: 704-825-6748; Tel: 704-461-6748.

Sacred Heart College, 101 Mercy Dr., Belmont, 28012-4805. Tel: 704-829-5100; Fax: 704-829-5137; Email: jhardin@mercysc.org. Sr. Rosalind Picot, R.S.M., Pres. Sisters of Mercy.College ceased academic operation, effective August 1987. Corporation intact.

Legal Title: Sisters of Mercy.

[B] HIGH SCHOOLS

KERNERSVILLE. *Bishop McGuinness Catholic High School*, 1725 N.C. Hwy. 66 S., Kernersville, 27284. Tel: 336-564-1010; Fax: 336-564-1060; Email: tshaw@bmhs.us; Web: www.bmhs.us. Tracy A. Shaw, M.Ed., Asst. Prin. & Dir., Studies; Sr. Anne Thomas Taylor, S.S.J., Dean of Students; Leslie Redmon, Librarian. Lay Teachers 35; Religious 2; Students 371.

[C] ELEMENTARY SCHOOLS, INTERPAROCHIAL

ASHEVILLE. *Asheville Catholic School*, (Grades PreK-8), 12 Culvern St., Asheville, 28804. Tel: 828-252-7896 ; Fax: 828-252-5708; Email: info@ashevillecatholic.org; Web: www.ashevillecatholic.org. Michael Miller, Prin.; Shonra McManus, Librarian. Lay Teachers 15; Students 168.

[D] REGIONAL SCHOOLS

CHARLOTTE. *Mecklenburg Area Catholic Schools (M.A.C.S.)*, (Grades PreK-12), Catholic School System of Nine Schools. 1123 S. Church St., 28203. Tel: 704-370-3265; Fax: 704-370-3292; Web: www.discovermacs.org; Email: mslenes@charlottediocese.org. Janice Ritter, Ed. D., Supt.; Ms. Mary Lenes, Dir.

Charlotte Catholic High School (Bishop Hafey Memorial), 7702 Pineville-Matthews Rd., 28226. Tel: 704-543-1127; Fax: 704-543-1217; Email: shcarpenter@charlottecatholic.com; Web: www.gocougars.org. Kurt Telford, Prin.; Steve Carpenter, Asst. Prin.; Angela Montague, Asst. Prin.; Randy Belk, Dean of Students; Terri Taylor, Librarian; Revs. Matthew K. Kauth, S.T.D., Chap.; Jason K. Barone, Asst. Chap. Clergy 1; Lay Teachers 92; Religious 1; Students 1,246.

Charlotte Catholic High School Athletic Association, Tel: 704-543-1127; Fax: 704-543-1217.

Charlotte Catholic High School Alumni Association, 7702 Pineville-Matthews Rd., 28226. Tel: 704-543-1127; Fax: 704-543-1217.

Charlotte Catholic High School Home School Association, 7702 Pineville-Matthews Rd., 28226. Tel: 704-543-1127; Fax: 704-543-1217.

Christ the King Catholic High School, 2011 Crusader Way, Huntersville, 28078. Tel: 704-799-4400; Fax: 704-799-4404; Email: frontdesk@ctkchs.org; Web: ctkchs.org. Carl Semmler, Prin.; Rev. Paul M. McNaulty, Chap. Lay Teachers 28; Students 289.

Holy Trinity Catholic Middle School, (Grades 6-8), 3100 Park Rd., 28209. Tel: 704-527-7822; Fax: 704-525-7288; Email: kparks@htcms.net. Kevin Parks, Prin.; Deb Robinson, Asst. Prin.; Kevin Glossner, Asst. Prin.; Gerda Letizia, Dean of Students; Elizabeth Wise, Librarian; Rev. Joseph Matlak, Chap. Lay Teachers 65; Students 894.

St. Matthew School, (Grades PreK-5), 11525 Elm Ln., 28277. Tel: 704-544-2070; Fax: 704-544-2184; Email: stmatthewschool@stmatthewschool.net; Web: www.stmattwildcats.com. Kevin O'Herron, Prin.; Suzanne Beasley, Asst. Prin. Lay Teachers 38; Students 545.

Our Lady of the Assumption School, (Grades PreK-6), 4225 Shamrock Dr., 28215. Tel: 704-531-0067; Fax: 704-531-7633. Allana-Rae Ramkissoon, Prin.; Mary Jean Mulligan, Librarian. Lay Teachers 14; Students 153.

St. Ann School, (Grades PreK-5), 600 Hillside Ave., 28209. Tel: 704-525-4938; Fax: 704-525-2640. Kathy McKinney, Prin.; Lisa Horton, Asst. Prin. Lay Teachers 20; Students 184.

St. Gabriel School, (Grades PreK-5), 3028 Providence Rd., 28211. Tel: 704-366-2409; Fax: 704-362-5063; Web: www.stgabrielcatholicschool.org. Michelle Snoke, Asst. Prin.; Ellen Chase, Librarian. Lay Teachers 37; Students 552.

St. Mark School, (Grades K-5), 14750 Stumptown Rd., Huntersville, 28078. Tel: 704-766-5000; Fax: 704-875-6377; Web: stmarkcatholicschool.net. Debbie Butler, Prin.; Philip Harrington, Asst. Prin.; Lisa Rox, Librarian. Lay Teachers 44; Students 751.

St. Patrick School, (Grades K-5), 1125 Buchanan St., 28203. Tel: 704-333-3174; Fax: 704-333-3178; Email: AMTobergte@stpatrickschool.net; Web: www.saintpatrickschool.org. Julie Thornley, Prin.; Amy Tobergte, Prin.; Julie Laney, Librarian. Lay Teachers 22; Students 239.

[E] GENERAL HOSPITALS

ASHEVILLE. *Sisters of Mercy Urgent Care, Inc. dba Mercy Urgent Care*, 1201 Patton Ave., Asheville, 28806-0367. Tel: 828-210-2121; Fax: 828-254-4102; Email: sharon@mercyurgentcare.org; Web: www.mercyurgentcare.org. P.O. Box 16367, Asheville, 28816. Tim Johnston, CEO. Tot Asst. Annually 60,610; Total Staff 84.

[F] SPECIAL CARE FACILITIES

BELMONT. **Holy Angels Services, Inc.*, 6600 Wilkinson Blvd., Belmont, 28012. Tel: 704-825-4161; Fax: 704-825-0401; Email: info@holyangelsnc.org; Web: www.holyangelsnc.org. Mailing Address: P.O. Box 710, Belmont, 28012. Mrs. Regina P. Moody, M.Ed., Pres. & CEO. Residential and developmental programs and services for children and adults with mental retardation and physical disabilities. Sisters of Mercy 2; Tot Asst. Annually 48; Total Staff 132; Capacity (All Programs) 48.

McAuley Residence IID Group Homes, Belmont. Tel: 704-825-4161; Fax: 704-825-0401. Bed Capacity 48.

[G] CATHOLIC CHARITIES

CHARLOTTE. *Catholic Charities Diocese of Charlotte*, The Pastoral Center: 1123 S. Church St., 28203. Tel: 704-370-3262; Fax: 704-370-3290; Email: ccdoc@charlottediocese.org; Web: www.ccdoc.org. Gerard A. Carter, Ph.D., Exec. Dir. Tot Asst. Annually 22,000.

Area Offices:

Catholic Charities-Charlotte Regional Office, 1123 S. Church St., 28203. Tel: 704-370-3262; Fax: 704-370-3290; Email: ccdoc@charlottediocese.org. Sandy Buck, Dir. Tot Asst. Annually 19,000; Total Staff 60.

Catholic Charities-Murphy Office, 27 Hatchett St., Murphy, 28906. Tel: 828-835-3535; Fax: 828-835-9794; Email: nwmcfaddin@charlottediocese.org; Web: www.ccdoc.org. Netta McFaddin, Prog. Coord.

Catholic Charities-Piedmont Triad Office, 1612 E. 14th St., Winston-Salem, 27105. Tel: 336-727-0705 ; Fax: 336-714-3232; Web: www.ccdoc.org.

Catholic Charities-Refugee Resettlement Office, 1123 S. Church St., 28203. Tel: 704-370-3262; Fax: 704-370-3290; Email: gacarter@charlottediocese.org; Web: www.ccdoc.org. Sandy Buck, Dir.

Catholic Charities-Western Regional Office, 50 Orange St., Asheville, 28801. Tel: 828-255-0146; Fax: 828-253-7339; Email: clrhodes@charlottediocese.org; Web: www.ccdoc.org. Mr. Mark Nash, Dir.

Social Concerns and Advocacy, 1123 S. Church St., 28203. Tel: 704-370-3225; Fax: 704-370-3290; Email: jtpurello@charlottediocese.org. Joseph Purello, Dir.

[H] NURSING HOMES

HIGH POINT. *Maryfield Nursing Home*, 1315 Greensboro Rd., High Point, 27260. Tel: 336-821-4000; Fax: 336-886-4036; Email: sisterlucy@pennybyrn.org; Web: www.pennybyrnatmaryfield.com. Sr. Lucy Hennessy, S.M.G., Chm. Bd. Bed Capacity 125; Sisters 5.

Pennybyrn at Maryfield, 1315 Greensboro Highway, High Point, 27260. Tel: 336-821-4000; Email: sisterlucy@pennybyrn.org; Web: www.pennybyrnliving.org. Deacon David E. King; Sr. Lucy Hennessy, S.M.G., Contact Person.

[I] MONASTERIES AND RESIDENCES OF PRIESTS AND BROTHERS

CHARLOTTE. *Jesuit Community*, 507 S Tryon St, 28202. Tel: 704-332-2901; Fax: 704-358-0050; Email: jmshea@charlottediocese.org; Web: www.stpeterscatholic.org/. Revs. Jim Bowler, Pastoral Min./ Coord.; James Shea, S.J.; John Michalowski, S.J., Parochial Vicar

Jesuit Community in Western North Carolina.

BELMONT. *Belmont Abbey*, 100 Belmont-Mount Holly Rd., Belmont, 28012-1802. Tel: 704-461-6675; Fax: 704-461-6242; Web: belmontabbey.org. Rt. Rev. Placid D. Solari, O.S.B., Abbot; Very Rev. Christopher A. Kirchgessner, O.S.B., Prior; Revs. David G. Brown, O.S.B.; Francis P. Forster, O.S.B.; David R. Kessinger, O.S.B.; Kieran A. Neilson, O.S.B.; Arthur J. Pendleton, O.S.B.; Elias Correa-Torres, O.S.B.; Bros. Tobiah Abbott, O.S.B.; Anselm Cundiff, O.S.B.; Edward Mancuso, O.S.B.; Gregory Marshall, O.S.B.; James Raber, O.S.B.; George Rumley, O.S.B.; Paul Shanley, O.S.B.; Emmanuel Slobodzian, O.S.B.; Andrew Spivey, O.S.B.; Anthony Swofford, O.S.B.

Southern Benedictine Society of North Carolina, Inc. Brothers 12; Priests 7; Abbot 1.

STONEVILLE. *Franciscan Friary*, 477 Grogan Rd., Stoneville, 27048. Tel: 336-573-3751; Fax: 336-573-3752. Revs. Louis Canino, O.F.M., Dir.; David Hyman, O.F.M.

[J] CONVENTS AND RESIDENCES FOR SISTERS

CHARLOTTE. *Missionaries of Charity*, 1625 Glenn St., 28205. Tel: 704-531-2943. Sisters M. Jonathan, MC, Regl. Supr.; M. Martinella, MC, Supr. Convent and Gift of Mary home for expectant mothers Sisters 4.

St. Joseph Adoration Monastery, 3452 Willow Oak Rd., 28209. Tel: 205-271-2917; Email: contact@olamnuns.com; Web: www.olamnuns.com/ . 3222 County Road 548, Hanceville, AL 35077. Mother Dolores Marie, P.C.P.A., Abbess. Total in Community 6.

BELMONT. *Sisters of Mercy of the Americas, South Central Community, Inc.*, Sacred Heart Convent: 500 Sacred Heart Cir., Belmont, 28012-7621. Tel: 704-829-5100; Fax: 704-829-5137; Email: ljordan@mercysc.org; Web: www.mercysc.org. Sr. Lillian Jordan, Admin. Sisters 33.

Sisters of Mercy of the Americas, South Central Community, Inc., Mercy Administration Center: 101 Mercy Dr., Belmont, 28012-2898. Tel: 704-829-5260; Fax: 704-829-5267; Email: support@mercysc.org; Web: www.mercysc.org. Sr. Jane Hotstream, R.S.M., Pres. Sisters 450.

HIGH POINT. *Congregation of the Sisters of Charity of St. Vincent De Paul*, St. Vincent Convent, 1225

Elon Pl., High Point, 27263. Tel: 336-687-7005; Fax: 336-884-4545; Email: scvsisters@northstate.net. Sr. Elsa Tom, Supr.

Poor Servants of the Mother of God Inc., 1315 Greensboro Rd., High Point, 27260. Tel: 336-454-3014; Fax: 336-886-4036; Email: sisterlucy@pennybyrn.org; Web: www.smgsisters.com. Sr. Lucy Hennessy, S.M.G., Mission Leader. Sisters 5.

VALE. *Maryvale Motherhouse*, 2522 June Bug Rd., Vale, 28168. Tel: 704-276-2626; Fax: 704-276-2626; Email: mvsrs1961@hughes.net. Mother Mary Louis, Supr., (Maryvale Sisters). Parish ministry, day-care center, spiritual/retreat center. Sisters 4.

WINSTON-SALEM. *Sisters of St. Joseph of Chestnut Hill, PA*, St. Leo Convent, 1975 Georgia Ave., Winston-Salem, 27104. Tel: 336-727-3778; Email: srann@bmhs.us. Sr. Ann Thomas, Contact Person. Sisters 4.

[K] CAMPUS MINISTRY CENTERS

CHARLOTTE. *Diocesan Office of Campus Ministry*, 1123 S. Church St., 28203. Tel: 704-370-3243; Fax: 704-370-3291; Email: campusministry@charlottediocese.org; Web: www.charlottediocese.org. Ms. Mary Wright, Diocesan Dir., Campus Ministry; Ms. Ann Kilkelly, Devel. Dir.; Darien Clark, Asst. Dir.

Appalachian State University, Catholic Campus Ministry Center, 232 Faculty St., Boone, 28607. Tel: 828-264-7087; Fax: 828-262-0970; Email: appstatecatholic@gmail.com. Erin Kotlowski, Catholic Campus Minister.

Belmont Abbey College, O'Connell Hall, 100 Belmont-Mount Holly Rd., Belmont, 28012. Tel: 704-461-5094; Email: patrickford@bac.edu. Patrick Ford, Dir. Catholic Student Leadership & Formation.

Davidson College, Catholic Campus Ministry, Campus Box 7196, Davidson, 28035-7181. Tel: 704-894-2423; Web: www.davidsonccm.com. Scott Salvato, Campus Min.

High Point University, Hayworth Memorial Chapel: 1 University Pkwy., High Point, 27262. Email: mnnjoh@charlottediocese.org. Rev. Moses Njoh, Campus Min.

NC Agricultural and Technical State University, Thea House, Thea House, 131 N. Dudley St., Greensboro, 27401. Tel: 646-546-6780; Email: mcamadi@charlottediocese.org. Rev. Marcel Amadi, Catholic Campus Min.

University of North Carolina-Asheville/Mars Hill College, Catholic Campus Ministry, UNC-Asheville, Catholic Campus Ministry UNC–Asheville, P.O. Box 8067, Asheville, 28814. Tel: 828-226-3809; Email: ashevilleccm@gmail.com; Web: ashevilleccm.com. David Mayeux, Campus Min.

University of North Carolina-Charlotte, Catholic Campus Ministry House, 1400 Suther Rd., 28213-0565. Tel: 347-445-1334; Email: ccmuncc@gmail.com. Rev. Innocent Amasiorah, Campus Min.

University of North Carolina-Greensboro, ACM Center, P.O. Box 24784, Greensboro, 27402-2617. Tel: 336-334-5130; Email: hello@greensborocatholic.com; Web: greensborocatholic.com. UNCG Catholic Campus Ministry, 500 Stirling St, Greensboro, 27402. Gregg Costanzo, Campus Min.

Wake Forest University, P.O. Box 7204, Reynolda Station, Winston-Salem, 27109. Tel: 336-758-5018; Email: orrej@wfu.edu; Web: wakeforestcatholic.com/. Liz Orr, Dir. Catholic Programming, Tel: 336-758-2507; Rev. Marcel Amadi, Catholic Campus Min.

Western Carolina University, Catholic Student Center, Speedwell Rd, P.O. Box 2766, Cullowhee, 28723-0364. Tel: 828-293-9374; Fax: 828-262-3721 ; Email: wcucatholic@gmail.com; Web: wcucatholic.org/. Deacon Matthew Newsome, Catholic Campus Min.

[L] RETREAT CENTERS

STONEVILLE. *St. Francis Springs Prayer Center*, 477 Grogan Rd., Stoneville, 27048. Tel: 336-573-3751; Fax: 336-573-3752; Email: ann@stfrancissprings.com; Web: www.stfrancissprings.com. Revs. Louis Canino, O.F.M.; David Hyman, O.F.M.

[M] REFLECTION CENTERS

HAMPTONVILLE. *Well of Mercy Inc.*, 181 Mercy Ln., Hamptonville, 27020. Tel: 704-539-5449; Fax: 704-539-4487; Email: mercy@wellofmercy.org; Web: www.wellofmercy.org. Ms. Sandra O'Brien, Dir. Retreats and psycho-spiritual development programs. Tot Asst. Annually 780; Total Staff 10.

MAGGIE VALLEY. *Living Waters Catholic Reflection Center*, 103 Living Waters Ln., Maggie Valley, 28751. Tel: 828-926-3833; Fax: 828-926-1997; Email: lwcrc@bellsouth.net; Web: www.catholicretreat.org. Sr. Frances Marie Grady, S.C.L., Dir. Retreats, days of recollection & continuing education.

[N] HISPANIC MINISTRY

CHARLOTTE. *Diocesan Hispanic Ministry*, 1123 S. Church St., 28203. Tel: 704-370-3269; Fax: 704-370-3291; Email: fmelo@charlottediocese.org. Very Rev. Fidel C. Melo, V.H., Vicar for Hispanic Ministry; Rev. Julio C. Dominguez, Hispanic Min. Coord.; Deacons Dario Garcia Ospina; Enedino S. Aquino; Dario Garcia.

[O] CONFERENCE CENTERS

HICKORY. *Catholic Conference Center*, 1551 Trinity Ln., Hickory, 28602-9247. Tel: 828-327-7441; Fax: 828-327-0872; Email: info@catholicconference.org; Web: www.catholicconference.org. Deacon Scott D. Gilfillan, Dir.; Cathy Webb, Business Mgr.

[P] MISCELLANEOUS

CHARLOTTE. *Catholic Diocese of Charlotte Advancement Corporation*, c/o Finance Department: 1123 S. Church St., 28203. Tel: 704-370-3313; Email: billw@charlottediocese.org. William G. Weldon, CPA, C.F.O.

Catholic Diocese of Charlotte Housing Corp., 1123 S. Church St., 28203. Tel: 704-370-3248; Fax: 704-971-4312; Email: cdchc@charlottediocese.org; Web: charlottediocese.org/housing/. Gerard C. Carter, Ph.D., Vice Pres.; William G. Weldon, CPA, Treas.; Adriel Cardenas, Dir. Develops housing facilities and services for seniors and individuals with special needs. Units 200.

Charlotte Catholic Women's Group, 1123 S. Church St., 28203. Tel: 704-370-3210; Email: rkarnsparger@charlottediocese.org; Web: www.charlottecatholicwomensgroup.org. Connie Hudack, Pres.; Very Rev. Roger K. Arnsparger, V.E., Chap.

DL Catholic, Inc., c/o Finance Department, 1123 S. Church St., 28203. William G. Weldon, CPA, Contact Person.

**MiraVia*, 3737 Weona Ave., 28209. Tel: 704-525-4673; Fax: 704-521-2751; Email: info@mira-via.org; Web: www.mira-via.org. Jeannie Wray, Exec. Dir. Long-term maternity and aftercare services for single, pregnant women, with their babies.

Triad Catholic Schools Foundation, 1123 S. Church St., 28203-4003. Tel: 800-560-6311; Tel: 704-370-3303; Fax: 704-370-3398; Email: RPerez@charlottediocese.org. Bro. Robert Perez, O.F.M.Cap., Contact Person.

ASHEVILLE. *Catherine McAuley Mercy Foundation, Inc.*, 1201 Patton Ave., Asheville, 28806. Tel: 828-281-2598; Fax: 828-254-4102; Email: sharon@mercyurgentcare.org; Email: lsingleton@mercyurgentcare.org; Web: www.mercyurgentcare.org. Mailing Address: P.O. Box 16367, Asheville, 28816. Tim Johnston, CEO.

BELMONT. **Catherine's House*, 141 Mercy Dr., P.O. Box 1633, Belmont, 28012. Tel: 704-825-9599; Fax: 704-825-2734; Email: janetblaylock@catherineshouseinc.org; Web: www.catherineshouse.org. Ed Paat, Pres. Transitional housing for women and women with children who are homeless.

Holy Angels Foundation, Inc., 6600 Wilkinson Blvd., Belmont, 28012. Tel: 704-825-4161; Fax: 704-825-0401; Email: info@holyangelsnc.org; Web: www.holyangelsnc.org/. Mailing Address: P.O. Box 710, Belmont, 28012-0710. Mrs. Regina P. Moody, M.Ed., Pres.

Holy Angels, Inc., 6600 Wilkinson Blvd., Belmont, 28012. P.O. Box 710, Belmont, 28012-0710. Tel: 704-825-4161; Fax: 704-825-0401. Mrs. Regina P. Moody, M.Ed., Pres. Total Bed Capacity 35; Tot Asst. Annually 125; Total Staff 175.

Holy Angels, Inc. Camp Hope Recreational opportunities for individuals with developmental disabilities.

Holy Angels, Inc. Carrabaun, 6600 Wilkinson Blvd., P.O. Box 710, Belmont, 28012-0710. Tel: 704-825-4161; Fax: 704-825-0401; Email: info@holyangelsnc.org; Web: holyangelsnc.org. Mrs. Regina P. Moody, M.Ed., Pres. Adult group home. Bed Capacity 3.

Holy Angels, Inc. Cherub Cafe, Gifts & Candy Bouquets, Tel: 704-825-0414; Fax: 704-825-0401. (Age 18+); Job coaching, work options.

Holy Angels, Inc. Gary Home, 6600 Wilkinson Blvd., P.O. Box 710, Belmont, 28012-0710. Tel: 704-825-4161; Fax: 704-825-0401; Email: info@holyangelsnc.org; Web: www.holyangelsnc.org. Mrs. Regina P. Moody, M.Ed., Pres. Adult group home. Bed Capacity 3.

Holy Angels, Inc. Great Adventures Social Club, 6600 Wilkinson Blvd., P.O. Box 710, Belmont, 28012-0710. Tel: 704-825-4161; Fax: 704-825-0401 ; Email: info@holyangelsnc.org; Web: www.holyangelsnc.org. Mrs. Regina P. Moody, M.Ed., Pres. Adults with Intellectual Development Disabilities.

Holy Angels, Inc. Lakewood, 6600 Wilkinson Blvd., P.O. Box 710, Belmont, 28012-0710. Tel: 704-825-4161; Fax: 704-825-0401; Email: info@holyangelsnc.org; Web: www.holyangelsnc.org. Mrs. Regina P. Moody, M.Ed., Pres. Adult group home. Bed Capacity 4.

Holy Angels, Inc. Life Choices, Market Street, Cramerton, 28032. Tel: 704-825-4161; Fax: 704-825-0401; Email: info@holyangelsnc.org; Web: www.holyangelsnc.org. P.O. Box 710, Belmont, 28012-0710. Mrs. Regina P. Moody, M.Ed., Pres. Total Staff 5; Day Supports 25; Day Activity 25; Total Assisted 50.

Holy Angels, Inc. Morrow Center, Belmont. Tel: 704-825-4161; Fax: 704-825-0401; Email: info@holyangelsnc.org; Web: www.holyangelsnc.org. 6600 Wilkinson Blvd., P.O. Box 710, Belmont, 28012-0710. Mrs. Regina P. Moody, M.Ed., Pres. (Children 0-20) Bed Capacity 45.

Holy Angels, Inc. South Point, 6600 Wilkinson Blvd., P.O. Box 710, Belmont, 28012-0710. Tel: 704-825-4161; Fax: 704-825-0401; Email: info@holyangelsnc.org; Web: www.holyangelsnc.org. Mrs. Regina P. Moody, M.Ed., Pres. Adult group home. Bed Capacity 5.

Holy Angels, Inc. Supported Living (Age 18+).

House of Mercy, Inc., 100 McAuley Circle, P.O. Box 808, Belmont, 28012. Tel: 704-825-4711; Fax: 704-825-9976; Email: houseofmercync@gmail.com; Web: www.thehouseofmercy.org. Emily Sharpe, CEO. Provides a home for persons living with AIDS in the advanced stages who have no other housing alternative in an 11 county region. Bed Capacity 6.

Mercy Community Housing North Carolina (MCHNC), 6531 Wilkinson Blvd., Belmont, 28012. Tel: 404-873-3887; Fax: 877-693-2333; Email: pgrant@mercyhousing.org; Web: www.mercyhousing.org. Paula Grant, Vice Pres.

Mercy Housing, South East, Inc., 6531 Wilkinson Blvd., Belmont, 28012. Tel: 404-873-3887; Fax: 877-693-2333; Email: pgrant@mercyhousing.org; Web: www.mercyhousing.org. Paula Grant, Contact Person. Purpose: provide housing and supportive services to low income, special needs populations and seniors.

Mercy Place Belmont, 6531 Wilkinson Blvd., Belmont, 28012. Tel: 404-873-3887; Fax: 877-698-2333; Email: pgrant@mercyhousing.org. Paula Grant, Vice Pres.; Patricia O'Roark, Legal Affairs Mgr. Provides housing and support services for very low-income seniors.

Sisters of Mercy of North Carolina Foundation, Inc., 100 McAuley Cir., P.O. Box 987, Belmont, 28012. Tel: 704-366-0087; Fax: 704-366-8850; Email: cheryl@sistersofmercyfoundation.org; Web: www.somncfdn.org. Ms. Cheryl Brownd, Exec.; Sisters Linda Falquette, R.S.M., Bd. Chm.; Paulette Williams, R.S.M., Vice Pres.

Sisters of Mercy of the Americas, South Central Community, Inc., Mercy Administration Center, 101 Mercy Dr., Belmont, 28012-2898. Tel: 704-829-5260; Fax: 704-829-5267; Email: support@mercysc.org; Web: www.mercysc.org. Sr. Jane Hotstream, R.S.M., Pres.

South Central FIDES, Inc., 101 Mercy Dr., Belmont, 28012. Tel: 704-829-5260; Fax: 704-829-5267; Email: jhardin@mercysc.org. Sr. Mary Rose Bumpus, R.S.M., Pres.

GASTONIA. **Seton Media House, Inc.*, 1520 S. York St., Gastonia, 28053. Email: setonhouse@aol.com; Email: pwilliams@mercysc.org. Richard G. Hoefling, Pres. & CEO. Purpose: Distribution of printed materials reflective of Catholic teaching to Catholic schools and religious educ. programs at no cost to students, family or school.

GREENSBORO. *Franciscan Center*, 233 N. Greene St., Greensboro, 27401. Tel: 336-273-2554; Fax: 336-273-2441; Email: franciscancenter233@gmail.com; Web: www.catholicgiftshoponline.com. Revs. Louis Canino, O.F.M., Dir.; David Hyman, O.F.M.

Room At The Inn, Inc., 734 Park Avenue, Greensboro, 27405. Tel: 336-996-3788; Fax: 336-275-9522; Email: RoomAtTheInn@triad.rr.com; Web: www.roominn.org. P.O. Box 13936, Greensboro, 27415. O. Albert Hodges, Pres.

Society of St. Vincent De Paul, 109 W. Smith St., Greensboro, 27401. Tel: 336-272-0336; Tel: 336-210-3745. Financial assistance, furniture and appliances.

HUNTERSVILLE. **Be Not Afraid, Inc.*, 8800 Glenside St., Huntersville. Tel: 704-651-9255; Email: sandy.buck@benotafraid.net; Web: www.benotafraid.net. Sandy Buck, Dir.; Tracy Winsor, Admin. Coord. Comprehensive support for parents carrying to term following a prenatal diagnosis, and Catholic service development and mentoring.

SALISBURY. *Cursillos in Christianity*, 218 W. Thomas St., Salisbury, 28144.

RELIGIOUS INSTITUTES OF MEN REPRESENTED IN THE DIOCESE

For further details refer to the corresponding bracketed number in the Religious Institutes of Men or Women section.

[0200]—*Benedictine Monks* (Belmont, NC)—O.S.B.
[0470]—*The Capuchin Friars Province of the Stigmata*—O.F.M.Cap.
[1330]—*Congregation of the Mission* (Eastern Prov.)—C.M.
[0480]—*Conventual Franciscans* (Union City, NJ)—O.F.M.Conv.
[0520]—*Franciscan Friars* (New York, NY)—O.F.M.
[0690]—*Jesuit Fathers and Brothers* (Maryland Prov.)—S.J.
[0920]—*Oblates of St. Francis De Sales* (Wilmington-Philadelphia)—O.S.F.S.
[1070]—*Redemptorist Fathers* (Richmond Vice Prov.)—C.Ss.R.

RELIGIOUS INSTITUTES OF WOMEN REPRESENTED IN THE DIOCESE

[2980]—*Congregation de Notre Dame*—C.N.D.
[3080]—*Congregation of Our Lady, Help of the Clergy*—C.L.H.C.
[1110]—*Dominican Sisters of St. Catherine of Siena*—O.P.
[1840]—*Grey Nuns of the Sacred Heart*—G.N.S.H.
[2470]—*Maryknoll Sisters*—M.M.
[2710]—*Missionaries of Charity*—M.C.
[2790]—*Missionary Servants of the Most Blessed Trinity*—M.S.B.T.
[3640]—*Poor Servants of the Mother of God*—S.M.G.
[2970]—*School Sisters of Notre Dame*—S.S.N.D.
[1680]—*School Sisters of St. Francis* (Milwaukee, WI)—O.S.F.
[0480]—*Sisters of Charity* (Leavenworth, KS)—S.C.L.
[0590]—*Sisters of Charity of Saint Elizabeth, Convent Station*—S.C.
[0655]—*Sisters of Charity of Saint Vincent de Paul*—S.C.V.
[]—*Sisters of Mercy of the Americas* (South Central Community, Inc.)—R.S.M.
[]—*Sisters of Mercy of the Americas* (Mid-Atlantic Community)—R.S.M.
[]—*Sisters of Mercy of the Americas* (West Midwest Community)—R.S.M.
[]—*Sisters of Providence*—S.P.
[]—*Sisters of St. Francis* (Philadelphia, PA)—O.S.F.
[3893]—*Sisters of St. Joseph* (Chestnut Hill, PA)—S.S.J.

An asterisk (*) denotes an organization that has established tax-exempt status directly with the IRS and is not covered by the USCCB Group Ruling.

Diocese of Cheyenne

(Dioecesis Cheyennensis)

Most Reverend

STEVEN R. BIEGLER, D.D., S.T.L.

Bishop of Cheyenne; ordained July 9, 1993; appointed Bishop of Cheyenne March 16, 2017; installed June 5, 2017. *Office: 2121 Capitol Ave., Cheyenne, WY 82001.*

Most Reverend

JOSEPH HART, D.D.

Retired Bishop of Cheyenne; ordained May 1, 1956; appointed July 1, 1976; appointed Titular Bishop of Timida Regia; episcopal ordination August 31, 1976; installed June 12, 1978; retired September 26, 2001. *Res.: P.O. Box 1468, Cheyenne, WY 82003.*

ESTABLISHED AUGUST 2, 1887.

Square Miles 97,548.

Comprises the State of Wyoming and Yellowstone National Park.

For legal titles of parishes and diocesan institutions, consult the Chancery Office.

Chancery Office: 2121 Capitol Ave., P.O. Box 1468, Cheyenne, WY 82003-1468. Tel: 307-638-1530; Fax: 307-637-7936.

Web: www.dioceseofcheyenne.org

Email: dmcintyre@dioceseofcheyenne.org

STATISTICAL OVERVIEW

Personnel	
Bishop	1
Retired Bishops	1
Priests: Diocesan Active in Diocese	37
Priests: Diocesan Active Outside Diocese	3
Priests: Retired, Sick or Absent	13
Number of Diocesan Priests	53
Religious Priests in Diocese	7
Total Priests in Diocese	60
Extern Priests in Diocese	7
Ordinations:	
Diocesan Priests	2
Permanent Deacons in Diocese	31
Total Sisters	10
Parishes	
Parishes	37
With Resident Pastor:	
Resident Diocesan Priests	26
Resident Religious Priests	1
Without Resident Pastor:	
Administered by Priests	4
Missions	34
Closed Parishes	1
Professional Ministry Personnel:	
Sisters	4
Lay Ministers	56
Welfare	
Homes for the Aged	2
Total Assisted	109
Residential Care of Children	1
Total Assisted	250
Other Institutions	2
Educational	
Diocesan Students in Other Seminaries	2
Total Seminarians	2
Elementary Schools, Diocesan and Parish	6
Total Students	935
Catechesis/Religious Education:	
High School Students	660
Elementary Students	3,101
Total Students under Catholic Instruction	4,698
Teachers in the Diocese:	
Sisters	2
Lay Teachers	103
Vital Statistics	
Receptions into the Church:	
Infant Baptism Totals	631
Minor Baptism Totals	86
Adult Baptism Totals	74
Received into Full Communion	92
First Communions	814
Confirmations	728
Marriages:	
Catholic	129
Interfaith	48
Total Marriages	177
Deaths	492
Total Catholic Population	50,138
Total Population	573,720

Former Bishops—Rt. Revs. MAURICE F. BURKE, D.D., cons. Oct. 28, 1887; transferred to the See of St. Joseph, MO, June 19, 1893; died March 17, 1923; THOMAS M. LENIHAN, D.D., cons. Feb. 24, 1897; died Dec. 15, 1901; Most Revs. JAMES J. KEANE, D.D., cons. Bishop of Cheyenne Oct. 28, 1902; raised to the archiepiscopal dignity and transferred to Archdiocese of Dubuque, Aug. 11, 1911; died Aug. 2, 1929; PATRICK A. MCGOVERN, D.D., LL.D., ord. Aug. 18, 1895; asst. at the Pontifical Throne; appt. Jan. 19, 1912; cons. April 11, 1912; died Nov. 8, 1951; HUBERT M. NEWELL, D.D., LL.D., ord. June 15, 1930; appt. Coadjutor Aug. 2, 1947; cons. Sept. 24, 1947; succeeded to the See Nov. 8, 1951; retired Jan. 3, 1978; died Sept. 8, 1987; HUBERT JOSEPH HART, D.D., ord. May 1, 1956; appt. Titular Bishop of Timida Regia July 1, 1976; cons. Aug. 31, 1976; installed June 12, 1978; retired Sept. 26, 2001; DAVID L. RICKEN, D.D., J.C.L., ord. Sept. 12, 1980; appt. Coadjutor Bishop of Cheyenne Dec. 14, 1999; Episcopal Ordination Jan. 6, 2000; succeeded to See Sept. 26, 2001; installed Bishop of Green Bay Aug. 28, 2008.; PAUL D. ETIENNE, D.D., S.T.L., ord. June 27, 1992; appt. Bishop of Cheyenne Oct. 19, 2009; episcopal ord. and installed Dec. 9, 2009; appt. Archbishop of Anchorage Oct. 4, 2016; installed Nov. 9, 2016.

Chancery Office—2121 Capitol Ave., P.O. Box 1468, Cheyenne, 82003-1468. Tel: 307-638-1530; Fax: 307-637-7936.

Vicar General—Mailing Address: P.O. Box 1468, Cheyenne, 82003. Tel: 307-638-1530. Very Rev. CARL J. GALLINGER.

Chancellor—Mailing Address: P.O. Box 1468, Cheyenne, 82003-1468. Tel: 307-638-1530. PATRICIA A. LOEHRER, M.A., M.C.A.

Judicial Vicar—Rev. THOMAS E. CRONKLETON JR., J.C.D., Mailing Address: P.O. Box 1468, Cheyenne, 82003-1468. Tel: 307-638-1530; Tel: 866-790-0014; Fax: 307-637-7936.

Adjutant Judicial Vicar—Rev. THOMAS R. KADERA, J.C.L., Mailing Address: P.O. Box 1468, Cheyenne, 82003-1468.

Vicar for Retired and Disabled Clergy—VACANT.

College of Consultors—Most Rev. STEVEN BIEGLER; Very Rev. CARL GALLINGER; Rev. THOMAS E. CRONKLETON JR., J.C.D.; Very Revs. SAMUEL W. HAYES; AUGUST KOEUNE; GARY J. RUZICKA; Revs. ROBERT SPAULDING; STEVEN TITUS.

Presbyteral Council—Most Rev. STEVEN BIEGLER; Very Rev. CARL J. GALLINGER; Rev. THOMAS E. CRONKLETON JR., J.C.D.; Very Revs. SAMUEL W. HAYES; JAMES HEISER; Rev. WILLIAM HILL; Very Revs. AUGUST KOEUNE; GARY J. RUZICKA; Revs. ROBERT SPAULDING; EMILIO CABRERA, (Colombia); HIEP NGUYEN.

Vicars Forane—Very Revs. AUGUST KOEUNE, Cheyenne Deanery; GARY RUZICKA, Casper Deanery; SAMUEL HAYES, Rock Springs Deanery; CLIFF JACOBSON, Sheridan Deanery; JAMES HEISER, Thermopolis Deanery.

Finance Officer—MR. JEFFREY V. NIETERS, Finance Officer, Mailing Address: P.O. Box 1468, Cheyenne, 82003-1468. Tel: 307-638-1530; Fax: 307-637-7936.

Finance Council—Most Rev. STEVEN BIEGLER. Ex Officios, Voting: Very Rev. AUGUST KOEUNE; CHARLES HARKINS; CONNIE JANNEY; Rev. THOMAS E. CRONKLETON JR., J.C.D.; Very Rev. CARL GALLINGER. Appointed Members, Voting: MR. AARON COURTNEY; LINDY PASKETT; FRED HARRISON.

Diocesan Pastoral Council—VACANT.

Tribunal Office—All marriage correspondence are to be directed to: *Mailing Address: The Tribunal Office, P.O. Box 1468, Cheyenne, 82003-1468.* Tel: 307-638-1530; Tel: 866-790-0014; Fax: 307-637-7936.

Judicial Vicar—Rev. THOMAS E. CRONKLETON JR., J.C.D.

Adjutant Judicial Vicar—Rev. THOMAS R. KADERA, J.C.L.

Tribunal Case Instructor—PAMELA MILLER.

Ecclesiastical Notary—MARIA HENSCHEL.

Promoter of Justice—DIANE L. BARR, J.D., J.C.D., Ph. D.

Judges—Revs. THOMAS E. CRONKLETON JR., J.C.D.; THOMAS R. KADERA, J.C.L.

Defenders of the Bond—Very Revs. SAMUEL HAYES; CARL GALLINGER; Rev. JOHN E. LIST, J.C.L.; MRS.

ROBERTA SMALL, J.D., J.C.L.; Rev. ROBERT RODGERS, J.C.L.; MRS. CONNIE KASSAHN.

Advocates—SUSAN SIMON; BONNIE BAUMBERGER; Deacon KIM CARROLL; Very Rev. JAMES HEISER; Sr. GLADYS NOREEN, O.S.B.; DORENE MCINTYRE; MR. CAMERON SMITH; TAMRA HENDRICKSON; MRS. STEPHANIE DENNING; DONALD CLAUNCH; SHEREEN KUHBACHER.

Diocesan Administrative Offices and Boards

Development—MR. MATTHEW N. POTTER, C.F.P., C.I.M.A., Dir.; MRS. DENISE HAWKINS, Exec. Asst., P.O. Box 1468, Cheyenne, 82003-1468. Tel: 307-638-1530; Tel: 866-790-0014.

Education Office—VACANT, P.O. Box 1468, Cheyenne, 82003-1468. Tel: 307-638-1530; JOANN ANDERSON, Media Consultant, St. Rose of Lima, 605 E. 22nd Ave., Torrington, 82240. Tel: 307-532-5556; Fax: 307-534-2329.

Diocesan Schools Advisory Group—Most Rev. STEVEN BIEGLER; Revs. WILLIAM HILL; LOUIS M. SHEA; GLENN WHEWELL; Very Revs. AUGUST KOEUNE; CLIFFORD JACOBSON; Revs. KEVIN BARRETT; THOMAS INNYA GEORGE, (India); Very Rev. GARY RUZICKA; LINDA MARCOS, Prin. Holy Spirit School; NICHOLAS SCHAFER, Prin. St. Margaret School; PATRICK LANE, Prin. St. Mary's School; CYNDY NOVOTNY, Prin. St. Anthony Tri-Parish Catholic School; MARY LEGLER, Prin. Holy Name School; MRS. VANESSA GEMAR, Prin. John Paul II School.

Pastoral Ministries—Mailing Address: P.O. Box 1468, Cheyenne, 82003-1468. Tel: 307-638-1530; Fax: 307-637-7936. VACANT, Dir.; MARIA WARD, Asst. Dir.

Human Resources—TAMMY SKALA, Dir., P.O. Box 1468, Cheyenne, 82003-1468. Tel: 307-638-1530; Fax: 307-637-7936.

Legislative Liaison—Deacon MICHAEL LEMAN, P.O. Box 1468, Cheyenne, 82003. Tel: 307-638-1530; Fax: 307-638-4818.

Beginning Experience for Divorced or Widowed—CURTIS WEST, Mailing Address: P.O. Box 9953, Casper, 82609. Tel: 307-463-2677.

Marriage Encounter—MARIA WARD.

Natural Family Planning—MARIA WARD.

Respect Life Catholic Pro-Life Ministry—Deacon MICHAEL LEMAN; MARIA WARD.

Retrouvaille, Ministry for Hurting Marriages—MARIA WARD.

Newspaper "Wyoming Catholic Register"—Editorial Advisory Board: MR. MATTHEW N. POTTER, C.F.P., C.I.M.A.; MRS. DENISE HAWKINS; Deacon MICHAEL LEMAN; MARIA WARD; PAMELA MILLER.

Stewardship Committee—Deacon DOUG VLCHEK; JANET MATERI; CAREY HARTMANN; ROXIE HARRIS; VICKIE JOHNSTON.

Vocation Office—Rev. STEVEN TITUS, Mailing Address: Diocese of Cheyenne, P.O. Box 1468, Cheyenne, 82003. Tel: 307-638-1530; Fax: 307-638-4818.

Youth Office—Mailing Address: P.O. Box 1468, Cheyenne, 82003-1468. Tel: 307-638-1530; Fax: 307-637-7936. VACANT, Dir. Pastoral Ministries; MARIA WARD, Asst. Dir. Pastoral Ministries.

Other Diocesan Boards, Councils and Programs

Diocese of Cheyenne, Board of Directors—Most Rev. STEVEN BIEGLER; Very Revs. AUGUST KOEUNE; CARL GALLINGER; CONNIE JANNEY; CHARLES HARKINS.

Living & Giving in Christ: Diocesan Appeal—MR. MATTHEW N. POTTER, C.F.P., C.I.M.A.; MR. JEFFREY V. NIETERS, Mailing Address: P.O. Box 1468, Cheyenne, 82003-1468. Tel: 307-638-1530; Fax: 307-637-7936.

Boy Scouts—CHRIS JONES, St. Margaret, 618 E. Fremont, Riverton, 82501. Tel: 307-856-6986; Email: plugintothespirit@gmail.com.

Building Committee—Most Rev. STEVEN BIEGLER; Very Rev. GARY RUZICKA; RANDY BYERS; HERBERT W. STOUGHTON, Ph.D., Chm.; MR. JEFFREY V. NIETERS, Sec.; PATRICIA A. LOEHRER, M.A., M.C.A.; Deacon DAVID ZELENKA; Very Rev. CARL GALLINGER.

Catholic Relief Services—

Clergy Continuing Education Grants—Rev. WILLIAM HILL, Mailing Address: Holy Spirit Catholic Community, 116 Broadway, Rock Springs, 82901.

Confraternity of Christian Doctrine—P.O. Box 1468, Cheyenne, 82003-1468. Tel: 307-638-1530. VACANT.

Council of Religious—Sr. RUTH ANN HEHN, S.C.L.

Cursillo Board—VACANT.

Permanent Diaconate—Deacon JOSEPH BUSH, 2345 Larkspur Ct., Cody, 82414.

Diaconate Formation Director—Deacon JOSEPH SANDRINI, Mailing Address: P.O. Box 615, Newcastle, 82701-0615.

Housing—MELISSA CASTILLO, Admin., St. Anthony Manor, 211 E. 6th, Casper, 82601. Tel: 307-237-0843; DANIEL SCHMIDT, Admin., Holy Trinity Manor, 2516 E. 18th St., Cheyenne, 82001. Tel: 307-778-8850.

June Priests' Retreat—Rev. STEVEN TITUS, Mailing Address: P.O. Box 1468, Cheyenne, 82003. Tel: 307-638-1530; Fax: 307-638-4818.

Office of Worship—Rev. ROBERT SPAULDING.

Office of Hispanic Ministry—Rev. RAY RODRIGUEZ.

Propagation of the FaithP.O. Box 1468, Cheyenne, 82003-1468. Very Rev. CARL GALLINGER.

Pastoral Ministries—Mailing Address: P.O. Box 1468, Cheyenne, 82003-1468. Tel: 307-638-1530; Fax: 307-637-7936. VACANT, Dir.; MARIA WARD, Asst. Dir.

St. Joseph's Society: Clergy Retirement Fund of the Diocese of Cheyenne—Most Rev. STEVEN BIEGLER; Revs. THOMAS OGG, Vice Pres., (Retired); MICHAEL CARR, (Retired); Very Rev. SAMUEL W. HAYES; Revs. ROBERT RODGERS, J.C.L., Sec.; THOMAS E. CRONKLETON JR., J.C.D., Pres.; JAMES SCHUMACHER; ANDREW KINSTETTER; PHILIP VASKE; MR. LEO RILEY, Admin.; MR. MATTHEW N. POTTER, C.F.P., C.I.M.A., Dir. Devel.

Victim Assistance Coordinator—PATRICIA A. LOEHRER, M.A., M.C.A., Tel: 307-638-1530; Email: ploehrer@dioceseofcheyenne.org.

CLERGY, PARISHES, MISSIONS AND PAROCHIAL SCHOOLS

CITY OF CHEYENNE

(LARAMIE COUNTY)

1—ST. MARY'S CATHEDRAL (1868) [CEM]
2107 Capitol Ave., 82001. Tel: 307-635-9261; Fax: 307-635-5723; Email: stewardship@stmarycathedral.com; Web: www.stmarycathedral.com. Mailing Address: P.O. Box 1268, 82003-1268. Very Rev. August Koeune; Revs. Andrew Kinstetter; Jaimon Dominic, (India); Deacon Carroll Schell.
School—St. Mary's Cathedral School, (Grades PreK-8), Tel: 307-638-9268; Fax: 307-635-2847; Email: plane@stmaryswyo.org; Web: stmaryswyo.org. Patrick Lane, Prin. Lay Teachers 26; Students 232.
Catechesis Religious Program—100 West 21st St., 82001. Email: rcudney@stmarycathedral.com; Email: Bhart@stmarycathedral.com. Kara Clay, D.R.E.; Renee Cudney, D.R.E.; Becky Hart, D.R.E. Students 222.

2—HOLY TRINITY (1957)
1836 Hot Springs Ave., 82001-5337.
Tel: 307-632-5872; Fax: 307-632-1810; Web: www.holytrinitycheyenne.org. Revs. Thomas E. Cronkleton Jr., J.C.D., Email: frtom@holytrinitycheyenne.org; Joseph P. Fraher, In Res., (Retired); Steven Titus, In Res.; Deacons David Zelenka; Michael Leman.
Catechesis Religious Program—Email: holytrinitycheyenne@gmail.com. Amy Deibert, Pastoral Min./Coord.; Ms. Molly Spiering, Pastoral Min./Coord. Students 258.

3—ST. JOSEPH'S (1929) (Hispanic)
603 House Ave., 82007. Tel: 307-634-4625; Email: cgallinger@dioceseofcheyenne.org; Web: www.stjosephscheyenne.org. Mailing Address: P.O. Box 1141, 82003-1141. Very Rev. Carl J. Gallinger; Deacon Thomas Niemann.
Office—Office: 314 E. 6th St., 82007.
Res.: 515 House, 82007.
Catechesis Religious Program—Email: Dav63impala@yahoo.com. Ambee Gregorio, Dir. of Faith Formation; Eva Estorga, Regional Coord. Hispanic Ministry. Students 185.

OUTSIDE CITY OF CHEYENNE

BUFFALO, JOHNSON CO., ST. JOHN THE BAPTIST (1885) [CEM]
532 N. Lobban, Buffalo, 82834. Tel: 307-684-7268; Email: sjbc532@gmail.com; Web: www.sjbc-buffalo.com. Rev. Peter Johnson.
Catechesis Religious Program—Tel: 307-278-0193. Carol Gagliano, D.R.E. Students 115.
Missions—St. Mary—Clearmont, Johnson Co. 82834.
St. Hubert, Kaycee, Johnson Co. 82834.

CASPER, NATRONA CO.

1—ST. ANTHONY OF PADUA (1903)
604 S. Center St., Casper, 82601. Tel: 307-266-2666; Email: pastor@stanthonyscasper.org; Email: finance@stanthonyscasper.org; Email: secretary@stanthonyscasper.org; Web: stanthonyscasper.org. Rev. Kevin S. Barrett; Deacon David Johnson; Ms. LaVonne Carlson, Business Mgr.; Mrs. Sheila Wiggins, D.R.E.; Clareesa King, Music Min.; Ms. Trina Medina, Sec.
School—St. Anthony Tri-Parish School, (Grades PreK-8), 1145 W. 20th St., Casper, 82604.
Tel: 307-234-2873; Fax: 307-235-4946; Web: sascasper.com. Cyndy Novotny, Prin. Clergy 3; Lay Teachers 22; Students 264.
Catechesis Religious Program—Email: dre226@outlook.com. Mrs. Sheila Wiggins, D.R.E.; Jansen Bagwell, Dean Students. Students 65.

2—OUR LADY OF FATIMA (1954)
1401 CY Ave., Casper, 82604. Tel: 307-265-5586; Email: church@fatimaincasper.org; Web: www.fatimaincasper.org. Rev. Thomas Innya George, (India).
Catechesis Religious Program—Tel: 307-473-2076; Email: olfreligioused@outlook.com. Carol O'Hearn, C.R.E. Students 90.

3—SAINT PATRICK'S (1963) (Irish)
400 Country Club Rd., Casper, 82609.
Tel: 307-235-5535; Email: msnyderstpat@gmail.com; Web: www.stpatricks-casper.com. P.O. Box 51010, Casper, 82605-1010. Very Rev. Gary J. Ruzicka; Rev. Hiep Nguyen, Parochial Vicar.
Catechesis Religious Program—Email: beth@stpatricks-casper.com. Beth Peterson-Detrick, D.R.E. Students 222.

CODY, PARK CO., ST. ANTHONY (1942)
1333 Monument St., Cody, 82414-3406.
Tel: 307-587-3388; Email: apadua@stanthonycody.org; Web: www.stanthonycody.org. Very Rev. Vernon F. Clark; Revs. Brian J. Hess, Parochial Vicar; Charles Heston Joseph, Parochial Vicar; Deacons Gerald Boydston; Joseph Bush; Richard Moser.
Catechesis Religious Program—Tel: 307-587-2567; Email: info@stanthonycody.org. Tom Caudle, D.R.E. Students 147.
Missions—Tel: 307-587-3388.
St. Therese, 1406 State, Meeteetse, Park Co. 82433.
Our Lady of the Valley, 35 Rd. 1 AFW, Clark, Park Co. 82435.

DOUGLAS, CONVERSE CO., ST. JAMES (1907)
311 S. 5th St., Douglas, 82633-1500.
Tel: 307-358-2338; Email: stjames@stjamesdouglas.com; Web: www.stjamesdouglas.org. P.O. Box 1500, Douglas, 82633. Rev. Demetrio Penascoza, (Philippines).
Catechesis Religious Program—302 S. 5th St., Douglas, 82633. Email: faithformation@stjamesdouglas.com. Nicole Boner, D.R.E. Students 86.
Mission—Our Lady of Lourdes, Glendo, 82213.

EVANSTON, UINTA CO., ST. MARY MAGDALEN (1878) [JC]
849 Center St., Evanston, 82930. Tel: 307-789-2189; Fax: 307-313-4730; Email: stmmagdalen@questoffice.net; Web: www.stmmagdalen.moonfruit.com. Mailing Address: Box 163, Evanston, 82931-0163. Rev. Jesryll Intes.
Catechesis Religious Program—825 Center St., Evanston, 82930. Students 68.
Mission—St. Helen, 37117 I-80 Business Loop, Fort Bridger, Uinta Co. 82933. Tel: 307-333-3937; Email: intesjw@yahoo.com. P.O. Box 183, Fort Bridger, 82933.
Catechesis Religious Program—Students 15.

GILLETTE, CAMPBELL CO., ST. MATTHEW'S (1926) [JC]
1000 Butler Spaeth Rd., Gillette, 82716.
Tel: 307-682-3319; Email: stmatthews@stmatthewswy.org; Web: www.stmatthewswy.weconnect.com. Very Rev. Clifford Jacobson; Rev. Augustine Carrillo.
School—John Paul II Catholic School, (Grades PreSchool-8), Tel: 307-686-4114; Web: johnpauliicatholicschool.com. Mrs. Vanessa Gemar, Prin. Lay Teachers 20; Students (K-6) 197.
Catechesis Religious Program—Ms. Christie Hloucal, D.R.E.; Mrs. Theresa Meuer, Youth MIn. Students 313.
Missions—Blessed Sacrament—624 Wright Blvd., Wright, Campbell Co. 82732.
St. Patrick, 216 N. Belle Fourche, Moorcroft, Crook Co. 82721.

GLENROCK, CONVERSE CO., ST. LOUIS CATHOLIC CHURCH (1920) [JC]
601 S. 5th St., Glenrock, 82637-0027.
Tel: 307-436-9529; Email: church@stlouisglenrock.org. P.O. Box 27, Glenrock, 82637. Rev. Robert L. Fox; Deacon Kevin Halvorsen.
Catechesis Religious Program—Students 30.

GREEN RIVER, SWEETWATER CO., IMMACULATE CONCEPTION (1884) [JC]
Mailing Address: 900 Hitching Post Dr., Green River, 82935. Tel: 307-875-2184; Tel: 307-875-2441; Email: icc@wyoming.com. Rev. Denis D'Souza; Deacon Wes Nash.
Catechesis Religious Program—Students 110.

GREYBULL, BIG HORN CO., CHURCH OF THE SACRED

HEART (1919)
544 5th Ave. N., Greybull, 82426-0231.
Tel: 307-765-2438; Fax: 307-765-2249; Email: sacredheartgreybull@gmail.com; Web: sacredheartgreybull.com. P.O. Box 231, Greybull, 82426-0231. Rev. Glen Szczechowski.
Catechesis Religious Program—Students 50.
GUERNSEY, PLATTE CO., ST. ANTHONY'S (1969)
397 W. Whalen St., Guernsey, 82214-0430.
Tel: 307-836-2586; Email: stanthonyguernsey@embarqmail.com. P.O. Box 430, Guernsey, 82214-0430. Revs. Raymond B. Moss; Andrew Duncan.
Res.: 96 N. Kansas, P.O. Box 430, Guernsey, 82214-0430.
Catechesis Religious Program—Tel: 307-534-5002; Email: sseyfang82214@gmail.com. Sarah Seyfang, D.R.E. Students 26.
JACKSON, TETON CO., OUR LADY OF THE MOUNTAINS (1955) [JC]
201 S. Jackson St., Jackson, 83001-0992.
Tel: 307-733-2516; Email: answers@olmcatholic.org; Web: www.olmcatholic.org. P.O. Box 992, Jackson, 83001. Very Rev. Lucas K. Simango, (Zambia); Rev. Philip Vanderlin, O.S.B.; Deacons Doug Vlchek; Bill Hill; Harry Flavin; Philip Wanek.
Catechesis Religious Program—Email: sarahbeth@olmcatholic.org. Sarah Beth Barnett, D.R.E. Students 280.
Mission—Holy Family, 78 Friesian Cir., P.O. Box 1036, Thayne, Lincoln Co. 83127.
Chapel—The Chapel of the Sacred Heart, (Grand Teton National Park) Teton Park Rd., Jackson, 83001.
Catechesis Religious Program—Students 38.
KEMMERER, LINCOLN CO., ST. PATRICK'S (1901) [JC] (Italian—Slovak)
65 McGovern Ave., Diamondville, 83116.
Tel: 307-877-4573; Email: stpatrickkemm@yahoo.com. Mailing Address: Box 311, Kemmerer, 83101-0311. Rev. Arulanandu David.
Catechesis Religious Program—Students 69.
Mission—LaBarge Community.
LANDER, FREMONT CO., HOLY ROSARY (1882) [JC]
163 Leedy Rd., Lander, 82520-1047.
Tel: 307-332-4952; Email: eshields4hr@gmail.com; Web: holyrosarylander.org. P.O. Box 1047, Lander, 82520. Rev. James Schumacher; Deacon Rich Miller; Mrs. Eliner Shields, Admin.
Catechesis Religious Program—Mrs. Sarah Susanka, D.R.E. Students 87.
Missions—Church of the Ascension—Ohio St., Hudson, 82515. Tel: 307-332-4952; Email: landerplebisparochus@gmail.com.
St. Brendan, Jeffrey City, Freemont Co.
LARAMIE, ALBANY CO.
1—ST. LAURENCE O'TOOLE (1872) [JC]
319 E. Grand Ave., Laramie, 82070-1045.
Tel: 307-745-3115; Email: slotoole@bresnan.net; Web: www.stlaurenceotoole.org. Mailing Address: 617 S. Fourth St., Laramie, 82070. Rev. David Erickson.
Catechesis Religious Program—Students 35.
2—ST. PAUL'S NEWMAN CENTER (1957)
Mailing Address: Parish, 1800 E. Grand Ave., Laramie, 82070-4316. Tel: 307-745-5461; Email: newman@newmancenter.org; Web: www.newmancenter.org. Rev. Robert Spaulding; Lillie Romeiser, Campus Min.; Anthony Allen, Pastoral Min./Coord.; Thomas Quinlivan, Liturgy Dir.; Sandy Gaddis, Business Mgr.
LOVELL, BIG HORN CO., ST. JOSEPH'S (1979)
1141 Shoshone Ave., Lovell, 82431-0185.
Tel: 307-548-2282; Email: stjosephlovell@gmail.com. P.O. Box 185, Lovell, 82431-0185. Rev. Glen Szczechowski.
Rectory—1161 Shoshone Ave., Lovell, 82431.
Catechesis Religious Program—Students 32.
LUSK, NIOBRARA CO., ST. LEO'S (1911) [JC] (German—Irish)
900 W. Fifth St., Lusk, 82225-0959.
Tel: 307-334-2702; Email: stleochurch@gmail.com. P.O. Box 959, Lusk, 82225-0959. Revs. Raymond B. Moss; Andrew Duncan.
Catechesis Religious Program—Elaine Sednek, D.R.E. Students 11.
NEWCASTLE, WESTON CO., CORPUS CHRISTI (1890) [JC]
19 W. Winthrop, Newcastle, 82701.
Tel: 307-746-4219; Email: corpus@rtconnect.net. Revs. Timothy James Martinson; Hiep Nguyen; Deacons Kenneth Pitlick; Joseph Sandrini.
Catechesis Religious Program—Students 40.
Missions—St. Paul—P.O. Box 28, Sundance, Crook Co. 82729. Email: stpaul@rangeweb.net.
Catechesis Religious Program—Students 20.
St. Anthony, P.O. Box 177, Upton, Weston Co. 82730.
Catechesis Religious Program—Students 14.
St. Matthew's, 26 Hunter, Hulett, Crook Co. 82720.
Catechesis Religious Program—Students 2.
PINE BLUFFS, LARAMIE CO., ST. PAUL'S (1913)
Mailing Address: P.O. Box 97, Pine Bluffs, 82082-0097. Tel: 307-245-3761; Email: stpaulschurch@rtconnect.net. Rev. Kevin A. Koch.
Rectory—307 Beech St., Pine Bluffs, 82082-0097.
Church: 501 E. 4th St., Pine Bluffs, 82082.
Catechesis Religious Program—Riley Petry, D.R.E. Students 29.
Missions—St. Joseph—Hwy., Albin, Laramie Co.
St. Peter, 316 4th St., Carpenter, Laramie Co. 82054.
PINEDALE, SUBLETTE CO., OUR LADY OF PEACE (1940)
112 S. Sublette Ave., Pinedale, 82941.
Tel: 307-367-2359; Fax: 307-367-3553; Email: pinedalecatholicchurch@gmail.com. P.O. Box 70, Pinedale, 82941-0070. Rev. Peter James Mwaura; Deacon Daniel Kostelc.
Catechesis Religious Program—Jennifer Hayward, D.R.E. (K-12). Students 87.
Mission—St. Anne, 411 Piney Dr., Big Piney, Sublette Co. 83113. Rev. Peter James Mwaura, Contact Person.
Catechesis Religious Program—Students 27.
POWELL, PARK CO., ST. BARBARA (1910)
115 E. Third, Powell, 82435-0818. Tel: 307-754-2480; Fax: 307-316-0309; Email: stbarb@tctwest.net. P.O. Box 818, Powell, 82435. Rev. Phillip C. Wagner; Deacon Steven Penwell; Mrs. Leslie Cannon, Admin.
Catechesis Religious Program—Email: stbarbs.religiousedu@gmail.com. Tom Spiering, D.R.E.; Janet Spiering, D.R.E. Students 95.
RAWLINS, CARBON CO., ST. JOSEPH'S (1867) [JC]
Mailing Address: 219 W. Pine St., P.O. Box 68, Rawlins, 82301-0068. Tel: 307-324-4631; Email: cachurcsaj@qwestoffice.net. Very Rev. Samuel Hayes.
Catechesis Religious Program—Patricia Perez, D.R.E. Students 70.
Mission—Our Lady of the Sage, P.O. Box 116, Baggs, Carbon Co. 82321.
RIVERTON, FREMONT CO., ST. MARGARET'S (1908)
Mailing Address: 618 Fremont Ave., Riverton, 82501. Tel: 307-856-3757; Email: stmargchurch@wyoming.com. Revs. Louis M. Shea; Robert Rodgers, J.C.L.
Res.: 622 E. Park, Riverton, 82501.
Tel: 307-856-6226.
School—St. Margaret's School, (Grades PreK-5), 220 N. 7th E., Riverton, 82501. Tel: 307-856-5922; Email: stmarg@wyoming.com; Web: stmargaretriverton.com/school/. Nicholas Schaffer. Lay Teachers 14; Students 86; Clergy / Religious Teachers 2.
Catechesis Religious Program—Tel: 307-850-8164; Email: brythoman@hotmail.com. Bryan Thoman, D.R.E. Students 36.
Missions—St. Joseph—211 Wyoming St., Shoshoni, Fremont Co. 82649. Tel: 307-876-2760.
Our Lady of the Woods, 4 S. Riverton St., P.O. Box 1134, Dubois, Fremont Co. 82513. Tel: 307-455-2533.
St. Edward, Kinnear Rectory, 11350 US Hwy. 26, Kinnear, Fremont Co. 82516. Tel: 307-856-5502.
ROCK SPRINGS, SWEETWATER CO.
1—SS. CYRIL AND METHODIUS (1910) Merged with Our Lady of Sorrows Church, Rock Springs to form Holy Spirit Catholic Community.
2—HOLY SPIRIT CATHOLIC COMMUNITY (1887)
116 Broadway, Rock Springs, 82901.
Tel: 307-362-2611; Fax: 307-382-4911; Email: info@theholyspiritparish.com. Revs. William Hill III; Emilio Cabrera, (Colombia); Deacon Charles Lux.
Res.: 633 Bridger Ave., Rock Springs, 82901.
School—Holy Spirit Catholic School, (Grades PreK-6), 210 A St., Rock Springs, 82901. Tel: 307-362-6077; Email: hscsoffice@wyoming.com. Linda Marcos, Prin. Clergy 2; Lay Teachers 6; Sisters 2; Students 63.
Catechesis Religious Program—Email: amandamontoya@theholyspiritparish.com. Mrs. Amanda Sheehan, D.R.E. & Youth Min. Students 153.
Missions—St. Vivian—Superior, Sweetwater Co.
St. Anthony of the Desert, Wamsutter, Sweetwater Co.
St. Christopher, Eden, Sweetwater Co. 82926.
3—OUR LADY OF SORROWS, Merged with SS. Cyril and Methodius to form Holy Spirit Catholic Community.
SAINT STEPHENS, FREMONT CO., ST. STEPHEN'S (1884) [CEM] (Native American) Indian Mission for the Shoshone and Arapaho Indians. St. Stephen's Indian Mission, Inc.
Mailing Address: 33 St. Stephens Rd., Box 250, St. Stephens, 82524. Tel: 307-856-7806;
Fax: 307-856-3853; Email: melissa.brown@saintstephensmission.com; Web: www.saintstephensmission.com. Very Rev. James Heiser; Rev. Bryce Lungren, Parochial Vicar; Sisters Teresa Frawley, O.S.F., Pastoral Assoc.; Monica Suhayda, C.S.J., Pastoral Assoc.
Catechesis Religious Program—Email: patti.mcmahon@saintstephensmission.com. Patti McMahon, D.R.E. Students 61.
Missions—St. Joseph—Box 8358, Ethete, Fremont Co. 82520.
Blessed Sacrament.
SARATOGA, CARBON CO., ST. ANN'S (1957)
218 W. Spring St., Saratoga, 82331-0667.
Tel: 307-326-5461; Email: stannssaratoga@gmail.com. P.O. Box 667, Saratoga, 82331. Rev. Jason Marco.
Catechesis Religious Program—Rev. Jason Marco, D.R.E. Students 38.
Mission—St. Joseph, 3 Heather Dr., Hanna, Carbon Co. 82327.
SHERIDAN, SHERIDAN CO., HOLY NAME (1885) [JC]
260 E. Loucks, Sheridan, 82801. Tel: 307-672-2848; Fax: 307-672-5105; Web: www.holynamesheridan.org. Mailing Address: 9 S. Connor, Sheridan, 82801. Revs. Glenn Whewell; Clark Lenz, Parochial Vicar; Deacon John Bigelow.
School—Holy Name School, (Grades PreK-8), 121 S. Connor, Sheridan, 82801. Tel: 307-672-2021;
Fax: 307-673-4474; Email: holynamesch@bresnan.net; Web: www.hncswy.org. Mary Legler, Prin. Lay Teachers 15; Students 93.
Catechesis Religious Program—Tel: 307-672-2848. Stacy Preszler, D.R.E. Lay Teachers 19; Students 118.
Missions—Our Lady of the Pines—34 Wagon Box Rd., Story, Sheridan Co. 82842.
St. Edmund, 310 Historic Hwy. 14, Ranchester, Sheridan Co. 82839. Tel: 307-751-6619; Email: stedmundschurch@qwestoffice.net. Monique Barron, Sec.
Catechesis Religious Program—Students 25.
THERMOPOLIS, HOT SPRINGS CO., ST. FRANCIS (1906)
808 Arapahoe, Thermopolis, 82443-0272.
Tel: 307-864-2458; Email: frrandy1956@gmail.com; Web: sfthermop.droppages.com. P.O. Box 272, Thermopolis, 82443. Rev. Randall J. Oswald.
Catechesis Religious Program—Sharon Cordingly, C.R.E.; Kent Cordingly, C.R.E. Students 30.
TORRINGTON, GOSHEN CO., ST. ROSE (1906)
Mailing Address: 605 E. 22nd Ave., Torrington, 82240. Tel: 307-532-5556; Tel: 307-532-3177;
Tel: 307-532-3155; Email: strose.torrington@gmail.com. Revs. Raymond B. Moss; Andrew Duncan; Deacon Rolland Raboin.
Res.: 700 E. 22nd Ave., Torrington, 82240.
Catechesis Religious Program—Patricia Amberg, D.R.E. Students 70.
WHEATLAND, PLATTE CO., ST. PATRICK'S (1891) [JC]
1009 Ninth St., Wheatland, 82201. Tel: 307-322-2070; Email: stpatrick1009@gmail.com; Web: www.stpatricks-wheatland.com. Rev. Thomas R. Kadera, J.C.L.; Deacon Terry Archbold.
Catechesis Religious Program—Tel: 307-322-4213. Students 63.
Mission—Mary Queen of Heaven, 401 5th St., Chugwater, Platte Co. 82201.
WORLAND, WASHAKIE CO., ST. MARY MAGDALEN (1949) [JC]
Mailing Address: 1099 Charles Ave., P.O. Box 901, Worland, 82401-0901. Tel: 307-347-2820;
Fax: 307-347-2450; Email: stmarym@rtconnect.net; Web: www.worland.com/magdalen. Rev. Ray Rodriguez; Deacon Michael Martinson.
Catechesis Religious Program—Students 97.

Chaplains of Public Institutions

CHEYENNE. *U.S. Veterans Administration Hospital 1*, 90 MW/HC, F.E. Warren AFB, 82005. Vacant.
EVANSTON. *Wyoming State Hospital*. Vacant.
LUSK. *Wyoming Women's Center (Correctional Facility)*. Rev. Raymond B. Moss.
RAWLINS. *Wyoming State Penitentiary*, P.O. Box 468, Rawlins, 82301-0068. Tel: 307-324-4631. Rev. Jason Marco.
SHERIDAN. *U.S. Veterans Administration Hospital*. Vacant.

In Res.:
Revs.—
Gibbons, Joseph Marie of Jesus, M.Carm., Monks of the Most Blessed Virgin Mary of Mt. Carmel, 31 Rd. AFW, Powell, 82435
Maroney, Simon Mary, M.Carm., Monks of the Most Blessed Virgin Mary of Mt. Carmel, 31 Rd. AFW, Powell, 82435
Schneider, Daniel Mary, M.Carm., Prior, Monks of the Most Blessed Virgin Mary of Mt. Carmel, 31 Rd. AFW, Powell, 82435
Wright, Michael, M.Carm., Monks of the Most Blessed Virgin Mary of Mt. Carmel, 31 Rd. AFW, Powell, 82435.

Retired:
Rev. Msgr.—
O'Neill, James, (Retired)
Revs.—
Beavers, Carl, (Retired)
Carr, Michael, (Retired)
Chleborad, Gerald, (Retired)
Cook, Robert W., (Retired)
Fahey, Thomas C., Chap., (Retired)

Fraher, Joseph P., (Retired)
Gianola, William, (Retired)
Murray, John, (Retired)
Ogg, Thomas, (Retired)
Reid, Malcolm, (Retired)
Sheridan, Thomas, (Retired)
Stolcis, Ronald, (Retired).

Permanent Deacons:
Archbold, Terry, St. Patrick, Wheatland
Bigelow, John, (Retired)
Boydston, Gerald, St. Anthony, Cody
Burke, Michael, (Retired)
Bush, Joseph, St. Anthony, Cody
Carroll, Kim, St. Matthew, Gillette
Deti, John, (Retired)
Flavin, Harry, Our Lady of the Mountains, Jackson
Halvorsen, Kevin, St. Louis, Glenrock
Hill, Bill, Our Lady of the Mountains, Jackson
Hruska, Randy
Humphreys, Russ, (Retired)
Johnson, David, St. Anthony, Casper
Juarez, Jesus, (Retired)
Kostelc, Daniel, Our Lady of Peace, Pinedale
Lancaster, Al, (Retired)
Leman, Michael, Holy Trinity, Cheyenne
Lux, Charles, Holy Spirit, Rock Springs
Martinson, Michael, St. Mary Magdalen, Worland
McCarthy, Ed, (Retired)
Miller, Rich, Holy Rosary, Lander
Moser, Richard, St. Anthony, Cody
Nash, Wes, Immaculate Conception, Green River
Niemann, Thomas, St. Joseph, Cheyenne
Penwell, Steven, St. Barbara, Powell
Pitlick, Ken, (Retired), (Retired)
Raboin, Rolland, St. Rose of Lima, Torrington
Sandrini, Joseph, Corpus Christi, Newcastle
Schell, Carroll, (Retired)
Vlchek, Douglas, Our Lady of the Mountains, Jackson
Wanek, Philip, Our Lady of the Mountains, Jackson
Zelenka, David, Holy Trinity, Cheyenne.

INSTITUTIONS LOCATED IN DIOCESE

[A] PROTECTIVE INSTITUTIONS

TORRINGTON. *St. Joseph's Children's Home* (1930) 1419 Main St., Torrington, 82240-3340. Tel: 307-532-4197; Fax: 307-532-8405; Email: bmayor@stjoseph-wy.org; Email: rmeyer@stjoseph-wy.org; Web: www.stjoseph-wy.org. Box 1117, Torrington, 82240-1117. Robert C. Mayor, Exec. Dir.; Paula Krotz, Prin. Children 62; Clergy 1; Students 55; Total Staff 127; Clergy / Religious Teachers 1; Total Assisted 250.

[B] COLLEGES AND UNIVERSITIES

LANDER. **Wyoming Catholic College*, 306 Main St., Lander, 82520. Tel: 307-332-2930; Fax: 307-332-2918; Email: info@wyomingcatholic.org; Web: www.wyomingcatholic.org. Dr. Glenn Arbery, Pres.; Ms. Hillary Rowney, Librarian. Lay Teachers 17; Priests 1; Students 187.

[C] HOUSING FOR THE ELDERLY (LOW INCOME)

CHEYENNE. *Holy Trinity Manor* (1989) 2516 E. 18th St., 82001. Tel: 307-778-8850; Fax: 307-634-2451; Email: dschmidt@archhousing.com; Email: holytrinitymanor@archdiocesanhousing.org. Daniel Schmidt, Property Mgr. Total in Residence 30; Total Staff 2; Total Assisted 45.

CASPER. *St. Anthony Manor* (1983) 211 E. Sixth St., Casper, 82601. Tel: 307-237-0843; Fax: 307-237-3516; Email: tfunch@archhousing.com; Email: kstruble@archhousing.com. Mrs. Tonja Funch, Admin. Tot Asst. Annually 64; Total in Residence 64; Total Staff 3.

[D] MONASTERIES AND RESIDENCES FOR PRIESTS AND BROTHERS

POWELL. *Monks of the Most Blessed Virgin Mary of Mt. Carmel* aka Carmelite Monks (2004) 31 Road AFW, Powell, 82435. Tel: 307-645-3310; Fax: 307-645-3085; Email: cloisteredmonk@gmail.com; Web: www.carmelitemonks.org. Revs. Daniel Mary Schneider, M.Carm., Prior; Michael Wright, M.Carm., Subprior; Joseph Marie of Jesus Gibbons, M.Carm., Vocations Dir.; Nicholas Maroney, Novice Master. Novices 3; Priests 4; Temporary Vows 3; Perpetual Vows 12; Postulants 5.

[E] CAMPUS MINISTRY

CASPER. *St. Francis Newman Center* (1984) 1732 S. Elm St., Casper, 82601. Tel: 307-266-2666; Fax: 307-266-4127; Email: finance@stanthonyscasper.org. 9: 604 S. Center, Casper, 82601. Rev. Kevin Barrett, Dir.

LARAMIE. *St. Paul's Newman Center, University Catholic Community (University of Wyoming)*, 1800 E. Grand Ave., Laramie, 82070-4316. Tel: 307-745-5461; Email: newman@newmancenter.org; Web: www.newmancenter.org. Rev. Robert Spaulding; Lillie Romeiser, Campus Min.; Anthony Allen, Pastoral Min./Coord.; Thomas Quinlivan, Liturgy Dir.; Sandy Gaddis, Business Mgr. Total Staff 8.

POWELL. *John Henry Newman Center, Northwest College*, 674 N. Absaroka St., Powell, 82435. Tel: 307-754-9220; Email: nwcnewmancenter@gmail.com. P.O. Box 818, Powell, 82435. Rev. Phillip C. Wagner; Ms. Eliza Higgins, Campus Min.; Ms. Katy Spiering, Campus Min. Attended by St. Barbara, Powell. Students 10.

[F] MISCELLANEOUS LISTINGS

CHEYENNE. *Catholic Charities of Wyoming, Inc.*, 507 East 18th St., 82001. Tel: 307-637-0554; Fax: 307-632-2346; Email: bmayor@charitieswyoming.org. P.O. Box 907, 82003-0907. Most Rev. Steven Biegler, Pres.; Very Rev. Carl Gallinger, Vice Pres.; Ann Norwood, Bd. Member; Rev. Robert L. Fox, Bd. Member; Robert C. Mayor, Agency Dir. Tot Asst. Annually 850; Total Staff 7.

Holy Trinity Youth Education Trust, c/o Fr. Thomas E. Cronkleton, Jr., 1836 Hot Springs Ave., 82001-5337. Tel: 307-632-5872; Email: tcronkleton@holytrinitycheyenne.org. Rev. Thomas E. Cronkleton Jr., J.C.D., Trustee; Mr. Aaron Courtney, Trustee; Mr. James Dahill, Trustee; Ms. Amy Deibert, Trustee; Mr. Jeffrey V. Nieters, Trustee; Ms. Carly Rando, Trustee; Ms. Tammy Tschacher, Trustee; Ms. Molly Spiering, Trustee; Ms. Randi Losalu, Trustee.

Mall at St. Vincent DePaul (1998) c/o St. Mary Cathedral, P.O. Box 1268, 82003. Tel: 307-514-0365; Email: dpindara@stmarycathedral.com; Web: www.stmarycathedral.com. Diane Pindara, Mgr. Total Staff 5.

St. Mary's School Foundation, 100 West 21st St., 82001-3651. Tel: 307-635-9261; Fax: 307-635-5723; Email: akoeune@stmarycathedral.com; Web: www.stmarysschoolfoundation.org. P.O. Box 1268, 82003-1268. Rev. Thomas E. Cronkleton Jr., J.C.D., Pres.; Debra Hoblit-Hirsig, Vice Pres.; Keith G. Zabka, Sec. & Treas.

The Wyoming Catholic Ministries Foundation, 2121 Capitol Ave, 82001. Tel: 307-638-1530; Fax: 307-637-7936; Email: mpotter@wycmf.org; Web: www.wycmf.org. P.O. Box 227, 82003. Mr. Matthew N. Potter, C.F.P., C.I.M.A., CEO. Board of Directors Most Rev. Steven Biegler, Pres.; Mr. Jim Magagna; Deacon Harry Flavin; Mr. William N. Willingham; Mr. Jack Adams; Mrs. Esther McGann; Mrs. Gay Woodhouse, Treas.; Mr. Stuart Palmer; Mr. Mike Lovelett, Vice President; Mrs. Mary Kugler.

CASPER. *St. Anthony Tri-Parish Catholic School Foundation*, 1145 W. 20th St., Casper, 82604. Tel: 307-337-1361; Fax: 307-235-4946; Email: foundation@sascasper.com; Web: www.stanthonyschoolfoundation.org. Ron Morris, Pres.; Very Rev. Gary J. Ruzicka, Pastor.

Knights of Columbus Charitable Trust for Seminarian Education and Priests' Retirement (1991) P.O. Box 20243, 82003. Tel: 307-638-7016; Email: douggasseling@centurylink.net. Mr. Douglas Gasseling, Contact Person.

St. Vincent De Paul Thrift Store (1965) 301 E. H St., Casper, 82601. Tel: 307-237-2607; Email: msnyderstpat@gmail.com. Gloria Perez, Mgr. Tot Asst. Annually 9,100; Volunteers 24.

ROCK SPRINGS. *Rock Springs Catholic School Foundation*, 116 Broadway St., Rock Springs, 82901. Tel: 307-362-2611; Fax: 307-382-4911. Rev. William Hill III; Linda Marcos, Prin.

SAINT STEPHENS. *St. Stephens Indian Mission Foundation* (1974) P.O. Box 278, St. Stephens, 82524-0278. Tel: 307-856-6797; Fax: 307-857-1802; Email: ssimf@wyoming.com. Ronald Mamot, Dir.

RELIGIOUS INSTITUTES OF MEN REPRESENTED IN THE DIOCESE

For further details refer to the corresponding bracketed number in the Religious Institutes of Men or Women section.

[0200]—*Benedictine Monks*—O.S.B.
[]—*Monachi Carmelitarm*—M.Carm.
[0975]—*Society of Our Lady of the Most Holy Trinity*—S.O.L.T.

RELIGIOUS INSTITUTES OF WOMEN REPRESENTED IN THE DIOCESE

[1070-03]—*Dominican Sisters* (Sinsinawa)—O.P.
[]—*Dominican Sisters of Hope*—O.P.
[1680]—*School Sisters of St. Francis* (Milwaukee, WI)—O.S.F.
[0480]—*Sisters of Charity of Leavenworth, Kansas*—S.C.L.
[1650]—*Sisters of St. Francis of Philadelphia*—O.S.F.
[3830]—*Sisters of St. Joseph*—C.S.J.

DIOCESAN CEMETERIES

CHEYENNE. *Olivet Cemetery*, Tel: 307-635-9261; Email: akoeune@stmarycathedral.com; Web: www.stmarycathedral.com. Very Rev. August Koeune, P.O. Box 1268, 82003. Tel: 307-635-9261

NECROLOGY

† Savio, John, (Retired), Died Oct. 22, 2018

An asterisk (*) denotes an organization that has established tax-exempt status directly with the IRS and is not covered by the USCCB Group Ruling.

Archdiocese of Chicago

(Archidioecesis Chicagiensis)

His Eminence

BLASE CARDINAL CUPICH

Archbishop of Chicago; ordained August 16, 1975; appointed Bishop of Rapid City July 7, 1998; ordained and installed September 21, 1998; appointed Bishop of Spokane June 30, 2010; installed September 3, 2010; appointed Archbishop of Chicago September 11, 2014; installed November 18, 2014; created Cardinal Priest November 19, 2016.

Archbishop Quigley Center & Cardinal Meyer Center: P.O. Box 1979, Chicago, IL 60690-1979. Tel: 312-534-8200

Web: www.archchicago.org

Most Reverend

JOHN R. MANZ

Auxiliary Bishop of Chicago; ordained May 12, 1971; appointed Auxiliary Bishop of Chicago and Titular Bishop of Mulia January 13, 1996; consecrated March 5, 1996. *Mailing Address: 1400 S. Austin Blvd., Cicero, IL 60804.* Tel: 708-329-4040; Fax: 708-222-8854.

Most Reverend

JOSEPH N. PERRY

Auxiliary Bishop of Chicago; ordained May 24, 1975; appointed Auxiliary Bishop of Chicago and Titular Bishop of Lead May 5, 1998; consecrated June 29, 1998. *Mailing Address: 3525 S. Lake Park Ave., Chicago, IL 60653.* Tel: 312-534-8376; Fax: 312-534-5317.

Most Reverend

ANDREW P. WYPYCH

Auxiliary Bishop of Chicago; ordained April 29, 1979; appointed Auxiliary Bishop of Chicago and Titular Bishop of Naraggara June 13, 2011; Episcopal ordination August 10, 2011. *Mailing Address: 2330 W. 118th St., Chicago, IL 60643.* Tel: 773-779-8440; Fax: 773-779-8469.

Most Reverend

ALBERTO ROJAS

Auxiliary Bishop of Chicago; ordained May 24, 1997; appointed Auxiliary Bishop of Chicago and Titular Bishop of Marazanae June 13, 2011; Episcopal ordination August 10, 2011. *Mailing Address: 200 N. Milwaukee Ave., Ste. 200, Libertyville, IL 60048.* Tel: 847-549-0160.

Most Reverend

MARK A. BARTOSIC

Auxiliary Bishop of Chicago; ordained May 21, 1994; appointed Auxiliary Bishop of Chicago and Titular Bishop of Naratcata July 3, 2018; Episcopal ordination September 17, 2018. *Mailing Address: 1641 W. Diversey Pkwy., Chicago, IL 60614.* Tel: 773-388-8670; Fax: 773-388-8672.

Most Reverend

ROBERT G. CASEY

Auxiliary Bishop of Chicago; ordained May 21, 1994; appointed Auxiliary Bishop of Chicago and Titular Bishop of Thuburbo Maius July 3, 2018; Episcopal ordination September 17, 2018. *Mailing Address: 1850 S. Throop St., Chicago, 60611.* Tel: 312-534-8399; Fax: 312-243-4970.

Most Reverend

RONALD A. HICKS

Auxiliary Bishop of Chicago; ordained May 21, 1994; appointed Auxiliary Bishop of Chicago and Titular Bishop of Munatiana July 3, 2018; Episcopal ordination September 17, 2018. *Mailing Address: 835 N. Rush St., Chicago, 60611.* Tel: 312-534-8271.

Most Reverend

JOHN R. GORMAN

Retired Auxiliary Bishop of Chicago and Titular Bishop of Catula; ordained May 1, 1952; appointed February 16, 1988; consecrated April 11, 1988; retired January 24, 2003. *Res.: Our Lady of the Woods, 10731 W. 131st St., Orland Park, IL 60462.* Tel: 708-361-4754.

Most Reverend

RAYMOND E. GOEDERT

Retired Auxiliary Bishop of Chicago; ordained May 1, 1952; appointed Auxiliary Bishop of Chicago and Titular Bishop of Tamazeni July 8, 1991; consecrated August 29, 1991; retired January 24, 2003. *Res.: 1555 N. State Pkwy., Chicago, IL 60610.* Tel: 312-534-8271.

Most Reverend

GEORGE J. RASSAS

Retired Auxiliary Bishop of Chicago; ordained May 2, 1968; appointed Auxiliary Bishop of Chicago and Titular Bishop of Reperi December 1, 2005; consecrated February 2, 2006; retired September 18, 2018. *Mailing Address: 200 N. Milwaukee Ave., Ste. 200, Libertyville, IL 60048-2250.* Tel: 847-549-0160; Fax: 847-549-0163.

Most Reverend

FRANCIS J. KANE

Retired Auxiliary Bishop of Chicago; ordained May 14, 1969; appointed Auxiliary Bishop of Chicago and Titular Bishop of Sault Sainte Marie in Michigan January 24, 2003; consecrated March 19, 2003; retired September 18, 2018. *Mailing Address: 1555 N. State Pkwy., Chicago, IL 60610.* Tel: 312-337-5952.

ESTABLISHED NOVEMBER 28, 1843; CREATED 1880.

Square Miles 1,411.

Comprises the Counties of Cook and Lake in the State of Illinois.

Legal Title: The Catholic Bishop of Chicago, a Corporation Sole.
For legal titles of institutions, consult The Pastoral Center.

STATISTICAL OVERVIEW

Personnel	
Cardinals	1
Auxiliary Bishops	7
Retired Bishops	4
Priests: Diocesan Active in Diocese	523
Priests: Diocesan Active Outside Diocese	16
Priests: Diocesan in Foreign Missions	1
Priests: Retired, Sick or Absent	206
Number of Diocesan Priests	746
Religious Priests in Diocese	531
Total Priests in Diocese	1,277
Extern Priests in Diocese	167
Ordinations:	
Diocesan Priests	8
Religious Priests	11
Transitional Deacons	8
Permanent Deacons	19
Permanent Deacons in Diocese	653
Total Brothers	175
Total Sisters	1,296
Parishes	
Parishes	336
With Resident Pastor:	
Resident Diocesan Priests	258
Resident Religious Priests	41
Without Resident Pastor:	
Administered by Priests	37
Missions	11
Pastoral Centers	7
New Parishes Created	6
Closed Parishes	14
Professional Ministry Personnel:	
Brothers	2
Sisters	35
Lay Ministers	335
Welfare	
Catholic Hospitals	15
Total Assisted	2,390,000
Health Care Centers	2
Total Assisted	101,394
Homes for the Aged	43
Total Assisted	11,478
Residential Care of Children	2
Total Assisted	340
Day Care Centers	9
Total Assisted	2,609
Specialized Homes	2
Total Assisted	183
Special Centers for Social Services	107
Total Assisted	451,516
Residential Care of Disabled	6
Total Assisted	1,375
Other Institutions	7
Total Assisted	2,544
Educational	
Seminaries, Diocesan	2
Students from This Diocese	63
Students from Other Diocese	162
Diocesan Students in Other Seminaries	1
Seminaries, Religious	1
Students Religious	98
Total Seminarians	162
Colleges and Universities	5
Total Students	47,150
High Schools, Diocesan and Parish	4
Total Students	422
High Schools, Private	29
Total Students	19,860
Elementary Schools, Diocesan and Parish	169
Total Students	49,104
Elementary Schools, Private	7
Total Students	2,461
Non-residential Schools for the Disabled	2
Total Students	114
Catechesis/Religious Education:	
High School Students	6,285
Elementary Students	54,940
Total Students under Catholic Instruction	180,498
Teachers in the Diocese:	
Priests	39
Brothers	8
Sisters	51
Lay Teachers	4,930
Vital Statistics	
Receptions into the Church:	
Infant Baptism Totals	23,654

Adult Baptism Totals	1,588	Marriages:		Deaths	11,844
Received into Full Communion	1,396	Catholic	4,013	Total Catholic Population	2,183,000
First Communions	22,025	Interfaith	738	Total Population	5,900,365
Confirmations	19,346	Total Marriages	4,751		

Former Bishops—Rt. Revs. WILLIAM QUARTER, D.D., cons. March 10, 1844; died April 10, 1848; JAMES O. VAN DE VELDE, D.D., cons. Feb. 11, 1849; transferred to Natchez, July 29, 1853; died Nov. 13, 1855; ANTHONY O'REGAN, D.D., cons. July 25, 1854; resigned 1858; died Nov. 13, 1866; JAMES DUGGAN, D.D., cons. Bishop of Antigone, and Coadjutor to the Archbishop of St. Louis, May 1, 1857; transferred to Chicago, Jan. 21, 1859; hospitalized, 1869; died March 27, 1899; THOMAS FOLEY, D.D., Coadjutor-Bishop and Administrator of the diocese; cons. Bishop of Pergamus, Feb. 27, 1870; died Feb. 19, 1879; Most Revs. PATRICK A. FEEHAN, D.D., First Archbishop of Chicago; cons. Bishop of Nashville, Nov. 1, 1865; promoted to Chicago, Sept. 10, 1880; died July 12, 1902; JAMES EDWARD QUIGLEY, D.D., Archbishop of Chicago; ord. April 12, 1879; cons. Bishop of Buffalo, Feb. 24, 1897; promoted to Archbishop of Chicago, Jan. 8, 1903; died July 10, 1915; His Eminence GEORGE CARDINAL MUNDELEIN, Archbishop of Chicago; ord. June 8, 1895; cons. Titular Bishop of Loryma and Auxiliary Bishop of Brooklyn, Sept. 21, 1909; promoted to the See of Chicago, Dec. 9, 1915; created Cardinal Priest, March 24, 1924; died Oct. 2, 1939; SAMUEL CARDINAL STRITCH, Archbishop of Chicago; ord. May 21, 1910; appt. Bishop of Toledo, Aug. 10, 1921; promoted to Archbishop of Milwaukee, Aug. 26, 1930; transferred to Archbishop of Chicago, Dec. 27, 1939; created Cardinal Priest Feb. 18, 1946; elevated to the Roman Curia, Sacred Congregation for the Propagation of the Faith, March 1, 1958; died in Rome, May 27, 1958; ALBERT CARDINAL MEYER, Archbishop of Chicago; ord. July 11, 1926; appt. Bishop of Superior, Feb. 18, 1946; promoted to Archbishop of Milwaukee, July 21, 1953; transferred to Archbishop of Chicago, Sept. 19, 1958; created Cardinal Priest, Dec. 24, 1959; died April 9, 1965; JOHN CARDINAL CODY, S.T.D., D.D., Archbishop of Chicago; ord. Dec. 8, 1931; appt. Auxiliary Bishop of St. Louis, May 14, 1947; cons. July 2, 1947; promoted to Coadjutor of St. Joseph, Jan. 27, 1954; transferred to Kansas City-St. Joseph, Aug. 29, 1956; promoted to Coadjutor Archbishop of New Orleans, Aug. 14, 1961; acceded to the See of New Orleans, Nov. 8, 1964; transferred to the Archdiocese of Chicago, June 16, 1965; created Cardinal Priest in the Consistory, June 26, 1967; died April 25, 1982; JOSEPH CARDINAL BERNARDIN, D.D., Archbishop of Chicago; ord. April 26, 1952; appt. Auxiliary Bishop of Atlanta, March 9, 1966; cons. April 26, 1966; appt. Archbishop of Cincinnati, Nov. 21, 1972; appt. Archbishop of Chicago, July 10, 1982; installed Aug. 25, 1982; created Cardinal Priest, Feb. 2, 1983; died Nov. 14, 1996; FRANCIS CARDINAL GEORGE, O.M.I., Ph.D., S.T.D., Profession of Perpetual Vows Sept. 8, 1961; ord. a priest Dec. 21, 1963; appt. Bishop of Yakima July 10, 1990; Episcopal Ordination and Installation Sept. 21, 1990; appt. Archbishop of Portland in Oregon April 30, 1996; installed May 27, 1996; appt. Archbishop of Chicago April 8, 1997; installed May 7, 1997; created Cardinal Priest Feb. 21, 1998; retired Nov. 18, 2014; died April 17, 2015.

Vicar General—Most Rev. RONALD A. HICKS, D.Min.

Episcopal Vicars—Most Rev. ALBERTO ROJAS, Vicariate I (Deaneries A, B, C, D, E, F); Revs. MARK A. BARTOSIC, Vicariate II (Deaneries A, B, C, D, E, F); ROBERT G. CASEY, Vicariate III (Deaneries A, B, C, D, E); Most Revs. JOHN R. MANZ, Vicariate IV (Deaneries A, B, C, D, E); ANDREW P. WYPYCH, Vicariate V (Deaneries A, B, C, D, E); JOSEPH N. PERRY, Vicariate VI (Deaneries A, B, C, D).

Deans—Revs. MICHAEL G. MCGOVERN, Deanery I-A; PATRICK J. RUGEN, S.T.L., M.Div., M.A., Deanery I-B; VINCENT F. COSTELLO, Deanery I-C; EDWARD R. FIALKOWSKI, Deanery I-D; JOHN W. DEARHAMMER, Deanery I-E; EDWARD B. PANEK, Deanery I-F; KEVIN MCCRAY, Deanery II-A; JAMES L. BARRETT, Deanery II-B, (Retired); Rev. Msgr. JAMES T. KACZOROWSKI, Deanery II-C; Revs. LAWRENCE M. LISOWSKI, Deanery II-D; RONALD N. KALAS, Deanery II-E, (Retired); DANIEL R. FALLON, Deanery II-F; ROBERT LOMBARDO, C.F.R., Deanery III-A; JOHN R. WAISS, Deanery III-B; THOMAS E. CIMA, Deanery III-C; LAWRENCE R. DOWLING, Deanery III-D; DONALD J. NEVINS, Deanery III-E; THOMAS P. MAY, Deanery IV-A; JAMES F. HURLBERT, Deanery IV-B; JOSE MARIA GARCIA-MALDONADO, Deanery IV-C; ROBERT J. LOJEK, Deanery IV-D; ROBERT J. CLARK, Deanery IV-E; JOHN CELICHOWSKI, O.F.M.Cap., Deanery V-A; JOHN T. NOGA, Deanery V-B; THOMAS P. CONDE, M.Div., S.T.B., M.B.A., Deanery V-C; DENNIS A. ZIOMEK, Deanery V-D; WILLIAM T. CORCORAN, Ph. D., Deanery V-E; DAVID A. JONES, Deanery VI-A; THOMAS G. BELANGER, Deanery VI-B; CHARLES W. WATKINS, Deanery VI-C; KAROL TYBOR, Deanery VI-D.

College of Consultors—Revs. KENNETH A. BUDZIKOWSKI; JOSE MARIA GARCIA-MALDONADO; ROBERT M. FEDEK; JEROME J. JACOB; MICHAEL P. KNOTEK; THADEO E. MGIMBA; EDWARD M. MIKOLAJCZYK, (Retired); RICHARD MILEK; MATTHEW O'DONNELL; Rev. Msgr. PATRICK J. POLLARD, (Retired); Rev. THOMAS PROVENZANO, S.D.B.

Presbyteral Council—Revs. LOUIS TYLKA, Chm.; JAMES ANDREW MUELLER; JAMES A. HENEGHAN; EDWARD M. MIKOLAJCZYK, (Retired).

Finance Council—Vice Chairmen: Most Rev. RONALD A. HICKS, D.Min.; MR. EDWARD J. WEHMER; MR. MICHAEL O'GRADY. Members: MS. SALLY BLOUNT; MR. MARTIN CABRERA JR.; MR. BRENDAN CARROLL; MR. JEROME A. CASTELLINI; MR. JOHN W. CROGHAN; MR. GENO FERNANDEZ; MS. MARY LOU GORNO; MR. WARD R. HAMM; MR. ROBERTO R. HERENCIA; MR. JAMES P. HICKEY; MR. HARRY M. JANSEN KRAEMER JR.; MR. MICHAEL A. KERR; MR. CHARLES W. MULANEY JR.; MR. OLIVER NICKLIN; Rev. MARTIN E. O'DONOVAN; MR. MICHAEL O'GRADY; MR. CHRISTOPHER J. PERRY; MR. JIM PERRY; Rev. MICHAEL D. PLACE, S.T.D.; Rev. Msgr. PATRICK J. POLLARD, (Retired); MS. LISA POLLINA; MR. JOSEPH SCOBY; MR. TIMOTHY SULLIVAN; MR. SCOTT C. SWANSON; MR. KEVIN WILLER.

Pastoral Council—MS. NAOMI O'MALLEY, Chm.; MS. SABINA FERRARA-MULLIN, Vice Chm.

Women's Committee—MS. ANNE MARIE FINGER, Chm.; MS. AGGIE STEPNIAK; MR. ARI GUZMAN, Youth Rep.

Pastoral Youth Council—Co Chairs: KAROLINA NOWOBILSKA; MATTHEW PUDZISZ.

Provincial Offices

Catholic Conference of Illinois—ROBERT F. GILLIGAN, 65 E. Wacker Pl., Ste. 1620, Chicago, 60601. Tel: 312-368-1066; Fax: 321-368-1090; Web: catholicconferenceofillinois.org.

Archdiocesan Offices

Archdiocesan Departments can be contacted through the Archbishop Quigley Center, 835 N. Rush St., Chicago, IL 60611-2030 or the Cardinal Meyer Center, 3525 S. Lake Park Ave., Chicago, IL 60653-1402 (street & package delivery addresses). Address all mail to P.O. Box 1979, Chicago, IL 60690-1979. Tel: 312-534-8200.

Office of the Archbishop—Rev. KEVIN M. BIRMINGHAM, Administrative Sec. for the Archbishop, Tel: 312-534-8219.

Mundelein Seminary/University of St. Mary of the Lake—Very Revs. JOHN F. KARTJE, Ph.D., S.T.D., Rector/Pres.; THOMAS A. BAIMA, S.T.D., M.B.A., Vice Rector Academic Affairs.

Archdiocesan Vocations—Tel: 312-534-8298; Fax: 312-867-0357; Email: vocations@archchicago.org; Web: www.chicagopriest.com. Rev. TIMOTHY F. MONAHAN, Dir.

Casa Jesus—Rev. TIMOTHY F. MONAHAN, Dir.

Bishop Abramowicz Seminary—Rev. RICHARD MILEK, Chm.

St. Joseph College Seminary at Loyola University—Very Rev. PETER SNIEG JR., S.T.L., Rector & Pres., 1120 W. Loyola Ave., Chicago, 60626. Tel: 773-973-9700.

Office of Catholic Schools—MR. JIM RIGG, Ph.D., Supt., 835 N. Rush St., Chicago, 60611-2030. Tel: 312-534-5210; Fax: 312-534-5392; BENJAMIN POTTS, Assoc. Supt., Tel: 312-534-5221; MATTHEW WALTER, COO, Tel: 312-534-5200.

Canonical Affairs—835 N. Rush St., Chicago, 60611-2030. Tel: 312-534-5256; Fax: 312-534-5307; Email: jgrob@archchicago.org. Very Rev. JEFFREY S. GROB, J.C.D., Vicar for Canonical Affairs. Associate Vicars: Revs. RONALD P. STAKE, J.C.L., M.Div., Tel: 312-534-5284; Email: rstake@archchicago.org; FRANCIS Q. KUB, Tel: 312-534-8242; Email: fkub@archchicago.org; Very Rev. JEFFREY S. GROB, J.C.D., Archbishop's Delegate to Independent Review Bd. & Archbishop's Liaison - Lay Ecclesial Movements/New Communities, Tel: 312-534-5256; Deacon DANIEL G. WELTER, J.D., Auditor, Tel: 312-534-8283; Email: dwelter@archchicago.org; SUZETTE CASH, Administrative Asst., Tel: 312-534-8207; Fax: 312-534-5307; Email: scash@archchicago.org.

Chancellor—835 N. Rush St., Chicago, 60611-2030. Tel: 312-534-8283. Deacon DANIEL G. WELTER, J.D.

Archives and Records—MS. MEG HALL, Archivist, 711 W. Monroe St., Chicago, 60661. Tel: 312-534-4400; Fax: 312-831-0610.

Metropolitan Tribunal

Metropolitan Tribunal—Tel: 312-534-8280; Fax: 312-534-8314; Email: tribunal@archchicago.org.

Judicial Vicar—Very Rev. JEFFREY S. GROB, J.C.D., Tel: 312-534-8255; Email: tribunal@archchicago.

Adjutant Judicial Vicars—Very Rev. MICHAEL BRADLEY, J.C.D., Tel: 312-534-8205; Rev. JOHN LUCAS, J.C.L., Tel: 312-534-8403.

Promoter of Justice—Rev. WILLIAM H. WOESTMAN, O.M.I., J.C.D.

Judges—Revs. RAMIL E. FAJARDO, J.C.L.; JOHN M. GRIFFITHS, J.C.D.; MICHAEL A. HACK, J.C.D., (Retired); JOHN C. HERGENROTHER; ROBETH O. MOLINA TORRES, J.C.L.; ALEC J. WOLFF, J.C.L.; Sisters CHRISTINE M. KUB, O.P., J.C.L.; STEFANIA GALKA, M.Ch.R., J.C.L.; MR. RAPHAEL FRACKIEWICZ, J.C.D.; MRS. MONICA MAVRIC DE BELTRAMI, Esq.

Defenders of the Bond—Rev. Msgr. PETER GALEK, J.C.D.; Revs. WOJCIECH A. MARAT, J.C.D.; GRZEGORZ PODWYSOCKI, J.C.L.; WILLIAM H. WOESTMAN, O.M.I., J.C.D.; JAMES WALLACE, J.C.L.; Sr. TRACEY SHARP, S.C.R.H.; MRS. RENATA BABICZ-BARATTO, J.U.D.; MR. JESUS CABRERA, J.C.L.

Delegate of the Archbishop for Privilege Cases—Rev. JOSEPH C. MOL.

Auditors—Sr. BARBARA KOSINSKA, M.Ch.R.; Rev. JOSEPH C. MOL; MR. LUIS FLORES VEGA, J.C.L.; Deacon DANIEL G. WELTER, J.D.

Advocates—MR. R. DOUGLAS BOND, J.C.L.; MR. LUIS FLORES VEGA, J.C.L.

Vicar General

Vicar General—Most Rev. RONALD A. HICKS, D.Min., 835 N. Rush St., Chicago, 60611-2030. Tel: 312-534-8271.

Vicar for the Personal and Professional Development of Priests—980 N. Michigan Ave., Ste. #1525, Chicago, 60611. Tel: 312-642-1837. Rev. KENNETH C. SIMPSON, B.S., M.Div., D.Min.

Diocesan Priests' Placement Board—Rev. MICHAEL P. KNOTEK, Exec. Sec., Tel: 312-534-5276; Fax: 312-534-5281.

Archbishop's Delegate for Extern and International Priests—Tel: 312-534-5276. Rev. MICHAEL P. KNOTEK.

Vicar for Priests—980 N. Michigan Ave., Ste. #1525, Chicago, 60611. Tel: 312-534-7051; Fax: 312-642-4933. Rev. JEREMY THOMAS; Rev. Msgr. DENNIS J. LYLE, S.T.D.

Vicar for the Diaconate Community—816 Marengo, Forest Park, 60130. Tel: 708-366-8900; Fax: 708-366-8968. Deacons RICHARD F. HUDZIK, Vicar for Deacons; DAVID BRENCIC, Assoc. Dir. Diaconate; ENRIQUE ALONSO, Assoc. Dir. Hispanic Diaconate.

Religious, Office for—Sisters JOAN MCGLINCHEY, M.S.C., Dir., Tel: 312-534-8360; KATHLEEN MCNULTY, O.S.F., Asst. Dir., Tel: 312-534-3877; Bro. MICHAEL SEGVICH, C.F.C., Retirement Collection, Tel: 312-534-8234; Sr. LOVINA PAMMIT, O.S.F., Coord. Rel. Vocation Ministries, Tel: 312-534-5240.

Lay Ecclesial Ministry, Office for—CAROL A. WALTERS, Dir., Tel: 312-534-5263; Fax: 312-534-5281.

Vicar for Senior Priests—Revs. CHARLES T. RUBEY, (Retired); RONALD N. KALAS, (Retired).

Office for Protection of Children and Youth—MS. MARY JANE DOERR, Tel: 312-534-5319; Fax: 312-534-8307.

Assistance Ministry—TOM THARAYIL, Dir., Tel: 312-534-8267; Fax: 312-534-8307.

Child Abuse Investigations and Review—MS. LEAH R. MCCLUSKEY, Dir., Tel: 312-534-5205; Fax: 312-534-5279; Email: lmccluskey@archchicago.org.

Safe Environment—MYRA FLORES, Coord., Tel: 312-534-5238; Fax: 312-534-5307.

Ecumenical and Interreligious Affairs, Office for—Tel: 312-534-3867. Very Rev. THOMAS A. BAIMA, S.T.D., M.B.A., Vicar; DR. DANIEL OLSEN, Dir.

Health/Hospital Affairs—Rev. WILLIAM P. GROGAN, Archbishop's Delegate for Hospitals, Tel: 312-534-8339; Rev. Msgr. MICHAEL M. BOLAND, Archbishop's Delegate for Nursing Homes & Senior Svcs., Tel: 312-655-7460; Fax: 312-655-0219.

Bio Ethics Commission—Rev. WILLIAM P. GROGAN, Chair, Tel: 312-534-8339.

Chaplaincies/Chaplain Affairs—Most Rev. RONALD A. HICKS, D.Min., Tel: 312-534-8271.

Chicago Airports Catholic Chaplaincy—Rev. MICHAEL G. ZANIOLO, S.T.L., C.A.C., Chap., Mailing Address: P.O. Box 66353, Chicago, 60666-0353. Tel: 773-686-2636; Fax: 773-686-0130; Email: ordchapel@aol.com; Web: www.airportchapels.org.

Fire Department Chaplain—1140 W. Jackson Blvd., Chicago, 60607. Tel: 312-738-9246. Rev. JOHN P. MCNALIS, Interim Chap.

Police Department Chaplain—Rev. DANIEL J. BRANDT, Dir.

Department of Parish Vitality and Mission

Office for the Evangelization and Missionary Discipleship—MS. ELIZABETH WHITE, Dir., Cardinal Meyer Center, 3525 S. Lake Park Ave., Chicago, 60653-1402. Tel: 312-534-8037; Rev. JAMES P. MCILHONE, S.T.L., Ph.D., Dir. Biblical Formation, (Retired), Tel: 312-534-8014.

Office of Lifelong Formation—MR. KEVIN FOY, Interim Dir., Tel: 312-534-3317; Fax: 312-534-3801; CLARISSA ALJENTERA, Senior Coord. Family Ministries, Tel: 312-534-8051; ANNA DUDEK, Senior Coord. Youth & Young Adult Ministries, Tel: 312-534-8107; KENNETH VELASQUEZ, Senior Coord. Catechist Formation, Tel: 312-534-8043; PATRICIA MALINOWSKI, Senior Coord. Catechetical Ministry, Tel: 312-534-8053.

Marriage and Family Ministries—LAURA PALAFOX, Marriage Prep, Tel: 312-534-8381; VICTOR VALLEJO, Marriage Prog., Tel: 312-534-5355; MARYVEL TORRES, Family Ministries, Tel: 312-534-8353.

Youth and Young Adult Ministries—Tel: 312-534-8600.

Special Religious Education (SPRED)—Rev. JAMES H. MCCARTHY, Dir. Emeritus, (Retired), 2956 S. Lowe, Chicago, 60616. Tel: 312-842-1039; Fax: 312-842-4449; Sisters MARY THERESE HARRINGTON, S.H.; SUSANNE GALLAGHER, S.P.

Divine Worship and Sacraments, Office for—Cardinal Meyer Center, 3525 Lake Park Ave., Chicago, 60653-1402. MR. TODD WILLIAMSON, Dir.; WENDY BARTON SILHAVY, Dir. Liturgies & Music, Tel: 312-534-5153; Fax: 312-534-5158; Web: www.odw.org.

Office of Human Dignity and Solidarity—RYAN LENTS, Dir., Cardinal Meyer Center, 3525 S. Lake Park Ave., Chicago, 60653-1402. Tel: 312-534-8057.

Catholic Campaign for Human Development/Parish Sharing—MS. ELENA SEGURA.

Immigration Ministries—MS. ELENA SEGURA, Dir., Tel: 312-534-5333.

Catholic Relief Services and Justice Education—RYAN LENTS.

Respect Life/Pro-Life Office—DAWN FITZPATRICK, Dir., Tel: 312-534-5355; Fax: 312-534-1554.

Project Rachel—Tel: 312-337-1962; Tel: 800-456-4673 (800-456-HOPE).

Chastity Education Initiative—Tel: 312-534-5355.

Jail Ministry/Kolbe House—Rev. MARK A. BARTOSIC, 2434 S. California, Chicago, 60608. Tel: 773-247-0070; Fax: 773-247-0665.

Domestic Violence Outreach—Tel: 312-226-6161, Ext. 224. Rev. CHARLES W. DAHM, O.P.

Amate House/Young Adult Volunteer Program—JEANNIE A. BALANDA, Exec. Dir., 3600 S. Seeley, Chicago, 60609. Tel: 773-376-2445; Web: www.amatehouse.org.

Mission Office, The Society for the Propagation of the Faith, Missionary Childhood AssociationMEGAN MIO, M.Div., Dir., Tel: 312-534-3322; Fax: 312-534-1599; Email: missions@archchicago.org; Web: weaeremissionary.org.

Ethnic Initiatives—

Asian Catholic Initiative - St. Henry—Rev. PHI H. NGUYEN.

Black Catholic Initiative—MR. CLIFF BARBER, Tel: 312-534-5397.

Consejo Hispano—Rev. ISMAEL SANDOVAL, Tel: 773-523-3917.

Native American Initiative—Kateri Ctr., 3938 N. Leavitt St., Chicago, 60618. Very Rev. STEPHEN F. KANONIK, (St. Benedict), Tel: 773-588-6484.

Polish Initiative—Rev. MAREK MACIEJ SMOLKA, Tel: 312-787-8040.

Ethnic Apostolates—

Haitian Catholic Apostolate—7851 S. Jeffery Blvd., Chicago, 60649. Tel: 773-721-6365.

Indochinese Catholic Center—Rev. PETER HUNG, Dir., (Retired), 4827 N. Kenmore, Chicago, 60640. Tel: 773-784-1932.

Archdiocesan Council of Catholic Women (ACCW)—EVELYN GETTY, Pres., Tel: 312-534-8325.

Liturgy Training Publications (LTP)—3943 S. Racine Ave., Chicago, 60690. Tel: 773-579-4900; Fax: 773-579-4929. DEANNA KEEFE, Dir. Orders: Tel: 800-933-2800; Fax: 800-933-7094; Email: orders@ltp.org.

Strategic Planning and Implementation—MR. TIM WEISKE, Dir., Tel: 312-534-8125; Fax: 312-534-8766.

Renew My Church—Tel: 312-534-5010. Rev. JASON A. MALAVE, Cardinal's Delegate; MR. CLIFF BARBER, Chief Strategy Officer, Tel: 312-534-5397.

Office of the Chief Operating Officer

Chief Operating Officer—MS. BETSY BOHLEN, 835 N. Rush St., Chicago, 60611-2030. Tel: 312-534-8218.

Chief of Parish and School Ops.—Tel: 312-534-8357. MR. TIM CAWLEY.

Capital Assets—ERIC WOLLAN, Dir., Tel: 312-534-8394.

Facilities and Construction—KEVIN O'MALLEY, Dir.

Communications and Public Relations—MS. PAULA WATERS, Chief Communications Officer, 835 N. Rush St., Chicago, 60611-2030. Tel: 312-534-8289; Fax: 312-534-5306.

Office of Radio & Television—MR. JIM DISCH, Dir., Tel: 312-534-8277.

New World Publications—GRANT GALLICHO, Dir. Publications & Media, 835 N. Rush St., Chicago, 60611-2030. Tel: 312-534-7110; Fax: 312-534-7310.

Chicago Catholic—JOYCE DURIGA, Editor, Tel: 312-534-7577.

Hispanic Communications—ALEJANDRO CASTILLO, Dir., Tel: 312-534-7880; Fax: 312-534-7310.

Chicago Catolico—ALEJANDRO CASTILLO, Gen. Mgr., Tel: 312-534-7880.

Financial Services—PAUL MANNINO, CFO, Tel: 312-534-8293.

Controller's Operations—MS. CHRISTINE DUSZYNSKI, Controller, Tel: 312-534-5266.

Parish Finance and Administration—JESSE ESTRADA, Dir., Tel: 312-534-5312.

Information Technology—MR. JOHN DICELLO, Dir., Tel: 312-534-5330; Fax: 312-534-5346; MR. GANG CHEN, Mgr. Applications Svcs., Tel: 312-534-8331; Fax: 312-534-5346.

Insurance and Risk Management—Tel: 312-534-8295; Fax: 312-534-8302. MR. RICHARD RABS, Mgr.

Priests' Retirement and Mutual Aid Association (PRMAA)—4951 Harrison St., Hillside, 60162. Tel: 708-449-8026; Fax: 708-449-8148. MR. KEVIN J. MARZALIK, Dir.

St. Benedict's Technology Consortium—3525 S. Lake Park Blvd., Chicago, 60653. Web: www.sbtcsupport.org. SCOTT BELL, Dir.

Catholic Cemeteries—Rev. LAWRENCE J. SULLIVAN, Archdiocesan Dir.; MR. ROMAN SZABELSKI, CCCE, Exec. Dir., 1400 S. Wolf Rd., Hillside, 60162. Tel: 708-449-6100; Fax: 708-449-3419.

Legal Services and Policy Development—Tel: 312-534-8303. MR. WILLIAM KUNKEL, Gen. Counsel.

Personnel Services—835 N. Rush St., Chicago, 60611-2030. Tel: 312-534-8349. MS. CLAUDIA MANN, Dir.

Human Resources—VACANT.

Department of Stewardship and Development—Archbishop Quigley Ctr.: 835 N. Rush St., Chicago, 60611-2030. Tel: 312-534-5271. BRENDAN KEATING, Interim Chief Devel. Officer.

Development Services/Annual Catholic Appeal—MS. BARBARA SHEA COLLINS, Dir., Tel: 312-534-7944.

Joseph and Mary Retreat House—Rev. Msgr. JOHN F. CANARY, S.T.L., Dir., 1300 Stritch Dr., P.O. Box 455, Mundelein, 60060-0455. Tel: 847-566-6060; Fax: 847-566-6082.

Food Service Professionals, Archdiocese—5150 Northwest Hwy., Chicago, 60638. Tel: 773-385-5100; Fax: 773-385-5070; Web: www.fspro.com. MR. BRADLEY BLACK, Dir.

Department of Human Services

Director—Rev. Msgr. MICHAEL M. BOLAND, 721 N. LaSalle St., Chicago, 60654-3574. Tel: 312-655-7460; Fax: 312-655-0219.

Catholic Charities of Chicago—Rev. Msgr. MICHAEL M. BOLAND, Admin., Pres. & CEO; MS. ELIDA HERNANDEZ, CFO; MICHELE BIANCHI, Sr. Vice Pres. HR & Gen. Counsel; MS. KATHY DONAHUE, Sr. Vice Pres. Prog. Devel. & Evaluation; JOHN J. RYAN, Chief of Staff. Associate Administrators: Revs. RICHARD E. BULWITH, (Retired); GERARD P. KELLY, C.M.; CHARLES T. RUBEY, (Retired), 721 N. LaSalle St., Chicago, 60654-3574. Tel: 312-655-7000 Central Intake Phone; Tel: 800-244-0505. (Refer to Catholic Charities section under the Institutions located in the Archdiocese for further listings.).

Maternity Fund—NORENE CHESEBRO, 721 N. LaSalle St., Chicago, 60654-3574. Tel: 312-655-7596.

Office for Persons with Disabilities—721 N. LasSalle St., Chicago, 60654-3574. Tel: 312-401-1754. ANNE GROSKLAUS.

Catholic Office of the Deaf—Rev. JOSEPH A. MULCRONE, Dir., (Retired); MS. MARGARET SWATEK, D.R.E., Cardinal Meyer Center, 3525 S. Lake Park Ave., Chicago, 60653-1402. Tel: 312-534-7899; Tel: 312-534-8368 TTY; Fax: 312-534-0394; Email: cathdeafch@archchicago.org; Web: www.deafchurchchicago.parishesonline.com.

Mercy Home for Boys and Girls—Rev. SCOTT DONAHUE, Pres. & CEO, 1140 W. Jackson, Chicago, 60607. Tel: 312-738-9240.

CLERGY, PARISHES, MISSIONS AND PAROCHIAL SCHOOLS

CITY OF CHICAGO

(COOK COUNTY)

1—HOLY NAME CATHEDRAL (1849) Very Rev. Gregory Sakowicz, Rector; Revs. John P. Boivin; Don Einars Cambe; Marek Maciej Smolka; Deacons Michael McCloskey; Stan Strom; Daniel G. Welter, J.D.; Revs. Kevin M. Birmingham, In Res.; Louis J. Cameli, In Res.; Ramil E. Fajardo, J.C.L., In Res.; William J. Moriarity, In Res., (Retired); William H. Woestman, O.M.I., In Res.

Rectory—730 N. Wabash Ave., 60611.
Tel: 312-787-8040; Email: holyname-cathedral@archchicago.org.

Archbishop's Residence—1555 N. State Pkwy., 60610.

SEMINARY FORMATION HOUSE-CASA JESUS, 750 N. Wabash, 60611. Tel: 312-640-1065.

SEMINARY FORMATION HOUSE-BISHOP ABRAMOWICZ SEMINARY, Tel: 312-915-0598; Fax: 312-640-1066. Very Rev. Jacek Wrona, (Poland) Rector.

Catechesis Religious Program—Thomas Aspell, D.R.E. Students 143.

Convent—Oblate Sisters of Jesus the Priest.

2—ST. AGATHA, Rev. Lawrence R. Dowling; Deacons Gregory Shumpert; Robert Carlton.
Res.: 3147 W. Douglas Blvd., 60623.
Tel: 773-522-3050; Email: stagatha@archchicago.org.
Catechesis Religious Program—Students 107.

3—ST. AGNES OF BOHEMIA, Revs. Donald J. Nevins; Luis Santos Parra; Jose Alvarado Pasillas; Deacons Angel Favila; Juan Carlos Bautista.
Res.: 2651 S. Central Park Ave., 60623.
Tel: 773-522-0142; Email: stagnes-central@archchicago.org.
School—St. Agnes of Bohemia School, 2643 S. Central Park Ave., 60623. Tel: 773-522-0143; Fax: 773-522-0132; Email: kkysiak@school.stagnesofbohemia.org. Ms. Kaitlin K. Kysiak, Prin. Lay Teachers 23; Students 426.
Catechesis Religious Program—Tel: 773-277-5446. Students 368.
Convent—Misioneras de San Pio X, 2658 S. Central Park Ave., 60623. Tel: 773-762-3229.

4—ALL SAINTS-ST. ANTHONY, Revs. Peter B. McQuinn, M.Div.; John W. Parker, Pastor Emeritus, (Retired).
Res.: 518 W. 28th Pl., 60616. Tel: 312-842-2744; Email: allsaints@archchicago.org.
See Bridgeport Catholic Academy, Chicago under Consolidated Elementary Schools, located in the Institution section.
Catechesis Religious Program—Students 62.

5—ST. ALOYSIUS, Rev. Claudio Diaz Jr.; Deacons Adolfo Lopez; Ramon Arroyo; William Smyser; Ramon Navarro.
Res.: 2300 W. Le Moyne St., 60622.
Tel: 773-278-4808; Email: staloysius@archchicago.org.
Catechesis Religious Program—Students 119.

6—ST. ALPHONSUS, (German) Revs. Bartholomew S. Winters; Michael W. O'Connell, S.T.L.
Res.: 1429 W. Wellington Ave., 60657.
Tel: 773-525-0709; Email: stalphonsus-wellington@archchicago.org.
School—Alphonsus Academy and Center for the Arts, Tel: 773-348-4629; Email:

cbadynee@alphonsusacademy.org. Dr. Casimer Badynee, Prin. Lay Teachers 38; Students 492.
Catechesis Religious Program—Catherine Crino, D.R.E. Students 159.

7—ST. AMBROSE, Rev. John Owusu-Achiaw.
Res.: Congregation of the Holy Ghost (Spiritans), 1012 E. 47th St., 60653. Tel: 773-624-3695; Email: stambrose@archchicago.org.
Catechesis Religious Program—Students 28.

8—ST. ANDREW, Revs. Sergio Romo; John A. Farry, Pastor Emeritus, (Retired); Arlin J. Louis, O.M.I., In Res.; Deacons Eric Sorensen; Mark J. Purdome; David Heimann.
Res.: 3546 N. Paulina St., 60657. Tel: 773-525-3016; Email: standrew@archchicago.org.
School—St. Andrew School, 1710 W. Addison, 60613. Tel: 773-248-2500; Fax: 773-248-2709; Email: allenackermann@gosaintandrew.com. Mr. Allen Ackermann, Prin. Lay Teachers 37; Students 519.
Catechesis Religious Program—Students 145.

9—ANNUNCIATA (1941) Rev. Vidal M. Martinez, O.S.M., Admin.
Res.: 11128 S. Avenue G, 60617. Tel: 773-221-1040; Email: annunciata@archchicago.org.
School—Annunciata School, 3750 E. 112th St., 60617. Tel: 773-375-5711; Fax: 773-375-5704; Email: erenasannunciatags@gmail.com. Mr. Ed Renas, Prin. Lay Teachers 12; Students 176.
Catechesis Religious Program—Students 162.

10—ST. ANSELM, Rev. Robert M. Kelly, O.P.; Deacon Ivan Lazcano.
Res.: 6045 S. Michigan Ave., 60637.
Tel: 773-493-5959; Email: stanselm@archchicago.org.
Catechesis Religious Program—Students 19.

11—ST. ANTHONY OF PADUA (1903) Rev. Mark J. Krylowicz.
Res.: 11533 S. Prairie Ave., 60628. Tel: 773-468-1200 ; Email: stanthony-prairie@archchicago.org.
Catechesis Religious Program—

12—ASSUMPTION, Rev. Jason A. Malave, Admin.
Res.: 2434 S. California Ave., 60608.
Tel: 773-247-6644; Email: assumption-california@archchicago.org.
Convent—2831 W. 24th St. Blvd., 60623.
Catechesis Religious Program—Students 100.

13—ASSUMPTION OF THE BLESSED VIRGIN MARY, Revs. Joseph Chamblain, O.S.M.; Michael Doyle, O.S.M., Senior Priest; Timothy M. Kremen, O.S.M., In Res.; John M. Pawlikowski, O.S.M., Ph.D., In Res.; Deacon Kevin Zajdel.
Res.: 323 W. Illinois St., 60654-7812.
Tel: 312-644-0036; Email: assumption-illinois@archchicago.org.
Catechesis Religious Program—Students 100.

14—ST. BARBARA, Rev. Wojciech A. Marat, J.C.D.
Res.: 2859 S. Throop St., 60608. Tel: 312-842-7979; Email: stbarbara@stbarbarachicago.org.
School—St. Barbara School, Tel: 312-326-6243; Email: nnolazco@stbarbarachicago.org. Nicole Nolazco, Prin. Lay Teachers 10; Students 132.
Catechesis Religious Program—Students 4.

15—ST. BARNABAS, Revs. James J. Donovan Jr.; Augustine Mahonge; Raymond J. Tillrock, Pastor Emeritus, (Retired); William G. Kenneally, Senior Priest, (Retired); William Malloy, In Res., (Retired); Deacons James L. Conway; Andrew Neu; Ms. Kitty T. Ryan, Pastoral Assoc. & Liturgy Dir.
Res.: 10134 S. Longwood Dr., 60643.
Tel: 773-779-1166; Email: stbarnabas@archchicago.org.
School—St. Barnabas School, 10121 S. Longwood Dr., 60643. Tel: 773-445-7711; Fax: 773-445-9815; Email: egaffney@stbarnabasparish.org. Mrs. Elaine Gaffney, Prin. Lay Teachers 36; Students 581.
Catechesis Religious Program—Tel: 773-445-3450. Matt Furjanic, D.R.E. Students 181.

16—ST. BARTHOLOMEW, Revs. Ricardo Castillo; Thomas E. Lamping; Deacon Faustino Santiago, .
Res.: 4949 W. Patterson Ave., 60641.
Tel: 773-286-7871; Email: stbartholomew@archchicago.org.
School—St. Bartholomew School, 4941 W. Patterson Ave., 60641. Tel: 773-282-9373; Fax: 773-282-4757; Email: krebhancsuk@stbartholomew.net. Mrs. Karen Rebhan-Csuk, Prin. Lay Teachers 10; Students 206.
Catechesis Religious Program—Students 699.

17—ST. BASIL/VISITATION, Rev. Norman H. Moran-Rosero, M.Div., Admin.
Res.: 843 W. Garfield Blvd., 60621.
Tel: 773-846-3570; Email: stbasil@archchicago.org.
School—Visitation School, 900 W. Garfield Blvd., 60609. Tel: 733-373-5200; Fax: 733-373-5201; Email: elem.visitation@archchicago.org. Ms. Jennifer Markoff, Prin. Lay Teachers 13; Students 137.
Catechesis Religious Program—

18—ST. BEDE THE VENERABLE, Revs. Carlos Aranciba Bermudez, Admin.; Patrick La Pacz; Deacon Miguel Luevano; Rev. Charlie Plovanich; Deacon Ramiro Serna.
Res.: 8200 S. Kostner Ave., 60652. Tel: 773-884-2000; Email: stbede-venerable@archchicago.org.
School—St. Bede the Venerable School, 4440 W. 83rd St., 60652. Tel: 773-884-2020; Fax: 773-582-3366; Email: sstewart@stbedechicago.org. Sherry Stewart, Prin. Lay Teachers 14; Students 259.
Catechesis Religious Program—Tel: 773-884-2038; Fax: 773-884-2037. Students 284.

19—ST. BENEDICT (1902) Very Rev. Stephen F. Kanonik; Revs. Robert W. Beaven, Pastor Emeritus, (Retired); Robert M. Pajor; John A. Farry, In Res., (Retired); Richard P. Hynes, In Res.; Deacon David Reyes; Ms. Elaine Lindia, Pastoral Assoc.
Res.: 2215 W. Irving Park Rd., 60618.
Tel: 773-588-6484; Email: stbenedict-irvingpark@archchicago.org.
School—St. Benedict School, 3920 N. Leavitt St., 60618. Tel: 773-463-6797; Fax: 773-463-0782; Email: info@stbenedict.com; Web: sbps.stbenedict.com. Lay Teachers 47; Students 716.
High School—St. Benedict High School, 3900 N. Leavitt St., 60618. Tel: 773-539-0066;
Fax: 773-539-3397. Lay Teachers 22; Sisters 2; Students 175.
Catechesis Religious Program—Students 84.

20—ST. BENEDICT THE AFRICAN, Rev. David A. Jones, Email: djones@archchicago.org.
Res.: 340 W. 66th St., 60621. Tel: 773-873-4464; Email: stbenedict-66th@archchicago.org.
School—Academy of St. Benedict the African, 6020 S. Laflin, 60636. Tel: 773-776-3316; Email: info@academystbenedict.org. Patricia Murphy, Prin. Lay Teachers 15; Students 224.
Catechesis Religious Program—Students 2.

21—BLESSED ALOJZIJE STEPINAC CROATIAN MISSION, Rev. Drazan Boras, Dir.; Deacon Ivan M. Mikan. (Independent Mission)
Res.: 6346 N. Ridge, 60660. Tel: 773-262-0535; Email: blessedaloysius-mission@archchicago.org.
Catechesis Religious Program—Students 36.

22—BLESSED SACRAMENT, Revs. Ismael Sandoval; Cristian Cuevas Jara; Deacons Dismas Fernandez; Juan Rosales.
Office: 3528 S. Hermitage Ave., 60609-1217.
Tel: 773-523-3917; Email: blessedsacrament@archchicago.org.
Catechesis Religious Program—Students 160.

23—ST. BRIDE (1893) Rev. Robert J. Roll.
Res.: 7811 S. Coles Ave., 60649. Tel: 773-731-8822; Email: st-bride@archchicago.org.
Catechesis Religious Program—Students 29.

24—ST. BRUNO, Rev. Antoni Bury; Deacon Sal Villa.
Res.: 4751 S. Harding Ave., 60632. Tel: 773-523-3467 ; Email: stbruno@archchicago.org.
School—St. Bruno School, 4839 S. Harding Ave., 60632. Tel: 773-847-0697; Fax: 773-847-1620; Email: office@stbruno.com. Ms. Carla Sever, Prin. Lay Teachers 15; Students 183.
Catechesis Religious Program—Students 152.

25—ST. CAJETAN, Revs. Steven G. Dombrowski, M.Div.; William A. Burke, Pastor Emeritus; Deacon Joseph J. Roccasalva.
Parish Center Office—2445 W. 112th St., 60655.
Tel: 773-474-7800; Email: stcajetan@archchicago.org.
Res.: 11234 S. Artesian Ave., 60655.
School—St. Cajetan School, 2447 W. 112th St., 60655. Tel: 773-233-8844; Email: info@cajetan.org. Mrs. Michelle Nitsche, Prin. Lay Teachers 24; Students 406.
Catechesis Religious Program—Students 128.

26—ST. CAMILLUS, Revs. Waclaw L. Lech, O.C.D.; Jacek Chodzynski, O.C.D., In Res.
Res.: 5426 S. Lockwood Ave., 60638.
Tel: 773-767-8183; Email: stcamillus@archchicago.org.
Catechesis Religious Program—Students 554.

27—CHRIST THE KING (1936) Rev. Msgr. Michael J. Adams, Senior Priest, (Retired); Revs. Lawrence J. Sullivan; Matthew Litak; Deacon Alfred Antonsen.
Res.: 9235 S. Hamilton Ave., 60643-6360.
Tel: 773-238-4877; Email: christtheking@archchicago.org.
School—Christ the King School, 9240 S. Hoyne Ave., 60643-6303. Tel: 773-779-3329; Fax: 773-779-3390; Email: info@ck-school.org. Dr. Ann Marie Riordan, Prin. Lay Teachers 25; Students 385.
Catechesis Religious Program—Students 61.

28—ST. CHRISTINA
Tel: 773-779-7181. Revs. Thomas P. Conde, M.Div., S.T.B., M.B.A.; Binu Varghese; Deacons John Mutnansky; Stanley Rakauskas; Alfredo Adolfo.
Res.: 11005 S. Homan Ave., 60655. Tel: 773-779-7181 ; Email: stchristina@archchicago.org.
School—St. Christina School, 3333 W. 110th St., 60655. Tel: 773-445-2969; Fax: 773-445-0444; Email: schooloffice@stchristina.org. Mrs. Mary E. Stokes, Prin. Lay Teachers 26; Students 433.
Catechesis Religious Program—Students 368.

29—ST. CLARE OF MONTEFALCO, Rev. John Celichowski, O.F.M.Cap.; Deacons Felix Patino; Vincente Haro.
Res.: 5443 S. Washtenaw Ave., 60632.
Tel: 773-436-4422; Email: stclare@archchicago.org.
Catechesis Religious Program—Tel: 773-434-5599. Students 253.

30—ST. CLEMENT, Revs. Paul G. Seaman; Joseph Anthony Pillai, C.Ss.R.; Przemyslaw Wojcik, In Res.; Deacon Timothy P. Sullivan.
Res.: 642 W. Deming Pl., 60614. Tel: 773-281-0371; Email: stclement@archchicago.org.
School—St. Clement School, 2524 N. Orchard St., 60614. Tel: 773-348-8212; Fax: 773-348-4712; Email: info@stclementschool.org. Ms. Mari Jo Hanson, Prin. Lay Teachers 42; Students 447.
Catechesis Religious Program—
Tel: 773-281-0371, Ext. 14. Rachel Espinoza, D.R.E. Students 208.

31—ST. CLOTILDE, Rev. John B. Atoyebi.
Res.: 8430 Calumet Ave., 60619. Tel: 773-874-1022; Email: stclotilde@archchicago.org.
Catechesis Religious Program—

32—ST. COLUMBA (1884) Revs. Charles W. Watkins; Kilian J. Knittel, (Retired).
Res.: 13323 S. Greenbay Ave., 60633.
Tel: 773-646-2660; Email: stcolumba@archchicago.org.

33—ST. COLUMBANUS, Rev. Matthew O'Donnell.
Res.: 331 E. 71st St., 60619. Tel: 773-224-1022; Email: stcolumbanus@archchicago.org.
School—Augustus Tolton Catholic Academy, (Grades PreK-8), (Ministry of St. Dorothy and St. Columbanus) 7120 S. Calumet, 60619.
Tel: 773-224-3811; Fax: 773-224-3810; Email: dsmith@toltonacademy.org. Mr. Philip Bazile, Prin. Lay Teachers 14; Students 128; Clergy 1.
Catechesis Religious Program—Students 14.

34—ST. CONSTANCE (1916) Revs. Richard Milek; Pawel Barwikowski; James F. Heyd, S.T.L., In Res.; Deacons Rudolf Kotleba; James Schiltz; Mr. Roman Hamata, Pastoral Assoc.
Res.: 5843 W. Strong St., 60630. Tel: 773-545-8581; Email: stconstance@archchicago.org.
School—St. Constance School, 5841 W. Strong St., 60630. Tel: 773-283-2311; Fax: 773-283-3515; Email: office@stconstanceschool.org. Mrs. Eva M. Panczyk, Prin. Clergy 1; Lay Teachers 14; Students 147.
Catechesis Religious Program—81 English; 351 Polish. Students 574.

35—ST. CORNELIUS, Revs. Daniel R. Fallon; Edwin D. Pacocha, (Retired); Deacon John Rottman.
Res.: 5205 N. Lieb Ave., 60630. Tel: 773-283-5222; Email: stcornelius@archchicago.org.
Catechesis Religious Program—Students 95.

36—CORPUS CHRISTI, Revs. Anthony Anike; Peter Okojie, In Res.
Corpus Christi Friary, 4920 King Dr., 60615-2306.
Tel: 773-285-7720; Email: corpuschristi@archchicago.org.
Catechesis Religious Program—

37—ST. DANIEL THE PROPHET, Revs. John T. Noga; Slawomir Kurc; Deacons Richard Voytas; Rudolf Hess; Adam Danielewicz; Robert Montelongo.
Parish Office & Res.: 5300 S. Natoma Ave., 60638.
Tel: 773-586-1223; Email: stdaniel@archchicago.org.
School—St. Daniel the Prophet School, (Grades PreK-8), Tel: 773-586-1225; Email: principal@stdan.net. Ms. Cynthia Zabilka, Prin. Lay Teachers 29; Students 646.
Catechesis Religious Program—Tel: 773-229-8794. Students 293.

38—ST. DENIS, Rev. Theodore L. Ostrowski.
Res.: 8301 S. St. Louis Ave., 60652.
Tel: 773-434-3313; Email: stdenis@archchicago.org.
Catechesis Religious Program—Students 91.

39—ST. DOROTHY, Rev. Robert J. Miller; Deacons Wallace Harris; Leroy Gill Jr.
Res.: 450 E. 78th St., 60619. Tel: 773-651-7000; Email: stdorothy@archchicago.org.
School—Augustus Tolton Catholic Academy, (Grades PreK-8), (Ministry of St. Dorothy and St. Columbanus) 7120 S. Calumet Ave., 60619.
Tel: 773-224-3811; Email: dsmith@toltonacademy.org. Diana Smith, Prin. Clergy 1; Lay Teachers 14; Students 149.
Catechesis Religious Program—Mr. Mark Nimo, D.R.E.

40—ST. EDWARD, Revs. Kenneth Anderson; Dominic Clemente Jr.; James P. McIlhone, S.T.L., Ph.D., In Res., (Retired); Joseph C. Taylor, In Res., (Retired).
Res.: 4350 W. Sunnyside Ave., 60630-4146.
Tel: 773-545-6496; Email: stedward@archchicago.org.
School—St. Edward School, 4343 W. Sunnyside Ave., 60630-4146. Tel: 773-736-9133;
Fax: 773-736-9280; Email: office@stedwardschool.com. Ms. Sara Lasica, Prin. Lay Teachers 25; Students 333.
Catechesis Religious Program—Students 147.

41—ST. ELIZABETH, Rev. Robert M. Kelly, O.P.

Res.: 50 E. 41st St., 60653. Tel: 773-268-1518; Email: stelizabeth-41st@archchicago.org.
Catechesis Religious Program—
Convent—4117 S. Michigan, 60653.
42—EPIPHANY, Rev. Daniel Long.
Res.: 2524 S. Keeler Ave., 60623. Tel: 773-521-1112; Email: epiphany@archchicago.org.
School—Epiphany School, 4223 W. 25th St., 60623. Tel: 773-762-1542; Email: martinez@epiphanychicago.org. Mr. Scott J. Ernst, Prin. Lay Teachers 11; Students 264.
Catechesis Religious Program—Students 442.
43—ST. EUGENE, Revs. Richard Yanos; James J. O'Brien, M.A., Pastor Emeritus, (Retired); Grzegorz Wojcik; John G. Hetland; Philip J. Grib, S.J., In Res.
Res.: 7958 W. Foster Ave., 60656-1651.
Tel: 773-775-6659; Email: steugene@archchicago.org.
School—St. Eugene School, (Grades PreK-8), 7930 W. Foster Ave., 60656-1651. Tel: 773-763-2235; Fax: 773-763-2775; Email: school@st-eugene.org. Ms. Catherine Scotkovsky, Prin. Lay Teachers 17; Students 188.
Catechesis Religious Program—Students 131.
44—ST. FERDINAND (1927) Revs. Zdzislaw J. Torba; Lukasz Pyka; Pawel Zazuniak.
Res.: 5900 W. Barry Ave., 60634. Tel: 773-622-5900; Email: stferdinand@archchicago.org.
School—St. Ferdinand School, (Grades PreK-8), 3131 N. Mason Ave., 60634. Tel: 773-622-3022; Fax: 773-622-2807; Email: School@saintferdinand.org. Ms. Denise H. Akana, Prin. Lay Teachers 11; Students 223.
Catechesis Religious Program—
Tel: 773-622-5900, Ext. 366. Students 1,900.
Convent—5936 W. Barry Ave., 60634. Missionary Sisters of Christ the King for Polonia 4.
45—FIVE HOLY MARTYRS, Rev. Bronislaw Chmiel, Admin., (Retired).
Res.: 4327 S. Richmond St., 60632. Tel: 773-254-3636 ; Email: fiveholymartyrs@archchicago.org.
School—Pope John Paul II School, Five Holy Martyrs Campus, (Grades PreK-8), 4325 S. Richmond St., 60632. Tel: 773-523-6161; Fax: 773-254-9194; Email: principal@pjpiischool.org. Mrs. Deborah Coffey, Prin. Lay Teachers 14; Students 132.
Catechesis Religious Program—Students 28.
46—ST. FLORIAN (1905) Rev. David J. Simonetti.
Res.: 13145 S. Houston Ave., 60633.
Tel: 773-646-4877; Email: stflorian@archchicago.org.
Catechesis Religious Program—Students 58.
47—ST. FRANCIS BORGIA (1949) Revs. Robert J. Lojek; Robert Fraczek.
Res.: 8033 W. Addison St., 60634. Tel: 773-625-1118; Email: stfrancis-borgia@archchicago.org.
School—St. Francis Borgia School, (Grades PreK-8), Tel: 773-589-1000; Email: sbetzolt@sfborgia.org. Mrs. Susan L. Betzolt, Prin. Lay Teachers 14; Students 192.
Catechesis Religious Program—Tel: 773-625-1705; Fax: 773-625-1774. Students 155.
Convent—3521 N. Panama St., 60634.
48—ST. FRANCIS DE SALES, Revs. Armand Ramirez Ruiz; Francisco Luna; Deacon Faustino Ramos.
Res.: 10201 S. Ewing Ave., 60617. Tel: 773-734-1383; Email: stfrancisdesales-ewing@archchicago.org.
Catechesis Religious Program—Students 138.
49—ST. FRANCIS OF ASSISI, (Hispanic) Rev. Walter D. Mallo, I.V.E.; Deacon J. Zeferino Ochoa.
Res.: 813 W. Roosevelt Rd., 60608. Tel: 312-226-7575 ; Email: stfrancisassisi-roosevelt@archchicago.org.
Catechesis Religious Program—Students 734.
50—ST. GABRIEL (1880) Revs. Thomas E. Griffin, O.S.A.; James E. Merold, Pastor Emeritus, (Retired); Richard C. Creagh; Christopher C. Steinle, O.S.A., In Res.; Deacon Robert F. Morris II.
Res.: 4522 S. Wallace St., 60609. Tel: 773-268-9595; Email: stgabriel@archchicago.org.
Church: 45th St. & Lowe Ave., 60609.
School—St. Gabriel School, (Grades PreSchool-8), 607 W. 45th St., 60609. Tel: 773-268-6636; Fax: 773-268-2501; Email: info@stgabrielchicago.com. Mr. Stephen J. Adams, Prin. Lay Teachers 11; Students 173.
Catechesis Religious Program—Students 87.
51—ST. GALL, Revs. Rene Mena Beltran, M.Div.; Agustin Garza Candanosa; Deacons Miguel Arellano; Albert Herrera; John Bumbul.
Res.: 5511 S. Sawyer Ave., 60629. Tel: 773-737-3113; Email: stgall@archchicago.org.
School—St. Gall School, 5515 S. Sawyer Ave., 60629. Tel: 773-737-3454; Email: info@stgallschool.com. Caitlin Lee, Prin. Lay Teachers 15; Students 232.
Catechesis Religious Program—Students 1,489.
52—ST. GENEVIEVE, Revs. Sergio Tamayo; Yorman A. Beltran Arias; Deacons Antonio Delgado; Faustino Villasenor; Leonel Segura.
Res.: 4835 W. Altgeld St., 60639. Tel: 773-237-3011; Email: stgenevieve@archchicago.org.
School—St. Genevieve School, 4854 W. Montana St., 60639. Tel: 773-237-7131; Fax: 773-237-7265; Email: mcorrigan@stgschool.org. Ms. Mary M. Corrigan, Prin. Lay Teachers 12; Students 212.
Catechesis Religious Program—Tel: 773-637-6086. Students 491.
53—ST. GEORGE, (Slovenian) Revs. Armando Morales Martinez, M.Div.; Raphael A. Makori, In Res.
Res.: 9546 S. Ewing Ave., 60617. Tel: 773-734-0554; Email: stgeorge-ewing@archchicago.org.
Catechesis Religious Program—Tel: 773-734-1383. Students 82.
54—ST. GERTRUDE, Revs. Richard J. Prendergast; William G. Kenneally, Pastor Emeritus, (Retired); Mr. Kevin Chears, Pastoral Assoc.; Mr. Arthur Blumberg, Pastoral Assoc. In Res., Very Rev. Michael Bradley, J.C.D.
Res.: 1420 W. Granville Ave., 60660.
Tel: 773-764-3621; Email: stgertrude-granville@archchicago.org.
See Northside Catholic Academy under Consolidated Elementary Schools, located in the Institution Section.
Catechesis Religious Program—
55—GOOD SHEPHERD
2735 S. Kolin Ave., 60623. Rev. Jose Maria Garcia-Maldonado. In Res., Most Rev. John R. Manz.
Res.: 2719 S. Kolin Ave., 60623. Tel: 773-762-2322; Email: goodshepherd@archchicago.org.
Catechesis Religious Program—Students 428.
56—ST. GREGORY, THE GREAT, Revs. Paul H. Wachdorf, M.C.Sp.; Brian J. Fischer.
Office: 5545 N. Paulina St., 60640.
Res.: 1634 W. Gregory St., 60640. Tel: 773-561-3546; Email: stgregory@archchicago.org.
See Northside Catholic Academy, Chicago under Consolidated Elementary Schools, located in the Institution Section.
Catechesis Religious Program—Students 75.
57—ST. HEDWIG, Rev. Tomasz Wojciechowski, C.R.; Deacons Daniel Cabrera; Rodolfo Urquiza.
Res.: 2226 N. Hoyne Ave., 60647. Tel: 773-486-1660; Email: sthedwig@archchicago.org.
Catechesis Religious Program—Students 87.
58—ST. HELEN, Rev. Franciszek Florczyk, (Poland).
Res.: 2315 W. Augusta Blvd., 60622.
Tel: 773-235-3575; Email: sthelen@archchicago.org.
School—St. Helen School, (Grades PreK-8), 2347 W. Augusta Blvd., 60622. Tel: 773-486-1055; Email: info@sthelenchicago.org. Mrs. Marianne I. Johnson, Prin. Clergy 1; Lay Teachers 21; Students 400.
Catechesis Religious Program—
59—ST. HENRY, Rev. Phi H. Nguyen; Deacons David Pham; Duc Van Nguyen; Joseph T. Than.
Res.: 6335 N. Hoyne Ave., 60659. Tel: 773-764-7413; Email: sthenry@archchicago.org.
See Northside Catholic Academy, Chicago under Consolidated Elementary Schools, located in the Institution section.
Catechesis Religious Program—Students 256.
60—ST. HILARY (1926) Revs. Aloysius Funtila; Robert G. Darow, Pastor Emeritus, (Retired); Roger J. Caplis, Pastor Emeritus, (Retired); Thomas A. Libera, In Res., (Retired); Deacons Donald Wehling; Juan Ramirez.
Res.: 5600 N. Fairfield Ave., 60659.
Tel: 773-561-3474; Email: sthilary@archchicago.org.
School—St. Hilary School, (Grades PreK-8), 5614 N. Fairfield Ave., 60659. Tel: 773-561-5885; Fax: 773-561-6409; Email: donovan@sthilarychicago.org. Mrs. Kathleen M. Donovan, Prin. Lay Teachers 16; Students 181.
Catechesis Religious Program—Students 92.
61—HOLY ANGELS, Rev. Andrew Charles Smith Jr.; Deacons Mervin O. Johnson; Bruce McElrath.
Res.: 615 E. Oakwood Blvd., 60653.
Tel: 773-624-5375; Email: holyangels@archchicago.org.
School—Holy Angels School, (Grades PreK-8), 750 E. 40th St., 60653. Tel: 772-624-0727; Fax: 773-538-9683; Email: sstalling@holyangelschicago.org. Mr. Sean Stalling, Prin. Lay Teachers 12; Students 281.
Catechesis Religious Program—
62—HOLY CROSS/IMMACULATE HEART OF MARY, Rev. Fernando Cuevas, C.S., Admin.
Res.: 4557 S. Wood St., 60609. Tel: 773-376-3900; Email: holycross-ihm@archchicago.org.
Catechesis Religious Program—Students 623.
63—HOLY FAMILY, Rev. Michael A. Gabriel, Admin.; Deacon David J. Keene.
Res.: 1080 W. Roosevelt Rd., 60608.
Tel: 312-492-8442; Email: holyfamily-may@archchicago.org.
Catechesis Religious Program—Students 23.
64—HOLY INNOCENTS, Rev. Juan Carlos Arrieta Correa.
Res.: 743 N. Armour St., 60622. Tel: 312-666-3675; Email: holyinnocents@archchicago.org.
Catechesis Religious Program—1448 W. Superior St., 60622. Students 148.
65—HOLY NAME OF MARY, Revs. Robert J. Gilbert; James F. Flynn, Pastor Emeritus, (Retired).
Res.: 11159 S. Loomis St., 60643. Tel: 773-238-6800; Email: holyname-mary@archchicago.org.
Mission—Sacred Heart, 11652 S. Church St., Cook Co. 60643.
Catechesis Religious Program—
66—HOLY ROSARY, Rev. Michael V. Kalck; Deacon Timothy Donovan.
Res.: 612 N. Western Ave., 60612. Tel: 773-278-4820; Email: holyrosary-western@archchicago.org.
Catechesis Religious Program—Students 68.
67—HOLY TRINITY MISSION, (Polish) Revs. Andrzej Totzke, S.Ch.; Mariusz Lis; Wojciech Baryski, S.Ch., In Res.
Res.: 1118 N. Noble St., 60642. Tel: 773-489-4140; Email: holytrinity-mission@archchicago.org.
Catechesis Religious Program—Sr. Anna Strycharz, M.Ch.R., D.R.E. Students 333.
68—ST. HYACINTH BASILICA, Revs. Stanislaw Jankowski, C.R.; Steven Bartczyszyn, C.R.; Adam Piasecki, C.R., (Poland); Stanislaw Lasota, C.R., (Poland); Deacon Frank Girjatowicz.
Res.: 3636 W. Wolfram St., 60618. Tel: 773-342-3636; Email: sthyacinth@archchicago.org.
Catechesis Religious Program—Students 605.
69—ST. IGNATIUS, Rev. Joseph P. Tito; Deacons Raul Mora; Rogelio Soto; Lawrence Rossow.
Res.: 6559 N. Glenwood Ave., 60626.
Tel: 773-764-5936; Email: stignatius@archchicago.org.
See Northside Catholic Academy, Chicago under Consolidated Elementary Schools, located in the Institution section.
Catechesis Religious Program—Students 111.
70—IMMACULATE CONCEPTION, Revs. Robert M. Fedek; Matthew Heinrich; Deacons Ron Gronek, Senior Deacon; Richard H. Moritz.
Res.: 7211 W. Talcott Ave., 60631. Tel: 773-775-3833; Email: ic-talcott@archchicago.org.
School—Immaculate Conception School, (Grades PreK-9), 7263 W. Talcott Ave., 60631.
Tel: 773-775-0545; Fax: 773-775-3822; Email: info@iccowboys.net. Mrs. Susan Canzoneri, Prin. Lay Teachers 30; Students 517.
Catechesis Religious Program—
Tel: 773-775-0545, Ext. 216. Students 223.
71—IMMACULATE CONCEPTION (1912) (Lithuanian) Revs. Manuel Dorantes; Miguel Venegas.
Res.: 2745 W. 44th St., 60632-1999.
Tel: 773-523-1402; Email: ic-44th@archchicago.org.
See Pope John Paul II School, Five Holy Martyrs Campus under Five Holy Martyrs, Chicago.
Catechesis Religious Program—Students 504.
72—IMMACULATE CONCEPTION AND ST. JOSEPH
1107 N. Orleans St., 60610. Tel: 312-787-7174; Fax: 312-787-9825; Email: info@icsjparish.org; Web: www.icsjparish.org. Rev. Lawrence M. Lisowski; Ms. Kim Rak, D.R.E.
School—Immaculate Conception St. Joseph School, North Park Campus, 1431 N. Park, 60610.
Tel: 312-944-0304; Email: ksullivan@icsjschool.org. Catherine Sullivan, Prin. Lay Teachers 42; Students 466.
73—IMMACULATE CONCEPTION OF THE BLESSED VIRGIN MARY, Revs. Xamie M. Reyes; Flavio V. Gonzalez, In Res.; Deacons Abraham Chavez; Jose M. Sandoval.
Parish Office and Rectory—2944 E. 88th St., 60617.
Tel: 773-768-2100; Email: ic-88th@archchicago.org.
Church: 88th & Commercial Ave., 60617.
School—Immaculate Conception of the Blessed Virgin Mary School, 8739 S. Exchange, 60617.
Tel: 773-375-4674; Email: principal@immaculateconceptionsouth.org. Sr. Katia Alcantar, H.M.I.G., Prin. Lay Teachers 7; Students 222.
Catechesis Religious Program—Tel: 773-221-1423.
74—IMMACULATE HEART OF MARY, Rev. James A. Heneghan. In Res., Rev. John P. McNalis.
Res.: 3834 N. Spaulding, 60618. Tel: 773-478-1157; Email: ihm@archchicago.org.
Catechesis Religious Program—
Tel: 773-478-1157, Ext. 16. Students 232.
75—SAINT ITA (1900) Revs. Robert Cook, O.F.M.Conv.; Arturo Felix; Paulino Matus Castillo; Deacons Antonio Rodriguez; Ronald Stricker; Jamie Rios; Sr. Mary Jeanne Hayes, S.N.D.deN., Pastoral Assoc.
Res.: 1220 W. Catalpa Ave., 60640.
Tel: 773-561-5343; Email: stita@archchicago.org.
See Northside Catholic Academy, Chicago under Consolidated Elementary Schools, located in the Institution section.
Catechesis Religious Program—Students 258.
76—ST. JAMES (1855)
Mailing Address: 2907 S. Wabash Ave., 60616. Rev. John S. Edmunds, S.T.; Deacon Alfred Coleman II.
Res.: 2942 S. Wabash Ave., 60616. Tel: 312-842-1919 ; Email: stjameswabash@archchicago.org.
Catechesis Religious Program—Students 5.
St. James Food Pantry—
77—ST. JAMES, Revs. Andrzej A. Bartos; Andrzej Juszczec; Deacons Salvador Sanchez; Orlando Perez.
Res.: 5730 W. Fullerton Ave., 60639.

Tel: 773-237-1474; Email: stjames-fullerton@archchicago.org.
Catechesis Religious Program—Students 107.
Convent—2441 N. Menard Ave., 60639. Missionary Sisters of Christ the King for Polonia 2.

78—St. Jane de Chantal, Revs. Edward J. Cronin; Joseph J. Wojcik, Pastor Emeritus, (Retired); Jon M. Wachala; Deacon Ron Morowczynski.
Res.: 5252 S. Austin Ave., 60638. Tel: 773-767-2411; Email: stjane@archchicago.org.
School—St. Jane de Chantal School, (Grades PreK-8), 5201 S. McVicker Ave., 60638. Tel: 773-767-1130; Fax: 772-767-1387; Email: school@stjanedechantal.com. Ms. Nancy A. Andrasco, Prin. Lay Teachers 12; Students 202.
Catechesis Religious Program—Students 181.

79—St. Jerome, Revs. Noel Beltran Reyes, M.Div.; Ronaldo Paulino, R.C.J.; Harold A. Bonin, Pastor Emeritus, (Retired); Deacons Fritz Jean-Pierre; Elisco Ramos; Francisco Marin.
Res.: 1709 W. Lunt Ave., 60626. Tel: 773-262-3170; Email: stjerome-lunt@archchicago.org.
See Northside Catholic Academy, Chicago under Consolidated Elementary Schools, located in the Institution section.
Catechesis Religious Program—1706 W. Morse Ave., 60626. Students 290.

80—St. Jerome (1912) (Croatian) Revs. Ivica Majstorovic, O.F.M.; Antonio Musa.
Res.: 2823 S. Princeton Ave. (Cardinal Stepinac Way), 60616. Tel: 312-842-1871; Email: stjerome-princeton@archchicago.org.
School—St. Jerome School, 2801 S. Princeton Ave., 60616. Tel: 312-842-7668; Fax: 312-842-6427; Email: j.segvich@stjeromeschool.net. Mr. Tom Smyth, Prin. Lay Teachers 10; Students 147.
Catechesis Religious Program—2716 S. Princeton Ave., 60616. Students 406.

81—St. John Berchmans, Revs. Wayne F. Watts; William B. Gubbins, Pastor Emeritus, (Retired); A. Paul Reicher, In Res., (Retired); Deacons Jorge Cabrera; Guillermo Mendizabal.
Res.: 2517 W. Logan Blvd., 60647. Tel: 773-486-4300; Email: stjohn-berchmans@archchicago.org.
School—St. John Berchmans School, 2511 W. Logan Blvd., 60647. Tel: 773-486-1334; Fax: 773-486-1782; Email: info@stjohnberchmans.org. Mrs. Margaret A. Roketenetz, Prin. Lay Teachers 21; Students 222.
Catechesis Religious Program—Students 144.

82—St. John Bosco (1934) Revs. Thomas Provenzano, S.D.B.; Louis Aineto, S.D.B.; Richard Alejunas; Marco Riveros; Thomas Brennan; Richard Rosin; Deacons Victor M. Moreno; Ronald Swiatek.
Res.: 2250 N. McVicker Ave., 60639.
Tel: 773-622-4620; Email: stjohn-bosco@archchicago.org.
Catechesis Religious Program—2310 N. McVicker Ave., 60639. Students 819.

83—St. John Cantius, Revs. Scott Thelander, S.J.C., Admin.; Joshua Caswell, S.J.C.; Scott Haynes, S.J.C.; Albert Tremari, S.J.C.; Brendan Gibson, S.J.C.; Dennis Kolinski, S.J.C.; Robin Kwan, S.J.C.; Trenton Rauck, SJC.
Res.: 825 N. Carpenter St., 60642. Tel: 312-243-7373; Email: stjohn-cantius@archchicago.org.
Catechesis Religious Program—Judith Keefe, D.R.E. Students 159.

84—St. John de la Salle, Rev. Avitus L. Rukuratwa Kiguta.
Res.: 10205 King Dr., 60628. Tel: 773-785-2022; Email: stjohndelasalle@archchicago.org.
School—St. John de la Salle Catholic Academy,
Tel: 773-785-2331; Email: ssantellano@johndls.org. Sally Santellano, Prin. Lay Teachers 12; Students 130.
Catechesis Religious Program—Students 34.

85—St. John Fisher (1948) Revs. Kenneth A. Budzikowski; Daniel M. Tomich; Deacons Clayton Kort; Raymond Reilly; Thomas Siska; Robert Carroll.
Res.: 10234 S. Washtenaw Ave., 60655.
Tel: 773-445-6565; Email: stjohn-fisher@archchicago.org.
School—St. John Fisher School, 10200 S. Washtenaw Ave., 60655. Tel: 773-445-4737;
Fax: 773-233-3012; Email: jmcgrath@sjfschool.net. Sr. Jean Anne McGrath, C.S.J.; Mr. James Fornaciari, Prin. Lay Teachers 37; Students 670.
Catechesis Religious Program—Tel: 773-238-1851. Elena Chermak, D.R.E. Students 120.

86—St. Josaphat (1883) Revs. Francis M. Bitterman; Roberto Mercado Jr., In Res.; Deacon Patrick S. Casey.
Res.: 2311 N. Southport Ave., 60614.
Tel: 773-327-8955; Email: stjosaphat@archchicago.org.
School—St. Josaphat School, 2245 N. Southport Ave., 60614. Tel: 773-549-0909; Fax: 773-549-3127; Email: nmullens@stjosaphat.net. Nel Mullens, Prin. Lay Teachers 30; Students 384.
Catechesis Religious Program—Students 88.

87—St. Joseph (1887) Revs. Hugo Leon Londono, M.S.C.; Jon M. Wachala.
Res.: 4821 S. Hermitage Ave., 60609.
Tel: 773-254-2366; Email: stjoseph-hermitage@archchicago.org.
Catechesis Religious Program—Students 773.

88—St. Juliana, Revs. James Wallace, J.C.L.; Jesus Torres-Fuentes; Roger J. Caplis, In Res., (Retired); Deacons Robert Ryan; Edward Dolan.
Office: 7200 N. Osceola, 60631. Tel: 773-631-4127; Email: stjuliana@archchicago.org.
Res.: 7158 N. Osceola Ave., 60631.
School—St. Juliana School, 7400 W. Touhy, 60631. Tel: 773-631-2256; Email: mmarshall@stjuliana.org. Ms. Marjorie A. Marshall, Prin. Lay Teachers 27; Students 473.
Catechesis Religious Program—Students 352.

89—St. Katharine Drexel, Revs. Paul D. Whittington, O.P.; Thomas M. Jackson, O.P.; Patrick M. Wangai; Deacons Herbert Johnson; Roscoe B. Dixon Jr.
St. Joachim, 700 E. 91st St., 60619.
Tel: 773-374-2345; Email: StKatharineDrexelChgo@gmail.com.
St. Felicitas—1526 E. 84th St., 60619.
St. Ailbe—9015 S. Harper Ave., 60619.
School—St. Ailbe School, 9037 S. Harper Ave., 60619. Tel: 773-734-1386; Fax: 773-734-1440; Email: amostyn@stailbeschool.org. Alyssa Mostyn, Prin. Lay Teachers 12; Students 134.

90—St. Kevin, Rev. Pedro Campos.
Res.: 10509 S. Torrence Ave., 60617.
Tel: 773-721-2563; Email: stkevin@archchicago.org.
Catechesis Religious Program—Tel: 708-862-1087; Fax: 773-721-2563. Students 181.

91—St. Kilian, Revs. Donald Eruaga, M.S.P.; William Vanecko, Pastor Emeritus, (Retired); Alvin Jordan.
Res.: 8725 S. May St., 60620. Tel: 773-651-4000; Email: stkilian@archchicago.org.
School—St. Ethelreda, (Grades PreK-8), 8734 S. Paulina St., 60620. Tel: 773-238-1757;
Fax: 773-238-6059; Email: welcome@stethelreda.org. Denise Spells, Prin. Lay Teachers 12; Students 271.
Catechesis Religious Program—Students 19.

92—St. Ladislaus (1914) Revs. Marek Janowski; William J. Lisowski, Pastor Emeritus, (Retired); Jan F. Kaplan, Pastor Emeritus, (Retired); Damian Mazurkiewicz; Deacon Robert Cyran.
Res.: 5345 W. Roscoe St., 60641. Tel: 773-725-2300; Email: stladislaus@archchicago.org.
Catechesis Religious Program—Tel: 773-545-5809; Fax: 773-545-4340. Students 49.
Convent—5330 W. Henderson St., 60641.

93—St. Malachy + Precious Blood, Revs. Matthew Eyerman; Moses Agorjesu; Deacons Mario Avila; David Castaneda; Dexter Watson.
Res.: 2248 W. Washington Blvd., 60612.
Tel: 312-733-1068; Email: stmalachy@archchicago.org.
School—St. Malachy + Precious Blood School, (Grades PreK-8), 2252 W. Washington Blvd., 60612. Tel: 312-733-2252; Fax: 312-733-5703; Email: b.miller@stmalachychicago.com. Ms. Mary B. Miller, Prin. Lay Teachers 16; Students 228.
Catechesis Religious Program—Students 680.

94—St. Margaret Mary, Rev. Tirso S. Villaverde Jr.; Deacon Neba Ambe.
Res.: 2324 W. Chase Ave., 60645. Tel: 773-764-0615; Email: stmargaretmary@archchicago.org.
Catechesis Religious Program—Students 81.

95—St. Margaret of Scotland
9830 S. Vincennes Ave., 60643. Revs. Donald Eruaga, M.S.P.; Alvin Jordan.
Res.: 9837 S. Throop St., 60643. Tel: 773-779-5151; Email: stmargaretofscotland@archchicago.org.
School—St. Margaret of Scotland School, 9833 S. Throop St., 60643. Tel: 773-238-1088;
Fax: 773-238-1049; Email: sdavis@smoschicago.org. Ms. Shauntae Davis, Prin. Lay Teachers 16; Students 230.
Catechesis Religious Program—Students 12.

96—St. Mark, Revs. Martin D. Ibarra; John J. Sanaghan, In Res., (Retired); Deacons Antonio Navarro; Ramon Cazales.
Res.: 1048 N. Campbell Ave., 60622.
Tel: 773-342-1516; Email: stmark@archchicago.org.
Catechesis Religious Program—Students 85.

97—St. Martin De Porres, Rev. Thomas P. Walsh; Deacon William Pouncy.
Res.: 5112 W. Washington Blvd., 60644.
Tel: 773-287-0206; Email: stmartin@archchicago.org.
Catechesis Religious Program—Ms. Christine Riley, D.R.E. Students 19.

98—Mary, Mother of Mercy, Rev. Jose Antonio Murcia Abellan; John F. Villa-Holguin; Deacons Juan J. Valdez; Marcial Herrera.
Queen of the Universe—7114 S. Hamlin Ave., 60629. Tel: 773-582-4662; Web: mmmparish.org.
St. Adrian, 70th and S. Washtenaw Ave., 60619.
School—Queen of the Universe School, 7130 S. Hamlin Ave., 60629. Tel: 773-582-4266;
Fax: 773-585-7254; Email: mporod@qofu.org. Mrs. Mary F. Porod, Prin. Lay Teachers 11; Students 185.

99—St. Mary of Perpetual Help, Revs. Thomas G. Aschenbrener; Bartholomew J. Juncer.
Res.: 1039 W. 32nd St., 60608. Tel: 773-927-6646; Email: stmary-perpetualhelp@archchicago.org.
Catechesis Religious Program—Students 67.

100—St. Mary of the Angels, Revs. John R. Waiss; Hilary F. Mahaney; Charles M. Ferrer; Deacon Glenn Tylutki.
Res.: 1850 N. Hermitage Ave., 60622.
Tel: 773-278-2644; Email: stmary-angels@archchicago.org.
School—St. Mary of the Angels School, 1810 N. Hermitage Ave., 60622. Tel: 773-486-0119;
Fax: 773-486-0996; Email: bdolack@sma-school.org. Ms. Elizabeth M. Dolack, Prin. Lay Teachers 17; Students 231.
Catechesis Religious Program—Students 176.

101—St. Mary of the Lake (1901) Revs. James J. Kastigar; Daniel J. Collins, Senior Priest, (Retired); Biran Straus, In Res.; Joseph Zhu, In Res.; Deacons Paul Spalla; Ubaldo Munoz; William Pyrek; Mr. Brian Carpenter, In Res.
Res.: 4200 N. Sheridan Rd., 60613. Tel: 773-472-3711 ; Email: stmary-lake@archchicago.org.
School—St. Mary of the Lake School, 1026 W. Buena Ave., 60613. Tel: 773-281-0018; Fax: 773-281-0112; Email: cboyd@stmary-stthomas.org. Ms. Christine M. Boyd, Prin. Lay Teachers 12; Students 227.
Catechesis Religious Program—Students 95.

102—St. Mary of the Woods (1952) Revs. Aidan O'Boyle, Admin.; Donald J. Headley, In Res., (Retired); Deacon James Thompson.
Res.: 7033 N. Moselle Ave., 60646. Tel: 773-763-0206 ; Email: stmary-woods@archchicago.org.
School—St. Mary of the Woods School,
Tel: 773-763-7577; Email: myamoah@smow.org. Ms. Geralyn Lawler, Prin. Lay Teachers 26; Students 348.
Catechesis Religious Program—Students 232.

103—St. Mary, Star of the Sea (1948) Rev. Roger A. Corrales-Diaz; Rev. Msgr. Michael J. Adams, Pastor Emeritus, (Retired); Revs. Victor Correa-Roballo, (Colombia); Jesus Romero-Galan; Deacons Jesse Navarro; Jesus Ochoa; Angelo Cordoba.
Res.: 6435 S. Kilbourn Ave., 60629.
Tel: 773-767-1246; Email: stmary-sea@archchicago.org.
School—St. Mary, Star of the Sea School, 6424 S. Kenneth Ave., 60629. Tel: 773-767-6160; Email: cusauskas@stmarystaroftheseaschool.org. Ms. Candice M. Usauskas, Prin. Lay Teachers 14; Students 249.
Catechesis Religious Program—Tel: 773-767-7078; Fax: 773-767-7077. Therese A. Navarro, D.R.E. Students 276.

104—St. Matthias, Rev. Lawrence R. McNally; Deacon Dennis Ramos.
Res.: 2310 W. Ainslie St., 60625. Tel: 773-506-2191; Email: stmatthias@archchicago.org.
School—St. Matthias School, 4910 N. Claremont Ave., 60625. Tel: 773-784-0999; Fax: 773-784-3601; Email: sheila.klich@stmatthiasschool.org. Ms. Kathleen A. Carden, Prin. Lay Teachers 23; Students 300.
Catechesis Religious Program—Students 79.

105—St. Michael in Old Town (1852)
Tel: 312-642-2498; Fax: 312-642-9283; Email: jsteigerwald@st-mikes.org; Web: www.st-mikes.org. Revs. Ted Lawson, C.Ss.R.; Kenneth Sedlak, C.Ss.R.; Joseph J. Morin, C.Ss.R.; James Keena, C.Ss.R., In Res., (Retired); John Phelps, C.Ss.R., In Res.
Res.: 1633 N. Cleveland Ave., 60614.
Tel: 312-642-2498; Email: stmichael-cleveland@archchicago.org. Revs. Stephen Rehrauer, C.Ss.R., Prov.; John Fahey Guerra, Vicar; John Steingraeber, C.Ss.R., Admin.; Gregory May, C.Ss.R., Treas.; Bro. Lawrence Lujan Angel, Ordinary Consultor; Rev. Joseph P. Dorcey, C.Ss.R., In Res.
Catechesis Religious Program—Tel: 312-943-4767. Students 62.

106—St. Michael the Archangel
8235 S. Shore Dr., 60617. Revs. Louis M. Mboe; Mathieu Mboudou Abina, In Res.
Res.: 8237 S. Shore Dr., 60617. Tel: 773-734-4921; Email: stmichael-southshore@archchicago.org.
School—St. Michael the Archangel School, 8231 S. Shore Dr., 60617. Tel: 773-221-0212;
Fax: 773-734-8732; Email: vikkistokes.vs@gmail.com. Vikki Stokes, Prin. Lay Teachers 8; Students 77.
Catechesis Religious Program—Students 84.

107—St. Michael the Archangel, (Slovak) Rev. Thomas E. Cima.
Res.: 4821 S. Damen Ave., 60609. Tel: 773-523-1248; Email: stmichael-damen@archchicago.org.
Catechesis Religious Program—Students 173.

108—St. Monica, Revs. Mariusz P. Stefanowski; Andrew Izyk, (Retired); William M. Holbrook, In

Res., (Retired); Deacons Ron Gronek; Edward Podgorski.
Office: 5136 N. Nottingham Ave., 60656.
Tel: 773-763-1661; Email: stmonica@archchicago.org.
Res.: 5135 N. Mont Clare Ave., 60656.
School—St. Monica Academy, Tel: 773-631-7880; Email: rcoleman@stmonicachicago.com. Raymond Coleman, Prin. Lay Teachers 17; Students 257.
Catechesis Religious Program—Tel: 773-631-7810; Fax: 773-763-4917. Students 223.

109—NATIVITY OF OUR LORD (1868) Rev. William M. McFarlane, M.Div.; Deacons Francis Henry; Erik Zeimys.
Res.: 653 W. 37th St., 60609. Tel: 773-927-6263; Email: nativity-lord@archchicago.org.
See Bridgeport Catholic Academy, Chicago under Consolidated Elementary Schools, located in the Institution section.
Catechesis Religious Program—Students 131.

110—NATIVITY OF THE BLESSED VIRGIN MARY, Revs. Jaunius Kelpsas, (Lithuania); Gediminas Kersys; Thomas J. Mescall, In Res., (Retired).
Res.: 6812 S. Washtenaw Ave., 60629.
Tel: 773-776-4600; Email: nativity-bvm@archchicago.org.
Catechesis Religious Program—Students 14.
Convent—6804 S. Washtenaw Ave., 60629.

111—ST. NICHOLAS OF TOLENTINE (1909) Rev. Salvador Den Hallegado.
Res.: 3721 W. 62nd St., 60629. Tel: 773-735-1121; Email: stnicholas-tolentine@archchicago.org.
School—St. Nicholas of Tolentine School, 3743 W. 62nd St., 60629. Tel: 773-735-0772;
Fax: 773-735-5414; Email: mmenden@stnicksschool.com. Ms. Mariagnes Menden, Prin. Lay Teachers 20; Students 395.
Catechesis Religious Program—Tel: 773-284-2635. Students 433.

112—NOTRE DAME DE CHICAGO (1864) Revs. A. Paul Reicher, Pastor Emeritus, (Retired); Kevin W. Hays; Robert L. Tuzik, In Res., (Retired); Deacon Lawrence E. Segers.
Res.: 1335 W. Harrison St., 60607-3318.
Tel: 312-243-7400; Email: notredame@archchicago.org.
Schools—Children of Peace School—1900 W. Taylor St., 60612. Tel: 312-243-8186; Fax: 312-243-8479; Email: cnovak@childrenofpeaceschool.org. Carrie Novak, Prin. Lay Teachers 16; Students 137.
Holy Trinity School for the Deaf, (Grades PreK-8), Tel: 312-243-0785; Email: ktarello@childrenofpeaceschool.org. Kathy Tarello, Dir.
Catechesis Religious Program—Students 76.

113—OLD ST. MARY, Revs. Paul D. Huesing, C.S.P.; Patrick D. Johnson, C.S.P.; Steven Petroff.
Res.: 1500 S. Michigan, 60605. Tel: 312-922-3444; Email: oldstmarys@archchicago.org.
School—Old St. Mary School, (Grades PreK-8), 1532 S. Michigan Ave., 60605. Tel: 312-386-1560;
Fax: 312-386-1560; Email: jmartin@osmschool.com; Web: www.osmschool.com. Ms. Julie L. Martin, Prin. Lay Teachers 42; Students 475.
Catechesis Religious Program—Students 105.

114—OLD ST. PATRICK'S (1846) Revs. Thomas J. Hurley; John J. Wall, In Res.
Res.: 700 W. Adams St., 60661. Tel: 312-648-1021; Email: oldstpatricks@archchicago.org.
Shrine—Shrine of Our Lady of Pompeii,
Tel: 312-421-3757; Fax: 312-421-3756. Rev. Richard Fragomeni, Ph.D., Rector.
Catechesis Religious Program—Students 681.

115—OUR LADY GATE OF HEAVEN (1848) Revs. Collins Kisaka Nyache; Peter E. Muojekwu, In Res.
Res.: 2338 E. 99th St., 60617. Tel: 773-375-3059; Email: OL-GateOfHeaven@archchicago.org.
Catechesis Religious Program—Students 33.

116—OUR LADY HELP OF CHRISTIANS, Closed. Consult Archives and Records Center for parish and school records.

117—OUR LADY OF AGLONA, (Latvian), Closed. Consult Archives and Records Center for mission records.

118—OUR LADY OF FATIMA, Rev. Nestor Saenz, (Peru); Deacon Jose Negrete.
Res.: 2751 W. 38th Pl., 60632. Tel: 773-927-2421; Email: ol-fatima@archchicago.org.
Catechesis Religious Program—Students 55.
Shrine—Shrine of St. Anne.

119—OUR LADY OF GOOD COUNSEL, Closed. Consult Archives and Records Center for parish and school records.

120—OUR LADY OF GRACE, Revs. Elvio Baldeon Lope; Lawrence E. Gorski, In Res.; Deacons Enrique Alonso, Senior Deacon; Ernesto Robles; Miguel A. Santillan.
Res.: 2455 N. Hamlin Ave., 60647. Tel: 773-772-5900; Email: ol-grace@archchicago.org.
School—Our Lady of Grace School, 2446 N. Ridgeway Ave., 60647. Tel: 773-342-0170;
Fax: 773-342-5305; Email: ritarangeop@yahoo.com. Sr. Rita Marie Range, O.P., Prin. Lay Teachers 12; Dominican Sisters (Springfield, IL) 1; Students 169.
Catechesis Religious Program—Students 310.

121—OUR LADY OF GUADALUPE, Revs. Hector M. Navalo, C.M.F.; Steve Niskanon, C.M.F.; Jose Luis Chung Martinez; Ferdinand Okorie, C.M.F., In Res.; Deacons Raul Nunez; Jose M. Estrada; Ramon Jimenez.
Res.: 3200 E. 91st, 60617. Tel: 773-768-0793; Email: ol-guadalupe@archchicago.org.
School—Our Lady of Guadalupe School, 9050 S. Burley, 60617. Tel: 773-768-0999; Fax: 773-768-0529; Email: cploense@olgschicago.org. Ms. Hall Bonnie, Prin. Lay Teachers 12; Students 142.
Shrine—National Shrine of St. Jude,
Tel: 312-236-7782; Fax: 312-236-7230. (Claretian Missionaries).
Catechesis Religious Program—9049 S. Brandon, 60617. Students 367.

122—OUR LADY OF LOURDES, Revs. Michael J. Shanahan; Bolivar G. Molina-Ramirez; Dominic Vinh Van Ha; Deacons Daniel Patino; Leo Restrepo.
Res.: 4640 N. Ashland Ave., 60640.
Tel: 773-561-2141; Email: ol-lourdes-ashland@archchicago.org.
Catechesis Religious Program—Students 453.

123—OUR LADY OF MERCY, Revs. Nicholas R. Desmond; Donald J. Headley, Pastor Emeritus, (Retired); Deacons Robert Janega; Aurelio Garcia; Ramiro B. Carrion.
Res.: 4432 N. Troy St., 60625. Tel: 773-588-2620; Email: ol-mercy@archchicago.org.
Catechesis Religious Program—4414 N. Troy St. (2nd door bell), 60625. Tel: 773-588-1637;
Fax: 773-588-1638. Students 574.

124—OUR LADY OF MOUNT CARMEL, Revs. Patrick J. Lee; Thomas I. Healy, Pastor Emeritus, (Retired); Phillip F. Cioffi; Deacons Edmund Gronkiewicz; Richard Johnson; Thomas Lambert.
Office: 708 W. Belmont, 60657. Tel: 773-525-0453; Email: ol-mtcarmel-belmont@archchicago.org.
Res.: 690 W. Belmont, 60657.
School—Our Lady of Mount Carmel School, 720 W. Belmont Ave., 60657. Tel: 773-525-8779;
Fax: 773-525-7810; Email: staszcuk@olmca.org. Mr. Shane P. Staszcuk, Prin. Lay Teachers 15; Students 263.
Catechesis Religious Program—Razia S. Khokhar, D.R.E. Students 112.

125—OUR LADY OF PEACE, Rev. Collins Kisaka Nyache; Deacon Rameau Buissereth.
Res.: 7851 S. Jeffery Blvd., 60649. Tel: 773-768-0105; Email: ol-peace@archchicago.org.
Catechesis Religious Program—

126—OUR LADY OF POMPEII, See separate listing. See Old St. Patrick, Shrine of Our Lady of Pompeii Rev. Richard Fragomeni, Ph.D., Rector.

127—OUR LADY OF SORROWS, BASILICA OF, Rev. Christopher M. Krymski, O.S.M.; Deacon James E. Norman.
Res.: 3121 W. Jackson Blvd., 60612.
Tel: 773-638-0159; Email: ol-sorrows@archchicago.org.
Catechesis Religious Program—Students 32.
Shrine—National Shrine of St. Peregrine,
Tel: 773-638-5800; Fax: 773-533-8307.

128—OUR LADY OF TEPEYAC, Rev. Alejandro Marca Mansilla, O.C.D., Admin.
Res.: 2226 S. Whipple St., 60623. Tel: 773-521-8400; Email: ol-tepeyac@archchicago.org.
School—Our Lady of Tepeyac School, 2235 S. Albany, 60623. Tel: 773-522-0024; Fax: 773-522-4577; Email: pkrielaart@ourladyoftepeyac.org; Web: www.tepeyacelementary.org. Mrs. Patricia Y. Krielaart, Prin. Lay Teachers 10; Students 180.
High School—Our Lady of Tepeyac High School, 2228 S. Whipple St., 60623. Tel: 773-522-0023;
Fax: 773-522-0508; Email: info@ourladyoftepeyac.org; Web: www.ourladyoftepeyac.org. Rebecca Noonan, Prin. Lay Teachers 15; Sisters 1; Students 142.
Catechesis Religious Program—Tel: 773-277-0320. Students 206.

129—OUR LADY OF THE SNOWS, Rev. Stanley G. Rataj; Deacon Francisco Foti.
Res.: 4858 S. Leamington Ave., 60638.
Tel: 773-582-2266; Email: ol-snows@archchicago.org.
School—Our Lady of the Snows School, 4810 S. Leamington Ave., 60638. Tel: 773-735-4810; Email: joyce_willenborg@yahoo.com. Mrs. Eileen C. Sheedy, Prin. Lay Teachers 12; Students 183.
Catechesis Religious Program—Tel: 773-582-4904. Students 250.

130—OUR LADY OF VICTORY, Revs. Michael Wyrzykowski; Abraham M. Jacob, In Res.; Deacons Robert Leck; Michael Ahern.
Res.: 5212 W. Agatite Ave., 60630. Tel: 773-286-2950; Email: ol-victory@archchicago.org.
Catechesis Religious Program—Mary Beth Frystak, D.R.E. Students 185.

131—OUR LADY, MOTHER OF THE CHURCH (1966) Rev. Andrzej Bartosz; Deacons Christopher Virruso; August J. Annoreno; Theodore D. Marszalek.
Res.: 8747 W. Lawrence Ave., 60656.
Tel: 773-625-3369; Email: ol-mother@archchicago.org.
Catechesis Religious Program—Students 138.

132—ST. PANCRATIUS (1924) Rev. Felipe Vaglienty.
Res.: 4025 S. Sacramento Ave., 60632.
Tel: 773-523-5666; Email: stpancratius@archchicago.org.
Catechesis Religious Program—Students 400.

133—ST. PASCAL, Revs. Elliott Richard Dees; Mariusz P. Stefanowski; Thomas M. Dore, In Res., (Retired); Deacon Eugene Dorgan.
Res.: 3935 N. Melvina Ave., 60634. Tel: 773-725-7641; Email: stpascal@archchicago.org.
School—Pope Francis Global Academy - South Campus, (Regional School) 6143 W. Irving Park Rd., 60634. Tel: 773-763-7080; Email: torourke@pfgacademy.org. Ms. Margaret Kinel, Prin. Lay Teachers 30; Students 450.
Ciezadlo Center—3954 N. Meade Ave., 60634.
Catechesis Religious Program—
Tel: 773-725-7641, Ext. 22.

134—ST. PAUL (1876) Rev. Arturo Perez-Rodriguez, Admin., (Retired); Deacons Juan Dominguez; Rodrigo Silva.
Res.: 2127 W. 22nd Pl., 60608. Tel: 773-847-6100; Email: stpaul-22nd@archchicago.org.
Catechesis Religious Program—Students 78.

135—SS. PETER AND PAUL, Rev. Honoratus C. Mwageni, (Rwanda) Admin. In Res., Rev. Joseph Kaye.
Res.: 12433 S. Halsted St., 60628. Tel: 773-785-1200; Email: sspp-halsted@archchicago.org.

136—ST. PETER CANISIUS, Closed. Consult Archives and Records Center for parish and school records.

137—ST. PETER'S, Rev. Kurt Hartrich, O.F.M.
St. Peter's Friary, 110 W. Madison St., 60602.
Tel: 312-372-5111; Email: stpeter-madison@archchicago.org; Web: stpetersloop.org. (For complete listing of residents see Section N Residences of Priests and Brothers.) Brothers 6; Priests 14.

138—ST. PHILIP NERI, Rev. Thomas G. Belanger.
Res.: 2132 E. 72nd St., 60649. Tel: 773-363-1700; Email: stphilip-neri@archchicago.org.
School—St. Philip Neri School, 2110 E. 72nd St., 60649. Tel: 773-288-1138; Fax: 773-288-8252; Email: lsanders@spnschoolchicago.org. Mr. Kenneth Koll, Prin. Lay Teachers 9; Students 117.
Catechesis Religious Program—Lay Teachers 37.

139—ST. PIUS V
Tel: 312-226-6161. Revs. Thomas P. Lynch, O.P.; Raymond Bryce; Steven Bryce; Daniel Tobin; Brian G. Bricker, O.P., In Res.; Charles W. Dahm, O.P., In Res.; Mark R. Paraday, O.P., In Res.; Gabriel Torretta, In Res.
Office: 1919 S. Ashland Ave., 60608.
Tel: 312-226-6161; Email: stpiusv@archchicago.org.
Res.: 1914 S. Ashland Ave., 60608.
School—St. Pius V School, Tel: 312-226-1590; Email: nnasko@saintpiusv.org. Mrs. Nancy Nasko, Prin. Lay Teachers 11; Students 166.
Catechesis Religious Program—Sisters 422.
Shrine—Shrine of St. Jude Thaddeus,
Tel: 312-226-0020; Fax: 312-226-6440; Web: www.shrineofsaintjude.com.

140—ST. PRISCILLA, Revs. Maciej D. Galle, J.C.L.; Marcin M. Gladysz.
Res.: 6949 W. Addison St., 60634. Tel: 773-545-8840; Email: stpriscilla@archchicago.org.
Catechesis Religious Program—Tel: 773-685-3785. Students 87.

141—ST. PROCOPIUS, Rev. Adan Sandoval Duron; Deacon Candelario Rodriguez.
Res.: 1641 S. Allport St., 60608. Tel: 312-226-7887; Email: stprocopius@archchicago.org.
School—St. Procopius School, Tel: 312-421-5135; Email: griselda.ferguson@stprocopiusschool.org. Griselda Ferguson, Prin. Lay Teachers 14; Students 248.
Catechesis Religious Program—Students 177.

142—QUEEN OF ALL SAINTS BASILICA, Revs. Simon F. Braganza; Michael Trail; Rev. Msgr. Wayne F. Prist, Pastor Emeritus, (Retired); Rev. Edward D. Grace, In Res., (Retired).
Res.: 6280 N. Sauganash Ave., 60646.
Tel: 773-736-6060; Email: queen-saints@archchicago.org.
School—Queen of All Saints Basilica School,
Tel: 773-736-0567; Email: kreyes@qasparish.org. Mrs. Kristina L. Heidkamp-Reyes, Prin. Lay Teachers 36; Sisters 1; Students 636.
Catechesis Religious Program—Students 443.

143—QUEEN OF ANGELS (1909) Rev. Msgr. James T. Kaczorowski; Rev. Joseph S. Thomas, (In Res,), (Retired); Deacon Bienvenido Nieves.
Parish Office—4412 N. Western Ave., 60625.
Tel: 773-539-7510; Email: queen-angels@archchicago.org.

Res.: 2330 W. Sunnyside Ave., 60625.
School—Queen of Angels School, 4520 N. Western Ave., 60625. Tel: 773-769-4211; Fax: 773-769-4289; Email: jkelly@queenofangelschicago.org. Mrs. Julia B. Kelly, Prin. Lay Teachers 34; Students 416.
Catechesis Religious Program—Students 229.

144—ST. RENE GOUPIL, Revs. Robert Regan; Peter P. Paurazas, (Retired).
Res.: 6949 W. 63rd Pl., 60638. Tel: 773-229-8523; Email: strene@archchicago.org.
Catechesis Religious Program—Students 117.

145—RESURRECTION
Web: www.rescatholic.org. Rev. Msgr. James T. Kaczorowski, Admin.; Revs. Thomas A. Tivy, Pastor Emeritus, (Retired); Daniel J. Brandt, In Res.; Deacons Uriol Rodriguez; Efrain Lopez; Juan Gonzalez; Francisco Rivera.
Business Office—3043 N. Francisco Ave., 60618.
Tel: 773-478-9705; Email: resurrection@archchicago.org.
Catechesis Religious Program—Students 226.

146—ST. RICHARD, Revs. Krzysztof Janczak, M.Div.; Jon M. Wachala; Deacon Lawrence J. Chyba.
Office: 5030 S. Kostner Ave., 60632.
Res.: 5032 S. Kostner Ave., 60632. Tel: 773-585-1221; Email: strichard@archchicago.org.
School—St. Richard School, 5025 S. Kenneth Ave., 60632. Tel: 773-582-8083; Fax: 773-582-8330; Email: mnapier@strichard.net. Michelle Augustyn-Napier, Prin. Lay Teachers 13; Students 254.
Catechesis Religious Program—Students 6.

147—ST. RITA OF CASCIA, Rev. Homero Sanchez Gomez, O.S.F.; Deacons David D. Andrade; Oscar Gonzalez; Jenny Meehan, Pastoral Assoc.
Res.: 6243 S. Fairfield Ave., 60629.
Tel: 773-434-9600; Email: strita@archchicago.org.
Catechesis Religious Program—Juan C. Roca, D.R.E. Students 211.

148—ST. ROBERT BELLARMINE, Revs. Neil E. Fackler; Michael A. Goergen, Pastor Emeritus, (Retired); Leroy A. Wickowski, Pastor Emeritus, (Retired); L. Scott Donahue, In Res.; Deacon William J. Frere.
Res.: 4646 N. Austin Ave., 60630-3157.
Tel: 773-777-2666; Email: strobert@archchicago.org.
School—St. Robert Bellarmine School, (Grades PreK-8), 6036 W. Eastwood Ave., 60630.
Tel: 773-725-5133; Email: cmijal@srb-chicago.org. Ms. Deanne Roy, Prin. Lay Teachers 23; Students 334.
Catechesis Religious Program—Tel: 773-286-0956. Students 103.

149—ST. ROMAN, Rev. Walter Yepes.
Res.: 2311 S. Washtenaw Ave., 60608.
Tel: 773-247-6645; Email: stroman@archchicago.org.
Catechesis Religious Program—Students 98.

150—ST. SABINA, Revs. Michael L. Pfleger; Thulani D. Magwaza; Deacons Leonard M. Richardson; William J. Hynes; Ms. Kimberly Lymore, Pastoral Assoc.
Res.: 1210 W. 78th Pl., 60620. Tel: 773-483-4300; Email: stsabina@archchicago.org.
School—St. Sabina Academy, 7801 S. Throop St., 60620. Tel: 773-483-5000; Email: office@stsabinaacademy.org. Mrs. Helen Dumas, Prin. Lay Teachers 15; Students 229.
Catechesis Religious Program—Students 201.

151—SACRED HEART, (Croatian) Rev. Stephen Bedenikovic, O.F.M.
Res.: 2864 E. 96th St., 60617. Tel: 773-768-1423; Email: sacredheart-croatian@archchicago.org.
School—Sacred Heart School, 2906 E. 96th St., 60617. Tel: 773-773-3728; Fax: 773-768-5034; Email: lgriffiths@sacredheartschool96.org. Dr. Lisa J. Griffiths, Prin. Lay Teachers 11; Students 186.
Catechesis Religious Program—Students 26.

152—SACRED HEART MISSION OF HOLY NAME OF MARY, Rev. James F. Flynn, (Retired).
Res.: 11652 S. Church St., 60643. Tel: 773-233-3955; Email: sacredheart-mission@archchicago.org.
Catechesis Religious Program—Students 34.

153—SAN JOSE LUIS SANCHEZ DEL RIO
3647 W. North Ave., 60647-4745. Tel: 773-772-9401; Web: sanjosesanchezdelrio.org. Most Rev. Robert Casey, Admin.; Deacons Jorge Garcia; Felipe Gonzalez; Floro Hita; Milton Rodriguez; Jose Vazquez; Francisco Ramos.
St. Philomena, 1921 N. Kedvale Ave., 60639.
St. Francis of Assisi, 932 N. Kostner, 60651.
School—Maternity of the Blessed Virgin Mary School, 1537 N. Lawndale Ave., 60651.
Tel: 773-227-1140; Fax: 773-227-2939; Email: cmolina@maternitybvmchicago.com. Ms. Christine Molina, Prin. Lay Teachers 15; Students 190.

154—SANTA LUCIA-SANTA MARIA INCORONATA, Rev. Stipe Renic, O.F.M.
Res.: 3022 S. Wells St., 60616. Tel: 312-842-6115; Email: santalucia-santamaria@archchicago.org.
School—Santa Lucia-Santa Maria Incoronata School, 3017 S. Wells St., 60616. Tel: 312-326-1839; Fax: 312-326-1945; Email: office@santaluciaschool.net. Mr. Tom J. Clausing, Interim Prin. Lay Teachers 10; Students 42.
Catechesis Religious Program—Students 41.

155—SANTA MARIA ADDOLORATA (1903) Revs. Firmo Mantovani, C.S.; Gino Dalpiaz, C.S.; Most Rev. Lawrence P. Sabatini, C.S., In Res.; Deacon Luis Perez.
Res.: 528 N. Ada St., 60642. Tel: 312-421-3122; Email: santamariaaddolorata@archchicago.org.
Catechesis Religious Program—Students 150.

156—ST. SIMON THE APOSTLE, Revs. Thomas Boharic; Francis Q. Kub, Pastor Emeritus; Deacon Manuel Salgado.
Res.: 5157 S. California Ave., 60632.
Tel: 773-436-1045; Email: stsimon@archchicago.org.
Catechesis Religious Program—Students 293.

157—ST. STANISLAUS KOSTKA, (Polish—Spanish) Rev. Anthony Bus, C.R.; Deacons Nicolas Flores; Jorge Salinas.
Res.: 1351 W. Evergreen Ave., 60622.
Tel: 773-278-2470; Email: ststanislaus-evergreen@archchicago.org.
School—St. Stanislaus Kostka School, 1255 N. Noble St., 60622. Tel: 773-278-4560; Fax: 773-278-9097; Email: principal@ststanschicago.org. Mrs. Michele Alday-Engelman, Prin. Lay Teachers 12; Students 147.
Catechesis Religious Program—Students 42.

158—ST. STANISLAUS, BISHOP AND MARTYR, Revs. Anthony Dziorek, C.R.; Richard Balazs, C.R.
Res.: 5352 W. Belden Ave., 60639. Tel: 773-237-5800; Email: ststanislaus-belden@archchicago.org.
Catechesis Religious Program—Students 38.

159—ST. STEPHEN, KING OF HUNGARY, Rev. Michael P. Knotek, Admin.
Res. & Office: 2015 W. Augusta Blvd., 60622-6062.
Tel: 773-486-1896; Email: ststephen-augusta@archchicago.org.
Catechesis Religious Program—Students 10.

160—ST. SYLVESTER (1884) Rev. Samson Ngatia Mukundi; Deacons Sigifredo Ortiz; Benjamnin Diaz.
Res.: 2915 W. Palmer St., 60647. Tel: 773-235-3646; Email: stsylvester@archchicago.org.
School—St. Sylvester School, (Grades PreK-8), 3027 W. Palmer Blvd., 60647. Tel: 773-772-5222;
Fax: 773-722-0352; Email: doyle@stsylvesterschool.org. Allyn Doyle, Prin. Lay Teachers 14; Students 248.
Catechesis Religious Program—Tel: 773-772-9082. Students 358.

161—ST. SYMPHOROSA AND SEVEN SONS, Rev. Idzi Stacherczak.
Res.: 6135 S. Austin Ave., 60638. Tel: 773-767-1523; Email: stsymphorosa@archchicago.org.
School—St. Symphorosa and Seven Sons School, 6125 S. Austin Ave., 60638. Tel: 773-585-6888;
Fax: 773-585-8411; Email: kberry@stsymphorosaschool.org. Mrs. Kathleen M. Berry, Prin. Lay Teachers 11; Students 209.
Catechesis Religious Program—Students 189.

162—ST. TARCISSUS (1926) Revs. Michael Grisolano; Daniel P. McCarthy, Pastor Emeritus, (Retired); John M. Griffiths, J.C.D., In Res.; Deacon Gregory M. Bzdon.
Res.: 6020 W. Ardmore Ave., 60646.
Tel: 773-763-8228; Email: sttarcissus@archchicago.org.
School—Pope Francis Global Academy - North Campus, (Regional School) 6040 W. Ardmore, 60646. Tel: 773-736-8806; Email: torourke@pfgacademy.org. Mr. Terrence K. O'Rourke, Prin. Lay Teachers 30; Students 461.
Catechesis Religious Program—Students 135.

163—ST. TERESA OF AVILA, Rev. Frank J. Latzko.
Parish Office: 1930 N. Kenmore, 60614-4139.
Tel: 773-528-6650; Email: stteresa@archchicago.org.
Child Care—Cardinal Bernardin Montessori Academy, 1651 W. Diversey Pkwy., 60614. Michelle Mirecki, Prin. Students 180.
Catechesis Religious Program—Students 156.

164—ST. THECLA, Revs. Daniel R. Fallon, Admin.; Gerald E. Rogala, Pastor Emeritus, (Retired); Ronald P. Stake, J.C.L., M.Div., In Res.; Deacons Robert Cnota; Steven Wagner; Michael McManus.
Res.: 6725 W. Devon Ave., 60631. Tel: 773-792-3077; Email: stthecla@archchicago.org.
School—St. Thecla School, 6323 N. Newcastle Ave., 60631. Tel: 773-763-3380; Fax: 773-763-6151; Email: tomalley@saintthecla.org. Tim O'Malley, Prin. Lay Teachers 17; Students 195.
Catechesis Religious Program—Students 186.

165—ST. THERESE CATHOLIC CHINESE CHURCH, Rev. Dong Ping F. Li.
Res.: 218 W. Alexander St., 60616. Tel: 312-842-6777 ; Email: sttherese@archchicago.org.
School—St. Therese Catholic Chinese Church School, 247 W. 23rd St., 60616. Tel: 312-326-2837;
Fax: 312-326-6068; Email: principal@sttheresechicago.org. Ms. Lisa Oi, Prin. Lay Teachers 20; Students 297.
Catechesis Religious Program—Mr. Thomas Howard, D.R.E. Students 367.

166—ST. THOMAS APOSTLE, Revs. Elias O'Brien, O.Carm.; Aliaksandr Audziayuk; Deacon Kurt Davis.
Res.: 5472 S. Kimbark Ave., 60615.
Tel: 773-324-2626; Web: stthomasapostle@archchicago.org.
School—St. Thomas Apostle School, 5467 S. Woodlawn Ave., 60615. Tel: 773-667-1142;
Fax: 773-753-7434; Email: tgallo@stapostleschool.com. Mr. Timothy Gallo, Prin. Lay Teachers 16; Students 342.
Catechesis Religious Program—Students 59.

167—ST. THOMAS MORE, Rev. Msgr. Richard M. Zborowski; Rev. Matthew Ross Compton; Deacon George Borha.
Res.: 2825 W. 81st St., 60652. Tel: 773-436-4444; Email: stthomas-more@archchicago.org.
Catechesis Religious Program—Students 37.

168—ST. THOMAS OF CANTERBURY (1916) Revs. Robert Cook, O.F.M.Conv.; James L. Barrett, In Res., (Retired); Anthony Gittins, C.S.Sp., Ph.D., In Res.; Deacon Antonio Rodriguez.
Res.: 4827 N. Kenmore Ave., 60640.
Tel: 773-878-5507; Email: stthomas-canterbury@archchicago.org.
School—St. Thomas of Canterbury School,
Tel: 773-271-8655; Email: cboyd@stmary-stthomas.org. Ms. Christine M. Boyd, Prin. Lay Teachers 10; Students 227.
Catechesis Religious Program—
Convent—8120 S. California, 60652. Congregation of the Mother of Carmel 6; Sinsinwa Dominicans 1.

169—ST. TIMOTHY, Rev. Harold B. Murphy, Pastor Emeritus, (Retired).
Res.: 6326 N. Washtenaw Ave., 60659.
Tel: 773-262-6600; Email: sttimothy@archchicago.org.
Catechesis Religious Program—Students 60.

170—TRANSFIGURATION OF OUR LORD, Rev. Fernando Zuleta.
Res.: 2609 W. Carmen Ave., 60625.
Tel: 773-561-7953; Email: transfiguration-carmen@archchicago.org.
Catechesis Religious Program—Students 195.

171—ST. TURIBIUS, Revs. William E. Lego, O.S.A.; John J. Dowling, O.S.A., (Res.); Deacons Thomas Christensen; Javier Pineda.
Res.: 5646 S. Karlov Ave., 60629. Tel: 773-581-2730; Email: stturibius@archchicago.org.
Catechesis Religious Program—Sr. Mary Beth Bromer, C.S.S.F., D.R.E. Students 430.

172—ST. VIATOR (1888) Revs. Patrick W. Render, C.S.V.; Moises L. Mesh, C.S.V.; Deacons Mario Hernandez; Victor Flores; William Burns.
Res.: 4170 W. Addison St., 60641. Tel: 773-286-4040; Email: stviator@archchicago.org.
School—St. Viator School, 4140 W. Addison St., 60641. Tel: 773-545-2173; Fax: 773-794-1697; Email: Principal@StViatorChicago.org. Ms. Colleen Brewer, Prin. Lay Teachers 18; Students 292.
Catechesis Religious Program—Students 214.

173—ST. VINCENT DE PAUL (1875) Rev. Jeremy R. Dixon, C.M.
Res.: 1010 W. Webster Ave., 60614.
Tel: 773-325-8610; Email: stvincent-depaul@archchicago.org.

174—ST. WALTER, Rev. James A. Mezydlo.
Res.: 11722 S. Oakley Ave., 60643. Tel: 773-779-1515 ; Email: stwalter@archchicago.org.
School—St. Walter School, 11741 S. Western Ave., 60643. Tel: 773-445-8850; Fax: 773-445-0277; Email: sotoole@stwalter.com. Ms. Sharon M. O'Toole, Prin. Lay Teachers 12; Sisters 3; Students 118.
Catechesis Religious Program—Students 16.

175—ST. WENCESLAUS, Revs. Benjamin Lupercio; John H. Nowak, C.R.; Deacons Miguel A. Valle; Jamie Rios.
Res.: 3400 N. Monticello Ave., 60618.
Tel: 773-588-1135;
Fax: stwenceslaus@archchicago.org.
Catechesis Religious Program—Students 180.

176—ST. WILLIAM (1916) Revs. Ryszard Gron; Stanislaw Czarnecki, S.J.; Jaroslaw Maciejewski; Deacons Edward Simola; Juan Ponce De Leon.
Res.: 2600 N. Sayre Ave., 60707. Tel: 773-637-6565; Email: stwilliam@archchicago.org.
School—St. William School, 2559 N. Sayre Ave., 60707. Tel: 773-637-5130; Fax: 773-745-4208; Email: msegvich@stwilliamschool.org. Mrs. Nancy M. Zver, Prin. Lay Teachers 11; Students 194.
Catechesis Religious Program—Alicja Pozwio, D.R.E. Students 187.

OUTSIDE THE CITY OF CHICAGO

ALSIP, COOK CO., ST. TERRENCE, Rev. Edward J. Barrett; Deacon Richard Miska.
Res.: 4300 W. 119th Pl., Alsip, 60803.
Tel: 708-597-0970; Email: stterrence@archchicago.org.
Catechesis Religious Program—Tel: 708-597-0754. Students 406.

ARGO, COOK CO., ST. BLASE (1924) Rev. Wojciech Kwiecien; Deacon Jesus Chavez.
Res.: 6101 S. 75th Ave., Argo, 60501.
Tel: 708-458-0007; Email: stblase@archchicago.org.
Catechesis Religious Program—
Tel: 708-458-0246 (Spanish & English);
Tel: 708-458-8772 (Polish);
Fax: 708-458-8554 (Spanish & English);
Fax: 708-458-9560 (Polish). Students 667.

ARLINGTON HEIGHTS, COOK CO.

1—ST. EDNA (1965) Revs. Darrio L. Boscutti; Rodolfo Gaytan Ramirez; Deacons James Pauwels; Gregory M. Beeber; Joseph Yannotta; Ms. Loretta Crepeau, Pastoral Assoc.
Res.: 2525 N. Arlington Heights Rd., Arlington Heights, 60004. Tel: 847-398-3362; Email: stedna@archchicago.org.
Catechesis Religious Program—Students 583.

2—ST. JAMES, Revs. Matthew E. Foley; William J. Zavaski, Pastor Emeritus, (Retired); Derek Ho; Deacons Paul Schmidt; Pierce Sheehan; James R. Bannon; Thomas Westerkamp.
Office: 820 N. Arlington Heights Rd., Arlington Heights, 60004. Tel: 224-345-7200; Email: stjames-arlington@archchicago.org.
School—St. James School, Tel: 224-345-7145; Email: secretaries@stjamesschoolah.org. Judy Pappas, Prin. Lay Teachers 35; Students 492.
Catechesis Religious Program—Students 535.

3—MISION SAN JUAN DIEGO, Revs. Matthew E. Foley, Admin.; Javier Garcia Vasquez; Deacons Hector Soto; Luis Zaragoza.
Res.: 2323 N. Wilke Rd., Arlington Heights, 60004.
Tel: 847-590-9332; Email: juandiego-mission@archchicago.org.
Catechesis Religious Program—Students 263.

4—OUR LADY OF THE WAYSIDE, Revs. Edward R. Fialkowski; Nagothu Vinod; Daniel J. Brady, In Res., (Retired); Deacons Thomas Corcoran; Donald Grossnickle; Michael Madison; Paul Onischuk; Peter Letourneau.
Res.: 432 W. Park St., Arlington Heights, 60005.
Tel: 847-253-5353; Email: ol-wayside@archchicago.org.
School—Our Lady of the Wayside School,
Tel: 847-253-0050; Email: dwood@olwschool.org. Mr. David W. Wood, Prin. Lay Teachers 25; Students 408.
Catechesis Religious Program—432 S. Mitchell, Arlington Heights, 60005. Tel: 847-398-5011;
Fax: 847-253-0050. Students 591.

BARRINGTON, LAKE CO., ST. ANNE, Revs. Bernard J. Pietrzak; John W. Dewes, Pastor Emeritus, (Retired); Balajoji Thanugundla; Krzysztof D. Ciaston; Deacon Robert Powers.
Res.: 120 N. Ela St., Barrington, 60010.
Tel: 847-382-5300; Email: stanne-ela@archchicago.org.
School—St. Anne School, 319 E. Franklin St., Barrington, 60010. Tel: 847-381-0311;
Fax: 847-381-0384; Email: DKapka@stannschoolbarrington.org. Mrs. Dawn M. Kapka, Prin. Lay Teachers 22; Students 288.
Catechesis Religious Program—Students 480.

BARTLETT, COOK CO., ST. PETER DAMIAN, Rev. Christopher Ciomek, D.Min.; Deacon David Sattler.
Res.: 109 S. Crest Ave., Bartlett, 60103.
Tel: 630-837-5411; Email: stpeter-damian@archchicago.org.
Catechesis Religious Program—Tel: 630-830-2295. Students 889.

BELLWOOD, COOK CO., ST. SIMEON, Rev. Jose Sequeira; Deacons Victor Chairez; Sergio Lopez.
Res.: 430 Bohland Ave., Bellwood, 60104.
Tel: 708-547-6868; Email: stsimeon@archchicago.org.
Catechesis Religious Program—Students 120.

BERWYN, COOK CO.

1—ST. LEONARD, Rev. Robert Krueger; Deacon Jose Cisneros.
Res.: 3318 S. Clarence Ave., Berwyn, 60402.
Tel: 708-484-0015; Email: stleonard@archchicago.org.
School—St. Leonard School, 3322 S. Clarence Ave., Berwyn, 60402. Tel: 708-749-3666;
Fax: 708-749-7981; Email: vcash@stleonardschool.org. Mrs. Veronica Skelton-Cash, Prin. Lay Teachers 13; Students 204.
Catechesis Religious Program—Tel: 708-795-5919. Students 145.

2—ST. MARY OF CELLE, Revs. Hugo Morales; William J. Stenzel, Pastor Emeritus, (Retired); Deacons Philip Gianatasio; Hans P. Goeckner.
Res.: 1428 Wesley Ave., Berwyn, 60402.
Tel: 708-788-0876; Email: stmary-celle@archchicago.org.
Catechesis Religious Program—Tel: 708-795-6460;
Fax: 708-749-2120. Ms. Elisangela Guidice, D.R.E. Students 163.

3—ST. ODILO, Rev. Anthony J. Brankin; Rev. Msgr. Richard T. Saudis, In Res., (Retired); Deacon Alfonso Salgado.
Res.: 2244 East Ave., Berwyn, 60402.
Tel: 708-484-2161; Email: stodilo@archchicago.org.
School—St. Odilo School, 2301 S. Clarence Ave., Berwyn, 60402. Tel: 708-484-0755;
Fax: 708-484-0088; Email: donegan@saintodilo.org. William Donegan, Prin. Lay Teachers 12; Sisters of Charity B.V.M. 2; Students 201.
Catechesis Religious Program—Students 414.
Shrine—Poor Souls.

BLUE ISLAND, COOK CO.

1—ST. BENEDICT, Deacons Juan Limon; Abundio Valadez.
Res.: 2339 York St., Blue Island, 60406.
Tel: 708-385-8510; Email: stbenedict-york@archchicago.org.
School—St. Benedict School, 2324 New St., Blue Island, 60406. Tel: 708-385-2016; Fax: 708-385-4490; Email: stbenbengals@hotmail.com. Melissa Wilson, Prin. Lay Teachers 14; Students 176.
Catechesis Religious Program—Ernesto Vargas, D.R.E. Students 217.
Mission—St. Peter Claver, 14125 Claire Blvd., Robbins, Cook Co. 60472.

2—ST. DONATUS (1909) Rev. Deogratias Mbonyumugenzi, Admin.; Deacon Tomas Herrera.
Res.: 1939 Union St., Blue Island, 60406.
Tel: 708-385-2890; Email: stdonatus@archchicago.org.
Catechesis Religious Program—12905 Division St., Blue Island, 60406. Students 417.

BRIDGEVIEW, COOK CO., ST. FABIAN, Revs. Grzegorz Warmuz; Jan Bukowski, COr, (Poland); Deacons Thomas Hyde; Charles Tipperreiter; Ronald Zielinski; Joseph Stalcup Sr.
Res.: 8300 S. Thomas Ave., Bridgeview, 60455.
Tel: 708-599-1110; Email: stfabian@archchicago.org.
Catechesis Religious Program—7450 83rd St., Bridgeview, 60455. Students 817.

BROOKFIELD, COOK CO.

1—ST. BARBARA, Rev. Edgar Rodriguez, Admin.; Deacons John Debnar; Thomas Carlson.
Res.: 4008 Prairie Ave., Brookfield, 60513.
Tel: 708-485-2900; Email: stbarbara-prairie@archchicago.org.
Catechesis Religious Program—Tel: 708-485-4610. Students 224.

2—CZECH MISSION OF SAINTS CYRIL AND METHODIUS, Revs. Dusan Hladik, (Czech Republic); Drahomir Dvoulety, In Res.
Res.: 9415 Rochester Ave., Brookfield, 60513.
Tel: 708-656-7472; Email: sscyril-methodius-mission@archchicago.org.
Catechesis Religious Program—

BUFFALO GROVE, LAKE CO., ST. MARY, [CEM] Revs. Daniel R. Whiteside; Richard E. Sztorc, Pastor Emeritus, (Retired); Denis Carneiro; Deacons Eugene Kukla, Senior Deacon; Gary Long, Senior Deacon.
Res.: 10 N. Buffalo Grove Rd., Buffalo Grove, 60089.
Tel: 847-541-1450; Email: stmary-buffalogrove@archchicago.org.
School—St. Mary School, 50 N. Buffalo Grove Rd., Buffalo Grove, 60089. Tel: 847-459-6270;
Fax: 847-537-2810; Email: sstoneberg@stmarybg.org. Lynne Strutzel, M.A., Prin. Lay Teachers 28; Students 415.
Catechesis Religious Program—Tel: 847-537-9423;
Fax: 847-808-0548. Students 451.

BURBANK, COOK CO., ST. ALBERT THE GREAT, Revs. Mariusz J. Nawalaniec, (Poland); Bernardo Lozano; Leslaw Prebendowski, Sch.; Deacons Raul Duque; Irvin Bryce; Raymundo Diaz De Leon.
Res.: 5555 W. State Rd., Burbank, 60459.
Tel: 708-423-0321; Email: stalbert@archchicago.org.
School—St. Albert the Great School, 5535 W. State Rd., Burbank, 60459. Tel: 708-424-7757; Email: jmclawhorn@satgschool.org. Mrs. Jodi McLawhorn, Prin. Lay Teachers 13; Students 176.
Catechesis Religious Program—Tel: 708-636-0406. Students 813.

BURNHAM, COOK CO., MOTHER OF GOD
13323 S. Green Bay Ave., Burnham, 60633. Rev. Charles W. Watkins, Admin.
Res.: 14207 S. Green Bay Ave., Burnham, 60633.
Tel: 773-646-2660; Email: motherofgod@archchicago.org.

CALUMET CITY, COOK CO.

1—ST. ANDREW THE APOSTLE (1992) Rev. Jacek A. Dada; Deacon Lawrence J. Smith.
Res.: 768 Lincoln Ave., Calumet City, 60409.
Tel: 708-862-4165; Email: standrew-apostle@archchicago.org.
Catechesis Religious Program—Students 72.

2—OUR LADY OF KNOCK, Revs. David P. Pavlik; Patrick M. Lyons, Pastor Emeritus, (Retired); Donald J. Fenske, Pastor Emeritus, (Retired); Deacon Thomas Knetl.
Res.: 501 163rd St., Calumet City, 60409.
Tel: 708-862-3011; Email: ol-knock@archchicago.org.
School—Christ Our Savior, (Inter-Parish School)
Tel: 708-333-8173; Fax: 708-339-3336; Web: www.christoursaviorcatholicschool.org. Karen Brodzik, Prin. Students 162.
Catechesis Religious Program—Tel: 708-868-1711. Students 36.

3—ST. VICTOR, Revs. David P. Pavlik; Leonard A. Dubi, Pastor Emeritus, (Retired); Luis Valerio Romero; Deacon Dan Ragonese.
Res.: 553 Hirsch Ave., Calumet City, 60409.
Tel: 708-891-8920; Email: stvictor@archchicago.org.
School—Christ Our Savior, (Inter-Parish School)
Tel: 708-333-8173; Fax: 708-333-3247.
Catechesis Religious Program—Students 186.

CALUMET PARK, COOK CO., SEVEN HOLY FOUNDERS, Closed. Consult Archives and Records Center for parish records.

CHICAGO HEIGHTS, COOK CO.

1—ST. AGNES, Revs. John S. Siemianowski; Thomas R. Kasputis; Deacon David Brothers.
Res.: 1501 Chicago Rd., Chicago Heights, 60411.
Tel: 708-709-2694; Web: stagnes-chicago@archchicago.org.
School—St. Agnes School, Email: Admin@SaintAgnes.us. Mr. Matthew T. Lungaro, Prin. Clergy 1; Lay Teachers 9; Students 191.
Catechesis Religious Program—Students 102.

2—ST. KIERAN, Rev. John S. Siemianowski; Deacon David Dutko.
Res.: 724 W. 195th St., Chicago Heights, 60411.
Tel: 708-755-0074; Email: stkieran@archchicago.org.
Catechesis Religious Program—Tel: 708-754-0484;
Fax: 708-754-0484. Students 55.

3—ST. PAUL, Revs. Orlando Flores Orea; Misabet Garcia Gil; Deacon Joseph Kudra.
Res.: 206 E. 25th St., Chicago Heights, 60411.
Tel: 708-754-3120; Email: stpaul-25th@archchicago.org.
Catechesis Religious Program—Tel: 708-754-7720. Students 171.

CHICAGO RIDGE, COOK CO., OUR LADY OF THE RIDGE, Revs. Wayne A. Svida; Philip E. Cyscon, In Res.; Deacons Edwin Hill; John Orzechowski.
Res.: 10811 S. Ridgeland Ave., Chicago Ridge, 60415.
Tel: 708-425-3800; Email: ol-ridge@archchicago.org.
Catechesis Religious Program—Tel: 708-424-4949. Students 168.

CICERO, COOK CO.

1—ST. ANTHONY OF PADUA
1510 S. 49th Ct., Cicero, 60804. Rev. Sergio Solis; Deacon Manuel Orozco. In Res., Rev. Alejandro Garrido.
Res.: 1515 S. 50th Ave., Cicero, 60804.
Tel: 708-652-0231; Email: stanthony-49th@archchicago.org.
St. Anthony Center—1510 S. 49th Ct., Cicero, 60804.
Catechesis Religious Program—Students 416.

2—ST. FRANCES OF ROME, Very Rev. Paul Stein, S.T.L.; Deacon Jesus Blanco.
Res.: 1428 S. 59th Ct., Cicero, 60804.
Tel: 708-652-2140; Email: stfrances-rome@archchicago.org.
School—St. Frances of Rome School, 1401 S. Austin Blvd., Cicero, 60804. Tel: 708-652-2277; Email: office@sfr-school.org; Web: www.sfr-school.org. Dr. Anthony Clishem, Prin. Lay Teachers 14; Students 208.
Catechesis Religious Program—Tel: 708-656-8632. Ms. Sandra L. Dominguez-Herrera, D.R.E. Students 56.

3—ST. MARY OF CZESTOCHOWA (1895) (Polish—Spanish) Revs. Waldemar Wieladek, C.Ss.R.; Marian Furca, C.Ss.R.; Zbigniew Pienkos, C.Ss.R., In Res.
Res.: 3010 S. 48th Ct., Cicero, 60804.
Tel: 708-652-0948; Email: stmary-czestochowa@archchicago.org.
Catechesis Religious Program—Students 174.

4—MARY, QUEEN OF HEAVEN (1911) Rev. Sergio De la Torre Carrillo, M.Div., Admin.; Deacons Martin Enciso; Jesus Garcia.
Res.: 5300 W. 24th St., Cicero, 60804.
Tel: 708-863-6608; Email: mary-heaven@archchicago.org.
Catechesis Religious Program—Students 394.

5—OUR LADY OF CHARITY (1954) Rev. Sergio Mena-Mena; Deacon Maximino Montalvo
Res.: 3600 57th Ct., Cicero, 60804-4235.
Tel: 708-863-1207; Email: ol-charity@archchicago.org.
School—Our Lady of Charity School, 3620 57th Ct., Cicero, 60804. Tel: 708-652-0262; Fax: 708-652-0601; Email: lletourneau@olc-school.org; Web: www.olc-school.org. Mrs. Lynn M. Letourneau, Prin. Lay Teachers 10; Students 251.
Catechesis Religious Program—Ms. Sandra L. Dominguez-Herrera, D.R.E. Students 33.

6—OUR LADY OF THE MOUNT, Rev. Juan Luis Andrade-Limon, Admin.; Deacon Benito Gallegos.
Res.: 2414 S. 61st Ave., Cicero, 60804.
Tel: 708-652-2791; Email: ol-mount@archchicago.org.
Catechesis Religious Program—Students 206.

COUNTRY CLUB HILLS, COOK CO., ST. EMERIC, Rev. Edmond Aristil; Deacon Philip DuBrownik.
Res.: 4330 W. 180th St., Country Club Hills, 60478.
Tel: 708-798-0757; Email: stemeric@archchicago.org.
Catechesis Religious Program—Tel: 708-799-4430; Fax: 708-798-0799. Students 44.

DEERFIELD, LAKE CO., HOLY CROSS, Revs. Vincent F. Costello; John M. Thinnes, Pastor Emeritus, (Retired); Deacons Edward Melton; Stewart I. Adams; Kevin Garvey; Michelle Shaffer, Pastoral Assoc.; Rev. Kenneth J. Fischer, In Res., (Retired).
Res.: 724 Elder Ln., Deerfield, 60015.
Tel: 847-945-0430; Email: holycross-elder@archchicago.org.
Catechesis Religious Program—Tel: 847-945-0581; Fax: 847-945-0582. Students 425.

DES PLAINES, COOK CO.
1—ST. MARY, Revs. Lawrence Collins; Paul F. Rosemeyer, Pastor Emeritus, (Retired); Roy Belocura; Deacons James O'Malley, (Retired); James J. O'Leary.
Res.: 794 Pearson St., Des Plaines, 60016.
Tel: 847-824-8144; Email: stmarypearson@archchicago.org.
Catechesis Religious Program—Tel: 847-298-1435; Fax: 847-824-3906. Students 346.
2—ST. PAUL CHONG HASANG, Rev. Sang Sup Bing, Dir.
Res.: 725 Dursey Ln., Des Plaines, 60016.
Tel: 847-699-6334; Email: stpaul-mission@archchicago.org.
Catechesis Religious Program—Students 259.
3—ST. STEPHEN PROTOMARTYR
1267 Everett Ave., Des Plaines, 60018-2398.
Tel: 847-824-2026; Fax: 847-824-3842; Email: ststephen@sbcglobal.net; Web: www.ststephen-desplaines.org. Revs. Manuel Arcila; Michael G. Zaniolo, S.T.L., C.A.C., In Res.; Deacons Anthony Towey; William H. Warmouth; Conrad Wojnar.
Catechesis Religious Program—Tel: 847-297-3844; Fax: 847-824-3842. Students 316.
4—ST. ZACHARY (1961) Revs. Piotr Rapcia; Lawrence F. Springer, In Res., (Retired); Deacons John J. Smith; David Brezinski; Mariusz J. Kosla.
Res.: 567 W. Algonquin Rd., Des Plaines, 60016.
Tel: 847-956-7020; Email: stzachary@archchicago.org.
School—St. Zachary School, Tel: 847-437-4022; Email: principal@saintzachary.org. Ms. Caroline R. Forestor, Prin. Lay Teachers 13; Students 140.
Catechesis Religious Program—Tel: 847-956-1175. Students 253.

ELK GROVE VILLAGE, COOK CO.
1—ST. JULIAN EYMARD, Rev. Brian Kean, M.Div.; Deacon Ted Czarnecki.
Res.: 601 Biesterfield Rd., Elk Grove Village, 60007.
Tel: 847-956-0130; Email: stjulian@archchicago.org.
Catechesis Religious Program—Tel: 847-593-8938. Students 419.
2—QUEEN OF THE ROSARY, Rev. Fred Pesek Jr.; Deacons Jerrold S. Szostak; Keith F. Strohm; Lawrence J. Smith; Revs. Anthony Nyong, In Res.; Ignatius Okonkwo, In Res.
Res.: 750 Elk Grove Blvd., Elk Grove Village, 60007.
Tel: 847-437-0403; Email: queen-rosary@archchicago.org.
School—Queen of the Rosary School, 690 Elk Grove Blvd., Elk Grove Village, 60007. Tel: 847-437-3322; Fax: 847-437-3290; Email: kmcginn@qrcougars.org. Ms. Kathleen McGinn, Prin. Lay Teachers 17; Students 267.
Catechesis Religious Program—680 Elk Grove Blvd., Elk Grove Village, 60007. Tel: 847-437-3346. Students 181.

ELMWOOD PARK, COOK CO., ST. MOTHER THEODORE GUERIN, Revs. Paul D. Cao; Jacque B. Beltran, S.T.B., D.Min. (Cand.); Very Rev. Jeffrey S. Grob, J.C.D., In Res.; Rev. Filbert Ngwila, In Res.; Deacon Ronald Pilarski; Mr. Ruthanne Swiatkowski, D.R.E.
St. Cyprian—2601 Clinton St., River Grove, 60171.
St. Celestine, 3020 N. 76th Ct., Elmwood Park, 60707. Tel: 708-453-2555; Email: office@stguerinparish.org; Web: stguerinparish.org.
School—St. Celestine School, 3017 N. 77th Ave., Elmwood Park, 60707. Tel: 708-453-8234; Fax: 708-452-0237; Email: jjrocchi@stcelestineschool.org. Mrs. Jeanine L. Rocchi, Prin. Lay Teachers 26; Students 443.

EVANSTON, COOK CO.
1—ST. ATHANASIUS, Revs. Thomas A. Libera, Pastor Emeritus, (Retired); Hernan Cuevas-Contreras.
Res.: 1615 Lincoln St., Evanston, 60201.
Tel: 847-328-1430; Email: stathanasius@archchicago.org.
School—St. Athanasius School, 2510 Ashland Ave., Evanston, 60201. Tel: 847-864-2650; Fax: 847-475-7385; Email: jberg@saintas.net. Carol McClay, Prin. Lay Teachers 22; Students 219.
Catechesis Religious Program—Ms. Margaret Waldron, D.R.E. Students 136.
2—ST. MARY, Revs. Kevin McCray; Antony A. Joseph; Deacon Dennis R. Robak.
Parish Center—Res.: 1012 Lake St., Evanston, 60201. Tel: 847-864-0333; Email: stmary-lakestreet@archchicago.org.
School—Pope John XXIII, Tel: 847-475-5678; Email: gail.hulse@popejohn23.org. Mrs. Gail F. Hulse, Prin. Consolidated with St. Nicholas Parish to form Pope John XXIII School. See St. Nicholas for further details. Lay Teachers 23; Students 237.
Catechesis Religious Program—Students 204.
3—ST. NICHOLAS, Revs. Joseph P. Tito; Robert H. Oldershaw, Pastor Emeritus, (Retired); Deacons Jaime Rojas; Christopher Murphy.
Res.: 806 Ridge Ave., Evanston, 60202.
Tel: 847-864-1185; Email: stnicholas@archchicago.org.
School—Pope John XXIII, 1120 Washington, Evanston, 60202. Tel: 847-475-5678; Fax: 847-475-5683; Email: gail.hulse@popejohn23.org. Mrs. Gail F. Hulse, Prin. Consolidated with St. Mary Parish to form Pope John XXIII School. Lay Teachers 23; Students 237.
Catechesis Religious Program—Sr. Christina Fuller, D.R.E. Students 411.

EVERGREEN PARK, COOK CO.
1—ST. BERNADETTE, Rev. Benedykt M. Pazdan; Deacon Kevin O'Donnell.
Res.: 9343 Francisco Ave., Evergreen Park, 60805.
Tel: 708-422-8995; Email: stbernadette@archchicago.org.
Catechesis Religious Program—Tel: 708-425-7697. Students 99.
2—MOST HOLY REDEEMER, Revs. James M. Hyland; Paul Guzman; Albert R. Adamich, Senior Priest, (Retired); Joseph F. Hardy, In Res.; Deacon Mark Phelan.
Res.: 9525 S. Lawndale Ave., Evergreen Park, 60805.
Tel: 708-425-5354; Email: holyredeemer@archchicago.org.
School—Most Holy Redeemer School, 9536 S. Millard Ave., Evergreen Park, 60805. Tel: 708-422-8280; Fax: 708-422-4193; Email: nharmening@mhrschool.com. Mrs. Nancy A. Harmening, Prin. Lay Teachers 18; Students 351.
Catechesis Religious Program—Tel: 708-346-8185. Students 289.
3—QUEEN OF MARTYRS, Revs. Martin T. Marren; Christopher Kituli, M.Div.; Deacon Robert J. Landuyt.
Res.: 10233 S. Central Park, Evergreen Park, 60805-3799. Tel: 708-423-8110; Email: queen-martyrs@archchicago.org.
School—Queen of Martyrs School, 3550 W. 103rd St., 60655. Tel: 708-422-1540; Fax: 708-422-1811; Email: ktomaszewski@qmschool.com. Ms. Kathleen M. Tomaszewski, Prin. Lay Teachers 20; Students 259.
Catechesis Religious Program—Tel: 708-422-1647. Bernadine Smierciak, D.R.E. Students 197.

FLOSSMOOR, COOK CO., INFANT JESUS OF PRAGUE, Revs. Jacek A. Jura; Michael A. Hack, J.C.D., Pastor Emeritus, (Retired); William J. Flaherty, Pastor Emeritus, (Retired).
Res.: 1131 Douglas Ave., Flossmoor, 60422.
Tel: 708-799-5400; Email: infantjesus@archchicago.org.
School—Infant Jesus of Prague School, 1101 Douglas Ave., Flossmoor, 60422. Tel: 708-799-5200; Email: pdull@ijpschool.org. Ms. Natalie Formica, Prin. Lay Teachers 20; Students 298.
Catechesis Religious Program—Patricia Kahl, D.R.E. Students 186.

FOREST PARK, COOK CO., ST. BERNARDINE, Rev. Stanislaw Kuca; Deacon Lendell Richardson.
Res.: 7246 Harrison St., Forest Park, 60130.
Tel: 708-366-0839; Email: stbernardine@archchicago.org.
Catechesis Religious Program—Tel: 708-366-3553. Ms. Ann Stauffer, D.R.E. Students 45.

FRANKLIN PARK, COOK CO., ST. GERTRUDE, Revs. Eryk Czarnecki, (Poland); Alfred P. Corbo, Pastor Emeritus, (Retired); Krzysztof T. Pankanin, (Poland); Deacon Robert Murphy.
Res.: 9613 Schiller Blvd., Franklin Park, 60131.
Tel: 847-455-1100; Email: stgertrude-schiller@archchicago.org.
Catechesis Religious Program—9617 Schiller Blvd., Franklin Park, 60131. Students 240.

GLENVIEW, COOK CO.
1—ST. CATHERINE LABOURE, Revs. Paul Maina Waithaka; James A. Murphy, Pastor Emeritus; Deacons Ray Gavin; Frank Beil; Michael Bretz.
Res.: 3535 Thornwood Ave., Glenview, 60026.
Tel: 847-729-1414; Email: stcatherine-laboure@archchicago.org.
School—St. Catherine Laboure School, 3425 Thornwood Ave., Glenview, 60026. Tel: 847-724-2240 ; Fax: 847-724-5805; Email: administrator@sclschool-glenview.org. Mrs. Jodi Reuter, Prin. Lay Teachers 19; Students 193.
Catechesis Religious Program—Students 326.
2—OUR LADY OF PERPETUAL HELP, Revs. Jeremiah M. Boland, S.T.L.; Thomas E. Hickey, Pastor Emeritus, (Retired); John E. Flavin, Pastor Emeritus, (Retired); Patrick Tyrrell, S.J.; John M. Thinnes, Senior Priest, (Retired); Isaac Lara; Nicholas Kostyk; Deacons James Revord; David Kalina; Weiland Christopher.
Res.: 1775 Grove St., Glenview, 60025.
Tel: 847-729-1525; Email: OL-Help@archchicago.org.
School—Our Lady of Perpetual Help School, 1123 Church St., Glenview, 60025. Tel: 847-724-6990; Fax: 847-724-7025; Email: amills@olph-il.org. Dr. Amy Mills, Prin. Lay Teachers 60; School Sisters of St. Francis 1; Students 837.
Catechesis Religious Program—Tel: 847-998-5289; Fax: 847-729-6194. Students 1,033.

GLENWOOD, COOK CO., ST. JOHN, Rev. Karol Tybor; Deacon James Detloff.
Res.: 301 S. Cottage Grove Ave., Glenwood, 60425.
Tel: 708-758-5098; Email: stjohn-cottagegrove@archchicago.org.
Catechesis Religious Program—Students 60.

GRAYSLAKE, LAKE CO., ST. GILBERT (1930) Revs. John P. Chrzan, M.Div.; Eugene J. Nowak, Pastor Emeritus, (Retired); Christian Shiu; Deacons Richard Globis; Mark Plaiss; Alan Biegel.
Res.: 301 E. Belvidere Rd., Grayslake, 60030.
Tel: 847-223-4731; Email: stgilbert@archchicago.org.
School—St. Gilbert School, 231 E. Belvidere Rd., Grayslake, 60030. Tel: 847-223-8600; Email: Brian.tekampe@stgilbertschool.org. Mr. Brian Tekampe, Prin. Clergy 1; Lay Teachers 23; Students 382.
Catechesis Religious Program—Tel: 847-223-3071; Fax: 847-223-6545. Sr. Donna Schmitt, O.S.F., D.R.E. Students 556.

GURNEE, LAKE CO., ST. PAUL THE APOSTLE, Revs. Gregory Houck; David Genders, O.Carm.; Deacons Michael Penich; Ivan Siap; Robert Birck.
Res.: 6401 Gages Lake Rd., Gurnee, 60031.
Tel: 847-918-0600; Email: stpaul-apostle@archchicago.org.
Catechesis Religious Program—Tel: 847-816-8677. Students 1,071.

HANOVER PARK, COOK CO., ST. ANSGAR (1968) Revs. Eduardo Garcia-Ferrer; Mario Pelayo Corona; Deacon Alberto Contreras.
Res.: 2040 Laurel Ave., Hanover Park, 60133.
Tel: 630-837-5553; Email: stansgar@archchicago.org.
Catechesis Religious Program—Students 605.

HARVEY, COOK CO.
1—ASCENSION-ST. SUSANNA, Rev. James F. Flynn, Admin., (Retired); Deacon Thomas R. Carvlin.
Res.: 15234 Myrtle Ave., Harvey, 60426.
Tel: 708-333-0931; Email: ascension-myrtle@archchicago.org.
Catechesis Religious Program—Students 49.
2—ST. JOHN THE BAPTIST, (Polish) Rev. Edward Romanski, (Poland) Admin.
Res.: 15746 Union Ave., Harvey, 60426.
Tel: 708-333-0184; Email: stjohn-baptist@archchicago.org.
Catechesis Religious Program—Students 214.

HARWOOD HEIGHTS, NORRIDGE , COOK CO., ST. ROSALIE, Revs. Marcim Mikulski; Marek Kreis.
Res.: 4401 N. Oak Park Ave., Harwood Heights-Norridge, 60706. Tel: 708-867-8817; Email: strosalie@archchicago.org.
Catechesis Religious Program—6750 W. Montrose, Harwood Hts., 60706. Students 64.

HAZEL CREST, COOK CO., ST. ANNE, Rev. Ralph H. Zwirn; Deacon Gary Miarka.
Res.: 16802 S. Lincoln St., Hazel Crest, 60429.
Tel: 708-355-1792; Email: stanne-lincoln@archchicago.org.
Child Care—Early Learning Center, (Grades PreK-Day Care), 16777 Dixie Hwy., Hazel Crest, 60429. Students 82.
Catechesis Religious Program—Tel: 708-335-2286. Students 69.

HICKORY HILLS, COOK CO., ST. PATRICIA, Rev. Marcel J. Pasciak; Deacons Charles Keegan; Norbert Weitendorf.
Res.: 9050 S. 86th Ave., Hickory Hills, 60457.
Tel: 708-598-5222; Email: stpatricia@archchicago.org.
School—St. Patricia School, 9000 S. 86th Ave., Hickory Hills, 60457. Tel: 708-598-8200; Fax: 708-598-8233; Email: jnowinski@stpatriciaparish.com. Ms. Jamie L. Nowinski, Prin. Lay Teachers 14; Students 177.
Catechesis Religious Program—Tel: 708-599-1221. Students 279.

HIGHLAND PARK, LAKE CO., IMMACULATE CONCEPTION, Revs. Michael F. McMahon; Terrence A. McCarthy, Pastor Emeritus, (Retired); Deacon Louis Vignocchi; Mary Nelson, Pastoral Assoc.
Res.: 770 Deerfield Rd., Highland Park, 60035.
Tel: 847-433-0130; Email: ic-greenbay@archchicago.org.
Catechesis Religious Program—Tel: 847-433-2224. Students 203.

HIGHWOOD, LAKE CO., ST. JAMES, Revs. Thomas F.

Baldonieri; Ronald E. Scarlata, Pastor Emeritus, (Retired); Deacon Luis R. Lara.
Res.: 134 North Ave., Highwood, 60040.
Tel: 847-433-1494; Email: stjames-north@archchicago.org.
Catechesis Religious Program—Tel: 847-432-2570. Mrs. Judy Cullen, D.R.E.; Miriam Chan, D.R.E. Students 234.

HILLSIDE, COOK CO., ST. DOMITILLA, Rev. Julio Jimenez Soto.
Res.: 4940 Washington St., Hillside, 60162.
Tel: 708-449-8430; Fax: stdomitilla@archchicago.org.
Catechesis Religious Program—Tel: 708-449-1558. Students 140.

HOFFMAN ESTATES, COOK CO., ST. HUBERT, Revs. Michael G. Scherschel; Fred T. Licciardi, C.PP.S.; Deacons Richard Lawson; Steven Baldasti; Allen Tatara.
Res.: 729 Grand Canyon St., Hoffman Estates, 60169. Tel: 847-885-7700; Email: sthubert@archchicago.org.
School—St. Hubert School, 255 Flagstaff Ln., Hoffman Estates, 60169. Tel: 847-885-7702; Fax: 847-885-0604; Email: office@sthubertschool.org. Kelly Bourrell, Prin. Lay Teachers 24; Students 287.
Catechesis Religious Program—Tel: 847-855-7703. Mr. Michael Keenan, D.R.E. Students 480.

HOMETOWN, COOK CO., OUR LADY OF LORETTO (1951) Rev. Thomas S. Cabala.
Res.: 8925 S. Kostner Ave., Hometown, 60456.
Tel: 708-424-7471; Email: ol-loretto@archchicago.org.
Catechesis Religious Program—Tel: 708-499-0832. Students 81.

HOMEWOOD, COOK CO., ST. JOSEPH, Revs. Robert J. Kyfes; Daniel Jarosewic; Deacon George Maddock.
Res.: 17951 Dixie Hwy., Homewood, 60430.
Tel: 708-798-0622; Email: stjoseph-dixie@archchicago.org.
Catechesis Religious Program—Tel: 708-798-6311. Students 223.

INDIAN CREEK, LAKE CO., ST. MARY OF VERNON (1978) Revs. Joseph C. Curtis; John P. Finnegan, Pastor Emeritus, (Retired); Deacons Mark R. Zwolski; James Wogan; Philip Pagnotta Jr.; John Glenn; Daniel Moore; Gerald Nora; Ms. Maureen Evers, Pastoral Assoc.
Res.: 236 U.S. Hwy. 45, Indian Creek, 60061.
Tel: 847-362-1005; Email: mary-heaven@archchicago.org.
Catechesis Religious Program—Tel: 847-362-0653. Students 582.

INGLESIDE, LAKE CO., OUR LADY OF THE LAKES, Rev. Shawn Gould; Deacons Lawrence Spohr; Gregory Zeifert; David Bresemann.
St. Peter—557 W. Lake St., Antioch, 60002.
St. Bede, 36455 N. Wilson Rd., Ingleside, 60041.
Tel: 847-587-2251; Email: parishoffice@ollonline.org; Web: ourladyofthelakesparish.org.
School—St. Bede School, 36399 N. Wilson Rd., Ingleside, 60041. Tel: 847-587-5541; Fax: 847-587-2713; Email: pstrang@stbedeschool.com. Mrs. Patricia J. Strang, Prin. Lay Teachers 13; Students 189.
Catechesis Religious Program—Tel: 847-587-2301. Mark Buckley, D.R.E. Students 247.

INVERNESS, COOK CO., HOLY FAMILY, Revs. Terence M. Keehan; Medard P. Laz, Pastor Emeritus; Richard Jakubik; Marsha Adamczyk, Pastoral Assoc.; Deacon Dennis G. Brown.
Res.: 2515 W. Palatine Rd., Inverness, 60067.
Tel: 847-359-0042; Email: holyfamily-palatine@archchicago.org.
School—Holy Family Catholic Academy, Tel: 847-907-3452; Email: info@holyfamilycatholicacademy.net. Mrs. Catherine A. O'Brien, Prin. Lay Teachers 32; Students 474.
Catechesis Religious Program—Tel: 847-359-0572. Students 825.

LA GRANGE, COOK CO.
1—ST. CLETUS
Tel: 708-352-6209. Revs. Robert J. Clark; Lorenzo Gamboa Cadena; Kenneth Baker; Deacon Stuart Heyes.
School—St. Cletus School, 700 W. 55th St., La Grange, 60525. Tel: 708-352-4820; Fax: 708-352-0788; Email: tchinske@stcletusparish.com. Mr. Thomas Chinske, Prin. Lay Teachers 31; Students 397.
Catechesis Religious Program—Tel: 708-352-2383. Students 604.

2—ST. FRANCIS XAVIER, Revs. William Tkachuk; William E. Killeen; Deacon Andrew Allison; Ms. Katherine Devries, Pastoral Assoc.
Res.: 124 N. Spring Ave., La Grange, 60525.
Tel: 708-352-0168; Email: stfrancisxavier-spring@archchicago.org.
School—St. Francis Xavier School, 145 N. Waiola Ave., La Grange, 60525. Tel: 708-352-2175; Fax: 708-352-2057; Email: sfxmain@sfxlg.org. Mrs. Sharon Garcia, Prin. Lay Teachers 38; Students 495.
Catechesis Religious Program—Tel: 708-352-4555. Students 980.

LA GRANGE PARK, COOK CO., ST. LOUISE DE MARILLAC (1955)
600 W. 55th St., La Grange, 60525.
Tel: 708-352-6209; Email: stcletus@archchicago.org. Revs. Denis Condon; John C. Hergenrother, Pastor Emeritus; Joseph W. Altman; Deacon David Brencic.
School—St. Louise de Marillac School, (Grades PreK-8), Tel: 708-352-2202; Email: info@slmschool.org. Ms. Annmarie N. Mahay, Prin. Lay Teachers 9; Students 144.
Child Care—Youth Ministry, 1144 Harrison Ave., La Grange Park, 60526. Tel: 708-352-7388; Email: stlouise-marillac@archchicago.org.
Catechesis Religious Program—1125 Harrison Ave., La Grange Park, 60526. Students 195.

LAKE FOREST, LAKE CO.
1—ST. MARY, Revs. Michael A. Nacius; Mark Augustine; Deacons John Herrmann; Robert J. Thomas; Ms. Loretta Nugent, Pastoral Assoc.
Res.: 175 E. Illinois Rd., Lake Forest, 60045.
Tel: 847-234-0205; Email: stmary-illinois@archchicago.org.
School—St. Mary School, 185 E. Illinois Rd., Lake Forest, 60045. Tel: 847-234-0371; Fax: 847-234-9593; Email: dwieters@schoolofstmary.org. David Wieters, Prin. Lay Teachers 40; Students 409.
Catechesis Religious Program—Tel: 847-234-0090; Fax: 847-234-2755. Ms. Jean Brunk, D.R.E. Students 376.

2—ST. PATRICK, Rev. Msgr. Robert J. Dempsey; Rev. William J. McNulty, Pastor Emeritus, (Retired); Deacons Frank DeFrank; John V. Lucas; Raymond C. Loman.
Res.: 991 S. Waukegan Rd., Lake Forest, 60045.
Tel: 847-234-1401; Email: stpatrick-waukegan@archchicago.org.
Catechesis Religious Program—Tel: 847-234-2179; Fax: 847-234-2313. Students 469.

LAKE VILLA, LAKE CO., PRINCE OF PEACE (1955) Revs. Gerald G. Walsh, M.Div.; Adam Blatt; Daniel F. Sullivan, In Res., (Retired); Deacons Timothy Leonard; Jeff Barton; Christopher Savage; Jim Minor; James Even.
Res.: 135 S. Milwaukee Ave., Lake Villa, 60046.
Tel: 847-356-7915; Email: princeofpeace@archchicago.org.
School—Prince of Peace School, Tel: 847-356-6111; Email: bbaldassano@princeofpeacelv.org. Stephanie Stoneberg, Prin. Lay Teachers 12; Students 275.
Catechesis Religious Program—Tel: 847-356-5850. Students 363.

LAKE ZURICH, LAKE CO., ST. FRANCIS DE SALES (1949) Rev. David Ryan; Deacons Robert Arvidson; George Flaherty.
Res. & Rectory: 227 E. Main St., Lake Zurich, 60047.
Church: 135 S. Buesching Rd., Lake Zurich, 60047.
Tel: 847-438-6622; Email: stfrancisdesales-main@archchicago.org.
School—St. Francis de Sales School, 11 S. Buesching Rd., Lake Zurich, 60047. Tel: 847-438-7921; Fax: 847-438-7114; Email: schoolinfo@stfrancislz.org. Kyle Schmitt, Prin. Lay Teachers 16; Students 348.
Catechesis Religious Program—Tel: 847-726-4850. Kathy Brady-Murfin, D.R.E. Students 713.

LANSING, COOK CO., ST. ANN, Rev. Mark Kalema.
Parish Office—3010 Ridge Rd., Lansing, 60438.
Tel: 708-895-6700; Email: stann-ridge@archchicago.org.
Res.: 3026 Ridge Rd., Lansing, 60438.
School—St. Ann School, 3014 Ridge Rd., Lansing, 60438. Tel: 708-895-1661; Fax: 708-865-6923; Email: janicesummerrise@saintannschool.com. Kelly Rojas, Prin. Lay Teachers 10; Students 169.
Catechesis Religious Program—Tel: 708-895-5970. Ms. Barbara Antoskiewicz, D.R.E. Students 218.

LEMONT, COOK CO.
1—ST. ALPHONSUS, Revs. Brian Ardagh; Thomas Hoffman; Deacons Daniel Rittenhouse; Terrance McGuire; William Lubben.
Res.: 210 E. Logan, Lemont, 60439.
Tel: 630-257-2414; Email: stalphonsus-logan@archchicago.org.
School—St. Alphonsus-St. Patrick Consolidated, (Grades K-8), Admin. Office: 20 W. 145 Davey Rd., Lemont, 60439. Tel: 630-783-2220; Email: schooloffice@stals-stpats.org. Robert Priest, Prin. Lay Teachers 15; Students 144.
Catechesis Religious Program—Tel: 630-257-2371; Fax: 630-257-2381. Kevin Cody, D.R.E. Students 316.

2—BLESSED JURGIS MATULAITIS MISSION
Mailing Address: 14915-127th St., Unit 101, Lemont, 60439. Rev. Algis Baniulis, S.J.
Lithuanian Catholic Mission, 14911 127th St., Lemont, 60439-7417. Tel: 630-257-5613; Email: blessedjurgis-mission@archchicago.org.
Catechesis Religious Program—Students 868.

3—SS. CYRIL AND METHODIUS (1884) Rev. Waldemar Stawiarski; Deacons Neil Rogers; Michael Ciciura.
Res.: 608 Sobieski St., Lemont, 60439.
Tel: 630-257-2776; Email: sscm@archchicago.org.
School—SS. Cyril and Methodius School, 607 Sobieski St., Lemont, 60439. Tel: 630-257-6488; Fax: 630-257-6465; Email: shirleyt@stcyril.org. Mrs. Shirley A. Tkachuk, Prin. Lay Teachers 18; Students 228.
Catechesis Religious Program—Tel: 630-257-9314; Fax: 630-257-9805. Students 497.

4—ST. JAMES AT SAG BRIDGE, [CEM] Revs. Thomas R. Koys, S.T.L.; Edward D. Gleeson, Pastor Emeritus, (Retired); Deacons Douglas Szarzynski; John M. Wilkinson.
Res.: 10600 South Archer Ave., Lemont, 60439-9344.
Tel: 630-257-7000; Email: stjames-archer@archchicago.org.
Catechesis Religious Program—Students 30.

5—ST. PATRICK (1839) Revs. Kurt D. Boras; Richard J. Shannon, Pastor Emeritus, (Retired); Thomas Hoffman; Deacons Joseph Winblad; Lawrence A. Oskielunas.
Res.: 200 Illinois St., Lemont, 60439.
Tel: 630-257-6134; Email: stpatrick-illinois@archchicago.org.
School—St. Alphonsus-St. Patrick Consolidated, (Grades PreK-8), Admin. Office: 20 W. 145 Davey Rd., Lemont, 60439. Tel: 630-783-2220; Fax: 630-783-2230; Email: schooloffice@stals-stpats.org. Robert Priest, Prin. Lay Teachers 15; Students 144.
Catechesis Religious Program—Tel: 630-257-8012; Fax: 630-257-0401. Students 110.

6—SLOVENIAN CATHOLIC MISSION (1994) (Dedicated to Bl. A.M. Slomsek)
Tel: 630-257-2068. Rev. Metod Ogorevc, O.F.M.; Deacon John Vidmar.
Res.: 14246 Main St., P.O. Box 608, Lemont, 60439-0608. Tel: 630-257-2068; Email: blessedslomsek@archchicago.org.

LIBERTYVILLE, LAKE CO., ST. JOSEPH, Revs. John Trout, S.P.S.; John E. Hennessey, Pastor Emeritus, (Retired); Robinson Ortiz; Martin Luboyera; Deacons David Tiemeier; George Kashmar; Dennis Mudd Sr.; Mr. David Retseck, Pastoral Assoc.
Res.: 121 E. Maple Ave., Libertyville, 60048.
Tel: 847-362-2073; Email: stjoseph-maple@archchicago.org.
School—St. Joseph School, 221 Park Pl., Libertyville, 60048. Tel: 847-362-0730; Fax: 847-362-8130; Email: aphoenix@sjslibertyville.org. Ms. Anne Phoenix, Prin. Lay Teachers 29; Students 449.
Catechesis Religious Program—116 Hurlburt Ct., Libertyville, 60048. Mr. Terence Zawacki, D.R.E. Students 1,029.

LYONS, COOK CO., ST. HUGH, Revs. Robert Marchwiany; Edward S. Stockus, Pastor Emeritus, (Retired); Robert J. Burnell, Pastor Emeritus, (Retired); Deacon Frank Mamolella.
Res.: 7939 W. 43rd St., Lyons, 60534.
Tel: 708-447-3108; Email: sthugh@archchicago.org.
Catechesis Religious Program—Tel: 708-447-5711. Students 80.

MARKHAM, COOK CO., ST. GERARD MAJELLA, Rev. James F. Flynn, Admin., (Retired).
Res.: 16130 Clifton Park, Markham, 60426.
Tel: 708-331-8400; Email: stgerard-majella@archchicago.org.
Catechesis Religious Program—Students 151.

MATTESON, COOK CO., ST. LAWRENCE O'TOOLE (1959) Rev. Michael Novick; Deacons John Rangel; Edward Winter; William A. Doerr.
Res.: 4101 St. Lawrence Ave., Matteson, 60443.
Tel: 708-748-6090; Email: stlawrenceotoole@archchicago.org.
Catechesis Religious Program—Students 69.

MAYWOOD, COOK CO., ST. EULALIA
1845 S. 9th Ave., Maywood, 60153. Rev. Michael J. Arkins, S.S.S.; Deacons Giulio Camerini; Dwight Sullivan. In Res., Revs. Christian Christopher, S.S.S.; Nguyen D. Thang, S.S.S.
Res.: 1851 S. 9th Ave., Maywood, 60153.
Tel: 708-343-6120; Email: steulalia@archchicago.org.
Catechesis Religious Program—Students 55.

MELROSE PARK, COOK CO.
1—ST. CHARLES BORROMEO, Rev. Jesus Ramirez Cerda, Admin.; Deacon Freddy Palacios.
Res.: 1637 N. 37th Ave., Melrose Park, 60160.
Tel: 708-343-7646; Email: stcharles@archchicago.org.
Catechesis Religious Program—Students 605.

2—OUR LADY OF MOUNT CARMEL, (Italian) Revs. Giovanni Bizzotto, In Res.; August Feccia, C.S.; Yosef Sadipun; Colon Jackson, In Res.; Deacons John P. Battisto; Jose Ramon Arenas.
Res.: 1101 N. 23rd Ave., Melrose Park, 60160.
Tel: 708-344-4140; Email: ol-mtcarmel23rd@archchicago.org.

Catechesis Religious Program—Modesta Martinez, D.R.E. Students 775.

Shrine—Shrine of Our Lady of Mt. Carmel.

3—SACRED HEART, Revs. Francisco I. Ortega Munoz; Erwin J. Friedl, Pastor Emeritus, (Retired); Benedict Ezeoke, (Nigeria) In Res.; Herbert J. Meyr, In Res., (Retired); Deacons Raymond Behrendt; Norberto Ojeda; Michael K. Barnish; Eduardo Rodriguez.
Res.: 819 N. 16th Ave., Melrose Park, 60160.
Tel: 708-344-0757; Email: sacredheart-16th@archchicago.org.
School—Sacred Heart School, 815 N. 16th Ave., Melrose Park, 60160. Tel: 708-681-0240;
Fax: 708-681-0454; Email: school@shsmelrosepark.com. Mrs. Barbara J. Ciconte, Prin. Lay Teachers 10; Students 184.
Catechesis Religious Program—Students 293.
Convent—1503 W. Rice St., Melrose Park, 60160.

MIDLOTHIAN, COOK CO., ST. CHRISTOPHER (1922) Rev. Krzysztof Paluch.
Res.: 4130 W. 147th St., Midlothian, 60445.
Tel: 708-388-8190; Email: stchristopher@archchicago.org.
School—St. Christopher School, 14611 S. Keeler Ave., Midlothian, 60445. Tel: 708-385-8776;
Fax: 708-385-8102; Email: info@stchrisschool.org. Dr. Michelle Walthers, Prin. Lay Teachers 11; Students 192.
Catechesis Religious Program—Tel: 708-388-4040. Students 160.

MORTON GROVE, COOK CO., ST. MARTHA, Rev. Dennis B. O'Neill; Deacon Joseph Tony R. Valdez.
Res.: 8523 Georgiana Ave., Morton Grove, 60053.
Tel: 847-965-0262; Email: stmartha@archchicago.org.
Catechesis Religious Program—Tel: 847-965-6861. Students 155.
Shrine—The Shrine of All Saints.

MT. PROSPECT, COOK CO.

1—ST. CECILIA, Revs. Oswaldo Guillen, S.D.B., (Venezuela); Daniel J. Brady, Pastor Emeritus, (Retired); Damasus C. Okoro, C.S.Sp., In Res.; Deacon Valdemar Silva.
Res.: 700 S. Meier Rd., Mt. Prospect, 60056.
Tel: 847-437-6208; Email: stcecilia@archchicago.org.
Catechesis Religious Program—Tel: 847-437-6310; Fax: 847-437-5730. Lisa Mersereau, D.R.E. Students 109.

2—ST. EMILY, Revs. James Presta, M.Div., S.T.L., S.T.D.; Rafal Stecz; William J. McNulty, (Retired); John W. Roller, In Res., (Retired); Sr. M. Danielle Jacob, Pastoral Assoc.; Gail Goleas, Pastoral Assoc.
Office: 1400 E. Central Rd., Mt. Prospect, 60056.
Res.: 101 N. Horner Ln., Mt. Prospect, 60056.
Tel: 847-824-5049; Email: stemily@archchicago.org.
School—St. Emily School, 1400 E. Central Rd., Mt. Prospect, 60056. Tel: 847-296-3490;
Fax: 847-296-1155; Email: schoolinfo@stemily.org. Mrs. Mary K. Hemmelman, Prin. Lay Teachers 23; Students 289.
Catechesis Religious Program—Tel: 847-299-5865. Students 345.

3—ST. RAYMOND DE PENAFORT, Revs. Edward B. Panek; Gilbert Mashurano; Deacons David Babczak; John Lorbach; Ms. Rosemarie Rosado, Pastoral Assoc.
Res.: 301 S. I Oka St., Mt. Prospect, 60056.
Tel: 847-253-8600; Email: straymond@archchicago.org.
School—St. Raymond de Penafort School, 300 S. Elmhurst Ave., Mt. Prospect, 60056.
Tel: 847-253-8555; Fax: 847-253-8939; Email: maryeileen.ward@st-raymond.org. Ms. Mary Eileen Ward, Prin. Lay Teachers 33; Students 518.
Catechesis Religious Program—
Tel: 847-253-8600, Ext. 150. Students 383.

4—ST. THOMAS BECKET (1969) Rev. John W. Roller, Pastor Emeritus, (Retired); Deacon Anthony Jannotta.
Res.: 1321 Burning Bush Ln., Mt. Prospect, 60056.
Tel: 847-827-9220; Email: stthomas-becket@archchicago.org.
Catechesis Religious Program—Tel: 847-296-9051. Students 83.

MUNDELEIN, LAKE CO.

1—SANTA MARIA DEL POPOLO (1935) Revs. Miguel Angel Martinez; James W. Kinn, Pastor Emeritus, (Retired); Gerald K. O'Reilly; Deacons Dave Auld; Efrain Flores-Zamora; Felipe Vasquez.
Res.: 116 N. Lake St., Mundelein, 60060.
Tel: 847-949-8300; Web: samtamariadelpopolo@archchicago.org.
See Frassati Catholic Academy(Grades 6-8) located at Transfiguration, Wauconda.
Catechesis Religious Program—Tel: 847-990-6865. Students 439.
Convent—133 N. Lincoln Ave., Mundelein, 60060.
Tel: 847-566-7343. Ms. Aida Munoz, D.R.E.

2—ST. MARY OF THE ANNUNCIATION (Fremont Center) (1864) Rev. Jerome J. Jacob; Deacons Robert A. Poletto; Alan Sedivy; Gary L. Kupsak; Miguel Alandy.
Res.: 22333 W. Erhart Rd., Mundelein, 60060.
Tel: 847-223-0010; Email: stmary-erhart@archchicago.org.
School—Frassati Catholic Academy-Mundelein Campus, (Grades PreK-5), 22277 W. Erhart Rd., Mundelein, 60060. Tel: 847-223-4021;
Fax: 847-223-3489; Email: tkleckner@frassaticatholicacademy.org. Mrs. Tammy A. Kleckner, Prin. Member of Catholic Consortium of Lake County. Lay Teachers 25; Students 314.
See Frassati Catholic Academy(Grades 6-8) located at Transfiguration, Wauconda.
Catechesis Religious Program—Students 517.

3—OUR LADY OF SILUVA LITHUANIAN MISSION
116 N. Lake St., Mundelein, 60060.
Tel: 773-776-4600. Mailing Address: 6812 S. Washtenaw, 60629. Rev. Jaunius Kelpsas, (Lithuania) Dir.

NILES, COOK CO.

1—ST. ISAAC JOGUES, Revs. Mario J. Pereira, S.F.X.; Carlos P. Pereira, S.F.X.; Deacon Paul Stanton.
Res.: 8149 Golf Rd., Niles, 60714. Tel: 847-967-1060; Email: stisaac@archchicago.org.
Catechesis Religious Program—Tel: 847-966-1180; Fax: 847-966-0159. Delores Stanton, D.R.E. Students 115.

2—ST. JOHN BREBEUF, Revs. Michael G. Meany; Robert S. Banzin, Pastor Emeritus, (Retired); Piotr Samborski; Przemyslaw Tomczyk; Deacons Andrew J. Beierwaltes; Lawrence Skaja.
Res.: 8307 N. Harlem Ave., Niles, 60714.
Tel: 847-966-8145; Email: stjohn-brebeuf@archchicago.org.
School—St. John Brebeuf School, 8301 Harlem Ave., Niles, 60714. Tel: 847-966-3266; Fax: 847-966-5351; Email: office@sjbschool.org. Mary Maloney, Prin. Lay Teachers 20; Students 252.
Catechesis Religious Program—Tel: 847-966-3269. Students 270.

3—OUR LADY OF RANSOM (1960) Revs. Christopher M. Gustafson; Matthew Bozovsky; Deacons Charles O'Donnell; James Fruge; Ms. Constance Mottley, Pastoral Assoc.
Ministry Center—Parish Office: 8624 W. Normal, Niles, 60714. Tel: 847-823-2550; Web: ol-ransom@archchicago.org.
Catechesis Religious Program—Tel: 847-696-2994. Students 212.

NORRIDGE, COOK CO., DIVINE SAVIOR (1955) Revs. Richard J. LoBianco; William M. Holbrook, Senior Priest, (Retired); James D. Beath.
Res.: 7740 W. Montrose, Norridge, 60706.
Tel: 708-456-9000; Email: divinesavior@archchicago.org.
Catechesis Religious Program—Mr. Mary Coban, D.R.E. Students 150.

NORTH RIVERSIDE, COOK CO., MATER CHRISTI, Revs. Matthew Nemchausky; M. Cyril Nemecek, Pastor Emeritus, (Retired).
Res.: 2431 S. 10th Ave., North Riverside, 60546.
Tel: 708-442-5611; Email: materchristi@archchicago.org.
Catechesis Religious Program—2400 S. 10th Ave., North Riverside, 60546. Students 121.
Shrine—Mother of Mothers.

NORTHBROOK, COOK CO., ST. NORBERT AND OUR LADY OF THE BROOK PARISH (1899) Revs. Robert P. Heinz; Dan Ignatius Folwaczny; Laurence J. Dunn, (Res.), (Retired).
Res.: 1809 Walters Ave., Northbrook, 60062.
Tel: 847-272-7090; Email: parishoffice@stnorbertparish.org.
School—St. Norbert School, 1817 Walters Ave., Northbrook, 60062. Tel: 847-272-0051;
Fax: 847-272-5274; Email: glawler@stnorbertschool.org. Mr. Stephen Schacherer, Prin. Lay Teachers 19; Students 177.
Catechesis Religious Program—Tel: 847-272-3086; Fax: 847-513-6761. Students 473.

NORTHLAKE, COOK CO., ST. JOHN VIANNEY, CURE OF ARS, Revs. Luke E. Winkelmann; Phillip T. Owen; George C. Gonzalez; Deacons Pedro Sedano; James Sinacore; Thomas G. Imbordino.
Res.: 46 N. Wolf Rd., Northlake, 60164.
Tel: 708-562-0500; Email: stjohn-vianney@archchicago.org.
School—St. John Vianney, Cure of Ars School, 27 N. Lavergne Ave., Northlake, 60164. Tel: 708-562-1466; Fax: 708-562-0142; Email: info@sjvsonline.org. Ms. Heidi Reith, Prin. Lay Teachers 10; Students 177.
Catechesis Religious Program—
Tel: 708-562-1466, Ext. 120. Students 321.

OAK FOREST, COOK CO., ST. DAMIAN (1961) Revs. Joseph T. Noonan, B.A., CPA, M.Div.; Michael Olson; Francis G. Scanlan, In Res., (Retired); Deacons Thomas Hipelius; William Stearns; John Rex; Thomas J. Ruzevich; Richard Korepanow.
Res.: 5220 W. 155th St., Oak Forest, 60452.
Tel: 708-687-1370; Email: stdamian@archchicago.org.
School—St. Damian School, 5300 W. 155th St., Oak Forest, 60452. Tel: 708-687-4230; Fax: 708-687-8347; Email: m_stockhausen@stdamianschool.org. Marian Stockhausen, Prin. Lay Teachers 24; Students 443.
Catechesis Religious Program—Tel: 708-687-7788; Fax: 708-687-1735. Mary Jo Landuyt, D.R.E. Students 462.

OAK LAWN, COOK CO.

1—ST. CATHERINE OF ALEXANDRIA, Revs. Dennis A. Ziomek; George P. McKenna, Pastor Emeritus, (Retired); Edward S. Stockus, Senior Priest, (Retired); Nicholas Cavallari.
Res.: 4100 W. 107th St., Oak Lawn, 60453.
Tel: 708-425-2850; Email: stcatherine-107th@archchicago.org.
School—St. Catherine of Alexandria School, 10621 S. Kedvale Ave., Oak Lawn, 60453. Tel: 708-425-5547; Fax: 708-425-3701; Email: medwards@scaoaklawn.org. Mrs. Arlene A. Baumann, Interim Prin. Lay Teachers 25; Students 469.
Catechesis Religious Program—Tel: 708-425-5747; Fax: 708-425-3701. Students 114.

2—ST. GERALD (1934) Revs. Lawrence J. Malcolm, (Retired); Michael E. Flynn; William Browne, (Jamaica) In Res.; Deacons Richard Feltes; Michael Fekete.
Parish Office—9310 S. 55th Ct., Oak Lawn, 60453.
Tel: 708-422-0234; Email: stgerald@archchicago.org.
Res.: 9349 S. Central Ave., Oak Lawn, 60453.
School—St. Gerald School, 9320 S. 55th Ct., Oak Lawn, 60453. Tel: 708-422-0121; Fax: 708-422-9216; Email: school@stgerald.com. Mr. Al P. Theis, Prin. Clergy 2; Lay Teachers 23; Students 446.
Catechesis Religious Program—Tel: 708-423-0458. Students 359.

3—ST. GERMAINE (1962)
Mailing Address: 9711 S. Kolin, Oak Lawn, 60453. Rev. Michael J. Furlan; Deacons Joseph Gonzalez; John L. Malone.
Res.: 4240 W. 98th St., Oak Lawn, 60453.
Tel: 708-636-5060; Email: stgermaine@archchicago.org.
School—St. Germaine School, 9735 S. Kolin, Oak Lawn, 60453. Tel: 708-425-6063; Email: mrkreedy@stgol.org. Mr. Kevin Reedy, Prin. Lay Teachers 13; Students 220.
Catechesis Religious Program—Jeanne Lassandrello, D.R.E. Students 240.

4—ST. LINUS (1955) Revs. Mark J. Walter; Joseph E. Auer, Pastor Emeritus, (Retired); Joseph T. Cook; Gene F. Smith, In Res., (Retired); Deacons Edward Gadomski; Robert L. Cislo.
Res.: 10300 S. Lawler Ave., Oak Lawn, 60453.
Tel: 708-422-2400; Email: stlinus@archchicago.org.
School—St. Linus School, 10400 S. Lawler Ave., Oak Lawn, 60453. Tel: 708-425-1656; Fax: 708-425-1802; Email: mhayes@stlinusschool.org. Ms. Margaret Hayes, Prin. Lay Teachers 21; Students 363.
Catechesis Religious Program—Tel: 708-636-4373. Cheryl A. Antos, D.R.E. Students 212.

5—ST. LOUIS DE MONTFORT, Rev. Stanley Stuglik; Deacon William L. Sullivan.
Res.: 8808 S. Ridgeland, Oak Lawn, 60453.
Tel: 708-599-5300; Email: stlouis-monfort@archchicago.org.
Catechesis Religious Program—8840 S. Ridgeland, Oak Lawn, 60453. Students 116.

OAK PARK, COOK CO.

1—ASCENSION (1907) Rev. James F. Hurlbert; Mrs. Mary Catherine Meek, Pastoral Assoc.
Parish Office: 808 S. East Ave., Oak Park, 60304.
Tel: 708-848-2703; Email: ascension-east@archchicago.org.
School—Ascension School, 601 Van Buren, Oak Park, 60304. Tel: 708-386-7282; Fax: 708-524-4796; Email: school@ascensionoakpark.com. Mrs. Maryanne J. Polega, Prin. Lay Teachers 25; Students 430.
Catechesis Religious Program—Tel: 708-848-3099. Students 417.

2—ST. CATHERINE OF SIENA-ST. LUCY, Rev. George O. Omwando; Shelby Boblick, Pastoral Assoc.
Res.: 38 N. Austin Blvd., Oak Park, 60302.
Tel: 708-386-8077; Email: stcatherine-stlucy@archchicago.org.
School—St. Catherine of Siena-St. Lucy School, 27 Washington Blvd., Oak Park, 60302.
Tel: 708-386-5286; Fax: 708-386-7328; Email: info@catherinelucy.org. Mrs. Sharon Leamy, Prin. Lay Teachers 10; Students 177.
Catechesis Religious Program—Students 53.

3—ST. EDMUND, Revs. John W. McGivern; John P. Lucas, In Res.; Deacon Thomas M. Dwyer; Ms. Margaret Leddy, Pastoral Assoc.
Res.: 188 S. Oak Park Ave., Oak Park, 60302.
Tel: 708-848-4417; Email: stedmund@archchicago.org.
Catechesis Religious Program—Tel: 708-848-7220. Students 113.

4—ST. GILES (1927) Revs. Carl Morello; Thomas M. Dore, Pastor Emeritus, (Retired); Edward P. Salmon, In Res., (Retired); Thomas E. Unz, In Res., (Retired); Deacons John A. Henricks; Gerald Zych; Loretto J. Madonia.
Office: 1025 Columbian Ave., Oak Park, 60302.
Tel: 708-383-3430; Email: stgiles@archchicago.org.
Res.: 1045 Columbian Ave., Oak Park, 60302.
School—St. Giles School, 1034 Linden Ave., Oak Park, 60302. Tel: 708-383-6279; Fax: 708-383-9952; Email: office@stgilesschool.org. Meg Bigane, Prin. Lay Teachers 32; Students 406.
Catechesis Religious Program—Tel: 708-383-4185; Fax: 708-383-8669. Students 375.

OLD MILL CREEK, LAKE, ST. RAPHAEL THE ARCHANGEL 40000 N. U.S. Hwy. 45, Old Mill Creek, 60046.
Tel: 847-395-3474; Fax: 847-395-3552; Email: rectory@straphaelcatholic.org; Web: www.straphaelcatholic.org. Rev. Michael G. McGovern; Deacon Gregory Webster.
Catechesis Religious Program—Students 186.

ORLAND HILLS, COOK CO., ST. ELIZABETH SETON, Revs. William T. Corcoran, Ph.D.; William T. O'Mara, Pastor Emeritus, (Retired); John Zurek; William B. Gubbins, In Res., (Retired); Deacons Dennis Cristofaro; Frank Gildea.
Res.: 9300 W. 167th St., Orland Hills, 60477.
Tel: 708-403-0101; Email: stelizabeth-seton@archchicago.org.
School—Cardinal Joseph Bernardin, 9250 W. 167th St., Orland Hills, 60477. Tel: 708-403-6525; Fax: 708-403-8621; Email: info@cjbschool.org. Mary Iannueilli, Prin. Inter-Parish School serving St. Elizabeth Seton, St. Francis of Assisi, St. Julie Billiart and St. Stephen, Deacon and Martyr. Lay Teachers 35; Students 570.
Catechesis Religious Program—Tel: 708-403-0101; Fax: 708-403-9810. Students 407.

ORLAND PARK, COOK CO.

1—ST. FRANCIS OF ASSISI, Revs. Artur J. Sowa; Gael Gensler; Edward F. Upton, Pastor Emeritus, (Retired); Deacons Daniel Carroll; Michael J. Pindelski; John Donahue.
Res.: 15050 S. Wolf Rd., Orland Park, 60467.
Tel: 708-460-0042; Email: stfrancisassisi-wolf@archchicago.org.
Catechesis Religious Program—15010 S. Wolf Rd., Orland Park, 60467. Mary Kay Burberry, D.R.E. Students 960.

2—ST. MICHAEL, Revs. Paul C. Burak; Edward McLaughlin, Pastor Emeritus, (Retired); Geofrey Andama; Miguel Angel Flores Andrade; William J. Finnegan, Senior Priest, (Retired); Sr. Marietta Umlor, C.S.C., Pastoral Assoc.; Deacons Michael McDonough; Thomas Bartholomew; Tony Cocco; Jim Janicek; Saul Vazquez; Abel B. Trujillo; Patricia A. Chuchla, Pastoral Assoc.
Res.: 14310 Highland Ave., Orland Park, 60462.
Tel: 708-349-0903; Email: stmichael-highland@archchicago.org.
School—St. Michael School, 14355 Highland Ave., Orland Park, 60462. Tel: 708-349-0068; Fax: 708-349-2658; Email: psmith@saintmike.org. Mr. Paul W. Smith, Prin. Lay Teachers 34; Students 542.
Catechesis Religious Program—14345 Highland Ave., Orland Park, 60462. Students 419.

3—OUR LADY OF THE WOODS, Revs. Michael G. Foley; William J. Finnegan, Pastor Emeritus, (Retired); Andrew Wawrzyn, S.T.L.; Most Rev. John R. Gorman, In Res., (Retired); Rev. Edward M. Mikolajczyk, In Res., (Retired); Deacon John Macarol.
Res.: 10731 W. 131st St., Orland Park, 60462.
Tel: 708-361-4754; Email: ol-woods@archchicago.org.
Catechesis Religious Program—Tel: 708-361-9435. Colleen Walery, D.R.E. Students 778.

PALATINE, COOK CO.

1—ST. THERESA, Revs. Timothy J. Fairman; Thomas Bishop; Michael J. Wanda; Matthew Jamesson; Deacons Stephen Norys; Richard Pizzato; Lou Riccio; Lawrence R. Schumacher; Gregory Vogt; James Devine.
Res.: 455 N. Benton, Palatine, 60067.
Tel: 847-358-7760; Email: sttheresa@archchicago.org.
Church: 465 N. Benton, Palatine, 60067.
Pauline Center / Ministry Center—
School—St. Theresa School, 445 N. Benton, Palatine, 60067. Tel: 847-359-1820; Fax: 847-705-2084; Email: mkeenley@sttheresaschool.com. Ms. Mary Kay J. Keenley, Prin. Lay Teachers 28; Students 379.
Catechesis Religious Program—Tel: 847-358-2846. Elizabeth Vogt, D.R.E. Students 368.

2—ST. THOMAS OF VILLANOVA, Revs. Thomas R. Rzepiela; Raymond A. Yadron, Pastor Emeritus, (Retired); Marcin Zasada; Deacons Thomas Dunne; Len Marturano; Richard Willer; John Breit; Mark Duffey; William T. Karstenson.
Office: 1201 E. Anderson Dr., Palatine, 60074.
Tel: 847-358-6999; Email: stthomas-villanova@archchicago.org.
School—St. Thomas of Villanova School, 1141 E. Anderson Dr., Palatine, 60074. Tel: 847-358-2110; Fax: 847-776-1435; Email: stvprincipal@stvschool.org. Mrs. Mary Brinkman, Prin. Lay Teachers 19; Students 169.
Catechesis Religious Program—Tel: 847-358-2386. Students 635.

PALOS HEIGHTS, COOK CO., ST. ALEXANDER (1959) Revs. Martin E. Michniewicz; Patrick J. O'Neill; Deacons Timothy Keating; James Horton.
Res.: 7025 W. 126th St., Palos Heights, 60463.
Tel: 708-448-4861; Email: stalexander@archchicago.org.
School—St. Alexander School, 126th St. at 71st Ave., Palos Heights, 60463. Tel: 708-448-0408; Fax: 708-448-5947; Email: info@stalexanderschool.com. Mrs. Catherine Biel, Prin. Lay Teachers 15; Students 297.
Catechesis Religious Program—Tel: 708-448-6624. Students 405.

PALOS HILLS, COOK CO., SACRED HEART, Very Rev. Jacek Wrona, (Poland); Revs. Robert F. McGinnity, Pastor Emeritus, (Retired); David R. Straub; Deacons Richard Werner; Thomas J. Rzendzian.
Res.: 8245 W. 111th St., Palos Hills, 60465.
Tel: 708-974-3336; Email: sacredheart-111th@archchicago.org.
Catechesis Religious Program—Tel: 708-974-3900; Fax: 708-974-3922. Students 284.

PARK FOREST, COOK CO., ST. IRENAEUS (1948) Rev. Terrance Johnson.
Res.: 78 Cherry St., Park Forest, 60466.
Tel: 708-748-6891; Email: stirenaeus@archchicago.org.
Catechesis Religious Program—Tel: 708-748-7997. Students 40.

PARK RIDGE, COOK CO.

1—MARY, SEAT OF WISDOM (1955) Revs. Gerald T. Gunderson; Ronald N. Kalas, Pastor Emeritus, (Retired); Tomy Abraham; Timothy Anastos; Deacon Kevin Blindauer.
Res.: 920 Granville Ave., Park Ridge, 60068.
Tel: 847-825-3153; Email: mary-wisdom@archchicago.org.
School—Mary, Seat of Wisdom School, (Grades PreK-8), 1352 S. Cumberland, Park Ridge, 60068.
Tel: 847-825-2500; Fax: 847-825-1943; Email: jdue@mswschool.org. Mrs. Julie T. Due, Prin. Lay Teachers 34; Students 523.
Catechesis Religious Program—Tel: 847-825-8763; Fax: 847-825-8658. Ms. Regina M. Thibeau, D.R.E. Students 306.

2—ST. PAUL OF THE CROSS (1911) Revs. Britto Berchmans, Ph.D.; Piotr Gnoinski, M.Div.; Matthew Kowalski, O.S.B.; Very Rev. Daniel A. Smilanic, J.C.D., In Res.; Deacons Robert T. Bulger; Andrew P. Cameron.
Res.: 320 S. Washington St., Park Ridge, 60068.
Tel: 847-825-7605; Email: stpaul-cross@archchicago.org.
School—St. Paul of the Cross School, 140 S. Northwest Hwy., Park Ridge, 60068.
Tel: 847-825-6366; Fax: 847-825-2466; Email: nagnew@spc-school.net. Dr. Erika Mickelburgh, Prin. Lay Teachers 39; Students 540.
Catechesis Religious Program—215 S. Ridge Ter., Park Ridge, 60068. Anna Mae Parkhill, D.R.E. Students 1,301.

POSEN, COOK CO., ST. STANISLAUS BISHOP AND MARTYR, Revs. Pius Eusebius Kokose, C.S.Sp., (Ghana); Casimir Eke, C.S.Sp., In Res.; Lukas Ouda, In Res.; Deacon Daniel Dutkiewicz.
Res.: 14414 McKinley Ave., Posen, 60469.
Tel: 708-597-4910; Email: ststanislaus-mckinley@archchicago.org.
Catechesis Religious Program—Juan C. Roca, D.R.E. Students 218.

PROSPECT HEIGHTS, COOK CO., ST. ALPHONSUS LIGUORI, Revs. Joseph Le; John W. Hurley, In Res.; Deacons Calvin Blickle Jr.; Steve Stecker.
Res.: 411 N. Wheeling Rd., Prospect Heights, 60070.
Tel: 847-255-7452; Email: stalphonsus-liguori@archchicago.org.
School—St. Alphonsus Liguori School,
Tel: 847-255-5538; Email: l.chorazy@saintalphonsus.com. Ms. Janice M. Divincenzo, Prin. Lay Teachers 13; Students 159.
Catechesis Religious Program—Tel: 847-255-9490. Students 217.

RIVER FOREST, COOK CO.

1—ST. LUKE (1887) Revs. John S. Szmyd, M.Div., S.T.B.; Steven Bauer, S.T.L.; Deacons John Baier; Terrance Norton; Robert Slobig.
Res.: 528 Lathrop Ave., River Forest, 60305-1835.
Tel: 708-771-8250; Email: stluke@archchicago.org.
School—St. Luke School, 519 Ashland Ave., River Forest, 60305-1824. Tel: 708-366-8587; Fax: 708-366-3831; Email: twesley@stlukeparish.org. Ms. Kristine Gritzmacher, Interim Co-Prin.; Mr. Bob Ballenger, Interim Co-Prin. Lay Teachers 29; Students 313.
Catechesis Religious Program—Tel: 708-771-5959; Fax: 708-771-5960. Students 261.

2—ST. VINCENT FERRER, Revs. Thomas K. McDermott, O.P.; Raphael Christianson; Kevin R. Fane, O.P., In Res.; Peter J. Hereley, O.P., In Res.; John J. O'Malley, O.P., In Res.; Deacons John Gaughan; Jerome J. Trakszelis.
Res. & Church: 1530 Jackson Ave., River Forest, 60305. Tel: 708-366-7090; Email: stvincent-ferrer@archchicago.org.
School—St. Vincent Ferrer School, 1515 Lathrop Ave., River Forest, 60305. Tel: 708-771-5905; Fax: 708-771-7114; Email: jglimco@svfschool.org. John Glimco, Prin. Lay Teachers 17; Students 261.
Catechesis Religious Program—1527 Lathrop, River Forest, 60305. Students 73.

RIVERDALE, COOK CO., ST. MARY QUEEN OF APOSTLES, Rev. Gosbert Rwezahura; Deacon Gerald Hahn.
Res.: 207 W. 145th St., Riverdale, 60827.
Tel: 708-849-4901; Email: stmary-apostles@archchicago.org.
School—Christ Our Savior, (Inter-Parish School)
Tel: 708-333-8173; Web: www.christoursaviorcatholicschool.org.
Catechesis Religious Program—Ms. Ann Hilsen, D.R.E. Students 22.

RIVERSIDE, COOK CO., ST. MARY, Revs. Thomas P. May; Leon R. Wagner, Pastor Emeritus, (Retired); Deacons Robert Boharic; Randy Belice.
Res.: 126 Herrick Rd., Riverside, 60546.
Tel: 708-447-1020; Email: stmary-herrick@archchicago.org.
School—St. Mary School, 97 Herrick Rd., Riverside, 60546. Tel: 708-442-5747; Fax: 708-442-0125; Email: principal@stmaryriverside.org. Mrs. Barbara A. Rasinski, Prin. Lay Teachers 28; Students 391.
Catechesis Religious Program—Tel: 708-447-6812. Barbara M. Slipek, D.R.E. Students 387.

ROLLING MEADOWS, COOK CO., ST. COLETTE, Rev. John Ekwoanya, In Res.; Deacons John Connor; Raul Trejo.
Res.: 3900 S. Meadow Dr., Rolling Meadows, 60008.
Tel: 847-394-8100; Email: stcolette@archchicago.org.
School—St. Colette School, (Grades PreK-8),
Tel: 847-392-4098; Email: vzemko@stcolette.com. Mr. Joseph Quinlan, Prin. Lay Teachers 11; Students 132.
Catechesis Religious Program—Students 354.

ROSEMONT-DES PLAINES, COOK CO., OUR LADY OF HOPE, Rev. Wojciech Jan Oleksy; Rev. Msgr. Kenneth Velo, In Res.; Deacon James J. Ernst.
Res.: 9711 W. Devon Ave., Rosemont, 60018.
Tel: 847-825-4673; Email: ol-hope@archchicago.org.
Catechesis Religious Program—Students 174.

ROUND LAKE, LAKE CO., ST. JOSEPH, Rev. Michael L. Zoufal; Deacon Joel Ruiz.
Res.: 114 N. Lincoln Ave., Round Lake, 60073.
Tel: 847-546-3610; Web: stjoseph-lincoln@archchicago.org.
School—St. Joseph School, 118 N. Lincoln Ave., Round Lake, 60073. Tel: 847-546-1720; Email: amillersjs@gmail.com. Ms. Kari Rybarczyk, Prin. Lay Teachers 22; Students 130.
Catechesis Religious Program—Tel: 847-546-3554. Students 928.

SAUK VILLAGE, COOK CO., ST. JAMES, Rev. David B. Krolczyk.
Res.: 22400 S. Torrence Ave., Sauk Village, 60411-5144. Tel: 708-757-2170; Email: stjames-torrence@archchicago.org.
Catechesis Religious Program—Tel: 708-757-2174. Students 68.
Convent—21903 Orion St., Sauk Village, 60411.

SCHAUMBURG, COOK CO.

1—CHURCH OF THE HOLY SPIRIT, Revs. John W. Dearhammer; George J. Kane, Pastor Emeritus, (Retired); Sr. Marianne Supan, O.P., Pastoral Assoc.; Deacons Wayne Beyer; Mario Contreras; Mike Enger; Sung Han; Xavier Carrera; Raymond Doud.
Res.: 1451 W. Bode Rd., Schaumburg, 60194.
Tel: 847-882-7580; Email: holyspirit@archchicago.org.
Catechesis Religious Program—Tel: 847-882-7584. Students 505.

2—ST. MARCELLINE (1968) Rev. Harold B. Stanger; Deacons Thomas LaMantia; Michael Filipucci; Paul Migala; Don Maiers; Howard P. Lanctot.
Res.: 822 Springinsguth Rd., Schaumburg, 60193.
Tel: 847-524-4429; Email: stmarcelline@archchicago.org.
Catechesis Religious Program—Students 219.

3—ST. MATTHEW, Rev. Joseph Glab, C.R.; Ms. Milissa Bartold, Pastoral Assoc.
Res.: 1001 E. Schaumburg Rd., Schaumburg, 60194.
Tel: 847-891-1220; Web: stmatthew@archchicago.org.
Catechesis Religious Program—1005 Schaumburg Rd., Schaumburg, 60194. Students 422.

SCHILLER PARK, COOK CO.

1—ST. BEATRICE (1926) Revs. Robert Schultz; John J. Bresnahan, (Retired).
Res.: 4157 Atlantic Ave., Schiller Park, 60176.
Tel: 847-678-0138; Email: stbeatrice@archchicago.org.
Catechesis Religious Program—Students 96.
2—ST. MARIA GORETTI (1962) Rev. James F. Blazek.
Res.: 3929 N. Wehrman Ave., Schiller Park, 60176.
Tel: 847-678-3988; Email: stmariagoretti@archchicago.org.
School—St. Maria Goretti School, Tel: 847-678-2560; Email: cmendez@gorettischool.org. Mrs. Claudia M. Mendez, Prin. Lay Teachers 10; Students 152.
Catechesis Religious Program—Students 71.
SKOKIE, COOK CO.
1—ST. JOAN OF ARC, Revs. Daniel F. Costello; James P. Kehoe, (Retired); Ms. Valerie Walker, Pastoral Assoc.
Res.: 9248 N. Lawndale Ave., Evanston, 60203-1509.
Tel: 847-673-0409; Email: stjoan@archchicago.org.
School—St. Joan of Arc School, Tel: 847-679-0660; Email: sjaemail@gmail.com. Mr. Craig R. Scanlon, Prin. Lay Teachers 17; Students 183.
Catechesis Religious Program—Students 112.
2—ST. LAMBERT, Rev. Richard T. Simon; Deacon John C. O'Leary.
Res.: 8148 Karlov Ave., Skokie, 60076.
Tel: 847-673-5090; Email: stlambert@archchicago.org.
Catechesis Religious Program—Tel: 847-329-1201. Students 176.
3—ST. PETER, Revs. Henry C. Kricek, M.A., S.T.L.; Edward D. Grace, Pastor Emeritus, (Retired); Mariano Rondael; Rev. Msgr. Stephen Osci-Duah, In Res.; Rev. Paul O. Adaja, In Res.; Sr. Kathleen Maloney, O.S.B., Pastoral Assoc.
Res.: 8116 Niles Center Rd., Skokie, 60077.
Tel: 847-673-1492; Email: stpeter-nilescenter@archchicago.org.
Catechesis Religious Program—Tel: 847-679-1202; Fax: 847-673-6469. Sr. Kathleen Maloney, O.S.B., D.R.E. Students 162.
SOUTH HOLLAND, COOK CO.
1—HOLY GHOST (1962) Rev. Gosbert Rwezahura, Admin.; Deacon James Renwick.
Res.: 700 E. 170th St., South Holland, 60473.
Tel: 708-333-7011; Email: holyghost@archchicago.org.
School—Christ Our Savior, (Inter-Parish School) Tel: 708-333-8173. Karen Brodzik, Prin. Students 162.
Catechesis Religious Program—Students 18.
2—ST. JUDE THE APOSTLE, Rev. Ignatius I. Anaele; Deacons Mel Stasinski; Timothy Springer.
Res.: 880 E. 154th St., South Holland, 60473.
Tel: 708-333-3550; Email: stjude@archchicago.org.
School—Christ Our Savior Catholic School, Inter-Parish school serving St. Andrew, Our Lady of Knock, St. Victor, Holy Ghost, St. Jude and St. Mary Queen of Apostles. 900 E. 154th St., South Holland, 60473-1106. Tel: 708-333-8173; Email: cosmainoffice@gmail.com. Karen Brodzik, Prin. Lay Teachers 14; Students 162.
Catechesis Religious Program—Tel: 708-225-1180. Students 39.
STICKNEY, COOK CO., ST. PIUS X (1954) Rev. Anthony L. Markus; Deacon Juan Valencia.
Res.: 4314 S. Oak Park Ave., Stickney, 60402.
Tel: 708-484-7951; Email: stpiusx@archchicago.org.
Catechesis Religious Program—4300 S. Oak Park Ave., Stickney, 60402. Students 97.
STREAMWOOD, COOK CO., ST. JOHN THE EVANGELIST (1962)
502 S. Park Blvd., Streamwood, 60107. Revs. Grzegorz P. Gorczyca, M.Div.; William J. Moriarity, Pastor Emeritus, (Retired); Nathaniel Payne, M.Div.; Deacons James Furey; Larry Rybicki; Jozef S. Mika; Robert Pasdiora; Michael S. Benoit; Joseph L. Esposito.
Res.: 540 S. Park Blvd., Streamwood, 60107.
Tel: 630-837-6500; Email: stjohn-evangelist@archchicago.org.
School—St. John the Evangelist School, 513 Parkside Cir., Streamwood, 60107.
Fax: 630-289-3026; Email: school@mystjohns.org. Mrs. Mary Ellyn Billmeyer, Prin. Lay Teachers 15; Students 235.
Catechesis Religious Program—Tel: 630-837-1060. Students 364.
SUMMIT, COOK CO., ST. JOSEPH, Revs. Robert Stuglik; William J. Lisowski, Senior Priest, (Retired).
Res.: 7240 W. 57th St., Summit, 60501.
Tel: 708-458-0501; Email: stjoseph-57th@archchicago.org.
School—St. Joseph School, 5641 S. 73rd Ave., Summit, 60501. Tel: 708-458-2927; Email: Stjosephcatholicschool@stjosephsummit.com. Mr. Lawrence Manetti, Prin. Lay Teachers 11; Students 167.
Catechesis Religious Program—Students 142.
TINLEY PARK, COOK CO.
1—ST. GEORGE (1934) Revs. Kenneth J. Fleck; Brendan Guilfoil; Deacons Thomas Schutzius; Joseph Panek; Gregory Bartos; Peter Manning; Joseph Truesdale.
Res.: 6707 W. 175th St., Tinley Park, 60477.
Tel: 708-532-2243; Email: stgeorge-175th@archchicago.org.
School—St. George School, 6700 W. 176th St., Tinley Park, 60477. Tel: 708-532-2626; Fax: 708-532-2025; Email: info@stgeorgeschool.org. Mrs. Charlotte A. Pratl, Prin. Lay Teachers 15; Mantellate Sisters 1; Students 190.
Catechesis Religious Program—6670 W. 176th St., Tinley Park, 60477. Students 250.
2—SAINT JULIE BILLIART, Rev. Louis Tylka; Deacon Edward Pluchar.
Res.: 7399 W. 159th St., Tinley Park, 60477.
Tel: 708-429-6767; Email: stjulie@archchicago.org.
Catechesis Religious Program—Tel: 708-429-1044. Patricia Kmak, D.R.E. Students 588.
3—ST. STEPHEN, DEACON AND MARTYR (1999) Revs. Thomas A. Bernas; Miroslaw Kulesa; Deacons Kenneth Zawadzki; William Engler; Charles McFarland; Peter Van Merkestyn; William Schultz; Robert Conlin.
Res.: 17500 S. 84th Ave., Tinley Park, 60487.
Tel: 708-342-2400; Email: ststephen-84th@archchicago.org.
Catechesis Religious Program—Leslie Krauledis, D.R.E. Students 1,417.
VOLO, LAKE CO., ST. PETER
Mailing Address: 27551 Volo Village Rd., Volo, 60073. Revs. Anthony Rice, S.J.C.; Nathan Caswell, S.J.C.
Res.: 27570 Volo Village Rd., Volo, 60073.
Tel: 815-385-5496; Email: stpeter-volovillage@archchicago.org.
Catechesis Religious Program—Students 146.
WADSWORTH, LAKE CO., ST. PATRICK
Mailing Address: 15000 Wadsworth Rd., Wadsworth, 60083. Revs. James E. Merold, (Retired); Michael J. Owen; Deacons Louis Abboud; William Gibbons; Edward Tomkowiak; Todd M. Benzschawel; Joseph Casey; Jeremy N. Carter; Richard Holevoet.
Res.: 15040 Wadsworth Rd., Wadsworth, 60083.
Tel: 847-244-4161; Web: stpatrick-wadsworth@archchicago.org.
School—St. Patrick School, 15020 Wadsworth Rd., Wadsworth, 60083. Tel: 847-623-8446;
Fax: 847-623-3119; Email: mvitulli@stpatrickwadsworth.org. Mrs. Mary A. Vitulli, Prin. Lay Teachers 27; Students 454.
Catechesis Religious Program—Tel: 847-236-9131; Fax: 847-336-0630. Students 248.
WAUCONDA, LAKE CO., TRANSFIGURATION, Rev. Juan Pablo Avila-Ibarra; Deacons Feliks Pezowicz; Jose Mancilla-Martinez.
Res.: 316 W. Mill St., Wauconda, 60084.
Tel: 847-526-2400; Email: transfiguration-mill@archchicago.org.
Schools—Frassati Catholic Academy- Wauconda Campus—Tel: 847-487-5600; Email: tkleckner@frassaticatholicacademy.org. Mrs. Tammy Klechner, Prin. Lay Teachers 25; Students 314.
Frassati Catholic Academy, (Grades 6-8),
Tel: 847-487-5600; Email: tkleckner@frassaticatholicacademy.org. Mrs. Tammy A. Kleckner, Prin. Ministry of St. Mary of the Assumption; Santa Maria del Popolo, Mundelein. Member of Catholic Consortium of Lake County. Lay Teachers 25; Students 314.
Catechesis Religious Program—Tel: 847-526-6400. Students 543.
WAUKEGAN, LAKE CO.
1—ST. ANASTASIA, Revs. Dennis M. Zalecki; Radley Alcantara; Deacons Genaro Mendez; Pedro Martinez; Victor Ruiz.
Res.: 624 Douglas Ave., Waukegan, 60085.
Tel: 847-623-2875; Email: stanastasia@archchicago.org.
School—St. Anastasia School, Tel: 847-623-8320; Email: khillmann@stanastasiaschool.org. Mrs. Kristine A. Hillmann, Prin. Lay Teachers 14; Students 258.
Catechesis Religious Program—Students 88.
2—ST. DISMAS, Revs. Patrick J. Rugen, S.T.L., M.Div., M.A.; John M. Ryan, Pastor Emeritus, (Retired); Deacon Anthony Sacramento.
Res.: 2600 Sunset Ave., Waukegan, 60087.
Tel: 847-623-5050; Email: stdismas@archchicago.org.
Catechesis Religious Program—2226 McAree Rd., Waukegan, 60087. Students 332.
3—MOST BLESSED TRINITY
450 Keller Ave., Waukegan, 60085-5030.
Tel: 847-623-2655; Email: blessedtrinity@archchicago.org. Revs. Timothy J. O'Malley, J.D.; Moises Navarro; Julio Lam; Deacons Gary Munda; Irvin Boppart; Fredy Munoz; Pablo Albarran.
School—Most Blessed Trinity Academy, 510 Grand Ave., Waukegan, 60085. Tel: 847-623-4110;
Fax: 847-599-0477; Email: lsaccaro@mostblessedtrinityacademy.org. Dr. Lynne Saccaro, Prin. Lay Teachers 16; Students 191.
Catechesis Religious Program—Students 1,099.
WESTCHESTER, COOK CO.
1—DIVINE INFANT JESUS, Revs. Marcin D. Szczypula; Gerald P. Joyce, Pastor Emeritus, (Retired); Thomas Winikates; Deacon James R. Sponder.
Res.: 1601 Newcastle Ave., Westchester, 60154.
Tel: 708-865-8071; Email: divineinfant@archchicago.org.
School—Divine Infant Jesus School,
Tel: 708-865-0122; Email: elem.divineinfant@archchicago.org. Mr. Kristine Owens, Prin. Lay Teachers 10; Students 160.
Catechesis Religious Program—Sr. Susan Majcen, O.P., D.R.E. Students 209.
2—DIVINE PROVIDENCE, Revs. Timothy R. Fiala, S.T.L.; Thomas E. Unz, Pastor Emeritus, (Retired); Deacon Richard F. Hudzik.
Res.: 2550 S. Mayfair Ave., Westchester, 60154.
Tel: 708-562-3364; Email: divineprovidence@archchicago.org.
School—Divine Providence School, 2500 S. Mayfair Ave., Westchester, 60154. Tel: 708-562-2258;
Fax: 708-562-9171; Email: kfoleno@divineprovidenceschool.org. Mrs. Karen Foleno, Prin. Lay Teachers 15; Students 229.
Catechesis Religious Program—Tel: 708-562-3422. Christine Schweihs-Defoe, D.R.E. Students 96.
WESTERN SPRINGS, COOK CO., ST. JOHN OF THE CROSS (1960) Rev. Marc Reszel; Rev. Msgr. Peter Galek, J.C.D.; Rev. David Dowdle, Senior Priest; Deacons Joseph Pepitone; John E. Schopp IV.
Res.: 5005 Wolf Rd., Western Springs, 60558.
Tel: 708-246-4404; Email: stjohn-cross@archchicago.org.
School—St. John of the Cross School, 705 51st St., Western Springs, 60558. Tel: 708-246-4454;
Fax: 708-246-9010; Email: gorman@sjc.pvt.k12.il.us. Mrs. Kathleen A. Gorman, Prin. Lay Teachers 39; Students 631.
Catechesis Religious Program—51st St. & Wolf Rd., Western Springs, 60558. Ms. Janet Caschetta, D.R.E. Students 1,038.
WHEELING, COOK CO., ST. JOSEPH THE WORKER, Revs. Jerzy Gawlik, S.V.D.; Krzysztof B. Pipa, S.V.D.; Francis Rayappan; Jesus Mata Martinez; Deacon Martin Carrillo.
Res.: 181 W. Dundee Rd., Wheeling, 60090.
Tel: 847-537-2740; Email: stjoseph-worker@archchicago.org.
Polska Parafialna Szkola Im. Juliusza Slowackiego, NFP—Web: www.juliuszlowacki.com.
Catechesis Religious Program—Tel: 847-537-4182. Students 1,031.
WILLOW SPRINGS, COOK CO., OUR LADY, MOTHER OF THE CHURCH POLISH MISSION
Mailing Address: Box 334, Argo, 60501. Revs. Michael Blicharski, O.Cist.; Piotr Rogusz, In Res.; Ludwik Zyla, O.Cist., In Res.
Church: 116 Hilton St., Willow Springs, 60480-0479.
Tel: 708-467-0436; Email: ol-mother-mission@archchicago.org.
Catechesis Religious Program—
Shrine—Shrine of Saint John Paul II.
WILMETTE, COOK CO.
1—ST. FRANCIS XAVIER, Revs. William J. Sheridan, S.T.L.; Rodlin Rodrigue; Edward F. Harnett, Pastor Emeritus, (Retired); Dr. Patty Jane Pelton, Pastoral Assoc.; Deacon Robert Kerls.
Office: 524 Ninth St., Wilmette, 60091.
Tel: 847-256-4250; Email: stfrancisxavier-9th@archchicago.org.
School—St. Francis Xavier School, 808 Linden Ave., Wilmette, 60091-2714. Tel: 847-256-0644;
Fax: 847-256-0753; Email: colleenbarrett@sfx-school.org. Ms. Colleen M. Barrett, Prin. Lay Teachers 35; Students 460.
Catechesis Religious Program—Tel: 847-251-6730; Fax: 847-256-4254. Kieran Lyons, D.R.E.; Sr. Mary Ann Casey, D.R.E. Students 474.
2—ST. JOSEPH, Rev. Msgr. Daniel G. Mayall; Revs. Laurent K. Mhagama; Robeth Molina Torres, In Res.; Deacon Derald Shinkle.
Res.: 1747 Lake Ave., Wilmette, 60091.
Tel: 847-251-0771; Email: stjoseph-lake@archchicago.org.
School—St. Joseph School, 1740 Lake Ave., Wilmette, 60091. Tel: 847-256-7870; Email: mkendrick@stjosephwilmette.com. Michael Kendrick, Prin. Lay Teachers 18; Students 163.
Catechesis Religious Program—Tel: 847-851-3734. Students 319.
WINNETKA, COOK CO.
1—DIVINE MERCY, Revs. Steven M. Lanza, S.T.L.; Dean F. Semmer; Michael J. Solazzo; Daniel J. Cassidy, In Res.; Ms. Susan Lehocky, D.R.E.
St. Philip the Apostle, Res.: 1962 Old Willow Rd., Northfield, 60093.
Sacred Heart, 1077 Tower Rd., Winnetka, 60093.

Tel: 847-446-0856; Email: office@stphilipparish.org; Web: divinemercynorthshore.org.
School—Sacred Heart School, 1095 Gage St., Winnetka, 60093. Tel: 847-446-0005; Email: kfink@shwschool.org. Ms. Kristen E. Fink, Prin. Lay Teachers 25; Students 190.

2—SS. FAITH, HOPE AND CHARITY, Revs. Martin E. O'Donovan; Thomas Philip, (India); William J. Flaherty, In Res., (Retired); Deacon Dr. Michael Cavanaugh.
Res.: 191 Linden St., Winnetka, 60093.
Tel: 847-446-7646; Email: ssfhc@archchicago.org.
School—SS. Faith, Hope and Charity School, 180 Ridge Ave., Winnetka, 60093. Tel: 847-446-0031; Fax: 847-446-9064; Email: office@faithhopeschool.org. Dr. Thomas Meagher, Prin. Lay Teachers 27; Students 327.
Catechesis Religious Program—200 Ridge Rd., Winnetka, 60093. Tel: 847-446-1828; Fax: 847-446-2145. Students 549.

ZION-BEACH PARK, LAKE CO., OUR LADY OF HUMILITY, Revs. Paul G. Stemn; Michael J. Owen; Deacons James Askew; Marcelino Hernandez; Michael Mercure; Joseph Krame.
Res.: 10655 W. Wadsworth Rd., Zion-Beach Park, 60099-3558. Tel: 847-872-8778; Email: olhumility@archchicago.org.
School—Our Lady of Humility School, 10601 Wadsworth Rd., Zion-Beach Park, 60099.
Tel: 847-746-3722; Fax: 847-731-2870; Email: pbrowne@olhschool.org. Ms. Dolan Margaret, Prin. Lay Teachers 16; Students 290.

Syro-Malabar Rite

BELLWOOD, COOK CO., SYRO-MALABAR CATHOLIC MISSION OF THE ARCHDIOCESE OF CHICAGO, See separate listing. Under the Diocese of St. Thomas Syro-Malabar.

CHICAGO, COOK CO., KNANITE SYRO-MALABAR CATHOLIC MISSION OF THE ARCHDIOCESE OF CHICAGO, See separate listing. Under the Diocese of St. Thomas Syro-Malabar.

Syro-Malankara Rite

CHICAGO, COOK CO., SYRO-MALANKARA CATHOLIC MISSION,
Legal Name: Syro-Malankara Catholic Mission of the Archdiocese of Chicago
St. Mary's Malankara Catholic Church—1208 Ashland Ave., Evanston, 60202. Tel: 847-332-1794; Fax: 847-424-0889. Revs. Babu Madathilpambil-Thomas, Dir.; Joseph Kandathikudy, In Res.

Chaplains of Public Institutions

CHICAGO. *Chicago Airports Catholic Chaplaincy*, P.O. Box 66353, 60666. Rev. Michael G. Zaniolo, S.T.L., C.A.C.
Hines V.A. Hospital. Revs. James Burnett, Benjamin Chinnappan, (India).
John H. Stroger, Jr. Hospital of Cook County, Tel: 312-864-1246. Revs. James Chambers, S.J., Robert E. Finn, S.J., Eugene J. Nevins, S.J., Dir., Sr. Marie Louise Jilk, S.Sp.S.

NORTH CHICAGO. *Veterans Affairs Medical Center*. Rev. William F. Vander Heyden, (Retired).

OAK FOREST. *Oak Forest Hospital*, 4700 W. 159th St., Oak Forest, 60452. Tel: 708-687-2035. Rev. Wayne H. Wurst.

On Duty Outside the Archdiocese:
Rev. Msgrs.—
Brankin, Patrick M., St. Theresa, P.O. Box 297, Collinsville, OK 74021-0297
Dobes, George E., J.C.L., 3370 S. 2nd St., Arlington, VA 22204-1709
Trisco, Robert F., Hist.Eccl.D., (Retired), Curley Hall, Catholic University of America, Washington, DC 20064
Very Rev.—
Kasperczuk, Marek, Pontifical College Josephinum, 7625 N. High St., Columbus, OH 43235
Revs.—
Carcaga, Jose Martin, Nuestros Peguenos Hermanos
Gavancho, Juan C., S.T.L., 14435 Uhl Ave., Clearlake, CA 95422
Grunow, Stephen E., S.T.L., Word on Fire Catholic Ministries, Santa Barbara, CA 93105
Lefebure, Leo D., Our Lady of Victory, 4835 Mac Arthur Way, Washington, DC 20007
Lesniewski, Stephen F., Diocese of Orange, Santiago De Compostela, 21682 Lake Forest Dr., Lake Forest, CA 92630
Sullivan, John J., Cape Girardeau, Sacred Heart, Salem, MO 65560.

Military Chaplains:
Revs.—
Barkemeyer, John F., c/o Mr. & Mrs. Barkemeyer, 120 Fourth St., Wilmette, 60091
Beltran, Jacque B., S.T.B., D.Min. (Cand.), 540 Keller Ave., Waukegan, 60060
Doering, Christopher, c/o Mrs. Alice Deering, 7932 W. Grand Ave. Apt 1w, Elmwood Park, 60707
Greschel, Mark, PCS 704, Box 3203, Apo, AP 96338
Hannigan, John T., VA Medical Center, 650 Indian School Rd., Phoenix, AZ 85012
Keener, Robert J., 5159 Aqua Marine Way, Oceanside, CA 92057. USN
Kilian, Waldemar A., Chap., Naval Station Command, 7849 Geneva Dr., Gurnee, 60031. USN
Kloak, David G., Chap., 3525 N. Nora Ave., 60634
Musula, Charles E., 256 Michigan Ave., #406D, Watertown, NY 13601
Nguyen, Hoang H., Hckiam AB, 180 Kuntz Ave., P.O. Box 8311, Hickam AFB, HI 96853
Zemczak, Pawel, 7300 Blackstone Ave., #3, Justice, 60458.

Missionary Work:
Rev.—
Cleary, Philip C., 5503 Danbury Cir., Lake In The Hills, 60156.

Other Assignments:
Rev. Msgr.—
Velo, Kenneth, DePaul University, 1 E. Jackson, 60604
Revs.—
Becker, Charles P., P.O. Box 633, Wauconda, 60084
Cyson, Philip, 11826 Stewart Ave., 60628
Falkenthal, Thomas W., Chap., (Retired), 4000 Island Blvd. Ste. 1902, Aventura, FL 33160
Gilligan, Michael J., Ph.D., S.T.L., San Rocco Oratory of St. Agnes, 315 E. 22nd St & San Rocco Pl., Chicago Hts., 60411
Heyd, James F., Priests for Life, Maryville, 5843 W. Strong St., 60630
Hurtado-Badillo, Domingo, Chap., St. Alexius Medical Center, Hoffman Estates, 60194
Joslyn, James W., Recruiter, (Retired), 1 N. Dee Rd., #2C, Park Ridge, 60068
Kiley, J. Cletus, Special Advisor, 950 N. Michigan, Apt. 5301, 60611
Kondziolka, Ronald L., Chap., St. James Hospital, Olympia Fields, 60461
McQuaid, Thomas W., 100 N. Hermitage #914, 60612
Muraya, Anthony, Student Priest, University of St. Mary of the Lake, 1000 E. Maple Ave., Mundelein, 60060
Nguyen, Joseph Thai, Vietnamese Catholic Center, 1538 Century Blvd., Santa Ana, CA 92703
Place, Michael D., S.T.D., 1671 Missioin Hill Dr. #308, Northbrook, 60062
Ploplis, Theodore, St. Joseph Hospital, 2900 N. Lakeshore Dr., 60657
Santiago, Leoncia, James Lovell Healthcare Center, 3001 Green Bay Rd., North Chicago, 60064
Spiess, Kevin J., 1401 Burr Oak Rd., #202B, Hinsdale, 60521
Steiner, Daniel R., Villa Scalabrini, Northlake, 60164
Zimmer, William E., 1428 S. 59th Ct., Cicero, 60804.

Retired:
Rev. Msgrs.—
Adams, Michael J., (Retired), Christ the King, 9235 S. Hamilton Ave., 60620
Canary, John, (Retired), Notre Dame De Chicago, 1335 W. Harrison St., 60607
Coughlin, Daniel P., (Retired), 5100 N. Marine Dr. #27M, 60640
Hynes, Richard P., (Retired), 5100 N. Marine Dr., #15a, 60640
Meyer, Charles R., M.A., S.T.D., (Retired), St. Benedict Nursing Home, 6930 W. Touhy, Niles, 60714
Pollard, John E., S.T.L., (Retired), Queen of All Saints, 6280 N. Sauganash Ave., 60646
Pollard, Patrick J., (Retired), 12375 W. McCarthy Rd., Palos Park, 60464
Prist, Wayne F., (Retired), Queen of All Saints, Chicago, 6280 N. Sauganash Ave., 60646
Sarauskas, George, (Retired), 67 Kimbark Rd., Apt. 3, Riverside, 60546
Saudis, Richard T., (Retired), St. Odilo, 22-44 East Ave., Berwyn, 60402
Revs.—
Adamich, Albert R., (Retired), Most Holy Redeemer, 9525 S. Lawndale Ave., Evergreen Park, 60042
Ahlstrom, Michael P., (Retired), St. Barbara, 4008 Prairie Ave., Brookfield, 60513
Anglim, Ronald H., (Retired), 15619 Mount Carmel Dr., Apt. 8, Homer Glen, 60491
Auer, Joseph E., (Retired), Bishop Lyne Home, 12210 S. Will-Cook Rd., Palos Park, 60464-7332
Bacchi, Robert A., (Retired), Bishop Lyne Residence, 12280 S. Willicook Rd., Palos Park, 60464
Baldwin, John F., CHC, USN, (Retired), 1002 Fontana Dr., Alameda, CA 94502
Banzin, Robert S., (Retired), 5100 Marine Dr., #13 M, 60640
Barrett, James L., (Retired), St. Thomas of Canterbury, 4827 N. Kenmore Ave., 60640
Beaven, Robert W., (Retired), 205 Amendola Way, Grayslake, 60035
Bedoya, Martin, (Retired), 905 Center St., Des Plaines, 60016
Bojczuk, Thaddeus J., (Retired), Mercy Circle, 3659 W. 99th St., 60655
Bonin, Harold A., (Retired), 905 Center Ave., Lyons, 60534
Bowler, Michael J., (Retired), 3211 S. Racine 2nd Flr Front, 60608
Brady, Daniel J., (Retired), 432 W. Park St., Arlington Heights, 60005
Bresnahan, John J., (Retired), 1675 Mill St., Apt. 504, Des Plaines, 60018
Broccolo, Gerard T., (Retired), 7865 E. Mississippi Ave., #903, Denver, CO 80247
Bulwith, Richard E., (Retired), Bishop Lyne Residence, 12210 S. Will-Cook Rd., Palos Park, 60464
Burke, Frank J., (Retired), Bp. Lyne Residence, 12230 S. Will Cook Rd., Palos Park, 60464
Burke, William A., (Retired), 16826 81st Ave. 1-S, Tinley Park, 60477
Burnell, Robert J., (Retired), 10494 E. Stony Ridge Cr., Sister Bay, WI 54234
Canavan, Mark P., (Retired), 500 Castle Rd., McHenry, 60050
Caplis, Roger J., (Retired), P.O. Box 656, Williams Bay, WI 53191-0656
Chmiel, Bronislaw, (Retired), 5848 S. Lawndale Ave., 1st Fl., 60629
Clements, George H., (Retired), 10226 S. Trumbull St., Evergreen Park, 60805
Coleman, Robert P., (Retired), St. James, 10600 S. Archer Ave., Lemont, 60439
Collins, Daniel J., (Retired), St. Mary of the Lake, 4200 N. Sheridan Rd., 60613
Corbo, Alfred P., (Retired), 321 Bryn Mawr, Itasca, 60143
Corcoran, Edward G., (Retired), 6333 Rancho Mission Rd., San Diego, CA 92128
Costello, William J., (Retired), 7110 Balboa Lane, Fox Lake, 60020
Cusick, John C., (Retired), 266 Pottawatomi Dr., Fontana, WI 53125
Darow, Robert G., (Retired), 5901 N. Sauganash Ln., 60646
Dewes, John W., (Retired), St. Anne, 120 N. Ela St., Barrington, 60010
Dore, Thomas M., (Retired), St. Pascal, 3935 N. Melvina Ave., 60634-2527
Doyle, John J., (Retired), Bethlehem Woods, 1571 W. Ogden, La Grange, 60526
Dubi, Leonard A., (Retired), 3505 Lakeview Dr., Hazel Crest, 60429
Dunn, Laurence J., (Retired), St. Norbert and OL Brook, 1809 Walters Ave., Northbrook, 60062
Ebrom, Robert L., (Retired), 912 Ridge Sq., #206, Elk Grove Village, 60007
Egan, Gerard P., (Retired), 310 S. Michigan Ave., #1905, 60604
Fanelli, Charles V., (Retired), St. John Vianney, 46 N. Wolf Rd., Northlake, 60164
Farry, John A., (Retired), Mercy Circle, 3659 W. 99th St., 60655
Fenske, Donald J., (Retired), Our Lady of Knock, 501 163rd St., Calumet City, 60409
Finnegan, John P., (Retired), 10 E. Hawthorne Pkwy., Vernon Hills, 60061
Finnegan, William J., (Retired), Bishop Lyne Residence, 12280 S. Will-Cook Rd., Palos Park, 60464
Fischer, Kenneth J., (Retired), Holy Cross, 724 Elder Ln., Deerfield, 60015
Flaherty, William J., (Retired), Ss. Faith, Hope & Charity, 191 Linden St., Winnetka, 60093-3832
Flavin, John E., (Retired), St. Benedict Nursing and Rehab., 6930 Touhy Ave., Niles, 60714
Flynn, James F., (Retired), Ascension - St. Suanna, 15234 Myrtle Ave., Harvey, 60426
Friedl, Erwin J., (Retired), St. Benedicts Nursing and Rehab, 6930 W. Touhy, Niles, 60714
Gallagher, James R., (Retired), 2108 S. Scoville, Berwyn, 60402
Gleeson, Edward D., (Retired), 1275 Bonaventure Ct., Lemont, 60439
Goergen, Michael A., (Retired), Bishop Lyne Residence, 12280 S. Will-Cook Rd., Palos Park, 60464
Grace, Edward D., (Retired), Queen of All Saints, 6280 N. Sauganash, 60646
Grace, James N., (Retired), 1833 E. Wildberry Dr., Glenview, 60025
Grassi, Dominic J., (Retired), 5555 N. Sheridan Rd. #1612, 60640

Gratkowski, Eugene W., (Retired), N. Addison Ave., #B2, Elmhurst, 60126
Gubbins, William B., (Retired), 9440 Seton Pl., Orland Park, 60459
Harnett, Edward F., (Retired), St. Francis Xavier, 524 Ninth St., Wilmette, 60091
Headley, Donald J., (Retired), St. Mary of the Woods, 7033 N. Moselle Ave., 60646
Healy, Thomas I., (Retired), St. Bonaventure Oratory, 1641 W. Diversey Pkwy., 60614
Hebda, Martin J., (Retired), 1719 Boulder Dr., Darien, 60561
Heidenreich, Robert J., (Retired), 3639 Bell, 60618
Hennessey, John E., (Retired), 5100 N. Marine Dr. #15A, 60640
Hickey, Thomas E., (Retired), 6334 N. Sheridan Rd., 60660
Hoffman, John R., (Retired), 96 Lake Ln., Fox Lake, 60020
Hung, Peter, (Retired), St. Benedict Nursing & Rehab, 6930 W. Touhy Ave., Niles, 60714
Huske, Leonard G., (Retired), 347 Daffodil Ln., Matteson, 60443
Izyk, Andrew, (Retired), St. Constance, 5843 W. Strong St., 60630
Jackson, Joseph M., Ph.D., (Retired), SS. Faith, Hope, and Charity, 191 Linden St., Winnetka, 60093
Jamnicky, John, (Retired), St. John Paul II Residence, 2550 E. University Ave. #401, Georgetown, TX 78626
Jankowski, Daniel C., 6301 N. Sheridan Rd., #17g, 60660
Jasinski, Raymond J., (Retired), Rosary Hill Nursing Home, 9000 W. 81st St., Justice, 60458
Joslyn, James W., (Retired), 1 North Dee Rd., #2C, Park Ridge, 60068
Joyce, Gerald P., (Retired), Divine Infant, 1601 Newcastle Ave., Westchester, 60154
Kalas, Ronald N., (Retired), 7258 W. Gregory, 60656
Kane, George J., (Retired), 1700 Cambourne, Schaumburg, 60194
Kaplan, Jan F., (Retired), 6101 S. 75th Ave., Argo, 60501
Kastigar, John J., (Retired), Bishop Lyne Residence, 12230 S. Will Cook Rd., Palos Park, 60464
Kehoe, James P., (Retired), 1101 S. State St. #407, 60605
Kenneally, William G., (Retired), 10427 S. Hoyne, 60643
Kiepura, Kenneth, (Retired), 254 Cerromar Way S., Venice, FL 34293
Kiley, Philip, (Retired), St. Benedict Home, 6930 W. Touhy, Niles, 60714
Kinn, James W., (Retired), Bishop Lyne Residence, 12280 S. Will-Cook Rd., Palos Park, 60464
Kissane, Maurice J., (Retired), 21663 Howell Dr., Cassopolis, MI 49031
Klees, Raymond F., (Retired), 1524 S. Sangamon Unit 505, 60608
Knittel, Kilian J., (Retired), P.O. Box 9408, Michigan City, IN 46361
Kozak, Richard J., (Retired), 3000 Columbine Cr., Unit #E, Valparaiso, FL 46383
Lagges, Patrick, (Retired), 7915 Harrison Pl., Merrillville, IN 46410
Laini, Valerian, (Retired), St. Benedict Nursing Home & Rehab, 6930 W. Touhy Ave., Niles, 60714
Laske, Kenneth S., (Retired), 4032 W. Nelson St., 60641
Laz, Medard P., (Retired), 3015 N. Ocean Blvd., #18H, Fort Lauderdale, FL 33308
Libera, Thomas A., (Retired), St. Hillary, 5600 N. Fairfield, 60659
Lisowski, William J., (Retired), 12230 Will-Cook Rd., Palos Park, 60464
Lorenz, Matthais E., (Retired), 5531 E. Lake Dr., #31C, Lisle, 60532
Luczak, Andrew E., (Retired), 8137 N. Washington, Niles, 60714
Lyons, Patrick M., (Retired), Our Lady of Knock, 501 163rd St., Calumet City, 60409
Mair, Robert G., (Retired), c/o Thomas Place, 2200 Patriot Blvd., Glenview, 60026
Malcolm, Lawrence J., (Retired), St. Gerald, 9310 S. 55th Ct., Oak Lawn, 60453
Malloy, William, (Retired), St. Barnabas, 10134 S. Longwood Dr., 60643
Maloney, Edward J., (Retired), 7417 Channahon Ct., Fox Lake, 60020
Mass, Ronald J., (Retired), 15417 Aster Ln., Orland Park, 60462
McBrady, Lawrence P., (Retired), 1400 N. Lake Shore Dr. #175, 60610
McCarthy, Daniel P., (Retired), St. Tarcissus, 6020 W. Ardmose Ave., 60646
McCarthy, James H., (Retired), SPRED, 2953 S. Lowe Ave., 60616
McCarthy, Terrence A., (Retired), Bishop Lynne Residence, 12230 S. Will Cook Rd., Palos Park, 60464
McGinnity, Robert F., (Retired), Bishop Lyne Residence, 12280 S. Will-Cook Rd., Palos Hills, 60464
McGlinn, Robert J., (Retired), St. Hyacinth, 1414 W. Becher St., Milwaukee, WI 53215
McIlhone, James P., S.T.L., Ph.D., (Retired), St. Edward, 4350 W. Sunnyside Ave., 60630
McKenna, Edward J., (Retired), c/o Mrs. Geraldvilt, 714 Walnut Dr., Darien
McKenna, George P., (Retired), Bishop Lyne Home, 12230 S. Will-Cook Rd., Palos Park, 60464
McLaughlin, Edward, (Retired), 5757 W. 127th St., Palos Heights, 60463
McNulty, William J., (Retired), 1433 Perry St., #402, Des Plaines, 60016
Merold, James E., (Retired), 217 Sheridan Ct., Waukegan, 60085
Mescall, Thomas J., (Retired), 11340 S. Washtenaw, 60655
Meyr, Herbert J., (Retired), Sacred Heart, 819 N. 16th Ave., Melrose Park, 60160-3828
Michelini, Michael S., (Retired), c/o Therese Rooney, 7504 N. Octavia Ave., 60654
Mikolajczyk, Edward M., (Retired), Our Lady of the Woods, 1073 W. 131st. St., Orland Park, 60462
Millea, Thomas V., (Retired), 317 West Wood Oaks Ct., Kankakee, 60109
Moran, Thomas A., (Retired), 500 Castle Rd., McHenry, 60050
Moriarity, William J., (Retired), Holy Name Cathedral, 730 N. Wabash, 60661
Mulcrone, Joseph A., (Retired), St. Francis Borgia, 8033 W. Addison, 60634
Mulvihill, John E., (Retired), St. James, 134 N. Ave, Highwood, 60040
Murphy, Harold B., (Retired), St. Margaret Mary, 2324 W. Chase Ave., 60645
Murphy, James P., (Retired), 1623 Ashland, Apt. 5E, Des Plaines, 60016
Murray, John W., (Retired), 1804 N. Riverwoods Dr., Melrose Park, 60160
Mysliwiec, Haldane, (Retired), 41955 Smith St., Antioch, 60002
Nangle, Thomas R., (Retired), N. 5574 Johnson, Delavan, WI 53115
Navoy, Ronald W., (Retired), 1709 Lakecliff Dr. #8, Wheaton, 60187
Nemecek, M. Cyril, (Retired), 2333 S. 8th Ave., North Riverside, 60546
Nicola, John J., (Retired), Holy Family Villa, 12220 S. Will-Cook Rd., Palos Park, 60646
Nowak, Eugene J., (Retired), N 1222 Tombeau Rd., Genoa City, WI 53128
O'Brien, James J., M.A., (Retired), St. Eugene, 7958 W. Foster Ave, 60656-3696
O'Mara, William T., (Retired), 9765 Cambridge Cir., Mokena, 60448
Oldershaw, Robert H., (Retired), 2244 Sherman Ave. #1, Evanston, 60201
Pacocha, Edwin D., (Retired), 2712 N. Western Ave., 60647
Parker, John W., (Retired), 8239 Holly Ct., Palos Hills, 60465
Patte, Steven W., (Retired), St. Raymond De Pentafort, 301 S. I-Oka Ave., Mount Prospect, 60056
Paurazas, Peter P., (Retired), St. Patricia, 9050 S. 86th Ave., Hickory Hills, 60457
Peng, John B., (Retired), c/o Stephanie Leung, 6833 N. Minnetonka, 60646
Perez-Rodriguez, Arturo, (Retired), 27105 Sacramento Ave., 60623
Plotkowski, John S., (Retired), St. Zachary, 567 W. Algonquin Rd., Des Plaines, 60016
Price, John R., (Retired), N4195 Lake View Dr., Markesan, WI 53946
Quinlan, James V., (Retired), 3050 NE. 47th Ct., #202, Ft. Lauderdale, FL 33308
Reicher, A. Paul, (Retired), St. John Berchmans, 2517 W. Logan Blvd., 60647
Rezula, Leon J., (Retired), 436 Drake Cr., Schaumburg, 60193
Rizzo, Robert C., (Retired), 5100 N. Marine Dr., Apt. 21G, 60640
Rogala, Gerald E., (Retired), 500 Lakeview Ave., Apt. 1A, Highwood, 60040
Roller, John W., (Retired), St. Emily, 1400 E. Central Rd., Mount Prospect, 60056
Rosemeyer, Paul F., (Retired), St. Benedict Home, 6930 W. Touhy Ave., Niles, 60714
Rudnik, John J., (Retired), St. Benedict Home, 6930 W. Touhy Ave., Niles, 60714
Ryan, John M., (Retired), 26 N. Pistakee Lake Rd., #2A, Fox Lake, 60020
Salera, Alfredo J., (Retired), 122 N. Metropolitan Ave., Waukegan, 60085
Salmon, Edward P., (Retired), St. Giles, 1045 Columbian Ave., Oak Park, 60302
Sanaghan, John J., (Retired), St. Mark, 1048 N. Campbell Ave., 60622
Sasso, Frank M., (Retired), 519 Eastwood, Michigan City, IN 46360
Scanlan, Francis G., (Retired), St. Damian, 5220 W. 155th St., Oak Forest, 60452
Scarlata, Ronald E., (Retired), Our Lady of Angels Retirement, 1201 Wyoming Ave. #0123, Joliet, 60435
Schlax, Charles H., (Retired), Nazarethville, 300 N. River Rd., Des Plaines, 60016
Schopp, George L., (Retired), 403 Sand Creek Dr., Chesterton, IN 46304
Schouten, Francis L., (Retired), 3755 W. 112th Pl., 60655
Shannon, Richard J., (Retired), 709 79th St., Unit 107, Darien, 60561
Simpson, Brian L., (Retired), St. Colette, 3100 Town Square Dr. #302, Rolling Meadows, 60008
Smilanic, Daniel, J.C.D., (Retired), 401 S. Ascot Dr., Unit 2H, Park Ridge, 60068
Smith, Gene F., (Retired), St. Linus, 10300 S. Lawles Ave., Oak Lawn, 60453
Springer, Lawrence F., (Retired), St. Zachary, 567 W. Algonquin Rd., Des Plaines, 60016
Srenn, Thomas E., (Retired), 716 Territory Dr., Galena, 61036
Stafford, Dennis, M.Div., (Retired), 39103 92nd St., Genoa City, WI 53128
Stenzel, William J., (Retired), 12915 N. Ivy St., Cedar Lake, IN 46303
Stockus, Edward S., (Retired), 10508 S. Keeler, Oak Lawn, 60453
Sullivan, Daniel F., (Retired), c/o Mrs. Joan Rizzo,185 E. Old Mill Tr., Antioch, 60002
Sztorc, Richard E., (Retired), St. Mary, 10 N. Buffalo Grove Rd., Buffalo Grove, 60089
Talarico, Anthony M., (Retired), Holy Ghost, 700 E. 170th St., South Holland, 60473
Taylor, Joseph C., (Retired), St. Edward, 4350 W. Sunnyside Ave., 60630
Thinnes, John M., (Retired), St. Benedict Home, 6930 W. Toughy, Niles, 60714
Tillrock, Raymond J., (Retired), 5346 S. Cornell, Apt. 201, 60615
Tivy, Thomas A., (Retired), 77 N. Wolf Rd., Northlake, 60164
Tonelli, Robert F., (Retired), 9343 S. Francisco Ave., Evergreen Park, 60805
Trela, Norman J., (Retired), St. Symphorosa, 6135 S. Austin, 60638
Tucker, Patrick M., (Retired), 519 Eastwood, Michigan City, IN 46360
Tuzik, Robert L., (Retired), Notre Dame De Chicago, 1335 W. Harrison St., 60607
Unz, Thomas E., (Retired), St. Giles, 1025 Columbian Ave., Oak Park, 60302
Upton, Edward F., (Retired), 17816 New Hampshire Ct., Orland Park, 60467
Vanecko, William, (Retired), St. Columbanus, 331 E. 71st St., 60619
Vitro, Thomas J., (Retired), P.O. Box 932, Lake Geneva, WI 53147
Wagner, Leon R., (Retired), Holy Family Villa, 12230 S. Will-Cook Rd., Palos Park, 60464
Walsh, Michael J., (Retired), Bishop Lyne Home, 12230 S. Will-Cook Rd., Palos Park, 60464
Welsh, William P., (Retired), 8340 Callie Ave., #314, Morton Grove, 60053
Wickowski, Leroy A., (Retired), St. Luke, 528 Lathrop Ave., River Forest, 60305
Winters, Martin N., (Retired), Benedictine Monastery of Our Lady of Sorrows, 5800 W. 147th St., Oak Forest, 60452
Wojcik, Joseph J., (Retired), 1762 W. Peterson Ave., #E203, 60631
Wulsch, Michael A., (Retired), 13033 Penefield Ln., Huntley, 60143
Yadron, Raymond A., (Retired), 1152 E. Anderson Dr., Palatine, 60074
Zake, Louis J., Ph.D., (Retired), 310 S. Michigan Ave., Unit 704, 60604
Zavaski, William J., (Retired), St. James, 820 N. Arlington Heights Rd., Arlington Heights, 60004
Zizzo, Robert, (Retired), 729 Grand Canyon St., Hoffman Estates, 60169.

Permanent Deacons:
Abboud, Louis, St. Patrick, Wadsworth
Adolfo, Alfredo, St. Christina, Chicago
Aguilar, Ruben, Mary, Mother of Mercy, Chicago
Ahern, Michael, Our Lady of Victory
Alandy, Miguel, St. Mary of the Annunciation, Mundelein
Albarran, Pablo, Most Blessed Trinity, Waukegan
Allison, Andrew, St. Francis Xavier, La Grange
Alonso, Enrique, Our Lady of Grace, Chicago; Office of the Diaconate
Alvarez, Jose, (Retired), Chicago
Ambe, Neba, St. Margaret Mary, Chicago
Amberg, John, (Retired), Frankfort, IL
Andrade, David D., St. Rita of Cascia, Chicago

Annoreno, August J., Our Lady Mother of the Church, Chicago
Antiss, Robert S., (Retired), Hoffman Estates
Antonsen, Larry, Christ the King, Chicago
Arellano, Miguel, St. Gall, Chicago
Arenas, Jose Ramon, Our Lady of Mount Carmel, Melrose Park
Arndt, John, (Retired), Evanston, IL
Arroyo, Ramon, St. Aloysius, Chicago
Arvidson, Robert, St. Francis de Sales, Lake Zurich
Askew, James, Our Lady of Humility, Beach Park/Zion
Auld, David D., Santa Maria Del Popolo, Mundelein
Avila, Mario, St. Malachy & Precious Blood, Chicago
Ayala, Efrain, (Retired), Downers Grove, IL
Babczak, David, St. Raymond DePenafort, Mt. Prospect
Baier, John, St. Luke, River Forest
Baldasti, Steven, St. Hubert, Hoffman Estates
Bannon, James R., St. James, Arlington Hts.
Barnish, Michael K., Sacred Heart, Melrose Park
Barone, Louis, (Retired), Woodstock, IL
Bartholomew, Thomas, St. Michael, Orland Park
Barton, Jeffrey, Prince of Peace, Lake Villa
Bartos, Gregory, St. George, Tinley Park
Battisto, John P., Our Lady of Mount Carmel, Melrose Park
Bautista, Juan Carlos, St. Agnes of Bohemia, Chicago
Beeber, Gregory M., St. Edna, Arlington Heights
Behrendt, Raymond J., Sacred Heart, Melrose Park
Beierwaltes, Andrew J., St. John Brebeuf, Niles
Beil, Frank, St. Catherine Laboure, Glenview
Belanger, James, (Retired), Niles, IL
Belice, Randy, St. Mary, Riverside
Benoit, Michael S., St. John the Evangelist, Streamwood
Benzschawel, Todd M., St. Patrick, Wadsworth
Bergquist, Bernard, (Retired), Cheswick, PA
Beyer, Wayne, Church of Holy Spirit, Schaumburg
Bickle, Calvin, St. Alphonsus Liguori, Wheeling
Biegel, Alan, St. Gilbert, Grayslake
Birck, Robert, St. Paul the Apostle, Gurnee
Bishop, Joseph, (Retired), St. James, Sauk Village; Orland Hills
Blanco, Jesus, St. Frances of Rome, Cicero
Blindauer, Kevin, Mary, Seat of Wisdom, Park Ridge
Boharic, Robert, St. Mary, Riverside
Boppart, Irvin, Most Blessed Trinity, Waukegan
Borha, George, St. Thomas More, Chicago
Bovyn, Paul, (Retired)
Breit, John, St. Thomas of Villanova, Palatine
Brencic, David, St. Louise de Marillac, La Grange Park; Office of the Diaconate
Brenner, Patrick, St. Monica, Chicago
Bresemann, David, Our Lady of the Lakes, Ingleside
Bretz, Michael, Glenview, IL; St. Catherine, Laboure
Brezinski, David, St. Zachary, Des Plaines
Brooks, George, J.D., (Retired), Tinley Park
Brothers, David, St. Agnes, Chicago Heights
Brown, Dennis G., Dept. of Human Services, Chicago
Bryce, Irvin, St. Albert the Great, Burbank
Buckley, Mark, Our Lady of Lakes, Ingleside
Buissereth, Rameau, Our Lady of Peace, Chicago
Bulger, Robert, St. Paul of the Cross, Park Ridge
Bumbul, John, St. Gall, Chicago
Burns, William, St. Viator, Chicago
Burt, John D., (Retired), Chicago, IL
Bzdon, Gregory M., St. Tarcissus, Chicago
Cabrera, Daniel, St. Hedwig, Chicago
Cabrera, Jorge, St. John Berchmans, Chicago
Camerini, Guilio, St. Eulalia, Maywood
Cameron, Andrew P., St. Paul of the Cross, Park Ridge
Carlson, Thomas, St. Barbara, Brockfield
Carrera, Xavier, Church of the Holy Spirit, Schaumburg
Carrillo, Martin, St. Joseph the Worker, Wheeling
Carrion, Ramiro B., Our Lady of Mercy, Chicago
Carroll, Daniel, St. Francis of Assisi, Orland Park
Carroll, Robert O. Jr., St. John Fisher, Chicago
Carter, Jeremy N., St. Patrick, Wadsworth
Carvlin, Thomas, Ascension St. Susanna, Harvey
Cascino, Joseph Jr., (Retired), Huntley, IL
Casey, Joseph, St. Patrick, Wadsworth
Casey, Patrick S., St. Josaphat, Chicago
Castaneda, David, St. Malachy & Precious Blood, Chichago
Dr. Cavanaugh, Michael, SS. Faith, Hope, and Charity, Winnetka
Cazales, Ramon, St. Mark, Chicago
Chairez, Victor, St. Simeon, Bellwood
Chausse, Joseph, (Retired), Tinley Park
Chavez, Abraham, Immaculate Conception, 88th, Chicago
Chavez, Jesus, St. Blase, Argo
Chrastka, Joel, (Retired), Berwyn, IL
Christensen, Thomas, St. Turibius, Chicago
Churilla, William, (Retired), Joliet, IL
Chyba, Lawrence J., St. Richard, Chicago
Ciciura, Michael, Ss. Cyril and Methodius, Lemont
Ciesil, Norbert, (Retired), Schaumburg, IL
Cintron, Gilberto, (Retired), Chicago
Cislo, Robert L., St. Linus, Oak Lawn
Cisneros, Jose, St. Leonard, Berwyn
Clark, William, (Retired)
Cnota, Robert, St. Thecla, Chicago
Cocco, Anthony, St. Michael, Orland Park
Coleman, Alfred II, St. James, Chicago
Colgan, Dennis L., St. Mother Theodore Guerin, Elmwood Park
Condill, James, (Retired), Barrington
Conlin, Robert, St. Stephen, Deacon and Martyr, Tinley Park
Connor, John, St. Colette, Rolling Meadow
Contreras, Alberto, St. Ansgar, Hanover Park
Contreras, Mario, Church of the Holy Spirit, Schaumburg
Conway, James, St. Barnabas, Chicago
Cook, John, St. Katharine Drexel, Chicago
Corcoran, Thomas, Our Lady of the Wayside, Arlington Heights
Cordoba, Angelo, St. Mary Star of the Sea, Chicago
Crane, Walter James, (Retired), Arlington Hts., IL
Cristofaro, Dennis, St. Elizabeth Seton, Orland Hills
Cunalata, Oswaldo, (Retired), Elmhurst, IL
Cyran, Robert, Transfiguration, Wauconda
Czarnecki, Thaddeus, St. Julian Eymard, Elk Grove Village
Dahl, Earl, (Retired), Streamwood
Damian, Eugene P., (Retired), Spring Grove, IL
Danielewicz, Adam, St. Daniel the Prophet, Chicago
Davis, Kurt, St. Thomas the Apostle, Chicago
De Frank, Frank, St. Patrick, Lake Forest
De Rose, Ronald
Debnar, John, St. Barbara, Brookfield
DeFiore, Robert, (Retired), Huntley
Dehler, Thomas, (Retired), O'Fallon, MI
DeLarco, Michael, St. Mother Theodore Guerin, Elmwood Park
Delgado, Antonio, St. Genevieve, Chicago
DeLorenzo, Edward, (Retired), Westchester
Detloff, James, St. Emeric, Country Club Hills
Devine, James, St. Theresa, Palatine
Devona, James, (Retired), Woodstock
Diaz, Benjamin, St. Sylvester, Chicago
Diaz De Leon, Raymundo, St. Albert the Great, Burbank
Dixon, Roscoe B. Jr., St. Katharine Dexel, Chicago
Doerr, William A., St. Lawrence O'Toole, Matteson
Dolan, Edward, St. Juliana, Chicago
Dominguez, Juan, St. Paul, Chicago
Donahue, John, St. Francis of Assisi, Orland Park
Donovan, Timothy, Holy Rosary, Chicago
Dorgan, Eugene J., St. Pascal, Chicago
Doud, Raymond, Church of the Holy Spirit, Schaumburg
Dubrownik, Phillip, St. Emeric, Country Club Hills
Duderstadt, Peery, St. Norbert Our Lady of the Brook, Northbrook
Duffey, Mark, St. Thomas of Villanova, Palatine
Dunne, Thomas, St. Thomas of Villanova, Palatine
Duque, Raul, St. Albert the Great, Burbank
Duszynski, Thomas, (Retired), Schaumburg
Dutkiewicz, Daniel, St. Stanislaus Bishop and Martyr, Posen
Dutko, David, St. Kieran, Chicago Heights
Dwyer, Thomas M., St. Edmund, Oak Park
Encisco, Martin, Mary Queen of Heaven, Circero
Ende, Gilbert, Lemont, IL
Enger, Michael, Church of the Holy Spirit, Schaumburg
Engler, William, St. Stephen, Deacon & Martyr, Tinley Park
Ernst, James, Our Lady of Hope, Rosemont
Esposito, Robert F., St. John the Evangelist, Streamwood, IL
Estrada, Jose M., Our Lady of Guadalupe, Chicago
Even, James, Prince of Peace, Lake Villa
Faherty, Paul, (Retired), River Forest
Fair, Davis, (Retired), Westchester, IL
Favila, Angel, St. Agnes of Bohemia, Chicago, IL
Fekete, Michael, St. Gerald, Oak Lawn
Feltes, Richard, St. Gerald, Oak Lawn
Fernandez, Dismas, Blessed Sacrament, Chicago
Filipucci, Michael, St. Marcelline, Schaumburg
Flaherty, George, St. Francis DeSales, Lake Zurich
Flam, Richard, (Retired), San Antonio, TX
Flewellen, James, (Retired), Chicago, IL
Flores, Nicolas, St. Stanislaus Kostka, Chicago
Flores, Victor, St. Viator, Chicago
Flores-Zamora, Efrain, Santa Maria Del Popolo, Mundelein
Foti, Francisco, Our Lady of the Snows, Chicago
Fox, Gerald, (Retired), Sleepy Hollow, IL
Frere, William J., St. Robert Bellarmine, Chicago
Fronczek, Casimir, (Retired), Niles, IL
Fruge, James, Our Lady of Ransom, Niles
Furey, James, St. John the Evangelist, Streamwood
Gagnon, Robert, (Retired), Lakewood, IL
Gaida, Thomas, National Shrine of Maximilian Kolbe, Libertyville
Gallegos, Benito, Our Lady of the Mount, Cicero
Garcia, Aurelio, Our Lady of Mercy, Chicago
Garcia, Jesus, Mary Queen of Heaven, Cicero
Garcia, Jorge, San Jose Luis Sanchez del Rio, Chicago
Garvey, Kevin, Holy Cross, Deerfield
Gaughan, John, St. Vincent Ferrer, River Forest
Gavin, Raymond, St. Catherine Laboure, Glenview
Gianatasio, Philip, St. Mary of Celle, Berwyn
Gibbons, William, St. Patrick, Wadsworth
Gietl, Richard, (Retired), Springfield, IL
Gildea, Francis, St. Elizabeth Seton, Orland Park
Gill, Leroy Jr., St. Dorothy, Chicago
Girjatowicz, Frank, St. Hyacinth Basilica, Chicago
Glenn, John, St. Mary of Vernon, Indian Creek
Globis, Richard J., St. Gilbert, Grayslake
Goeckner, Hans P., St. Mary of Celle, Berwyn
Gonzalez, Felipe, San Jose Luis Sanchez del Rio, Chicago
Gonzalez, Joseph, St. Germaine, Oak Lawn
Gonzalez, Juan, Resurrection, Chicago
Gonzalez, Oscar, St. Rita of Cascia, Chicago
Gregory, Gregory, St. Theresa, Palatine
Gronek, Ronald, Immaculate Conception, Chicago
Gronkiewicz, Edmund, Our Lady of Mount Carmel, Chicago
Grossnickle, Donald R., Our Lady of the Wayside, Arlington Heights
Hahn, Gerald, St. Mary Queen of the Apostles, Riverdale
Hahn, Matthew, St. James, Arlington Heights
Halt, Thomas, (Retired), Ft. Myer, FL
Han, Sung, Church of the Holy Spirit, Schaumburg
Haro, Vincente, St. Clare of Montefalco, Chicago
Harris, Wallace, St. Dorothy, Chicago
Henricks, John, St. Giles, Oak Park
Henry, Francis, Nativity of Our Lord, Chicago
Hernandez, Marcelino, Our Lady of Humility, Zion
Hernandez, Mario, St. Viator, Chicago
Herrera, Albert, St. Gall, Chicago
Herrera, Marcial, Mary, Mother of Mercy, Chicago
Herrera, Tomas, St. Donatus, Blue Island
Herrmann, John, St. Mary, Lake Forest
Hess, Rudolf, St. Daniel the Prophet, Chicago
Heyes, Stuart, St. Cletus, LaGrange
Hill, Edwin, Our Lady of the Ridge, Chicago Ridge
Hinch, Ralph, Office of the Deaf, Chicago
Hipelius, Thomas, St. Damian, Oak Forest
Hita, Floro, San Jose Luis Sanchez del Rio, Chicago
Holevoet, Richard, St. Patrick, Wadsworth
Horton, James, St. Alexander, Palos Heights
Hotcaveg, Irwin E., (Retired), Chicago
Hudzik, Richard F., Divine Providence, Westchester, IL
Huie, Colin, St. Michael, Orland Park
Hyde, Thomas, St. Fabian, Chicago
Hynes, William J., St. Sabina, Chicago
Imbordino, Thomas G., St. John Vianney, Northlake
Janega, Robert, Our Lady of Mercy
Janicek, James, St. Michael, Orland Park
Jannotta, Anthony, St. Thomas Becket, Mt. Prospect
Jean-Pierre, Fritz, St. Jerome, Chicago
Jimenez, Ramon, Our Lady of Guadalupe, Chicago
Johnson, Herbert, St. Katharine Drexel, Chicago
Johnson, Mervin O., Holy Angels, Chicago
Johnson, Richard, Our Lady of Mount Carmel, Chicago
Joynt, William, (Retired), Tucson, AZ
Kalina, David J., Our Lady of Perpetual Help, Glenview
Kalivoda, Bill, (Retired), Crystal Lake, IL
Karstenson, William T., St. Thomas of Villanova, Palatine
Kashmar, George, St. Joseph, Libertyville
Keating, Timothy, St. Alexander, Palos Heights
Keegan, Charles, St. Patricia, Hickory Hills
Keenan, Gerald M., Divine Mercy, Winnetka
Keene, David J., Holy Family, Chicago
Kerls, Robert, St. Francis Xavier, Wilmette
Kiley, Michael E., Palos Community Hospital
Knetl, Thomas, Our Lady of Knock, Calumet City
Kocar, Marvin, (Retired), Lyons, IL
Korepanow, Richard, St. Damian, Oak Forest
Kort, Clayton, Evergreen Park, IL
Kosla, Mariusz J., St. Zachary, Des Plaines
Kotleba, Rudolf, St. Constance, Chicago
Krakora, Joseph, (Retired), Lake Forest
Krame, Joseph, Our Lady of Humility, Zion
Krueger, William J., (Retired), Tucson, AZ
Kudra, Joseph, St. Paul, Chicago, Heights
Kukla, Eugene, St. Mary, Buffalo Grove
Kupsak, Gary L., St. Mary of the Annunciation, Mundelein
Kush, Michael G., (Retired), Deltona, FL

LaMantia, Thomas, St. Marcelline Schaumburg
Lambert, Thomas, Our Lady of Mt. Carmel, Chicago
Lanctot, Howard P., St. Marcelline, Schaumburg
Landuyt, Robert J., Queen of Martyrs, Evergreen Park
Langwell, James E., Incarnation, Palos Heights
Lara, Luis R., St. James, Highwood
Lawson, Richard, St. Hubert, Hoffman Estates
Lazcano, Ivan, St. Anselm, Chicago
Leck, Robert, Our Lady of Victory, Chicago
Leonard, Timothy, Prince of Peace, Lake Villa
Letourneau, Peter, Our Lady of the Wayside, Arlington Hts.
Limon, Juan, St. Benedict, Blue Island
Loman, Raymond C., St. Patrick, Lake Forest
Long, Gary, St. Mary, Buffalo Grove
Lopez, Adolfo, St. Aloysius, Chicago
Lopez, Efrain, Resurrection, Chicago
Lopez, Sergio, St. Simeon, Bellwood
Lorbach, John, St. Raymond de Penafort, Mt. Prospect
Lubben, William, St. Alphonsus, Lemont
Lucas, John V., St. Patrick, Lake Forest
Luevano, Miguel, St. Bede the Venerable, Chicago
Macarol, John, Our Lady of the Woods, Orland Park
Maddock, George, St. Joseph, Homewood
Madison, Michael, Our Lady of the Wayside, Arlington Heights
Madonia, Loretto, St. Giles, Oak Park
Maiers, Donald R., St. Marcelline, Schaumburg
Maldonado, Meliquides, (Retired), Chicago, IL
Malone, John L., St. Germaine, Oak Lawn
Mamolella, Frank, St. Hugh, Lyons
Mancilla-Martinez, Jose, Transfiguration, Wauconda
Manning, Peter, St. Albert the Great, Burbank
Marin, Francisco, St. Jerome, Chicago
Marquez, J. Frank, (Retired), Chicago
Marrero, Jose, (Retired), Chicago, IL
Marszalek, Theodore D., Our Lady, Mother of the Church, Chicago
Martinez, Francisco, (Retired), Mt. Dora, FL
Martinez, Pedro, St. Anastasia, Waukegan
Marturano, Leonard, St. Thomas of Villanova, Palatine
McAllister, Dennis F., St. Norbert and Our Lady of the Brook
McCloskey, Michael, Holy Name Cathedral, Chicago
McDonough, Michael, St. Michael, Orland Park
McElrath, Bruce, Holy Angels
McFarland, Charles, St. Stephen, Deacon and Martyr, Tinley Park
McGuire, Terrance, St. Alphonsus, Lemont
McLynn, Michael, (Retired), La Grange Park
McManus, Michael, St. Thecla, Chicago
McNulty, Michael, Divine Mercy, Winnetka
Medina, Salvador, Shrine of Our Lady of Guadalupe, Des Plaines
Mellon, Jon, (Retired)
Melton, Edward, Holy Cross, Deerfield
Mendez, Genaro, St. Anastasia, Waukegan
Mendieta, Raul, (Retired), Chicago
Mendizabal, Guillermo, St. John Berchmans, Chicago
Mercure, Michael, Our Lady of Humility, Zion-Beach Park
Metallo, Arthur, (Retired), Morton Grove, IL
Miarka, Gary, St. Anne, Hazel Crest
Migala, Paul, St. Marcelline, Schaumberg
Mika, Jozef S., St. John the Evangelist, Streamwood
Mikan, Ivan M., Blessed Alojzije Stepinac Croatian Mission, Chicago
Minor, James R., Prince of Peace, Lake Villa
Miska, Richard, St. Terrence, Alsip
Monnelley, Michael, (Retired)
Montalvo, Maximino, Our Lady of Charity, Chicago
Montelongo, Robert, St. Daniel the Prophet, Chicago
Moore, Daniel, St. Mary of Vernon, Indian Creek
Mora, Raul, St. Ignatius, Chicago
Moreno, Victor M., St. John Bosco, Chicago
Moritz, Richard H., Immaculate Conception, Chicago
Morowczynski, Romuald, St. Jane de Chantal, Chicago
Morris, Robert F. II, St. Gabriel, Chicago
Mudd, Dennis Sr., St. Joseph, Libertyville, IL
Mullaney, Roger, (Retired), Highwood
Munda, Gary, Most Blessed Trinity, Waukegan
Munoz, Fredy, Most Blessed Trinity, Waukegan
Munoz, Romeo, (Retired), St. Jude the Apostle, South Holland; Scottsdale, AZ
Munoz, Ubaldo, St. Mary of the Lake, Chicago
Murphy, Christopher, St. Nicholas, Evanston
Murphy, Robert, St. Gertrude, Franklin Park
Mutnansky, John, St. Christina, Chicago
Navarro, Antonio, St. Mark, Chicago
Navarro, Jesse, St. Mary, Star of the Sea, Chicago
Navarro, Ramon, St. Aloysius, Chicago
Navolio, John, (Retired), Chicago, IL
Negrete, Jose, Our Lady of Fatima, Chicago
Negron, Miguel A., St. Mother Theodore Guerin, Elmwood Park
Neu, Andrew, St. Barnabas
Newman, Jeffrey, (Retired)
Newton, Robert, (Retired), Fulton, IL
Nguyen, Duc Van, St. Henry, Chicago
Nieves, Bienvenido, Queen of Angels, Chicago
Nora, Gerald, St. Mary of Vernon, Indian Creek
Norman, James E., Our Lady of Sorrows Basilica, Chicago
Norton, Terrence, St. Luke, River Forest
Nunez, Raul, Our Lady of Guadalupe, Chicago
O'Donnell, Charles, Our Lady of Ransom, Niles
O'Donnell, Kevin, St. Bernadette, Evergreen Park
O'Leary, Edward, (Retired), Fredericksburg, VA
O'Leary, James J., St. Mary, Des Plaines
O'Leary, John C., St. Lambert, Skokie
O'Malley, James, St. Mary, Des Plaines
Ochoa, J. Zeferino, St. Francis of Assisi, Chicago
Ochoa, Jesus, St. Mary, Star of the Sea, Chicago
Ojeda, Norberto, Sacred Heart, Melrose Park
Onischuk, Paul, Our Lady of the Wayside, Arlington Hts.
Orozco, Manuel, St. Anthony, Cicero
Orzechowski, John, Our Lady of the Ridge, Chicago Ridge
Oskielunas, Lawrence A., St. Patrick, Lemont
Pagnotta, Philip Jr., St. Mary of Vernon, Indian Creek
Palacios, Freddy, St. Charles Borromeo, Melrose Park
Panek, Joseph, St. George, Tinley Park
Pasdiora, Robert, St. John the Evangelist, Streamwood
Patino, Daniel, Our Lady of Lourdes
Patino, Felix, St. Clare of Montefalco, Chicago
Patton, James M., (Retired)
Pauwels, James, St. Edna, Arlington Heights
Pena, Leonardo, Mt. Prospect Hispanic Ministry
Penich, Michael Jr., St. Paul the Apostle, Gurnee
Perez, Luis, Santa Maria Addolorata, Chicago
Perez, Orlando, St. James, Chicago
Peters, Bruce, Holy Angels, Chicago
Peterson, George A., (Retired), (Retired); Mt. Prospect, IL
Pezowicz, Feliks, Transfiguration, Wauconda
Pham, David, St. Henry, Chicago
Phelan, Mark, Most Holy Redeemer, Evergreen Park
Pilarski, Ronald, St. Mother Theodore Guerin, Elmwood Park
Pincich, Samuel, (Retired), Glenview, IL
Pindelski, Michael J., St. Francis of Assisi, Orland Park
Pineda, Javier, St. Turibius
Pizzato, Richard, St. Theresa, Palatine
Plaiss, Mark, St. Gilbert, Grayslake, IL
Pluchar, Edward, St. Julie Billiart, Tinley Park
Podgorski, Edward, St. Monica, Chicago
Poletto, Robert, St. Mary of the Annunciation, Mundelein
Ponce De Leon, Juan, St. William, Chicago
Pouncy, William, St. Martin de Porres, Chicago
Powers, Robert, St. Anne, Barrington
Pozo, Guido, (Retired), Chicago
Principe, Michael, (Retired), Franklin Park
Puhala, Robert, M.A., Divine Mercy, Northfield
Purdome, Mark J., St. Andrew, Chicago
Pyrek, William, St. Mary of the Lake, Chicago
Quackenbush, Edward, (Retired)
Ragonese, Dan, St. Victor, Calumet City
Rakauskas, Stanley, St. Christina, Chicago
Ramirez, Juan, St. Hilary, Chicago
Ramos, Dennis, St. Matthias, Chicago
Ramos, Eliseo, St. Jerome, Chicago
Ramos, Faustino, St. Francis De Sales, Chicago
Ramos, Francisco, San Jose Luis Sanchez del Rio, Chicago
Rangel, John, St. Lawrence O'Toole, Matteson
Reilly, Raymond, St. John Fisher, Chicago
Renk, Dennis A., (Retired), Bourbonnais, IL
Renwick, James, Holy Ghost, South Holland
Restrepo, Leo, Our Lady of Lourdes, Chicago
Revord, James, Our Lady of Perpetual Help, Glenview
Rex, John, St. Damian, Oak Forest
Reyes, David, St. Benedict, Chicago
Riccio, Louis, St. Theresa, Palatine
Richard, Leonard, St. Sabina, Chicago
Richardson, John, (Retired), Zion, IL
Richardson, Lendell, St. Bernardine, Forest Park
Riffner, Joseph, (Retired), Zion, IL
Rios, Jamie, St. Ita, Chicago
Rittenhouse, Daniel, St. Alphonsus, Lemont
Rivera, Francisco, Resurrection, Chicago
Robak, Dennis R., St. Mary, Evanston
Robles, Ernesto, Our Lady of Grace, Chicago
Roccasalva, Joseph J., St. Cajetan, Chicago
Rodriguez, Antonio, St. Thomas of Canterbury, Chicago
Rodriguez, Candelario, St. Procopius, Chicago
Rodriguez, Eduardo, Sacred Heart, Melrose Park
Rodriguez, Emiliano, (Retired), Chicago
Rodriguez, Juan, (Retired), Crown Point, IN
Rodriguez, Manuel, (Retired), Chicago
Rodriguez, Milton, San Jose Luis Sanchez del Rio, Chicago
Rodriguez, Uriol, Resurrection, Chicago
Rogers, Neil, Ss. Cyril and Methodius, Lemont
Rojas, Jaime, St. Nicholas, Evanston
Rossow, Lawrence, St. Ignatius, Chicago
Rottman, John, St. Cornelius, Chicago
Rueth, William, (Retired), Crest Hill, IL
Ruiz, Angel, (Retired), Margate, FL
Ruiz, Joel, St. Joseph, Round Lake
Ruiz, Victor, St. Anastasia, Waukegan
Ruzevich, Thomas, St. Damian
Ryan, Edward, (Retired), Calumet City
Ryan, Robert E. Sr., St. Juliana, Chicago
Ryan, Thomas, (Retired), Chicago
Rybicki, Lawrence, St. John the Evangelist, Streamwood
Rzendzian, Thomas J., Sacred Heart, Palos Hills
Sacramento, Anthony, St. Dismas, Waukegan
Salgado, Alfonso, St. Odilo, Berwyn
Salgado, Manuel, St. Simon the Apostle, Chicago
Salinas, Jorge, St. Stanislaus Kostka, Chicago
Sanchez, Salvador, St. James, Fullerton Ave., Chicago
Sandoval, Jose M., Immaculate Conception, Chicago
Santiago, Faustino, St. Bartholomew, Chicago
Santillan, Miguel A., Our Lady of Grace, Chicago
Sattler, David, St. Peter Damian, Bartlett
Savage, Christopher, Prince of Peace, Lake Villa
Schiltz, James, St. Constance, Chicago
Schmidt, Paul, St. James, Arlington Hts.
Schopp, John E. IV, St. John of the Cross, Western Springs
Schultz, William, St. Stephen, Deacon and Martyr, Tinley Park
Schumacher, Lawrence R., St. Theresa, Palatine
Schutzius, Thomas, St. George, Tinley Park
Sedano, Pedro, St. John Vianney, Northlake
Sedivy, Alan, St. Mary of the Annunciation, Mundelein
Segers, Lawrence E., Notre Dame De Chicago, Chicago
Segura, Leonel, St. Genevieve, Chicago
Serna, Francisco, (Retired), Chicago
Serna, Ramiro, St. Bede the Venerable, Chicago
Serratore, Gregory, (Retired), Chicago
Seveska, Richard, (Retired), Foristell, MO
Sheehan, Patrick P., St. James, Arlington Hts.
Shinkle, Derald, St. Joseph, Wilmette
Shumpert, Gregory, St. Agatha
Siap, Ivan, St. Paul the Apostle, Gurnee
Silva, Rodrigo, St. Paul, Chicago
Silva, Valdemar, St. Cecilia
Simola, Edward, St. William, Chicago
Sinacore, James M., St. John Vianney, Northlake
Siranovic, Joseph, (Retired), Elmhurst, IL
Siska, Thomas, St. John Fisher, Chicago
Skaja, Lawrence, St. John Brebeuf, Niles
Slobig, Robert, St. Luke, River Forest
Smith, John J., St. Zachary, Des Plaines
Smith, Lawrence J., St. Andrew the Apostle, Calumet City
Smyser, William, St. Aloysius, Chicago
Sorensen, Eric, St. Andrew, Chicago
Soria, Carlos, (Retired), Chicago, IL
Soto, Hector, Mision San Juan Diego, Arlington Heights
Soto, Rogelio, St. Ignatius, Chicago
Soto, Santos, (Retired), Chicago
Spalla, Paul, St. Mary of the Lake, Chicago
Spohr, Lawrence, Our Lady of the Lakes, Ingleside
Sponder, James R., Divine Infant Jesus, Westchester
Springer, Timothy, St. Jude the Apostle, South Holland
Stalcup, Joseph Sr., St. Fabian, Bridgeview
Stanton, Paul, St. Isaac Jogues, Niles
Stasinski, Melvin, St. Jude the Apostle, South Holland
Stearns, William, St. Damian, Oak Forest
Stecker, Stephen, St. Alphonsus Liguori, Prospect Hts.
Steinbeigle, Francis, (Retired), Oak Forest
Stricker, Ronald, St. Ita, Chicago
Strohm, Keith F., Queen of the Rosary, Elk Grove Village
Strom, Stanley, Holy Name Cathedral, Chicago
Sullivan, Dwight, St. Eulalia, Maywood
Sullivan, Timothy P., St. Clement, Chicago
Sullivan, William L., (Retired), Chicago
Sullivan, William T., St. Louis De Montfort, Oak Lawn
Sutton, Daniel, (Retired), Oak Lawn, IL
Swiatek, Ronald, St. John Bosco, Chicago
Szarzynski, Douglas, St. James at Sag Bridge, Lemont

Szostak, Jerrold S., Queen of the Rosary, Elk Grove Village
Tatara, Allen, St. Hubert, Hoffman Estates
Tecruceno, Cornelio, San Jose Luis Sanchez del Rio, Chicago
Telle, Paul, (Retired), Park City, IL
Than, Joseph T., St. Henry, Chicago
Thomas, Robert J., St. Mary, Lake Forest
Thompson, James, St. Mary of the Woods, Chicago
Tiemeier, David, St. Joseph, Libertyville
Tipperreiter, Charles, St. Fabian, Bridgeview
Tomkowiak, Edward, St. Patrick, Wadsworth
Towey, Anthony, St. Stephen Protomartyr, Des Plaines
Trakszelis, Jerome J., St. Vincent Ferrer, River Forest
Trejo, Raul, St. Colette, Rolling Meadows
Troy, Daniel J., (Retired)
Truesdale, Joseph, St. George, Tinley Park
Trujillo, Abel B., St. Michael, Orland Park
Tylutki, Glenn, St. Mary of the Angels, Chicago
Urquiza, Rodolfo, St. Hedwig, Chicago
Valadez, Abundio, St. Benedict, Blue Island
Valadez, Juan, Mary, Mother of Mercy, Chicago
Valdez, Joseph Tony R., St. Martha, Morton Grove
Valdivia, Juan, (Retired)
Valencia, Juan, St. Pius X, Stickney
Valle, Miguel A., St. Wenceslaus, Chicago
Van Merkestyn, Peter, St. Stephen, Deacon and Martyr, Tinley Park
Vargas, Miguel, Shrine of Our Lady of Guadalupe, Des Plaines
Vasek, Emil, St. Kieran, Chicago Heights
Vazquez, Gilberto, Santa Maria Del Popolo, Mundelein
Vazquez, Jose, San Jose Luis Sanchez del Rio, Chicago
Vidmar, John, Bl. A.M. Slomsek Slovenian Catholic Mission, Lemont
Vignocchi, Louis, Immaculate Conception, Highland Park
Villa, Salvatore, St. Bruno, Chicago
Villalobos, Antonio, (Retired), Chicago
Villasenor, Faustino, St. Genevieve, Chicago, IL
Virruso, Christopher, Our Lady Mother of the Church, Chicago
Voytas, Richard, St. Daniel the Prophet, Chicago
Wagner, Steve J., St. Thecla, Chicago
Walters, John, Mother Theodore Guerin, Elmwood Park
Warfield, Richard, (Retired), Orland Park
Warmouth, William H., St. Stephen Protomartyr, Des Plaines
Watson, Dexter, St. Malachy + Precious Blood, Chicago
Webster, Gregory, St. Raphael the Archangel, Old Mill Creek
Wehling, Donald, St. Hilary, Chicago
Weiland, Christopher, Our Lady of Perpetual Help, Glenview
Weitendorf, Norbert, St. Patricia, Hickory Hills
Welter, Daniel G., J.D., Holy Name Cathedral, Chicago
Werner, Richard, Sacred Heart, Palos Hills
Westerkamp, Thomas, St. James, Arlington Heights
Wilkinson, John M., St. James at Sag Bridge, Lemont
Willer, Richard, St. Thomas of Villanova, Palatine
Winblad, Joseph, St. Patrick, Lemont
Winter, Edward, St. Lawrence O'Toole, Matteson
Wogan, James, St. Mary of Vernon, Indian Creek
Wojnar, Conrad, St. Stephen Protomartyr, Des Plaines
Yannotta, Joseph, St. Edna, Arlington Heights
Zajdel, Kevin, Assumption, Chicago
Zanardo, Ronald, (Retired), Inverness, IL
Zaragoza, Luis, Mision San Juan Diego, Arlington Heights, IL
Zawadzki, Kenneth, St. Stephen, Deacon & Martyr, Tinley Park
Zeifert, Gregory, Our Lady of Lakes, Ingleside
Zeimys, Erik, Nativity of Our Lord, Chicago
Zielinski, Ronald, St. Fabian, Bridgeview
Zima, Robert, (Retired), Winter Garden, FL
Zwolski, Mark, St. Mary of Vernon, Indian Creek
Zych, Gerald, St. Giles, Oak Park.

INSTITUTIONS LOCATED IN DIOCESE

[A] SEMINARIES, ARCHDIOCESAN

CHICAGO. *St. Joseph College Seminary*, 1120 W. Loyola Ave., 60626-6198. Tel: 773-973-9700; Fax: 773-973-9750; Email: pam.ferrarini@cometojoseph.org; Web: www.cometojoseph.com. Very Rev. Peter Snieg Jr., S.T.L., Pres.; Ms. Pamela Ferrarini, Admin.; Revs. Tom Krettek, Dean; Matthew Alexander, Dir.; Robert S. Flack, S.J., Dir.; Daniel A. Flens, Dir.; Dr. Christian Stirling, Dir.; Mrs. Dawn Zamora, Dir.; Revs. Britto Berchmans, Ph.D.; Timothy R. Fiala, S.T.L.; Mariusz P. Stefanowski; Mr. Alberto Bertozzi; Mrs. Diana Kozojed; Mrs. Yuvanka Zavala-Juarez, B.A. Clergy 3; Lay Teachers 2; Priests 5; Students 25; Clergy / Religious Teachers 3.

MUNDELEIN. *University of Saint Mary of the Lake / Mundelein Seminary*, 1000 E. Maple Ave., Mundelein, 60060-1174. Tel: 847-566-6401; Fax: 847-566-7330; Email: jkartje@usml.edu; Web: www.usml.edu. Very Revs. John F. Kartje, Ph.D., S.T.D., Rector; Thomas A. Baima, S.T.D., M.B.A., Vice Rector; Rev. Brian T. Welter, M.Div., Vice Rector; Mr. John Lehocky, C.P.A., M.B.A., Vice Pres. Fin.; Mr. Jim Heinen, COO; Dr. Deborah Armenta, Assoc. Dean of Formation; Revs. August J. Belauskas, M.A., S.T.L., Assoc. Dean of Formation; Thomas Byrne, Assoc. Dean of Formation; Sr. Judith Anne Haase, O.P., Assoc. Dean of Formation; Rev. Dennis Kasule, S.T.D., Assoc. Dean Formation; Ms. Patricia Klein, M.A., Assoc. Dean Formation; Sr. Kathleen Mitchell, Assoc. Dean of Formation; Rev. Edward S. Pelrine, Assoc. Dean of Formation; Deacon Pat Quagliana, Assoc. Dean of Formation; Revs. Elmer Romero, M.Div., Assoc. Dean Formation; Dennis Spies, S.T.L., M.Div., Assoc. Dean of Formation; Marie Pitt-Payne, Asst. Dean; Ms. Linda Cerabona, M.A., Dir. of Music; Ms. Linda Couri, M.S.W., L.C.S.W., D.Min. (cand.), Dir.; Mr. Thomas Dougherty, Dir. for Center for Speech & Writing; Ms. Nelly Lorenzo, M.Div., Dir.; Deacon Robert Puhala, M.A., Dir. of Deacon Formation; Revs. Carlos Rodriguez, M.Div., Dir.; Bradley Angelo Zamora, M.Div., Liturgy Dir.; Dr. Christopher Rogers, Library Dir.; Revs. Joseph C. Henchey, C.S.S., S.T.D., Adjunct Spiritual Dir.; Emery de Gaal, Prof.; Lawrence R. Hennessey, M.A., S.T.L., Ph.D., Prof.; Dr. Matthew Levering, Prof.; Rev. John G. Lodge, S.S.L., S.T.D., Prof.; Dr. Elizabeth Sung, Prof.; Revs. Raymond J. Webb, S.T.L., Ph.D., Prof.; Patrick M. Boyle, O.S.M., Assoc. Prof.; Sr. Mila Diaz Solano, Assoc. Prof.; Dr. Denis R. McNamara, Ph.D., Assoc. Prof.; Rev. Robert Schoenstene, Assoc. Prof.; Dr. Steven Smith, Assoc. Prof.; Revs. Martin Zielinski, M.Div., Ph.D., Assoc. Prof.; Marek J. Duran, S.T.L., S.T.D., Asst. Prof.; W. Scott Hebden, Asst. Prof.; Dr. Paul Hillard, Asst. Prof.; Revs. Ronald T. Kunkel, S.T.D., Asst. Prof.; Brendan P. Lupton, S.T.D., Pres., Pontifical Faculty; David Olson, Asst. Prof.; Patricia Pintado-Murphy, Ph.D., Asst. Prof.; Revs. David Mowry, Instructor; Daniel S. Siwek, S.T.L., Instructor. Clergy 25; Lay Teachers 11; Priests 26; Seminarians 200; Students 400; Clergy / Religious Teachers 3.

The Liturgical Institute, 1000 E. Maple Ave., Mundelein, 60060. Tel: 847-837-4542; Fax: 847-837-4545; Web: www.liturgicalinstitute.org. Very Rev. Thomas A. Baima, S.T.D., M.B.A., Acting Dir.; Dr. Denis R. McNamara, Ph.D., Assoc. Dir.; Jesse Weiler, Assoc. Dir. Mktg. & Comm.; Kevin Thornton, Publications Mgr.

Ministry Formation, 1000 E. Maple Ave., Mundelein, 60060-1174. Tel: 847-970-4866; Fax: 847-932-3305. Very Rev. Thomas A. Baima, S.T.D., M.B.A., Archbishop's Liaison Formation Progs.

Institute for Diaconal Studies, 1000 E. Maple Ave., Mundelein, 60060-1174. Tel: 847-837-4563; Fax: 847-837-4565. Deacon Robert Puhala, M.A., Dir.; Rev. Bernard Kennedy, O.F.M., M.Div., Dir. Spiritual Formation; Ms. Katarzyna Kasiarz, M.A., Assoc. Dir.

Instituto De Liderazgo Pastoral (Hispanic Programs for Lay Ministry and Permanent Diaconate), 1000 E. Maple Ave., Mundelein, 60060-1174. Tel: 847-837-4556; Fax: 847-837-4565. Ms. Nelly Lorenzo, M.Div., Dir.; Rev. Gerardo Carcar, (Paraguay) Dir. of Spiritual Formation; Graciela Contreras, Asst. Dir.; Daniel Ramirez-Florez, S.T.L., Assoc. Dir.; Luz Alvarez, Assoc. Dir.; Aura Martinez, Assoc. DIr.

Institute for Lay Formation, 1000 E. Maple Ave., Mundelein, 60060-1174. Tel: 847-837-4550; Fax: 847-837-4565. Ms. Linda Couri, M.S.W., L.C.S.W., D.Min. (cand.), Dir.; Ms. Catherine S. Sims, M.Div., Assoc. Dir.; Mr. Bob Alexander, Assoc. Dir.

Conference Center, 1000 E. Maple Ave., Mundelein, 60060-1174. Tel: 847-837-4505; Fax: 847-837-4505. Michelle Perez, Dir.

Institute for Ongoing Formation, 1000 E. Maple Ave., Mundelein, 60060-1174. Tel: 847-837-4558; Fax: 847-837-4565. Ms. Megan Diechl, M.A.P.S., Assoc. Dir.

Feehan Memorial Library.

[B] SEMINARIES, RELIGIOUS OR SCHOLASTICATES

CHICAGO. *Catholic Theological Union*, 5401 S. Cornell Ave., 60615. Tel: 773-371-5400; Fax: 773-324-8490; Web: www.ctu.edu. Rev. Mark R. Francis, C.S.V., Pres.; Mr. Michael W. Connors, C.P.A., Vice Pres. Admin. & Fin.; Colleen Kennedy, Vice Pres.; Ms. Regina Wolfe, Ph.D., Vice Pres. & Prof.; Ronald Brown, Dir.; Marian Diaz, Dir.; Rev. Edward Foley, O.F.M.Cap., Dir.; Christine Henderson, Dir.; Rachel Kuhn, Dir.; Mr. Marco Lopez, Dir.; Ms. Kimberly Lymore, Dir.; Mr. Richard Mauney, Dir.; Steve Millies, Dir.; Ms. Carmen Nanko-Fernandez, D.Min., Dir.; Rev. John M. Pawlikowski, O.S.M., Ph.D., Dir.; Sr. Lucianne Siers, Dir.; Kellene Urbaniak, Dir.; Kris Veldheer, Dir.; Ms. Vanessa White, M.T.S., Dir.; Diane Healy, Business Mgr.; Mrs. Maria de Jesus Lemus, Registrar; Rev. John Barker, O.F.M., Prof.; Sr. Dianne Bergant, C.S.A., Ph.D., Prof.; Rev. Stephen B. Bevans, S.V.D., Prof.; Sisters Maria Cimperman, R.S.C.J., Prof.; Mary Frohlich, R.S.C.J., Ph.D., Prof.; Rev. Anthony Gittins, C.S.Sp., Ph.D., Prof.; Mr. Richard E. McCarron, Ph.D., Prof.; Sr. Dawn Nothwehr, O.S.F., Ph. D., Prof.; Rev. Gilbert Ostdiek, O.F.M., S.T.D., Prof.; Sr. Barbara Reid, O.P., Ph.D., Prof. New Testament Studies; Revs. Robert Schreiter, C.PP.S., Th.D., Prof.; Roger P. Schroeder, S.V.D., Prof.; Donald P. Senior, C.P., S.T.D., Prof.; Antonio Sison, C.PP.S., Prof.; Mr. Scott C. Alexander, Ph.D.; Mr. Michel Andraos, Ph.D.; Sr. Laurie A. Brink, O.P.; Ms. Eileen Crowley, Ph.D.; Revs. Richard Fragomeni, Ph.D.; vanThanh Nguyen, S.V.D. Major Seminary. Serving the following: Franciscans, Servites, Passionists, Augustinians, Norbertines, Society of the Divine Word, Missionaries of the Precious Blood, Claretians, Crosier Fathers, Spiritans, Missionaries of the Sacred Heart, Viatorians, Redemptorists, Maryknoll, Blessed Sacrament Clergy 15; Lay Teachers 10; Priests 13; Sisters 8; Students 310; Lay Administrators 15; Non-Catholic Clergy 1; Clergy / Religious Teachers 19.

[C] COLLEGES AND UNIVERSITIES

CHICAGO. *De Paul University*, One E. Jackson Blvd., 60604. Tel: 312-362-8000; Email: eudovic@depaul.edu; Web: www.depaul.edu. Revs. Dennis H. Holtschneider, C.M., Chancellor; Edward R. Udovic, C.M., Sec. of the Univ.; Mr. Jeff Bethke, Exec. Vice Pres. & CFO; Dr. Marten denBoer, Provost; Dan Allen, Vice Pres. for Advancement; Erin Archer, Treas.; Steve Stoute, Chief of Staff; A. Gabriel Esteban, Pres.; Linda Blakley, Vice Pres. for Public Relations and Communications; Mr. Robert Janis, Vice Pres. Facility Operations; Dr. David Kalsbeek, Senior Vice Pres. for Enrollment Management and Marketing; Mr. Robert McCormick, Vice Pres. Information Svcs.; Dr. Elizabeth Ortiz, Vice Pres. for Institutional Diversity and Equity; Mr. Jose D. Padilla, Vice Pres. and General Counsel; Sherri Sidler, Controller; Ms. Stephanie Smith, Vice Pres. for Human Resources; Dr. Gene Zdziarski, Vice Pres. of Student Affairs. Sponsored by the Congregation of the Mission (Vincentian Fathers and Brothers).Campuses: Downtown, Lincoln Park, Oak Forest, Naperville, Rolling Meadows. Faculty 914; Students 22,769; University Staff 1,590.

Administrative Officers of the University: Mr. Jose D. Padilla, Vice Pres. and General Counsel; Mr. Santino Caringella, Treas.; Dr. Gene Zdziarski, Vice Pres. Student Affairs; Mr. Robert Janis, Vice Pres. Facilities Operations; Dr. David Kalsbeek, Senior Vice Pres. Enrollment Mgmt. & Mktg.; Linda Blakley, Vice Pres. Public Relations & Communications; Mr. Robert McCormick, Vice Pres. Information Svcs.; Ms. Stephanie Smith, Vice Pres. Human Resources; Dr. Jay Braatz, Senior Exec.& Vice Pres., Planning & Presidential Admin.; Ms. Erin Minne, Senior Vice Pres., Advancement; Dr. Elizabeth Ortiz, Vice Pres. Institutional Diversity & Equity; Rev. Edward R. Udovic, C.M., Sr. Exec. Univ. Mission & Vice Pres. Teaching & Learning Resources; Sherri Sidler, Controller.

College of Liberal Arts and Sciences, 990 W. Fullerton Ave., Ste. 4200, 60614. Tel: 773-325-7310; Fax: 773-325-7304. Dr. Guillermo Vasquez de Velasco, Dean.

College of Law, 931 Lewis Center, 25 E. Jackson Blvd., 60604. Tel: 312-362-8701; Fax: 312-362-5826. Ms. Jennifer Rosato Perea, Dean.

Kellstadt Graduate School of Business Driehaus College of Business, 7103 DePaul Center, One E. Jackson Blvd., 60604. Tel: 312-362-6783; Fax: 312-362-6677. Misty Johanson, Interim Dean.

College of Communication, 14 E. Jackson Blvd., Ste. 1800, 60604. Tel: 312-362-8000; Fax: 312-362-7584. Dr. Salma Ghanem, Dean.

School of Music, 200 Music Bldg., 804 W. Belden, 60614. Tel: 773-325-7260; Fax: 773-325-7263. Dr. Ronald Caltabiano, Dean.

School for New Learning, 14 E. Jackson Blvd., 60604. Tel: 312-362-8001; Fax: 312-362-8809. Don Opitz, Dean.

College of Computing and Digital Media, 243 S. Wabash Ave., 60604-2302. Tel: 312-362-8381. Dr. David Miller, Dean.

College of Science and Health, 1110 W. Belden Ave., 60614. Tel: 773-325-8300. Dorothy Kozlowski, Interim Dean.

The Theatre School, 2135 N. Kenmore Ave., 60614. Tel: 773-325-7917. Mr. John Culbert, Dean.

College of Education, 2320 N. Kenmore Ave., 60614. Tel: 773-325-7740. Dr. Paul Zionts, Dean.

Jesuit Community at Loyola University Chicago, 6324 N. Kenmore, 60660. Tel: 773-508-8800; Fax: 773-508-2098; Email: lujc.minister@gmail.com; Web: www.luc.edu. Revs. G. Krettek, Dean; Thomas J. Regan, S.J., Dean; David A. Godleski, S.J., Supr.; John J. O'Callaghan, S.J., S.T.D., Supr.; Stephen N. Katsouros, S.J., Dir.; Robert S. Flack, S.J., Dir. Spiritual Life; James S. Prehn, S.J., Rector; John Belmonte, S.J., Supt.; Mark W. Andrews, S.J., Pastoral Min./Coord; Daniel F. Hartnett, S.J., Pastoral Min.; Thomas Chillikulam, Campus Min.; Michael Christiana, Campus Min.; Mitchell C. Pacwa, S.J., Television Ministry; John F. Costello, S.J., Special Asst. to Pres.; Glen Chun, S.J., Prov. Asst.; James A. Stoeger, S.J., Prov. Asst.; Patrick Tyrrell, S.J.; William E. Creed, S.J., Chap.; Mark G. Henninger, S.J., Chap.; Tuan Le, S.J., Chap.; Dennis McNeilly, Chap.; T. Jerome Overbeck, S.J., Chap.; Peter J. Bernardi, S.J., Prof.; Peter W. Breslin, S.J., Prof.; David G. DeMarco, S.J., Prof.; D. Scott Hendrickson, S.J., Prof.; Charles Jurgensmeier, S.J., Prof.; John M. McManamon, S.J., Prof.; Jose A. Mesa, S.J., Prof.; Stephen F. Mitten, S.J., Prof.; Keith F. Muccino, S.J., Prof.; James G. Murphy, S.J., Prof.; Stephen Schloesser, S.J., Prof.; Thomas H. Tobin, S.J., Prof.; Patrick M. Boyle, O.S.M., Prof.; Harry J. Gensler, S.J., Prof.; Frank LaRocca, S.J., Prof.; Peter Banda, Graduate Student; Bernard Jado, Graduate Student; Pravid Severekar, Graduate Student; Tho Vu, Graduate Student; Cristian Contreras, Graduate Student; Marlon Innis, Graduate Student; Junseong Park, S.J., Graduate Student; Mamy Randriamanantena, S.J., Graduate Student; Gail G. Bohr, S.J.; Paul J. Faulstich, S.J.; John J. Foley, S.J.; John J. Kilgallen, S.J.

The Jesuit Community Corporation at Loyola University Clergy 44; Priests 30; Sisters 3; Students 16,429; Full Time Faculty 1,674; Clergy / Religious Teachers 44.

**Loyola University-Chicago*, 1032 W. Sheridan Rd., 60660. Tel: 773-274-3000; Web: www.luc.edu. Mr. Robert Parkinson Jr., Chm.

Loyola University of Chicago, Illinois Students 17,007; Total Enrollment 17,007; Clergy / Religious Teachers 28.

President's Office, 820 N. Michigan Ave., 60611. Tel: 312-915-6400; Fax: 312-915-6414; Email: president@luc.edu; Web: www.luc.edu. Ms. Erin Moriarty, Dean of Admissions; Rev. Patrick M. Boyle, O.S.M., Vice Provost Global Initiatives; Ms. Pamela G. Costas Esq., Vice Pres. & Gen. Counsel; Mr. Thomas M. Kelly, Sr. Vice Pres. Administrative Svcs.; Mr. Wayne Magdziarz, Sr. Vice Pres. & Capital Planning & Campus Mgmt.; Jane Neufeld, Vice Pres. Student Devel.; Rev. James S. Prehn, S.J., Vice Pres., Chief of Staff; Mr. Paul Roberts, M.B.A., Vice Pres., Enrollment Mgmt. & Student Success; Mr. Philip D. Hale, Vice Pres. Govt. Affairs; Kana Henning, Assoc. Vice Pres. Facilities Mgmt.; Badia Ahad, Faculty Dir. of Univ. Core Curriculum; Richard Albright, Dir. of Vietnam Center; Michael Andrews, Dir. of Rome Center; Gabrielle Buckley, Dir. of Gannon Center for Woman & Leadership; Anthony Cardoza, Dir. of Ricci Scholars Prog.; Jennifer Engel, Exec. Dir for the Office of Intl. Prog,; Mr. Tobyn Friar, Dir. of Fin. Aid; Patrick Green, Exec. Dir. for the Center of Experiential Learning; Timothy Heuer, Dir. of Enrollment Systems, Research & Reporting; Claudio Katz, Faculty Dir. of the Intersciplinary Honors Prog.; Virginia Ginny McCarthy, Dir. of Campus Min., Medical School; Michael Murphy, Dir. of Hank Center for the Catholic Intellectual Heritage; Lisa Reiter, Ph.D., Dir. Campus Ministry, Lake Shore Campus; Anne Reuland, Asst. Provost & Dir. of Faculty Admin.; Brigid Schultz, Faculty Dir. of Dual Credit Prog.; Jill Schur, Dir. of Graduate & Professional Enrollment Mgmt.; Rachel Shefner, Assoc. Dir. of Center for Science & Math Education; Adam Shorter III, Dir. of Fin. & Opers.; Heather Taylor, Dir. of Enrollment Mktg.; Matthew Thibeau, Interim Dir. for Ignation Pedagogy; Ping Tsui, Interim Dir. of Inst. Effectiveness; Fraser Turner, Dir. of the Office of Global Initiatives; Angelina Vaca, Dir. of the Office of Research Svcs.; David Van Zytveld, Dir. of Center for Urban Research & Learning; Dr. Margaret Callahan, Ph. D., Acting Provost Academic Affairs; Shawna Cooper-Gibson, Asst. Provost for Student Academic Svcs,; Jo Beth D'Agostino, Assoc. Provost for Academic Prog. & Planning; Dr. John Frendreis, Special Asst. for Collective Bargaining Agreement; Christopher Manning, Asst. Provost for Academic Diversity; Joanna Pappas, Assoc. Provost for Fin. & Opers.; Rita Vazquez, Univ. Registrar; Mr. Robert Parkinson Jr., Bd. Chm.; Dr. John J. Hardt, Ph.D., Assoc. Provost Mission & Identity; Dr. Richard S. Hurst, Ph.D., Dir. Inst. Research; Ms. Claire Korinek, Dir. Registration & Records; Ms. Diane Hullinger, Sr. Assoc. Registrar; Mr. Damon Cates, Sr. Vice Pres.; Ms. Colleen Newquist, Vice Pres. University Mktg.&Communications.

The following are the Schools and Colleges which compose the University:.

The College of Arts and Sciences (1870) 1032 W. Sheridan Rd., 60660. Tel: 773-508-3500; Fax: 773-508-3514; Email: casloyola@luc.edu; Web: www.luc.edu/cas. Rev. Thomas J. Regan, S.J., Dean. Students 6,802; Clergy / Religious Teachers 28.

The School of Law (1908) 25 E. Pearson St., 60611. Fax: 312-915-7906; Web: www.luc.edu/law. Michael Kaufman, J.D., Dean. Students 1,111.

Loyola University Stritch School of Medicine (1909) 2160 S. First Ave., Maywood, 60153. Tel: 708-216-3229; Email: ssom-admissions@luc.edu; Web: www.ssom.luc.edu. Dr. Steve Goldstein, Dean & Chief Diversity Officer, Stritch School of Medicine; Rev. Keith F. Muccino, S.J., Asst. Provost for Educ. Resources; Greg Gruener, Vice Dean of Education; Mitch Denning, Vice Dean for Research; Leanne Cribbs, Assoc. Dean of Graduate Programs; James Mendez, Assoc. Dean for Student Affairs; Freager Williams, Interim Asst. Dean for Diversity & Inclusion; Lee Schmidt, Sr. Assoc Dean for Educ.; Karen Saban, Assoc. Dean of Graduate Prog.; Janet Campbell, Dir. of Student Affairs; Edward Gricius, Dir. of Student Affairs, NSON; Gail Hendler, Dir. of Health Sciences Library; Donna Quinones, Dir. for Simulation Educ.; Antonio Valero, Dir. of Animal Research Protection; Ruben Mestril, Dir. of Research Integrity; Matt Hejna, Dir. of Safety Compliance; Martha King, Dir. of Faculty Admin.; Ron Price, Assoc. Vice Pres. for Informatics & System Devel. Students 662.

School of Social Work (1914) 1 E. Pearson St., 60611. Tel: 312-915-7005; Email: admission@luc.edu; Web: www.luc.edu/socialwork/admission/undergrad. 820 N. Michigan Ave., 60611. Dr. Goutham Menon, Dean. Students 671.

School of Continuing & Professional Studies, 820 N. Michigan Ave., 60611. Tel: 312-915-8900; Web: www.luc.edu/adult-education. Jeanne Widen, Dean. Students 370.

The Quinlan School of Business (1922) 820 N. Michigan Ave., 60611. Tel: 312-915-6113; Fax: 312-915-6118; Email: Quinlanubus@luc.edu. Kevin T. Stevens, DBA, Dean. Students 2,641.

The Graduate School (1926) 1032 W. Sheridan Rd., 60660. Tel: 773-508-3396; Email: admissions@luc.edu; Web: www.luc.edu/gradschool. Rev. Thomas Regan, S.J., Ph.D., Interim Dean. Students 1,246.

The School of Nursing (1935) 1032 W. Sheridan Rd., 60660. Tel: 773-508-3249; Email: schoolofnursing@luc.edu; Web: www.luc.edu/nursing. Dr. Vicki Keough, R.N., Ph.D., Dean. Students 1,235.

The School of Education (1969) 820 N. Michigan Ave., 60611. Tel: 312-915-6800; Fax: 312-915-6660 ; Email: SchlEduc@luc.edu; Web: www.luc.edu/education. Dr. David Slavsky, Interim Dean. Students 758.

School of Communication (2008) 820 N. Michigan Ave., 60611. Tel: 312-915-6548; Fax: 312-915-8593 ; Web: www.luc.edu/soc. John Slania, Dean. Students 817.

Arrupe College, 820 N. Michigan Ave., 60611. Tel: 800-262-2373; Email: arrupeadmission@luc.edu; Web: www.luc.edu/arrupe. Rev. Stephen N. Katsouros, S.J., Dean. Students 349.

**Resurrection University*, 1431 N. Claremont Ave., 60622.

Saint Xavier University, 3700 W. 103rd St., 60655-3105. Tel: 773-298-3000; Fax: 773-779-9061; Web: www.sxu.edu. Christine M. Wiseman, J.D., Pres. Sponsorship: Institute of the Sisters of Mercy of the Americas.Campus locations: Chicago & Orland Park. Full-Time 173; Part-Time 258; Sisters 1; Students 3,887; Staff 248.

Administrative Officers of the University: Kathleen Alaimo, Ph.D., Interim Provost; Anthony Campbell, Ph.D., Vice Pres. Student Affairs & Dean, Students; Joan Knox, Assoc. Pres. University & Community Relations, Vice Pres. Univ. & Community Relations; Robert H. Fisher, M.B.A., CFO; Kathleen A. Rinehart, J.D., Gen. Counsel & Sec. Corporation, Email: rinehart@sxu.edu; John R. Bass, Assoc. Vice Pres. Univ. Advancement; Graziano Marcheschi, D.Min., Vice Pres. Univ. Mission & Ministry; Deborah Rodriguez, Assoc. Vice Pres. Mktg. & Communications.

College of Arts and Sciences, Tel: 773-298-3091; Fax: 773-298-3872. Greg Coutts, Ph.D., Interim Dean.

School of Nursing, Tel: 773-298-3701; Fax: 773-298-3704. Gloria Jacobson, R.N., Ph.D., Dean, Email: jacobson@sxu.edu.

Graham School of Management, Tel: 773-298-3600; Fax: 773-298-3610. Asghar Sabbaghi, Ph.D., Dean.

School of Education, Tel: 773-298-3200; Fax: 773-298-3201. E. Suzanne Lee, Ph.D., Interim Dean.

Graduate and Continuing Education, Tel: 708-802-6205; Fax: 708-802-6202. Becky Copper-Glenz, Ed.D., Dean.

RIVER FOREST. *Dominican University (Formerly Rosary College)*, 7900 W. Division St., River Forest, 60305. Tel: 708-366-2490; Fax: 708-524-5990; Email: webmaster@email.dom.edu; Web: www.dom.edu. Dr. Donna M. Carroll, Pres.; Sr. Jean Crapo, O.P., Prioress; Dr. Jeffrey R. Breese, Provost & Vice Pres. Academic Affairs; Ms. Amy McCormack, Senior Vice Pres. Finance & Admin. Dominican Sisters of Sinsinawa, WI.

Dominican University Faculty 167; Priests 1; Sisters 6; Total Enrollment 3,676; Staff 224.

Rosary College of Arts and Sciences at Dominican University, Tel: 708-524-6816; Fax: 708-524-5990. Dr. Jeffrey Carlson, Assoc. Provost Undergraduate Education & Dean.

Brennan School of Business, Tel: 708-524-6810; Fax: 708-524-6939. Dr. Roberto Curci, Dean.

School of Education, Tel: 708-524-6922; Fax: 708-524-6665. Therese Hogan, Div. Chair.

Graduate School of Library and Information Science, Tel: 708-524-6845; Fax: 708-524-6657. Dr. Kate Marek, Dean.

Graduate School of Social Work, Tel: 708-366-3463; Fax: 708-366-3446. Dr. Charles Stoops Jr., Dean.

School of Professional and Continuing Studies, Tel: 708-714-9125; Fax: 708-714-9126. Mr. Matt Hlinak, Asst. Provost.

[D] HIGH SCHOOLS, PRIVATE

CHICAGO. *Brother Rice High School*, 10001 S. Pulaski Rd., 60655-3356. Tel: 773-429-4300; Fax: 773-779-5239; Email: kburns@brrice.org; Web: www.brotherrice.org. Dr. Kevin Burns, Pres.; Mr. James P. Antos, Prin.; Ms. Beverly Buciak, Librarian. Congregation of Christian Brothers & Edmund Rice Brothers. Brothers 1; Lay Teachers 52; Priests 1; Students 740.

Christ the King Jesuit College Preparatory School, 5088 W. Jackson Blvd., 60644. Tel: 773-261-7505; Fax: 773-261-7507; Email: cmartin@ctkjesuit.org; Web: www.ctkjesuit.org. Clement V. Martin, Pres.; Temple Payne, Prin. Participant in the Cristo Rey Work/Study Program, Inc. Lay Teachers 24; Priests 1; Students 353.

Cristo Rey Jesuit High School, Inc., 1852 W. 22nd Pl., 60608. Tel: 773-890-6800; Fax: 773-890-6801; Email: info@cristorey.net; Web: www.cristorey.net. Antonio Ortiz, Pres.; Lucas Schroeder, Prin. Lay Teachers 30; Priests 1; Sisters 1; Students 600; Clergy / Religious Teachers 1.

Cristo Rey Work/Study Program, Inc., 1852 W. 22nd Pl., 60608. Tel: 773-890-6800; Fax: 773-890-6880; Email: lsellers@cristorey.net. Lillie Sellers, Dir.

De La Salle Institute, 3434 S. Michigan Ave., 60616. Tel: 312-842-7355; Email: webmaster@dls.org; Web: www.dls.org. Mrs. Diane Brown, Prin.; Rev. Paul E. Novak, O.S.M., Pres. Brothers of the Christian Schools.

De La Salle Institute Brothers 1; Lay Teachers 60; Students 825.

DePaul College Prep, 3633 N. California Ave., 60618-4602. Tel: 773-539-3600; Fax: 773-539-9158; Email: lpilcher@depaulprep.org; Email: mdempsey@depaulprep.org; Web: www.depaulprep.org. Ms. Mary Dempsey, Pres.; Dr. Megan Stanton-Anderson, Prin.; Ms. Amy Golden, Dir.; Ms. Lisa Pilcher, Dir.; Ms. Flo Merkl-Deutsch, Dir.; Mr. Patrick Mahoney, Dir.; Ms. Marsha Blake, Business Mgr.; Mr. Patrick Dwyer, Campus Min. Lay Teachers 46; Sisters 1; Students 495; Staff 30.

St. Francis de Sales High School, 10155 S. Ewing Ave., 60617. Tel: 773-731-7272; Fax: 773-731-7888; Email: info@sfdshs.org; Web: www.sfdshs.org. Mary Kay Ramirez, Prin. Lay Teachers 18; Students 183.

**Hales Franciscan High School, Inc.*, 4930 Cottage Grove Ave., 60615. Tel: 773-285-8400; Fax: 773-285-7025. Nichole M. Jackson, Prin.;

Friar Johnpaul Cafiero, O.F.M., D.Min., M.A., M.Div., Trustee of Bd.; Rev. David Rodriguez, O.F.M., M.F.A., Trustee of Bd. Lay Teachers 5; Priests 1; Students 81.

Hales Services, Inc., 4930 S. Cottage Grove, 60615. Tel: 773-285-8400, Ext. 255; Fax: 773-285-7025. Rev. Edouard Kalubi, O.de.M.

Holy Trinity High School, 1443 W. Division St., 60642. Tel: 773-278-4212; Fax: 773-278-0144; Email: mlynch@holytrinity-hs.org; Web: www.holytrinity-hs.org. Mr. Timothy Bopp, Pres.; Ms. Marianne Lynch, Prin. Brothers of Holy Cross. Brothers 1; Lay Teachers 26; Students 290.

St. Ignatius College Prep, 1076 W. Roosevelt Rd., 60608-1594. Tel: 312-421-5900; Fax: 312-421-7124; Email: john.chandler@ignatius.org; Web: www.ignatius.org. Rev. Michael P. Caruso, S.J., Pres.; John. J. Chandler, Vice Pres.; Ms. Brianna Latko, Prin.; Rev. Lukas Laniauskas, Pastoral Min./Coord. Lay Teachers 96; Sisters 1,420; Students 1,390; Clergy / Religious Teachers 3.

St. Ignatius Jesuit Community, 1025 W. Taylor, 60607. Tel: 312-829-2297; Fax: 312-829-9552; Email: dfmastrangelo@gmail.com. Revs. David Mastrangelo, S.J., Supr.; Algis Baniulis, S.J.; Michael P. Caruso, S.J., High School Pres.; Philip J. Grib, S.J., Assoc. Pastor; Lukas Lanaiuskas, S.J., Vice Pres.; Mr. Eric T. Immel, S.S., Asst. Dean, Student Success & Seminarian; Mr. James R. Shea, S.J., Adult Faith Formation; Rev. Bradley M. Schaeffer, S.J., Prov. Asst.; Bro. John L. Moriconi, S.J., Sec. to Prov.; Revs. Keith J. Esenther, S.J., Province Records; Michael Rossmann, Vocation Promoter; Jose Aponte, Graduate Student; Gregory Lynch, Min.; Brian Taber, Teacher; Mr. Patrick Hyland, Teacher; Mr. W. Pierce Gibson IV, Teacher. Lay Teachers 94; Priests 3; Sisters 4; Students 1,450; Clergy / Religious Teachers 5.

Josephinum Academy, 1501 N. Oakley Blvd., 60622. Tel: 773-276-1261; Fax: 773-292-3963; Email: lourdes.weber@josephinum.org; Web: www.josephinum.org. Lourdes Weber, Prin.; Susan McGowan, Librarian. High School (Grades 9-12)

Josephinum, Inc. Girls 205; Lay Teachers 25; Sisters 3.

Leo High School, 7901 S. Sangamon, 60620. Tel: 773-224-9600; Fax: 773-224-3856; Email: admin@leohighschool.org; Web: www.leohighschool.org. Philip Mesina, Prin. Boys 322.

Marist High School, 4200 W. 115th St., 60655-4306. Tel: 773-881-5300; Fax: 773-881-0595; Email: laurencell.karen@marist.net; Web: www.marist.net. Bro. Patrick McNamara, F.M.S., Pres.; Larry N. Tucker, Prin.; Kristen Rademacher, Librarian. Brothers 3; Lay Teachers 116; Students 1,767.

Marist Brothers, Tel: 773-881-5300; Fax: 773-881-0595. Larry N. Tucker, Prin.

Mother McAuley Liberal Arts High School, 3737 W. 99th St., 60655. Tel: 773-881-6500; Fax: 773-881-6562; Email: eboyce@mothermcauley.org; Email: mklingenberger@mothermcauley.org; Web: www.mothermcauley.org. Mary Acker Klingenberger, Pres.; Mrs. Eileen Boyce O'Reilly, Prin. Sisters of Mercy. Lay Teachers 83; Sisters 2; Students 886; Clergy / Religious Teachers 1.

Mount Carmel High School, 6410 S. Dante Ave., 60637. Tel: 773-324-1020; Email: ehughes@mchs.org; Web: www.mchs.org. John Haggerty, Prin.; Mr. Ned Hughes, Pres. Carmelites. Lay Teachers 40; Students 580; Clergy / Religious Teachers 8.

Res.: 6401 S. Harper Ave., 60637. Revs. Leopold Gluckhert, O.Carm.; Benjamin Aguilar, O.Carm.; James Lewis, O.Carm. Lay Teachers 42; Sisters 1; Students 640; Carmelites in Residence 3.

St. Patrick High School, 5900 W. Belmont Ave., 60634. Tel: 773-282-8844; Fax: 773-282-2361; Web: www.stpatrick.org. Dr. Joseph Schmidt, Pres.; Jonathon P. Baffico, Prin.; Mr. Jeffrey Troxell, Asst. Prin.; Ms. Rachele R. Esola, Librarian. Brothers of the Christian Schools.

St. Patrick High School Brothers 2; Lay Teachers 56; Students 700.

Resurrection College Prep High School, 7500 W. Talcott Ave., 60631. Tel: 773-775-6616; Fax: 773-775-0611; Web: www.reshs.org. Sr. Donna Marie Wolowicki, C.R., Pres.; Richard Piwowarski, Prin.; Mrs. Barbara Petrovich, Treas. Sisters of the Resurrection. Girls 465; Lay Teachers 36; Sisters 4; Students 476; Clergy / Religious Teachers 1.

St. Rita of Cascia High School, 7740 S. Western Ave., 60620. Tel: 773-925-6600; Fax: 773-925-2451; Email: strita@stritahs.com; Web: www.stritahs.com. Mr. Ernest J. Mrozek, Pres.; Brendan Conroy, Prin.; Mrs. Robyn Kurnat, Librarian. (See Section N for Monastery listing)

St. Rita of Cascia High School Corporation Brothers 1; Lay Teachers 36; Priests 1; Students 636.

St. Rita of Cascia High School Foundation, 7740 S. Western Ave., 60620. Tel: 773-925-6600; Fax: 773-925-2451; Email: mgallagher@stritahs.com. Mike Gallagher, CFO.

St. Rita of Cascia High School Facilities, Inc., 7740 S. Western Ave., 60620. Tel: 773-925-6600; Fax: 773-925-2451.

ARLINGTON HEIGHTS. *St. Viator High School*, 1213 E. Oakton St., Arlington Heights, 60004. Tel: 847-392-4050; Tel: 224-625-1216; Fax: 847-392-8305; Email: cabrahamian@saintviator.com; Email: cwillard@saintviator.com; Email: bliedlich@saintviator.com; Web: www.saintviator.com. Mr. Brian Liedlich, Pres.; Revs. Daniel R. Hall, C.S.V., Vice Pres.; Arnold E. Perham, C.S.V., Email: aperham@saintviator.com; Charles G. Bolser, C.S.V., Chap.; Bro. Peter N. Lamick, C.S.V.; Mrs. Karen Love, Prin.; Mrs. Catherine Abrahamian, Contact Person. Clerics of St. Viator. Brothers 1; Lay Teachers 75; Priests 4; Students 889; Clergy / Religious Teachers 11.

BURBANK. *St. Laurence High School, Inc.*, 5556 W. 77th St., Burbank, 60459. Tel: 708-458-6900; Fax: 708-458-6908; Email: atucker@stlaurence.com; Web: www.stlaurence.com. Joseph Martinez, Pres.; James C. Muting Jr., Prin. Congregation of Christian Brothers. Brothers 1; Lay Teachers 55; Students 700; Clergy / Religious Teachers 1.

CHICAGO HEIGHTS. *Marian Catholic High School* aka Marian Catholic High School, 700 Ashland Ave., Chicago Heights, 60411. Tel: 708-755-7565; Fax: 708-756-9758; Email: mchsinfo@marianchs.com; Web: www.marianchs.com. Vince Krydynski, Pres.; Steve Tortorello, Prin. Dominican Sisters (Springfield, IL). Lay Teachers 85; Sisters 4; Students 1,001; Clergy / Religious Teachers 1.

DES PLAINES. **Willows Academy*, 1015 Rose Ave., Des Plaines, 60016. Tel: 847-824-6900; Email: petros@willowsacademy.org. Jeanne Petros, Dir.

LAGRANGE PARK. *Nazareth Academy*, 1209 W. Ogden Ave., La Grange Park, 60526. Tel: 708-354-0061; Fax: 708-354-0109; Email: dtracy@nazarethacademy.com; Web: www.nazarethacademy.com. Mrs. Deborah Tracy, Pres.; Therese Hawkins, Prin. Congregation of St. Joseph. Lay Teachers 47; Sisters 1; Students 769.

LAKE FOREST. *Woodlands Academy of the Sacred Heart*, 760 E. Westleigh Rd., Lake Forest, 60045-3298. Tel: 847-234-4300; Fax: 847-234-4348; Email: info@woodlandsacademy.org; Web: www.woodlandsacademy.org. Mr. Gerald Grossman, Head of School; Ms. Madonna L. Edmunds, Prin.; Ms. Ellen Hines, Librarian. Religious of Sacred Heart. Lay Teachers 21; Students 177.

MUNDELEIN. *Carmel Catholic High School*, One Carmel Pkwy., Mundelein, 60060. Tel: 847-566-3000; Fax: 847-566-8465; Email: (name)@carmelhs.org; Web: www.carmelhs.org. Bradley Bonham, Ph.D., Pres.; Mr. Jason Huther, Prin.; Eric Franklin, Librarian; Joseph Nemmers, Chm. Lay Teachers 77; Students 1,145.

NILES. *Notre Dame College Prep.* (Boys) 7655 Dempster St., Niles, 60714. Tel: 847-965-2900; Fax: 847-965-2975; Web: www.nddons.org. Ralph J. Elwart, Pres., Email: relwart@nddons.org; Peter J. Newell, Exec. Chair; Mr. Mick Swanson, Dean of Students, Email: mswanson@nddons.org; Mr. Daniel Tully, Prin., Email: dtully@nddons.org; Mr. Scott L. Dutton, Dir. Campus Ministry, Email: sdutton@nddons.org; Mrs. Fran Pelrine, Asst. Prin. Academics; Ms. MaryAnn Malartsik, Business Mgr., Email: maryann@nddons.org; Mr. Michael Hennessey, Dir. Athletics, Email: mhennessey@nddons.org; Rev. Richard Conyers, C.S.C., Email: rconyers@nddons.org; Mrs. Karyn Kozyra, Fin. Dir. Lay Teachers 67; Priests 2; Sisters 1; Students 800.

OAK PARK. *Fenwick High School*, 505 Washington Blvd., Oak Park, 60302. Tel: 708-386-0127; Fax: 708-386-3052; Email: admin@fenwickfriars.com; Web: www.fenwickfriars.com. Rev. Richard C. LaPata, O.P., Asst. Dir., Annual Funds; Richard Borsch, Dir. of Student Svcs.; Bro. Paul M. Byrd, O.P.; Peter Groom, Prin.; Revs. Joseph Ekpo; Richard A. Peddicord, O.P., Pres.; Michael A. Winkels, O.P.; Dennis C. Woerter, O.P., Dir., Campus Min.; R. Douglas-Adam Greer, O.P.; Nancy M. Bufalino, COO; Rev. Nicholas Monco, O.P.; Elizabeth McKinley, Librarian; Bro. Joseph Trout. Dominican Order. Lay Teachers 86; Students 1,191; Dominican Order Priests 6; Dominican Brothers 2; Diocesan Priests 1.

RIVER FOREST. *Trinity High School*, 7574 W. Division St., River Forest, 60305. Tel: 708-771-8383; Email: micgerm@trinityhs.org; Web: www.trinityhs.org. Noreen Powers, Prin. Dominican Sisters (Sinsinawa, WI). Lay Teachers 45; Sisters 1; Students 491.

RIVER GROVE. *Guerin College Preparatory High School*, 8001 Belmont Ave., River Grove, 60171. Tel: 708-453-6233; Fax: 708-453-6296; Email: sbaldwin@guerinprep.org; Web: www.guerinprep.org. Mr. Steven Baldwin, Pres.; Ms. Karen Booth, Prin.; Sr. Jan Ostrowski, S.P., Librarian. Sisters of Providence. Lay Teachers 50; Sisters 4; Students 435.

WAUKEGAN. *Cristo Rey St. Martin College Prep*, 3106 Bevidere Rd., Waukegan, 60085. Tel: 224-215-9400 ; Fax: 224-219-9737; Email: pkendall@cr-sm.org; Web: www.cr-sm.org. Mr. G. Preston Kendall, Pres., Email: pkendall@cristoreystmartin.org; Mr. Michael Odiotti, Prin., Email: modiotti@cristoreystmartin.org; Marlene Eby, Asst. Prin.; Pierre Edmonds, Dean Students, Email: pedmonds@cristoreystmartin.org; Jim Dippold, Campus Min. Lay Teachers 26; Students 406.

CRSM Work Study, Inc., 3106 Belvidere, Waukegan, 60085. Tel: 847-244-6895; Fax: 847-244-8237; Email: pkendall@cr-sm.org; Web: www.cr-sm.org. Ms. Michelle Mehlis, Dir. of Corporate Work Study.

WESTCHESTER. *St. Joseph High School*, 10900 W. Cermak Rd., Westchester, 60154-4299. Tel: 708-562-4433; Fax: 708-562-4459; Email: ronald.hoover@stjoeshs.org; Web: stjoeshs.org. Bro. Thomas Harding, F.S.C., Pres.; Mr. Ronald Hoover, Prin. De La Salle Christian Brothers. Lay Teachers 24; Students 381.

WILMETTE. *Loyola Academy*, 1100 Laramie Ave., Wilmette, 60091-1021. Tel: 847-256-1100; Fax: 847-251-4031; Email: pmcgrath@loy.org; Email: adabu@loy.org; Web: www.goramblers.org. Rev. Patrick E. McGrath, S.J., Pres.; Charles Heintz, Prin.; Ms. Lauren Bonner, Prin.; Phillip Nieman, Prin.; Ms. Margaret Culhane, Dean of Students; David Behof, Registrar/Institutional Researcher; Geryl Cerney, Controller; Brian Hake, CFO. Lay Teachers 181; Priests 4; Scholastics 1; Students 2,000; Clergy / Religious Teachers 2.

Regina Dominican High School, 701 Locust Rd., Wilmette, 60091. Tel: 847-256-7660; Fax: 847-256-3726; Web: www.rdhs.org. Elizabeth Schuster, Pres.; Kathleen Porreca, Prin. Sisters of St. Dominic (Adrian, MI).(Catholic School for Women) Lay Teachers 31; Sisters 1; Students 250; Clergy / Religious Teachers 4.

[E] ELEMENTARY SCHOOLS, PRIVATE

CHICAGO. *St. Angela School*, 1332 N. Massasoit Ave., 60651-1108. Tel: 773-626-2655; Fax: 773-626-8156; Email: KWittenberg@saintangela.org; Web: www.saintangela.org. Ms. Geralyn Lawler, Prin. Clergy 2; Lay Teachers 15; Students 253.

Chicago Jesuit Academy, (Grades 3-8), at Resurrection Campus, 5058 W. Jackson Blvd., 60644-4324. Tel: 773-638-6103; Fax: 773-638-6107; Email: info@cjacademy.org; Web: www.cjacademy.org. Matthew Lynch, Pres.; Megan Mortensen, Vice Pres.; Mrs. Maria Lefkow Sorenson, Vice Pres.; Thomas Van Grinsven, Vice Pres.; Jenna Boyle, Headmaster; Mr. Thomas Beckley, Prin. Full-scholarship, college prep, Roman Catholic, Jesuit middle school for young men with educational and economic needs on Chicago's West Side; serving 166 3rd-8th graders and 206 alumni through College-Persistence Programs; small class sizes, 9.5-hour day Lay Teachers 20; Students 166; Tot Asst. Annually 372; Total Staff 57.

The Frances Xavier Warde School, 120 S. Des Plaines St., 60661-3515. Tel: 312-466-0700; Fax: 312-466-0711; Email: fxw@fxw.org; Web: www.fxw.org. Mr. Michael Kennedy, Head of School, Email: kennedym@fxw.org; Mrs. Erin Horne, Prin. Old St. Patrick's Campus (Preschool & Kindergarten); Mrs. Danielle Kelly, Prin., Old St. Patrick's Campus (Grades 1-3); Katie Gallagher, Prin. Holy Name Campus (Grades 4-8). Lay Teachers 91; Students 974.

Sacred Heart Schools (Academy of the Sacred Heart for Girls, Hardey Prep. for Boys), (Grades K-8), 6250 N. Sheridan Rd., 60660-1730. Tel: 773-262-4446; Fax: 773-262-6178; Email: sacred.heart@shschicago.org; Web: www.shschicago.org. Mr. Nat Wilburn, Head of Schools; Mrs. Mary Ann Ligon, Head of Lower School, (Grades 3-5); Ms. Carolyn Rownd, Head of Middle School, (Grades 6-8); Ms. Lisa Zimmer, Head of Primary School, (Grades K-2); Mrs. Jean Brunder, Library Media Specialist. Religious of the Sacred Heart. Lay Teachers 58; Students 704.

San Miguel Febres Cordero School, Inc. aka San Miguel School and Community Center, (Grades 6-8), 1954 W. 48th St. 4th Flr., 60609. Tel: 773-890-0233; Fax: 773-304-1984; Web: www.sanmiguelchicago.org. 1936 W. 48th St, 60609. Mr. Eric Serrano, Pres.; Bro. Mark Snodgrass, Prin. Operated by DeLaSalle Christian Brothers. Catholic Middle School for at risk youth; graduate support through high school ; adult education (physical fitness, ESL, financial mgmt., citizenship, and parenting skills); after school youth development programs for ages 11-18. Brothers 1;

Lay Teachers 8; Students 87; Clergy / Religious Teachers 1.

Back of the Yards Campus, 1954 W. 48th St., 60609. Tad Smith, Exec. Dir.

LAKE FOREST. **East Lake Academy*, (Grades PreK-8), 13911 W. Laurel Dr., Lake Forest, 60045. Tel: 847-247-0035; Fax: 847-247-1937; Email: rechavez@eastlakeacademy.org; Web: www.eastlakeacademy.org. Rosario Echavez, Prin. Priests 1; Students 113; Teachers 18.

LEMONT. *Everest Academy of Lemont, Inc.*, 11550 Bell Rd., Lemont, 60439-7417. Tel: 630-243-1995; Fax: 630-243-1988; Email: everestbusinessoffice@everestlemont.com; Web: www.everestadvantage.com. Mary DeRoche, Prin. Clergy 1; Lay Teachers 21; Sisters 1; Students 223; Total Staff 30.

[F] CONSOLIDATED ELEMENTARY SCHOOLS

CHICAGO. *Bridgeport Catholic Academy*, (Grades PreK-8), 3700 S. Lowe, 60609. Tel: 773-376-6223; Email: ckoster@bcachicago.org; Web: www.bcachicago.org. Caroline Koster, Prin. Serving the following parishes: All Saints-St. Anthony (518 W. 28th Pl.); Nativity of Our Lord (653 W. 37th St.). Lay Teachers 15; Students 275.

Northside Catholic Academy, Primary School Campus, 6216 N. Glenwood Ave., 60660. Tel: 773-743-6277; Fax: 773-743-6174; Email: chuzenis@ncaweb.org; Web: www.northsidecatholic.org. Mrs. Christine Huzenis, Prin. Lay Teachers 37; Students 521.

Middle School Campus, 5525 N. Magnolia, 60640-1306. Tel: 773-271-2008; Fax: 773-271-3101. Serving the following parishes: St. Gertrude; St. Ita; St. Ignatius; St. Henry; St. Jerome; St. Gregory.

[G] CATHOLIC CHARITIES

CHICAGO. *Catholic Charities of the Archdiocese of Chicago-Archdiocesan Offices*, 721 N. LaSalle St., 60654. Tel: 312-655-7000; Fax: 312-655-0219; Email: spodder@catholiccharities.net; Web: catholiccharities.net. Steve Podder, Dir.; Rev. Msgr. Michael M. Boland, Admin., Pres. & CEO; Rev. Charles T. Rubey, Assoc. Dir. Programs, (Retired); Ms. Kathy Donahue, Sr. Vice Pres. Prog. Devel. & Evaluation; Ms. Elida Hernandez, C.F.O.; Revs. Richard E. Bulwith, Assoc. Admin., (Retired); Wayne F. Watts, Assoc. Admin.; John J. Ryan, Chief of Staff; Michele Bianchi, Sr. Vice Pres. HR & Gen. Counsel; Rev. Gerard P. Kelly, C.M., Assoc. Admin.

Development, 721 LaSalle St., 60654. Tel: 312-655-7289; Fax: 312-655-0605; Email: jsilekis@catholiccharities.net. Judith M. Silekis, Dir.

Facilities Operations, 721 N. LaSalle St., 60654. Tel: 312-655-7920; Fax: 312-943-8741; Email: spodder@catholiccharities.net. Steve Podder, Dir.

Finance, 721 N. LaSalle St., 60654. Tel: 312-655-7326; Fax: 312-266-4276; Email: ehernand@catholiccharities.net. Ms. Elida Hernandez, Dir.

Human Resources, 721 N. LaSalle St., 60654. Tel: 312-655-7538; Fax: 312-654-0849; Email: mbianchi@catholiccharities.net. Michele Bianchi, Senior Vice Pres.

Government Relations, 721 N. LaSalle, 60654. Tel: 312-655-7020; Fax: 312-654-0849; Email: smjohnson@catholiccharities.net. Stephanie Johnson, Dir.

Legal and Compliance Services, 721 N. LaSalle, 60654. Tel: 312-655-7538; Fax: 312-654-0849; Email: mbianchi@catholiccharities.net. Michele Bianchi, General Counsel.

Board Relations, 721 N. LaSalle St., 60654. Tel: 312-655-8492; Fax: 312-930-0425; Email: drocotel@catholiccharities.net. Dalia Rocotello, Dir.

Communications, 721 N. LaSalle St., 60654. Tel: 312-655-7019; Fax: 312-930-0425; Email: kkappel@catholiccharities.net. Kristin Kappel, Dir.

Performance Quality Improvement and Data Analysis, 721 N. LaSalle, 60654. Tel: 312-655-7305 ; Email: kdonahue@catholiccharities.net. Ms. Kathy Donahue, Dir.

Legal Assistance, 721 N. LaSalle St., 60654. Tel: 312-948-6983; Fax: 312-559-1530 0; Email: hbahena@catholiccharities.net. Hilda Bahena, Dept. Dir.

Housing Development, 721 N. LaSalle St., 60654. Tel: 312-948-6820; Fax: 312-948-6899; Email: asmith@catholiccharities.net. Antwaun L. Smith, Contact Person.

Catholic Charities Housing Development Corporation, 721 N. LaSalle St., 60654. Tel: 312-655-2007; Fax: 312-944-1550; Email: ehiggins@catholiccharities.net. Eileen Higgins, Vice Pres.

Sisters of St. Casimir Center, 2601 W. Marquette Rd., 60629. Tel: 312-655-7920; Fax: 312-943-8741; Email: spodder@catholiccharities.net. Steve Podder, Dir., Facilities.

Cook County Regional Services:.

Chicago Services, 721 N. LaSalle St., 60654. Tel: 312-655-7700; Fax: 312-655-0219; Email: kmulvaney@catholiccharities.net. Kate Mulvaney, Regl. Svc. Rep. Dir.

North Suburban Services, 1717 Rand Rd., Des Plaines, 60016. Tel: 847-376-2100; Fax: 847-390-8214. Karen Daniels, Regl. Svcs. Dir.

Northwest Suburban Services, 1717 Rand Rd., Des Plaines, 60016. Tel: 847-376-2100; Fax: 847-390-8214; Email: mwaters@catholiccharities.net. Michael Waters, Regl. Svcs. Dir.

South Suburban Services, 12732 Wood St., Calumet Park, 60827. Tel: 708-333-8379; Fax: 708-333-9519 ; Email: cltorres@catholiccharities.net. Christopher Torres, Regl. Svcs. Dir.

Southwest Suburban Services, 12731 South Wood St., Blue Island, 60827. Tel: 708-586-1355; Fax: 708-430-0502; Email: cltorres@catholiccharities.net. Christopher Torres, Regl. Svcs. Dir.

West Suburban Services, 1400 S. Austin Blvd., Cicero, 60804. Tel: 708-329-4022; Fax: 708-222-1491; Email: ezepeda@catholiccharities.net. Esmeralda Zepeda, Regl. Svc. Dir.

Lake County Regional Services:.

Joseph Cardinal Bernardin Center for Lake County Services, 671 S. Lewis Ave., Waukegan, 60085. Tel: 847-782-4000; Fax: 847-782-1040; Email: tdenny@catholiccharities.net. Teresa Denny, Senior Dir. LC & Regl. Svcs.

Community Development and Outreach Services:.

Office, 721 N. La Salle, 60654. Tel: 312-655-7508; Fax: 312-642-9716; Email: agutierrez@catholiccharities.net. Angel Gutierrez, Vice Pres.

Community Based Violence Intervention and Prevention Program, 5645 W. Lake St., 60644.

Maternal Child and Health Services:.

Women, Infants and Children (WIC) Food and Nutrition Centers Program, 6202 S. Halsted, 60621. Tel: 773-729-3908; Fax: 773-783-1342; Email: warached@catholiccharities.net. William Abi Rached, Program Dir. WIC Warehouse: 4500 W. Chicago Ave., Chicago, IL 60651, Eric Young, Dir.; WIC Food Centers: 416 E. 43rd St., Chicago, IL 60653; 6202 S. Halsted St., Chicago, IL 60621; 2310 W. Roosevelt Rd., Chicago, IL 60608; 5332 S. Western, Chicago, IL 60609; 3110 W. Armitage, Chicago, IL 60647; 1643 W. Cermak Rd., Chicago, IL 60608; 1734 W. Chicago Ave., Chicago, IL 60622; 3932 W. Madison St., Chicago, IL 60624; 5125 W. Chicago, Chicago, IL 60651; 1802 E. 71st St., Chicago IL 60649; 11255 S. Michigan Ave., Chicago, IL 60628; 4622 W. Diversey Ave., Chicago, IL 60639; 8959 S. Commercial Ave., Chicago, IL 60617; 2400 S. Kedzie Ave., Chicago, IL 60623, 1106 W. 79th St., Chicago, IL 60620 and 2907 S. Wabash Ave., Chicago, IL 60616.

Special Supplemental Food & Nutrition Programs-Senior Programs, Tel: 773-729-3912. Diane Nunley, Assoc. Vice Pres. Congregate Meals; Home Delivered Meals; Summer Food Program; Child Adult Care Food Program (CACFP); Safe Haven.

Senior Food and Nutrition Program (SNFP), 1965 W. Pershing Rd., 60609. Tel: 773-523-5758; Email: eirizarr@catholiccharities.net. Eliu Irizarry, Prog. Dir.

Senior Food and Nutrition Program (SNFP) Warehouse, 1965 W. Pershing Rd., 60609. Tel: 773-523-0299; Email: eirizarr@catholiccharities.net. Eliu Irizarry, Program Dir.

SNFP Distribution Sites:.

Korean Self-Help Center, 4934 N. Pulaski Rd., 60630. Tel: 773-545-8348.

Logan Square Service Center, 3110 W. Armitage Ave., 60647. Tel: 773-395-4207.

Austin Peoples Action Center, 5125 W. Chicago Ave., 60651. Tel: 773-378-8760.

Pilsen Service Center, 1643 W. Cermak Rd., 60608. Tel: 773-523-0409.

Bronzeville Service Center, 2907 S. Wabash Ave., 60616. Tel: 312-326-5020; Email: eirizarr@catholiccharities.net. Eliu Irizarry, Dir.

Englewood Service Center, 6202 S. Halsted, 60621. Tel: 773-488-6800; Email: eirizarr@catholiccharities.net. Eliu Irizarry, Dir.

Southeast Service Center, 8959 S. Commercial Ave., 60617. Tel: 773-978-6235.

Calumet Park Service Center, 12420 S. Ada St., Calumet Park, 60827. Tel: 708-597-7088; Email: eirizarr@catholiccharities.net. Eliu Irizarry, Dir.

St. Blase Service Center, 7438 W. 61st St., Summit, 60501. Tel: 708-563-2407; Email: eirizarr@catholiccharities.net. Eliu Irizarry, Dir.

South Regional Services, 16100 Seton Dr., South Holland, 60473. Tel: 708-333-8379; Email: cltorres@catholiccharities.net. Christopher Torres, Dir.

North/Northwest Regional Family Service Center, 1717 Rand Rd., Des Plaines, 60016. Tel: 847-376-2100; Email: eirizarr@catholiccharities.net. Eliu Irizarry, Dir.

West Regional Services, 1400 S. Austin Blvd., Cicero, 60804. Tel: 708-329-4023; Email: eirizarr@catholiccharities.net. Eliu Irizarry, Dir.

SNFP Outreach Yolanda James, Contact Person, Tel: 773-924-7041. Sites 160.

Seniors Farmers Market Nutrition Program (SFMNP), 416 E. 43rd St., 60653. Tel: 773-924-7043; Email: yjames@catholiccharities.net. Yolanda James, Contact Person.

The Peace Corner, Inc., 5022 W. Madison St., 60644.

Special Supplemental Food & Nutrition Programs-Children Programs:.

Summer Food Service; Child and Adult Care Food Program, Tel: 773-729-3912. Diane Nunley, Assoc. Vice Pres.

Employment and Training:.

CHA Family Works, Regional Family Works Office, 4802 N. Broadway, Ste. 205, 60640. Tel: 773-409-4754; Email: mlucas@catholiccharities.net. Melissa Lucas, Regional Dir.

Summer Youth Employment Program, 6202 S. Halsted St., 60621. Tel: 312-655-7330; Email: gcleggs@catholiccharities.net. Gina Cleggs, Assoc. Vice Pres.

One Summer Chicago Plus Program, 6202 S. Halsted St., 60621. Tel: 312-655-7330. Gina Cleggs, Assoc. Vice Pres.

EPIC Program, 6202 S. Halsted St., 60621. Tel: 312-655-7330; Email: gcleggs@catholiccharities.net. Gina Cleggs, Assoc. Vice Pres.

Youth Services:.

Youth Employment Services; Mentoring Plus Jobs, Tel: 773-729-3864. Gina Cleggs, Assoc. Vice Pres.

Social Enterprises:.

Lunch-N-More Catering and Food Service Enterprise; Painting Enterprise; Veterans Independent Painting, 6202 S. Halsted St., 60621. Tel: 312-655-7330; Email: gcleggs@catholiccharities.net. Gina Cleggs, Assoc. Vice Pres.

Translation and Interpretation Network (TIN), 721 N. La Salle St., 7th Fl., 60654. Tel: 312-655-7483; Email: mmoiron@catholiccharities.net. Michael Moiron, Dir.

Family and Parish Support Services:.

Office, 721 N. LaSalle St., 60654. Tel: 312-655-7151; Fax: 312-948-6987; Email: parizzi@catholiccharities.net. Peggy Arizzi, Vice Pres.; Bob Haennicke, Assoc. Vice Pres.; Maureen Murphy, Assoc. Vice Pres.

Addiction Consultation and Educational Services, 721 N. LaSalle St., 60654. Tel: 312-655-7725; Email: pdavis@catholiccharities.net. Pamela Davis, Dept. Dir.

Augustus Tolton Peace Center, 5645 W. Lake St., 60644.

Casa Catalina, 4533-37 S. Ashland Ave., 60609. Tel: 773-376-9425; Email: jtumas@catholiccharities.net. Sr. Jo Ellen, Prog. Dir.

Central Information and Referral Services, 2601 W. Marquette Rd., 60629. Tel: 312-655-7700; Fax: 312-655-0678; Email: nwatson@catholiccharities.net. Nedra Watson, Prog. Dir.

Central States Institute of Addiction, 1800 N. Hermitage Ave., 60622. Tel: 312-655-7533; Fax: 312-266-9027; Email: kdoyle@catholiccharities.net. Kevin J. Doyle, Dept. Dir.

Community Family Service Center, 1100 S. May, 60607. Tel: 312-733-5661; Fax: 312-733-5211; Email: lrios@catholiccharities.net. Laura Rios, Vice Pres.

Emergency Assistance Department, 721 N. LaSalle St., 60654. Tel: 312-655-7500; Fax: 312-654-9861; Email: stillmon@catholiccharities.net. Sharon Tillmon, Dept. Dir.

Community Casework and Counseling, 1800 N. Hermitage Ave., 60622. Tel: 312-655-7140; Fax: 312-382-1612; Email: pdavis@catholiccharities.net. Pamela Davis, Dept. Dir.

Archdiocesan AIDS Ministry Office, 1800 N. Hermitage Ave., 60622. Tel: 312-948-6500; Fax: 312-382-1612; Email: pdrott@catholiccharities.net. Patricia Drott, Program Dir.

Holbrook Center for Counseling and Psychotherapy, 730 N. Wabash Ave., Courtyard Bldg., 60611. Tel: 312-655-7725; Fax: 312-573-7719; Email: vjames@catholiccharities.net. Deborah Hammond, Dir.; Valorie James, Dir.

Lake County HIV/AIDS Case Management, 671 S. Lewis, Waukegan, 60085. Tel: 847-782-4100; Fax: 847-782-1030; Email: dfries@catholiccharities.net. David Fries, Dept. Dir.

Immigration & Naturalization Services, 205 W. Monroe St., 60606. Tel: 312-427-7078; Fax: 312-427-3130; Email: ngavilan@catholiccharities.net. Nancy Gavilanes, Prog. Dir.

Inspiring Hope Program, 5645 W. Lake St., 60644.

Maternity/Adoption Services, 1800 N. Hermitage Ave., 60622. Tel: 312-454-1717; Fax: 312-382-1612 ; Email: nchesebr@catholiccharities.net. Norene Chesebro, Dept. Dir.

Mobile Outreach, 10 S. Kedzie Ave., 60612. Tel: 312-746-7213; Fax: 312-746-4863. Renee Rouse, Prog. Dir.

Refugee Resettlement Program, 4827 N. Kenmore Ave., 60640. Tel: 312-655-7856; Fax: 312-879-0208 ; Email: ekulovic@catholiccharities.net. Elmida Kulovic, Prog. Dir.

LOSS (Loving Outreach to Survivors of Suicide), 721 N. LaSalle St., 60654. Tel: 312-655-7283; Fax: 312-948-3340; Email: dmajor@catholiccharities.net. Rev. Charles T. Rubey, Founder, (Retired); Deborah Major, Dept. Dir.

Homelessness Prevention Call Center, 1800 N. Hermitage St., 60622. Tel: 312-744-5000; Fax: 312-698-5078; Email: wavila@catholiccharities.net. Wendy Avila, Dir.

Lake County Family Self-Sufficiency, 671 S. Lewis, Waukegan, 60085. Tel: 847-782-4100; Fax: 847-782-1030; Email: astyx@catholiccharities.net. Ashley Styx, Prog. Supvr.

Lake County Emergency Assistance, 671 S. Lewis, Waukegan, 60085. Tel: 847-782-4100; Fax: 847-782-1030; Email: akon@catholiccharities.net. Alicia Kon, Prog. Supv.

Lake County Housing Case Management, 671 S. Lewis, Waukegan, 60085. Tel: 847-782-4100; Fax: 847-782-1030; Email: ddrinka@catholiccharities.net. Donna Drinka, Prog. Supv.

Child, Youth and Family Services:.

Office, 721 N. LaSalle St., 60654. Tel: 312-655-8570; Fax: 312-879-0293; Email: lrios@catholiccharities.net. Laura Rios, Vice Pres.

Youth and Family Therapeutic Services, 2310 W. Roosevelt Rd., 2nd Fl., 60608. Tel: 312-655-7984; Fax: 312-236-5384. Margaret Monahan, Dept. Dir.

Intact Family Services, 1800 N. Hermitage Ave., 60622. Tel: 312-382-2505; Fax: 312-258-1839; Email: mhenderson@catholiccharities.net. Mary J. Henderson, Dept. Dir.

Adoption Preservation and Respite Services, 2601 W. Marquette Rd., 60629. Tel: 312-655-8357; Fax: 773-349-8080; Email: lmolina@catholiccharities.net. Laura Molina, Supvr.

Jadonal E. Ford Center for Adolescent Parenting, 2310 W. Roosevelt Rd., 2nd Fl., 60608. Tel: 312-236-5384; Fax: 773-995-0125; Email: vwalker@catholiccharities.net. Velma Brown-Walker, Dept. Dir.

Arts of Living Institute, 2601 W. Marquette Rd., 60629. Tel: 312-948-6003; Fax: 773-349-8080; Email: mursetta@catholiccharities.net. Meaghan Ursetta, Prog. Dir.

Administration - Head Start Centers, 2601 W. Marquette Rd., 60629. Tel: 312-651-2061; Fax: 773-349-8080; Email: tajohnso@catholiccharities.net. Tasha Johnson, Dept. Dir.

Administration - Child Care Centers, 1100 S. May St., 60607. Tel: 312-948-6170; Fax: 312-666-3562; Email: drodrigu@catholiccharities.net. Diane Rodriguez, Prog. Dir.

Community Family Service Center, 1100 S. May St., 60607. Tel: 312-602-1467; Fax: 312-733-5211; Email: fmalone@catholiccharities.net. Frederica Malone, Prog. Dir.

Childhood Development Programs, Daycare/Head Start:.

St. Blase Child Development Center, 7438 W. 61st Pl., Summit, 60501. Tel: 708-496-1193; Fax: 708-496-1246; Email: cmccall@catholiccharities.net. Carolyn McCall, Site Dir.

Chicago Lawn Child Development Center, 3001 W. 59th St., 60629. Tel: 773-925-1085; Fax: 773-925-1170.

Cordi-Marian Child Development Center, 1100 S. May St., 60607. Tel: 312-666-3787; Fax: 312-666-3562.

St. Joseph Child Development Center, 4800 S. Paulina, 60609. Tel: 773-927-2524; Fax: 773-247-9170; Email: lrios@catholiccharities.net. Laura Rios, Vice Pres.

St. Mary of Celle, 1428 S. Wesley Ave., Berwyn, 60402. Tel: 708-303-3650; Fax: 708-303-3655.

Our Lady of Tepeyac Child Development Center, 2414 S. Albany Ave., 60623. Tel: 773-277-5222; Fax: 773-522-2403; Email: pgutierr@catholiccharities.net. Petra Gutierrez, Site Dir.

Housing Services:.

Office, 721 N. LaSalle 5th FL., 60654. Tel: 312-655-7490; Fax: 312-944-1550; Email: trodriguez@catholiccharities.net; Email: ehiggins@catholiccharities.net. Eileen Higgins, Vice Pres.; Roberta Magurany, Assoc. Vice Pres.; Millicent Ntiamoah, Assoc. Vice Pres.; Antwaun Smith, Assoc. Vice Pres.

Ailbe Assisted Housing Corporation
Ailbe Senior Housing Corporation
All Saints Senior Housing, NFP
Bernardin Senior Housing Corporation
Brendan Senior Housing Corporation
Catholic Charities Housing Development Corporation
Cortland Manor Development Corporation
Frances Senior Housing Corporation
Goedert Senior Housing Corporation
Lawrence Senior Housing Corporation
Hayes Senior Housing Corporation
St. Leo Assisted Housing, NFP
St. Leo Development Association
Matthew Senior Housing Corporation
North Center Senior Housing, NFP
Northlake Senior Housing, NFP
Options for Housing, Inc.
Palos Park Senior Housing, NFP
Porta Coeli Senior Housing, NFP
St. Peter Claver Senior Housing Corporation
Roseland Senior Housing Corporation
Sabina Senior Housing Corporation
Tolton Senior Housing Corporation
Holy Family Villa
House of the Good Shepherd of Chicago.

Affordable Senior Housing:.

All Saints Residence, 11701 S. State St., 60628. Tel: 773-995-9000; Fax: 773-995-1310.

Bishop Goedert Residence, Bldg. 53, Hines VA Campus, Hines, 60141. Tel: 708-273-6600; Fax: 708-273-6609; Email: sgonzale@catholiccharities.net. Sonya Gonzalez, Property Mgr.

Hayes Manor, 1211 W. Marquette Rd., 60636. Tel: 773-873-7400; Fax: 773-873-1709; Email: lmyles@catholiccharities.net. Linda Myles, Dir.

Matthew Manor, 271 N. Albany Ave., 60612. Tel: 773-533-0001; Fax: 773-533-0622.

Ozanam Village, 251 N. Albany Ave., 60612. Tel: 773-533-0001; Fax: 773-533-0622; Email: sgonzale@catholiccharities.net. Sonya Gonzalez, Property Mgr.

Roseland Manor, 11717 S. State St., 60628. Tel: 773-995-9000; Fax: 773-995-1310; Email: oharris@catholiccharities.net. Onita Harris, Property Mgr.

St. Peter Claver Courts, 14115 S. Claire Blvd., Robbins, 60472. Tel: 708-389-1570; Fax: 708-389-1571.

St. Ailbe Faith Apartments, 1244 E. 93rd St., 60619. Tel: 773-721-0903; Fax: 773-721-0920; Email: bhawkins@catholiccharities.net. Belinda Hawkins, Property Mgr.

St. Ailbe Love Apartments, 9240 S. Kimbark Ave., 60619. Tel: 773-721-0903; Fax: 773-721-0920; Email: bhawkins@catholiccharities.net. Belinda Hawkins, Property Mgr.

St. Brendan Apartments, 6718 S. Racine Ave., 60636. Tel: 773-846-8600; Fax: 773-846-0873; Email: tlatham@catholiccharities.net. Linda Myles, Property Mgr.

St. Francis of Assisi Residence, 12218 S. Will-Cook Rd., Palos Park, 60464. Tel: 630-343-1880; Fax: 630-343-1890.

St. Sabina Elders Village, 1222 W. 79th St., 60620. Tel: 773-994-7850; Fax: 773-994-7945; Email: lmyles@catholiccharities.net. Linda Myles, Property Mgr.

Tolton Manor, 6345 S. Stewart Ave., 60621. Tel: 773-783-7800; Fax: 773-846-0868; Email: ajackson@catholiccharities.net. Andiera Jackson, Property Mgr.

Frances Manor, 1270 E. Golf Rd., Des Plaines, 60016. Tel: 847-390-1270; Fax: 847-390-9331.

Lawrence Manor, 21425 Southwick Dr., Matteson, 60443. Tel: 708-481-1200; Fax: 708-481-3168; Email: ccamp@catholiccharities.net. Casie Camp, Property Mgr.

Bernardin Manor, 1700 Memorial Dr., Calumet City, 60409. Tel: 708-832-1700; Fax: 708-832-9160; Email: sreddick@catholiccharities.net. Sandra Reddick, Property Mgr.

Donald W. Kent Residence, 100 S. Wolf Rd., Northlake, 60164. Tel: 708-409-4710; Fax: 708-409-4712; Email: ycastro@catholiccharities.net. Yadira Castro, Dir.

St. Vincent de Paul Residence, 4040 N. Oakley Ave., 60618. Tel: 773-539-2660; Fax: 312-681-7701.

Porta Coeli Residence, 2260 E. 99th St., 60617. Tel: 773-374-2470; Fax: 773-374-2472; Email: bhawkins@catholiccharities.net. Belinda Hawkins, Property Mgr.

Affordable Housing for Persons with Disabilities:.

Pope John Paul II Residence, 7741 S. Emerald Ave., 60620. Tel: 773-651-9950; Fax: 773-651-9970; Email: csteen@catholiccharities.net. Cynthia Steen, Property Mgr.

St. Ailbe Hope Apartments, 9101-9103 S. Harper, 60619. Tel: 773-721-0903; Fax: 773-721-0920; Email: bhawkins@catholiccharities.net. Belinda Hawkins, Property Mgr.

Senior Care Skilled Nursing Home:.

Holy Family Villa, 12220 S. Will-Cook Rd., Palos Park, 60464-7332. Tel: 630-257-2291; Fax: 630-257-2334; Email: kgraben@catholiccharities.net; Web: www.holyfamilyvilla.net. Roberta Magurany, Admin.

Home for Retired Priests:.

Bishop T.J. Lyne Residence for Retired Priests, 12230 South Will-Cook Rd., Palos Park, 60464-7332. Tel: 630-257-2291; Fax: 630-257-2334; Email: rmaguran@catholiccharities.net. Roberta Magurany, Admin. & Contact Person.

Supportive Housing:.

Bishop Edwin M. Conway Residence, 1900 N. Karlov Ave., 60639. Tel: 773-252-9941; Fax: 773-525-9946; Email: gsaldana@catholiccharities.net. Gabriela Saldana, Prog. Dir.

Transitional Housing:.

Cooke's Manor Transitional Housing For Men, Tel: 312-655-7235; Fax: 312-648-1034. Millicent Ntiamoah, Assoc. Vice Pres.

Madonna House, 1114 W. Grace St., 60613. Tel: 773-327-1605; Fax: 773-248-1497. Sharita Sloan, Supervisor.

House of the Good Shepherd, P.O. Box 13453, 60613. Tel: 312-655-7000; Email: jkielty@catholiccharities.net. Sr. Jean Kielty, Dir.

Homeless Housing Programs:.

New Hope Apartments, 2601 W. Marquette Rd., 60629. Tel: 312-655-7235; Fax: 312-648-1034. Millicent Ntiamoah, Assoc. Vice Pres.

Streets to Home, 2601 W. Marquette Rd., 60629. Tel: 312-655-7719; Fax: 773-374-2177. Sharon Love, Dept. Dir.

St. Joseph Apartments, 2601 W. Marquette Rd., 60629. Tel: 312-655-7235; Fax: 312-648-1034; Email: mntiamoa@catholiccharities.net. Millicent Ntiamoah, Assoc. Vice Pres.

Bridge Subsidy Program, 2601 W. Marquette Rd., 60629. Tel: 312-948-6503; Fax: 312-906-8265; Email: jumartinez@catholiccharities.net. Judith Martinez, Program Dir.

Veterans Housing and Programs:.

St. Leo Residence for Veterans, 7750 S. Emerald Ave., 60620. Tel: 773-651-9950; Fax: 773-651-9970 ; Email: csteen@catholiccharities.net. Cynthia Steen, Property Mgr.

Veterans Employment Program, 2601 W. Marquette Rd., 60629. Tel: 773-808-2958; Fax: 773-808-2960; Email: akochevar@catholiccharities.net. Anthony Kochevar, Prog. Dir.

Veterans Lake County, 671 S. Lewis Ave., Waukegan, 60085. Tel: 312-655-7235; Fax: 312-648-1034; Email: mntiamoa@catholiccharities.net. Millicent Ntiamoah, Assoc. Vice Pres.

Supportive Services for Veterans Families, 2601 W. Marquette Rd., 60629. Tel: 312-948-6898; Fax: 312-648-1034; Email: moscar@catholiccharities.net. Magalie Oscar, Dept. Dir.

Senior Services:.

Office, 721 N. La Salle Dr., 60654. Tel: 312-948-7412; Fax: 312-640-1587; Email: mbibat@catholiccharities.net. Mary Ann Bibat, Vice Pres.; Angela Taylor, Assoc. Vice Pres.; Meisha Lyons, Vice Pres.

Northeast/Northwest Chicago Case Management Services, 3125 N. Knox, 60641. Tel: 773-583-9224; Fax: 773-583-2373; Email: wwalker@catholiccharities.net. Wyvonnia Walker, Dept. Dir.

South Suburban Senior Services, 15300 S. Lexington, Harvey, 60426. Tel: 708-596-2222; Fax: 708-596-9567; Email: umcintosh@catholiccharities.net. Umekia McIntosh, Dept. Dir.

Northwest Suburban Senior Services, 1801 W.

Central, Arlington Heights, 60005.
Tel: 847-253-5500; Fax: 847-253-9597; Email: cgunders@catholiccharities.net. Ms. Cynthia Gunderson, Dept. Dir.

Lake County Senior Case Management Services, 116 N. Lincoln, Round Lake, 60073. Tel: 847-546-5733; Fax: 847-546-7114; Email: mharris@catholiccharities.net. Marla Harris, Dept. Dir.

Round Lake Home Delivered Meals Distribution Site, 116 N. Lincoln, Round Lake, 60073.
Tel: 847-740-6714; Email: mbibat@catholiccharities.net. Mary Ann Bibat, Vice Pres.

Lake County Nutrition Program Sites (Congregate and Home Delivered Meals), 671 S. Lewis Ave., Waukegan, 60085. Tel: 847-782-4268; Fax: 847-782-1041; Email: bandress@catholiccharities.net. Barbara Andress, Nutrition Dir.

Grayslake Senior Center and Congregate Site, 50 Library Ln., Grayslake, 60030. Tel: 847-543-1041; Email: mbibat@catholiccharities.net. Mary Ann Bibat, Vice Pres.

Antioch/Lake Villa Home Delivered Meal Distribution and Congregate Site, 1625 Deep Lake Rd., Lake Villa, 60046. Tel: 847-838-6415; Email: mbibat@catholiccharities.net. Mary Ann Bibat, Vice Pres.

Park Place Home Delivered Meal Distribution and Congregate Site, 414 S. Lewis Ave., Waukegan, 60085. Tel: 847-662-0085.

Adult Day Care Sites:.

Accolade Adult Day Care, 112 S. Humphrey, Oak Park, 60302-2704. Tel: 708-445-1300;
Fax: 708-445-9595. Angela Reese, Site Dir.

Ada S. Niles Adult Day Care, 6717 S. Elizabeth, 60639. Tel: 773-488-5400; Fax: 773-488-5878; Email: debjohnson@catholiccharities.net. Debora Johnson, Site Dir.

St. Ailbe Adult Day Care, 9249 S. Avalon, 60619.
Tel: 773-721-0177; Fax: 773-721-1228; Email: ltennent@catholiccharities.net. LaDonna Tennet, Site Dir.

Senior Centers:.

Ada S. Niles Senior Center and Adult Day Care Services, 653 W. 63rd St., 60621.
Tel: 312-745-3307; Fax: 312-745-3330; Email: dking@catholiccharities.net. Denise King, Senior Center Supvr.

Josephine P. Argento Senior Center, 1700 N. Memorial Dr., Calumet City, 60409.
Tel: 708-832-1208; Email: rboyd@catholiccharities.net. Rob Boyd, Senior Center Coord.

Kelvyn Park Senior Center Satellite, 2715 N. Cicero Ave., 60639. Tel: 312-744-3350; Fax: 312-744-3803 ; Email: mbibat@catholiccharities.net. Martha Lavaire, Contact Person.

St. Vincent De Paul Residence North Center Senior Satellite, 4040 N. Oakley St., 60618.
Tel: 312-744-4029; Fax: 312-744-8812. Liza Martin, Senior Center Dir.

Senior Aid Programs:.

Senior Aides Employment Program, 2601 W. Marquette Rd., 60629. Tel: 773-349-8035; Fax: 773-349-8081; Email: sjohnigan@catholiccharities.net. Stephanie Johnigan, Prog. Dir.

Catholic Home Care, Inc., 1100 S. May St., 60607.
Tel: 312-655-7415; Fax: 312-337-2705; Email: cbrooks@catholiccharities.net. Carla Turner-Brooks, Dept. Dir.

Non-Service Area Listing:.

Christ Child Society of Chicago, 9515 Callan Dr., Orland Park, 60462. Tel: 708-671-0105. Dorothy Pauly, Contact Person.

Keenager News, 721 N. LaSalle St., 60654.
Tel: 312-655-7425; Fax: 312-930-0425; Email: ahamilton@catholiccharities.net. Amanda Hamilton, Editor.

Mission of the Holy Cross, 721 N. LaSalle St., 60654. Tel: 312-655-7000; Fax: 312-655-0219. Rev. Msgr. Michael M. Boland.

Options for Housing, Inc. f/k/a Shelter for the Homeless, Inc., 721 N. LaSalle St., 60610.
Tel: 312-655-7305. Ms. Kathy Donahue, Contact Person.

St. Josephs Carondelet Child Center, 721 N. LaSalle St., 60654.

Society of St. Vincent De Paul of Chicago, 651 N. Lake St., 60661. Tel: 312-655-7181;
Fax: 312-454-0101; Web: www.svdpchicago.org. James D. Lonergan, CEO.

Affiliated Agencies:.

Maryville Academy, 1150 N. River Rd., Des Plaines, 60016. Tel: 847-824-6126; Fax: 847-824-7190. Sr. Catherine M. Ryan, O.S.F., Exec. Dir.

Mercy Home for Boys & Girls, 1140 W. Jackson Blvd., 60607. Tel: 312-738-7590;
Fax: 312-738-0484. Rev. Scott Donahue, Pres.

Misericordia Home, Misericordia/Heart of Mercy Center, 6300 N. Ridge, 60660. Tel: 773-973-6300; Fax: 773-973-5214. Sr. Rosemary Connelly, R.S.M., Exec. Dir.

St. Coletta's of Illinois, 18350 Crossing Dr., Tinley Park, 60477. Tel: 708-342-5200; Fax: 708-342-2579 . Wayne A. Kottmeyer, Exec. Dir.

[H] RESIDENTIAL CHILD-YOUTH CARE

CHICAGO. *Mission of Our Lady of Mercy-Mercy Home for Boys and Girls*, 1140 W. Jackson Blvd., 60607. Tel: 312-738-7560; Fax: 312-738-0484; Email: mhinfo@mercyhome.org; Web: www.mercyhome.org. Rev. L. Scott Donahue, Pres. & CEO; Cheryl Murphy, CFO, Vice Pres. Facilities & Human Resources; Tom Gilardi, Vice Pres. Youth Programs; Joseph Wronka, Vice Pres. The Academy & Agency Advancement; Patrick Bittorf, Vice Pres. The Academy; Lori Kinast, Vice Pres. Organizational Devel.; Nicolette Prepura, Dir. Mission Press; Steve Snyder, Vice Pres. Information Systems. Religious 5; Total Staff 309; Youths 400.

DES PLAINES. *Maryville Academy*, 1150 N. River Rd., Des Plaines, 60016. Tel: 847-294-1999;
Fax: 847-824-7288; Web: www.maryvilleacademy.org. Sr. Catherine M. Ryan, O.S.F., Exec. Dir.; Cheryl M. Heyden, Asst. Exec. Dir.; Mr. Mark Nufer, Vice Pres.
Maryville Academy Bed Capacity 135; Patients Asst Anual. 4,200.

Casa Imani Program, 951 W. Bartlett Rd., Bartlett, 60103. Tel: 630-736-7450; Fax: 630-736-7478. Evelyn Smith, Prog. Dir.

Children's HealthCare Center, 4015 N. Oak Park Ave., 60634. Tel: 773-205-3600; Fax: 773-205-3630 . Shawn Pickett, Prog. Dir.

Crisis Nursery, 4015 N. Oak Park Ave., 60634.
Tel: 773-205-3600; Fax: 773-205-3633. Amy Kendal-Lynch, Prog. Dir.

Casa Salama Program, 951 W. Bartlett Rd., Bartlett, 60103. Tel: 630-736-7450;
Fax: 630-736-7485. Sabrina Gaston, Prog. Dir.

CYO (Catholic Youth Organization) Program, 1658 W. Grand Ave., 60622. Tel: 312-491-3500;
Fax: 312-491-3501. Kimberly Williams, Prog. Dir.

Family Engagement Program, 1658 W. Grand Ave., 60622. Tel: 312-491-3500; Fax: 312-491-3501; Email: ryanc@maryvilleacademy.org. Nina Aliprandi, Prog. Dir.

Casa Imani, 1150 N. River Rd., Des Plaines, 60016. Tel: 630-736-7488; Email: gastons@maryvilleacadmey.org. Sabrina Gaston, Dir. Girls 10.

Maryville Madden Shelter, 1658 W. Grand Ave., 60622. Tel: 312-491-3500; Fax: 312-491-3501. LaTanya Carter, Prog. Dir.

Maryville CYO, 1658 W. Grand Ave., 60622.
Tel: 312-491-3500; Fax: 312-491-3501. Kimberly Williams, Prog. Coord.

Maryville Jen School, 1150 N. River Rd., Des Plaines, 60016. Tel: 847-390-3020;
Fax: 847-294-1738. Ann Craig, Chief Educ. Officer.

Maryville Saint George Program, Tel: 847-294-2815;
Fax: 847-294-1916. Sabrina Gaston, Prog. Dir.

St. Monica Program, 1658 West Grand Ave, 60622.
Tel: 312-491-3514; Fax: 312-491-3501; Email: jacksond2@maryvilleacademy.org. Donita Jackson, Dir. Families 65; Tot Asst. Annually 65; Total Staff 20.

Maryville Behavioral Health Hospital, 555 Wilson Ln., Des Plaines, 60016. Tel: 847-768-5430;
Fax: 847-768-5478. Joseph Novak, Hospital CEO.

Maryville Family Behavioral Health Clinic, 1455 Golf Rd., Ste. 105, Des Plaines, 60016.

Casa Esperanza, 951 W. Barlett Rd., Bartlett, 60103. Tel: 847-294-2815; Fax: 847-294-7288; Email: mccannm@maryvilleacademy.org. Jose Sanchez-Argueta, Community Relations Dir. Children 20.

Maryville Stephen Sexton Training Institute,
Tel: 847-294-1970; Fax: 847-294-2788; Email: heydenc@maryvilleacademy.org. Cheryl M. Heyden, Dir.

Supervised Visitation Program, 1150 N. River Rd., Des Plaines, 60016. Tel: 847-294-1999;
Fax: 312-491-3501; Email: ryanc@maryvilleacademy.org. Nina Aliprandi, Prog. Dir.

San Francisco Program, 1150 N. River Rd., Des Plaines, 60016. Tel: 847-294-2815;
Fax: 847-294-1737; Email: mccannm@maryvilleacademy.org. Mary Sanchez, Dir.

St. Dominic Savio Program, 1150 N. River Rd., Des Plaines, 60016. Tel: 847-390-3056;
Fax: 847-294-7288; Email: kajcicl@maryvilleacademy.org. Liliana Kajcic, Prog. Dir.

[I] DAY NURSERIES, SETTLEMENTS AND SOCIAL CENTERS

CHICAGO. **Claver House of Renewal, Inc.*, 8514 S. Avalon St., 60619. Tel: 773-731-3294. Edward Chatman, Pres. Food pantry, soup kitchen, homebound senior citizen care, after-school youth recreational programs; mentoring; tutoring and scholarship assistance to elementary and high school graduates continuing studies at Catholic educational institutions. Outreach to the homeless: clothing, toys and basic toiletries for local shelters.

**Port Ministries*, 5013 S. Hermitage Ave., 60609.
Tel: 773-778-5955; Fax: 773-778-2451; Email: info@theportministries.org; Web: www.theportministries.org. A Franciscan outreach to the poor and homeless; mobile soup kitchen, GED, ESL, family svcs., neighborhood gym and free clinic. Tot Asst. Annually 3,000; Total Staff 6.

[J] HOSPITALS

CHICAGO. *Saint Anthony Hospital*, 2875 W. 19th St., 60623. Tel: 773-484-1000; Fax: 773-521-7902. Mr. Peter V. Fazio Jr., Bd. Chm.; Mr. Guy A. Medaglia, Pres. & CEO; Sr. Benigna Morais, M.S.C., Chap.; Revs. Benedict Ezeoke, (Nigeria); Cajetan Ebuziem, (Nigeria)
Saint Anthony Health Ministries Patients Asst Anual. 146,108; Total Staff 1,005; Total Licensed Beds 151.

St. Bernard Hospital & Health Care Center, 326 W. 64th St., 60621. Tel: 773-962-3900;
Fax: 773-602-3849; Email: cholland@stbh.org; Web: stbh.org. Charles Holland, Pres. & CEO. Religious Hospitallers of St. Joseph/Catholic Health International.
St. Bernard Hospital Bed Capacity 210; Patients Asst Anual. 120,000; Sisters 1; Total Staff 850.

Holy Cross Hospital Affiliated with Sinai Health System 2701 W. 68th St., 60629. Tel: 773-884-9000 ; Web: www.holycrosshospital.org. Ms. Karen Teitelbaum, Pres. & CEO; Sr. Laura Parker, S.P., Dir. Spiritual Care Dept. Sisters of St. Casimir of Chicago.
Holy Cross Hospital Patients Asst Anual. 187,000; Sisters 4; Total Staff 840; Licensed Beds 274.

Mercy Hospital and Medical Center, 2525 S. Michigan Ave., 60616-2477. Tel: 312-567-2100;
Fax: 312-567-6575; Web: www.mercy-chicago.org. Carol Schneider, Pres. & CEO, Tel: 312-567-2580; Fax: 312-567-6575; Rev. Martin J. Hebda, Vice Pres., Spirituality & Mission, (Retired), Tel: 312-567-2045; Fax: 312-328-7741. Bed Capacity 449; Patients Asst Anual. 93,615; Staffed Beds 199.
Affiliates:.
Mercy Health System of Chicago.
Mercy Services Corp.
Mercy Foundation, Inc.
Mercy Health System of Chicago Liability Self-Insurance Trust.
Mercy Medical at Dearborn Station (Outpatient Physician Offices) 47 W. Polk St., 60605.
Tel: 312-922-3011.
Mercy Works at Dearborn Station, 47 W. Polk St., 60605. Tel: 312-922-3011; Fax: 312-922-5860.
Mercy Medical in Chinatown (Outpatient Physician Offices) 2347 S. Wentworth, 60616.
Tel: 312-842-0100.
Mercy Medical on Pulaski (Outpatient Satellite Facility) 5525 S. Pulaski Rd., 60629.
Tel: 773-585-1955; Tel: 773-284-5268.
Mercy Works on Pulaski, 5635 S. Pulaski Rd., 60629. Tel: 773-284-5278; Fax: 773-585-0395.
Mercy Works on Ashland, 3316 S. Ashland, 60608.
Tel: 773-254-2133.
Mercy Medical in Chatham, 8541 S. State St., 60619. Tel: 773-994-2300.

Presence Resurrection Medical Center, 7435 Talcott Ave., 60631. Tel: 773-774-8000; Fax: 773-792-8958; Web: www.presencehealth.org. Robert Dahl, CEO; Leszek Baczkura, Spiritual Care Mgr. Sponsored by Ascension Health Ministries (Ascension Sponsor), a public juridic person.
Presence Chicago Hospitals Network dba Presence Resurrection Medical Center Bed Capacity 337; Tot Asst. Annually 148,839; Staff 1,620.

Presence Saint Joseph Hospital Chicago, 2900 N. Lake Shore Dr., 60657. Tel: 773-665-3000;
Fax: 773-665-4859; Web: www.presencehealth.org. Kenneth Jones, Pres.; Revs. Theodore Ploplis, Coord. Spiritual Svcs.; Arlin Jean Louis, O.M.I.; Rabbi Norm Lewison; Dr. Sharon Barchman. Sponsored by Ascension Health Ministries (Ascension Sponsor), a public juridic person.
Legal Title: Presence Chicago Hospitals Network dba Presence St. Joseph Hospital Bed Capacity 361; Tot Asst. Annually 92,123; Staff 1,364.

Presence Saints Mary and Elizabeth Medical Center, 2233 W. Division, 60622. Tel: 312-770-2000;
Fax: 312-770-2392; Web: www.presencehealth.org/presence-saints-mary-and-elizabeth-medical-center-chicago. Martin Judd, Regl. Pres. & CEO; Isidro Gallegos Rodriguez, Mgr. Spiritual Care; Revs. John J. Sanaghan, Chap., (Retired); Raphael A. Makori, Chap.; Rachel Daly, Chap.; Sr. Dorothy Nkuba, S.T.H., Chap.; Rev. Linda Clum, Chap.;

William F. Kramer, Chap.; Rev. Fernando Zuleta, Chap. Sponsored by Ascension Health Ministries (Ascension Sponsor), a public juridic person.

Legal Title: Presence Chicago Hospitals Network dba Presence Saints Mary and Elizabeth Medical Center. Bed Capacity 495; Patients Asst Anual. 177,788; Total Staff 1,684.

DES PLAINES. *Presence Holy Family Medical Center*, 100 N. River Rd., Des Plaines, 60016. Tel: 847-297-1800; Fax: 847-297-1863; Web: www.presencehealth.org. Michael Gordon, Pres.; Leszek Baczkura, Regl. Coord. Spiritual Care. Sponsored by Ascension Health Ministries (Ascension Sponsor), a juridic person.

Legal Title: Presence Chicago Hospitals Network dba Presence Holy Family Medical Center Bed Capacity 178; Tot Asst. Annually 20,218; Staff 617.

ELK GROVE VILLAGE. *Alexian Brothers Medical Center*, 800 Biesterfield Rd., Elk Grove Village, 60007-3392. Tel: 847-437-5500; Fax: 847-981-5774; Web: www.amitahealth.org. Stan Kedzior, Dir.; Beth Collier, Chap. Mgr.; James Gullickson, Business Mgr.; Rev. Ignatius Okonkwo, Priest Chap.; Phyllis Harman, Chap.; Ora Schnitzer, Chap.; Janet Ronchetti, Chap.; Revs. John Ekwoanya, Chap.; William E. Veith, Chap.; Anne Windholz, Staff Chap. Ascension Health Ministries (Ascension Sponsor), a public juridic personParent Institution: Alexian Brothers Hospital Network Bed Capacity 401; Tot Asst. Annually 464,471; Total Staff 2,190.

EVANSTON. *Presence Saint Francis Hospital*, 355 Ridge Ave., Evanston, 60202. Tel: 847-316-4500; Fax: 847-316-7733; Email: Judy.MacPhersonSchumacher@presencehealth.org; Web: www.presencehealth.org. Sr. Hanna Paradowska, C.S.F.N., Chap.; Rabbi Ilene Melemad, Chap.; Deacon Don Wehling, Chap.; Sr. Judith Belser, Chap.; Kenneth Jones, Pres.; Rev. Christopher LeBlanc, Chap.; Bob Shuford, Chap.; Natalie Nyberg, Chap. Sponsored by Presence Health Ministries.An Affiliate of Presence Health.

Presence Chicago Hospitals Network dba Presence Saint Francis Hospital Bed Capacity 215; Patients Asst Anual. 99,136; Priests 1; Sisters 1; Total Staff 719.

EVERGREEN PARK. *Little Company of Mary Hospital and Health Care Centers*, 2800 W. 95th St., Evergreen Park, 60805. Tel: 708-422-6200; Fax: 708-425-9756; Email: dreilly@lcmh.org; Web: www.lcmh.org. Sr. Sharon Ann Walsh, L.C.M., Bd. Chm.; Dr. John Hanlon, Pres. & CEO; Mary Jo Quick, Vice Pres. Mission & Spirituality; Rev. James R. Gallagher, Chap., (Retired); Carol Ehler, Chap.; Sr. Christa Henrich, Chap.; Pamela Palmer, Chap.; Rebecca McDaniel, Chap.; Eileen McNicholas, Dir. Health Educ. Center, Pastoral Care Dept.; Solveiga Palionis, Chap.; Deacon Richard Warfield, Mgr. Pastoral Care

The Little Company of Mary Hospital and Health Care Centers Bassinets 34; Bed Capacity 238; Sisters of the Little Company of Mary 13.

Affiliates:.

Little Company of Mary Affiliated Services, Inc., 2800 W. 95th St., Evergreen Park, 60805. Tel: 708-422-6200; Fax: 708-425-9756; Email: dreilly@lcmh.org. Dr. Kent Armbruster, Dir.; Violet Clark, Dir.; Thomas Fahey, Chm.; Irving Fuld, Dir.; Ann Haskins, Dir.; Ken Herlin, Dir.; Rev. James W. Miller, Dir.; Kevin Rehder, Dir.; Dennis Reilly; Dr. Daniel Rowan, Dir.; Marie Ruff, Dir.; Randy Ruther, Treas.

Palos Office Center, 12450 S. Harlem, Palos Heights, 60463. Tel: 708-448-1207; Fax: 708-448-7827; Email: bmeller@lcmh.org. 2800 W. 95th Street, Evergreen Park, 60805. Dennis Reilly.

Oak Lawn Care Station, 5660 W. 95th St., Oak Lawn, 60453. Tel: 708-499-2273; Fax: 708-857-3705; Email: bmeller@lcmh.org. Dennis Reilly.

Burbank Office Building, 4901 W. 79th St., Burbank, 60459. Tel: 708-422-0300; Fax: 708-422-7460; Email: bmeller@lcmh.org. Dennis Reilly.

Mary Potter Pavilion, 2850 W. 95th St., Evergreen Park, 60805. Tel: 708-229-5785; Email: bmeller@lcmh.org. Dennis Reilly.

Little Company of Mary Hospital Foundation, 2800 W. 95th St., Evergreen Park, 60805. Tel: 708-229-5067; Fax: 708-229-6525; Email: blepacek@lcmh.org; Web: www.lcmh.org/home/foundation. Brian Lepacek, Exec. Dir.

Little Company of Mary Health Systems of Evergreen Park, 2800 W. 95th St., Evergreen Park, 60805. Tel: 708-422-6200; Fax: 708-425-9756; Email: dreilly@lcmh.org. Dennis Reilly, Pres.; Dennis Day, Dir.; Jack Faber, Dir.; Kevin Egan, Sec.

HOFFMAN ESTATES. *Alexian Brothers Behavioral Health Hospital*, 1650 Moon Lake Blvd., Hoffman Estates, 60169. Tel: 847-882-1600; Fax: 847-755-8060; Web: www.amitahealth.org. Clayton Ciha, CEO & Pres.; Stan Kedzior, Dir. Mission Integration; Alan Schmitt, Staff Chap; Cindy Wallace, Dir.; Dorothy Symonds, Staff Chap.; Michael Szydlowski, Chap. Sponsored by Ascension Health Ministries (Ascension Sponsor), a public juridic person. Bed Capacity 141; Tot Asst. Annually 11,632; Total Staff 621.

Parents:.

Alexian Brothers Health System, Tel: 847-385-7147; Fax: 847-483-7036.

Alexian Brothers Hospital Network, Tel: 847-385-7147; Fax: 847-483-7036.

St. Alexius Medical Center, 1555 Barrington Rd., Hoffman Estates, 60169. Tel: 847-843-2000; Fax: 847-490-2570; Email: len.wilk@amitahealth.org; Web: www.amitahealth.org. Len Wilk, Pres. & CEO; Stan Kedzior, Dir. Mission Integration; Sr. N. Noemia Silva, Staff Chap.; Rev. Domingo Hurtado-Badillo, Coord. & Chap.; Gina Lyke, Chap.; Blessed Madugba, Staff Chap. Sponsored by Ascension Health Ministries (Ascension Sponsor), a public juridic person. Bed Capacity 318; Tot Asst. Annually 231,922; Total Staff 1,518.

Parent Institutions:.

Alexian Brothers Health System, Tel: 847-385-7147; Fax: 847-483-7036.

Alexian Brothers Hospital Network, Tel: 847-385-7147; Fax: 847-483-7036.

MAYWOOD. **Loyola University Medical Center* aka Foster G. McGaw Hospital, 2160 S. First Ave., Maywood, 60153. Tel: 708-216-9000; Fax: 708-216-1121; Web: loyolamedicine.org. Mr. Larry M. Goldberg, Pres. & CEO; Wendy Leutgens, B.S., R.N., M.S., CEO, LUMC; Dr. John J. Hardt, Ph.D., Vice Pres., Mission & Integration; Jill M. Rappis, J.D., Sr. Vice Pres., Gen. Counsel & Sec.; Marie Coglianese, M.P.S., Dir. Pastoral Care & Educ.; Rev. Tuan Le, S.J.; Mr. Jerry Kaelin, M.Div., M.A., Chap. CPE Supvr., CPE Mgr.; Ms. Kathleen Brannigan, M.T.S.; Revs. Matthew Eaton, M.Div.; Alin Dogaru, Romanian Catholic Diocese of U.S.; Mr. Robert Andorka; Kevin Cassidy, M.P.S.; Rev. Michael Hayes, M.Div., Chap.; Diana Durkin, Chap.; Felipe Legarreta, Ph.D., Chap.; Mark G. Henninger, S.J., Ph.D., Chap. Bed Capacity 559; Patients Asst Anual. 141,658; Total Staff 5,848.

OLYMPIA FIELDS. *Franciscan Health Olympia Fields*, Franciscan Health Chicago Heights, 20201 S. Crawford Ave., Olympia Fields, 60461. Tel: 708-747-4000; Fax: 708-503-3270; Email: allan.spooner@franciscanalliance.org; Web: www.franciscanhealth.org/south-suburban-chicago. Allan Spooner, Pres.; Sr. M. Ruth Luthman, O.S.F., Vice Pres. Mission Integration; Revs. Ronald L. Kondziolka, Chap.; Philip E. Cyscon, Chap.

Franciscan Alliance, Inc. Bassinets 36; Bed Capacity 214; Sisters 2; Tot Asst. Annually 71,996; Total Staff 1,555.

[K] HEALTH CARE CENTERS

CHICAGO. *St. Basil Health Service - Free People's Clinic*, 1850 W. Garfield, 60609. Tel: 773-436-4758; Fax: 773-436-2749. Patients Asst Anual. 5,000.

BROADVIEW. **Presence Behavioral Health* dba ProCare Centers; Employee Resource Center, 1820 S. 25th Ave., Broadview, 60155. Tel: 708-681-2324; Fax: 708-681-1289; Web: www.presencehealth.org. Mr. Frank C. Perham, Vice Pres., Behavioral Health. Sponsored by Ascension Health Ministries (Ascension Sponsor), a public juridic person.An Affiliate of Presence Health. Tot Asst. Annually 101,394; Total Staff 200.

[L] PROTECTIVE INSTITUTIONS

CHICAGO. *House of the Good Shepherd*, Mailing Address: P.O. Box 13453, 60613. Tel: 773-935-3434 ; Fax: 773-935-3523. Catholic Charities of the Archdiocese of Chicago.Shelter for abused women with children.

House of the Good Shepherd Capacity (Families) 14; Tot Asst. Annually 117; Total Staff 16.

**L'Arche Chicago*, 1011 Lake St., Ste. 403, Oak Park, 60301. Tel: 708-660-1600; Fax: 708-416-1346; Email: office@larchechicago.org; Web: www.larchechicago.org. Michael Altena, Community Leader & Dir. L'Arche is people with and without intellectual disabilities sharing life in communities of faith. Mutual relationships and trust in God is at the heart of our life together. Bed Capacity 10; Tot Asst. Annually 10; Total Staff 20; Served Annually 10; Staff 15.

St. Mary of Providence, 4200 N. Austin Ave., 60634. Tel: 773-545-8300; Fax: 773-545-8035; Email: srritab@sbcglobal.net; Web: www.smopchicago.org. Sr. Rita Butler, Dir.; Darlene Zdanowski, Admin.; Rev. Thomas A. Mulcrone, Chap. Developmental training and residential care of developmentally disabled adults.

St. Mary of Providence Bed Capacity 96; Sisters 6; Tot Asst. Annually 120; Total Staff 150.

Misericordia Home, 6300 N. Ridge, 60660-1017. Tel: 773-973-6300; Fax: 773-973-5214; Web: www.misericordia.com. Sr. Rosemary Connelly, R.S.M., Exec. Dir.; Rev. John J. Clair, Asst. Exec. Dir. Children and adults with developmental disabilities. Bed Capacity 612; Priests 1; Sisters 13; Tot Asst. Annually 820; Total Staff 1,006.

BARTLETT. *Bartlett Learning Center*, 801 Carillon Dr., Bartlett, 60103. Tel: 630-289-4221; Fax: 630-289-4390. Michael Meis, Prin.; Moisette McNerney, Librarian. Sponsored by the Sisters of St. Joseph, Third Order of St. Francis.Operates Bartlett Learning Center Day School Program and the Cupertino Home, Warrenville, IL. Day School program serves developmentally delayed and multiple handicapped individuals ages 3 to 21. Day School Program accepts youth identified LD, BD, EMH, TMH, and TBI Speech/Language Impaired, Autistic. Community Integrated Living Arrangement Serves developmentally delayed gentlemen ages 18 to 45.

Barlett Learning Center, Inc. dba Clare Woods Academy and Cupertino Home. Lay Staff 88; Patients Asst Anual. 115; Sisters 2.

LAKE ZURICH. *Mt. St. Joseph Home*, 24955 North Hwy. 12, Lake Zurich, 60047. Tel: 847-438-5050; Fax: 847-438-6313; Email: msjlz@aol.com; Web: mtstjosephhome.com. Sr. Lucy Tarolivo, Exec. Dir., Web: mtstjosephhome.com. Operated by the Daughters of St. Mary of Providence.Intermediate care for developmentally disabled women. Bed Capacity 129; Sisters 6; Tot Asst. Annually 130; Total Staff 180.

RIVER FOREST. *Big Sisters*, P.O. Box 5728, River Forest, 60305. Tel: 708-488-8893. Mrs. Caroline Brogan, Pres.; Mrs. Mary Alice Jovan, Past Pres.

TINLEY PARK. *St. Coletta's of Illinois, Inc.*, 18350 Crossing Dr., Tinley Park, 60487. Tel: 708-342-5200; Fax: 708-342-2579; Email: mconerty@stcil.org; Email: askafgaard@stcil.org; Web: www.stcil.org. Annette Skafgaard, Dir. Sponsored by the Sisters of St. Francis of Assisi. Residential care, education, job training & job placement for developmentally disabled children and adults. Bed Capacity 160; Capacity 450; Tot Asst. Annually 400; Total Staff 325.

Divisions:.

Lt. Joseph P. Kennedy Jr. School, Tinley Park, Tel: 708-342-5200; Fax: 708-342-2579.

Kennedy Vocational Job Training Center, Tinley Park, Tel: 708-342-5200; Fax: 708-342-2579.

St. Coletta's of Illinois Foundation, Tel: 708-342-5246; Fax: 708-342-2579; Email: bsiwinski@stcolettail.org. Affiliate.

[M] SENIOR CARE INSTITUTIONS

CHICAGO. *Cortland Manor Retirement Home*, 1900 N. Karlov, 60639. Tel: 773-235-3670; Email: gsaldana@catholiccharities.net. Gabriela Saldana, Dir. Catholic Charities Housing Development Corporation. Capacity 48.

St. Joseph Village of Chicago, 4021 W. Belmont Ave., 60641. Tel: 773-328-5500; Fax: 773-328-5502; Email: sjvinfo@franciscanministries.org; Web: www.stjosephvillageofchicago.com; Web: franciscancommunities.com. 11500 Theresa Dr., Lemont, 60439. Daniel Lunney, Dir. Mission Integration & Pastoral Care; Mr. Brian Celerio, Exec. Dir. Sponsored by Franciscan Sisters of Chicago-Franciscan Communities Inc. d/b/a St. Joseph Village of Chicago Priests 3; Sisters 1; Skilled Nursing Beds 54; Total Apartments 40; Annually Assisted 210; Total Staff 125.

Jugan Terrace, 2300 N. Racine Ave., 60614. Tel: 773-935-9600; Fax: 773-935-9614; Email: mschicago@littlesistersofthepoor.org.

Little Sisters of the Poor of Chicago, Inc. Senior Housing Apartments 50.

Little Sisters of the Poor Center for the Aging, 2325 N. Lakewood Ave., 60614. Tel: 773-935-9600; Fax: 773-935-9614. Sr. Marcel Joseph McCanless, L.S.P., Pres. Intermediate and skilled care facility.

Little Sisters of the Poor of Chicago, Inc. Bed Capacity 76; Residents 76; Sisters 11; Assisted Annually 100; Staff 112.

Mercy Circle, 3659 W. 99th St., 60655. Tel: 773-253-3600; Fax: 773-253-3700; Web: www.mercycircle.org. Frances Lachowicz, Exec. Dir. Sponsored by Sisters of Mercy of the Americas West Midwest Community. Managed by Trinity Senior Living Communities.Independent living apartments, licensed assisted living apartments, licensed skilled nursing units. Resident Capacity 111.

Presence Resurrection Life Center, 7370 W. Talcott Ave., 60631. Tel: 773-594-7400; Fax: 773-594-7402; Email: N.Razo@Presencehealth.org; Email: deana.wilson@presencehealth.org; Web: www.presencehealth.org/presence-resurrection-medical-center-chicago-life-center-skilled-nursing-care. Michael Gordon, Pres.; Nancy Razo, Admin.; Mark Wolski, Chap. A division of Presence Senior Services-Chicagoland; Skilled intermediate and sheltered nursing care. Bed Capacity 162; Tot Asst. Annually 461; Staff 163.

Presence Resurrection Retirement Community, 7262 W. Peterson Ave., 60631. Tel: 773-792-7930; Fax: 773-792-8316; Web: www.presencehealth.org. Mr. Kenneth Kolich, Exec. Dir.; Judy Reyes, Spiritual Care Dir. A division of Presence Chicago Hospitals Network managed by Presence Senior Services-Chicagoland. Total Apartments 473; Tot Asst. Annually 615; Total Staff 43.

DES PLAINES. *Presence Nazarethville*, 300 N. River Rd., Des Plaines, 60016. Tel: 847-297-5900; Fax: 847-297-0504; Email: Judy.MacPhersonSchumacher@presencehealth.org; Email: Maryann.McKeogh@presencehealth.org; Web: www.presencehealth.org. Sr. Maryann McKeogh, C.S.F.N., Admin.; Deacon Jack Smith, Spiritual Care Dir. Sponsored by Presence Health. Parent: Ascension Health Senior Care

Presence Senior Services-Chicagoland dba Presence Nazarethville Bed Capacity 83; Tot Asst. Annually 92; Total Staff 72.

EVANSTON. *Saint Francis Nursing and Rehabilitation Center*, 500 Ashbury Ave., Evanston, 60202. Tel: 847-316-3320; Fax: 847-316-3337; Web: www.seniors.reshealth.org. Sandra Bruce, Pres.; Michael Kaplan, Admin.; Leszek Baczkura, Coord. Spiritual Svcs.; Lauren Ivory, Chap. Sponsored by the Franciscan Sisters of the Sacred Heart, Servants of the Holy Heart of Mary, Sisters of Mercy of the Americas, Sisters of the Holy Family of Nazareth & Sisters of the Resurrection.A division of Resurrection Senior Services; Comprehensive nursing, rehabilitation and social services. Bed Capacity 127.

GLENVIEW. *Presence Maryhaven Nursing and Rehabilitation Center*, 1700 East Lake Ave., Glenview, 60025. Tel: 847-729-1300; Fax: 847-729-9620; Email: marcus.shaw@presencehealth.org. Michael Gordon, Pres.; Marcus Shaw, Admin.; Michael Stacy, Chap. Sponsored by Presence Health Ministries.A division of Presence Senior Services-Chicagoland.; Parent: Ascension Health Senior Care; Home for Aged, intermediate and skilled care facilities, Medicare, Therapy. Capacity 135; Tot Asst. Annually 287; Total Staff 119.

JUSTICE. *Rosary Hill Home*, 9000 W. 81st St., Justice, 60458. Tel: 708-458-3040; Fax: 708-458-7230; Email: rosaryhill@sbcglobal.net; Web: www.sistersop.org. Sr. M. Natalie, O.P., Admin.; Rev. Raymond J. Jasinski, (Retired). Operated by the Dominican Sisters Immaculate Conception Province Bed Capacity 60; Sisters 13; Number Under Care 60; Staff 71.

LAGRANGE PARK. *Presence Bethlehem Woods Retirement Community*, 1571 Ogden Ave., La Grange Park, 60526. Tel: 708-579-3663; Fax: 708-579-7159; Web: www.presencehealth.org. Mary Jester, Admin.; Maria Brantman, Dir. Sponsored by Presence Health Ministries.A division of Presence Chicago Hospitals Network, managed by Presence Senior Services-Chicagoland. Independent living apartments and Licensed assisted living apartments. Bed Capacity 334; Tot Asst. Annually 382; Total Staff 60.

LEMONT. *Alvernia Manor Senior Living*, 13950 Main St., Lemont, 60439. Tel: 630-257-7721; Fax: 630-257-0338; Email: info@alverniamanor.org; Web: www.alverniamanor.org. Sr. Cynthia Drozd, O.S.F., Admin. Sponsored by The School Sisters of St. Francis of Christ the King. Residents 50.

Franciscan Village, 1270 Village Dr., Lemont, 60439. Tel: 630-243-3400; Fax: 630-257-5823; Email: MGarbacz@franciscancommunities.org; Web: www.franciscancommunities.com. 11500 Theresa Dr., Lemont, 60439. Rev. Robert D. Lucas, C.M., Priest/Chap.; Daniel Bannon, Exec. Dir.; Juanita Liepelt, Chap.; Margaret M. Garbacz, Dir. of Mission Integration/Pastoral Care. Sponsored by the Franciscan Sisters of Chicago.Continuing Care Retirement Community.

Legal Titles: Franciscan Communities, Inc. / Franciscan Ministries Sponsored by the Franciscan Sisters of Chicago. Franciscan Communities, Inc. d/b/ a Franciscan Village Tot Asst. Annually 600; Total Staff 325; Independent Living 184; Assisted Living 81; Skilled Nursing 124.

LINDENHURST. *The Village at Victory Lakes*, 11500 Theresa Dr., Lemont, 60439. Tel: 847-356-4600; Email: MMcVey@franciscancommunities.org; Web: www.franciscancommunities.com. Rev. Anselm Ibe; Calvin Isaacson, Exec. Dir.; Mary Kay McVey, Dir. of Mission Integration & Pastoral Care. Franciscan Communities, Inc. d/b/a The Village at Victory Lakes Tot Asst. Annually 992; Total Staff 300; Assisted Living 60; Independent Living 140; Skilled Nursing 120.

NILES. *Presence Saint Benedict Nursing and Rehabilitation Center* dba Presence Saint Benedict Nursing and Rehabilitation Center, 6930 W. Touhy Ave., Niles, 60714. Tel: 847-647-0003; Fax: 847-588-2515; Web: www.seniors.presencehealth.org. Mr. Richard Nash, Chap.

Legal Title: Presence Senior Services - Chicagoland. Bed Capacity 123; Tot Asst. Annually 400; Staff 125.

NORTHLAKE. *Presence Casa San Carlo Retirement Community*, 420 N. Wolf Rd., Northlake, 60164. Tel: 708-562-4300; Fax: 708-492-0682; Email: deana.wilson@presencehealth.org; Web: www.seniors.presencehealth.org. Deana Wilson, Admin.; Elvenord Vertus, Dir. Sponsored by Presence Health Ministries.Now a part of Ascension Health Senior Care.

Legal Name: Presence Senior Services-Chicagoland d.b.a. Presence Casa San Carlo Retirement Community Bed Capacity 184; Residents 173; Total Staff 23.

Presence Villa Scalabrini Nursing and Rehabilitation Center, 480 N. Wolf Rd., Northlake, 60164-1667. Tel: 708-562-0040; Fax: 708-562-5180; Email: Daryce.Fields@presencehealth.org; Web: www.seniors.presencehealth.org. Daryce Fields, Admin.; Rev. Daniel R. Steiner, Spiritual Care Dir. Sponsored by the Franciscan Sisters of the Sacred Heart, Servants of the Holy Heart of Mary, Sisters of Mercy of the Americas, Sisters of the Holy Family of Nazareth & Sisters of the Resurrection.Organization name: Ascension Health Senior Care, Diocese: St Louis and Entity type: Missouri Nonprofit. Bed Capacity 229; Priests 1; Tot Asst. Annually 579; Staff 175.

PALATINE. *St. Joseph's Home for the Elderly*, 80 W. Northwest Hwy., Palatine, 60067. Tel: 847-358-5700; Fax: 847-358-5763; Email: mspalatine@littlesistersofthepoor.org. Sr. Margaret Charles Hogarty, L.S.P., Supr. Operated by the Little Sisters of the Poor.

Little Sisters of the Poor of Palatine, Inc. Bed Capacity 95; Sisters 12; Tot Asst. Annually 103; Total Staff 117.

PALOS PARK. *Holy Family Villa*, 12220 S. Will-Cook Rd., Palos Park, 60464. Tel: 630-257-2291; Fax: 630-257-2334; Email: hfv12375@aol.com. Roberta Magurany, Admin. Catholic Charities, Archdiocese of Chicago. Bed Capacity 129; Residents 109; Sisters 5; Total Staff 120; Total Assisted 140.

PARK RIDGE. *Presence Resurrection Nursing and Rehabilitation Center*, 1001 N. Greenwood, Park Ridge, 60068. Tel: 847-692-5600; Fax: 847-692-2305; Email: Judy.MacPhersonSchumacher@presencehealth.org; Web: www.seniors.presencehealth.org. Michael Gordon, Pres.; Lisa Orzada, Admin.; Sr. Philomina Jose, Chap.; Michael Stacy, Chap. Sponsored by Presence Health Ministries.Organization Name Ascension Health Senior Care, Entity Type Missouri nonprofit corporation, Diocese St Louis. Bed Capacity 298; Sisters 1; Tot Asst. Annually 980; Total Staff 216.

WHEELING. **Addolorata Villa*, 555 McHenry Rd., Wheeling, 60090-3899. Tel: 847-537-2900; Fax: 847-215-5805; Email: tong@franciscancommunities.com; Web: www.addoloratavilla.com; Web: www.franciscancommunities.com. 11500 Theresa Drive, Lemont, 60439. Ms. Dawn Cohn, Exec. Dir. & Admin., Email: dcohn@franciscancommunities.com; Ms. Maureen Tokar, Dir. Residential Svcs.; Rev. Antonio Ong, Dir. Mission Integration & Pastoral Care, Email: tong@franciscancommunities.com; Mr. Leo Jaboni, Chap. Sponsored by the Franciscan Sisters of Chicago, a continuing care retirement community.Sponsored by the Franciscan Sisters of Chicago, a continuing care retirement community. Franciscan Communities, Inc. d/b/a Addolorata Villa.

Legal Title: Franciscan Communities, Inc. Sisters (Servants of Mary) 5; Skilled 88; Intermediate 10; Sheltered 31; Independent Living Apartments 100; Assisted Living 61; Assisted Living - Memory Lane 22.

[N] MONASTERIES AND RESIDENCES OF PRIESTS AND BROTHERS

CHICAGO. *Annunciata Priory*, 11128 S. Avenue G, 60617-6925. Tel: 773-221-1043; Fax: 773-221-1556; Email: annunciatachurch@yahoo.com; Web: www.servite.org. Rev. Vidal M. Martinez, O.S.M., Admin.

Assumption Priory, 323 W. Illinois St., 60654. Tel: 312-644-0036; Fax: 312-644-1838; Email: pastor@assumption-chgo.org; Web: www.assumption-chgo.org. Revs. Joseph Chamblain, O.S.M.; Lawrence Michael Doyle, O.S.M.; John M. Pawlikowski, O.S.M., Ph.D.

St. Augustine Friary, 5413 S. Cornell Ave., 60615-5603. Tel: 773-358-6500; Fax: 773-358-6501; Email: ttaylor11406@gmail.com. Rev. James G. Thompson, O.S.A., Prior; Bro. Thomas Taylor, O.S.A., Formation Team Member & Sub-Prior; Rev. Joseph Mostardi, Dir.

The Augustinians-Provincialate, Augustinian Province Offices, 5401 S. Cornell Ave., 60615-5664. Tel: 773-595-4000; Fax: 773-595-4004; Email: secretary@midwestaugustinians.org; Web: www.midwestaugustinians.org. Very Rev. Bernard C. Scianna, O.S.A., Prior Prov.; Bro. Thomas Taylor, O.S.A., Prov. Sec.; Revs. Thomas R. McCarthy, O.S.A., Vocation Dir., Tel: 773-776-3044; John D. Merkelis, O.S.A., Personnel Dir. & Vicar Prov.; Richard J. McGrath, O.S.A., Province Treas.; Sr. Mary Ann Hamer, O.S.F., Asst. Treas.; Mr. Michael W. Gerrity, Advancement Dir.; Deacon Robert O. Carroll Jr., Treas.

Chicago Province of the Society of Jesus, 1010 N. Hooker St., 60642. Tel: 773-975-6363; Tel: 773-975-6888; Fax: 773-975-0230; Email: UMISocius@jesuits.org; Web: www.jesuitsmidwest.org. Very Rev. Brian G. Paulson, S.J., Prov.; Rev. Glen Chun, S.J., Prov. Asst.

St. Clare Friary, 3407 S. Archer Ave., 60608-6817. Tel: 773-890-1238; Fax: 773-847-7409; Web: www.capuchinfranciscans.org. Rev. John Scherer, Pastoral Min./Coord.; Bros. Michael Dorn, Pastoral Assoc.; Truong Nguyen, Pastoral Assoc.; Revs. Edward Foley, O.F.M.Cap., Vice Postulator, Blessed Solanus Casey; William Cieslak, O.F.M.-Cap., Itinerant Preacher; John Celichowski, O.F.-M.Cap., Contact Person; Worku Yohannes Gabre, O.F.M.Cap., Student; Anish Cleetus Palliyil, O.F.-M.Cap., Student; Bro. Truong Dinh, O.F.M.Cap., Temporary Professed; Friar Steven Kropp, O.F.M.-Cap., Vicar; Bros. Brenton Ertel, O.F.M.Cap., Temporary Professed; Fred Cabras, O.F.M.Cap., Temporary Professed; Joseph Babcock, In Res.; Faris Najor, In Res.; Nathan Linton, In Res.

Claretian Missionaries-U.S.A. Province, Inc., 205 W. Monroe St., 7th Fl., 60606. Tel: 312-544-8220; Fax: 312-768-4056; Email: petersg@claretians.org. Very Rev. Rosendo Urrabazo, C.M.F., Prov. Supr.; Most Rev. Placido Rodriguez; Revs. Milton E. Alvarez, C.M.F.; Robert Billett; Robert Bishop; Salvatore Bonano; Mark Brummel; Thomas Brummel; Agustin Carrillo; Carlos Castillo; Theodore Cirone; Beauplan Derilus; Alberto Domingo; Frank Ferrante; John Hampsch; Frank Iacona; Paul Keller; Donald Lavelle; Byron Macias; Paulis Marandi; Steve Niskanen; Gilles Njobam; Raymond O'Connor; Malachy Osunwa; Sahaya Peter; James Raphel; Javier Reyes; Benjamin Romero-Arrieta; Benjamin Romero-Arrieta; Raymond Smith; Richard Todd; Manuel Villalobos; Richard Wozniak; Bros. Rene LePage; Daniel Magner, C.M.F.; Paul Roy; Richard Wilga, C.M.F. Brothers 9; Postulants 4; Priests 90; Professed Students 4.

Claretian Formation Houses:

Provincial Residence, 400 N. Euclid Ave., Oak Park, 60302. Tel: 708-848-2076; Fax: 708-848-2069. Very Rev. Rosendo Urrabazo, C.M.F.; Revs. Richard Bartlett, C.M.F.; Thomas Brummel, C.M.F.; Raymond E. O'Connor, C.M.F., Supr.; Wayne Schimmelmann, C.M.F.; Richard J. Todd, C.M.F.; Bros. Daniel Magner, C.M.F.; Richard Paquette, C.M.F.; Richard Wilga, C.M.F.

Claret House (Formation Residence), 5540 S. Everett St., 60637. Tel: 773-493-8119; Fax: 773-493-8411. Revs. Mark J. Brummel, C.M.F.; Theodore Cirone, C.M.F.; Steve Niskanon, C.M.F., Novice Master & Prefect of Students; Manuel Villalobos, C.M.F.

Claret Center, Inc., 5536 S. Everett Ave., 60637. Tel: 773-643-6259; Fax: 773-643-6929; Email: office@claret.org; Web: www.claretcenter.org. Mary Hogan, Exec. Dir.

Claretians, Inc., 205 W. Monroe, 60606. Tel: 312-544-8220; Fax: 312-768-4056; Email: petersg@claretians.org; Web: www.claretians.org. Rev. Mark J. Brummel, C.M.F., Treas.

Claretian Missionaries Community Support Trust, 400 N. Euclid Ave., Oak Park, 60302. Tel: 708-848-2076; Fax: 708-848-2069. Very Rev. Rosendo Urrabazo, C.M.F., Pres.; Revs. Leonard Brown, C.M.F.; Mark J. Brummel, C.M.F., Treas.; Jose Sanchez, C.M.F.; Bruce L. Wellems, C.M.F., Sec.

Claretian Missionaries Charitable Property Trust, 205 W. Monroe St., 7th Fl., 60606. Tel: 312-544-8221. Rev. Mark J. Brummel, C.M.F., Trustee.

Claretian Missionaries Continuing Care Trust, 205 W. Monroe St., 7th Fl., 60606. Tel: 312-544-8221. Rev. Mark J. Brummel, C.M.F., Trustee.

Claretian Missionaries Endowment Trust, 205 W. Monroe St., 7th Fl., 60606. Tel: 312-544-8221. Rev. Mark J. Brummel, C.M.F., Trustee.

Claretian Missionaries Service Corporation, 205 W. Monroe St., 7th Fl., 60606. Tel: 312-544-8220; Fax: 312-768-4056. Rev. Mark J. Brummel, C.M.F., Treas.

Claretian Volunteers and Lay Missionaries, 205 W. Monroe St., 60606. Tel: 312-544-8176, Ext. 479; Fax: 312-236-7756; Email: volunteers@claretians.

org; Web: www.claretianvolunteers.org. Rev. Mark J. Brummel, C.M.F., Provincial Treas.

Columban Fathers Theologate, 5103 S. Ellis Ave., 60615. Tel: 773-955-0660; Fax: 773-955-0805. Very Rev. Timothy Mulroy, S.S.C., Rector; Rev. Leo Distor, S.S.C., Vice Rector. Priests 2; Seminarians 14.

Congregation of Christian Brothers, Brother Rice Community, 10001 S. Pulaski Rd., 60655.
Tel: 773-429-4300; Email: bropathayes@gmail.com. Bros. Thomas J. Collins, C.F.C., Community Leader; George G. Gremley, C.F.C.; R.L. Stanish, C.F.C.; Patrick T. Varilla, C.F.C. Brothers 4.

Conventual Franciscans of St. Bonaventure Province, 6107 N. Kenmore Ave., 60660. Tel: 773-274-7681; Fax: 773-274-9751; Email: dmk9271@gmail.com. Rev. Michael Zielke, O.F.M.Conv., Min. Prov.
The Conventual Franciscans of Saint Bonaventure Province Corporation
The Conventual Franciscans of Saint Bonaventure Province Charitable Continuing Care Trust Fund
Franciscan Friars Educational Corporation
St. Hedwig Cemetery and Mausoleum Corporation
Franciscan Friars Retirement CorporationSaint Bonaventure Friary, 6107 N. Kenmore Ave., 60660. Tel: 773-764-8811. Revs. Anthony Lajato, O.F.M.-Conv., Guardian & Co-Dir., Postulants; Justin Kusibab, O.F.M.Conv.; Bros. Joseph Graff; Joseph Schenk, O.F.M.Conv.; Rev. Robert Cook, O.F.M.-Conv., Sec. Province.
Assigned but serving elsewhere: Revs. Bernard Geiger, O.F.M.Conv., Apostolate for Family Consecration, 3375 County Rd. 36, Bloomingdale, OH 43910-7903; John Calgaro, O.F.M.Conv., Milwaukee, WI.

Croatian Franciscan Custody of the Holy Family, 4851 S. Ellis Ave., 60615. Tel: 773-536-0552;
Fax: 773-536-2094; Email: jgrbes@gmail.com; Web: www.crofranciscans.com. Rev. Jozo Grbes, O.F.M., Custos, Croatian Franciscan Custody of the Holy Family. *St. Anthony's Friary*, 4848 S. Ellis Ave., 60615. Tel: 773-373-3463; Fax: 773-268-7744. Revs. Josip N. Galic, O.F.M., Guardian; Ljubo Krasic, O.F.M.; Zvonimir Kutlesa, O.F.M.; Philip Pavich, O.F.M.

Croatian Franciscan Fathers, 6346 N. Ridge, 60660. Tel: 773-262-0535; Fax: 773-262-4603; Email: bastepinacchicago@sbcglobal.net. Rev. Paul Maslach, O.F.M., Croatian Catholic Mission Blessed Alojzije Stepinac.

Crosier Community of Chicago, 5401 S. Cornell Ave., 60615. Tel: 773-684-6975; Fax: 773-684-8357. Rev. Thomas Enneking, O.S.C.; Bro. David Donnay, O.S.C.

DePaul Vincentian Residence, 2233 N. Kenmore Ave., 60614-3594. Tel: 773-325-8700; Email: pmcdevi1@depaul.edu. Revs. Patrick McDevitt, C.M., Supr.; Jeremy R. Dixon, C.M.; Dan Borlik, Campus Min.; William Piletic, Chap.; Thomas Gao, International Priest in Res.; Stanislav Bindas, C.M., In Res.; Woldekidan Desalegn, In Res.; Jose Maria Garcia, In Res.; Fanta Getahun, In Res.; Ranjan Lima, In Res.; Andreas Mueller, In Res.; Hugh O'Donnell, In Res.; Joseph Van Diem Pham, In Res.; Michael Njeru, C.M.; Robert R. Rohrich, C.M.; Paul Sisul, C.M.; Mark Pranaitis, C.M., Admin.; Mr. Greg Hallam, Treas. Congregation of the Mission, Society of Priests.

Divine Word Theologate, 5342 S. University, 60615-5106. Tel: 773-288-2777 (office);
Tel: 773-288-7923 (residence); Fax: 773-288-6307. Revs. Michael Hutchins, S.V.D., Rector; Brandon Hiep Nguyen, S.V.D., Dir. Formation Admonitor & Vice Rector; vanThanh Nguyen, S.V.D.; Roger P. Schroeder, S.V.D., Admonitor; Dominikus Moi, S.V.D.; Bro. Michael Decker, S.V.D., Dir. Brother Formation & Dir. Ministries; Rev. Stephen B. Bevans, S.V.D. Brothers 1; Priests 6; Students 24.

Dominican Community, 1914 S. Ashland Ave., 60608. Tel: 312-829-1931; Fax: 312-226-6119; Email: bcurran@stpiusvparish.org. Revs. Charles W. Dahm, O.P.; Matthias R. Mueller, O.P.; Brendan A. Curran, O.P.

Dominicans (Provincial Office), 1910 S. Ashland Ave., 60608-2904. Tel: 312-243-0011;
Fax: 312-829-8471; Email: office@opcentral.org; Web: www.opcentral.org. Revs. James V. Marchionda, O.P., Prov.; Jude McPeak, O.P., Dir.; Paul de Porres Whittington, O.P., Dir.; Thomas H. Tobin, S.J., Dir.; Very Rev. Louis S. Morrone, O.P., Vicar; Rev. Andrew Wisdom, Vicar
Dominicans, Province of St. Albert the Great, U.S.A. (Central Dominican Province)
Provincial Staff: Very Rev. James V. Marchionda, O.P., Prior Prov.; Revs. Michail Ford, O.P., Spiritual Dir. Shrine of St. Jude; Steven F. Kuhlmann, O.P., Promoter of Dominican Laity; Very Rev. Louis S. Morrone, O.P., Socius & Vicar Prov.; Revs. Andrew-Carl Wisdom, O.P., Vicar for Devel.; Jay Harrington, O.P., Ph.D., S.T.D., Regent of Studies. *The New Priory Press*, 1910 S. Ashland Ave., 60608-2904. Tel: 312-243-0011;
Fax: 312-829-8471; Email: newpriorypress@opcentral.org; Web: www.newpriorypress.com. Very Rev. Charles E. Bouchard, O.P., Dir. *St. Pius V Priory*, 1909 S. Ashland Ave., 60608-2904. Tel: 312-226-0074;
Fax: 312-226-6199; Email: stpiusv@gmail.com. Very Rev. Louis S. Morrone, O.P., Socius & Vicar Provincial & Prior; Revs. William J. Bernacki, O.P.; Joseph E. Bidwill, O.P.; John Vincent Blake, O.P.; Brian G. Bricker, O.P.; Gerard B. Cleator, O.P.; Rapael A. Fabish, O.P.; Michail Ford, O.P.; John M. Gambro, O.P.; Thomas M. Jackson, O.P.; Albert G. Judy, O.P.; Thomas P. Lynch, O.P.; James V. Marchionda, O.P.; Michael J. Monshau, O.P.; Walter T. O'Connell, O.P.; Mark Paraday, O.P.; Patrick R. Rearden, O.P.; Edward H. Riley, O.P.; Michael B. Ruthenberg, O.P.; Jose Santiago, O.P.; Brian G. Walker, O.P.; Paul de Porres Whittington, O.P.; Jude McPeak, O.P.; Peter Otillio, O.P.; Bro. Stephen D. Lucas, O.P.; Revs. Jon Alexander, (Retired); James Barnett, (Retired); David Delich, O.P.; Francis X. Dyer, O.P., (Retired); Jordan A. McGrath, O.P., (Retired); Nicholas Monco, O.P., Chap.; Daniel W. Morrissey, O.P., (Retired); Christopher Saliga, Campus Min.
Shrine of St. Jude Thaddeus; Society for Vocational Support, Inc.; St. Dominic Mission Society; Dominican Social Action Fund; Dominican Laity; The Bolivian Trust of the Dominicans; Office for Mission Advancement; The New Priory Press.

Federation of Augustinians of North America, 5401 S. Cornell Ave., 60615-5664. Tel: 773-595-4036;
Tel: 610-203-9272 (Exec. Dir.); Fax: 773-595-4004; Email: director@fanaosa.org; Web: www.fanaosa.org. Revs. Michael F. DiGregorio, O.S.A., Prior; Gary McCloskey, O.S.A., Exec. Dir.; Kevin Mullins, Council Member; Anthony B. Pizzo, O.S.A., Council Member.

Franciscan House of Studies, 6107 N. Kenmore Ave., 60660. Tel: 773-764-8811; Fax: 773-274-9751; Email: dmk9271@gmail.com. Rev. Anthony Lajato, O.F.M.Conv., Guardian & Co-Dir., Postulants. A Formation House of Conventual Franciscan Friars.

Holy Evangelists Friary Order of Friars Minor. 4513 N. Ashland Blvd., 60651-5401. Tel: 773-878-3723; Fax: 773-878-1382; Email: friarjpc@gmail.com. Friar Johnpaul Cafiero, O.F.M., D.Min., M.A., M.Div.; Revs. Robert Pawell, M.Div.; Eulogio Roselada, O.F.M. Priests 3.

Holy Name Friary, Assumption BVM Province, 3800 W. Peterson Ave., 60659-3116. Tel: 708-209-6889. Revs. Bernard Kennedy, O.F.M., M.Div., Guardian; Dir. Spiritual Formation, Institute for Diaconal Studies, Mundelein Seminary; Camillus Janas, O.F.M., Chaplain to Felician Sisters; Lawrence Janowski, O.F.M., Chap. Felician Sisters.

Holy Spirit Friary, Order of Friars Minor, 5225 S. Greenwood Ave., 60615-4335. Tel: 773-753-1920. Revs. Gilberto Cavazos-Gonzales, O.F.M., S.L.T., Faculty, Catholic Theological Union; Albert Haase, O.F.M., Staff, Mayslake Ministries; Phil D. Hogan, O.F.M., Faculty, Hales Franciscan High School; Gilbert Ostdiek, O.F.M., S.T.D., Faculty, Catholic Theological Union; Charles E. Payne, O.F.M., Ph. D., Adjunct Faculty, Catholic Theological Union; Bro. Charles Reid, O.F.M., Theological Student; Rev. David Rodriguez, O.F.M., M.F.A., Faculty, St. Rita of Cascia High School.

Institute of Christ the King Sovereign Priest, 6415 S. Woodlawn Ave., 60637-3817. Tel: 773-363-7409;
Fax: 773-363-7824; Email: info@institute-christ-king.org; Web: www.institute-christ-king.org. Very Rev. Msgr. R. Michael Schmitz; Revs. Matthew L. Talarico, Prov.; Joel Estrada, Vicar; Jean-Baptiste Commins, (French Guiana) Rector; Matthew Weaver, Sec. *Shrine of Christ the King Sovereign Priest*, Church: 64th and Woodlawn. Res.: Priory of the Infant Jesus.

St. John Stone Friary, 1165 E. 54th Pl., 60615-5109. Tel: 773-684-6510; Fax: 773-684-9830; Web: www.midwestaugustinians.org. Revs. Karl A. Gersbach, O.S.A., Prior; Reinhard J. Sternemann, O.S.A., Treas.; John Szura, O.S.A.; Bros. Fred R. Kaiser, O.S.A., Subprior; John Patrick Currier, O.S.A.; Rev. James J. Sheridan; Bro. David W. Adelsbach, O.S.A.; Rev. Michael J. O'Connor, O.S.A.

St. Joseph Interprovincial Post-Novitiate Formation House (A Franciscan House of the Sacred Heart Province) 5495 S. Hyde Park Blvd., 60615.
Tel: 773-363-0072; Fax: 773-363-0076; Email: jrozanskyofm@gmail.com. Rev. Joseph Rozansky, Guardian&Formation Staff. Professed 5; Students 13.

St. Jude League, 205 W. Monroe, 60606.
Tel: 312-236-7782; Fax: 312-236-7230; Web: www.claretians.org. Rev. Mark J. Brummel, C.M.F., Dir. Editorial Offices: "U.S. Catholic" and other Claretian Publications.

Korean Catholic Center, 4115 N. Kedvale, 60641.
Tel: 773-283-3979. Rev. John Smith, S.S.C., Dir.

La Salette Theologate, 4541 S. Greenwood Ave., 60653. Tel: 678-258-5661.

Lithuanian American Jesuits (Della Strada Residence and Lithuanian Youth Center) 2345 W. 56th St., 60636. Tel: 630-257-5570; Email: baniulisa@gmail.com; Web: www.jezuitai.lt. Rev. Algis Baniulis, S.J., Pres.
Jesuit Fathers of Della Strada Inc.Baltic Jesuits Advancement Project, 1380 Castlewood Dr., Lemont, 60439-6732. Tel: 630-243-6234; Email: lithjesuit@hotmail.com. Revs. Antanas Grazulis, S.J., Sec.; Algis Baniulis, S.J., Chap. Dir. *Blessed Jurgis Matulaitis Mission*, 14911 E. 127th St., Lemont, 60439. Tel: 630-257-5613; Email: matulaitismission@gmail.com; Web: www.matulaitismission.com. Priests 1. *Lithuanian Youth Center Inc.*, 5620 S. Claremont Ave., 60636. Tel: 773-778-7500.

Marist Brothers, Monastery Community, 4200 W. 115th St., 60655. Tel: 773-881-6380;
Fax: 773-881-0595; Email: moran.kevin@marist.net; Web: www.marist.net. Bros. Julian Roy; Paul Forgues; Richard Grenier; Christopher Shannon.

Marist Brothers, St. Ann Residence, 10114 S. Leavitt, 60643. Tel: 773-239-4116. Bros. Vito Aresto, Dir.; Stephen Synan; Hugh Turley, F.M.S.; Henry Hammer; Brendan Brennan.

Maryknoll Fathers & Brothers, 5128 S. Hyde Park Blvd., 60615-4217. Tel: 773-493-3367;
Fax: 773-493-3427; Email: chicago@maryknoll.org; Web: maryknollsociety.org. Mr. Kevin Foy, Assoc. Regl. Dir.; Mr. Gregory Darr, Regl. Promoter; Mr. Jay Weingarten, Major Gift Officer; Revs. William J. Donnelly, M.M.; John W. Eybel, M.M.; William Mullan, M.M.; Stephen Booth, M.M.; Thomas A. Tiscornia, M.M.; Bro. Mark Gruenke, M.M.
Legal Title: The Catholic Foreign Mission Society of America.

Monastery of the Holy Cross, 3111 S. Aberdeen St., 60608-6503. Tel: 773-927-7424; Fax: 773-927-5734; Email: edward@chicagomonk.org; Web: www.chicagomonk.org. Revs. Peter Funk, O.S.B., Conventual Prior; Brendan D. Creeden, O.S.B., Novice Master; Edward J. Glanzmann, O.S.B., Porter; Guests; Bros. Timothy Ferrell, O.S.B., Asst. Cellarer; Ignatius Isaac, O.S.B., Librarian, Grounds; Augustine Jusas, O.S.B., Property Mgr.; Joseph Woudenberg, O.S.B., Gift Shop Mgr; Grounds; Gabriel Sumeral, O.S.B., Sacristan; Web Master. Benedictine Monks (Subiaco Cassinese Congregation). Non-Professed 1; Solemnly Professed Monks 8.

Order of Friar Servants of Mary (Servites) United States of America Province, Inc., Servite Provincial Center, 3121 W. Jackson Blvd, 60612-2729.
Tel: 773-533-0360; Fax: 773-533-8307; Email: michaelcallary@servitesUSA.org; Web: www.servite.org. Very Rev. John M. Fontana, O.S.M., Prov.; Revs. Gerald M. Horan, O.S.M., Prov. Asst.; Eugene M. Smith, O.S.M., Prov. Councilor; Donald M. Siple, O.S.M., Prov. Councilor; Michael M. Pontarelli, O.S.M., Prov. Councilor; Bro. Michael M. Callary, O.S.M., Sec.; Revs. Christopher M. Krymski, O.S.M., Dir. National Shrine of St. Peregrine; Paul M. Gins, O.S.M., Prov. Archivist; Mr. Eddie Murphy, Vocation Dir. Brothers 7; Priests 46. *National Shrine of St. Peregrine, O.S.M.*, 3121 W. Jackson Blvd., 60612-2729.
Tel: 773-638-0189, Ext. 100; Email: chriskrymski@aol.com; Web: www.servite.org. Rev. Christopher M. Krymski, O.S.M., Dir. *Servants of Mary (Servite) Development Office*, 1439 S. Harlem Ave., Berwyn, 60402. Tel: 708-795-8885;
Fax: 708-795-8892; Email: lchoate@servitedevelopment.org; Web: www.servite.org. Mr. James Foerster, Dir.; Rev. Lawrence M. Choate, O.S.M., Dir. Devel. Office. *Monastery of Our Lady of Sorrows*, 3121 W. Jackson Blvd., 60612-2729. Tel: 773-638-5800;
Fax: 773-533-8307; Web: www.servite.org. Bros. Edmund M. Baran, O.S.M.; Robert M. Fandel, O.S.M.; Joseph Fundak, O.S.M.; Leonardus Hambur, O.S.M.; Sebastianus Soy Mulu, O.S.M.; Revs. Lawrence M. Choate, O.S.M.; Frank M. Falco, O.S.M.; Thomas M. Greaney, O.S.M.; Michael M. Guimon, O.S.M.; Christopher M. Krymski, O.S.M.; Vidal M. Martinez, O.S.M.; David M. Brown, O.S.M.

Passionist Community of St. Vincent Strambi, 5417 S. Cornell Ave., 60615. Tel: 773-324-2704;
Fax: 773-324-2557; Email: jconley@passionist.org. Revs. John Schork, C.P., Vicar Prov. & Treas.; Donald Webber, C.P., Dir. Office Mission Effectiveness; Donald P. Senior, C.P., S.T.D., CTU Faculty; Bro. Enno Dango, C.P., CTU Faculty; Revs. John Conley, C.P., Supr., Dir. Ofc Mission Effectiveness; Alfredo Ocampo, C.P., M.Div., Formator, Formation Dir.; Robin Ryan, C.P., Ph.D., CTU Faculty; Francis X. Keenan, C.P., Resident Presence St. Benedict Nursing/Rehab Center; Tu-Jin Paul Kim, C.P., Pastor, Korean Martyrs Catholic Center; Bros. Nicholas Divine, Student; Phillip Donlan, Student; Soohoon Hur, Student
Congregation of the Passion: St. Vincent Strambi Community Priests 9; Seminarians 3.

St. Patrick's Missionary Society, 8422 W. Windsor Ave., 60656-4252. Tel: 773-887-4741; Email: spsil@spms.org; Web: spms.org. Revs. Michael Madigan, S.P.S., Office Manager; Michael Moore, S.P.S., Office Mgr. *St. Patrick's Fathers Guilds and Associates*.

St. Peter's Friary, 110 W. Madison St., 60602-4196. Tel: 312-372-5111; Fax: 312-853-2361; Web: www.stpetersloop.org. Revs. Arthur Anderson, O.F.M., Guardian; William Burton, O.F.M.; Kenneth Capalbo, O.F.M., Confessor; Wenceslaus Church, Confessor; Mario DiCicco, O.F.M., Confessor; Thomas Ess, O.F.M., Confessor; Kurt Hartrich, O.F.M., Pastor, St. Peter's Parish; James A. Hoffman, O.F.M., Confessor, Franciscan Outreach Ministry; Robert Hutmacher, O.F.M.; James Hwang, O.F.M., Student; Robert Karris, O.F.M.; George Musial, O.F.M., Confessor; Michael Perry, O.F.M.; Glenn Phillips, O.F.M., Confessor; Juan Carlos Ruiz Guerrero, O.F.M, Confessor; Elric Sampson, O.F.M., Confessor; Edward Shea, O.F.M., Vicar, Confessor; Peter Minh Van Dau, O.F.M.; Bros. Leo Geurts, O.F.M., Front Office, Book Store; Dot Hoang, O.F.M., Student; Clarence Klingert, O.F.M., Gift Shop Dir.; Thomas Krull, O.F.M., Maintenance Dir.; William Lanning, O.F.M., Business Office; Joseph Middleton, O.F.M., Front Office, Guest Master; Herbert Rempe, O.F.M., Business Mgr.; William Schulte, O.F.M., Librarian; Raymond Shuhert, O.F.M. Order of Friars Minor.

Premonstratensian Fathers and Brothers (Norbertines), 4841 S. Woodlawn Ave., 60615. Tel: 773-548-8020; Fax: 773-548-8023; Web: www.norbertines.org. Revs. James Baraniak, Supr.; A. Gerard Jordan, In Res.; Patrick LaPacz, In Res.; Binu Varghese, In Res.; Bro. Johnathan Turba, In Res.; Rev. Patrick Bergin, In Res.; Deacon Jordan Neeck, In Res. Holy Spirit House of Studies. Priests 4; Students 3.

Provincial Office of the Congregation of the Resurrection, 3601 N. California Ave., 60618-4602. Tel: 773-463-7506; Fax: 773-463-7512. Very Rev. Eugene Szarek, C.R., Prov. Supr.; Revs. Gary Hogan, C.R., Vicar Prov.; Steve Bartczyszyn, C.R., Prov. Councilor; Paul Sims, C.R., Ph.D., Prov. Councilor; George Zieba, C.R., Prov. Councilor; James Gibson, C.R., General Curia, Rome, Italy.

Redemptorist Fathers (1914) The Redemptorists/Denver Province, 1633 N. Cleveland Ave., 60614. Tel: 312-248-8894; Fax: 303-370-0036; Email: archives@redemptorists-denver.org; Web: www.redemptorists-denver.org. Rev. Stephen Rehrauer, C.Ss.R., Prov.

Redemptorist Society of Alaska (1964) c/o The Redemptorists/Denver Province, 1633 N. Cleveland Ave., 60614. Tel: 312-248-8894; Fax: 312-248-8852; Email: admin@redemptorists-denver.org. Rev. Stephen Rehrauer, C.Ss.R., Prov.

Redemptorist Fathers of Chicago, 1633 N. Cleveland Ave., 60614. Tel: 312-642-2498; Fax: 312-642-9283; Email: stmichael-cleveland@archchicago.org; Web: www.st-mikes.org. Revs. Stephen Rehrauer, C.Ss.R., Prov.; John Steingraeber, C.Ss.R., Admin.; Ramon Dompke, C.Ss.R.; John Fahey Guerra, Vicar; Bro. Lawrence Lujan Angel, Ordinary Consultor; Revs. Joseph P. Dorcey, C.Ss.R., Mission Procurator; Theodore J. Lawson, C.Ss.R., Rector, Pastor, St. Michael in Old Town; Gregory May, C.Ss.R., Treas.; J. Robert Fenili, C.Ss.R., In Res., (Retired); James Keena, C.Ss.R., In Res., (Retired); John Phelps, C.Ss.R., In Res.; Kenneth Sedlak, C.Ss.R., In Res.; Joseph J. Morin, C.Ss.R., In Res., Assoc. Pastor, St. Michael in Old Town.

Redemptorist Fathers of Iowa (1908) c/o The Redemptorist/Denver Province, 1633 N. Cleveland Ave., 60614. Tel: 312-248-8894; Fax: 312-248-8852; Email: admin@redemptorists-denver.org. Rev. Stephen Rehrauer, C.Ss.R., Prov.

The Redemptorists/Denver Province (1996) 1633 N. Cleveland Ave., 60614. Tel: 312-248-8894; Fax: 312-248-8852; Email: ljlacssr@hotmail.com; Web: www.redemptoristsdenver.org. Revs. Stephen Rehrauer, C.Ss.R., Prov.; John Fahey, C.Ss.R., Vicar; Gregory May, C.Ss.R., Treas.; John Steingraeber, C.Ss.R., Dir.; Bro. Laurence Lujan Angel, C.Ss.R, Prov. Brothers 22; Deacons 4; Priests 137; Cardinal 1.

The Redemptorists of Denver, Colorado (1981) 1633 N. Cleveland Ave., 60614. Tel: 312-248-8894; Fax: 312-248-8852; Email: OPC@redemptorists-denver.org; Web: www.redemptorists-denver.org. Rev. Stephen Rehrauer, C.Ss.R., Prov.

The Redemptorists of Glenview, Illinois, 1633 N. Cleveland Ave., 60614. Tel: 312-248-8894; Fax: 312-248-8852. Rev. Gregory May, C.Ss.R., Treas.

The Redemptorists of Greeley, Colorado, Inc. (1983) c/o The Redemptorists/Denver Province, 1633 N. Cleveland Ave., 60614. Tel: 312-248-8894; Fax: 312-248-8852; Email: OPC@redemptorists-denver.org; Web: www.redemptorists-denver.org. Rev. Stephen Rehrauer, C.Ss.R., Prov.

Redemptorist Society of Oregon (1906) c/o The Redemptorists/Denver Province, 1633 N. Cleveland Ave., 60614. Tel: 312-248-8894; Fax: 312-248-8852; Email: OPC@redemptorists-denver.org. Rev. Stephen Rehrauer, C.Ss.R., Prov.

St. Rita Monastery, 7740 S. Western Ave., 60620-5867. Tel: 773-476-3879; Fax: 773-925-2451. Very Rev. Bernard C. Scianna, O.S.A., Provincial; Revs. Alfred M. Burke, O.S.A.; Stephen M. Curry, O.S.A.; Bernard Danber, O.S.A., Prior; Edwin J. Dodge, O.S.A.; Thomas R. McCarthy, O.S.A.; John P. Tasto, O.S.A.; Gerald J. Van Overbeek, O.S.A.; Bros. Lawrence Sparacino, O.S.A.; Joe Ruiz, O.S.A. (See High Schools, Private).

Sacred Heart Mission House, 4105 N. Avers Ave., 60618. Tel: 773-588-7476; Fax: 773-588-6517; Email: agendajomu@gmail.com; Web: www.jezuici.org. Revs. Tomasz Oleniacz, S.J., Supr., Editor, The Messenger of The Sacred Heart in Polish language; Jerzy Brzoska; Jerzy Mordarski, S.J.; Bro. Adam Poreba; Jakub Spiewak

The Polish Messenger of The Sacred Heart, Inc. Brothers 1; Priests 5. *Jesuit Millennium Center*, 5835 W. Irving Park Rd., 60634. Tel: 773-777-7000; Fax: 773-427-0126; Email: agendajomu@gmail.com; Web: www.jezvici.org. *Jan Beyzym Society, Inc.*, 4105 N. Avers Ave., 60618. Tel: 773-588-7476; Fax: 773-588-6517; Email: agendajomu@gmail.com. Rev. Tomasz Oleniacz, S.J. (Polish Jesuit Foreign Missions).

Sant'Angelo Community at St. Cyril Priory, 6401 S. Harper Ave., 60637. Tel: 773-324-0020; Email: baguilar@carmelnet.org; Web: www.mchs.org. Revs. Benjamin Aguilar, O.Carm., Prior; Carl J. Markelz, O.Carm.; Bro. Neil Conlisk; Leopold Glueckert; Tracy O'Sullivan, (Retired); Enrique Varela.

Residing here are all the priests who teach at Mt. Carmel High School: Revs. Benjamin Aguilar, O.Carm.; Tony Mazurkiewicz, O.Carm.

Scalabrini House of Theology, 5121 S. University Ave., 60615. Tel: 773-684-5230; Tel: 773-684-1706; Fax: 773-684-5240; Email: scalajmr@hotmail.com. Revs. Jesus Reyes, C.S., Rector; Mauro Lazzarato, C.S., Animator; Gino Dalpiaz, C.S., Spiritual Dir. Priests 2; Students 8.

USA Midwest Province of the Society of Jesus, Inc., 1010 N. Hooker St., 60642. Tel: 773-975-6363; Fax: 773-975-0230; Email: UMISocius@jesuits.org; Web: www.jesuitsmidwest.org. Very Rev. Brian G. Paulson, S.J., Prov. USA Midwest Province of the Society of Jesus, Email: umiprovincial@jesuits.org; Revs. Albert J. Di Ulio, S.J., Treas.; Glen Chun, S.J., Socius; Timothy R. Lannon, S.J., Dir. Brothers 28; Priests 406; Scholastics 77. Jesuits Serving Abroad: Revs. Richard J. Baumann, S.J., (Nairobi); Keith J. Esenther, S.J., (Zimbabwe); Kevin L. Flannery, S.J., (Rome); Robert J. Geisinger, S.J., (Rome); Charles Rodrigues, S.J.; Jacob D. Martin, S.J., (London); J. Thomas McClain, S.J., (Rome); Paul R. Mueller, S.J., (Rome); Joseph E. Mulligan, S.J., (Managua); Lewis C. Murtaugh, S.J., (Peru); Eduardo Pinzon-Umana, S.J., (Retired); James M. O'Leary, S.J., (Spain); Bernard J. Owens, S.J., (Kenya); John R. Sima, S.J., (Peru); Mark J. George, S.J. Members in the U.S. not listed elsewhere: Revs. Thomas S. Acker, S.J., (Youngstown, OH); Paul J. Nienaber, S.J., (Winona, MN); Robert J. Ochs, S.J., (Cerrito, CA); Mitchell C. Pacwa, S.J., (Birmingham, AL); Donald Vettese, S.J., (Ann Arbor).

USA Midwest Province of the Society of Jesus Aged and Infirmed Trust, 1010 N. Hooker St., 60642. Tel: 773-975-6870; Tel: 773-975-6363; Fax: 773-975-2042; Email: UMISocius@jesuits.org. Rev. Albert J. Di Ulio, S.J., Contact Person.

USA Midwest Province of the Society of Jesus Formation Trust, 1010 N. Hooker St., 60642. Tel: 773-975-6363; Tel: 773-975-6888; Fax: 773-975-0230; Email: UMISocius@jesuits.org. Rev. Albert J. Di Ulio, S.J., Contact Person.

USA Midwest Province of the Society of Jesus Apostolic Works Trust, 1010 N. Hooker St., 60642. Tel: 773-975-6363; Tel: 773-975-6888; Fax: 773-975-0230; Email: UMISocius@jesuits.org. Rev. Albert J. Di Ulio, S.J., Contact Person.

USA Midwest Province of the Society of Jesus Foundation Trust, 1010 N. Hooker St., 60642. Tel: 773-975-6363; Tel: 773-975-6888; Fax: 773-975-0230; Email: UMISocius@jesuits.org. Rev. Albert J. Di Ulio, S.J., Contact Person.

USA Midwest Province of the Society of Jesus St. Ignatius Trust, 1010 N. Hooker St., 60642. Tel: 773-975-6363; Tel: 773-975-6888; Fax: 773-975-0230; Email: UMISocius@jesuits.org. Rev. Albert J. Di Ulio, S.J., Contact Person. *Clark Street Jesuit Residence Community*, 357 W. Dickens Ave., 60614. Tel: 773-975-6363; Tel: 773-975-6888; Fax: 773-975-0230; Email: UMISocius@jesuits.org. Revs. Albert J. Di Ulio, S.J.; John P. Foley, S.J.; Stephen T. Krupa, S.J., Prof. Pastoral Studies; Timothy R. Lannon, S.J., Asst. to Prov.; Glen Chun, S.J., Prov. Asst.; Lawrence Biondi, S.J.; Daniel McDonald, Prov. Asst. Priests 12. *Woodlawn Jesuit Community*, 5554 S. Woodlawn, 60637. Tel: 773-975-6363; Tel: 773-975-6888; Fax: 773-975-0230; Email: UMISocius@jesuits.org. Revs. James M. Dixon, S.J.; Paul V. Mankowski, S.J.; Robert T. Sears, S.J.; James F. Vorwoldt, S.J.; James W. Schulzi, S.J. Priests 5.

Vincentian Community, Congregation of the Mission, Western Province, 2210-12 N. Racine Ave., 60614. Email: eudovic@depaul.edu. Revs. Richard B. Benson, C.M.; Gerard P. Kelly, C.M.; Robert D. Lucas, C.M.; J. Patrick Murphy, C.M.; Christopher S. Robinson, C.M.; Edward R. Udovic, C.M., Supr.; Bro. Mark Elder, C.M.

ARLINGTON HEIGHTS. *Viatorian Province Center-Clerics of St. Viator*, 1212 E. Euclid Ave., Arlington Heights, 60004-5747. Tel: 847-398-1354; Fax: 847-637-2145; Web: www.viatorians.com. Rev. Donald J. Fitzsimmons, C.S.V.; Bro. James E. Lewnard, C.S.V.; Revs. James E. Michaletz, C.S.V., 308 E. Marsile St., Bourbonnais, 60914; George J. Auger, C.S.V.; Robert T. Bolser, C.S.V.; John E. Eck, C.S.V.; John W. Milton, C.S.V.; Charles G. Bolser, C.S.V.; Arnold E. Perham, C.S.V.; Simon P. Lefebvre, C.S.V.; John E. Van Wiel, C.S.V.; Bros. Carlos Ernesto Florez, C.S.V.; Donald P. Houde, C.S.V.; Deacon Dale A. Barth, C.S.V.

Priests & Brothers of the Province Serving Abroad: Revs. Alejandro Adame, C.S.V.; Gustavo C. Lopez, C.S.V.; John A. Pisors, C.S.V.; Pedro E. Herrera, C.S.V.; Bro. Fredy Contreras, C.S.V., Clerigos de San Viator, Avenida Universitatire #62-100, Barrio La Villita, Tunja, Colombia; Revs. Jose Felipe Montes, C.S.V.; Albeyro Vanegas, C.S.V., Clerigos de San Viator, Autopista Norte #209-51, Bogota D.C., Colombia; Rafael Sanabria, C.S.V.; Edgar Suarez, C.S.V., Parroquia San Viator, Torremolinos, Lote 3, Vía Arrayanes, Bogota D.C., Colombia; Frank Encisco, C.S.V.; Edwin J. Ruiz, C.S.V., Parroquia Santa Ines de Guaymaral, Km 5 via Guaymaral, Bogota, D.C., Bogota D.C. Colombia; Carlos Luis Claro, C.S.V., Fraternidad Sacedotal, Carrera 8 #75-80, Bogota D.C., Colombia; Bros. Elkin A. Mendoza, C.S.V.; E. Jhobany Orduz, C.S.V.; Jhon Avellaneda, C.S.V.; Edwin Barreto, C.S.V.; Parmenio Medina, C.S.V., Clergios de San Viator, Autopista Norte #209-51, Bogota D.C., Colombia; Juan Carlos Ubaque, C.S.V., Tel: 011-571-676-0296; Juan Ramirez, C.S.V., Coligio San Viator, Avenida Universitaria #62-100, Barrio LaVillita, Tunja, Colombia.

Priests & Brothers Serving Elsewhere In The Archdiocese of Chicago: Revs. Corey D. Brost, C.S.V.; Mark R. Francis, C.S.V.; Thomas E. Long, C.S.V.; Moises L. Mesh, C.S.V.; Patrick W. Render, C.S.V.; Fredy L. Santos, C.S.V.; Bros. Peter N. Lamick, C.S.V.; John R. Eustice, C.S.V.; Michael T. Gosch, C.S.V.

Priests & Brothers Serving Elsewhere In U.S.A.: Revs. Daniel R. Belanger, C.S.V., 52742 E. 5000 N. Rd., Bourbonnais, 60914; James F. Fanale, C.S.V., 230 N. Sixth Ave., P.O. Box 470, Saint Anne, 60964; William F. Haesaert, C.S.V., 4219 Pinecrest Cir. E., Las Vegas, NV 89121; Michael P. Keliher, C.S.V., 2736 Legend Hollow Ct., Henderson, NV 89074; Lawrence D. Lentz, C.S.V., 2093 Heritage Oaks St., Las Vegas, NV 89119; Daniel J. Lydon, C.S.V., 308 E. Marsile St., Bourbonnais, 60914; Daniel J. Mirabelli, C.S.V., 1303 40th St., Rock Island, 61201; Jason P. Nesbit, C.S.V., 308 E. Marsile St., Bourbonnais, 60914; Daniel T. Nolan, C.S.V., 2501 Wigwam Pkwy., Apt. 728, Henderson, NV 89074; John M. Palmer, C.S.V., 1861 Portsmouth Dr., Lisle, 60532; John N. Peeters, C.S.V., 428 S. Indiana Ave., Kankakee, 60901; Richard J. Pighini, C.S.V., 428 S. Indiana Ave., Kankakee, 60901; Richard A. Rinn, C.S.V., 2461 E. Flamingo Rd., Las Vegas, NV 89121; Erwin M. Savela, C.S.V., 1601 Barton Rd., Apt. 1203, Redlands, CA 92373; Alan M. Syslo, C.S.V., 2736 Legend Hollow Ct., Henderson, NV 89074; Thomas R. von Behren, C.S.V., 2028 Heritage Oaks St., Las Vegas, NV 89119; Donald R. Wehnert, C.S.V., 428 S. Indiana Ave., Kankakee, 60901; Bros. John J. Dodd, C.S.V., 1916 Heritage Oaks St. #2040, Las Vegas, NV 89119; Patrick T. Drohan, C.S.V., Villa Desderata, 3015 N. Bayview Ln., McHenry, 60051; Carlos Ernesto Florez, C.S.V., 1932 Heritage Oaks St., Las Vegas, NV 89119; Michael A. Rice, C.S.V., 2461 E. Flamingo Rd., Las Vegas, NV 89121; Rob Robertson, C.S.V., 4219 Pinecrest Cir. E., Las Vegas, NV 89121; Daniel J. Tripamer, C.S.V., 4219 Pinecrest Cir. E., Las Vegas, NV 89121.

BLUE ISLAND. *Marist Brothers*, 12212 Irving Ave., Blue Island, 60406. Tel: 708-385-1488; Email: brown.

gerry@yahoo.com. Bros. Gerard Brown, F.M.S.; Christopher Shannon.

BURBANK. *Congregation of Christian Brothers* dba Christian Brothers of Ireland, Inc., 5550 W. 87th St., Burbank, 60459-2914. Tel: 773-429-4353; Fax: 773-429-4381; Email: bropathayes@gmail.com. Bro. Patrick Hayes, C.F.C., Sec.; Charles McKenna, In Res.; Donald McGovern, In Res.; Thomas Mahoney, In Res.; Peter Martin, In Res.; Paul Messick, In Res.

COUNTRYSIDE. *St. Gratian Friary, Franciscan Friars*, 5536 S. Edgewood Ln., Countryside, 60525-3426. Tel: 708-482-4546; Fax: 708-482-8676; Email: stgratian@aol.com. Revs. Charles Faso, O.F.M.; Dennis Koopman, O.F.M., Vicar; James Walton, O.F.M.; Bros. Leon Beranek, O.F.M.; Clarence Klingert, O.F.M., Guardian. Brothers 2; Priests 3.

ELK GROVE VILLAGE. *Congregation of Alexian Brothers Immaculate Conception Province, Inc.*, 600 Alexian Way, Elk Grove Village, 60007. Tel: 847-264-8704; Fax: 847-264-8697; Email: Adeline.Dzierozynski@alexian.net; Web: www.alexianbrothers.org. Bros. Daniel McCormick, C.F.A., Prov.; Richard Lowe, C.F.A., Prov. Asst.; Lawrence Krueger, C.F.A., Treas.; Jeffrey Callander, C.F.A., Sec.

Provincial Councilors: Bros. Daniel McCormick, C.F.A., Provincial; Jeffrey Callander, C.F.A., Sec.; Lawrence Krueger, C.F.A., Treas. & Asst. Sec.; Richard Lowe, C.F.A. *Brothers of St. Alexius Health and Welfare Fund, Inc.*, Tel: 847-385-7147; Fax: 847-483-7036.

EVANSTON. *Canisius House Jesuit Community*, 201 Dempster St., Evanston, 60201-4704. Tel: 847-475-1825; Email: canisiushouse201@gmail.com. Very Rev. Brian G. Paulson, S.J., Provincial; Revs. Patrick E. McGrath, S.J., Supr.; Stanislaw Czarnecki, S.J.; Wojciech Bojanowski, Campus Min.; Minh-Hoang Le, Campus MIn.

HICKORY HILLS. *Legion of Christ*, 8601 W. 89th St., Hickory Hills, 60457. Tel: 773-372-5142; Email: chicago@legionaries.org. Revs. Michael Mitchell, L.C., Supr.; Michael Moriarty, L.C.; Deacon Peter Krezelec, L.C.; Rev. Joshua West, L.C.; Deacon Brett Taira, L.C.; Revs. Bruce Wren, L.C.; John Brender, L.C.

LA GRANGE PARK. *Comboni Missionaries*, 1615 E. 31st St., La Grange Park, 60526-1377. Tel: 708-354-1999; Fax: 708-354-2006; Email: cmcoffice@sbcglobal.net; Web: www.combonimissionaries.org; Web: www.laymission-comboni.org. Revs. Jose Manuel Garcia Oviedo, M.C.C.J., Supr., Ministry; Chris Aleti, Ministry; John Paul Pezzi, M.C.C.J., Busar; Angelo Biancalana, M.C.C.J., (Retired).

LEMONT. *The Slovene Franciscan Fathers, Order of Friars Minor, Commissariat of the Holy Cross*, 14246 Main St., P.O. Box 608, Lemont, 60439. Tel: 630-257-2494; Fax: 630-257-2359; Email: metodofm@sbcglobal.net. Revs. Metod Ogorevc, O.F.M., Guardian & Pres.; Bernard Karmanocky, Vicar. Priests 3.

**Slovenian Catholic Center*, 14252 Main St., P.O. Box 634, Lemont, 60439. Tel: 708-204-4390; Email: jvidmar@archchicago.org; Web: www.sloveniancenter.org. Deacon John Vidmar, Bd. Member.

LIBERTYVILLE. *Marytown, Our Lady of Fatima Friary*, 1600 W. Park Ave., Libertyville, 60048-2593. Tel: 847-367-7800; Fax: 847-367-7831; Email: broaug510@aol.com; Email: mail@kolbeshrine.org; Web: www.kolbeshrine.org. Bro. Augustine Kelly, O.F.M.Conv., Guardian; Rev. Hans Flonder, O.F.M.Conv., Vocation Dir.; John Clote, Admin. *Conventual Franciscan Friars of Marytown*, Tel: 847-367-7800; Fax: 847-367-7831. *National Shrine of St. Maximilian Kolbe*, Tel: 847-367-7800; Fax: 847-367-7831. Conventual Franciscan Friars 17.

MATTESON. *Austin Friary*, 5245 Stoneridge Ct., Matteson, 60443-2269. Tel: 708-747-2732; Fax: 708-747-3549. Revs. Terry A. Deffenbaugh, O.S.A., Prior; Michael J. O'Connor, O.S.A., Dir. Senior Care; Edward Andrews, O.S.A., (Retired); Bro. David W. Adelsbach, O.S.A. Brothers 1; Priests 3.

OAK PARK. *Dominican Community of St. Martin de Porres*, 204 S. Humphrey, Oak Park, 60302. Tel: 708-848-4271; Email: stmartin@dominicans.org; Web: www.domcentral.org. Revs. Michael A. Winkels, O.P.; James V. Marchionda, O.P.

Missionaries of Saint Charles, Provincial Residence, 546 N. East Ave., Oak Park, 60302. Tel: 708-386-4430; Fax: 708-386-4457; Email: sjbprovince@comcast.net; Web: www.scalabrinians.org. Very Rev. Miguel Alvarez-Galindo, Prov.
Fathers of St. CharlesScalabrini Development Office, 546 N. East Ave., Oak Park, 60302. Tel: 708-848-1616; Fax: 708-848-2525. *Scalabrinians Community Support Corporation, Oak Park*, Tel: 708-386-4430; Fax: 708-386-4457. *Scalabrinians Community Formation Corporation, Oak Park*, Tel: 708-386-4430; Fax: 708-386-4457.

PARK RIDGE. *Passionist Provincial Office*, 660 Busse Hwy., Park Ridge, 60068. Tel: 847-518-8844; Fax: 847-518-0461; Email: moonsjoe@yahoo.com; Web: www.passionist.org. Revs. Joseph Moons, C.P., Prov. Supr.; David Colhour, C.P., Consultor; Philip Paxton, C.P., Consultor; Alexander Steinmiller, C.P., Consultor; James Strommer, C.P., Prov. Asst.; John B. Ormechea, C.P.
The Congregation of the Passion, Holy Cross ProvincePassionist Missions, Inc., 660 Busse Hwy., Park Ridge, 60068. Tel: 847-518-8844; Fax: 847-518-0461. Sr. Loretta Ciesielski, Dir. *Holy Cross Province Development Office*, 660 Busse Hwy., Park Ridge, 60068. Tel: 847-518-8844; Fax: 847-518-0461. Mr. Keith Zekind, Exec. Dir.; Mrs. Angela Kwasinski, Dir. Donor Relations; Claire Smith, Dir. Communications. *Province Finance Office*, 660 Busse Hwy., Park Ridge, 60068. Tel: 847-518-8844; Fax: 847-518-0461; Email: keith@cppo.org. Mr. Keith Zekind, Dir. Finance; Mrs. Susan Arvanitis, Controller; Rev. John Schork, C.P., Prov. Treas. *Passionist Archives*, 660 Busse Hwy., Park Ridge, 60068. Tel: 847-518-8844; Fax: 847-518-0461. Sr. Loretta Ciesielski, Archivist.

TECHNY. *Divine Word Residence*, 1901 Waukegan Rd., P.O. Box 6000, Techny, 60082-6000. Tel: 847-412-1100; Fax: 847-753-7456; Email: rector@techny.org; Web: www.divineword.org. Revs. Lukas Batmomolin, S.V.D.; John Bergin, S.V.D.; Andrew Biller, S.V.D.; James Braband, S.V.D.; Stephan Brown, S.V.D.; Joseph Bugner, S.V.D.; Peter DeTaVo, S.V.D.; Joseph Detig, S.V.D.; Very Rev. Quang Duc Dinh, S.V.D., Rector; Revs. Francis Drzaic, S.V.D.; Felix Eckerman, S.V.D.; John Fincutter, S.V.D.; Dariusz Garbaciak, S.V.D.; Kazimierz Garbacz, S.V.D.; Paul Gootee, S.V.D.; Joseph Guidry, S.V.D.; William Halvey, S.V.D.; Kenneth Hamilton, S.V.D.; Charles Heskamp, S.V.D.; Janusz Horowski; Robert Jones, S.V.D.; Robert Kelly, S.V.D.; Arnold Lang, S.V.D.; Ronald Lange, S.V.D.; Joseph Logue, S.V.D.; Robert Mertes, S.V.D.; Walter Miller, S.V.D.; Tan Viet Nguyen, S.V.D.; Carlos Paniagua-Monroy, S.V.D.; Stanley Plutz, S.V.D.; Matheus Ro, S.V.D.; Alexander Rodlach, S.V.D.; John Rodney, S.V.D.; Derek Simons, S.V.D.; David Streit, S.V.D.; Gerald Theis, S.V.D.; Nhan Tran, S.V.D.; Gerhard Vogel, S.V.D.; Bros. Raymond Albers, S.V.D.; Joachim Brignac, S.V.D.; Rene Gawlik, S.V.D.; Patrick Hegarty, S.V.D.; Daniel Holman, S.V.D.; Stephen Kerekes, S.V.D.; Kenneth Valois, S.V.D.; Revs. Michael J. Bonner, S.V.D.; Walter Bunofsky, S.V.D.; Bro. Mathew Zemel, S.V.D.; Revs. Dennis Callan, S.V.D.; John Farley, S.V.D.; Raymond Hannah, S.V.D.; Raymond Hober, S.V.D.; James Henry, S.V.D.; Arnold Steffen, S.V.D.; Joseph Fertal; Robert Fisher; Bro. George Haegele, S.V.D.; Revs. James Heiar; Michael Hutchins, S.V.D., Rector; Antoine Leason, S.V.D.; Timothy Lenchak, S.V.D.; Robert Mallonee; Gerard O'Doherty; Richard Thibeau, S.V.D. (Formerly Divine Word Seminary-St. Mary's Mission House)
Divine Word Techny Community Corporation Brothers 9; Priests 56.

Society of the Divine Word, Provincial Headquarters-Chicago Prov. (Province of Saint Joseph Freinademetz, S.V.D.) 1985 Waukegan Rd., P.O. Box 6038, Techny, 60082-6038. Tel: 847-272-2700; Fax: 847-412-9505; Email: provincial@uscsvd.org; Web: www.divineword.org. Revs. Dariusz Garbaciak, S.V.D., Prov. Treas.; James Braband, S.V.D., Sec. Education, Recruitment & Formation; Very Rev. Quang Duc Dinh, S.V.D., Prov. *Vocation Office*, Tel: 800-553-3321; Fax: 563-876-5515; Email: svdvocations@dwci.edu; Web: www.svdvocations.org. Mr. Len Uhal, National Dir. *Blessed Arnold Charitable Trust*, 1985 Waukegan Rd., P.O. Box 6067, Techny, 60082-6067. Tel: 847-272-2700; Fax: 847-753-7464; Email: treasurer@uscsvd.org; Web: www.divineword.org. Rev. Dariusz Garbaciak, S.V.D., Sec. *DWTCRE Charitable Trust*, 1901 Waukegan Rd., P.O. Box 6067, Techny, 60082. Tel: 847-272-2700; Fax: 847-753-7464; Email: dgarbaciak@uscsvd.org; Web: www.divineword.org. Rev. Dariusz Garbaciak, S.V.D., Sec. *Divine Word Funds, Inc.*, 1985 Waukegan Rd., P.O. Box 6067, Techny, 60082-6067. Tel: 847-272-2700; Fax: 847-753-7464; Email: treasurer@uscsvd.org; Web: www.annuitysvd.org. Rev. Dariusz Garbaciak, S.V.D., Prov. Treas.; Very Rev. Quang Duc Dinh, S.V.D., Pres. *S.V.D. Funds, Inc.*, 1985 Waukegan Rd., P.O. Box 6067, Techny, 60082-6067. Tel: 847-272-2700; Fax: 847-753-7464; Email: treasurer@uscsvd.org; Web: www.annuitysvd.org. Rev. Dariusz Garbaciak, S.V.D., Prov. Treas.; Very Rev. Quang Duc Dinh, S.V.D., Pres. *Divine Word Novitiate*, 1945 Waukegan Rd., P.O. Box 6000, Techny, 60082-6000. Tel: 847-412-1444; Fax: 847-412-1454. Rev. Timothy Lenchak, S.V.D., Dir.; Bro. Mathew Zemel, S.V.D., Dir. Novices 4.

WILLOW SPRINGS. *Cistercian Fathers, Our Lady Mother of the Church Polish Mission*, 116 Hilton St., Willow Springs, 60480-1697. Tel: 708-467-0436; Fax: 708-467-0479; Email: cistercianmission@gmail.com. Revs. Michael Blicharski, O.Cist., Dir.; Konrad Ciechanowski, O.Cist., Assoc. Pastor. Cistercian Priory dependant monastery of the Abbey in Szczyrzyc, Poland (Polish Congregation) est. 1982.
Cistercian Fathers, Our Lady Mother of the Church Polish Mission Priests 2.

[O] CONVENTS AND RESIDENCES FOR SISTERS

CHICAGO. *Adrian Dominican Sisters, Dominican Midwest Mission Chapter*, 10024 S. Central Park Ave., 60655-3132. Tel: 773-253-3827; Fax: 773-779-6094; Email: kklingen@adriandominicans.org; Web: www.adriandominicans.org. Sr. Kathleen Klingen, O.P., Chapter Prioress.

Benedictine Sisters of Chicago, St. Scholastica Monastery, 7430 N. Ridge Blvd., 60645. Tel: 773-764-2413; Fax: 773-761-5131; Email: prioress@osbchicago.org; Web: www.osbchicago.org. Sisters Judith Murphy, O.S.B., Prioress; Virginia Jung, O.S.B., Archivist. Sisters 36.

Congregation of the Albertine Sisters, 1550 N. Astor, 60610. Tel: 312-642-5838; Email: dpekala@archchicago.org. Sisters Domicela Pekala, Contact Person; Theodosia Lichosyt, Supr. Sisters 3.

Daughters of St. Mary of Providence, Provincialate: 4200 N. Austin Ave., 60634-1615. Tel: 773-205-1313; Fax: 773-205-1316; Email: dsmpchi@sbcglobal.net; Email: srritab@sbcglobal.net; Web: www.dsmpic.org. Sr. Rita Butler, Prov. Sisters 65.

Providence Soup Kitchen, 1350 W. Evergreen Ave., 60642. Tel: 773-205-1313.

Daughters of St. Paul, 172 N. Michigan, 60601. Tel: 312-346-4902 (convent); Tel: 312-346-4228 (center); Fax: 312-346-2587; Email: chicago@pauline.org; Web: www.pauline.org. Sr. Majorina Zamatta, F.S.P., Supr. Sisters 4.

St. Elizabeth Convent, 1356 N. Claremont Ave., 60622. Web: www.poorhandmaids.org. Sr. Bonnie Boilini, P.H.J.C., Contact Person. Poor Handmaids of Jesus Christ.

Little Sisters of Jesus, 1529 S. Sawyer St., 60623. Tel: 773-277-5061; Email: littlesrs.chg@juno.com; Web: www.rc.net/org/littlesisters. Sisters 3.

Little Sisters of the Poor, The, 2325 N. Lakewood Ave., 60614. Tel: 773-935-9600; Fax: 773-935-9614. Sr. Marcel Joseph McCanless, L.S.P., Supr.
Little Sisters of the Poor of Chicago, Inc. Sisters 10.

Mary Ward Center, 3215 E. 91st St., 60617. Housing for Institute of the Blessed Virgin Mary (Loretto Sisters).

Medical Missionaries of Mary, 3410 W. 60th Pl., 60629. Tel: 773-737-3458; Email: mmmchi2015@gmail.com; Web: www.mmmworldwide.org. Sr. Joanne Bierl, M.M.M., Rel Order Leader. Sisters 2.

Medical Missionaries of Mary Development Office. Mission Development Office, 4425 W. 63rd St., Ste. 100, 60629-5565. Tel: 773-735-3712; Fax: 773-735-4661; Email: mdommm2014@gmail.com; Web: www.mmmworldwide.org. Sr. Joanne Bierl, M.M.M., Devel. Dir.

Missionaries of Charity, 2325 W. 24th Pl., 60608. Tel: 773-847-8771. Sisters M. Jonathan, M.C., Regl. Supr.; M. Justus, M.C., Supr. Sisters 7.

Missionary Sisters of Christ the King, 4910 N. Menard Ave., 60630. Tel: 773-481-1831; Fax: 773-545-4171; Email: annablauciak@gmail.com; Email: katarzynazar17@gmail.com. Sisters Anna Blauciak, M.Ch.R., Delegate of the General Supr.; Malgorzata Tomalka; Katarzyna Zaremba, M.Ch.R., Treas. Sisters 230. 1118 N. Noble St., 60622. Tel: 773-489-0714. Sr. Gertruda Szymanska, M.Ch.R., Supr. 5936 W. Barry Ave., 60634-5130. Tel: 773-889-7979. Sr. Dorota Domin, M.Ch.R., Supr. 2441 N. Menard Ave., 60639-2334. Tel: 773-637-9187. Sr. Stefania Galka, M.Ch.R., J.C.L., Supr. 3651 W. George St., 60618. Tel: 773-395-3520. Sr. Iwona Boronska, M.Ch.R., Supr. 5555 W. State St., Burbank, 60459. Tel: 708-458-8556. Sr. Weronika Ilnicka, M.Ch.R., Supr.

Missionary Sisters of the Sacred Heart, 434 W. Deming Pl., 60614. Tel: 773-883-7302; Fax: 773-525-0513. Sr. Joaquina Costa, M.S.C., Treas.

Mother of Good Counsel Convent, 3800 W. Peterson Ave., 60659-3116. Tel: 773-463-3020; Fax: 773-463-3567; Email: sconniet@feliciansisters.org; Web: www.feliciansistersna.org. Sr. Mary Christopher Moore,

C.S.S.F., Prov. Min. Felician Sisters: Mother of Good Counsel Convent; Our Lady of the Angels Convent; Archives; (*) Felician Services, Inc.

The Felician Sisters of the United States of America, Incorporated, Chicago Province Sisters 92.

Felician Volunteers in Mission, Inc.

North American Province of the Congregation of Our Lady of the Cenacle, Inc., 513 W. Fullerton Pkwy., 60614-6428. Tel: 773-528-6300; Fax: 773-549-0554; Email: cenacleprovincialate@usa.net; Web: www.cenaclesisters.org. Sr. Rose Hoover, R.C., Prov. Professed Sisters 74.

Cenacle Sisters, 513 W. Fullerton Pkwy., 60614-6428. Tel: 773-528-6300; Fax: 773-528-2456; Email: cenacleprovincialate@usa.net; Web: www.cenaclesisters.org. Sr. Marguerite Gautreau, R.C., Local Leader. Professed Sisters 17.

Religious Hospitallers of St. Joseph, 12251 South, 80th Ave., P.O. Box 82, Palos Heights, 60463. Tel: 708-448-9278; Fax: 708-448-9318; Email: adoyle9657@aol.com. Sr. Anna Doyle, Local Contact. Sisters 2.

Sisters of Mercy of the Americas West Midwest Community, Inc., 10024 S. Central Park, 60655-3132. Tel: 773-779-6011; Fax: 773-779-6094; Email: sistersofmercy@mercywmw.org; Web: www.sistersofmercy.org/west-midwest. Sisters Laura Reicks, R.S.M., Pres.; Susan M. Sanders, R.S.M., Pres.; Ana María Pineda, Vice Pres.; Maria Klosowski, R.S.M., Leadership Team; Margaret Maloney, Leadership Team; Margaret Mary Hinz, R.S.M., Leadership Team; Ms. Rebecca Vandenbosch, CFO. Sisters 531; Associates 605.

Sisters of Our Lady of LaSalette, 4220 N. Sheridan Rd., 60613. Tel: 773-248-4047; Email: marijosnds@starpower.com; Email: sr_emie@yahoo.com. Sisters Josephine S. Valenton, S.N.D.S., U.S.A. Mission in Charge; Emelita S. Sobrepena, S.N.D.S., Local Supr. Sisters (Chicago Community) 2; Sisters (Virginia Community) 3; Sisters (Miami, FL Community) 3.

Sisters of St. Casimir, Motherhouse and Novitiate, 2601 W. Marquette Rd., 60629-1817. Tel: 773-776-1324; Fax: 773-776-8755; Email: mzalot@ssc2601.com; Web: www.ssc2601.com. Sr. Regina Dubickas, S.S.C., Gen. Supr. Sisters 54.

Sisters of the Good Shepherd, 1114 W. Grace St., 60613. Tel: 773-935-3434; Fax: 773-935-3523. Sr. Lakshmie Napagoda, Contact. Sisters 3.

Sisters of the Holy Cross, 7422 N. Harlem, 60631-4409. Tel: 574-284-5660; Email: sbrennan@cscsisters.org. Sr. Suzanne Brennan, Treas. Sisters 1.

Other Residences:*Sisters of the Holy Cross*, 9964 W. 153rd St., Orland Park, 60462. Tel: 708-403-5134; Email: sbrennan@cscsisters.org. Sr. Suzanne Brennan, Treas. Sisters 1.

Sisters of the Resurrection Provincial House and Novitiate, 7260 W. Peterson Ave., E-216, 60631. Tel: 773-792-6363; Email: svawanzek@gmail.com. Sr. Virginia Ann Wanzek, C.R., Prov. Supr. Congregation of the Sisters of the Resurrection, Chicago Province.

Sisters of the Resurrection Sisters 26.

Society of Helpers (1956) 2226 W. Pratt Blvd., 60645. Tel: 773-405-9884; Fax: 773-548-5026; Email: jeankielty@yahoo.com. Sr. Jean Kielty, Prov. Team. Professed Sisters 23.

Other residences:

Society of Helpers, 2043 N. Humboldt Blvd., 1st Fl., 60647. *Society of Helpers*, 2043 N. Humboldt Blvd., 2nd Fl., 60647. Tel: 773-342-8832. *Society of Helpers*, 2226 W. Pratt Blvd., 60645. Tel: 773-405-9884; Fax: 872-806-2231. *Society of Helpers*, 4541 S. Wood, 60609. Tel: 773-807-8561; Fax: 773-376-8929. *Society of Helpers*, 2258 S. Marshall Blvd., 60623. Tel: 773-522-9160; Fax: 773-522-9161.

Society of Helpers, 2648 Pershing Rd., 60632. Tel: 872-444-5315.

ARLINGTON HEIGHTS. *Missionaries of the Sacred Heart of Jesus and Our Lady of Guadalupe M.S.C.Gpe.*, 1212 E. Euclid Ave., Arlington Heights, 60004. Tel: 847-255-5616.

Sisters of the Living Word, 800 N. Fernandez Ave. B, Arlington Heights, 60004-5336. Tel: 847-577-5972; Fax: 847-577-5980; Email: slw@slw.org; Web: www.slw.org. Sr. Sharon Glumb, S.L.W., Leadership. Sisters 55.

BARTLETT. *Immaculata Congregational Home*, 801 W. Bartlett Rd., Bartlett, 60103-4401. Tel: 630-837-4061; Fax: 630-837-0052; Email: ssj801@sbcglobal.net. Sr. Patricia Schafke, S.S.J.-T.O.S.F., Coord. Congregational Home of the Sisters of St. Joseph, T.O.S.F. Sisters in Residence 19.

BLUE ISLAND. *Mother of Sorrows Convent*, 13811 S. Western Ave., Blue Island, 60406-4172. Tel: 708-385-2103; Fax: 708-824-0688; Email: srloustu@yahoo.com. Sr. Louise Staszewski, O.S.M., Regl. Supr. Motherhouse of the Servants of Mary.

Mantellate Sisters Servants of Mary Sisters 4.

DES PLAINES. *Monastery of Discalced Carmelites*, 949 N. River Rd., Des Plaines, 60016. Tel: 847-298-4241; Fax: 847-298-4242. Mother Anne of Jesus, O.C.D., Prioress. Attended by priests of the Archdiocese.

Sisters of the Holy Family of Nazareth, Holy Family Province, 310 N. River Rd., Des Plaines, 60016. Tel: 847-298-6760; Fax: 847-803-1941; Email: info@nazarethesfn.org; Web: www.nazarethcsfn.org. Sr. Kathleen Maciej, Supr. Sisters 225.

EVERGREEN PARK. *Little Company of Mary Sisters - USA* (Little Company of Mary Sisters) 9350 S. California, Evergreen Park, 60805. Tel: 708-422-0130; Fax: 708-422-2212; Email: lguest@lcmh.org; Web: www.lcmsistersusa.org. Sr. Sharon Ann Walsh, L.C.M., Prov. Leader. Charitable Trust: American Province of Little Company of Mary Sisters Charitable Trust. Sisters 13; Total in Community 13.

HOFFMAN ESTATES. *Poor Handmaids of Jesus Christ, Annunciation Convent*, 1480 Ashley Rd., Hoffman Estates, 60169-4818. Email: phjcashley@aol.com; Web: www.poorhandmaids.org. Sr. Patricia Kolas, Contact Person.

JUSTICE. *Dominican Sisters Immaculate Conception Province*, 9000 W. 81st St., Justice, 60458. Tel: 708-458-3040; Fax: 708-458-7230; Email: rosaryhill@sbcglobal.net; Web: www.sistersop.org. Mother Helena Cempa Sr., O.P., Prov. Sisters 39.

LA GRANGE PARK. *Sisters of St. Joseph of La Grange*, 1515 W. Ogden Ave., La Grange Park, 60526. Tel: 708-354-9200; Fax: 708-354-9573; Web: csjoseph.org. Sr. Chris March, Contact Person. Sponsored ministries include secondary education, Christ in the Wilderness (retreat center), School and Tutors on Wheels, an adult literacy program, The Well (spirituality center) and Taller de Jose (outreach program), St. Joseph Press, and Ministry of the Arts.

Nazareth Academy, Sisters of St. Joseph Charitable Trust. Sisters 52; Total in Community 52.

LAKE VILLA. *Handmaids of the Precious Blood*, 724 Petite Lake Rd., Lake Villa, 60046-9619. Tel: 423-241-7065. Rev. Mother Marietta, H.P.B., Mother Prioress.

LEMONT. *Franciscan Sisters of Chicago, General Administration Building*, 11500 Theresa Dr., Lemont, 60439-2727. Tel: 630-243-3600; Fax: 630-243-3576; Email: bbajuscik@chicagofranciscans.com; Web: www.chicagofranciscans.org. Sr. M. Bernadette Bajuscik, O.S.F., Gen. Min.

Legal Title: Franciscan Sisters of Chicago, previously Franciscan Sisters of Blessed Kunegunda Sisters 23.

Mount Assisi Convent, School Sisters of St. Francis of Christ the King, 13900 Main St., Lemont, 60439-9736. Tel: 630-257-7495; Fax: 630-257-2618; Email: lemontfranciscans1909@gmail.com; Web: lemontfranciscans.org. Sr. Patricia Kolenda, S.S.-F.C.R., Prov. Supr. Sisters 32.

Our Lady of Victory Convent, 11400 Theresa Dr., Lemont, 60439-2728. Tel: 630-243-3600; Fax: 630-243-3601; Email: bbajuscik@chicagofranciscans.com; Web: www.chicagofranciscans.org. Sr. M. Bernadette Bajuscik, O.S.F., Gen. Min. General Motherhouse of the Franciscan Sisters of Chicago.

Legal Titles: Franciscan Sisters of Blessed Kunegunda Sisters 23.

MELROSE PARK. *Missionary Sisters of St. Charles Borromeo* Provincialate and Bishop Scalabrini Community. 1414 N. 37th Ave., Melrose Park, 60160. Tel: 708-343-2162; Fax: 708-343-6452; Email: provincialmscs@sbcglobal.net; Web: www.scalabriniane.org. Sisters Marissonia Daltoe, M.S.C.S., Prov. Supr.; Rodita P. Rogador, M.S.C.S., Councilor & Sec.; Noemie E. Digo, M.S.C.S., Councilor & Prov. Coord. on Formation; Leticia Valderrama, M.S.C.S., Prov. Councilor & Prov. Coord., Apostolate; Maria Manuela Amaral, M.S.C.S., First Councilor. Missionary Sisters of St. Charles Borromeo (Scalabrinians). Sisters 59.

NORRIDGE. *School Sisters of Notre Dame*, 2148 W Foster Ave., 60625. Tel: 773-561-7290; Email: ckrohe@amssnd.org; Web: www.ssnd.org. Sr. Charmaine Krohe, Prov. Sisters 30.

NORTHFIELD. *Provincial House of the Missionary Sisters Servants of the Holy Spirit*, 319 Waukegan Rd., P.O. Box 6026, Northfield, 60093-2719. Tel: 847-441-0126; Fax: 847-441-5587; Email: provinceleader@live.com. Sr. Monica Mabel Balbuena, S.Sp.S., Province Leader. Professed Sisters 73.

Arnold Janssen Foundation.

Helena Stollenwerk Foundation.

NORTHLAKE. *Daughters of Divine Love Congregation*, 133 N. Prater Ave., Northlake, 60164. Tel: 708-223-4260; Fax: 708-223-0262; Email: ddloveus@aol.com. Sr. Mary Agbakoba, S.R.M.O., Regional Superior. A Pontifical Religious Institute.

OAK FOREST. *Missionary Sisters of St. Benedict of Illinois, Inc.*, 5900 W. 147th St., Oak Forest, 60452. Tel: 708-535-9623; Email: missionarysis@sbcglobal.net. Sr. Assumpta Wrobel, Supr.; Rev. Martin N. Winters, In Res., (Retired).

OAK PARK. *Daughters of the Heart of Mary*, 140 N. Euclid Ave., #401, Oak Park, 60302-1684. Tel: 708-386-0190; Email: anitadhm@att.net; Web: www.dhm.org. Sr. Marilyn Smith, D.H.M., Supr.

Ephpheta Center Bed Capacity 2; Sisters 3; Total Staff 1.

PALOS PARK. *Poor Clare Monastery of the Immaculate Conception of Illinois*, 12210 S. Will Cook Rd., Palos Park, 60464-7332. Tel: 708-361-1810; Fax: 708-361-1816; Email: info@chicagopoorclares.org; Web: www.chicagopoorclares.org. Mother M. Teresita, P.C.C., Abbess. Sisters 7.

WESTERN SPRINGS. *Loretto Convent*, 5103 Carolina, Western Springs, 60558. Housing for Institute of the Blessed Virgin Mary (Loretta Sisters).

WAUKEGAN. *Franciscan Missionaries of Mary*, 4311 S. Grove Ave., Stickney, 60402. Tel: 708-317-5075; Email: bcfmm29@gmail.com; Web: www.fmmusa.org. Sr. Beatrice Costagliolia, F.M.M., Coord. Sisters 5.

WILMETTE. *Maria Immaculata Convent-The SCC Center* The Society of the Sisters of Christian Charity, Corporation of Mallinckrodt College of the North Shore 2041 Elmwood Ave., Wilmette, 60091-1431. Tel: 847-920-9341; Fax: 847-920-9346; Email: srjanice@sccwilmette.org; Web: www.sccwilmette.org. Sr. Janice Boyer, S.C.C., Major Supr. Sisters 5.

Sacred Heart Convent, 2221 Elmwood Ave., Wilmette, 60091-1435. Tel: 847-251-3770; Fax: 847-251-8040; Email: srjanice@sccwilmette.org. Sr. Eleanor Ann Ortmann, Supr. A home for aged and infirm Sisters of Christian Charity, Motherhouse in Wilmette, Illinois. Sisters in Residence 25.

[P] PIOUS UNIONS AND OTHER SOCIETIES

CHICAGO. **Canons Regular of Saint John Cantius*, 825 N. Carpenter St., 60642-5499. Tel: 312-243-7373; Fax: 312-243-4545; Email: pastor@cantius.org; Web: www.canons-regular.org. Revs. C. Frank Phillips, C.R., Moderator; Joshua Caswell, S.J.C.; Nathan Caswell, S.J.C.; Brendan Gibson, S.J.C.; Scott Haynes, S.J.C.; James Isaacson, S.J.C.; Dennis Kolinski, S.J.C.; Robin Kwan, S.J.C.; Kevin Mann, S.J.C.; Anthony Rice, S.J.C.; Scott Thelander, S.J.C.; Albert Tremari, S.J.C.; Joseph Brom, S.J.C.; Nathan Ford, S.J.C.; Juan Garcia, S.J.C.; Quin Huston, S.J.C.; Nicholas Kalinowski, S.J.C.; Kevin Menard, S.J.C.; Andrew Panzer, S.J.C.; Rev. Trenton Rauck, SJC; Michael Sanders, S.J.C.; Matthew Schuster, S.J.C.; Perry Smith, S.J.C.; Mark Visconti, S.J.C.; David Yallaly, S.J.C. A public diocesan association of the Christian Faithful. Brothers 5; Novices 3; Priests 13; Seminarians 4.

[Q] PUBLIC ASSOCIATIONS OF THE FAITHFUL

LIBERTYVILLE. *U.S. National Center of the Militia of the Immaculata Movement*, 40 N. Seymour Avenue, Mundelein, 60060. Tel: 331-223-5564; Email: minational@missionimmaculata.com; Web: www.missionimmaculata.com; Web: miyouth.org. P.O. Box 7645, Libertyville, 60048-2593. John W. Galten, M.I. Natl. Pres.; Roy Samson, Natl. Dir. M.I. Youth & Young Adults. International Latin name: Militia Immaculatae (MI).; An international public association of the faithful comprised of clergy, religious and laity dedicated to Catholic evangelization and promotion of Marian consecration MY youths and young adults. Founded in 1917 in Rome by St. Maximilian Kolbe.

[R] VISITING AND NURSING OF THE SICK IN THEIR HOMES

CHICAGO. *Catholic Home Care*, 721 N. LaSalle St., 60654. Tel: 312-655-8368; Fax: 312-337-2705; Email: cbrooks@catholiccharities.net. Carla Turner-Brooks, Dept. Dir. Home health agency, Medicare certified, JCAHO accredited, providing health care to individuals in their homes in Cook and Lake Counties.

Catholic Home Care Home Services, 721 N. LaSalle St., 60610. Tel: 312-655-7415; Email: cbrooks@catholiccharities.net. Carla Turner-Brooks, Dir. Home health agency, private duty, JCAHO accredited.

DES PLAINES. **Presence Home Care Chicagoland*, 2380 E. Dempster St., Des Plaines, 60016. Tel: 847-493-4800; Fax: 847-493-4804; Web: www.presencehealth.org. Rosann Prosser, Dir. Clinical Operations; Michael Gordon, Pres. Sponsored by Presence Health MinistriesSponsored by Ascension Health Ministries (Ascension Sponsor), a public juridic person.

Legal Title: Presence Home Care dba Presence Home Care-Chicagoland Patients Asst Anual. 3,663; Staff 95.

[S] SOCIETIES, CLUBS AND RESIDENCES

CHICAGO. **The Catholic Kolping Society of Chicago*, 5826 N. Elston, 60646. Tel: 773-792-2190; Fax: 773-792-0062; Email: chicagokolping@aol.com; Web: www.kolping.org. Rev. Michael G. Scherschel, Praeses.

RIVER FOREST. *Equestrian Order of the Holy Sepulchre of Jerusalem* North Central Lieutenancy 7575 Lake St., River Forest, 60305. Tel: 708-771-6886; Email: dr.tort@comcast.net; Web: www.eohsjnorthcentral.org. Sir Max Douglas Brown, KC, HS, Lieutenant.

[T] RETREAT HOUSES

CHICAGO. *Cenacle Retreat and Conference Center*, 513 Fullerton Pkwy., 60614. Tel: 773-528-6300; Fax: 773-528-0361; Email: crcc@cenaclechicago.org; Email: csisters@cenaclechicago.org (ministry office); Email: prayercardoffice@cenaclechicago.org (prayer enrollment office); Web: www.cenaclechicago.org. Mr. Robert J. Raccuglia, Dir.

Focolare Movement-Mariapolis Center, 5001 S. Greenwood Ave., 60615. Tel: 773-285-2746; Fax: 773-536-5054; Email: mplscenter.chicago@focolare.us; Web: www.focolare.us. Daytime Capacity 60; Overnight Capacity 30.

Monastery of the Holy Cross/Ascension Guest House, 3111 S. Aberdeen St., 60608. Tel: 773-927-7424; Tel; 888-539-4261 (toll free); Fax: 773-927-5734; Email: fatheredwardglanzmann@gmail.com; Web: www.chicagomonk.org. Rev. Edward J. Glanzmann, O.S.B., Guestmaster.

BARRINGTON. *Bellarmine Jesuit Retreat House, Inc.*, 420 W. County Line Rd., Barrington, 60010. Tel: 847-381-1261; Fax: 847-381-4695; Email: info@jesuitretreat.org; Web: www.jesuitretreat.org. Revs. Richard H. McGurn, S.J., Supr.; James P. Gschwend, S.J., Retreat Dir.; J. Michael Sparough, S.J., Retreat Dir.; Karl J. Voelker, S.J., Retreat Dir. Guests 5,000.

DES PLAINES. *Cabrini Retreat Center* (Formerly St. Frances Cabrini Retreat House) 9430 Golf Rd., Des Plaines, 60016. Tel: 847-297-6530; Fax: 847-297-6544; Email: info@cabrinicenter.org; Web: www.cabrinicenter.org. Nancy A. Golen, Dir.; Sr. Grace Waters, M.S.C., Mission Integration Dir. Retreats for youth, laity, religious and immigrants. Sponsored by the Missionary Sisters of the Sacred Heart of Jesus. Sisters 2.

LEMONT. *St. Mary's Retreat House*, 14230 Main St., P.O. Box 608, Lemont, 60439. Tel: 630-257-5102; Tel: 630-257-2494; Fax: 630-257-2359; Email: baragasmrh@gmail.com. Rev. Metod Ogorevc, O.F.M., Dir.

MUNDELEIN. *Cardinal Stritch Retreat House*, 1300 Stritch Dr., P.O. Box 455, Mundelein, 60060-0455. Tel: 847-566-6060; Fax: 847-566-6082; Web: www.stritchretreat.org. Rev. Msgr. Dennis J. Lyle, S.T.D., Dir.; Ms. Eva Schopper, Office Mgr. Serves the clergy, Catholic laity and ministers of Chicago and Region VII. Retreatants during year 2,300.

TECHNY. *Techny Towers Retreat and Conference Center*, 2001 Waukegan Rd., P.O. Box 176, Techny, 60082-0176. Tel: 847-272-1100; Fax: 847-272-9363; Email: info@technytowers.org; Web: www.technytowers.org. Donald P. Van Arsdale, Exec. Dir.; Julie Hoffman, Conference Mgr. A full-service conference facility used by parish groups, religious communities, nonprofit organizations and schools. Accommodations for 250 (daytime) and 125 (overnight). Chapel seats 750.

[U] NATIONAL INSTITUTIONS

CHICAGO. *Catholic Church Extension Society*, 150 S. Wacker Dr., 20th Fl., 60606-4200. Tel: 312-236-7240; Fax: 312-236-5276; Email: info@catholicextension.org; Web: www.catholicextension.org. His Eminence Blase J. Cupich, S.T.L., S.T.D., Chancellor; Rev. John J. Wall, Pres.; Ms. Julie Turley, Vice Pres. Devel.; Mr. Joseph Boland, Vice Pres. Mission; Ms. Angela D'Antonio, Vice Pres. Marketing; Mr. Meinrad Scherer-Emunds, Vice Pres. Content; Mr. Thomas Gordon, COO; Mr. Kevin P. McGowan, CFO

The Catholic Church Extension Society of the United States of America.

Catholic Kolping Society of America-National Endowment Fund, 5826 N. Elston Ave., 60646-5544. Tel: 877-659-7237; Fax: 973-478-8049; Email: patfarkas@optonline.net; Web: www.kolping.org. Lisa Brinkmann, Treas.

Catholic League for Religious Assistance to Poland, 2330 W. 118th St., 60643. Tel: 312-534-5050; Fax: 773-779-8469; Email: awypych@archchicago.org. Most Rev. Andrew P. Wypych, D.D., Exec. Dir.; Rev. Idzi Stacherczak, Asst. Dir.

Center for the Study of Religious Life, 5401 S. Cornell Ave., 60615-5698. Tel: 773-752-2720; Fax: 773-752-2723; Email: csrl@religious-life.org; Web: www.religious-life.org. Sr. Mary Charlotte Chandler, R.S.C.J., Dir. Sponsored by the Conference of Major Superiors of Men, the Leadership Conference of Women Religious and Catholic Theological Union at Chicago to conduct interdisciplinary and intercultural reflection on U.S. religious life and serve as a resource to religious leadership.

Jan Beyzym Society, Inc., 4105 N. Avers Ave., 60618. Tel: 773-588-7476; Fax: 773-588-6517; Email: agendajomu@gmail.com; Web: www.jezuicichicago.org. Revs. Tomasz Oleniacz, S.J., Pres.; Jerzy Mordarski, S.J., Sec.; Jerzy Brzoska; Bro. Adam Poreba; Jakub Spiewak. Polish Jesuits Foreign Missions.

Lumen Christi Institute, 1220 E. 58th St., 60637-1507. Tel: 773-955-5887; Fax: 773-955-5233; Email: info@lumenchristi.org; Web: www.lumenchristi.org. Mr. Thomas Levergood, Exec. Organized by Catholic scholars at the University of Chicago in 1997, The Lumen Christi Institute promotes Catholic thought and culture among students and faculty at the University of Chicago through lectures, courses, conferences and other programs. It also sponsors a national Catholic Scholars Program that works with faculty from across the nation in fields such as law, theology, philosophy and science and religion to renew Catholic thought and mentor the next generation of college teachers.

**The National Center for the Laity*, P.O. Box 291102, 60629. Tel: 773-776-9036; Fax: 773-776-9036; Email: wdroel@cs.com; Web: www.catholiclabor.org/ncl.htm. Mrs. Terry Mambu Rauch, Pres. Founded in 1977, the NCL is dedicated to advancing a key insight of Vatican II: that the church is the people of God in service to the modern world. NCL publishes a newsletter, INITIATIVES, hosts conferences and retreats and maintains a speakers' bureau.

National Organization for Continuing Education of Roman Catholic Clergy, Inc., 333 N. Michigan Ave., Ste. 1205, 60601. Tel: 312-781-9450; Fax: 312-442-9709; Email: nocercc@nocercc.org; Web: www.nocercc.org. Rev. Richard L. Chiola, Ph. D., Pres., (Retired); Mr. James H. Alphen, M.B.A., Exec. Dir. Founded in 1973, a membership association of dioceses, religious communities, and other interested organizations and individuals committed to the Church's mission to promote and support ongoing formation for priests and presbyterates. Professional and formational services include an annual convention; an annual orientation workshop; regional meetings; programs that dioceses and religious communities can host for clergy and other pastoral ministers; a quarterly newsletter; and other practical resources in diverse media.

National Religious Vocation Conference, 5401 S. Cornell, Ste. 207, 60615-5664. Tel: 773-363-5454; Fax: 773-363-5530; Web: www.nrvc.net. Sr. Kristin Matthes, Chm. The National Religious Vocation Conference is a professional organization of vocation ministers that presents religious life as a viable option in the Catholic Church. NRVC promotes vocation awareness, invitation, and discernment to life as a religious sister, brother, or priest. NRVC reflects all forms of religious life and provides educational opportunities, resources, and other supportive services for spiritual, professional, and personal growth.

National Shrine of St. Frances Xavier Cabrini, Inc., 2520 N. Lakeview Ave., 60614. Tel: 773-360-5115; Fax: 773-432-7043; Email: admin@cabrinishrinechicago.com; Web: www.cabrinishrinechicago.com. Rev. Theodore Ploplis, Rector; Sr. Bridget Zanin; M.S.C., Dir.

**NPH USA*, 134 N. LaSalle St., Ste. 500, 60602. Tel: 312-386-7499; Fax: 312-658-0040; Email: info@nphusa.org; Web: www.nphusa.org. Casey Guevara-Lehker, Exec. Asst. Dedicated to improving the lives of orphaned, abandoned and disadvantaged children through the support of the Nuestros Pequenos Hermanos (NPH) network of orphanages in Latin America and the Caribbean.

Radio Maryja, 6965 W. Belmont Ave., 60634. Tel: 773-385-8472; Fax: 773-385-5631; Email: admin@radiomaryjachicago.org; Web: www.radiomaryja.pl; Web: www.radiomaryjachicago.org. 6965 W. Belmont Ave., 60634. Redemptorist religious radio.

**Second Sense*, 65 E. Wacker Pl., Ste. 1010, 60601. Tel: 312-236-8569; Fax: 312-236-8128; Web: www.second-sense.org. Mr. David J. Tabak, Exec. Dir. Provides devotional services including large print Mass, library, scholarships for Catholic Students; the liturgy of the Hours in large print or audio cassette; the sacramental rites in large print; and large print Bibles.

Serra International, 70 E. Lake St., Ste. 1210, 60601. Tel: 312-419-7411; Tel: 800-488-4008 (toll free); Fax: 312-419-8077; Fax: 800-377-7877 (toll free); Email: serra@serra.org; Web: www.serra.org. Mr. John W. Woodward, Exec. Dir., Serra International & Serra International Foundation.

USA Council of Serra International, Tel: 312-201-6549; Tel: 888-777-6681 (toll free); Fax: 312-201-6548; Fax: 888-777-6803 (toll free); Email: serraus@serraus.org; Web: www.serraus.org. Mr. E.V. Verbeke, Exec. Dir.

ARLINGTON HEIGHTS. **Foundation For Children In Need*, 725 N. Pine Ave., Arlington Heights, 60004. Tel: 847-670-1145; Email: tomchitta@hotmail.com; Web: www.fcn-usa.org. P.O. Box 1247, Arlington Heights, 60006-1247. Tom Chitta, Co-founder. FCN is a Catholic lay organization established to reach out to the neediest in the rural villages of India. The main focus is to provide sponsorship help for education and health care for the poor.

EVANSTON. **Solidarity Bridge, Inc.*, 1703 Darrow Ave., #1, Evanston, 60201. Tel: 847-328-7748; Fax: 847-574-7491; Email: info@solidaritybridge.org; Web: www.solidaritybridge.org. Juan L. Hinojosa, Founding Dir. Provides short term international mission opportunities utilizing secular callings as vehicles of service to the poor in partnership with local counterparts in Bolivia.

GLENVIEW. **Coalition in Support of Ecclesia Dei, Ltd.*, P.O. Box 2071, Glenview, 60025-6071. Tel: 847-724-7151; Fax: 847-724-7158; Email: ecclesiadei@sbcglobal.net; Web: www.ecclesiadei.org. Mary M. Kraychy, Pres. & Exec. Dir. The Coalition assists priests, seminarians and laity in the implementation of Pope Benedict XVI's Summorum Pontificum, providing Latin-English Booklet Missals and other inspirational/educational materials (electronic media DVD's/videos) and printed material, eg. Atlar Cards).

GURNEE. **Caritas For Children, Inc.*, 5250 Grand Ave., PMB 105, Gurnee, 60031-1877. Tel: 312-944-7070; Fax: 414-771-3528; Email: cthoar@caritas.us; Web: www.caritas.us. Christopher T. Hoar, Contact Person. A private juridic person in the Archdiocese of Chicago, Caritas for Children promotes and supports inter-country adoptions from Poland through Catholic Charities of Chicago and provides financial assistance for the health, education and general welfare of orphaned and other disadvantaged children located worldwide under a variety of Child-Sponsorship programs in partnership with the services of Catholic Religious communities.

LIBERTYVILLE. **Institute on Religious Life*, P.O. Box 7500, Libertyville, 60048-7500. Tel: 847-573-8975; Email: IRLstaff@religiouslife.com; Web: www.religiouslife.com. Rev. Thomas Nelson, O.Praem., Nat'l. Dir.; Michael D. Wick, Exec. Dir.; Anne Tschanz, Coord. IRL promotes and supports the growth, development, and renewal of the consecrated life-particularly vowed religious life-as a gift to the Church and an evangelical witness to the world.

RIVER FOREST. *Dominican Leadership Conference*, 533 Park Ave., River Forest, 60305. Tel: 708-771-5280; Email: sisters@domlife.org; Web: www.dominicansistersconference.org. Sr. Patricia Farrell, O.P., Exec. Dir.

Dominican Leadership Conference of Dominican Men and Women Religious in the United States of America.

TECHNY. *Divine Word Missionaries, Inc.*, 1835 Waukegan Rd., Box 6099, Techny, 60082-6099. Tel: 847-272-7600; Fax: 847-272-8572; Email: info@svdmissions.org; Web: www.svdmissions.org. Revs. Richard Vaz, S.V.D., Pres.; Lukas Batmomolin, S.V.D., Supr. Delegate; Mr. David Gallagher, Treas.

S.V.D., Catholic Universities, Inc., Box 6099, Techny, 60082-6099.

[V] MINISTRY IN HIGHER EDUCATION

CHICAGO. *Campus Ministries*, 835 N. Rush St., 60611. Tel: 312-534-8271.

Non-Catholic Institutions:

Northwestern University, Sheil Center, 2110 N. Sheridan Rd., Evanston, 60201. Tel: 847-328-4648; Fax: 847-328-4660. Rev. Kevin J. Feeney, M.A.S., D.Min. (Cand.), Dir. & Chap.

University of Chicago Calvert House, 5735 S. University Ave., 60637. Tel: 773-288-2311; Email: calvert.uchicago@gmail.com; Web: www.uofccatholic.com. Rev. Andrew Liaugminas, S.T.D., Dir. and Chap.

University of Illinois at Chicago - John Paul II Newman Center, 700 S. Morgan St., 60607-3429. Tel: 312-226-1880; Fax: 312-226-2361; Web: www.jp2newman.com. Revs. Patrick M. Marshall, Chap. & Exec. Dir.; Michal Lewon, Assoc. Chap.

[W] PERSONAL PRELATURE

CHICAGO. *Midtown Residence* Prelature of the Holy Cross and Opus Dei 1825 N. Wood St., 60622.

Tel: 773-292-5450; Tel: 773-292-0660; Fax: 773-292-0996; Email: CoordinatorChicago@gmail.com; Web: www.opusdei.org. Revs. Charles M. Ferrer; Hilary F. Mahaney; Deogracias Rosales; John R. Waiss.

Northview University Center Prelature of the Holy Cross and Opus Dei 7225 N. Greenview Ave., 60626. Tel: 773-465-3468; Fax: 773-465-1195; Web: www.opusdei.org. Rev. Juan R. Velez.

Prelature of the Holy Cross and Opus Dei, 5800 N. Keating Ave., 60646. Tel: 773-283-5800; Fax: 773-202-8179; Email: CoordinatorChicago@gmail.com; Web: www.opusdei.org. Revs. Peter V. Armenio, B.S., Ph.D.; Leo Agustina; Frank J. Hoffman; Very Rev. F. Javier del Castillo, Vicar for the Midwest. Office of the Vicar for the Midwest.

[X] MISCELLANEOUS LISTINGS

CHICAGO. **Aid for Women, Inc.*, 8 S. Michigan Ave., Ste. 812, 60603-3311. Tel: 312-621-1107; Fax: 312-621-1972; Email: info@aidforwomen.org; Web: www.helpaidforwomen.org. Susan Barrett, Exec. Dir. Dedicated to upholding the principles of Humanae Vitae and Evangelium Vitae, the organization maintains a crisis center where any pregnant woman will find help and encouragement to choose life for her unborn child through pregnancy testing, ultrasound exam, confidential counseling and referral to community resources. Long-term support is also available through residential programs, Heather's House and Monica's House.

Alexian Brothers Bonaventure House, 825 W. Wellington Ave., 60657. Tel: 773-327-9921; Fax: 773-327-9113; Web: www.alexianbrothershousing.org. Korrey Kooistra, Exec. Housing and supportive services for otherwise homeless persons with HIV/AIDS. Sponsored by Ascension Health Ministries (Ascension Sponsor), a public juridic person.

Alexian Brothers Bettendorf Place, LLC.

Alexian Brothers Health System dba Alexian Brothers Foundation, 200 S. Wacker Dr., Ste. 1213, 60606. Tel: 223-273-2334; Fax: 630-505-1314 ; Web: www.amitahealth.org. Mark A. Frey, CEO. Ascension Health Ministries (Ascension Sponsor), a public juridic person.

Amate House Foundation, 3600 S. Seeley, 60609-1148.

The Aquin Guild, c/o Office for Catechesis & Youth Ministry, Cardinal Meyer Center, 3525 S. Lake Park Ave., 60653-1402. Tel: 312-534-3700; Fax: 312-534-3801. Rev. John W. Clemens, Dir. Provides spiritual direction to Catholics engaged in public and parochial education.

Aquinas Literacy Center (ESL), 1751 W. 35th St., 60609. Tel: 773-927-0512; Email: info@aquinasliteracycenter.org; Web: www.aquinasliteracycenter.org. Alison Altmeyer, Admin.

St. Bernard Health Network, 326 W. 64th St., 60621.

St. Bernard Housing Development Corp., 326 W. 64th St., 60621. Tel: 773-962-4165; Web: www.stbh.org. Diahann Sinclair, Exec. Dir. A subsidy of St. Bernard Hospital, Chicago.

**Bethany Trust Fund*, Brown Brothers Harriman Trust Company, N.A., 150 S. Wacker Dr., Ste. 3250, 60606. Tel: 312-781-7140.

**Big Shoulders Fund*, 212 W. Van Buren St., Ste. 900, 60607. Tel: 312-751-8337; Fax: 312-751-5235; Web: www.bigshouldersfund.org. Joshua Hale, Pres. & CEO. Provides support to the Catholic Schools in the neediest areas of inner-city Chicago.

The Bolivian Trust of the Dominicans, 1910 S. Ashland Ave., 60608-2904. Tel: 312-243-0011; Fax: 312-829-8471; Email: office@opcentral.org. Rev. James V. Marchionda, O.P., Prov.

St. Bonaventure Oratory, Res.: 1641 W. Diversey Pkwy., 60614. Tel: 773-281-6588; Fax: 773-388-8676; Email: stbonaventure@archchicago.org. Rev. Thomas I. Healy, Rector, (Retired).

**Brother David Darst Center for Justice and Peace, Spirituality and Education*, 2834 S. Normal Ave., 60616. Tel: 312-225-3099; Fax: 312-842-4178; Email: director@darstcenter.org; Web: www.darstcenter.org. Keith Donovan, Exec. Dir.

**Brothers and Sisters of Love*, c/o St. James Church, 2907 W. Wabash, 60616. Tel: 312-842-1919, Ext. 208; Fax: 312-842-3612; Web: brothersandsistersoflove.com. Bro. Jim Fogarty, Exec. Dir.

The Catholic Education Institute, c/o Hinshaw and Culbertson, 222 N. LaSalle St., 60601. Tel: 718-823-8565; Fax: 718-823-8072; Email: johnpiderit@me.com; Web: www.catholicexcellence.org. Rev. John J. Piderit, S.J., Pres.

Catholic Education Scholarship Trust, 50 S. LaSalle St., 60603.

Catholic Office of the Deaf, 3525 S. Lake Park Ave., 60653-1402. Tel: 312-534-7899 (Voice); Tel: 312-751-8368 (TDD); Fax: 312-957-4766; Email: cathdeafch@archchicago.org; Web: www.deafchurchchicago.org. Rev. Joseph A. Mulcrone, Dir., (Retired).

**Central American Martyrs Center (Su Casa Catholic Worker Community)*, 5045 S. Laflin, 60609. Tel: 773-376-9263; Fax: 773-376-9241; Email: sucasacw@gmail.com; Web: www.sucasacw.org. Bro. Denis Murphy, F.S.C.

Charitable Trust of the Order of Friar Servants of Mary, United States of America Province, Inc., 3121 W. Jackson Blvd., 60612-2729. Tel: 773-533-0360; Fax: 773-533-8307; Email: michaelcallary@servitesusa.org; Web: www.servite.org. Rev. Michael Doyle, O.S.M., Treas.

Chicago Airports Catholic Chaplaincy, P.O. Box 66353, 60666-0353. Tel: 773-686-2636; Fax: 773-686-0130; Email: ordchapel@aol.com; Web: www.airportchapels.org. Rev. Michael G. Zaniolo, S.T.L., C.A.C., Chap.

Claretian Associates, Inc., 9108 S. Brandon Ave., 60617. Tel: 773-734-9181; Fax: 773-734-9221; Email: angelah@claretianassociates.org; Web: www.claretianassociates.org. Angela Hurlock, Exec. Dir. Organization to provide affordable housing and encourage neighborhood improvement in South Chicago.

**Communicators for Women Religious (CWR)*, 5401 S. Cornell Ave., 60615. Email: nschaefer@c4wr.org; Web: www.c4wr.org. Nicholas Schaefer, Exec. Dir.

**Cristo Rey Network*, 14 E. Jackson Blvd., Ste. 1200, 60604. Tel: 312-784-7200; Fax: 312-784-7217; Email: egoettl@cristoreynetwork.org; Web: www.cristoreynetwork.org; Email: bmelton@cristoreynetwork.org. Rev. John P. Foley, S.J., Chief Mission Officer & Board Chair Emeritus; Elizabeth Goettl, CEO. The Cristo Rey Network supports and helps establish Catholic high schools where students work to earn tuition and gain business experience. Each school is modeled after Cristo Rey Jesuit High School of Chicago.

CRI, INC., 14 E. Jackson Blvd., Ste. 1200, 60604. Tel: 312-784-7217; Email: bmelton@cristoreynetwork.org; Web: cristoreynetwork.org. Brian Melton, Contact Person.

**DeSales Charitable Trust*, Brown Brothers Harriman Trust Company, N.A., 150 S. Wacker Dr., Ste. 3250, 60606. Tel: 312-781-7140.

**Dominican Volunteers USA*, 533 Ashland Ave., River Forest, 60305. Tel: 312-226-0919; Email: info@dvusa.org; Web: www.dvusa.org. Megan Rupp, Exec. Dir. Dominican Volunteers USA provides full-time volunteer opportunities for lay people. Volunteers live and work with Dominican (Order of Preachers) ministries and communities across the United States, serving those who are in most need.

**Felician Services, Inc.*, 3800 W. Peterson Ave., 60659-3116. Tel: 773-463-3806; Fax: 773-463-2059. Sr. Mary Barbara Ann Bosch, C.S.S.F., CEO.

Focolare Movement, 5001 S. Greenwood Ave., 60615. Tel: 773-536-7873; Fax: 773-536-5054; Email: czfchicago@focolare.us; Web: www.focolare.us. Cristina Outeirinho, Admin. Work of Mary founded in Trent, Italy in 1943. International headquarters are in Rome, Italy; national formation center in New York.

Women, 5017 S. Greenwood Ave., 60615. Tel: 773-536-7873; Fax: 773-536-5054. Erika Croatto, Co-Dir.

Men, 7018 W. 34th St., Berwyn, 60402. Tel: 708-484-9771; Fax: 708-484-4998. Mr. Gary Brandl, Co-Dir.

Franciscan Friars Retirement Corporation, 6107 Kenmore Ave., 60660-2797. Tel: 773-274-7681; Fax: 773-274-9751; Email: dmk9271@gmail.com. Rev. Michael Zielke, O.F.M.Conv., Prov.

Franciscan Outreach, 1645 W. LeMoyne St., 60622. Tel: 773-278-6724; Fax: 773-278-7120; Web: www.franoutreach.org. Diana Faust, O.F.S., Exec. Dir. Owns & operates: Marquard Center (dining room for the homeless), Franciscan House of Mary & Joseph (shelter), Franciscan Annex (shelter), a day program, housing programs, and a Case Management Program for the homeless in Chicago. Bed Capacity 330; Tot Asst. Annually 3,000; Total Staff 53.

**Franciscan Works*, P.O. Box 607781, 60660. Tel: 773-809-4008; Email: joan@franciscanworks.org; Web: www.franciscanworks.org. Joseph Sehnert, Exec. Dir. &Interim Board Pres. Serving Liberia Mission Incorporated, Blacktom Town, Montserrado County, Liberia, West Africa. Franciscan Works is dedicated to breaking the cycle of poverty for the poorest of poor children in developing countries through education rooted in Gospel values in the spirit of St. Francis of Assisi.

Franciscans of the Eucharist of Chicago, 3808 W. Iowa St., 60651. Tel: 773-486-8431; Fax: 773-486-8432; Email: FEVocations@gmail.com; Web: www.franciscansoftheeucharistofchicago.org. Rev. Robert Lombardo, C.F.R., Pres. A new Franciscan community dedicated to serving the poor, evangelization and teaching, retreat work and Eucharistic Adoration.

Freres des Ecoles Chretiennes, c/o Locke Lord LLP, 111 S. Wacker Dr., 60606. Tel: 312-443-1823; Email: MRenetzky@lockelord.com. Kenneth Payne, Pres.

General Assistance, Inc. aka Daughters of Charity International Project Services, 131 S. Dearborn Ste. 1700, 60603. Tel: 312-324-8439; Fax: 312-324-9439; Email: dcoyne@perkinscoie.com. Daniel W. Coyne, Contact Person. Support organization for the Daughters of Charity.

**Hermitage Charitable Trust*, Brown Brothers Harriman Trust Company, N.A., 150 S. Wacker Dr., Ste. 3250, 60606. Tel: 312-781-7140.

Holy Family Church, Inc., 1010 N. Hooker St., 60642. Tel: 773-975-6363; Tel: 773-975-6888; Fax: 773-975-0230; Email: UMISocius@jesuits.org. Revs. Michael A. Gabriel; Glen Chun, S.J., Contact Person.

The Holy Spirit Life Learning Center, 2020 W. Morse Ave., Unit 1S, 60645. Tel: 773-764-3000; Email: hsllcenter@gmail.com; Web: www.ssps-usa.org/b_ministries/llc. Sr. Angelica Oyarzo-Chavol, Exec. Dir. The mission is to support individuals, especially women & children, to reach a better standard of living by improving learning skills & developing self-confidence.

**Home to Enhance African Life, Inc.*, 340 W. Superior St., Unit 612, 60654. Tel: 312-952-4855; Email: nick@healnigeria.org; Web: www.healnigeria.org. Nicola Costello, Pres.

Hopebound Ministries, Inc., 3800 W. Peterson Ave., 60659. Tel: 773-463-3806; Fax: 773-463-2059; Email: mrparrillo@felicianservices.org. Sr. Mary Clarette Stryzewski, C.S.S.F., Pres.

Ignatian Spirituality Project, 1641 S. Allport, 60608. Tel: 312-226-9184; Email: info@ispretreats.org; Email: catherine@ispretreats.org; Email: tom@ispretreats.org; Web: www.ispretreats.org. Thomas Drexler, Exec. The project works with the homeless through retreats and spiritual companionship in the belief that by claiming their spiritual life they can recover from addiction and other problems associated with homelessness.

Ignatius Productions, Inc., 1010 N. Hooker St., 60642. Tel: 773-975-6363; Fax: 773-975-0230; Email: UMISocius@jesuits.org; Web: www.fathermitchpacwa.org. Rev. Albert DiUlio, S.J., Treas.

Illinois Catholic Health Association, 65 E. Wacker Pl., Ste. 1620, 60601. Tel: 312-368-0011; Fax: 312-368-1701; Email: pcacchione@il-cha.org; Web: www.il-cha.org. Patrick J. Cacchione, Exec. Dir.

The Illinois Patrons of the Arts in the Vatican Museums, c/o Archdiocese of Chicago Office of Vicar General, 835 N. Rush, 60611. Tel: 312-534-5351; Fax: 312-534-5391; Email: illinoispatrons@gmail.com; Web: www.vaticanpatronschicago.org. His Eminence Blase J. Cupich, S.T.L., S.T.D., Chm.; Anne Shea, Pres.

Intercommunity Housing Corporation, c/o Law Offices of Edward T. Joyce & Associates, 135 S. LaSalle St., Ste. 2200, 60603. Tel: 312-641-2600; Email: ejoyce@joycelaw.com. David E. Myles, Pres.; Edward T. Joyce, Sec. The Intercommunity Housing Corporation promotes the development and establishment of affordable residential retirement housing for religious, clergy and laity; a design for 21st century living.

Italian Catholic Federation, 2825 W. 81st St., 60652. Tel: 773-436-4444; Fax: 773-778-9087; Email: info@icf.org; Web: www.icf.org. Rev. Charles V. Fanelli, Chap., (Retired).

Jesuit International Missions, Inc., 1010 N. Hooker St., 60642. Tel: 773-975-6363; Tel: 773-975-6888; Fax: 773-975-0230; Email: UMItreasurer@jesuits.org; Email: UMISocius@jesuits.org. Revs. Glen Chun, S.J., Socius; Albert DiUlio, S.J., Treas.

The Jesuit Partnership, 1010 N. Hooker St., 60642. Tel: 773-975-6888; Fax: 743-975-0230; Email: UMISocius@jesuits.org. Revs. Thomas A. Lawler, S.J., Pres.; Albert DiUlio, S.J., Treas.; Glen Chun, S.J., Sec.

Jesuit Seminary Association, 1010 N. Hooker St., 60642. Tel: 773-975-6363; Tel: 773-975-6888; Fax: 773-975-0230; Email: UMISocius@jesuits.org; Web: www.jesuitsmidwest.org. Rev. Albert J. Di Ulio, S.J., Treas.

John McKniff Peruvian Formation Charitable Trust, 5401 S. Cornell Ave., 60615.

Kolbe House, 2434 S. California Ave., 60608. Tel: 773-247-0070; Fax: 773-247-0665; Email: jailkolbe@aol.com. Revs. David A. Kelly, C.PP.S.;

Arturo Perez-Rodriguez, Dir., (Retired); Deacon Pablo A. Perez, Asst. Dir. Catholic jail ministry.

LaSalle Pastoral Foundation, 111 S. Wacker Dr., 60606. Tel: 312-443-1823.

Le Royer Foundation, 326 W. 64th St., 60621. Tel: 773-962-4073; Fax: 773-962-9276.

Loyola Press, 3441 N. Ashland Ave., 60657. Tel: 773-281-1818; Fax: 773-281-0555; Email: cicciarelli@loyolapress.com; Email: jdubbs@hinshawlaw.com; Web: www.loyolapress.com. 222 N. LaSalle St., Ste. 300, 60601. Joeylln Cicciarelli, Pres.

Maria Kaupas Center, 2740 W. 68th St., 60629. Tel: 773-925-8686; Email: info@mariakaupascenter.org; Web: www.mariakaupascenter.org. Melinda Rueden, Exec.

Marillac St. Vincent Family Services, Inc., 2145 N. Halsted St., PO Box 14699, 60614. Tel: 312-943-6776; Fax: 312-278-4209; Web: www.marillacstvincent.org. Mr. Peter Beale-DelVecchio, CEO. Early childhood education for children ages 6 weeks to kindergarten; before and after school programs for ages kindergarten to 8th grade; anti-violence and arts programs for children ages 6 to 19 years; emergency assistance food for low-income families. Employees 220; Students 900; Clergy / Religious Teachers 2.

Marillac Social Center, 212 S. Francisco, 60612.

St. Vincent de Paul Center, 2145 N. Halsted St., 60614.

Marillac St. Vincent Ministries, Inc., 2145 N. Halsted St., 60614. Tel: 312-943-6776; Fax: 312-278-4209. Mr. Peter Beale-DelVecchio, CEO. Supports early childhood education for children 6weeks to kindergarten; before and after school programs for children from kindergarten to 8th grade; provides counseling and family support services, emergency assistance for food for low-income families; homebou, Supports case management, counseling, and emergency relief for senior citizens. Supports outreach to the homeless in the form of case management and other concrete services.

Marist Volunteer Program, 4200 W. 115th St., 60655-4306. Tel: 773-881-5343; Fax: 773-881-3667; Email: maristvolunteerprogram@yahoo.com. Bro. Hugh Turley, F.M.S., Contact Person.

Miles Jesu, P.O. Box 267989, 60626. Tel: 773-262-0861; Fax: 773-267-1093; Email: administration@milesjesu.com; Web: www.milesjesu.com. Maire Duggan, M.J., Admin.

Missionary Sisters of the Sacred Heart of Jesus - Holy Spirit Region, 434 W. Deming Pl., 60614. Tel: 773-388-7313; Email: joaquiac@comcast.net. Sr. Joaquina Costa, M.S.C., Supr.

Mother Cabrini League, 434 W. Deming Pl., 60614. Tel: 773-388-7329; Fax: 773-525-0513. Sr. Joaquina Costa, M.S.C., Dir.; Joyce Bandera, Office Supvr. The purpose of the League is to spread devotion to St. Frances Xavier Cabrini.

**Mughamba Scholarship Foundation*, 120 LaSalle St., Ste. 3800, 60602. Rev. Kombo L. Peshu, S.T.L., Pres.

Mundelein College, Office of the General Counsel of Loyola University-Chicago, 820 N. Michigan Ave., Ste. 750, 60611. Tel: 312-915-6239; Email: pcostas@luc.edu; Web: www.luc.edu. 6525 N. Sheridan Rd., 60626. Tel: 773-508-3029; Fax: 312-915-6208. Mr. Wayne Magdziarz, Pres. & Chm. Bd. Trustees; Ms. Pamela G. Costas Esq., Sec.; Janet W. Sisler, Vice Pres. & Treas.

National Fund for Catholic Religious Vocations (NFCRV), 5401 S. Cornell Ave., Ste. 207, 60615-5664. Tel: 773-595-4028; Email: ploftus@nfcrv.org; Web: www.nfcrv.org. Mr. Philip Loftus, Exec.

New World Publications, 835 N. Rush St., 60611. Tel: 312-534-7777; Fax: 312-534-7350; Email: mail@catholicnewworld.com; Web: www.catholicnewworld.com. Grant Gallicho, Dir. Publications & Media; Alejandro Castillo, Interim Gen. Mgr.; Joyce Duriga, Editor. Publishers of Catholic New World, Chicago Catolico, and the Archdiocesan Directory.

North American Conference of Associates and Religious (NACAR), 5417 S. Cornell Ave., 60615. Tel: 773-324-2704; Tel: 773-988-4597; Email: info@nacar.org; Web: www.nacar.org. Rev. Arthur Carrillo, C.P., J.C.L.

Oblates for International Pastoral aka Oblate International Pastoral Investment Trust, 161 N. Clark St., Ste. 4700, 60601. Tel: 210-421-3426; Fax: 410-510-1312; Email: rwhitley@oiptrust.org; Email: avandyke@oiptrust.org; Email: dessureault@omigen.org; Web: www.oiptrust.org. Revs. Marc Dessureault, O.M.I., Trustee & CEO; Warren A. Brown, O.M.I., Trustee; Rufus J. Whitley, O.M.I., Pres. & CIO; Seamus P. Finn, O.M.I., Chief, Faith Consistent Investing; Anne VanDyke, COO; Revs. James P. Brobst, O.M.I., Trustee; James Chambers, S.J., Trustee.

Office for Mission Advancement Dominicans: Province of St. Albert the Great. 1910 S. Ashland Ave., 60608-2904. Tel: 312-226-0020; Fax: 312-829-8471; Email: office@opcentral.org; Web: www.opcentral.org. Mr. Robert Dixon, Dir.

Order of Friar Servants of Mary United States of America Province, Inc., 3121 W. Jackson Blvd., 60612-2729. Tel: 773-533-0360; Fax: 773-533-8307; Email: michaelcallary@servitesusa.org; Web: www.servite.org. Very Rev. John M. Fontana, O.S.M., Prov. The Order of Friar Servants of Mary-U.S.A. Province, Inc., Chicago, IL.

Our Lady of the Angels Mission Center aka Mission of Our Lady of the Angels, 3808 W. Iowa St., 60651. Tel: 773-486-8431; Fax: 773-486-8432; Email: olamission@gmail.com; Web: www.missionola.com. Rev. Robert Lombardo, C.F.R., Dir. The mission establishes a Catholic outreach on Chicago's west side. The services include: food pantry, clothing room, senior citizens programs, after school programs, retreat space and prayer ministry.

The Peace Corner, Incorporated, P.O. Box 440113, 60644. Tel: 773-261-5330; Fax: 773-261-1523; Email: thepeacecorner@yahoo.com; Web: www.thepeacecorner.org. Angel Gutierrez, Vice Pres. A ministry of the Comboni Missionaries of the Heart of Jesus, Inc., The Peace Corner is a youth center in the Austin neighborhood of Chicago (5022 W. Madison Ave.) serving youth in need with no distinction of faith, race and background. The Peace Corner offers a safe and caring environment for youth while providing tutoring, computer classes, GED preparation, legal counseling, job training, support groups and recreational activities.

Precious Blood Ministry of Reconciliation, 5114 S. Elizabeth St, P.O. Box 09379, 60609-0379. Tel: 773-952-6643; Fax: 773-952-6739; Email: dkellycpps@gmail.com. Revs. David A. Kelly, C.PP.S., Exec. Dir.; Dennis Kinderman, C.PP.S. A ministry of the Cincinnati and Kansas City provinces of the Missionaries of the Precious Blood that responds to violence and conflict in the Back of the Yards neighborhood of Chicago (5114 S. Elizabeth St.) and fosters renewal of the church through reconciliation programs, retreats and training workshops for church communities.

Presence Care Transformation Corporation (1997) 200 S. Wacker, 11th Fl., 60606. Tel: 312-308-3200; Fax: 312-308-3396; Web: www.presencehealth.org. Dana Gilbert, Pres. Sponsored by Ascension Health Ministries (Ascension Sponsor), a public juridic person.

Presence Chicago Hospitals Network, 200 S. Wacker Dr., 60606. Tel: 312-308-3221; Fax: 312-308-3395; Web: www.presencehealth.org. Martin Judd, Pres. Sponsored by Ascension Health Ministries (Ascension Sponsor), a public juridic person.

Presence Health Foundation Board of Trustees, Tel: 847-813-3477; Fax: 847-813-3482.

**Presence Health Network*, 200 S. Wacker Dr., 60606. Tel: 312-308-3221. Dougal Hewitt, Chief Officer Mission&External Affairs.

Presence Healthcare Services, Tel: 773-774-8000; Fax: 773-792-9926.

Presence Senior Services - Chicagoland, Tel: 847-813-3176; Fax: 847-813-3876.

Ray Ryan Formation Charitable Trust, 5401 S. Cornell Ave., 60615.

Redemptorist Fathers of St. Alphonsus Parish of Chicago, c/o Redemptorists, 1633 N. Cleveland Ave., 60614. Tel: 312-642-2498; Fax: 312-642-9285; Email: srehrauer@redemptorists-denver.org. Revs. Ramon Dompke, C.Ss.R.; John Steingraeber, C.Ss.R., Admin.; John Fahey Guerra, Vicar; Joseph Fenili, (Retired); Gregory May, C.Ss.R., Treas.; James Keena, C.Ss.R., (Retired); Theodore J. Lawson, C.Ss.R.; Bro. Lawrence Lujan Angel, Prov. Asst.; Revs. Joseph Morin, C.Ss.R.; John Phelps, C.Ss.R.; Stephen Rehrauer, C.Ss.R., Prov.; Joseph P. Dorcey, C.Ss.R., Mission Procurator; Kenneth Sedlak, C.Ss.R., Pastoral Min./Coord.

The Redemptorists of Blessed Sacrament, 1633 N. Cleveland Ave., 60614. Tel: 312-248-8894; Email: OPC@redemptorists-denver.org. Rev. Gregory May, C.Ss.R., Treas.

Servite Secular Order, Inc., Tel: 872-216-6776; Email: osmsecular@gmail.com; Web: www.secularservites.org. Rev. Donald M. Siple, O.S.M., National Asst. Servite Secular Order.

S.F.V., Inc., 1645 W. LeMoyne St., 60622. Tel: 773-278-6724; Fax: 773-278-7021. Rev. Kurt Hartrich, O.F.M., Pres. Sponsor corporation of St. Francis Village (a retirement village) in Crowley, TX.

St. Joseph Services, Inc., 1501 N. Oakley Blvd., 60622. Tel: 773-278-0484; Fax: 773-278-0192. Ann Deuel, Exec. Supports the mission of the Daughters of Charity to serve persons in poverty.

**Society of Friends of the John Paul II Foundation*, 116 Hilton St., Western Springs, 60480. Tel: 630-308-2609; Email: fjp2chicago@gmail.com. Elizabeth Ceisel-Mikowska, Contact Person.

**Society of Jesus Worldwide*, 1010 N. Hooker St., 60642. Tel: 773-975-6363; Tel: 773-975-6888; Fax: 773-975-0230; Email: UMISocius@jesuits.org. Revs. Glen Chun, S.J., Contact Person; Albert DiUlio, S.J., Treas.

St. Anthony Hospital, 2875 W. 19th St., 60623. Tel: 773-484-4300; Fax: 773-521-7902; Web: www.saintanthonyhospital.org. Sponsored by Ascension Health and the Missionary Sisters of the Sacred Heart of Jesus to operate St. Anthony Hospital.

Saint Anthony Health Affiliates, 2875 W. 19th St., 60623. Tel: 773-484-4300; Fax: 773-521-7902.

Taller de Jose, 2831 W. 24th Blvd., 60623. Tel: 773-523-8320; Fax: 773-523-8421; Email: info@tallerdejose.org; Web: www.tallerdejose.org. Anna Mayer, Exec. Dir. Taller de Jose is a community resource center, offering accompaniment to people in need, connecting people to services and services to people. As a sponsored ministry of the Congregation of St. Joseph, Taller de José exists so that all may be one.

The Society for the Propagation of the Faith, 3525 S. Lake Park Ave., 60653-1402. Tel: 312-534-3322; Fax: 312-534-1599. Megan Mio, M.Div., Contact Person & Dir.

St. Thomas Aquinas Priory (STAF) (St. Albert the Great Prov.) 1910 S. Ashland Ave., 60608-2904. Tel: 312-243-0011; Fax: 312-829-8471; Email: office@opcentral.org. Rev. James V. Marchionda, O.P., Prov.

United Stand Family Center, 3731 W. 62nd St., 60629. Tel: 773-585-4499; Fax: 773-585-5615. Dr. Kim Mis, C.S.S.F., Exec. Dir. Education, Prevention, Problem Identification, Consultation, and Intervention with Children and Families. Total Staff 55.

Villa Guadalupe Senior Services Corporation, 3201 E. 91st St., 60617. Tel: 773-933-0344; Fax: 773-933-0827. Angela Hurlock, Exec. Dir.; Rev. Mark J. Brummel, C.M.F., Treas. Organization to provide affordable housing and related services for Senior Citizens in South Chicago. Apartments 53; Seniors Assisted 3,000; Staff 9.

Villa Redeemer, c/o Redemptorists, 1633 N. Cleveland Ave., 60614. Tel: 312-642-2498; Fax: 312-642-9283.

Westcourt Corporation, 5550 W. 87th St., Burbank, 60459. Tel: 773-429-4343; Fax: 773-429-4381; Email: bropathayes@gmail.com. Bro. Patrick Hayes, C.F.C.

Zaccheus House (2002) 12242 S. Parnell, 60628. Tel: 773-568-7822; Web: www.zacchaeushouse.org. Most Rev. Joseph N. Perry, Moderator, Email: deacon@zaccaeushouse.org. A ministry of Deacons offering hospitality and life skills education to men in transition to stability in their lives.

ARLINGTON HEIGHTS. **Alexian Brothers Center for Mental Health*, 3436 N. Kennicott Ave., Arlington Heights, 60004. Tel: 847-952-7460; Fax: 847-222-1754; Web: www.alexianbrothershealth.org/acmh. Mr. Rick Germann, Assoc. Vice Pres.; Revita DeChalus, Chap. *Legal Titles: Sponsored by Ascension Health Ministries (Ascension Sponsor), a public juridic person.* Tot Asst. Annually 3,650; Total Staff 96.

BARTLETT. **Bethany House of Hospitality*, 951 W. Bartlett Rd., Ste. Home F, Bartlett, 60103.

BLUE ISLAND. *St. Francis Hospital and Health Center*, 12935 S. Gregory St., Blue Island, 60406.

CHICAGO HEIGHTS. *Dominican Association of Secondary Schools, Inc.*, 700 S. Ashland Ave., Chicago Heights, 60411. Tel: 708-755-7565; Fax: 708-756-9759; Web: www.dominicanschools.org. Sr. Kathleen Anne Tait, O.P., Contact Person.

DES PLAINES. *Shrine of Our Lady of Guadalupe*, 1170 North River Rd., Des Plaines, 60016. Tel: 847-294-1806; Fax: 847-294-1981; Email: info@santuarioguadalupe.com; Web: www.solg.org. Very Rev. Esequiel Sanchez, Rector; Rev. Charlie Plovanich.

Sisters of the Holy Family of Nazareth - U.S.A., Inc., 310 N. River Rd., Des Plaines, 60016. Tel: 847-298-6760; Fax: 847-803-1941; Email: info@nazarethcsfn.org. Sr. Kathleen Maciej, Supr.

Viator House of Hospitality, 1150 N. River Rd., 100/150 Halpin Bldg., Des Plaines, 60016. Web: www.viatorhouseofhospitality.com. Rev. Corey D. Brost, C.S.V., Dir.; Bro. Michael T. Gosch, C.S.V., Dir.

ELK GROVE VILLAGE. *Alexian Brothers of America, Inc.*, 600 Alexian Way, Elk Grove Village, 60007. Tel: 847-264-8704; Fax: 847-264-8697; Web: www.alexianbrothers.org. Bro. Daniel McCormick, C.F.A., Prov. Congregation of Alexian Brothers, Immaculate Conception Province.

BLFR Foundation, LLC, 600 Alexian Way, Elk Grove Village, 60007. Tel: 847-264-8704; Fax: 847-264-8697. Bro. Daniel McCormick, C.F.A., CEO.

EVERGREEN PARK. *American Province of Little Company of Mary Sisters Charitable Trust*, 9350 S. California, Evergreen Park, 60805.

Tel: 708-422-0130; Fax: 708-422-2212; Email: swalsh@lcmh.org; Web: www.lcmsisters.org.

Network for Mercy Education, 10024 S. Central Park Ave., 60655. Tel: 708-295-6614; Email: cravenrsm@gmail.com. Sr. Corinne Raven, R.S.M., Dir.

GURNEE. *Aid for Women of Northern Lake County*, 4606 W. Old Grand Ave., Unit 4, Gurnee, 60031. Tel: 847-249-2700; Web: www.aidforwomenlakecounty.org. To give hope to women who are pregnant, explain the risks involved in abortion & offer life-affirming alternatives such as parenting or adoption. If the client is single, she is presented with the opportunity to change her lifestyle & begin a life of chastity until & within marriage. Each client is treated with respect, dignity & confidentiality. Appropriate referrals are made to afford the best prenatal care for herself & her child.

Assisi Homes of Gurnee, Inc., 3495 W. Grand Ave., Gurnee, 60031. Tel: 847-336-4428; Tel: 303-830-3300; Fax: 847-336-3778; Email: mrankin@mercyhousing.org; Web: www.mercyhousing.org. Melissa Clayton, Contact Person. Units 60.

JUSTICE. *Saint John Paul II Eucharistic Adoration Association, Inc.*, 9000 W. 81st. St., Justice, 60458. Tel: 708-728-0840; Tel: 312-444-1784; Email: information@pjp2ea.org; Web: www.pjp2ea.org. 20 N. Wacker Dr., Ste. 1700, 60606. Charles Smith, Treas.

LAGRANGE PARK. *Joyful Again*, 543 N. Dover Ave., P.O. Box 1365, La Grange Park, 60526-9465. Tel: 708-354-7211; Email: joyfulagain7211@gmail.com; Web: www.joyfulagain.org. Rev. Medard P. Laz, Exec. Dir., (Retired); Charlotte Hrubes, Dir. Support program for widowed men and women.

School and Tutors on Wheels aka Tutoring English to Advance Change (TEACH), 100 S. 6th Ave., La Grange, 60525. Tel: 708-354-9200; Fax: 708-609-0945; Web: www.teachempowers.org. Constantine Bitsas, Exec.

Sisters of St. Joseph of LaGrange Charitable Trust, 1515 W. Ogden Ave., La Grange Park, 60526-2721. Tel: 708-354-9200; Fax: 708-354-9573. Linda Talentowski, Contact Person.

The Well Spirituality Center, 1515 W. Ogden Ave., La Grange Park, 60526. Tel: 708-482-5088; Fax: 708-354-9573; Email: thewell@csjoseph.org; Web: www.csjthewell.org. Bridget Sperduto, Exec. Dir. The Well Spirituality Center is a regional Center for the telling of the Universe Story, where people of all faiths and cultures are invited to recognize and affirm our communion with God and all creation; to experience an atmosphere for spiritual, physical and emotional wholeness; and to participate in the sacred process of healing and caring for earth and her people.

LAKE FOREST. *Barat Education Foundation*, P.O. Box 457, Lake Forest, 60045. Tel: 847-501-1726; Fax: 847-234-4628; Email: alumni@thebaratfoundation.org; Web: www.thebaratfoundation.org. Maureen Ryan, Exec. Dir.

New Ethos, 825 S. Waukegan Rd. A8 #225, Lake Forest, 60045. Tel: 312-208-8777; Email: newethosfilm@gmail.com; Web: www.new-ethos.org. Rev. Donald C. Woznicki, Exec. Dir. Collaborates with the Entertainment Industry to bring the Catholic consumer true, good & beautiful entertainment.

LEMONT. *Franciscan Communities, Inc.*, 11500 Theresa Dr., Lemont, 60439. Tel: 331-318-5200; Fax: 331-318-5210; Email: jamiano@franciscanministries.org; Web: www.franciscanministries.org. Judy Amiano, Pres. & CEO; John Glover, Exec.; Daniel Noonan, CFO. A senior living and care ministry sponsored by the Franciscan Sisters of Chicago serving over 1900 residents through its independent living, assisted living, memory care and skilled care nursing services.

Franciscan Community Benefit Services, 11500 Theresa Dr., Lemont, 60439. Tel: 331-318-5200; Fax: 331-318-5210; Email: jamiano@franciscanministries.org; Web: www.franciscanministries.org. Judy Amiano, Pres. Sponsored by the Franciscan Sisters of Chicago.A charitable foundation, operating as the Madonna Foundation, focused on the ministry of the Franciscan Sisters of Chicago and increasing access to Catholic high schools by young women in urban areas through scholarships and program enhancement.

Franciscan Ministries Sponsored by the Franciscan Sisters of Chicago, 11500 Theresa Dr., Lemont, 60439. Tel: 331-318-5200; Email: jamiano@franciscanministries.org; Web: www.franciscanministries.org. Judy Amiano, Pres. & CEO; John Glover, COO; Daniel Noonan, CFO; Dawn Mayer, Vice Pres. of Mission Integration & Pastoral Care. Franciscan Sisters of Chicago Service Corporation d/b/a Franciscan Ministries Sponsored by the Franciscan Sisters of Chicago.

St. Joseph Property Trust, 11500 Theresa Dr., Lemont, 60439. Tel: 630-243-3554; Fax: 630-243-3576; Email: fradke@chicagofranciscans.com. Sr. Francis Clare Radke, Trustee.

Mother Theresa Care & Mission Trust, 11500 Theresa Dr., Lemont, 60439. Tel: 630-243-3554; Fax: 630-243-3576; Email: fradke@chicagofranciscans.com. Sr. Francis Clare Radke, Treas.

LISLE. *Alexian Brothers Community Services*, 2601 Navistar Dr., Bldg. 2, Fl. 3, Lisle, 60532. Tel: 224-273-2334; Fax: 630-505-1314; Web: www.amitahealth.org. Mark A. Frey, CEO. Alexian Brothers Community Services (Programs for the care of the elderly) in Chattanooga, TN and in St. Louis, MO.

Alexian Brothers Health System, Inc. Investment Trust, 2601 Navistar Dr., Bldg. 2, Fl. 3, Lisle, 60532. Tel: 224-273-2334; Fax: 630-505-1314; Email: melissa.kulik@amitahealth.org; Web: www.amitahealth.org. Mark A. Frey, CEO. Sponsored by Ascension Health Ministries (Ascension Sponsor), a public juridic person.

Alexian Brothers Senior Ministries, 2601 Navistar Dr., Bldg. 2, Fl. 3, Lisle, 60532. Tel: 224-273-2334; Fax: 630-505-1314; Email: melissa.kulik@amitahealth.org; Web: www.amitahealth.org. Mark A. Frey, CEO. Ascension Health. *Legal Title: Ascension Health.*

MELROSE PARK. *Dominican Literacy Center (ESL)*, 1503 Rice St., Melrose Park, 60160. Tel: 708-338-0659; Fax: 708-338-0659; Email: judithcurran@yahoo.com. Sr. Judith Curran, O.P., Dir.

MUNDELEIN. *Civitas Dei Foundation*, 1000 E. Maple Ave., Mundelein, 60060. Tel: 847-837-4516. Rev. Michael J. K. Fuller, M.Div., S.T.L., S.T.D., B.A. The Journal is named Chicago Studies.

Foundation for Adult Catechetical Teaching Aids, 22333 W. Erhart Rd., Mundelein, 60060. Tel: 847-223-0010; Fax: 847-223-5960; Email: FoundationACTA@gmail.com; Web: www.actafoundation.org. Revs. Donald P. Senior, C.P., S.T.D., Treas.; Lawrence R. Dowling, Pres.

NORTHLAKE. *Scalabrini Village*, 420-480 N. Wolf Rd., Northlake, 60164. Tel: 708-562-0040; Fax: 708-562-5180.

OLYMPIA FIELDS. *Franciscan Health Foundation - South Suburban Chicago*, 20201 S. Crawford Ave., Olympia Fields, 60461. Tel: 708-747-4000, Ext. 85470; Fax: 708-503-3270; Email: SSCFoundation@franciscanalliance.org; Web: www.franciscanalliance.org/foundation. Susan Linn, Exec. Dir. Staff 3.

PALATINE. *Friends of St. Thomas of Villanova School*, P.O. Box 2627, Palatine, 60078. Tel: 847-383-6480; Fax: 847-821-7142; Email: friends@fostovs.org; Web: www.fostovs.org. Our mission is to raise funds to support the Christian values and quality education offered by St. Thomas of Villanova School. We do so by seeking charitable gifts, which will be used by St. Thomas of Villanova School in accordance with priorities established by the school's administrators.

RIVER FOREST. *Education and Intervention, Inc.* dba ICAP (Inter Congregational Addictions Program), 7777 W. Lake St., Ste. 115, River Forest, 60305-1734. Tel: 773-612-5207; Fax: 773-852-3608; Email: lclose@bvmcong.org; Email: mgkinn2@aol.com; Web: Icaptoday.org. Sisters Letitia Close, Corp. Sec.; Mary Gene Kinney, B.V.M., Master Addictions Counselor (M.A.C.). National and International network for women religious recovering in 12 step programs; services of intervention, referral, follow-up and education to communities of women religious. *Education and Intervention, Inc.*

SOUTH HOLLAND. *American Catholic Press*, 16565 S. State St., South Holland, 60473. Tel: 708-331-5485; Fax: 708-331-5484; Email: acp@acpress.org; Web: www.americancatholicpress.org. Rev. Michael J. Gilligan, Ph.D., S.T.L., Exec. Dir. Founded in 1967, ACP makes available resources on liturgy and liturgical music, especially for parishes and dioceses. ACP was incorporated as a nonprofit organization in 1972.

TECHNY. *Blessed Arnold Religious Charitable Trust*, 1985 Waukegan Rd., P.O. Box 6067, Techny, 60082-6067. Tel: 847-272-2700; Fax: 847-753-7464; Email: treasurer@uscsvd.org; Web: www.divineword.org. Rev. Dariusz Garbaciak, S.V.D., Treas.; Bro. Mathew Zemel, S.V.D., Chm. Society of the Divine Word.

Divine Word Techny Community Corporation dba Divine Word Seminary/Divine Word Residence f/k/a DWTCRE Charitable Trusts, 1901 Waukegan Rd., P.O. Box 65, Techny, 60082. Tel: 847-272-2700; Fax: 847-753-7464; Email: housetreasurer@techny.org; Web: www.divineword.org. Bro. Mathew Zemel, S.V.D., Trustee; Revs. Dariusz Garbaciak, S.V.D., Sec.; Nhan Tran, S.V.D.

Techny Land Corporation, NFP, 1985 Waukegan Rd., P.O. Box 6038, Techny, 60082. Tel: 847-272-2700, Ext. 1670; Email: mzemel@uscsvd.org. Bro. Mathew Zemel, S.V.D., Pres.

Techny Land Investments, 1985 Waukegan Rd., P.O. Box 6038, Techny, 60082. Tel: 847-272-2700; Email: treasurer@uscsvd.org. Rev. Dariusz Garbaciak, S.V.D., Pres.; Bro. Mathew Zemel, S.V.D., Treas.

WAUKEGAN. *Alexian Brothers The Harbor*, c/o Bonaventure House, 825 W. Wellington Ave., 60657. Tel: 847-782-8015; Fax: 847-782-0822; Web: www.alexianbrothershousing.org. Korrey Kooistra, Exec. Operated by Alexian Brothers Bonaventure House, Inc., Housing and supportive services for otherwise homeless persons with HIV/AIDS. Sponsored by Ascension Health Ministries (Ascension Sponsor), a public juridic person.

WILMETTE. *Loyola Recreational Facility Corp.*, 1100 Laramie, Wilmette, 60091-1021. Tel: 847-256-1100; Fax: 847-251-4031; Web: www.goramblers.org. Rev. Patrick E. McGrath, S.J.

Musica Pacis, Office of the Treasurer, P.O. Box 969, Wilmette, 60091-0969. Tel: 708-624-2559; Email: musicapacis@attglobal.net. Rev. Alec J. Wolff, J.C.L., Treas.

[Y] CLOSED INSTITUTIONS

CHICAGO. *Archdiocese of Chicago's Joseph Cardinal Bernardin Archives and Records Center*, 711 W. Monroe St., 60661. Tel: 312-534-4400; Fax: 312-831-0610; Email: info@archchicago.org; Web: archives.archchicago.org. The following parish, school or institution records may be found at the above address unless otherwise indicated. Notations to sacramental records of closed parishes held by the Archives and Records Center should be directed to the Archives and Records Center and should specify the name of the parish. The location of records periodically changes. Inquiries for records of parishes, schools or institutions not on this list should be directed to the above address.

Academy of St. Benedict the African (May St.).
Academy of St. Benedict the African (Honore St.).
Academy of St. Benedict the African (Stewart St.).
Academy of the Immaculate Conception (Unknown).
Academy of the Sacred Heart, Sacred Heart Schools, 6250 N. Sheridan Rd., 60660. Tel: 773-262-4446; Email: brian.mcguinness@shschicago.org. Mr. Nat Wilburn, Headmaster.
Academy of Our Lady aka Longwood Academy.
Academy of Our Lady of Mount Carmel (Unknown) Became school for Our Lady of Mount Carmel.
Academy of St. Joseph (Unknown).
Academy of St. Priscilla at Divine Savior.
Academy of St. Scholastica Renamed St. Scholastica Academy.
Academy of the Holy Child aka Little Academy of the Holy Child St. Anastasia School.
ST. ADALBERT PARISH Records at St. Paul 22nd St.
St. Adalbert Commercial High School (Unknown).
St. Adalbert School.
St. Adrian Parish (7000 S. Fairfield Ave.).
St. Adrian School.
St. Agatha Catholic Academy (Douglas Ave. & Lexington Ave. Campuses)-Records at ARC.
St. Agatha Academy (Unknown).
St. Agatha School.
St. Agnes School (14th) (part of Holy Family, Chicago, Archives).
Blessed Agnes Commercial High School and School, St. Agnes of Bohemia School, 2643 S. Central Park, 60623. Tel: 773-522-0143.
Blessed Agnes of Bohemia Church, St. Agnes of Bohemia Parish, 2643 S. Central Park, 60623. Tel: 773-522-0143.
St. Agnes Academy (Unknown).
St. Agnes Parish (39th St.) (Pershing Rd.) (Archives).
St. Agnes School (39th St.).
St. Agnes High School (Unknown) (39th St.).
St. Albertus Academy (Waukegan) (Unknown).
Alexine Learning Center (school at ARC; sacramental records pre 1979 at Sisters of St. Joseph, 708-354-9200).
St. Ailbe Parish (9015 S. Harper Ave.).
All Saints Parish (State St.).
All Saints School (State St.).
All Saints Parish (Wallace St.).
All Saints School (Wallace).
All Saints / St. Anthony School (Wallace).
St. Aloysius School.
St. Aloysius School (Maxwell St.) (part of Holy Family, Chicago, ARC).
St. Aloysius Commercial High School (Boys) (Unknown).

St. Aloysius High School (Girls) (Unknown) (& St. Aloysius School).
St. Alphonsus School (Wellington) Renamed Alphonsus Academy and Center for the Arts.
St. Alphonsus School (Lemont) St. Alphonsus/St. Patrick School, 205 Cass St., Lemont, 60439. Tel: 630-257-2380; Fax: 630-257-4648.
St. Alphonsus High School (Chicago).
St. Alphonsus Commercial High School (Lemont) (Unknown).
Alvernia Conservatory of Music (Unknown).
Alvernia High School.
St. Ambrose High School (Unknown).
St. Ambrose School (47th St.).
St. Ambrose Parish (117th St.) See St. Louis de France Parish (117th St.).
St. Andrew High School.
St. Andrew Mission (Wadsworth) St. Patrick Parish, 15000 Wadsworth Rd., Wadsworth, 60083. Tel: 847-244-4161; Fax: 847-336-0630.
St. Andrew The Apostle School (Calumet City).
ANGEL GUARDIAN CROATIAN CATHOLIC MISSION, Blessed Alojzije Stepinac Croatian Catholic Mission, 6346 N. Ridge Ave., 60660. Tel: 773-262-0535; Fax: 773-262-4603.
Angel Guardian Orphanage.
St. Angela Parish.
St. Angela Academy (Unknown).
St. Ann Parish (Chicago Heights).
St. Ann School (Chicago Heights).
ST. ANN PARISH (Leavitt St.) - Records at St. Paul 22nd St.
St. Ann High School (Leavitt St.).
St. Anne Hospital and St. Anne's Tuberculosis Sanitarium, Saint Elizabeth Campus, Saints Mary and Elizabeth Medical Center, 1431 N. Claremont Ave., 60622. Tel: 773-278-2000.
St. Anne's School of Nursing, Ancilla College, 9601 Union Rd., Plymouth, IN 46563. Tel: 574-936-8898 ; Tel: 866-262-4552 (Toll Free).
St. Anne Parish (Garfield Blvd.).
St. Anne School (Garfield Blvd.).
St. Anne School (Hazel Crest).
St. Anne Parish, 711 W. Monroe St., 60661. Tel: 312-534-4400; Fax: 312-831-0610. (Waukegan); (Archives).
St. Anne Mission Chapel (Richton) St. Liborius Parish, 71 W. 35th St., Steger, 60475. Tel: 708-754-1363.
Annunciation Parish (Wabansia).
Annunciation School (Wabansia).
St. Anselm School.
St. Anthony of Padua Parish (24th Pl.).
St. Anthony of Padua School (24th Pl.).
St. Anthony School (Cicero).
St. Anthony High School & Commercial High School (24th Pl.).
St. Anthony School (Prairie).
Aquinas Catholic High School.
Aquinas Dominican High School.
Aquinas High School.
Archbishop Quigley Preparatory Seminary.
Ascension Parish (Harvey) at Ascension-St. Susanna Parish, 15234 Myrtle Ave., Harvey, 60426-3194. Tel: 708-333-0931; Fax: 708-333-3281 .
Ascension School (Harvey).
Ascension-St. Susanna School (Harvey).
Ascension of Our Lord Parish (Evanston).
Ascension of Our Lord School (Evanston).
Assumption School (24th St.).
Assumption Parish (Marshfield Ave.).
Assumption School (Marshfield Ave.).
Assumption BVM Parish (123rd St.).
Assumption BVM School (123rd St.).
Assumption School (Unknown) (Illinois St.).
Assumption / St. Catherine of Genoa School and Parish.
St. Attracta Parish (Cicero).
St. Attracta School (Cicero).
St. Attracta-St. Valentine Church (Cicero).
St. Augustine Parish (S. Laflin).
St. Augustine School & High School.
St. Beatrice School.
Barat College (Lake Forest) De Paul University, 1 E. Jackson Blvd., 60604. Tel: 312-362-8850.
St. Barbara High School.
St. Barbara School (Brookfield).
St. Bartholomew Parish (Waukegan).
St. Bartholomew School (Waukegan).
St. Basil Parish, St. Basil/Visitation Parish 5443 S. Honore, 60609.
St. Basil Parish (Ukrainian Rite), St. Michael Parish (Ukrainian Rite), 12205 S. Parnell, 60628. Tel: 773-291-0168.
St. Basil School.
St. Bede Parish (Ingleside).
St. Benedict the African West (Records at St. Benedict the African-East).
Bellarmine School of Theology, Loyola University of Chicago, Dean of Students of the Graduate School, 820 N. Michigan Ave., 60611.
St. Benedict High School (Coed 1919-1939) (Unknown).
St. Bernadette School (Evergreen Park).
St. Bernard Parish.
St. Bernard School.
St. Bernardine School (Forest Park).
Bishop Quarter Boarding School for Motherless Boys.
Bishop Quarter Junior Military School aka Bishop Quarter School for Little Boys.
St. Blase School (Argo).
Blessed Sacrament Parish (Millard St.).
Blessed Sacrament School (Millard St.).
Blessed Sacrament / Our Lady of Lourdes School.
SS. Benedict and Scholastica Academy.
St. Bonaventure Parish, St. Alphonsus Parish, 1429 W. Wellington Ave., 60657. Tel: 773-525-0709.
St. Bonaventure School (Diversey).
St. Boniface Parish (N. Noble).
St. Boniface School (N. Noble).
St. Boniface High School (Unknown).
St. Brendan Parish (Racine).
St. Brendan School (Racine).
St. Bride School.
St. Bridget Parish.
St. Bridget School & High School.
Bridgeport Industrial School for Boys See Illinois Industrial School for Boys.
Bridgeport Catholic Academy Middle School (St. Mary of Perpetual Help Campus).
Bridgeport Catholic Academy North Campus (All Saints/St. Anthony Campus).
St. Bronislava Parish (Sacramental Records at Immaculate Conception on 88th).
St. Bronislava School.
Brother Candidates High School (Techny) Box 107, East Troy, WI 53120. Tel: 414-642-3300.
Cabrini Green Alternative High School.
Cabrini Hospital Sacramental records - St. Anthony Hospital (Chicago); Medical records - St. Anthony Hospital.
St. Callistus Oratory (Records at Notre Dame de Chicago Parish).
St. Callistus Parish.
St. Callistus School (pre 1994 - ARC) (1994-2004 at Notre Dame Parish).
St. Camillus School.
Cardinal Stritch High School.
Carmel High School (Boys and Girls) (Boys' Carmel and Girls' Carmel merged to form 1 Carmel High School) Carmel High School, One Carmel Pkwy., Mundelein, 60060-2499. Tel: 847-566-3000.
St. Carthage Parish (73rd St.).
St. Carthage School.
St. Casimir Academy.
St. Casimir Parish (Chicago Heights).
St. Casimir School (Chicago Heights).
St. Casimir Parish (Whipple St.).
St. Casimir School (Whipple St.).
St. Casimir High School, Our Lady of Tepeyac High School, 2228 S. Whipple St., 60623. Tel: 773-522-0023; Fax: 773-522-0508. (Whipple St.).
St. Catherine Academy (See Siena High School)
St. Catherine High School (See Siena High School).
Cathedral College.
Cathedral High School.
Chrysalis Program.
Corpus Christi School.
St. Catherine of Genoa Parish.
St. Catherine of Genoa School.
St. Catherine of Siena Parish (Oak Park) Sacramental Records: St. Catherine/St. Lucy Parish, 38 N. Austin Blvd., Oak Park, 60302. Tel: 708-386-8077; Fax: 708-386-5190.
St. Catherine of Siena School (Oak Park) School Records: St. Catherine/St. Lucy School, 27 W. Washington Blvd., Oak Park, 60302. Tel: 708-386-5286.
St. Cecilia Parish (Wells St.).
St. Cecilia School (Wells St.).
St. Celestine (Elmwood Park).
St. Charles Borromeo Parish (Hoyne Ave.).
St. Charles Borromeo School (Hoyne Ave.).
St. Charles Borromeo School (Melrose Park).
St. Charles Lwanga Parish (W. Garfield).
St. Charles Lwanga School (W. Garfield).
Children of Peace School Holy Family site at ARC; St. Callistus site at Holy Trinity site.
Christ the Redeemer Church (Byzantine Rite).
St. Clara Parish (Woodlawn Ave.).
St. Clara School (Woodlawn).
St. Clara-St. Cyril Parish (S. Woodlawn).
St. Clare of Montefalco School.
St. Clement High School.
St. Clotilde School.
St. Columba Academy (Unknown).
St. Columba School (134th St.).
St. Columbanus High School (Unknown).
St. Columbanus School (71st St.) Records at ARC.
St. Columbkille Parish (Paulina).
St. Columbkille School & Commercial High School.
Columbus Hospital Sacramental Records - Archives, Medical Records - St. Anthony Hospital.
Columbus Hospital School of Nursing.
St. Constance High School.
Convent of the Holy Child Renamed Holy Child High School.
Convent of the Sacred Heart (Chicago) Sacred Heart Schools, 6250 N. Sheridan Rd., 60660. Tel: 773-262-4446.
Convent of the Sacred Heart High School (Lake Forest) Woodlands Academy of the Sacred Heart, 760 E. Westleigh Rd., Lake Forest, 60045-3298. Tel: 847-234-4300.
Cook County Hospital (Sacramental Records).
St. Cornelius School, (Grades PreK-8).
Corpus Christi High School, Hales Franciscan High School, 4930 S. Cottage Grove, 60615. Tel: 773-285-8400.
Cuneo Hospital Medical Records - St. Anthony Hospital Sacramental-Archives.
St. Cyprian Parish (River Grove).
St. Cyril College, Mt. Carmel High School.
St. Cyril Parish (Dante Ave.).
St. Cyril School.
Ss. Cyril & Methodius Church & School (Hermitage Ave.).
Ss. Cyril & Methodius Church & School (Walton St.).
St. David School.
ST. DAVID PARISH.
De Lourdes College (Des Plaines) Holy Family College, Registrar's Office, Grant Ave. & Frankford Ave., Philadelphia, PA 19114. Tel: 215-637-4851.
St. Denis School.
DePaul Academy & DePaul University Academy, DePaul University, Registrar's Office, 243 S. Wabash, 60604. Tel: 312-341-8610.
DePaul High School (Unknown).
DePaul University Loop High School (Unknown).
St. Dionysius Parish (Cicero).
St. Dionysius School (Cicero).
Divine Savior School.
St. Dionysius High School (Cicero) (Unknown).
St. Dominic Parish (Locust).
St. Domitilla School (Hillside).
St. Dominic School & High School.
St. Donatus School (Blue Island).
St. Dorothy School (78th St.) Records at ARC.
St. Edmund School (Oak Park).
St. Elizabeth High School (41st St.) Pre-1924 - Records Unknown; Post-1924 at Archives.
St. Elizabeth School Records at ARC.
ST. EMERIC CHURCH (Washtenaw Ave.) St. Stephen King of Hungary Parish, 2015 W. Augusta Blvd., 60622-4947. Tel: 773-486-1896; Fax: 773-486-1902 .
St. Emeric School (County Club Hills).
Englewood Catholic Academy (Honore St.).
Englewood Catholic Academy (Laflin St.).
Englewood Catholic Academy (May St.).
Englewood Catholic Academy (Princeton St.).
Englewood Catholic Academy (St. Basil site); Reopened as St. Basil School.
Englewood Catholic Academy (Visitation site); Reopened as Visitation School.
Ephpheta School for the Deaf.
ST. ETHELREDA PARISH.
St. Eulalia School.
Felician College.
St. Felicitas Parish (1526 E. 84th St.).
St. Felicitas High School (Unknown).
St. Felicitas School.
St. Fidelis Parish.
St. Fidelis School (N. Washtenaw).
St. Finbarr Parish.
St. Finbarr High School and School (Unknown).
Five Holy Martyrs School.
St. Florian Commerical High School (Unknown).
St. Florian Mission (52nd & Archer) St. Camillus, 5426 S. Lockwood Ave., 60638. Tel: 773-767-8183.
St. Florian School, (Grades PreK-8).
Ford City Catholic Center.
Fournier Institute of Technology, DePaul University, Registrar's Office, 243 S. Wabash, 60604. Tel: 312-341-8610.
Fornier Institute Viatorian Preparatory (Lemont) Viatorian Archives, Arlington Heights, 60006.
St. Frances Xavier Cabrini Parish (Lexington St.).
St. Frances Xavier Cabrini School (Lexington St.).
St. Frances Xavier Cabrini School of Nursing.
St. Francis Xavier Commercial High School (Unknown).
St. Francis de Paula Parish.
St. Francis de Paula School (S. Ellis).
St. Francis de Sales School.
ST. FRANCIS OF ASSISI CHURCH (Kostner Ave.).

St. Francis of Assisi High School (Roosevelt Rd.) (Unknown).
St. Francis of Assisi (932 N. Kostner).
St. Francis of Assisi School (Kostner Ave.).
St. Francis of Assisi School (Roosevelt Ave.).
St. Francis Hospital (Blue Island) Sacramental Records - Archives.
Our Lady of the Angels Mission Separated from St. Francis of Assisi/Our Lady of the Angel Parish Records at Our Lady of the Angels Mission (this is not closed).
St. Francis Xavier Parish (Nelson) (Archives).
St. Francis Xavier School (Nelson).
St. Gabriel Commercial High School St. Gabriel High School (Unknown).
St. Gabriel School (open) Records (1941-1965) at Archives.
Garfield Alternative High School.
St. Gelasius Parish and School.
St. George Parish (Wentworth Ave.).
St. George School & Commercial High School (Lituanica Ave.).
St. George School (Wentworth Ave.).
St. George Parish (Lituanica Ave.).
St. George School (Ewing St.).
St. George High School (Evanston).
St. Gerald High School (Oak Lawn) (Unknown).
St. Gerard Majella School (Markham).
St. Gertrude High School (Franklin Park) (Unknown).
St. Gertrude School (Chicago).
St. Gertrude School (Franklin Park).
Good Counsel High School.
Good Shepherd Chapel (Illinois Technical School for the Colored Girls).
Good Shepherd School.
Gordon Tech High School (California Ave.) Renamed DePaul College Prep.
St. Gregory the Great High School.
St. Gregory the Great School.
Guardian Angel School (part of Holy Family Parish, Chicago).
Hardey Preparatory, Sacred Heart Schools, 6250 N. Sheridan Rd., 60660. Tel: 773-262-4446.
Heart of Mary High School.
St. Hedwig Mission, St. John Berchmans Parish, 2517 W. Logan Blvd., 60647. Tel: 773-486-4300; Fax: 773-252-5346. (Washtenaw Ave.).
St. Hedwig Orphanage (Niles).
St. Hedwig School (Hoyne Ave.) (Archives).
St. Helen's Chapel (Unknown).
St. Helena of the Cross Parish (Records at ARC).
St. Helena of the Cross School (Parnell Ave.).
St. Henry School.
St. Henry Commercial High School (Unknown).
Holy Child High School (Waukegan).
Holy Cross Parish (65th St.).
Holy Cross School (65th St.).
Holy Cross School (Wood St.).
Holy Cross Parish (46th St.).
Holy Cross High School (River Grove)(ARC).
Holy Family Parish (North Chicago).
Holy Family Parish (Waukegan).
Holy Family High School (Unknown).
Holy Family School (North Chicago).
Holy Family School (May St.).
Holy Family Academy (Division St.).
Holy Family Extension High School (Des Plaines) Sisters of Holy Family of Nazareth, Provincial Archives, 310 N. River Rd., Des Plaines, 60016. Tel: 847-298-6760.
Holy Family Orphanage (Unknown).
Holy Ghost Parish & School (Adams St.).
Holy Ghost Academy (Techny) Convent of the Holy Spirit (Techny).
Holy Ghost School (South Holland).
Holy Guardian Angel Parish (Arthington/Cabrini).
Holy Guardian Angel School.
Holy Innocents School.
Holy Name Cathedral School.
Holy Name High School (Unknown).
Holy Name of Mary School.
Holy Rosary Commercial High School (North Chicago) (Unknown).
Holy Rosary Slovak Parish (108th St.).
Holy Rosary Slovak School (108th St.).
Holy Rosary Parish and School (113th St.).
Holy Rosary Parish (North Chicago).
Holy Rosary School (North Chicago).
Holy Rosary School (Western Ave.).
HOLY TRINITY PARISH, Holy Trinity Polish Mission, 1118 N. Noble St., 60622-4015. Tel: 773-489-4140; Fax: 773-489-5918.
Holy Trinity School (Noble St.).
Holy Trinity Parish (Wolcott).
Holy Trinity Parish (Throop).
Holy Trinity School (Throop).
Holy Trinity School (Wolcott).
Holy Trinity School (Taylor, Deaf Children).
House of the Good Shepherd.
St. Hugh School (Lyons).
St. Hyacinth Mission (Spaulding) St. Hyacinth Basilica Parish, 3636 N. Wolfram, 60618. Tel: 773-342-3636; Fax: 773-342-3638.
St. Hyacinth School (Wolfram) Records at ARC.
St. Ignatius College, St. Ignatius College Prep., 1073 W. Roosevelt Rd., 60608. Tel: 312-421-5900.
St. Ignatius School.
Illinois Industrial School for Boys (Unknown).
Illinois Technical School for Colored Girls.
Illinois Industrial School for Girls (ARC).
Immaculata High School.
Immaculate Conception School (Exchange Ave.; Open, 1884-1984 only).
Immaculate Conception Commercial High School (Aberdeen St.).
Immaculate Conception-St. Bridget School.
Immaculate Conception Parish (Aberdeen St.).
Immaculate Conception School (Aberdeen St.).
Immaculate Conception School (44th St.).
Immaculate Conception Parish (Waukegan).
Immaculate Conception School (Waukegan).
Immaculate Conception School (Highland Park).
Immaculate Conception School (North Park Ave.; Open, 1868-1986 only).
Immaculate Conception High School (Highland Park) (Unknown).
IMMACULATE CONCEPTION PARISH, 75 N. Buffalo Grove Rd., Buffalo Grove, 60089. (Buffalo Grove) Renamed St. Mary Parish (Buffalo Grove).
IMMACULATE CONCEPTION OF THE BLESSED VIRGIN MARY PARISH (1859) (North Park Ave.) - Records at Immaculate Conception St. Joseph Parish.
Immaculate Heart of Mary High School (Westchester).
Immaculate Heart of Mary School (Spaulding Ave.).
Immaculate Heart of Mary Vicariate Parish (Ashland).
Incarnation Parish (Palos Heights).
Industrial and Manual Labor School of the Sisters of the Holy Cross (Unknown).
Institute of Our Lady of the Sacred Heart aka Academy of Our Lady of the Sacred Heart Renamed Academy of Our Lady (Longwood Academy).
St. Irenaeus School (Park Forest).
St. Isaac Jogues School (Niles).
St. Isidore the Farmer School (Blue Island).
St. Isidore the Farmer Parish Records at St. Donatus, Blue Island.
St. Ita High School (Unknown).
St. Ita School.
St. James Academy (Lemont) (Unknown).
St. James Parish (Strassburg or New Strassburg) (Unknown).
St. James School (Wabash Ave.).
St. James Parish & School (Maywood).
St. James Parish (Mundelein or Fremont Center) St. Mary of the Annunciation Parish, 22333 W. Erhart Rd., Mundelein, 60060. Tel: 847-223-0010; Fax: 847-223-5960.
St. James Commercial High School (Maywood) (Unknown).
St. James School (Highwood) Records at ARC.
St. James School (Fullerton and Menard).
St. James School (Sauk Village).
St. James High School (Wabash) (Unknown).
St. Jarlath Parish (Jackson).
St. Jarlath School (Jackson).
ST. JEAN BAPTISTE CHURCH (33rd Pl.).
St. Jerome School (Lunt).
Jesuit School of Theology, Loyola University of Chicago, 820 N. Michigan Ave., 60611. Loyola University of Chicago, Office of the Dean of Graduate School.
Jesus, Our Brother School.
St. Joachim Parish (700 E. 91st St.).
St. Joachim School.
St. John Bosco School.
Old St. John Parish (18th St.).
Old St. John School, Christian Brothers University, 2455 Avery Ave., Memphis, TN 38112.
St. John Cantius Commercial High School (Unknown).
St. John Cantius School.
St. John Chrysostom Parish and School (Bellwood).
St. John De La Salle School Renamed St. John De La Salle Academy of Fine Arts (King Dr.).
St. John Nepomucene Church & School.
St. John of God Parish & School (S. Throop).
St. John the Baptist Parish (50th Pl.).
ST. JOHN THE BAPTIST CHURCH (Burley Ave.).
St. John the Baptist School (50th Pl.).
St. John the Baptist School (Harvey).
St. Josaphat Commerical High School (Hermitage Ave.).
St. Josaphat School (Pre-1961 at Archives).
St. Josaphat Parish Orphanage (Unknown).
St. Joseph Bohemian Orphanage, Maryville Academy, 1150 N. River Rd., Des Plaines, 60016. Tel: 708-824-6126; Fax: 847-824-7277. (Lisle); (Assumed location).
St. Joseph Commercial Business College (Waukegan) (Unknown).
St. Joseph Orphanage (Lisle) See St. Joseph Bohemian Orphanage (Lisle).
St. Joseph School (Wilmette) (Pre-1986 only at Archives).
St. Joseph the Worker School.
St. Joseph's Institute.
St. Joseph Parish (17th Pl.).
St. Joseph School (17th Pl.) (Unknown).
St. Joseph Parish and School (38th Pl.) (See St. Joseph and St. Anne Parish).
ST. JOSEPH PARISH (1846) (Orleans) - Records at Immaculate Conception & St. Joseph Parish.
St. Joseph School (Orleans).
St. Joseph School (Hermitage).
St. Joseph High School (Hermitage Ave.) 711 W. Monroe St., 60661. Tel: 312-534-4400; Fax: 312-831-0610.
St. Joseph Commercial High School (Hermitage) Unknown.
St. Joseph Parish (Chicago Heights).
St. Joseph School (Chicago Hts.).
St. Joseph Parish (Saginaw St.).
St. Joseph School (Saginaw St.).
St. Joseph's Orphan Asylum (35th St.).
St. Joseph Orphanage for Boys (destroyed by fire, post-1859 in archives).
St. Joseph Parish Orphanage (Unknown).
St. Joseph Provident Orphanage.
St. Joseph Military Academy (See St. Joseph's Institute).
St. Joseph Academy (Chicago) (records destroyed in 1871 fire).
St. Joseph Academy (See St. Joseph's Institute) (LaGrange Park).
St. Joseph Commercial High School (Waukegan) (Unknown).
St. Joseph Parish (Waukegan).
SS. Joseph & Bartholomew Parish Renamed Holy Family Parish (Waukegan).
St. Joseph School (Waukegan).
St. Joseph & St. Anne Parish.
St. Joseph & St. Anne Commercial High School and School (Unknown).
St. Joseph Mission (13th St.).
St. Joseph Mission School (13th St.).
St. Joseph Servite Seminary (Elgin-St. Charles) Provincial Archives, Servite Provincial Center, 3121 W. Jackson Blvd., 60612. Tel: 773-533-0360.
St. Joseph's Academy Renamed St. Scholastica Academy (Unknown).
St. Joseph's Carondelet Child Center (Records at Catholic Charities-Legal and Compliant Services).
St. Joseph's Home for the Friendless.
St. Joseph Technical High School (Techny) Divine Word Missionaries, East Troy, WI 53120.
St. Joseph School (Homewood).
Josephinum High School (Records at Josephinum) Renamed Josephinum Academy.
St. Jude the Apostle School (South Holland).
St. Justin Martyr Parish (71st St.).
St. Justin Martyr School.
St. Kevin School.
St. Kieran School (Chicago Heights).
St. Kilian School.
St. Kilian Junior High School (Unknown).
St. Ladislaus School.
Lake Shore Catholic Academy (Waukegan & North Chicago).
St. Lambert School (Skokie).
St. Laurence School and Parish.
St. Lawrence O'Toole School (Matteson) Records at ARC.
St. Leo High School, Mother Guerin Convent, 8001 Belmont Ave., River Grove, 60171. Tel: 708-453-6233.
St. Leo the Great School and Parish.
St. Leonard Commercial High School (Berwyn) St. Leonard School, 3322 S. Clarence, Berwyn, 60402. Tel: 708-749-1989; Fax: 708-749-7981.
Lewis Memorial Maternity Hospital.
Little Flower Parish & School see St. Therese of the Infant Jesus School.
Little Flower High School.
Longwood Academy see Academy of Our Lady.
Loretto Academy (Adams St., 1864-1871) (Unknown).
Loretto Academy (Woodlawn).
Loretto Academy (Englewood).
Loretto Adult Center (Englewood), Kennedy King College, 6800 S. Wentworth, Rm. 3571, 60621.
Loretto Extension Service (Unknown).
Loretto High School (Englewood).
St. Louis de France Parish (117th St.).
St. Louis de France School (117th St.).
St. Louis de Montfort School (Oak Lawn).
St. Louis Parish (Polk St.).
St. Louis School (Polk St.) (Unknown).
St. Louis Academy.
Lourdes High School Records located at De LaSalle

Institute 3455 S. Wabash, 60616.
Tel: 312-842-7355; Fax: 312-842-5640.
Loyola Academy (Chicago), 1100 N. Laramie Ave., Wilmette, 60091. Tel: 847-256-1100.
St. Lucy Parish, St. Catherine-St. Lucy Parish, 38 N. Austin Blvd., Oak Park, 60302.
Tel: 708-386-8077; Fax: 708-386-5190.
St. Lucy School.
St. Ludmilla Parish.
St. Ludmilla School.
St. Louise de Marillac High School.
Madonna High School.
St. Malachy High School, St. Malachy School, 2252 W. Washington, 60612. Tel: 312-733-2252;
Fax: 312-733-5703.
ST. MALACHY PARISH St. Malachy + Precious Blood Parish at St. Malachy Location.
Mallinckrodt High School.
Mallinckrodt College (Wilmette) (Unknown).
St. Margaret's Home & Hospital (Unknown).
St. Margaret Mary School, (Grades PreK-8), (Chase Ave.).
Maria High School (67th St. & California Ave.).
Santa Maria del Popolo School.
Maria Immaculata Academy (Wilmette).
Marian Hills Seminary (Hinsdale) (Unknown).
Marian School for Deaf (Catholic Charities).
St. Mark School (Cortez St.).
St. Mark the Evangelist School.
Marquette Institute (Clark St.).
St. Martha School (Morton Grove).
St. Martin Parish (Princeton St.).
St. Martin de Porres Academy (111th St.).
St. Martin de Porres School (Jackson Blvd.).
St. Martin School & Commercial High School (Princeton).
St. Mary Academy (Libertyville) (Unknown).
St. Mary Commercial High School (Mundelein) (Unknown).
St. Mary High School (Lake Forest) (Unknown).
St. Mary High School (Highland Park) (Unknown).
St. Mary High School (Grenshaw).
St. Mary School (Des Plaines).
St. Mary School (Evanston).
St. Mary School (1948-1995 at Archives) (Riverside) (Open).
St. Mary Parish (Lemont) St Patrick Parish, 200 Illinois St., Lemont, 60439. Tel: 708-257-6134;
Fax: 630-257-0401.
St. Mary Parish (Waukegan) 711 W. Monroe St., 60661. Tel: 312-534-4400; Fax: 312-831-0610.
St. Mary Center for Learning (Grenshaw).
St. Mary Alternative High School (Grenshaw) Records to 1976 at Archives. Records after 1976 or from the night school at Harold Washington College, 30 E. Lake St., 60601. Tel: 312-553-6065.
St. Mary Parish and St. Mary's Mission St. Mary (Seeley); St. Mary's Mission (90th St.); (Byzantine Rite) Annunciation Byzantine, 14610 Will-Cook Rd., Lockport, 60441-9212. Tel: 708-645-0214.
St. Mary Magdalen Parish (S. Marquette Ave.) Records at St. Michael on South Shore Dr.
St. Mary Magdalene School.
St. Mary of Celle School (Berwyn).
ST. MARY OF THE ASSUMPTION PARISH (137th St.).
St. Mary of the Assumption School (137th St.).
St. Mary of Czestochowa School (Cicero) 711 W. Monroe St., 60661. Tel: 312-534-4400;
Fax: 312-831-0610.
St. Mary of the Lake Parish (1870-1928, Ingleside) Renamed St. Bede Parish (Ingleside).
St. Mary of the Lake High School (1844-1867) Unknown, assumed destroyed.
St. Mary of Mt. Carmel Parish (Hermitage St.).
St. Mary of Mt. Carmel School (Hermitage).
Mary of Nazareth School (Harvey).
St. Mary of Perpetual Help School, Bridgeport Catholic Academy, 3700 S. Lowe, 60609-6507.
Tel: 773-376-6223; Fax: 773-376-3864.
St. Mary of Perpetual Help High School.
St. Mary of the Woods Mission School Renamed Immaculate Conception School (Highland Park).
St. Mary of the Woods Parish, Immaculate Conception Parish, 700 W. Deerfield Rd., Highland Park, 60035. Tel: 847-433-0130;
Fax: 847-433-0669. (Highland Park); Renamed Immaculate Conception Parish.
St. Mary Mission Seminary (Techny) Catholic Theological Union, 5401 S. Cornell, 60615-5698.
Tel: 773-324-8000.
St. Mary Orphanage for Girls (Destroyed in fire, some records exist in St. Joseph Orphanage registers).
Mary, Queen of Heaven School (Cicero).
St. Mary's Training School, Maryville Academy, 1150 N. River Rd., Des Plaines, 60016.
Tel: 847-824-6126; Fax: 847-824-7277. Several intake registers are at the archives.; Name changed to Maryville Jen School.
St. Mary's School of Nursing (Des Plaines) Holy Family College, Registrar's Office, Grant Ave. & Frankford Ave., Philadelphia, PA 19114.
Tel: 215-637-4851.
St. Mary's Academy, Christian Brothers University, 2455 Avery Ave., Memphis, TN 38112.
St. Mary's High School (Des Plaines) (Unknown).
St. Mary's Select School, Sisters of the Holy Cross, Notre Dame, IN 46556.
St. Mary's Seminary (Unknown).
Marywood High School (Evanston) Mother Guerin Convent, 8001 Belmont Ave., River Grove, 60171.
Tel: 773-625-3278; Tel: 708-453-6233.
Mater Christi School.
Mater Dolorosa Seminary (Hillside) 3121 W. Jackson Blvd., 60612.
Maternity B.V.M. Mission (92nd) Renamed St. Ailbe Parish.
Maternity of the Blessed Virgin Mary Parish (3647 W. North Ave.).
St. Matthew Parish (Walnut St.).
St. Matthew Commercial High School (Unknown).
St. Matthew School (Walnut St.).
St. Matthias School.
St. Maurice Parish (Archives) Consolidated into Blessed Sacrament (Hoyne Ave.).
St. Maurice School.
McKinley Park Catholic School (Hermitage site and Hoyne site).
St. Mel Parish.
St. Mel & St. Mel-Holy Ghost School.
St. Mel High School (Up to 1969).
Mendel High School.
Mercy High School.
Mercy Mission High School aka Mercy Mission Learning Center.
St. Michael School (Cleveland & Hudson) (1918-1949 only).
St. Michael Central High School (Cleveland & Hudson).
St. Michael School (South Shore Dr.) (Open) Pre-1949 only at Archives.
St. Michael Parish (Wabansia St.).
St. Michael School (Wabansia St.).
St. Michael Parish (24th Pl.).
St. Michael School (24th Pl.).
St. Michael the Archangel Mission (Bellwood) Renamed St. Simeon Parish (Bellwood).
St. Michael the Archangel School.
St. Michael the Archangel Commercial High School (Unknown).
St. Michael Commercial High School (South Shore Dr.).
Misericordia Hospital, Client Records & Adoption Placements: Catholic Charities, 651 N. LaSalle, 60611. Tel: 312-655-7073; Fax: 312-236-5172. Sacramental Records in registers of St. Agnes Parish, 39th St. and Catholic Charities.
Mission of the Holy Ghost (Northbrook) St. Norbert Parish, 1809 Walters Ave., Northbrook, 60062.
Tel: 847-272-7090; Fax: 847-272-7771.
St. Monica Parish (36th St.).
St. Monica School (36th St.) (Unknown).
St. Monica Mission (Harwood Heights) Renamed St. Rosalie Parish (Harwood Heights).
Monastery of Mt. St. Phillip Servite Novitiate, Provincial Archives, Servite Provincial Center, 3121 W. Jackson Blvd., 60612. Tel: 773-533-0360. (Granville, WI).
Montay College.
Mother Theodore Guerin High School (River Grove) at Guerin College Preparatory High School, 8001 W. Belmont, River Grove, 60171.
Tel: 708-453-6233; Fax: 708-453-6296.
Mother Theodore Guerin Convent, 8001 Belmont Ave., River Grove, 60171. Tel: 708-453-1275.
Mother of God Parish (Waukegan).
Mother of God School & High School (Waukegan).
Mother of Sorrows Institute (Blue Island) (Unknown).
Mother of Sorrows Grade and High School (Blue Island).
Mount Assisi Academy (Lemont).
Mount Carmel Academy (Part of St. Patrick Academy in Chicago, later Des Plaines)(Girls); (Unknown).
Mount Carmel School (Served St. Rocco) (Chicago Heights).
Mt. Assisi Academy.
Mundelein College, Office of Registration & Records, 820 N. Michigan Ave., Room 504, 60611.
Tel: 312-915-7221.
Mundelein Cathedral High School.
Mundelein Seminary See University of St. Mary of the Lake (Mundelein).
Municipal Tuberculosis Sanitarium (Sacred Heart Chapel).
Nativity of Our Lord High School (Unknown).
Nativity of Our Lord School & Commercial High School.
Nativity Early Childhood Center (S. Washtenaw).
NATIVITY BVM PARISH (Paulina St.) (Ukranian Rite: Moved to Palos Park).
Nativity BVM School (Washtenaw).
Nazareth Academy (Grammar School - Unknown, Renamed Our Lady of Bethlehem Academy),(High School still open as Nazareth Academy) (LaGrange).
St. Nicholas School (Evanston).
St. Nicholas Parish (State St.).
St. Nicholas School (State St.).
Niles College at St. Joseph Seminary, Loyola University Chicago.
St. Norbert Parish (Northbrook).
Northside Catholic Academy (St. Henry Campus & St. Gregory Campus) (Records split between two remaining campuses) St. Gertrude Campus, 6216 N. Glenwood Ave., 60660. Tel: 773-743-6277. St. Margaret Mary Campus, 7318 N. Oakley Ave., 60645. Tel: 773-271-2008.
Notre Dame Academy (Unknown).
Notre Dame de Chicago School.
Notre Dame High School for Girls (Mango Ave.).
Notre Dame High School (St. Ferdinand).
Our Lady of Aglona, 711 W. Monroe St., 60661.
Tel: 312-534-4400; Fax: 312-831-0610.
Our Lady of Bethlehem Academy (School records - ARC; sacramental records - Sisters of St. Joseph 708-354-9200).
Our Lady of Destiny (DesPlaines Campus & North Campus) Records at ARC.
Our Lady of Fatima Mission (Christina Ave.) St. Hyacinth Basilica Parish, 3636 N. Wolfram, 60618. Tel: 773-342-3636; Fax: 773-342-3638.
Our Lady of Fatima School (39th/Pershing Rd.).
Our Lady of the Gardens Parish.
Our Lady of the Gardens School, 711 W. Monroe St., 60661. Tel: 312-534-4400; Fax: 312-831-0610.
Our Lady Gate of Heaven School.
Our Lady of Good Counsel Parish (Western Ave.).
Our Lady of Good Counsel School (Western Ave.).
Our Lady of the Good Counsel Parish (Hermitage Ave.).
Our Lady of Good Counsel School (Hermitage Ave.).
Our Lady of Guadalupe Chapel (Ashland).
Our Lady Help of Christians Parish.
Our Lady Help of Christians School.
Our Lady of Hope School (Des Plaines).
Our Lady of Hungary Parish (93rd St.).
Our Lady of Hungary School (93rd St.).
Our Lady of Knock School (Calumet City).
Our Lady of Loretto School (Hometown).
Our Lady of Lourdes School (Ashland Ave.).
Our Lady of Lourdes Commercial High School (Keeler St.).
Our Lady of Lourdes Parish (Keeler St.).
Our Lady of Lourdes School (Keeler St.).
Our Lady of Lourdes High School (Ashland Ave.) (Unknown).
Our Lady of Mercy Commercial High School (Unknown).
Our Lady of Mercy School.
Our Lady of the Miraculous Medal Parish (Langley Ave.) Renamed Our Lady of the Gardens Parish.
Our Lady of the Mount School (Cicero).
Our Lady of Mt. Carmel School (Melrose Park).
Our Lady of Peace School.
Our Lady of Perpetual Help Vicariate (13th St.).
Our Lady of Perpetual Help Vicariate School (13th St.).
Our Lady of Providence Academy (Records destroyed in flood).
Our Lady of Ransom School.
Our Lady of Solace Parish (Sangamon).
Our Lady of Solace School (Sangamon).
Our Lady of Sorrows High School (1887-1897) Mother Guerin Convent, 8001 Belmont Ave., River Grove, 60171.
Our Lady of Sorrows School.
Our Lady of Sorrows Seminary, Servite Provincial Archives, 3121 W. Jackson, 60612.
Tel: 773-638-0159; Fax: 773-638-3036.
Our Lady of the Angels Parish, 711 W. Monroe St., 60661. Tel: 312-534-4400; Fax: 312-831-0610.
Our Lady of the Angels School.
OUR LADY OF THE BROOKMerged with St. Norbert to form St. Norbert and Our Lady of the Brook, Northbrook.
OUR LADY OF THE CROSS MISSION CHAPEL, St. Margaret Mary Parish, 2324 W. Chase, 60645.
Tel: 773-764-0615; Fax: 773-764-0941.
Our Lady of Pompeii School (Lexington Ave.).
OUR LADY OF POMPEII PARISH (Lexington Ave.).
Our Lady of Pompeii Parish (Chicago Heights) Renamed St. Rocco Parish (Chicago Heights).
Our Lady of Victory High School (Unknown).
Our Lady of Victory School.
Our Lady of Vilna Parish (23rd St.).
Our Lady of Vilna School (23rd St.).
Our Lady of the West Side School Renamed St. Agatha Catholic Academy.
St. Pancratius School.
St. Pascal School.
St. Patrick Academy (Chicago, later Des Plaines)

(Girls) Mother McAuley High School, 3737 W. 99th St., 60608. Tel: 773-881-6522.
St. Patrick School (pre 1967, post 1967 at Frances Xavier Ward School) (Adams St.).
St. Patrick School (Lemont) St. Alphonsus-St. Patrick School, 205 Cass St., Lemont, 60439. Tel: 630-257-2380.
St. Patrick Parish (Commercial Ave.).
St. Patrick School (Commercial Ave.).
St. Patrick Academy (Boys); at St. Patrick High School (Belmont Ave.).
St. Patrick High School (Boys, Adams St.) at St. Patrick High School (Belmont Ave.).
St. Patrick High School aka St. Patrick Female Academy (Adams St.) (Adams St.) (Girls).
St. Patrick High School (Commercial Ave.) (Unknown).
St. Paul - Our Lady of Vilna School (22nd Pl.).
St. Paul School (Chicago Heights) (Unknown).
St. Paul School (22nd St.).
St. Paul Commercial High School (Unknown).
St. Paul High School (Midway).
St. Paul Parish (Records destroyed in 1871 fire) (12th St.).
St. Paul School (12th St.) - destroyed.
St. Paul Select School (Unknown).
St. Peter Parish (Antioch).
St. Paul's Home for Working Boys (Renamed Mercy Mission).
St. Peter School (Antioch).
St. Peter School (Skokie) Records at ARC.
St. Peter School (Volo) St. Peter Parish, 27551 W. Hwy. 120, Round Lake, 60073. Tel: 815-385-5496; Fax: 631-514-4647.
St. Peter School (Unknown) (Madison).
St. Peter Canisius Parish, 711 W Monroe St., 60661. Tel: 312-534-4400; Fax: 312-831-0610.
St. Peter Canisius School.
St. Peter Commercial High School (Skokie) (Unknown).
SS. Peter and Paul Parish (Exchange St.).
SS. Peter and Paul School (Exchange St.).
St. Peter & Paul School (Halsted St.).
SS. Peter and Paul Parish (Paulina St.).
Ss. Peter & Paul School (Paulina St.).
SS. Peter & Paul Parish (Libertyville) St. Joseph Parish, 121 E. Maple, Libertyville, 60048. Tel: 847-362-2073; Fax: 847-362-6821.
SS. Peter & Paul High School (Exchange Ave.).
ST. PETER & PAUL CHURCH (Central Park Ave.) (Byzantine Rite) St. Nicholas Parish (Byzantine Rite), 8103 Columbia Ave., Munster, IN 46321-1802. Tel: 219-838-9380.
St. Philip Benizi Parish (later named St. Mel Parish) (Maypole St.).
St. Philip Benizi School (Unknown) (Maypole St.).
St. Philip Benizi Parish (Oak St.).
St. Philip Benizi School (Oak St.).
St. Philip Evening School (Unknown).
St. Philip Basilica High School.
St. Philip the Apostle Parish (Northfield).
St. Philip the Apostle School (Northfield).
St. Philomena Parish (1921 N. Kedvale Ave.).
St. Philomena School.
St. Philomena Commercial High School.
St. Pius V Commercial High School, St. Pius V School, 1919 S. Ashland, 60608. Tel: 312-226-1590; Fax: 312-226-7265.
St. Pius X School (Stickney).
Precious Blood School.
Presentation Parish.
Precious Blood Parish St. Malachy + Precious Blood Parish.
Presentation School.
Presentation-Precious Blood Unit School.
St. Priscilla School, 711 W. Monroe St., 60661. Tel: 312-534-4400; Fax: 312-831-0610.
St. Procopius College Academy (Chicago) Renamed St. Procopius College Academy (Lisle).
St. Procopius School (open) (pre-1983 records at ARC).
St. Procopius High School.
PROVIDENCE OF GOD PARISH Records at St. Procopius.
Providence Academy & High School (pre-1970) Mother Guerin Convent, 8001 Belmont Ave., River Grove, 60171. Tel: 312-625-3278.
Providence of God School and Commercial High School.
Providence-St. Mel High School (No longer under the authority of the Archdiocese) 119 S. Central Park Blvd., 60624. Tel: 773-722-4600.
Queen of Peace High School (Burbank).
Queen of Peace Parish (Waukegan).
Queen of Angels High School (Unknown).
QUEEN OF APOSTLES PARISH Consolidated into St. Mary Queen of Apostles.
Queen of Apostles School (Riverdale).
Queen of the Universe (7114 S. Hamlin Ave.).
Quigley Preparatory Seminary North.
Quigley Preparatory Seminary South.
Quigley Preparatory Seminary.
St. Raphael Parish (60th St.).
St. Raphael School (60th St.).
St. Rene Goupil School (New England Ave.) Records at ARC.
Resurrection Catholic Academy (Barry Ave.).
Resurrection Parish and School (Jackson Blvd.).
St. Rita College, St. Rita High School, 7740 S. Western Ave., 60620. Tel: 773-925-6600.
St. Rita of Cascia School.
St. Rocco Parish (For school records, see Mt. Carmel School.) (Chicago Heights).
St. Roman School.
St. Rosalie School (Harwood Heights).
Rosary House High School (River Forest) 7574 W. Division St., River Forest, 60305. Tel: 708-771-8383.
Rosary College, Dominican University, 7900 W. Division St., River Forest, 60305. Tel: 708-366-2490.
St. Rose of Lima Parish (W. 48th St.).
St. Rose of Lima School.
Sacred Heart Chapel (Municipal Tuberculosis Sanitarium) (ARC).
Sacred Heart Parish (1077 Tower Rd.).
Sacred Heart Parish (19th St.).
Sacred Heart School & High School (19th St.).
Sacred Heart Parish (May St.).
Sacred Heart School & High School (May St.).
Sacred Heart Parish (Oakley Blvd.).
Sacred Heart School (Oakley Blvd.).
Sacred Heart High School (Oakley) (Unknown).
Sacred Heart Parish (Church St.) Sacred Heart Mission, 11652 S. Church St., 60643. Tel: 773-233-3955.
Sacred Heart of Jesus Parish (46th St.).
Sacred Heart of Jesus School (46th St.).
Sacred Heart of Jesus High School (46th St.).
Sacred Heart of Mary High School (Arlington Heights) St. Viator High School, 1213 E. Oakton St., Arlington Heights, 60004. Tel: 847-392-4050.
Sacred Heart Seminary (Melrose Park) (Stone Park) Scalabrini Mission Center, 3800 W. Division St., Stone Park, 60165. Tel: 708-345-8270.
St. Salomea Parish (S. Indiana).
St. Salomea School (S. Indiana).
San Callisto Mission (Unknown).
San Marcello Mission (Evergreen) Immaculate Conception Parish, 1415 N. North Park, 60610. Tel: 312-944-1230; Fax: 312-944-0673.
Santa Lucia Mission, Santa Lucia-Santa Maria Incoronata Parish, 3022 S. Wells, 60616. Tel: 312-842-6115; Fax: 312-842-0103.
Santa Maria Addolorata School.
Santa Maria Incoronata Parish, Santa Lucia-Santa Maria Incoronata Parish, 3022 S. Wells, 60616. Tel: 312-842-6115. Sacramental Records:.
Santa Teresita Vicariate (Palatine) Mision San Juan Diego, 35 W. Wood St., Palatine, 60067. Tel: 847-358-6337; Fax: 847-202-4603.
St. Scholastica Academy.
St. Scholastica High School Renamed St. Scholastica Academy.
Seton Academy (South Holland).
St. Sebastian Parish (W. Wellington).
St. Sebastian School & High School.
Servite Seminary (Hillside) Provincial Archives, Servite Provincial Center, 3121 W. Jackson Blvd., 60612. Tel: 773-533-0360.
Seven Holy Founders Parish (Records at St. Donatus, Blue Island).
Seven Holy Founders School (Calumet Park).
Sheil Institute.
Siena High School, Mother McAuley High School, 3737 W. 99th St., 60642. Tel: 773-881-6522.
South Side Italian Mission (Alexander St.).
St. Simeon School (Bellwood).
St. Simon the Apostle School.
St. Stanislaus Bishop and Martyr School (Lorel Ave.).
St. Stanislaus Bishop and Martyr School (Posen).
St. Stanislaus College, DePaul College Prep, 3633 N. California, 60618. Tel: 773-539-3600.
St. Stanislaus Kostka High School, St. Stanislaus Kostka Elementary, 1255 N. Noble, 60622. Tel: 773-278-4560; Fax: 773-278-2471.
St. Stanislaus Parish and School (19th, renamed Sacred Heart).
St. Stephen School (22nd Pl.).
St. Stephen Protomartyr School (Des Plaines).
St. Stephen Parish (22nd Pl.).
Old St. Stephen Parish (Ohio St.).
Old St. Stephen School (Ohio St.).
St. Susanna Parish (Harvey) Ascension-St. Susanna Parish, 15234 Myrtle, Harvey, 60426-3194. Tel: 708-333-0931.
St. Susanna School (Harvey).
St. Sylvester Commercial High School.
St. Tarcissus School (Ardmore Ave.).
St. Thaddeus School.
St. Theodore Parish (S. Paulina).
St. Theodore School.
St. Therese Medical Center aka St. Therese Hospital (Waukegan) Sacramental Records Archives.
St. Teresa of Avila School.
ST. THERESE OF THE INFANT JESUS PARISH (Wood St.).
St. Therese of the Infant Jesus School aka Little Flower School (Wood St.).
St. Thomas Aquinas (Church and School) (Washington Blvd.).
St. Thomas More School.
St. Thomas Mission (River Forest) St. Luke Parish, 528 Lathrop, River Forest, 60305. Tel: 708-771-8250; Fax: 708-771-8809.
St. Thomas the Apostle High School, St. Thomas the Apostle School, 5467 S. Woodlawn, 60615. Tel: 773-667-1142; Fax: 773-753-7434.
St. Timothy School.
Transfiguration of Our Lord School.
St. Turbius School (Karlou Ave.) Records at ARC.
Unity Catholic High School.
Unity High School.
University of St. Mary of the Lake (Chicago, 1844-1866) (Unknown, assumed destroyed).
St. Valentine Parish (Cicero).
St. Valentine School (Cicero).
St. Veronica School (18th) (part of Holy Family Parish, Chicago) (Unknown).
St. Veronica Parish (Archives).
St. Veronica School (Whipple St.).
St. Viator High School (Unknown) (Addison).
Viatorian Preparatory School (Lemont) See Fournier Institute, Viatorian Preparatory School (Lemont).
St. Victor School (Calumet City) (ARC).
St. Victor High School (Unknown) (Calumet City).
Villa Nazareth High School (Des Plaines).
St. Vincent de Paul School.
St. Vincent de Paul Academy & St. Vincent Academy (Girls) (See DePaul High School).
St. Vincent de Paul High School Seminary (Lemont) Vincentians Academic Archives, 2233 N. Kenmore St., 60614. Tel: 312-362-8042.
St. Vincent Orphanage/St. Vincent Infant Hospital/St. Vincent Infant Asylum Client & School Records: Catholic Charities, Division of Services for Children and Youth, 651 N. LaSalle, Chicago, IL 60611. Tel: 312-655-7073 Sacramental Records: Holy Name Cathedral, 730 N. Wabash, Chicago, IL 60611 Tel: 312-787-8040 Fax: 312-787-9113.
St. Vincent Ferrer Orphanage (Unknown).
St. Vincent's Infant Hospital School of Child Care (Halsted) St. Vincent de Paul Center, 2145 N. Halsted, 60614. Tel: 312-943-6776.
Visitation Parish (Garfield Blvd.) St. Basil-Visitation Parish, 5443 S. Honore, 60609. Tel: 773-625-6311; Fax: 773-783-3348.
Visitation Academy See Marywood High School. (Records destroyed in flood.) (Evanston).
Visitation High School.
St. Vitus Parish.
St. Vitus School.
Weber High School, DePaul College Prep, 3633 N. California Ave., 60618. Tel: 773-539-3600.
Weber Technical High School Renamed Gordon Technical High School.
St. Wenceslaus School (Monticello St.).
ST. WENCESLAUS PARISH (DeKoven St.).
St. Wenceslaus School (Unknown) (DeKoven St.).
White Pines Academy (Lemont) Renamed Everest Academy.
St. Willibrord Parish (114th St.).
St. Willibrord School (114th St.).
St. Willibrord High School aka Willibrord Catholic High School.
St. Xavier Academy, Mother McAuley High School, 3737 W. 99th St., 60655. Tel: 773-881-6500.
Young Ladies' Seminary of the Sacred Heart Renamed Woodlands Academy of the Sacred Heart (Lake Forest).

RELIGIOUS INSTITUTES OF MEN REPRESENTED IN THE ARCHDIOCESE

For further details refer to the corresponding bracketed number in the Religious Institutes of Men or Women section.

[0120]—*Alexian Brothers*—C.F.A.
[0140]—*The Augustinians* Chicago—O.S.A.
[0200]—*Benedictine Monks*—O.S.B.
[0330]—*Brothers of the Christian Schools (Midwest Province)* (Burr Ridge, IL)—F.S.C.
[0600]—*Brothers of the Congregation of Holy Cross*—C.S.C.
[0900]—*Canons Regular of Premontre* (U.S. Circary)—O.Praem.
[]—*Canons Regular of St. John Cantius*—S.J.C.
[0400]—*Canons Regular of the Order of the Holy Cross* (Prov. of St. Odilia, Minneapolis, MN)—O.S.C.
[0470]—*The Capuchin Friars*—O.F.M.Cap.
[0270]—*Carmelite Fathers & Brothers* (Most Pure Heart of Mary)—O.Carm.

[0340]—*Cistercian Fathers* (Polish Congr.)—O.Cist.
[0360]—*Claretian Missionaries*—C.M.F.
[1320]—*Clerics of St. Viator* (Chicago, IL)—C.S.V.
[0380]—*Comboni Missionaries of the Heart of Jesus-Verona*—M.C.C.J.
[0310]—*Congregation of Christian Brothers*—C.F.C.
[0750]—*Congregation of Marianhill Missionaries*—C.M.M.
[0220]—*Congregation of the Blessed Sacrament* (Rome, Italy)—S.S.S.
[]—*Congregation of the Holy Spirit* (Eastern Prov.)—C.S.Sp.
[1330]—*Congregation of the Mission* (Western Prov.)—C.M.
[1210]—*Congregation of the Missionaries of St. Charles* (Western Prov.)—C.S.
[1000]—*Congregation of the Passion* (Western Prov.)—C.P.
[1130]—*Congregation of the Priests of the Sacred Heart*—S.C.J.
[1080]—*Congregation of the Resurrection* (Chicago Prov.)—C.R.
[0480]—*Conventual Franciscans* (St. Bonaventure, Our Lady of Consolation Provs.)—O.F.M.Conv.
[0260]—*Discalced Carmelite Friars*—O.C.D.
[0520]—*Franciscan Friars* (Sacred Heart, Assumption of B.V.M. Provs.; Commissariats of the Holy Cross, Holy Family)—O.F.M.
[0690]—*Jesuit Fathers and Brothers* (Chicago, Polish, Lithuanian Provs.)—S.J.
[0730]—*Legionnaires of Christ*—L.C.
[0740]—*Marian Fathers*—M.I.C.
[0770]—*The Marist Brothers*—F.M.S.
[0780]—*Marist Fathers*—S.M.
[0800]—*Maryknoll*—M.M.
[0830]—*Mill Hill Missionaries*—M.H.M.
[0860]—*Missionhurst Congregation of the Immaculate Heart of Mary*—C.I.C.M.
[0910]—*Oblates of Mary Immaculate*—O.M.I.
[0430]—*Order of Preachers-Dominicans*—O.P.
[1030]—*Paulist Fathers* (New York Prov.)—C.S.P.
[0610]—*Priests of the Congregation of Holy Cross* (Notre Dame, IN)—C.S.C.
[1070]—*Redemptorist Fathers* (Denver)—C.SS.R.
[1190]—*Salesians of Don Bosco*—S.D.B.
[1220]—*Servants of Charity*—S.C.
[1240]—*Servites* (Chicago, IL)—O.S.M.
[1260]—*Society of Christ*—S.Ch.
[0760]—*Society of Mary*—S.M.
[0370]—*Society of St. Columban*—S.S.C.
[1200]—*Society of the Divine Savior*—S.D.S.
[0420]—*Society of the Divine Word*—S.V.D.
[1060]—*Society of the Precious Blood* (Kansas City Prov.)—C.PP.S.
[1170]—*St. Patrick Missionary Society*—S.P.S.
[1360]—*Xaverian Missionary Fathers*—S.X.

RELIGIOUS INSTITUTES OF WOMEN REPRESENTED IN THE ARCHDIOCESE

[0100]—*Adorers of the Blood of Christ*—A.S.C.
[0230]—*Benedictine Sisters of Pontifical Jurisdiction* (Chicago, IL; Duluth, MN)—O.S.B.
[0690]—*Comboni Missionary Sisters*—C.M.S.
[3110]—*Congregation of Our Lady of the Retreat in the Cenacle*—R.C.
[1860]—*Congregation of the Handmaids of the Precious Blood*—H.P.B.
[2100]—*Congregation of the Humility of Mary*—C.H.M.
[]—*Congregation of the Mother of Carmel*—C.M.C.
[0460]—*Congregation of the Sisters of Charity of the Incarnate Word*—C.C.V.I.
[3710]—*Congregation of the Sisters of Saint Agnes*—C.S.A.
[3832]—*Congregation of the Sisters of St. Joseph*—C.S.J.
[1920]—*Congregation of the Sisters of the Holy Cross*—C.S.C.
[1780]—*Congregation of the Sisters of the Third Order of St. Francis of Perpetual Adoration*—F.S.P.A.
[1710]—*Congregation of the Third Order of St. Francis of Mary Immaculate, Joliet, IL*—O.S.F.
[1730]—*Congregation of the Third Order of St. Francis, Oldenburg, IN*—O.S.F.
[0760]—*Daughters of Charity of St. Vincent de Paul*—D.C.
[0793]—*Daughters of Divine Love*—D.D.L.
[0940]—*Daughters of St. Mary of Providence*—D.S.M.P.
[0810]—*Daughters of the Heart of Mary*—D.H.M.
[0420]—*Discalced Carmelite Nuns*—O.C.D.
[1070-03]—*Dominican Sisters*—O.P.
[1070-07]—*Dominican Sisters*—O.P.
[1070-27]—*Dominican Sisters*—O.P.
[1070-13]—*Dominican Sisters*—O.P.
[1070-10]—*Dominican Sisters*—O.P.
[1115]—*Dominican Sisters of Peace*—O.P.
[1170]—*Felician Sisters*—C.S.S.F.
[1370]—*Franciscan Missionaries of Mary*—F.M.M.
[1210]—*Franciscan Sisters of Chicago*—O.S.F.
[1230]—*Franciscan Sisters of Christian Charity*—O.S.F.
[1310]—*Franciscan Sisters of Little Falls, Minnesota*—O.S.F.
[1415]—*Franciscan Sisters of Mary*—F.S.M.
[1430]—*Franciscan Sisters of Our Lady of Perpetual Help*—O.S.F.
[1450]—*Franciscan Sisters of the Sacred Heart*—O.S.F.
[1240]—*Franciscan Sisters, Daughters of the Sacred Hearts of Jesus and Mary*—O.S.F.
[2370]—*Institute of the Blessed Virgin Mary (Loretto Sisters)*—I.B.V.M.
[2330]—*Little Sisters of Jesus*—L.S.J.
[2320]—*Little Sisters of the Holy Family*—P.S.S.F.
[2340]—*Little Sisters of the Poor*—L.S.P.
[3570]—*Mantellate Sisters, Servants of Mary of Blue Island*—O.S.M.
[2420]—*Marist Missionary Sisters*—S.M.S.M.
[2430]—*Marist Sisters Congregation of Mary*—S.M.
[2470]—*Maryknoll Sisters of St. Dominic*—M.M.
[2480]—*Medical Missionaries of Mary*—M.M.M.
[2680]—*Misericordia Sisters*—S.M.
[2710]—*Missionaries of Charity*—M.C.
[2865]—*Missionaries of the Sacred Heart of Jesus and Our Lady of Guadalupe*—M.S.C.Gpe.
[2790]—*Missionary Servants of the Most Blessed Trinity*—M.S.B.T.
[2715]—*Missionary Sisters of Christ the King for Polonia*—M.CHR.
[2900]—*Missionary Sisters of St. Charles Borromeo*—M.S.C.S.
[3990]—*Missionary Sisters of St. Peter Claver*—S.S.P.C.
[2860]—*Missionary Sisters of the Sacred Heart*—M.S.C.
[3530]—*Missionary Sisters Servants of the Holy Spirit*—S.Sp.S.
[]—*Oblate Sisters of Jesus the Priest*—O.J.S.
[3040]—*Oblate Sisters of Providence*—O.S.P.
[3130]—*Our Lady of Victory Missionary Sisters*—O.L.V.M.
[0950]—*Pious Society Daughters of St. Paul*—F.S.P.
[3230]—*Poor Handmaids of Jesus Christ*—P.H.J.C.
[3440]—*Religious Hospitallers of Saint Joseph*—R.H.S.J.
[2970]—*School Sisters of Notre Dame*—S.S.N.D.
[1680]—*School Sisters of St. Francis*—O.S.F.
[3590]—*Servants of Mary (Servite Sisters)*—O.S.M.
[3520]—*Servants of the Holy Heart of Mary*—S.S.C.M.
[0440]—*Sisters of Charity of Cincinnati, Ohio*—S.C.
[0570]—*Sisters of Charity of Seton Hill, Greensburg, Pennsylvania*—S.C.
[0630]—*Sisters of Charity of St. Vincent de Paul*—S.V.Z.
[0430]—*Sisters of Charity of the Blessed Virgin Mary*—B.V.M.
[0660]—*Sisters of Christian Charity*—S.C.C.
[0990]—*Sisters of Divine Providence*—C.D.P.
[2360]—*Sisters of Loretto at the Foot of the Cross*—S.L.
[2575]—*Sisters of Mercy of the Americas* (Chicago, IL)—R.S.M.
[3000]—*Sisters of Notre Dame de Namur*—S.N.D.deN.
[3080]—*Sisters of Our Lady Christian Doctrine*—R.C.D.
[3350]—*Sisters of Providence*—S.P.
[3360]—*Sisters of Providence of Saint Mary-of-the-Woods, IN*—S.P.
[1620]—*Sisters of Saint Francis of Millvale, Pennsylvania*—O.S.F.
[1540]—*Sisters of Saint Francis, Clinton, Iowa*—O.S.F.
[3780]—*Sisters of Saints Cyril and Methodius*—SS.C.M.
[3740]—*Sisters of St. Casimir*—S.S.C.
[1520]—*Sisters of St. Francis of Christ the King*—O.S.F.
[1640]—*Sisters of St. Francis of Perpetual Adoration*—O.S.F.
[1570]—*Sisters of St. Francis of the Holy Family*—O.S.F.
[1800]—*Sisters of St. Francis of the Third Order Regular*—O.S.F.
[3830-15]—*Sisters of St. Joseph*—C.S.J.
[3840]—*Sisters of St. Joseph of Carondelet*—C.S.J.
[3930]—*Sisters of St. Joseph of the Third Order of St. Francis*—S.S.J.-T.O.S.F.
[0260]—*Sisters of the Blessed Sacrament for Indians and Colored People*—S.B.S.
[2980]—*Sisters of the Congregation de Notre Dame*—C.N.D.
[1030]—*Sisters of the Divine Savior*—S.D.S.
[1830]—*Sisters of the Good Shepherd*—R.G.S.
[1970]—*Sisters of the Holy Family of Nazareth*—C.S.F.N.
[2140]—*Sisters of the Immaculate Conception of the Blessed Virgin Mary* (Lithuanian).
[2270]—*Sisters of the Little Company of Mary*—L.C.M.
[2350]—*Sisters of the Living Word*—S.L.W.
[3320]—*Sisters of the Presentation of the B.V.M*—P.B.V.M.
[3480]—*Sisters of the Resurrection*—C.R.
[1705]—*Sisters of the Third Order of St. Francis of Assisi*—O.S.F.
[1720]—*Sisters of the Third Order of St. Francis of the Congregation of Our Lady of Lourdes*—O.S.F.
[2150]—*Sisters, Servants of the Immaculate Heart of Mary*—I.H.M.
[1890]—*Society of Helpers*—H.H.S.
[4060]—*Society of the Holy Child Jesus*—S.H.C.J.
[4070]—*Society of the Sacred Heart*—R.S.C.J.

ARCHDIOCESAN CEMETERIES

CHICAGO. *Central Office*, Catholic Cemeteries: 1400 S. Wolf Rd., Hillside, 60162-2197. Tel: 708-449-6100; Fax: 708-449-3419; Web: www.cathcemchgo.org. Rev. Lawrence J. Sullivan, Arch. Dir.; Mr. Roman Szabelski, Exec. Dir.
St. Boniface
St. Casimir
St. Henry
Mt. Olivet
CALUMET CITY. *Holy Cross*
CRESTWOOD. *St. Benedict*
DES PLAINES. *All Saints*
EVANSTON. *Calvary*
EVERGREEN PARK. *St. Mary*
FOX LAKE. *St. Bede*
FREMONT CENTER. *St. Mary*
GLENWOOD. *Assumption*
HIGHLAND PARK. *St. Mary*
HILLSIDE. *Mt. Carmel*
Our Lady of Sorrows
Queen of Heaven
JUSTICE. *Resurrection*
LAKE FOREST. *St. Mary*
LEMONT. *St. Alphonsus*
SS. Cyril & Methodius
St. James, Sag Bridge
St. Patrick
LIBERTYVILLE. *Ascension*
NILES. *St. Adalbert*
Maryhill
NORTHBROOK. *Sacred Heart*
OAK FOREST. *St. Gabriel*
ORLAND PARK. *St. Michael*
PALATINE. *St. Michael the Archangel*
PARK FOREST. *St. Anne*
RIVER GROVE. *St. Joseph*
ROSENCRANS. *St. Patrick*
ROUND LAKE. *St. Joseph*
SAUK VILLAGE. *St. James*
SKOKIE. *St. Peter*
STEGER. *Calvary*
VOLO. *St. Peter*
WAUCONDA. *Transfiguration*
WAUKEGAN. *St. Mary*
WEST LAKE FOREST. *St. Patrick*
WILMETTE. *St. Joseph*
WORTH. *Holy Sepulchre*

NECROLOGY

† Adducci, Anthony J., Died Sep. 30, 2018
† Colleran, James A., (Retired), Died Jun. 2, 2018
† Gollatz, Ronald J., (Retired), Died Apr. 17, 2018
† Harvey, John L., Riverdale, IL St. Mary Queen of Apostles, Died Jun. 9, 2018
† Jabusch, Willard F., (Retired), Died Dec. 12, 2018
† Lewandowski, Ronald C., (Retired), Died Apr. 6, 2018
† McDonnell, John J., (Retired), Died Jul. 23, 2018
† Mulcahy, Gerald F., (Retired), Died Apr. 23, 2018
† O'Connor, James T., Pastor Emeritus, Lyons, IL St. Hugh, Died Apr. 27, 2018
† Olivero, Michael A., Mt. Prospect, IL St. Cecilia, Died Aug. 4, 2018
† Powers, John J., (Retired), Died Aug. 10, 2018
† Purtell, Thomas J., (Retired), Died Aug. 24, 2018
† Riley, Dennis S., Pastor Emeritus, Chicago, St. Angela, Died Apr. 15, 2018
† Roache, James P., (Retired), Died Nov. 21, 2018
† Rochford, John J., (Retired), Died Jun. 1, 2018
† Tapper, John W., Pastor Emeritus, Hanover Park, IL St. Ansgar, Died May. 20, 2018

Archdiocese of Cincinnati

(Archidioecesis Cincinnatensis)

Most Reverend

DENNIS M. SCHNURR, J.C.D., D.D.

Archbishop of Cincinnati; ordained July 20, 1974; appointed Bishop of Duluth January 18, 2001; ordained April 2, 2001; appointed Coadjutor Archbishop of Cincinnati October 17, 2008; installed December 7, 2008; Succeeded to the See December 21, 2009. *Office: 100 E. Eighth St., Cincinnati, OH 45202-2129.*

Most Reverend

DANIEL E. PILARCZYK, S.T.D., PH.D., D.D.

Archbishop Emeritus of Cincinnati; ordained December 20, 1959; appointed Titular Bishop of Hodelm and Auxiliary Bishop of Cincinnati November 12, 1974; consecrated December 20, 1974; appointed Archbishop of Cincinnati November 2, 1982; installed December 20, 1982; retired December 21, 2009. *Office: 100 E. Eighth St., Cincinnati, OH 45202-2129.*

Most Reverend

JOSEPH R. BINZER

Auxiliary Bishop of Cincinnati; ordained June 4, 1994; appointed Titular Bishop of Subbar and Auxiliary Bishop of Cincinnati April 6, 2011; consecrated June 9, 2011. *Office: 100 E. Eighth St., Cincinnati, OH 45202-2129.*

Square Miles 8,543.

Erected Diocese June 19, 1821; Archdiocese July 19, 1850.

Comprises that part of the State of Ohio lying south of 40 degrees, 41 minutes, being the 19 Counties south of the northern line of Mercer, Auglaize, and Logan, all west of the eastern line of Logan, Champaign, Clark, Greene, Clinton, Highland and Adams Counties.

For legal titles of parishes and archdiocesan institutions, consult the Chancery Office.

Archdiocesan Offices: 100 E. Eighth St., Cincinnati, OH 45202-2129. Tel: 513-421-3131; Fax: 513-421-6225.

Web: www.catholiccincinnati.org

STATISTICAL OVERVIEW

Personnel	
Archbishops	1
Retired Archbishops	1
Auxiliary Bishops	1
Priests: Diocesan Active in Diocese	142
Priests: Diocesan Active Outside Diocese	5
Priests: Retired, Sick or Absent	91
Number of Diocesan Priests	238
Religious Priests in Diocese	186
Total Priests in Diocese	424
Extern Priests in Diocese	18
Ordinations:	
Diocesan Priests	4
Religious Priests	1
Transitional Deacons	9
Permanent Deacons in Diocese	218
Total Brothers	100
Total Sisters	648
Parishes	
Parishes	211
With Resident Pastor:	
Resident Diocesan Priests	103
Resident Religious Priests	20
Without Resident Pastor:	
Administered by Priests	88
Professional Ministry Personnel:	
Brothers	33
Sisters	29
Lay Ministers	626
Welfare	
Catholic Hospitals	7
Total Assisted	1,330,640
Homes for the Aged	7
Total Assisted	2,523
Residential Care of Children	1
Total Assisted	196
Day Care Centers	1
Total Assisted	177
Special Centers for Social Services	7
Total Assisted	133,557
Other Institutions	2
Total Assisted	10,856
Educational	
Seminaries, Diocesan	1
Students from This Diocese	48
Students from Other Diocese	39
Diocesan Students in Other Seminaries	10
Total Seminarians	58
Colleges and Universities	5
Total Students	20,747
High Schools, Diocesan and Parish	12
Total Students	5,973
High Schools, Private	11
Total Students	6,666
Elementary Schools, Diocesan and Parish	81
Total Students	24,618
Elementary Schools, Private	7
Total Students	1,936
Non-residential Schools for the Disabled	1
Total Students	53
Catechesis/Religious Education:	
High School Students	1,872
Elementary Students	16,382
Total Students under Catholic Instruction	78,305
Teachers in the Diocese:	
Priests	7
Brothers	7
Sisters	31
Lay Teachers	2,156
Vital Statistics	
Receptions into the Church:	
Infant Baptism Totals	4,897
Minor Baptism Totals	497
Adult Baptism Totals	399
Received into Full Communion	549
First Communions	5,499
Confirmations	5,667
Marriages:	
Catholic	1,185
Interfaith	438
Total Marriages	1,623
Deaths	3,958
Total Catholic Population	451,045
Total Population	3,034,008

Former Bishops—Rt. Rev. EDWARD D. FENWICK, O.P., D.D., ord. Feb. 23, 1793; cons. Jan. 13, 1822; died Sept. 26, 1832; Most Revs. JOHN BAPTIST PURCELL, D.D., ord. May 20, 1826; cons. Oct. 13, 1833; appt. Archbishop, July 19, 1850; died July 4, 1883; WILLIAM HENRY ELDER, D.D., ord. March 29, 1846; cons. Bishop of Natchez May 3, 1857; appt. Titular Bishop of Avar, and Coadjutor to the Archbishop of Cincinnati cum jure successionis, Jan. 30, 1880; succeeded to the See of Cincinnati, July 4, 1883; died Oct. 31, 1904; HENRY K. MOELLER, D.D., ord. June 10, 1876; cons. Bishop of Columbus, Aug. 25, 1900; promoted to Archiepiscopal See of Areopolis and made Coadjutor to the Most Rev. William Henry Elder cum jure successionis, April 27, 1903; succeeded to the See of Cincinnati, Oct. 31, 1904; died Jan. 5, 1925; JOHN T. MCNICHOLAS, O.P., S.T.M., ord. Oct. 10, 1901; cons. Bishop of Duluth, MN Sept. 8, 1918; promoted to Archiepiscopal See of Cincinnati, July 8, 1925; appt. Assistant at the Pontifical Throne, Feb. 18, 1923; died April 22, 1950; KARL J. ALTER, D.D., LL.D., ord. June 4, 1910; cons. Bishop of Toledo, June 17, 1931; appt. Assistant to the Pontifical Throne, May 30, 1950; elevated to Archbishop of Cincinnati, June 21, 1950; retired July 23, 1969; died Aug. 23, 1977; PAUL F. LEIBOLD, D.D., J.C.D., ord. May 18, 1940; appt. Titular Bishop of Trebenna and Auxiliary of Cincinnati, April 10, 1958; cons. June 17, 1958; installed as Bishop of Evansville, June 15, 1966; appt. Archbishop of Cincinnati, July 23, 1969; installed Oct. 2, 1969; died June 1, 1972; His Eminence JOSEPH CARDINAL BERNARDIN, D.D., ord. April 26, 1952; appt. Titular Bishop of Lugura and Auxiliary Bishop of Atlanta, March 9, 1966; cons. April 26, 1966; appt. Archbishop of Cincinnati, Nov. 21, 1972; installed Dec. 19, 1972; appt. Archbishop of Chicago, July 10, 1982; installed Aug. 25, 1982; created Cardinal Priest, Feb. 2, 1983; died Nov. 14, 1996; Most Rev. DANIEL E. PILARCZYK, S.T.D., Ph.D., D.D., ord. Dec. 20, 1959; appt. Titular Bishop of Hodelm and Auxiliary Bishop of Cincinnati Nov. 12, 1974; cons. Dec. 20, 1974; appt. Archbishop of Cincinnati Nov. 2, 1982; installed Dec. 20, 1982; retired Dec. 21, 2009.

Vicars General—Most Rev. JOSEPH R. BINZER; Rev. STEVE J. ANGI, J.C.L.

Archdiocesan Department Directors—MR. H. THEODORE BERGH, Dir., Community Svcs.; MS. SUSAN M. GIBBONS, Dir. Educational Svcs.; Rev. STEVE J. ANGI, Dir., Exec. Svcs.; MR. RICHARD KELLY, Dir., Financial Svcs.; MR. ROBERT J. REID, J.D., Dir., Human Resources; Rev. JAN KEVIN SCHMIDT, Dir., Pastoral Svcs.; MR. DAVID W. KISSELL, Dir. Stewardship Svcs.; MICHAEL A. SCHAFER, Dir., Communication & Mission Promotion.

Pastoral Council Secretariat—Rev. RAYMOND E. LARGER, Exec. Sec.

Presbyteral Council—Most Revs. DENNIS M. SCHNURR, J.C.D., D.D.; JOSEPH R. BINZER; Revs. STEVE J. ANGI; MICHAEL L. BIDWELL; EDWARD T. PRATT; THOMAS H. MCCARTHY; ADAM D. PUNTEL; MATTHEW J. ROBBEN; BARRY J. STECHSCHULTE; JAMES R. SCHUTTE; JAMES M. WEDIG; DAVID A. SUNBERG; ANGELO ANTHONY, C.PP.S.; ERIC A. BOWMAN; JAMES F. FITZ, S.M.; AL HIRT, O.F.M.; MATTHEW K. LEE; ROBERT J. THESING, S.J.

Vicarri Foranei (Deans)—Revs. TODD O. GROGAN, Cathedral Deanery; BERNARD J. WELDISHOFER, St. Andrew Deanery; P. DEL STAIGERS, St. Francis de Sales Deanery; MICHAEL L. BIDWELL, St. Lawrence

Deanery; KYLE E. SCHNIPPEL, St. Margaret Mary Deanery; LARRY R. THARP, Hamilton Deanery; WILLIAM C. WAGNER, St. Martin Deanery; CHRISTOPHER J. WORLAND, Dayton Deanery; JOHN D. MACQUARRIE, Springfield Deanery; STEVEN L. SHOUP, Sidney Deanery; RICHARD W. WALLING, St. Mary's Deanery.

Consultors—Most Rev. JOSEPH R. BINZER; Revs. STEVE J. ANGI; JASON E. BEDEL; MICHAEL L. BIDWELL; THOMAS P. DIFOLCO, (Retired); TODD O. GROGAN; THOMAS W. KREIDLER; JOHN E. KRUMM, (Retired); EDWARD T. PRATT; PATRICK L. SLONEKER; BARRY J. STECHSCHULTE; PETER T. ST. GEORGE; JAMES M. WEDIG.

Archdiocesan Offices

Unless otherwise indicated, all Archdiocesan Offices and Directors are located at: *100 E. Eighth St., Cincinnati, 45202*. Tel: 513-421-3131; Fax: 513-421-6225.

Office of the Archbishop—LINDA CHOUTEAU, Exec. Sec. to the Archbishop, Tel: 513-421-3131, Ext. 2810; Fax: 513-421-7537.

Office of Mediation—EARL LEONHARDT JR., Admin., Tel: 513-421-3131, Ext. 2810.

Priestly Formation—Rev. ANDREW J. UMBERG, S.T.L., Dir.

Priests' Personnel Director—Most Rev. JOSEPH R. BINZER, J.C.L., Dir.

Vocations Office—Rev. DANIEL J. SCHMITMEYER, Dir.; MR. WAYNE TOPP, Asst. Dir.

Services for Senior Clergy—Rev. CLARENCE G. HEIS, Prog. Coord.

Department of Executive Services

Director—Rev. STEVE J. ANGI.

Chancery—

Chancellor—Rev. STEVE J. ANGI, J.C.L.

Archivist—SARAH L. ATER, M.L.S.

Imprimatur Censors—Revs. ANTHONY R. BRAUSCH, Ph.L.; EARL K. FERNANDES, S.T.D.; DR. MATTHEW C. GENUNG, S.S.D.; Revs. ROBERT J. HATER, (Retired); DAVID G. HOWARD, J.C.L.; J. ROBERT JACK, M.A.; PAUL JEROME KELLER, O.P., S.T.D.; ALEXANDER C. MCCULLOUGH; BENEDICT D. O'CINNSEALAIGH, S.T.D.; RYAN THOMAS RUIZ; PAUL A. RUWE, M.A.; TIMOTHY P. SCHEHR, Ph.D., (Retired); ANDREW J. UMBERG, S.T.L.; RICHARD W. WALLING; JOHN E. WESSLING, S.T.D., (Retired); JASON A. WILLIAMS; DAVID L. ZINK, M.A.

Office for Consecrated Life—Sr. MARILYN KERBER, S.N.D.deN., Dir.

Permanent Diaconate Office—Deacon MARK J. MACHUGA.

Office of Safe Environment for the Protection of Children & Youth—MR. JOSEPH RIEDE, Coord.

Coordinator of Ministry to Survivors of Abuse—Tel: 800-686-2724, Ext. 6623; Tel: 513-263-6623; Email: victimsassistance@catholiccincinnati.org.

Tribunal-Archdiocese of Cincinnati—Tel: 513-421-3131; Fax: 513-723-1035.

Director—Sr. VICTORIA VONDENBERGER, R.S.M., J.C.L.

Judicial Vicar—Rev. BARRY M. WINDHOLTZ, J.C.L.

Adjutant Judicial Vicar—Rev. STEVE J. ANGI, J.C.L.

Judges—Most Rev. JOSEPH R. BINZER; Deacon STEVEN R. BROWN, J.C.L.; Revs. JAMES A. BRAMLAGE, (Retired); DAVID J. ENDRES, Ph.D.; DAVID E. FAY; JOHN P. FISCHER, (Retired); GERALD R. HAEMMERLE, M.A., (Retired); TIMOTHY S. KALLAHER, (Retired); RAYMOND C. KELLERMAN; NORMAN LANGENBRUNNER, (Retired); THOMAS C. NOLKER; ROBERT A. OBERMEYER, (Retired); BENEDICT D. O'CINNSEALAIGH, S.T.D.; R. MARC SHERLOCK; THOMAS A. SNODGRASS, J.C.L., (Retired); LARRY R. THARP; JOHN R. WHITE, J.C.L.

Defenders of the Bond—Rev. DENNIS J. CAYLOR, J.C.L., (Retired); Sr. VICTORIA VONDENBERGER, R.S.M., J.C.L.; Rev. WILLIAM H. WYSONG, J.C.L.

Promoter of Justice—Sr. VICTORIA VONDENBERGER, R.S.M., J.C.L.

Assessors—MS. AMI R. QUINN; MRS. KELLY M. TERRY.

Notaries—MRS. SARA T. COOK; MRS. CANDY L. ENGELKE; MS. LYNN M. HERICKS.

Department of Communication & Mission Promotion

Director—MICHAEL A. SCHAFER.

Media Relations—JENNIFER SCHACK.

Newspaper-"The Catholic Telegraph"—Most Rev. DENNIS M. SCHNURR, J.C.D., D.D., Publisher; STEPHEN TROSLEY, Editor-in-Chief.

Department of Community Services

Director—MR. H. THEODORE BERGH.

Archdiocesan Office of Catholic Charities—MR. H. THEODORE BERGH, Dir.

Catholic Charities of Southwestern Ohio—MR. H. THEODORE BERGH, CEO, Cincinnati Office: 7162 Reading Rd., Ste. 600, Cincinnati, 45237. Tel: 513-241-7745; Email: tbergh@ccswoh.org; Web: www.ccswoh.org.

Su Casa Hispanic Center—GIOVANNA ALVAREZ, Contact Person, 7162 Reading Rd., Ste. 610, Cincinnati, 45237. Email: galvarez@ccswoh.org; Web: www.ccswoh.org.

Hamilton Office—1910 Fairgrove Ave., Ste. B, Hamilton, 45011. Tel: 513-863-6129.

Springfield Office—701 E. Columbia St., Springfield, 45503. Tel: 937-325-8715. TYRA JACKSON, Exec. Dir.

Catholic Social Services of Miami Valley—LAURA ROESCH, Exec. Dir., 922 W. Riverview Dr., Dayton, 45407. Tel: 937-223-7217.

Rural Life Conference—1436 Needmore Rd., Dayton, 45414. Tel: 937-224-3026. ANDREW MUSGRAVE, Dir.

Catholic Social Action—100 E. 8th St., Cincinnati, 45202. Tel: 513-421-3131. ANDREW MUSGRAVE, Dir. Dayton Office: PAM LONG, 1436 Needmore Rd., Dayton, 45414. Tel: 937-224-3026.

Department of Educational Services

Director—MS. SUSAN M. GIBBONS, Dir.

School Office—100 E. 8th St., Cincinnati, 45202. Tel: 513-421-3131, Ext. 2702; Fax: 513-421-6271. MS. SUSAN M. GIBBONS, Supt., Archdiocesan Schools.

CISE (Catholic Inner-City Schools Education) Office—100 E. 8th St., Cincinnati, 45202. Tel: 513-421-3131; Fax: 513-421-6271. MS. KRISTINA PHILLIPS; MRS. MABE RODRIGUEZ, Dir.

Department of Financial Services

Chief Financial Officer—MR. RICHARD KELLY.

Controller—MR. THOMAS L. TWILLING.

Assistant Controller—MR. DAVE ABELE.

Director of Benefits and Risk Management—CHARLOTTE T. CARPENTER.

Senior Auditor—MR. JOSEPH RIEDE.

Cemeteries—MS. DEBRA K. CRANE, Esq., Dir., The Archdiocese of Cincinnati Cemeteries Office, 11000 Montgomery Rd., Cincinnati, 45249. Tel: 513-489-0300.

Office of Property Management and Real Estate—JOSEPH H. MANGAN, Dir.

Department of Human Resources

Director—MR. ROBERT J. REID, J.D.

HR Consultant—MRS. MARGARET H. PAUL, SPHR.

HR Coordinator—MRS. KAREN A. BRANNON.

Department of Pastoral Life and Evangelization

Director—Rev. JAN KEVIN SCHMIDT, 100 E. 8th St., Cincinnati, 45202. Tel: 513-421-3131, Ext. 2655.

Associate Department Director for Evangelization—MR. SEAN ATER.

Associate Department Director for Pastoral Life—MRS. LEISA ANSLINGER, Tel: 513-421-3131.

Office for College and University Campus Ministry—MR. LUKE CAREY, Dir., Tel: 513-421-3131. (See Special Listing: Campus Ministry).

Office for African American Pastoral Ministries—Deacon ROYCE E. WINTERS, Dir.

Office for Health and Hospital Ministries—Rev. CLARENCE G. HEIS, Dir., Tel: 513-240-8384.

Office for Respect Life Ministries—MR. BOB WURZELBACHER, Dir.

Office for Marriage and Family Life—MR. DAN THIMONS, Dir.

Office for Evangelization and Discipleship—100 E. 8th St., Cincinnati, 45202. Tel: 513-421-3131. MR. SEAN ATER, Archdiocesan Dir.

Office for Pastoral and Regional Planning—MRS. LEISA ANSLINGER, Dir.

Office for Ethnic Initiatives and Apostolates—VACANT, Dir.

Office for Mission and Pontifical Mission SocietiesDR. MIKE GABLE, Dir.

Archdiocesan Office for Hispanic Pastoral Ministry—Rev. LOUIS GASPARINI, M.C.C.J., Dir., 100 E. Eighth St., Cincinnati, 45202. Tel: 513-421-3131.

Hispanic Catholic Ministry, Cincinnati—Rev. RODOLFO COAQUIRA HILAJE, M.C.C.J., 115 W. Seymour Ave., Cincinnati, 45216. Tel: 513-948-1760.

Hispanic Catholic Ministry, Dayton—MS. MARY ALICE ONDONEZ, Asst. Dir., Holy Family/ Nazareth Center, 310 Allen St., Dayton, 45410. Tel: 937-258-1309.

Hamilton Hispanic Ministry—MS. KARLA EYSOLDT, 224 Dayton St., Hamilton, 45011. Tel: 513-448-8994; Email: keysoldt@catholiccincinnati.org.

Office for Divine Worship and Sacraments—100 E. 8th St., Cincinnati, 45202. Tel: 513-421-3131. VACANT, Dir.

Office for Youth Evangelization and Discipleship—MR. BRADLEY BURSA, Dir., 100 E. Eighth St., Cincinnati, 45202. Tel: 513-421-3131.

Office for Young Adult Evangelization and Discipleship—MR. LUKE CAREY, Dir., 100 E. Eighth St., Cincinnati, 45202. Tel: 513-421-3131.

Department of Stewardship

Department of Stewardship—MR. DAVID W. KISSELL, Dir.

Office of Development Operations—MR. RYAN LOPEZ, Dir.

Office of Donor Relations—MRS. LESLIE W. ODIOSO, Mgr.

CLERGY, PARISHES, MISSIONS AND PAROCHIAL SCHOOLS

GREATER CINCINNATI

(HAMILTON COUNTY)

1—ST. PETER IN CHAINS CATHEDRAL (1822) 325 W. Eighth St., 45202. Tel: 513-421-5354; Email: office@cathedralaoc.org; Web: www.stpeterinchainscathedral.org. Revs. Jan Kevin Schmidt, Rector; Raymond E. Larger, Parochial Vicar; Deacon Michael A. Trimpe; Mr. Ed Birck, Business Mgr.; Mrs. Debbie Birck, Pastoral Assoc.; Mr. Anthony Dicello, M.M., Dir. Music; Mr. Blake Callahan, Music Min.; Mr. Bob Harpenau, Sacristan. In Res., Rev. Jan Kevin Schmidt.

2—ALL SAINTS (Kenwood) (1948) Revs. J. Dennis Jaspers; Jerome R. Bishop, Parochial Vicar; Deacons Amado Lim; Robert J. Leever, Pastoral Assoc.; Marianna Kuhn, Business Mgr.; Ron Miller, Dir. Music & Liturgy; Micki Harrell, Dir. Devel.; Mr. Brian Caperton Sr., Pastoral Assoc.; Kevan Hartman, Prin.; Emily Mulvey, D.R.E.

Res.: 8939 Montgomery Rd., 45236.

Tel: 513-792-4600; Email: parishoffice@allsaints.cc; Web: www.allsaints.cc.

School—All Saints School, (Grades K-8), Tel: 513-792-4732; Email: KHartman@Allsaints.cc. Kevan Hartman, Prin. Lay Teachers 32; Students 497.

Catechesis Religious Program—Tel: 513-792-4603. Ginny Rush, Dir. Faith Formation. Students 249.

3—ST. ALOYSIUS GONZAGA (Bridgetown) (1866) [CEM] Rev. W. Michael Hay.

Res.: 4366 Bridgetown Rd., 45211. Tel: 513-574-4840 ; Email: saintaloysuis5@gmail.com.

School—St. Aloysius Gonzaga School, (Grades K-8), 4390 Bridgetown Rd., 45211. Tel: 513-574-4035; Fax: 513-574-5421; Email: saintaloysius5@gmail.com. Sandi Staud, Prin. Lay Teachers 15; Students 172.

Catechesis Religious Program—Students 60.

4—ST. ALOYSIUS-ON-THE-OHIO (1873) Rev. Richard E. Dressman.

Res.: 134 Whipple St., 45233. Tel: 513-941-3445; Email: twagner.saoto@gmail.com.

5—ST. ANN (Groesbeck) (1953) Rev. Thomas H. McCarthy; Deacon John M. Quattrone.

Church & Res.: 2900 W. Galbraith Rd., 45239.

Tel: 513-521-8440; Email: info@saintannparish.org; Web: www.saintannparish.org.

See Our Lady of Grace, Cincinnati under Consolidated Elementary Schools located in the Institution section.

Catechesis Religious Program—Tel: 513-729-2810; Web: www.saintannparish.org/ReligiousEd/religious_education.htm. Mary Clare McLaughlin, D.R.E. Students 100.

6—ANNUNCIATION OF THE BLESSED VIRGIN MARY (1910) 3547 Clifton Ave., 45220. Tel: 513-861-1295; Email: pastor@annciationbvmparish.org; Web: www.annunciationbvmparish.org. Rev. Todd O. Grogan.

School—Annunciation of the Blessed Virgin Mary School, (Grades PreK-8), 3545 Clifton Ave., 45220. Tel: 513-221-1230; Fax: 513-281-8009; Email: aertel@abvmcincy.org; Web: www.school.annunciationbvmparish.org. Mr. Anthony Ertel, Prin. Lay Teachers 16; Students 148.

Catechesis Religious Program—Email: faithformation@annunciationbvmparish.org. Students 50.

7—ST. ANTHONY (Madisonville) (1858) [CEM]

St. Anthony Parish Center, 5122 Chapman St., 45227. Revs. James P. Weber; Jacob E. Willig, Parochial Vicar; Mary Anne Bressler, Pastoral Assoc.

Church & Office: 6104 Desmond St., 45227.

Tel: 513-261-0920; Email: Office@stanthonychurch.net; Web: www.stanthonychurch.net.

Catechesis Religious Program—Cody Egner, D.R.E., Tel: 513-871-5757, Ext. 215. Students 30.

8—ST. ANTONINUS (1944) Rev. Ronald C. Haft; Deacon Robert J. Schroeder, Pastoral Assoc.

Res.: 1500 Linneman Rd., 45238. Tel: 513-922-5400; Email: bollin@saintantoninus.org.
School—St. Antoninus School, (Grades K-8), 5425 Julmar Dr., 45238. Tel: 513-922-2500; Fax: 513-922-5519; Email: kahny@saintantoninus.org; Web: www.saintantoninus.org. Mrs. Shelly Kahny, Prin. Lay Teachers 23; Students 394.
Catechesis Religious Program—Tel: 513-922-2500, Ext. 2031. Students 27.

9—ST. BARTHOLOMEW (1961)
9375 Winton Rd., 45231. Tel: 513-522-3680; Email: Barts.Business@fuse.net; Web: eStBarts.org. Rev. Gerard P. Hiland; Deacons Gerald A. Flamm; Conrad C. Kolis; Kathleen Rothschild, Business Mgr.; Milt Goedde, Music Min.; Sandy Hornbach, Pastoral Assoc.; Amy Staubach, D.R.E.
See John Paul II Catholic School, Cincinnati under Consolidated Elementary Schools located in the Institution section.
Catechesis Religious Program—Email: amy.staubach@fuse.net. Students 28.

10—ST. BERNARD (1919) Rev. Joseph A. Robinson.
Res.: 740 Circle Ave., 45232. Tel: 513-541-3732; Email: stbernardwp@fuse.net.
Catechesis Religious Program—Twinned with Mother of Christ.

11—ST. BERNARD (Taylor's Creek) (1867) [CEM] Rev. Donald L. Siciliano.
Res.: 7130 Harrison Rd., 45247. Tel: 513-353-4207; Email: stbernard@stbernardtc.org; Web: stbernardtc.church.
School—St. Bernard School, (Grades K-8), 7115 Springdale Rd., 45247. Tel: 513-353-4224; Fax: 513-353-3958; Email: laib@stbernardtc.org; Web: www.stbernardtc.church. Courtney Brown, Prin. Lay Teachers 14; Students 208.
Catechesis Religious Program—Students 48.

12—ST. BONIFACE (1863) Rev. Joseph A. Robinson; Deacon Jerry Yetter; Jenni Lindgren, Business Mgr.
Res.: 1750 Chase Ave., 45223. Tel: 513-541-1563; Email: stboniface@cinci.rr.com; Web: www.stbonifacecincinnati.com.
See St. Boniface School, Cincinnati under Consolidated Elementary Schools located in the Institution section.
Catechesis Religious Program—Students 4.

13—ST. CATHARINE OF SIENA (1903)
Email: condren_p@stcatharinesiena.org. Rev. Anthony M. Dattilo; Therese Bower Hibdon, Pastoral Min.
Res.: 2848 Fischer Pl., 45211. Tel: 513-661-0651; Email: hafelestc@gmail.com; Web: stcathos.org.
School—St. Catharine of Siena School, (Grades PreK-8), 3324 Wunder Ave., 45211. Tel: 513-481-7683; Fax: 513-481-9438; Email: metz_j@stcatharinesiena.org. Jerry Metz, Prin. Lay Teachers 13; Students 159.
Catechesis Religious Program—Students 4.

14—ST. CECILIA (Oakley) (1908) Revs. James P. Weber, Email: jweber@stceciliacincinnati.org; Jacob E. Willig, Parochial Vicar.
Res.: 3105 Madison Rd., 45209. Tel: 513-871-5757, Ext. 208; Email: bkellison@stceciliacincinnati.org; Web: www.stceciliacincinnati.org.
School—St. Cecilia School, (Grades PreK-8), 4115 Taylor Ave., 45209. Tel: 513-533-6060; Fax: 513-533-6068; Web: www.school.stceciliacincinnati.org. Mr. Michael Goedde, Prin. Clergy 1; Lay Teachers 20; Students 269; Clergy / Religious Teachers 1.
Catechesis Religious Program—Tel: 513-871-5757, Ext. 215. Cody Egner, Faith Formation Dir. Students 38.

15—CHURCH OF THE ASSUMPTION (Mount Healthy) (1854) [CEM] Rev. Jerome J. Gardner; Deacons Richard J. Reder; Robert A. Staab Jr.
Res.: 7711 Joseph St., 45231. Tel: 513-521-7274; Email: parish.office@assumptionmthealthy.
See Our Lady of Grace, Cincinnati under Consolidated Elementary Schools located in the Institution section.
Catechesis Religious Program—Tel: 513-728-4940. Adam Couch, Pastoral Assoc. Faith Formation. Students 18.

16—CHURCH OF THE RESURRECTION (2010) Church of the Resurrection - Bond Hill Rev. David A. Lemkuhl; Deacon Royce E. Winters.
Church: 1619 California Ave., 45237.
Tel: 513-242-0400; Email: deacon@resurrectioncinci.org; Email: office@resurrectioncinci.org; Web: www.resurrectioncinci.org.

17—ST. CLARE (College Hill) (1909) Revs. George Jacquemin; Robert J. Hater, In Res., (Retired).
Res.: 1443 Cedar Ave., 45224. Tel: 513-541-2100; Email: office@saintclareparish.org; Web: www.saintclareparish.org.
See John Paul II Catholic, Cincinnati under Consolidated Elementary Schools located in the Institution section.
Catechesis Religious Program—Email: dbookr@saintclareparish.org. Donna Booker, D.R.E. Students 30.

18—ST. CLEMENT (St. Bernard) (1850) Rev. Fred Link, O.F.M.; Deacon John P. Gerke, Pastoral Assoc.; Marty Cunningham, Music Min.
St. Clement Friary: 4536 Vine St., 45217.
Tel: 513-641-3176 (Church); Email: office@stclementcincinnati.org; Web: www.stclementcincinnati.org.
School—St. Clement School, (Grades PreK-8), 4534 Vine St., 45217. Tel: 513-641-2137; Fax: 513-242-6036; Email: jeiser@stcschool.org; Web: www.stcschool.org. Mr. Jeff Eiser, Prin., Tel: 513-641-2137, Ext. 802. Clergy 1; Lay Teachers 21; Sisters 1; Students 296.
Catechesis Religious Program—Ms. Colleen Gerke, D.R.E. Students 7.

19—CORPUS CHRISTI (1958) Revs. Kyle E. Schnippel; J. Thomas Wray; Deacons John Corson; Larry H. Day, Pastoral Assoc.; William Marshall, Pastoral Assoc. Admin., Music & Liturgy; Pam McLaughlin, D.R.E.
Res.: 2014 Springdale Rd., 45231. Tel: 513-825-0618; Fax: 513-825-0182; Email: info@corpuschristicommunity.org; Web: corpuschristicommunity.org.
See St. John the Baptist Catholic School, Cincinnati under Consolidated Elementary Schools in the institution section.
Catechesis Religious Program—Email: pmclaughlin@corpuschristicommunity.org. Students 75.

20—ST. DOMINIC (Delhi Hills) (1933) Revs. Jim J. Walsh; Chris Lack; Deacon Mark A. Bardonaro, Admin.
Res.: 4551 Delhi Pike, 45238. Tel: 513-471-7741; Email: parishoffice@stdominicdelhi.org; Web: www.stdominicdelhi.org.
School—St. Dominic School, (Grades PreK-8), 371 Pedretti Ave., 45238. Tel: 513-251-1276; Fax: 513-251-6428; Email: bcavanaugh@stdominicdelhi.org; Web: www.stdominicdelhi.org. William S. Cavanaugh, Prin. Lay Teachers 25; Students 434.
Catechesis Religious Program—Tel: 513-471-7741, Ext. 481; Email: teagan@stdominicdelhi.org. Theresa Eagan, C.R.E. Students 62.

21—ST. FRANCIS DE SALES (1849) [CEM] Collaborative cluster - see St. Robert, Bellarmine.
Email: info@stfrancisds.com; Web: www.stfrancisds.com. Rev. J. Eugene Contadino, S.M., B.A., M.A., Ph. D.
Res.: 1600 Madison Rd., 45206. Tel: 513-961-1945; Email: info@saintfrancisdesalesparish.org; Web: www.stfrancisds.com/our-parish.html.
School—St. Francis de Sales School, (Grades PreK-8), 1602 Madison Rd., 45206. Tel: 513-961-1953; Fax: 513-961-2900; Email: browarsky_j@desalescincy.org; Web: www.desalescincy.org. Joanne Browarsky, Prin. Lay Teachers 22; Students 222; Clergy / Religious Teachers 1; Staff 9.
Catechesis Religious Program—Email: info@stfrancisds.com; Web: www.stfrancisds.com; Email: alliebrizzi@gmail.com. Allie Brizzi, Contact Person. Collaborative Cluster, see St. Robert Bellarmine. Students 5.

22—ST. FRANCIS SERAPH (1859) Rev. David Kohut, O.F.M.; Bro. Timothy Sucher, O.F.M., Pastoral Assoc.
St. Francis Friary: 1615 Vine St., 45202. Cell: 513-535-2719; Email: JPearce@SFSParish.org; Email: DRKohut52@hotmail.com; Email: tsucher@franciscan.org.
School—St. Francis Seraph School, (Grades PreSchool-8), 14 E. Liberty St., 45202.
Tel: 513-721-7778; Fax: 513-721-5445; Web: www.stfrancisseraphschool.org. Halsey Mabry, Prin.; Cindy George, Librarian; Jamie Klauke, Admin.; Anne Niehauser, Admin. Clergy 5; Lay Teachers 14; Sisters 1; Students 210.
Catechesis Religious Program—Students 4.

23—ST. FRANCIS XAVIER CHURCH (1819)
611 Sycamore St., 45202. Tel: 513-721-4045; Email: office@stxchurch.org; Web: www.stxchurch.org. Revs. Patrick A. Fairbanks, S.J.; Matthew T. Gamber, S.J.; Jerome Veigas; Robert J. Ross, S.J.

24—ST. GABRIEL (Glendale) (1857) Rev. David E. Fay; Deacon Herman H. Bryant.
Res.: 48 W. Sharon Ave., 45246. Tel: 513-771-4700; Email: gabrielglendale@fuse.net.
See St. Gabriel Consolidated School, Cincinnati under Consolidated Elementary Schools located in the Institution section.
Catechesis Religious Program—Rose Voulgarakis, D.R.E. Students 116.

25—ST. GERTRUDE (Madeira) (1923)
Offices & Parish Address: 6543 Miami Ave., 45243. Revs. Andre-Joseph LaCasse, O.P.; Clement Dickie, Parochial Vicar; Robert Stephan, S.J., Parochial Vicar; Zane Gabriel Torretta, O.P.; John Farren, Prior; Michael Mary Dosch, O.P., Novice Master; Edmund Augustino Ditton, O.P., In Res.; Joseph Alobaidi, In Res.; Paul Jerome Keller, O.P., S.T.D., In Res.
Priory Address: 7630 Shawnee Run Rd., 45243.
Tel: 513-561-5954; Fax: 513-527-3971; Email: parishoffice@stgertrude.org; Web: www.stgertrude.org.
School—St. Gertrude School, (Grades K-8), Tel: 513-561-8020; Fax: 513-561-7184; Email: office@stgertrudesch.org; Web: www.stgertrudesch.org. Sr. Maria Greve, Prin. Lay Teachers 24; Students 340; Clergy / Religious Teachers 4.
Catechesis Religious Program—Email: dre@stgertrude.org. Shari Siebert, D.R.E. Students 370.

26—GOOD SHEPHERD The Community of the Good Shepherd (1973) Revs. Thomas M. Mannebach; Jack W. Wehman; Deacons Dennis J. Berry, Dir. of Pastoral Care & Outreach; Richard W. Gallenstein, 55+ Min.; James Jones; Max Schellman; Mark Westendorf, Coord. of Outreach Ministries; Sr. Elaine Winter, S.N.D., D.R.E.; Teri Cunningham, Dir. Stewardship and Business Mgr.; Stephen P. Lindner, Dir. Liturgical Ministries; Walter Plummer, Coord. of Youth Formation; Doug Schmutte, Dir., Music Min.; Emily Weierman, Coord. of Adult Faith Formation; Nancy Dallas, Sac. Prep. & Children's Liturgy.
Church & Mailing Address: 8815 E. Kemper Rd., 45249. Tel: 513-489-8815; Fax: 513-489-8521; Email: gs.info@good-shepherd.org; Web: www.good-shepherd.org.

27—GUARDIAN ANGELS (Mt. Washington) (1892) [CEM] Rev. Thomas M. King; Deacons Paul W. Feie; Robert Fey; Rick Novick.
Res.: 6531 Beechmont Ave., 45230.
Tel: 513-231-7440; Email: office@gaparish.org; Web: www.gaparish.org.
School—Guardian Angels School, (Grades PreK-8), 6539 Beechmont Ave., 45230. Tel: 513-624-3141; Fax: 513-624-3150; Email: cstoops@gaschool.org; Web: www.gaschool.org. Corey Stoops, Prin.; Holly Leach, Librarian. Lay Teachers 31; Students 445.
Catechesis Religious Program—Tel: 513-624-3146; Web: www.gaparish.org. Kay Froehlich, D.R.E. Students 125.
Mission—St. Jerome, 131 Rhode Ave., Hamilton Co. 45230. Tel: 513-231-7042; Email: admin@st-jerome-cinci.org. 5858 Kellogg Ave., 45230.

28—HOLY CROSS-IMMACULATA (Mount Adams) (1859) Rev. Leonard J. Fecko; Deacon Tracy W. Jamison, Ph.D.
Res.: 30 Guido St., 45202. Tel: 513-721-6544; Email: holymac30@fuse.net; Web: www.hciparish.org.
Catechesis Religious Program—Students 2.

29—HOLY FAMILY (Price Hill) (1883) Includes Our Lady of Grace, Our Lady of Perpetual Help, Blessed Sacrament, St. Michael Parishes and San Antonio.
814 Hawthorne Ave., 45205. Tel: 513-921-7527; Email: office@holyfamilycincinnati.org; Web: www.holyfamilycincinnati.org. Parish Office & Mailing Address: 3006 W. 8th St., 45205. Rev. Leonard C. Wenke.
School—Holy Family School, (Grades PreK-8), 3001 Price Ave., 45205. Tel: 513-921-8483; Fax: 513-921-2460; Email: kputhoff@theholyfamilyschool.org. Ms. Katie Puthoff, Prin. Lay Teachers 13; Sisters 1; Students 211.
Chapel—San Antonio da Padova, 1950 Queen City Ave., 45214.

30—HOLY NAME (1904) Rev. Thomas Speier I, O.F.M., Parochial Admin., (Retired).
Church: 2422 Auburn Ave., 45219. Tel: 513-721-5608 ; Email: holynamecatholicchurch@gmail.com; Web: holynamemtauburn.com.
Catechesis Religious Program—

31—HOLY TRINITY CHURCH (Norwood) (1994) Rev. Raymond C. Kellerman.
Res.: 2420 Drex Ave., 45212. Tel: 513-366-4400; Fax: 513-366-4404; Email: HolyTrinityNorwood@gmail.com; Web: www.holytrinitynorwood.org.
See St. Nicholas Academy, Cincinnati under Consolidated Elementary Schools in the institution section.
Catechesis Religious Program—7121 Plainfield Rd., 45236. Tel: 513-791-3238; Fax: 513-686-2720; Email: ldavis821@aol.com. Laura E. Davis, D.R.E. Twinned with St. John the Evangelist, Cincinnati. Students 9.

32—ST. IGNATIUS OF LOYOLA (Monfort Heights) (1946) Revs. Geoffrey D. Drew; David Kobak, Parochial Vicar; Deacons Timothy M. Helmick; Michael C. Erb; Anthony Gagliarducci; John Homoelle; Richard Berning, Business Mgr.; Sr. Lucy Zientek, C.D.P., Pastoral Assoc.; Ms. Patty Stretch, Music Min.; Mrs. Kimberly Abele, D.R.E.; Ms. Emily Branscum, Youth Min.
Res.: 5222 North Bend Rd., 45247. Tel: 513-661-6565 ; Email: office@sainti.org.
School—St. Ignatius of Loyola School, (Grades K-8),

Tel: 513-389-3242; Email: office@saintischool.org; Web: www.saintischool.org. Kevin Vance, Prin. Lay Teachers 63; Students 1,046.
Catechesis Religious Program—Students 140.

33—IMMACULATE HEART OF MARY (Forestville) (1944) Rev. Thomas W. Kreidler; Deacons Michael J. Cassani; J. Russell Feldkamp; Mark U. Johnson; William Mullaney; David Shaffer; David Shea, D.Min.; Donna Wenstrup, D.R.E.; David Auxier, Music Min.; Marisue Naber, Parish Nurse; Mr. Michael Haley, Youth Min.; Tina Ramundo, PRP Coord.
Res.: 7820 Beechmont Ave., 45255.
Tel: 513-388-4466; Email: parish@ihom.org; Web: www.ihom.org.
School—Immaculate Heart of Mary School, (Grades PreSchool-8), 7800 Beechmont Ave., 45255.
Tel: 513-388-4086; Fax: 513-388-3026; Email: school@ihom.org; Web: www.ihomschool.org. Krista Devine, Prin. Brothers 1; Clergy 1; Lay Teachers 44; Students 615.
Catechesis Religious Program—Tel: 513-388-4093; Email: formation@ihom.org. Mr. Michael Haley, Youth Min.; Mr. Pete Taylor, Children's Formation. Students 427.

34—ST. JAMES OF THE VALLEY (Wyoming) (1886) St. James of the Valley is part of the Winton Wyoming Pastoral Region with Our Lady of the Rosary and St. Matthias, Cincinnati. Revs. Alexander C. McCullough; Lambert Ulinzwenimana, (Rwanda); Deacon Walter A. Hucke Jr.; David Crowe, Business Mgr.
Res.: 411 Springfield Pk., Wyoming, 45215.
Tel: 513-948-1218; Email: info@wintonwyomingpr.org; Web: www.wintonwyomingpr.org.
Catechesis Religious Program—Tel: 513-808-8515; Email: dnissen@wintonwyomingpr.org. David Nissen, D.R.E. Students 151.

35—ST. JAMES THE GREATER (White Oak) (1843) [CEM] 3565 Hubble Rd., 45247. Tel: 513-741-5300; Email: info@stjameswhiteoak.com; Web: www.stjameswhiteoak.com. Revs. Thomas C. Nolker; Bryan T. Reif; Deacon Tim A. Crooker, Pastoral Assoc.
School—St. James the Greater School, (Grades K-8), 6111 Cheviot Rd., 45247. Tel: 513-741-5333; Fax: 513-741-5312; Email: infosjs@stjameswo.org; Web: www.stjameswo.org. Jeffrey Fulmer, Prin. Lay Teachers 37; Students 556.
Catechesis Religious Program—Tel: 513-741-5339; Email: thayes@stjameswhiteoak.com. Theresa Hayes, D.R.E.

36—ST. JOHN FISHER (Newtown) (1947)
3227 Church St., 45244. Tel: 513-561-9431; Email: jimc@sjfchurch.org; Web: sjfchurch.org. Revs. P. Del Staigers; David A. Doseck, Parochial Vicar; Deacon Thomas M. Gaier; Jim Crosby, Pastoral Assoc.
Catechesis Religious Program—Tel: 513-527-5243. Students 122.

37—ST. JOHN NEUMANN (Springfield Township) (1978) Revs. Kyle E. Schnippel; J. Thomas Wray; Deacons John R. Gobbi, Pastoral Assoc.; Patrick A. Palumbo, Pastoral Assoc.; Ronald H. Risch, Pastoral Assoc.
Res.: 12191 Mill Rd., 45240.
Tel: 513-742-0953, Ext. 10; Email: cfuerbacher@sjnews.org; Web: www.sjnews.org.
See St. John the Baptist Catholic School, Cincinnati under Consolidated Elementary Schools located in the Institution section.
Catechesis Religious Program—Students 11.

38—ST. JOHN THE BAPTIST (Dry Ridge) (1860) [CEM] Rev. Peter T. St. George.
Res.: 5361 Dry Ridge Rd., 45252. Tel: 513-385-8010; Email: stjohns@stjohnsdr.org; Web: www.stjohnsdr.org.
See St. John the Baptist Catholic School, Cincinnati under Consolidated Schools in the Institution section.
Catechesis Religious Program—Students 105.

39—ST. JOHN THE BAPTIST (Harrison) (1851) [CEM] Office & Mailing Address: 509 Harrison Ave., Harrison, 45030. Tel: 513-367-9086; Email: jkemper@stjb.net; Email: aland@stjb.net; Web: www.stjb.net. Revs. Jeffrey M. Kemper, Ph.D.; Edward J. Shine, (Retired); William J. Dorrmann, (Retired); Deacon Donald J. Meyer Jr.
Res.: 110 N. Hill St., Harrison, 45030. Email: parishoffice@stjb.net; Web: www.stjb.net.
School—St. John the Baptist School, (Grades K-8), 508 Park Ave., Harrison, 45030. Tel: 513-367-6826; Fax: 513-367-6864; Email: meymann_s@sjbharrison.org; Web: sjbharrison.org. Susan Meymann, Prin.; Julia Koors, Librarian. Lay Teachers 24; Students 346.
Catechesis Religious Program—Email: jgemperline@stjb.net. Joy Gemperline, D.R.E. Students 180.

40—ST. JOHN THE EVANGELIST (1891) Revs. Timothy S. Bunch; Ryan Thomas Ruiz.
Res.: 7121 Plainfield Rd., 45236. Tel: 513-791-3238; Email: neilb@stjohndp.org; Web: www.stjohndp.org.
See St. Nicholas Academy, Cincinnati under Consolidated Schools in the Institution section.
Catechesis Religious Program—Laura E. Davis, Pastoral Min. Students 45.

41—ST. JOSEPH (1846) (African American)
745 Ezzard Charles Dr., 45203. Tel: 513-381-4526; Fax: 513-381-5244; Email: church@stjosephcincinnati.org; Web: www.saintjosephchurchandschool.com. Rev. Reynaldo S. Taylor; Deacon Dennis Edwards; Wylie G. Howell, Pastoral Assoc./Music Min.; William Jefferson, Business Mgr./Parish Finance; Lisa Massa, Coord. Communications; Mary Roberson, Business Mgr.; Mr. Shon Hubble, Music MIn.
Res.: Fatima Hall, 693 Bridle Path, 45231.
Tel: 513-284-4201.
School—St. Joseph School, (Grades PreK-8), St. Joseph Catholic School, A Seton Education Partner 745 Ezzard Charles Dr., 45203. Tel: 513-381-2126; Fax: 513-381-6513; Email: info@saintjoeschool.org. Dionne Partee, Prin.; Maureen Lechleiter, Librarian; Mr. V. Johnson, Primary Dean, Email: vjohnson@saintjoeschool.org; Mr. D. Montgomery, Intermediate Dean; Mr. J. Richardson, Jr. High Dean and Min. Coord.; Mrs. Gwendlyn Baskin, School Business Mgr.; Barbara Houston, School Sec.; Rickie Younger, Dean & IT Coord. Lay Teachers 14; Students 300.
Catechesis Religious Program—
Tel: 513-381-4526, Ext. 16. Joan R. Brunner, C.R.E. Students 140.

42—ST. JUDE THE APOSTLE (1956)
5924 Bridgetown Rd., 45248. Tel: 513-574-1230; Email: ken.schultz@stjudebridgetown.org. Rev. W. Michael Hay.
Res/Rectory: 5920 Bridgetown Rd., 45248.
School—St. Jude the Apostle School, 5940 Bridgetown Rd., 45248. Tel: 513-598-2100; Fax: 513-598-2118; Email: hornsby.m@stjudebulldogs.org. Louis Eichhold, Prin. Lay Teachers 30; Students 465.
Catechesis Religious Program—
Tel: 513-574-1230, Ext. 30. Students 50.

43—ST. LAWRENCE (Price Hill) (1868) Rev. Mark T. Watkins; Sr. Helen Julia Hahn, S.C., Pastoral Min.
Res.: 3680 Warsaw Ave., 45205. Tel: 513-921-0328; Email: rectory@stlawrenceparish.org; Web: www.stlawrenceparish.org.
School—St. Lawrence School, (Grades PreK-8), 1020 Carson Ave., 45205. Tel: 513-921-4996; Fax: 513-921-5108; Email: school@stlawrenceparish.org; Web: www.stlawrenceparish.org/school.htm. Mr. Richard A. Klus, Prin. Clergy 1; Lay Teachers 25; Students 365; Clergy / Religious Teachers 1.
Catechesis Religious Program—Students 341.

44—ST. LEO THE GREAT (1886)
Mailing Address: 2573 St. Leo Pl., 45225-1960.
Tel: 513-921-1044; Fax: 513-921-8048; Email: stleocinti@aol.com. Rev. James R. Schutte.
See St. Boniface School, Cincinnati under Consolidated Elementary Schools located in the Institution section.
Catechesis Religious Program—Students 118.

45—ST. LOUIS (1870) (German) Rev. Steve J. Angi.
Res.: 29 E. Eighth St., 45202-2086.
Tel: 513-263-6621.

46—ST. MARGARET - ST. JOHN PARISH (2008)
Mailing Address: 4100 Watterson St., 45227.
Tel: 513-271-0856; Fax: 513-271-1513; Email: marymathers@fuse.net; Web: www.smsjparish.com. Revs. James P. Weber; Jacob E. Willig, Parochial Vicar.
Res.: 3105 Madison Rd., 45209. Tel: 513-871-5757.
Worship Site: St. Margaret of Cortona Church, 6000 Murray Rd., 45227.
Catechesis Religious Program—St. Anthony, 6104 Desmond St., 45227. Cody Egner, Regional Dir. of Religious Educ. Students 18.

47—ST. MARGARET MARY (North College Hill) (1920) Rev. Jerome J. Gardner.
Res.: 1830 W. Galbraith Rd., 45239.
Tel: 513-521-7387; Email: parishoffice@stmargaretmaryparish.org.
See Our Lady of Grace, Cincinnati under Consolidated Elementary Schools located in the Institution section.
Catechesis Religious Program—Tel: 513-729-0222. Mrs. Wilma McGlasson, D.R.E. Students 10.

48—ST. MARTIN OF TOURS (Cheviot) (1911) Rev. Terence J. Hamilton.
Res.: 3720 St. Martin Pl., 45211. Tel: 513-661-2000; Email: lsundrup@fuse.net; Web: www.saintmartin.org.
School—St. Martin of Tours School, (Grades K-8), 3729 Harding Ave., 45211. Tel: 513-661-7609; Fax: 513-661-8102; Email: jfightmaster@saintmartin.org; Web: saintmartin.org/school. Mr. Jason Fightmaster, Prin. Lay Teachers 19; Students 292.
Catechesis Religious Program—Students 29.

49—ST. MARY (Hyde Park) (1898)
2853 Erie Ave., 45208. Tel: 513-321-1207; Email: jrinear@smshp.com; Web: www.smchp.com. Rev. Kenneth E. Schartz; Deacon John A. Schuler; Mrs. Michele Carle-Bosch, D.R.E.; Ms. Margaret Shank, Pastoral Assoc.; Jeff Rinear, Parish Admin.; Katie Barton, Music Min.
School—St. Mary School, (Grades K-8), 2845 Erie Ave., 45208. Tel: 513-321-0703; Fax: 513-533-5517; Email: lkoslovsky@smshp.com; Web: www.smshp.com. Miss Marianne Rosemond, Prin. Clergy 13; Lay Teachers 24; Students 467.

50—ST. MATTHIAS (Forest Park) (1967) St. Matthias is part of the Winton Wyoming Pastoral Region with Our Lady of the Rosary and St. James of the Valley, Cincinnati. Revs. Alexander C. McCullough; Lambert Ulinzwenimana, (Rwanda); Deacon Hoang Dominic Vu; David Crowe, Business Mgr.
Church: 1050 W. Kemper Rd., 45240.
Tel: 513-851-1930; Email: info@wintonwyomingpr.org; Web: www.wintonwyomingpr.org.
Rectory—1044 W. Kemper Rd., 45240.
Catechesis Religious Program—17 Farragut Rd., 45218. Tel: 513-808-8515; Email: dnissen@wintonwyomingpr.org. David Nissen, Youth Faith Formation Dir. Students 4.

51—ST. MICHAEL (1919) Rev. Edward M. Burns; Brian Bisig, Dir. Music; Scott Hungler, Business Mgr.; Tom Giordano, Pastoral Assoc. Min. & Care.
Church & Mailing Address: 11144 Spinner Ave., 45241. Tel: 513-563-6377, Ext. 307; Email: scott@saintmichaelchurch.net; Web: www.saintmichaelchurch.net.
School—St. Michael School, (Grades K-8), 11136 Oak St., 45241. Tel: 513-554-3555; Fax: 513-554-3551; Email: cmurphy@stmichaelsharonville.org; Web: www.stmichaelsharonville.org. Carolyn Murphy, Prin.; Frances Ablett, Librarian. Lay Teachers 24; Students 410.
Catechesis Religious Program—Students 410.

52—ST. MONICA-ST. GEORGE PARISH NEWMAN CENTER (1993)
328 W. McMillan St., 45219. Tel: 513-381-6400. Revs. Alan Hirt, O.F.M.; Clifford Hennings, O.F.M.; Mrs. Jill Kreinbrink, Music Min. & Dir. Liturgy; Michael Huffman, Business Mgr.; Sheila Murphy, Pastoral Assoc.; Ms. Holly O'Hara, Campus Min.; Michael Schreiner, Campus Min.
Res.: 1723 Pleasant Ave., 45202.
Catechesis Religious Program—Students 110.

53—MOTHER OF CHRIST (1946) (African American)
5301 Winneste Ave., 45232. Tel: 513-541-3732; Email: mniemer@oldenburgosf.com. Rev. Joseph A. Robinson.

54—NATIVITY OF OUR LORD (Pleasant Ridge) (1917) Rev. Paul F. DeLuca.
Res.: 5935 Pandora Ave., 45213-2017.
Tel: 513-531-3164; Email: parish@nativity-cincinnati.org; Web: www.nativity-cincinnati.org.
School—Nativity of Our Lord School, (Grades K-8), 5936 Ridge Ave., 45213-1699. Tel: 513-458-6767; Fax: 513-458-6769; Email: school@nativity-cincinnati.org. Chris Shisler, Prin. Lay Teachers 25; Students 375.
Catechesis Religious Program—Email: janet.schneider@nativity-cincinnati.org. Sr. Janet Schneider, C.D.P., D.R.E. Students 64.

55—OLD ST. MARY (1842) Very Rev. Jon-Paul Bevak; Revs. Adrian J. Hilton, Parochial Vicar, 123 E. 13th St., 45202; Lawrence Juarez, Parochial Vicar.
Res.: 123 E. 13th St., 45202. Tel: 513-721-2988; Email: secretary@oldstmarys.org; Web: www.oldstmarys.org.
Catechesis Religious Program—Students 75.

56—OUR LADY OF LOURDES (Westwood) (1927)
3426 Lumardo Ave., 45238. 3450 Lumardo Ave., 45238. Rev. Leonard C. Wenke; Deacon Thomas E. Westerfield; Mr. Robert Gerth, Ph.D., Pastoral Assoc.
Res.: 2832 Rosebud Dr., 45238. Tel: 513-922-0715; Email: parish@lourdes.org; Web: www.lourdes.org.
School—Our Lady of Lourdes School, (Grades K-8), 5835 Glenway Ave., 45238. Tel: 513-347-2660; Fax: 513-347-2663; Email: hbessler@lourdes.org; Web: www.lourdes.org. Ms. Heather Bessler, Prin.; Angela Hautman, Librarian. Lay Teachers 18; Students 295.
Catechesis Religious Program—5835 Glenway Ave., 45238. Tel: 513-347-2646; Email: kkrimm@lourdes.org. Kristina Krimm, D.R.E. Students 19.

57—OUR LADY OF THE ROSARY (Greenhills) (1938) Our Lady of the Rosary is part of Winton Wyoming Pastoral Region with St. James of the Valley and St. Matthias, Cincinnati.
17 Farragut Rd., 45218. Tel: 513-825-8626; Email: info@wintonwyomingpr.org; Web: www.wintonwyomingpr.org. Revs. Alexander C. McCullough; Lambert Ulinzwenimana, (Rwanda) Parochial Vicar; Deacons Walter A. Hucke Jr.; Steven A. Ryan; Matthew R. Skinner; David Crowe, Business Mgr.
See John Paul II Catholic, Cincinnati under

Consolidated Elementary Schools located in the Institution section.
Catechesis Religious Program—Tel: 513-825-8515; Email: dnissen@wintonwyomingpr.org. David Nissen, Youth Faith Formation Dir. Students 120.

58—OUR LADY OF THE SACRED HEART (Reading) (1874)
177 Siebenthaler Ave., 45215. Tel: 513-733-4950; Email: olsh@fuse.net; Web: olshcatholic.church. Rev. Matthew J. Robben; Angie Touvelle, Business Mgr.; Mrs. Beth Pettigrew, Pastoral Assoc.
Res.: 415 W. Vine St., 45215.
Catechesis Religious Program— Twinned with Sts. Peter and Paul, Reading Tel: 513-554-1010. Students 8.

59—OUR LADY OF THE VISITATION (Mack) (1947) Rev. Mark J. Burger; Deacon Marc. A. Alexander; Dave Feldman, Pastoral Assoc.; Leslee House, Pastoral Assoc.; Ken Meymann, Pastoral Assoc.; Kathy Parsons, Pastoral Assoc.; Bill Tonnis, Pastoral Assoc.
Res.: 3172 South Rd., 45248. Tel: 513-922-2056; Email: olvisitation@olvisitation.org.
School—Our Lady of the Visitation School, 3180 South Rd., 45248. Tel: 513-347-2222;
Fax: 513-347-2225; Email: haug@olvisitation.org; Web: olvisitation.org. Holly Aug, Prin. Lay Teachers 40; Students 738.
Catechesis Religious Program—Tel: 513-347-2228; Fax: 513-347-2225. Ms. Jeanne Hunt, Pastoral Assoc. Catechesis & Evangelization; Laura Hampel, Pastoral Assoc. for Youth Min. Students 74.

60—OUR LADY OF VICTORY (Delhi Hills) (1842) [CEM] Rev. Benedict D. O'Cinnsealaigh, S.T.D.; Deacons Charles Jenkins; Mark J. Machuga.
Res.: 810 Neeb Rd., 45233. Tel: 513-922-4460; Email: secretary@olv.org.
School—Our Lady of Victory School, (Grades K-8), 808 Neeb Rd., 45233. Tel: 513-347-2072;
Fax: 513-347-2073; Email: borgmana@olv-school.org; Web: school.olv.org. Ms. Amy Borgman, Prin. Clergy 19; Lay Teachers 24; Students 423.
Catechesis Religious Program—Tel: 513-347-2071. Mr. Jonathan Schaefer, D.R.E. Students 55.

61—OUR LORD, CHRIST THE KING (Mt. Lookout) (1926) Revs. Edward P. Smith, M.A.; Francis W. Voellmecke, Ph.D., In Res., (Retired); Deacon Donald Gloeckler.
Res.: 3223 Linwood Ave., 45226. Tel: 513-321-4121; Email: parish@olctk.org; Web: www.olctk.org.
School—Cardinal Pacelli, (Grades PreSchool-8), 927 Ellison, 45226. Tel: 513-321-1048; Fax: 513-533-6118 ; Email: cento_t@cardinalpacelli.org; Web: cardinalpacelli.org. Terri Cento, Prin. Lay Teachers 26; Students 378; Clergy / Religious Teachers 2.
Catechesis Religious Program—Students 60.

62—STS. PETER AND PAUL (Reading) (1850) [CEM]
330 W. Vine St., Reading, 45215. Tel: 513-554-1010; Email: Mike.schweitzer@catholicreading.church. Rev. Matthew J. Robben; Deacons Charles W. Roemer; Tom Lynd; Michael Schweitzer, Pastoral Admin.; Mrs. Beth Pettigrew, Pastoral Assoc. In Res., Rev. John P. Heim, S.J.
Catechesis Religious Program—Email: ppanzeca1@fuse.net. Students 49.

63—RESURRECTION OF OUR LORD (1919)
1744 Iliff Ave., 45205. Rev. Robert L. Keller.
Res.: 1744 Iliff Ave., 45205-1018. Tel: 513-471-2700; Email: bkeller@resurrectionschool.org.
School—Resurrection of Our Lord School, (Grades K-8), 1740 Iliff Ave., 45205-1018. Tel: 513-471-6600;
Tel: 513-471-6620; Fax: 513-471-2610; Email: dlooby@resurrectionschool.org; Web: www.resurrectionschool.org. Mrs. Dolores Heffner, Prin. Aides 3; Clergy 1; Lay Teachers 13; Students 192; Clergy / Religious Teachers 1.
Catechesis Religious Program—

64—ST. ROBERT BELLARMINE (1927)
3801 Francis Xavier Way, 45207-2211. Web: www.bellarminechapel.org. Rev. Tom Lawler; Liz Keuffer, Business Mgr.; Sue Antoinette, Youth Min., Tel: 513-745-4224; Karen Brandstetter, Pastoral Assoc., Tel: 513-745-3349; Jane Myers, D.R.E.; Brendan Hemmerle, Music Min.; Tim Severyn, Dir., Social Mission; Kathy Kohl, Dir., Marriage Min.
Xavier University: 3800 Victory Pkwy., 45207-2211.
Tel: 513-745-3398; Fax: 513-745-2031; Email: bellarminechapel@xavier.edu.
Catechesis Religious Program—Tel: 513-745-3317. Students 182.

65—ST. ROSE OF LIMA (1867)
2501 Riverside Dr., 45202. Tel: 513-871-1162; Email: rrbarone@fuse.net. Rev. Barry Windholtz.
Catechesis Religious Program—Students 40.

66—SACRED HEART (1870) (Italian) Very Rev. Jon-Paul Bevak; Rev. Adrian J. Hilton, Parochial Vicar.
Res.: 2733 Massachusetts Ave., 45225.
Tel: 513-541-4654; Email: secretary@sacredheartcincinnati.com; Web: www.sacredheartcincinnati.com.
1870 .
See Corryville Catholic Elementary School, Cincinnati under Consolidated Elementary Schools located in the Institution section.

67—ST. SAVIOUR (Deer Park) (1947) Revs. Timothy S. Bunch; Ryan Ruiz, S.L.D.; Deacon Jerome Cain. Parish Region with St. John the Evangelist, Deer Park
Res.: 4136 Myrtle Ave., 45236. Tel: 513-791-9004; Email: stsaviour@stsaviourparish.org; Web: www.stsaviourparish.org.
Catechesis Religious Program—Tel: 513-791-0119. Students 120.

68—ST. SIMON THE APOSTLE (1966)
Email: stsimon@fuse.net. Rev. Richard E. Dressman.
Res.: 825 Pontius Rd., 45233. Tel: 513-941-3656; Email: tgates@stsimonparish.org.
Catechesis Religious Program—Email: mbschumacher@fuse.net. Mary Beth Schumacher, D.R.E. Students 160.

69—ST. STEPHEN (1867)
3804 Eastern Ave., 45226. Tel: 513-871-3373; Email: parish@saintstephen.church; Web: www.saintstephen.church. 320 Donham Ave., 45226. Revs. Edward P. Smith, M.A., Canonical Pastor, Web: www.saintstephen.church; Benjamin Asibvo Kusi, In Res.; J. Thomas Fitzsimmons, In Res., (Retired); Beth Worland, Pastoral Admin.
Catechesis Religious Program—3806 Eastern Ave., 45226. Email: parish@saintstephenchurch.church. Students 13.

70—ST. TERESA OF AVILA (1916) Revs. Michael L. Bidwell; John Amankwah, (Ghana); Deacon David P. Steinwert; Mrs. Maria Williams, Dir., Pastoral Svcs. & D.R.E.
Res.: 1175 Overlook Ave., 45238. Tel: 513-921-9200; Email: office@stteresa-avila.org; Web: www.stteresa-avila.org. Priests 1.
School—St. Teresa of Avila School, (Grades K-8), 1194 Rulison Ave., 45238. Tel: 513-471-4530;
Fax: 513-471-1254; Email: willmes_s@stteresa.net; Web: www.stteresa.net. Mrs. Sharon Willmes, Prin.; Mrs. Chris Artmayer, Librarian. Lay Teachers 17; Students 220.
Catechesis Religious Program—
Tel: 513-921-9200, Ext. 117;
Tel: 513-921-9200, Ext. 105; Email: mwilliams@stteresa-avila.org; Email: dwurzelbacher@stteresa-avila.org. Mr. Donald Wurzelbacher, RCIA Coord. Students 31.

71—ST. THERESE LITTLE FLOWER Little Flower (Mt. Airy) (1926) Rev. Patrick M. McMullen, Parochial Admin.; Joyce Murray-Gerdes, Dir. of Faith Formation; Rebecca Wells, Dir. of Music; Michael Desmier, Business Admin.
Res.: 5560 Kirby Ave., 45239. Tel: 513-541-5560; Fax: 513-681-2631; Email: parishoffice@littleflower-church.org; Web: www.littleflower-church.org.
See Our Lady of Grace, Cincinnati under Consolidated Elementary Schools located in the Institution section.

72—ST. VINCENT DE PAUL (1861) Rev. Donald R. Rettig.
Res.: 4026 River Rd., 45204. Tel: 513-451-5714; Email: svdpcin@hotmail.com.
Catechesis Religious Program—Students 3.

73—ST. VINCENT FERRER (Kenwood) (1946)
7754 Montgomery Rd., 45236. Tel: 513-791-9030; Email: parishoffice@svfchurch.org; Web: www.svfchurch.org. Revs. J. Dennis Jaspers; Jerome R. Bishop, Parochial Vicar.
School—St. Vincent Ferrer School, (Grades K-8),
Tel: 513-791-6320; Email: roy_k@svf-school.org; Web: www.svf-school.org. Kim Roy, Prin. Lay Teachers 14; Students 177.
Catechesis Religious Program—Tel: 513-791-6321. Mr. Brian Caperton Sr., Pastoral Assoc. Students 79.

74—ST. VIVIAN (1943)
7600 Winton Rd., 45224. Tel: 513-728-4331; Email: rectory@stvivian.org; Web: stvivian.org. Rev. Gerard P. Hiland; Deacon Larry Maag; Kathleen Rothschild, Business Mgr.; Sandy Hornbach, Pastoral Assoc.; Amy Staubach, Youth Min.; Julie Borgerding, Music Min.
School—St. Vivian School, (Grades PreK-8), 885 Denier Pl., 45224. Tel: 513-522-6858;
Fax: 513-728-4336; Email: jane.brack@stvivian.org; Web: mystvivian.org. Jane Brack, Prin.; Cathy Bennett, Librarian; Kathleen Rothschild, Business Mgr. Lay Teachers 18; Students 240.
Catechesis Religious Program—Tel: 513-728-4339; Email: julie.zinser@stvivian.org. Julie Zinser, D.R.E. Students 18.

75—ST. WILLIAM (1909) Revs. Michael L. Bidwell; John Amankwah, (Ghana); Deacons George Bruce; Thomas Faeth.
Res.: 4108 W. Eighth St., 45205. Tel: 513-921-0247; Email: info@saintwilliam.com; Web: www.saintwilliam.com.
School—St. William School, (Grades K-8), 4125 St. William Ave., 45205. Tel: 513-471-2989;
Fax: 513-471-8226; Email: jzeiser@saintwilliam.com; Email: aschaefer@saintwilliam.com; Email: ssitzler@saintwilliam.com; Email: info@saintwilliam.com; Web: www.saintwilliam.com. Mr. Jarrod Zeiser, Prin.; Erin Rowland, Counselor; Mrs. Maria Schoeppner, Special Ed Coord. Lay Teachers 30; Students 236.

OUTSIDE THE CITY OF CINCINNATI

AMELIA, CLERMONT CO., ST. BERNADETTE (1944)
1479 Locust Lake Rd., Amelia, 45102-1798.
Tel: 513-753-5566; Email: tralston@stbameliaparish.org; Web: www.stbameliaparish.org. Rev. Timothy W. Ralston.
School—St. Bernadette School, (Grades K-8), 1453 Locust Lake Rd., Amelia, 45102-1703.
Tel: 513-753-4744; Fax: 513-753-9018; Email: lingram@stbernadetteamelia.org; Email: jell@stbernadetteamelia.org; Web: www.stbameliaschool.org. Mrs. Lizann Ingram, Prin. Clergy 1; Lay Teachers 18; Students 219.
Catechesis Religious Program—Email: azurlinden@stbameliaparish.org. Amy Zurlinden, Dir. of Faith Formation. Students 17.

ARNHEIM, BROWN CO., ST. MARY (1837) [CEM] Rev. Dohrman W. Byers; Deacon Ronald S. Dvorachek; Marilyn Fryer, Pastoral Assoc.
Res.: 6647 Van Buren St., Georgetown, 45121.
Tel: 937-446-2555; Email: stmaryarnheim@hughes.net.
Catechesis Religious Program—Tel: 937-446-1854; Email: lindamulvaney@frontier.com. Linda Mulvaney, D.R.E. Students 45.

BATAVIA, CLERMONT CO., HOLY TRINITY (1906)
140 N. 6th St., Batavia, 45103. Tel: 513-732-2024; Email: mbachman@cccatholics.org; Web: stlparish.org. Revs. Martin E. Bachman; J. Robert Jack, M.A., Parochial Vicar.
Catechesis Religious Program—Tel: 513-732-2218. Students 13.

BEAVERCREEK, GREENE CO., ST. LUKE (1955)
Mailing Address: 1440 N. Fairfield Rd., Beavercreek, 45432. Tel: 937-426-1733; Fax: 937-912-9952; Email: saintluke@saintlukeparish.org; Web: www.saintlukeparish.org. Rev. Terrance L. Schneider; Deacons Gerald M. Dupree; William K. LeCain; Richard D. Simpson.
School—St. Luke School, (Grades K-8), 1440 N. Fairfield Rd., Beavercreek, 45432. Tel: 937-426-8551 ; Fax: 937-426-6435; Email: sutton@saintlukeparishschool.org; Web: www.saintlukeparishschool.org. Mrs. Leslie Vondrell, Prin.; Jeannique Phillips, Librarian. Lay Teachers 23; Students 348.
Catechesis Religious Program—Fax: 937-912-9959; Email: CBarhorst@saintlukeparish.org. Students 177.

BELLEFONTAINE, LOGAN CO., ST. PATRICK (1852) [CEM]
Mailing Address: 316 E. Patterson Ave., Bellefontaine, 43311. Tel: 937-592-1656;
Fax: 937-592-0971; Email: catholicbellefontaine@gmail.com; Web: www.catholicbellefontaine.org. Rev. Shawn R. Landenwitch; Deacons Robert A. Crook; Harold Dipple.
Res.: 328 E. Patterson Ave., Bellefontaine, 43311. Students 96.
Church: 320 E. Patterson Ave., Bellefontaine, 43311.
Catechesis Religious Program—Email: ashleyroberts.dre@gmail.com. Ashley F. Roberts, D.R.E. Students 120.

BETHEL, CLERMONT CO., ST. MARY (1941)
3398 S.R. 125, Bethel, 45106. Tel: 513-734-4041; Email: sccr.parish@outlook.com; Web: ccc.city. Rev. James Reutter; Deacon Jerry Etienne.

BOTKINS, SHELBY CO., IMMACULATE CONCEPTION (1865) [CEM] (German)
P.O. Box 519, Botkins, 45306. Revs. Sean M. Wilson; Jarred L. Kohn, Parochial Vicar; Deacon Terrell Coleman.
Res.: 116 N. Mill St., Botkins, 45306.
Tel: 937-693-2561; Tel: 937-693-3535; Email: iccstlc@bright.net; Web: www.slicchurches.org.
Church: N. Main & Walnut Sts., Botkins, 45306.
Catechesis Religious Program—Tel: 937-693-3535; Email: ccdoffice@embarqmail.com; Email: lisafullenkamp@hotmail.com. Beth Klopfenstein, D.R.E.; Lisa Fullenkamp, RCIA Coord. Students 305.

BRADFORD, MIAMI CO., IMMACULATE CONCEPTION (1875) [JC]
200 Clay St., Bradford, 45308. Revs. James L. Simons; James S. Duell.
Res.: 14 E. Wood St., Versailles, 45380.
Tel: 937-526-4945; Email: jsimons@bfvcatholic.org.
Church & Mailing Address: 200 Clay St., Bradford, 45308. Tel: 937-448-6220.
Catechesis Religious Program—

BURKETTSVILLE, MERCER CO., ST. BERNARD (1874) (St. Henry Cluster)
Mailing Address: 272 E. Main St., Box 350, St. Henry, 45883. Revs. William O'Donnell, C.PP.S., (Retired); Jim Smith, C.PP.S., Parochial Vicar; Bro. Nicholas Renner, C.PP.S; Deacons Randy Balster; Jerry Buschur.

Church: 71 W. Main St., Burkettsville, 45310.
Tel: 419-678-4118; Email: shclusteroffice@hotmail.com; Web: www.sthenrycluster.com.
St. Henry Catechetical Center—Tel: 419-678-3811. See St. Henry, St. Henry for details.
Catechesis Religious Program—Students 136.

CAMDEN, PREBLE CO., ST. MARY (1942) Rev. Matthew Amoako-Attah, C.S.Sp.
Res.: 407 E. Main St., Eaton, 45320.
Tel: 937-456-3380.
Church & Mailing Address: 7721 N. Main St., P.O. Box 28, Camden, 45311. Tel: 937-452-3352; Email: jerrygrbr@aol.com.

CARTHAGENA, MERCER CO., ST. ALOYSIUS (1865) [CEM] (German) (St. Henry Cluster)
Mailing Address: P.O. Box 350, St. Henry, 45883-0350. Tel: 419-678-4118; Email: shclusteroffice@hotmail.com; Web: www.sthenrycluster.com. Revs. William O'Donnell, C.PP.S., (Retired); James Smith, C.P.P.S., Parochial Vicar; Bro. Nicholas Renner, C.PP.S; Deacon Randy Balster.
Res.: 1509 Cranberry Rd., St. Henry, 45883.
Tel: 419-925-4776; Fax: 419-678-8285; Email: tomhemm@hotmail.com.
Church: 6036 State Rte. 274, Carthagena, 45822.
St. Henry Catechetical Center—For details call Tel: 419-678-3811.
Catechesis Religious Program—Catherine Wenning, D.R.E. Students 22.

CASSELLA, MERCER CO., NATIVITY OF THE BLESSED VIRGIN MARY (1847) [CEM] (Marion Catholic Community)
6524 State Rte. 119, Maria Stein, 45860.
Tel: 419-925-4775; Email: marioncathcom@gmail.com; Web: marioncatholiccommunity.org. 7428 State Rte. 119, Maria Stein, 45860. Revs. Thomas Brenberger, C.PP.S.; Eugene H. Schnipke, C.PP.S.; Sharon Kremer, Parish Life Coord.; Sue Fortkamp, Business Mgr.
Catechesis Religious Program—Email: katiedippold@hotmail.com. Katie Dippold, C.R.E. Students 239.

CELINA, MERCER CO., IMMACULATE CONCEPTION OF THE BLESSED VIRGIN MARY (1864) [CEM] (German)
Email: kschnipke@celina-ic.org. Revs. Ken Schnipke, C.PP.S.; Vincent P. Wirtner III, C.PP.S., Parochial Vicar.
Res.: 229 W. Anthony St., Celina, 45822-1608.
Tel: 419-586-6648; Fax: 419-586-6649; Email: info@celina-ic.org; Web: celina-ic.org.
School—Immaculate Conception of the Blessed Virgin Mary School, (Grades PreK-6), 200 W. Wayne St., Celina, 45822-1469. Tel: 419-586-2379; Fax: 419-586-6649; Email: polly.muhlenkamp@icschool-celina.org; Web: icschool-celina.org. Mrs. Pauline Muhlenkamp, Prin. Lay Teachers 13; Students 172.
Catechesis Religious Program—Wayne & Walnut Sts., Celina, 45822. Tel: 419-586-2379; Email: jjohnson@celina-ic.org. Joyce Johnson, C.R.E.; Gary Locke, Youth Min. Students 221.

CENTERVILLE, MONTGOMERY CO.

1—ST. FRANCIS OF ASSISI (1969) Rev. Brian W. Phelps; Deacon Chris Rauch, Business Mgr.; Ms. Jeanne Sheppard, Sec.; Mary Ellen Singer, D.R.E.
Res.: 6245 Wilmington Pike, Centerville, 45459.
Tel: 937-433-1013; Email: bulletin@sfacc.org; Web: www.sfacc.org.

2—INCARNATION (1945) Revs. Patrick L. Sloneker; Andrew J. Smith, Parochial Vicar; Deacons Roger E. Duffy; Robert Zinck; Marilyn Porcino, Pastoral Assoc.; Stacy Stang, Pastoral Assoc.; Kevin Samblanet, Music Min.; Daniel Dunn, Youth Min.
Res.: 55 Williamsburg Ln., Centerville, 45459.
Tel: 937-433-1188; Fax: 937-433-3263; Web: www.incarnation-parish.com.
School—Incarnation School, (Grades PreK-8), 45 Williamsburg Ln., Centerville, 45459.
Tel: 937-433-1051; Fax: 937-433-9796; Email: info@incarnation-school.com; Web: www.incarnation-school.com. Cheryl Reichel, Prin. Lay Teachers 54; Students 915.
Catechesis Religious Program—Tel: 937-433-3377. Paula Weckesser, C.R.E.; Daniel Dunn, Youth & Young Adult Ministry. Students 885.

CHICKASAW, MERCER CO., MOST PRECIOUS BLOOD (1903) [CEM] (German) (Marion Catholic Community)
35 S. Maple St., Chickasaw, 45826. Revs. Eugene H. Schnipke, C.PP.S.; Thomas Brenberger, C.PP.S.; Deacon Clifton Perryman; Sharon Kremer, Parish Life Coord.; Sue Roeckner, Business Mgr.
Office: Marion Catholic Community Office, 7428 State Rte. 119, Maria Stein, 45860.
Tel: 419-925-4775; Email: marioncathcom@gmail.com.
Res.: 8533 State Rte. 119, Maria Stein, 45860.
Tel: 419-925-4522.
Church: 35 S. Maple St., Box 26, Chickasaw, 45826-0026.
Catechesis Religious Program—Missy Moeller, C.R.E. Students 122.

COLDWATER, MERCER CO., HOLY TRINITY (1867) [CEM] (Coldwater Cluster)
Mailing Address: 120 E. Main St., P.O. Box 107, Coldwater, 45828. Tel: 419-678-4802; Email: kphares@coldwatercluster.org; Web: www.coldwatercluster.org. Revs. Richard W. Walling; Alexander T. Witt, Parochial Vicar.
Res.: 116 E. Main St., P.O. Box 107, Coldwater, 45828.
Catechesis Religious Program—Email: cbettinger@coldwatercluster.org. Charmaine Bettinger, D.R.E. Students 850.

COVINGTON, MIAMI CO., ST. TERESA OF THE INFANT JESUS (1950) [JC] (German—French) Rev. James S. Duell.
Res.: 6925 W. U.S. Route 36, Covington, 45318.
Tel: 937-473-2970; Email: stteresacovington@yahoo.com; Web: www.stteresacovington.org.
Catechesis Religious Program—Mrs. Michelle Kuether, C.R.E. Students 38.

CRANBERRY PRAIRIE, MERCER CO., ST. FRANCIS (1858) [CEM] (German) (St. Henry Cluster)
P.O. Box 350, St. Henry, 45883. Revs. William O'Donnell, C.PP.S., (Retired); James Smith, C.P.P.S., Parochial Vicar; Bro. Nicholas Renner, C.PP.S; Deacon Randy Balster.
Church & Res.: 1509 Cranberry Rd., St. Henry, 45883. Tel: 419-678-4118; Email: shclusteroffice@hotmail.com; Web: www.sthenrycluster.com.
St. Henry Catechetical Center—Catherine Wenning, D.R.E. See St. Henry, St. Henry for details. Tel: 419-678-3811. E-mail: sthenryccd@bright.net Students 56.

DAYTON, GREENE CO., QUEEN OF APOSTLES (1973) Rev. Thomas A. Schroer, S.M.; Deacon Greg Cecere, Pastoral Assoc.
Church: Mount St John, 4435 E. Patterson Rd., Dayton, 45430-1033. Tel: 937-429-0510; Email: qacohio@sbcglobal.net; Web: www.qac-ohio.org.
Catechesis Religious Program—Erica Rudemiller, D.R.E. Students 32.

DAYTON, MONTGOMERY CO.

1—ST. ADALBERT (1903) (Polish)
1212 St Adalbert Ave., Dayton, 45404.
Tel: 937-233-1503; Email: acutcher@olrdayton.com. 6161 Chambersburg Rd., Huber Heights, 45424. Revs. Anthony E. Cutcher; Deepak D'Souza, Parochial Vicar; Ms. Joy Blaul, Pastoral Assoc.

2—ST. ALBERT THE GREAT (1939)
Email: kkowal@stalbertthegreat.net. Revs. Christopher J. Worland; Patrick J. Welsh; Deacon David E. Zink; Tom Hutchinson, Business Mgr.
Res.: 3033 Far Hills Ave., Dayton, 45429.
Tel: 937-293-1191; Fax: 937-293-1848; Email: parish@stalbertthegreat.net; Web: www.stalbertthegreat.net.
School—St. Albert the Great School, (Grades PreK-8), 104 W. Dorothy Ln., Kettering, 45429.
Tel: 937-293-9452; Fax: 937-293-7525; Email: sgabert@stag-school.org; Web: www.stalbertthegreat.net. Sherry Gabert, Prin. Lay Teachers 28; Students 310.
Catechesis Religious Program—Tel: 937-298-2402; Fax: 937-293-8292. Students 245.

3—ST. ANTHONY OF PADUA (1913)
830 Bowen St., Dayton, 45410.
Tel: 937-253-9132, Ext. 104; Email: gkonerman@stanthonydayton.org. Rev. Gregory J. Konerman; Bill Leibold, Dir. Admin.
School—St. Anthony of Padua School, (Grades K-8), 1824 St. Charles Ave., Dayton, 45410.
Tel: 937-253-6251; Fax: 937-253-1541; Email: acampion@stanthonydayton.org; Web: school.stanthonydayton.org. Ms. Alana Campion, Prin. Administrators 1; Faculty 3; Lay Teachers 11; Students 196.
Catechesis Religious Program—

4—ASCENSION (1955)
2025 Woodman Dr., Kettering, 45420.
Tel: 937-253-5171; Tel: 937-254-5411;
Tel: 937-254-0622; Email: epratt@ascensionkettering.org; Web: www.ascensionkettering.org. Rev. Edward T. Pratt; Deacon Victor B. Hildebrand, Pastoral Assoc.; Cathy Magness, Pastoral Assoc.; Christy Shanklin, Business Mgr.; Joseph Ollier, Parish Life Dir.; Jeanne Fairbanks, Youth Min.
School—Ascension School, (Grades K-8), 2001 Woodman Dr., Kettering, 45420. Tel: 937-254-5411; Fax: 937-254-1150; Email: sdigiorgio@ascensionkettering.org; Web: school.ascensionkettering.org. Susan Digiorgio, Prin.; Matthew Himes, Librarian. Lay Teachers 23; Students 310.
Catechesis Religious Program—2001 Woodman Dr, Kettering, 45420. Email: sgraham@ascensionkettering.org; Email: jfairbanks@ascensionkettering.org. Sue Graham, C.R.E.; Jeanne Fairbanks, Coord. Youth Min. Students 269.

5—ST. BENEDICT THE MOOR (2005) (African American) Rev. Francis Tandoh, C.S.Sp.; Janice Kwofie, Administrative Dir.
Rectory—130 Gramont Ave., Dayton, 45417.
Tel: 937-228-6123.
Office: 519 Liscum Dr., Dayton, 45417.
Tel: 937-268-6697; Email: sajares@yahoo.com; Email: janice1us@aol.com.
School—St. Benedict the Moor School, 138 Gramont Ave., Dayton, 45417. Tel: 937-268-6391;
Fax: 937-268-9775; Email: janice1us@aol.com. Marianne Pitts, Prin. Clergy 2; Lay Teachers 12; Students 133.
Catechesis Religious Program—Students 20.

6—ST. CHARLES BORROMEO (Kettering) (1962) Revs. Daniel J. Meyer; Timothy Fahey, Parochial Vicar; Deacon Thomas H. Miller; Christian Cosas, Music Min.; Chris Kreger, Pastoral Associate; Mr. Steve Morris, Business Mgr.; Tim Clarke, D.R.E.; Erin Fanning, Sacramental Min.; Heather Dunn, Youth Min.
Church: 4500 Ackerman Blvd., Kettering, 45429.
Tel: 937-434-6081; Email: business@stcharleskettering.org; Web: www.stcharles-kettering.org.
School—St. Charles Borromeo School, (Grades PreK-8), 4600 Ackerman Blvd., Dayton, 45429.
Tel: 937-434-4933; Fax: 937-434-6692; Email: office@stcharleskettering.org; Web: stcharleskettering.org/school. David Bogle, Prin.; Margaret Brown, Librarian; Nancy Cochran, Contact Person. Administrators 1; Aides 4; Lay Teachers 30; Students 486.
Catechesis Religious Program—Tel: 937-434-9272. Tim Clarke, Dir. Faith Formation. Students 169.

7—EMMANUEL (1837) Revs. Angelo Anthony, C.PP.S.; Matthew Keller; Michelle Carner, Liturgy & Music Dir.
Res.: 149 Franklin St., Dayton, 45402.
Tel: 937-228-2013; Email: parishoffice@emmanuelcatholic.com; Web: www.emmanuelcatholic.com.
Catechesis Religious Program—Email: brothermatt@emmanuelcatholic.com. Bro. Matt Schaefer, D.R.E. Students 81.

8—ST. HELEN (1953)
5000 Burkhardt Dr., Dayton, 45431.
Tel: 937-254-6233; Email: office@sthelenparish.org; Web: www.sthelenparish.org. 605 Granville Pl., Dayton, 45431. Rev. Satish Antony Joseph; Deacons John Danner; Susano Mascorro; Ralph O'Bleness; Mary Heider, Pastoral Assoc. Liturgy & Stewardship; Seanb Kelly, Pastoral Assoc.; Mel McWilliams, Pastoral Assoc.
School—St. Helen School, (Grades PreK-8), 5086 Burkhardt Rd., Dayton, 45431. Tel: 937-256-1761;
Fax: 937-254-4614; Email: cbuschur@sthelenschl.org; Web: www.sthelenschl.org. Christine Buschur, Prin. Lay Teachers 25; Students 423.
Catechesis Religious Program—Tel: 937-256-8815; Email: amy.mcentee@sthelenparish.org. Amy McEntee, Pastoral Assoc. Youth Evangelization. Students 71.

9—ST. HENRY (1960)
Mailing Address & Church: 6696 Springboro Rd., Dayton, 45449. Tel: 937-434-9231;
Fax: 937-434-6798; Email: akunka@sthenryparish.com; Web: www.sthenryparish.com. Revs. Thomas M. Shearer; Ronald Combs; James S. Romanello; Deacon Michael Mahoney; Mary Ehret, Pastoral Assoc.
Res.: 6340 Blossom Park Dr., West Carrollton, 45449-3021. Email: shearer@sthenryparish.com.
See Bishop Leibold School, Dayton under Consolidated Elementary Schools located in the Institution section.
Catechesis Religious Program—Students 234.

10—HOLY ANGELS (1901)
1322 Brown St., Dayton, 45409. Tel: 937-229-5911; Email: kdoran@holyangelsdayton.org; Web: hasadayton.org. Rev. Gregory J. Konerman; John Klobuka, Parochial Vicar.
Church: 211 L St., Dayton, 45409.
School—Holy Angels School, (Grades PreK-8), 223 L St., Dayton, 45409. Tel: 937-229-5959;
Fax: 937-229-5960; Email: bbauer@holyangels.cc. Jacob LaForge, Prin. Clergy 1; Lay Teachers 23; Students 306.
Catechesis Religious Program—Tel: 937-229-5909; Email: schristy@holyangelsdayton.org. Students 284.

11—HOLY CROSS (1914) (Lithuanian)
1924 Leo St., Dayton, 45404. Tel: 937-233-1503; Email: jbarbour@saintpeterparish.org. 6161 Chambersburg Rd., Huber Heights, 45424. Revs. Anthony E. Cutcher; Deepak D'Souza, Parochial Vicar; Ms. Joy Blaul, Pastoral Assoc.

12—HOLY FAMILY (1905)
Mailing Address: 140 S. Findlay, Dayton, 45403.
Tel: 937-938-6098; Email: pastor@daytonlatinmass.

org; Web: www.daytonlatinmass.org. Rev. George Gabet, F.S.S.P.
Catechesis Religious Program—Please call office for information.

13—HOLY TRINITY (1860) [JC] Revs. Angelo Anthony, C.PP.S.; Matthew Keller; Deacon Michael Leo; Ms. Lynda Middleton, Pastoral Assoc.; Shaughn Phillips, Youth Min.; Judith L. Trick, Business Mgr.
Parish Office: 272 Bainbridge St., Dayton, 45402.
Tel: 937-228-1223; Web: ht_busmgr@sbcglobal.net.

14—ST. JOSEPH (1847) Revs. Angelo Anthony, C.PP.S.; Matthew Keller, Pastoral Assoc.
Res.: 411 E. Second St., Dayton, 45402.
Tel: 937-228-9272; Email: stjosephday@sbcglobal.net.

15—ST. MARY (1859)
310 Allen St., Dayton, 45410-1818. Tel: 937-256-5633 ; Email: stmaryparish@stmarydayton.org; Web: www.stmarydayton.org. Revs. Francis Tandoh, C.S. Sp.; Ariel Rico Rincon, Chap.

16—OUR LADY OF GRACE (2014) Rev. Joshua Otusafo, C.S.Sp.; Deacon Skip Royer.
Office, Res. & Mailing Address: 220 W. Siebenthaler Ave., Dayton, 45405. Tel: 937-274-2107;
Fax: 937-274-4363; Email: info@ourladyofgracedayton.org; Web: www.ourladyofgracedayton.org.
Catechesis Religious Program—Students 12; Staff 1.
Worship Sites:—
Corpus Christi Church—527 Forest Ave., Dayton, 45405.
Our Lady of Mercy Church, 533 Odlin Ave., Dayton, 45405.

17—OUR LADY OF THE IMMACULATE CONCEPTION (1938) Rev. Satish Antony Joseph; Deacons Ralph Gutman; Michael Montgomery, O.F.M.
Res.: 2300 S. Smithville Rd., Dayton, 45420.
Tel: 937-252-9919; Email: cindyreaster@icparishdayton.org; Web: www.icparishdayton.org.
School—Our Lady of the Immaculate Conception School, (Grades PreK-8), 2268 S. Smithville Rd., Dayton, 45420. Tel: 937-253-8831; Email: jwalling@icsdayton.org; Web: www.icsdayton.org. Mr. Daniel Stringer, Prin. Lay Teachers 13; Students 232.
Catechesis Religious Program—Email: willmarsh@icparishdayton.org. Will Marsh, D.R.E.

18—OUR LADY OF THE ROSARY (1887)
22 Notre Dame Ave., Dayton, 45404.
Tel: 937-228-8802; Email: jbarbour@saintpeterparish.org; Web: daytonxii.org. 6161 Chambersburg Rd., Huber Heights, 45424. Revs. Anthony E. Cutcher; Deepak D'Souza, Parochial Vicar; Ms. Joy Blaul, Pastoral Assoc.
School—Our Lady of the Rosary School, (Grades K-8), 40 Notre Dame Ave., Dayton, 45404.
Tel: 937-222-7231; Fax: 937-222-7393; Email: school@olrdayton.com. Jacki Loffer, Prin. Lay Teachers 15; Students 191; Clergy / Religious Teachers 1.

19—ST. PETER (Huber Heights) (1959)
6161 Chambersburg Rd., Huber Heights, 45424.
Tel: 937-233-1503; Email: jbarbour@saintpeterparish.org; Web: daytonxii.org. Revs. Anthony E. Cutcher; Deepak D'Souza, Parochial Vicar; Ethan M. Moore, In Res.; Joseph Kindel, In Res.; Deacons Leo N. Cordonnier; Robert W. Gutendorf; Robert Kozlowski; David M. McCray; Daniel J. Wade; Ms. Joy Blaul, Pastoral Associate; Mr. Darren Backstrom, Business Mgr.
School—St. Peter School, (Grades PreK-8), 6185 Chambersburg Rd., Huber Heights.
Tel: 937-233-8710; Email: kmoorman@saintpeterparish.org; Web: daytonxii.org/saint-peter-school. Mr. Ron Albino, Prin.; Kellie Jobe, Business Mgr.; Mrs. Kathy Moorman, School Sec. Lay Teachers 43; Students 604.
Catechesis Religious Program—Tel: 937-237-3516;
Fax: 937-233-5717; Email: jrobbins@saintpeterparish.org. Ms. Joy Blaul, Pastoral Assoc.; Jackie Robbins, C.R.E. Students 130.

20—PRECIOUS BLOOD (1948)
Mailing Address: 4961 Salem Ave., Dayton, 45416.
Tel: 937-276-5954; Fax: 937-276-5955; Email: jhurr@preciousbloodchurch.org; Web: www.northwestdaytoncatholic.org. Revs. James C. Seibert, C.PP.S.; Timothy Knepper, C.PP.S, Parochial Vicar; Deacons Michael F. Prier; Andrew R. Rammel; Dale DeBrosse, D.R.E.; Debbie DeBrosse, D.R.E.; Curtis Kneblik, D.R.E.; Narisa Lao, Liturgy Dir.; Shane Legg, Youth Min.; Joseph Hurr, Business Mgr.
Res.: 1000 W. Wenger Rd., Englewood, 45322.
Tel: 937-836-7535; Fax: 937-836-1130.
School—Mother Maria Anna Brunner School, (Grades PreK-8), 4870 Denlinger Rd., Dayton, 45426.
Tel: 937-277-2291; Fax: 937-277-2217; Email: rjohnson@brunnercatholicschool.org; Web: www.brunnercatholicschool.org. Robin Johnson, Prin. Lay Teachers 15; Students 219.

21—QUEEN OF MARTYRS (Northridge) (1948)
4134 Cedar Ridge Rd., Dayton, 45414.
Tel: 937-277-2092; Email: awagner@qmdayton.org; Web: www.qmdayton.org. Rev. Joshua Otusafo, C.S. Sp., Parochial Admin.; Deacon Skip Royer.

22—ST. RITA (1922) Revs. James C. Seibert, C.PP.S.; Timothy Knepper, C.PP.S, Parochial Vicar; Deacon James C. Olinger; Matt Ruttle, Pastoral Assoc.; Joseph Hurr, Business Mgr.; Narisa Lao, Liturgy Dir.
Res.: 5401 N. Main St., Dayton, 45415.
Tel: 937-278-5815; Email: dhamby@stritadayton.org; Web: northwestdaytoncatholic.org.
School—Mother Maria Anna Brunner School, (Grades K-8), 4870 Denlinger Rd., Dayton, 45426.
Tel: 937-277-2291; Fax: 937-277-2217; Email: rjohnson@brunnercatholicschool.org; Web: www.brunnercatholicschool.org. Robin Johnson, Prin. Clergy 5; Lay Teachers 14; Students 212.
Catechesis Religious Program—Curtis Kneblic, D.R.E. Students 1.

EATON, PREBLE CO., VISITATION OF THE BLESSED VIRGIN MARY (1853) Rev. Matthew Amoako-Attah, C.S.Sp.
Res.: 407 E. Main St., Eaton, 45320.
Tel: 937-456-3380; Email: church@visitationstjohn.com.
Catechesis Religious Program—Tel: 937-456-3395. Sharon Stump, D.R.E.; Renee Piekutowski, Youth Min. Students 92.

ENGLEWOOD, MONTGOMERY CO., ST. PAUL (1972)
1000 W. Wenger Rd., Englewood, 45322.
Tel: 937-836-7535; Email: office@stpaulenglewood.org. Revs. James C. Seibert, C.PP.S.; Timothy Knepper, C.PP.S, Parochial Vicar; Deacons Joseph Subler; Dale DeBrosse, D.R.E.; Debbie DeBrosse, D.R.E.; Curtis Kneblik, D.R.E.; Narisa Lao, Liturgy Dir.; Shane Legg, Youth Mini.

FAIRBORN, GREENE CO., MARY HELP OF CHRISTIANS (1862) [CEM]
954 N. Maple Ave., Fairborn, 45324-5498.
Tel: 937-878-8353; Fax: 937-879-8800; Email: jsewellmhc@gmail.com; Web: www.mhcparish.com. Rev. Thomas A. Nevels; Deacon Max Roadruck.
Catechesis Religious Program—Tel: 937-878-7325; Email: mollymhc@gmail.com. Molly Hynes Collinsworth, D.R.E. Students 136.

FAIRFIELD, BUTLER CO., SACRED HEART OF JESUS (1957) Rev. Larry R. Tharp.
Church: 400 Nilles Rd., Fairfield, 45014.
Tel: 513-858-4210; Fax: 513-858-4211; Email: frtharp@sacredheart-fairfield.org; Web: www.sacredheart-fairfield.org.
Res.: 5202 Mississippi Dr., Fairfield, 45014.
Tel: 513-863-5318; Fax: 513-863-5318.
School—Sacred Heart of Jesus School, (Grades K-8), Tel: 513-858-4215; Email: jstclair@shjs.org; Web: www.shjs.org. Joseph Nagle, Prin. Clergy 1; Lay Teachers 25; Students 450.
Catechesis Religious Program—Tel: 513-858-4213; Email: bmiller@sacredheart-fairfield.org. Bryan Miller, D.R.E. Students 105.

FAYETTEVILLE, BROWN CO., ST. ANGELA MERICI (2003)
130 Stone Alley, P.O. Box 279, Fayetteville, 45118.
Tel: 513-875-5020; Fax: 513-875-5022; Email: stangelamericiparish@cinci.rr.com. Rev. Thomas L. Bolte.
Catechesis Religious Program—Students 128.
Chapels—St. Patrick Chapel—Fayetteville, 45118.
St. Martin Chapel, Fayetteville, 45118.

FORT LORAMIE, SHELBY CO., ST. MICHAEL (1838) [CEM] [JC3] Rev. Steven L. Shoup; Deacon Paul L. Timmerman; Ann Bollheimer, Pastoral Assoc.; Rose Meyer, Pastoral Assoc.; Kevin Schulze, Youth Min.; Mrs. Amy Noykos, Liturgy Dir.
Res.: 33 Elm St., P.O. Box 7, Fort Loramie, 45845.
Tel: 937-295-2891; Email: steves@nflregion.org; Web: www.nflregion.org.
Catechesis Religious Program—Tel: 937-295-2179; Fax: 937-295-3349. Deb Ranly, D.R.E.; Kate Boeke, D.R.E. Students 621.

FORT RECOVERY, MERCER CO., MARY HELP OF CHRISTIANS (1881) [CEM] (Fort Recovery Cluster)
Mailing Address: 403 Sharpsburg Rd., Fort Recovery, 45846. Tel: 419-375-4153; Email: mhc@fortrecoverycatholics.org; Web: www.fortrecoverycatholics.org. Revs. Ned J. Brown; Matthew S. Feist.
Catechesis Religious Program—Tel: 419-375-4153; Fax: 419-375-4154. Students 288.

FRANKLIN, WARREN CO., ST. MARY OF THE ASSUMPTION (1867)
9579 Yankee Rd., Springboro, 45066.
Tel: 937-557-1711; Email: cathyw@stmaryassumption.church; Web: www.stmaryassumption.church. Rev. James J. Manning; Deacons Thomas F. Platfoot; Richard Hobbs; Stephen Bermick III; Ms. Jan Donihoo, Business Mgr.; Mr. Mike Hoendorf, Youth MIn.; Mr. John Wright, Liturgy Dir.; Mrs. Cathy Waag, Sec.; Mr. Dave Bush, Facilitates Mgr.
Email: info@stmaryassumption.church.
Catechesis Religious Program—
Tel: 937-557-1711, Ext. 102. Mr. Chris Stier, D.R.E. Students 275.

FRENCHTOWN, DARKE CO., HOLY FAMILY (1846) [CEM]
11255 State Rte. 185, Versailles, 45380. Email: lindsey@bfvcatholic.org. Revs. James L. Simons; James S. Duell, Parochial Vicar.
Res.: 14 E. Wood St., Versailles, 45380-1440.
Tel: 937-526-4945; Email: jsimons@bfvcatholic.org.
Catechesis Religious Program—Email: ccd@bfvcatholic.org. Julie Meyer, D.R.E. Students 44.

FRYBURG, AUGLAIZE CO., ST. JOHN (1850) [CEM 2] (German)
11319 Van Buren St., Wapakoneta, 45895-8467.
Tel: 419-738-6043; Tel: 419-738-2115; Email: sjfadm@bright.net; Web: stjohnfryburg.org. 309 Perry St., Wapakoneta, 45895-2118. Revs. Sean M. Wilson; Jarred L. Kohn, Parochial Vicar; Deacon Nicholas Jurosic; Cathy Hengstler, Youth Min.; Denise Sheipline, D.R.E.; Mrs. Louise Westbay, Music Min.

GEORGETOWN, BROWN CO., ST. GEORGE (1902) Rev. Dohrman W. Byers; Deacon Ronald S. Dvorachek; Joan St. Clair, Pastoral Assoc.; Susan Caproni, Business Mgr.
Parish Office & Mailing Address: 16 N. 4th St., Ripley, 45167. Tel: 937-392-1116; Email: stmarymichaelgeorge@outlook.com.
Church: 509 E. State St. & Elm St., Georgetown, 45121.
Catechesis Religious Program—State & Elm Streets, Georgetown, 45121. Tel: 937-378-6453; Email: jstclair.sgchurch1@frontier.com. Joan St. Clair, D.R.E. Students 12.

GERMANTOWN, MONTGOMERY CO., ST. AUGUSTINE (1941) Rev. Francis Tandoh, C.S.Sp.; Deacon Kenneth R. Stewart, RCIA Coord.
Rectory—Rectory & Mailing Address: 6891 Weaver Rd., Germantown, 45237.
Res.: 130 Gramont Ave., Dayton, 45417.
Tel: 937-268-2747; Fax: 937-268-6698; Email: info@unitedinhope.org.
Church: 6939 Weaver Rd., Germantown, 45327-9378. Tel: 937-855-2289; Email: csaintaugustine@woh.rr.com; Web: www.catholicsmart.com.
Catechesis Religious Program—Diane Kessio, D.R.E. Students 26.

GLYNWOOD, AUGLAIZE CO., ST. PATRICK (1857) [CEM] (Irish)
Mailing Address: 511 E. Spring St., St. Marys, 45885. Rev. Barry J. Stechschulte.
Church: 6959 Glynwood Rd., St. Marys, 45885.
Tel: 419-394-5050; Email: busmgr@bright.net.
Catechesis Religious Program—Tel: 419-739-7839; Tel: 419-394-4001. Sara Ott, D.R.E.; Shannon Schwartz, D.R.E. Students 26.

GREENFIELD, HIGHLAND CO., ST. BENIGNUS (1856) [CEM]
Mailing Address: P.O. Box 399, Greenfield, 45123. Rev. Michael A. Paraniuk; Paula Miller, Business Mgr.; Susan Stuckey, RCIA Coord.
Res.: 218 S. Second St., Greenfield, 45123.
Church: 204 S. Second St., Greenfield, 45123.
Tel: 937-981-2785; Email: stbenignus@gmail.com.
Catechesis Religious Program—Susan Stuckey, C.R.E. Students 27.

GREENVILLE, DARKE CO., ST. MARY (1853) [CEM] Rev. John R. White, J.C.L.
Res.: 233 W. 3rd St., Greenville, 45331.
Tel: 937-548-1616; Email: stmjc@bizwoh.rr.com; Web: www.stmarysgreenville.org.
School—St. Mary School, (Grades PreK-8), 238 W. 3rd St., Greenville, 45331. Tel: 937-548-2345;
Fax: 937-548-0878; Email: cdetling@smsgvl.com. Vernon Rosenbeck, Prin. Lay Teachers 9; Students 73.
Catechesis Religious Program—Email: mmassorivetti@smsgvl.com. Monica Masso-Rivetti, D.R.E. Students 103.

HAMILTON, BUTLER CO.

1—ST. ANN (1909) Rev. Larry R. Tharp.
Church & Mailing Address: 646 Clinton Ave., Hamilton, 45015. Tel: 513-863-4963; Email: info@saintanncc.com; Web: www.saintanncc.com.
School—St. Ann School, (Grades PreK-8), 3064 Pleasant Ave., Hamilton, 45015. Tel: 513-863-0604; Email: info@saintannCS.com; Web: www.saintanncs.com. Sarah Bitzer, Prin. Lay Teachers 14; Students 203.
Catechesis Religious Program—Combined with Sacred Heart Church, Fairfield.

2—ST. JOSEPH (1867) (German) Revs. Robert K. Muhlenkamp; James H. Elsbernd, Sacramental Min.
Res. and Mailing Address: 171 Washington St., Hamilton, 45011. Tel: 513-863-1424;
Fax: 513-863-1451; Email: jhaubner@sjcshamilton.org.
School—St. Joseph School, (Grades K-8), 925 Second St., Hamilton, 45011. Tel: 513-863-8758;

Fax: 513-863-5772; Email: tstenger@sjcshamilton.org; Web: www.sjcshamilton.org. J. William Hicks, Prin. Lay Teachers 13; Students 216.

Catechesis Religious Program—Students 2.

3—ST. JULIE BILLIART (1989) [CEM 2] (This parish is the successor in interest to St. Mary, St. Stephen and St. Veronica parishes, formerly located in Hamilton, OH.) Rev. Robert K. Muhlenkamp; Deacon William B. Renneker; Mrs. Betty Meiner, Business Mgr.; Jonathan Alexander, Music Dir.

Church: 224 Dayton St., Hamilton, 45011-1634.

Tel: 513-863-1040; Email: sjbparish@stjulie.net; Web: www.stjulie.net.

Catechesis Religious Program—Email: mpausting@stjulie.net. Mrs. Mary Pat Austing, C.R.E. Students 217.

4—ST. PETER IN CHAINS (1894) (German) Revs. Robert K. Muhlenkamp; Richmond Dzekoe, Vicar; Deacon Jeff Merrell.

Church, Mailing & Office Address: 382 Liberty Ave., Hamilton, 45013. Tel: 513-863-3938; Email: parishoffice@stpeterinchains.org; Web: www.stpeterinchains.org.

School—St. Peter in Chains School, (Grades K-8), 451 Ridgelawn Ave., Hamilton, 45013.

Tel: 513-863-0685; Fax: 513-863-1859; Email: schooloffice@stpeterinchains.org. Michael Collins, Prin. Lay Teachers 16; Students 186.

Catechesis Religious Program—382 Liberty Ave., Hamilton, 45013. Tel: 513-863-1257, Ext. 302. Students 6.

HILLSBORO, HIGHLAND CO., ST. MARY CATHOLIC CHURCH (1853) [CEM]

212 S. High St., Hillsboro, 45133-1445.

Tel: 937-393-1742; Email: stmarycre@cinci.rr.com; Web: www.saintmaryhillsboro.org. Rev. Michael A. Paraniuk; Deacon Leonard Parker, (Retired).

School—St. Mary School, (Grades PreSchool-8), 119 E. Walnut St., Hillsboro, 45133. Tel: 937-840-9932; Email: stmaryprincipal@cinci.rr.com; Web: www.stmaryofhillsboro.com. Ms. Darlene Smith, Prin. Clergy 4; Lay Teachers 4; Students 35.

Catechesis Religious Program—119 E. Walnut St., Hillsboro, 45133. Email: stmarycre@cinci.rr.com. Michelle Vanzant-Salyer, C.R.E. Students 75.

JAMESTOWN, GREENE CO., ST. AUGUSTINE (1870)

P.O. Box 189, Jamestown, 45335. Rev. Andrew P. Cordonnier.

Res.: 265 Purcell Dr., Xenia, 45385. Cell: 937-409-9355.

Church: 44 E. Washington St., Jamestown, 45335. Cell: 937-675-2601; Email: csmith2039@aol.com.

Catechesis Religious Program—Tel: 937-675-2390. Della Weidel, D.R.E. Students 18.

LEBANON, WARREN CO., ST. FRANCIS DE SALES (1883) Revs. Bernard J. Weldishofer; Craig E. Best, Parochial Vicar; Deacon Jay Rettig; Tom Beckman, Business Mgr.; Paula Kern, Music Min.

Parish Office: 20 Desales Ave., Lebanon, 45036.

Tel: 513-932-2601; Email: parishoffice@stfrancisdesales-lebanon.org; Email: mhimes@stfrancisdesales-lebanon.org; Web: stfrancisdesales-lebanon.org.

Rectory: 15 Desales Ave., Lebanon, 45036. Email: pastor@stfrancisdesales-lebanon.org.

School—St. Francis de Sales Parish School,

Tel: 513-932-6501; Email: pmclaughlin@stfrancisdesales-lebanon.org. Mr. Paul McLaughlin, Prin. Lay Teachers 12; Students 185.

Catechesis Religious Program—Email: mkletzly@stfrancisdesales-lebanon.org. Mike Kletzly, D.R.E. Students 244.

LIBERTY TOWNSHIP, BUTLER CO., ST. MAXIMILIAN KOLBE (1989) Revs. James J. Riehle; Simon Peter Wankya, Parochial Vicar; Ron Piepmeyer, (In Res.); Deacons John Paul Back; Michael W. Hinger; Michael E. Lippman.

Church & Mailing: 5720 Hamilton-Mason Rd., Liberty Township, 45011. Tel: 513-777-4322; Email: web@saint-max.org; Web: www.saint-max.org.

Res.: 7168 St. Albans Way, Liberty Twp., 45011.

See St. Gabriel Consolidated School, Cincinnati under Consolidated Elementary Schools located in the Institution section.

Catechesis Religious Program—Email: zhinger@saint-max.org. Zack Hinger, D.R.E. Students 564.

LOVELAND, WARREN CO.

1—ST. COLUMBAN (1859)

894 Oakland Rd., Loveland, 45140.

Tel: 513-683-0105, Ext. 2104; Fax: 513-683-1389; Email: cnagy@stcolumban.org; Web: www.stcolumban.org. Rev. Lawrence R. Tensi; Deacons Michael H. Brock; Thomas Jabs; James Miller; Gerard J. Sasson; Jim Verhoff.

School—St. Columban School, (Grades PreK-8), 896 Oakland Rd., Loveland, 45140. Fax: 513-683-7904; Web: www.saintcolumbanschool.org. Mrs. Jo Rhoten, Prin. Lay Teachers 29; Students 532.

Catechesis Religious Program—(Grades K-8), Email: tkerley@stcolumban.org. Mrs. Terri Kerley, Admin.; Mr. Scott Mussari, D.R.E. Students 444.

2—ST. MARGARET OF YORK (1984)

9499 Columbia Rd., Loveland, 45140-1560.

Tel: 513-697-3100; Email: receptionist@smoy.org; Web: www.smoy.org. Revs. Jason E. Bedel; Maria Raju Pasala, Parochial Vicar; Deacons Paul H. Blessing; Raymond Kroger; Jeffrey M. Perkins; Michael Ott, Dir. Admin. & Finance; Melissa Capella, Youth Min.

Res.: 9483 Columbia Rd., Loveland, 45140-1560.

School—St. Margaret of York School, (Grades K-8), 9495 Columbia Rd., Loveland, 45140-1560.

Tel: 513-697-3100; Email: info@smoyschool.com; Web: www.smoyschool.com. Mrs. Kristin Penley, Prin. Clergy 2; Lay Teachers 33; Students 630.

MARIA STEIN, MERCER CO., ST. JOHN THE BAPTIST (1836) [CEM] (Marion Catholic Community)

7428 State Rte. 119, Maria Stein, 45860. Revs. Eugene H. Schnipke, C.PP.S.; Thomas Brenberger, C.PP.S., Sr. Assoc. Pastor; Deacon Clifton Perryman; Sharon Kremer, Parish Life Coord.

Marion Catholic Community Office: 8533 State Rt. 119, Maria Stein, 45860. Tel: 419-925-4775; Email: marioncathcom@gmail.com.

Res.: 8533 State Rte. 119, Maria Stein, 45860.

Tel: 419-925-4522.

Catechesis Religious Program—Email: wibbenmeyerchris@gmail.com. Chris Wibbenmeyer, D.R.E. Students 262.

MASON, WARREN CO., ST. SUSANNA (1938) Revs. Robert J. Farrell; Eric P. Roush; Deacon Louis F. Wong; Shannon Benvenuti, Business Mgr.

Church: 616 Reading Rd., Mason, 45040.

School—St. Susanna School, (Grades K-8), 500 Reading Rd., Mason, 45040. Tel: 513-398-3821; Fax: 513-398-1657; Email: albrinckd@stsusanna.org. Dan Albrinck, Prin. Clergy 14; Lay Teachers 37; Students 697.

Catechesis Religious Program—Students 932.

MCCARTYVILLE, SHELBY CO., SACRED HEART OF JESUS (1882) Rev. Stephen J. Mondiek; Deacon Paul Luthman.

Res. & Mailing Address: 9377 State Rte. 119 W., Anna, 45302-9520. Tel: 937-394-3823;

Tel: 419-628-2502; Email: office@sacredheartohio.org.

Catechesis Religious Program—Megan Jock, D.R.E. Students 404.

MECHANICSBURG, CHAMPAIGN CO., ST. MICHAEL CHURCH (1865)

40 Walnut St., Mechanicsburg, 43044.

Tel: 937-653-1375; Fax: 937-653-1383; Email: stmarychurchoffice@gmail.com; Web: www.champaigncatholics.org. Mailing Address: c/o St. Mary Church, 231 Washington Ave., Urbana, 43078. Revs. Matthew K. Lee; Ignatius Madanu, Parochial Vicar; Mrs. Amy Brinker, Business Mgr.

Catechesis Religious Program—Students 32.

MIAMISBURG, MONTGOMERY CO., OUR LADY OF GOOD HOPE (1852) [CEM] Revs. Thomas M. Shearer; James S. Romanello; Deacons Richard Martin; Terry Martin.

Res.: 6 S. Third St., Miamisburg, 45342.

Tel: 937-866-1432; Email: info@olghchurch.com.

See Bishop Leibold School, Dayton under Consolidated Elementary Schools located in the Institution section.

Catechesis Religious Program—Email: tstanley@olghchurch.com. Students 115.

MIDDLETOWN, BUTLER CO., HOLY FAMILY (1991) [JC] (This parish is the successor in interest to Holy Trinity, St. John the Baptist and St. Mary parishes, formerly located in Middletown, OH) Rev. John R. Civille; Deacon John T. Lyons.

Office: 201 Clark St., Middletown, 45042.

Tel: 513-422-0602; Email: jciville@holyfamilymiddletown.com; Web: www.holyfamilymiddletown.com.

See John XXIII Catholic Elementary School under Consolidated Elementary Schools located in the Institution section.

Catechesis Religious Program—Students 150.

MILFORD, CLERMONT CO., ST. ANDREW (1854) [CEM] Revs. Michael L. Cordier; Christopher M. Geiger; Deacon Timothy Schutte.

Res.: 552 Main St., Milford, 45150. Tel: 513-831-3353 ; Email: office@standrew-milford.org.

School—St. Andrew-St. Elizabeth Seton, (Grades PreK-8), 555 Main St., Milford, 45150.

Tel: 513-831-5277; Tel: 513-575-0093;

Fax: 513-831-8436; Email: reeds@saseas.org; Email: claytonp@saseas.org; Web: www.saseasschool.org. Mr. Mark Wilburn, Prin. Consolidated.

Legal Title: Consolidated school with St. Elizabeth Ann Seton Parish Clergy 20; Lay Teachers 26; Students 281.

Catechesis Religious Program—Email: ReligiousEd@standrew-milford.org. Kathy Bitzer, D.R.E. Students 253.

MILLVILLE, BUTLER CO., QUEEN OF PEACE (1941)

2550 Millville Ave., Hamilton, 45013.

Tel: 513-863-4344; Email: parishoffice@qpchurch.org; Web: www.queeofpeacechurch.net. Rev. James M. Wedig; Deacons Jeffrey P. Ehrnschwender; Michael E. Mignery.

School—Queen of Peace School, (Grades PreK-8),

Tel: 513-863-8705; Email: parishoffice@qpchurch.org; Web: queenofpeacehamilton.org. Tina Conners, Prin. Clergy 2; Lay Teachers 15; Preschool 20; Students 175; Pre K Enrollment 15.

Catechesis Religious Program—Students 92.

MINSTER, AUGLAIZE CO.

1—ST. AUGUSTINE (1832) [CEM] (German)

P.O. Box 93, Minster, 45865. Rev. Frankline Rayappa; Deacons Hal Belcher; Roger L. Klosterman; Sr. Marla Gipson, C.PP.S., Pastoral Assoc.

Res.: 48 N. Hanover St., Minster, 45865.

Tel: 419-628-2614; Email: info@staugie.com; Web: www.staugie.com.

Catechesis Religious Program—89 N. Lincoln St., P.O. Box 93, Minster, 45865. Tel: 419-628-3434; Fax: 419-628-3584. Clustered with St. Joseph Parish, Egypt, OH Students 654.

2—ST. JOSEPH (1852) [CEM] Clustered with St. Augustine, Minster.

02441 SR 364, Minister, 45865. Tel: 419-628-2614; Fax: 419-628-2614; Email: info@staugie.com. Mailing Address: P.O. Box 93, Minster, 45865. Rev. Frankline Rayappa.

Res.: 48 N. Hanover St., Minster, 45865.

Fax: 419-628-1078.

Catechesis Religious Program—Tel: 419-628-3434. Clustered with St. Augustine, Minster.

MONROE, BUTLER CO., OUR LADY OF SORROWS (1883) Revs. Paul L. Gebhardt; Stephen Lattner, O.S.B.; Deacon Jack Schaefer; Nora Neu, Pastoral Assoc.; Mrs. Ava Bertsch, Business Mgr.; Mr. Joseph Kiesewetter, Youth Min.; Mrs. Danielle Schrantz, Pastoral Musician.

Res.: 416 Lebanon St., Monroe, 45050.

Church: 330 Lebanon St., Monroe, 45050.

Tel: 513-539-8061; Fax: 513-539-0443; Email: olos@cinci.rr.com; Web: www.olosmonroe.com.

Catechesis Religious Program—Email: cd3.baum@gmail.com. Mrs. Christine Baumgardner, C.R.E. Students 137.

MONTEZUMA, MERCER CO., OUR LADY OF GUADALUPE (1904) [CEM]

P.O. Box 69, Montezuma, 45866. Rev. Alfons Minja, C.PP.S., (Tanzania).

Res.: 6701 State Rte. 219, Montezuma, 45866.

Tel: 419-268-2312; Email: ologlinda@yahoo.com.

Catechesis Religious Program—Ruth Wynk, C.R.E. Students 80.

MORROW, WARREN CO., ST. PHILIP THE APOSTLE (1965) [CEM] Revs. Bernard J. Weldishofer; Craig E. Best, Parochial Vicar; Deacons Paul F. Leibold; David M. Wallace; James H. Woeste.

Res.: 824 E. U.S. 22-3, Morrow, 45152-9690.

Tel: 513-899-9248.

Church: 944 E. U.S. 22-3, Morrow, 45152-9690.

Tel: 513-899-3601; Fax: 513-899-3785; Web: www.stphilipmorrow.org.

Catechesis Religious Program—Mrs. Mary Orite-Shea, C.R.E. Students 128.

MOUNT CARMEL, CLERMONT CO., ST. VERONICA (1949) Revs. P. Del Staigers; Patrick H. Crone, (Retired); David A. Doseck, Parochial Vicar; Deacon R. Daniel Murphy.

Church: 4473 Mt. Carmel-Tobasco Rd., 45244.

Tel: 513-528-1622; Email: office@stveronica.org; Web: www.stveronica.org.

School—St. Veronica School, (Grades PreK-8), 4475 Mt. Carmel-Tobasco Rd., 45244. Tel: 513-528-0442; Fax: 513-528-0513; Email: school@stveronica.org; Email: sharon.bresler@stveronica.org; Web: www.school.stveronica.org. Sharon Bresler, Prin.; Butch Keithley, Asst. Prin. Lay Teachers 31; Sisters 1; Students 480.

Catechesis Religious Program—Tel: 513-688-3155; Email: bill.frantz@stveronica.org. Bill Frantz, D.R.E. Students 44.

MOUNT ORAB, BROWN CO., ST. MICHAEL (1944)

P.O. Box 279, Fayetteville, 45118. Rev. Thomas L. Bolte.

130 Stone Alley, P.O. Box 279, Mount Orab, 45118.

Tel: 513-875-5020, Ext. 2.

Church: 220 S. High St., Mount Orab, 45154.

Catechesis Religious Program—Tel: 513-335-6277. Regina Pritchard, C.R.E. Students 12.

MOUNT REPOSE, CLERMONT CO., ST. ELIZABETH ANN SETON (1976) Revs. Michael L. Cordier; Christopher M. Geiger, Parochial Vicar; Deacon Steve R. Brown.

Res.: 5900 Buckwheat Rd., Milford, 45150.

Tel: 513-575-0119; Email: parishoffice@setonmilford.org; Web: www.setonmilford.org.

School—St. Elizabeth Ann Seton School, (Grades PreK-5), 5900 Buckwheat Rd., Milford, 45150.

Tel: 513-575-0093; Fax: 513-575-1078; Email: wilburnm@saseas.org; Web: www.saseasschool.org. Lay Teachers 10; Students 159.

Child Care—Preschool, Tel: 513-575-9900. Mrs. Aimee Limberg, Dir. Lay Teachers 8; Students 116.
Catechesis Religious Program—Email: dre@setonmilford.org. Patricia Norris, D.R.E. Students 145.

NEW BREMEN, AUGLAIZE CO., HOLY REDEEMER (1948) Rev. Thomas E. Dorn; Deacon Gregory Bornhorst.
Church: 120 S. Eastmoor Dr., P.O. Box 67, New Bremen, 45869. Tel: 419-629-2543; Email: holyredeemer@nktelco.net; Web: www.hrcatholic.org.
Catechesis Religious Program—Students 372.

NEW CARLISLE, CLARK CO., SACRED HEART (1950)
209 W. Lake Avenue, New Carlisle, 45434. Rev. Thomas A. Nevels; Mrs. Christina McGrath, Pastoral Assoc.; Mr. Richard Kraus, Business Mgr.; Mrs. Kristen Kosey, Music Min.; Mrs. Kelly Summers, D.R.E.
Res. & Mailing Address: 476 N. Scott St., New Carlisle, 45344. Tel: 937-845-3121; Email: office@sacredheartnc.com; Web: sacredheartnc.org.
Church: 209 W. Lake Ave., New Carlisle, 45344.
Catechesis Religious Program—Sacred Heart Religious Education Program, Email: catechism@sacredheartnc.net. Students 115.

NEW PARIS, PREBLE CO., ST. JOHN THE EVANGELIST (1870) [CEM]
400 N. Spring St., New Paris, 45347. Rev. Matthew Amoako-Attah, C.S.Sp.
Res. & Mailing Address: 407 E. Main St., Eaton, 45320. Tel: 937-456-3380; Email: church@visitationstjohn.com.
Church: N. Spring St., New Paris, 45347.
Catechesis Religious Program—Joint program with Visitation Parish, Eaton, OH.

NEW RICHMOND, CLERMONT CO., ST. PETER (1850) [CEM]
Email: sccr.parish@outlook.com. Rev. James Reutter; Deacon Ronald L. Stang.
Res.: 1192 Bethel-New Richmond Rd., New Richmond, 45157. Tel: 513-553-3267, Ext. 1; Email: jddepuccio2@gmail.com; Web: www.ccc.city.
Catechesis Religious Program—Email: dreyouthpastor@gmail.com. Mr. PJ Ehling, C.R.E. & Youth Min. Students 28.

NEWPORT, SHELBY CO., SS. PETER AND PAUL (1856) [CEM] Rev. Steven L. Shoup; Lisa Monnin, Pastoral Assoc.
Res.: 6788 State Rte. 66, P.O. Box 199, Fort Loramie, 45845. Tel: 937-295-2891; Email: steves@nflregion.org; Web: www.nflregion.org.
Catechesis Religious Program—Tel: 937-295-2536. Lisa Monnin, C.R.E. Students 77.

NORTH LEWISBURG, CHAMPAIGN CO., IMMACULATE CONCEPTION (1869)
164 W. Elm St., North Lewisburg, 43060.
Tel: 937-653-1375; Fax: 937-653-1383; Email: stmarychurchoffice@gmail.com; Web: www.champaigncatholics.org. c/o St. Mary Church, 231 Washington Ave., Urbana, 43078. Revs. Matthew K. Lee; Ignatius Madanu, Parochial Vicar; Mrs. Amy Brinker, Business Mgr.
Catechesis Religious Program—Students 4.

NORTH BEND, HAMILTON CO., ST. JOSEPH (1860) Rev. Andrew J. Umberg, S.T.L.
Church: 25 E. Harrison Ave., North Bend, 45052.
Tel: 513-941-3661, Ext. 10; Email: stjoseph@stjosephnorthbend.com; Web: www.stjosephnorthbend.com.
Res.: 162 Miami Ave., North Bend, 45052.
Tel: 513-375-1545.
Catechesis Religious Program—Tel: 513-941-3661; Email: bethscholl@stjosephnorthbend.com. BethAnn Scholl, D.R.E. Students 187.

NORTH STAR, DARKE CO., ST. LOUIS (1891) [CEM] Rev. David L. Zink, M.A.
Parish Office & Mailing Address: P.O. Box 9, Osgood, 45351. Tel: 419-582-2531; Email: stlouis.stnicholasoffice@gmail.com.
Church: 15 Star Rd., North Star, 45350.
Catechesis Religious Program—Linda Wehrkamp, D.R.E. Students 214.

OSGOOD, DARKE CO., ST. NICHOLAS (1909) [CEM] Rev. David L. Zink, M.A.
Office: 128 Church St., P.O. Box 9, Osgood, 45351.
Tel: 419-582-2531; Email: stlouis.stnicholasoffice@gmail.com.
Catechesis Religious Program—Sandra Mangen, D.R.E. Students 219.

OWENSVILLE, CLERMONT CO., ST. LOUIS (1856) [CEM]
Mailing Address: P.O. Box 85, Owensville, 45160. Revs. Martin E. Bachman; J. Robert Jack, M.A., Parochial Vicar.
Res.: 255 N. Broadway, Owensville, 45160.
Church: 210 N. Broadway, Owensville, 45160.
School—St. Louis School, (Grades PreK-8), 250 N. Broadway, P.O. Box 85, Owensville, 45160.
Tel: 513-732-0636; Email: leu.betsy@stlouischool.org. Mrs. Elizabeth Leu, Prin. Lay Teachers 12; Students 126.
Catechesis Religious Program—John Ivan, Dir. Students 220.

OXFORD, BUTLER CO., ST. MARY CHURCH AND CATHOLIC CAMPUS MINISTRY (1853) [CEM] (Miami Univ. OH)
111 E. High St., Oxford, 45056.
Tel: 513-523-2153, Ext. 126; Fax: 513-523-0559; Email: info@stmox.org; Web: www.stmox.org. Rev. Jeffrey P. Silver; Roberta L. Kinne, Pastoral Assoc.; Courtney Palcic, Pastoral Assoc.; Pam Burk, Business Mgr.; Holly Moran, Campus Min.

PEEBLES, ADAMS CO., ST. MARY QUEEN OF HEAVEN (1952) (Vicariate)
205 Wendell Ave., Peebles, 45660. Rev. Adam D. Puntel.
Church, Office & Mailing Address: Holy Trinity, 612 E. Mulberry St., West Union, 45693.
Tel: 937-544-2757; Email: office@holytrinity-ac.org.
Catechesis Religious Program—Students 21.

PHILOTHEA, MERCER CO., ST. MARY (1851) [CEM] (German) (Coldwater Cluster)
3821 Philothea Rd., Coldwater, 45828. Mailing Address: P.O. Box 107, Coldwater, 45828. Revs. Richard W. Walling; Alexander T. Witt.
Res.: 120 E. Main St., P.O. Box 107, Coldwater, 45828. Tel: 419-678-4802; Email: kphares@coldwatercluster.org; Web: www.coldwatercluster.org.
Catechesis Religious Program—Sue Homan, D.R.E. Students 51.

PIQUA, MIAMI CO.
1—ST. BONIFACE (1855)
310 S. Downing St., Piqua, 45356. Tel: 937-773-1656; Fax: 937-773-2665; Email: stboniface@piquaparishes.org; Web: www.piquaparishes.org. Revs. Daniel P. Hunt; Angelo C. Caserta, (Retired), Tel: 937-778-9526.
Res.: 528 Broadway, Piqua, 45356. Tel: 937-773-0075 ; Email: pastor@piquaparishes.org.
See Piqua Catholic School, Piqua under Consolidated Elementary Schools located in the Institution section.
Catechesis Religious Program—Email: diane@piquaparishes.org. Diane Mengos, D.R.E. Students 85.
2—ST. MARY (1843)
528 Broadway St., Piqua, 45356. Tel: 937-773-1327; Email: stmary@piquaparishes.org. Rev. Daniel P. Hunt; Deacon Michael Knight, RCIA Coord.
See Piqua Catholic School, Piqua under Consolidated Elementary Schools located in the Institution section.
Catechesis Religious Program—Email: dmengos@piquaparishes.org. Diane Mengos, D.R.E. Students 85.

RHINE, SHELBY CO., ST. LAWRENCE (1856) [CEM] (German)
P.O. Box 519, Botkins, 45306. Revs. Sean M. Wilson; Jarred L. Kohn, Parochial Vicar; Deacon Terrell Coleman.
Church & Res.: 16053 Botkins Rd., Botkins, 45306.
Tel: 937-693-2561; Tel: 937-639-3535; Email: iccstlc@bright.net; Web: www.slicchurches.org.
Catechesis Religious Program—Tel: 937-693-3535; Email: ccdoffice@embarqmail.com. Beth Klopfenstein, D.R.E. Students 88.

RIPLEY, BROWN CO., ST. MICHAEL (1840) Rev. Dohrman W. Byers; Deacon Ronald S. Dvorachek; Ruth Allen, Pastoral Assoc.; Susan Caproni, Business Mgr.
Church & Parish Office: 16 N. Fourth St., Ripley, 45167. Tel: 937-392-1116; Email: stmarymichaelgeorge@outlook.com.
School—St. Michael School, (Grades PreK-8), 300 Market St., Ripley, 45167. Tel: 937-392-4202; Email: andy.arn@stmichaelripley.com. Andrew Arn, Prin. Lay Teachers 7; Students 102.
Catechesis Religious Program—Tel: 937-378-6453; Fax: 937-378-6829; Email: jstclair.sgchurch1@frontier.com. Joan St. Clair, D.R.E. Students 7.

ROCKFORD, MERCER CO., ST. TERESA (1936)
P.O. Box 445, Rockford, 45882-0445. Revs. Ken Schnipke, C.PP.S.; Vincent P. Wirtner III, C.PP.S., Parochial Vicar.
Church: 4227 State Rte. 707, Rockford, 45882.
Tel: 419-363-2633; Email: stteresachurch@bright.net; Web: stteresa-rockford.org. Mrs. Diane Huber, Contact Person.
Catechesis Religious Program—Email: crestteresa@bright.net. Mrs. Cheryl Nichols. Students 79.

RUSSELLS POINT, LOGAN CO., ST. MARY OF THE WOODS (1927)
464 Madison Ave., Russells Point, 43348.
Tel: 937-843-3127; Email: office@saintmaryofthewoods.com; Web: www.saintmaryofthewoods.com. Rev. Shawn R. Landenwitch; Deacon Jeffrey D. Hall Sr.
Res.: P.O. Box 329, Russells Point, 43348-0329.
Catechesis Religious Program—Tel: 937-843-4227. Dona Fischer. Students 118.
Mission—St. George Chapel Marianists of Ohio, 9636 Lake Shore Dr., E., Huntsville, Logan Co. 43324.
Tel: 937-842-4902.

RUSSIA, SHELBY CO., ST. REMY (1846) [CEM] Rev. Martin E. Fox.
Res.: 108 E. Main St., Russia, 45363-9701.
Tel: 937-526-3437; Email: stremy@roadrunner.com; Web: www.stremychurch.com.
Catechesis Religious Program—Karen Rosenbeck, C.R.E. Students 325.

ST. ANTHONY, MERCER CO., ST. ANTHONY (1852) [CEM] (German) (Coldwater Cluster)
Mailing Address: P.O. Box 107, Coldwater, 45828. Revs. Richard W. Walling; Alexander T. Witt, Parochial Vicar.
Church: 471 St. Anthony Rd., Fort Recovery, 45846-9404. Tel: 419-678-4802; Fax: 419-678-4803; Email: kphares@coldwatercluster.org; Web: www.coldwatercluster.org.
Catechesis Religious Program—Email: cmuhlenkamp@coldwatercluster.org. Cindy Muhlenkamp, D.R.E. Students 71.

SAINT HENRY, MERCER CO., ST. HENRY (1839) [CEM] (St. Henry Cluster) Revs. William O'Donnell, C.PP.S., (Retired); Jim Smith, C.PP.S., Parochial Vicar; Bro. Nicholas Renner, C.PP.S, Outreach; Deacons Jerry Buschur; Randy Balster.
Res.: 1509 Cranberry Rd., Cranberry, 45883.
Tel: 419-925-4776.
Church & Mailing Address: 272 E. Main St., Box 350, St. Henry, 45883. Tel: 419-678-4118; Email: shclusteroffice@hotmail.com; Web: www.sthenrycluster.com.
Inter-parish Center—162 S. Walnut, St. Henry, 45883. Tel: 419-678-3811; Fax: 419-678-8285.
Catechesis Religious Program—Tel: 419-678-3811; Email: sthenryccd@bright.net. Catherine Wenning, D.R.E. Students 565.

ST. JOSEPH, MERCER CO., ST. JOSEPH (1839) [CEM] (German) (Fort Recovery Cluster)
403 Sharpsburg Rd., Fort Recovery, 45846. Revs. Ned J. Brown; Matthew S. Feist.
Church: 1689 St. Joseph Rd., Fort Recovery, 45846.
Catechesis Religious Program—Cassie Schemmel, D.R.E.; Holly Wuebker, D.R.E. Twinned with St. Peter Parish, St. Peter. Students 85.

ST. MARYS, AUGLAIZE CO., HOLY ROSARY (1852) [CEM] Rev. Barry J. Stechschulte; Deacon Martin J. Brown.
Res.: 511 E. Spring St., St. Marys, 45885.
Tel: 419-394-5050; Email: holyrosary@bright.net; Web: www.holyrosarychurch.us.
School—Holy Rosary School, (Grades PreK-8), 128 S. Pine St., Saint Marys, 45885. Tel: 419-394-5291; Email: lkrugh@holyrosaryschool.us; Web: www.holyrosaryschool.us. Lay Teachers 14; Students 184; Clergy / Religious Teachers 1.
Catechesis Religious Program—Email: mielkecrew@yahoo.com. Nan Mielke, D.R.E. Students 182.

ST. PARIS, CHAMPAIGN CO., SACRED HEART (ST. PARIS) (1868)
c/o St. Mary Church, 231 Washington Ave., Urbana, 43078. Tel: 937-653-1375; Fax: 937-653-1383; Email: stmarychurchoffice@gmail.com; Web: www.champaigncatholics.org. 121 East Walnut St., St. Paris, 43072. Revs. Matthew K. Lee; Ignatius Madanu, Parochial Vicar; Mrs. Amy Brinker, Business Mgr.

ST. PETER, MERCER CO., ST. PETER (1860) [CEM] (German) (Fort Recovery Cluster)
403 Sharpsburg Rd., Fort Recovery, 45846.
Tel: 419-375-4153; Email: stpeter@fortrecoverycatholics.org; Web: fortrecoverycatholics.org. Revs. Ned J. Brown; Matthew S. Feist
Legal Titles: St. Peter Catholic Church
Church: 1477 Philothea Rd., Fort Recovery, 45846.
Catechesis Religious Program—Cassie Schemmel, C.R.E.; Holly Wuebker, C.R.E. Twinned with St. Joseph Parish, St. Joseph. Students 159.

ST. ROSE, MERCER CO., ST. ROSE (1839) [CEM] (German) (Marion Catholic Community)
7428 State Rte. 119, Maria Stein, 45860.
Tel: 419-925-4775; Email: marioncathcom@gmail.com; Web: marioncatholiccommunity.org. Revs. Eugene H. Schnipke, C.PP.S.; Thomas Brenberger, C.PP.S.; Deacon Clifton Perryman; Sharon Kremer, Parish Life Coord.; Sue Fortkamp, Business Mgr.
Catechesis Religious Program—Jackie Garman, D.R.E. Students 56.

ST. SEBASTIAN, MERCER CO., ST. SEBASTIAN (1852) [CEM] (German) (Marion Catholic Community)
Mailing Address: 7428 St. Rt. 119, Maria Stein, 45860. Tel: 419-925-4775; Email: marioncathcom@gmail.com; Web: www.marioncatholiccommunity.org. Revs. Eugene H. Schnipke, C.PP.S.; Thomas Brenberger, C.PP.S.; Deacon Clifton Perryman; Sharon Kremer, Parish Life Coord.; Sue Roeckner, Business Mgr.
Church: 3280 Co. Rd. 716-A, Celina, 45822.
Catechesis Religious Program—Judy Forsthoefel, D.R.E. Students 59.

ST. WENDELIN, MERCER CO., ST. WENDELIN (1856) [CEM] (St. Henry Cluster)

2980 Ft Recovery-Minster Rd., Box 350, Wendelin, 45883. Tel: 419-678-4118; Fax: 419-678-8285; Email: shclusteroffice@hotmail.com; Web: www.sthenrycluster.com. P.O. Box 350, St. Henry, 45883. Revs. William O'Donnell, C.PP.S., (Retired); Jim Smith, C.PP.S., Parochial Vicar; Bro. Nicholas Renner, C.PP.S; Deacon Randy Balster.
Res.: 1509 Cranberry Rd., St. Henry, 45883.
Tel: 419-925-4776.
Catechesis Religious Program—Tel: 419-678-3811; Email: sthenryccd@bright.net. Students 39.

SHANDON, BUTLER CO., ST. ALOYSIUS (1867) [CEM]
P.O. Box 95, Shandon, 45063. Rev. James M. Wedig; Deacon Bill Brunsman.
Res.: 5484 Cinti Brookville Rd., Shandon, 45063.
Church: 3350 Chapel Rd., Shandon, 45063.
Tel: 513-738-1014; Email: npadgett_staloysius@fuse.net; Web: www.stalshandon.org.
Catechesis Religious Program—
Tel: 513-738-1014, Ext. 306. Students 175.

SHARPSBURG, MERCER CO., ST. PAUL (1868) [CEM] (Fort Recovery Cluster)
Mailing Address: 403 Sharpsburg Rd., Fort Recovery, 45846. Tel: 419-375-4153; Email: stpaul@fortrecoverycatholics.org; Web: www.fortrecoverycatholics.org. Revs. Ned J. Brown; Matthew S. Feist.
Res.: 517 Meiring Rd., Fort Recovery, 45846.
Fax: 419-375-4154.
Catechesis Religious Program—Tel: 419-375-2308. Students 123.

SIDNEY, SHELBY CO., HOLY ANGELS (1848)
324 S. Ohio Ave., Sidney, 45365-3012.
Tel: 937-498-2307; Email: jill@holyangelssidney.com; Web: www.holyangelssidney.com. Revs. Frank G. Amberger; Peter Langenkamp, Parochial Vicar; Deacon Philip Myers; Jill Heitmeyer, Business Mgr.
School—Holy Angels School, (Grades K-8), 120 E. Water St., Sidney, 45365-3199. Tel: 937-492-9293; Fax: 937-492-8578; Email: bspicer@holyangelscatholic.com; Email: mjbaker@holyangelscatholic.com; Web: www.holyangelscatholic.com. Beth Spicer, Prin. Lay Teachers 19; Students 220.
Catechesis Religious Program—c/o Office 121 E. Water St., Sidney, 45365-3199. Tel: 937-498-0433; Fax: 937-498-1448; Email: hareligioused@hotmail.com. Susan Anderson, C.R.E. Students 190.

SOUTH CHARLESTON, CLARK CO., ST. CHARLES BORROMEO (1866) [CEM]
31 S. Chillicothe St., P.O. Box F, South Charleston, 45368-0806. Tel: 937-462-8971; Email: stcdr@att.net. Rev. William J. Kramer.
Rectory—Rectory: 1908 Washington North Dr., Dayton, 45458. Tel: 937-470-9266.

SPRINGFIELD, CLARK CO.
1—ST. BERNARD (1860) [CEM] (German) Rev. John D. MacQuarrie.
Res.: 910 Lagonda Ave., Springfield, 45503.
Tel: 937-322-5243; Email: jherzog72@yahoo.com; Web: stbernard-springfield.org.
See Catholic Central School, Springfield under Consolidated Elementary Schools located in the Institution section.
Catechesis Religious Program—Tel: 937-324-2870. Trish Evans, A.R.E. Students 59.
2—ST. JOSEPH (1882)
801 Kenton St., Springfield, 45505.
Tel: 937-323-7523. Rev. William J. Kramer; Deacons John R. Collins; Norman G. Horstman, D.R.E.
See Catholic Central School, Springfield under Consolidated Elementary Schools located in the Institution section.
3—ST. RAPHAEL (1849) Rev. William J. Kramer; Deacons John R. Collins; Norman G. Horstman.
Res.: 1139 Pheasant Run, Springfield, 45503.
Tel: 937-460-7421.
Church: 225 E. High St., Springfield, 45505.
Tel: 937-323-7523; Email: plarger@catholicweb.com; Web: www.josephraphael.org.
See Catholic Central School, Springfield under Consolidated Elementary Schools located in the Institution section.
Catechesis Religious Program—Email: nhorstman@catholicweb.com. Twinned with St. Joseph, Springfield. Students 250.
4—ST. TERESA OF THE CHILD JESUS (1931)
1827 N. Limestone St., Springfield, 45503.
Tel: 937-342-8861; Email: stteresa.church@bizwoh.rr.com; Web: www.stteresaspgfldoh.org. Rev. John D. MacQuarrie.
Res.: 910 Lagonda Ave., Springfield, 45503.
See Catholic Central School, Springfield under Consolidated Elementary Schools located in the Institution section.
Catechesis Religious Program—
Tel: 937-342-8861, Ext. 16. Lucianne Lilienthal, Coord. Rel. Formation. Students 63.

STONELICK, CLERMONT CO., ST. PHILOMENA (1837) [CEM]
5240 Stonelick Williams Corner Rd., Box 85, Owensville, 45160. Tel: 513-732-2218; Fax: 513-732-2368; Email: smatthews@cccatholics.org. Revs. Martin E. Bachman; J. Robert Jack, M.A., Parochial Vicar.
Res.: 255 N. Broadway, Box 85, Owensville, 45160.
Church: Stonelick-Williams Corner Rd., Owensville, 45160.

TIPP CITY, MIAMI CO., ST. JOHN THE BAPTIST (1858) [CEM] Rev. R. Marc Sherlock.
Res.: 753 S. Hyatt St., Tipp City, 45371-1255.
Tel: 937-667-3419; Email: sjbsecretary@woh.rr.com; Web: www.stjohntippcity.org.
Catechesis Religious Program—Email: charleswright@woh.rr.com; Email: teriiverson@woh.rr.com. Deacon Charles O. Wright, Dir. Evangelization & Catechesis; Teri Iverson, Dir. Youth Min. Students 348.

TRENTON, BUTLER CO., HOLY NAME (1871) [CEM] Revs. Paul L. Gebhardt; Stephen Lattner, O.S.B.; Deacons Lawrence D. Gronas; William E. Schaefer.
Res.: 222 Hamilton Ave., Trenton, 45067.
Tel: 513-988-6335; Email: holynamercc@gmail.com; Web: www.holynameofjesuscatholicchurch.org.
Catechesis Religious Program—Tel: 513-988-9348. Students 53.

TROY, MIAMI CO., ST. PATRICK (1857)
409 E. Main St., Troy, 45373. Tel: 937-335-2833; Fax: 937-335-1453; Email: Stpatofficemgr@woh.rr.com; Web: www.stpattroy.org. Revs. Eric A. Bowman; Michael Samala; Deacons John Carlin; David B. Gillespie.
School—St. Patrick School, (Grades PreK-8), 420 E. Water St., Troy, 45373. Tel: 937-339-3705; Fax: 937-339-1158; Email: ccathcart@stpattroy.org; Web: www.stpattroyschool.org. Ms. Cyndi Cathcart, Prin. Clergy 1; Lay Teachers 14; Students 151.
Catechesis Religious Program—Students 178.

URBANA, CHAMPAIGN CO., ST. MARY (1853)
228 Washington Ave., Urbana, 43078.
Tel: 937-653-1375; Fax: 937-653-1383; Email: stmarychurchoffice@gmail.com; Web: www.champaigncatholics.org. 231 Washington Ave., Urbana, 43078. Revs. Matthew K. Lee; Ignatius Madanu, Parochial Vicar; Mrs. Amy Brinker, Business Mgr.
See Catholic Central School, Springfield under Consolidated Elementary Schools located in the Institution section.
Catechesis Religious Program—Students 84.

VANDALIA, MONTGOMERY CO., ST. CHRISTOPHER (1957) Rev. John W. Tonkin; Deacon Charles O. Wright; Andrea Parker, Pastoral Assoc.
Res.: 435 E. National Rd., Vandalia, 45377.
Tel: 937-898-3542, Ext. 101; Email: christophervandalia@stchristopheronline.com; Web: www.stchristopheronline.com.
School—St. Christopher School, (Grades K-8), 405 E. National Rd., Vandalia, 45377. Tel: 937-898-5104; Fax: 937-454-4790; Email: mkincaid@stchristopheronline.com; Web: school.stchristopheronline.com. Mary Kincaid, Prin.; Carrie Hartley, Librarian. Lay Teachers 24; Students 291.
Catechesis Religious Program—
Tel: 937-898-3542, Ext. 104; Email: esas@stchristopheronline.com. Elise Sas, D.R.E. Students 212.

VERSAILLES, DARKE CO., ST. DENIS (1839) [CEM] Revs. James L. Simons; James S. Duell, Parochial Vicar.
Res.: 14 E. Wood St., Versailles, 45380.
Tel: 937-526-4945; Email: jsimons@bfvcatholic.org.
Catechesis Religious Program—Email: ccd@bfvcatholic.org. Julie Meyer, D.R.E. Students 362.

WAPAKONETA, AUGLAIZE CO., ST. JOSEPH (1839) [CEM]
101 W. Pearl St., Wapakoneta, 45895.
Tel: 419-738-2115; Email: stjoe@bright.net; Web: www.stjoewapak.org. 309 Perry St., Wapakoneta, 45895-2197. Revs. Sean M. Wilson; Jarred L. Kohn, Parochial Vicar; Deacon Richard L. Westbay.

WAYNESVILLE, WARREN CO., ST. AUGUSTINE (1876) [JC] Rev. James J. Manning.
Res.: 5715 Lytle Rd., Waynesville, 45068.
Tel: 513-897-0545; Email: jcain@staugustinewaynesville.com.
Catechesis Religious Program—Email: amuth@staugustinewaynesville.com. Ann Muth, D.R.E. Students 70.

WEST CHESTER, BUTLER CO., ST. JOHN THE EVANGELIST (1880) Rev. Don J. West; Deacon Gerald L. Barney.
Church: 9080 Cincinnati-Dayton Rd., West Chester, 45069. Tel: 513-777-6433; Email: info@stjohnwc.org.
See St. Gabriel Consolidated School, Cincinnati under Consolidated Elementary Schools located in the Institution section.
Catechesis Religious Program—Tel: 513-755-4974. Students 210.

WEST MILTON, MIAMI CO., TRANSFIGURATION (1950) Revs. Eric A. Bowman; Michael Samala.
Res.: 972 S. Miami St., West Milton, 45383.
Tel: 937-698-4520; Email: office@tchurch.org; Web: www.transfigurationcatholicchurch.org.
Catechesis Religious Program—Students 153.

WEST UNION, ADAMS CO., HOLY TRINITY (1950) Rev. Adam D. Puntel.
Res.: 612 E. Mulberry St., West Union, 45693.
Tel: 937-544-2757; Email: office@holytrinity-ac.org.
Catechesis Religious Program—Email: a.barczak@holytrinity.org. Andy Barczak, D.R.E. Students 45.

WILLIAMSBURG, CLERMONT CO., ST. ANN (1947) Revs. Martin E. Bachman; J. Robert Jack, M.A., Parochial Vicar.
Res. & Mailing Address: 140 N. Sixth St., Batavia, 45103. Tel: 513-732-2024; Tel: 513-732-2218; Fax: 513-732-0049; Fax: 513-732-2368; Email: alleluia@fuse.net.
Church: 370 S. 5th St., Williamsburg, 45176.
Catechesis Religious Program—Marlene Bauer, D.R.E. Students 10.

WILMINGTON, CLINTON CO., ST. COLUMBKILLE (1866) Holy Name Chapel is part of St. Columbkille.
73 N. Mulberry St., Wilmington, 45177.
Tel: 937-382-2236; Email: parishoffice@stcolumbkille.org; Web: www.stcolumbkille.org. Rev. Michael J. Holloran; Deacons Robert G. Baker; Robert E. Meyer.
Catechesis Religious Program—Tel: 937-382-1596. Students 105.

WITHAMSVILLE, CLERMONT CO., ST. THOMAS MORE (1940)
800 Ohio Pike, 45245-2219. Tel: 513-752-2080; Email: sttm@sttm.org; Web: www.sttm.org. Rev. William C. Wagner; Deacons Robert L. Brazier; John J. Convery; Frederick J. Haas; Michael T. Thomas, Pastoral Assoc.
School—St. Thomas More School, (Grades K-8), 788 Ohio Pike, 45245-2156. Tel: 513-753-2540, Ext. 122; Fax: 513-753-2554; Email: principal@sttm.org; Web: www.sttmschool.org. Mrs. Candace Hurley, Prin. Clergy 1; Lay Teachers 17; Students 255.
Catechesis Religious Program—Email: bready@sttm.org. Mrs. Becky Ready, D.R.E. Students 104.

XENIA, GREENE CO., ST. BRIGID (1849) [CEM]
312 Fairground Rd., Xenia, 45385. Rev. Andrew P. Cordonnier; Deacon Dennis Kall.
Church & Mailing Address: 258 Purcell Dr., Xenia, 45385. Tel: 937-372-3193; Fax: 937-374-3622; Email: tpeters@stbrigidxenia.org; Web: www.stbrigidxenia.org.
Res.: 265 Purcell Dr., Xenia, 45385.
Tel: 937-409-9355.
School—St. Brigid School, (Grades PreK-8), 312 Fairground Rd., Xenia, 45385. Tel: 937-372-3222; Email: tadkins@stbrigidxenia.org; Web: www.stbrigidxenia.org. Terry Adkins, Prin. Lay Teachers 12; Students 186.
Catechesis Religious Program—Email: jklippel@stbrigidxenia.org. Janell Klippel, D.R.E. Students 74.

YELLOW SPRINGS, GREENE CO., ST. PAUL (1856) [CEM]
308 Phillips St., Yellow Springs, 45387.
Tel: 937-767-7450; Email: office@stpaulchurchyso.org; Email: finance@stpaulchurchyso.org; Email: cre@stpaulchurchyso.org; Email: cemetery@stpaulchurchyso.org; Web: www.stpaulchurchyso.org. Rev. Andrew P. Cordonnier.
Catechesis Religious Program—
Tel: 937-767-7450, Ext. 12; Email: cre@stpaulchurchyso.org. Sherry Malloy, D.R.E. Students 19.

Closed and Merged Parishes

GREATER CINCINNATI
1—ST. AGNES (Bond Hill) (1892) (African American), Merged with St. Andrew, St. Mark the Evangelist, and St. Martin de Porres, Cincinnati, to form Church of the Resurrection, Cincinnati. For inquiries for parish records contact the Chancery.
2—ST. ALOYSIUS CHURCH, Closed. For inquiries for parish records, contact St. Clement, (St. Bernard).
3—ST. ANDREW (1874) (African American), Merged with St. Agnes, St. Mark the Evangelist, and St. Martin de Porres, Cincinnati, to form Church of the Resurrection, Cincinnati. For inquiries for parish records contact the Chancery.
4—ASSUMPTION OF THE BLESSED VIRGIN MARY (Walnut Hills) (1872) Closed. For inquiries for parish records contact the chancery.
5—ST. BONAVENTURE (1869) Closed. For inquiries for parish records, contact St. Leo, Cincinnati.
6—ST. CHARLES BORROMEO CHURCH (Carthage) Closed. For inquiries for parish records, contact St. James of the Valley, (Wyoming).
7—COMMUNITY OF HOPE, Closed. For inquiries for parish records contact the chancery.
8—ST. ELIZABETH CHURCH (Norwood) Merged with St. Matthew Church, Norwood and Sts. Peter & Paul Church, Norwood to form Holy Trinity Church, Norwood. Records at Holy Trinity Church.
9—ST. GEORGE PARISH & NEWMAN CENTER, Closed. For inquiries for parish records contact St. Monica-St. George Newman Center.

10—HOLY ANGELS (1859) Merged with St. Francis de Sales, Cincinnati. Records at St. Francis de Sales.
11—ST. JEROME (1863) Closed. For inquiries for parish records contact Guardian Angels, Cincinnati.
12—ST. JOHN VIANNEY (Madison Pl.) (1949) Merged with St. Margaret of Cortona Parish, Cincinnati to form St. Margaret-St. John Parish, Cincinnati. For inquiries for parish records contact St. Margaret-St. John, Cincinnati.
13—ST. MARGARET OF CORTONA (Madisonville) (1921) Merged with St. John Vianney Parish, Cincinnati to form St. Margaret-St. John Parish, Cincinnati. For inquiries for parish records contact St. Margaret-St. John, Cincinnati.
14—ST. MARK THE EVANGELIST (1905) Merged with St. Agnes, St. Andrew, and St. Martin de Porres, Cincinnati, to form Church of the Resurrection, Cincinnati. For inquiries for parish records contact the Chancery.
15—ST. MARTIN DE PORRES (Lincoln Heights) (1935) (African American), Merged with St. Agnes, St. Andrew, and St. Mark the Evangelist, Cincinnati, to form Church of the Resurrection, Cincinnati. For inquiries for parish records contact the Chancery.
16—ST. MATTHEW CHURCH (Norwood) Merged with St. Elizabeth Church, Norwood and Sts. Peter & Paul Church, Norwood to form Holy Trinity Church, Norwood. Records at Holy Trinity Church.
17—ST. MICHAEL CHURCH (LOWER PRICE HILL), Closed. For inquiries for parish records, contact Holy Family Parish, (Price Hill).
18—OUR LADY OF GRACE (Price Hill) Consolidated with Holy Family Parish. Records at Holy Family. (Price Hill).
19—OUR LADY OF LORETTO (LINWOOD), Merged with St. Margaret of Cortona, Madisonville. For inquiries for parish records contact St. Margaret-St. John, Cincinnati.
20—OUR LADY OF PERPETUAL HELP, Consolidated with Holy Family Parish, Price Hill. Records at Holy Family Parish. (Price Hill).
21—OUR LADY OF PRESENTATION (ENGLISH WOODS), Closed. For inquiries for parish records contact St. Leo the Great, Cincinnati.
22—OUR MOTHER OF SORROWS (Roselawn) (1941) Closed. For inquiries for parish records, contact Nativity of Our Lord, Cincinnati.
23—ST. PATRICK, Merged with St. Boniface, Cincinnati. See listing for details. Records at St. Boniface (Northside).
24—STS. PETER AND PAUL CHURCH (Norwood) Merged with St. Elizabeth Church, Norwood and St. Matthew Church, Norwood to form Holy Trinity Church, Norwood. Records at Holy Trinity Church.
25—ST. PIUS CHURCH (CUMMINSVILLE), Closed. For inquiries for parish records contact the chancery.
26—ST. RICHARD OF CHICHESTER (College Hill) Merged with St. Therese, the Little Flower, Cincinnati. See listing for details. Records at St. Therese, the Little Flower.
27—SAN ANTONIO DI PADOVA (FAIRMOUNT), (Italian) Refer to Holy Family (Price Hill) for records.
28—ST. THOMAS AQUINAS (NORTH AVONDALE), Closed. For inquiries for parish records, contact St. Clement, St. Bernard.
BLANCHESTER, CLINTON CO., HOLY NAME (1853) Closed. For inquiries for parish records, see St. Columbkille, Wilmington.
BLUE CREEK, ADAMS CO., ST. JOSEPH, Closed. For inquiries for parish records contact Holy Trinity, West Union.
DAYTON, MONTGOMERY CO.
1—ST. AGNES (1915) Closed. For Sacramental records, please see Our Lady of Grace, Dayton.
2—ASSUMPTION (1949) Merged with Our Lady of Mercy, Dayton. For Sacramental records, please see Our Lady of Grace, Dayton.
3—CORPUS CHRISTI (1911) Merged with Our Lady of Mercy, Dayton to form Our Lady of Grace, Dayton. For inquiries for parish records, see Our Lady of Grace, Dayton.
4—ST. JAMES (1919) Closed. For Sacramental records, please see St. Benedict the Moor, Dayton.
5—OUR LADY OF MERCY (1928) Merged with Corpus Christi, Dayton to form Our Lady of Grace, Dayton. For inquiries for parish records, see Our Lady of Grace, Dayton.
6—SACRED HEART, Closed. For inquiries for parish records contact Emmanuel, Dayton.
7—ST. STEPHEN (North Dayton) (1906) (Hungarian), Closed. For inquiries for parish records, contact Our Lady of the Rosary, Dayton.
FAYETTEVILLE, BROWN CO., ST. PATRICK (1837) [CEM] Closed. For inquiries for parish records, see St. Angela Merici, Fayetteville.
FELICITY, CLERMONT CO., OUR MOTHER OF GOOD COUNSEL, Closed. For inquiries for parish records please see St. Mary Church, Bethel.
FRANKLIN, WARREN CO., ST. MARY (1867) Physical building closed. Renamed St. Mary of the Assumption, Springboro. For inquiries for parish records, contact St. Mary of the Assumption, Springboro.
HAMILTON, BUTLER CO.
1—ST. MARY, Merged now known as St. Julie Billiart. Records St. Julie Billiart, Hamilton.
2—ST. STEPHEN, Merged now known as St. Julie Billiart. Records St. Julie Billiart, Hamilton.
3—ST. VERONICA, Merged now known as St. Julie Billiart. Records St. Julie Billiart, Hamilton.
MANCHESTER, ADAMS CO., ST. MARY OF THE ASSUMPTION (1878) Closed. For inquiries for parish records please contact Holy Trinity, West Union.
SAINT MARTIN, BROWN CO., SAINT MARTIN (1830) [CEM] Closed. For inquiries for parish records, see St. Angela Merici, Fayetteville.
MIDDLETOWN, BUTLER CO.
1—HOLY TRINITY, Merged now known as Holy Family.
2—ST. JOHN THE BAPTIST, Merged now known as Holy Family.
3—ST. MARY, Merged now known as Holy Family.
NEW MIAMI, BUTLER CO., ST. LAWRENCE, Closed. For inquiries for parish records please see St. Julie Billiart, Hamilton.
NEW VIENNA, CLINTON CO., ST. MICHAEL (1874) Closed. For inquiries for parish records contact St. Benignus, Greenfield.
ST. PATRICK, SHELBY CO., ST. PATRICK, Closed. For inquiries for parish records contact St. Michael, Fort Loramie.
SARDINIA, BROWN CO., ST. ELIZABETH PARISH (1955) Closed. For inquiries for parish records, contact St. Mary, Arnheim.
SPRINGFIELD, CLARK, CO., ST. MARY (1921) Closed. For inquiries for parish records please see St. Raphael, Springfield.
VERA CRUZ, BROWN CO., HOLY GHOST (VICARIATE), Closed. For inquiries for parish records contact St. Angela Merici, Fayetteville.

On Special and Archdiocesan Assignment:
Revs.—
Elsbernd, James H., 6678 Paisley Dr., 45236. Tel: 513-865-1175
Gruenbauer, Hans H., P.O. Box 54541, 45254. Tel: 513-659-6446
Heis, Clarence G., 1140 Clifton Hills Ave., 45220. Tel: 513-240-8384
Hess, Daniel K., Via dell' Umilta 30, Rome, Italy 00187
Hilton, Adrian J., 123 E. 13th St., 45202. Tel: 513-721-2988
Kindel, Joseph, 6161 Chambersburg Rd., Dayton, 45424. Tel: 937-233-1503
Peterka, Dale C., 5418 Moeller Ave., 45212. Tel: 513-418-3055
Taylor, Reynaldo S., 745 Ezzard Charles Dr., 45203. Tel: 513-381-4526
Wood, Eric M., Via dell'Umilta 30, Roma, Italy 00187.

On Duty Outside the Archdiocese:
Revs.—
Armstrong, Christopher R., J.C.D., 1025 MI Ave., N.E., P.O. Box 4469, Washington, DC 20017
Fernandes, Earl K., S.T.D., 3339 Massachusetts Ave., N.W., Washington, DC 20008.

Priests On Personal Leave:
Rev.—
Do, Tuan Anh.

Priests Commended to a Life of Prayer and Penance:
Rev.—
Pater, Daniel R.

Retired:
Revs.—
Albietz, Henry F., (Retired), P.O. Box 343, Englewood, 45322. Tel: 937-836-5604
Axe, Thomas R., (Retired), 7010 Rowan Hill Dr., #435, 45227. Tel: 513-871-8906
Bader, Paul A., (Retired), 11677 Greenlawn Ave., 45246
Baker, Kenneth R., (Retired), 3505 Calumet Rd., Apt. 5B, Ludlow Falls, 45339. Tel: 937-307-7028
Beckman, Joseph F., (Retired), 6616 Beechmont Ave., 45230. Tel: 513-624-0554
Bensman, Gerald E., S.T.L., (Retired), 3505 Calumet Rd. #5A, Ludlow Falls, 45339. Tel: 937-999-8210
Birarelli, Carl A., (Retired), 5230 Wedgewood Lane, Sarasota, FL 45235. Tel: 914-210-3694
Bokenkotter, Thomas, (Retired), 4512 Hector Ave., 45227
Bramlage, James A., (Retired), 934 Mound St., 45203. Tel: 513-381-0327
Breaker, Donald J., (Retired), 1027 Kings Court, Venice, FL 34293-2025
Brinkmoeller, David E., (Retired), 3503 Calumet Rd., #4B, Ludlow Falls, 45339. Tel: 937-474-9257
Caserta, Angelo C., (Retired), P.O. Box 4008, Sidney, 45356-4008
Caserta, Charles W., (Retired), 655 Mumford St., #A, Troy, 45373
Caylor, Dennis J., J.C.L., (Retired), 1041 Sundown Rd., Springfield, 45503. Tel: 937-561-8632
Collins, James R., (Retired), 5222 Fox Ridge Dr., 45248. Tel: 513-325-6819
Crone, Patrick H., (Retired), 1201 Scottwood Dr., Batavia, 45103. Tel: 513-460-4293
Cross, William H., (Retired), 3426 Woodford Rd., #7, 45213
Dennemann, Thomas J., (Retired), 5210 Water St., Milford, 45150. Tel: 513-831-1151
Dettenwanger, Dennis, (Retired), 135 Garfield Pl., #617, 45202. Tel: 513-520-0126
DiFolco, Thomas P., (Retired), 985 Windsor St., 45206. Tel: 513-532-2914
Dorrmann, William J., (Retired), 1418 Stone Rd., Harrison, 45030. Tel: 513-202-1735
Duffy, Patrick P., (Retired), Fairfield Pavilion, 5251 Dixie Highway, Fairfield, 45014
Emerick, Stephen J., (Retired), 1960 Madison Rd., #115, 45206. Tel: 513-487-3515
Fischer, John P., (Retired), 3608 State Rte. 222, Batavia, 45103. Tel: 513-680-2881
Fitzsimmons, J. Thomas, (Retired), 320 Donham St., 45226. Tel: 513-871-3373
Flaherty, Michael T., (Retired), 1312 Twin Spires Dr., Batavia, 45103. Tel: 513-843-7859
Gaeke, Thomas M., (Retired), 4578 Swigart Rd., Dayton, 45440
Geraci, Anthony J., (Retired), 1908 Washington North Dr., Dayton, 45458
Goebel, Robert W., (Retired), 3324 Alicemont Ave., 45209. Tel: 513-604-0229
Hackman, Marvin R., (Retired), 121 Dover Rd., Springfield, 45504
Haemmerle, Gerald R., M.A., (Retired), 8240 St. Francis Ct., Dayton, 45458. Tel: 937-640-3127
Hater, Robert J., (Retired), 1443 Cedar Ave., 45224. Tel: 513-541-4611
Helmlinger, Peter M., (Retired), 3027 Summer Field Trail, Sidney, 45365
Hurst, Paul F., (Retired), 928 Bayley Dr., 45233. Tel: 513-347-5578
Hussey, Edmund M., (Retired), 3714 Falls Circle Dr., Hilliard, 43026. Tel: 614-771-2736
Kallaher, Timothy S., (Retired), 9891 Smart Rd., Hillsboro, 45133. Tel: 937-466-2450
Kammerer, Raymond, (Retired), 4210 Laura Marie Dr., Waynesville, 45068. Tel: 513-855-4018
Keferl, Francis J., (Retired), 86 E. Van Lake Dr., Vandalia, 45377
Kosse, Theodore C., (Retired), 3175 Island Creek Rd., West Union, 45693. Tel: 937-549-4178
Kroeger, John, (Retired), 409 Elizabeth St., 45203. Tel: 513-421-4221
Krumm, John E., (Retired), 5581 Charles Ln., Hillsboro, 45133. Tel: 937-409-9355
Kunkel, George C., (Retired), The Wellington at North Bend Crossing, 5156 North Bend, #331, 45247
Lang, Charles F., (Retired), P.O. Box 11, Fairborn, 45324-0011. Tel: 937-469-1629
Langenbrunner, Norman, (Retired), 7864 Gapstow Bridge, 45231. Tel: 513-376-8191
Leshney, Michael F., (Retired), 16 Arbor Circle, #1618, 45255. Tel: 513-515-7555
Meade, James W., (Retired), 140 Palisades Pointe #2, 45238. Tel: 513-382-0205
Meehan, Terence A., (Retired), 3171 Bridget St., Dayton, 45417
Meyer, Harry J., (Retired), 6210 Cleves-Warsaw, 45233. Tel: 513-373-8135
Mick, Lawrence E., (Retired), 3103 Observation Tr., Dayton, 45449. Tel: 937-434-4689
Mierenfeld, Lawrence E., (Retired), 96 Scarborough Village Dr., Centerville, 45458. Tel: 937-603-1165
Mueller, Eugene J., (Retired), 3055 Inwood Dr., 45241. Tel: 513-769-4908
Niemeier, Dennis A., (Retired), 1521 Nature Trail Way, 45231. Tel: 513-648-0976
O'Connor, James J., (Retired), 2806 US Rte., Celina, 45822
Obermeyer, Robert A., (Retired), 1279 S. Waynesville Rd., Oregonia, 45054. Tel: 513-265-9641
Piepmeyer, Ronald J., (Retired), 5720 Hamilton-Mason Rd., Hamilton, 45011
Porter, John E., (Retired), 3505 Calumet Rd., #3A, Ludlow Falls, 45339. Tel: 937-698-5989
Pucke, Michael U., (Retired), 2272 Mossy Grove, Hamilton, 45013. Tel: 513-863-6190
Reilly, David F., (Retired), 7228 S. Dwyer Rd., Okeana, 45053. Tel: 513-738-0470
Robisch, David C., (Retired), 3 Sheldon Close, 45227. Tel: 513-271-4246

Savino, Michael A., (Retired), 140 Palisades Pt., #2, 45238. Tel: 513-479-1241
Schehr, Timothy P., Ph.D., (Retired), 6616 Beechmont Ave., 45230
Schmidt, Thomas W., (Retired), 3505 Calumet Rd., #3B, Ludlow Falls, 45339
Schmitz, George R., (Retired), 135 Garfield Pl., #509, 45202. Tel: 513-662-1547
Schmitz, Robert E., (Retired), 10859 Ponds Ln., 45242
Seger, Oscar H., (Retired), 782 Osterloh Rd., Minster, 45865. Tel: 567-286-0274
Seher, Philip O., (Retired), 5536 Palisades Dr., 45238. Tel: 513-383-4486
Shelander, Donald E., (Retired), P.O. Box 11469, 45211
Shine, Edward J., (Retired), 212 George St., Harrison, 45030. Tel: 513-202-0179
Simone, Earl Francis, (Retired), 100 E. 8th St., 45202
Snodgrass, Thomas A., J.C.L., (Retired), 9037 Winton Rd., 45231. Tel: 513-313-0221
Stockelman, William R., (Retired), 3291 State Rt. 132, Amelia, 45102
Thorsen, Robert J., (Retired), 9157 Montgomery Rd., Ste. 203, 45242
Trippel, Edward G., (Retired), 476 Riddle Rd., #612, 45220
Vincent, David P., (Retired), 3505 Calumet Rd., Unit 2A, Ludlow Falls, 45339. Tel: 937-719-3114
Voellmecke, Francis W., Ph.D., (Retired), 3223 Linwood Rd., 45226. Tel: 513-321-4121
Vonderhaar, Eugene F., (Retired), 10560 Blocker Rd., Bradford, 45308. Tel: 937-448-3061
Wall, John E., (Retired), 5156 N. Bend Crossing, 45247
Waller, Robert C., (Retired), 3505 Calumet Rd., #1B, Ludlow Falls, 45339
Walter, Steven P., (Retired), 10340 Richland Park Dr., Loveland. Tel: 513-608-8489
Wessling, John E., S.T.D., (Retired), 8140 Walcot Ln., Unit E, 45249. Tel: 513-530-5350
Westerhoff, Ralph A., (Retired), 843 Neeb Rd. #1, 45233. Tel: 513-921-2021
Wilker, Ronald H., (Retired), 7001 Cottonwood Rd., Celina, 45822. Tel: 419-268-2842
Witsken, Gary J., (Retired), 6708 Verde Ridge, 45247
Wollering, Carl J., (Retired), 5858 Kellog Ave., 45228. Tel: 513-231-7042.

Permanent Deacons:
Alexander, Marc. A., Our Lady of the Visitation, Cincinnati
Ascolese, Michael A., (Retired), St. Bartholomew, Cincinnati
Back, John Paul, St. Maximilian Kolbe, Liberty Twp.
Baker, Robert, St. Columbkille, Wilmington
Baldwin, Russell O., Emmanuel, Holy Trinity & St. Joseph, Dayton
Balster, Randolph L., St. Henry Cluster Parishes, St. Henry
Bardonaro, Mark A., St. Dominic, Cincinnati
Barney, Gerald L., St. John the Evangelist, West Chester
Basye, Robert L., St. Timothy, Lady Lake, FL
Belcher, Halver L., St. Augustine, Minster
Bermick, Stephen III, St. Mary of the Assumption, Springboro
Berry, Dennis J., Good Shepherd, Cincinnati
Bertke, Omer H., (Retired)
Blessing, Paul H., St. Margaret of York, Loveland
Bornhorst, Gregory A., Holy Redeemer, New Bremen
Brazier, Robert L., St. Thomas More, Withamsville
Brock, Michael H., St. Columban, Loveland
Brodeur, Wilfred J., (Retired)
Brown, Martin J., Holy Rosary, St. Marys
Brown, Steven R., J.C.L., St. Elizabeth Ann Seton, Milford
Bruce, George R., St. William, Cincinnati
Brunsman, Willard, St. Aloysius, Shandon
Bryant, Herman, St. Gabriel, Cincinnati
Buschur, Jerome L., St. Henry Cluster Parishes, St. Henry
Cain, Jerome, St. Saviour, Cincinnati (Blue Ash)
Camele, David G., (Retired)
Campos, Brian M., Ascension, Dayton
Carlin, John K., St. Patrick, Troy
Cassani, Michael J., Immaculate Heart of Mary, Cincinnati
Cecere, Gregory, Queen of Apostles, Dayton
Cohen, Kim, Incarnation, Sarasota, FL
Coleman, Terrell, St. Lawrence, Rhine; Immaculate Conception, Botkins
Collins, John R., (Retired)
Collins, Robert, (Retired)
Convery, John J., (Retired), St. John Fisher, Cincinnati
Cordonnier, Leo N., St. Peter, Dayton
Corson, John, Corpus Christi, New Burlington
Couzins, Jerome, (Unassigned)
Crook, Robert A., St. Patrick, Bellefontaine
Crooker, Timothy, St. James the Greater, White Oak
Danner, Jonathan M., St. Helen, Dayton
Dawson, David A., (Retired)
Day, Larry H., Corpus Christi, New Burlington
De Brosse, Dale J., Precious Blood, Dayton; St. Rita, Dayton; St. Paul, Englewood
Deardorff, Roy L., (Retired)
DeHanes, Kenneth J. Sr., St. Michael, Sharonville
Dipple, Harold I., St. Patrick, Bellefontaine
Duffy, Roger E., Church of the Incarnation, Centerville
Dupree, Gerald M., St. Luke, Beavercreek
Dvorachek, Ronald S., St. George, Georgetown; St. Mary, Arnheim; St. Michael the Archangel, Ripley
Edwards, Dennis, St. Joseph, Cincinnati
Ehrnschwender, Jeffrey P., Queen of Peace, Millville
Erb, Michael C., St. Ignatius Loyola, Cincinnati
Etienne, Jerald F., (Retired)
Faeth, Thomas J., St. William, Cincinnati
Feie, Paul W., Guardian Angels, Cincinnati
Feldkamp, J. Russell, Immaculate Heart of Mary, Cincinnati
Fey, Robert, Guardian Angels, Cincinnati
Fischesser, Elmer, Mercy Hospital, Fairfield
Flamm, Gerald A., St. Bartholomew/St. Vivian, Cincinnati
Gagliarducci, Anthony, (Retired)
Gaier, Thomas M., St. John Fisher, Newtown
Gallenstein, Richard W., Good Shepherd, Cincinnati
George, Raymond W., (Retired)
Geraci, James L., (Retired)
Gerke, John P., St. Clement, Cincinnati
Gerstung, Carl H., St. Henry, Dayton
Gillespie, David B., St. Patrick, Troy
Gloeckler, Donald, Our Lord Christ the King, Cincinnati
Glynn, John T., (Retired)
Gobbi, John R., (Retired)
Graber, Thomas H., St. Mary, Greenville
Gronas, Lawrence D., Holy Name, Trenton
Gutendorf, Robert W., St. Peter, Huber Heights
Gutman, Ralph, Our Lady of the Immaculate Conception, Dayton
Haas, Frederick J., St. Thomas More, Withamsville
Hall, Jeffrey D. Sr., (Retired)
Harris, Timothy J., (Retired)
Helmick, Timothy M., St. Ignatius Loyola, Cincinnati
Hennessey, James F., Holy Trinity, Batavia
Hildebrand, Victor B., Ascension, Kettering
Hinger, Michael W., St. Maximilian Kolbe, Liberty Twp.
Hobbs, Richard, St. Mary of the Assumption, Franklin
Homoelle, John, St. Ignatius Loyola, Cincinnati
Horstman, Norman G., St. Raphael & St. Joseph, Springfield
Hucke, Walter A. Jr., Our Lady of the Rosary, Greenhills
Jabs, Thomas, St. Columban, Loveland
Jacquez, Henry L., Holy Trinity, Norwood
Jamison, Tracy W., Ph.D., Holy Cross-Immaculata & Old St. Mary, Cincinnati
Jenkins, Charles J., Our Lady of Victory, Cincinnati
Jernigan, Jacob, (Retired)
Johnson, Mark U., Immaculate Heart of Mary, Cincinnati
Jones, James E., (Retired)
Jurosic, Nicholas T., St. John Fryburg; St. Patrick, Glynwood
Kall, Dennis, St. Brigid, Xenia
Keller, David R., (Leave of Absence)
Kenzora, Phillip A., St. Teresa of the Child Jesus, Springfield
Klingshirn, David, (Retired)
Klosterman, Roger L., St. Augustine, Minster
Knight, Michael R., (Retired)
Kolis, Conrad C., St. Vivian, St. Bartholomew, Cincinnati
Kostic, Nicholas V. Jr., St. Brigid, Xenia
Kowalski, James, (Retired)
Kozlowski, Robert R., (Retired)
Kraus, Daniel E., Ascension, Kettering
Kroger, Raymond, (Retired)
LeCain, William K., St. Luke, Beavercreek
Leever, Robert J., All Saints, Cincinnati
Leibold, Paul F., St. Philip the Apostle, Morrow
Leo, Michael, Holy Trinity, Dayton
Lim, Amado L., All Saints, Cincinnati
Lippman, Michael E., St. Maximilian Kolbe, Liberty Twp.
Luthman, Paul, Sacred Heart of Jesus, McCartyville
Lutz, Vincent T., St. John the Baptist, Dry Ridge
Lynd, Thomas, Sts. Peter & Paul, Reading
Lyons, John T., Holy Family, Middletown
Lyons, Raymond, St. Leonard Senior Living Community, Centerville
Maag, Lawrence A., (Retired)
Machuga, Mark J., Our Lady of Victory, Cincinnati
Mahoney, Michael, (Retired)
Martin, Richard W., Our Lady of Good Hope, Miamisburg
Martin, Terrance A., Our Lady of Good Hope, Miamisburg
Martin, William, (Unassigned)
Mascorro, Susano, (Retired)
McCray, David M., (Retired)
Merrell, Jeffrey, St. Peter in Chains, Hamilton
Merritt, James A., St. John, West Chester
Meyer, David, St. Vincent Ferrer, Cincinnati
Meyer, Donald J. Jr., St. John the Baptist, Harrison
Meyer, Michael, St. Remy, Russia
Meyer, Robert E., St. Columbkille, Wilmington
Mignery, Michael E., Queen of Peace, Millville
Miller, James A., St. Columban, Loveland
Miller, Thomas H., St. Charles Borromeo, Kettering
Minnich, Patrick, (LOA)
Montgomery, Michael, Our Lady of the Immaculate Conception, Dayton
Moore, William F., (Retired)
Mullaney, William M., (Retired)
Murphy, Daniel R., St. Veronica, Cincinnati
Myers, Philip B., Holy Angels, Sidney
Nagy, Norbert, (Retired)
Novick, Rick, Guardian Angels, Cincinnati
O'Bleness, Ralph F., (Retired)
Olinger, James C., St. Rita, Dayton
Palumbo, Patrick A., St. John Neumann, Cincinnati
Parker, Leonard B., (Retired)
Perkins, Jeffrey M., St. Margaret of York, Loveland
Perryman, Clifton A., Marion Catholic Community, Maria Stein
Petrie, William J., (Retired)
Pitts, Joseph L. Jr., (Retired)
Platfoot, Thomas F., Our Lady of Mercy, Queen of Martyrs, & Corpus Christi, Dayton
Prier, Michael F., Precious Blood, Dayton
Quattrone, John M., St. Ann, Groesbeck
Rader, Daniel L., (Retired)
Rammel, Andrew R., Precious Blood, Dayton
Rauch, Christopher A., St. Francis of Assisi, Centerville
Reder, Richard J., Assumption, Mt. Healthy
Reising, Edward B., St. Joseph, North Bend
Renneker, William B., (Retired)
Rettig, John M., St. Francis de Sales, Lebanon
Richardson, Paul E., (Retired)
Risch, Ronald H., (Retired)
Riva-Saleta, Luis O., (Retired)
Roadruck, Max, (Retired)
Roemer, Charles W., Sts. Peter and Paul, Reading
Rogers, Earl, (Retired)
Royer, Milton W., (Retired)
Ryan, Steven A., Our Lady of the Rosary, Greenhills
Saluke, William M., (Retired)
Sasson, Gerard J., St. Columban, Loveland
Schaefer, John M., Our Lady of Sorrows, Monroe
Schaefer, William E., Holy Name, Trenton
Schellman, Leon, Good Shepherd, Cincinnati
Schmidl, George L., (Retired)
Schnur, Kenneth R., (Retired)
Schroeder, Robert J., St. Antoninus, Cincinnati
Schuler, John A., St. Mary, Hyde Park
Schutte, Timothy, St. Andrew, Milford
Shaffer, David, Immaculate Heart of Mary, Cincinnati
Shea, David J., Immaculate Heart of Mary, Cincinnati
Simpson, Richard D., St. Luke, Beavercreek
Sipniewski, Thomas M., Church of the Ascension, Kettering
Skinner, Matthew R., Our Lady of the Rosary, Greenhills
Slattery, John M., (Unassigned)
Sonnenberg, James J., (Retired)
Srode, Walter, (Retired)
Staab, Robert A. Jr., Assumption, Mt. Healthy
Stang, Ronald L., St. Peter, New Richmond
Stasiak, Mark, (Retired)
Staun, William J., Holy Trinity, Norwood
Steinwert, David P., St. Teresa of Avila, Cincinnati
Stewart, Kenneth R., St. Augustine, Germantown
Subler, Joseph, St. Paul, Englewood
Thamann, John D., (Retired)
Thomas, Dan, (Retired)
Thomas, Michael T., St. Thomas More, Withamsville
Timmerman, Paul L., St. Michael, Fort Loramie
Trimpe, Michael A., Cathedral of St. Peter in Chains, Cincinnati
Vilaboy, Manuel D., (Retired)
Vu, Hoang Dominic, St. Matthias, Cincinnati
Wade, Daniel J., St. Peter, Huber Heights
Wagner, Francis X., St. Peter in Chains Cathedral, Cincinnati

Walker, Harry S., (Retired)
Wallace, David M., St. Philip, Morrow
Walworth, James W. Sr., Holy Angels, Dayton
Westbay, Richard L., St. Joseph, Wapakoneta
Westendorf, Mark J., Good Shepherd, Cincinnati
Westerfield, Thomas E., (Retired)
Winters, Royce E., Church of the Resurrection, Cincinnati
Woeste, James H., St. Philip the Apostle, Morrow
Wong, Louis F., St. Susanna, Mason
Wright, Charles O., St. Christopher, Vandalia
Yetter, Jerry J., St. Boniface, Cincinnati
Zinck, Robert C. Jr., Church of the Incarnation, Centerville
Zink, David E., St. Albert the Great, Kettering
Zvonar, George J., (Retired).

INSTITUTIONS LOCATED IN DIOCESE

[A] THE ATHENAEUM OF OHIO

CINCINNATI. *The Athenaeum of Ohio* (1829) Mount St. Mary's Seminary, 6616 Beechmont Ave., 45230. Tel: 513-231-2223; Fax: 513-231-3254; Email: ath@athenaeum.edu; Web: www.athenaeum.edu. Most Rev. Dennis M. Schnurr, J.C.D., D.D., Archbishop of Cincinnati, Chancellor, Chm. of Bd. of Trustees; Revs. Anthony R. Brausch, Ph.L., Pres. & Rector; David J. Endres, Ph.D., Dean, Athenaeum of Ohio; Mr. Dennis K. Eagan, B.B.A., Vice Pres., Finance Admin. Incorporated March 24, 1928 by the State of Ohio and presently has three divisions: Mount St. Mary's Seminary of the West; the Lay Pastoral Ministry Program and the Special Studies Division. Clergy 2; Lay Teachers 29; Priests 14; Sisters 1; Students 242; Clergy / Religious Teachers 2.

Lay Pastoral Ministry Program, 6616 Beechmont Ave., 45230. Tel: 513-231-1200; Fax: 513-231-3254 ; Email: smcgurgan@athenaeum.edu. Dr. Susan McGurgan, D.Min., Dir.; Dr. Hal Belcher, Ph.D., Prog. Coord.; Barbara Yoder, Dir.

The St. Gregory Seminary Trust, 6616 Beechmont Ave., 45230. Tel: 513-231-2223; Email: ath@athenaeum.edu.

[B] SEMINARIES

CINCINNATI. *Mount St. Mary's Seminary of the West* (1829) (Diocesan) 6616 Beechmont Ave., 45230. Tel: 513-231-2223; Fax: 513-231-3254; Email: ath@mtsm.org; Web: www.athenaeum.edu. Revs. David J. Endres, Ph.D., Dean; Thomas McQuillen, M.A., Dean; Ryan Ruiz, S.L.D., Dir.; Paul A. Ruwe, M.A., Dir.; David A. Sunberg, Dir.; Jason A. Williams, Dir.; Anthony R. Brausch, Ph.L., Rector; Anthony Stephens, C.P.M., M.Div., Vice Rector/Dir. of Formation; Mr. Nicholas Jobe, B.S., Registrar; Mr. Dennis K. Eagan, B.B.A., Vice Pres., Finance & Admin.; Mrs. Connie Song, M.L.S., M.S.L.S., Librarian; Revs. Joseph F. Beckman, In Res., (Retired); Steven Beseau, S.T.D., In Res.; Timothy P. Schehr, Ph.D., In Res., (Retired); Daniel Schmitmeyer, In Res.; Rev. Paul Jerome Keller, O.P., S.T.D., Non-Res. Faculty; Deacon Tracy W. Jamison, Ph.D., Non-Res. Faculty; Dr. David Foster, Ph.D., Non-Res. Faculty; Dr. Matthew C. Genung, S.S.D., Non-Res. Faculty; Dr. Mary Catherine Levri, D.M.A., Non-Res. Faculty; Alan Mostrom, M.A., Non-Res. Faculty; Mr. Marco Mulattieri, S.S.L., Non-Res. Faculty; Bradford Manderfield, Non-Res. Faculty. Major seminary for students in Theology. Clergy 2; Lay Teachers 31; Priests 16; Seminarians 82; Sisters 1; Students 82.

[C] NOVITIATES AND HOUSES OF STUDY

CINCINNATI. *St. Anthony Shrine* (1888) 5000 Colerain Ave., 45223-1213. Tel: 513-541-2146; Fax: 513-541-9347. Revs. Daniel Kroger, O.F.M., CEO; Joseph Ricchini, O.F.M., Dir.; Bro. Vincent Delorenzo, O.F.M., Supr.; Revs. Kenan Freson, O.F.M., Vicar; Clifford Hennings, O.F.M.; David Kobak; Bros. Gabriel Balassone, O.F.M., In Res.; Jerome Beetz, O.F.M., In Res,; David Crank, O.F.M., In Res.; Rev. Frank Geers, O.F.M., (Retired); Bro. Scott Obrecht, O.F.M., (On Sabbatical). Brothers 5; Priests 8.

Dominican Novitiate, 7630 Shawnee Run Rd., 45243. Tel: 513-527-3972; Email: novicemaster@stgertrude.org; Web: www.opstjoseph.org. Rev. Michael Mary Dosch, O.P., Contact Person. Novices 13; Students 13; Clergy / Religious Teachers 3.

BEAVERCREEK. *Marianist Novitiate*, 4435 E. Patterson Rd., Beavercreek, 45430-1033. Tel: 937-426-5721; Fax: 937-429-4686; Email: cwittsm@gmail.com. Rev. Christopher T. Wittmann, S.M., Dir. of Novices, Email: cwittsm@gmail.com; Bros. Daniel L. Klco, S.M., M.S., Asst. Dir. of Novices; John Lemker, S.M., Marianist Rel.; Thomas Redmond, S.M., Marianist Rel.; Thomas Wendorf, S.M., Ph. D., Marianist Rel.; Magdaleno Ceballos, Novice; Juan Perez, Novice; Junghyeon Cho, Pre-Novice; Geunwoo Shim, Pre-Novice. Brothers 4; Novices 2; Priests 1; (Pre-Novice) 2.

[D] COLLEGES AND UNIVERSITIES

CINCINNATI. *Good Samaritan College of Nursing and Health Science*, 375 Dixmyth Ave., 45220. Tel: 513-862-2631; Fax: 513-862-3572; Email: james.hauschildt@email.gscollege.edu; Web: www.gscollege.edu. James A. Hauschildt, Pres.; Donna S. Nienaber, Sec. Good Samaritan College offers the following programs: Associates of Science in Health Science, Associates in Applied Science in Nursing and Bachelors of Science in Nursing (RN-BSN-Hybrid online & in-class flexibility). For Admissions call: (513) 862-2743. Students 404.

Mount St. Joseph University (1920) (Grades Associate-Doctorate), 5701 Delhi Rd., 45233-1670. Tel: 513-244-4200; Fax: 513-244-4654; Email: info@msj.edu; Web: www.msj.edu. Janet Cox, Dean of Students; Mr. Zachary Silka, Vice Pres.; Kathleen Cardwell, Dir. Mktg. & Commun.; Jeff Briggs, Treas.; Diana Davis, Provost; H Williams, Pres. Coed. Chartered by the State of Ohio. Employees 543; Faculty 112; Priests 1; Sisters 1; Students 2,062; Clergy / Religious Teachers 1.

Xavier University (1831) (Grades Associate-Doctorate), 3800 Victory Pkwy., 45207. Tel: 513-745-3501; Fax: 513-745-4223; Email: balloum@xavier.edu; Web: www.xavier.edu. Revs. Michael J. Graham, S.J., Pres.; Daniel F. Hartnett, S.J., Pastor & Rector, Bellarmine Chapel; Mr. Thomas Hayes, Ph.D., Dean, Williams College of Business; Dr. Steve Herbert, Dean of the Graduate School; Dr. Paul Gore, Dean, College of Professional Sciences; Mr. David Mengel, Dean, College of Arts and Sciences; Dr. John F. Kucia, Vice Pres., Emeritus; Mr. Gary R. Massa, Vice Pres., Univ. Rels.; Mr. Jeffery Coleman, Vice Pres., Risk Mgmt.; Mr. Phil Chick, Vice Pres., Chief Business Officer; Ms. Debra Mooney, Vice President/Chief Mission Officer; Mr. Gregory Christopher, Vice Pres., DIr. of Athletics; Melissa Baumann, Provost & Chief Academic Officer; Ms. Janice Walker, Chief Diversity and Inclusion Officer; Mr. David Johnson, Chief Student Affairs Officer; Mrs. Connie Perme, Assoc. VIce Pres., Human Resources; Ken Gibson, Library Dir.; Mr. Henry Saas, Bursar; Andrea Wawrzusin, Registrar; Ms. Mary Ballou, Contact Person. Lay Teachers 383; Sisters 2; Students 7,132; College of Arts & Sciences Enrollment 1,823; Williams College of Business Undergraduates 1,275; College of Professional Sciences Enrollment 1,858; Graduate Program Enrollment 2,135; Permanent Staff: Priests 4; ESL & Non-Degree Seeking Enrollment 41.

DAYTON. *The University of Dayton* (1850) (Grades Bachelors-Doctorate), (Coed) 300 College Park Ave., Dayton, 45469-1638. Tel: 937-229-1000; Fax: 937-229-4000; Web: www.udayton.edu. Paul H. Benson, Ph.D., Provost; Revs. James Fitz, S.M., M.Div., Vice Pres. for Mission & Rector; Joseph F. Kozar, S.M., Ph.D., Religious Studies; Thomas A. Thompson, S.M., Dir., Marian Library; Johan G. Roten, S.M., S.T.D., Dir., Research & Special Collections, Marian Library; James Schimelpfening, S.M., Campus Min.; Bakpenam Sebastien Abalodo, S.M., Intl. Marian Research Institute; Bros. Raymond L. Fitz, S.M., Ph.D., Social Justice; Thomas Giardino, S.M., Marianist Rel.; Robert H. Hughes, S.M., Printing & Design; M. Gary Marcinowski, S.M., M.F.A., Visual Arts; Andrew J. Kosmowski, S.M., Library-Marian Initiatives; Brandon Alana-Maugaotega, Marianist Rel.; Sisters Leanne Jablonski, F.M.I., Religious Studies; Laura M. Leming, F.M.I., Ph.D., Sociology & Anthropology; Gabby Bibeau, F.M.I. Society of Mary (Marianists). Brothers 14; Clergy 7; Priests 11; Sisters 3; Students 10,899.

The Marian Library/International Marian Research Institute (IMRI) (1943) 300 College Park, Dayton, 45469-1390. Tel: 937-229-4214; Email: ngerhard1@udayton.edu. Kathleen M. Webb, M.L.S., Dean; Rev. Thomas A. Thompson, S.M.; Bro. Andrew J. Kosmowski, S.M., Librarian; Nancy Gerhard, Staff; Rev. Bakpenam Sebastien Abalodo, S.M.

Institute for Pastoral Initiatives (1971) 1700 S. Patterson Blvd, Dayton, 45469. Tel: 937-229-3126; Email: azukowski1@udayton.edu; Web: https://udayton.edu/artssciences/ctr/ipi/index.php. 300 College Park, Dayton, 45469-7013. Sr. Angela Ann Zukowski, M.H.S.H., D.Min., Dir.

Libraries.

SAINT MARTIN. *Chatfield College* (1971) (Grades Associate-Associate), Brown County Ursulines, 20918 State Rte. 251, St. Martin, 45118. Tel: 513-875-3344; Fax: 513-875-3912; Email: john.tafaro@chatfield.edu; Web: www.chatfield.edu. John P. Tafaro, Pres.; Dolores Berish, Librarian. Faculty 5; Priests 2; Sisters 1; Students 250; Adjunct Faculty 53; Staff 32.

[E] HIGH SCHOOLS, INTER-PAROCHIAL

CINCINNATI. *Archbishop McNicholas High School*, 6536 Beechmont Ave., 45230. Tel: 513-231-3500; Fax: 513-231-1351; Email: dmueller@mcnhs.org; Web: www.mcnhs.org. Mr. David B. Mueller, Prin.; Mr. Jeffry Hutchinson-Smyth, Campus Min.; Mr. David Jackson, Exec. Dir.; Mrs. Shannon Kapp, Dir. of Communications and Marketing; Mrs. Roberta Veleta, Dir. of Finance. Lay Teachers 49; Students 545.

Elder High School (1922) 3900 Vincent Ave., 45205-1699. Tel: 513-921-3744; Fax: 513-921-8123; Email: ruffingkd@elderhs.net; Web: www.elderhs.org. Kurt Ruffing, Prin.; Ms. Monica Williams-Mitchell, Librarian. Lay Teachers 63; Students 768.

LaSalle High School (1960) 3091 N. Bend Rd., 45239-7696. Tel: 513-741-3000; Fax: 513-741-2666; Email: afrigge@lasallehs.net; Web: www.LaSalleHS.net. Aaron Marshall, Prin. Lay Teachers 46; Students 605.

Moeller High School (1959) 9001 Montgomery Rd., 45242-7780. Tel: 513-791-1680; Email: nbeiersdorfer@moeller.org; Web: www.moeller.org. Nathan Beiersdorfer, Dir. Bus. Opers.; Marshall Hyzdu, Pres.; Carl Kremer, Prin. Lay Teachers 65; Students 875; Marianist Brothers 2.

Mt. Notre Dame High School Mt. Notre Dame, 711 E. Columbia Ave., 45215. Tel: 513-821-3044; Fax: 513-821-6068; Email: mnd@mndhs.org; Web: www.mndhs.org. Mrs. Judy Gerwe, Pres.; Mrs. Karen Day, Prin. Lay Teachers 60; Sisters 1; Students 724.

Purcell Marian High School (East Walnut Hills) 2935 Hackberry St., 45206. Tel: 513-751-1230; Fax: 513-751-1395; Email: mspencer@purcellmarian.org; Web: www.purcellmarian.org. Mr. Andrew Farfsing, Prin.; Peggy Flick, Librarian. Lay Teachers 33; Priests 1; Sisters 1; Students 325.

Roger Bacon High School (1928) 4320 Vine St., 45217. Tel: 513-641-1300; Fax: 513-641-0498; Email: tburke@rogerbacon.org; Web: www.rogerbacon.org. Steve Schad, Prin.; Amy M. Wilson, Admin. Asst.; Thomas Burke, Pres.; Rev. Mark J. Hudak, O.F.M., Information and Technology Coord.; Brandon Cowans, Dir. of Admissions and Communications; Rev. Roger Lopez, O.F.M., Community Outreach; Michael Engel, Treas. & CFO; Pam Rosfeld, Dir.; Steve Rossi, Athletic Dir.; Rick Sollmann, Asst. Advancement Dir.; Julie Vehorn, Dir. of Academics; Paul Zlatic, Dean of Discipline. Franciscan Friars of the Cincinnati Province of St. John the Baptist. Brothers 2; Lay Teachers 41; Priests 2; Students 508; Clergy / Religious Teachers 2.

Seton High School (Price Hill) 3901 Glenway Ave., 45205. Tel: 513-471-2600; Fax: 513-557-7423; Email: whitek@setoncincinnati.org; Web: www.setoncincinnati.org. Mrs. Karen White, Prin.; Mrs. Kathy Ciarla, Pres.; Mrs. Susan Hollenbach, Vice Prin.; Marianne Ridiman, Retention Coord.; Mrs. Janice Linz, Campus Min. Lay Teachers 44; Sisters of Charity of Cincinnati 1; Students 516; Clergy / Religious Teachers 1.

DAYTON. *Archbishop Alter High School* (1962) 940 E. David Rd., Kettering, 45429. Tel: 937-434-4434; Fax: 937-434-0507; Web: www.alterhs.org. Mrs. Lourdes Lambert, Prin.; Mrs. Theresa Metter, Librarian. Lay Teachers 48; Sisters 1; Students 605; Clergy / Religious Teachers 1.

Carroll High School (1961) 4524 Linden Ave., Dayton, 45432. Tel: 937-253-8188; Fax: 937-424-9636; Email: msableski@carrollhs.org; Web: www.carrollhs.org. Mr. Matthew T. Sableski, Prin. Lay Teachers 58; Students 766.

Chaminade Julienne Catholic High School, 505 S. Ludlow St., Dayton, 45402. Tel: 937-461-3740; Fax: 937-461-6256; Email: Jmarshall@cjeagles.org; Web: www.cjeagles.org. Mr. Dan Meixner, Pres.; Mr. John Marshall, Prin.; Stephen Fuchs, Asst. Prin.; Greg Mueller, Asst. Prin.; Mrs. Kelli Kinnear, Dir. Campus Ministry; Gina Harrington, Librarian; Rev. Robert Jones, Chap. Conducted by the Society of Mary (Marianists) and Sisters of Notre Dame de Namur. Lay Teachers 54; Priests 1; Sisters 1; Students 659; Clergy / Religious Teachers 1.

HAMILTON. *Stephen T. Badin High School* (1966) 571 New London Rd., Hamilton, 45013. Tel: 513-863-3993; Fax: 513-785-2844; Email: bpendergest@badinhs.org; Web: badinhs.org. Brian

Pendergest, Prin. Lay Teachers 49; Students 610; Total Staff 85.

MIDDLETOWN. *Bishop Fenwick High School*, 4855 State Rte. 122, Franklin, 45005. Tel: 513-423-0723; Fax: 513-420-8690; Email: nwoodward@fenwickfalcons.org; Web: www.fenwickfalcons.org. Mr. Blane Collison, Prin. Lay Teachers 35; Students 534; Clergy / Religious Teachers 4.

SIDNEY. *Lehman Catholic High School* (1970) 2400 St. Mary's Ave., Sidney, 45365. Tel: 937-498-1161; Fax: 937-492-9877; Email: d.stauffer@lehmancatholic.com; Web: www.lehmancatholic.com. Denise Stauffer, Prin. & CEO; Peter Dunlap, Dean; Rev. Peter Langenkamp, Chap. Lay Teachers 15; Priests 1; Sisters 1; Students 180.

SPRINGFIELD. *Catholic Central School*, 1200 E. High St., Springfield, 45505-1124. Tel: 937-324-4551; Fax: 937-521-1352; Email: sdeweese@ccirish.org; Web: www.ccirish.org. David Fuller, Pres.; Shannon DeWeese, Prin. Lay Teachers 22; Students 349.

[F] HIGH SCHOOLS, PRIVATE

CINCINNATI. *DePaul Cristo Rey High School*, 1133 Clifton Hills Ave., 45220. Tel: 513-861-0600; Fax: 513-861-0900; Email: jeanne.bessette@dpcr.net; Web: www.discoverdepaul.org. Sr. Jeanne Bessette, O.S.F., Pres. & Contact Person; Abby Held, Dir.; Lisa Atkins, CFO; Margee Garbsch, Dir. Communications; Sparkle Worley, Vice Pres. Advancement; Paul Ebert, Prin. Sponsored by Sisters of Charity of Cincinnati Employees 62; Lay Teachers 24; Religious 3; Students 327.

Mercy McAuley High School, 6000 Oakwood Ave., 45224. Tel: 513-681-1800; Web: www.mercymcauley.org. Mrs. Connie Kampschmidt, Prin. Lay Teachers 56; Students 716.

The Summit Country Day School Also see The Summit Country Day school located under Elementary Schools, Private. 2161 Grandin Rd., 45208-3300. Tel: 513-871-4700; Fax: 513-533-5373; Email: wilson_r@summitcds.org; Web: www.summitcds.org. Richard Wilson, Head of School; John Thornburg, Div. Dir., Upper School (Grades 9-12). Lay Teachers 41; Priests 1; Students 416.

St. Ursula Academy, 1339 E. McMillan St., 45206. Tel: 513-961-3410; Fax: 513-961-3856; Email: lkramer@saintursula.org; Web: www.saintursula.org. Lelia Kramer, Pres.; Dr. Mari Thomas, Prin.; Jill Herald, Librarian. Lay Teachers 61; Students 650.

Ursuline Academy of Cincinnati (1896) Senior High School. 5535 Pfeiffer Rd., 45242. Tel: 513-791-5791 ; Fax: 513-791-5802; Email: tbarhorst@ursulineacademy.org; Web: www.ursulineacademy.org. Rev. John E. Wessling, S.T.D., (Retired); Sharon Redmond, Pres.; Thomas Barhorst, Prin.; Mary Bender, Asst. Prin.; Jill Hallahan, Asst. Prin.; Corey Holthaus, Librarian. Ursuline Sisters of Brown Co. Saint Martin, OH. Lay Teachers 70; Priests 1; Sisters 2; Students 621; Clergy / Religious Teachers 8.

St. Xavier High School, 600 W. North Bend Rd., 45224. Tel: 513-761-7600; Fax: 513-842-1610; Email: bschulte@stxavier.org; Web: www.stxavier.org. Timothy Reilly, Pres.; Mr. Terrence H. Tyrrell, Prin.; Mr. Michael J. Dehring, Admin.; Jason Ahlers, Admin.; Jennifer Ziebol, Admin.; Brian Schaeper, Admin.; Mr. James Schurrer, Admin.; Andrea Owens, Librarian. Lay Teachers 135; Priests 3; Students 1,580; Clergy / Religious Teachers 4.

[G] CONSOLIDATED ELEMENTARY SCHOOLS

CINCINNATI. *St. Boniface School* (1867) (Grades PreK-8), 4305 Pitts Ave., 45223. Tel: 513-541-5122; Fax: 513-541-3939; Email: school@stbonifaceschool.net; Web: www.stbonifaceschool.net. Sisters Miriam Kaeser, Prin.; Ann Gorman, R.S.M., Admin. Serving the parishes of St. Boniface, St. Leo and Mother of Christ, Cincinnati. Lay Teachers 13; Sisters 4; Students 202.

Corryville Catholic Elementary School, (Grades PreSchool-8), 108 Calhoun St., 45219. Tel: 513-281-4856; Fax: 513-281-6497; Email: lwestendorf@corryvillecatholic.org; Email: khesselbrock@corryvillecatholic.org; Web: www.corryvillecatholic.org. Ms. Linda Westendorf, Prin. Consolidated school serving the parishes of Holy Name, St. Andrew, Assumption, Sacred Heart and St. Monica-St. George. Clergy 1; Lay Teachers 13; Sisters 1; Students 206.

St. Gabriel Consolidated School, (Grades K-8), 18 W. Sharon Ave., 45246. Tel: 513-771-5220; Fax: 513-771-5133; Email: s.wendt@stgabeschool.org; Email: info@stgabeschool.org; Web: www.stgabeschool.org. Stacie Wendt, Prin. Consolidated school serving the parishes of St. Gabriel, Glendale; St. John, West Chester; St. Matthias, Forest Park; St. Maximilian Kolbe, West Chester. Lay Teachers 18; Students 330.

John Paul II Catholic School (1980) (Grades PreK-8), 9375 Winton Rd., 45231. Tel: 513-521-0860; Fax: 513-728-3101; Email: nroach@jpiics.org; Web: www.jpiics.org. Mrs. Leanora Roach, Prin.; Mrs. Nancy Acciani, Librarian. Lay Teachers 27; Students 431.

St. John the Baptist Catholic School, (Grades PreSchool-8), 5375 Dry Ridge Rd., 45252. Tel: 513-385-7970; Fax: 513-699-6964; Email: cdreyer@stjohnsdrschool.org; Web: www.stjohnsdrschool.org. Mr. Daniel A. Minelli, Prin. Clergy 13; Lay Teachers 26; Students 431.

St. Nicholas Academy, (Grades PreK-8), 170 Siebenthaler Ave., 45215. Tel: 513-686-2727; Fax: 513-686-2729; Email: cdunham@stnacademy.org; Web: stnacademy.org. Mrs. Aideen Briggs, Prin. An interparish elementary school sponsored by St. John the Evangelist, Deer Park, Holy Trinity, Norwood and Our Lady of the Sacred Heart, Reading parishes. Lay Teachers 20; Students 170.

Our Lady of Grace, (Grades K-8), 2940 W. Galbraith Rd., 45239. Tel: 513-931-3070; Fax: 513-931-3707; Email: mkirk@olgcs.org; Email: mdesmier@olgcs.org; Web: www.olgcs.org. Mrs. Mandy Kirk, Prin.; Michael Desmier, Business Mgr. Serving the parishes of St. Ann (Groesbeck), Church of the Assumption (Mount Healthy), St. Margaret Mary (North College Hill) & St. Therese, the Little Flower (Mt. Airy). Lay Teachers 26; Students 402.

DAYTON. *Bishop Leibold School*, (Grades PreSchool-8), 24 S. Third St., Miamisburg, 45342. Tel: 937-866-3021; Fax: 937-866-5680; Email: twallace@bishopleibold.org; Web: www.bishopleibold.com. Dr. Theodore Wallace, Prin. Consolidated school of St. Henry, Dayton and Our Lady of Good Hope, Miamisburg. Lay Teachers 27; Students 350.

West Campus, (Grades PreSchool-8), 24 S. Third St., Miamisburg, 45342. Tel: 937-866-3021; Fax: 937-866-5680; Email: twallace@bishopleibold.org; Web: www.bishopleibold.org. Dr. Theodore Wallace, Prin.; Julie Wehner, Sec. (West Campus). Lay Teachers 12; Students 190.

East Campus, (Grades 4-8), 6666 Springboro Pike, Dayton, 45449. Tel: 937-434-9343; Fax: 937-436-3048; Email: twallace@bishopleibold.org; Web: www.bishopleibold.org. Dr. Theodore Wallace, Prin.; Amy Hart, Sec. (East Campus); Kathy Stonecash, Librarian. Lay Teachers 15; Students 193.

HAMILTON. *St. Joseph Consolidated School*, (Grades K-8), 925 S. Second St., Hamilton, 45011. Tel: 513-863-8758; Fax: 513-863-5772; Email: info@sjcshamilton.org; Web: www.sjcshamilton.org. J. William Hicks, Prin.; Theresa Stenger, Contact Person; Kathy Brossart, Librarian. Serving the parishes of St. Aloysius, Shandon and St. Joseph, Hamilton. Lay Teachers 11; Students 196; Total Staff 35.

MIDDLETOWN. *St. John XXIII Catholic School*, (Grades PreK-8), 3806 Manchester Rd., Middletown, 45042. Tel: 513-424-1196; Fax: 513-672-2114; Email: pfairbanks@stjohn23school.org; Email: dpickerill@stjohn23school.org; Email: info@stjohn23school.org; Web: stjohn23school.org. Dawn Pickerill, Prin.; Terri Mulhall, Librarian. Serving the parishes of Holy Family, Middletown; St. Mary, Franklin; Holy Name, Trenton; Our Lady of Sorrows, Monroe. Lay Teachers 30; Students 420.

PIQUA. *Piqua Catholic School*, (Grades PreK-8), 503 W. North St., Piqua, 45356. Tel: 937-773-1564; Fax: 937-773-0380; Email: zimmermanb@piquacatholic.org; Web: www.piquacatholic.org. Bradley Zimmerman, Prin.; Jessica Rank, Business Mgr.; Tweetie Duer, Admin. Asst.; Rachel Birman, Librarian. Serving the parishes of St. Boniface and St. Mary. Lay Teachers 9; Sisters 1; Students 121; Clergy / Religious Teachers 1.

SPRINGFIELD. *Catholic Central School*, (Grades 9-12), 1200 E. High St., Springfield, 45505-1124. Tel: 937-328-7427, Ext. 101; Fax: 937-328-7426; Web: www.ccirish.org. David Fuller, Pres.; Patrick Rizer, Prin.; Dr. Karen M. Juliano, CEO. Lay Teachers 14; Students 141.

[H] ELEMENTARY SCHOOLS, PRIVATE

CINCINNATI. **The Good Shepherd Catholic Montessori School*, (Grades PreK-8), 4460 Berwick St., 45227. Tel: 513-271-4171; Fax: 513-271-4680; Web: www.gscmontessori.org. Anne Marie Vega, Prin.; Daniel Teller, Exec. Faculty 42; Students 195.

The Summit Country Day School (1890) (Grades PreK-8), 2161 Grandin Rd., 45208-3300. Tel: 513-871-4700; Fax: 513-533-5373; Email: wilson_r@summitcds.org; Web: www.summitcds.org. Richard Wilson, Head of School; Mr. Mike Johnson, Div. Dir., Middle School (Grades 5-8); Kathy Scott, Dir. Affiliated with the Sisters of Notre Dame de Namur. Lay Teachers 81; Priests 1; Students 616.

St. Ursula Villa (1990) (Grades PreK-8), 3660 Vineyard Pl., 45226. Tel: 513-871-7218; Fax: 513-871-0082; Email: p.duplace@stursulavilla.org; Web: www.stursulavilla.org. Polly Duplace, Prin. & Contact Person; Susan Hall, Librarian. Clergy 20; Lay Teachers 53; Students 460.

LIBERTY TOWNSHIP. *Mother Teresa Catholic Elementary School* (1998) (Grades K-8), 7197 Mother Teresa Ln., Liberty Township, 45044-9426. Tel: 513-779-6585; Fax: 513-779-6468; Email: sranne@mtces.org; Web: www.mtces.org. Jim Samocki, Bd. Chm.; Ms. Angie McGraw, Devel. Dir.; Sr. Anne Mary Schulz, C.PP.S., Prin.; Mrs. Mary Stas, Asst. Prin.; Angie Timms, Librarian. Lay Teachers 23; Sisters 1; Students 517.

[I] CHILD CARE INSTITUTIONS

CINCINNATI. *St. Joseph Infant and Maternity Home* dba St. Joseph Home (1876) 10722 Wyscarver Rd., 45241. Tel: 513-563-2520; Fax: 513-563-1958; Email: dconnors@stjosephhome.org; Email: tcook@stjosephhome.org; Web: www.stjosephhome.org. Mr. Dan Connors, Pres. & CEO and Contact Person. Sisters of Charity of Cincinnati, OH.Adult Day Program, 10875 Indeco Dr., Blue Ash, OH 45241. Respite Beds 8; Residential 48.

St. Joseph Orphanage (1829) 5400 Edalbert Dr., 45239-7695. Tel: 513-741-3100; Fax: 513-741-5686; Email: info@SJOkids.org; Web: www.sjokids.org. Eric Cummins, M.A., CEO. Archdiocesan Children and Adult Behavioral Health, Education and Residential Treatment Center. Students 147; Served Daily 4,580; Clergy / Religious Teachers 17; Staff 297.

St. Joseph Orphanage Outpatient Community Case Management, 5400 Edalbert Dr., 45239. Tel: 513-741-3100; Fax: 513-741-5686; Email: info@sjokids.org. Eric Cummins, M.A., CEO.

St. Joseph Orphanage-Villa Campus, 5400 Edalbert Dr., 45239. Tel: 513-741-3100; Fax: 513-741-5686; Email: info@sjokids.org; Web: www.sjokids.org. Eric Cummins, M.A., CEO. Behavioral Health and Education. Students 93.

St. Joseph Orphanage Foster Care-Cincinnati, Tel: 513-481-7350; Fax: 513-481-7360. Foster Care Service, Birth to 21.

St. Joseph Orphanage-Altercrest Campus, 274 Sutton Rd., 45230. Tel: 513-231-5010; Fax: 513-231-8651; Email: info@sjokids.org; Web: www.sjokids.org. Eric Cummins, M.A., CEO. Comprehensive services for adolescents including Community Transition Programs, Special Education, Outpatient, Day Treatment, Residential Mental/Behavioral Healthcare and Crisis Stabilization Unit. Students 54; Clergy / Religious Teachers 6.

St. Joseph Orphanage Butler County Case Management, 6975 Dixie Hwy., Ste. A, Fairfield, 45014. Tel: 513-887-2100; Fax: 513-887-2101; Email: info@sjokids.org. Eric Cummins, M.A., CEO.

St. Joseph Orphanage Foster Care-Dayton, 6680 Poe, Ste. 450, Dayton, 45414. Tel: 937-643-0398; Fax: 937-643-9961; Email: info@sjokids.org. Eric Cummins, M.A., CEO.

[J] SPECIAL SCHOOLS

CINCINNATI. *St. Rita School for the Deaf* (1915) (Grades PreK-12), 1720 Glendale-Milford Rd., 45215. Tel: 513-771-7600; Fax: 513-326-8264; Email: afrith@srsdeaf.org; Email: mhavens@srsdeaf.org; Email: nmarsh@srsdeaf.org; Web: www.srsdeaf.org. Mrs. Angela Frith, Pres.; Rev. William H. Wysong, J.C.L.; Megan Havens, Prin. K-6; Natalie Marsh, Prin. 7-12. Day school for deaf and hard of hearing, and hearing children with special communication needs. Clergy 1; Lay Teachers 25; Preschool 43; Students 122; High School Students 31; Elementary Students 48; Clergy / Religious Teachers 3.

[K] GENERAL HOSPITALS

CINCINNATI. *The Good Samaritan Hospital of Cincinnati, Ohio*, 375 Dixmyth Ave., 45220. Tel: 513-862-1400; Tel: 513-862-2601; Fax: 513-862-1190; Email: james_plichta@trihealth.com; Web: www.trihealth.com. Mark Clement, Pres. & CEO; Jamie Easterling, Admin.; Frank Nation, Vice Pres., Tel: 513-569-6248; Fax: 513-569-6233. Catholic Health Initiatives (CHI). Bassinets 65; Bed Capacity 562; Tot Asst. Annually 320,000; Total Staff 3,300.

Registered Training College of Nursing Please see listing under Colleges and Universities located in the Institution section.

[L] HEALTH CARE SYSTEMS

CINCINNATI. *Mercy Health*, 1701 Mercy Health Pl.,

45237. Tel: 513-952-5000; Tel: 513-952-4765; Fax: 513-562-9576; Web: www.mercy.com. John M. Starcher, Pres. & CEO. Mercy Health is sponsored by Bon Secours Mercy Ministries. Bed Capacity 3,646; Tot Asst. Annually 3,042,787; Total Staff 33,406.

Mercy Health Cincinnati LLC, 1701 Mercy Health Pl., 45237. Tel: 513-952-4747; Fax: 513-952-5571; Email: laknauf@mercy.com; Web: www.e-mercy.com. David Fikse, Pres. Tot Asst. Annually 1,385,902; Total Staff 2,246.

Mercy Health-Anderson Hospital LLC, 7500 State Rd., 45255. Tel: 513-624-4500; Tel: 513-952-4747; Fax: 513-624-3299; Fax: 513-952-5571; Email: laknauf@mercy.com; Web: www.e-mercy.com. Mailing Address: 1701 Mercy Health Pl., 45237. Mr. Kenneth James, Pres. Bed Capacity 286; Tot Asst. Annually 162,622; Total Staff 1,248.

Mercy Health-Clermont Hospital LLC, 3000 Hospital Dr., Batavia, 45103. Tel: 513-732-8200; Tel: 513-952-4747; Fax: 513-732-8537; Fax: 513-952-5571; Email: laknauf@mercy.com; Web: www.e-mercy.com. Mailing Address: 1701 Mercy Health Pl., 45237. Mr. Justin Krueger, Pres.; Sr. Cheryl Erb, R.S.M., Senior Vice Pres. Mission Integration. Bed Capacity 160; Tot Asst. Annually 155,787; Total Staff 766.

Mercy Health-Fairfield Hospital LLC, 3000 Mack Rd., Fairfield, 45014. Tel: 513-870-7000; Tel: 513-952-4747; Fax: 513-870-7065; Fax: 513-952-5571; Email: laknauf@mercy.com; Web: www.e-mercy.com. Mailing Address: 1701 Mercy Health Pl., 45237. Thomas S. Urban, Market Pres. & CEO, North Market, Cincinnati Region; Sr. Cheryl Erb, R.S.M., Sr. Vice Pres. Mission Integration. Bed Capacity 262; Tot Asst. Annually 222,018; Total Staff 1,414.

Mercy Health-West Hospital LLC, 3300 Mercy Health Blvd., 45211. Tel: 513-853-5000; Tel: 513-952-4747; Fax: 513-853-9141; Fax: 513-952-5571; Email: laknauf@mercy.com; Web: www.e-mercy.com. Mailing Address: 1701 Mercy Health Pl., 45237. Michael Kramer, Market Pres. & CEO, West Market, Cincinnati Region; Sr. Cheryl Erb, R.S.M., Senior Vice Pres. Mission Integration. Bed Capacity 252; Tot Asst. Annually 192,269; Total Staff 1,314.

Mercy Franciscan Senior Health and Housing Services, Inc. dba Mercy Health-West Park, 2950 West Park Dr., 45238. Tel: 513-451-8900; Fax: 513-451-3728; Email: laknauf@mercy.com; Web: www.e-mercy.com. Mailing Address: 1701 Mercy Health Pl., 45237. Jamie J. Houseman, Market Dir. Long Term Care; Rachel Wirth, Exec. Dir. Bed Capacity 299; Residents 215; Tot Asst. Annually 472; Total Staff 175.

Mercy Franciscan Social Ministries, Inc. dba Mercy Health-St. John & Mercy Health-St. Raphael, 1701 Mercy Health Pl., 45237. Tel: 513-952-4747; Fax: 513-952-5571; Email: laknauf@mercy.com; Web: www.e-mercy.com. Gina Hemenway, Dir. Tot Asst. Annually 7,856; Total Staff 10.5.

SPRINGFIELD. *Community Mercy Health Partners* Mercy Health Springfield, 100 Medical Center Dr., Springfield, 45504. Tel: 937-523-1000; Fax: 937-523-5950; Email: mpotina@mercy.com; Web: www.mercy.com. Matthew Caldwell, Pres. Bed Capacity 250; Tot Asst. Annually 215,981; Total Staff 2,300.

Mercy Memorial Hospital, 904 Scioto St., Urbana, 43078. Tel: 937-484-6112; Fax: 937-484-6105; Email: mpotina@mercy.com. Rev. Emmanuel Nyong, Dir. Bed Capacity 25; Tot Asst. Annually 51,215; Total Staff 135; Staff 148.

Springfield Regional Medical Center (1950) 100 Medical Center Dr., Springfield, 45504. Rev. Emmanuel Nyong, Dir. Bed Capacity 254; Tot Asst. Annually 226,729; Total Staff 1,733; Staff 1,733.

Oakwood Village, 1500 Villa Rd., Springfield, 45503. Tel: 937-390-9000; Fax: 937-390-9333; Web: www.oakwoodvillage.com. Jamie J. Houseman, Exec. Dir. Bed Capacity 305; Tot Asst. Annually 306; Total Staff 240.

Mercy McAuley Center, 906 Scioto St., Urbana, 43078. Tel: 937-653-5432; Fax: 937-652-2072. Bed Capacity 129; Residents 112; Tot Asst. Annually 217; Total Staff 148.

[M] SENIOR RESIDENCES

CINCINNATI. *Archbishop Leibold Home for the Aged*, 476 Riddle Rd., 45220-2493. Tel: 513-281-8001; Fax: 513-281-4943; Email: mscincinnati@littlesistersofthepoor.org. Sr. Mary Karl, Supr. The Little Sisters of the Poor. Bed Capacity 100; Residents 95; Sisters 9; Total Staff 120; Total Assisted 140.

St. Margaret Hall, 1960 Madison Rd., 45206-1896. Tel: 513-751-5880; Fax: 513-751-9813; Email: contact@stmargarethall.com; Web: www.stmargarethall.com. Janet Murphy, Admin. & Contact Person. Bed Capacity 134; Residents 114; Carmelite Sisters for the Aged and Infirm 4; Tot Asst. Annually 240; Total Staff 200.

Sisters of Charity Senior Care Corp. dba Bayley, 990 Bayley Dr., 45233. Tel: 513-347-5500; Fax: 513-347-5553; Email: patty.lingg@bayleylife.org; Web: www.bayleylife.org. Adrienne Walsh, Pres. & CEO. Also includes Bayley Adult Day Program and Bayley Village. Bed Capacity 195; Total Staff 397; Total Assisted Living 78; Independent Cottages 78; Health Care 110; Licensed Nursing 110.

CENTERVILLE. **St. Leonard*, 8100 Clyo Rd., Centerville, 45458. Tel: 937-433-0480; Fax: 937-439-7165; Email: jegibbs@chilivingcomm.org; Web: www.homeishere.org. Prentice Lipsey, Exec. Dir. A facility of Sylvania Franciscan Health, an affiliate of Catholic Health Initiatives. Residents 700; Skilled Nursing Beds 150; Total Staff 425.

[N] MONASTERIES AND RESIDENCES OF PRIESTS AND BROTHERS

CINCINNATI. *Brothers of the Poor of St. Francis*, 7831 Ayerdayl Ln., 45255. Tel: 513-924-0111; Fax: 513-321-3777; Email: hibrothers@fuse.net. Bro. Edward Kesler, C.F.P., Supr. Brothers of the Poor of St. Francis.

Cincinnati Jesuit Community, 3844 Victory Pkwy., 45207. Tel: 513-745-3858; Email: victoryparkwayjesuits@gmail.com. Revs. Michael J. Graham, S.J., Pres.; Patrick A. Fairbanks, S.J.; Tom Lawler; Jerome Veigas, Parochial Vicar; Nathan Wendt, Chap.; Albert J. Bischoff, S.J., (Retired); Richard W. Bollman, S.J., Parish Priest, Bellarmine Chapel; Bro. Darrell J. Burns, S.J., Mission & Identity, Activities Coord.; Revs. Robert E. Hurd, S.J.; Thomas P. Kennealy, S.J., Librarian; John J. LaRocca, S.J.; Kenneth R. Overberg, S.J., Prof. of Theology; Robert J. Ross, S.J.; Benjamin J. Urmston, S.J.; George B. Wilson, S.J.; Walter C. Deye, S.J., Rector; Matthew T. Gamber, S.J. Members of the Jesuit Community (Society of Jesus, S.J.). Brothers 1; Priests 14.

St. Clare Friary, 5831 Saranac Ave., 45224. Tel: 513-541-0488; Fax: 513-541-2424; Email: drkohut52@hotmail.com. Revs. David Kohut, O.F.M.; Patrick McCloskey, O.F.M., Vicar.

St. Clement Friary (1850) 4536 Vine St., 45217. Tel: 513-641-2257; Fax: 513-641-2262; Email: vincedel@franciscan.org. Revs. Fred Link, O.F.M., Pastor; Frank Jasper, O.F.M., Supr.; Louis Bartko, O.F.M., (Retired); John Paul Flajole, O.F.M., (Retired); William Ollendick, O.F.M.; James Van Vurst, O.F.M., Vicar, Assoc. Pastor; Valentine Young, O.F.M., (Retired); Thomas Richstatter, O.F.M., (Retired); Ric Sheider, O.F.M., (Retired); Roger Lopez, O.F.M., Instr., Roger Bacon HS; Bros. Marcel Groth, O.F.M., (Retired); Louis Lamping, O.F.M., (Retired); Kenneth Beetz, O.F.M., Maintenance; Kevin Duckson, O.F.M., (Retired); Michael Charron, O.F.M., Studies; Thomas Gerchak, O.F.M. St. John the Baptist Province. Residence for Retired Friars, Pastor of St. Clement Parish and other Friars. Brothers 6; Priests 10.

Comboni Missionaries (Verona Fathers)-Comboni Mission Center, 1318 Nagel Rd., 45255-3120. Tel: 513-474-4997; Fax: 513-474-0382; Email: info@combonimissionaries.org; Web: www.combonimissionaries.org. Revs. John M. Converset, M.C.C.J., Prov.; Kenneth Gerth, M.C.C.J.; Ruffino Ezama, M.C.C.J., Dir. Mission Office; Joseph Bragotti, M.C.C.J.; Jose Angel Romero, M.C.C.J.; Louis Gasparini, M.C.C.J., Supr.; Rodolfo Coaquira Hilaje, M.C.C.J.; Modi Nyorko. Houses Comboni Missionaries of the Heart of Jesus, Inc., The Offices of the Province of North America, including the Office of the Provincial. Priests 8.

De Sales Crossings Marianist Community, 1600 Madison Rd., 45206-1815. Tel: 513-961-1945; Tel: 513-961-2257; Fax: 513-221-4907; Email: ccca@fuse.net. Bros. William I. Grundish, S.M., (Retired); Robert P. Donovan, S.M.; Rev. J. Eugene Contadino, S.M., B.A., M.A., Ph.D.; Bros. Robert S. Dzubinski, S.M., Dir.; Giancarlo Bonutti, S.M.; Robert A. Politi, S.M., Librarian; Edward Longbottom, Marianist Religious. Brothers 6; Priests 1. *De Sales Crossings Marianist Community*, 1600 Madison Rd., 45206-1815. Tel: 513-961-2257. Bros. Robert A. Politi, S.M.; Giancarlo Bonutti, S.M.; Rev. J. Eugene Contadino, S.M., B.A., M.A., Ph.D.; Bros. Robert P. Donovan, S.M.; Robert S. Dzubinski, S.M.; William I. Grundish, S.M., (Retired). Brothers 5; Priests 1.

St. Francis Seraph Friary, 1615 Vine St., 45202-6400. Tel: 513-721-4700; Fax: 513-421-9672; Email: sjbsec@franciscan.com; Web: www.franciscan.org. Rev. Mark Soehner, O.F.M., Prov.; Mr. David O'Brien, CFO; Rev. Daniel J. Anderson, O.F.M., Sec.; Ms. Toni Cashnelli, Dir.; Rev. John Bok, O.F.M., Dir.; Ms. Colleen Cushard, Dir.; Revs. Patrick McCloskey, O.F.M., Dir.; Francis S. Tebbe, O.F.M., Dir.; Cyprian Berens, O.F.M., Chap., (Retired); Robert Bruno, O.F.M., Chap.; Matthias Crehan, O.F.M., Chap.; Ricardo Russo, O.F.M., Chap.; Bro. Bill Spond, O.F.M., Chap.; Rev. David Kohut, O.F.M.; Bro. Timothy Sucher, O.F.M., Pastoral Assoc.; Revs. William Farris, O.F.M., Vicar; Hilarion Kistner, O.F.M., (Retired); Thomas Speier I, O.F.M., (Retired); Bros. Scott Obrecht, O.F.M.; John Carey, O.F.M.; Phillips Robinette, O.F.M.; Rev. Bonaventure Bai, O.F.M.; Bro. Daniel Barrett, O.F.M.; Revs. James M. Bok, O.F.M.; Larry Dunham, O.F.M.; Arthur Espelage, O.F.M., J.C.D.; Harold Geers, O.F.M.; Bro. Thomas Gerchak, O.F.M.; Revs. Blane Grein, O.F.M.; Bruce Hausfeld, O.F.M., (Retired); Bryant Hausfeld, O.F.M., (Retired); Carl Hawver, O.F.M., (Retired); Bert Heise, O.F.M., (Retired); Donald E. Holtgrewe, O.F.M., (Retired); Bro. Timothy Lamb, O.F.M.; Rev. Max Langenderfer, O.F.M., (Retired); Bros. Dominic Lococo, O.F.M.; Christopher Meyer, O.F.M.; Rev. Miles Pfalzer, O.F.M., (Retired); Bros. Stephen Richter, O.F.M., (Retired); Giovanni Ried, O.F.M.; Revs. Manuel Viera, O.F.M., J.C.L.; Valens J. Waldschmidt, O.F.M., (Retired); Jack R. Wintz, O.F.M., (Retired); Bros. Louis Zant, O.F.M.; Brian Maloney, O.F.M., In Res.; Josef Anderlohr, O.F.M., In Res. Provincial Headquarters of the Province of St. John the Baptist of the Order of Friars Minor. Brothers 6; Priests 11. *Brother Juniper Friary*, 4344 Sullivan Ave., 45217-1747. Rev. Donald A. Miller, O.F.M., Ph.D., Franciscan Media Staff; Bro. Chris Cahill, O.F.M., Faculty, Roger Bacon High Sch.

St. Gertrude Priory, 7630 Shawnee Run Rd., 45243. Tel: 513-561-5954; Email: john.farren@opeast.org; Web: www.stgertrude.org. Revs. John Farren, Prior; Andre-Joseph LaCasse, O.P.; Henry Stephan, Parochial Vicar; Clement Dickie, Parochial Vicar; Michael Mary Dosch, O.P., Novice Master; Joseph Alobaidi, In Res.; Paul Jerome Keller, O.P., S.T.D., In Res.; Edmund Augustino Ditton, O.P., In Res. Brothers 14.

Headquarters of Glenmary Home Missioners Home Missioners of America (1939) Glenmary Home Missioners: P.O. Box 465618, 45246-5618. Tel: 513-874-8900; Fax: 513-881-7485; Email: rprzybylowicz@glenmary.org; Email: cartysiewicz@glenmary.org; Web: www.glenmary.org. 4119 Glenmary Trace, Fairfield, 45246-5618. Revs. Chet Artysiewicz, Pres.; Bruce C. Brylinski, G.H.M., Candidacy Dir., Post Novitiate Dir.; Bro. Dennis Craig; Rev. Robert Dalton, Sacramental Min. in Houston, MS, (Retired); Bro. Craig Digmann, Outreach Ministry - Catholic Presence Ministry in Sneedville, Tennessee; Revs. Daniel Dorsey, Dir. of Formation, Dir. of Novitiate; Dominic R. Duggins, House Dir., (Retired); David Glockner, Admin., (Retired); Ed Gorny, (Retired); Robert Hare, (Retired); Roland Hautz, (Retired); Bros. David Henley, Vocation Dir.; Jack Henn, Dir. of Senior and Disabled Members; Rev. Dennis Holly, (Retired); Bros. Larry Johnson, Vice Pres.; Curt Kedley, Residing in Windsor, NC; Rev. Thomas Kirkendoll, Asst. Dir. of Formation, (Retired); Bro. Levis Kuwa, Nursing Missionary in Blakely, GA; Rev. Fid Levri, In Reed, Ky, (Retired); Bro. Jason Muhlenkamp, Outreach Ministry in Blakely, GA; Revs. Francois Pellissier, G.H.M., Outreach Ministry; Gerald Peterson, (Retired); Neil Pezzulo, Vice Pres.; Frank Ruff, Works with UNBOUND ministry and liturgical substitutes in Trenton, KY, (Retired); Leo Schloemer, (Retired); Bros. Thomas Sheehy, Outreach Ministry in Erwin, TN; Virgil Siefker, Outreach Ministry in Windsor, NC; Mike Springer; Revs. Wil Steinbacher, National Ministries in Madison, TN, (Retired); Don Tranel, Dir. of Development; Bro. Ken Woods, In Kingsport, TN; Rev. John Rausch, G.H.M., Human/Economics Ministry in Stanton, KY. Also known as The Home Missioners of America.

Jesuit Community at St. Xavier High School, Jesuit Community, 7361 View Pl., 45224. Tel: 513-761-5522; Email: robert.thesing@gmail.com. Revs. Robert J. Thesing, S.J., Supr.; Thomas Manahan, Prof.; Edward L. Pigott, S.J.; John P. Heim, S.J.; Richard Millbourn, S.J.; Mr. Richard E. Schuckman, S.J., Teacher; Revs. James Ackerman; Terrance Baum, Admin.; Joseph D. Folzenlogen, S.J., Pastoral Min./Coord.; Paul Macke, Spiritual Advisor/Care Services.

St. John the Baptist Friary, 10722 Wyscarver Rd., 45241-3083. Tel: 513-769-1613; Fax: 513-769-1650; Email: johnpbok@gmail.com. Revs. John Bok, O.F.M., Guardian; Bruno Kremp, O.F.M., Vicar; Anthony Walter, O.F.M.; Bros. Martin Humphreys, O.F.M.; Gene Mayer, O.F.M.; Revs. Damian Cesanek, O.F.M., (Retired); Max Langenderfer, O.F.M., (Retired).

Pleasant Street Friary (1969) 1723 Pleasant St., 45202-6413. Tel: 513-739-3969; Email:

jquigleyofm@gmail.com. Revs. Murray L. Bodo, O.F.M.; John Quigley, O.F.M.

CELINA. *St. Charles*, Society of the Precious Blood, 2860 U.S. Rte. 127, Celina, 45822.
Tel: 419-925-4516; Fax: 419-925-4800; Email: hrmanager@cpps-preciousblood.org. Bro. Theophane Woodall, C.PP.S., Vicar; Revs. John Butler, Res.; James O'Connor, Res.; Kenneth J. Schroeder, C.PP.S., (Retired); Thomas Beischel, C.PP.S., (Retired); Joseph Brown, C.PP.S., (Retired); Robert Conway, C.PP.S., (Retired); James Dugal, C.PP.S., (Retired); Linus Evers, C.PP.S., (Retired); Juan Acuna Gonzalez, C.PP.S., (Retired); Joseph Hinders, C.PP.S., (Retired); John Hoying, C.PP.S., (Retired); Vincent Hoying, C.PP.S., (Retired); William Hoyng, C.PP.S., (Retired); Edgar Jutte, C.PP.S., (Retired); Leonard Kostka, C.PP.S., (Retired); Robert Kunisch, C.PP.S., (Retired); Frederick Lang, C.PP.S., (Retired); James McCabe, C.PP.S., (Retired); James Miller, C.PP.S., (Retired); William Miller, C.PP.S., (Retired); Charles Mullen, C.PP.S., (Retired); Alfred Naseman, C.PP.S.; Patrick Patterson, C.PP.S., (Retired); Louis Schmit, C.PP.S., (Retired); James Schrader, C.PP.S., (Retired); Donald J. Thieman, C.PP.S., (Retired); Ralph Verdi, C.PP.S., (Retired); Paul W. Wohlwend, C.PP.S., (Retired); Bros. Paul Chase; Daniel Eisenman; Gregory Frantz; Revs. Philip Gilbert; Peter M. Helmlinger, (Retired); Thomas Hemm, C.PP.S.; David Hoying; Bro. Joe Mary Hrezo; Rev. Ernest Krantz, C.PP.S.; Bro. Charles McCafferty; Revs. Fred Nietfeld; Edward Oen; Bro. Nick Renner; Rev. Alphonse Spilly, C.PP.S.; Bros. Jerome Schulte, C.PP.S.; Timothy Cahill, C.PP.S.; Rev. James E. Franck, C.PP.S. Brothers 7; Priests 37.

DAYTON. *Marianist Community*, 100 Chambers St., Dayton, 45409-2817. Tel: 937-627-8998. Revs. Robert Jones, S.M., Dir.; Thomas A. Schroer, S.M., Campus Min.; Charles J. Stander, S.M., Univ. Chap.; Bros. Justin Quiroz, S.M.; Robert H. Hughes, S.M.; Tchamie Thierry Kadja, S.M.; Julius Muthusi; Thomas Njari. Brothers 5; Priests 3. *Marianist Community*, Meyer Hall, 4435 E. Patterson Rd., Dayton, 45430-1033.
Tel: 937-426-7852; Fax: 937-426-7858; Email: sullivanj3@udayton.edu. Bros. A. Joseph Barrish, S.M., Artist, Marianist Network for the Arts; Donald R. Geiger, S.M., Ph.D., (Retired); Andrew J. Kosmowski, S.M., Librarian, Marian Library; J. Mitchell Schweickart, S.M., (Retired); Jeffrey Sullivan, S.M., Dir.; Kenneth Thompson, S.M. Brothers 6. *Marianist Community, Novitiate*, 4435 E. Patterson Rd., Dayton, 45430-1033.
Tel: 937-426-5721; Fax: 937-429-4686. Rev. Christopher T. Wittmann, S.M., Dir. & Master of Novices; Bros. Sung Yung Kim, S.M., Novice; John Lemker, S.M., (Retired); Joseph Nugent, S.M., Novice; Thomas Wendorf, S.M., Ph.D., Dir. Vocations, Marianist Prov. of U.S.; Daniel L. Klco, S.M., M.S.; Juan Perez, Pre-Novice. Brothers 4; Novices 2; Priests 1; (Pre-Novice) 1. *Marianist Community*, 312 Stonemill Rd., Dayton, 45409-2543.
Tel: 937-627-1553. Revs. Ignase Arulappen, S.M., Doctoral Student; Bertrand A. Buby, S.M., Ph.D., S.T.D., (Retired); Theodore K. Cassidy, S.M., (Retired); Bros. Raymond Fitz, S.M., Ph.D., Prof. & Pres. Emeritus; Blaise Mosengo, S.M., Doctoral Student; Brandon Alana-Maugaotega. Brothers 3; Priests 3. *Marianist Community*, 121 Sawmill Rd., Dayton, 45409-2524. Tel: 937-222-4928. Rev. Norbert C. Burns, S.M., S.T.D., (Retired); Bros. James Facette, S.M., (Retired); Alex J. Tuss, S.M., Ph.D., (Retired); Lawrence Cada, S.M., (Retired); Philip Aaron, S.M., (Retired). Brothers 4; Priests 1. *Marianist Community*, University of Dayton, Alumni Hall, 300 College Pk., Dayton, 45469-0300. Tel: 937-229-3556. Revs. Bakpenam Sebastien Abalodo, S.M.; Joseph F. Kozar, S.M., Ph.D., Dir. & Asst. Rector; Johan G. Roten, S.M., S.T.D., Dir. Research, Marian Library; James A. Russell, S.M., (Retired); Thomas A. Thompson, S.M., Dir., Marian Library; Bros. James Brown, S.M.; Victor M. Forlani, S.M., M.B.A., D.B.A.; Louis Fournier, S.M.; Charles Gausling, S.M.; John Habjan, S.M.; M. Gary Marcinowski, S.M., M.F.A.; David L. Schmitz, S.M.; John Klobuka. Brothers 7; Priests 6. *Mercy Siena Cottages*, 5124 Old Dublin Ct., Dayton, 45415-3171. Tel: 937-279-2106. Bros. Paul Jablinski, S.M., (Retired); Edward E. Zamierowski, S.M., (Retired). Brothers 2. *Mercy Siena Support Community*, 5112 Old Dublin Ct., Dayton, 45415-3194. Tel: 937-274-4626. Bros. John Laudenbach, S.M., Dir.; Nicholas Rufo, S.M.; Robert N. Wiethorn, S.M.; Paul Hoffman, S.M., Dir. Brothers 4; Priests 1. *Assisted Living Siena Gardens*, 6015 N. Main St., Dayton, 45415-3110. Tel: 937-274-4626. Rev. John Bakle, S.M., (Retired); Bro. Wilbert Hamm, S.M.; Revs. James Kunes, S.M., (Retired); Paul A. Reich, S.M., (Retired); Kenneth J. Sommer, S.M.; Bros. Edward Unferdorfer; Bernard Zalewski, S.M. Brothers 3; Priests 4. *Marianist Community*, 301 Kiefaber St., Dayton, 45409-2537.
Tel: 937-627-8091. Rev. James F. Fitz, S.M., Vice Pres., Mission & Rector; Bros. Thomas O'Neill Farnsworth, S.M., Psy.D., Faculty; Thomas J. Pieper, S.M., Dir., Campus Min. Brothers 2; Priests 1. *Marianist Network for the Arts*, 4400 Shakertown Rd., Dayton, 45430-1075.
Tel: 937-320-5405. Bros. A. Joseph Barrish, S.M., Artist; John Lemker, S.M., Artist; Donald Smith, S.M., Artist. Religious 3; Total Staff 3. *North American Center for Marianist Studies*, 4435 E. Patterson Rd., Dayton, 45430-1083.
Tel: 937-429-2521. George Lisjak, Dir. Religious 2. *Marianist Mission*, P.O. Box 340998, Dayton, 45434-0998. Linda Hayes, Dir. Religious 3; Total Staff 38. *Marianist Environmental Education Center*, 4435 E. Patterson Rd., Dayton, 45430-1095.
Tel: 937-429-3582; Fax: 937-429-3195; Email: meec@udayton.edu. Sr. Leanne Jablonski, F.M.I., Dir. Religious 1; Total Staff 3.

Provincial Office of the Cincinnati Province of the Society of the Precious Blood, 431 E. Second St., Dayton, 45402-1764. Tel: 937-228-9263;
Fax: 937-228-6878; Email: prodirsec@cpps-preciousblood.org; Web: www.cpps-preciousblood.org. Revs. Jeffrey S. Kirch, C.PP.S., Prov. Dir.; Kenneth Schnipke, C.PP.S., Vice Prov.; Bro. Joseph J. Fisher, C.PP.S., Prov. Treas.; Revs. Benjamin Berinti, C.PP.S., 1st Councilor; Stephen Dos Santos, C.PP.S., 2nd Councilor, Prov. Sec.; Timothy McFarland, 3rd Councilor; Juan Acuna Gonzalez, C.PP.S., 4th Councilor, (Retired); Bros. Thomas Bohman, C.PP.S., 5th Councilor; Matthew Schaefer, C.PP.S, Admin; Very Revs. Larry J. Hemmelgarn, C.PP.S., Admin.; William Nordenbrock, C.PP.S., Mod. Gen.; Rev. Dennis Chriszt, C.PP.S., Dir. of Interprovincial Advanced Form.; Bro. Antonio Sison, C.PP.S., Prof.; Revs. Andrew O'Reilly, C.PP.S., Retreat Dir.; John Mencsik, C.PP.S., Semi-Retired Supply Help; Richard Nieberding, C.PP.S.; John Kalicky, (Retired); LeRoy Moreeuw; William J. Beuth, C.PP.S.; Bro. Brian Boyle, C.PP.S.; Revs. Gerald G. Dreiling, C.PP.S.; Joseph F. Deardorff, C.PP.S.; Leon Flaherty, C.PP.S.; James E. Gaynor, C.PP.S.; Joseph Rodak, C.PP.S.; Jerome P. Stack, C.PP.S.; Jerome Steinbrunner, C.PP.S. Brothers 23; Clergy 114; Deacons 2; Non-Professed 15; Professed 9.

HUNTSVILLE. *Marianist Community* (1953) 9636 Lakeshore Dr., E., Huntsville, 43324-9520.
Tel: 937-842-4902; Email: rogerbau45@live.com. Rev. Michael F. Nartker, S.M.; Bros. Roger Bau, S.M., Dir. & Contact Person; William Schlosser, S.M.; Donald Smith, S.M.; Roy McLoughlin; Rev. James Schimelpfening, S.M., D.Min. Brothers 4; Priests 2.

[O] CONVENTS AND RESIDENCES FOR SISTERS

CINCINNATI. *Franciscan Monastery of St. Clare (Poor Clares)* (1990) 1505 Miles Rd., 45231-2427.
Tel: 513-825-7177; Fax: 513-825-4071; Email: amcovely@juno.com; Web: www.poorclarescincinnati.org. Sr. Pia Malaborbor, Abbess. Sisters 10.

Franciscan Sisters of the Poor U.S. Area Office Franciscan Sisters of the Poor 60 Compton Rd., 45215. Tel: 513-761-9040; Fax: 513-761-6703; Email: office@franciscansistersofthepoor.org; Web: www.franciscansistersofthepoor.org. Sisters Marilyn Trowbridge, S.F.P., Rel Order Leader; Ann Cecile Albers, S.F.P., Community Min. Sisters in Archdiocese 37.

Provincial House, Health Center of Sisters of Notre Dame de Namur, 699 E. Columbia Ave., 45215. Sisters Carol Lichtenberg, S.N.D.deN., Prov.; Donna Wisowaty, S.N.D.deN., Admin.; Marie Kelly, Mod.; Grace Escobar, Mod. Sisters 76.

Sisters of Charity of Cincinnati, Ohio (1852) 5900 Delhi Rd., Mount St. Joseph, 45051.
Tel: 513-347-5201; Fax: 513-347-5228; Email: j.cook@srcharitycinti.org; Web: www.srcharitycinti.org. Sr. Joan Elizabeth Cook, S.C., Pres. Sisters 267.

Sisters of Charity Novitiate, Tel: 513-347-5471;
Fax: 513-347-5228. Sr. Donna Steffen, S.C., Novice Dir. Novices 2.

Ursulines of Cincinnati (1910) 1339 E. McMillan St., 45206-2164. Tel: 513-961-3410, Ext. 139;
Fax: 513-872-7177; Email: sisters@ursulinesofcincinnati.org; Web: http://cincinnatiursuline.org. Sr. Margaret Mary Efkeman, O.S.U. Ursuline Sisters.Sisters of this community sponsor one high school and one grade school. They also work in social service, communications, adult education, parish work and social justice. Sisters 6.

DAYTON. *Sisters of the Precious Blood Generalate* (1834) 4000 Denlinger Rd., Dayton, 45426.
Tel: 937-837-3302; Fax: 937-837-8825; Email: jlehman@cppsadmin.org; Web: www.preciousbloodsistersdayton.org. Sisters Joyce Lehman, C.PP.S., Pres.; Nancy Kinross, C.PP.S., Councilor & Sec.; Linda Pleiman, C.PP.S., Councilor & Treas.; Cecilia Taphorn, C.PP.S., Councilor & Vice Pres.; Patricia Kremer, Councilor; Noreen Jutte, C.PP.S., Archivist. Sisters 103.

Sisters of the Precious Blood, Salem Heights Convent, 4960 Salem Ave., Dayton, 45416-1797.
Tel: 937-278-0871; Fax: 937-278-8722; Email: jkroeger@cppsdayton.org; Web: www.preciousbloodsistersdayton.org. Sisters Judy Kroeger, C.PP.S, Admin.; Nancy Wolf, C.PP.S., Coord. Sr. Svcs. Sisters 50.

SAINT MARTIN. *Ursulines of Brown County* (1845) 20860 State Rt. 251, St. Martin, 45118.
Tel: 513-875-2020, Ext. 27; Fax: 513-875-2311; Email: pkemper@tds.et; Web: www.ursulinesofbc.org. Sr. Phyllis Kemper, O.S.U., Congregational Minister. Ursuline Order, Congregation of Paris. Sisters 21.

[P] RESIDENCES FOR ADULTS AND YOUTHS

CINCINNATI. *Friars Club*, 4300 Vine St., 45217.
Tel: 513-488-8777; Email: atimmons@friarsclubinc.org; Web: www.friarsclubinc.org. Annie Timmons, Exec. Dir. Tot Asst. Annually 1,000; Total Staff 7.

[Q] RETREAT HOUSES, CONFERENCE AND RENEWAL CENTERS

CINCINNATI. **Our Lady of the Holy Spirit Center*, 5440 Moeller Ave., 45212. Tel: 513-351-9800;
Fax: 513-351-9885; Email: info@olhsc.org; Web: www.olhsc.org. Mr. Tom Leibel, Dir.

DAYTON. *Bergamo Center for Lifelong Learning* (1967) 4400 Shakertown Rd., Dayton, 45430-1075.
Tel: 937-426-2363; Fax: 937-426-1090; Email: info@bergamocenter.org; Web: www.bergamocenter.org. Brent Devitt, Exec. Dir.; Gina Gregory, Conference Planning.

MILFORD. *Jesuit Spiritual Center at Milford*, 5361 S. Milford Rd., Milford, 45150-9746.
Tel: 513-248-3500; Email: tgillman@jesuitspiritualcenter.com; Web: www.jesuitspiritualcenter.com. Sr. Therese Gillman, O.S.F., Exec. Dir. & Contact Person.

[R] CAMPUS MINISTRY AND NEWMAN CENTERS

CINCINNATI. *Mount St. Joseph University Mission and Ministry* (1920) 5701 Delhi Rd., 45233-1670.
Tel: 513-244-4844; Email: Karen.Elliott@msj.edu; Web: www.msj.edu. Sr. Karen Elliot, C.PP.S., Dir.; Charissa Qiu, Coord. Campus Ministry.

University of Cincinnati Newman Center, 328 W. McMillan St., 45219-1224. Tel: 513-381-6400;
Fax: 513-381-2540; Email: smsgnewman@gmail.com; Web: www.smsgonline.com. Ms. Holly O'Hara, Campus Min.; Rev. Alan Hirt, O.F.M.; Michael Schreiner, Campus Min.

Xavier University Dorothy Day Center for Faith & Justice, Gallagher Student Center: 3815 St. Francis Xavier Way, Rm. 310, 45207.
Tel: 513-745-3567; Fax: 513-745-1959; Email: minning@xavier.edu; Web: www.xavier.edu/cfj. Mr. Greg Carpinello, Sr. Dir.; Revs. Abigal King-Kaiser, Assoc. DIr.; Nelson Pierce, Dir. Gospel Choir; Albert J. Bischoff, S.J., Retired Campus Min., (Retired); Roberta Whitely, Coord. Liturgy & Music; Ms. Katie Minning, Contact Person; Greg Mellor, Coord. Fatih & Ministry (Part-time); Shannon Hughes, Sr. Asst. Dir., Svc., Justice & Immersion; Angela Gray, Asst. Dir., Svc. & Justice; Abby Anderson, Asst. Dir., Faith & Min.; Tala Ali, Muslim Chap.; Mr. Spencer Liechty, Coord. Faith & Justice.

DAYTON. *Sinclair Community College Campus Ministry*, 444 W. Third St., Dayton, 45402.
Tel: 937-512-2768; Email: jane.steinhauser@sinclair.edu; Web: www.sinclaircampusministry.org. Dr. V. Jane Steinhauser, Archdiocesan Dir. of Campus Ministry.

University of Dayton Campus Ministry, 300 College Park, Dayton, 45469-0408. Tel: 937-229-3339;
Fax: 937-229-2035; Email: campus-ministry@udayton.edu; Web: www.udayton.edu/ministry. Revs. Charles J. Stander, S.M., Univ. Chap.; Thomas A. Schroer, S.M., Campus Min., Faculty/Staff; Bro. Thomas Pieper, S.M., Campus Min. Stuart Hall/Marianist Hall; Sr. Kathleen Rossman, O.S.F., Campus Min., Sophomore/VWK; Crystal Sullivan, Dir.; Jennifer Morin-Williamson, Residence Hall Campus Min. Marycrest; Nick Cardilino, Campus Min.; Bridget Ebbert, Campus Min., Sophomore/South Quad/Founders; Dawn Oppy, Sr. Admin. Sec. to Campus Ministry; Mary Niebler, Campus Min.; Mr. Scott Paeplow, Campus Min., Liturgical/Pastoral Music; Kelly Adamson, Campus Min.; Colleen Brown, Campus Min., Liturgies & Sacraments; Teri Dickison, Asst. to Dir.

Campus Min.; Kathy Sales, Assoc. Dir., Liturgy; Mike Bennett, Campus Min., Retreats & Faith Communities; Samantha Kennedy, Campus Min.; Elizabeth Montgomery, Campus Min.; Brad Seligmann, Campus Min.; Dustin Pickett, Campus Min.; Katie Mathews, Campus Min.; Karen Rolfe, Sec.

FAIRBORN. *Catholic Campus Ministry* (1968) 3650 Colonel Glenn Hwy., Fairborn, 45324-2096. Tel: 937-426-1836; Email: eburns@wsucampusministryaoc.org; Email: cfarmer@wsucampusministryaoc.org; Email: nkovatch@wsucampusministryaoc.org; Web: www.raidercatholics.com. Rev. Ethan M. Moore, Dir.; Mr. Nic Kovatch, Campus Min.; Ms. Joan LaPore, Admin.; Denise Jasek, Music Min.

OXFORD. *Miami University Catholic Campus Ministry*, 111 E. High St., Oxford, 45056. Tel: 513-523-2153; Fax: 513-523-0559; Email: info@stmox.org; Web: www.stmox.org. Rev. Jeffrey P. Silver; Roberta L. Kinne, Pastoral Assoc.; Courtney Palcic, Pastoral Assoc. for Rel. Ed.; Pam Burk, Business Mgr.

WILMINGTON. *Wilmington College Campus Ministry*, 73 N. Mulberry St., Wilmington, 45177. Tel: 937-382-2236; Fax: 937-382-3234; Email: parishoffice@stcolumbkille.org; Web: www.stcolumbkille.org. Rev. Michael J. Holloran. Pastoral care available through St. Columbkille Parish.

[S] COMMUNITY CENTERS

CINCINNATI. *Healthy Moms & Babes, Inc.* (1985) 2270 Banning Rd., Ste. 200, 45239. Tel: 513-591-5600; Fax: 513-591-5604; Email: tcruise@healthymomsandbabes.org; Web: www.healthymomsandbabes.org. Sr. Patricia Cruise, S.C., Pres. & CEO. Annual Participants 3,000; Staff 18.

[T] FOUNDATIONS AND ENDOWMENTS

CINCINNATI. **Catholic Community Foundation for the Archdiocese of Cincinnati, Inc.*, 100 E. 8th St., 45202. Tel: 513-421-3131; Fax: 513-421-6225; Email: dkissell@catholiccincinnati.org; Web: www.1faith1hope1love.org. Mr. David W. Kissell, Dir.

Community Support Charitable Trust (1987) 1615 Vine St., 45202. Tel: 513-721-4700; Fax: 513-421-9672; Email: sjbcfo@franciscan.org; Web: franciscan.org. David P. O'Brien, Admin.; Revs. Kenan Freson, O.F.M., Trustee; Jeremy Harrington, O.F.M., Trustee; Bro. Vincent Delorenzo, O.F.M., Trustee

Community Support Charitable Trust for the Province of St. John the Baptist of the Order of Friars Minor.

Friars Club Foundation, Inc., 1615 Vine St., 45202. Tel: 513-721-4700; Fax: 513-421-9672, Ext. 3211; Email: sjbcfo@franciscan.org. Mr. John O'Connor, Vice Pres., Sec. & Trustee; Brian Veith, Treas. & Trustee.

Good Samaritan Hospital Foundation of Cincinnati, Inc., 375 Dixmyth Ave., 45220-2489. Tel: 513-862-3786; Fax: 513-862-3788; Email: mary_rafferty@trihealth.com; Web: www.gshfoundation.com. Mary L. Rafferty, Contact Person.

Roger Bacon High School Endowment, 4320 Vine St., 45217. Tel: 513-641-1300; Fax: 513-641-0498; Email: mengel@rogerbacon.org; Web: www.rogerbacon.org. Thomas Burke, Pres. & Contact Person; Steve Schad, Prin.; Michael Engel, Treas.

SC Ministry Foundation, Inc. (1986) 345 Neeb Rd., 45233. Tel: 513-347-1122; Fax: 513-347-1017; Email: dsmiley@scministryfdn.org; Web: www.scministryfdn.org. Ms. Amelia Riedel, Exec.

Sisters of Charity of Cincinnati-Charitable Trust (1988) 5900 Delhi Rd., Mount Saint Joseph, 45051. Tel: 513-347-5201; Fax: 513-347-5228; Email: j.cook@srcharitycinti.org; Web: www.srcharitycinti.org. Sr. Joan Elizabeth Cook, S.C., Pres. A designated trust fund to primarily support older and infirm members of the congregation.

Sisters of Notre Dame De Namur, Ohio Province, Charitable Trust, 701 E. Columbia Ave., 45215-3999. Tel: 513-761-7636; Fax: 513-761-6159; Email: ohprovoff@ohsnd.org; Web: www.sndohio.org. Sr. Carol Lichtenberg, S.N.D.deN., Prov. & Contact Person.

The Summit Country Day School Foundation (1994) 2161 Grandin Rd., 45208. Tel: 513-871-4700; Fax: 513-871-6558; Email: Lottman_B@SummitCDS.org. Charles Crowther, Pres.; Tom Theobald, Chm.; Bernadette Lottman.

Ursulines of Cincinnati, Ohio Charitable Trust, 1339 E. McMillan St., 45206-2164. Tel: 513-961-3410, Ext. 139; Fax: 513-872-7177; Email: sisters@ursulinesofcincinnati.org. Carol Beyersdorfer, Chairperson; Sr. Margaret Mary Efkeman, O.S.U.

DAYTON. *Community Support Charitable Trust* (1994) 431 E. Second St., Dayton, 45402. Tel: 937-228-9263; Fax: 937-228-6878; Email: provtreas@cpps-preciousblood.org. Bro. Joseph J. Fisher, C.PP.S., Admin.; Revs. Matthew Jozefiak, Trustee; Angelo Anthony, C.PP.S., Trustee; Bro. Thomas R. Bohman, C.PP.S., Trustee; Mr. John York, Trustee; Ms. Cynthia Hill, Trustee; Rev. Eugene H. Schnipke, C.PP.S., Trustee.

FAIRFIELD. *Glenmary Home Missioners Charity, Inc.*, 4119 Glenmary Trace, Fairfield, 45014. Tel: 513-874-8900; Email: mschneider@glenmary.org. Revs. Daniel Dorsey, Pres.; Dominic R. Duggins, Vice Pres. & Sec., (Retired).

[U] MISCELLANEOUS LISTINGS

CINCINNATI. *St. Andrew Kim Korean Catholic Community* (1980) 3171 Struble Rd., 45251. Tel: 513-903-6003; Web: www.cincykoreancatholic.org. Rev. Dong-Hyuk Jeon, Admin.; Hodon Ryu, Contact Person; Jung Ja Kim, Contact Person.

The Angela Foundation for Ursuline Education, 7659 Montgomery Rd., Ste. 2, 45236. Tel: 513-221-5500; Email: jwimberg@ursuline-education.com. Ms. Judith Wimberg, Exec. Dir.

Catholic Cursillo of Cincinnati (1962) P.O. Box 317655, 45231. Tel: 937-773-2700; Email: tylerjdr4@gmail.com; Web: www.cincinnaticursillo.org. Julie Tyler, Dir.

**The Catholic Social Workers National Association Foundation*, P.O. Box 498531, 45249. Tel: 317-416-8285; Email: cswna@cswna.org; Web: www.cswna.org. Kathleen Neher, Pres. & Contact Person.

Cincinnati Catholic Women's Association (1917) 958 Marion Ave., 45229. Tel: 513-961-3566; Fax: 513-745-9244; Email: teddie@fuse.net; Web: cincinnaticatholicwomen.org. Susan Dorward, Pres.; Teddie Curry, Treas.

Claver Jesuit Ministry, 5301 Winneste Ave., 45232-1132. Tel: 513-319-3865; Email: clavmin@gmail.com; Web: www.claverjesuit.org. Rev. Joseph D. Folzenlogen, S.J., Dir.

The Comboni Lay Missionaries Association, 1318 Nagel Rd., 45255-3120. Tel: 513-474-4997; Fax: 513-474-0382; Email: info@laymission-comboni.org; Web: www.laymission-comboni.org. Ms. Jeannie Zeitlin, Pres.; Mr. Chuck Carey, Vice Pres., Treas.; Mr. Paul Wheeler, Dir.; Ms. Cynthia Britton, Sec.

The Comboni Missionaries Auxiliary, Inc., 1318 Nagel Rd., 45255-3120. Tel: 513-474-4997; Fax: 513-474-0382; Email: info@combonimissionaries.org; Web: www.combonimissionaries.org. Olga Baldwin, Pres.; Mrs. Jane Fronk; Rev. Louis Gasparini, M.C.C.J., Spiritual Advisor / Care Services; Ms. Maria Lanzot, Vice Pres.; Mrs. Mary Catherine Meyer, Treas.

**The Couple to Couple League International* (1971) 4290 Delhi Pk., 45238. Tel: 513-471-2000; Fax: 513-557-2449; Email: ccli@ccli.org; Web: www.ccli.org. Christopher Reynolds, M.B.A., Exec. Dir.; Don Regan, Dir. Finance.

De Paul Cristo Rey Work Study Program Corporation, 1133 Clifton Hills Ave., 45220. Tel: 513-861-0600; Fax: 513-861-0900; Email: jeanne.bessette@dpcr.net; Web: www.discoverdepaul.org. Sr. Jeanne Bessette, O.S.F., Pres. & CEO; Abby Held, Dir. Sponsored by Sisters of Charity of Cincinnati.

St. Dymphna Ministry, c/o Summit Behavioral Healthcare, 1101 Summit Rd., 45237. Rev. Valens J. Waldschmidt, O.F.M., (Retired).

**St. Francis Seraph Ministries*, 1615 Republic St., 45202. Tel: 513-549-0542; Fax: 513-721-1152; Email: team@sfsministries.org; Email: aanderson@sfsministries.org; Web: www.sfsministries.org. Annise Anderson, Office Mgr.

Franciscan Central Purchasing (1965) St. Clement Friary, 4536 Vine St., 45217. Tel: 513-641-2257; Fax: 513-641-2262. Rev. Maynard Tetreault, O.F.M., Dir.

Franciscan Media, LLC, 28 W. Liberty St., 45202. Tel: 513-241-5615; Fax: 513-241-0399; Email: magazineeditors@franciscanmedia.org; Web: www.FranciscanMedia.org. Kelly McCracken, Pres.; Rev. Daniel Kroger, O.F.M., Publisher.

Franciscan Missionary Union, 1615 Vine St., 45202. Tel: 513-721-4700, Ext. 3222; Fax: 513-421-9672; Email: sjbcfo@franciscan.org; Web: www.franciscan.org. Revs. Damien Cesanek, O.F.M., Pres. & Trustee; Michael Chowning, O.F.M., Trustee; John Bok, O.F.M., Vice Pres. & Trustee; Bro. Gene Mayer, O.F.M., Sec., Treas. & Trustee; Mr. David O'Brien, Treas.

Franciscans Network, 1605 Main St., 45202. Tel: 513-739-3969; Email: franciscansnetwork@cinci.rr.com; Email: jquigleyofm@gmail.com; Web: www.franciscansnetwork.org. Diane H. Laake, Contact Person; Revs. John Quigley, O.F.M., Bd. of Trustees; Murray L. Bodo, O.F.M., Bd. of Trustees; Alan Hartman, S.F.O., Bd. of Trustees.

Jesuit Advancement Office, 10945 Reed Hartman Hwy., Ste. 119, 45242. Jeff Meyrose, Dir.

St. Joseph Housing Corporation, 10722 Wyscarver Rd., 45241. Tel: 513-563-2520; Fax: 513-563-1958; Email: tcook@stjosephhome.org. Matt Cooksey, Treas.

Marian Center of Cincinnati, 5862 Harvey Cir., 45233. Tel: 513-922-1250; Fax: 859-441-0641. Mr. Robert E. Hater, Lay Dir.; Lois A. Hater, Sec.

St. Mark's Chaplaincy for the Extraordinary Form, P.O. Box 1, Harrison, 45030. Ashley Paver, Pres.

Mercy Education Collaborative of Cincinnati (Collaborative), 6000 Oakwood Ave., 45224. Tel: 513-681-1802; Fax: 513-681-1811; Email: wmorse@mercysc.org. Mr. Robert Morse, Vice Pres.

**Mercy Neighborhood Ministries, Inc.*, 1602 Madison Rd., 45206. Tel: 513-751-2500; Fax: 513-221-5498; Email: ashinkle@mnministries.org; Web: www.mercyneighborhoodministries.org. Suzanne M. Kathman, Exec. Dir.

Ministers of Service, 745 Ezzard Charles, 45203. Tel: 513-381-0630; Fax: 513-742-9096; Email: church3824@cs.com. Mr. Jack D. McWilliams, Dir. The Ministers of Service Program, which began in 1979, provides training in urban ministry, primarily but not exclusively for African American laypersons. The Ministers of Service Program focuses on parish/community ministry to prepare laypersons to take active roles in church ministry.

National Fraternity of the Secular Franciscan Order, U.S.A., 1615 Vine St., 45202. Tel: 636-734-9979; Email: jansfo@yahoo.com; Web: www.secularfranciscansusa.org. Jan Parker, Pres.

**Natural Family Planning International Inc.*, 2911 Werk Rd., 45211-7018. Tel: 740-457-9663; Email: s.craig@nfpandmore.org; Web: www.nfpandmore.org. Mr. John F. Kippley, Pres.; Sheila Kippley, Sec. & Treas.; Steve Craig, Exec. Dir.

New Jerusalem Community, 745 Derby Ave., 45232. Tel: 513-541-4748; Fax: 513-541-4748; Email: njcommunity@juno.com. Paul Moore, Pres. & Leadership Council; Mary Howard, Leadership Council.

**Pregnancy Center West, Inc.*, 4900 Glenway Ave., 45238. Tel: 513-244-5700; Fax: 513-244-2886; Email: pcwest@fuse.net; Email: info@pc-west.org; Web: www.pc-west.org. Ms. Laura Caporaletti, Exec.

**Presentation Ministries, Inc.*, 3230 McHenry Ave., 45211. Tel: 513-662-5378; Email: orders@presentationministries.com; Web: www.presentationministries.com. Deacon George Schmidl, Pres. & Contact Person.

**Ruah Woods* Ruah Woods helps men and women live their vocation to love, according to God's plan, as informed by the Theology of the Body. This is accomplished by providing on-site Theology of the Body education, marriage prep, psychological therapy integrated with the Catholic faith and writing curriculum: ROOTED: K-12 Theology of the Body Curriculum. 6675 Wesselman Rd., 45248. Tel: 513-407-8672; Fax: 513-417-8955; Email: lesliekuhlman@ruahwoods.org; Web: www.ruahwoods.org; Web: www.ruahwoodspress.com; Web: www.rwpsych.org. Leslie Kuhlman, Exec. Dir.

Secular Franciscan Order, 4012 Ryland, Springfield, 45503. Tel: 937-399-7531; Email: sfopax@mindspring.com. Stephen White, O.F.S. Regl. Min., (Cincinnati, OH); Ray Richter, Vice-Min. Holy Trinity Regional Fraternity, Inc.; Founded by St. Francis of Assisi before A.D. 1215.

**Society of Saint Philip Neri, Inc.* The Cincinnati Oratory The Cincinnati Oratory 123 E. 13th St., 45202. Tel: 513-721-2988; Email: provost@cincinnatioratory.com; Web: www.cincinnatioratory.com. Very Rev. Jon-Paul Bevak, Provost; Revs. Adrian J. Hilton, Vicar; Lawrence Juarez; Bro. Brent Stull. Brothers 1; Novices 1; Priests 3.

The Company of St. Ursula - USA, 3021 Fairfield Ave., Apt. B-7, 45206. Tel: 513-961-0667; Email: csu@fuse.net; Web: www.companyofstursula.org. Ms. Mary-Cabrini Durkin, Pres.

Ursuline Education Network, 7659 Montgomery Rd., Ste. 2, 45236. Tel: 513-221-5300; Email: jwimberg@ursuline-education.com; Web: www.ursuline-education.com. Ms. Judith Wimberg, Exec. Dir. UEN is a service to all Ursuline Schools.

Vietnamese Catholic Community of Our Lady of Lavang, 314 Township Ave., 45216. Tel: 513-242-2933; Email: lavangcinti@gmail.com. Rev. Chau Pham, S.V.D., Chap. Tot in Congregation 500.

St. Xavier Church Property Corporation, 611 Sycamore St., 45202. Tel: 513-721-4045; Fax: 513-723-0451; Email: office@stxchurch.org; Web: www.stxchurch.org. Revs. Patrick A. Fairbanks, S.J., Pres.; Albert DeUlio, S.J., Treas.;

Brian G. Paulson, S.J., Provincial; Walter C. Deye, S.J., Rector.

CARTHAGENA. *The Society of the Precious Blood Senior Housing Corporation*, 2860 U.S. Rte. 127, Celina, 45822. Tel: 419-925-4516; Fax: 419-925-4800; Web: www.st-charles-cpps.org. Rev. Kenneth J. Schroeder, C.PP.S., Pres. & Contact Person, (Retired).

CELINA. **St. Marys Deanery Center*, 2860 U.S. Rte. 127, Celina, 45822. Tel: 419-925-5022; Email: smdeanery@bright.net; Web: www.stmarysdeanery.com. Rev. Richard W. Walling, Dean; Mr. Tom Kueterman, Dir.

CENTERVILLE. *St. Leonard Faith Community*, 8100 Clyo Rd., Centerville, 45458. Tel: 937-435-3626; Email: slfc.pa01@gmail.com; Email: slfc.office@gmail.com; Web: www.stleonardfaithcommunity.org. Rev. Lawrence E. Mick, Moderator/Chap., (Retired). Families 181.

DAYTON. *Catholic Vietnamese Community of Dayton*, 217 W. Fourth St., Dayton, 45402.
Tel: 937-224-3904; Email: sacredheartdayton@yahoo.com. Rev. Leo Vu, Chap.

FAIRBORN. *National Diaconate Institute for Continuing Education, Inc.*, 330 Chatham Dr., Fairborn, 45324. Tel: 937-879-5332; Email: maxroadruck2@ameritech.net; Web: www.ndice.org. Max J. Roadruck Jr., Past Pres.

MARIA STEIN. *Maria Stein Shrine of the Holy Relics* (1846) 2291 St. Johns Rd., PO Box 128, Maria Stein, 45860. Tel: 419-925-4532;
Fax: 513-925-5044; Web: www.mariasteinshrine.org. Donald C. Rosenbeck, Pres. & Admin. Includes Maria Stein Shrine of the Holy Relics, The Heritage Museum, and The Pilgrim Gift Shop.

MASON. **Royalmont Academy*, (Grades PreK-12), 200 Northcrest Dr., Mason, 45040. Tel: 513-754-0555; Fax: 513-754-0009; Email: vmurphy@royalmont.org; Web: www.royalmontacademy.org. Mrs. Veronica Murphy, Head of School. Member of Regnum Christi Education Lay Teachers 25; Students 142; Clergy / Religious Teachers 2.

MOUNT SAINT JOSEPH. *Archivists for Congregations of Women Religious*, ACWR National Office, 5900 Delhi Rd., Mount St. Joseph, 45051.
Tel: 513-347-4080; Email: archivistsacwr@gmail.com; Web: www.archivistsacwr.org. Purpose: Professional Preservation of the archives of Roman Catholic women religious congregations and collaboration with historians in making known the lives and works of women religious.

XENIA. **Change and Be Changed, Inc.*, P.O. Box 221, Xenia, 45385. Cell: 937-657-7474; Email: thomas.hangartner@wright.edu; Email: ehangart@gmail.com. Rev. Thomas A. Schroer, S.M.

RELIGIOUS INSTITUTES OF MEN REPRESENTED IN THE ARCHDIOCESE

For further details refer to the corresponding bracketed number in the Religious Institutes of Men or Women section.

[0200]—*Benedictine Monks.*
[0460]—*Brothers of the Poor of St. Francis*—C.F.P.
[0380]—*Comboni Missionaries of the Heart of Jesus (Verona)*—M.C.C.J.
[0650]—*Congregation of the Holy Spirit* (Province of the United States)—C.S.Sp.
[0865]—*Congregation of the Mother of the Redeemer*—C.R.M.
[0520]—*Franciscan Friars* (Province of St. John the Baptist, Cincinnati)—O.F.M.
[0570]—*Glenmary Home Missioners*—G.H.M.
[0690]—*Jesuit Fathers and Brothers* U.S.A. Midwest Province, Northeast Province)—S.J.
[0730]—*Legionaries of Christ* (New York)—L.C.
[0800]—*Maryknoll Fathers and Brothers.*
[]—*Oratory of St. Philip Neri Society of Apostolic Life.*
[0430]—*Order of Preachers (Dominicans)* (St. Joseph Province)—O.P.
[1065]—*Priestly Fraternity of St. Peter.*
[0760]—*Society of Mary (Marianists)* (United States Province)—S.M.
[0420]—*Society of the Divine Word* (Chicago Province)—S.V.D.
[1060]—*Society of the Precious Blood* (Cincinnati Province)—C.PP.S.

RELIGIOUS INSTITUTES OF WOMEN REPRESENTED IN THE ARCHDIOCESE

[0230]—*Benedictine Sisters of Pontifical Jurisdiction* (Beech Grove, IN; Villa Hills, KY)—O.S.B.
[0330]—*Carmelite Sisters for the Aged and Infirm*—O.Carm.
[1000]—*Congregation of Divine Providence of Kentucky*—C.D.P.
[0870]—*Congregation of the Daughters of Mary Immaculate (Marianist Sisters)*—F.M.I.
[3832]—*Congregation of the Sisters of St. Joseph*—C.S.J.
[1730]—*Congregation of the Sisters of the Third Order of St. Francis, Oldenburg, IN*—O.S.F.
[1070-07]—*Dominican Sisters* (Adrian, MI)—O.P.
[1070-16]—*Dominican Sisters* (Nashville, TN)—O.P.
[1070-15]—*Dominican Sisters of Hope*—O.P.
[1115]—*Dominican Sisters of Peace* (Columbus, OH)—O.P.
[1430]—*Franciscan Sisters of Our Lady Perpetual Help* (St. Louis, MO)—O.S.F.
[1440]—*Franciscan Sisters of the Poor*—S.F.P.
[2340]—*Little Sisters of the Poor*—L.S.P.
[2470]—*Maryknoll Sisters of St. Dominic*—M.M.
[2720]—*Mission Helpers of the Sacred Heart*—M.H.S.H.
[3760]—*Order of St. Clare-Poor Clares*—O.S.C.
[3230]—*Poor Handmaids of Jesus Christ*—P.H.J.C.
[0440]—*Sisters of Charity of Cincinnati, Ohio*—S.C.
[0570]—*Sisters of Charity of Seton Hill, Greensburg, Pennsylvania*—S.C.
[1710]—*Sisters of St. Francis of Mary Immaculate* (Joliet, IL)—O.S.F.
[2575]—*Sisters of Mercy of the Americas* (South Central Community, Belmont, NC)—R.S.M.
[2990]—*Sisters of Notre Dame* (Covington Prov.)—S.N.D.
[3000]—*Sisters of Notre Dame de Namur*—S.N.D.deN.
[3360]—*Sisters of Providence of Saint Mary-of-the-Woods, Indiana*—S.P.
[1530]—*Sisters of St Francis of the Congregation of Our Lady of Lourdes* (Sylvania, OH)—O.S.F.
[3840]—*Sisters of St. Joseph of Carondelet* (Latham, NY)—C.S.J.
[1830]—*The Sisters of the Good Shepherd*—R.G.S.
[3260]—*Sisters of the Precious Blood* (Dayton, OH)—C.PP.S.
[4120]—*Ursuline Nuns of the Congregation of Paris* (Brown Co.)—O.S.U.
[4120-01]—*Ursuline Nuns of the Congregation of Paris* (Cincinnati, OH)—O.S.U.

CEMETERIES

CINCINNATI. *Catholic Calvary Cemetery Association*, 1721 Duck Creek Rd., 45207. Tel: 513-704-6261; Fax: 513-961-0062; Email: Jayccc576@gmail.com; Email: larry.ungerer@juno.com. Ronald Hibbard, Supt.

Gate of Heaven Cemetery, 11000 Montgomery Rd., 45249. Tel: 513-489-0300; Fax: 513-489-1817; Email: info@gateofheaven.org; Web: www.gateofheaven.org. Ms. Debra K. Crane, Esq., Dir., Cemeteries

St. John, Administrative Office Address: 3819 W. 8th St., 45205. Tel: 513-557-2306; Tel: 513-242-4191; Fax: 513-557-2310; Email: steve@cccsohio.org; Web: www.cccsohio.org. 4423 Vine St., 45217. Stephen E. Bittner, Pres.; Jerome Auer, Dir. Operated by Cincinnati Catholic Cemetery Society

St. Joseph, Administrative Office Address: 3819 W. 8th St., 45205.
Tel: 513-557-2306 (Administrative Office);
Tel: 513-921-3050 (St. Joseph Office);
Fax: 513-557-2310 (Admin. Office); Email: steve@cccsohio.org; Web: www.cccsohio.org. Stephen E. Bittner, Pres.; Jerome Auer, Dir. Operated by Cincinnati Catholic Cemetery Society

St. Joseph New Cemetery Association, 4500 Foley Rd., 45238. Tel: 513-251-3110; Fax: 513-251-1075; Email: rwinter@stjoenew.com; Web: www.stjoenew.com. Robert Winter, Gen. Mgr.

St. Mary, 701 E. Ross Ave., 45217.
Tel: 513-242-4191 (St. Mary Office);
Tel: 513-557-2306, Ext. 319 (Administrative Office); Fax: 513-557-2310 (Administrative Office); Email: steve@cccsohio.org; Web: www.cccsohio.org. Administrative Office Address: 3819 W. 8th St., 45205. Stephen E. Bittner, Pres.; Jerome Auer, Dir. Part of Cincinnati Catholic Cemetery Society

DAYTON. *The Calvary Cemetery Association*, 1625 Calvary Dr., Dayton, 45409. Tel: 937-293-1221; Fax: 937-293-7316; Email: terrih@ccadayton.org. Terri Hailey, Business Mgr.; Rick Meade, Exec. Dir.

SPRINGFIELD. *Calvary*, 3155 E. Possum Rd., Springfield, 45502. Tel: 937-323-7474; Email: matthewspat7@yahoo.com. James P. Matthews, Supt.

NECROLOGY

† Bensman, John L., (Retired), Died May. 25, 2018
† Espelage, Thomas, (Retired), Died Oct. 2, 2018
† Meyer, Thomas E., (Retired), Died Dec. 6, 2018

An asterisk (*) denotes an organization that has established tax-exempt status directly with the IRS and is not covered by the USCCB Group Ruling.

Diocese of Cleveland

(Dioecesis Clevelandensis)

Most Reverend

NELSON J. PEREZ

Bishop of Cleveland; ordained May 20, 1989; appointed Titular Bishop of Catrum and Auxiliary Bishop of Rockville Centre June 8, 2012; installed July 25, 2012; appointed Bishop of Cleveland July 11, 2017; installed September 5, 2017. *Office: 1404 E. Ninth St., Cleveland, OH 44114.* Tel: 216-696-6525.

Cathedral Square Plaza: 1404 E. Ninth St., Cleveland, OH 44114. Tel: 216-696-6525; Tel: 800-869-6525 (Ohio only); Fax: 216-621-7332.

Web: www.dioceseofcleveland.org

Email: info@dioceseofcleveland.org

Most Reverend

RICHARD GERARD LENNON

Retired Bishop of Cleveland; ordained priest May 19, 1973; appointed Titular Bishop of Sufes and Auxiliary Bishop of Boston June 29, 2001; ordained September 14, 2001; appointed Bishop of Cleveland April 4, 2006; installed May 15, 2006; retired December 28, 2016.

Most Reverend

ANTHONY M. PILLA, D.D., M.A.

Retired Bishop of Cleveland; ordained May 23, 1959; appointed Auxiliary and Titular Bishop of Scardona June 30, 1979; consecrated August 1, 1979; named Apostolic Administrator of Cleveland July 29, 1980; appointed Bishop of Cleveland November 18, 1980; installed January 6, 1981; retired May 15, 2006. *Office: 28700 Euclid Ave., Wickliffe, OH 44092.* Tel: 440-943-7600; Fax: 440-943-2428.

Most Reverend

ROGER W. GRIES, O.S.B.

Retired Auxiliary Bishop of Cleveland; ordained May 16, 1963; appointed Auxiliary and Titular Bishop of Presidio April 3, 2001; consecrated June 7, 2001; retired November 1, 2013. *Office: 1230 Ansel Rd., Cleveland, OH 44109.* Tel: 216-721-0676; Fax: 216-721-0903.

ESTABLISHED APRIL 23, 1847.

Square Miles 3,414.

Comprises, since July 22, 1943, eight counties in the north-central part of the State of Ohio, namely Ashland, Cuyahoga, Geauga, Lake, Lorain, Medina, Summit and Wayne Counties.

For legal titles of parishes and diocesan institutions, consult the Chancery Office.

STATISTICAL OVERVIEW

Personnel	
Bishop	1
Retired Bishops	3
Abbots	1
Retired Abbots	2
Priests: Diocesan Active in Diocese	232
Priests: Diocesan Active Outside Diocese	7
Priests: Diocesan in Foreign Missions	2
Priests: Retired, Sick or Absent	115
Number of Diocesan Priests	356
Religious Priests in Diocese	83
Total Priests in Diocese	439
Extern Priests in Diocese	18
Ordinations:	
Diocesan Priests	3
Religious Priests	1
Transitional Deacons	9
Permanent Deacons	4
Permanent Deacons in Diocese	209
Total Brothers	24
Total Sisters	772
Parishes	
Parishes	185
With Resident Pastor:	
Resident Diocesan Priests	165
Resident Religious Priests	11
Without Resident Pastor:	
Administered by Priests	11
Missions	1
Pastoral Centers	1
Welfare	
Catholic Hospitals	4
Total Assisted	497,879
Health Care Centers	1
Total Assisted	752
Homes for the Aged	2
Total Assisted	790
Residential Care of Children	1
Total Assisted	47
Day Care Centers	3
Total Assisted	987
Specialized Homes	3
Total Assisted	927
Special Centers for Social Services	17
Total Assisted	179,734
Residential Care of Disabled	1
Total Assisted	47
Other Institutions	5
Total Assisted	25,434
Educational	
Seminaries, Diocesan	2
Students from This Diocese	63
Students from Other Diocese	14
Diocesan Students in Other Seminaries	2
Students Religious	16
Total Seminarians	81
Colleges and Universities	3
Total Students	6,724
High Schools, Diocesan and Parish	5
Total Students	2,584
High Schools, Private	15
Total Students	9,756
Elementary Schools, Diocesan and Parish	82
Total Students	26,212
Elementary Schools, Private	5
Total Students	1,702
Non-residential Schools for the Disabled	2
Total Students	174
Catechesis/Religious Education:	
High School Students	2,206
Elementary Students	24,891
Total Students under Catholic Instruction	74,330
Teachers in the Diocese:	
Priests	24
Brothers	22
Sisters	117
Lay Teachers	3,404
Vital Statistics	
Receptions into the Church:	
Infant Baptism Totals	4,891
Minor Baptism Totals	334
Adult Baptism Totals	284
Received into Full Communion	714
First Communions	5,865
Confirmations	6,332
Marriages:	
Catholic	1,293
Interfaith	534
Total Marriages	1,827
Deaths	6,956
Total Catholic Population	663,919
Total Population	2,769,738

Former Bishops—Rt. Revs. AMADEUS RAPPE, D.D., ord. March 14, 1829; cons. Oct. 10, 1847; resigned July 29, 1870; died Sept 8, 1877; RICHARD GILMOUR, D.D., ord. Aug. 30, 1852; cons. April 14, 1872; died April 13, 1891; IGNATIUS F. HORSTMANN, D.D., ord. June 10, 1865; cons. Feb. 25, 1892; died May 13, 1908; JOHN P. FARRELLY, D.D., ord. May 22, 1880; cons. May 1, 1909; died Feb. 12, 1921; Most Revs. JOSEPH SCHREMBS, S.T.D., Archbishop-Bishop of Cleveland; cons. Feb. 22, 1911; transferred to the See of Cleveland, June 16, 1921; installed Sept. 8, 1921; appt. Archbishop, March 25, 1939; died November 2, 1945; EDWARD F. HOBAN, S.T.D., Ph. D., L.L.D., Archbishop-Bishop of Cleveland; cons. Dec. 21, 1921; transferred to Cleveland as Coadjutor Bishop "cum jure successionis" Nov. 14, 1942; succeeded to See of Cleveland, Nov. 2, 1945; appt. Archbishop, July 23, 1951; died Sept. 22, 1966; CLARENCE G. ISSENMANN, S.T.D., cons. May 25, 1954; transferred to Cleveland as Coadjutor Bishop "cum jure successionis" and Titular Bishop of Filaca. Ap-Adm. Oct. 7, 1964; succeeded to See of Cleveland, Sept. 22, 1966; retired June 5, 1974; died July 27, 1982; JAMES A. HICKEY, S.T.D., J.C.D., cons. April 14, 1967; appt. Bishop of Cleveland, June 5, 1974; installed July 16, 1974; appt. Archbishop of Washington, DC June 17, 1980; created Cardinal by Pope John Paul II in the consistory on June 28, 1988; retired Nov. 21, 2000; died Oct. 24, 2004; ANTHONY M. PILLA, ord. May 23, 1959; appt. Auxiliary and Titular Bishop of Scardona June 30, 1979; cons. Aug. 1, 1979; named Apostolic Administrator of Cleveland July 29, 1980; appt. Bishop of Cleveland Nov. 18, 1980; installed Jan. 6, 1981.; RICHARD G. LENNON, Retired Bishop of Cleveland, (Retired), ord. priest May 19, 1973; appt. Titular Bishop of Sufes and Auxiliary Bishop of Boston June 29, 2001; ord. Sept. 14, 2001; appt. Bishop of Cleveland April 4, 2006; installed May 15, 2006; retired Dec. 28, 2016.

Vicar General/Moderator of the Curia—Rev. DONALD P. OLEKSIAK, 1404 E. Ninth St., 6th Fl., Cleveland, 44114. Tel: 216-696-6525, Ext. 3800.

Vicar General—Rev. GARY D. YANUS, J.C.D., 1404 E. Ninth St., 7th Fl., Cleveland, 44114. Tel: 216-696-6525, Ext. 4000.

College of Consultors—Revs. EDWARD T. ESTOK, M.Div.; DONALD P. OLEKSIAK; DOUGLAS T. BROWN; ERIC S. GARRIS; LAWRENCE JURCAK, J.C.L.; JOSEPH R. MAMICH; WILLIAM A. THADEN; JOSEPH G. WORKMAN.

Presbyteral Council—Most Rev. NELSON J. PEREZ, D.D., M.Div., M.A., Pres.; Revs. VINCENT J. HAWK; THOMAS J. BEHREND; JOSEPH P. BOZNAR; DOUGLAS T. BROWN; JAMES L. CADDY, (Retired); THOMAS M. DRAGGA, D.Min.; ERIC S. GARRIS; GERALD J. KELLER, (Retired); JOHN THOMAS LANE, S.S.S.;

JOSEPH D. MCNULTY; LAWRENCE JURCAK, J.C.L.; ROBERT J. JASANY; EDWARD T. ESTOK, M.Div.; JOSEPH R. MAMICH, Moderator; JOSEPH G. WORKMAN; DONALD P. OLEKSIAK, (ex officio); MARK A. LATCOVICH, Ph.D., (ex officio); MATTHEW E. PFEIFFER; JOHN C. RETAR; PAUL J. ROSING; TIMOTHY J. ROTH, M.A., M.Div.; DANIEL F. SCHLEGEL, M.Div., M.A., Ex Officio; A. JONATHAN ZINGALES, J.C.L.; ANTHONY J. SUSO; WILLIAM A. THADEN. Presbyteral Conveners: Revs. DOUGLAS T. BROWN; JOHN C. RETAR; THOMAS M. DRAGGA, D.Min.; VINCENT J. HAWK; MATTHEW E. PFEIFFER; THOMAS J. BEHREND; JOSEPH P. BOZNAR; LAWRENCE JURCAK, J.C.L.; JOHN THOMAS LANE, S.S.S.; JOSEPH D. MCNULTY; JOSEPH G. WORKMAN; ROBERT J. JASANY; A. JONATHAN ZINGALES, J.C.L.

Diocesan Finance Council—MICHAEL MEEHAN, Chm.; KAREN KLEINHENZ; THOMAS J. PERCIAK; WILLIAM J. REIDY; DONALD DAILEY; THOMAS RICHLOVSKY; JANET MILLER; PATRICK MCMAHON; LAURA GALLAGHER, Judge; JEFFREY MIKLICH.

Diocesan Pastoral Council—Most Rev. NELSON J. PEREZ, D.D., M.Div., M.A.; SHERRI MOYER, Chair; STEPHANIE PRITTS, Vice Chair.

Conference of Religious Leadership—Sisters MARGARET TAYLOR, S.I.W.; CAROL TOBLER, S.I.W.; MARGARET MARY MC AULIFFE, S.I.W.

Diocese of Cleveland—Cathedral Square Plaza, 1404 E. Ninth St., Cleveland, 44114.

All Diocesan Offices are in the Cathedral Square Plaza at 1404 E. Ninth St. and may be reached at: Tel: 216-696-6525;
Tel: 800-869-6525 (Ohio only); Fax: 216-781-8243
.

Matrimonial dispensations and permissions should be addressed to the Tribunal.

Chancellor—Tel: 216-696-6525, Ext. 2080;
Fax: 216-621-7332. MR. VINCENT GARDINER, J.C.L.

Office for Worship—1404 E. Ninth St., 6th Fl., Cleveland, 44114. Tel: 216-696-6525, Ext. 4120. JEANNE MARIE MILES, Dir.

Tribunal—1404 E. Ninth St., Ste. 700, Cleveland, 44114-2555. Tel: 216-696-6525, Ext. 4000;
Tel: 800-869-6525 (Ohio only);
Tel: 800-676-4431 (Outside Ohio);
Fax: 216-696-3226.

Judicial Vicar—Rev. GARY D. YANUS, J.C.D.

Adjunct Judicial Vicars—Revs. LAWRENCE JURCAK, J.C.L.; CHARLES F. STREBLER, J.C.L.; RICHARD BONA, J.C.D.

Judges—MS. LYNETTE TAIT, J.C.L.; MR. VINCENT GARDINER, J.C.L.

Defenders of the Bond—Revs. JOSEPH A. BACEVICE; A. JONATHAN ZINGALES, J.C.L.; WILLIAM M. JERSE, J.C.L.; MR. CARL A. CALDWELL, M.A., J.C.B.

Staff Advocate—MR. CARL A. CALDWELL, M.A., J.C.B.

Auditors—MRS. KATE F. FIALA; MRS. JUDY R. LIEDERBACH, M.A.; MRS. AMY E. RIGGLE; Revs. TIMOTHY J. ROTH, M.A., M.Div.; ADAM A. ZAJAC, M.A., M.Div.

Promoters of Justice—Revs. A. JONATHAN ZINGALES, J.C.L.; MARK Q. FEDOR, J.C.D.

Ecclesiastical Notaries & Notaries Public—MRS. LEE ANN CALVERT; MRS. AMANDA L. HOCKENBERRY.

Ecclesiastical Notary—MRS. KATHRYN C. TEMPESTELLI.

Translators—Revs. BEDE KOTLINSKI, O.S.B.; JOHN F. WESSEL, (Retired); MICHAEL J. TROHA, M.A.; RICHARD BONA, J.C.D.

Archives—MR. VINCENT GARDINER, J.C.L., Chancellor; MR. PHILIP HAAS, Dir. Archives, Cathedral Square Plaza, 4th Fl.. Tel: 216-696-6525, Ext. 3450.

Catholic Cemeteries Association—ANDREJ N. LAH, Pres., 10000 Miles Ave., Cleveland, 44105. Tel: 216-641-7575.

Callistian Guild—Mailing Address: P.O. Box 605125, Cleveland, 44105. Tel: 216-641-7575.

Catholic Community Foundation—MR. PATRICK J. GRACE, Exec. Dir., 1404 E. 9th St., Ste. 810, Cleveland, 44114-1722. Tel: 216-696-6525, Ext. 5750; Fax: 216-348-0740.

Stewardship Office—1404 E. 9th St., 8th Fl., Cleveland, 44114. MRS. TERRI PRESKAR, Dir., Tel: 216-696-6525, Ext. 5090; Email: tpreskar@catholiccommunity.org.

Central Purchasing—JAMES P. TERESI, Dir., 9000 Town Centre Dr., Broadview Heights, 44147. Tel: 440-717-9700.

Communications Department—Deacon JAMES J. ARMSTRONG, Exec. Dir., Tel: 216-696-6525, Ext. 3130; Email: jarmstrong@dioceseofcleveland.org.

Mission Office, Society for the Propagation of the FaithRev. R. STEPHEN VELLENGA, Dir., 1404 E. 9th St., Cleveland, 44114. Tel: 216-696-6525, Ext. 4280.

Pontifical Programs—Society for the Propagation of the Faith; Society of St. Peter the Apostle; Missionary Union of the Clergy; Missionary Childhood Assoc.

Diocesan Programs—Missionary Cooperation Plan; St. Francis Xavier Mission Assoc.; Cleveland Diocesan Mission, C.A.

Finance Office—1404 E. 9th St., 8th Fl., Cleveland, 44114. JAMES P. GULICK, Finance Officer.

Diocesan Legal Office—KEVIN T. BURKE, Gen. Counsel, 1404 E. 9th St., 7th Fl., Ste. 701, Cleveland, 44114.

Diocesan Building Commission—MR. LAWRENCE E. MURTAUGH, 1404 E. 9th St., 3rd Fl., Cleveland, 44114.

Diocesan Insurance Office—JOHN C. EASTON, Dir. Risk Mgmt. & Asst. Finance Officer; KATHLEEN PIERCE, 1404 E. 9th St., 8th Fl., Cleveland, 44114.

Benefit Plans - Health Benefits, Group Life, and Pension—1404 E. 9th St., 8th Fl., Cleveland, 44114. DONNA B. SPEAGLE.

Human Resources Office—1404 E. 9th St., 8th Fl., Cleveland, 44114. MARY ANN BLAKELEY; DONNA B. SPEAGLE.

Workers' Compensation Office—1404 E. 9th St., 8th Fl., Cleveland, 44114. JOHN C. EASTON, Dir. Risk Mgmt. & Asst. Finance Officer; KATHLEEN PIERCE.

Diocese of Cleveland Facilities Services Corp.—MR. LAWRENCE E. MURTAUGH, Exec. Dir., 1404 E. 9th St., 3rd Fl., Cleveland, 44114.

Secretariat for Catechetical Formation and Education

Interim Secretary for Catechetical Formation and Education/Superintendent—1404 E. 9th St., 2nd Fl., Cleveland, 44114. Tel: 216-696-6525, Ext. 1022 . DR. FRANK O'LINN.

Departments—

Catholic Education Endowment Trust—CINDY WILLIAMS, 1404 E. 9th St., Cleveland. Tel: 216-696-6525, Ext. 2830.

Newman Campus Catholic Ministry—1404 E. 9th St., Cleveland, 44114. Rev. VINCENT J. HAWK, Dir., Tel: 216-696-6525, Ext. 3225; JOANN PIOTRKOWSKI, Asst. Dir., Tel: 216-696-6525, Ext. 3226.

Newman Campus Ministers—JOHN SZARWARK, Akron University, Tel: 216-696-6525, Ext. 3000; STEVE PERRY, Case Western Reserve Univ., Tel: 216-421-9614, Ext. 302; ANDREW J. HOY, College of Wooster & Oberlin College, Tel: 330-263-2262; VACANT, Cleveland State Univ.; NATE EDIGER, Ashland University, Tel: 419-289-5481; STEVE EYERMAN, Baldwin Wallace College, Tel: 440-243-4955.

Catechesis—PATRICIA PATTERSON, Dir., 1404 E. Ninth St., Cleveland, 44114. Tel: 216-696-6525, Ext. 1148.

Associate Director of Catechesis/Catechetical Formation Leader (East)—WILLIAM CHRISTOPHER HOAG, D.Min., 1404 E. 9th St., Cleveland, 44114. Tel: 216-696-6525, Ext. 2880.

Catechetical Formation Leaders—DENISE SMITHBERGER, (South), Tel: 216-696-6525, Ext. 8910; LAURA BASTULLI-PARRAN, (Central), Tel: 216-696-6525, Ext. 3380; HORTENSIA RODRIGUEZ, (West & Hispanic Parishes), 1404 E. 9th St., Cleveland, 44114. Tel: 216-696-6525, Ext. 1028.

Elementary Schools—1404 E. 9th St., Cleveland, 44114.

Associate Superintendent—MRS. TRACEY ARNONE, Tel: 216-696-6525, Ext. 1280.

Assistant Superintendent—SUSAN BIGGS, Tel: 216-696-6525, Ext. 1290.

Special Education Coordinator—MOLLY BULLOCK, Tel: 216-696-6525, Ext. 2480.

Special Projects/Voucher Programs—PAMELA OUZTS, Coord., 1404 E. 9th St., Cleveland, 44114. Tel: 216-696-6525, Ext. 3250.

Finance/School Controller—1404 E. 9th St., Cleveland, 44114. Tel: 216-696-6525. JOHN SZARWARK, Tel: 216-696-6525, Ext. 3000; DENNIS BECKSTROM, Tel: 216-696-6525, Ext. 5310.

Secondary Schools—1404 E. 9th St., Cleveland, 44114. Tel: 216-696-6525, Ext. 2460. DR. FRANK O'LINN, Assoc. Supt.

Government Programs—PAM OUZTS, Dir., 1404 E. 9th St., Cleveland, 44114. Tel: 216-696-6525, Ext. 3250.

Teacher Personnel Services—MELISSA HOKANSON, Dir., 1404 E. 9th St., Cleveland, 44114. Tel: 216-696-6525, Ext. 3360.

Nutrition Services/Summer Food Program—EDWARD MOREL, Dir., 1404 E. 9th St., Cleveland, 44114. Tel: 216-696-6525, Ext. 3110.

Curriculum—JENNIFER MIROGLOTTA, Coord., 1404 E. 9th St., Cleveland, 44114. Tel: 216-696-6525, Ext. 3240.

Educational Technology—DOLORES BRUNO, 1404 E. 9th St., Cleveland, 44114. Tel: 216-696-6525, Ext. 8990.

Tuition Assistance—1404 E. 9th St., Cleveland, 44114. Tel: 216-696-6525, Ext. 1032. MELANIE GALIZIO, Coord.

Technology—THOMAS MCBRIDE, Dir., 1404 E. 9th St., Cleveland, 44114. Tel: 216-696-6525, Ext. 3200.

Mandated Services—Consultant: PAMELA OUZTS, Coord., 1404 E. 9th St., Cleveland, 44114. Tel: 216-696-6525, Ext. 3250.

Secretariat for Parish Life

Secretary—Sr. RITA MARY HARWOOD, S.N.D., 1404 E. 9th St., 3rd Fl., Cleveland, 44114. Tel: 216-696-6525, Ext. 2200.

African Ministry—Sr. RITA MARY HARWOOD, S.N.D., Tel: 216-696-6525, Ext. 3500.

Apostleship of the Sea Chaplain for the Diocese of Cleveland (Port Chaplain)—Sr. RITA MARY HARWOOD, S.N.D., Interim, Tel: 216-696-6525, Ext. 3500.

Asian Ministry—Sr. RITA MARY HARWOOD, S.N.D., Tel: 216-696-6525, Ext. 3500.

World Apostolate of Fatima, USA, Inc.—(also known as the Blue Army) *Cleveland Diocesan Division, 3785 Independence Rd., Cleveland, 44105.*
Tel: 440-223-8570. KATHRYN DECAPITE, Pres.; Rev. ROBERT J. JASANY, Spiritual Dir.

Catholic Renewal Ministries—Rev. ROBERT J. FRANCO, 35777 Center Ridge Rd., North Ridgeville, 44039-3097. Tel: 440-327-2201 Bishop's Delegate. Presentation House, 28706 Euclid Ave., #4, Wickliffe, 44092. Tel: 440-944-9445.

Central City Ministry with Poor—3675 W. 165th St., Cleveland, 44111-5750. Tel: 216-566-0531. Rev. JAMES P. O'DONNELL, (Retired).

Diocesan Interfaith Commission—Rev. JOSEPH T. HILINSKI, Delegate, Tel: 216-696-6525, Ext. 5110.

Enthronement of the Sacred Heart—MRS. DONNA ZAK, Sec. & Treas., Tel: 440-232-7725.

Ethnic Ministries—For the Pastoral Care of Migrants and Refugees and for any ethnic communities not listed below, please contact Sr. Rita Mary Harwood, S.N.D., The Parish Life Office. Tel: 216-696-6525, Ext. 3500.

Diocesan Hispanic Office—MISAEL MAYORGA, Dir., 1404 E. 9th St., Cleveland, 44114. Tel: 216-696-6525, Ext. 4300.

Korean Catholic Apostolate—Rev. SANG-JUN PARK, St. Andrew Kim (Korean Pastoral Center), 2310 W. 14th St., Cleveland, 44113. Tel: 216-861-4630.

Native American Ministry—Sr. RITA MARY HARWOOD, S.N.D., Dir., 1404 E. 9th St., Cleveland, 44114. Tel: 216-696-6525, Ext. 3500.

Office of Ministry to African American Catholics—Tel: 216-696-6525, Ext. 3020. MR. CARY DABNEY, Dir.

Philippine-American Ministry—1007 Superior Ave., Cleveland, 44114. Tel: 216-771-6666. Rev. ARNEL A. LAGMAN.

Vietnamese-American Apostolate—St. Boniface Parish, 3545 W. 54th St., Cleveland, 44102.
Tel: 216-961-2713, Ext. 2540. Rev. HILARY KHANH KAI NGUYEN, C.R.M.

Office of Evangelization—TERRIE BALDWIN, Dir., Tel: 216-696-6525, Ext. 2540.

Holy Name Societies, Cleveland Diocesan Union—Rev. THOMAS A. HAREN, Spiritual Dir., 13623 Rockside Rd., Garfield Heights, 44125-5197. Tel: 216-662-8685.

Office of Lay Ecclesial Ministry—PATRICIA BATCHMAN, Dir., Center for Pastoral Leadership, 28700 Euclid Ave., Wickliffe, 44092. Tel: 440-943-7672.

Office for the Protection of Children and Youth—SHARON MINSON, Dir., Tel: 216-696-6525, Ext. 1157.

Secretariat for Clergy and Religious

Secretary—1404 E. 9th St., 6th Fl., Cleveland, 44114. Tel: 216-696-6525, Ext. 2440. Rev. DANIEL F. SCHLEGEL, M.Div., M.A., Sec. & Vicar for Clergy & Relg.

Borromeo Seminary—See Seminaries.

Delegate for Religious—Sr. M. ROCHELLE GUERTAL, O.SS.T., 1404 E. 9th St., 6th Fl., Cleveland, 44114. Tel: 216-696-6525, Ext. 2920.

Continuing Education for Formation of Ministers—The Center for Pastoral Leadership, 28700 Euclid Ave., Wickliffe, 44092. Tel: 440-943-7474. Rev. MICHAEL K. GURNICK, M.A., M.Div., Dir., Pastor: St. Patrick Parish, 3602 Bridge Ave., Cleveland, 44113-3314. Tel: 216-631-6872.

Permanent Diaconate Formation Office—Deacon DAVID S. KUSHNER, Dir., The Center for Pastoral Leadership, 28700 Euclid Ave., Wickliffe, 44092. Tel: 440-943-7652.

Retirement Board—Revs. MICHAEL D. AUSPERK, Chm., Holy Family Parish, 3450 Sycamore Dr., Stow, 44224. Tel: 330-688-6411; JOSEPH PREVITE, Corresponding Sec., Holy Rosary Parish, 12021 Mayfield Rd., Cleveland, 44106-1996. Tel: 216-421-2995; GARY D. YANUS, J.C.D., Recording Sec., c/o Tribunal: 1404 E. 9th St., Cleveland, 44114. Tel: 216-696-6525.

St. Mary Seminary—See Seminaries.

Delegate for Senior Priests—Rev. JOHN MANNING, Delegate, 1404 E. 9th St., 6th Fl., Cleveland, 44114. Tel: 216-696-6525, Ext. 3850.

Delegate for Senior Deacons—Deacon EDMUND A. GARDIAS, 1404 E. 9th St., 6th Fl., Cleveland, 44114. Tel: 216-696-6525, Ext. 2910.

Vocation Office—Rev. MICHAEL P. MCCANDLESS, M.Div., M.A., Dir., The Center for Pastoral Leadership, 28700 Euclid Ave., Wickliffe, 44092. Tel: 440-943-7660.

Avilas of the Diocese of Cleveland—1295 Haverston Rd., Lyndhurst, 44124. Tel: 440-473-6107. MRS. VIRGINIA KOVACINA, Pres.

Parents of Priests—MR. DONALD TRASK, Pres., 13355 Foxmoor Trail, Chesterland, 44026. Tel: 440-729-4684.

Serra District 85 Governor—MRS. COLETTE SISLAK, District Governor, 17724 Lomond Blvd., Shaker Heights, 44120. Tel: 216-752-8873.

Catholic Charities Corporation

Catholic Charities Corporation—MR. PATRICK GAREAU, Pres. & CEO, 7911 Detroit Ave., Cleveland, 44102. Tel: 216-334-2901.

Catholic Charities Annual Appeal—MR. PATRICK J. GRACE, 1404 E. Ninth St., 8th Fl., Cleveland, 44114. Tel: 216-696-6525, Ext. 5750; Fax: 216-348-0740.

Catholic Charities Parish Outreach—Executive Director: *7911 Detroit Ave., Cleveland, 44102.* Tel: 216-334-2959; Fax: 216-334-2983. MR. TERRENCE FLANAGAN.

Office for Human Life—PEGGY GEROVAC, Dir., 7911 Detroit Ave., Cleveland, 44102. Tel: 216-334-2965; Fax: 216-334-2976.

Office of Ministry for Persons with Disabilities—Rev. JOSEPH D. MCNULTY, Exec. Dir., 2486 W. 14th St., Cleveland, 44113. Tel: 216-781-5530; Fax: 216-781-1124.

Marriage and Family Office—WILLIAM BOOMER, M.A., Dir., 7911 Detroit Ave., Cleveland, 44102. Tel: 216-334-2971.

Youth and Young Adult Ministry and CYO Office—GREG MOSER, Dir., 7911 Detroit Ave., Cleveland, 44102. Tel: 216-334-1261, Ext. 32.

Migration and Refugee Services—TOM MROSKO, Dir., 7800 Detroit Ave., Cleveland, 44102. Tel: 216-939-3731.

Catholic Charities Treatment, Prevention, and Recovery Services—3135 Euclid Ave., Rm. 202, Cleveland, 44115. MAUREEN DEE, Tel: 216-391-2030; Fax: 216-291-8946.

Catholic Charities Family Services—7911 Detroit Ave., Cleveland, 44102. Tel: 216-334-2937; Fax: 216-334-2907. MS. JOAN HINKELMAN, Sr. Dir.

Catholic Charities Regional Services—6753 State Rd., Parma, 44134. Tel: 440-843-5649. ANGELA IVANCIC, Chief Clinical Officer.

Disabilities Services—7911 Detroit Ave., Cleveland, 44102. Tel: 216-939-2962; Fax: 216-939-2905. MARILYN SCOTT, Sr. Dir.

Emergency Assistance Services—MELISSA SIRAK, Dir., 7911 Detroit Ave., Cleveland, 44102. Tel: 216-334-2984.

Older Adult Services—MATHEW CUBA, 7801 Detroit Ave., Cleveland, 44102. Tel: 216-634-7405.

Pastoral Care Services—7911 Detroit Ave., Cleveland, 44102. Tel: 216-334-2960. Rev. WILLIAM A. SMITH.

Catholic Charities Housing Corporation—c/o 1404 E. 9th St., Cleveland, 44114. MARYELLEN STAAB, Dir., Tel: 216-696-6525, Ext. 1506.

Diocesan Social Action Office—Tel: 216-939-3843; Fax: 216-334-2907. DIANE ZBASNIK, Dir.

Commission on Catholic Community Action—7911 Detroit Ave., Cleveland, 44102. Tel: 216-939-3843 ; Fax: 216-334-2907. DIANE ZBASNIK, Dir.

Catholic Action Commission of Lorain County—VACANT, Dir., 628 Poplar St., Lorain, 44052. Tel: 440-366-1106.

Catholic Commission of Lake and Geauga Counties—MS. KELLY DAVIS, 28700 Euclid Ave., Wickliffe, 44092. Tel: 440-943-7612.

Catholic Commission (Summit County)—795 Russell Ave., Akron, 44307. Tel: 330-535-2787; Fax: 330-535-9040. VACANT, Dir.

Catholic Commission of Wayne, Ashland and Medina Counties—MR. JEFF CAMPBELL, Dir., 4210 N. Jefferson St., #A, Medina, 44256. Tel: 330-723-9615; Fax: 330-764-8795.

Catholic Campaign for Human Development—MRS. ANN CLARK, 7911 Detroit Ave., Cleveland, 44102.

Catholic Relief Services—MS. KELLY DAVIS, 28700 Euclid Ave., Wickliffe, 44092. Tel: 440-943-7612.

Bishop William M. Cosgrove Family Center—1736 Superior Ave., Cleveland, 44114. Tel: 216-781-8262 ; Fax: 216-566-9161. MR. ERIC MILKIE, Prog. Dir.

Rose-Mary, The Johanna Grasselli Rehabilitation and Education Center—GINA KERMAN, Exec. Dir., 2346 W. 14th St., Cleveland, 44113. Tel: 216-481-4823; Fax: 216-481-4154.

St. Augustine Corporation—RICK MESERINI, Exec. Dir. & Pres., 7801 Detroit Ave., Cleveland, 44102. Tel: 216-634-7400; Fax: 216-634-7483.

Catholic Lawyers' Guild of Cleveland—The Catholic Diocese of Cleveland Foundation.

Catholic Lawyers' Guild of Cleveland Endowment Trust—The Catholic Diocese of Cleveland Foundation.

CLERGY, PARISHES, MISSIONS AND PAROCHIAL SCHOOLS

CITY OF CLEVELAND

(CUYAHOGA COUNTY)

1—CATHEDRAL OF ST. JOHN THE EVANGELIST (1848) Revs. Arnel A. Lagman, Parochial Vicar; Sean P. Ralph, M.Div., M.A.; Deacon John P. Sferry Sr., (Retired); Rev. John Manning, In Res.
Res.: 1007 Superior Ave. E., 44114-2582.
Tel: 216-771-6666; Fax: 216-781-5646; Email: stjohns@dioceseofcleveland.org; Web: SaintJohnCathedral.com.
Church: E. 9th St. & Superior Ave., N.E., 44114.
Catechesis Religious Program—Email: capperson-hansen@dioceseofcleveland.org. Carolyn Apperson-Hansen, D.R.E. Students 8.

2—ST. ADALBERT (1883)
2347 E. 83rd St., 44104. Rev. Gary D. Chmura.
Res.: 12503 Buckingham Ave., 44120.
Tel: 216-881-7647; Email: garychmura@stadalbertschool.net; Web: stadalbertschool.net/st-adalbert-parish.
School—St. Adalbert School, (Grades PreK-8), 2345 E. 83rd St., 44104. Tel: 216-881-6250; Fax: 216-881-9030; Email: jdsmith@stadalbertschool.net; Web: www.stadalbertschool.net. James Smith, Prin. Clergy 3; Lay Teachers 30; Students 438; Clergy / Religious Teachers 3.
Catechesis Religious Program—Lisa Johnson, D.R.E. Students 17.

3—ST. AGNES - OUR LADY OF FATIMA (1980) Rev. Robert Marva, O.F.M.Cap.; Deacon Hardin M. Martin.
Res.: 6805 Quimby Ave., 44103. Tel: 216-391-1655; Fax: 216-391-7919.
Church: 6800 Lexington Ave., 44103.
Tel: 216-391-1655; Email: brotherbob@saolf.org.
Catechesis Religious Program—Students 44.

4—ST. ALOYSIUS - ST. AGATHA (1898) Rev. J. Mark Hobson, D.Min.; Deacon James Paul Jr.
Res.: 10932 St. Clair Ave., 44108-1939.
Tel: 216-451-3262; Email: jhobson@dioceseofcleveland.org.
School—St. Aloysius - St. Agatha School, 640 Lakeview Rd., N.E., 44108. Tel: 216-451-2050; Fax: 216-541-1601; Email: sch_stagathastal@dioceseofcleveland.org. Dennis Kless, Prin. Lay Teachers 13; Sisters 1; Students 155.
Catechesis Religious Program—Students 10.

5—ST. ANDREW (1906) (Slovak), Closed. For inquiries for parish records, contact the Archives, Diocese of Cleveland.

6—ST. ANDREW KIM PASTORAL CENTER (1988) (Korean) Rev. Sang-Jun Park; Deacon Charles C. Shin.
Res.: 2310 W. 14th St., 44113-3613.
Tel: 216-861-4630; Email: spark@dioceseofcleveland.org.
Catechesis Religious Program—Students 51.

7—ANNUNCIATION (1924) Closed. For inquiries for parish records contact Blessed Trinity Parish, Cleveland.

8—ASCENSION (1946) Closed. For inquiries for parish records contact Blessed Trinity Parish, Cleveland.

9—ST. AUGUSTINE (1860) Revs. Joseph D. McNulty; Benjamin P. Jimenez, S.J., Parochial Vicar; Sr. Corita Ambro, C.S.J., Pastoral Assoc.; Deacon John M. Rivera, Pastoral Assoc.; Mary Smith, Pastoral Assoc.; Deacon David Mayer.
Res.: 2486 W. 14th St., 44113-4449.
Tel: 216-781-5530.
Catechesis Religious Program—Mrs. Kathleen Ulintz, C.R.E. Students 227.
Convent—2432 W. 14th St., 44113.

10—ST. BARBARA (1905) (Polish)
Tel: 216-661-1191; Fax: 216-661-1148; Email: st.barbara@att.net. Rev. Joseph Hilinski, M.Div.
Res.: 1505 Denison Ave., 44109-2890.
Tel: 216-661-1191; Email: st.barbara@att.net.

11—ST. BENEDICT, Closed. For inquiries for parish records contact the chancery.

12—BLESSED SACRAMENT (1903) Closed. For inquiries for parish records contact the Archives of the Diocese of Cleveland.

13—BLESSED TRINITY PARISH (2010)
14040 Puritas Ave., 44135-2822. Tel: 216-671-5890; Fax: 216-938-9843; Email: office@blessedtrinitycleveland.org; Web: www.blessedtrinitycleveland.org. Rev. Douglas H. Koesel, M.Div.; Deacon Richard C. Beercheck; Kathleen Corbett, Pastoral Assoc.
Catechesis Religious Program—Students 16.

14—ST. BONIFACE (1903)
Tel: 216-961-2713; Email: stboniface3545@gmail.com. Rev. Hilary Khanh Kai Nguyen, C.R.M.
Res.: 3545 W. 54th St., 44102.
See Metro Catholic School, Cleveland under Elementary Schools, Parochial and Diocesan located in the Institution section.
Catechesis Religious Program—Tel: 216-926-5116. Katherine Stary, D.R.E.

15—ST. CASIMIR (1891) (Polish)
8223 Sowinski Ave., 44103-2298. Tel: 216-303-9182; Email: pastorkaz@hotmail.com. Rev. Eric S. Orzech. Polish
Catechesis Religious Program—

16—ST. CASIMIR (2009)
18022 Neff Rd., 44119-2644. Tel: 216-481-3157; Fax: 216-481-3734; Web: www.saintcasimirparish.org. Rev. Joseph A. Bacevice.

17—ST. CATHERINE (1898) Closed. For inquiries for parish records, contact the Archives, Diocese of Cleveland.

18—ST. CECILIA (1915) Closed. For inquiries for parish records contact the Archives of the Diocese of Cleveland.

19—ST. COLMAN (1880)
Tel: 216-651-0550. Revs. Caroli Borromeo Shao, A.J.; Benjamin Koka, A.J., Parochial Vicar; Sr. Audrey Koch, C.S.J., Pastoral Assoc.; Deacon William H. Corrigan; Eileen Kelly, Outreach Ministry.
Res.: 2027 W. 65th St., 44102-4394.
Catechesis Religious Program—Students 34.
Convent—2007 W. 65th St., 44102.

20—COMMUNITY OF ST. MALACHI (1975) Closed. For inquiries for parish records contact St. Malachi, Cleveland. (Personal Parish).

21—CONVERSION OF ST. PAUL (1931) Closed. For inquiries for parish records contact the Archives of the Diocese of Cleveland.

22—CORPUS CHRISTI (1935) Closed. For inquiries for parish records contact Mary Queen of Peace Parish, Cleveland.

23—CRISTO REY, CAPILLA DE (1983) (Hispanic), Closed. For inquiries for parish records contact La Sagrada Familia.

24—ST. ELIZABETH OF HUNGARY (1892) (Hungarian)
Mailing Address: P.O. Box 20175, 44104-0175.
Tel: 216-231-0325; Fax: 216-421-0461; Email: ELIZABETHCLEV@dioceseofcleveland.org; Web: www.stelizabethcleveland.org/. Rev. Andras Mezei, Admin.
Church: 9016 Buckeye Rd., 44104.
Catechesis Religious Program—Students 4.

25—ST. EMERIC (1904 & Territorial 1964) (Magyar)
Tel: 216-861-1937. Rev. Andras Mezei, Admin.
Res.: 1860 W. 22nd St., 44113-3185.

26—EPIPHANY (1944) Closed. For inquiries for parish records contact the chancery.

27—ST. FRANCIS (1887) Closed. For inquiries for parish records contact the chancery.

28—ST. GEORGE (1895) (Lithuanian), Closed. For inquiries for parish records contact St. Casimir, Cleveland.

29—ST. HENRY (1946) Closed. For inquiries for parish records, contact the Archives, Diocese of Cleveland.

30—HOLY FAMILY (1911) Closed. For inquiries for parish records contact the chancery.

31—HOLY NAME (1854)
Tel: 216-271-4242; Email: holyname2@att.net. Rev. Msgr. Richard C. Antall.
Res.: 8328 Broadway Ave., S.E., 44105-3931.
School—Holy Name School, Tel: 216-341-0084; Email: jones@holyname-elementary.org. Lorenzo Jones, Prin. Lay Teachers 17; Students 188.
Catechesis Religious Program—Students 219.

32—HOLY REDEEMER (1924) (Italian) Rev. Martin F. Polito.
Res.: 15712 Kipling Ave., 44110-3104.
Tel: 216-531-3313; Email:

holyredeemerparish@gmail.com; Web: www.holyredeemer-cleveland.weconnect.com.
Catechesis Religious Program—Sandi Shell, D.R.E. Students 15.
Convent—924 Ruple Rd., 44110. Tel: 216-481-2740.
33—HOLY ROSARY (1892) (Italian)
Tel: 216-421-2995; Fax: 216-421-2258; Email: info@holy-rosary.org; Web: www.holy-rosary.org. Rev. Joseph Previte; Deacon Bruce J. Battista; Laura Bastulli-Parran, Pastoral Assoc.; Tammy Moore, Pastoral Assoc.; Lorenzo Salvagni, Music Min.
Res.: 12021 Mayfield Rd., 44106-1996.
Catechesis Religious Program—Students 102.
34—HOLY TRINITY - ST. EDWARD (1975) Closed. For inquiries for parish records contact the chancery.
35—ST. HYACINTH (1906) (Polish), Closed. For inquiries for parish records contact the chancery.
36—ST. IGNATIUS OF ANTIOCH (1902)
Tel: 216-251-0300; Email: stignatiusparish@aol.com; Web: www.sioa.weconnect.com. Rev. Kevin E. Estabrook; Sr. Dianne Piunno, S.N.D., Pastoral Assoc.
Res.: 10205 Lorain Ave., 44111-5435.
School—St. Ignatius of Antioch School,
Tel: 216-671-0535; Email: sch_stignatiuses@dioceseofcleveland.org. Margaret Ricksecker, Prin. Lay Teachers 22; Students 308.
Catechesis Religious Program—Students 20.
37—IMMACULATE CONCEPTION (1865) Revs. Frank G. Godic; John J. Hayes, In Res., (Retired).
Res.: 4129 Superior Ave., 44103-1179.
Tel: 216-431-5900; Email: fgodic@dioceseofcleveland.org.
Catechesis Religious Program—Students 4.
38—IMMACULATE HEART OF MARY (1894) [CEM] (Polish) Revs. Ralph Hudak; Andrzej Panek, Parochial Vicar.
Res.: 6700 Lansing Ave., 44105-3797.
Tel: 216-341-2734; Tel: 216-341-2735;
Fax: 216-341-7200; Email: ihmpol@mainet.net; Web: www.immaculateheartchurch.org.
Catechesis Religious Program—Students 25.
Convent—6804 Lansing Ave., 44105.
39—ST. JEROME (1919)
Tel: 216-481-8200; Fax: 216-481-6459; Email: jeromeclev@dioceseofcleveland.org; Web: www.stjeromecleveland.org. Rev. William M. Jerse, J.C.L.; Deacon Peter Travalik.
Res.: 15000 Lake Shore Blvd., 44110-1298.
School—St. Jerome School, 15100 Lake Shore Blvd., 44110. Tel: 216-486-3587; Fax: 216-486-4288; Email: sch_stjerome@dioceseofcleveland.org. Mrs. Susan Coan, Prin. Lay Teachers 14; Students 250.
Catechesis Religious Program—Email: ministrysj@gmail.com. Marguerite DiPenti, D.R.E. Students 10.
Convent—15025 Ridpath Ave., 44110.
40—ST. JOHN CANTIUS (1898) (Polish)
Tel: 216-781-9095. Revs. Lucjan Stokowski, (Retired); Andrzej Knapik, Parochial Vicar.
Res.: 906 College Ave., S.W., 44113-4494. Web: stjohncantiuschurch.org.
Catechesis Religious Program—
41—ST. JOHN NEPOMUCENE (1902) (Bohemian)
Tel: 216-641-8444; Tel: 216-641-8445;
Fax: 216-641-8824; Email: fatherjasany@st-john-nepomucene.org; Email: sjnpkowalski@st-john-nepomucene.org; Web: st-john-nepomucene.org. Rev. Robert J. Jasany.
Res.: 3785 Independence Rd., 44105-3357.
Church: Fleet Ave. & E. 50th St., 44105.
Catechesis Religious Program—Students 17.
42—ST. JOSAPHAT (1908) Closed. For inquiries for parish records contact the chancery.
43—ST. JOSEPH (Woodland) Closed. For inquiries for parish records contact the chancery.
44—ST. JOSEPH (Collinwood) (1877) Closed. For inquiries for parish records contact St. Aloysius, Cleveland.
45—ST. LAWRENCE (1901) Closed. For inquiries for parish records contact the chancery.
46—ST. LEO THE GREAT (1948)
Tel: 216-661-1006; Email: info@leothegreat.org. Rev. James P. Schmitz; Mrs. Joan Berigan, Pastoral Min./Coord.
Res.: 4940 Broadview Rd., 44109-5799. Email: mlhauck@leothegreat.org; Email: jschmitz@leothegreat.org; Web: www.leothegreat.org.
School—St. Leo the Great School, 4900 Broadview Rd., 44109. Tel: 216-661-2120; Fax: 216-661-7125; Email: dburns@leothegreat.org. Denise Burns, Prin. Lay Teachers 15; Students 272.
Catechesis Religious Program—Email: mperry@leothegreat.org. Mrs. Mary Perry, D.R.E. Students 61.
47—ST. MALACHI (1865) Closed. For inquiries for parish records contact St. Malachi, Cleveland.
48—ST. MALACHI (2009)
Tel: 216-861-5343; Email: rectory@stmalachi.org; Email: jeanette.s@stmalachi.org; Email: charlene.m@stmalachi.org; Email: stephanie.p@stmalachi.org; Email: backdoor@stmalachi.org; Web: www.stmalachi.org. Rev. Thomas Mahoney, Admin.; Deacon Leo Bistak. In Res., Rev. Neil Walters.
Res.: 2459 Washington Ave., 44113-2380. Email: aschuerger@dioceseofcleveland.org.
School—Urban Community School, Intermediate School, formerly St. Malachi, St. Patrick (Bridge) and St. Wendelin Parochial Schools. 4909 Lorain Ave., 44102. Tel: 216-939-8441; Fax: 216-939-8198; Email: amitchell@urbancommunityschool.org; Web: www.urbancommunityschool.org. Mr. Tom Gill, Pres.; Lisa DeCore, Prin. Aides 25; Lay Teachers 31; Sisters 4; Students 560.
Catechesis Religious Program—Stephanie Pritts, D.R.E. Students 37.
Convent—2456 Vermont Ave., 44113.
49—ST. MARK (1945)
Tel: 216-226-7577; Email: cbirchfield@stmarkcleveland.com. Rev. Adam A. Zajac, M.A., M.Div.; Deacons David J. Lundeen, Business Mgr.; Howard Masony.
Res.: 15800 Montrose Ave., 44111-1084. Web: www.stmarkcleveland.com.
School—St. Mark School, 15724 Montrose Ave., 44111. Tel: 216-521-4115; Fax: 216-221-8664; Email: cocita@stmarkwestpark.com. Mrs. Karen Cocita. Lay Teachers 25; Students 421.
Catechesis Religious Program—Tel: 216-226-7577; Email: jpuckett@stmarkcleveland.com. Students 89.
50—ST. MARY (1905) (Slovenian)
Tel: 216-761-7740. Rev. John M. Kumse, Email: johnkumse@yahoo.com; Deacon David S. Kushner.
Res.: 15519 Holmes Ave., 44110-2497.
Catechesis Religious Program—Students 60.
51—ST. MARY OF CZESTOCHOWA (1913) (Polish), Closed. For inquiries for parish records contact the chancery.
52—MARY QUEEN OF PEACE (2010)
4423 Pearl Rd., 44109-4266. Tel: 216-749-2323;
Fax: 216-741-7183; Email: frbrown@maryqop.org; Web: www.maryqop.org. Rev. Douglas T. Brown; Deacon Patrick F. Berigan; Revs. Richard Bona, J.C.D., In Res.; Joseph Rodak, C.PP.S., In Res.
School—Mary Queen of Peace Elementary School, 4419 Pearl Rd., 44109-4268. Tel: 216-741-3685;
Fax: 216-741-5534; Email: sch_mqp@dioceseofcleveland.org. Jessica Robertson, Prin.; Mr. Nicholas Blazek, Vice Prin. Lay Teachers 26; Students 305.
Catechesis Religious Program—Mrs. Joan Berigan, D.R.E. Students 44.
53—ST. MEL (1945)
Tel: 216-941-4313; Tel: 216-941-4314;
Fax: 216-941-1093; Email: church@stmel.net. Rev. Mark Q. Fedor, J.C.D.
Res.: 14436 Triskett Rd., 44111-2263. Web: stmelparish.net.
Catechesis Religious Program—Students 29.
54—ST. MICHAEL THE ARCHANGEL (1882)
Tel: 216-621-3847; Email: michaelclev@dioceseofcleveland.org; Web: www.smacleveland.net. Revs. Mark R. Riley; Dennis R. O'Grady, Pastor Emeritus, (Retired); Sr. Miriam Fidelis, Pastoral Min./Coord.; Deacon Gonzalo Lopez; Ms. Nory Maldonado, Sec.; Mrs. Maribel Claudio, Receptionist; Ms. Lydia Fernandez, Social Justice Coord.; Mrs. Mary Balog, Outreach Coord.; Mr. Robert Dillon, Organist/Music Coord.
Res.: 3114 Scranton Rd., 44109-1632.
See Metro Catholic School, Cleveland under Elementary Schools, Parochial and Diocesan located in the Institution section.
Catechesis Religious Program—Students 66.
55—NATIVITY OF THE BLESSED VIRGIN MARY, Closed. For inquiries for parish records contact the chancery.
56—OUR LADY OF ANGELS (1922)
Email: eme@olangels.org; Web: www.olangels.org. Rev. Russell P. Lowe.
Res.: 3644 Rocky River Dr., 44111-3998.
Tel: 216-252-2332; Email: rpllowe@yahoo.com.
School—Our Lady of Angels Parish, (Grades PreK-8), Tel: 216-251-6841; Email: kkrupar@olangels.org; Web: www.olangels.org. Mrs. Kathy Krupar, Prin. Lay Teachers 31; Students 425; Clergy / Religious Teachers 1.
Catechesis Religious Program—Katherine Stary, D.R.E. Students 18.
57—OUR LADY OF GOOD COUNSEL (1873) Closed. For inquiries for parish records contact Mary Queen of Peace Parish, Cleveland.
58—OUR LADY OF LOURDES (1883)
Tel: 216-641-2829; Email: olol@ourladyoflourdes-cle.com; Web: ourladyoflourdes-cle.org. Rev. Joseph H. Callahan; Sr. Charlotte Hobelman, Pastoral Min./Coord.; Ms. Eileen Murray, Business Mgr.; Sr. Charlotte Hocevar, Sec.
Legal Title: Our Lady of Lourdes Parish
Res.: 3395 E. 53rd St., 44127-1692. Email: jcallahan@dioceseofcleveland.org.
Church: 3396 E. 55th St., 44127-1692.
Catechesis Religious Program—Students 91.
Convent—3401 E. 53rd St., 44127.
59—OUR LADY OF MERCY (1922) (Slovak), Closed. For inquiries for parish records contact the Archives of the Diocese of Cleveland.
60—OUR LADY OF MOUNT CARMEL (East) (1936) Closed. For inquiries for parish records contact the chancery.
61—OUR LADY OF MOUNT CARMEL (West) (1926) (Italian)
Tel: 216-651-6641; Email: jeddy@dioceseofcleveland.org. Revs. Joseph Eddy; Arcangelo Manzi, O.de.M., Parochial Vicar; Richard S. Rasch, O.de.M., In Res.; Kirun Kunar, O.de.M., In Res.
Res.: 6928 Detroit Ave., 44102-3093.
Tel: 216-651-5043; Email: rrasch@dioceseofcleveland.org.
School—Our Lady of Mount Carmel School, 1355 W. 70th St., 44102. Tel: 216-281-7146;
Fax: 216-281-7001; Email: sch_olmtcarmelclev@dioceseofcleveland.org. Michelle Schenek, Prin. Lay Teachers 15; Sisters 2; Students 228.
Catechesis Religious Program—Students 8.
Convent—Tel: 216-281-9304.
62—OUR LADY OF PEACE (1919)
Email: office@olpchurch.com. Rev. Gary Chmura; Mrs. Nancy McIntosh, Pastoral Assoc.; Revs. Damian Ezeani, In Res.; Jerome Silayo, In Res.; Nicholas Mtei, In Res.
Res.: 12503 Buckingham Ave., 44120-1498.
Tel: 216-421-4211; Fax: 216-421-1612; Email: pastor@olpchurch.com; Web: www.olpchurch.com.
Church: 12601 Shaker Blvd., 44120.
Catechesis Religious Program—Tel: 216-233-1713; Email: jlpekoc@yahoo.com. Jean Pekoc, D.R.E. Students 52.
63—OUR LADY OF PERPETUAL HELP (1929) (Lithuanian), Closed. For inquiries for parish records contact St. Casimir, Cleveland.
64—ST. PATRICK (1853)
Tel: 216-639-6872. Rev. Michael K. Gurnick, M.A., M.Div.; Deacon William Merriman.
Res.: 3602 Bridge Ave., 44113-3314. Email: patrickbridge@dioceseofcleveland.org.
School—Urban Community School, 4909 Lorain Avenue, 44102. Tel: 216-939-8330; Email: amitchell@urbancommunityschool.org. Lisa DeCore, Prin. Lay Teachers 37; Students 572.
Catechesis Religious Program—Students 23.
65—ST. PATRICK (Rocky River Drive) (1848) [CEM]
Tel: 216-251-1200; Email: stpatrickparishwp@gmail.com; Web: www.stpatrickwp.org. Rev. James R. Ols.
Res.: 4427 Rocky River Dr., 44135-2551.
Tel: 216-251-9900; Email: frjamesols@gmail.com.
Catechesis Religious Program—Students 18.
66—ST. PAUL (1902) (Croatian)
Tel: 216-431-1895. Rev. Zvonko Blasko.
Res.: 1369 E. 40th St., 44103-1194.
Catechesis Religious Program—Students 22.
67—ST. PETER (1853) (German)
Tel: 216-344-2999. Rev. Robert J. Kropac.
Res.: 1533 E. 17th St., 44114.
68—SS. PHILIP AND JAMES (1950) Closed. For inquiries for parish records contact the Archives of the Diocese of Cleveland.
69—ST. PHILIP NERI (1914) Closed. For inquiries for parish records, contact the Archives, Diocese of Cleveland.
70—ST. PROCOP (1872) (Bohemian), Closed. For inquiries for parish records contact the chancery.
71—ST. ROCCO (1922) (Italian)
Tel: 216-961-8331, Ext. 7008; Email: mbuhaley@stroccocleveland.com. Revs. James Mayer, O.de.M.; Paschal Rosca, O.de.M., Parochial Vicar.
Res.: 3205 Fulton Rd., 44109-1495.
Tel: 216-961-8331.
School—St. Rocco School, Tel: 216-961-8557; Email: sch_strocco@dioceseofcleveland.org. Matthew Daniels, Prin. Lay Teachers 17; Students 166.
Catechesis Religious Program—Email: Marydrip@cox.net. Mary Ripepi, D.R.E. Students 14.
72—ST. ROSE OF LIMA (1899) Closed. For inquiries for parish records contact the chancery.
73—SACRED HEART OF JESUS (1888) (Polish), Closed. For inquiries for parish records contact the Archives of the Diocese of Cleveland.
74—SAGRADA FAMILIA (1997) (Hispanic)
Tel: 216-631-2888; Email: rreidy@dioceseofcleveland.org. Rev. Robert J. Reidy; Deacons Epifanio Torres; Victor R. Colon; Ignacio Miranda; Frederick Simon.
Church: 7719 Detroit Ave., 44102-2811. Email: sagrada1997@yahoo.com.
Catechesis Religious Program—Marylin Caraballo, D.R.E. (Children). Students 70.
75—SAN JUAN BAUTISTA (1975) (Spanish), Closed. For inquiries for Parish Records contact La Sagrada Familia.
76—ST. STANISLAUS (1873) (Polish)
Tel: 216-341-9091; Tel: 216-341-9092; Email: ststans@ameritech.net. Revs. Eric S. Orzech; Joseph

R. Spolny, Parochial Vicar; Dan Kane, Business Mgr.; David Krakowski, Dir. Music.
Res.: 3649 E. 65th St., 44105-1293.
Church: Forman Ave. & E. 65th St., 44105.
School—St. Stanislaus School, 6615 Forman Ave., 44105. Tel: 216-883-3307; Fax: 216-883-0514; Email: martind@ststanislaus.us. Mrs. Deborah Martin, Prin. Lay Teachers 16; Students 186.
Catechesis Religious Program—Students 2.

77—ST. STEPHEN (1869) (German)
Tel: 216-631-5033. Revs. Caroli Borromeo Shao, A.J.; Benjamin Koka, A.J., Parochial Vicar; Deacon Moises Cruz.
Res.: 1930 W. 54th St., 44102-3298.
Tel: 216-631-5633; Fax: 216-631-5634; Web: www.ststephencleveland.org.
See Metro Catholic School, Cleveland under Elementary Schools, Parochial and Diocesan located in the Institution section.
Catechesis Religious Program—
Convent—1891 W. 57th St., 44102.

78—ST. THOMAS AQUINAS, Closed. For inquiries for parish records contact the chancery.

79—TRANSFIGURATION (1943) Closed. For inquiries for parish records contact the chancery.

80—ST. VINCENT DE PAUL St. Vincent de Paul Church (1922)
Tel: 216-252-2626; Fax: 216-252-6993; Email: church@svdpcleveland.org; Web: www.svdpcleveland.org. Revs. Kenneth F. Wallace; Robert E. Clancy, Sr. Parochial Vicar; Deacon Kenneth J. Hill.
Res.: 13400 Lorain Ave., 44111-3470. Email: kwallace@svdpcleveland.org.
Church: Lorain Ave. & Berea Rd., 44111.
Catechesis Religious Program—Students 16.

81—ST. VITUS (1893) (Slovenian)
Tel: 216-361-1444. Rev. Joseph P. Boznar; Sr. Mary Avsec, S.N.D., Pastoral Assoc.
Res.: 6019 Lausche Ave., 44103-1455.
Catechesis Religious Program—Students 70.

82—ST. WENDELIN PARISH (1903) (Slovak)
Tel: 216-696-1926. Rev. Robert J. Kropac.
Res.: 2281 Columbus Rd., 44113-4230.
School—Urban Community School, 4909 Lorain Ave., 44102. Tel: 216-939-8330; Fax: 216-939-8360; Email: ldecore@urbancommunityschool.org. Lisa DeCore, Prin. (Primary and Junior High) (See St. Malachi listing for Intermediate Level) Lay Teachers 37; Students 571.
Catechesis Religious Program—Students 63.

OUTSIDE THE CITY OF CLEVELAND

AKRON, SUMMIT CO.

1—ANNUNCIATION (1907) Closed. For inquiries for parish records contact Visitation of Mary, Akron.

2—ST. ANTHONY OF PADUA (1933) (Italian)
Tel: 330-762-7277; Tel: 330-762-7278;
Fax: 330-762-2229; Email: rectory@stanthony-akron.org; Web: www.stanthony-akron.com. Rev. Edward A. Burba.
Res.: 83 Mosser Pl., Akron, 44310-3184.
School—St. Anthony of Padua School, (Grades K-8), 80 E. York St., Akron, 44310. Tel: 330-253-6918;
Fax: 330-253-6999; Email: sch_stanthonyakron@dioceseofcleveland.org. Sr. Elizabeth Szilvasi, M.P.F., Prin. Lay Teachers 13; Religious 1; Students 147.
Catechesis Religious Program—Students 29.
Convent—93 Mosser Pl., Akron, 44310.

3—ST. BERNARD PARISH (2010) [CEM]
44 University Ave., Akron, 44308-1609.
Tel: 330-253-5161; Fax: 330-253-6949; Email: info@stbernardstmary.org. Rev. Christopher J. Zerucha; Deacon Ramon DiMascio.
Catechesis Religious Program—Students 40.

4—BLESSED TRINITY (2009)
300 E. Tallmadge Ave., Akron, 44310-2399.
Tel: 330-376-5144; Fax: 330-376-5311; Email: blessedtrinityakron@dioceseofcleveland.org; Web: www.blessedtrinityakron.org. Rev. Joseph A. Warner; Deacon John J. Hirnikl.
Catechesis Religious Program—Terri Bullock, D.R.E. Students 27.

5—CHRIST THE KING (1935) Closed. For inquiries for parish records contact Blessed Trinity, Akron.

6—ST. FRANCIS DE SALES (1948)
Tel: 330-644-2225; Tel: 330-644-2226; Email: jschleicher@neo.rr.com; Web: stfparish.com. Revs. G. David Bline; Jacob Bearer, Parochial Vicar; Deacons Richard C. Butz; Raymond S. Herrick.
Res.: 4019 Manchester Rd., Akron, 44319-2193.
School—St. Francis de Sales School, 4009 Manchester Rd., Akron, 44319. Tel: 330-644-0638;
Fax: 330-644-2663; Email: msbuzzelli@stfparishschool.org. Kathryn Buzzelli, Prin. Lay Teachers 28; Students 313.
Catechesis Religious Program—Students 208.

7—ST. HEDWIG (1912) (Polish), Closed. For inquiries for parish records contact the chancery.

8—ST. HILARY (1958)
Tel: 330-867-1055; Email: church@sthilarychurch.org. Revs. Steven K. Brunovsky; Matthew Jordan, Parochial Vicar.
Res.: 615 Moorfield Rd., Fairlawn, 44333-4236. Email: sbrunovsky@sthiliarychurch.org.
Church: 2750 W. Market St., Fairlawn, 44333-4236.
School—St. Hilary School, 645 Moorfield Rd., Fairlawn, 44333. Tel: 330-867-8720;
Fax: 330-867-5081; Email: tarnone@st-hilary.com. Mrs. Tracey Arnone, Prin. Lay Teachers 38; Students 592.
Catechesis Religious Program—Students 290.

9—IMMACULATE CONCEPTION (1923)
Tel: 330-753-8429; Email: ickenmore@yahoo.com; Web: www.ickenmore.org. Rev. Michael B. Smith; Melissa Keegan, Pastoral Assoc.
Res.: 2101 17th St., S.W., Akron, 44314-2315. Email: melkeegan44314@gmail.com.
Church: 2100 16th St., S.W., Akron, 44314.
Catechesis Religious Program—Email: info@ickenmore.org. Students 7.

10—ST. JOHN THE BAPTIST (1907)
1044 Brown St., Akron, 44301-1596.
Tel: 330-535-4502; Fax: 330-475-0054; Email: azingales@dioceseofcleveland.org. 87 Broad St., Akron, 44305. Revs. A. Jonathan Zingales, J.C.L.; Dismas Byarugaba, A.J., In Res.; Bernard P. Kyara, A.J., In Res.; Mr. Edward Coia, Business Mgr.

11—ST. MARTHA (1919) Closed. For inquiries for parish records contact Blessed Trinity, Akron.

12—ST. MARY (1887)
44 University Ave., Akron, 44308. Rev. Christopher J. Zerucha.
Church: 750 S. Main St., Akron, 44311-1094.
School—St. Mary School, (Grades K-8),
Tel: 330-253-1233; Email: pnugent@stmaryakron.com. Dr. Patricia Nugent, Ed.D., Prin. Clergy 2; Lay Teachers 13; Students 175; Clergy / Religious Teachers 2.

13—ST. MATTHEW (1943)
Tel: 330-733-9944. Revs. G. Michael Williamson; Thomas A. McGovern, Pastor Emeritus, (Retired).
Res.: 2603 Benton Ave., Akron, 44312-1694. Email: info@stmatthewparish.net; Web: www.stmatthewparish.net.
Church: Berne & Woolf St., Akron, 44312.
School—St. Matthew School, 2580 Benton Ave., Akron, 44312. Tel: 330-784-1711; Fax: 330-733-1004; Email: jczaplicki@stmatthewparish.net. John Czaplicki, Prin. Lay Teachers 17; Students 177.
Catechesis Religious Program—Tel: 330-784-7328; Email: jplaspohl@stmatthewparish.net. Students 158.

14—NATIVITY OF THE LORD JESUS (1977)
2425 Myersville Rd., Akron, 44312-4951. Email: father@nativityofthelord.org. Rev. Zachary M. Kawalec; Deacon Dennis L. Smith.
Res.: 2499 Killian Rd., Uniontown, 44685.
Tel: 330-699-5086; Email: office@nativityofthelord.org; Web: www.nativityofthelord.org.
Catechesis Religious Program—Students 67.

15—ST. PAUL (1919)
1580 Brown St., Akron, 44301. Tel: 330-724-1263;
Fax: 330-724-7680; Email: stpaulakr@sbcglobal.net; Web: www.stpaulakron.org. Revs. Matthew E. Pfeiffer; William D. Kang, In Res., (Retired); Deacon John Amedeo; Therese Nesline, Pastoral Min./Coord.; Mrs. Patty Hogue, Sec.
Res.: 433 Mission Dr., Akron, 44301-2798.
Catechesis Religious Program—Mrs. Kathleen Ott, D.R.E. & Faith Formation. Students 30.

16—ST. PETER (1917) Closed. For inquiries for parish records contact St. Mary Parish, Akron.

17—SACRED HEART OF JESUS (1915) (Hungarian), Closed. For inquiries for parish records contact the Archives of the Diocese of Cleveland.

18—ST. SEBASTIAN (1928)
Tel: 330-836-2233; Email: church@stsebastian.org. Revs. John A. Valencheck; Anthony Simone, Parochial Vicar; Deacon Terry W. Peacock.
Res.: 476 Mull Ave., Akron, 44320-1299. Email: jonesj@stsebastian.org; Web: www.stsebastian.org.
School—St. Sebastian School, 500 Mull Ave., Akron, 44320. Tel: 330-836-9107; Fax: 330-836-7690; Email: sch_stsebastian@dioceseofcleveland.org. Anthony Rohr, Prin. Lay Teachers 28; Students 373.
Catechesis Religious Program—Email: sivecc@stsebastian.org. Mrs. Cathy Sivec, D.R.E. Students 362.

19—ST. VINCENT DE PAUL PARISH (1837) [CEM]
Tel: 330-535-3135; Email: support@stvincentchurch.com. Rev. Norman K. Douglas; Deacon Robert C. Bender; Rev. David J. Halaiko, (Retired); (In Res.), (Retired).
Res.: 164 W. Market St., Akron, 44303-2373. Email: peggy@stvincentchurch.com; Email: frnorm@stvincentchurch.com; Web: stvincentchurch.com.
Church: W. Market St. & Maple St., Akron, 44303.
School—St. Vincent de Paul Parish School, (Grades PreK-8), 17 S. Maple St., Akron, 44303.
Tel: 330-762-5912; Fax: 330-535-2515. Diane Salamon, Prin. Lay Teachers 18; Students 204.
Catechesis Religious Program—Email: ellen@stvincentchurch.com. Ellen Dies, D.R.E. Students 76.

20—VISITATION OF MARY (2009)
87 Broad St., Akron, 44305. Tel: 330-535-4141;
Fax: 330-475-0054; Email: azingales@dioceseofcleveland.org; Web: www.visitationofmary.org. Rev. A. Jonathan Zingales, J.C.L.; Diana Herhold, Pastoral Min.; Deacon Scott T. Proper; Rev. Bernard P. Kyara, A.J., In Res.
*Legal Title: Church of the Annunciation*In Res., Rev. Dismas Byarugaba, A.J.

AMHERST, LORAIN CO., ST. JOSEPH (1864) [CEM]
Tel: 440-988-2848; Email: parishoffice@StJosephAmherst.com; Web: stjosephamherst.com. Rev. Timothy J. O'Connor; Sr. Stefana Osredkar, Pastoral Min.; Ms. Sharon Angell, Business Mgr.
Res.: 200 St. Joseph Dr., Amherst, 44001-1663.
Fax: 440-984-2301; Email: FrTimOconnor@StJosephAmherst.com. Clergy 1.
School—St. Joseph School, (Grades PreK-8), 175 St. Joseph Dr., Amherst, 44001. Tel: 440-988-4244;
Fax: 440-988-5249; Email: sch_stjosephamherst@dioceseofcleveland.org; Web: www.sjsamherst.org. Amy Makruski, Prin. Lay Teachers 15; Students 190.
Catechesis Religious Program—
Tel: 440-988-2848, Ext. 242; Email: DRE@StJosephAmherst.com. Carol Wallington, D.R.E. Students 224.
Convent—151 St. Joseph Dr., Amherst, 44001.
Tel: 440-988-2621; Email: SrStefana@StJosephAmherst.com. Sisters 2.

ASHLAND, ASHLAND CO., ST. EDWARD (1853) [JC]
Tel: 419-289-7224; Email: church@stedwardashland.org. Rev. Rodney A. Kreidler; Deacon Joseph R. Dietz.
Res. & Administration Center: 501 Cottage St., Ashland, 44805-2167. Web: www.stedwardashland.org.
School—St. Edward School, 433 Cottage St., Ashland, 44805. Tel: 419-289-7456;
Fax: 419-289-9474; Email: principal@stedwardashland.org; Email: school@stedwardashland.org; Web: www.stedwardashland.org. Suellen Valentine, Prin. Lay Teachers 15; Students 170.
Catechesis Religious Program—Students 37.

AVON, LORAIN CO.

1—HOLY TRINITY (1833) [CEM] Revs. John A. Misenko; John J. Gorski, Pastor Emeritus, (Retired).
Res.: 33601 Detroit Rd., Avon, 44011-1999.
Tel: 440-937-5363; Email: holytrinityavon@aol.com; Web: holytrinityavon.com.
School—Holy Trinity School, (Grades PreK-8), 2610 Nagel Rd., Avon, 44011. Tel: 440-937-6420;
Fax: 440-937-1029; Email: michael.modzeleski@htsavon.org. Kim Kuchta, Co-Prin.; Michael Modzeleski, Co-Prin. Lay Teachers 27; Students 587.
Catechesis Religious Program—Students 504.

2—ST. MARY OF THE IMMACULATE CONCEPTION (1841) [CEM]
Tel: 440-934-4212; Email: Parish@stmaryavon.org; Web: www.stmaryavon.org. Revs. C. Thomas Cleaton; Arthur B. Egan, Pastor Emeritus, (Retired); Deacon Daniel J. Hancock.
Res.: 2640 Stoney Ridge Rd., Avon, 44011-1899. Email: tcleaton@yahoo.com.
School—St. Mary of the Immaculate Conception School St. Mary - Avon, (Grades PreK-8), 2680 Stoney Ridge Rd., Avon, 44011-1899.
Tel: 440-934-6246; Fax: 440-934-6250; Email: cschager@stmayravon.org. Colleen Schager, Prin. Clergy 3; Lay Teachers 14; Students 222.
Catechesis Religious Program—Students 238.
Convent—Tel: 440-934-5173.

AVON LAKE, LORAIN CO.

1—HOLY SPIRIT (1965)
Tel: 440-933-3777; Email: hsp@holyspiritavonlake.org; Web: www.holyspiritavonlake.org. Rev. Charles F. Strebler, J.C.L.; Patricia A. Kassay, Pastoral Assoc.; Deacon Robert K. Walling; Mr. Leonard Gnizak, Music Min.; Mrs. Sarah Hamski, Youth Min.; Mr. Robert Mishlan, Business Mgr.; Mrs. Lauralyn Stuebner, Sec.; Ms. Terri Pastura, D.R.E.
Res.: 410 Lear Rd., Avon Lake, 44012-2004. Email: rawalling@twc.com.

2—ST. JOSEPH (1949)
Tel: 440-933-3152; Email: office@stjosephavonlake.org. Rev. Ronald Wearsch; Deacon Keith A. Jenkins.
Res.: 32929 Lake Rd., Avon Lake, 44012-1497. Email: pastor@stjosephavonlake.org; Web: www.stjosephavonlake.org.
School—St. Joseph School, 32946 Electric Blvd., Avon Lake, 44012. Tel: 440-933-6233;
Fax: 440-933-2463; Email:

principal@stjosephavonlake.org. Mrs. Joan Hazen, Prin. Lay Teachers 21; Students 290.
Catechesis Religious Program—Email: dre@stjosephavpnlake.org. Rozann Swanson, D.R.E. Students 0.
BARBERTON, SUMMIT CO.
1—ST. AUGUSTINE (1898) Revs. David J. Majikas; William E. Browne, Parochial Vicar; Deacon Robin Adair.
Res.: 204 Sixth St., N.W., Barberton, 44203-2198.
Tel: 330-745-0011; Email: augustine1898@rrbiznet.com.
Church: Corner of Sixth St., N.W. & Lake Ave., Barberton, 44203.
School—St. Augustine School, 195 Seventh St., N.W., Barberton, 44203. Tel: 330-753-6435;
Fax: 330-753-4095; Email: sch_staugustine@dioceseofcleveland.org; Web: www.staugschool.net. Elaine Faessel, Prin. Lay Teachers 12; Students 235.
Catechesis Religious Program—Students 59.
2—SS. CYRIL AND METHODIUS (1906) (Slovak), Closed. For inquiries for parish records contact the chancery.
3—HOLY TRINITY (1911) (Magyar), Closed. For inquiries for parish records contact the chancery.
4—ST. MARY'S (1912) (Polish), Closed. For inquiries for parish records contact the chancery.
5—SACRED HEART (1916) (Slovenian), Closed. For inquiries for parish records contact the chancery.
BAY VILLAGE, CUYAHOGA CO., ST. RAPHAEL (1946)
Tel: 440-871-1100; Email: info@saintraphaelparish.com. Revs. Timothy W. Gareau; Eric S. Garris, Parochial Vicar; Deacon Larry D. Gregg; Terri Telepak, Pastoral Assoc.; Dr. Andrew Kereky, Pastoral Assoc.
Res.: 525 Dover Center Rd., Bay Village, 44140-2366.
Web: www.saintraphaelparish.com.
School—St. Raphael School, Tel: 440-871-6760; Email: amiller@saintraphaelparish.com. Ann Miller, Prin. Lay Teachers 38; Students 722.
Catechesis Religious Program—Students 622.
BEDFORD, CUYAHOGA CO.
1—ST. MARY (1910)
300 Union St., Bedford, 44146-4594.
Tel: 440-359-8205; Fax: 440-359-0727; Email: jseebauer@dioceseofcleveland.org. Rev. Joseph G. Seebauer; Deacon William R. Starkey.
2—OUR LADY OF HOPE (2009)
400 Center Rd., Bedford, 44146-2296.
Tel: 400-232-8166; Fax: 440-786-9929; Email: jseebauer@dioceseofcleveland.org. Rev. Joseph G. Seebauer; Mrs. Louise Martin, Pastoral Assoc.
Catechesis Religious Program—Students 31.
3—ST. PIUS X (1952) Closed. For inquiries for parish records contact Our Lady of Hope, Bedford.
BEDFORD HEIGHTS, CUYAHOGA CO., HOLY TRINITY (1965) Closed. For inquiries for parish records contact Holy Trinity, Bedford Heights.
BEREA, CUYAHOGA CO.
1—ST. ADALBERT (1873) [CEM] (Polish) Rev. Charles M. Butkowski; Deacon Edmund A. Gardias.
Res.: 66 Adalbert St., Berea, 44017-1799.
Tel: 440-234-6830; Email: office@saintadalbertparish.org; Web: www.saintadalbertparish.org.
School—Academy of St. Adalbert, (Grades K-8), 56 Adalbert St., Berea, 44017. Tel: 440-234-5529;
Fax: 440-234-2881; Email: gmitchell@saintadalbert.org. Mr. George Mitchell, Prin. Lay Teachers 11; Students 109.
Catechesis Religious Program—Email: aklanac@saintadalbertparish.org. Annette Klanac, D.R.E. Students 128.
2—ST. MARY (1852) [CEM]
Tel: 440-359-8205. Revs. John P. Singler; Michael J. Feldtz, Parochial Vicar; G. Max Cole, In Res.; Deacon Thomas A. Cully.
Res.: 250 Kraft St., Berea, 44017-1449.
Tel: 440-243-3877.
School—St. Mary School, 265 Baker St., Berea, 44017-1515. Tel: 440-243-4555; Fax: 440-243-6214; Email: info@smsberea.org. Andrew Carner, Prin. Lay Teachers 18; Students 272.
Catechesis Religious Program—Students 124.
BRECKSVILLE, CUYAHOGA CO., ST. BASIL THE GREAT (1960)
Tel: 440-526-1686. Revs. Walter H. Jenne; David D. Liberatore, Senior Parochial Vicar; John S. Mulhollan, Parochial Vicar; Deacon Louis M. Primozic; Sr. Judith Wood, S.S.J.-T.O.S.F., Pastoral Assoc.; Mrs. Robin Youngs, Pastoral Assoc.; Nancy Jovanov, Dir. Music; Diane Stuczynski, Office Mgr.
Res.: 8700 Brecksville Rd., Brecksville, 44141-1999.
Catechesis Religious Program—Tel: 440-526-3520;
Tel: 440-526-3587. Mrs. Mary Ann Webb, D.R.E.; Tommy Dome, Dir. Evangelization; Tim Dollard, Dir. Youth Ministry. Students 693.
BROADVIEW HEIGHTS, CUYAHOGA CO., ASSUMPTION (1857) Rev. Justin Dyrwal, O.S.B.; Deacon David A. Streeter.
Res.: 9183 Broadview Rd., Broadview Heights, 44147-2596. Tel: 440-526-1177; Email: coarectory@att.net; Web: www.coabvm.org.
School—Assumption School, Tel: 440-526-4877; Email: sch_assumption@dioceseofcleveland.org. Mrs. Joanne LoPresti, Prin. Clergy 1; Lay Teachers 23; Students 179.
Catechesis Religious Program—Tel: 440-526-6690; Email: batomusko@gmail.com. Mrs. Barbara Tomusko, D.R.E. Students 360.
Convent—
BROOK PARK, CUYAHOGA CO.
1—ASSUMPTION OF MARY (1860) [CEM] Closed. For inquiries for parish records contact Mary Queen of the Apostles Parish, Brook Park.
2—MARY QUEEN OF THE APOSTLES PARISH (2010)
6455 Engle Rd., Brook Park, 44142-3503.
Tel: 216-433-1440; Fax: 216-433-1434; Email: frjstenger@ameritech.net; Email: mqabrookpark@gmail.com. Revs. James R. Stenger; James J. Kulway, Parochial Vicar; Deacon Thomas P. Bizon; Sr. Therese Horan, O.S.U., Pastoral Assoc.; Bob Huczel, Admin. & Pastoral Assoc.; Elaine Gaughan, Pastoral Assoc.
Catechesis Religious Program—Email: Trish_Solon@ameritech.net. Patricia Solon, D.R.E. Students 154.
3—ST. PETER THE APOSTLE (1968) Closed. For inquiries for parish records contact Mary Queen of the Apostles Parish, Brook Park.
BROOKLYN, CUYAHOGA CO., ST. THOMAS MORE (1946)
Tel: 216-749-0414; Email: stmore@sbcglobal.net. Revs. William G. Bouhall; James J. Vesely, Pastor Emeritus, (Retired).
Res.: 4170 N. Amber Dr., Brooklyn, 44144-1399.
School—St. Thomas More School, 4180 N. Amber Dr., Brooklyn, 44144. Tel: 216-749-1660;
Fax: 216-398-4265; Email: jfrancis@stmschool.com. Mrs. Jennifer Francis, Prin. Lay Teachers 17; Students 268.
Catechesis Religious Program—Email: PSR.STM@gmail.com. Colleen DeVenney, D.R.E. Students 40.
BRUNSWICK, MEDINA CO.
1—ST. AMBROSE (1957) Revs. Robert G. Stec, M.A., M.Div.; Robert C. Ramser, Parochial Vicar; Deacons Clement J. Belter; Thomas J. Sheridan; Gary R. Tomazic; Frank Weglicki.
Res.: 929 Pearl Rd., Brunswick, 44212-2597.
Tel: 330-460-7300; Email: office@stambrose.us; Web: www.stambrose.us.
School—St. Ambrose School, 923 Pearl Rd., Brunswick, 44212. Tel: 330-460-7301;
Fax: 330-225-5425; Email: LCinadr@StASchool.us; Web: www.SaintAmbroseSchool.us. Mrs. Lisa Cinadr, Prin. Clergy 6; Lay Teachers 25; Students 500.
Catechesis Religious Program—Tel: 330-460-7321; Email: jmajka@stambrose.us. Janet Majka, D.R.E. Students 779.
2—ST. COLETTE (1977)
Tel: 330-273-5500; Email: lradey@stcoletteparish.com; Web: stcolettecatholicchurch.com. Revs. William R. Krizner; Thomas G. Montavon, Pastor Emeritus, (Retired); Deacon Thomas J. Grasson; Lisa Radey, Pastoral Assoc.
Res.: 330 W. 130th St., Brunswick, 44212-2309.
Catechesis Religious Program—Email: cmpizon@gmail.com. Larry Pizon, D.R.E.; Chris Pizon, D.R.E. Students 279.
CHAGRIN FALLS, CUYAHOGA CO.
1—HOLY ANGELS (1977)
Tel: 440-708-0000; Email: office@holyangelschurch.com; Web: www.holyangelschurch.com. Rev. G. Max Cole, Admin.; Sr. Susan Javorek, S.N.D., Pastoral Assoc.; Deacon Vincent L. Belsito.
Res.: 8580 Taylor May Rd., Chagrin Falls, 44023-4879. Email: holyangels@dioceseofcleveland.org.
Church: 18205 Chillicothe Rd., Chagrin Falls, 44023-4879.
Catechesis Religious Program—Tel: 440-708-0808; Email: cathy@holyangelschurch.com. Cathleen Lamanna, Sec. Students 674.
2—ST. JOAN OF ARC (1948)
Tel: 440-247-7183; Fax: 440-247-2327; Email: stjoanchagrin@gmail.com; Web: stjoanofarcchurch.org. Revs. Gary J. Malin; John R. Olsavsky, J.C.L., Pastor Emeritus, (Retired); Sr. Ann Marie Kanusek, S.N.D., Pastoral Assoc.; Deacons Jeffrey Dunlop; Dennis A. Guritza.
Res.: 496 E. Washington St., Chagrin Falls, 44022-2999. Tel: 440-247-7183, Ext. 10.
School—St. Joan of Arc School, 498 E. Washington St., Chagrin Falls, 44022-2998. Tel: 440-247-6530;
Fax: 440-247-2045; Email: sdibacco@stjoanofarc.org. Shelley DiBacco, Prin. Lay Teachers 15; Students 173.
Catechesis Religious Program—498 E. Washington Street, Chagrin Falls, 44022-2929. Tel: 440-247-3606 ; Email: officeoffaithformation@stjoanofarc.org. Sr. Judith Bucco, D.R.E. Students 335.
Convent—456 E. Washington St., Chagrin Falls, 44022.
CHARDON, GEAUGA CO., ST. MARY (1909)
Tel: 440-285-7051; Email: frredmond@stmarychardon.org. Rev. Daniel P. Redmond; Deacons Lawrence Boehnlein; Thomas J. Peshek.
Res.: 401 North St., Chardon, 44024-1087.
School—St. Mary School, Tel: 440-286-3590; Email: mpetelin@stmarychardon.org. Mary Petelin, Prin. Lay Teachers 14; Students 224.
Catechesis Religious Program—Students 563.
Convent—315 North St., Chardon, 44024.
CHESTERLAND, GEAUGA CO., ST. ANSELM (1961)
Tel: 440-729-9575; Fax: 440-729-9103; Email: anselmst@aol.com; Web: www.stanselm.org. Revs. Thomas M. Sweany; Stephen M. Spisak, Parochial Vicar; Deacon Robert Kovach.
Church: 12969 Chillicothe Rd., Chesterland, 44026-3115.
School—St. Anselm School, 13013 Chillicothe Rd., Chesterland, 44026. Tel: 440-729-7806;
Fax: 440-729-3524; Email: office@stanselmschool.org; Web: stanselmschool.org. Miss Joan Agresta, Prin. Lay Teachers 16; Students 223.
Catechesis Religious Program—Email: nmarra@ursulinesisters.org. Sr. Noel Marra, D.R.E. Students 313.
Convent—13055 Chillicothe Rd., Chesterland, 44026.
CLEVELAND HEIGHTS, CUYAHOGA CO.
1—ST. ANN (1915) Closed. For inquiries for parish records contact Communion of Saints Parish, Cleveland Heights.
2—COMMUNION OF SAINTS PARISH (2010)
Email: jmcnulty@dioceseofcleveland.org. Revs. John P. McNulty; Patrick R. Schultz, Parochial Vicar; Matthew M. Cortnik, Parochial Vicar; Deacon Raymond L. Daull; Meg Matuska, Dir., Music Ministry.
Res.: 2175 Coventry Rd., Cleveland Heights, 44118-2898. Tel: 216-321-0024; Email: communionofsaints@dioceseofcleveland.org.
Worship Site of Communion of Saints Parish at St. Philomena Church— (2010) 13824 Euclid Ave., East Cleveland, 44112.
School—Communion of Saints Parish School, 2160 Stillman Rd., Cleveland Heights, 44118.
Tel: 216-932-4177; Fax: 216-932-7439; Email: gwhiteley@olleuclid.org. Mrs. Gerry Whiteley, Prin. Lay Teachers 15; Students 225.
Catechesis Religious Program—Mrs. Nell Ginley, Dir. & Pastoral Min.; Zak Jester, Youth Min. Students 55.
3—ST. LOUIS (1947) Closed. For inquiries for parish records contact Communion of Saints Parish, Cleveland Heights.
CLINTON, SUMMIT CO., ST. GEORGE (1908) Closed. For inquiries for parish records, contact SS. Peter & Paul Parish, Doylestown, OH.
COLUMBIA STATION, LORAIN CO., ST. ELIZABETH ANN SETON (1976)
Mailing Address: P.O. Box 968, Columbia Station, 44028-0968. Rev. Edward T. Holland.
Res.: 25777 Royalton Rd., Columbia Station, 44028-0968.
Church: 25801 Royalton Rd., Columbia Station, 44028.
Catechesis Religious Program—Tel: 440-236-3711. Students 64.
CONCORD TWP., LAKE CO., ST. GABRIEL (1966)
Tel: 440-352-8282; Web: www.st-gabriel.org. Revs. Frederick F. Pausche; Jeremy D. Merzweiler; Jozef A. Bozek, (Poland); Deacons Ronald Adkins; Daniel P. Clavin; Robert H. Grgic; Maureen Dowd, Pastoral Assoc.; Paul Kelly, Pastoral Assoc.; Mrs. Susan Kuchenbecker, Business Mgr.
Res.: 9925 Johnnycake Ridge Rd., Concord Twp., 44060-6294.
School—St. Gabriel School, (Grades PreK-8), 9935 Johnnycake Ridge Rd., Concord Twp., 44060.
Tel: 440-352-6169; Fax: 440-639-0143; Email: sgsoffice@st-gabrielschool.org; Web: www.st-gabrielschool.org. Mrs. Ann Ulrich, Prin.; Robert M. Kumazec III, Vice Prin.; Mrs. Susan Kuchenbecker, Business Mgr. Lay Teachers 34; Students 573.
Catechesis Religious Program—9935 Johnnycake Ridge Rd., Concord Twp., 44060. Email: pkelly@st-gabriel.org. Students 1,162.
Convent—9918 Johnnycake Ridge Rd., Concord Twp., 44060.
COPLEY, SUMMIT CO., GUARDIAN ANGELS (1964)
Tel: 330-666-1373; Email: office@guardianangels-copley.org; Email: keithk@guardianangels-copley.org; Web: www.guardianangels-copley.org. Rev. James F. Kramer; Rev. Msgr. Robert C. Wolff, Pastor Emeritus, (Retired).
Church & Res.: 1686 Cleveland-Massillon Rd., Copley, 44321-1976.
Catechesis Religious Program—Keith Kepes, D.R.E. Students 88.
CUYAHOGA FALLS, SUMMIT CO.

1—ST. EUGENE (1963)
Tel: 330-923-5244. Rev. Peter Colletti.
Res.: 1821 Munroe Falls Ave., Cuyahoga Falls, 44221-3699. Email: ncrosby@dioceseofcleveland.org.
Catechesis Religious Program—Students 77.

2—IMMACULATE HEART OF MARY Immaculate Heart of Mary (1952) Revs. James E. Singler; Thomas W. McCann, Pastor Emeritus, (Retired); Deacons Gregory Hoefler; William J. Yoho Jr.; Mary Murphy, Pastoral Assoc. & RCIA Dir.; Jennifer Ricard, Pastoral Assoc.; Erin Hogan, Youth Min.; Mr. Jeff Mills, Liturgy Dir.; Jeff Andrea, Music Min.; Kira Andrea, Music Min.; Kathleen Friess, Prin.; Julie Bowling, Sec.
Res.: 1905 Portage Tr., Cuyahoga Falls, 44223-1792. Tel: 330-929-8361; Fax: 330-929-8496; Email: jbowling@ihmcfo.org; Web: www.ihmcfo.org.
School—Immaculate Heart of Mary School, (Grades PreK-8), 2859 Lillis Dr., Cuyahoga Falls, 44223. Tel: 330-923-1220; Email: kfriess@ihmgradeschool.org; Web: www.ihmgradeschool.org. Kathleen Friess, Prin. Lay Teachers 23; Students 303.
Catechesis Religious Program—Email: mmurphy@ihmcfo.org. Mary Murphy, PSR Prin. Students 140.

3—ST. JOSEPH (1831)
Tel: 330-928-2173. Rev. Jared P. Orndorff; Deacon Kent L. Davis.
Res.: 215 Falls Ave., Cuyahoga Falls, 44221-3999.
Church: 1761 Second St., Cuyahoga Falls, 44221.
School—St. Joseph School, 1909 Third St., Cuyahoga Falls, 44221-3894. Tel: 330-928-2151;
Fax: 330-928-3139; Email: stjoe@saintjoe.org; Web: www.saintjoe.org. Mrs. Carrie DePasquale, Prin. Clergy 11; Lay Teachers 15; Students 196.
Catechesis Religious Program—Students 39.

DOYLESTOWN, WAYNE CO., SS. PETER AND PAUL (1827) [CEM] [JC] Revs. Robert E. Stein; David J. McCarthy, Pastor Emeritus, (Retired); Deacon Dale A. Youngblood.
Res.: 161 W. Clinton St., Doylestown, 44230-1297. Tel: 330-658-2145; Email: churchbulletin26@yahoo.com.
School—SS. Peter and Paul School, 169 W. Clinton St., Doylestown, 44230. Tel: 330-658-2804;
Fax: 330-658-2287; Email: sch_peternpauldoy@dioceseofcleveland.org. Jeanine Marsilia, Prin. Clergy 1; Lay Teachers 8; Students 97.
Catechesis Religious Program—Students 127.

EAST CLEVELAND, CUYAHOGA CO.
1—CHRIST THE KING (1928) Closed. For inquiries for parish records contact Communion of Saints Parish, Cleveland Heights.
2—ST. PHILOMENA (1902) Closed. For inquiries for parish records contact Communion of Saints Parish, Cleveland Heights.

EASTLAKE, LAKE CO., ST. JUSTIN MARTYR (1962)
Tel: 440-946-1177; Tel: 440-946-1178;
Fax: 440-946-9126; Email: sjmoffice@stjustin.net; Email: justinmartyr@dioceseofcleveland.org; Web: www.stjustin.net. Rev. Kevin M. Liebhardt; Deacon Timothy J. Shell; Beth Rossetti, Pastoral Assoc.
Administration Center—35781 Stevens Blvd., Eastlake, 44095-5095.
Catechesis Religious Program—Tel: 440-946-3287; Email: charles@stjustin.net. Charles Hunt, D.R.E. Students 153.

ELYRIA, LORAIN CO.
1—ST. AGNES (1914)
611 Lake Ave., Elyria, 44035-3541.
Tel: 440-322-5622; Fax: 440-322-0231; Email: saintagnes@oh.rr.com; Web: www.saintagneselyria.church. Rev. Albert Veigas; Deacon Bruce H. Tennant.
2—HOLY CROSS (1922) (Polish), Closed. For inquiries for parish records contact the chancery.
3—ST. JUDE (1943)
Tel: 440-366-5711; Email: sjwebmaster@saintjudeparish.org. Revs. Frank P. Kosem; Richard A. Gonser, In Res., (Retired); Deacon Patrick J. Humphrey.
Res.: 590 Poplar St., Elyria, 44035-3999.
Tel: 440-366-5711; Fax: 440-366-1916; Email: sjwebmaster@saintjudeparish.org; Email: fpk@saintjudeparish.org; Web: www.saintjudeparish.org.
School—St. Jude School, (Grades PreK-8), 594 Poplar St., Elyria, 44035. Tel: 440-366-1681;
Fax: 440-366-5238; Email: mhibler@stjudejaguars.org; Web: www.stjudejaguars.org. Molly Hibler, Prin. Lay Teachers 42; Students 490.
Catechesis Religious Program—
Tel: 440-366-5711, Ext. 113; Email: kristen@saintjudeparish.org. Mrs. Kristen Craig, D.R.E. Students 72.
4—ST. MARY (1845) [CEM]
Tel: 440-323-5539; Tel: 440-323-5530;
Fax: 440-322-2329; Email: stmaryelyria@windstream.net; Web: www.stmaryelyria.org. Rev. Charles T. Diedrick; Sr. Mary Dorothy Tecca, C.S.A., Pastoral Assoc.; Deacon Frank A. Humphrey III.
School—St. Mary School, 237 Fourth St., Elyria, 44035. Tel: 440-322-2808; Fax: 440-322-1423; Email: surig@smselyria.org. Sharon Urig, Prin. Lay Teachers 18; Students 128.
Catechesis Religious Program—Tel: 440-322-3054. Students 92.
5—SACRED HEART OF JESUS (1922) (Hungarian), Closed. For inquiries for parish records contact the chancery.

ELYRIA TOWNSHIP, LORAIN CO., ST. VINCENT DE PAUL (1949)
Tel: 440-324-4212; Email: frjcretar@gmail.com; Web: www.svdpelyria.com. Rev. John C. Retar, Admin.; Deacons John K. Slatcoff; Edgar Gonzalez.
Res.: 41295 N. Ridge Rd., Elyria Township, 44035-1098. Email: svdp@parishmail.com.
Catechesis Religious Program—Jackie Prosak, D.R.E. Students 70.

EUCLID, CUYAHOGA CO.
1—ST. CHRISTINE (1925) Closed. For inquiries for parish records contact Our Lady of the Lake Parish, Euclid.
2—ST. FELICITAS (1950) Closed. For inquiries for parish records contact St. John of the Cross, Euclid.
3—HOLY CROSS (1924) Closed. For inquiries for parish records contact Our Lady of the Lake Parish, Euclid.
4—ST. JOHN OF THE CROSS (2009)
140 Richmond Rd., Euclid, 44143-1299.
Tel: 216-289-0770; Tel: 216-289-0771;
Tel: 216-289-0772; Email: secretary@saintjohnofthecross.org; Web: www.saintjohnofthecross.org. Rev. John D. Betters; Deacon Charles Doerpers, C.A.C.; Dr. Francesco Binda, Music Min.; Jim Granito, Business Mgr.; Ms. Anita Linsky, Sec. St. Felicitas & St. Paul merged 2009
Catechesis Religious Program—Anney Roach, D.R.E. Students 24.
5—OUR LADY OF THE LAKE PARISH (2010)
19951 Lake Shore Blvd., Euclid, 44119.
Tel: 216-486-0850; Fax: 216-486-0851; Email: joe@olleuclid.org. Rev. Joseph J. Fortuna; Mr. Shawn Witmer, Pastoral Assoc.; Mrs. Dana Heil, Pastoral Assoc., Email: dana@olleuclid.org.
School—Our Lady of the Lake Elementary School, 175 E. 200th St., Euclid, 44119. Tel: 216-481-6824; Fax: 216-481-9841; Email: rkingsbury@olleuclid.org. Mrs. Rita Kingsbury, Prin. Lay Teachers 24; Students 320.
Catechesis Religious Program—Students 30.
6—ST. PAUL (1860) [CEM] Closed. For inquiries for parish records contact St. John of the Cross, Euclid.
7—SS. ROBERT & WILLIAM (2010)
367 E. 260th St., Euclid, 44132-1495.
Tel: 216-731-1515; Fax: 216-731-0300; Email: info@srweuclid.cc; Web: www.srweuclid.cc. Revs. John D. Betters; Thomas Kowatch; Timothy J. Roth, M.A., M.Div.; Ms. Renee Barber, Pastoral Assoc.
School—SS. Robert & William, 351 E. 260 St., Euclid, 44132. Tel: 216-731-3060; Email: mcosgriff@srwschool.cc; Web: www.srwschool.cc. Margaret Cosgriff, Prin.; Martha Dodd, Prin. Clergy 2; Lay Teachers 33; Students 464.
Catechesis Religious Program—Email: gmonroe@srweuclid.cc. Mrs. Gail Monroe, D.R.E. Students 50.
8—ST. ROBERT BELLARMINE (1950) Closed. For inquiries for parish records contact SS. Robert & William, Euclid.
9—ST. WILLIAM (1946) Closed. For inquiries for parish records contact SS. Robert & William, Euclid.

FAIRPORT HARBOR, LAKE CO., ST. ANTHONY OF PADUA (1887)
Email: father.pete@stafh.org. Rev. Peter M. Mihalic; Deacon John T. Wenzel; Steve Biro, Youth Min.
Res.: 316 Fifth St., Fairport Harbor, 44077-5696.
Tel: 440-354-4525; Email: stafh@ameritech.net; Web: www.stafh.org.
Catechesis Religious Program—Email: steve@stafh.org. Students 3.

FAIRVIEW PARK, CUYAHOGA CO., ST. ANGELA MERICI (1923)
Tel: 440-333-2133; Fax: 440-333-8061; Email: secretary@samparish.org; Email: business@samparish.org; Email: pastor@samparish.org; Web: www.samparish.org. Rev. Michael J. Lanning; Deacons James L. Agrippe, (Retired); Erick Lupson.
Res.: 20970 Lorain Rd., Fairview Park, 44126-2096.
School—St. Angela Merici School, 20830 Lorain Rd., Fairview Park, 44126. Tel: 440-333-2126;
Fax: 440-333-8480; Email: sch_stangela@dioceseofcleveland.org. Elizabeth Andrachik, Prin.; Lisa Whelan, Prin. Lay Teachers 24; Students 439.
Catechesis Religious Program—Email: dre@samparish.org. Miss Kathleen A. Lynch, D.R.E. Students 280.

GARFIELD HEIGHTS, CUYAHOGA CO.
1—HOLY SPIRIT PARISH (2008)
Email: pastor@holyspiritcleveland.org. Rev. David Nestler; Deacons Shelby Friend; Ronald R. James.
Res.: 4341 E. 131st St., Garfield Heights, 44105-5563. Tel: 216-581-0981; Fax: 216-581-8222; Email: secretary@holyspiritcleveland.org; Web: www.holyspiritcleveland.org.
See Archbishop James P. Lyke Elementary School, Cleveland under Elementary Schools, Parochial and Diocesan located in the Institution section.
Catechesis Religious Program—Students 20.
2—ST. MONICA (1952)
Tel: 216-662-8685; Email: sshepka@saintmonicachurch.net. Revs. Thomas A. Haren; Theodore Marszal, S.T.D., Parochial Vicar; Jerome A. Lukachinsky, In Res., (Retired); Thomas G. Montavon, In Res., (Retired); Deacon Stan Drozell.
Res.: 13623 Rockside Rd., Garfield Heights, 44125-5197. Email: frharen@saintmonicachurch.net.
See St. Benedict Catholic School, Garfield Heights under Elementary Schools, Parochial and Diocesan located in the Institution section.
Catechesis Religious Program—Students 50.
3—SS. PETER AND PAUL (1927) (Polish)
Tel: 216-429-1515; Email: gkoenig@peterandpaulcleveland.com. Rev. John J. Schneider.
Res.: 4750 Turney Rd., Garfield Heights, 44125-1448. Email: joh.j.schneider@icloud.com.
Catechesis Religious Program—St. Therese Church, 5276 E. 105th St., Garfield Heights, 44125. Students 9.
4—ST. THERESE (1927)
Tel: 216-581-2852; Email: sttheresegarfield@gmail.com; Web: www.sttheresegarfield.org. Rev. John J. Schneider; Deacon Robert J. Bugaj; Frank Kozuch, Music Min.
Res.: 5276 E. 105th St., Garfield Heights, 44125-2698. Email: fatherjohn@theresegarfield.org.
Catechesis Religious Program—Nancy Heineke, D.R.E. Students 30.
5—ST. TIMOTHY (1923) Closed. For inquiries for parish records, contact the Archives, Diocese of Cleveland.

GATES MILLS, CUYAHOGA CO., ST. FRANCIS OF ASSISI (1943)
Tel: 440-461-0066; Email: info@stfrancisgm.org; Web: www.stfrancisgm.org. Revs. Stephen A. Flynn; Russell G. Rauscher, Parochial Vicar; Deacon William T. Elwood; Sr. Maureen Grady, O.S.U., Pastoral Assoc.
Res.: 6850 Mayfield Rd., Gates Mills, 44040-9635.
School—St. Francis of Assisi School,
Tel: 440-442-7450; Email: apublicover@stfrancisgm.org. Adrienne Publicover, Prin. Lay Teachers 25; Students 366.
Catechesis Religious Program—Students 312.

GRAFTON, LORAIN CO.
1—ASSUMPTION (1894) (Polish), Closed. For inquiries for parish records contact the chancery.
2—IMMACULATE CONCEPTION (1835) [CEM] Closed. For inquiries for parish records contact the chancery.
3—OUR LADY QUEEN OF PEACE PARISH (2006) [CEM]
708 Erie St., Grafton, 44044. Tel: 440-926-2364;
Fax: 440-926-3783; Email: info@olqpgrafton.org; Web: www.olqpgrafton.org. Rev. John P. Seabold.
Catechesis Religious Program—Email: gogonek@olqpgrafton.org. Grace Ogonek, D.R.E. Students 145.

HIGHLAND HEIGHTS, CUYAHOGA CO., ST. PASCHAL BAYLON (1953)
Tel: 440-442-3410; Email: parishoffice@saintpaschal.com. Revs. John Thomas Lane, S.S.S.; John Christman, S.S.S., Parochial Vicar; Juancho Ramos, Parochial Vicar; Deacons Robert J. Bowers; Joseph Bourgeois; Ms. Michelle Mazza, Business Mgr.; George Peko, RCIA Coord.; Anna Peko, RCIA Coord.
Res.: 5384 Wilson Mills Rd., Highland Heights, 44143-3023. Fax: 440-442-2001; Web: www.saintpaschal.com.
School—St. Paschal Baylon School, 5360 Wilson Mills Rd., Highland Heights, 44143.
Tel: 440-442-6766; Fax: 440-446-9037; Email: cjansky@saintpaschal.com. Carol Jansky, Prin. Lay Teachers 27; Students 374.
Catechesis Religious Program—Students 219.

HINCKLEY, MEDINA CO., OUR LADY OF GRACE (1965)
Rev. William A. Smith; Deacon Bruce Dobbins Jr.
Res.: 1088 Ridge Rd., Hinckley, 44233-9602.
Tel: 330-278-4121; Email: ourladygrace@roadrunner.com.
Catechesis Religious Program—Email: ologpsr@gmail.com. Bridget Smith, D.R.E.; Mary Gabriel, Music Min. Students 162.

HUDSON, SUMMIT CO., ST. MARY (1860) [CEM]
Tel: 330-653-8118. Revs. Edward J. Kordas; Scott D. Goodfellow, Parochial Vicar; Mr. Michael Schwark, Pastoral Assoc.; Deacon Carl H. Winterich; Rose Gordyan, Pastoral Assoc.
Church & Res.: 340 N. Main St., Hudson, 44236-4720. Fax: 330-463-5759; Email:

maryhudson@dioceseofcleveland.org; Web: www.stmaryhudson.cc.
Catechesis Religious Program—Email: ldavidson@stmaryhudson.cc; Email: vroman@stmaryhudson.cc; Email: Rnowak@stmaryhudson.cc. Lisa Davidson, D.R.E.; Mr. Vince Roman, D.R.E.; Mr. Ron Nowak, D.R.E. Students 1,247.

INDEPENDENCE, CUYAHOGA CO., ST. MICHAEL (1851) [CEM]
Tel: 216-524-1394; Tel: 216-524-1395; Fax: 216-328-8537; Email: administrator@stmichaelchurchindependence.org; Web: stmichaelchurchindependence.org. Rev. John J. Mullee; Janice M. Wisnieski, Pastoral Assoc.; Deacon James Vincent. In Res., Rev. John G. Vrana, (Retired).
Res.: 6912 Chestnut Rd., Independence, 44131-3399.
Church: 6540 Brecksville Rd., Independence, 44131.
School—St. Michael School, 6906 Chestnut Rd., Independence, 44131. Tel: 216-524-6405; Fax: 216-524-7538; Email: sch_stmichael@dioceseofcleveland.org. Margaret Campisi, Prin. Lay Teachers 23; Students 381.
Catechesis Religious Program—Tel: 216-524-4212. Students 313.

KIRTLAND, LAKE CO., DIVINE WORD (1977) Revs. David G. Woost; James L. Caddy, (Retired); Deacon Carl M. Varga; John Gaydos, Business Mgr.; Debbie Lokar, Pastoral Assoc.; Rebecca Harper, Music Min.
Res.: 8100 Eagle Rd., Kirtland, 44094-9714.
Tel: 440-256-1412; Email: dgermano@divinewordkirtland.org; Email: frdave@divinewordkirtland.org.
Catechesis Religious Program—Email: grensi@divinewordkirtland.org. Gina Rensi, D.R.E. Students 275.

LAKEWOOD, CUYAHOGA CO.
1—ST. CLEMENT (1922)
Tel: 216-226-5116; Email: stclementlakewood@cox.net. Rev. Joseph G. Workman; Deacon Daniel L. Bryan; Rev. Deogratias M. Ruwaainenyi, In Res.
Res.: 2022 Lincoln Ave., Lakewood, 44107-6099.
Church: 14401 Madison Ave., Lakewood, 44107.
See Lakewood Catholic Academy, Lakewood under Elementary Schools Parochial and Diocesan in the Institution Section.
Catechesis Religious Program—Students 48.
2—SS. CYRIL AND METHODIUS (1902) (Slovak), Closed. For inquiries for parish records contact the chancery.
3—ST. HEDWIG (1905) (Polish), Closed. For inquiries for parish records contact the Archives of the Diocese of Cleveland.
4—ST. JAMES (1908)
Mailing Address: 17400 Northwood Ave., Lakewood, 44107. Tel: 216-712-6755; Email: stjameslakewood@ohiocoxmail.com. Rev. Joseph G. Workman.
Res.: 2022 Lincoln Ave., Lakewood, 44107.
Church: Detroit & Granger Ave., Lakewood, 44107.
Catechesis Religious Program—
5—ST. LUKE (1922)
Tel: 216-521-0184; Fax: 216-521-9360; Email: frkevin@stlukelakewood.org; Web: www.stlukelakewood.org. Revs. Kevin P. Elbert; Gary D. Yanus, J.C.D., In Res.; Marilyn Streeter, Pastoral Assoc.; Deacon John D. Henderson; Lawrence Wallace, Music Min.
Res.: 1212 Bunts Rd., Lakewood, 44107-2699.
See Lakewood Catholic Academy, Lakewood under the Elementary Schools, Parochial and Diocesan in the Institution Section.
Catechesis Religious Program—Anna Buckley, P.C.L.; Vicki Pierce, Youth Min. Students 149.
6—TRANSFIGURATION (2010)
12608 Madison Ave., Lakewood, 44107.
Tel: 216-521-7288; Tel: 216-521-9091; Fax: 216-521-7005; Email: transfiguration@ohiocoxmail.com. Rev. Theodore Haag, O.F.M.
Catechesis Religious Program—Deacon David A. Streeter, D.R.E. Students 32.

LITCHFIELD, MEDINA CO., OUR LADY HELP OF CHRISTIANS PARISH (1976) Rev. Edward F. Suszynski Jr.; Deacon Michael F. Jervis Sr.; Sandra J. Lynn, Pastoral Assoc.
Administration Center—9608 Norwalk Rd., Litchfield, 44253-9598. Tel: 330-722-1180; Email: fathereds@gmail.com.
Worship Sites:—
Our Lady Help of Christians in Litchfield—Litchfield, Medina Co.
Our Lady Help of Christians in Nova, 240 State Rte. 511, Nova, Medina Co. 44859.
Our Lady Help of Christians in Seville, 60 High St., Seville, Medina Co. 44273.
Our Lady Help of Christians in Lodi, 8240 Buffham Rd., Lodi, Medina Co. 44254.
Catechesis Religious Program—Students 84.
Convent—9608 Norwalk Rd., Litchfield, 44253.

LORAIN, LORAIN CO.
1—ST. ANTHONY OF PADUA (1923)
Tel: 440-288-0106; Email: info@stanthonylorain.com; Web: www.stanthonylorain.org. Rev. Edward J. Smith; Deacon Paul R. Heise.
Res.: 1305 E. Erie Ave., Lorain, 44052-2226. Email: smithfr@stanthonylorain.com.
School—St. Anthony of Padua School, 1339 E. Erie Ave., Lorain, 44052. Tel: 440-288-2155; Fax: 440-288-2159; Email: akosij@stanthonylorain.com. Joseph M. Akosi, Prin. Lay Teachers 15; Students 246.
Catechesis Religious Program—Students 82.
2—SS. CYRIL AND METHODIUS (1905) (Slovenian), Closed. For inquiries for parish records contact St. John, Lorain.
3—ST. FRANCES XAVIER CABRINI PARISH (2010)
2143 Homewood Dr., Lorain, 44055-2799.
Tel: 440-277-7266; Email: jretar@dioceseofcleveland.org; Web: www.saintfrancesxcabrini.org. Rev. John C. Retar
Legal Titles: St. John the Baptist, St. Vitus, Saints Cyril and Methodius
Catechesis Religious Program—Students 41.
4—HOLY TRINITY (1906) (Slovak), Closed. For inquiries for parish records contact Mary Mother of God, Lorain.
5—ST. JOHN THE BAPTIST (1900) Closed. For inquiries for parish records contact the chancery.
6—ST. JOSEPH (1896) (German), Closed. For inquiries for parish records contact the chancery.
7—ST. LADISLAUS (1890) (Hungarian), Closed. For inquiries for parish records contact the chancery.
8—ST. MARY (1873)
309 Seventh St., Lorain, 44052-1879.
Tel: 440-245-5283; Fax: 440-246-0804. Rev. Daniel O. Divis; Mrs. Patricia Shullick, Pastoral Min.
9—NATIVITY OF THE BLESSED VIRGIN MARY (1898) (Polish) Rev. Robert J. Glepko; Deacon Robert J. Dybo.
Res.: 418 W. 15th St., Lorain, 44052-3597.
Tel: 440-244-9090; Email: nbvmlorain@dioceseofcleveland.org; Web: nativitybvmlorain.org.
Church: 1454 Lexington Ave., Lorain, 44052.
Catechesis Religious Program—Email: lmh111066@yahoo.com. Ms. Lenore Hales, D.R.E. Students 31.
10—ST. PETER (1909)
Tel: 440-282-9103; Email: stpeterchurch@stpeterlorain.org. Rev. Craig M. Hovanec; Deacon Jay R. Ogan.
Res.: 3655 Oberlin Ave., Lorain, 44053-2759. Web: www.stpeterlorain.org.
School—St. Peter School, 3601 Oberlin Ave., Lorain, 44053. Tel: 440-282-9909; Email: sch_stpeterlorain@dioceseofcleveland.org. Rebecca Brown, Prin. Lay Teachers 23; Students 372.
Catechesis Religious Program—Students 184.
Convent—3651 Oberlin Ave., Lorain, 44053.
11—SACRED HEART CHAPEL (1952) (Hispanic)
Mailing Address: 4301 Pearl Ave., Lorain, 44055-3311. Tel: 440-277-7231; Fax: 440-277-4886; Email: sacredheartchapellorain@gmail.com; Web: sacredheartchapel.org. Rev. William A. Thaden; Sr. Catherine McConnell, H.M., Pastoral Assoc.
Res.: 3921 Seneca Ave., Lorain, 44055.
12—ST. STANISLAUS (1908) (Polish), Closed. For inquiries for parish records contact the chancery.
13—ST. VITUS (1922) (Croatian), Closed. For inquiries for parish records contact the chancery.

LOUDONVILLE, ASHLAND CO., ST. PETER (1870) [CEM]
220 E. Butler St., Loudonville, 44842-1235.
Tel: 419-994-4396; Email: frvhawk@loudonvillecatholic.org; Email: linda@loudonvillecatholic.org; Email: kkuruc@loudonvillecatholic.org; Web: www.loudonvillecatholic.org. Rev. Vincent J. Hawk.
Res.: 132 N. Wood St., Loudonville, 44842-1235.
Tel: 419-994-5263; Email: vhawk@dioceseofcleveland.org.
Catechesis Religious Program—Students 35.

LYNDHURST, CUYAHOGA CO., ST. CLARE (1944)
Tel: 440-449-4242, Ext. 101; Email: parishsecretary14@att.net; Web: www.saintclare.net. Revs. Stanley J. Klasinski; James Cosgrove, Parochial Vicar; Mrs. Lori Mascia, Pastoral Assoc.
Res.: 5659 Mayfield Rd., Lyndhurst, 44124-2981.
School—Corpus Christi Academy (2016) 5655 Mayfield Rd., Lyndhurst, 44124. Fax: 440-449-1497; Email: principal@corpuschristiacad.org; Web: www.corpuschristiacad.org. Kenneth Mitskavich, Prin. Lay Teachers 15; Students 203.
Catechesis Religious Program—Students 152.

MACEDONIA, SUMMIT CO., OUR LADY OF GUADALUPE (1967)
9080 Shepard Rd., Macedonia, 44056.
Tel: 330-468-2194; Fax: 330-468-2196; Email: secretary@olg.cc; Web: www.olg.cc. Rev. Kevin C. Shemuga; Deacon David Govern; Mrs. Nancy Freibott, Pastoral Assoc.
Res.: 10419 Ravenna Rd., Twinsburg, 44087.
Catechesis Religious Program—9080 Shepard Rd., Macedonia, 44056. Students 145.

MADISON, LAKE CO., IMMACULATE CONCEPTION (1863)
2846 Hubbard Rd., Madison, 44057-2934.
Tel: 440-428-5164; Fax: 440-428-3075; Email: office@iccmadison.com; Web: www.iccmadison.com. Rev. Sean J. Donnelly; Deacons Thomas G. Hupertz; Kenneth C. Meade; Richard F. Kuhlman.
Catechesis Religious Program—6599 River Rd., Madison, 44057. Tel: 440-428-1083; Email: pcl_immaculatemad@dioceseofcleveland.org. Students 215.

MAPLE HEIGHTS, CUYAHOGA CO.
1—ST. MARTIN OF TOURS (1960) [CEM]
Tel: 216-475-4300; Email: vlreeve-smt44137@sbcglobal.net. Rev. Luigi C. Miola.
Rectory: 14600 Turney Rd., Maple Heights, 44137-4788. Email: lcmiola-smt44137@sbcglobal.net.
See St. Bendict Catholic School under Elementary Schools, Parochial and Diocesan in the Institution Section.
Catechesis Religious Program—Students 52.
2—ST. WENCESLAS (1923) Closed. For inquiries for parish records contact the chancery.

MEDINA, MEDINA CO.
1—ST. FRANCIS XAVIER (1860) [CEM]
Tel: 330-725-4968; Email: francismedina@dioceseofcleveland.org; Web: sfxmedina.com/parish. Revs. Anthony F. Sejba, Email: tsejba@sfxmedina.org; Christopher H. Weber, Parochial Vicar; Deacons Bob Cavanaugh; Joseph E. Loutzenhiser; Paul Kipfstuhl.
Res.: 606 E. Washington St., Medina, 44256-2183.
St. Francis Xavier ParishChurch: 606 E. Washington St., Medina, 44256-2183.
School—St. Francis Xavier School, 612 E. Washington St., Medina, 44256. Tel: 330-725-3345; Fax: 330-721-8626; Email: bseislove@sfxmedina.org. Bibiana Seislove, Prin. Lay Teachers 28; Students 493.
Catechesis Religious Program—Tel: 330-722-7700; Email: skish@sfxmedina.org. Summer Kish, D.R.E. Students 474.
2—HOLY MARTYRS (1980)
Tel: 330-722-6633; Email: churchoffice@holymartyrs.net; Web: www.holymartyrs.net. Rev. Stephen J. Dohner; Sr. Marie Ellen Kuhel, O.S.U., Spiritual Advisor/Care Svcs.; Janet Payton, Pastoral Assoc.; Diane Bruce, D.R.E.; Darrell McQuate, Youth Min.
Res.: 3100 Old Weymouth Rd., Medina, 44256-9207.
Tel: 330-722-6633; Email: churchoffice@holymartyrs.net; Web: www.holymartyrs.net.
Catechesis Religious Program—Diane Bruce, Dir. Faith Formation; Adam Nestor, Youth Min. Students 581.

MENTOR, LAKE CO.
1—ST. BEDE THE VENERABLE (1964)
Tel: 440-257-5544; Email: office@stbedementor.org; Web: www.stbedementor.org. Rev. Timothy J. Plavac; Mrs. Karen J. Roman, Pastoral Assoc.; Deacons Kenneth Knight, Pastoral Assoc.; John Burke Jr., Pastoral Assoc.; Laura Ruque, C.R.E.; Marjorie Zager, Music Min.
Res.: 9114 Lake Shore Blvd., Mentor, 44060-1697.
Catechesis Religious Program—Tel: 440-257-6988. Students 291.
2—ST. JOHN VIANNEY (1969)
7575 Bellflower Rd., Mentor, 44060-3948.
Tel: 440-255-0600; Email: frjohns@sjvmentor.org. Revs. Thomas W. Johns; Peter Morris, Parochial Vicar; Clyde K. Foster, Parochial Vicar; Deacon Gregory A. Leisure; Laura McBride; Mary Kovach, Pastoral Assoc.
See All Saints of St. John Vianney School, Wickliffe under Elementary Schools, Parochial and Diocesan located in the Institution section.
Catechesis Religious Program—Students 612.
3—ST. MARY OF THE ASSUMPTION (1857)
Tel: 440-255-3404; Email: parishoffice@stmarysmentor.org; Web: www.stmarysmentor.org. Rev. Thomas G. Elsasser; Deacon William A. Brys.
Res.: 8560 Mentor Ave., Mentor, 44060-5853.
School—St. Mary of the Assumption School, (Grades PreK-8), 8540 Mentor Ave., Mentor, 44060.
Tel: 440-255-9781; Fax: 440-974-8107; Email: principal@stmarysmentor.org. Mrs. Mary Benns, Prin. Lay Teachers 28; Students 413.
Catechesis Religious Program—Email: angela.collins@stmarysmentor.org. Angela Collins, D.R.E. Students 229.

MIDDLEBURG HEIGHTS, CUYAHOGA CO., ST. BARTHOLOMEW (1956)
Tel: 440-842-5400. Rev. Leonard M. Bacik.
Res.: 14865 E. Bagley Rd., Middleburg Heights, 44130-5502.
School—Academy of St. Bartholomew, 14875 E. Bagley Rd., Middleburg Heights, 44130-5502.
Tel: 440-845-6660; Fax: 440-845-6672; Email: sch_stbartholomew@dioceseofcleveland.org. Elizabeth Palascak, Prin. Lay Teachers 18; Students 132.

Catechesis Religious Program—Students 150.
MIDDLEFIELD, GEAUGA CO., ST. LUCY (1958)
16280 East High St., Middlefield, 44062.
Tel: 440-548-3812; Web: www.edwardlucy.com. P.O. Box 709, Parkman, 44080. Rev. John T. Burkley.
Catechesis Religious Program—Students 73.
NEWBURY, GEAUGA CO., ST. HELEN (1949)
Tel: 440-564-5805. Rev. James G. McPhillips; Deacons Willard Payne; Lawrence Somrack.
Res.: 12060 Kinsman Rd., Newbury, 44065-9678. Email: frjay@sthelen.com.
School—St. Helen School, Tel: 440-564-7125; Email: srmargaret@sthelen.com. Sr. Margaret Hartman, S.N.D., Prin. Sisters of Notre Dame 1; Lay Teachers 14; Students 202.
Catechesis Religious Program—Email: mflauto@sthelen.com. maria Flauto, Contact Person. Students 137.
NORTH OLMSTED, CUYAHOGA CO.
1—ST. BRENDAN (1964)
Tel: 440-777-7222; Fax: 440-779-7997; Email: stbrendannolmsted@yahoo.com; Web: www.StBrendanNorthOlmsted.org. Revs. Thomas G. Woost; Cornelius J. Murray, Pastor Emeritus, (Retired); Terrence M. Grachanin, Parochial Vicar; Deacon Robert D. Herron, Chap.
Church & Mailing Address: 4242 Brendan Ln., North Olmsted, 44070-2999.
Res.: 3920 Brendan Ln., North Olmsted, 44070.
Tel: 440-777-3702; Tel: 440-777-8433; Email: stbrendannolmsted@yahoo.com.
School—St. Brendan School, Tel: 440-777-8433; Email: jonacila@stbrendannortholmsted.org. Miss Julie Onacila, M.A., Prin. Lay Teachers 19; Students 195.
Catechesis Religious Program—Email: stbrendanreo@yahoo.com. Mary Oldja, D.R.E.; Rachel May Kut, Dir. Youth Min. Students 168.
2—ST. CLARENCE (1978)
Tel: 440-734-2414; Email: popremcak@st-clarence.org. Rev. Neil P. Kookoothe; Deacon Neal J. Novak.
Res.: 30106 Lorain Rd., North Olmsted, 44070-3986.
Fax: 440-734-4255; Email: clarencenolmsted@dioceseofcleveland.org; Web: www.st-clarence.org.
Catechesis Religious Program—Email: staff@st-clarence.org. Theresa Rosenhamer, D.R.E. Students 262.
Youth Ministry House—30072 Lorain Rd., North Olmsted, 44070. Tel: 440-665-6615.
3—ST. RICHARD (1950)
Tel: 440-777-5050; Tel: 440-777-5051;
Tel: 440-777-5052; Fax: 440-777-3577; Email: richardnolmsted@dioceseofcleveland.org; Web: www.st-richard.org. Rev. Charles J. Stollenwerk, M.Div.; Deacon F. Gregory Noveske; Sr. M. Jerome Fitzgerald, S.I.W., Pastoral Assoc.
Res.: 26855 Lorain Rd., North Olmsted, 44070-3260.
Catechesis Religious Program—Tel: 440-779-7529; Email: psrdirector@st-richard.org. Maureen Coughlin, D.R.E. Students 39.
Convent—5053 Whitethorn Ave., North Olmsted, 44070. Tel: 440-777-2168; Email: secretary@st-richard.org. Sisters 1.
NORTH RIDGEVILLE, LORAIN CO.
1—ST. JULIE BILLIART (1978) [JC]
Tel: 440-324-1978. Rev. Robert Franco, Admin.; Deacons John M. Rivera; Kenneth A. DeLuca.
Res.: 5545 Opal Dr., North Ridgeville, 44039-2025. Email: frgv@windstream.net.
Church: 5500 Lear Nagle Rd., North Ridgeville, 44039.
Catechesis Religious Program—Students 133.
2—ST. PETER (1875) [CEM]
Tel: 440-327-2201; Email: parishoffice@stpeternr.org. Revs. Robert J. Franco; Andrew J. Hoover, Parochial Vicar; Deacon Donald M. Jankowski.
Res.: 35777 Center Ridge Rd., North Ridgeville, 44039-3097. Web: www.stpeternr.org.
School—St. Peter School, 35749 Center Ridge Rd., North Ridgeville, 44039. Tel: 440-327-3212;
Fax: 440-327-6843; Email: rogerbrooks@stpeterschoolnr.org. Mr. Roger Brooks, Prin. Lay Teachers 13; Sisters of Notre Dame 1; Students 218.
Catechesis Religious Program—Email: groh@stpeternr.org. Sr. Sean Groh, S.N.D., D.R.E. Students 307.
NORTH ROYALTON, CUYAHOGA CO., ST. ALBERT THE GREAT (1959) Revs. Edward T. Estok Jr., M.A., M.Div.; John M. Pfeifer; Joe H. Kim; Mrs. Mary Pat Frey, Pastoral Assoc.
Res.: 6667 Wallings Rd., North Royalton, 44133-3067. Tel: 440-237-6760; Email: frete@saint-albert.org.
School—St. Albert the Great School,
Tel: 440-237-1032; Email: schooloffice@saint-albert.org; Web: www.saint-albert.org. Mr. Edward A. Vittardi, Prin. Lay Teachers 38; Students 908.
Catechesis Religious Program—Sr. Kathryn Mary O'Brien, O.S.U., D.R.E. Students 355.
NORTHFIELD, SUMMIT CO., ST. BARNABAS (1956) Revs. Ralph E. Wiatrowski, J.C.D.; Matthew J. Byrne, Parochial Vicar; Deacon Gerald Butler.
Res.: 9451 Brandywine Rd., Northfield, 44067-2484. Tel: 330-467-7959; Web: www.stbarnabasfamily.org.
School—St. Barnabas School, (Grades PreK-8), 9200 Olde Eight Rd., Northfield, 44067. Tel: 330-467-7921; Fax: 330-468-1926; Email: sch_stbarnabas@dioceseofcleveland.org. Erin Faetanini, Prin. Lay Teachers 25; Students 407.
Catechesis Religious Program—Tel: 330-467-7601. Toni Zobel, D.R.E. Students 305.
NORTON, SUMMIT CO.
1—ST. ANDREW THE APOSTLE (1951)
Email: standrewsecr@rrbiznet.com. Rev. James G. Maloney; Deacon Gregory A. Wunderle.
Res. & Church: 4022 Johnson Rd., Norton, 44203-5998. Tel: 330-825-2617; Email: jmaloney@dioceseofcleveland.org.
Catechesis Religious Program—Tel: 330-825-8264. Students 68.
2—PRINCE OF PEACE (2002)
Tel: 330-825-9543; Fax: 330-706-1437; Email: ppeacechurch@neo.rr.com; Web: www.princeofpeaceparish.org. Rev. Robert H. Jackson; Deacon Robert A. Youngblood; Lawrence G. Lauter, Pastoral Assoc.
Res.: 1263 Shannon Ave., Norton, 44203-6792.
Tel: 330-825-9543; Email: ppeacechurch@neo.rr.com.
Catechesis Religious Program—Students 174.
OBERLIN, LORAIN CO., SACRED HEART (1880)
Email: secretary@sacredheartoberlin.org; Web: sacredheartoberlin.org. Revs. Robert J. Cole, Pastor Emeritus, (Retired); William B. Padavick, Pastor Emeritus, (Retired); David Trask; Deacon Thomas B. Daw.
Res.: 410 W. Lorain St., Oberlin, 44074-1002. Email: sacredheart@oberlin.net.
Catechesis Religious Program—Students 63.
OLMSTED FALLS, CUYAHOGA CO., ST. MARY OF THE FALLS (1854) [CEM]
Tel: 440-235-2222; Tel: 440-235-2223;
Tel: 440-235-2808; Fax: 440-235-2937; Email: stmaryofc@aol.com; Web: www.stmaryofthefalls.org. Revs. Walter J. Hyclak; Ryan J. Cubera, Vicar; Deacon Richard Mueller, Business Mgr.
Res.: 25615 Bagley Rd., Olmsted Falls, 44138-1915.
School—St. Mary of the Falls School, (Grades PreK-8), 8262 Columbia Rd., Olmsted Falls, 44138-2242. Tel: 440-235-4580; Fax: 440-235-6833; Email: sch_stmaryfalls@dioceseofcleveland.org; Email: annemarie.rajnicek@stmaryofthefallsschool.com; Web: www.stmaryofthefallsschool.com. Annemarie Aquaviva Rajnicek, Prin. Lay Teachers 18; Students 270.
Catechesis Religious Program—Tel: 440-235-2808. Students 621.
ORANGE VILLAGE, CUYAHOGA CO., ST. MARGARET OF HUNGARY (1921) (Hungarian), Closed. For inquiries for parish records contact the chancery.
ORRVILLE, WAYNE CO., ST. AGNES (1879)
Tel: 330-682-3606; Tel: 330-682-2611; Email: stagnesorrv@embarqmail.com. Rev. Ronald J. Turek, Admin.
Res.: 541 Spring St., Orrville, 44667-2414. Email: agnesorrville@dioceseofcleveland.org.
Church: E. Oak St. & Lake St., Orrville, 44667.
Catechesis Religious Program—Students 59.
PAINESVILLE, LAKE CO., ST. MARY (1850) [CEM]
Tel: 440-354-6200. Rev. R. Stephen Vellenga; Deacon Thomas B. deHaas Jr.
Administrative Building: 242 N. State St., Painesville, 44077-4095.
Clergy Res.: 339 E. Erie St., Painesville, 44077-4095.
Catechesis Religious Program—Students 413.
PARKMAN, GEAUGA CO., ST. EDWARD (1928)
P.O. Box 709, Parkman, 44080. Rev. John T. Burkley.
Church & Res.: 16150 Center St., Parkman, 44080.
Catechesis Religious Program—Students 73.
Mission—St. Lucy, 16280 E. High St., Middlefield, Geauga Co. 44062.
PARMA, CUYAHOGA CO.
1—ST. ANTHONY OF PADUA (1959)
Tel: 440-842-2666; Email: office@stanthonypaduaparma.org; Web: www.stanthonypaduaparma.org. Revs. Dale W. Staysniak; Peter T. Kovacina; Deacon Gerard Blanda.
Res.: 6750 State Rd., Parma, 44134-4518.
School—St. Anthony of Padua School, 6800 State Rd., Parma, 44134-4632. Tel: 440-845-3444;
Fax: 440-884-4548; Email: pklimkewicz@stanthonypaduaschool.org. Mr. Patrick Klimkewicz, Prin. Lay Teachers 17; Students 225.
Catechesis Religious Program—Email: randyharris@stanthonypaduaparma.org. William R. Harris, D.R.E. Students 225.
Convent—6834 State Rd., Parma, 44134.
2—ST. BRIDGET OF KILDARE (1956)
Tel: 440-886-4434; Fax: 440-886-4431; Email: bridgetparma@dioceseofcleveland.org; Email: stbridget5620@yahoo.com; Web: www.stbridgetparma.com. Revs. Robert W. Wisniewski, Email: stbridget5620@yahoo.com; Lawrence J. Bayer, Pastor Emeritus, (Retired); Robert J. Kraig, Assiting Priest, (Retired); Deacon James J. Armstrong; Steven Malec, Business Mgr. & Pastoral Assoc.; Christina Harrison, Parish Catechetical Leader.
Res.: 5620 Hauserman Rd., Parma, 44130-1698.
School—St. Bridget of Kildare School,
Tel: 440-886-1468;
Fax: sch_stbridget@dioceseofcleveland.org; Web: www.stbridget-parma.com. Heather Hawk Frank, Prin.; Tracey Bresnahan, Sec. Lay Teachers 12; Students 246.
3—ST. CHARLES BORROMEO (1923)
Tel: 440-884-3030; Email: teh@stcharlesonline.org; Web: www.stcharlesonline.org. Revs. John T. Carlin; Louis H. Thomas, Parochial Vicar; Christopher A. Cox; Deacons John A. Talerico; Daniel M. Galla; Brian Pelcin, Pastoral Assoc.; Thomas Holzheimer, Business Mgr./Music Min.; Paula Leigh, D.R.E.
Res.: 5891 Ridge Rd., Parma, 44129-3642.
School—St. Charles Borromeo School, 7107 Wilber Ave., Parma, 44129-3445. Tel: 440-886-5546;
Fax: 440-886-1163; Email: sch_stcharlesbor@dioceseofcleveland.org. Mrs. Eileen Updegrove, Prin. Lay Teachers 23; Students 401.
Catechesis Religious Program—Students 192.
Convent—6811Wilber Ave., Parma, 44129.
Tel: 440-558-4024. Sisters 1.
4—ST. COLUMBKILLE (1956)
6740 Broadview Rd., Parma, 44134-4898.
Tel: 216-524-1987; Tel: 216-524-1988; Email: stcolumbkilleparish@gmail.com. Revs. Anthony J. Suso; Edwin M. Leonard, Parochial Vicar; James F. Mazanec, Parochial Vicar; Deacon Paul C. Kutolowski.
School—St. Columbkille School, Tel: 216-524-4816; Email: rcernystcolumbkille@ohiocoxmail.com. Mrs. Renee Cerny, Prin. Lay Teachers 25; Students 405.
Catechesis Religious Program—
Tel: 216-524-4816, Ext. 43; Email: schmura@stcolumbkilleparish.org. Shari Chmura, D.R.E. Students 169.
5—ST. FRANCIS DE SALES (1931)
Tel: 440-884-2319; Email: church_sfds@sbcglobal.net; Web: stfrancisdesales-church.org. Rev. Mark J. Peyton.
Res.: 3434 George Ave., Parma, 44134-2904.
Church: State & Snow Rd., Parma, 44134.
6—HOLY FAMILY (1872) [CEM]
Tel: 440-842-5533; Email: amihaloew@holyfamparma.org; Email: scudney@holyfamparma.org; Web: www.HolyFamParma.org. Revs. Richard A. Evans; Edward N. Schwet, Parochial Vicar; Deacons Joseph P. Litke; Charles E. Tweddell.
Res.: 7367 York Rd., Parma, 44130-5162.
Tel: 440-842-5533; Email: scudney@holyfamparma.org.
School—Holy Family School, (Grades K-8),
Tel: 440-842-7785; Email: office@holyfamilyschoolparma.org; Web: www.HolyFamilySchoolParma.org. Mr. Tom Brownfield, Prin. Lay Teachers 15; Students 196.
Catechesis Religious Program—
Tel: 440-842-5533, Ext. 347; Email: sryvonne@holyfamparma.org. Sr. Yvonne Spenoso, I.H.M., D.R.E.; Ms. Dara Hoffman, Prin. Students 90.
7—ST. JOHN BOSCO (1963)
Tel: 440-886-3500; Fax: 440-886-0966; Email: sjbinfo@sjbparmaheights.org; Web: www.sjbparmaheights.org. Rev. Lawrence Jurcak, J.C.L.; Deacon Roger Polefko, Pastoral Min./Coord.; Norman Cotone, Dir., Music & Liturgy.
Res.: 6480 Pearl Rd., Parma Heights, 44130-2997.
Catechesis Religious Program—Tel: 440-886-0061; Email: ckall@sjbparmaheights.org. Mrs. Christine Kall, D.R.E. Students 97.
8—ST. MATTHIAS (1980)
1200 W. Sprague Rd., Parma, 44134-6801.
Tel: 440-888-8220; Email: matthiasparma@dioceseofcleveland.org; Web: www.stmatthiaschurch.org. Rev. Raymond A. Sutter, M.Div.; Deacon Thomas A. Litwinowicz.
Catechesis Religious Program—
Tel: 440-888-8220, Ext. 24; Email: dlaheta@stmatthiaschurch.org. Dianne Laheta, D.R.E. Students 3.
PENINSULA, SUMMIT CO., MOTHER OF SORROWS (1882)
Rev. John D. Terzano.
Res.: 6034 S. Locust St., Peninsula, 44264-9726.
Tel: 330-657-2631; Email: mospenoh@windstream.net.
Catechesis Religious Program—Brian Quieser, D.R.E. Students 93.
PERRY, LAKE CO., ST. CYPRIAN (1968)

Tel: 440-259-2344. Rev. Jerzy Kusy, Admin.; Deacons Andrew Novak, Email: andrewnovak82@yahoo.com; James F. Daley Jr.; George P. Malec.
Res.: 4217 Middle Ridge Rd., Perry, 44081-9794.
Catechesis Religious Program—Students 184.

RICHFIELD, SUMMIT CO., ST. VICTOR (1964)
Tel: 330-659-6591; Email: stvictor@roadrunner.com; Web: www.saintvictorparish.org. Revs. Allen F. Corrigan; Arthur A. Bacher, Pastor Emeritus, (Retired); Mrs. Darlene Bednarz, Pastoral Min./Coord.
Church: 3435 Everett Rd., Richfield, 44286-0461.

RITTMAN, WAYNE CO., ST. ANNE (1855) [CEM] Rev. Michael D. Ausperk, Admin.
Res.: 139 S. First St., Rittman, 44270-1492.
Tel: 330-927-2941; Email: stannerittman@gmail.com.
Church: E. Ohio & S. First St., Rittman, 44270.
Catechesis Religious Program—

ROCKY RIVER, CUYAHOGA CO., ST. CHRISTOPHER (1922)
Tel: 440-331-4255; Email: info@stchrisparish.com; Web: stchrisparish.com. Revs. John C. Chlebo; Timothy M. Daw, Parochial Vicar; Deacons Thomas Long; Dennis A. Conrad; Ms. Gayle Cilimburg, Pastoral Assoc.
Res.: 20141 Detroit Rd., Rocky River, 44116-2420.
School—St. Christopher School, (Grades K-8), 1610 Lakeview Ave., Rocky River, 44116-2409.
Tel: 440-331-3075; Fax: 440-331-0674; Email: stchrisschool@scsrr.org; Web: www.scsrr.org. Mr. Scott Raiff, Prin. Lay Teachers 17; Students 291.
Catechesis Religious Program—Tel: 440-331-6226. Dr. Debra Dacone, D.R.E. Students 514.

SHAKER HEIGHTS, CUYAHOGA CO., ST. DOMINIC (1945)
Tel: 216-991-1444; Email: kmcdevitt@stdominicchurch.net; Email: parishoffice@stdominicchurch.net; Web: www.stdominicchurch.net. Rev. Thomas G. Fanta; Gerald Bowers, Pastoral Assoc.; Jen Deshpande, Pastoral Assoc.
Res.: 3450 Norwood Rd., Shaker Heights, 44122-4967.
Church: 19000 Van Aken Blvd., Shaker Heights, 44122.
School—St. Dominic School, 3455 Norwood Rd., Shaker Heights, 44122-4901. Tel: 216-561-4400; Fax: 216-561-1573; Email: info@stdominicschool.net; Web: www.stdominicschool.net. Susan Biggs, Prin. Lay Teachers 18; Students 192.
Catechesis Religious Program—Tel: 216-658-3672; Email: lwoconish@stdominicschurch.net. Liz Woconish, D.R.E. Students 500.

SHEFFIELD, LORAIN CO., ST. TERESA OF AVILA (1845) [CEM]
Tel: 440-934-4227; Email: st.teresa.church@neohio.twcbc.com; Web: www.stteresaparish.com. Rev. Edward J. Smith.
Church: 1878 Abbe Rd., Sheffield, 44054-2322.
Catechesis Religious Program—Students 51.

SHEFFIELD LAKE, LORAIN CO., ST. THOMAS THE APOSTLE (1962)
Tel: 440-949-7744. Rev. Stephen L. Shields.
Res.: 521 Harris Rd., Sheffield Lake, 44054-1409. Web: saintthomaschurch.net.
Catechesis Religious Program—Students 28.

SOLON, CUYAHOGA CO.
1—RESURRECTION OF OUR LORD (1971) Rev. Thomas M. Dragga, D.Min.; Ms. Elisabeth Frey, Pastoral Assoc.; Theresa Battaglia, Pastoral Assoc.; Julie Parrotta, Dir. Music Ministry.
Res. & Church: 32001 Cannon Rd., Solon, 44139-1699. Tel: 440-248-0980; Email: tdragga@churchofresurrection.org.
Catechesis Religious Program—Students 167.
2—ST. RITA (1929)
Tel: 440-248-1350; Email: strita@stritaparish.com; Web: www.stritaparish.com. Revs. Richard Burchell; Edward J. Janoch, Parochial Vicar; Deacons Robert H. Grgic, D.R.E.; Mark D. Janezic; Mr. Albert E. Leko, Pastoral Assoc.
Res.: 32820 Baldwin Rd., Solon, 44139-4098. Email: rburchell@stritaschool.com.
School—St. Rita School, 33200 Baldwin Rd., Solon, 44139. Fax: 440-248-9442; Email: dgrgic@stritaschool.com. Deborah Grgic, Prin. Lay Teachers 25; Students 325.
Catechesis Religious Program—32940 Parkway, Solon, 44139. Kelly Foraker, D.R.E. Students 463.

SOUTH AMHERST, LORAIN CO., NATIVITY OF BLESSED VIRGIN MARY (1933)
Email: toconnor@dioceseofcleveland.org. Rev. Timothy J. O'Connor, Admin.
Res.: 333 S. Lake St., South Amherst, 44001-2013.
Tel: 440-986-7011; Email: nativitysouthamherst@gmail.com.

SOUTH EUCLID, CUYAHOGA CO.
1—ST. GREGORY THE GREAT (1922) Closed. For inquiries for parish records contact the chancery.
2—ST. MARGARET MARY (1948) Closed. For inquiries for parish records contact the Archives of the Dioceses of Cleveland.
3—SACRED HEART OF JESUS PARISH (2010)
1545 S. Green Rd., South Euclid, 44121-4085.
Tel: 216-382-7601; Fax: 216-382-4992; Email: office@sacredheartofjesusparish.org. Revs. Dave R. Ireland; Thomas J. Winkel, Parochial Vicar; Deacon David N. Chordas.
School—Corpus Christi Academy, 5655 Mayfield Rd., Lyndhurst, 44121. Tel: 440-449-4242;
Fax: 440-449-1497; Email: principal@corpuschristiacad.org. Kenneth Mitskavich, Prin. Lay Teachers 15; Students 203.
Catechesis Religious Program—Students 8.

STOW, SUMMIT CO., HOLY FAMILY (1946)
Tel: 330-688-6412; Email: pjrosing@holyfamilystow.org; Web: www.holyfamilystow.org. Revs. Paul J. Rosing; Michael D. Ausperk, Parochial Vicar; Kevin J. Klonowski; Deacon John D. Green; Mrs. Barbie Byrne, Spiritual Advisor/Care Svcs.; Mrs. Judy Dobos, Liturgy Dir.; Mrs. Sandy Michaels, Music Min.; ms. Abby Gresser, Youth Min.; Mrs. Amy Rich, Admin.; Mr. Edward Coia, Admin.; Mrs. Jamie Heinl, Parish Life Coord.; Mrs. Diane Hurtuk, D.R.E.
Res.: 3450 Sycamore Dr., Stow, 44224-3999.
Church: 3179 Kent Rd., Stow, 44224.
School—Holy Family School, 3163 Kent Rd., Stow, 44224. Tel: 330-688-3816; Fax: 330-688-3474; Email: sfournier@holyfamilyschoolstow.org. Mrs. Sharon Fournier, Prin. Lay Teachers 26; Students 413; Clergy / Religious Teachers 1.

STRONGSVILLE, CUYAHOGA CO.
1—ST. JOHN NEUMANN (1977)
Tel: 440-238-1770; Email: secretary@sjnohio.com. Revs. Barry T. Gearing; Robert A. Lorkowski, Parochial Vicar; Ryan J. Mann, Parochial Vicar; Sr. Patricia Sylvester, S.N.D., Pastoral Assoc.; Deacons Keith A. Walcutt; Kenneth J. Piechowski.
Res.: 16271 Pearl Rd., Strongsville, 44136-6095.
See SS. Joseph & John Interparochial, Strongsville under St. Joseph, Strongsville.
Catechesis Religious Program—Students 504.
2—ST. JOSEPH (1946)
Tel: 440-238-5555; Email: jmamich@sjohio.org. Revs. Joseph R. Mamich; Robert McWilliams, Parochial Vicar; Deacons Pete Moore; Robert Lester.
Res.: 12700 Pearl Rd., Strongsville, 44136-3484.
School—SS. Joseph and John Interparochial, 12580 Pearl Rd., Strongsville, 44136-3422.
Tel: 440-238-4877; Fax: 440-238-8745; Email: dthomas@sjjschool.com. Mrs. Darlene Thomas, Prin. Lay Teachers 33; Students 680.
Catechesis Religious Program—Tel: 440-238-5231. Students 227.

TALLMADGE, SUMMIT CO., OUR LADY OF VICTORY (1944)
Mailing Address: Administration Center, 73 North Ave., Tallmadge, 44278-1996. Tel: 330-633-3637;
Tel: 330-633-3672; Fax: 330-633-6978; Web: www.ourladyofvictory.net. Rev. Michael A. Matusz.
Rectory—55 North Ave., Tallmadge, 44278.
Church: 105 North Ave., Tallmadge, 44278.
Catechesis Religious Program—73 North Ave., Tallmadge, 44278. Email: jpasko@ourladyofvictory.net. Mrs. Joanne Pasko, D.R.E. Students 73.

THOMPSON, GEAUGA CO., ST. PATRICK (1854) [CEM]
Tel: 440-298-1327; Email: stpatrickofficethompson@gmail.com. Rev. Daniel P. Redmond; Deacons Phillip P. Kraynik; Robert F. Schwartz.
Res.: 16550 Rock Creek Rd., Thompson, 44086-8753. Email: frredmond@gmail.com.

TWINSBURG, SUMMIT CO., SS. COSMAS AND DAMIAN (1963) Rev. Michael J. Stalla; Deacon Edward J. Chernick; Mrs. Darlene Bednarz, Pastoral Assoc.; Joni Smith, Pastoral Assoc.
Res.: 10419 Ravenna Rd., Twinsburg, 44087-1726.
Church: 10439 Ravenna Rd., Twinsburg, 44087-1726. Tel: 330-425-8141; Email: frmichael@sscosmas-damian.org.
Catechesis Religious Program—Students 131.

UNIONTOWN, SUMMIT CO., QUEEN OF HEAVEN (1964)
Email: office@queenofheavenparish.org. Revs. David R. Durkee; Robert E. Pahler, Pastor Emeritus, (Retired).
Res.: 1800 Steese Rd., Uniontown, 44685-9555.
Tel: 330-896-2345; Email: maggies@queenofheavenparish.org; Web: www.queenofheavenparish.org.
Catechesis Religious Program—Students 441.

UNIVERSITY HEIGHTS, CUYAHOGA CO., GESU (1926)
2470 Miramar Blvd., University Heights, 44118-3896. Tel: 216-932-0617; Email: gesucleveland@churchofthegesu.org; Web: churchofthegesu.org. Revs. Karl J. Kiser; Michael A. Vincent, S.J.; Nathaniel Romano; Deacon James K. O'Donnell; Sr. Kathleen Flannery, O.S.U., Pastoral Assoc.
Church: 2490 Miramar Blvd., University Heights, 44118.
School—Gesu School, 2450 Miramar Blvd., University Heights, 44118. Tel: 216-932-0620; Fax: 216-932-8326; Email: liemmolo@gesu.com; Web: gesu.com. Ms. Lucy Iemmolo, Prin. Lay Teachers 42; Students 631.
Catechesis Religious Program—Mary Von Carlowitz, Co-Dir. Faith Formation; Marcia Leous, Co-Dir. Faith Formation. Students 145.
Convent—4070 Meadowbrook Blvd., University Heights, 44118. Sisters 2.

VALLEY CITY, MEDINA CO., ST. MARTIN OF TOURS (1840) [CEM]
Mailing Address: 1800 Station Rd., Valley City, 44280-9522. Tel: 330-483-3808; Fax: 330-483-3848. Rev. Daniel J. Reed; Deacon William H. Perkins; Mary Takacs, Pastoral Assoc.; Colene Conley, Pastoral Assoc.; Steve Dickson, Music Min.; Rosie Strack, Business Mgr.; Terri Yohman, Youth Min.; Cheryl Lasch, Sec.
Res.: 1824 Station Rd., Valley City, 44280-9522.
Catechesis Religious Program—Students 289.

WADSWORTH, MEDINA CO., SACRED HEART OF JESUS (1886) [JC]
Tel: 330-336-3049; Email: church@shofjesus.com; Web: shofjesus.com. Revs. Joseph L. Labak; Patrick A. Spicer, Parochial Vicar; Deacons Roger N. Klaas; Richard Michney.
Res.: 260 Broad St., Wadsworth, 44281-2113.
Tel: 330-319-6340; Email: church@shofjesus.com.
School—Sacred Heart of Jesus School, 110 Humbolt Ave., Wadsworth, 44281. Tel: 330-334-6272;
Fax: 330-334-3236; Email: sah_badams@tccsa.net; Email: sch_sacredheart@dioceseofcleveland.org; Web: www.shswadsworth.org; Web: www.sacredheartexcellence.org. Mr. William Adams, Prin. Lay Teachers 22; Students 275; Clergy / Religious Teachers 1.
Catechesis Religious Program—Tel: 330-336-3049; Email: annette@shofjesus.com. Annette Bernard, D.R.E. Students 258.

WARRENSVILLE HEIGHTS, CUYAHOGA CO., ST. JUDE (1945) Closed. For inquiries for parish records contact the chancery.

WELLINGTON, LORAIN CO., ST. PATRICK (1851)
Tel: 440-647-4375; Email: secretary@stpatrickwellington.com; Web: stpatrickwellington.com. Rev. David Trask; Deacon Dean R. Paoletta.
Res.: 512 N. Main St., Wellington, 44090-1198. Cell: 440-987-9873; Fax: 440-987-9287.
Catechesis Religious Program—Students 73.

WEST SALEM, WAYNE CO., ST. STEPHEN (1952)
Tel: 419-853-4946. Rev. Thomas E. Stock.
Res.: 44 Britton St., West Salem, 44287-9318.
Catechesis Religious Program—Students 37.

WESTLAKE, CUYAHOGA, CO.
1—ST. BERNADETTE (1950)
Tel: 440-734-1300; Email: info@stbern.net; Web: www.saintbernadetteparish.org. Revs. Philip G. Racco; Jeffrey W. Barnish, Parochial Vicar; Deacon Mark A. Cunningham; Sr. Donna Marie Bradesca, Dir. of Adult Faith Formation; Mrs. Christine Krysiak, Pastoral Assoc.; Monica Dietz, Prin.; Mrs. Diana Lipfird, D.R.E./RCIA; Ms. Mary Egan, Fin. Mgr./ Inst. Mgr.
Res.: 2256 Clague Rd., Westlake, 44145-4328. Email: maryegan@msn.com.
School—St. Bernadette School, 2300 Clague Rd., Westlake, 44145. Tel: 440-734-7717;
Fax: 440-734-9198; Email: office@stbern.net. Monica Dietz, Prin. Lay Teachers 24; Students 470.
2—ST. LADISLAS (1973)
Tel: 440-835-2300; Email: stlads@stlads.org. Rev. Donald E. Snyder, M.Div.; Deacon John Travis; Sisters Johnica D'amico, Pastoral Assoc. & D.R.E.; Mary Joan, O.S.U., Music Min.; Mary Ellen Downs, Pastoral Assoc.; Mr. Robert Hertl, Pastoral Assoc.; Mike McClain, Youth Min.
Res. & Church Address: 2345 Bassett Rd., Westlake, 44145-2999.
Catechesis Religious Program—Mike McClain, Youth Min. Students 295.

WICKLIFFE, LAKE CO., OUR LADY OF MOUNT CARMEL (1921) Revs. Thomas J. Behrend; David L. McCafferty, Pastor Emeritus, (Retired); Joseph P. O'Donnell, Parochial Vicar; Gregory J. Olszewski, Parochial Vicar; David G. Baugh, In Res., (Retired); Gregory F. Schaut, In Res.; Edward N. Schwet, In Res.
Res.: 1730 Mount Carmel Dr., Wickliffe, 44092-1835.
Tel: 440-585-0700; Email: staraska@olmcwickliffe.org.
Church: 29850 Euclid Ave., Wickliffe, 44092.
See Mater Dei Academy under Elementary Schools, Parochial & Diocesan located in the institution section.
Catechesis Religious Program—Students 162.

WILLOUGHBY, LAKE CO., IMMACULATE CONCEPTION PARISH (1865) Rev. Dennis M. McNeil, Parochial Vicar; Sr. Josephine Rasoamampionona, D.R.E.; Mr. Michael Kelley, Music Min.; Ms. Elayne Kramer, Business Mgr.; Joanie Klemens, Prin.; Ms. Kathleen Doles, Sec.; Ms. Eileen Fleisher, Sec.
Res.: 37940 Euclid Ave., Willoughby, 44094-5899.
Tel: 440-942-4500; Email: parish@immaculate.net; Web: www.immaculate.net.

See Mater Dei Academy under Elementary Schools, Parochial & Diocesan located in the institution section.
Catechesis Religious Program—Students 154.

WILLOUGHBY HILLS, LAKE CO., ST. NOEL (1980)
35200 Chardon Rd., Willoughby Hills, 44094-9193. Tel: 440-946-0887. Rev. George Smiga; Deacon David T. Nethery.
Res.: 2676 Som Center, Willoughby Hills, 44094.
Catechesis Religious Program—Michele Baetzold, Coord. Faith Formation. Students 92.

WILLOWICK, LAKE CO., ST. MARY MAGDALENE (1949)
Tel: 440-943-2133; Email: MToomey@smmwillowick.org; Web: smmwillowick.org. Rev. Steven H. Breck; Deacon Carl Toomey.
Res.: 32010 Vine St., Willowick, 44095-3581.
Fax: 440-943-3780; Email: FrBreck@smmwillowick.org.
Church: 32114 Vine St., Willowick, 44095.
Catechesis Religious Program—
Tel: 440-943-2133, Ext. 6013. Students 77.

WOOSTER, WAYNE CO., ST. MARY OF THE IMMACULATE CONCEPTION (1846) [CEM]
Tel: 330-264-8824; Fax: 330-262-4633; Email: stmarywoosteroffice@gmail.com; Web: stmarywooster.org. Revs. Stephen P. Moran; Richard J. Samide, Parochial Vicar.
Res.: 527 Beall Ave., P.O. Box 109, Wooster, 44691-0109. Email: spfgm@aol.com.

School—St. Mary of the Immaculate Conception School, (Grades PreK-8), 515 Beall Ave., Wooster, 44691. Tel: 330-262-8671; Fax: 330-262-0967; Email: stm_lmarvin@tccsa.net. Laura Marvin, Prin. Lay Teachers 8; Students 95; Clergy / Religious Teachers 7.
Catechesis Religious Program—Tel: 330-264-5838; Tel: 330-264-8824, Ext. 208; Email: cmatesich.stmarywooster@gmail.com. Mrs. Carol Matesich, D.R.E.; Mrs. Donna Lohnes, Sec.; Ms. Rachel Teague, Youth Min. Students 143.

Cleveland Diocesan Mission

EL SALVADOR, C.A.. *Casa Parroquial Inmaculada Concepcion*. Rev. Paul E. SchindlerLa Libertad Dept. La Libertad El Salvador, Central America.
Casa Parroquial San Pedro Teotepeque. Rev. John T. OstrowskiLa Libertad El Salvador, Central America.

Chaplains of Public Institutions

CLEVELAND. *Children's Rehab Hospital*. Contact: St. Andrew Abbey, Cleveland; Tel: 216-721-5300.
Cleveland Clinic Foundation. Rev. Cirilo A. Nacorda, Tel: 216-361-1444.
Cuyahoga County Jail. Rev. Neil Walters, Tel: 216-443-6182.
Cuyahoga County Juvenile Justice Center. Rev. Gary Chmura, Tel: 216-421-4211Parish Life Office; Tel: 216-696-6525, Ext. 3500.
Euclid Hospital. Rev. Joseph Fortuna, Tel: 216-486-0850.
Fairview General Hospital. Rev. Deogratias M. Ruwaainenyi, Tel: 216-476-4929.
Hillcrest Hospital. Attended from St. Francis of Assisi, Tel: 216-461-0066.
Lutheran Medical Center. Rev. Arcangelo Manzi, O.de.M., Tel: 216-651-5043.
Metro Health Medical Center & Rehabilitation Center. Rev. Kiran Kumar, O.de.M., Tel: 216-651-5043(Hospital).
Northcoast Behavioral Healthcare System North Campus. Rev. Gary Chmura, Tel: 216-421-4211.
Northeast Reintegration Center. Rev. J. Mark Hobson, D.Min., Tel: 216-451-3262.
Parma Community Hospital. Rev. James R. Semonin, Tel: 440-886-4434.
Rainbow Hospital. Rev. Matthew J. Glaros, Tel: 216-641-8444(See University Hospitals).
Richmond UHHS Medical Center. Rev. John D. Betters, Tel: 216-731-1515Attended from St. John of the Cross, Tel: 216-288-0770.
South Pointe Hospital. Mr. Charles Sidoti, Tel: 216-491-7924Attended from Pastoral Care Office, Tel: 216-491-7924.
SouthWest General Hospital. Rev. Caesar Amandua, A.J., Tel: 440-816-8000Pastoral Care Office; Tel: 440-816-8000.
University Hospitals. Rev. Matthew J. Glaros, Tel: 216-641-8444.
University Hospitals Bedford Medical Center. Attended from Our Lady of Hope Parish, Tel: 440-232-8166.
Veterans Medical Center, Louis Stokes V.A., 10701 East Blvd., 44106. Tel: 216-791-3800, Ext. 305. Attended from Parish Life Office, Tel: 216-696-6525, Ext. 3500.

AKRON. *Akron City Hospital*. Rev. Dismas Byarugaba, A.J., Tel: 330-535-4141.
Akron General Hospital. Rev. Bernard P. Kyara, A.J., Tel: 330-535-4141.
Summit County Jail, Akron. St. Bernard Parish, Akron; Tel: 330-253-5161.

ASHLAND. *Ashland County Jail*, Ashland. Attended from St. Edward, Tel: 419-289-7224.
Samaritan Hospital, Ashland. Rev. Rodney A. Kreidler, Tel: 419-548-3812Attended from St. Edward, Tel: 419-289-7224.

BARBERTON. *Summa Barberton Citizens Hospitals*, Barberton. Rev. David J. Majikas, Tel: 330-745-0011Attended from St. Augustine, Tel: 330-745-0011.

CHAGRIN FALLS. *Windsor Hospital*, Chagrin Falls. Attended from St. Joan of Arc, Tel: 440-247-7183.

CHARDON. *Geauga Community Hospital*, Chardon. Rev. James G. McPhillips, Tel: 440-564-5805Attended from St. Helen, Newbury, Tel: 440-564-5805.
Geauga County Jail, Chardon. Tel: 440-279-2009. Rev. John T. Burkley, Tel: 440-548-3812, Deacon Willard C. Payne, Tel: 440-564-5805.

CONCORD. *Tri Point Medical Center*, Concord. Rev. Gregory F. Schaut, Tel: 440-585-0700A Lake Health Hospital.

CUYAHOGA FALLS. *Fallsview Mental Health Center*, Cuyahoga Falls. Attended from St. Eugene, Tel: 330-923-5244.
Summa Western Reserve, Cuyahoga Falls. Rev. James P. Orndorf, Tel: 330-928-2173Attended from St. Joseph, Tel: 330-928-2173.

ELYRIA. *Elyria Memorial Hospital*, Elyria. Laity Robin Hughes, Chap., Pastoral Care, Tel: 440-284-8440.

GRAFTON. *Grafton Correctional Institution*. Rev. Charles J. Ryba, (Retired), Tel: 440-657-5828, Deacon John Rivera, Tel: 440-327-4426.

LODI. *Lodi Hospital*, Lodi. Attended from Our Lady Help of Christians, Tel: 330-722-1180; 330-273-1500 (Cleveland).

LORAIN. *Lorain Correctional Institution*, Lorain. Rev. Charles J. Ryba, (Retired), Tel: 440-657-5728.

LOUDONVILLE. *Kettering-Mohican Area Medical Center*, Loudonville. Rev. Vincent J. Hawk, Tel: 419-994-4396Attended from St. Peter, Tel: 419-994-4396.

MEDINA. *Medina Community Hospital*, Medina. Attended from St. Francis Xavier, Tel: 330-725-4968.
Medina County Jail, Medina. Attended by St. Francis Xavier Parish, Medina; Tel: 330-725-4968.

NORTHFIELD. *Northcoast Behavioral Healthcare System South*, Northfield, 44067. Rev. Gary Chmura, Tel: 216-421-4211.

OBERLIN. *Mercy Health-Allen Hospital*, Oberlin. Rev. David Trask, Tel: 440-775-1211Attended from Sacred Heart, Tel: 330-774-6791.

ORRVILLE. *Aultman-Orville Hospital*, Orrville. Rev. Ronald J. Turek, Tel: 330-682-3606Attended from St. Agnes, Tel: 330-682-3010.

SMITHVILLE. *Village Network*, Smithville. Rev. Stephen P. Moran, Tel: 330-264-8824Attended from St. Mary of the Immaculate Conception, Wooster, Tel: 330-264-8824.

WADSWORTH. *Wadsworth-Rittman Hospital*, Wadsworth. Attended from Sacred Heart of Jesus, Tel: 330-336-3049.

WILLOUGHBY. *Lake Health Hospital, Willoughby Campus*, Willoughby. Rev. Gregory F. Schaut, Tel: 440-585-0700.

WOOSTER. *Wayne County Jail*, Wooster. Rev. Stephen P. Moran, Tel: 330-264-8824Attended from St. Mary of the Immaculate Conception, Tel: 330-264-8824.
Wooster Community Hospital, Wooster. Attended from St. Mary of the Immaculate Conception, Tel: 330-264-8824.

Released from Diocesan Assignment:
Revs.—
Conroy, Kevin M., Maryknoll Fathers & Brothers, Maryknoll, NY 10545
Denk, Michael J., Institute of Voluntas Dei, New York, NY 10001
Patrick, William J., (Retired), 3733 N. Harbor #15, Fullerton, CA 92835.

Military Chaplains:
Revs.—
Brankatelli, Joseph R.
Kondik, Curtis L.

Absent on Leave:
Revs.—
Dickinson, William R.
Dool, Franz C.
Miceli, John P.
Ruggeri, Salvatore M.
Schuerger, Anthony J.

Absent on Sick Leave:
Revs.—
Dunson, Donald H.
Vrabel, George A.

Administrative Leave:
Revs.—
Brodnick, Joseph
Ischay, Matthew A.
Kalista, Timothy D.
Lucas, Theodore
McGonegal, James R.

Life of Prayer and Penance:
Revs.—
Lieberth, Joseph
Rupp, Edward F.

Retired:
Most Revs.—
Lennon, Richard G., D.D., M.A., M.Th., (Retired), 8736 Brecksville Rd., Brecksville, 44141
Pilla, Anthony M., D.D., M.A., (Retired), 4955 Clubside Rd., Lyndhurst, 44124
Rev. Msgr.—
Wolff, Robert C., (Retired), 5232 Broadview Rd., Richfield, 44286
Revs.—
Bacher, Arthur A., (Retired), 47 Forest Cove Dr., Akron, 44319
Baugh, David G., (Retired), 1730 Mt. Carmel Dr., Wickliffe, 44092
Bayer, Lawrence J., (Retired), 13372 Olympus Way, Strongsville, 44149
Becherer, James R., (Retired), 4963 E. Lake Rd., Sheffield Lake, 44054
Begin, Robert T., (Retired), 12500 Edgewater Dr. #1506, Lakewood, 44107
Bryda, Ronald J., (Retired), 28283 Center Ridge Rd., E-16, Westlake, 44140
Bryk, John J., (Retired), 7867 Daniel Dr., Seven Hills, 44131
Burge, Robert, (Retired), 10082 Granger Rd., Garfield Heights, 44125
Caddy, James L., (Retired), 8100 Eagle Rd., Kirtland, 44094
Cappelletti, Joseph, (Retired), 7054 Austin Point Dr., Concord, 44077
Cassidy, James M., (Retired), 5232 Broadview Rd., Richfield, 44286
Ciccolini, Samuel R., (Retired), 2101 17th St. S.W., Akron, 44314
Cole, Robert J., (Retired), 250 Kraft St., Berea, 44017
Colletta, Ralph V., (Retired), P.O. Box 605, Bath, 44210-0605
Cozzens, Donald, (Retired), 2650 University Blvd., Apt. 104, Shaker Heights, 44118
Crawford, John G., (Retired), 3434 George Ave., Parma, 44134
Czech, Edward M., (Retired), 7821 Lake Ave., 44102
Duke, Jerome J., (Retired), P.O. Box 32, Addison, PA 15411
Egan, Arthur B., (Retired), 378 French Creek Rd., Avon, 44011
Franz, S. Michael, (Retired), 5323 Broadview Rd., Richfield, 44286
Gajdzinski, Norman A., (Retired), 20341 Brookstone Tr., Middleburg Heights, 44130
Gilles, Thomas C., (Retired), 5232 Broadview Rd., Richfield, 44286
Gonsor, Richard A., (Retired), 590 Poplar St., Elyria, 44035
Gorski, John J., (Retired), 2820 N. Bay Dr., Apt. P-9, Westlake, 44145-6020
Hagedorn, Thomas J., (Retired), 312 4th St., Elyria, 44035
Halaiko, David J., (Retired), 164 W. Market St., Akron, 44303
Hayes, John J., (Retired), 4129 Superior Ave., 44103
Hengle, John R., (Retired), 3155 Englewood Dr., Stow, 44224
Hepner, Ernest C., (Retired), 101 Single Tree Ln., Aiken, SC 29803
Hudak, Richard E., (Retired), 1931 King James Pkwy., #424, Westlake, 44145
Karg, William D., (Retired), St. Paul Parish, 433 Mission Dr., Akron, 44301
Keller, Gerald J., (Retired), 33896 Maple Ridge Rd., Avon, 44011
Klein, James T., (Retired), 27441 Westown Blvd., Westlake, 44145
Kraig, Robert J., (Retired), 6900 Paradise Way, North Ridgevelle, 44039
Kraker, Joseph H., (Retired), 3479 Copely Rd., Copley, 44321
Kristancic, Dennis J., (Retired), 3977 Osage St., Stow, 44224

Krupp, Albert A., (Retired), 5232 Broadview Rd., Richfield, 44286
Lajack, Jerome M., (Retired), 1485 Hollow Wood, Avon, 44011
Lan, Augustine Pham Van, (Retired), 20860 Fairpark Dr., Fairview Park, 44126
Laubenthal, Allan R., S.T.D., (Retired), 28700 Euclid Ave., Wickliffe, 44092
Lukachinsky, Jerome A., (Retired), 13623 Rockside Rd., Garfield Heights, 44125
Lusoski, Thomas J., (Retired), 21108 Franklin Rd., Maple Heights, 44137
Mahoney, Thomas D., (Retired), 15555 Hillard Rd., #805, Lakewood, 44107
Marquard, Elmer E., (Retired), 5232 Broadview Rd., Richfield, 44286
Marsick, James J., (Retired), 3430 Wooster Rd., #209-B, Rocky River, 44116
Martello, Lawrence N., M.A., M.Div., (Retired), 3290 Cooper Foster Rd., Lorain, 44053
McCafferty, David L., (Retired), 39 N. Portage Path, Akron, 44303
McCann, Thomas W., (Retired), 401 E. Heritage Dr., Cuyahoga Falls, 44223
McCarthy, David J., (Retired), St. Joseph Parish, 215 Falls Ave., Cuyahoga Falls, 44221
McCreight, James H., (Retired), 15555 Hillard Rd., Unit 403, Lakewood, 44107
McGovern, Thomas A., (Retired), 1986 Village Pkwy., Tallmadge, 44278-3036
Mecir, Joseph S., (Retired), 15101 Howe Rd., Apt. 423, Strongsville, 44136
Montavon, Thomas G., (Retired), St. Monica Parish, 13623 Rockside Rd., Garfield Heights, 44125-5197
Mueller, John J., (Retired), 1746 Pine St. S. Apt H, Columbus, 43229
Murphy, John F., (Retired), 283 Union St., Bedford, 44146
Murray, Cornelius J., (Retired), 36550 Chester Rd., #1401, Avon, 44011
O'Connor, Neil D., (Retired), 12334 Corinth Ct., Strongsville, 44149
O'Donnell, James P., (Retired), 3675 W. 165 St., 44111
O'Donnell, Thomas V., (Retired), 283 Union St., #236, Bedford, 44146
O'Grady, Dennis R., (Retired), 7096 Pearl Rd., Parma Heights, 44130
O'Neill, William P., J.C.L., (Retired), 283 Union St., Bedford, 44146
Obloy, Leonard G., (Retired), 4291 Richmond Rd., Warrensville Heights, 44122
Ocilka, John A., (Retired), 8323 Greenlawn Ave. Down, Parma, 44129
Olsavsky, John R., J.C.L., (Retired), 215 Village Dr., Seven Hills, 44131-5713
Padavick, William B., (Retired), 4291 Richmond Rd., Warrensville Heights, 44122
Pahler, Robert E., (Retired), 5232 Broadview Rd., Richfield, 44286
Pajk, Thomas J., (Retired), 1851 King James Pkwy. #107, Westlake, 44145
Pfeiffer, Robert F., J.C.L., (Retired), 4300-B Hudson Dr., Stow, 44201
Piskura, Joseph, (Retired), 29050 Detroit Rd., Apt. 329, Westlake, 44145
Pizmoht, Louis A., (Retired), 8276 Deepwood Blvd., Unit 1, Mentor, 44060
Proehl, Douglas, (Retired), 1544 Cedarwood Dr., #156, Westlake, 44145
Reymann, James J., (Retired), 123 McKinley St., Wellington, 44090
Ryba, Charles J., (Retired), 6860 Savannah Dr., North Ridgevelle, 44039
Sanson, Robert J., J.C.D., (Retired), 5252 Park Dr., Vermilion, 44089
Schorr, James D., (Retired), Light of Hearts Villa, 283 Union St., Bedford, 44146
Seminatore, Joseph, (Retired), 12600 Rockside Rd., #111, Garfield Heights, 44105
Severt, William H., (Retired), 3131 Smith Rd., Fairlawn, 44333
Sheil, James E., (Retired), 35755 Detroit Rd., Avon, 44011
Snedeker, Arthur, (Retired), 1200 W. Sprague Rd., Parma, 44134
Stokowski, Lucjan, (Retired), 18340 River Valley Blvd., North Royalton, 44133
Sullivan, John J., (Retired), 7575 Bellflower Rd., Mentor, 44060
Szudarek, Ronald J., (Retired), 7194 Marko Ln., Parma, 44134
Tezie, John M., (Retired), 3290 Cooper Foster Rd., Lorain, 44053
Thomas, Ralph W., (Retired), 1905 Portage Tr., Cuyahoga Falls, 44223
Tomicky, Ronald, (Retired), 7821 Lake Ave., #504, 44102
Uhler, Carl A., (Retired), 5100 Marymount Village Dr., #232, Garfield Heights, 44125
Valley, John, (Retired), 37825 Lakeshore Blvd., Eastlake, 44095
Vesely, James J., (Retired), 6756 State Rd., Parma, 44134
Vrana, John G., (Retired), 6912 Chestnut Rd., Independence, 44131
Walsh, Francis P., (Retired), 26322 Lake Rd., Bay Village, 44140
Weber, Thomas L., (Retired), 22222 Calverton Rd., Shaker Heights, 44122
Weist, Edward F., J.C.D., (Retired), 28367 Center Ridge Rd., #15, Westlake, 44145
Wenz, Robert F., (Retired), 15101 Howe Rd. #309, Strongsville, 44136
Wessel, John F., (Retired), 2451 Crimson Dr., Westlake, 44145
Wysocki, Paul, (Retired), 8274 Stanhope Rd., Williamsfield, 44093.

Permanent Deacons:
Adair, Robin, St. Augustine, Barberton
Adkins, Ronald M., St. Gabriel, Concord Township
Agrippe, James L., (Retired)
Amedeo, John, St. Paul, Akron
Anderson, Robert C., (Retired)
Armstrong, James J., St. Bridget, Parma Heights, Deacon Representative Clergy Personnel Board
Bacik, Dale A., Apollo Beach, FL (Released from Dio. Assignment)
Battista, Bruce J., Holy Rosary, Cleveland
Beercheck, Richard C., Blessed Trinity, Cleveland
Belsito, Vincent L., Holy Angels, Chagrin Falls
Belter, Clement J., St. Ambrose, Brunswick
Bender, Robert C., St. Vincent de Paul, Akron
Berigan, Patrick F., (Retired)
Bizon, Thaddeus C. Jr., St. Albert the Great, N. Royalton
Bizon, Thomas P., Mary Queen of the Apostles, Brook Park
Blanda, Gerard, St. Anthony of Padua, Parma
Boehnlein, Lawrence A., St. Mary, Chardon
Bosau, Wayne A., (Retired)
Bowers, Robert J., St. Paschal Baylon, Highland Heights
Bryan, Daniel L., St. Clement, Lakewood
Brys, William A., St. Mary of the Assumption, Mentor
Bubnick, Robert C. Sr., (Retired)
Bugaj, Robert J., St. Therese, Garfield Heights; St. Martin of Tours, Maple Heights
Burke, John Jr., St. Bede the Venerable, Mentor
Butkovic, Donald P., (Retired)
Butz, Richard C., (Retired)
Cavanaugh, Robert A., St. Francis Xavier, Medina
Chernick, Edward J., SS. Cosmas & Damian, Twinsburg
Chordas, David N., Sacred Heart of Jesus, South Euclid
Clavin, Daniel P., St. Gabriel, Concord
Colon, Victor R., Sagrada Familia, Cleveland
Conrad, Dennis A., St. Christopher, Rocky River
Croniger, James D., (Retired)
Cruz, Moises, St. Stephen, Cleveland
Cully, Thomas A., St. Mary, Berea
Cunningham, Mark A., St. Bernadette, Westlake
Daley, James F. Jr., St. Cyprian, Perry
Daull, Raymond L., Communion of Saints, Cleveland Heights
Davis, Kent L., St. Joseph, Cuyahoga Falls
Daw, Thomas B., Sacred Heart, Oberlin
DeGracia, Jose A., (Retired)
DeHaas, Thomas B. Jr., St. Mary, Painesville
DeLuca, Kenneth A., St. Julie Billiart, North Ridgeville
Di Mascio, Ramon J., St. Bernard, Akron
Dietz, Joseph R., St. Edward, Ashland
Dillon, Edward R., (Retired)
Dirk, William E., (Retired)
Dobbins, Bruce E., Our Lady of Grace, Hinckley
Doerpers, Charles B., St. John of the Cross, Euclid
Dunlop, Jeffrey F., St. Joan of Arc, Chagrin Falls
Dybo, Robert J., Nativity of the Blessed Virgin Mary, Lorain
Elwood, William T., St. Francis of Assisi, Gates Mills
Feldkamp, Edward J., (Retired)
Figueroa, Miguel A., (Retired)
Flores, Jose A., (Retired)
Foradori, Peter J., St. Mary of the Immaculate Conception, Wooster
Frania, Gregory C., (Retired)
Friend, Shelby, Holy Spirit, Garfield Heights
Galla, Daniel M., St. Charles Borromeo, Parma
Gardias, Edmund A., Delegate for Senior Deacons; St. Adalbert, Berea
Golonka, Kenneth A., (Retired)
Gonzalez, Edgar, St. Vincent de Paul, Elyria
Govern, David, Our Lady of Guadalupe, Macedonia
Grasson, Thomas J., (Retired)
Gregg, Larry D., St. Raphael, Bay Village
Grgic, Robert H., St. Gabriel, Concord Township
Guritza, Dennis A., St. Joan of Arc, Chagrin Falls
Hancock, Daniel J., St. Mary of the Immaculate Conception, Avon
Heise, Paul R., St. Anthony of Padua, Lorain
Henderson, John D., St. Luke, Lakewood
Herrick, Raymond S., St. Francis de Sales, Akron
Herron, Robert D., St. Brendan, North Olmsted
Hill, Kenneth J., St. Vincent de Paul, Cleveland
Hirnikl, John J., Blessed Trinity, Akron
Hlabse, Paul J., (Retired)
Hoefler, Gregory, Immaculate Heart of Mary, Cuyahoga Falls
Humphrey, Frank A. III, St. Mary, Elyria
Humphrey, Patrick J., St. Jude, Elyria
Hupertz, Thomas G., Immaculate Conception, Madison
James, Ronald R., Holy Spirit, Garfield Heights
Janezic, Mark D., St. Rita, Solon
Jankowski, Donald M., Dir. Pastoral Care, St. Mary of the Woods, Avon; St. Peter, North Ridgeville
Jenkins, Keith A., St. Joseph, Avon Lake
Jervis, Michael F., Our Lady Help of Christians, Litchfield
Kamlowsky, Philip P., (Retired), Holy Family, Stow
Kaniecki, James A., (Retired)
Kipfstuhl, Paul J., St. Francis Xavier, Medina; Assoc. Dir., Office of Continuing Education for Ministers
Klaas, Roger N., (Retired)
Knight, Kenneth, St. Bede the Venerable, Mentor
Knox, Steven K., (Retired)
Kovach, Robert C. Jr., St. Anselm, Chesterland
Kovitch, Joseph R., (Retired)
Kraynik, Phillip P., St. Patrick, Thompson
Kuhlman, Richard F., Immaculate Conception, Madison
Kushner, David S., St. Mary, Cleveland; Dir. of the Permanent Diaconate Formation Office
Kutolowski, Paul C., St. Columbkille, Parma
Leisure, Gregory A., St. John Vianney, Mentor
Lester, Robert J., St. Joseph, Strongsville
Litke, Joseph P., Holy Family, Parma
Litwinowicz, Thomas A., St. Matthias, Parma
Long, Thomas T., St. Christopher, Rocky River
Lonteen, Francis R., (Retired)
Lopez, Gonzalo, St. Michael the Archangel, Cleveland
Loutzenhiser, Joseph E., (Retired)
Lozada, Frank, (Retired)
Lundeen, David J., St. Mark, Cleveland
Lupson, Erick N., St. Angela Merici, Fairview Park
Makara, Stephen C. Jr., Queen of Heaven, Green
Maldonado, Louis, (Retired)
Malec, George P., St. Cyprian, Perry
Martin, Hardin M., St. Agnes-Our Lady of Fatima, Cleveland
Masony, Howard J., St. Mark, Cleveland
Matoney, Robert Jr., (Retired)
Matusicky, Daniel J., (Retired)
McGraw, Joseph E., (Released from Dio. Assignment); Union, KY
McKenna, J. Kevin, (Retired)
Meade, Kenneth C., Immaculate Conception, Madison
Medina, Ceferino, (Retired)
Merriman, William C., St. Patrick, Cleveland
Michney, Richard, Sacred Heart of Jesus, Wadsworth
Miranda, Ignacio, Sagrada Familia, Cleveland
Mueller, Richard A., St. Mary of the Falls, Olmstead Falls
Nethery, David T., St. Noel, Willoughby
Netzband, Ralph W., (Retired)
Norris, Daniel F., (Retired)
Novak, Andrew J., St. Cyprian, Perry
Novak, Neal J., St. Clarence, North Olmsted
Noveske, F. Gregory, St. Richard, North Olmsted
O'Donnell, James K., Gesu, University Heights
Ogan, Jay R., St. Peter, Lorain
Ortiz, Juan, (Retired)
Paoletta, Dean R., St. Patrick, Wellington
Paul, James Jr., St. Aloysius-St. Agatha, Cleveland
Payne, Willard C., St. Helen, Newbury
Peacock, Terry W., St. Sebastian, Akron
Pecek, Louis G., Ph.D., (Retired)
Pecot, David E., (Retired)
Pennypacker, Lindley W., (Retired), North Port, FL.
Perkins, William H., St. Martin of Tours, Valley City
Peshek, Thomas J., St. Mary, Chardon
Piechowski, Kenneth J., St. John Neumann, Strongsville
Piskach, Robert J., (Retired)
Polefko, Roger F., St. John Bosco, Parma Heights
Primozic, Louis M., St. Basil the Great, Brecksville
Proper, Scott T., Visitation of Mary, Akron
Ramos, Jose L., (Leave of Absence)
Reiland, George J. Jr., (Retired)
Rivera, Carlos, (Retired)

Rivera, John M., St. Augustine, Cleveland; St. Julie Billiart, North Ridgeville
Sabol, Robert G., St. Elizabeth Ann Seton, Columbia Station
Sanchez, Reinaldo, (Retired), Puerto Rico
Schill, William E., (Retired)
Schwartz, Robert F., St. Patrick, Thompson
Seal, J. David, (Retired)
Senn, Thomas J., (Retired)
Sferry, John P. Sr., (Retired)
Shell, Timothy J., St. Justin Martyr, Eastlake
Sheridan, Thomas, St. Ambrose, Brunswick
Sherman, Homer L., (Retired)
Shin, Charles C., St. Andrew Kim Pastoral Center, Cleveland
Simon, Frederick F., Sagrada Familia, Cleveland
Slatcoff, John K., St. Vincent De Paul, Elyria Township
Smith, Dennis L., Nativity of the Lord Jesus, Akron
Snyder, Wayne W., (Retired)
Somrack, Lawrence A., St. Helen, Newbury
Staab, William M., Blessed Trinity, Cleveland
Starkey, William R., St. Mary, Bedford
Stewart, James, (Retired)
Stokes, Troy F., (Retired)
Streeter, David A., Assumption, Broadview Heights; Deacon Representative, Clergy Personnel Board
Talerico, John A., St. Charles Borromeo, Parma
Tatulinski, Frank E., (Leave of Absence)
Tennant, Bruce H., St. Agnes, Elyria
Tomazic, Gary R., St. Ambrose, Brunswick
Toomey, Carl M., St. Mary Magdalene, Willowick
Torres, Epifanio, Sagrada Familia, Cleveland
Travalik, Peter M., St. Jerome, Cleveland
Travis, John, St. Ladislas, Westlake
Tweddell, Charles E., Holy Family, Parma
Varga, Carl M., Divine Word, Kirtland
Vincent, James C., St. Michael, Independence
Volek, Ronald J., (Released from Dio. Assignment); Lancaster, SC
Vrabel, Jerome B., (Retired)
Walcutt, Keith A., St. John Neumann, Strongsville
Walling, Robert K., Holy Spirit, Avon
Weglicki, Frank L. Jr., St. Ambrose, Brunswick
Wenzel, John T., St. Anthony of Padua, Fairport Harbor
Wilson, Francis B., (Retired)
Winterich, Carl H., St. Mary, Hudson
Woods, Richard E., (Retired)
Woyton, Louis M., (Retired)
Wunderle, Gregory A., St. Andrew the Apostle, Norton
Yantek, Mark C., Our Lady of Angels, Cleveland
Yates, Stephen L., (Released from Dio. Assignment); Chapel Hill, NC
Yoho, William J. Jr., Immaculate Heart of Mary, Cuyahoga Falls
Youngblood, Dale A., S.S. Peter and Paul, Doylestown
Youngblood, Robert A., Prince of Peace, Norton
Zawadzki, Charles W., (Retired)
Zdolshek, John R., (Retired)
Zerrer, Robert A., St. Mary of the Immaculate Conception, Wooster.

INSTITUTIONS LOCATED IN DIOCESE

[A] SEMINARIES, DIOCESAN

WICKLIFFE. *Borromeo Seminary* (1954) 28700 Euclid Ave., Wickliffe, 44092-2585. Tel: 440-943-7600; Fax: 440-943-7577; Email: mal@dioceseofcleveland.org; Web: www.borromeoseminary.org. Revs. Mark A. Latcovich, Ph.D., Pres. & Rector & Prof. Theology; Patrick S. Anderson, Dir.; Damian J. Ference, M.A., Ph.L., Dir.; John F. Loya, M.Div., M.A., Spiritual Dir.; Mr. Philip J. Guban, B.A., Treas.; Sr. Mary Quinlan, S.N.D., Registrar; Mr. Alan K. Rome, M.L.S., Librarian; Rev. Michael Joyce, O.F.M.Cap., Vicar Prov.; Dr. Ed Kaczuk, Ph.D., Music Dir.; Revs. Lester Knoll, O.F.M.Cap., CFP Staff/Spiritual Advisor; Anthony J. Marshall, S.S.S., Teacher, Religious Studies; Beth Rath, Ph.D., Teacher, Philosophy; Revs. Brian Stacy, OFM Cap, Spiritual Advisor/ Care Svcs.; Andrew B. Turner, M.Div., M.A., Vice Rector; Joel Johnson, Prof. Lay Teachers 3; Priests 9; Religious 1; Seminarians 48; Students 48; Clergy / Religious Teachers 3.

St. Mary Seminary and Graduate School of Theology (1948) (Our Lady of the Lake) 28700 Euclid Ave., Wickliffe, 44092-2585. Tel: 440-943-7600; Fax: 440-943-7577; Email: mal@dioceseofcleveland.org; Web: stmarysem.edu. Rev. Mark A. Latcovich, Ph.D., Pres. & Rector; Sr. Brendon Zajac, S.N.D., D.Min., Registrar & Asst. Academic Dean; Revs. Gerald J. Bednar, Ph.D., Vice Pres.; Andrew B. Turner, M.Div., M.A., Dir.; Mark L. Hollis, M.Div., Spiritual Dir.; Sr. Mary McCormick, O.S.U., Ph.D., Academic Dean; Revs. Michael G. Woost, S.T.L., Dean, Students; Mark S. Ott, Prof.; Lorenzo Tosco, C.S.J., S.S.L., Prof.; Joseph M. Koopman, S.T.D., Prof.; Sr. Lisa Belz, Prof.; Dr. Edward J. Kaczuk, Ph.D., Liturgy Dir.; Mr. Alan K. Rome, M.L.S., Librarian; Mr. Philip J. Guban, B.A., Treas. Clergy 11; Priests 11; Religious 4; Sisters 3; Students 111; Adjunct Faculty 9; Students for Priesthood, Diocesan 48; Permanent Diaconate 13; Other Dioceses 13; Clergy / Religious Teachers 24.

[B] COLLEGES AND UNIVERSITIES

CLEVELAND. *Notre Dame College* (1922) 4545 College Rd., South Euclid, 44121. Tel: 216-381-1680; Fax: 216-381-3802; Email: bjohnston@ndc.edu; Web: www.notredamecollege.edu. Thomas G. Kruczek, Pres.; Deborah Sheren, Chief Information Officer; Karen Zoller, Dir. Clara Fritzsche Library. Lay Teachers 59; Priests 1; Sisters of Notre Dame 6; Students 2,000; Total Staff 227.

Ursuline College (1871) 2550 Lander Rd., Pepper Pike, 44124. Tel: 440-449-4200; Fax: 440-646-8102; Email: ann.mcguire@ursuline.edu; Web: www.ursuline.edu. Sr. Christine DeVinne, O.S.U., Pres.; Timothy Reardon, Vice Pres. & CFO; Deanne Hurley, Vice Pres. Enrollment & Student Affairs; Richard Konisiewicz, Vice. Pres. Inst. Advancement. Students 1,124; Total Staff 231; Ursuline Sisters of Cleveland 7; Lay Professors 76.

UNIVERSITY HEIGHTS. *John Carroll Jesuit Community* (1886) 2520 Miramar Blvd., University Heights, 44118-3821. Tel: 216-397-1886; Email: jesuits@jcu.edu; Web: www.jcu.edu. Revs. Karl J. Kiser; Thomas Pipp, Rector; Nathaniel Romano, Pastoral Assoc.; Andrea Bianchini, Prof.; Paul C. O'Connor, S.J., Teacher; Angelo Munduni; Gerald J. Sabo, S.J.; William J. Murphy, S.J.; Michael A. Vincent, S.J.; Jayme Stayer, S.J.; Bernard F. McAniff, S.J. Priests 10; Students 3,800; Total Enrollment 3,724; Clergy / Religious Teachers 11; Clergy / Religious Teachers 11.

**John Carroll University* (1886) 1 John Carroll Blvd., University Heights, 44118. Tel: 216-397-1886; Tel: 216-397-4281; Email: jkrukones@jcu.edu; Web: www.jcu.edu. Michael Johnson, Pres.; Mr. Mark D. McCarthy, Vice Pres., Student Affairs; Dr. Edward J. Peck, Vice Pres., Univ. Mission & Identity; Ms. Doreen Riley, Vice Pres., Univ. Advancement; Dennis F. Hareza, Vice Pres., Fin. & CFO; Stephanie Levenson, Vice Pres.; Dr. Margaret Farrar, Dean, College of Arts & Sciences; Dr. Alan Miciak, Dean, Boler College of Business; Todd Bruce, Asst. Provost, IEA; Dr. James H. Krukones, Interim Academic Vice Pres.; Anne Kugler, Assoc. Dean, College of Arts & Sciences; Michael Martin, Assoc. Dean, College of Arts & Sciences; Dr. Walter Simmons, Assoc. Dean, Boler College of Business; Scott Moore, Assoc. Dean, Boler College of Business; Dr. Sherri Crahen, Assoc. Vice Pres., Student Affairs; Dr. Maryclaire Moroney, Asst. Provost, Academic Advising & Student Success; Ms. Michelle Millet, Dir., Grasselli Library. Priests 2; Students 3,600; Total Staff 410; Lay Faculty 177; Clergy / Religious Teachers 2.

[C] HIGH SCHOOLS, DIOCESAN

CLEVELAND. *Cleveland Central Catholic High School* (1968) 6550 Baxter Ave., 44105. Tel: 216-441-4700; Fax: 216-441-8353; Fax: 216-641-2045; Email: allisonmarie@centralcatholichs.org; Web: www.centralcatholichs.org. Sr. Allison Marie Gusdanovic, S.N.D., Prin.; Leo Hyland, Pres. Lay Teachers 46; Sisters 5; Students 545; Clergy / Religious Teachers 3.

Villa Angela-St. Joseph High School (1990) 18491 Lakeshore Blvd., 44119. Tel: 216-481-8414; Fax: 216-486-1035; Email: dcsank@vasj.com; Web: www.vasj.com. Mr. Bill Cervenik, Pres.; Mr. David M. Csank, Prin. Lay Teachers 40; Sisters 1; Students 461.

ELYRIA. *Elyria Catholic High School* (1948) (Coed) 725 Gulf Rd., Elyria, 44035. Tel: 440-365-1821; Fax: 440-365-7536; Web: www.elyriacatholic.com. Mrs. Amy Butler, M.A., Pres.; Suzanne Lester, Prin. Serving Elyria, Avon, Sheffield, North Ridgeville, Grafton, Oberlin, Amherst, Lorain, Avon Lake, Columbia Station, LaGrange, Litchfield, Medina, N. Olmsted, New London, Olmsted Falls, Valley City, Vermilion, Wakeman, Wellington and Westlake. Lay Teachers 33; Students 399; Clergy / Religious Teachers 3.

MENTOR. *Lake Catholic High* (1970) 6733 Reynolds Rd., Mentor, 44060. Tel: 440-578-1020; Fax: 440-974-9087; Email: info@lakecatholic.org; Web: www.lakecatholic.org. Mr. Mark Crowley, Pres.; Richard Koenig, Prin. Lay Teachers 40; Students 592.

PARMA HEIGHTS. *Holy Name High School* (Coed) 6000 Queens Hwy., Parma Heights, 44130. Tel: 440-886-0300; Fax: 440-886-1267; Email: shelbreyblanc@holynamehs.com; Email: kmulac@holynamehs.com; Web: www.holynamehs.com. Shelbrey Blanc, Prin.; Sr. Paula Greggila, Librarian. Lay Teachers 42; Sisters 1; Students 595; Administration 3.

[D] HIGH SCHOOLS, PRIVATE

CLEVELAND. *Benedictine High School*, 2900 Martin Luther King Dr., 44104-4898. Tel: 216-421-2080; Fax: 216-421-1100; Fax: 216-421-0107; Email: cbhs@cbhs.edu; Web: www.cbhs.edu. Rt. Rev. Gary Hoover, O.S.B., Chancellor; Frank Bossu, Pres.; Revs. Michael Brunovsky, O.S.B., Prof.; Bede Kotlinski, O.S.B., Classics Teacher; Finbar Ramsak, O.S.B, Theology Teacher; Anselm Zupka, O.S.B., German Teacher; Sue Zulandt, Prin.; Ms. Terri Wysocki, Business Mgr.; Mr. Christopher Lorber, Athletic Dir. Lay Teachers 29; Priests 4; Students 344; Clergy / Religious Teachers 2.

St. Edward High School (Boys) 13500 Detroit Ave., Lakewood, 44107. Tel: 216-221-3776; Fax: 216-221-4609; Email: jkubacki@sehs.net; Web: www.sehs.net. James P. Kubacki, Pres.; James Reed III, Prin.; Mrs. Jacqueline Wagner, Librarian. Brothers 1; Lay Teachers 85; Students 938; Total Staff 134.

St. Ignatius High School (1886) 1911 W. 30th St., 44113. Tel: 216-651-0222; Fax: 216-651-6313; Email: mcosgriff@ignatius.edu; Web: www.ignatius.edu. Revs. Raymond P. Guiao, S.J., Pres.; Paul Shelton, S.J., Teacher; Ross T. Pribyl, S.J.; Mr. Daniel Bradesca, Prin.; Mrs. Milena Streen, Librarian. Lay Teachers 120; Priests 5; Students 1,515; Clergy / Religious Teachers 4.

Saint Joseph Academy (1890) 3470 Rocky River Dr., 44111. Tel: 216-251-6788; Fax: 216-251-5809; Email: info@sja1890.org; Web: www.sja1890.org. Mary Ann Corrigan-Davis, Pres.; Jeff Sutliff, Prin. Lay Teachers 68; Students 719; Total Staff 117.

Magnificat High School (Girls) 20770 Hilliard Blvd., Rocky River, 44116. Tel: 440-331-1572; Fax: 440-331-7257; Web: www.magnificaths.org. Moira Clark, Pres.; Marilyn Arundel, Dean, Faculty & Academics; Ms. Jennifer Kirallah, Dir. Lay Teachers 70; Sisters 1; Students 690.

**St. Martin de Porres High School* (2003) 6202 St. Clair Ave., 44103. Tel: 216-881-1689; Fax: 216-881-8303; Web: www.saintmartincleveland.org. Charles Napoli, Pres.; John Fay, Prin. Lay Teachers 28; Students 400.

**St. Martin de Porres High School Work Study Program* (2004) 6111 Lausche Ave., 44103. Tel: 216-881-1689; Fax: 216-881-8303; Email: adavis@stmdphs.org. Martha Solarz, Admin.

AKRON. *Archbishop Hoban High School* (Coed) One Holy Cross Blvd., Akron, 44306. Dr. Todd R. Sweda, Pres.; Emily Ramos, Prin. Brothers of Holy Cross. Brothers 4; Deacons 1; Lay Teachers 63; Students 836.

Our Lady of the Elms School, (Grades PreK-12), 1375 W. Exchange St., Akron, 44313-7697. Tel: 330-867-0880; Fax: 330-864-6488; Email: dfarquharjones@theelms.org; Web: www.theelms.org. Deborah Farquhar-Jones, Pres.; Michael Gavin, Academic Dean. Lay Teachers 24; Sisters 1; Students 230; Clergy / Religious Teachers 1.

St. Vincent-St. Mary High School, 15 N. Maple St., Akron, 44303. Tel: 330-253-9113; Fax: 330-996-0020; Email: webmaster@stvm.com; Web: www.stvm.com. Thomas M. Carone, Pres.; Robert Brownfield, Prin; Ms. Amy Barcelo, Dir.; Stella Weigand, Dir., Fin.; Mr. Gino D'Andrea, Dir.; Mr. Thomas McKrill, Dean; Christopher Salvatore, Campus Min.; Pamela Godshalk, Librarian. Lay Teachers 50; Students 639.

CHARDON. *Notre Dame-Cathedral Latin School*, 13000 Auburn Rd., Chardon, 44024. Tel: 440-286-6226; Fax: 440-286-7199; Email: ndcl@ndcl.org; Web: www.ndcl.org. Mr. Joseph A. Waler, M.A., M.Ed., Prin.; Mrs. Denice Teeples, M.S., M.A.T., Asst. Prin.; Mr. Christopher Poulos, Asst. Prin.; Sarah Reed, Co-Dir. Campus Ministry; Beth Davis, Co-Dir., Campus Ministry. Sisters of Notre Dame. Lay Teachers 68; Sisters 5; Students 704; Clergy / Religious Teachers 1.

CLEVELAND HEIGHTS. *Beaumont School*, 3301 N. Park Blvd., Cleveland Heights, 44118. Tel: 216-321-2954; Fax: 216-321-3947; Email: advancement@beaumontschool.org; Web: www.beaumontschool.org. Mrs. Wendy Hoke, Pres.; Mr. Nicholas Beyer, Prin.; Ms. Lisa Andreani, Treas. Ursuline Sisters. Lay Teachers 40; Sisters 4; Students 326.

CUYAHOGA FALLS. *Walsh Jesuit High School*, 4550 Wyoga Lake Rd., Cuyahoga Falls, 44224. Tel: 330-929-4205; Tel: 800-686-4694 (Cleveland);

Fax: 330-929-9749; Email: info@walshjesuit.org; Web: www.walshjesuit.org. Rev. Mark Carr, Prin.; Karl Ertle, Pres.; Revs. Donald J. Petkash, S.J., Religious Supr. & Vice Pres. Mission & Identity; Paul C. O'Connor, S.J., Pastoral Ministry; Kenneth A. Styles, S.J., Pastoral Ministry. Lay Teachers 79; Priests 5; Students 1,010; Clergy / Religious Teachers 4.

GARFIELD HEIGHTS. *Trinity High School*, 12425 Granger, Garfield Heights, 44125.
Tel: 216-581-1644; Fax: 216-581-9348; Email: bachol@ths.org; Web: www.ths.org. Sr. Shawn Lee, S.S.J.-T.O.S.F., Pres.; Dennise Strobl, Dir. of Fin.; Ms. Carla E. Fritsch, Spec. Asst. to Pres.; Mrs. Linda Bacho, Prin.; Mr. William Svoboda, Asst. Prin. & Dir. of Rel. Form.; Patrick Straffen, Dir. of Advancement. Sisters of St. Joseph of the Third Order of St. Francis. Lay Teachers 30; Sisters 3; Students 360.

GATES MILLS. *Gilmour Academy*, (Grades PreK-12), 34001 Cedar Rd., Gates Mills, 44040-9356.
Tel: 440-473-8000; Email: admission@gilmour.org; Email: kennyk@gilmour.org; Web: www.gilmour.org. Mark Haag, Dir. Lower School; Ryan Ryzner, Dir.; Kathleen C. Kenny, Head of School; Mr. Fred G. Botek, Chm., Bd. of Trustees; J. Brian Horgan, Dir.; Rev. John Blazek, C.S.C., Campus Min. Congregation of Holy Cross.Day and Resident College Preparatory School. Brothers 3; Lay Teachers 69; Priests 1; Residents 70; Students 642; Clergy / Religious Teachers 2.

PARMA. *Padua Franciscan High School* (1961) 6740 State Rd., Parma, 44134. Tel: 440-845-2444;
Fax: 440-845-5710; Email: padua@paduafranciscan.com; Web: www.paduafranciscan.com. Rev. Allan DaCorte, O.F.M., Pres.; Tom Harkness, Vice Pres. of Institutional Advancement; David G. Stec, Prin.; Bro. Tom Carroll, O.F.M., Vice Prin.; Matthew Harley, Campus Minister; Alexandra Frech, Librarian. Brothers 1; Lay Teachers 66; Priests 1; Students 784.

[E] ELEMENTARY SCHOOLS

AKRON. *Our Lady of the Elms School*, (Grades PreK-12), 1375 W. Exchange St., Akron, 44313-7108.
Tel: 330-867-0880; Tel: 330-864-7210;
Fax: 330-836-9351; Fax: 330-867-1262; Email: mgavin@theelms.org; Web: www.theelms.org. Deborah Farquhar-Jones, Pres.; Michael Gavin, Prin. Lay Teachers 34; Students 239; Clergy / Religious Teachers 1.

CHARDON. *Notre Dame Elementary School* (1957) (Grades PreK-8), 13000 Auburn Rd., Chardon, 44024. Tel: 440-279-1127; Fax: 440-286-1235; Web: www.ndes.org. Barbara Doering, Prin.; Mrs. Sabrina Mysyk, Librarian. Clergy 2; Lay Teachers 36; Sisters 10; Students 490; Clergy / Religious Teachers 3.

Notre Dame PreSchool (2000) 13000 Auburn Rd., Chardon, 44024. Tel: 440-279-0575; Web: ndes.org. Barbara Doering, Prin.; Ms. Jessica Tvergyak, Preschool Dir. Lay Teachers 6; Sisters of Notre Dame 1; Students 57; Clergy / Religious Teachers 1.

HUDSON. *Seton Catholic School* (1997) 6923 Stow Rd., Hudson, 44236. Tel: 330-342-4200;
Fax: 330-342-4276; Email: fritzp@setoncatholicschool.org; Web: www.setoncatholicschool.org. Mrs. Karen Alestock, Prin.; Tim Conti, Chm.; Mrs. Annie Deemer, Asst. Prin.; Lisa Garrison, Librarian. Lay Teachers 32; Students 423.

PARMA HEIGHTS. *Incarnate Word Academy* (1930) (Grades PreK-8), 6620 Pearl Rd., Parma Heights, 44130. Tel: 440-842-6818; Fax: 440-888-1377; Email: jcicerchi@incarnatewordacademy.org; Email: cmiller@incarnatewordacademy.org; Web: incarnatewordacademy.org. Mrs. Janette Cicerchi, Prin.; Carli Kistler-Miller, Admin.; Sr. Rosemarie Burke, S.I.W., Campus Min. Lay Teachers 26; Students 396; Clergy / Religious Teachers 1.

[F] ELEMENTARY SCHOOLS, PAROCHIAL AND DIOCESAN

CLEVELAND. *Archbishop James P. Lyke Elementary School*, 18230 Harvard Ave., 44128.
Tel: 216-991-9644; Fax: 216-991-9470; Email: schlykesthenry@dioceseofcleveland.org; Web: www.archbishoplykeschool.org. Mrs. Margarete W. Smith, Prin. Students 162.

St. Francis School, 7206 Myron Ave., 44103.
Tel: 216-361-4858; Fax: 216-361-1673; Email: embachers@stfranciscleveland.org. Scott Embacher, Prin.; Liz Niehaus, Librarian. Lay Teachers 15; Students 215.

Metro Catholic School (1988) (Grades PreK-8), 3555 West 54, 44102. Tel: 216-631-5733;
Fax: 216-634-2853; Email: metro@leeca.org; Web: www.metrocatholic.org. Sr. Anne Maline, S.N.D., Co-Dir.; Mary Lou Toler, Co-Dir. Lay Teachers 50; Preschool 42; Ursuline Nuns 12; Students (K-8) 502; Clergy / Religious Teachers 12.

St. Stephen Bldg. (Grade 5-8), (Grades 5-8), 1910 W. 54th St., 44102. Tel: 216-281-4044;
Fax: 216-634-2853; Email: malinea@metrocatholic.net; Web: www.metrocatholic.org. Robert Finkovich, Admin. Clergy 14; Lay Teachers 18; Students 250.

St. Michael Bldg. (Grades 2-4), 1910 W. 54th St., 44102. Tel: 216-281-4044; Fax: 216-634-2853; Email: metro@leeca.org; Web: www.metrocatholic.org. Sr. Karen Bohan, O.S.U., Asst. to Dir. Clergy 4; Lay Teachers 12; Students 150.

St. Boniface Bldg. (PreK-1), 3555 W. 54th St., 44102. Tel: 216-631-5733; Fax: 216-634-2853; Email: sch_metro@dioceseofcleveland.org; Web: www.metrocatholic.org. Angela Weinrich, Asst. to Dir.; Jeanna Forhan, Librarian. Students 152.

St. Thomas Aquinas School (2010) (Grades K-8), 9101 Superior Ave., 44106. Tel: 216-421-4668;
Fax: 216-721-8444; Email: sch_stthomasaquinas@dioceseofcleveland.org. Katy Rankin, Prin.; Sr. Domicele Yestonsky, S.N.D., Librarian. Lay Teachers 16; Students 187.

Urban Community School, 4909 Lorain Ave., 44102.
Tel: 216-939-8441; Fax: 216-939-8198; Email: mdoyle2401@aol.com. Sr. Maureen Doyle, O.S.U., Dir.; Mrs. Elizabeth DeCore, Prin.; Elizabeth Allard, Librarian. Lay Teachers 37; Students 571.

GARFIELD HEIGHTS. *St. Benedict Catholic School*, (Grades K-8), 13633 Rockside Rd., Garfield Heights, 44125. Tel: 216-662-9380;
Fax: 216-662-3137; Email: loriti@stbenedictohio.com; Web: www.stbenedictohio.com. Lisa Oriti, Prin.; Christine Malone, Admin. Lay Teachers 24; Sisters 2; Students 384; Clergy / Religious Teachers 2.

LAKEWOOD. *Lakewood Catholic Academy* (includes Holy Family Learning Center) 14808 Lake Ave., Lakewood, 44107. Tel: 216-521-0559;
Fax: 216-521-0515; Email: info@lcasaints.com; Web: www.lakewoodcatholicacademy.com. Mr. Brian Sinchak, Pres.; Brenna Warrell, Prin. Clergy 1; Lay Teachers 80; Students 630.

LYNDHURST. *Corpus Christi Academy*(2016)5655 Mayfield Rd., Lyndhurst, 44124. Tel: 440-449-4244 ; Fax: 440-449-1497; Email: office@corpuschristiacad.org; Web: www.corpuschristiacad.org. Kenneth Mitskavich, Prin. Lay Teachers 17; Students 205.

WICKLIFFE. *All Saints of St. John Vianney School* (1977) (Grades PreK-8), 28702 Euclid Ave., Wickliffe, 44092. Tel: 216-943-1395;
Fax: 216-943-4468; Email: info@allsaintssjv.com; Web: www.allsaintssjv.org. Terri Armelli, Prin.; Mrs. Paula Kirchner, Librarian; Mrs. Debra Sobkowich, Sec. Lay Teachers 24; Sisters 1; Students 337.

Mater Dei Academy (2010) (Grades PreK-8), Formerly Immaculate Conception School, Willoughby and Our Lady of Mt. Carmel School, Wickliffe 29840 Euclid Ave., Wickliffe, 44092.
Tel: 440-585-0800; Fax: 440-569-1438; Email: info@MaterDeiAcademy.us; Web: www.MaterDeiAcademy.us. Joanie Klemens, Prin.; Marietta Hrach, Librarian. Clergy 3; Lay Teachers 28; Students 416.

[G] SPECIAL SCHOOLS AND CENTERS For Exceptional Children

CLEVELAND.

Julie Billiart School (1954) 4982 Clubside Rd., Lyndhurst, 44124-2596. Tel: 216-381-1191;
Fax: 216-381-2216; Email: ldavis@jbschool.org; Web: www.juliebilliartschool.org. Lannie Davis-Frecker, M.Ed., Pres. School for children with special learning needs. Lay Teachers 30; Sisters 3; Students 126.

CHARDON.

Julie Billiart Network (2016) 4982 Clubside Rd., Lyndhurst, 44124. Tel: 216-381-1191; Email: ssweigert@jbschool.org; Web: www.juliebilliartschool.org. Alaine Davis, Contact Person.

AKRON.

Julie Billiart School of St. Sebastian Parish, Akron (2015) (Grades K-5), 380 Mineola Ave., Akron, 44320. Tel: 234-206-0941; Tel: 216-381-1191; Email: ssweigert@jbschool.org; Web: www.juliebilliartschool.org. 4982 Clubside Rd., Lyndhurst, 44124. Jason Wojnicz, Prin. School for children with special learning needs Clergy 1; Lay Teachers 12; Students 51; Clergy / Religious Teachers 1.

[H] PRESCHOOL AND DAY CARE CENTERS

GARFIELD HEIGHTS. *Marymount Child Care Center* (1991) 12215 Granger Rd., Garfield Heights, 44125. Tel: 216-581-3540; Fax: 216-518-2188; Email: marymountcare@aol.com. Michelle C. Kreiger, Dir. Sisters 1; Tot Asst. Annually 120; Total Staff 15.

LAKEWOOD. *Holy Family Learning Center*, 14808 Lake Ave., Lakewood, 44107. Tel: 216-521-4352;
Fax: 216-521-0515; Email: hflcsko@yahoo.com; Web: www.holyfamilylearningcenter.com. Sr. Kathleen Ogrin, O.S.U., Dir., H.F.L.C. Lay Teachers 32; Sisters 1; Total Staff 33; Total Assisted 115.

[I] GENERAL HOSPITALS

(For information on other Catholic related hospitals please contact the Chancery Office.)

CLEVELAND.

St. John Hospital, 2475 E. 22nd St., 44115.
Tel: 216-696-5560; Fax: 216-696-2204; Web: www.sistersofcharityhealth.org. Thomas Strauss, Pres. & CEO.

Marymount Hospital, Inc., 12300 McCracken Rd., Garfield Heights, 44125. Tel: 216-587-8080;
Fax: 216-587-8212; Email: napierd@ccf.org; Web: www.marymount.org. Dr. Daniel Napierkowski, Pres.; Rev. Dennis Mrosso; Joseph Rinderknecht, Dir. Pastoral Care; Sr. Jo Ann Poplar, S.S.J.-T.O.S.F., Staff Chap.; Ms. Janet Elaine McDonald, Staff Chap. Bed Capacity 277; Sisters of St. Joseph of the Third Order of St. Francis 3; Tot Asst. Annually 82,847; Total Staff 1,175.

St. Vincent Charity Medical Center, 2351 E. 22nd St., 44115. Tel: 216-861-6200; Fax: 216-696-2204; Web: www.stvincentcharity.org. David Perse, M.D., Pres. & CEO.

LORAIN.

Mercy Health - Allen Hospital, LLC (Ministry/Activity of Mercy Health of the Archdiocese of Cincinnati) 200 W. Lorain Street, Oberlin, 44074. Email: catherine.woskobnick@mercy.com. 3700 Kolbe Rd., Lorain, 44053. Tel: 440-776-7000. Catherine Bartek-Woskobnick, Admin.; Ms. Charlotte Wray, Admin. Bed Capacity 25; Tot Asst. Annually 39,032; Total Staff 195.

Mercy Health - Regional Medical Center, LLC (Ministry/Activity of Mercy Health of the Archdiocese of Cincinnati) 3700 Kolbe Rd., Lorain, 44053. Tel: 440-960-4000; Email: catherine.woskobnick@mercy.com. Catherine Bartek-Woskobnick, Admin.; Edwin Oley, Admin. Bed Capacity 317; Tot Asst. Annually 135,000; Total Staff 2,000.

[J] SPECIAL HOSPITALS

CLEVELAND. *Rose Mary, The Johanna Grasselli Rehabilitation and Education Center*, 2346 W. 14th St., 44113. Tel: 216-481-4823;
Fax: 216-481-4154; Email: contact@rosemarycenter.com; Web: rose-marycenter.com. Gina Kerman, Contact Person. Bed Capacity 98; Children 21; Residents 98; Tot Asst. Annually 200; Total Staff 300.

[K] HOMES FOR AGED

CLEVELAND. *St. Augustine Manor* dba St. Augustine Health Ministries (1969) 7801 Detroit Ave., 44102.
Tel: 216-634-7400; Fax: 216-634-7483; Email: advancement@st-aug.org; Web: www.staugministries.org. Rick Meserini, Pres. & CEO; Mark Seryak, Chair; Frank Huba, CFO; Dana Carns, Dir. Advancement; Rev. Januarius Lyimo, A.J., Chap. Provides a continuum of residential and community based services primarily for chronically ill and older adults. Sisters 5; Tot Asst. Annually 1,796; Total Staff 445.

St. Augustine Health Campus Skilled Nursing Facility (1969) 7801 Detroit Ave., 44102.
Tel: 216-939-7602; Fax: 216-939-7483. Anita Gerrasch, Admin. Skilled nursing, rehabilitation and long-term care. Total in Residence 234.

St. Augustine Towers Assisted Living Residencies (1996) 7821 Lake Ave., 44102. Tel: 216-634-7444;
Fax: 216-634-2717. Brigid Nolan, Dir. Total Apartments 99.

Holy Family Home Health Care & Hospice (1956) 6707 State Rd., Parma, 44134. Tel: 440-888-7722;
Fax: 440-866-6040; Email: info@holyfamilyhome.com; Web: www.holyfamilyhome.com. Kristin Graham, Dir.; Rev. Simon Kimaryo, Chap. Home health care, private duty care at home, palliative care and inpatient & community-based hospice care. Bed Capacity 30; Patients Asst Anual. 752.

Older Adult Services, 7801 Detroit Ave., 44102. Mary Jo Zeller, Prog. Coord. West Rose/Mt. Carmel, Tel.: 216-631-7717, Fax: 216-631-3006. Home delivered and congregate meals to home-bound seniors.; Broadway Golden Hours, Tel.: 216-441-0111, Fax: 216-441-6290. Home delivered meals to home-bound seniors. West Rose/Mt. Carmel Participants 150; Broadway Golden Hours Participants 94.

St. Augustine Child Enrichment Center (1999) 7801 Detroit Ave., 44102. Tel: 216-939-7681;
Fax: 216-939-7298. Stephanie Moore, Dir. Early learning and child day care for children ages 6 weeks to preschool. Capacity 102.

Little Sisters of the Poor dba Sts. Mary and Joseph

Home for the Aged, 4291 Richmond Rd., 44122-6199. Tel: 216-450-1225; Fax: 216-464-8435; Email: devcleveland@littlesistersofthepoor.org; Web: www.littlesistersofthepoorcleveland.org. Sr. Loraine Maguire, Prov. Little Sisters of the Poor. Sisters 3; Total Staff 2.

Mount St. Joseph, 21800 Chardon Rd., 44117. Tel: 216-531-7426; Fax: 216-531-4033; Email: sister-raphael@msjorg.net. Sr. M. Raphael Gregg, NHA. Conducted by Sisters of St. Joseph of St. Mark - Mount St. Joseph. Bed Capacity 100; Residents 100; Sisters 7; Tot Asst. Annually 201; Total Staff 147.

AKRON. *Francesca Residence*, 39 N. Portage Path, Akron, 44303. Tel: 330-867-6334; Fax: 330-867-6334; Email: martinovich00@hotmail.com. Sr. M. Martin Green, F.D.C., Admin. Daughters of Divine Charity 6; Tot Asst. Annually 30; Total in Residence 25; Total Staff 11.

BEDFORD. *Light of Hearts Villa, Inc.*, 283 Union St., Bedford, 44146. Tel: 440-232-1991; Fax: 440-735-3429; Web: www.lightofheartsvilla.org. Elizabeth J. Hickle, Exec. Dir. Bed Capacity 90; Total in Residence 90; Total Staff 80; Total Assisted 68.

FAIRLAWN. *The Village at St. Edward* (1964) 3131 Smith Rd., Fairlawn, 44333. Tel: 330-666-1183; Email: danielle.maur@vased.org; Web: www.vased.org. John P. Stoner, Pres. & CEO; Rev. David A. Novak, Chap. Sisters 1; Total Staff 300; Nursing Care Residents 81; Assisted Living Residents 90.

The Village at St. Edward (1990) 3131 Smith Rd., Fairlawn, 44333. Tel: 330-668-2828; Email: danielle.maur@vased.org; Web: www.vsecommunities.org. John P. Stoner, Pres. & CEO; Rev. David A. Novak, Chap. The Village at St. Edward was changed to The Village of St. Edward (this is a dba of St. Edward Home) Bed Capacity 259; Tot Asst. Annually 400; Total in Residence 259; Total Staff 260.

GARFIELD HEIGHTS. *Jennings Center for Older Adults* Jennings (1942) 10204 Granger Rd., Garfield Heights, 44125. Tel: 216-581-2900; Fax: 216-581-4505; Web: www.jenningscenter.org. Allison Q. Salopeck, Pres. & CEO. Sponsored by the Sisters of the Holy Spirit, Jennings offers a continuum of residences and services for adults, including independent and assisted living, long-term care, skilled nursing and rehabilitation, and community-based services in four locations. Sisters 2; Tot Asst. Annually 1,100; Total Staff 348.

Jennings Assisted Living, 10204 Granger Rd., Garfield Heights, 44125. Tel: 216-581-2900; Fax: 216-581-4505; Email: welcome@jenningscenter.org; Web: www.jenningscenter.org. Allison Q. Salopeck, Contact Person. Studio 1; One Bedroom Suites 51; Two Bedroom Suites 2.

Jennings Hall Skilled Nursing Facility, 10204 Granger Rd., Garfield Heights, 44125. Tel: 216-581-2900; Fax: 216-581-4505; Email: welcome@jenningscenter.org; Web: www.jenningscenter.org. Allison Q. Salopeck, Contact Person. Skilled Nursing Facility Bed Capacity 174.

Jennings Manor Housing Corporation (1998) 10204 Granger Rd., Garfield Heights, 44125. Tel: 216-581-2900; Fax: 216-581-4505; Email: welcome@jenningscenter.org; Web: www.jenningscenter.org. Allison Q. Salopeck, Contact Person. Apartment Building for HUD Section 202 Supportive Housing for the Elderly Total Apartments 61.

Jennings Operating, LLC, 10204 Granger Rd., Garfield Heights, 44125. Tel: 216-581-2900; Fax: 216-581-4505; Email: allison.salopeck@jenningsohio.org; Web: www.jenningsohio.org. Allison Q. Salopeck, Contact Person.

Jennings Real Estate, LLC, 10204 Granger Rd., Garfield Heights, 44125. Tel: 216-581-2900; Fax: 216-581-4505; Email: allison.salopeck@jenningsohio.org; Web: www.jenningsohio.org. Allison Q. Salopeck, Contact Person.

Holy Spirit Villas (1998) 10204 Granger Rd., Garfield Heights, 44125. Tel: 216-581-2900; Fax: 216-581-4505; Email: welcome@jenningscenter.org; Web: www.jenningscenter.org. Allison Q. Salopeck, Contact Person. Independent Housing Units 10.

St. Agnes Terrace Apartments Independent Housing 10204 Granger Rd., Garfield Heights, 44125. Tel: 216-581-2900; Fax: 216-581-4505; Email: welcome@jenningscenter.org; Web: www.jenningscenter.org. Allison Q. Salopeck, Contact Person. Apartments 42.

St. Rita Apartments, 10204 Granger Rd., Garfield Heights, 44125. Tel: 216-581-2900; Fax: 216-581-4505; Email: welcome@jenningscenter.org; Web: www.jenningscenter.org. Allison Q. Salopeck, Contact Person. Apartments 63.

Eva L. Bruening Adult Day Center (2003) 10204 Granger Rd., Garfield Heights, 44125. Tel: 216-581-2900; Fax: 216-581-4505; Email: welcome@jenningscenter.org; Web: www.jenningscenter.org. Allison Q. Salopeck, Contact Person. Bed Capacity 50; Clients Per Day Capacity 50.

The Learning Circle Child Day Care Center (1999) 10204 Granger Rd., Garfield Heights, 44125. Tel: 216-581-2900; Fax: 216-581-4505; Email: welcome@jenningscenter.org; Web: www.jenningscenter.org. Allison Q. Salopeck, Contact Person. Infant to before and after school care. Capacity 75.

Village at Marymount, 5200 Marymount Village Dr., Garfield Heights, 44125. Tel: 216-332-1100; Fax: 216-332-1619; Email: jmyers@ccf.org; Web: www.villageatmarymount.org. Mr. Jeffry Myers, Pres.; Sr. Mary Alice Jarosz, S.S.F.-T.O.S.F., Dir. Mission Svcs.; Rev. Ted Haag, O.F.M., Priest Chap. Village at Marymount provides comprehensive health care services in response to the needs of the local community by leasing and operating health care facilities and services, including Marymount Place, a 104-unit Senior Living Community for the Well-Elderly/Assisted Living and Villa St. Joseph, a 142-bed long-term facility (under an Operating Agreement with Marymount Health Care Systems within the philosophy and objectives of the Sisters of St. Joseph of the Third Order of St. Francis.) Bed Capacity 246; Tot Asst. Annually 1,173; Total Staff 360.

PARMA. *Mount Alverna Village* (Ministry/Activity of Franciscan Communities, Inc. of the Archdiocese of Chicago). Franciscan Communities, Inc. d/b/a Mount Alverna Village 11500 Theresa Dr., Lemont, IL 60439. Tel: 440-843-7800; Fax: 440-843-7107; Email: pwelsh@franciscancommunities.com; Web: www.franciscancommunities.com/facilities/mtalverna. Patrick M. Welsh, Exec. Dir.; Peggy McNulty, Dir. of Mission Integration; Joseph McCartney, Dir. of Pastoral Care. Capacity 183; Residents 153; Total Staff 253; Assisted Living 30; Total Assisted 183.

RICHFIELD. *Regina Health Center* (1992) 5232 Broadview Rd., Richfield, 44286-9608. Tel: 330-659-4161; Fax: 330-659-5113; Email: myantek@reginahealthcenter.org. Mark Yantek, Exec. Dir. Sponsored by Sisters of Charity of St. Augustine. Bed Capacity 155; Total in Residence 143; Total Staff 185; Nursing Home Beds 101; Assisted Living Units 54; Total Assisted 44.

[L] MONASTERIES AND RESIDENCES OF PRIESTS AND BROTHERS

CLEVELAND. *Benedictine Order of Cleveland* St. Andrew Abbey, St. Andrew Abbey, 10510 Buckeye Rd., 44104-3725. Tel: 216-721-5300; Fax: 216-721-1253; Email: wysocki@cbhs.edu; Web: www.standrewabbey.org. Rt. Rev. Gary Hoover, O.S.B., Abbot; Most Rev. Roger W. Gries, O.S.B., D.D., M.Ed., Auxiliary Bishop of Cleveland, (Retired). Brothers 7; Priests 18. 1230 Ansel Rd., 44108. Tel: 216-721-0676; Fax: 216-721-0903. Rt. Rev. Clement Zeleznik, O.S.B., Chap., Loyola Retreat House, (Retired); Revs. Bede Kotlinski, O.S.B.; Joachim Pastirik, O.S.B.; Gerard Gonda, O.S.B., Pres. Benedictine High School; Timothy Buyansky, O.S.B., Prior; Dominic Mondzelewski, O.S.B.; Placid Pientek, O.S.B.; Rt. Rev. Gary Hoover, O.S.B., Admin. Abbot; Revs. Paschal Petcavage, O.S.B.; Justin Dyrwal, O.S.B., Pastor of Assumption. *Assumption Church*, 9183 Broadview Rd., Broadview Heights, 44147. Tel: 440-526-1177; Fax: 440-526-2838; Email: finbar@cbhs.edu. Rev. Finbar Ramsak, O.S.B, Contact Person.

Other Assignments: Rev. Finbar Ramsak, O.S.B, Vocation Dir.; Rt. Rev. Christopher Schwartz, O.S.B., Abbot, (Retired), Incarnate Word Academy, 6634 Pearl Rd., 44130-3898. Tel: 440-886-6996; Revs. Michael Brunovsky, O.S.B., Prin., Benedictine High School, St. Andrew, 5135 Superior Ave., 44130. Tel: 216-431-2057; Dismas Boeff, O.S.B., St. Peter, 6455 Engle Rd., 44142. Tel: 216-433-1440; Fax: 216-433-1434; Kenneth J. Katricak, O.S.B., St. Andrew Abbey, 2900 M.L. King Dr., 44104. Tel: 216-721-5300; Anselm Zupka, O.S.B.

Congregation of the Blessed Sacrament, 5384 Wilson Mills Rd., 44143-3092. Tel: 440-442-6311; Fax: 440-442-2001; Email: susandwork@yahoo.com; Web: blessedsacrament.com. Very Rev. Anthony Schueller, S.S.S., Prov. Supr.; Revs. John Thomas Lane, S.S.S., Pastor; John Christman, S.S.S.; Roger Bourgeois, S.S.S.; Rev Robert Chabot, Sac. Min.; Revs. Joselito Hitosis, S.S.S.; Paul Bernier, S.S.S.; Deacon Joseph Bourgeois; Bros. Gary L. Laverdiere, S.S.S.; Allen Boeckman, S.S.S. Brothers 3; Deacons 1; Priests 12. *Regina Health Center*, 5232 Broadview Rd., Richfield, 44286-9608. Tel: 330-659-4161; Email: myantek@reginahealthcenter.org. Rev. Andrew Beaudoin, S.S.S.; Bro. Eugene Blee, S.S.S. Brothers 3; Priests 4.

Congregation of the Blessed Sacrament Provincial House, 5384 Wilson Mills Rd., Highland Heights, 44143-3092. Tel: 440-442-6311; Fax: 440-442-4752; Email: susandwork@blessedsacrament.com; Web: www.blessedsacrament.com. Very Rev. Anthony Schueller, S.S.S., Prov. Supr. Province of St. Ann.

Priests attached to Provincialate: Revs. Andrew Beaudoin, S.S.S., 11487 Kerridale Ave., Spring Hill, FL 34608-3111. Tel: 352-686-8078; John Christman, S.S.S.

Maryknoll Fathers & Brothers (1911) 10309 Edgewater Dr., 44102. Tel: 216-651-2121; Fax: 216-651-8242; Email: mklcleve@aol.com; Web: www.maryknoll.org. Rev. James H. Huvane, M.M., Dir. Total in Residence 1; Total Staff 1.

Mercedarians (1218) 6928 Detroit Ave., 44102-3093. Tel: 216-651-5043; Fax: 216-651-6641; Email: olmc.cleveland@gmail.com; Web: orderofmercy.org. Rev. Richard S. Rasch, O.de.M., Contact Person. Order of the B.V.M. of Mercy. Priests 3; Mercedarian Sisters (H.M.S.S.) 5; Total Staff 35. In Res. Revs. Richard S. Rasch, O.de.M., Vicar Provincial & Pastor; Jerome P. Laubacker, O.de.M.; Justin Freeman, O.de.M., Chap., Metro Hospital; Bro. Martin J. Jarocinski, O.de.M., Sec. & Sacristan.

St. Paul Friary, 4120 Euclid Ave., 44103. Tel: 216-431-8854; Email: Stpaulshrine@sbcglobal.net; Web: www.saintpaulshrine.com. Bro. Robert Toomey, Vicar; Revs. David Nestler; Robert Marva, O.F.M.Cap.; Samuel Driscoll, O.F.M.Cap., Confessor; Roger Massawe, O.F.M.Cap., Chap.; Deacon Akolla Etuge. Brothers 1; Priests 5.

St. Agnes-Our Lady of Fatima, 6800 Lexington Ave., 44103. Tel: 216-391-1655; Fax: 216-391-7919; Email: brotherbob@saolf.org. Rev. Robert Marva, O.F.M.Cap.; Deacon Hardin M. Martin. Capuchin Franciscan Friars.

St. Stanislaus Friary (1906) 3649 E. 65th St., 44105-1293. Tel: 216-341-9091; Fax: 216-341-2688; Email: ststans@ameritech.net; Web: www.ststanislaus.org. Rev. Eric S. Orzech. The Franciscan Friars, Province of the Assumption of the Blessed Virgin.(Please see St. Stanislaus, Cleveland in the parish section for additional information.)*Marymount Convent*, Garfield Heights, 44125. Tel: 216-587-8376.

AVON. *Congregation of St. Joseph* (1873) 4076 Case Rd., Avon, 44011. Tel: 440-934-6270; Email: lato@roadrunner.com; Web: www.murialdo.org. Revs. Angelo Zonta, C.S.J., Dir.; Lawrence Tosco, C.S.J., Treas.

Legal Titles: Fathers and Brothers of St. Joseph Brothers 3; Priests 2.

BROOKLYN. *St. Anthony of Padua Friary* (1960) 4185 Brookway Ln., Brooklyn, 44144. Tel: 314-409-1111; Email: allanofm@me.com. Revs. Allan DaCorte, O.F.M.; Theodore Haag, O.F.M.; James Kelly, O.F.M.; Bro. Thomas Carroll, O.F.M., Guardian. Brothers 1; Priests 3.

[M] CONVENTS AND RESIDENCES FOR SISTERS

CLEVELAND. *Carmel of the Holy Family* (1923) 2541 Arlington Rd., 44118-4009. Tel: 216-321-6568; Email: barb.carmel@gmail.com; Web: www.clevelandcarmel.org. Sr. Barbara Losh, O.C.D., Prioress. Discalced Carmelite Nuns. Sisters 8.

Congregation of the Sisters of St. Joseph, Inc. dba Congregation of St. Joseph, Cleveland Center, 3430 Rocky River Dr., 44111-2997. Tel: 216-252-0440; Fax: 216-941-3430; Web: www.csjoseph.org. Sisters Kathleen Brazda, Pres.; Patricia Warbritton, Treas. Sisters 476.

Monastery of the Poor Clares (1877) Poor Clare Nuns (Colettine) 3501 Rocky River Dr., 44111-2998. Tel: 216-941-2820; Fax: 216-941-9298; Email: ppcnuns@gmail.com. Mother Mary Dolores Warner, PCC, Supr. Observing the Primitive Rule of St. Clare (strictly cloistered, solemn vows). Perpetual exposition of the Blessed Sacrament. Cloistered Nuns 15; Extern Sisters 2.

Motherhouse and Novitiate of the Sisters of the Holy Spirit (1932) 10102 Granger Rd., 44125. Tel: 216-581-2941; Fax: 216-581-1207; Email: sisterpatricia.raelene@jenningscenter.org. Sr. Patricia Raelene Peters, C.S.Sp., Supr. Gen. Professed Sisters 2.

Motherhouse and Novitiate of the Ursuline Sisters (1850) 2600 Lander Rd., 44124. Tel: 440-449-1200; Fax: 440-449-3588; Email: sdurkin@ursulinesisters.org; Web: www.ursulinesisters.org. Sr. Susan Durkin, O.S.U., Pres.

The Ursuline Academy of Cleveland Professed Nuns 141.

Poor Clares of Perpetual Adoration, 4108 Euclid

Ave., 44103. Tel: 216-361-0783; Email: angelspcpa@sbcglobal.net; Web: thepoorclares.com. Mother Mary James, P.C.P.A., Supr. Monastery adjoins Conversion of St. Paul Shrine, where they maintain Perpetual Adoration. Cloistered Sisters 21.

Provincial House of Sisters of the Most Holy Trinity, 21281 Chardon Rd., 44117. Tel: 216-481-8232; Fax: 216-481-6577; Email: osst@srstrinity.com; Web: www.srstrinity.com. Sr. M. Rochelle Guertal, O.S.S.T., Regl. Delegate. Attended from Center for Pastoral Leadership. Sisters 17; Total in Residence 15.

Sisters of St. Joseph of St. Mark General Motherhouse and Novitiate of Sisters of St. Joseph of St. Mark-Generalate, Diocese of Cleveland 21800 Chardon Rd., 44117-2199. Tel: 216-531-7426 ; Fax: 216-383-0511; Email: sr_mpaschal_msj@yahoo.com. Sr. M. Raphael Gregg, Gen. Supr. Sisters 5.

AKRON. *Dominican Sisters of Peace* (1929) Our Lady of the Elms Convent, 1230 W. Market St., Akron, 44313-7108. Tel: 330-836-4908; Fax: 330-836-5913; Web: www.oppeace.org. 1375 W Exchange St., Akron, 44313-7619. Sr. Valerie Shaul, O.P., Motherhouse & Mission Group Coord. Sisters 451; Total in Akron Motherhouse 26.

CHARDON. *Provincial House of the Sisters of Notre Dame, Juniorate, Novitiate* (1874) Notre Dame Education Center, 13000 Auburn Road, Chardon, 44024. Tel: 440-286-7101; Fax: 440-286-3377; Email: mgorman@ndec.org; Web: www.sndchardon.org. Sr. M. Patricia Teckman, Admin. Sisters 270.

GARFIELD HEIGHTS. *Marymount Congregational Home* (1926) 12215 Granger Rd., Garfield Heights, 44125. Tel: 216-581-2101; Fax: 216-518-2187; Web: www.ssj-tosf.org. Sr. Joyce Hollkamp, S.S.J.-T.O.S.F., Business & Facilities Coord. Residence of the Sisters of St. Joseph, Third Order of St. Francis. Sisters 23.

PARMA HEIGHTS. *Sisters of the Incarnate Word and Blessed Sacrament* (1625) 6618 Pearl Rd., Parma Heights, 44130-3808. Tel: 440-886-6440, Ext. 401; Email: smtaylor.incarnatewordorder@yahoo.com. Sr. Margaret Taylor, S.I.W., Congregational Leader

Sisters of the Incarnate Word and Blessed Sacrament Sisters 18.

6634 Pearl Rd., Parma Heights, 44130-3808. Tel: 440-886-6440.

RICHFIELD. *The Sisters of Charity of St. Augustine* (1851) 5232 Broadview Rd., Richfield, 44286-9608. Tel: 330-659-5100; Fax: 330-659-3899; Email: jak@srsofcharity.org; Web: www.srsofcharity.org. Sr. Judith Ann Karam, C.S.A., Congregational Leader. Final Professed Sisters 28.

Regina Health Center (1993) Tel: 330-659-4161; Fax: 330-659-5113. Skilled Nursing Beds 101; Religious Congregations 22; Total Assisted Care 54.

[N] SECULAR INSTITUTES

NORTH ROYALTON. *Society of Our Lady of the Way/ Madonna della Strada* (1936) c/o Mary Ann Tady, 12750 N. Star Dr., North Royalton, 44133, Tel: 216-381-5502; Email: matslow@aol.com; Web: www.saecimds.com. Miss Mary Ann Tady, Member. Secular Institute for Single Women.

[O] HOMES FOR WOMEN

AKRON. *Leonora Hall* (1946) 39 N. Portage Path, Akron, 44303. Tel: 330-867-1752; Fax: 330-867-6334; Email: martinorich00@hotmail.com. Sr. M. Antoinette, F.D.C., Exec. Dir. Leonora Hall Residence "is a Home Away From Home" for Women who are working, going to school or unable to live independently. Semi-independent/supported living services are also provided for women with mild/moderate developmental disabilities in collaboration with Summit County Board of Developmental Disabilities Residents 11; Daughters of Divine Charity 2; Personnel 4.

[P] LAY ASSOCIATIONS

CLEVELAND. *Community of Little Brothers and Sisters of the Eucharist, Inc.* (1977) 2182 E. 35th St., 44115-3039. Tel: 216-566-0531; Fax: 216-566-0531; Email: littlesismaggie@gmail.com. Rev. James P. O'Donnell, Dir., (Retired).

**Society of St. Vincent de Paul, Diocesan Council*, Cathedral Square Plaza, 1404 E. 9th St., 3rd Fl., 44114. Tel: 216-696-6525; Fax: 216-861-3200; Email: JPatton@svdpcle.org. Robert Reuter, Pres.; John Patton, Exec.

[Q] RETREAT HOUSES

CLEVELAND. *Jesuit Retreat House* Jesuit Retreat Center (1898) 5629 State Rd., Parma, 44134. Tel: 440-884-9300; Fax: 440-885-1055; Email: jrhcleve@att.net; Web: www.jrh-cleveland.org. Richard S. Krivanka, Dir.

AVON. *St. Leonard Youth Retreat Center* (1998) 4076 Case Rd., Avon, 44011. Tel: 440-934-6735; Email: stleonardyrc@gmail.com; Web: www.stleonardyrc.com. Mr. Robert O'Donnell, Dir.; Rev. Lorenzo Tosco, C.S.J., S.S.L., Contact Person. Capacity 80.

[R] SOCIAL SERVICE AGENCIES AND INSTITUTIONS

CLEVELAND. *Catholic Charities Corporation*, 7911 Detroit Ave., 44102. Tel: 216-334-2900; Fax: 216-334-2907; Email: pgareau@ccdocle.org; Web: www.ccdocle.org. Mr. Patrick Gareau, Pres. & CEO; Wayne Peel, CFO; Lisa Black, Gen. Counsel; Patricia Holian, Exec. Vice Pres.; Fredy Robles, Exec.; Samantha Mealy, Dir. Mktg. & Communications. Tot Asst. Annually 419,073; Total Staff 900.

Catholic Charities Annual Appeal, 7911 Detroit Ave., 44102. Tel: 216-334-2900; Fax: 216-334-2983 ; Email: smealy@ccdocle.org; Web: www.ccdocle.org. Total Staff 1.

Catholic Charities Community Services, 7911 Detroit Ave., 44102. Tel: 216-334-2937; Fax: 216-334-2907; Email: gawurstner@ccdocle.org; Web: www.ccdocle.org. Ms. Joan Hinkelman, Exec. Tot Asst. Annually 5,290; Total Staff 108.

Catholic Charities Community Services of Ashland County, 34 W. Second St., Ste. 18, Ashland, 44805-2000. Tel: 419-289-1903; Fax: 419-281-8342; Email: svillegas@ccdocle.org. Ms. Sheryl Villegas, Dir.

Catholic Charities of Cuyahoga County, 3135 Euclid Ave., 44115-2507. Tel: 216-391-2030; Fax: 216-391-8946; Email: medee@clevelandcatholiccharities.org; Web: www.ccdocle.org. Maureen Dee, Exec. Dir. A multi-function social service agency which offers social service programs. Individual, family, and group counseling; marital counseling, psychiatric consultations; and outpatient psychiatric services for children, youth, and adults. Chemical dependency assessments and outpatient counseling for youth and families having alcohol and other drug-related problems. Bilingual services for Hispanic youth and families. Tot Asst. Annually 6,433; Total Staff 59.

Catholic Charities Community Services of Geauga County, 602 South St., Ste. D1, Chardon, 44024. Tel: 800-242-9755; Fax: 440-285-4909; Email: mbertman@ccdocle.org; Web: www.ccdocle.org. Ms. Michelle Bertman, Dir.; James Clements, Dir. Tot Asst. Annually 2,151; Total Staff 11.

Catholic Charities Community Services of Lake County, 8 N. State St., Ste. 455, Painesville, 44077-3954. Tel: 440-946-7264; Fax: 440-953-1608 ; Email: ecurriemanring@ccdocle.org; Web: www.ccdocle.org. Emily Currie-Manring, Dir. Tot Asst. Annually 4,562; Total Staff 18.

Catholic Charities Community Services of Lorain County, 628 Poplar St., Elyria, 44035. Tel: 440-366-1106; Fax: 440-366-5645. Bonita Shumpert, Dir. Tot Asst. Annually 354; Total Staff 24.

Catholic Charities Community Services of Medina County, 4210 N. Jefferson, Ste. A, Medina, 44256. Tel: 330-723-9615 (Medina); Fax: 330-764-8795 (Medina); Email: makipfstuhl@ccdocle.org; Web: www.ccdocle.org. Michelle Kipfstuhl, Dir. Tot Asst. Annually 2,432; Total Staff 21.

Catholic Charities Community Services of Summit County, 812 Biruta St., Akron, 44307-1104. Tel: 330-762-2961; Fax: 330-762-2001; Email: contactus@ccdocle.org; Web: www.ccsummitcounty.org. Ms. Catherine Thier, Dir. Total Staff 179; Total Assisted 15,273.

Catholic Charities Community Services of Wayne County, 521 Beall Ave., Wooster, 44691-3523. Tel: 330-262-7836; Fax: 330-262-2867; Email: svillegas@ccdocle.org. Ms. Sheryl Villegas, Dir.

Camp Christopher, Ira & Hametown Rd., Bath, 44210. Tel: 800-296-2267; Fax: 330-762-2001; Email: campchristopher@ccdocle.org. Ms. Catherine Thier, Dir.

Family Centers & Early Learning Programs, Tel: 216-334-2936; Email: jhinkelman@ccdocle.org. Ms. Joan Hinkelman, Sr. Dir. Tot Asst. Annually 5,290; Total Staff 108.

Parmadale (1925) 6753 State Rd., Parma, 44134. Tel: 440-845-7700; Fax: 440-845-5910; Email: pdale@clevelandcatholiccharities.org; Web: www.ccdocle.org. Maureen Dee, Dir. Chemical Dependency Treatment; Community-Based Family Services; Specialized Foster Care; Outpatient Services; Training and Consultation Services; and Volunteer Program; Adoption Services; Head Start.

St. Phillip Neri Family Center, 799 E. 82nd St., 44103. Tel: 216-391-4415; Email: awinfield@ccdocle.org. Autumn Winfield, Dir.

Fatima Family Center, 6600 Lexington Ave., 44103. Tel: 216-391-0505; Fax: 216-391-1118; Email: ljray@ccdocle.org. LaJean Ray, Dir.

St. Martin de Porres Family Center, 1264 E. 123rd St., 44108-4042. Tel: 216-268-3909; Fax: 216-268-0207; Email: mmckenzie@ccdocle.org. Karnese McKenzie, Dir.

Hispanic Senior Center, 7800 Detroit Ave., 44102. Tel: 216-939-3714; Fax: 216-631-3654; Email: esantos@ccdocle.org. Evelyn Santos, Prog. Dir.

Employment & Training Services, 799 E. 82nd St., 44103. Tel: 216-426-9870; Fax: 216-426-9932; Email: awinfield@ccdocle.org. Autumn Winfield, Dir.

Head Start, 7911 Detroit Ave., 44102-2815. Tel: 216-334-2942; Fax: 216-334-2948. Linda Schettler, Dir. Children 722; Lay Teachers 50.

Catholic Charities Early Learning Centers

Arbor Park, 3750 Fleming Ave., 44115. Tel: 216-431-4818; Fax: 216-431-4255; Email: jhinkelman@ccdocle.org. Linda Schettler, Dir.

Catholic Charities Emergency and Specialized Services, 7911 Detroit Ave., 44102. Tel: 216-334-2961; Fax: 216-334-2983; Email: tjflanagan@ccdocle.org; Web: www.ccdocle.org. Melissa Sirak, Dir. Emergency assistance, hunger network, parish partnerships. Tot Asst. Annually 119,741; Total Staff 22.

Bishop William M. Cosgrove Center (1994) 1736 Superior Ave., 44114. Tel: 216-781-8262; Fax: 216-566-9161; Email: contactus@ccdocle.org. Mr. Eric Milkie, Dir. Tot Asst. Annually 5,210; Total Staff 8.

Marriage & Family Office, 7911 Detroit Ave., 44102. Tel: 216-334-2978; Fax: 216-334-2976; Email: whboomer@ccdocle.org; Web: ccdocle.org/mfm. William Boomer, M.A., Dir. Total Staff 5.

Office for Human Life, 7911 Detroit Ave., 44102. Tel: 216-334-2965; Fax: 216-334-2976; Email: pmgerovac@clevelandcatholiccharities.org. Peggy Gerovac, Dir.

Migration & Refugee Services, 7800 Detroit Ave., 44102. Tel: 216-281-7005; Fax: 216-939-3890; Email: contactus@ccdocle.org. Tom Mrosko, Dir. Tot Asst. Annually 1,561; Total Staff 32.

Ministry to Persons with Disabilities, 2486 W. 14th St., 44113. Tel: 216-781-5530; Email: mjscott@ccdocle.org. Marilyn Scott, Contact Person.

Catholic Charities Disabilities Services, 7911 Detroit Ave., 44102. Tel: 216-334-2962; Fax: 216-334-2905; Email: mjscott@ccdocle.org. Marilyn Scott, Contact Person. Tot Asst. Annually 15,414; Total Staff 5.

Youth and Young Adult Ministry & CYO, 7911 Detroit Ave., 44102. Tel: 216-334-1261; Fax: 216-334-1270; Email: dxmoser@ccdocle.org. Dobie Moser, Dir. Tot Asst. Annually 41,272; Total Staff 19.

Catholic Charities Treatment, Prevention and Recovery Services, 3135 Euclid Ave., Rm. 202, 44115-2507. Tel: 216-391-2030; Fax: 216-391-8946; Email: medee@clevelandcatholiccharities.org; Web: www.ccdocle.org. Maureen Dee, Exec. Dir., Email: medee@ccdocle.org. Catholic Charities-Treatment, Prevention and Recovery Services is part of the health and human services delivery system of the Diocese. Utilizing a holistic approach to healing, the system focuses on meeting the behavioral health needs of children and families in Cuyahoga County. Tot Asst. Annually 6,433; Total Staff 59.

LaProvidencia Family Center, 1515 W. 29th St., 44113. Tel: 216-696-2197; Fax: 216-696-2088; Email: medee@ccdoclev.org. Ms. Ramonita Rodriguez-Johnson, Dir.

Matt Talbot for Recovering Men, 6753 State Rd., Parma, 44134. Tel: 440-345-3020; Fax: 440-345-3019. Ms. Jennifer Tulli, Dir. Tot Asst. Annually 97; Total Staff 15.

Matt Talbot Inn, 6753 State Rd., Parma, 44134. Tel: 440-843-5522; Fax: 440-843-1627; Email: jtulli@ccdocle.org. Ms. Jennifer Tulli, Dir. Tot Asst. Annually 871; Total Staff 21.

Matt Talbot for Women, 7901 Detroit Ave., 44115. Tel: 216-634-7500; Fax: 216-939-7720; Email: jtmarinich@ccdoclev.org. Judy Marinich, Clinical Suprv. Tot Asst. Annually 210; Total Staff 38.

The Covenant, 1515 W. 29th St., 44113. Tel: 216-574-9000; Fax: 216-664-6534; Email: medee@ccdoclev.org. Maureen Dee, Exec. Dir. Youth & family mental health & chemical dependency counseling. Tot Asst. Annually 722; Total Staff 22.

Diocesan Social Action Office, 7911 Detroit Ave., 44102. Tel: 216-939-3843. Diane Zbasnik, Contact Person.

Catholic Action Commission of Lorain County, 628 Poplar St., Lorain, 44052. Tel: 440-366-1106; Web: www.ccdocle.org/dsao. Mr. Daniel Alonso, Dir.

Catholic Campaign for Human Development, 7911 Detroit Ave., 44102. Tel: 216-939-3841; Email:

amclark@ccdocle.org; Web: www.ccdocle.org/dsao. Mrs. Ann Clark, Dir.

Catholic Commission of Lake/Geauga Counties, 28700 Euclid Ave., Wickliffe, 44092. Tel: 440-943-7612; Web: www.ccdocle.org/dsao. Ms. Kelly Davis, Dir.

Catholic Commission of Summit County, 795 Russell Ave., Akron, 44307. Tel: 330-535-2787. Diane Zbasnik, Dir.

Catholic Commission of Wayne, Ashland and Medina Counties, 4210 N. Jefferson St., Ste. A, Medina, 44256. Tel: 330-723-9615, Ext. 11. Mr. Jeff Campbell, Dir.

Catholic Relief Services - Operation Rice Bowl, 28700 Euclid Ave., Wickliffe, 44092. Tel: 440-943-7612. Ms. Kelly Davis, Dir.

Diocese of Cleveland Facilities Services Corp., 1404 E. 9th St., 44114. Tel: 216-696-6525; Fax: 216-902-1314; Email: lmurtaugh@dioceseofcleveland.org. Mr. Lawrence E. Murtaugh, Exec. Dir. Total Staff 20.

St. Malachi Center, Inc., 2416 Superior Viaduct, 44113. Tel: 216-771-3036; Fax: 216-771-3659; Email: anita@stmalachicenter.org; Web: www.stmalachicenter.org. Anita Branan, Contact Person. Total Staff 10; Medical Clinic (Fridays) for the Homeless Annual Patients 144; Total Assisted Daily 100.

Malachi House, Inc., 2810 Clinton Ave., 44113. Tel: 216-621-8831; Fax: 216-621-8841; Email: jhilow@malachihouse.org; Email: vrains@malachihouse.org; Web: www.malachihouse.org. Mrs. Judy Ghazoul Hilow, Dir.; Veronica Rains, Sec. Malachi House provides unskilled, family-like care to the dying poor without cost. Serves individuals who need an available caregiver, who have limited or no financial resources and are in need of special home care in the final stages of life. Tot Asst. Annually 110; Total Staff 25.

AKRON. *Interval Brotherhood Home* dba I.B.H. Addiction Recovery Center (1970) 3445 S. Main St., Akron, 44319. Tel: 330-644-4095; Fax: 330-645-2031; Email: dpfinn@ibh.org. Donald P. Finn, Dir. Bed Capacity 65; Tot Asst. Annually 365; Total Staff 88; Total in Residential Treatment 367.

LORAIN. *St. Elizabeth Center*, 2726 Caoline Ave., Lorain, 44055. Tel: 440-242-0056; Email: lwricehead@ccdocle.org. Lynn Wrice-Head, Contact Person. Tot Asst. Annually 2,856; Total Staff 16.

NORTHFIELD. *St. Barnabas Villa, Inc.* (1985) 9234 Olde Eight Rd., Northfield, 44067. Tel: 330-467-3758; Fax: 330-908-1186; Email: stbarnabasvilla@yahoo.com. Natalie Priest, Dir.; Mary Anne Cody, Asst. Mgr. A shared living facility for 11 people over 60 years of age. Bed Capacity 11; Total in Residence 11; Total Staff 16.

PARMA. *Parkview*, 5210 Loya Pkwy., Parma, 44134. Tel: 440-345-3001; Email: lschettler@ccdocle.org. Linda Schettler, Contact Person.

Regional Services, 6753 State Rd., Parma, 44134. Tel: 440-843-5649; Email: aivancic@ccdocle.org. Angela Ivancic, Chief Clinical Officer.

WELLINGTON. **St. Patrick Manor, Inc. c/o Humility of Mary Housing, Inc.*, 2251 Front St. Ste. 210, Cuyahoga Falls, 44221. Tel: 234-525-6400; Fax: 330-384-2144; Email: fberry@hmhousing.org; Web: www.hmhousing.org. 120 Maple St., Wellington, 44090. Dolly Lee, Site Mgr. Bed Capacity 50; Tot Asst. Annually 60; Total Staff 3; Units (Independent Living) 50.

[S] SHRINES

CLEVELAND. *Our Lady of Lourdes Shrine* Euclid, (U.S. Rtes. 20 & 6). Administered by the Sisters of the Most Holy Trinity. 21281 Chardon Rd., 44117. Tel: 216-481-8232; Fax: 216-481-6577; Email: osst@srstrinity.com; Web: www.srstrinity.com. Sr. M. Rochelle Guertal, O.SS.T., Regl. Supr. Total in Residence 15.

St. Paul Shrine The Conversion of St. Paul Shrine, 4120 Euclid Ave., 44103. Tel: 216-431-8854; Email: srcarmelpcpa@gmail.com. Revs. Roger Massawe, O.F.M.Cap., Rector; Samuel Driscoll, O.F.M.Cap., Confessor Asst. to Rector.

GARFIELD HEIGHTS. *Our Lady of Czestochowa Shrine* (Ohio Rte. 17). Administered by the Sisters of St. Joseph Third Order of St. Francis (S.S.J.-T.O.S.F.) 12215 Granger Rd., Garfield Heights, 44125. Fax: 216-518-2187; Tel: 216-518-2101. Sr. Joyce Hollkamp, S.S.J.-T.O.S.F., Business & Facilities Coord.

PARMA HEIGHTS. *Queen of the Holy Rosary Shrine* (U.S. Rte. 42). Administered by the Sisters of the Incarnate Word and Blessed Sacrament (S.I.W.) 6618 Pearl Rd., Parma Heights, 44130-3808. Tel: 440-886-6440, Ext. 401; Email: smtaylor.incarnatewordorder@yahoo.com; Web: www.incarnatewordorder.org. Sr. Margaret Taylor, S.I.W., Supr.

[T] MINISTRY TO THE SPANISH SPEAKING

CLEVELAND. *Office of Hispanic Ministry*, Diocese of Cleveland, 1404 E. 9th St., 44114. Tel: 216-696-6525; Fax: 216-861-3200; Email: mmayorga@dioceseofcleveland.org; Web: www.dioceseofcleveland.org/hispanicministry. Misael Mayorga, Dir.

Hispanic Parishes: Iglesia La Sagrada Familia, 7719 Detroit Ave., 44102. Tel: 216-631-6817; Fax: 216-631-3305; Email: sagrada1997rob@yahoo.com. Rev. Robert J. Reidy.

Sacred Heart Chapel, 4301 Pearl Ave., Lorain, 44055. Tel: 440-277-7231; Tel: 440-277-7232; Fax: 440-277-4886; Email: sacredheartchapellorain@gmail.com. Rev. William A. Thaden, Admin.

Parishes with Ministry to Spanish Speaking: St. Bernard, 44 University Ave., Akron, 44308. Tel: 330-253-5161; Fax: 330-253-6949; Email: djreed@stbernardstmary.org. Rev. Daniel J. Reed.

St. Michael, 3114 Scranton Rd., 44109. Tel: 216-621-3847; Web: smarcangel.wixsite.com/44109. Revs. Dennis R. O'Grady, (Retired); Mark R. Riley; Sr. Miriam Fidelis, Sacramental Min.; Ms. Nory Maldonado, Sec. Religious 1; Tot Asst. Annually 7,200; Total Staff 7; Registered Parishioner Households 803; Infant Baptisms (up to age 7) 34; Minor Baptisms (ages 7 to 17) 13; Adult Baptisms (18 & older) 1.

St. Mary's - Painesville, 242 N. State St., Painesville, 44077. Tel: 440-354-4381; Fax: 440-354-9174; Email: stevevellenga@yahoo.com. Rev. R. Stephen Vellenga.

Our Lady of Lourdes, 3395 E. 53rd St., 44127. Tel: 216-641-2829 (Rectory & Office); Fax: 216-641-0043; Email: ourladyoflourdescle@yahoo.com; Web: www.ourladyoflourdes-cle.org. Rev. Joseph H. Callahan. Tot Asst. Annually 1,000; Total Staff 4.

St. Mary of the Immaculate Conception, 527 Beall Ave., P.O. Box 109, Wooster, 44691. Tel: 330-264-8824; Tel: 330-264-8822; Fax: 330-262-4633; Email: stmarywoost@embarqmail.com. Judith Caraballo-Arzuaga, Dir., Hispanic Ministry, (Wayne, Ashland & Medina Districts); Rev. Stephen P. Moran.

[U] NEWMAN CENTERS

CLEVELAND. *Office of Newman Catholic Campus Ministry*, 1404 E. 9th St., 44114. Tel: 216-696-6525, Ext. 2450; Fax: 216-579-9655; Email: jszarwark@dioceseofcleveland.org; Web: www.ocfecleveland.org. Rev. Vincent J. Hawk, Dir.; Joann Piotrkowski, Asst. DIr. Total Staff 8; Newman Centers 7.

Case-Western Reserve University, 11205 Euclid Ave., 44106. Tel: 216-421-9614, Ext. 302; Email: sperry@dioceseofcleveland.org. Steve Perry, Campus Min.

University of Akron, Newman Center, 44 University Ave., Akron, 44308. Tel: 330-376-3585; Tel: 216-696-6525; Fax: 216-696-8646; Email: jszarwark@dioceseofcleveland.org. John Szarwark, Campus Min. & Asst. Dir., Newman Campus Min. (Akron).

Baldwin-Wallace College Newman Center, 170 E. Center St., Berea, 44017. Tel: 440-243-4955; Email: seyerman@dioceseofcleveland.org. Steve Eyerman, Campus Min. (Berea).

Oberlin College, Tel: 216-696-6525; Email: jszarwark@dioceseofcleveland.org. Andrew J. Hoy, Campus Min.; John Szarwark, Contact Person.

The College of Wooster, 1473 Beall Ave., Wooster, 44691. Tel: 330-263-2364; Fax: 330-263-2534; Email: jtrejo@dioceseofcleveland.org. Andrew J. Hoy, Campus Min. (Wooster).

University of Ashland, 220 E. Butler St., Loudonville, 44842. Tel: 419-994-4396; Email: nediger@dioceseofcleveland.org. Rev. Vincent J. Hawk, Campus Min.; Nate Ediger, Campus Min.

Cleveland State University, 1404 E. 9th Street, 44114.

[V] ENDOWMENT TRUSTS

CLEVELAND. *St. John Cathedral Endowment Trust*, 1007 Superior Ave. E., 44114-2582. Tel: 216-771-6666; Fax: 216-781-5646; Email: stjohns@dioceseofcleveland.org; Web: www.saintjohncathedral.com. Revs. Arnel A. Lagman, Parochial Vicar; Sean P. Ralph, M.Div., M.A.

Poor Clares Perpetual Adoration Foundation of Cleveland, Ohio, 4108 Euclid Ave., 44103. Tel: 330-996-4090; Email: Barb@pcpafnd.org; Web: www.pcpafnd.org. 134 Western Ave, Akron, 44313. Sharon Deitrick, Pres.

The Thomas C. and Sandra S. Sullivan Foundation, 1404 E. 9th St., 8th Fl., 44114. Tel: 216-696-6525, Ext. 4080; Fax: 216-348-0740; Email: crigo@catholiccommunity.org; Web: www.catholiccommunity.org. Mr. Patrick J. Grace, Exec. Dir.; Mrs. Terri Preskar, Dir., Stewardship.

Villa Angela-St. Joseph High School Education Endowment Trust (1990) 18491 Lakeshore Blvd., 44119. Tel: 216-481-8414; Fax: 216-486-1035; Email: bcervenik@vasj.com; Web: www.vasj.com. Mr. Bill Cervenik, Pres.; Mr. David M. Csank, Prin.; Timothy Neary, Dean, Academics; Mr. Thomas Erzen, Dean.

AKRON. *The Daughters of Divine Charity, St. Mary Province, Charitable Trust*, 39 N. Portage Path, Akron, 44303-1183. Tel: 330-867-4960; Fax: 330-867-6334; Email: mmmissy@outlook.com. Sr. M. Martin Green, F.D.C., Contact Person.

CUYAHOGA FALLS. *HMH Foundation*, 2251 Front St., Ste. 210, Cuyahoga Falls, 44221. Tel: 234-525-6400; Fax: 330-384-2144; Email: fberry@hmhousing.org; Web: www.hmhousing.org. Fred Berry, Pres.

CHARDON. *The Sisters of Notre Dame Charitable Trust*, 13000 Auburn Rd., Chardon, 44024. Tel: 440-286-7101; Fax: 440-286-3377; Email: mgorman@ndec.org; Web: www.sndchardon.org. Sr. Margaret Mary Gorman, S.N.D., Chm.

FAIRLAWN. *St. Hilary Parish Foundation*, 2750 W. Market St., Fairlawn, 44333. Cell: 330-608-4787; Fax: 330-869-2312; Email: d.sarkis@sthilaryfoundation.org; Web: www.StHilaryFoundation.org. Frederick M. Lombardi, Pres.; Diane Sarkis, Devel. Dir.

MENTOR. *St. Mary of the Assumption Parish Endowment Trust* (1857) 8560 Mentor Ave., Mentor, 44060-5853. Tel: 440-255-3404; Fax: 440-255-4194; Email: tgelsass@ameritech.net; Web: www.stmarysmentor.org. Karen Goebel, Contact Person. Priests 1.

PARMA HEIGHTS. *Incarnate Word Academy Student and Faculty Advancement Endowment (IWA Endowment)* (2002) 6620 Pearl Rd., Parma Heights, 44130. Tel: 440-842-6818; Fax: 440-888-1377; Email: cmiller@incarnatewordacademy.org; Web: www.incarnatewordacademy.com. Carli Kistler-Miller, Dir. Advancement; Janette Cicerchi, Prin.

Incarnate Word Endowment Trust (1986) 6618 Pearl Rd., Parma Heights, 44130-3808. Tel: 440-886-6440, Ext. 401; Email: smtaylor.incarnatewordorder@yahoo.com; Web: www.incarnatewordorder.org. Sr. Margaret Taylor, S.I.W., Congregational Leader.

ROCKY RIVER. *Friends of the Poor Clares Foundation*, 3701 Hunting Run Rd., Medina, 44256. Tel: 216-903-9080. John Grillo, Pres.

SHAKER HEIGHTS. *St. Dominic Endowment Fund* (2003) 3450 Norwood Rd., Shaker Heights, 44122. Tel: 216-991-1444; Fax: 216-491-0190; Email: kmqua@yahoo.com; Web: www.stdominicchurch.net. Rev. Thomas G. Fanta, Pres.

WELLINGTON. *St. Patrick Church Endowment Trust* (1990) 512 N. Main St., Wellington, 44090. Tel: 440-647-4375; Email: secretary@stpatrickwellington.com. Rev. David Trask, Contact Person.

WOOSTER. *St. Mary of the Immaculate Conception Elementary Day School Endowment Trust* (1990) 527 Beall Ave., P.O. Box 109, Wooster, 44691. Tel: 330-264-8824; Fax: 330-262-4633; Email: stmarywoosteroffice@gmail.com; Web: stmarywooster.org. Karen Goebel, Contact Person.

[W] MISCELLANEOUS

CLEVELAND. **St. Augustine Services Corporation*, 7801 Detroit Ave., 44102. Tel: 216-634-7400; Fax: 216-634-7483; Email: rmeserini@st-aug.org. Rick Meserini, Pres. Total Staff 7.

Catholic Charities Housing Corporation (CCHC), 1404 E. Ninth St., 44114. Tel: 216-696-6525, Ext. 1501; Fax: 216-902-1314; Email: lmurtaugh@dioceseofcleveland.org. Mr. Lawrence E. Murtaugh, Exec. Dir.

Catholic Community Connection, 2475 E. 22nd St., 5th Fl., 44115. Tel: 216-875-4613; Tel: 216-875-4606; Fax: 216-696-2204; Email: vhawkins@sistersofcharityhealth.org. Marian R. Rubin, M.B.A., Pres.

Congregation of the Sisters of St. Joseph Charitable Trust, 3430 Rocky River Dr., 44111-2997. Tel: 216-252-0440. Sr. Marguerite O'Brien, Chm.

Congregation of the Sisters of St. Joseph Ministries, Inc. CSJ Ministries, 3430 Rocky River Rd., 44111-2997. Tel: 269-492-9390; Email: jfleischhacker@csjoseph.org. Janet Fleischhacker, Dir.

CSJ Initiatives, Inc. (2014) 3430 Rocky River Dr., 44111-2997. Tel: 316-689-4005; Email: kdavis@csjinitiatives.org; Web: www.csjinitiatives.org. 3700 East Lincoln St., Wichita, KS 67218. Mr. Denise Gannon, C.E.O.

First Friday Club of Cleveland, Inc., 1404 E. Ninth St., Ste. 100, 44114. Tel: 440-390-0172; Email: firstfridayofcleveland@gmail.com. Greg Spielman, Pres.; Cheryl Zelenka, Sec.

Joseph House of Cleveland, Inc. (1914) 6108 St. Clair Ave., 44103. Tel: 440-256-1412; Tel: 216-431-7200;

Fax: 440-256-4929; Web: josephhouseofcleveland.org. Rev. David G. Woost, Pastor, Divine Word, Kirtland. (Partnership 1993) Total Staff 1.

L'Arche, Cleveland (1975) P.O. Box 20450, 44120. Tel: 216-721-2614; Fax: 216-229-2311; Email: office@larchecleveland.org; Web: www.larchecleveland.org. Ms. April Boone, Dir. An ecumenical community providing homes for adults with developmental disabilities. Residents 14; Total Staff 33.

Mercedarian Apartments, Inc., 1404 E. Ninth St., 44114. Tel: 216-696-6525; Fax: 216-902-1314; Email: lmurtaugh@dioceseofcleveland.org. 329 Fulton Avenue, 44109. Mr. Lawrence E. Murtaugh, Pres.

Ninth Street CDC, 1404 E. Ninth St., Ste. 701, 44114-1722. Tel: 216-696-6525; Fax: 216-781-7732; Email: kburke@dioceseofcleveland.org. James Gulick, Pres.

Pulaski Franciscan Community Development Corp. (2001) 3649 E. 65th St., 44105. Tel: 216-341-9091. Rev. Eric S. Orzech.

River's Edge A Place for Reflection and Action, 3430 Rocky River Dr., 44111. Tel: 216-688-1111; Email: maureen@riversedgecleveland.com; Web: www.riversedgecleveland.com. Maureen S. Powers, Exec. Dir.

Sisters of Charity Foundation of Cleveland (1996) 2475 E. 22nd St., 4th Fl., 44115. Tel: 216-241-9300; Web: www.socfcleveland.org. Susanna H. Krey, Pres.

Sisters of Charity of St. Augustine Health System, 2475 E. 22nd St., 44115. Tel: 216-696-5560; Fax: 216-696-2204; Web: www.sistersofcharityhealth.org. Thomas Strauss, Pres. & CEO. Serves as the Member of St. Vincent Charity Medical Center and foundations and health and human service corporations sponsored by Sisters of Charity Health System Ministries, a public juridic person of pontifical right. Serves as one of two members of the joint venture corporation operating St. John Medical Center.

Sisters of St. Joseph, 3430 Rocky River Dr., 44111-2997. Tel: 216-252-0440; Fax: 216-941-3430. Mary Zavoda, Contact Person.

St. Vincent Charity Development Foundation, 2351 E. 22nd St., 44115. Tel: 216-875-4624; Email: foundation@stvincentcharity.com; Web: stvincentcharity.com. Timothy O'Callahan, Exec.

**St. Vitus Development Corporation* (2000) 6019 Lausche Ave., 44103. Tel: 216-361-1444; Fax: 216-361-1445; Email: skuhar@hotmail.com. Stane Kuhar, Sec. & Contact Person; Rev. Joseph P. Boznar, Pres.; Joseph V. Hocevar, Treas.

AKRON. *Christ Child Society of Akron*, P.O. Box 13411, Akron, 44334-8811. Tel: 330-922-3700; Email: presidentakronchristchild@gmail.com; Web: www.christchildsocietyakron.org. Sally Olszewski, Vice Pres.; Nancy Parks, Asst. Treas.

First Friday Club of Greater Akron (2000) 795 Russell Ave., Akron, 44307. Tel: 330-535-7668; Fax: 330-535-9040; Email: ffcofga@neo.rr.com; Web: www.firstfridayclubofgreaterakron.org. Mike Herhold, Pres.

BATH. **Crown Point Ecology Center*, 3220 Ira Rd., Akron, 44333. Tel: 330-668-8992; Web: www.crownpt.org. P.O. Box 484, Bath, 44210. Mrs. Monica Bongue, Dir.

BEREA. **The Community of Jesus, The Living Mercy*, P.O. Box 694, Berea, 44017. Tel: 800-482-4100; Email: BethesdaHouse@aol.com. Rachel Benda, Dir.

CHARDON. *Christ Child Society-Geauga Chapter*, P.O. Box 1133, Chardon, 44024. Tel: 440-290-0432. Linda Yanko, Vice Pres.

Notre Dame Schools (2015) 13000 Auburn Rd., Chardon, 44024. Tel: 440-286-6226; Email: Maria.Injic@ndcl.org. Dr. Michael Bates, Pres.

Notre Dame Village (2016) 13000 Auburn Rd., Chardon, 44024. Tel: 440-279-1117; Fax: 440-286-9364; Email: mgorman@ndec.org. Sr. Margaret Mary Gorman, S.N.D., Contact Person.

COPLEY. *Faith and Light U.S.A., Inc.*, 6152 State St., Louisville, 44641. Tel: 330-875-3433; Tel: 314-865-3733; Email: beckihaller@aol.com; Email: kwakukirt@gmail.com. Loyola Retreat House, 700 Killinger Rd., Loyola Retreat House, Inc., Clinton, 44216-9653. Mrs. Elizabeth R. Haller, Treas., Faith and Light U.S.A. East.

CUYAHOGA FALLS. *Humility of Mary Housing, Inc.*, 2251 Front St. Ste. 210, Cuyahoga Falls, 44221. Tel: 234-525-6400; Fax: 330-384-2144; Email: fberry@hmhousing.org; Web: www.hmhousing.org. Fred Berry, Pres. & CEO. Affordable housing and housing related services for low and moderate income individuals. Total Staff 35; Total Assisted 1,200.

Walsh Jesuit High School Foundation, 4550 Wyoga Lake Rd., Cuyahoga Falls, 44224. Tel: 330-929-4205; Email: ganza@walshjesuit.org. Mr. Thomas Orr, Chm.; Mrs. Colleen Joyce, Treas.; Mr. Charles Abraham, Sec.

ELYRIA. *First Friday Forum of Lorain County*, 320 Middle Ave., Elyria, 44035. Tel: 440-213-2133; Tel: 440-244-0643; Email: ffflorain@gmail.com. Larry Kowalski, Pres.

FAIRLAWN. *H M Housing Development Corporation*, 3250 W. Market St., Ste. 204, Fairlawn, 44333. Tel: 234-525-6400; Fax: 330-384-2144; Email: fberry@hmhousing.org; Web: www.hmhousing.org. Fred Berry, Pres. & CEO.

H.M. Life Opportunity Services (1987) 2251 Front St. Ste. 210, Cuyahoga Falls, 44221. Tel: 330-376-5600 ; Fax: 330-384-2144; Email: fberry@hmhousing.org; Web: www.hmhousing.org. Fred Berry, Pres.

Central Office - Humility of Mary Housing, Inc., Tel: 234-525-6400; Fax: 330-384-2144; Email: fberry@hmhousing.org; Web: www.hmhousing.org. Fred Berry, Pres.

GARFIELD HEIGHTS. *Jennings Manor Housing Corporation* (1996) 10204 Granger Rd., Garfield Heights, 44125. Tel: 216-581-2900; Fax: 216-581-4505; Email: welcome@jenningscenter.org; Web: www.jenningscenter.org. Allison Q. Salopeck, Pres. & CEO; Jim Patena, Exec. Dir., Home & Community Based Svcs. 61 unit apartment building - HUD 202 Supportive Housing for Older Adults.

Marymount Health Care Systems, 12300 McCracken Rd., Garfield Heights, 44125. Tel: 216-587-8080; Fax: 216-587-8212; Email: jmyers@ccf.org. 5200 Marymount Village Dr., Garfield Heights, 44125. Dr. Daniel Napierkowski, Pres. Provides comprehensive health and human services in response to the needs of the local community by owning, leasing and operating health care facilities and services consistent with the philosophy and objectives of the Roman Catholic religious congregation.

MHCS Real Estate Holding Company, 12300 McCracken Rd., Garfield Heights, 44125-2975. Tel: 216-587-8627; Fax: 212-469-9179; Email: jmyers@ccf.org. 5200 Marymount Village Dr., Garfield Heights, 44125. Dr. Daniel Napierkowski, Pres. To assist in the provision of comprehensive health care services by acquiring, holding, owning, and leasing real estate (and interests therein) and health care facilities, including but not limited to leasing such as real estate and facilities to Marymount.

Village Property Holding Company, LLC, 5200 Marymount Village Dr., Garfield Heights, 44125. Tel: 216-332-1100; Fax: 216-332-1619; Email: jmyers@ccf.org. Mr. Jeffry Myers, CEO.

LORAIN. *H M Housing Development Corp. - Faith House*, 1561 E. East 30th St., Lorain, 44055. Tel: 440-277-4430; Fax: 440-277-4452; Email: fberry@hmhousing.org. 2251 Front St., Ste. 210, Cuyahoga Falls, 44221. Fred Berry, Pres.

Mercy Health - Lorain, LLC (Ministry/Activity of Mercy Health of the Archdiocese of Cincinnati) 3700 Kolbe Rd., Lorain, 44053. Tel: 440-960-3295; Fax: 440-960-4630; Email: ed.oley@mercy.com. Edwin Oley, Pres.; Catherine Bartek-Woskobnick, Admin. Total Assisted 240,164.

PAINESVILLE. *Christ Child Society of the Western Reserve*, 1509 Mentor Ave., Painesville Township, 44077. Tel: 440-350-9836; Email: shetzer@gmail.com. Susan Hetzer, Pres.

**Retrouvaille of Cleveland, Inc.*, 5470 N. Woods Ln., Solon, 44139. Tel: 440-349-2135; Email: shelly@peet-martinko.com; Web: retrouvailleofcleveland.catholicweb.com. Rev. Ryan J. Mann, Chap.; Rob Martinko, Contact Person; Shelly Peet, Contact Person.

PARMA. **Christ Child Society of Cleveland* (1916) 7901 Detroit Avenue, Ste. 300, 44102. Tel: 216-939-3859 ; Email: christchildcleveland@yahoo.com; Web: www.christchildsocietycleveland.org. Mrs. Cathy Caruso, Pres.

Society of St. Joseph the Worker Brothers of St. Joseph the Worker (1979) 7033 State Rd., Parma, 44134-4952. Tel: 440-888-4872; Fax: 440-888-6825; Email: bsjw@msn.com; Web: www.bsjw.org. Lawrence R. Verbiar, Dir.

WICKLIFFE. *Center for Pastoral Leadership Services, Inc.* (1991) 28700 Euclid Ave., Wickliffe, 44092-2585. Tel: 440-943-7600; Fax: 440-943-7577; Email: pguban@dioceseofcleveland.org. Rev. Mark A. Latcovich, Ph.D., CEO; Mr. Philip J. Guban, B.A., COO.

COAR Peace Mission, Inc. (1980) 28700 Euclid Ave., Wickliffe, 44092. Tel: 440-943-7615; Fax: 440-943-7618; Email: coarpm@gmail.com; Web: www.coarpeacemission.org. Mary Stevenson, Exec. Dir. Total Staff 100; Total Assisted 1,000.

COAR Children's Village Ms. Mary Stevenson, Exec. (Zaragoza, El Salvador, C.A.); Comunidad Oscar Arnulfo Romero (COAR) provides housing, education and health care for orphaned, abandoned and street children in Zaragoza, El Salvador, Central America. The Children's Village can house up to 120 children under the supervision and guidance of a housemother in fifteen home-like cottages. The COAR school provides a kindergarten to grade twelve school education to about 800 children from Zaragoza and neighboring villages. State approved vocational training is offered to high school students. The COAR Clinic, a quality medical clinic in an area with little other access to health care, serves the health and dental needs of up to 25-50 patients (adults and children) weekly. The Archdiocese of San Salvador through its Caritas ministries administers COAR Children's Village. The COAR Peace Mission in Cleveland, OH is the support and development office for the Children's Village in El Salvador. COAR was founded in August 1980 by Rev. Ken Myers, a priest of the Cleveland Diocese.

RELIGIOUS INSTITUTES OF MEN REPRESENTED IN THE DIOCESE

For further details refer to the corresponding bracketed number in the Religious Institutes of Men or Women section.

[]—*Apostles of Jesus* (Karen, Kenya)—A.J.
[0200]—*Benedictine Monks* (St. Andrew Abbey)—O.S.B.
[0600]—*Brothers of the Congregation of Holy Cross* (Midwest Prov.)—C.S.C.
[0470]—*The Capuchin Friars*—O.F.M.Cap.
[1150]—*Congregation of St. Joseph*—C.S.J.
[0220]—*Congregation of the Blessed Sacrament*—S.S.S.
[0865]—*Congregation of the Mother of the Redeemer*—C.R.M.
[0690]—*Jesuit Fathers and Brothers* (Detroit Prov.)—S.J.
[0485]—*Missionaries of St. Francis de Sales*—M.S.F.S.
[0520]—*Order of Friars Minor*—O.F.M.
[0970]—*Order of Our Lady of Mercy*—O.de.M.
[0610]—*Priests of the Congregation of the Holy Cross* (Indiana Prov.)—C.S.C.

RELIGIOUS INSTITUTES OF WOMEN REPRESENTED IN THE DIOCESE

[0230]—*Benedictine Sisters of Pontifical Jurisdiction* (Erie, PA)—O.S.B.
[3832]—*Congregation of the Sisters of St. Joseph*—C.S.J.
[0790]—*Daughters of Divine Charity*—F.D.C.
[0420]—*Discalced Carmelite Nuns* (Carmel of the Holy Family)—O.C.D.
[1070]—*Dominican Sisters of Adrian*—O.P.
[1115]—*Dominican Sisters of Peace*—O.P.
[]—*Evangelizing Sisters of Mary*—E.S.M.
[1210]—*Franciscan Sisters of Chicago*—O.S.F.
[2590]—*Mercedarian Sisters of the Blessed Sacrament*—H.M.S.S.
[3760]—*Order of St. Clare-Poor Clare Colettine Nuns*—P.C.C.
[3210]—*Poor Clares of Perpetual Adoration*—P.C.P.A.
[3420]—*Religious of the Eucharist*—R.E.
[3430]—*Religious Teachers Filippini*—M.P.F.
[0440]—*Sisters of Charity of Cincinnati, Ohio*—S.C.
[0580]—*Sisters of Charity of St. Augustine*—C.S.A.
[2580]—*Sisters of Mercy of the Americas* (South Central)—R.S.M.
[2990]—*Sisters of Notre Dame* (Cleveland)—S.N.D.
[]—*Sisters of Our Lady of Kilimanjaro*—C.D.N.K.
[3360]—*Sisters of Providence*—S.P.
[1530]—*Sisters of St. Francis* (Sylvania)—O.S.F.
[3910]—*Sisters of St. Joseph of St. Mark* (Cleveland)—S.J.S.M.
[3930]—*Sisters of St. Joseph of the Third Order of St. Francis*—S.S.J.-T.O.S.F.
[]—*Sisters of St. Michael the Archangel*—S.S.M.A.
[1970]—*Sisters of the Holy Family of Nazareth*—C.S.F.N.
[2030]—*Sisters of the Holy Spirit*—C.S.Sp.
[2110]—*Sisters of the Humility of Mary*—H.M.
[2210]—*Sisters of the Incarnate Word and Blessed Sacrament*—S.I.W.
[2060]—*Sisters of the Most Holy Trinity*—O.SS.T.
[3260]—*Sisters of the Precious Blood* (Dayton, Ohio)—C.PP.S.
[2150]—*Sisters Servants of Immaculate Heart of Mary*—I.H.M.
[3620]—*Sisters, Servants of Mary Immaculate*—S.S.M.I.
[]—*Social Mission Sisters*—S.M.
[4120-04]—*Ursuline Nuns of the Congregation of Paris* (Cleveland)—O.S.U.
[4120-07]—*Ursuline Sisters of Youngstown*—O.S.U.

DIOCESAN CEMETERIES

CLEVELAND. *Assumption of Mary Cemetery*, Mailing Address: Calvary Cemetery, P.O. Box 605310, 44105. Tel: 216-641-7575, Ext. 3; Email: alah@clecem.org; Web: www.clecem.org. 14900 Brookpark Rd., 44135. Andrej N. Lah, C.E.O.

St. John Cemetery, 7000 Woodland Ave., 44104. Andrej N. Lah, Dir.

St. Joseph Cemetery, 7916 Woodland Ave, 44104. Tel: 216-641-7575, Ext. 2; Email: alah@clecem.org;

Web: www.clecem.org. Mailing Address: P.O. Box 605310, 44105. Andrej N. Lah, Dir.

St. Mary Cemetery, 2677 W. 41st St., 44113. Tel: 216-641-7575, Ext. 3; Email: alah@clecem.org; Web: www.clecem.org. Mailing Address: P.O. Box 605310, 44105. Andrej N. Lah, Dir.

St. Mary of the Falls Cemetery, 1260 West Bagley Rd., Berea, 44017. Tel: 216-641-7575, Ext. 3; Email: alah@clecem.org; Web: www.clecem.org. Mailing Address: P.O. Box 605310, 44105. Andrej N. Lah, Dir.

Holy Trinity Cemetery, 33843 Detroit Rd., Avon, 44011. Tel: 216-641-7575, Ext. 8; Email: alah@clecem.org; Web: www.clecem.org. Mailing Address: P.O. Box 605310, 44105. Andrej N. Lah, Dir.

St. Joseph Cemetery, 32789 Detroit Rd., Avon, 44011. Tel: 216-641-7575, Ext. 8; Email: alah@clecem.org; Web: www.clecem.org. Mailing Address: P.O. Box 605310, 44105. Andrej N. Lah, Dir.

Calvary Cemetery, 10000 Miles Ave., P.O. Box 605310, 44105. Tel: 216-641-7575, Ext. 2; Email: alah@clecem.org; Web: www.clecem.org. Andrej N. Lah, Dir.

AKRON. *Holy Cross Cemetery*, Mailing Address: P.O. Box 605310, 44105. Tel: 216-641-7575, Ext. 7; Email: alah@clecem.org; Web: www.clecem.org. 100 E. Waterloo Rd., Akron, 44319. Andrej N. Lah, Dir.

AVON. *Elmhurst Park Cemetery*, Mailing Address: P.O. Box 605310, 44105. Tel: 216-641-7575, Ext. 8; Email: alah@clecem.org; Web: www.clecem.org. 32787 Detroit Rd., Avon, 44011. Andrej N. Lah, Dir. (Non-Sectarian)

Holy Trinity Cemetery, Mailing Address: P.O. Box 605310, 44105. Tel: 216-641-7575, Ext. 8; Email: alah@clecem.org; Web: www.clecem.org. 2886 Jaycox Rd., Avon, 44011. Andrej N. Lah, Dir.

BROOK PARK. *Holy Cross Cemetery*, 14609 Brookpark Rd., Brook Park, 44142. Tel: 216-641-7575, Ext. 3; Email: alah@clecem.org; Web: www.clecem.org. Mailing Address: 10000 Miles Ave., 44105. Andrej N. Lah, Dir.

CUYAHOGA HEIGHTS. *St. Mary Cemetery*, Mailing Address: P.O. Box 605310, 44105. Tel: 216-641-7575, Ext. 2; Email: alah@clecem.org; Web: www.clecem.org. 4720 E. 71st St., Cuyahoga Heights, 44125. Andrej N. Lah, Dir.

CHARDON. *All Souls Cemetery*, 10366 Chardon Rd., Chardon, 44024. Tel: 216-641-7575; Email: alah@clecem.org; Web: www.clecem.org. Mailing Address: P.O. Box 605310, 44105. Andrej N. Lah, Dir.

ELYRIA. *St. Mary Cemetery*, Mailing Address: 7284 Lake Ave., Elyria, 44035. Tel: 216-641-7575, Ext. 6 ; Email: alah@clecem.org; Web: www.clecem.org. P.O. Box 605310, 44105. Andrej N. Lah, Dir.

EUCLID. *St. Paul Cemetery*, 1231 Chardon Rd., Euclid, 44117. Tel: 216-641-7575; Email: alah@clecem.org; Web: www.clecem.org. Mailing Address: P.O. Box 605310, 44105. Andrej N. Lah, Dir.

LORAIN. *Calvary Cemetery*, P.O. Box 605310, 44105. Tel: 216-641-7575, Ext. 6; Email: alah@clecem.org; Web: www.clecem.org. 555 N. Ridge Rd. West, Lorain, 44053. Andrej N. Lah, Dir.

NORTHFIELD. *All Saints Cemetery*, Mailing Address: P.O. Box 605310, 44105. Tel: 216-641-7575, Ext. 5; Email: alah@clecem.org; Web: www.clecem.org. 480 W. Highland Rd., Northfield, 44067. Andrej N. Lah, Dir.

VALLEY CITY. *Resurrection Cemetery*, Mailing Address: P.O. Box 605310, 44105. Tel: 216-641-7575, Ext. 9; Email: alah@clecem.org; Web: www.clecem.org. 6303 Center Rd., Valley City, 44280. Andrej N. Lah, Dir.

NECROLOGY

† Crosby, Neil A., Cuyahoga Falls, OH St. Eugene, Died May. 16, 2018
† DiNardo, Mark A., (Retired), Died Jan. 21, 2018
† Flynn, Thomas A., Pastor Emeritus, North Olmsted, OH St. Clarence Parish, Died Aug. 26, 2018
† Friedel, Robert E., Pastor Emeritus, Twinsburg, OH Ss. Cosmas & Damian, Died Nov. 8, 2018
† Goebel, Joseph A., (Retired), Died Aug. 21, 2018
† Juhas, John J., (Retired), Died Jan. 1, 2018
† Pritt, Philip P., Pastor Emeritus, Rittman, OH St. Anne Parish, Died Feb. 3, 2018
† Rath, Thomas V., (Retired), Died May. 14, 2018
† Rathfon, John R., Pastor Emeritus, Cuyahoga Falls, Immaculate Heart of Mary, Died Jul. 19, 2018
† Viall, James A., (Administrative Leave), Died Jul. 18, 2018
† Wright, John J., (Retired), Died May. 3, 2018

An asterisk (*) denotes an organization that has established tax-exempt status directly with the IRS and is not covered by the USCCB Group Ruling.

Diocese of Colorado Springs

Most Reverend

MICHAEL J. SHERIDAN, S.TH.D.

Bishop of Colorado Springs; ordained May 29, 1971; appointed Titular Bishop of Tibiuca and Auxiliary Bishop of Saint Louis July 9, 1997; ordained September 3, 1977; appointed Coadjutor Bishop of Colorado Springs December 4, 2001; succeeded to the See January 30, 2003.

Most Reverend

RICHARD C. HANIFEN, D.D., J.C.L.

Bishop Emeritus of Colorado Springs; ordained June 6, 1959; appointed Titular Bishop of Abercorn and Auxiliary of Denver July 6, 1974; consecrated September 20, 1974; appointed First Bishop of Colorado Springs November 10, 1983; installed January 30, 1984; retired January 30, 2003. *Office: 228 N. Cascade Ave., Colorado Springs, CO 80903-1498.*

Diocesan Offices: 228 N. Cascade Ave., Colorado Springs, CO 80903-1498. Tel: 719-636-2345; Fax: 719-636-1216.

ESTABLISHED AND CREATED A DIOCESE JANUARY 30, 1984.

Square Miles 15,493.

Comprising the Counties of Chaffee, Cheyenne, Douglas, Elbert, El Paso, Kit Carson, Lake, Lincoln, Park and Teller.

For legal titles of parishes and diocesan institutions, consult the Diocesan Offices.

STATISTICAL OVERVIEW

Personnel	
Bishop	1
Retired Bishops	1
Priests: Diocesan Active in Diocese	31
Priests: Diocesan Active Outside Diocese	5
Priests: Retired, Sick or Absent	11
Number of Diocesan Priests	47
Religious Priests in Diocese	20
Total Priests in Diocese	67
Extern Priests in Diocese	17
Permanent Deacons in Diocese	65
Total Brothers	2
Total Sisters	76
Parishes	
Parishes	39
With Resident Pastor:	
Resident Diocesan Priests	34
Resident Religious Priests	5
Without Resident Pastor:	
Administered by Priests	7
Pastoral Centers	4
Professional Ministry Personnel:	
Sisters	3
Lay Ministers	40
Welfare	
Catholic Hospitals	2
Total Assisted	365,762
Health Care Centers	2
Total Assisted	340
Homes for the Aged	1
Total Assisted	254
Special Centers for Social Services	4
Total Assisted	31,169
Educational	
Diocesan Students in Other Seminaries	12
Students Religious	13
Total Seminarians	25
High Schools, Private	1
Total Students	255
Elementary Schools, Diocesan and Parish	5
Total Students	950
Catechesis/Religious Education:	
High School Students	1,334
Elementary Students	5,422
Total Students under Catholic Instruction	7,986
Teachers in the Diocese:	
Priests	1
Sisters	1
Lay Teachers	116
Vital Statistics	
Receptions into the Church:	
Infant Baptism Totals	669
Minor Baptism Totals	114
Adult Baptism Totals	75
Received into Full Communion	248
First Communions	1,271
Confirmations	1,409
Marriages:	
Catholic	164
Interfaith	65
Total Marriages	229
Deaths	478
Total Catholic Population	183,150
Total Population	1,144,689

Former Bishops—Most Rev. RICHARD C. HANIFEN, D.D., J.C.L., (Retired), ord. June 6, 1959; appt. Titular Bishop of Abercorn and Auxiliary of Denver July 6, 1974; cons. Sept. 20, 1974; appt. first Bishop of Colorado Springs Nov. 10, 1983; installed Jan. 30, 1984; retired Jan. 30, 2003.

Diocesan Offices—228 N. Cascade Ave., Colorado Springs, 80903-1498. Tel: 719-636-2345; Fax: 719-636-1216. Office Hours: Mon.-Fri. 8-5.

Vicar General—Rev. Msgr. ROBERT E. JAEGER, V.G.

Vicar for Clergy—Rev. BRADFORD NOONAN.

Vicar for Religious—Rev. Msgr. RICARDO CORONADO-ARRASCUE, J.C.D.

Judicial Vicar and Chancellor—Rev. Msgr. RICARDO CORONADO-ARRASCUE, J.C.D.

Vice Chancellor—Rev. JAIMES PONCE, J.C.D.

Presbyteral Council—Rev. Msgrs. ROBERT E. JAEGER, V.G.; RICARDO CORONADO-ARRASCUE, J.C.D.; Revs. MICHAEL GOODYEAR; MARK ZACKER, V.F.; JAMES M. WILLIAMS; NATHANIEL HINDS; BRADFORD NOONAN; GEORGE V. FAGAN, J.C.L., V.F.; JAMES J. GORDON, F.S.S.P.

College of Consultors—Rev. Msgrs. ROBERT E. JAEGER, V.G.; RICARDO CORONADO-ARRASCUE, J.C.D.; Revs. GEORGE V. FAGAN, J.C.L., V.F.; NATHANIEL HINDS; JAMES J. GORDON, F.S.S.P.

Vicars Forane—Rev. Msgr. ROBERT E. JAEGER, V.G.; Revs. GEORGE V. FAGAN, J.C.L., V.F.; MARK ZACKER, V.F.; BRADFORD J. NOONAN, V.F.; STEPHEN J. PARLET, V.F.

Deaneries—Metro-North Deanery (Colorado Springs): Rev. MARK ZACKER, V.F., Vicar. Metro-South Deanery (Colorado Springs): Rev. Msgr. ROBERT E. JAEGER, V.G., Vicar. Eastern Deanery: Rev. GEORGE V. FAGAN, J.C.L., V.F., Vicar. Northern Deanery: Rev. BRADFORD J. NOONAN, V.F., Vicar. Western Deanery: Rev. STEPHEN J. PARLET, V.F., Vicar.

Diocesan Tribunal

Diocesan Tribunal—228 N. Cascade Ave., Colorado Springs, 80903. Tel: 719-636-2345.

Judicial Vicar—Rev. Msgr. RICARDO CORONADO-ARRASCUE, J.C.D.

Auditor—CASEY STATON, Email: cstaton@diocs.org.

Defender of the Bond—Rev. SEAN MCCANN, J.C.L., Email: smccann@diocs.org.

Tribunal Secretary and Assistant to the Judicial Vicar and Ecclesiastical Notary—MARIA MAGALONG, Email: mmagalong@diocs.org.

Auditor and Ecclesiastical Notary—MR. NICHOLAS DILLON, Email: ndillon@diocs.org.

Advocates—Appointed individually for particular cases Very Rev. DAVID RAMSEY PRICE; Rev. C. JOSEPH DYGERT; Deacon RICHARD BOWLES; Rev. JOSEPH P. MINH VU; Deacons MICHAEL D. CILETTI; THOMAS F. LIOTTA; FRANK J. RICOTTA JR.; LYNN C. SHERMAN; MR. MATT CASSADY; MR. TRACY ESTES; MR. LAURENCE E. GARRETT; MS. CATHY GREENLAW; MS. VICKI HEFFNER; MR. RICHARD KATNIK; MR. RICHARD W. KAUTT; MR. GARY MESWARD; MRS. BARBARA SHERMAN.

Diocese of Colorado Springs, a Colorado Corporation Sole

Diocesan Offices and Ministries

Unless otherwise indicated offices and ministries are located in the Pastoral Center, 228 N. Cascade Ave., Colorado Springs, CO 80903. Tel. 719-636-2345. Web: www.diocs.org.

Office of the Bishop—

Bishop—Most Rev. MICHAEL J. SHERIDAN, S.Th.D., Tel: 719-636-2345.

Vicar General—Rev. Msgr. ROBERT E. JAEGER, V.G., Tel: 719-636-2345.

General Counsel and Chief of Staff—Deacon DOUGLAS M. FLINN, Esq., Tel: 719-636-2345; Email: dflinn@diocs.org.

Executive Assistant to the Bishop and Director of the Propagation of the Faith—ESPERANZA A. GRIFFITH, Tel: 719-636-2345; Email: egriffith@diocs.org.

College Campus Ministry—Rev. KYLE INGELS, Dir., Tel: 719-636-2345; Email: kingels@diocs.org.

Special Projects Director—MRS. MARY THERESA THOMAS, Dir., Tel: 719-636-2345; Email: mthomas@diocs.org.

Diocesan Senior Staff—

Vicar General—Rev. Msgr. ROBERT E. JAEGER, V.G., Tel: 719-636-2345.

Judicial Vicar and Chancellor—Rev. Msgr. RICARDO CORONADO-ARRASCUE, J.C.D., Tel: 719-636-2345.

Finance Officer—MR. ROBERT G. DOERFLER JR., Tel: 719-636-2345; Email: rgdoerfler@diocs.org.

General Counsel and Chief of Staff—Deacon DOUGLAS M. FLINN, Esq., Tel: 719-636-2345; Email: dflinn@diocs.org.

President and CEO of Catholic Charities of Central Colorado—ANDY BARTON, Tel: 719-636-2345; Email: abarton@ccharitiescc.org.

Director Mission Effectiveness—MR. EDWARD GAFFNEY, Email: edgaffney@diocs.org.

Superintendent of Catholic Education—MRS. HOLLY GOODWIN, Tel: 719-636-2345; Email: hgoodwin@diocs.org.

Diocesan Pastoral Council—MR. PAUL SPREHE,

Chm.; Ms. Margie McCarthy, Vice Chair; Mr. Gary Caragao; Mrs. Jackie Staton; Ms. Joan Kilman; Mr. John Chaffin; Mr. John Colgan; Ms. Lori Bertagnolli; Mr. Marc Lanning; Matt Bahnemann; Ms. Megan Nagel; Susan Corliss; Mr. Thad Wolfe; Mr. Robert Burns; Revs. Joe Dygert; Donald Dilg, C.S.C.; Sr. Naomi Rosenburger, O.S.B.; Deacon Matthias J. Kasper; Rev. Msgr. Robert E. Jaeger, V.G., Ex Officio; Mr. Edward Gaffney, Staff.

Diocesan Finance Council—Mr. Robert G. Doerfler Jr., Staff; Mr. John Colgan; Mr. Jason P. Homec; Mr. Michael Wolf; Mr. Jon Paukovich; Mr. Gary Beres.

Buildings and Properties Committee—Mr. Steve Lepine; Mr. Dennis Palsgrove; Mr. Gary Beres; Mr. Gene Zimmer; Mr. Joseph Novak; Mr. Michael Wolf; Rev. Msgr. Robert E. Jaeger, V.G., Ex Officio. Staff: Mr. Robert G. Doerfler Jr.; Mrs. Janis Balentine.

Diocesan Offices and Ministries—

Catholic Charismatic Renewal Services—Deacon Charles Matzker, Liaison, Tel: 719-597-4249; Fax: 719-591-1816; Email: freshfire@q.com; Email: deaconchuck@holyapostlescc.org. CCRS c/o Holy Apostles Catholic Church, 4925 N. Carefree Cir., Colorado Springs, 80917.

Chancellor—

Chancellor and Judicial Vicar—Rev. Msgr. Ricardo Coronado-Arrascue, J.C.D., Tel: 719-636-2345.

Vice Chancellor—Rev. Jaimes Ponce, J.C.D., Tel: 719-636-2345.

Assistant to the Chancellor and Ecclesiastical Archivist—Mr. Nicholas Dillon, Email: ndillon@diocs.org.

The Colorado Catholic Herald—Mrs. Veronica Ambuul, Editor, Tel: 719-636-2345; Email: veronica@coloradocatholicherald.com.

Colorado Springs Council of Black Catholics—Ms. Aisha Young, Pres., Tel: 719-822-7861.

Office of Continuing Formation of Clergy—Rev. Lawrence C. Brennan, S.Th.D., Dir., Tel: 719-636-2345; Email: lbrennan@diocs.org.

Office of Permanent Diaconate—Deacon David Illingworth, Dir., Email: dillingworth@diocs.org; Rev. Lawrence C. Brennan, S.Th.D., Dir., Tel: 719-636-2345; Email: lbrennan@diocs.org.

Finance Office—Mr. Robert G. Doerfler Jr., Dir., Tel: 719-636-2345; Email: rgdoerfler@diocs.org.

Accounting—Mr. Robert Corker, Dir., Tel: 719-636-2345; Email: rcorker@diocs.org.

Buildings & Properties—Mrs. Janis Balentine, Dir., Tel: 719-636-2345; Email: janisbalentine@diocs.org.

Benefits—Ms. Janet Hutchinson, Coord., Tel: 719-636-2345; Email: jhutchinson@diocs.org.

Hispanic Ministry—Mr. Javier Cervantes, Dir., Tel: 719-636-2345; Email: jcervantes@diocs.org.

Human Resources—Mrs. Nancy Stromer, Dir., Tel: 719-636-2345; Email: nstromer@diocs.org.

Information Technology—Mr. Gary Schuck, Dir., Tel: 719-636-2345; Email: gschuck@diocs.org; Ms. Amelia Saldariagga, IT Support Analyst/Engineer, Tel: 719-636-2345; Email: asaldariagga@diocsorg; Andrea Bekurs, Webmaster & Social Media Content Coord., Tel: 719-636-2345; Email: abekurs@diocs.org.

Jail Ministry—Deacon Cliff Donnelly, Dir., Tel: 719-636-2345; Email: cliff.donnelly@gmail.com.

Mission Effectiveness—Mr. Edward Gaffney, Dir., Tel: 719-636-2345; Email: edgaffney@diocs.org.

Development and Planned Giving—Jaime Crane, Dir., Tel: 719-636-2345; Email: jcrane@diocs.org.

Donor Relations Manager—Mr. Wayne Paton, Tel: 719-636-2345; Email: wpaton@diocs.org.

Appeal & Grants Coordinator—Mrs. Marie Vanremortel, Tel: 719-636-2345; Email: mvanremortel@diocs.org.

Administrative Assistant & Event Coordinator—Mrs. Kathy Rowlands, Dir., Tel: 719-636-2345; Email: krowlands@diocs.org.

Office of Marriage and Family Life—Coordinators: Mr. Christian Meert; Mrs. Christine Meert, Tel: 719-471-9702; Email: christian@cmeert.com.

Total Catholic Education—Mrs. Holly Goodwin, Supt., Tel: 719-636-2345; Email: hgoodwin@diocs.org.

Catechesis, Youth Ministry, and Evangelization—Mrs. Michelle Maher-Lyons, Dir., Tel: 719-636-2345; Email: michelle@diocs.org.

Traumatic Brain Injury Ministry—Deacon Patrick Jones, Coord., Email: lamontglen@mac.com.

Victim Assistance—Vacant.

Vocations—Most Rev. Michael J. Sheridan, S.Th.D., Tel: 719-636-2345. Team: Revs. Kyle Ingels; James Baron.

CLERGY, PARISHES, MISSIONS AND PAROCHIAL SCHOOLS

CITY OF COLORADO SPRINGS

(County of El Paso)

1—St. Mary's Cathedral (1887)
22 W. Kiowa St., 80903. Tel: 719-473-4633; Email: Staff@stmaryscathedral.org; Web: www.stmaryscathedral.org. Very Rev. David Ramsey Price, Rector; Rev. Roylan Recio, Parochial Vicar; Deacons Mark Griffith; Frank J. Ricotta Jr.
Catechesis Religious Program—Email: rlserenity@outlook.com. Rebecca Longoria, Coord. Rel. Educ. Students 161.

2—St. Andrew Kim Parish (1984) (Korean)
4515 E. Pikes Peak Ave., 80916. Tel: 719-638-0100; Email: sakcolorado@yahoo.com. Rev. Kyeong Sik Choi.
Catechesis Religious Program—Helen Hwang, D.R.E. Students 22.

3—Corpus Christi (1916)
2318 N. Cascade Ave., 80907. Tel: 719-633-1457; Email: parish@corpuschristicos.org. Rev. Mark Zacker, V.F.; John Kraus, Contact Person.
School—Corpus Christi School, (Grades PreK-8), 2410 N. Cascade Ave., 80907. Tel: 719-632-5092; Fax: 719-578-9124; Email: jkraus@corpuschristicos.org. John Kraus, Prin. Lay Teachers 25; Students 230.
Catechesis Religious Program—
Tel: 719-633-1457, Ext. 15; Email: gniemerg@CorpusChristiCOS.org. Gary Niemerg, D.R.E. Students 0.

4—Divine Redeemer (1950) [JC]
926 Farragut Ave., 80909. Tel: 719-633-5559; Email: memick@divineredeemer.net; Web: www.divineredeemer.net. Rev. Brian Roeseler; Deacons David Bull; Andre Mason.
School—Divine Redeemer School, (Grades PreK-8), 901 N. Logan, 80909. Tel: 719-471-7771; Fax: 719-234-0300; Email: ksmith@divineredeemer.net; Email: jdamerell@divineredeemer.net; Web: www.divineredeemer.net/school. Kari Smith, Prin. Clergy 6; Lay Teachers 16; Students 207.
Catechesis Religious Program—Tel: 719-234-0342; Tel: 719-234-0334; Email: kbull@divineredeemer.net; Email: cstowe@divineredeemer.net. Kathy Bull, D.R.E.; Cody Stowe, D.R.E. Students 20.

5—St. Francis of Assisi (1981)
2650 Parish View, 80919. Tel: 719-599-5031; Email: parish@stfranciscs.org; Web: stfranciscs.org. Rev. Kenneth E. Przybyla; Deacons Patrick J. Bidon; Gerald Lachiewicz.
Catechesis Religious Program—Jennifer Lehrman, Dir. Adult & Elementary Faith Formation; Terrie Hernandez, Dir. Middle School Faith Formation & H.S. Young Adult Min. Students 175.

6—St. Gabriel the Archangel (1998)
8755 Scarborough, 80920. Tel: 719-528-8407; Email: office@saintgabriel.net; Web: www.saintgabriel.net. Rev. Kirk Slattery; Deacons David Geislinger; Mike McGrady, D.R.E.; Mr. Marc Lanning, Business Mgr.
Catechesis Religious Program—Students 449.

7—Holy Apostles (1973)
4925 N. Carefree Cir., 80917. Tel: 719-597-4249; Fax: 719-591-1816; Email: office@holyapostlescc.org; Web: www.holyapostlescc.org. Revs. James Baron; Lawrence Mulinda, Parochial Vicar; Deacons Rick Athey; Patrick O'Connor; Charles Matzker.
Child Care—Preschool, Tel: 719-591-1566; Fax: 719-591-1816; Email: hapreschool@holyapostlescc.org; Web: www.ucsdcs.org/holyapostles. Del Rose, Dir. Lay Teachers 8; Students 62.
Catechesis Religious Program—Tel: 719-597-4249; Email: miversen@holyapostlescc.org. Mike Iverson, Dir., Evangelization & Discipleship; Lara Dyer, Youth Min. Students 165.

8—Holy Trinity (1959)
3122 Poinsetta Dr., 80907. Tel: 719-633-2132; Email: holytrinitycatholicparish@comcast.net; Web: www.holytrinitycos.org. Deacons David Boroff; Andrew Dunnam.
Catechesis Religious Program—Students 34.

9—St. Joseph's (Southgate) (1968)
1830 S. Corona Ave., 80905.
Tel: 719-632-9903, Ext. 107; Email: felix@stjosephcos.org; Web: saintjosephcs.com. Rev. Nathaniel Hinds; Deacons Albert E. Kimminau, Sacramental Min.; Michael Bowen, M.D., Sacramental Min.
Catechesis Religious Program—Email: faithformation@saintjosephcs.com. Catherine Kusman, D.R.E. Students 158.

10—Our Lady of Guadalupe (1948) (Hispanic)
2715 E. Pikes Peak, 80909. Tel: 719-633-7204; Email: office@olgcos.org; Web: olgcos.org. Revs. John Toepfer, O.F.M.Cap.; Homero Cardozo Vargas; Deacons Clifford Donnelly; Ernesto Romero.
Res.: 22 S. Garland, 80909. Email: fjtoepfer@olgcos.org; Web: vcarriedo@olgcos.org.
Catechesis Religious Program—Email: promero@olgcos.org. Patricia Romero, D.R.E. Students 468.

11—Our Lady of the Pines-Black Forest (1965)
Mailing Address: 11020 Teachout Rd., 80908.
Tel: 719-495-2351; Fax: 719-495-9062; Email: office@ourladyofthepines.org; Web: ourladyofthepines.org. Rev. Andrzej Szczesnowicz; Deacons Gene Eastham; Joseph Forgue; Charles W. Specht; Bill Bollwerk.
Catechesis Religious Program—Email: evangelization@ourladyofthepines.org. Students 566.

12—St. Patrick (1981)
6455 Brook Park Dr., 80918. Tel: 719-598-3595; Email: stpatscs@stpatscs.org; Web: www.stpatscs.org. Revs. Michael Goodyear; Sean McCann, J.C.L., Parochial Vicar; Deacons James Bachta; Richard Brown, Colorado Springs; Thomas Tenpenny; Matthias J. Kasper.
Catechesis Religious Program—Email: MHKasper@stpatscs.org. Martha Kasper, D.R.E. Students 440.

13—Saint Paul (1925)
9 El Pomar Rd., 80906. Tel: 719-471-9700; Email: stpaul@stpaulcos.org. Rev. Msgr. Robert E. Jaeger, V.G.; Rev. Jack Fitzpatrick; Deacons Richard J. Bowles; Gregory Papineau.
School—St. Paul Catholic School, (Grades PreK-8), Tel: 719-632-1846; Email: cbench@stpaulcos.org. Jim Welte, Prin. Clergy 2; Lay Teachers 17; Students 168.
Catechesis Religious Program—Tel: 719-219-2704. Evenly Cedrun, D.R.E. Students 210.

14—Sacred Heart (1891)
2021 W. Pikes Peak Ave., 80904. Tel: 719-633-8711; Email: office@tricommunity.org. Revs. Ronald P. Raab, C.S.C.; Robert E. Roetzel, C.S.C.
Catechesis Religious Program—
Tel: 719-633-8711, Ext. 105; Email: formationdirector@tricommunity.org. Roberto Chavez, Dir.; Sue Gerlach, Dir. Students 170.
Missions—Our Lady of Perpetual Help—218 Ruxton Ave., Manitou Springs, El Paso Co. 80829.
Holy Rosary, 4435 Holiday Tr., Cascade, El Paso Co. 80809.

15—The Vietnamese Holy Martyrs Parish (1993) [CEM] (Vietnamese)
1133 N. Wahsatch Ave., 80903. Tel: 719-351-1845; Email: rev.j.p.minh.vu@gmail.com. Rev. Joseph P. Minh Vu.
Catechesis Religious Program—Students 10.

OUTSIDE THE CITY OF COLORADO SPRINGS

Bailey, Park Co., St. Mary of the Rockies (1990)
224 Buggy Whip Rd., P.O. Box 319, Bailey, 80421-8319. Tel: 303-838-2375; Email: stmaryrockies@gmail.com; Web: www.stmaryrockies.org. Rev. Bogdan Siewiera, (Poland).
Catechesis Religious Program—Students 14.

Buena Vista, Chaffee Co., St. Rose of Lima (1880)
118 S. Gunnison, P.O. Box 458, Buena Vista, 81211. Tel: 719-395-8424; Email: Office@strosebuenavista.org; Web: strosebuenavista.org. Rev. Stephen J. Parlet, V.F.; Deacons Richard Willburn, (Retired); Roger Metzinger.
Catechesis Religious Program—Email: nicolletteabc123g@gmail.com. Nicole Kirst, D.R.E. Students 18.
Mission—St. Joseph, 455 Castello Ave., Fairplay, Park Co. 80440. Val White, Contact Person. (Send all correspondence to Buena Vista address.).

Burlington, Kit Carson Co., St. Catherine of Siena (1916)
Tel: 719-346-7156; Email: nohnmacht@stcharlesborromeocos.org. Rev. Carlos Gallardo Morales; Deacon Norbert Ohnmacht.
Res. & Mailing Address: 513 Colorado Ave., P.O. Box 266, Stratton, 80836. Tel: 719-348-5336. Rev. Carlos Gallardo, Contact Person.
Church: 450 3rd St., Burlington, 80807.
Tel: 719-346-7156; Email: strattonstcharles@yahoo.com.
Catechesis Religious Program—Students 92.

Calhan, El Paso Co., St. Michael's (1905)
574 8th St., Box 199, Calhan, 80808.
Tel: 719-347-2290; Email: jponce@diocs.org; Web: www.diocs.org/Parishes/St-Michael. Rev. Jaimes Ponce, J.C.D.; Deacon Lynn C. Sherman.
Catechesis Religious Program—Students 26.

Castle Rock, Douglas Co., St. Francis of Assisi (1888)
2746 E. Fifth St., Castle Rock, 80104.
Tel: 303-688-3015; Tel: 720-215-4540;
Fax: 303-405-6808; Email: mmccann@stfranciscr.org; Web: www.stfranciscr.org. Revs. Bradford J.

Noonan, V.F.; Ricardo Rosales, L.C.; Deacon Thomas F. Liotta.
Catechesis Religious Program—Andrew Koumis, D.R.E.; Sylvia Werner, D.R.E.; Tod Masters, D.R.E.; Michel Goldman, D.R.E. Students 778.

CHEYENNE WELLS, CHEYENNE CO., SACRED HEART (1912)
105 W. 5th N., Cheyenne Wells, 80810.
Tel: 719-767-5272; Email: jmkeas@yahoo.com; Web: www.cheyennecountycatholicco.org. P.O. Box 819, Cheyenne Wells, 80810. Rev. Jason Keas.
Mission—St. Augustine (1918) 301 Church St., Kit Karson, WY 80825.

ELIZABETH, ELBERT CO., OUR LADY OF THE VISITATION (1996) [CEM]
P.O. Box 1689, Elizabeth, 80107. Tel: 303-646-4964; Fax: 303-646-9811; Email: olvoffice@olv.cc; Email: olvpastor@olv.cc; Email: olvre@olv.cc; Web: www. ourladyofthevisitation.org. Rev. Robert G. Newbury Jr.; Randall Brungardt, Rel. Order Leader; Mrs. Mary Pimental, Sec.
Church: 34201 County Rd. 33, Kiowa, 80117.
Catechesis Religious Program—Students 30.

FALCON, EL PASO CO., ST. BENEDICT CATHOLIC CHURCH (2005)
12130 Falcon Hwy., Falcon, 80831.
Tel: 719-495-1426; Email: stbeninfo@qwestoffice.net; Web: stbenedictfalcon.org. Rev. Jaimes Ponce, J.C.D.
Catechesis Religious Program—Harriet Bauer, D.R.E. Students 63.

FOUNTAIN, EL PASO CO., ST. JOSEPH (1936) Merged with Holy Family, Security to form St. Dominic, Security.

HIGHLANDS RANCH, DOUGLAS CO., ST. MARK CATHOLIC CHURCH (2000)
Mailing Address: 9905 Foothills Canyon Blvd., Highlands Ranch, 80129. Tel: 720-348-9700; Fax: 720-344-6847; Email: juanitam@stmarkhr.org; Email: juliea@stmarkhr.org; Web: www.stmarkhr. org. Revs. Gregory W. Bierbaum; Brian Q. Mohan, Parochial Vicar; Deacons Garrett Christnacht; Edward DeMattee.
Catechesis Religious Program—Email: karols@stmarkhr.org. Karol Seydel, D.R.E. Students 437.

LEADVILLE, LAKE CO., HOLY FAMILY PARISH (1878) [CEM] [JC]
609 Poplar St., Leadville, 80461. Tel: 719-486-1382; Fax: 719-486-3930; Email: himtnchurch@hotmail. com; Web: holyfamilyleadville.com. Rev. Rafael Torres-Rico; Deacon Anthony Werckman.
Res.: 424 W. 2nd, Leadville, 80461.
Catechesis Religious Program—Students 96.

LIMON, LINCOLN CO., OUR LADY OF VICTORY (1925)
425 H Ave., P.O. Box 790, Limon, 80828.
Tel: 719-775-2118; Email: gfagan@diocs.org. Rev. George V. Fagan, J.C.L., V.F.
Catechesis Religious Program—Limon & Missions, Fax: 719-775-9406. Students 43.
Missions—St. Anthony of Padua—133 Fifth St., P.O. Box 275, Hugo, Lincoln Co. 80821. (Send all correspondence to Limon address.).
St. Mary, [CEM] Flagler, Kit Carson Co. 80815. (Send all correspondence to Limon address.).

LITTLETON, DOUGLAS CO., PAX CHRISTI CATHOLIC CHURCH (1988)
5761 McArthur Ranch Rd., Littleton, 80124.
Tel: 303-799-1036; Email: supportstaff@paxchristi. org; Web: www.paxchristi.org. Rev. Marek Krol; Joanne Lafond, Sec.; Lisa Walker, Business Mgr.
Catechesis Religious Program—Ginger Gieser, Dir. Discipleship. Students 594.

MONUMENT, EL PASO CO., ST. PETER (1911)
Mailing Address: 55 N. Jefferson St., Monument, 80132. Tel: 719-481-3511; Fax: 719-266-3404; Email: april.charlton@petertherock.org; Web: www. petertherock.org. Revs. Gregory Golyzniak; Donald P. Brownstein, V.F.; Michael Holmquist; Deacons Douglas Flinn; G. Scott Bowen; Thomas Dickinson.
Res.: 25 S. Jefferson St., Monument, 80132.
School—St. Peter School, (Grades PreSchool-8), Tel: 719-481-1855; Email: sheila. whalen@petertherock.org; Web: www. petertherockschool.org. Rev. Gregory Golyzniak. Lay Teachers 19; Students 195.
Catechesis Religious Program—Email: claire. ramos@petertherock.org. Claire Ramos, D.R.E. (Pre-K-12) Students 311.

PARKER, DOUGLAS CO., AVE MARIA (1983)
9056 E. Parker Rd., Parker, 80138-7209.
Tel: 303-841-3750; Email: parishoffice@avemariacatholicparish.org; Web: www.avemariacatholicparish.org. Revs. August Stewart, V.F.; Thomas Jamka; Deacons Peter McCann; Gregory Archunde; Bill Korty.
School—Ave Maria School (2000) (Grades PreK-8), Tel: 720-842-5000; Email: tloiselle@avemariacatholicparish.org. Mrs. Theresa Loiselle, Prin. Lay Teachers 28; Students 435.
Catechesis Religious Program—Lynne K. Lane, D.R.E.; Angelle Schott, Youth Min.; Nancy Hartshorn, Youth Min. Students 665.

SALIDA, CHAFFEE CO., ST. JOSEPH (1907)
320 E. 5th St., Salida, 81201. Tel: 719-539-6419; Fax: 719-539-7127; Email: stjosephsalida@q.com; Web: www.stjosephsalida.org. P.O. Box 847, Salida, 81201. Rev. James M. Williams.
Catechesis Religious Program—Nicole Kirst, D.R.E. Students 45.

SECURITY, EL PASO CO.
1—ST. DOMINIC (2008)
5354 S. Hwy. 85/87, Security, 80911.
Tel: 719-392-7653; Email: stdominic@stdominiconline.org; Web: www. stdominiconline.org. Rev. John David Stearns; Deacons Robert Cole; Douglas Marsh; Andre Mason; Sr. Ann Cassidy, F.M.A., D.R.E.
Rectory—Security, 80911.
Catechesis Religious Program—Sherry Staatz, D.R.E. Students 281.
2—HOLY FAMILY (1957) Merged with St. Joseph, Fountain to form St. Dominic, Security.
3—IMMACULATE CONCEPTION PARISH (2008)
626 Aspen Dr., Security, 80911. Mailing Address: P.O. Box 5211, 80931-5211. Tel: 719-382-0121; Email: sanctealphonse@gmail.com. Rev. James J. Gordon, F.S.S.P.
Catechesis Religious Program—

STRATTON, KIT CARSON CO., ST. CHARLES BORROMEO (1910)
Mailing Address: 513 Colorado Ave., P.O. Box 266, Stratton, 80836. Rev. Carlos Gallardo Morales; Deacon Norbert Ohnmacht.
Church: P.O. Box 266, Stratton, 80836.
Catechesis Religious Program—Students 43.

WOODLAND PARK, TELLER CO., OUR LADY OF THE WOODS CATHOLIC PARISH (1954) (Our Lady of the Woods Church)
Mailing Address: 116 S. West St., P.O. Box 5590, Woodland Park, 80866-5590. Rev. Timothy L. Corbley, I.V. Dei, D.Min.
Catechesis Religious Program—Students 87.

Chaplains of Public Institutions

COLORADO SPRINGS. *Fire Department*. Deacon Christopher Phelps.
Penrose-St. Francis Hospital & Health Services. Rev. Stephen Akujobi, Deacon David Geislinger.
Police Department.
CASTLE ROCK. *Fire Department*. Rev. Bradford J. Noonan, V.F.

Retired:
Most Rev.—
Hanifen, Richard C., D.D., J.C.L., (Retired), 228 N. Cascade Ave., 80903
Rev. Msgr.—
Dunn, Donald F., (Retired), 411 Lakewood Cir., # A-8-7, 80910
Revs.—
Auer, John, (Retired), P.O. Box 55, Bailey, 80421
Battiato, Patrick, (Retired), P.O. Box 5402, 80931
Bond, Ernest W., (Retired), P.O. Box 307, Terry, MT 59349
Grabrian, Dennis, (Retired), 7172 Regional St., PMB 434, Dublin, CA 94568
Krenzke, John W., (Retired), 2626 Osceola St., Apt. 912 W., Denver, 80212
Vollmer, William C., (Retired), 35 Tilly Ln., Castle Rock, 80104.

Permanent Deacons:
Antinora, Richard, (Serving Archdiocese of Denver)
Archunde, Gregory, Ave Maria, Parker
Athey, Rick, St. Francis of Assisi, Colorado Springs
Bachta, James, St. Patrick, Colorado Springs
Balchus, Michael, (Orlando, FL)
Barrow, Russ, St. Rose of Lima, Buena Vista
Bauer, Richard, (Serving Archdiocese Military Services, USA)
Bidon, Patrick J., Dir., Jail Ministry, St. Francis of Assisi, Colorado Springs
Bollwerk, William, Our Lady of the Pines
Bothern, Derek, (Washington State)
Bowen, Michael, M.D., St. Joseph, Colorado Springs
Bowen, Scott, St. Peter, Monument
Bowles, Richard, St. Paul, Colorado Springs; Fort Carson, Colorado Springs
Broussard, Robert, (Retired), Colorado Springs
Brown, Richard, (Retired), Colorado Springs
Bull, David, Divine Redeemer, Colorado Springs
Camous, Dave, (Serving in Florida)
Carpio, Francisco, (Retired), Philippines
Christnacht, Garrett, St. Mark, Highlands Ranch
Ciletti, Michael D., (Retired), Colorado Springs
Cole, Robert, St. Dominic, Security
Corley, Mel, (Retired)
Cruise, Benedict, (Retired), Colorado Springs
DeMattee, Edward, St. Mark, Highlands Ranch
Dickinson, Thomas, St. Peter, Monument
Donnelly, Clifford, Dir. Jail Ministry, Our Lady of Guadalupe
Dunnam, Andrew, Holy Trinity, Colorado Springs
Eastham, Eugene S., (Retired), Colorado Springs
Estey, Russell, Fort Carson, Colorado Springs
Evanitz, David, (Retired), Colorado Springs
Flinn, Douglas, Chief of Staff & Gen. Counsel, Diocese of Colorado Springs, St. Peter, Monument
Forgue, Joseph, (Retired), Colorado Springs
Geislinger, David, St. Gabriel the Archangel, Colorado Springs
Gonzales, Rudy, Corpus Christi, Colorado Springs
Griffith, Mark, St. Mary's Cathedral, Colorado Springs
Hancock, John, (Retired), Colorado Springs
Harden, Richard, (Serving in Illinois)
Huard, Kenneth, (Retired), Colorado Springs
Illingworth, David, Dir. Diaconate Life Ministry, Corpus Christi
Jones, Patrick, (Medically Retired), Coord., Traumatic Brain Injury Ministry
Kasper, Matthias J., (Retired), St. Patrick, Colorado Springs
Kimminau, Albert E., (Retired), Colorado Springs
Lachiewicz, Gerald, St. Francis of Assisi, Colorado Springs
Leverington, Michael, (Retired), (Arizona)
Liotta, Thomas F., St. Francis of Assisi, Castle Rock
Marsh, Douglas, St. Dominic, Colorado Springs
Mason, Andre, St. Dominic, Colorado Springs
Matzker, Charles, Catholic Charismatic Renewal Svcs.; Holy Apostles Church, Colorado Springs
McCann, Peter, Ave Maria, Parker
McGrady, Michael, St. Gabriel the Archangel, Colorado Springs
McKee, Anthony, (Retired), Woodland Park
Milberg, Raymond, (Retired), Colorado Springs
Moss, Charles J. III, (Retired), (Arizona)
O'Connor, Patrick, Holy Apostles, Colorado Springs
Ohnmacht, Norbert, St. Charles, Stratton; St. Catherine, Burlington
Papineau, Gregory, St. Paul, Colorado Springs
Phelps, Christopher, Campus Ministry, Colorado Springs
Ricotta, Frank J. Jr., St. Mary's Cathedral, Colorado Springs
Rishavy, Kevin, Corpus Christi, Colorado Springs
Romero, Ernesto, Our Lady of Guadalupe, Colorado Springs
Ross, David, AFA Cadet Chapel, Colorado Springs
Sago, Bruce, (Serving in Arcadia, CA)
Sandusky, Tom, Pax Christi, Littleton
Shafer, Jacob, (Retired), Colorado Springs
Sherman, Lynn C., St. Michael, Calhan
Specht, Charles W., (Retired), Colorado Springs
Tenpenny, Tom, St. Patrick, Colorado Springs
Tomich, Daniel, St. Dominic, Security
Waller, Robert L., (Serving Archdiocese Military Services, USA)
Walsh, Timothy, (Retired), Castle Rock
Werckman, Anthony, Holy Family, Leadville
Willburn, Richard, (Retired), Buena Vista.

INSTITUTIONS LOCATED IN DIOCESE

[A] HIGH SCHOOLS

COLORADO SPRINGS. **St. Mary's High School*, 2501 E. Yampa, 80909. Tel: 719-635-7540;
Fax: 719-471-3490; Email: jtrechter@smhscs.org; Web: www.smhscs.org. Mr. Rob Rysavy, Pres.; Mr. David Hyland, Prin.; Mr. Joe Trechter, Dir., Advancement. Lay Teachers 25; Students 260; Clergy / Religious Teachers 2.

[B] GENERAL HOSPITALS

COLORADO SPRINGS. *Penrose-St. Francis Health Services*, 2222 N. Nevada, 80907.
Tel: 719-776-5007; Fax: 719-776-2131; Email: krisordelheide@centura.org; Web: www.centura. org. 9100 E. Mineral Cir,, Centennial, 80112. Brian Erling, CEO; Kris Ordelheide, Contact Person. An operating unit of Catholic Health Initiatives Colorado (an affiliate of Catholic Health Initiatives) Bed Capacity 522; Tot Asst. Annually 550,731; Total Staff 2,858.
Penrose Hospital, 2222 N. Nevada, 80907.
Tel: 719-776-5000; Fax: 719-776-2131; Email: krisordelheide@centura.org. 9100 E. Mineral Cir., Centennial, 80112. Margaret Sabin, CEO; Revs. Stephen Akujobi, Sacramental Min.; Dan Ayers, Sacramental Min.; Theresa Gregoire, Catholic Chap.; Kris Ordelheide, Contact Person. An oper-

ating unit of Catholic Health Initiatives Colorado (an affiliate of Catholic Health Initiatives) Bed Capacity 327; Priests 2; Tot Asst. Annually 230,450; Total Staff 2,157.

St. Francis Medical Center, 6001 E. Woodmen Rd., Colorado, 80923. Tel: 719-571-1000; Email: markhartman@centura.org; Email: krisordelheide@centura.org. 9100 E. Mineral Cir., Centennial, 80112. Tel: 303-673-8104. Mark Hartman, Admin.; Kris Ordelheide, Contact Person. An operating unit of Catholic Health Initiatives Colorado (an affiliate of Catholic Health Initiatives) Bed Capacity 195; Tot Asst. Annually 135,050; Total Staff 1,062.

[C] NURSING HOMES

COLORADO SPRINGS. **St. Francis Nursing Center*, 7550 Assisi Hts., 80919. Tel: 719-598-1336; Fax: 719-955-7031; Email: jerry@stfrancis.org; Web: stfrancis.org/mt-st-francis-nursing-center/. Randy May, Exec. Dir.; Gerald Wintz, Chap.; Almaz Berhe, Admin. Sisters of St. Francis of Perpetual Adoration. Tot Asst. Annually 155; Total Staff 158; Beds 110.

[D] SPECIAL CARE FACILITIES

COLORADO SPRINGS. *Namaste Alzheimer Center*, 2 Penrose Blvd., 80906. Tel: 719-442-4240; Email: afellows@chilivingcomm.org; Web: www.homeishere.org. Marga Callender, Chap.; Ashley Fellows, Admin. CHI Living Communities, a subsidiary of Catholic Health Initiatives, programs for seniors with Alzheimer's or dementia. Bed Capacity 64; Staff 90.

[E] RESIDENCES FOR MEN RELIGIOUS

COLORADO SPRINGS. *Our Lady of the Angels Friary*, 8095 Walker Rd., 80908. Tel: 719-495-2228. Revs. Curtis Carlson, O.F.M.Cap., Supr.; Cyrus Gallagher, O.F.M.Cap.; David Gottschalk, O.F.M.Cap.; Matthew Gross, O.F.M.Cap.; Bro. Felix Shinsky, O.F.M.Cap., Vicar.

Solanus Casey Friary, 5 University Dr., 80910. Tel: 719-632-7584; Email: frank.grinko@capuchins.org. Revs. Frank X. Grinko, O.F.M. Cap., Supr.; Gene Emrisek, O.F.M.Cap., Vicar; Vittorio Boria, O.F.M.Cap.; John Toepfer, O.F.M.Cap., Bursar.

CASCADE. *Holy Cross Novitiate*, 7872 W. Hwy. 24, Cascade, 80809. Tel: 719-684-9277; Email: kmolinaro@holycrossusa.org. P.O. Box 749, Cascade, 80809-0749. Revs. Kenneth M. Molinaro, C.S.C., Novice Master; Donald W. Dilg, C.S.C., Asst. Novice Master; Bro. James Blasak, C.S.C., Procurator. Congregation of Holy Cross, United States Province. Brothers 3; Novices 13; Priests 2.

SEDALIA. *Sacred Heart Jesuit Community*, 4801 N. Hwy. 67, Sedalia, 80135. Tel: 303-688-4198; Fax: 303-688-9633; Email: reservations@sacredheartretreat.org; Web: www.sacredheartretreat.org. P.O. Box 185, Sedalia, 80135-0185. Revs. Hanh D. Pham, S.J., Supr.; Vincent E. Hovley, S.J., Retreat Dir.; Edward Kinerk, S.J., Dir.; Paul B. Patin, S.J., Retreat Dir.

[F] RESIDENCES FOR WOMEN RELIGIOUS

COLORADO SPRINGS. **Benet Hill Monastery*, 3190 Benet Ln., 80921-1509. Tel: 719-633-0655; Fax: 719-471-0403; Email: info@benethillmonastery.org; Web: www.benethillmonastery.org. Sisters Clare Carr, O.S.B., Prioress; Margaret Meaney, Community Archivist. Motherhouse of the Benedictine Sisters (1963)., Properties owned: Benet Hill Monastery and Retreat Houses Professed Sisters 29.

Sisters of St. Francis of Perpetual Adoration, 7665 Assisi Hts., 80919-3837. Tel: 719-598-5486; Fax: 719-598-1578; Web: www.stfrancis.org. Sr. Marietta Spenner, Prov. Provincial House. Sisters of St. Francis of Perpetual Adoration, Province of St. Joseph (The Sisters of St. Francis of Colorado Springs). Professed Sisters 39.

[G] RETREAT CENTERS

COLORADO SPRINGS. **Benedictine Spirituality Center in the Pines*, 3190 Benet Ln., 80921-1509. Tel: 719-633-0655; Fax: 719-471-0403; Email: info@benethillmonastery.org; Web: www.benethillmonastery.org. Sr. Clare Carr, O.S.B., Prioress. Full-time, paid 11; Sisters 30; Tot Asst. Annually 1,186; Retreatants 476.

Franciscan Retreat Center, Inc., 7740 Deer Hill Grove, 80919-3836. Tel: 719-955-7025; Fax: 719-260-8044; Email: frc@stfrancis.org; Web: www.franciscanretreatcenter.org. Kathleen M. Tillman, Dir. Bed Capacity 70; Total Staff 8; Total Guests 18,000.

SEDALIA. *Sacred Heart Jesuit Retreat House*, 4801 N. Hwy. 67, P.O. Box 185, Sedalia, 80135-0185. Tel: 303-688-4198; Fax: 303-688-9633; Web: www.sacredheartretreat.org. Revs. Edward Kinerk, S.J., Spiritual Dir.; Hanh D. Pham, S.J., Spiritual Dir.; Vincent E. Hovley, S.J., Spiritual Dir.; Paul B. Patin, S.J., Spiritual Dir.; Sr. Eileen Currie, M.S.C., Spiritual Dir. Total in Residence 4.

[H] MISCELLANEOUS LISTINGS

COLORADO SPRINGS. *All for the Glory of God Ministry*, 5885 Del Paz Dr., 80918. Tel: 719-593-2120; Fax: 719-593-2120; Email: pjoy1948@icloud.com. Paula Joy, Dir.

Ave Maria Catholic School Corporation, 9056 E. Parker Rd., Parker, 80138. Tel: 720-842-5400; Fax: 720-842-5402; Email: tloiselle@avemariacatholicparish.org; Web: school.avemariacatholicparish.org. Mrs. Holly Goodwin, Supt. Catholic Educ.; Terri Loiselle, Prin.

Catholic Center at the Citadel, 750 Citadel Dr. E., Ste. 3056, 80909. Tel: 719-573-7364; Email: ccarlson@diocs.org; Web: www.catholiccitadel.org. Revs. Curtis Carlson, O.F.M.Cap., Dir.; Cyrus Gallagher, O.F.M.Cap.; Gene Emrisek, O.F.M.Cap.; Vittorio Boria, O.F.M.Cap.; Frank X. Grinko, O.F.M. Cap.

Catholic Charities of Central Colorado, Inc. dba Catholic Charities of Colorado Springs, 228 N. Cascade Ave., 80903. Tel: 719-636-2345; Fax: 719-636-1216; Email: info@ccharitiescc.org; Web: www.ccharitiescc.org. Andy Barton, CEO. Tot Asst. Annually 31,000; Total Staff 63; Volunteers 21,550.

The Catholic Foundation of the Diocese of Colorado Springs, Inc., 228 N. Cascade Ave., 80903. Tel: 719-636-2345; Fax: 719-636-1216; Email: rgdoerfler@diocs.org; Web: www.diocs.org. Mr. Robert G. Doerfler Jr., Dir.

Colorado Springs Cursillo Movement, 228 N. Cascade Ave., 80903. Cinthia Lopez, Dir.

Fostering Hope Foundation, 3055 Sunnybrook Ln., 80904. Tel: 719-635-6756; Cell: 414-915-9026; Email: njc9@comcast.net; Email: angela.carron@fosteringhopefoundation.org. Dr. Angela Carron, Exec.

Franciscan Community Counseling, Inc., 7665 Assisi Hts., 80919. Tel: 719-955-7008; Fax: 719-598-0346; Email: lizr@stfrancis.org; Web: www.franciscancommunitycounseling.org. Ms. Elizabeth Ryan, Exec. Tot Asst. Annually 450; Total Staff 6.

The Franciscan Foundation of Colorado Springs, 7665 Assisi Hts., 80919-3836. Tel: 719-598-5486; Fax: 719-532-0567; Email: marietta@stfrancis.org. Sr. Marietta Spenner, Pres.

St. Katharine Drexel Catholic Preschool, 5761 McArthur Ranch Rd., Littleton, 80124. Tel: 720-214-0691; Email: mlupher@paxchristi.org. Mandi Lupher, Dir. Lay Teachers 5; Students 34.

**St. Mary's Catholic Education Foundation*, 2501 E. Yampa St., 80909. Tel: 719-635-7540; Fax: 719-471-3490; Email: jtrechter@smhscs.org. Mr. Michael Pepper, Pres.; Mr. Joe Trechter, Exec.

**Partners in Housing, Inc.*, 455 Gold Pass Hts., 80906. Tel: 719-473-8890; Fax: 719-635-9360; Web: www.partnersinhousing.org. Mary Stegner, Exec. Dir. Tot Asst. Annually 374; Total Staff 22; Total Families Assisted Annually 121.

**S.E.T. of Colorado Springs* dba S.E.T Family Medical Clinic; Health S.E.T., 2864 S. Circle Dr., Ste. 450, 80906. Tel: 719-776-8850; Fax: 719-776-8854; Email: krisordelheide@centura.org; Web: www.setofcs.org. Mr. Jeffrey Porter, Dir.; Kris Ordelheide, Contact Person.

**St. Thomas Aquinas Society*, P.O. Box 62908, 80962-2908. Tel: 719-448-0020; Fax: 877-207-3707; Email: contact@stthomasaquinassociety.org; Web: www.StThomasAquinasSociety.org. Therese Lorentz, Dir.

**Villa Santa Maria, Inc.*, 405 E. St. Elmo Ave., 80905. Tel: 719-632-7444; Fax: 719-520-9345; Email: mvancel@archdiocesesanhousing.org; Web: www.archhousing.com. Kathy Vannerson, Dir. Total in Residence 50; Total Staff 8.

**The Villas in Southgate*, 405 E. St. Elmo Ave., 80905. Tel: 719-632-7444; Fax: 719-520-9345; Email: mvancel@archdiocesanhousing.org; Web: www.archhousing.com. Kathy Vannerson, Dir. Part of Archdiocesan Housing (an affiliate of Catholic Charities). Total in Residence 100; Total Staff 7.

Women Partnering, 961 E. Colorado Ave., 80903. Tel: 719-577-9404; Fax: 719-577-9407; Email: womenpart@gmail.com; Web: stfrancis.org. Sr. Jeannette Kneifel, O.S.F., Pres.

WOODLAND PARK. *Magnificat - Pikes Peak Region, Colorado Chapter*, 647 Lovell Gulch Rd., Woodland Park, 80863. Tel: 719-428-2101; Email: magnificatofpikespeak@gmail.com. Mrs. Heather Davis, Dir.

NECROLOGY

† Slattery, John F., (Retired), Died Nov. 28, 2018
† Butler, Michael, (Retired), Died Mar. 23, 2018

An asterisk (*) denotes an organization that has established tax-exempt status directly with the IRS and is not covered by the USCCB Group Ruling.

Diocese of Columbus

(Dioecesis Columbensis)

Most Reverend

ROBERT J. BRENNAN

Bishop of Columbus; ordained May 27, 1989; appointed Titular Bishop of Erdonia and Auxiliary Bishop of Rockville Centre June 8, 2012; ordained July 25, 2012; appointed Bishop of Columbus January 31, 2019; installed March 29, 2019.

Chancery Office: 198 E. Broad St., Columbus, OH 43215. Tel: 614-224-2251; Fax: 614-224-6306.

Web: www.columbuscatholic.org

Most Reverend

FREDERICK F. CAMPBELL, PH.D., D.D.

Retired Bishop of Columbus; ordained May 31, 1980; appointed Titular Bishop of Afufenia and Auxiliary Bishop of St. Paul and Minneapolis March 2, 1999; consecrated May 14, 1999; appointed Eleventh Bishop of Columbus October 14, 2004; installed January 13, 2005; retired January 31, 2019. *Res.: 198 E. Broad St., Columbus, OH 43215.* Tel: 614-224-2251.

Most Reverend

JAMES A. GRIFFIN, J.D., J.C.L.

Retired Bishop of Columbus; ordained May 28, 1960; consecrated Titular Bishop of Holar and Auxiliary to the Bishop of Cleveland August 1, 1979; appointed Tenth Bishop of Columbus February 7, 1983; installed April 25, 1983; retired October 14, 2004; named Diocesan Administrator October 18, 2004 to January 12, 2005. *Mailing Address: 198 E. Broad St., Columbus, OH 43215.*

ESTABLISHED 1868.

Square Miles 11,310.

Comprises the following 23 Counties in the State of Ohio: Hardin, Marion, Morrow, Knox, Holmes, Tuscarawas, Union, Delaware, Licking, Coshocton, Madison, Franklin, Muskingum, Fayette, Pickaway, Fairfield, Perry, Ross, Hocking, Pike, Jackson, Vinton and Scioto.

For legal titles of parishes and diocesan institutions, consult the Chancery Office.

STATISTICAL OVERVIEW

Personnel	
Bishop	1
Retired Bishops	2
Priests: Diocesan Active in Diocese	94
Priests: Diocesan Active Outside Diocese	1
Priests: Retired, Sick or Absent	47
Number of Diocesan Priests	142
Religious Priests in Diocese	33
Total Priests in Diocese	175
Extern Priests in Diocese	20
Ordinations:	
Diocesan Priests	5
Transitional Deacons	5
Permanent Deacons in Diocese	109
Total Brothers	2
Total Sisters	217
Parishes	
Parishes	105
With Resident Pastor:	
Resident Diocesan Priests	63
Resident Religious Priests	7
Without Resident Pastor:	
Administered by Priests	30
Administered by Deacons	3
Missions	3
Professional Ministry Personnel:	
Brothers	2
Sisters	20
Lay Ministers	97
Welfare	
Catholic Hospitals	6
Total Assisted	1,358,057
Homes for the Aged	21
Total Assisted	6,915
Residential Care of Children	3
Total Assisted	4,032
Specialized Homes	6
Total Assisted	8,399
Special Centers for Social Services	10
Total Assisted	284,948
Educational	
Seminaries, Diocesan	1
Students from This Diocese	33
Students from Other Diocese	113
Diocesan Students in Other Seminaries	3
Total Seminarians	36
Colleges and Universities	2
Total Students	4,422
High Schools, Diocesan and Parish	11
Total Students	4,712
Elementary Schools, Diocesan and Parish	41
Total Students	10,569
Elementary Schools, Private	1
Total Students	165
Catechesis/Religious Education:	
High School Students	1,726
Elementary Students	14,162
Total Students under Catholic Instruction	35,792
Teachers in the Diocese:	
Brothers	1
Sisters	5
Lay Teachers	962
Vital Statistics	
Receptions into the Church:	
Infant Baptism Totals	3,157
Minor Baptism Totals	320
Adult Baptism Totals	439
Received into Full Communion	358
First Communions	3,311
Confirmations	3,553
Marriages:	
Catholic	445
Interfaith	281
Total Marriages	726
Deaths	1,813
Total Catholic Population	280,878
Total Population	2,740,672

Former Bishops—Rt. Revs. SYLVESTER HORTON ROSECRANS, D.D., ord. June 5, 1852; cons. Titular Bishop of Pompeiopolis and Auxiliary to the Bishop of Cincinnati, March 25, 1862; transferred to Columbus, March 3, 1868; died Oct. 21, 1878; JOHN AMBROSE WATTERSON, D.D., ord. Aug. 9, 1868; cons. Aug. 8, 1880; died April 17, 1899; Most Revs. HENRY MOELLER, D.D., cons. Bishop of Columbus, Aug. 25, 1900; promoted to the Archiepiscopal See of Areopolis and made Coadjutor to the Archbishop of Cincinnati, with the right of succession, April 27, 1903; succeeded to the See of Cincinnati, Oct. 31, 1904; died Jan. 5, 1925; JAMES JOSEPH HARTLEY, D.D., cons. Feb. 25, 1904; died Jan. 12, 1944; MICHAEL JOSEPH READY, D.D., cons. Dec. 14, 1944; died May 2, 1957; CLARENCE GEORGE ISSENMANN, S.T.D., cons. Titular Bishop of Phytea and Auxiliary Bishop of Cincinnati May 25, 1954; appt. Bishop of Columbus Dec. 5, 1957; transferred to Cleveland as Apostolic Administrator. "cum jure successionis," Oct. 7, 1964; died July 27, 1982; His Eminence JOHN CARDINAL CARBERRY, D.D., S.T.D., J.C.D., Ph.D., appt. Titular Bishop of Elis and Coadjutor of Lafayette in Indiana "cum jure successionis," May 3, 1956; cons. July 25, 1956; succeeded to See Nov. 20, 1957; transferred to Columbus Jan. 20, 1965; transferred to the Archdiocese of St. Louis, March 24, 1968; created Cardinal April 28, 1969; died June 17, 1998.; Most Revs. CLARENCE E. ELWELL, D.D., cons. Dec. 21, 1962; appt. to Columbus May 29, 1968; died Feb. 16, 1973; EDWARD J. HERRMANN, D.D., appt. Auxiliary Bishop of Washington and Titular Bishop of Lamzella, March 4, 1966; cons. April 26, 1966; appt. Ninth Bishop of Columbus, June 26, 1973; installed Aug. 21, 1973; retired Sept. 18, 1982; named Apostolic Administrator Sept. 1982 to April 1983; died Dec. 22, 1999; JAMES A. GRIFFIN, J.D., J.C.L., ord. May 28, 1960; cons. Titular Bishop of Holar and Auxiliary to the Bishop of Cleveland Aug. 1, 1979; appt. Tenth Bishop of Columbus Feb. 7, 1983; installed April 25, 1983; retired Oct. 14, 2004; FREDERICK F. CAMPBELL, Ph. D., D.D., ord. May 31, 1980; appt. Titular Bishop of Afufenia and Auxiliary Bishop of St. Paul and Minneapolis March 2, 1999; cons. May 14, 1999; appt. Eleventh Bishop of Columbus Oct. 14, 2004; installed Jan. 13, 2005; retired Jan. 31, 2019.

Vicar General—Very Rev. Msgr. STEPHAN J. MOLONEY, M.A., M.Div., J.C.L.

Vicar for Priests—Very Rev. MICHAEL J. LUMPE.

Episcopal Moderator for Administration—MR. DOMINIC PRUNTE.

Episcopal Moderator for Charities and Social Concerns—MARK H. HUDDY, J.D.

Episcopal Moderator for Education and the Superintendent of Schools—ADAM J. DUFAULT.

Episcopal Moderator for Spiritual Life and Parish Ministry—Deacon THOMAS M. BERG JR., B.A., M.J., M.P.S.

Chancery Office—198 E. Broad St., Columbus, 43215. Tel: 614-224-2251; Fax: 614-224-6306; Email: chomailbox@columbuscatholic.org. Office Hours: Mon.-Fri. 8-4:30.

Chancellor—Deacon THOMAS M. BERG JR., B.A., M.J., M.P.S.

Consultative Bodies

College of Consultors—Most Rev. ROBERT J. BRENNAN; Very Rev. Msgr. STEPHAN J. MOLONEY, M.A., M.Div., J.C.L.; Rev. Msgr. WILLIAM A. DUNN, (Retired); Revs. MARK J. HAMMOND, J.C.L., S.T.L.; ROBERT PENHALLURICK; JOSEPH T. YOKUM; Very Rev. MICHAEL J. LUMPE.

Parochial Examiners—Very Rev. Msgr. STEPHAN J. MOLONEY, M.A., M.Div., J.C.L.; Very Rev. MICHAEL J. LUMPE; Revs. THOMAS G. PETRY; DONALD E. FRANKS; CRAIG R. EILERMAN; ROBERT PENHALLURICK; JONATHAN F. WILSON; THOMAS J.

BUFFER, S.T.D.; JOSEPH T. YOKUM; WILLIAM A. METZGER, B.A.; JEFFREY J. CONING.

Deaneries—Deanery 1: Center-South Columbus: Very Rev. MICHAEL J. LUMPE, St. Joseph Cathedral, 212 E. Broad St., Columbus, 43215. Deanery 2: Northwest: Rev. ROBERT PENHALLURICK, 4475 Dublin Rd., Hilliard, 43026-2243. Deanery 3: North High: VACANT. Deanery 4: Northland: Rev. THOMAS G. PETRY, St. Anthony, 1300 Urban Dr., Columbus, 43229-5132. Deanery 5: West: Rev. WILLIAM A. METZGER, B.A., Ss. Simon & Jude Church, 9350 High Free Pike, West Jefferson, NC 43162-9704. Deanery 6: East: VACANT. Deanery 7: Marion: Rev. THOMAS J. BUFFER, S.T.D., 251 N. Main St., Marion, 43302-3031. Deanery 8: Muskingum-Perry: Rev. DONALD E. FRANKS, St. Ann Church, P.O. Box 107, Dresden, 43821. Deanery 9: Knox Licking: Rev. JONATHAN F. WILSON, Blessed Sacrament, 394 E. Main St., Newark, 43055-6529. Deanery 10: Tuscarawas-Holmes-Coshocton: Rev. JEFFREY J. CONING, Sacred Heart Church, 139 Third St., N.E., New Philadelphia, 44663-3900. Deanery 11: Fairfield/Hocking/Pickaway: Rev. CRAIG R. EILERMAN, St. Mary Church, 132 S. High St., Lancaster, 43130. Deanery 12: Southern: Rev. JOSEPH T. YOKUM, St. Peter in Chains Church, 2167 Lick Run Lyra Rd., Wheelersburg, 45694-8882.

Presbyteral Council—Most Rev. ROBERT J. BRENNAN; Revs. JOSEPH T. YOKUM, Chm.; THOMAS J. BUFFER, S.T.D., Vice Chm.; THOMAS G. PETRY; JONATHAN F. WILSON, Sec.; ROBERT PENHALLURICK; DONALD E. FRANKS; CRAIG R. EILERMAN; WILLIAM A. METZGER, B.A.; JEFFREY J. CONING; Rev. Msgr. WILLIAM A. DUNN, Bishop's Appointee, (Retired); Very Rev. MICHAEL J. LUMPE, Bishop's Appointee. Ex Officio: Very Rev. Msgr. STEPHAN J. MOLONEY, M.A., M.Div., J.C.L.

Diocesan Pastoral Council—Most Rev. ROBERT J. BRENNAN, Pres.; DAN EISENHAUER, Chm.

Bishop's Council—Very Rev. Msgr. STEPHAN J. MOLONEY, M.A., M.Div., J.C.L., Vicar Gen.; Deacon THOMAS M. BERG JR., B.A., M.J., M.P.S., Chancellor & Episcopal Moderator for Spiritual Life and Parish Ministry; MR. MARK H. HUDDY, Episcopal Moderator for Catholic Charities & Social Concerns; MR. WILLIAM S. DAVIS, Dir. Finance; MR. DOMINIC PRUNTE, Dir. Personnel & Episcopal Moderator for Admin.; ANDREA PANNELL, Dir. Devel. & Planning; ADAM J. DUFAULT, Episcopal Moderator for Educ. & Supt. Schools.

Diocesan Board of Review for the Protection of Children—198 E. Broad St., Columbus, 43215. Tel: 614-224-2251. Very Rev. Msgr. STEPHAN J. MOLONEY, M.A., M.Div., J.C.L., Victims Asst. Coord.; MRS. MARY THOMPSON; MR. DOMINIC J. CAVELLO; DR. PAULA COMPTON; DR. KATHLEEN WODARCYK; MRS. CINDY KELLEY; DR. MARY ANN MURPHY; MR. ROBERT TAYLOR; Rev. WILLIAM P. HAHN; MR. H. TIM MERKLE; MR. JED MORISON, Chm.

Diocesan Commission for Ecumenical and Interreligious Affairs—VACANT.

Diocesan Finance Council—Very Rev. Msgr. STEPHAN J. MOLONEY, M.A., M.Div., J.C.L.; Deacon THOMAS M. BERG JR., B.A., M.J., M.P.S.; MR. WILLIAM S. DAVIS; MRS. INGRID SOTAK, Sec.; KATHY HOUCK; CHERYL TURNBULL; TIMOTHY BOTTS; MICHAEL DEASCENTIS JR.; CHRISTOPHER FIDLER, Chm.; ROBERT HETTERSCHEIDT; ED WALSH; Rev. ROBERT PENHALLURICK.

Building Commission—MR. BRUCE BOYLAN, Chm.

Council for Religious—198 E. Broad St., Columbus, 43215. Tel: 614-224-2251. Sisters MAUREEN ANNE SHEPARD, O.S.F.; EILEEN FITZSIMMONS, O.Carm., Pres.; Rev. RAMON MACOY OWERA, C.F.I.C.; Sisters JEAN WELLING, S.C.; JOHN PAUL MAHER, O.P.; BARBARA KOLESAR, O.P.

Diocesan Offices

Tribunal—197 E. Gay St., Ste. 500, Columbus, 43215-3290. Tel: 614-241-2500; Fax: 614-241-2522.

Judicial Vicar—Rev. ROBERT J. KITSMILLER, M.Div., J.C.L.

Adjutant Judicial Vicar—Rev. DENNIS E. STEVENSON, M.A., M.Div., J.C.L.

Diocesan Judges—Rev. Msgrs. JOHN K. CODY, M.Div., J.C.L., (Retired); JOHN G. JOHNSON, J.C.D.; Rev. JOSEPH N. BAY, M.A., M.Div., J.C.L.; Deacon JOHN R. CRERAND, M.A., J.C.L.; Revs. ROBERT J. KITSMILLER, M.Div., J.C.L.; DENNIS E. STEVENSON, M.A., M.Div., J.C.L.

Promoter of Justice, Vicar General—Very Rev. Msgr. STEPHAN J. MOLONEY, M.A., M.Div., J.C.L.

Defenders of the Bond—Revs. MARK J. HAMMOND, J.C.L., S.T.L.; HILARY C. IKE, (Nigeria) J.C.L.; MR. DANIEL M. SHAKAL, M.Div., M.C.L., J.C.L.

Advocates—Deacons THOMAS M. BERG JR., B.A., M.J., M.P.S.; DAVID BEZUSKO; CHRISTOPHER CAMPBELL; JEFFREY D. FORTKAMP; DANIEL W. HANN; FRANK A. IANNARINO; ROBERT A. JOSEPH; JAMES W. KELLY; PETER C. LABITA; MICHAEL T. KOPCZEWSKI; ROGER MINNER; DAVID LOZOWSKI; JAMES MORRIS; DEAN W. RACINE; THOMAS D. PHILLIPS; JAMES A. ROUSE, A.E., M.S., P.E.; KEVIN P. MURRIN; MARK A. SCARPITTI; THOMAS J. ROWLANDS; JASON MINH NGUYEN; CRAIG SMITH; RONALD E. ONSLOW; STEPHEN A. PETRILL; MARION E. SMITHBERGER; FRANK K. SULLIVAN; CHARLES G. WAYBRIGHT; PATRICK WILSON; MARK R. WEINER; PAUL J. ZEMANEK.

Tribunal Auditors/Notaries—MS. MARY BETH KRECSMAR; MS. PATRICIA SMITH; MRS. SUE ULMER.

Tribunal Notary—SR. RAYMUNDA BROOKS, O.P., M.A.

Tribunal Psychologists—TIMOTHY M. LUIS, Ph.D.; DAVID DEITZ PH.D.

Catholic Record Society—TOM FLEMING, Chm. Research Com.; DONALD SCHLEGEL, Sec., 197 E. Gay St., Columbus, 43215. Tel: 614-241-2571.

The Catholic Times, Inc.—197 E. Gay St., Columbus, 43215. Tel: 614-224-5195. DOUG BEAN, Editor.

Censor of Books—Revs. WILLIAM THOMAS KESSLER, (Retired); THOMAS J. BUFFER, S.T.D.

Communications Office—GEORGE A. JONES, B.S., Dir., 197 E. Gay St., Columbus, 43215. Tel: 614-241-2555; Fax: 614-241-2557.

Development and Planning Office—197 E. Gay St., Columbus, 43215. Tel: 614-241-2550; Fax: 614-241-2567. ANDREA PANNELL, Exec. Dir.

Diocesan Finance Office—MR. WILLIAM S. DAVIS, Dir. Finance, 197 E. Gay St., Columbus, 43215. Tel: 614-224-1221; Fax: 614-241-2573.

Real Estate—Diocesan Finance Office, 197 E. Gay St., Columbus, 43215. Tel: 614-224-1221.

Insurance Office—MR. DOMINIC PRUNTE, Dir.; JULIENNE BIALT, Mgr., 197 E. Gay St., Columbus, 43215. Tel: 614-224-1221.

Safe Environment Office—REGINA E. QUINN, Dir., 197 E. Gay St., Columbus, 43215. Tel: 614-241-2568.

Victim Assistance Coordinator—Very Rev. Msgr. STEPHAN J. MOLONEY, M.A., M.Div., J.C.L., Tel: 614-224-2251; Tel: 866-448-0217 (Toll Free); Email: helpisavailable@columbuscatholic.org.

Health Affairs Department—Rev. MARK J. HAMMOND, J.C.L., S.T.L., 303 E. High St., Mount Vernon, 43050-3419. Tel: 740-392-4711.

Office of the Diaconate—Deacon FRANK A. IANNARINO, Dir., 197 E. Gay St., Columbus, 43215. Tel: 614-241-2545; Email: fiannarino@columbuscatholic.org. School: 7625 N. High St., Columbus, 43235. Tel: 614-885-5585.

Office of Vocations—Rev. PAUL A. NOBLE, M.A., Ph.D., Dir., 197 E. Gay St., Columbus, 43215. Tel: 614-221-5565.

Priests Continuing Education—Very Rev. MICHAEL J. LUMPE, 212 E. Broad St., Columbus, 43215. Tel: 614-224-1295.

Priests Personnel Board—Rev. JAMES P. BLACK, St. Joan of Arc Church, 10700 Liberty Rd. S., Powell, 43065.

Catholic Conference of Ohio

Catholic Conference of Ohio—CAROLYN JURKOWITZ, Dir., 9 E. Long St., Ste. 201, Columbus, 43215. Tel: 614-224-7147; Fax: 614-224-7150; Email: general@ohiocathconf.org; Web: ohiocathconf.org.

Diocesan Departments

Department of Administration

Catholic Center—MR. BRUCE BOYLAN, Dir. Facilities & Supt. Bldgs., Diocesan Office Building, 197 E. Gay St., Columbus, 43215. Tel: 614-228-2453.

Cemeteries—RICHARD FINN, Dir., 6440 S. High St., Lockbourne, 43137. Tel: 614-491-2751; Fax: 614-491-4264; Email: rfinn@columbuscatholic.org.

Central Purchasing Service—STEVE DEEDRICK, Dir., 197 E. Gay St., Columbus, 43215. Tel: 614-262-0010; Tel: 800-842-8319; Fax: 614-262-0013.

Diocesan Charities Membership Corporation—MARK H. HUDDY, J.D., Trustee & Sec., 198 E. Broad St., Columbus, 43215. Tel: 614-224-2251.

Information Technology Office—MR. STEVE NASDEO, Dir., 197 E. Gay St., Columbus, 43215. Tel: 614-221-1182.

Personnel Office—MR. DOMINIC PRUNTE, Dir., 197 E. Gay St., Columbus, 43215. Tel: 614-241-2590.

Retreats—MARY E. MURPHY, Dir., St. Therese's Retreat Center, 5277 E. Broad St., Columbus, 43213-1389. Tel: 614-866-1611. Ss. Peter and Paul Retreat Center, 2734 Seminary Rd., S.E., Newark, 43056-9339. Tel: 740-928-6400; Fax: 740-928-1512.

Department for Catholic Charities and Social Concerns

Catholic Charities and Social Concerns—MARK H. HUDDY, J.D., Episcopal Moderator, 197 E. Gay St., Columbus, 43215. Tel: 614-241-2540; Fax: 614-228-7302.

Catholic Campaign for Human Development—ERIN CORDLE, Dir., 197 E. Gay St., Columbus, 43215-3229. Tel: 614-241-2540; Fax: 614-228-7302; Email: ecordle@columbuscatholic.org.

Catholic Relief Services—ERIN CORDLE, Dir., Office for Social Concerns, 197 E. Gay St., Columbus, 43215. Tel: 614-241-2540; Fax: 614-228-7302; Email: ecordle@columbuscatholic.org.

J.O.I.N. (Joint Organization for Inner-City Needs)—LISA KEITA, Dir., 578 E. Main St., Columbus, 43215. Tel: 614-241-2530.

Office for Social Concerns—197 E. Gay St., Columbus, 43215. Tel: 614-241-2540; Fax: 614-228-7302. JERALD FREEWALT, Dir.

Rural Life Apostolate—JERALD FREEWALT, Dir., 197 E. Gay St., Columbus, 43215. Tel: 614-241-2540; Fax: 614-228-7302.

St. Francis Evangelization Center—LISA KEITA, Dir., 108 W. Mill St., McArthur, 45651-1229. Tel: 740-596-4316; Fax: 740-596-4316.

Diocesan Sponsored Catholic Social Agencies—

Catholic Social Services—RACHEL LUSTIG, Pres. & CEO, 197 E. Gay St., Columbus, 43215. Tel: 614-221-5891.

St. Stephen's Community House—1500 E. 17th Ave., Columbus, 43219. Tel: 614-294-6347; Fax: 614-294-0258. MARILYN MEHAFFIE.

St. Vincent Family Center—1490 E. Main St., Columbus, 43205. Tel: 614-252-0731; Tel: 614-252-2069 (TDD & TTY); Fax: 614-252-8468. SUSAN LEWIS KAYLOR.

Department for Education

Department for Education—197 E. Gay St., Columbus, 43215. Tel: 614-221-5829. ADAM J. DUFAULT, Episcopal Moderator & Supt.

Office of Religious Education & Catechesis—BARBARA ROMANELLO-WICHTMAN, Ph.D., Dir., 197 E. Gay St., Columbus, 43215. Tel: 614-221-4633.

Office of Youth and Young Adult Ministry—197 E. Gay St., Columbus, 43215. Tel: 614-241-2565. MR. MICHAEL HALL, Dir.

Diocesan Scouting Program—Deacon CHRISTOPHER J. REIS, Chap.

Department for Spiritual Life and Parish Ministry

Marriage and Family Life Office—MRS. STEPHANIE RAPP, Dir., 197 E. Gay St., Columbus, 43215. Tel: 614-241-2560; Email: flomailbox@columbuscatholic.org.

Catholic Ethnic Ministries Office—197 E. Gay St., Columbus, 43215. Tel: 614-221-7990; Email: pharris@columbuscatholic.org. PAMELA HARRIS, Dir.

Office for Divine Worship—MICHELLE LEMIESZ, M.Div., Dir., 197 E. Gay St., Columbus, 43215. Tel: 614-221-4640.

Liturgical Commission—MICHELLE LEMIESZ, M.Div., Dir., 197 E. Gay St., Columbus, 43215. Tel: 614-221-4640.

Pontifical Mission SocietiesThe Society for the Propagation of the Faith, Holy Childhood Association, The Society of St. Peter Apostle, Missionary Union of Priests & Religious MR. LEANDRO M. TAPAY, M.A., Dir., 197 E. Gay St., Columbus, 43215. Tel: 614-228-8603; Email: mismailbox@columbuscatholic.org.

Diocesan Council of Catholic Women—197 E. Gay St., Columbus, 43215. Tel: 614-228-8601. KATHLEEN BOESCH, Pres.

CLERGY, PARISHES, MISSIONS AND PAROCHIAL SCHOOLS

CITY OF COLUMBUS

(FRANKLIN COUNTY)

1—ST. JOSEPH CATHEDRAL (1878) Very Rev. Michael J. Lumpe, Rector; Revs. Cyrus M. Haddad, Parochial Vicar; Adam A. Streitenberger, Parochial Vicar; Deacon James Gorski. In Res., Revs. Robert J. Kitsmiller, M.Div., J.C.L.; Hilary C. Ike, (Nigeria) J.C.L.

Res.: 212 E. Broad St., 43215. Tel: 614-224-1295; Email: cathedral@stjosephcathedral.org; Web: www.saintjosephcathedral.org.

Church: E. Broad St. & N. Fifth St., 43215.

Catechesis Religious Program—Email:

jneal@saintjosephcathedral.org. Jake Neal, D.R.E. Students 2.

2—ST. AGATHA (Upper Arlington) (1940) Rev. Daniel L. Ochs; Deacon Maurice N. Milne III.
Res.: 1860 Northam Rd., 43221. Tel: 614-488-6149; Email: stagatha@st-agatha.org; Web: www.st-agatha.org.
School—St. Agatha School, (Grades K-8), 1880 Northam Rd., 43221. Tel: 614-488-9000; Fax: 614-488-5783; Email: lalshara@cdeducation.org; Web: www.saintagathaschool.org. Mrs. Luna Alsharaiha, Prin. Lay Teachers 22; Students 293.
Catechesis Religious Program—Tel: 614-488-4975. Mrs. Jeanne Altiero, D.R.E. Students 300.

3—ST. AGNES (1954) Revs. Patrick A. Toner, (Retired); Brett Garland, Parochial Vicar; Deacon Paul Deshaies.
Res.: 2364 W. Mound St., 43204-2903.
Tel: 614-276-5413; Email: saintagnes1954@yahoo.com; Web: StAgnesColumbus.Com.
Catechesis Religious Program—478 S. Roys Ave., 43204. Students 8.

4—ST. ALOYSIUS (1906)
Mailing Address: 2165 W. Broad St., 43204-2903. 473 Roys Ave., 43204. Revs. Patrick A. Toner, (Retired); Brett Garland, Parochial Vicar.
Res.: 32 Clarendon Ave., 43223. Tel: 614-276-6587; Email: stals32@yahoo.com; Web: StAloysiusColumbus.org.
Catechesis Religious Program—478 S. Roys Ave., 43204. Students 9.

5—ST. ANDREW (1955) Very Rev. Msgr. Stephan J. Moloney, M.A., M.Div., J.C.L.; Rev. Todd Lehigh, Parochial Vicar; Deacon Thomas M. Berg Jr., B.A., M.J., M.P.S.
Res.: 1899 McCoy Rd., 43220. Tel: 614-451-4290; Fax: 614-451-8300; Email: jfrilling@standrewparish.cc; Web: www.standrewparish.cc.
School—St. Andrew School, (Grades PreSchool-8), 4081 Reed Rd., 43220. Tel: 614-451-1626; Fax: 614-451-0272; Email: jwichtma@cdeducation.org; Web: www.standrewschool.com. Joel Wichtman, Prin. Lay Teachers 26; Students 433.
Catechesis Religious Program—Tel: 614-451-2855. Kris Pellissier, Pre School Dir.; Suzanne Emsweller, D.R.E. Students 255.

6—ST. ANDREW KIM TAEGON KOREAN CATHOLIC COMMUNITY (1978) (Korean)
Mailing Address: 221 Hanford St., 43206-3656.
Tel: 614-732-0714; Web: www.kcolumbus.org. Rev. Dukwoo Antonio Kim.
Catechesis Religious Program—Kwangju Kwak, D.R.E. Students 23.

7—SAINT ANTHONY (1963) Rev. Thomas G. Petry; Deacon Craig Smith.
Church: 1300 Urban Dr., 43229. Tel: 614-885-4857; Email: st.anthony@sbcglobal.net.
School—Saint Anthony School, (Grades K-8), Tel: 614-888-4268; Fax: 614-888-4435; Email: ciaconis@cdeducation.org; Web: stanthonycolumbus.org. Chris Iaconis, Prin. Lay Teachers 9; Students 200.
Catechesis Religious Program—Tel: 614-888-8190. Judy McElwee, D.R.E. Students 60.

8—STS. AUGUSTINE AND GABRIEL (1984) Rev. Joseph N. Bay, M.A., M.Div., J.C.L.; Deacon Jason Minh Nguyen.
Office: 1567 Loretta Ave., Ste. 111, 43211-1677.
Tel: 614-268-3123; Email: duson07@yahoo.com; Web: www.staugustinegabriel.com.
Church: 1550 E. Hudson St., 43211.
Catechesis Religious Program—Students 11.

9—ST. CATHARINE (1931) Rev. Daniel J. Dury; Deacon Christopher J. Reis; Rev. William Thomas Kessler, (In Res.), (Retired).
Res.: 500 S. Gould Rd., 43209. Tel: 614-231-4509; Fax: 614-231-8366; Email: info@stcatharine.com; Web: www.stcatharine.com.
School—St. Catharine School, (Grades PreSchool-8), 2865 Fair Ave., 43209. Tel: 614-235-1396; Fax: 614-235-9708; Email: jweisner@cdeducation.org. Mrs. Janet Weisner, Prin. Lay Teachers 19; Students 276.
Catechesis Religious Program—Tel: 614-231-4500. Mrs. Chris Schleicher, D.R.E. Students 232.

10—ST. CECILIA (1882) Rev. Leo L. Connolly, M.Div.; Deacon John R. Malone Jr.
Res.: 434 Norton Rd., 43228. Tel: 614-878-5353; Fax: 614-878-0459; Email: email@saintceciliachurch.org; Web: www.saintceciliachurch.org.
School—St. Cecilia School, (Grades K-8), 440 Norton Rd., 43228. Tel: 614-878-3555; Fax: 614-878-6852; Email: jbeattie@cdeducation.org. Deb Adamczak, Prin. Lay Teachers 17; Students 208.
Catechesis Religious Program—Tel: 614-878-0133. Mr. Jim Martin, PSR Dir. Students 167.

11—CHRIST THE KING (1946) Rev. David A. Schalk, M.Div., S.T.B.; Deacon Peter C. Labita. In Res., Revs. Ramon Macoy Owera, C.F.I.C.; Dennis E. Stevenson, M.A., M.Div., J.C.L.
Res.: 2770 Dover Rd., 43209. Tel: 614-237-0401; Email: christthekingcolumbus@gmail.com.
Church: 2777 E. Livingston Ave., 43209.
School—All Saints Academy, (Grades PreSchool-8), 2855 E. Livingston Ave., 43209. Tel: 614-231-3391; Fax: 614-338-2170; Email: lmiller@cdeducation.org. Laura Miller, Prin. St. Thomas, St. Phillip & Christ the King. Lay Teachers 19; Students 315.
Catechesis Religious Program—Students 294.

12—ST. CHRISTOPHER (1947) Rev. David A. Poliafico; Deacon Byron Phillips.
Res.: 1420 Grandview Ave., 43212. Tel: 614-754-8888 ; Fax: 614-486-0433; Email: stchris@aol.com; Web: saintchristophercc.com.
School—Trinity, (Grades PreSchool-8), 1440 Grandview Ave., 43212. Tel: 614-488-7650; Fax: 614-488-4687; Web: trinity.education.org; Email: kmoehrma@cdeducation.org. Ms. Kimber Moehrman, Prin. Lay Teachers 18; Students 195.
Catechesis Religious Program—Linda Wolfe, Catechetical Leader. Students 63.

13—COLUMBUS VIETNAMESE CATHOLIC COMMUNITY (1994)
1567 Loretta Ave., Ste. 111, 43211-1677.
Tel: 614-268-3123; Fax: 614-268-8130; Email: duson07@yahoo.com; Web: www.staugustinegabriel.com. Rev. Joseph N. Bay, M.A., M.Div., J.C.L., Chap.

14—COMMUNITY OF HOLY ROSARY AND ST. JOHN (1979)
648 S. Ohio Ave., 43205. Tel: 614-252-5926; Email: hrsjoffice@gmail.com; Web: www.hrsj.org. Rev. Ramon Macoy Owera, C.F.I.C., Admin.
Catechesis Religious Program—
Tel: 614-252-5926, Ext. 226. Students 37.

15—CORPUS CHRISTI (1923)
1111 Stewart Ave., 43206. 277 Reeb Ave, 43207.
Tel: 614-443-2828; Fax: 614-444-0523; Email: parishccslcolumbus@gmail.com; Web: www.ccslcolumbus.org/. Rev. Vincent T. Nguyen, Admin.
Catechesis Religious Program—Clustered with St. Ladislas, Columbus. Students 110.

16—ST. DOMINIC (1889) Rev. Ramon Macoy Owera, C.F.I.C., Admin.
Administrative Offices: 648 S. Ohio Ave., 43205.
Tel: 614-252-5926; Fax: 614-252-1655.
Church: 453 N. 20th St., 43203-0572. Email: stdominic@stdominic-church.org; Web: www.stdominic-church.org.
Catechesis Religious Program—Students 48.

17—ST. ELIZABETH (1967) Revs. Antony Varghese, C.F.I.C., Admin.; Sudehakar Reddy Thirumalareddy, C.F.I.C., Asst. Admin.; Jesse Chi Chick, C.F.I.C., Assoc. Admin.; Deacon Dean W. Racine.
Church: 6077 Sharon Woods Blvd., 43229.
Tel: 614-891-0150; Email: secretary@stelcc.org; Web: www.stelizabethchurch.org.
Res.: 1682 Lynnhurst Rd., 43229.
Catechesis Religious Program—Email: stelizabethreled@sbcglobal.net. Dave Gruber, D.R.E. & RCIA Coord. Students 98.

18—ST. FRANCIS OF ASSISI (1892) Rev. Fritzner Valcin, (Haiti) Admin.
Res.: 386 Buttles Ave., 43215. Tel: 614-299-5781; Fax: 614-299-1987; Email: office@sfacolumbus.org; Web: www.sfacolumbus.org.

19—HOLY CROSS (1833) Rev. Dwayne A. McNew, Admin.
Res.: 204 S. Fifth St., 43215. Tel: 614-224-3416; Email: admmike@columbus.rr.com; Web: www.holycrosscatholic.com.
Catechesis Religious Program—Email: MATTHEWS9244@SBCGLOBAL.NET. Debi Matthews, C.R.E. Students 9.

20—HOLY FAMILY (1877) Rev. Stanley L. (Stash) Dailey, Admin.; Deacon W. Earl McCurry.
Res.: 584 W. Broad St., 43215-2710.
Tel: 614-221-4323; Fax: 614-221-9818; Email: holyfamilycolumbus@gmail.com; Web: www.holyfamilycolumbus.org.
Catechesis Religious Program—Students 70.

21—HOLY NAME OF JESUS (1905) Rev. Antonio Carvalho, Admin.
Res.: 154 E. Patterson Ave., 43202.
Tel: 614-262-0390; Email: holynamechurchcolumbus@gmail.com; Web: www.holynamercc.info.
Catechesis Religious Program—

22—HOLY SPIRIT (Whitehall) (1947) Rev. William L. Arnold, M.E., M.Ed.; Sr. Joan Popovits, O.P., Pastoral Min.; Deacon George A. Zimmermann Jr.
Res.: 4383 E. Broad St., 43213. Tel: 614-861-1521; Email: info@holyspiritcolumbus.org; Web: www.holyspiritcolumbus.org.
School—Holy Spirit School, (Grades K-8), 4382 Duchene Ln., 43213. Tel: 614-861-0475; Fax: 614-861-8608; Email: info@holyspiritcolumbus.org; Web: www.holyspiritcolumbus.org. Amy Chessler, Prin. Lay Teachers 14; Students 260.
Catechesis Religious Program—Mark Butler, D.R.E. Students 84.

23—IMMACULATE CONCEPTION (1916) Rev. Matthew N. Hoover; Sr. Ruth Hamel, O.P., Pastoral Min.; Deacon Christopher Campbell.
Res.: 414 E. North Broadway, 43214.
Tel: 614-267-9241; Fax: 614-267-7720; Email: icoffice@iccols.org.
School—Immaculate Conception School, (Grades K-8), 366 E. North Broadway, 43214. Tel: 614-267-6579 ; Fax: 614-267-2549; Email: cokent@cdeducation.org; Web: www.iccols.org. Colleen Kent, Prin.; Rick Logue, Asst. Prin. Lay Teachers 24; Students 370.
Catechesis Religious Program—Email: pudrey@iccols.org. Paulette Mudrey, D.R.E. Students 71.

24—ST. JAMES THE LESS (1947) Rev. Antonio Baus; Bro. Tom Bohman, C.PP.S., Pastoral Assoc.
Res.: 1652 Oakland Park Ave., 43224.
Tel: 614-262-1179; Email: sjamesless@yahoo.com; Web: www.stjames-cpps.org.
School—St. James the Less School, (Grades K-8), 1628 Oakland Park Ave., 43224. Tel: 614-268-3311; Fax: 614-268-1808; Email: scecchetti@cdeducation.org; Web: www.saintjamestheless.com. Samary Cecchetti, Prin. Lay Teachers 21; Students 500.
Catechesis Religious Program—Students 160.

25—ST. JOHN THE BAPTIST (1896) (Italian) Revs. Robert J. Kitsmiller, M.Div., J.C.L., Admin.; Joseph C. Klee, (In Res.).
Rectory—720 Hamlet St., 43215-1534.
Tel: 614-294-5319; Fax: 614-294-4303; Email: info@sjbitaliana.com; Web: www.sjbitaliana.org.
Church: 168 E. Lincoln, 43215.

26—ST. LADISLAS (1908)
Mailing Address: 277 Reeb Ave., 43207-1978.
Tel: 614-443-2828; Fax: 614-444-0523; Email: parishccslcolumbus@gmail.com; Web: www.ccslcolumbus.org. Rev. Vincent T. Nguyen, Admin.
Catechesis Religious Program—(Clustered with Corpus Christi.) Students 78.

27—ST. LEO (1903) Closed. For inquiries for parish records please see St. Mary, Columbus.

28—ST. MARGARET OF CORTONA (1922) Rev. Jeffrey J. Rimelspach; Deacons Andrew W. Naporano; Thomas J. Rowlands.
Res.: 1600 Hague Ave., 43204-1606.
Tel: 614-279-1690; Fax: 614-279-2386;
Tel: 614-274-1922; Email: stmargaretcol@yahoo.com; Web: www.stmargaretcolumbus.org.
Catechesis Religious Programs—Tel: 614-272-7571; Email: stmargaretpsr@yahoo.com. Kenneth Hagy, Dir. Students 116.
Catechesis of the Good Shepherd, Students 18.

29—ST. MARY (1865) Rev. Kevin F. Lutz; Deacon Roger Minner.
Office: 672 S. Third St., 43206. Tel: 614-445-9668; Email: ann@stmarygv.org; Web: www.stmarygv.com.
School—St. Mary School, (Grades PreSchool-8), 700 S. Third St., 43206. Tel: 614-444-8994; Fax: 614-445-2853; Email: kwalton@cdeducation.org; Web: www.stmaryschoolgv.com. Ms. Kayla Walton, Prin. Lay Teachers 15; Students 283; Religious Teachers 2.

30—ST. MARY MAGDALENE (1928) Revs. Patrick A. Toner, (Retired); Brett Garland, Parochial Vicar.
Res.: 473 S. Roys Ave., 43204. Tel: 614-274-1121; Email: twurst@saintmarymag.org; Web: www.saintmarymag.org.
School—St. Mary Magdalene School, (Grades PreSchool-8), 2940 Parkside Rd., 43204.
Tel: 614-279-9935; Fax: 614-279-9575; Email: rfumi@cdeducation.org. Mark Watts, Prin. Lay Teachers 10; Students 225.
Catechesis Religious Program—Tel: 614-279-9291. Students 20.

31—ST. MATTHIAS (1956) Rev. Anthony Davis; Sr. Marie Shields, S.N.D.deN., Pastoral Assoc.
Res.: 1582 Ferris Rd., 43224. Tel: 614-267-3406; Email: stmatthiascolumbus@sbcglobal.net; Web: www.stmatthiascolumbus.com.
School—St. Matthias School, (Grades K-8), 1566 Ferris Rd., 43224. Tel: 614-268-3030; Fax: 614-268-4681; Email: dkinley@cdeducation.org. Mr. Daniel Kinley, Prin. Lay Teachers 12; Students 260; Religious Teachers 1.
Catechesis Religious Program—Maria Gillan, D.R.E. Students 35.

32—OUR LADY OF PEACE (1946) Rev. Msgr. John G. Johnson, J.C.D.; Deacon Jeffrey D. Fortkamp; Sisters Martha Langstaff, O.P., Pastoral Min.; Barbara Kolesar, O.P., Pastoral Min.
Res.: 20 E. Dominion Blvd., 43214. Tel: 614-263-8824 ; Fax: 614-263-3383; Email: olp@rrohio.com; Web: www.olp-parish.org.
School—Our Lady of Peace School, (Grades K-8), 40 Dominion Blvd., 43214. Tel: 614-267-4535; Fax: 614-267-2333; Email: olp@cdeducation.org; Web: www.olpcolumbus.org. James Silcott, Prin. Lay Teachers 14; Students 240.
Catechesis Religious Program—Students 90.
Convent—60 E. Dominion Blvd., 43214.

33—OUR LADY OF THE MIRACULOUS MEDAL (1967) Rev.

James Coleman; Deacon Stephen A. Venturini, Pastoral Assoc.
Church & Office: 5225 Refugee Rd., 43232-5398.
Tel: 614-861-1242; Fax: 614-861-1499; Email: cool5225@sbcglobal.net; Web: www.churchofourladycolumbus.org.
Catechesis Religious Program—Tel: 614-868-1414. Students 57.

34—OUR LADY OF VICTORY (1922) Rev. Msgr. Romano Ciotola; Deacon Rob Joseph.
Res.: 1559 Roxbury Rd., 43212. Tel: 614-488-2428; Fax: 614-488-0507; Email: office@ourladyofvictory.cc; Web: www.ourladyofvictory.cc.
See Trinity, Columbus under St. Christopher, Columbus for details.
Catechesis Religious Program—Tel: 614-486-7678; Fax: 614-488-0507. Krista Joseph, D.R.E. Students 347.

35—ST. PATRICK (1852) Revs. Stephen Alcott, O.P.; Charles Shonk, O.P., Parochial Vicar; Paul Snyder, O.P., Parochial Vicar; Bro. Paul Kennedy, O.P. In Res., Rev. Bernard Mulcahy, O.P.
Res.: 280 N. Grant Ave., 43215. Tel: 614-224-9522; Email: office@stpatrickcolumbus.org; Web: www.stpatrickcolumbus.org.
Catechesis Religious Program—Tel: 614-240-5925. Sr. Maria Vianney Kysley, O.P., D.R.E. Students 382.
Shrine—Blessed Margaret Guild, Tel: 614-240-5915; Email: director@littlemargaret.org; Web: www.littlemargaret.org/guild.html.

36—ST. PETER (1970) Rev. Mark S. Summers; Deacon Philip M. Paulucci, M.S.W., L.I.S.W.
Res.: 6899 Smoky Row Rd., 43235-2034.
Tel: 614-889-2221; Fax: 614-889-6612; Email: fr.summers@stpetercolumbus.com; Web: www.stpetercolumbus.com.
Catechesis Religious Program—Tel: 614-889-1407. Students 600.

37—ST. PHILIP THE APOSTLE (1956)
1555 Elaine Rd., 43227. Revs. William L. Arnold, M.E., M.Ed.; Stephen Akange, (In Res.).
Administrative Offices: 4383 E. Broad St., 43213-1357.
Church: 1573 Elaine Rd., 43227. Tel: 614-237-1671; Fax: 614-231-8416; Email: stphilip1573@att.net; Web: www.stphilipcolumbus.org.

38—SACRED HEART (1875) Rev. Robert J. Kitsmiller, M.Div., J.C.L.
Church: 893 Hamlet St., 43201. Tel: 614-299-4191; Fax: 614-294-4303; Email: info@SJBitaliana.org; Web: www.sacredheartchurchcolumbus.org.
Administrative Offices: 168 E. Lincoln, 43215.

39—SANTA CRUZ PARISH (1993) (Spanish) Rev. Antonio Carvalho, Admin. Pro-tem.
Church: 143 E. Patterson Ave., 43202. Email: santacruzcols@gmail.com.
Catechesis Religious Program—Celia Palma, D.R.E. Students 69.

40—SAINT STEPHEN THE MARTYR (1963) Revs. Eduardo Velazquez, M.S.P., Admin.; Saul Alonso Garcia, M.S.P., Asst. Admin.
Res.: 4131 Clime Rd., 43228. Tel: 614-272-5206; Fax: 614-272-5200; Email: ststephenchurch2011@gmail.com; Web: ststephenmartyr.org.
Catechesis Religious Program—
Tel: 614-272-5206, Ext. 105. Students 300.

41—ST. THOMAS THE APOSTLE (1900) Rev. Michael C. Gentry; Deacon Thomas D. Phillips. In Res., Rev. Dean Mathewson, part-time Chap., Riverside Hospital.
Res.: 2692 E. Fifth Ave., 43219. Tel: 614-252-0976; Fax: 614-252-7519; Email: secretary@saintthomasapostle.com; Web: www.saintthomasapostle.com.
Catechesis Religious Program—Students 117.

42—ST. TIMOTHY (1961) Rev. Timothy M. Hayes, S.T.L.; Deacon Marion E. Smithberger.
Res.: 1088 Thomas Ln., 43220. Tel: 614-451-2671; Fax: 614-451-4181; Email: sttimothy@rrohio.com; Web: www.sttimchurch.org/.
School—St. Timothy School, (Grades K-8), 1070 Thomas Ln., 43220. Tel: 614-451-0739;
Fax: 614-451-3108; Email: gmoshold@cdeducation.org; Web: www.sttimschool.org. George Mosholder, Prin. Lay Teachers 13; Students 253.
Catechesis Religious Program—Tel: 614-451-3867; Fax: 614-451-3108. Rita Feige, D.R.E. Students 75.

OUTSIDE THE CITY OF COLUMBUS

ADA, HARDIN CO., OUR LADY OF LOURDES (1874) Revs. William J. Ferguson; Jeffrey E. Tigyer, Parochial Vicar; Deacon J. Michael Hood.
Res.: 222 E. Highland Ave., Ada, 45810.
Tel: 419-634-2626; Email: oll@wcoil.com; Web: www.oll-ada.com.
Catechesis Religious Program—Students 61.

BREMEN, FAIRFIELD CO., ST. MARY (1917) [CEM] Rev. Tyron J. Tomson.
Res.: 600 Marietta St., Bremen, 43107.
Tel: 740-569-7738; Email: stbernparish@yahoo.com.
Church: 602 Marietta St., Bremen, 43107.
Tel: 740-569-7738; Email: stbernparish@yahoo.com.
Catechesis Religious Program—Tel: 740-862-8839. Jim Barlow, D.R.E. Students 30.

BUCKEYE LAKE, LICKING CO., OUR LADY OF MT. CARMEL (1928)
Mailing Address: P.O. Box 45, Buckeye Lake, 43008.
Tel: 740-928-3266; Email: olmc@midohio.twcbc.com; Web: www.olmcbuckeyelake.org. Rev. William A. Hritsko; Deacon Richard B. Busic, Pastoral Assoc.
Church: 5133 Walnut Rd. S.E., Buckeye Lake, 43008.
Catechesis Religious Program—Tel: 740-928-3264. Leslie Niedzielski, D.R.E. Students 70.

CANAL WINCHESTER, FAIRFIELD CO., ST. JOHN XXIII (2000) Rev. Brian O'Connor; Deacons Roger Pry; Charles J. Miller.
Office: 5170 Winchester Southern Rd., N.W., Canal Winchester, 43110. Tel: 614-920-1563;
Fax: 614-920-1564; Email: stjohn@sjxxiiiparish.org; Web: www.sjxxiiiparish.com.
Res.: 7820 White Ash Ct., Canal Winchester, 43110.
Catechesis Religious Program—Students 291.

CARDINGTON, MORROW CO., SACRED HEARTS (1868) Revs. Thomas J. Buffer, S.T.D.; Ryan M. Schmit, Parochial Vicar.
Res.: 4680 U.S. Hwy. 42, Cardington, 43315.
Tel: 419-946-3611; Email: sacredheartschurch@gmail.com; Web: www.sacredheartschurch.org.
Catechesis Religious Program—Students 15.

CHILLICOTHE, ROSS CO.

1—ST. MARY (1837) [CEM] [JC] Rev. Lawrence L. Hummer.
Res.: 61 S. Paint St., Chillicothe, 45601.
Tel: 740-772-2061; Email: saintmary@roadrunner.com; Web: www.stmarychillicothe.com.
School—Bishop Flaget Elementary, (Grades PreSchool-8), 570 Parsons Ave., Chillicothe, 45601.
Tel: 740-774-2970; Fax: 740-774-2998; Email: lcorcora@cdeducation.org; Web: www.bishopflaget.org. Laura Corcoran, Prin. Lay Teachers 20; Students 204; Religious Teachers 1.
Catechesis Religious Program—Email: saintmary@roadrunner.com. Kathleen Boesch, D.R.E. Students 41.

2—ST. PETER (1846) [CEM] [JC]
118 Church St., Chillicothe, 45601.
Tel: 740-774-1407; Email: secretary@stpeterchillicothe.com; Web: www.stpeterchillicothe.com. Revs. William P. Hahn; Sean Dooley, Parochial Vicar; Michael Hartge, Parochial Vicar; Deacon Reed T. Hauser.
Catechesis Religious Program—Email: yec@stpeterchillicothe.com. Tess Hatmacher, D.R.E.; Chris Hiles, D.R.E. Students 58.

CIRCLEVILLE, PICKAWAY CO., ST. JOSEPH (1840) [CEM] Rev. Theodore F. Machnik.
Res.: 134 W. Mound St., Circleville, 43113.
Church Offices: 777 E. Ohio St., P.O. Box 40, Circleville, 43113. Tel: 740-477-2549; Email: office@saintjosephcircleville.com; Web: saintjosephcircleville.com.
Catechesis Religious Program—Vanessa Butterbaugh, C.R.E. Students 245.

CORNING, PERRY CO., ST. BERNARD (1882)
Mailing Address: 309 N. Main St., New Lexington, 43764-1204. Tel: 740-342-1348; Fax: 740-342-9133; Email: strose@columbus.rr.com; Web: strosepcc.org. Revs. Michael Hartge; Daniel Swartz, Parochial Vicar; Deacon Mark R. Weiner.
Church: 425 Adams St., Corning, 43730.
Catechesis Religious Program—

COSHOCTON, COSHOCTON CO., SACRED HEART (1857) [CEM] Rev. Victor R. Wesolowski; Deacon Douglas Mould.
Res.: 805 Main St., Coshocton, 43812.
Tel: 740-622-8817; Fax: 740-623-8824; Email: parishoffice@sacredheartcoshocton.org; Web: www.sacredheartcoshocton.org.
School—Sacred Heart School, (Grades PreK-6), 39 Burt Ave., Coshocton, 43812. Tel: 740-622-3728;
Fax: 740-622-9151; Email: mkobel@sacredheartschool.edu. Mary Kobel, Prin. Lay Teachers 6; Students 77.
Catechesis Religious Program—Deacon Douglas Mould, D.R.E. Students 66.

CROOKSVILLE, PERRY CO., CHURCH OF THE ATONEMENT (1896) [CEM]
Mailing Address: 309 N. Main St., New Lexington, 43764-1204. Tel: 740-342-1348; Fax: 740-342-9133; Email: strose@columbus.rr.com; Web: www.strosepcc.org. 320 Winter St., Crooksville, 43731. Revs. Michael Hartge; Daniel Swartz, Parochial Vicar; Deacon Mark R. Weiner, Sacramental Min.
Catechesis Religious Program—Students 38.

DANVILLE, KNOX CO., ST. LUKE (1820) [CEM] Revs. Mark J. Hammond, J.C.L., S.T.L.; Daniel Olvera, Parochial Vicar; Deacon Tim Birie.
Res.: 307 S. Market St., P.O. Box P, Danville, 43014.
Tel: 740-599-6362; Email: stluke@ecr.net; Web: stlukedanvilleoh.org.
Catechesis Religious Program—St. Luke Community Center, 7 W. Rambo, P.O. Box P, Danville, 43014-0616. Tel: 740-507-1731; Email: smickley@knoxcc.org. Sheryl Mickley, D.R.E. Students 157.

DELAWARE, DELAWARE CO., ST. MARY (1856) [CEM] Rev. Sylvester Onyeachonam; Deacons Todd M. Tucky; Feliz F. Azzola.
Res.: 82 E. William St., Delaware, 43015.
Tel: 740-363-4641; Fax: 740-363-9915; Email: stmary@delawarestmary.org; Web: www.delawarestmary.org.
School—St. Mary School, (Grades PreK-8), 66 E. William St., Delaware, 43015. Tel: 740-362-8961;
Fax: 740-362-3733; Email: gstull@cdeducation.org; Web: www.stmarydelaware.org. Gina Stull, Prin. (Grades K-8). Lay Teachers 26; Students 399.
Catechesis Religious Program—66 E. William St., Delaware, 43015. Tel: 740-369-8228; Email: twhite@delawarestmary.org; Web: www.delawarestmary.org/faith-formation/parish-school-of-religion/. Diana Toth, Dir. Students 314.

DENNISON, TUSCARAWAS CO., IMMACULATE CONCEPTION (1870) [CEM] Revs. Jeffrey J. Coning; Thomas Gardner, Parochial Vicar.
Res.: 206 N. First St., Dennison, 44621.
Tel: 740-922-3533; Fax: 740-922-2486; Email: icdennison@sbcglobal.net; Web: icdennison.com.
School—Immaculate Conception School, (Grades PreSchool-6), 100 Sherman St., Dennison, 44621.
Tel: 740-922-3539; Email: mritzert@cdeducation.org. Matthew Ritzert, Prin. Lay Teachers 7; Students 90.
Catechesis Religious Program—Cyndy Host, D.R.E. Students 32.

DOVER, TUSCARAWAS CO., ST. JOSEPH (1849) [CEM 2] Rev. James H. Hatfield III.
Res.: 613 N. Tuscarawas Ave., Dover, 44622.
Tel: 330-364-6661; Fax: 330-602-7488; Email: stjosephchurch@roadrunner.com; Web: www.stjosephdover.org.
School—Tuscarawas Central Catholic Elementary, (Grades PreK-6), 600 N. Tuscarawas Ave., Dover, 44622. Tel: 330-343-9134; Fax: 330-364-6509; Email: mritzert@cdeducation.org. Matthew Ritzert, Prin. Lay Teachers 12; Students 190.
Catechesis Religious Program—Ms. Cindy Teynor, D.R.E. Students 135.

DRESDEN, MUSKINGUM CO., ST. ANN (1889) Rev. Donald E. Franks; Deacon David Lozowski.
Res.: 405 Chestnut St., Box 107, Dresden, 43821.
Tel: 740-754-2221; Email: saintann@columbus.rr.com.
Catechesis Religious Program—Students 30.
Mission—St. Mary, [CEM] 6280 St. Mary's Rd., Dresden, Muskingum Co. 43821.

DUBLIN, FRANKLIN CO., ST. BRIGID OF KILDARE (1987) Rev. Msgr. Joseph M. Hendricks; Rev. Matthew B. Morris, Parochial Vicar; Deacons Frank A. Iannarino; Donald Poirier; Paul J. Zemanek; Sr. Teresa Tuite, O.P., Pastoral Care/Bereavement.
Res.: 7179 Avery Rd., P.O. Box 3130, Dublin, 43016-0062. Tel: 614-761-3734; Email: kcremeans@stbrigidofkildare.org; Web: www.stbrigidofkildare.org.
School—St. Brigid of Kildare School, (Grades PreSchool-8), 7175 Avery Rd., Dublin, 43017.
Tel: 614-718-5825; Fax: 614-718-5831; Email: koreilly@cdeducation.org. Ms. Kathleen O'Reilly, Prin. Lay Teachers 32; Students 557.
Catechesis Religious Program—Tel: 614-761-1176. Tina White, D.R.E.; Andrea Komenda, D.R.E. Students 1,334.

GAHANNA, FRANKLIN CO., ST. MATTHEW aka St. Matthew the Apostle Catholic Church & School (1959) Revs. Theodore K. Sill, M.Div., M.Th.; Peter Asantebwana, (Tanzania) Parochial Vicar; Deacon Joseph C. Meyer
St. Matthew Inc.
Res.: 807 Havens Corners Rd., Gahanna, 43230.
Tel: 614-471-0212; Email: Lgrimes@stmatthew.net; Web: www.stmatthew.net.
School—St. Matthew School, (Grades PreK-8), 795 Havens Corners Rd., Gahanna, 43230.
Tel: 614-471-4930; Fax: 614-471-1673; Email: smaloy@cdeducation.org; Web: www.cdstmatthew.org/. Susan Maloy, Prin. Clergy 8; Lay Teachers 27; Students 599.
Catechesis Religious Program—795 Havens Corners Rd., Gahanna, 43230. Tel: 614-471-2067;
Fax: 614-471-1693. Ashley Hettinger, D.R.E. Students 319.

GRANVILLE, LICKING CO., ST. EDWARD THE CONFESSOR (1947) Rev. Msgr. Paul P. Enke; Deacon John C. Barbour.
Res.: 785 Newark-Granville Rd., Granville, 43023-1450. Tel: 740-587-3254; Fax: 740-587-0149; Email:

church@saintedwards.org; Web: www.saintedwards.org.
Catechesis Religious Program—Tel: 740-587-4160; Email: reled@saintedwards.org. Students 453.
GROVE CITY, FRANKLIN CO., OUR LADY OF PERPETUAL HELP (1954) Rev. Daniel J. Millisor, M.Div.; Deacon Michael T. Kopczewski. In Res., Rev. James L. Colopy, (Retired).
Church & Mailing Address: 3730 Broadway, Grove City, 43123. Tel: 614-875-3322; Fax: 614-875-6779; Email: info@ourladyofperpetualhelp.net; Web: www.ourladyofperpetualhelp.net.
School—Our Lady of Perpetual Help School, (Grades PreK-8), 3752 Broadway, Grove City, 43123.
Tel: 614-875-6779; Fax: 614-539-5719; Email: jfreeman@cdeducation.org. Julie Freeman, Prin. Lay Teachers 19; Students 340.
Catechesis Religious Program—3730 Broadway, Grove City, 43123. Tel: 614-875-9345. Students 327.
GROVEPORT, FRANKLIN CO., ST. MARY (1871) Very Rev. Msgr. Stephan J. Moloney, M.A., M.Div., J.C.L., Priest Mod.; Rev. John M. Reade, Pastoral Min.
Res.: 5684 Groveport Rd., Groveport, 43125.
Tel: 614-497-1324; Email: stmarygroveport@hotmail.com; Web: www.stmarygroveport.org.
Catechesis Religious Program—Tel: 614-497-1437; Email: stmarypsrgroveport@msn.com. Alice Doran, D.R.E. Students 75.
HEATH, LICKING CO., ST. LEONARD (1962)
57 Dorsey Mill Rd., Heath, 43056. Tel: 740-522-5270; Fax: 740-522-5261; Email: stleonard-heath@roadrunner.com; Web: www.saintleonard-heath.com. Rev. William A. Hritsko; Deacon Larry Wilson.
HILLIARD, FRANKLIN CO., ST. BRENDAN (1956) Revs. Robert Penhallurick; Edward Shikina, Parochial Vicar; Deacons James Morris; Douglas A. Saunders.
Res.: 4475 Dublin Rd., Hilliard, 43026.
Tel: 614-876-1272; Email: parish@stbrendans.net; Web: www.stbrendans.net.
School—St. Brendan School, (Grades K-8),
Tel: 614-876-6132; Email: wgruber@cdeducation.org. William T. Gruber, Prin. Lay Teachers 22; Students 475.
Catechesis Religious Program—Tel: 614-876-9533. Drew Snyder, Dir. Evang. & Catechesis. Students 603.
JACKSON, JACKSON CO., HOLY TRINITY (1875) [CEM]
215 Columbia St., Jackson, 45640. Tel: 740-286-1428; Email: jacksonholytrinity@frontier.com. Revs. Joseph T. Yokum; Nicola Ventura, Parochial Vicar; Christopher Tuttle, Parochial Vicar.
Catechesis Religious Program—Students 38.
JOHNSTOWN, LICKING CO., CHURCH OF THE ASCENSION (1912) [CEM]
555 S. Main St., Johnstown, 43031-1231.
Tel: 740-967-7871; Fax: 740-967-0321; Email: ascensionjohnstown@gmail.com; Web: www.johnstownascension.org. Rev. Mark V. Ghiloni; Deacon William J. Andrews.
Catechesis Religious Program—Tel: 740-967-1338. Kelly Pertee, D.R.E. Students 80.
JUNCTION CITY, PERRY CO., ST. PATRICK (1820) [CEM]
Mailing Address: 309 N. Main St., New Lexington, 43764-1204. Tel: 740-342-1348; Fax: 740-342-9133; Email: strose@columbus.rr.com; Web: strosepcc.org. 1170 State Route 668 S, Junction City, 43748. Revs. Michael Hartge; Daniel Swartz, Parochial Vicar; Deacon Mark R. Weiner.
Catechesis Religious Program—1170 State Rte. 668 S., Junction City, 43748.
KENTON, HARDIN CO., IMMACULATE CONCEPTION (1866) [CEM] Revs. William J. Ferguson; Jeffrey E. Tigyer, Parochial Vicar; Deacon J. Michael Hood.
Res.: 215 E. North St., Kenton, 43326.
Tel: 419-675-1162; Email: iccatholic@windstream.net; Web: www.immaculateconceptionkenton.org.
Parish Center—220 E. North St., Kenton, 44326.
Catechesis Religious Program—Stacy Stacklin, D.R.E. Students 30.
LA RUE, MARION CO., ST. JOSEPH'S (1864) Closed. For inquiries for parish records contact the Chancery.
LANCASTER, FAIRFIELD CO.
1—ST. BERNADETTE (1963) Rev. Tyron J. Tomson; Deacons Mark A. Scarpitti; Jeffrey P. Carpenter.
Church & Office: 1343 Wheeling Rd., Lancaster, 43130-8701. Tel: 740-654-1893; Email: stbernparish@yahoo.com; Web: www.stbernadetteparish.net.
School—St. Bernadette School, (Grades PreSchool-5), 1325 Wheeling Rd., Lancaster, 43130.
Tel: 740-654-3137; Fax: 740-654-1602; Email: stbernlan@cdeducation.org; Web: www.stbernadetteschool.com. Pam Eltringham, Prin. Lay Teachers 8; Students 140.
Catechesis Religious Program—Students 44.
2—ST. MARK (1959) [JC] Rev. Peter M. Gideon.
Res.: 324 Gay St., Lancaster, 43130.
Tel: 740-653-1229; Fax: 740-653-8329; Email: tbrunney@stmarklancaster.com; Web: www.stmarklancaster.com.
Catechesis Religious Program—331 Gay St., Lancaster, 43130. Students 63.
3—ST. MARY (1818) [CEM] Rev. Craig R. Eilerman; Deacon Frank K. Sullivan, Pastoral Assoc.
Res.: 132 S. High St., Lancaster, 43130.
Tel: 740-653-0997; Fax: 740-653-0337; Email: creilerman@stmarylancaster.org; Web: www.stmarylancaster.org.
School—St. Mary School, (Grades PreSchool-8), 309 E. Chestnut St., Lancaster, 43130. Tel: 740-654-1632; Fax: 740-654-0877; Email: eschorna@cdeducation.org; Web: www.saintmarylancaster.org. Erin Schornack, Prin. Lay Teachers 14; Students 300.
Catechesis Religious Program—Tel: 740-653-5054. Brian McCauley, P.S.R. Dir. Students 167.
LOGAN, HOCKING CO., ST. JOHN (1841) [CEM] Rev. Stephen L. Krile; Deacon Donald Robers.
Res.: 351 N. Market St., Logan, 43138.
Tel: 740-385-2549; Fax: 740-380-2837; Email: marian@stjohnlogan.com; Web: www.stjohnlogan.com.
School—St. John School, (Grades PreSchool-6), 321 N. Market St., Logan, 43138. Tel: 740-385-2767; Fax: 740-385-9727; Email: selder@cdeducation.org; Web: www.stjohn.cdeducation.org. Mr. Andy Potter, Prin. Lay Teachers 4; Students 67.
Catechesis Religious Program—Jennifer Indoden, P.S.R. Students 70.
LONDON, MADISON CO., ST. PATRICK (1866) [CEM] Rev. Michael J. Hinterschied; Deacon Daniel W. Hann.
Res.: 61 S. Union St., London, 43140.
Tel: 740-852-0942; Fax: 740-852-5008; Email: julie@stpatricklondon.org; Web: www.stpatricklondon.org.
School—St. Patrick School, (Grades PreSchool-8), 226 Elm St., London, 43140. Tel: 740-852-0161; Fax: 740-852-0602; Email: jfroning@cdeducation.org. Deb Adamczak, Prin. Lay Teachers 11; Students 173.
Catechesis Religious Program—Maria Berryhill, D.R.E. Students 33.
MARION, MARION CO., ST. MARY (1864) [CEM] Revs. Thomas J. Buffer, S.T.D.; Ryan M. Schmit, Parochial Vicar.
Res.: 251 N. Main St., Marion, 43302.
Tel: 740-382-2118; Email: stmaryinfo@marionstmary.org; Web: www.marionstmary.org.
School—St. Mary School, (Grades PreSchool-8), 274 N. Prospect St., Marion, 44302. Tel: 740-382-1607; Fax: 740-382-6577; Email: jmental@cdeducation.org. Jack Mental, Prin. Lay Teachers 7; Students 81.
Catechesis Religious Program—Tel: 740-382-2262. Students 150.
MARYSVILLE, UNION CO., OUR LADY OF LOURDES (1866) [CEM] Rev. Kevin J. Kavanagh, S.T.L., M.Div.; Deacons Charles Knight; David Bezusko; John Westover.
Res.: 1033 W. Fifth St., Marysville, 43040.
Tel: 937-644-6020; Tel: 937-644-6030;
Fax: 937-644-3297; Email: olol.marysville@rrohio.com; Web: www.olol.cc.
Catechesis Religious Program—Jill Turner, D.R.E. Students 396.
MILLERSBURG, HOLMES CO., ST. PETER (1877) [CEM] [JC] Rev. Ronald J. Aubry.
Res.: 379 S. Crawford St., Millersburg, 44654-1463.
Tel: 330-674-1671; Fax: 330-674-1673; Email: holmescountycatholicchurches@gmail.com; Web: holmescatholic.net.
Catechesis Religious Program—Fax: 330-674-1673. Students 31.
Mission—SS. Peter and Paul (1857) 139 Main St., Glenmont, 44628.
Catechesis Religious Program—Students 6.
MT. VERNON, KNOX CO., ST. VINCENT DE PAUL (1842) [CEM] Revs. Mark J. Hammond, J.C.L., S.T.L.; Daniel Olvera, Parochial Vicar; Deacon Timothy J. Birie.
Res.: 303 E. High St., Mt. Vernon, 43050.
Tel: 740-392-4711; Fax: 740-392-4714; Email: gregmhenkel@gmail.com; Web: www.stvincentmountvernon.org.
School—St. Vincent de Paul School, (Grades PreSchool-8), 206 E. Chestnut St., Mt. Vernon, 43050. Tel: 740-393-3611; Fax: 740-393-0236; Email: mdowns@cdeducation.org. Martha Downs, Prin. Lay Teachers 9; Students 190.
Catechesis Religious Program—Susan Birie, A.R.E. Students 102.
MURRAY CITY, HOCKING CO., ST. PHILIP NERI, Closed. For inquiries for sacramental records contact St. John, Logan.
NEW ALBANY, FRANKLIN CO., CHURCH OF THE RESURRECTION (1983)
6300 E. Dublin-Granville Rd., New Albany, 43054.
Tel: 614-855-1400; Email: slarson@cotrna.org; Web: www.cotrna.org. Rev. Jerome P. Rodenfels, (Retired); Deacon David Murrin.
Res.: 5575 Morgan Rd., New Albany, 43054.
Catechesis Religious Program—Email: pkehres@cotrna.org. Peggy Kehres, C.C.M. Students 500.
NEW BOSTON, SCIOTO CO., ST. MONICA (1916) [CEM]
Mailing Address: 514 Market St., Portsmouth, 45662. Revs. Joseph T. Yokum; Nicola Ventura, Parochial Vicar; Christopher Tuttle, Parochial Vicar; Deacon James M. Sturgeon.
Church: 4252 Pine St., New Boston, 45662.
Tel: 740-354-4551; Email: office@sciotocatholic.org; Web: www.sciotocatholic.org.
Catechesis Religious Program—Students 39.
NEW LEXINGTON, PERRY CO., ST. ROSE OF LIMA (1867) [JC]
309 N. Main St., New Lexington, 43764.
Tel: 740-342-1348; Fax: 740-342-9133; Email: strose@columbus.rr.com; Web: strosepcc.org. Revs. Michael Hartge; Daniel Swartz, Parochial Vicar; Deacon Mark R. Weiner.
School—St. Rose of Lima School, (Grades PreK-8), 119 W. Water St., New Lexington, 43764.
Tel: 740-342-3043; Fax: 740-342-1082; Email: mlollo2@cdeducation.org; Web: stroselimaschool.org. Michael Lollo, Prin. Religious Teachers 2; Lay Teachers 7; Students 79.
Catechesis Religious Program—
NEW PHILADELPHIA, TUSCARAWAS CO., SACRED HEART (1895) [CEM 2] Revs. Jeffrey J. Coning; Thomas Gardner, Parochial Vicar; Deacon Ronald E. Onslow; Rev. Jonathan Kathenge, (Kenya) (In Res.).
Res.: 139 3rd St., N.E., New Philadelphia, 44663-3900. Tel: 330-343-6876; Fax: 330-343-1406; Email: shchurch@neohio.twcbc.com; Web: www.sacredheartnewphila.org.
Catechesis Religious Program—Students 85.
NEWARK, LICKING CO.
1—CHURCH OF THE BLESSED SACRAMENT (1904) [JC]
Mailing Address: 394 E. Main St., Newark, 43055.
Tel: 740-345-4290; Fax: 740-345-3890; Email: office@blsac.net; Web: www.blsac.net. 378 E. Main St., Newark, 43055. Rev. Jonathan F. Wilson; Deacon Patrick Wilson.
School—Church of the Blessed Sacrament School, (Grades K-8), Tel: 740-345-4125; Email: mpackham@cdeducation.org. Josh Caton, Prin. Lay Teachers 10; Students 180.
Catechesis Religious Program—Tel: 740-763-4304. Students 50.
2—ST. FRANCIS DE SALES (1842) [CEM 2]
Mailing Address: 40 Granville St., Newark, 43055.
Tel: 740-345-9874; Email: info@stfrancisparish.net; Web: www.stfrancisparish.net. Rev. David W. Sizemore; Deacon Steven DeMers.
School—St. Francis de Sales School, (Grades PreK-8), Tel: 740-345-4049; Fax: 740-345-9768; Email: smummey@cdeducation.org; Web: www.stfrancisparish.net/school/home. Sally Mummey, Prin.; Dr. Kelly Cahill Roberts, Vice Prin. Lay Teachers 18; Students 371.
NEWCOMERSTOWN, TUSCARAWAS CO., ST. FRANCIS DE SALES (1918) [JC] Rev. Victor R. Wesolowski, Priest Moderator; Deacon Frank A. Duda, Admin.
Church: 440 River St., Newcomerstown, 43832.
Tel: 740-498-7368; Email: stfran10@att.net.
Catechesis Religious Program—Denise Thompson, C.R.E. Students 14.
OTWAY, SCIOTO CO., OUR LADY OF LOURDES (1916) [CEM]
Mailing Address: 2215 Galena Pike, West Portsmouth, 45663. Rev. Nicholas L. Droll, Admin.
Church: 16 W. Main St., Otway, 45657.
Tel: 740-858-4600; Fax: 740-858-4600.
Catechesis Religious Program—Students 19.
Otway Community Service Center—P.O. Box 8, Otway, 45657.
PICKERINGTON, FAIRFIELD CO., SETON PARISH (1978) Rev. James A. Klima; Deacon Hector Raymond, Pastoral Min.
Res.: 600 Hill Rd. N., Pickerington, 43147-9201.
Tel: 614-833-0482; Fax: 614-833-4154; Email: hello@setonparish.com; Web: www.setonparish.com.
Catechesis Religious Program—Tel: 614-833-0485. Mary Jane Sobczyk, D.R.E.; Barbara Serrano, Youth Min.
PLAIN CITY, UNION CO., ST. JOSEPH (1864)
Mailing Address: 670 W. Main St., Plain City, 43064.
Tel: 614-873-8850; Fax: 614-873-0735; Email: office@saintjosephplaincity.com; Web: www.saintjosephplaincity.com. Rev. Joseph J. Trapp II; Deacon Anthony Bonacci.
Church: 140 West Ave., Plain City, 43064.
Catechesis Religious Program—Renee Dvorsky, D.R.E. Students 273.
PORTSMOUTH, SCIOTO CO.
1—HOLY REDEEMER (1853) [CEM] [JC]
Mailing Address: 514 Market St., Portsmouth, 45662. Tel: 740-354-4551; Fax: 740-354-2716; Email: office@portsmouthcatholic.org; Web: www.portsmouthcatholic.org. Revs. Joseph T. Yokum; Christopher Tuttle, Parochial Vicar; Nicola Ventura, Parochial Vicar; Deacons Terrance A. Acox; Christopher Veracalli; James M. Sturgeon.

Church: 1325 Gallia St., Portsmouth, 45662.
School—Notre Dame Elementary, (Grades PreK-6), 1401 Gallia St., Portsmouth, 45662.
Tel: 740-353-2354; Fax: 740-353-6769; Email: jmcmackin@cdeducation.org; Web: www.notredameschools.com. Josh McMackin, Prin. Serving all 7 parishes in Scioto County. Lay Teachers 15; Students 228; Religious Teachers 1.
Catechesis Religious Program—Students 18.
2—ST. MARY (1842) [CEM] Revs. Joseph T. Yokum; Nicola Ventura, Parochial Vicar; Deacons James M. Sturgeon; Christopher Varacalli; Terrance A. Acox.
Res.: 514 Market St., Portsmouth, 45662.
Tel: 740-354-4551; Fax: 740-354-5797; Email: office@sciotocatholic.org; Web: www.sciotocatholic.org.
Catechesis Religious Program—Students 15.
POWELL, DELAWARE CO., ST. JOAN OF ARC (1987)
10700 Liberty Rd. S., Powell, 43065-9303.
Tel: 614-761-0905; Email: contactus@stjoanofarcpowell.org; Web: www.stjoanofarcpowell.org. Revs. James P. Black; Stephen Smith, Parochial Vicar; Deacons Thomas M. Berg Sr., (Retired); James A. Rouse, A.E., M.S., P.E., (Retired); Stephen A. Petrill.
REYNOLDSBURG, FRANKLIN CO., ST. PIUS X (1958) Rev. David J. Young; Deacons John Vellani; James W. Kelly; Rev. Process Milton Kiocha, A.J., (In Res.).
Res.: 1051 Waggoner Rd., Reynoldsburg, 43068.
Tel: 614-866-2859; Fax: 614-866-1499; Email: stpiusx@stpiusxreynoldsburg.org; Web: www.spxreynoldsburg.com.
School—St. Pius X School, (Grades PreSchool-8), 1061 Waggoner Rd., Reynoldsburg, 43068.
Tel: 614-866-6050; Fax: 614-866-6187; Email: dasmith@cdeducation.org; Web: www.coeducation.org/schools/px/index.html. Mr. Darren Smith, Prin. Lay Teachers 18; Students 530.
Catechesis Religious Program—Tel: 614-864-3505. De Bukowski, C.R.E.; Judie Bryant, Dir. Youth Ministry. Students 255.
SOMERSET, PERRY CO.
1—HOLY TRINITY (1826) [CEM]
Mailing Address: P.O. Box 190, Somerset, 43783.
Tel: 740-743-1317; Email: stjoe-holytrinity@columbus.rr.com. Rev. Stephen F. Carmody, O.P.; Deacon Eugene C. Dawson.
Church: 228 S. Columbus St., Somerset, 43783.
School—Holy Trinity School, (Grades PreK-8), 225 S. Columbus St., Somerset, 43783. Tel: 740-743-1324; Fax: 740-743-3870; Email: stjoe-holytrinity@columbus.rr.com; Web: holytrinitypacers.com. William Noll, Prin. Lay Teachers 11; Students 144.
Catechesis Religious Program—Tel: 740-743-1855. Melissa Sipos, D.R.E. Students 58.
2—ST. JOSEPH (1818) [CEM]
Mailing Address: P.O. Box 190, Somerset, 43783. Rev. Stephen F. Carmody, O.P.; Deacon Eugene C. Dawson.
Church: 5757 State Rte. 383, N.E., Somerset, 43783.
Tel: 740-743-1317; Email: stjoe-holytrinity@columbus.rr.com.
Catechesis Religious Program—Tel: 740-743-1855. Students 12.
SUGAR GROVE, FAIRFIELD CO., ST. JOSEPH (1853) [CEM] [JC] Rev. James A. Walter.
Res.: 308 N. Elm St., P.O. Box 209, Sugar Grove, 43155-0209. Tel: 740-746-8302; Email: stjosephsugargrove@gmail.com; Web: saintjosephchurch.homedns.org.
Catechesis Religious Program—Tel: 740-746-8302. Students 31.
SUNBURY, DELAWARE CO., ST. JOHN NEUMANN (1982) Rev. Paul A. Noble, M.A., Ph.D.; Deacon Carl A. Calcara Jr.
Church: 9633 E. State Rte. 37, Sunbury, 43074.
Tel: 740-965-1358; Email: saintjohnneumannsunbury@gmail.com; Email: jsutton.saintjohn@gmail.com; Web: www.saintjohnsunbury.org.
Catechesis Religious Program—Robert M. Steinbauer, D.R.E. Students 731.
UTICA, LICKING CO., CHURCH OF THE NATIVITY (1909) Closed. For inquiries for parish records please see St. Vincent de Paul, Mount Vernon.
WASHINGTON COURT HOUSE, FAYETTE CO., ST. COLMAN (1885) [CEM] Revs. William P. Hahn; Sean Dooley, Parochial Vicar; Thomas Herge, Parochial Vicar.
Office: 219 S. North St., Washington Court House, 43160. Tel: 740-335-5000; Email: office@stcolmanwch.org; Web: www.stcolmanwch.org.
Catechesis Religious Program—Tel: 740-335-5005. Stephanie Robinson, R.E.C. Students 119.
WAVERLY, PIKE CO., ST. MARY, QUEEN OF THE MISSIONS (1878) [JC] Revs. William P. Hahn; Sean Dooley, Parochial Vicar; Thomas Herge, Parochial Vicar.
Res.: 407 S. Market St., Waverly, 45690.
Tel: 740-947-2436; Email: stmary_qm@frontier.com; Web: www.stmarywaverly.com.
Catechesis Religious Program—Students 6.
WELLSTON, JACKSON CO., SS. PETER AND PAUL (1881) [CEM] Revs. Joseph T. Yokum; Nicola Ventura, Parochial Vicar; Christopher Tuttle, Parochial Vicar.
Res.: 227 S. New York Ave., Wellston, 45692.
Tel: 740-384-2359; Email: jacksoncountycatholi1@yahoo.com.
School—SS. Peter and Paul School, (Grades PreSchool-8), 229 S. New York Ave., Wellston, 45692. Tel: 740-384-6354; Email: kfulton@cdeducation.org. Kristyl Fulton, Prin. Lay Teachers 9; Students 98.
Catechesis Religious Program—Students 90.
WEST JEFFERSON, MADISON CO., SS. SIMON AND JUDE (1867) [CEM]
9350 High Free Pike, West Jefferson, 43162-9704.
Tel: 614-879-8562; Fax: 614-879-7373; Email: frmetzger@stsimonjude.org; Web: stsimonjude.org. Rev. William A. Metzger, B.A.; Deacon Joseph A. Knapke.
Catechesis Religious Program—Email: kjones@stsimonjude.org. Katie Jones, D.R.E. Students 31.
WEST PORTSMOUTH, SCIOTO CO., OUR LADY OF SORROWS (1945) [CEM] Rev. Nicholas L. Droll, Admin.
Res.: 2215 Galena Pike, West Portsmouth, 45663.
Tel: 740-858-4600; Email: fatherndroll@gmail.com.
New To You Service Center—
Catechesis Religious Program—P.O. Box 31, Otway, 45657. Students 10.
Mission—Holy Trinity, 9493 Carey's Run, Pond Creek, Scioto Co. 45663.
WESTERVILLE, DELAWARE CO., ST. PAUL THE APOSTLE (1913) Revs. Charles F. Klinger, M.A., M.Div., Ph.D.; Anthony P. Lonzo, Parochial Vicar; Emmanuel Adu Addai, Parochial Vicar; Deacons Mickey B. Hawkins; Joseph W. Ciaciura; Carl Jerzyk; Thomas Barford; Rev. David E. Gwinner, (In Res.), (Retired).
Church: 313 N. State St., Westerville, 43082.
Tel: 614-882-2109; Email: stpaulchurch@stpacc.org; Web: www.stpaulcatholicchurch.org.
School—St. Paul the Apostle School, (Grades K-8), 61 Moss Rd., Westerville, 43082. Tel: 614-882-2710; Fax: 614-882-5998; Email: kanorris@cdeducation.org. John Hocker, Dean of Students; Kathleen Norris, Ph.D., Prin. Lay Teachers 40; Students 841.
Catechesis Religious Program—Tel: 614-882-5045; Email: mputman@stpacc.org. Mary Ann Putman, D.R.E. Students 1,000.
WHEELERSBURG, SCIOTO CO., ST. PETER (1855) [CEM]
2167 Lick Run Lyra Rd., Wheelersburg, 45694. Email: office@sciotocatholic.org; Web: www.sciotocatholic.org. Mailing Address: 514 Market St., Portsmouth, 45662. Tel: 740-345-4551. Revs. Joseph T. Yokum, St. Peter in Chains, 2167 Lick Run Lyra Rd., Wheelersburg, 45694-8882; Christopher Tuttle, Parochial Vicar; Nicola Ventura, Parochial Vicar; Deacons Terrance A. Acox; James M. Sturgeon; Christopher Veracalli.
Catechesis Religious Program—Theresa Metzler, Family Life Coord. Students 50.
WILLS CREEK, COSHOCTON CO., OUR LADY OF LOURDES, Closed. For sacramental records contact Sacred Heart, Coshocton.
WORTHINGTON, FRANKLIN CO., ST. MICHAEL aka St. Michael the Archangel Catholic Church (1946) Revs. Anthony A. Dinovo Jr.; Timothy Lynch, Parochial Vicar; Deacons John R. Crerand, M.A., J.C.L.; Klaus Fricke; William F. Demidovich Jr.
Res.: 5750 N. High St., Worthington, 43085.
Tel: 614-885-7814; Fax: 614-885-8060; Email: office@saintmichael-cd.org; Web: www.saintmichael-cd.org.
School—St. Michael School, (Grades PreSchool-8), 64 E. Selby Blvd., Worthington, 43085-3986.
Tel: 614-885-3149; Fax: 614-885-1249; Email: srjp@cdeducation.org; Web: www.cdeducation.org/schools/mi. Sr. John Paul Maher, O.P., Prin. Lay Teachers 25; Students 375; Religious Teachers 4.
Catechesis Religious Program—Tel: 614-888-5384. Kathleen Henry, D.R.E. Students 286.
ZALESKI, VINTON CO., ST. SYLVESTER (1861) [CEM] (Irish) Revs. William P. Hahn; Sean Dooley, Parochial Vicar; Michael Hartge, Parochial Vicar; David E. Young, B.A., M.Div., (In Res.), (Retired).
Res.: 119 N. Second St., P.O. Box 264, Zaleski, 45698-0264. Tel: 740-774-1407; Tel: 740-596-5474; Email: secretary@stpeterchillicothe.com; Web: www.stpeterchillicothe.com/st-sylvester-zaleski.
Catechesis Religious Program—Students 11.
ZANESVILLE, MUSKINGUM CO.
1—ST. NICHOLAS (1842) [CEM] (German)
955 E. Main St., Zanesville, 43701. Rev. Martin J. Ralko; Deacon Burdette N. (Pete) Peterson Jr., Pastoral Assoc.
Res.: 925 E. Main St., Zanesville, 43701.
Tel: 740-453-0597; Email: dginikos@stnickparish.org; Web: www.stnickparish.org.
School—Bishop Fenwick School, (Grades PreSchool-8), 1030 E. Main St., Zanesville, 43701.
Tel: 740-453-2637; Fax: 740-454-0653; Email: ksagan@cdeducation.org. Kelly Sagan, Prin. Lay Teachers 22; Students 285.
Catechesis Religious Program—Tel: 740-450-7461. Becky Cade, C.R.E. Students 52.
2—ST. THOMAS AQUINAS (1820) [CEM 2]
Tel: 740-453-3301; Email: parish@saintthomaszanesville.org; Web: www.saintthomaszanesville.org. Rev. Jan C. Sullivan; Lori Mazzone, Dir.
School—Bishop Fenwick Early Childhood Center, (Grades PreSchool-PreK), School: 139 N. Fifth St., Zanesville, 43701. Tel: 740-454-9731; Email: bschiele@cdeducation.org. Bethany Schiele, Dir.
Catechesis Religious Program—Email: azurface@saintthomaszanesville.org. Amanda Zurface, J.C.L., D.R.E. Students 45.
ZOAR, TUSCARAWAS CO., CHURCH OF THE HOLY TRINITY (1995) [CEM 4]
1835 Dover Zoar Rd., N.E., Bolivar, 44612.
Tel: 330-874-4716; Email: bulletin@holytrinityzoar.net; Web: www.holytrinityzoar.net. Revs. Jeffrey J. Coning; Thomas Gardner, Parochial Vicar; Deacon Lyn Houze. In Res., Rev. Jonathan Kathenge, (Kenya).
Catechesis Religious Program—Students 72.

Chaplains of Public Institutions

COLUMBUS. *Children's Hospital*. Rev. Sylvester Onyeachonam.
Corrections Medical Center. Mrs. Rose Hamilton.
OSU Hospital East. Vacant.
OSU Medical Center. Vacant.
CHILLICOTHE. *Chillicothe Correctional Institution*, P.O. Box 5500, Chillicothe, 45601.
Tel: 740-773-2616, Ext. 248. Rev. Lawrence L. Hummer.
Ross Correctional Institution, P.O. Box 7010, Chillicothe, 45601. Tel: 740-774-4182, Ext. 2519. Rev. Joseph C. Klee, Tel: 614-372-5249 (Parish).
Veteran's Affairs Medical Center, 17273 S.R. 104, Chillicothe, 45601. Tel: 740-773-1141, Ext. 7203. Rev. William P. Hahn.
LANCASTER. *Southeastern Correctional Institution*, Lancaster. Tel: 740-653-4324. Deacon Paul Deshaies.
LONDON. *London Correctional Institution*,
Tel: 740-852-2454, Ext. 451. Rev. Michael J. Hinterschied, Chap.
Madison Correctional Institution. Deacon Daniel W. Hann, Chap.
LUCASVILLE. *Southern Ohio Correctional Facility*, Lucasville. Tel: 740-259-5544. Deacons James M. Sturgeon, Christopher Varacalli.
MARION. *Marion Correctional Institution*,
Tel: 740-382-5781. Rev. Joseph C. Klee, Tel: 614-372-5249 (Parish).
MARYSVILLE. *Ohio Reformatory for Women*. Rev. Joseph J. Trapp II, Chap.
ORIENT. *Corrections Reception Center*. Rev. Joseph J. Trapp II, Sacramental Min.
Pickaway Correctional Institution, Tel: 614-877-4362. Deacon Donald Robers.

On Duty Outside the Diocese:
Rev.—
Ascencio, Joseph A., Chap., Federal Prison System, Florence, CO 81226.

Hospital Ministry:
Revs.—
Chick, Jesse Chi, C.F.I.C.
Faustner, William J., (Retired)
Mathewson, Dean, Tel: 614-252-0976
Owera, Ramon Macoy, C.F.I.C.
Thirumalareddy, Sudehakar Reddy, C.F.I.C.

Retired:
Rev. Msgrs.—
Clagett, Carl P., (Retired), 25 Noe Bixby Rd., 43213
Cody, John K., M.Div., J.C.L., (Retired), 173 Charleston Ave., 43214
Dreese, John J., S.S.L., S.T.L., (Retired), P.O. Box 39, New Straitsville, 43766
Dunn, William A., (Retired), 3697 MillStream Dr., Hilliard, 43026
Fairchild, Edward, (Retired), 3306 Beachworth Dr., 43232
Frecker, A. Anthony, M.Div., M.Th., (Retired), 71291 Shea Rd., Mc Arthur, 45651
Funk, David R., B.A., S.T.B., (Retired)
Geiger, James A., M.A., Ph.D., (Retired)
Lane, Frank P., Ph.D., (Retired), 5459 Hanover Cir., Cincinnati, 45230
Meagher, Frank J., (Retired), 5253 E. Broad St., Apt. 207, 43213
Missimi, Anthony N., (Retired), 1374 Lakeshore Dr., Apt. B, 43204

Noon, Robert L., (Retired), 5253 E. Broad St. #127, 43213
Sorohan, David V., M.A., S.T.L., Ph.D., (Retired), 25 Noe Bixby #148, 43213

Revs.—
Benecki, Stanley, (Retired), 5253 E. Broad St. #202, 43213
Blubaugh, Homer D., (Retired), P.O. Box 33, Danville, 43014
Colopy, James L., (Retired), 3730 Broadway, Grove City, 43123-2235
Cotton, Charles E., (Retired), 515 Milford Ave., 43202
DeVille, William H., (Retired), 196 S. Grant Ave., Unit 304, 43215-8365
Ehwald, Joseph A., (Retired)
Engle, Richard F., (Retired), 25 Noe Bixby Rd. #146, 43213
Faustner, William J., (Retired), 4590 Knightsbridge #104, 43214
Gribble, G. Michael, M.Div., (Retired), 13644 Juniper Rd., Thornville, 43076
Gwinner, David E., (Retired), 313 N. State St., Westerville, 43082
Keck, Edward, (Retired), 626 Hannah Cir., Canton, 44709
Kessler, William Thomas, (Retired), 500 S. Gould, 43209
Larussa, Raymond, (Retired)
Maroon, Donald M., (Retired), P.O. Box 273, New Straitsville, 43766
Metzger, Richard L., (Retired), 6643 Retton Rd., Reynoldsburg, 43068. 6643 Retton Rd., Reynoldsburg, 43068
Metzger, Stephen A., (Retired), 690 State Rte. 6685, Junction City, 43748
Nimocks, Michael F., (Retired), 5253 E. Broad St. #212, 43213
Reis, Justin J., (Retired), 25 Noe Bixby Rd., 43213
Reis, Michael J., (Retired)
Rodenfels, Jerome P., (Retired), P.O. Box 119, Russells Point, 43348
Schilder, David M., (Retired), 192 Grand Ave., Chillicothe, 45601
Snoke, F. Richard, (Retired)
Stanton, Francis M., (Retired), 5253 E. Broad St., # 124, 43213-3834
Stattmiller, John E., (Retired), P.O. Box 31, Otway, 45657
Stluka, Jerome D., (Retired), 25 Noe Bixby Rd. #110, 43213
Swickard, John L., (Retired), 500 Capitol Ct., Williamsburg, VA 23185
Virginia, Stephen G., (Retired), 1018 27th St., Portsmouth, 45662
Young, David E., B.A., M.Div., (Retired), 119 N. 2nd St., Zaleski, 45698.

Permanent Deacons:
Acox, Terrance A., Scioto Co. Parish Consortium
Allison, Mark D., (Ministering Outside the Diocese)
Andrews, William J., Church of the Ascension, Johnstown
Azzola, Feliz F., (Retired)
Barbour, John C., St. Edward the Confessor Church, Granville
Barford, Thomas M., (Retired)
Baumann, Richard L., (Retired)
Berg, Thomas M. Sr., (Retired)
Berg, Thomas M. Jr., B.A., M.J., M.P.S., St. Andrew, Columbus; Chancellor, Diocese of Columbus
Bezusko, David, Our Lady of Lourdes Church, Marysville
Birie, Timothy J., St. Vincent de Paul Church, Mount Vernon
Bonacci, Anthony C., St. Joseph, Plain City
Busic, Richard B., Our Lady of Mt. Carmel, Buckeye Lake
Butts, Jerome J., (Retired)
Cain, Albert E., (Retired)
Calcara, Carl A. Jr., St. John Neumann, Sunbury
Campbell, Christopher, Immaculate Conception, Columbus; Prin., Bishop Watterson High School
Carpenter, Jeffrey P., St. Bernadette Church, Lancaster
Christ, Edward, Perry County Consortium
Ciaciura, Joseph W., St. Paul, Westerville
Crerand, John R., M.A., J.C.L., St. Michael, Worthington; Mod., Tribunal & Judge, Diocesan Tribunal
Dawson, Eugene C., (Retired)
DeMers, Steven, St. Francis DeSales, Newark
Demidovich, William F. Jr., St. Michael, Worthington
Deshaies, Paul, (Retired)
Duda, Frank A., Deacon Admin., St. Francis de Sales, Newcomerstown
DuPrey, John L., (Retired)
Eiden, Gregory L., (Retired)
Elam, Jack W., (Retired)
Fondriest, Ronald H., (Retired)
Fortkamp, Jeffrey D., Our Lady of Peace, Columbus
Fricke, Klaus, St. Michael, Worthington
Ghiloni, Robert W., (Retired)
Gorman, William J., (Retired)
Gorski, James, St. Joseph Cathedral, Columbus
Gundrum, Henry, (Retired)
Hann, Daniel W., St. Patrick, London
Hauser, Reed T., St. Peter Church, Chillicothe
Hawkins, Mickey, St. Paul, Westerville
Hood, J. Michael, Our Lady of Lourdes, Ada; Immaculate Conception, Kenton
Houze, Lester, Holy Trinity, Zoar
Iannarino, Francis A., Dir. Diaconate Office; St. Brigid of Kildare, Dublin; Chap., Bishop Watterson High School, Columbus
Jerzyk, Carl, St. Paul, Westerville
Johnston, Thomas V., (Retired)
Joseph, Robert A., Our Lady of Victory, Columbus
Kelly, James W., St. Pius X, Reynoldsburg
Knapke, Joseph A., Ss. Simon & Jude Church, West Jefferson
Knight, Charles, (Retired)
Koebel, Lawrence F., (Retired)
Kopczewksi, Michael, Our Lady of Perpetual Help Church, Grove City
Krick, Richard T., (Retired)
Kunkler, Gordon T., (Retired)
Labita, Peter C., Christ the King, Columbus
Lampe, Elmer L., (Retired)
Larcomb, Dwight T., (Retired)
Lozowski, David, St. Ann Church, Dresden
Malone, John R. Jr., St. Cecilia Church, Columbus
McCurry, William E., Holy Family, Columbus
Meyer, Joseph C., St. Matthew the Apostle Church, Gahanna
Miller, Charles J., St. John XXIII, Canal Winchester
Milne, Maurice N. III, St. Agatha, Columbus
Minner, Roger, St. Mary, Columbus
Morris, James, St. Brendan, Hilliard
Mould, Douglas, Sacred Heart, Coshocton
Mueller, Martin, (Retired)
Murrin, Kevin P., Church of the Resurrection, New Albany
Naporano, Andrew W., St. Margaret of Cortona, Columbus
Nguyen, Jason Minh, St. Augustine & Gabriel Church, Columbus
Onslow, Ronald E., Sacred Heart Church, NewPhiladelphia
Paniccia, Frank A., (Retired)
Parsons, Ralph L., (Retired)
Paulucci, Philip M., M.S.W., L.I.S.W., St. Peter, Columbus
Peterson, Burdette N., St. Nicholas, Zanesville
Petrill, Stephen A., St. Joan of Arc Church, Powell
Phillips, Byron, St. Christopher, Columbus
Phillips, Thomas D., St. Thomas the Apostle Church, Columbus
Plummer, Gil L. Sr., (Retired)
Poirier, Donald, St. Brigid of Kildare, Dublin
Pry, Roger F., St. John XXIII, Canal Winchester
Racine, Dean W., St. Elizabeth, Columbus; Business Mgr., St. Paul, Westerville
Rankin, John, (Retired)
Raymond, Hector, Seton Parish, Pickerington
Reis, Christopher J., St. Catharine Church, Columbus; Chap., Diocesan Scouting Prog.
Robers, Donald, St. John, Logan; Chaplain, Pickaway Correctional
Ross, Michael D., Ph.D., (Retired)
Rouse, James A., A.E., M.S., P.E., (Retired)
Rowlands, Thomas J., St. Margaret of Cortona Church, Columbus
Rzewnicki, Phil E., (Ministering Outside the Diocese)
Saunders, Douglas A., St. Brendan the Navigator Church, Hilliard
Scarpitti, Mark A., St. Bernadette, Lancaster
Schermer, Joseph E., (Retired)
Smith, Craig, St. Anthony, Columbus
Smithberger, Marion E., St. Timothy, Columbus
Smoulder, George, (Unassigned)
Sturgeon, James M., Scioto County Parish Consortium
Sullivan, Frank, St. Mary, Lancaster; Chap., Bishop Hartley High School
Supino, Bart, (Retired)
Tucky, Todd M., St. Mary Church, Delaware
Turner, Harry, (Retired)
Varacalli, Christopher, Scioto County Parish Consortium
Vellani, Albert J., St. Pius X, Reynoldsburg
Venturini, Stephen A., Our Lady of the Miraculous Medal, Columbus
Waybright, Charles G., Seton Parish, Pickerington; Seton Parish, Pickerington
Weiner, Mark R., Perry County Consortium
Westover, John, (Retired)
Wiggins, Patrick J., (Retired)
Wilson, Larry, St. Leonard, Heath
Wilson, Patrick, Blessed Sacrament, Newark
Zemanek, Paul J., St. Brigid of Kildare, Dublin
Zimmermann, George A. Jr., Holy Spirit, Columbus; St. Phillip, Columbus.

INSTITUTIONS LOCATED IN DIOCESE

[A] SEMINARIES, PONTIFICAL COLLEGES

COLUMBUS. *Pontifical College Josephinum* (1888) 7625 N. High St., 43235-1498. Tel: 614-885-5585; Fax: 614-885-2307; Email: bcheek@pcj.edu; Web: www.pcj.edu. Dr. Perry J. Cahill, Academic Dean, College of Theology. Faculty 42; Students 170; Clergy Religious Teachers 12.

Chancellor & Vice Chancellor: Most Revs. Christophe Pierre, Apostolic Nuncio to the United States, Chancellor; Frederick F. Campbell, D.D., Ph.D., Vice Chancellor & Bishop of Columbus.

General Administration: Rev. Msgrs. Christopher J. Schreck, Ph.D., S.T.D., S.S.L., Rector & Pres.; Kevin T. McMahon, S.T.D., Vice Rector, Admin.; Revs. Raymond N. Enzweiler, Ph.D., Be.L., Vice Rector; John A. Allen, S.T.B., Vice Pres., Advancement & Dir., Alumni Rels.; Dr. David J. DeLeonardis, Ph.D., Academic Dean, College of Liberal Arts; John O. Erwin, M.B.A., C.P.A., Vice Pres., Admin.; Treas.; Dir., Human Resources.

Administrative Officers: Sam Dean, M.B.A., Registrar; Carolyn A. Dinovo, B.A., Dir. Communications; Mr. Donald D. Frye, M.S., Dir. Information Technology; Rev. Marek Kasperczuk, Dir.; Marky Leichtnam, B.S., Financial Aid Dir.; Janet Jenkins, M.S., R.D.N., L.D., Coord. Nutrition & Wellness; Alisa K. Schlabig, Coord. Health Svcs.; Deacon Tom Dubois, Exec. Dir., National Assoc. Diaconate Directors.

College of Liberal Arts: Alma M. Amell, Ph.D., Prof. & Dir. Hispanic Formation; Loyann W. Brush, M.A., Asst. Prof.; Marisa D. Cahall, Ph.D., Lecturer (Adjunct); Lisa Ciminillo, M.S., Lecturer (Adjunct); David J. De Leonardis, Ph.D., Assoc. Prof., Academic Dean & Dir. Intellectual Formation; Rev. Raymond N. Enzweiler, Ph.D., Be.L., Assoc. Prof. & Asst. Dir. Pastoral & Apostolic Formation, Dean, Community Life, Dir. Human Formation; Douglas C. Fortner, Ph.D., Asst. Prof.; Eric S. Graff, Ph.D., Asst. Prof., Dir. Strategic Planning & Dir. Accreditation; Rev. John F. Heisler, M.A., Instructor & Dir. Spiritual Formation & Dir. Sacred Liturgy; Jason J. Keefer, D.M.A., Asst. Prof. & Dir. Sacred Music; Dr. Kevin Poole, Ph.D., Asst. Prof.; Beverly S. Lane, M.L.S., Asst. Librarian; Marny S. Lemmel, Ph.D., Asst. Prof.; Joseph T. Papa, Ph.D., Asst. Prof.; Patricia A. Polko, M.A., Instructor & Dir. Josephinum English Language Prog.; Rev. John M. Rozembajgier, J.C.L., S.T.L., Lecturer; Vice Rector, College Liberal Arts; Athletic Dir.;, Asst. Vice Rector, Formation; Daniel Shields, Ph.D., Asst. Prof.; Elizabeth V. Stilp, M.A., Lecturer (Adjunct) & Dir. Academic Support Svcs.; Rev. John Sims Baker, Dean of Community Life; Mr. William L. Little, Adjunct Prof.; Rev. Eric Wagner, Prof.

School of Theology: Rev. John A. Allen, S.T.B., Vice Pres. Advancement & Dir. Alumni Rels.; Perry J. Cahall, Ph.D., Assoc. Prof., Academic Dean & Dir. Intellectual Formation; Rev. Louis V. Iasiello, O.F.M., Ph.D., RADM, CHC, USN, Ret., Prof. & Dir. Pastoral & Apostalic Formation; Grzegorz Ignatik, S.T.L., M.T.S., Lecturer (Adjunct); Timothy M. Luis, Ph.D., Lecturer (Adjunct), Dir. Counseling Svcs.; Rev. Msgr. Kevin T. McMahon, S.T.D., Prof. & Vice Rector, Administration; Revs. David G. Monaco, C.P., Ph.D., Assoc. Prof., Sacred Scripture; Joseph A. Murphy, S.J., S.T.D., Assoc. Prof., Dir. Admissions; Dir. Community Support Svcs.; William F. Murphy Jr., S.T.D., Prof. & Editor, Josephinum Journal of Theology; Rev. David A. Schalk, M.Div., S.T.B., Lecturer (Adjunct); Rev. Msgr. Christopher J. Schreck, Ph. D., S.T.D., S.S.L., Prof., Rector & Pres.; Rev. W. Becket Soule, O.P., J.C.D., Prof., Bishop James A. Griffin Chair of Canon Law; Peter G. Veracka, M.S.L.S., Assoc. Prof. & Dir. Library Svcs.; Rev. Michael Kelly, Dir. of Spiritual Formation.

[B] COLLEGES AND UNIVERSITIES

COLUMBUS. *Ohio Dominican University*, 1216 Sunbury Rd., 43219. Tel: 614-251-4500; Fax: 614-252-0776;

Email: admissions@ohiodominican.edu; Web: www.ohiodominican.edu. Dr. Robert Gervais, Pres.; Dr. Theresa Holleran, Ph.D., Vice Pres. Academic Affairs; Alvin Rodack, Vice Pres., Fin. & Admin. & CFO; Sharon Reed, Dean of Student Life; John W. Naughton, M.B.A., Dir., Graduate Admissions; Sr. Diane Traffas, O.P., Vice Pres.; Julie Burdick, V.P. Enrollment & Student Success; Mark Cooper, Vice Pres. Advancement & External Rels.; Rev. Paul H. Colloton, O.S.F.S., D.Min., Chap.; Michelle Sarff, Librarian. Dominican Sisters of Peace Lay Teachers 61; Students 1,716; Religious Teachers 3; Adjuncts 100.

[C] HIGH SCHOOLS, DIOCESAN OR INTERPAROCHIAL

COLUMBUS. *Bishop Hartley High School*, 1285 Zettler Rd., 43227. Tel: 614-237-5421; Fax: 614-237-3809; Email: hartley@cdeducation.org; Web: bishop-hartley.org. Mike Winters, Prin., Email: mwinters@cdeducation.org; Christopher Kowalski, Vice Prin. Clergy 1; Lay Teachers 55; Students 683.

Bishop Ready High School (1961) 707 Salisbury Rd., 43204. Tel: 614-276-5263; Fax: 614-276-5116; Email: cseamen@cdeducation.org; Web: www.brhs.org. Celene A. Seamen, Prin.; Jeri Rod, Asst. Prin. Administrators 2; Lay Teachers 30; Priests 1; Sisters 1; Students 400.

Bishop Watterson High School (1954) 99 E. Cooke Rd., 43214. Tel: 614-268-8671; Fax: 614-268-0551; Email: ccampbel@cdeducation.org; Web: www.cd.education.org/schools/bw. Deacon Christopher Campbell, Prin.; Ryan P. Schwieterman, Asst. Prin.; Andrea Pore, Asst. Prin.; Deacon Frank A. Iannarino, Chap. Deacons 2; Lay Teachers 90; Students 901.

St. Charles Preparatory School, 2010 E. Broad St., 43209. Tel: 614-252-6714; Fax: 614-251-6800; Email: jlower@cdeducation.org; Web: www.stcharlesprep.org. James Lower, Prin. Lay Teachers 35; Sisters 1; Students 640.

St. Francis de Sales High School, 4212 Karl Rd., 43224. Tel: 614-267-7808; Fax: 614-265-3375; Email: dgarrick@cdeducation.org; Web: sfdstallions.org. Mr. Dan Garrick, Prin.; Jim Jones, Asst. Prin. Lay Teachers 70; Students 847.

LANCASTER. *William V. Fisher Catholic High School*, 1803 Granville Pike, Lancaster, 43130. Tel: 740-654-1231; Fax: 740-654-1233; Email: dburley@cdeducation.org; Web: fishercatholic.org. Jim Globokar, Prin. Lay Teachers 14; Students 168.

NEW PHILADELPHIA. *Tuscarawas Central Catholic Junior/Senior High School*, (Grades 7-12), 777 Third St., N.E., New Philadelphia, 44663. Tel: 330-343-3302; Fax: 330-343-6388; Email: aciviello@cdeducation.org; Web: www.tccsaints.com. Annette Civiello, B.A., M.A., Ph.D., Prin. Lay Teachers 13; Students 153.

NEWARK. *Newark Catholic High School* (1958) 1 Green Wave Dr., Newark, 43055. Tel: 740-344-3594; Fax: 740-344-0421; Email: bhill@cdeducation.org; Web: www.newarkcatholic.org/. Beth Hill, Prin. Lay Teachers 21; Students 215.

PORTSMOUTH. *Notre Dame High School* (1953) (Grades 7-12), (Junior/Senior High School) 2220 Sunrise Ave., Portsmouth, 45662. Tel: 740-353-2354; Fax: 740-353-2526; Email: twalker@cdeducation.org. Tom Walker, Prin. Lay Teachers 13; Students 153.

ZANESVILLE. *Bishop Rosecrans High School* (1950) 1040 E. Main St., Zanesville, 43701. Tel: 740-452-7504; Fax: 740-455-5080; Email: ksagan@cdeducation.org; Web: www.rosecrans.cdeducation.org. Chelsea Toliver, Prin.; Kelly Sagan, Dir. Lay Teachers 12; Students 110.

[D] MONTESSORI SCHOOLS

COLUMBUS. *St. Joseph Montessori School* (1968) 933 Hamlet St., 43201-3595. Tel: 614-291-8601; Fax: 614-291-7411; Email: sjmsoffice@cdeducation.org; Email: sjmsdev@cdeducation.org; Web: www.sjms.net. Matthew Brenner, Headmaster. Lay Teachers 30; Students 275.

[E] PRIVATE SCHOOLS

COLUMBUS. *Our Lady of Bethlehem School and Childcare*, 4567 Olentangy River Rd., 43214. Tel: 614-459-8285; Fax: 614-451-3706; Email: lebling@cdeducation.org; Email: ldulin@cdeducation.org; Web: www.ourladyofbethlehem.org. Lori Dulin, Prin. Infant and Toddler Care; Totally Terrific Twos; Preschool; Pre-Kindergarten; Full & Half Day Kindergarten; Full & Part Time Childcare; Summer Program.

Our Lady of Bethlehem Schools, Inc. Students 126; Total Staff 23.

[F] GENERAL HOSPITALS

COLUMBUS. *Mohun Health Care Center* (1956) 2340 Airport Dr., 43219. Tel: 614-416-6132; Fax: 614-251-0338; Email: aqueener@mohun.org. April Queener, Admin.; Friar Michael DeTemple, Chap. Bed Capacity 72; Tot Asst. Annually 93; Total Staff 94.

Mount Carmel Health System, 6150 E. Broad St., 43213-1574. Tel: 614-546-4533; Fax: 614-546-4573; Email: communitybenefit@mchs.com; Web: mountcarmelhealth.com. Edward Lamb, Pres. & CEO; Sr. Barbara Hahl, Vice Pres.

dba Mount Carmel East Hospital, Mount Carmel West Hospital, Mount Carmel St Anns Hospital, Mount Carmel New Albany Surgical Hospital, Mount Carmel Grove City, Mount Carmel Fitness and Health Bed Capacity 1,424; Tot Asst. Annually 1,207,068; Total Staff 10,360; Volunteers 884.

Legal Holdings:.

Mount Carmel College of Nursing, 127 S. Davis Ave., 43222. Tel: 614-234-5800; Fax: 614-234-2875 ; Email: admissions@mccn.edu; Web: www.mccn.edu. Ann Marie T. Brooks, Pres. Faculty 86; Students 1,063; Volunteers 18.

Mount Carmel Health System Foundation, 6150 E. Broad St, 43231-1574. Tel: 614-546-4500; Fax: 614-546-4501; Email: givetomc@mchs.com; Web: www.mountcarmelfoundation.org. Deanna Stewart, Pres. Tot Asst. Annually 3,664,207.

DENNISON. *Trinity Hospital Twin City, an Affiliate of Catholic Health*, 819 N. First St., Dennison, 44621. Tel: 740-922-2800; Fax: 740-922-6945; Email: mrainsberger@trinitytwincity.org. Rev. Thomas Gardner, Spiritual Care Svcs. Bed Capacity 25; Tot Asst. Annually 46,248; Total Staff 231.

ZANESVILLE. **Genesis HealthCare System*, 2951 Maple Ave., Zanesville, 43701. Tel: 740-454-4633; Fax: 740-455-4914; Email: sfuller@genesishcs.org. Mr. Matthew Perry, CEO & Pres. Bed Capacity 321; Franciscan Sisters of Christian Charity 2; Total Staff 3,500.

Genesis Hospital, 2951 Maple Dr., Zanesville, 43701. Tel: 740-454-4633; Email: mperry@genesishc.org. Mr. Matthew Perry, CEO.

[G] HOMES FOR AGED AND HOUSING FOR ELDERLY

COLUMBUS. *Mother Angeline McCrory Manor, Inc.* (2005) 5199 E. Broad St., 43213. Tel: 614-751-5700 ; Fax: 614-751-8311; Email: kdrufke@carmeliteseniorliving.org; Web: www.carmeliteseniorliving.org. Sr. Ann Brown, O.-Carm., CEO.

Seton South Columbus, Inc. (1995) 155 Highview Blvd., 43207. Tel: 614-492-9944; Fax: 614-492-9955; Email: coneal@borror.com. Connie O'Neal, Admin. Total in Residence 60; Total Staff 2.

Seton Square, North, 1776 Drew Ave., 43235. Tel: 614-451-1995; Fax: 614-451-3793; Email: fhinklin@borror.com. Fawn Hinklin, Admin. Total in Residence 242; Total Staff 6.

Seton Square, West, 3999 Clime Rd., 43228. Tel: 614-274-8550; Fax: 614-308-1550; Email: vthomas@borror.com. Vikki Thomas, Admin. Total in Residence 48; Staff 3.

The Villas at St. Therese, Inc., 25 Noe Bixby Rd., 43213. Tel: 614-864-3576; Email: srann@carmeliteseniorliving.org. Sr. Ann Brown, O.Carm., CEO.

**Villas at St. Therese Plain City Assisted Living*, 7025 Club Park Dr., Plain City, 43064. Tel: 614-761-3734; Email: jhendricks@stbrigidofkildare.org. P.O. Box 3130, Dublin, 43016. Rev. Msgr. Joseph M. Hendricks, Contact Person.

**The Villas at St. Therese Plain City Independent Living*, 7079 Club Park Dr., Plain City, 43064. Tel: 614-761-3734; Email: jhendricks@stbrigidofkildare.org. P.O. Box 3130, Dublin, 43016. Sr. Ann Brown, O.Carm., CEO.

COSHOCTON. *Seton Coshocton, Inc.*, 377 Clow Ln., Coshocton, 43812. Tel: 740-622-7664 (Coshocton No.); Fax: 740-622-4635; Email: RCONKLE@BORROR.COM. Roxana Conkle, Property Mgr.; Katie Grubbs, Svc. Coord. Total in Residence 40; Total Staff 3; Apartments 40.

DOVER. *Seton Development, Inc.*, 501 S. James St., Dover, 44622. Tel: 330-343-3611; Fax: 330-364-3147; Email: thoover@borror.com. Tina Hoover, Admin. Total in Residence 50; Total Staff 4.

Seton Square Dover, II, Inc., 139 Filmore Ave., Dover, 44622. Tel: 330-343-3611; Fax: 330-364-3147; Email: thoover@borror.com. Tina Hoover, Admin. Total in Residence 40; Total Staff 4.

KENTON. *Seton Kenton, Inc.*, 699 Morningside Dr., Kenton, 43326. Tel: 419-673-7202; Fax: 419-673-7202; Email: kmelton@borror.com. Karen Melton, Admin. Total in Residence 50; Total Staff 2; In Residence 48.

LANCASTER. *Seton Lancaster, Inc.*, 232 Gay St., Lancaster, 43130. Tel: 740-681-1403; Fax: 740-681-9178; Email: drose@borror.com. Diana Rose, Admin. Total in Residence 35; Total Staff 2.

LONDON. *Seton London, Inc.*, 350 Cambridge Dr., London, 43140. Tel: 740-852-4233; Email: vthomas@borror.com. Vikki Thomas, Admin. Total in Residence 50; Total Staff 3.

MARION. *Seton Square Marion, Inc.*, 255 Richland Rd., Marion, 43302. Tel: 740-389-4746; Fax: 740-389-9780; Email: dreyneke@borror.com. Deborah Reyneke, Admin. Total in Residence 67; Total Staff 4.

REYNOLDSBURG. *Seton Square East, Inc.*, 1235 Briarcliff Rd., Reynoldsburg, 43068. Tel: 614-861-4860; Fax: 614-861-8022; Email: jclipner@borror.com. Jonda Clipner, Admin. Total in Residence 106; Total Staff 3.

WASHINGTON COURT HOUSE. *Seton Washington Court House*, 400 N. Glenn Ave., Washington Court House, 43160. Tel: 740-335-2292; Fax: 740-335-2291; Email: khoty@borror.com. Kimberly Hoty, Admin. Total in Residence 40; Total Staff 3.

WELLSTON. *Seton Square Wellston, Inc.* (1980) 570 W. First St., Wellston, 45692. Tel: 740-384-6174; Fax: 740-384-1514; Email: npetersen@borror.com. Nyla Petersen, Admin. Total in Residence 48; Total Staff 2.

ZANESVILLE. *Seton Housing, Inc.*, 516 Sheridan St., Zanesville, 43701. Tel: 740-453-4422; Fax: 740-453-4950; Email: kmendenhall@borror.com. Kellie Mendenhall, Admin. Total in Residence 45; Total Staff 1.

[H] CONVENTS AND RESIDENCES FOR SISTERS

COLUMBUS. *Congregation of the Sisters of the Holy Cross*, Mount Carmel East Convent, 266 McNaughton Rd., 43213-2139. Tel: 614-866-9397; Email: sbrennan@cscsisters.org. Sr. Suzanne Brennan, Treas.

Sisters of the Holy Cross, Inc. Sisters 2.

Dominican Sisters of Peace, Inc., 2320 Airport Dr., 43219-2098. Tel: 614-416-1900; Fax: 614-252-7435; Email: srpeace@oppeace.org; Web: www.oppeace.org. Sisters 451.

Leadership Team: Sisters Patricia Twohill, O.P., Prioress; Anne Lythgoe, O.P., Gen. Councilor; Gene Poore, O.P., Gen. Councilor; Therese Leckert, O.P., Gen. Councilor, Sec.-General; Gemma Doll, O.P., Gen. Councilor.

Sisters' Residence:.

Dominican Sisters of Peace Columbus Motherhouse, 2320 Airport Dr., 43219-2098. Tel: 614-416-1092; Fax: 614-416-1379; Email: mdelaney@oppeace.org. Sr. Germaine Conroy, O.P., Mission Group Coord. Sisters 68.

Mother Angeline McCrory Manor Convent, 5199 E. Broad St., 43213. Tel: 614-751-5700; Email: srann@carmeliteseniorliving.org. Sr. Ann Brown, O.Carm., Supr. Carmelite Sisters for the Aged and Infirm. Sisters 6.

GROVE CITY. *Daughters of Mary Mother of Mercy Convent*, 5754 Daisy Trail Dr., Grove City, 43123. Tel: 267-237-5614; Email: laboure_okoroafor@yahoo.com. Sister Laboure Okoroafor, Prioress. Religious order Sisters 2.

[I] NEWMAN CENTERS

COLUMBUS. *St. Thomas More Newman Center at The Ohio State University*, St. Thomas More Newman Center at The Ohio State Univ., 64 W. Lane Ave., 43201. Tel: 614-291-4674; Fax: 614-291-2065; Email: mailbox@buckeyecatholic.com; Web: www.buckeyecatholic.com. Revs. Edward Nowak, Dir.; Stuart Wilson-Smith, Assoc. Dir.; Vincent W. McKiernan, C.S.P., Assoc. Dir.; Charlie Donahue, C.S.P., Assoc. Dir. Priests 4.

[J] FOUNDATIONS

COLUMBUS. **The Foundation of the Catholic Diocese of Columbus* dba The Catholic Foundation, 257 E. Broad St., 43215. Tel: 614-443-8893; Fax: 614-443-8894; Email: lbrown@catholic-foundation.org; Email: kshuey@catholic-foundation.org; Web: www.catholic-foundation.org. Loren P. Brown, Pres. & CEO.

LANCASTER. **William V. Fisher Catholic High School Endowment Fund*, 1803 Granville Pike, Lancaster, 43130. Tel: 740-654-1231; Fax: 740-654-1233; Email: dburley@cdeducation.org; Web: fishercatholic.org. Jim Globokar, Prin.

MARION. *Marion Catholic School Endowment Fund*, c/o St. Mary Church, 251 N. Main St., Marion, 43302-3031. Tel: 740-382-2118; Email: stmaryinfo@marionstmary.org; Web: www.marioncatholicschools.com. Mr. Joe Devany, Contact Person.

NEW PHILADELPHIA. *Tuscarawas Central Catholic High School Endowment Fund*, 777 Third St. N.E., New

Philadelphia, 44663. Tel: 330-343-3302; Fax: 330-343-6388; Email: aciviello@cdeducation.org. Annette Civiello, B.A., M.A., Ph.D., Prin.

NEWARK. **Newark Catholic High School Foundation*, One Green Wave Dr., Newark, 43055. Tel: 740-344-5671; Fax: 740-344-0421; Email: nbourne@newarkcatholic.org. Nancy Bourne, Contact Person.

ZANESVILLE. *Bishop Rosecrans High School Foundation* (1986) 1040 E. Main St., Zanesville, 43701. Tel: 740-452-7504; Fax: 740-455-5080; Email: Ksagan@cdeducation.org; Web: www.rosecrans.cdeducation.org. Kelly Sagan, Dir.

[K] MISCELLANEOUS

COLUMBUS. *Catholic Men's Ministry*, 7080 Westview Dr., Worthington, 43085. Tel: 614-505-6605; Email: mail@catholicmensministry.com; Web: catholicmensministry.com. Chuck Wilson, Dir.

The Christ Child Society of Columbus, Inc., P.O. Box 340091, 43234-0091. Tel: 614-436-5518; Email: columbus@christchildsociety.org; Web: www.christchildsociety.org. Bethany Kistler, Pres.

Columbus Catholic Women's Conference, 2280 W. Henderson Rd., #205, Upper Arlington, 43220. Tel: 614-398-2292; Email: info@columbuscatholicwomen.com; Web: www.columbuscatholicwomen.com. Mrs. Michele Faehnle, Chm.; Julie Naporano, Chm.

Cristo Rey Columbus High School Work Study Program, 400 E. Town St., 43215. Tel: 614-223-9261; Email: jfoley@cristoreycolumbus.org; Web: cristoreycolumbus.org. Mr. F. James Foley, Pres.; John Petro, Work-Study Dir.

Diocesan Charities Membership Corporation, 198 E. Broad St., 43215. Tel: 614-224-2251; Email: chomailbox@columbuscatholic.org. Rev. Msgr. Joseph M. Hendricks, Contact Person.

Diocesan Retirement Community Corp., 198 E. Broad St., 43215. Tel: 614-224-2251; Fax: 614-224-6306; Email: chomailbox@columbuscatholic.org. Rev. Msgr. Joseph M. Hendricks, Pres. & CEO.

Haitian Catholic Coalition of Ohio, 1582 Ferris Rd., 43224. Tel: 614-778-0459; Email: frval2@yahoo.com. Nedy Melidor, Founder & Counselor; Rev. Fritzner Valcin, (Haiti) Counselor.

**The Jubilee Museum and Catholic Cultural Center*, 57 S. Grubb St., 43215-2747. Tel: 614-746-4407; Email: kenneyshawn@yahoo.com; Web: jubileemuseum.org. Shawn Kenney, Admin. Holy Family Parish.

The Nigerian Catholic Community in Columbus, Ohio, Inc., P.O. Box 248401, 43224. Tel: 614-267-3406; Email: hike@columbuscatholic.org. Rev. Hilary C. Ike, (Nigeria) J.C.L., Chap.

Shrine of Blessed Margaret of Castello, 280 N. Grant Ave., 43215. Tel: 614-240-5915; Fax: 614-240-5928; Email: director@littlemargaret.org; Web: www.littlemargaret.org. Rev. Stephen Alcott, O.P., Dir. Shrine dedicated to promoting the sanctity of life, and the cause of canonization of Blessed Margaret of Castello, O.P.

St. Stephen's Community House, 1500 E. 17th Ave., 43219. Tel: 614-294-6347; Fax: 614-294-0258; Email: jpegues@saintstephensch.org; Web: www.saintstephensch.org. Marilyn Mehaffie, Admin. Total Staff 60; Total Assisted 30,000.

HILLIARD. **Catholic Medical Association of Central Ohio*, 4475 Dublin Rd., Hilliard, 43026. Tel: 614-806-2222; Email: jp2cmacolumbus@gmail.com; Web: www.cmacbus.com. Anthony Casey, M.D., Pres.; Dr. Marian K. Schuda, Sec.

LANCASTER. **St. Mary of the Assumption Foundation*, 132 S. High St., Lancaster, 43130. Tel: 740-653-0997; Fax: 740-653-0337; Email: info@stmarylancaster.org. Rev. Craig R. Eilerman, Contact Person.

ZANESVILLE. *St. Nicholas Foundation* (1842) 955 E. Main St., Zanesville, 43701. Tel: 740-453-0597; Fax: 740-453-0590; Email: tomcstnick@rrohio.com; Web: www.stnickparish.org. Rev. Martin J. Ralko, Pres.

RELIGIOUS INSTITUTES OF MEN REPRESENTED IN THE DIOCESE

For further details refer to the corresponding bracketed number in the Religious Institutes of Men or Women section.

[]—*Apostles of Jesus*—A.J.
[1080]—*Congregation of the Resurrection*—C.R.
[]—*Congregation of the Sons of the Immaculate Conception*—C.F.I.C.
[0520]—*Franciscan Friars*—O.F.M.
[0685]—*Institute of the Incarnate Word*—I.V.E.
[0690]—*Jesuit Fathers and Brothers* (Detroit and Maryland Provs.)—S.J.
[]—*Missionary Servants of the Word*—M.S.P.
[0920]—*Oblates of St. Francis DeSales*—O.S.F.S.
[0270]—*Order of Carmelites* (North American Prov. of St. Elias).
[0430]—*Order of Preachers-Dominicans* (Prov. of St. Joseph; Prov. of St. Albert)—O.P.
[1030]—*Paulist Fathers*—C.S.P.
[1050]—*Pontifical Institute for Foreign Missions*—P.I.M.E.
[1060]—*Society of the Precious Blood* (Cincinnati Prov.)—C.PP.S.

RELIGIOUS INSTITUTES OF WOMEN REPRESENTED IN THE DIOCESE

[0280]—*The Bridgettine Sisters*—O.Ss.S.
[0330]—*Carmelite Sisters for the Aged and Infirm*—O.Carm.
[3710]—*Congregation of the Sisters of St. Agnes*—C.S.A.
[1920]—*Congregation of the Sisters of the Holy Cross*—C.S.C.
[1710]—*Congregation of the Third Order of St. Francis of Mary Immaculate, Joliet, IL*—O.S.F.
[0885]—*Daughters of Mary, Mother of Mercy*.
[1070-27]—*Dominican Sisters, Congregation of the Immaculate Conception*.
[]—*Dominican Sisters of Mary, Mother of the Eucharist* (Ann Arbor, MI)—O.P.
[1115]—*Dominican Sisters of Peace, Inc.*—O.P.
[1230]—*Franciscan Sisters of Christian Charity* (Manitowoc, WI)—O.S.F.
[]—*Franciscan Sisters of the Immaculate Heart of Mary*—F.I.H.
[2300]—*Little Servant Sisters of the Immaculate Conception*—L.S.I.C.
[]—*Missionary Servants of the World (Hermanas Misioneras Servidores de la Palabra)*—H.M.S.P.
[0440]—*Sisters of Charity of Cincinnati, Ohio*—S.C.
[0500]—*Sisters of Charity of Nazareth, Kentucky*—S.C.N.
[3000]—*Sisters of Notre Dame de Namur*—S.N.D.deN.
[1630]—*Sisters of St. Francis of Penance and Christian Charity* (Stella Niagara, NY)—O.S.F.
[1530]—*Sisters of St. Francis of the Congregation of Our Lady of Lourdes* (Sylvania, OH)—O.S.F.
[3260]—*Sisters of the Precious Blood* (Dayton, OH)—C.PP.S.
[1720]—*Sisters of the Third Order Regular of St. Francis of the Congregation of Our Lady of Lourdes* (Rochester, NY)—O.S.F.

DIOCESAN CEMETERIES

COLUMBUS. *Mount Calvary*, 581 Mt. Calvary Ave., 43223-2217. Tel: 614-491-2751; Fax: 614-491-4264; Email: ccocsj@aol.com. Mailing Address: 6440 S. High St., Lockbourne, 43137-9208. Rich Finn, Dir. & Gen. Mgr.

LEWIS CENTER. *Resurrection Cemetery*, 9571 N. High St., Lewis Center, 43035-9413. Tel: 614-888-1805; Fax: 614-888-1810; Email: ccocres@aol.com. Rich Finn, Dir. & Gen. Mgr.

LOCKBOURNE. *St. Joseph*, 6440 S. High St., Lockbourne, 43137-9208. Tel: 614-491-2751; Fax: 614-491-4264; Email: ccocsj@aol.com. Rich Finn, Dir. & Gen. Mgr.

PATASKALA. *Holy Cross Cemetery*, 11539 National Rd., S.W., Pataskala, 43062-8304. Tel: 740-927-4442; Fax: 740-927-4645; Email: ccochc@aol.com. Rich Finn, Dir. & Gen. Mgr.

NECROLOGY

† Schlegel, George J., (Retired), Died Apr. 12, 2018
† Serraglio, Mario, (Retired), Died May. 25, 2018
† Laurinaitis, Saulius P., (Retired), Died Sep. 7, 2018
† Ogurchock, James A., (Retired), Died Jul. 7, 2018
† Reichert, Lawrence J., (Retired), Died Jun. 30, 2018

An asterisk (*) denotes an organization that has established tax-exempt status directly with the IRS and is not covered by the USCCB Group Ruling.

Diocese of Corpus Christi

(Dioecesis Corporis Christi)

Most Reverend

WM. MICHAEL MULVEY, S.T.L., D.D.

Eighth Bishop of Corpus Christi; ordained June 29, 1975; appointed Bishop of Corpus Christi January 18, 2010; ordained March 25, 2010. *Mailing Address: P.O. Box 2620, Corpus Christi, TX 78403-2620. Res.: 4650 Ocean Dr., #503, Corpus Christi, TX 78412.*

Most Reverend

EDMOND CARMODY, D.D.

Bishop Emeritus of Corpus Christi; ordained June 8, 1957; appointed Auxiliary Bishop of the Archdiocese of San Antonio November 8, 1988; consecrated December 15, 1988; appointed Bishop of the Diocese of Tyler March 24, 1992; installed May 25, 1992; appointed Bishop of the Diocese of Corpus Christi February 3, 2000; installed March 17, 2000; retired Jan. 18, 2010. *Res.: 4126 Ocean Dr., Corpus Christi, TX 78411-1224.* Tel: 361-882-6191. *Mailing Address: P.O. Box 2620, Corpus Christi, TX 78403.*

Most Reverend

RENE H. GRACIDA, D.D.

Bishop Emeritus of Corpus Christi; ordained May 23, 1959; appointed Titular Bishop of Masuccaba and Auxiliary of Miami December 6, 1971; consecrated January 25, 1972; appointed Bishop of Pensacola-Tallahassee October 1, 1975; transferred to Corpus Christi May 19, 1983; installed July 11, 1983; retired April 1, 1997. *Res.: 609 Maldonado Dr., Sinton, TX 79387-3647. Mailing Address: P.O. Box 2620, Corpus Christi, TX 78403.* Tel: 361-882-6191.

Square Miles 10,951.

Erected a Vicariate Apostolic in 1874; elevated to a Diocese March 23, 1912.

The territory embraced by the Diocese of Corpus Christi comprises the Counties of Aransas, Bee, Brooks, Duval, Jim Wells, Kleberg, Kenedy, Live Oak, Nueces, Refugio, San Patricio, and parts of McMullen in the State of Texas.

The Chancery Office: 555 N. Carancahua, Ste. 750, Corpus Christi, TX 78401. Mailing Address: P.O. Box 2620, Corpus Christi, TX 78403-2620. Tel: 361-882-6191; Fax: 361-882-1018.

For legal titles of parishes and diocesan institutions, consult the Chancery Office.

Web: www.diocesecc.org

Email: chancery@diocesecc.org

STATISTICAL OVERVIEW

Personnel	
Bishop	1
Retired Bishops	2
Priests: Diocesan Active in Diocese	65
Priests: Diocesan Active Outside Diocese	5
Priests: Retired, Sick or Absent	31
Number of Diocesan Priests	101
Religious Priests in Diocese	30
Total Priests in Diocese	131
Extern Priests in Diocese	7
Ordinations:	
Transitional Deacons	2
Permanent Deacons in Diocese	100
Total Brothers	2
Total Sisters	143
Parishes	
Parishes	69
With Resident Pastor:	
Resident Diocesan Priests	52
Resident Religious Priests	3
Without Resident Pastor:	
Administered by Priests	14
Missions	32
Professional Ministry Personnel:	
Brothers	2
Sisters	21
Lay Ministers	76
Welfare	
Catholic Hospitals	6
Total Assisted	449,345
Health Care Centers	8
Total Assisted	70,962
Homes for the Aged	1
Total Assisted	54
Residential Care of Children	1
Total Assisted	248
Day Care Centers	1
Total Assisted	4
Special Centers for Social Services	1
Total Assisted	85,336
Educational	
Diocesan Students in Other Seminaries	13
Total Seminarians	13
High Schools, Diocesan and Parish	1
Total Students	311
High Schools, Private	1
Total Students	255
Elementary Schools, Diocesan and Parish	13
Total Students	2,086
Elementary Schools, Private	2
Total Students	426
Catechesis/Religious Education:	
High School Students	3,307
Elementary Students	8,604
Total Students under Catholic Instruction	15,002
Teachers in the Diocese:	
Sisters	11
Lay Teachers	228
Vital Statistics	
Receptions into the Church:	
Infant Baptism Totals	1,459
Minor Baptism Totals	374
Adult Baptism Totals	140
Received into Full Communion	133
First Communions	1,936
Confirmations	1,293
Marriages:	
Catholic	397
Interfaith	53
Total Marriages	450
Deaths	1,598
Total Catholic Population	354,946
Total Population	581,879

Former Bishops—Rt. Revs. DOMINIC MANUCY, ord. Aug. 15, 1850; cons. Dec. 8, 1874; transferred to Mobile March 9, 1884; reappointed to Vicariate Apostolic of Brownsville Feb. 1, 1885; died Dec. 4, 1885, before taking possession; PETER VERDAGUER, ord. Dec. 12, 1862; cons. Nov. 9, 1890; died Oct. 26, 1911; PAUL JOSEPH NUSSBAUM, C.P., D.D., ord. May 30, 1894; cons. May 20, 1913; resigned March 26, 1920; Bishop of Marquette; appt. Nov. 14, 1922; died June 24, 1935; Most Revs. EMMANUEL B. LEDVINA, D.D., LL.D., appt. April 30, 1921; cons. June 14, 1921; Assistant at Pontifical Throne May 30, 1931; resigned March 15, 1949; died Dec. 15, 1952; MARIANO S. GARRIGA, D.D., LL.D., Coadjutor cum jure successionis,; appt. June 20, 1936; cons. Sept. 21, 1936; succeeded to See March 15, 1949; assistant at Pontifical Throne April 14, 1951; died Feb. 21, 1965; THOMAS J. DRURY, D.D., LL.D., Fourth Bishop of Corpus Christi; Bishop of San Angelo; appt. Oct. 16, 1961; cons. Jan. 24, 1962; fourth Bishop of Corpus Christi; appt. July 19, 1965; installed Sept. 1, 1965; retired Bishop of Corpus Christi; appt. May 19, 1983; died July 22, 1992; RENE H. GRACIDA, D.D., (Retired), Bishop Emeritus; Fifth Bishop of Corpus Christi; appt. Titular Bishop of Masuccaba and Auxiliary of Miami Dec. 6, 1971; cons. Jan. 25, 1972; appt. Bishop of Pensacola-Tallahassee Oct. 1, 1975; transferred to Corpus Christi May 19, 1983; installed July 11, 1983; retired April 1, 1997; ROBERTO O. GONZALEZ, O.F.M., Sixth Bishop of Corpus Christi; appt. Titular Bishop of Ursona and Auxiliary Bishop of Boston July 19, 1988; ord. Oct. 3, 1988; appt. Coadjutor Bishop of Corpus Christi May 16, 1995; transferred to Corpus Christi June 26, 1995; succeeded to See April 1, 1997; appt. Apostolic Administrator to Corpus Christi and Archbishop of San Juan, March 26, 1999; installed Archbishop of San Juan, Puerto Rico May 8, 1999; EDMOND CARMODY, D.D., ord. June 8, 1957; appt. Auxiliary Bishop of the Archdiocese of San Antonio Nov. 8, 1988; cons. Dec. 15, 1988; appt. Bishop of the Diocese of Tyler March 24, 1992; installed May 25, 1992; appt. Bishop of the Diocese of Corpus Christi Feb. 3, 2000; installed March 17, 2000; retired Jan. 18, 2010.

Diocesan Curia—555 N. Carancahua, Ste. 750, Corpus Christi, 78401. Mailing Address: P.O. Box 2620, Corpus Christi, 78403-2620.

Office of the Bishop—Most Rev. WM. MICHAEL MULVEY, S.T.L., D.D.; Very Rev. JAMES G. STEMBLER, V.G., Vicar Gen.; BENEDICT NGUYEN, M.T.S., J.D./J.C.L., D.Min. (ABD), Chancellor; DAVID CAMPA, Chief of Staff/Gen. Counsel; Rev. Msgr. THOMAS P. FEENEY, J.C.L., Judicial Vicar.

Bishop's Office—Mailing Address: P.O. Box 2620, Corpus Christi, 78403-2620. Tel: 361-882-6191; Fax: 361-693-6726. BENEDICT NGUYEN, M.T.S., J.D./J.C.L., D.Min. (ABD), Canonical Counsel & Theological Adviser; Sr. GLORIA RODRIGUEZ, M.J.M.J., Dir. Office of Consecrated Life & Women Vocations; Deacon MICHAEL MANTZ, Dir. Office of the Permanent Diaconate; Rev. Msgrs. ROGER R. SMITH, Vicar for Priests; TOM MCGETTRICK, Vicar for Retired Priests, (Retired); Rev. ROMEO SALINAS, Dir. Vocations.

Bishops Emeriti—Most Revs. EDMOND CARMODY, D.D., (Retired); RENE H. GRACIDA, D.D., (Retired).

Consultative Bodies—Mailing Address: P.O. Box 2620, Corpus Christi, 78403-2620.

Council of Religious—Sr. GLORIA RODRIGUEZ, M.J.M.J., Dir. Consecrated Life & Women Vocations.

Deans—Very Revs. PEDRO T. ELIZARDO JR., V.F., Alice Deanery; RICHARD GONZALES, V.F., Beeville Deanery; VACANT, Corpus Christi Central Deanery; VACANT, Corpus Christi Five Points

Deanery; Very Revs. JOSE A. SALAZAR, V.F., Corpus Christi Westside Deanery; RICHARD A. LIBBY, V.F., Southside Deanery; JOSEPH A. LOPEZ, J.C.L., V.F., Kingsville Deanery; WILLIAM JOSEPH MARQUIS, V.F., Refugio Deanery.

College of Consultors—Very Revs. PEDRO T. ELIZARDO JR., V.F.; RICHARD GONZALES, V.F.; JOSE A. SALAZAR, V.F.; RICHARD A. LIBBY, V.F.; JOSEPH A. LOPEZ, J.C.L., V.F.; WILLIAM JOSEPH MARQUIS, V.F.; JAMES G. STEMBLER, V.G.

Diaconate Formation Screening Committee—ELVA MANTZ, Recording Sec.; Deacons MICHAEL MANTZ, Dir. Office of the Permanent Diaconate; ALLEN CICORA.

Finance Council—Most Rev. WM. MICHAEL MULVEY, S.T.L., D.D.; Very Rev. JAMES G. STEMBLER, V.G.; DAVID CAMPA, Chief of Staff/Gen. Counsel; BENEDICT NGUYEN, M.T.S., J.D./J.C.L., D.Min. (ABD), Chancellor; Rev. ROMEO SALINAS; Deacon ADELFINO PALACIOS JR.; MR. MIKE MCLELLAN; MR. TOM CARLISLE; MR. GARY A. RAMIREZ; MR. FRED MCCUTCHON; Sr. MARY ANN KORCZYNSKI, I.W.B.S.; MARY JEANNE (MJ) OLSEN. Consultants: TERESA CONVILLE, Chair, Finance Council; PAUL A. DAMEROW, CPA.

Building Commission—Most Rev. WM. MICHAEL MULVEY, S.T.L., D.D.; ORLANDO ZEPEDA, Chm.; Very Rev. JAMES G. STEMBLER, V.G.; TERESA CONVILLE, Ex Officio; MR. BUD COLWELL, P.E.; MR. JAMES ROME, ARCH., (Retired); MR. MIKE LIPPINCOTT; MR. TED STEPHENS; MR. JIMMY EARNEST; MR. LEO FARIAS. Consultants: MR. JEFF KISEL, Catholic Mutual; TERESA CONVILLE, Fiscal Officer; BENEDICT NGUYEN, M.T.S., J.D./J.C.L., D.Min. (ABD), Chancellor; DAVID CAMPA, Chief of Staff/Gen. Counsel.

Presbyteral Council—Most Rev. WM. MICHAEL MULVEY, S.T.L., D.D., Bishop; Rev. Msgr. ROGER R. SMITH, Vicar for Priests; Very Rev. JAMES G. STEMBLER, V.G.; Rev. Msgrs. THOMAS P. FEENEY, J.C.L.; TOM MCGETTRICK, Vicar for Retired Priests, (Retired); Revs. ROBERT DUNN; GABRIEL P. COELHO, Ph.D., LPC-S; JAMES VASQUEZ; RAJU THOTTANKARA, (India); RAYNALDO YRLAS JR.; ROMEO SALINAS; JOSE ANGEL SALAZAR; Very Revs. PEDRO T. ELIZARDO JR., V.F.; RICHARD GONZALES; RICHARD A. LIBBY, V.F.; WILLIAM JOSEPH MARQUIS, V.F.; JOSEPH A. LOPEZ, J.C.L., V.F.; Rev. JEROME DROLSHAGEN, S.O.L.T.

Tribunal—Rev. Msgr. THOMAS P. FEENEY, J.C.L., Judicial Vicar.

Judges—Rev. Msgrs. THOMAS P. FEENEY, J.C.L.; LEONARD PIVONKA, J.C.D.; Very Rev. JOSEPH A. LOPEZ, J.C.L., V.F.; Rev. Msgrs. MICHAEL HOWELL; ROGER R. SMITH; MARK CHAMBERLIN.

Promoter of Justice—BENEDICT NGUYEN, M.T.S., J.D./J.C.L., D.Min. (ABD).

Defender of the Bond—Rev. ANGEL MONTANO, J.C.L.

Notary-Secretary—BELINDA HARRIS.

Instructor—VACANT.

Administrative Offices

The Chancery Office—555 N. Carancahua, Ste. 750, P.O. Box 2620, Corpus Christi, 78403-2620. Office Hours: Mon.-Fri. 8:30-5. Closed Holy Days and holidays.

Office of the Bishop—Most Rev. WM. MICHAEL MULVEY, S.T.L., D.D.

Bishops Emeriti—Most Revs. EDMOND CARMODY, D.D., (Retired); RENE H. GRACIDA, D.D., (Retired).

Theological Advisor to the Bishop—BENEDICT NGUYEN, M.T.S., J.D./J.C.L., D.Min. (ABD).

Canonical Counsel to the Bishop—BENEDICT NGUYEN, M.T.S., J.D./J.C.L., D.Min. (ABD).

Executive Administrative Assistant to the Bishop—CECILIA FUENTES.

Vicar General—Very Rev. JAMES G. STEMBLER, V.G.

Executive Administrative Assistant to Vicar General—SANDRA CASTELLANOS.

Judicial Vicar—Rev. Msgr. THOMAS P. FEENEY, J.C.L.

Chancellor—BENEDICT NGUYEN, M.T.S., J.D./J.C.L., D.Min. (ABD).

Executive Administrative Assistant to the Chancellor—NANCY ALEMAN.

Director Human Resources and Personnel—DAVID CAMPA, Chief of Staff/Gen. Counsel.

Office of the Permanent Diaconate—Deacons MICHAEL MANTZ, 1200 Lantana St., Kolbe Center, Corpus Christi, 78407-2454. Tel: 361-289-2343; Fax: 361-289-2454; PAUL MOORE, Dir. Diaconate.

Vicar for Priests—Rev. Msgr. ROGER R. SMITH, Vicar for Priests.

Family Life Office—LESLIE BROWN; ELIZABETH NGUYEN, Dir.

Fiscal Officer—TERESA CONVILLE.

Controller—PAUL A. DAMEROW, CPA.

Office of Parish Stewardship and Development—Deacon MARK ARNOLD.

Information Technology Services—LEE ALVARADO, MIS Technical Dir.

Web Development Office—MADELYN CALVERT.

Real Property Office—Deacon MICHAEL MANTZ.

Propagation of the Faith Office—Rev. RAYNALDO YRLAS JR.

Archives—PATRICIA ROESER, Ph.D., Records Admin.

Catholic Schools Office—DR. ROSEMARY J. HENRY.

Catholic Cemeteries—JILL HUNDLEY.

Office for Child and Youth Protection (OCYP)—STEPHANIE BONILLA, Dir.

Victim Assistance Coordinator—KRISTI SKROBARCZYK.

Office of Communications—MARGIE RIVERA, Dir.

The South Texas Catholic—Most Rev. WM. MICHAEL MULVEY, S.T.L., D.D., Publisher; MARY COTTINGHAM, Mng. Editor; BENEDICT NGUYEN, M.T.S., J.D./J.C.L., D.Min. (ABD), Theological Consultant.

Office of Pastoral Parish Services—555 N. Carancahua., Ste. 750, Corpus Christi, 78401.

Ministry & Life Enrichment for Persons with Disabilities—CELIA MENDEZ, Mgr., 615 Oliver Ct., Corpus Christi, 78408. Mailing Address: P.O. Box 9056, Corpus Christi, 78469. Tel: 361-884-0651.

Department of Religious Education—THERESE RECINELLA, D.Min., D.R.E.

Office of Youth Ministry—ZACH EVERETT, Dir.

Diocese of Corpus Christi Perpetual Benefit Endowment Fund, Inc.—Mailing Address: P.O. Box 2620, Corpus Christi, 78403-2620. Tel: 361-882-6191.

Diocese of Corpus Christi Deposit and Loan Fund, Inc.—Mailing Address: P.O. Box 2620, Corpus Christi, 78403-2620. Tel: 361-882-6191.

Office of Divine Worship—Very Rev. PEDRO T. ELIZARDO JR., V.F., Dir.

Office of Multicultural and Social Ministry—JAIME REYNA, Dir.

Vocations Director & Seminary Formation—Rev. ROMEO SALINAS, Dir.

Assistant Vocations Director—BOB CUMMINGS.

Consecrated Life & Women Vocations—Sr. GLORIA RODRIGUEZ, M.J.M.J., Dir.

Other Offices and Organizations

Alhambra—ED ROTTER, Grand Commander, 225 Ocean View Pl., Corpus Christi, 78411. Tel: 361-854-6581; TERESE PETERSON, Grand Sultana, 5922 Grassmere, Corpus Christi, 78415. Tel: 361-854-7470; Email: teresepeterson@hotmail.com.

Campus Ministries—Texas A&M Kingsville, St. Thomas Aquinas Newman Center and Chapel, P.O. Box 2193, Kingsville, 78363. Tel: 361-221-1103; Fax: 361-221-1104. *Del Mar College, St. Thomas More, 2045 18th St., Corpus Christi, 78404.* Tel: 361-888-9308. *The Cardinal John Henry Newman Catholic Student Center at Texas A&M Univ., Corpus Christi, 78412.* Tel: 361-879-5448. NINA JOINER, Campus Min., Texas A&M Kingsville, Del Mar College, St. Thomas More, 2045 18th St., Corpus Christi, 78404. Tel: 361-888-9308. The Cardinal John Henry Newman Catholic Student Center at Texas A&M Univ., Corpus Christi, 78412. Tel: 361-879-5448; AMY BARRAGREE, Campus Min. for Texas A&M in Corpus Christi and Del Mar College; SANTOS R. JONES III, Campus Min. for Coastal Bend College, Beeville.

Catholic Daughters of the Americas—ERICA LOZANO, Dist. 16, Corpus Christi, Dist. 41, Corpus Christi, Tel: 361-548-6344; BERTIE ALMENDAREZ, Dist. 36, Corpus Christi, Tel: 361-548-4377; DELMA CANTU, Dist. 47, Odem, Tel: 361-365-2385; EVE TREVINO, State Regent, Corpus Christi, Tel: 361-994-8553; Email: evetrevino@yahoo.com; CHRIS MORIN, Dist. 48, Corpus Christi, Tel: 361-991-8975; SUSIE SAENZ, Dist. 57, Falfurrias, Tel: 361-325-5861; DOROTHY VILLARREAL, Dist. 23, Alice, Tel: 361-668-3421; TINA SAENZ, Dist. 43, San Diego, Tel: 361-279-7903.

Catholic Charities—615 Oliver Ct., Corpus Christi, 78408. Mailing Address: P.O. Box 9056, Corpus Christi, 78469. KEVIN BRANSON, Exec. Dir.

The Catholic Charismatic Renewal Movement—JAY DILLASHAW, Tel: 361-438-0935.

Cursillo Movement—BLANCA FLORES, Pres.

English Cursillo—JERRY FRANCO, Dir. School, Tel: 361-563-8562.

Spanish Cursillo—MANUEL RANGEL, Dir. School, Tel: 361-877-5048.

Diocesan Council of Catholic Women—ANN DUGGINS, Pres., Tel: 361-664-6613; Tel: 361-227-1130; Very Rev. JAMES G. STEMBLER, V.G., Spiritual Advisor, Tel: 361-592-7351.

Diocesan Telecommunications Corporation—MARTY WIND, Exec. Vice Pres. & Gen. Mgr., 1200 Lantana, Corpus Christi, 78407. Tel: 361-289-6437; Fax: 361-289-1420.

Disaster Response Program—615 Oliver Ct., Corpus Christi, 78408. Mailing Address: P.O. Box 9056, Corpus Christi, 78469. Tel: 361-884-0651, Ext. 245 . DOREYA (YIYI) DEAN, Grant Writer/Admin.

Emergency Aid—ELMA ORTIZ, Mgr., 615 Oliver Ct., Corpus Christi, 78408. P.O. Box 9056, Corpus Christi, 78469.

Family Counseling—GLORIA GARCIA, M.S., L.P.C.S., L.M.F.T., Mgr., 615 Oliver Ct., Corpus Christi, 78408. Mailing Address: P.O. Box 9056, Corpus Christi, 78469.

Housing Counseling—DOREYA (YIYI) DEAN, Mgr., 615 Oliver Ct., Corpus Christi, 78408. Mailing Address: P.O. Box 9056, Corpus Christi, 78469.

Representative Payee—ELSA ORTIZ, Mgr., 615 Oliver Ct., Corpus Christi, 78408. Mailing Address: P.O. Box 9056, Corpus Christi, 78469.

Immigration Services—KIMBERLEY SEGER, Mgr. & Attorney, 615 Oliver Ct., Corpus Christi, 78408. Mailing Address: P.O. Box 9056, Corpus Christi, 78469.

Knights of Columbus—MIKELL WEST, 6533 Patti Dr., Apt. #1108, Corpus Christi, 78414. Tel: 361-215-8487.

Legion of Mary—DELMA TORRES, Curia Pres.; Deacon SOLOMON WILLIS, Spiritual Dir., Tel: 361-877-1598.

Marriage Encounter—Contact Person: ROB JOHNSON; CRIS JOHNSON, 510 Meadowbrook Dr., Corpus Christi, 78412. Tel: 361-537-4997; Email: georob6316@sbcglobal.net.

Radio Stations - KLUX FM HD—1200 Lantana St., Corpus Christi, 78407. Tel: 361-289-2487. MARTY WIND, Gen. Mgr.

Serra International—RON ALONZO, Pres., 1222 Morgan, Corpus Christi, 78404. Tel: 361-947-1346.

CLERGY, PARISHES, MISSIONS AND PAROCHIAL SCHOOLS

CITY OF CORPUS CHRISTI

(NUECES COUNTY)

1—CORPUS CHRISTI CATHEDRAL (1853) [CEM] Very Rev. Hanh Van Pham, Rector; Rev. Jose M. Gutierrez, Parochial Vicar; Deacons Michael Mantz; Adelfino Palacios Jr.; Amando Leal.
Res.: 505 N. Upper Broadway, 78401.
Tel: 361-883-4213, Ext. 101; Email: info@cccathedral.com; Email: elda.garcia@cccathedral.com; Web: www.cccathedral.com.
Catechesis Religious Program—Email: religiousedcccathedral.com. Orfelinda Hernandez, D.R.E. Students 170.
Chapels—Emmanuel—(Crypt).
Blessed Sacrament.

2—SAINT ANDREW BY THE SEA PARISH (1986)
14238 Encantada Ave., 78418-6432.
Tel: 361-949-7193; Email: standrewcc@stx.rr.com; Web: standrewbytheseacctx.org. Rev. Msgr. Michael Howell.
Catechesis Religious Program—Tel: 361-949-8834; Email: standrewdreoffice@gmail.com. Cheryl Hooper, D.R.E. Students 120.

3—ST. ANSELM ANGLICAN USE COMMUNITY (1992) (Suffragan to: Our Lady of Guadalupe Chapel, NAS, Corpus Christi)
Mailing Address: 15849 Grenadine Dr, 78413.
Tel: 361-961-4999. Rev. John Vidal.
Church: Naval Air Station Corpus Christi.

4—CHRIST THE KING (1946) (Hispanic)
3423 Rojo, 78415. Tel: 361-883-2821; Email: churchoffice@ctk-cc.org; Web: www.ctk-cc.org. Rev. William K. Bakyil, S.O.L.T., (Ghana); Deacon Manuel Marroquin.
Catechesis Religious Program—Sr. Mary Handmaid, D.R.E. Students 83.
Convent—

5—SS. CYRIL AND METHODIUS (1947) (Hispanic)
3210 S. Padre Island Dr., 78415. Tel: 361-853-7371; Email: sscyrilandmethodius@sscmc.org; Web: sscmc.org. Rev. Msgr. Lawrence E. White, Pastor; Rev. Sanish Mathew, Parochial Vicar; Deacons Fernando Perez; Albert Galvan.
Catechesis Religious Program—Email: kmjgarcia@sscmc.org. Kiki Garcia, D.R.E. Students 85.

6—HOLY CROSS (1914) (African American)
1109 N. Staples St., 78401. Tel: 361-888-4012; Email: hcrosstx@gmail.com; Web: www.holycrosscc.net. Rev. Roy Kalayil, (India).
Catechesis Religious Program—Students 20.

7—HOLY FAMILY CHURCH (1946)
3157 MacArthur Street, 78416. Tel: 361-882-3245; Fax: 361-882-4968; Email: church@holyfamilycc.net; Web: www.holyfamilycc.net. 2509 Nogales St., 78416. Revs. Darryl J. D'Souza; Rene Meier, Parochial Vicar; Deacon Tomas Gallegos.
Priest's Res.: 2530 Presa, 78416.
Catechesis Religious Program—
Tel: 361-882-3245, Ext. 13; Email: irene@holyfamilycc.net. Irene Anes, D.R.E. Students 205.

8—SAINT JOHN THE BAPTIST (2001)
Mailing Address: 7522 Everhart Rd., 78413.
Tel: 361-991-4400; Fax: 361-991-4401; Email: churchoffice@sjbcctx.org; Web: www.sjbcctx.org. Rev. Rodolfo D. Vasquez; Deacons Jesse Lee Hinojosa; Julio Dimas.
Rectory—4809 Lake Nocona, 78413.
Catechesis Religious Program—Students 335.

9—ST. JOSEPH (1950) (Hispanic) Revs. Rogel Rosalinas, S.O.L.T.; Terencio Ayo, S.O.L.T., (Philippines) Parochial Vicar; Bro. Martin McGough, Music Min.; Deacons Reynaldo Rojas; Juan Carlos Ayala.
Res.: 710 S. 19th St., P.O. Box 5196, 78465-5196.
Tel: 361-882-7912; Fax: 361-882-6853; Email: stjoseph@stx.rr.com; Web: www.stjosephcctx.org.
Catechesis Religious Program—Debra A. Martinez, D.R.E. Students 115.

10—MOST PRECIOUS BLOOD (1966)
3502 Saratoga Blvd., 78415. Tel: 361-854-3800; Email: mpb@mpbchurch.org; Web: www.mpbchurch.org. Revs. Robert Dunn; David Javier Bayardo, Parochial Vicar; Deacons Ken Bockholt; David Castillo; Frank N. Newchurch; Erick Simeus.
Catechesis Religious Program—Tel: 361-945-0811; Email: kenbuckfam@yahoo.com. Lee Bockholt, D.R.E. Students 814.

11—NUESTRA SENORA DE SAN JUAN DE LOS LAGOS (2010) (Hispanic)
Mailing Address: 1755 Frio St., 78417.
Tel: 361-852-0249; Fax: 361-852-8463; Email: sanjuanlagos3@yahoo.com. Rev. Jose Angel Salazar; Deacon Manuel Maldonado
Legal Name: Nuestra Senora de San Juan de Los Lagos, Madre de la Iglesia
Catechesis Religious Program—Students 141.

12—OUR LADY OF GUADALUPE aka OLG (1969)
540 Hiawatha St., 78405. Tel: 361-882-1951; Email: olgcctx@gmail.com; Web: olgcctx.com. Rev. Salvatore James Farfaglia; Deacon Armando Botello.
Catechesis Religious Program—Margarita Valdez, D.R.E.; Juan Antonio Valdez, D.R.E. Students 81.

13—OUR LADY OF MOUNT CARMEL (1969) Rev. Gabriel P. Coelho, Ph.D., LPC-S.
Our Lady of the Rosary, Church: 1080 S. Clarkwood Rd., 78406. Tel: 361-241-2004; Fax: 361-242-1099; Email: ourladyofrosary@stx.rr.com.
Catechesis Religious Program—Students 6.
Mission—St. Vivian, 3516 FM 665 W., Robstown, 78380.

14—OUR LADY OF PERPETUAL HELP (1954)
Mailing Address: 5830 Williams Dr., 78412.
Tel: 361-991-7891; Fax: 361-993-1211; Email: olphoffice@olphcctx.org; Web: www.olphcctex.org. Rev. Frank X. Martinez; Deacons Vic Benys; Arnold Marcha; Armando Sanchez; Fred Castillo; Rodolfo R. Martinez.
Catechesis Religious Program—Students 171.

15—OUR LADY OF PILAR (1964) (Hispanic) Rev. Msgr. Marcos Martinez; Deacon Armando M. Bolanos.
Res.: 1101 Bloomington St., 78416. Email: pillarchurch@stx.rr.com.
Catechesis Religious Program—Students 325.

16—OUR LADY OF THE ROSARY (1967)
1123 Main Dr., 78409. Tel: 361-241-2004; Email: ourladyoftherosary@stx.rr.com. Rev. Gabriel P. Coelho, Ph.D., LPC-S.
Catechesis Religious Program—Students 17.
Missions—Our Lady of Mt. Carmel Mission—Mission: 1080 S. Clarkwood Rd., 78406.
St. Vivian Mission, Petronila 3516 FM 665, Robstown, 78380.

17—OUR LADY STAR OF THE SEA (1950)
3110 E. Causeway Blvd., 78403. Tel: 361-883-4507; Email: olss.church@gmail.com; Web: www.olsscc.org. Rev. Roy Kalayil, (India) Admin.
Catechesis Religious Program—Leah Wiggins, D.R.E. Students 30.

18—ST. PATRICK CHURCH (1944)
3350 S. Alameda St., 78411. Tel: 361-855-7391; Email: stpatrickschurch@bizstx.rr.com; Web: www.stpatrickchurchcc.org. Rev. Msgr. Roger R. Smith; Rev. Christopher E. Becerra, Parochial Vicar; Deacon Eleazar (Larry) Rodriguez.
Catechesis Religious Program—Tel: 361-855-7567; Email: mrswetish@hotmail.com. Marian Rose Swetish, D.R.E. Students 100.

19—ST. PAUL THE APOSTLE (1967)
2233 Waldron Rd., 78418. Tel: 361-937-3864; Email: office@stpaultheapostlecc.com. Rev. Joseph T. Nguyen, Admin.; Deacon Francisco Rodriguez.
Catechesis Religious Program—Tel: 361-937-6908; Email: scxoop2013@gmail.com. Sr. Claudia X. Ongpin, O.P., D.R.E. Students 158.

20—ST. PETER, PRINCE OF APOSTLES (1967)
3901 Violet Rd., 78410-2924. Tel: 361-241-3249; Web: www.stpeterprince.net. Rev. Emilio Jimenez.
Mission—St. Mary, 4849 Cynthia, Nueces Co. 78410.

21—ST. PHILIP THE APOSTLE (1982)
3513 Cimarron Rd., 78414. Tel: 361-991-5146; Email: info@stphilipcc.com; Web: www.stphilipcc.com. Rev. Luis Alfredo Villarreal; Deacons Bob Allen; Dan Shaunessey; Narciso Ortiz.
Catechesis Religious Program—Tel: 361-993-1710. Katie Tipton, D.R.E. Students 575.

22—ST. PIUS X (1963)
5620 Gollihar Rd., 78412. Tel: 361-993-4053; Email: phesse@stpiusxcc.org; Web: stpiusxcc.org. Revs. Paul A. Hesse, B.A., M.Div.; Eric G. Chapa, Parochial Vicar; Deacons Salvador Alvarado; Stacy Milsap; Bryan Krnavek, Prin.
Please see St. Pius X Catholic School under the Institutions Located in the Diocese section.
Catechesis Religious Program—Tel: 361-993-9024. Students 205.

23—SACRED HEART (1916) [CEM] (Hispanic)
1322 Comanche St., 78415. Tel: 361-883-6082; Email: sacredheartchurch001@stx.rr.com; Web: www.mpbchurch.org. Rev. Angel Montana, J.C.L.; Deacon Feliz Muniz.
Catechesis Religious Program—Email: ibarra60@yahoo.com. Nelda Ibarra, D.R.E. Students 66.
Stations—Nueces County Jail—Tel: 361-887-2300.
Navarro Place.

24—SAINT HELENA OF THE TRUE CROSS OF JESUS aka St. Helena (2001)
7634 Wooldridge Rd., 78414. Tel: 361-974-8783; Email: sthelenasecretary@gmail.com; Web: sthelenacc.com. Very Rev. Richard A. Libby, V.F.; Deacon Richard Longoria, Tel: 361-446-2291.
Catechesis Religious Program—
Tel: 361-994-8783, Ext. 22; Email: arsegovia15@gmail.com. Catalina Longoria, D.R.E. Students 66.

25—ST. THERESA (1947) Rev. Donald Downey, J.C.L.; Deacon Stephen Nolte.
Res.: 1302 Lantana St., 78407. Tel: 361-289-2759; Fax: 361-299-2018.
Catechesis Religious Program—Tel: 361-289-2238. Mrs. Josie Martinez, D.R.E. Students 58.

26—ST. THOMAS MORE PARISH (1990)
2045 18th St., 78404-3862. Tel: 361-888-9308; Email: stthomasmorecc@corpus.twcbc.com; Web: www.stthomasmorecc.org. Rev. Tomasz Kozub, (Poland).
Catechesis Religious Program—Email: sandramcc@stx.rr.com; Email: lisagodinez322@gmail.com; Email: jer_arch@hotmail.com. Sandra McCutchon, D.R.E.; Jonathan Eric Rivera, RCIA Coord.; Lisa Godinez, D.R.E. Students 80.

OUTSIDE THE CITY OF CORPUS CHRISTI

AGUA DULCE, NUECES CO., ST. FRANCES OF ROME (1934) (Czech—Hispanic)
Mailing Address: P.O. Box 598, Agua Dulce, 78330.
Tel: 361-998-2216; Fax: 361-998-9038. 410 Simmons St., Agua Dulce, 78330. Rev. Jacob John Valayath.
Catechesis Religious Program—Students 64.

ALICE, JIM WELLS CO.
1—ST. ELIZABETH OF HUNGARY (1918) Rev. Msgr. Leonard Pivonka, J.C.D.; Deacons James A. Carlisle; Ernesto Gutierrez.
Office: 603 E. 5th St., Alice, 78332. Tel: 361-664-6481 ; Fax: 361-664-7243; Email: st.elizabeth1918@gmail.com.
Res.: 518 N. Almond St., P.O. Box 1009, Alice, 78333.
Catechesis Religious Program—Tel: 361-664-7719. Students 114.

2—ST. JOSEPH (1911)
801 S. Reynolds St., Alice, 78332. Tel: 361-664-7551; Email: info@sjcatholicchurch.org; Web: www.sjcatholicchurch.org. Very Rev. Pedro T. Elizardo Jr., V.F.; Rev. Jaison Mathew, Parochial Vicar.
Catechesis Religious Program—311 Dewey St. & 801 S. Reynolds, Alice, 78332. David Guerrero, D.R.E. Students 220.
Chapel—Perpetual Eucharistic Adoration.

3—OUR LADY OF GUADALUPE (1969) (Hispanic)
1300 Guerra St., Alice, 78332. Rev. E. Julian Cabrera.
Res.: 1318 Guerra St., P.O. Box 411, Alice, 78333.
Tel: 361-664-2953;
Fax: 361-664-4001 (Church Office).
Church: 1010 Beam Station Rd., Alice, 78332.
Catechesis Religious Program—Tel: 361-664-0437. Students 450.
Mission—Santo Nino De Atocha, 918 CR 122 (Tecolote), P.O. Box 411, Alice, Jim Wells Co. 78333. Email: pastor@olgalice.org.

ARANSAS PASS, SAN PATRICIO CO., ST. MARY, STAR OF THE SEA (1948) Rev. James Vasquez, Admin.
Res.: 342 S. Rife St., Aransas Pass, 78336.
Tel: 361-758-2662; Fax: 361-758-3964.
Catechesis Religious Program—Cynthia Vasquez. Students 209.

BANQUETE, NUECES CO., SAINT MICHAEL THE ARCHANGEL (1857) [JC]
Mailing Address: 4325 Fourth St., P.O. Box 9, Banquete, 78339. Tel: 361-387-8371;
Fax: 361-387-7607; Email: stmichaelbanquete@gmail.com. Rev. John Chavarria, Parochial Admin.; Deacon Pilar M. Gonzalez.
Catechesis Religious Program—Students 107.

BEEVILLE, BEE CO.
1—ST. JAMES (Alta Vista) (1966) (Hispanic) Rev. Paul Kottackal; Deacon Juan Vasquez.
Res.: 605 S. Alta Vista, Beeville, 78102.
Tel: 361-358-4825; Email: stjameschurchbeeville@twc.com.
Catechesis Religious Program—Juanita L. Martinez, D.R.E. Students 70.

2—ST. JOSEPH (1895) [CEM] Very Rev. Richard Gonzales, V.F.; Deacons Paul Matula; Luis Trevino; Rolando R. Salazar.
Res.: 609 E. Gramman St., Beeville, 78102.
Tel: 361-358-3239; Fax: 361-358-4270; Email: office@stjosephbeeville.org; Web: www.stjosephbeeville.org.
Catechesis Religious Program—Santos R. Jones III, Pastoral Assoc.; Debra Olivares, Dir. Faith Formation; Victor Gomez, Youth Min.; Linda Mae Gomez, Youth Min. Students 131.

3—OUR LADY OF VICTORY (1908) [CEM 2]
Mailing Address: 707 North Ave. E., Beeville, 78102.
Tel: 361-358-0088; Fax: 361-358-2028; Email: churcholv@yahoo.com. Very Rev. Lukose Thirunelliparamabil, (India); Deacon Rogelio Rosenbaum.
Rectory—403 W. Carter St., Beeville, 78102.
Catechesis Religious Program—Tel: 361-542-9409; Fax: 361-358-2820; Email: lalyarteaga@yahoo.com. Laly Arteaga, D.R.E. Students 198.
Mission—Sacred Heart Mission - Pettus, Pettus, 78146.

BENAVIDES, DUVAL CO., SANTA ROSA DE LIMA (1941) (Hispanic) Rev. P. George Thomas.
Res.: 203 Santa Rosa de Lima St., P.O. Box W, Benavides, 78341. Tel: 361-256-3427; Email: benavideschurch@yahoo.com.
Catechesis Religious Program—Beatriz Canas, D.R.E. Students 130.
Missions—St. Joseph—P.O. Box W, San Jose Ranch, Duval Co. 78341.
Sacred Heart, P.O. Box W, Realitos, Duval Co. 78376.

BEN BOLT, JIM WELLS, CO., ST. PETER MISSION (1927)
Mailing Address: 221 Salazar Ave., P.O. Box 678, Ben Bolt, 78342. Tel: 361-664-1688;
Fax: 361-664-1688; Email: benboltcatholicparish@gmail.com; Web: www.stpeterparishofbenbolt.com. Very Rev. Pedro T. Elizardo Jr., V.F.
Catechesis Religious Program—Students 74.

BISHOP, NUECES CO., ST. JAMES (1938) [CEM] Rev. John Xaviour, Admin.
Res.: 601 W. 3rd St., P.O. Box 843, Bishop, 78343.
Tel: 361-584-3250; Fax: 361-584-1046; Email: ryszardkoziol@poczta.onet.pl.
Catechesis Religious Program—Students 149.
Mission—St. James, 310 W. Ave. B, Driscoll, Nueces Co. 78351.

EDROY, SAN PATRICIO CO., OUR LADY OF GUADALUPE MISSION (1934) See Sacred Heart of Jesus Parish, Odem.
Mailing Address: 18012 CR 1598, P.O. Box 127, Edroy, 78352. Tel: 361-368-9156; Email: sacredheartodem@yahoo.com. Rev. Isaias Estepa, (Colombia) Admin.
Catechesis Religious Program—Students 19.

FALFURRIAS, BROOKS CO., SACRED HEART (1914) [CEM] (Hispanic) Rev. Dennis P. Zerr; Deacon Ricardo E. Costley.
Res.: 304 S. Caldwell St., Falfurrias, 78355.
Tel: 361-325-3455; Email: shcfal@hotmail.com.
Catechesis Religious Program—Email: shcfal@outlook.com. Joan Bostwick, D.R.E. Students 303.
Mission—St. Ann, c/o Sacred Heart Parish, Encino, Brooks Co. 78355.

FREER, DUVAL CO., ST. MARY (1968) Rev. Francis Sebastian, M.S.T., Admin.; Deacons Eluterio Bitoni; Pete Trevino Jr.; Mary Alice Casas, Sec. & Bookkeeper.
Res.: 1500 Duval St., P.O. Drawer B, Freer, 78357.
Tel: 361-394-6832; Fax: 361-394-6568.
Catechesis Religious Program—Students 199.

GEORGE WEST, LIVE OAK CO., ST. GEORGE (1924) [CEM] Rev. George Johnson; Deacon Shayne Katzfey.
Oratory, [CEM] [JC] 304 Crockett St., P.O. Box 580, George West, Live Oak Co. 78022. Tel: 361-447-2893;

Fax: 361-447-2886; Email: stgeorge_west@yahoo.com.
Catechesis Religious Program—Deacon Shayne Katzfey, D.R.E.; Lori Katzfey, D.R.E. Students 113.
Mission—St. Joseph, [CEM] [JC] Gussetville, Live Oak Co.

GREGORY, SAN PATRICIO CO., IMMACULATE CONCEPTION (1926) (Hispanic)
107 Church St., Gregory, 78359-0108.
Tel: 361-643-4505; Web: www.iccgregory.org. P.O. Box 108, Gregory, 78359-0108. Rev. Andrew Hejdak, (Poland).
Catechesis Religious Program—Students 276.

INGLESIDE, SAN PATRICIO CO., OUR LADY OF THE ASSUMPTION (1970)
2414 Main, Ingleside, 78362. Tel: 361-776-2446; Email: morin@cableone.net. Rev. Patrick G. Higgins, (Ireland) Admin.; Deacon Art Provencio.
Catechesis Religious Program—Students 247.

KINGSVILLE, KLEBERG CO.
1—ST. GERTRUDE (1908)
1120 S. 8th St., Kingsville, 78363. Tel: 361-592-7351; Email: stgertrude@sbcglobal.net; Web: www.stgertrudekingsville.org. Very Rev. Joseph A. Lopez, J.C.L., V.F.; Deacons John R. Joiner; Edwin N. Rowley.
Please see St. Gertrude School under the Institutions Located in the Diocese section.
Catechesis Religious Program—Tel: 361-592-2443. Students 150.
2—ST. JOSEPH (1973) (Hispanic)
1400 Brookshire, P.O. Box 1602, Kingsville, 78364-1602. Rev. Juan Fernando Gamez, (Colombia) Admin.; Deacons Ricardo Gonzalez; Richard B. Morin.
Catechesis Religious Program—Fax: 361-516-1397. Sylvia Molina, D.R.E. Students 207.
3—ST. MARTIN (1914) (Hispanic)
715 N. Eighth St., Kingsville, 78363.
Tel: 361-592-4602; Fax: 361-221-8751; Email: stmartincatholic@sbcglobal.net; Web: www.stmartinkingsville.org. Rev. Jose Naul Ordonez, (Colombia); Deacons Danny L. Herrera; Tiburcio Garcia; Raul G. Rosales.
Catechesis Religious Program—Tel: 361-219-4665. Gloria DeLeon, D.R.E. Students 240.
Convent—919 N. Ninth St., Kingsville, 78363.
Mission—Christ the King, King Ranch, Kleberg Co.
4—OUR LADY OF GOOD COUNSEL (1954) [CEM 3] [JC]
Rev. Peter Thenan, (India) Admin.
Res.: 1102 E. Kleberg, Kingsville, 78363.
Tel: 361-592-3489; Fax: 361-592-6370; Email: ourlady78363@gmail.com; Web: ourladykingsville.org.
Catechesis Religious Program—Mary A. Pena, D.R.E. Students 151.
5—ST. THOMAS AQUINAS NEWMAN CENTER AND CHAPEL, Very Rev. Joseph A. Lopez, J.C.L., V.F.
Legal Name: St. Thomas Aquinas Newman Center and Chapel (Texas A&M University Kingsville)
Tel: 361-221-1103; Email: njoiner@diocesecc.org.
Church: 1457 Retama, P.O. Box 2193, Kingsville, 78363.

MATHIS, SAN PATRICIO CO.
1—SAINT PATRICK MISSION (1829) [CEM]
20742 Magnolia St., San Patricio, 78368.
Tel: 361-387-1312; Tel: 361-387-7842;
Fax: 361-387-9311; Email: stthomastheapostle@christon624.com; Email: aramos@christon624.com; Web: www.christon624.com. Mailing Address: c/o St. Thomas the Apostle, 16602 FM 624, Robstown, 78380. Very Rev. Philip Panackal, (India).
Catechesis Religious Program—Tel: 361-244-2138; Email: pmhoelscher@aol.com. Michele Hoelscher, D.R.E. Students 15.
2—ST. PIUS X MISSION - SANDIA (1955)
Mailing Address: c/o Sacred Heart, 217 W. San Patricio Ave., Mathis, 78368. Tel: 361-547-9181;
Fax: 361-547-6111; Email: sacredheartchurchmathis@gmail.com. Rev. Raju Thottankara, (India); Deacon Walter Noel Breland, D.R.E.
Catechesis Religious Program—Tel: 361-249-0087; Email: noelbrel@gmail.com. Students 19.
3—SACRED HEART (1942) [JC]
217 W. San Patricio Ave., Mathis, 78368-2259.
Tel: 361-547-9181; Email: sacredheartchurchmathis@gmail.com. Rev. Raju Thottankara, (India).
Catechesis Religious Program—Tel: 361-537-5461; Email: lauriemolivarez@gmail.com. Laurie Olivarez, D.R.E. Students 400.

ODEM, SAN PATRICIO CO., SACRED HEART (1934)
401 W. Willis St., Odem, 78370. Cell: 361-368-9156; Email: sacredheartodem@yahoo.com. P.O. Box 276, Odem, 78370. Rev. Isaias Estepa, (Colombia) Admin.; Deacon Robert Flores.
Catechesis Religious Program—Tel: 361-368-2746. Students 268.
Mission—Our Lady of Guadalupe Mission, Edroy, 78352.

ORANGE GROVE, JIM WELLS CO., ST. JOHN OF THE CROSS (1925) [CEM]
Mailing Address: 200 S. Metz St., P.O. Box 329, Orange Grove, 78372. Tel: 361-384-2795;
Fax: 361-384-0056; Email: saintjohn0003@aol.com. Rev. Prince Kuruvila, (India).
Catechesis Religious Program—Terrie Silva, D.R.E. Students 212.
Mission—St. Francis of Assisi Mission, Mailing Address: 303 FM 534, Sandia, Jim Wells Co. 78383.

PETTUS, BEE CO., SACRED HEART MISSION (1916)
Suffragan to Our Lady of Victory, Beeville.
Mailing Address: c/o Our Lady of Victory, 707 North Ave. E., Beeville, 78102. Tel: 361-358-0088. 104 N. Bee Ave, Pettus, 78102. Very Rev. Lukose Thirunellipparamabil, (India).

PORT ARANSAS, NUECES CO., ST. JOSEPH (1860) [JC]
Mailing Address: 412 Lantana St., P.O. Box 1546, Port Aransas, 78373. Tel: 361-749-5825;
Fax: 361-749-5509; Email: stjosephportaransas@stx.rr.com; Web: www.stjosephportaransas.com. Rev. Romeo Salinas; Deacon Mark Arnold.
Catechesis Religious Program—Students 33.

PORTLAND, SAN PATRICIO CO., OUR LADY OF MOUNT CARMEL (1961)
1008 Austin St., Portland, 78374. Tel: 361-643-7533; Email: parish@olmcportland.com; Web: olmcportland.com. Very Rev. Piotr A. Koziel, S.T.L., V.F.; Deacon Robert Rosales.
Catechesis Religious Program—Tel: 361-643-3548. Mrs. Melanee Warner, D.R.E.; Margaret Alarilla, D.R.E. Students 501.

PREMONT, JIM WELLS CO., ST. THERESA OF THE INFANT JESUS (1958) Very Rev. John C. Ouellette; Deacons Ramiro Davila, Sacramental Min.; Ruben Maldonado.
Res.: 235 S.W. 4th St., P.O. Box 569, Premont, 78375. Tel: 361-348-2202; Fax: 361-348-3533; Email: sttheresaij@gmail.com; Web: sttheresaij.com.
Catechesis Religious Program—Students 78.
Missions—Immaculate Conception—Concepcion, Duval Co.
Our Lady of Guadalupe, Ramirez, Duval Co.

REFUGIO, REFUGIO CO.
1—ST. JAMES THE APOSTLE (1886) [CEM] [JC]
Mailing Address: 202 E. Santiago St., Refugio, 78377. Tel: 361-526-4454; Fax: 361-526-2336. Rev. John McKenzie.
Catechesis Religious Program—Students 99.
Mission—St. Catherine Mission, Hwy. 2441, Blanconia, 78377.
2—OUR LADY OF REFUGE (1795) [CEM] [JC]
1008 S. Alamo St., Refugio, 78377. Tel: 361-526-2083 ; Email: olrefuge@yahoo.com; Web: christonhwy77.com. Rev. Bill Marquis.
Catechesis Religious Program—106 W. Roca, Refugio, 78377. Students 64.

RIVIERA, KLEBER CO., OUR LADY OF CONSOLATION (1914) [CEM] [JC] (German)
204 Palm Ave., Riviera, 78379. Tel: 361-297-5255; Fax: 361-297-5155; Email: ourlady@rivnet.com; Web: ourladyatriviera.tripod.com. Rev. Varghese K. Ethappiri; Deacon Michael Valenzuela.
Catechesis Religious Program—Students 67.
Missions—Our Lady of Guadalupe—111 S. Second St., Riviera, Kleberg Co. 78379.
Sacred Heart, W. County Rd. 2160, Ricardo, Kleberg Co. 78363.

ROBSTOWN, NUECES CO.
1—ST. ANTHONY (1914) [CEM] (Hispanic)
204 Dunne St., Robstown, 78380-0792.
Tel: 361-387-2774; Email: stanthonyparish@gmail.com; Web: stanthonyrobstown.org. P.O. Box 792, Robstown, 78380. Revs. Gerard J. Sheehan, S.O.L.T.; Michael Edward Crump, S.O.L.T., Parochial Vicar; John M. Patterson II, S.O.L.T., Parochial Vicar; Deacons Emilio Flores; Homer Martinez.
Catechesis Religious Program—Email: katherine.lopez@stanthonyrobstown.org. Katherine L. Castro, D.R.E. Students 252.
Mission—St. Mary, 911 Garcia St., Robstown, Nueces Co. 78380.
2—ST. JOHN NEPOMUCENE (1924) [JC] (Czech) Rev. Mark Wheelan, S.O.L.T.
Res.: 603 N. First St., Robstown, 78380.
Tel: 361-387-3705; Fax: 361-387-3681; Email: frgerrysheehan@gmail.com.
Catechesis Religious Program—Sr. Patricia Burns, D.R.E. Students 51.
3—ST. THOMAS THE APOSTLE (1980)
16602 FM 624, Robstown, 78380. Tel: 361-387-1312;
Tel: 361-387-7842; Fax: 361-387-9311; Email: stthomastheapostle@christon624.com; Email: aramos@christon624.com; Web: www.christon624.com. Very Rev. Philip Panackal, (India).
Catechesis Religious Program—
Mission—St. Patrick Mission, 20742 Magnolia St., Mathis, 78368.

ROCKPORT, ARANSAS CO.
1—ST. PETER'S PARISH (1989) [JC2] (Vietnamese)
Mailing Address: P.O. Box 1060, Rockport, 78382.
Tel: 361-729-3008. Rev. John Tran Nugyen, O.F.M.
Catechesis Religious Program—2761 FM 1781, Rockport, 78381-1060. Students 29.
2—SACRED HEART (1838)
209 N. Church St., Rockport, 78382.
Tel: 361-729-9203; Email: shrockport@rockport.twcbc.com. 114 N. Church St., Rockport, 78382. Rev. Raynaldo Yrlas Jr.; Deacons Jerre H. Ledbetter; George Joe Wiest; Daniel Joseph Boehm; Ronald Janota.
Res.: 704 E. Cornwall St., Rockport, 78382.
Tel: 361-729-2174; Fax: 361-729-1989; Email: shpastor@rockport.twcbc.com; Web: www.shcrockport.org.
Catechesis Religious Program—Tel: 361-729-8283; Email: reled@rockport.twcbc.com. Gloria J. Scott, D.R.E. Students 410.
Convent—114 N. Church St., Rockport, 78382.
Tel: 361-729-5311.
3—STELLA MARIS CHAPEL (1858)
222 Hagey Dr., Lamar, 78382. P.O. Box 1980, Fulton, 78358.

SAN DIEGO, DUVAL CO., ST. FRANCIS DE PAULA (1866)
Rev. Balaswamy Pasala, (India).
Res.: 401 S. Victoria St., P.O. Box 279, San Diego, 78384. Tel: 361-279-3596; Fax: 361-279-8288.
Catechesis Religious Program—411 S. Victoria St., San Diego, 78384. Students 410.
Mission—St. Joseph, 2688 FM 735, Palito Blanco, Jim Wells Co. 78384. Email: stfrancisdepaulachurch@yahoo.com.

SARITA, KENEDY CO., OUR LADY OF GUADALUPE (1935)
103 S. Main St., Sarita, 78385. Tel: 361-294-5350;
Fax: 361-294-5406; Email: lebhshomea@omiusa.org. P.O. Box 6, Sarita, 78385. Rev. James Foelker, O.M.I., Admin.; Deacon Michael Valenzuela.
Catechesis Religious Program—Students 13.
Mission—Santa Elena, Norias Ranch, Kenedy Co.

SINTON, SAN PATRICIO CO.
1—OUR LADY OF GUADALUPE (1954) [CEM] [JC] (Hispanic)
725 Sodville Ave., Sinton, 78387. Tel: 361-364-2210; Email: office@olgsinton.org; Web: olgsinton.org. Rev. Glen F. Mullan.
Catechesis Religious Program—Tel: 361-364-4007. Students 180.
2—SACRED HEART (1916) Rev. Ignatius C. Nwankwocha, Admin.
Res. & Office: 906 E. Sinton St., P.O. Box 266, Sinton, 78387. Tel: 361-364-1768; Email: shsinton@yahoo.com.
Catechesis Religious Program—Gloria Luna, D.R.E.; Deacon Solomon T. Willis III, C.R.E. Students 270.
Mission—St. Paul, P.O. Box 266, St. Paul, San Patricio Co. 78387.

SKIDMORE, BEE CO., IMMACULATE CONCEPTION (1915) [JC] Rev. Thomas L. Goodwin, Admin.
Res.: 300 First St., P.O. Box 189, Skidmore, 78389.
Tel: 361-287-3256; Fax: 361-287-3696.
Catechesis Religious Program—Students 82.
Mission—St. Francis Xavier, Frio St., Tynan, Bee Co. 78384.

TAFT, SAN PATRICIO CO.
1—HOLY FAMILY (1957) [JC]
702 McIntyre Ave., Taft, 78390-0173.
Tel: 361-528-3132; Email: holyfamilytaft@cableone.net. Mailing Address: P.O. Box 173, Taft, 78390. Rev. John McKenzie.
Office: 701 Fetick, Taft, 78390. Tel: 361-528-3132.
Res.: 646 McIntyre Ave., Taft, 78390.
Catechesis Religious Program—Students 85.
2—IMMACULATE CONCEPTION (1928)
120 E. Escobedo, P.O. Box 868, Taft, 78390.
Tel: 361-528-2626; Email: immaculate.conception.taft@gmail.com. Rev. Peter E. Stanley.
Catechesis Religious Program—Students 221.

THREE RIVERS, LIVE OAK CO., SACRED HEART (1948)
303 E. Alexander St., P.O. Box 729, Three Rivers, 78071-0729. Tel: 361-786-3398; Email: sh.threerivers@diocesecc.org; Web: www.shthreerivers.org. Rev. Ryszard Zielinski, (Poland).
Catechesis Religious Program—Students 69.
Mission—Our Lady of Guadalupe, P.O. Box 729, Pawnee, Bee Co. 78071.

TIVOLI, REFUGIO CO., OUR LADY OF GUADALUPE (1936)
Mailing Address: 501B William St., P.O. Drawer I, Tivoli, 77990. Tel: 361-237-3634. Rev. Ponnuswamy R. Victor.
Catechesis Religious Program—Students 20.
Missions—St. Anthony of Padua—Austwell, Refugio Co.
St. Dennis, O'Connor Ranch, Refugio Co.

VIOLET, NUECES CO., ST. ANTHONY (1910) [CEM]
3894 Co. Rd. 61, Robstown, 78380-5737.
Tel: 361-387-4434; Email: stanthonyviolet@yahoo.com. Rev. Zenon Konowalek, (Poland); Yvette Cavazos, Sec. & Bookkeeper.
Catechesis Religious Program—Nova Ordner, D.R.E. Students 26.

WOODSBORO, REFUGIO CO., ST. THERESE, THE LITTLE FLOWER (1915) [CEM] (Hispanic) Rev. Andrew Hejdak, (Poland).
Res.: 315 Pugh St., P.O. Box 1076, Woodsboro, 78393. Tel: 361-543-4166; Fax: 361-543-5922; Email: sttherese1076@gmail.com.
Catechesis Religious Program—Students 89.
Mission—St. Mary, Bayside, Refugio Co.

On Special Assignment:
Revs.—
Ethappiri, Varghese K.
Mathias, Arularasu
Nwachukwu, Thomas Kizito, Chap.
Onuoha, Silas, Chap.

On Duty Outside the Diocese:
Revs.—
McGerity, Francis X.
Taurasi, David.

Military Chaplains:
Revs.—
Gajda, Piotr J., Green Beret Chap., 5395 Wolfe Dr., Oklahoma City, OK 73145
Shuley, Keith, C.C., Command Chap., U.S. Merchant Marine Academy, 300 Steamboat Rd., Kings Point, NY 11024
Tran, Tung T., St. Rose of Lima, 268 Alvardo St., Chula Vista, CA 91910.

Retired:
Most Revs.—
Carmody, Edmond, D.D., (Retired)
Gracida, Rene H., D.D., (Retired)
Rev. Msgrs.—
Anders, Arnold, (Retired)
Chamberlin, Mark
Chilen, Michael D., (Retired)
Killeen, John P., (Retired)
McGettrick, Tom, (Retired)
McGowan, Seamus, (Retired)
Shirley, Richard, P.A., V.E., (Retired)
Revs.—
Bergin, Paschal, (Retired)
Feminelli, John, (Retired)
Fidalgo, Federico, (Retired)
Hamilton, James, (Retired)
Heese, Henry, (Retired)
Hernandez, Manuel Jr., (Retired)
Lenihan, Michael, (Retired)
Mikolajczyk, Bruno, (Retired)
O'Donovan, Thomas P., (Retired)
Stephan, Matthew J., (Retired)
Vega, John Michael, (Retired)
Walsh, Arthur, (Retired)
Wellar, Thomas, (Retired)
Zurovetz, Jerome G., (Retired).

Deacons:
Allen, Bob, (Retired/ Active), Philip the Apostle, Corpus Christi
Alvarado, Carlos, (Inactive), St. Joseph, Corpus Christi
Alvarado, Salvador, St. Pius X, Corpus Christi
Arnold, Mark, St. Joseph, Port Aransas
Ayala, Juan C., St. Joseph, Corpus Christi
Benys, Victor, (Retired), Our Lady of Perpetual Help, Corpus Christi
Blanco, Israel, (Retired)
Bockholt, Ken, Most Precious Blood, Corpus Christi
Boehm, Daniel Joseph, Sacred Heart, Rockport
Bolanos, Armando M., Our Lady of Pilar, Corpus Christi
Boostrom, William, Holy Family, Taft
Botello, Armando, Our Lady of Guadalupe, Corpus Christi
Breland, Walter Noel, (Retired)
Carlisle, James A., (Retired/ Active), St. Elizabeth, Alice
Castillo, Alfredo, OLHP, Corpus Christi
Castillo, David, Most Precious Blood, Corpus Christi
Cavada, Armando, St. John of the Cross, Orange Grove
Christoph, Mark, Sacred Heart, Mathis
Cicora, Allen, St. Peter Prince of the Apostles, Corpus Christi
Cleavelin, William, St. Thomas the Apostle, Calallen
Costley, Ricardo E., Sacred Heart, Falfurrias
Davila, Ramiro, St. Theresa of the Infant Jesus, Premont, TX
Dimas, Julio, St. John the Baptist, Corpus Christi
Duggins, Russell W., (Retired), St. Joseph, Beeville
Farias, Eluterio, (Retired/ Active), St. Peter Prince of the Apostles, Corpus Christi
Flores, Emilio, St. Anthony of Padua, Robstown
Flores, Robert, Sacred Heart, Odem
Gallegos, Tomas, Holy Family, Corpus Christi
Galvan, Alberto III, Saints Cyril & Methodius, Corpus Christi
Garcia, Tiburcio, St. Martin, Kingsville
Garza, Jose A. Jr., St. James, Driscoll
Gonzalez, Emede, St. Joseph, Alice
Gonzalez, Pilar M., St. Michael the Archangel, Banquete
Gonzalez, Ricardo, St. Joseph, Kingsville
Grassedonio, Roy M., (Retired)
Gutierrez, Ernesto, St. Elizabeth, Alice
Herrera, Danny L., St. Martin, Kingsville
Janota, Ron, Sacred Heart, Rockport
Joiner, John R., (Retired/ Active), St. Gertrude, Kingsville
Katzfey, Shayne, St. George, George West
Landagan, Sebastian, (Retired)
Lara, Antonio S., St. Francis Xavier Mission, Tynan
Leal, Amando, Corpus Christi Cathedral, Corpus Christi
Ledbetter, Jerre H., Sacred Heart, Rockport (Inactive)
Lickteig, Wayne, S.O.L.T., Dir., Lay Council of Society, St. Anthony, Robstown
Longoria, Richard, St. Helena, Corpus Christi
Lugo, Loni, (Retired), Nuestra Señora de San Juan de Los Lagos, Madre de la Iglesia Parish, Corpus Christi
Luna, Cristobal E. Jr., (Inactive)
Maldonado, Jesus R., (Retired), St. Theresa of the Infant Jesus, Premont
Maldonado, Manuel, (Retired)
Mantz, Michael, (Retired/ Active), Dir. Deacons, Corpus Christi Cathedral, Corpus Christi
Marcha, Arnold, Our Lady of Perpetual Help, Corpus Christi
Marroquin, Manuel, Christ the King, Corpus Christi
Martinez, Homer, St. Anthony, Robstown
Martinez, Rodolfo R., Our Lady of Perpetual Help, Corpus Christi
Matula, Paul, St. Joseph, Beeville
Millsap, Stacey, St. Pius X, Corpus Christi
Millsap, Stanley Amos, (Retired)
Morin, Richard B., St. Joseph, Kingsville
Muniz, Felix, Sacred Heart, Corpus Christi
Newchurch, Frank N., Most Precious Blood, Corpus Christi
Nolte, Stephen, St. Theresa, Corpus Christi
Ortiz, Narciso, St. Philip the Apostle, Corpus Christi
Ouellette, Roland, (Retired)
Palacios, Adelfino Jr., Corpus Christi Cathedral, Corpus Christi
Perez, Fernando, Sts. Cyril & Methodius, Corpus Christi
Phillips, George, (Retired)
Postert, Anthony K., (Retired), St. Mary Star of the Sea, Aransas Pass
Provencio, Arthur, Our Lady of the Assumption, Ingleside
Ramirez, Rudy, (Inactive)
Rauen, Mike, (Retired)
Rodriguez, Eleazar (Larry), St. Patrick, Corpus Christi
Rodriguez, Francisco Jr., St. Paul the Apostle, Corpus Christi
Rodriguez, Reynaldo Jr., (Retired)
Rojas, Reynaldo, St. Joseph, Corpus Christi
Rosales, Raul G., St. Martin, Kingsville
Rosales, Robert, Our Lady of Mt. Carmel, Portland
Rosenbaum, Rogelio, Our Lady of Victory, Beeville
Rowley, Edwin N., (Retired/ Active), St. Gertrude, Kingsville
Salazar, Rolando R., (Retired), St. Joseph, Beeville
Salinas, Hector, St. Patrick, Corpus Christi
Sanchez, Armando, Our Lady of Perpetual Help Parish, Corpus Christi
Shaunessy, Daniel P., St. Philip the Apostle, Corpus Christi
Simeus, Erick, Most Precious Blood, Corpus Christi
Trevino, Luis, St. Joseph, Beeville
Trevino, Pedro R. Jr., St. Mary, Freer
Valenzuela, Michael, Our Lady of Consolation, Riviera
Vargas, Bernardo, (Retired), Sacred Heart, Corpus Christ
Vasquez, Juan, St. James, Beeville
Vasquez, Lupe, (Retired), (Inactive)
Washburn, Marc, St. Andrew by the Sea, Corpus Christi
Wiest, George Joe, (Inactive), Sacred Heart, Rockport
Willis, Solomon T. III, Spiritual Dir. for Legion of Mary, Corpus Christi; Sacred Heart, Sinton.

INSTITUTIONS LOCATED IN DIOCESE

[A] HIGH SCHOOLS

CORPUS CHRISTI. *Incarnate Word Academy High School* (1871) (Private) 2910 S. Alameda, 78404.
Tel: 361-883-0857; Fax: 361-881-8742; Email: retas@iwacc.org; Web: www.iwacc.org. Sammie Grunwald, Pres.; Mr. Jose Torres, Prin.; LaQuita Hilzinger, Librarian. Lay Teachers 24; Sisters 3; Students 255; Clergy / Religious Teachers 3; Staff 9.

St. John Paul II High School (2006) 3036 Saratoga Blvd., 78415. Tel: 361-855-5744;
Fax: 361-855-1343; Email: frmartinez@jpiihighschool.org; Web: www.jpiihighschool.org. Jim Brannigan, Prin.; Rev. Peter G. Martinez, Pres.; Mrs. Priscilla Vela, Dean. Lay Teachers 20; Sisters 3; Students 311.

[B] JUNIOR HIGH AND ELEMENTARY SCHOOLS

CORPUS CHRISTI. *Bishop Garriga Middle Preparatory School* (1987) (Grades 6-8), (Diocesan) 3114 Saratoga Blvd., 78415. Tel: 361-851-0853;
Fax: 361-853-5145; Email: rgonzalez@bgmps.org; Email: mderocher@bgmps.org; Web: www.bgmps.org. Rev. Peter G. Martinez, Pres.; Mr. Rene Gonzalez, Prin.; Christine Stanley, Librarian, Email: cstanley@jpiihighschool.org. Lay Teachers 10; Students 177.

SS. Cyril and Methodius School (1957) (Grades PreK-5), (Parochial) 5002 Kostoryz Rd., 78415.
Tel: 361-853-9392; Email: lsamaniego@sscmcschool.org; Web: www.sscmc.org. Lilly Samaniego, Prin.; Carol Sanchez, Librarian; Cassie Vaiz, Sec. Lay Teachers 10; Students 154.

Holy Family Catholic School (1946) (Parochial) 2526 Soledad St., 78416. Tel: 361-884-9142;
Fax: 361-884-1750. Mrs. Maria Elena Zavala, Prin.; Cerna Ramirez, Librarian. Lay Teachers 6; Sisters 1; Students 89.

Incarnate Word Academy Elementary Level (1950) (Private) 450 Chamberlain St., 78404.
Tel: 361-883-0857; Fax: 361-881-9519; Email: garciado@iwacc.org; Web: www.iwacc.org. Sammie Grunwald, Pres.; Pamela Carrillo, Prin. Lay Teachers 20; Sisters 2; Students 256; Clergy / Religious Teachers 2.

Incarnate Word Academy Middle School, (Grades 6-8), (Private) 2917 Austin St., 78404.
Tel: 361-883-0857, Ext. 113; Fax: 361-882-9193; Email: agarza@iwacc.org; Web: www.iwacc.org. Sammie Grunwald, Pres.; LaQuita Hilzinger, Librarian. Lay Teachers 20; Sisters 1; Students 170; Clergy / Religious Teachers 1.

Most Precious Blood School, (Grades PreK-5), (Parochial) 3502 Saratoga Blvd., 78415.
Tel: 361-852-4800; Fax: 361-855-8707; Email: nebazan@yahoo.com; Web: www.mpbcs.net. Nelda Bazan, Prin.; Lana Wilhelm, Librarian. Clergy 1; Lay Teachers 15; Students 201.

Our Lady of Perpetual Help Academy aka OLPH Academy (1955) (Parochial) 5814 Williams Dr., 78412. Tel: 361-991-3305; Tel: 361-992-5951;
Fax: 361-994-1806; Email: rramon@olphacademycc.org; Web: www.olphacademycc.org. Raul Ramon, Prin.; Iliana Ortiz, Librarian. Lay Teachers 16; Students 206.

St. Patrick School (1949-1950) (Grades PreK-6), (Parochial) 3340 S. Alameda St., 78411.
Tel: 361-852-1211; Fax: 361-852-4855; Email: eburton@stpatrickschoolcc.org; Email: rbaysinger@stpatrickschoolcc.org; Email: cburkart@stpatrickschoolcc.org; Web: www.stpatrickschoolcc.org. Evelyn Burton, Prin.; Mrs. Constance Burkart, Librarian & Tuition Mgmt.; Veronica Baysinger, Sec. Lay Teachers 22; Students 264.

St. Pius X Catholic School (1965) (Grades PreK-6), (Parochial) 737 St. Pius Dr., 78412.
Tel: 361-992-1343; Fax: 361-992-0329; Web: www.stpiusxschoolcc.org. Bryan Krnavek, Prin. Lay Teachers 16; Students 172.

ALICE. *St. Elizabeth School* (1949) (Parochial) 615 E. Fifth, Alice, 78332. Tel: 361-664-6271;
Fax: 361-668-4250; Web: sesalice.org. Patricia Garcia, Prin.; Kim Garcia, Librarian. Clergy 1; Faculty 11; Lay Teachers 10; Students 162.

St. Joseph School (Parochial) 311 Dewey, Alice, 78332. Tel: 361-664-4642; Fax: 361-664-5511; Email: school@sjcatholicchurch.org. Mrs. Mary Sandoval, Prin. Lay Teachers 11; Students 190.

KINGSVILLE. *St. Gertrude School*, (Grades PreK-4), (Parochial) 400 E. Caesar St., Kingsville, 78363.
Tel: 361-592-6522; Fax: 361-592-0100; Web: www.stgschoolktx.org. Very Rev. Joseph A. Lopez, J.C.L., V.F., Pastor. Lay Teachers 6; Students 62.

ROBSTOWN. *St. Anthony School* (1916) (Grades PreK-8), (Parochial) 203 Dunne Ave., Robstown, 78380. Tel: 361-387-3814; Fax: 361-387-7110; Email: anthonyschoolsaint@yahoo.ca; Web: www.stanthonysaints.org. Norma Castaneda, Prin.; Delia Morales, Parent Involvement Liaison; Norma Hernandez, Sec. Lay Teachers 12; Sisters 4; Students 131.

ROCKPORT. *Sacred Heart School*, (Grades PreK-5), (Parochial) 213 S. Church St., Rockport, 78382. Tel: 361-729-2672; Fax: 361-729-9382; Email: shsprin@shsrockport.org; Web: www.shsrockport.org. Rev. Raynaldo Yrlas Jr.; Katherine K. Barnes, Prin.; Mrs. Gwen Novosad, Dir.; Randall E. Barnes, Librarian; Mrs. Maricruz Gonzalez, Sec. Lay Teachers 10; Students 120; Clergy / Religious Teachers 5.

[C] DAY NURSERY, PRE-KINDER, KINDER

CORPUS CHRISTI. *Our Lady of the Rosary Catholic School* (1992) 2237 Waldron Rd., 78418. Tel: 361-939-9847; Fax: 361-937-0890; Email: rosary1512@yahoo.com. Sr. Josephine Taban-ud, Prin. Lay Staff 2; Sisters 6; Students 56.

ROBSTOWN. *St. Joseph's Dream*, 3660 Jack Dr., Robstown, 78380. Tel: 361-387-9598; Email: paxsolt@aol.com. Sisters 2; Total Staff 2; Total Assisted 4.

[D] GENERAL HOSPITALS

CORPUS CHRISTI. *CHRISTUS Spohn Family Health Center - Northside*, 2606 Hospital Blvd., 78405. Tel: 361-887-8811; Fax: 361-887-8874; Email: humberto.ramos@christushealth.org. Mailing Address: 5802 Saratoga Blvd., Ste. 300, 78414. Humberto Ramos, Dir.; Linda McClung, Corp. Sec. Sisters of Charity of the Incarnate Word (San Antonio, TX). Tot Asst. Annually 23,607; Total Staff 15.

CHRISTUS Spohn Family Health Center - Padre Island, 14202 S. Padre Island Dr., 78418. Tel: 361-949-7660; Fax: 361-949-9372; Email: humberto.ramos@christushealth.org. Mailing Address: 5802 Saratoga Blvd., Ste. 300, 78414. Linda McClung, Corp. Sec. Sisters of Charity of the Incarnate Word (San Antonio, TX). Tot Asst. Annually 1,303; Total Staff 2.

CHRISTUS Spohn Family Health Center - Westside, 4617 Greenwood Dr., 78416. Tel: 361-857-2872; Fax: 361-857-2946; Email: humberto.ramos@christushealth.org. Mailing Address: 5802 Saratoga Blvd., Ste. 300, 78414. Linda McClung, Corp. Sec. Sisters of Charity of the Incarnate Word (San Antonio, TX). Tot Asst. Annually 9,339; Total Staff 11.

CHRISTUS Spohn Health System Corporation, 5802 Saratoga Blvd., Ste. 300, 78404. Tel: 361-985-5566; Fax: 361-985-5592; Email: l.mcclung@christushealth.org. Dominic Dominguez, CEO; Stpehen Kazanjian, Vice Pres., Mission Integration; Linda McClung, Corp. Sec. Sisters of Charity of the Incarnate Word (San Antonio, TX). Bed Capacity 776; Tot Asst. Annually 449,345; Total Staff 3,355.

CHRISTUS Spohn Hospital Corpus Christi - Memorial, 5802 Saratoga Blvd., Ste. 300, 78414. Tel: 361-985-5566; Fax: 361-985-5592; Email: justin.doss@christushealth.org. 2606 Hospital Blvd., 78405. David LeMonte, Admin. Sisters of Charity of the Incarnate Word (San Antonio, TX). Bed Capacity 25; Tot Asst. Annually 79,708; Total Staff 334.

CHRISTUS Spohn Hospital Corpus Christi - Shoreline, 5802 Saratoga Blvd., Ste. 300, 78414. Tel: 361-985-5566; Fax: 361-985-5592; Email: l.mcclung@christushealth.org. 600 Elizabeth St., 78404. Rev. Aloysius Ezenwata, Dir.; David LeMonte, Admin.; Revs. Mathias Arularasu, Chap.; Matthew Click, Chap.; Silas Onuoha, Chap.; Ephraim Udeagbala, Chap.; Lynne Blackler, Chap.; Rev. Efren Cruzada, Chap.; Ernest Mills, Chap.; Christy J. Woods, Chap. Sisters of Charity of the Incarnate Word (San Antonio, TX). Bed Capacity 420; Tot Asst. Annually 134,615; Total Staff 1,807.

CHRISTUS Spohn Hospital Corpus Christi - South, 5802 Saratoga Blvd., Ste. 300, 78414. Tel: 361-985-5566; Email: l.mcclung@christushealth.org. 5950 Saratoga Blvd., 78414. Mark Casanova, Admin.; Rev. Thomas Kizito Nwachukwu, Chap.; Lynette Blackler, Chap. Sisters of Charity of the Incarnate Word (San Antonio, TX). Bed Capacity 152; Tot Asst. Annually 82,892; Total Staff 590.

5950 Saratoga Blvd., 78414. Tel: 361-985-5000; Fax: 361-985-5173. Mark Casanova, Pres.; Rev. Silas Onuoha, Chap.; Griselda Escobar, Chap.; Linda McClung, Corp. Sec.; Revs. Ephraim Udeabala; Joseph V. Varghese. Bed Capacity 129; Patients Asst Anual. 67,264; Total Staff 523.

CHRISTUS Spohn Medical Group Family Medicine Academic Center - Central, 2601 Hospital Blvd., Ste. 117 & 112, 78405. Tel: 361-902-4789; Fax: 361-902-4746. Jose R. Hinojosa, Prog. Dir.; Linda McClung, Corp. Sec. Sisters of Charity of the Incarnate Word (San Antonio, TX). Tot Asst. Annually 14,000; Total Staff 34.

CHRISTUS Spohn Memorial - Specialty Clinic, 2606 Hospital Blvd., 78405. Tel: 361-902-4765; Fax: 361-881-1439; Email: humberto.ramos@christushealth.org. Mailing Address: 5802 Saratoga Blvd., Ste. 300, 78414. Dominic Dominguez, Pres. & CEO; Linda McClung, Corp. Sec. Sisters of Charity of the Incarnate Word (San Antonio, TX). Tot Asst. Annually 6,088; Total Staff 6.

ALICE. *CHRISTUS Spohn Hospital Alice*, 5802 Saratoga Blvd., Ste. 300, 78414. Tel: 361-985-5566; Fax: 361-985-5592; Email: l.mcclung@christushealth.org; Web: www.christusspohn.org. 2500 E. Main St., Alice, 78404. Thomas McKinney, Admin.; Rev. Jacob John Valayath, Chap. Sisters of Charity of the Incarnate Word (San Antonio, TX). Bed Capacity 80; Tot Asst. Annually 56,176; Total Staff 220.

2500 E. Main St, Alice, 78332. Tel: 361-661-8016; Fax: 361-661-8073. David LeMonte, Pres.; Linda McClung, Corp. Sec.; Rev. Jacob John Valayath. Bed Capacity 73; Patients Asst Anual. 53,386; Total Staff 250.

BEEVILLE. *CHRISTUS Spohn Hospital Beeville*, 5802 Saratoga Blvd., Ste. 300, 78414. Tel: 361-985-5566; Fax: 361-985-5592; Email: l.mcclung@christushealth.org; Web: www.christusspohn.org. 1500 E. Houston Hwy., Beeville, 78102. Genifer Rucker, Admin.; Very Rev. Lukose Thirunelliparamabil, (India) Chap. Sisters of Charity of the Incarnate Word (San Antonio, TX). Bed Capacity 49; Tot Asst. Annually 45,031; Total Staff 168.

1500 E. Houston Hwy., Beeville, 78102. Tel: 361-354-2125; Fax: 361-358-9322. Nathan Tudor, Pres.; Linda McClung, Corp. Sec.; Rev. Luke Thirunelliparambil, Chap. Bed Capacity 43; Patients Asst Anual. 41,882; Total Staff 164.

CHRISTUS Spohn Medical Clinic, 5802 Saratoga Blvd., Ste. 300, 78414. 1602 E. Houston Hwy., Ste A, Beeville, 78102. Tel: 361-358-6249; Fax: 361-358-4098; Email: l.mcclung@christushealth.org; Web: www.christusspohn.org. Genifer Rucker, Admin. Sisters of Charity of the Incarnate Word (San Antonio, TX). Tot Asst. Annually 3,411; Total Staff 5.

FREER. *CHRISTUS Spohn - Freer Clinic*, 5802 Saratoga Blvd., Ste. 300, 78414. 111 E. Riley, Freer, 78357. Tel: 361-394-7311; Fax: 361-394-7158; Email: l.mcclung@christushealth.org; Web: www.christusspohn.org. Humberto Ramos, Dir. Sisters of Charity of the Incarnate Word (San Antonio, TX). Tot Asst. Annually 5,490; Total Staff 6.

KINGSVILLE. *CHRISTUS Spohn Hospital Kleberg*, 1311 General Cavazos Blvd., Kingsville, 78363. Tel: 361-985-5566; Fax: 361-985-5592; Email: l.mcclung@christushealth.org; Web: www.christusspohn.org. Mailing Address: 5802 Saratoga Blvd., Ste. 300, 78414. Thomas McKinney, Admin.; Rev. John Xaviour, Chap. Sponsorship: Sisters of Charity of the Incarnate Word (San Antonio, TX). Bed Capacity 50; Tot Asst. Annually 50,923; Total Staff 236.

1311 General Cavazos Blvd., Kingsville, 78363. Tel: 361-595-1661; Fax: 361-595-5005. David LeMonte, Vice Pres. & COO; Marcia Kline, Chap.; Rev. John Xaviour, Chap. Bed Capacity 50; Patients Asst Anual. 39,190; Total Staff 221.

ROBSTOWN. *CHRISTUS Spohn Family Health Center - Robstown*, 1038 Texas Yes Blvd., Robstown, 78380. Tel: 361-767-1200; Fax: 361-387-5184; Email: humberto.ramos@christushealth.org. Mailing Address: 5802 Saratoga Blvd., Ste. 300, 78414. Tel: 361-985-5566; Fax: 361-855-0566. Linda McClung, Corp. Sec. Sisters of Charity of the Incarnate Word (San Antonio, TX). Tot Asst. Annually 7,724; Total Staff 9.

[E] HOMES FOR THE AGED

CORPUS CHRISTI. *Villa Maria, Inc.*, 3146 Saratoga Blvd., 78415. Tel: 361-857-6171; Fax: 361-857-6173; Email: villamaria@corpus.twcbc.com. Patricia Cantu, Exec. Dir. Apartment complex for senior adults. Bed Capacity 60; Total in Residence 54; Total Staff 3.

[F] RETREAT HOUSES

CORPUS CHRISTI. *Our Lady of Corpus Christi Retreat Center*, 1200 Lantana, Bldg. C, 78407. Tel: 361-289-9095, Ext. 321; Fax: 361-289-0087. Rev. Samuel Medley, S.O.L.T.

Pax Christi Liturgical Retreat Center, 4601 Calallen Dr., 78410-4940. Tel: 361-241-5479; Fax: 361-241-0569; Web: www.paxchristisisterscc.org. Sr. Teresa Diaz, Admin.

SARITA. *Lebh Shomea House of Prayer* (1973) 500 La Parra Ranch Rd., Sarita, 78385. Tel: 361-294-5369; Fax: 361-294-5791; Email: lebhshomea@omiusa.org; Web: www.lebhshomea.org. Missionary Oblates of Mary Immaculate, P.O. Box 9, Sarita, 78385-0009. Maurice Lange, Dir.; Regina Lange, Admin.; Revs. Jack Lau, In Res.; Andrew Sensenig, In Res.; Sr. Marie Combs, In Res. Priests 2; Total Staff 6.

[G] MONASTERIES AND RESIDENCES OF PRIESTS AND BROTHERS

BENAVIDES. *Catholic Solitudes* (1994) 11053 Hwy. 16 N., P.O. Box 211, Benavides, 78341. Tel: 361-527-4636; Email: catholic.solitudes@gmail.com. Rev. Patrick Meaney, Moderator. Special Apostolate: A fraternal community stressing eremitical contemplative prayer. Priests 1; Total in Residence 2; Total Staff 2.

ROBSTOWN. *Society of Our Lady of the Most Holy Trinity*, 1200 Lantana, Robstown, 78407. Tel: 361-387-2754; Fax: 361-387-3818; Email: gpservant@gmail.com; Web: www.solt.net. Revs. Zaldy Abainza, S.O.L.T.; Terencio Ayo, S.O.L.T., (Philippines); William K. Bakyil, S.O.L.T., (Ghana); Jerome Drolshagen, S.O.L.T., Regl. Priest Servant; Michael Edward Crump, S.O.L.T.; John Gaffney, S.O.L.T., Gen. Procurator; James R. Kelleher, S.O.L.T.; Peter Marsalek, S.O.L.T., Gen. Priest Servant; Benjamin Martin, S.O.L.T.; John McHugh, S.O.L.T.; John M. Patterson II, S.O.L.T.; Peter Nghi Duc Pham, S.O.L.T.; Edward Roche, S.O.L.T.; Rogel Rosalinas, S.O.L.T.; Gerard J. Sheehan, S.O.L.T.; Michael Slovak, S.O.L.T.; Brady Williams, S.O.L.T., Gen. Sec. & Novice Servant; Dominic Zimmermann, S.O.L.T.; Deacons Wayne Lickteig, S.O.L.T.; Bernard Vessa, S.O.L.T.

[H] CONVENTS AND RESIDENCES FOR SISTERS

CORPUS CHRISTI. *Blessed Sacrament Chapel* (1970) 4105 Ocean Dr., 78411-1223. Tel: 361-852-6212; Fax: 361-852-8815; Email: sspsap.corpuschristi@gmail.com; Web: www.mountgraceconvent.org. Sr. Mary Leticia Acayan, Supr. Sister-Servants of the Holy Spirit of Perpetual Adoration (Motherhouse, Steyl, Holland) 7.

Dominicas de Santo Tomas de Aquino (DSTA) (1913) 12217 Hearn Rd., 78410. Tel: 361-242-8829; Fax: 361-241-3621. Sisters Maria P. Vega, Local Supr.; Ma. Elena Banderas Rangel; Maria Carmen Tabares Garcia, D.S.T.A. Sisters 2.

Incarnate Word Convent (1871) 5201 Lipes Blvd., 78413. Tel: 361-882-5413; Fax: 361-880-4152; Email: sawagner@iwbscc.org; Email: STrespeces@iwbscc.org; Web: www.iwbscc.org. Sr. Anne Brigid Schlegel, I.W.B.S., Local Sister in Charge. Sisters of the Incarnate Word and Blessed Sacrament.

Convent Academy of the Incarnate Word. Sisters 29; Total in Residence 29; Total Staff 15.

Missionaries of Christ's Charity, 6333 N. Washam, 78414. Tel: 361-815-4974; Email: ttbheip@yahoo.com. Sr. Mary Ann Hiep Truong, Supr. Sisters 6.

Mount Tabor Convent, 12940 Leopard St., 78410. Tel: 361-241-1955; Fax: 361-241-2271; Email: mounttabormjmj@gmail.com. Sisters Gloria Rodriguez, M.J.M.J.; Milagros Tormo, M.J.M.J., Local Supr. Central Regional House of the Missionary Sisters of Jesus, Mary, and Joseph. Sisters 6.

The Ark Assessment Center & Emergency Shelter for Youth (1994) 12960 Leopard St., 78410. Tel: 361-241-6566; Fax: 361-241-5279. Sr. Milagros Tormo, M.J.M.J., Pres.

Pax Christi Institute (1969) 4601 Calallen Dr., 78410. Tel: 361-241-2833; Fax: 361-241-2140; Email: paxchristisisters@gmail.com; Web: www.paxchristisisterscc.org. Mother Maria Elva Reyes, P.C.I., Supr. Gen. Sisters 11; Total Staff 9; Total Assisted 3,200.

Religious Missionaries of St. Dominic, Inc. (1986) 2237 Waldron Rd., 78418. Tel: 361-937-5978 (Community); Fax: 361-367-3814; Email: martiresterry@gmail.com. Sisters 9.

Sisters of Adoration of Blessed Sacrament, Saint Alphonsa Convent, 454 Haroldson Dr., 78412. Tel: 361-288-7353. Sisters Jassamol Pallikizhakethil, S.A.B.S, Supr.; Jessamma George, S.A.B.S.; Rosy Joseph. Sisters 3.

Sisters of Adoration of the Blessed Sacrament, 5313 Grayford Pl., 78413. Tel: 361-884-7136; Email: sabs2000@sbcglobal.net. Sr. Roalia Aricatt, Supr. Sisters 3.

Sisters of Adoration of the Blessed Sacrament, SABS, 222 Ocean View, 78411. Tel: 361-854-2820; Email: srrosepaul@yahoo.co.uk. Sisters Merlin Poothavelil, Supr.; Rose Paul Madassery, S.A.B.S., Contact Person. Sisters 6.

Sisters of the Incarnate Word Incarnate Word Residence 3002 Austin St., 78404-2413. Cell: 361-688-2654; Web: iwbscc.org. Sr. Barbara Netek, I.W.B.S., Contact Person. Sisters of the Incarnate Word and Blessed Sacrament 2.

KINGSVILLE. *Missionary Daughters of the Most Pure Virgin Mary* (1916) 919 N. Ninth St., Kingsville, 78363. Tel: 361-595-1087; Fax: 361-221-9763; Email: aduba@hotmail.com. Sr. Agueda Durazo, M.D.P.V.M., Supr. Sisters 8.

ROBSTOWN. *Incarnate Word Ranch - Bluntzer*, Mailing Address: 5201 Lipes Blvd., 78413.
Tel: 361-882-5413; Fax: 361-880-4152;
Tel: 361-877-1232; Email: smas@iwbscc.org; Email: Strespeces@iwbscc.org. Sr. Annette Wagner, I.W.B.S., Supr. Sisters of the Incarnate Word and Blessed Sacrament 2.

Sisters of the Society of Our Lady of the Most Holy Trinity, Regl. Headquarters - Casa Santo Tomas, P.O. Box 152, Robstown, 78380. Tel: 361-387-8090; Fax: 361-387-3818; Email: sorelena@solt.net; Web: www.solt.net. Sr. Megan Mary Thibodeau, S.O.L.T., Gen. Sister Servant.

ROCKPORT. *Schoenstatt Sisters of Mary* (1926) 130 Front St., Rockport, 78382-7800. Tel: 361-729-1868 ; Email: schoenstattlamartx@corpus.twcbc.com. Sr. Gloria Mauricio Pina, I.S.S.M., Supr. Secular Institute of the Schoenstatt Sisters of Mary. Sisters 10.

SARITA. *Lebh Shomea House of Prayer*, 500 La Parra Ranch Rd., Sarita, 78385. Tel: 361-294-5369;
Fax: 361-294-5791; Email: admin@lebhshomea.org; Web: www.lebhshomea.org. P.O. Box 9, Sarita, 78385-0009. Sr. Marie Combs, Contact Person. Sisters 1; Total in Residence 4; Total Staff 10.

[I] MISCELLANEOUS

CORPUS CHRISTI. *The Cathedral Concert Series* (1985) Diocese of Corpus Christi, P.O. Box 2620, 78403.
Tel: 361-882-6191; Email: lgwozdz@diocesecc.org; Web: www.ccseries.org. Mr. Lee Gwozdz, Exec. Dir.

Fannie Bluntzer Nason Renewal Center, Inc. (2000) 5201 Lipes Blvd., 78413. Tel: 361-882-5413;
Fax: 361-880-4152; Email: sawagner@iwbscc.org; Email: strespeces@iwbscc.org. Sr. Annette Wagner, I.W.B.S., Pres.; Syivia Basaldu, Admin. Asst. Bed Capacity 96.

Incarnate Word Academy Foundation (1989) 5201 Lipes Blvd., 78413. Tel: 361-882-5413;
Fax: 361-880-4152; Email: sawagner@iwbscc.org; Email: STrespeces@iwbscc.org; Email: DTamez@iwbscc.org; Email: smasnapka@iwbscc.org; Web: www.iwacc.org. Sr. Annette Wagner, I.W.B.S., Pres.

Journey to Damascus, Inc., P.O. Box 948, 78403.
Tel: 361-244-2138; Email: j2damascus@yahoo.com; Web: www.journeytodamascus.org. Revs. Paul A. Hesse, B.A., M.Div., Corpus Christi Chap.; Thomas L. Goodwin, Board of Trustees Chap. Assisted 250 men and women in 2014, including approximately 60 on partial or full scholarship.

Mother Teresa Shelter, Inc. (2003) 513 Sam Rankin, 78401. Tel: 361-883-7372; Fax: 361-881-1373; Email: mteresashelter@diocesecc.org; Web: motherteresashelter.org. Sr. Rose Paul Madassery, S.A.B.S., Opers. Supvr. A day shelter used as a homeless gathering facility; providing bath, laundry, limited eating facilities and counseling services. Tot Asst. Annually 77,224; Staff 11.

Natural Family Planning Outreach, P.O. Box 2620, 78403. Tel: 361-882-6191. Elizabeth Nguyen, Dir. of Family, Laity & Life.

Secular Institute of the Schoenstatt Fathers aka Schoenstatt Fathers, 4343 Gaines St., 78412-2541.
Tel: 361-992-9841; Fax: 361-992-9842; Email: frgerold@hotmail.com.

RELIGIOUS INSTITUTES OF MEN REPRESENTED IN THE DIOCESE

For further details refer to the corresponding bracketed number in the Religious Institutes of Men or Women section.

[]—*Catholic Solitudes (Hermits)*.
[]—*Heralds of the Good News, Mary Queen of Apostles Prov. (India)*—H.G.N.
[]—*Missionary Society of St. Thomas the Apostle (Society of Apostolic Life)* (India).
[0910]—*Oblates of Mary Immaculate*—O.M.I.
[]—*Secular Institute*.
[0975]—*Society of Our Lady of the Most Holy Trinity, Society of Apostolic Life*—S.O.L.T.

RELIGIOUS INSTITUTES OF WOMEN REPRESENTED IN THE DIOCESE

[0360]—*Carmelite Sisters of the Divine Heart of Jesus*—Carmel D.C.J.
[]—*Congregation of Sisters of St. Joseph of 'St. Marc'*—S.J.S.M.
[0460]—*Congregation of the Sisters of Charity of the Incarnate Word* (San Antonio, TX)—C.C.V.I.
[]—*Dominican Sisters of St. Thomas Aquinas*—O.P.
[]—*Missionaries of Christ's Charity*.
[2690]—*Missionary Catechists of Divine Providence* (San Antonio, TX)—M.C.D.P.
[]—*Missionary Daughters of the Most Pure Virgin Mary* (U.S. Foundation-Mexico)—M.D.P.V.M.
[2770]—*Missionary Sisters of Jesus, Mary, and Joseph*—M.J.M.J.
[]—*Pax Christi Institute*—P.C.I.
[]—*Religious Missionaries of St. Dominic* (Spanish Prov.)—O.P.
[]—*Schoenstatt Sisters of Mary (Secular Institute)*—I.S.S.M.
[3540]—*Sister Servants of the Holy Spirit of Perpetual Adoration*—S.Sp.S.deA.P.
[]—*Sisters for Christian Community*—S.F.C.C.
[]—*Sisters of Adoration of the Blessed Sacrament* (India)—S.A.B.S.
[3360]—*Sisters of Providence of Saint Mary-of-the-Woods, IN*—S.P.
[3718]—*Sisters of St. Anne*—S.S.A.
[2205]—*Sisters of the Incarnate Word and Blessed Sacrament* (Corpus Christi)—I.W.B.S.
[]—*Sisters of the Society of Our Lady of the Most Holy Trinity (Society of Apostolic Life)*—S.O.L.T.

NECROLOGY

† Antony, Paul Peter, (India) Died Jul. 31, 2017
† Ashe, Michael B., (Retired), Died Oct. 5, 2018
† Doherty, Charles, (Retired), Died May. 9, 2018
† Jones, Ralph O., Died Feb. 3, 2018

An asterisk (*) denotes an organization that has established tax-exempt status directly with the IRS and is not covered by the USCCB Group Ruling.

Diocese of Covington

(Dioecesis Covingtonensis)

Most Reverend

ROGER J. FOYS, D.D.

Bishop of Covington; ordained May 16, 1973; appointed Bishop of Covington May 31, 2002; consecrated and installed July 15, 2002. *Mailing Address: 1125 Madison Ave., Covington, KY 41011-3115.* Tel: 859-392-1512; Fax: 859-392-1508.

1125 Madison Ave., KY 41011-3115. Tel: 859-392-1500; Fax: 859-392-1589.

Web: www.covdio.org

Email: porecchio@covdio.org

ESTABLISHED JULY 29, 1853.

Square Miles 3,359.

Comprises 14 Counties of the Commonwealth of Kentucky in the north and east of the Commonwealth, including Bracken, Boone, Campbell, Carroll, Fleming, Gallatin, Grant, Harrison, Kenton, Lewis, Mason, Owen, Pendleton and Robertson Counties.

For legal titles of parishes and diocesan institutions, consult the Chancery Office.

STATISTICAL OVERVIEW

Personnel	
Bishop	1
Priests: Diocesan Active in Diocese	56
Priests: Diocesan Active Outside Diocese	4
Priests: Retired, Sick or Absent	31
Number of Diocesan Priests	91
Religious Priests in Diocese	8
Total Priests in Diocese	99
Extern Priests in Diocese	4
Ordinations:	
Diocesan Priests	2
Transitional Deacons	2
Permanent Deacons in Diocese	40
Total Brothers	4
Total Sisters	242
Parishes	
Parishes	48
With Resident Pastor:	
Resident Diocesan Priests	37
Resident Religious Priests	2
Without Resident Pastor:	
Administered by Priests	8
Administered by Religious Women	1
Missions	5
Professional Ministry Personnel:	
Brothers	3
Sisters	13
Lay Ministers	179
Welfare	
Catholic Hospitals	5
Total Assisted	958,852
Health Care Centers	1
Total Assisted	2,973
Homes for the Aged	3
Total Assisted	946
Residential Care of Children	1
Total Assisted	776
Day Care Centers	1
Total Assisted	70
Special Centers for Social Services	9
Total Assisted	194,103
Other Institutions	1
Total Assisted	4,593
Educational	
Diocesan Students in Other Seminaries	12
Total Seminarians	12
Colleges and Universities	1
Total Students	2,828
High Schools, Diocesan and Parish	7
Total Students	2,269
High Schools, Private	2
Total Students	820
Elementary Schools, Diocesan and Parish	28
Total Students	5,707
Elementary Schools, Private	2
Total Students	322
Catechesis/Religious Education:	
High School Students	143
Elementary Students	2,901
Total Students under Catholic Instruction	15,002
Teachers in the Diocese:	
Priests	1
Sisters	9
Lay Teachers	752
Vital Statistics	
Receptions into the Church:	
Infant Baptism Totals	853
Minor Baptism Totals	232
Adult Baptism Totals	182
Received into Full Communion	102
First Communions	1,264
Confirmations	1,193
Marriages:	
Catholic	243
Interfaith	92
Total Marriages	335
Deaths	698
Total Catholic Population	89,035
Total Population	529,445

Former Bishops—Rt. Revs. GEORGE ALOYSIUS CARRELL, S.J., D.D., ord. Dec. 20, 1827; cons. Nov. 1, 1853; died Sept. 25, 1868; AUGUSTUS MARIA TOEBBE, D.D., ord. Sept. 14, 1854; cons. Jan. 9, 1870; died May 2, 1884; CAMILLUS PAUL MAES, D.D., ord. Dec. 19, 1868; cons. Jan. 25, 1885; died May 11, 1915; FERDINAND BROSSART, D.D., ord. Sept. 1, 1872; cons. Jan. 25, 1916; retired March 14, 1923; died Aug. 6, 1930; Most Revs. FRANCIS WILLIAM HOWARD, D.D., ord. June 16, 1891; cons. July 15, 1923; died Jan. 18, 1944; WILLIAM THEODORE MULLOY, D.D., LL.D., ord. June 7, 1916; cons. Jan. 10, 1945; died June 1, 1959; RICHARD HENRY ACKERMAN, C.S.Sp., D.D., cons. May 22, 1956; transferred to Covington April 6, 1960; retired Nov. 28, 1978; died Nov. 18, 1992; WILLIAM ANTHONY HUGHES, D.D., ord. April 6, 1946; cons. Sept. 12, 1974; appt. April 13, 1979; retired July 4, 1995; died Feb. 7, 2013.; ROBERT W. MUENCH, D.D., ord. May 18, 1968; cons. June 29, 1990; appt. Bishop of Covington, Jan. 5, 1996; installed March 19, 1996; transferred to Baton Rouge, Dec. 15, 2001; installed Bishop of Baton Rouge March 14, 2002.

Vicars General—Very Revs. RYAN L. MAHER, V.G.; DANIEL L. SCHOMAKER, V.G.

Chancellor—MRS. JAMIE N. SCHROEDER.

Vice Chancellor—VACANT.

Administrative Assistant to the Bishop, Episcopal Master of Ceremonies, & Assistant to the Chancellor—Rev. JOSEPH C. SHELTON.

Diocesan Tribunal—Very Rev. JAMES M. RYAN, J.C.L., Judicial Vicar. Adjutant Judicial Vicar: VACANT; Sr. MARGARET STALLMEYER, C.D.P., J.C.L., Dir. & Judge; MS. KAREN A. GUIDUGLI, Case Promoter & Notary; MS. ELIZABETH DJORDJEVIC, Case Promoter & Notary; Sr. MARY SHANNON KRIEGE, S.N.D., Sec. & Notary.

Judges—Very Revs. MICHAEL D. BARTH, J.C.L.; BARRY M. WINDHOLTZ, J.C.L.; Rev. RYAN L. STENGER, J.C.L.

Defenders of the Bond—Revs. GREGORY E. OSBURG; GERALD E. TWADDELL, Ph.D.; Sr. MARY CATHERINE WENSTRUP, O.S.B., J.C.L.; Rev. Msgr. JOHN R. SCHULTE, J.C.L.; Rev. JAMES M. RYAN, J.C.L., (Retired).

Promoter of Justice—Rev. Msgr. WILLIAM B. NEUHAUS, J.C.L.

Diocesan Consultors—Very Revs. RYAN L. MAHER, V.G.; DANIEL L. SCHOMAKER, V.G.; Rev. Msgr. DOMINIC K. FOSU, V.F.; Revs. STEPHEN M. BANKEMPER; BAIJU KIDAAGEN, V.C.; NICHOLAS E. C. ROTTMAN.

Deans—Very Revs. RYAN L. MAHER, V.G., Covington; MARK A. KEENE, V.F., Northern Kenton County; MATTHEW A. CUSHING, V.F., South West; GERALD L. REINERSMAN, V.F., Campbell County; Rev. Msgr. DOMINIC K. FOSU, V.F., South East.

Deanery Pastoral Council—Very Rev. RYAN L. MAHER, V.G.

Presbyteral Council—Very Rev. DANIEL L. SCHOMAKER, V.G., Chancery Contact.

Due Process Board of Administrative Review—MR. STEPHEN KOPLYAY, Sec.

Diocesan Offices and Directors

1125 Madison Ave., Covington, 41011-3115. Tel: 859-392-1500; Fax: 859-392-1589; Email: porecchio@covdio.org. Office Hours: Mon.-Fri. 8:30-4:30.

Archives—MR. THOMAS S. WARD, Archivist.

Board of Total Catholic Education—MR. MICHAEL T. CLINES.

Campus Ministry-Newman Center—Rev. LAWRENCE A. SCHAEPER, Chap.; MRS. DONNA HEIM, Campus Min., Northern Kentucky Univ., 19 Clearview Dr., Highland Heights, 41076-1403. Tel: 859-261-5340; Email: heimd2@nku.edu.

Catholic Charities—MR. ALAN B. PICKETT, Dir., 3629 Church St., Covington, 41015-1499. Tel: 859-581-8974; Fax: 859-581-9595.

Catholic Scouting—MR. ISAAK A. ISAAK, Dir.

Cemeteries—MR. DONALD KNOCHELMANN, Dir.

Centro de Amistad—Sr. JUANA MENDEZ, S.C., Dir., 25 Cavalier Blvd., Florence, 41042-1684. Tel: 859-282-1392; Fax: 859-818-0694; Email: jmendez@covdio.org.

Censor Librorum—Revs. JAMES E. QUILL, S.T.D., (Retired); RYAN L. STENGER, J.C.L.

Charismatic Renewal—MS. CAROL HODGE, Contact Person, Tel: 859-341-5932.

Communication—MRS. LAURA KEENER, Dir.

Continuing Education of Priests—Very Rev. GERALD L. REINERSMAN, V.F.

Cursillo Movement—MR. DAN HECK SR., Lay Dir.

Disabilities Committee—MR. STEPHEN KOPLYAY, Chm.

Ecumenism—Rev. RONALD M. KETTELER, Thomas

More College, 333 Thomas More Pkwy., Crestview Hills, 41017-3428. Tel: 859-344-3393.

Initiation—Chancery VACANT.

Family Ministry—MR. ISAAK A. ISAAK, Dir.

Finance—MR. DALE HENSON, Dir.

Hispanic Ministry—Sr. JUANA MENDEZ, S.C., Dir., 25 Cavalier Blvd., Florence, 41042-1684. Tel: 859-282-1392; Fax: 859-818-0694.

Legion of Mary—Rev. MARIO J. TIZZIANI.

Liaison for Retired Priests—Rev. JOHN H. KROGER, (Retired).

Ministry Development Program for Deacons—Rev. Msgr. WILLIAM B. NEUHAUS, J.C.L.

Mission Services—See Stewardship and Missions.

Missions Among Black and Native Americans—Sr. JANET BUCHER, C.D.P., Tel: 859-491-5872; Fax: 859-431-8444.

Mustard Seed Community—MS. CAROL HODGE, Tel: 859-341-5932.

Newspaper "Messenger"—MRS. LAURA KEENER, Editor & Gen. Mgr., Tel: 859-392-1500, Ext. 1571.

Deaf Ministry—Mother of God Parish, 119 W. Sixth St., Covington, 41011-1409. Tel: 859-291-2288.

Permanent Diaconate Formation—Rev. Msgr. WILLIAM B. NEUHAUS, J.C.L.

Priest Personnel—VACANT.

Priests' Retirement Committee—Very Rev. MARK A. KEENE, V.F., Chm.

Pro Life—MS. FAYE ROCH, Dir.

Religious—Sr. FRANCES MOORE, C.D.P., Dir.

Religious Education—MR. ISAAK A. ISAAK, Dir.

Serra Club for Vocations of Diocese of Covington—MR. MICHAEL MURRAY, Pres.; Rev. ANDREW L. YOUNG, Chap.

St. Vincent de Paul Community Pharmacy, Inc.—aka Faith Community Pharmacy. MS. JILL HILGEFORT, Dir.

Stewardship and MissionsMR. MICHAEL MURRAY, Dir., Includes Pontifical Aid Societies, Campaign for Human Development, Catholic Relief Services, Holy Childhood Assoc., Inner City Missions.

Catholic Schools—MR. MICHAEL T. CLINES, Supt., Includes the Alliance for Catholic Urban Education (A.C.U.E.).

Vocations Office—Rev. ANDREW L. YOUNG, Vocations Promoter.

Worship—Deacon PETER J. (PETE) FREEMAN, Dir.

Youth and Young Adult Ministry—MR. ISAAK A. ISAAK, Dir., Tel: 859-392-1500, Ext. 1533. Includes the Covington Youth Retreat Committee.

Victim Assistance Coordinator—MS. MARGARET M. SCHACK, Tel: 859-392-1515; Email: mschack@covdio.org.

CLERGY, PARISHES, MISSIONS AND PAROCHIAL SCHOOLS

CITY OF COVINGTON

(KENTON COUNTY)

1—CATHEDRAL, BASILICA OF THE ASSUMPTION aka St. Mary's Cathedral (1837)
1130 Madison Ave., Covington, 41011-3116.
Tel: 859-431-2060; Fax: 859-431-8444; Email: tbrundage@covcathedral.com; Web: www.covcathedral.com. 1101 Madison Ave., Covington, 41011-3116. Very Rev. Ryan L. Maher, V.G., Rector; Rev. Andrew L. Young, Vice Rector; Deacon Gerald R. Franzen.
Catechesis Religious Program—Email: srwoeste@covcathedral.com. Sr. Barbara Woeste, O.S.B., D.R.E.

2—ST. AGNES (1930)
1680 Dixie Hwy., Fort Wright, 41011-2779.
Tel: 859-431-1802; Fax: 859-291-7017; Email: parishoffice@saintagnes.com; Web: www.saintagnes.com. Very Rev. Mark A. Keene, V.F.; Revs. Jason M. Bertke, Parochial Vicar; James E. Quill, S.T.D., In Res., (Retired); Deacons Robert Stoeckle; Gary R. Scott; Ralph B. Grieme Jr.
School—St. Agnes School, (Grades K-8),
Tel: 859-261-0543; Email: saintagnes@saintagnes.com; Web: www.saintagnes.com. Richard Hoyt, Prin. Clergy 1; Lay Teachers 26; Students 388.
Catechesis Religious Program—Students 79.

3—ST. AUGUSTINE (1870)
1839 Euclid Ave., Covington, 41014-1162.
Tel: 859-431-3943; Email: dschomaker@covdio.org. Very Rev. Daniel L. Schomaker, V.G.; Rev. Britton Hennessey, Parochial Vicar.
School—St. Augustine School, (Grades K-8), 1840 Jefferson Ave., Covington, 41014-1165.
Tel: 859-261-5564; Fax: 859-261-5402; Email: knienaber@staugustines.net; Web: www.staugustines.net. Mrs. Kathleen Nienaber, Prin.; Amy Becker, Librarian. Clergy 1; Lay Teachers 11; Students 138.
Catechesis Religious Program—
St. Augustine Outreach Center—2523 Todd Ct., Covington, 41011. Tel: 859-491-4584; Email: asmith@staugustines.net. Anika Smith, Dir.

4—ST. BENEDICT (1885)
338 E. 17th St., Covington, 41014-1315.
Tel: 859-431-5607; Email: stbenedict@zoomtown.com. Rev. Joshua L. Lange; Deacon Phillip J. Racine.

5—CHURCH OF OUR SAVIOR (1943) (African American)
246 E. 10th St., Covington, 41011-3026.
Tel: 859-491-5872; Email: jbucher@fuse.net. Sr. Janet Marie Bucher, C.D.P., Parish Life Collaborator.
Catechesis Religious Program—

6—HOLY CROSS (1890)
3612 Church St., Covington, 41015-1431.
Tel: 859-431-0636; Email: info@holycrosscov.org; Web: holycrosscov.org. Rev. Thomas C. Barnes; Sr. Helen Charles Wilke, C.D.P., Pastoral Assoc.; Mr. David Arnold, Pastoral Assoc.; Mrs. Donna Foltz, Pastoral Assoc.
School—Holy Cross School, (Grades K-8), 3615 Church Street, Covington, 41015. Tel: 859-581-6599; Email: main@holycrosselem.com; Web: www.holycrosselem.com. Mrs. Lisa Timmerding, Prin. Lay Teachers 15; Students 183.
Catechesis Religious Program—Students 165.

7—ST. JOHN (1854)
627 Pike St., Covington, 41011-2148.
Tel: 859-431-5314; Email: lindagob88@gmail.com. Rev. G. Michael Greer; Deacon Steven I. Durkee; Linda O'Bryan, Business Mgr.
Catechesis Religious Program—Students 20.
Mission—St. Ann (1860) 1274 Parkway, Covington, Kenton Co. 41011-1060.

8—MOTHER OF GOD (1841) Rev. Michael E. Comer.
Res.: 119 W. 6th St., Covington, 41011-1409.
Tel: 859-291-2288; Email: motherofgod@insightbb.com; Email: motherofgod@mother-of-god.org.
Catechesis Religious Program—

OUTSIDE THE CITY OF COVINGTON

ALEXANDRIA, CAMPBELL CO., ST. MARY OF THE ASSUMPTION (1860) [CEM]
Mailing Address: 8246 E. Main St., Alexandria, 41001. Revs. Joseph A. Gallenstein; Edward J. Brodnick, Parochial Vicar; Deacon Timothy A. Britt.
Res.: 8 Stillwater Dr., Alexandria, 41001.
Tel: 859-635-4188; Email: stmaryalex@fuse.net; Web: saintmaryparish.com.
School—St. Mary of the Assumption School, (Grades PreSchool-8), 9 S. Jefferson St., Alexandria, 41001-1394. Tel: 859-635-9539; Fax: 859-448-4824; Email: matt.grosser@saintmaryparish.com. Matt Grosser, Prin. Lay Teachers 30; Students 458.
Catechesis Religious Program—Students 157.

AUGUSTA, BRACKEN CO., ST. AUGUSTINE (1859) [JC]
215 E. Fourth St., Augusta, 41002-1117.
Tel: 606-756-2377; Email: msgrfosu@saintaugustine-augusta.org; Web: www.saintaugustine-augusta.org. Rev. Msgr. Dominic K. Fosu, V.F., Parochial Admin.; Deacon Frank Estill.
School—St. Augustine School, (Grades PreSchool-5), 203 E 4th Street, Augusta, 41002-1117.
Tel: 606-756-3229; Email: school@saintaugustine-augusta.org; Web: www.saintaugustine-augusta.org. Mrs. Jane Walton, Prin. Clergy 1; Lay Teachers 4; Students 50.
Catechesis Religious Program—Students 6.

BELLEVUE, CAMPBELL CO.
1—ST. ANTHONY (1889) Merged with Sacred Heart, Bellevue to form Divine Mercy, Bellevue.
2—DIVINE MERCY (2003)
318 Division St., Bellevue, 41073-1104.
Tel: 859-261-6172; Email: divinemercyoffice@gmail.com; Web: dmsbcatholic.com. Rev. Martin John Pitstick; Deacon David W. Klingenberg.
Res.: 320 Poplar St., Bellevue, 41073-1198.
Catechesis Religious Program—
3—SACRED HEART (1874) Merged with St. Anthony, Bellevue to form Divine Mercy, Bellevue.

BROOKSVILLE, BRACKEN CO., ST. JAMES (1868) [CEM]
122 Garrett Ave., Brooksville, 41004-0027.
Tel: 606-735-2271; Email: dfosu@covdio.org. Rev. Msgr. Dominic K. Fosu, V.F., Parochial Admin.
Catechesis Religious Program—Students 45.

BURLINGTON, BOONE CO., IMMACULATE HEART OF MARY (1954)
5876 Veterans Way, Burlington, 41005-8824.
Tel: 859-689-5010; Tel: 859-689-4303; Email: ihms@ihm-ky.org; Web: ihm.org. Revs. Nicholas E. C. Rottman; James P. Schaeper, Parochial Vicar; Deacons Richard S. Malsi; Gregory L. Meier, Pastoral Assoc.; Sr. Armella Pietrowski, D.R.E.; Karen Gutzeit, Youth Min.; Mark Krzywonos, Parish Council Chariperson; John Doubrava, Business Mgr.; Kathy Donahue, Parish Sec.
School—Immaculate Heart of Mary School, (Grades PreK-8), Tel: 859-689-4303; Email: kthorburn@ihm-ky.org; Web: www.ihm-ky.org. Nancy Marcos, Prin.; Kristin Harper, Vice Prin.; Krista Thorburn, Sec. Lay Teachers 31; Students 500.
Catechesis Religious Program—Email: rickpegwells@yahoo.com; Email: srarmella@ihm-ky.org; Email: ltippett@ihm-ky.org; Email: gmeier@ihm-ky.org. Lisa Tippett, C.R.E.; Peggy Wells. Students 320.

CALIFORNIA, CAMPBELL CO., STS. PETER AND PAUL (1854) [CEM 2]
2162 California Crossroads, California, 41007-9713.
Tel: 859-635-2924; Tel: 859-636-2999;
Fax: 859-635-0294; Email: parishoffice@stspp.com; Web: www.parish.stspp.com. Rev. Jacob Varghese, V.C.
School—Sts. Peter and Paul School, (Grades PreK-8), 2160 California Crossroads, California, 41007.
Tel: 859-635-4382; Email: office@stspp.com; Web: stspp.com. Nicole Herrmann, Prin. Clergy 1; Lay Teachers 12; Students 108.
Catechesis Religious Program—Tel: 859-635-4382; Email: lstenlencdp@yahoo.com. Sr. Lynn Stenken, C.D.P., D.R.E. Students 35.
Mission—Immaculate Conception, 174 Stepstone Church Rd., Butler, 41006. Email: frjacobv@gmail.com.

CAMP SPRINGS, CAMPBELL CO., ST. JOSEPH (1845) [CEM]
Mailing Address: 6833 Four Mile Rd., Camp Springs, 41059-9746. Tel: 859-635-2491; Fax: 859-635-7336; Email: parishoffice@stjosephcampsprings.org; Web: www.stjosephcampsprings.org. Rev. Ryan L. Stenger, J.C.L.
School—St. Joseph School, (PreK) Tel: 859-635-2491; Email: parishoffice@stjosephcampsprings.org; Web: www.stjosephcampsprings.org. Clergy 1; Lay Teachers 2; Students 30.

CARROLLTON, CARROLL CO., ST. JOHN THE EVANGELIST (1853) [CEM]
503 Fifth St., Carrollton, 41008-1203.
Tel: 502-732-5776; Email: dwrightsr@hotmail.com; Web: stjohncarrollton.org. Rev. Thomas F. Picchioni; Deacon Michael J. Keller.
Catechesis Religious Program—Students 142.
Mission—Transfiguration, 260 Inverness Rd., Perry Park, Owen Co. 40363. Email: dwrightsr@hotmail.com. Don Wright, Contact Person.

COLD SPRING, CAMPBELL CO., ST. JOSEPH (1870) [CEM]
4011 Alexandria Pk., Cold Spring, 41076-1895.
Tel: 859-441-1604; Email: Email@stjoeparish.net; Web: stjosephcoldspring.com. Very Rev. Gerald L. Reinersman, V.F.; Deacons Steve Bennett III; Timothy B. Schabell.
School—St. Joseph School, (Grades K-8),
Tel: 859-441-2025; Email: sgreis@stjoeschool.net; Web: www.stjosephcoldspring.com. Lay Teachers 27; Students 437.
Catechesis Religious Program—Students 73.

CRESCENT SPRINGS, KENTON CO., ST. JOSEPH (1916)
2470 Lorraine Ct., Crescent Springs, 41017-1406.
Tel: 859-341-6609; Email: apappas@stjosephcsky.org; Email: jmarshall@stjosephcsky.org; Email: pdevous@stjosephcsky.org; Email: hhenry@stjosephcsky.org; Email: tklare@stjosephcsky.org; Web: www.stjosephcrescent.com. Revs. Phillip W. DeVous; Augustine Aidoo, Parochial Vicar; Deacon Hudson L. Henry; Mrs. Andrea Pappas, Business Mgr.
School—St. Joseph School, (Grades PreK-8), 2474 Lorraine Ave., Crescent Springs, 41017.
Tel: 859-578-2742; Fax: 859-578-2754; Email: lbarbian@sjscrescent.org; Web: www.sjscrescent.com. Sally Zeck, Prin. Lay Teachers 26; Students 335.
Catechesis Religious Program—
Tel: 859-341-6609, Ext. 4023. Ms. Tina Klare, D.R.E. Students 55.

CYNTHIANA, HARRISON CO., ST. EDWARD (1864) [CEM]
107 N. Walnut St., Cynthiana, 41031-1225.
Tel: 859-234-5444; Email: churchoffice@stedwardky.org. Rev. Harry A. Settle Jr.
School—St. Edward School, (Grades PreSchool-5),
Tel: 859-234-2731; Email: schooloffice@stedwardky.org; Email: ssowder@stedwardky.org. Clergy 1; Lay Teachers 5; Students 33; Clergy / Religious Teachers 2.
Catechesis Religious Program—Email: hsettle@covdio.org. Students 26.

DAYTON, CAMPBELL CO., ST. BERNARD (1853)
401 Berry St., Dayton, 41074-1139.
Tel: 859-261-8506; Email: saintbernardoffice@gmail.com; Web: dmsbcatholic.com. Rev. Martin John Pitstick; Deacon David W. Klingenberg.
Res.: 318 Division St., Bellevue, 41073-1198.
Catechesis Religious Program—Students 15.

EDGEWOOD, KENTON CO., ST. PIUS X (1958) [CEM]

348 Dudley Rd., Edgewood, 41017-2609.
Tel: 859-341-4900; Email: jcasson@staff.stpiusx.com; Web: parish.stpiusx.com. Revs. Baiju Kidaagen, V.C.; Michael C. Hennigen, Parochial Vicar; Matthias M. Wamala, In Res.; Deacon James S. Fedor.
School—St. Pius X School, (Grades K-8),
Tel: 859-341-4900; Web: school.stpiusx.com; Email: jlonnemann@teachers.stpiusx.com. Jill Lonnemann, Prin. Clergy 3; Lay Teachers 52; Students 696; Clergy / Religious Teachers 17.
Catechesis Religious Program—Students 90.

ELSMERE, KENTON CO., ST. HENRY (1890)
3813 Dixie Hwy., Elsmere, 41018-1809.
Tel: 859-727-2035; Email: mbraun@sthenryel.com; Web: sthenryel.com. Revs. Gregory J. Bach; Eric L. Andriot, Parochial Vicar; Deacons Jack Alexander, Pastoral Assoc.; Michael T. Lyman; Patrick Mason, Music Min.
School—St. Henry School, (Grades K-8),
Tel: 859-342-2551; Email: clageman@sthenryel.com; Web: www.sthenryel.com. Mr. Dennis Wolff, Prin. Lay Teachers 30; Students 348.
Catechesis Religious Program—Students 340.

ERLANGER, BOONE CO.
1—CRISTO REY (2004) (Hispanic)
25 Cavalier Blvd., Florence, 41042-1684.
Tel: 859-538-1175; Tel: 859-538-1176;
Fax: 859-538-1181; Email: cristorey@nkymail.net; Web: www.micristorey.com. Rev. Allan R. Frederick; Deacon Antonio L. Escamilla; Ms. Griselda Castrellon, Sec.
Catechesis Religious Program—Email: afrederick@covdio.org. Students 175.
2—MARY, QUEEN OF HEAVEN (1955)
1150 Donaldson Hwy., Erlanger, 41018-1048.
Tel: 859-525-6909; Email: kkahmann@mqhparish.com; Web: www.mqhparish.com. Revs. Kevin James Kahmann; Niby Kannai, C.M.I., Parochial Vicar; Deacons Richard J. Dames, Sacramental Min.; Lawrence L. Kleisinger.
School—Mary, Queen of Heaven School, (Grades K-8), 1130 Donaldson Rd., Erlanger, 41018.
Tel: 859-371-8100; Fax: 859-371-3362. Meg Piatt, Prin. Lay Teachers 14; Students 156.
Catechesis Religious Program—Email: lkleisinger@mqhparish.com. Students 47.

ERLANGER, KENTON CO., ST. BARBARA (1967)
4042 Turkeyfoot Rd., Erlanger, 41018-2921.
Tel: 859-371-3100; Email: stb@stbarbaraky.org; Web: www.stbarbaraky.org. Rev. John J. Sterling; Deacons Bernard J. Kaiser; Charles J. Melville.
Catechesis Religious Program—Email: jkoop@stbarbaraky.org. Jackie Koop, D.R.E. Students 221.

FALMOUTH, PENDLETON CO., ST. FRANCIS XAVIER (1880) [CEM]
202 W. Second St., Falmouth, 41040-1118.
Tel: 859-444-2605; Email: stxoffice@gmail.com. Rev. Michael B. Norton.
Catechesis Religious Program—Tel: 859-609-4501; Email: stfxcre@gmail.com. Scotty Zelensky, D.R.E. Students 45.

FLEMINGSBURG, FLEMING CO., ST. CHARLES BORROMEO (1859)
211 Mt. Carmel Ave., Flemingsburg, 41041-1315.
Tel: 606-849-9415; Email: stcharlesandstrose@gmail.com. Rev. Eric M. Boelscher, Admin.
Catechesis Religious Program—Students 8.

FLORENCE, BOONE CO., ST. PAUL (1872)
7301 Dixie Hwy., Florence, 41042-2126.
Tel: 859-371-8051; Email: stpaul@stpaulnky.org; Web: www.stpaulnky.org. Very Rev. Michael D. Barth, J.C.L.; Revs. Trinity P. Knight, Parochial Vicar; David B. Gamm, In Res., (Retired); Deacons Nicholas J. Schwartz; Thomas E. Kathman; Scott A. Folz.
School—St. Paul School, (Grades PreSchool-8),
Tel: 859-647-4070; Fax: 859-647-0644; Email: stpaul1@stpaulnky.org. Mrs. Kemberly Markham, Prin. Clergy 6; Lay Teachers 22; Students 291.
Catechesis Religious Program—
Tel: 859-371-8051, Ext. 222. Students 130.

FORT MITCHELL, KENTON CO., BLESSED SACRAMENT (1920)
2409 Dixie Hwy., Fort Mitchell, 41017-2993.
Tel: 859-331-4302; Email: parish@bscky.org; Web: bscky.org. Revs. Daniel J. Vogelpohl, V.F.; Josiah N. Booth; Very Rev. James M. Ryan, J.C.L., In Res.; Deacon James J. Bayne.
Res.: 2415 Dixie Hwy., Fort Mitchell, 41017-2993.
School—Blessed Sacrament School, (Grades K-8), School: 2407 Dixie Hwy., Fort Mitchell, 41017.
Tel: 859-331-3062; Fax: 859-344-7323; Email: bssoffice@bssky.org. Daniel Steffen, Prin.; Emily Bradley, Librarian. Lay Teachers 38; Students 532.
Catechesis Religious Program—
Tel: 859-331-4302, Ext. 22; Email: rthomas@bscky.org. Rosanne Thomas, D.R.E. Students 156.

FORT THOMAS, CAMPBELL CO.
1—ST. CATHERINE OF SIENA (1930)
Mailing Address: 1803 N. Ft. Thomas Ave., Fort Thomas, 41075-1170. Tel: 859-441-1352;
Fax: 859-572-2686; Email: church@stcatherineofsiena.org; Web: stcatherineofsiena.org. Rev. Stephen M. Bankemper.
School—St. Catherine of Siena School, (Grades K-8), St. Catherine of Siena School, 23 Rossford Ave, Fort Thomas, 41075-1170. Tel: 859-572-2680; Email: bstegner@stcatherineofsiena.org. Ms. Julie Scherer, Prin. Lay Teachers 17; Students 170.
Catechesis Religious Program—Students 102.
2—ST. THOMAS (1902)
26 E. Villa Pl., Fort Thomas, 41075-2223.
Tel: 859-441-1282; Fax: 859-572-4640; Email: josbu@sttschool.org; Web: www.saintthomasfortthomas.org. Rev. Msgr. John R. Schulte, J.C.L.; Revs. David R. Ludwig, Parochial Vicar; Albert E. Ruschman, In Res., (Retired); Deacon Charles J. Hardebeck.
School—St. Thomas School, (Grades PreSchool-8), 428 S. Fort Thomas Ave., Fort Thomas, 41075.
Tel: 859-572-4641; Fax: 859-572-4644; Email: dflam@sttschool.org; Web: sttschool.org. Mrs. Deborah A. Flamm, Prin.; Sarah Erickson, Librarian. Clergy 1; Lay Teachers 20; Students 222; Clergy / Religious Teachers 1.
Catechesis Religious Program—Cell: 859-638-4133; Email: cmark@sttschool.org. Charles Marks, Pastoral Assoc. Students 104.

INDEPENDENCE, KENTON CO., ST. CECILIA (1880) [CEM]
5313 Madison Pk., Independence, 41051-0186.
Tel: 859-363-4311; Fax: 859-363-4312; Email: stcsecretary@stcindependence.org; Web: saintceciliaparish.net. Revs. Mario J. Tizziani; Aby Thampi, Parochial Vicar. Fr Mario J Tizziani noted "St. Cecilia Roman Catholic Church"
School—St. Cecilia School, (Grades PreK-8),
Tel: 859-363-4314; Fax: 859-363-4315; Email: drankin@stcindependence.org; Web: saintceciliaschool.net. Mr. Robert Detzel, Prin. Clergy 2; Lay Teachers 21; Students 282.
Catechesis Religious Program—Students 103.

KENTON, KENTON CO., ST. MATTHEW (1909) [CEM] Rev. Aby Thampi, Admin.
Res.: 13782 Decoursey Pk., Morning View, 41063-9707. Tel: 859-356-6530; Fax: 859-356-1695; Email: stmatthew13782@gmail.com.
Catechesis Religious Program—Tel: 859-356-3650; Email: stmattew@zoomtown.com. Roseanne Rawe, D.R.E. Students 0.
Mission—Assumption of the Blessed Virgin, 3711 St. Mary Rd., Morning View, Kenton Co. 41063.

LUDLOW, KENTON CO., STS. BONIFACE AND JAMES (1872)
304 Oak St., Ludlow, 41016-1417. Tel: 859-261-5340; Email: stbonjames@fuse.net; Web: bonifaceandjames.org. Rev. Lawrence A. Schaeper.
Catechesis Religious Program—Email: stbonjames@fuse.net. Students 11.

MAY'S LICK, MASON CO., ST. ROSE OF LIMA (1864)
Mailing Address: 211 Mt. Carmel Ave., Flemingsburg, 41041-1315. Tel: 606-849-9415; Email: eboelscher@covdio.org. Rev. Eric M. Boelscher, Admin.
Church: 5011 Raymond Rd., May's Lick, 41055-8821.

MAYSVILLE, MASON CO., ST. PATRICK (1847) [CEM]
110 E. Third St., Maysville, 41056-0248.
Tel: 606-564-9015; Email: lwilson@stpatschool.com. Revs. Jacob E. Straub; Michael A. Black, Parochial Vicar.
School—St. Patrick School, (Grades K-8), 318 Limestone St., Maysville, 41056-0248.
Tel: 606-564-5949; Email: sfaris@stpatschool.com; Web: www.stpatschool.com. Mrs. Sarah Kalb, Prin.; Rev. Jacob E. Straub, Admin. Clergy 1; Lay Teachers 19; Students 150; Clergy / Religious Teachers 1.
High School—St. Patrick High School, 318 Limestone St., Maysville, 41056-0248.
Tel: 606-564-5949; Email: skalb@stpatschool.com. Mrs. Sarah Kalb, Prin. Lay Teachers 11; Students 53; Clergy / Religious Teachers 1.
Catechesis Religious Program—Students 42.
Mission—St. James, Kentucky Rd. 435, Minerva, Mason Co. 41062.

MELBOURNE, CAMPBELL CO., ST. PHILIP (1910)
1402 Mary Ingles Hwy., Melbourne, 41059-9766.
Tel: 859-441-8949; Email: recphilip@stphilipky.org. Rev. Robert A. Rottgers; Deacon Peter J. (Pete) Freeman.
School—St. Philip School, (Grades K-8),
Tel: 859-441-3423; Email: recphilip@stphilipky.org. Mrs. Kimberly Brewer, Prin. Lay Teachers 6; Students 72.
Catechesis Religious Program—Students 20.

NEWPORT, CAMPBELL CO.
1—ST. FRANCIS DE SALES, Closed. For sacramental records contact Holy Spirit, Newport.
2—HOLY SPIRIT (1997)
825 Washington Ave., Newport, 41071-1999.
Tel: 859-431-2533; Email: office@holyspiritnky.org; Web: holyspiritnky.org. Rev. Msgr. William F. Cleves, V.F.; Mr. R. Alex Bramel, Business Mgr.; Mr. Seth Cutter, Music Min.; Mrs. M. Elaine Hennekes, Sec.
Child Care—Holy Spirit Child Development Center, 840 Washington Ave., Newport, 41071-1946.
Tel: 859-491-7612; Email: childcare@holyspiritnky.org. Mrs. Michelle Mabrey, Dir.; Mrs. Sharon Meyer, Sec. Lay Teachers 13; Students 58.
3—ST. STEPHEN, Closed. For sacramental records contact Holy Spirit, Newport.
4—ST. VINCENT DE PAUL, Closed. For sacramental records contact Holy Spirit, Newport.

PARK HILLS, OUR LADY OF LOURDES QUASI-PARISH (2016)
1101 Amsterdam Rd., Park Hills, 41011.
Tel: 859-291-1854; Fax: 859-291-1917; Email: info@ourladyoflourdes.info; Web: www.ourladyoflourdes.info. Revs. Shannon M. Collins, M.S.J.B.; Sean P. Kopczynski, M.S.J.B., Parochial Vicar; Daniel G. Kluge, Parochial Vicar.

SOUTHGATE, CAMPBELL CO., ST. THERESE OF THE INFANT JESUS (1927)
11 Temple Pl., Southgate, 41071-3133.
Tel: 859-441-1654; Fax: 859-441-2395; Email: rectory@sainttherese.ws; Web: sainttherese.ws. Very Rev. Douglas J. Lauer, V.F.; Rev. Clarence J. Heitzman, Pastor Emeritus, (Retired); Deacons Joseph E. McGraw; William R. Theis.
School—St. Therese of the Infant Jesus School, (Grades K-8), 2516 Alexandria Pike, Southgate, 41071. Tel: 859-441-0449; Fax: 859-441-0449; Email: olearyd@sainttherese.ws. Dot O'Leary, Prin.; Mrs. Ellen Lonneman, Librarian. Lay Teachers 15; Students 197.
Catechesis Religious Program—Students 60.

TAYLOR MILL, KENTON CO.
1—ST. ANTHONY (1878)
485 Grand Ave., Taylor Mill, 41015-0219.
Tel: 859-431-1773; Tel: 859-431-5987 School; Email: vschweitzer@stanth.org; Email: saintanthonychurch@fuse.net; Web: saintanthonytaylormill.org. Rev. Benton Clift Sr., Parochial Admin. Pro Tem.
School—St. Anthony School, (Grades K-8),
Tel: 859-431-5987; Email: school@stanth.org; Web: www.saintanthonytaylormill.org/school. Ms. Veronica Schweitzer, Prin. Lay Teachers 8; Students 51.
Catechesis Religious Program—Students 6.
2—ST. PATRICK (1966)
Mailing Address: 3285 Mills Rd., Covington, 41015-2480. Tel: 859-356-5151; Fax: 859-344-7042; Email: parishoffice@stpatrickchurch.us; Web: www.stpatrickchurch.us. Rev. Jeffrey D. Von Lehmen; Deacon Carl A. Ledbetter.
Catechesis Religious Program—Students 313.

UNION, BOONE CO., ST. TIMOTHY (1989)
10272 Hwy. 42, P.O. Box 120, Union, 41091-0120.
Tel: 859-384-1100; Fax: 859-384-1709; Email: lprofitt@saint-timothy.org; Web: www.saint-timothy.org. Revs. Richard G. Bolte, V.F.; V. Ross Kelsch, Parochial Vicar; Deacons Thomas L. Nolan; Steven E. Alley; Dave Philbrick; Dave Profitt.
Catechesis Religious Program—Tel: 859-384-5100; Email: dthomas@saint-timothy.org. Deb Thomas, D.R.E. Students 142.

VANCEBURG, LEWIS CO., HOLY REDEEMER (1965)
239 KY 59, P.O. Box 8, Vanceburg, 41179-0008.
Tel: 606-796-3052. Rev. David Glockner, Parochial Admin., (Glenmary).
Catechesis Religious Program—Tel: 606-796-2830; Email: tericantor@aol.com. Students 7.

WALTON, BOONE CO., ALL SAINTS (1951) [CEM 2]
1 Beatrice Ave., Walton, 41094-1029.
Tel: 859-485-4476; Fax: 859-485-6476; Email: allsaints.walton.ky@gmail.com; Web: allsaintswalton.com. Rev. Matthew Cushing; Deacon Paul V. Yancey, Curia; All Saints, Walton.
Catechesis Religious Program—62 Needmore St., Walton, 41094. Students 135.

WARSAW, GALLATIN CO., ST. JOSEPH (1864) [CEM]
602 Main Cross, P.O. Box 495, Warsaw, 41095-0495.
Tel: 859-567-2425; Email: gwitzeman@covdio.org. Rev. B. Gerald Witzemann, Parochial Admin., (Retired).
Res.: 203 Hackberry, Warsaw, 41095-0495. Email: porecchio@covdio.org.
Catechesis Religious Program—Students 30.
Mission—St. Edward (1958) 1335 Hwy. 22 E., R.R. 4, Owenton, Owen Co. 40359-9003.

WILDER, CAMPBELL CO., ST. JOHN THE BAPTIST (1847)
1307 John's Hill Rd., Wilder, 41076-9129.
Tel: 859-781-2117; Email: stjohnwilder@gmail.com. Rev. Gregory E. Osburg.

WILLIAMSTOWN, GRANT CO., ST. WILLIAM (1912) [CEM 2]
6 Church St., Williamstown, 41097-9454.
Tel: 859-824-5351; Email: stwilliamstjohn@gmail.com. Rev. Damian J. Hils.
Catechesis Religious Program—Tel: 859-824-5381; Email: suzinoel17@gmail.com. Suzi Noel, D.R.E. Students 51.

Mission—St. John's (1956) 834 Center Ridge Rd. (Hwy. 3184), De Mossville, 41033.

PILGRIMAGE SHRINES

COVINGTON, SHRINE OF ST. ANN, Attached to St. Ann Mission.

SOUTHGATE, SHRINE OF THE LITTLE FLOWER, Attached to St. Therese Church.

Chaplains of Public Institutions

FORT THOMAS. *Veterans Hospital*. Revs. Jerome Steinbrunner, C.PP.S., Reynaldo S. Taylor.

Leave of Absence:
Very Rev.—
McDole, Ian P., J.C.L.
Rev.—
Witte, Mark G.

Retired:
Rev. Msgrs.—
Cooney, Roger P., (Retired), 3532 Myrtle Ave, Covington, 41015-1514
Meier, Allen J., P.A., (Retired), 600 Farrell Dr., Rm. 25, Covington, 41011-2798
Neuhaus, William B., (Retired), 3813 Dixie Hwy, Elsmere, 41018-1809
Rutz, Gilbert J., J.D., M.A., M.Ed., M.Div., (Retired), 4633 N. 54th St., Phoenix, AZ 85018
Revs.—
Berschied, Paul L., (Retired), 3516 Misty Creek Dr., Erlanger, 41017
Delange, Maurice, (Retired), 114 Church St., Aurora, IN 47001-1700
Dickmann, Louis H., (Retired), 6660 Licking Pike, Cold Spring, 41076-8807
Gamm, David B., (Retired), St. Paul Rectory, 7301 Dixie Hwy., Florence, 41042-2126
Gerrety, James P., (Retired), St. Charles Community, 600 Farrell Dr., Covington, 41011
Hartman, Raymond S., (Retired), Atria Summit Hills, 2625 Legends Way, Crestview Hills, 41017
Heitzman, Clarence J., (Retired), St. Therese Rectory, 11 Temple Pl., Southgate, 41071-3133
Henderson, Robert J., (Retired), 202 Thornbush Ct., Cold Spring, 41076-1939
Hogan, Verne F., (Retired), 474 Farrell Dr., Covington, 41011-3980
Kroger, John H., (Retired), 320 Poplar St., Bellevue, 41073-1109
Quill, James E., S.T.D., (Retired), 1680 Dixie Hwy., Park Hills, 41011
Reinke, Robert J., (Retired), St. Charles Community, 600 Farrell Dr., #302, Covington, 41011-3798
Riesenberg, John J., (Retired), Madonna Manor, 2344 Amsterdam Rd., Villa Hills, 41017-3712
Robbins, Thomas P., (Retired), 5375 Millstone Ct., Taylor Mill, 41015
Rosing, Robert C., (Retired), St. Charles Community, 600 Farrell Dr., #309, Covington, 41011-3798
Ruschman, Albert E., (Retired), 26 E. Villa Pl., Fort Thomas, 41075-2223
Ryan, James M., J.C.L., (Retired), Blessed Sacrament Rectory, 2415 Dixie Hwy., Ft Mitchell, 41017-2936
Schmidt, Leo C., (Retired), St. Charles Lodge, 600 Farrell Dr., Covington, 41011-3798
Urlage, Robert J., (Retired), 2327 Rolling Hills Dr., Crestview Hills, 41017-5136
Witzemann, B. Gerald, (Retired), P.O. Box 495, Warsaw, 41095-0495.

Permanent Deacons:
Alexander, John N., St. Henry, Elsmere
Alley, Steven E., St. Timothy, Union
Bayne, James L., Blessed Sacrament, Ft. Mitchell
Bennett, Stephen J., St. Joseph, Cold Spring
Britt, Timothy A., St. Mary, Alexandria
Dames, Richard J., Mary, Queen of Heaven, Erlanger
Durkee, Steven I., St. John, Covington
Dushney, Thomas M., Mother of God, Covington
Escamilla, Antonio L., Cristo Rey, Florence
Estill, Andrew (Frank), St. Augustine, Augusta
Fedor, James S., St. Pius X, Edgewood
Folz, Scott A., St. Paul, Florence
Franzen, Gerald R., Cathedral, Covington
Freeman, Peter J. (Pete), Curia; St. Timothy, Union
Grieme, Ralph B. Jr., St. Agnes, Ft. Wright
Hardebeck, Charles J., St. Thomas, Ft. Thomas
Henry, Hudson L., St. Joseph, Crescent Springs
Kaiser, Bernard, St. Barbara, Erlanger
Kathman, Thomas E., St. Paul, Florence
Keller, Michael J., St. John the Evangelist, Carrollton
Kleisinger, Lawrence L., Mary, Queen of Heaven, Erlanger
Klingenberg, David W., Divine Mercy, Bellevue & St. Bernard, Dayton
Leardon, John D., St. Augustine, Covington
Ledbetter, Carl A., Chaplain, St. Elizabeth Hospice; St. Patrick, Taylor Mill
Lyman, Michael T., St. William, Williamstown
Malsi, Richard S., Immaculate Heart of Mary, Burlington
McGraw, Joseph E., Holy Spirit, Newport
Meier, Gregory L., Immaculate Heart of Mary, Burlington
Melville, Charles J., St. Barbara, Erlanger
Nolan, Thomas L., St. Timothy, Union
Norris, Eugene F., (Retired)
Philbrick, James (Dave), St. Timothy, Union
Profitt, Randall D., St. Anne Retreat Center, Melbourne; St. Timothy, Union
Racine, Phillip J., St. Benedict, Covington
Schabell, Timothy B., St. Joseph, Cold Spring
Schwartz, Nicholas J., St. Paul, Florence
Scott, Gary R., St. Agnes, Ft. Wright
Stoeckle, Robert A., St. Agnes, Ft. Wright
Theis, William R., St. Therese, Southgate
Yancey, Paul V., All Saints, Walton.

INSTITUTIONS LOCATED IN DIOCESE

[A] COLLEGES AND UNIVERSITIES

CRESTVIEW HILLS. *Thomas More University* (Coed) 333 Thomas More Pkwy., Crestview Hills, 41017. Tel: 859-341-5800; Fax: 859-344-3649; Email: admissions@thomasmore.edu; Web: www.thomasmore.edu. Dr. Kathleen Jagger, Pres.; Rev. Gerald E. Twaddell, Ph.D., Chap.; Mr. Andrew Cole, Campus Min. Faculty 153; Priests 2; Sisters 1; Students 2,828; Clergy / Religious Teachers 3; Staff 124.

[B] HIGH SCHOOLS, DIOCESAN

COVINGTON. *Covington Catholic High School*, 1600 Dixie Hwy., Covington, 41011-2797. Tel: 859-491-2247; Fax: 859-448-2242; Email: browe@covcath.org; Web: www.covcath.org. Mr. Robert J. Rowe, Prin.; Mrs. Theresa Guard, Dean of Students; Mr. Michael Guidugli, Asst. Prin., Dir. of Building & Grounds; Mr. Anthony Zechella, Asst. Prin., Dean of Academics; Very Rev. Mark A. Keene, V.F., Pastoral Admin.; Rev. Michael C. Hennigen, Chap. Boys 597; Lay Teachers 51; Students 597.

Covington Latin School (1923) (Grades 7-12), 21 E. 11th St., Covington, 41011-3196. Tel: 859-291-7044; Fax: 859-291-1939; Email: headmaster@covingtonlatin.org; Web: www.covingtonlatin.org. Mr. Michael T. Clines, Headmaster; Mr. Matt Krebs, Dean; Very Rev. Ryan L. Maher, V.G., Pastoral Admin.; Rev. Ryan L. Stenger, J.C.L., Chap.; Ms. Stephanie Tewes, Dean. Boys 104; Girls 103; Lay Teachers 23; Students 207.

Holy Cross High School, 3617 Church St., Covington, 41015-1498. Tel: 859-431-1335; Fax: 859-655-2184; Email: mike.holtz@hchscov.com; Web: hchscov.com. Mr. Michael Holtz, Prin.; Revs. Thomas P. Robbins, Pastoral Admin. & Chap., (Retired); Jeffrey D. Von Lehmen, Chap. Lay Teachers 34; Priests 2; Religious 1; Students 335; Clergy / Religious Teachers 3.

ALEXANDRIA. *Bishop Brossart High School* (1950) 4 Grove St., Alexandria, 41001-1295. Tel: 859-635-2108; Fax: 859-635-2135; Email: info@bishopbrossart.org; Web: www.bishopbrossart.org. Mr. Dan Ridder, Prin.; Very Rev. Gerald L. Reinersman, V.F., Pastoral Admin.; Rev. Edward J. Brodnick, Chap. Lay Teachers 24; Sisters of Notre Dame 1; Students 276.

ERLANGER. *St. Henry District High School*, 3755 Scheben Dr., Erlanger, 41018-3597. Tel: 859-525-0255; Fax: 859-525-5855; Email: dmotte@shdhs.org; Web: www.shdhs.org. Mr. David M. Otte, Prin.; Revs. Gregory J. Bach, Pastoral Admin.; Niby Kannai, C.M.I., Chap. Lay Teachers 43; Students 525.

MAYSVILLE. *St. Patrick High School*, 318 Limestone St., Maysville, 41056-1248. Tel: 606-564-5949; Fax: 606-564-8795; Email: sfaris@stpatschool.com. Mr. Wesley Cooper Jr., Prin.; Revs. Jacob E. Straub, Admin.; Michael A. Black, Chap. Lay Teachers 11; Students 53; Clergy / Religious Teachers 1.

NEWPORT. *Newport Central Catholic High School*, 13 Carothers Rd., Newport, 41071-2497. Tel: 859-292-0001; Fax: 859-292-0656; Email: mdaley@ncchs.com; Web: www.ncchs.com. Mr. Ron Dawn, Prin.; Stephanie Piegols, Admin.; Rev. Michael E. Comer, Admin.
Legal Titles: Newport Catholic High School Our Lady of Providence High School Lay Teachers 25; Students 300; Clergy / Religious Teachers 1.

[C] HIGH SCHOOLS, PRIVATE

COVINGTON. *Villa Madonna Academy High School / Junior High*, (Grades 7-12), 2500 Amsterdam Rd., Villa Hills, 41017-3798. Tel: 859-331-6333; Fax: 859-331-8615; Email: pmcqueen@villamadonna.net; Web: www.villamadonna.net. Ms. Pamela McQueen, Pres. & Prin.; Rev. Baiju Kidaagen, V.C., Chap. Lay Teachers 25; Sisters 1; Students 242.

PARK HILLS. *Notre Dame Academy, Inc.*, 1699 Hilton Dr., Park Hills, 41011-2796. Tel: 859-261-4300; Fax: 859-292-7722; Email: koehll@ndapandas.org; Web: www.ndapandas.org. Dr. Laura Koehl, Pres.; Mr. Jack Von Handorf, M.Ed., Prin.; Rev. Michael C. Hennigen, Chap. Sisters of Notre Dame. Girls 578; Lay Teachers 44; Sisters 4; Students 578; Clergy / Religious Teachers 1.

[D] ELEMENTARY SCHOOLS, INTERPAROCHIAL

COVINGTON. *Holy Family Catholic School* (1988) (Grades K-8), 338 E. 16th St., Covington, 41014-1398. Tel: 859-581-0290; Fax: 859-581-0624; Email: evieth@holyfamilycovington.org; Web: www.holyfamilycovington.org. Beth Vieth, Prin.; Sylvia Wilson, Librarian. Lay Teachers 5; Students 45.

Prince of Peace School, (Grades PreK-8), 625 Pike St., Covington, 41011-2798. Tel: 859-431-5153; Fax: 859-291-8632; Email: khandorf@popcov.com; Web: www.popcov.com. Mrs. Kathy Handorf, Prin. Montessori Pre Primary (Age 3) Clergy 1; Lay Teachers 10; Sisters of Notre Dame 1; Students 118; Clergy / Religious Teachers 1.

BELLEVUE. *Holy Trinity Elementary School*, (Grades K-5), 235 Division St., Bellevue, 41073-1101. Tel: 859-291-6937; Fax: 859-291-6970; Email: jhubbard@holytrinity-school.org; Web: holytrinity-school.org. Mr. James Hubbard, Prin.; Ms. Liz Enzweiler, Librarian. Clergy 5; Lay Teachers 4; Sisters 2; Students 76; Clergy / Religious Teachers 3.

NEWPORT. *Holy Trinity Junior High School*, (Grades 6-8), 840 Washington Ave., Newport, 41071-2485. Tel: 859-292-0487; Fax: 859-431-8745; Email: jhubbard@holytrinity-school.org; Web: holytrinity-school.org. Mr. James Hubbard, Prin.; Mrs. Pat Lauer, Librarian. Clergy 3; Lay Teachers 4; Students 40; Clergy / Religious Teachers 1.

[E] ELEMENTARY SCHOOLS, DIOCESAN

FORT MITCHELL. *Guardian Angel* aka Beechwood Independent Schools (1966) (Grades K-8), 75 Orphanage Rd., P.O. Box 17007, Fort Mitchell, 41017-0007. Tel: 859-331-2040; Fax: 859-344-5022. Ms. Nikki Benson, Educ. Prog. Dir. School for the Emotional Behavioral Disabled. Lay Teachers 4; Students 39.

[F] ELEMENTARY SCHOOLS, PRIVATE

COVINGTON. *Villa Madonna Academy*, (Grades K-6), 2500 Amsterdam Rd., Villa Hills, 41017-3798. Tel: 859-331-6333; Fax: 859-331-8615; Email: sbosley@villamadonna.net; Web: www.villamadonna.org. Mrs. Soshana Bosley, Prin.; Mr. Ben Tilley, Librarian. Lay Teachers 22; Students 210; Clergy / Religious Teachers 9.

WALTON. *St. Joseph Academy* (1976) (Grades PreK-8), 48 Needmore St., Walton, 41094-1028. Tel: 859-485-6444; Fax: 859-485-4262; Email: principal@sjawalton.com; Web: www.sjawalton.com. Sr. Elizabeth Ann Barkett, Prin.; Mrs. Michelle Jones, Librarian. Sisters of St. Joseph the Worker. Lay Teachers 15; Sisters 3; Students 138; Clergy / Religious Teachers 3.

[G] MONTESSORI SCHOOLS (PRESCHOOL)

VILLA HILLS. *Villa Madonna Montessori*, 2402 Amsterdam Rd., Covington, 41017-5316. Tel: 859-341-5145; Fax: 859-331-2136; Email: villamadonnamontessori@gmail.com; Web: villamadonnamontessori.org. Stacey R. Brosky, Admin. Lay Teachers 6; Students 89.

[H] PRESCHOOLS

PARK HILLS. *Julie Learning Center, Inc.*, 1601 Dixie Hwy., Park Hills, 41011. Tel: 859-392-8231; Fax: 859-291-1774; Email: directorjlc2014@gmail.com. Mrs. Mary Hedger, Exec. Dir. Preschool with educational emphasis for ages 4-6. Lay Teachers 9; Students 36.

[I] GENERAL HOSPITALS

COVINGTON. *St. Elizabeth, Covington*, 1500 James Simpson Jr. Way, Covington, 41011-0800. Tel: 859-301-2000; Email: joseph.bozzelli@stelizabeth.com; Web: www.stelizabeth.com. Mr. Garren Colvin, Pres.; Mr. Joseph Bozzelli, Vice Pres.; Mr. Gary Blank, Exec.; Rev. Robert J. Henderson, (Retired)
St. Elizabeth Medical Center, Inc. Tot Asst. Annually 76,629; Total Staff 152.

EDGEWOOD. *St. Elizabeth, Edgewood*, 1 Medical Village Dr., Edgewood, 41017-3441. Tel: 859-301-2000; Email: joseph.bozzelli@stelizabeth.com; Web: www.stelizabeth.com. Mr. Garren Colvin, Pres.; Mr. Gary Blank, Exec. Vice Pres. & COO; Mr. Joseph Bozzelli, Pastoral Min./Coord.; Rev. Robert J. Henderson, (Retired)
Saint Elizabeth Medical Center, Inc. Bed Capacity 534; Tot Asst. Annually 595,449; Total Staff 4,144.

FLORENCE. *St. Elizabeth, Florence*, 4900 Houston Rd., Florence, 41042-4824. Tel: 859-212-5200; Email: joseph.bozzelli@stelizabeth.com; Web: www.stelizabeth.com. Mr. Garren Colvin, Pres.; Mr. Joseph Bozzelli, Vice Pres.; Mr. Gary Blank, Exec.; Rev. Robert J. Henderson, Pastor, (Retired)
Saint Elizabeth Medical Center, Inc. Bed Capacity 169; Tot Asst. Annually 140,018; Total Staff 1,054.

FORT THOMAS. *St. Elizabeth, Fort Thomas*, 85 N. Grand Ave., Fort Thomas, 41075-1793. Tel: 859-301-2000; Email: joseph.bozzelli@stelizabeth.com; Web: www.stelizabeth.com. Mr. Garren Colvin, Pres.; Mr. Joseph Bozzelli, Vice Pres.; Mr. Gary Blank, Exec.; Rev. Robert J. Henderson, Pastor, (Retired)
Saint Elizabeth Medical Center, Inc. Bed Capacity 332; Tot Asst. Annually 98,363; Total Staff 854.

WILLIAMSTOWN. *St. Elizabeth, Grant County*, 238 Barnes Rd., Williamstown, 41097-9482. Tel: 859-824-8240; Email: rosanne.nields@stelizabeth.com. Mr. Garren Colvin, Pres.; Mr. Joseph Bozzelli, Vice Pres.; Rev. Robert J. Henderson, (Retired); Mr. Gary Blank, Exec.
Saint Elizabeth Medical Center, Inc. Bed Capacity 25; Tot Asst. Annually 43,284; Total Staff 124.

[J] NURSING HOMES

COVINGTON. *St. Charles Care Center, Inc.* (1960) 600 Farrell Dr., Covington, 41011-3798. Tel: 859-331-3224; Fax: 859-292-1670; Email: lbender@stcharlescommunity.org; Web: www.stcharlescommunity.org. Nicole Smith, Admin. Adult Day Health Program; Licensed In and Outpatient Occupational Speech and Physical Therapy Department; Private Duty Nursing; In Home Care, Licensed Personal Care and Senior Living Accommodations. Employees 96; Sisters of Notre Dame 2; Tot Asst. Annually 681; Nursing Bed Capacity 32; Senior Living Apartments 71; Cottages 62.
Madonna Manor (1966) 2344 Amsterdam Rd., Villa Hills, 41017-3712. Tel: 859-426-6400; Fax: 859-578-7472; Email: jhaney@chilivingcomm.org; Web: www.homeishere.org. Josie Browning Haney, Exec.; Rev. John J. Riesenberg, Chap., (Retired); Krista Powers, Spiritual Advisor/ Care Svcs. CHI Living Communities, a subsidiary of Catholic Health Initiatives Bed Capacity 84; Skilled Nursing Beds 60; Tot Asst. Annually 40; Staff 150.

[K] PROTECTIVE INSTITUTIONS

COVINGTON. *Diocesan Catholic Children's Home* aka DCCH Center for Children and Families (1961) 75 Orphanage Rd., P.O. Box 17007, Fort Mitchell, 41017-2730. Tel: 859-331-2040; Fax: 859-344-5022; Email: bwilson@dcchcenter.org; Web: www.dcchcenter.org. Mr. Robert J. Wilson, M.A., Exec. Dir.; Ms. Nikki Benson, Prin. (Full-time, paid) 90; Sisters 1; Students 39; Children in Residence 39.

[L] HOMES FOR AGED

FORT THOMAS. *Carmel Manor*, 100 Carmel Manor Rd., Fort Thomas, 41075-2395. Tel: 859-781-5111; Fax: 859-781-2337; Email: msetters@carmelmanor.org; Web: carmelmanor.com. Sr. Diane Mack, O.Carm., Admin. Carmelite Sisters for the Aged and Infirm. Bed Capacity 175; Residents 175; Tot Asst. Annually 225; Total Staff 180.

[M] CONVENTS AND RESIDENCES FOR SISTERS

COVINGTON. *The Franciscan Daughters of Mary (F.D.M.)* (Public Association of the Faithful) St. Benedict Convent, 336 E. 16th St., Covington, 41014. Tel: 859-491-3899; Fax: 859-491-4900; Cell: 859-512-0333; Email: fdmsisters@gmail.com; Email: rosegardenmission@gmail.com; Web: www.fdofmary.org. P.O. Box 122070, Covington, 41012-2070. Mother Seraphina Marie Quinlan, F.D.M., Supr.; Sr. Clare Borchard, Vicar. Sisters 7.
St. Walburg Monastery, 2500 Amsterdam Rd., Covington, 41017-5316. Tel: 859-331-6324; Fax: 859-331-2136; Web: www.stwalburg.org. Sr. Aileen Bankemper, Prioress. Benedictine Sisters, Villa Madonna Academy, Villa Madonna Montessori.
Villa Madonna Academy, Villa Madonna Montessori Professed Sisters 39.

ERLANGER. *Monastery of the Sacred Passion*, 1151 Donaldson Hwy., Erlanger, 41018-1000. Tel: 859-371-8568; Fax: 859-371-8568; Email: mother.margaretmary@outlook.com; Web: www.erlangerpassionists.org. Sr. Margaret Mary, C.P., Supr.; Rev. Gerald E. Twaddell, Ph.D., Chap. Passionist Nuns. Professed 6; Sisters 6.

MELBOURNE. *St. Anne Province Center*, 5300 St. Anne Dr., Melbourne, 41059-9603. Tel: 859-441-0700; Fax: 859-441-1510; Email: info@cdpkentucky.org; Web: www.cdpkentucky.org. Sr. Alice Gerdeman, C.D.P., Prov. Supr.; Rev. Elmer Nadicksbernd, S.V.D., Chap., (Retired). Provincial House and Novitiate of the Sisters of Divine Providence of Kentucky. Sisters in Community 94.
Holy Family Home, 5300 St. Anne Dr., Melbourne, 41059-9604. Tel: 859-781-0712; Fax: 859-781-8854; Email: cschumacher@cdpkentucky.org. Sr. Carleen Schumacher, Admin.; Rev. Elmer Nadicksbernd, S.V.D., Chap., (Retired). Sisters in Residence 50.

PARK HILLS. *Provincial Center of the Sisters of Notre Dame* Juniorate, Novitiate (1924) 1601 Dixie Hwy., Park Hills, 41011-2701. Tel: 859-291-2040; Fax: 859-291-1774; Email: shemmer@sndky.org; Web: www.sndky.org. Sr. Mary Ethel Parrott, S.N.D., Prov. Supr.; Rev. Robert J. Ross, S.J., Chap., (Retired). Sisters 98.

WALTON. *St. William Convent* aka Sisters of St. Joseph the Worker, 1 St. Joseph Ln., Walton, 41094-1026. Tel: 859-485-4256; Fax: 859-485-4914; Email: motherchristina@ssjw.org. Mother Christina Murray, S.J.W., Supr. Sisters of St. Joseph the Worker. Sisters 9.

[N] SOCIAL SERVICES

COVINGTON. *Catholic Charities*, 3629 Church St., Covington, 41015-1499. Tel: 859-581-8974; Fax: 859-581-9595; Email: apickett@covingtoncharities.org; Email: vbauerle@covingtoncharities.org; Web: www.covingtoncharities.org. Mr. Alan Pickett, Exec. Dir.; Mrs. Vicky Bauerle, Contact Person. Tot Asst. Annually 10,000; Total Staff 32.
Parish Kitchen (1974) 141 West Pike St., Covington, 41011. Tel: 859-581-7745; Email: parishkitchen@fuse.net; Web: parishkitchen.org. P.O. Box 1234, Covington, 41012. Mr. Alan Pickett, Exec. Dir.; Maria Meyer, Dir. Tot Asst. Annually 65,000; Total Staff 3.
Rose Garden Home Mission, 2040 Madison Ave., PO Box 122070, Covington, 41012. Tel: 859-491-7673; Fax: 859-491-4900; Email: rosegardenmission@gmail.com; Web: www.fdofmary.org. Mother Seraphina Marie Quinlan, F.D.M., Dir. Tot Asst. Annually 42,500; Total Staff 3.
**Society of St. Vincent de Paul, Council of Northern Kentucky*, 2655 Crescent Springs Rd., Covington, 41017. Tel: 859-446-7723; Tel: 859-446-7727; Email: karen.zengel@svdpnky.org; Email: lou.settle@svdpnky.org; Web: www.svdpnk.org. Karen Zengel, Exec. Dir. Tot Asst. Annually 32,000; Parish Conferences 30; Volunteers 500.

[O] DIOCESAN RETREAT HOUSES

MELBOURNE. *St. Anne Retreat Center for the Diocese of Covington*, 5275 St. Anne Dr., Melbourne, 41059-1101. Tel: 859-441-2003; Fax: 859-441-7955; Email: dprofitt@covdio.org; Email: klittle@covdio.org; Web: www.stanneretreatcenter.org. Deacon Dave Profitt, Dir.; Karen Little, Contact Person. Retreatants 4,593.

[P] NEWMAN CLUBS

HIGHLAND HEIGHTS. *Catholic Newman Club - Northern Kentucky University*, 19 Clearview Dr., Highland Heights, 41076-1449. Tel: 859-261-5340; Email: larry29609@lycos.com; Web: www.newmanconnection.com. Rev. Lawrence A. Schaeper, Chap.; Mrs. Donna Heim, Campus Min.

[Q] MISCELLANEOUS

COVINGTON. *Notre Dame Urban Education Center, Inc.*, 14 E. 8th St., Covington, 41011. Tel: 859-261-4487; Fax: 859-261-4437; Email: smtherese@sndky.org. Sr. Maria Therese Schappert, S.N.D., Dir.

MELBOURNE. *Congregation of Divine Providence of Melbourne KY Inc.*, 5300 St. Anne Dr., Melbourne, 41059-9601. Tel: 859-441-0700; Fax: 859-441-1510; Email: agerdeman@cdpkentucky.org; Web: www.cdpkentucky.org. Sr. Alice Gerdeman, C.D.P., Prov. Sisters 94.

PARK HILLS. *Sisters of Notre Dame International, Inc.*, 1601 Dixie Hwy., Covington, 41011. Tel: 859-291-2040, Ext. 102; Email: mmeadows@sndky.org. Sr. Kristin Battles, Supr.

RELIGIOUS INSTITUTES OF MEN REPRESENTED IN THE DIOCESE

For further details refer to the corresponding bracketed number in the Religious Institutes of Men or Women section.

[0460]—*Brothers of the Poor of St. Francis* (Aachen, Germany)—C.F.P.
[0275]—*Carmelites of Mary Immaculate* (Devamatha, India Province)—C.M.I.
[0570]—*Glenmary Home Missioners* (Cincinnati, Ohio)—G.H.M.
[0690]—*Jesuit Fathers and Brothers* (U.S.A. Midwest Prov.)—S.J.
[0730]—*Legionaries of Christ* (Thornwood, New York)—L.C.
[0420]—*Society of the Divine Word* (Chicago Prov.)—S.V.D.
[1335]—*Vincentian Congregation* (Padra, Rewa, India)—V.C.

RELIGIOUS INSTITUTES OF WOMEN REPRESENTED IN THE DIOCESE

[0230]—*Benedictine Sisters of Pontifical Jurisdiction* (Covington, Kentucky)—O.S.B.
[0330]—*Carmelite Sisters for the Aged and Infirm* (Germantown, NY)—O.Carm.
[3180]—*Congregation of the Passion of Jesus Christ* (Covington, Kentucky)—C.P.
[0440]—*Sisters of Charity of Cincinnati, Ohio*—S.C.
[1000]—*Sisters of Divine Providence of Kentucky* (Covington, Kentucky)—C.D.P.
[2990]—*Sisters of Notre Dame* (Covington, Kentucky)—S.N.D.
[1530]—*Sisters of St. Francis of the Congregation of Our Lady of Lourdes* (Sylvania, Ohio)—O.S.F.
[3920]—*Sisters of St. Joseph the Worker* (Covington, Kentucky)—S.J.W.

DIOCESAN CEMETERIES

COLD SPRING. *St. Joseph*
FORT MITCHELL. *St. John*
St. Mary
FORT THOMAS. *St. Stephen*
WILDER. *St. Joseph*

NECROLOGY

† Hinds, William H., (Retired), Died Apr. 12, 2018

An asterisk (*) denotes an organization that has established tax-exempt status directly with the IRS and is not covered by the USCCB Group Ruling.

Diocese of Crookston

(Dioecesis Crookstoniensis)

Most Reverend

MICHAEL J. HOEPPNER, D.D., J.C.L.

Bishop of Crookston; ordained June 29, 1975; appointed seventh Bishop of Crookston September 28, 2007; Episcopal ordination November 30, 2007. *Chancery Office: 1200 Memorial Dr., Crookston, MN 56716.* Tel: 218-281-4533; Email: mhoeppner@crookston.org.

Most Reverend

VICTOR H. BALKE, D.D., PH.D.

Bishop Emeritus of Crookston; ordained May 24, 1958; appointed July 7, 1976; Episcopal ordination September 2, 1976; retired September 28, 2007. *Res.: 1200 Memorial Dr., Crookston, MN 56716.* Tel: 218-281-4533; Email: vhbalke@crookston.org. *Res.: 200 3rd St., N.W., East Grand Forks, MN 56721.*

Chancery Office: 1200 Memorial Dr., P.O. Box 610, Crookston, MN 56716. Tel: 218-281-4533; Fax: 218-281-5991.

Web: www.crookston.org

Email: mfoltz@crookston.org

ESTABLISHED BY HIS HOLINESS PIUS X, DECEMBER 31, 1909.

Square Miles 17,210.

Comprises the Counties of Becker, Beltrami, Clay, Clearwater, Hubbard, Kittson, Lake of the Woods, Marshall, Mahnomen, Norman, Pennington, Polk, Red Lake and Roseau in the State of Minnesota.

Patroness of the Diocese: The Immaculate Conception.

Legal Title: Diocese of Crookston.
For legal titles of parishes and diocesan institutions, consult the Chancery Office.

STATISTICAL OVERVIEW

Personnel	
Bishop	1
Retired Bishops	1
Priests: Diocesan Active in Diocese	31
Priests: Diocesan Active Outside Diocese	2
Priests: Retired, Sick or Absent	12
Number of Diocesan Priests	45
Religious Priests in Diocese	3
Total Priests in Diocese	48
Extern Priests in Diocese	2
Ordinations:	
Diocesan Priests	1
Transitional Deacons	1
Permanent Deacons in Diocese	23
Total Sisters	41
Parishes	
Parishes	66
With Resident Pastor:	
Resident Diocesan Priests	26
Resident Religious Priests	2
Without Resident Pastor:	
Administered by Priests	38
Professional Ministry Personnel:	
Sisters	1
Lay Ministers	29
Welfare	
Catholic Hospitals	3
Total Assisted	111,930
Homes for the Aged	3
Total Assisted	869
Day Care Centers	1
Total Assisted	49
Educational	
Diocesan Students in Other Seminaries	5
Total Seminarians	5
High Schools, Diocesan and Parish	1
Total Students	175
Elementary Schools, Diocesan and Parish	8
Total Students	1,223
Catechesis/Religious Education:	
High School Students	1,001
Elementary Students	2,976
Total Students under Catholic Instruction	5,380
Teachers in the Diocese:	
Lay Teachers	138
Vital Statistics	
Receptions into the Church:	
Infant Baptism Totals	402
Minor Baptism Totals	11
Adult Baptism Totals	13
Received into Full Communion	99
First Communions	455
Confirmations	405
Marriages:	
Catholic	106
Interfaith	66
Total Marriages	172
Deaths	458
Total Catholic Population	35,014
Total Population	277,690

Former Bishops—Most Revs. TIMOTHY CORBETT, D.D., ord. June 12, 1886; ord. May 19, 1910; resigned See Aug. 6, 1938; appt. Titular Bishop of Vita; died July 20, 1939; JOHN H. PESCHGES, D.D., ord. April 15, 1905; ord. Nov. 9, 1938; died Oct. 30, 1944; FRANCIS J. SCHENK, D.D., ord. June 13, 1926; ord. May 24, 1945; transferred to Duluth Jan. 27, 1960; died Oct. 28, 1969; LAURENCE A. GLENN, D.D., ord. June 11, 1927; ord. Sept. 12, 1956; appt. Bishop of Crookston Feb. 3, 1960; retired July 28, 1970; died Jan. 26, 1985; KENNETH J. POVISH, D.D., ord. June 3, 1950; appt. Bishop of Crookston July 28, 1970; ord. Sept. 29, 1970; transferred to Lansing Oct. 21, 1975; died Sept. 5, 2003; VICTOR H. BALKE, D.D., (Retired), ord. May 24, 1958; appt. July 7, 1976; Episcopal ord. Sept. 2, 1976; retired Sept. 28, 2007.

Vicar General & Moderator of the Curia—Very Rev. Msgr. MICHAEL H. FOLTZ, V.G., J.C.L., 1200 Memorial Dr., P.O. Box 610, Crookston, 56716. Tel: 218-281-4533, Ext. 419; Email: mfoltz@crookston.org.

Chancery Office—1200 Memorial Dr., P.O. Box 610, Crookston, 56716. Tel: 218-281-4533;
Fax: 218-281-5991; Web: www.crookston.org. Most Rev. MICHAEL J. HOEPPNER, D.D., Bishop, Fax: 218-281-5991 (Bishop's Office); Very Rev. Msgr. MICHAEL H. FOLTZ, V.G., J.C.L., 1200 Memorial Dr., P.O. Box 610, Crookston, 56716. Tel: 218-281-4533, Ext. 419 (office); Fax: 218-281-5991; Email: mfoltz@crookston.org. Office Hours Mon.-Fri. 8am-noon & 1-5pm. All official business should be directed to this office.

Chancellor—BONNIE SULLIVAN, 1200 Memorial Dr., Crookston, 56716. Tel: 218-281-4533, Ext. 416; Email: bsullivan@crookston.org.

Information Officer—Very Rev. Msgr. MICHAEL H. FOLTZ, V.G., J.C.L., Tel: 218-281-4533, Ext. 419; Email: mfoltz@crookston.org.

Finance Officer—MR. CHAD RYAN, Tel: 218-281-4533, Ext. 417; Email: cryan@crookston.org.

Diocesan Tribunal—Very Rev. JOSEPH RICHARDS, 1200 Memorial Dr., P.O. Box 610, Crookston, 56716-0610. Tel: 218-281-4533, Ext. 420; Tel: 218-281-4050; Email: tribunal@crookston.com.

Judicial Vicar—Very Rev. JOSEPH RICHARDS.

Adjutant Judicial Vicar—Very Rev. Msgr. MICHAEL H. FOLTZ, V.G., J.C.L.

Defenders of the Bond—Rev. VIRGIL HELMIN, J.C.L.

Promoter of Justice—Very Rev. Msgr. MICHAEL H. FOLTZ, V.G., J.C.L.

Notaries—BONNIE SULLIVAN; MRS. RENEE TATE.

Psychological Consultant—GERALDINE CARIVEAU, M.S., C.C.M.H.C.

Diocesan Offices And Directors

Diocesan Consultors—Very Rev. Msgr. MICHAEL H. FOLTZ, V.G., J.C.L., Tel: 218-281-4533, Ext. 419; Email: mfoltz@crookston.org; Rev. Msgr. ROGER GRUNDHAUS, J.C.L., (Retired); Rev. TOM FRIEDL; Very Rev. RAUL PEREZ-COBO; Revs. XAVIER ILANGO; VINCENT MILLER.

Finance Council—Most Rev. MICHAEL J. HOEPPNER, D.D.; Very Rev. Msgr. MICHAEL H. FOLTZ, V.G., J.C.L., Tel: 218-281-4533, Ext. 419; Email: mfoltz@crookston.org; Revs. CHUCK HUCK; WILLIAM DECRANS; CHRISTIE CLARK; TIM HAGL; NICK STROMSODT; MARK KLINKHAMMER; BONNIE SULLIVAN.

Adoption Referral/Post Adoption Search—BONNIE SULLIVAN, Mailing Address: P.O. Box 610, Crookston, 56716. Tel: 218-281-4533; Email: bsullivan@crookston.org.

Boy Scouts—DON VOTAVA, 32077 State Hwy. #1 N.W., Warren, 56762. Tel: 218-745-5423; Rev. THOMAS FRIEDL.

Catholic Campaign for Human Development—Mailing Address: P.O. Box 610, Crookston, 56716. Tel: 218-281-4533, Ext. 439. MR. ROBERT NOEL, Email: bnoel@crookston.org.

Catholic Charities—MR. ROBERT NOEL, Dir., Tel: 218-281-4533, Ext. 439; Email: bnoel@crookston.org.

Catholic Relief Services—Mailing Address: P.O. Box 610, Crookston, 56716. Tel: 218-281-4533, Ext. 439 . MR. ROBERT NOEL, Dir., Email: bnoel@crookston.org.

Commission on Building and Planning—Very Rev. JOSEPH RICHARDS; DON SCHOFF; CURT BLOCK; ROGER WINTER; MARY DAHL, Chm.

Commission on Liturgy, Sacred Music and Art—Rev. AUGUST GOTHMAN; MARY DAHL; JULIE MAREK; JULIE HARDMEYER; SHERRY KNOTT; AANA FREIHAMMER; GAYLE GULBRANSON.

Cursillo—ROSE E. WEBER, Lay Dir., Rte. 3, P.O. Box 116, Crookston, 56716. Tel: 218-281-6679.

Deans—Very Revs. JOSEPH RICHARDS, Northwest; RICHARD D. LAMBERT, Northeast; RAUL PEREZ-COBO, Southwest; Rev. TOM FRIEDL, Southeast; Very Rev. Msgr. TIMOTHY H. MCGEE, South-Central.

Diaconate Office—Mailing Address: 1200 Memorial Dr., P.O. Box 610, Crookston, 56716. Tel: 218-281-4533, Ext. 425. Deacon MARK KREJCI, Email: mkrejci@crookston.org.

Diocesan Board of Conciliation and Arbitration— Tel: 218-281-4533, Ext. 419. VACANT.

Director of Schools—MR. ANDREW HILLIKER, Tel: 218-236-5066; Email: ahilliker@crookston.org.

Holy Childhood Association—Very Rev. Msgr. MICHAEL H. FOLTZ, V.G., J.C.L., Dir., Mailing Address: 1200 Memorial Dr., P.O. Box 610, Crookston, 56716-0610. Tel: 218-281-4533, Ext. 419; Email: mfoltz@crookston.org.

Native American Indian Commission—KEN PERRAULT, Mailing Address: P.O. Box 965, Cass Lake, 56633-0965. Tel: 218-244-6393.

Office of Formation in Discipleship—Deacon MARK KREJCI, Dir. Ministries of Marriage, Family & Respect for Life, Mailing Address: 1200 Memorial Dr., P.O. Box 610, Crookston, 56716-0610. Tel: 218-281-4533, Ext. 425; Email: mkrejci@crookston.org.

Formator; Adult, Emerging Adult & Youth Formation—Mailing Address: 1200 Memorial Dr., P.O. Box 610, Crookston, 56716-0610. Tel: 218-281-4533, Ext. 439. MR. ROBERT NOEL, Email: bnoel@crookston.org.

Newspaper, "Our Northland Diocese"—1200 Memorial Dr., P.O. Box 610, Crookston, 56716-0610. Tel: 218-281-4533, Ext. 425. MRS. JANELLE GERGEN, Editor.

Pastoral Office of Administration—MR. CHAD RYAN, 1200 Memorial Dr., P.O. Box 610, Crookston, 56716-0610. Tel: 218-281-4533, Ext. 417.

Pastoral Office of Worship—MARY DAHL, Dir., 1200 Memorial Dr., P.O. Box 610, Crookston, 56716-0610. Tel: 218-281-4533, Ext. 455.

Priests' Council—Most Rev. MICHAEL J. HOEPPNER, D.D., Pres.; Revs. VINCENT MILLER, Chm.; ANTONY FERNANDO, Vice Chm.; Very Rev. Msgr. MICHAEL H. FOLTZ, V.G., J.C.L., Mailing Address: P.O. Box 610, Crookston, 56716. Tel: 218-281-4533, Ext. 419; Email: mfoltz@crookston.org; Revs. XAVIER ILANGO; JOHN COX, O.M.I.; JOHN KLEINWACHTER; PATRICK SULLIVAN; ADAM A. HAMNESS; Rev. Msgr. ROGER GRUNDHAUS, J.C.L., (Retired).

Priests' Personnel Board—Most Rev. MICHAEL J. HOEPPNER, D.D.; Very Rev. Msgr. MICHAEL H. FOLTZ, V.G., J.C.L.; Revs. LARRY DELANEY; XAVIER ILANGO; Very Rev. JERRY ROGERS; Rev. BRYAN KUJAWA.

Priests Retirement Board of Trustees—Revs. LARRY DELANEY; VINCENT MILLER; GEORGE E. NOEL.

Propagation of the FaithMailing Address: 1200 Memorial Dr., P.O. Box 610, Crookston, 56716-0610. Tel: 218-281-4533. MR. ROBERT NOEL.

TEC (Teens Encounter Christ)—TERESA STEEN, 1200 Memorial Dr., Crookston, 56716.

Vocations—Revs. XAVIER ILANGO, Dir., 1200 Memorial Dr., Crookston, 56716. Tel: 701-893-5006; MATTHEW SCHMITZ, Promotions, 200 3rd St., N.W., East Grand Forks, 56721. Tel: 218-773-0877.

Youth Events Coordinator—1200 Memorial Dr., P.O. Box 610, Crookston, 56716-0610. Tel: 218-281-4533, Ext. 435. BRADY BORSLIEN.

Diocesan Board of Review for the Protection of Young Children—Very Rev. Msgr. MICHAEL H. FOLTZ, V.G., J.C.L.; JUDITH MEYER, Chm.; JIM REMER; Rev. VINCENT MILLER; JENNIFER MESSELT; PHIL HODAPP; JACKIE GADDIE.

Victim Assistance Coordinator—Mailing Address: P.O. Box 610, Crookston, 56716. Tel: 218-281-7895. MRS. CINDY HULST, Email: chulst@crookston.org.

Safe Environment—Mailing Address: P.O. Box 610, Crookston, 56716. Tel: 218-281-4224. MRS. RENEE TATE, Email: rtate@crookston.org.

CLERGY, PARISHES, MISSIONS AND PAROCHIAL SCHOOLS

CITY OF CROOKSTON

(POLK COUNTY)

1—CATHEDRAL OF THE IMMACULATE CONCEPTION, Revs. Vincent Miller, Rector; Augie Gothman; Deacons Dennis Bivens; Daniel Hannig.
Church: 702 Summit Ave., 56716-2736.
Tel: 218-281-1735; Email: vmiller.cathedral@midconetwork.com; Web: crookstoncathedral.com.
School—The Cathedral School, (Grades K-6), Tel: 218-281-1835; Email: pjones.cathedral@midconetwork.com. Patricia Jones, Prin. Clergy 2; Lay Teachers 9; Students 70.
Catechesis Religious Program—Email: cathedral@midconetwork.com. Students 275.
Mission—St. Peter, Gentilly, Polk Co.

2—ST. ANNE'S, Closed. For inquiries for parish records contact the Cathedral of the Immaculate Conception, Crookston.

OUTSIDE THE CITY OF CROOKSTON

ADA, NORMAN CO., ST. JOSEPH'S (1895) [JC] Revs. William DeCrans; Joseph DeCrans, (In Res.).
Res.: 405 E. Thorpe Ave., Ada, 56510.
Tel: 218-784-4131; Email: stjoseph@loretel.net; Web: nccatholicchurch.com.
Catechesis Religious Program—(Grades K-12), Email: sjchurchlady@yahoo.com. Teresa Steen, D.R.E. Students 67.
Missions—Holy Family—Halstad, Norman Co.
St. William, Twin Valley, Norman Co.

AKELEY, HUBBARD CO., ST. JOHN, Merged with Immaculate Conception, Nevis to form Our Lady of the Pines, Akeley/Nevis Community.

ALMA, MARSHALL CO., ST. JOHN THE BAPTIST, Closed. For inquiries for parish records contact St. Stephen, Stephen. Tel: 218-478-2231.

ARGYLE, MARSHALL CO., ST. ROSE OF LIMA, [CEM] Served by St. Stephen, Stephen. Rev. Luis Segundo Buitron.
501 W. 3rd St., P.O. Box 277, Argyle, 56713.
Tel: 218-437-6341; Email: stroser@wiktel.com.
Catechesis Religious Program—Dawn Hoeper, D.R.E. Students 28.

BADGER, ROSEAU CO., ST. MARY'S (BADGER) (1899) Served by Sacred Heart, Roseau. Tel: 218-463-2441, Fax: 218-463-2443.
504 N. Main St., Badger, 56714. Tel: 218-463-2441; Email: shcroseau@centurylink.com; Email: frjohn@centurylink.net. Mailing Address: 403 Main Ave. N., Roseau, 56751. Rev. John Kleinwachter.

BAGLEY, CLEARWATER CO., ST. JOSEPH (1912) Served by St. Mary, Fosston.
Mailing Address: 16 Red Lake Ave., P.O. Box 67, Bagley, 56621. Tel: 218-694-6416; Fax: 218-694-6416 ; Email: stjoseph@gvtel.com. Rev. John Melkies Suvakeen.
Catechesis Religious Program—Clarissa Dowhower, D.R.E. Students 38.

BARNESVILLE, CLAY CO., ASSUMPTION (1883) [CEM]
112 4th Ave. N.W., P.O. BOX 339, Barnesville, 56514. Rev. Gary LaMoine.
Res.: 307 Front St. N., P.O. Box 339, Barnesville, 56514. Tel: 218-354-7320; Email: assumption@bvillemn.net.
Catechesis Religious Program—Phyllis Peppel, D.R.E. Students 114.
Mission—St. Cecilia, Sabin, Clay Co.

BAUDETTE, LAKE OF THE WOODS CO., SACRED HEART (1908) Served by St. Mary's, Warroad.
104 1st St. S.W., Baudette, 56623. Tel: 218-386-1178; Email: ourlady@mncable.net; Web: sacredheartbaudette.org. P.O. Box 738, Baudette, 56623. Rev. Todd Arends; Deacon James Lukenbill.
Catechesis Religious Program—Students 27.
Mission—St. Joseph, [CEM] 400 Park Ave., Williams, Lake of the Woods Co. 56686.

BEAULIEU, MAHNOMEN CO., ST. JOSEPH PARISH (BEAULIEU) (1895) [CEM] Served by St. Michael, Mahnomen. Tel: 218-935-2503; Fax. 218-935-2503.
Mailing Address: 120 W. Jefferson, Mahnomen, 56557. Tel: 218- 935-2503; Email: stmikes@arvig.net. Rev. David J. Super.
Catechesis Religious Program—Jolynn Pribula, D.R.E. (Senior High School); Peggy Darco, D.R.E. (Elementary School).

BEJOU, MAHNOMEN CO., IMMACULATE CONCEPTION, Closed. For inquiries for parish records contact St. Michael's, Mahnomen.

BEMIDJI, BELTRAMI CO., ST. PHILIP'S, [CEM]
Mailing Address: 702 Beltrami Ave., N.W., Bemidji, 56601-3046. Tel: 218-444-4262; Email: rector@stphilipsbemidji.org; Email: chuck@stphilipsbemidji.org. Revs. Chuck Huck; Bryan Kujawa; Deacons Kermit Erickson; Robb Naylor.
School—St. Philip's School, (Grades PreK-8), Tel: 218-444-4938; Email: school@stphilipsbemidji.org. Rev. Chuck Huck, Supt. Clergy 2; Lay Teachers 24; Students 327.
Catechesis Religious Program—Tel: 218-441-4944. Kris Jensen, D.R.E., (Grades PreK-8). 220 246.
Mission—St. Charles, Pennington, Beltrami Co.

BENWOOD, ROSEAU CO., ST. JOSEPH THE WORKER, Closed. For inquiries for parish records please contact Sacred Heart, Roseau.

BIG ELBOW LAKE, BECKER CO., ST. FRANCES CABRINI (BIG ELBOW LAKE), Served by St. Ann, Waubun.
39719 County Hwy. 35, Waubun, 56589. Mailing Address: 1112 3rd St., Waubun, 56589.
Tel: 218-473-2101; Email: 1112sta@arvig.net; Web: whiteearthcatholiccommunity.com. Rev. John Cox, O.M.I.

BLACKDUCK, BELTRAMI CO., ST. ANN'S (BLACKDUCK) (1905) Served by St. Patrick's, Kelliher. Tel: 218-647-8392.
388 1st St. E., Blackduck, 56650. Tel: 218-647-8300; Email: stpatrick@catholicexchange.com; Email: frjohn@triparish.org. Mailing Address: P.O. Box 187, Kelliher, 56650. Rev. John Christianson.
Catechesis Religious Program—Ginger Kaiser, D.R.E. Students 45.

BROOKS, RED LAKE CO., ST. JOSEPH (CHURCH OF BROOKS) (1916) [CEM]
Mailing Address: P.O. Box 400, Red Lake Falls, 56750-0400. Tel: 218-253-2188; Email: frschreiner@go2joseph.org; Web: www.rlccatholic.org. Rev. Robert Schreiner. Served by St. Joseph's, Red Lake Falls. Tel: 218-253-2188; Fax. 218-253-2195.
Catechesis Religious Program—Students 28.

CALLAWAY, BECKER CO., ASSUMPTION (1912) [CEM] Served by Sacred Heart, Frazee
206 Dakota St., P.O. Box 67, Callaway, 56521.
Tel: 218-375-3571; Email: shfre@loretel.net. Rev. Msgr. David Baumgartner, V.G., J.C.L.
Catechesis Religious Program—Students 25.

DETROIT LAKES, BECKER CO.

1—HOLY ROSARY, [CEM] Very Rev. Msgr. Timothy H. McGee; Rev. Andrew Obel; Deacons James Thomas; Gary Hager.
Office: 1043 Lake Ave., Detroit Lakes, 56501-3499.
Tel: 218-847-1393; Email: parish@holyrosarycc.org; Web: www.holyrosarycc.org.
School—Holy Rosary School, (Grades PreK-8), Tel: 218-847-1393; Email: tmcgee@holyrosarycc.org. Very Rev. Msgr. Timothy H. McGee, Supt. Lay Teachers 13; Students 147.
Catechesis Religious Program—Jean Olson, D.R.E.; JoAnne Knuttila, D.R.E.; Barbara Schmidt, D.R.E. (Grades 7-12). Students 208.

2—ST. MARY OF THE LAKES
20996 County Hwy. 20, Detroit Lakes, 56501.
Tel: 218-439-3937; Email: stmaryofthelakes@loretel.net; Web: stmaryofthelakes.cc. Rev. Bob J. LaPlante.
Catechesis Religious Program—Sue Livermore, D.R.E. Students 15.
Mission—St. Francis Xavier, Lake Park, Becker Co.

DILWORTH, CLAY CO., ST. ELIZABETH (1910)
Mailing Address: 207 Main St. N., P.O. Box 307, Dilworth, 56529-0307. Tel: 218-287-2705; Email: karen@stlizdilworth.org; Web: www.stlizdilworth.org. Rev. Patrick Sullivan.
Catechesis Religious Program—Email: joyce@stlizdilworth.org. Joyce Hajostek, D.R.E. Students 130.
Mission—St. Andrew, Hawley, Clay Co. 56549.

DOROTHY, RED LAKE CO., ST. DOROTHY, Closed. For inquiries for parish records contact St. Joseph's, Red Lake Falls.

EAST GRAND FORKS, POLK CO., SACRED HEART, [CEM]
200 Third St. N.W., East Grand Forks, 56721-1806.
Tel: 218-773-0877; Email: mfoltz@sacredheartegf.net; Email: jguzman@sacredheartegf.net; Web: www.sacredheartegf.net/parish/. Very Rev. Msgr. Michael H. Foltz, V.G., J.C.L.; Revs. Matthew Schmitz; Maschio Mascarenghas; Deacons Mark LeTexier, Pastoral Min./Coord.; Steve Thomas, RCIA Coordinator.
School—Sacred Heart School, (Grades PreK-12), Tel: 218-773-0877. Jodi Vanderhaiden, Prin. Clergy 3; Lay Teachers 46; Students 368.
Catechesis Religious Program—Email: rkingsbury@sacredheartegf.net. Renata Kingsbury, D.R.E. (Grades PreK-9). Students 241.
Missions—St. Francis—P.O. Box 161, Fisher, Polk Co. 56723. Tel: 218-893-2335; Email: mpniknox@rrv.net. Nancy Knox, Contact Person.
Holy Trinity, 130 St. N.W., Angus, 56762.
Tel: 218-289-0591; Email: Taus.janice84@gmail.com. Janice Taus, Contact Person.

EUCLID, POLK CO., ST. MARY (EUCLID), Served by Sts. Peter & Paul, Warren. Tel: 218-281-5422.
Mailing Address: 208 N. 7th St., Warren, 56762.
Tel: 218-745-4511; Email: donnag@invisimax.com. 13439 U.S. Hwy. 75SW, Euclid, 56717. Rev. Emmanuel Sylvester.
Catechesis Religious Program—Patsy Zammert, D.R.E. Students 1.

FALUN, ROSEAU CO., ST. PHILIP (FALUN) (1910) Served by Sacred Heart, Roseau.

Mailing Address: 403 Main Ave. N., Roseau, 56751. Tel: 218-463-2441; Email: shcroseau@centurylink.net. Rev. John Kleinwachter.

Catechesis Religious Program—Tracy Borowicz, D.R.E. Students 8.

FELTON, CLAY CO., ST. LAWRENCE, Closed. For inquiries for parish records contact St. Joseph's, Ada.

FERTILE, POLK CO., ST. JOSEPH, [CEM]

Mailing Address: 10480 438th St. S.W., Fertile, 56540. Tel: 218-945-6649; Email: StJoesFertile@gvtel.com; Web: www.stjosephsfertile.com. Very Rev. Joseph Richards.

Catechesis Religious Program—Students 46.

FISHER, POLK CO., ST. FRANCIS OF ASSISI (1881) [CEM] (Fisher). Served by Sacred Heart, East Grand Forks. Tel: 218-773-0877.

Mailing Address: 302 Park Ave., P.O. Box 161, Fisher, 56723-0161. Tel: 218-891-2249; Fax: 218-773-0877; Email: mpnjknox@rrv.net. Very Rev. Msgr. Michael H. Foltz, V.G., J.C.L.; Revs. Matthew Schmitz; Maschio Mascarenghas.

Catechesis Religious Program—Students 35.

FLORIAN, MARSHALL CO., ASSUMPTION - CHURCH OF FLORIAN (1881) [CEM] Served by St. Stephen, Stephen.

Mailing Address: 26932 390th St. N.W., Strandquist, 56758. Tel: 218-478-3578; Fax: 218-478-3578; Email: assumptionchurch@wiktel.com; Web: www.wiktel.net/assumption. Rev. Luis Segundo Buitron; Michelle Kostrzewski, Sec.

Catechesis Religious Program—Mary Stusynski, D.R.E. Students 33.

FOSSTON, POLK CO., ST. MARY'S (1901) [CEM 2]

Mailing Address: 725 6th St., N.E., Fosston, 56542. Tel: 218-435-6484; Email: frjohnstmstj@gmail.com; Email: stmarysfosston@gmail.com; Web: stmarysfosston.org. Rev. John Melkies Suvakeen.

Res.: 725 10th St., N.E., Fosston, 56542.

Catechesis Religious Program—Email: stmarys@gvtel.com. Students 41.

FRAZEE, BECKER CO., SACRED HEART (1892) [CEM]

Mailing Address: 202 W. Maple Ave., Frazee, 56544. Tel: 218-334-4221; Email: shfre@loretel.net; Web: frazeesacredheart.org. Rev. Msgr. David Baumgartner, V.G., J.C.L.

Res.: 306 W. Walnut Ave., Frazee, 56544.

Catechesis Religious Program—Students 168.

Mission—Assumption, 206 Dakota St., Callaway, Becker Co. 56521. Tel: 218-334-4226; Email: frdavid.shfre@arvig.net.

GENTILLY, POLK CO., ST. PETER'S (GENTILLY), [CEM]

Mailing Address: 25723-185th Ave., S.W., 56716. Tel: 218-281-1735; Email: dmbivens.cathedral@midconetwork.com. 702 Summit Ave., 56651. Rev. Vincent Miller; Deacon Dennis Bivens. Served by Cathedral of the Immaculate Conception, Crookston. Tel: 218-281-1735.

Catechesis Religious Program—Students 35.

GEORGETOWN, CLAY CO., ST. JOHN (1885) Served by St. Francis de Sales, Moorhead. Tel: 218-233-4780.

308 Probstfield St., P.O. Box 248, Georgetown, 56546. Tel: 218-233-4780; Email: jherm@feltontel.net; Email: fatherraul@gmail.com. Mailing Address: St. Francis de Sales Parish, 601 15th Ave. N, Moorhead, 56560. Very Rev. Raul Perez-Cobo.

Catechesis Religious Program—Students 13.

GOODRIDGE, PENNINGTON CO., ST. ANNE (GOODRIDGE) (1915) Served by St. Francis Xavier, Oklee.

202 Osmund Ave., Goodridge, 56725. Mailing Address: c/o St. Francis Xavier Parish, P.O. Box 126, Oklee, 56742. Tel: 218-378-4529; Email: parishstaff@oggcatholic.org; Web: www.oggcatholic.org. Rev. Adam A. Hamness, Admin.

GREENBUSH, ROSEAU CO., BLESSED SACRAMENT, [CEM]

342 4th St. S., P.O. Box A, Greenbush, 56726. Tel: 218-782-2467; Email: blessedsacrament@wiktel.com. Rev. George E. Noel.

Catechesis Religious Program—Tel: 218-556-6090; Email: jess.foss@hotmail.com. Jess Foss, D.R.E. Students 90.

Missions—St. Joseph—Middle River, Marshall Co.

St. Edward, Karlstad, Marshall Co.

GRYGLA, MARSHALL CO., ST. CLEMENT (GRYGLA), Served by St. Francis Xavier, Oklee.

130 N. Marshall Ave., Grygla, 56727. Tel: 218-796-5844; Email: parishstaff@oggcatholic.org; Web: www.oggcatholic.org. Mailing Address: c/o St. Francis Xavier Parish, P.O. Box 126, Oklee, 56742. Rev. Adam A. Hamness, Admin.

HALLOCK, KITTSON CO., ST. PATRICK'S

Mailing Address: 170 5th St. S., P.O. Box 596, Hallock, 56728-0596. Tel: 218-843-2323; Email: stpatrickshallock@gmail.com. Rev. Xavier Ilango.

Catechesis Religious Program—Karen Gubbels, D.R.E. Students 20.

Mission—Holy Rosary, P.O. Box 596, Lancaster, Kittson Co. 56735.

HALSTAD, NORMAN CO., HOLY FAMILY (HALSTAD) (1984) Served by St. Joseph, Ada. Tel: 218-784-4131. [JC]

307 5th St. E., Halstad, 56548. Tel: 218-784-4131; Email: stjoseph@loretel.net; Web: nccatholicchurch.com. Mailing Address: Pastoral Administrative Office, 405 E. Thorpe Ave., Ada, 56510. Rev. William DeCrans.

Catechesis Religious Program—Teresa Steen, D.R.E. Students 71.

HAWLEY, CLAY CO., ST. ANDREW, [JC] Served by St. Elizabeth, Dilworth. Tel: 218-287-2705.

Mailing Address: 1418 Main St., Hawley, 56549-0129. Tel: 218-483-4264; Email: parish@standrewshawley.org; Web: www.standrewshawley.org. P.O. Box 129, Hawley, 56549. Rev. Patrick Sullivan; Deacon Tom Jirik.

Catechesis Religious Program—Bev Samuelson, D.R.E. Students 140.

KARLSTAD, KITTSON CO., ST. EDWARD THE CONFESSOR (KARLSTAD), Served by Blessed Sacrament, Greenbush. Tel: 218-782-2467.

119 Harding St. S., Karlstad, 56732. c/o Blessed Sacrament, P.O. Box A, Greenbush, 56726. Tel: 218-782-2467; Email: blessedsacrament@wiktel.com. Rev. George E. Noel.

Catechesis Religious Program—Students 15.

KELLIHER, BELTRAMI CO., ST. PATRICK (1909) [JC]

131 5th St. N.E., P.O. Box 187, Kelliher, 56650. Tel: 218-647-8300; Email: frjohn@triparish.org; Email: stpatrick@catholicexchange.com; Web: triparish.org. Rev. John Christianson.

Catechesis Religious Program—Sissy Neft, D.R.E. Students 35.

Missions—St. Ann—Blackduck, Beltrami Co.

St. John, Nebish, Beltrami Co.

LAKE ITASCA, CLEARWATER CO., ST. CATHERINE, Closed. For inquiries for parish records contact St. Peter's, Park Rapids.

LAKE PARK, BECKER CO., ST. FRANCIS XAVIER'S, [CEM] Served by St. Mary of the Lakes, Detroit Lakes.

2066 Second St., Lake Park, 56554. Tel: 218-239-6639. Rev. Bob J. LaPlante.

Catechesis Religious Program—Rich Veit, D.R.E. (Grades 7-12); Toni Grabinger, D.R.E. (Grades K-6).

LANCASTER, KITTSON CO., HOLY ROSARY

Mailing Address: St. Patrick's, 170 5th St. S., P.O. Box 596, Hallock, 56728. Tel: 218-843-2323; Email: stpatrickshallock@gmail.com. Rev. Xavier Ilango, Admin. Served by St. Patrick, Hallock. Tel: 218-843-2323.

Catechesis Religious Program—Students 2.

LAPORTE, HUBBARD CO., ST. THEODORE OF TARSUS (LAPORTE) (1988) [CEM 2] Served by Our Lady of the Pines Church, Nevis.

580 County Rd. 39, Laporte, 56461. Tel: 218-652-4005; Tel: 218-224-3135 (Church); Email: parishofficenevis@gmail.com; Web: www.ccnevislaporte.org. Mailing Address: 205 Main St., P.O. Box 378, Nevis, 56467. Rev. Antony Fernando.

Catechesis Religious Program—Email: olpfaithform@gmail.com. Sandy Roerick, D.R.E. Students 28.

LEO, ROSEAU CO., ST. ALOYSIUS, Closed. For inquiries for parish records contact Blessed Sacrament, Greenbush.

MAHNOMEN, MAHNOMEN CO., ST. MICHAEL'S PARISH (1908) [CEM]

120 W. Jefferson Ave., Mahnomen, 56557. Tel: 218-935-2503; Email: stmikes@arvig.net; Email: dsuper@stmichaelmahnomen.org. Rev. David J. Super.

School—St. Michael's Parish School, (Grades PreK-8), Tel: 218-935-5222; Email: schalich@stmichaelmahnomen.org. Sarah Chalich, Prin. Clergy 1; Lay Teachers 8; Students 44.

Catechesis Religious Program—Jolynn Pribula, D.R.E. (High School); Peggy Darco, D.R.E. (Elementary School). Students 102.

Mission—St. Joseph, [CEM] Beaulieu, Mahnomen Co.

MENTOR, POLK CO., ST. LAWRENCE (1920) [CEM]

16180 336th St. S.E., Mentor, 56736. Tel: 218-637-8178; Email: stlawrence@gvtel.com; Web: www.stlawrencementor.org. Very Rev. Joseph Richards.

Church & Mailing Address: P.O. Box 51, Mentor, 56736.

Catechesis Religious Program—Anita Revier, D.R.E.; Amy Kolden, D.R.E. Students 36.

MIDDLE RIVER, MARSHALL CO., ST. JOSEPH, HUSBAND OF MARY (MIDDLE RIVER), [CEM] Served by Blessed Sacrament, Greenbush.

535 N 1st St., Middle River, 56737. Tel: 218-782-2467; Email: blessedsacrament@wiktel.com. Mailing Address: P.O. Box A, Greenbush, 56726. Rev. George E. Noel.

Catechesis Religious Program—Students 7.

MOORHEAD, CLAY CO.

1—ST. FRANCIS DE SALES (1948) [JC]

601 15th Ave. N., Moorhead, 56560. Tel: 218-233-4780; Fax: 218-227-0021; Email: info@stfrancismhd.org; Web: www.stfrancismhd.org. Very Rev. Raul Perez-Cobo; Deacon Dean Roberts; Sr. Lucy Perez-Calizto, Guadalupe Min. Coord.; Bonnie Lee, Liturgy Dir.

Catechesis Religious Program—Lisa Eggert, D.R.E. & Youth Min. Students 147.

Mission—St. John the Baptist, Georgetown, Clay Co. 56546. Email: fatherraul@gmail.com.

2—ST. JOSEPH'S (1873) [JC]

218 10th St. S., Moorhead, 56560. Tel: 218-236-5066; Fax: 218-233-0717; Email: louderkirk@stjoesmhd.com; Web: www.stjoesmhd.com. Revs. Larry Delaney; Nate Brunn; Deacons Allen Kukert; Bill Beutler; Courtney Abel; Paul Erickson; Mark Krejci; Tom Cerar; John Biby, Admin.

School—St. Joseph's School, (Grades PreK-8), 1005 2nd Ave. S., Moorhead, 56560. Tel: 218-233-0553; Tel: 218-233-0556; Fax: 218-291-9479; Email: saints@stjoesmhdschool.com; Web: www.stjoesmhdschool.com. Mr. Andrew Hilliker, Prin.; Heidi Huus, Sec. Clergy 2; Lay Teachers 28; Students 222.

Catechesis Religious Program—

Tel: 218-284-6230 Youth Faith Formation;

Tel: 218-284-6229 Middle School & High School Faith Formation;

Tel: 218-284-6222 Adult Faith Formation; Email: khendrickx@stjoesmhd.com Youth Faith Formation; Email: mhundcerna@stjoesmhd.com Middle School & High School Faith Formation; Email: serickson@stjoesmhd.com Adult Faith Formation. Kate Hendrickx, D.R.E. (PreK-5); Melissa Hund-Cerna, D.R.E. (6-12); Shawn Erickson, RCIA Coord. Students 188.

Mission—St. Thomas Aquinas Newman Center.

NAYTAHWAUSH, MAHNOMEN CO., ST. ANNE (1917) (Naytahwaush). Served by St. Ann's, Waubun.

202 County Rd. 4, Naytahwaush, 56566. Mailing Address: 1112-3rd St., Waubun, 56589. Tel: 218-473-2101; Email: 1112sta@arvig.net; Web: whiteearthcatholiccommunity.com. Rev. John Cox, O.M.I.

NEBISH, BELTRAMI CO., ST. JOHN (NEBISH), Served by St. Patrick, Kelliher.

Mailing Address: P.O. Box 187, Kelliher, 56650. Tel: 218-647-8300; Email: frjohn@triparish.org; Email: stpatrick@catholicexchange.com. 27867 Irvine Ave., N.E., Nebish, 56667. Rev. John Christianson.

Catechesis Religious Program—Students 26.

NEVIS, HUBBARD CO.

1—IMMACULATE CONCEPTION, Closed. Merged with St. John's, Akeley to form Our Lady of the Pines, Nevis.

2—OUR LADY OF THE PINES (2003) [CEM 2]

Mailing Address: 205 Main St. W., Nevis, 56467. Tel: 218-652-4005 (Office); Tel: 218-652-4022; Tel: 218-652-2785 (Rectory); Email: parishofficenevis@gmail.com; Email: ccnevis@gmail.com; Web: www.ccnevislaporte.org. P.O. Box 378, Nevis, 56467. Rev. Antony Fernando.

Catechesis Religious Program—Mary Schiebe, D.R.E. Students 61.

Mission—St. Theodore of Tarsus Church, 580 County Rd. 39, Laporte, Hubbard Co. 56461. Email: ccnevis@gmail.com.

OGEMA, BECKER CO., MOST HOLY REDEEMER, [CEM]

106 Ontario St., P.O. Box 57, Ogema, 56569-0057. Tel: 218-983-3261; Email: owep@tvutel.com. Revs. Joseph Hitpas, O.M.I.; Daniel Nassaney, O.M.I.

Catechesis Religious Program—1112 3rd St., Waubun, 56589. Tel: 218-473-2101; Email: 1113sta@arvig.net. Janet Lhotka, D.R.E. Students 33.

Missions—St. Benedict—White Earth, Becker Co. 56591.

St. Theodore, Ponsford, Becker Co. 56575.

OKLEE, RED LAKE CO., ST. FRANCIS XAVIER'S (OKLEE) (1881) [CEM]

301 Governor St., Oklee, 56742. Tel: 218-796-5844; Email: parishstaff@oggcatholic.org; Email: frhamness@oggcatholic.org; Web: www.oggcatholic.org. P.O. Box 126, Oklee, 56742. Rev. Adam A. Hamness, Admin.

Missions—St. Anne—Goodridge, Pennington Co. 56725.

St. Clement, Grygla, Marshall Co. 56727.

OSLO, MARSHALL CO., ST. JOSEPH, [CEM] Served by SS. Peter and Paul, Warren. Tel: 218-745-4511.

515 Main St., P.O. Box 97, Oslo, 56744. Tel: 218-695-2641; Tel: 218-745-4533; Email: stjosephoslo1@gmail.com; Email: stjoseph@wiktel.com. Mailing Address: Sts. Peter & Paul Parish, 208 N. 7th St., Warren, 56762. Rev. Emmanuel Sylvester.

Catechesis Religious Program—Sr. Marguerite Streifel, D.R.E. Students 9.

PARK RAPIDS, HUBBARD CO., ST. PETER THE APOSTLE (1887) [CEM]

305 W. 5th St., Park Rapids, 56470-0353. Tel: 218-732-5142; Email: fr.tom@arvig.net; Web: www.stpeterpr.org. P.O. Box 353, Park Rapids, 56470-0353. Rev. Thomas Friedl; Deacon John Zinniel.

Res.: 506 W. 7th St., Park Rapids, 56470-0353. Tel: 218-237-5881.

Catechesis Religious Program—Email: annette@arvig.net. Annette Haas, D.R.E. & Youth Min. (PreK-12). Students 146.

Mission—St. Mary, Two Inlets, Becker Co., MN. Email: sm2inlets@arvig.net. Lynn Gartner, Contact Person.

PENNINGTON, BELTRAMI CO., ST. CHARLES CATHOLIC CHURCH OF PENNINGTON, Served by St. Philip's, Bemidji. Tel: 218-444-4262
Scenic Hwy. 39, Pennington, 56663.
Tel: 218-444-4262; Email: chuck@stphilipsbemidji.org. Mailing Address: St. Philip's, 702 Beltrami Ave., N.W., Bemidji, 56601-3046. Rev. Chuck Huck.
Catechesis Religious Program—

PLUMMER, RED LAKE CO., ST. VINCENT DE PAUL, Closed. For inquiries for parish records contact St. Francis Xavier, Oklee.

PONSFORD, BECKER CO., ST. THEODORE OF PONSFORD, Served by Most Holy Redeemer, Ogema. Tel: 218-936-3261.
Mailing Address: 106 Ontario St., Ogema, 56569-0057. Tel: 218-983-3261; Email: owep@tvutel.com; Web: whiteearthcatholiccommunity.com. P.O. Box 57, Ogema, 56569-0057. Rev. Joseph Hitpas, O.M.I.
Catechesis Religious Program—

RED LAKE, BELTRAMI CO., ST. MARY'S MISSION CHURCH (1858) [CEM]
Hwy. 1, P.O. Box 189, Red Lake, 56671-0189.
Tel: 218-679-3615; Tel: 218-679-3614; Email: frjerry@stmarysmission.org. Very Rev. Jerry Rogers.
School—St. Mary's Mission Church School, (Grades PreK-6), Tel: 218-679-3388; Email: frjerry@stmarysmission.org. Very Rev. Jerry Rogers, Supt. Clergy 1; Lay Teachers 10; Students 106.
Catechesis Religious Program—
Mission—Sacred Heart, Wilton, Beltrami Co.

RED LAKE FALLS, RED LAKE CO., ST. JOSEPH (1879) [CEM]
112 Edward Ave., P.O. Box 400, Red Lake Falls, 56750-0400. Tel: 218-253-2188; Email: deb@go2joseph.org; Web: go2joseph.org. Rev. Robert Schreiner.

Catechesis Religious Program—Students 135.
Mission—St. Joseph, [CEM] Brooks, Red Lake Co. 56715.

ROSEAU, ROSEAU CO., SACRED HEART, [CEM]
403 Main Ave. N., Roseau, 56751. Tel: 213-463-2441; Email: shcroseau@centurylink.net; Email: frjohn@centurylink.net; Web: roseaucatholic.org. Rev. John Kleinwachter.
Catechesis Religious Program—Tel: 218-242-4053. Tracy Borowicz, D.R.E. Students 73.
Missions—St. Philip—Falun, Roseau Co.
St. Mary's, [CEM] Badger, Roseau Co.

SABIN, CLAY CO., ST. CECILIA (SABIN) (1910) Served by Assumption, Barnesville. Tel: 218-354-7320.
Mailing Address: Assumption, P.O. Box 339, Barnesville, 56514-0339. Tel: 218-354-7320; Email: assumption@bvillemn.net. 20 Halloway Ave. S., Sabin, 56580. Rev. Gary LaMoine.
Catechesis Religious Program—Students 38.

SHEVLIN, CLEARWATER CO., OUR LADY OF VICTORY, Closed. For inquiries for parish records contact St. Joseph's, Bagley.

STEPHEN, MARSHALL CO., ST. STEPHEN'S, [CEM]
Mailing Address: P.O. Box 507, Stephen, 56757.
Tel: 218-478-2231; Email: ststephens@wiktel.com. 515 5th St., Stephen, 56757. Rev. Luis Segundo Buitron.
Catechesis Religious Program—Students 30.
Missions—Assumption Church of Florian—Florian, Marshall Co.
St. Rose of Lima, Argyle, Marshall Co. 56713.

TABOR, POLK CO., HOLY TRINITY CATHOLIC (TABOR), Served by Sacred Heart, East Grand Forks. Tel: 218-773-0877.
Mailing Address: 37639 140th St., N.W., Angus, 56762-8929. Tel: 218-745-5853; Tel: 218-773-0877; Email: mfoltz@sacredheartegf.net; Web: www.rc.net/crookston/holytrinity. Sacred Heart, 200 3rd St., N.W., East Grand Forks, 56721. Very Rev. Msgr. Michael H. Foltz, V.G., J.C.L.; Revs. Maschio Mascarenghas; Matthew Schmitz.
Catechesis Religious Program—Students 26.

TERREBONNE, RED LAKE CO., ST. ANTHONY, Closed. For inquiries for parish records contact St. Joseph's, Red Lake Falls.

THIEF RIVER FALLS, PENNINGTON CO., ST. BERNARDS (1896) [CEM]
105 Knight Ave. N., Thief River Falls, 56701.
Tel: 218-681-3571; Email: laura.brickson@stbernardstrf.com; Email: rdplambert@hotmail.com; Web: www.stbernardscc.org/. Very Rev. Richard D. Lambert.
School—St. Bernards School, (Grades PreK-5), Tel: 218-681-1539; Email: randy.schantz@stbernardstrf.com. Laura Brickson, Prin. Clergy 1; Lay Teachers 10; Students 102.
Catechesis Religious Program—Email: margaret.rasmussen@stbernardstrf.com; Email: rdplambert@hotmail.com; Web: www.stbernardstrf.org. Margaret Rasmussen, D.R.E.; Jayne Miller, Youth Min. Students 245.

TWIN VALLEY, NORMAN CO., ST. WILLIAM (TWIN VALLEY), Served by St. Joseph Pastoral Administrative Office, Ada. Tel: 218-784-4131.
500 Lincoln Ave. N.W., Twin Valley, 56584.
Tel: 218-784-4131; Email: stjoseph@loretel.net; Web: nccatholicchurch.com. Mailing Address: 405 E. Thorpe Ave., Ada, 56510. Rev. William DeCrans; Deacon Nick Revier.
Catechesis Religious Program—Students 33.

TWO INLETS, BECKER CO., ST. MARY'S (TWO INLETS) (1907) [CEM]
55744 County Hwy. 44, P.O. Box 353, Park Rapids, 56470. Tel: 218-732-4046; Tel: 218-732-5142; Fax: 218-237-6919; Email: sm2inlets@arvig.net; Email: fr.tom@arvig.net; Web: www.stmarys-twoinlets-churchandgrotto.com. Mailing Address: 305 W. 5th St., P.O. Box 353, Park Rapids, 56470. Rev. Thomas Friedl. Served by St. Peter, Park Rapids.
Catechesis Religious Program—Tel: 218-732-5142; Email: annette@arvig.net. Annette Haas, D.R.E. Students 12.

WARREN, MARSHALL CO., SS. PETER AND PAUL (1909) [CEM] Rev. Emmanuel Sylvester.
Res.: 208 N. Seventh St., Warren, 56762.
Tel: 218-745-4511; Email: donnag@invisimax.com.
Catechesis Religious Program—Students 83.
Missions—St. Joseph - Oslo—P.O. Box 97, Oslo, Marshall Co. 56744.
St. Mary, Euclid, Polk Co. 56722.

WARROAD, ROSEAU CO., ST. MARY'S, [CEM]
511 Cedar Ave. N.W., Warroad, 56763.
Tel: 218-386-1178; Email: tarenda@saintmarywarroad.org; Email: stmarys@mncable.net; Web: stmaryswarroad.org. Mailing Address: P.O. Box 33, Warroad, 56763. Rev. Todd Arends.

WAUBUN, MAHNOMEN CO., ST. ANN (1912) [CEM]
1112 3rd St., Waubun, 56589-9402.
Tel: 218- 473-2101; Email: 1112sta@arvig.net; Web: whiteearthcatholiccommunity.com. Revs. John Cox, O.M.I.; Daniel Nassaney, O.M.I.
Catechesis Religious Program—Janet Lhotka, D.R.E. Students 91.
Missions—St. Anne—204 County Rd. #4, Naytahwaush, Mahnomen Co. 56566.
St. Frances Cabrini, 39719 County Hwy. 35, Big Elbow Lake, Becker Co. 56589.

WHITE EARTH, BECKER CO., ST. BENEDICT (WHITE EARTH), [CEM] Served by Most Holy Redeemer, Ogema. Tel: 218-936-3261.
106 Ontario St., Ogema, 56569-0057.
Tel: 218-983-3261; Email: owep@tvutel.com; Web: whiteearthcatholiccommunity.com. P.O. Box 57, Ogema, 56569-0057. Rev. Joseph Hitpas, O.M.I.
Catechesis Religious Program—1112 3rd St., Waubun, 56589. Tel: 218-473-2101; Email: 1112sta@arvig.net. Janet Lhotka, D.R.E. Students 21.

WILLIAMS, LAKE OF THE WOODS CO., ST. JOSEPH (WILLIAMS), Served by Sacred Heart, Baudette. Tel: 218-634-2689.
104 - 1st St., S.W., P.O. Box 738, Baudette, 56623. Tel: 218-634-2689; Email: ourlady@mncable.net; Email: jim@lukenbill.net. P.O. Box 33, Warroad, 56763. Deacon James Lukenbill, Pastoral Assoc.

WILTON, BELTRAMI CO., SACRED HEART (WILTON), Served by St. Mary's Mission, Red Lake. Tel: 218-679-3614.
Mailing Address: P.O. Box 1897, Bemidji, 56619-1897. Tel: 218-751-8446; Email: frjerry@stmarysmission.org. 135 - 3rd St., N.W., Wilton, 56619. Very Rev. Jerry Rogers.
Catechesis Religious Program—Students 30.

On Duty Outside the Diocese:
Revs.—
Bushy, Timothy F.
Silva, Luis
Vasek, Craig J.

Retired:
Most Rev.—
Balke, Victor H., D.D., (Retired), 200 3rd St. N.W., East Grand Forks, 56721. Tel: 218-289-0389
Rev. Msgrs.—
Grundhaus, Roger, J.C.L., (Retired), 620 Summit Ave., 56716. Tel: 218-281-5951
Krebs, Donald H., (Retired), 3344-38th St., S., Moorhead, 56560. Tel: 218-236-6644
Noesen, Gerald, (Retired), 620 Summit Ave., 56716. Tel: 218-281-3060
Patnode, Michael, (Retired), 1103 Bunchberry Ln. NE, Bemidji, 56601. Tel: 701-318-1395
Revs.—
Palcisko, Raymond, (Retired), P.O. Box 81, Warren, 56762. Tel: 651-276-0205
Prada, Mario, (Retired), 1409 St. John's Dr., 56716. Tel: 218-289-3355
Pribula, Duane, (Retired), 5220-12th St. S., #201C, Fargo, ND 58104. Tel: 218-790-0091
Pryor, G. Robert, (Retired), The Glenn Minnetonka, 5300 Woodhill Rd., Unit CSG, Minnetonka, 55345. Tel: 702-249-2709
Stone, Bob, (Retired), 3301 Michelson Dr., Irvine, CA 92612
Wieseler, Larry, (Retired), 15 Cassidy Hill Rd., Coventry, CT 06238-1386. Barrio Los Coscos, Calle Buenos Aires #29, Maracay, EDO, Aragua Venezuela.

Permanent Deacons:
Abel, Courtney, St. Joseph, Moorhead
Bauer, Randy, (On Duty Outside the Diocese)
Beutler, Bill, St. Joseph, Moorhead
Bivens, Dennis, St. Peter, Gentilly
Bruggeman, John A., St. Joseph's, Red Lake Falls
Cerar, Tom, St. Elizabeth, Dilworth
Eisbrenner, John, (Retired), St. Bernard, Thief River Falls
Erickson, Kermit, St. Philip, Bemidji
Erickson, Paul, St. Joseph, Moorhead
Hager, Gary, Holy Rosary, Detroit Lakes
Hannig, Daniel, Cathedral, Crookston
Jirik, Tom, St. Andrew, Hawley
Kaiser, Aaron, St. Joseph, Bagley
Krejci, Mark, St. Joseph, Moorhead
Kukert, Allen, St. Joseph, Moorhead
LeTexier, Mark, Sacred Heart, East Grand Forks
Lukenbill, James, Sacred Heart, Baudette
Muller, John, (On Duty Outside the Diocese)
Naylor, Robb, St. Philip, Bemidji
Pribula, Timothy, St. Michael, Mahnomen
Revier, Nick, St. William, Twin Valley
Roberts, Dean, St. Francis de Sales, Moorhead
Thomas, James, Holy Rosary, Detroit Lakes
Thomas, Steve, Sacred Heart, East Grand Forks
Vande Kamp, James, (On Duty Outside the Diocese)
Zinniel, John, St. Peter's, Park Rapids.

INSTITUTIONS LOCATED IN DIOCESE

[A] GENERAL HOSPITALS

BAUDETTE. *CHI LakeWood Health*, 600 Main Ave. S., Baudette, 56623. Tel: 218-634-2120; Fax: 218-634-3487; Email: christinadraper@catholichealth.net; Web: www.lakewoodhealthcenter.org. Jeffry Stampohar, Pres. Affiliate of Catholic Health Initiatives. Bed Capacity 36; Patients Asst Anual. 20,613; Total Apartments 10; Bed Capacity: Acute 15; Long Term Care 47; Staff 141.
CHI Lakewood Health Care Center, 600 Main Ave. S., Baudette, 56623. Tel: 218-634-2120; Fax: 218-634-3416; Email: benkoppelman@catholichealth.net; Web: www.lakewoodhealthcenter.org. Mr. Ben Koppelman, Admin. Affiliate of Catholic Health Initiatives. Bed Capacity 36; Tot Asst. Annually 22,835; Total Staff 165; Residents Assisted Annually 47.

DETROIT LAKES. **Essentia Health St. Mary's*, 1027 Washington Ave., Detroit Lakes, 56501. Tel: 218-847-5611; Email: linda.wainright@essentiahealth.org; Web: www.essentiahealth.org. Peter Jacobson, Pres.; Tim Cook, Chap.; Linda Wainright, Chap. Bed Capacity 87; Total Staff 850.

PARK RAPIDS. *St. Joseph Area Health Services*, 600 Pleasant Ave., Park Rapids, 56470. Tel: 218-732-3311; Fax: 218-732-1368; Email: benkoppelman@catholichealth.net; Web: chisjh.org. Mr. Ben Koppelman, Pres. & CEO. Affiliate of Catholic Health Initiatives. Bed Capacity 25; Tot Asst. Annually 48,060; Total Staff 299.

[B] HOMES FOR THE AGED

CROOKSTON. *Villa St. Vincent*, 516 Walsh St., 56716. Tel: 218-281-3424; Fax: 218-281-4755; Email: judy.hulst@bhshealth.org. Ms. Judith Hulst, Admin. Residents 170; Skilled Nursing Beds 80; Assisted Living Apts. 71; Alzheimer's Beds 24; Staff 240.

ADA. *Bridges Care Center* dba Benedictine Living Community of Ada Subs. of Benedictine Health System. 201 9th St. W., Ste. 2, Ada, 56510. Tel: 218-784-5500; Fax: 218-784-5245; Email: jean.bienek@bhshealth.org. Jean Bienek, Admin. Sponsored by the Benedictine Sisters Benevolent Association, Duluth. Residents 73; Skilled Nursing Beds 49; Staff 91.

DETROIT LAKES. *St. Mary's Nursing Center*, 1027 Washington Ave., Detroit Lakes, 56501.

Tel: 218-844-0776; Fax: 218-544-0780; Email: tthompson@trustedcareforlife.com. Christy Brinkman, Admin., Sr. Housing. Attended by Staff of St. Mary's Regional Health Center. Transitional Care 23; Long Term Care 73; Assisted Living 30; Independent Living 58.

[C] CONVENTS AND RESIDENCES FOR SISTERS

CROOKSTON. *Mount St. Benedict Monastery*, 620 Summit Ave. E., 56716-2799. Tel: 218-281-3441; Fax: 218-281-6966; Email: crxbenedictines@gmail.com; Web: www.msb.net. Sisters Shawn Carruth, O.S.B., Prioress; Kathleen McGeary, O.S.B., Subprioress. Motherhouse of the Order of the Sisters of St. Benedict of Pontifical Jurisdiction-The Federation of St. Gertrude. Sisters in Community 45; Total in Community 45.

Sunrise Center for Children and Families, Tel: 218-281-6540; Email: sunrisecenterforchildren@gmail.com. Susan Murphy, Admin.; Sr. Kathy Kuchar, O.S.B., Trustee. Students 49.

[D] NEWMAN CENTERS

CROOKSTON. *Newman Outreach*, 702 Summit Ave., 56716. Tel: 218-281-1735; Email: hbach.cathedral@midconetwork.com. Hope Bach, Dir.

BEMIDJI. *Holy Spirit Newman Center*, 702 Beltrami Ave., N.W., Bemidji, 56601-2607. Tel: 218-444-4262; Email: ncenter@paulbunyan.net; Email: chuck@stphilipsbemidji.org; Web: www.newmancenterbsu.org. Rev. Bryan Kujawa, Parochial Vicar.

MOORHEAD. *St. Thomas Aquinas Newman Center*, 218 S. 10th St., Moorhead, 56560. Tel: 218-236-5066; Email: nate.brunn@stjoesmhd.com. Rev. Nate Brunn, Parochial Vicar.

[E] MISCELLANEOUS

CROOKSTON. **The Diocese of Crookston Catholic Community Foundation*, 1200 Memorial Dr., 56716. Tel: 218-281-4533; Fax: 218-281-3328; Email: ccf@crookston.org; Web: www.crookston.org/ccf. Very Rev. Msgr. Michael H. Foltz, V.G., J.C.L., Vicar.

**Mount Saint Benedict Foundation*, 620 Summit Ave., 56716-2799. Tel: 218-281-3441; Fax: 218-281-6966; Email: crxbenedictines@gmail.com. Sr. Jennifer Kehrwald, O.S.B., Dir.

RELIGIOUS INSTITUTES OF MEN REPRESENTED IN THE DIOCESE

For further details refer to the corresponding bracketed number in the Religious Institutes of Men or Women section.

[0910]—*Oblates of Mary Immaculate*—O.M.I.

RELIGIOUS INSTITUTES OF WOMEN REPRESENTED IN THE DIOCESE

[0230]—*Benedictine Sisters of Pontifical Jurisdiction* (Congregation of St. Gertrude)—O.S.B.

[0230]—*Benedictine Sisters of Pontifical Jurisdiction (Federation of St. Benedict)*—O.S.B.

[3832]—*Congregation of the Sisters of St. Joseph*—C.S.J.

[]—*Congregation of the Sisters of the Third Order of St. Francis*—O.S.F.

[]—*Franciscan Sisters*—O.S.F.

[2450]—*Sisters of Mary of the Presentation* (Valley City, ND)—S.M.P.

[]—*Sisters of St. Joseph of Concordia* (KS)—C.S.J.

An asterisk (*) denotes an organization that has established tax-exempt status directly with the IRS and is not covered by the USCCB Group Ruling.

Diocese of Dallas

(Dioecesis Dallasensis)

Most Reverend

EDWARD J. BURNS

Bishop of Dallas; ordained June 25, 1983; appointed Bishop of Juneau January 19, 2009; ordained March 3, 2009; installed April 2, 2009; appointed Bishop of Dallas December 13, 2016; installed February 9, 2017.

Most Reverend

J. GREGORY KELLY

Auxiliary Bishop of Dallas; ordained May 15, 1982; appointed Auxiliary Bishop of Dallas and Titular Bishop of Jamestown December 16, 2015; installed February 11, 2016.

Diocesan Pastoral Center: 3725 Blackburn, P.O. Box 190507, Dallas, TX 75219. Tel: 214-528-2240; Fax: 214-526-1743.

Web: www.cathdal.org

ESTABLISHED DIOCESE OF DALLAS ON JULY 15, 1890.

Square Miles 7,523.

Redesignated Diocese of Dallas-Fort Worth on October 20, 1953.

Redesignated Diocese of Dallas on August 27, 1969.

Comprises the following nine Counties in the State of Texas: Collin, Dallas, Ellis, Fannin, Grayson, Hunt, Kaufman, Navarro and Rockwall.

Legal Corporate Title: Roman Catholic Diocese of Dallas.

For legal titles of parishes and diocesan institutions, consult the Diocesan Pastoral Center.

STATISTICAL OVERVIEW

Personnel	
Bishop	1
Auxiliary Bishops	1
Abbots	1
Retired Abbots	1
Priests: Diocesan Active in Diocese	76
Priests: Diocesan Active Outside Diocese	6
Priests: Retired, Sick or Absent	29
Number of Diocesan Priests	111
Religious Priests in Diocese	79
Total Priests in Diocese	190
Extern Priests in Diocese	31
Ordinations:	
Diocesan Priests	5
Religious Priests	2
Permanent Deacons	24
Permanent Deacons in Diocese	170
Total Brothers	10
Total Sisters	95
Parishes	
Parishes	69
With Resident Pastor:	
Resident Diocesan Priests	47
Resident Religious Priests	13
Without Resident Pastor:	
Administered by Priests	8
Administered by Deacons	1
Missions	5
Pastoral Centers	3
Professional Ministry Personnel:	
Brothers	6
Sisters	11
Lay Ministers	529
Welfare	
Homes for the Aged	3
Total Assisted	332
Special Centers for Social Services	12
Total Assisted	27,840
Educational	
Seminaries, Diocesan	2
Students from This Diocese	44
Students from Other Diocese	50
Diocesan Students in Other Seminaries	28
Seminaries, Religious	1
Students Religious	4
Total Seminarians	76
Colleges and Universities	1
Total Students	2,542
High Schools, Diocesan and Parish	3
Total Students	2,253
High Schools, Private	5
Total Students	2,935
Elementary Schools, Diocesan and Parish	26
Total Students	8,832
Elementary Schools, Private	2
Total Students	316
Non-residential Schools for the Disabled	1
Total Students	146
Catechesis/Religious Education:	
High School Students	6,610
Elementary Students	37,455
Total Students under Catholic Instruction	61,165
Teachers in the Diocese:	
Priests	15
Scholastics	2
Sisters	12
Lay Teachers	1,452
Vital Statistics	
Receptions into the Church:	
Infant Baptism Totals	12,150
Adult Baptism Totals	860
Received into Full Communion	457
First Communions	11,529
Confirmations	10,839
Marriages:	
Catholic	1,576
Interfaith	331
Total Marriages	1,907
Deaths	1,630
Total Catholic Population	1,226,031
Total Population	4,054,985

Former Bishops—Rt. Revs. THOMAS F. BRENNAN, D.D., cons. April 5, 1891; resigned Nov. 17, 1892; died March 21, 1916; EDWARD JOSEPH DUNNE, D.D., cons. Nov. 30. 1893; died Aug. 5, 1910; Most Revs. JOSEPH PATRICK LYNCH, D.D., LL.D., appt. June 8, 1911; cons. July 12, 1911; Assistant at Pontifical Throne, May 13, 1936; died Aug. 19, 1954; THOMAS K. GORMAN, D.D., D.Sc.Hist., ord. June 23, 1917; Bishop of Reno; appt. April 24, 1931; cons. July 22, 1931; Assistant at the Pontifical Throne, May 4, 1942; appt. Titular Bishop of Rhasus and Coadjutor to the Bishop of Dallas, Feb. 8, 1952; succeeded to Aug. 19, 1954; resigned and appointed Titular Bishop of Pinhel, Aug. 27, 1969. (Title rescinded); died Aug. 16, 1980; THOMAS TSCHOEPE, D.D., ord. May 30, 1943; appt. Bishop of San Angelo, Jan. 12, 1966; cons. March 9, 1966; appt. Bishop of Dallas, Aug. 27, 1969; installed Oct. 29, 1969; retired July 14, 1990; died Jan. 24, 2009; CHARLES V. GRAHMANN, ord. March 17, 1956; appt. Titular Bishop of Equilio and Auxiliary of San Antonio June 30, 1981; cons. Aug. 29, 1981; appt. First Bishop of Victoria April 14, 1982; installed May 29, 1982; appt. Coadjutor of Dallas Dec. 18, 1989; Reception as Coadjutor of Dallas Feb. 21, 1990; appt. Bishop of Dallas July 14, 1990; retired March 6, 2007; died Aug. 14, 2018.; KEVIN J. FARRELL, (Retired), ord. Dec. 24, 1978; appt. Auxiliary Bishop of Washington and Titular Bishop of Rusuccuru Dec. 28, 2001; ord. Feb. 11, 2002; appt. Bishop of Dallas March 6, 2007; installed May 1, 2007; appt. Prefect of Vatican Dicastery for the Laity, Family, and Life Aug. 17, 2016.

Vicar General—Most Rev. J. GREGORY KELLY, V.G.

Diocesan Pastoral Center—3725 Blackburn St., P.O. Box 190507, Dallas, 75219. Tel: 214-528-2240; Fax: 214-526-1743. Office Hours: 9-5.

Vicar for Clergy—Most Rev. J. GREGORY KELLY, V.G.

Interim Chancellor and Delegate for Canonical and Civil Law—Most Rev. J. GREGORY KELLY, V.G., Fax: 214-526-1743.

Diocesan Tribunal—Mailing Address: P.O. Box 190507, Dallas, 75219. Tel: 214-379-2840; Fax: 214-523-2437.

Judicial Vicar—Rev. Msgr. JOHN P. BELL, J.C.L.

Director of the Tribunal—WILLIAM C. HARE III, J.C.L.

Assessor—MARGARET GILLETT.

Defensor Vinculi—JOHN P. GARGAN, J.C.D., J.D.; DANIELA KNEPPER, J.C.L.; Very Rev. DONALD ZEILER, V.F., M.Div., M.A.; CHRISTINA HIP-FLORES, M.P.P.; KELLY E. O'DONNELL, J.C.D.

Adjutant Judicial Vicar—Very Rev. JOHN LIBONE, V.F., J.C.L.

Auditors—CAROL CROCHET PHILLIPS; NORA D. SMITH; MARY MARGARET HERNANDEZ.

Notaries—DALILA CRUZ; MARIA LONGORIA CHAVEZ; DIANA E. GARCIA; ELVIA RAMIREZ.

Diocesan Judges—WILLIAM C. HARE III, J.C.L.; LYNDA ROBITAILLE, J.C.D.; DIANE L. BARR, J.C.D., J.D.; Sr. VIRGINIA LOUISE BARTOLAC, S.C.L., J.C.D.; Rev. Msgrs. MARK A. PLEWKA, J.C.L.; MILAM JOSEPH, M.A., (Retired); ANNE KIRBY, J.C.L.; Rev. PAUL HAI NGUYEN, C.Ss.R., J.C.L.

Procurator-Advocates—SUSAN C. BOYD; JUDY CLARK; THERESA ETCHEVERRY; JEANNE MARIE GIRSCH; SANDRA WARNE GIST; Sr. MARY PAUL HAASE, C.S.F.N.; CECILIA LYNNE JONES; Deacon JOHN PAUL KELLY; BARBARA LANDREGAN; DONALD LENZ; PRISCILLA MAHAFFEY; MARGIE MEDLIN; Rev. JOSEPH A. MEHAN JR.; LINDA MOSES; DENISE G. PHILLIPS; Deacon KENNETH REISOR; MARY ROBINSON; Deacon CARL H. THELIN; GERALD F. PERRYMAN JR.; Rev. TIMOTHY A. GOLLOB.

Pastors Consultors—Most Rev. J. GREGORY KELLY, V.G.; Rev. Msgr. HENRY V. PETTER.

College of Consultors—Most Rev. J. GREGORY KELLY, V.G., Ex Officio; Rev. Msgr. HENRY V. PETTER; Very Rev. JASON CARGO, V.F.; Revs. MICHAEL D. FORGE; FRAY LUIS G. ARRAIZA, O.F.M.Cap.; Very Rev. JOHN LIBONE, V.F., J.C.L.; Revs. JOSHUA WHITFIELD; ALAN PAUL MCDONALD; JESUS BELMONTES; MICHAEL GUADAGNOLI; STEPHEN W. BIERSCHENK; Very Rev. J. EDUARDO GONZALEZ, V.F.

Presbyteral Council—Rev. Msgr. HENRY V. PETTER; Revs. JOSHUA WHITFIELD; ALAN PAUL MCDONALD; ANTHONY F. LACKLAND; JESUS BELMONTES; ROBERT WILLIAMS.

Deans—Very Revs. JAMES YAMAUCHI, V.F., Eastern Deanery; RUSSELL MOWER, V.F., Southwest Deanery; WILMER DE JESUS DAZA, V.F., Southeast Deanery; THOMAS CLOHERTY, V.F., Northern Deanery; JOHN LIBONE, V.F., J.C.L., Central Deanery; J. EDUARDO GONZALEZ, V.F., Northeast Deanery; JASON CARGO, V.F., North Central.

At-Large Members—Revs. MARTIN MORENO; ANDREW V. SEMLER; ARTHUR UNACHUKWU; MICHAEL D. FORGE; MICHAEL GUADAGNOLI; STEPHEN W. BIERSCHENK.

Ex Officio Member—Most Rev. J. GREGORY KELLY, V.G.

Censor Librorum—VACANT.

Diocesan Boards

Finance Council—Most Revs. J. GREGORY KELLY, V.G.; EDWARD J. BURNS, D.D.; WILLIAM KEFFLER, COO; CECILIA COLBERT, CFO; FRANK HUBACH; HARRY J. LONGWELL; JAMES MORONEY III; KATHY MULDOON; LYDIA NOVAKOV; JACK PRATT; ED SCHAFFLER; DENIS SIMON.

Building Commission—Rev. Msgr. JEROME P. DUESMAN, (Retired); LUIS CARRERA; WILLIAM KEFFLER, COO; MARK HIGHTOWER; CECILIA COLBERT, CFO; MATT SISCO.

Personnel Board—Most Revs. EDWARD J. BURNS, D.D.; J. GREGORY KELLY, V.G.; Very Rev. THOMAS CLOHERTY, V.F.; Rev. STEPHEN W. BIERSCHENK; Rev. Msgr. HENRY V. PETTER; Rev. MICHAEL GUADAGNOLI.

Diocesan Offices and Directors

Judicial Vicar—Rev. Msgr. JOHN P. BELL, J.C.L.

Tribunal—

Vicar General/Moderator of the Curia—Most Rev. J. GREGORY KELLY, V.G.

Liaison for Statistical Data—RITA V. GRACIA, M.T.S.

Chief Operating Officer—WILLIAM KEFFLER, COO.

I. Vicar for Clergy—Most Rev. J. GREGORY KELLY, V.G.

Priest Personnel—Most Rev. J. GREGORY KELLY, V.G., P.O. Box 190507, Dallas, 75219. Tel: 214-379-2848.

Vocations—Rev. EDWIN LEONARD IV, Dir.

Diaconate—Deacons JOHN O'LEARY, Dir., Diaconal Ministry & Formation; MICHAEL PICARD, Formation Dir. (English); LEOPOLDO CORTINAS III, Formation Dir. (Spanish), P.O. Box 190507, Dallas, 75219. Tel: 214-379-2859.

II. Catholic Schools Office—Mailing Address: P.O. Box 190507, Dallas, 75219. Tel: 214-379-2831. DR. MATTHEW VEREECKE, Supt. Associate Superintendents: Sr. DAWN ACHS, S.S.N.D.; DR. VERONICA ALONZO.

III. Director of Ministries—Sr. THERESA KHIRALLAH, S.S.N.D., Mailing Address: P.O. Box 190507, Dallas, 75219. Tel: 214-379-2897.

Catechetical Services—CHERYL WHAPHAM, M.T.S., Dir., Mailing Address: P.O. Box 190507, Dallas, 75219. Tel: 214-379-2848.

Youth and Young Adult and Campus Ministry Office—JASON DEUTERMAN, M.T.S., Dir., Mailing Address: P.O. Box 190507, Dallas, 75219. Tel: 214-379-2843.

Pastoral Services—Deacon CHARLES STUMP JR., M.S., M.P.M., Dir., Tel: 214-379-2882.

Substance Addictions Ministry—CLAUDIO MORA, Dir., Tel: 214-379-2877.

Ministries to People with Disabilities and Their Caregivers and to the Deaf—MELISSA WALDON, M.S., Coord. & Catechesis, Tel: 214-379-2895.

Hospital Ministry—Deacon CHARLES STUMP JR., M.S., M.P.M., Dir., Tel: 214-379-2882.

Prison Ministry—Deacon JOSE TREVINO, Coord., Tel: 214-379-2883.

Liturgy Office—DR. PATRICIA HUGHES, Dir. Worship, Tel: 214-379-2860.

Family Life Ministry—CLAUDIO MORA, Dir.

IV. Chief Financial Officer—CECILIA COLBERT.

Business Office—Tel: 214-379-2807. BARRY HANNER, Dir. Financial Svcs.; JAMES PICHA, Controller.

Retreat/Conference Center—Catholic Conference and Formation Center BERTHA ESCARZAGA, Dir., 901 S. Madison Ave., Dallas, 75208. Mailing Address: P.O. Box 190507, Dallas, 75219. Tel: 214-943-6585.

V. Director of Construction and Real Estate—MARK HIGHTOWER.

Office of Purchasing and Contracts—CINDY HERNDON, Dir.

VI. Director of Human Resources—JAY SALEM.

VII. Diocesan Risk Management—JOHN A. SMITH, Dir.

VIII. IT/Network Administrator—DEBRA HUTCHINGS, Dir.

IX. Director of Parish & School Financial Reporting—FRED VILLELA.

X. Director of Catholic Charities—DAVE WOODYARD, Pres. & CEO, Tel: 214-520-6590.

XI. Director of Communications—ANNETTE GONZALES TAYLOR, Dir., Mailing Address: P.O. Box 190507, Dallas, 75219. Tel: 214-379-2873; CYNTHIA GILL BATES, New Media Specialist, Tel: 214-379-2889.

The Texas Catholic and La Revista Catolica—Official Catholic Publications of the Diocese of Dallas Tel: 214-528-8792; Fax: 214-528-3411; Web: www.texascatholic.com. Most Rev. EDWARD J. BURNS, D.D., Publisher; DAVID SEDENO, Editor; CONSTANZA MORALES, Mng. Editor La Revista Catolica; LAURIE CLUCK, Sales Account Exec., Tel: 214-379-2891; Fax: 214-528-3411.

XII. Director of Development—JIM URBANUS, Dir.

Interim Chancellor—Mailing Address: P.O. Box 190507, Dallas, 75219. Most Rev. J. GREGORY KELLY, V.G.

Archives—JOYCE HIGGINS, Archivist.

Safe Environment Office—BARBARA LANDREGAN, Dir., Mailing Address: P.O. Box 190507, Dallas, 75219. Tel: 214-379-2812.

Victim Assistance Coordinator—BARBARA LANDREGAN.

CLERGY, PARISHES, MISSIONS AND PAROCHIAL SCHOOLS

CITY OF DALLAS

(DALLAS COUNTY)

1—CATHEDRAL SANTUARIO DE GUADALUPE (1869)
2215 Ross Ave., 75201. Tel: 214-871-1362; Email: info@cathedralguadalupe.org; Web: www.cathedralguadalupe.org. Revs. Oscar Mora, Parochial Vicar; Stephen W. Bierschenk, Rector; Deacons Roberto Alvarez; Chris Volkmer; Benito Garcia; Charles Stump Jr.; Hector Rodriguez.
Catechesis Religious Program—Imelda Ramirez, D.R.E. Students 932.

2—ALL SAINTS CATHOLIC PARISH (1976)
5231 Meadowcreek, 75248. Tel: 972-661-9282; Fax: 972-233-5401; Email: sholmes@allsaintsdallas.org; Web: www.allsaintsdallas.org. Revs. Alfonse Nazzaro; Jovita Okoli; Paul Nguyen; Deacons Denis Simon; Robert Rayner; Michael Bolesta.
School—All Saints Catholic School, (Grades PreK-8), 7777 Osage Plaza Pkwy., 75252. Tel: 214-217-3300; Web: www.allsaintsk8.org. Shana Druffner, Prin.; Gabriel Moreno, Dir. Advancement & Mission; Kristen Theisen, Librarian. Lay Teachers 25; Students 290.
Catechesis Religious Program—Students 723.

3—ST. ANDREW KIM CATHOLIC PARISH (1977) (Korean)
2111 Camino Lago, Irving, 75039. Tel: 972-620-9150; Fax: 972-484-4628; Email: office@dallaskoreancatholic.org; Web: www.dallaskoreancatholic.org. Rev. Dominic Kim, Pastoral Admin.; Deacon John Lee.
Catechesis Religious Program—John S. Lee, D.R.E. Sisters 2; Students 178.

4—ST. ANTHONY CATHOLIC PARISH - DALLAS (1938) (African American)
3788 Myrtle Street, 75215. Deacon Denis D. Corbin, Pastoral Admin.
Res.: 2711 Romine St., 75215. Tel: 214-428-6926; Email: deacondeniscorbin@sbcglobal.net.
Catechesis Religious Program—Students 16.

5—ST. AUGUSTINE CATHOLIC PARISH (1937)
1054 N. St. Augustine Dr., 75217. Tel: 214-398-1583; Fax: 214-398-2580; Email: churchoffice@stadallas.com; Web: staugustinedallas.org. Rev. Luca Simbula, Admin.; Deacons Jorge Castillo; Rosendo Gloria.
Res.: 1047 N. St. Augustine Dr., 75217.
Tel: 214-391-1513.
Catechesis Religious Program—Arabelia Martinez, P.C.L. Students 750.

6—ST. BERNARD OF CLAIRVAUX CATHOLIC PARISH (1947) (Hispanic)
1404 Old Gate Ln., 75218. Tel: 214-321-0454; Fax: 214-320-0119; Email: NZuniga@sbdallas.org; Web: www.stbernards.us. 1423 San Saba Dr., 75218. Revs. Gaston Giacinti, I.V.E.; Delfin Condori, I.V.E.
School—St. Bernard of Clairvaux Catholic School, (Grades PreK-8), 1420 Old Gate Ln., 75218. Tel: 214-321-2897; Fax: 214-321-4060; Email: mdavies@stbernardccs.org. Michael Davies, Prin.; Sally Walsh, Librarian. Clergy / Religious Teachers 2; Lay Teachers 22; Students 190.
Catechesis Religious Program—Elizabeth Torres, D.R.E. Students 953.

7—BLESSED SACRAMENT CATHOLIC PARISH (1901)
231 N. Marsalis Ave., 75203. Tel: 214-948-6535; Fax: 214-948-1660; Email: lmartinez@bsdallas.org. Revs. Jimwell Goyo; Agustin Fuertes; Deacons Jose L. Hernandez; Randy Nease.
Catechesis Religious Program—Students 493.

8—ST. CECILIA CATHOLIC PARISH (1933) (Hispanic)
1845 W. Davis St., 75208. Tel: 214-941-5821; Fax: 214-272-9950; Email: info@stceciliadallas.org; Web: stceciliadallas.org. Mailing Address: 1809 W. Davis St., 75208. Revs. Martin Moreno; Daniel Rendon; Deacons Gonzalo Gonzales; Gerardo Porras.
School—St. Cecilia Catholic School, (Grades PreK-8), 635 Marycliff Rd., 75208. Tel: 214-948-8628; Fax: 214-948-4956; Email: info@stceciliadallas.org. Guadalupe Moreno, Librarian. Lay Teachers 19; Sisters of St. Mary of Namur 1; Students 236.
Catechesis Religious Program—Students 701.

9—CHRIST THE KING CATHOLIC PARISH (1941)
8017 Preston Rd., 75225. Tel: 214-365-1200; Fax: 214-365-1205; Email: parishmail@ctkdallas.org; Web: www.ctkdallas.org. Rev. Msgr. Donald F. Zimmerman; Rev. Arthur Unachukwu, In Res.; William C. Hare III, J.C.L., Pastoral Assoc.
School—Christ the King Catholic School, (Grades PreK-8), 4100 Colgate St., 75225. Tel: 214-365-1234; Fax: 214-365-1236; Email: ereiman@cksdallas.org. Lay Teachers 47; Students 420; Religious Teachers 2.
Catechesis Religious Program—Students 614.

10—ST. EDWARD CATHOLIC PARISH (1903)
4001 Elm St., 75226. Tel: 214-823-1291; Fax: 214-823-7535; Email: faguilar@stedwardparish.rog; Web: www.stedwardparish.org. Mailing Address: 4014 Simpson St., 75246. Revs. Edison Vela; Robert Brawanski, Parochial Vicar.
Res.: 4007 Elm St., 75226.
Catechesis Religious Program—Tel: 214-887-1484; Email: rlopez@stedwardparish.org. Rita Lopez, D.R.E. Students 1,013.

11—ST. ELIZABETH OF HUNGARY CATHOLIC PARISH (1956)
4015 S. Hampton Rd., 75224. Tel: 214-331-4328; Fax: 214-331-2464; Email: ghudgins@stelizabethdallas.org. Very Rev. Russell Mower, V.F.; Rev. Emmett Hall; Deacons Frank Kozarevich; Douglas Boyd.
School—St. Elizabeth of Hungary Catholic School, (Grades PreK-8), 4019 S. Hampton Rd., 75224. Tel: 214-331-5139; Fax: 214-467-4346; Email: stelizabethpastor@gmail.com; Web: saintspride.com. Rachel Robb, Prin.; Monica Connelly, Librarian. Lay Teachers 20; Students 220.
Catechesis Religious Program—Elizabeth Seidemann, P.C.L. Students 238.

12—HOLY CROSS CATHOLIC PARISH (1956)
4910 Bonnie View Rd., 75241. Tel: 214-374-7952; Fax: 214-375-7457; Email: office.holycrosscc@gmail.com; Email: tgollob25@gmail.com; Web: www.holycrosscatholicdallas.org. Mailing Address: 2926 E. Ledbetter Dr., 75216. Rev. Timothy A. Gollob; Deacons Salvador Pina; Charles Osborne.
Catechesis Religious Program—Email: dre.holycross@sbcglobal.net. Paula Martinez, D.R.E. Students 4.

13—HOLY TRINITY CATHOLIC PARISH (1907)
3811 Oak Lawn Ave, 75219. Tel: 214-526-8555; Email: general@htccd.org; Web: www.htccd.org. 3826 Gilbert Ave., 75219. Revs. Milton Ryan; Michael Walsh, C.M.; Deacon Roberto Loera.
School—Holy Trinity Catholic School, (Grades PreK-8), 3815 Oak Lawn Ave., 75219. Tel: 214-526-5113; Email: mdavis@htcsdallas.org; Web: www.htcsdallas.org. Marion Davis, Prin.; Nina Little, Librarian. Lay Teachers 18; Students 130; Lay Ministers 4; Religious Teachers 1.
Catechesis Religious Program—Email: elizabethd@htccd.org. Elizabeth Delgado, D.R.E. Students 213.

14—ST. JAMES CATHOLIC CHURCH (1934)
1002 E. Saner Ave., 75376. Tel: 214-371-9209; Email: secretary@stjamescath.org. Mailing Address: P.O. Box 763338, 75376. Revs. Lauro Gonzalez, M.N.M.; Mauricio Sosa, M.N.M.; Deacons Vincent F. Jimenez; Filemon Villegas.
Catechesis Religious Program—Email: faithformation@stjamescath.org. Juan Calixto, D.R.E. Students 936.

15—ST. JUDE CHAPEL (Downtown Dallas) (1968)
1521 Main St., 75201. Tel: 214-353-0517; Email: stjude@sbcglobal.net. Rev. Jonathan Austin.

16—MARY IMMACULATE CATHOLIC PARISH (1956)
2800 Valwood Pkwy., 75234. Tel: 972-243-7104; Fax: 972-406-1254; Email: aliciag@maryimmaculatechurch.org; Web: www.maryimmaculatechurch.org. Revs. Michael D. Forge; Guiseppe Spoto, Parochial Vicar; Deacons Dennis Duffin; Michael Weston; Fidel Alvarez.
School—Mary Immaculate Catholic School, (Grades K-8), 14032 Dennis Ln., 75234. Tel: 972-243-7105; Fax: 972-241-7678; Email: mkrause@mischool.org. Matthew Krause, Prin. Lay Teachers 20; Students 485.
Catechesis Religious Program—Email: carolinew@maryimmaculatechurch.org. Caroline Wilks, P.C.L. Students 1,501.

17—ST. MARY OF CARMEL CATHOLIC PARISH (1944)
2900 Vilbig Rd., 75212. Tel: 214-747-1433; Email: secsmc@gmail.com; Web: smcparishdallas.org. Revs. Jenaro de la Cruz, O.C.D.; James A. Curiel, O.C.D., Parochial Vicar.
School—St. Mary of Carmel School, (Grades PreK-8), 1716 Singleton Blvd., 75212. Tel: 214-748-2934; Fax: 214-760-9052; Email: rita.deleon@smcschool.org; Web: smcschool.org. Kaetlyn Aguilar, Prin. Lay Teachers 15; Students 176.
Catechesis Religious Program—Students 257.

18—ST. MONICA CATHOLIC PARISH (1954)
9933 Midway Rd., 75220. Tel: 214-358-1453; Fax: 214-351-1887; Email: ddiaz@stmonicachurch.org. Rev. Michael Guadagnoli; Rev. Msgr. John F. Meyers, Pastor Emeritus, (Retired); Rev. Wade Bass, Parochial Vicar; Deacons Bob Marrinan; Brian Mitchell; Abel Cortes; Peter Raad.
School—St. Monica Catholic School, (Grades PreK-8), 4140 Walnut Hill Ln., 75229. Tel: 214-351-5688; Email: ddiaz@stmonicachurch.org. Philip Riley, Prin. Lay Teachers 57; Students 808; Religious Teachers 2.
Catechesis Religious Program—Marianela Byrne, Dir. Faith Formation. Students 699.

19—NUESTRA SENORA DEL PILAR (2001) (Hispanic)
4455 W. Illinois Ave., 75211. Tel: 214-467-9116; Fax: 214-339-7249; Email: pilarchurch@gmail.com; Web: www.nuestrasenoradelpilar.com. Very Rev. Wilmer de Jesus Daza, V.F. In Res.
Catechesis Religious Program—Students 995.

20—OUR LADY OF LOURDES CATHOLIC PARISH (1954)
5605 Bernal Dr., 75212. Tel: 214-637-6673; Fax: 214-637-2454; Email: lourdesdallas@tx.rr.com; Web: www.lourdesdallas.org. Rev. Fray Luis G. Arraiza, O.F.M.Cap.; Deacon Pete Nanez.
Catechesis Religious Program—Tel: 214-678-0487. Olivia Cruz, P.C.L. Students 684.

21—OUR LADY OF PERPETUAL HELP CATHOLIC PARISH (1942) (Hispanic)
7617 Cortland Ave., 75235. Tel: 214-352-6012; Fax: 214-351-9883; Email: olph@olphdallas.org; Web: www.olphdallas.org. Rev. Msgr. Milam Joseph, M.A., Pastor Emeritus, (Retired); Revs. Inigo Lopez, Admin.; Rafael M. Ramirez, S.S.D., In Res.; Deacon Gerardo Garza.
School—Our Lady of Perpetual Help Catholic School, (Grades PreK-8), 7625 Cortland Ave., 75235. Tel: 214-351-3396; Fax: 214-351-9889; Email: info@olphdallas.org. Sr. Moly Kurien, D.S.H., Librarian. Lay Teachers 11; Students 197; Religious Teachers 4.
Catechesis Religious Program—Students 579.
Convent—Daughters of the Sacred Heart, Sisters 5.

22—OUR LADY OF SAN JUAN DE LOS LAGOS - ST. THERESA CATHOLIC PARISH (1928)
2601 Singleton Blvd., 75212. Tel: 214-631-9627; Fax: 214-631-9627; Email: HSalinas78132@hotmail.com; Web: www.OLSanJuanDallas.org. Deacon Hugo A. Salinas
Legal Name: Quasi-Parish of Our Lady of San Juan De Los Lagos - St. Theresa
Catechesis Religious Program—Tel: 214-688-0942; Email: Susanna.Ramirez@gpisd.org. Susanna Ramirez, D.R.E. Students 200.

23—ST. PATRICK CATHOLIC PARISH - DALLAS (1963)
9643 Ferndale Rd., 75238. Tel: 214-348-7380; Fax: 214-340-5956; Email: office@stpatrickdallas.org; Web: www.stpatrickdallas.org. Revs. Josef Vollmer-Konig; Tuan Le; Ignacio Olvera; Deacons David Banowsky; Doug Breckenridge.
School—St. Patrick Catholic School, (Grades PreK-8), 9635 Ferndale Rd., 75238. Tel: 214-348-8070; Fax: 214-503-7230; Web: www.stpatrickschool.org; Email: jhendry@spsdallas.org. Julie Hendry, Prin. Lay Teachers 38; Students 489.
Catechesis Religious Program—Mrs. Martha Noel, P.C.L. Students 559.

24—ST. PETER THE APOSTLE CATHOLIC PARISH (1905)
2907 Woodall Rodgers Fwy., 75204. Tel: 214-855-1384; Fax: 214-855-1309; Email: saintpeter@stpeterdal.com; Web: www.stpeterdal.com. Rev. Jacek Nowak, S.Ch.
Catechesis Religious Program—Marcella Savala-Hamilton, P.C.L. Students 110.

25—ST. PETER VIETNAMESE CATHOLIC PARISH (1996)
10123 Garland Rd., 75218. Tel: 214-321-9493. Rev. Pham M. Joseph, C.M.
Catechesis Religious Program—Students 95.

26—ST. PHILIP THE APOSTLE CATHOLIC PARISH (1954)
8131 Military Pkwy., 75227. Tel: 214-388-5464; Fax: 214-388-2839; Web: www.stphilipcatholicchurch.org. Very Rev. J. Eduardo Gonzalez, V.F.; Deacons Marco Antonio Cruz; Roy Mellon Jr.
School—St. Philip & St. Augustine Catholic Academy, (Grades PreK-8), 8151 Military Pkwy., 75227. Tel: 214-381-4973; Fax: 214-381-0466; Email: eromero@stsacatholic.org. Erica Romero, Prin.; Ashley Curts, Librarian. Lay Teachers 26; Students 334.
Catechesis Religious Program—Email: clazo@stphilipcatholicchurch.org. Sr. Carmen Lazo, S.S.N.D., P.C.L. Students 449.

27—ST. PIUS X CATHOLIC PARISH (1954)
3030 Gus Thomasson Rd., 75228. Tel: 972-279-6155; Fax: 972-686-7510; Email: cpierotti@spxdallas.org; Web: www.spxdallas.org. Revs. Salvador Guzman; Ramiro Alvarez, Parochial Vicar; Patrick Olaleye; Deacons John A. Schell; Victor Carpio.
School—St. Pius X Catholic School, (Grades PreK-8), Tel: 972-279-2339; Email: tscott@spxdallas.org. Tana Scott, Prin. Lay Teachers 28; Students 327.
Catechesis Religious Program—Students 796.

28—ST. RITA CATHOLIC PARISH (1961)
12521 Inwood Rd., 75244. Tel: 972-934-8388; Fax: 972-934-8965; Email: dcorbin@stritaparish.net; Web: www.stritaparish.net. Revs. Joshua Whitfield, Admin.; Michal Markiewicz, Parochial Vicar; Deacons Charles T. Sylvester; Bill Fobes; Doug Breckenridge; Chris Knight.
Res.: 12626 Planters Glen, 75244.
School—St. Rita Catholic School, (Grades PreK-8), 12525 Inwood Rd., 75244. Tel: 972-239-3203; Fax: 972-934-3657; Web: www.strita.net. Dr. Carol Walsh, Prin. Lay Teachers 59; Students 684.
Catechesis Religious Program—Susan Sheetz, Coord., Children's Faith Formation. Students 512.

29—SAN JUAN DIEGO CATHOLIC PARISH (2006)
10919 Royal Haven, 75229. Tel: 214-271-4691; Fax: 214-271-4696; Email: aortiz@sanjuandiegodallas.org; Web: www.sanjuandiegodallas.org. Rev. Jesus Belmontes.
Catechesis Religious Program—Lupita Frausto, P.C.L.; Maria Martinez, P.C.L. Students 2,001.

30—SANTA CLARA OF ASSISI CATHOLIC PARISH (1993) (Hispanic)
321 Calumet Ave., 75211. Tel: 214-337-3936; Fax: 214-333-9148; Email: info@santaclararcc.org; Web: santaclaracatholicchurch.org. Mailing Address: P.O. Box 210888, 75211. Very Rev. Cruz Calderon, V.F.; Rev. Angel Torres, Vicar; Deacon Felicito Laguna.
School—Santa Clara of Assisi Catholic Academy, (Grades PreK-8), Tel: 214-333-9423; Email: dpuga@santaclararcc.org. Stephanie Matous, Prin. Lay Teachers 18; Students 246; Religious Teachers 1.
Catechesis Religious Program—Email: dpuga@santaclararcc.org; Email: mlimon@santaclararcc.org. Students 1,274.

31—ST. THOMAS AQUINAS CATHOLIC PARISH (1952)
6306 Kenwood Ave., 75214. Tel: 214-821-3360; Email: campise@stadallas.org; Web: www.stthomasaquinas.org. Very Rev. John Libone, V.F., J.C.L.; Rev. James Dorman, Parochial Vicar; Deacon Kenneth Reisor.
Schools—St. Thomas Aquinas Catholic School - Upper School—(Grades 5-8), 3741 Abrams Rd., 75214. Tel: 214-826-0566; Fax: 214-826-0251; Email: jwatts@staschool.org. Patrick Magee, Pres. Lay Teachers 92; Students 889; Religious Teachers 1.
St. Thomas Aquinas Catholic School - Lower School, (Grades PreK-4), 6255 E. Mockingbird, 75214. Tel: 469-341-0911; Email: pmagee@staschool.org. Patrick Magee, Prin. Lay Teachers 68; Students 850; Religious Teachers 1.
Catechesis Religious Program—Email: barker@stadallas.org. Brandon Barker, P.C.L. Students 661.

OUTSIDE THE CITY OF DALLAS

ALLEN, COLLIN CO.
1—ST. JUDE CATHOLIC PARISH (1981)
1515 N. Greenville Ave., Allen, 75002. Tel: 972-727-1177; Fax: 972-727-1401; Email: shawthorne@stjudeparish.com; Web: www.stjudeparish.com. Revs. Andrew V. Semler; Joel Bako, Parochial Vicar; Abraham Thomas, Parochial Vicar; Deacons Ronald Fejeran; Robert Holladay; Al Karcher; John Boyle.
Res.: 404 Spring Leaf Ct., Allen, 75002.
Catechesis Religious Program—Julie Buchanan, P.C.L. Students 2,055.

2—OUR LADY OF ANGELS CATHOLIC PARISH (2000)
1914 Ridgeview Dr., Allen, 75013. Tel: 469-467-9669; Email: pchisolm@ourladyofangels.com; Web: www.ourladyofangels.com. Rev. Msgr. John P. Bell, J.C.L.; Deacons Mike Picard; David Rekieta.
Catechesis Religious Program—Email: Shernandez@ourladyofangels.com. Sandy Hernandez, C.R.E. (Grade School); Sheila Tullier, Dir. Youth Min.; Christian Oregines, Youth Min. Coord.; Jennifer Hardee, Early Childhood Min. Coord. Students 917.

BONHAM, FANNIN CO., ST. ELIZABETH CATHOLIC PARISH - BONHAM
916 Maple St., Bonham, 75418. Tel: 903-583-7734; Fax: 903-583-7702; Email: info@se-bonham.com. Rev. Paolo Capra; Deacon Joseph Culling.
Catechesis Religious Program—Maria Macias, D.R.E. Students 109.

CARROLLTON, DALLAS CO., SACRED HEART OF JESUS CHRIST CATHOLIC PARISH (1999)
2121 N. Denton Dr., Carrollton, 75006. Tel: 972-446-3461; Fax: 972-446-9551; Email: info@thanhtamdallas.org; Web: thanhtamdallas.org. Rev. Dominic Phuc Pham, C.Ss.R.
Catechesis Religious Program—3949 Legacy Tr., Carrollton, 75010. Tel: 469-289-7922; Email: trungtran65@hotmail.com. Trung Tran, P.C.L. Students 416.

COMMERCE, HUNT CO., ST. JOSEPH CATHOLIC PARISH - COMMERCE (1895)
2207 Monroe St., Commerce, 75428. Email: admasst.stj@gmail.com. Mailing Address: P.O. Box 832, Commerce, 75429. Rev. Marcus Chidozie; Deacon Joe Webber.
Catechesis Religious Program—Natalie Salisbury, P.C.L. Students 68.

COPPELL, DALLAS CO., ST. ANN CATHOLIC PARISH - COPPELL (1985)
180 Samuel Blvd., Coppell, 75019. Tel: 972-393-5544; Fax: 973-462-1617; Email: parishoffice3@stannparish.org; Web: www.stannparish.org. Rev. Msgr. Henry V. Petter; Revs. Martin Castañeda; Francisco Orozco, O.C.D.; Deacons Ron Blanton; Ed Scarbrough; Eduardo Barajas; Fidel Alvarez; Kory Killgo.

CORSICANA, NAVARRO CO., IMMACULATE CONCEPTION CATHOLIC PARISH - CORSICANA (1871)
3000 Hwy. 22 W., Corsicana, 75110. Tel: 903-874-4473; Fax: 903-874-2619; Email: pastor@iccorsicana.org; Web: www.iccorsicana.org. Mailing Address: P.O. Box 798, Corsicana, 75151. Rev. Marco Rangel; Deacon Lewis J. Palos.
School—James L. Collins Catholic School, (Grades PreK-8), Tel: 903-872-1751; Email: vmorrison@collinscatholicschool.org. Vicky Morrison, Prin. Lay Teachers 27; Students 108.
Catechesis Religious Program—Email: arosas@iccorsicana.org. Ana Rosas, P.C.L. Students 414.

DENISON, GRAYSON CO., ST. PATRICK CATHOLIC PARISH - DENISON (1872) [CEM]
314 N. Rusk Ave., Denison, 75020. Tel: 903-463-3275; Fax: 903-463-3447; Email: parishoffice@saintpats.net; Web: www.saintpats.net. Rev. Stephen J. Mocio.
Catechesis Religious Program—Dale Sullivan, P.C.L. & Youth Min. Students 155.

DUNCANVILLE, DALLAS CO., HOLY SPIRIT CATHOLIC PARISH (1974)
1111 W. Danieldale Rd., Duncanville, 75137-3719. Tel: 972-298-4971; Web: holyspiritcatholic.com. Revs. Joseph C. Lee; Eugene Okoli; Deacons Al Evans; Charles Ruelas; Paul Wood.
Catechesis Religious Program—Deborah Pearson, P.C.L. Students 688.

ENNIS, ELLIS CO., ST. JOHN NEPOMUCENE CATHOLIC PARISH (1902) [CEM]
401 E. Lampasas St., Ennis, 75119. Tel: 972-878-2834; Fax: 972-875-2452; Email: joannag@stjohncc.net; Email: marial@stjohncc.net; Web: stjohncc.net. Revs. John Dick; Antonio Liberman-Ormaza; Deacon Don Griffith.
Rectory & Res.: 505 E. Lampasas, Ennis, 75119.
Catechesis Religious Program—Karim Sullivan, D.R.E.; Stephen Thompson, D.R.E.; Seth Wright, D.R.E. Students 1,600.

FERRIS, ELLIS CO., CORPUS CHRISTI CATHOLIC PARISH (1977) (Hispanic)
111 N. Wood, Ferris, 75125. Tel: 972-544-2161; Email: corpuschristiferris@yahoo.com; Web: corpuschristiferris.org. Rev. Anibal Adorno, V.F.; Deacon Jose Muniz, Admin.
Res.: 117 N. Wood, Ferris, 75125.
Catechesis Religious Program—Email: jccorpuschristi@yahoo.com. Juan Cadena, P.C.L. Students 154.

FORNEY, KAUFMAN CO., ST. MARTIN OF TOURS CATHOLIC PARISH (1891)
9470 C.R. 213, Forney, 75126. Tel: 972-564-9114; Email: office@stmartinforney.org; Email: stmchurchoff@aol.com; Web: www.stmartinforney.org. Very Rev. James Yamauchi, V.F.
Catechesis Religious Program—Email: stmreleducation@aol.com. Beth Wright, P.C.L. Students 403.

FRISCO, COLLIN CO., ST. FRANCIS OF ASSISI CATHOLIC PARISH - FRISCO (1966)
8000 El Dorado Pkwy., Frisco, 75033.
Tel: 972-712-2645; Fax: 972-712-1087; Email: receptionist@stfoafrisco.org; Web: www.stfoafrisco.org. Revs. Rodolfo Garcia; Artemio Patino, Parochial Vicar; Charles Githinji, Parochial Vicar; Deacons John R. Costello; Martin Armendariz; Gregg Kahrs; Alex Barbieri.
Catechesis Religious Program—Students 2,050.

GARLAND, DALLAS CO.
1—GOOD SHEPHERD CATHOLIC PARISH (1944)
1304 Main St., Garland, 75040. Tel: 972-276-8587; Email: info@gschurch.org; Web: www.gschurch.org. Mailing Address: 1224 Main St., Garland, 75040. Revs. Jose Luis Esparza, F.N.; Israel Gonzalez; Americo Lozano; Deacons Jim Harris; Jose E. Lopez. Res.: 1123 W Ave A, Garland, 75040.
School—Good Shepherd Catholic School, (Grades PreK-8), 214 S. Garland Ave., Garland, 75040. Tel: 972-272-6533; Fax: 972-272-0512; Email: goodsh@airmail.net; Email: grichardsonbassett@gscschool.org; Web: www.gscschool.org. Gail R. Bassett, Prin. Lay Teachers 13; Students 248.
Catechesis Religious Program—Email: prodriguez@gschurch.org. Patricia Rodriguez, D.R.E. Students 3,383.
2—ST. MICHAEL THE ARCHANGEL CATHOLIC PARISH - GARLAND (1980)
950 Trails Pkwy., Garland, 75043.
Tel: 972-279-6581, Ext. 10; Fax: 972-279-6647; Email: parishoffice@stmichaelgarland.org. Revs. Joseph A. Mehan Jr.; Joseph Nedumankuzhiyil, In Res.; Deacons Joe Perez; Andrew Pena.
Catechesis Religious Program—Email: swilliams@stmichaelgarland.org. Sherri Williams, P.C.L. Students 7,478.
3—MOTHER OF PERPETUAL HELP CATHOLIC PARISH (1992) (Vietnamese)
2121 W. Apollo Rd., Garland, 75044.
Tel: 972-414-7073; Email: dmhcggarland@gmail.com. Rev. Paul Hai Nguyen, C.Ss.R., J.C.L.
Catechesis Religious Program—Students 1,009.

GRAND PRAIRIE, DALLAS CO.
1—IMMACULATE CONCEPTION CATHOLIC PARISH - GRAND PRAIRIE (1916)
610 N.E. 17th St., Grand Prairie, 75050.
Tel: 972-262-5137; Fax: 972-264-7657; Email: fhawkins@icgrandprairie.org; Web: www.icgrandprairie.org. Very Rev. Joseph Son Van Nguyen, V.F.; Rev. Luis Fermin Sierra; Deacon David Maida.
School—Immaculate Conception Catholic School, (Grades PreK-8), 400 N.E. 17th St., Grand Prairie, 75050. Tel: 972-264-8777; Fax: 972-264-7742; Email: fhawkins@icgrandprairie.org; Web: school.icgrandprairie.org. Linda Santos, Prin. Lay Teachers 11; Sisters of the Holy Family of Nazareth 2; Students 137.
Catechesis Religious Program—Tel: 972-264-8385; Email: ctanaka@icgrandprairie.org. Cecilia Tamaka, P.C.L. Students 639.
2—ST. JOSEPH VIETNAMESE PARISH (1993)
Email: dhpham2000@yahoo.com. Rev. Bartholomew Dat Pham.
Res.: 1902 S. Beltline Rd., Grand Prairie, 75051.
Tel: 972-264-9441; Email: dhpham2000@yahoo.com.
Catechesis Religious Program—Students 351.
3—ST. MICHAEL THE ARCHANGEL CATHOLIC PARISH - GRAND PRAIRIE (1985)
2910 Corn Valley, Grand Prairie, 75052.
Tel: 972-262-0552; Tel: 972-262-6590;
Fax: 972-642-5429; Email: smgptxpete@sbcglobal.net; Web: www.stmichaelgptx.org. Rev. Joseph Hoa Duc Trinh; Deacons Pete Rodriguez; J. Robert Miller.

GREENVILLE, HUNT CO., ST. WILLIAM CATHOLIC PARISH (1892)
4300 Stuart St., Greenville, 75401. Tel: 903-450-1177 ; Email: st.william@aol.com; Web: www.saintwilliamtheconfessor.org. Rev. Paul L. Weinberger; Deacons Lee B. Davis; Ismael A. Guerra.
Catechesis Religious Program—Students 375.

IRVING, DALLAS CO.
1—CHURCH OF THE INCARNATION (1973)
1845 E. Northgate Dr., Irving, 75062.
Tel: 972-721-5375; Tel: 972-721-5118; Email: udcampmin@gmail.com; Web: www.udallas.edu/offices/campusministry/church-incarnation.php. Rev. Thomas More Barba, O.P., Rector; Nick Lopez, Dir.; Carol Norris, Dir. Music Ministry.
2—HOLY FAMILY OF NAZARETH CATHOLIC PARISH (1964)
2323 Cheyenne St., Irving, 75062. Tel: 972-252-5521; Fax: 972-252-5523; Email: info@holyfamilychurch.net; Web: www.holyfamilychurch.net. Mailing Address: 2330 Cheyenne St., Irving, 75062. Revs. Albert B. Becher; Peter Chinnappan, Parochial Vicar; Deacons Kenneth Hale; Ron Morgan; Larry Harmon; James Baird.
School—Holy Family Catholic Academy, (Grades PreK-8), 2323 Cheyenne St., Irving, 75062. Tel: 972-255-0205; Fax: 972-252-0448; Email: admin@hfca-irving.org; Web: www.hfca-irving.org. Mrs. Kathryn Carruth, Prin. Lay Teachers 19; Students 236.
Catechesis Religious Program—Tel: 972-252-5521; Fax: 972-252-5523; Email: kjohnson@holyfamilychurch.net. Lou Ann Kemper, D.R.E. Students 523.
3—ST. LUKE CATHOLIC PARISH (1902)
1015 Schulze Dr., Irving, 75060. Tel: 972-259-3222; Fax: 972-259-3339; Email: mary.osullivan@stlukeirving.org; Web: www.stlukeirving.org. Revs. Ernesto Esqueda Sanchez; Richard Bezzegato, C.S.; Jose Cervera Araujo; Deacons Jose Trevino; Daniel D. Segovia; Patrick Lamers.
Catechesis Religious Program—1009 Schulze Dr, Irving, 75060. Tel: 972-259-1832; Email: dsegovia@stlukeirving.org. Deacon Daniel D. Segovia, P.C.L. Students 2,645.
4—MATER DEI PERSONAL PARISH
2030 E. Hwy. 356, Irving, 75060. Tel: 972-438-7600; Email: info@materdeiparish.com; Web: www.materdeiparish.com. Revs. Peter Bauknecht; James Buckley; Brian McDonnell; Timothy O'Brien.
Catechesis Religious Program—Tracy Numley, P.C.L. Students 42.

ITALY, ELLIS CO., EPIPHANY CATHOLIC PARISH
434 S. Ward, Italy, 76651. Tel: 972-875-2834;
Fax: 972-875-2452; Email: marial@stjohncc.net. Mailing: 401 E. Lampasas St., Ennis, 75119. Revs. Antonio Liberman-Ormaza; John Dick.
Catechesis Religious Program—Gloria Rodriguez, D.R.E. Students 46.

KAUFMAN, KAUFMAN CO., ST. ANN CATHOLIC PARISH - KAUFMAN (1935)
806 N. Washington St., Kaufman, 75142.
Tel: 972-962-3247; Email: sapkau@mycvc.net. Rev. Jet Garcia; Deacon William Jasmin.
Catechesis Religious Program—Alma Sipriano, P.C.L. Students 429.

LANCASTER, DALLAS CO., ST. FRANCIS OF ASSISI CATHOLIC PARISH - LANCASTER (1973)
1537 Rogers Ave., Lancaster, 75134.
Tel: 972-227-4124; Tel: 972-227-7080;
Fax: 972-227-2882; Email: stfran@swbell.net; Web: www.stfrancislancaster.org. Rev. Manuel Sabando; Deacons Sergio Carranza; Lawrence Seidemann.
Catechesis Religious Program—Tel: 972-227-0770; Email: sfre@swbell.net; Web: www.stfrancislancaster.org. Gabriela Vela, P.C.L. Students 483.

MCKINNEY, COLLIN CO.
1—ST. GABRIEL THE ARCHANGEL CATHOLIC PARISH (1996)
110 St. Gabriel Way, McKinney, 75071.
Tel: 972-542-7170; Fax: 972-542-7756; Email: generalmailbox@stgabriel.org; Web: www.stgabriel.org. Very Rev. Donald Zeiler, V.F., M.Div., M.A.; Rev. Robert Williams; Deacons Michael Seibold, Business Mgr.; Robert Boduch; Victor M. Machiano; Michael Begala, (Leave of Absence); Barry Schliesmann; John Rapier
Legal Titles: St. Gabriel the Archangel Catholic Parish, previously St. Gabriel the Archangel Catholic Community.
2—ST. MICHAEL CATHOLIC PARISH - MCKINNEY (1892)
411 Paula Rd., McKinney, 75069. Tel: 972-542-4667; Fax: 972-542-4641; Email: stmichael@stmichaelmckinney.org; Web: www.stmichaelmckinney.org. Revs. Eugene Azorji, Admin.; Juan Carlos Marín, Parochial Vicar; Deacons George Polcer; Sidney Little; Andrew Tanner.

MESQUITE, DALLAS CO., DIVINE MERCY OF OUR LORD CATHOLIC PARISH (2002)
1585 E. Cartwright Rd., Mesquite, 75149.
Tel: 972-591-5294; Fax: 972-289-7445; Email: carmen@divinemercytx.org; Web: www.divinemercyofourlord.org. Revs. Ernesto Torres; Gil Mediana, Vicar; Agustin Torm, Vicar; Deacons Steve Marco; Ismael Reyes.
Rectory—510 Elderwood Loop, Mesquite, 75181.
Tel: 972-222-0436.
Catechesis Religious Program—
Tel: 972-591-5294, Ext. 228; Email: faithformation@divinemercytx.org. Ana L. Dávila, P.C.L. Students 622.

PLANO, COLLIN CO.
1—ST. ELIZABETH ANN SETON CATHOLIC PARISH (1976)
2700 West Spring Creek Pkwy, Plano, 75023.
Tel: 972-596-5505; Fax: 972-985-7573; Email: mlarson@eseton.org; Web: www.setonparish.org. Mailing Address: 2701 Piedra Dr., Plano, 75023. Revs. Bruce Bradley; Jacob Dankasa; Javier Diaz-Servin; Deacons Michael Seibold; Thomas Roche; Anthony Silvestro; Douglas Biglen; Vince Vaillancourt. Res.: 2800 Piedra Dr., Plano, 75023.
Catechesis Religious Program—3100 W. Spring Creek Pkwy., Plano, 75023. Email: bbaumann@eseton.org. Bruce Baumann, P.C.L. Students 996.
2—ST. MARK THE EVANGELIST CATHOLIC PARISH (1966)
1105 W. 15th St., Plano, 75075. Tel: 972-423-5600; Fax: 972-423-5024; Email: vfonseca@stmarkplano.org; Web: www.stmarkplano.org. Revs. Clifford G. Smith; Henry Erazo Herrea; John Hopka; Deacons Edward Putonti; Federico Marquez; Dominic T. Hoang; Shawn French; Luis Garzon; Henry Wiechman; Fred Rotchford.
School—St. Mark Catholic School, (Grades PreK-8), 1201 Alma Dr., Plano, 75075. Tel: 972-578-0610; Fax: 972-423-3299; Email: patricia.opon@stmcs.net; Web: www.stmcs.net. Patricia Opon, Prin. Lay Teachers 44; Students 553.
Catechesis Religious Program—Tel: 972-423-5600; Email: vfonseca@stmarkplano.org. Students 1,901.
3—PRINCE OF PEACE CATHOLIC PARISH (1991)
5100 W. Plano Pkwy., Plano, 75093.
Tel: 972-380-2100; Email: lwhitney@pplano.org; Web: www.popplano.org. Very Rev. Thomas Cloherty, V.F.; Rev. Stephen Ingram; Deacons Eugene T. Kowalski; David E. Tompsett; John O'Leary; John Gorman; Joe Coleman.
School—Prince of Peace Catholic School, (Grades PreK-8), Tel: 972-380-5505; Email: mosullivan@popschool.net. Linda Whitney, Contact Person. Lay Teachers 85; Students 823.
Catechesis Religious Program—Students 457.
4—SACRED HEART OF JESUS CATHOLIC PARISH - PLANO (1993) (Chinese)
4201 14th St., Plano, 75074. Tel: 972-516-8500; Email: webmaster@chinese-catholic.org; Web: www.chinese-catholic.org. Rev. Vincent Lin Yu Ming.
Catechesis Religious Program—Kevin McGills, P.C.L. Students 73.

QUINLAN, HUNT CO., OUR LADY OF FATIMA CATHOLIC PARISH
1579 E. Quinlan Pkwy., Quinlan, 75474.
Tel: 903-450-1177; Email: stwilliam@aol.com. 4300 Stuart St., Greenville, 75401. Rev. Paul L. Weinberger.

RICHARDSON, DALLAS CO.
1—ST. JOSEPH CATHOLIC PARISH - RICHARDSON (1976)
600 S. Jupiter Rd., Richardson, 75081.
Tel: 972-231-2951; Fax: 972-231-2875; Email: church@stjosephcc.net. Very Rev. Jason Cargo, V.F.; Revs. Michael Baynham; Martin Mwangi; Deacons Randall L. Engel; Timothy J. Vineyard; Richard Nelson; Jose Mendez.
School—St. Joseph Catholic School, (Grades K-8), Tel: 972-692-4594; Email: fthompson@stjosephccschool.net. Fran Thompson, Prin. Lay Teachers 39; Students 274.
Catechesis Religious Program—Tel: 972-690-5588; Fax: 972-692-4575. Students 567.
2—ST. PAUL THE APOSTLE CATHOLIC PARISH (1956)
720 S. Floyd Rd., Richardson, 75080.
Tel: 972-235-6105; Email: adrianne@saintpaulchurch.org; Web: www.saintpaulchurch.org. Mailing Address: 900 St. Paul Dr., Richardson, 75080. Revs. John Szatkowski; Benito Tamez, Parochial Vicar; Deacon Bob Bonomi.
School—St. Paul the Apostle Catholic School, (Grades PreK-8), Tel: 972-235-3263; Email: d.safford@spsdfw.org. Lay Teachers 35; Students 278.
Catechesis Religious Program—Tel: 972-235-2598; Email: beckie@saintpaulchurch.org. Becky Soto, P.C.L. Students 481.

ROCKWALL, ROCKWALL CO., OUR LADY OF THE LAKE CATHOLIC PARISH (1978)
1305 Damascus Rd., Rockwall, 75087.
Tel: 972-771-6671; Fax: 972-771-7283; Email: receptionist@ourladyrockwall.org; Web: www.ourladyrockwall.org. Revs. George P. Monaghan; Antonio Hernandez, Parochial Vicar; Deacons Randy Wilson; Oscar Miranda; Paul Husting.
Catechesis Religious Program—Tel: 972-961-9384; Email: pcl@ourladyrockwall.org. Sara Campbell, P.C.L. Students 1,218.

ROWLETT, DALLAS CO., SACRED HEART CATHOLIC PARISH (1899) [CEM]
3905 Hickox Rd., Rowlett, 75089.
Tel: 972-475-4405, Ext. 10; Email: parishoffice@sacredheartrowlett.org; Web: www.sacredheartrowlett.org. Rev. Danilo Ramos; Deacons Kenneth Melston; Jack Hopkins.
Res.: 3502 Andrea, Rowlett, 75088.
Catechesis Religious Program—Nancy Hampton, P.C.L. Students 327.

SHERMAN, GRAYSON CO., ST. MARY CATHOLIC PARISH (1872) [CEM]
727 S. Travis, Sherman, 75090. Tel: 903-893-5148;
Fax: 903-813-5489; Email: ndobbs@stmarych.org; Web: www.stmarych.org. Rev. Esteban D. Antes, Parochial Vicar; Deacon Albert Miller.
School—St. Mary Catholic School, (Grades PreK-8), 713 Travis St., Sherman, 75090. Tel: 903-893-2127; Fax: 903-892-3233; Email: pscheibmeir@stmarys-sch.org; Web: www.stmarys-sch.org. Phillip Scheibmeir, Prin.; Karen Martin, Sec. Lay Teachers 14; Students 162.
Catechesis Religious Program—Annie Kremer, P.C.L. & D.R.E. Students 503.

TERRELL, KAUFMAN CO., ST. JOHN THE APOSTLE CATHOLIC PARISH (1876)
702 N. Frances St., Terrell, 75160. Email: chsectr701@sbcglobal.net. Very Rev. James P. Orosco, V.F.; Deacon James Starr.
Catechesis Religious Program—Michelle Gobert, D.R.E. Students 556.

VAN ALSTYNE, GRAYSON CO., HOLY FAMILY CATHOLIC PARISH (1980)
919 Spence Rd., Van Alstyne, 75495.
Tel: 903-482-6322; Email: office@holyfamily-vanalstyne.org; Web: www.holyfamily-vanalstyne.org. Mailing Address: P.O. Box 482, Van Alstyne, 75495. Revs. Juan Marin, Parochial Vicar; Eugene Azorji, Admin.; Deacon Patrick Hayes.
Catechesis Religious Program—Janis Hicks, P.C.L. Students 245.

WAXAHACHIE, ELLIS CO., ST. JOSEPH CATHOLIC PARISH - WAXAHACHIE (1875)
609 Kaufman St., Waxahachie, 75165.
Tel: 972-938-1953; Email: receptionist@stjosephwaxahachie.com; Web: www.saintjosephwaxahachie.com. Rev. Ivan Asencio, Admin.; Deacons Hugo Monsanto; Dennis Phillip Bryant; Michael Friske.
School—St. Joseph Catholic School, (Grades 9-12), 506 E. Marvin St., Waxahachie, 75165.
Tel: 972-937-0956; Fax: 972-937-1742; Email: receptionist@stjosephwaxahachie.com. Debbie Timmermann, Prin.; Penny Walden, Librarian. Lay Teachers 14; Students 182.
Catechesis Religious Program—James Speelman, P.C.L. Students 392.

WHITESBORO, GRAYSON CO., ST. FRANCIS OF ASSISI CATHOLIC PARISH - WHITESBORO
807 N. Union, Whitesboro, 76273. Mailing Address: 727 S. Travis St., Sherman, 75090. Tel: 903-893-5148 ; Fax: 903-813-5489; Web: www.stmarych.org. Rev. Esteban D. Antes.
Catechesis Religious Program—Hanna Ferguson. Students 73.

WYLIE, COLLIN CO., ST. ANTHONY CATHOLIC PARISH - WYLIE (1858) [CEM]
401 N. Ballard Ave., Wylie, 75098. Tel: 972-442-2765 ; Fax: 972-429-9215; Email: frtony@saint-anthony.com. Very Rev. Anthony M. Densmore, V.F.; Rev. Sinu Puthenpurackal Joseph; Deacon Jose Arturo Perez.
Catechesis Religious Program—Students 975.

Chaplains of Public Institutions

DALLAS. *Baylor Scott and White Health*, 3500 Gaston Ave., 75246. Tel: 214-820-2558. Deacons Michael Bolesta, Chap., Hugo A. Salinas, Chap.
Children's Medical Center of Dallas, 1935 Motor St., 75235. Tel: 214-456-2822. Ryan Campbell, Chap.
City Hospital at White Rock, 9440 Poppy Dr., 75218. Tel: 214-321-0454. Revs. Delfin Condori, I.V.E., Gaston Giacinti, I.V.E.
Dallas/Fort Worth Airport Catholic Chaplain, 12521 Inwood Rd., 75244. Tel: 214-379-2821. Vacant.
Hutchins State Jail, 1500 E. Langdon Rd., 75241. Tel: 972-227-4124. Rev. Manuel Sabando.
Medical City Dallas Hospital, 7777 Forest Ln., 75230. Tel: 972-235-6105. Rev. John Szatkowski.
Methodist Charlton Medical Center, 3500 W. Wheatland Rd., 75237. Tel: 214-947-2470. Rev. Louis Chijioke, Chap., Sr. Maria Gomez, S.S.N.D., Chap.
Methodist Dallas Medical Center, 1441 N. Beckley Ave., 75265. Tel: 214-947-2470. Rev. Louis Chijioke, Chap., Sr. Maria Gomez, S.S.N.D., Chap.
Parkland Health & Hospital System, 5200 Harry Hines Blvd., 75235. Tel: 214-590-8512. Rev. Alfred Asuncion, Chap.
Texas Health Presbyterian Hospital - Dallas, 8200 Walnut Hill Ln., 75231. Tel: 214-345-7158. Deacon Gregg Kahrs.
UT Southwestern University Medical Center and William P. Clements Jr. University Hospital, 6201 Harry Hines, 75390. Phyllis Carr, Chap.
VA - North Texas Health Care System, 2926 E. Ledbetter Dr., 75216. Tel: 214-374-7952. Rev. Timothy A. Gollob.
Zale Lipsky Hospital, 5151 Harry Hines Blvd., 75390. Phyllis Carr, Chap.

BONHAM. *Buster Cole State Jail*, 3901 Silo Rd., Bonham, 75418. Tel: 903-583-7734. Rev. Paolo Capra.
Choice Moore Transfer Facility, 1700 N. FM 87, Bonham, 75418. Tel: 903-583-4464. Rev. Paolo Capra.
Sam Rayburn Memorial Veterans Center, 1201 E. 9th St., Bonham, 75418. Tel: 903-583-7734. Rev. Paolo Capra.

PLANO. *Children's Medical Center - Legacy*, 7609 Preston Rd., Plano, 75024. Tel: 469-303-2822. Mr. Witek Nowosiad, Chap.

SEAGOVILLE. *Federal Correctional Institution*, 2113 N. Hwy. 75, Seagoville, 75159. Tel: 214-398-1583. Rev. Luca Simbula.

TERRELL. *Terrell State Hospital*, 702 N. Frances St., Terrell, 75160. Tel: 972-563-3643. Very Rev. James P. Orosco, V.F.

On Duty Outside the Diocese:
Revs.—
Anyama, Vincent C., St. Mary Seminary, 9845 Memorial Dr., Houston
Becker, Paul, Pontifical North American College, Ufficio Merci, Governatorato, 00120 Vatican City State
Brown, Richard
Martin, Sean, 23 S. Spring Ave., St. Louis, MO 63108
Phan, Cho Dinh Peter, P.O. Box 571135, Washington, DC
Riemer, Lawrence H., 1803 Laurel Oak Dr., Valrico, FL 33596.

On Leave of Absence:
Revs.—
Alphonso, John
Alvarez, Ramon
Chen, Reuben
Crisp, Robert R.
Dugan, T. Michael
Heines, Timothy
Iverson, Paul
Myers, Jeremy B.
Paredes, Edmundo B.
Speiser, Thomas M.

Retired:
Rev. Msgrs.—
Duesman, Jerome P., (Retired)
Duesman, Leon, J.C.B., (Retired)
Fischer, Don L., (Retired), 10754 Wyatt Cir., 75218
Joseph, Milam, M.A., (Retired)
Meyers, John F., (Retired), 6211 W. Northwest Hwy., Ste. 2205, 75225
Pichard, Lawrence, (Retired)
Rehkemper, Robert C., (Retired), 1111 E. Sandy Lake Rd., Coppell, 75019
Revs.—
Buitrago, Alejandro, (Retired)
Caldwell, Fred, (Retired), 2508 Dewberry Ct., Melissa, 75454
Clayton, Daniel, (Retired)
Diez, Oscar, (Retired)
Drozd, Henry J., (Retired), P.O. Box 42063, Savannah, GA 31409-0001
Flori, David J., (Retired)
Haugh, John, (Retired), 1139 E. Sandy Lake Rd., Coppell, 75019
Morris, Loyd, (Retired), 7406 Summit View Ln., Sachse, 75048
Ortega, Efren, (Retired)
Rodriguez, Salvador, (Retired)
Sharp, James, (Retired), 5621 Cornerstone Dr., Garland, 75043. Tel: 973-681-8915
Slovacek, Emil C., (Retired), P.O. Box 190507, 75219.

Permanent Deacons:
Pichard, Lawrence, (Retired)
Hawley, Gregorio
Alvarez, Fidel
Alvarez, Roberto
Andrade, Rafael
Armendariz, Martin
Ashley, Frank B., (On Duty Outside the Diocese)
Baca, Tomas, (Retired)
Baird, James
Banowsky, David
Barajas, Eduardo
Barbieri, Alex
Begala, Michael, (Leave of Absence)
Biglen, Douglas
Blanton, Ron
Boduch, Robert, (Retired)
Bolesta, Michael
Bonomi, Bob
Bourland, Fred, (On Duty Outside the Diocese)
Boyd, Douglas
Boyle, John
Breckenridge, Doug
Bryant, Dennis Phillip
Burke, James, (Inactive)
Burkel, James, (On Duty Outside the Diocese)
Carlisle, John, (On Duty Outside the Diocese)
Carpio, Victor
Carranza, Sergio
Castillo, Jorge
Catsoris, John A., (Retired)
Chou, George
Chung, Hoan Moses, (Retired)
Coleman, Joe
Corbin, Denis D.
Cortes, Abel
Cortinas, Leopoldo III
Costello, John R.
Crawley, Denver, (On Duty Outside the Diocese)
Cruz, Marco Antonio
Culling, Joseph
Dam, Thu
Daniels, James, (On Duty Outside the Diocese)
Davis, Lee B.
Dennis, Duffin
Engel, Randall L.
Evans, Al
Fejeran, Ronald
Fobes, Bill
Forbrich, Don, (Retired)
Freeman, Gene
French, Shawn
Friske, Michael
Garcia, Benito
Garza, Gerardo
Garzon, Luis
Gloria, Asuncion
Gonzales, Gonzalo
Gorman, John
Grant, Richard
Griffith, Don
Guerra, Ismael A.
Gutting, Justin, (Retired Outside the Diocese)
Gutting, Paul, (On Duty Outside the Diocese)
Hale, Kenneth, (Retired)
Hancock, John, (On Duty Outside the Diocese)
Harmon, Larry
Harrington, Richard, (Leave of Absence)
Harris, Jim
Hayes, Patrick
Hernandez, Jose L.
Hernandez, Juan Jorge
Hoang, Dominic T.
Holladay, Robert
Hopkins, Jack
Husting, Paul, (Retired)
Huynh, Huy Francis
Ibarra, Juan, (On Duty Outside the Diocese)
Jasmin, William
Jimenez, Vincent F.
Jones, Edward S., (On Duty Outside the Diocese)
Kahrs, Gregg
Karcher, Al
Kelly, John Paul
Killgo, Kory
Knight, Chris
Kowalski, Eugene, (Retired)
Kozarevich, Frank, (Retired)
Laguna, Felicito
Lamers, Patrick
LeBlanc, John D., (Retired)
Lee, John
Leicht, Robert R. Jr., (On Duty Outside the Diocese)
Leyden, Edward, (Retired)
Little, Sidney
Loera, Roberto
Lopez, Al, (Retired)
Lopez, Jose E.
Lucido, Larry, (Retired)
Maida, David
Marcoe, Steven
Markwald, Pete, (Retired)
Marquez, Federico
Marrinan, Robert Sr.
Marroquin, Joseph, (On Duty Outside the Diocese)
McAlister, Craig, (On Duty Outside the Diocese)
McDermott, Robert
Mellon, Roy Jr.
Melston, Kenneth, (Retired)
Miller, Albert
Miller, J. Robert
Miranda, Oscar
Mitchell, Brian
Monsanto, Hugo
Montes, Jesus Alberto, (Retired)
Moreno, Ricardo, (On Duty Outside the Diocese)
Morgan, Ron
Muldoon, Tim, (Retired Outside the Diocese)
Muniz, Jose
Nanez, Pete
Nease, Randy
Nelson, William
O'Leary, John
Olivarez, Jesse, (Leave of Absence)
Olvera, Isidro, (On Duty Outside the Diocese)
Orozco, Adolph Jr., (Retired)
Osborne, Charles E.
Palomeque, Roberto
Palos, Lewis J.
Pena, Andrew
Perez, Joe R., (Retired)

Perez, Jose Arturo
Petkovsek, James C., (On Duty Outside the Diocese)
Picard, Michael
Pina, Salvador
Polcer, George
Porras, Gonzalo
Powers, Paul, (Retired)
Putonti, Edward
Raad, Peter
Rapier, John
Rayner, Robert
Reisor, Kenneth
Reittinger, Paul W., (Retired)
Rekieta, David
Rener, Bonnie Leo, (Retired)
Reyes, Ismael
Ricard, Robert, (Retired)
Riojas, Ricardo
Roche, Thomas, (Retired)
Rodriguez, Hector
Rodriguez, Pete
Rotchford, Fred
Ruelas, Charles
Salinas, Hugo A.
Sanchez, Robert, (Retired)
Scarbrough, Ed
Schell, John A.
Schliesmann, Barry
Schroepfer, Jake
Schuster, William J., (Retired)
Segovia, Daniel D.
Seibold, Michael
Seidemann, Lawrence
Shaw, Michael, (Retired)
Silvestro, Anthony
Simon, Denis
Starr, James
Stump, Charles Jr., M.S., M.P.M.
Sykora, Richard, (Retired Outside the Diocese)
Sylvester, Charles T.
Tanner, Andrew
Thelin, Carl H., (Retired)
Tompsett, David E.
Tran, Anthony, (Retired)
Trevino, Antonio D., (Retired)
Trevino, Jose
Vaillancourt, Vince
Van Pham, Hao
Vazquez, Jose Antonio
Vega, Frutos, (On duty outside the Diocese)
Villegas, Filemon
Vineyard, Timothy J.
Vogel, Gary M.
Volkmer, Chris
Washington, Warner, (Retired)
Webb, Philip E., (Retired)
Webber, Joe
Weston, Michael
Wiechman, Henry
Wilson, Randy
Wong, Peter, (Retired)
Wood, Paul.

INSTITUTIONS LOCATED IN DIOCESE

[A] SEMINARIES, DIOCESAN

DALLAS. *The Redemptoris Mater House of Formation* Redemptoris Mater Seminary, P.O. Box 211669, 75211. Tel: 214-467-2255; Fax: 214-467-5440; Web: www.rmdallas.org. 419 N. Cockrell Hill Rd., 75211. Revs. Daniel Rendon, Spiritual Dir.; Juan Marin, Spiritual Dir.; Very Rev. Fernando Carranza, Rector & Contact Person; Rev. Alan Paul McDonald, Vice Rector. Clergy / Religious Teachers 4; Priests 4; Students 30; Lay Missionaries 7.

IRVING. *Holy Trinity Seminary* Diocesan College and Pre-Theology Seminary. 3131 Vince Hagan Dr., Irving, 75062. Tel: 972-438-2212; Fax: 972-438-6530; Web: www.holytrinityseminary.org. Rev. Jesudoss Thomas, Res. Spiritual Dir.; Very Rev. James E. Swift, C.M., Rector; Theresa Frank, Dir. Pastoral Form.; Dr. Gregory Hamilton, Music Dir.; Dr. Matthew Walz, Dir. Intellectual Formation; Revs. Zachary Webb, Assoc. Dir. of Formation; Anthony F. Lackland, Dir.; Kevin Wilwert, Dir. Clergy / Religious Teachers 4; Priests 5; Seminarians 73; Students 73; Total Staff 5; Lay Faculty 4.

[B] COLLEGES AND UNIVERSITIES

IRVING. *University of Dallas*, President's Office, 1845 E. Northgate, Irving, 75062. Tel: 972-721-5203; Email: president@udallas.edu; Web: www.udallas.edu. Dr. John Plotts, Interim Pres.; Dr. Jonathan Sanford, Provost; Revs. Roch Kereszty, O.Cist., S.T.D.; James Lehrberger, O.Cist., Ph.D.; Robert Maguire, O.Cist., Ph.D. Clergy 10; Students 2,542.

[C] HIGH SCHOOLS, DIOCESAN

DALLAS. *Bishop Dunne Catholic School, Inc.*, (Grades 6-12), (Coed) 3900 Rugged Dr., 75224. Tel: 214-339-6561; Fax: 214-339-1438; Email: ltorrez@bdcs.org; Web: www.bdcs.org. Mrs. Mary Marchiony, Prin.; Lydia Torrez, Dir. Devel. & Alumni; Melanie Gibson, Librarian. Administrators 12; Lay Teachers 62; Priests 1; Students 535; Total Staff 16; Sisters (S.S.N.D.) 1.

Bishop Lynch High School, Inc., 9750 Ferguson Rd., 75228. Tel: 214-324-3607; Fax: 214-324-3600; Email: jennifer.adamcik@bishoplynch.org; Web: www.bishoplynch.org. Alison Bednarczyk, Librarian; Christopher Rebuck, Pres.; Dr. Chad Riley, Prin. Clergy 1; Deacons 2; Lay Teachers 80; Priests 0.5; Sisters 1; Students 1,010; Total Staff 64.

PLANO. *John Paul II High School, Inc.*, 900 Coit Rd., Plano, 75075. Tel: 972-867-0005; Fax: 972-867-7555; Email: marlenehammerle@johnpauliihs.org; Web: www.johnpauliihs.org. Deacon Jake Schroepfer, Pres.; Dr. Marlene Hammerle, Prin.; Debra Goheen, Coord. Media Svcs. Deacons 2; Lay Teachers 63; Students 690.

[D] HIGH SCHOOLS, PRIVATE

DALLAS. **Cristo Rey Dallas High School, Inc.*, 1064 N. St. Augustine Dr., 75217. Tel: 469-844-7956; Email: kwoodard@cristoreydallas.org; Email: ccampbell@cristoreydallas.org; Web: cristoreydallas.org. Christine Roman, Prin.; Kelby Woodard, Pres.; Colin Campbell, Dir. of Mission. Lay Teachers 31; Students 475.

Jesuit College Preparatory School (Boys) 12345 Inwood Rd., 75244. Tel: 972-387-8700; Fax: 972-661-9349; Email: wsidney@jesuitcp.org; Web: www.jesuitcp.org. Rev. Philip S. Postell, S.J., Chap.; Mr. Michael A. Earsing, Pres.; Mr. Thomas Garrison, Prin.; Mr. Thomas Croteau, S.J., Scholastic; Revs. Leo V. Leise, S.J.; Walter T. Sidney, S.J., Rector; Mark Wester, Librarian. Society of Jesus. Clergy / Religious Teachers 130; Lay Teachers 125; Priests 3; Scholastics 2; Students 1,108; Total Staff 160.

Ursuline Academy of Dallas, Inc. (Girls) 4900 Walnut Hill Ln., 75229-6599. Tel: 469-232-1800; Fax: 469-232-1836; Email: gkane@ursulinedallas.org; Web: www.ursulinedallas.org. Ms. Gretchen Z. Kane, Pres.; Elizabeth Smith, Dean; Andrea Shurley, Prin.; Jim Koehler, Bus. Mgr.; Catherine Maurer, Admin. Lay Teachers 159; Students 851; Religious Sisters 2.

IRVING. *Cistercian Preparatory School*, (Grades 5-12), 3660 Cistercian Rd., Irving, 75039-4500. Tel: 469-499-5400; Fax: 469-499-5440; Email: admissions@cistercian.org; Web: www.cistercian.org. Rev. Paul McCormick, O.Cist., B.A., M.B.A., S.T.L., M.A., Headmaster; Jacqulyn Dudasko, Librarian. Cistercian Fathers of Our Lady of Dallas Abbey.(Boys) Clergy/Religious Teachers 15; Lay Teachers 39; Students 345.

The Highlands School, (Grades PreK-12), 1451 E. Northgate Dr., Irving, 75062. Tel: 972-554-1980; Fax: 972-721-1691; Email: info@thehighlandsschool.org; Web: www.TheHighlandsSchool.org. Ms. Dora Barrera, Exec. Asst.; Ms. Jennifer Denney, Admissions; Rev. Daniel Ray, L.C., Pres.; Michael Pennell, Prin. Brothers 2; Clergy / Religious Teachers 1; Lay Teachers 42; Priests 3; Students 355; High School Students 118; Elementary & Middle School Students 237; Consecrated Women 5.

[E] ELEMENTARY SCHOOLS DIOCESAN

DALLAS. *St. Philip & St. Augustine Catholic Academy, Inc.*, 8151 Military Pkwy., 75227. Tel: 214-381-4973; Fax: 214-381-0466; Email: sshirley@spsacatholic.org; Web: spsacatholic.org. Erica Romero, Prin. Lay Teachers 26; Students 350.

[F] ELEMENTARY SCHOOLS, PRIVATE

DALLAS. **Mount St. Michael Catholic School*, (Grades PreK-8), 4500 W. Davis St., 75211. Tel: 214-337-0244; Fax: 214-339-1702; Email: info@msmcatholic.org; Web: www.msmcatholic.org. P.O. Box 225159, 75222-5159. Judy Munchrath, Prin. Lay Teachers 16; Priests 2; Students 128; Total Staff 24.

[G] SPECIAL SCHOOLS, PRIVATE

DALLAS. *Notre Dame of Dallas Schools, Inc.* Notre Dame School, (Grades 1-12), 2018 Allen St., 75204. Tel: 214-720-3911; Fax: 214-720-3913; Email: tfrancis@notredameschool.org; Web: www.notredameschool.org. Carmen Fernandez, Asst. Prin.; Ms. Theresa Francis, Prin. Day School: Provides instructional education for children with developmental disabilities, ages 6-15; Vocational Center: Provides vocational training for young adults, ages 16-21. (Full-time, paid) 45; Lay Teachers 18; Students 162; Assistants 13; Religious Teachers 1.

[H] CATHOLIC CHARITIES

DALLAS. *Catholic Charities Endowment Trust*, 1421 W. Mockingbird Ln., 75247. Tel: 214-520-6590; Fax: 214-520-6595; Email: dwoodyard@ccdallas.org; Web: ccdallas.org. David Woodyard, Pres. & CEO.

Catholic Charities of Dallas (Collins Estate / St. Joseph Orphanage) Trust, 3725 Blackburn St., P.O. Box 190507, 75219. Tel: 214-379-2803; Email: bhanner@cathdal.org. Barry Hanner, Dir. of Financial Svcs.

Catholic Charities of Dallas, Inc., 1421 W. Mockingbird Ln., 75247. Tel: 866-223-7500; Fax: 214-520-6595; Email: info@ccdallas.org; Web: www.ccdallas.org. David Woodyard, Pres. & CEO. Tot Asst. Annually 38,000; Total Staff 140.

CCD - PM Corporation (2018) 1421 W. Mockingbird Ln., 75243. Tel: 469-801-8110. David Woodyard.

Children, Family & Senior Services, 1421 W. Mockingbird Ln., 75247. Tel: 214-520-6590; Fax: 214-520-6595; Email: dwoodyard@ccdallas.org; Web: ccdallas.org/need-help/children-family-senior-services/. David Woodyard, CEO. Tot Asst. Annually 2,473; Total Staff 35.

Santa Clara Community Center, 321 Calumet Ave., 75211. Tel: 214-333-1525; Fax: 214-333-1439; Email: jbrogdon@ccdallas.org. David Woodyard, CEO.

Immigration and Legal Services, 1421 W. Mockingbird Ln., 75247. Tel: 214-634-7182; Fax: 214-634-2531; Email: dwoodyard@ccdallas.org; Web: ccdallas.org/need-help/immigration-legal-services/. David Woodyard, CEO. Tot Asst. Annually 28,760; Total Staff 33.

St. Martin Family Service Center, Inc., 1421 W. Mockingbird Ln., 75247. Tel: 214-520-6590; Fax: 214-520-6595; Email: dwoodyard@ccdallas.org. David Woodyard, CEO.

Refugee Services, 1421 W. Mockingbird Ln., 75247. Tel: 214-553-9909; Fax: 214-553-8116; Email: dwoodyard@ccdallas.org; Web: ccdallas.org/need-help/refugee-services/. David Woodyard, CEO. Tot Asst. Annually 1,631; Total Staff 21.

[I] EDUCATION CENTERS

DALLAS. *Mount Carmel Center*, 4600 W. Davis St., 75211-3498. Tel: 214-331-6224; Fax: 214-330-0844; Email: admin@mountcarmelcenter.org; Web: www.mountcarmelcenter.org. Friar Jorge Cabrera-Marrero, Supr.; Rev. Stephen Sanchez, O.C.D., Prov. Sponsored by Discalced Carmelite Fathers of the Southwestern Province.Adult center for Catholic spirituality.

Legal Title: Discalced Carmelite Fathers of the Oklahoma Province. Clergy / Religious Teachers 4.

[J] PERSONAL PRELATURES

IRVING. *Opus Dei* Prelature of the Holy Cross and Opus Dei. 3610 Wingren, Irving, 75062. Tel: 972-650-0064; Fax: 972-717-3580; Email: wingrencenter@gmail.com; Web: www.opusdei.org. Rev. Joseph Thomas.

[K] MONASTERIES AND RESIDENCES OF PRIESTS

DALLAS. *St. Aloysius Gonzaga Jesuit Community*, 5024 Sugar Mill Rd., 75244. Tel: 214-484-6056; Email: wsidney@jesuits.org. Revs. Philip S. Postell, S.J., School Chap.; Walter T. Sidney, S.J., Supr.; Carlos Esparza, Graduate Student; Leo V. Leise, S.J., Sacramental Min.; Very Laity W. Tucker Redding, Teacher; Mr. Thomas Croteau, S.J., Teacher. Priests 5; Scholastics 2.

Capuchin Franciscan Friars, Custody Mexico - Texas, 2911 Lapsley St., 75212. Tel: 214-377-7643; Email: gerardoirigoyen@yahoo.com. Rev. Fray Luis G. Arraiza, O.F.M.Cap. Priests 1.

Congregation of the Mission, Western Province, 3826 Gilbert Ave., 75219. Tel: 214-526-0234; Email: cmsouth@sbcglobal.net; Web: www.vincentian.org. Revs. Milton Ryan; F. Patrick Hanser, C.M.; Minh J. Pham, C.M.; Michael Walsh, C.M., Parochial Vicar; Paul Sauerbier, C.M.; James E. Swift, C.M. Priests 6.

St. John Neumann Formation House Vietnamese Redemptorist Mission. 3912 S. Ledbetter Dr., 75236. Tel: 972-296-6735; Email: haidinh1@juno.com; Web: www.dccthaingoai.com. Revs. Dominic Hai Dinh, C.Ss.R., Formation Dir. & Contact Person; Dien Tran, C.S.S.R., Vicar; Duy Le, Chap.; Rev. Hung Quoc Pham, Chap. Total in Residence 16.

Mt. Carmel Center, 4600 W. Davis St., 75211.

Tel: 214-331-6224; Fax: 214-330-0844; Email: admin@mountcarmelcenter.org; Web: www.mountcarmelcenter.org. Friar Jorge Cabrera, Supr.; Rev. Stephen Sanchez, O.C.D., Prov.

HUBBARD. *Domus Dei Clerical Society of Apostolic Life*, 22822 N. FM 709, Hubbard, 76648. Cell: 360-909-8516; Email: francisqbui@yahoo.com; Web: www.nhachua.net. P.O. Box 313, Hubbard, 76648. Rev. Francis Bui, Supr.; Bros. Phuong Tran, Member; James Ngo, Member.

IRVING. *Cistercian Abbey of Our Lady of Dallas*, 3550 Cistercian Rd., Irving, 75039. Tel: 972-438-2044; Fax: 972-579-7637; Email: pverhalen@cistercian.com; Web: www.cistercian.org. Bro. Christopher Kalan; Rev. Paul McCormick, O.Cist., B.A., M.B.A., S.T.L., M.A., Prior; Rt. Revs. Denis M. Farkasfalvy, O.Cist., S.S.L., M.S., S.T.D., Abbot Emeritus; Peter Verhalen, O.Cist., M.A., M.Th., Abbot; Revs. Thomas Esposito, O.Cist., B.A., S.T.B., S.S.L., S.S.D., Subprior; Bernard Marton, O.Cist., S.T.D., M.A., Member; Bro. Benedict Lacombe, Member; Revs. Bede Lackner, O.Cist., Ph.D.; Roch Kereszty, O.Cist., S.T.D.; Augustine Hoelke, O.Cist., M.T.H.; Philip Neri Lastimosa, O.-Cist., B.A., M.T.H.; Julius Leloczky, O.Cist., S.T.D.; James Lehrberger, O.Cist., Ph.D.; Robert Maguire, O.Cist., Ph.D.; Gregory Schweers, O.-Cist., M.A.; Mark Ripperger, O.Cist., M.A.; Joseph Van House, O.Cist., S.T.L.; John Bayer, O.Cist., B.A.; Anthony Bigney, O.Cist., B.A.; Ignatius Peacher, O.Cist., B.A.; Ambrose Strong, O.Cist., B.A., M.Th., S.T.L.; Stephen Gregg, O.Cist., B.A.; Lawrence Brophy, O.Cist., M.S., B.A., S.T.B.; Justin McNamara, O.Cist., B.A.; Bros. Francis Gruber, O.Cist.; Rafael Schaner, O.Cist.; Matthew Hegemann, O.Cist. Brothers 6; Priests 22.

Dominican Priory of St. Albert the Great and Novitiate, 3150 Vince Hagan St., Irving, 75062-4701. Tel: 972-438-1626; Fax: 972-438-6948; Email: ibordenave@opsouth.org; Web: opdallas.com. Revs. Donald Dvorak, O.P.; Andrew Kolzow, O.P.; Arthur Kirwin, O.P.; Thomas More Barba, O.P., Campus Min.; Ian G. Bordennave, O.P., Prior; Jude Siciliano, O.P., Subprior; Bertrand Ebben, O.P.; Brian Pierce, O.P. Priests 7.

Our Lady of the Rosary of Pompeii Dominican Laity Chapter, 3150 Vince Hagan St., Irving, 75062. Tel: 469-682-6605; Email: cdpumphrey@gmail.com. Cheryl Pumphrey, Contact Person.

Legionaries of Christ, 3813 Cabeza de Vaca Cir., Irving, 75062. Tel: 214-529-3324; Email: foduill@legionaries.org; Web: www.dfw-rc.org. Revs. Fergal O'Duill, L.C., Supr.; Ryan Richardson, Chap.; Edward Bentley, L.C.; Michael Picard, L.C.; Daniel Ray, L.C.; Bro. Paul Ruedas, L.C.; Revs. Owens Kearns, L.C.; Simon Clearly, L.C.; Bro. Josef Babuin, L.C. Brothers 3; Priests 7.

KERENS. **Benedictine Monastery of Thien Tam*, 13055 S.E. CR 4271, Kerens, 75144. Tel: 903-396-3201; Email: danvienthientam@gmail.com. Revs. Dominic Hanh Nguyen, O.S.B., Prior; Paulavang Vuong, O.S.B. Brothers 7; Priests 5.

[L] CONVENTS AND RESIDENCES FOR SISTERS

DALLAS. *Carmelite Nuns of Dallas*, 600 Flowers Ave., 75211. Tel: 214-330-7440; Fax: 214-623-1885; Email: rgracia@cathdal.org. Mother Juanita Marie Horan, O.C.D., Prioress. Professed Sisters 2.

Daughters of the Sacred Heart, 7621 Cortland Ave., 75235. Tel: 214-351-4338. Molly Kurin, Supr. Sisters 4.

Missionaries of Charity, 2704 Harlandale Ave., 75216. Tel: 214-374-3351. Sisters M. Jonathan, M.C., Regl. Supr.; M. Sujaya, M.C., Supr. Convent and Our Lady of Guadalupe home for expectant mothers Sisters 5.

School Sisters of Notre Dame, P.O. Box 227275, 75222. Tel: 214-330-9152; Fax: 214-330-9197; Email: tkirallah@cathdal.org; Web: www.ssnd.org. Sr. Juliette Daigle, S.N.D. Sisters 15.

Sisters of Our Lady of Charity of the Good Shepherd - Dallas Inc., 4500 W. Davis St., 75211. Tel: 214-331-1754; Fax: 214-333-1659; Email: dallasolc@hotmail.com. Sr. Yolanda Martinez, O.L.C., Supr. Sisters 4.

Ursuline Sisters of Dallas, 9905 Inwood Rd., 75220. Tel: 214-799-2454; Email: lmcarter2@gmail.com; Web: www.osucentral.org. Sr. Lois Castillo, Dir. Sisters 9.

GRAND PRAIRIE. *Sisters of the Holy Family of Nazareth* (Holy Family Province) 1814 Egyptian Way, Grand Prairie, 75050. Tel: 972-641-4496; Fax: 972-641-1668; Email: smariettao@yahoo.com. Sr. Marrietta Osinska, C.S.F.N., Local Supr. Sisters 14.

IRVING. *Congregation of Mary, Queen-American Region (CMR)*, 723 Sunset Dr., Irving, 75061. Tel: 469-417-0123; Email: cmrvocation@yahoo.com; Web: www.trinhvuong.org. Sisters Janine Tran, C.M.R., P.C.L.; Irene Dinh, P.C.I.; Teresita Au, C.M.R., Teacher; Sr, Marie Nguyen, C.M.R., Teacher. Sisters 4; Perpetually Professed Religious 4.

[M] CAMPUS MINISTRY

DALLAS. *Southern Methodist University-Catholic Campus Ministry*, Neuhoff Catholic Student Ctr., 3057 University Blvd., 75205. Tel: 214-987-0044; Fax: 214-987-3731; Email: smucatholic@smu.edu; Web: smucatholic.org. Cody Borras, Campus Min.; Dave Moore, Music Min.; Rev. Arthur Unachukwu, Chap.

IRVING. *University of Dallas-Campus Ministry*, 1845 E. Northgate Dr., Irving, 75062. Tel: 972-721-5375; Email: tbarba@udallas.edu; Web: www.udallas.edu/offices/campusministry/church-incarnation.php. Rev. Thomas More Barba, O.P., Rector; Nick Lopez, Dir.

[N] MISCELLANEOUS LISTINGS

DALLAS. *Bishop Dunne Catholic School Building and Endowment Fund*, 3900 Rugged Dr., 75224. Tel: 214-339-6561; Fax: 214-339-1438; Email: ltorrez@bdcs.org; Web: www.bdcs.org. Kate Dailey, Pres.

Bishop Lynch High School Building and Endowment Trust, 9750 Ferguson Rd., 75228. Tel: 214-324-3607; Fax: 214-327-8242; Email: chris.rebuck@bishoplynch.org; Email: jaynie.poff@bishoplynch.org; Web: www.bishoplynch.org. Christopher Rebuck, Pres.; Jaynie Poff, Treas., (Retired).

Carmelite Nuns Foundation, 600 Flowers Ave., 75211. Tel: 214-330-7440; Fax: 214-623-1885; Email: dallascarmelites@yahoo.com. Mother Juanita Marie Horan, O.C.D., Prioress.

**Catholic Charismatic Services of Dallas Texas, Inc.* dba Christian Community of God's Delight, 4500 W. Davis, 75211. Tel: 214-333-2337; Fax: 214-339-1702. P.O. Box 225008, 75222. Mr. David Peterman Jr., Pres. Charismatic Covenant Community

Christian Community of God's Delight, Culture of Life Network.

Catholic Community Appeal, Inc. dba Bishop's Annual Appeal for Catholic Ministries, 3725 Blackburn St., P.O. Box 190507, 75219. Tel: 214-379-2803; Fax: 214-521-0840; Email: bhanner@cathdal.org; Web: www.cathdal.org. Barry Hanner, Dir. of Financial Svcs.

Catholic Community Educational Services of Dallas, Inc., 3725 Blackburn St., P.O. Box 190507, 75219-4404. Tel: 214-379-2873; Fax: 214-520-3247; Email: agtaylor@cathdal.org. Annette G. Taylor, Dir. Communications.

**Catholic Crisis Pregnancy Centers of Dallas, Texas* Birth Choice of Dallas, 8610 Greenville Ave., Ste. 200, 75243. Tel: 214-631-2402. Ryan Harkin, Dir. *Legal Title: DBA Birth Choice of Dallas.*

Catholic Physicians Guild of Dallas (2015) 11220 Shelterwood Ln., 75229. Tel: 214-750-9153; Fax: 888-256-9526; Email: jeffrey.thompson@cathmeddallas.org; Email: cathmeddallas@gmail.com; Web: www.cathmeddallas.org. Deacon Charles Stump Jr., Chap.; Dr. Jeffrey Thompson, Pres. Estimated Number of Catholics 200.

The Catholic Pro-Life Committee, Inc. dba The Catholic Pro-Life Committee of North Texas, Inc., 14675 Midway Rd., #121, Addison, 75001. Tel: 972-267-LIFE; Fax: 972-385-3851; Email: cplc@prolifedallas.org; Web: www.prolifedallas.org. Rebecca Visosky, Exec. Dir.

Commission on Ecumenism, 3725 Blackburn St., P.O. Box 190507, 75219-4404. Tel: 214-528-2240; Email: lrossol@cathdal.org. Lynn Rossol, Contact Person, Tel: 214-379-2854; Rev. Robert Williams, Chm.

Dallas Diocesan Council of Catholic Women, 1700 Bertino Way, Rockwall, 75032. Tel: 972-771-4715; Web: nccw.org. Mrs. Stacy Cuzick, Pres.; Sr. Theresa Khirallah, S.S.N.D., Spiritual Advisor.

Dallas Diocesan Education Endowment Trust, P.O. Box 190507, 75219. Tel: 214-379-2800. Barry Hanner, Dir.

Dallas Vocation Guild, 6638 Harlgarlinghouse Ln., 75252. Tel: 972-612-5764; Email: cahead57@att.net. Mrs. Robyn Mathews, Contact Person.

Diocesan Seminary Burse Endowment Fund Trust, 3725 Blackburn St., P.O. Box 190507, 75219. Tel: 214-379-2803; Fax: 214-521-0840; Email: bhanner@cathdal.org. Barry Hanner, Dir. Trust Fund for education of seminarians for Diocese of Dallas.

Focolare Movement - Women's Branch, Texas (Work of Mary), 2437 Crow Creek Dr., 75233. Tel: 214-333-8162; Email: southwest.w@focolare.us. Therese Lee, Pres.

James L. Collins Catholic School Education Trust, 3725 Blackburn St., P.O. Box 190507, 75219. Tel: 214-379-2803; Fax: 214-523-2422; Email: bhanner@cathdal.org. Barry Hanner, Dir.

**Jesuit College Preparatory School of Dallas Foundation, Inc.*, 12345 Inwood Rd., 75244. Tel: 972-387-8700. Rev. Walter T. Sidney, S.J., Supr.

St. Joseph Residence, Inc., 330 W. Pembroke, 75208-6532. Tel: 214-948-3597; Fax: 214-948-1209; Email: richard@stjr.org; Email: ron@stjr.org. Sr. Carolina Botero, Admin. For elderly ladies, gentlemen, and couples. Conducted by Daughters of the Sacred Heart of Jesus (Bethlemitas). Residents 48; Sisters 4.

Ladies of Charity of Dallas, 8448 Walnut Hill Ln., P.O. Box 595666, 75359-0666. Tel: 214-821-5775; Email: mmgriggs@swbell.net. Mary Griggs, Pres.

St. Mary of Carmel Building Trust, 2900 Vilbig Rd., 75212. Tel: 214-747-1433; Email: secsmc@gmail.com. Rev. Jenaro de la Cruz, O.C.D.

**New Evangelization of America*, 3316 Parkhurst Ln., Richardson, 75082. Tel: 469-867-9650; Email: neamail@msn.com; Email: mary.wilson@deospace.com; Web: deospace.com. Gracie Stanford, Sec.; Mary Wilson, Treas.

Our Faith - Our Future Trust, 3725 Blackburn St., P.O. Box 190507, 75219. Tel: 214-379-28003; Email: bhanner@cathdal.org. Barry Hanner, Dir. Financial Svcs.

Santa Clara School Endowment Fund Trust, 3725 Blackburn St., P.O. Box 190507, 75219. Tel: 214-379-2803; Fax: 214-523-2422; Email: bhanner@cathdal.org. Barry Hanner, Dir. Trust Fund to support Santa Clara School.

Texas Catholic Publishing Company, 3725 Blackburn St., P.O. Box 190347, 75219. Tel: 214-379-2893; Fax: 214-528-3411; Email: lharbour@cathdal.org; Web: www.texascatholic.com. David Sedeno, Editor.

St. Thomas More Society of Diocese of Dallas, Texas, 3251 Cambrick St. #17, 75204. Tel: 214-448-4200; Email: ariagnoconnie@yahoo.com. Connie Ariagno, Pres.

Ursuline Academy of Dallas Foundation, Inc., 4900 Walnut Hill Ln., 75229. Tel: 469-232-3584; Fax: 469-232-3593; Email: cmaurer@ursulinedallas.org; Email: gkane@ursulinedallas.org; Web: www.ursulinedallas.org. Ms. Gretchen Z. Kane, Pres.; Catherine Maurer, Dir.

**Young Catholic Professionals*, 6060 N. Central Expwy., Ste. 500, 75206. Tel: 832-306-1919; Email: national@youngcatholicprofessionals.org; Web: www.youngcatholicprofessionals.org. Peter Blute, Contact Person.

ALLEN. *St. Jude Parish Building Trust*, 1515 N. Greenville Ave., Allen, 75002. Tel: 972-727-1177; Fax: 972-727-1401; Email: shawthorne@stjudeparish.com; Web: www.stjudeparish.com. Rev. Andrew V. Semler.

Our Lady of Angels Building Trust, 1914 Ridgeview Dr., Allen, 75013. Tel: 469-467-9669; Email: fsantos@ourladyofangels.com; Web: www.ourladyofangels.com. Fernando Santos, Bus. Mgr. Families 1,248.

HONEY GROVE. *One America International, Inc.*, 2236 CR 2415, Honey Grove, 75446. Tel: 903-378-7073; Email: mary@matasso.com. Thomas Matasso, Pres.

IRVING. *CHRISTUS Health*, 919 Hidden Ridge, Irving, 75038-3813. Tel: 469-282-2649; Email: elaine.harrison@christushealth.org; Web: www.Christushealth.org. Ernie W. Sadau, M.H.A., Pres. & CEO; Linda McClung, Exec. Vice Pres. & Chief Admin. Officer. Bed Capacity 5,718; Tot Asst. Annually 5,678,866; Total Staff 25,000.

CHRISTUS St. Joseph Village, 1201 E. Sandy Lake Rd., Coppell, 75019. Tel: 972-304-0300; Email: mitchell.george@christushealth.org. Mitchell D. George, Dir. CHRISTUS Health is the Parent Entity; this facility is for Senior Residential Care Tot Asst. Annually 187.

CHRISTUS Health Liability Retention Trust, 919 Hidden Ridge, Irving, 75038. Tel: 469-282-2000. Linda McClung, Exec.

CHRISTUS Health Foundation, 919 Hidden Ridge, Irving, 75038-3813. Tel: 713-803-1813; Fax: 713-652-0760; Email: jeannette.baughman@christushealth.org. P.O. Box 1919, Houston, 77251. Jeannette Baughman, Pres.

**Disaster Services Corporation - Society of St. Vincent de Paul USA*, 320 Decker Dr., Ste. 100, Irving, 75062. Cell: 214-717-1802; Email: ldisco@svdpdisaster.org; Web: www.svdpdisaster.org. Elizabeth Disco-Shearer, CEO. Tot Asst. Annually 100,000; Total Staff 204.

**Explore Your Faith*, 400 E. Royal Ln., Ste. 290, Irving, 75039-3602. Tel: 972-725-9306; Cell: 469-417-9797; Email: info@exploreyourfaith.org; Web: www.exploreyourfaith.org. Mrs. Maria Bocalandro, Pres.

Holy Trinity Seminary Scholarship Trust, 3131

Vince Hagan Dr., Irving, 75062. Tel: 214-379-2800; Email: bhanner@cathdal.org. P.O.Box 190507, 75219. Barry Hanner, Contact Person.

Theology of the Body Evangelization Team, Inc. (TOBET), 948 Blaylock Cir., Irving, 75061. Tel: 972-849-6543; Email: scollmer@tobet.org; Web: tobet.org. His Excelency Samuel Aquila, Spiritual Advisor/Care Svcs.; Monica Ann Ashour, Exec. Volunteers 30; Staff 7.

PLANO. *St. Elizabeth Ann Seton Parish Building Trust*, 2701 Piedra Dr., Plano, 75023. Tel: 972-596-5505; Email: mlarson@eseton.org; Web: www.setonparish.org. Marianne Larson, Dir. Finance.

John Paul II High School Building and Endowment Fund, 900 Coit Rd., Plano, 75075. Tel: 972-867-0005; Tel: 469-229-5112; Fax: 972-867-7555; Email: doreenhewes@johnpauliihs.org; Web: www.johnpauliihs.org. Deacon Jake Schroepfer, Trustee; Mr. Brian McPheeters, Admin.

3701 Cardinals, LLC, 900 Coit Rd., Plano, 75075. Tel: 972-867-0005; Email: brianmcpheeters@johnpauliihs.org. Mr. Brian McPheeters, Admin.

RICHARDSON. *St. Paul Parish Endowment Trust Fund*, 900 St. Paul Dr., Richardson, 75080. Tel: 972-235-6105; Fax: 972-480-8528; Email: adrianne@saintpaulchurch.org. Rev. John Szatkowski.

RELIGIOUS INSTITUTES OF MEN REPRESENTED IN THE DIOCESE

For further details refer to the corresponding bracketed number in the Religious Institutes of Men or Women section.

[0200]—*Benedictine Monks*—O.S.B.
[0470]—*The Capuchin Friars*—O.F.M.Cap.
[0340]—*Cistercian Fathers*—O.Cist.
[0260]—*Discalced Carmelite Friars* (Oklahoma Prov.)—O.C.D.
[]—*Divine Word Missionaries*—S.V.D.
[]—*Fuego Nuevo*—F.N.
[0685]—*Institute of Incarnate Word*—I.V.E.
[0690]—*Jesuit Fathers and Brothers* (USA Central & Southern Province)—S.J.
[0730]—*Legionaries of Christ*—L.C.
[]—*Misioneros de la Natividad de Maria*—M.N.M.
[1210]—*Missionaries of St. Charles-Scalabrinians*—C.S.
[0430]—*Order of Preachers (Dominicans)* (Southern Dominican Prov.)—O.P.
[1065]—*Priestly Fraternity of St Peter*—F.S.S.P.
[1070]—*Redemptorists, Congregation of Most Holy Redeemer*—C.SS.R.
[1260]—*Society of Christ*—S.Ch.
[]—*Society of Domus Dei*—S.D.D.
[1330]—*Vincentian Fathers* (Southern Prov.)—C.M.

RELIGIOUS INSTITUTES OF WOMEN REPRESENTED IN THE DIOCESE

[0910]—*Bethlemita, Daughters of the Sacred Heart of Jesus*—Bethl.
[0370]—*Carmelite Sisters of the Sacred Heart*—O.C.D.
[]—*Congregation of Mary Queen*—C.M.R.
[]—*Daughters of the Sacred Heart*—D.S.H.
[0420]—*Discalced Carmelite Nuns*—O.C.D.
[]—*Dominican Sisters of Saint Cecilia Congregation*—O.P.
[1070-03]—*Dominican Sisters of Sinsinawa*—O.P.
[2710]—*Missionaries of Charity*—M.C.
[2690]—*Missionary Catechists of Divine Providence*—M.C.D.P.
[2970]—*School Sisters of Notre Dame*—S.S.N.D.
[]—*Sisters of Blessed Korean Martyrs*—S.B.K.M.
[]—*Sisters of Our Lady of Charity of the Good Shepherd* (Dallas, Inc.)—R.G.S.
[3950]—*Sisters of Saint Mary of Namur* (Western Prov.)—S.S.M.N.
[1970]—*Sisters of the Holy Family of Nazareth* (Sacred Heart Vice Prov.)—C.S.F.N.
[4110]—*Ursuline Nuns (Roman Union)* (Central Prov.)—O.S.U.

DIOCESAN CEMETERIES

DALLAS. *Calvary Hill Cemetery*, 3235 Lombardy Ln., 75220. Tel: 214-357-5754; Fax: 214-523-2422; Email: bhanner@cathdal.org; Web: www.calvaryhillcemetery.com. Mailing Address: P.O. Box 190507, 75219. Tel: 214-379-2803. Barry Hanner, Dir. A corporation that owns and operates Diocesan cemeteries.

Holy Redeemer Cemetery, 1500 S. Westmoreland, Desoto, 75115. Email: bhanner@cathdal.org; Web: www.holyredeemerdesoto.com. Mailing Address: 3725 Blackburn St., P.O. Box 190507, 75219. Tel: 214-357-5754. Barry Hanner, Dir.

Old Calvary Hill, 2500 N. Hall St., 75201. Tel: 214-357-5754; Fax: 214-523-2422; Email: bhanner@cathdal.org. Mailing Address: 3725 Blackburn St., P.O. Box 190507, 75219. Tel: 214-379-2803. Barry Hanner, Dir.

Sacred Heart Cemetery, 3900 Rowlett Rd., Rowlett, 75088. Tel: 214-379-2803; Email: bhanner@cathdal.org. Mailing Address: 3725 Blackburn St., P.O. Box 190507, 75219. Tel: 214-357-5754; Fax: 214-523-2422. Barry Hanner, Dir.

PARISH COLUMBARIA

ALLEN. *St. Jude Parish Columbarium*, 1515 N. Greenville, Allen, 75002. Tel: 972-727-1177; Fax: 972-727-1401; Email: shawthorne@stjudeparish.com. Rev. Andrew V. Semler.

FARMERS BRANCH. *Mary Immaculate Church - Columbarium*, 2800 Valwood Pkwy., Farmers Branch, 75234. Tel: 972-243-7104; Email: marisaw@maryimmaculatechurch.org. Revs. Michael D. Forge; Guiseppe Spoto, Parochial Vicar.

GARLAND. *Mother of Perpetual Help Church - Columbarium*, 2121 W. Apollo Rd., Garland, 75044. Tel: 972-414-7073; Email: dmhcggarland@gmail.com. Rev. Paul Hai Nguyen, C.Ss.R., J.C.L.

PLANO. *St. Elizabeth Ann Seton Parish Columbarium*, 2700 W. Spring Creek Pkwy., Plano, 75023. Tel: 972-596-5505; Email: cchristenson@eseton.org; Web: www.setonparish.org. 2701 Piedra Dr., Plano, 75023. Rev. Bruce Bradley.

Prince of Peace Church - Columbarium, 5100 Plano Pkwy., Plano, 75093. Tel: 972-380-2100; Fax: 972-380-5162; Email: l.whitney3a@popplano.org. Linda Whitney, Contact Person.

St. Mark the Evangelist Parish - Columbarium, 1201 Alma Dr., Plano, 75075. Tel: 972-423-5600; Fax: 972-423-5024; Email: church@stmarkplano.org; Web: stmarkplano.org. Revs. John Hopka, Pastoral Assoc.; Clifford G. Smith; Deacons Shawn French; Luis Garzon; Federico Marquez; Rev. Henry Erazo, Pastoral Assoc.; Deacons Ed Putoni; Fred Rotchford; Henry Wiechman.

RICHARDSON. ST. JOSEPH CHURCH - COLUMBARIUM, 600 S. Jupiter Rd., Richardson, 75081. Tel: 972-231-2951; Email: lsmith@stjosephcc.net. Loretta Smith, Contact Person.

PARISH CEMETERIES

CORSICANA. *Calvary Catholic Cemetery*, c/o Immaculate Conception Parish, 2100 Block of W. 2nd Ave., Corsicana, 75110. Tel: 903-874-4473; Email: mhensley@iccorsicana.org. Rev. Marco Rangel, Pastor

DENISON. *St. Patrick Parish-Calvary Cemetery*, St. Patrick Parish, 314 N. Rusk Ave., Denison, 75020. Tel: 903-463-3275; Fax: 903-463-3447; Email: parishoffice@saintpats.net. Rev. Stephen J. Mocio

ENNIS. *St. Joseph Cemetery*, St. John Nepomucene Parish, 401 E. Lampasas, Ennis, 75119. Tel: 972-878-2834; Fax: 972-875-2452; Email: bhanner@cathdal.org. Barry Hanner, Contact Person

SHERMAN. *St. Mary Parish-St. Mary Cemetery*, 727 S. Travis St., Sherman, 75090. Tel: 903-893-5148; Fax: 903-813-5489. Rev. Esteban D. Antes

WYLIE. *St. Paul Cemetery*, St. Anthony Parish, 404 N. Ballard Ave., Wylie, 75098. Tel: 972-442-2765; Fax: 972-429-9215; Email: frtony@saint-anthony.com. Rev. Anthony M. Densmore

NECROLOGY

† Grahmann, Charles V., Retired Bishop of Dallas, Died Aug. 14, 2018
† Church, Timothy A., (Retired), Died Aug. 15, 2018
† Roberts, Kenneth, (Retired), Died Dec. 20, 2018
† Villaroya, Ernesto, (Retired), Died May. 31, 2018

An asterisk (*) denotes an organization that has established tax-exempt status directly with the IRS and is not covered by the USCCB Group Ruling.

Diocese of Davenport

(Dioecesis Davenportensis)

Most Reverend

THOMAS R. ZINKULA, D.D.

Bishop of Davenport; ordained May 26, 1990; appointed Bishop of Davenport April 19, 2017; ordained and installed June 22, 2017. *Chancery: 780 W. Central Park Ave., Davenport, IA 52804-1901.*

Chancery: 780 W. Central Park Ave., Davenport, IA 52804-1901. Tel: 563-324-1911; Fax: 563-324-5842.

Web: www.davenportdiocese.org

Email: communication@davenportdiocese.org

Most Reverend

MARTIN J. AMOS

Bishop Emeritus of Davenport; ordained May 25, 1968; appointed Titular Bishop of Meta and Auxiliary Bishop of Cleveland April 3, 2001; ordained June 7, 2001; appointed Bishop of Davenport October 12, 2006; installed November 20, 2006; retired April 19, 2017. *3101 River Glen Dr., Austinburg, OH 44010-9761.*

Most Reverend

WILLIAM E. FRANKLIN, D.D.

Bishop Emeritus of Davenport; ordained February 4, 1956; appointed Titular Bishop of Surista and Auxiliary Bishop of Dubuque January 29, 1987; ordained April 1, 1987; appointed Bishop of Davenport November 12, 1993; installed January 20, 1994; retired October 12, 2006. *780 W. Central Park Ave., Davenport, IA 52804-1901.*

ERECTED MAY 8, 1881.

Square Miles 11,438.

Comprises that part of the State of Iowa bounded on the east by the Mississippi River; on the west by the western boundaries of the counties of Jasper, Marion, Monroe and Appanoose; on the south by the State of Missouri; on the north by the northern boundaries of the Counties of Jasper, Poweshiek, Iowa, Johnson, Cedar and Clinton.

For legal titles of diocesan institutions, consult the Chancery.

STATISTICAL OVERVIEW

Personnel	
Bishop	1
Retired Bishops	2
Priests: Diocesan Active in Diocese	56
Priests: Diocesan Active Outside Diocese	3
Priests: Retired, Sick or Absent	38
Number of Diocesan Priests	97
Religious Priests in Diocese	4
Total Priests in Diocese	101
Extern Priests in Diocese	7
Ordinations:	
Diocesan Priests	1
Transitional Deacons	2
Permanent Deacons in Diocese	56
Total Brothers	2
Total Sisters	99
Parishes	
Parishes	77
With Resident Pastor:	
Resident Diocesan Priests	42
Resident Religious Priests	4
Without Resident Pastor:	
Administered by Priests	28
Administered by Deacons	2
Administered by Lay People	1
Professional Ministry Personnel:	
Sisters	8
Lay Ministers	79
Welfare	
Catholic Hospitals	1
Total Assisted	409,607
Health Care Centers	2
Total Assisted	187,339
Homes for the Aged	3
Total Assisted	1,288
Special Centers for Social Services	2
Total Assisted	465
Residential Care of Disabled	1
Total Assisted	17
Educational	
Students from This Diocese	13
Total Seminarians	13
Colleges and Universities	1
Total Students	2,852
High Schools, Diocesan and Parish	5
Total Students	1,244
Elementary Schools, Diocesan and Parish	13
Total Students	3,568
Catechesis/Religious Education:	
High School Students	1,956
Elementary Students	5,439
Total Students under Catholic Instruction	15,072
Teachers in the Diocese:	
Priests	2
Lay Teachers	563
Vital Statistics	
Receptions into the Church:	
Infant Baptism Totals	1,137
Minor Baptism Totals	105
Adult Baptism Totals	83
Received into Full Communion	112
First Communions	1,415
Confirmations	1,261
Marriages:	
Catholic	205
Interfaith	131
Total Marriages	336
Deaths	920
Total Catholic Population	94,225
Total Population	783,834

Former Bishops—Rt. Revs. JOHN MCMULLEN, D.D., ord. June 20, 1858; cons. July 25, 1881; died July 4, 1883; HENRY COSGROVE, D.D., ord. Aug. 27, 1857; cons. Sept. 14, 1884; died Dec. 22, 1906; JAMES DAVIS, D.D., ord. June 21, 1878; cons. Nov. 30, 1904; died Dec. 2, 1926; Most Revs. HENRY P. ROHLMAN, D.D., ord. Dec. 21, 1901; cons. Bishop of Davenport July 26, 1927; appt. Coadjutor-Archbishop of Dubuque and Titular Archbishop of Macra in Rhodope, June 15, 1944; Archbishop of Dubuque, Nov. 21, 1946; appt. Titular Archbishop of Cotrada and retired, Dec. 2, 1954; died Sept. 13, 1957; RALPH LEO HAYES, D.D., ord. Sept. 18, 1909; appt. Bishop of Helena June 23, 1933; cons. Sept. 21, 1933; appt. Rector of North American College in Rome and transferred to Titular See of Hierapolis Sept. 1935; appt. Bishop of Davenport Nov. 16, 1944; appt. Assistant at the Pontifical Throne April 30, 1958; transferred to Titular See of Naraggara and retired Oct. 20, 1966; died July 4, 1970; GERALD FRANCIS O'KEEFE, D.D., ord. Jan. 29, 1944; appt. Auxiliary Bishop of St. Paul and Titular Bishop of Candyba May 5, 1961; cons. July 2, 1961; appt. Bishop of Davenport Oct. 20, 1966; installed Jan. 4, 1967; retired Nov. 12, 1993; died April 12, 2000; WILLIAM E. FRANKLIN, ord. Feb. 4, 1956; appt. Titular Bishop of Surista and Auxiliary Bishop of Dubuque Jan. 29, 1987; ord. April 1, 1987; appt. Bishop of Davenport Nov. 12, 1993; installed Jan. 20, 1994; retired Oct. 12, 2006.; MARTIN J. AMOS, ord. May 25, 1968; appt. Titular Bishop of Meta and Auxiliary Bishop of Cleveland April 3, 2001; ord. June 7, 2001; appt. Bishop of Davenport Oct. 12, 2006; installed Nov. 20, 2006; retired April 19, 2017.

Vicar General—Very Rev. ANTHONY J. HEROLD, V.G.

Chancellor/Chief of Staff—Deacon DAVID MONTGOMERY, Send marriage matters to Tribunal.; To locate sacramental records of parishes that have closed consult the list under the Diocesan Archives on our website.

Vice-Chancellor—Very Rev. PAUL J. APPEL, J.C.L.

Diocesan Tribunal—

Judicial Vicar—Very Rev. PAUL J. APPEL, J.C.L.

Promoters of Justice—Rev. Msgr. FRANCIS C. HENRICKSEN, (Retired); Rev. JOSEPH M. WOLF, J.C.L., V.F.

Defenders of the Bond—Revs. NICHOLAS O. AKINDELE; JOHN P. GALLAGHER, J.C.L., (Retired); Very Rev. WILLIAM E. REYNOLDS, J.C.L., V.F.

Notaries—Deacon DAVID MONTGOMERY; Very Rev. PAUL J. APPEL, J.C.L.; Rev. THOMAS J. HENNEN; Very Rev. ANTHONY J. HEROLD, V.G.; THOMAS TALLMAN; BETH BLOUGH; KATHY LANTZKY.

Judges—Very Revs. PAUL J. APPEL, J.C.L.; RUDOLPH T. JUAREZ, J.C.L., E.V., V.F.; Revs. JOSEPH M. WOLF, J.C.L., V.F.; ROBERT J. BUSHER, (Retired); EDWARD J. FITZPATRICK, (Retired); ROBERT T. MCALEER, (Retired).

Diocesan Consultors—Revs. NICHOLAS J. ADAM; PAUL E. CONNOLLY; DAVID G. STEINLE; JOSEPH M. SIA; Rev. Msgr. JOHN M. HYLAND, (Retired); Very Revs. ANTHONY J. HEROLD, V.G.; KENNETH E. KUNTZ, V.F.; RUDOLPH T. JUAREZ, J.C.L., E.V., V.F.

Deans—Very Revs. JAMES J. VRBA, V.F., Davenport; MARTIN G. GOETZ, V.F., Keokuk; KENNETH E. KUNTZ, V.F., Clinton; PATRICK J. HILGENDORF, V.F., Ottumwa; WILLIAM E. REYNOLDS, J.C.L., V.F., Grinnell; RUDOLPH T. JUAREZ, J.C.L., E.V., V.F., Iowa City.

Diocesan Corporate Board—Most Reverend THOMAS R. ZINKULA, D.D.; Very Rev. ANTHONY J. HEROLD, V.G.; Deacon DAVID MONTGOMERY; TERRENCE KILBURG, CPA; ROGER REILLY.

Finance Officer—THOMAS TALLMAN.

Finance Council—Most Reverend THOMAS R. ZINKULA, D.D.

Diocesan Offices and Directors

Finance—THOMAS TALLMAN.

Director of Development and Stewardship—MICHAEL HOFFMAN.

Director of Parish Planning—DAN EBENER, D.B.A.

Director of Communication—Deacon DAVID MONTGOMERY.

Director of Technology—ROBERT BUTTERWORTH.

Director of Faith Formation—DON BOUCHER.

Superintendent of Schools—LEE MORRISON, Ph.D.

Director of Social Action—KENT FERRIS.

Immigration Program Counselors—GRICELDA GARNICA; KARINA GARNICA.

Director of Liturgy—Deacon FRANCIS L. AGNOLI, D.Min.

Director of Catholic Charities—KENT FERRIS.

Catholic Relief Services—KENT FERRIS.

Catholic Campaign for Human Development—LOXI HOPKINS.

Newspaper—The Catholic Messenger BARB ARLAND-FYE, Editor & Gen. Mgr., 780 W. Central Park Ave., Davenport, 52804-1901. Tel: 563-323-9959; Fax: 563-888-4382; Email: messenger@davenportdiocese.org; Web: catholicmessenger.net.

Pastoral Council—Most Reverend THOMAS R. ZINKULA, D.D.

Diaconate—Deacon TERRY L. STARNS.

Deacon Formation—Deacon FRANCIS L. AGNOLI, D.Min.

Presbyteral Council—Most Reverend THOMAS R. ZINKULA, D.D.

The Priests' Aid Society, Inc.—Mailing Address: P.O. Box 1478, Newton, 50208-1478. Tel: 641-792-2050. Most Rev. THOMAS R. ZINKULA.

Propagation of the FaithKENT FERRIS.

Vicar for Priests—Very Rev. STEPHEN P. EBEL, E.V., (Retired), 1522 W. Garfield St., Davenport, 52804. Tel: 563-349-4033.

Vicar for Hispanics—Very Rev. RUDOLPH T. JUAREZ, J.C.L., E.V., V.F., 4330 St. Patrick Dr., Iowa City, 52240-4733.

Victim Assistance Coordinator—ALICIA OWENS, Mailing Address: P.O. Box 232, Bettendorf, 52722-0004. Tel: 563-349-5002; Email: vac@diodav.org.

Vocations—Rev. JOSEPH M. SIA.

CLERGY, PARISHES, MISSIONS AND PAROCHIAL SCHOOLS

CITY OF DAVENPORT

(SCOTT COUNTY)

1—ST. ALPHONSUS CHURCH OF DAVENPORT, IOWA (1903)
2618 Boies Ave., 52802. Tel: 563-322-0987; Fax: 563-323-1458; Email: davstalfin@diodav.org; Web: www.stalphonsusdav.org. Very Rev. Paul J. Appel, J.C.L.
See All Saints Catholic School, Davenport under Elementary Schools, Interparochial located in the Institution Section.
Catechesis Religious Program—Email: davstaldre@diodav.org. Mary Ann Hagemann, D.R.E. Students 42.

2—ST. ANTHONY CHURCH OF DAVENPORT, IOWA (1837)
417 N. Main St., 52801. Tel: 563-322-3303; Fax: 563-322-5136; Email: davstanthony@diodav.org; Web: www.stanthonysdavenportiowa.org. Rev. Apo T. Mpanda; Mr. John Cooper; Denise Hoteling, D.R.E.; Deb Williams, Accountant; Mrs. Jan Streit, Sec.
Catechesis Religious Program—Email: davstanthonydre@diodav.org. Students 56.

3—HOLY FAMILY CHURCH OF DAVENPORT, IOWA (1897)
1315 W. Pleasant St., 52804. Tel: 563-322-0901; Tel: 563-322-0902; Fax: 563-884-4965; Email: davholyfamily@diodav.org; Web: holyfamilydavenport.com. Rev. H. Robert Harness, V.F.
See All Saints Catholic School, Davenport under Elementary Schools, Interparochial located in the Institution Section.
Child Care—Holy Family Teddy Bear Club, 1923 N. Fillmore St., 52804. Tel: 563-322-6648; Email: davholyfamily@diodav.org. Lisa Conger, Dir. (Preschool & daycare program) Students 26.
Catechesis Religious Program—Diane Lannan, D.R.E. Students 50.

4—ST. MARY CHURCH OF DAVENPORT, IOWA (1867)
516 Fillmore St., 52802. Tel: 563-322-3383; Email: davstmary@diodav.org; Web: stmarydavenport.org. Revs. Christopher R. Young; Joseph M. Sia, Sacramental Min.
Catechesis Religious Program—Tel: 563-322-1450; Email: davstmarydre@diodav.org. Kay Steele, D.R.E.; Jasmin Tone, Youth Min. Students 160.

5—OUR LADY OF VICTORY CHURCH OF DAVENPORT, IOWA (1962)
4105 N. Division St., 52806. Tel: 563-391-4245; Fax: 563-445-1003; Email: davolv@diodav.org; Web: www.olvjfk.com. Rev. Jacob M. Greiner; Deacons Francis L. Agnoli, D.Min.; Marcel G. Mosse; Albert G. Boboth; John J. Wagner.
School—John F. Kennedy Catholic School, (Grades PreK-8), 1627 W. 42nd St., 52806. Tel: 563-391-3030; Fax: 563-388-5206; Email: chad.steimle@olvjfkmail.com; Web: www.olvjfk.com. Chad Steimle, Prin. Lay Teachers 34; Students 449.
Catechesis Religious Program—1627 W 42nd St, 52806. Tel: 563-391-8384; Email: davolvrek6@diodav.org. Jennifer Wemhoff, D.R.E., K-8. Students 82.

6—ST. PAUL THE APOSTLE CHURCH OF DAVENPORT, IOWA (1909)
916 E. Rusholme St., 52803. Tel: 563-322-7994; Fax: 563-322-7995; Email: davstpaul@diodav.org; Web: www.stpaulcatholicparish.org. Very Rev. Anthony J. Herold, V.G.; Rev. Nicholas O. Akindele, Parochial Vicar; Deacon Robert W. Shaw.
School—St. Paul the Apostle Church of Davenport, Iowa School, (Grades PreK-8), 1007 E. Rusholme St., 52803. Tel: 563-322-2923; Fax: 563-322-9359; Email: julie.delaney@st-paul.pvt.k12.ia.us. Mrs. Julie Delaney, Prin. Lay Teachers 30; Students 475.
Catechesis Religious Program—Email: davstpauldre@diodav.org. Jen Brooke, D.R.E. Students 138.

7—SACRED HEART CATHEDRAL OF DAVENPORT, IOWA (1856) [JC]
422 E. 10th St., 52803-5499. Tel: 563-324-3257; Fax: 563-326-6014; Email: davsacredheart@diodav.org; Web: www.shcdavenport.org. Very Rev. Richard A. Adam; Deacon Daniel L. Huber.
See All Saints Catholic School, Davenport under Elementary Schools, Interparochial located in the Institution Section.
Catechesis Religious Program—Students 21.

OUTSIDE THE CITY OF DAVENPORT

ALBIA, MONROE CO., ST. MARY CHURCH OF ALBIA, IOWA (1874) [CEM]
730 Benton Ave., W., Albia, 52531. Tel: 641-932-5130 ; Email: stmaryalbia@iowatelecom.net; Email: albiastmary@diodav.org. P.O. Box 365, Albia, 52531. Rev. Michael Volkmer, C.PP.S., Admin.
Catechesis Religious Program—Email: scrallalbia@iowatelecom.net. Sharon Crall, D.R.E. Students 180.

BAUER, MARION CO., ST. JOSEPH'S CHURCH OF BAUER, IOWA, [CEM] Contact Tina Schneider, 454 Vermont Dr., Lacona, IA, 50139.
780 W. Central Park Ave., 52804-1901. Email: hoefling@davenportdiocese.org. Rev. Kevin J. Anstey, Admin.

BETTENDORF, SCOTT CO.

1—ST. JOHN VIANNEY CHURCH OF BETTENDORF, IOWA (1967) [JC]
4097 18th St., Bettendorf, 52722-2120.
Tel: 563-332-7910; Fax: 563-332-0833; Email: bettsjv@diodav.org; Web: www.sjvbett.org. Very Rev. James J. Vrba, V.F.; Deacons John R. Weber, Sacramental Min.; Charles A. Metzger, Sacramental Min.; Daryl G. Fortin.
School—St. John Vianney Church of Bettendorf School, Tel: 563-332-5308; Email: preschool@sjvbett.org; Web: www.sjvbett.org. Christy Barnum, Dir. Lay Teachers 5; Students 45.
Catechesis Religious Program—Email: re@sjvbett.org. Jeanne Moran, D.R.E. Students 714.

2—OUR LADY OF LOURDES CHURCH OF BETTENDORF, IOWA (1903)
1506 Brown St., Bettendorf, 52722.
Tel: 563-359-0345; Fax: 563-344-6017; Email: bettlourdes@diodav.org; Web: www.lourdescatholic.com. 1414 Mississippi Blvd., Bettendorf, 52722-4915. Revs. Jason K. Crossen; Christopher Weber, Parochial Vicar; Deacons Dennis L. Duff; Charles A. Metzger; Michael D. Snyder; John R. Weber.
School—Our Lady of Lourdes Church of Bettendorf, Iowa School aka Lourdes Catholic School, (Grades PreSchool-8), 1453 Mississippi Blvd., Bettendorf, 52722. Tel: 563-359-3466; Fax: 563-823-1595; Email: bettlourdesbiz@diodav.org; Email: jennifer.alongi@lourdes.pvt.k12.ia.us; Web: www.lourdescatholic.org. Jennifer Alongi, Prin. Lay Teachers 23; Students 220.
Catechesis Religious Program—Email: bettlourdesdre@diodav.org. Emily Andes, D.R.E. Students 126.

BLOOMFIELD, DAVIS CO., ST. MARY MAGDALEN CHURCH OF BLOOMFIELD, IOWA (1953)
108 Weaver Rd., Bloomfield, 52537.
Tel: 641-682-4212; Email: bloomstmarymag@diodav.org. Mailing Address: 222 N. Ward St., Ottumwa, 52501. Very Rev. Patrick J. Hilgendorf, V.F.
Catechesis Religious Program—Tel: 641-980-8808; Email: angela.hunter@operint.com. Angela Hunter, D.R.E. Students 23.

BLUE GRASS, SCOTT CO., ST. ANDREW CHURCH OF BLUE GRASS, IOWA (1976) [JC]
333 W. Lotte St., Blue Grass, 52726.
Tel: 563-381-1363; Email: bluegrassstandrew@diodav.org; Web: www.standrewbluegrass.org. Revs. Apo T. Mpanda, Priest Mod.; Robert L. Grant, Sacramental Min.; Deacons Terry L. Starns, Parish Life Coord.; Dan E. Freeman.
Catechesis Religious Program—Email: smschmidt@centurylink.net. Phyllis Avesing, D.R.E.; Shirley Schmidt, RCIA Coord. Students 90.

BROOKLYN, POWESHIEK CO., ST. PATRICK CHURCH OF BROOKLYN, IOWA, [CEM]
215 Jackson St., Brooklyn, 52211-0512.
Tel: 641-522-4323; Email: brooklynstpat@diodav.org; Web: stpatrick-stbridget.org. P.O. Box 512, Brooklyn, 52211. Rev. Corey C. Close.
Catechesis Religious Program—Tel: 847-594-2868; Email: brooklynstpatdre@diodav.org. Angie Gritsch, D.R.E. Students 69.

BUFFALO, SCOTT CO., ST. PETER CHURCH OF BUFFALO, IOWA (1912) [CEM]
406 4th St., Buffalo, 52728. Tel: 563-322-0987; Fax: 563-323-1458; Email: buffalostpeter@diodav.org. P.O. Box 488, Buffalo, 52728. Very Rev. Paul J. Appel, J.C.L.; Deacon Larry F. Dankert.
Catechesis Religious Program—Email: davstalfin@diodav.org. Nancy Stalder, D.R.E. Students 44.

BURLINGTON , DES MOINES CO.

1—SS. JOHN & PAUL CHURCH OF BURLINGTON, IOWA (1842) [JC] Merged with SS. Mary & Patrick, West Burlington to form Divine Mercy Parish of Burlington-West Burlington.

2—ST. MARY CHURCH OF SPERRY, IOWA (1850) [CEM]
13204 Dodgeville Rd., Sperry, 52650.
Tel: 319-752-8771; Email: dodgevillestmary@diodav.org; Web: www.dmcountycatholic.org. Mailing Address: 502 W. Mt. Pleasant Ave., West Burlington, 52655. Very Rev. Martin G. Goetz, V.F.; Rev. Daniel Dorau, Parochial Vicar; Deacon Robert J. Glaser.
Catechesis Religious Program—Tel: 319-752-6733; Email: dodgevillestmarydre@diodav.org. Cindy Pfeiff, D.R.E. Students 65.

CAMANCHE, CLINTON CO., CHURCH OF THE VISITATION OF CAMANCHE, IOWA (1966)
1028 Middle Rd., Camanche, 52730-1032.
Tel: 563-259-1188; Fax: 563-259-4462; Email: camanchevisitation@diodav.org. Rev. Joseph M. Wolf, J.C.L., V.F.
Catechesis Religious Program—Cell: 563-613-2921. Sandra Campie, D.R.E. Students 37.

CENTERVILLE, APPANOOSE CO., ST. MARY CHURCH OF CENTERVILLE, IOWA (1870)
828 S. 18th St., Centerville, 52544.
Tel: 641-437-1984; Email: centervillestmary@diodav.org. Rev. William G. Hubmann, C.PP.S.
Catechesis Religious Program—Email: awesangels@gmail.com. Kathy Allen, D.R.E.; Ms. Tanya Moore, D.R.E.; Ms. Sonja Carson, Youth Min. Students 60.

CHARLOTTE, CLINTON CO., ASSUMPTION AND ST. PATRICK CHURCH OF CHARLOTTE, IOWA (1993) [CEM 2]
147 Broadway St., Charlotte, 52731.
Tel: 563-677-2758; Email: charlotteassumstpat@diodav.org. Rev. Scott G. Lemaster.
Catechesis Religious Program—Tel: 563-357-7276; Email: eberhart19@yahoo.com. Erin Meyermann, D.R.E. Students 33.

CLINTON, CLINTON CO., JESUS CHRIST, PRINCE OF PEACE ROMAN CATHOLIC CHURCH OF CLINTON, IOWA (1990) [CEM 2]
1105 LaMetta Wynn Dr., Clinton, 52732.
Tel: 563-242-3311; Fax: 563-242-3323; Email: clintonjcpop@diodav.org; Web: www.jcpop.org. Very Rev. Kenneth E. Kuntz, V.F.; Rev. John J. Stack; Deacons Jeffrey C. Schuetzle; Ramon Hilgendorf; Annette Lyons; Deb Jacobsen, RCIA Coord.; David Schnier, Business Mgr.; Angie Ahlberg, Sec.
School—Jesus Christ, Prince of Peace Roman Catholic Church of Clinton, Iowa School, (Grades PreK-12), 312 S. 4th St., Clinton, 52732.
Tel: 563-242-1663; Fax: 563-243-8272; Email: n.peart@staff.prince.pvt.k12.ia.us; Web: www.prince.pvt.k12.ia.us. Mrs. Nancy Peart, Prin.
Legal Title: Prince of Peace Catholic Education System Lay Teachers 21; Students 204.
Catechesis Religious Program—Brenda Bertram, D.R.E. & Youth Min. Students 141.

COLFAX, JASPER CO., IMMACULATE CONCEPTION CHURCH OF COLFAX, IOWA (1898)
305 E. Howard, Colfax, 50054-1025.
Tel: 515-674-3711; Email: colfaximmconc@diodav.org; Web: www.immaculateconceptioncolfax.org. Rev. Ross M. Epping, Mod.; Very Rev. William E. Reynolds, J.C.L., V.F., Sacramental Min.; Deacon Joseph F. Dvorak, Parish Life Coord.
Catechesis Religious Program—Tel: 515-490-6883; Email: peggy.dvorakia@gmail.com. Peggy Dvorak, D.R.E. Students 49.

COLUMBUS JUNCTION, LOUISA CO., ST. JOSEPH CHURCH OF COLUMBUS JUNCTION, IOWA (1853)
815 Second St., Columbus Junction, 52738.
Tel: 319-728-8210; Email: coljctstjoseph@diodav.org; Web: www.saintjosephcj.webs.com. Rev. Troy A. Richmond.
Catechesis Religious Program—Email: coljctstjosephdre@diodav.org. Catalina Valdez, D.R.E. Students 46.

CORALVILLE, JOHNSON CO., ST. THOMAS MORE CHURCH OF CORALVILLE, IOWA (1944) [JC]
3000 12th Ave., Coralville, 52241. Tel: 319-337-2173; Fax: 319-337-2174; Email: crlvlsttmore@diodav.org; Web: www.stmparishfamily.com. Rev. Charles Adam; Deacon David L. Krob, Sacramental Min.
Catechesis Religious Program—Tel: 319-337-4231; Email: redirector@stthomasmoreic.com. Shannon Duffy, D.R.E. Students 534.

COSGROVE, JOHNSON CO., ST. PETER CHURCH OF COSGROVE, IOWA (1878)
4022 Cosgrove Rd., S.W., Oxford, 52322.
Tel: 319-828-4180; Tel: 319-545-2077; Email: cosgrovestpeter@diodav.org; Web: www.stpetercosgrove.weebly.com. Revs. Edmond J. Dunn, Ph.D., Sacramental Min.; Robert J. Cloos, Parochial Vicar; Deacons David Montgomery; Joseph T. Rohret.
Catechesis Religious Program—Email: kyouthgroup@gmail.com. Jodi Suther, D.R.E. Students 34.

DEWITT, CLINTON CO., ST. JOSEPH CHURCH OF DEWITT, IOWA (1850) [CEM]
417 6th Ave., DeWitt, 52742. Tel: 563-659-3514; Fax: 563-659-2599; Email: dewittstjoseph@diodav.org; Email: sjc@gmtel.net; Web: www.stjoseph-dewitt.weconnect.com. Rev. Stephen C. Page; Sr. Janet Heiar, S.S.N.D., Pastoral Assoc.; Deacon Mark A. Comer.
School—St. Joseph Church of DeWitt School, Iowa, (Grades PreK-8), Tel: 563-659-3812; Email: sharon.roling@st-joseph-dwt.pvt.k12.ia.us; Web: www.st-joseph-dwt.pvt.k12.ia.us. Sharon Roling, Prin. Lay Teachers 16; Students 203.
Catechesis Religious Program—Email: sjyouth@gmtel.net. Pat Sheil, D.R.E. Students 160.

DELMAR, CLINTON CO., ST. PATRICK CHURCH OF DELMAR, IOWA (1882) [CEM]
405 Delmar Ave., Delmar, 52037. Tel: 563-677-2758; Email: charlotteassumstpat@diodav.org. 147 Broadway St., Charlotte, 52731. Rev. Scott G. Lemaster.
Catechesis Religious Program—Email: d.bowman@fbcom.net. Jane Bowman, D.R.E. Students 26.

DODGEVILLE, DES MOINES CO.

FAIRFIELD, JEFFERSON CO., ST. MARY'S CHURCH OF FAIRFIELD, IOWA (1864)
3100 W. Madison Ave., Fairfield, 52556-2466.
Tel: 641-472-3179; Email: fairfieldstmary@diodav.org; Web: www.fairfieldstmary.org. Rev. Nicholas J. Adam.
Catechesis Religious Program—Jean Dorothy, D.R.E. Students 110.

FARMINGTON, VAN BUREN CO., ST. BONIFACE CHURCH OF FARMINGTON, IOWA (1862) [CEM]
609 Washington St., Farmington, 52626.
Tel: 319-837-6808; Fax: 319-837-8112; Email: westpointstmary@diodav.org. P.O. Box 247, Farmington, 52626. Rev. Dennis L. Hoffman.
Catechesis Religious Program—Tel: 319-837-8905; Email: westpointstmarydre@diodav.org. Dixie Booten, D.R.E. Students 18.

FORT MADISON, LEE CO., HOLY FAMILY PARISH OF FORT MADISON, IOWA (2009) [CEM]
1111 Ave. E., Fort Madison, 52627. Email: fortmadholyfamily@diodav.org; Web: fortmadisoncatholiccommunity.com. Revs. Joseph P. V. Phung; Mark P. Spring, Parochial Vicar; Sr. Peggy Duffy, S.S.N.D., Pastoral Assoc.; Deacons Ronald K. Stein; Robert R. Gengengbacher; David U. Sallen
Legal Title: Sacred Heart Church, Ss. Mary & Joseph Church
Catechesis Religious Program—
Tel: 319-372-2127, Ext. 107; Email: fortmadholyfamilydre@diodav.org. Students 80.

GEORGETOWN, MONROE CO., ST. PATRICK CHURCH OF GEORGETOWN, IOWA (1851) [CEM]
Hwy. 34 W., Albia, 52531. Tel: 641-932-5589; Email: georgetownstpat@diodav.org. P.O. Box 183, Albia, 52531. Rev. Mark Yates, C.PP.S.; Deacon Edwin D. Kamerick; Sharon Crall, Pastoral Assoc.
Catechesis Religious Program—Email: scrallalbia@iowatelecom.net. Students 11.

GRAND MOUND, CLINTON CO., SS. PHILIP AND JAMES CHURCH OF GRAND MOUND, IOWA (1876) [CEM]
606 Fulton St., P.O. Box 7, Grand Mound, 52751-0007. Tel: 563-847-2271; Email: grandmssphilipjames@diodav.org. Rev. Francis V. Odoom; Deacon Michael D. Sheil.
Catechesis Religious Program—Maureen Schrader, D.R.E. Students 48.

GRINNELL, POWESHIEK CO., ST. MARY CHURCH OF GRINNELL, IOWA (1924) [CEM]
1002 Broad St., Grinnell, 50112. Tel: 641-236-7486; Email: grinnellstmary@diodav.org; Web: www.stmarygrinnell.com. P.O. Box 623, Grinnell, 50112. Rev. Ross M. Epping; Deacon John S. Osborne.
Catechesis Religious Program—Tel: 641-236-8838; Email: grinnellstmarydre@diodav.org. Ms. Crystal DeNeve, D.R.E. Students 138.

HILLS, JOHNSON CO., ST. JOSEPH CHURCH OF HILLS, IOWA (1902) [CEM]
Mailing Address: 209 Brady St., P.O. Box 187, Hills, 52235. Tel: 319-679-2271; Email: hillsstjoseph@diodav.org; Web: stsmaryandjoseph.com. Rev. Michael J. Spiekermeier; Mrs. Carol Kaalberg, Pastoral Min./Coord.
Catechesis Religious Program—109 Jayne St., Lone Tree, 52755. Mrs. Trudi Westfall, D.R.E. Students 54.

HOUGHTON, LEE CO., ST. JOHN CHURCH OF HOUGHTON, IOWA (1895) [CEM]
205 Denning St., P.O. Box 100, Houghton, 52631.
Tel: 319-469-2001; Web: stjj.weconnect.com. Rev. Bruce A. DeRammelaere.
Catechesis Religious Program—Tel: 319-837-8905; Email: westpointstmarydre@diodav.org. Dixie Booten, D.R.E. Students 8.

IOWA CITY, JOHNSON CO.

1—ST. MARY CHURCH OF IOWA CITY, IOWA (1840) [CEM 2] [JC]
228 E. Jefferson St., Iowa City, 52245.
Tel: 319-337-4314; Email: icstmary@diodav.org; Web: www.icstmary.org. Mailing Address: 302 E. Jefferson St., Iowa City, 52245-2137. Revs. Stephen J. Witt; Robert J. Cloos, Parochial Vicar; Deacon Joseph B. Welter; Sr. Mary Agnes Giblin, B.V.M., Pastoral Assoc.
Catechesis Religious Program—Tel: 319-351-7638; Email: carolyn.brandt@regina.org. Carolyn Brandt, D.R.E. See Regina Inter-Parish Catholic Education Center under Education Centers in the Institutions Section.

2—ST. PATRICK CHURCH OF IOWA CITY, IOWA (1872) [CEM]
4330 St. Patrick Dr., Iowa City, 52240.
Tel: 319-337-2856; Fax: 319-354-5590; Email: icstpat@diodav.org; Web: www.stpatsic.com. Very Rev. Rudolph T. Juarez, J.C.L., E.V., V.F.; Rev. Guillermo Trevino Jr., Parochial Vicar.
Catechesis Religious Program—Tel: 319-351-7638; Email: carolyn.brandt@regina.org. Carolyn Brandt, D.R.E. See Regina Inter-Parish Catholic Education Center under Education Centers in the Institutions Section.

3—ST. WENCESLAUS CHURCH OF IOWA CITY, IOWA (1893) [JC]
618 E. Davenport St., Iowa City, 52245.
Tel: 319-337-4957; Fax: 319-337-5822; Email: icstwenc@diodav.org; Web: stwenc-ic.com. 630 E. Davenport St., iowa city, 52245. Rev. Gary L. Beckman; Deacon Christopher L. Kabat.
Catechesis Religious Program—Tel: 319-351-7638; Email: carolyn.brandt@regina.org. Carolyn Brandt, D.R.E. See Regina Inter-Parish Catholic Education Center under Education Centers in the Institutions Section.

KEOKUK, LEE CO., CHURCH OF ALL SAINTS OF KEOKUK, IOWA (1982)
310 S. 9th St., Keokuk, 52632. Tel: 319-524-8334; Email: keokukallsaints@diodav.org; Web: www.allsaintskeokuk.org. Rev. Robert A. Lathrop.
School—Keokuk Catholic Schools, Inc., (Grades PreK-5), 2981 Plank Rd., Keokuk, 52632-2399.
Tel: 319-524-5450; Fax: 319-524-7725; Email: darren.macarthur@keokukcatholic.org; Web: www.keokukcatholicschools.org. Darren MacArthur, Prin. Lay Teachers 10; Students 90.
Child Care—St. Vincent's Extended Day Care Program, 2981 Plank Rd., Keokuk, 52632-5452.
Tel: 319-524-5450; Fax: 319-524-7725; Email: darren.macarthur@keokukcatholic.org; Web: www.keokukcatholicschools.org. Darren MacArthur, Prin. Lay Teachers 10; Students 92.
Catechesis Religious Program—Trevor Pullinger, D.R.E. Students 67.

KEOTA, KEOKUK CO., HOLY TRINITY CHURCH OF KEOTA/HARPER, IOWA (1992) [CEM 3]
109 N. Lincoln St., Keota, 52248-9757.
Tel: 641-636-3883; Email: keotaholytrinity@diodav.org; Web: www.holytrinityparish-keota.com. Rev. Charles J. Fladung, V.F.
Catechesis Religious Program—Cell: 641-660-3063; Email: shannon.greiner@sigourneyschools.com. Shannon Greiner, D.R.E. Students 169.

KNOXVILLE, MARION CO., ST. ANTHONY CHURCH OF KNOXVILLE, IOWA (1870) [CEM]
1202 Woodland St., Knoxville, 50138.
Tel: 641-828-7050; Fax: 641-842-2338; Email: knoxvillestanthony@diodav.org; Web: www.stanthonyknoxville.com. 1201 Woodland St., Knoxville, 50138. Rev. Kevin J. Anstey; Deacon Thomas A. Hardie.
Catechesis Religious Program—Email: knoxvillestanthonydre@diodav.org. Laura Hollinrake, Dir. Faith Formation. Students 35.

LE CLAIRE, SCOTT CO., OUR LADY OF THE RIVER CHURCH OF LE CLAIRE-PRINCETON, IOWA (1969)
28200 226th St., P.O. Box 32, LeClaire, 52753.
Tel: 563-289-5736; Fax: 563-289-3688; Email: leclaireolor@diodav.org; Web: www.ourladyoftheriver.com. Rev. Joseph M. Wolf, J.C.L., V.F.
Catechesis Religious Program—Roberta Pegorick, D.R.E. Students 109.

LONE TREE, JOHNSON CO., ST. MARY CHURCH OF LONE TREE, IOWA (1853) [CEM] [JC]
216 West Jayne St., Lone Tree, 52755.
Tel: 319-679-2271. Mailing Address: Sts. Mary & Joseph Cluster Office, P.O. Box 187, Hills, 52235. Email: lonetreestmary@diodav.org; Web: stsmaryandjoseph.com. Rev. Michael J. Spiekermeier, Admin.; Mrs. Carol Kaalberg, Pastoral Min./Coord.
Catechesis Religious Program—Mrs. Trudi Westfall, D.R.E. Students 48.

LONG GROVE, SCOTT CO., ST. ANN CHURCH OF LONG GROVE, IOWA (1853) [CEM]
16550 290th St., Long Grove, 52756.
Tel: 563-285-4596; Fax: 563-285-4897; Email: longrovestann@diodav.org; Web: www.stannslonggrove.org. Rev. Msgr. Drake R. Shafer.
Catechesis Religious Program—Email: jkloft@stannslonggrove.org. Joyce Kloft, D.R.E. Students 303.

LOST NATION, CLINTON CO., OUR LADY OF THE HOLY ROSARY CATHOLIC CHURCH OF LOST NATION, IOWA aka Sacred Heart Catholic Church (2015) [CEM]
903 Main St., P.O. Box 127, Lost Nation, 52254-0127. Tel: 563-678-2200; Email: lostnationholyrosary@diodav.org. Rev. Francis V. Odoom.
Catechesis Religious Program—Beverly Brauer, D.R.E. Students 19.

LOVILIA, MONROE CO., ST. PETER CHURCH OF LOVILIA, IOWA (1904) [CEM]
601 W. 6th St., Lovilia, 50150. Tel: 641-946-8298; Email: loviliastpeter@diodav.org. P.O. Box 8, Lovilia, 50150. Rev. Mark Yates, C.PP.S.; Deacon Edwin D. Kamerick.
Catechesis Religious Program— Clustered with St. Mary, Albia and St. Patrick, Georgetown. 730 Benton Ave. W, Albia, 52531. Tel: 641-932-5589. Mailing Address: P.O. Box 365, Albia, 52531. Sharon Crall, D.R.E.

MARENGO, IOWA CO., ST. PATRICK CHURCH OF MARENGO, IOWA (1878) [CEM]
957 Western Ave., Marengo, 52301.
Tel: 319-642-5438; Fax: 319-642-5648; Email: marengostpat@diodav.org; Email: marengostpatdre@diodav.org. P.O. Box 183, Marengo, 52301. Rev. David F. Wilkening, V.F.
Catechesis Religious Program—Tel: 319-560-8476; Email: angela.carney@mercer.com. Angie Carney, D.R.E. Students 39.

MECHANICSVILLE, CEDAR CO., ST. MARY CHURCH OF MECHANICSVILLE, IOWA (1872)
302 W. Reeder St., Mechanicsville, 52306-0457.
Tel: 563-886-2506; Email: Tiptonstmary@diodav.org; Web: www.stmarystipton.net. P. O. Box 309, Tipton, 52772. Rev. Richard U. Okumu.
Catechesis Religious Program—Tel: 563-432-6236. Lori Crock, D.R.E. Students 34.

MELCHER, MARION CO., SACRED HEART CHURCH OF MELCHER, IOWA (1912) [CEM] [JC]
204 S.W. D St., Melcher, 50163. Tel: 641-947-4981; Email: melchersacredheart@diodav.org. P.O. Box 277, Melcher Dallas, 50163. Rev. Kevin J. Anstey; Deacon Thomas A. Hardie.
Catechesis Religious Program—Email: sacredheartmd@iowatelecom.net. Ms. Shari Schneider, D.R.E. Students 47.

MELROSE, MONROE CO., ST. PATRICK CHURCH OF MELROSE, IOWA (1870) [CEM]
200 Trinity Ave., Melrose, 52569. Tel: 641-732-3531; Email: melrosestpat@diodav.org. Rev. Mark Yates, C.PP.S.; Deacon Edwin D. Kamerick.
Catechesis Religious Program—Tel: 641-726-3246; Email: melrosestpatdre@diodav.org. Jane Kamerick, D.R.E. Students 21.

MONTROSE, LEE CO., ST. JOSEPH CHURCH OF MONTROSE, IOWA (1860) [JC]
Mailing Address: 1111 Ave. E., Fort Madison, 52627.
Tel: 319-372-2127; Fax: 319-372-2083; Email: montrosestjoseph@diodav.org; Web: www.fortmadisoncatholiccommunity.com. 508 Cedar St., Montrose, 52639. Revs. Joseph P. V. Phung; Mark P. Spring, Parochial Vicar; Deacon David U. Sallen.
Catechesis Religious Program— Combined with Holy Family, Fort Madison. Email: fortmadholyfamilyre@diodav.org. Sr. Peggy Duffy, S.S.N.D., D.R.E.

MOUNT PLEASANT, HENRY CO., ST. ALPHONSUS CHURCH OF MT. PLEASANT, IOWA (1862) [CEM]
607 S. Jackson St., Mount Pleasant, 52641-2696. Tel: 319-385-8410; Fax: 319-385-0545; Email: mtpleasantstal@diodav.org; Web: www.stalphonsus.weconnect.com. Rev. Paul E. Connolly.
Catechesis Religious Program—Email: stalphonsus@windstream.net. Margi Mountz, D.R.E. & Adult Faith Formation. Students 139.

MUSCATINE, MUSCATINE CO., SS. MARY AND MATHIAS CHURCH OF MUSCATINE, IOWA, [CEM]
215 W. Eighth St., Muscatine, 52761. Email: muscssmarymathias@diodav.org; Web: marymathias.org. Revs. Troy A. Richmond; Hai D. Dinh, Parochial Vicar; Deacons Dennis H. McDonald; M. Anthony Mouzon.
School—Saints Mary and Mathias Catholic School, (Grades PreK-8), 2407 Cedar St., Muscatine, 52761-2696. Tel: 563-263-3264; Email: ben.nietzel@muscatinesaints.org; Web: www.muscatinesaints.org. Benjamin Nietzel, Prin. Lay Teachers 20; Students 309.
Catechesis Religious Program—Tel: 563-263-3848; Email: srcheryl@marymathias.org. Sr. Mary Cheryl Demmer, P.B.V.M., D.R.E. Students 338.

NEWTON, JASPER CO., SACRED HEART CHURCH OF NEWTON, IOWA (1867) [CEM]
1115 S. Eighth Ave. E., Newton, 50208-1478. Tel: 641-792-2050; Tel: 641-792-4625; Fax: 641-792-8639; Email: newtonsacredheart@diodav.org; Web: shcnewton.org. P.O. Box 1478, Newton, 50208-1478. Very Rev. William E. Reynolds, J.C.L., V.F.
Catechesis Religious Program—Email: shlifelongff@gmail.com. Students 148.

NICHOLS, MUSCATINE CO., ST. MARY CHURCH OF NICHOLS, IOWA (1874) [CEM] [JC]
201 Short St., Nichols, 52766. Tel: 319-679-2271; Email: nicholsstmary@diodav.org; Web: stsmaryandjoseph.com. Mailing Address: Sts. Mary & Joseph Cluster Office, 209 Brady St., P.O. Box 187, Hills, 52235-0187. Rev. Michael J. Spiekermeier, Admin.; Mrs. Carol Kaalberg, Pastoral Min./Coord.
Catechesis Religious Program—Tel: 319-679-2274. Mrs. Trudi Westfall, D.R.E.

NORTH ENGLISH, IOWA CO., ST. JOSEPH CHURCH OF NORTH ENGLISH, IOWA (1896) [JC]
221 N. Knollridge St., North English, 52316. Tel: 319-664-3325; Email: stjosephne@yahoo.com; Email: northenglishstjoseph@diodav.org. P.O. Box 219, North English, 52316. Rev. David F. Wilkening, V.F.
Catechesis Religious Program—Tel: 319-325-6086; Email: awestphal@english-valleys.k12.ia.us. Amanda Westphal, D.R.E. Students 51.

OSKALOOSA, MAHASKA CO., ST. MARY CHURCH OF OSKALOOSA, IOWA (1871) [CEM]
315 1st Ave. E., Oskaloosa, 52577. Tel: 641-673-0659 ; Tel: 641-673-6680; Web: stmarysosky.com. 301 High Ave. E., Oskaloosa, 52577. Rev. John D. Spiegel, V.F.; Deacons Donald L. Efinger; Lowell W. Van Wyk.
Catechesis Religious Program—Tel: 641-673-0659; Email: oskystmarydre@diodav.org. Samantha Ridder, D.R.E. Students 103.

OTTUMWA, WAPELLO CO.
1—CHURCH OF ST. MARY OF THE VISITATION (1851)
216 N. Court St., Ottumwa, 52501-2586. Tel: 641-682-4559; Fax: 641-682-4433; Email: ottstmary@diodav.org; Web: www.stmaryofthevisitationinottumwa.net. Rev. James G. Betzen, C.PP.S.; Deacon James J. Vonderhaar.
Catechesis Religious Program—117 E 4th St., Ottumwa, 52501. Tel: 641-682-4496; Email: ottstmarydre@diodav.org. Lisa Canny, D.R.E. Students 226.
2—ST. PATRICK CHURCH OF OTTUMWA, IOWA (1880)
222 N. Ward St., Ottumwa, 52501. Tel: 641-682-4212 ; Fax: 641-682-7915; Email: ottstpat@diodav.org; Web: www.stpatrickottumwa.com. Very Rev. Patrick J. Hilgendorf, V.F.
Catechesis Religious Program—Ottumwa Regional Catholic Religious Education, Tel: 641-682-0320; Email: stpatedu@hotmail.com. Gail Bates, D.R.E. Students 40.

OXFORD, JOHNSON CO., ST. MARY CHURCH OF OXFORD, IOWA (1860) [CEM]
215 Summit St., Oxford, 52322. Tel: 319-828-4180; Email: oxfordstmary@diodav.org; Web: sites.google.com/site/stmaryoxford/. P.O. Box 80, Oxford, 52322-0080. Rev. Robert J. Cloos; Deacons David Montgomery; Joseph T. Rohret.
Catechesis Religious Program—Tel: 319-668-9532; Email: oxfordstmaryDRE@diodav.org. Dorene Francis, D.R.E. Students 116.

PELLA, MARION CO., ST. MARY CHURCH OF PELLA, IOWA (1869) [CEM]
726 218th Pl., Pella, 50219-7500. Tel: 641-628-3078; Email: pellastmary@diodav.org; Web: www.stmarypella.org. Rev. John D. Spiegel, V.F.; Deacons Lowell W. Van Wyk; Donald L. Efinger.
Catechesis Religious Program—Email: pellastmarydre@diodav.org. Carol Laughlin, D.R.E. Students 214.

PETERSVILLE, CLINTON CO., IMMACULATE CONCEPTION CHURCH OF PETERSVILLE, IOWA (1853) [CEM]
147 Broadway St., Charlotte, 52731. Tel: 563-677-5728; Email: charlotteassumstpat@diodav.org. 2885 145th St., Petersville, 52731. Rev. Scott G. Lemaster.
Catechesis Religious Program—405 Delmar Ave., P. O. Box 293, Delmar, 52037. Tel: 563-677-2758. Jane Bowman, D.R.E.

RICHLAND, KEOKUK CO., SS. JOSEPH AND CABRINI CATHOLIC CHURCH (2008) [CEM]
308 W. Main St., P.O. Box 130, Richland, 52585-0130. Tel: 319-456-3161; Email: richlandssjosephcabrini@diodav.org; Web: ssjosephandcabriniparish.weconnect.com. Revs. Nicholas J. Adam; Damian Ilokaba, Sacramental Min.; Shirley Van Dee, Parish Life Coord.
Catechesis Religious Program—Tel: 319-456-3161. Students 8.

RICHMOND, WASHINGTON CO., HOLY TRINITY CHURCH OF RICHMOND, IOWA (1854) [CEM]
571 Howard St., Kalona, 52247-9558. Tel: 319-656-2802; Tel: 319-648-2331; Email: richmondholytrinity@diodav.org; Web: www.clusterparishes.org. PO Box C, Riverside, 52327. Rev. William D. Roush; Deacon Derick K. Cranston.
Catechesis Religious Program—Email: cranstond@diodav.org. Students 70.

RIVERSIDE, WASHINGTON CO., ST. MARY CHURCH OF RIVERSIDE, IOWA (1877) [CEM]
360 Washburn St., Riverside, 52327. Tel: 319-648-2331; Email: clusterparish@gmail.com. P.O. Box C, Riverside, 52327. Rev. William D. Roush.
Catechesis Religious Program—Email: cranstond@diodav.org. Students 90.

ST. PAUL, LEE CO., ST. JAMES CHURCH OF ST. PAUL, IOWA (1838) [CEM]
Mailing Address: 205 Denning St., P.O. Box 100, Houghton, 52631-0100. Tel: 319-469-2001; Email: stpaulstjames@diodav.org; Web: stjj.weconnect.com. 2044 Locust St., St. Paul, 52657. Rev. Bruce A. DeRammelaere.
Catechesis Religious Program— (Clustered with St. John, Houghton.) Tel: 319-837-8905; Email: westpointstmarydre@diodav.org. Dixie Booten, D.R.E. Students 11.

SIGOURNEY, KEOKUK CO., ST. MARY CHURCH OF SIGOURNEY, IOWA (1873) [CEM] [JC]
415 E. Pleasant Valley St., Sigourney, 52591. Tel: 641-622-3426; Fax: 641-622-2316; Email: sigourneystmary@diodav.org; Web: www.holytrinityparish-keota.com. Rev. Charles J. Fladung, V.F.; Deacon James L. Striegel.
Catechesis Religious Program—Tel: 641-622-3698; Email: sigourneystmarydre@diodav.org. Jenny Thompson, C.R.E. Students 102.

SOLON, JOHNSON CO., ST. MARY CHURCH OF SOLON, IOWA (1858) [CEM]
1749 Racine Ave., Solon, 52333-0069. Tel: 319-624-2228; Fax: 319-624-3564; Email: solonstmary@diodav.org; Web: www.solonstmary.org. Rev. Timothy J. Sheedy; Deacons Mitchell A. Holte; David L. Krob.
Catechesis Religious Program—Email: solonstmaryDRE@diodav.org. Julie Agne, D.R.E. Students 280.

SUGAR CREEK, CLINTON CO., SS. MARY AND JOSEPH CHURCH OF SUGAR CREEK, IOWA (1993) [CEM 2]
147 Broadway, Charlotte, 52731. Tel: 563-677-2758; Email: charlotteassumstpat@diodav.org. 3218 110th St, Preston, 52069. Rev. Scott G. Lemaster.
Catechesis Religious Program—Erin Meyermann, D.R.E.

TIPTON, CEDAR CO., ST. MARY CHURCH OF TIPTON, IOWA (1856) [CEM]
208 Meridian St., Tipton, 52772. P.O. Box 309, Tipton, 52772-0309. Tel: 563-886-2506; Fax: 563-886-6326; Email: tiptonstmary@diodav.org; Web: www.stmarystipton.net. Rev. Richard U. Okumu.
Catechesis Religious Program—Tel: 319-321-0715; Email: Stmarymaryb@gmail.com. Mary Barnum, D.R.E. Students 93.

VICTOR, IOWA CO., ST. BRIDGET CHURCH OF VICTOR, IOWA (1886) [CEM] [JC]
104 Third St., Victor, 52347. Tel: 319-647-2220; Tel: 319-647-2294; Fax: 319-647-7721; Email: victorstbridget@diodav.org; Web: www.stpatrick-stbridget.org. Rev. Corey C. Close.
Catechesis Religious Program—Tel: 319-350-2974; Email: victorstbridgetdre@diodav.org. Stephanie Thys, D.R.E. Students 32.

WASHINGTON, WASHINGTON CO., ST. JAMES CHURCH OF WASHINGTON, IOWA (1860) [JC]
602 W. 2nd St., Washington, 52353-1994. Tel: 319-653-4504; Email: info@stjameswashington.org; Email: washstjames@diodav.org; Web: www.stjameswashington.org. Rev. Bernard E. Weir.
School—St. James Church of Washington School, Iowa, (Grades PreK-5), Tel: 319-653-3631; Email: bmcbride@stjameswashington.org; Web: www.stjameswashington.org. Mrs. Beth McBride, Prin. Clergy 1; Lay Teachers 12; Students 107; Clergy / Religious Teachers 1.
Catechesis Religious Program—Email: washstjamesdre@diodav.org. Lori Fritz, Faith Formation Coord. Students 238.

WELLMAN, WASHINGTON CO., ST. JOSEPH CHURCH OF WELLMAN, IOWA (1969) [CEM]
235 11th St., Wellman, 52356. Tel: 319-648-2331; Fax: 319-648-5024; Email: wellmanstjoseph@diodav.org; Web: www.clusterparishes.org. P.O. Box 145, Wellman, 52356. Rev. William D. Roush; Deacon Derick K. Cranston, Pastoral Assoc.
Catechesis Religious Program—Email: cranstond@diodav.org. Students 45.

WEST BRANCH, CEDAR CO., ST. BERNADETTE CHURCH OF WEST BRANCH, IOWA (1960)
507 E. Orange, West Branch, 52358-0103. Tel: 319-643-2095; Email: westbranchstbern@diodav.org. P.O. Box 103, West Branch, 52358. Rev. David G. Steinle.
Catechesis Religious Program—Email: westbranchstbernDRE@diodv.org. Joanne Salemink, D.R.E. Students 52.

WEST BURLINGTON, DES MOINES CO.
1—DIVINE MERCY PARISH OF BURLINGTON-WEST BURLINGTON
502 W. Mt. Pleasant St., West Burlington, 52655. Tel: 319-752-6733; Tel: 319-752-8771; Fax: 319-753-5211; Email: burldivinem@diodav.org; Web: www.dmcountrycatholic.org. Very Rev. Martin G. Goetz, V.F.; Rev. Daniel Dorau, Parochial Vicar; Deacon Robert J. Glaser.
Catechesis Religious Program—700 S. Roosevelt Ave., Burlington, 52601. Tel: 319-752-8690; Email: burldivinedre@diodav.org. Cease Cady, D.R.E. Students 115.
2—SS. MARY & PATRICK CHURCH OF WEST BURLINGTON, IOWA (1870) [CEM] Merged with SS. John & Paul Church of Burlington, Iowa to form Divine Mercy Parish of Burlington-West Burlington.

WEST LIBERTY, MUSCATINE CO., ST. JOSEPH CHURCH OF WEST LIBERTY, IOWA (1892) [CEM]
107 W. Sixth St., West Liberty, 52776-1246. Tel: 319-627-2229; Fax: 319-627-2552; Email: westlibstjoseph@diodav.org; Web: www.stjosephwestliberty.org. Very Rev. Rudolph Juarez, E.V., J.C.L.; Rev. Guillermo Trevino Jr., Parochial Vicar.
Catechesis Religious Program—Email: angellymiahdamian1964@gmail.com. Rosemary Gonzalez, D.R.E. Students 176.

WEST POINT, LEE CO., ST. MARY CHURCH OF WEST POINT, IOWA, [CEM]
116 4th St., West Point, 52656. Tel: 319-837-6808; Fax: 319-837-6808; Email: westpointstmary@diodav.org; Web: www.westpointstmary.org. Rev. Dennis L. Hoffman.
Catechesis Religious Program—Tel: 319-837-8905; Email: westpointstmarydre@diodav.org. Dixie Booten, D.R.E. Students 14.

WILLIAMSBURG, IOWA CO., ST. MARY CHURCH OF WILLIAMSBURG, IOWA (1891) [CEM]
102 E. Penn St., Williamsburg, 52361. Tel: 319-668-1397; Email: williamsburgstmary@diodav.org. P.O. Box 119, Williamsburg, 52361. Rev. David F. Wilkening, V.F.
Catechesis Religious Program—Tel: 319-668-2757; Email: williamsburgstmarydre@diodav.org. Trilby Owens, D.R.E. Students 163.

WILTON, MUSCATINE CO., ST. MARY CHURCH OF WILTON, IOWA (1857) [CEM]
701 E. 3rd St., Wilton, 52778. Email: wiltonstmary@diodav.org; Web: www.stmarywilton.org. Rev. David G. Steinle.
Catechesis Religious Program—Tel: 641-715-4004; Email: steinled@diodav.org. Lynette Fagner, D.R.E. Students 70.

Chaplains of Public Institutions

IOWA CITY. *Mercy Hospital*.
University of Iowa Hospitals and Clinics. Revs. Timothy J. Regan, Gregory A. Steckel.
VA Medical Center. Rev. Damian O. Ilokaba, (Nigeria).

On Duty Outside the Diocese:
Rev.—
Nguyen, Joseph T., 1525 Sheridan Dr., Kenmore, NY 14217-1211.

Graduate Studies:
Rev.—
Lamansky, John D., Pontifical Gregorian University, Rome.

Retired:
Rev. Msgrs.—
Burnett, James E., (Retired), 8505 Hemlock Ln., Darien, IL 60561-8416
Henricksen, Francis C., (Retired), 1113 1st Cedar Bluff St., Tipton, 52772-9289
Hyland, John M., (Retired), 780 W. Central Park Ave., 52804-1901
Schmidt, W. Robert, Ph.D., (Retired), 6701 Jersey Ridge Rd., 52807-3203
Spiegel, Robert H., (Retired), 2021 Edmundson Dr., Oskaloosa, 52577-4311
Walter, Robert J., (Retired), 6701 Jersey Ridge Rd., 52807-3203
Very Rev.—
Ebel, Stephen P., E.V., (Retired), 1522 W. Garfield St., 52804-1745
Revs.—
Busher, Robert J., (Retired), 780 W. Central Park Ave., 52804-1901
Doyle, Thomas R., (Retired), 780 W. Central Park Ave., 52804-1901
Fitzpatrick, Edward J., (Retired), 15 Montgomery Pl., Iowa City, 52240-3092
Gallagher, John P., J.C.L., (Retired), 104 E. Gleneagles Rd. Apt. B, Ocala, FL 34472-8476
Helms, Walter B., (Retired), 202 Village Dr., Apt. 4, Tiffin, 52340
Hitch, David, (Retired), Prairie Hills Senior Living, 219 S. Cedar St., Tipton, 52722-1764
Kaska, E. William, (Retired), 104 Jefferson St., Iowa City, 52245
Kelly, Andrew E., (Retired), 1005 W. 8th St., Yankton, SD 57078-3389
Leonhardt, Louis J., (Retired), P.O. Box 454, Lone Tree, 52755
Lumsden, Patrick L., (Retired), 480 Madison Ave. N., Unit 2, North Liberty, 52317-2321
Martin, Dennis C., (Retired), 114 E. Maxson Ave., West Liberty, 52776-1053
McAleer, Robert T., (Retired), 5370 Kilt Ct., Bettendorf, 52722
McDaniel, George W., Ph.D., (Retired), 518 W. Locust, 52803-2898
O'Melia, Edward A., (Retired), 780 W. Central Park Ave., 52804-1901
Parlette, Thomas L., (Retired), 780 W. Central Park Ave., 52804-1901
Phillips, Michael T., (Retired), 212 Sweeny Ave., Burlington, 52601-6246
Reilman, Thomas J., (Retired), 264 Angela Jean Cir., Peosta, 52068-9726
Roost, Joseph F., (Retired), 1910 Grand Ave., Keokuk, 52632-2942
Ryan, Philip V., (Retired), 207 W. Green St., Apt. A2, P.O. Box 263, Brooklyn, 52211-0263
Spiegel, Thomas J., (Retired), 2021 Edmundson Dr., Oskaloosa, 52577-4311
Stecher, John E., (Retired), 780 W. Central Park Ave., 52804-1901
Stratman, Thomas F., (Retired), 780 W. Central Park Ave., 52804-1901
Wiegand, William R., (Retired), 608 2nd St., Apt. 316, Pella, 50219.

Permanent Deacons:
Barton, Steven E., Davenport
Becker, James L., Muscatine
Beckman, Clifford C., Sperry
Boboth, Albert G., Davenport
Comer, Mark A., Grand Mound
Cranston, Derick K., Kalona
Dankert, Larry F., Davenport
Donnelly, William G., Bettendorf
Duff, Dennis L., Bettendorf
Dvorak, Joseph F., Colfax
Freeman, Dan E., Davenport
Frericks, Donald E., Blue Grass
Gengenbacher, Robert R., Fort Madison
Glaser, Robert J., Burlington
Hardie, Thomas A., Knoxville
Hilgendorf, Ramon C., Clinton
Holte, Mitchell A., Solon
Huber, Daniel L., Davenport
Jacobsen, John E., Bettendorf
Kabat, Christopher L., Iowa City
Kamerick, Edwin D., Melrose
Krob, David L., Ely
McDonald, Dennis H., Muscatine
Metzger, Charles A., Bettendorf
Miller, Jerome A., Iowa City
Montgomery, David, Oxford
Mosse, Marcel G., Davenport
Osborne, John S., Grinnell
Rasmussen, Richard J., Bettendorf
Reha, David, Wellman
Rohret, Joseph T., Parnell
Rosenthal, Joseph I., Davenport
Sallen, David U., Ft. Madison
Schuetzle, Jeffrey C., Clinton
Shaw, Robert W., Davenport
Sheil, Michael D., DeWitt
Snavely, Robert E., Tipton
Snyder, Michael D., Bettendorf
Starns, Terry L., Blue Grass
Stein, Ronald K., Donnellson
Strader, George D., Davenport
Striegel, James L., Delta
Van Wyk, Lowell W., Pella
Vonderhaar, James J., Ottumwa
Wagner, John J., Davenport
Weber, John R., Bettendorf
Welter, Joseph B., Kalona.

Incardinated in the Diocese and Working or Retired Outside the Diocese:
Deacons—
Cadena, Juan J., Ferris, TX
Donart, Arthur C., Thomson, IL; Thomson, IL
Gutierrez, Julian, Alexandria, VA
Lennon, Patrick, Oswego, IL
McCoy, Robert C., Grimes, IA
Schroeder, William E., West Des Moines, IA.

Incardinated Elsewhere While Working in the Diocese:
Deacons—
Agnoli, Francis L., Davenport
Efinger, Donald L., Pella
Fortin, Daryl G., Bettendorf
Mouzon, Anthony M., Muscatine
Thompson, Ward B., Lone Tree.

INSTITUTIONS LOCATED IN DIOCESE

[A] COLLEGES AND UNIVERSITIES

DAVENPORT. **St. Ambrose University*, (Grades Bachelors-Doctorate), 518 W. Locust St., 52803-2898. Tel: 563-333-6300; Fax: 563-333-6243; Email: officeofthepresident@sau.edu; Web: www.sau.edu. Dr. Joan Lescinski, C.S.J., Pres.; Dr. Sandra Cassady, Dean College of Health & Human Svcs., Vice Pres. Strategic Initiatives; Dr. Paul Koch, Provost & Vice Pres., Academic & Student Affairs; Dr. James Loftus, Vice Pres. for Enrollment Mgmt.; Michael Poster, CPA, Vice Pres. Finance; James Stangle, Vice Pres. Advancement; Revs. Thomas J. Hennen, Chap.; Brian Miclot, Ph. D., Prof.; Robert L. Grant, Prof. Clergy 1; Lay Teachers 211; Priests 3; Sisters 1; Students 2,852; Total Faculty & Staff 483; Clergy / Religious Teachers 2.

[B] HIGH SCHOOLS, INTERPAROCHIAL

DAVENPORT. *Assumption High School*, 1020 W. Central Park Ave., 52804-1899. Tel: 563-326-5313; Fax: 563-326-3510; Email: andy.craig@assumptionhigh.org; Web: www.assumptionhigh.org. Mr. Andrew Craig, Pres.; Mrs. Bridget Murphy, Prin.; Mike Frieden, Dean of Students. Lay Teachers 27; Students 460; Clergy / Religious Teachers 3.

BURLINGTON. *Notre Dame Middle School - High School*, (Grades 6-12), 702 S. Roosevelt Ave., Burlington, 52601-1602. Tel: 319-754-8431; Fax: 319-752-8690; Email: bill.maupin@bnotredame.org; Web: burlingtonnotredame.org. Bill Maupin, Prin. Lay Teachers 16; Students 228; Clergy / Religious Teachers 2.

FORT MADISON. *Holy Trinity Jr./Sr. High School* aka Holy Trinity Catholic Schools, Inc., (Grades 7-12), 2600 Ave. A, Fort Madison, 52627.
Tel: 319-372-2486; Tel: 319-837-6131, Ext. 102; Fax: 319-837-8112; Fax: 319-372-6310; Email: michael.sheerin@holytrinityschools.org; Email: mindy.goldie@holytrinityschools.org; Web: www.holytrinityschools.org. Michael Sheerin, Prin. Holy Trinity Jr/Sr High School educates children in grades 7-12 and is located in Fort Madison, Iowa. Holy Trinity Elementary School educates children in grades K-6 and is located in West Point, Iowa.
Holy Trinity Catholic Schools, Inc. Lay Teachers 15; Students 139; Elementary School Students 173.

[C] EDUCATION CENTERS

IOWA CITY. *The Regina Inter-Parish Catholic Education Center*, 2140 Rochester Ave., Iowa City, 52245. Tel: 319-337-2580; Fax: 319-337-4109; Email: alan.opheim@icregina.com; Web: regina.org. Rev. Charles A. Adam.
Regina Junior Senior High School, (Grades 7-12), 2150 Rochester Ave., Iowa City, 52245.
Tel: 319-338-5436; Fax: 319-887-3817; Email: glenn.plummer@icregina.com; Web: regina.org. Glenn Plummer, Prin. Lay Teachers 32; Students 353.
Regina Elementary School, (Grades K-6), 2120 Rochester Ave., Iowa City, 52245-3527.
Tel: 319-337-5739; Fax: 319-337-4109; Email: celeste.vincent@icregina.com; Web: regina.org. Ms. Celeste Vincent, Prin. Lay Teachers 32; Students 441.
Regina Religious Education, 2140 Rochester Ave., Iowa City, 52245. Tel: 319-351-7638;
Fax: 319-337-4109; Email: carolyn.brandt@icregina.com; Web: www.regina.org. Carolyn Brandt, D.R.E. Students 79.
Regina Special Events Office, 2140 Rochester Ave., Iowa City, 52245. Tel: 319-358-2455;
Fax: 319-337-4109; Email: trish.kohl@icregina.com. Trish Kohl, Contact Person.
Regina Preschool-Daycare, 2140 Rochester Ave., Iowa City, 52245. Tel: 319-337-6198;
Fax: 319-337-4109; Email: mary.pechous@icregina.com; Web: regina.org. Ms. Mary Pechous, Dir. Students 75.

[D] ELEMENTARY SCHOOLS, INTERPAROCHIAL

DAVENPORT. *All Saints Catholic School*, (Grades PreK-8), 1926 N. Marquette St., 52804-2199.
Tel: 563-324-3205; Fax: 563-324-9331; Email: jeanne.vonfeldt@saints.pvt.k12.ia.us; Web: ascsdav.org. Jeanne Von Feldt, Prin. Lay Teachers 27; Students 441.

BURLINGTON. *Notre Dame Elementary School*, (Grades PreK-5), 700 S. Roosevelt Ave., Burlington, 52601-1602. Tel: 319-752-3776; Tel: 319-754-4417;
Fax: 319-752-8690; Email: bill.maupin@bnotredame.org; Web: www.burlingtonnotredame.org. Bill Maupin, Prin. Lay Teachers 15; Students 228; Clergy / Religious Teachers 5.

OTTUMWA. *Seton Catholic School*, (Grades PreK-5), 117 E. 4th St., Ottumwa, 52501-2992.
Tel: 641-682-8826; Fax: 641-682-6202; Email: james.wessling@oseton.com; Web: www.oseton.com. James A. Wessling, Prin. Lay Teachers 13; Students 138.

[E] CATHOLIC STUDENT CENTERS

IOWA CITY. *Newman Catholic Student Center*, 104 E. Jefferson St., Iowa City, 52245. Tel: 319-337-3106; Fax: 319-337-6858; Email: newman-center@uiowa.edu; Web: www.newman-ic.org. Rev. Jeffry Belger, Dir.

[F] RESIDENTIAL ADOLESCENT CARE CENTERS

CLINTON. *L'Arche Clinton*, 715 S. 3rd St, Lower Level, Clinton, 52732. P.O. Box 278, Clinton, 52733-0278. Tel: 563-243-9035; Fax: 563-243-7796; Email: communityleader.larcheclinton@gmail.com; Web: www.larcheclinton.org. Dr. Jaret Land, Exec. Dir.; April Burken, Dir.; Mrs. Jean Bormann, Dir. Devel. & Communications; Mrs. Hilary Graham, Admin.
Arch, Inc. Bed Capacity 15; Tot Asst. Annually 17; Total Staff 30.

[G] GENERAL HOSPITALS

CENTERVILLE. *Mercy Medical Center - Centerville*, 1 St. Joseph's Dr., Centerville, 52544. Tel: 641-437-4111 ; Fax: 641-437-3304; Web: www.mercycenterville.org. Ann Young, Pres. Owned by Mercy Medical Center, Des Moines. Attended from St. Mary's, Centerville. Bed Capacity 25; Tot Asst. Annually 150,000; Total Staff 270.

CLINTON. *Mercy Medical Center - Clinton* A subsidiary of Trinity-Health, Inc. 1410 N. Fourth St., Clinton, 52732. Tel: 563-244-5609, Ext. 5609; Email: melissa.free@mercyhealth.com. Amy Berentes, Admin. Bed Capacity 163; Tot Asst. Annually 37,339; Staff 953.
Mercy Living Center - North, 600 14th Ave. N., Clinton, 52732. Tel: 563-244-3884;
Fax: 563-244-3882; Email: melissa.free@mercyhealth.com; Web: www.mercyclinton.com. Julie Eggers, Admin. Bed Capacity 86.

IOWA CITY. *Mercy Hospital*, 500 E. Market St., Iowa City, 52245. Tel: 319-339-0300; Web: www.mercyiowacity.org. Sean J. Williams, CEO. Bed Capacity 234; Tot Asst. Annually 409,607; Total Staff 1,141.

[H] HOMES FOR AGED

DAVENPORT. *Kahl Home for the Aged and Infirm*, 6701 Jersey Ridge Rd., 52807. Tel: 563-324-1621;
Fax: 563-324-1723; Email: lmcdonald@kahlhomedav.com; Web: kahlhomedav.com. Mrs. Kimberly Hufsey, Admin. Carmelite Sisters for the Aged and Infirm. Bed Capacity 135; Residents 128; Sisters 4; Total Staff 195.

CLINTON. *The Alverno Health Care Facility, Trinity Health*, 849 13th Ave. N., Clinton, 52732.
Tel: 563-242-1521; Fax: 563-243-3016; Email: alvernoinfo@mercyhealth.com; Web: www.thealverno.com. Libby Goodman, Admin. Bed Capacity 132; Total Staff 180; Total Assisted 434.

[I] MONASTERIES AND RESIDENCES FOR PRIESTS AND BROTHERS

DAVENPORT. *St. Vincent Center*, 780 W. Central Park Ave., 52804-1901. Tel: 563-324-1911;
Fax: 563-324-5842; Email: montgomery@davenportdiocese.org. Most Reverend Thomas R. Zinkula, D.D., Ordinary; Revs. Nicholas O. Akindele, Res.; Robert J. Busher, Res., (Retired); Thomas R. Doyle, Res., (Retired); Denis Hatungimana, Res.; Rev. Msgr. John M. Hyland, Res., (Retired); Revs. Edward A. O'Melia, Res., (Retired); Fortunatus Rwehikiza, Res.; Joseph M. Sia, Res.; Thomas F. Stratman, Res., (Retired).

WEVER. *Brothers of the Poor of Saint Francis*, 3405 190th St., Wever, 52658. Tel: 319-372-9543;
Fax: 319-372-9543; Email: markgast@gmail.com. Bros. Mark Gastel, Member; Austin Schroeder, Member.

[J] CONVENTS AND RESIDENCES FOR SISTERS

DAVENPORT. *Franciscan Sisters of Christ the Divine Teacher*, 2605 Boies Ave., 52802. Tel: 563-323-1502 ; Web: www.divineteacher.org. Sr. Susan Rueve, O.S.F., Supr. Sisters 2.

Humility of Mary Center - Motherhouse of the Congregation of the Humility of Mary, 820 W. Central Park Ave., 52804-1900. Tel: 563-323-9466; Fax: 563-323-5209; Email: sisters@chmiowa.org; Web: chmiowa.org. Sr. Mary Ann Vogel, C.H.M., Pres. Sisters 74.

Our Lady of the Prairie Retreat, 2664 145th Ave., Wheatland, 52777. Tel: 563-323-9466;
Fax: 563-323-5209; Email: olpretreat@gmail.com; Web: www.chmiowa.org. Sr. Mary Ann Vogel, C.H.M., Pres.

CLINTON. *The Canticle*, 841 13th Ave. N., Clinton, 52732-5162. Tel: 563-242-7903; Fax: 563-242-8024; Email: jcebula@clintonfranciscans.com; Web: www.clintonfranciscans.com. Sr. Janice I. Cebula, O.S.F. Residence of the Sisters of St. Francis, Clinton, Iowa. Sisters 29; Total in Residence 33.

Sisters of St. Francis, Clinton, Iowa, Administrative Center, 843 13th Ave. N., Clinton, 52732-5115.
Tel: 563-242-7611; Fax: 563-243-0007; Email: jcebula@clintonfranciscans.com; Web: www.clintonfranciscans.com. Sr. Janice I. Cebula, O.S.F., Pres. Sisters 52.

ELDRIDGE. *Carmel of the Queen of Heaven Discalced Carmelite Nuns*, 17937 250th St., Eldridge, 52748-9425. Tel: 563-285-8387; Fax: 563-285-7467; Email: solitude@netins.net; Web: www.carmelitesofeldridge.org. Sr. Lynne Elwinger, O.C.D., Prioress. Professed Sisters 7.

[K] MISCELLANEOUS

DAVENPORT. **Assumption Foundation for K-12 Schools*, 1020 W. Central Park Ave., 52804.
Tel: 563-326-5313; Fax: 563-326-3510; Email: andy.craig@assumptionhigh.org. Mr. Andrew Craig, Pres.

Catholic Foundation for the Diocese of Davenport, 780 W. Central Park Ave., 52804-1901.
Tel: 563-324-1911; Fax: 563-324-5842; Email: hoffman@davenportdiocese.org; Web: www.davenportdiocese.org. Michael Hoffman, Exec.

Catholic Service Board, 230 W. 35th St., 52806.
Tel: 563-323-1923; Email: chrisgallin@msn.com. Mary Gallin, Pres.

Congregation of the Humility of Mary Charitable Trust, 820 W. Central Park Ave., 52804-1900.
Tel: 563-323-9466; Fax: 563-323-5209; Email: sisters@chmiowa.org; Web: www.chmiowa.org. Sr. Mary Ann Vogel, C.H.M., Contact Person.

Eagles' Wings Incorporated, 5816 Telegraph Rd., 52804. Tel: 563-324-7263; Email: marcia@eagleswings.ws; Web: www.eagleswings.ws. Marcia Moore, Dir.

St. Paul the Apostle Foundation, 916 E. Rusholme St., 52803. Tel: 563-322-7994; Fax: 363-322-7995; Email: davstpaul@diodav.org. Very Rev. Anthony J. Herold, V.G., Contact Person.

Project Renewal of Davenport, Inc., 906 W. Fifth St., 52802. Tel: 563-324-0800; Email: projectrenewal@revealed.net; Web: www.projectrenewal.net. Ann Schwickerath, Dir.; Carl Callaway, Site Supvr. In Res. Ann Schwickerath; Carl Callaway.

Roman Catholic Ministries of Iowa City, Iowa (2002) 780 W. Central Park Ave., 52804.
Tel: 563-324-1911; Fax: 563-324-5842; Email: communication@davenportdiocese.org. Very Rev. Anthony J. Herold, V.G., Contact Person.

Sacred Heart Cathedral Foundation, Inc., 422 E. 10th St., 52803. Tel: 563-324-3257;
Fax: 563-326-6014; Email: davsacredheart@diodav.org; Web: www.shcdavenport.org. Very Rev. Richard Adam, Pres.

School Tuition Organization of Southeast Iowa, 1850 E. 54th St., 52807. Tel: 563-391-1845; Email: steve.roling@roling.tax; Web: stoseiowa.org. Steven M. Roling, Exec. Dir.

Scott County Catholic Education Services, Inc. dba All Saints Catholic School, 1926 Marquette St., 52804. Tel: 563-324-3205; Fax: 530-324-9331; Email: mvardeman@saints.pvt.k12.ia.us; Web: www.ascsdav.org. Jeanne Von Feldt, Prin.
DBA All Saints Catholic School.

Spirit, Inc., 2214 Harrison St., 52803.
Tel: 563-324-1776; Tel: 563-323-5499; Email: pdroe61@gmail.com. Paul Roe, Pres.; Timothy Heinrichs, Vice Pres.; Diane Roe, Sec.

**St. Thomas Aquinas Guild of the Quad Cities*, 2939 E. 44th Ct., 52807. Tel: 563-343-6647; Email: stthomasaquinasguild@gmail.com; Web: www.stthomasaquinasguildqc.com. Tim Millea, M.D., Contact Person.

**Cafe on Vine*, 932 W. 6th St., 52802. P.O. Box 3375, 52808. Tel: 563-324-4472; Email: cafeonvine2@aol.com; Web: www.cafeonvine.org. Waunita Sullivan, Exec. Dir.

Vietnamese Catholic Community of Our Lady of Mong Trieu, 422 E. 10th St., 52803.
Tel: 563-324-3257; Fax: 563-326-6014; Email: davsacredheart@diodav.org. Very Rev. Richard A. Adam.

St. Vincent's Home, 780 W. Central Park Ave., 52804-1901. Tel: 563-324-1911; Fax: 563-324-5842; Email: ferris@davenportdiocese.org; Web: www.davenportdiocese.org. Kent Ferris, Contact Person.

BETTENDORF. *Catholic Endowment of Bettendorf, Iowa, Inc.*, P.O. Box 4, Bettendorf, 52722.
Tel: 309-314-1998; Email: bboeye@melfosterco.com. Bradley W. Boeye.

BURLINGTON. *Burlington Notre Dame Foundation*, 702 S. Roosevelt Ave., Burlington, 52601.
Tel: 319-752-8690; Fax: 319-752-8690; Email: val.giannettino@bnotredame.org; Web: burlingtonnotredame.com. Val Giannettino, Devel. Dir.

St. Vincent De Paul Society, St. John the Baptist Church Conference, 700 Division St., Ste. 1, Burlington, 52601. Tel: 319-752-9332; Email: burldivinemfin@diodav.org. Jim Wade, Contact Person.

CENTERVILLE. *St. Mary's Foundation of Centerville*, 828 S. 18th St., Centerville, 52544.
Tel: 641-437-1984; Email: centervillestmary@diodav.org. Rev. William G. Hubmann, C.PP.S.

CLINTON. *Mercy Home Care and Hospice*, 638 S. Bluff, Clinton, 52732. Tel: 563-244-3766;
Fax: 563-244-3719; Email: Timothy.Shinbori@trinity-health.com; Email: Lisa.Mason-Hagen@mercyhealth.com; Web: www.mercyclinton.com. Timothy T. Shibori, Exec. Dir. Tot Asst. Annually 200; Total Staff 50.

Sisters of St. Francis, Clinton, Iowa, Charitable Trust, 843 13th Ave. N., Clinton, 52732.
Tel: 563-242-7611; Fax: 563-243-0007; Email: jcebula@clintonfranciscans.com; Web: www.clintonfranciscans.com. Sr. Janice I. Cebula, O.S.F., Pres.

CORALVILLE. **John Paul II Medical Research Institute*, 2500 Crosspark Rd., Ste. W230, Coralville, 52241.
Tel: 319-665-3001; Email: jay.kamath@jp2mri.org; Web: jp2mri.org. Mr. Jay Kamath, Devel. Dir.

St. Thomas More New Season Charitable Trust, 3000 12th Ave., Coralville, 52241. Tel: 319-337-2173;
Fax: 319-337-2174; Email: parishoffice@stthomasmoreic.com; Web: www.stmparishfamily.com. Rev. Charles A. Adam.

GRINNELL. *St. Mary's Parish Foundation, Grinnell, Iowa*, 814 4th Ave., Grinnell, 50112.
Tel: 641-236-3174; Fax: 641-236-4329; Email: mike.thorndike@grinnellbank.com. P.O. Box 744, Grinnell, 50112. J. Michael Thorndike, Treas.

IOWA CITY. *Mercy Hospital Foundation*, 500 E. Market St., Iowa City, 52245-2689. Tel: 319-339-3657;
Fax: 319-358-2624; Email: michelle.marks@mercyic.org; Web: www.mercyiowacity.org/MercyFoundation. Margaret N. Reese, Pres.

Mercy Hospital Guild of Iowa City, Iowa, 500 E. Market St., Iowa City, 52245. Tel: 319-339-3659; Email: jenna.maxson@mercyic.org; Web: www.mercyiowacity.org. Jenna Maxson, Contact Person.

Mercy Outreach Iowa City, Inc., 500 E. Market St., Iowa City, 52245. Tel: 319-339-3540; Email: Margaret.Reese@mercyic.org. Margaret N. Reese, Pres.

Regina Foundation, 2140 Rochester Ave., Iowa City, 52245. Tel: 319-354-5866; Email: foundation@regina.org; Web: www.regina.org/foundation. Ms. Kecia Boysen, Dir.

KEOKUK. *Ladies of Charity of Keokuk*, 814 Main St., Keokuk, 52632. Tel: 319-524-2991; Cell: 319-520-7874; Email: hb.blickhan@gmail.com. Madonna Kirchner, Pres.

RELIGIOUS INSTITUTES OF MEN REPRESENTED IN THE DIOCESE

For further details refer to the corresponding bracketed number in the Religious Institutes of Men or Women section.

[0460]—*Brothers of the Poor of St. Francis*—C.F.P.
[1060]—*Society of the Precious Blood*—C.PP.S.

RELIGIOUS INSTITUTES OF WOMEN REPRESENTED IN THE DIOCESE

[0330]—*Carmelite Sisters for the Aged and Infirm*—O.Carm.
[2100]—*Congregation of Humility of Mary*—C.H.M.
[0420]—*Discalced Carmelite Nuns*—O.C.D.
[]—*Franciscan Sisters of Christ the Divine Teacher*—O.S.F.
[2392]—*Lovers of the Holy Cross Sisters* Vietnam—L.H.C.
[2970]—*School Sisters of Notre Dame, Central Pacific*—S.S.N.D.
[0430]—*Sisters of Charity of Blessed Virgin Mary*—B.V.M.
[2575]—*Sisters of Mercy of the Americas*—R.S.M.
[1540]—*Sisters of Saint Francis, Clinton, Iowa*—O.S.F.
[1705]—*Sisters of St. Francis of Assisi*—O.S.F.
[3840]—*Sisters of St. Joseph of Carondelet*—C.S.J.
[3320]—*Sisters of the Presentation of the B.V.M.*—P.B.V.M.
[4120-03]—*Ursuline of Louisville, KY*—O.S.U.

NECROLOGY

† Beyer, Richard J., Chap., Mercy Hospital, Iowa City, Died Dec. 20, 2018

An asterisk (*) denotes an organization that has established tax-exempt status directly with the IRS and is not covered by the USCCB Group Ruling.

Archdiocese of Denver

Archidioecesis Denveriensis

Most Reverend

SAMUEL J. AQUILA

Archbishop of Denver; ordained June 5, 1976; appointed Coadjutor Bishop of Fargo June 12, 2001; ordained August 24, 2001; Succeeded to the See March 18, 2002; appointed Archbishop of Denver May 29, 2012; installed July 18, 2012. *Pastoral Center: 1300 S. Steele St., Denver, CO 80210.*

Most Reverend

JORGE H. RODRIQUEZ

Auxiliary Bishop of Denver; ordained December 24, 1987; appointed Titular Bishop of Azura and Auxiliary Bishop of Denver August 25, 2016; installed November 4, 2016. *Pastoral Center: 1300 S. Steele St., Denver, CO 80210.*

Pastoral Center: 1300 S. Steele St., Denver, CO 80210. Tel: 303-722-4687

Web: www.archden.org

ESTABLISHED A VICARIATE-APOSTOLIC IN 1868.

Square Miles 40,154.

Erected a Diocese August 16, 1887; created an Archdiocese November 15, 1941.

Comprises the northern part of the State of Colorado, including the 25 Counties of Adams, Arapahoe, Boulder, Broomfield, Clear Creek, Denver, Eagle, Garfield, Gilpin, Grand, Jackson, Jefferson, Larimer, Logan, Moffat, Morgan, Phillips, Pitkin, Rio Blanco, Routt, Sedgwick, Summit, Washington, Weld and Yuma.

STATISTICAL OVERVIEW

Personnel	
Retired Cardinals	1
Archbishops	1
Auxiliary Bishops	1
Priests: Diocesan Active in Diocese	144
Priests: Diocesan Active Outside Diocese	7
Priests: Diocesan in Foreign Missions	2
Priests: Retired, Sick or Absent	51
Number of Diocesan Priests	204
Religious Priests in Diocese	108
Total Priests in Diocese	312
Extern Priests in Diocese	44
Ordinations:	
Diocesan Priests	5
Transitional Deacons	5
Permanent Deacons in Diocese	180
Total Brothers	16
Total Sisters	182
Parishes	
Parishes	124
With Resident Pastor:	
Resident Diocesan Priests	89
Resident Religious Priests	17
Missions	19
Pastoral Centers	4
New Parishes Created	2
Welfare	
Catholic Hospitals	4
Total Assisted	843,709
Health Care Centers	6
Total Assisted	29,028
Homes for the Aged	3
Total Assisted	291
Day Care Centers	6
Total Assisted	541
Specialized Homes	2
Total Assisted	1,158
Special Centers for Social Services	28
Total Assisted	107,706
Residential Care of Disabled	2
Total Assisted	48
Other Institutions	29
Total Assisted	3,756
Educational	
Seminaries, Diocesan	2
Students from This Diocese	58
Students from Other Diocese	59
Diocesan Students in Other Seminaries	7
Total Seminarians	65
Colleges and Universities	2
Total Students	12,026
High Schools, Diocesan and Parish	2
Total Students	1,057
High Schools, Private	4
Total Students	3,232
Elementary Schools, Diocesan and Parish	35
Total Students	7,572
Elementary Schools, Private	2
Total Students	596
Catechesis/Religious Education:	
High School Students	3,147
Elementary Students	21,847
Total Students under Catholic Instruction	49,542
Teachers in the Diocese:	
Priests	7
Brothers	4
Sisters	17
Lay Teachers	930
Vital Statistics	
Receptions into the Church:	
Infant Baptism Totals	7,525
Minor Baptism Totals	543
Adult Baptism Totals	349
Received into Full Communion	391
First Communions	6,803
Confirmations	11,743
Marriages:	
Catholic	1,460
Interfaith	264
Total Marriages	1,724
Deaths	2,508
Total Catholic Population	599,086
Total Population	3,762,667

Former Bishops—Most Revs. JOSEPH PROJECTUS MACHEBEUF, D.D., cons. Titular Bishop of Epiphania and Vicar Apostolic of Colorado and Utah, Aug. 16, 1868; first Bishop of Denver in 1887; died July 10, 1889; NICHOLAS CHRYSOSTOM MATZ, D.D., cons. Titular Bishop of Telmessa and Coadjutor of Denver cum jure successionis, Oct. 28, 1887; succeeded to the See of Denver, July 10, 1889; died Aug. 9, 1917; J. HENRY TIHEN, D.D., ord. April 26, 1886; cons. Bishop of Lincoln, July 6, 1911; transferred to the See of Denver, Sept. 21, 1917; resigned Jan. 6, 1931; Apostolic Admin. until July 16, 1931; died Jan. 14, 1940.

Former Archbishops—Most Revs. URBAN J. VEHR, D.D., ord. May 29, 1915; Bishop of Denver; appt. April 17, 1931; cons. June 10, 1931; installed July 16, 1931; elevated to Archiepiscopal dignity, Nov. 15, 1941; appt. Jan. 6, 1942; installed as Archbishop of Denver; resigned Feb. 22, 1967; died Sept. 19, 1973; JAMES V. CASEY, D.D., J.C.D., ord. Dec. 8, 1939; Titular Bishop of Citium and Auxiliary of Lincoln; appt. Auxiliary Bishop April 5, 1957; cons. April 24, 1957; appt. Bishop of Lincoln June 14, 1957; promoted to Archbishop of Denver, Feb. 22, 1967; died March 14, 1986; His Eminence J. FRANCIS CARDINAL STAFFORD, D.D., ord. Dec. 15, 1957; cons. Auxiliary Bishop of Baltimore, Feb. 29, 1976; installed Bishop of Memphis Jan. 18, 1983; appt. Nov. 16, 1982; installed Archbishop of Denver July 31, 1986; appt. June 3, 1986; appt. President of the Pontifical Council for the Laity in Rome, Aug. 1996; elevated to Cardinal Feb. 21, 1998; Most Rev. CHARLES J. CHAPUT, O.F.M.Cap., D.D., ord. Aug. 29, 1970; Episcopal ordination July 26, 1988; appt. Bishop of Rapid City April 11, 1988; appt. Archbishop of Denver Feb. 18, 1997; appt. Archbishop of Philadelphia July 19, 2011.

The Pastoral Center—1300 S. Steele St., Denver, 80210-2599. Tel: 303-722-4687.

Secretary to the Archbishop—Rev. MATTHEW MAGEE.

Auxiliary Bishop of Denver—Most Rev. JORGE RODRIGUEZ, Ph.D.

Vicar General and Moderator of the Curia—Very Rev. RANDY M. DOLLINS, V.G.

Vicar for Clergy—Most Rev. JORGE RODRIGUEZ, Ph.D.

Chancellor/Special Assistant to the Archbishop—DAVID UEBBING.

Archivist—KARYL KLEIN.

Chief Financial Officer—MR. KEITH A. PARSONS, CPA.

Presbyteral Council—Most Rev. SAMUEL J. AQUILA, S.T.L., Pres.; Very Rev. RANDY M. DOLLINS, V.G.; Most Rev. JORGE RODRIGUEZ, Ph.D.; Very Rev. GIOVANNI CAPUCCI, J.C.D.; Revs. PETER MUSSETT; EDWARD J. POEHLMANN; MICHAEL J. O'BRIEN; ENRIQUE SALAZAR; CARLOS WILSON BELLO-AYALA; NATHAN GOEBEL; JASON F. WUNSCH; JOSE DE JESUS GARCIA; WARLI DE ARAUJO CASTRO; SCOTT BAILEY; SAMUEL MOREHEAD; TIMOTHY GAINES; RICHARD NAKVASIL; DAVID BLUEJACKET; DARRICK LEIER; DANIEL CARDO, S.C.V.

College of Consultors—Most Revs. SAMUEL J. AQUILA, S.T.L., Archbishop; JORGE RODRIGUEZ, Ph.D., Vicar for Clergy; Revs. DAVID BLUEJACKET; JOSE DE JESUS GARCIA; NATHAN GOEBEL; SAMUEL MOREHEAD; MICHAEL J. O'BRIEN; JASON F. WUNSCH.

Archdiocesan Finance Council—LAURIE BARELA, CFP; Most Rev. SAMUEL J. AQUILA, S.T.L., Archbishop; Very Rev. RANDY M. DOLLINS, V.G.; MR. KEITH A. PARSONS, CPA, CFO; ERIC ZELLWEGER, C.F.A., Chm.; JODI THOMAS, C.R.C.M., C.B.A.; GREG GERKEN, M.A.I.; KEVIN KUHN, Esq.; MICK BLEYLE, CFA; BRIAN CALLAHAN, CPA; KELLY KOZELISKI,

CPA; MICHELLE MILES, C.A.M.S.; TOM MAY; WALT COUGHLIN; PAUL KLUCK, S.I.O.R.

Deaneries—Very Revs. MATTHEW BOOK, V.F., Southwest Denver; BRIAN S. MORROW, V.F., Northeast Denver; CHRISTOPHER A. RENNER, V.F., Northwest Denver; JAMES E. FOX, V.F., Central East Denver; HENRI TSHIBAMBE, V.F., West Denver; ANDREW KEMBERLING, V.F., Southeast Denver; TERRENCE KISSELL, V.F., East; MICHAEL CARVILL, F.S.C.B., V.F., Boulder; ROCCO PORTER, V.F., Fort Collins; MICHAEL BODZIOCH, V.F., Eastern Plains; JAMES H. CRISMAN, V.F., Greeley; ELBERT CHILSON, V.F., Western Slope; THOMAS COYTE, V.F., Central West Denver.

Metropolitan Tribunal & Office of Canonical Affairs

Metropolitan Tribunal & Office of Canonical Affairs—1300 S. Steele St., Denver, 80210. Tel: 303-894-8994.

Judicial Vicar—Very Rev. GIOVANNI CAPUCCI, J.C.D.

Metropolitan Judges—MR. CARLOS VENEGAS, J.C.L.; MR. ANTHONY ST. LOUIS-SANCHEZ, J.C.L.; MR. STEPHEN HANCOCK, J.D., J.C.L.; Rev. Msgr. J. ANTHONY MCDAID, J.C.D., (Retired).

Defenders of the Bond—Sr. FRANCISCA IGWEILO, O.P., J.C.L.; Rev. VINCENT PHUNG, J.C.L.; MRS. SHANNON C. FOSSETT, J.C.L.; Very Rev. ROBERT M. HERBST, O.F.M.Conv., J.C.D.; CHRISTOPHER J. BEAUDET, J.C.D.

Promoter of Justice—Rev. VINCENT PHUNG, J.C.L.

Judicial Auditors—MR. ANDREW SHEA; MS. SORAYA GONZALEZ.

Advocates—Advocates appointed individually for particular cases.

Ecclesiastical Notaries—MRS. RONDA WHITEHURST; MRS. LUCINDA MARQUES; MRS. LAURA NASH; MR. PETER WAYMEL.

Coordinator of Second Instance—MRS. RONDA WHITEHURST.

Coordinator of the Tribunal Chancery—MRS. RONDA WHITEHURST.

The Archdiocese of Denver, a Colorado Corporation Sole

Archdiocesan Offices and Ministries

Unless otherwise indicated, offices and ministries are located in the Pastoral Center on the campus of The Saint John Paul II Center for the New Evangelization, 1300 S. Steele St., Denver, Colorado 80210. Tel: 303-722-4687; Web: www.archden.org.

Office of Archbishop—
Archbishop—Most Rev. SAMUEL J. AQUILA, S.T.L.
Secretary to the Archbishop—Rev. MATTHEW MAGEE, Tel: 303-715-3210; Email: father.magee@archden.org.

Auxiliary Bishop—Most Rev. JORGE RODRIGUEZ, Ph.D., Tel: 303-715-3100; Email: bishop.rodriguez@archden.org.

Executive Assistant to the Auxiliary Bishop—JANETH CHAVEZ, Tel: 303-715-3100; Email: janeth.chavez@archden.org.

Moderator of the Curia—Very Rev. RANDY M. DOLLINS, V.G., Tel: 303-715-3263; Email: father.dollins@archden.org.
Administrative Assistant to the Moderator of the Curia—CARRIE SIGMAN, Tel: 303-715-3263; Email: carrie.sigman@archden.org.

Vicar for Clergy—Most Rev. JORGE RODRIGUEZ, Ph.D., Tel: 303-715-3100; Email: bishop.rodriguez@archden.org.
Administrative Assistant—JANETH CHAVEZ, Tel: 303-715-3100; Email: janeth.chavez@archden.org.

Chancellor—DAVID UEBBING, Tel: 303-715-3185; Email: david.uebbing@archden.org.

Secretary—HATTY ARENIVER, Tel: 303-715-3185; Email: hatty.areniver@archden.org.

Scheduling Assistant and Coordinator of the Holy Trinity Center—SANDRA MILEY, Tel: 303-715-3129; Email: sandra.miley@archden.org.

Archives—
Archivist—KARYL KLEIN, Tel: 303-715-3144; Email: archives@archden.org.

Black Catholics—
Director—MARY LEISRING, Tel: 303-715-3165; Email: mary.leisring@archden.org.

Catholic Schools—
Superintendent—ELIAS MOO, Tel: 303-715-3132; Email: elias.moo@archden.org.
Special Programs Director and Assistant to the Superintendent—BARBARA ANGLADA, Tel: 303-715-3132; Email: barbara.anglada@archden.org.

Child and Youth Protection—
Victim Assistance Coordinator—JIM LANGLEY, Psy. D., Tel: 720-239-2832; Email: victim.assistance@archden.org.
Safe Environment Coordinator—CHRISTI SULLIVAN, Tel: 303-715-3241; Email: christi.sullivan@archden.org.

Colorado Catholic Conference—1535 Logan St., Denver, 80203. Tel: 303-894-8808; Email: ccc@cocatholicconference.org; Web: cocatholicconference.org.
Executive Director—JENNIFER KRASKA.
Coordinator—DIANE CHAVEZ.

Development—
Office of Development—3801 E. Florida Ave., Ste. 909, Denver, 80210.
Chief Development Officer—PAUL DUDZIC, Tel: 720-476-7468; Email: paul.dudzic@archden.org.

Diaconate—
Director of Deacon Personnel—Deacon JOSEPH H. DONOHOE, Tel: 303-715-3198; Email: deacon.donohoe@archden.org.
Diaconate Coordinator—AMY VIGIL, Tel: 303-715-3198; Email: amy.vigil@archden.org.

Diaconate Formation—(See section A, Seminaries, Religious or Scholasticates: Saint John Vianney Theological Seminary).

Evangelization and Family Life Ministries—
Executive Director—SCOTT ELMER, Tel: 303-715-3203; Email: scott.elmer@archden.org.

Director of Hispanic Evangelization—ALFONSO LARA, Tel: 303-715-3169; Email: alfonso.lara@archden.org.

Centro San Juan Diego—2830 Lawrence St., Denver, 80205. Tel: 303-295-9470; Web: www.centrosanjuandiego.org.

Finance, Administration and Planning—
CFO and Executive Director—MR. KEITH A. PARSONS, CPA, Tel: 303-715-3258; Email: keith.parsons@archden.org.
Executive Assistant—AMANDA ULLMAN, Tel: 303-715-3258; Email: amanda.ullman@archden.org.

Lay Formation—(See section A, Seminaries, Religious or Scholasticates: Saint John Vianney Theological Seminary).

Liturgy—
Director—Rev. HUNG PHAM, S.J., Tel: 303-715-3162; Email: hung.pham@archden.org.

Priestly Vocations—
Director—Rev. RYAN O'NEILL.

Consecrated Life—
Director—Sr. SHARON FORD, R.S.M.

Seminaries—
Saint John Vianney Theological Seminary—Rev. DANIEL LEONARD, V.F., Rector.
The Redemptoris Mater House of Formation—Very Rev. TOBIAS RODRIGUEZ-LASA, Rector.

Social Ministry—AL HOOPER, Dir., Tel: 303-715-3220; Email: al.hooper@archden.org.

Strategy Integration—
Chief Strategy Officer—JOSHUA KARABINOS, Tel: 303-715-3160; Email: joshua.karabinos@archden.org.

The Archdiocese of Denver Management Corporation—
President—MR. KEITH A. PARSONS, CPA, Tel: 303-715-3258.
Executive Assistant—AMANDA ULLMAN, Tel: 303-715-3258; Email: amanda.ullman@archden.org.
Accounting—TIMOTHY TODD, Dir., Tel: 303-715-3181; Email: timothy.todd@archden.org.
Cemeteries and Mortuary—GARY SCHAAF, Exec. Dir., Tel: 303-425-9511; Email: gary.schaaf@archden.org.
Construction and Planning—MIKE WISNESKI, Dir., Tel: 303-715-3297; Email: mike.wisneski@archden.org.
Human Resources—Deacon CLARENCE G. MCDAVID, Dir., Tel: 303-715-3193; Email: deacon.mcdavid@archden.org.
Information Systems—MICHAEL MCKEE, Dir., Tel: 303-715-3299; Email: michael.mckee@archden.org.
Insurance and Risk Management—PETER CRONAN, Dir., Tel: 303-715-3150; Email: peter.cronan@archden.org.
Internal Audit—JOHN VUNOVICH, Dir., Tel: 303-715-3174; Email: john.vunovich@archden.org.
Legal Department—REBECCA N. WELBORN, Esq., Dir., Tel: 303-715-3273; Email: rebecca.welborn@archden.org.
Parish Finance—ERNEST W. ARMSTRONG, CPA, Dir., Tel: 303-715-3120; Email: ernie.armstrong@archden.org.
Real Estate—LINDA BISHOP, Esq., Dir., Tel: 303-715-3194; Email: lou.bishop@archden.org.

CLERGY, PARISHES, MISSIONS AND PAROCHIAL SCHOOLS

CITY OF DENVER

(COUNTY OF DENVER)

1—CATHEDRAL BASILICA OF THE IMMACULATE CONCEPTION CATHOLIC PARISH IN DENVER (1860)
1535 Logan St., 80203. Tel: 303-831-7010; Email: CBIC2016@denvercathedral.org. Revs. Ronald Cattany; Joseph Hearty, F.S.S.P.; Deacons Robert E. Finan; Robert Rinne.
Mission—St. Elizabeth of Hungary Catholic Church, 1060 St. Francis Way, 80204. Tel: 303-534-4014; Email: saintelizabeth@qwestoffice.net. Lauretta Proulx, Contact Person.

2—ALL SAINTS CATHOLIC PARISH IN DENVER (1950)
2559 S. Federal Blvd., 80219. Tel: 303-922-3758; Fax: 303-922-3750; Email: Msgr.NguyenP@archden.org. Mailing Address: 2560 S. Grove St., 80219. Rev. Msgr. Peter Quang Nguyen, V.F.; Rev. Vincent Bui, Parochial Vicar; Deacon Charles W. Parker Jr.

3—ANNUNCIATION CATHOLIC PARISH IN DENVER (1883)
3601 Humboldt St., 80205. Tel: 303-296-1024; Email: Father.Polifka@archden.org. Mailing Address: 1408 E. 36th Ave., 80205. Rev. Charles J. Polifka, O.F.M.-Cap.
School—Annunciation Catholic School, (Grades K-8), 3536 Lafayette St., 80205. Tel: 303-295-2515; Fax: 303-295-2516; Email: info@annunciationk8.org; Web: www.annunciationk8.org. Deborah Roberts, Prin. Lay Teachers 17; Students 180; Clergy / Religious Teachers 1.

4—ST. ANTHONY OF PADUA CATHOLIC PARISH IN DENVER (1947)
3801 W. Ohio Ave., 80219. Tel: 303-935-2431; Fax: 303-935-8969; Email: Father.Gierasimczyk@archden.org; Web: www.stanthonysdenver.org. Revs. Wojciech Gierasimczyk; Miljenko Pavkovic, Parochial Vicar.

5—ASSUMPTION OF THE BLESSED VIRGIN MARY CATHOLIC PARISH IN DENVER (1912)
2361 E. 78th Ave., 80229. Tel: 303-288-2442; Fax: 303-289-2713; Email: pklopfenstein@assumptiondenver.org; Web: www.assumptiondenver.org. Very Rev. Brian S. Morrow, V.F.
School—Assumption of the Blessed Virgin Mary Catholic School, (Grades PreK-8), 2341 E. 78th Ave., 80229. Tel: 303-288-2159; Fax: 303-288-4716; Email: pklopfenstein@assumptiondenver.org; Email: sgrey@assumptiondenver.org; Web: assumptiondenver.org. Sarah Grey, Prin. Lay Teachers 17; Religious Teachers 1; Students 180.
Catechesis Religious Program—Email: lblincow@assumptiondenver.org. Linda Blincow, D.R.E. Students 170.

6—BLESSED SACRAMENT CATHOLIC PARISH IN DENVER (1912)
4900 Montview Blvd., 80207. Tel: 303-355-7361; Email: Father.Wilborn@archden.org; Web: www.blessedsacrament.net. Mailing & Office Address: 1912 Eudora St., 80220. Rev. Jeffrey Wilborn.
School—Blessed Sacrament Catholic School, (Grades PreSchool-8), 1958 Elm St., 80220. Tel: 303-377-8835 ; Email: info@bscs-denver.net. Dr. Carla Dire Capstick, Prin.

7—ST. CAJETAN CATHOLIC PARISH IN DENVER (1922) (Hispanic)
299 S. Raleigh St., 80219. Tel: 303-922-6306; Fax: 303-936-8285; Email: Father.Velaquez@archden.org; Web: stcajetan.denverparish.com. Mailing Address & Office: 299 S. Stuart St., 80219. Revs. Heriberto Torres-Velazquez, C.R., Admin.; Miguel Guzman, C.R., Parochial Vicar.

8—ST. CATHERINE OF SIENA CATHOLIC PARISH IN DENVER (1912)
4200 Federal Blvd., 80211. Tel: 303-455-9090; Fax: 303-455-6651; Email: stcatherineofsiena@comcast.net; Web: saintcatherine.us. Rev., Nilson Leal de Sá, C.B.; Rev. Luc-Marie Vaillant, C.B., Parochial Vicar.
School—St. Catherine of Siena Catholic School, (Grades PreK-8), Tel: 303-477-8035; Fax: 303-477-0110; Email: stcatinfo@comcast.net. Douglas Sandusky, Prin. Lay Teachers 13; Students 164.
Catechesis Religious Program—Email: coleman.colin@gmail.com. Students 226.

9—CHRIST THE KING CATHOLIC PARISH IN DENVER (1947)
830 Elm St., 80220-4313. Tel: 303-388-1643; Email: ChurchOffice@ChristTheKingDenver.org; Web: www.ChristTheKingDenver.org. Very Rev. Gregory Cioch, S.T.L., V.F.
School—Christ the King Catholic School, (Grades PreK-8), 860 Elm St., 80220. Tel: 303-321-2123; Fax: 303-321-2191; Email: HDignan@CKRCS.org; Web: www.ckrcs.org. Bernadette Hensen, Prin. Lay Teachers 27; Students 254.

10—Church of the Ascension Catholic Parish in Denver (1972)
14050 Maxwell Pl., 80239. Tel: 303-373-4950; Fax: 303-373-4954; Email: Father.Norick@archden.org; Web: www.acpden.com. Revs. Daniel J. Norick, V.F.; Roberto Rodriguez Cruz, Parochial Vicar.
11—Cure d'Ars Catholic Parish in Denver (1952)
3201 Dahlia St., 80207. Email: curedarschurchoffice@gmail.com; Web: curedarschurch.org. Mailing & Office Address: 4701 Martin Luther King Blvd., 80207-1862. Rev. Joseph Cao; Deacon Clarence G. McDavid.
12—St. Dominic Parish (1889)
2905 Federal Blvd., 80211. Tel: 303-455-3613; Email: info@stdominicdenver.org. Mailing Address & Office: 3053 W. 29th Ave., 80211. Very Rev. Edward Ruane, O.P.; Revs. Christopher Saliga, O.P., Parochial Vicar; Robert Keller, O.P., In Res.; Very Rev. David F. Wright, O.P., In Res.; Revs. Thomas Poulsen, O.P., In Res.; James Karepin, O.P., In Res.; Andrew Wisdom, O.P., In Res.; Robert Barry, O.P., In Res.; Deacon Antonio Guerrero.
13—St. Francis de Sales Catholic Parish in Denver (1892)
300 S. Sherman St., 80209. Tel: 303-744-7211; Fax: 303-777-0305; Email: busmgr@sfdsdenver.com; Web: www.sfdsdenver.com. Mailing Address & Office: 301 S. Grant St., 80209. Rev. Kenneth J. Liuzzi, V.F.
School—St. Francis de Sales Catholic STEM School, (Grades PreK-8), 235 S. Sherman St., 80209.
Tel: 303-744-7231; Fax: 303-744-1028; Email: School-office@sfdsdenver.com. Sr. Mary Rose Lieb, O.S.F., M.S.A., Ms.Ed., Prin.
14—Saint Gianna Beretta Molla Catholic Parish
4905 Cathay St., 80249. Tel: 303-968-0533; Email: father.wunsch@archden.org; Web: stgiannadenver.org. Mailing Address: P.O. Box 39015, 80239. Rev. Jason F. Wunsch.
15—Good Shepherd Catholic Parish in Denver (1981)
2626 E. Seventh Ave. Pkwy., 80206-3809.
Tel: 303-322-7706; Fax: 303-399-1382; Email: goodshep@aol.com; Web: www.goodshepherdchurchdenver.org. Very Rev. James E. Fox, V.F.; Deacon Patrick Whaley.
School—Good Shepherd Catholic School, (Grades PreK-8), 620 Elizabeth St., 80206. Tel: 303-321-6231; Fax: 303-261-1059; Email: Mark.Strawbridge@goodshepherddenver.org; Web: www.goodshepherddenver.org. Mr. Mark Strawbridge, Prin. Lay Teachers 30; Students 463; Religious Teachers 3.
16—Guardian Angels Catholic Parish in Denver (1954)
1843 W. 52nd Ave., 80221. Tel: 303-433-8361; Fax: 303-477-2066; Email: gangelsdenver@gmail.com; Web: GuardianAngelsChurchDenver.org. Rev. Daniel Zimmerschied.
School—Guardian Angels Catholic School, (Grades PreK-8), Tel: 303-433-8361; Email: gangelsdenver@gmail.com. Mary Gold, Prin.
17—Holy Family Catholic Parish in Denver (1889)
4380 Utica St., 80212. Tel: 303-455-1664; Email: office@holyfamilydenver.com. Mailing Address & Office: 4377 Utica St., 80212. Rev. Martin Lally.
18—Holy Ghost Catholic Parish in Denver (1905)
1900 California St., 80202. Tel: 303-292-1556; Email: Father.Uhl@archden.org; Web: www.holyghostchurch.org. Revs. Christopher W. Uhl, O.M.V.; Andrew Huhtanan, O.M.V., Parochial Vicar.
19—Holy Rosary Catholic Parish in Denver (1918)
Mailing Address & Office: 4688 Pearl St., 80216.
Tel: 303-297-1962; Fax: 303-297-1682; Email: holy.rosary@live.com; Web: holyrosarydenver.com. Rev. Luis Escandon-Farrera.
Catechesis Religious Program—Students 124.
20—St. Ignatius Loyola Catholic Parish in Denver (1924)
2301 York St., 80205. Tel: 303-322-8042; Email: parish@loyoladenver.org; Web: www.loyoladenver.org. Mailing Address & Office: 2309 Gaylord St., 80205. Revs. Dirk Dunfee, S.J.; Roy Joseph, S.J., Parochial Vicar; Joseph Tuoc Nguyen, S.J., In Res.
21—St. James Catholic Parish in Denver (1904)
1311 Oneida St., 80220. Tel: 303-322-7449; Email: Father.GarciaJ@archden.org; Web: www.stjamesdenver.org. Mailing Address: 1314 Newport St., 80220. Rev. Jose de Jesus Garcia.
School—St. James Catholic School, (Grades PreK-8), 1250 Newport St., 80220. Tel: 303-333-8275; Email: school.office@stjamesdenver.org. Carol Hovell-Genth, Prin.
22—St. Joseph Catholic Parish in Denver (1888)
600 Galapago St., 80204. Tel: 303-534-4408; Fax: 303-534-0177; Email: Lupe.Rucker@stjosephdenver.org; Email: Magdalena.Harrach@stjosephdenver.org; Web: www.StJosephDenver.org. Mailing Address & Office: 623 Fox St., 80204. Rev. Msgr. Bernard A. Schmitz.
23—St. Joseph Polish Catholic Parish in Denver (1902)
517 E. 46th Ave., 80216. Tel: 303-296-3217; Email: st.joephpolish@gmail.com. Rev. Stanislaw Michalek.
24—St. Mary Magdalene Catholic Parish in Denver (1907)
2771 Zenobia St., 80212. Tel: 303-455-1968; Email: stmarymagdalenedenver@gmail.com; Web: saintmarymagdenver.org. Rev. Robert Barry, O.P.
25—Most Precious Blood Catholic Parish in Denver (1952)
3959 E. Iliff Ave., 80210. Tel: 303-756-3083; Email: Father.Dolan@archden.org; Web: www.mpbdenver.org. Mailing Address & Office: 2250 S. Harrison, 80210. Revs. Patrick Dolan; Peter Dinh, Parochial Vicar.
School—Most Precious Blood Catholic School, (Grades K-8), Tel: 303-757-1279; Email: swyatt@mpbdenver.org. Colleen McManamon, Prin.
26—Mother of God Catholic Parish in Denver (1949)
475 Logan St., 80203. Tel: 303-744-1715; Fax: 303-744-1716; Email: stephanie@motherofgoddenver.com. Rev. Vincent Phung, J.C.L.
27—Notre Dame Catholic Parish in Denver (1957)
2190 S. Sheridan Blvd., 80219. Tel: 303-935-3900; Email: Msgr.Buelt@archden.org; Web: www.denvernotredame.org. Mailing Address & Office: 5100 W. Evans Ave., 80219. Rev. Msgr. Edward Buelt, J.C.L.; Deacons Kevin Leiner; Ernest Martinez.
School—Notre Dame Catholic School, (Grades PreK-8), 2165 S. Zenobia St., 80219. Tel: 303-935-3549; Fax: 303-937-4868; Email: cmolis@notredamedenver.org; Web: www.notredamedenver.org. Mr. Greg Caudle, Prin. Lay Teachers 19; Students 265; Religious Teachers 3.
28—Our Lady of Grace Catholic Parish in Denver (1951)
2645 E. 48th Ave., 80216. Tel: 303-297-3440; Fax: 303-296-3486; Email: Father.Zermeno-Martin@archden.org. Rev. Felix Zermeno-Martin.
29—Our Lady of Guadalupe Catholic Parish in Denver (1936)
1209 W. 36th Ave., 80211. Tel: 303-477-1402; Fax: 303-477-4013; Email: Father.Hernandez@archden.org; Web: www.ologdenver.org. Rev. Benito A. Hernandez, C.R.
30—Our Lady of Lourdes Catholic Parish in Denver (1947)
2298 S. Logan St., 80210. Tel: 303-722-6861; Email: Father.Larkin@archden.org; Web: www.lourdesdenver.org. Mailing Address & Office: 2200 S. Logan St., 80210. Rev. Brian Larkin; Mary Rogers, Pastoral Assoc.
School—Our Lady of Lourdes Catholic School, (Grades PreK-8), 2256 S. Logan St., 80210.
Tel: 303-722-7525; Fax: 303-765-5305; Email: ololoffice@gmail.com; Web: lourdesclassical.org. Rosemary Anderson, Prin. Lay Teachers 17; Students 223.
Catechesis Religious Program—John O'Brien, D.R.E.
31—Our Lady of Mount Carmel Catholic Parish in Denver (1894)
3549 Navajo St., 80211-3040. Tel: 303-455-0447; Fax: 303-455-5487; Email: Father.Guentner@archden.org; Web: ourladymountcarmel.com. Revs. Hugh M. Guentner, O.S.M.; Mark Franceschini, O.S.M., In Res.
32—Presentation of Our Lady Catholic Parish in Denver (1913)
695 Julian St., 80204. Tel: 303-534-4882; Email: Father.Poehlmann@archden.org; Web: www.presentationdenver.org. Mailing Address & Office: 665 Irving St., 80204. Rev. Edward J. Poehlmann.
33—Risen Christ Catholic Parish in Denver (1967)
3060 S. Monaco Pkwy., 80222. Tel: 303-758-8826; Fax: 303-782-9667; Email: Father.Bailey@archden.org; Web: www.risenchristchurch.org. Bailey Scott.
34—St. Rose of Lima Catholic Parish in Denver (1924)
Church: 355 S. Navajo St., 80223. Tel: 303-778-7673; Email: Father.ThompsonN@archden.org; Web: www.srldenver.org. Mailing Address & Office: 1320 W. Nevada Pl., 80223. Rev. Nicholas Thompson, Admin.; Deacon Don Tracy.
School—St. Rose of Lima Catholic School, (Grades PreK-8), 1345 W. Dakota Ave., 80223.
Tel: 303-733-5806; Fax: 303-733-0125; Email: strosedenver@gmail.com; Web: srldenver.org/school. Mr. Tomas Gallegos, Prin. Lay Teachers 12; Students 275.
35—Sacred Heart Catholic Parish in Denver (1879)
2760 Larimer St., 80205. Tel: 303-294-9830; Fax: 303-296-0171; Email: sacredheartdenver@gmail.com. Rev. Alvaro Panqueva.
Catechesis Religious Program—Graciela Vazquez, D.R.E. Students 302.
36—St. Vincent De Paul Catholic Parish in Denver (1926)
2375 E. Arizona Ave., 80210. Tel: 303-744-6119; Fax: 303-744-6124; Email: mila@saintvincents.org; Web: www.saintvincents.org. Very Rev. Andrew Kemberling, V.F.; Rev. Douglas Grandon, Parochial Vicar; Deacons Marvin Hagarty; Timothy Kelly; Hal Goldwire.
School—St. Vincent De Paul Catholic School, (Grades PreK-8), 1164 S. Josephine St., 80210.
Tel: 303-777-3812; Fax: 303-773-9528; Email: info@svdpk8.com; Web: www.svdpk8.com. Sr. Dominic Quinn, O.P., Prin.; Mary Cohen, Asst. Prin. Lay Teachers 26; Students 409; Religious Teachers 3.

OUTSIDE THE CITY OF DENVER

Akron, Washington Co., St. Joseph Catholic Parish in Akron (1917) [CEM]
551 W. 6th St., Akron, 80720. Email: pastor@stmarybrush.org. Rev. Marek Ciesla, S.Chr.
Arvada, Jefferson Co.
1—St. Joan of Arc Catholic Parish in Arvada (1967)
12735 W. 58th Ave., Arvada, 80002.
Tel: 303-420-1232; Fax: 303-420-0126; Email: Father.Goebel@archden.org; Web: www.stjoanarvada.org. Rev. Nathan Goebel; Deacons Joseph Gerber; Rex Pilger; Matt Archer.
2—Shrine of St. Anne Catholic Parish in Arvada (1920) [CEM]
7555 Grant Pl., Arvada, 80002. Tel: 303-420-1280; Fax: 303-420-1341; Email: dcapra@shrineofstanne.org; Web: www.shrineofstanne.org. Rev. Sean J. McGrath; Deacons Richard Borda; Ron Beck.
School—Shrine of St. Anne Catholic School, (Grades K-8), 7320 Grant Pl., Arvada, 80002.
Tel: 303-422-1800; Fax: 303-422-1011; Email: info@stannescatholic.org; Web: www.stannescatholic.com. Theresa Donahue, Prin. Lay Teachers 19; Students 285.
3—Spirit of Christ Catholic Parish in Arvada (1974)
7400 W. 80th Ave., Arvada, 80003. Tel: 303-422-9173; Fax: 303-422-8251; Email: staff@spiritofchrist.org; Web: www.spiritofchrist.org. Very Rev. Christopher A. Renner, V.F., Pastor; Rev. Gregory Ames, V.F., Parochial Vicar; Deacon Charles Hahn.
Aspen, Pitkin Co., St. Mary Catholic Parish in Aspen (1882)
533 E. Main St., Aspen, 81611. Tel: 970-925-7339; Email: admin@stmaryaspen.org; Web: www.stmaryaspen.org. Rev. John L. Hilton, V.F.
Ault, Weld Co., St. Mary in Ault (1953) Administered by Our Lady of the Valley, Windsor.
267 E. 4th St., Ault, 80610. Tel: 970-834-1609; Email: Father.Pedersen@archden.org; Web: www.stmarysault.com. Mailing Address: P.O. Box 1373, Ault, 80610. Rev. Gregg Pedersen.
Aurora, Arapahoe Co.
1—St. Lawrence Korean Catholic Parish in Aurora (1981)
4310 S. Pitkin St., Aurora, 80015-1974.
Tel: 303-617-7400; Fax: 303-617-8265; Email: Father.Chae@archden.org. Rev. Dong Ho Chae.
2—St. Michael the Archangel Catholic Parish in Aurora (1978)
19099 E. Floyd Ave., Aurora, 80013.
Tel: 303-690-6797; Email: stmtac@aol.com; Web: www.stmichael-aurora.org. Very Rev. Terrence Kissell, V.F.; Rev. Mauricio Bermudez, Parochial Vicar; Deacons Willie Liwanag; Anthony Pierson; Craig Fucci; Christopher Pomrening; Gregory Persinski.
Catechesis Religious Program—Email: jj.peters@comcast.net. Jim Peters, D.R.E. Students 1,009.
3—St. Pius X Catholic Parish in Aurora (1954)
13670 E. 13th Pl., Aurora, 80011. Email: Father.Aguera@archden.org; Web: www.stpiusxparish.org. Rev. Jorge Aguera, D.C.J.M., (Spain).
School—St. Pius X Catholic School, (Grades PreK-8), 13680 E. 14th Pl., Aurora, 80011. Tel: 303-364-6515; Email: emichalczyk@stpiusxschool.net; Web: stpiusxschool.net. Eileen Michalczyk, Prin. Lay Teachers 16; Students 250.
4—Queen of Peace Catholic Parish in Aurora (1968)
13120 E. Kentucky Ave., Aurora, 80012.
Tel: 303-364-1056; Fax: 303-340-8915; Email: Father.Medina@archden.org; Web: www.queenofpeace.net. Rev. Felix Medina-Algaba.
5—St. Therese Catholic Parish in Aurora (1926)
1243 Kingston St., Aurora, 80010. Tel: 303-344-0132; Fax: 303-344-0133; Email: sbeat@comcast.net; Web: sttheresechurch-aurora.org. Rev. Hector Chiapa-Villarreal.
School—St. Therese Catholic School, (Grades PreK-8), 1200 Kenton St., Aurora, 80010.
Tel: 303-364-7494; Fax: 303-364-1340; Email: admin@sttheresechool.com; Web: www.sttheresechool.com. Antonia Vaeth, Prin. Lay Teachers 13; Students 210; Religious Teachers 1.
Catechesis Religious Program—Tel: 303-344-0132;

Email: judithv995@gmailcom. Judith Villanueva, D.R.E. Students 754.

BASALT, EAGLE CO., ST. VINCENT CATHOLIC PARISH IN BASALT (1970)
Church: 250 Midland Ave., Carbondale, 81621.
Tel: 970-704-0820; Fax: 970-704-0830; Email: office@stvincentstmary.com; Web: www.stvincentstmary.com. Mailing Address & Office: 397 White Hill Rd., Carbondale, 81623. Rev. Richard Nakvasil.
Catechesis Religious Program—Email: education@stvincentstmary.com. Margaretta Bruegger, D.R.E. Students 146.

BOULDER, BOULDER CO.

1—ST. MARTIN DE PORRES CATHOLIC PARISH IN BOULDER (1968)
3300 Table Mesa Dr., Boulder, 80305.
Tel: 303-499-7744; Fax: 303-494-8754; Email: Father.Baird@archden.org; Web: www.smdpchurch.org. Very Rev. James Baird, V.F.

2—SACRED HEART OF JESUS CATHOLIC PARISH IN BOULDER (1875) [JC]
1318 Mapleton Ave., Boulder, 80304.
Tel: 303-442-6158; Fax: 303-442-7905; Web: www.shjboulder.org. Mailing Address & Office: 2312 14th St., Boulder, 80304. Very Rev. Mark S. Kovacik, V.F.; Rev. Jose Anibal Chicas, Parochial Vicar; Deacons David Luksch; Chris Byrne.
School—Sacred Heart of Jesus Catholic School, (Grades PreK-8), 1317 Mapleton Ave., Boulder, 80304. Tel: 303-447-2362; Email: mecseyt@shjboulder.org; Web: www.school.shjboulder.org. Tom Mecsey, Prin. Lay Teachers 15; Students 203.
Mission—St. Rita in Nederland, 326 CO-119, Nederland, 80466. Tel: 720-984-9712.

3—SACRED HEART OF MARY CATHOLIC PARISH IN BOULDER (1873) [CEM]
6739 S. Boulder Rd., Boulder, 80303.
Tel: 303-494-7572; Email: admin@sacredheartofmary.com. Rev. Cliff J. McMillan.

4—ST. THOMAS AQUINAS UNIVERSITY CATHOLIC PARISH IN BOULDER (1950) University of Colorado, Campus Ministry.
898 14th St., Boulder, 80302. Tel: 303-443-8383; Fax: 303-443-8399; Email: Father.Mussett@archden.org; Web: www.thomascenter.org. Mailing Address: 904 14th St., Boulder, 80302. Revs. Peter Mussett; Shaun Galvin, Parochial Vicar.
Catechesis Religious Program—Email: patty.quinn@thomascenter.org. Patty Quinn, D.R.E. Students 4.

BRECKENRIDGE, SUMMIT CO., ST. MARY CATHOLIC PARISH IN BRECKENRIDGE (1875) Administered by Our Lady of Peace Mission, Silverthorne.
109 S. French St., Breckenridge, 80424.
Tel: 970-668-0250; Email: carol@summitcatholic.org; Web: www.summitcatholic.org. Mailing Address: P.O. Box 23109, Silverthorne, 80498. Revs. Stephen A. Siebert; Emmanuel Osigwe, Parochial Vicar; Deacons James Doyle; Charles Lamar.
Mission—Our Lady of Peace Silverthorne, 89 Smith Ranch Rd., Silverthorne, 80498.

BRIGHTON, ADAMS CO., ST. AUGUSTINE CATHOLIC PARISH IN BRIGHTON (1887)
178 S. 6th Ave., Brighton, 80601. Tel: 303-659-1410; Fax: 303-659-6449; Email: Father.SequeiraA@archden.org; Web: www.staugustinebrighton.org. Rev. Franklin Sequeira-Treminio; Deacon Bill Jordan.

BROOMFIELD, BOULDER CO., NATIVITY OF OUR LORD CATHOLIC PARISH IN BROOMFIELD (1958)
900 W. Midway Blvd., Broomfield, 80020.
Tel: 303-469-5171; Fax: 303-469-5172; Email: m.carvill@nool.us; Web: www.nool.us. Very Rev. Michael Carvill, F.S.C.B., V.F.; Rev. Accursio Ciaccio, F.S.C.B., Parochial Vicar.
School—Nativity: Faith and Reason, (Grades PreK-8), Tel: 303-466-4177; Email: m.mott@nool.us. Dr. Holly Peterson, Prin. Lay Teachers 25; Students 419.

BRUSH, MORGAN CO., ST. MARY CATHOLIC PARISH IN BRUSH (1911) Administered by St. Joseph, Akron.
340 Stanford St., Brush, 80723. Tel: 970-842-2216; Fax: 970-842-4461; Email: Father.Ciesla@archden.org; Web: www.stmarybrush.org. Rev. Marek Ciesla, S.Chr.
Mission—St. John in Stoneham, Stoneham, Weld Co. 80754.

BYERS, ARAPAHOE CO., OUR LADY OF THE PLAINS CATHOLIC PARISH IN BYERS (1972)
186 N. McDonnell St., Byers, 80103.
Tel: 303-822-5880; Fax: 303-822-5780; Email: Father.Green@archden.org; Web: ourladyoftheplains.org. Rev. John Green.

CARBONDALE, GARFIELD, CO., ST. MARY OF THE CROWN CATHOLIC PARISH IN CARBONDALE (1980)
397 White Hill Rd., Carbondale, 81623.
Tel: 970-704-0820; Fax: 970-704-0830; Email: Father.Nakvasil@archden.org; Web: www.stvincentstmary.com. Rev. Richard Nakvasil. Administered by St. Vincent, Basalt.
Catechesis Religious Program—Email: education@stvincentstmary.com. Margaretta Bruegger, D.R.E. Students 154.

CENTENNIAL, ARAPAHOE CO., ST. THOMAS MORE CATHOLIC PARISH IN CENTENNIAL (1971)
8035 S. Quebec St., Centennial, 80112.
Tel: 303-770-1155; Fax: 303-770-1160; Email: stm@stthomasmore.org; Web: www.stthomasmore.org. Rev. Msgr. Thomas S. Fryar, V.G.; Revs. Rohan Miranda, O.C.D., Parochial Vicar; Gregory Lesher, Parochial Vicar; Deacons George Brown; Alan Rastrelli, M.D.; Steven Stemper; Timothy Kenny; Robert Cropp; George C. Morin Jr.; Dick Rapp, Business Mgr.
School—St. Thomas More Catholic School, (Grades PreK-8), 7071 E. Otero Ave., Centennial, 80112.
Tel: 303-770-0441; Fax: 303-267-1899; Email: laurao@stthomasmore.org; Web: www.stmcatholic.org. Jan Altevogt, Prin.
Catechesis Religious Program—Tel: 303-770-0531; Email: yifats@stthomasmore.org. Yifat Shahrabani, D.R.E. Students 1,783.

CENTRAL CITY, GILPIN CO., ST. MARY ASSUMPTION IN CENTRAL CITY (1865) Administered by St. Paul, Idaho Springs.
135 Pine St., Central City, 80427. Tel: 303-567-4662; Email: Father.Kopczynski@archden.org; Web: www.godrushcatholic.org. Mailing Address & Office: 1632 Colorado Blvd., P.O. Box 848, Idaho Springs, 80452. Rev. Tadeusz Kopczynski.

COMMERCE CITY, ADAMS CO., OUR LADY MOTHER OF THE CHURCH CATHOLIC PARISH IN COMMERCE CITY (1954)
6690 E. 72nd Ave., Commerce City, 80022.
Tel: 303-289-6489; Fax: 303-289-6480; Email: Msgr.Santos@archden.org; Web: www.parisholmc.org. Rev. Msgr. Jorge de los Santos.

CONIFER, JEFFERSON CO., OUR LADY OF THE PINES CATHOLIC PARISH IN CONIFER (1979)
Mailing Address & Office: 9444 Eagle Cliff Rd., Conifer, 80433. Tel: 303-838-0338; Email: Father.Gaines@archden.org; Web: www.olpconifer.org. Rev. G. Timothy Gaines.
Mission—St. Elizabeth in Buffalo Creek, Buffalo Creek, Jefferson Co. 80425.

CRAIG, MOFFAT CO., ST. MICHAEL CATHOLIC PARISH IN CRAIG (1920)
678 School St., Craig, 81625. Tel: 970-824-5330; Fax: 970-824-7870; Email: nwtriparish@gmail.com; Web: nwtriparish.com. Revs. Geraldo Puga; Shannon Thurman, Parochial Vicar.

EDWARDS, EAGLE CO., ST. CLARE OF ASSISI CATHOLIC PARISH IN EDWARDS (1993)
31622 U.S. Hwy. 6, Edwards, 81632.
Tel: 970-926-2821; Email: Father.Quera@archden.org; Web: stclareparish.com. Mailing Address: P.O. Box 1390, Edwards, 81632. Revs. Jose Maria Quera, (Spain); Darrick Leier, Parochial Vicar; Patrick Geo, Parochial Vicar; Salvador Sanchez, Parochial Vicar.
School—St. Clare of Assisi Catholic School, (Grades K-8), Tel: 970-926-8980; Email: admin@stclareparish.com. Sr. Mary Glady, Prin.
Mission—St. Mary in Eagle, Eagle, Eagle Co. 81631.

ENGLEWOOD, ARAPAHOE CO.

1—ALL SOULS CATHOLIC PARISH IN ENGLEWOOD (1954)
Mailing Address & Office: 4950 S. Logan St., Englewood, 80113-6847. Tel: 303-789-0007; Fax: 720-833-2777; Email: allsouls@allsoulscatholic.org; Web: allsoulscatholic.org. Rev. Samuel Morehead; Deacons Kevin R. Brath; Martin A. Wager.
School—All Souls Catholic School, (Grades PreSchool-8), 4951 S. Pennsylvania, Englewood, 80113. Tel: 303-789-2155; Web: talarcon@allsoulsschool.com; Web: allsoulsschool.com. Tracy Alarcon, Prin.
Catechesis Religious Program—Email: rgoelitz@allsouls55.org. Roger Goelitz, D.R.E. Students 32.

2—HOLY NAME CATHOLIC PARISH IN ENGLEWOOD (1894)
3290 W. Milan Ave., Englewood, 80110.
Tel: 303-781-6093; Email: business@holynamedenver.org; Web: www.holynamedenver.org. Rev. Daniel Cardo, S.C.V.

3—ST. LOUIS-KING OF FRANCE CATHOLIC PARISH IN ENGLEWOOD (1911)
3310 S. Sherman St., Englewood, 80113.
Tel: 303-761-3940; Fax: 303-806-5394; Email: Father.Jungmann@archden.org; Web: www.stlouiscatholicparish.org. Rev. William Jungmann.

ERIE, WELD CO., ST. SCHOLASTICA CATHOLIC PARISH IN ERIE (1899)
Church: 615 Main St., Erie, 80516. Tel: 303-828-4221; Email: Father.Wedow@archden.org; Web: www.stscholasticaerie.org. Mailing Address & Office: 575 Wells St., P.O. Box 402, Erie, 80516. Rev. Robert L. Wedow. Administered by St. Theresa, Frederick.

ESTES PARK, LARIMER CO., OUR LADY OF THE MOUNTAINS CATHOLIC PARISH IN ESTES PARK (1915)
920 Big Thompson Ave., Estes Park, 80517.
Tel: 970-586-8111; Fax: 970-586-8112; Email: info@olmestes.org; Web: www.olmestes.org. Rev. Faustinus Anyamele.

EVERGREEN, JEFFERSON CO., CHRIST THE KING CATHOLIC PARISH IN EVERGREEN (1932)
4291 Evergreen Pkwy., Evergreen, 80439-7723.
Tel: 303-674-3155; Fax: 303-674-3285; Email: Father.FoxR@archden.org; Web: www.ctkevergreen.com. Rev. James R. Fox, V.F.; Deacons Michael Grafner; Robert Hoffman.

FORT COLLINS, LARIMER CO.

1—ST. ELIZABETH ANN SETON CATHOLIC PARISH IN FT. COLLINS (1981)
5450 S. Lemay Ave., Fort Collins, 80525.
Tel: 970-226-1303; Email: Father.Toledo@archden.org; Web: www.seas-parish.org. Revs. Joseph Toledo, V.F.; Edison Chinnappan, Parochial Vicar; Deacons William Trewartha; Donald Weiss.

2—HOLY FAMILY CATHOLIC PARISH IN FT. COLLINS (1924)
328 N. Whitcomb St., Fort Collins, 80521.
Tel: 970-482-6599; Fax: 970-482-8045; Email: holyfamily.ftcollins@comcast.net. Mailing Address & Office: 326 N. Whitcomb St., Fort Collins, 80521. Rev. Enrique Salazar.

3—ST. JOHN XXIII CATHOLIC PARISH IN FT. COLLINS (1967)
1220 University Ave., Fort Collins, 80521.
Tel: 970-484-3356; Fax: 970-658-5003; Email: sandy@john23.com; Web: www.saintjohn.church. Rev. Rocco S. Porter.

4—ST. JOSEPH CATHOLIC PARISH IN FT. COLLINS (1879)
300 W. Mountain Ave., Fort Collins, 80521.
Tel: 970-482-4148; Fax: 970-221-0635; Email: jlcoleman@stjosephfc.org; Web: www.stjosephfc.org. Mailing Address & Office: 101 N. Howes St., Fort Collins, 80521. Revs. Simon Kalonga; Joseph A. Hartmann, Parochial Vicar; Deacons Gregg Reynolds; Warren G. Lybarger; Jerome Kraft.
School—St. Joseph Catholic School, (Grades PreK-8), 127 N. Howes St., Fort Collins, 80521.
Tel: 970-484-1171; Email: dklein@gosaintjoseph.org. Nick Blanco, Prin.

FORT LUPTON, WELD CO., ST. WILLIAM CATHOLIC PARISH IN FT. LUPTON (1909)
1025 Fulton Ave., Fort Lupton, 80621.
Tel: 303-857-6642; Fax: 303-857-6643; Email: Father.Wojcik@archden.org; Web: www.saintwilliamchurch.org. Rev. Grzegorz Wojeik.
Mission—Our Lady of Grace in Wattenburg, Wattenburg, Weld Co. 80621.

FORT MORGAN, MORGAN CO., ST. HELENA CATHOLIC PARISH IN FT. MORGAN (1910)
917 W. 7th Ave., Fort Morgan, 80701.
Tel: 970-867-2885; Email: Father.Vigil@archden.org; Web: www.sthelenachurch.org. Rev. Erik Vigil-Reyes.
Missions—St. Francis of Assisi in Weldona—Weldona, 80653.
Our Lady of Lourdes in Wiggins, Wiggins, Morgan Co. 80654.

FOXFIELD, ARAPAHOE CO., OUR LADY OF LORETO CATHOLIC PARISH IN FOXFIELD (1998)
18000 E. Arapahoe Rd., Foxfield, 80016.
Tel: 303-766-3800; Fax: 303-766-3700; Email: Father.Bluejacket@archden.org; Web: /www.ourladyofloreto.org. Revs. David Bluejacket; Lourda Inbaraj, Parochial Vicar; Nicholas Larkin, Parochial Vicar; Deacons Richard Miller; Michael Magee.
School—Our Lady of Loreto Catholic School, (Grades PreK-8), Tel: 303-951-8330; Email: SAdm@ourladyofloreto.org; Web: www.OLOLCatholicSchool.org. Mr. Andrew McDonald, Prin. Lay Teachers 14; Students 240.

FREDERICK, WELD CO., ST. THERESA CATHOLIC PARISH IN FREDERICK (1923)
Church: 502 Walnut St., Frederick, 80530.
Tel: 303-833-2966; Email: Father.Florez@archden.org; Web: www.sttheresafred.org. Mailing Address & Office: 501 Walnut St., P.O. Box 418, Frederick, 80530. Revs. Hernan Florez; Tomislav Tomic, Parochial Vicar.

GLENWOOD SPRINGS, GARFIELD CO., ST. STEPHEN CATHOLIC PARISH IN GLENWOOD SPRINGS (1885)
1885 Blake Ave., Glenwood Springs, 81601.
Tel: 970-945-6673; Fax: 970-945-6677; Email: ststephen1885@sopris.net; Web: www.ststephen1885.org. Very Rev. Elbert Chilson, V.F.; Deacons Victor Kimminau; Charles Sprick, (Retired).
School—St. Stephen Catholic School, (Grades PreK-8), 414 S. Hyland Park Dr., Glenwood Springs, 81601. Tel: 970-945-7746; Fax: 970-945-1208; Email: glendaoliver@scsglenwood.org; Web: www.scsglenwood.org. Glenda Oliver, Prin. Lay Teachers 16; Students 165.

GOLDEN, JEFFERSON CO., ST. JOSEPH CATHOLIC PARISH IN GOLDEN (1859)
969 Ulysses St., Golden, 80401. Tel: 303-279-4464; Fax: 303-273-9811; Email: terrih@stjoegold.org;

Web: www.stjoegold.org. Rev. Joseph Tran; Deacons Dennis J. Langdon; Edward Clements.

GRAND LAKE, GRAND CO., ST. ANNE CATHOLIC PARISH IN GRAND LAKE (1944)
360 Hancock St., Grand Lake, 80446.
Tel: 970-887-0032, Ext. 5; Email: admin@grandcatholic.com; Web: grandcatholic.com. Mailing Address: P.O. Box 2029, Granby, 80446. Revs. Michael Freihofer; Peter Wojda, Parochial Vicar; Deacon James R. Moat.
Missions—Our Lady of the Snow in Grandby—300 11th St., Granby, Grand Co. 80446.
St. Bernard of Montjoux in Fraser / Winter Park, 275 E. Rendezvous Rd., Fraser, Grand Co. 80482.
Catechesis Religious Program—Tel: 303-815-0055; Email: mtnval2@gmail.com. Students 53.

GREELEY, WELD CO.
1—ST. MARY CATHOLIC PARISH IN GREELEY (1965)
2222 23rd Ave., Greeley, 80634. Tel: 970-352-1724; Fax: 970-352-1729; Email: susan.benke@stmarygreeley.org; Web: www.stmarygreeley.org. Very Rev. James K. Goggins, V.F.; Susan Benke, Business Mgr.; Deacons John Volk; Frederick L. Torrez.
School—St. Mary Catholic School, (Grades PreK-8), 2351 22nd Ave., Greeley, 80631. Tel: 970-353-8100; Fax: 970-353-8102; Email: principal@stmarycs.net; Web: www.stmarycs.net. Donna Bornhoft, Prin. Lay Teachers 15; Students 157; PreK Enrollment 29.
Catechesis Religious Program—
Tel: 970-352-1724, Ext. 119; Email: youthminister@stmarygreeley.org. Briana LaFrance, D.R.E. Students 86.
2—OUR LADY OF PEACE CATHOLIC PARISH IN GREELEY (1948)
1311 3rd St., Greeley, 80631. Tel: 970-353-1747; Fax: 970-353-4830; Email: Father.RamirezM@archden.org; Web: www.ourladyofpeacegreeley.org. Rev. Mario Ramirez, S.T.B.; Deacon Cesar Perez.
Catechesis Religious Program—1303 3rd St., Greeley, 80631.
3—ST. PETER CATHOLIC PARISH IN GREELEY (1903)
915 12th St., Greeley, 80631. Email: cheryl@stpetergreeley.org; Web: www.stpetergreeley.org. Very Rev. James H. Crisman, V.F.

HOLYOKE, PHILLIPS CO., ST. PATRICK CATHOLIC PARISH IN HOLYOKE (1893)
541 S. Interocean Ave., Holyoke, 80734.
Tel: 970-854-2762; Tel: 970-859-2866; Email: patrickpeterctk@gmail.com. Mailing Address & Office: 519 S. Interocean Ave., Holyoke, 80734. Rev. Jerry Rohr.
Missions—Christ the King in Haxtun—Haxtun, Phillips Co. 80731. Tel: 970-774-7640.
St. Peter the Apostle in Fleming, Fleming, Logan Co. 80728. Tel: 970-265-2792.

IDAHO SPRINGS, CLEAR CREEK CO., ST. PAUL CATHOLIC PARISH IN IDAHO SPRINGS (1881)
1632 Colorado Blvd., Idaho Springs, 80452.
Tel: 303-567-4662; Email: Father.Kopczynski@archden.org; Web: www.godrushcatholic.org. Mailing Address: P.O. Box 848, Idaho Springs, 80452. Rev. Tadeusz Kopczynski.
Mission—Our Lady of Lourdes in Georgetown, [CEM] Georgetown, Clear Creek Co. 80452.

ILIFF, LOGAN CO., ST. CATHERINE IN ILIFF (1927)
Administered by St. Anthony, Sterling.
111 S. Fifth St., Iliff, 80736. Tel: 970-522-6422; Email: Father.Bodzioch@archden.org; Web: www.saintanthonyssterling.org. Mailing Address: 326 S. 3rd St., Sterling, 80751. Very Rev. Michael Bodzioch, V.F.

JOHNSTOWN, WELD CO., ST. JOHN THE BAPTIST CATHOLIC PARISH IN JOHNSTOWN (1937)
1000 Country Acres Dr., Johnstown, 80534.
Tel: 970-587-2879; Email: Father.Bonilla@archden.org; Web: www.sjbjohnstown.org. Revs. Juan Manuel Bonilla; Angel Perez-Brown, Parochial Vicar.

JULESBURG, SEDGWICK CO., ST. ANTHONY OF PADUA CATHOLIC PARISH IN JULESBURG (1907)
606 W. 3rd St., Julesburg, 80737. Tel: 970-474-2655; Fax: 970-474-2655; Email: Father.O'Brien@archden.org. Rev. Michael J. O'Brien.
Mission—St. Peter in Crook, 612 E. 3rd Ave., Crook, 80726.

KREMMLING, GRAND CO., ST. PETER CATHOLIC PARISH IN KREMMLING (1944)
106 S. 5th St., Kremmling, 80459.
Tel: 970-887-0032, Ext. 5; Email: admin@grandcatholic.com. Mailing Address: P.O. Box 2029, Granby, 80446. Revs. Michael Freihofer; Peter Wojda, Parochial Vicar. Administered by St. Anne, Grand Lake.

LAFAYETTE, BOULDER CO., IMMACULATE CONCEPTION CATHOLIC PARISH IN LAFAYETTE (1907)
Mailing Address & Office: 715 Cabrini Dr., Lafayette, 80026-2676. Tel: 303-665-5103;
Fax: 303-604-9077; Email: Msgr.Amundsen@archden.org; Web: lafayettecatholic.org. Rev. Msgr. Robert L. Amundsen; Rev. Jose Saenz, Parochial Vicar.
Catechesis Religious Program—Tel: 303-665-5103; Email: kathleen@lafayettecatholic.org. Kathleen Donohoe, D.R.E. Students 599.

LAKEWOOD, JEFFERSON CO.
1—ST. BERNADETTE CATHOLIC PARISH IN LAKEWOOD (1947)
W. 12th Ave. & Teller St., Lakewood, 80214.
Tel: 303-233-1523; Fax: 303-233-7285; Email: stbernparish@gmail.com; Web: www.stbernadettelakewood.org. Mailing Address & Office: 7240 W. 12th Ave., Lakewood, 80214. Very Rev. Thomas Coyte, V.F.
School—St. Bernadette Catholic School, (Grades PreK-8), 1100 Upham St., Lakewood, 80214.
Tel: 303-237-0401; Email: office@stbcs.net. Anna-Marie Murillo, Prin.
2—CHRIST ON THE MOUNTAIN CATHOLIC PARISH IN LAKEWOOD (1975)
13922 W. Utah Ave., Lakewood, 80228-4110.
Tel: 303-988-2222; Email: Father.Allen@archden.org; Fax: 303-986-6956; Web: www.christonthemountain.net. Rev. David Allen; Deacon Michael Fletcher.
3—ST. JUDE CATHOLIC PARISH IN LAKEWOOD (1967)
9405 W. Florida Ave., Lakewood, 80232-5111.
Tel: 303-988-6435; Fax: 303-988-6438; Email: mail@saintjudelakewood.org; Web: www.saintjudelakewood.org. Rev. Msgr. Robert J. Kinkel; Deacons Michael L. Bunch; Jay Garland; Alan C. Spears.
4—OUR LADY OF FATIMA CATHOLIC PARISH IN LAKEWOOD (1958)
1985 Miller St., Lakewood, 80215. Tel: 303-233-6236; Fax: 303-237-6097; Email: frhenri@fatimalakewood.com; Web: Fatimalakewood.com. Very Rev. Henri Tshibambe, V.F.; Rev. Francisco J. Garcia, Parochial Vicar; Deacons Joseph W. Hawley; Rich Boyd; Glenn Allison; Michael Daly; Carl Zarlengo, Business Mgr.
School—Our Lady of Fatima Catholic School, (Grades PreK-8), 10530 W. 20th Ave., 80215.
Tel: 303-233-2500; Email: ltaylor@olfcs.com; Email: czarlengo@fatimalakewood.com; Web: www.olfcs.com. Miss Lisa Taylor, Prin. Lay Teachers 23; Students 150; Religious Teachers 3.

LITTLETON, ARAPAHOE CO.
1—ST. MARY CATHOLIC PARISH IN LITTLETON (1901) [JC]
6853 S. Prince, Littleton, 80120. Tel: 303-798-8506; Fax: 303-347-2270; Email: kathy.reuter@stmarylittleton.org; Web: www.stmarylittleton.org. Revs. Javier Nieva, D.C.J.M., (Spain); Armando Marsal, D.C.J.M., (Spain) Parochial Vicar; Juan Espino, D.C.J.M., Parochial Vicar; Luis Granados, D.C.J.M., (Spain) In Res.; Deacons Timothy M. Kilbarger; Anthony Dudzic; Greg Frank.
School—St. Mary Catholic School, (Grades PreK-8), 6833 S. Prince St., Littleton, 80120.
Tel: 303-798-2375; Fax: 720-283-4756; Email: jbaker@stmarylittleton.com; Web: www.littletoncatholicschool.com. Jim Baker, Prin.; Rev. Jamie de Cendra, D.C.J.M., (Spain) Chap. Lay Teachers 36; Students 467; Clergy / Religious Teachers 1.
2—OUR LADY OF MOUNT CARMEL CATHOLIC PARISH IN LITTLETON (1997)
5612 S. Hickory St., Littleton, 80120.
Tel: 303-703-8538; Email: secretary@olmcfssp.org; Web: olmcfssp.org. Mailing Address & Office: 5620 S. Hickory Cir., Littleton, 80120. Revs. James Jackson, F.S.S.P.; Caleb Kick, Parochial Vicar; Daniel Nolan, Parochial Vicar.

LITTLETON, JEFFERSON CO.
1—ST. FRANCES CABRINI CATHOLIC PARISH IN LITTLETON (1972)
6673 W. Chatfield Ave., Littleton, 80128.
Tel: 303-979-7688; Fax: 303-972-8566; Email: jdonnelly@sfcparish.org; Web: www.sfcparish.org. Revs. John Paul Leyba; Ronald Sequeira, Parochial Vicar; Israel Gonsalves, O.C.D., Parochial Vicar; Deacons Chet Ubowski; Marc Nestorick; Brian Kerby.
2—LIGHT OF THE WORLD ROMAN CATHOLIC PARISH IN LITTLETON (1979)
10316 W. Bowles Ave., Littleton, 80127.
Tel: 303-973-3969; Fax: 303-973-2122; Email: jennifer@lotw.org; Web: lotw.org. Very Rev. Matthew Book, V.F.; Rev. Joseph LaJoie, Parochial Vicar; Deacons Joseph H. Donohoe; Rick Montagne; Mark Wolbach.

LONGMONT, BOULDER CO.
1—ST. FRANCIS OF ASSISI CATHOLIC PARISH IN LONGMONT (1982) [JC]
3791 Pike Rd., Longmont, 80503. Tel: 303-772-6322; Fax: 303-772-9415; Email: father@sfassisi.org; Web: www.sfassisi.org. Rev. Frank Maroney.
2—ST. JOHN THE BAPTIST CATHOLIC PARISH IN LONGMONT (1882) [JC]
Mailing Address & Office: 323 Collyer St., Longmont, 80501. Tel: 303-776-0737; Email: info@johnthebaptist.org; Web: www.johnthebaptist.org. Revs. Humberto Marquez; Daniel Ciucci, Parochial Vicar; Deacons Mike Berens; Robert J. Howard; Jose Rodriguez.
School—St. John the Baptist Catholic School, (Grades PreK-8), 350 Emery St., Longmont, 80501.
Tel: 303-776-8760; Email: schooloffice@johnthebaptist.org; Web: school.johnthebaptist.org. Kemmery Hill, Prin. Lay Teachers 25; Students 275.
Catechesis Religious Program—Cell: creed@johnthebaptist.org. Students 425.

LOUISVILLE, BOULDER CO., ST. LOUIS CATHOLIC PARISH IN LOUISVILLE (1884)
902 Grant Ave., Louisville, 80027. Tel: 303-666-6401; Fax: 303-666-0826; Email: parishoffice@stlp.org; Web: www.stlp.org. Revs. Timothy Hjelstrom; John Robert Mrozek II, Parochial Vicar; Deacon Ronald Darschewski.
School—St. Louis Catholic School, (Grades PreK-8), 925 Grant Ave., Louisville, 80027. Tel: 303-666-6220; Fax: 303-666-5244; Email: lwelty@stlp.org; Web: school.stlp.org. Kathy Byrnes, Prin. Lay Teachers 15; Students 180; Clergy / Religious Teachers 3.

LOVELAND, LARIMER CO., ST. JOHN THE EVANGELIST CATHOLIC PARISH IN LOVELAND (1902)
1730 W. 12th St., Loveland, 80537.
Tel: 970-635-5800; Fax: 970-669-5743; Email: info@saintjohns.net; Web: www.saintjohns.us. Mailing Address & Office: 1515 Hilltop Dr., Loveland, 80537. Revs. Stephen E. Adams, V.F.; David Gomez, Parochial Vicar; Deacons Dennis Wallisch; August Cordova; Pat Travis.
School—St. John the Evangelist Catholic School, (Grades PreK-8), Tel: 970-635-5830; Email: saintjohnsschool@saintjohns.net; Web: www.school.saintjohns.net. Nichole Rottinghaus, Prin. Lay Teachers 15; Students 197.

MEAD, WELD CO., GUARDIAN ANGELS CATHOLIC PARISH IN MEAD (1911)
109 S. 3rd St., Mead, 80542. Tel: 970-535-0721; Email: Father.Hartway@archden.org; Web: www.meadangels.org. Mailing Address: P.O. Box 444, Mead, 80542. Rev. Alan Hartway, C.PP.S.

MEEKER, RIO BLANCO CO., HOLY FAMILY IN MEEKER (1905)
889 Park Ave., Meeker, 81641. Tel: 970-878-3300; Email: nwtriparish@gmail.com; Web: nwtriparish.com. Mailing Address: P.O. Box 866, Meeker, 81641. Revs. Geraldo Puga; Shannon Thurman, Parochial Vicar. Administered by St. Michael, Craig.

MINTURN, EAGLE CO., ST. PATRICK CATHOLIC PARISH IN MINTURN (1913)
476 Pine St., Minturn, 81645. Tel: 970-926-2821; Email: Father.Quera@archden.org; Web: www.saintpatrickminturn.com. Mailing Address: P.O. Box 219, Minturn, 81645-0219. Revs. Jose Maria Quera, (Spain); Darrick Leier, Parochial Vicar. Administered by St. Clare of Assisi, Edwards.

NORTHGLENN, ADAMS CO., IMMACULATE HEART OF MARY CATHOLIC PARISH IN NORTHGLENN (1967)
11385 Grant Dr., Northglenn, 80233.
Tel: 303-452-2041; Email: deacontaylor@ihmco.org; Web: www.ihmco.org. Rev. James Spahn; Deacons Mason Fraley, Parochial Vicar; Taylor Elder; Jerome Durnford; Paul Louderman; Louis Arambula.

PEETZ, LOGAN CO., SACRED HEART IN PEETZ (1914) [CEM] Administered by St. Anthony, Sterling.
621 Logan St., Peetz, 80747. Tel: 970-522-6422; Email: Father.Bodzioch@archden.org; Web: www.saintanthonyssterling.org. Mailing Address & Office: 326 S. 3rd St., Sterling, 80751. Very Rev. Michael Bodzioch, V.F.

PLATTEVILLE, WELD CO., ST. NICHOLAS CATHOLIC PARISH IN PLATTEVILLE (1889)
Church: 514 Marion Ave., Platteville, 80651.
Tel: 970-785-2143; Email: stnickschurch@qwestoffice.net; Web: www.stnicholasplatteville.org. Mailing Address & Office: 520 Marion Ave., P.O. Box 576, Platteville, 80651. Revs. Juan Manuel Bonilla; Angel Perez-Brown, Parochial Vicar. Administered by St. John the Baptist, Johnstown.

RANGELY, RIO BLANCO CO., ST. IGNATIUS OF ANTIOCH IN RANGELY (1931)
109 S. Stanolind Ave., Rangely, 81648.
Tel: 970-675-8935; Fax: 970-824-5330; Email: nwtriparish@gmail.com; Web: nwtriparish.com. Mailing Address: 678 School St., Craig, 81625. Revs. Geraldo Puga; Shannon Thurman, Parochial Vicar.

RIFLE, GARFIELD CO., ST. MARY CATHOLIC PARISH IN RIFLE (1910)
761 Birch Ave., Rifle, 81650. Tel: 970-625-5125; Email: Father.GarciaG@archden.org; Web: www.stmaryrifle.com. Mailing Address: P.O. Box 191, Rifle, 81650. Rev. Gerardo Garcia Jimenez, Admin.
Mission—Sacred Heart in Silt, Silt, Garfield Co. 81652.

ROGGEN, WELD CO., SACRED HEART CATHOLIC PARISH IN ROGGEN (1924)
38044 Weld County Rd. 16, Roggen, 80652.

Tel: 303-849-5313; Fax: 303-849-5674; Email: Father.Bello@archden.org; Web: www.thesacredheartchurch.org. Rev. Carlos Wilson Bello-Ayala.

Mission—Holy Family in Keenesburg, Keenesburg, Weld Co. 80643.

STEAMBOAT SPRINGS, ROUTT CO., HOLY NAME CATHOLIC PARISH IN STEAMBOAT SPRINGS (1907)

Church: 524 Oak St., Steamboat Springs, 80477.

Tel: 970-879-0671; Fax: 970-879-7406; Email: Father.Bayer@archden.org; Web: www.catholicsteamboat.com. Mailing Address & Office: 504 Oak St., P.O. Box 774198, Steamboat Springs, 80477-4198. Rev. Ernest Bayer.

Mission—St. Martin in Oak Creek, Oak Creek, Routt Co. 80467.

STERLING, LOGAN CO., ST. ANTHONY CATHOLIC PARISH IN STERLING (1888)

331 S. 3rd St., Sterling, 80751. Tel: 970-522-6422; Email: Father.Bodzioch@archden.org; Web: www.saintanthonyssterling.org. Mailing Address & Office: 326 S. 3rd St., Sterling, 80751. Very Rev. Michael Bodzioch, V.F.

THORNTON, ADAMS CO.

1—HOLY CROSS CATHOLIC PARISH IN THORNTON (1957)

Tel: 303-289-2258; Email: Father.Castro@archden.org; Web: www.holycrossthornton.com. Rev. Warli de Araujo Castro.

2—SAINT JOHN PAUL II CATHOLIC PARISH IN THORNTON

3951 Cottonwood Lakes Blvd., Thornton, 80241.

Tel: 303-452-2041; Email: father.spahn@archden.org; Web: stjohnpaul2.org. Mailing Address: c/o Immaculate Heart of Mary Catholic Parish, 11385 Grant Dr., Northglenn, 80241. Rev. James Spahn.

WALDEN, JACKSON CO., ST. IGNATIUS CATHOLIC PARISH IN WALDEN, Administered by St. Anne, Grand Lake.

448 LaFever St., Walden, 80430.

Tel: 970-887-0032, Ext. 5; Web: www.grandcatholic.com. P.O. Box 2029, Granby, 80446. Rev. Michael A. Freihofer.

WESTMINSTER, ADAMS CO.

1—HOLY TRINITY CATHOLIC PARISH IN WESTMINSTER (1956)

7595 N. Federal Blvd., Westminster, 80030.

Tel: 303-428-3594; Fax: 303-427-4125; Email: Parishoffice@htcatholic.org; Web: www.htcatholic.org. Revs. Piotr Mozdyniewicz; Miguel Enriquez, Parochial Vicar; Deacon Geoff Bennett.

School—Holy Trinity Catholic School, (Grades PreK-8), 3050 W. 76th Ave., Westminster, 80030.

Tel: 303-427-5632; Email: dkline@htcatholic.org. David Kline, Prin. Lay Teachers 14; Students 138; Unique 1.

Mission—Our Lady of Visitation in Denver, Denver Co. 80221.

2—ST. MARK CATHOLIC PARISH IN WESTMINSTER (1973)

3141 W. 96th Ave., Westminster, 80031.

Tel: 303-466-8720; Fax: 303-466-0998; Email: Father.Koehler@archden.org; Web: www.saintmarkcc.org. Very Rev. Kenneth Koehler, V.F.

WHEAT RIDGE, JEFFERSON CO.

1—STS. PETER & PAUL CATHOLIC PARISH IN WHEAT RIDGE (1949)

3900 Pierce St., Wheat Ridge, 80033.

Tel: 303-424-3706; Fax: 303-424-0819; Email: info@peterandpaulcatholic.org; Web: www.peterandpaulcatholic.org. Revs. Jason M. Thuerauf, V.F.; Victor Raj, H.G.N., Parochial Vicar.

School—Sts. Peter & Paul Catholic School, (Grades PreSchool-8), 3920 Pierce St., Wheat Ridge, 80033.

Tel: 303-420-0402; Fax: 303-456-1888; Email: mgosage@sppscatholic.com; Web: www.sppscatholic.com. Sr. Faustia Deppe, O.C.D., Prin. Lay Teachers 13; Priests 2; Sisters 4; Students 217; Clergy / Religious Teachers 4.

Convent—Carmelite Sisters of the Most Sacred Heart of Los Angeles, 4040 Pierce St., Wheat Ridge, 80033. Tel: 303-422-6419.

2—QUEEN OF VIETNAMESE MARTYRS CATHOLIC PARISH IN WHEATRIDGE (1976)

Tel: 303-431-0382; Fax: 303-431-1876; Email: Father.CaiMyLoc@archden.org; Web: qvm.ktvd.org. Rev. Bonaventure Cai My Loc, C.M.C.

WINDSOR, WELD CO., OUR LADY OF THE VALLEY CATHOLIC PARISH IN WINDSOR (1969)

1250 7th St., Windsor, 80550. Tel: 970-686-5084; Fax: 970-686-9169; Email: office@ourladyofthevalley.net; Web: www.ourladyofthevalley.net. Revs. Gregg Pedersen; Boguslaw Rebacz, Parochial Vicar; Deacons Harold Kimble; John Riviera.

WRAY, YUMA CO., ST. ANDREW THE APOSTLE CATHOLIC PARISH IN WRAY (1888)

412 Dexter St., Wray, 80758. Tel: 970-332-5858; Email: standrewapostlewray@gmail.com; Web: www.stjohnstandrew.org. Rev. Felicien Mbala.

YUMA, YUMA CO., ST. JOHN THE EVANGELIST CATHOLIC PARISH IN YUMA (1888) Administered by St. Andrew the Apostle, Wray.

508 S. Ash St., Yuma, 80759. Tel: 970-848-5973; Fax: 970-848-2817; Email: Father.Mbala@archden.org; Web: www.stjohnstandrew.org. Rev. Felicien Mbala.

Military Chaplains:

Revs.—

Dwyer, Curtiss, LT, CHC, USN, 15 Cypress Ln., Fredericksburg, VA 22406

Lesher, Gregory, LTJG, CHC, USN, CLB6 H&S Co. RMT, PSC Box 20181, Camp Lejeune, NC 28542-0181

Romero, Donald, Ch. Major, AF Chaplain Corps College, 155 N. Twining Rd. Bldg. 693, Mazwell AFB, AL 36112.

Other Archdiocesan Assignment:

Revs.—

Bustillos, Guillermo, Chap., Hispanic Apostolic Movement

Claver, James, Chap. Bishop Machebeuf High School

Frank, Chrysostom, Prof., Regis University

Hellstrom, Christopher, Chap., Spiritual Formation & Healing Prayer Ministry

Ignatius, John, Supr., Servants of Christ Jesus

Kostka, Paul, Chap., University of Denver

McLagan, Joseph, Chap. Holy Family High School

Sanchez, Salvador, Ministerial Duties, St. Clare of Assisi Parish.

On Duty Outside the Archdiocese:

Revs.—

Chagala, Arturo, Parochial Admin., St. Michael Parish, 1445 North 2nd St., Philadelphia, PA 19122

Dellinger, Jonathan, Pastor, St. Nicholas Parish, 707 St. Nicholas Dr., North Pole, AK 99705

Ricci, Lorenzo, Missionary Work, Cape Town, South Africa.

Graduate Studies:

Revs.—

Eusterman, Daniel

Nepil, John

Rapp, Michael.

Retired:

Rev. Msgrs.—

Croak, David P., (Retired), 13952 E. Marina Dr., #603, Aurora, 80014

Glenn, Michael G., S.T.L., (Retired), c/o Office of the Vicar for the Clergy: 1300 S. Steele St., 80210

Jones, Raymond N., V.E., (Retired), 700 S. Yarrow St., Lakewood, 80226

Leone, Kenneth J., (Retired), 2850 Classic Dr., #2803, Highlands Ranch, 80126

McDaid, J. Anthony, J.C.D., (Retired), c/o Office of the Vicar for Clergy: 1300 S. Steele St., 80210

Schroeder, George, (Retired), Blessed Sacrament Parish, 11300 N. 64th St., Scottsdale, AZ 85254

Revs.—

Blach, Leo M., (Retired), 2515 E. 104th, Unit H, Thornton, 80233

Blanco, Joseph, (Retired), c/o Office of the Vicar for Clergy: 1300 S. Steele St., 80210

Breslin, William E., (Retired), 3434 E. Arizona Ave., 80210

Brock, William, (Retired), P.O. Box 948, Cheyenne, WY 82003

Cuneo, James J., (Retired), 6991 Nile Ct., Arvada, 80007

DeLazzer, Dorino, (Retired), c/o Office of the Vicar for Clergy: 1300 S. Steele St., 80210

Denig, Philip P., (Retired), 9B Ardsley Ave., Whitting, NJ 08759

Fisher, Robert D., (Retired), 1223 Race St., #503, 80206

Freeman, Roland P., In Res., (Retired), All Saints Parish, 2560 S. Grove St., 80219

Garrou, Dennis, (Retired), c/o Office of the Vicar for Clergy: 1300 S. Steele St., 80210

Gass, Michael W., (Retired), 12605 Madison Wy., Thornton, 80241

Geilenkirchen, Jude, (Retired), 9300 E. Center Ave., Unit 10-C, 80210

Jayachandra, Hermanagild, S.T.D., (Retired), B-105 Sri Ganesh Dharshan, 4A Sankaran Pillai Rd., Tiruchirapalli, India 620002

Kerrigan, Michael F., (Retired), Mother of God Parish, 475 Logan St., 80210

Kleiner, James E., (Retired), c/o Office of the Vicar for Clergy: 1300 S. Steele St., 80210

Lascelle, Roger L., (Retired), 7550 W. Fremont Ave., Littleton, 80128

McCormick, Thomas, (Retired), 9300 E. Center Ave., Unit 10-C, 80247

Medrano, Marcus, (Retired), 2576 104th Cir., Westminster, 80234

Mirto, Gregorio, In Res., (Retired), St. Theresa Parish, 705 St. Theresa Blvd., Sugar Land, TX 77498

Monahan, Joseph E., (Retired), 12605 Madison Wy., Thornton, 80241

Moreno, James, (Retired), c/o Office of the Vicar for Clergy: 1300 S. Steele St., 80210

Murphy, John, In Res., (Retired), St. Luke Catholic Church, 421 E. 38th St., Erie, PA 16504

Pfister, Neal A., (Retired), c/o Office of the Vicar for Clergy: 1300 S. Steele St., 80210

Purfield, James R., (Retired), 2835 W. 32nd Ave., 80211

Revello, James K.I., (Retired), c/o Office of the Vicar for Clergy: 1300 S. Steele St., 80210

Reycraft, Robert J., (Retired), 7505 W. Yale Ave., #2602, 80227

Schaffer, Darrell, In Res., (Retired), Sts. Peter & Paul Parish, 3900 Pierce St., Wheat Ridge, 80033

Smith, Vincent Leo, (Retired), P.O. Box 82, Fairplay, 80440

Stahl, David, (Retired), 231 Applewood Ct., Brush, 80723

Urban, Peter, In Res., (Retired), St. Anthony of Padua Parish, 3801 W. Ohio Ave., 80219

Weissbeck, Reinhold, (Retired), 675 S. Alton Way, Unit 10-B, 80247

Willette, Donald, (Retired), 2211 W. Mulberry Ave., Unit 67, Fort Collins, 80521

Woerth, Thomas, (Retired), c/o Office of the Vicar for Clergy: 1300 S. Steele St., 80210.

Permanent Deacons:

Allison, Glenn, Our Lady of Fatima, Lakewood

Ansay, Ronald J., (Retired)

Antinora, Richard, St. Elizabeth Ann Seton, Ft. Collins

Arambula, Louis, Immaculate Heart of Mary, Northglenn

Archer, Matthew, St. Joan of Arc, Arvada

Arling, David, Nativity of Our Lord, Broomfield

Armijo, Edward, (Retired)

Atencio, Sidney, Presentation of Our Lady, Denver

Babish, Joseph, St. Elizabeth of Hungary, Denver

Baker, Richard, (Retired)

Barrows, Russell D., Mt. Carmel, Denver

Beck, Ron, Shrine of St. Anne, Arvada

Benedetto, Joseph, St. Bernadette, Lakewood

Benjamin, Joseph G., St. Joseph Church, Akron

Bennett, Geoff, Holy Trinity, Westminster

Berens, Michael, St. John the Baptist, Longmont

Blume, James W., Annunciation, Denver

Borda, Richard S., Shrine of St. Anne, Arvada

Boyd, Richard M., Our Lady of Fatima, Lakewood

Brath, Kelvin, All Souls, Englewood

Brown, George, St. Thomas More, Centennial

Bunch, Michael L., St. Jude, Lakewood

Byrne, Christopher, Sacred Heart of Jesus, Boulder

Casados, Ross, (Retired)

Clements, Edward R., St. Joseph, Golden

Coleman, Colin, St. Catherine of Siena, Denver

Concha, Henry, Annunciation, Denver

Cordova, August, St. John the Evangelist, Loveland

Corley, Mel, (Retired)

Creel, Rodger L., (Retired)

Criste, Phil, (Retired)

Cropp, Robert, St. Thomas More, Centennial

Cuevas, Robert, St. Mary Magdalene, Denver

Daly, Michael, Our Lady of Fatima, Lakewood

Dang, Peter Hung Phi, Queen of Vietnamese Martyrs, Denver

Daniels, James, St. William, Ft. Lupton

Darschewski, Ronald, St. Louis, Louisville

Decker, Myles, Charlotte, NC

Del Real, Harold, (Retired)

DelVillar, Oscar, Immaculate Conception, Lafayette

DeProfio, Dominic, St. Mary Magdalene, Denver

Donohoe, Joseph H., Office of Diaconate, Dir. of Deacon Personnel

Dorwart, Jason, (Retired)

Downey, Hugh, St. Joan of Arc & Missionary Deacon in Africa

Doyle, James, Our Lady of Peace, Dillon

Dreiling, Kenneth, (Retired)

Dudzic, Anthony, (Retired), St. Mary, Littleton

Duran, Ruben, Church of the Ascension, Denver

Durnford, Jerome, Immaculate Heart of Mary, Northglenn

Elder, R. Taylor, Immaculate Heart of Mary, Northglenn

Engel, Witold, (Retired)

Ertmer, William, St. Francis de Sales, Denver

Estrada, Ruben, Church of the Ascension, Denver

Finan, Robert E., Cathedral Basilica of the Immaculate Conception, Denver

Fletcher, Michael, Christ on the Mountain, Lakewood

Fortunato, George R., St. Ignatius of Antioch, Rangely

Fox, Thomas, (Diocese of Tucson)

Frank, Gregory L., St. Mary, Littleton

Franklin, John, (Retired)
Fucci, Craig, St. Michael the Archangel, Aurora
Gallagher, Michael, (Retired)
Garcia, Modesto, St. Nicholas, Platteville
Garland, Jay, St. Jude, Lakewood
Gerber, Joseph, St. Joan of Arc, Arvada
Gingerich, Cecil, St. Peter, Greeley
Goldwire, Hal, St. Vincent De Paul, Denver
Grafner, Michael, Christ the King, Evergreen
Gregorius, Robert, (Retired)
Grimm, R. Paul, (Retired)
Guerrero, Antonio, St. Dominic, Denver
Hahn, Charles, Spirit of Christ, Arvada
Haigh, Robert, (Retired)
Halpine, Russell, (Retired)
Harrington, Philip, St. Mary, Aspen
Hastings, William O., St. Peter, Greeley
Hathaway, Timothy, Our Lady of Loreto, Foxfield
Hawkins, Ken, (Retired)
Hawley, Joseph W., (Retired)
Heckman, Kevin, Blessed Sacrament, Denver
Hegarty, Marvin A., (Retired)
Hetzel, Martin, Nativity of Our Lord, Broomfield
Hoffman, Robert, Christ the King, Evergreen
Howard, Robert J., (Retired)
Hudec, Gordon D., St. Mark, Westminster
Jordan, Bill, St. Augustine, Brighton
Kelly, Timothy M., St. Vincent de Paul, Denver
Kenny, Timothy, St. Thomas More, Centennial
Kerby, Brian J., St. Frances Cabrini, Littleton
Kilbarger, Timothy M., St. Mary, Littleton
Kimble, Harold, Our Lady of the Valley, Windsor
Kimminau, Victor H., (Retired)
Kraft, Jerome, St. Joseph, Ft. Collins
Lamar, Charles, St. Mary, Breckenridge
Lanciotti, Robert, St. Elizabeth Ann Seton, Ft. Collins
Langdon, Dennis J., St. Joseph, Golden
Le, Joseph Tam Van, (Retired)
Leiner, Kevin, Notre Dame, Denver
Liwanag, Wilfredo B., St. Michael the Archangel, Aurora
Lopez, Samuel, St. Francis de Sales, Denver
Louderman, Paul, Immaculate Heart of Mary, Northglenn
Luksch, David, Sacred Heart of Jesus, Boulder
Lybarger, Warren G., (Retired)
Mackin, James, Sacred Heart of Mary, Boulder
Magee, Michael, Our Lady of Loreto, Foxfield
Martha-Pro, Mario, St. William, Ft. Lupton
Marthe, Daniel M., (Retired)
Martin, Gregory, (Retired)
Martin, Richard, (Miamisburg, OH)
Martinez, Ernest, Notre Dame, Denver
Martinez, William, Our Lady of Guadalupe, Denver
Martinovic, Mladen, St. Louis, Englewood
Matz, Karl T., (Retired)
McClellan, William, (Retired)
McDavid, Clarence G., Cure D'Ars, Denver
Meilinger, Joseph H., (Retired)
Menogan, Guffie E., (Retired)
Michieli, Ronald, St. Anthony, Sterling
Milhone, Gordon G., Gilbert, AZ
Miller, Gary E., Guardian Angels, Denver
Miller, Richard, Our Lady of Loreto, Foxfield
Moat, James, St. Anne, Grand Lake
Montagne, Eric, Light of the World, Littleton
Mooneyham, Gene, (Retired)
Morales, Dennis, (Retired)
Morin, George C. Jr., St. Thomas More, Centennial
Mota, Pedro, Our Lady of Peace, Greeley
Mumby, David, Christ the King, Denver
Nepil, Darell, Our Lady of Lourdes, Denver
Nestorick, Marc, St. Frances Cabrini, Littleton
Ngo, Lawrence Tong, Queen of Vietnamese Martyrs, Denver
Onesky, Leonard, (Retired)
Parker, Charles W. Jr., All Saints, Denver
Parrilli, James, Cathedral Basilica of the Immaculate Conception, Denver
Patino, Hugo, (Monterey, CA)
Pelis, Richard F., (Retired)
Perez, Cesar, Our Lady of Peace, Greeley
Perzinski, Greg, St. Michael the Archangel, Aurora
Peverley, David, St. John XXIII, Ft. Collins
Pierson, Anthony, St. Michael the Archangel, Aurora
Pilger, Rex H. Jr., St. Joan of Arc, Arvada
Plevak, David, Church of the Ascension, Denver
Pomrening, Christopher, St. Michael the Archangel, Aurora
Pontillo, John E., Immaculate Conception, Lafayette
Pruneda, Efra, Queen of Peace, Aurora
Quinlan, Thomas, (Retired)
Quintana, Lloyd, (Retired)
Rastrelli, Alan, M.D., St. Thomas More, Centennial
Reynolds, Gregg, St. Joseph, Ft. Collins
Ridder, Norm, Spirit of Christ, Arvada
Rinne, Robert, Cathedral Basilica of Immaculate Conception, Denver
Riviera, John J., Lady of the Valley, Windsor
Roderick, Ronald II, St. Paul, Idaho Springs
Rodriguez, Jose, St. John the Baptist, Longmont
Rogge, Gary, (Retired)
Rompot, Vernon L., Cedar Rapids, IA
Rymes, Stan, Our Lady of the Mountain, Estes Park
Salas, Pablo, Presentation of Our Lady, Denver
Salvato, Mark, Risen Christ, Denver
Sanchez, Alfredo, (Retired)
Sanchez, Andrew, St. John XXIII, Ft. Collins
Sanchez, Maclovio, (Retired)
Sandoval, Alfonso M., (Retired)
Sandoval, Henry, Guardian Angels, Denver
Schaefer, Donald, Holy Name, Englewood
Schultz, Charles, St. Mark, Westminster
Sedlevicius, John, St. John Paul II, Thornton
Smith, John L., Mesquite, NV
Spears, Alan C., St. Jude, Lakewood
Sprick, Charles B., (Retired)
Stemper, Steven, St. Thomas More, Centennial
Stow, William J., St. Bernadette, Lakewood
Thierjung, George, Our Lady of the Mountains, Estes Park
Thompson, David, Queen of Peace, Aurora
Torrez, Frederick L., St. Mary, Greeley
Tracy, Don, St. Rose of Lima, Denver
Tran, John, Christ on the Mountain, Lakewood
Travis, Pat, St. John the Evangelist, Loveland
Trewartha, William, (Retired)
Ubowski, Chester W., St. Frances Cabrini, Littleton
Unger, Timothy, Risen Christ, Denver
Usera, Andrew, New Boston, NH
Valle, Edgar, Presentation of Our Lady, Denver
Vallero, Steven J., Nativity of Our Lord, Broomfield
Vielma, Mario, Our Lady Mother of the Church, Commerce City
Vieria, Richard, Holy Family, Denver
Vigil, Arthur A., (Retired)
Volk, John, St. John the Baptist, Johnstown
Wager, Martin A., All Souls, Englewood
Wall, James R., (Retired)
Wallisch, Dennis, St. John the Evangelist, Loveland
Walsh, Timothy, (Retired)
Webster, Earl, (Retired)
Wehrman, John J., St. William, Fort Lupton
Weiss, Donald, St. Elizabeth Ann Seton, Fort Collins
Whaley, Patrick, Church of the Good Shepherd, Denver
Wilson, Richard, St. Helena, Ft. Morgan
Wolbach, Mark, Light of the World, Littleton
Zajac, Paul M., St. Anthony of Padua, Denver.

INSTITUTIONS LOCATED IN DIOCESE

[A] SEMINARIES, RELIGIOUS OR SCHOLASTICATES

DENVER. *Saint John Vianney Theological Seminary*, 1300 S. Steele St., 80210. Tel: 303-282-3427; Fax: 303-715-2007; Email: Father.Leonard@archden.org; Web: www.sjvdenver.edu. Revs. Daniel Leonard, V.F., Rector; Jason Wallace, Vice Rector; Joel Barstad, Academic Dean; Ms. Denise Seery, Registrar; Rev. Daniel Barron, Dir. Spiritual Formation; Paul Villamaria, Dir. Finance; Dr. Sean Innerst, Cycle Dir. Theology; Christina Lynch, Dir. Psychological Svcs.; Stephen Sweeney, Dir. Cardinal Stafford Theological Library; Dr. Nicholas Lebish, Dir. Catholic Biblical & Catechetical Schools; Deacon Robert Hoffman, Dir.; Rev. James Thermos, Dir. Spirituality Year; Mr. Tom McLaughlin, Dir.; Tamara Conley, Reference Librarian. Faculty 16; Seminarians 123; Students 123; Staff/Administrators 14; Faculty/Staff/Administrators - Catholic Biblical and Catechetical Schools 21; Staff/Administrators - St. Francis School of Theology for Deacons 4; Staff/Administrators - Cardinal Stafford Theological Library 4; Clergy / Religious Teachers 18.

Redemptoris Mater House of Formation, 3434 E. Arizona Ave., 80210. Tel: 303-733-2220; Fax: 303-733-2223; Email: redemptoris.mater@archden.org; Web: www.rmsdenver.org. Very Revs. Tobias Rodriguez-Lasa, Rector; Giovanni Capucci, J.C.D., Vice Rector; Revs. William Clemence, Prefect of Studies; Emilio Franchomme, Spiritual Dir. Priests 5; Students 30; Clergy / Religious Teachers 5.

[B] COLLEGES AND UNIVERSITIES

DENVER. *Regis University* (1877) 3333 Regis Blvd., 80221-1099. Tel: 303-458-4100; Fax: 303-458-4921; Email: president@regis.edu; Web: www.regis.edu. Rev. John P. Fitzgibbons, S.J., Pres., Email: president@regis.edu. A university conducted under the auspices of the Society of Jesus. Faculty 814; Priests 6; Students 11,600; Clergy / Religious Teachers 4.

GREENWOOD VILLAGE. **Augustine Institute, Inc.*, 6160 S. Syracuse Way, Ste. 310, Greenwood Village, 80111. Tel: 303-937-4420; Fax: 303-468-2933; Email: info@augustineinstitute.org; Web: www.augustineinstitute.org. Dr. Tim Gray, Pres.

[C] DIOCESAN HIGH SCHOOLS

DENVER. *Bishop Machebeuf High School*, 458 Uinta Way, 80230-6934. Tel: 303-344-0082; Fax: 303-344-1582; Email: kgreiner@machebeuf.org; Email: dnestorick@machebeuf.org; Web: www.machebeuf.org. Deacon Marc Nestorick, Prin.; Rev. James Claver, Chap. Lay Teachers 27; Sisters 2; Students 365; Clergy / Religious Teachers 3.

BROOMFIELD. *Holy Family High School*, 5195 W. 144th Ave., Broomfield, 80023. Tel: 303-410-1411; Fax: 303-466-1935; Email: matt.hauptly@holyfamilyhs.com; Web: www.holyfamilyhs.com. Matthew Hauptly, Prin.; Rev. Joseph McLagan, Chap.; Ms. Dana St. John, Librarian. Lay Teachers 55; Priests 1; Students 641.

[D] HIGH SCHOOLS, INDEPENDENT

DENVER. *Arrupe Jesuit High School* (2003) 4343 Utica St., 80212. Tel: 303-455-7449; Fax: 888-868-6548; Email: dhug@arrupejesuit.com; Web: www.arrupejesuit.com. Michael O'Hagan, Pres.; Rev. John R. Nugent, S.J., Prin. Administrators 9; Lay Teachers 22; Priests 2; Students 430; Clergy / Religious Teachers 3; Volunteers 5.

J K Mullen High School (1931) 3601 S. Lowell Blvd., 80236. Tel: 303-761-1764; Fax: 303-761-0502; Email: Howard@mullenhigh.com; Web: www.mullenhigh.com. Mr. Jeffrey Howard, Prin. Brothers of the Christian SchoolsCoed High School

The Christian Brothers of J.K. Mullen High School Lay Teachers 58; Students 879.

AURORA. **Regis Jesuit High School Corporation* (1877) 6400 S. Lewiston Way, Aurora, 80016.
Tel: 303-269-8000 (Boys Div.);
Fax: 303-766-2240 (Boys Div.);
Fax: 303-221-4772 (Girls Div.); Email: communications@regisjesuit.com; Web: www.regisjesuit.com. Mr. David Card, Pres.; Mr. Jimmy Tricco, Prin. Co-divisional school, offering single-gender instruction by operating as two separate Divisions - the Boys Division and the Girls Division. Lay Teachers 167; Seminarians 2; Students 1,186; Clergy / Religious Teachers 5; Students - Boys Division 948; Students - Girls Division 738.

ENGLEWOOD. *St. Mary's Academy High School* (1864) 4545 S. University Blvd., Englewood, 80113.
Tel: 303-762-8300; Fax: 303-783-6201; Email: jcleaver@smanet.org; Web: stmarys.academy. Bill Barrett, Pres.; Iswari Natarajan, Prin. Sisters of Loretto at the Foot of the Cross. Lay Teachers 27; Students 251; Clergy / Religious Teachers 1.

[E] ELEMENTARY SCHOOLS, DIOCESAN

THORNTON. *Frassati Catholic Academy*, (Grades PreK-7), 3951 Cottonwood Lakes Blvd., Thornton, 80241. Tel: 303-451-9607; Email: sylvia.prusinowska@gofrassati.org; Email: Sara.Alkayali@gofrassati.org; Web: gofrassati.org. Sara Alkayali, Prin. Lay Teachers 17; Students 248.

[F] ELEMENTARY SCHOOLS, INDEPENDENT

ENGLEWOOD. *St. Mary's Academy Lower School* (1864) (Grades PreK-5), 4545 S. University Blvd., Englewood, 80113. Tel: 303-762-8300;
Fax: 303-783-6201; Email: ksmith@smanet.org; Web: stmarys.academy. Karen Smith, Prin.; Missy McConnell, Librarian. Sisters of Loretto at the Foot of the Cross. Lay Teachers 20; Students 198; Clergy / Religious Teachers 1.

St. Mary's Academy Middle School (1864) (Grades 6-8), 4545 S. University Blvd., Englewood, 80113.
Tel: 303-762-8300; Fax: 303-783-6201; Email: jcleaver@smanet.org; Email: bbarrett@smanet.org; Web: stmarys.academy. Bill Barrett, Pres.; Martha Ashley, Prin.; Geoff McVie, Librarian. Sisters of Loretto at the Foot of the Cross Lay Teachers 20; Students 216; Clergy / Religious Teachers 1.

[G] ELEMENTARY SCHOOLS, PRIVATE

DENVER. *Escuela De Guadalupe*, (Grades PreK-8), 660 Julian St., 80204. Tel: 303-964-8456; Email: natalie_tabor@escuelaguadalupe.org; Web: www.escuelaguadalupe.org. Ms. Mariella Robledo, Prin.; Sr. Vicki Schwartz, Pres. Lay Teachers 18; Students 215.

[H] THERAPEUTIC CHILD CARE FACILITIES/ SPECIAL EDUCATION

DENVER. *Mount St. Vincent Home, Inc.* (1883) (Grades K-8), Therapeutic Residential Child Care Facility; Special Education. 4159 Lowell Blvd., 80211.

Tel: 303-458-7220; Fax: 303-477-7559; Email: cliverance@msvhome.org; Web: www.msvhome.org. Kirk Ward, Exec. Dir.; Cindy Liverance, Dir.

[I] MINISTRY TO THE HANDICAPPED

DENVER. *The Bridge Community, Inc.*, 3101 W. Hillside Pl., 80219. Tel: 303-935-4740; Fax: 303-935-7795; Email: rishabridge@comcast.net. Risha Dimas, Contact Person & Dir. Lay Staff 6; Priests 1; Sisters 1; Bed Group Home 8.

Special Religious Education-Pastoral Care of Developmentally Disabled Persons (1976) Religious education of intellectually disabled children and adults (a ministry of the Archdiocese of Denver). 3101 W. Hillside Pl., 80219. Tel: 303-934-1999; Email: smcbridge@comcast.net; Web: www.bridge-community.org. Rev. Roland P. Freeman, Dir. Special Educ. & Chap., (Retired); Sr. Mary Catherine Widger, S.L., Assoc. Dir. Spec. Educ.; Veronica Saykally, Contact Person. Priests 1; Tot Asst. Annually 400; Total Staff 3.

[J] GENERAL HOSPITALS

DENVER. *Saint Joseph Hospital*, 1375 E. 19th Ave., 80218. Tel: 303-812-2000; Fax: 303-812-4296; Email: SJHCommunications@sclhealth.org; Web: www.SaintJosephDenver.org. Jameson Smith, CEO; Rev. Gabriel Okafor, Chap. Bed Capacity 374; Tot Asst. Annually 285,597; Total Staff 2,473.

FRISCO. *St. Anthony Summit Medical Center* (1968) 9100 E. Mineral Cir., Centennial, 80112. Lee Boyles, CEO; Kris Ordelheide, Contact Person. An operating unit of Catholic Health Initiatives Colorado (an affiliate of Catholic Health Initiatives). Tot Asst. Annually 27,423.

LAKEWOOD. *St. Anthony Hospital*, 11600 W. 2nd Pl., Lakewood, 80112. Tel: 720-321-0000; Fax: 720-321-0011; Email: krisordelheide@centura.org; Email: EdwardSim@centura.org. Mailing Address: 9100 E. Mineral Cir., Centennial, 80112. Edward Sim, CEO; Kris Ordelheide, Contact & Gen. Counsel. An operating unit of Catholic Health Initiatives Colorado (an affiliate of Catholic Health Initiatives). Bed Capacity 237; Tot Asst. Annually 296,186; Total Staff 1,732.

WESTMINSTER. *St. Anthony North Health Campus*, 14300 Orchard Pkwy., Westminster, 80023. Tel: 303-804-8103; Fax: 303-804-8198; Email: krisordleheide@centura.org. Mailing Address: 9100 E. Mineral Cir., Centennial, 80112. Kevin Jenkins, CEO; Kris Ordelheide, Contact Person. An operating unit of Catholic Health Initiatives Colorado (an affiliate of Catholic Health Initiatives). Bed Capacity 100; Tot Asst. Annually 234,503; Total Staff 706.

[K] HOSPICE AND HOMEBOUND SERVICE

DENVER. *St. Anthony Hospice* (1968) 2551 W. 84th Ave., Westminster, 80031. Tel: 303-804-8103; Fax: 303-804-8198; Email: krisordelheide@centura.org; Email: Shellyjaynes-heideman@centura.org. Mailing Address: 9100 E. Mineral Cir., Centennial, 80112. Kris Ordelheide, Gen. Counsel & Contact. An operating unit of Catholic Health Initiatives Colorado (an affiliate of Catholic Health Initiatives). Bed Capacity 17; Tot Asst. Annually 250; Total Staff 18.

Dominican Home Health Agency, Inc., 2501 Gaylord St., 80205. Tel: 303-322-1413; Fax: 303-322-2702; Email: info@dominicanhha.org; Email: iwicker@dominicanhha.org; Web: www.dominicanhha.org. Allen Ross, Chairman of Board; Daniel Grey, Admin. Serving the poor, sick and elderly of Denver with no cost in-home nursing visits, durable medical equipment loans and wellness clinics. Tot Asst. Annually 2,225.

[L] INDEPENDENT AND ASSISTED LIVING

DENVER. *Gardens at St. Elizabeth* (1968) 2835 W. 32nd Ave., 80211. Tel: 303-383-2746; Fax: 303-383-2695; Email: peggymartin@catholichealth.net; Web: www.catholichealthinit.org. Mailing Address: 198 Inverness Dr. W., Englewood, 80112. Sr. Peggy Ann Martin, O.P., J.C.L., Contact person. An operating unit of CHI Living Communities (an affiliate of Catholic Health Initiatives). Sisters 3; Total Staff 110; Independent Living Units 131; Independent Living Residents 135; Assisted Living Units 123; Assisted Living Residents 83.

Little Sisters of the Poor - Mullen House (1918) 3629 W. 29th Ave., 80211. Tel: 303-433-7221; Fax: 303-455-9184; Email: msdenver@littlesistersofthepoor.org; Web: www.littlesistersofthepoordenver.org. Sr. Patricia Metzgar, I.S.P., Mother Supr.; Rev. Thomas Poulson, O.P. Total Staff 95; Total Assisted 65.

AURORA. *St. Anna's Home (Congregation of Sisters of Charity of St. Vincent de Paul, Colorado Chapter Inc.)*, 13901 E. Quincy Ave., Aurora, 80015. Tel: 303-627-2986; Fax: 303-627-6308; Email: st.annashome@hotmail.com. Sisters Johanna (Hyun Sook) Soh, Dir.; Stephanie (Kwangmi) Lee, Dir.; Ambrosia (Hyeonok) Ham, Dir. Bed Capacity 16; Tot Asst. Annually 8; Total Staff 3.

[M] SPECIAL TRANSITIONAL HOUSING

DENVER. *Sacred Heart House of Denver* (1980) 2844 Lawrence St., 80205. Tel: 303-296-6686; Fax: 303-296-2903; Email: jlmdenver45@gmail.com; Web: sacredhearthouse.org. Ms. Janet L. Morris, Exec. Dir. Housing and services for mothers with children and for single women experiencing homelessness. Homeless Women & Children Served Annually 1,150; Staff 8.

[N] AFFORDABLE HOUSING AND SERVICES FOR SENIORS, FAMILIES, AND THE DISABLED

DENVER. *Archdiocesan Family Housing, Inc.* (1968) 6240 Smith Rd., 80216. Tel: 303-830-0215; Email: jraddatz@archhousing.com. Justin Raddatz, Exec. Dir. Bed Capacity 98; Tot Asst. Annually 98.

Archdiocesan Housing, Inc. (1968) 6240 Smith Rd., 80216. Tel: 303-830-0215; Fax: 303-830-2885; Email: jraddatz@archhousing.com; Web: www.archdiocesanhousing.com. Justin Raddatz, Exec. Dir. Bed Capacity 1,719; Tot Asst. Annually 3,145; Total Staff 85; Entities 24.

Cathedral Plaza Inc. (1980) c/o 6240 Smith Rd., 80216. Justin Raddatz, Exec. Dir. Bed Capacity 154.

**Clare Gardens, Inc.* (1972) 2626 Osceola St., 80212. Tel: 303-830-3300; Fax: 303-830-3301; Email: dbendell@mercyhousing.org; Web: www.mercyhousing.org. Mailing Address: 1600 Broadway, Ste. 2000, 80202. Melissa Clayton, Pres. Affordable housing. Total Staff 9; Housing Units 128.

Colorado Affordable Catholic Housing Corp. (1991) 6240 Smith Rd., 80216. Tel: 303-830-0215; Email: jraddatz@archhousing.com. Justin Raddatz, Exec. Dir. Affordable housing financing services.

**Francis Heights, Inc.* (1970) 2626 Osceola St., 80212. Tel: 303-830-3300; Fax: 303-830-3301; Email: dbendell@mercyhousing.org. Mailing Address: 1600 Broadway Ste. 1000, 80202. Melissa Clayton, Pres. Affordable Housing. Housing Units 383.

Golden Spike, Inc., c/o 6240 Smith Rd., 80216. Tel: 303-830-0215; Fax: 303-830-2885; Email: jraddatz@archhousing.com; Web: www.archdiocesanhousing.org. Justin Raddatz, Exec. Dir. Affordable housing. Bed Capacity 200; Tot Asst. Annually 200.

Higgins Plaza, Inc. (1990) c/o 6240 Smith Rd., 80216. Justin Raddatz, Exec. Dir. Affordable housing. Bed Capacity 90.

Holy Cross Village, Inc., c/o 6240 Smith Rd., 80216. Tel: 303-830-0215; Email: jraddatz@archhousing.com; Web: www.archdiocesanhousing.org. Justin Raddatz, Exec. Dir. Affordable housing. Bed Capacity 61; Tot Asst. Annually 61.

Holy Family Plaza, Inc. (1981) c/o 6240 Smith Rd., 80216. Justin Raddatz, Exec. Dir. Affordable housing. Bed Capacity 79.

Housing Management Services, Inc. (1986) 6240 Smith Rd., 80216. Tel: 303-830-0215; Email: jraddatz@archhousing.com. Justin Raddatz, Exec. Dir. Affordable housing. Bed Capacity 1,719; Tot Asst. Annually 3,145; Total Staff 85.

Immaculata Plaza, Inc., c/o 6240 Smith Rd., 80216. Tel: 303-830-0215; Fax: 303-830-2885; Email: jraddatz@archhousing.com; Web: www.archdiocesanhousing.org. Justin Raddatz, Exec. Dir.

Machebeuf Apartments, Inc., c/o 6240 Smith Rd., 80216. Tel: 303-830-0215; Email: jraddatz@archhousing.com; Web: www.archdiocesanhousing.org. Justin Raddatz, Exec. Dir. Afforable housing. Bed Capacity 55; Tot Asst. Annually 55.

Madonna Plaza, Inc. (1989) c/o 6240 Smith Rd., 80216. Justin Raddatz, Exec. Dir. Affordable housing. Bed Capacity 50.

Marian Plaza, Inc. (1983) c/o 6240 Smith Rd., 80216. Justin Raddatz, Exec. Dir. Bed Capacity 120.

St. Martin Plaza, Inc. (1988) c/o 6240 Smith Rd., 80216. Justin Raddatz, Exec. Dir. Affordable housing. Bed Capacity 50.

Prairie Rose Plaza, c/o 6240 Smith Rd., 80216. Tel: 303-830-0215; Email: jraddatz@archhousing.com; Web: www.archdiocesanhousing.org. Justin Raddatz, Exec. Dir. Affordable housing. Bed Capacity 19; Tot Asst. Annually 19.

The Sacred Heart of Jesus Housing Foundation (1999) 1300 S. Steele St., 80210. Lou Bishop, Dir. Independent Living 16.

Villa Sierra Madre, Inc., c/o 6240 Smith Rd., 80216. Tel: 303-830-2885; Email: jraddatz@archhousing.com; Web: www.archdiocesanhousing.org. Justin Raddatz, Exec. Dir. Affordable housing. Bed Capacity 60; Tot Asst. Annually 60.

Villas de Santa Lucia, Inc., 6240 Smith Rd., 80216. Tel: 303-830-0215; Email: jraddatz@archhousing.com; Web: www.archdiocesanhousing.org. Justin Raddatz, Dir. Affordable housing. Bed Capacity 61.

Westminster

*Clare of Assisi Homes - Westminster, Inc. (1995) 2451 W. 82 Pl., Westminster, 80031-4099. Tel: 303-830-3300; Fax: 630-830-3301; Email: dbendell@mercyhousing.org; Web: www.mercyhousing.org. Mercy Housing, 1600 Broadway, Ste. 2000, 80202. Melissa Clayton, Pres. Affordable housing. Total Apartments 60; Total Staff 5.

*Villa Maria, Inc. (1996) 2461 W. 82nd Pl., Westminster, 80031-4099. Tel: 303-830-3300; Fax: 630-830-3301; Email: dbendell@mercyhousing.org; Web: www.mercyhousing.org. Mailing Address: 1600 Broadway, Ste. 2000, 80202. Melissa Clayton, Pres. Affordable housing. Units 40.

[O] CATHOLIC CHARITIES & COMMUNITY SERVICES

DENVER. *Catholic Charities and Community Services of the Archdiocese of Denver, Inc.*, 6240 Smith Rd., 80216. Tel: 303-742-0828; Fax: 720-502-5673; Email: info@ccdenver.org; Web: www.ccdenver.org. Darren Walsh, CEO. Shelters for the Homeless, Emergency Assistance Services, Individual & Family Counseling Services, Pregnancy Counseling, Senior Services, Early Education, Immigration Services, Respect Life Resources. Tot Asst. Annually 102,956; Total Staff 485.

Catholic Charities Samaritan House, 2301 Lawrence St., 80205. Tel: 303-294-0241; Fax: 303-294-9523; Email: msinnett@ccdenver.org; Web: www.ccdenver.org. Mailing Address: 6240 Smith Rd., 80216. Mike Sinnett, Exec. Dir. Homeless Shelter.

Catholic Charities Marisol Home, c/o 6240 Smith Rd., 80216. Tel: 720-799-9400; Fax: 720-598-9910; Email: jmcintosh@ccdenver.org; Web: www.ccdenver.org. Jan McIntosh, Exec. Dir. Homeless Shelter.

Catholic Charities Margery Reed Mayo Day Nursery, 1128 28th St., 80205. Tel: 303-308-1420; Fax: 303-308-1421; Email: akeough@ccdenver.org; Web: www.ccdenver.org. Mailing Address: 6240 Smith Rd., 80216. Alison Keough, Dir. Child Care, Colorado Preschool & Kindergarten Program, Head Start & Early Head Start.

Catholic Charities Child Development Center, 1155 Decatur St., 80204. Tel: 720-299-9440; Fax: 303-629-6710; Email: akeough@ccdenver.org; Web: www.ccdenver.org. Mailing Address: 6240 Smith Rd., 80216. Alison Keough, Dir. Child Care, Colorado Preschool & Kindergarten Program, Head Start & Early Head Start.

Catholic Charities Early Childhood Education, 4045 Pecos St., 80211. Tel: 303-742-0828; Fax: 303-742-4373; Email: akeough@ccdenver.org; Web: www.ccdenver.org. Mailing Address: 6240 Smith Rd., 80216. Alison Keough, Dir.

Catholic Charities Family Services, 4045 Pecos St., 80211. Tel: 303-742-4971; Fax: 303-742-4373; Email: gbennett@ccdenver.org; Web: www.ccdenver.org. Mailing Address: 6240 Smith Rd., 80216. Deacon Geoff Bennett, Dir. Respect Life, Adoption, Adult Services, Kinship, Homebased Counseling.

Catholic Charities Immigration Services, c/o 6240 Smith Rd., 80216. Tel: 303-742-0828; Fax: 303-742-4410; Email: cmartinezgloria@ccdenver.org; Web: www.ccdenver.org. Deacon Geoff Bennett, Exec. Dir.

Catholic Charities Larimer Regional Office, 460 Linden Center Dr., Fort Collins, 80524. Tel: 970-484-5010; Fax: 970-484-0259; Email: jdomko@ccdenver.org; Web: www.ccdenver.org. Mailing Address: 6240 Smith Rd., 80216. Mike Sinnett, Exec. Dir. The Mission Shelter for Homeless, Emergency Assistance, Senior Services, Immigration Services.

Catholic Charities Guadalupe Shelter for Homeless, 1442 N. 11th Ave., Greeley, 80631. Tel: 970-353-6433; Fax: 970-353-3861; Email: ekearnshout@ccdenver.org; Web: www.ccdenver.org. Mailing Address: 6240 Smith Rd., 80216. Mike Sinnett, Exec. Dir. Emergency Assistance, Senior Services, Case Management, Immigration Services.

Catholic Charities Western Slope Office, 1004 Grand Ave., Glenwood Springs, 81601. Tel: 970-384-2060; Fax: 970-945-2089; Email: mmcdonough@ccdenver.org; Web: www.ccdenver.org. Mailing Address: 6240 Smith Rd., 80216. Mike Sinnett, Exec. Dir. Community Integration Services, Emergency Assistance, Transitional Housing.

Catholic Charities St. Veronica Outreach, 4045 Pecos St., 80211. Tel: 303-742-0828;

Fax: 303-455-9008; Email: aeurek@ccdenver.org; Web: www.ccdenver.org. Mailing Address: 6240 Smith Rd., 80216. Deacon Geoff Bennett, Exec. Dir. Serving Adams, Arapahoe, Denver & Jefferson Counties.

Catholic Charities Mulroy Senior Center, 3550 W. 13th Ave., 80204. Tel: 303-892-1540; Fax: 303-825-0712; Email: gbennett@ccdenver.org; Web: www.ccdenver.org. Mailing Address: 6240 Smith Rd., 80216.

Catholic Charities Plaza Del Milagro, 2500 1st Ave., Greeley, 80631. Tel: 970-346-2888; Fax: 970-378-1176; Email: wwolberg@ccdenver.org; Web: www.ccdenver.org. Mailing Address: 6240 Smith Rd., 80216. Wayne Wolberg, Exec. Dir. Migrant & Seasonal Housing.

Catholic Charities Plaza Del Sol, 2501 Ash Ave., #36, Greeley, 80631. Tel: 970-378-1171; Fax: 970-378-1176; Email: wwolberg@ccdenver.org; Web: www.ccdenver.org. 6240 Smith Rd., 80216. Wayne Wolberg, Exec. Dir. Migrant & Seasonal Housing.

Marisol Health - Denver East, 3894 Olive St., 80207. Tel: 303-320-8352; Fax: 303-321-1626; Email: slugo@ccdenver.org; Web: www.ccdenver.org. Mailing Address: 6240 Smith Rd., 80216. Jan McIntosh, Exec. Dir. Pregnancy counseling, education and medical care.

Marisol Health - Lafayette, 1285 Centaur Village Dr., Lafayette, 80026. Tel: 303-665-2341; Email: slugo@ccdenver.org; Web: www.ccdenver.org. Mailing Address: 6240 Smith Rd., 80216. Jan McIntosh, Exec. Dir.

Boulder Gabriel House, 6739 S. Boulder Rd., Boulder, 80303. Tel: 303-449-0122; Email: meckstein@ccdenver.org; Web: www.ccdenver.org. Mailing Address: 6240 Smith Rd., 80216. Jan McIntosh, Exec. Dir.

Denver Gabriel House, 1341 Oneida St., 80022. Tel: 303-377-1577; Email: meckstein@ccdenver.org; Web: www.ccdenver.org. Mailing Address: 6240 Smith Rd., 80216. Jan McIntosh, Exec. Dir.

Aurora Gabriel House, 13101 E. Mississippi Ave., #280, Aurora, 80012. Tel: 303-364-9929; Email: meckstein@ccdenver.org; Web: www.ccdenver.org. Mailing Address: 6240 Smith Rd., 80216. Jan McIntosh, Dir.

Jefferson County Gabriel House, 1980 Nelson St., Lakewood, 80215. Tel: 720-459-8783; Email: meckstein@ccdenver.org; Web: www.ccdenver.org. Mailing Address: 6240 Smith Rd., 80216. Jan McIntosh, Exec. Dir.

Centro San Juan Diego Gabriel House, 2830 Lawrence St., 80205. Tel: 720-450-0788; Email: meckstein@ccdenver.org; Web: www.ccdenver.org. 6240 Smith Rd., 80216. Jan McIntosh, Exec. Dir.

St. Francis de Sales Gabriel House, 301 S. Grant St., 80209. Tel: 303-744-7211; Email: meckstein@ccdenver.org; Web: www.ccdenver.org. Mailing Address: 6240 Smith Rd., 80216. Jan McIntosh, Exec. Dir.

Fort Collins Gabriel House, 101 N. Howes St., Fort Collins, 80521. Tel: 970-581-8803; Email: meckstein@ccdenver.org; Web: www.ccdenver.org. Mailing Address: 6240 Smith Rd., 80216. Jan McIntosh, Exec. Dir.

All Saints Gabriel House, 2559 S. Federal Blvd., 80219. Tel: 720-325-4338; Email: meckstein@ccdenver.org; Web: www.ccdenver.org. Mailing Address: 6240 Smith Rd., 80216. Jan McIntosh, Exec. Dir.

Summit/Frisco Gabriel House, 18 School Rd., Ste. 100, Frisco, 80443. Tel: 720-584-0299; Email: meckstein@ccdenver.org; Web: www.ccdenver.org. Mailing Address: 6240 Smith Rd., 80216. Jan McIntosh, Exec. Dir.

Annunciation Gabriel House, 3621 Humboldt St., 80205. Tel: 303-817-4916; Email: meckstein@ccdenver.org; Web: www.ccdenver.org. Mailing Address: 6240 Smith Rd., 80216. Jan McIntosh, Exec. Dir.

Eagle Gabriel House, 127 E. 3rd St., Eagle, 81631. Tel: 970-445-7198; Email: meckstein@ccdenver.org; Web: www.ccdenver.org. Mailing Address: 6240 Smith Rd., 80216. Jan McIntosh, Exec. Dir.

Catholic Charities Farm Labor Housing Corporation, 6240 Smith Rd., 80216. Tel: 970-378-1171; Fax: 970-378-1176; Email: wwolberg@ccdenver.org; Web: www.ccdenver.org. Wayne Wolberg, Exec. Dir.

[P] MONASTERIES AND RESIDENCES OF PRIESTS AND BROTHERS

DENVER. *Capuchin Province of Mid-America, Inc.* (1977) 3613 Wyandot St., 80211-2950. Tel: 303-477-5436; Fax: 303-477-6925; Email: contact@capuchins.org; Web: www.capuchins.org. Revs. Christopher Popravak, O.F.M.Cap., Prov.; John Cousins, O.F.M.Cap., Vicar; David Songy, O.F.M.Cap., Treas.; Blaine Burkey, O.F.M.Cap., Archivist. Order of Friars Minor Capuchin, Province of St. Conrad Novices 2; Postulants 1; Priests 47; Professed 8; Solemnly Professed 10. *St. Francis of Assisi Friary*, 3553 Wyandot St., 80211-2948. Tel: 303-477-5542; Fax: 303-477-1676; Email: sojan.parapilly@capuchins.org. Rev. Sojan Parapilly, O.F.M.Cap., Contact Person. (Order of Friars Minor Capuchin) Total in Residence 9; Total Staff 1. *San Antonio Friary*, 3554 Humboldt St., 80205-3940. Tel: 303-477-5436; Email: contact@capuchins.org. Rev. Charles J. Polifka, O.F.M.Cap., Guardian. Order of Friars Minor Capuchin Total in Residence 4. *St. Anthony of Padua Friary*, 3805 W. Walsh Pl., 80219-3241. Tel: 303-936-6242; Fax: 303-936-6255; Email: contact@capuchins.org. Revs. Christopher Popravak, O.F.M.Cap., Prov.; Mahder Hasema, O.F.M.-Cap.; Christopher Gama, O.F.M.Cap., Guardian; Bros. Joseph Ignowski, O.F.M.Cap.; Luke Jordan, O.F.M.Cap.; Jude Quinto, O.F.M.Cap.; Anthony Monahan, O.F.M.Cap.; Jordan Schmeldler, O.F.-M.Cap.; Marshall Schmidt, O.F.M.Cap. Total in Residence 10; Post-Novitiates 3.

Congregation of the Mission Western Province: De Paul House, 2499 S. Colorado Blvd., Apt. 503, 80222. Cell: 303-717-9858; Email: paul@goldenconsulting.com. Rev. Paul L. Golden, C.M., Acting Supr.; Bro. F. Joseph Hess, C.M., Treas.; Rev. Thomas J. Nelson, C.M. Congregation of the Mission, Missouri.

Dominican Friars, St. Dominic Priory, 3005 W. 29th Ave., 80211-3701. Tel: 303-455-3614; Fax: 303-455-3087; Email: wrightop@gmail.com. Very Rev. David F. Wright, O.P., Prior; Rev. Robert Keller, O.P., Novice Master and Sub. Prior; Very Rev. Edward Ruane, O.P., In Res.; Revs. Robert Barry, O.P., In Res.; Thomas Poulsen, O.P., In Res.; Christopher Saliga, O.P., In Res.; James Karepin, O.P., In Res.; Andrew Wisdom, O.P., In Res. St. Dominic Priory & Dominican Novitiate; Province of St. Albert the Great Novices 4; Priests 8.

Maryknoll Fathers and Brothers, Mailing Address: 9300 E. Center Ave., #10-C, 80247. Web: www.maryknoll.org. Rev. Thomas McCormick, Mission Promoter, (Retired). Catholic Foreign Mission Society of America, Inc., New York.

Regis High Jesuit Community, 16810 E. Caley Ave., Centennial, 80016-1005. Tel: 303-690-4782; Email: jgoeke@jesuits.org. Revs. James Goeke, S.J., Supr.; Eric Ramirez, S.J., Pastoral Dir.; Thomas Rochford, S.J., Faculty Chap.; John Craig, S.J., Chap. (Society of Jesus, Missouri).

Regis Jesuit Community (The Jesuits at Regis University), Regis University Jesuit Community M-12, 3333 Regis Blvd., 80221-1154. Tel: 303-964-5500; Fax: 303-964-5525; Email: woulvey@jesuits.org. Revs. John P. Fitzgibbons, S.J., Pres.; Kevin F. Burke, S.J., Vice Pres.; John R. Nugent, S.J., Prin.; William T. Oulvey, S.J., Rector; Mark D. McGregor, S.J., Dir. Military & Veterans Svcs.; Patrick T. Quinn, S.J., Mission Coord., Staff; Revs. Marcus C. Fryer, S.J., Pastoral Min.; Eustace Sequeira, S.J., Pastoral Min.; Fernando Álvarez-Lara, S.J., Prof.; Daniel J. Everson, S.J., Religion Teacher; Timothy M. McMahon, S.J. Society of Jesus, U.S. Central & Southern Province.

Servants of Christ Jesus (2011) 4022 S. Olive St., 80237. Tel: 720-458-3038; Email: servants@scjesus.org; Web: www.scjesus.org. Rev. John Ignatius Little, Dir.

Society of Jesus - St. Ignatius Loyola Jesuit Community (1944) 2309 Gaylord St., 80205-5627. Tel: 303-322-8042; Fax: 303-322-2927; Email: parish@loyoladenver.org; Web: www.loyoladenver.org. Revs. Roy Joseph, S.J.; Dirk Dunfee, S.J.; Joseph Tuoc Nguyen, S.J.

The Theatine Fathers (1923) 1050 S. Birch St., 80246. Tel: 303-757-4280; Email: 1906.ccrr@gmail.com; Web: www.theatinesusa.com. Very Rev. Patrick Valdez, C.R., Prov. Theatine Fathers. Priests 1.

Xavier Jesuit Center (1993) 3450 W. 53rd, 80221-6568. Tel: 303-480-3900; Fax: 303-480-3913; Email: jguyer@jesuits.org. Revs. James B. Guyer, S.J., Supr.; Edward F. Flaherty, S.J.; C. Thomas Jost, S.J.; John J. Waters, S.J.; E. Eugene Arthur, S.J.; Joseph E. Damhorst, S.J.; Bros. Glenn Kerfoot, S.J.; Donald R. Schlichter, S.J. Society of Jesus, Central & Southern (UCS).

BROOMFIELD. *Priestly Fraternity of St. Charles Borromeo (F.S.C.B.)* Massachusetts 900 W. Midway Blvd., Broomfield, 80020. Tel: 508-369-2197; Email: m.carvill@gmail.com; Web: www.fraternityofsaintcharles.org. Very Rev. Michael Carvill, F.S.C.B., V.F.; Rev. Accursio Ciaccio, F.S.C.B.; Deacon Emaneule Fadini.

GREELEY. *Societas Matris Dolorosissimae*, 2132 22nd St., Greeley, 80631. Tel: 970-370-7933. P.O. Box 311, Keenesburg, 80643. Rev. Chad Ripperger, Moderator.

LITTLETON. *Disciples of the Hearts of Jesus and Mary*, St. Mary Parish, 6853 S. Prince St., Littleton, 80120. Tel: 303-798-8506; Email: luisgranados@dcjm.org; Web: www.dcjm.org. Revs. Javier Nieva, D.C.J.M., (Spain); Armando Marsal, D.C.J.M., (Spain); Juan Espino, D.C.J.M.; Luis Granados, D.C.J.M., (Spain) In Res.

SNOWMASS. *St. Benedict's Monastery* (1956) 1012 Monastery Rd., Snowmass, 81654. Tel: 970-279-4400; Fax: 970-927-3399; Email: retreat@rof.net; Web: www.snowmass.org. Rt. Rev. Joseph Boyle, O.C.S.O., Abbot; Revs. Charles Albanese, O.C.S.O.; Edward Hoffman, O.C.S.O.; Thomas Keating, O.C.S.O.; William Meninger, O.C.S.O.; Micah Schonberger, O.C.S.O. Cistericians Order of the Strict Observance (Trappists) Professed Monks 12.

[Q] CONVENTS AND RESIDENCES FOR SISTERS

DENVER. *Missionaries of Charity*, 633 Fox St., 80204. Tel: 303-860-8040; Email: raymond.kelley@archden.org. Sr. M. Damascene, M.C., Supr. & Contact. Shelter for Homeless Women (8 Beds).

Monastery of Our Lady of Light (Capuchin Poor Clares) (1989) 3325 Pecos, 80211. Tel: 303-458-6339; Fax: 303-477-6925; Email: denver.capclares@gmail.com; Web: www.ourladyoflightmonastery.com. Sr. Maria de Cristo Palafox, O.S.C.Cap., Abbess

Capuchin Poor Clares of Denver, Colorado Sisters 7.

Sisters of St. Francis of Penance and Christian Charity (1939) 5314 Columbine Rd., 80221-1277. Tel: 303-458-6270; Fax: 303-477-4105; Email: sueaf@franciscanway.org; Web: www.franciscanway.org. Sr. Rita Cammack, Prov. Min. *Sisters of St. Francis, Denver, Colorado* Sisters in Province 26.

Casa Chiara (Provincial offices, sisters' residences & ministries) 5312-5326 Columbine Rd., 80221. Tel: 303-458-6270; Email: sueaf@franciscanway.org; Email: patty@franciscanway.org. Sisters Rita Cammack, Prov.; Patricia Podhaisky, O.S.F., Treas. Sisters 6.

GOLDEN. *Mother Cabrini Shrine*, 20189 Cabrini Blvd., Golden, 80401. Tel: 303-526-0758; Fax: 303-526-9795; Email: jefflewis@mothercabrinishrine.org; Web: www.mothercabrinishrine.org. Jeff Lewis, Admin. Missionary Sisters of the Sacred Heart of Jesus (M.S.C.) 3.

LITTLETON. *Carmel of Holy Spirit* (1947) 6138 S. Gallup St., Littleton, 80120-2702. Tel: 303-798-4176. Mother Mary of Jesus Doran, O.C.D., Prioress. Discalced Carmelites (O.C.D.). *Corporate Name: The Discalced Carmelite Nuns of Colorado* Sisters 10.

VIRGINIA DALE. *Abbey of St. Walburga* (1935) 1029 Benedictine Way, Virginia Dale, 80536-7633. Tel: 970-472-0612; Fax: 970-484-4342; Email: aswabbey@gmail.com; Web: www.walburga.org. Rev. Michael Philen, Chap., (Priest in Residence); Mother Maria-Michael Newe, O.S.B., Abbess *Corporate Name: Abbey of St. Walburga, Incorporated* Novices 2; Sisters 23; Claustral Oblate 1.

[R] RETREAT CENTERS

DENVER. *Annunciation Heights*, 7400 Hwy. 7, Estes Park, 80517. Tel: 970-586-5689; Email: Brenda.Brown@Annunciationheights.org. Mailing Address: c/o 1300 S. Steele St., 80210. Kyle Mills, Exec. Dir.

LITTLETON. *Jesus Our Hope Hermitage*, 10519 S. Deer Creek Rd., Littleton, 80127. Tel: 303-697-7539; Fax: 303-697-7539; Email: Jesusourhoperetreat@gmail.com; Web: www.jesus-our-hope.org. Deacon Robert Hoffman, Chm.; Sr. Monica Tauiliili, Contact Person.

PINE. *Emmaus Catholic Retreat and Conference Center*, 13034 U.S. Hwy. 285, Pine, 80470. Mailing Address: c/o 1300 S. Steele St., 80210. Mr. Keith A. Parsons, CPA, Pres.

[S] CAMPUS MINISTRY

GOLDEN. **Fellowship of Catholic University Students (FOCUS)* (1999) 603 Park Point Dr. #200, Genesee, 80401. Tel: 303-962-5750; Fax: 303-565-5738; Email: info@focus.org; Web: www.focus.org. Mailing Address: P.O. Box 17408, Golden, 80402. Craig Miller, Pres.

[T] ASSOCIATIONS OF CONSECRATED LIFE

DENVER. *The Catholic Community of the Beatitudes*, 2924 W. 43rd Ave., 80211. Tel: 720-855-9412; Fax: 303-455-6651; Email: beatitudesinfo@gmail.com; Web: www.beatitudes.us. Rev., Nilson Leal de Sá, C.B., Supr.

Companions of Christ, 1050 Pennsylvania St., 80203. Tel: 720-933-4185; Web: www.denvercompanionsofchrist.org; Email: denver.companions@gmail.com. Rev. Braden Wagner, Mod.

**Marian Community of Reconciliation (Fraternas)*

(2012) 1060 St. Francis Way, 80204. Tel: 303-629-0500; Email: Denver@fraternas.org; Web: www.fraternas.org. Sr. Luciane Urban, Supr.

[U] MISCELLANEOUS LISTINGS

DENVER. *St. Anthony Health Foundation*, 11600 W. 2nd Pl., Lakewood, 80228. Tel: 720-321-4310; Fax: 720-321-4311; Email: krisordelheide@centura.org. Mailing Address: 9100 E. Mineral Cir., Centennial, 80112. Kris Ordelheide, Contact Person. An operating unit of Catholic Health Initiatives Colorado Foundation.

The Archdiocese of Denver Cemeteries Perpetual Care Trust, 1300 S. Steele St., 80210. Tel: 303-722-4687; Email: keith.parsons@archden.org. Mr. Keith A. Parsons, CPA, Admin.

The Archdiocese of Denver Irrevocable Revolving Fund Trust, 1300 S. Steele St., 80210. Tel: 303-722-4687; Email: Keith.Parsons@archden.org. Mr. Keith A. Parsons, CPA, Admin.

The Archdiocese of Denver Management Corporation, 1300 S. Steele St., 80210. Tel: 303-722-4687; Email: Keith.Parsons@archden.org. Mr. Keith A. Parsons, CPA, Pres.

The Archdiocese of Denver Risk Management Property/Casualty Insurance Trust, 1300 S. Steele St., 80210. Tel: 303-722-4687; Email: Peter.Cronan@archden.org. Peter Cronan, Dir.

The Archdiocese of Denver Welfare Benefits Trust, 1300 S. Steele St., 80210. Tel: 303-722-4687; Email: Deacon.McDavid@archden.org. Deacon Clarence McDavid, Dir.

Arrupe Corporate Work-Study Program (2003) 4343 Utica St., 80212. Tel: 303-455-7449, Ext. 237; Fax: 888-868-6548; Email: rninneman@arrupejesuit.com; Web: www.arrupejesuit.com. Richard Ninneman, Dir.

Ask A Bishop, P.O. Box 12436, 80212. Tel: 402-202-3762; Email: anand@askabishop.com; Web: www.askabishop.com. 4570 Julian St., 80211. Anand Bheemarasetti, Pres.

Catholic Education Capital Corporation (2010) 1535 Logan St., 80203-7939. Tel: 303-894-8808; Fax: 303-894-7939. Jennifer Kraska, Exec. Dir.

Catholic Health Initiatives Colorado Foundation, Catholic Health Initiatives, 2525 S. Downing St., Mason Hall, 3rd Fl., 80210. Tel: 303-673-8104; Email: krisordelheide@centura.org. 9100 E. Mineral Cir., Centennial, 80112. Mr. Josh Bailey, Pres.; Kris Ordelheide, Gen. Council.

Penrose-St. Francis Health Foundation
An affiliate division of Catholic Health Initiatives Colorado Foundation (an affiliate of Catholic Health Initiatives).

Christ Child Society of Denver, 2754 E. Amherst Ave., 80210. Tel: 303-995-6467; Email: denverchristchild@gmail.com. P.O. Box 100869, 80250-0869. Elizabeth Haskell, Vice Pres.

**Catholic Young Adult Sports* (CYAS) 4775 S. Pearl St., Englewood, 80113. Tel: 720-924-6333; Email: info@catholicyoungadultsports.com; Web: www.catholicyoungadultsports.com. Mailing Address: P.O. Box 102584, 80250. Paul Spotts, Pres.

**Christ in the City*, 3401 N. Pecos St., 80211. Tel: 303-952-9743; Email: info@christinthecity.org; Web: www.christinthecity.co. Linda Weigand, Contact Person.

**Christian Life Movement, Inc.* (1985) 1060 11th St., 80204. Tel: 303-629-5100; Email: denverclm@clmusa.org; Web: www.clmusa.org. Maye J. Agama, Pres.

Colorado Catholic Education Conference, 1535 Logan St., 80203-7939. Tel: 303-894-8808; Fax: 303-894-7939. Jennifer Kraska, Exec. Dir.

**Colorado Vincentian Volunteers* (1994) 1732 Pearl St., 80203. Tel: 303-863-8141; Email: cvv@covivo.org; Web: www.covivo.org. Bill Jaster, Dir.; Mary Frances Jaster, Dir.

**Highlight Catholic Ministries* dba Frassati Sports & Adventure; Badano Sports 5850 W. Warren Ave., 80227. Tel: 720-593-1903. P.O. Box 19684, 80227. Ryan O'Connor, Pres.

Saint John Paul II Center for the New Evangelization, 1300 S. Steele St., 80210. Tel: 303-722-4687; Email: michael.mcKee@archden.org. Michael McKee, Pres.

**Saint Joseph Hospital Foundation* (1977) 1375 E. 19th Ave., 80218. Tel: 303-812-6437; Email: nicholas.lopez@sclhs.net; Web: www.sclhealth.org/locations/saint-joseph-hospital-foundation. Nicholas Lopez, Exec. Dir.

Magnificat-Denver, CO Chapter, 5418 S. Iris St., Littleton, 80123. Tel: 303-884-3902; Email: magnificatofdenver@gmail.com. Celia Kulbe, Coord.

Mercy Housing Management Group, Inc. (1983) 1600 Broadway, Ste. 2000, 80202. Tel: 303-830-3300; Fax: 303-830-3301. Cheryll O'Bryan, Pres.

**Mercy Housing, Inc.* (1981) 1600 Broadway, Ste. 2000, 80202. Tel: 303-830-3300; Fax: 303-830-3301 ; Email: dbendell@mercyhousing.org; Web: www.mercyhousing.org. Ron Jackson, Vice Pres. Affordable Housing Properties.

Seeds of Hope Charitable Trust (1996) 1300 S. Steele St., 80210. Tel: 303-715-3127; Email: info@seedsofhopedenver.org; Web: www.seedsofhopedenver.org. Jay Clark, Admin.

Seeds of Hope of Northern Colorado, Inc., 1300 S. Steele St., Ste. 345, 80210. Tel: 303-715-3127; Email: info@seedsofhopedenver.org; Web: www.seedsofhopedenver.org. Jay Clark, Exec. Dir.

ALLENSPARK. *Camp St. Malo Visitor and Heritage Center*, 10758 Hwy. 7, Allenspark, 80510. Tel: 303-747-0201. Mailing Address: 1300 S. Steele St., 80210. Nancy Lang, Contact Person.

AURORA. *St. Simeon Cemetery Association* (2003) 22001 E. State Hwy. 30, Aurora, 80018. Tel: 303-502-9179; Email: Gary.Schaaf@archden.org; Web: cfcscolorado.org. Gary Schaaf, Dir.

BOULDER. *Sacred Heart School Foundation*, Mailing Address: 2242 Juniper Ct., Boulder, 80304. Tel: 303-442-2520, Ext. 224; Fax: 303-442-0930; Email: tmullen@cigarettestore.com; Web: shjsf.org. 2312 14th St., Boulder, 80304. Tel: 303-444-3478. Mr. James Mullen, Contact.

BROOMFIELD. *SCL Health Foundation*, 500 Eldorado Blvd., Ste. 4300, Broomfield, 80021. Tel: 303-812-6460; Email: chellie.panzera@sclhealth.org; Email: megan.mahncke@sclhealth.org. Megan Mahncke, Pres.

Sisters of Charity of Leavenworth Health System, Inc. dba SCL Health, 500 Eldorado Blvd., Ste. 4300, Broomfield, 80021. Tel: 303-813-5190; Email: OCD-Contact@sclhs.net; Web: sclhealthsystem.org. Lydia Jumonville, CEO.

ENGLEWOOD. **Association for the Promotion of Apostolate, Inc.*, 3290 W. Milan Ave., Englewood, 80110. Tel: 303-547-5132; Email: eregal@gmail.com. Eduardo Regal, Exec. Dir.

Bella Natural Women's Care dba Bella Natural Women's Care & Family Wellness, 180 E. Hampden Ave., Ste. 100, Englewood, 80113. Tel: 303-789-4968; Email: info@BellaNWC.org. Dede Chism, CEO. Patients Asst Anual. 12,200.

Catholic Health Initiatives (2004) 198 Inverness Dr. W., Englewood, 80112. Tel: 303-383-2746; Fax: 303-383-2695; Email: peggymartin@catholichealth.net; Web: www.catholichealthinit.org. Kevin Lofton, Pres. & CEO; Sr. Peggy Ann Martin, O.P., J.C.L., Contact.

Catholic Health Initiatives Colorado (1968) 9100 E. Mineral Cir., Centennial, 80112. Tel: 303-290-6500 ; Fax: 303-673-8198; Email: krisordelheide@centura.org. Peter Banko, CEO; Kris Ordelheide, Contact. An affiliate of Catholic Health Initiatives.

CHI Health at Home, 198 Inverness Dr. W., Englewood, 80112. Tel: 303-383-2746; Fax: 303-383-2695; Email: peggymartin@catholichealth.net; Web: www.catholichealthinit.org. Sr. Peggy Ann Martin, O.P., J.C.L., Sr. Vice Pres. Sponsorship & Governance.

CHI National Services, 198 Inverness Dr. W., Englewood, 80112. Tel: 303-383-2746; Fax: 303-383-2695; Email: peggymartin@catholichealth.net; Web: www.catholichealthinit.org. Sr. Peggy Ann Martin, O.P., J.C.L., Sr. Vice Pres. Sponsorship & Governance.

**Creatio, Inc.*, 3290 W. Milan Ave., Englewood, 80110. Tel: 720-441-2927; Email: info@creatio.org; Web: www.creatio.org. Adam Henrichs, Dir.

Family of Nazareth, Inc., 4790 E. Mansfield Ave., Englewood, 80113. Tel: 303-949-1764; Email: stevewaymel@actioncoach.com. Steven Waymel, Pres.

**OneBillionStories.com*, 4324 S. Jason St., Englewood, 80110. Tel: 720-295-2125; Email: seth@onebillionstories.com; Web: www.onebillionstories.com. Seth DeMoor, Pres.

Source and Summit Institute, 3230 S. Gilpin St., Englewood, 80113. Tel: 800-215-5049; Email: info@sourceandsummit.com; Web: www.sourceandsummit.com. Adam Bartlett, Pres.

ESTES PARK. **Our Lady of Tenderness, Poustinia* (1983) 1190 Soul Shine Rd., Estes Park, 80517. Tel: 303-877-0728; Email: oltadmin@oltpoustinia.org. Mailing Address: P.O. Box 4311, Estes Park, 80517. Revs. Robert L. Wedow, Dir.; Joel Barstad, Dir.; Mrs. Ilene Gleason, Dir. Volunteers 18.

GREELEY. **Catholic Psychotherapy Association, Inc.*, 7251 W. 20th St., M-2, Greeley, 80634. Tel: 907-590-1424; Email: gcreed@catholicpsychotherapy.org; Email: vconzett@catholicpsychotherapy.org; Web: www.catholicpsychotherapy.org. Dr. Gerry Crete, Pres.; Dr. Gregory Creed, Treas.

**International Missionary Foundation*, P.O. Box 8, Greeley, 80632. Tel: 970-616-0411; Email: jwilliams@imfmission.org; Email: info@imfmission.org; Web: www.imfmission.org. Joseph Williams, Exec. Dir.

St. Mary's Catholic Education Foundation Greeley, 2222 23rd Ave., Greeley, 80634. Tel: 970-352-1724; Fax: 970-352-1729; Email: susan.benke@stmarygreeley.org. Susan Benke, Treas.

GREENWOOD VILLAGE. **The Catholic Foundation for the Roman Catholic Church in Northern Colorado* dba The Catholic Foundation of Northern Colorado, 6160 S. Syracuse Way, Ste. 211, Greenwood Village, 80111. Tel: 303-468-9885; Fax: 303-468-9889; Email: info@thecatholicfoundation.com; Web: www.thecatholicfoundation.com. Deacon Steven Stemper, Pres.

**Endow*, 6160 S. Syracuse Way, Ste. 210, Greenwood Village, 80111. Tel: 720-382-5242; Fax: 720-382-5145; Email: info@endowgroups.org; Web: www.endowgroups.org. Martha Reichert, Pres.; Katherine Meeks, Exec. Women's Ministry.

**Real Life Catholic*, 6160 S. Syracuse Way, Ste. B160C, Greenwood Village, 81111. Tel: 330-732-5228; Email: info@reallifecatholic.com; Web: www.reallifecatholic.com. Chris Stefanick, Pres.

**The Vine Foundation* dba The Amazing Parish, 6160 S. Syracuse Way, Ste. 220, Greenwood Village, 80111. Tel: 303-481-4320; Email: randy@amazingparish.org; Web: www.amazingparish.org. Bill Weingartner, Exec. Dir.

LAKEWOOD. *Apostolate of Our Lady of Hope* dba St. Rafka Mission of Hope & Mercy, 2301 Wadsworth Blvd., Lakewood, 80214. Tel: 310-848-3132; Tel: 303-238-1028; Email: info@missionofhopeandmercy.org; Web: www.saintrafkamission.com; Web: www.missionofhopeandmercy.org. Rev. Andre Mahanna, Pres.

LITTLETON. **St. Andrew Missionaries*, 7128 S. Lafayette Way, Littleton, 80122. Tel: 303-909-2736 ; Email: everett@standrewmissionaries.org; Web: www.standrewmissionaries.org. Everett Fritz, Exec. Dir.

**In Ipso, Inc.*, 8818 W. Glasgow Pl., Littleton, 80128. Tel: 720-934-1353; Cell: 720-231-2660; Email: danainipso12@gmail.com; Email: peter@in-ipso.org; Web: www.in-ipso.org. Peter Stur, Pres.

**L'Alto Catholic Institute, NFP*, 2881 W. Long Cir., Ste. #A, Littleton, 80120. Tel: 630-384-9031. Timothy Glemkowski, Pres.

LONGMONT. **From Mission To Mission*, 303 Atwood St., Longmont, 80501. Tel: 720-494-7211; Email: missiontomission@hotmail.com; Web: www.missiontomission.org. Julie Lupien, Dir.

SHERIDAN. *Association for Catholic Formation and Leadership, Inc.*, 3290 W. Milan Ave., Sheridan, 80110. Tel: 303-902-4233; Email: bermudez@aciprensa.com; Web: www.institutotepeyac.com. Alejandro Bermudez, Exec. Dir.

THORNTON. *Archbishops Guild*, 4363 E. 93rd Pl., Thornton, 80229. Annie Elizalde, Admin.

WHEAT RIDGE. *Archdiocese of Denver Mortuary at Mount Olivet, Inc.* (1981) 12801 W. 44th Ave., Wheat Ridge, 80033. Tel: 303-425-9511; Email: Gary.Schaaf@archden.org. Gary Schaaf, Dir.

The Mount Olivet Cemetery Association, 12801 W. 44th Ave., Wheat Ridge, 80033. Tel: 303-425-9511; Email: Gary.Schaaf@archden.org. Gary Schaaf, Dir.

RELIGIOUS INSTITUTES OF MEN REPRESENTED IN THE ARCHDIOCESE

For further details refer to the corresponding bracketed number in the Religious Institutes of Men or Women section.

[0200]—*Benedictine Fathers*—O.S.B.
[0470]—*Capuchin Friars*—O.F.M.Cap.
[]—*Carmelite Fathers*—O.C.D.
[0350]—*Cistercian Order of the Strict Observance* (Trappists)—O.C.S.O.
[]—*Claretian Missionaries*—C.M.F.
[]—*Community of the Beatitudes*—C.B.
[]—*Congregation of St. John*—C.S.J.
[1330]—*Congregation of the Mission (Vincentians)*—C.M.
[]—*Congregation of the Mother of the Redeemer*—C.R.M.
[]—*Disciples of the Hearts of Jesus and Mary*—D.C.J.M.
[0535]—*Franciscan Friars of the Renewal*—C.F.R.
[]—*Heralds of the Good News*—H.G.N.
[0690]—*Jesuit Fathers and Brothers*—S.J.
[]—*Legionaries of Christ*—L.C.
[]—*Miles Christi Religious Order*—M.C.
[0940]—*Oblates of the Virgin Mary*—O.M.V.
[]—*Order of Friar Servants of Mary*—O.S.M.
[0430]—*Order of Preachers* (Dominicans)—O.P.
[1030]—*Paulist Fathers* (Sacred Heart of Jesus)—C.S.P.
[1065]—*Priestly Fraternity of St. Peter*—F.S.S.P.
[1205]—*Priestly Fraternity of the Missionaries of St. Charles Borromeo*—F.S.C.B.
[1260]—*Society of Christ*—S.Ch.
[]—*Society of the Precious Blood*—C.PP.S.

[]—*Sodalitium Christianae Vitae*—S.C.V.
[1300]—*Theatine Fathers*—C.R.
[1335]—*Vincentian Congregation*—V.C.

RELIGIOUS INSTITUTES OF WOMEN REPRESENTED IN THE ARCHDIOCESE

[]—*Allied Discalced Carmelites of the Holy Trinity*—A.C.D.SS.T.
[0190]—*Benedictine Nuns*—O.S.B.
[0230]—*Benedictine Sisters of Pontifical Jurisdiction*—O.S.B.
[3765]—*Capuchin Poor Clares*—O.S.C.Cap.
[0370]—*Carmelite Sisters of the Most Sacred Heart of Los Angeles*—O.C.D.
[]—*Community of the Beatitudes*—C.B.
[0420]—*Discalced Carmelite Nuns*—O.C.D.
[1070-14]—*Dominican Sisters* (Grand Rapids, MI)—O.P.
[1070-03]—*Dominican Sisters* (Sinsinawa, WI)—O.P.
[1105]—*Dominican Sisters of Hope*—O.P.
[1115]—*Dominican Sisters of Peace*—O.P.
[]—*Dominican Sisters of St. Catherine of Siena*—O.P.
[1070-07]—*Dominican Sisters of the Congregation of St. Cecilia* (Nashville, TN)—O.P.
[2340]—*Little Sisters of the Poor*—L.S.P.
[2710]—*Missionaries of Charity*—M.C.
[]—*Missionaries of Charity of Mary Immaculate*—M.C.M.I.
[]—*Missionary Sisters of St. Charles Borromeo.*
[2860]—*Missionary Sisters of the Sacred Heart of Jesus*—M.S.C.
[]—*Order of St. Francis*—O.S.F.
[3130]—*Our Lady of Victory Missionary Sisters*—O.L.V.M.
[]—*Religious of the Cenacle*—R.C.
[2519]—*Religious Sisters of Mercy of Alma, Michigan*—R.S.M.
[2970]—*School Sisters of Notre Dame*—S.S.N.D.
[0440]—*Sisters of Charity of Cincinnati, Ohio*—S.C.
[0480]—*Sisters of Charity of Leavenworth, Kansas*—S.C.L.
[0430]—*Sisters of Charity of the Blessed Virgin Mary*—B.V.M.
[]—*Sisters of Life*—S.V.
[2360]—*Sisters of Loretto at the Foot of the Cross* (Nerinx, KY)—S.L.
[2575]—*Sisters of Mercy of the Americas*—R.S.M.
[]—*Sisters of Our Lady of Mercy*—S.O.L.M.
[1705]—*Sisters of St. Francis of Assisi* (Milwaukee, WI)—O.S.F.
[1630]—*Sisters of St. Francis of Penance and Christian Charity*—O.S.F.
[3840]—*Sisters of St. Joseph of Carondelet*—C.S.J.
[]—*Sisters of St. Vincent de Paul*—S.C.
[3260]—*Sisters of the Precious Blood* (Dayton, OH)—C.PP.S.

ARCHDIOCESAN CEMETERIES AND MORTUARIES

AURORA. *St. Simeon Cemetery Association* (2003) 22001 E. State Hwy. 30, Aurora, 80018.
Tel: 303-502-9179; Email: Gary.Schaaf@archden.org. Gary Schaaf, Dir.

WHEAT RIDGE. *Archdiocese of Denver Mortuary at Mount Olivet, Inc.* (1981) 12801 W. 44th Ave., Wheat Ridge, 80033. Tel: 303-425-9511; Email: Gary.Schaaf@archden.org. Gary Schaaf, Dir.

The Mount Olivet Cemetery Association, 12801 W. 44th Ave., Wheat Ridge, 80033. Tel: 303-502-9179; Email: Gary.Schaaf@archden.org. Gary Schaaf, Dir.

NECROLOGY

† Bradtke, Thomas, (Retired), Died Jun. 2, 2018
† Mucha, Jan, (Retired), Died Mar. 21, 2018
† Ossino, Angelo, (Retired), Died Feb. 13, 2018
† Ryan, Dennis K., (Retired), Died Mar. 4, 2018

An asterisk (*) denotes an organization that has established tax-exempt status directly with the IRS and is not covered by the USCCB Group Ruling.

Diocese of Des Moines

(Dioecesis Desmoinensis)

Most Reverend

RICHARD E. PATES

Bishop of Des Moines; ordained December 20, 1968; appointed Titular Bishop of Suacia and Auxiliary Bishop of Saint Paul and Minneapolis December 22, 2000; ordained March 26, 2001; appointed Bishop of Des Moines April 10, 2008; installed May 29, 2008. *Office: 601 Grand Ave., Des Moines, IA 50309.*

Most Reverend

JOSEPH L. CHARRON, C.PP.S., S.T.D.

Retired Bishop of Des Moines; ordained June 3, 1967; appointed Titular Bishop of Bencenna and Auxiliary Bishop of Saint Paul and Minneapolis November 6, 1989; consecrated January 25, 1990; appointed Bishop of Des Moines November 12, 1993; installed January 21, 1994; retired April 10, 2007.

Chancery: *601 Grand Ave., Des Moines, IA 50309.* Tel: 515-243-7653; Fax: 515-237-5070.

Web: www.dmdiocese.org

Email: bishop@dmdiocese.org

ERECTED BY POPE ST. PIUS X, AUGUST 12, 1911.

Square Miles 12,446.

Comprises that part of the State of Iowa which is bounded on the east by the eastern boundaries of the Counties of Polk, Warren, Lucas and Wayne; on the south by the State of Missouri; on the west by the Missouri River; and on the north by the northern boundaries of the Counties of Harrison, Shelby, Audubon, Guthrie, Dallas and Polk.

Patrons of the Diocese: I. Blessed Virgin Mary Queen; II. Pope Saint Pius X. Diocese solemnly consecrated to the Immaculate Heart of Mary on May 16, 1948.

Legal Title: "The Roman Catholic Diocese of Des Moines."
For legal titles of parishes and diocesan institutions, consult the Chancery Office.

STATISTICAL OVERVIEW

Personnel	
Bishop	1
Retired Bishops	1
Priests: Diocesan Active in Diocese	53
Priests: Diocesan Active Outside Diocese	1
Priests: Retired, Sick or Absent	34
Number of Diocesan Priests	88
Religious Priests in Diocese	7
Total Priests in Diocese	95
Extern Priests in Diocese	15
Ordinations:	
Diocesan Priests	1
Transitional Deacons	1
Permanent Deacons	17
Permanent Deacons in Diocese	106
Total Sisters	48
Parishes	
Parishes	80
With Resident Pastor:	
Resident Diocesan Priests	48
Resident Religious Priests	5
Without Resident Pastor:	
Administered by Priests	26
Administered by Deacons	1
Professional Ministry Personnel:	
Sisters	9
Lay Ministers	179
Welfare	
Catholic Hospitals	4
Total Assisted	1,824,791
Homes for the Aged	1
Total Assisted	128
Special Centers for Social Services	7
Total Assisted	30,000
Educational	
Diocesan Students in Other Seminaries	16
Total Seminarians	16
Colleges and Universities	1
Total Students	714
High Schools, Diocesan and Parish	2
Total Students	1,571
Elementary Schools, Diocesan and Parish	15
Total Students	4,490
Catechesis/Religious Education:	
High School Students	2,962
Elementary Students	8,412
Total Students under Catholic Instruction	18,165
Teachers in the Diocese:	
Priests	2
Lay Teachers	644
Vital Statistics	
Receptions into the Church:	
Infant Baptism Totals	1,430
Minor Baptism Totals	145
Adult Baptism Totals	144
Received into Full Communion	196
First Communions	1,790
Confirmations	1,492
Marriages:	
Catholic	258
Interfaith	145
Total Marriages	403
Deaths	722
Total Catholic Population	109,307
Total Population	898,915

Former Bishops—Most Revs. AUSTIN DOWLING, D.D., first Bishop of Des Moines; ord. June 24, 1891; appt. Bishop Jan. 31, 1912; cons. April 25, 1912; promoted to the See of St. Paul, Jan. 1919; THOMAS W. DRUMM, D.D., Bishop of Des Moines; ord. Dec. 21, 1901; cons. May 21, 1919; died Oct. 24, 1933; GERALD T. BERGAN, D.D., ord. Oct. 28, 1915; appt. March 24, 1934; cons. June 13, 1934; Enthroned June 21, 1934; elevated to Archiepiscopal dignity and promoted to Omaha Feb. 9, 1948; EDWARD C. DALY, O.P., S.T.M., Bishop of Des Moines; ord. June 12, 1921; appt. March 13, 1948; cons. May 13, 1948; named Asst. at Papal Throne, May 23, 1958; died Nov. 23, 1964; GEORGE J. BISKUP, D.D., ord. March 19, 1937; appt. Auxiliary Bishop of Dubuque, March 9, 1957; cons. April 24, 1957; appt. Bishop of Des Moines, Feb. 3, 1965; appt. Coadjutor Archbishop of Indianapolis, July 26, 1967; succeeded to See Jan. 14, 1970; MAURICE J. DINGMAN, D.D., Bishop of Des Moines; ord. Dec. 8, 1939; appt. Bishop of Des Moines April 2, 1968; cons. June 19, 1968; installed July 7, 1968; retired Oct. 14, 1986; died Feb. 1, 1992; WILLIAM H. BULLOCK, ord. June 7, 1952; appt. Auxiliary Bishop of St. Paul and Minneapolis and Titular Bishop of Natchez June 3, 1980; cons. Aug. 12, 1980; appt. Bishop of Des Moines Feb. 10, 1987; installed April 2, 1987; appt. to Diocese of Madison April 13, 1993; died April 3, 2011.; JOSEPH L. CHARRON, C.PP.S., (Retired), ord. June 3, 1967; appt. Titular Bishop of Bencenna and Auxiliary Bishop of Saint Paul and Minneapolis Nov. 6, 1989; cons. Jan. 25, 1990; appt. Bishop of Des Moines Nov. 12, 1993; installed Jan. 21, 1994; retired April 10, 2007.

Vicar General—Rev. MICHAEL A. AMADEO.

Chancery—601 Grand Ave., Des Moines, 50309. Tel: 515-243-7653; Fax: 515-237-5070. Office Hours: Mon.-Fri. 8:30-4:30.

Chancellor's Office—MR. JASON KURTH, Chancellor, Email: jkurth@dmdiocese.org; MR. ADAM STOREY, Vice Chancellor, Fax: 515-237-5070. All Matrimonial Correspondence to Tribunal.

Executive Assistant to the Bishop—ANGIE HEMMINGSEN, 601 Grand Ave., Des Moines, 50309. Tel: 515-237-5039; Fax: 515-237-5071; Email: ahemmingsen@dmdiocese.org.

Finance Officer—PAUL CARLSON, 601 Grand Ave., Des Moines, 50309. Tel: 515-237-5008; Email: pcarlson@dmdiocese.org.

Vicar for Finance—Tel: 515-223-4577. Rev. Msgr. EDWARD HURLEY, (Retired).

Tribunal—Please send all dispensation requests to the Tribunal Office.

Judicial Vicar—Rev. CHRISTOPHER PISUT.

Coordinator of Tribunal—CATHY GEARHART, Email: cgearhart@dmdiocese.org.

Defenders of the Bond—Revs. LAWRENCE R. HOFFMANN, (Retired); DAVID J. POLICH; Deacon ROBERT L. HOWE.

Judges—Revs. CHRISTOPHER PISUT; CHRISTOPHER HARTSHORN; DANIEL F. KRETTEK, (Retired); Rev. Msgr. STEPHEN L. ORR.

Notary—CATHY GEARHART.

Advocates—Revs. JOHN P. LUDWIG, (Retired); JOHN DORTON, (Retired); MRS. SARAH LUFT; Deacon DENNIS LUFT.

Diocesan Consultors—Rev. Msgrs. EDWARD HURLEY, (Retired); STEPHEN ORR, (Retired); Revs. MICHAEL A. AMADEO; CHRISTOPHER FONTANINI; LAZARUS KIRIGIA; LUIS ALONSO MEJIA; ROSS PARKER; JOSEPH PINS.

Diocesan Corporation Board—Most Rev. RICHARD PATES; Rev. MICHAEL AMADEO; MR. JASON KURTH; MRS. KATHLEEN ZIMPLEMAN; MR. DENNIS PURDUM.

Diocesan Offices and Directors

Administrative Services—601 Grand Ave., Des Moines, 50309. Tel: 515-237-5048; Fax: 515-237-5071. Sr. JUDE FITZPATRICK, C.H.M., Dir., Email: jfitzpatrick@dmdiocese.org.

Campus Ministry—Rev. MARK OWUSU, Dir.

Charismatic Renewal Liaison—Rev. Msgr. FRANK CHIODO, St. Anthony Parish, 15 Indianola Rd., Des Moines, 50315. Tel: 515-244-4709.

Communications, Office of—MRS. ANNE MARIE COX, Dir., 601 Grand Ave., Des Moines, 50309. Tel: 515-237-5057; Fax: 515-237-5070; Email: acox@dmdiocese.org.

Continuing Education for Clergy—Rev. THOMAS THAKADIPURAM.

Deaf-Handicapped, Office of—MRS. PEGGY CHICOINE, Coord., Tel: 515-289-1311; Email: dpchicoine@msn.com.

Stewardship Office—601 Grand Ave., Des Moines, 50309. Tel: 515-237-5079; Email: mkenney@dmdiocese.org. MAUREEN KENNEY, Dir.

Diocesan Council of Catholic Women—MRS. NANCY LARSON, Pres., 604 Maple St., Shenandoah, 51601. Tel: 712-246-2452.

Diaconate (Permanent)—601 Grand Ave., Des Moines, 50309. Deacon JAMES OBRADOVICH, Dir.

Diaconate Formation—Directors: Deacon RON MYERS; TAMMY MYERS, 601 Grand Ave., Des Moines, 50309. Tel: 515-237-5037.

Holy Childhood, Pontifical Association—DR. TRACY BONDAY, 601 Grand Ave., Des Moines, 50309. Tel: 515-237-5013; Email: tbonday@dmdiocese.org.

Legislative Activities, Office of—VACANT.

Newspaper—The Catholic Mirror MRS. ANNE MARIE COX, Editor, 601 Grand Ave., Des Moines, 50309. Tel: 515-237-5057; Email: acox@dmdiocese.org.

Priests' Pension Fund Society—Most Rev. RICHARD PATES; Rev. JOSEPH PINS; Rev. Msgr. EDWARD HURLEY, (Retired); Revs. MICHAEL AMADEO; ROBERT L. SCHOEMANN, (Retired); GREGORY LEACH; KENNETH A. GROSS; Rev. Msgr. STEPHEN ORR, (Retired).

Propagation of the FaithSr. JUDE FITZPATRICK, C.H.M.

St. Vincent de Paul Society—Rev. JOHN BERTOGLI, Spiritual Dir., 607 High St., Des Moines, 50309. Tel: 515-288-7411.

Schools—601 Grand Ave., Des Moines, 50309. DR. TRACY BONDAY, Supt. & Dir. Educ., Tel: 515-237-5040; Email: tbonday@dmdiocese.org; MS. DENISE MULCAHY, Dir. Teaching & Learning, Tel: 515-237-5035; Email: dmulcahy@dmdiocese.org; MRS. JULIE MELCHER, Dir. Educational Svcs., Tel: 515-237-5015; Email: jmelcher@dmdiocese.org; MRS. NICOLE CASTILLO WALLER, Hispanic Advocate, Tel: 515-237-5088; Email: nwaller@dmdiocese.org; MR. JOHN HUYNH, Dir. Faith Journey, Tel: 515-237-5006; Email: jhuynh@dmdiocese.org.

Faith Journey—601 Grand Ave., Des Moines, 50309. Tel: 515-237-5006; Email: jhuynh@dmdiocese.org. MR. JOHN HUYNH, Dir.

Seminarians—Rev. ROSS PARKER, Dir.

Vocations—601 Grand Ave., Des Moines, 50309. Tel: 515-237-5014. Rev. ROSS PARKER, Dir.

Office for Worship (Liturgy, Music, Art and Architecture)—601 Grand Ave., Des Moines, 50309. Tel: 515-237-5046. VACANT, Dir.

Youth Ministry/Young Adult Ministry, Office of—MR. JUSTIN WHITE, Dir., 601 Grand Ave., Des Moines, 50309. Tel: 515-237-5098; Email: jwhite@dmdiocese.org.

St. Thomas More Center—6177 Panorama Rd., Panora, 50216. Tel: 515-755-3164. MS. ALEX KAUTZKY, Exec. Dir.

Office of Evangelization and Catechesis—MR. JOHN GAFFNEY, Dir., 601 Grand Ave., Des Moines, 50309. Tel: 515-237-5026; Email: jgaffney@dmdiocese.org.

Office of Marriage Ministry—MR. ADAM STOREY, 601 Grand Ave., Des Moines, 50309. Tel: 515-237-5056; Email: astorey@dmdiocese.org.

Victim Assistance Coordinator—MR. SAM PORTER, Tel: 515-286-2015; Email: advocate@dmdiocese.org.

CLERGY, PARISHES, MISSIONS AND PAROCHIAL SCHOOLS

CITY OF DES MOINES

(POLK COUNTY)

1—ST. AMBROSE CATHEDRAL (1856) [JC]
607 High St., 50309. Tel: 515-288-7411; Fax: 515-288-3969; Email: nancy@saintambrosecathedral.org. Revs. John Bertogli, Rector; Ambrose Ladu Daniel, Parochial Vicar; Deacons Francis Chan, Refugee Min.; Chris Rohwer; Lee Pao Yang; Michael McCarthy; James Obradovich; Debbie S. Rohrer, Liturgy Coord. & Wedding Dir.; Vern S. Rash, RCIA Coord.; Peter Relyea, Business Mgr.
Catechesis Religious Program—Students 193.

2—ALL SAINTS (1914) [JC]
Mailing Address: 650 N.E. 52nd Ave., 50313. Tel: 515-265-5001; Fax: 515-265-5636; Email: info@dmallsaints.org; Email: office@dmallsaints.org; Web: www.dmallsaints.org. Rev. Robert Harris; Mark Burdt; William Connet, Liturgy Coord. & Music Min.; Mary Treanor, Pastoral Asst.; Sue A. Christensen, Contact Person.
Catechesis Religious Program—Email: mandie@dmallsaints.org. Students 101.
Nick R. and Carole P. Zagar Endowment Scholarship Fund—

3—ST. ANTHONY'S (1905)
15 Indianola Rd., 50315. Tel: 515-244-4709; Fax: 515-280-6959; Email: info@stanthonydsm.org. Rev. Msgr. Frank Chiodo; Deacon Daniel Gehler, Parochial Vicar; Rev. Jose Reynaldo Hernandez Minero, Hispanic Chap.; Deacons Juan Bustamante; Thomas Hunkele; Quang (Quan) Tong; Mark Paris, Accountant/Bookkeeper.
School—St. Anthony's School, (Grades PreK-8), 16 Columbus Ave., 50315. Tel: 515-243-1874; Fax: 515-243-4467; Email: saschool@stanthonydsm.org. Jennifer Raes, Prin. Lay Teachers 26; Students 340.
Catechesis Religious Program—Tel: 515-244-1119. Chris Corrice, D.R.E. Students 285.

4—ST. AUGUSTIN'S (1920)
545 42nd St., 50312. Tel: 515-255-1175; Fax: 515-255-7969; Email: info@staugustin.org; Web: www.staugustin.org. Revs. Christopher Pisut; James Livingston, Asst. Priest, Homebound Ministry; Deacons Kevin Heim, RCIA Coord.; Joe Coan; Fred Pins; Kent Fieldsend, Music Min.; Deacon Kurt Heinrich; Sybil Sullivan Heilman, Business Mgr.; Cindy Sullivan, Sec.
School—St. Augustin's School, (Grades K-8), 4320 Grand Ave., 50312. Tel: 515-279-5947; Fax: 515-279-8049; Email: ndowdle@staugustinschool.org; Web: staugustinschool.org. Dr. Nancy Dowdle, Prin. Lay Teachers 21; Students 242; Religious Teachers 1.
Catechesis Religious Program—Religious Education Program, Email: janis@staugustin.org. Janis Falk, D.R.E.; Ben Cohen, Youth Min. Students 166.

5—BASILICA OF SAINT JOHN (1905)
1915 University Ave., 50314. Tel: 515-244-3101; Fax: 515-244-3165; Email: basilicadm@msn.com; Web: basilicaofstjohn.org. Rev. Aquinas Nichols; Deacons Luke Tieskoetter; Mark Campbell, Youth Min.; Jennifer Parsons, RCIA Coord.; Charles Stastny, Business Mgr.; Gail Johll, Music Min.
Catechesis Religious Program—Tel: 515-244-3101, Ext. 220; Email: margarets@basilicaofstjohn.org. Margaret Stastny, D.R.E. Students 103.
Basilica of St. John Foundation—Email: charless@basilicaofstjohn.org.

6—ST. CATHERINE OF SIENA CATHOLIC STUDENT CENTER (1969) (Non-Territorial University Parish)
1150 128th St., 50311-4142. Tel: 515-271-4747; Fax: 515-271-1918; Email: office@stcatherinedrake.org; Web: stcatherinedrake.org. Rev. Mark Owusu; Deacon Rick Condon; Robert L. VanGilder, Business Mgr., Accountant & Bookkeeper; Smith Erin, Campus Min.; Dennis Hendrickson, Music Min.; Teresa Smith, Sec.
Catechesis Religious Program—Email: laird.teresa@yahoo.com. Teresa Laird, D.R.E. Students 35.
St. Catherine of Siena Foundation—

7—CHRIST THE KING (1939)
5711 S.W. 9th St., 50315. Tel: 515-285-2888; Fax: 515-285-8182; Email: michellem@christthekingparish.org; Web: www.christthekingparish.org. Rev. Patrick McManus; Deacons Larry Kehoe, RCIA Coord.; Charles Putbrese; Tony Valdez; Steven Reed; Deanna Mathias, Business Mgr.
School—Christ the King School, (Grades K-8), 701 Wall St., 50315. Tel: 515-285-3349; Fax: 515-285-0381; Email: cgeilenfeld@cksdesmoines.com. Chuckie Geilenfeld, Prin. Lay Teachers 23; Students 210.
Catechesis Religious Program—Margaret Stastny, D.R.E. Students 239.
Christ the King Housing Services—
Christ the King Foundation—

8—CHURCH OF ST. PETER VIETNAMESE CATHOLIC COMMUNITY
Mailing Address: 618 E. 18th St., 50316. Tel: 515-266-1160; Email: office@stpeterdesmoines.org; Web: www.stpeterdesmoines.org. Rev. Joseph Ly Quy Chu; Deacons Gene Jager; Paul Tran; Mrs. Kelly Truong Tong, Accountant/Bookkeeper.
Catechesis Religious Program—Students 66.

9—HOLY TRINITY (1920)
2926 Beaver Ave., 50310-4040. Tel: 515-255-3162; Fax: 515-255-1361; Email: parishoffice@holytrinitydm.org. Rev. Mark Neal; Deacons Randy Kiel; James Obradovich; Douglas Renze; Sandy Stacy, Pastoral Care Min.; Regina Montgomery, Business Mgr.; Jim Wilwerding, RCIA Coord.; Diane Tellis, Accountant & Bookkeeper; Carolyn Rainey, Sec.
School—Holy Trinity School, (Grades PreK-8), Mrs. Anne Franklin, Prin. Lay Teachers 28; Students 429.
Catechesis Religious Program—Email: johnm@holytrinitydm.org. John Mertes, D.R.E. Students 218.

10—ST. JOSEPH'S (1924)
3300 Easton Blvd., 50317. Tel: 515-266-2226; Fax: 515-266-2227; Email: debbie@stjosephdsm.org. Rev. Joseph Pins; Deacons Marvin Brewer; William Hare, RCIA Coord.; Randy Lynch; Paula Fastenau, Business Mgr.; Debbie Muse, Accountant/Bookkeeper.
School—St. Joseph's School, (Grades PreK-8), 2107 E. 33rd St., 50317. Tel: 515-266-3433; Fax: 515-266-2860; Email: debbie@stjosephdsm.org. Phyllis Konchar, Prin. Lay Teachers 17; Students 210.
Catechesis Religious Program—Tel: 515-266-2449. Stacy Halbach, D.R.E.; Deb Ryan, Youth Min. Students 161.
St. Joseph Foundation—
St. Joseph School Foundation—

11—ST. MARY OF NAZARETH (1964)
4600 Meredith Dr., 50310. Tel: 515-276-4042; Fax: 515-252-1995; Email: stmarys@stmarysdsm.org; Web: www.stmarysdsm.org. Rev. Gregory Leach.
Catechesis Religious Program—Tel: 515-276-7589; Email: debr@stmarysdsm.org. Deb Richards, Catechetical Leader. Students 335.

12—OUR LADY OF THE AMERICAS (1882)
Mailing Address: 1271 E. 9th St., 50316. Tel: 515-266-6695; Fax: 515-266-9803; Email: vcalderon@oloadsm.com; Web: oloadsm.com. Rev. Fabian Moncada; Deacon Troy Thompson; Sr. Maria Elena Roman Aguilar, Prov.; Mr. Wilfrido Matamoros, Business Mgr.; Mrs. Victoria Calderon, Sec.
Catechesis Religious Program—Email: csalas@oloadsm.com; Email: lcontreras@oloadsm.com. Students 297.

13—ST. PETER'S (1915) Merged with Visitation, Des Moines to form Our Lady of the Americas, Des Moines.

14—ST. THERESA OF THE CHILD JESUS (1951) [JC]
1230 Merle Hay Rd., 50311-2098. Tel: 545-279-4654; Fax: 515-277-0838; Email: sfitz@sainttheresaiowa.org; Email: mgisler@sainttheresaiowa.org; Web: www.sainttheresaiowa.org. Rev. Raymond Higgins; Mary Gisler, Business Mgr.
School—St. Theresa of the Child Jesus School, (Grades PreK-8), 5810 Carpenter Ave., 50311. Tel: 515-277-0178; Fax: 515-255-2415; Email: estemler@sainttheresaiowa.org; Web: www.sainttheresaiowa.org. Ellen Stemler, Prin. Lay Teachers 23; Students 288.
Catechesis Religious Program—Email: jbecicka@sainttheresaiowa.org. Jane Ann Becicka, D.R.E.; Megan Howes, Youth Min.; Barbara Woods, RCIA Coord. Students 184.
Endowments—St. Theresa of the Child Jesus Foundation—
St. Theresa's School Foundation.

15—VISITATION (1882) Merged with St. Peter's, Des Moines to form Our Lady of the Americas, Des Moines.

OUTSIDE THE CITY OF DES MOINES

ADAIR, ADAIR CO., ST. JOHN (1879) Attended by All Saints, Stuart
Mailing Address: c/o All Saints, 216 All Saints Dr., P.O. Box 605, Stuart, 50250. Tel: 515-523-1943. Rev. Antony Mathew; Tammy Doud, Business Mgr.
Church: 501 Adair St., Adair, 50002.
Catechesis Religious Program—Tel: 641-742-3325; Email: annie68164@hotmail.com. Annie Brincks, Catechetical Leader. Students 14.

ADEL, DALLAS CO., ST. JOHN (1917)
24043 302nd Pl., Adel, 50003-0185. Tel: 515-993-4482; Fax: 515-993-3973; Email: saintjc3@gmail.com; Web: www.stjohnsadel.org. Mailing Address: P.O. Box 185, Adel, 50003-0185. Rev. Remigius C. Okere, C.S.Sp.; Jacque Seidl, Youth Min.; Lori Glanz, Business Mgr.; Michael Cooper, Music Min.
Catechesis Religious Program—Tel: 515-993-4590. Mrs. Kelly Howard, D.R.E. Students 230.

AFTON, UNION CO., ST. EDWARD (1878) Attended by Holy Spirit Parish from Creston.
104 W. Union St., Afton, 50830. Tel: 641-782-5278; Email: holyspiritst.edward@iowatelecom.net; Web: www.stedwardafton.parishesonline.com. Mailing Address: 406 W. Clark, Creston, 50801. Rev. Kenneth Halbur.
Catechesis Religious Program—Tel: 641-347-7115; Email: jgjvalencia@gmail.com. Jennifer Valencia, D.R.E. Students 42.

ALTOONA, POLK CO., SS. JOHN AND PAUL (1983)
Mailing Address: 1401 1st Ave. S., Altoona, 50009. Tel: 515-967-3796; Fax: 515-967-7197; Email:

ssjohnpaul@ssjohnpaul.org; Web: www.ssjohnpaul.org. Rev. Timothy Fitzgerald; Deacon Dennis Luft; John Mineart, Business Mgr.; Elizabeth Donner, Youth Min.; Patty Hormann, Liturgy Coord. & Music Min.

Catechesis Religious Program—Tel: 515-967-8047; Email: pchapman@ssjohnpaul.org. Paulette Chapman, D.R.E. Students 317.

ANITA, CASS CO., ST. MARY (1924) Attended by 302 Chestnut St., Anita, 50020. Tel: 712-243-4721; Email: petepaul@metc.net; Web: www.peterpaulandmary.org. Mailing Address: 600 Locust St., Atlantic, 50022. Rev. Chinnappan M. Devaraj, O.F.M.; Mary Jo Robinson, Business Mgr.

ANKENY, POLK CO.

1—ST. LUKE THE EVANGELIST CATHOLIC CHURCH
1102 N.W. Weigel Dr., Ankeny, 50023.
Tel: 515-964-1278; Email: douglas.jones@slte.org; Email: fradam@slte.org; Email: pete@slte.org; Web: www.slte.org. Deacons Fred Cornwell; Dan McGuire; Matthew Halbach; Rev. Adam Westphal; Deacon Donald Shannon.

School—St. Luke the Evangelist School, (Grades K-6), 2110 N.W. Weigel Dr., Ankeny, 50023.
Tel: 515-985-7074; Email: tonya.eaton@slte-school.org; Email: kendra.smith@slte-school.org; Web: www.slte.org. Tonya Eaton, Prin.; Sue Fitzpatrick, Sec.; Mrs. Kendra Jorgensen, Sec. Lay Teachers 18; Students 162.

Catechesis Religious Program—Peter Haack, D.R.E. Students 343.

2—OUR LADY'S IMMACULATE HEART (1961)
510 E. First St., Ankeny, 50021. Tel: 515-964-3038; Fax: 515-964-5997; Email: olih@olih.org; Web: www.olih.org. Rev. Michael A. Amadeo; Deacons Jeffrey Boehlert; Gregory Kolbinger; Steven Udelhofen; Sr. Susan Widdel, RCIA Coord. & Pastoral Min.; Becky J. Robovsky, Business Mgr.; Kyle Lechtenberg, Liturgy Dir.; Mr. Randy Henderson, Youth Min.; Mrs. Amy Wall, Sec.

Catechesis Religious Program—Tel: 515-964-3545; Email: tomp@olih.org. Tom Primmer, D.R.E. Students 1,099.

Our Lady's Immaculate Heart Charitable Foundation—

ATLANTIC, CASS CO., SS. PETER AND PAUL (1871)
106 West 6th St., Atlantic, 50022. Tel: 712-243-4721; Email: petepaul@metc.net; Web: www.sspeterpaulandmary.org. Mailing Address: 600 Locust St., Atlantic, 50022. Rev. Chinnappan M. Devaraj, O.F.M.; Mary Jo Robinson, Business Mgr.

Catechesis Religious Program—Email: jwmson@metc.net. Julie Williamson, Catechetical Leader. Students 133.

AUDUBON, AUDUBON CO., ST. PATRICK (1918) [CEM]
116 E. Division St., Audubon, 50025.
Tel: 712-563-2283; Fax: 712-563-3238; Email: spht@iowatelecom.net; Web: www.sphtdm.org. Rev. David Nkrumah; Linda Blomme, Accountant & Bookkeeper; Katie Yager, Sec.

Catechesis Religious Program—Jennifer Mosinski, D.R.E. Students 82.

AVOCA, POTTAWATTAMIE CO., ST. MARY, MEDIATRIX OF ALL GRACES (1882)
109 N. Maple St., P.O. Box 38, Avoca, 51521-0038.
Tel: 712-343-6948; Email: smpavoca@walnutel.net; Web: stmaryavoca.org. Rev. Seth Owusu; Pamela Paulson, Liturgy Coord.; Ann Koster, Liturgy Coord.; Jane True, Accountant Bookkeeper.

Catechesis Religious Program—Mary Lou Goettsch, D.R.E. Students 74.

BAYARD, GUTHRIE CO., ST. PATRICK (1882)
214 Prairie St., Bayard, 50029. Tel: 641-747-2569; Email: stmstc@netins.net; Web: showcase.netins.net/web/pgcatholic. Mailing Address: 603 Main St., Guthrie Center, 50115. Rev. Thomas Kunnel; Judee Vaughan, Business Mgr.

Catechesis Religious Program—Students 44.

BEDFORD, TAYLOR CO., SACRED HEART, Attended by St. Clare, Clarinda.
707 Main St., Bedford, 50833. Tel: 712-542-2030; Email: stclareclarinda@mchsi.com; Web: www.dmdiocese.org/mass.htm. Mailing Address: 300 E. Lincoln Blvd., Clarinda, 51632. Rev. Eze Venantius Umunnakwe, C.S.Sp.; Glenda Stockwell, Accountant/Bookkeeper.

Catechesis Religious Program—James Rogers, D.R.E. Students 14.

CARLISLE, WARREN CO., ST. ELIZABETH SETON (1979)
2566 N Scotch Ridge Rd., Carlisle, 50047.
Tel: 515-989-0659; Email: steliz256@g.com; Web: www.stelizabethcarlisle.com. Mailing Address: P.O. Box 35, Carlisle, 50047. Rev. Jim Kirby; Kevin Sinclair, Pres.; Keith Churchill, Treas.; Richard Harmon, RCIA Coord. & Adult Faith Formation Coord.; Molly Lauer, Sec.

Catechesis Religious Program—Stacie Henkelman, Catechetical Leader. Students 123.

CARTER LAKE, POTTAWATTAMIE CO., OUR LADY OF CARTER LAKE (1970) Merged with Our Lady Queen of the Apostles, Council Bluffs and Holy Family, Council Bluffs to form Corpus Christi, Council Bluffs.

CASEY, GUTHRIE CO., ST. JOSEPH (1898) Closed. For inquiries for parish records contact the chancery.

CHARITON, LUCAS CO., SACRED HEART (1869)
407 N. Main, Chariton, 50049. Tel: 681-774-4978; Email: shch@iowatelecom.net. Rev. Felix A. Onuora, C.S.Sp.; Mary Chapman, Business Mgr.

Catechesis Religious Program—Tel: 641-344-3100; Email: pontieradams@aol.com. Sheila Adams, D.R.E. Students 62.

CLARINDA, PAGE CO., ST. CLARE (1942)
300 E. Lincoln Blvd., Clarinda, 51632.
Tel: 712-542-2030; Email: stclareclarinda@mchsi.com. Rev. Eze Venantius Umunnakwe, C.S.Sp.

Catechesis Religious Program—Mark Baldwin, Catechetical Leader; Emily Akers, Catechetical Leader. Students 30.

CORNING, ADAMS CO., ST. PATRICK'S (1869) [CEM]
504 Grove Ave., Corning, 50841. Tel: 515-322-3363; Fax: 515-322-4370; Email: pat_corning@yahoo.com; Web: www.dmdiocese.org/mass.htm. Rev. Michael G. Peters; Beth Waddle, Liturgy Coord.; Lisa Allison, Office Mgr., Bookkeeper & Accountant; Melody Miller, Music Min.; Ms. Nancy Rychnovsky, Sec.

Catechesis Religious Program—901 Grove Ave., Corning, 50841-1343. Tel: 641-322-4089; Email: rych@mchsi.com. Jane Rychnoysky, D.R.E. Students 39.

CORYDON, WAYNE CO., ST. FRANCIS (1969) Attended by Chariton of the South Central Catholic Ministry Team.
Mailing Address: c/o 407 N. Main St., Chariton, 50049. Tel: 641-774-4978; Fax: 641-774-4978; Web: www.dmdiocese.org/mass.htm. Rev. Felix A. Onuora, C.S.Sp.; Mary Chapman, Business Mgr.
Church: c/o United Methodist Church of Corydon, 213 W. Jackson St., Corydon, 50060.

Catechesis Religious Program—Tel: 712-328-7272. Sheila Adams, Catechetical Leader. Classes held at Methodist Church.

COUNCIL BLUFFS, POTTAWATTAMIE CO.

1—CORPUS CHRISTI
3304 4th Ave., Council Bluffs, 51501.
Tel: 712-323-2916; Email: pastor@corpuschristiia.com; Email: officemanager@corpuschristiia.com; Web: www.corpuschristiparishiowa.org. Rev. Thomas Thakadipuram; Deacons Darwin Kruse; Monty Montagne; Bob McClellan; Maureen Kruse, RCIA Coord.

Worship Sites—

Our Lady, Queen of Apostles—3304 4th Ave., Council Bluffs, 51501.

Holy Family, 2217 Ave. B, Council Bluffs, 51501.

Our Lady of Carter Lake, 3501 N. 9th St., Carter Lake, 51510.

Catechesis Religious Program—Tel: 712-323-1163; Email: dre@corpuschristiia.com. Students 158.

2—HOLY FAMILY (1908) Merged with Our Lady, Queen of Apostles, Council Bluffs and Our Lady of Carter Lake, Carter Lake to form Corpus Christi, Council Bluffs.

3—OUR LADY, QUEEN OF APOSTLES (1957) Merged with Holy Family, Council Bluffs and Our Lady of Carter Lake, Carter Lake to form Corpus Christi, Council Bluffs.

4—ST. PATRICK (1924)
4 Valley View Dr., Council Bluffs, 51503.
Tel: 712-323-1484; Email: stpatrickscb@gmail.com; Web: www.dmdiocese.org/mass.htm. Rev. Glen Wilwerding; Deacons Charles Hannan; James Mason; Emmet Tinley, Business Mgr.; John Pfenning, RCIA Coord.

Catechesis Religious Program—Email: luannb223@gmail.com. LuAnn Baumker, D.R.E. Students 144.

Saint Patrick Church of Council Bluffs Iowa Foundation—

5—ST. PETER (1887) (German)
One Bluff St., Council Bluffs, 51503.
Tel: 712-322-8889; Fax: 712-323-8267; Email: ckottas@aol.com; Web: www.dmdiocese.org/mass.htm. Rev. Charles Kottas; Deacons Stephen Rallis; Dennis Kirlin; Patrick Snook; Jean Thomas, Treas.; Dolores Kral, Sec.

St. Francis Worship Center—238 6th St., Council Bluffs, 51501.

Catechesis Religious Program—Email: dolokral@msn.com. Jean Thomas, Youth Min.; Dolores Kral, Catechetical Leader. Students 153.

CRESTON, UNION CO., HOLY SPIRIT (1975)
107 W. Howard St., Creston, 50801.
Tel: 641-782-5278; Email: holyspiritstedward@windstream.net; Web: www.holyspiritcreston.parishesonline.com. Mailing Address: 406 W. Clark St., Creston, 50801. Rev. Kenneth Halbur.
Res. & Mailing Address: 407 W. Clark St., Creston, 50801.
Church: 107 W. Howard St., Creston, 50801. Also serving the parish of St. Edward, Afton.

School—St. Malachy School, (Grades PreK-8), 403 W. Clark St., Creston, 50801. Tel: 641-782-7125; Fax: 641-782-5924; Email: frken@windstream.net. Jennifer Simmons, Prin.; Rev. Kenneth Halbur, Canonical Admin. Lay Teachers 16; Students 198.

Catechesis Religious Program—Email: bhudson@iowatelecom.net. Barb Hudson, D.R.E. Students 84.

St. Malachy School Foundation—

CUMBERLAND, CASS CO., ST. TIMOTHY (Reno) (1883)
69488 Wichita Rd., Cumberland, 50843.
Tel: 712-243-4721; Email: charlie@metc.net. Mailing Address: 600 Locust St., Atlantic, 50022. Rev. Michael Berner; Charlotte Schroeder, Business Mgr.

Catechesis Religious Program—Faith Formation, Tel: 712-762-3456; Email: mccurdyfarms@gmail.com. John McCurdy, D.R.E. Students 12.

DEFIANCE, SHELBY CO., ST. PETER (1882) Served from Earling.
501 Fifth St., P.O. Box 127, Defiance, 51527.
Tel: 712-748-3501; Fax: 712-748-3500; Email: stpeters@netins.net; Web: www.dmdiocese.org/mass.htm. Rev. Guthrie Dolan; Nancy Schaben, Business Mgr.

Catechesis Religious Program—Email: drestpeters@fmctc.com. Diane Mulligan, Liturgy Coord.; Mary Gross, D.R.E. Students 20.

DUNLAP, HARRISON CO., ST. PATRICK
509 S. 3rd St., Dunlap, 51529. Tel: 712-643-5808; Tel: 712-643-5115; Email: dwchurch@iowatelecom.net; Web: www.dmdiocese.org/mass.htm. Rev. Joel McNeil; Deacon Marvin Klein, (Retired); Debbie Gaul-Rusch, Accountant/Bookkeeper.

Catechesis Religious Program—Students 100.

EARLING, SHELBY CO., ST. JOSEPH (1882) (German)
212 2nd St., P.O. Box 225, Earling, 51530.
Tel: 712-747-2091; Fax: 712-747-9501; Email: stjoseph@fmctc.com; Web: www.dmdiocese.org/mass.htm. Rev. Guthrie Dolan; Elaine Kramer, Business Mgr.
See Shelby County Board of Catholic Education, Panama under Education Centers located in the Institution section.

Catechesis Religious Program—Tel: 712-747-2781. Mrs. Susie Fah, D.R.E. Students 58.

ELKHART, POLK CO., ST. MARY/HOLY CROSS (1885)
460 N.W. Washington Ave., P.O. Box 110, Elkhart, 50073. Tel: 515-367-2685; Fax: 515-367-7028; Email: smhc@saintmaryhc.org; Web: www.saintmaryhc.org. Rev. Andrew Windschitl; Deacon Terry Schleisman; Nicole Cory, Sacramental Min.; Peter Relyea, Business Mgr.; Celeste Muehlenthaler, Music Min.; Barb Liske, Sec.

Rectory—

Catechesis Religious Program—Email: shergenreter@saintmaryhc.org; Email: mkahler@saintmaryhc.org; Email: afisher@saintmaryhc.org. Stacie Hergenreter, D.R.E.; Andrea Fisher, Youth Min.; Melissa Kahler, Youth Min. Students 196.

EXIRA, AUDUBON CO., HOLY TRINITY, Attended by 218 N. Kilworth St., Exira, 50076. Tel: 712-563-2283; Fax: 712-268-3238; Email: spht@iowatelecom.net; Web: www.sphtdm.org. Mailing Address: 116 E. Division St., Audubon, 50025. Rev. David Nkrumah; Linda Blomme, Business Mgr.; Judy Bintner, Sec.; Katie Yager, Sec.

Catechesis Religious Program—Jennifer Mosinski, D.R.E.

GLENWOOD, MILLS CO., OUR LADY OF THE HOLY ROSARY (1955)
24116 Marian Ave., Glenwood, 51534-5291.
Tel: 712-527-5211; Fax: 712-527-3829; Email: holyrosarych@msn.com; Web: www.holyrosaryglenwood. Rev. Daniel E. Siepker; Deacon Ronald Kohn.

Catechesis Religious Program—Theresa Romens, D.R.E. Students 246.

GRAND RIVER, DECATUR CO., ST. PATRICK, Served from St. Bernard, Osceola
460 Wabonsey St., Grand River, 50108.
Tel: 641-342-2850; Email: stbernardiowa@gmail.com; Email: davidjpolich@hotmail.com; Web: www.dmdiocese.org. Rev. David J. Polich.

GRANGER, DALLAS CO., ASSUMPTION OF THE BLESSED VIRGIN MARY (1871) [CEM]
1906 Sycamore, Granger, 50109. Tel: 515-999-2239; Fax: 515-999-2208; Email: parish@assumptiongranger.org; Web: www.assumptiongranger.com. P.O. Box 159, Granger, 50109. Rev. Dominic Assim; Deacons Dennis Wright; Thomas Schenk Sr., RCIA Coordinator; Anita Meiners-Stahowick, Business Mgr.; William (Shannon) Stokes, Accountant; Brenda Erps, Sec.; Dr. Lori Ancona, Music Dir.; Dan Merry, Trustee; Rose Slack, Trustee.

Catechesis Religious Program—
Tel: 515-999-2239, Ext. 16; Email: cdavidson@assumptiongranger.org. Cathy Davidson, D.R.E.; Elizabeth Godwin, Youth Min. Students 254.

GREENFIELD, ADAIR CO., ST. JOHN (1907)

303 N.E. Elm St., Greenfield, 50849.
Tel: 641-343-7065; Web: stjohnsgreenfieldia@gmail.com; Web: stjohns3.wixsite.com/home. Rev. James Ahenkora; Bethany Kintigh, Liturgy Dir.; Mrs. Molly Jo Kilborn, Treas.; Christine Rubio, Business Mgr.
Catechesis Religious Program—Tel: 641-745-0960; Email: tmphillippi1@gmail.com. Mrs. Tina Phillippi, D.R.E. Students 71.

GRISWOLD, CASS CO., OUR LADY OF GRACE (1911)
203 Adair St., Griswold, 51535. Tel: 712-243-4721; Email: charlie@metc.net; Web: www.dmdiocese.org/mass.htm. Mailing Address: 600 Locust St., Atlantic, 50022. Rev. Michael Berner; Charlotte Schroeder, Business Mgr.

GUTHRIE CENTER, GUTHRIE CO., ST. MARY (1906) [JC]
603 Main St., Guthrie Center, 50115.
Tel: 515-747-2569; Fax: 641-747-3843; Email: stmstc@netins.net. Rev. Thomas Kunnel; Judee Vaughan, Business Mgr.; Misean Hernandez, Sec.; Courtney Redfern, Sec.
Catechesis Religious Program—Cynthia Ahrens, Catechetical Leader. Students 69.

HAMBURG, FREMONT CO., ST. MARY (1874) Attended by St. Mary, Shenandoah.
1306 Washington St., Hamburg, 51640.
Tel: 712-382-2871; Email: stmaryshamburg@gmail.com; Web: www.parishesonline.com. Mailing Address: P.O. Box 67, Hamburg, 51640. Rev. Raphael Assamah; Anne Hendrickson, Accountant/Bookkeeper.
Catechesis Religious Program—Scott Mayberry, Youth Min. & Catechetical Leader. Students 49.

HARLAN, SHELBY CO., ST. MICHAEL (1888)
Mailing Address: 1912 18th St., Harlan, 51537.
Tel: 712-755-5244; Email: stmike@harlannet.com. Rev. John M. Frost; Deacons Patrick Davitt; James DeBlauw; John Rosman, Liturgy Coord. & Music Min.; Kathy Hull, Accountant & Bookkeeper; Cindy Marcin, Bookkeeper; Brenda Blum, Sec.
Church & Res.: 2001 College Pl., Harlan, 51537.
School—St. Michael School, (Grades PreK-6), 2005 College Pl., Harlan, 51537. Tel: 712-755-5634; Email: jerlbach@shelcocath.pvt.k12.ia.us. Mrs. Ann Anderson, Prin.; Joanne Erlbacher, Bus. Mgr. Lay Teachers 11; Students 104; Religious Teachers 3.
See Shelby County Board of Catholic Education, Panama under Education Centers located in the Institution section.
Catechesis Religious Program—Tel: 712-755-5366; Email: stmikere@harlannet.com. Veronica Wright, D.R.E. Students 158.
St. Michael Parish Foundation—

IMOGENE, FREMONT CO., ST. PATRICK (1880) (Irish)
304 Third St., Imogene, 51645. Tel: 712-386-2277; Email: stpatsimogene@gmail.com; Web: www.stpatrickchurchimogeneiowa.weebly.com. Rev. Lazarus Kirigia.
Catechesis Religious Program—Tel: 712-386-2239. Linda Laughlin, Catechetical Leader. Students 46.

INDIANOLA, WARREN CO., ST. THOMAS AQUINAS (1958)
210 R63 Hwy., Indianola, 50125. Tel: 515-961-3026; Fax: 515-961-3458; Email: bintners@msn.com; Web: www.stthomasindianola.com. Rev. Christopher Fontanini; Steph Binter, Business Mgr., Accountant & Bookkeeper.
Catechesis Religious Program—Email: jsayredre@gmail.com. Jo Ann Sayre, D.R.E. Students 296.

IRISH SETTLEMENT, MADISON CO., ST. PATRICK dba St. Patrick Catholic Church, Irish Settlement (1852)
3396 155th St., Cumming, 50061. Tel: 515-462-1083; Email: office@saintjosephchurch.net; Web: www.dmdiocese.org. Mailing Address: 1026 N. 8th St., Winterset, 50273. Rev. Thomas V. Dooley; Marilyn Connor, Liturgy Coord.; Mike Drysdale, Business Mgr.; Rose Anderson, Adult Faith Formation Coord.; Mary Ellen Krantz, Adult Faith Formation Coord.
Catechesis Religious Program—Students 39.

JAMAICA, GUTHRIE CO., ST. JOSEPH (1903) Closed. For inquiries for parish records contact the chancery.

LACONA, WARREN CO., HOLY TRINITY CHURCH OF SOUTHEAST WARREN COUNTY (1978)
222 Washington Ave, Lacona, 50139.
Tel: 641-534-4691; Fax: 641-534-4691; Email: wilmethc@yahoo.com; Email: nimerichterdean@yahoo.com; Web: www.dmdiocese.org/mass.htm. Mailing Address: 14844 Kennedy St, Indianola, 50125. Rev. Dean Nimerichter; Chris Willmeth, Business Mgr.
Res.: 304 N. Washington Ave., Lacona, 50139-0145.
Worship Centers—
St. Mary of the Assumption Church—St. Mary of the Assumption Church: Lacona, 50139.
St. Augustine, St. Augustine Church: Milo, 50166.
Catechesis Religious Program—Amy Welch, Catechetical Leader; Barb Ripperger, Youth Min. Students 36.

LENOX, TAYLOR CO., ST. PATRICK (1872) Attended by St. Patrick, Corning.
600 W. Michigan, Lenox, 50851. Tel: 641-333-2565; Email: stpatl@frontiernet.net; Web: www.dmdiocese.org/mass.htm. Rev. Michael G. Peters; Kathy Ecklin, Bookkeeper.
Catechesis Religious Program—107 E. Kansas St., Lenox, 50851. Kathy Ecklin, D.R.E. Students 25.

LEON, DECATUR CO., ST. BRENDAN (1856) (Irish)
1001 N.W. Church St., Leon, 50144.
Tel: 641-446-4789; Email: southch3@grm.net; Web: www.dmdiocese.org/mass.htm. Rev. Felix A. Onuora, C.S.Sp.; Deacon Reinhold Kunze; Marilyn Arndorfer, Accountant/ Bookkeeper.
Catechesis Religious Program—Tel: 641-414-2278; Email: rmpoush@yahoo.com. Renae Poush, D.R.E. Students 39.

LOGAN, HARRISON CO., ST. ANNE (1920)
104 W. 3rd St., Logan, 51546. Tel: 712-644-2520; Email: stanne@iowatelecom.net; Web: www.dmdiocese.org/mass.htm. Rev. Raphael Masabakhwa; Deacon Dennis Lovell; Annette Lorenz, Business Mgr.; Kathy Lovell, Liturgy Coord.
Res.: 112 W. 3rd St., Logan, 51546.
Catechesis Religious Program—Kyle Haffey, D.R.E. Students 85.

MALOY, RINGGOLD CO., IMMACULATE CONCEPTION (1874) [CEM] Closed. For inquiries for parish records contact the chancery.

MASSENA, CASS CO., ST. PATRICK (1888) Served from Greenfield.
503 Main St., P.O. Box 61, Massena, 50853.
Tel: 712-779-3397; Fax: 712-779-3397; Email: st.patricksmassena@gmail.com; Web: www.dmdiocese.org. Rev. James Ahenkora; Linda Reineke, Sec.
Catechesis Religious Program—Email: thensley21@yahoo.com. Theresa Hensley, Catechetical Leader. Students 46.

MISSOURI VALLEY, HARRISON CO., ST. PATRICK (1877)
215 N. Seventh St., Missouri Valley, 51555.
Tel: 712-642-3155; Email: stpatsch@loganet.net; Web: movalleycatholics.wordpress.com; Web: www.dmdiocese.org. Rev. Raphael Masabakhwa; Deacon Michael Carney; Michele Wilson, Sec.
Catechesis Religious Program—Email: rep.annettel@gmail.com. Annette Lorenzen, D.R.E. Students 47.

MONDAMIN, HARRISON CO., HOLY FAMILY (1970) Attended by St. Patrick.
97 Mulberry, Mondamin, 51557. Tel: 712-644-2092; Email: jzahner@windstream.net; Email: churchspsh@gmail.com. Mailing Address: 509 S. 3rd St., Dunlap, 51529. Rev. Joel McNeil; John Davie, Accountant/Bookkeeper; Loene Herman, Liturgy Coord.; Ruth Zahner, Music Coord.; Susan Maule, Accountant & Bookkeeper.
Church: 307 Mulberry, Mondamin, 51557.
Tel: 712-643-5115.

MT. AYR, RINGGOLD CO., ST. JOSEPH (1913) Served from St. Bernard, Osceola.
100 N. Polk St., Mt. Ayr, 50854. Tel: 641-464-2826; Email: stbernardiowa@gmail.com; Email: davidjpolich@hotmail.com; Web: www.dmdiocese.org. Mailing Address: 222 E. Pearl St., Osceola, 50213. Rev. David J. Polich; Donna Watson, Accountant/Bookkeeper.
Catechesis Religious Program—Liz Schafer, D.R.E. Students 35.

NEOLA, POTTAWATTAMIE CO., ST. PATRICK (1882)
308 4th St., P.O. Box 127, Neola, 51559.
Tel: 712-485-2124; Email: stpats@wiaw.net; Web: www.stpatricksneola.com. Rev. Daniel Aboagye Danso; RaeShelle Jensen, Business Mgr.
Catechesis Religious Program—Tel: 402-680-3797; Tel: 712-325-9397; Email: amyaus74@gmail.com; Email: hiltopturf@aol.com. Amy Ausdemore, D.R.E.; Bernadette Koch, D.R.E. Students 224.
Saint Patrick Foundation—

NORWALK, WARREN CO., ST. JOHN THE APOSTLE CHURCH (1892)
720 Orchard St., Norwalk, 50211. Tel: 515-981-4855; Fax: 515-981-9475; Email: stjohns@stjohnsnorwalk.org; Web: www.stjohnsnorwalk.org. Rev. John P. Ludwig, (Retired); Deacon David Miller; Michele Miller, Music Coord.; Timothy Mineart, Business Mgr.; Kathleen Ballard, Accountant/Bookkeeper; Alayne Pieper, Sec.
Catechesis Religious Program—Email: melissahillstjohns@hotmail.com. Melissa Hill, D.R.E. Students 330.
Shrine—Shrine of the Assumption, Churchville.

ORIENT, ADAIR CO., ST. MARK, Closed. For inquiries for parish records contact the chancery.

OSCEOLA, CLARKE CO., ST. BERNARD (1885)
222 E. Pearl, Osceola, 50213. Tel: 641-342-2850; Fax: 641-342-2850; Email: stbernardiowa@gmail.com; Email: davidjpolich@hotmail.com; Web: www.dmdiocese.org. Rev. David J. Polich; Ms. Perla Rosales, Sec.
Catechesis Religious Program—Tel: 641-414-1755; Email: schade.maryjo@gmail.com. Mrs. Mary Jo Schade, D.R.E. Students 117.

PANAMA, SHELBY CO., ST. MARY OF THE ASSUMPTION (1895)
200 N. 2nd St., Panama, 51562. Tel: 712-489-2030; Fax: 712-489-2030; Email: smpanama@fmctc.com; Web: www.stmarypanama.parishesonline.com. Mailing Address: P.O. Box 203, Panama, 51562. Rev. David L. Smith, S.J.; Laura Arkfeld-Mohr, Accountant & Bookkeeper.
See Shelby County Board of Catholic Education, Panama under Education Centers located in the Institution section.
Catechesis Religious Program—Laura Gubbels, D.R.E. Students 52.
St. Mary Parish Religious Education Foundation—

PANORA, GUTHRIE CO., ST. CECILIA (1907) [JC] Attended by St. Mary, Guthrie Center.
Mailing Address: 603 Main St., Guthrie Center, 50115. Tel: 641-747-2569; Fax: 641-747-3843; Email: stcstmstp@netins.net; Web: www.showcase.netins.net/web/pages. Rev. Thomas Kunnel; Judee Vaughan, Business Mgr.
Church: 221 N. First St., Panora, 50216.
Catechesis Religious Program—Students 44.

PERRY, DALLAS CO., ST. PATRICK (1881)
1312 3rd St., Perry, 50220. Tel: 515-465-4387; Fax: 515-465-4232; Email: stpatsperry@gmail.com; Web: www.stpatsperry.com. Rev. Christopher Reising; Mark Paris, Business Mgr.
School—St. Patrick School, (Grades K-8), 1302 5th St., Perry, 50220. Tel: 515-465-4186; Fax: 515-465-9808; Email: stpatrickschool@stpatricks-perry-ia.org; Web: www.stpatricks-perry-ia.org. Kandice Roethler, Prin. Lay Teachers 11; Students 114.
Catechesis Religious Program—Barbara Wolter, D.R.E. Students 91.

PORTSMOUTH, SHELBY CO., ST. MARY, OUR LADY OF FATIMA (1885)
412 4th St., P.O. Box 98, Portsmouth, 51565.
Tel: 712-743-2625; Fax: 712-743-2625; Email: hankhu@iowatelecom.net; Web: www.dmdiocese.org. Rev. David L. Smith, S.J.; Henrietta Hughes, Business Mgr. & Liturgy Coord.
Catechesis Religious Program—Henrietta Hughes, Catechetical Leader. Students 34.

RED OAK, MONTGOMERY CO., ST. MARY (1902)
1510 Highland Ave., Red Oak, 51566.
Tel: 712-623-2744; Email: stmarysrosecretary@gmail.com; Web: www.stmaryredoak.parishesonline.com. Rev. Lazarus Kirigia; Cindy Joneson, Accountant/Bookkeeper; Jean Anderson, Sec.
Catechesis Religious Program—Virgnia Bueno, D.R.E.; Emily Comfort, Youth Min. Students 47.

ST. MARYS, WARREN CO., IMMACULATE CONCEPTION (1871)
101 St. James, P.O. Box 88, St. Marys, 50241.
Tel: 515-961-3026, Ext. 6; Email: immacula@netins.net; Email: lcs3garr@yahoo.com; Web: www.dmdiocese.org. Rev. Christopher Fontanini; Deacon David O'Brien; Leasa Garrett, Accountant/Bookkeeper; Suzanne Stills, Liturgy Coord.
Catechesis Religious Program—220 Iowa St., P.O. Box 113, St. Marys, 50241. Email: joro23@juno.com. Michelle Fick, D.R.E. Students 59.

SHENANDOAH, PAGE CO., ST. MARY
Mailing Address: 512 W. Thomas Ave., Shenandoah, 51601. Tel: 712-246-1718; Email: shenrectory@msn.com; Web: www.dmdiocese.org. Rev. Raphael Assamah; Sue Hanna, Music Min. & Liturgy Coord.; Bruce Baldwin, Accountant/Bookkeeper.
Catechesis Religious Program—Lynda Marshall, Catechetical Leader; Brad Johnson, Youth Min. Students 74.

STUART, GUTHRIE CO., ALL SAINTS (1876)
216 All Saints Dr., P.O. Box 605, Stuart, 50250.
Tel: 515-523-1943; Email: allsaintsoffice@gmail.com. Rev. Antony Mathew; Brenda Wedemeyer, RCIA Contact; Tammy Daud, Business Mgr.
Catechesis Religious Program—Email: cabinmn@gmail.com. Cathy Hicks, D.R.E. Students 69.

URBANDALE, POLK CO., ST. PIUS X (1955)
Mailing Address: 3663 66th St., Urbandale, 50322.
Tel: 515-276-2059; Fax: 515-276-8351; Email: eharlan@saintpiuschurch.org; Web: www.stpiushome.org. Revs. David Fleming; John Harmon, Parochial Vicar, (Retired); Deacon James Houston; Vicki Ferin, Pastoral Min./Coord.; Erica Harlan, Sec.
School—St. Pius X School, (Grades PreK-8), 3601 66th St., Urbandale, 50322. Tel: 515-276-1061; Fax: 515-276-0350; Email: eharlan@saintpiuschurch.org; Web: www.stpiusxschool.org. Ms. Mary Jo Kever, Prin. Lay Teachers 31; Students 349.
Catechesis Religious Program—Tel: 515-278-5684; Email: cfournier@saintpiuschurch.org. Dr. Cheryl Fournier, D.R.E.; Mary Sue Lone, RCIA Coord. Students 274.
St. Pius X Parish Foundation—

VILLISCA, MONTGOMERY CO., ST. JOSEPH (1947) Attended by St. Clare, Clarinda.
131 W. High St., Villisca, 50864. Tel: 712-542-2030; Email: stclareclarinda@mchsi.com; Web: www.dmdiocese.org/mass.htm. Mailing Address: 300 E.

Lincoln Blvd., Clarinda, 51632. Rev. Eze Venantius Umunnakwe, C.S.Sp.; Gary Poen, Accountant & Bookkeeper; Becky Poen, Music Dir.

WALNUT, POTTAWATTAMIE CO., ST. PATRICK dba St. Patrick Catholic Church (1882) Attended by St. Mary, Mediatrix of All Graces, Avoca.
718 Antique City Dr., Walnut, 51521.
Tel: 712-343-6948; Email: smpavoca@walnutel.net; Web: www.stmarysavoca.org. Mailing Address: 109 N. Maple St., P.O. Box 38, Avoca, 51521. Rev. Seth Owusu; Donna Muell, Liturgy Coord.; Jane True, Accountant/Bookkeeper.
Catechesis Religious Program—109 N. Maple, Avoca, 51521. Tel: 712-343-6951. Mary Lou Goettsch, D.R.E. Students 6.

WAUKEE, DALLAS CO., ST. BONIFACE (1880)
1200 Warrior Ln., Waukee, 50263-9587.
Tel: 515-987-4597; Fax: 515-987-5272; Email: office@stbonifacechurch.org; Web: stbonifacechurch.org. Rev. Vince G. Rosonke; Catherine Bellis, Finance & Facilities Mgr.; Sara Krohnke, Health Min.
Catechesis Religious Program—Amy Slick, Catechetical Leader; Deb Purcell, RCIA Coord.; T.J. Irvin, Youth Min.; Scott Fitzgerald, Liturgical Music. Students 1,205.

WEST DES MOINES, POLK CO.

1—ST. FRANCIS OF ASSISI (1991)
Mailing Address: 7075 Ashworth Rd., West Des Moines, 50266. Tel: 515-223-4577; Fax: 515-223-4768; Email: info@saintfrancischurch.org; Web: www.saintfrancischurch.org. Revs. Raymond McHenry, M.B.A.; Trevor Chicoine; Deacon William Richer; Emily Schmid, Music Min.; Christopher Aldinger, Business Mgr.; Debbie Muse, Accountant; Sheila Timmerman, Exec.
School—St. Francis of Assisi School, (Grades K-8), Tel: 515-457-7167; Email: sfaschool@saintfrancisschool.org; Web: www.saintfrancisschool.org. Mrs. Misty Hade, Prin.; Jon Aldrich, Asst. Prin. Lay Teachers 44; Students 638.
Catechesis Religious Program—Tel: 515-440-1030. Christen Cota, D.R.E.; Faye Akers, RCIA Coord.; Jill Klubek-Alonzo, Pre-K Faith Formation Coord. Students 778.

2—SACRED HEART (1892)
Mailing Address: 1627 Grand Ave., West Des Moines, 50265. Tel: 515-225-6414; Fax: 515-225-0286; Email: office@sacredheartwdm.org; Web: www.sacredheartwdm.org. Revs. Christopher Hartshorn; Luis Alonso Mejia, Parochial Vicar; Deacons Ed Garza, Pastoral Min.; Ron Myers; Randy Horn; Leah Mohlman, Music Min.; Nancy Gion, Business Mgr., Accountant & Bookkeeper.
School—Sacred Heart School, (Grades PreK-8), 1601 Grand Ave., West Des Moines, 50265.
Tel: 515-223-1284; Fax: 515-223-9413; Email: Jane.kinney@sacredheartwdm.org. Jane Kinney, Prin.; Tiffany Bayless, Librarian. Lay Teachers 35; Students 583.
Catechesis Religious Program—Kayla Richer, D.R.E.; Deb Chalik, D.R.E., Coord.; Sarah Sheerin, Youth Min.; Paul Conner, RCIA & Adult Faith Formation Coord.; Casey Conner, RCIA & Adult Faith Formation Coord.; Karla Willis, Hispanic Min.; Marcia Schaul, Catechetical Leader. Students 440.

WESTON, POTTAWATTAMIE CO., ST. COLUMBANUS (1883) Served from St. Patrick, Neola.
22720 Weston Ave, Underwood, 51576.
Tel: 712-485-2124; Email: stpats@wiaw.net; Web: stpatricksneola.com. Mailing Address: P.O. Box 127, Neola, 51559. Rev. Daniel Aboagye Danso; RaeShelle Jensen, Business Mgr.; Jan Reineke, Accountant/Bookkeeper.
Catechesis Religious Program—Tel: 712-325-9397; Email: hiltopturf@aol.com. Bernadette Koch, D.R.E. Students 15.

WESTPHALIA, SHELBY CO., ST. BONIFACE (1873)
305 Duren Strasse, Westphalia, 51578.
Tel: 712-627-4255; Email: stboniface@fmctc.com. Mailing Address: P.O. Box 86, Westphalia, 51578. Rev. David L. Smith, S.J.; Lorene Kaufmann, Business Mgr. & Music Coord.
Catechesis Religious Program—Students 24.

WINTERSET, MADISON CO., ST. JOSEPH (1893)
1026 N. 8th Ave., Winterset, 50273.
Tel: 515-462-1083; Fax: 515-462-2378; Email: office@saintjosephchurch.net; Web: www.saintjosephchurch.net. Rev. Thomas V. Dooley; Deacon Sam Sullivan; Patricia Barker, Sec.; Mike Drysdale, Accountant/Bookkeeper.
Catechesis Religious Program—Heather Honkomp, D.R.E.; Tiffany Bond, Youth Min. Students 137.

WOODBINE, HARRISON CO., SACRED HEART (1902) Attended by St. Patrick's, Dunlap.
33 7th St., Woodbine, 51579. Tel: 712-643-5115;
Tel: 712-643-5808; Email: churchspsh@gmail.com; Web: www.dmdiocese.org. Mailing Address: 509 S. 3rd St., Dunlap, 51529. Rev. Joel McNeil; Deacon Marvin Klein; Debbie Gaul-Rusch, Sec.; Mary Weis, Liturgy Coord.; Kelly Mikels, Accountant/Bookkeeper; Mary Kay Eby, Music Min.
Catechesis Religious Program—Students 42.

WOODWARD, DALLAS CO., ST. ANN (1934) Closed. For inquiries for parish records contact Assumption Church, Granger.

Chaplains of Public Institutions

DES MOINES. *Des Moines City Chaplaincy Program*, 1390 Buffalo Rd., West Des Moines, 50265. Email: michael.mclaughlin1746@gmail.com. Rev. Michael R. McLaughlin.
Des Moines Area Detention Facility Chaplain, P.O. Box 110, Elkhart, 50073. Tel: 513-367-2685; Email: awindschitl@saintmaryhc.org. Rev. Andrew Windhcittl.
United States Veterans Hospital, 3600 30th St., 50310.

CLARINDA. *State Hospital*. Served from St. Clare Church, Clarinda.

GLENWOOD. *Glenwood State School*. Vacant.

MITCHELLVILLE. *Iowa Correctional Institution for Women*. Ms. Kay Kopatich, Chap. & Coord., Svcs. to Catholic Residents.

On Special Assignment:
Revs.—
Kirby, Daniel J., Diocesan Dir. Seminarians
McLaughlin, Michael R., Des Moines City Chaplaincy
Owusu, Mark, Diocesan Dir. Campus Ministry
Parker, Ross, Diocesan Dir. Seminarians & Vocations
Tran, Tan Van, Hospital & Nursing Home Chaplaincy in Council Bluffs; Special Liturgical Ministry, Council Bluffs Region.

On Duty Outside the Diocese:
Rev.—
Grant, Robert, St. Ambrose University, Davenport, 52803.

Retired:
Rev. Msgrs.—
Beeson, Lawrence A., J.C.D., (Retired), 1390 Buffalo Rd., West Des Moines, 50265
Bognanno, Frank E., (Retired), 3663 Grand Ave., Unit 207, 50312
Chamberlain, Robert J., (Retired), 739 33rd St., 50312
Hess, Michael, (Retired), 786 Glen Oaks Terrace, West Des Moines, 50266
Hurley, Edward, (Retired), 280 S. 79th St., Unit 1308, West Des Moines, 50266
Orr, Stephen, (Retired), 4773 Woodland Ave., #5, West Des Moines, 50266
Pfeffer, Edward B., J.C.L., (Retired), 5815 Winwood Dr., Apt. 325, Johnston, 50131
Revs.—
Acrea, John, (Retired), 2115 Summit Ave., Saint Paul, MN 55105
Aiello, Anthony, (Retired), 3422 S.W. 13th St., 50315
Aubrey, Robert J., (Retired), 3429 Belmar Dr., 50317
Bruck, Donald, (Retired), 1110 Elm St., Harlan, 51537
Chevalier, Martin G., (Retired), 2929 Beaver Ave., Apt. 102, 50310
Coenen, Thomas, (Retired), 1109 Normal St., Woodbine, 51579
Dorton, John, (Retired), 3614 SW 37th St., 50321
Freeman, James, (Retired), 207 N. Wilmont Rd., #454, Tucson, AZ 85711
Gittons, Gordon, (Retired), 5837 Winwood Dr., Johnston, 50131
Gross, Ken, (Retired), 1390 Buffalo Rd., West Des Moines, 50265
Gubbels, Wayne, (Retired), 1620 Victoria St., Harlan, 51537
Harmon, John, (Retired), 3663 66th St., Urbandale, 50322
Hoffmann, Lawrence R., (Retired), 1390 Buffalo Rd., West Des Moines, 50265
Kenkel, Benedict J., (Retired), 2108-12th St., Apt. 151, Harlan, 51537
Kenkel, Leonard A., (Retired), 2108 12th St., Apt. 151, Harlan, 51537
Kleffman, James, (Retired), Bethany Hts., Rm. 217, 11 Eliott St., Council Bluffs, 51503
Koch, Eugene R., (Retired), 1390 Buffalo Rd., West Des Moines, 50265
Koch, Paul M., (Retired), 238 S. 6th St., Council Bluffs, 51501
Krettek, Daniel F., (Retired), 125 NE Maple St., Elkhart, 50073
Laurenzo, James, (Retired), 1205 Lewis, 50315
Leto, Nelo A., (Retired), 5837 Winwood Dr., Rm. 240, Johnston, 50131
Ludwig, John P., (Retired), 1390 Buffalo Rd., West Des Moines, 50265
Maier, John, (Retired), 507 Spencer Pl., Leavenworth, KS 66048
Monahan, Paul, (Retired), 1801 E. Kanesville Blvd., #107, Council Bluffs, 51503
Palmer, Frank S., (Retired), 4460 - 88th St., Urbandale, 50322
Schoemann, Robert L., (Retired), 1390 Buffalo Rd., West Des Moines, 50265
Sherbo, Albert, (Retired), 811 - 3rd St., P.O. Box 508, Anita, 50020
Smith, Vernon, (Retired), 3459 Lindenwood St., Sioux City, 51104.

Permanent Deacons:
Barnwell, Jerry, (Retired)
Bartemes, David, (Retired)
Bertrand, Eric
Boehlert, Jeffrey
Bradley, Thomas
Bray, Robert, (Retired)
Brewer, Marvin, (Retired)
Brooks, Darrl (Scott)
Burdt, Mark
Bustamante, Juan
Campbell, Mark
Carney, Michael
Chan, Francis
Coan, Joseph II, (Retired)
Condon, Rick
Cornwell, Fred
Cortese, Joseph II
Davitt, Patrick, (Retired)
DeBlauw, James, (Retired)
Doyle, James, (Retired)
Erickson, Gregg
Garza, David, (Retired)
Garza, Ed
Gaul, Leo, (Retired)
Halbach, Matthew
Hannan, Charles, (Retired)
Hare, William
Heim, Kevin
Heinrich, Kurt
Herman, James, (Retired)
Horn, Randy
Houston, James
Howe, Robert, (Retired)
Hunkele, Thomas
Huntsman, Michael
Huynh, Joseph, (Retired)
Inman, Jack, (Retired)
Jacobi, Donald, (Retired)
Jager, Gene, (Retired)
Kehoe, Laurence
Kiel, Randy
Kirkman, Patrick, (Retired)
Kirlin, Dennis, (Retired)
Klein, Marvin
Knotek, Lawrence, (Retired)
Kohn, Ronald
Kolbinger, Gregory
Kruse, Darwin
Kunze, Reinhold
Lopez, Frank
Lovell, David, (Retired)
Lovell, Dennis
Luft, Dennis M.
Lynch, Randy
Maly, Thomas, (Retired)
Manno, Michael
Mason, James, (Retired)
McCarthy, Michael, (Retired)
McClellan, Robert
McGuire, Dan
Miller, Dave
Montagne, Monty
Myers, Ron
O'Brien, David
Obradovich, James
Pantaloni, Ed, (Retired)
Patrick, Dennis
Pfenning, John
Pins, Fred
Plourde, Jean
Putbrese, Charles
Rallis, Stephen
Reed, Steven
Renze, Douglas
Richardson, Alan, (Retired)
Richer, William
Rohwer, Chris, (Retired)
Romeo, Tony, (Retired)
Schenk, Thomas Sr.
Schleisman, Terry
Schmidt, David
Schmidt, Joel
Scurlock, Joseph, (Retired)
Seeman, Hans, (Retired)

Shannon, Donald
Snook, Patrick
Starbuck, Tom
Stark, Raymond (Rob)
Stessman, Gail
Stone, Kelly
Sullivan, Robert, (Retired)
Sullivan, Sam
Thompson, Troy
Tieskoetter, Luke
Tinley, Emmet
Tong, Quang (Quan)
Tran, Paul
Udelhofen, Steven
Valdez, Tony
Webering, James, (Retired)
Weisenhorn, Earl
Wolford, Charles, (Retired)
Woltanski, Mike, (Retired)
Wright, Dennis
Yang, LyPao
Ziller, Richard, (Retired).

INSTITUTIONS LOCATED IN DIOCESE

[A] EDUCATION CENTERS

DES MOINES. *Holy Family School*, (Grades PreK-8), 1265 E. 9th St., 50316. Tel: 515-262-8025; Fax: 515-262-9665; Email: mpflaherty@hfsdm.org; Email: doriger@hfsdm.org; Web: hfsdm.org. Martin P. Flaherty, Prin.; Mr. Darin Origer, Business Mgr.; Traci Rogo, Librarian. Participating parishes: Our Lady of the Americas, Des Moines; Basilica of St. John, Des Moines; St. Ambrose Cathedral, Des Moines; All Saints, Des Moines; St. Peter, Des Moines. Lay Teachers 18; Students 234; Religious Teachers 1.

COUNCIL BLUFFS. *Council Bluffs Area Catholic Education Systems, Inc.* dba Saint Albert Catholic Schools, (Grades PreK-12), 400 Gleason Ave., Council Bluffs, 51503. Tel: 712-329-9000; Fax: 712-328-8316; Email: schweitzerd@saintalbertschools.org; Web: www.saintalbertschools.org. David Schweitzer, Pres. Child care to Grade 12 diocesan regional Catholic school system. Lay Teachers 49; Priests 1; Students 668; Total Staff 133; Total Enrollment (PreK-12) 746.

St. Albert Middle & High School, 400 Gleason Ave., Council Bluffs, 51503. Tel: 712-328-2316; Fax: 712-328-8316; Email: schweitzerd@saintalbertschools.org; Web: saintalbertschools.org/. Cecilia Hallstrom, Office Mgr. Lay Teachers 27; Priests 1; Students 310; Total Staff 39.

St. Albert Elementary School, (Grades PreK-5), 400 Gleason Ave., Council Bluffs, 51503. Tel: 712-323-3703; Fax: 712-328-2316; Email: jensena@saintalbertschools.org; Web: saintalbertschools.org. Anne Jensen, Prin. Lay Teachers 25; Students 359.

HARLAN. *Elementary School: Shelby County Catholic School*, (Grades PreK-6), 2005 College Pl., Harlan, 51537. Tel: 712-755-5634; Fax: 712-755-3332; Email: jerlbach@shelcocath.com; Web: www.shelcocath.pvt.k12.ia.us. Ann Andersen, Prin.; Rev. John M. Frost, Canonical Admin.; Joanne Erlbacher, Business Mgr. Lay Teachers 11; Students 104; Total Staff 20; Religious Teachers 3.

WEST DES MOINES. *St. Joseph Educational Center*, 1400 Buffalo Rd., West Des Moines, 50265. Tel: 515-225-1092; Web: www.sjeciowa.org; Email: sjec.dsm@gmail.com. Deacon Matthew Halbach, Dir. Lay Teachers 2; Religious Teachers 1.

Religious Education, West Des Moines. Tel: 515-222-1084.

[B] COLLEGES AND UNIVERSITIES

DES MOINES. *Mercy College of Health Sciences* (1995) 928-6th Ave., 50309-1239. Tel: 515-643-3180; Fax: 515-643-6698; Email: ministry@mercydesmoines.org; Email: foundation@mercydesmoines.org; Web: www.mchs.edu. Douglas Fiore, Pres.; Nancy Kertz, Ph.D., A.P.R.N., Dean of Nursing; Jeannine Matz, Ph.D., Dean of Liberal Arts & Sciences; Robert Loch, Ph.D., Dean of Allied Health; Thomas Leahy, J.D., Vice Pres.; Jennifer Miller, Vice Pres.; Matthew Romkey, Vice Pres.; Anne Dennis, Sr. Dir. Human Resources; Bo Bonner, Dir. Mission and Ministry. Sponsored by Catholic Health Initiatives. Lay Teachers 60; Students 714; Total Staff 113.

[C] HIGH SCHOOLS, INTERPAROCHIAL

COUNCIL BLUFFS. *Saint Albert Catholic Schools*, 400 Gleason Ave., Council Bluffs, 51503. Tel: 712-329-9000; Fax: 712-328-0228; Email: businessoffice@saintalbertschools.org; Web: www.saintalbertschools.org. Paul Hans, Prin. (6-12); Anne Jensen, Prin. (PreK-5); David Schweitzer, Pres. Serving all parishes in Council Bluffs; St. Patrick, Missouri Valley; St. Patrick, Neola; Holy Rosary, Glenwood; St. Columbanus, Weston. Lay Teachers 52; Priests 1; Students 698; Total Staff 84.

WEST DES MOINES. *Dowling Catholic High School*, 1400 Buffalo Rd., West Des Moines, 50265. Tel: 515-225-3000; Fax: 515-222-1056; Email: dryan@dowlingcatholic.org; Web: www.dowlingcatholic.org. Dr. Dan Ryan, Pres.; Matt Meedering, Prin.; Carol Aina, Registrar; Rev. Zachary Kautzky, Chap.; Megan Anderson, Librarian. Serving all parishes in Des Moines; Sacred Heart, West Des Moines; St. Francis of Assisi, West Des Moines; St. Boniface, Waukee; Assumption, Granger; St. John, Cumming; St. Mary, Elkhart; Holy Cross, Elkhart; SS. John and Paul, Altoona; Immaculate Heart, Ankeny; St. Luke the Evangelist, Ankeny; St. John, Adel; St. John the Apostle, Norwalk; St. Pius X, Urbandale. Lay Teachers 96; Clergy/Religious Teachers 1; Students 1,406.

[D] GENERAL HOSPITALS

DES MOINES. *Mercy Medical Center*, 1111 Sixth Ave., 50314-2611. Tel: 515-247-3121; Fax: 515-247-4259; Email: wenman@mercydesmoines.org; Web: www.mercydesmoines.org. Bob Ritz, Pres.; Rev. Anthony Adibe, C.S.Sp. Catholic Health Initiatives Denver, CO. Bed Capacity 802; Tot Asst. Annually 1,504,820; Total Staff 7,100.

Iowa Heart Center.

Mercy Children's Hospital & Clinics.

Mercy Clinics, Inc.

Mercy Court.

Mercy College of Health Sciences, 928 6th Ave., 50309-1239. Tel: 515-643-3180; Email: ministry@mercydesmoines.org; Web: www.mchs.edu. Barbara Q. Decker, J.D., Pres.

Mercy Foundation.

Mercy Foundation of Des Moines dba Mercy Foundation, Bishop Drumm Retirement Center, Mercy Hospice-Johnston.

Mercy Hospice and Home Care.

Mercy Park Apartments.

Mercy Professional Practice Associates.

Clark Street House of Mercy, 1409 Clark St., 50314. Tel: 515-643-6588. Rebecca Peterson, Dir.

Graduate Medical Education.

CORNING. *Alegent Health Mercy Hospital*, 603 Rosary Dr., Corning, 50841. Tel: 641-322-3121; Fax: 651-322-4872; Email: info@alegent.org. Debra Goldsmith, Pres. Bed Capacity 14; Tot Asst. Annually 3,749; Total Staff 92.

COUNCIL BLUFFS. *CHI Health: Mercy Hospital*, 800 Mercy Dr., Council Bluffs, 51503. Tel: 712-328-5000; Web: info@alegent.org; Web: www.alegent.org. Marie Knedler, Pres.; Colleen Leise, Div. Mgr. Pastoral Care. Bed Capacity 146; Distinct Patients (Inpatient & Outpatient) 30,947; Total Staff 591.

MISSOURI VALLEY. **Alegent Health Community Hospital of Missouri Valley, IA*, 631 N. 8th St., Missouri Valley, 51555. Tel: 712-642-2784; Email: info@alegent.org. Ms. Kandy Do, Admin. Bed Capacity 25; Distinct Patients (Inpatient & Outpatient) 6,275; Total Staff 119.

[E] HOMES FOR AGED

JOHNSTON. *Bishop Drumm Retirement Center* (1939) 5837 Winwood Dr., Johnston, 50131-1651. Tel: 515-270-1100; Fax: 515-276-1714; Email: heather.rehmer@chilivingcomm.org; Web: www.homeishere.org. Mrs. Heather Rehmer, Exec.; Adam Braden, Admin.; April Young, Chap. CHI Living Communities, a subsidiary of Catholic Health Initiatives Residents 74; Skilled Nursing Beds 128; Total Staff 250; Total Assisted 60. In Res. Rev. Thomas M. DeCarlo, Resident Chap.

McAuley Terrace Apts. (1981) 5921 Winwood Dr., Johnston, 50131-1670. Tel: 515-270-6640; Fax: 515-331-8875; Email: heather.rehmer@chilivingcomm.org; Web: homeishere.org. Mrs. Heather Rehmer, Dir. Bishop Drumm Retirement Center is part of CHI Living Communities, a subsidiary of Catholic Health Initiatives Independent Living 74.

Martina Place Assisted Living Residence (1997) 5815 Winwood Dr., Johnston, 50131-1666. Tel: 515-251-7999; Fax: 515-331-8860; Email: gail.christie@chilivingcomm.org; Web: homeishere.org. Mrs. Heather Rehmer, Dir. CHI Living Communities, a subsidiary of Catholic Health Initiatives Assisted Living Residents 60.

[F] SPECIAL CARE FACILITIES

DES MOINES. *House of Mercy*, 1409 Clark St., 50314-1964. Tel: 515-643-6500; Fax: 515-643-6598; Email: RPeterson@mercydesmoines.org; Web: houseofmercydesmoines.org. Rebecca Peterson, Dir. Substance abuse residential treatment. Bed Capacity 80; Tot Asst. Annually 2,500; Total Staff 100.

[G] SPIRITUAL MINISTRY TO THE DIOCESE

DES MOINES. *Emmaus House*, 1521 Center St., 50314. Tel: 515-282-4839; Email: Director@TheEmmausHouse.org; Web: www.TheEmmausHouse.org. Rev. Daniel F. Krettek, Co-Dir., (Retired); Mr. Kevin O'Donnell, Co-Dir.

[H] NEWMAN CENTERS

DES MOINES. *St. Catherine of Siena Catholic Student Center* (Drake Newman Community) 1150-28th St., 50311-4142. Tel: 515-271-4747; Fax: 515-271-1918; Email: office@stcatherinedrake.org; Email: campusminister@stcatherinedrake.org; Email: pastor@stcatherinedrake.org; Web: stcatherinedrake.org. Rev. Mark Owusu; Erin Smith, Campus Min.; Teresa Smith, Sec. Students 700; Non-Students 311.

[I] MISCELLANEOUS LISTINGS

DES MOINES. *Catholic Council for Social Concern* aka Catholic Charities, 601 Grand Ave., 50309. Tel: 515-237-5045; Tel: 515-237-5096; Fax: 515-237-5099; Email: sstarbuck@catholiccharitiesdm.org; Email: bdecker@catholiccharitiesdm.org; Web: www.CatholicCharitiesDM.org. Barbara Q. Decker, J.D., Exec.; Shelly Starbuck, Dir.

The Catholic Foundation of Southwest Iowa (2012) 601 Grand Ave., 50309. Tel: 515-237-5044; Email: cmccarville@catholicfoundationiowa.org; Web: www.catholicfoundationiowa.org. Rachel Seidl, Dir.; Chris McCarville, Exec.; Brooke Pulliam, Dir. Planned Giving.

Catholic Tuition Organization, Diocese of Des Moines, 601 Grand Ave., 50309. Tel: 515-237-5010; Fax: 515-237-5070; Email: jwells@dmdiocese.org. Jeanne Wells, Exec. Dir.

Dowling-St. Joseph Alumni Association Investment Co. L.L.C., 1400 Buffalo Rd., West Des Moines, 50265. Tel: 515-225-3000; Fax: 515-222-1056; Email: dryan@dowlingcatholic.org; Web: www.dowlingcatholic.org. Dr. Dan Ryan, Pres.

Dowling-St. Joseph Alumni Foundation, 1400 Buffalo Rd., West Des Moines, 50265. Tel: 515-225-3000; Fax: 515-222-1056; Email: dryan@dowlingcatholic.org; Web: www.dowlingcatholic.org. Brian Laurenzo, Pres.; Dr. Dan Ryan, Sec.

**St. Gabriel Communications* dba Iowa Catholic Radio, 2900 Westown Pkwy., Ste. 220, West Des Moines, 50266. Tel: 515-223-1150; Email: contact@kwky.com. Mr. Brian Sweeney, Business Mgr.

St. Gregory Centers Charitable Fund, Inc., 5875 Fleur Dr., 50321.

Holy Family School Inner-City Youth Foundation, P.O. Box 8437, 50301. Tel: 515-262-7466; Email: hfcsfoundation@gmail.com; Web: www.hfcsdm.org. Sarah Wiser, Admin.

Iowa Catholic Conference, 530-42nd St., 50312-2707. Tel: 515-243-6256; Fax: 515-243-6257; Email: info@iowacatholicconference.org; Web: www.iowacatholicconference.org. Thomas Chapman, Exec. Dir.

Life in the Spirit Community, Inc., Saint Ambrose Cathedral, 607 High St., 50309. 6815 Brookview Dr., Urbandale, 50322. Tel: 515-276-6614; Email: jos44eph@aol.com. Joe Russo, Contact Person.

Mercy Child Development Center, 6th & University, 50314. Tel: 515-243-6232. Diane Engelking, Dir.

Mercy Foundation of Des Moines - Affiliate of Catholic Health Initiatives, 411 Laurel St., Ste. 2250, 50314. Tel: 515-247-3248; Email: foundation@mercydesmoines.org; Web: foundation.mercydesmoines.org. Shannon Cofield, Pres.

Senior Housing Corporation - Diocese of Des Moines (2010) 601 Grand Ave., 50309. Tel: 515-237-5061; Email: jkurth@dmdiocese.org. Mr. Jason Kurth, Sec.

COUNCIL BLUFFS. *St. Albert Educational Foundation*, 400 Gleason Ave., Council Bluffs, 51503. Tel: 712-329-9000, Ext. 339; Fax: 712-328-0228; Email: faurotc@saintalbertschools.org; Web: www.saintalbertschools.org. Rev. Charles Kottas, Pastor; Martin Shudak, Chm.

Mercy Hospital Foundation, Council Bluffs, Iowa, 800 Mercy Dr., Council Bluffs, 51503. Tel: 712-328-5000; Fax: 712-325-2425; Email: info@alegent.org. Kathy Bertolini, Division Vice Pres. Philanthropy.

St. Joseph Catholic Cemetery Association, 1 Bluff St.,

Council Bluffs, 51503. Tel: 712-322-8889 (Office); Email: jeanthomas@cox.net. Rev. Charles Kottas, Mgr.

CUMMING. *City Hospital Chaplaincy Service*, 1495 Warren Ave., Cumming, 50061. Tel: 515-681-1746; Email: michael.mclaughlin1746@gmail.com. Rev. Michael R. McLaughlin. Serving all non-Catholic hospitals in Des Moines.

GRISWOLD. *Creighton University Retreat Center* (1967) 16493 Contrail Ave., Griswold, 51535.
Tel: 712-778-2466; Email: curc@netins.net; Web: www.creighton.edu/ministry/retreatcenter/. Amy K. Hoover, Dir. & Contact Person.

HARLAN. *Shelby County Catholic Education Foundation*, 2005 College Pl., Harlan, 51537.
Tel: 712-755-5634; Fax: 712-755-3332; Email: aanderse@shelcocath.pvt.k12.ia.us; Email: jerlbach@shelcocath.pvt.k12.ia.us; Web: shelcocath.pvt.k12.ia.us. Mrs. Ann Anderson, Admin.; Rev. John M. Frost, Canon. Admin.; Joanne Erlbacher, Bus. Mgr.

PANORA. *St. Thomas More Center*, 6177 Panorama Rd., Panora, 50216. Tel: 515-309-1936;
Fax: 515-309-1885; Email: office@stmcenter.com; Email: alex@stmcenter.com; Web: www.stmcenter.com. Rev. Ross Parker, Chap. Home of Catholic Youth Camp (Iowa).

WEST DES MOINES. *St. Francis of Assisi Roman Catholic School Foundation*, 7075 Ashworth Rd., West Des Moines, 50266. Tel: 515-223-4577;
Fax: 515-223-4768; Email: info@saintfrancischurch.org; Web: www.saintfrancischurch.org. Rev. Raymond McHenry, M.B.A., Pastor.

St. Thomas Classical Academy, 1723 Thornwood Rd., West Des Moines, 50265. Tel: 515-237-5046; Email: sriesberg@dmdiocese.org. Mrs. Wendy Ogden, Dir.

RELIGIOUS INSTITUTES OF MEN REPRESENTED IN THE DIOCESE

For further details refer to the corresponding bracketed number in the Religious Institutes of Men or Women section.

[0600]—*Brothers of the Congregation of the Holy Cross*—C.S.C.

[]—*Congregation of the Holy Ghost* (Nigeria).

[0690]—*Jesuit Fathers and Brothers* (Wisconsin Prov.)—S.J.

[0430]—*Order of Preachers-Dominicans*—O.P.

[0200]—*Order of St. Benedict* (Conception, MO)—O.S.B.

RELIGIOUS INSTITUTES OF WOMEN REPRESENTED IN THE DIOCESE

[2100]—*Congregation of the Holy Humility of Mary*—C.H.M.

[]—*Congregation of the Little Missionaries of the Sacred Heart*—L.M.S.H.

[]—*Franciscan Sisters of Perpetual Adoration*—F.S.P.A.

[2575]—*Institute of the Sisters of Mercy of the Americas* (Cedar Rapids, IA; Omaha, NE; Chicago, IL)—R.S.M.

[]—*Missionary Catechists of the Sacred Heart of Jesus and Mary*.

[]—*Order of St. Clare (Poor Sisters of St. Clare)*—O.S.C.

[1680]—*School Sisters of St. Francis*—O.S.F.

[3580]—*Servants of Mary*—O.S.M.

[]—*Servants of the Immaculate Heart of Mary*—I.H.M.

[]—*Sisters for Christian Community*—S.F.C.C.

[0430]—*Sisters of Charity of the Blessed Virgin Mary*—B.V.M.

[3320]—*Sisters of Presentation of the Blessed Virgin Mary*—P.B.V.M.

[1540]—*Sisters of Saint Francis* (Clinton, IA)—O.S.F.

[1705]—*The Sisters of St. Francis of Assisi*—O.S.F.

[1570]—*Sisters of St. Francis of the Holy Family*—O.S.F.

An asterisk (*) denotes an organization that has established tax-exempt status directly with the IRS and is not covered by the USCCB Group Ruling.

Archdiocese of Detroit

(Archidioecesis Detroitensis)

His Eminence

ADAM CARDINAL MAIDA, J.C.L., J.D., S.T.L.

Archbishop Emeritus of Detroit; ordained May 26, 1956; appointed to Green Bay November 8, 1983; consecrated January 25, 1984; installed as Archbishop of Detroit June 12, 1990; created Cardinal on November 26, 1994; retired January 5, 2009.

Most Reverend

THOMAS J. GUMBLETON, D.D.

Retired Auxiliary Bishop of Detroit; ordained June 2, 1956; appointed Auxiliary Bishop of Detroit and Titular Bishop of Ululi March 8, 1968; consecrated May 1, 1968; retired February 2, 2006. *Office: 12 State St., Detroit, MI 48226.*

Most Reverend

FRANCIS R. REISS, D.D.

Retired Auxiliary Bishop of Detroit; ordained June 4, 1966; appointed Auxiliary Bishop of Detroit and Titular Bishop of Remesiana July 7, 2003; consecrated August 12, 2003; retired November 11, 2015. *Office: 12 State St., Detroit, MI 48226.*

Most Reverend

DONALD FRANCIS HANCHON

Auxiliary Bishop of Detroit; ordained October 19, 1974; appointed Auxiliary Bishop of Detroit and Titular Bishop of Horreomargum March 22, 2011; consecrated May 5, 2011. *Office: 4311 Central Ave., Detroit, MI 48210-2785.*

Most Reverend

ALLEN H. VIGNERON, D.D.

Archbishop of Detroit; ordained July 27, 1975; appointed Auxiliary Bishop of Detroit and Titular Bishop of Sault Ste. Marie June 12, 1996; consecrated July 9, 1996; appointed Coadjutor Bishop of Oakland January 10, 2003; installed February 26, 2003; succeeded to See October 1, 2003; appointed Archbishop of Detroit January 5, 2009; installed January 28, 2009.

Archbishop's Office: 12 State St., Detroit, MI 48226. Tel: 313-237-5816; Fax: 313-237-4642.

Most Reverend

JOSE ARTURO CEPEDA ESCOBEDO

Auxiliary Bishop of Detroit; ordained June 1, 1996; appointed Auxiliary Bishop of Detroit and Titular Bishop of Tagase April 18, 2011; consecrated May 5, 2011. *Office: 241 Pearson St., Ferndale, MI 48220-1824.*

Most Reverend

ROBERT JOSEPH FISHER

Auxiliary Bishop of Detroit; ordained June 27, 1992; appointed Titular Bishop of Forum Popilii and Auxiliary Bishop of Detroit November 23, 2016; installed January 25, 2017. *Office: 23965 23 Mile Rd., Macomb, MI 48042-4511.*

Most Reverend

GERARD WILLIAM BATTERSBY

Auxiliary Bishop of Detroit; ordained May 30, 1998; appointed Titular Bishop of Eguga and Auxiliary Bishop of Detroit November 23, 2016; installed January 25, 2017. *Office: 35637 Cherry Hill Rd., Westland, MI 48186-3474.*

Square Miles 3,901.

Established March 8, 1833; Created An Archbishopric August 3, 1937.

Comprises the Counties of Lapeer, Macomb, Monroe, Oakland, St. Clair and Wayne.

For legal titles of parishes and archdiocesan institutions, consult the Archbishop's Office.

STATISTICAL OVERVIEW

Personnel	
Retired Cardinals	1
Archbishops	1
Auxiliary Bishops	4
Retired Bishops	2
Priests: Diocesan Active in Diocese	225
Priests: Diocesan Active Outside Diocese	5
Priests: Retired, Sick or Absent	112
Number of Diocesan Priests	342
Religious Priests in Diocese	205
Total Priests in Diocese	547
Extern Priests in Diocese	46
Ordinations:	
Diocesan Priests	3
Religious Priests	1
Transitional Deacons	3
Permanent Deacons	7
Permanent Deacons in Diocese	217
Total Brothers	73
Total Sisters	718
Parishes	
Parishes	218
With Resident Pastor:	
Resident Diocesan Priests	160
Resident Religious Priests	23
Without Resident Pastor:	
Administered by Priests	14
Pastoral Centers	1
New Parishes Created	1
Closed Parishes	5
Professional Ministry Personnel:	
Brothers	11
Sisters	51
Lay Ministers	671
Welfare	
Catholic Hospitals	9
Total Assisted	2,024,722
Health Care Centers	2
Total Assisted	2,655
Homes for the Aged	21
Day Care Centers	1
Total Assisted	232
Specialized Homes	15
Total Assisted	12,945
Special Centers for Social Services	28
Total Assisted	33,225
Other Institutions	8
Total Assisted	10,864
Educational	
Seminaries, Diocesan	2
Students from This Diocese	36
Students from Other Diocese	80
Diocesan Students in Other Seminaries	3
Seminaries, Religious	2
Students Religious	22
Total Seminarians	61
Colleges and Universities	3
Total Students	9,893
High Schools, Diocesan and Parish	4
Total Students	1,478
High Schools, Private	18
Total Students	7,976
Elementary Schools, Diocesan and Parish	59
Total Students	16,861
Elementary Schools, Private	3
Total Students	1,208
Catechesis/Religious Education:	
High School Students	3,396
Elementary Students	39,544
Total Students under Catholic Instruction	80,417
Teachers in the Diocese:	
Priests	45
Brothers	12
Sisters	31
Lay Teachers	2,129
Vital Statistics	
Receptions into the Church:	
Infant Baptism Totals	6,604
Minor Baptism Totals	383
Adult Baptism Totals	384
Received into Full Communion	743
First Communions	7,347
Confirmations	7,727
Marriages:	
Catholic	1,621
Interfaith	498
Total Marriages	2,119
Deaths	7,554
Total Catholic Population	1,130,271
Total Population	4,273,000

Former Bishops—Rt. Revs. FREDERIC RESE, D.D., cons. Oct. 6, 1833; resigned Aug. 19, 1840; died Dec. 30, 1871; PETER PAUL LEFEVERE, D.D., cons. Nov. 22, 1841; Bishop of Zela, coadjutor and admin. of Detroit; died March 4, 1869; CASPAR HENRY BORGESS, D.D., cons. April 24, 1870; Bishop of Calydon, coadjutor and admin. of Detroit; became Bishop of Detroit Dec. 30, 1871; resigned April 16, 1887; died May 3, 1890; JOHN SAMUEL FOLEY, D.D., cons. Nov. 4, 1888; died Jan. 5, 1918; Most Rev. MICHAEL JAMES GALLAGHER, D.D., cons. Sept. 8, 1915; Bishop of Tipasa, coadjutor of Grand Rapids; became Bishop of Grand Rapids Dec. 26, 1916; transferred to Detroit July 18, 1918; died Jan. 20, 1937; His Eminence EDWARD CARDINAL MOONEY, D.D., appt. Apostolic Delegate in India Jan. 8, 1926; appt. Titular Archbishop of Irenopolis Jan. 18, 1926; cons. Jan. 31, 1926; appt. Apostolic Delegate in Japan Feb. 25, 1931; transferred to the Diocese of Rochester Aug. 28, 1933; transferred to the Archdiocese of Detroit Aug. 3, 1937; created Cardinal Priest of the title of S. Susanna Feb. 18, 1946; died Oct. 25, 1958; JOHN CARDINAL DEARDEN, D.D., S.T.D., ord. Dec. 8, 1932; cons. Titular Bishop of Sarepta and Coadjutor Bishop of Pittsburgh Dec. 22, 1950; installed Archbishop of Detroit Jan. 29, 1959; created Cardinal April 28, 1969; resigned as Archbishop July 15, 1980; died Aug. 1, 1988; EDMUND CARDINAL SZOKA, J.C.L., D.D., Archbishop Emeritus of Detroit; ord. June 5, 1954; appt. Bishop of Gaylord June 15, 1971; cons. July 20, 1971; installed July 20, 1971; promoted to See of Detroit March 28, 1981; installed May 17, 1981; created Cardinal June 28, 1988; appt. Pres., Prefecture for Economic Affairs of the Holy See June 25, 1990; Pres., Pontifical Commission for Vatican City State Oct. 14, 1997; Pres. emeritus of the Pontifical Commission for Vatican City State; Pres. of the government of Vatican City State Feb. 22, 2001; resigned Sept. 15, 2006; died Aug. 20, 2014.; ADAM CARDINAL MAIDA, J.C.L., J.D., S.T.L., ord. May 26, 1956; appt. to Green Bay Nov. 8, 1983; cons. Jan. 25, 1984; installed as Archbishop of Detroit June 12, 1990; created Cardinal on Nov. 26, 1994; retired Jan. 5, 2009.

College of Consultors—Rev. BRIAN K. COKONOUGHER; Rev. Msgr. H. THOMAS JOHNSON; Rev. GERALD A. MCENHILL; Rev. Msgrs. MICHAEL HRYDZIUSZKO; MICHAEL C. LEFEVRE; ROBERT J. MCCLORY; Rev. ANTHONY RICHTER; Rev. Msgrs. DANIEL J. TRAPP; JOHN P. ZENZ.

Presbyteral Council—Revs. PAUL K. BALLIEN, Chair; DOUGLAS BIGNALL; ROBERT H. BLONDELL, (Retired); Rev. Msgr. JOHN G. BUDDE; Revs. DAVID A. BUERSMEYER; JAMES E. COMMYN; JEFFREY DAY; MARC A. GAWRONSKI; PATRICK GONYEAU, Vice Chair; JOSEPH R. HORN; Rev. Msgrs. MICHAEL HRYDZIUSZKO; H. THOMAS JOHNSON; Revs. JAMES F. KEAN; ALEXANDER KRATZ, O.F.M.; SHAFIQUE

MASIH; TIMOTHY P. MAZUR; CHRISTOPHER MUER; ROMAN PASIECZNY; Very Rev. SALVATORE PALAZZOLO; Revs. PHILIP PAXTON, C.P.; JOHN PHELPS, C.Ss.R.; EDWARD J. PRUS, (Retired); Very Rev. Canon WALTER J. PTAK; Revs. ANTHONY RICHTER; PAUL M. SNYDER; ROBERT R. SPEZIA; DAVID M. TOMASZYCKI; Rev. Msgr. DANIEL J. TRAPP; Revs. RICHARD L. TREML; MICHAEL A. WORONIEWICZ; EDWARD F. ZAORSKI.

Archdiocesan Vicars Forane—Revs. PAUL K. BALLIEN, Northwest Wayne; DOUGLAS BIGNALL, Central Macomb; Rev. Msgr. JOHN G. BUDDE, Lakes; Revs. JAMES E. COMMYN, Serf; MARC A. GAWRONSKI, Southwest; ALEXANDER KRATZ, O.F.M., Genesis; JAMES F. KEAN, Pontiac Area; SHAFIQUE MASIH, Renaissance; ROMAN PASIECZNY, North Macomb; Very Rev. SALVATORE PALAZZOLO, Blue Water; Rev. JOHN PHELPS, C.Ss.R., Trinity; Very Rev. Canon WALTER J. PTAK, West Wayne; Revs. PAUL M. SNYDER, South Oakland; RICHARD L. TREML, Thumb; MICHAEL A. WORONIEWICZ, Monroe; EDWARD F. ZAORSKI, Downriver.

Archdiocesan Pastoral Council—MR. LUIS AGUIRRE, At-Large; MRS. JACLYN ALLOR, Central Macomb; MS. MARILYN BACHELOR, At-Large; MR. ROBERT BARRETTE JR., SERF; MR. NICKOLAS CRAANEN, Monroe; MS. TRESSA KOMARA, Southwest; MR. RICHARD LARKINS, Renaissance; MR. MARK NEMECEK, At-Large; MRS. KYM NUMMER, Vice Chair, At-Large; MR. RICHARD RICE, Northwest Wayne; MR. WALTER ROBERTS, North Macomb; MR. JAMES TINGAY, Thumb. Contact: MRS. LORY MCGLINNEN, Dir., Parish Life & Svcs., Tel: 313-237-5934.

Archdiocesan Departments and Offices

General Information and Reference—Tel: 313-237-5800

Office of the Archbishop—All official mail should be directed to this office. *12 State St., Detroit, 48226.* Tel: 313-237-5816; Fax: 313-237-4642. Rev. JAMES CHRISTOPHER GRAU, Personal Sec. to Archbishop.

Moderator of the Curia—Rev. JEFFREY DAY, Tel: 313-237-5783; Fax: 313-237-4642; MRS. KRISTA BAJOKA, Adjunct to Moderator of the Curia, Tel: 313-596-7147; Fax: 313-237-4642; MR. MARCO DECAPITE, Adjunct to Moderator of the Curia for Technology, Tel: 313-596-7157; Fax: 775-361-1541.

Office of the Chancellor—MR. MICHAEL R. TRUEMAN, Chancellor, Tel: 313-237-5847; Fax: 313-237-4643; Fax: 313-237-4642.

Archives—Tel: 313-237-5864; Fax: 313-596-7199. MR. STEVEN WEJROCH, Archivist.

Marriage Permissions/Dispensations—Rev. PAUL CZARNOTA, J.D., J.C.L., Tel: 313-237-5848; Fax: 313-237-4642.

The Metropolitan Tribunal—12 State St., Detroit, 48226. Tel: 313-237-5865; Fax: 313-237-5872. Office Hours: Mon.-Fri. 8:30-4:30.

Judicial Vicar—Rev. Msgr. RONALD T. BROWNE, J.C.L.

Adjutant Judicial Vicar—Rev. ROBERT HAYES WILLIAMS, J.C.L.

Administrative Director—VACANT.

Judges—Revs. TIMOTHY F. BABCOCK, (Retired); JAMES L. BJORUM, J.C.L.; MRS. HEIDI KRUPP-GONZALES, J.C.L.; Revs. JEROME SLOWINSKI, J.C.L.; THOMAS E. URBAN, J.C.L.

Defenders of Bond—Revs. PAUL CZARNOTA, J.D., J.C.L.; MICHAEL LOYSON; MRS. PATRICIA MKRTUMIAN.

Advocates—Rev. RONALD J. JOZWIAK; Rev. Msgr. MICHAEL C. LEFEVRE; Revs. MICHAEL MOLNAR, J.C.L.; NORMAN D. NAWROCKI, J.C.L.; EDWARD PETERS, J.C.D., Other priests, deacons and certified lay advocates (ad actum).

Notaries—MR. ADAM DWORNICK; MS. JACQUELINE L. LOVE; MRS. DOLORES PAULL; MS. LINDSAY MARTINEZ; MRS. ALLISON KOT; MS. SONIA LOPEZ.

Coordinator of Administrative Support Staff—MS. JACQUELINE L. LOVE.

Office for Clergy and Consecrated Life—12 State St., Detroit, 48226. Tel: 313-596-7155; Fax: 313-237-4643. Rev. ROBERT R. SPEZIA, Episcopal Vicar, Dir.

Permanent Diaconate Program—Deacon KEVIN BREEN, Assoc. Dir., Tel: 313-596-7142; Fax: 313-237-4643.

Delegate for Consecrated Life—Sr. ROSE MARIE KUJAWA, C.S.S.F., Tel: 313-596-7143.

Immigration Legal Services for Clergy, Consecrated Life and Schools—MS. VIVIANA LANDE, Esq., Immigration Lawyer, 12 State St., Detroit, 48226. Tel: 313-596-7148.

Office of Priestly Vocations—Rev. JOSEPH R. HORN, Dir., 2701 Chicago Blvd., Detroit, 48206. Tel: 313-237-5875; Fax: 313-883-6070; MS. CARRIE KUHAR, Prog. Coord., Fax: 313-237-5839.

Department of Communications—12 State St., Detroit, 48226. Tel: 313-237-5943; Fax: 313-237-4644. MR. EDMUNDO REYES.

Public Relations—MR. NED MCGRATH, Dir., Tel: 313-237-4677; Fax: 313-237-4644.

Media Relations—MS. HOLLY FOURNIER, Mgr., Tel: 313-237-5802; Fax: 313-237-4644; MS. PATRICIA MALDONADO, Dir. Opers., Tel: 313-237-5938; Fax: 313-237-5928; MR. MICHAEL STECHSCHULTE, The Detroit Catholic, Mng. Editor, Tel: 313-596-7109.

Office of Printing and Publications—MR. BOB PAWLAK, Dir., Tel: 313-237-5967; Fax: 313-965-8471.

Department of Development and Stewardship—MR. DAVID KELLEY, Dir., 12 State St., Detroit, 48226. Tel: 313-596-7400; Fax: 313-883-8785.

Planned Giving—MR. THOMAS P. SCHOLLER, Assoc. Dir. Devel. & Stewardship, Tel: 313-596-7408.

Special Services—Deacon DAVID P. CASNOVSKY, Assoc. Dir., Tel: 313-596-7412.

Institutional Advancement—MR. DAVID ZANITSCH, Dir., Tel: 313-596-7421; MS. CATHLEEN ARSENAULT, Annual Giving Mgr., Tel: 313-596-7422; MR. JONATHAN FRANCIS, Communications Mgr., Tel: 313-596-7425; MRS. EMILY BERSCHBACK, Event Mgr., Tel: 313-596-7424.

Charitable Gift Planning—MR. DARREN HOGAN, Assoc. Dir., Tel: 313-596-7404.

Major Gifts—MRS. MARITA COWAN, Assoc. Dir., Tel: 313-596-7409.

Catholic Services Appeal—MS. THERESA J. KACH, Assoc. Dir., Tel: 313-596-7405.

Development Services—MS. JESSICA I. ORZECHOWSKI, Mgr., Tel: 313-596-7407.

Department of Evangelization, Catechesis and Schools—12 State St., Detroit, 48226. Tel: 313-596-7140; Fax: 313-237-5867. Rev. STEPHEN PULLIS, Dir.

Office of Catholic Schools—MR. KEVIN KIJEWSKI, J.D., Supt., Tel: 313-237-5775. Regional Associate Superintendents: DR. KAREN WHITE, Tel: 313-237-5776; MS. MELISSA LIPSMEIER, Tel: 313-237-5772; MR. JAMES ABERCROMBIE, Tel: 313-237-4654.

Health, Athletics and Physical Safety—Tel: 313-237-5960. MR. VICTOR MICHAELS, Admin.; MR. MICHAEL EVOY, Assoc. Admin.

Office of Evangelization—Tel: 313-237-5908. MR. NICHOLAS JORGENSEN, Assoc. Dir. Evangelization.

Office of Catechesis—Tel: 313-237-4667. Sr. KATHLEEN MATZ, C.D.P., Assoc. Dir. Catechesis.

Ministerial Certification—Tel: 313-596-7312. SEAN CALVIN, Assoc. Dir. Ministerial Certification.

Marriage and Family Life—MR. DAVID P. GROBBEL, Assoc. Dir.; MS. GRETCHEN MENA, Natural Family Planning, Tel: 313-237-5894.

Cultural Ministries—MR. LEON DIXON, Coord. Black Catholic Ministries, Tel: 313-596-7103; MRS. KARLA FLORES, Coord. Hispanic Ministries, Tel: 313-596-7309.

Youth, Young Adults and Campus Ministries—MS. LAURA PICCONE HANCHON, Assoc. Dir. Youth Ministry, Tel: 313-237-5953; MR. PATRICK HOWARD, Young Adult Campus Liaison; Revs. JOHN FLETCHER, C.C., Wayne State Univ. Campus Min., Tel: 313-577-3462; ANTHONY FOX, O.F.M.Conv., UM-Dearborn Campus Min., Tel: 313-271-6000.

Department of Finance and Administration—MR. RICHARD AUSTIN, Dir., 12 State St., Detroit, 48226. Tel: 313-237-5834; Fax: 313-237-5868; MR. FREDERICK BARTEL, Treas., Tel: 313-596-7132.

Audit and Business Management—MRS. FRANCES ASHE, Dir., Tel: 313-237-5903.

Accounting Services—MR. DONALD GENOTTI, Controller, Tel: 313-237-5825.

Audit/Financial Services—MR. MICHAEL FELCYN, Mgr., Tel: 313-596-7163; MR. MICHAEL SMYKOWSKI, Assoc. Dir., Tel: 313-237-5841.

Office of Facilities Services - Sacred Heart Major Seminary and Cathedral Campus—MR. JOHN DUNCAN, Dir., Tel: 313-883-8599; Fax: 313-883-8699; Deacon LAZARUS DER-GHAZARIAN, Assoc. Dir., Tel: 313-883-8506.

Office of Real Estate—MS. JILL HAINES, Assoc. Dir. Real Estate, Tel: 313-596-7139; Fax: 313-237-5791; MR. MICHAEL MCINERNEY, Consultative Dir. Archdiocesan Properties, Tel: 313-237-5830; Fax: 313-237-5791; MR. FRANK MACDONELL, Contractor, PMNet Bldgs., Tel: 313-237-5829; Fax: 313-596-7187.

Department of Process, Data and Technology—Blue Rock Technologies, Contractual. Tel: 313-237-5797; Fax: 313-237-5979.

Department of Human Resources—MS. CHANTALE STEVENSON, Dir., 12 State St., Detroit, 48226. Tel: 313-237-5948; Fax: 313-596-7194.

Human Resources Manager—MS. ERIN TAFT, Tel: 313-596-7156; Fax: 313-596-7478; Rev. Msgr. G. MICHAEL BUGARIN, Episcopal Vicar, Archbishop's Delegate to the Archdiocesan Review Bd.

Safe Environments—MS. SHARON GORMAN, Coord., Tel: 313-596-5826; Fax: 313-596-7197.

Department of Parish Life—

Office of Pastoral Planning and Leadership Services—MR. ANTHONY LATARSKI, Assoc. Dir. & Regl. Coord. Pastoral Planning and Leadership Svcs., Tel: 313-237-5765; Fax: 313-237-5869; MS. MARY MARTIN, Regl. Coord., Tel: 313-237-7327; MS. CHRISTINA HALL, Regl. Coord., Tel: 313-237-4650; MR. GIANLUCA SPERONE, Data Analyst; MS. MEGAN TYMRAK, Mapping and Surveys Coord., Tel: 313-237-8011.

Office of Christian Worship—MR. DANIEL MCAFEE, Dir., Tel: 313-237-4697; Fax: 313-237-5869; Sr. GEORGETTE ZALESKA, Coord., Tel: 313-237-6064; MR. JOSEPH BALISTRERI, Coord. Worship & Music, Tel: 313-237-5782; MS. STACEY MASON, Coord. Music Ministries - St. John Ctr., Tel: 734-414-1161; Fax: 734-414-1150.

Christian Service and Health Care Ministries—MS. JOYCE HYTTINEN, Dir. Catholic Charities of Southeast Michigan, Tel: 313-237-5905; Fax: 313-237-5869.

Ecumenical/Interfaith Relations—Rev. Msgr. JOHN C. KASZA, Archbishop's Ecumenical/Interfaith Advisor, St. James Parish, 46325 W. 10 Mile Rd., Novi, 48374; MR. DAVID J. CONRAD, Coord., Tel: 313-237-4678; Fax: 313-237-5869.

Victim Assistance Coordinator—MS. MARGARET A. HUGGARD, M.S.W., Tel: 866-343-8055.

Promoter of Ministerial Standards—MS. INA GRANT, Tel: 313-237-4813; Fax: 313-237-5844.

Propagation of the Faith (Missions)Rev. Msgr. JAMES A. MOLONEY, P.A., 17650 W. Outer Dr., Dearborn Heights, 48127. Tel: 313-237-5807.

Association of the Holy Childhood—17650 W. Outer Dr., Dearborn Heights, 48127. Tel: 313-237-5807. Rev. Msgr. JAMES A. MOLONEY, P.A.

Catholic Youth Organization—12 State St., Detroit, 48226. Tel: 313-963-7172; Fax: 313-963-7179. MS. CHRISTOPHER WERNER, Dir.

Archdiocesan Theological Commission—Rev. Msgr. ROBERT J. MCCLORY, Tel: 313-237-5783.

Priests Conference for Polish Affairs of the Archdiocese of Detroit—Rev. STANLEY A. ULMAN, Pres.

CLERGY, PARISHES, MISSIONS AND PAROCHIAL SCHOOLS

CITY OF DETROIT

(WAYNE COUNTY)

1—CATHEDRAL, CHURCH OF THE MOST BLESSED SACRAMENT
Tel: 313-865-6300; Fax: 313-867-4613; Email: cathedral@aod.org; Web: cathedral.aod.org. Revs. John J. Mech, Rector; Patrick Gonyeau.
Res.: 9844 Woodward Ave., 48202.
Catechesis Religious Program—Email: Graves.Yvonne@aod.org. Yvonne Graves, D.R.E. Students 16.

2—ALL SAINTS, Merged with St. Gabriel, Detroit.

3—ST. ALOYSIUS
1234 Washington Blvd., 48226. Tel: 313-237-5810; Fax: 313-963-9076; Email: st.al.office@gmail.com; Web: www.stalsdetroit.com. Rev. Loren Connell, O.F.M.
St. Dominic Outreach Center—4826 Lincoln, 48208. Tel: 313-831-6070; Fax: 313-831-1224; Email: stdominiccenter@aol.com. Sharon Jenkins, Dir.
Catechesis Religious Program—Students 19.

4—ST. ANDREW, (Polish), Merged into Our Lady Queen of Angels, Detroit.

5—SS. ANDREW AND BENEDICT
Tel: 313-381-1184; Fax: 313-381-0416; Email: smmparish@comcast.net. Rev. Edward F. Zaorski.
Res.: 2430 S. Beatrice St., 48217. Email: madazsiwallace@yahoo.com.
Catechesis Religious Program—Mary Ann Wallace, D.R.E. Students 26.

6—ST. ANTHONY, Merged with Our Lady of Sorrows, Detroit to form Good Shepherd, Detroit.

7—ST. ANTHONY, (Lithuanian), Merged into Divine Providence, Southfield.

8—ASSUMPTION GROTTO (1832) [CEM]
Tel: 313-372-0762; Fax: 313-372-2064; Email: grottorectory@ameritech.net; Web: www.assumptiongrotto.com. Revs. Eduard Perrone; John Christopher Bustamante.
Res.: 13770 Gratiot Ave., 48205.
Catechesis Religious Program—Students 25.

9—ST. AUGUSTINE AND ST. MONICA, Rev. Msgr. Daniel J. Trapp.
Res.: 4151 Seminole St., 48214.
Catechesis Religious Program—Students 9.

10—ST. BARTHOLOMEW, Merged with St. Rita, Detroit to form St. Bartholomew/St. Rita, Detroit.

11—ST. BARTHOLOMEW/ST. RITA, Closed. Merged into Our Lady Queen of Heaven, Detroit.

12—ST. BRENDAN, Closed. For inquiries for parish records contact the chancery.

13—ST. CATHERINE OF SIENA, Closed. For inquiries for parish records contact the chancery.

14—ST. CECILIA, Merged with St. Leo, Detroit to form St. Charles Lwanga, Detroit.

15—ST. CHARLES BORROMEO (1886) Bro. Raymond Stadmeyer, O.F.M.Cap.
Res.: 1491 Baldwin Ave., 48214. Tel: 313-331-0253; Fax: 313-331-4834; Email: stcharlesborremeodetroit@yahoo.com; Web: www.stcharleasdetroit.org.
Catechesis Religious Program—Students 47.

16—ST. CHARLES LWANGA, Merged with St. Leo and St. Cecilia
Tel: 313-933-6788; Fax: 313-933-1439; Email: Stcharleslwanga@outlook.com; Web: saintcharleslwanga.org. Rev. Theodore K. Parker.
Res.: 10400 Stoepel Ave., 48204.
Church: Livernois at Stearns, 48204.
Catechesis Religious Program—Patricia Dixon, D.R.E. Students 84.

17—CHRIST THE KING, Rev. Victor Clore; Deacons Christian Remus, Pastoral Min./Coord.; Joseph Urbiel, Faith Formation Dir.; Mrs. Maureen Northrup, M.S.W., Outreach.
Res.: 16805 Pierson, 48219. Tel: 313-532-1211; Fax: 313-532-1216; Email: christking@ameritech.net; Web: www.ChristTheKingCatholicDetroit.org.
Church: 20800 Grand River & Burt Rd., 48219.
School—Christ the King School, (Grades 1-8), 16800 Trinity, 48219. Tel: 313-532-1213; Fax: 313-532-1050 ; Email: alund.ctk@gmail.com; Email: schooloffice.ctk@gmail.com. Amanda Lund, Prin. Clergy 1; Lay Teachers 9; Students 140; Clergy / Religious Teachers 1; Parish Population 12.
St. Christine Christian Services—22261 Fenkell, 48223. Tel: 313-535-7272; Fax: 313-535-3439.
Catechesis Religious Program—Students 44.

18—ST. CHRISTINE, Closed. For inquiries for parish records contact the chancery.

19—ST. CHRISTOPHER, Merged with St. Thomas Aquinas, Detroit to form St. Christopher-St. Thomas Aquinas.

20—ST. CHRISTOPHER-ST. THOMAS AQUINAS, Closed. For inquiries for parish records contact the chancery.

21—CHURCH OF THE MADONNA, Merged with St. Benedict, Highland Park and St. Gregory the Great, Detroit to form St. Moses the Black, Detroit.

22—CORPUS CHRISTI (2006)
19800 Pembroke Ave., 48219-2145.
Tel: 313-537-5773; Email: corpuschristidetroit@comcast.net; Web: www.corpuschristi-detroit.org. Revs. Donald Archambault; Patrick Gonyeau; Deacon Paul Mueller, Pastoral Assoc.

23—ST. CUNEGUNDA
Tel: 313-843-4717; Fax: 313-841-4255; Email: saintbarbara@sbcglobal.net; Web: saintbarbarasaintcunegunda.org. Rev. Zbigniew Grankowski.
Res.: 5900 St. Lawrence Ave., 48210.
Catechesis Religious Program—Michael Peck, D.R.E. Students 105.

24—ST. ELIZABETH
Tel: 313-921-9225; Fax: 313-921-9475; Email: lovette4318@att.net. Rev. Norman P. Thomas, Admin.
Res.: 3138 E. Canfield Ave., 48207.
Catechesis Religious Program—Velma Coleman, D.R.E. Students 25.

25—ST. FRANCIS D'ASSISI, Merged with St. Hedwig, Detroit to form St. Francis D'Assisi-St. Hedwig, Detroit.

26—ST. FRANCIS D'ASSISI-ST. HEDWIG, Merged with St. Francis D'Assisi & St. Hedwig Parishes.
3245 Junction, 48210. Tel: 313-894-5409; Email: stfrancis.sthedwigparish@gmail.com; Web: www.stfrancis-sthedwig.com. Rev. Bernardo Cruz.
Res.: 4500 Wesson St., 48210.
Catechesis Religious Program—Students 241.

27—ST. FRANCIS DE SALES, Merged with Precious Blood, Detroit to form St. Peter Claver, Detroit.

28—ST. GABRIEL
8118 W. Vernor Hwy., 48209-1524.
Tel: 313-841-0753; Fax: 313-841-0916; Email: julia@archangel-gabriel.org; Web: www.archangel-gabriel.org. Rev. Marc A. Gawronski.
Catechesis Religious Program—
Tel: 313-841-0753, Ext. 400. Mrs. Allen Santisteban, D.R.E. Students 465.

29—ST. GEMMA GALGANI, Closed. For inquiries for parish records contact the chancery.

30—ST. GERARD, Merged with Immaculate Heart of Mary, Detroit to form Corpus Christi, Detroit.

31—GESU
17180 Oak Dr., 48221. Tel: 313-862-4400; Fax: 313-862-1083; Email: gesudet@aol.com; Web: gesudetroit.com. Revs. Peter Etzel; Phillip T. Cooke, S.J.; Sr. Angela Hibbard, I.H.M., Pastoral Assoc.
School—Gesu School, (Grades PreK-8), 17139 Oak Dr., 48221. Tel: 313-863-4677; Fax: 313-862-4395; Email: laurin.c@gesudetroit.org; Web: www.gesuschool.udmercy.edu/. Mrs. Christa Laurin, Prin. Lay Teachers 13; Students 281.
Catechesis Religious Program—Email: gesuamh@aol.com. Students 91.

32—GOOD SHEPHERD (2006) Merged with Our Lady Queen of Heaven, Detroit to form Our Lady Queen of Heaven-Good Shepherd, Detroit.

33—ST. GREGORY THE GREAT, Merged with Church of the Madonna, Detroit and St. Benedict, Highland Park to form St. Moses the Black, Detroit.

34—GUARDIAN ANGELS, Closed. For inquiries for parish records contact the chancery.

35—ST. HEDWIG, Merged with St. Francis D'Assisi, Detroit to form St. Francis D'Assisi-St. Hedwig, Detroit.

36—HOLY CROSS HUNGARIAN, (Hungarian)
Tel: 313-842-1133; Email: holycross1905@att.net; Web: www.holycrosshungarian.com. Revs. Barnabas G. Kiss, O.F.M.; Angelus Ligeti, O.F.M.
Res.: 8423 South St., 48209. Email: sztkereszt@comcast.net.
Catechesis Religious Program—Emma T. Mahar, D.R.E. Students 12.

37—HOLY FAMILY, (Italian)
641 Walter P. Chrysler Dr., 48226. Tel: 313-963-2046 ; Email: holyfamilypd@gmail.com; Web: www.holyfamilydetroitwebs.com. Rev. Giuseppe Licciardi, (Italy) Admin. Latin and Italian Mass

38—HOLY REDEEMER
Tel: 313-842-3450; Fax: 313-842-0539; Email: 1880mhredeemer@gmail.com. Revs. Dennis Walsh, S.O.L.T.; Anthony Blount; Mark Wendling, S.O.L.T., (Canada) In Res.
Res.: 1721 Junction Ave., 48209.
School—Holy Redeemer School, (Grades 1-8), 1711 Junction Ave., 48209. Tel: 313-841-5230; Email: hredeemer72@yahoo.com. Clergy 2; Lay Teachers 7; Students 164; Parish Population 1.
Catechesis Religious Program—Tel: 313-841-5230; Email: hredeemer72@yahoo.com. Marcela Solis, D.R.E. Students 520.

39—ST. HYACINTH (1907) (Polish)
3151 Farnsworth Ave., 48211. Tel: 313-922-1507; Email: st.hyacinth@att.net; Web: www.sainthyacinth.com. Rev. Janusz Iwan.

40—IMMACULATE HEART OF MARY, Merged with St. Gerard, Detroit to form Corpus Christi, Detroit.

41—ST. JUAN DIEGO PARISH
7800 Woodmont Ave., 48228. Tel: 313-584-7460; Fax: 313-584-6361. Rev. Jaime Hinojos.

42—ST. JOHN CANTIUS, (Polish), Closed. For inquiries for parish records contact the chancery.

43—ST. JOSAPHAT, (Polish), Merged with St. Joseph, Detroit and Sweetest Heart of Mary, Detroit to form Mother of Divine, Detroit.

44—ST. JOSEPH, Merged with St. Josaphat, Detroit and Sweetest Heart of Mary, Detroit to form Mother of Divine Mercy, Detroit.

45—ST. JOSEPH ORATORY PARISH St. Joseph Roman Catholic Church
1828 Jay St., 48207. Tel: 313-784-9152; Email: sjdetroit@institute-christ-king.org; Web: www.institute-christ-king.org/detroit. Rev. Canon Michael Stein, Rector; Rev. Adrian Sequeira.
Catechesis Religious Program—Students 52.

46—ST. JUDE
Tel: 313-527-0380; Fax: 313-527-3511; Email: stjudedetroit@hotmail.com; Web: www.stjudedetroit.org. Rev. Shafique Masih.
Res.: 15889 E. Seven Mile Rd., 48205.
Tel: 313-527-0380; Fax: 313-527-3511; Email: stjudedetroit@hotmail.com; Web: stjudedetroit.org.

47—ST. LADISLAUS, (Polish), Merged with St. Louis, Detroit & Transfiguration-Our Lady of Help of Christians, Detroit to become St. John Paul II, Detroit.

48—ST. LEO, Merged with St. Cecilia, Detroit to form St. Charles Lwanga, Detroit.

49—ST. LOUIS THE KING, Merged with St. Ladislaus, Detroit & Transfiguration-Our Lady of Help of Christians, Detroit to become St. John Paul II, Detroit.

50—ST. LUKE, Closed. For inquiries for parish records contact the chancery.

51—MARTYRS OF UGANDA, Closed. For inquiries for parish records contact the chancery.

52—ST. MARY
Tel: 313-961-8711; Fax: 313-961-4994; Email: rectory@oldstmarysdetroit.com; Web: www.oldstmarysdetroit.com. Rev. Wayne Epperly, C.S.Sp.
Res.: 646 Monroe Ave., 48226.
Catechesis Religious Program—

53—ST. MARY'S OF REDFORD
Mailing Address: 14601 Mansfield, 48227.
Tel: 313-273-1100; Email: stmaryspa@gmail.com. Rev. Charles M. Morris, Admin.
Catechesis Religious Program—Annette Wright, D.R.E. Students 25.

54—ST. MATTHEW
Tel: 313-884-4470; Fax: 313-884-4276; Email: stmatthew27@aol.com; Web: stmatthewdetroit.com. Rev. Duane R. Novelly.
Res.: 6021 Whittier Ave., 48224.
Catechesis Religious Program—

55—ST. MOSES THE BLACK
1125 Oakman Blvd., 48238. Tel: 313-868-4308; Email: cathedral@aod.org. Revs. John J. Mech; Patrick Gonyeau.
Res.: 9844 Woodward, 48202. Tel: 313-865-6300; Fax: 313-867-4613.
Catechesis Religious Program—Email: cubcake01@aol.com. Yvonne Graves, D.R.E. Students 35.

56—MOST HOLY TRINITY
Tel: 313-965-4450; Fax: 313-965-4453; Email: businessoffice@mhtdetroit.org; Web: mhtdetroit.org. Rev. Msgr. Charles G. Kosanke; Rev. Ryan J. Adams; Deacon Kenneth Fry; Mrs. Anne-Marie Marie Fry, Contact Person; Ms. Rebecca Vogel, Christian Svc. & Outreach Coord.
Res.: 1050 Porter St., 48226. Email: grace@mostholytrinityministries.org.
School—Most Holy Trinity School, (Grades 1-8), 1229 Labrosse, 48226. Tel: 313-961-8855; Fax: 313-961-5797; Email: businessoffice@mhtdetroit.org; Web: www.mhtdetroit.org. Christopher Camilleri, Prin. Lay Teachers 14; Students (K-8) 146; Parish Population 1.
Catechesis Religious Program— Classes held at Ste. Anne, Detroit.

57—MOTHER OF DIVINE MERCY
Tel: 313-831-6659; Fax: 313-831-8522; Email: MotherofDivineMercy2@gmail.com; Web: www.motherofdivinemercy.org. Rev. Gregory Tokarski; Deacon Joseph Lennon; Mark Baker, Business Mgr.
Res.: 4440 Russell St., 48207.
Catechesis Religious Program—Carol Sniezyk, D.R.E.

58—NATIVITY OF OUR LORD
Tel: 313-922-0033; Fax: 313-922-8553; Email: nativityol@sbcglobal.net; Web: nativitydetroit.org. Bro. Raymond Stadmeyer, O.F.M.Cap.; Frances Carnaghi, Pastoral Min./Coord.; Christine McLaughlin, Pastoral Min./Coord.
Res.: 5900 McClellan Ave., 48213.
Catechesis Religious Program—Students 35.

59—OUR LADY GATE OF HEAVEN, Closed. For inquiries for parish records please see St. Suzanne/Our Lady Gate of Heaven, Detroit.

60—OUR LADY HELP OF CHRISTIANS, (Polish), Merged with Transfiguration, Detroit to form Transfiguration-Our Lady Help of Christians, Detroit.

61—OUR LADY OF GOOD COUNSEL, Merged with St. Raymond, Detroit June 2011.

62—OUR LADY OF GUADALUPE
4329 Central St., 48210-2736. Tel: 313-841-0783; Tel: 586-596-2779. Rev. Adalberto Espinoza.
Catechesis Religious Program—4330 Central St., 48210. Students 270.

63—OUR LADY OF MT. CARMEL, Closed. For inquiries for parish records contact the chancery.

64—OUR LADY OF THE ROSARY
5930 Woodward Ave., 48202. Tel: 313-875-6011. Revs. Daniel J. Jones; Marko Djonovic.

65—OUR LADY QUEEN OF ANGELS, Merged with St. Stephen-Mary Mother of the Church, Detroit to form Our Lady of Guadalupe, Detroit.

66—OUR LADY QUEEN OF HEAVEN, Merged with Good Shepherd, Detroit to form Our Lady Queen of Heaven-Good Shepherd, Detroit.

67—OUR LADY QUEEN OF HEAVEN-GOOD SHEPHERD
Tel: 313-891-4553; Fax: 313-891-5782; Email: ladyofgoodshepherd@att.net; Web: www.ourladyofgoodshepherd.net. Revs. Michael C. Nkachukwu; Tyrone Robinson.
Res.: 8200 Rolyat Ave., 48234.
Catechesis Religious Program—Ms. Gayle Koyton, D.R.E. Students 6.

68—SS. PETER AND PAUL (West Side) (Polish)
Tel: 313-846-2222; Fax: 313-584-1484; Web: ssppdetroit.net. Rev. Jaroslaw Pilus.
Res.: 7685 Grandville Ave., 48228.
Catechesis Religious Program—Gloria Yarber, D.R.E. Students 25.

69—SS. PETER AND PAUL JESUIT
629 E. Jefferson Ave., 48226. Tel: 313-961-8077; Email: office@ssppjesuit.org; Web: www.ssppjesuit.org. 438 St. Antoine St., 48226. Revs. Gary R. Wright, S.J.; Timothy McCabe, S.J.; Mrs. Lydia

Maola, Business Mgr.; Ms. Mara Rutten, Parish Life Coord.; Julie Ford, Liturgy Dir.

70—ST. PETER CLAVER
13305 Grove Ave., 48235. Tel: 313-342-5292; Fax: 313-342-3513; Email: parishoffice@spcccdetroit.org; Web: www.spcccdetroit.org. Rev. John Phelps, C.Ss.R.

71—ST. PHILOMENA, Closed. For inquiries for parish records contact the chancery.

72—PRECIOUS BLOOD, Merged with St. Francis de Sales, Detroit to form St. Peter Claver, Detroit.

73—PRESENTATION/OUR LADY OF VICTORY
17305 Ashton Ave., 48219. Tel: 313-255-9000, Ext. 0; Email: hubertsand@sbcglobal.net. Rev. Stephen Burr; Deacon Hubert Sanders, Pastoral Admin.
Catechesis Religious Program—Email: hubertsanders60@icloud.com; Web: www.presentationourladyofvictory.org. Mrs. Wanda Sanders, D.R.E. Students 12.

74—ST. RAYMOND-OUR LADY OF GOOD COUNSEL
20103 Joann Ave., 48205. Tel: 313-527-0525; Fax: 313-527-9776; Email: infosaintraymond@gmail.com; Web: www.straymondolgc.org. Revs. Michael C. Nkachukwu; Tyrone Robinson.
Community Center—20055 Joann Ave., 48205. Tel: 313-372-0437.
Catechesis Religious Program—Students 14.

75—ST. RITA, Merged with St. Bartholomew, Detroit to form St. Bartholomew/St. Rita, Detroit.

76—SACRED HEART OF JESUS
Tel: 313-831-1356; Fax: 313-831-8603; Email: info@sacredheartdetroit.com; Email: npt@sacredheartdetroit.com; Web: www.sacredheartdetroit.com. Rev. Norman P. Thomas, Admin.
Res.: 1000 Eliot St., 48207.

77—ST. SCHOLASTICA
8201 W. Outer Drive, 48219. Revs. John Bolger; James Lowe, C.C.; John Fletcher, C.C.; Pierre Ingram, C.C.; Carlos Martins; Charles Orchard, C.C.; John Vandenakker, C.C.; Michael Minifie; Terence Donahue.
Res. & Church: 17320 Rosemont Ave., 48219.
Tel: 313-531-0140; Fax: 313-531-0739; Email: scholastica@sbcglobal.net; Web: stscholasticachurch.org.
Catechesis Religious Program—
Convent—17305 Ashton, 48219.

78—STE. ANNE DE DETROIT Ste. Anne Parish de Detroit, Rev. Msgr. Charles G. Kosanke; Rev. Ryan J. Adams; Deacon Kenneth Fry; Mrs. Anne-Marie Marie Fry, Pastoral Assoc.
Res.: 1000 Ste. Anne St., 48216-2027.
Tel: 313-496-1701; Fax: 313-496-0429; Email: businessoffice@steannedetroit.org; Web: ste-anne.org.
Catechesis Religious Program—Students 116.

79—ST. STEPHEN-MARY MOTHER OF THE CHURCH, Merged with Our Queen of Angels, Detroit to form Our Lady of Guadalupe, Detroit.

80—ST. SUZANNE/OUR LADY GATE OF HEAVEN
19321 West Chicago, 48228. Rev. Victor Clore.
Res.: 9357 Westwood Ave., 48228. Tel: 313-838-6780; Fax: 313-838-1063; Email: ssolgh@sbcglobal.net.

81—SWEETEST HEART OF MARY, [CEM] (Polish), Merged with St. Josaphat, Detroit and St. Joseph, Detroit to form Mother of Divine Mercy, Detroit.

82—ST. THOMAS AQUINAS, Merged with St. Christopher, Detroit to form St. Christopher-St. Thomas Aquinas, Detroit.

83—TRANSFIGURATION-OUR LADY HELP OF CHRISTIANS, Merged with St. Louis, Detroit & St. Ladislaus, Detroit to become St. John Paul II, Detroit.

OUTSIDE THE CITY OF DETROIT

ALGONAC, ST. CLAIR CO., ST. CATHERINE OF ALEXANDRIA, [CEM] Merged with Holy Cross, Marine City & St. Mark, Harsens Island to form Our Lady on the River, Marine City.

ALLEN PARK, WAYNE CO., ST. FRANCES CABRINI
Tel: 313-381-5601; Fax: 313-381-7837; Email: office@cabriniparish.com; Web: cabriniparish.org. Revs. Timothy P. Birney; Dominic Macioce.
Res.: 9000 Laurence Ave., Allen Park, 48101. Email: jillferraiuolo@gmail.com.
School—St. Frances Cabrini Elementary and Middle School, (Grades 1-8), 15300 Wick Ave., Allen Park, 48101. Tel: 313-928-6610; Fax: 313-928-8502; Email: lpacholski@cabrinicatholicschools.com. Ms. Lisa Pacholski, Admin. Lay Teachers 30; Students 373.
High School—St. Frances Cabrini High School, 15305 Wick Rd., Allen Park, 48101.
Tel: 313-388-0110; Email: dsweeney@cabrinicatholicschools.com. Donna Sweeney, Prin. Lay Teachers 28; Students 271.
Catechesis Religious Program—Tel: 313-928-4727; Email: scollins@cabriniparish.com. Shanon Collins, D.R.E. Students 291.

ALLENTON, ST. CLAIR CO., ST. JOHN THE EVANGELIST
P.O. Box 10, Allenton, 48002. Tel: 810-796-2926; Fax: 810-796-9713; Email: office@fmsaints.com; Web: fmsaints.com. Rev. Michael R. Gawlowski. Clustered with St. Cornelius, Dryden
Res.: 872 Capac Rd., Allenton, 48002. Email: secretaryst.john@yahoo.com.
Catechesis Religious Program—883A Capac Rd., Allenton, 48002. Tel: 810-395-2301; Email: faithformation-east@fmsaints.com. Christine Medly, D.R.E. Students 121.

ARMADA, MACOMB CO., ST. MARY MYSTICAL ROSE (1946)
24040 Armada Ridge Rd., Armada, 48005.
Tel: 586-784-5966; Web: www.stmarymysticalrose.org. Rev. George Patauave.
Catechesis Religious Program—
Tel: 586-784-5966, Ext. 107; Email: kglowicki@stmarymysticalrose.org. Kim Glowicki, D.R.E. Students 55.

AUBURN HILLS, OAKLAND CO.

1—ST. JOHN FISHER CHAPEL UNIVERSITY PARISH
3665 Walton Blvd., Auburn Hills, 48326.
Tel: 248-373-6457; Fax: 248-373-5479; Email: frontoffice@sjfcup.com; Web: stjohnfisherparish.org. Rev. Msgr. Michael C. LeFevre; Mr. Paul Borucki, Pastoral Assoc.; Mrs. Susan Buratto, Pastoral Assoc.; Andrew Peters, Campus Min.
Catechesis Religious Program—Tel: 248-373-3130; Email: familyfaithsharing@sjfcup.com. Kathleen Susalla Rochon, D.R.E. Students 146.

2—SACRED HEART
Tel: 248-852-4170; Fax: 248-852-5745; Email: sacredheartauburnhills@gmail.com; Web: esacredheart.org. Rev. Richard Cavellier, J.C.L.
Res.: 3400 S, Adams Rd., Auburn Hills, 48326.
Catechesis Religious Program—Email: maryalice.mike@sbcglobal.net. Michael Merlo, D.R.E. Students 40.

BELLEVILLE, WAYNE CO., ST. ANTHONY
Tel: 734-697-1211; Fax: 734-697-6217; Email: stanthony48111@yahoo.com; Web: www.stanthonybelleville.com. Rev. John J. Kiselica; Deacon John Burke.
Res.: 409 W. Columbia Ave., Belleville, 48111.
Catechesis Religious Program—Tel: 734-699-3373; Email: stanthonycf@yahoo.com. Ms. Joyce Hansen, D.R.E. Students 147.

BERKLEY, OAKLAND CO., OUR LADY OF LA SALETTE
Tel: 248-541-3762; Fax: 248-541-4250;
Fax: office@lasalette-church.org; Web: www.lasalette-church.org. Rev. Patrick J. Connell; Deacons Daniel M. Darga, Pastoral Assoc.; Clement Stankiewicz, Senior Active Deacon.
Res.: 2600 Harvard Rd., Berkley, 48072.
Catechesis Religious Program—Email: amascia@lasalette-church.org. Bro. Al Mascia, O.F.M., D.R.E. Students 95.

BEVERLY HILLS, OAKLAND CO., OUR LADY QUEEN OF MARTYRS
32340 Pierce St., Beverly Hills, 48025.
Tel: 248-644-8620; Fax: 248-644-8623; Email: kwolff@olqm-parish.org; Web: www.olqm-parish.org. Rev. James A. Smalarz; Sr. Francesca Therese Bozzo, O.S.F., Pastoral Min.; Deacon Christopher Beltowski.
School—Our Lady Queen of Martyrs School, (Grades 1-8), 32460 Pierce Ave., Beverly Hills, 48025.
Tel: 248-642-2616; Fax: 248-642-3671; Email: jmojeske@olqm-parish.org; Web: www.olqmcatholicschool.org. Jacqueline Mojeske, Prin. Lay Teachers 20; Students 195; Clergy / Religious Teachers 1.
Catechesis Religious Program—32460 Pierce St., Beverly Hills, 48025. Tel: 248-647-6068; Email: mgarlow@olqm-parish.org. Mary Garlow, D.R.E. Students 286.

BIRMINGHAM, OAKLAND CO.

1—ST. COLUMBAN, Merged with St. Alan, Troy to form Christ Our Light, Troy.

2—HOLY NAME
Tel: 248-646-2244; Fax: 248-646-2286; Email: info@hnchurch.org; Web: www.hnchurch.org. Rev. Msgr. John P. Zenz; Deacon Michael J. McKale; Deborah Shinder, Pastoral Assoc.; Mrs. Kim Shepard, Business Mgr.; Brandon Gauvin, Music Min.; DeAnn Brzezinski, Prin.
Parish Office—630 Harmon St., Birmingham, 48009.
School—Holy Name School, (Grades 1-8), 680 Harmon St., Birmingham, 48009. Tel: 248-644-2722; Fax: 248-644-1191; Email: dbrzezinski@hnschool.com; Web: school.hnchurch.org. DeAnn Brzezinski, Prin. Lay Teachers 26; Students 270; Parish Population 1.
Catechesis Religious Program—Tel: 248-642-4130; Email: meib@hnchurch.org. Meg Eib, D.R.E. Students 370.

BLOOMFIELD HILLS, OAKLAND CO.

1—ST. HUGO OF THE HILLS
2215 Opdyke Rd., Bloomfield Hills, 48304.
Tel: 248-644-5460; Tel: 248-283-2213;
Fax: 248-644-1758; Email: patty.sinta@sthugo.org; Web: www.sthugo.org. Rev. Msgr. Anthony M. Tocco; Rev. Timothy J. Wezner; Deacons Oscar A. Brown; Michael T. Smith; Sr. Barbara Rund, O.P., Pastoral Assoc.; Brian Bartkowiak, Business Mgr.
School—St. Hugo of the Hills School, (Grades 1-8), 380 E. Hickory Grove, Bloomfield Hills, 48304.
Tel: 248-642-6131; Fax: 248-642-4457; Email: kelly.ryan@sthugoschool.org. Joseph Vincler, Pres. Lay Teachers 45; Students 490; Parish Population 1.

2—ST. OWEN (1962) Rev. James F. Cronk; Deacon Michael VonEnde.
Res.: 6869 Franklin Rd., Bloomfield Hills, 48301.
Tel: 248-626-0840; Fax: 248-626-0345; Email: parishoffice@stowen.org; Web: www.stowen.org.
Catechesis Religious Program—Tel: 248-626-2300. Jarrod Dillon, D.R.E.; Mary Mills, Youth Min. Students 274.

3—ST. REGIS St. Regis Catholic Church and School
3695 Lincoln Rd., Bloomfield Hills, 48301-4055.
Tel: 248-646-2686; Fax: 248-646-4643; Email: cynthia.neer@stregis.org; Web: www.stregis.org. Rev. David A. Buersmeyer.
School—St. Regis School St. Regis Catholic School, (Grades PreK-8), 3691 Lincoln Rd., Bloomfield Hills, 48301-4055. Tel: 248-724-3377; Fax: 248-644-0944; Email: BusinessOffice@stregis.org; Web: www.stregis.org. Ms. Katie Brydges, Prin. Lay Teachers 26; Students 430; Clergy / Religious Teachers 1; Parish Population 4,000.

CANTON, WAYNE CO.

1—SAINT JOHN NEUMANN
Mailing Address: 44800 Warren Rd., Canton, 48187.
Tel: 734-455-5986, Ext. 114. Revs. Paul K. Ballien; Mark A. Livingston, Parochial Vicar.
Res.: 44745 Windmill Dr., Canton, 48187.
Tel: 734-453-9434.
Catechesis Religious Program—Tel: 734-455-5910; Email: pballien@sjncanton.org. Sabrina S. Queen, D.R.E. Students 57.

2—RESURRECTION
48755 Warren Rd., Canton, 48187-1216.
Tel: 734-451-0444; Email: resoffice@resurrectionparish.net; Web: www.resurrectionparish.net. Rev. Thomas J. Kramer.
Catechesis Religious Program—Email: plipard@aol.com. Deacon Paul Lippard, D.R.E. Students 100.

3—ST. THOMAS A'BECKET (1977) Rev. Christopher P. Maus; Deacon James Ward.
Res.: 555 S. Lilley Rd., Canton, 48188.
Tel: 734-981-1333; Fax: 734-981-1481; Email: grace.pellerito@abecket.org; Web: www.abecket.org.
Catechesis Religious Program—Tel: 734-981-6680. Students 838.

CAPAC, ST. CLAIR CO., ST. NICHOLAS
4331 Capac Rd., Box 129, Capac, 48014.
Tel: 810-395-7572; Web: fmsaints.com. Rev. Noel Emmanuel Cornelio.
Catechesis Religious Program—

CARLETON, MONROE CO.

1—DIVINE GRACE, [CEM 5]
Tel: 734-654-2500; Fax: 734-654-6594; Email: divinegraceparish@yahoo.com. Rev. Giancarlo Ghezzi, P.I.M.E., Admin.
Res.: 2996 W. Labo Rd., Carleton, 48117.
School—St. Patrick School, (Grades 1-8),
Tel: 734-654-2522; Email: saintpatrick@chartermi.net. Carl Lenze, Prin. Lay Teachers 6; Students 108; Parish Population 1.
Catechesis Religious Program—Tel: 734-654-6444. Janice Doederlien, D.R.E. Students 115.

2—ST. PATRICK (1847) [CEM 3] Merged with St. Joseph, Maybee to form Divine Grace, Carleton.

CENTER LINE, MACOMB CO., ST. CLEMENT, [CEM] Merged with St. Teresa, Warren to form St. Mary, Our Lady Queen of Families, Warren.

CLARKSTON, OAKLAND CO., ST. DANIEL
Tel: 248-625-4580; Fax: 248-620-9839; Email: mwiencko@stdanielclarkston.org. Rev. Ronald J. Babich.
Res.: 7010 Valley Park Dr., Clarkston, 48346.
Catechesis Religious Program—Colleen Snyder, D.R.E. Students 486.

CLAWSON, OAKLAND CO., GUARDIAN ANGELS
Email: michaelk@guardiana.com; Web: www.guardiana.com. Rev. Tony Richter, Admin.; Deacon Robert Schwartz.
Res.: 581 E. 14 Mile Rd., Clawson, 48017. Email: frgerry@guardiana.com.
School—Guardian Angels School, (Grades PreK-8), 521 E. 14 Mile Rd., Clawson, 48017.
Tel: 248-588-5545; Fax: 248-589-7356; Email: OrtisiT@gaschool.com; Web: www.gaschool.com. Mr. Stephen Turk, Prin. Lay Teachers 16; Students 230; Parish Population 1.
Catechesis Religious Program—Email: johndavidk@guartdiana.com. John David Kuhar, D.R.E. Students 125.

CLINTON TWP., MACOMB CO.

1—ST. CLAUDE, Merged with St. Thecla, Clinton Twp.

2—ST. LOUIS
Tel: 586-468-8734; Fax: 586-468-9647; Email: stlouischurchslc@comcast.net; Web: www.

stlouiscatholiccommunity.com. Rev. Lawrence A. Pettke.
Res.: 24415 Crocker Blvd., Clinton Township, 48036. Email: parishofficeslc@comcast.net.
Catechesis Religious Program—39140 Ormsby St., Clinton Township, 48036.
Tel: 586-468-8734, Ext. 104; Email: barbaracillislc@comcast.net. Linda Bauer, RCIA Coord.; Kathy Huebener, Co-Coord.; Barbara Cilli, Office Mgr. Students 75.
3—St. Paul of Tarsus, Rev. Jerome Slowinski, J.C.L. 41218 Whispering Oaks Dr., Clinton Township, 48038. Tel: 586-228-1210; Fax: 586-228-8935; Email: parishoffice@stpauloftarsus.com; Web: www.stpauloftarsus.com. Res.: 41300 Romeo Plank Rd., Clinton Township, 48038.
Catechesis Religious Program—
Tel: 586-228-6651, Ext. 4; Email: pdeclercq@stpauloftarsus.com. Peggy Declercq, D.R.E. Students 300.
4—St. Ronald (1971)
17701 15 Mile Rd., Clinton Township, 48035-2401.
Tel: 586-792-1190; Fax: 586-792-0765;
Tel: 586-792-1191; Email: parishoffice@stronald.com; Web: www.stronald.com. Rev. William J. Herman.
Catechesis Religious Program—Tel: 586-792-1276; Email: kjacob.stronald@gmail.com. Kimberly Jacob, D.R.E. Students 179.
5—San Francesco Community
Tel: 586-792-5346; Fax: 586-792-5119; Email: giulioschiavi79@gmail.com. Rev. Dino Vanin, P.I.M.E., Admin.
Res.: 22870 S. Nunneley Rd., Clinton Township, 48035.
Catechesis Religious Program—Email: rburrell@comcast.net. Ann Burrell, D.R.E. Students 47.
6—St. Thecla, Merged with St. Claude, Clinton Twp. Revs. Brian K. Cokonougher; Radoslaw A. Zablocki; Deacon Thomas Houle.
Res.: 20740 S. Nunneley Rd., Clinton Township, 48035-1628. Tel: 586-791-3930; Fax: 586-791-3890; Email: barond@stthecla.com.
School—St. Thecla School, (Grades 1-8), 20762 S. Nunneley Rd., Clinton Township, 48035.
Tel: 586-791-2170; Fax: 586-791-2356; Email: maloneyd@stthecla.com; Web: stthecla.com/school. Geoffrey Fisher, Prin. Lay Teachers 21; Students 296; Parish Population 1.
Catechesis Religious Program—Tel: 586-792-0550. Students 160.
7—St. Valerie of Ravenna, Merged into St. Louis, Clinton Township.
Columbus, St. Clair Co., St. Philip Neri, [CEM] Merged with All Saints, Memphis & Holy Rosary Mission, Smiths Creek to form Holy Family, Memphis.
Davisburg, Oakland Co., Divine Mercy, Closed. For inquiries for parish records contact the chancery.
Dearborn, Wayne Co.
1—St. Alphonsus, Merged with St. Clement, Dearborn to form St. Alphonsus-St. Clement, Dearborn.
2—St. Alphonsus-St. Clement
13540 Gould St., Dearborn, 48126. Tel: 313-581-7495 ; Tel: 313-581-5218; Fax: 313-581-4233; Email: sta-stc@att.net; Email: info@sta-stc.comcastbiz.net. 7469 Calhoun St., Dearborn, 48126. Revs. Linus Kinyua, (Kenya); Aaron J. DePeyster.
3—St. Barbara
Tel: 313-582-8383; Fax: 313-582-1581; Email: saintbarbara@sbcglobal.net; Web: www.saintbarbarasaintcunegunda.org. Rev. Zbigniew Grankowski. Clustered with Saint Cunegunda in Detroit, MI
Res.: 13534 Colson Ave., Dearborn, 48126.
Catechesis Religious Program— Twinned with St. Cunegunda, Detroit. 5874 St. Lawrence, 48210. Michael Peck, D.R.E. Students 90.
4—St. Clement (1927) Merged with St. Alphonsus, Dearborn to form St. Alphonsus-St. Clement, Dearborn.
5—Divine Child (1950)
1055 N. Silvery Ln., Dearborn, 48128.
Tel: 313-277-3110; Fax: 313-277-3211; Email: lil@divinechild.org; Web: www.divinechild.org. Revs. James D. Bilot; Matthew Hood.
School—Divine Child School, (Grades 1-8), 25001 Herbert Weier Dr., Dearborn, 48128.
Tel: 313-562-1090; Fax: 313-562-9306; Email: dccbondy@yahoo.com; Web: www.divinechildelementaryschool.org. Sr. Cecilia Bondy, O.S.F., Elementary Prin. Lay Teachers 33; Bernardine Sisters 2; Students 547; Parish Population 1.
High School—Divine Child High School, 1001 N. Silvery Ln., Dearborn, 48128. Tel: 313-562-1990; Fax: 313-562-9361; Email: blicharzm@divinechild.org; Web: www.divinechildhighschool.org. Mr. Eric Haley, High School Prin. Lay Teachers 61; Students 855.
Catechesis Religious Program—Tel: 313-562-8667; Email: dwyerd@dces.info. Mrs. Dawn Dwyer, D.R.E. Students 122.
Convent—1045 N. Silvery Ln., Dearborn, 48128.
Tel: 313-561-5455.
6—St. Joseph, Merged with St. Martha, Dearborn to form St. Kateri Tekakwitha, Dearborn.
7—St. Kateri Tekakwitha
Tel: 313-336-3227; Fax: 313-441-6769; Email: info@stkateridearborn.org; Web: www.stkateridearborn.org. Rev. Terrence D. Kerner; Deacon Thomas Leonard.
Res.: 16101 Rotunda Dr., Dearborn, 48120. Email: fr.tdk@stkateridearborn.org.
Catechesis Religious Program—Email: dre@stkateridearborn.org. Grace Lakatos, D.R.E. Students 31.
8—St. Martha, Merged with St. Joseph, Dearborn to form St. Kateri Tekakwitha, Dearborn.
9—Sacred Heart, [CEM] We manage Mt. Kelly Cemetery.
Office: 912 South Military St., Dearborn, 48124. Revs. Kenneth M. Chase; John F. Child, Weekend Assoc., (Retired).
Res.: 22430 W. Michigan Ave., Dearborn, 48124.
School—Sacred Heart School, (Grades K-8), 22513 Garrison, Dearborn, 48124. Tel: 313-561-9192; Fax: 313-561-1598; Email: principal@shparish.org; Web: www.shparish.org. Gary Yee, Prin. Lay Teachers 12; Students 228; Parish Population 101.
Catechesis Religious Program—Tel: 313-565-1020; Email: REdirector@shparish.org. Julie Wieleba-Milkie, D.R.E. Students 100.
10—St. Sebastian, Very Rev. Canon Walter J. Ptak; Deacon Lawrence Girard.
Res.: 20710 Colgate, Dearborn Heights, 48125.
Tel: 313-562-5356; Fax: 313-562-0058; Email: parishoffice@stsebastiancatholicchurch.org; Web: www.saintsebastiancatholicchurch.org.
School—St. Sebastian School, (Grades 1-8), 3997 Merrick, Dearborn Heights, 48125.
Tel: 313-563-6640; Fax: 313-563-6641; Email: stsebastian@comcast.net. Sr. Geraldine Kaczynski, F.S.S.J., Prin. Lay Teachers 11; Franciscan Sisters of St. Joseph 2; Students 186; Parish Population 1.
Catechesis Religious Program—Tel: 313-563-0960. Jan Russell, D.R.E. Students 226.
Convent—20700 Colgate Ave., Dearborn Heights, 48125. Tel: 313-562-7733.
Dearborn Heights, Wayne Co.
1—St. Albert the Great
Tel: 313-292-0430; Email: info@stalberts.org. Rev. Daniel Zaleski; Deacon Regis Buckley.
Res.: 4855 Parker, Dearborn Heights, 48125.
Catechesis Religious Program—Tel: 313-292-9370; Email: dkscobey@yahoo.com. Dana Scobey, D.R.E. Students 58.
2—St. Anselm
Tel: 313-565-4808; Fax: 313-565-7514; Email: MsgrMoloney@gmail.com; Web: www.SaintAnselmParish.org. Rev. Msgr. James A. Moloney, P.A., Pastor & Dir., Society for The Propagation of The Faith.
Res.: 17650 W. Outer Dr., Dearborn Heights, 48127.
School—St. Anselm School, (Grades 1-8),
Tel: 313-563-3430; Email: akraetke@saintanselmschool.org; Web: www.SaintAnselmSchool.org. Mrs. Angela Kraetke, Prin. Lay Teachers 14; Students 121; Parish Population 1.
Catechesis Religious Program—17700 W. Outer Dr., Dearborn Heights, 48127. Tel: 313-561-0512; Email: Mwalkuski@stanselmschool.org. Mrs. Maryanne Walkuski, D.R.E. Students 20.
3—St. John the Baptist
26123 McDonald Ave., Dearborn Heights, 48125.
Tel: 313-292-9693; Fax: 313-292-1755; Email: pastor@stjohnbaptistcatholicchurch.org. Very Rev. Canon Walter J. Ptak, Admin.
4—St. Linus
6466 Evangeline, Dearborn Heights, 48127-2086.
Tel: 313-274-4500; Fax: 313-562-2821; Email: frpatrick@stlinusparish.org; Web: stlinus.info. Rev. Patrick Stoffer; Deacon Daniel Gonos, Pastoral Assoc.
School—St. Linus School, (Grades 1-8),
Tel: 313-274-5320; Email: stlinuscatholicschoolmi@gmail.com; Web: www.stlinuscatholicchurch.org/school. Christine Sagert, Prin. Lay Teachers 9; Students 180; Clergy / Religious Teachers 1; Parish Population 1,979.
Catechesis Religious Program—Tel: 313-274-5778; Email: dredonna@stlinusparish.org. Donna Stachulski, D.R.E. Students 118.
5—St. Sabina, Rev. James F. Lopez.
Res.: 25605 Ann Arbor Tr., Dearborn Heights, 48127.
Tel: 313-561-1977; Fax: 313-561-1315; Email: secretary@saintsabinaparish.org; Email: pastor@saintsabinaparish.org; Web: www.stsabina.weconnect.com.
Dryden, Lapeer Co., St. Cornelius
Tel: 810-796-2926; Fax: 810-796-9713; Email: office@fmsaints.com; Web: www.fmsaints.com. Rev. Michael R. Gawlowski. Clustered with St. John the Evangelist, Allenton
Res.: 3834 Mill St., P.O. Box 208, Dryden, 48428.
Catechesis Religious Program—Tel: 810-796-4701; Email: faithformation-west@fmsaints.com. Julie Allison, D.R.E. Students 150.
Dundee, Monroe Co., St. Irene, Merged with St. Joseph, Ida to form St. Gabriel, Ida.
Eastpointe, Macomb Co.
1—St. Barnabas, Merged with Holy Innocents, Roseville to form Holy Innocents-St. Barnabas, Roseville.
2—St. Basil
22800 Schroeder Ave., Eastpointe, 48021.
Tel: 586-777-5610; Fax: 586-779-3341; Email: stbasileastpoint@comcast.net. 22851 Lexington Ave., Eastpointe, 48021. Rev. Eric Fedewa.
Catechesis Religious Program—Tel: 586-772-5434; Email: stbasilreligioused@comcast.net. Mary Fortunate, D.R.E. Students 48.
3—St. Veronica
21440 Universal Ave., Eastpointe, 48021-2998.
Tel: 586-777-0331; Fax: 586-777-0615. Revs. Stanley L. Pachla Jr.; Kulan-Daisamy Arokiasamy, (India) Priest in Res.
Catechesis Religious Program—Tel: 586-772-5434. Mary Fortunate, D.R.E. Students 57.
Ecorse, Wayne Co.
1—St. Andre Bessette Parish
4250 W. Jefferson Ave., Ecorse, 48229-1597.
Tel: 313-383-8514; Fax: 313-383-7508; Email: frontofficesab@yahoo.com. Rev. Cornelius Okeke.
Catechesis Religious Program—Email: reledsab@yahoo.com. Avelia Tapia, D.R.E. Students 164.
2—St. Francis Xavier, [CEM] Merged with Our Lady of Lourdes, River Rouge to form St. Andre Bessette, Ecorse.
Emmett, St. Clair Co., Our Lady of Mount Carmel
Tel: 810-384-1338; Fax: 810-384-8708; Email: olmcshydre@gmail.com. Rev. Thomas Kuehnemund; Deacon William Kolarik.
Rectory—10828 Brandon Rd., Emmett, 48022.
Catechesis Religious Program—Brenda Krzak. Students 130.
Erie, Monroe Co., St. Joseph, [CEM]
Tel: 734-848-6125; Fax: 734-848-2784; Email: parish@stjosepherie.com. Rev. Mark P. Prill, Admin.
Res.: 2214 Manhattan Ave., Erie, 48133.
School—St. Joseph School, (Grades PreSchool-8), 2238 Manhattan St., Erie, 48133. Tel: 734-848-6985; Email: julie.miazgowicz@stjosepherie.com. Mrs. Julie Miazgowicz, Prin. Lay Teachers 9; Sisters 1; Students 106.
Catechesis Religious Program—Students 61.
Convent—Manhattan Ave., Erie, 48133.
Farmington, Oakland Co.
1—St. Colman, Merged into St. Fabian, Farmington Hills.
2—St. Gerald (1964)
21300 Farmington Rd., Farmington, 48336.
Tel: 248-477-7470; Fax: 248-477-3878; Web: stgeraldparish.org. Rev. Krzysztof Nowak.
Catechesis Religious Program—Tel: 248-476-7677; Fax: 248-381-5803; Email: marytaylor.sgp@gmail.com. Mary Taylor, D.R.E. Students 126.
3—Our Lady of Sorrows
Tel: 248-474-5720; Fax: 248-474-1340; Email: info@olsorrows.com; Web: www.olsorrows.com. Revs. Mark S. Brauer; Paul W. Graney; Deacon Donald Quigley.
Res.: 23815 Power Rd., Farmington, 48336-2461.
School—Our Lady of Sorrows School, (Grades 1-8), 24040 Raphael, Farmington, 48336-2465.
Tel: 248-476-0977; Fax: 248-615-5567; Email: awhitfield@olsorrows.com; Web: www.olsorrows.com. Ann Whitfield, Prin. Lay Teachers 56; Students 860.
Catechesis Religious Program—24040 Raphael Rd., Farmington, 48336. Tel: 248-474-6480; Email: reled@olsorrows.com. Mr. Gregory Crachiolo, D.R.E. Students 169.
Farmington Hills, Oakland Co.
1—St. Alexander, Merged into St. Gerald, Farmington.
2—St. Clare of Assisi (1967) Merged into Our Lady of Sorrows, Farmington.
3—St. Fabian
Tel: 248-553-4610; Fax: 248-553-6296; Email: ppyrkosz@stfabian.org; Web: www.stfabian.org. Rev. Msgr. Timothy D. Hogan; Rev. Andrew Dawson.
Church & Office: 32200 W. 12 Mile Rd., Farmington Hills, 48334.
School—St. Fabian School, (Grades 1-8),
Tel: 248-553-2750; Email: info@stfabian.org; Web: www.stfabian.org/school. Sharon Szuba, Prin. Lay Teachers 15; Students 240; Parish Population 1.
Catechesis Religious Program—Tel: 248-553-4860; Fax: 248-553-2041; Email: npawlukiewicz@stfabian.org. Nancy Pawlukiewicz, D.R.E.; Matthew Hunt, Youth Min.; Peggy Aoun, Middle School Coord. Students 250.

FERNDALE, OAKLAND CO., ST. JAMES, Merged with Our Lady of Fatima, Oak Park to form Our Mother of Perpetual Help, Oak Park.

FLAT ROCK, WAYNE CO., ST. ROCH, Rev. Raymond H. Lewandowski, M.Div., M.A.
Res.: 25022 Gibraltar Rd., Flat Rock, 48134.
Tel: 734-782-4471; Fax: 734-782-5450; Email: stroch@strochflatrock.com; Web: www.strochflatrock.com.
Catechesis Religious Program—MaryAnn Dobbs, D.R.E. Students 449.

FRASER, MACOMB CO., OUR LADY QUEEN OF ALL SAINTS, Merged with Sacred Heart, Roseville & St. Athanasius, Roseville to form St. Pio of Pietrelcina, Roseville.

GARDEN CITY, WAYNE CO.
1—ST. DUNSTAN, Merged with St. Raphael the Archangel, Garden City to form St. Thomas the Apostle, Garden City.
2—ST. RAPHAEL THE ARCHANGEL, Merged with St. Dunstan, Garden City to form St. Thomas the Apostle, Garden City.
3—ST. THOMAS THE APOSTLE, Rev. Simeon T. Iber; Deacon Leon Rodgers; Cindy Portis, Business Mgr.; Missy Taylor, D.R.E.; Catherine Borsh, RCIA Coord., Sec.; Paul Shafer, Music Min.
Parish Center—31530 Beechwood, Garden City, 48135-1935. Tel: 734-427-1533 (Office); Email: cborsh@thomastheapostle.org; Web: thomastheapostle.org.
Catechesis Religious Program—Tel: 734-425-5550; Fax: 734-956-6808. Missy Taylor. Students 112.

GIBRALTAR, WAYNE CO., ST. VICTOR, Merged with St. Mary, Rockwood to form St. Mary, Our Lady of the Annunciation, Rockwood.

GROSSE ILE, WAYNE CO., SACRED HEART, [CEM]
Tel: 734-676-1378; Fax: 734-676-3623. Rev. Michael Molnar, J.C.L.
Parish Center—21599 Parke Ln., Grosse Ile, 48138. Email: frmike@sacredheartgi.com.
Catechesis Religious Program—Students 276.

GROSSE POINTE, WAYNE CO., OUR LADY STAR OF THE SEA
Tel: 313-884-5554; Fax: 313-885-5591; Email: l.garazsi@stargp.org. Rev. Msgr. Gary T. Smetanka.
Church: 467 Fairford, Grosse Pointe Woods, 48236.
School—Our Lady Star of the Sea School, (Grades 1-8), Tel: 313-884-1070; Email: l.garazsi@stargp.org. Julie Aemisegger, Prin. Lay Teachers 25; Students 237; Parish Population 1.
Catechesis Religious Program—Tel: 313-884-7407; Email: j.zedaa@stargp.org. Judith Zedan, D.R.E. Students 254.

GROSSE POINTE FARMS, WAYNE CO., ST. PAUL ON THE LAKE CATHOLIC CHURCH, [CEM] Rev. Msgr. Patrick F. Halfpenny; Revs. Craig F. Marion; Thomas F. Slowinski; Deacon William E. Jamieson, Pastoral Assoc.
Res.: 157 Lake Shore Rd., Grosse Pointe Farms, 48236. Tel: 313-884-8761; Tel: 313-885-8855; Fax: 313-886-6467; Email: info@stpaulonthelake.org; Web: stpaulonthelake.org.
School—St. Paul on the Lake Catholic Church School, (Grades PreK-8), 170 Grosse Pointe Blvd., Grosse Pointe Farms, 48236. Tel: 313-885-3430; Fax: 313-885-9357; Email: office@stpaulonthelake.org; Email: tforsythe@stpaulonthelake.org; Web: www.stpaulonthelake.com. Tina Forsythe, Prin. Lay Teachers 27; Students 304.
Catechesis Religious Program—Tel: 313-885-7022; Fax: 313-885-9316; Email: jjones@stpaulonthelake.org. Mrs. Judith Jones, D.R.E. Students 480.

GROSSE POINTE PARK, WAYNE CO.
1—ST. AMBROSE
Tel: 313-822-2814; Fax: 313-822-9838; Email: stambrose@comcast.net; Web: stambrosechurch.net. Rev. Timothy R. Pelc; Mr. Charles J. Dropiewski, Pastoral Assoc.
Res.: 15020 Hampton, Grosse Pointe Park, 48230.
Catechesis Religious Program—Tel: 313-822-1248; Email: reled.stambrose@comcast.net. Mrs. Kelly Wollums, D.R.E. Students 241.
2—ST. CLARE OF MONTEFALCO
1401 Whittier Rd., Grosse Pointe Park, 48230.
Tel: 313-647-5000; Fax: 313-647-5005; Web: stclarem.org. Rev. Andrzej Kowalczyk, C.S.M.A.
School—St. Clare of Montefalco School, (Grades PreK-8), 16231 Charlevoix, Grosse Pointe Park, 48230. Tel: 313-647-5100; Fax: 313-647-5105; Email: atonissen@stclarem.org; Web: stclareschool.net. Ann Tonissen, Prin. Clergy 2; Lay Teachers 10; Sisters 2; Students 119.
Catechesis Religious Program—Sr. Kathleen Jo Avery, O.S.M., D.R.E.; David Troiano, Music Min. Students 103.

HAMTRAMCK, WAYNE CO.
1—ST. FLORIAN
Tel: 313-871-2778; Fax: 313-871-5947; Email: office@stflorianparish.org. Rev. Miroslaw Frankowski, S.Ch.
Res. & Church: 2626 Poland Ave., Hamtramck, 48212.
Catechesis Religious Program—Students 135.
2—ST. JOHN PAUL II PARISH
5830 Simon K, 48212. Tel: 313-305-7394; Fax: 313-305-7396; Email: sjp2parish@gmail.com. Rev. Andrew Wesley.
Catechesis Religious Program—Tel: 313-891-1520. Debbie Warren, D.R.E. Students 55.
3—OUR LADY QUEEN OF APOSTLES, (Polish)
Mailing Address: 3851 Prescott Ave., Hamtramck, 48212-3115. Tel: 313-891-1520; Fax: 313-891-3552; Email: qofaparish1917@gmail.com. Rev. Janusz Iwan.
Catechesis Religious Program—Debbie Warren, D.R.E. Students 17.

HARPER WOODS, WAYNE CO.
1—OUR LADY QUEEN OF PEACE, Closed. For inquiries for parish records contact the chancery.
2—ST. PETER THE APOSTLE (1952) Merged into St. Veronica, Eastpointe.

HARRISON TWP., MACOMB CO., ST. HUBERT
Tel: 586-463-5877; Web: www.sthubertchurch.com. Rev. Douglas Bignall.
Res.: 38775 Prentiss St., Harrison Township, 48045.
Catechesis Religious Program—Tel: 586-463-5875; Fax: 586-463-4520. Nicole Fournier, C.R.E. Students 207.

HARSENS ISLAND, ST. CLAIR CO., ST. MARK, Merged with Holy Cross, Marine City & St. Catherine of Alexandria, Algonac to form Our Lady on the River, Marine City.

HAZEL PARK, OAKLAND CO.
1—ST. JUSTIN, Merged with St. Mary Magdalen, Hazel Park to form St. Justin, Hazel Park.
2—ST. JUSTIN-ST. MARY MAGDALEN
50 E. Annabelle, Hazel Park, 48030.
Tel: 248-542-8060; Fax: 248-542-4563; Email: doris-sjsmm@comcast.net. Rev. Robert Hayes Williams, J.C.L.
Res.: 1631 E. Elza St., Hazel Park, 48030.
Tel: 248-542-2129; Fax: 248-542-2715.
Catechesis Religious Program—Connie M. Grden, D.R.E. Students 17.
3—ST. MARY MAGDALEN, Merged with St. Justin, Hazel Park to form St. Justin-St. Mary Magdalen, Hazel Park.

HIGHLAND, OAKLAND CO., CHURCH OF THE HOLY SPIRIT
Web: www.holyspirithighland.com. Rev. Wayne G. Ureel; Deacon Michael Somervell.
Church: 3700 Harvey Lake Rd., Highland, 48356. Email: chspirit78@aol.com.
Catechesis Religious Program—Tel: 248-887-1634; Tel: 248-887-5888; Email: Jillian@holyspirithighland.com. Jillian Peck, D.R.E. Students 136.

HIGHLAND PARK, WAYNE CO., ST. BENEDICT, Merged with Church of the Madonna, Detroit and St. Gregory the Great, Detroit to form St. Moses the Black, Detroit.

HOLLY, OAKLAND CO., ST. RITA
302 E. Maple, Holly, 48442. Rev. David J. Blazek.
Res.: 309 E. Maple, Holly, 48442. Tel: 248-634-4841; Fax: 248-634-4858; Email: stritaholly@sbcglobal.net; Web: www.stritaholly.org.
Catechesis Religious Program—Nicole Hagle, D.R.E. Students 191.

IDA, MONROE CO.
1—ST. GABRIEL, [CEM]
8295 Van Aiken St., Ida, 48140. Tel: 734-269-3895; Email: parish@stgabrielida.org. P.O. Box F, Ida, 48140. Rev. Gerard J. Cupple.
Res.: 576 Main St., Dundee, 48131.
Tel: 734-529-2160; Fax: 734-529-3463; Email: stirene@frontier.com.
Catechesis Religious Program—Tel: 734-529-2097; Email: stgabrieldre@aol.com. Catherine Anderson, D.R.E. Students 143.
2—ST. JOSEPH, [CEM] Merged with St. Irene, Dundee to form St. Gabriel, Ida.

IMLAY CITY, LAPEER CO., SACRED HEART, [CEM]
Tel: 810-724-1135; Email: staff@imlaysacredheart.org; Web: imlaysacredheart.org. Rev. Noel Emmanuel Cornelio. Clustered with St. Nicholas, Capac
Res.: 700 Maple Vista, Imlay City, 48444.
Catechesis Religious Program—Tel: 586-382-7532; Email: lkbrestov@gmail.com. Laura Brestovansky, D.R.E. Students 111.

INKSTER, WAYNE CO., HOLY FAMILY PARISH, Most Rev. Walter A. Hurley, J.C.L., Admin.; Rev. Sean P. Bonner.
Res.: 27800 Annapolis Rd., Inkster, 48141.
Tel: 313-563-8242; Fax: 313-563-0696; Email: holyfamilyink@comcast.net; Email: frsean-SMSRHF@usa.net.
Catechesis Religious Program— Religious Ed combined with St. Mary, Wayne.

IRA TOWNSHIP, ST. CLAIR CO., IMMACULATE CONCEPTION, [CEM]
Mailing Address: 9764 Dixie Hwy., Ira Township, 48023. Tel: 586-725-3051; Fax: 586-725-8240; Email: parish@iccatholic.org. Rev. Joseph M. Esper; Deacons Kenneth Nowicki; Lawrence Paczkowski.
School—Immaculate Conception School, (Grades 1-8), 7043 Church Rd., Ira Township, 48023.
Tel: 586-725-0078; Fax: 586-725-8240; Email: martinelli@iccatholic.org. Lawrence Ricard, Prin. Clergy 4; Lay Teachers 12; Students 159; Parish Population 1.
Catechesis Religious Program—Tel: 586-725-1762; Email: kovalcik@iccatholic.org. Tina Kovalcik, D.R.E., Tel: 586-725-1762. Students 335.

LAKE ORION, OAKLAND CO., ST. JOSEPH
Tel: 248-693-0440; Fax: 248-693-3724; Email: secretary@stjosephlakeorion.org; Web: www.stjoelo.org. Revs. C. Michael Verschaeve; John Maksym, Parochial Vicar; Deacon John Manera; Kathy Hasty, Pastoral Assoc.; Leszek Bartkiewicz, Music Min.
Res.: 715 N. Lapeer Rd., Lake Orion, 48362.
School—St. Joseph School, (Grades 1-8), 703 N. Lapeer Rd., Lake Orion, 48362. Tel: 248-693-6215; Fax: 248-693-0958; Email: jzmikly@stjosephlakeorion.org; Web: school.stjoelo.org. Joe Zmilky, Prin. Lay Teachers 29; Students 355; Parish Population 1.
Catechesis Religious Program—Tel: 248-693-9555; Email: boley@stjosephlakeorion.org; Email: snyebrothers@stjosephlakeorion.org. Beth A. Oley, D.R.E.; Susan Nye-Brothers, RCIA Coord. Students 781.

LAKEPORT, ST. CLAIR CO., ST. EDWARD'S ON THE LAKE, [CEM]
Tel: 810-385-4340; Fax: 810-385-6972; Web: stedwardonthelake.org. Rev. Lee E. Acervo.
Res.: 6945 Lakeshore Rd., Lakeport, 48059.
School—St. Edward's on the Lake School, (Grades 1-5), 6995 Lakeshore Rd., Lakeport, 48059.
Tel: 810-385-4461; Fax: 810-385-6070; Email: stedwardschool@hotmail.com. Mrs. Nancy Appel, Prin. For grades 6-8 please refer to St. Mary/McCormick Catholic Academy, Port Huron, under Elementary Schools, Inter-Parochial in the Institutions Located in the Archdiocese section. Clergy 2; Lay Teachers 7; Students 84; Parish Population 1.
Catechesis Religious Program—Email: stedwarddre@hotmail.com. Paula McCarthy, D.R.E. Students 60.
Convent—6975 Lakeshore Rd., Lakeport, 48059.

LAPEER, LAPEER CO., IMMACULATE CONCEPTION OF THE BLESSED VIRGIN MARY, [CEM]
Tel: 810-664-8594; Fax: 810-644-4564; Email: office@lapeercatholic.org; Web: www.lapeercatholic.org. Revs. Brian K. Hurley; Joseph W. Tuskiewicz.
Res.: 814 W. Nepessing St., Lapeer, 48446.
School—Bishop Kelley School, (Grades 1-8), 926 W. Nepessing St., Lapeer, 48446. Tel: 810-664-5011; Fax: 810-664-5606; Email: gwilloughy@bishopkelleylapeer.org; Web: www.bishopkelleylapeer.org. Gar Willoughby, Prin. Clergy 3; Lay Teachers 19; Students 159; Clergy / Religious Teachers 9; Parish Population 1,900.
Catechesis Religious Program—Email: kbotello@bishopkelleylapeer.org. Mrs. Kenlin Botello, D.R.E. Students 285.

LINCOLN PARK, WAYNE CO.
1—CHRIST THE GOOD SHEPHERD
Tel: 313-928-1324; Fax: 313-928-1326; Email: parish@christgoodsheherd.org; Web: www.christgoodshepherd.org. Rev. David Bechill.
Res.: 1540 Riverbank Ave., Lincoln Park, 48146.
School—John Paul II Catholic School, (Grades 1-8), 1590 Riverbank St., Lincoln Park, 48146.
Tel: 313-386-0633; Email: school@jp2catholic.com; Web: jp2catholic.com. Mrs. Mariann Lupinacci, Prin. Sponsored by Christ the Good Shepherd, Our Lady of the Scapulor & St. Vincent Pallotti Parishes. Clergy 4; Lay Teachers 20; Students 175; Parish Population 1.
Catechesis Religious Program—Students 85.
2—ST. HENRY, Merged into Christ the Good Shepherd, Lincoln Park.

LIVONIA, WAYNE CO.
1—ST. AIDAN
Tel: 734-425-5950; Fax: 734-425-3687; Email: bulletin@staidanlivonia.org; Web: www.saintaidanlivonia.org. Rev. Kevin Thomas.
Res.: 17500 Farmington Rd., Livonia, 48152.
Catechesis Religious Program—Tel: 734-425-9333. Mr. David J. Conrad, D.R.E. Students 244.
2—ST. COLETTE (1970)
Tel: 734-464-4433; Fax: 734-464-1694; Email: parishoffice@stcolette.net; Web: www.stcolette.net. Rev. Gary Michalik; Deacon Gary Pardo.
Res.: 17600 Newburgh Rd., Livonia, 48152-2699.
Catechesis Religious Program—Tel: 734-464-4435; Email: religioused@stcolette.net. Theresa Lisiecki, D.R.E. Students 485.
3—ST. EDITH
Tel: 734-464-1222; Fax: 734-464-7582; Email: parishoffice@stedith.org; Web: www.stedith.org. Rev. James McNulty.
Res.: 15089 Newburgh Rd., Livonia, 48154.

School—St. Edith School, (Grades PreK-8), Tel: 734-464-1250; Email: gwojciechowski@stedith.org; Web: www.stedithschool.com. Mrs. Georgene Wojciechowski, Prin. Lay Teachers 12; Students 219.
Catechesis Religious Program—Tel: 734-464-2020; Email: cmisiak@stedith.org. Colleen Misiak, Dir. Faith Formation. Students 341.

4—ST. GENEVIEVE, Merged with St. Maurice, Livonia to form St. Genevieve-St. Maurice, Livonia.

5—ST. GENEVIEVE-ST. MAURICE, Merged with St. Genevieve and St. Maurice.
Tel: 734-427-5220; Email: cbiddinger@stgenevieve.org; Web: www.stgenevieve-stmaurice.org. Rev. Howard L. Vogan; Deacon Kevin Breen.
Res.: 29015 Jamison St., Livonia, 48154-4021. Email: rectory@stgenevieve.org; Web: www.saintgenevieve.org.
Catechesis Religious Program—Tel: 734-261-5920; Email: pchudzinski@stgenevieve.org. Kathleen Morasso, Pastoral Min./Coord.; Phyllis Chudzinski, D.R.E. Students 60.

6—ST. MAURICE, Merged with St. Genevieve, Livonia to form St. Genevieve-St. Maurice, Livonia.

7—ST. MICHAEL, Revs. William Tindall; Anthony Camilleri.
Res.: 11441 Hubbard Ave., Livonia, 48150.
Tel: 734-261-1455; Fax: 734-522-1123; Email: parish@livoniastmichael.org; Web: www.livoniastmichael.org.
School—St. Michael School, (Grades 1-8), 11311 Hubbard, Livonia, 48150. Tel: 734-421-7360; Fax: 734-466-9713; Email: parish@livonaistmichael.org. Mrs. Nancy Kuszczak, Prin. Lay Teachers 28; Students 540.
Catechesis Religious Program—Email: jpawelski@livoniastmichael.org. Janine Pawelski, D.R.E. Students 90.
Family Life Center—11400 Fairfield, Livonia, 48154. Tel: 734-421-7522.

8—ST. PRISCILLA
19120 Purlingbrook St., Livonia, 48152.
Tel: 248-476-4700; Fax: 248-476-7831; Email: maryjo@saintpriscilla.org; Web: saintpriscilla.org. Rev. Theodore D'Cunha, S.A.C.; Deacon Robert C. Fitzgerald.
Catechesis Religious Program—Tel: 248-476-4702; Email: dre@saintpriscilla.org. Alyssa Choraszewski, D.R.E.

MACOMB, MACOMB CO.

1—ST. ISIDORE
Tel: 586-286-1700; Fax: 586-286-8753; Email: info@stisidore.church. Revs. Ronald Victor; Mark George, S.J.; Deacons Thomas Carter; Jeffrey Loeb.
Res.: 18201 Twenty-Three Mile Rd., Macomb, 48042. Email: chris@stisidore.church; Web: stisidore.church.
Catechesis Religious Program—Email: ann@stisidore.church. Ann DeRey, D.R.E. Students 969.

2—ST. MAXIMILIAN KOLBE, Merged with St. Francis of Assisi, Ray Township to form St. Francis of Assisi-St. Maximilian Kolbe, Ray Township.

MADISON HEIGHTS, OAKLAND CO., ST. VINCENT FERRER
28353 Herbert St., Madison Heights, 48071.
Tel: 248-542-8720; Email: sheryl@stvincentferrer. Rev. John C. Esper; Deacons Andrew Fairbanks; Francis X. Chau Ngoc Doan.
Res.: 1087 E. Gardenia Ave., Madison Heights, 48071.
Catechesis Religious Program—Tel: 248-398-1743; Email: sisternancy@stvincentferrer.net. Sr. Nancy Zajac, O.P., D.R.E. Students 175.

MARINE CITY, ST. CLAIR CO.

1—HOLY CROSS, [CEM] Merged with St. Catherine of Alexandria, Algonac & St. Mark, Harsens Island to form Our Lady on the River, Marine City.

2—OUR LADY ON THE RIVER
610 S. Water St., Marine City, 48039-1557.
Tel: 810-765-3568; Fax: 810-765-2974; Email: parish@ourladyontheriver.net; Web: www.ourladyontheriver.net. Revs. Douglas J. Terrien; Bradley Forintos; Deacon Michael Oldani.
School—Holy Cross Catholic School, (Grades 1-8), 618 S. Water St., Marine City, 48039.
Tel: 810-765-3591; Fax: 810-765-9074; Email: school@holycrossonline.net; Web: www.holycrossonline.net. Carl Wagner, Prin. Lay Teachers 8; Students 94; Parish Population 1.
Catechesis Religious Program—Tel: 810-765-8300; Email: dre@ourladyontheriver.net. Mr. Joseph Kuligowski, D.R.E. Students 228.

MARYSVILLE, ST. CLAIR CO., ST. CHRISTOPHER
Tel: 810-364-4100; Fax: 810-364-5947; Email: kgamalski@stchrismi.org; Email: htenyer@stchrismi.org; Web: www.stchrismi.org. Rev. James Fredrick Arwady.
Res.: 1000 Michigan Ave., Marysville, 48040.
Catechesis Religious Program—
Tel: 810-364-4100, Ext. 7; Email: kristi.socha@gmail.com. Kristi Socha, D.R.E. Students 147.

MAYBEE, MONROE CO., ST. JOSEPH, [CEM] Merged with St. Patrick, Carleton to form Divine Grace, Carleton.

MELVINDALE, WAYNE CO.

1—ST. CONRAD, Merged into St. Mary Magdalen, Melvindale.

2—ST. MARY MAGDALEN
Tel: 313-381-8566; Fax: 313-381-1319; Email: smmparish@comcast.net. Rev. Edward F. Zaorski.
Res.: 19624 Wood St., Melvindale, 48122.
Catechesis Religious Program—
Tel: 313-381-8566, Ext. 104; Email: armandobv729@hotmail.com. Armando Bravo, D.R.E. Students 148.

MEMPHIS, MACOMB CO.

1—ALL SAINTS, Merged with St. Philip Neri, Columbus & Holy Rosary Mission, Smiths Creek to form Holy Family, Memphis.

2—HOLY FAMILY
Tel: 810-392-2056; Email: bbquig@holyfamily-online.org; Web: holyfamily-online.org. Revs. Joseph Mallia; John Nedumcheril; Deacon Alan Gwozdz.
Church: 79780 Main St., Memphis, 48041.
Catechesis Religious Program—Email: sfinely@holyfamily-online.org. Susan Finley, D.R.E. Students 181.

MILFORD, OAKLAND CO., ST. MARY, OUR LADY OF THE SNOWS, [CEM]
1955 E. Commerce, Milford, 48381.
Tel: 248-685-1482; Fax: 248-684-5642; Email: parishoffice@stmarymilfordmi.org; Web: www.stmarymilfordmi.org. Rev. Msgr. John G. Budde; Valerie Thompson, Pastoral Assoc.
Catechesis Religious Program—Tel: 248-685-2702. Colleen Gonzalez, D.R.E. Students 626.

MONROE, MONROE CO.

1—ST. ANNE
2420 N. Dixie Hwy., Monroe, 48162.
Tel: 734-289-2910; Fax: 734-289-1098; Email: stanneparish@sbcglobal.net. Rev. Henry Rebello, S.A.C.
Catechesis Religious Program—Email: dre@stcharlesnewport.com. Mrs. Janice Doederlein, D.R.E. Students 52.

2—ST. JOHN THE BAPTIST
Tel: 734-241-8910; Fax: 734-241-1943; Email: parishoffice@stjohnmonroe.com; Web: www.stjohnmonroe.com. Rev. Raymond E. Arwady, Admin.
Res.: 511 S. Monroe St., Monroe, 48161. Email: lmorgel@stjohnmonroe.com.
See Monroe Catholic Elementary Schools under Elementary Schools, Interparochial located in the Institution section.
Catechesis Religious Program—Email: mquick@stjohnmonroe.com. Mrs. Mary Quick, Dir. Faith Formation. Students 61.

3—ST. JOSEPH, [JC] Closed. For inquiries for parish records contact the chancery.

4—ST. MARY, [JC]
Tel: 734-241-1644; Fax: 734-241-3077; Email: parishoffice@stmarymonroe.org; Web: www.stmarymonroe.org. Revs. David G. Burgard; Giancarlo Ghezzi, P.I.M.E.; Robert K. Singelyn, In Res., (Retired).
Res.: 127 N. Monroe St., Monroe, 48162.
See Monroe Catholic Elementary Schools under Elementary Schools, Interparochial located in the Institution section.
Catechesis Religious Program—Tel: 734-241-6097; Email: faithformation@stmarymonroe.org. Mrs. Mary Quick, D.R.E. Students 135.

5—ST. MICHAEL THE ARCHANGEL, [JC] Rev. Philip Ching.
Res.: 502 W. Front St., Monroe, 48161.
Tel: 734-241-8645; Email: stmichaelmonroe@yahoo.com; Web: www.stmichaelmonroe.com.
See Monroe Catholic Elementary Schools under Elementary Schools, Interparochial located in the Institution section.
Catechesis Religious Program—151 N. Monroe St., Monroe, 48162. Tel: 734-241-6097. Mrs. Mary Quick, D.R.E. Students 77.

MOUNT CLEMENS, MACOMB CO., ST. PETER (1843) [CEM]
95 Market St., Mount Clemens, 48043. Rev. Michael N. Cooney; Sheila Roy, Pastoral Assoc.; Moira Shaum, Business Mgr.
Admin. Bldg.—110 New St., Mount Clemens, 48043.
Tel: 586-468-4578; Fax: 586-684-1868; Email: info@saintpeterchurch.us; Email: sroy@saintpeterchurch.us; Web: stpetermtclemens.weconnect.com.
School—St. Mary, (Grades 1-8), 2 Union St., Mount Clemens, 48043. Tel: 586-468-4570;
Fax: 586-468-6454; Email: mmiscavish@stmarymtclemens.com; Web: www.stmarymtclemens.com. Maureen Miscavich, Prin. Lay Teachers 27; Students 410.
Catechesis Religious Program—Email: religioused@saintpeterchurch.us. Judy Coll, D.R.E. Students 320.

NEW BALTIMORE, MACOMB CO., ST. MARY QUEEN OF CREATION, [CEM]
50931 Maria St., New Baltimore, 48047.
Tel: 586-725-2441; Web: www.smqoc.com. Revs. Charles White IV; Louis Charles Lapeyre; Deacon Anthony Lewandoski, (Retired).
Res.: 51041 Maria St., New Baltimore, 48047.
Catechesis Religious Program—36254 Main St., New Baltimore, 48047. Tel: 586-725-7579. Students 561.

NEW BOSTON, WAYNE CO., ST. STEPHEN, [CEM] Rev. John P. Hedges.
Res.: 18858 Huron River Dr., New Boston, 48164-9272. Tel: 734-753-5268; Fax: 734-753-5828; Email: parishoffice@ststephennewboston.org; Web: ststephennewboston.org.
School—St. Stephen School, (Grades 1-8), 18800 Huron River Dr., New Boston, 48164-9272.
Tel: 734-753-4175; Email: principal@ststephennb.org; Web: www.ststephennb.org. Lay Teachers 10; Students 184; Parish Population 1.
Catechesis Religious Program—Tel: 734-753-4722; Email: joniebop@outlook.com. Joan M. Gutierrez, D.R.E. Students 106.
Convent—Tel: 734-753-9937.

NEWPORT, MONROE CO., ST. CHARLES BORROMEO, [CEM]
8109 Swan Creek Rd., Newport, 48166.
Tel: 734-586-2531, Ext. 1; Email: secretary@stcharlesnewport.com; Web: stcharlesnewport.org. 8033 N. Dixie Hwy., Newport, 48166. Rev. Henry Rebello, S.A.C.
School—St. Charles Borromeo Catholic Academy, (Grades 1-8), 8125 Swan Creek Rd., Newport, 48166.
Tel: 734-586-2531, Ext. 2; Email: scs@stcharlesnewport.com. Gina Baker, Prin. Lay Teachers 10; Students 204.
Catechesis Religious Program—
Tel: 734-586-2531, Ext. 4; Email: dre@stcharlesnewport.com. Mrs. Janice Doederlein, D.R.E. Students 67.

NORTH BRANCH, LAPEER CO.

1—ST. MARY'S BURNSIDE (1854) [CEM]
5622 Summers Rd., North Branch, 48461.
Tel: 810-688-3797; Fax: 810-688-2969; Email: sspeterpaul@northbranchcatholic.com; Web: www.sspeterpaulnb.org. P.O. Box 268, North Branch, 48461. Revs. Richard L. Treml; Sama Muma.

Catechesis Religious Program—7090 Cade Rd., Brown City, 48416. Michael Vinande, D.R.E. Twinned with SS. Peter and Paul, North Branch. Students 150.
Mission—Sacred Heart Mission, 7090 Cade Rd., Brown City, 48416. Tel: 810-346-3036; Fax: 810-346-3036.

2—SS. PETER AND PAUL (1906) [CEM]
P.O. Box 208, North Branch, 48461. Revs. Richard L. Treml; Sama Muma.
Res.: 6645 Washington, North Branch, 48461.
Catechesis Religious Program—6650 Sherman St., North Branch, 48461. Lisa Verellen, D.R.E. Twinned with St. Mary's Burnside, North Branch. Students 105.
Chapel—St. Patrick's, 9851 Main St., Clifford, Lapeer Co. 48727.

NORTHVILLE, WAYNE CO.

1—ST. ANDREW KIM KOREAN CATHOLIC CHURCH
Tel: 248-442-9026; Fax: 248-442-9020; Email: email@standrewkimdetroit.org. Rev. Jae Woo Park.
Res.: 21177 Halsted Rd., Northville, 48167.
Catechesis Religious Program—Students 142.

2—OUR LADY OF VICTORY
Tel: 248-349-2621; Email: olvoffice@olvnorthville.net; Web: olvnorthville.org. Rev. Denis B. Theroux; Deacon Ric Misiak.
Church & Res.: 133 Orchard Dr., Northville, 48167. Email: jlupo@olvnorthville.net.
School—Our Lady of Victory School, (Grades 1-8), 132 Orchard Dr., Northville, 48167.
Tel: 248-349-3610; Fax: 248-380-7247; Email: lzelek@olvnorthville.net. Dan Timmis, Prin. Lay Teachers 29; Students 427; Parish Population 1.
Catechesis Religious Program—Tel: 248-349-2559; Email: mskene@olvnorthville.net. Kelly Bruno, D.R.E. Students 455.

NOVI, OAKLAND CO.

1—HOLY FAMILY Church of the Holy Family
Tel: 248-349-8847; Fax: 248-349-3711; Email: admin@hfnovi.com; Web: www.holyfamilynovi.org. Revs. Robert A. LaCroix; James Houbeck; Deacon Robert Ervin.
Res.: 24505 Meadowbrook, Novi, 48375.
Catechesis Religious Program—Tel: 248-349-8837. Students 417.

2—ST. JAMES St James of Novi
Tel: 248-347-7778; Fax: 248-347-9625; Web: www.sjnovi.net. Rev. Msgr. John C. Kasza; Rev. Radoslaw A. Zablocki.
Church: 46325 Ten Mile Road, Novi, 48374.
Catechesis Religious Program—Mrs. Gretchen Hennen, D.R.E. Students 878.

OAK PARK, OAKLAND CO.
1—OUR LADY OF FATIMA, Merged with St. James, Ferndale to form Our Mother of Perpetual Help, Oak Park.
2—OUR MOTHER OF PERPETUAL HELP (1950)
Tel: 248-545-2310; Fax: 248-545-2310; Email: fatimaofficeolofsj@gmail.com; Web: www.omoph.org. Revs. Paul Chateau; Jeffrey D. Allan, In Res.; Felix S. Alsola, (Philippines) In Res.
Res.: 13500 Oak Park Blvd., Oak Park, 48237-2099.
Catechesis Religious Program—Email: natalielacroix@ymail.com. Natalie LaCroix, D.R.E. Students 44.
ORCHARD LAKE, OAKLAND CO., OUR LADY OF REFUGE
3700 Commerce Rd., Orchard Lake, 48324.
Tel: 248-682-0920; Fax: 248-682-3794; Email: cbishop@olorcc.org; Web: www.olorcc.org. Parish Office: 3725 Erie Dr., Orchard Lake, 48324-1527. Rev. Gerald A. McEnhill.
Res.: 3663 Erie Dr., Orchard Lake, 48324.
Tel: 248-682-0933.
School—Our Lady of Refuge School, (Grades 1-8), 3750 Commerce Rd., Orchard Lake, 48324.
Tel: 248-682-3422; Fax: 248-683-2265; Email: drichards@olr-school.net; Web: www.olr-school.net. Mr. Robert Pyles, Prin. Lay Teachers 25; Students 291; Parish Population 1.
Catechesis Religious Program—Email: dre@olorcc.org. Bonnie Degen, D.R.E. Students 100.
ORION TOWNSHIP, OAKLAND CO., CHRIST THE REDEEMER (1989)
Tel: 248-391-1621; Fax: 248-391-3412; Email: officemgr@ctredeemer.org. Rev. Joseph E. Dailey.
Res.: 2700 Waldon Rd., Lake Orion, 48360.
Catechesis Religious Program—Tel: 248-391-4074; Email: dre@ctredeemer.org. Mrs. Lisa Brown, D.R.E. Students 611.
ORTONVILLE, OAKLAND CO., ST. ANNE
Tel: 248-627-3965; Fax: 248-627-5153; Email: anne@churchofstanne.org; Web: www.churchofstanne.org. Rev. Gerard Frawley, S.A.C. Spanish baptisms available upon request
Res.: 825 S. Ortonville Rd., Ortonville, 48462.
Catechesis Religious Program—Email: marianne@churchofstanne.org. Marianne Boesch, D.R.E. Students 160.
PLYMOUTH, WAYNE CO.
1—ST. KENNETH
14951 N. Haggerty Rd., Plymouth, 48170.
Tel: 734-420-0288; Fax: 734-420-2921; Email: padretom@stkenneth.org. Rev. Thomas A. Belczak.
Catechesis Religious Program—Tel: 734-420-3031; Email: recoordinator@stkenneth.org. Betty Berryman, D.R.E. Students 412.
2—OUR LADY OF GOOD COUNSEL
47650 North Territorial Rd., Plymouth, 48170.
Tel: 734-453-0326; Fax: 734-416-9257. Revs. John Riccardo; Prentice Tipton; David M. Tomaszycki; Deacon David Carignan.
Office: 1062 Church St., Plymouth, 48170. Email: keithk@olgcparish.net.
School—Our Lady of Good Counsel School, (Grades 1-8), 1151 William St., Plymouth, 48170.
Tel: 734-453-3053; Email: oconnort@olgcparish.net. Lay Teachers 23; Students 428; Parish Population 1.
Catechesis Religious Program—1160 Penniman, Plymouth, 48170. Email: oshaughnessys@olgcparish.net. Sandy O'Shaughnessy, D.R.E. Students 479.
PONTIAC, OAKLAND CO.
1—ST. DAMIEN OF MOLOKAI PARISH (2009) [CEM]
120 Lewis St., Pontiac, 48342. Tel: 248-332-0283; Web: www.st-damien.org. Revs. James F. Kean; Grayson D. Heenan.
Catechesis Religious Program—Email: mcharria@st-damien.org. Ms. Maria Charria, D.R.E. Students 425.
2—ST. JOSEPH, Merged with St. Vincent de Paul, Pontiac & St. Michael, Pontiac, to form St. Damien of Molokai, Pontiac.
3—ST. MICHAEL, Merged with St. Vincent de Paul, Pontiac & St. Joseph, Pontiac to form St. Damien of Molokai, Pontiac.
4—ST. VINCENT DE PAUL, Merged with St. Michael, Pontiac & St. Joseph, Pontiac to form St. Damien of Molokai, Pontiac.
PORT HURON, ST. CLAIR CO.
1—HOLY TRINITY, [CEM]
325 32nd St., Port Huron, 48060. Tel: 810-984-2689; Fax: 810-984-8559; Email: denise@holytrinityph.org; Email: frsal@holytrinityph.org; Web: holytrinityph.org. Very Rev. Salvatore Palazzolo; Deacons Dennis Crimmins; John J. Connors.
Catechesis Religious Program—2865 Henry St., Port Huron, 48060. Tel: 810-985-9609; Email: karen@holytrinityph.org. Karen Clor, D.R.E. Students 135.
2—ST. JOSEPH, [JC] Merged with St. Stephen, Port Huron & Our Lady of Guadalupe Mission, Port Huron to form Holy Trinity, Port Huron.
3—ST. MARY
Tel: 810-982-7906; Fax: 810-982-8255; Email: stmaryporthuron@gmail.com; Web: www.stmaryporthuron.com. Rev. Zbigniew Zomerfeld; Deacon Timothy Maxwell.
Res.: 1505 Ballentine St., Port Huron, 48060.
School—St. Mary School, Michael Green, Prin. Lay Teachers 12; Students 117.
Catechesis Religious Program—Email: maryshoudy@yahoo.com. Mary Shoudy, D.R.E. Students 140.
4—OUR LADY OF GUADALUPE MISSION, Merged with St. Joseph, Port Huron & St. Stephen, Port Huron to form Holy Trinity, Port Huron.
5—ST. STEPHEN, Merged with St. Joseph, Port Huron & Our Lady of Guadalupe Mission, Port Huron to form Holy Trinity, Port Huron.
RAY TOWNSHIP, MACOMB CO.
1—ST. FRANCIS OF ASSISI, Merged with St. Maximilian Kolbe, Macomb Township to form St. Francis of Assisi-St. Maximilian Kolbe, Ray Township.
2—ST. FRANCIS OF ASSISI-ST. MAXIMILIAN KOLBE
62811 New Haven Rd., Ray Township, 48096.
Tel: 586-598-3314; Email: stfrancisnh@comcast.net; Web: stfrancis-stmaximilian.com. Rev. Christopher Talbot.
Catechesis Religious Program—
Tel: 586-598-3314, Ext. 302; Email: wordist@msn.com. Jane Van Belle, D.R.E. Students 305.
REDFORD, WAYNE CO.
1—ST. AGATHA, Closed. For inquiries for parish records contact the chancery.
2—ST. HILARY, Merged into St. John Bosco, Redford.
3—ST. JOHN BOSCO, Merged with St. Robert Bellarmine to form St. John XXIII, Redford.
4—ST. JOHN XXIII
12100 Beach Daly Rd., Redford, 48239.
Tel: 248-800-6081. Rev. Gregory A. Piatt, Admin.
5—OUR LADY OF LORETTO
Tel: 313-534-9000; Fax: 313-534-6744; Email: oll48240@gmail.com; Web: www.ourladyofloretto.com. Revs. Socorro Fernandes, S.A.C.; Kishore Battu; Sr. Margretta Wojcik, O.S.F., Pastoral Assoc.
Res.: 17116 Olympia Ave., Redford, 48240.
Catechesis Religious Program—Tel: 313-532-3707; Email: MRKohn@aol.com. Donna Kohn, D.R.E. Students 45.
6—ST. ROBERT BELLARMINE, Merged with St. John Bosco, Redford.
7—ST. VALENTINE
14841 Beech Daly Rd., Redford, 48239. Revs. Socorro Fernandes, S.A.C.; Kishore Battu; Deacon Lawrence Toth.
Res.: 25881 Dow, Redford, 48239. Tel: 313-532-4394; Fax: 313-537-2237; Email: stvalsparish@stvalentineschool.com.
School—St. Valentine School, (Grades 1-8), 25875 Hope St., Redford, 48239. Tel: 313-533-7149; Fax: 313-533-3060; Email: rdamuth@stvalentineschool.com; Web: stvalentineschool.com. Rachel Damuth, Prin.; Maureen Kelly, Librarian. Lay Teachers 14; Preschool 30; Students 178; Parish Population 1.
Catechesis Religious Program—Tel: 313-538-9161. Students 58.
RICHMOND, MACOMB CO., ST. AUGUSTINE, [CEM]
68035 Main St., Richmond, 48062. Tel: 586-727-5215; Fax: 586-727-3760; Email: staugustinerichmond@comcast.net; Web: www.staugustinecatholicparish.org. Revs. Joseph Mallia; John Nedumcheril; Deacon Alan Gwozdz.
School—St. Augustine School, (Grades PreK-8), 67901 Howard, Richmond, 48062. Tel: 586-727-9365; Fax: 586-727-6502; Email: info@mysaints.net; Web: www.staugustinecatholicschool.com. Mrs. Emily Lenn, Prin. Lay Teachers 11; Students 159; Clergy / Religious Teachers 11.
Catechesis Religious Program—68035 Main St., Richmond, 48062. Tel: 586-727-9290. Susan Finley, D.R.E. Students 147.
RIVER ROUGE, WAYNE CO., OUR LADY OF LOURDES, Merged with St. Francis Xavier, Ecorse to form St. Andre Bessette, Ecorse.
RIVERVIEW, WAYNE CO., ST. CYPRIAN
13249 Pennsylvania, Riverview, 48193.
Tel: 734-283-1366; Fax: 734-283-2809; Email: dtraeder@stcyprian.com. Rev. William J. Promesso.
Catechesis Religious Program—
Tel: 734-283-1366, Ext. 118; Email: sshurtz@stcyprian.com. Mrs. Stacey Sutowski-Shurtz, D.R.E. Students 194.
ROCHESTER, OAKLAND CO., ST. ANDREW
Tel: 248-651-7486; Fax: 248-651-3950; Email: contact@standrewchurch.org; Web: www.standrewchurch.org. Rev. Msgr. Michael Hrydziuszko; Rev. Tomasz Wilisowski, C.S.M.A.; Deacons Marc Gemellaro; Thomas Sliney.
Res.: 1400 Inglewood, Rochester, 48307.
Catechesis Religious Program—Tel: 248-651-6571; Email: maureens@standrewchurch.org. Mrs. Maureen Schreffler, D.R.E. Students 970.
ROCHESTER HILLS, OAKLAND CO.
1—ST. IRENAEUS
771 Old Perch Rd., Rochester Hills, 48309.
Tel: 248-651-9595; Fax: 248-651-1504; Web: www.stirenaeus.org. Rev. Brian J. Chabala.
Catechesis Religious Program—Tel: 248-651-2443. Patricia Egan-Myers, D.R.E. Students 612.
Mission—St. Rosa-O.C.I.M.A., P.O. Box 952, Bloomfield Hills, Oakland Co. 48303-0952.
Tel: 248-651-2443, Ext. 115; Email: info@ocimaya.org; Web: www.ocimaya.org/orphanagesantaelena.html.
2—ST. MARY OF THE HILLS
Tel: 248-853-5390; Fax: 248-853-7989; Email: stmary89@smoth.org; Web: www.smoth.org. Rev. Stanley A. Ulman.
Church: 2675 John R., Rochester Hills, 48307-4652.
Catechesis Religious Program—Tel: 248-844-8662. Peggy Casing, D.R.E. Students 547.
3—ST. PAUL ALBANIAN CATHOLIC CHURCH, Rev. Frederik Kalaj.
Office: 525 Auburn Rd., Rochester Hills, 48307.
Tel: 248-844-2150; Email: fatherfredkalaj@gmail.com; Web: www.stpaulalbaniancatholicchurch.org.
Catechesis Religious Program—Tel: 586-207-1235. Franz Grishaj, D.R.E. Students 290.
ROCKWOOD, WAYNE CO.
1—ST. MARY, [CEM] Merged with St. Victor, Gibraltar to form St. Mary, Our Lady of the Annunciation, Rockwood.
2—ST. MARY, OUR LADY OF THE ANNUNCIATION, [CEM]
Tel: 734-379-9248; Fax: 734-379-6548; Email: stmaryrockwood@sbcglobal.net; Web: www.stmaryannunciation.org. Rev. James R. Rafferty.
Res.: 32477 Church, Rockwood, 48173.
Catechesis Religious Program—Email: ljswayze@yahoo.com. Leslie Swayze, Catechism Coord. Students 96.
ROMEO, MACOMB CO., ST. CLEMENT OF ROME
343 S. Main St., Romeo, 48065. Tel: 586-752-9611; Fax: 586-752-1601. Rev. Stephen C. Reckker.
Catechesis Religious Program—Tel: 586-752-6591; Fax: 586-752-7093; Email: dknoblock@stclementromeo.com. Deborah Knoblock, D.R.E. Students 504.
ROMULUS, WAYNE CO., ST. ALOYSIUS
Tel: 734-941-5056; Fax: 734-941-6018; Email: st_aloysiuschurch@yahoo.com; Web: www.staloysiusromulus.org. Rev. John Dumas.
Res.: 11280 Ozga St., Romulus, 48174.
Church: 37200 Neville St., Romulus, 48174.
Catechesis Religious Program—Tel: 734-941-3730; Email: dre.st.aloysiuschurch@gmail.com. Kimberly Gilliland, D.R.E. Students 35.
ROSEVILLE, MACOMB CO.
1—ST. ANGELA, Merged into St. Isaac Jogues, St. Clair Shores.
2—ST. ATHANASIUS, Merged with Sacred Heart, Roseville & Our Lady Queen of All Saints, Fraser to form St. Pio of Pietrelcina, Roseville.
3—ST. DONALD, Closed. For inquiries for parish records contact the chancery.
4—HOLY INNOCENTS-ST. BARNABAS
16359 Frazho, Roseville, 48066. Tel: 586-777-7543; Web: www.HISBParish.us. Rev. John Wynnycky; Deacon Michael Lang Sr.
Res. & Mailing Address: 26100 Ridgemont St., Roseville, 48066.
Catechesis Religious Program—24800 Phlox, Eastpointe, 48021. Tel: 586-775-4650;
Fax: 586-775-6933. Maureen Romeo, Dir., Faith Formation. Students 46.
5—HOLY INNOCENTS, Merged with St. Barnabas, Eastpointe to form Holy Innocents-St. Barnabas, Roseville.
6—ST. PIO OF PIETRELCINA
18720 13 Mile Rd., Roseville, 48066. 18430 Utica Rd., Roseville, 48066. Tel: 586-777-9116, Ext. 0; Fax: 586-776-7208; Email: stpioparishsec@gmail.com. Rev. Grzegorz Rozborski; Deacon Arthur Majkowski.
Catechesis Religious Program—Fax: 586-776-2945; Email: stpioyouthmin@gmail.com. Janice Pazuchowski, Faith Formation Coord. Students 95.
7—SACRED HEART, Merged with St. Athanasius, Roseville & Our Lady Queen of All Saints, Fraser to form St. Pio of Pietrelcina, Roseville.
ROYAL OAK, OAKLAND CO.
1—ST. DENNIS, Merged into St. Vincent Ferrer, Madison Heights.
2—ST. MARY, [CEM]
Tel: 248-547-1818; Tel: 247-547-1819;
Fax: 248-547-4577; Email: parishoffice@st-mary.org. Rev. Paul M. Snyder; Deacon Thomas Avery; Christine Wagberg, Pastoral Assoc.; Mrs. Linda Maccarone, Dir. of Parish Mission.
Res.: 730 Lafayette Ave. S., Royal Oak, 48067. Email: bwojcik@st-mary.org.
School—St. Mary School, (Grades 1-8), 628 Lafayette Ave. S., Royal Oak, 48067. Tel: 248-545-2140;
Fax: 248-545-2303; Email: gbala@st-mary.org. Gabriela Bala, Prin. Clergy 9; Lay Teachers 19; Students 339; Parish Population 1.

Catechesis Religious Program—628 S. Lafayette, Royal Oak, 48067. Tel: 248-547-1810; Email: dtrudell@st-mary.org. Donna Trudell, Dir. Faith Formation. Students 248.

3—NATIONAL SHRINE OF THE LITTLE FLOWER BASILICA
Tel: 248-541-4122; Fax: 248-541-2838; Web: www.shrinechurch.com. Rev. Msgr. Robert J. McClory, Rector; Revs. John D. Kopson; Joseph Lang; Kevin Roelant.
Res. & Church: 2100 W. 12 Mile Rd., Royal Oak, 48073-3973.
School—National Shrine of the Little Flower Basilica School, (Grades 1-6), 1621 Linwood, Royal Oak, 48067. Tel: 248-541-4622; Fax: 248-541-6969; Email: fotiu@shrineschools.com; Web: www.shrineschools.com. Katie Fotiu, Prin.; Jennifer Bero, Asst. Prin. Clergy 4; Lay Teachers 35; Students 429; Pre-K Enrollment 161.
High School—National Shrine of the Little Flower Basilica High School, 3500 W. Thirteen Mile Rd., Royal Oak, 48073. Tel: 248-549-2925;
Fax: 248-549-2953; Email: jmio@shrineschools.com; Web: www.shrineschools.com. James Mio, Prin.; Julia Mazanka, Asst. Prin.; Mrs. Pamela Olejniczak, Asst. Prin., Dean of Students. Lay Teachers 25; Students 250; Academy Students (7th & 8th Grades) 119; 7th & 8th Grades 16.
Catechesis Religious Program—Tel: 248-541-5133; Email: jlynch@shrinechurch.com. Janie Lynch, D.R.E. Students 322.

ST. CLAIR, ST. CLAIR CO., ST. MARY, [CEM]
415 N. 6th St., St. Clair, 48079. Tel: 810-329-2255;
Fax: 810-329-5997. Rev. Michael Christopher Zuelch.
School—St. Mary School, (Grades 1-5), 800 Orchard St., St. Clair, 48079. Tel: 810-329-4150;
Fax: 810-329-5705; Email: cnesbitt@stmarystclair.org. LeeAnn Brennan, Prin. Lay Teachers 6; Students 47; Clergy / Religious Teachers 6.
Catechesis Religious Program—Tel: 810-329-7801. Lisa Yamin, D.R.E. Students 150.
Community Center—

ST. CLAIR SHORES, MACOMB CO.

1—ST. GERMAINE, Merged with St. Gertrude, St. Clair Shores to form Our Lady of Hope, St. Clair Shores.

2—ST. GERTRUDE, [CEM] Merged with St. Germaine, St. Clair Shores to form Our Lady of Hope, St. Clair Shores.

3—ST. ISAAC JOGUES
21100 Madison, St. Clair Shores, 48081.
Tel: 586-778-5100; Email: parishoffice@saintisaacjogues.com; Web: www.saintisaacjogues.com. 25001 Chippendale, Roseville, 48066. Rev. David Cybulski.
Parish Center—25001 Chippendale, Roseville, 48066.
School—St. Isaac Jogues School, (Grades 1-8), 21100 Madison St., Saint Clair Shores, 48081.
Tel: 586-771-3525; Fax: 586-778-8183; Email: cmaniaci@saintisaacjogues.com. Sr. Catherine Marie, O.P., Prin. Lay Teachers 13; Sisters 4; Students 240; Parish Population 1.
Catechesis Religious Program—Email: laroth@saintisaacjogues.com. Lisa Ann Roth, Dir. Catechesis & Evangelization.

4—ST. JOAN OF ARC
Tel: 586-777-3670; Fax: 586-774-5528; Email: info@sjascs.org; Web: www.sjascs.org. Rev. Msgr. G. Michael Bugarin; Rev. John Bettin; Deacon Thomas Strasz; Ms. Dina Ciaffone, Business Mgr.
Parish Center—22412 Overlake, St. Clair Shores, 48080.
School—St. Joan of Arc School, (Grades 1-8), 22415 Overlake, St. Clair Shores, 48080. Tel: 586-777-8370; Fax: 586-447-3574; Email: info@stjoan.net; Web: www.stjoan.net. Katherine Kalich, Prin.; Ms. Mary Pat Brennan, Vice Prin. Lay Teachers 30; Students 394; Parish Population 1.
Catechesis Religious Program—22415 Overlake St., St. Clair Shores, 48080. Tel: 586-772-1282;
Fax: 586-775-8374; Email: repoffice@sjascs.org. Mrs. Jean Hartman, D.R.E. Students 240.

5—ST. LUCY St. Lucy Catholic Church
Tel: 586-771-8300; Fax: 586-447-4220; Email: parish@stlucychurch.com; Web: www.stlucychurch.com. Rev. James E. Commyn; Deacon John Thompson
St. Lucy Catholic Church
Res.: 23401 Jefferson, St. Clair Shores, 48080.
Catechesis Religious Program—Tel: 586-771-8300. Students 19.

6—ST. MARGARET OF SCOTLAND
21201 Thirteen Mile Rd., St. Clair Shores, 48082.
Tel: 586-293-2240, Ext. 121; Email: thehighlander@sms-scs.org; Web: www.stmargaretscsmi.org. Rev. Ronald DeHondt; Deacons Ronald Channell; Michael P. O'Keefe; Deacon Emeritus Val Buyle.
Catechesis Religious Program—Students 243.

7—OUR LADY OF HOPE
Tel: 586-771-1750; Fax: 586-771-7634; Email: jhamlin@olohscs.org; Web: www.olohscs.org. Rev. James L. Bjorum, J.C.L.
Office: 28301 Little Mack, St. Clair Shores, 48081. Email: revjlb@olohscs.org.
School—St. Germaine, (Grades PreK-8), 28250 Rockwood, St. Clair Shores, 48081.
Tel: 586-771-0890; Email: jdegrez@stgermaine.org; Web: www.stgermaine.org. Mrs. Julie DeGrez, Prin. Lay Teachers 16; Students 190.
Catechesis Religious Program—
Tel: 586-771-1750, Ext. 125; Email: sgudenau@olohscs.org. Susan Gudenau, D.R.E. Students 86.

SHELBY TWP., MACOMB CO.

1—ST. JOHN VIANNEY CHURCH
Tel: 586-781-6525; Fax: 586-781-6527; Email: dkennard@catholicweb.com; Web: www.sjvshelby.ord. Rev. Timothy P. Mazur; Mrs. Patricia Boik, Business Mgr.; Mr. John Lajiness, Pastoral Assoc.; Barbara Bakotich, Youth Min.; Sarah Dudek, Music Min.
Res.: 54045 Schoenherr Rd., Shelby Twp., 48315. Email: sjvparishmail@catholicweb.com.
Catechesis Religious Program—Email: kristineboor@catholicweb.com. Kristine Boor, D.R.E. Students 151.

2—ST. KIERAN
Tel: 586-781-4901; Fax: 586-781-6516. Rev. Msgr. H. Thomas Johnson; Patricia Radacsy, Pastoral Assoc.
Res.: 53600 Mound Rd., Shelby Twp., 48316. Email: jeanee@stkieran.org; Web: www.stkieran.org.
Catechesis Religious Program—Tel: 586-781-6515; Email: sue@stkieran.org. Susan Weyland, D.R.E.; Rose Churilla, D.R.E. Students 735.

3—ST. THERESE OF LISIEUX, Revs. Lawrence Zurawski; Charles D. Fox; Deacon Gregory Willoughby.
Church: 48115 Schoenherr Rd., Shelby Twp., 48315-4225. Tel: 586-254-4433; Fax: 586-254-5463; Email: info@sttheresepari sh.ws; Web: StThereseParish.ws.
Catechesis Religious Program—Tel: 586-254-2944; Email: brendamanzo@sttheresepari sh.ws. Brenda Manzo, D.R.E. Students 742.

SOUTH LYON, OAKLAND CO., ST. JOSEPH
Tel: 248-446-8700; Fax: 248-446-8746; Email: Office@saintjosephsouthlyon.org; Web: saintjosephsouthlyon.org. Revs. Stan Tokarski; Gregory J. Deters; Deacon Chris Booms.
Church: 830 S. Lafayette, South Lyon, 48178. Email: theresa.durant@saintjosephsouthlyon.org.
Res.: 810 S. Lafayette, South Lyon, 48178.
Tel: 248-437-2042.
Catechesis Religious Program—Email: kim.donahue@saintjosephsouthlyon.org. Ms. Kimberly Donahue, D.R.E. Students 731.

SOUTHFIELD, OAKLAND CO.

1—ST. BEATRICE, Merged with St. Bede, Southfield, St. Ives, Southfield & St. Michael, Southfield to form Church of the Transfiguration, Southfield.

2—ST. BEDE, Merged with St. Beatrice, Southfield, St. Ives, Southfield & St. Michael, Southfield to form Church of the Transfiguration, Southfield.

3—CHURCH OF THE TRANSFIGURATION
25225 Code Rd., Southfield, 48033.
Tel: 248-356-8787; Fax: 248-356-1240; Email: scheelerj@transfigsfld.org; Web: www.transfigsfld.org. Revs. Jeffrey Scheeler, O.F.M.; Jeremy Harrington.
Catechesis Religious Program—Diane Klucka, D.R.E. Students 35.

4—DIVINE PROVIDENCE, (Lithuanian)
Tel: 248-354-3429; Email: dpLithuanianchurch@gmail.com. Rev. Gintaras Jonikas.
Res.: 25335 W. 9 Mile Rd., Southfield, 48033-3933.
Catechesis Religious Program—Tel: 248-347-0832; Email: dsiredas@hotmail.com. Vitas Sirgedas, D.R.E.; Danute Sirgedas, D.R.E. Students 25.

5—ST. IVES, Merged with St. Beatrice, Southfield, St. Bede, Southfield & St. Michael, Southfield to form Church of the Transfiguration, Southfield.

6—ST. MICHAEL, Merged with St. Beatrice, Southfield, St. Bede, Southfield & St. Ives, Southfield to form Church of the Transfiguration, Southfield.

7—OUR LADY OF ALBANIANS
29350 Lahser Rd., Southfield, 48034.
Tel: 248-353-3410; Fax: 248-353-5412; Email: olalbanians@yahoo.com. Rev. Nue Gjergji, Admin.
Catechesis Religious Program—Dr. Gjecka Gjelaj, D.R.E.

SOUTHGATE, WAYNE CO.

1—ST. HUGH, Merged into St. Francis Cabrini Parish, Allen Park.

2—ST. PIUS X (1950) Rev. Robert J. McCabe.
Office: 14101 Superior Ave., Southgate, 48195.
Tel: 734-285-1100; Fax: 734-285-5310; Email: church@saintpius-x.org; Web: saintpius-x.org.
Res.: 14160 Longtin Ave., Southgate, 48195.
School—St. Pius X School, (Grades 1-8), 14141 Pearl St., Southgate, 48195. Tel: 734-284-6500;
Fax: 734-285-6525; Email: mseward@saintpius-x.org; Web: www.saintpiusschool.org. Michelle E. Seward, Elementary Prin. Lay Teachers 18; Students 369.
Catechesis Religious Program—Tel: 734-284-6562; Email: dsolis@saintpius-x.org. Philippa Monteleon, D.R.E. Students 103.

STERLING HEIGHTS, MACOMB CO.

1—ST. BLASE
Tel: 586-268-2244; Fax: 586-268-1174; Email: office@stblase.org; Web: www.stblase.org. Rev. Randall Phillips; Dr. Mary Dumm, Pastoral Assoc.; Deacon Edwin McLeod.
Res.: 12151 E. 15 Mile Rd., Sterling Heights, 48312-5120. Email: Parishstaff@stblase.org.
Catechesis Religious Program—Students 162.

2—SS. CYRIL AND METHODIUS
41233 Ryan Rd., Sterling Heights, 48314.
Tel: 586-726-6911; Fax: 586-685-1070; Email: parishoffice@saintcyrils.org. Revs. Libor Marek, Admin.; Juraj Nuota; Deacons Phil McCown; Gerald Smigell.
Catechesis Religious Program—Paul Schuller, D.R.E.; Carroll Schuller, D.R.E. Students 388.

3—ST. EPHREM
Tel: 586-264-1230; Fax: 586-264-2757; Email: office@stephrems.org; Web: www.saintephremchurch.org. Rev. Craig Giera.
Res.: 38900 Dodge Rd., Sterling Heights, 48312.
Catechesis Religious Program—Tel: 586-264-2777; Fax: 586-264-2783; Email: ReligiousEd@stephrems.org; Email: RobL@stephrems.org. Mr. Robert Leonardi, D.R.E. Students 98.

4—ST. JANE FRANCES DE CHANTAL
38750 Ryan Rd., Sterling Heights, 48310.
Tel: 586-977-8080; Fax: 586-977-9305; Email: jgazo@sjfparish.org; Web: sjfparish.org.
Catechesis Religious Program—Tel: 586-977-0310. Students 84.

5—ST. MALACHY
Tel: 586-264-1220; Fax: 586-264-1656; Email: contact@stmalachychurch.org. Rev. Joseph J. Gembala.
Res.: 14115 E. 14 Mile Rd., Sterling Heights, 48312-6506. Email: business@stmalachychurch.org; Web: www.saintmalachychurch.org.
Catechesis Religious Program—Tel: 586-268-4430. Mrs. Joan Marjan, D.R.E. Students 321.

6—ST. MATTHIAS
Mailing Address: 12311 Nineteen Mile Rd., Sterling Heights, 48313. Tel: 586-731-1300; Email: parishoffice@stmatthiaschurch.net. Rev. Francisco Restrepo.
Res.: 12509 Nineteen Mile Rd., Sterling Heights, 48313.
Catechesis Religious Program—Tel: 586-731-0650. Donna Latimer, D.R.E. Students 120.

7—ST. MICHAEL, Revs. Michael W. Quaine; Artemio Galos; Deacons Jerome Campernel; Franz Hoffer.
Church: 40501 Hayes Rd., Sterling Heights, 48313.
Tel: 586-247-0020; Fax: 586-247-4081; Web: WWW.stmichaelcc.org.
Res.: 39443 Heatherheath, Clinton Township, 48038. Tel: 313-268-6379.
Catechesis Religious Program—Tel: 586-247-0098. Claudia Welbes, D.R.E. Students 370.

8—OUR LADY OF CZESTOCHOWA
Tel: 586-977-7267; Fax: 586-977-2074; Email: info@parisholc.org; Web: www.parisholc.org. Very Rev. Andrzej Maslejak, S.Chr.; Revs. Siarhei Anhur, S.Chr.; Robert Wojslaw, S.Chr.
Res.: 3100 18 Mile Rd., Sterling Heights, 48314-3810.
Catechesis Religious Program—Sr. Wioletta Koltun, D.R.E. Students 320.

9—ST. RENE GOUPIL
Mailing Address: 35955 Ryan Rd., Sterling Heights, 48310. Tel: 586-939-7500; Fax: 586-939-7839; Email: MMay@StRene.org. Rev. Steven C. Koehler; Deacon David Fleming.
Res.: 35670 Ryan Rd., Sterling Heights, 48310.
Catechesis Religious Program—Michael Novak, D.R.E. Students 139.

TAYLOR, WAYNE CO.

1—ST. ALFRED
24175 Baske St., Taylor, 48180. Tel: 313-291-6464;
Fax: 313-291-2700; Email: stalfredchurchtaylormi@gmail.com; Web: stalfredtaylor.org. Rev. Charles K. Altermatt; Deacon Scott LaForest.
Catechesis Religious Program—
Tel: 313-291-6464, Ext. 105; Email: stalfredreligioused@gmail.com. Kathleen Operhall, D.R.E. Students 108.

2—ST. CONSTANCE
Tel: 313-291-4050; Fax: 313-291-5655; Email: ctwiggstconstance@comcast.net. Rev. Leo F. Sabourin.
Res.: 21555 Kinyon Rd., Taylor, 48180.
Catechesis Religious Program—Bernadine Shook, D.R.E. Students 139.

3—ST. CYRIL OF JERUSALEM, Merged with St. Paschal, Taylor to form Our Lady of the Angels, Taylor.

4—OUR LADY OF THE ANGELS
Tel: 313-381-3000; Fax: 313-381-5528; Email: mail@loacc.org. Rev. Dariusz Strzalkowski; Deacon William A. Thome.
Church: 6442 Pelham Rd., Taylor, 48180.
Catechesis Religious Program—Karen Kerr, D.R.E. Students 135.

5—ST. PASCHAL, Merged with St. Cyril of Jerusalem, Taylor to form Our Lady of the Angels, Taylor.

TEMPERANCE, MONROE CO.

1—ST. ANTHONY, [CEM]
4605 St. Anthony Rd., Temperance, 48182.
Tel: 734-854-1143; Fax: 734-854-4622; Email: stanthony@bex.net; Web: stanthonytemperance.org. Rev. Robert J. Slaton. English Masses; Latin Masses
Catechesis Religious Program—4609 St. Anthony Rd., Temperance, 48182. Tel: 734-854-1160; Email: dredu@stanthonytemperance.org. Virginia Stout, D.R.E. Students 31.

2—OUR LADY OF MOUNT CARMEL
8330 Lewis Ave., Temperance, 48182.
Tel: 734-847-2805; Fax: 734-847-8970; Email: olmc@bex.net; Web: mountcarmeltemperance.org. Rev. Don A. LaCuesta; Deacon Martin Selmek.
Catechesis Religious Program—
Tel: 734-847-1725, Ext. 21. Ms. Mary Urbanski, D.R.E. Students 270.

TRENTON, WAYNE CO.

1—ST. JOSEPH, [JC]
Tel: 734-676-9082; Fax: 734-676-6255; Email: dpetrlich@stjosephtrenton.com. Rev. Stephen Rooney; Donald Scott Anastasia, Pastoral Assoc.
Parish Center—2565 Third St., Trenton, 48183. Email: frbrad@stjosephtrenton.com.
School—St. Joseph School, (Grades 1-1), 2675 Third St., Trenton, 48183. Tel: 734-676-2565; Web: www.stjosephschooltrenton.com; Fax: 734-676-9744; Email: principal@stjosephschooltrenton.com. Christen McMillan, Prin. Lay Teachers 11; Students 157; Parish Population 1.
Catechesis Religious Program—Tel: 734-676-9082; Fax: 734-676-6255. Dennae Petrlich, D.R.E. Students 220.

2—ST. TIMOTHY, Rev. David Lesniak.
Parish Office—Parish Office: 2901 Manning Dr., Trenton, 48183. Tel: 734-676-5115;
Fax: 734-676-6863; Web: www.sttimothytrenton.org.
Catechesis Religious Program—Email: re.st.timothy@gmail.com. Denise Murray, D.R.E.; Theresa Kramer, Adult Faith Formation Coord. Students 85.

TROY, OAKLAND CO.

1—ST. ALAN, Merged with St. Columban, Birmingham to form Christ Our Light, Troy.

2—ST. ANASTASIA
Tel: 248-689-8380; Fax: 248-689-7489; Email: hmichelcavage@stanastasia.org; Email: office@stanastasia.org; Web: www.stanastasia.org. Revs. Steven A. Wertanen; Jacob A. Van Assche; Deacon Tommaso Caporuscio.
Res.: 4571 John R. Rd., Troy, 48085.
Catechesis Religious Program—Email: espencer@stanastasia.org. Elizabeth Spencer, D.R.E. Students 661.

3—CHRIST OUR LIGHT
Tel: 248-649-5510; Fax: 248-649-6729; Email: christourlight@comcast.net; Web: christourlight.weconnect.com. Rev. Donald L. Demmer, Admin.
Res.: 2345 Coolidge Rd., Troy, 48084.
Tel: 248-649-5511.
Church: 3077 Glouchester, Troy, 48084.
Catechesis Religious Program—
Tel: 248-649-5510, Ext. 107; Email: joann.bonahoom@coltroy.org. JoAnn Bonahoom, D.R.E. Students 308.

4—ST. ELIZABETH ANN SETON
Tel: 248-879-1310; Fax: 248-879-2886; Email: Secretary@saintliz.org; Web: www.saintliz.org. Rev. Norman D. Nawrocki, J.C.L.; Deacon Gregory Formanczyk.
Church: 280 E. Square Lake Rd., Troy, 48085.
Catechesis Religious Program—Email: TKonwinski@saintliz.org. Terri Konwinski, D.R.E. Students 96.

5—ST. LUCY, (Croatian)
Tel: 248-619-9910; Fax: 248-619-9912. Rev. Antun Orsolic.
Catechesis Religious Program—Mr. Leonardo Ljuljduraj, D.R.E., Organist. Students 20.

6—ST. THOMAS MORE
4580 Adams Rd., Troy, 48098. Tel: 248-647-2222; Fax: 248-647-8192; Email: inquiry@stmoffice.com; Web: stthomasmoretroy.org. Rev. Msgr. Thomas G. Rice; Deacons Michael Stach, Pastoral Assoc.; Christopher Stark.
Catechesis Religious Program—Tel: 248-647-4680; Email: josylin@stmoffice.com. Josylin Mateus, D.R.E. Students 415.

UTICA, MACOMB CO., ST. LAWRENCE
44633 Utica Rd., Utica, 48317. Tel: 586-731-5347; Fax: 586-731-5393; Web: www.stlawrenceparish.com. Revs. Roman Pasieczny; Matthew Ellis; Timothy J. Wezner.
School—St. Lawrence School, (Grades PreK-8), 44429 Utica Rd., Utica, 48317. Lisa Dimercurio, Prin. Lay Teachers 36; Students 697.
Catechesis Religious Program—Tel: 586-731-5072; Email: lrajnicek@stlawrenceparish.com. Mrs. Lisa Rajnicek, M.Ed., D.R.E. Students 344.

WALLED LAKE, OAKLAND CO., ST. WILLIAM, Rev. Michael G. Savickas; Deacons Charles R. Dreyer; John Liddle; Mrs. Deborah Diviny, Business Mgr.; Mrs. Karen Trojniak, Youth Min.; Mrs. Mary Dreyer, Music Min.; Mrs. Nancy Thomas, RCIA Coord.
Res.: 531 Common St., Walled Lake, 48390-3417.
Tel: 248-624-1421; Email: Rectory1@StWilliam.com; Web: www.StWilliam.com.
School—St. William School, (Grades PreK-8), 135 O'Flaherty, Walled Lake, 48390. Tel: 248-669-4440; Email: ljackson@stwilliam.com; Web: www.stwilliam-school.com. Linda Jackson, M.A., Prin. Lay Teachers 12; Students 110.
Catechesis Religious Program—Tel: 248-624-1371; Email: mmccrandall@stwilliam.com. Deacon Michael McCrandall, D.R.E. Students 186.

WARREN, MACOMB CO.

1—ST. ANNE
32000 Mound Rd., Warren, 48092. Tel: 586-264-0713 ; Fax: 586-264-0718; Email: jackie@st-anne.net. Rev. Alberto P. Bondy.
School—St. Anne School, (Grades 1-8), 5920 Arden, Warren, 48092. Tel: 586-264-2911; Email: mainoffice@st-anne.net; Web: st-anne.net. Clergy 1; Lay Teachers 30; Students 527; Parish Population 1.
Catechesis Religious Program—Tel: 586-268-3434; Email: dhathaway@st-anne.net. Debbie Hathaway, D.R.E. Students 15.

2—ASCENSION, Merged into St. Clement, Center Line.

3—ST. CLETUS, Closed. For inquiries for parish records contact the chancery.

4—ST. DOROTHY, Merged with St. Leonard of Port Maurice, Warren to form St. Teresa of Avila, Warren.

5—ST. EDMUND (1961) Merged with St. Sylvester, Warren to form St. Faustina, Warren.

6—ST. FAUSTINA
Tel: 586-772-2720; Fax: 586-772-5576; Email: stfaustina@comcast.net; Web: stfaustinawarren.org. Rev. Bogdan Milosz.
Res.: 14025 Twelve Mile Rd., Warren, 48088. Web: stfaustina-mi.org.
Catechesis Religious Program—Tel: 586-773-9220; Fax: 586-772-5021; Email: sandyjacord@gmail.com. Sandy Acord, D.R.E. Students 83.

7—ST. LEONARD OF PORT MAURICE, [CEM] Merged with St. Dorothy, Warren to form St. Teresa of Avila, Warren.

8—ST. LOUISE
2500 E. Twelve Mile Rd., Warren, 48092.
Tel: 586-751-3340; Email: fathermichael@saintlouisedm.org; Web: www.saintlouisedm.org. Revs. Michael (Clement) Suhy, O.S.B.; Pathrose Panuvel; Deacon Charles Pace.
Catechesis Religious Program—Ms. Julia Czarnecki, Campus Min.

9—ST. MARK
4401 Bart Ave., Warren, 48091. Tel: 586-759-3020; Email: parishcenter@stmarkparishwarren.org. Rev. Stanley Obloj; Deacon Brian Carroll.
Res.: 4362 Kendall, Warren, 48091.
Catechesis Religious Program—Email: abrewer@stmarkparishwarren.org. Amanda Brewer, D.R.E. Students 45.

10—ST. MARTIN DE PORRES
Tel: 586-264-7515; Fax: 586-264-4013; Email: parishoffice@smdeporres.com; Web: www.smdeporres.com. Rev. Nicholas Zukowski.
Res.: 31555 Hoover Rd., Warren, 48093.
Catechesis Religious Program—Tel: 586-264-7970. Mrs. Christine Cabe, D.R.E. Students 292.

11—ST. MARY, OUR LADY QUEEN OF FAMILIES PARISH
25320 Van Dyke, Center Line, 48015.
Tel: 586-757-3306; Fax: 586-757-5390; Email: stccpsrishoffice@gmail.com; Web: www.ourladyqueenoffamilies.net. 12255 Frazho Rd., Warren, 48089-1200. Rev. Robert A. Bauer; Deacon Stanley Avery.
Res.: 8050 Engelman, Center Line, 48015.
Catechesis Religious Program— Religious education now held at St. Dorothy Site. 12251 Frazho Rd., Warren, 48089. Tel: 586-427-2759; Email: smolqf.reled@gmail.com. Alice Baron, D.R.E.; Donna Van Gheluwe, D.R.E. Students 7.

12—OUR LADY OF GRACE VIETNAMESE PARISH Our Lady of Grace Parish (1999)
Tel: 586-755-1313; Web: www.ologwarren.org. Rev. Hoang Chi Lam.
Church & Res.: 26256 Ryan Rd., Warren, 48091.
Fax: 586-393-6623.
Catechesis Religious Program— Religious Education ProgramDeacon Kevin Tietz, D.R.E. Students 16.

13—ST. SYLVESTER, Merged with St. Edmund, Warren to form St. Faustina, Warren.

14—ST. TERESA OF AVILA, Merged with St. Clement, Center Line to form St. Mary, Our Lady Queen of Families, Warren.

WASHINGTON, MACOMB CO., SS. JOHN AND PAUL
Tel: 586-781-9010; Fax: 586-781-7061; Email: ssjohnandpaul@sbcglobal.net; Web: www.ssjohnandpaul.org. Rev. Festus N. Ejimadu.
Res.: 61847 Glenwood Trail, Washington, 48094.
Church: 7777 W. 28 Mile Rd., Washington, 48094.
Catechesis Religious Program—Tel: 586-781-9488; Email: klocke@ssjohnandpaul.org. Kathryn Locke, D.R.E. Students 238.

WATERFORD, OAKLAND CO.

1—ST. BENEDICT
40 S. Lynn Ave., Waterford, 48328.
Tel: 248-681-1534; Email: stbenz80@gmail.com. Rev. James A. Mayworm, (Retired); Joyce Miracle, Contact Person.
Parish Center—80 S. Lynn Ave., Waterford, 48328. Tel: 248-681-1534, Ext. 200; Web: stbencc.org.
Catechesis Religious Program—Email: gloria.armstrong.stben@gmail.com. Gloria Armstrong, D.R.E. Students 87.

2—OUR LADY OF THE LAKES
Mailing Address: 5481 Dixie Hwy., Waterford, 48329. Tel: 248-623-0274; Fax: 248-623-2723; Email: parishoffice@ollonline.org; Web: ollonline.org. Revs. Scott A. Thibodeau; Christopher Muer, Parochial Vicar; Deacons John Schulte; Stephen Talbot.
School—Our Lady of the Lakes School, (Grades PreK-8), 5495 Dixie Hwy., Waterford, 48329.
Tel: 248-623-0340; Fax: 248-623-2274;
Fax: 248-623-6550; Email: jeanine.kenny@ollonline.org; Web: www.ollonline.org. Jeanine Kenny, Prin.; Mrs. Kitty Farkas, Vice Pres. Clergy 2; Lay Teachers 16; Students 200; Clergy / Religious Teachers 2.
High School—Our Lady of the Lakes High School, Rev. Christopher Muer; Jeanine Kenny, Prin.; Mr. Jared Kullman, Athletic Dir./Dir. of AP & Curriculum. Lay Teachers 17; Students 102; Clergy / Religious Teachers 2.
Catechesis Religious Program—Email: ollreligiouseducation@parishmail.com. Artha Horowitz, D.R.E.; Mrs. Vicki Asai, RCIA Coord. Students 301.

3—ST. PERPETUA
134 Airport Rd., Waterford, 48327. Tel: 248-682-6431 ; Fax: 248-682-7088; Email: stper682@aol.com. Rev. Jack H. Baker; Deacon Robert Gajda.
Catechesis Religious Program—Pauline Zorza, D.R.E. Students 136.

WAYNE, WAYNE CO., ST. MARY, [CEM]
34530 W. Michigan Ave., Wayne, 48184-1748.
Tel: 734-721-8745; Fax: 734-721-0260; Email: parishoffice@stmarywayne.org; Web: www.stmarywayne.org. Rev. Sean P. Bonner, Admin.
Catechesis Religious Program—
Tel: 734-721-8745, Ext. 42; Email: faithformation@stmarywayne.org. Priscilla Steenburg, D.R.E. Students 128.

WEST BLOOMFIELD, OAKLAND CO., PRINCE OF PEACE
Email: parishsecretary@princeofpeacecatholic.church; Web: princeofpeacecatholic.church. Rev. Ronald J. Jozwiak.
Res.: 4300 Walnut Lake Rd., West Bloomfield, 48323.
Catechesis Religious Program—Tel: 248-681-5070. Karen Schroder, D.R.E. Students 128.

WESTLAND, WAYNE CO.

1—ST. BERNARDINE, Closed. For inquiries for parish records contact the chancery.

2—CHURCH OF THE DIVINE SAVIOR, Merged with St. Damian, Westland & St. Theodore of Canterbury, Westland to form St. Mary, Cause of Our Joy Parish, Westland.

3—ST. DAMIAN, Merged with Church of the Divine Savior, Westland & St. Theodore of Canterbury, Westland to form St. Mary, Cause of Our Joy Parish, Westland.

4—ST. MARY, CAUSE OF OUR JOY
Tel: 734-425-4421; Email: office@stmarycooj.org; Web: www.stmarycooj.org. Rev. Kenneth Mazur, P.I.M.E.
Res.: 8200 N. Wayne Rd., Westland, 48185.
Catechesis Religious Program—Email: faithformation@stmarycooj.org. Sr. Gemma Legel, O.S.F., Faith Formation Dir. Students 96.

5—ST. RICHARD, Most Rev. Walter A. Hurley, J.C.L.
Res. & Church Office: 35851 Cherry Hill, Westland, 48186. Tel: 734-729-2240; Fax: 734-727-0466; Email: frsean-SMSRHF@usa.net.
Catechesis Religious Program—Tel: 734-729-4411; Fax: 734-727-0466. Religious Ed now held at St. Mary, Wayne.

6—SS. SIMON AND JUDE (1959)
Tel: 734-722-1343; Fax: 734-326-5466; Email: pastor@stssimonandjude.com. Rev. Gerard V. Bechard.
Office: 32500 Palmer Rd., Westland, 48186.

Catechesis Religious Program—Mary Ann Kocsis, D.R.E., Email: psr@stssimonandjude.com; Margaret Reyez, D.R.E. Students 80.

7—ST. THEODORE OF CANTERBURY (1963) Merged with Church of the Divine Savior, Westland & St. Damian, Westland to form St. Mary, Cause of Our Joy, Westland.

WHITE LAKE, OAKLAND CO., ST. PATRICK, Revs. Thomas L. Meagher; John Peter Arul, M.S.F.S.; Deacon Michael Chesley.
Res.: 9086 Hutchins Rd., White Lake, 48386.
Tel: 248-698-3100; Fax: 248-698-2350; Web: www.stpatrickwhitelake.org.
School—St. Patrick School, (Grades 1-8), 9040 Hutchins Rd., White Lake, 48386. Tel: 248-698-3240; Fax: 248-698-4339; Email: jclark@stpwl.org. Jeremy Clark, Prin.; Bridget Page, Librarian. Lay Teachers 26; Students 458; Parish Population 1.
Catechesis Religious Program—Students 646.

WOODHAVEN, WAYNE CO., OUR LADY OF THE WOODS
Tel: 734-671-5101; Fax: 734-671-2901; Email: Fra@olow.org; Web: olow.org. Rev. Andrew Czarnecki.
Res.: 21892 Gudith Rd., Woodhaven, 48183. Email: rgonzalez@olow.org.
Catechesis Religious Program—Colleen Ontko, D.R.E. Students 102.

WYANDOTTE, WAYNE CO.

1—ST. ELIZABETH, [JC] Merged into St. Joseph, Wyandotte.

2—ST. HELENA, Closed. For inquiries for parish records contact the chancery.

3—ST. JOSEPH, Merged with St. Patrick, Wyandotte to form St. Vincent Pallotti.

4—OUR LADY OF MT. CARMEL, [CEM] (Polish), Merged (High school closed on June 30, 2011. Contact Parish for records) with St. Stanislaus Kostka, Wyandotte to form Our Lady of the Scapular, Wyandotte.

5—OUR LADY OF THE SCAPULAR
Tel: 734-284-9135; Fax: 734-284-1367; Email: ourladyofthescapular@wyan.org; Web: www.ourladyofthescapular.org. Rev. Mark Borkowski
Legal Title: Our Lady of Mount Carmel and St. Stanislaus Kostka
Church, Mailing Address & Res.: 976 Pope John Paul II Ave. (Superior Blvd.), Wyandotte, 48192-3496.
Catechesis Religious Program— Program held at Our Lady of the Scapular, Wyandotte Email: Frmarkb@aol.com. Mr. David Carle, Diocesan D.R.E. Students 51.

6—ST. PATRICK, [JC] Merged with St. Joseph, Wyandotte to form St. Vincent Pallotti, Wyandotte.

7—ST. STANISLAUS KOSTKA, (Polish), Merged with Our Lady of Mt. Carmel, Wyandotte to form Our Lady of the Scapular, Wyandotte.

8—ST. VINCENT PALLOTTI
334 Elm St., Wyandotte, 48192. Tel: 734-285-9840; Fax: 734-285-9745; Email: parish@stvpp.org; Web: www.stvpp.org. Revs. Michael Cremin, S.A.C.; Brendan McCarrick.
See Pope John Paul II Regional School at Christ the Good Shepherd, Lincoln Park.
Catechesis Religious Program—
Tel: 734-285-9840, Ext. 102; Email: dre@stvpp.org. Julie Dzanbazoff, D.R.E. Students 195.

YALE, ST. CLAIR CO., SACRED HEART, [CEM]
Tel: 810-387-9800; Email: olmcshydre@gmail.com. Rev. Thomas Kuehnemund; Deacon William Kolarik.
Res.: 310 N. Main St., Yale, 48097-2845.
Catechesis Religious Program—Brenda Krzak, D.R.E. Students 76.

Chaplains of Public Institutions

DETROIT. *Children's Hospital*, Tel: 313-745-5917. Sr. Beverly Hindson, I.H.M.
Cottage Hospital, Tel: 810-785-8855. VacantAttended from St. Paul on the Lake Parish, Grosse Pointe Farms, MI.
Detroit Osteopathic Hospital, Tel: 313-865-6300. Attended from Cathedral of the Most Blessed Sacrament, Detroit.
Detroit Receiving Hospital, 48226. Tel: 313-745-3000. Vacant.
DMC Sinai-Grace Hospital, Tel: 313-966-3300. Vacant.
Harper University Hospital, Tel: 313-745-6000. Vacant.
Henry Ford Hospital, Tel: 800-436-7936. Sr. Ellen Burke, O.S.F.
Hutzel Hospital, Tel: 313-831-3139. Vacant.
John D. Dingell Veterans Administration Medical Center, Tel: 313-576-1000. Rev. Chrysanthus Udoh, Chap.
St. John Hospital, 22101 Moross Rd., 48236.
Tel: 313-343-7850; Email: regina.burton2@ascension.org. Rev. Joseph Mahoney, Sr. Jane Dutkiewicz.
Karmanos Cancer Institute, Tel: 800-527-6266. Vacant.
Mound Correctional Facility, 17601 Mound Rd., 48212. Rev. Michael Chesley, Tel: 855-878-3754; Web: www.svdpji.org.
Ryan Correctional Facility, 17600 Ryan Rd., 48212. Rev. Michael Chesley, Tel: 855-878-3754; Web: www.svdpji.org.
Wayne County Jail, 1231 St. Antoine, 48226. Rev. Michael Chesley, Tel: 855-878-3754; Web: www.svdpji.org.
Wayne County Juvenile Detention Facility, 1326 St. Antoine, 48226. Ida Johns, Tel: 313-237-6056.

DEARBORN. *Oakwood Hospital*, Dearborn.
Tel: 313-593-7000. Rev. Luke Iwuji.

FARMINGTON HILLS. *Botsford Hospital*, Farmington Hills. Tel: 248-471-8000. Rev. Dennis J. Nowinski.

GARDEN CITY. *Garden City Hospital*, Garden City.
Tel: 734-421-3300. Rev. Bernard Pilarski, (Retired).

GROSSE POINTE. *Beaumont Hospital*, Grosse Pointe.
Tel: 313-343-1000. Rev. Richard Bartoszek.

LAPEER. *Lapeer County Jail*, 3231 John Conley Dr., Lapeer, 48446. Rev. Michael Chesley, Chap., Tel: 855-878-3754; Web: www.svdpji.org.
Thumb Correctional Facility, 3225 John Conley Dr., Lapeer, 48446. Rev. Michael Chesley, Tel: 855-878-3754; Web: www.svdpji.org.

MONROE. *Monroe County Jail*, 100 E. Second St., Monroe, 48161. Rev. Michael Chesley, Tel: 855-878-3754; Web: www.svdpji.org.

MOUNT CLEMENS. *Macomb County Jail*, 43565 Elizabeth Rd., Mount Clemens, 48043.
Tel: 586-307-9326. Jo Kudela.
Macomb County Juvenile Justice Center, 400 N. Rose Rd., Mount Clemens, 48043. Ida Johns, Tel: 313-237-6056Attended from St. Peter's, Mount Clemens.
Mount Clemens General Hospital, Mount Clemens.
Tel: 586-493-8500. Vacant.

NEW HAVEN. *Macomb Correctional Facility*, 26 Mile Rd, New Haven, 48048. Rev. Michael Chesley, Tel: 855-878-3754; Web: www.svdpji.org.

PONTIAC. *St. Clair County Jail*, 1170 Michigan Rd., Port Huron, 48060. Rev. Michael Chesley, Tel: 855-878-3754; Web: www.svdpji.org.
Doctors' Hospital of Michigan, 461 W. Huron, Pontiac, 48341. Tel: 248-857-7200. Vacant.
Oakland County Children's Village, 1200 N. Telegraph Rd., Pontiac, 48341. Tel: 313-237-6056. Ida Johns, Coord. of Ministry to Youth in Detention, Carleen Ward, Chap., Tel: 248-858-1183.
Oakland County Jail, 1201 N. Telegraph, Pontiac, 48341. Tel: 248-338-9310; Fax: 248-338-2695. Sr. Margaret Devaney.
Pontiac Osteopathic Hospital, Pontiac.
Tel: 248-338-5000. Vacant.

PORT HURON. *St. Clair County Juvenile Intervention Center*, 1170 Michigan, Port Huron, 48060.
Tel: 313-237-6056. Ida Johns, Coord. of Ministry to Youth in Detention, Kevin Totty, Chap., Tel: 810-966-4106.
Port Huron Hospital, Port Huron. Tel: 810-985-7750. Attended from Holy Trinity Parish, Port Huron.

PLYMOUTH. *Robert Scott Correctional Facility*, 47500 Five Mile Rd., Plymouth, 48170. Rev. Michael Chesley, Tel: 855-878-3754; Web: www.svdpji.org.

ROCHESTER. *Crittendon Hospital*, Rochester.
Tel: 248-652-5000. Rev. Joy Chakian.

ROYAL OAK. *Beaumont Hospital*, Royal Oak.
Tel: 248-898-5000. Rev. Christopher Welsh.

TRENTON. *Oakwood Southshore Medical Center*, Trenton. Tel: 734-671-7779. Beverly M. Beltramo.

TROY. *Beaumont Hospital*, Troy. Tel: 248-964-5000. Rev. Joy Chakian.

WARREN. *Henry Ford Macomb Hospital*, Warren.
Tel: 586-759-7300. Rev. Luke Krotkiewicz.

WAYNE. *Oakwood Annapolis Hospital*, Wayne.
Tel: 734-467-4000.

WHITE LAKE. *Camp White Lake*, 8110 E. White Lake, White Lake, 48386. Rev. Michael Chesley, Tel: 855-878-3754; Web: www.svdpji.org.

WYANDOTTE. *Henry Ford Wyandotte Hospital*, Wyandotte. Tel: 734-246-6000. Karen Gorski.

YALE. *Yale Community Hospital*, Yale.
Tel: 810-387-2998. Attended from Sacred Heart Parish, Yale, MI.

Special Assignment:
Revs.—
Babcock, Timothy F., Asst. Dir. Intl. Priests & Archbishop's Liaison, Catholic Funeral & Cemetery Svcs., (Retired)
Fox, Charles D., Sacred Heart Major Seminary, Detroit
Laboe, Timothy A., Sacred Heart Major Seminary, Detroit
McDonell, Clint W., Sacred Heart Major Seminary, Detroit.

Graduate Studies:
Rev.—
Kirkconnell, Joseph D., Catholic University of America, Washington.

On Duty Outside the Archdiocese:
Rev. Msgr.—
Sable, Robert M., Prelate Auditor of the Roman Rota, Vatican
Revs.—
Maka, Tomasz, Archdiocese for Military Service
Sands, Maurice Henry, United States Conference of Catholic Bishops.

Currently Without Assignment:
Revs.—
Shafer, Robert J.
Ventline, Lawrence M.

Absent on Leave:
Revs.—
Belczak, Edward
Brady, Reginald
Brewczynski, Jacek M.
Bucon, Raymond H.
Casey, Patrick P.
Crepeau, John
Currin, John M.
Fraser, Bernard
Hogan, Richard
Kaczmarczyk, Pawel
Livingston, James
Mateja, Steven J.
Mistor, Todd C.
Mondragon, Ezequiel
Petroske, Peter
Prince, Michael J.
Quinlan, Jack
Roman, Victor
Schulte, Gary W.
Schuster, Robert C.
Siroskey, Paul Larry
Sopiak, Donald A.
Stochmal, Marek
Tomasko, Andrew J.
Vileo, Stephen L.
Wilkes, Michael.

Retired:
Rev. Msgrs.—
Bass, Ricardo E., (Retired), 2350 Watkins Lake Rd., Apt. 200, Waterford, 48328
Humitz, Robert S., (Retired), 2350 Watkins Lake Rd., Apt. 213, Waterford, 48328
Monticello, Robert V., (Retired), 14469 Levan Rd., Apt. D, Livonia, 48154-5094
Schweder, John F., (Retired), 900 N. 70th Ave., Hollywood, FL 33024
Revs.—
An Ninh, Vincent Nguyen, (Retired), 6318 Briar Ter., Houston, TX 77072
Anderson, Ronald, (Retired), 5126 Sandalwood Cir., Grand Blanc, 48439
Babcock, Timothy F., (Retired)
Baranowski, Arthur R., (Retired), 23375 Spring Creek Dr., Macomb, 48042
Blondell, Robert H., (Retired), 53256 Pineridge Dr., Chesterfield, 48051
Bodde, Frederick A., (Retired), 6116 River Rd., East China, 48054-4731
Briffa, Salvino P., (Retired), 14465 Levan Rd., Apt. D, Livonia, 48150
Brzezinski, Jerome A., (Retired), 2655 Patrick Henry St., Auburn Hills, 48042
Charnley, George, (Retired), 7468 Wilshire, West Bloomfield, 48322
Child, John F., (Retired), 11453 Levan Rd., Apt. C, Livonia, 48154
Chmura, Julian, (Retired), 41842 Lindsay Dr., Plymouth, 48170
Complo, Daniel C., (Retired), 38 E. Willow, Apt. C, Monroe, 48162-2644
Cusick, Thomas H., (Retired), 14453 Levan Rd., Apt. D, Livonia, 48154
D'Achille, Arnold V., (Retired), 4287 27th Ct. S. W., #103, Naples, FL 34116
Delonnay, Lawrence, (Retired), 1107 Lakeshore Dr., Columbiaville, 48421
Eckert, Sidney J., (Retired), P.O. Box 610827, Port Huron, 48061
Essman, Ronald, (Retired), 45817 Heather Ridge Dr., Macomb Township, 48044
Fabian, Jack V., (Retired), 12161 Whitefish Point Dr., Paradise, 49768
Fares, Lawrence T., (Retired), 31980 Mark Adam Lange, Warren, 48093
Flynn, Thomas P., (Retired), 22034 Sunnyside, St. Clair Shores, 48080
Gagala, John, J.C.L., (Retired), 22750 Ten Mile Rd., Southfield, 48033
Gagnon, Joseph A., (Retired), 1660 River Rd., #48, Marysville, 48040
Hall, John F., (Retired), 2701 Chicago Blvd., 48206

Hartmann, Richard A., (Retired), 14465 Levan Rd., Apt. A, Livonia, 48154
Jackson, Lawrence J., (Retired), 24348 Eastwood Village Ct., Apt. 106, Clinton Twp., 48035
Kaiser, Lawrence H., (Retired), 14465 Levan Rd., Apt. A, Livonia, 48154-5092
Kaucheck, Kenneth R., J.C.D., (Retired)
Kaul, John L., (Retired), 11453 Levan Rd., Livonia, 48154
Kcira, Anton P., (Retired), 417 Meadow Bridge Dr., Rochester Hills, 48307
Klettner, Frederick J., (Retired), 2208 Bowman Rd., Franklin, TN 37064
Kotlarz, Robert J., (Retired), 20103 Joann Ave., 48205
Kowalski, George, (Retired), 12765 Walnut St., Southgate, 48195
Kurzawa, Ronald, (Retired), 14469 Levan Rd., Apt. A, Livonia, 48154
Maciejewski, Norbert F., (Retired), 1480 Hammock Ridge Rd., Apt. 4207, Clermont, FL 34711
MacLennan, Donald B., (Retired), 30105 Avenida Alvera, Cathedral City, CA 92234-2869
Meyer, James, (Retired), 4600 Woodward Ave., Ste. 308, 48201-1894
Miller, George, (Retired), 38827 Horton Dr., Farmington Hills, 48331
Mitchell, Edward J., (Retired), 24661 Westhampton, Royal Oak, 48237
Murphy, William J., (Retired), 14455 Levan Rd., Apt. B, Livonia, 48154-5091
O'Sullivan, Daniel, (Retired), 3941 Crooks Rd., Troy, 48084
Page, Leon J., (Retired), 12109 Avondale, Warren, 48089-3922
Perfetto, Richard A., (Retired), 37610 Barkridge, Westland, 48185
Phalen, John L., (Retired), 9314 Top Flight Dr., Lakeland, FL 33810
Pilarski, Bernard, (Retired), 40695 Newport Dr., Plymouth, 48170
Prus, Edward J., (Retired), 241 Pearson, Ferndale, 48220-1896
Puzio, Thomas, (Retired), 14453 Levan Rd., Apt. A, Livonia, 48154
Rakoczy, Richard S., (Retired), 999 Stratton Dr., Waterford, 48328
Redwanski, Dale H., O.S.C., (Retired), 4223 Shari Ln., Mount Clemens, 48043
Romano, Joseph L., (Retired), 14453 Levan Rd., Apt. B, Livonia, 48154-5090
Roodbeen, Henry W., (Retired), 4663 Norfold Dr., Northville, 48167
Ruedisueli, Robert A., (Retired), 6306 Custer Rd., P.O. Box 64, Port Sanilac, 48469
Sayers, Raymond J., (Retired)
Sayes, Ronald E., (Retired), 4200 W. Utica Rd., Apt. 429, Shelby Township, 48317
Scheick, James C., (Retired), 14469 Levan Rd., Apt. C, Livonia, 48154-5094
Siebert, William P., (Retired), 16041 Vergi Ct., Clinton Township, 48038
Sinatra, William D., (Retired), 43225 Polo Cir., Sterling Heights, 48313-2064
Singelyn, Robert K., (Retired), 127 N. Monroe St., Monroe, 48162-2686
Strain, Eugene R., (Retired), 320 Elm, Rochester, 48307
Sullivan, John J., (Retired), 19624 Wood St., Melvindale, 48122
Sutherland, Thomas J., (Retired), 49230 Arlington Ct., Shelby Township, 48315-3903
Taube, Sylvester, (Retired), 14455 Levan Rd., Apt. A, Livonia, 48154
Tierney, Gary M., J.C.L., (Retired), 14455 Levan Rd., Apt. B, Livonia, 48154
Treppa, Terence, (Retired), 36076 Abbey Dr., Westland, 48185
Walsh, Jerome, (Retired), 3736 Trinity Terrace Ln., Euless, TX 76040
Weingartz, Francis A., (Retired), 900 Cook Rd., Apt. 312, Grosse Pointe Woods, 48236
Welsh, Richard C., (Retired), 26560 Burg Rd., Apt. B324, Warren, 48089-3503
Wieging, James F., (Retired), 4601 Allen Rd., Rm. 616, Allen Park, 48101
Witkowski, Robert J., (Retired), 5971 Fordham Dr., Shelby Township, 48316
Wojcicki, Wojciech, (Retired), 14453 Levan Rd., Apt. C, Livonia, 48154-5090
Wojtewicz, Eugene E., (Retired), 24612 Rock Lake Ct., Brownstown, 48134
Worthy, Donald L., (Retired), 4281 Marseilles, 48224
Zielinski, Francis A., (Retired), 2477 Yordy Rd., Mio, 48647.

Permanent Deacons:
Anaya-Busto, Hector, National Shrine of the Little Flower Basilica, Royal Oak
Avery, Stanley, St. Mary Our Lady Queen of Families, Warren
Avery, Thomas, On one-year leave
Ball, John H., St. Rene Goupil, Sterling Heights
Barbera, John, St. Louis, Clinton Twp.; Macomb Correctional Facility, New Haven
Bark, Kenneth, St. Patrick, White Lake
Baross, Donald, St. Rene Goupil, Sterling Heights
Barthel, Michael, Unassigned
Baughman, Jene, (Moved to Port Austin - Incardinating to Saginaw)
Beltowski, Christopher, Our Lady Queen of Martyrs Parish, Beverly Hills
Berch, James, St. Isaac Jogues, St. Clair Shores
Bloomfield, Richard, Our Lady of the Scapular, Wyandotte
Booms, Chris, St. Joseph, South Lyon
Bousamra, Thomas, (Serving in the Gaylord Diocese)
Bovitz, Robert, St. Pius X, Southgate
Breen, Kevin, St. Genevieve-St. Maurice, Livonia
Brown, Oscar A., St. Hugo of the Hills, Bloomfield Hills
Bruen, Patrick T., Senior Status
Buckley, Regis, St. Albert the Great, Dearborn Heights
Burke, John, St. Anthony, Belleville
Burrell, Frederick, St. Mark, Warren, Senior Status
Bussa, Stephen, St. Alphonsus - St. Clement, Dearborn
Butler, Lenard, Our Lady of Hope, St. Clair Shores
Buyle, Val, St. Margaret of Scotland, St. Clair Shores
Campernel, Jerome, St. John Vianney, Shelby Twp.
Caporuscio, Tommaso, St. Anastasia, Troy
Carigan, David, Our Lady of Good Counsel, Plymouth
Carroll, Brian, Senior Status
Carter, Thomas, St. Isidore, Macomb
Casnovsky, David P., National Shrine of the Little Flower Basilica, Royal Oak
Channell, Ronald, St. Margaret of Scotland, St. Clair Shores
Chesley, Michael, St. Patrick, White Lake
Clark, K. Perry, St. Fabian, Farmington Hills
Conlen, Patrick, St. John Neumann, Canton
Connors, John J., Holy Trinity, Port Huron
Cook, Ronald W., Senior Status
Cornell, Peter, Senior Status
Cousino, George, Divine Grace, Carleton
Cox, Donald J., Sr. Status
Crimmins, Dennis, Holy Trinity, Port Huron
Darga, Daniel M., Our Lady of La Salette, Berkley
Delbeke, Robert G., Senior Status
Desjarlais, Eugene B., Senior Status
DeWitt, Robert, Our Lady of Grace, Dearborn Heights
Doan, Francis X. Chau Ngoc, St. Vincent Ferrer, Madison Heights
Donnelly, Thomas, (Unassigned) Resident of Florida
Dreyer, Charles R., St. William, Walled Lake; St. Patrick, White Lake
Drysdale, David, St. Mary, Our Lady of the Annunciation, Rockwood
Ervin, Robert, Holy Family, Novi
Esler, Donald, St. Edith, Livonia
Esper, Tracy, St. Michael, Monroe
Fairbanks, Andrew, St. Vincent Ferrer, Madison Heights
Feliciano, Raul, Our Lady of Guadalupe, Detroit
Fitzgerald, Robert C., St. Priscilla, Livonia
Fitzmaurice, John, St. Mary, St. Clair
Fleming, David, St. Rene Goupil, Sterling Hts.
Flores, Luis A., St. Frances Cabrini, Allen Park
Formanczyk, Gregory, St. Elizabeth Ann Seton, Troy
Friend, Harry, (Serving in the Gaylord Diocese)
Fry, Kenneth, St. Anne, Detroit
Gabel, Raymond, Senior Status
Gajda, Robert, St. Perpetua, Waterford
Gardner, Jack F. Jr., Residing in Texas
Gemellaro, Marc, St. Andrew, Rochester
Gennette, James, Senior Status
Gergosian, Edward, (Serving in the Phoenix Diocese)
Girard, Lawrence, St. Sebastian, Dearborn
Godfryd, Kurt, St. Clement of Rome, Romeo
Goetz, Robert, Senior Status (Serving in the Diocese of Gaylord)
Gonos, Daniel, St. Linus, Dearborn
Goodhue, Harold, (Serving in the Gaylord Diocese)
Grenda, Ronald, St. Joseph, South Lyon
Gwozdz, Alan, Holy Family, Memphis
Hammond, Michael, St. Gabriel, Ida
Healy, Lawrence, St. Michael, Sterling Heights
Hensel, James L., Senior Status
Herta, Robert, Senior Status
Hoffer, Franz, St. Michael, Sterling Heights
Houghton, Michael, St. John Vianney, Shelby Township
Houle, Thomas, St. Thecla, Clinton Township
Hulan, Richard, St. Irenaeus, Rochester Hills
Hulway, Joseph A., Immaculate Conception, Lapeer
Hurley, Daniel J., Senior Status
Igoe, James, Sr. Status
Ingels, Michael M., Senior Status
Iskra, Joseph, SS. Augustine & Monica, Detroit
Jablonowski, Alexander, Senior Status
Jamieson, William E., St. Paul on the Lake, Grosse Point Farms
Jimenez, Rafael, St. Francis D'Assisi - St. Hedwig, Detroit
Junak, Donald C., Senior Status
Jurewicz, Marion, St. Martin de Porres, Warren
Karle, Joseph III, St. Mary of the Hills, Rochester Hills
Kessler, Wilhelm, Senior Status
Kibit, Henry J., Unassigned
King, Francis, St. Regis, Bloomfield Hills
Kolarik, William, Our Lady of Mt. Carmel, Emmett
Krzeminski, Eugene, (Serving in the Las Vegas Diocese)
Kucharek, Zigment, Senior Status
Kunik, Raymond L., (Serving in the Lansing Diocese); St. Priscilla, Livonia
LaForest, Scott, St. Alfred, Taylor
Lalone, Norman, Senior Status (Serving in the Diocese of San Diego)
Lang, Michael Sr., Holy Innocents & St. Barnabas, Roseville
Lennon, Joseph, Mother of Divine Mercy, Detroit
Leonard, Tom, St. Kateri Tekakwitha, Dearborn
Lewandoski, Anthony, St. Mary Queen of Creation
Liddle, John, St. William, Walled Lake
Lippard, Paul, Resurrection, Canton
Loeb, Jeffrey, St. Isadore, Macomb Township
Loffreda, Dennis, St. Hubert, Harrison Twp.
Luddecke, Ralph, St. Mary, Wayne
Lynch, Peter, SS. Peter and Paul, North Branch
Maciolek, Leo, St. James, Novi
Majkowski, Arthur, St. Pio of Pietrelcina, Roseville
Malloy, John Jr., St. Roch, Flat Rock
Manera, John, St. Joseph the Worker, Waterford
Marks, Stephen
Marku, John, Senior Status
Maxwell, Timothy, St. Mary, Port Huron
McCown, Phil, SS. Cyril and Methodius, Sterling Heights
McCrandall, Michael, St. Florian, Hamtramck, Incardinated in Lansing
McGowan, Gerard, Christ the Good Shepherd, Lincoln Park
McIntyre, Ronald L., Senior Status
McKale, Michael J., Holy Name, Birmingham
McLeod, Edwin, St. Blase, Sterling Heights
McLeod, Robert E., Senior Status
Meerschaert, Gary, St. Francis Assisi-St. Maximilian Kolbe, Ray Township
Melenyk, Glenn, St. James, Novi
Meyer, Edward, St. Patrick, White Lake
Misiak, Richard, Our Lady of Victory, Northville
Mitchell, Steven, Our Lady of Good Counsel, Plymouth
Modes, Robert, Senior Status
Mohan, Thomas, St. Benedict, Waterford
Morad, Alfred J., Senior Status
Morello, Steven, St. James, Novi
Morici, Anthony, St. Anne, Ortenville
Motowski, Norbert, SS. Andrew and Benedict, Detroit
Mouro, Joseph, Senior Status
Mueller, Paul, Corpus Christi, Detroit
Murphy, Thomas P., Our Lady of the Woods, Woodhaven
Nelson, Joseph, (Retired), (Serving in the Diocese of Gaylord)
Nickels, Paul, St. Mary of the Snows Parish, Milford
Nicola, James, St. Cyprian, Riverview
Nowicki, Kenneth, Immaculate Conception, Ira Twp.
O'Brien, Michael, Serving in the Diocese of Arlington
O'Donnell, C. Roger, Divine Child, Dearborn; Chaplain, Angela Hospice
O'Keefe, Michael P., St. Margaret of Scotland, St. Clair Shores
Oldani, Michael, Our Lady on the River, Marine City
Ortisi, Rosario, St. Kieran, Utica
Ovies, Robert, Senior Status
Paczkowski, Lawrence, Immaculate Conception, Ira Township
Pardo, Gary, St. Colette, Livonia
Parent, John, Sacred Heart, Auburn Hills
Pastore, Dominick, St. Isaac Jogues, St. Clair Shores
Pelchat, Paul F., Senior Status
Pilon, Timothy, Senior Status
Piro, Rudolph P., St. Genevieve - St. Maurice, Livonia
Posavetz, George R., Senior Status
Quigley, Donald, Our Lady of Sorrows, Farmington

Rabaut, Christopher, St. Augustine & St. Monica, Detroit
Redwine, Mark, St. Timothy, Trenton
Remus, Christian, Christ the King, Detroit
Rhein, Richard, St. Francis of Assisi - St. Maximilian Kolbe, Ray Township
Riopelle, Ernest, Senior Status
Rodgers, Leon, St. Thomas the Apostle, Garden City
Root, Joseph, (Retired), (Serving in the Diocese of Phoenix)
Ruehlen, Lawrence, St. John Vianney, Shelby Township
Rybinski, Marc, St. Paul of Tarsus, Clinton Township
Sanders, Hubert, Presentation/Our Lady of Victory, Detroit
Sandstrom, Donald, St. Therese of Lisieux, Shelby Twp.
Santeramo, John, Sabbatical
Schiffer, Gerald, St. Linus, Dearborn Hts.
Schlesser, Peter, (Retired), (Serving in the Diocese of Miami)
Schulte, John, Inactive
Schwartz, Robert, Guardian Angels, Clawson
Selmek, Martin, Our Lady of Mt. Carmel, Temperance
Shubik, Richard, St. Clare Montefalco, Grosse Point Park
Skladanowski, John L., St. Pio of Pietrelcina, Roseville
Sliney, Thomas, St. Andrew Parish, Rochester
Small, Vincent, Our Lady of Good Counsel, Plymouth
Smigell, Gerald, Ss. Cyril & Methodius, Sterling Heights
Smith, Lee, St. Isaac Jogues, St. Clair Shores
Smith, Michael T., St. Hugo of the Hills, Bloomfield Hills
Smith, Richard T., (Serving in the Phoenix Diocese)
Sobolewski, Don, (Serving in the Grand Rapids Diocese)
Somervell, Michael, Holy Spirit, Highland
Springer, Mark, Unassigned
Stach, Michael, St. Thomas More, Troy
Stanaj, Aleksander, St. Paul Albanian, Rochester Hills
Stankiewicz, Clement, Our Lady of LaSalette, Berkley
Stark, Christopher, St. Thomas Moore, Troy
Stevens, Paul, Blessed John Paul II, Detroit
Stevens, Truman, (Serving in the Diocese of Lafayette)
Stewart, Michael, St. Mary, Monroe
Stimpson, Bill, Senior Status
Strasz, Thomas, St. Joan of Arc, St. Clair Shores
Sullivan, Lawrence, Senior Status
Swartz, Edward, (Serving in the Altoona-Johnstown Diocese)
Talbot, Stephen, Our Lady of the Lakes, Waterford
Thibodeau, James, St. Mary, Pinckney, Lansing Diocese (Incardinated in Detroit)
Thomas, Thomas, St. Mary Our Lady Queen of Families, Warren
Thome, William A., Our Lady of the Angels, Taylor
Thompson, John, St. Lucy, St. Clair Shores
Tietz, Kevin, Our Lady of Grace Parish, Warren
Tombler, Eugene, Guardian Angels, Clawson
Toth, Lawrence, St. Valentine, Redford
Trabbic, Kenneth, St. Joseph, Erie
Tremmel, Robert, Senior Status
Urbiel, Joseph, Christ the King, Detroit
Vader, Ronald, Our Lady of Loretto, Redford
Valade, Ronald, St. Irenaeus, Rochester Hills
Vanneste, Johnny, Senior Status
Vasquez, Jesus, Senior Status
VonEnde, Michael, St. Owen, Bloomfield Hills
Ward, James, St. Thomas a'Becket, Canton
White, Brian S., Sacred Heart, Imlay City
Wilder, James, Assumption Grotto, Detroit
Willoughby, Gregory, St. Therese of Lisieux, Shelby Township
Wilson, Edward C. Jr., St. Paul of Tarsus, Clinton Township
Wisniewski, Matthew, Christ the Good Shepherd, Lincoln Park
Wright, John, St. Irenaeus, Rochester Hills
Yezak, Thomas, Senior Status.

INSTITUTIONS LOCATED IN DIOCESE

[A] SEMINARIES, ARCHDIOCESAN

DETROIT. *Sacred Heart Major Seminary, Inc.*, 2701 Chicago Blvd., 48206. Tel: 313-883-8500; Fax: 313-868-8685; Email: information@shms.org; Web: www.shms.edu. Rev. Msgr. Todd J. Lajiness, Rector & Pres.; Rev. Timothy A. Laboe, Dean of Studies; Dr. Matthew Gerlach, Dean; Mr. Ryan Cahill, Dir. Admissions & Enrollment; Ms. Astrid Caicedo, Asst. Dean & Dir. Accreditation; Ms. Ann Marie Connolly, Dir. Finance & Treas.; Mr. David Kelley, Dir. Devel.; Dr. John Gresham, Dir.; Dr. David Twellman, Registrar & Dir. Institutionalized Research; Rev. Stephen Burr, Vice Rector & Dean of Seminarian Formation; Kathryn Luberski, Dir. Students 480; Clergy / Religious Teachers 18.

The College of Liberal Arts Revs. Stephen Burr, Dir. Undergraduate Seminarians; Robert Spezia, Spiritual Dir. Undergraduate Seminarians; Mr. Christopher Spilker, Dir. Libraries; Dr. Ronald Prowse, Dir. Music. Students 480; Clergy / Religious Teachers 18.

The School of Theology Rev. Msgr. Daniel J. Trapp, Spiritual Dir. Graduate Students; Revs. John Vandenakker, C.C., Dir. Graduate Pastoral Formation; Daniel J. Jones, Dir. Graduate Seminarians.

*The Institute for Lay Ministry (ILM)*Priests 14; Sisters 1; Students 463; Lay Faculty 17.

ORCHARD LAKE. *SS. Cyril and Methodius Seminary*, 3535 Indian Tr., Orchard Lake, 48324. Tel: 248-683-0311; Fax: 248-738-6735; Web: www.sscms.edu. Rev. Msgr. Thomas C. Machalski, Rector/Pres.; Dr. Joshua Genig, Dir. Lay Ministry Programs; Rev. Msgr. Francis Koper, Dean Pastoral Formation; Rev. Tomasz Seweryn, Dean Pastoral Formation; Timothy Bailey, Comptroller; Revs. Pawel Lis, Dean Discipline & Prefect; Leonard Obloy, Dean Studies; Ms. Caryn Noel, Librarian; Very Rev. Canon Walter J. Ptak, Dean Human Formation; Sr. Karen Shirilla, S.J., Dir. Assessment; Mrs. Joanne Olejniczak-Caushaj, Registrar & Student Svcs. Lay Teachers 1; Priests 9; Sisters 1; Students 36.

Full-Time Faculty: Revs. Bryan J. Patterson, S.T.L.; Gregory Banazak, S.T.D.; Stanislaus Flis, (Poland) S.T.D.; Louis Madey, S.T.D., Ph.D.

[B] SEMINARIES, RELIGIOUS OR SCHOLASTICATES

OXFORD. *St. Benedict Monastery, House of Formation*, 2711 Drahner Rd., Oxford, 48370. Tel: 248-628-2249; Web: www.benedictinemonks.com. Rev. Damien Gjonaj, O.S.B., Conventual Prior. Headquarters Novitiate House of Sylvestrine Benedictine Monks in the United States. Brothers 3; Priests 4; Students 1.

[C] COLLEGES AND UNIVERSITIES

DETROIT. *Marygrove College* (Coed) Incorporated 8425 W. McNichols Rd., 48221. Tel: 313-927-1200; Fax: 313-927-1345; Email: info@marygrove.edu; Web: www.marygrove.edu. Dr. Elizabeth Burns, Pres.; Dr. Denise Williams Mallett, Ed.D., Vice Pres. of Enrollment Management; Jacqueline El-Sayed, Vice Pres. Academic Affairs; Linda Taylor, C.P.A., Controller, & C.F.O.; Jon Calderwood, Registrar. Sisters, Servants of the Immaculate Heart of Mary. Lay Staff 49; I.H.M. 2; Students 355.

University of Detroit Mercy, 4001 W. McNichols Rd., 48221-3038. Tel: 313-993-1455; Fax: 313-993-1229; Email: president@udmercy.edu; Web: www.udmercy.edu. Dr. Antoine M. Garibaldi, Pres. Clergy 14; Faculty 348; Lay Staff 569; Priests 9; Sisters 5; Students 5,110; Total Enrollment 5,110; Clergy / Religious Teachers 14.

LIVONIA. *Madonna University*, 36600 Schoolcraft Rd., Livonia, 48150. Tel: 734-432-5300; Tel: 800-852-4951; Fax: 734-432-5393; Web: www.madonna.edu. Michael A. Grandillo, Ph.D., Pres.; Cameron Cruickshank, Ph.D., Exec. V.P. for Enrollment Mgmt. & Univ. Advancement; Dr. Lewis Walker, Provost & Vice Pres. Academic Affairs; Dr. Connie Tingson-Gatuz, Vice Pres. Student Affairs; Ms. Dina Dubuis, Asst. V.P. and Registrar; David Boyd, Vice Pres. Finance; Phillip Hang, Dir. Coeducational; Single-sex Residential Halls; Conducted by the Felician Sisters. Lay Staff 420; Priests 2; Sisters 3; Students 4,428; Faculty: Full-time 120; Faculty: Part-time 266.

Madonna Outreach Centers:

SWEEP Center, 5716 Michigan Ave., 48210. Tel: 313-965-5334. Lay Staff 3; Students 35.

Macomb University Center, 44575 Garfield Rd., UC-1, Rm. 120, Clinton Township, 48038-1139. Tel: 586-263-6330; Fax: 586-226-4974; Email: lmcintyre@madonna.edu. Linda McIntyre, Coord. Lay Staff 1.

[D] HIGH SCHOOLS, INTER-PAROCHIAL

MADISON HEIGHTS. *Bishop Foley Catholic High School*, 32000 Campbell Rd., Madison Heights, 48071. Tel: 248-585-1210; Fax: 248-585-3667; Email: accavitti@bishopfoley.org; Web: www.bishopfoley.org. Frank Accavitti III, Prin. Lay Teachers 24; Priests 2; Students 317; Clergy / Religious Teachers 2.

MARINE CITY. *Cardinal Mooney Catholic School*, 660 S. Water St., Marine City, 48039. Tel: 810-765-8825; Fax: 810-765-7164; Email: secretary@cardinalmooney.org; Web: www.cardinalmooney.org. Mr. Jason Petrella, Prin.; Mrs. Beth Engel, Business Mgr.; Mrs. Kathleen Meyers, Exec. Admin. Lay Teachers 16; Students 140; Clergy / Religious Teachers 2.

MONROE. *St. Mary Catholic Central High School* (Coed) 108 W. Elm Ave., Monroe, 48162. Tel: 734-241-7622; Fax: 734-241-9042; Email: advancement@smccmonroe.com; Web: www.smccmonroe.com. Jason Linster, Prin.; Mr. Sean Jorgensen, Pres.; Chad Myers, Athletic Dir.; Mr. Timothy Magg, Campus Minister. Lay Teachers 21; Students 348; Clergy / Religious Teachers 1.

RIVERVIEW. *Gabriel Richard Catholic High School*, 15325 Pennsylvania Rd., Riverview, 48193. Tel: 734-284-1875; Fax: 734-284-9304; Email: admissions@gabrielrichard.org; Web: www.gabrielrichard.org. Mr. Joseph Whalen, Prin. Lay Teachers 25; Students 316.

[E] HIGH SCHOOLS, PRIVATE

DETROIT. *Detroit Cristo Rey High School, Inc.*, 5679 Vernor Hwy., 48209. Tel: 313-843-2747; Fax: 313-843-2750; Web: www.detroitcristorey.org. Michael J. Khoury, Pres.; Mr. Kevin Cumming, Prin.; Naomi Howrani, Dir. Devel.; Lori Kuhn, Dir. Admin. & CFO; Ines Leal, Dir. Admissions; Fred Lumpkin, Dir. CWSP; Torrey Henry, Dean Students. Lay Teachers 22; Priests 1; Students 340.

Detroit Cristo Rey High School Corporate Work Study Program, Inc., 5679 W. Vernor Hwy., 48209. Tel: 313-843-2747; Fax: 313-843-2750; Email: mkhoury@detroitcristorey.org; Web: www.detroitcristorey.org. Pamela Jackson, CWSP Sales Dir., Email: pjackson@detroitcristorey.org.

Loyola High School, 15325 Pinehurst, 48238-1633. Tel: 313-861-2407; Fax: 313-861-4718; Email: loyola@loyolahsdetroit.org; Web: www.loyolahsdetroit.org. Rev. Mark W. Luedtke, S.J., Pres.; Mr. Wyatt Jones III, Prin. Faculty 23; Lay Teachers 15; Priests 2; Students 145; Clergy / Religious Teachers 1.

Loyola Work Experience Program, Inc., 15325 Pinehurst, 48238. Tel: 313-861-2407; Fax: 313-861-4718; Email: mluedtke@loyolahsdetroit.org; Web: www.loyolahsdetroit.org. Rev. Mark W. Luedtke, S.J., Pres.; Mr. Wyatt Jones III, Prin.

University of Detroit Jesuit High School and Academy, (Grades 7-12), 8400 S. Cambridge, 48221-1699. Tel: 313-862-5400; Fax: 313-862-3299; Email: Anthony.trudel@uofdjesuit.org; Web: www.uofdjesuit.org. Revs. Ted Munz, S.J., Pres.; Mark W. Luedtke, S.J., Pres. Loyola High School; Brian J. Lehane, S.J., Supr. & Theology Teacher; Bro. James J. Boynton, S.J., Asst. to Prov., Vocations; Mr. Anthony Trudel, Prin.; Mrs. Erin Chekal, Librarian; Rev. Adam DeLeon, S.J., Theology Teacher Loyola High School. Brothers 1; Lay Teachers 64; Priests 1; Students 934; Regents 2; Clergy / Religious Teachers 4.

BLOOMFIELD HILLS. *Academy of the Sacred Heart*, 1250 Kensington Rd., Bloomfield Hills, 48304-3029. Tel: 248-646-8900; Fax: 248-646-4143; Web: www.ashmi.org. Sr. Bridget Bearss, R.S.C.J., Prin.; Margaret Butzier, Librarian. Religious of the Sacred Heart. Lay Teachers 21; Students 130.

The Brother Rice Endowment Fund (The "Foundation") 7101 Lahser Rd., Bloomfield Hills, 48301-4045. Tel: 248-833-2000; Fax: 248-833-2001; Email: clack@brrice.edu; Email: mcnamara@brrice.edu; Web: www.brrice.edu. Mr. Mike Tyranski, Bd. Pres.

Brother Rice High School, 7101 Lahser Rd., Bloomfield Hills, 48301-4045. Tel: 248-833-2000; Fax: 248-833-2001; Web: www.brrice.edu. Mr. Thomas Reidy, Pres.; Ed Okuniewski, Prin. Congregation of Christian Brothers. Brothers 3; Lay Teachers 42; Sisters 2; Students 586.

Marian High School for Young Women, 7225 Lahser Rd., Bloomfield Hills, 48301. Tel: 248-644-1750; Fax: 248-644-6107; Web: www.marian-hs.org. Rev. Mario V. Amore, Chap.; Sr. Lenore Pochelski, I.H.M., Head of School; Stacey Cushman, Vice Prin. Lay Teachers 38; Sisters 2; Students 456; Clergy / Religious Teachers 1.

FARMINGTON HILLS. *Mercy High School for Girls*, 29300 W. Eleven Mile Rd., Farmington Hills, 48336. Tel: 248-476-8020; Fax: 248-476-3691; Email: mhs@mhsmi.org; Web: www.mhsmi.org. Dr. Cheryl Delaney Kreger, Pres.; Patricia Sattler, Prin. Religious Sisters of Mercy. Lay Teachers 49; Students 685.

LIVONIA. *Ladywood High School*, 14680 Newburgh Rd., Livonia, 48154. Closed in 2018.

NOVI. *Catholic Central High School*, 27225 Wixom Rd., Novi, 48374. Tel: 248-596-3810; Fax: 248-596-3811 ; Email: dnoelke@catholiccentral.net; Web: www.catholiccentral.net. Revs. Dennis P. Noelke, C.S.B., Prin.; Richard J. Elmer, C.S.B.; William Riegel, C.S.B.; Robert W. Moslosky, C.S.B.; James M. O'Neill, C.S.B.; Dennis Kauffman, C.S.B.; John B. Huber, C.S.B., Pres.; Patrick W. Fulton, C.S.B. Basilian Fathers. Lay Teachers 68; Priests 8; Students 1,020; Clergy / Religious Teachers 5.

ORCHARD LAKE. *St. Mary's Preparatory*, 3535 Commerce Rd., Orchard Lake, 48324.
Tel: 248-683-0530; Fax: 248-683-1740; Email: lkosco@stmarysprep.com; Web: www.stmarysprep.com. Mr. Cormac Lynn, Headmaster; Rev. Msgr. Thomas C. Machalski, Chancellor; Candice Knight, Dir. Admissions. Deacons 1; Lay Teachers 46; Students 489.

PONTIAC. *Notre Dame Preparatory School and Marist Academy*, (Grades PreSchool-12), 1300 Giddings Rd., Pontiac, 48340. Tel: 248-373-5300;
Fax: 248-373-8024; Email: lolszamowski@ndpma.org; Email: aguest@ndpma.org; Email: ndpma@ndpma.org; Web: www.ndpma.org. Rev. Leon M. Olszamowski, S.M., Pres.; Mr. Andrew Guest, Headmaster. Notre Dame Preparatory School and Marist Academy is an Independent, Catholic Co-ed School with three divisions, Grades JrK-3 through 12, sponsored by the Society of Mary, USA Province and owned by the 22 members of the Board of Trustees under the corporate name: Notre Dame Preparatory School and Marist Academy. Clergy 6; Employees 158; Faculty 96; Families 780; Lay Teachers 94; Religious 6; Students 1,085; Elementary School Students 370; High School Students 701; Clergy / Religious Teachers 6.

Notre Dame Preparatory - High School,
Tel: 248-373-5300; Web: www.ndpma.org. Revs. Leon M. Olszamowski, S.M., Pres.; Joseph C. Hindelang, S.M., Prin.; Mr. Andrew Guest, Exec. Brothers 2; Clergy 6; Lay Teachers 55; Priests 4; Religious 6; Students 705; Total Staff 158; Clergy / Religious Teachers 6; Staff 96.

Notre Dame Marist Academy - Middle Division, (Grades PreSchool-5), Tel: 248-373-5371; Web: www.ndpma.org. Rev. Leon M. Olszamowski, S.M., Pres.; Mr. Brandon Jezdimir, Prin. Lay Teachers 14; Students 189; Clergy / Religious Teachers 6.

Notre Dame Marist Academy - Lower Division, (Grades PreK-5), Tel: 248-373-2573; Web: www.ndpma.org. Rev. Leon M. Olszamowski, S.M., Pres.; Mr. Andrew Guest, Exec.; Ms. Diana C. Atkins, Prin. Pre-School (Age 3) Lay Teachers 14; Students 156; Clergy / Religious Teachers 5.

RAY TOWNSHIP. *Austin Catholic High School*, 25925 23 Mile Rd., Chesterfield, 48051. Tel: 586-200-0143;
Fax: 586-408-6034; Email: jcoppens@austincatholichighschool.org. Janel M. Coppens, Prin. Lay Teachers 21; Students 80; Clergy / Religious Teachers 1.

WARREN. *De La Salle Collegiate*, 14600 Common Rd., Warren, 48088-3387. Tel: 586-778-2207;
Fax: 586-498-1628; Email: sstewart@delasallehs.com; Web: www.delasallehs.com. Mr. John M. Knight, Pres.; Mr. Stephen Stewart, Prin.; Dennis Parks, Media Specialist/IT; Sheryl Anderson, Media Specialist/IT. High School Brothers of the Christian Schools. Brothers 3; Lay Teachers 52; Sisters 1; Students 737; Clergy / Religious Teachers 1.

Regina High School for Girls, 13900 Masonic Blvd., Warren, 48088. Tel: 586-585-0500;
Fax: 586-585-0507; Email: adiamond@reginahs.com; Web: www.reginahs.com. Sr. Mary Leanne, S.S.J.-T.O.S.F., Pres.; Ms. Ann E. Diamond, Prin.; Mrs. Karen Forys, Asst. Prin.; Kyle J. Smith, Business Mgr.; Scott Manteuffel, Librarian. Lay Teachers 21; Sisters 4; Students 283; Clergy / Religious Teachers 3.

WIXOM. *St. Catherine of Siena Academy* A private Catholic high school for girls. 28200 Napier Rd., Wixom, 48393. Tel: 248-946-4848;
Fax: 248-438-1679; Email: info@saintcatherineacademy.org; Web: www.saintcatherineacademy.org. Karen Ervin, Prin. Faculty 25; Lay Teachers 22; Students 265; Total Enrollment 228; Campus Minister 1; Chaplain 1; Clergy / Religious Teachers 2.

[F] ELEMENTARY SCHOOLS, INTER-PAROCHIAL

CANTON. *All Saints Catholic School*, (Grades PreK-8), 48735 Warren Rd., Canton, 48187-1233.
Tel: 734-459-2490; Fax: 734-459-0981; Email: office@allsaintscs.com; Web: www.allsaintscs.com. Ms. Kristen Strausbaugh, Prin.; Scott Wisniewski, Admin. Lay Teachers 34; Students 557; Total Enrollment 557.

CLARKSTON. *Everest Academy*, (Grades PreK-12), 5935 Clarkston Rd., Clarkston, 48348.
Tel: 248-620-3390; Fax: 248-922-2082; Email: mnalepa@everestacademy.org; Email: ccarter@everestacademy.org; Web: www.everestcatholic.org. Greg Reichert, Prin., Middle & High School; Ms. Susan Ender, Prin., Elementary School; Julie Werner, Librarian; Ms. Michelle Reiff, Chm. Lay Teachers 38; Priests 3; Students 415; Consecrated Women 3.

MONROE. *Monroe Catholic Elementary Schools*, (Grades 1-8), 151 N. Monroe St., Monroe, 48162.
Tel: 734-241-6335; Fax: 734-241-0497; Email: amarting@monroecatholicschools.com; Web: www.mcesmonroe.com. Mrs. Alicia Marting, Dir. Clergy 4; Lay Teachers 28; Students 516; Parish Population 4,418.

St. Michael Archangel Campus, (Grades Day Care-1), 510 W. Front St., Monroe, 48161.
Tel: 734-241-3923; Fax: 734-241-7314; Email: kubik@monroecatholicschools.com; Web: www.mcesmonroe.com. Mrs. Alicia Marting, Exec. Dir.; Kyle Kubik, Prin. Clergy 1; Lay Teachers 8; Students 195; Parish Population 1.

St. John the Baptist Campus, (Grades 2-4), 521 S. Monroe St., Monroe, 48161. Tel: 734-241-1670;
Fax: 734-241-8782; Email: kubik@monroecatholicschools.com; Web: www.mcesmonroe.com. Kyle Kubik, Prin.; Mrs. Alicia Marting, Dir. Clergy 1; Lay Teachers 8; Students 129; Parish Population 1.

St. Mary Campus, (Grades 5-8), 151 Monroe St., Monroe, 48162. Tel: 734-241-3377;
Fax: 734-241-0497; Email: zawistowicz@monroecatholicschools.com; Web: www.mcesmonroe.com. Mrs. Alicia Marting, Exec. Dir.; Sheena Zawistowicz, Prin. Clergy 1; Lay Teachers 12; Students 194; Parish Population 1.

PORT HURON. *St. Mary/McCormick Catholic Academy*, (Grades 1-8), 1429 Ballentine St., Port Huron, 48060. Tel: 810-982-7906; Fax: 810-987-8255; Email: office@stmarymccormick.com; Web: www.stmarymccormick.com. Mr. Michael Gibson, Prin. (2 schools merged) Lay Teachers 12; Students 117; Parish Population 1.

ROCHESTER. *Holy Family Regional School - South Campus & North Campus*, (Grades 1-8), 2633 John R. Rd., (South Campus), Rochester Hills, 48307.
Tel: 248-299-3798; Tel: 248-656-1234;
Fax: 248-299-3843; Fax: 248-656-3494; Email: myers.jon@holyfam.org; Web: www.holyfam.org. Mr. Jon R. Myers, Prin. Lay Teachers 47; Students 858.

[G] ELEMENTARY, PRIVATE

BLOOMFIELD HILLS. *Academy of the Sacred Heart*, (Grades PreK-12), 1250 Kensington Rd., Bloomfield Hills, 48304-3029. Tel: 248-646-8900;
Fax: 248-646-4143; Web: www.ashmi.org. Damian Hermann, Prin. Religious of the Sacred Heart. Lay Teachers 80; Students 448.

PONTIAC. *Notre Dame Preparatory School and Marist Academy*, (Grades PreK-12), 1300 Giddings Rd., Pontiac, 48340. Tel: 248-373-5300;
Fax: 248-373-8024; Web: www.ndpma.org. Revs. Leon M. Olszamowski, S.M., Pres.; Joseph C. Hindelang, S.M., Prin.; Ronald Nikodem, S.M., Campus Min.; James Strasz, S.M., Campus Min.; Mr. Andrew Guest, Headmaster; Ms. Diana C. Atkins, Prin.; Mr. Brandon Jezdimir, Prin. Notre Dame Marist Academy, Lower Division (JK - 5th grade); Notre Dame Marist Academy, Middle Division (6th - 8th grade); Notre Dame Preparatory School (9th - 12th grade) Clergy 6; Lay Teachers 150; Students 1,049; Clergy / Religious Teachers 2.

[H] GENERAL HOSPITALS

DETROIT. *Ascension St. John Hospital* (A unit of St. John Health System) 22101 Moross Rd., 48236.
Tel: 313-343-4000; Fax: 313-343-7533. Robert Haban, Pres. Bed Capacity 714; Ascension Health 12; Tot Asst. Annually 28,306; Total Staff 2,731; Outpatients 1,032,535.

BRIGHTON. *Ascension Brighton Center for Recovery* (A unit of St. John Providence) 12851 Grand River Rd., Brighton, 48116. Tel: 877-967-2371; Web: www.brightonhospital.org. Raymond Waller, Dir. Bed Capacity 99; Tot Asst. Annually 6,077; Total Staff 223.

EAST CHINA. *Ascension River District Hospital* (A unit of St. John Health) 4100 River Rd., East China, 48054. Tel: 810-329-7111; Fax: 810-329-8920; Web: www.stjohn.org/riverdistrict. Robert Hoban, Pres. Bed Capacity 68; Tot Asst. Annually 2,000; Total Staff 400.

LIVONIA. *St. Mary Mercy Hospital* (A division of Trinity Health-Michigan) 36475 W. Five Mile Rd., Livonia, 48154. Tel: 734-655-4800; Fax: 734-655-1620; Web: www.stmarymercy.org. Mr. David Spivey, Pres. & CEO; Revs. Luke Iwuji; Peter Ben Opara; David E. Nantais, Mission Leader. Bed Capacity 304; Patients Asst Anual. 270,427; Total Staff 1,764; Total Inpatient Days 77,870; RN's 559; LPN's 3.

MADISON HEIGHTS. *St. John Macomb-Oakland Hospital, Oakland Center* (A unit of St. John Health) 27351 Dequindre, Madison Heights, 48071. Tel: 248-967-7000; Email: paula.caruso@ascension.org; Web: www.stjohn.org/macomb-oakland. Mr. Michael Beaubien, COO; Mr. Joseph Tasse, Pres. Bed Capacity 180; Tot Asst. Annually 88,804; Total Staff 1,077.

NOVI. *Ascension Providence Hospital* (A unit of St. John Health) 47601 Grand River Ave., Novi, 48374. Tel: 248-465-4500; Fax: 248-465-4501. Joseph Hurshe, Pres. Bed Capacity 200; Staff 1,629.

PONTIAC. *St. Joseph Mercy Oakland* (A division of Trinity Health-Michigan) 44405 Woodward Ave., Pontiac, 48341-2985. Tel: 248-858-3000;
Fax: 248-858-3299; Web: www.stjoesoakland.com. Ms. Shannon Striebich, Pres. & CEO; Charles Kibirgie, Chap.; Beverly M. Beltramo, Chief Mission Officer; Ms. Linda Thompson, Chap. Bed Capacity 438; Tot Asst. Annually 21,000; Total Staff 3,000.

PORT HURON. *St. Joseph Mercy Port Huron* (A division of Trinity Health-Michigan) 2601 Electric, Port Huron, 48060-6518. Tel: 810-985-1510;
Fax: 810-985-1579. Mr. Peter Karadjoff, Pres. & CEO. Bed Capacity 119; Patients Asst Anual. 154,019; Total Staff 775.

SOUTHFIELD. *Ascension Providence Hospital* (A unit of St. John Health) 16001 W. Nine Mile Rd., Southfield, 48037. Tel: 248-849-3000;
Fax: 248-849-3035. Rev. Felix S. Alsola, (Philippines) Chap.; Joseph Hurshe, Pres. Bassinets 65; Bed Capacity 365; Lay Staff 3,160; Daughters of Charity of St. Vincent de Paul 6; Tot Asst. Annually 23,794; Total Staff 3,282.

WARREN. *Ascension Macomb-Oakland Hospital* (a unit of St. John Providence) 11800 E. 12 Mile Rd., Warren, 48093. Tel: 586-573-5000;
Fax: 586-573-5541; Web: www.stjohn.org/macomb. Terence Hamilton, Pres.; William Mott Jr., COO. Bed Capacity 376; Tot Asst. Annually 233,000; Total Staff 3,400.

[I] SPECIAL HOSPITALS AND SANATORIA FOR INVALIDS

FRASER. *Fraser Villa*, 33300 Utica Rd., Fraser, 48026.
Tel: 586-293-3300; Email: delaneye@trinity-health.org; Web: www.trinityhealthseniorcommunities.org/fraser-villa-fraser. Libby Delaney, Exec. Part of St. Joseph Mercy Senior Communities. Bed Capacity 170; Tot Asst. Annually 750; Total Staff 230.

LAKE ORION. *Guest House, Inc.*, 1601 Joslyn Rd., Lake Orion, 48360. Tel: 800-626-6910;
Fax: 248-391-0210; Email: info@guesthouse.org; Web: www.guesthouse.org. Jeff Henrich, Pres. State licensed, CARF-accredited residential addiction treatment center for priests, brothers, deacons, seminarians, sisters and women in formation. Bed Capacity 26; Employees 48; Total Assisted 70.

Guest House - Men's Program, 1720 W. Scipps Rd., Lake Orion, 48360. Tel: 800-626-6910;
Tel: 248-393-0186; Email: mensdirector@guesthouse.org; Web: GuestHouse.org. Jeff Henrich, Pres. Bed Capacity 16; Tot Asst. Annually 65; Total Staff 48.

Guest House for Women Religious, 1740 W. Scripps Rd., Lake Orion, 48360. Tel: 800-626-6910;
Fax: 248-393-0186; Email: womensdirector@guesthouse.org; Web: www.guesthouse.org. Sr. MaryEllen Merrick, I.H.M., Exec. Dir., Women's Program. A state-licensed and CARF accredited endorsed residential treatment center for Catholic sisters and women in formation. Central Admissions Office, from U.S. & Canada call: 800-626-6910. Bed Capacity 10; Tot Asst. Annually 65; Total Staff 48.

Guest House Recovery Residence, 444 Nakomis Rd., Lake Orion, 48362. Tel: 248-693-8973;
Fax: 248-693-8973.

LIVONIA. *Marycrest Manor*, 15475 Middlebelt Rd., Livonia, 48154. Tel: 734-427-9175;
Fax: 734-427-5044. Mr. James Butler, Admin. Served by Marianhill Fathers.Ownership: Franciscan Sisters of St. Joseph. Bed Capacity 55; Residents 55; Sisters 3; Tot Asst. Annually 172; Total Staff 85.

Marywood Nursing Care Center, 36975 W. Five Mile Rd., Livonia, 48154. Tel: 734-464-0600;
Fax: 734-464-4846; Email: j.mimnaugh@marywoodncc.com; Web: www.marywoodnursingcarecenter.org. Mr. John Mimnaugh, N.H.A., Admin. Skilled Nursing Facility. Capacity 103; Sisters 4; Total Staff 200.

ROCHESTER HILLS. *Bellbrook*, 873 W. Avon Rd., Rochester Hills, 48307. Tel: 248-656-6300; Email: steven.kastner@trinity-health.org; Web: www.trinityhealthseniorcommunities.org/bellbrook-rochester-hills. Mr. Steven Kastner, Pres. Part of

St. Joseph Mercy Senior Communities. Bed Capacity 275; Total Staff 220.

ROYAL OAK. *The Neighborhoods of White Lake*, 10770 Elizabeth Lake Rd., White Lake, 48386. Tel: 248-618-4100; Email: steven.kastner@trinity-health.org; Web: www.trinityhealthseniorcommunities.org/neighborhoods-of-white-lake. Mr. Steven Kastner, Pres. Part of St. Joseph Mercy Senior Communities. Bed Capacity 79; Total Staff 100.

WATERFORD. *Lourdes Alzheimers Special Care Center* Clausen Manor Memory Care, 2400 Watkins Lake Rd., Waterford, 48328. Tel: 248-674-4732; Fax: 248-618-6269; Email: racho@lourdes-sc.org; Web: www.lourdesseniorcommunity.org. Sr. Maureen Comer, O.P., CEO; Mr. Rich Acho, CFO. Bed Capacity 20; Tot Asst. Annually 29; Total Staff 35.

Lourdes Nursing Home Lourdes Rehabilitation and Healthcare Center, 2300 Watkins Lake Rd., Waterford, 48328. Tel: 248-886-5600; Email: cburke@lourdes-sc.org; Email: racho@lourdes-sc.org; Web: www.lourdesseniorcommunity.org. Sr. Maureen Comer, O.P., CEO. Skilled & basic nursing facility for men and women rehabilitation and 24 hour nursing care. Bed Capacity 108; Residents 99; Tot Asst. Annually 499; Total Staff 244.

[J] HOUSING AND/OR COMMUNITY FACILITIES FOR THE AGING

BLOOMFIELD HILLS. *St. Elizabeth Briarbank Home for the Aged*, 39315 Woodward Ave., Bloomfield Hills, 48304. Tel: 248-644-1011; Fax: 248-644-1596; Email: sebh@att.net; Web: www.briarbank.com. Sr. Mary Toth, Supr.; Mrs. Katarina Zefic, Admin. Daughters of Divine Charity. Aged Residents 30; Bed Capacity 30; Sisters 4; Tot Asst. Annually 40; Total Staff 23.

CLINTON TOWNSHIP. *A Friend's House Adult Day Services*, 15945 Canal, Clinton Township, 48038. Tel: 586-412-8494; Fax: 586-416-2311; Web: www.ccsem.org. 26238 Ryan, Warren, 48091. Tel: 586-759-8700; Fax: 586-759-8789. Hershell Masten, Prog. Dir. Daytime care for older adults. Support services for caregiving families. A service of Catholic Services of Southeast Michigan. Tot Asst. Annually 200; Total Staff 11.

Clinton Villa, 17825 Fifteen Mile Rd., Clinton Township, 48035. Tel: 586-792-0358; Email: kaylsj@trinity-health.org; Web: www.trinityhealthseniorcommunities.org/clinton-villa-clinton-township. Ms. Sheri Kayl, Admin. Part of St. Joseph Mercy Senior Communities. Tot Asst. Annually 1,032; Total Staff 12; Units 77.

FARMINGTON HILLS. *Marian Oakland*, 29250 W. Ten Mile Rd., Farmington Hills, 48336. Tel: 248-474-7204; Email: Angela.Walton@trinity-health.org; Web: www.trinityhealthseniorcommunities.org/marian-oakland-farmington-hills. Angela Walton, Admin. Part of St. Joseph Mercy Senior Communities. Units 81.

FORT GRATIOT. *Sanctuary at Mercy Village* (A member of Trinity Senior Living Communities) 4170 24th Ave., Fort Gratiot, 48059. Tel: 810-989-7440; Email: warshekk@trinity-health.org; Web: tp://www.trinityhealthseniorcommunities.org/sanctuary-at-mercy-village-fort-gratiot. Kelsey Warshefski, Admin. Bed Capacity 135.

IMLAY CITY. *Maple Vista*, 600 Maple Vista, Imlay City, 48444. Tel: 810-724-6300; Email: campagnc@trinity-health.org; Web: www.trinityhealthseniorcommunities.org/maple-vista-imlay-city. Ms. Crystal Campagne, Housing Mgr. Part of St. Joseph Mercy Senior Communities. Units 69.

LIVONIA. *Villa Marie*, 15131 Newburgh, Livonia, 48154. Tel: 734-464-9494; Email: sharon.cuddington@trinity-health.org; Web: www.trinityhealthseniorcommunities.org/villa-marie-livonia. Sharon Cuddington, Housing Mgr. Part of St. Joseph Mercy Senior Communities. Units 69.

Senior Clergy Village of Livonia, Inc., 14461 Levan Rd., Livonia, 48154. Tel: 734-838-0457; Email: info@seniorclergyvillage.org; Web: www.seniorclergyvillage.org. Sr. Beatrice Marie Plamondon, Dir. Residents 20; Total Staff 3.

Trinity Continuing Care Services dba Trinity Senior Living Communities, 17410 College Pkwy., Ste. 200, Livonia, 48152-2363. Tel: 734-542-8300; Email: Steven.Kastner@trinity-health.org; Web: www.trinityhealthseniorcommunities.org. Mr. Steven Kastner, Pres. Bed Capacity 3,515; Tot Asst. Annually 6,000; Total Staff 2,300.

MONROE. *Marian Place*, 408 W. Front St., Monroe, 48161. Tel: 734-241-2414; Email: steven.kastner@trinity-health.org; Web: www.trinityhealthseniorcommunities.org/marian-place-monroe. Mr. Steven Kastner, Pres. Part of St. Joseph Mercy Senior Communities. Units 51.

SOUTHGATE. *Maryhaven*, 11350 Reeck Rd., Southgate, 48195. Tel: 734-287-2111; Email: dewyerm@trinity-health.org; Web: www.trinityhealthseniorcommunities.org/maryhaven-southgate. Melissa Dewyer, Admin. Part of St. Joseph Mercy Senior Communities. Units 79.

WATERFORD. *Fox Manor, Inc.*, 2350 Watkins Lake Rd., Waterford, 48328. Tel: 248-674-9590; Email: cburke@lourdes-sc.org; Web: www.lourdes-sc.org. Sr. Maureen Comer, O.P., CEO. Dominican Sisters of Peace.Residential facility for independent senior citizens of moderate or limited means. Bed Capacity 57; Tot Asst. Annually 75; Total Staff 16.

Lourdes Assisted Living Corporation Joseph T. Mendelson Assisted Living Home, 2450 Watkins Lake Rd., Waterford, 48328. Tel: 248-886-5100; Fax: 248-618-6361; Email: racho@lourdes-sc.org; Web: www.lourdesseniorcommunity.org. Sr. Maureen Comer, O.P., CEO; Ms. Cori Sharrard, Dir.; Mr. Rich Acho, CFO. Bed Capacity 80; Tot Asst. Annually 122; Total Staff 58.

[K] MONASTERIES AND RESIDENCES OF PRIESTS AND BROTHERS

DETROIT. *St. Bonaventure Friary*, 1740 Mt. Elliott Ave., 48207-3496. Tel: 313-579-2100; Fax: 313-579-5388; Email: ljlacross@thecapuchins.org. Bro. Jerome Johnson, O.F.M.Cap., Dir.; Revs. David Preuss, O.F.M.Cap., Dir.; William R. Hugo, O.F.M.Cap., Vicar; Very Rev. Michael Sullivan, O.F.M.Cap., Prov.; Bro. Larry LaCross, O.F.M.Cap., Pastoral Min./Coord.; Revs. Jose Savior, Pastoral Min./Coord.; Begashaw Tadesse, Pastoral Min./Coord.; Daniel Crosby, Pastoral Assoc.; George Kooran, Pastoral Assoc.; Bro. Anthony Kote-Witah, Pastoral Assoc.; Revs. Alfredo Gundrum, Sacramental Min.; John Hascall, Sacramental Min.; Patrick McSherry, O.F.M.Cap., Rome Assignment; Bro. Richard Merling, O.F.M.Cap., Solanus Casey History; Revs. Art Cooney, In Res.; Bede Louzon, O.F.M.Cap., In Res.; Joseph Maloney, O.F.M.Cap., In Res.; Philip Naessens, O.F.M.Cap., In Res.; Albert Sandor, O.F.M.Cap., In Res.

Province of St. Joseph of the Capuchin Order, Inc. Provincialate, 1820 Mt. Elliott Ave., 48207-3485. Tel: 313-579-2100; Fax: 313-579-2275; Email: dpiontkowski@thecapuchins.org. Very Rev. Michael Sullivan, O.F.M.Cap., Prov. Min.; Rev. Steven R. Kropp, O.F.M.Cap., Vicar; Bro. Jerome Johnson, O.F.M.Cap., Councilor; Revs. Patrick McSherry, O.F.M.Cap., Archivist; James Andres, O.F.M.Cap., CAP Retreat; Very Rev. Daniel J. Fox, O.F.M.Cap., Councilor; Bro. Larry LaCross, O.F.M.Cap., Pastoral Min./Coord.; Revs. Perry McDonald, Sec.; David Preuss, O.F.M.Cap., Councilor; Bro. TL Michael Auman, Communications; Ms. Brenda Boatman, HR Generalist; Ms. Leslie Burrows, Fin. Specialist; Ms. Hannah Costello, HR Mgr.; Ms. Kristi Hassouna, Devel. Dir.; Mr. Tim Hinkle, Public Relations; Ms. Sally McCuen, Hospitality Coord.; Ms. Angela Morris, Solanus Casey Center Mgr.; Ms. Stephanie Murray, HR Generalist; Mr. David Orzechowski, IT; Mr. John Parker, IT Mgr.; Mr. Jeffrey Parrish, Ministries/HR Dir.; Mr. Christopher Pelak, HR Generalist; Ms. Debi Piontkowski, Prov. Asst.; Ms. Diane Simpkins, Treas.; Mr. Jose Soberal, Buildings Mgr.; Ms. Antoinette White, Fin. Specialist; Ms. Junia Yasenov, Archivist.

Detroit Province of the Society of Jesus-Provincial Office, 1010 N. Hooker St., Chicago, IL 60642. Tel: 773-975-6888; Fax: 733-975-0230; Email: UMISocius@jesuits.org; Web: www.jesuitsmidwest.org. Rev. Albert DiUlio, Treas.

Jesuit Community at the University of Detroit Mercy, Lansing-Reilly Hall, 4001 W. McNichols Rd., 48221-3038. Tel: 313-993-1625; Fax: 313-993-1653; Email: LRJesuit@gmail.com. Revs. Peter Etzel; Mark George, S.J.; Gary R. Wright, S.J.; Phillip T. Cooke, S.J., Parochial Vicar; Gilbert Sunghera, S.J., Rector; Donald Vettese, S.J., Chap.; R. Gerard Albright, S.J.; Gerald F. Cavanagh, S.J.; Thomas W. Florek, S.J.; Simon J. Hendry, S.J.; J. Timothy Hipskind, S.J.; Stephen F. Hurd, S.J.; Justin J. Kelly, S.J.; Timothy McCabe, S.J.; Joel G. Medina, S.J.; Raphael Shen, S.J., (China); John M. Staudenmaier, S.J.; Robert A. Ytsen, S.J.; Bros. Richard D. Hittle, S.J.; Denis Weber, S.J.; Damian Torres-Botello, Regent. (Corporate Title: The Jesuit Community Corporation at the University of Detroit).

St. Mary's Friary, 1057 Parker, 48214-2612. Tel: 313-821-5883; Email: jhast@thecapuchins.org; Web: www.thecapuchins.org. Rev. Tom Nguyen, In Res.; Bros. Michael Gaffney, O.F.M.Cap., In Res.; Joseph Monachino, O.F.M.Cap., In Res.

St. Paul of the Cross Community, Congregation of the Passion, 23335 Schoolcraft, 48223. Tel: 313-531-0562; Fax: 313-535-8468; Email: ppaxton@stpaulretreat.org. Revs. Peter Berendt, C.P.; Patrick Brennan, C.P., Retreat Dir.; Randal Joyce, C.P.; Philip Paxton, C.P., Rev. Supr.; Bro. Raymond Sanchez, C.P. A center for the Passionist Fathers & Brothers in mid-western & north central United States. Members of this community conduct parish missions, renewals & retreats for laity, clergy & religious, Forty Hours Devotion & other ministries. Brothers 1; Priests 4.

PIME Missionaries (Pontifical Institute for Foreign Missions) 17330 Quincy St., 48221. Tel: 313-342-4066; Fax: 313-342-6816; Email: info@pimeusa.org; Web: www.pimeusa.org. Revs. Phillip Mayfield, P.I.M.E., Rector; Dino Vanin, P.I.M.E., Treas.; George Berendt, P.I.M.E.; Very Rev. George Palliparambil, PIME, U.S. Region Supr.; Revs. Giancarlo Ghezzi, P.I.M.E., Vice Regional Supr.; Daniele Criscione; Shanthi Chacko Puthussery, Outreach Coord.

BERKLEY. *Dun Scotus Frairy*, 2599 Harvard Rd., Berkley, 48072. Tel: 313-727-9784; Email: abunaalex@yahoo.com. Rev. Alexander Kratz, O.F.M., Contact Person. Postulants 2; Friars 5.

BLOOMFIELD HILLS. *Congregation of Christian Brothers, Mater Dei Community*, 7350 Parkstone Ln., Bloomfield Hills, 48301. Tel: 248-258-1186; Cell: 815-272-7742; Fax: 248-833-2001; Email: bromaccfc@yahoo.com. Bros. James McDonald, Community Contact; David A. MacIntyre, C.F.C.; Arthur M. Arndt, C.F.C. Brothers 3.

CLARKSTON. *Colombiere Center*, 9075 Big Lake Rd., Clarkston, 48346-1015. Tel: 248-625-5611; Fax: 248-625-3526; Email: colombiere@colombiere.com; Web: www.colombierejesuits.com. Revs. John F. Libens, S.J., Supr. & Dir.; Jerome K. Odbert, S.J., Asst. Supr.; Raymond C. Baumhart, S.J.; Carl A. Bonk, S.J.; Francis E. Canfield, S.J.; John P. Coakley, S.J.; James J. Creighton, S.J.; Matthew E. Creighton, S.J.; John R. Crocker, S.J.; John T. Dillon, S.J.; John E. Dister, S.J.; Eugene F. Dwyer, S.J.; Daniel Flaherty, S.J.; Dennis T. Glasgow, S.J.; Joseph B. Kappes, S.J.; John H. Kleinhenz, S.J.; James V. Lewis, S.J.; Daniel P. Liderbach, S.J.; Edward J. Mattimoe, S.J.; Frank M. Oppenheim, S.J.; Cletus H. Pfab, S.J.; Thomas H. Radloff, S.J.; Theodore C. Ross, S.J.; L. Harold Sanford, S.J.; James K. Serrick, S.J.; Timothy J. Shepard, S.J.; Jerome F. Treacy, S.J.; Bros. Henry C. Kuhn, S.J.; John P. Martin, S.J.; Daniel J. McCullough, S.J.; Jerome Pryor, S.J.; Robert W. Schneider, S.J.; James E. Small, S.J.; Revs. Dennis Ahern, S.J.; Casimir Bukala, S.J.; Eugene Carmichael, S.J.; P. Joseph Casey, S.J.; Frederick Deters, S.J.; George Lane, S.J.; Charles Niehaus; Robert Thul; Richard H. Twohig, S.J.; Bro. Michael O'Grady, S.J.; Revs. Denis Dirscherl; Patrick Peppard; James F. Riley, S.J.; John A. Saliba, S.J.; Thomas Schubeck; Robert J. Scullin, S.J., Supr.; George Von Kaenel; David E. Watson, S.J.; John White; W. Jared Wicks. Jesuit Health Care Community for the United States Midwest Province.

DEARBORN HEIGHTS. *All Saints Friary*, 23755 Military Rd., Dearborn Heights, 48127. Tel: 313-278-5129; Fax: 313-278-5828; Email: mariebernardolol@hotmail.com; Web: www.franciscancommunity.com. Bro. James O'Brien, O.F.M.Conv., Guardian; Rev. Anthony Fox, O.F.M.Conv., Vicar All Saints Friary. (This is a subsidiary of St. Bonaventure, Chicago, IL.) Brothers 1; Priests 1.

Mariannhill Mission Society, Our Lady of Grace Monastery, 23715 Ann Arbor Tr., Dearborn Heights, 48127-1449. Tel: 313-561-7140; Tel: 313-561-8888; Tel: 313-561-2330; Fax: 313-561-9486; Email: cmm-usa@juno.com; Web: www.mariannhill.us. Revs. Thomas Heier, C.M.M., Editor; Vergil Heier, C.M.M., Contact Person; Raymond Lucasinsky, C.M.M., Supr.; Bro. James Miller, C.M.M., Business Mgr.; Revs. Timothy Mock, C.M.M.; Kevin O'Doherty, C.M.M.; Michael Sheehy, C.M.M., Contact Person; Thomas Szura, C.M.M., Supr. Leaves Magazine, Congregation of the Missionaries of Mariannhill, Mariannhill Fathers, Mariannhill Missionaries Brothers 1; Priests 7; Tot in Congregation 317; Total in Community 8.

GROSSE POINTE. *Order of Canons Regular of the Holy Cross*, 576 Neff Rd., Grosse Pointe, 48230. Tel: 313-884-1121; Email: frludwig@opusangelorum.org; Web: www.cruzios.org. Revs. Wolfgang Seitz, O.R.C.; Matthew Hincks, O.R.C.; Titus Kieninger, O.R.C.; Ludwig M. Oppl, O.R.C.

GROSSE POINTE PARK. *Congregation of St. Michael the Archangel - Michaelite Fathers*, 1401 Whittier Rd., Grosse Pointe Park, 48230. Tel: 313-647-5030; Fax: 313-647-5005; Web: WWW.michaelites.ca. Revs. Andrzej Kowalczyk, C.S.M.A., Vice Provincial & Pastor; Tomasz Wilisowski, C.S.M.A., Assoc. Pastor.

OXFORD. *St. Benedict Monastery*, 2711 Drahner Rd., Oxford, 48370. Tel: 248-628-2249. Rev. Damien Gjonaj, O.S.B., Prior; Bro. Gregory David Jones, O.S.B., Subprior; Revs. John Martin Shimkus, O.S.B., Treas.; Michael R. Green, O.S.B.

REDFORD. *Society of the Catholic Apostolate-Indian Province of the State of Michigan*, 17116 Olympia, Redford, 48240. Tel: 313-534-9000;

Fax: 313-534-6744; Email: theodore.dcunha61@gmail.com. Rev. Theodore D'Cunha, S.A.C., Local Rector.

SOUTH LYON. *Miles Christi*, 25300 Johns Rd., South Lyon, 48178. Tel: 248-596-9677; Email: infousa@mileschristi.org; Web: www.mileschristi.org. Rev. John Ezratty, M.C., Supr.

WYANDOTTE. *Society of the Catholic Apostolate (Pallottine Fathers)* Irish Pallottine Fathers (Irish Province) 3352 Fourth St., Wyandotte, 48192. Tel: 734-285-2966; Fax: 734-285-1059; Email: pallottine@wyan.org; Web: www.irishpallottines.org. Revs. Michael Cremin, S.A.C., Pres.; Brendan McCarrick, Sec.; Bro. Faustino Paez, S.A.C., In Res.; Rev. John Casey, S.A.C., In Res., (Retired).

Pallottine Missionary Center (Irish Province) Irish Pallottine Fathers, 424 Orange St., Wyandotte, 48192. Tel: 734-282-3019; Fax: 734-285-1059; Email: pallottine@wyan.org; Web: www.irishpallottines.org. Revs. Derry Murphy, S.A.C., Prov.; John Kelly, S.A.C., Prov. Bursar, Treas.; Noel O'Connor, S.A.C., Pres.; Brendan McCarrick. Employees 2.

[L] CONVENTS AND RESIDENCES FOR SISTERS

DETROIT. *Missionaries of Charity*, 1917 Cabot St., 48209. Tel: 313-841-1394. Sisters M. Jonathan, MC, Regl. Supr.; M. Brunetta, M.C., Supr. Sisters 4.

Sisters, Home Visitors of Mary Convent, 121 E. Boston, 48202. Tel: 313-869-2160; Email: homevisitors@att.net; Email: brcwolff@wowway.com. Sr. Barbara Dakoske, H.V.M., Admin. Sisters 28.

BLOOMFIELD HILLS. *Daughters of Divine Charity - Holy Family Province* (1972) 39315 Woodward Ave., Bloomfield Hills, 48304. Tel: 248-644-1011; Tel: 248-644-8052; Fax: 248-644-1596; Email: sebh@att.net; Email: sredwardfdc@gmail.com; Web: www.briarbank.com. Sr. Mary Toth, Supr.

Legal Title: Daughters of Divine Charity of Detroit, Inc. Sisters 3.

CLINTON TOWNSHIP. *Monastery of St. Therese of the Child Jesus*, 35750 Moravian Dr., Clinton Township, 48035-2138. Tel: 586-790-7255; Fax: 586-790-7271; Email: carmelctwp@sbcglobal.net; Web: www.carmelctwp.org. Mother Mary Therese, Prior. Discalced Carmelite Nuns. Postulants 1; Sisters 13; Solemnly Professed 7; Temporary Professed 3.

DEARBORN HEIGHTS. *Servants of Jesus*, 8080 Kinmore, Dearborn Heights, 48127. Tel: 313-562-6156. Sr. Karen Shirilla, S.J., Sec.

Sisters of the Good Shepherd (RGS), 20651 W. Warren Ave., Dearborn Heights, 48127-2622. Tel: 313-253-2090; Email: srjanicergs@gmail.com.

EASTPOINTE. *Marist Sisters, Inc.*, 16057 Hauss, Eastpointe, 48021. Tel: 586-772-2577; Fax: 586-772-8302; Email: constance56@comcast.net. Sisters Linda Sevcik, S.M., Unit Leader; Constance Dodd, S.M., Sec. & Treas.

FARMINGTON HILLS. *Bernardine Franciscan Sisters of Michigan*, Our Lady of the Rosary Convent, 27405 W. 10 Mile Rd., Farmington Hills, 48336-2201. Tel: 248-476-4111; Fax: 248-476-6950; Email: selenaosf@gmail.com; Web: www.bfranciscan.org. Sr. Marilisa da Silva, O.S.F., Congregational Min. Bernardine Sisters of the Third Order of St. Francis. Sisters 19.

Monastery of the Blessed Sacrament, 29575 Middlebelt Rd., Farmington Hills, 48334-2311. Tel: 248-626-8253; Fax: 248-626-8724; Email: opnunsfh@sbcglobal.net; Web: www.opnuns-fh.org. Sr. Mary Peter, O.P., Prioress; Rev. David J. Santoro, O.P, Chap. Nuns of the Order of Preachers (Cloistered Dominican Nuns, Perpetual Adoration). Sisters 26.

Sisters of Mercy of the Americas West Midwest Community, Inc., 29000 Eleven Mile Rd., Farmington Hills, 48336. Tel: 248-476-8000; Fax: 248-476-4222; Email: sistersofmercy@mercywmw.org; Web: www.sistersofmercy.org/west-midwest. Sisters Susan Sanders, R.S.M., Pres., Email: ssanders@mercywmw.org; Ana María Pineda, Vice Pres.; Rebecca VandenBosch, CFO; Sisters Margaret Mary Hinz, R.S.M., Leadership Team; Maria Klosowski, R.S.M., Leadership Team; Margaret Maloney, Leadership Team. Sisters 531; Associates 605.

West Midwest FIDES, Inc., 29000 Eleven Mile Rd., Farmington Hills, 48336. Tel: 248-476-8000; Fax: 248-476-4222; Web: www.sistersofmercy.org/west-midwest. Sisters Lillian Murphy, R.S.M., Vice Pres.; Margaret Mary Hinz, R.S.M., Sec.; Katherine Glosenger, R.S.M., Treas.; Christine McCann, R.S.M., Governing Bd. Member.

LIVONIA. *Presentation of the BVM Convent*, 36800 Schoolcraft Rd., Livonia, 48150-1172. Tel: 734-591-1730; Fax: 734-591-1710; Email: sconniet@feliciansisters.org; Web: www.feliciansistersna.org. Sr. Mary Christopher Moore, C.S.S.F., Prov. Min.

Provincial House of the Congregation of the Sisters of St. Felix, C.S.S.F., Felician Sisters Sisters 71; Professed Sisters in North America, Our Lady of Hope Province 511.

MONROE. *Sisters, Servants of the Immaculate Heart of Mary, Leadership Council*, 610 W. Elm Ave., Monroe, 48162-7909. Tel: 734-240-9700; Fax: 734-240-9784; Web: www.ihmsisters.org. Sisters Mary Jane Herb, I.H.M., Pres.; Marianne Gaynor, Vice Pres.; Margaret Chapman, Treas.; Ellen Rinke, Mission Councilor; Patricia McCluskey, I.H.M., Mission Councilor. Sisters 285.

Institute for Communal Contemplation and Dialogue, 8531 W. McNichols, 48221. Tel: 313-971-3668; Fax: 313-342-7421; Email: circles@engagingimpasse.org; Web: engagingimpasse.org. Sr. Nancy Sylvester, I.H.M., Exec. Dir.

ORTONVILLE. *Our Lady of Mt. Thabor Monastery* Dominican Nuns, 1295 Bald Eagle Lake Rd., Ortonville, 48462. Tel: 248-627-4355; Email: mtthabor@aol.com; Web: www.mtthabornunsop.com. Sr. Anne Mary, O.P., Prioress. Dominican Nuns of Mt. Thabor. Sisters 7.

OXFORD. *Dominican Sisters of Peace* (2009) Oxford Motherhouse, 775 W. Drahner Rd., Oxford, 48371-4866. Tel: 248-628-2872; Fax: 248-628-1725; Email: srpeace@oppeace.org; Web: www.oppeace.org. Sr. Sheila Marie McIntyre, Mission Group Coord. Sisters 19; Sisters in Congregation 451; Sisters in Diocese 31.

RIVERVIEW. *Sisters of Mary Reparatrix*, 10065 Northway Ave., Allen Park, 48101. Tel: 313-383-3312; Email: kasparek@comcast.net. Sr. Ann Kasparek, S.M.R., Admin. Bed Capacity 4; Sisters 3.

[M] HOMES FOR MEN AND WOMEN

DETROIT. *St. Mary's Residence Adult Foster Care*, 2120 Orleans St., 48207. Tel: 313-259-6874; Tel: 313-259-0459; Fax: 313-259-2001. Sr. M. Hyacinthe, F.D.C., Admin. Daughters of Divine Charity.A residence for women desiring home-like surroundings. Residents 25; Sisters 4; Lay Associate 1.

[N] CATHOLIC SOCIAL SERVICE AGENCIES

ROYAL OAK. *Catholic Charities of Southeast Michigan*, 15945 Canal Rd., Clinton Township, 48038. Tel: 855-882-2736; Web: www.ccsem.org. David Bartek, CEO.

[O] SPECIALIZED CHILD CARE FACILITIES AND SCHOOLS

DETROIT. *Holy Cross Services-Bowman House* (part of HCCS, Diocese of Lansing) 17200 Rowe St., 48205. Tel: 313-469-8152; Tel: 989-596-3557; Fax: 313-469-8254; Email: cdevaux@hccsnet.org; Web: www.holycrossservices.org. Sharon Berkobien, CEO. Clergy 3; Students 15; Tot Asst. Annually 27.

Christ Child House, 15751 Joy Rd., 48228. Tel: 313-584-6077; Fax: 313-584-1148; Email: jyablonky@christchildhouse.org; Web: www.christchildhouse.org. Mr. John Yablonky, A.C.S.W, M.S.W., L.M.S.W., Exec. Dir. Educational Coordinator 1; Volunteer Tutors 8.

Don Bosco Hall, Inc., 2340 Calvert, 48206. Tel: 313-869-2200; Fax: 313-869-8220; Email: csmall@donboscohall.org; Web: www.donboscohall.org. Mr. Charles Small, Pres. & CEO. Residential treatment center for boys, ages 12-17, in need of care, guidance and therapy. Lay Staff 125; Residents 140; Transitional Services 180; Mentoring Program 155.

St. Vincent and Sarah Fisher Center SVSF Center, 16800 Trinity, 48219. Tel: 313-535-9200; Fax: 313-535-7804; Email: diane.renaud@svsfcenter.org; Email: renee.pouget@svsfcenter.org; Web: www.svsfcenter.org. Diane Renaud, Exec. Dir. & CEO. Free personalized educational programs for children and adults Students 1,100; Volunteers 200; Staff 14.

CLINTON TWP.. *King House-Holy Cross Services* (part of HCCS, Diocese of Lansing) 24455 Crocker Blvd., Clinton Twp, 48036. Tel: 586-463-7130; Tel: 989-596-3557; Fax: 586-463-7131; Email: cdevaux@hccsnet.org; Web: www.holycrossservices.org. Sharon Berkobien, CEO. Clergy 3; Students 15; Tot Asst. Annually 37.

DEARBORN HEIGHTS. *Vista Maria*, 20651 W. Warren Ave., Dearborn Heights, 48127. Tel: 313-271-3050; Fax: 313-271-6250; Email: info@vistamaria.org; Web: www.vistamaria.org. Angela Aufdemberge, Pres. & CEO. Residential treatment programs for adolescent girls, and community-based programs, including foster care and after school programs for boys and girls involved in The Juvenile Justice & Child Welfare Systems. Sponsored by the Sisters of the Good Shepherd. Lay Staff 271; Sisters 2; Students 265; Foster Care 89; Girls & Women Residential 135; Adoptions 16.

LIVONIA. *Felician Sisters Child Care Centers, Inc.* dba Montessori Center of Our Lady Child Care Center and Montessori School; St. Mary Child Care Center, 14200 Newburgh Rd., Livonia, 48154. Tel: 734-793-3853; Tel: 734-793-3852; Email: k.richter@feliciansisters.org; Email: g.jones@feliciansisters.org; Web: www.montessoricenterofourlady.org; Web: www.stmarychildcarecenter.org. Karen Richter, Pres. Felician Sisters (C.S.S.F.) Sisters 2; Students 250; Clergy / Religious Teachers 1; Lay Teachers and Care Givers 58.

[P] RETREAT HOUSES

DETROIT. *St. Paul of the Cross Passionist Retreat and Conference Center* Conducted by the Passionist Community. 23333 Schoolcraft Rd., 48223-2499. Tel: 313-535-9563; Fax: 313-535-9207; Email: info@stpaulretreat.org; Web: stpaulretreat.org. Revs. Pat Brennan, C.P., Retreat Dir.; Philip Paxton, C.P., Staff Member; Faith Offman, Assoc. Retreat Dir.; Ms. Sandra Arnould, Business Admin.

BLOOMFIELD HILLS. *Manresa Jesuit Retreat House*, 1390 Quarton Rd., Bloomfield Hills, 48304-3554. Tel: 248-644-4933; Fax: 248-644-8291; Email: office@manresa-sj.org; Web: www.manresa-sj.org. Revs. Leo P. Cachat, S.J., Retreat Dir. & Spiritual Dir.; Peter J. Fennessy, S.J., Supr.; Retreat & Spiritual Dir.; Francis J. Daly, S.J., Exec. Dir. Priests 3.

Visitation North Spirituality Center, 7227 Lahser Rd., Bloomfield Hills, 48301. Tel: 248-433-0950; Fax: 248-433-0952; Email: visitationnorth@ihmsisters.org; Web: www.visitationnorth.org. Sr. Kathleen Budesky, I.H.M., Dir. Sisters 5.

MONROE. *River House - IHM Spirituality Center*, 805 W. Elm Ave., Monroe, 48162. Tel: 734-240-5494; Fax: 734-240-5495; Email: riverhouse@ihmsisters.org; Web: www.ihmsisters.org. Sisters Carol Quigley, I.H.M., Spiritual Dir.; Judith Bonini, Spiritual Dir.; Ms. Cristy Smith, Coord. Sponsorship of I.H.M. Congregation. Sisters 4.

OXFORD. *Queen of the Family Retreat Center*, 751 W. Drahner Rd., Oxford, 48371. Tel: 248-628-5560; Fax: 248-628-4898; Email: qfrc@queenofthefamily.org; Web: www.queenofthefamily.org. Ms. Michelle Reiff, Dir.

PLYMOUTH. *St. John Chapel*, 44045 Five Mile Rd., Plymouth, 48170-2555. Tel: 734-414-0600; Fax: 734-414-0606. Rev. John Riccardo

Legal Title: The Retreat Center at St. John or St. John Seminary.

WASHINGTON. *Capuchin Retreat*, 62460 Mt. Vernon Rd., P.O. Box 396, Washington, 48094. Tel: 248-651-4826; Fax: 248-650-4910; Email: info@capretreat.org; Web: www.capretreat.org. Revs. Gerald Kessel, O.F.M.Cap., Dir.; Biju Parakkalayil, Pastoral Min./Coord.; Binoy Nedumparampil, Pastoral Assoc.; Thomas Zelinski, Pastoral Assoc.; James Andres, O.F.M.Cap., In Res.; Bro. Joseph Howe, O.F.M.Cap., In Res.; Rev. James C. Hast, O.F.M.Cap., In Res.; Linda Andrews, Admin.; Leslie Healy, Admin. Asst.

[Q] SPECIAL SERVICES

DETROIT. *Capuchin Soup Kitchen*, 1820 Mt. Elliott, 48207. Tel: 313-579-2100; Fax: 313-571-1822; Email: jjohnson@cskdetroit.org. Bro. Jerome Johnson, O.F.M.Cap., Exec. Tot Asst. Annually 566,000; Total Staff 65.

On the Rise Bakery, 6110 McClellan, 48213. Tel: 313-922-8510; Email: jjohnson@cskdetroit.org. Bro. Raymond Stadmeyer, O.F.M.Cap., Dir.

Conner Kitchen, 4390 Conner, 48215. Tel: 313-822-8606; Fax: 313-822-9163; Email: jjohnson@cskdetroit.org. Jay Brown, Site Dir.; Nancyann Turner, O.P., Mgr. Children & Youth Program, Tel: 313-822-8606, Ext. 21. Tot Asst. Annually 336,000; Total Staff 17.

Capuchin Services, 6333 Medbury, 48211. Tel: 313-925-1730, Ext. 100; Fax: 313-925-1944; Email: jjohnson@cskdetroit.org. Reggie Huff, Opers. Mgr. Tot Asst. Annually 56,100; Total Staff 20.

Meldrum Kitchen, 1264 Meldrum, 48207. Tel: 313-579-2100; Fax: 313-571-1822; Email: jjohnson@cskdetroit.org. Alison Costello, Site Dir.; Ed Conlin, S.W., Chap.; Bro. Bob Malloy, O.F.M.-Cap., Chap. Tot Asst. Annually 178,000; Total Staff 17.

Jefferson House, 8311 E. Jefferson, 48214. Tel: 313-331-8900; Fax: 313-331-2322; Email: jjohnson@cskdetroit.org. Amy Kinner, Site Dir. Transitional alcohol-drug residence. Tot Asst. Annually 30; Total Staff 6.

Manna Community Meal (Soup Kitchen) 1050 Porter St., 48226. Tel: 313-963-8708; Email: mariannearbogast@gmail.com. Marianne Arbogast, Co-Mgr.; Rev. Thomas Lumpkin, Co-Mgr. Tot Asst. Annually 700; Total Staff 5.

Pope John XXIII Hospitality House, 3977 2nd Ave., 48201. Tel: 313-965-4450; Fax: 313-965-4453. Cancer outpatient-residents, Transportation for Area Pediatric Cancer Patients.

Society of St. Vincent de Paul, 3000 Gratiot Ave., 48207. Tel: 313-393-2930; Fax: 313-393-3015; Email: rplaywin@svdpdetroit.org; Web: www.svdpdet.org. Mr. Roger Playwin, CEO. Tot Asst. Annually 300,000; Total Staff 101.

EASTPOINTE. *St. John's Deaf Center*, 16103 Chesterfield Ave., Eastpointe, 48021. Tel: 586-439-0146 (VP); Fax: 586-774-8476; Email: sjdcnewsletter@gmail.com; Web: www.sjdc-oll.org. Rev. Michael Depcik, O.S.F.S., Dir.; Annmarie Kowalcyzk, Pastoral Min./Coord.; Paul Kuplicki, Business Mgr. Tot Asst. Annually 150; Total Staff 3.

ONSTED. *St. Patrick's Retreat*, 11528 Killarney Hwy., Onsted, 49265. Tel: 313-965-4450; Fax: 313-965-4453; Email: corktown99@sbcglobal.net. Retreats for Family with cancer outpatient; small groups of handicapped-developmentally disabled; small parish team meetings; hospice & chaplain's meetings and offers assistance for patient visits to world shrines.

St. Patrick's Chapel, Tipton, Michigan, 4345 US12, Tipton, 49287. Tel: 313-965-4450; Fax: 313-965-4453; Email: corktown99@sbcglobal.net. 14-acre site for children's chapel and nature sanctuary to memorialize victims of childhood cancer and programs of aftercare for bereaved family members.

[R] CAMPS AND COMMUNITY CENTERS

DETROIT. *C.Y.O. Boys Camp*, 12 State St., 48226. Tel: 313-963-7172, Ext. 6; Tel: 810-622-8744; Fax: 810-622-0570; Email: ckrucker@cyodetroit.org; Web: www.cyocamps.org. 7303 Walker Rd., Carsonville, 48419. Mrs. Caroline Krucker, Dir. Students 155; Clergy / Religious Teachers 1.

C.Y.O. Girls Camp, 12 State St., 48226. Tel: 313-963-7172; Tel: 810-622-8744; Fax: 810-622-0570; Email: ckrucker@cyodetroit.org; Web: www.cyocamps.org. Mrs. Caroline Krucker, Dir. Students 162; Clergy / Religious Teachers 1.

Camp Ozanam, 3000 Gratiot Ave., 48207. Tel: 810-622-8744; Tel: 313-393-2930; Fax: 810-622-0570; Email: ckrucker@svdpdetroit.org; Web: www.svdpdet.org. Mrs. Caroline Krucker, Dir. A free week-long Christian camping experience for boys 8-14. Recruitment through Parish Conferences of the Society of St. Vincent de Paul. Clergy / Religious Teachers 1; Clergy / Religious Teachers 1.

Camp Stapleton, 3000 Gratiot Ave., 48207. Tel: 313-393-2930; Tel: 810-622-8744; Fax: 810-622-0570; Email: ckrucker@svdpdetroit.org; Web: www.svdpdet.org. Mrs. Caroline Krucker, Dir. A free week long Christian camping experience for girls 8-12. Recruitment through Parish Conferences of the Society of St. Vincent de Paul. Students 100; Clergy / Religious Teachers 1.

[S] CAMPUS MINISTRIES

DETROIT. *Center for Creative Studies Campus Ministry*, 5221 Gullen Mall, #761, 48202. Tel: 313-577-3462; Email: faithformation@aod.org.

Marygrove College Campus Ministry, 8425 W. McNichols Rd., 48221. Tel: 313-927-1208; Fax: 313-927-1315; Email: eburns@marygrove.edu; Web: www.marygrove.edu. Dr. Elizabeth Burns, Pres.

University of Detroit Mercy University Ministry, University Ministry UC106, 4001 W. McNichols Rd., 48221-3038. Tel: 313-993-1560; Email: ministry@udmercy.edu; Web: www.udmercy.edu/ministry. Ms. Anita Klueg, Dir.

McNichols Campus, Tel: 313-993-1560. David E. Nantais, Dir.; Sr. Beth Ann Finster, S.S.J., Asst. Dir.; Meg Marshall, Campus Min.

Wayne County Community College, 12 State St., 48226. Tel: 313-237-4647; Email: yacm@aod.org. Mr. Patrick Howard, Young Adult & Campus Ministry.

Wayne State Medical School, 5221 Gullen Mall, #761, 48202. Tel: 313-577-3462. Revs. James Lowe, C.C., Chap.; John Fletcher, C.C., Chap.

Wayne State University, Newman Center, 5221 Gullen Mall, #761, 48202. Tel: 313-577-3462; Fax: 313-577-8580. Revs. James Lowe, C.C., Chap.; John Fletcher, C.C.

DEARBORN. *Archdiocesan Catholic Campus Ministry Association, Gabriel Richard Campus Ministry Center*, University of Michigan-Dearborn, Gabriel Richard Campus Ministry Center, 5001 Evergreen, Dearborn, 48128. Tel: 313-271-6000; Email: Fox.Anthony@aod.org; Web: www.grcnewmancenterdearborn.org. Rev. Anthony Fox, O.F.M.Conv., Campus Min.

University of Michigan-Dearborn, Henry Ford Community College Newman Center aka Gabriel Richard Catholic Newman Center, 5001 Evergreen Rd., Dearborn, 48128. Tel: 313-271-6000; Email: Fox.Anthony@aod.org; Web: www.grcnewmancenterdearborn.org. Rev. Anthony Fox, O.F.M.Conv., Campus Min.

FARMINGTON HILLS. *Oakland Community College*, 12 State St., 48226. Tel: 313-237-4647; Email: yacm@aod.org. Mr. Patrick Howard, Young Adult & Campus Ministry Liaison.

LIVONIA. *Madonna University Campus Ministry*, 36600 Schoolcraft, Livonia, 48150. Tel: 734-432-5839; Email: jdcox@madonna.edu; Web: www.madonna.edu. Mr. Jesse Cox, Dir.

Schoolcraft College, 36600 Schoolcraft Rd, Livonia, 48150. Tel: 734-432-5839; Email: cmws@madonna.edu.

MONROE. *Monroe Community College*, 12 State St., 48226. Tel: 313-237-4647; Email: yacm@aod.org. Mr. Patrick Howard, Young Adult & Campus Ministry Liasion.

PORT HURON. *Blue Water/Thumb Regional Campus Ministry*, 12 State St., 48226. Tel: 313-237-4647; Email: yacm@aod.org. Mr. Patrick Howard, Young Adult & Campus Min. Liaison. (Baker College and St. Clair Community College).

ROCHESTER. *St. John Fisher Campus Ministry-Oakland University, Rochester*, 3665 Walton Blvd., Auburn Hills, 48326. Tel: 248-370-2189; Web: www.oucampusministry.com. Mrs. Lisa Brown, Pastoral Assoc.

SOUTHFIELD. *Lawrence Technological University*, 21000 W 10 Mile Rd, Southfield, 48075. Tel: 313-237-4647. Patrick Carzon, Pres.

WARREN. *Macomb Community College Campus Ministry*, 12 State St., 48226. Tel: 313-237-4647; Email: yacm@aod.org. Mr. Patrick Howard, Young Adult & Campus Ministry Liaison.

[T] MISCELLANEOUS LISTINGS

DETROIT. *All Saints Literacy Center* (2014) 3553 W. Vernor Hwy., 48216. Tel: 313-297-1399; Email: allsaintsliteracy@gmail.com. Mr. Roger Frank, Dir.

Ste. Anne Restoration Fund, 1000 Ste. Anne St., 48216. Tel: 313-496-1701; Fax: 313-496-0429; Email: businessoffice@steannedetroit.org. Rev. Msgr. Charles G. Kosanke, Contact Person.

Annunciation Institute, 2701 Chicago Blvd., 48206. Tel: 313-980-0622; Email: annunciation.net@me.com; Web: annunciationvirtues.com. Gerald Rauch, Pres.

Archdiocese of Detroit Endowment Foundation, Inc., 12 State St., 48226. Tel: 313-596-7401; Fax: 313-883-8681. Mr. David Kelley, Sec.

Archdiocese of Detroit Priests' Pension Plan, Inc., 12 State St., 48226. Tel: 313-596-7151; Fax: 313-596-7186. Rev. Robert R. Spezia, Vicar.

Cabrini Clinic, 1050 Porter St., 48226. Tel: 303-965-4450. Rev. Msgr. Charles G. Kosanke, Contact Person.

Capuchin Franciscan Volunteer Corps, 1820 Mt. Eliott St., 48207. Closed in 2017.

Christ Child Society, 15751 Joy Rd., 48228. Tel: 313-584-6077. Rev. Msgr. John P. Zenz, Spiritual Dir.; Ms. Pamela Hildebrand, Pres.

Priest Health Plan, Chancery Building, 12 State St., 48226. Tel: 313-237-5803; Email: Austin.Richard@aod.org. Mr. Richard Austin, Dir.

Detroit Catholic Charismatic Renewal Center, 2322 Ford Ave, Wyandotte, 48192-2317. Tel: 734-282-6244; Fax: 734-282-6284; Email: dccrcenter@aol.com; Web: www.dccr.info. Arlene Apone, Assoc. Liaison/Dir.

THE DETROIT ORATORY, P.O. Box 2129, 48202. Tel: 313-910-8575; Email: frdanieljones@gmail.com. Rev. Daniel J. Jones, Contact Person.

Dominican Literacy Center, 5555 Conner Ave., Ste. 1414, 48213. Tel: 313-267-1000; Email: dominicanliteracy@yahoo.com. Kimberly Williams, Exec.

Gabriel Richard Historical Society, 1000 Ste. Anne St., 48216. Tel: 313-496-1701; Fax: 313-496-0429; Email: businessoffice@steannedetroit.org. Rev. Msgr. Charles G. Kosanke.

Institute for Communal Contemplation and Dialogue, 8531 W. McNichols, 48221. Tel: 313-971-3668; Email: nsylvester@aol.com; Web: www.iccdinstitute.org. Sr. Nancy Sylvester, I.H.M., Exec. Dir.

Jesuit Volunteer Corps., 7333 W. Seven Mile Rd., 48221. Tel: 313-345-3480; Fax: 313-345-5410; Email: jvcmw@jesuitvolunteers.org; Web: www.jesuitvolunteers.org. P.O. Box 21936, 48221-0936. Angela Moloney, Exec. Dir.

Latino Cultural Pastoral Center, 4329 Central, 48210. Tel: 248-398-4565.

**Mercy Education Project*, 1450 Howard St., 48216. Tel: 313-963-5881; Fax: 313-963-0209; Email: mep@mercyed.net; Web: www.mercyed.net. Mrs. Janette Phillips, Contact Person.

Mooney Real Estate Holdings, 12 State St., 48226. Tel: 313-596-7146. Mr. Richard Austin, Treas.

**St. Patrick Senior Center, Inc.*, 58 Parsons St., 48201-2202. Tel: 313-833-7080; Fax: 313-833-0128; Email: info@stpatsrctr.org; Web: www.stpatsrctr.org. Mrs. SaTrice Coleman-Betts, Exec. Dir.

Pontiac Vision 2000 Schools, Inc., 12 State St., 48226. Tel: 313-237-5803. Mr. Richard Austin, Sec. & Treas.

**Pope Francis Center*, 438 Saint Antoine St., 48226. Tel: 313-964-2823; Email: info@popefranciscenter.org; Web: www.popefranciscenter.org. Rev. Timothy McCabe, S.J.

Siena Literacy Center, 16888 Trinity St., 48219. Tel: 313-532-8404; Fax: 313-532-8409; Email: dnesbitt@sienaliteracy.org; Web: www.sienaliteracy.org. Donna J. Nesbitt, Dir.

Solanus Casey Center, 1780 Mt. Elliott, 48207-3596. Tel: 313-579-2100; Fax: 313-579-5365; Email: dpcap@thecapuchins.org; Web: www.solanuscaseycenter.org. Rev. David Preuss, O.F.M.Cap., Dir.

BIRMINGHAM. *The Cardinal Club of Detroit*, 417 Baldwin Rd., Birmingham, 48009. Mr. Charles Moore, Contact Person.

BLOOMFIELD HILLS. **The Catholic Foundation of Michigan*, 1145 W. Long Lake Rd., Ste. 201, Bloomfield Hills, 48302. Tel: 248-204-0332. Angela Moloney, Pres. & CEO.

Clarkston Pastoral Center, Inc., 2460 Opdyke Rd., Bloomfield Hills, 48304. Tel: 248-644-2954; Email: fformolo@legionaries.org. Revs. Benjamin O'Loughlin, L.C., Admin.; Daniel Pajerski, L.C., Everest Academy Boys School Dir.

**Ladies of Charity of St. Vincent de Paul Oakland County Association*, P.O. Box 602, Bloomfield Hills, 48303. Tel: 248-646-0920. Mary Glantz, Contact Person.

Logos, Inc. (Michigan), 2460 Opdyke Rd., Bloomfield Hills, 48304. Tel: 248-644-2954; Email: fformolo@legionaries.org. Revs. Benjamin O'Loughlin, L.C., Admin.; Daniel Pajerski, L.C.

Mercy Homecare - Oakland, 34505 W. 12 Mile Rd, Ste. 100, Farmington Hills, 48331. Tel: 855-559-7178; Email: Erin.Denholm@trinity-health.org; Web: www.trinityhealthathome.org/st-joseph-mercy-home-care-and-hospice. Ms. Erin Denholm, Pres.

**Cranbrook Hospice Care*, 34505 W. 12 Mile Rd, Ste. 100, Farmington Hills, 48331. Tel: 855-559-7178; Email: erin.denholm@trinity-health.org; Web: www.trinityhealthathome.org/st-joseph-mercy-home-care-and-hospice. Ms. Erin Denholm, Pres. *dba St. Joseph Mercy Home Care and Hospice.*

Opdyke, Inc., 2460 Opdyke Rd., Bloomfield Hills, 48304. Tel: 248-644-2954; Email: fformolo@arcol.org. Rev. Frank Formolo.

BROWNSTOWN. *Magnificat - Detroit, MI Chapter*, 24353 Sand Lake Ln., Brownstown, 48134. Tel: 734-771-4151; Email: gramma627@hotmail.com. Virginia Shaffer, Coord.

CLINTON TOWNSHIP. *Servants of Jesus of The Divine Mercy*, 33826 Beaconsfield, Clinton Township, 48035. Tel: 586-777-8591; Fax: 586-777-7989; Email: info@divinemercy.org; Web: www.sjdivinemercy.org. Mrs. Catherine M. Lanni, Spiritual Moderator/Pres.

DEARBORN. *Leo XIII Society*, 1840 N. Melborn, Dearborn, 48128. Tel: 313-359-1499; Fax: 313-359-1767. P.O. Box 213, Elmore, OH 43416. Ernie Scarano, Pres.

DEARBORN HEIGHTS. *Council of Catholic Women Archdiocese of Detroit*, P.O. Box 10, Dearborn Heights, 48127. Tel: 586-772-1976; Email: krpkath@hotmail.com. Kathleen Penno, Pres.

Servants of Jesus Charitable Trust, 8080 Kinmore, Dearborn Heights, 48127. Tel: 313-562-6156. Sr. Karen Shirilla, S.J., Sec.

FARMINGTON HILLS. *Dominican Center for Religious Development*, 29000 W. 11 Mile Rd., Farmington Hills, 48336. Tel: 248-536-3142; Email: director@dominicancenter.org; Web: www.dominicancenter.org. Sr. Adrienne Schaffer, O.P., Dir.; Rev. Victor Clore.

Living Faith - Fine Arts Apostolate, 36703 Kenmore Dr., Farmington Hills, 48335. Tel: 248-444-1034; Email: kelly@crossandlight.com; Web: www.crossandlight.com. Kelly Nieto, Pres. & Contact Person.

LIVONIA. **Angela Hospice Home Care, Inc.*, 14100 Newburgh Rd., Livonia, 48154-5010. Tel: 734-464-7810; Email: ahospice@aol.com; Email: thrubiak@angelahospice.us; Web: www.angelahospice.org. Mrs. Margot Parr, CEO. Bed Capacity 32; Total Assisted Annually (with home care) 2,200; Total Staff 229.

CHE Trinity, Inc., 20555 Victor Pkwy., Livonia, 48152. Tel: 734-343-1392; Fax: 734-343-3450.

**Christ Medicus Foundation*, P.O. Box 530901, Livonia, 48153. Tel: 248-478-5959. Mr. Michael J. O'Dea, Exec. Dir.

Felician Sisters of Livonia Foundation, 36800 Schoolcraft, Livonia, 48150. Tel: 734-591-1730; Fax: 734-591-1710; Email: sconniet@feliciansisters.org; Web: www.feliciansistersna.org. Sr. Mary Christopher Moore, C.S.S.F., Pres.

Marian Village Corporation dba Marywood Nursing Care Center, Marywood Nursing Care Center: 36975 Five Mile Rd., Livonia, 48154. Tel: 734-464-0600; Fax: 734-464-4846; Email: j.mimnaugh@marywoodncc.com; Web: www.marywoodnursingcarecenter.org. Mr. John Mimnaugh, N.H.A., Pres.

Mercy Services for Aging, Non-profit Housing Corporation Wholly owned subsidiary of Trinity Continuing Care Services 17410 College Pkwy., Ste. 200, Livonia, 48152-2363. Tel: 248-656-6300; Email: Steven.Kastner@trinity-health.org; Web: www.trinityhealthseniorcommunities.org/. Mr. Steven Kastner, Pres.

Trinity Continuing Care Services - Indiana, Inc., 17410 College Pkwy., Ste. 200, Livonia, 48152-2363. Tel: 734-343-6600; Email: Steven.Kastner@trinity-health.org; Web: www.trinityhealthseniorcommunities.org/. Mr. Steven Kastner, Pres.

Trinity Continuing Care Services - Massachusetts, 17410 College Pkwy., Ste. 200, Livonia, 48152. Tel: 734-343-6600. Mr. Steven Kastner, Pres.

**Trinity Health Corporation*, 20555 Victor Pkwy., Livonia, 48152. Tel: 734-343-1000; Fax: 734-343-3057; Email: moorej@trinity-health.org; Web: www.trinity-health.org. Richard J. Gilfillan, M.D., Pres. & CEO.

Trinity Health PACE, 20555 Victor Pkwy., Livonia, 48152-7018. Tel: 734-343-1000; Email: kelly.hopkins@trinity-health.org; Web: www.trinityhealthpace.org/. Ms. Kelly Hopkins, Vice Pres. PACE & Long Term Managed Care.

**Trinity Health-Michigan*, 20555 Victor Pkwy., Livonia, 48152. Tel: 734-343-1000; Fax: 734-343-3057; Email: moorej@trinity-health.org; Web: www.trinity-health.org. Roger Spoelman, Pres. Organization owns & operates 6 hospital divisions in Michigan. In addition to acute care facilities, Trinity Health - Michigan operates other related health care programs and facilities. Trinity Health - Michigan is part of Trinity Health, a multi-state health care organization.

Trinity Home Health Services, 17410 College Pkwy., Ste. 150, Livonia, 48152. Tel: 877-827-0788; Email: erin.denholm@trinity-health.org; Web: www.trinityhomehealth.org. Ms. Erin Denholm, CEO *dba Trinity Health at Home*.

MACOMB. *National Alliance of Parishes Restructuring into Communities (NAPRC)*, 23375 Spring Creek Dr., Macomb, 48042. Rev. Arthur R. Baranowski, Dir., (Retired).

MONROE. *IHM Senior Living Community, Inc.*, 610 W. Elm Ave., Monroe, 48162. Tel: 734-240-9700; Email: mtylinski@ihmsisters.org.

SSIHM Charitable Trust, 610 W. Elm Ave., Monroe, 48162-7909. Tel: 734-240-9700; Fax: 734-240-9784; Email: mtylinski@ihmsisters.org. Sr. Margaret Chapman, Treas.

PLYMOUTH. **New Leaven Inc.*, Administrative Office, 17174 Summit Dr., Northville, 48168. Tel: 313-268-7265; Email: NewLeavenFinance@gmail.com; Web: newleaven.org. Deacon Robert Ervin, Pres.; Francisco Gavrilides, Vice Pres.; Edward Connolly, Treas.

**Retrouvaille of Metro Detroit*, 44011 Five Mile Rd., Plymouth, 48170. Tel: 313-531-7275. Steve Fenbert, Contact Person; Sheila Fenbert, Contact Person.

PONTIAC. *Mt. Hope Catholic Cemetery Association*, 120 Lewis, Pontiac, 48342. Tel: 248-350-1900; Fax: 248-350-1737; Email: AODCemeteries@aod.org. Rev. Timothy F. Babcock, Cemetery Liaison, (Retired).

**Terra Sancta Pilgrimages*, 400 South Blvd., W., Pontiac, 48341. Tel: 248-514-1747; Email: terrasanctapontiac@gmail.com; Web: mothermarypontiac.org. Patricia Giangrande, O.F.S., Exec. Dir.

PORT HURON. *Port Huron Mercy Family Care*, 2601 Electric Ave., P.O. Box 610669, Port Huron, 48061-0669. Tel: 810-985-1868. Ms. Nancy Mason, Dir. (A unit of Trinity Health).

REDFORD. *Catholic Biblical School of Michigan, Ltd.*, 26234 Graham Rd., Redford, 48239. Tel: 313-570-8105; Fax: 586-774-4040; Email: fmorath@msn.com; Web: cbsmich.org. 14200 East Ten Mile Rd, Warren, Warren. Frederick Morath, Pres.

ROMEO. **Blessed Virgin Mary Foundation* BVM Foundation, 11070 W. Gates, Romeo, 48065. Tel: 586-752-6744; Tel: 586-281-4110; Fax: 888-950-3329; Email: b.v.m.foundation.edu@gmail.com. 119 Church St. #236, Romeo, 48065. Mr. Brian Palmer, Pres.

SHELBY TWP.. *Holy Trinity Apostolate*, 53565 Sherwood Ln., Shelby Twp., 48315. Tel: 586-781-6051; Fax: 568-781-6099; Email: barbaramm@sbcglobal.net. Barbara Middleton, Pres. Founded by Servant of God, Rev. John A. Hardon, S.J.

SOUTHFIELD. **Mary's Mantle*, Tel: 248-376-5338; Fax: 248-376-5338; Email: info@marysmantle.net; Web: www.marysmantle.net. Mrs. Katie Montes, Dir.

**Mother and Unborn Baby Care Inc.*, 23712 Clarkston, Southfield, 48034.

SOUTHGATE. *Divine Mercy Academy Foundation*, 27555 Executive Dr., Ste. 165, Farmington Hills, 48331. Tel: 248-347-6800; Fax: 248-347-6808; Email: ddoyle@doylecpa.net. Michael Dewan, Pres.; Todd Nadeau, Vice Pres.; Daniel Doyle, Treas.

STERLING HEIGHTS. *Catholic Kolping Society of America, Detroit Branch, Inc.*, 1201 Rock Valley Dr., Rochester, 48307. Tel: 248-650-6275; Email: CJL961@aol.com. Mrs. Mary Dolland, Treas.; Matthew Tiza, Pres.

WARREN. *St. John Providence* dba St. John Health System, 28000 Dequindre Rd., Warren, 48092. Tel: 586-753-0911; Fax: 586-753-1228. Jean Meyer, Pres. & CEO. Holding Company sponsored by Ascension Health, which provides services supportive of the following entities: Ascension St. John Hospital; Medical Resources Group; Affiliated Health Services, Inc.; Eastwood Community Clinics; Ascension River District.

WATERFORD. *Dominican Health Care Corporation*, 2300 Walkins Lake Rd., Waterford, 48328. Tel: 248-886-5600; Fax: 248-674-1211; Email: cburke@lourdes-sc.org; Web: www.lourdes-sc.org. Sr. Maureen Comer, O.P., CEO.

Lourdes Campus Fund, 2300 Watkins Lake Rd., Waterford, 48328. Tel: 248-674-2241; Fax: 248-674-1211; Email: cburke@lourdes-sc.org; Web: www.lourdes-sc.org. Sr. Maureen Comer, O.P., CEO.

WIXOM. *St. Catherine of Siena Academy Foundation*, 28200 Napier Rd., Wixom, 48393. Tel: 248-946-4848; Fax: 248-438-1679; Email: jgould@saintcatherineacademy.org. Karen Ervin, Prin.

WESTLAND. *Chinese Catholic Society of Michigan, Inc.*, 39375 Joy Rd., Westland, 48185. Tel: 248-855-4517 ; Fax: 248-647-7736. Mr. Francis G. King, Pres.; Mr. Thomas McGuire, Spiritual Dir.

[U] ARCHDIOCESAN CEMETERIES

DETROIT. *Holy Cross*, 8850 Dix Ave., 48209. Tel: 734-285-2155; Fax: 734-285-6510; Email: Cortese.Deanna@aodcemeteries.org. Deanna Cortese, Outreach Dir. (owned by the Archdiocese of Detroit); Cemetery now inactive. All mail and inquiries should be sent to: c/o Our Lady of Hope..

Mt. Elliott, 1701 Mt. Elliott Ave., 48207. Tel: 313-567-0048; Tel: 313-365-5650; Fax: 313-365-6460; Email: mgracely@mtelliott.com; Email: mchilcote@mtelliott.com; Web: www.mtelliott.com. Mr. Michael Chilcote, Exec.; Mr. Mark Gracely, Dir. (owned & operated by the Mt. Elliott Cemetery Assoc.)

Mt. Olivet, 17100 Van Dyke, 48234. Tel: 313-365-5650; Tel: 313-365-6460; Email: mgracely@mtelliott.com; Email: mchilcote@mtelliott.com; Web: www.mtelliott.com. Mr. Michael Chilcote, Exec.; Mr. Mark Gracely, Dir. (owned & operated by the Mt. Elliott Cemetery Assoc.)

BROWNSTOWN. *Our Lady of Hope*, 18303 Allen Rd., Brownstown, 48193. Tel: 734-285-2155; Fax: 734-285-6510; Email: Cortese.Deanna@aodcemeteries.org; Web: www.cfcsdetroit.org/locations/our-lady-of-hope. Deanna Cortese, Outreach Dir. (owned & operated by the Archdiocese of Detroit)

CLINTON TOWNSHIP. *Resurrection*, 18201 Clinton River Rd., Clinton Township, 48038. Tel: 586-286-9020; Fax: 586-286-2441; Email: tburrows@mtelliott.com; Email: mchilcote@mtelliott.com; Web: www.mtelliott.com. Mr. Timothy Burrows, Dir.; Mr. Michael Chilcote, Exec. (owned & operated by the Mt. Elliott Cemetery Assoc.)

DEARBORN HEIGHTS. *St. Hedwig Cemetery*, 23755 Military, Dearborn Heights, 48127. Tel: 313-562-1900; Fax: 313-562-8238; Email: shcdaz@aol.com. David Zielinski, Exec. (owned & operated by the Conventual Franciscan Friars)

MONROE. *St. Joseph Cemetery*, 909 N. Monroe St., Monroe, 48162. Tel: 734-241-1411; Fax: 734-241-1422; Email: Cortese.Deanna@aodcemeteries.org. Deanna Cortese, Outreach Dir.

ROCHESTER. *Guardian Angel*, 4701 Rochester Rd., Rochester, 48306. Tel: 800-275-9574; Tel: 248-601-2900; Fax: 248-601-1711; Email: wmann@mtelliott.com; Email: mchilcote@mtelliott.com; Web: www.mtelliott.com. Mr. Michael Chilcote, Exec.; Mrs. Wendy Mann, Dir. (owned & operated by the Mt. Elliott Cemetery Assoc.)

SOUTHFIELD. *Holy Sepulchre*, 25800 W. Ten Mile Rd., Southfield, 48033. Tel: 248-350-1900; Fax: 248-350-1737; Email: Cortese.Deanna@aodcemeteries.org; Web: www.cfcsdetroit.org/locations/holy-sepulchre. Deanna Cortese, Outreach Dir.; Bill Hoeft, Location Mgr. (owned & operated by the Archdiocese of Detroit)

WATERFORD. *All Saints*, 4401 Nelsey Rd., Waterford, 48329. Tel: 248-623-9633; Fax: 248-623-2311; Email: rburns@mtelliott.com; Email: mchilcote@mtelliott.com; Web: www.mtelliott.com. Mr. Russ Burns, Dir.; Mr. Michael Chilcote, Exec. (owned & operated by the Mt. Elliott Cemetery Assoc.)

[V] CLOSED INSTITUTIONS

DETROIT. *Archdiocesan Archives*, 12 State St., 48226. Tel: 313-237-5846; Fax: 313-596-7199; Email: archives@aod.org. Mr. Steve Wejroch, Archivist. Sacramental records from the following institutions are in the custody of the Archdiocese of Detroit Archives.

Suppressed Parishes:

Assumption of the Blessed Virgin Mary, Detroit.
Corpus Christi (1923-1984), Detroit.
Divine Mercy, Davisburg Records at Archdiocesan Archives.
Epiphany, Detroit.
Guardian Angels, Detroit.
Holy Ghost, Detroit.
Immaculate Conception, Detroit.
Martyrs of Uganda, Detroit.
Most Holy Name of Jesus, Detroit.
Mother of Our Savior, Detroit.
Our Lady of Guadalupe (1920-1957), Detroit.
Our Lady of Help, Detroit.
Our Lady of Mt. Carmel, Detroit.
Our Lady Queen of Hope, Detroit.
Our Lady Queen of Peace, Harper Woods Records in Archdiocesan Archives.
Patronage of St. Joseph, Detroit.
Resurrection, Detroit.
Santa Maria, Detroit.
SS. Kevin & Norbert, Inkster.
St. Agatha, Redford / Detroit.
St. Agnes, Detroit.
St. Albertus, Detroit.
St. Augustine, Detroit.
St. Benedict the Moor, Detroit.
St. Bernadette, Dearborn.
St. Bernard of Clairvaux, Detroit.
St. Bernardine of Siena, Westland Records at Archives, Archdiocese of Detroit.
St. Boniface, Detroit.
St. Boniface-St. Vincent, Detroit.
St. Brendan, Detroit.
St. Brigid, Detroit.
St. Camillus, Eloise.
St. Casimir, Detroit.
St. Catherine of Siena (1912-1990), Detroit.
St. Catherine of Siena (2005-2009), Detroit.
St. Catherine-St. Edward, Detroit.
St. Christine, Detroit.
St. David of Wales, Detroit.
St. Dominic, Detroit.
St. Donald, Roseville Records at Archives, Archdiocese of Detroit.
St. Edward, Detroit.
St. Eugene, Detroit.
St. Gemma, Detroit.
St. George, Detroit.
St. Helena, Wyandotte.
St. Ignatius of Antioch, Detroit.
St. Joachim, Detroit.
St. John Berchmans, Detroit.
St. John Berchmans-St. Juliana, Detroit.
St. John Cantius, Detroit.
St. John Nepomucene, Detroit.
St. John the Evangelist, Detroit.
St. John Vianney, Highland Park.
St. Juliana, Detroit.
St. Kevin, Inkster.
St. Lawrence, Detroit.
St. Luke, Detroit.
St. Margaret Mary, Detroit.
St. Martin of Tours, Detroit.
St. Mel, Dearborn Heights.
St. Monica, Detroit.
St. Norbert, Inkster.
St. Patrick, Detroit.
St. Paul, Detroit.
St. Peter, Detroit.
St. Philip Neri, Detroit.
St. Robert Bellarmine.

St. Rose of Lima, Detroit.
St. Stanislaus, Detroit.
St. Theresa of Avila, Detroit.
St. Thomas the Apostle, Detroit.
St. Vincent de Paul, Detroit.
St. Wenceslaus, Detroit.
Visitation, Detroit.

Other Closed Institutions (Sacramental records in Archdiocesan Archives):
Anawim Community, Grosse Pointe.
Bon Secours Hospital, Grosse Pointe.
Cardinal Leger Community, Detroit.
Emmaus Community, Nori / Northville.
Episcopal Residence, Detroit.
Grace Hospital, Detroit.
Henry Ford Hospital, Detroit.
Mother of Consolation Mission, Detroit.
Mount Carmel Hospital, Detroit.
Our Lady of the Hills, Troy.
St. Bernadette Chapel (Detroit Osteopathic Hospital), Detroit.
St. Francis Hospital, Hamtramck.
St. John Senior Community, Detroit.
St. Joseph Hospital (East & West), Mount Clemens.
St. Joseph Mercy Hospital, Detroit.
St. Joseph Retreat House, Dearborn.
St. Mary Hospital / Detroit Memorial Hospital, Detroit.
Vida Nueva Community, Utica.

Merged Parishes (Sacramental records from the following institutions can be found at the location indicated):
All Saints, Memphis Records at Holy Family, Memphis.
Annunciation, Detroit Records at Good Shepherd, Detroit.
Annunciation-Our Lady of Sorrows, Detroit Records at Good Shepherd, Detroit.
Ascension, Warren Records at St. Mary, Our Lady Queen of Families, Warren.
Church of the Madonna, Detroit Records at St. Moses the Black, Detroit.
Divine Savior Parish, Westland Records at St. Mary, Cause of Our Joy Parish, Westland.
Good Shepherd Parish, Detroit Records at Our Lady Queen of Heaven-Good Shepherd Parish, Detroit.
Holy Cross, Marine City Records at Our Lady on the River, Marine City.
Holy Innocents, Roseville Records at Holy Innocents-St. Barnabas, Roseville.
Holy Rosary Mission, Smith's Creek Records at Holy Family, Memphis.
Immaculate Heart of Mary, Detroit Records at Corpus Christi, Detroit.
Mary Mother of the Church Mission, Detroit Records at Our Lady of Guadalupe, Detroit.
Our Lady Gate of Heaven, Detroit Records at St. Suzanne-Our Lady Gate of Heaven, Detroit.
Our Lady Help of Christians, Detroit Records at St. John Paul II, Hamtramck.
Our Lady of Fatima, Oak Park Records at Our Mother of Perpetual Help, Oak Park.
Our Lady of Good Counsel, Detroit Records at St. Raymond-Our Lady of Good Counsel, Detroit.
Our Lady of Grace, Dearborn Heights Records kept at St. Sabine, Dearborn Heights.
Our Lady of Guadalupe Mission, Port Huron Records at Holy Trinity, Port Huron.
Our Lady of Lourdes, River Rouge Records at St. Andre Bessette, Ecorse.
Our Lady of Mount Carmel, Wyandotte Records at Our Lady of Scapular, Wyandotte.
Our Lady of Sorrows, Detroit Records at Good Shepherd, Detroit.
Our Lady of Victory Parish, Detroit Records at Presentation-Our Lady of Victory Parish, Detroit.
Our Lady Queen of All Saints, Fraser Records at St. Pio of Pietrelcina, Roseville.
Our Lady Queen of Angels, Detroit Records at Our Lady of Guadalupe, Detroit.
Our Lady Queen of Heaven Parish, Detroit Records at Our Lady Queen of Heaven=Good Shepherd Parish, Detroit.
Precious Blood, Detroit Records at St. Peter Claver, Detroit.
Presentation Parish, Detroit Records at Presentation-Our Lady of Victory Parish, Detroit.
Sacred Heart, Roseville Records at St. Pio of Pietrelcina, Roseville.
San Francesco Parish, Detroit Records at San Francesco Parish, Clinton Township.
SS. Cyril & Methodius Parish, Detroit Records at SS. Cyril and Methodius Parish, Sterling Heights.
St. Alan, Troy Records at Christ our Light, Troy.
St. Alexander Parish, Farmington Hills Records at St. Gerald Parish, Farmington.
St. Alphonsus Parish, Dearborn Records at St. Alphonsus-St. Clement Parish, Dearborn.
St. Andrew, Detroit Records at Our Lady of Guadalupe, Detroit.
St. Angela, Roseville Records at St. Isaac Jogues, Roseville.
St. Anthony (Lithuanian), Detroit Records at Divine Providence, Southfield.
St. Anthony of Padua, Detroit Records at Good Shepherd, Detroit.
St. Athanasius, Roseville Records at St. Pio of Pietrelcina, Roseville.
St. Barnabas, Eastpointe Records at Holy Innocents-St. Barnabas, Roseville.
St. Bartholomew, Detroit Records at Our Lady Queen of Heaven, Detroit.
St. Bartholomew-St. Rita, Detroit Records at Our Lady Queen of Heaven, Detroit.
St. Beatrice, Southfield Records at Church of the Transfiguration, Southfield.
St. Bede, Southfield Records at Church of the Transfiguration, Southfield.
St. Benedict, Highland Park Records at St. Moses the Black, Detroit.
St. Catherine, Algonac Records at Our Lady on the River, Marine City.
St. Cecilia, Detroit Records at St. Charles Lwanga, Detroit.
St. Christopher Parish, Detroit Records at St. Christopher-St. Thomas Aquinas Parish, Detroit.
St. Clare of Assisi, Farmington Hills Records at Our Lady of Sorrows, Farmington.
St. Clement, Center Line Records at St. Mary, Our Lady Queen of Families, Warren.
St. Clement Parish, Dearborn Records at St. Alphonsus-St. Clement Parish, Dearborn.
St. Cletus, Warren Records at Our Lady of Grace (Vietnamese), Warren.
St. Colman, Farmington Hills Records at St. Fabian, Farmington Hills.
St. Columban, Birmingham Records at Christ Our Light, Troy.
St. Conrad, Melvindale Records at St. Mary Magdalen, Melvindale.
St. Christopher, Detroit Records at St. Christopher-St. Thomas Aquinas, Detroit.
St. Claude, Mount Clemens Records at St. Thecla, Clinton Twp.
St. Cyril of Jerusalem, Taylor Records at Our Lady of the Angels, Taylor.
St. Damian Parish, Westland Records at St. Mary, Cause of Our Joy Parish, Westland.
St. Dennis, Royal Oak Records at St. Vincent Ferrer, Madison Heights.
St. Dorothy, Warren Records at St. Mary, Our Lady Queen of Families, Warren.
St. Dunstan, Garden City Records at St. Thomas the Apostle, Garden City.
St. Edmund, Warren Records at St. Faustina, Warren.
St. Elizabeth, Wyandotte Records at St. Vincent Pallotti, Wyandotte.
St. Francis D'Assisi, Detroit Records at St. Francis D'Assisi-St. Hedwig, Detroit.
St. Francis de Sales, Detroit Records at St. Peter Claver, Detroit.
St. Francis of Assisi, Ray Records at St. Francis of Assisi-St. Maximilian Kolbe, Ray.
St. Francis Xavier, Ecorse Records at St. Andre Bessette, Ecorse.
St. Genevieve, Livonia Records at St. Genevieve-St. Maurice, Livonia.
St. Gerard, Detroit Records at Corpus Christi, Detroit.
St. Germaine, St. Clair Shores Records at Our Lady of Hope, St. Clair Shores.
St. Gertrude, St. Clair Shores Records at Our Lady of Hope, St. Clair Shores.
St. Gregory the Great, Detroit Records at St. Moses the Black, Detroit.
St. Hedwig, Detroit Records at St. Francis D'Assisi-St. Hedwig, Detroit.
St. Henry, Lincoln Park Records at Christ the Good Shepherd, Lincoln Park.
St. Hilary, Redford Records at St. John Bosco, Redford.
St. Hugh, Southgate Records at St. Frances Cabrini, Allen Park.
St. Irene, Dundee Records at St. Gabriel, Ida.
St. Ives, Southfield Records at Church of the Transfiguration, Southfield.
St. James, Ferndale Records at Our Mother of Perpetual Help, Oak Park.
St. Jerome, Detroit Records at St. Lucy, Troy.
St. Josaphat, Detroit Records at Mother of Divine Mercy, Detroit.
St. Joseph, Dearborn Records at St. Kateri Tekakwitha, Dearborn.
St. Joseph, Detroit Records at Mother of Divine Mercy, Detroit.
St. Joseph Parish, Ida Records at St. Gabriel Parish, Ida.
St. Joseph, Maybee Records at Divine Grace, Carleton.
St. Joseph Parish, Monroe Records at St. John the Baptist Parish, Monroe.
St. Joseph, Pontiac Records at St. Damien of Molokai, Pontiac.
St. Joseph, Port Huron Records at Holy Trinity, Port Huron.
St. Joseph, Wyandotte Records at St. Vincent Pallotti, Wyandotte.
St. Justin Parish, Hazel Park Records at St. Justin-St. Mary Magdalen Parish, Hazel Park.
St. Ladislaus, Hamtramck Records at St. John Paul II, Detroit.
St. Leo, Detroit Records at St. Charles Lwanga, Detroit.
St. Leonard of Port Maurice, Warren Records at St. Mary, Our Lady Queen of Families, Warren.
St. Louis the King, Detroit Records at St. John Paul II, Detroit.
St. Mark, Harsens Island Records at Our Lady of the River, Marine City.
St. Martha, Dearborn Records at St. Kateri Tekakwitha, Dearborn.
St. Mary, Rockwood Records at St. Mary, Our Lady of the Annunciation, Rockwood.
St. Mary Magdalen Parish, Hazel Park Records at St. Justin-St. Mary Magdalen Parish, Hazel Park.
St. Maurice, Livonia Records at St. Genevieve-St. Maurice, Livonia.
St. Maximilian Kolbe, Macomb Records at St. Francis of Assisi-St. Maximilian Kolbe, Ray.
St. Michael, Pontiac Records at St. Damien of Molokai, Pontiac.
St. Michael, Southfield Records at Church of the Transfiguration, Southfield.
St. Paschal Baylon, Taylor Records at Our Lady of the Angels, Taylor.
St. Patrick, Carleton Records at Divine Grace, Carleton.
St. Patrick, Wyandotte Records at St. Vincent Pallotti, Wyandotte.
St. Patrick Mission, North Branch Records at SS. Peter & Paul, North Branch.
St. Peter Apostle, Harper Woods Records at St. Veronica, Eastpointe.
St. Philip Neri, Columbus Records at Holy Family, Memphis.
St. Raphael, Garden City Records at St. Thomas the Apostle, Garden City.
St. Raymond Parish, Detroit Records at St. Raymond-Our Lady of Good Counsel Parish , Detroit.
St. Rita, Detroit Records at Our Lady Queen of Heaven, Detroit.
St. Stanislaus Kostka, Wyandotte Records at Our Lady of the Scapular, Wyandotte.
St. Stephen, Detroit Records at Our Lady of Guadalupe, Detroit.
St. Stephen, Port Huron Records at Holy Trinity, Port Huron.
St. Stephen-Mary Mother of the Church, Detroit Records at Our Lady of Guadalupe, Detroit.
St. Suzanne, Detroit Records at St. Suzanne/Our Lady Gate of Heaven, Detroit.
St. Sylvester, Warren Records at St. Faustina, Warren.
St. Teresa of Avila, Warren Records at St. Mary, Our Lady Queen of Families, Warren.
St. Theodore Parish, Westland Records at St. Mary, Cause of Our Joy Parish, Westland.
St. Thomas Aquinas, Detroit Records at St. Christopher-St.Thomas Aquinas, Detroit.
St. Valerie of Ravenna, Clinton Township Records at St. Louis, Clinton Twp.
St. Victor, Gibraltar Records at St. Mary, Our Lady of the Annunciation, Rockwood.
St. Vincent de Paul, Pontiac Records at St. Damien of Molokai, Pontiac.
Sweetest Heart of Mary, Detroit Records at Mother of Divine Mercy, Detroit.
Transfiguration, Detroit Records at St. John Paul II, Detroit.
Transfiguration-Our Lady Help of Christians, Detroit Records at St. John Paul II, Hamtramck.

RELIGIOUS INSTITUTES OF MEN REPRESENTED IN THE ARCHDIOCESE

For further details refer to the corresponding bracketed number in the Religious Institutes of Men or Women section.

[0170]—*Basilian Fathers* (Toronto, Ont.)—C.S.B.
[0200]—*Benedictine Monks* (Detroit Prov.)—O.S.B.
[0330]—*Brothers of the Christian Schools* (District of Eastern North America)—F.S.C.
[0470]—*The Capuchin Friars* (St. Joseph Prov.)—O.F.M.Cap.
[]—*Companions of the Cross*—C.C.
[0310]—*Congregation of Christian Brothers* (American Prov.)—C.F.C.
[0750]—*Congregation of Mariannhill Missionaries*—C.M.M.
[]—*Congregation of St. Michael the Archangel*—C.S.M.A.

[]—*Congregation of the Holy Spirit*—C.S.Sp.
[1000]—*Congregation of the Passion* (Western Prov. & Holy Cross Prov.)—C.P.
[0480]—*Conventual Franciscans*—O.F.M.Conv.
[0520]—*Franciscan Friars (Custody of the Holy Family/Croatian)* (Prov. of St. John the Baptist; Prov. of St. Stephen, King of Hungary; Assumption Prov.)—O.F.M.
[]—*Institute of Christ the King Sovereign Priest*.
[0690]—*Jesuit Fathers and Brothers* (Midwest, New York, Maryland Provinces)—S.J.
[0730]—*Legionaries of Christ*—L.C.
[]—*Little Brothers of Jesus*—L.B.J.
[0780]—*Marist Fathers* (Northeastern Prov.)—S.M.
[]—*Maryknoll Fathers and Brothers*—M.M.
[]—*Miles Christi Institute*—M.C.
[]—*Missionaries of St. Francis de Sales* Visakhapatnam Province, India—M.S.F.S.
[0920]—*Oblates of St. Francis De Sales*—O.S.F.S.
[0430]—*Order of Preachers-Dominicans* (Prov. of St. Albert the Great)—O.P.
[0180]—*Order of St. Basil the Great*—O.S.B.M.
[1050]—*Pontifical Institute for Foreign Missions*—P.I.M.E.
[1070]—*Redemptorist Fathers* (Denver Prov.)—C.SS.R.
[1260]—*Society of Christ* (American-Canadian Prov.)—S.Ch.
[]—*Society of Our Lady of the Most Holy Trinity*—S.O.L.T.
[0990]—*Society of the Catholic Apostolate* (Assumption B.V.M. Prov.; Bangalore Prov.; Mother of Divine Love.; Irish Prov.)—S.A.C.

RELIGIOUS INSTITUTES OF WOMEN REPRESENTED IN THE ARCHDIOCESE
[1810]—*Bernardine Sisters of the Third Order of St. Francis*—O.S.F.
[3810]—*Catholic Mission Sisters of St. Francis Xavier*—X.S.
[]—*Congregation of the Sisters of Divine Providence*—C.D.P.
[3832]—*Congregation of the Sisters of St. Joseph*—C.S.J.
[1730]—*Congregation of the Sisters of the Third Order of St. Francis in Oldenburg, IN.*
[0760]—*Daughters of Charity of Province of St. Louise*—D.C.
[0790]—*Daughters of Divine Charity*—F.D.C.
[]—*Daughters of Mary* (India)—D.M.
[]—*Daughters of Mary Immaculate (Chaldean)*—D.M.I.
[]—*Daughters of Mary, Mother of Mercy*—D.M.M.M.
[0420]—*Discalced Carmelite Nuns*—O.C.D.
[1050]—*Dominican Contemplative Nuns*—O.P.
[1070-13]—*Dominican Sisters (Adrian, MI)*—O.P.
[1070-14]—*Dominican Sisters (Grand Rapids, MI)*—O.P.
[]—*Dominican Sisters of Mary, Mother of the Eucharist*.
[]—*Dominican Sisters of Mt. Thabor*—O.P.
[1115]—*Dominican Sisters of Peace*—O.P.
[1170]—*Felician Sisters*—C.S.S.F.
[]—*Franciscan Sisters of the Immaculate Conception* (Albanian).
[2430]—*Marist Sisters Congregation of Mary*—S.M.
[2710]—*Missionaries of Charity*—M.C.
[M.Chr.]—*Missionary Sisters of Christ the King for Polonia*.
[]—*Order of St. Basil the Great*—O.S.B.M.
[]—*Racine Dominicans*—O.P.
[2970]—*School Sisters of Notre Dame*—S.S.N.D.
[3560]—*Servants of Jesus*—S.J.
[3590]—*Servants of Mary (Servite Sisters)*—O.S.M.
[0440]—*Sisters of Charity of Cincinnati, Ohio*—S.C.
[2245]—*Sisters of Jesus the Savior*—S.J.S.
[2575]—*Sisters of Mercy of the Americas* (Mid-Atlantic Community; West Midwest Community)—R.S.M.
[2990]—*Sisters of Notre Dame*—S.N.D.
[1530]—*Sisters of St. Francis of the Congregation of Our Lady of Lourdes* (Sylvania, OH & Tiffin, OH)—O.S.F.
[3930]—*Sisters of St. Joseph of the Third Order of St. Francis*—S.S.J.-T.O.S.F.
[1830]—*Sisters of the Good Shepherd*—R.G.S.
[1970]—*Sisters of the Holy Family of Nazareth*—C.S.F.N.
[2160]—*Sisters, Servants of the Immaculate Heart of Mary* (Scranton, PA).
[1760]—*Sisters of the Third Order of St. Francis of Penance and Charity* (Tiffin, OH).
[2090]—*Sisters, Home Visitors of Mary*—H.V.M.
[2150]—*Sisters, Servants of the Immaculate Heart of Mary* (Monroe, MI; Scranton, PA)—I.H.M.
[2460]—*Society of Mary Reparatrix*—S.M.R.
[4070]—*Society of the Sacred Heart*—R.S.C.J.

NECROLOGY
† Blaska, John A., (Retired), Died Feb. 26, 2018
† Kowalczyk, Sigismund C., (Retired), Died Apr. 19, 2018
† Schmidberger, Richard, (Retired), Died Apr. 17, 2018

An asterisk (*) denotes an organization that has established tax-exempt status directly with the IRS and is not covered by the USCCB Group Ruling.

Diocese of Dodge City

(Dioecesis Dodgepolis)

Most Reverend

JOHN B. BRUNGARDT

Bishop of Dodge City; ordained May 23, 1998; appointed Bishop of Dodge City December 15, 2010; installed February 2, 2011. *Office: 910 Central Ave., P.O. Box 137, Dodge City, KS 67801-0137.*

Catholic Church Offices: 910 Central Ave., P.O. Box 137, Dodge City, KS 67801-0137. Tel: 620-227-1500; Fax: 620-227-1545.

Web: www.dcdiocese.org

Email: dcdiocese@dcdiocese.org

Most Reverend

RONALD M. GILMORE, S.T.L., D.D.

Bishop Emeritus of Dodge City; ordained June 7, 1969; appointed Bishop of Dodge City May 12, 1998; installed July 16, 1998; retired December 15, 2010. *Office: 910 Central Ave., P.O. Box 137, Dodge City, KS 67801.*

Most Reverend

STANLEY G. SCHLARMAN, D.D.

Bishop Emeritus of Dodge City; ordained July 13, 1958; appointed to the Titular See of Capri and Auxiliary Bishop of Belleville, March 13, 1979; consecrated May 14, 1979; appointed Bishop of Dodge City March 1, 1983; installed May 4, 1983; retired May 12, 1998. *Res.: 2620 Lebanon Ave., Belleville, IL 62221.*

ESTABLISHED MAY 19, 1951.

Square Miles 23,000.

Comprises the following Counties in the State of Kansas: Barton, Stafford, Pratt, Barber, Rush, Ness, Lane, Scott, Wichita, Greeley, Hamilton, Kearny, Finney, Hodgeman, Pawnee, Edwards, Ford, Gray, Haskell, Grant, Stanton, Morton, Stevens, Seward, Meade, Clark, Kiowa and Comanche.

Principal Patron: Our Lady of Guadalupe.

Secondary Patron: St. John the Baptist.

For legal titles of parishes and diocesan institutions, consult the Chancery Office.

STATISTICAL OVERVIEW

Personnel	
Bishop	1
Retired Bishops	2
Priests: Diocesan Active in Diocese	16
Priests: Retired, Sick or Absent	15
Number of Diocesan Priests	31
Religious Priests in Diocese	3
Total Priests in Diocese	34
Extern Priests in Diocese	8
Permanent Deacons in Diocese	8
Total Sisters	64
Parishes	
Parishes	47
With Resident Pastor:	
Resident Diocesan Priests	12
Resident Religious Priests	2
Without Resident Pastor:	
Administered by Priests	24
Administered by Lay People	1
Completely Vacant	1
Missions	1
Professional Ministry Personnel:	
Sisters	8
Lay Ministers	33
Welfare	
Catholic Hospitals	1
Total Assisted	262,340
Special Centers for Social Services	3
Total Assisted	6,830
Educational	
Diocesan Students in Other Seminaries	7
Total Seminarians	7
Elementary Schools, Diocesan and Parish	6
Total Students	826
Catechesis/Religious Education:	
High School Students	631
Elementary Students	3,505
Total Students under Catholic Instruction	4,969
Teachers in the Diocese:	
Lay Teachers	86
Vital Statistics	
Receptions into the Church:	
Infant Baptism Totals	782
Minor Baptism Totals	95
Adult Baptism Totals	60
Received into Full Communion	83
First Communions	928
Confirmations	805
Marriages:	
Catholic	140
Interfaith	41
Total Marriages	181
Deaths	425
Total Catholic Population	47,859
Total Population	214,144

Former Bishops—Most Revs. JOHN BAPTIST FRANZ, D.D., cons. Aug. 29, 1951; transferred to the See of Peoria Aug. 8, 1959; retired June 1, 1971; died July 3, 1992.; MARION F. FORST, D.D., cons. March 24, 1960; transferred to See of Kansas City, KS as Auxiliary Oct. 16, 1976; retired as Auxiliary Bishop Dec. 23, 1986; died June 2, 2007; EUGENE J. GERBER, D.D., cons. Dec. 14, 1976; transferred to See of Wichita, KS Nov. 23, 1982; installed Bishop of Wichita Feb. 9, 1983; resigned Oct. 4, 2001; died Sept. 29, 2018.; STANLEY G. SCHLARMAN, D.D., (Retired), cons. May 14, 1979; appt. Bishop of Dodge City March 1, 1983; installed May 4, 1983; retired May 12, 1998; RONALD M. GILMORE, ord. June 7, 1969; appt. Bishop of Dodge City May 12, 1998; installed July 16, 1998; retired Dec. 15, 2010.

Chancery Office and Administration—Unless otherwise noted, the mailing address is: P.O. Box 137, Dodge City, 67801-0137. Tel: 620-227-1500; Fax: 620-227-1545. Office Hours: Mon.-Fri. 9-4:30.

Vicar General and Moderator of the Curia—Rev. ROBERT A. SCHREMMER, V.G., Tel: 620-227-1555; Email: rschremmer@dcdiocese.org.

Chancellor—Sr. JANICE GROCHOWSKY, C.S.J., J.C.L., Tel: 620-227-1527; Email: jgrochowsky@dcdiocese.org.

Diocesan Archivist Emeritus—MR. TIMOTHY F. WENZL, Tel: 620-227-1556; Email: twenzl@dcdiocese.org.

Finance Officer—MR. DANIEL M. STREMEL, CPA, CDFM, Tel: 620-227-1517; Email: dmstremel@dcdiocese.org.

Seminarians—Rev. WESLEY W. SCHAWE, Dir., Tel: 620-227-1533; Fax: 620-227-1545; Email: vocations@dcdiocese.org. Priestly Vocation Promotion: Revs. JUAN SALAS, Dir., 509 St. John St., Garden City, 67846. Tel: 620-275-4204; Email: jsalas@stmarygc.com; TED D. STOECKLEIN, V.F., Asst. Dir., P.O. Box 87, Great Bend, 67530-0087. Tel: 620-792-1396; Fax: 620-792-3642; Email: frstoecklein@gmail.com; JACOB SCHNEIDER, Asst. Dir., 1510 N. Calhoun St., Liberal, 67901. Tel: 620-624-4135; Fax: 620-624-3553; Email: fr.schneider17@gmail.com.

Executive Secretary to the Bishop—MRS. GAYLA KIRMER, Tel: 620-227-1525; Fax: 620-227-1545; Email: gkirmer@dcdiocese.org.

Receptionist—MS. ANA GAYTAN, Tel: 620-227-1500; Fax: 620-227-1545; Email: agaytan@dcdiocese.org.

Safe Environment—

Coordinator—MRS. TAMMY LAMPE, Tel: 620-227-1534; Fax: 620-227-1545; Email: tlampe@dcdiocese.org.

Reports of Suspected Abuse Made To—MR. CHARLES BEFORT, Tel: 620-285-3219; Email: crbefort@cox.net.

Kansas Department for Children and Families—Tel: 800-922-5330.

Diocesan Fitness Review Administrator—MR. DAVID H. SNAPP, Tel: 620-225-5051 (Office); Tel: 620-225-2412 (Home).

Assistance Minister—MRS. DONNA STAAB, M.S.N., R.N., B.C., Tel: 620-792-2098; Tel: 620-786-5785; Email: donna@cpcis.net.

Office of Stewardship—MR. ERIC HASELHORST, Dir., Tel: 620-227-1537; Email: ehaselhorst@dcdiocese.org.

Office of Development—MR. MARK ROTH, Dir., Tel: 620-227-1535; Email: mroth@dcdiocese.org.

Assistant & Database Manager—MRS. HEIDY RAMIREZ, Tel: 620-227-1530; Fax: 620-227-1545; Email: hramirez@dcdiocese.org.

Office of Finance—MR. DANIEL M. STREMEL, CPA, CDFM, Dir., Tel: 620-227-1517; Email: dmstremel@dcdiocese.org.

Controller—MRS. GEORGINA PAZ, Tel: 620-227-1531; Fax: 620-227-1545; Email: gpaz@dcdiocese.org.

Human Resources Coordinator—MRS. TAMMY LAMPE, Tel: 620-227-1534; Fax: 620-227-1545; Email: tlampe@dcdiocese.org.

Tribunal—

Judicial Vicar—Rev. JOHN V. HOTZE, J.C.L., (WCH).

Defender of the Bond—Rev. PETER TRONG TRAN, J.C.L., Tel: 620-355-6405; Email: petertrong@hotmail.com.

Judge—Rev. JAMES E. BAKER, J.C.L., (Retired).

Notary—Sr. JANICE GROCHOWSKY, C.S.J., J.C.L.

Promoter of Justice—VACANT.

All matrimonial correspondence may be sent to the attention of Sr. Janice Grochowsky, C.S.J., J.C.L. Tel: 620-227-1527; Fax: 620-227-1545; Email: jgrochowsky@dcdiocese.org.

Catholic Education and Formation—

Catholic Elementary Schools—MRS. TRINA DELGADO, Supt., Tel: 620-227-1513; Fax: 620-227-1545; Email: tdelgado@gckschools.com.

Pastoral Ministry Formation—MRS. COLEEN STEIN, Coord. (English), Tel: 620-227-1538; Fax: 620-227-1545; Email: cstein@dcdiocese.org; MS. MATILDA SCHEURER, Assoc. Coord. (Spanish).
Youth/Family Ministry and Religious Formation—MR. ADAM URBAN, Dir., Tel: 620-227-1540; Fax: 620-227-1545; Email: aurban@dcdiocese.org.
Catechist Support—MR. ERIC HASELHORST, Coord. English, Tel: 620-227-1537; Fax: 620-227-1545; Email: ehaselhorst@dcdiocese.org.
Young Adult Ministry—GENTRY HEIMERMAN, Dir., Tel: 620-227-1550; Fax: 620-227-1545; Email: gheimerman@dcdiocese.org.
Curia Intern—DIANA RAMIREZ, Tel: 620-227-1500; Fax: 620-227-1545; Email: dramirez@dcdiocese.org.

Catholic Charities of Southwest Kansas—Web: www.catholiccharitiesswks.org/. DEBBIE SNAPP, Exec. Dir., 906 Central, Dodge City, 67801. Tel: 620-227-1588; Fax: 620-227-1572; Email: dsnapp@catholiccharitiesswks.org. Mailing Address: P.O. Box 137, Dodge City, 67801-0137.
Satellite Offices—Garden City: 603 N. 8th, Garden City, 67846. Tel: 620-272-0010. *Great Bend: 2201 16th St., Great Bend, 67530*. Tel: 620-792-1393. *Family Crisis Center, 1924 Broadway, P.O. Box 1543, Great Bend, 67530*. Fax: 620-793-9941; Tel: 620-792-1885 (Crisis Line); Tel: 620-793-9943. *Sommerset Place, 5830 16th Ter., Great Bend, 67530*. Tel: 620-793-8075; Fax: 620-793-7417. *Community Immigration Svcs., 1510 Taylor Plaza E., Garden City, 67846*. Tel: 620-276-6710; Fax: 620-276-9228.
Pro-Life Activities/Respect Life Activities—MRS. GAYLA KIRMER, Tel: 620-227-1525; Fax: 620-227-1545; Email: gkirmer@dcdiocese.org.
Office of Matrimony, Family Life & Natural Family Planning—MRS. JENEE BERNAL, Dir., Tel: 620-227-1500; Fax: 620-227-1545; Email: jbernal@dcdiocese.org.

Hispanic Ministry—Sr. ANGELA EREVIA, M.C.D.P., Dir., Tel: 620-227-1542; Email: aerevia@dcdiocese.org.

Vietnamese Ministry—Rev. PETER TRONG TRAN, J.C.L., Chap., P.O. Box 983, Lakin, 67860-0983. Tel: 620-355-6405; Email: petertrong@hotmail.com.

Mission Outreach and Propagation of the Faith—MRS. GAYLA KIRMER, Dir.

Media and Communications—
Diocesan Newspaper—semi-monthly, "Southwest Kansas Catholic" MR. DAVID MYERS, Editor, Tel: 620-227-1519; Fax: 620-227-1545; Email: skregister@dcdiocese.org.
Interactive Television Network—MRS. COLEEN STEIN, Coord., Tel: 620-227-1538; Fax: 620-227-1545; Email: cstein@dcdiocese.org.
Media/Press Liaison—MR. TIMOTHY F. WENZL, Tel: 620-227-1556; Fax: 620-227-1545; Email: twenzl@dcdiocese.org.

Scouting—
Catholic Committee on Scouting—MR. DAVE GEIST, Tel: 620-225-8230; Tel: 620-225-0161; Email: dave.geist@swkaging.org.

Legal Services—
Diocesan Attorney—TAMARA L. DAVIS, P.A., 107 Layton, Ste. A, Dodge City, 67801. Tel: 620-225-1674; Fax: 620-227-2770.

Consultative Bodies—
Presbyteral Council—Most Rev. JOHN B. BRUNGARDT; Revs. ROBERT A. SCHREMMER, V.G.; TED A. SKALSKY, V.F.; MARK BRANTLEY; ANSELM EKE, M.S.P.; ANEESH PARAPPANATTU, M.S.F.S.; JAMES P. DIEKER, V.F.; CHARLES J. MAZOUCH, V.F., (Retired).
College of Consultors—Revs. BERNARD H. FELIX; TED A. SKALSKY, V.F.; ROBERT A. SCHREMMER, V.G.; TED D. STOECKLEIN, V.F.; RENE LABRADOR; WARREN L. STECKLEIN, V.F.; WESLEY W. SCHAWE; PETER TRONG TRAN, J.C.L.
Diocesan Finance Council—Most Rev. JOHN B. BRUNGARDT, Ex Officio; MR. DANIEL M. STREMEL, CPA, CDFM, Ex Officio & Sec.; MRS. GEORGINA PAZ, Ex Officio; Rev. ROBERT A. SCHREMMER, V.G.; MR. JOHN SMITHHISLER; MR. BILL BAALMANN; Rev. DONALD E. BEDORE; MR. LEONARD MOEDER; MRS. LINDA MOEDER.
Diocesan Review Board—MR. DAVID H. SNAPP, Chair; MRS. DEBBIE SCHARTZ-ROBINSON; Rev. JOHN R. STRASSER; MR. MIKE MARTINEZ; MR. JAMES KARLAN; MR. CHARLES BEFORT; MR. REGIS LOPATA.
Deans—Revs. TED D. STOECKLEIN, V.F., Great Bend; TED A. SKALSKY, V.F., Dodge City; JAMES P. DIEKER, V.F., Garden City.

Priest Continuing Formation Commission—Revs. REGINALD A. URBAN, (Retired); WESLEY W. SCHAWE; JOHN FORKUOH, (Ghana); TERRANCE W. KLEIN; ROBERT A. SCHREMMER, V.G.

CLERGY, PARISHES, MISSIONS AND PAROCHIAL SCHOOLS

CITY OF DODGE CITY

(FORD COUNTY)

1—CATHEDRAL OF OUR LADY OF GUADALUPE (2001) [JC]
Mailing Address: P.O. Box 670, 67801.
Tel: 620-225-4802; Tel: 620-227-3442;
Fax: 620-338-8268; Email: info@dodgecitycathedral.com; Web: www.dodgecitycathedral.com. 3231 N. 14th St., 67801. Revs. Wesley W. Schawe; Aneesh Parappanattu, M.S.F.S., Parochial Vicar; Sisters Gregoria Bueno, Hispanic Pastoral Min.; Yolanda Maria Figueroa, Hispanic Pastoral Min.; Jodi D. Lix, Dir. Finance & Admin.; Sr. Julieta Mondragon, Hispanic Pastoral Min.
Legal Name: Cathedral of Our Lady of Guadalupe Catholic Church of Dodge City, Kansas
School—Sacred Heart Cathedral School, (Grades 1-8), Tel: 620-227-6532; Fax: 620-227-3221; Email: lynee.habiger@dcshcs.com. Lynee Habiger, Prin. Lay Teachers 20; Students 167.
Catechesis Religious Program—Email: nalvarez@dodgecitycathedral.com. Norma Alvarez, D.R.E.; Anne Shaughnessy, Family Formation; David McHugh, Youth Ministry. Students 567.

2—CHURCH OF THE SACRED HEART, Closed. For inquiries for sacramental records, please contact The Cathedral of Our Lady of Guadalupe, Dodge City.

OUTSIDE THE CITY OF DODGE CITY

ASHLAND, CLARK CO., ST. JOSEPH CATHOLIC CHURCH OF ASHLAND, KANSAS (1886) [JC]
P.O. Box 577, Ashland, 67831-0577.
Tel: 620-635-2338; Email: stjosephashland@yahoo.com. 512 Cedar St., Ashland, 67831-0577. Rev. Prakash Kola.
Res.: 514 Main St., P.O. Box 577, Ashland, 67831-0577.
Catechesis Religious Program—Tel: 620-200-7258. Trisha Elliott, D.R.E. Students 27.

BEAVER, BARTON CO., ST. JOSEPH, Closed. Sacramental records can be found at St. John, Hoisington.

BELPRE, EDWARDS CO., ST. BERNARD CATHOLIC CHURCH OF BELPRE, KANSAS (1901)
203 Hudson St., Belpre, 67519. Tel: 620-285-2035; Email: office@sacredheartlarned.org. 1111 State St., Larned, 67550. Rev. Bernard H. Felix.
Catechesis Religious Program—Tel: 620-348-4725; Email: eleenduncan@embarqmail.com. Eileen Duncan, D.R.E. Students 20.

BUCKLIN, FORD CO., ST. GEORGE, Closed. Sacramental records can be found at Our Lady of Guadalupe, Dodge City.

BURDETT, PAWNEE CO., HOLY ROSARY, Closed. Sacramental records can be found at Sacred Heart, Larned.

CLAFLIN, BARTON CO., IMMACULATE CONCEPTION CATHOLIC CHURCH OF CLAFLIN, KANSAS (1904) [JC]
310 Main St., Claflin, 67525. Tel: 620-587-3628;
Tel: 620-587-2339 (Parish Center);
Fax: 620-588-3628; Email: sschachle@hotmail.com; Web: www.IccClaflin.com. Mailing Address: P.O. Box 197, Claflin, 67525. Rev. Terrance W. Klein; Mr. Steven Schachle, Admin.
Legal Name: Immaculate Conception Catholic Church of Claflin, Kansas
Catechesis Religious Program—Email: lfeist@usd355.org. Laurie Feist, D.R.E. Students 67.

COLDWATER, COMANCHE CO., HOLY SPIRIT, Quasi-parish. Sacramental records can be found at St. Joseph, Ashland.
200 N. Philadelphia, Coldwater, 67029.
Tel: 620-582-2154; Fax: 620-582-2153; Email: kolaprakash01@gmail.com. P.O. Box 332, Coldwater, 67029. Rev. Prakash Kola.
Catechesis Religious Program—Kim Alexander, D.R.E. Students 10.

DEERFIELD, KEARNEY CO., CHRIST THE KING CATHOLIC CHURCH OF DEERFIELD, KANSAS (1937)
Mailing Address: 812 Main St., P.O. Box 455, Deerfield, 67838. Tel: 620-355-6405; Email: rk_1315@yahoo.com. Rev. Peter Trong Tran, J.C.L.
Legal Name: Christ the King Catholic Church of Deerfield, Kansas.

DIGHTON, LANE CO., ST. THERESA CATHOLIC CHURCH OF DIGHTON, KANSAS (1927) [JC]
322 S. First St., Dighton, 67839. Tel: 620-397-5357; Email: gcvonl02@gmail.com. P.O. Box 787, Dighton, 67839-0787. Rev. George Fajardo.
Catechesis Religious Program—Rene Roberts, D.R.E. Students 45.

DUBUQUE, BARTON CO., ST. CATHERINE, Closed. Sacramental records can be found at St. John the Evangelist, Hoisington.

ELKHART, MORTON CO., ST. JOAN OF ARC CATHOLIC CHURCH OF ELKHART, KANSAS (1921) [JC] Rev. Francis Khoi Nguyen.
Res.: 723 S. Baca Ave., P.O. Box 570, Elkhart, 67950-0570. Tel: 620-697-4622; Email: fknguyen58@gmail.com.
Catechesis Religious Program—Tel: 620-697-4587. Traci O'Hanlon, D.R.E. Students 58.

ELLINWOOD, BARTON CO., ST. JOSEPH CATHOLIC CHURCH OF ELLINWOOD, KANSAS (1876) [JC] Rev. Terrance W. Klein.
Res.: 214 N. Main St., Ellinwood, 67526.
Tel: 620-564-2534; Web: www.stjosephellinwood.com.
School—St. Joseph Catholic School, (Grades 1-8), Tel: 620-564-2721; Fax: 620-564-2714; Email: mclayton@stjosephellinwood.com. Marlene Clayton, Prin. Lay Teachers 6; Students 71.
Catechesis Religious Program—Sean O'Neill, Youth Min. Students 20.

FOWLER, MEADE CO., ST. ANTHONY CATHOLIC CHURCH OF FOWLER, KANSAS (1910) [JC]
Mailing Address: 411 Fourth St., P.O. Box 80, Fowler, 67844. Tel: 690-646-5297; Email: pastorccmc@gmail.com; Web: meadecocatholic.com. Rev. Ted A. Skalsky, V.F.; Judy Dewell, Pastoral Assoc.; Steve Dewell, Pastoral Assoc.
Res.: 412 W. Carthage St., Box 1207, Meade, 67864. Tel: 620-873-2003.
Catechesis Religious Program—28121 N. Rd., Fowler, 67844. Tel: 620-430-1627; Email: sweber655@gmail.com. Sarah Weber, D.R.E., 28121 N Rd., Fowler, 67844. Students 26.

GARDEN CITY, FINNEY CO.
1—ST. DOMINIC CATHOLIC CHURCH OF GARDEN CITY, KANSAS (1965) Rev. Warren L. Stecklein, V.F.; Lola Wilson, Dir. Adult Formation & Stewardship.
Office: 615 J. C. St., Garden City, 67846.
Tel: 620-276-2024; Fax: 620-276-2086; Email: stdomoffice@st-dominic.org.
School—St. Dominic Catholic School, (Grades 1-6), Tel: 620-276-8981; Fax: 620-276-2086; Email: ldrevnick@st-dominic.org; Web: www.st-dominic.org/school/. LeaAnn Drevnick, Sec.; Mrs. Trina Delgado, Prin. Lay Teachers 12; Students 166.
Catechesis Religious Program—Tel: 620-276-3500; Email: rformation@st-dominic.org. Sr. Myra Arney, O.P., D.R.E.; Kristie Ritter, Youth Min. Students 188.

2—ST. MARY CATHOLIC CHURCH OF GARDEN CITY, KANSAS (1898) [CEM 2] [JC2] Revs. Charles F. Seiwert, J.C.L.; Juan Manuel Salas Alanis, Parochial Vicar.
Res.: 509 St. John St., Garden City, 67846.
Tel: 620-275-4204; Fax: 620-272-9971; Email: jmoreno@stmarygc.com.
School—St. Mary Catholic School, (Grades 1-6), Tel: 620-276-2241; Fax: 620-276-7067; Email: Mmead@gckschools.com. Mrs. Michelle Mead, Prin. Lay Teachers 11; Students 105.
Catechesis Religious Program—Tel: 620-276-2716. Hector Rivera, D.R.E. Students 430.

GREAT BEND, BARTON CO.
1—ST. PATRICK (1960) [JC] Merged with St. Rose to form Prince of Peace, Great Bend.

2—PRINCE OF PEACE CATHOLIC CHURCH OF GREAT BEND, KANSAS (2006)
4100 Broadway, Great Bend, 67530-0087.
Tel: 620-792-1396; Fax: 620-792-3642; Email: secretary@gbpeace.kscoxmail.com; Web: www.greatbendcatholic.com. P.O. Box 87, Great Bend, 67530-0087. Revs. Donald E. Bedore; Ted D. Stoecklein, V.F., Parochial Vicar; Louis Trung Dinh Hoang, Parochial Vicar
Legal Name: Prince of Peace Catholic Church of Great Bend, Kansas
Res. & Mailing Address: 1423 Holland, P.O. Box 87, Great Bend, 67530-0087.
School—Holy Family School, (Grades PreK-6), 4200 Broadway, Great Bend, 67530. Tel: 620-793-3265; Fax: 620-792-2798; Email: office@gbholyfamily.org; Web: gbholyfamily.eduK12.net. Mrs. Karen Moeder, Prin. Lay Teachers 33; Students 249.
Catechesis Religious Program—Email: dregbpeace@kscoxmail.com. Jaclyn Brown, D.R.E. Students 97.

3—ST. ROSE OF LIMA (1878) [JC] Merged with St. Patrick, Great Bend to form Prince of Peace, Great Bend.

GREENSBURG, KIOWA CO., ST. JOSEPH CATHOLIC CHURCH OF GREENSBURG, KANSAS (1952)
820 Walnut, Greensburg, 67054. Tel: 620-552-3636; Email: ellenpeters0715@gmail.com. Rev. Robert A. Schremmer, V.G., Priest Supvr. & Sacramental Min.; Ellen Peters, Parish Life Coord.; Katie Vigness, Sec.
Catechesis Religious Program—Students 6.

HANSTON, HODGEMAN CO., ST. ANTHONY CATHOLIC CHURCH OF HANSTON, KANSAS (1908) [CEM]

102 S. Douglas, Hanston, 67849. Tel: 620-357-8791; Email: frjohn47@yahoo.com. P.O. Box 54, Hanston, 67849. Rev. John Forkuoh, (Ghana).
Catechesis Religious Program—Jaimi Burke, D.R.E. Students 26.

HOISINGTON, BARTON CO., ST. JOHN THE EVANGELIST CATHOLIC CHURCH OF HOISINGTON, KANSAS (1892) [CEM] Rev. Anselm Eke, M.S.P.; Judy Spangler, RCIA Coord.
Legal Name: St. John the Evangelist Catholic Church of Hoisington, Kansas
Office: 122 E. 5th St., Hoisington, 67544.
Tel: 620-653-2963; Email: stjohnevangel@dc.kscoxmail.com.
Rectory—108 E. 5th St., Hoisington, 67544.
Catechesis Religious Program—Email: stjohnreligioused@dc.kscoxmail.com. Rose Debes, D.R.E. Students 93.

HUGOTON, STEVENS CO., ST. HELEN CATHOLIC CHURCH OF HUGOTON, KANSAS (1948) Rev. Francis Khoi Nguyen.
Parish Office—1011 S. Jefferson St., Hugoton, 67951-2823. Tel: 620-544-2551; Email: fknguyen58@gmail.com.
Catechesis Religious Program—Tel: 316-544-7544. Carrie Baeza, D.R.E. Students 119.

INGALLS, GRAY CO., ST. STANISLAUS CATHOLIC CHURCH OF INGALLS, KANSAS (1909) [JC]
Mailing Address: P.O. Box 175, Ingalls, 67853.
Tel: 620-335-5202; Email: pastor@st-dominic.org; Web: Ststanislausingalls.com. 200 N. Rush, Ingalls, 67853. Rev. Warren L. Stecklein, V.F.
Catechesis Religious Program—Kathy Massoth, D.R.E.; Anne Shaughnessy, D.R.E. Students 67.

JETMORE, HODGEMAN CO., ST. LAWRENCE CATHOLIC CHURCH OF JETMORE, KANSAS (1923) [CEM]
Mailing Address: P.O. Box 278, Jetmore, 67854-0278. Tel: 620-357-8791; Email: frjohn47@yahoo.com. Rev. John Forkuoh, (Ghana); Sr. Catherine Therese Paulie, C.S.J., Pastoral Min.
Catechesis Religious Program—Jenny Goebel, D.R.E. Students 13.

JOHNSON, STANTON CO., ST. BERNADETTE CATHOLIC CHURCH OF JOHNSON, KANSAS (1949)
Mailing Address: c/o Mary, Queen of Peace Church, 804 N. Colorado, Ulysses, 67880. Rev. Peter Fernandez Jr.; Deacon Apolonio Rodriguez.
Catechesis Religious Program—105 N. Chestnut, Johnson, 67855. Tel: 620-492-1454. Mrs. Blanca Corrales, D.R.E. Students 80.

KINSLEY, EDWARDS CO., ST. NICHOLAS CATHOLIC CHURCH OF KINSLEY, KANSAS (1883)
706 E. Sixth St., Kinsley, 67547. Tel: 620-659-2692; Fax: 620-659-2049; Email: stkinsley@hotmail.com. P.O. Box 285, Kinsley, 67547. Rev. John R. Strasser.
Catechesis Religious Program—Beth Frame, D.R.E. Twinned with St. Joseph, Offerle. Students 27.

KIOWA, BARBER CO., ST. JOHN THE APOSTLE CATHOLIC CHURCH OF KIOWA, KANSAS (1885) [JC]
920 E. Main St., Kiowa, 67070. Tel: 620-825-4361; Email: ccbc@sctelcom.net. Rev. Mark Brantley
Legal Name: St. John the Apostle Catholic Church of Kiowa, Kansas
Church: 410 N. Main St., Sharon, 67138.
Res.: 300 Curry Ln., Medicine Lodge, 67104.
Catechesis Religious Program—Tel: 620-825-4361. Lindsey McMoran, D.R.E. Students 9.

LACROSSE, RUSH CO., ST. MICHAEL CATHOLIC CHURCH OF LACROSSE, KANSAS (1911) [JC]
P.O. Box 309, LaCrosse, 67548. Tel: 785-222-2561; Email: church@gbta.net; Web: rushcountycatholicchurches.com. 918 Lincoln St., LaCrosse, 67548-0309. Rev. Eric Gyamfi.
Catechesis Religious Program—Tel: 785-222-2869; Email: rbbaalmann@gbta.net. Ruth Baalmann, D.R.E. Students 51.

LAKIN, KEARNY CO., ST. ANTHONY OF PADUA CATHOLIC CHURCH OF LAKIN, KANSAS (1909) [JC]
600 Soderberg St., P.O. Box 983, Lakin, 67860.
Tel: 620-355-6405; Email: petertrong@hotmail.com. Rev. Peter Trong Tran, J.C.L.
Legal Name: St. Anthony of Padua Catholic Church of Lakin, Kansas
Catechesis Religious Program—Tel: 620-355-6405. Molly Shelden, D.R.E., Tel: 620-640-2742. Students 144.

LARNED, PAWNEE CO., SACRED HEART OF JESUS CATHOLIC CHURCH OF LARNED, KANSAS (1912) [CEM] [JC]
1119 State St., Larned, 67550. Rev. Bernard H. Felix
Legal Name: Sacred Heart of Jesus Catholic Church of Larned, Kansas
Res.: 1111 State St., Larned, 67550.
Tel: 620-285-2035; Fax: 620-285-3025; Email: office@sacredheartlarned.org; Web: sacredheartlarned.org.
Catechesis Religious Program—Email: stacysanger@hotmail.com. Stacy Sanger, D.R.E. Students 71.

LEOTI, WICHITA CO., ST. ANTHONY OF PADUA OF LEOTI, KANSAS (1887) [JC]
600 S. 4th St., P.O. Box D, Leoti, 67861.
Tel: 620-379-4431; Fax: 620-379-4428; Email: office@wbsnet.org. Rev. Timothy Hickey
Legal Name: St. Anthony of Padua Catholic Church of Leoti, Kansas
Res.: 208 N. 2nd St., Marienthal, 67863.
Catechesis Religious Program—Tel: 620-379-4427. Julie Conard, D.R.E. Students 53.

LIBERAL, SEWARD CO., ST. ANTHONY OF PADUA OF LIBERAL, KANSAS (1916)
1510 N. Calhoun, Liberal, 67901. Tel: 620-624-4135; Fax: 620-624-3553; Email: clarissa@sapliberal.org; Web: www.stanthonyliberalks.org. Revs. James P. Dieker, V.F.; Jacob Schneider, Parochial Vicar; Deacons Victor Mencos; Ruben Sigala; Oscar Rodriguez; Hector Rios; Sr. Rosa Maria Martinez Solis, Hispanic Pastoral Min.; Ms. Matilda Scheurer, Pastoral Min.; Clarissa Carrillo, Youth Min.; Daniel Diepenbrock, Business Mgr.; Araceli LaPoint, Sec.
Legal Name: St. Anthony of Padua Catholic Church of Liberal, Kansas
Rectory—1230 N. Pershing, Liberal, 67901.
Catechesis Religious Program—Email: frjacob@sapliberal.org. Students 503.

LIEBENTHAL, RUSH CO., ST. JOSEPH CATHOLIC CHURCH OF LIEBENTHAL, KANSAS (1876) [CEM] Rev. Eric Gyamfi, Admin.
Church: 202 Main St., Liebenthal, 67553.
Tel: 785-222-3292; Email: church@gbta.net.
Catechesis Religious Program—Ruth Baalmann, D.R.E. (attending St. Michael's Program at LaCrosse, KS).

LORETTO, RUSH CO., ST. MARY, HELP OF CHRISTIANS, Closed. Sacramental records can be found at St. Joseph, Liebenthal.

MARIENTHAL, WICHITA CO., ST. MARY CATHOLIC CHURCH OF MARIENTHAL, KANSAS (1886) [CEM]
Mailing Address: 208 N. Second St., Marienthal, 67863. Tel: 620-379-4427; Fax: 620-379-4428; Email: office@wbsnet.org. Rev. Timothy Hickey.
Catechesis Religious Program—Lisa Ridder, D.R.E. Students 28.

MCCRACKEN, RUSH CO., ST. MARY (1886) Closed. For inquiries for sacramental records please contact St. Michael, La Crosse.

MEADE, MEADE CO., ST. JOHN THE BAPTIST CATHOLIC CHURCH OF MEADE, KANSAS (1889) [JC] Rev. Ted A. Skalsky, V.F.
Legal Name: St. John the Baptist Catholic Church of Meade, Kansas
Res.: 412 W. Carthage St., P.O. Box 1207, Meade, 67864. Tel: 620-873-2003; Email: pastorccmc@gmail.com; Web: meadecocatholic.org.
Catechesis Religious Program—Heather Flavin, D.R.E. Students 33.

MEDICINE LODGE, BARBER CO., HOLY ROSARY CATHOLIC CHURCH OF MEDICINE LODGE, KANSAS (1952) [JC]
300 Curry Ln., Medicine Lodge, 67104. Email: holyrosaryml@gmail.com; Web: barbercountycatholic.org. Rev. Mark Brantley
Legal Name: Holy Rosary Catholic Church of Medicine Lodge, Kansas
Catechesis Religious Program—Cheri Dohrmann, D.R.E. Students 29.

NESS CITY, NESS CO., SACRED HEART CATHOLIC CHURCH OF NESS CITY, KANSAS (1912) [CEM] Rev. Pascal L. Klein.
Res.: 510 S. School St., Ness City, 67560.
Tel: 785-798-3195; Fax: 785-798-3004; Email: shschool@gbta.net.
School—Sacred Heart School, (Grades 1-8),
Tel: 785-798-3530; Fax: 785-798-3004; Email: shschool@gbta.net. Debbie Hagans, Prin.; Kathy Whitley, Librarian. Lay Teachers 4; Students 69.
Catechesis Religious Program—Adair Hemel, D.R.E. Students 6.

NORTH ELLINWOOD, BARTON CO., STS. PETER & PAUL, Closed. Sacramental records can be found at St. Joseph, Ellinwood.

NORTH KINSLEY, EDWARDS CO., SS. PETER AND PAUL, Closed. Sacramental records can be found at St. Nicholas, Kinsley.

ODIN, BARTON CO., HOLY FAMILY CATHOLIC CHURCH OF ODIN, KANSAS (1879) [CEM]
1387 N.E. 90th Ave., Odin, 67525. Tel: 620-587-3628; Fax: 620-588-3628; Email: sschachle@hotmail.com; Web: www.holyfamilyodin.com. Mailing Address: c/o Immaculate Conception Parish, P.O. Box 197, Claflin, 67525. Mr. Steven Schachle, Parish Admin.

OFFERLE, EDWARDS CO., ST. JOSEPH CATHOLIC CHURCH OF OFFERLE, KANSAS (1876) [CEM 2]
P.O. Box 285, Kinsley, 67547. Tel: 620-659-2692; Email: stkinsley@hotmail.com. 111 W. 1st, Offerle, 67563. Rev. John R. Strasser.
Catechesis Religious Program— Twinned with St. Nicholas, Kinsley. Beth Frame, D.R.E.

OLMITZ, BARTON CO., ST. ANN CATHOLIC CHURCH OF OLMITZ, KANSAS (1889) [CEM] Rev. Anselm Eke, M.S.P.
Res.: 115 Cleveland St., P.O. Box 8, Olmitz, 67564.
Tel: 620-653-2963; Email: linda.bahr@linde.com.
Catechesis Religious Program—Lisa Starr, D.R.E. Students 32.

PLAINS, MEADE CO., ST. PATRICK CATHOLIC CHURCH OF PLAINS, KANSAS (1916) [JC]
601 Superior St., Plains, 67869-0247.
Tel: 620-873-2003; Email: pastorccmc@gmail.com; Web: meadecocatholic.org. P.O. Box 247, Plains, 67869-0247. Rev. Ted A. Skalsky, V.F.
Res.: 412 W. Carthage St., Meade, 67864.
Tel: 620-338-6547; Email: tedsky59@gmail.com.
Catechesis Religious Program—Tel: 620-563-6199; Email: carellano@usd483.net. Carla Arellano, D.R.E.; Carmen Puentes, D.R.E. Students 107.

PRATT, PRATT CO., SACRED HEART CATHOLIC CHURCH OF PRATT, KANSAS (1887) [CEM] Rev. Michael A. Klag.
Parish Offices: 332 N. Oak St., Pratt, 67124.
Tel: 620-672-6352; Fax: 620-672-3748; Email: mikeatmount@yahoo.com.
Rectory—240 Edgeford Dr., Pratt, 67124.
Catechesis Religious Program—Erin Crouch, D.R.E. Students 89.

RANSOM, NESS CO., ST. ALOYSIUS CATHOLIC CHURCH OF RANSOM, KANSAS (1903) [CEM]
107 Vermont, Ransom, 67572-0096.
Tel: 785-731-2497; Email: shschool@gbta.net. P.O. Box 96, Ransom, 67572-0096. Rev. Pascal L. Klein.
Catechesis Religious Program—Troyette Lawson, D.R.E. Students 9.

ST. JOHN, STAFFORD CO., ST. JOHN THE APOSTLE CATHOLIC CHURCH OF ST. JOHN, KANSAS (1949) Rev. Michael A. Klag
Legal Name: St. John the Apostle Catholic Church of St. John, Kansas
Res., Church & Office: 609 E. Fourth St., Box 475, St. John, 67576. Tel: 620-549-3847; Email: mikeatmount@yahoo.com.
Catechesis Religious Program—Tel: 620-549-3847. Johnna Stanford, D.R.E. Students 44.

ST. MARY, HODGEMAN CO., ST. MARY, Closed. Sacramental records can be found at St. John the Baptist, Spearville.

SATANTA, HASKELL CO., ST. ALPHONSUS CATHOLIC CHURCH OF SATANTA, KANSAS (1946)
603 Tecumseh, Satanta, 67870. Tel: 620-649-2692; Email: catholic@pld.com; Web: www.stanthonyliberalks.com. Box 65, Satanta, 67870. Revs. James P. Dieker, V.F.; Jacob Schneider, Parochial Vicar; Sr. Marie Elena Martinez-Sifuentes, M.C.M.I., Pastoral Min.
Church: 601 Tecumseh, Satanta, 67870.
Catechesis Religious Program—Email: hildamacias32@hotmail.com. Hilda Macias, D.R.E. Students 69.

SCOTT CITY, SCOTT CO., ST. JOSEPH CATHOLIC CHURCH OF SCOTT CITY, KANSAS (1911) [JC]
Mailing Address: P.O. Box 228, Scott City, 67871-0228. Tel: 620-872-3644; Email: sjscsecretary@att.net. 1006 S. Main St., Scott City, 67871-0228. Rev. George Fajardo.
Res.: 606 W. 10th, P.O. Box 228, Scott City, 67871-0228.
Catechesis Religious Program—Email: kykaye@hotmail.com. Challie Metzger, D.R.E.; Kylie Stoecklein, D.R.E. Students 171.

SEWARD, STAFFORD CO., ST. FRANCIS XAVIER CATHOLIC CHURCH OF SEWARD, KANSAS (1886) Closed. For inquiries for sacramental records, contact Sacred Heart Parish, Pratt.
Legal Name: St. Francis Xavier Catholic Church of Seward, Kansas.

SHARON, BARBER CO., ST. BONIFACE CATHOLIC CHURCH OF SHARON, KANSAS (1904) [CEM]
410 N. Main St., Sharon, 67138. Tel: 620-294-5526; Email: ccbc@sctelcom.net; Web: barbercountycatholic.org. P.O. Box 118, Sharon, 67138-0118. Rev. Mark Brantley.
Res.: 300 Curry Ln., Medicine Lodge, 67104.
Catechesis Religious Program—Kathy Dohm, D.R.E. Students 36.

SPEARVILLE, FORD CO., ST. JOHN THE BAPTIST CATHOLIC CHURCH OF SPEARVILLE, KANSAS (1904) [CEM] [JC2] Rev. John Forkuoh, (Ghana)
Legal Name: St. John the Baptist Catholic Church of Spearville, Kansas
Res.: 100 S. Main St., P.O. Box 187, Spearville, 67876. Tel: 620-385-2212; Email: frjohn47@yahoo.com.
Catechesis Religious Program—Judy Gleason, D.R.E. Students 83.

SYRACUSE, HAMILTON CO., ST. RAPHAEL CATHOLIC CHURCH OF SYRACUSE, KANSAS (1906) [CEM] [JC]
Mailing Address: P.O. Box 731, Syracuse, 67878-0731. Tel: 620-384-7357; Fax: 620-355-6406; Email: church@straphaelsyracuse.org. 506 E. Ave. F, Syracuse, 67878-0731. Rev. Peter Trong Tran, J.C.L.
Catechesis Religious Program—Email: locution95@yahoo.com. Logie Asebedo, D.R.E. Students 89.

TIMKEN, RUSH CO., HOLY TRINITY CATHOLIC CHURCH OF TIMKEN, KANSAS (1904) [CEM] [JC]
103 S. Main, LaCrosse, 67548. Tel: 785-222-2561; Email: church@gbta.net. Rev. Eric Gyamfi.
Catechesis Religious Program—Tel: 785-356-2238;

Email: 5flaxs@gbta.net. Lydia Flax, D.R.E. Students 12.

TRIBUNE, GREELEY CO., ST. JOSEPH THE WORKER CATHOLIC CHURCH OF TRIBUNE, KANSAS (1950) [JC] Mailing Address: 801 N. Broadway, Box 67, Tribune, 67879. Tel: 620-379-4431; Email: St. Josephtribune@hotmail.com. Rev. Timothy Hickey
Legal Name: St. Joseph the Worker Catholic Church of Tribune, Kansas
Catechesis Religious Program—Trista Shafer, D.R.E. Students 56.

ULYSSES, GRANT CO., MARY, QUEEN OF PEACE CATHOLIC CHURCH OF ULYSSES, KANSAS (1948) Rev. Peter Fernandez Jr.; Deacon Apolonio Rodriguez
Legal Name: Mary, Queen of Peace Catholic Church of Ulysses, Kansas
Res.: 804 N. Colorado, Ulysses, 67880.
Tel: 620-356-1532; Fax: 620-424-1065; Email: mqop@pld.com.
Catechesis Religious Program—Email: mqopdre@pld.com. Toney Hernandez, D.R.E. Students 207.

WINDTHORST, FORD CO., IMMACULATE HEART OF MARY, Closed. Sacramental records can be found at St. John the Baptist, Spearville.

WRIGHT, FORD CO., ST. ANDREW CATHOLIC CHURCH OF WRIGHT, KANSAS (1909) [CEM]
10893 St. Andrew Rd., Wright, 67882.
Tel: 620-227-3363; Email: rschremmer@dcdiocese.org; Web: saintandrewwright.org. P.O. Box 125, Wright, 67882. Rev. Robert A. Schremmer, V.G.
Parish Center—11792 Jewel Rd., Wright, 67882.
Catechesis Religious Program—Email: regina.lix@gmail.com. Regina Lix, D.R.E. Students 14.

Retired:
Revs.—
Baker, James E., J.C.L., (Retired), 1707 Belmont Pl., Garden City, 67846
Fiedler, Donald J., (Retired)
Helms, Michael L., (Retired), 950 N. Jenny Barker Rd., Lot #43, Garden City, 67846
LeBlanc, Gregory, (Retired)
Maes, John J., (Retired), P.O. Box 165, Spearville, 67876
Martin, Benjamin, (Retired), 212 E. Grant Ave., Marienthal, 67863
Mazouch, Charles J., V.F., (Retired), 5216 Ridgeway Dr., Great Bend, 67530
Moore, Brian R., Ph.D., (Retired), 200 Campus Dr., Apt 2-D, 67801
Murphy, Ultan P., (Retired), 3820 Broadway Ave., Riverbend Rm. 23, Great Bend, 67530-3649
Pottorff, Lisle J., (Retired), 6900 E. 45th St. N., Apt. D2, Bel Aire, 67226
Suellentrop, Anthony J., (Retired), 22052 W. 66th St., #173, Shawnee Mission, 66226
Tighe, Dermot F., (Retired), 6700 E. 45th St. N., Apt. 117, Bel Aire, 67226
Urban, Reginald A., (Retired), 1327 Harvest Rd., Apt. B, Hays, 67601.

Permanent Deacons:
Hermocillo, Martin, Diaconate Convenor
Lampe, Dwaine, (Retired)
Mencos, Victor A., St. Anthony, Liberal
Rael, Gilbert E., Larned State Hospital/Larned Mental Health Correctional Facility, Larned
Rios, Hector, St. Anthony, Liberal
Rodriguez, Apolonio, Mary Queen of Peace, Ulysses
Rodriguez, Erasmo, (Retired)
Rodriguez, Oscar, St. Anthony, Liberal
Rondeau, Richard, (Retired)
Sigala, Ruben, St. Anthony, Liberal.

INSTITUTIONS LOCATED IN DIOCESE

[A] GENERAL HOSPITALS

GARDEN CITY. *St. Catherine Hospital*, 401 E. Spruce, Garden City, 67846-5679. Tel: 620-272-2222; Fax: 620-272-2566; Email: jostarkey@centura.org; Email: krisordelheide@centura.org; Web: www.stcatherinehosp.com. Scott Taylor, Pres. & CEO; Joben Rieth, R.N., M.B.A., Vice Pres., Clinical Svcs. & Opers.; Amanda Vaughan, CFO; Kris Ordelheide, Contact Person. Affiliated with Catholic Health Initiatives. Bed Capacity 100; Tot Asst. Annually 262,340; Total Staff 672.

[B] RETREAT CENTERS

DODGE CITY. *Grace That Reigns Society USA* (2014) 2002 Fairway Dr., 67801. Tel: 620-338-3334. Most Rev. Ronald M. Gilmore, Tel: 620-338-3334. Offering retreats for clergy, laity or parishes; days of recollection; conferences.

GREAT BEND. *Heartland Center for Spirituality* (1985) 3600 Broadway, Great Bend, 67530-3692.
Tel: 620-792-1232; Fax: 620-792-1746; Email: office@heartlandspirituality.org; Web: www.heartlandspirituality.org. Sr. Renee Dreiling, O.P., Dir. Retreat Center. Total Staff 8.

PAWNEE ROCK. *Heartland Farm* (1988) 1049 County Rd. 390, Pawnee Rock, 67567-7002.
Tel: 620-923-4585; Fax: 620-923-4313; Email: hfarm@gbta.net. Sr. Jane Belanger, Contact Person. A Ministry of the Dominican Sisters of Peace. Organic sustainable agriculture, body massage, retreat opportunities in rural setting; monthly programs. Total Membership 3.

[C] EDUCATIONAL ENDOWMENT FUNDS

DODGE CITY. *Sacred Heart Cathedral School Endowment Fund*, 3231 N. 14th St., 67801.
Tel: 620-225-4802; Fax: 620-338-8268; Email: info@dodgecitycathedral.com. P.O. Box 670, 67801. Rev. Wesley W. Schawe.

ELLINWOOD. *St. Joseph School Education Endowment Fund*, 109 W. 3rd, Ellinwood, 67526.
Tel: 620-564-2534; Fax: 620-564-2613; Email: church@stjosephellinwood. Rev. Terrance W. Klein, 109 W. 3rd, Ellinwood, 67526. Tel: 620-564-2290.

GARDEN CITY. *St. Dominic Grade School Endowment Fund*, 615 J.C. St., Garden City, 67846.
Tel: 620-276-2024; Fax: 620-276-2086; Email: stdomoffice@st-dominic.org. Chris Heiman, Chm.
St. Mary Catholic Education Endowment Fund, 509 St. John St., Garden City, 67846.
Tel: 620-275-4204; Fax: 620-272-9971; Email: cseiwert@stmarygc.com. Rev. Charles Seiwert.

GREAT BEND. *The Holy Family Grade School Education Endowment Fund*, 4200 Broadway, Great Bend, 67530. Tel: 620-792-1396; Fax: 620-792-3642; Email: bookkeeper@gbpeace.kscoxmail.com. Rev. Donald E. Bedore.

LARNED. *Sacred Heart Endowment Fund, Inc.*, 1111 State St., Larned, 67550. Tel: 620-285-2035; Fax: 620-285-3025; Email: office@sacredheartlarned.org. Rev. Bernard H. Felix.

LIBERAL. *St. Anthony School Endowment Fund*, 1510 N. Calhoun St., Liberal, 67901. Tel: 620-624-4135; Fax: 620-624-3553; Email: matilda@sapliberal.org. Rev. James P. Dieker, V.F.

NESS CITY. *The Sacred Heart School Endowment Fund*, 510 S. School St., Ness City, 67560.
Tel: 785-798-3530; Fax: 785-798-3004; Email: shschool@gbta.net. Christy Seib, Sec.

PRATT. *The Sacred Heart Endowment, Inc.*, 332 N. Oak St., Pratt, 67124. Tel: 620-672-6352; Fax: 620-672-3748; Email: mikeatmount@yahoo.com. Rev. Michael A. Klag.

[D] CONVENTS AND RESIDENCES FOR SISTERS

GREAT BEND. *Dominican Sisters of Peace*, 3600 Broadway Ave., Great Bend, 67530-3692.
Tel: 620-792-1232; Fax: 620-792-1746; Email: ehertel@oppeace.org; Web: www.oppeace.org. Sr. Eloise Hertel, O.P., Mission Group Coord. Dominican Sisters of Peace.
Dominican Sisters of Peace, Inc. Perpetually Professed Sisters in Diocese 52; Lay Associates in Diocese 53.

ST. JOHN. *Congregation of the Sisters of the Third Order of St. Francis of Perpetual Adoration (LaCrosse, WI)*, 609 E. 4th St., P.O. Box 475, St. John, 67576. Tel: 620-377-5006. Sisters 2.

[E] SERVICES FOR THE ELDERLY

GREAT BEND. *Cedar Park Place, Inc.*, 3910 Cedar Park Pl., Great Bend, 67530-3692. Tel: 620-793-8115; Fax: 620-793-6702; Email: jmurray@mercyhousing.org. Jana Murray, Admin. Low and Middle Income Housing for Elderly and Disabled. Bed Capacity 66; Tot Asst. Annually 63; Total Staff 2.

[F] MISCELLANEOUS

DODGE CITY. *Catholic Social Service Endowment Fund* (1989) 906 Central Ave., 67801. Tel: 620-227-1562; Fax: 620-227-1572; Email: mlegleiter@catholiccharitiesswks.org. Deborah Snapp, Dir.
Dechant Foundation, 107 Layton St., Ste. A, P.O. Box 741, 67801. Tel: 620-225-1674; Email: tdavis@tldavispa.com. Most Rev. John B. Brungardt, Ordinary.
Deposit and Loan Fund of the Catholic Diocese of Dodge City, 107 Layton, Ste. A, P.O. Box 863, 67801. Tel: 620-225-1674; Email: tdavis@tldavispa.com. Most Rev. John B. Brungardt, Ordinary.
The Diocese of Dodge City Priest Retirement Fund, Inc., 2210 1st Ave., 67801. Tel: 620-227-6792; Email: rdechant@sbcglobal.net. Raymond Dechant, Contact Person.
Manna House, 1012 First Ave., 67801.
Tel: 620-227-6707; Email: stevetabor1952@yahoo.com. Steve Tabor, Dir.; John Askew, Pres.; Zach Schneweis, Treas.; Marsha Morrison, 925 Club View, 67801. Tel: 620-227-6767; Maria Musick; Nancy Freeland; Jose Vargas; Kathy Redman; Gerald May, Bd. Member. Short-term housing and food distribution need. Part-Time Staff 3; Full-Time Staff 1; Total Assisted 4,742.
Newman University, Western Kansas Center, 236 San Jose, Ste. 39, 67801. Tel: 620-227-9616; Fax: 620-227-9688; Email: birdj@newmanu.edu; Web: www.newmanu.edu. Jessica Bird, Dir., Western Kansas Center.

GARDEN CITY. *St. Catherine Hospital Development Foundation*, 401 E. Spruce, Garden City, 67846.
Tel: 620-272-2376; Fax: 620-272-2180; Email: paigekraus@centura.org; Email: krisordelheide@centura.org; Web: www.schdf.org. Mrs. Paige Kraus, Exec.; Kris Ordelheide, Contact Person.

HUTCHINSON. *St. Rose - Dominican Nurses Alumnae Association*, 609 W. 24th Ave., Hutchinson, 67502.
Tel: 620-793-3679; Email: mkchacon@cox.net. Kathleen Chacon, R.N., Treas. & Contact Person.

RELIGIOUS INSTITUTES OF MEN REPRESENTED IN THE DIOCESE

For further details refer to the corresponding bracketed number in the Religious Institutes of Men or Women section.

[]—*Missionaries of St. Francis de Sales*—M.S.F.S.
[]—*Missionaries of St. Paul*—M.S.P.

RELIGIOUS INSTITUTES OF WOMEN REPRESENTED IN THE DIOCESE

[3832]—*Congregation of St. Joseph*—C.S.J.
[1780]—*Congregation of the Sisters of the Third Order of St. Francis of Perpetual Adoration* (La Crosse, WI)—F.S.P.A.
[1115]—*Dominican Sisters of Peace*—O.P.
[]—*Mexican Passionist Sisters*—C.F.P.
[]—*Missionaries of the Charity of Mary Immaculate*—M.C.M.I.
[2690]—*Missionary Catechists of Divine Providence*—M.C.D.P.

An asterisk (*) denotes an organization that has established tax-exempt status directly with the IRS and is not covered by the USCCB Group Ruling.

Archdiocese of Dubuque

(Archidioecesis Dubuquensis)

Most Reverend

MICHAEL OWEN JACKELS

Archbishop of Dubuque; ordained May 30, 1981; appointed Bishop of Wichita January 28, 2005; ordained April 4, 2005; appointed Archbishop of Dubuque April 8, 2013; installed May 30, 2013.

Most Reverend

JEROME HANUS, O.S.B., D.D.

Archbishop Emeritus of Dubuque; ordained July 30, 1966; appointed Bishop of St. Cloud July 6, 1987; ordained and installed August 24, 1987; appointed Coadjutor Archbishop of Dubuque August 23, 1994; welcomed October 27, 1994; succeeded to the See October 16, 1995; retired April 8, 2013.

Chancery-Archdiocesan Center: P.O. Box 479, Dubuque, IA 52004-0479. Tel: 563-556-2580; Fax: 563-556-5464.

Web: www.dbqarch.org

Email: dbqcco@dbqarch.org

Square Miles 17,403.

Established July 28, 1837; Created an Archdiocese June 15, 1893.

Patrons of the Archdiocese: Primary: St. Raphael, the Archangel; Secondary: St. John Mary Vianney, Cure of Ars.

Corporate Title: The Archdiocese of Dubuque.

Comprises 30 Counties, that part of the State of Iowa north of the Counties of Polk, Jasper, Poweshiek, Iowa, Johnson, Cedar and Clinton and east of the Counties of Kossuth, Humboldt, Webster and Boone.

For legal titles of parishes and archdiocesan institutions, consult the Chancery.

STATISTICAL OVERVIEW

Personnel	
Archbishops	1
Retired Archbishops	1
Abbots	1
Retired Abbots	2
Priests: Diocesan Active in Diocese	78
Priests: Diocesan Active Outside Diocese	1
Priests: Retired, Sick or Absent	75
Number of Diocesan Priests	154
Religious Priests in Diocese	32
Total Priests in Diocese	186
Extern Priests in Diocese	15
Ordinations:	
Diocesan Priests	2
Transitional Deacons	5
Permanent Deacons in Diocese	118
Total Brothers	20
Total Sisters	527
Parishes	
Parishes	166
With Resident Pastor:	
Resident Diocesan Priests	67
Without Resident Pastor:	
Administered by Priests	94
Administered by Lay People	5
Pastoral Centers	1

Professional Ministry Personnel:	
Sisters	8
Lay Ministers	540
Welfare	
Catholic Hospitals	7
Total Assisted	1,107,590
Health Care Centers	2
Total Assisted	214
Homes for the Aged	4
Total Assisted	730
Special Centers for Social Services	4
Total Assisted	36,155
Other Institutions	1
Total Assisted	16
Educational	
Seminaries, Diocesan	1
Students from This Diocese	9
Diocesan Students in Other Seminaries	15
Seminaries, Religious	1
Students Religious	105
Total Seminarians	129
Colleges and Universities	3
Total Students	4,367
High Schools, Diocesan and Parish	7
Total Students	2,049

Elementary Schools, Diocesan and Parish	42
Total Students	9,184
Catechesis/Religious Education:	
High School Students	3,710
Elementary Students	9,184
Total Students under Catholic Instruction	28,623
Teachers in the Diocese:	
Priests	1
Sisters	3
Lay Teachers	885
Vital Statistics	
Receptions into the Church:	
Infant Baptism Totals	1,788
Minor Baptism Totals	490
Adult Baptism Totals	75
Received into Full Communion	203
First Communions	2,358
Confirmations	2,092
Marriages:	
Catholic	497
Interfaith	288
Total Marriages	785
Deaths	2,103
Total Catholic Population	192,374
Total Population	1,010,471

Former Bishops—Most Revs. MATHIAS LORAS, D.D., cons. Dec. 10, 1837; died Feb. 19, 1858; CLEMENT SMYTH, O.C.S.O., D.D., named Coadjutor Bishop of Dubuque Jan. 9, 1857; cons. May 3, 1857; Succeeded Feb. 19, 1858; died Sept. 22, 1865; JOHN HENNESSY, D.D., First Archbishop; named Bishop of Dubuque April 24, 1866; cons. Sept. 30, 1866; raised to the Archiepiscopal Dignity, June 15, 1893; died March 4, 1900; JOHN J. KEANE, D.D., cons. Bishop of Richmond, Aug. 25, 1878; transferred to the Titular See of Jasso, Aug. 12, 1888; elevated to the Archiepiscopal Dignity with the title of Archbishop of Damascus, Jan. 29, 1897; transferred to the See of Dubuque, July 24, 1900; resigned April 3, 1911; appt. Titular Archbishop of Cios, April 28, 1911; died June 22, 1918; JAMES JOHN KEANE, D.D., ord. Dec. 23, 1882; cons. Bishop of Cheyenne, Oct. 28, 1902; elevated to the Archiepiscopal Dignity and transferred to Dubuque, Aug. 11, 1911; died Aug. 2, 1929; FRANCIS J. L. BECKMAN, S.T.D., Titular Archbishop of Phulli; ord. June 20, 1902; appt. Bishop of Lincoln, Dec. 23, 1923; cons. Bishop of Lincoln, May 1, 1924; Apostolic Administrator of Omaha, June 1, 1926 to July 4, 1928; elevated to Archiepiscopal Dignity and transferred to Dubuque, Jan. 17, 1930; appt. Assistant at the Pontifical Throne, April 21, 1928; resigned Nov. 11, 1946; died Oct. 17, 1948; HENRY P. ROHLMAN, D.D., appt. Bishop of Davenport, May 20, 1927; cons. July 25, 1927; appt. Coadjutor Archbishop of Dubuque "cum jure successionis" and Apostolic Administrator, June 15, 1944; installed Sept. 12, 1944; succeeded Nov. 11, 1946; named Assistant at Pontifical Throne, Sept. 2, 1950; resigned and named Titular Archbishop of Cotrada, Dec. 2, 1954; died Sept. 13, 1957; LEO BINZ, D.D., ord. March 15, 1924; appt. Titular Bishop of Pinara, Coadjutor Bishop and Apostolic Administrator of Winona, Nov. 21, 1942; cons. Dec. 21, 1942; named Titular Archbishop of Silyum and Coadjutor to the Archbishop of Dubuque "cum jure successionis," Oct. 15, 1949; named Assistant at the Pontifical Throne, June 11, 1954; Archbishop of Dubuque, Dec. 2, 1954; Pallium conferred, June 12, 1958; appt. Archbishop of St. Paul, Dec. 16, 1961; retired July, 1975; died Oct. 9, 1979; JAMES J. BYRNE, S.T.D., appt. Titular Bishop of Etenna and Auxiliary Bishop of St. Paul, May 10, 1947; ord. Bishop, July 2, 1947; transferred to Boise, ID, June 16, 1956; appt. Archbishop of Dubuque, March 19, 1962; retired Aug. 23, 1983; named Apostolic Administrator; died Aug. 2, 1996; DANIEL W. KUCERA, O.S.B., Ph.D., D.D., ord. May 26, 1949; appt. Titular Bishop of Natchez and Auxiliary Bishop of Joliet, June 6, 1977; ord. Bishop, July 21, 1977; appt. Bishop of Salina, KS, March 11, 1980; installed May 7, 1980; named Archbishop of Dubuque, Dec. 20, 1983; installed Feb. 23, 1984; retired Oct. 16, 1995; died May 30, 2017.; JEROME HANUS, O.S.B., (Retired), ord. July 30, 1966; appt. Bishop of St. Cloud July 6, 1987; ord. and installed Aug. 24, 1987; appt. Coadjutor Archbishop of Dubuque Aug. 23, 1994; welcomed Oct. 27, 1994; succeeded to the See Oct. 16, 1995; retired April 8, 2013.

Unless otherwise indicated, all Archdiocesan office addresses and telephone numbers are: Archdiocesan Pastoral Center, 1229 Mt. Loretta Ave., Dubuque, 52003-7826. Tel: 563-556-2580; Fax: 563-556-5464. *Mailing Address: P.O. Box 479, Dubuque, 52004-0479*. Office Hours: Mon.-Thurs. 8-4:30; Fri. 8-2 (Central Time).

(For letters of good standing please contact the Vicar General's Office). (Please send all dispensation requests to the Tribunal).

Archbishop—Most Rev. MICHAEL OWEN JACKELS. Executive Secretary: SARAH OTTING, M.A.P.S.

Vicar General—Rev. Msgr. THOMAS E. TOALE, Ph.D. Secretary: SARAH OTTING, M.A.P.S.

Chancellor—Sr. Maureen McPartland, O.P., J.C.L. Secretary: Sarah Otting, M.A.P.S.

Judicial Vicar—Rev. Scott E. Bullock, J.C.L.

Moderator of the Curia—Rev. Msgr. Thomas E. Toale, Ph.D.

Director of the Pastoral Center—Lynn Osterhaus.

Finance Officer—Richard L. Runde, CPA.

College of Consultors—Rev. Msgr. Thomas E. Toale, Ph.D.; Revs. Philip E. Thompson; Greg E. Bahl; James Bergin, S.V.D.; Raymond A. Burkle; Noah J. Diehm; Jeffrey A. Dole; Rev. Msgr. Daniel J. Knepper, (Retired); Rev. Neil J. Manternach; Rev. Msgrs. James L. Miller; Carl L. Schmitt, (Retired).

Deans—Very Rev. Mark A. Ressler, Cedar Rapids; Rev. John A. Moser, Decorah; Very Revs. Dwayne J. Thoman, Dubuque; Dennis J. Quint, Dyersville; Michael J. Mescher, Marshalltown; Kenneth B. Gehling, Co Dean, Mason City; Stephen L. Meyer, Co Dean, Mason City; Brian M. Dellaert, New Hampton; Dennis J. Colter, Waterloo.

Archdiocesan Offices

Archives—Dan Burns, Dir.

Campaign for Human Development—Tracy Morrison, M.S., L.M.H.C., Dir.

Catholic Cemeteries of the Archdiocese of Dubuque—Richard L. Runde, CPA, Dir.

Catholic Schools—(see also Bureau of Education under Miscellaneous) Kim Hermsen, M.A., Supt. Schools; Itza Heim, Sec.; Mindy Hart, M.A., Assoc. Dir. Educ.; Alice Conlon, M.A., Assoc. Dir. Educ.; Cathy Walz, M.S., Assoc. Dir. Educ.

Communications—John Robbins, Dir.; John Nigg, IT Admin.; Jeremy Jones, IT Admin.; Dan Burns, Print Shop Technician.

Newspaper "The Witness"—Dan Russo, Editor, P.O. Box 917, Dubuque, 52004-0917. Tel: 563-588-0556; Fax: 563-588-0557. Staff: Jill Kruse-Domeyer, Editorial Asst.; Bret Fear, Production, Design & Advertising; Barb Gleason, Circulation & Sec.

Council of Catholic Women—Rev. Daniel J. Knipper, Spiritual Advisor, (Retired); Florine Swanson, Pres., 2796 290th St., Galt, 50101. Tel: 563-852-4360.

Development Office—Jeff Henderson, Ed.S., Dir.; Jeff Schneider, Assoc. Dir.; Mark Schmidt, M.S.W., M.A., Devel. Project Coord.; Denise Aird, Sec.

Education Resource Center—Kim Feldman, Dir.; Tricia Tranel, Resource Center Specialist.

Faith Formation Division—Kevin Feyen, M.T.S., Chair; Jim Betzner, M.S., Faith Formation Project Coord.; Lynne Chapman, Faith Formation Project Coord.

Adolescent Faith Formation—Kevin Feyen, M.T.S., Dir.

Adult Faith Formation—Mary Pedersen, D.Min., Dir.

Catechetical Services—Joanne Pohland, M.A., Dir.

Disability Inclusion—Mindy Hart, M.A., Dir.; Jim Betzner, M.S., Coord. Retreats/Renewal Days.

Family Life Office—Matthew Selby, M.A., Dir.

Finance Office—Richard L. Runde, CPA, Finance Officer; Penny Minnihan, CPA, Auditor; Kathy Wuertzer, Controller; Peggy Thill, Accounting Clerk; Julie Sanders, Staff Accountant; Patricia Neises, Insurance Billing Specialist; Jennie Pothour, Insurance Billing Clerk.

Health Care Ethics—Janine Marie Idziak, Ph.D., Consultant.

Human Resources—Lynn Osterhaus, Dir.

Insurance: Property and Liability (Dubuque Archdiocesan Protection Program)—Rich Earles, Claims Risk Mgr., Archdiocesan Ctr.; Patricia Neises, Sec.

Leadership Development and Pastoral Planning—Dan Rohner, Dir.; Kim Schmidt, Sec.

Maintenance—Bob Runde, Dir.; Jim Foust, Assoc. Dir.; Bob Hancock, Assoc. Dir.

Metropolitan Tribunal—Mailing Address: P.O. Box 479, Dubuque, 52004-0479. Tel: 563-556-2580. (Please send all dispensation requests to the Tribunal).

Director—Sr. Maureen McPartland, O.P., J.C.L.

Judicial Vicar—Rev. Scott E. Bullock, J.C.L.

Defenders of the Bond—Rev. Msgrs. James O. Barta, Ph.D., (Retired); Richard P. Funke, J.C.L., (Retired); Rev. Donald J. Plamondon, J.C.L., (Retired).

Judges—Revs. Scott E. Bullock, J.C.L.; Joseph L. Hauer, J.C.D.; Deacon Gerald T. Jorgensen, Ph.D., J.C.L.; Revs. Douglas J. Loecke, J.C.L.; Mark R. Nemmers, (Retired); Very Rev. Brian M. Dellaert; Sisters Maureen McPartland, O.P., J.C.L.; Francine Quillin, P.B.V.M., J.C.L.; Rev. Msgr. W. Dean Walz, J.C.D., (Retired).

Promoters of Justice—Deacon Gerald T. Jorgensen, Ph.D., J.C.L., (regarding Penal Matters); Rev. Msgr. Richard P. Funke, J.C.L., (Retired), (regarding Matrimonial Matters).

Secretary and Notary—Carla Kasal.

Permanent Diaconate Program—Deacon Tom Lang, Dir.; Kim Schmidt, Sec. Assistant Directors: Deacons Richard Wallace; Gerald T. Jorgensen, Ph.D., J.C.L.; Raymond Larsen.

Protection of Children and Young People—Lynn Osterhaus.

Recently Ordained Program—St. John XXII Parish, 8100 Roncalli Dr., S.W., Cedar Rapids, 52404. Rev. Dustin L. Vu, Dir.

Respect Life - Social Justice—Mark Schmidt, M.S.W., M.A., Dir.

Stewardship & Mission Awareness—Sr. Lynn Fangman, P.B.V.M., Dir.; Barb Gleason, Sec.

Vocations/Seminarians—Rev. Jon M. Seda, Dir.; Carmen Lappe, Vocations Coord., St. Stephen the Witness Catholic Student Ctr., 1019 W. 23rd St., Cedar Falls, 50613. Tel: 563-580-0027. Associate Vocation Directors: Revs. Kyle M. Digmann; Dustin L. Vu.

Worship Office—Rev. Greg E. Bahl, Dir.; Kim Schmidt, Sec.

Archdiocesan Boards, Commissions and Councils

The Archdiocese of Dubuque Corporate Board—Most Rev. Michael Owen Jackels; Rev. Msgr. Thomas E. Toale, Ph.D.; Richard L. Runde, CPA, Treas.; Sarah Otting, M.A.P.S., Recording Sec.; Chris Corken; Sr. Maureen McPartland, O.P., J.C.L.

Archdiocese of Dubuque Deposit & Loan Fund Board—Most Rev. Michael Owen Jackels; Rev. Msgr. Thomas E. Toale, Ph.D.; Chris Corken; Sr. Maureen McPartland, O.P., J.C.L.; Richard L. Runde, CPA, Treas.; Sarah Otting, M.A.P.S., Recording Sec.

Archdiocese of Dubuque Education Fund Board—Most Rev. Michael Owen Jackels, Pres.; Richard L. Runde, CPA; Rev. Msgr. Thomas E. Toale, Ph.D.; Chris Corken; Sr. Maureen McPartland, O.P., J.C.L.; Sarah Otting, M.A.P.S., Recording Sec.

Archdiocese of Dubuque Perpetual Care Fund Board—Most Rev. Michael Owen Jackels; Rev. Msgr. Thomas E. Toale, Ph.D.; Sr. Maureen McPartland, O.P., J.C.L.; Richard L. Runde, CPA, Treas.; Deacon John Stierman; Sarah Otting, M.A.P.S., Recording Sec.

Archdiocese of Dubuque Seminarian Education Fund Board—Most Rev. Michael Owen Jackels; Rev. Msgr. Thomas E. Toale, Ph.D.; Chris Corken; Sr. Maureen McPartland, O.P., J.C.L.; Richard L. Runde, CPA, Treas.; Sarah Otting, M.A.P.S., Recording Sec.

American Martyrs Retreat House Advisory Board—Tom Hoag, Chm.; Jackie Hoggins; Luke Jenson; Julie Paladino; Lynn Ptacek; Dale Roethler; Rev. Msgr. Lyle L. Wilgenbusch, (Retired); Deacon Alan Weber, Dir.

Archdiocesan Catholic School Board—Ex-Officio: Kim Hermsen, M.A., Exec. Officer; Matthew Chizek; Laurie Field; Angie Long; Kim Reiter; Jake Schaeffer, Vice Chair; Sherry Schulte; Rev. James L. Secora; Cathy Stierman; Michelle Tressel, Chair.

Building Commission—Rev. Greg E. Bahl; Rev. Msgr. Russell M. Bleich, S.T.L., Chair, (Retired); Milt Dakovich; Deacon Ray Larsen; Ron Leibold; Rev. Neil J. Manternach; Jeff Morrow; John J. Negro; James Osterberger; Jim Betzner, M.S., Recording Sec.; Richard L. Runde, CPA, Exec. Sec.; Rev. Msgr. Carl L. Schmitt, (Retired); Ed Wineinger.

Church Design/Renovation Commission—Revs. John S. Haugen; Greg E. Bahl, Exec. Sec.; Pam Johnston; Revs. Neil J. Manternach, Chm.; Dennis D. Juhl, (Retired); Gary A. Mayer; Anastasia Nicklaus.

Due Process Board—Rev. Gabriel C. Anderson; Sr. Jean Gordon, B.V.M.; Chris Corken; David Heiar; Brendan Quann, Chair; Lynn Osterhaus, Staff, (non-voting); Julie Niemeyer.

Finance Council—Most Rev. Michael Owen Jackels, Chm.; Richard L. Runde, CPA, Exec. Sec.; Kathy Wuertzer; Donald Bergan; Deacon Matthew F. Berry; Sr. Margaret Mary Cosgrove, B.V.M.; Thomas W. Hanley; Rev. Joseph L. Hauer, J.C.D.; Jason McDermott; Karen Sturm; Rev. Msgr. Thomas E. Toale, Ph.D.; Steve Weiss.

Medical-Moral Commission—Janine Marie Idziak, Ph.D., Chm.; Brian Fagan, J.D.; Rev. John S. Haugen; Janice Loecke, R.N., B.S.; Eileen McSperrin, B.S.N.; Sr. Susan O'Connor, R.S.M., M.S.W., M.A.; Deacon Michael Schemmel; Mark Valliere, M.D., M.M.M.

PAMAD (Pastoral Associates/Ministers of the Archdiocese of Dubuque)—Nancy Strub, Pres.; Karen Bonfig, Vice Pres.; Karen Newman, Sec.; Marsha Hauser, Treas.

Pastoral Council—Most Rev. Michael Owen Jackels, Pres.; Dan Rohner, Exec. Sec.; Rev. Msgr. Thomas E. Toale, Ph.D., Ex Officio; Bob Buschette; Susan Keune; Sr. Carla Popes, P.B.V.M.; Deacon Rigoberto Real; Marcia Reilly; Sharon Rettinger; Sue Salow, Chair; Michael Schnurr; Pauline Shatek; Deacon Michael Ward; Marie Ware, Sec.

Personnel Advisory Board—Revs. Steven J. Rosonke, Age Group II; Philip E. Thompson, Age Group I; Steven M. Garner, Age Group III; Gary A. Mayer, Age Group IV; Mark Osterhaus, At Large; Rev. Msgr. Thomas E. Toale, Ph.D., Ex Officio.

Priests' Council—Most Rev. Michael Owen Jackels, Pres.; Rev. G. Robert Gross, Chair. Ex Officio Member: Rev. Msgr. Thomas E. Toale, Ph.D. Appointed by the Archbishop: Rev. Msgr. James L. Miller.

Retired Priests' Representatives—Rev. Msgr. Carl L. Schmitt, (Retired); Rev. Bernard C. Grady, (Retired).

Religious Priests' Representative—Rev. James Bergin, S.V.D.

Deanery Representatives—Revs. Philip E. Thompson, Cedar Rapids Deanery; G. Robert Gross, Decorah Deanery; Greg E. Bahl, Dubuque Deanery; Rev. Msgr. James L. Miller, Dubuque Deanery; Revs. Noah J. Diehm, Dyersville Deanery; Bernard C. Grady, Marshalltown Deanery, (Retired); Raymond A. Burkle, New Hampton Deanery; Jeffrey A. Dole, Waterloo Deanery; Neil J. Manternach, Mason City Deanery.

Priestly Life and Ministry Committee—(Standing Committee of the Priests' Council) Revs. Greg E. Bahl; Steven M. Garner; Dustin L. Vu; Very Rev. Brian M. Dellaert.

Review Board for the Protection of Minors—Dr. Tom Andregg; Stephen Brackett, Pastor; Deacon Michael Klappholz; Janel Kluesner; Geri Konrady; Randal Nigg, Dubuque, Chair; Deacon Gerald T. Jorgensen, Ph.D., J.C.L., Promoter of Justice regarding Penal Matters; Rev. Michael G. Schueller; Stefani Weber.

Seminary Admissions and Advisory Board—Rev. David A. Schatz, M.A.; Wendy Mulert; Very Rev. Dwayne J. Thoman; Rev. Jon M. Seda, Chm.

Victim Assistance Coordinator—Dr. Thomas Ottavi, Tel: 563-584-3000.

Worship Commission—Rev. Greg E. Bahl; Amy Dolan; Rev. G. Robert Gross; Bob Hauser; Lori Knuth; Deacon Edward Martin; Anastasia Nicklaus; Mollie Muntefering; Very Rev. Dennis J. Quint; Marcia Reilly.

CLERGY, PARISHES, MISSIONS AND PAROCHIAL SCHOOLS

CITY OF DUBUQUE

(Dubuque County)

1—St. Raphael's Cathedral Church, Dubuque, Iowa (1833) [JC]

231 Bluff St., 52001-6918. Tel: 563-582-7646; Fax: 563-556-6796; Email: DBQ054@dbqarch.org; Web: www.cathedralstpats.org. Rev. Msgr. Thomas E. Toale, Ph.D.; Rev. Greg E. Bahl; Deacons Jim Luksetich; Paul Peckosh; James Mandralla, Music Dir. & Liturgist.

See Holy Family Catholic Schools under Consolidated K-12 Systems located in the Institution section.

2—St. Anthony Church (Dubuque, Iowa) (1867) [JC]

1880 St. Ambrose St., 52001-4196. Tel: 563-588-0571 ; Fax: 563-588-0572; Email: dbq060@dbqarch.org; Web: www.stanthony-dubuque.org. 1870 St. Ambrose St., 52001-4196. Rev. Steven J. Rosonke; Deacons William Hickson; William Mauss.

See Holy Family Catholic Schools under Consolidated K-12 Systems located in the Institution Section.

3—The Church of the Nativity, Dubuque, Iowa (1923) [JC]

1225 Alta Vista St., 52001. Tel: 563-582-1839; Fax: 563-582-1830; Email: dbq057@dbqarch.org;

Web: www.nativity.weconnect.com. Rev. Msgr. James L. Miller; Deacon Steve Whiteman.
See Holy Family Catholic Schools under Consolidated K-12 Systems located in the Institution section.
4—CHURCH OF THE RESURRECTION, DUBUQUE, IOWA (1857) [CEM]
Church & Office: 4300 Asbury Rd., 52002.
Tel: 563-556-7511; Email: dbq058@dbqarch.org; Web: www.res-dbq.org. Very Rev. Phillip G. Gibbs; Rev. Andrew J. Upah; Deacons Mike Ellis; Gerald T. Jorgensen, Ph.D., J.C.L.; Jim Schmidt.
See Holy Family Catholic Schools under Consolidated K-12 Systems located in the Institution Section.
5—ST. COLUMBKILLE CHURCH, DUBUQUE, IOWA (1887) [JC]
1230 Rush St., 52003-7598. Tel: 563-583-9117; Email: dbq062@dbqarch.org; Web: www.stcolumbkille.net. 1240 Rush St., 52003-7598. Revs. Thomas J. McDermott; Paul Attah-Nsiah; David A. Schatz, M.A., Pastor in Solidum; Deacons William Biver; Travis King.
See Holy Family Catholic Schools under Consolidated K-12 Systems located in the Institution Section.
6—HOLY SPIRIT CHURCH, DUBUQUE, IOWA
2215 Windsor Ave., 52001. Tel: 563-583-1709; Email: dbq059@dbqarch.org; Web: www.holyspiritdbq.org. Very Rev. Dwayne J. Thoman; Rev. Andrew Awotwe-Mensah; Deacons Dave Brinkmoeller; Stephen MacDonald; John Stierman; James J. Thill, Pastoral Assoc.
Holy Ghost Church—2921 Central Ave.
Holy Trinity Church, 1701 Rhomberg Ave., 52001.
Sacred Heart Church, 2215 Windsor Ave., 52001.
7—ST. JOSEPH THE WORKER CHURCH OF DUBUQUE, DUBUQUE, IOWA (1949) [JC]
2001 Saint Joseph St., 52001. 60 S. Algona St., 52001-5605. Tel: 563-588-1433; Email: dbq062@dbqarch.org; Web: www.theworker.org. Revs. Gabriel C. Anderson; Ralph E. Davis; David A. Schatz, M.A., Pastor in Solidum; Deacons William Biver; Travis King.
See Holy Family Catholic Schools under Consolidated K-12 Systems located in the Institution Section.
8—ST. PATRICK'S CHURCH, DUBUQUE, IOWA (1862) [JC]
15th & Iowa Streets, 52001. Tel: 563-583-9749; Email: dbq054@dbqarch.org; Web: www.cathedralstpats.org. 1425 Iowa St., 52001. Rev. Msgr. Thomas E. Toale, Ph.D.; Rev. Greg E. Bahl; Deacons Jim Luksetich; Paul Peckosh.
See Holy Family Catholic Schools under Consolidated K-12 Systems located in the Institution Section.

OUTSIDE THE CITY OF DUBUQUE

ACKLEY, FRANKLIN CO., ST. MARY'S CHURCH OF ACKLEY, ACKLEY, IOWA (1891) [CEM]
Mailing Address: 611 Sherman Ave., P.O. Box 2, Ackley, 50601. Tel: 641-847-2329; Email: DBQ108@dbqarch.org; Web: www.franklinhardincatholic.org. Rev. Kevin R. Earleywine; Deacon Robin Claypool.
ALTA VISTA, CHICKASAW CO., SAINT BERNARD'S CHURCH, ALTA VISTA, IOWA (1897) [CEM]
116 E. Washington St., Alta Vista, 50603. 203 7th St., Elma, 50628. Tel: 641-393-2520; Web: www.holyrosarycluster.org. Very Rev. Jerry F. Kopacek.
AMES, STORY CO.
1—ST. CECILIA CHURCH, AMES, IOWA (1899)
2900 Hoover Ave., Ames, 50010-4498.
Tel: 515-233-3092; Fax: 515-233-6423; Email: dbq003@dbqarch.org; Web: www.stceciliaparish.org. Rev. James L. Secora; Deacons John McCully, (Retired), Hispanic Min. Coord.; Charles Bernhard; Mark Bortle; Alan Christy; Ron Smith.
School—St. Cecilia School, (Grades PreK-5), 2900 Hoover Ave., Ames, 50010-4498. Tel: 515-232-5290; Email: dbqe01@dbqarch.org. Sara Rooney, Prin. Lay Teachers 16; Students 184.
2—ST. THOMAS AQUINAS CHURCH, AMES, IOWA (1947)
2210 Lincoln Ave., Ames, 50014-7184.
Tel: 515-292-3810; Fax: 515-292-3841; Email: dbq004@dbqarch.org; Web: www.staparish.net. Rev. Kyle M. Digmann.
ANAMOSA, JONES CO., ST. PATRICK'S CHURCH, ANAMOSA, IOWA (1861) [CEM]
215 N. Garnavillo St., Anamosa, 52205-1121.
Tel: 319-462-2141; Email: dbq005@dbqarch.org; Web: www.stpatchurch.com. Rev. Nicholas B. March.
School—St. Patrick School, (Grades PreK-6), 216 N. Garnavillo St., Anamosa, 52205-1122.
Tel: 319-462-2688; Email: dbqe02@dbqarch.org. Jayne Intlekofer, Prin. Lay Teachers 8; Students 85.
BALLTOWN, DUBUQUE CO., ST. FRANCIS CHURCH, BALLTOWN, IOWA (1891) [CEM]
468 Balltown Rd., Balltown, 52073.
Tel: 563-870-4041; Email: dbq104@dbqarch.org; Web: www.lasallepastorate.com. 835 Church St., P.O. Box 398, Holy Cross, 52053. Rev. Noah J. Diehm.
See LaSalle Catholic Schools, Holy Cross under Elementary School Systems located in the Institution section.
BANKSTON, DUBUQUE CO., ST. CLEMENT CHURCH, BANKSTON, IOWA (1859) [CEM]
24287 New Vienna Rd., Epworth, 52045-9732.
Tel: 563-876-5540; Email: dbq076@dbqarch.org; Web: www.stelizabethpastorate.com. P.O. Box 286, Epworth, 52045-0286. Revs. Michael G. Schueller; Phillip F. Kruse, Sacramental Priest; Deacons Gerald Koopmann; Dan O'Connell; John Wolfe.
See Seton Catholic Schools, Farley under Elementary School Systems located in the Institution section.
BARCLAY, BLACKHAWK CO., ST. FRANCIS CHURCH, BARCLAY, IOWA (1862) [CEM]
7830 E. Airline Hwy., Dunkerton, 50626-9715.
Tel: 319-822-7477; Email: dbq109@dbqarch.org. 7837 E. Airline Hwy., Dunkerton, 50626-9715. Rev. Jeffrey A. Dole.
BELLE PLAINE, BENTON CO., ST. MICHAEL CHURCH, BELLE PLAINE, IOWA (1885)
1304 Ninth Ave., Belle Plaine, 52208. Mailing Address: 900 Park St., Tama, 52339.
Tel: 641-484-3039; Email: dbq197@dbqarch.org; Web: www.circleofsaints.weconnect.com. Very Rev. Michael J. Mescher; Deacons Joseph Behounek; Stan Upah.
BELLEVUE, JACKSON CO., ST. JOSEPH'S CHURCH, BELLEVUE, IOWA (1841) [CEM]
405 Franklin St., Bellevue, 52031. Tel: 563-872-3234; Email: dbq012@dbqarch.org; Web: www.stjosephbellevue.org. Rev. Dennis W. Miller; Deacons Loras Weber; Robert Wood.
See Bellevue, Marquette High School under Consolidated K-12 Systems located in the Institution section.
BELMOND, WRIGHT CO., ST. FRANCIS CHURCH, BELMOND, IOWA (1870) [CEM]
1207 3rd St. N.E., Belmond, 50421.
Tel: 515-532-3586; Email: dbq039@dbqarch.org; Web: www.holyfamilycluster.org. 608 2nd Ave., N.E., Clarion, 50525. Rev. Jerry W. Blake; Deacons Pedro Garcia; Michael Whitters.
BLAIRSTOWN, BENTON CO., ST. JOHN'S CHURCH, BLAIRSTOWN, IOWA (1948)
105 West St. N.W., Blairstown, 52209.
Tel: 319-228-8131; Email: dbq150@dbqarch.org; Web: www.queenofsaints.com. 405 4th Ave., P.O. Box 250, Van Horne, 52346-0250. Rev. Craig E. Steimel; Deacon Robert Pailthorpe.
BRITT, HANCOCK CO., ST. PATRICK CHURCH, BRITT, IOWA (1880) [CEM]
335 1st Ave. S.E., Britt, 50423. 660 Bush Ave., Garner, 50438. Tel: 641-923-2329; Email: dbq088@dbqarch.org; Web: www.archangelscc.org. Revs. James W. Dubert; Paul E. Lippstock, Sacramental Priest; Deacon Tom Blomme.
BUFFALO CENTER, WINNEBAGO CO., ST. PATRICK'S CHURCH, BUFFALO CENTER, IOWA (1899)
115 5th Ave. N.W., Buffalo Center, 50424. Web: www.archangelscc.org. 660 Bush Ave., Garner, 50438. Tel: 641-923-2329; Email: dbq088@dbqarch.org. Revs. James W. Dubert; Paul E. Lippstock, Sacramental Priest; Deacon Tom Blomme.
CALMAR, WINNESHIEK CO., ST. ALOYSIUS CHURCH (CALMAR, IOWA) (1875) [CEM]
306 S. Maryville, Calmar, 52132. Tel: 563-562-3045; Email: dbq019@dbqarch.org. P.O. Box 819, Calmar, 52132-0819. Rev. G. Robert Gross; Deacon Dan O'Brien.
See Calmar-Festina-Spillville Catholic School, Calmar under Elementary School Systems located in the Institution section.
CASCADE, DUBUQUE CO., ST. MATTHIAS PARISH, CASCADE, IOWA (1995) [CEM]
410 Third Ave. N.W., Cascade, 52033.
Tel: 563-852-3524; Email: dbqcmt1@dbqarch.org; Web: www.stapastorate.org. 408 Third Ave., N.W., P.O. Box 699, Cascade, 52033. Rev. Douglas J. Loecke, J.C.L.; Deacons Ray Noonan; Joe Schockemoehl; Steven W. Strang.
See Aquin Educational System, Cascade under Consolidated K-12 Systems located in the Institution section.
CEDAR FALLS, BLACKHAWK CO., ST. PATRICK'S CHURCH, CEDAR FALLS, IOWA (1855)
8th & Washington Sts, Cedar Falls, 50613.
Tel: 319-266-3523; Email: dbq025@dbqarch.org; Web: www.saintpatrickcf.org. 705 Main St., Cedar Falls, 50613. Very Rev. Dennis J. Colter; Deacon Alan Weber.
School—St. Patrick School, (Grades PreK-8), 615 Washington St., Cedar Falls, 50613.
Tel: 319-277-6781; Email: dbqe07@dbqarch.org. Lynette Hackett, Prin. Lay Teachers 20; Students 266.
CEDAR RAPIDS, LINN CO.
1—ALL SAINTS CHURCH, CEDAR RAPIDS, IOWA (1947) [JC]
Church, Parish Office & Mailing Address: 720 29th St., S.E., Cedar Rapids, 52403-3099.
Tel: 319-363-6130; Email: dbq026@dbqarch.org; Web: www.allsaintscr.com. Rev. John R. Flaherty; Deacons Michael Klappholz; Edward Martin.
School—All Saints Catholic School, (Grades PreK-5), 720 29th St., S.E., Cedar Rapids, 52403.
Tel: 319-363-4110; Fax: 319-363-9547. Megan Boomgarden, Prin. Lay Teachers 16; Students 229.
2—IMMACULATE CONCEPTION CHURCH, CEDAR RAPIDS, IOWA (1858) [JC]
857 3rd St. S.E., Cedar Rapids, 52406-1247.
Tel: 319-362-7181; Email: dbq027@dbqarch.org; Web: www.iccr.church. Mailing Address: P.O. Box 1247, Cedar Rapids, 52406-1247. Rev. Christopher R. Podhajsky; Deacons Robert F. Hurych; Vern Rompot.
3—ST. JOHN XXIII PARISH, CEDAR RAPIDS, IOWA, [CEM]
8100 Roncalli Dr., S.W., Cedar Rapids, 52404-9178.
Tel: 319-846-3139; Fax: 319-846-3159; Email: dbq227@dbqarch.org; Web: www.stjohn23cr.org. Rev. Dustin L. Vu; Deacon Stanley Scheiding.
4—ST. JUDE CHURCH, CEDAR RAPIDS, IOWA (1962) [JC]
50 Edgewood Rd. N.W., Cedar Rapids, 52405.
Tel: 319-390-3520; Email: dbq028@dbqarch.org; Web: www.judes.org. Rev. Mark D. Murphy; Deacon John Winkel.
See Holy Family School, Cedar Rapids under Elementary School Systems located in the Institution section.
5—ST. LUDMILA'S CHURCH, CEDAR RAPIDS, IOWA (1922) [JC]
211 21st Ave. S.W., Cedar Rapids, 52404. 2107 J St., S.W., Cedar Rapids, 52404-3615. Tel: 319-362-7282; Fax: 319-398-0352; Email: dbq029@dbqarch.org; Web: www.stludmila.org. Rev. Kenneth J. Glaser; Deacons Paul Jim Berger; Mark Sandersfeld.
See Holy Family School, Cedar Rapids under Elementary School Systems located in the Institution section.
6—ST. MATTHEW'S CHURCH, CEDAR RAPIDS, IOWA (1922) [JC]
2310 First Ave. N.E., Cedar Rapids, 52402-4999.
Tel: 319-363-8269; Email: dbq030@dbqarch.org; Web: www.stmatthewcr.org. Rev. Steven M. Garner; Deacons John Kauffman; Richard Wallace.
School—St. Matthew School, (Grades PreK-5), 2244 1st Ave. NE, Cedar Rapids, 52402. Tel: 319-362-3021 . Amy Conlon, Prin. Lay Teachers 16; Students 256.
7—ST. PATRICK CHURCH, CEDAR RAPIDS, IOWA (1886) [JC]
500 1st Ave. N.W., Cedar Rapids, 52405.
Tel: 319-362-7966; Fax: 319-247-7260; Email: dbq031@dbqarch.org; Web: ww.stpatrickscr.org. 120 5th St., N.W., Cedar Rapids, 52405. Rev. Ivan R. Nienhaus; Deacon Daniel Hoeger.
8—ST. PIUS THE X CHURCH, CEDAR RAPIDS, IOWA (1959) [JC]
4949 Council St. N.E., Cedar Rapids, 52402-2492.
Tel: 319-393-4445; Fax: 319-393-9424; Email: dbq032@dbqarch.org; Web: www.crpiusx.org. Rev. Philip E. Thompson; Deacons Ron Ridder; Paul Zimmerman.
See St. Pius and St. Elizabeth Ann Seton Schools under Elementary School Systems located in the Institution section.
9—ST. WENCESLAUS CHURCH, CEDAR RAPIDS, IOWA (1874) [JC]
1230 5th St. S.E., Cedar Rapids, 52401.
Tel: 319-362-8061; Email: dbq027@dbqarch.org; Web: www.stwenceslauscr.com. Mailing Address: 1224 5th St., S.E., Cedar Rapids, 52401. Rev. Christopher R. Podhajsky; Deacons Robert F. Hurych; Vern Rompot.
CENTRAL CITY, LINN CO., ST. STEPHEN'S CHURCH, CENTRAL CITY, IOWA (1932)
Mailing Address: 4700 Valley Farm Rd., P.O. Box 496, Central City, 52214-0496. Tel: 319-438-6625; Web: www.northlinncc.org. Rev. Nicholas B. March.
CHARLES CITY, FLOYD CO., THE IMMACULATE CONCEPTION CHURCH, CHARLES CITY, IOWA (1857) [CEM]
106 Chapel Ln., Charles City, 50616-2810.
Tel: 641-228-1071; Email: dbq035@dbqarch.org; Web: www.iccharlescity.com. Rev. Gary A. Mayer; Deacon Michael Ward.
School—Immaculate Conception School, (Grades PreK-6), 1203 Clark St., Charles City, 50616.
Tel: 641-228-1225; Email: dbqe14@dbqarch.org. Laurie Field, Prin. Lay Teachers 16; Students 224.
CHELSEA, TAMA CO., ST. JOSEPH CHURCH, CHELSEA, IOWA (1867) [CEM]
307 Station St., Chelsea, 52215. Tel: 641-484-3039; Email: dbq197@dbqarch.org; Web: www.circleofsaints.weconnect.com. Mailing Address: 900 Park St., Tama, 52339. Very Rev. Michael J. Mescher; Deacons Joseph Behounek; Stan Upah.
CLARION, WRIGHT CO., ST. JOHN CHURCH, CLARION, IOWA (1883) [CEM]

608 Second Ave., N.E., Clarion, 50525-0026.
Tel: 515-532-3586; Fax: 515-532-2153; Email: dbq039@dbqarch.org; Web: www.holyfamilycluster.org. Rev. Jerry W. Blake; Deacons Pedro Garcia; Michael Whitters.

CLEAR LAKE, CERRO GORDO CO., ST. PATRICK CHURCH, CLEAR LAKE, IOWA (1901)
1001 Ninth Ave. S., Clear Lake, 50428-2615.
Tel: 641-357-3214; Fax: 641-357-3210; Email: dbq040@dbqarch.org; Web: www.stpatrick.weconnect.com. Rev. John A. Gossman; Deacon Darrel Courrier.

CLERMONT, FAYETTE CO., ST. PETER CHURCH, CLERMONT, IOWA (1855) [CEM]
608 Larrabee, Clermont, 52135. Tel: 563-423-6007; Email: dbq195@dbqarch.org; Web: www.stjosephtheworkercluster.com. P.O. Box 25, Clermont, 52135-0025. Rev. Donald T. Komboh, (Nigeria); Deacon Michael Schemmel.

COGGON, LINN CO., ST. JOHN'S CHURCH, COGGON, IOWA (1912) [CEM]
211 N. 3rd St., Coggon, 52218. Tel: 319-438-6625; Email: dbq005@dbqarch.org; Web: www.northlinncc.org. Mailing Address: 4700 Valley Farm Rd., P.O. Box 496, Central City, 52214. Rev. Nicholas B. March.

COLESBURG, DELAWARE CO., ST. PATRICK'S CHURCH, COLESBURG, IOWA (1862) [CEM]
708 Delaware St., Colesburg, 52035.
Tel: 563-928-7200; Email: dbq072@dbqarch.org; Web: www.vibrantcatholic.com. Mailing Address: 203 S. Locust, P.O. Box 365, Edgewood, 52042-0365. Rev. John S. Haugen.

COLO, STORY CO., ST. MARY CHURCH, COLO, IOWA, [CEM]
422 4th St., Colo, 50056. Tel: 641-377-2710; Email: dbq192@dbqarch.org. 410 Bailey St., P.O. Box 236, Colo, 50056-0236. Rev. Rick D. Dagit; Deacons Steven Van Kerckvoorde; Mark Wyant.

CRESCO, HOWARD CO., NOTRE DAME CHURCH, CRESCO, IOWA (1999) [JC]
223 2nd Ave. E., Cresco, 52136. Tel: 563-547-3565; Email: dbq047@dbqarch.org; Web: www.notredameparish.weebly.com. 116 Third St. E., Cresco, 52136. Rev. Dennis R. Cain.
School—Notre Dame School, (Grades K-6), 221 Second Ave. E., Cresco, 52136. Tel: 563-547-4513; Email: dbqe15@dbqarch.org. Renee Cuvelier, Prin. Lay Teachers 15; Students 212.

DECORAH, WINNESHIEK CO., ST. BENEDICT CHURCH, DECORAH, IOWA (1864) [CEM]
307 W. Main St., Decorah, 52101-1778.
Tel: 563-382-9631; Email: dbq049@dbqarch.org; Web: www.stbenedictcc.com. Rev. Donald A. Hertges; Deacon Nick Francois.
School—St. Benedict School, (Grades K-8), 402 Rural Ave., Decorah, 52101. Tel: 563-382-4668; Email: dbqe16@dbqarch.org. Stephen Haluska, Prin. Lay Teachers 15; Students 133.

DELHI, DELAWARE CO., ST. JOHN CHURCH, DELHI, IOWA (1872) [CEM]
303 South St., Delhi, 52223. Tel: 563-922-2251; Email: dbq050@dbqarch.org. 307 South St., P.O. Box 187, Delhi, 52223-0187. Rev. John R. Kremer.

DORCHESTER, ALLAMAKEE CO., ST. MARY'S CHURCH, DORCHESTER, IOWA (1865) [CEM]
594 Waterloo Creek Dr., Dorchester, 52140.
Tel: 563-568-3671; Email: dbq216@dbqarch.org; Web: www.stpatrickwaukon.weconnect.com. Mailing Address: 109 2nd St., S.W., P.O. Box 146, Waukon, 52172. Rev. Mark Osterhaus; Deacon Jeff Molitor.

DUNCAN, HANCOCK CO., ST. WENCESLAUS CHURCH, DUNCAN, IOWA (1900) [CEM]
2343 Navy Ave., Britt, 50423. Mailing Address: 660 Bush Ave., Garner, 50438-1513. Tel: 641-923-2329; Email: dbq088@dbqarch.org; Web: www.archangelscc.org. Revs. James W. Dubert; Paul E. Lippstock, Sacramental Priest; Deacon Tom Blomme.

DYERSVILLE, DUBUQUE CO., BASILICA OF ST. FRANCIS XAVIER, DYERSVILLE, IOWA (1859) [CEM]
104 Third St. S.W., Dyersville, 52040-1696.
Tel: 563-875-7325; Email: dbq067@dbqarch.org; Web: www.spiresoffaith.com. Very Rev. Dennis J. Quint; Revs. Dennis C. Conway; Ralph E. Davis; Deacons Roger Riesberg; James Steger.
See St. Xavier School under Elementary School Systems located in the Institution section.

EAGLE CENTER, BLACKHAWK CO., ST. MARY'S CHURCH, EAGLE CENTER, IOWA (1859) [CEM]
1435 E. Eagle Rd., Waterloo, 50703. Mailing Address: 1102 Walnut St., Traer, 50675.
Tel: 319-478-2222; Email: dbq199@dbqarch.org; Web: www.princeofpeacecluster.com. Rev. Michael O. Hutchison.

EAGLE GROVE, WRIGHT CO., THE SACRED HEART CHURCH, (EAGLE GROVE, IOWA) (1882) [CEM]
204 S. Jackson Ave., Eagle Grove, 50533.
Tel: 515-532-3586; Fax: 515-532-2153; Email: dbq039@dbqarch.org; Web: www.holyfamilycluster.org. 608 2nd Ave. N.E., Clarion, 50525. Rev. Jerry W. Blake; Deacons Pedro Garcia; Michael Whitters.

EARLVILLE, DELAWARE CO., ST. JOSEPH'S CHURCH, EARLVILLE, IOWA (1887) [CEM]
303 Mary St., Earlville, 52041. Tel: 563-923-3135; Email: dbq067@dbqarch.org; Web: www.spiresoffaith.com. Mailing Address: 307 Mary St., Earlville, 52041. Very Rev. Dennis J. Quint; Revs. Dennis C. Conway; Ralph E. Davis; Deacons Roger Riesberg; James Steger.

EDGEWOOD, DELAWARE CO., ST. MARK'S CHURCH, EDGEWOOD, IOWA (1916) [CEM]
203 S. Locust St., P.O. Box 365, Edgewood, 52042.
Tel: 563-928-7200; Email: dbq072@dbqarch.org; Web: www.vibrantcatholic.com. Rev. John S. Haugen.

ELDORA, HARDIN CO., ST. MARY'S CHURCH, ELDORA, IOWA (1868) [CEM]
614 Washington, Eldora, 50627-1257.
Tel: 641-939-5545; Email: dbq108@dbqarch.org; Web: www.communityofdisciples.net. Rev. Kevin R. Earleywine; Deacon Robin Claypool.

ELKADER, CLAYTON CO., ST. JOSEPH'S CHURCH, ELKADER, IOWA (1844) [CEM]
330 First St., P.O. Box 626, Elkader, 52043-0626.
Tel: 563-245-2548; Email: dbq072@dbqarch.org; Web: www.vibrantcatholic.com. Rev. John S. Haugen.

ELMA, HOWARD CO., THE IMMACULATE CONCEPTION CHURCH, ELMA, IOWA (1887) [CEM]
207 Seventh St., Elma, 50628. Tel: 641-393-2520; Web: www.holyrosarycluster.org. 203 Seventh St., Elma, 50628. Very Rev. Jerry F. Kopacek.

EPWORTH, DUBUQUE CO., ST. PATRICK CHURCH, EPWORTH, IOWA (1879) [CEM]
102 First St. S.E., Epworth, 52045. 104 First St., S.E., P.O. Box 286, Epworth, 52045-0286.
Tel: 563-876-5540; Email: dbq076@dbqarch.org; Web: www.stelizabethpastorate.com. Revs. Michael G. Schueller; Phillip F. Kruse, Sacramental Priest; Deacons Gerald Koopmann; Dan O'Connell; John Wolfe.
See Seton Catholic Schools, Farley under Elementary School Systems located in the Institution section.

FAIRBANK, BUCHANAN CO., IMMACULATE CONCEPTION CHURCH, FAIRBANK, IOWA (1858) [CEM]
106 Iowa St., Fairbank, 50629. Tel: 319-635-2211; Email: dbq151@dbqarch.org; Web: www.icfairbank.weebly.com. P.O. Box 505, Fairbank, 50629-0505. Rev. Ray E. Atwood; Deacon Jim Patera.

FARLEY, DUBUQUE CO., SAINT JOSEPH'S CHURCH, FARLEY, IOWA (1914) [CEM]
202 2nd Ave S.E., Farley, 52046. 104 First St., S.E., P.O. Box 286, Epworth, 52045. Tel: 563-876-5540; Email: dbq076@dbqarch.org; Web: www.stelizabethpastorate.com. Revs. Michael G. Schueller; Phillip F. Kruse, Sacramental Priest; Deacons Gerald Koopmann; Dan O'Connell; John Wolfe.
See Seton Catholic Schools, Farley under Elementary School Systems located in the Institution section.

FAYETTE, FAYETTE CO., ST. FRANCIS CHURCH, FAYETTE, IOWA (1879) [CEM]
205 Lovers Ln., Fayette, 52142. Tel: 563-578-8227; Email: dbq195@dbqarch.org; Web: www.stjosephtheworkercluster.com. Mailing Address: P.O. Box 276, Fayette, 52142-0276. Rev. Donald T. Komboh, (Nigeria); Deacon Michael Schemmel.

FESTINA, WINNESHIEK CO., OUR LADY OF SEVEN DOLORS CHURCH, FESTINA, IOWA (1843) [CEM]
2348 County Rd. B32, Fort Atkinson, 52144.
Tel: 563-562-3045; Email: dbq019@dbqarch.org; Web: www.CFOparishes.org. Mailing Address: P.O. Box 819, Calmar, 52132-0819. Rev. G. Robert Gross; Deacon Dan O'Brien.
See Calmar-Festina-Spillville Catholic School, Calmar under Elementary School Systems located in the Institution section.

FILLMORE, DUBUQUE CO., THE SACRED HEART CHURCH, FILLMORE, IOWA (1890) [CEM]
19661 Sacred Heart Ln., Bernard, 52032.
Tel: 563-852-3524; Email: dbqcmt1@dbqarch.org; Web: www.stapastorate.org. Mailing Address: 408 Third Ave., N.W., P.O. Box 699, Cascade, 52033-0699. Rev. Douglas J. Loecke, J.C.L.; Deacons Ray Noonan; Joe Schockemoehl; Steven W. Strang.
See Aquin Educational System, Cascade under Consolidated K-12 Systems located in the Institution section.

FOREST CITY, WINNEBAGO CO., ST. JAMES CATHOLIC CHURCH, FOREST CITY, IOWA (1870) [CEM]
906 W. O St., Forest City, 50436. Tel: 641-923-2329; Email: dbq088@dbqarch.org; Web: www.archangelscc.org. 660 Bush Ave., Garner, 50438-1513. Revs. James W. Dubert; Paul E. Lippstock, Sacramental Priest; Deacon Tom Blomme.

FORT ATKINSON, WINNESHIEK CO., ST. JOHN CHURCH, FORT ATKINSON, IOWA (1875) [CEM]
201 Oak St., Fort Atkinson, 52144. Tel: 563-569-8259; Email: dbq166@dbqarch.org; Web: www.christourhopecluster.com. Office & Mailing Address: 110 Commercial Ave., P.O. Box 205, Protivin, 52163. Rev. Kyle M. Digmann; Deacon Jim Zajicek.
See Trinity Catholic School, Protivin under Elementary School Systems located in the Institution section.

GARNAVILLO, CLAYTON CO., ST. JOSEPH CHURCH, GARNAVILLO, IOWA (1846) [CEM]
204 W. Oak, Garnavillo, 52049. Tel: 563-252-1247; Email: dbq096@dbqarch.org; Web: www.maryicjoseph.org. 520 2nd St., P.O. Box 847, Guttenberg, 52052-0847. Rev. Marvin J. Bries; Deacon James Pfaffly.

GARNER, HANCOCK CO., ST. BONIFACE CHURCH, GARNER, IOWA (1883) [CEM]
600 Bush Ave., Garner, 50438. Tel: 641-923-2329; Email: dbq088@dbqarch.org; Web: www.archangelscc.org. 660 Bush Ave., Garner, 50438-1513. Revs. James W. Dubert; Paul E. Lippstock, Sacramental Priest; Deacon Tom Blomme.

GARRYOWEN, JACKSON CO., ST. PATRICK CHURCH, GARRYOWEN, BERNARD, IOWA (1840) [CEM]
28914 46th Ave., Bernard, 52032. 408 3rd Ave., N.W., P.O. Box 699, Cascade, 52033-0699.
Tel: 563-852-3524; Email: dbqcmt1@dbqarch.org; Web: www.stapastorate.org. Rev. Douglas J. Loecke, J.C.L.; Deacons Ray Noonan; Joe Schockemoehl; Steven W. Strang.
See Aquin Educational System, Cascade under Consolidated K-12 Systems located in the Institution section.

GILBERT, STORY CO., S.S. PETER AND PAUL CHURCH, GILBERT, IOWA (1882) [CEM]
14238 500th Ave., Ames, 50014. 1110 11th St., Nevada, 50201. Tel: 515-382-2974; Email: dbq192@dbqarch.org; Web: www.ssppgilbert.net. Rev. Rick D. Dagit.

GILBERTVILLE, BLACKHAWK CO., IMMACULATE CONCEPTION CHURCH, GILBERTVILLE, IOWA (1875) [CEM]
325 15th Ave., Gilbertville, 50634. Tel: 319-296-1092; Email: dbq092@dbqarch.org; Web: www.icsjchurch.com. 311 15th Ave., P.O. Box 136, Gilbertville, 50634-0136. Rev. Henry P. Huber.
See Bosco Catholic School System, Gilbertville, Iowa under Consolidated K-12 Systems located in the Institution section.

GREENE, BUTLER CO., ST. MARY CHURCH, GREENE, IOWA (1872) [CEM]
105 N. Main, P.O. Box 480, Greene, 50636-0480.
Tel: 641-823-4146; Email: dbq094@dbqarch.org. Rev. Msgr. Walter L. Brunkan; Deacon Matt Miller.

GUTTENBERG, CLAYTON CO., ST. MARY CHURCH, GUTTENBERG, IOWA (1851) [CEM]
518 S. Second St., Guttenberg, 52052.
Tel: 563-252-1247; Email: dbq096@dbqarch.org; Web: www.maryicjoseph.org. 502 S. Second St., P.O. Box 847, Guttenberg, 52052-0847. Rev. Marvin J. Bries; Deacon James Pfaffley.
See St. Mary and Immaculate Conception School System, Guttenberg under Elementary School Systems located in the Institution section.

HAMPTON, FRANKLIN CO., ST. PATRICKS CHURCH, HAMPTON, IOWA (1870)
1405 N. Federal, Hampton, 50441. Tel: 641-456-4857; Email: dbq108@dbqarch.org; Web: www.franklinhardincatholic.org. Rev. Kevin R. Earleywine.

HANOVER, ALLAMAKEE CO., ST. MARY'S CHURCH, HANOVER, IOWA (1875) [CEM]
2096 Hwy. 76, Waukon, 52172. Tel: 563-568-3671; Email: dbq216@dbqarch.org; Web: www.stpatrickwaukon.weconnect.com. Mailing Address: c/o St. Patrick Parish, 109 Second St. S.W., Waukon, 52172. Rev. Mark Osterhaus; Deacon Jeff Molitor.

HARPERS FERRY, ALLAMAKEE CO., ST. ANN-ST. JOSEPH CHURCH, HARPERS FERRY, IOWA (1855) [CEM]
307 W. Orange St., Harpers Ferry, 52146. 648 Main St., Lansing, 52151. Tel: 563-538-4171; Email: dbq115@dbqarch.org; Web: www.holyfamilyofthebluffs.org. Rev. John A. Moser.

HIAWATHA, LINN CO., ST. ELIZABETH ANN SETON CHURCH, HIAWATHA, IOWA (1989) [JC]
1350 Lyndhurst Dr., Hiawatha, 52233.
Tel: 319-393-3778; Email: dbq103@dbqarch.org; Web: www.seasp.org. Very Rev. Mark A. Ressler; Deacons Frank Easton; Dennis Mulherin; Scott Zogg.
See St. Pius and St. Elizabeth Ann Seton Schools under Elementary School Systems located in the Institution section.

HOLY CROSS, DUBUQUE CO., HOLY CROSS CHURCH, HOLY CROSS, IOWA (1845) [CEM]
Church & Office: 875 Church St., Holy Cross, 52053.
Tel: 563-870-4041; Email: dbq104@dbqarch.org; Web: www.lasallepastorate.com. 835 Church St., P.O. Box 398, Holy Cross, 52053-0398. Rev. Noah J. Diehm.
See LaSalle Catholic Schools, Holy Cross under Elementary School Systems located in the Institution section.

HOPKINTON, DELAWARE CO., ST. LUKE'S CHURCH, HOPKINTON, IOWA (1922)
206 First St., S.E., P.O. Box 159, Hopkinton, 52237-0159. Tel: 563-926-2613; Email: dbq136@dbqarch.org; Web: www.sacredheartstluke.com. Rev. Paul C. Baldwin.

INDEPENDENCE, BUCHANAN CO., ST. JOHN'S CHURCH, INDEPENDENCE, IOWA (1856) [CEM]
209 Fifth Ave. N.E., Independence, 50644-1998. Tel: 319-334-7191; Email: dbq106@dbqarch.org. Rev. David M. Beckman; Deacon Tim Post.
School—St. John School, (Grades PreK-8), 314 Third St., NE, Independence, 50644. Tel: 319-334-7173; Email: dbqe35@dbqarch.org. Jim Gieryng, Prin. Lay Teachers 13; Students 183.

IONIA, CHICKASHAW CO., ST. BONIFACE CHURCH (IONIA, IOWA) (1899) [CEM]
204 E. Prairie, Ionia, 50645. Web: www.goodshepherdcluster.com. 313 W. Court St., New Hampton, 50659. Tel: 641-394-2105; Email: dbq141@dbqarch.org. Very Rev. Brian M. Dellaert; Deacon Victor J. DeSloover.

IOWA FALLS, HARDIN CO., ST. MARK'S CHURCH, IOWA FALLS, IOWA (1855) [CEM]
415 Main St., P.O. Box 368, Iowa Falls, 50126-0368. Tel: 641-648-9547; Email: dbq108@dbqarch.org; Web: www.communityofdisciples.net. Rev. Kevin R. Earleywine; Deacon Robin Claypool.

JESUP, BUCHANAN CO., ST. ATHANASIUS CHURCH, JESUP, IOWA (1880) [CEM]
623 Stevens St., Jesup, 50648. Tel: 319-827-6682; Email: dbq109@dbqarch.org; Web: www.saintaparish.com. 635 Stevens St., P.O. Box 316, Jesup, 50648-0316. Rev. Jeffrey A. Dole.
School—St. Athanasius School, (Grades K-8), 641 Stevens St., P.O. Box 288, Jesup, 50648-0288. Tel: 319-827-1314; Email: dbqe36@dbqarch.org. Jennifer Sornson, Prin. Lay Teachers 12; Students 127.

KEY WEST, DUBUQUE CO., ST. JOSEPH'S CHURCH, KEY WEST, IOWA (1872)
10270 Key West Dr., 52003. 10204 Key West Dr., 52003-8936. Tel: 563-582-7392; Email: dbq111@dbqarch.org; Web: www.stjosephkeywest.com. Rev. Rodney M. Allers; Deacon Tom Lang.
See Holy Family Catholic Schools under Consolidated K-12 Systems located in the Institution Section.

LA PORTE CITY, BLACKHAWK CO., SACRED HEART CHURCH (LAPORTE CITY, IOWA) (1887)
1021 Poplar St., La Porte City, 50651. Tel: 319-478-2222; Email: dbq199@dbqarch.org; Web: www.princeofpeacecluster.com. 1102 Walnut St., Traer, 50675. Rev. Michael O. Hutchison.

LAKE MILLS, WINNEBAGO CO., ST. PATRICK'S CHURCH, LAKE MILLS, IOWA (1870) [CEM]
406 S. Grant St., Lake Mills, 50450. Mailing Address: 660 Bush Ave., Forest City, 50436-1131. Tel: 641-923-2329; Email: dbq088@dbqarch.org; Web: www.archangelscc.org. Revs. James W. Dubert; Paul E. Lippstock, Sacramental Priest; Deacon Tom Blomme.

LANSING, ALLAMAKEE CO., THE IMMACULATE CONCEPTION CHURCH, LANSING, IOWA (1855) [CEM]
660 Main St., Lansing, 52151. Tel: 563-538-4171; Email: dbq115@dbqarch.org; Web: www.holyfamilyofthebluffs.org. 648 Main St., Lansing, 52151. Rev. John A. Moser.

LAWLER, CHICKASAW CO., OUR LADY OF MT. CARMEL CHURCH, LAWLER, IOWA (1869) [CEM]
3030 IA Hwy. 24, Lawler, 52154. 110 Commercial Ave., P.O. Box 205, Protivin, 52163-0205. Tel: 563-569-8259; Email: dbq166@dbqarch.org; Web: www.christourhopecluster.com. Rev. Aaron R. Junge; Deacon Jim Zajicek.

LITTLE TURKEY, CHICKASAW CO., ASSUMPTION CHURCH, LITTLE TURKEY, LAWLER, IOWA (1902) [CEM]
3303 160th St., Lawler, 52154. Tel: 563-569-8259; Email: dbq166@dbqarch.org; Web: www.christourhopecluster.com. 110 Commercial Ave., P.O. Box 205, Protivin, 52163. Rev. Aaron R. Junge; Deacon Jim Zajicek.

LOURDES, HOWARD CO., OUR LADY OF LOURDES CHURCH, LOURDES, IOWA (1875) [CEM]
14068 17th St., Elma, 50628. Tel: 641-393-2520; Email: dbq075@dbqarch.org; Web: www.holyrosarycluster.org. 203 7th St., Elma, 50628. Very Rev. Jerry F. Kopacek.

LUXEMBURG, DUBUQUE CO., HOLY TRINITY CHURCH, LUXEMBURG, IOWA (1865) [CEM]
103 S. Andres St., Luxemburg, 52065. Tel: 563-870-4041; Email: dbq104@dbqarch.org; Web: sites.google.com/site/lasallepastorate. 835 Church St., P.O. Box 398, Holy Cross, 52053. Rev. Noah J. Diehm.
See LaSalle Elementary Schools, Holy Cross under Elementary School Systems located in the Institution section.

MANCHESTER, DELAWARE CO., ST. MARY'S CHURCH, MANCHESTER, IOWA (1872) [CEM]
119 W. Fayette St., Manchester, 52057-1596. Tel: 563-927-4710; Email: dbq123@dbqarch.org; Web: www.blessedtrinitycluster.org. Revs. Gabriel C. Anderson; John R. Kremer, Sacramental Min.; Deacon Dave Loecke.
School—St. Mary School, (Grades K-6), 132 W. Butler, Manchester, 52057-1502. Tel: 563-927-3689; Email: dbqe37@dbqarch.org. Kelley Harbach, Prin. Lay Teachers 15; Students 199.

MANLY, WORTH CO., SACRED HEART CHURCH, MANLY, IOWA (1883) [CEM]
412 N. Broadway, P.O. Box 160, Manly, 50456-0160. Tel: 641-454-2586; Email: dbq130@dbqarch.org. Revs. Neil J. Manternach; Jacob D. Rouse; Deacons Matthew F. Berry; Michael G. Byrne; Charles Cooper.

MAQUOKETA, JACKSON CO., THE SACRED HEART CHURCH, MAQUOKETA, IOWA (1873) [CEM]
200 S. Vermont St., Maquoketa, 52060. Tel: 563-652-6931; Email: dbq125@dbqarch.org; Web: www.sacredheartparishmaquoketa.webs.com. Rev. Austin J. Wilker; Deacon Greg Michel.
School—Sacred Heart School, (Grades PreK-6), 806 Eddy St., Maquoketa, 52060. Tel: 563-652-3743; Email: dbqe38@dbqarch.org. Jennifer Litterer, Prin. Lay Teachers 11; Students 154.

MARION, LINN CO., ST. JOSEPH CHURCH, MARION, IOWA (1890) [JC]
1790 14th St., Marion, 52302-2267. Tel: 319-377-4869; Email: dbq126@dbqarch.org; Web: www.stjoesmarion.org. Revs. David H. O'Connor; Mark Kwenin; Deacons Kenneth Bauer; Dennis Ternes.
School—St. Joseph School, (Grades PreK-8), 1430 14th St., Marion, 52302-2499. Tel: 319-377-6348; Email: dbqe39@dbqarch.org. Casey Kettmann, Prin. Lay Teachers 16; Students 193.

MARSHALLTOWN, MARSHALL CO.
1—ST. HENRY'S CHURCH, MARSHALLTOWN, IOWA (1959)
221 W. Olive St., Marshalltown, 50158-4248. Tel: 641-753-7374; Email: dbq127@dbqarch.org; Web: www.sthenrychurch.com. Rev. Donald J. Czapla; Deacons Mark Dolash; Roger Polt; Gary Pusillo.
See St. Francis Catholic School, Marshalltown under Elementary School Systems located in the Institution section.
2—ST. MARY'S CHURCH, MARSHALLTOWN, IOWA (1869)
11 W. Linn St., Marshalltown, 50158. Tel: 641-752-6378; Email: dbq128@dbqarch.org; Web: www.stmarymarshalltown.weconnect.com. 107 S. 1st St., Marshalltown, 50158. Revs. Alan J. Dietzenbach; Donald J. Czapla, Sacramental Priest; Deacons Jeff Harris; Felix Hernandez; Tom Renze.
See St. Francis Catholic School, Marshalltown under Elementary School Systems located in the Institution section.

MASON CITY, CERRO GORDO CO., EPIPHANY PARISH, MASON CITY, IOWA (2012)
Mailing & Parish Office: 300 Fifth St., S.E., Mason City, 50401. Revs. Neil J. Manternach; Aaron R. Junge; Jacob D. Rouse; Deacons Matthew F. Berry; Michael G. Byrne; Charles Cooper.
Holy Family Church—716 N. Adams Ave., Mason City, 50401.
St. Joseph Church, 302 Fifth St. S.E., Mason City, 50401.
See Newman Catholic School System, Mason City under Consolidated K-12 Systems located in the Institution section.

MASONVILLE, DELAWARE CO., IMMACULATE CONCEPTION CHURCH, MASONVILLE, IOWA (1883) [CEM]
606 Bernhart St., Masonville, 50654. Email: dbq123@dbqarch.org; Web: www.blessedtrinitycluster.org. 119 W. Fayette St., Manchester, 52057. Tel: 563-927-4710. Revs. Gabriel C. Anderson; John R. Kremer, Sacramental Priest; Deacon Dave Loecke.

MCGREGOR, CLAYTON CO., ST. MARY'S CHURCH, MCGREGOR, IOWA (1873) [CEM]
311 7th St., McGregor, 52157. 405 S. East St., P.O. Box 1521, Monona, 52159. Tel: 563-539-4442; Email: dbq134@dbqarch.org; Web: www.trinitycluster.com. Rev. Nils Hernandez; Deacon Patrick J. Malanaphy.

MONONA, CLAYTON CO., ST. PATRICK'S CHURCH, MONONA, IOWA (1856) [CEM]
405 East St. S., P.O. Box 1521, Monona, 52159-0557. Tel: 563-539-4442; Email: dbq134@dbqarch.org; Web: www.trinitycluster.com. Rev. Nils Hernandez; Deacon Patrick J. Malanaphy.

MONTICELLO, JONES CO., SACRED HEART CHURCH (MONTICELLO, IOWA) (1868) [CEM]
302 N. Sycamore St., Monticello, 52310. Tel: 319-465-5994; Email: dbq136@dbqarch.org; Web: www.sacredheartstluke.com. 210 E. Third St., Monticello, 52310-1535. Rev. Paul C. Baldwin; Deacon Ed Goldsmith.
School—Sacred Heart School, (Grades PreK-6), 234 N. Sycamore, Monticello, 52310-1515. Tel: 319-465-4605; Email: dbqe42@dbqarch.org. Laura Herbers, Prin. Lay Teachers 10; Teachers 138.

MOUNT VERNON, LINN CO., ST. JOHN'S CHURCH, MT. VERNON, IOWA (1843) [CEM]
212 7th St., S.E., Mount Vernon, 52314. Tel: 319-895-6246; Email: dbq137plc@dbqarch.org; Web: www.stjohnmv.org. Revs. Philip E. Thompson, Priest Supvr.; John R. Flaherty, Sacramental Priest; Susan M. Schettler, Parish Life Coord.

NASHUA, CHICKASAW CO., ST. MICHAEL'S CHURCH, NASHUA, IOWA (1870) [CEM]
602 Cedar St., Nashua, 50658. Mailing Address & Parish Office: 612 Cedar St., P.O. Box 308, Nashua, 50658-0308. Tel: 641-435-2070; Email: dbq035@dbqarch.org. Rev. Gary A. Mayer; Deacon Michael Ward.

NEVADA, STORY CO., ST. PATRICK CHURCH, NEVADA, IOWA (1870) [CEM]
1127 10th St., Nevada, 50201. 1110 11th St., Nevada, 50201. Tel: 515-382-2974; Email: dbq192@dbqarch.org; Web: www.stpatricknevada.org. Rev. Rick D. Dagit; Deacons Steven Van Kerckvoorde; Mark Wyant.

NEW ALBIN, ALLAMAKEE CO., ST. JOSEPH CHURCH, NEW ALBIN, IOWA (1910) [CEM]
154 3rd St. N.E., New Albin, 52160. 648 Main St., Lansing, 52151. Tel: 563-538-4171; Email: dbq115@dbqarch.org; Web: www.holyfamilyofthebluffs.org. Rev. John A. Moser.

NEW HAMPTON, CHICKASAW CO., HOLY FAMILY CHURCH, NEW HAMPTON, IOWA (2002) [CEM]
202 N Broadway, New Hampton, 50659. Tel: 641-394-2105; Email: dbq141@dbqarch.org; Web: www.goodshepherdcluster.com. Parish Office & Mailing Address: 313 W. Court St., New Hampton, 50659. Very Rev. Brian M. Dellaert; Deacon Victor J. DeSloover.
School—St. Joseph Community School, (Grades PreK-8), 216 N. Broadway, New Hampton, 50659. Tel: 641-394-2865; Email: dbqe43@dbqarch.org. Christina Carlton, Prin. Lay Teachers 15; Students 169.

NEW HAVEN, MITCHELL CO., ST. PETER'S CHURCH, NEW HAVEN, IOWA (1876) [CEM]
2985 360th St., Osage, 50461. 203 7th St., Elma, 50628. Tel: 641-393-2520; Web: www.holyrosarycluster.org. Very Rev. Jerry F. Kopacek.

NEW MELLERAY, DUBUQUE CO., HOLY FAMILY CHURCH, NEW MELLERAY, PEOSTA, IOWA (1850) [CEM]
16318 Holy Family Ln., Peosta, 52068. Combined Parish Office: 10204 Key West Dr., 52003. Tel: 563-582-7392; Email: dbq111@dbqarch.org; Web: www.stjosephkeywest.com. Rev. Rodney M. Allers; Deacon Tom Lang.

NEW VIENNA, DUBUQUE CO, ST. BONIFACE CHURCH OF NEW VIENNA, NEW VIENNA, IOWA (1845) [CEM]
7401 Columbus St., New Vienna, 52065. Tel: 563-875-7325; Email: dbq067@dbqarch.org; Web: www.spiresoffaith.com. 104 Third St. S.W., Dyersville, 52040. Very Rev. Dennis J. Quint; Revs. Dennis C. Conway; Ralph E. Davis; Deacons Roger Riesberg; James Steger.

NEWHALL, BENTON CO., ST. PAUL'S CHURCH, NEWHALL, IOWA (1914)
306 3rd Ave., Newhall, 52315. 405 Fourth Ave., P.O. Box 250, Van Horne, 52346-0250. Tel: 319-228-8131; Email: dbq150@dbqarch.org; Web: www.queenofsaints.com. Rev. Craig E. Steimel; Deacon Robert Pailthorpe.

NORTH BUENA VISTA, CLAYTON CO., IMMACULATE CONCEPTION CHURCH, NORTH BUENA VISTA, IOWA (1898) [CEM]
218 Main St., North Buena Vista, 52066. Tel: 563-252-1247; Email: dbq096@dbqarch.org; Web: www.maryicjoseph.org. Mailing Address & Office: 520 S. 2nd St., P.O. Box 847, Guttenberg, 52052-0847. Rev. Marvin J. Bries; Deacon James Pfaffly, Dir. Faith Formation.
See St. Mary & Immaculate Conception School System, Guttenberg under Elementary School Systems located in the Institution Section.

NORTH WASHINGTON, CHICKASAW CO., IMMACULATE CONCEPTION CHURCH, NORTH WASHINGTON, IOWA (1868) [CEM]
114 N. Wapsi, North Washington, 50659. Tel: 641-394-2105; Email: dbq141@dbqarch.org; Web: www.goodshepherdcatholiccluster.com. 313 W. Court St., New Hampton, 50659. Very Rev. Brian M. Dellaert; Deacon Victor J. DeSloover.

NORWAY, BENTON CO., ST. MICHAEL CHURCH, NORWAY, IOWA (1867) [CEM]
512 Evergreen St., Norway, 52318. 405 Fourth Ave., P.O. Box 250, Van Horne, 52346-0250. Tel: 319-228-8131; Email: dbq150@dbqarch.org; Web: www.queenofsaints.com. Rev. Craig E. Steimel; Deacon Robert Pailthorpe.

OELWEIN, FAYETTE CO., SACRED HEART CHURCH, OELWEIN, IOWA (1876) [CEM]
626 S. Frederick Ave., Oelwein, 50662. Tel: 319-283-3743; Email: dbq150@dbqarch.org; Web: www.sacredheartoelwein.com. 600 1st Ave. S.W., Oelwein, 50662. Rev. Ray E. Atwood; Deacon Jim Patera.
School—Sacred Heart School, (Grades K-6), 601 First Ave., S.W., Oelwein, 50662. Tel: 319-283-1366;

Email: dbqe44@dbqarch.org. Deacon Michael Ward, Prin. Lay Teachers 10; Students 108.

OSAGE, MITCHELL CO., SACRED HEART CHURCH (OSAGE, IOWA) (1878) [CEM]
1204 State St., Osage, 50461. Tel: 641-732-4342; Email: dbq152@dbqarch.org; Web: www.stisidorecluster.org. 218 S. 12th St., Osage, 50461. Rev. Raymond A. Burkle.

OSSIAN, WINNESHIEK CO., ST. FRANCIS CHURCH, OSSIAN, IOWA (1876) [CEM]
420 E. Main St., Ossian, 52161. Tel: 563-562-3045; Email: dbq019@dbqarch.org; Web: www.CFOparishes.org. Mailing Address: P.O. Box 819, Calmar, 52132-0819. Rev. G. Robert Gross; Deacon Dan O'Brien.
School—St. Francis de Sales School, (Grades K-8), 414 E. Main St., Ossian, 52161. Tel: 563-532-9353; Email: dbqe46@dbqarch.org. Kristin Kriener, Prin. Lay Teachers 12; Students 109.

OTTER CREEK, JACKSON CO., ST. LAWRENCE CHURCH, OTTER CREEK, IOWA (1854) [CEM]
17434 Bellevue-Cascade Rd., Zwingle, 52079.
Tel: 563-652-6931; Email: dbq125@dbqarch.org. 200 S. Vermont, Maquoketa, 52060. Rev. Austin J. Wilker; Deacon Greg Michel.

OXFORD JUNCTION, JONES CO., SACRED HEART CHURCH (OXFORD JUNCTION, IOWA) (1890) A parish within the territory of the Archdiocese of Dubuque, but served by the Diocese of Davenport.
309 Church St., Oxford Junction, 52323.
Tel: 563-678-2200; Email: dbq155@dbqarch.org; Web: www.sacredheartoj.org. 903 Main St., P.O. Box 127, Lost Nation, 52254-0127. Rev. Francis Odoom, (Ghana).

PEOSTA, DUBUQUE CO., ST. JOHN THE BAPTIST CHURCH OF PEOSTA, IOWA (1874) [CEM]
235 Peosta St., Peosta, 52068. Tel: 563-876-5540; Email: dbq076@dbqarch.org; Web: www.stelizabethpastorate.com. 104 First St., S.E., P.O. Box 286, Epworth, 52045-0286. Revs. Michael G. Schueller; Phillip F. Kruse, Sacramental Priest; Deacons Gerald Koopmann; Dan O'Connell; John Wolfe.
See Seton Catholic Schools, Farley under Elementary School Systems located in the Institution section.

PETERSBURG, DELAWARE CO., S.S. PETER AND PAUL CHURCH, PETERSBURG, IOWA (1867) [CEM]
1625 300th Ave., Dyersville, 52040.
Tel: 563-875-7992; Email: dbq067@dbqarch.org; Web: www.spiresoffaith.com. 104 Third St. S.W., Dyersville, 52040. Very Rev. Dennis J. Quint; Revs. Dennis C. Conway; Ralph E. Davis; Deacons Roger Riesberg; James Steger.

PLACID, DUBUQUE CO., ST. JOHN CHURCH, PLACID, EPWORTH, IOWA (1874) [CEM]
22481 E. Pleasant Grove Rd., Epworth, 52045.
Tel: 563-876-5540; Email: dbq076@dbqarch.org; Web: www.stelizabethpastorate.com. 104 1st St. S.E., P.O. Box 286, Epworth, 52045-0286. Revs. Michael G. Schueller; Phillip F. Kruse, Sacramental Priest; Deacons Gerald Koopmann; Dan O'Connell; John Wolfe.
See Seton Catholic Schools, Farley under Elementary School Systems located in the Institution section.

POSTVILLE, ALLAMAKEE CO., ST. BRIDGET CHURCH (POSTVILLE, IOWA) (1872)
135 W. Williams St., Postville, 52162.
Tel: 563-539-4442; Email: dbq134@dbqarch.org; Web: www.trinitycluster.com. Mailing Address & Parish Office: 405 S. East St., P.O. Box 1521, Monona, 52159-0557. Rev. Nils Hernandez; Deacon Patrick J. Malanaphy.

PRAIRIEBURG, LINN CO., ST. JOSEPH'S CHURCH, PRAIRIEBURG, IOWA (1874) [CEM]
300 West Ave., Prairieburg, 52219. 4700 Valley Farm Rd., P.O. Box 496, Central City, 52214-0496.
Tel: 319-438-6625; Email: dbq005@dbqarch.org; Web: www.northlinncc.org. Rev. Nicholas B. March.

PRESTON, JACKSON CO., ST. JOSEPH'S CHURCH, PRESTON, IOWA (1881) [CEM]
250 S. Faith St., P.O. Box 309, Preston, 52069-0309.
Tel: 563-689-5161; Email: dbq125@dbqarch.org; Web: www.stjosephprestonia.com. Rev. Austin J. Wilker; Deacon Greg Michel.

PROTIVIN, HOWARD CO., HOLY TRINITY CHURCH, PROTIVIN, IOWA (1878) [CEM]
124 N. Main St., Protivin, 52163. Tel: 563-569-8259; Email: dbq166@dbqarch.org; Web: www.christourhopecluster.com. Mailing Address: 110 Commercial Ave., P.O. Box 205, Protivin, 52163-0205. Rev. Aaron R. Junge; Deacon Jim Zajicek.
See Trinity Catholic School, Protovin under Elementary School Systems located in the Institution Section.

RAYMOND, BLACKHAWK CO., ST. JOSEPH'S CHURCH, RAYMOND, IOWA (1905) [CEM]
313 E. Central St., Raymond, 50667. 311 15th Ave., P.O. Box 136, Gilbertville, 50634. Tel: 319-296-1092; Email: dbq092@dbqarch.org; Web: www.icsjchurch.com. Rev. Henry P. Huber.
See Bosco Catholic School System, Gilbertville, Iowa under Consolidated K-12 Systems located in the Institution section.

REINBECK, GRUNDY CO., HOLY FAMILY CHURCH, REINBECK, IOWA (2004)
Tel: 319-345-2006; Email: dbq169@dbqarch.org; Web: www.holyfamilycatholicparish.com. Rev. David G. Kucera; Deacons Greg Lievens; John Schwennen.
St. Gabriel Church—21275 U Ave., Reinbeck, 50669.
St. Patrick Church, 302 Second St., Parkersburg, 50665.

RICEVILLE, HOWARD CO., IMMACULATE CONCEPTION CHURCH, RICEVILLE, IOWA (1879) [CEM]
211 E. Main St., Riceville, 50466. Tel: 641-393-2520; Web: www.holyrosarycluster.org. 203 7th St., Elma, 50628. Very Rev. Jerry F. Kopacek.

RICKARDSVILLE, DUBUQUE CO., ST. JOSEPH CHURCH, RICKADSVILLE, IOWA (1840) [CEM]
20249 St. Joseph Dr., Durango, 52039. 835 Church St., P.O. Box 398, Holy Cross, 52053.
Tel: 563-870-4041; Email: dbq104@dbqarch.org; Web: sites.google.com/site/lasallepastorate. Rev. Noah J. Diehm.
See LaSalle Elementary Schools, Holy Cross under Elementary School Systems located in the Institution section.

ROCKFORD, FLOYD CO., THE HOLY NAME CHURCH, ROCKFORD, IOWA (1910)
507 First Ave. N.W., Rockford, 50468.
Tel: 641-756-3569; Email: dbq094@dbqarch.org. Rev. Msgr. Walter L. Brunkan; Deacon Matt Miller.

ROCKWELL, CERRO GORDO CO., SACRED HEART CHURCH (ROCKWELL, IOWA) (1878) [CEM]
305 Elm St. E., P.O. Box 30, Rockwell, 50469.
Tel: 641-822-4950; Email: dbq040@dbqarch.org; Web: www.sacredheartrockwell.org. 316 3rd St. N., Rockwell, 50469-0030. Rev. John A. Gossman.

ROSEVILLE, FLOYD CO., ST. MARY CHURCH (ROSEVILLE), MARBLE ROCK, IOWA (1867) [CEM]
2397 Hwy. 14, Marble Rock, 50653.
Tel: 641-823-4146; Email: dbq094@dbqarch.org. 105 N. Main, P.O. Box 480, Greene, 50636-0480. Rev. Msgr. Walter L. Brunkan; Deacon Matt Miller.

RYAN, DELAWARE CO., ST. PATRICK'S CHURCH, RYAN, IOWA (1882) [CEM]
600 Franklin St., Ryan, 52330. 119 W. Fayette St., Manchester, 52057. Tel: 563-927-4710; Email: dbq123@dbqarch.org; Web: www.blessedtrinitycluster.org. Revs. Gabriel C. Anderson; John R. Kremer, Sacramental Priest; Deacon Dave Loecke.

ST. CATHERINE, DUBUQUE CO., ST. CATHERINE CHURCH, ST. CATHERINE, IOWA (1887) [CEM]
5189 St. Catherine Rd, 52003. Tel: 563-582-7392; Email: dbq111@dbqarch.org; Web: www.stjosephkeywest.com. 10204 Key West Dr., 52003. Rev. Rodney M. Allers; Deacon Tom Lang.
See Marquette High School Bellevue under Consolidated K-12 Systems located in the Institution section.

ST. DONATUS, JACKSON CO., ST. DONATUS CHURCH, ST. DONATUS, IOWA (1853) [CEM]
97 1st St. E., St. Donatus, 52071. 10204 Key West Dr., 52003. Tel: 563-582-7392; Email: dbq111@dbqarch.org; Web: www.stjosephkeywest.com. Rev. Rodney M. Allers; Deacon Tom Lang.
See Marquette High School, Bellevue under Consolidated K-12 Systems located in the Institution section.

ST. LUCAS, FAYETTE CO., ST. LUKE'S CHURCH, ST. LUCAS, IOWA (1855) [CEM]
215 E. Main, St. Lucas, 52166. Mailing Address: 110 Commercial Ave., P.O. Box 205, Protivin, 52163-0205. Tel: 563-569-8259; Email: dbq166@dbqarch.org; Web: www.christourhopecluster.com. Rev. Aaron R. Junge; Deacon Jim Zajicek.
See Trinity Catholic School, Protivin under Elementary School Systems located in the Institution section.

SHERRILL, DUBUQUE CO., S.S. PETER AND PAUL CHURCH, SHERRILL, IOWA (1852) [CEM]
5131 Sherrill Rd., Sherrill, 52073. Tel: 563-870-4041; Email: dbq104@dbqarch.org; Web: sites.google.com/site/lasallepastorate. 835 Church St., P.O. Box 398, Holy Cross, 52053-0398. Rev. Noah J. Diehm.
See LaSalle Catholic Schools, Holy Cross under Elementary School Systems located in the Institution section.

SPILLVILLE, WINNESHIEK CO., ST. WENCESLAUS CHURCH, SPILLVILLE, IOWA (1860) [CEM]
207 Church St., Spillville, 52168. Tel: 563-562-3045; Email: dbq019@dbqarch.org; Web: www.CFOparishes.org. Mailing Address: P.O. Box 819, Calmar, 52132-0819. Rev. G. Robert Gross; Deacon Dan O'Brien.
See Calmar-Festina-Spillville Catholic School, Calmar under Elementary School Systems located in the Institution section.

SPRINGBROOK, JACKSON CO., SS. PETER AND PAUL CHURCH, SPRINGBROOK, IOWA (1864) [CEM]
107 E. Main St., Springbrook, 52075.
Tel: 563-872-3875; Email: dbq012@dbqarch.org; Web: www.stjosephbellevue.org. Mailing Address: 105 E. Main St., P.O. Box 97, Springbrook, 52075. Rev. Dennis W. Miller; Deacons Loras Weber; Robert Wood.
See Marquette High School, Bellevue under Consolidated K-12 Systems located in the Institution section.

SPRINGVILLE, LINN CO., SAINT ISIDORE CHURCH, SPRINGVILLE, IOWA (1961)
603 6th St. S., P.O. Box 318, Springville, 52336.
Tel: 319-854-6141; Email: dbq137PLC@dbqarch.org; Web: www.stisidorespringville.org. Revs. Philip E. Thompson, Priest Supvr.; Jack R. Flaherty, Sacramental Priest; Susan M. Schettler, Parish Life Coord.

STACYVILLE, MITCHELL CO., VISITATION CHURCH, STACYVILLE, IOWA (1894) [CEM]
604 N Broad St., Stacyville, 50476. Web: www.stisidorecluster.org. Parish Office & Mailing Address: 218 S. 12th St., Osage, 50461.
Tel: 641-732-4342; Email: dbq152@dbqarch.org. Rev. Raymond A. Burkle.

STATE CENTER, MARSHALL CO., ST. JOSEPH'S CHURCH, STATE CENTER, IOWA (1870) [CEM]
610 3rd St. S.W., State Center, 50247.
Tel: 641-377-2710; Email: dbq192@dbqarch.org. 410 Bailey St., P.O. Box 236, Colo, 50056. Rev. Rick D. Dagit; Deacons Steven Van Kerckvoorde; Mark Wyant.

STRAWBERRY POINT, CLAYTON CO., ST. MARY CHURCH, STRAWBERRY POINT, IOWA (1876) [CEM]
320 W. Mission St., Strawberry Point, 52076-9432.
Tel: 563-933-6166; Email: dbq072@dbqarch.org; Web: www.vibrantcatholic.com. Mailing Address: 314 W. Mission St., Strawberry Point, 52076-9432. Rev. John S. Haugen.

SUMNER, BREMER CO., IMMACULATE CONCEPTION CHURCH, SUMNER, IOWA (1894) [CEM]
413 W. First St., Sumner, 50674-1313.
Tel: 563-578-5366; Email: dbq195@dbqarch.org; Web: www.stjosephtheworkercluster.com. Rev. Donald T. Komboh, (Nigeria); Deacon Michael Schemmel.

TAMA, TAMA CO., ST. PATRICK'S CHURCH, TAMA, IOWA (1864) [CEM]
900 Park St., Tama, 52339. Tel: 641-484-3039; Email: dbq197@dbqarch.org; Web: www.circleofsaints.weconnect.com. Very Rev. Michael J. Mescher; Deacons Joe Behounek; Stan Upah.

TEMPLE HILL, JONES CO., ST. PETER'S CHURCH, TEMPLE HILL, CASCADE, IOWA (1852) [CEM]
20123 Temple Hill Rd., Cascade, 52033. 408 Third Ave. N.W., P.O. Box 699, Cascade, 52033-0699.
Tel: 563-852-3524; Email: dbqcmt1@dbqarch.org; Web: www.stapastorate.org. Rev. Douglas J. Loecke, J.C.L.; Deacons Ray Noonan; Joe Schockemoehl; Steven W. Strang.
See Aquin Educational System, Cascade under Consolidated K-12 Systems located in the Institution section.

TRAER, TAMA CO., ST. PAUL CHURCH, TRAER, IOWA (1912) [CEM]
1102 Walnut St., Traer, 50675-1440.
Tel: 319-478-2222; Email: dbq199@dbqarch.org; Web: www.princeofpeacecluster.com. Rev. Michael O. Hutchison.

URBANA, BENTON CO., ST. MARY'S CHURCH, URBANA, IOWA (1872) [JC]
402 Ash Ave., Urbana, 52345. Mailing Address: 516 Rowley St., P.O. Box 116, Walker, 52352-0116.
Tel: 319-448-4241; Email: dbq203PLC@dbqarch.org; Web: www.heartofmary.org. Very Rev. Mark A. Ressler, Priest Supvr.; Rev. James P. Brokman, Sacramental Priest; Deacon Steven Ford; Marcia Reilly, Parish Life Coord.

VAN HORNE, BENTON CO., IMMACULATE CONCEPTION CHURCH, VAN HORNE, IOWA (1869) [CEM]
405 Fourth Ave., P.O. Box 250, Van Horne, 52346-0250. Tel: 319-228-8131; Email: dbq150@dbqarch.org; Web: www.queenofsaints.com. Rev. Craig E. Steimel; Deacon Robert Pailthorpe.

VINTON, BENTON CO., ST. MARY CHURCH, VINTON, IOWA (1878) [CEM]
2200 Second Ave., Vinton, 52349. Tel: 319-472-3368; Email: dbq203PLC@dbqarch.org; Web: www.heartofmary.org. Very Rev. Mark A. Ressler, Priest Supvr.; Rev. James P. Brokman, Sacramental Priest; Deacon Steven Ford; Marcia Reilly, Parish Life Coord.

VOLGA, CLAYTON CO., SACRED HEART CHURCH (VOLGA CITY, IOWA) (1889) [CEM]
306 White St., Volga, 52077. Tel: 563-928-7200; Email: dbq072@dbqarch.org; Web: www.vibrantcatholic.com. Mailing Address: P.O. Box 135, Volga, 52077-0135. Rev. John S. Haugen.

WALKER, LINN CO., SACRED HEART CHURCH, WALKER, IOWA (1885) [CEM]
518 Rowley St., Walker, 52352. Tel: 319-448-4241; Email: dbq203PLC@dbqarch.org; Web: www.heartofmary.org. 516 Rowley St., P.O. Box 116,

Walker, 52352. Very Rev. Mark A. Ressler, Priest Supvr.; Rev. James P. Brokman, Sacramental Priest; Deacon Steven Ford; Marcia Reilly, Parish Life Coord.

WATERLOO, BLACKHAWK CO.

1—BLESSED SACRAMENT CHURCH, WATERLOO, IOWA (1947) [JC]
Church, Res. & Office: 650 Stephan Ave., Waterloo, 50701. Tel: 319-233-6179; Email: dbq208@dbqarch.org; Web: www.blessedsacramentwaterloo.org. Rev. Anthony J. Kruse; Deacons Chris Evans; Robert Stirm.
See Cedar Valley Catholic Schools under Consolidated K-12 Systems located in the Institution Section.

2—ST. EDWARD'S CHURCH, WATERLOO, IOWA (1945) [JC]
1425 Kimball Ave., Waterloo, 50702.
Tel: 319-233-8060; Email: dbq210@dbqarch.org; Web: www.sted.org. 1423 Kimball Ave., Waterloo, 50702. Rev. Scott E. Bullock, J.C.L.; Deacons Raymond Larsen; Richard Lynch.
See Cedar Valley Catholic Schools under Consolidated K-12 Systems located in the Institution Section.

3—QUEEN OF PEACE CHURCH, WATERLOO, IOWA (2002) [JC]
320 Mulberry St., Waterloo, 50703.
Tel: 319-226-3655; Email: dbq213@dbqarch.org; Web: www.cedarnet.org/dbq213. Rev. Pierre Louis Joseph; Deacon Rigoberto Real.
See Cedar Valley Catholic Schools under Consolidated K-12 Systems located in the Institution Section.

4—SACRED HEART CHURCH, WATERLOO, IOWA (1909) [JC]
623 W. Fourth St., Waterloo, 50702.
Tel: 319-234-4996; Email: dbq209@dbqarch.org; Web: www.sacredheartwloo.org. 627 W. Fourth St., Waterloo, 50702. Revs. Kenneth C. Stecher; Luigi Htya Ruh, (Myanmar); Deacon Dan Rigel.
See Cedar Valley Catholic Schools under Consolidated K-12 Systems located in the Institution Section.

WATKINS, BENTON CO., ST. PATRICK CHURCH, WATKINS, IOWA (1880) [CEM]
109 2nd St., Watkins, 52354. Cluster Office & Mailing Address: 405 Fourth Ave., P.O. Box 250, Van Horne, 52346. Tel: 319-228-8131; Email: dbq150@dbqarch.org; Web: www.queenofsaints.com. Rev. Craig E. Steimel; Deacon Robert Pailthorpe.

WAUCOMA, FAYETTE CO., ST. MARY CHURCH, WAUCOMA, IOWA (1898) [CEM]
218 3rd St. N.W., Waucoma, 52171. 110 Commercial Ave., P.O. Box 205, Protivin, 52163-0205.
Tel: 563-569-8259; Email: dbq166@dbqarch.org; Web: www.christourhopecluster.com. Rev. Aaron R. Junge; Deacon Jim Zajicek.

WAUKON, ALLAMAKEE CO., ST. PATRICK'S CHURCH, WAUKON, IOWA (1851) [CEM]
101 Second St., S.W., Waukon, 52172. 109 Second St., S.W., P.O. Box 146, Waukon, 52172.
Tel: 563-568-3671; Email: dbq216@dbqarch.org; Web: www.stpatrickwaukon.weconnect.com. Rev. Mark Osterhaus; Deacon Jeff Molitor.
School—St. Patrick School, (Grades K-6), 200 Second St., S.W., Waukon, 52172. Tel: 563-568-2415; Email: dbqe54@dbqarch.org. Katherine Fahey, Prin. Lay Teachers 16; Students 232.

WAVERLY, BREMER CO., ST. MARY'S CHURCH, WAVERLY, IOWA (1856) [CEM]
2700 Horton Rd., Waverly, 50677. Tel: 319-352-2493; Email: dbq217@dbqarch.org; Web: www.stmarysfamily.com. Rev. David J. Ambrosy; Deacon Phil Paladino.

WEBSTER CITY, HAMILTON CO., ST. THOMAS AQUINAS CHURCH, WEBSTER CITY, IOWA (1870) [CEM]
1008 Des Moines St., Webster City, 50595-2147.
Tel: 515-832-1190; Email: dbq218@dbqarch.org; Web: www.stthomaswc.org. 1000 Des Moines St., Webster City, 50595-2147. Very Rev. Stephen L. Meyer.
School—St. Thomas Aquinas School, (Grades K-6), 624 Dubuque St., Webster City, 50595-2245.
Tel: 515-832-1346; Email: dbqe55@dbqarch.org. Duane Siepker, Prin. Lay Teachers 9; Students 104.

WEST UNION, FAYETTE CO., HOLY NAME CHURCH, WEST UNION, IOWA (1870) [CEM]
128 N. Walnut St., West Union, 52175.
Tel: 563-422-3184; Email: dbq195@dbqarch.org; Web: www.stjosephtheworkercluster.com. Rev. Donald T. Komboh, (Nigeria); Deacon Michael Schemmel.

WEXFORD, ALLAMAKEE CO., IMMACULATE CONCEPTION CHURCH, WEXFORD, IOWA (1851) [CEM]
1416 Great River Rd., Lansing, 52151.
Tel: 563-538-4171; Email: dbq115@dbqarch.org; Web: www.icwexford.org. 648 Main St., Lansing, 52151. Rev. John A. Moser.

WILLIAMS, HAMILTON CO., ST. MARY CHURCH, WILLIAMS, IOWA (1875) [CEM]
404 4th St., Williams, 50271. 1000 Des Moines St., Webster City, 50595-2147. Tel: 515-832-1190; Email: dbq218@dbqarch.org; Web: www.sthomaswc.org. Very Rev. Stephen L. Meyer.

WINTHROP, BUCHANAN CO., ST. PATRICK CHURCH, WINTHROP, IOWA (1894) [CEM]
555 1st St. S., Winthrop, 50682. 209 5th Ave. N.E., Independence, 50644. Tel: 319-334-7191; Email: dbq106@dbqarch.org. Rev. David M. Beckman; Deacon Tim Post.

WORTHINGTON, DUBUQUE CO., ST. PAUL CHURCH, WORTHINGTON, IOWA (1875) [CEM]
301 2nd Ave., S.W., Worthington, 52078. 309 3rd Ave., S.W., P.O. Box 68, Worthington, 52078-0068.
Tel: 563-855-2125; Email: dbq067@dbqarch.org; Web: www.spiresoffaith.com. Very Rev. Dennis J. Quint; Revs. Dennis C. Conway; Ralph E. Davis; Deacons Roger Riesberg; James Steger.

ZEARING, STORY CO., ST. GABRIEL CHURCH, ZEARING, IOWA (1904)
302 N. Center St., Zearing, 50278. Tel: 641-377-2710; Email: dbq192@dbqarch.org. Mailing Address: 410 Bailey St., P.O. Box 236, Colo, 50056-0236. Rev. Rick D. Dagit; Deacons Steven Van Kerckvoorde; Mark Wyant.

Military Chaplains:
Rev.—
Lawrence, Andrew, Chap. COL, 8235 Forrester Blvd., Springfield, VA 22152.

On Special or Other Archdiocesan Assignment:
Rev. Msgr.—
Toale, Thomas E., Ph.D., Vicar General
Very Rev.—
Gehling, Kenneth B., Chap., Mercy Medical Center, North Iowa, Mason City
Revs.—
McDermott, Thomas J., Spiritual Dir., St. Pius X Seminary, 1235 Mt. Loretta Ave., 52003. Tel: 563-556-1054
Schatz, David A., M.A., Rector, St. Pius X Seminary, 1235 Mt. Loretta Ave., 52003
Seda, Jon M., Vocations Dir., St. Stephen the Witness Catholic Student Center, 1019 W. 23rd St., Cedar Falls, 50613. Tel: 319-266-9863.

International Priests Serving in the Archdiocese of Dubuque:
Revs.—
Adawu, Anthony, (Archdiocese of the Cape Coast, Ghana); Chap., Mt. Mercy University, Cedar Rapids
Attah-Nsiah, Paul, (Diocese of Konongo-Mampong, Ghana); Dubuque
Awotwe-Mensah, Andrew, (Archdiocese of the Cape Coast, Ghana); Dubuque
Farinto, Solomon, (Diocese of Illorin, Nigeria); Chap., Covenant Medical Center, Waterloo
Htya Ruh, Luigi, (Diocese of Loikaw, Myanmar); Sacred Heart, Waterloo
Hutchison, Michael O., (Diocese of Konongo-Mampong, Ghana); Traer
Joseph, Pierre Louis, (Diocese of Hinche, Haiti); Queen of Peace, Waterloo
Komboh, Donald T., (Nigeria) (Diocese of Jalingo, Nigeria); Sumner
Kwenin, Mark, (Archdiocese of the Cape Coast, Ghana); Marion
Mensah, Philip, (Archdiocese of the Cape Coast, Ghana); Chap., Stonehill Franciscan Services, Dubuque
Nana Andoh, Raphael, (Archdiocese of the Cape Coast, Ghana); Chap., Mercy Medical Center, Dubuque.

Retired:
Rev. Msgrs.—
Barta, James O., Ph.D., (Retired), 1155 Mt. Loretta Ave., 52003. Tel: 563-583-2321
Bleich, Russell M., S.T.L., (Retired), 1155 Mount Loretta Ave., 52003. Tel: 319-366-1070
Dalton, John W., (Retired), 1400 Brookdale Rd., Naperville, IL 60563. Tel: 630-355-2664
Funke, Richard P., J.C.L., (Retired), 7974 Sailboat Key Blvd., #602, South Pasadena, FL 33707. Tel: 727-363-1754
Glovik, Karl L., (Retired), 1155 Mt. Loretta Ave., 52003. Tel: 563-556-4378
Hawes, Cletus J., (Retired), 2423 Wexford Hollow Dr., Lansing, 52151. Tel: 563-568-2154
Hemann, John W., (Retired), 481 N. Shore Dr., Apt. #301, Clear Lake, 50428-1368. Tel: 641-357-4539
Knepper, Daniel J., (Retired), 1155 Mount Loretta Ave., 52003
Laughlin, Martin T., (Retired), IN. 376 W. Hayden Dr., #914, Carmel, IN 46032
Lechtenberg, Edward W., (Retired), 321 Diagonal St., P.O. Box 104, Lansing, 52151. Tel: 563-538-4773
McClean, John R., (Retired), 1155 Mt. Loretta Ave., 52003. Tel: 563-556-1922
Ressler, Wayne A., (Retired), 3485 Windsor Ave., 52001
Schmitt, Carl L., (Retired), 619 Rural St., New Hampton, 50659. Tel: 641-330-4030
Simington, Ralph P., (Retired), 931 E. Ridgeway Ave., Waterloo, 50702. Tel: 319-236-6638
Slepicka, Joseph J., (Retired), 313 N. 13th St., Clear Lake, 50428. Tel: 641-357-2448
Steimel, Paul T., (Retired), 3709 W. 9th St., Apt. 8, Waterloo, 50702. Tel: 319-233-5287
Walz, W. Dean, J.C.D., (Retired), 24701 207th Ave., P.O. Box 182, Delhi, 52223-0182. Tel: 563-927-6672
Wilgenbusch, Lyle L., (Retired), 10204 Key West Dr., Apt. A, 52003. Tel: 319-230-0443
Revs.—
Bakewell, Donald V., (Retired), 4010 Mount Alpine, 52001. Tel: 563-845-0672
Barta, Ardel H., (Retired), 1155 Mt. Loretta Ave., 52003. Tel: 563-581-6720
Beck, Robert R., (Retired), 1220 N. Booth, 52001. Tel: 563-583-4230
Braak, Thomas E., (Retired), 205 W. Ingledue St., Marshalltown, 50158. Tel: 641-752-3846
Cahill, Dennis H., (Retired), 1155 Mt. Loretta Ave., 52003. Tel: 563-556-0180
Carpender, John W., (Retired), 720 Duggan Dr., #1, 52003-0250. Tel: 563-582-6993
Chappell, James T., (Retired), 17486 Bellevue Cascade Rd., Zwingle, 52079. Tel: 563-590-0280
Condon, Gerald A., (Retired), 130 Thompson Dr., S.E., #120, Cedar Rapids, 52403. Tel: 319-366-1287
Drexler, Harold J., (Retired), 3485 Windsor Ave., 52001. Tel: 563-556-7197
Droessler, Wayne J., (Retired), P. O. Box 365, Central City, 52214-0365. Tel: 319-540-0651
Fangmann, Frederick C., (Retired), 3485 Windsor Ave., 52001. Tel: 563-557-3717
Friedell, Ronald G., (Retired), 1001 Assisi Dr., #301, 52001. Tel: 563-556-1285
Gaul, Richard G., (Retired), 114 N. 1st St., Guttenberg, 52052. Tel: 563-880-2898
Grady, Bernard C., (Retired), 610 E. Boone St., Marshalltown, 50158
Hauer, Joseph L., J.C.D., 2301 Matthew John Dr., 52002. Tel: 563-542-4148
Hawes, Donald J., (Retired), 2423 Wexford Hollow Dr., Lansing, 52151. Tel: 563-568-2154
Hemann, Melvin D., (Retired), 29 Lincoln Ln., Palm Coast, FL 32137. Tel: 319-230-4957
Herzog, John M., (Retired), 1004 Mesa Verde Pl., Ames, 50014. Tel: 515-292-0558
Jaeger, Louis M., (Retired), 200 McCarren Dr., Apt. 201, Manchester, 52057. Tel: 319-215-9234
Juhl, Dennis D., (Retired), 2709 29th Ave., Marion, 52302. Tel: 319-432-5433
Karnik, George W., (Retired), 750 River Forest Rd., #35, Evansdale, 50707. Tel: 319-226-5412
Klein, Donald L., (Retired), 3492 Laurel Ln., Marion, 52302-8000. Tel: 319-377-1530
Kleinfehn, Walter J., (Retired), 4850 16th Ave., S.W., Apt. 103, Cedar Rapids, 52404. Tel: 319-390-0643
Knipper, Daniel J., (Retired), 502 Valley Dr., #24, Decorah, 52101. Tel: 563-568-7913
Koelker, Harry H., (Retired), 1155 Mt. Loretta Ave., 52001. Tel: 563-556-5024
Krapfl, Gary F., (Retired), 1960 Great River Rd., Lansing, 52151. Tel: 563-380-4682
Kuhn, Richard W., (Retired), P.O. Box 286, Epworth, 52045-0286
Kutsch, Eugene C., (Retired), 1155 Mt. Loretta Ave., 52003. Tel: 563-583-1638
Lundgren, Stephen A., (Retired), 255 Avenida Grenada, Unit 811, Palm Springs, CA 92264. Tel: 815-281-0125
Manternach, Carl J., (Retired), P.O. Box 479, 52004
McAndrew, Thomas F., (Retired), 1005 Lincoln Ave., Apt. 327, 52001. Tel: 563-588-3389
McGovern, Mark J., (Retired), 1014 O Ave., N.W., Cedar Rapids, 52405. Tel: 563-543-5178
McManus, Paul C., (Retired), 335 W. Jefferson, Winthrop, 50682. Tel: 319-935-3399
Nemmers, Mark R., (Retired), 801 Davis St., #212, 52001. Tel: 563-557-5094
O'Connor, John J., (Retired), P.O. Box 242, New Vienna, 52065. Tel: 563-590-7598
Otting, Loras C., (Retired), 3485 Windsor Ave., 52001. Tel: 563-556-3143
Otting, Paul J., (Retired), 1155 Mt. Loretta Ave., 52003. Tel: 563-582-2709
Ouderkirk, Lloyd Paul, (Retired), 1001 Assisi Dr., #215, 52001
Paisley, John C., (Retired), 816 Euclid St., 52001-8123. Tel: 563-583-9242
Peters, Paul R., (Retired), P.O. Box 348, Prairie Du Chien, WI 53821. Tel: 608-874-4533

Plamondon, Donald J., J.C.L., (Retired), 1155 Mt. Loretta Ave., 52003. Tel: 563-556-5095
Ptacek, John P., (Retired), 206 7th St. S.E., Farley, 52046. Tel: 563-744-9105
Recker, Philip F., (Retired), 1155 Mount Loretta Ave., 52003. Tel: 563-556-5262
Remy, David P., (Retired), 1746 Sunset Pl., Fort Myers, FL 33901. Tel: 850-207-0474
Reuter, Lloyd E., (Retired), 1905 5th St., P.O. Box 114, Gilbertville, 50634. Tel: 319-296-0848
Ries, Carl A., (Retired), 614 9th Ave., S.E., Dyersville, 52040. Tel: 563-875-9142
Salz, Marvin C., (Retired), 504 Short Ave., #135, New Hampton, 50659. Tel: 641-257-7805
Schaefer, Richard L., (Retired), P.O. Box 3014, 52004. Tel: 563-582-4030
Schmitt, Phillip E., (Retired), 212-1/2 7th St., S.E., Mt. Vernon, 52314-1518. Tel: 319-895-0404
Schneider, Joseph M., (Retired), P.O. Box 324, Brownsville, MN 55919
Tauke, Michael L., (Retired), 1127 Elizabeth Dr., Waverly, 50677. Tel: 319-483-5214
Tegeler, Herbert L., (Retired), 813 Tyler St., Cascade, 52033. Tel: 563-852-7224
Tilp, John R., (Retired), 2700 Matthew John Dr., Apt. 111, Des Moines, 52002. Tel: 515-279-0866
Vorwald, Aloysius J., (Retired), 203 3rd St., S.W. #2, Dyersville, 52040. Tel: 563-875-2627
Wild, Alexander, (Retired), 815 Duke Dr., #410, Grand Forks, ND 58201
Zee, Louis C., (Retired), 3315 Country Club Blvd., Stafford, TX 77477. Tel: 281-967-1912.

Permanent Deacons:
Aitchison, Gary, (Retired), Ames
Bauer, Kenneth, Marion
Behounek, Joseph, Chelsea; Belle Plaine; Tama
Berger, Paul Jim, St. Ludmila, Cedar Rapids
Bernhard, Charles, St. Cecilia, Ames
Berry, Matthew F., Manly; Mason City
Biver, William, St. Columbkille, Dubuque; St. Joseph the Worker, Dubuque
Blomme, Tom, Britt; Buffalo Center; Duncan; Forest City; Garner; Lake Mills
Bortle, Mark, St. Cecilia Parish, Ames
Brinkmoeller, Dave, Holy Spirit, Dubuque
Byrne, Michael G., Mason City; Manly
Christy, Alan, St. Cecilia, Ames
Cisler, William J., (Retired), Cedar Rapids
Cooper, Charles, Mason City; Manly
Courrier, Darrel, Clear Lake
DeSloover, Vic, New Hampton; Ionia; North Washington
Dolash, Mark, St. Henry, Marshalltown
Dunn, Frank, (Retired), Dubuque
Easton, Frank, Hiawatha
Evans, Chris, Blessed Sacrament, Waterloo
Flagel, LaVerne, (Retired), Marion
Ford, Steve, Urbana; Walker; Vinton
Francois, Nick, Decorah
Froyen, Leonard, Ph.D., (Retired), Cedar Falls
Garcia, Pedro, Belmond; Clarion; Eagle Grove
Gehrke, Richard, (Retired), Oelwein
Harris, Jeff, St. Mary, Marshalltown
Head, Robert, (Retired), Maquoketa
Herman, John, (Retired), Waterloo
Hickson, William, St. Anthony, Dubuque
Hoeger, Daniel, St. Patrick, Cedar Rapids
Hurych, Robert F., Immaculate Conception & St. Wenceslaus, Cedar Rapids
Jorgensen, Gerald T., Ph.D., J.C.L., Resurrection, Dubuque
Kauffman, John, St. Matthew, Cedar Rapids
Kean, James, (Retired), Epworth
King, Travis, St. Columbkille & St. Joseph the Worker, Dubuque
Klappholz, Mike, All Saints, Cedar Rapids
Koopmann, Gerald, Placid; Epworth; Bankston; Farley; Peosta
Lang, Tom, Key West; New Melleray; St. Catherine & St. Donatus
Larsen, Raymond, St. Edward, Waterloo
Lievens, Greg, Reinbeck
Loecke, Dave, Manchester; Masonville; Ryan
Luksetich, Jim, Cathedral of St. Raphael & St. Patrick Parish, Dubuque
Lynch, Richard, St. Edward, Waterloo
MacDonald, Stephen, Holy Spirit, Dubuque
Malanaphy, Patrick J., McGregor; Monona; Postville
Malone, John, (Retired), Cedar Rapids
Manning, Richard, (Retired), Cedar Rapids
Martin, Edward, All Saints Parish, Cedar Rapids
Mauss, William, St. Anthony, Dubuque
McCully, John, (Retired), Ames
McGhee, David, (Retired)
Michel, Greg, Maquoketa, Otter Creek; Preston
Miller, Matt, Greene; Rockford; Roseville
Moetsch, Michael P., Cedar Falls
Molitor, Jeff, Dorchester; Hanover; Waukon
Mulherin, Dennis, Hiawatha
Noonan, Ray, Cascade; Fillmore; Garryowen; Temple Hill
O'Brien, Dan, Calmar; Festina; Ossian; Spillville
O'Connell, Dan, Bankston; Epworth; Farley; Peosta; Placid
Pailthorpe, Robert, Blairstown; Newhall; Norway; Van Horne; Watkins
Paladino, Phil, Waverly
Patera, Jim, Oelwein; Fairbank
Peckosh, Paul, St. Raphael Cathedral & St. Patrick, Dubuque
Pfaffly, James, Guttenberg; North Buena Vista; Garnavillo
Polt, Roger, St. Henry, Marshalltown
Post, Tim, Independence; Winthrop
Pusillo, Gary, St. Henry, Marshalltown
Real, Rigoberto, Queen of Peace, Waterloo
Recker, Marvin, (Retired), Bernard
Renze, Tom, St. Mary Parish, Marshalltown
Riesberg, Roger, Dyersville; Earlville; New Vienna; Petersburg; Worthington
Rigel, Dan, Sacred Heart, Waterloo
Sandersfeld, Mark, St. Ludmila, Cedar Rapids
Saunders, Phil, (Retired), Cedar Rapids
Scharosch, Albert, (Retired), Cedar Rapids
Scheiding, Stanley, St. John XXIII Parish, Cedar Rapids
Schemmel, Michael, Clermont; Fayette; Sumner; West Union
Schmidt, Jim, Resurrection, Dubuque
Schockemoehl, Joe, Cascade; Fillmore; Garryowen; Temple Hill
Schwennen, John, Reinbeck
Sink, Tom, (Retired), Cedar Falls
Smith, Ron, St. Cecilia, Ames
Steger, James, Earlville; Dyersville; New Vienna; Petersburg; Worthington
Stierman, John, Holy Spirit, Dubuque
Stirm, Bob, Blessed Sacrament, Waterloo
Strang, Steven W., (Retired)
Ternes, Dennis, Marion
Thill, James J., Holy Spirit, Dubuque
Tondra, Richard, (Retired), Ames
Upah, Stan, Belle Plaine; Chelsea; Tama
Van Kerckvoorde, Steven, Colo; Nevada; State Center; Zearing
Wallace, Richard, St. Matthew, Cedar Rapids
Walsh, Tom, (Retired), Springville
Ward, Mike, Charles City; Nashua
Weber, Alan, Cedar Falls
Weber, Ed, (Retired), Waterloo
Weber, Loras, Bellevue, Springbrook
Whiteman, Steve, Nativity, Dubuque
Whitters, Michael, Belmond; Clarion; Eagle Grove
Wilson, James, (Retired), Waterloo
Winkel, John, St. Jude, Cedar Rapids
Wolfe, John, Bankston, Epworth; Farley, Peosta; Placid
Wood, Robert, Springbrook; Bellevue
Zajicek, Jim, Ft. Atkinson; Lawler; Little Turkey; Protivin; St. Lucas; Waucoma
Zimmerman, Paul, St. Pius X, Cedar Rapids
Zogg, Scott, Hiawatha.

Deacons Living Outside the Archdiocese:
Deacons—
Brock, Cary, Kennewick, WA
Brown, Paul, Auburn, AL
DiPietre, Dennis, Columbia, MO
Fortin, Daryl G., LeClaire, IA
Jenney, William E., (Retired), Brooklyn, MN
Jones, David, (Retired), Box Elder, SD
Pantaloni, Ed, (Retired), Grimes, IA
Quiles, Horacio, Springfield, MO
Ramirez, Diego, Canatillo Dgo, Mexico
Smith, Sean, Mundelein Seminary, IL.

Deacons from Other Dioceses Living in the Archdiocese:
Deacons—
Carroll, James, (Retired, Archdiocese of Chicago), Dubuque
Claypool, Robin, (Diocese of Sioux City), Ackley, Eldora, Hampton, Iowa Falls
Ellis, Mike, (Diocese of Winona-Rochester); Resurrection, Dubuque
Goldsmith, Ed, (Archdiocese of Omaha); Monticello; Hopkinton
Ridder, Ron, (Diocese of Grand Island); St. Pius X, Cedar Rapids
Rompot, Vern, (Retired, Archdiocese of Denver)
Wood, Robert A., (Archdiocese of St. Louis); Springbrook; Bellevue
Wyant, Mark, (Diocese of Sioux City); Colo, NV; State Center & Zearing.

INSTITUTIONS LOCATED IN DIOCESE

[A] SEMINARIES, ARCHDIOCESAN

DUBUQUE. *Seminary of St. Pius X*, 1235 Mt. Loretta Ave., 52003. Tel: 563-556-2580; Email: dbqspx@dbqarch.org. Revs. David A. Schatz, M.A., Rector; Thomas J. McDermott, Spiritual Dir. Students for Archdiocese of Dubuque 10; Students 2; Clergy / Religious Teachers 2.

[B] SEMINARIES, RELIGIOUS OR SCHOLASTICATES

EPWORTH. *Divine Word College* Divine Word College, 102 Jacoby Dr., S.W., P.O. Box 380, Epworth, 52045-0380. Tel: 563-876-3353; Fax: 563-876-3407; Email: tascheman@dwci.edu; Web: www.dwci.edu. Revs. Thomas J. Ascheman, S.V.D., Pres.; Sam Cunningham, Counselor; Cong Bang Tran, S.V.D., Vice Pres. Formation & Dean Students; Thang Hoang, S.V.D., Rector SVD Community; William Shea, S.V.D.; Pio Estepa, S.V.D., Teacher; Kenneth Anich, S.V.D.; Joseph McDermott, S.V.D.; James Bergin, S.V.D.; Paul Malinit Aquino, S.V.D.; Paul Chen, S.V.D.; Edmundus Yosef Soni De Class, S.V.D.; Ky Ngoc Dinh, S.V.D.; Adam MacDonald, S.V.D.; Anthony Cong Nguyen, S.V.D.; Son Peter Le, S.V.D.; Khoa Nguyen, S.V.D.; Nick Hien Nguyen, S.V.D.; Stephen Kha Nguyen, S.V.D.; Long Phi Nguyen, S.V.D.; Linh Pham, S.V.D.; John Szukalski, S.V.D.; Pablito Tagura, S.V.D.; Aris Pilapil Martin, S.V.D.; Xuan Hien Pham, S.V.D.; Alexander Roedlach, S.V.D.; Bros. Tony Kreinus, S.V.D.; Duy Linh Tran, S.V.D.; Vinh Vincent Trinh, S.V.D.; Michael Decker, S.V.D.; Daniel Yunck, S.V.D.; Rev. Francis Rayappan, In Res.; Bro Larry Kieffer, In Res. Society of the Divine Word (S.V.D.). Brothers 5; Lay Teachers 23; Priests 28; Sisters 2; Students 108; Clergy / Religious Teachers 9.

[C] COLLEGES AND UNIVERSITIES

DUBUQUE. *Clarke University of Dubuque, Iowa*, (Grades Associate-Doctorate), 1550 Clarke Dr., 52001. Tel: 563-588-6300; Email: presidentsoffice@clarke.edu; Web: www.clarke.edu. Rev. Andrew D. Marr, Chap.; Elizabeth McGrath, Vice Pres.; Kristi Bagstad, Registrar; Susan Burns, Vice Pres. Academic Affairs; Kate Zanger, Vice Pres. Student Life; Bill Biebuyck, Vice Pres., Inst. Advancement; Susanne Leibold, Dir. Library. Liberal Arts College. (Coed); Conducted by Sisters of Charity, B.V.M. Lay Teachers 83; Sisters 1; Students 1,004; Clergy / Religious Teachers 1.

Loras College, (Grades Bachelors-Masters), 1450 Alta Vista St., 52001. Tel: 563-588-7100; Fax: 563-588-7964; Email: jim.collins@loras.edu; Web: www.loras.edu. Mr. Jim Collins, Pres.; Revs. William M. Joensen, Ph.D., Dean of Campus Spiritual Life; Andrew D. Marr, Chap.; Douglas O. Wathier, S.T.D. (Accredited by the North Central Assoc. of Colleges and Secondary Schools) Priests 3; Sisters 1; Students 1,528; Clergy / Religious Teachers 2; Full Time Professors 91; Adjunct Professors 33.

CEDAR RAPIDS. *Mount Mercy University*, (Grades Bachelors-Masters), 1330 Elmhurst Dr. N.E., Cedar Rapids, 52402-4797. Tel: 319-363-8213; Fax: 319-363-5270; Email: president@mtmercy.edu; Web: www.mtmercy.edu. Rev. Anthony Adawu, Res. Chap., (Archdiocese of the Cape Coast, Ghana); Laurie Hamen, J.D., Pres.; Sr. Linda Bechen, R.S.M., Vice Pres., Mission & Min.; Brenda Haefner, Vice Pres., Development & Alumni Relations; Dr. Nate Klein, Vice Pres., Student Success; Dr. Terri Crumley, Vice Pres., Enrollment & Mktg.; Ms. Anne Gillespie, Vice Pres., Business & Fin.; Dr. Timothy Laurent, Provost & Vice Pres., Academic Affairs. Priests 1; Students 1,835; Full-time Faculty 84; Part-time Faculty 77; Clergy / Religious Teachers 3.

[D] HIGH SCHOOLS, INTERPAROCHIAL

CEDAR RAPIDS. *Xavier High School, Cedar Rapids, Iowa* Serving St. John XXIII; St. Jude, St. Ludmila, St. Patrick, Immaculate Conception, St. Wenceslaus, St. Matthew, All Saints, St. Pius X, Cedar Rapids; St. Joseph, Marion; St. Elizabeth Ann Seton, Hiawatha. (Coed) 6300 42nd St., N.E., Cedar Rapids, 52411. Tel: 319-294-6635. Revs. Philip E. Thompson, Pastoral Coord.; Dustin L. Vu, Spiritual Advisor/Care Svcs.; Tom Keating, Pres.; Angela Olson, Prin.; Gerry Miller, Asst. Prin. Lay

Teachers 48; Students 662; Clergy / Religious Teachers 1.

Xavier High School Foundation, P.O. Box 10956, Cedar Rapids, 52410-0956. Tel: 319-378-4571; Email: mharken@xavierfoundation.org. Mary Harken, Dir.; Rev. Philip E. Thompson, Pastoral Coord. Financially supports Xavier High School, Cedar Rapids, Iowa.

DYERSVILLE. *Beckman Catholic High School, Dyersville, Iowa*, (Grades 7-12), (Coed) 1325 Ninth St. S.E., Dyersville, 52040. Tel: 563-875-7188; Email: dbqh05@dbqarch.org. Marcel Kielkucki, Prin.; Ryan Devereux, Asst. Prin.; Very Rev. Dennis J. Quint, Pastoral Coord. Serving the following parishes: St. Francis Xavier, Dyersville; St. Joseph, Earlville; St. Boniface, New Vienna; Ss. Peter and Paul, Petersburg; St. Paul, Worthington. Lay Teachers 29; Students 378.

[E] SCHOOLS OF RELIGION

CALMAR. *Christian Family School of Religion, Calmar, Iowa* Serving: St. Aloysius, Calmar; Our Lady of Seven Dolors, Festina; St. Francis de Sales, Ossian; St. Wenceslaus, Spillville 107 E. South St., P.O. Box 819, Calmar, 52132. Tel: 563-562-3045; Email: dbqrt1@dbqarch.org. Rev. G. Robert Gross, Pastoral Coord.; Patty Frana, D.R.E. Lay Teachers 1; Priests 1; Students 96; Clergy / Religious Teachers 1.

MANCHESTER. *St. Paul School of Religion, Manchester, Iowa*, (Grades 7-12), Serving: St. Mary, Manchester; Immaculate Conception, Masonville; St. Patrick, Ryan Mailing Address: 119 W. Fayette St., Manchester, 52057. Tel: 563-927-4710. Rev. Gabriel C. Anderson, Pastoral Coord.; Kathy Oberrueter, Dir. of Faith Formation. Lay Teachers 2; Students 170.

NEW HAMPTON. *St. John School of Religion, New Hampton, Iowa* Serving: St. Bernard, Alta Vista; St. Boniface, Ionia; Our Lady of Lourdes, Lourdes; Holy Family, New Hampton; Immaculate Conception, North Washington 313 W. Court St., New Hampton, 50659. Tel: 641-394-2404; Email: dbqrt4@dbqarch.org. 823 W. Main St., New Hampton, 50659. Amanda Husak, Dir.; Very Rev. Brian M. Dellaert, Pastoral Coord. Lay Teachers 1; Students 100.

[F] ELEMENTARY SCHOOL SYSTEMS

CALMAR. *Calmar-Festina-Spillville Catholic Schools, Calmar, Iowa*, (Grades PreK-8), P.O. Box 815, Calmar, 52132. Tel: 563-562-3291. Kathryn Schmitt, Prin.; Rev. G. Robert Gross, Pastoral Coord. Formerly Our Lady of Seven Dolors (St. Mary), Festina; St. Wenceslaus, Spillville; St. Aloysius, Calmar; St. Wenceslaus (Grades K-3); St. Aloysius (Grades 4-8).

Legal Name: Calmar-Festina-Spillville Catholic Schools, Calmar, Iowa Lay Teachers 12; Students 147.

CEDAR RAPIDS. *Holy Family Consolidated School, Cedar Rapids, Iowa*, (Grades PreK-8), Tel: 319-396-7818; Email: dbqe12@dbqarch.org. Zach Zeckser, Admin.; Rev. Ivan R. Nienhaus, Pastoral Coord. Parishes Served: St. John XXIII, St. Jude, St. Ludmila and St. Patrick, Cedar Rapids. Lay Teachers 36; Students 384.

LaSalle Middle School, (Grades 6-8), 3700 First Ave. N.W., Cedar Rapids, 52405. Tel: 319-396-7792; Email: dbqe12@dbqarch.org. Janet Whitney, Asst. Prin.

St. Jude Elementary, (Grades PreK-5), 3700 First Ave. N.W., Cedar Rapids, 52405. Tel: 319-396-7818; Email: dbqe09@dbqarch.org. Jamie Larson, Prin.

St. Pius and St. Elizabeth Ann Seton Schools, Cedar Rapids, Iowa, (Grades PreK-5), 4901 Council St. N.E., Cedar Rapids, 52402-2402. Tel: 319-393-4507 ; Email: dbqe13@dbqarch.org. Rev. Philip E. Thompson, Pastoral Min./Coord.; Brian O'Donnell, Prin. Lay Teachers 26; Students 445.

Regis Middle School, Cedar Rapids, Iowa, (Grades 6-8), Parishes Served: All Saints, Immaculate Conception, St. Matthew, St. Pius X, and St. Wenceslaus, Cedar Rapids; St. Elizabeth Ann Seton, Hiawatha. 735 Prairie Dr. N.E., Cedar Rapids, 52402. Tel: 319-363-1968; Email: dbqm02@dbqarch.org. Rev. John R. Flaherty, Pastoral Coord.; Elizabeth Globokar, Prin.; Matthew Svare, Asst. Prin. Lay Teachers 23; Students 312.

DYERSVILLE. *St. Francis Xavier School, Dyersville, Iowa*, (Grades PreK-6), 203 Second St., S.W., Dyersville, 52040. Tel: 563-875-7376; Email: dbqe26@dbqarch.org. Peter Smith, Prin.; Very Rev. Dennis J. Quint, Pastoral Coord. Lay Teachers 28; Students 366.

FARLEY. *Seton Catholic Schools, Farley, Iowa*, (Grades PreK-8), 7597 Burds Rd., Peosta, 52068. Tel: 563-556-5967; Email: dbqe28@dbqarch.org. Mary Smock, Prin.; Rev. Michael G. Schueller, Pastoral Coord. Serving the following parishes: St. Clement, Bankston; St. Patrick, Epworth; St. Joseph, Farley; St. John the Baptist, Peosta; and St. John, Placid. Lay Teachers 27; Students 376.

GUTTENBERG. *St. Mary and Immaculate Conception School System, Guttenberg, Iowa*, (Grades PreK-8), 502 Second St. S., Guttenberg, 52052. Tel: 563-252-1577. P.O. Box 100, Guttenberg, 52052. Joanne Hedemann, Prin.; Rev. Marvin J. Bries, Pastoral Coord. Serves: St. Mary, Guttenberg & Immaculate Conception, North Buena Vista. Lay Teachers 7; Students 82.

HOLY CROSS. *LaSalle Elementary Schools, Holy Cross, Iowa* dba LaSalle Catholic Schools, (Grades K-6), Holy Cross Center, 835 Church St., P.O. Box 368, Holy Cross, 52053-0368. Tel: 563-870-2405; Email: dbqe34@dbqarch.org. Susan Hucker, Prin.; Rev. Noah J. Diehm, Pastoral Coord. Serves the following parishes: St. Francis of Assisi, Balltown; Holy Cross, Holy Cross; Holy Trinity, Luxemburg; St. Joseph, Rickardsville; and SS. Peter and Paul, Sherrill. Lay Teachers 6; Students 53.

MARSHALLTOWN. *St. Francis Catholic School, Marshalltown, Iowa*, (Grades PreK-6), 310 Columbus Dr., Marshalltown, 50158. Tel: 641-753-8744; Email: dbqe40@dbqarch.org. Matthew Herrick, Prin.; Rev. Donald J. Czapla, Pastoral Coord. Serving the following parishes: St. Mary, Marshalltown; St. Henry, Marshalltown. Lay Teachers 18; Students 213.

PROTIVIN. *Trinity Catholic School, Protivin, Iowa*, (Grades K-6), 116 N. Main St., Protivin, 52163. Tel: 563-569-8556; Fax: 563-569-8477; Email: dbqe47@dbqarch.com. Jerry Brown, Prin.; Rev. Aaron R. Junge, Pastoral Min./Coord. Serves: Holy Trinity, Protivin; St. Luke, St. Lucas; St. John, Fort Atkinson. Lay Teachers 6; Students 45.

[G] CONSOLIDATED K-12 SYSTEMS

DUBUQUE. *Holy Family Catholic Schools, Dubuque, Iowa*, (Grades PreK-12), 2005 Kane St., 52001. Tel: 563-582-5456; Email: dbqmd01@dbqarch.org. Carol Trueg, Chief Admin.; Rev. Steven J. Rosonke, Pastoral Coord. Serves the parishes of Dubuque and St. Joseph, Key West. Lay Teachers 133; Students 1,937; Clergy / Religious Teachers 2.

St. Joseph the Worker Early Childcare Center, 2105 Saint Joseph St., 52001. Tel: 563-582-1246; Email: dbqmd01@dbqarch.org.

Holy Ghost School, (Grades K-5), 2981 Central Ave., 52001. Tel: 563-556-1511; Email: dbqe17@dbqarch.org. Todd Wessels, Prin. Lay Teachers 8; Students 132.

Resurrection School, (Grades PreK-5), 4320 Asbury Rd., 52002. Tel: 563-583-9488; Email: dbqe20@dbqarch.org. Denise Grant, Prin. Lay Teachers 18; Students 302.

St. Anthony School/Our Lady of Guadalupe, (Grades PreK-5), 2175 Rosedale, 52001. Tel: 563-556-2820; Email: dbqe21@dbqarch.org. Lori Apel, Prin. Lay Teachers 25; Students 357.

St. Columbkille School, (Grades K-5), 1198 Rush St., 52003. Tel: 563-582-3532; Email: dbqe22@dbqarch.org. Barb Roling, Prin. Lay Teachers 19; Students 287.

Mazzuchelli Catholic Middle School, (Grades 6-8), 2005 Kane St., 52001. Tel: 563-582-1198; Email: dbqm03@dbqarch.com. Phillip Bormann, Prin.; Doug Varley, Asst. Prin. Lay Teachers 28; Students 358; Clergy / Religious Teachers 1.

Wahlert High School, 2005 Kane St., 52001. Tel: 563-583-9771; Email: dbqh04@dbqarch.org. Ronald Meyers, Prin.; Cindy Wagner, Asst. Prin. Parishes Served: The Parishes in Dubuque; Holy Family, New Melleray; St. Joseph's, Key West. Lay Teachers 36; Students 501; Clergy / Religious Teachers 2.

BELLEVUE. *Marquette High School, Bellevue, Iowa*, (Grades PreK-12), 502 Franklin St., Bellevue, 52031. Tel: 563-872-3356; Email: dbqe04@dbqarch.org. Geoffrey Kaiser, Prin.; Rev. Dennis W. Miller, Pastoral Coord. Parishes Served: St. Joseph, Bellevue; St. Catherine, St. Catherine; St. Donatus, St. Donatus; SS. Peter and Paul, Springbrook. Lay Teachers 9; Students 74.

Bellevue Area Consolidated School, (Grades Day Care-8), 403 Park St., Bellevue, 52031. Tel: 563-872-3284; Email: dbqe04@dbqarch.org. Geoffrey Kaiser, Prin.; Rev. Phillip F. Kruse, Pastoral Coord. Parishes Served: St. Joseph, Bellevue; SS. Peter & Paul, Springbrook; St. Donatus, St. Donatus. Lay Teachers 14; Students 165.

CASCADE. *Aquin Educational System*, (Grades PreK-8), Serving: St. Matthias, Cascade; Sacred Heart, Fillmore; St. Patrick, Garryowen; St. Peter, Temple Hill 608 Third Ave., N.W., P.O. Box 460, Cascade, 52033-0460. Tel: 563-852-3331; Email: dbqe06@dbqarch.org. Deacon Ray Noonan, Pastoral Coord.

Legal Name: Aquin Educational System, Cascade, Iowa Lay Teachers 23; Students 263.

Little Angels, 608 Third Ave., N.W., P.O. Box 460, Cascade, 52033-0460. Tel: 563-852-7020.

Aquin Elementary School, (Grades PreK-8), 608 Third Ave., N.W., P.O. Box 460, Cascade, 52033-0460. Tel: 563-852-3331; Email: dbqe06@dbqarch.org. Vicki Palmer, Prin. Lay Teachers 23; Students 263.

Aquin School of Religion, 608 Third Ave., N.W., P.O. Box 460, Cascade, 52033-0460. Tel: 563-852-3331; Email: dbq023ff@dbqarch.org. Nicole Casey, Dir. Faith Formation. Lay Teachers 1; Students 39.

GILBERTVILLE. *Bosco Catholic School System, Gilbertville, Iowa*, (Grades K-12), 405 16th Ave., Gilbertville, 50634. Tel: 319-296-1692; Email: dbqh06@dbqarch.org. Rev. Henry P. Huber, Pastoral Coord. Lay Teachers 33; Students 333.

Immaculate Conception School, (Grades 3-8), 311 16th Ave., Gilbertville, 50634. Tel: 319-296-1089; Email: dbqe31@dbqarch.org. Shelby Douglas, Prin.

St. Joseph School, (Grades K-2), 6916 Lafayette Rd., P.O. Box 158, Raymond, 50667. Tel: 319-233-5980; Email: dbqe31@dbqarch.org. Shelby Douglas, Prin. Parishes served: Immaculate Conception, Gilbertville; St. Joseph, Raymond.

Don Bosco High School, 405 16th Ave., Gilbertville, 50634. Tel: 319-296-1692; Email: dbqh06@dbqarch.org. Casey Redmond, Prin.; Rev. Henry P. Huber, Spiritual Dir. Parishes Served: St. Francis, Barclay; St. Mary of Mt. Carmel, Eagle Center; Immaculate Conception, Gilbertville; St. Athanasius, Jesup; Sacred Heart, LaPorte City; St. Joseph, Raymond. Lay Teachers 15; Students 108.

MASON CITY. *Newman Catholic School System*, (Grades PreK-12), 2445 19th St. S.W., Mason City, 50401. Tel: 641-423-6939. Rev. John A. Gossman, Pastoral Coord. Lay Teachers 42; Students 590.

Newman Child Care, 2050 S. McKinley Ave., Mason City, 50401. Tel: 641-423-0168; Email: dbqe41@dbqarch.org. Kathy Lloyd, Early Childhood Dir.

Newman Elementary School, (Grades K-8), 2000 S. McKinley Ave., Mason City, 50401. Tel: 641-423-3101; Email: dbqe41@dbqarch.org. Jan Avery, Admin. Lay Teachers 17; Students 306.

Newman High School, 2445 19th St. S.W., Mason City, 50401. Tel: 641-423-6939; Email: dbqh07@dbqarch.org. Tony Adams, Prin. Parishes Served: St. Patrick, Clear Lake; Sacred Heart, Manly; Epiphany, Mason City; Sacred Heart, Rockwell. Lay Teachers 25; Students 284.

WATERLOO. *Cedar Valley Catholic Schools, Waterloo, Iowa*, (Grades PreK-12), 3231 W. 9th St., Waterloo, 50702. Tel: 319-232-1422; Email: dbqmw01@dbqarch.org. Thomas Novotney, Admin.; Rev. Scott E. Bullock, J.C.L., Pastoral Coord. Serving the parishes of Waterloo. Lay Teachers 81; Students 1,023.

Blessed Sacrament School, (Grades PreK-5), 600 Stephan Ave., Waterloo, 50701. Tel: 319-233-7863. Aaron Becker, Prin.; Heather Williams, Asst. Prin.; Aaron Ferrie, Asst. Prin. Lay Teachers 12; Students 154.

Sacred Heart School, (Grades PreK-5), 620 W. 5th St., Waterloo, 50702. Tel: 319-234-6593. Aaron Becker, Prin.; Heather Williams, Asst. Prin.; Aaron Ferrie, Asst. Prin. Lay Teachers 9; Students 70.

St. Edward School, (Grades PreK-5), 139 E. Mitchell, Waterloo, 50702. Tel: 319-233-6202; Email: dbqe51@dbqarch.org. Aaron Becker, Prin.; Heather Williams, Asst. Prin. Lay Teachers 21; Students 283.

Blessed Maria Assunta Pallotta Middle School, (Grades 6-8), 3225 W. 9th St., Waterloo, 50702. Tel: 319-232-6592; Email: dbqm04@dbqarch.org. Nick Satterlee, Prin.; Thomas Novotney, Prin. Parishes served: the parishes of Waterloo. Lay Teachers 18; Students 225.

Columbus High School, 3231 W. 9th St., Waterloo, 50702. Tel: 319-233-3358; Email: dbqh08@dbqarch.org. Daniel Thole, Prin. Parishes Served: St. Patrick, Cedar Falls; Blessed Sacrament, Queen of Peace, Sacred Heart and St. Edward, Waterloo. Lay Teachers 22; Students 291.

[H] GENERAL HOSPITALS

DUBUQUE. *Mercy Medical Center-Dubuque* (A member of Mercy Health Network) 250 Mercy Dr., 52001. Tel: 563-589-8000; Fax: 563-589-8073; Email: mercydubuque@mercyhealth.com; Web: www.mercydubuque.com. Kay Takes, Pres.; Ms. Colleen M. Walters, Regional Vice Pres. Mission Integration; Deb Fleming, Chap.; Rev. Raphael Nana Andoh, Chap. Bed Capacity 247; Tot Asst. Annually 50,794; Total Staff 1,293.

CEDAR FALLS. *Sartori Memorial Hospital, Inc.* (Formerly known as S.F.H., Inc., a member of Mercy Health Network.) 515 College St., Cedar Falls, 50613. Tel: 319-268-3000; Fax: 319-268-3270

; Email: jack.dusenbery@wfhc.org. Jack Dusenbery, Contact Person; Ms. Colleen M. Walters, Vice Pres. Bed Capacity 101; Tot Asst. Annually 41,679; Total Staff 212.

CEDAR RAPIDS. *Mercy Medical Center, Endowment Foundation, Inc., Cedar Rapids, IA*, 701 Tenth St. S.E., Cedar Rapids, 52403. Tel: 319-398-6206; Email: kcrist@mercycare.org. Julie Crockett, Pres.; Sr. Susan O'Connor, R.S.M., M.S.W., M.A., Chairwoman of the Board.

Mercy Medical Center-Cedar Rapids (Sisters of Mercy-Regional Community of Cedar Rapids) 701 Tenth St. S.E., Cedar Rapids, 52403.
Tel: 319-398-6011; Email: kcrist@mercycare.org; Web: www.mercycare.org. Timothy Charles, Pres. & CEO; Mark McDermott, Dir. Pastoral Care Office; Tammy Buseman, Chap.; Rev. James P. Brokman, Chap.; Ryan Buchmueller, Chap.; Sr. Martha Donnelly, Chap. Sponsored by the Sisters of Mercy, West Midwest Community. Bed Capacity 369; Tot Asst. Annually 168,000; Total Staff 2,403; Skilled Nursing 21.

Mercycare Service Corporation (Parent Corp.) 701 10th St. S.E., Cedar Rapids, 52403.
Tel: 319-398-6011; Email: kcrist@mercycare.org. Timothy Charles, CEO & Pres. Sponsored by the Sisters of Mercy, West Midwest Community. Bed Capacity 369; Tot Asst. Annually 166,000; Total Staff 2,886.

DYERSVILLE. *Mercy Medical Center-Dubuque (Dyersville)* (A Member of Mercy Health Network) 1111 Third St. S.W., Dyersville, 52040.
Tel: 563-875-7101; Fax: 563-875-2957; Email: mercydyersville@mercyhealth.com; Web: www.mercydubuque.com. Kay Takes, Pres.; Ms. Colleen M. Walters, Vice Pres. Bed Capacity 20; Tot Asst. Annually 4,202; Total Staff 66.

MASON CITY. *Mercy Medical Center-North Iowa* (Member of Mercy Health Network) 1000 4th St. S.W., Mason City, 50401. Tel: 641-428-7000;
Fax: 641-428-7827; Email: northiowa@mercyhealth.com. Mr. Rod Schlader, Pres.; Very Rev. Kenneth B. Gehling, Chap.; Ms. Colleen M. Walters, Vice Pres., Mission Integration; Ross Erickson, Spiritual Care Leader (Evangelical). Bed Capacity 342; Tot Asst. Annually 551,434; Total Staff 2,673.

NEW HAMPTON. *Mercy Medical Center-New Hampton* (Member of Mercy Health Network) 308 N. Maple Ave., New Hampton, 50659. Tel: 641-394-4121;
Fax: 641-394-1669; Email: newhampton@mercyhealth.com; Web: www.mercynewhampton.com. Aaron Flugum, Pres. & CEO; Ms. Colleen M. Walters, Vice Pres.; Sr. Victoria Arndorfer, R.S.M., Chap. Bed Capacity 17; Patients Asst Anual. 40,835; Tot Asst. Annually 40,895; Total Staff 139.

OELWEIN. *Mercy Hospital of Franciscan Sisters, Inc.* Member of Mercy Health Network. 201 8th Ave. S.E., Oelwein, 50662. Tel: 319-283-6000;
Fax: 319-283-6004; Email: infowheatoniow@mercyhealth.com. Jack Dusenbery, Contact Person, Pres. & CEO; Ms. Colleen M. Walters, Vice Pres. Franciscan Sisters. Daughters of the Sacred Hearts of Jesus and Mary, Wheaton, IL. Bed Capacity 64; Tot Asst. Annually 23,896; Total Staff 119.

WATERLOO. *Covenant Medical Center, Inc.* Member of Mercy Health Network. 3421 W. Ninth St., Waterloo, 50702. Tel: 319-272-8000;
Fax: 319-272-7313; Email: jack.dusenbery@wfhc.org; Web: www.wheatoniowa.org. Jack Dusenbery, Pres. & Contact Person; Ms. Colleen M. Walters, Vice Pres. Franciscan Sisters. Daughters of the Sacred Hearts of Jesus and Mary, Wheaton, IL. Bed Capacity 346; Tot Asst. Annually 228,750; Total Staff 2,706.

[I] SPECIAL HEALTH CENTERS

DUBUQUE. *Clare House*, 3340 Windsor Ave., 52001-1300. Tel: 563-583-9786; Fax: 563-583-6080; Email: info@osfdbq.org; Web: www.osfdbq.org. Sisters Cathy Katoski, O.S.F., Pres.; Bertha Bonert, O.S.F., Dir.; Rev. Ronald G. Friedell, Chap., (Retired). Sisters of St. Francis, Dubuque. Bed Capacity 76; Patients Asst Anual. 100; Tot Asst. Annually 100; Total Staff 147; Professed Sisters 74.

Marian Hall Infirmary, 1050 Carmel Dr., 52003-7999. Tel: 563-556-5474; Fax: 563-588-1975. Rev. Msgr. James O. Barta, Ph.D., Chap., (Retired); Sarah Rentz, Admin. Bed Capacity 46; Tot Asst. Annually 43; Total Staff 94.

Caritas Center, 1130 Carmel Dr., 52003-7911.
Tel: 563-556-3240; Web: www.bvmsisters.org. Sarah Rentz, Admin. Bed Capacity 53; Tot Asst. Annually 45; Total Staff 95.

[J] HOMES FOR AGED

DUBUQUE. *Stonehill Franciscan Services, Inc.*, 3485 Windsor Ave., 52001-1312. Tel: 563-557-7180; Fax: 563-584-9282; Email: gbrown@stonehilldbq.com; Web: www.stonehilldbq.com. Sr. Kathy Knipper, O.S.F., Board Chm.; Gretchen Brown, Pres. & CEO; Rev. Philip Mensah, Chap. Bed Capacity 214; Residents 285; Tot Asst. Annually 530; Total Staff 450; Apartments & Villas 54.

Stonehill Benevolent Foundation, Tel: 563-557-7180 ; Fax: 563-584-9282. Danielle Gratton, Chair, Stonehill Benevolent Foundation Board. Sponsored by Sisters of St. Francis of the Holy Family.

CEDAR RAPIDS. *Hallmar-Mercy Medical Center*, 701 Tenth St. S.E., Cedar Rapids, 52403.
Tel: 319-398-6241; Email: kcrist@mercycare.org. Tim Charles, CEO/Pres. Sisters of Mercy, West Midwest Community.Cedar Rapids Regional, owned and operated by Mercy Medical Center. Residents 53; Total Staff 53; Total Assisted 80.

DYERSVILLE. *Ellen Kennedy Living Center*, 1177 7th St., S.W., Dyersville, 52040. Tel: 563-875-6323;
Fax: 563-875-6268; Email: oakcrest@mercyhealth.com. Kari A. Wittmeyer, Dir. & Contact Person. Sponsor: Mercy Medical Center.; Purpose: to provide funds to assure persons of limited resources will be able to access programs and services at the Ellen Kennedy Living Center. Total Staff 29; Assisted Living 32; Independent Living 26.

Mercy Medical Center-Dubuque-Dyersville-Oakcrest Manor (A Division of Mercy Health Services - Iowa) 1111 Third St. S.W., Dyersville, 52040.
Tel: 563-875-7101; Fax: 563-875-2957; Email: mercydyersville@mercyhealth.com; Web: www.mercydubuque.com. Kay Takes, Pres.; Mr. Joseph Norris, Dir. Bed Capacity 40; Patients Asst Anual. 62; Total Staff 40.

[K] MONASTERIES AND RESIDENCES OF PRIESTS AND BROTHERS

PEOSTA. *New Melleray Abbey, Order of Cistercians of the Strict Observance*, 6632 Melleray Cir., Peosta, 52068. Tel: 563-588-2319; Fax: 563-588-4117; Email: monks@newmelleray.org; Web: www.newmelleray.org. Rt. Revs. David R. Bock, O.C.S.O., Prior; Mark A. Scott, O.C.S.O., S.S.L., Abbot; Revs. Alberic R. Farbolin, O.C.S.O., Cantor; Thomas A. MacMaster, O.C.S.O., Confessor; Xavier L. Dieter, O.C.S.O., Confessor; Ephrem Poppish, O.C.S.O., Subprior; Stephen Verbest, O.C.S.O., Novice & Vocation Dir.; Jonah Wharff, O.C.S.O., Guest Master; David Hereshko; Bros. Gilbert B. Cardillo, O.C.S.O.; Juan Diego Lavado, O.C.S.O.; Cyprian Griffith, O.C.S.O.; Paul Halaburt, O.C.S.O.; Nicholas Koenig, O.C.S.O.; Joseph Kronebusch, O.C.S.O.; Charles Oberholzer, O.C.S.O.; John O'Driscoll, O.C.S.O.; Tobias Shanahan, O.C.S.O.; Robert Simon, O.C.S.O.; Paul Andrew Tanner, O.C.S.O.; Dennis Vavra, O.C.S.O.; Thomas Imhoff; Rt. Revs. David Wechter, O.C.S.O., Retired Abbot; Brendan J. Freeman, O.C.S.O., Retired Abbot; Revs. James E. O'Connor, O.C.S.O., Retired; Kenneth F. Tietjen, O.C.S.O., Retired
Corporation of New Melleray Brothers 13; Priests 13; Total in Residence 22; Absent on Medical Leave 2; Chaplains 2.

[L] CONVENTS AND RESIDENCES FOR SISTERS

DUBUQUE. *St. Joseph's Convent, Mount Carmel*, 1150 Carmel Dr., 52003. Tel: 563-556-3240; Web: www.bvmsisters.org. Sarah Rentz, Admin.; Rev. Msgr. Russell M. Bleich, S.T.L., Chap., (Retired); Christine Olsem, Contact Person. Motherhouse of the Sisters of Charity of the Blessed Virgin Mary. Bed Capacity 69; Sisters 64; Total Staff 51.

Mt. Loretto Convent, 2360 Carter Rd., 52001-2997.
Tel: 563-588-2008; Fax: 563-588-4463; Web: www.dubuquepresentations.org. Sisters Carmen Hernandez, P.B.V.M., Pres.; Rita Menart, P.B.V.M., M.A., L.M.H.C., Vice Pres.; Rev. Douglas O. Wathier, S.T.D., Chap. Motherhouse and Novitiate of the Sisters of the Presentation of the B.V.M. Sisters 97.

Mt. St. Francis, 3390 Windsor Ave., 52001-1311.
Tel: 563-583-9786; Fax: 563-583-3250; Email: info@osfdbq.org; Web: www.osfdbq.org. Sisters Cathy Katoski, O.S.F., Pres.; Kathy Knipper, O.S.F., Vice Pres.; Stacy Francois, Sec.; Rev. Robert R. Beck, Chap., (Retired). Motherhouse and Novitiate of the Sisters of St. Francis of the Holy Family.
Legal Title: Sisters of St. Francis of the Holy Family Charitable Trust Sisters 72.

Our Lady of the Mississippi Abbey, 8400 Abbey Hill Ln., 52003. Tel: 563-582-2595; Fax: 563-582-5511; Email: sisters@olmabbey.org; Web: www.mississippiabbey.org. Mother Rebecca Stramoski, O.C.S.O., Abbess. The Cistercian Nuns of the Strict Observance.Iowa Cistercians of the Strict Observance
Legal Name: Trappistine Nuns, Inc. Novices 2; Postulants 1; Sisters 17.

Sisters of Charity of the Blessed Virgin Mary, BVM Center, Mount Carmel, 1100 Carmel Dr., 52003-7991. Tel: 563-588-2351; Fax: 563-588-4832; Web: www.bvmsisters.org. Sisters Teri Hadro, B.V.M., Pres. Congregation; Lou Anglin, B.V.M., 1st Vice Pres.; LaDonna Manternach, B.V.M., 2nd Vice Pres.; Jennifer Head, Archivist. Total Staff 33.

Sisters of the Visitation, 2950 Kaufmann Ave., 52001-1631. Tel: 563-556-2440; Email: dbqsvm@dbqarch.org; Web: sistersofthevisitationdbq.org. Sr. Patricia Clark, S.V.M., Pres. & Contact Person. Sisters of the Visitation of the Immaculate Heart of Mary. Sisters 4.

CEDAR RAPIDS. *Sisters of Mercy of the Americas West Midwest Community, Inc. Sacred Heart Convent*, 1125 Prairie Dr., N.E., Cedar Rapids, 52402-4737.
Tel: 319-364-5196; Fax: 319-364-7383; Email: sistersofmercy@mercywmw.org; Web: www.sistersofmercy.org/west-midwest. Sisters Laura Reicks, R.S.M., Pres.; Susan Sanders, R.S.M., Vice Pres.; Rebecca Vandenbosch, C.F.O.; Sisters Margaret Mary Hinz, R.S.M., Leadership Team; Maria Klosowski, R.S.M., Leadership Team; Margaret Maloney, Leadership Team. Residence for the Sisters of Mercy of the Americas - West Midwest Community. Sisters 531; Associates 605.

Catherine McAuley Center, Cedar Rapids, 866 4th Ave. SE, Cedar Rapids, 52403. Tel: 319-363-4993; Fax: 319-363-8332; Email: paula@cmc-cr.org. Paula Land, Exec. Dir. Bed Capacity 15; Tot Asst. Annually 600; Total Staff 22.

[M] RETREAT HOUSES

DUBUQUE. *Shalom Spirituality Center*, 1001 Davis St., 52001-1398. Tel: 563-582-3592; Fax: 563-582-5872; Email: info@shalomretreats.org; Web: www.shalomretreats.org. Sr. Marci Blum, O.S.F., Dir. Retreatants 8,000; Total Staff 9.

CEDAR FALLS. *American Martyrs Retreat House*, 2209 North Union Rd., Cedar Falls, 50613-9441.
Tel: 319-266-3543; Email: dbqamrh@dbqarch.org; Web: www.americanmartyrsretreathouse.com. Deacon Alan Weber, Dir.

HIAWATHA. *Prairiewoods Franciscan Spirituality Center*, 120 E. Boyson Rd., Hiawatha, 52233-1277.
Tel: 319-395-6700; Email: ecospirit@prairiewoods.org; Web: www.prairiewoods.org. Jenifer A. Hanson, Dir. & Contact Person.

PEOSTA. *New Melleray Guest House*, 6632 Melleray Cir., Peosta, 52068. Tel: 563-588-2319;
Fax: 563-588-4117; Email: guesthouse@newmelleray.org; Web: www.newmelleray.org. Rev. Jonah Wharff, O.C.S.O., Contact Person.

[N] NEWMAN CENTERS

AMES. *St. Thomas Aquinas Church, Ames, Iowa*, 2210 Lincoln Way, Ames, 50014-7184. Tel: 515-292-3810 ; Fax: 515-292-3841; Email: dbq004@dbqarch.org; Web: www.staparish.net. Rev. Jon M. Seda; Joe Weyers, Dir. Evangelization; Shari Reilly, Dir. Campus Ministry & Liturgy; Eric Evans, Dir. Music & Campus Min.; Robert LeBlanc, Business Mgr. & Contact Person; Tom Budnik, Coord. Ministries; Brenda Neppel, RCIA Coord. & Marriage Prep.; Joe Leisz, Dir. of Devel. Serves the campus of Iowa State University, Ames.

CEDAR FALLS. *Catholic Student Center of Cedar Falls, Iowa*, 1019 W. 23rd St., Cedar Falls, 50613-3550.
Tel: 319-266-9863; Fax: 319-266-3706; Web: www.ststephenuni.org. Rev. Nicholas B. March, Dir. Campus Ministry; Deacon Leonard Froyen, Ph.D.; Dr. Bill Rocha, Campus Min.; Clare Hanson, Music Min.; Molly Scullin, Sec.; Carol Jacobi, Business Mgr. Serves the campus of the University of Northern Iowa, Cedar Falls. Total Staff 6.

[O] CATHOLIC CHARITIES

DUBUQUE. *Catholic Charities of the Archdiocese of Dubuque*, 1229 Mt. Loretta Ave., P.O. Box 1309, 52004-1309. Tel: 563-588-0558; Fax: 563-557-3140; Email: dbqcccced@dbqarch.org; Web: www.catholiccharitiesdubuque.org. Tracy Morrison, M.S., L.M.H.C., Exec. Dir.; Stacy Sherman, Dir. Grant Writing & Community Rels.; Lindsay Firzlaff, Exec. Asst.; Debra Jasper, Exec. Asst. Tot Asst. Annually 13,980. Catholic Charities Board of Directors Most Reverend Michael Owen Jackels, Pres.; Rev. Msgr. Thomas E. Toale, Ph.D., Vice Pres.; Deacon William Biver; Sisters Margaret Mary Cosgrove, B.V.M.; Susan O'Connor, R.S.M., M.S.W., M.A.; Tracy Morrison, M.S., L.M.H.C., (Staff Non-Voting); Jerry Fox; James Jackson; Ruth Palmer; Paul Sigwarth; Judy Wolf; Gabriela Vega-Bauerly.
Branch Offices.
Catholic Charities - Ames Office, St. Thomas Aquinas Parish, 2210 Lincoln Way, Ames, 50014.
Tel: 515-296-2759; Email: dbqccps@dbqarch.org. Catholic Charities of the Archdiocese of Dubuque, P.O. Box 1309, 52004-1309. Lisa Turner, L.M.F.T., Counselor

Legal Name: Catholic Charities of the Archdiocese of Dubuque.

Catholic Charities - Cedar Rapids Office, 420 Sixth St., S.E., Ste. 220, Cedar Rapids, 52401. Tel: 319-364-7121; Email: dbqccced@dbqarch.org. Catholic Charities of the Archdiocese of Dubuque, P.O. Box 1309, 52004-1309. Ellen Blocker, Admin. Asst.; Denise Patters, Immigration Attorney; Emily Rebelskey, Immigration Attorney; Yer Vang, J.D., Immigration Attorney; Catherine Clark, Immigration Legal Asst.; Claudia Rodriguez De Nuñez, Immigration Legal Asst.

Catholic Charities - Decorah Office, St. Benedict Parish, 307 W. Main St., Decorah, 52101. Tel: 563-382-9631; Email: dbqccced@dbqarch.org. Catholic Charities of the Archdiocese of Dubuque, P.O. Box 1309, 52004. Lori Eastwood, L.M.S.W., Counselor.

Catholic Charities - Dubuque, 1229 Mount Loretta Ave, 52003. Tel: 563-588-0558; Email: dbqccced@dbqarch.org. P.O. Box 1309, 52004. Lynne Lutze, Ph.D., L.M.H.C., N.C.C., Clinical Dir. & Counselor.

Catholic Charities - Mason City Office, Epiphany Parish, 300 Fifth St., S.E., Mason City, 50401. Tel: 641-424-9683; Email: dbqccced@dbqarch.org. Catholic Charities of the Archdiocese of Dubuque, P.O. Box 1309, 52004.

Catholic Charities - Waterloo Office, 2101 Kimball Ave., Ste. 138, Waterloo, 50702. Tel: 319-272-2080; Email: dbqccced@dbqarch.org. Catholic Charities of the Archdiocese of Dubuque, P.O. Box 1309, 52004. Teresa King, Community Outreach Coord.; Rachel Blough, Counselor; Miryam Antunez De Mayolo, Immigration Attorney.

Catholic Charities Housing, 1229 Mt. Loretta Ave., 52004-1309. Tel: 563-556-8476; Email: dbqcchss@dbqarch.org. Catholic Charities Housing, P.O. Box 1309, 52004-1309. Matthew Roddy, Housing Dir.; Aaron Gerrard, Kennedy Park West Site Mgr.; Pat Huseman, Maintenance Supvr.; Kayci Schumacher, Ecumenical Tower Site Mgr.; Aaron Wenzel, Ecumenical Tower Maintenance. Carter Plaza (2520 Carter Rd., Dubuque, 52001) and Alabar Plaza (1110 Doreen Ct., Waterloo, 50701) are housing properties owned by Catholic Charities. Kennedy Park West (2671 Owen Ct., Dubuque, 52002); and Ecumenical Tower (250 W. 6th St., Dubuque 52001) are housing properties managed by Catholic Charities.

Catholic Charities Foundation aka St. Mary's Home (Catholic Charities Housing) 1229 Mt. Loretta Ave., 52004-1309. Tel: 563-556-2580; Email: dbqccced@dbqarch.org. Most Reverend Michael Owen Jackels, Pres.; Rev. Msgr. Thomas E. Toale, Ph.D., Vice Pres.; Tracy Morrison, M.S., L.M.H.C., Exec. Dir.; Sr. Margaret Mary Cosgrove, B.V.M.; Greg Burbach; Michael Coyle; Nicholas Schrup III; Judy Wolf. Supports the works of Catholic Charities of the Archdiocese of Dubuque.

Housing Projects.

[P] MISCELLANEOUS

DUBUQUE. *Archdiocese of Dubuque Alternative Investments Grantor Trust*, 1229 Mt. Loretta Ave., 52003. Tel: 563-556-2580; Email: dbqcfo@dbqarch.org. Archdiocese of Dubuque, P.O. Box 479, 52004-0479. Richard L. Runde, CPA, Contact Person.

Archdiocese of Dubuque Deposit and Loan Fund, 1229 Mt. Loretta Ave., 52003-8787. Tel: 563-556-2580; Fax: 563-556-5464; Email: DBQCFO@dbqarch.org. Richard L. Runde, CPA, Contact Person.

Archdiocese of Dubuque Education Fund, 1229 Mt. Loretta Ave., 52003-8787. Tel: 563-556-2580; Fax: 563-556-5464; Email: DBQCFO@dbqarch.org. Richard L. Runde, CPA, Contact Person.

Archdiocese of Dubuque Perpetual Care Fund, 1229 Mt. Loretta Ave., 52003-8787. Tel: 563-556-2580; Fax: 563-556-5464; Email: DBQCFO@dbqarch.org. Richard L. Runde, CPA, Contact Person.

Archdiocese of Dubuque Seminarian Education Fund, 1229 Mt. Loretta Ave., 52003-8787. Tel: 563-556-2580; Fax: 563-556-5464; Email: DBQCFO@dbqarch.org. Richard L. Runde, CPA, Contact Person.

Bureau of Education of the Archdiocese of Dubuque, 1229 Mt. Loretta Ave., 52003. Tel: 563-556-2580; Email: dbqsup@dbqarch.org. Kim Hermsen, M.A., Supt. Schools.

Metropolitan Office of Catholic Education, Cedar Rapids Metro Office, 120 5th St., N.W., Cedar Rapids, 52405. Tel: 319-366-2517; Email: dbqsup@dbqarch.org. Kim Hermsen, M.A., Supt. Schools; Julie Kapsch, Sec.

**Catholic Foundation for the Archdiocese of Dubuque* Catholic Foundation in the Archdiocese of Dubuque, 1229 Mt. Loretta Ave., P.O. Box 357, 52003. Tel: 563-556-2580, Ext. 307; Email: dbqcdevdir@dbqarch.org; Web: www.ourCatholicFoundation.org. Jeff Henderson, Ed.S., Exec. Dir.; Jeff Schneider, Asst. Dir.

Cistercian Studies Quarterly, Inc., New Melleray Abbey, 6632 Melleray Cir., Peosta, 52068. Tel: 563-588-2319, Ext. 100; Fax: 563-582-5511; Email: csq@newmelleray.org; Web: www.cistercian-studies-quarterly.org. Bro. Paul Andrew Tanner, O.C.S.O., Book Review Editor & Contact Person. Sponsor: Cistercian Order of the Strict Observance of the USA Region.

Declaration of Trust of the Paul & Janet Auterman Charitable Educational Trust, 4300 Asbury Rd., 52002. Tel: 563-556-7511; Fax: 563-556-7419; Email: DBQ058S3@DBQARCH.ORG; Email: DBQ058@DBQARCH.ORG. Very Rev. Phillip G. Gibbs. Purpose: To establish a fund to assist students in attending Catholic schools, Pre-K through grade 12, and for such related purposes as allowed by Internal Revenue code Section 501(c)(3) of the 1986 Internal Revenue Code, as amended, or any successor section.

Hennessy Charitable Trust, 2360 Carter Rd., 52001-2997. Tel: 563-588-2008; Fax: 563-588-4463; Email: lynn@dubuquepresentations.org. Virginia Foletta, Chm.; Faye Fangman, Treas.; Joetta Venneman, Sec.; Marjorie Healy, Trustee; Elaine Hoye, Trustee; Ann Jackson, Trustee; Patricia Lickteig, Trustee; Margaret Kuhn, Trustee; Maureen Quillin, Trustee. Sponsored by the Sisters of the Presentation.Sponsored by the Sisters of the Presentation.

Opening Doors, 2100 Asbury Rd., Ste. 8, 52001. Tel: 563-582-7480; Fax: 563-582-7467; Email: cgebhart@openingdoorsdbq.org; Web: www.openingdoorsdbq.org. Carol Gebhart, M.A., Exec. Dir. Sponsors: Sinsinawa Dominicans, Sisters of the Presentation, Sisters of Charity, B.V.M, Sisters of the Visitation and Dubuque Franciscan Sisters. Purpose: Teresa Shelter provides emergency shelter and extended stay housing for women and children at 1111 Bluff Street. Maria House provides transitional housing and related support services for women and children at 1561 Jackson Street. A supportive housing program is operated at Francis Apartments. Tot Asst. Annually 320.

Maria House, 1561 Jackson St., 52001. Tel: 563-582-6286; Email: cgebhart@openingdoorsdbq.org; Web: www.openingdoorsdbq.org. Carol Gebhart, M.A., Dir.

Teresa Shelter, 1111 Bluff St., 52001. Tel: 563-690-0086; Cell: cgebhart@openingdoorsdbq.org; Web: www.openingdoorsdbq.org. Carol Gebhart, M.A., Dir.

Our Faith, Our Children, Our Future, School Tuition Organization, 1229 Mt. Loretta Ave., P.O. Box 479, 52004-0479. Tel: 563-556-2580; Fax: 563-556-5464; Email: dbqcfo@dbqarch.org; Web: www.ourfaithsto.org. Jennifer Decker, Bd. Member. Purpose: to provide tuition assistance to students enrolled in accredited non-public schools located within the Archdiocese of Dubuque in conformance with Iowa law.Board of Directors Mike Hulme, Pres.; Kim Hermsen, M.A., Vice Pres.; Jeff Henderson, Ed.S., Sec.; Katherine Fahey; Lynn Ptacek; Rev. Michael G. Schueller; Lori Thielen.

Presentation Lantern, Schmid Innovation Center, 900 Jackson St., Ste. LL5-1, 52001. Tel: 563-557-7134; Email: directorlantern@gmail.com; Web: www.presentationlanterndbq.org. Megan Ruiz, Dir. Tot Asst. Annually 100.

St. Raphael Priest Fund Society of the Archdiocese of Dubuque, 1229 Mt. Loretta Ave., 52003. Tel: 563-556-2580; Email: dbqcfo@dbqarch.org. Most Rev. Michael Owen Jackels, Pres.; Rev. Msgr. Thomas E. Toale, Ph.D., Vice Pres.; Richard L. Runde, CPA, Plan Admin.; Rev. Richard J. Ament, Dir.; Very Rev. Dennis J. Colter, Dir.; Revs. Jeffrey A. Dole, Dir.; Douglas J. Loecke, J.C.L., Dir.; Nicholas B. March, Dir.; Rev. Msgr. John R. McClean, Dir., (Retired); Revs. Thomas J. McDermott, Dir.; Mark D. Murphy, Dir.; Very Rev. Dennis J. Quint, Dir.; Rev. Steven J. Rosonke, Sec.; Rev. Msgr. Carl L. Schmitt, Dir., (Retired); Kathy Wuertzer, Recording Sec. To assist the Archdiocese of Dubuque in the support and care of its retired, disabled & infirm priests.

Villa Raphael, 1155 Mt. Loretta Ave., 52003. Tel: 563-588-2049; Email: dbqvilla@dbqarch.org. Patricia Flores, Dir. Administered by the Archdiocese of Dubuque. Total Apartments 16; Total in Residence 15; Total Staff 5.

Society of St. Vincent de Paul Particular Council of the City of Dubuque, Iowa, 4990 Radford Rd., 52002. Tel: 563-584-2226; Email: svdpdubuqueiowa@gmail.com. Mike Elliott; Tracy Ede, Exec.

CEDAR FALLS. **Sartori Health Care Foundation, Inc.*, 515 College St., Cedar Falls, 50613. Tel: 319-268-3161; Email: sartori@mercyhealth.com. Heather Bremer-Miller, Exec. Dir.; Ms. Colleen M. Walters, Vice Pres.

CEDAR RAPIDS. *Metro Catholic Outreach*, Sister Mary Lawrence Community Center, 420 6th St., S.E., #120, Cedar Rapids, 52401. Tel: 319-739-5490; Email: info@metrocatholicoutreach.org; Web: www.metrocatholicoutreach.org. Kate Getty, Exec. Dir. Social Justice organization including food pantry and financial assistance Tot Asst. Annually 21,755.

St. Vincent de Paul Particular Council of Cedar Rapids, Iowa, 928 7th St., S.E., Cedar Rapids, 52401. Tel: 319-365-5091; Email: store.crsvdp@gmail.com; Web: www.crsvdp.org. Kyle Flynn, Manager.

HAMPTON. *La Luz Hispana*, 116 1st Ave., N,W., Hampton, 50441. Tel: 641-812-1090; Email: laluzhispana@gmail.com; Web: www.laluzhispana.org. Ms. Claudia Rivera, Dir.; Mrs. Aimee Hanson, Assoc. Dir.

WATERLOO. *Covenant Foundation, Inc.*, 3421 W. Ninth St., Waterloo, 50702. Tel: 319-272-7676; Email: heather.bremermiller@wfhc.org. Heather Bremer-Miller, Exec. Dir.; Colleen Walters, Vice Pres.

Society of St. Vincent de Paul District Council of Waterloo, Iowa, 320 Broadway St., Waterloo, 50703. Tel: 319-232-3366; Fax: 319-232-5114; Email: prusso329@gmail.com. Patrick A. Russo, Exec. Dir.; William McGrane, Pres.

Wheaton Franciscan Healthcare-Iowa, Inc., 3421 W. Ninth St., Waterloo, 50702. Tel: 319-272-8000; Fax: 319-272-7313; Email: wheatonhealth@mercyhealth.com. Jack Dusenbery, Pres. & Contact Person; Ms. Colleen M. Walters, Vice Pres.

WEBSTER CITY. *St. Thomas Aquinas Foundation of Webster City, Iowa, St. Thomas Aquinas Parish*, 1000 Des Moines St., Webster City, 50595-2147. Tel: 515-832-1190; Fax: 515-832-3757; Web: www.stthomaswc.org. Very Rev. Stephen L. Meyer, Contact Person. St. Thomas Aquinas Parish.

[Q] CLOSED PARISHES

DUBUQUE. HOLY GHOST (1896) [JC] Merged with Holy Trinity and Sacred Heart, Dubuque to form Holy Spirit Parish, Dubuque. For sacramental records contact Holy Spirit, Dubuque.

HOLY TRINITY (1910) [JC] Merged with Holy Ghost and Sacred Heart, Dubuque to form Holy Spirit Parish, Dubuque. For sacramental records contact Holy Spirit, Dubuque.

ST. MARY (1850) [JC] Closed. For sacramental records contact Cathedral of St. Raphael, Dubuque.

SACRED HEART (1879) [JC] Merged with Holy Ghost and Holy Trinity, Dubuque to form Holy Spirit Parish, Dubuque. For sacramental records contact Holy Spirit, Dubuque.

ALLISON, BUTLER CO.. IMMACULATE CONCEPTIONClosed. For sacramental records, contact St. Mary, Greene.

ANDREW, JACKSON CO.. ST. JOHN (1914) [CEM] Closed. For sacramental records, please contact Sacred Heart Parish, Maquoketa.

BALDWIN, JACKSON CO.. HOLY TRINITY[CEM] Closed. For sacramental records, contact Sacred Heart, Maquoketa.

BLESSING, BLACKHAWK CO.. IMMACULATE CONCEPTION (1875) [CEM] Closed. For sacramental records, contact St. Mary of Mt. Carmel, Eagle Center.

BLUFFTON, WINNESHIEK CO.. ST. BRIDGET (1858) [CEM] Closed. For sacramental records, contact Notre Dame, Cresco.

CARROLL TOWNSHIP, CARROLL CO.. ST. WENCESLAUSClosed. For sacramental records, contact St. Paul, Traer.

CARTERSVILLE, CERRO GORDO CO.. ST. JOHNClosed. For sacramental records, contact Sacred Heart, Rockwell.

CASCADE, DUBUQUE CO.. ST. MARTIN (1848) Closed. Merged with St. Mary, Cascade to form St. Matthias, Cascade. For sacramental records, contact St. Matthias, Cascade.

ST. MARY (1857) Closed. Merged with St. Martin, Cascade to form St. Matthias, Cascade. For sacramental records, contact St. Matthias, Cascade.

CASTLE GROVE, JONES CO.. IMMACULATE CONCEPTION (1877) [CEM] Closed. For sacramental records contact Sacred Heart, Monticello.

CEDAR RAPIDS, LINN CO.. JOHN XXIII (2000) [JC] Merged with St. Patrick, Fairfax to form St. John XXIII, Cedar Rapids.

CHERRY MOUND, ALLAMAKEE CO.. ST. PIUS (1863) [CEM] Closed. For sacramental records contact Immaculate Conception, Lansing.

CHESTER, HOWARD CO.. ST. STEPHEN (1916) Closed. For sacramental records, contact Immaculate Conception, Elma.

CLUTIER, TAMA CO.. IMMACULATE CONCEPTION (1900) Closed. For sacramental records, contact St. Paul, Traer.

CORWITH, HANCOCK CO.. ST. MARY (1912) [CEM]

Closed. For sacramental records, please contact St. Patrick, Britt.

CRESCO, HOWARD CO.. ASSUMPTION OF THE BLESSED VIRGIN MARY (1858) Closed. Merged with St. Joseph, Cresco to form Notre Dame, Cresco. For sacramental records, please contact Notre Dame, Cresco.

ST. JOSEPH (1870) Closed. Merged with Assumption of the Blessed Virgin Mary, Cresco to form Notre Dame, Cresco. For sacramental records, please contact Notre Dame, Cresco.

DIKE, GRUNDY CO.. ST. MARY (1880) Closed. Merged with Sacred Heart, Grundy Center; St. Patrick, Parkersburg; Queen of Heaven, Reinbeck to form Holy Family, Reinbeck. For sacramental records, contact Holy Family, Reinbeck.

DOUGHERTY, CERRO GORDO CO.. ST. PATRICK (1870) [CEM] Closed. For sacramental records, please contact Sacred Heart Parish, Rockwell.

DUMONT, BUTLER CO.. ST. FRANCIS (1890) Closed. For sacramental records please contact St. Patrick, Hampton.

DYSART, TAMA CO.. ST. JOSEPH (1878) [CEM] Closed. For sacramental records, please contact St. Paul, Traer.

EVANSDALE, BLACKHAWK CO.. ST. NICHOLAS (1951) Closed. Merged with St. Mary, St. John & St. Joseph, Waterloo to form Queen of Peace, Waterloo. For sacramental records, please contact Queen of Peace, Waterloo.

FAIRFAX, LINN CO.. ST. PATRICK (1875) [CEM] Merged with John XXIII, Cedar Rapids to form St. John XXIII, Cedar Rapids. For sacramental records, contact St. John XXIII, Cedar Rapids.

GARBER, CLAYTON CO.. ST. MICHAEL (1917) [CEM] Closed. For sacramental records, please contact St. Joseph, Garnavillo.

GARWIN, TAMA CO.. ST. BONIFACE (1884) Closed. For sacramental records, please contact St. Patrick Parish, Tama.

GENEVA, FRANKLIN CO.. ST. PAUL[CEM] Closed. For sacramental records, contact St. Mary, Ackley.

GREELEY, DELAWARE CO.. ST. JOSEPH (1870) [CEM] Closed. For sacramental records, contact St. Mary, Manchester.

GREEN ISLAND, JACKSON CO.. SACRED HEARTClosed. For sacramental records, please contact St. Joseph, Preston.

GRUNDY CENTER, GRUNDY CO.. SACRED HEART (1885) Closed. Merged with St. Mary, Dike; St. Patrick, Parkersburg; & Queen of Heaven, Reinbeck to form Holy Family, Reinbeck. For sacramental records, contact Holy Family, Reinbeck.

HAVERHILL, MARSHALL CO.. IMMACULATE CONCEPTION (1877) Closed. For sacramental records, contact St. Henry, Marshalltown.

HAWKEYE, FAYETTE CO.. ST. FRANCIS XAVIER (1891) Closed. For sacramental records, contact Immaculate Conception, Sumner.

HAZLETON, BUCHANAN CO.. ST. MARY (1881) [CEM] Closed. For sacramental records, contact Sacred Heart, Oelwein.

JEWELL, HAMILTON CO.. GOOD SHEPHERD (1915) Closed. For sacramental records, contact St. Cecilia, Ames.

LA MOTTE, JACKSON CO.. HOLY ROSARY (1893) [CEM] Closed. For sacramental records please contact Sacred Heart, Maquoketa.

LAMONT, BUCHANAN CO.. ST. MARY (1894) [CEM] Closed. For sacramental records, contact St. Mary, Strawberry Point.

LATTNERVILLE, DUBUQUE CO.. ANNUNCIATIONClosed. Parish closed. For sacramental records, contact St. Patrick, Epworth.

LITTLEPORT, CLAYTON CO.. SACRED HEART[CEM] Closed. For sacramental records, please contact St. Joseph, Garnavillo.

LYCURGUS, ALLAMAKEE CO.. ST. MARY (1859) Closed. For sacramental records please contact St. Patrick, Waukon.

MASON CITY, CERRO GORDO CO.. HOLY FAMILY (1908) Merged with St. Joseph, Mason City to form Epiphany Parish, Mason City. For sacramental records contact Epiphany Parish, Mason City.

ST. JOSEPH (1873) Merged with Holy Family, Mason City to form Epiphany Parish, Mason City. For sacramental records contact Epiphany Parish, Mason City.

MCINTIRE, MITCHELL CO.. ST. MELClosed. For sacramental records, please contact Sacred Heart, Osage.

MEYER, MITCHELL CO.. SACRED HEART (1900) [CEM] Closed. Parish closed. For sacramental records, please contact, Sacred Heart, Osage. Church: 2695 480th St., McIntire, IA.

MONTI, BUCHANAN CO.. ST. PATRICK (1855) [CEM] Closed. For sacramental records, contact, St. John the Evangelist, Independence. Church: 2856 Washington Ave., Masonville, IA.

NEW HAMPTON, CHICKASAW CO.

St. Joseph (1870) Closed. Merged with St. Mary, New Hampton to form Holy Family, New Hampton. For sacramental records, contact Holy Family, New Hampton.

St. Mary (1894) Closed. Merged with St. Joseph, New Hampton to form Holy Family, New Hampton; for sacramental records please contact Holy Family, New Hampton.

NEW HARTFORD, BUTLER CO.. ST. JOSEPHClosed. For sacramental records, contact Holy Family, Reinbeck.

PARKERSBURG, BUTLER CO.. ST. PATRICKClosed. Merged with St. Mary, Dike, Sacred Heart, Grundy Center & Queen of Heaven, Reinbeck to form Holy Family, Reinbeck. For sacramental records, contact Holy Family, Reinbeck.

PINHOOK, BREMER CO.. ST. BRIDGET[CEM] Closed. For sacramental records, contact Immaculate Conception, Sumner.

PLYMOUTH ROCK, WINNESHIEK CO.. ST. AGNES (1857) [CEM] Closed. For sacramental records, contact Notre Dame, Cresco.

PLYMOUTH, CERRO GORDO CO.. ST. MICHAELClosed. For sacramental records, contact Sacred Heart, Manly.

PRAIRIE, DUBUQUE CO.. ST. JOSEPH[CEM] Closed. For parish records, contact St. Joseph, Key West.

REILLY SETTLEMENT, CHICKASAW CO.. SACRED HEART [CEM] Closed. For sacramental records, please contact Holy Trinity, Protivin.

REINBECK, GRUNDY CO.. QUEEN OF HEAVEN (1958) Closed. Merged with St. Mary, Dike, Sacred Heart, Grundy Center & St. Patrick, Parkersburg to form Holy Family, Reinbeck. For sacramental records, contact Holy Family, Reinbeck.

RHODES, MARSHALL CO.. ST. JOSEPH[CEM] Closed. For sacramental records, please contact St. Joseph, State Center.

ROWLEY, BUCHANAN CO.. ALL SAINTS (1896) Closed. For sacramental records, contact St. John the Evangelist, Independence.

ST. ANSGAR, MITCHELL CO.. ST. ANSGAR (1951) Closed. For sacramental records, contact Sacred Heart, Osage.

ST. ANTHONY, MARSHALL CO.. SACRED HEART (1878) [CEM] Closed. For sacramental records contact St. Mary, Colo.

ST. CECILIA, HOWARD CO.. ST. PATRICK[CEM] Closed. For sacramental records, contact Immaculate Conception, Elma.

ST. THERESA, JACKSON CO.. ST. THERESA (1853) [CEM] Closed. For sacramental records, contact Sacred Heart, Maquoketa.

SABULA, JACKSON CO.. ST. PETER (1840) [CEM] Closed. For sacramental records, please contact St. Joseph, Preston.

SAND SPRINGS, DELAWARE CO.. IMMACULATE CONCEPTIONClosed. For sacramental records, please contact St. Luke, Hopkinton.

SCHLEY, HOWARD CO.. HOLY CROSS[CEM] Closed. For sacramental records, contact Holy Trinity, Protivin.

SHELL ROCK, BUTLER CO.. HOLY NAMEClosed. For sacramental records, contact St. Mary, Waverly.

SOUTH GARRYOWEN, JACKSON CO.. ST. ALOYSIUS[CEM] Closed. For sacramental records, contact St. Matthias Parish, Cascade.

STONE CITY, JONES CO.. ST. JOSEPHClosed. For sacramental records, contact St. Patrick, Anamosa.

SWALEDALE, CERRO GORDO CO.. ST. LAWRENCEClosed. For sacramental records, contact Sacred Heart, Rockwell.

SYLVIA, DUBUQUE CO.. ASSUMPTION (1896) [CEM] Closed. For sacramental records, please contact Sacred Heart, Maquoketa.

VINING, TAMA CO.. ST. MARY (1874) [CEM] Closed. For sacramental records, contact St. Paul, Traer.

WADENA, FAYETTE CO.. ST. JOSEPH[CEM] Closed. Parish closed. For sacramental records, contact St. Joseph, Elkader.

WALFORD, LINN CO.. HOLY TRINITY (1890) Closed. For sacramental records, contact St. John XXIII, Cedar Rapids.

WATERLOO, BLACKHAWK CO.. ST. JOHN (1923) Closed. Merged with St. Mary & St. Joseph, Waterloo and St. Nicholas, Evansdale to form Queen of Peace, Waterloo. For sacramental records, contact Queen of Peace, Waterloo.

ST. JOSEPHClosed. Merged with St. Mary & St. John, Waterloo and St. Nicholas, Evansdale to form Queen of Peace, Waterloo. For sacramental records, contact Queen of Peace, Waterloo.

ST. MARY (1898) Closed. Merged with St. John & St. Joseph, Waterloo and St. Nicholas, Evansdale to form Queen of Peace, Waterloo. For sacramental records contact Queen of Peace, Waterloo.

WEST RIDGE, ALLAMAKEE CO.. ST. JOHN THE BAPTIST [CEM] Closed. For sacramental records, contact St. Patrick, Waukon.

WODEN, HANCOCK CO.. SACRED HEART (1900) Closed. For sacramental records, please contact St. Patrick, Britt.

RELIGIOUS INSTITUTES OF MEN REPRESENTED IN THE ARCHDIOCESE

For further details refer to the corresponding bracketed number in the Religious Institutes of Men or Women section.

[0330]—*Brothers of the Christian Schools* (Midwest Prov.)—F.S.C.

[0350]—*Order of Cistercians of the Strict Observance-Trappists* (Our Lady of New Melleray)—O.C.S.O.

[0420]—*Society of the Divine Word* (Northern Prov.)—S.V.D.

RELIGIOUS INSTITUTES OF WOMEN REPRESENTED IN THE ARCHDIOCESE

[0670]—*Cistercian Nuns of the Strict Observance*—O.C.S.O.

[1780]—*Congregation of the Sisters of the Third Order of St. Francis of Perpetual Adoration*—F.S.P.A.

[1070-03]—*Dominican Sisters Congregation of the Most Holy Rosary* (Sinsinawa, WI)—O.P.

[3530]—*Missionary Sisters Servants of the Holy Spirit*—S.Sp.S.

[2960]—*Notre Dame Sisters* (Omaha, NE)—N.D.

[2970]—*School Sisters of Notre Dame* (Mankato, MN)—S.S.N.D.

[1680]—*School Sisters of St. Francis* (Milwaukee, WI)—O.S.F.

[0440]—*Sisters of Charity of Cincinnati, Ohio.*

[0430]—*Sisters of Charity of the Blessed Virgin Mary*—B.V.M.

[0660]—*Sisters of Charity* (Wilmette, IL)—S.C.C.

[2575]—*Sisters of Mercy of the Americas* (West Midwest Community)—R.S.M.

[1540]—*Sisters of St. Francis* (Clinton, IA)—O.S.F.

[1705]—*Sisters of St. Francis* (St. Francis, WI).

[1570]—*Sisters of St. Francis of the Holy Family*—O.S.F.

[3320]—*Sisters of the Presentation of the B.V.M.* (Dubuque, IA; Fargo, SD)—P.B.V.M.

[4200]—*Sisters of the Visitation of the Immaculate Heart of Mary* (Dubuque, IA)—S.V.M.

CEMETERIES

DUBUQUE. *Catholic Cemeteries, Incorporated, of the Archdiocese of Dubuque*, P.O. Box 479, 52004-0479. Tel: 563-556-2580; Fax: 563-556-5464; Email: dbqcfo@dbqarch.org. Richard L. Runde, CPA, Contact Person

Mount Calvary Cemetery Association, Mailing Address: 1111 Davis St., 52001. Tel: 563-583-4329

Mount Olivet Cemetery Association, Mailing Address: 10556 Military Rd., 52003. Tel: 563-582-7059

CEDAR RAPIDS. *St. John's Cemetery Association, Cedar Rapids, Iowa*, Mailing Address: c/o St. Ludmila Parish, 2107 J St., S.W., Cedar Rapids, 52404. Tel: 319-362-8894

St. Joseph's Cemetery Association, Clinton Township, Linn County, Iowa, c/o St. Jude Parish, Sisley Grove Rd., Cedar Rapids, 52405. 50 Edgewood Rd., N.W., Cedar Rapids, 52405

Mt. Cavalry Cemetery Association, Cedar Rapids, Iowa, Mailing Address: c/o St. Matthew Parish, 2310 1st. Ave., Cedar Rapids, 52402. Tel: 319-362-4659

MCINTIRE. *St. Patrick's Cemetery Association, McIntire, Mitchell County, Iowa*, c/o Sacred Heart Parish, Timber Ave, Osage, 50461. 218 S. 12th St., Osage, 50461

WATERLOO. *Catholic Cemeteries of Waterloo, Waterloo, Iowa*, Mailing Address: 3912 W. 4th St., Waterloo. Tel: 319-233-0746

NECROLOGY

† Lang, Charles E., (Retired), Died Apr. 5, 2018

† Bruggeman, Donald R., (Retired), Died Jun. 25, 2018

† Levenhagen, Robert J., (Retired), Died Nov. 24, 2018

† Reasoner, Mark J., Cedar Rapids, St. Jude, Died Mar. 18, 2018

Diocese of Duluth

(Dioecesis Duluthensis)

Most Reverend

PAUL D. SIRBA

Bishop of Duluth; ordained May 31, 1986; appointed Bishop of Duluth October 15, 2009; ordained December 14, 2009. *Pastoral Center: 2830 E. Fourth St., Duluth, MN 55812.*

Pastoral Center: 2830 E. Fourth St., Duluth, MN 55812. Tel: 218-724-9111; Fax: 218-724-1056.

Web: www.dioceseduluth.org

ESTABLISHED OCTOBER 3, 1889.

Square Miles 22,354.

Corporate Title: Diocese of Duluth.

Comprises the counties of Aitkin, Carlton, Cass, Cook, Crow Wing, Itasca, Koochiching, Lake, Pine and St. Louis in the State of Minnesota.

For legal titles of parishes and diocesan institutions, consult the Chancery Office.

STATISTICAL OVERVIEW

Personnel	
Bishop	1
Priests: Diocesan Active in Diocese	43
Priests: Diocesan Active Outside Diocese	2
Priests: Retired, Sick or Absent	26
Number of Diocesan Priests	71
Religious Priests in Diocese	1
Total Priests in Diocese	72
Extern Priests in Diocese	6
Ordinations:	
Permanent Deacons	2
Permanent Deacons in Diocese	64
Total Sisters	59
Parishes	
Parishes	73
With Resident Pastor:	
Resident Diocesan Priests	35
Without Resident Pastor:	
Administered by Priests	38
Pastoral Centers	1
Professional Ministry Personnel:	
Sisters	2
Lay Ministers	30
Welfare	
Catholic Hospitals	2
Total Assisted	376,528
Homes for the Aged	3
Total Assisted	556
Day Care Centers	1
Total Assisted	85
Educational	
Diocesan Students in Other Seminaries	9
Total Seminarians	9
Colleges and Universities	1
Total Students	4,406
Elementary Schools, Diocesan and Parish	7
Total Students	1,274
Catechesis/Religious Education:	
High School Students	1,755
Elementary Students	2,244
Total Students under Catholic Instruction	9,688
Teachers in the Diocese:	
Sisters	2
Lay Teachers	118
Vital Statistics	
Receptions into the Church:	
Infant Baptism Totals	464
Minor Baptism Totals	33
Adult Baptism Totals	30
Received into Full Communion	79
First Communions	488
Confirmations	429
Marriages:	
Catholic	123
Interfaith	67
Total Marriages	190
Deaths	808
Total Catholic Population	45,283
Total Population	447,896

Former Bishops—Rt. Revs. JAMES MCGOLRICK, D.D., cons. Dec. 27, 1889; died Jan. 23, 1918; JOHN T. MCNICHOLAS, O.P., S.T.D., cons. Sept. 8, 1918; appt. Archbishop of Cincinnati July 8, 1925; died April 22, 1950; Most Revs. THOMAS A. WELCH, D.D., cons. Feb. 3, 1926; died Sept. 9, 1959; FRANCIS J. SCHENK, D.D., cons. May 24, 1945; appt. to Duluth Jan. 19, 1960; resigned April 30, 1969; died Oct. 28, 1969; PAUL F. ANDERSON, D.D., appt. Titular Bishop of Polignando and Coadjutor Bishop with right of succession July 19, 1968; cons. Oct. 17, 1968; succeeded to See April 10, 1969; resigned Aug. 7, 1982; appt. Apostolic Administrator Aug. 7, 1982; appt. Auxiliary Bishop of Sioux Falls, SD March 25, 1983; died Jan. 4, 1987; ROBERT H. BROM, D.D., cons. May 23, 1983; appt. Coadjutor Bishop of San Diego, CA, May 9, 1989; ROGER L. SCHWIETZ, O.M.I., D.D., ord. Dec. 20, 1967; appt. Bishop of Duluth Dec. 12, 1989; cons. Feb. 2, 1990; appt. Coadjutor Archbishop of Anchorage, Jan. 18, 2000; installed March 24, 2000; succeeded to See March 3, 2001; DENNIS M. SCHNURR, ord. July 20, 1974; appt. Bishop of Duluth Jan. 18, 2001; ord. April 2, 2001; appt. Coadjutor Archbishop of Cincinnati Oct. 17, 2008.

Pastoral Center—2830 E. Fourth St., Duluth, 55812. Tel: 218-724-9111; Fax: 218-724-1056. Office Hours: Mon.-Thurs. 8-12 & 12:30-4:30, Fri. 8-1.

Vicar General—Rev. JAMES B. BISSONETTE, J.C.L.

Finance Officer—MR. FRANZ HOEFFERLE.

Moderator of the Curia—VACANT.

Safe Environment—Rev. JAMES B. BISSONETTE, J.C.L.

Chancellor—Rev. STEVEN LAFLAMME, J.C.L.

Diocesan Tribunal Coordinator—MRS. SHAWNA HANSEN.

Judicial Vicar—Rev. STEVEN LAFLAMME, J.C.L.

Defenders of the Bond—MS. HEATHER EICHHOLS, J.C.L.; MS. ASHLEY VOELLER, J.C.L.

Promoter of Justice—Rev. JAMES B. BISSONETTE, J.C.L.

Procurator—VACANT.

Notaries—MRS. ROSE MARIE EICHMUELLER; MRS. SHAWNA HANSEN; MRS. MICHELLE LYNN WRIGHT.

College of Consultors—Revs. JAMES B. BISSONETTE, J.C.L.; PETER MUHICH; GABRIEL WAWERU; JUSTIN FISH; MICHAEL GARRY; ANTHONY WROBLEWSKI.

Diocesan Deans—Revs. PETER MUHICH; GABRIEL WAWERU; MICHAEL GARRY; JUSTIN FISH; ANTHONY WROBLEWSKI.

Diocesan Corporate Board—Most Rev. PAUL D. SIRBA; Revs. JAMES B. BISSONETTE, J.C.L.; STEVEN LAFLAMME, J.C.L.; CATHERINE VONRUDEN; MR. DOUGLAS HILDENBRAND.

Diocesan Finance Council Chair—Most Rev. PAUL D. SIRBA.

Diocesan Offices and Departments

Archivist (Historical)—2830 E. Fourth St., Duluth, 55812. Tel: 218-724-9111. MRS. LAURIE BISEL.

Boy Scouts—Rev. THOMAS GALARNEAULT.

Campus Ministry—Rev. MICHAEL SCHMITZ, 421 St. Marie St., Duluth, 55811. Tel: 218-728-3757.

Cemeteries—Rev. JAMES B. BISSONETTE, J.C.L., 2830 E. Fourth St., Duluth, 55812. Tel: 218-724-9111.

Censor of Books—Rev. STEVEN LAFLAMME, J.C.L.

Council of Catholic Women—Rev. PAUL FRUTH, Moderator, (Retired), P.O. Box 823, Crosslake, 56442. Tel: 218-768-2702.

Department of Catechesis, RCIA, and Lay Apostolate—2830 E. Fourth St., Duluth, 55812. Tel: 218-724-9111. MS. GRACE MCDONOUGH.

Department of Catholic Schools—MS. CYNTHIA ZOOK, 2830 E. Fourth St., Duluth, 55812. Tel: 218-724-9111.

Department of Communications—2830 E. Fourth St., Duluth, 55812. Tel: 218-724-9111. Deacon KYLE ELLER, 2830 E. Fourth St., Duluth, 55812. Tel: 218-724-9111.

Department of Continuing Formation of Clergy—Rev. STEVEN LAFLAMME, J.C.L.

Department of Stewardship—MR. JOSEPH LITCHTY.

Department of Indian Ministry—Sr. MARIE ROSE MESSINGSCHLAGER, C.D.P., 2830 E. Fourth St., Duluth, 55812. Tel: 218-724-9111.

Department of Liturgy—Rev. JOEL HASTINGS, 2830 E. Fourth St., Duluth, 55812. Tel: 218-724-9111.

Department of Marriage and Family Life—2830 E. 4th St., Duluth, 55812. MRS. BETSY KNEEPKENS, Dir.; Rev. ANTHONY JOHN CRAIG.

Department of Vocations and Priestly Formation—Rev. RYAN MORAVITZ.

Department of Permanent Diaconate—Deacon JOHN WEISKE, 2830 E. Fourth St., Duluth, 55812. Tel: 218-724-9111.

Department of Protection of Children & Young People—MR. ERNIE STAUFFENECKER, 2830 E. Fourth St., Duluth, 55812. Tel: 218-724-9111.

Victim Assistance Coordinators—MRS. ESTHER REAGAN, Tel: 218-820-9220; MR. TAB BAUMGARTNER, Tel: 218-249-5495.

Department of Social Apostolate and CHD—MS. PATRICE CRITCHLEY-MENOR, 2830 E. Fourth St., Duluth, 55812. Tel: 218-724-9111.

Department of Youth and Young Adult Ministry—Rev. MICHAEL SCHMITZ, 2830 E. Fourth St., Duluth, 55812. Tel: 218-724-9111.

Mission Outreach and Propagation of the FaithDeacon WILLIAM STEIN, 2830 E. Fourth St., Duluth, 55812. Tel: 218-724-9111.

Diocesan Newspaper "The Northern Cross"—Deacon KYLE ELLER, Editor, 2830 E. Fourth St., Duluth, 55812. Tel: 218-724-9111.

CLERGY, PARISHES, MISSIONS AND PAROCHIAL SCHOOLS

CITY OF DULUTH

(ST. LOUIS COUNTY)

1—CATHEDRAL OF OUR LADY OF THE ROSARY (1919)
2801 E. 4th St., 55812. Tel: 218-728-3646; Email: duluth.cathedral@duluthcatholic.org; Web: duluthcathedral.com. Revs. Peter Muhich, Rector; Jeremy Bock, Parochial Vicar; Deacon Rodger Brannan.
Catechesis Religious Program—David Walsh, Jr./ High School Dir. Evangelization & Faith Formation. Students 111.

2—ST. ANTHONY, Closed. For inquiries for parish records contact St. Benedict Church, Duluth.

3—ST. BENEDICT (1950)
1419 St. Benedict St., 55811. Tel: 218-724-4828; Email: secretary@stbensduluth.org; Web: www.stbensduluth.org. Rev. Joel Hastings; Deacons John Foucault; John Weiske; Jim Philbin; John Specht; Kyle Eller.
Res.: 1419 Arrowhead Rd., 55811.
Catechesis Religious Program—Email: faithformation@stbensduluth.org; Email: youth@stbensduluth.org. Elizabeth Cyr, Dir. Parish Engagement & Family Faith Formation; Ms. Grace McDonough, D.R.E. (Gr. 6-12). Students 49.

4—SS. CLEMENT AND JEAN, Closed. For inquiries for parish records contact Holy Family Church, Duluth.

5—ST. ELIZABETH (1913) Revs. James B. Bissonette, J.C.L.; Steven Langenbrunner.
Office: 721 N. 57th Ave. W., 55807.
Tel: 218-624-0125; Email: slaveau@stjamesduluth.org; Web: www.stjamesparishduluth.com.

6—GOOD SHEPHERD, Closed. For inquiries for parish records contact St. James Church, Duluth.

7—HOLY FAMILY
2430 W. 3rd St., 55806-1801. Tel: 218-722-4445; Email: holyfamilyduluth@yahoo.com; Web: catholicduluth.org. Rev. Ryan Moravitz; Deacon Timothy Kittelson.
Catechesis Religious Program—Karen Ball, D.R.E. Students 48.

8—ST. JAMES (1888)
721 N. 57th Ave. W., 55807. Tel: 218-624-0125; Email: slaveau@stjamesduluth.org; Web: stjamesparishduluth.com. Rev. Richard Kunst.
Catechesis Religious Program—Email: djhackett@stjamesduluth.org. Mary Ann Rotondi, D.R.E. Students 75.

9—ST. JOHN (Woodland) (1915)
3 W. Chisholm St., 55803. Tel: 218-724-6332; Web: www.saintjohnsduluth.org. 4230 St. John's Ave., 55803. Rev. Drew Braun; Deacon Walt Beier.
Catechesis Religious Program—Students 122.

10—ST. JOSEPH (1921)
2410 Morris Thomas Rd., 55811. Tel: 218-722-2259; Email: stlawrencechurch@msn.com; Web: www.catholicduluth.org. 151 W. Linden St., 55811. Rev. Ryan Moravitz; Deacon Chico Anderson.
Catechesis Religious Program— Coordinated with St. Lawrence, Duluth. Karen Ball, D.R.E. Students 20.

11—ST. LAWRENCE (1959)
2410 Morris Thomas Rd., 55811. Tel: 218-722-2259; Email: stlawrencechurch@msn.com; Web: www.catholicduluth.org. Rev. Ryan Moravitz; Deacon Chico Anderson.
Catechesis Religious Program—Karen Ball, D.R.E. (PreK-12). Students 238.

12—ST. MARGARET MARY (1917) Closed. for parish records contact St. James Church, Duluth.

13—ST. MARY STAR OF THE SEA (1883)
325 E. Third St., 55805. Tel: 218-722-3078; Email: office@stmarystaroftheseaduluth.com. Revs. Peter Muhich; Jeremy Bock, Parochial Vicar.
Catechesis Religious Program—David Walsh, Faith Formation Coord. Students 25.

14—ST. MICHAEL (1914)
4901 E. Superior St., 55804. Tel: 218-525-1902; Email: office@stmichaelsduluth.org. Rev. William C. Graham.
School—St. Michael Lakeside School, (Grades PreSchool-5), 4628 Pitt St., 55804. Tel: 218-525-1931 ; Fax: 218-525-0296; Email: fr.francis@stmichaelsduluth.org; Web: www.smlsduluth.org. Mrs. Peggy Fredrickson, Prin.; Angela Mejdrich, Vice Prin. Students 109; Teachers 10.
Catechesis Religious Program—Students 104.

15—OUR LADY OF MERCY (1922) Closed. For inquiries for parish records contact the chancery.

16—SS. PETER AND PAUL, Closed. For inquiries for parish records contact Holy Family Church, Duluth.

17—ST. RAPHAEL (1959)
5779 Seville Rd., 55811. Tel: 218-729-7537; Email: raphaelchurch@yahoo.com; Web: www.straphaelandstrose.com. Rev. James B. Bissonette, J.C.L.
Catechesis Religious Program—Rita Sherepa, Dir., Faith Formation. Students 112.

OUTSIDE THE CITY OF DULUTH

AITKIN, AITKIN CO., ST. JAMES (1881) [CEM]
299 Red Oak Dr., Aitkin, 56431. Tel: 218-927-6581; Email: aggie@aitkincatholic.org; Web: aitkincatholic.org. Rev. David Forsman; Deacons William Stein; Michael Eisenbraun.
Catechesis Religious Program—Students 79.

AURORA, ST. LOUIS CO., OUR LADY OF HOPE (1908)
16 W. Fifth Ave. N., Aurora, 55705.
Tel: 218-229-3210; Email: secretary@olhp.org. Rev. Peter S. Lambert.
Catechesis Religious Program—Email: education@olhp.org. Linda Erickson, D.R.E. Students 45.

BABBITT, ST. LOUIS CO., ST. PIUS X (1957)
15 Ash Blvd., Babbitt, 55706. Tel: 218-827-2291; Email: stpiusx@midco.net. Rev. William Skarich; Deacon Gregory Hutar, Parish Coord.
Res.: 231 E. Camp St., Ely, 55731.
Catechesis Religious Program—Students 19.

BALL CLUB, ITASCA CO., ST. JOSEPH, [CEM]
51061 Wolf Dr., Deer River, 56636.
Tel: 218-246-8582; Email: stmarys@paulbunyan.net; Web: deerrivercatholic.com. P.O. Box 98, Deer River, 56636. Rev. Steven Daigle.

BAXTER, CROW WING CO., ALL SAINTS (2007)
411 N. 10th St., Brainerd, 56401-0327.
Tel: 218-822-4040; Fax: 218-829-8754; Email: office@blccnorth.org; Web: www.blccnorth.org. 16898 Carlson Lake Rd, Brainerd, 56401. Revs. Anthony Wroblewski; Paul Strommer; Deacons David Brown; Michael Knuth; Thomas Freece; Joseph Des Marais; Ralph Bakeberg.
Catechesis Religious Program—Students 39.

BENA, CASS CO., ST. ANNE, [CEM] Closed. For inquiries for parish records contact St. Joseph, Ball Club.

BEROUN, PINE CO., ST. JOSEPH (1896) [CEM]
535 8th St. S.W., Pine City, 55063. Tel: 320-629-2935 . Rev. Msgr. Aleksander Suchan.
Church: 19390 Praha Ave., Beroun, 55063.
Tel: 320-629-3442.

BIGFORK, ITASCA CO., OUR LADY OF THE SNOWS (1960)
320 Golf Course Ln., Bigfork, 56628.
Tel: 218-743-3255; Email: olschurch@bigfork.net. Mailing Address: P.O. Box 11, Bigfork, 56628. Rev. Thomas Galarneault.
Catechesis Religious Program—Students 13.

BIWABIK, ST. LOUIS CO., ST. JOHN (1893) (Civilly merged with Our Lady of Hope, Aurora.)
Tel: 218-229-3210; Email: secretary@olhp.org. Rev. Peter S. Lambert.

BRAINERD, CROW WING CO.

1—ST. ANDREW (1963)
1108 Willow St., Brainerd, 56401. Tel: 218-829-1340; Fax: 218-454-1625; Email: st.andrews@lakescatholic.org; Web: www.blccsouth.org. Rev. Daniel Weiske; Deacons Mike Koecheler; Gerald Bock; Keith Grow.
Catechesis Religious Program—

2—ST. FRANCIS, [CEM]
411 N. 10th St., Brainerd, 56401-3027.
Tel: 218-822-4040; Fax: 218-829-8754; Email: office@blccnorth.org; Web: www.blccnorth.org. Revs. Anthony Wroblewski; Paul Strommer; Deacons Michael Knuth; David Brown; Joseph Des Marais; Thomas Freece; Ralph Bakeberg.
Res.: 416 9th St. N., Brainerd, 56401.
Tel: 218-828-0184.
Church: 404 9th St., N., Brainerd, 56401.
Tel: 218-822-4040; Fax: 218-829-8754.
School—St. Francis of the Lakes, (Grades PreK-8), 817 Juniper St., Brainerd, 56401. Tel: 218-829-2344; Fax: 218-828-4157; Email: office@stfranciscatholicschool.org; Web: www.stfranciscatholicschool.org. Debra Euteneuer, Prin. Lay Teachers 16; Students 247.
Catechesis Religious Program—1108 Willow St., Brainerd, 56401. Tel: 218-829-1340; Email: djohnson@lakescatholic.org. Dan Johnson, D.R.E. Students 228.

BUHL, ST. LOUIS CO., OUR LADY OF THE SACRED HEART (1905)
118 Pennsylvania Ave., P.O. Box 27, Buhl, 55713-0027. Tel: 218-254-5703; Tel: 218-969-4043;
Fax: 218-254-3636; Email: stjoes@cpinternet.com. Rev. Anthony John Craig.
Pastor Res.: 113 4th St. S.W., Chisholm, 55719-2017.

CARLTON, CARLTON CO., ST. FRANCIS (1928) [CEM]
509 Sunrise Dr., Carlton, 55718. Tel: 218-384-4563. Rev. David Tushar.
Catechesis Religious Program—Students 42.

CASS LAKE, CASS CO., ST. CHARLES (1900)
308 Central Ave. N., Cass Lake, 56633.
Tel: 218-335-2359; Email: stchas@arvig.net; Web: stcharleschurch.weconnect.com. P.O. Box 368, Cass Lake, 56633. Rev. Steven Daigle.
Catechesis Religious Program—Maria Patten, D.R.E. Students 24.

CHISHOLM, ST. LOUIS CO., ST. JOSEPH (1905) [CEM]
113 Fourth St. S.W., Chisholm, 55719.
Tel: 218-254-5703; Tel: 218-969-4043;
Fax: 218-254-3636; Email: stjoes@cpinternet.com. Rev. Anthony John Craig.
Catechesis Religious Program—Students 86.

CLOQUET, CARLTON CO.

1—HOLY FAMILY (1889) [CEM]
280 Reservation Rd., Cloquet, 55720.
Tel: 218-879-6793; Email: qopoffice@gmail.com. 102 4th St., Cloquet, 55720. Rev. Justin Fish.

2—QUEEN OF PEACE (1881) [CEM 2]
102 4th St., Cloquet, 55720. Tel: 218-879-6793; Email: qopoffice@gmail.com. Rev. Justin Fish.
School—Queen of Peace School, (Grades PreK-6),
Tel: 218-879-8516; Fax: 218-879-8930; Email: bvanloh@queenofpeaceschool.org. Mr. William VanLoh, Prin. Lay Teachers 12; Students 92.
Catechesis Religious Program—Students 148.

COHASSET, ITASCA CO., ST. AUGUSTINE (1908)
315 S.W. 21st St., Grand Rapids, 55744.
Tel: 218-326-2843; Email: info@stjosephscatholic.org. 601 NW 2nd Ave., Cohasset, 55721. Revs. Seth Gogolin; Charles Friebohle.

COLERAINE, ITASCA CO., MARY IMMACULATE (1964)
10 Corey St., Coleraine, 55722. Tel: 218-885-1126; Email: fr.joseph.sobolik@duluthcatholic.org; Web: www.scmicatholic.com. P.O. Box 290, Coleraine, 55722. Rev. Joseph T. Sobolik.
Catechesis Religious Program—Tel: 218-885-6321; Email: christina.serena@duluthcatholic.org. Christina Serena, D.R.E. & Youth Min. Students 31.

COOK, ST. LOUIS CO., ST. MARY (1906) [CEM]
P.O. Box 609, Cook, 55723. Tel: 218-666-5334; Email: stmaryscook@q.com. Rev. Drew Braun.
Catechesis Religious Program—Students 12.

CROMWELL, CARLTON CO., IMMACULATE CONCEPTION, [CEM]
P.O. Box 378, Floodwood, 55736. Tel: 218-476-2367; Email: churchstlouis@gmail.com. Rev. Pio Atonio.
Church: 5944 Hwy 210, Cromwell, 55726.
Tel: 218-476-2367; Email: churchstlouis@gmail.com.

CROSBY, CROW WING CO., ST. JOSEPH
617 Poplar St., Crosby, 56441. Tel: 218-546-6559; Email: crosby@catholic.org. 23753 Forest Rd, Deerwood, 56444. Rev. Elias Gieske; Deacons Philip Mayer; Daniel Goshey; Roger Marks. Deerwood and Crosby are Clustered. They are both called St. Joseph
Catechesis Religious Program—(Combined with Deerwood) Students 132.

CROSSLAKE, CROW WING CO., IMMACULATE HEART CHURCH (1955)
35208 Co Rd 37, Crosslake, 56442. Tel: 218-692-3731 ; Email: ihc@crosslake.net. P.O. Box 155, Crosslake, 56442. Rev. Blake Edward Rozier; Deacons James Kirzeder; Barry Olson; Timothy Richardson; Charles Welte.
Res.: 35162 County Rd. 37, Crosslake, 56442.
Fax: 218-692-3732; Web: www.crosslakecatholic.com.
Chapel—Our Lady of Snows.

DEER RIVER, ITASCA CO., ST. MARY (1908)
15 1st Ave. NW, Deer River, 56636.
Tel: 218-246-8582; Email: stmarys@paulbunyan.net; Web: deerrivercatholic.com. P.O. Box 98, Deer River, 56636. Rev. Steven Daigle.
Catechesis Religious Program—Tel: 218-246-2180; Email: gwenn@paulbunyan.net. Gwenn Smith, D.R.E. Students 44.

DEERWOOD, CROW WING CO., ST. JOSEPH
617 Poplar St., Crosby, 56441. Tel: 218-546-6559; Email: crosby@catholic.org; Web: www.cuyunacatholic.org. Rev. Elias Gieske; Deacons Philip Mayer; Daniel Goshey; Roger Marks.

ELY, ST. LOUIS CO., ST. ANTHONY (1888)
231 E. Camp St., Ely, 55731. Tel: 218-365-4017. Rev. William Skarich.
Catechesis Religious Program—Email: StAnthonyDEF@gmail.com. Students 116.

EMILY, CROW WING CO., ST. EMILY (1951)
39922 Lake St., Emily, 56447. Tel: 218-763-2101; Email: 2stemily@gmail.com; Web: www.emilycatholic.com. P.O. Box 25, Emily, 56447. Rev. Blake Edward Rozier; Deacons Barry Olson; Jim Kirzeder; Timothy Richardson; Charles Welte.
Catechesis Religious Program—Combined with Immaculate Heart Church, Crosslake. Students 2.

EVELETH, ST. LOUIS CO., RESURRECTION (1899)
301 Adams Ave., Eveleth, 55734. Tel: 218-744-3277; Email: nicole.nguyen@duluthcatholic.org. Mailing Address: P.O. Box 586, Eveleth, 55734. Rev. Michael Garry.
Catechesis Religious Program—Email: pam@resj.org. Pam Rapacz, D.R.E., (Grades K-11). Students 131.

FEDERAL DAM, CASS CO., SACRED HEART, Closed. For inquiries for parish records contact St. Mary, Deer River.

FLOODWOOD, ST. LOUIS CO., ST. LOUIS, [CEM]
105 4th Ave. E., Floodwood, 55736.

Tel: 218-476-2367; Email: churchstlouis@gmail.com. P.O. Box 378, Floodwood, 55736. Rev. Pio Atonio.
Catechesis Religious Program—Jessica Rich, D.R.E. Students 45.

FORT RIPLEY, CROW WING CO., ST. MATHIAS, [CEM]
4529 County Rd. 121, Fort Ripley, 56449.
Tel: 218-829-1340; Fax: 218-454-1625; Email: st.andrews@lakescatholic.org; Web: www.blccsouth.org. Parish Office of St. Andrew's & St. Mathias: 1108 Willow St., SE, Brainerd, 56401. Rev. Daniel Weiske; Deacons Gerald Bock; Keith Grow; Michael Koecheler.
Catechesis Religious Program—Students 55.
Station—Crow Wing State Park, St. Mathias.

GARRISON, CROW WING CO., OUR LADY OF FATIMA (1954)
27332 Central St., Garrison, 56450.
Tel: 218-546-6559; Email: crosbycatholic@gmail.org. 617 Poplar St., Crosby, 56441. Rev. Elias Gieske; Deacons Roger Marks; Daniel Goshey; Philip Mayer.

GILBERT, ST. LOUIS CO., ST. JOSEPH (1909)
Mailing Address: Box 586, Eveleth, 55734.
Tel: 218-744-3277; Email: nicole.nguyen@duluthcatholic.org. 515 Summit and Lousianna Ave W, Gilbert, 55741. Rev. Michael Garry.
Catechesis Religious Program—Email: pam@resj.org. Pam Rapacz, D.R.E. Students 31.

GNESEN, ST. LOUIS CO., ST. JOSEPH (1896) [CEM]
4230 St. John's Ave., 55803. Tel: 218-724-6332. 6110 Church Rd., 55803. Rev. Drew Braun; Deacon Walt Beier.
Catechesis Religious Program—Students 8.

GRAND MARAIS, COOK CO., ST. JOHN (1933) [CEM]
10 E. 5th St., P.O. Box 549, Grand Marais, 55604.
Tel: 218-387-1409; Email: stjohns@boreal.org; Web: www.stjohns-holyrosary.org. Rev. Steven Langenbrunner; Deacon Peter Mueller.
Catechesis Religious Program—Sharon Dorr, D.R.E. Students 31.

GRAND PORTAGE, COOK CO., HOLY ROSARY, [CEM]
Upper Rd., Grand Portage, 55605. Tel: 218-387-1409; Email: stjohns@boreal.org; Web: www.stjohns-holyrosary.org. P.O. Box 549, Grand Marais, 55604. Rev. Steven Langenbrunner; Deacon Peter Mueller.
Catechesis Religious Program—Sharon Dorr, D.R.E. Students 4.

GRAND RAPIDS, ITASCA CO., ST. JOSEPH
315 S.W. 21st St., Grand Rapids, 55744.
Tel: 218-326-2843; Fax: 218-326-1663; Email: info@stjosephscatholic.org; Web: www.stjosephscatholic.org. Revs. Seth Gogolin; Charles Friebohle.
School—St. Joseph School, (Grades PreK-6), Tel: 218-326-6232; Email: principal@stjosephscatholic.org; Web: www.stjosephscatholic.org. Teresa Matetich, Prin. Administrators 1; Lay Teachers 13; Students 190.
Catechesis Religious Program—Lisa Neary, D.R.E., (Grades 6-12); Mandy Foss, D.R.E. (Grades K-5). Students 242.

HACKENSACK, CASS CO., SACRED HEART (1915)
Box 874, Walker, 56484. Tel: 218-547-1054; Email: stagnes@arvig.net. 300 First St. N., Hackensack, 56452. Rev. Timothy John Lange.

HIBBING, ST. LOUIS CO., BLESSED SACRAMENT
2310 7th Ave. E., Hibbing, 55746. Tel: 218-262-5541; Email: parish@blsachibbing.org; Web: www.blsachibbing.org. Revs. Gabriel Waweru; Beau Braun.
Res.: 2328 7th Ave. E., Hibbing, 55746.
School—Blessed Sacrament School, (Grades PreSchool-6), Tel: 218-263-3054; Email: secretary@acshibbing.org; Web: www.acshibbing.org. Lay Teachers 11; Students 140; Religious Teachers 2.
Catechesis Religious Program—Deborah Toma, Youth Programs; Jennifer Steinbrecher, Sunday School. Students 115.
Chapel—Side Lake, Blessed Sacrament Chapel.

HILLMAN, CROW WING CO., HOLY FAMILY (1925) [CEM]
1182 Co. Rd. 8, Hillman, 56338. 617 Poplar St., Crosby, 56441. Rev. Elias Gieske; Deacons Daniel Goshey; Philip Mayer; Roger Marks.

HINCKLEY, PINE CO., ST. PATRICK (1875) [CEM]
203 Lawler Ave. S., P.O. Box 490, Hinckley, 55037-0490. Tel: 320-384-6313, Ext. 3; Email: saintpatricks@scicable.com; Web: stpatrick-luke.org. Rev. Joseph A. Sirba; Deacons James Mostek, D.R.E.; Steven Odegard.
Catechesis Religious Program—Tel: 952-221-1183; Email: jimmostek@yahoo.com. Students 54.

HOYT LAKES, ST. LOUIS CO., QUEEN OF PEACE (1955) (Civilly merged with Our Lady of Hope, Aurora.)
16 W. 5th Ave., N., Aurora, 55705. Tel: 218-229-3210 ; Email: secretary@olhp.org. Rev. Peter S. Lambert.

INTERNATIONAL FALLS, KOOCHICHING CO., ST. THOMAS AQUINAS, [CEM]
810 Fifth St., International Falls, 56649.
Tel: 218-283-3293; Email: parishoffice@stthomasifalls.org. Rev. Benjamin Hadrich.
School—St. Thomas Aquinas School, (Grades PreSchool-4), Tel: 218-283-3430; Fax: 218-283-3553; Email: principal@stthomascatholicschool.com. Dawn Flesland, Prin. Lay Teachers 6; Students 44.
Catechesis Religious Program—Sabrina Etienne, D.R.E. Students 62.

LITTLEFORK, KOOCHICHING CO., ST. COLUMBAN
810 Fifth St., International Falls, 56649.
Tel: 218-283-3293; Email: parishoffice@stthomasifalls.org. Rev. Benjamin Hadrich.
Church: Box 44, Littlefork, 56653.
Catechesis Religious Program—Students 4.

LONGVILLE, CASS CO., ST. EDWARD (1917)
P.O. Box 38, Longville, 56655-0038.
Tel: 218-363-2799; Email: stedwardlongville@yahoo.com. Rev. Keith Bertram.

MCGRATH, AITKIN CO., OUR LADY OF FATIMA (1910) [CEM] Clustered with St. James, Aitkin.
102 S. Hwy. 65, McGrath, 56350. Tel: 218-927-6581; Web: www.mcgregorcatholicchurch.org. Mailing Address: 299 Red Oak Dr., Aitkin, 56431. Rev. David Forsman; Deacon Michael Barta.

MCGREGOR, AITKIN CO., HOLY FAMILY, Clustered with St. James, Aitkin.
2 S. Maddy St., McGregor, 55760. Mailing Address: Box 156, Aitkin, 56431. Tel: 218-927-6581; Email: aggie@aitkincatholic.org; Web: www.mcgregorcatholicchurch.org. Rev. David Forsman; Deacon Michael Barta.
Catechesis Religious Program—Students 20.

MEADOWLANDS, ST. LOUIS CO., ST. MARY, [CEM]
P.O. Box 378, Floodwood, 55736. Tel: 218-476-2367; Email: churchstlouis@gmail.com. Rev. Pio Atonio.
Church: 9999 Hwy 133, Meadowlands, 55765.
Catechesis Religious Program—Students 5.

MOOSE LAKE, CARLTON CO., HOLY ANGELS (1926) [CEM]
60 Hartman Dr., P.O. Box 487, Moose Lake, 55767.
Tel: 218-485-8214; Tel: 218-485-4909; Email: holyangelschurch@hotmail.com. Rev. Kristoffer McKusky.
Catechesis Religious Program—Tel: 218-485-8214. Kari Janz, D.R.E. & Sec.; Jean Marie Blair, D.R.E. & Youth Min. Students 125.

MOUNTAIN IRON, ST. LOUIS CO., SACRED HEART (1925) Closed. For inquires for parish records contact Holy Spirit, Virginia.

NASHWAUK, ITASCA CO., ST. CECILIA'S (1905)
326 Second St., Nashwauk, 55769. Tel: 218-885-1126 . Rev. Joseph T. Sobolik; Deacon Richard Johnston.
Catechesis Religious Program—Tel: 218-885-6321; Email: christina.serena@duluthcatholic.org. Christina Serena, D.R.E. & Youth Min. Students 64.

NISSWA, CROW WING CO., ST. CHRISTOPHER (1949) Merged civilly with Our Lady of the Lakes, Pequot Lakes.

NORTHOME, KOOCHICHING CO., ST. MICHAEL (1906)
12026 Lake St., Northome, 56661. Tel: 218-743-3255. c/o Our Lady of the Snows, P.O. Box 11, Bigfork, 56628. Rev. Thomas Galarneault; Deacon James Vande Kamp.
Catechesis Religious Program—Students 23.

ORR, ST. LOUIS CO., HOLY CROSS (1958)
P.O. Box 218, Orr, 55771. Tel: 218-757-3273; Email: holyc@centurytel.net. Rev. Drew Braun.
Church: 10696 Shady Grove Ln. S., Box 218, Orr, 55771.
Catechesis Religious Program—Students 27.

PEQUOT LAKES, CROW WING CO., OUR LADY OF THE LAKES (1931)
30918 Rasmussen Rd, P.O. Box 759, Pequot Lakes, 56472. Tel: 218-562-4760; Email: stalicechurch@gmail.com; Web: Ourladyofthelakes.weconnect.com. Rev. Michael Patullo; Deacons David Craig; Richard Paine; Joe Sechser; Mike Marvin.
Catechesis Religious Program—Students 205.

PINE BEACH, CROW WING CO., ST. THOMAS, [CEM]
411 N. 10th St., Brainerd, 56401-0327.
Tel: 218-822-4040; Email: office@blccnorth.org. Revs. Anthony Wroblewski; Paul Strommer; Deacons Joseph DesMarais; Thomas Freece; David Brown; Michael Knuth; Ralph Bakeberg. Summer Mission Chapel.

PINE CITY, PINE CO., IMMACULATE CONCEPTION (1910) [CEM]
535 8th St. S.W., Pine City, 55063. Tel: 320-629-2935 ; Email: deb.bombard@duluthcatholic.org. Rev. Msgr. Aleksander Suchan; Deacons Eugene Biever; Mark Pulkrabek.
Catechesis Religious Program—Tel: 320-629-3911. Students 175.

PINE RIVER, CASS CO., OUR LADY OF LOURDES (1917) Merged civilly with Our Lady of the Lakes, Pequot Lakes.

PROCTOR, ST. LOUIS CO., ST. ROSE
3 Sixth Ave., Proctor, 55810. Tel: 218-624-0007; Email: saintroseproctor@qwestoffice.net. Rev. James B. Bissonette, J.C.L.
Catechesis Religious Program—Email: beckykubat@hotmail.com. Becky Kubat, D.R.E. Students 24.

REMER, CASS CO., ST. PAUL
101 3rd Ave. SE, P.O. Box 38, Longville, 56655.
Tel: 218-363-2799; Email: stedwardlongville@yahoo.com. Rev. Keith Bertram.
Catechesis Religious Program—Students 20.

SAGINAW, ST. LOUIS CO., ST. PHILIP NERI, Closed. For inquires for parish records contact St. Rose, Proctor.

SANDSTONE, PINE CO., ST. LUKE, [CEM]
122 Commercial Ave. N., Sandstone, 55072. Mailing Address: P.O. Box 644, Sandstone, 55072.
Tel: 320-245-5175; Email: saintlukes@scicable.com. Rev. Joseph A. Sirba; Deacon James Mostek.
Catechesis Religious Program—Tel: 952-221-1183; Email: jimmostek@yahoo.com. Students 44.

SAWYER, CARLTON CO., SS. MARY & JOSEPH (1859)
509 Sunrise Dr., Carlton, 55718. Tel: 218-384-4563. Rev. David Tushar.
Catechesis Religious Program—1225 Mission Rd., Sawyer, 55780. Students 29.

SILVER BAY, LAKE CO., ST. MARY (1955)
57 Horn Blvd., Silver Bay, 55614. Tel: 218-226-3100; Email: stmarysilverbay@outlook.com. Revs. Steven Laflamme, J.C.L.; Michael J. Lyons, In Res., (Retired); Deacon Fred Wright.
Catechesis Religious Program—Students 34.

SQUAW LAKE, ITASCA CO., ST. CATHERINE (1942)
52265 State Hwy. 46, Squaw Lake, 56681.
Tel: 218-743-3255. Mailing Address: c/o Our Lady of the Snows, P.O. Box 11, Bigfork, 56628. Rev. Thomas Galarneault.

STURGEON LAKE, PINE CO., ST. ISIDORE (1887) [CEM]
9010 Main St., Sturgeon Lake, 55783.
Tel: 218-372-3284; Email: st.mary.church@frontiernet.net; Web: stisidoresturgeonlake.org. Mailing Address: c/o St. Mary Church, 8118 Lake St., Willow River, 55795-0097. Rev. Kristoffer McKusky.
Catechesis Religious Program—60 Hartman Dr., Moose Lake, 55767. Tel: 218-485-8214; Email: holyangelschurch@hotmail.com. Kari Janz, D.R.E.; Liz Mascarenas, D.R.E. Students 10.

TOWER, ST. LOUIS CO., ST. MARTIN (1884)
107 N. 3rd St., Tower, 55790. Mailing Address: P.O. Box 757, Tower, 55790. Tel: 218-753-4310; Email: stmartins@frontiernet.net. Rev. Nicholas Nelson.
Catechesis Religious Program—Erin Peitso, D.R.E. Students 19.

TWO HARBORS, LAKE CO., HOLY SPIRIT, [CEM]
227 Third St., Two Harbors, 55616.
Tel: 218-834-4659; Email: hspirit@outlook.com; Web: www.holyspirittwoharbors.org. Rev. Steven Laflamme, J.C.L.
Catechesis Religious Program—Students 83.

VIRGINIA, ST. LOUIS CO.
1—HOLY SPIRIT
306 S. Second St., Virginia, 55792. Tel: 218-741-6344 ; Fax: 218-741-6345; Web: www.holyspiritvirginia.com. Rev. Brandon James Moravitz; Deacon Daniel Schultz.
School—Marquette Catholic School, (Grades PreK-6), 311 Third St. S., Virginia, 55792.
Tel: 218-741-6811; Fax: 218-741-2158; Email: mcsprincipal01@gmail.com; Web: www.marquettecatholicschool.com. Jean Virant, Prin. Lay Teachers 12; Students 125.
Catechesis Religious Program—Email: b.frost@mediacombb.net; Email: h.milani@mediacombb.net. Students 156.
2—SACRED HEART (1950) Closed. For inquiries for parish records contact Holy Spirit Church, Virginia.

WALKER, CASS CO., ST. AGNES (1918)
210 Division St., P.O. Box 874, Walker, 56484.
Tel: 218-547-1054; Email: stagnes@arvig.net. Rev. Timothy John Lange.
Catechesis Religious Program—Dan Schuler, D.R.E. & Youth Min. Students 61.

WILLOW RIVER, PINE CO., ST. MARY (1907) [CEM]
8118 Lake St., Willow River, 55795.
Tel: 218-372-3284; Email: st.mary.church@frontiernet.net. Rev. Kristoffer McKusky.
Catechesis Religious Program—60 Hartman Dr., Moose Lake, 55767. Tel: 218-485-8214; Email: holyangelschurch@hotmail.com. Kari Janz, D.R.E.; Liz Mascarenas, D.R.E. Students 4.

INDIAN MISSIONS

DULUTH, ST. LOUIS CO., INDIAN MISSIONS
c/o Chancery Office, 2830 E. Fourth St., 55812.
Tel: 218-724-9111; Fax: 218-724-1056; Email: mmessingschlager@dioceseduluth.org. Sr. Marie Rose Messingschlager, C.D.P.

Chaplains of Public Institutions.

Hospitals

DULUTH. *St. Luke's Hospital*, Tel: 218-249-5555. Rev. John C. Petrich, Chap., 915 E. 1st St., 55805.
St. Mary's Medical Center, 407 E. 3rd St., 55805. Tel: 218-786-4000. Rev. Thomas J. Foster, Chap.

MOOSE LAKE. *Moose Lake State Hospital*. Rev. Kris McKuskey, Chap.

Correctional Institutions

SAGINAW. *Northeast Regional Correctional Institution*. Rev. John C. Petrich, Chap., Tel: 218-722-0613.

SANDSTONE. *Sandstone Federal Prison*. Rev. Kris McKuskey.

WILLOW RIVER. *Challenge Incarceration Program*. Rev. Kris McKuskey, Chap.

On Duty Outside the Diocese:
Revs.—
Deutsch, Timothy, 2569 W. Victoria Dr., Alpine, CA 91901-3662
Johnson, Lawrence P., 1820 Froude St., San Diego, CA 92107.

Assignment Pending:
Rev.—
Solors, Stephen.

Leave of Absence:
Rev.—
Lederer, Brian.

Retired:
Revs.—
Antus, Roland, (Retired), 221 Boulder Dr., Cloquet, 55720. Tel: 218-348-3734
Arimond, Vincent, (Retired), 4195 Westberg Rd., Bldg. 5, Rm. C1, Hermantown, 55811. Tel: 218-491-3989
Boland, Eamonn, (Retired), 424 Jones St., Eveleth, 55734. Tel: 218-248-0369
Doyle, John, (Retired), 330 E. 3rd St., Rm. 430, 55805. Tel: 218-740-5038
Fournier, William, (Retired), 17404 N. 99th Ave., #124, Sun City, AZ 85373. Tel: 623-692-7592
Fruth, Paul, (Retired), P.O. Box 823, Crosslake, 56442. Tel: 218-692-2440
Gagne, Ronald, (Retired), 6894 Paulson Rd., Cotton, 55724. Tel: 218-482-3415
Hoffman, Dennis H., (Retired), P.O. Box 913, Ely, 55731. Tel: 218-591-5668
La Patka, Gerald, (Retired), 1125 9th St. S.E. Apt# 241, Wilmar, AZ 56201. Tel: 602-741-9305
Lyons, Michael J., (Retired), 57 Horn Blvd., Silver Bay, 55614. Tel: 218-830-1600
Mudrak, Lloyd, (Retired), 4195 Westberg Rd., Rm. 6A, Hermantown, 55811. Tel: 218-722-1062
Partika, Richard, (Retired), 925 Kenwood Ave., #2132, 55811. Tel: 218-728-3498
Schultz, Brian, (Retired)
Stretton, Noel, (Retired), 1902 St. Louis Ave., #218, 55802. Tel: 218-464-1292
Walsh, Seamus, (Retired), 35 2nd St., #3, Proctor, 55810
Wild, Jon Anthony, (Retired), 935 Kenwood Ave., #313, 55811
Zeck, George, (Retired), 500 Heartwood Dr., Rm. 311, Crosby, 56441. Tel: 218-821-6121.

Permanent Deacons:
Anderson, Dennis, (Retired)
Anderson, H. L., St. Lawrence, Duluth
Bakeberg, Ralph, St. Francis, Brainerd; All Saints, Baxter
Barta, Michael, Holy Family, McGregor; Our Lady of Fatima, McGrath
Bassa, Bryan, SS, Mary & Joseph, Sawyer
Beier, Walter, St. John, Duluth; St. Joseph, Gnesen
Biever, Eugene, Immaculate Conception, Pine City; St. Joseph, Beroun
Bock, Gerald, St. Andrew, Brainerd
Brannan, Rodger, Cathedral of Our Lady of the Rosary & St. Mary Star of the Sea, Duluth
Brown, David, St. Francis, Brainerd; All Saints, Baxter
Clack, James, St. Agnes, Walker
Craig, David, St. Alice, Pequot Lakes
Des Marais, Joseph, St. Francis, Brainerd; All Saints, Baxter
Egan, Timothy, Holy Spirit, Two Harbors
Eisenbraun, Michael, St. James, Duluth
Eller, Kyle, St. Benedict, Duluth
Ferris, Jack, (Retired)
Foucault, John, St. Benedict, Duluth
Freece, Thomas, St. Francis, Brainerd; All Saints, Baxter
Goshey, Daniel, St. Joseph, Grand Rapids
Griffiths, James, (Retired)
Grow, Keith, St. Andrew/St. Mathias, Brainerd
Hedlund, Steven, St. Francis, Carlton
Hutar, Gregory, St. Anthony, Ely; St. Pius, Babbitt
Johnson, Lyle, St. James, Duluth
Johnston, Richard, Nashwauk, Keewatin, Pengilly
Kirzeder, James, Immaculate Heart, Crosslake; St. Emily, Emily
Kittelson, Timothy, Holy Family, Duluth
Klick, Don, St. Anthony, Ely; St. Pius, Babbitt
Knuth, Michael, St. Francis, Brainerd; All Saints, Baxter
Koecheler, Michael, St. Andrew/St. Mathias, Brainerd
Kubat, Thomas, St. Rose, Proctor; St. Raphael, Duluth
Laumeyer, Richard, St. Mary Star of the Sea, Duluth
Marks, Roger, St. James, Aitkin; Our Lady of Fatima, Garrison; Holy Family, Hillman
Mayer, Philip, St. Joseph, Crosby; St. Joseph, Deerwood
Moravitz, Richard, St. Anthony, Ely; St. Pius, Babbitt
Mostek, Jim, St. Luke, Sandstone; St. Patrick, Hinckley
Mueller, Peter, St. John, Grand Marais; Holy Rosary, Grand Portage
Odegard, Steven, St. Patrick, Hinckley
Olson, Barry, St. Emily, Emily
Paine, Richard, Our Lady of the Lakes, Pequot Lakes
Peters, Scott, Holy Spirit, Two Harbors
Philbin, James, St. Benedict, Duluth
Provost, Carl, St. Rose, Proctor
Pulkrabek, Mark, Immaculate Conception, Pine City; St. Joseph, Beroun
Ramsey, Herbert, St. Agnes, Walker
Sampson, Ray, (Retired)
Schuler, Steve, St. Joseph, Grand Rapids
Schultz, Daniel, Holy Spirit, Virginia
Sechser, Joseph, Our Lady of the Lakes, Pequot Lakes
Skala, Mark, Our Lady of Hope, Aurora
Skansgaard, Jon, Queen of Peace & Holy Family, Cloquet
Specht, John, St. Benedict, Duluth
Stein, William, St. James, Aitkin; Holy Family, Hillman; Our Lady of Fatima, McGrath & Garrison
Toma, Grant, Blessed Sacrament, Hibbing
Vande Kamp, James, St. Michael's, Northome
Weiske, John, St. Benedict, Duluth
Windus, Theodore Sr., (Retired)
Woznick, Gregory, (Retired)
Wright, Fred, St. Mary, Silver Bay
Zaren, Francis, St. Thomas, International Falls; St. Columban, Littlefork.

INSTITUTIONS LOCATED IN DIOCESE

[A] COLLEGES AND UNIVERSITIES

DULUTH. *College of St. Scholastica*, (Grades Bachelors-Doctorate), 1200 Kenwood Ave., 55811. Tel: 218-723-6000; Fax: 218-723-6290; Web: www.css.edu. Dr. Colette Geary, Pres.; Steve Lyons, Vice Pres. for Student Affairs; Kevin McGrew, Dir. Library. A coed Benedictine college for resident, day, evening, and online students. Lay Staff 308; Sisters 4; Students 4,406; Lay Faculty 205.

[B] ELEMENTARY SCHOOLS, INTERPAROCHIAL

DULUTH. *Stella Maris Academy*, (Grades PreK-8), 2802 E. Fourth St., 55812. Tel: 218-724-8565; Email: michael.mazzio@stellamaris.academy; Web: www.stellamaris.academy. Mrs. Hilaire Hauer, Pres.; Jesse Murray, Prin.; Peggy Frederickson, Prin.; Julianne Blazevic, Prin.; Mr. Michael Mazzio, Business Mgr.
Legal Title: Duluth Area Catholic Schools, Holy Rosary School, St. James School, St. John's School. Aides 4; Lay Teachers 39; Students 453; Principals 3; Clergy / Religious Teachers 2; Staff 19.
Holy Rosary School, (Grades K-4), 2801 E. 4th St., 55812. Tel: 218-724-8565; Email: peggy.frederickson@stellamaris.academy. Mrs. Peggy Fredrickson, Prin. Lay Teachers 23; Students 222.
St. James Catholic School, (Grades PreSchool-8), 715 N. 57th Ave., W., 55807. Tel: 218-624-1511; Email: slaveau@stjamesduluth.org; Web: www.stellamaris.academy. Julianne Blazevic, Prin. Lay Teachers 15; Students 152; Religiuos Teachers 3.
St. John's School, (Grades 5-8), 1 W. Chisholm St., 55803. Tel: 218-724-9392; Fax: 218-724-9368; Email: jesse.murray@stellamaris.academy. Peggy Frederickson, Prin. Lay Teachers 10; Students 125.

[C] GENERAL HOSPITALS

DULUTH. *St. Mary's Medical Center*, 407 E. Third St., 55805. Tel: 218-786-4000; Fax: 218-786-4888; Email: james.garvey@essentiahealth.org; Web: www.essentiahealth.org. James Garvey, SVP Hospital Opers. East Region & Admin. SMMC; Mr. John Gibbs, M.Div., Dir. of Chap. Svcs.; Rev. Thomas J. Foster, Chap. Bed Capacity 329; Nurses 1,005; Sisters 3; Tot Asst. Annually 140,917; Total Staff 2,976.

BRAINERD. *St. Joseph's Medical Center*, 523 N. Third St., Brainerd, 56401. Tel: 218-829-2861; Email: info@essentiahealth.org; Web: www.essentiahealth.org. Adam Rees, Pres. Bed Capacity 162; Nurses 457; Tot Asst. Annually 235,611; Total Staff 1,502.

[D] HOMES FOR AGED

DULUTH. *Benedictine Living Community of Duluth* (Sub. of Benedictine Health System) 935 Kenwood Ave., 55811. Tel: 218-723-6408; Fax: 218-723-6449; Email: brian.pattock@bhshealth.org. Brian Pattock, Admin. Children 85; Senior Housing Apartments 45; Assisted Living Apartments 35; Skilled Nursing Beds 96; Short Term Stay/Rehabilitative Beds 30; Day Care (Adults) 25; Westwood Terrace Memory Care 21.

EVELETH. *Arrowhead Senior Living Community* dba St. Raphael's Health and Rehab Center, 601 Grant Ave., Eveleth, 55734. Tel: 218-744-9800; Fax: 218-744-9829; Email: cheri.high@bhshealth.org. Cheri High, Admin. Total Staff 100; Assisted Units 14; Skilled Beds 76.

VIRGINIA. *Arrowhead Senior Living Community* dba St. Michael's Health and Rehabilitation Center, 1201 8th St., S., Virginia, 55792. Tel: 218-748-7800; Fax: 218-748-7890; Email: cheri.high@bhshealth.org. Cheri High, Admin. Residents 250; Total Staff 100; Skilled Beds 83.

[E] CONVENTS AND RESIDENCES FOR SISTERS

DULUTH. *Motherhouse and Novitiate of the Sisters of Saint Benedict*, St. Scholastica Monastery, 1001 Kenwood Ave., 55811. Tel: 218-723-6555; Fax: 218-723-5902; Email: braway@css.edu; Web: www.duluthbenedictines.org. Sr. Luce Marie Dionne, O.S.B., Archivist. Professed Sisters 54.

[F] NEWMAN CENTERS

DULUTH. *Newman Catholic Campus Ministry*, 421 W. Marie St., 55811. Tel: 218-728-3757; Email: hserena@dioceseduluth.org; Email: fathermikeschmitz@gmail.com; Web: www.bulldogCatholic.org. Heather Serena, Coord.; Rev. Michael Schmitz, Dir., Web: www.umdcatholic.org.

[G] MISCELLANEOUS LISTINGS

DULUTH. *Benedictine Sisters Benevolent Association* (Parent Co.) 1001 Kenwood Ave., 55811-2300. Tel: 218-723-6089; Fax: 218-723-5902; Email: braway@css.edu; Web: www.duluthbenedictines.org. Sr. Beverly Raway, O.S.B., Pres.
Benedictine Health System, 4560 Norway Pines Pl., Hermantown, 55811. Tel: 218-786-2370; Fax: 218-786-2373; Email: jerry.carley@bhshealth.org; Web: www.bhshealth.org. Sponsored by Benedictine Sisters Benevolent Association.Benedictine Health System Subsidiaries and Sponsored Entities Not Located In The Diocese: Benedictine Care Centers; (St. Crispin Living Community, Red Wing, MN; Benedictine Health Center at Innsbruck, New Brighton, MN); Benedictine Health Dimensions, Inc.; Benedictine Living Communities-Bismarck, Inc. dba St. Gabriel's Community, Bismarck, ND; Benedictine Living Communities, Inc. (Benedictine Living Center of Garrison, Garrison, ND; Prince of Peace Care Center and Evergreen Place, Ellendale, ND; St. Benedict's Health Center and Benedict Court, Dickinson, ND; Benedictine Living Community of Wahpeton, Wahpeton, ND; St. Rose Care Center and Rosewood Court, LaMoure, ND); Benedictine Living Community of St. Peter, St. Peter, MN; Bridges Care Center dba Benedictine Living Community of Ada, Ada, MN; Madonna Towers of Rochester, Inc., Rochester, MN; Saint Anne of Winona and Callista Ct., Winona, MN; St. Gertrude's Health and Rehabilitation Center, Shakopee, MN; Villa St. Vincent, Crookston, MN; Benedictine Health Center of Minneapolis, Minneapolis, MN; Madonna Meadows of Rochester, Rochester, MN; Living Community of St. Joseph, St. Joseph, MO; Benedictine Senior

Living at Steeple Pointe, Osseo, MN; Benedictine Senior Living Community of New London dba Grace Living Community of GlenOaks, New London, MN; Benedictine Senior Living Community of Winsted dba St. Mary's Care Center, Winsted, MN. Catholic Residential Services, Inc.; (Benedictine Living Community of La Crosse, La Crosse, WI; Benedictine Living Community of Wausau, Wausau, WI).

Benedictine Health System Foundation, Inc., 4560 Norway Pines Pl., Hermantown, 55811.
Tel: 218-786-2370; Fax: 218-786-2373; Email: lee.larson@bhshealth.org. Jerry Carley, CEO; Lee Larson, Pres. (Sub. of Benedictine Health System) Comprised of the following Associated Foundations: Benedictine Living Community of Duluth Foundation, Duluth, MN; Benedictine Health Center of Minneapolis Foundation, Minneapolis, MN; Benedictine Living Center of Garrison, Foundation, Garrison, ND; Prince of Peace and Evergreen Foundation, Ellendale, ND; St. Benedict's Health Center Foundation, Dickinson, ND; Benedictine Living Community of Wahpeton Foundation, Wahpeton, ND; St. Gabriel's Community Foundation, Bismarck, ND; St. Rose Foundation, LaMoure, ND; Benedictine Living Community of St. Peter Foundation, St. Peter, MN; Benedictine Living Community of Ada Foundation, Ada, MN; Cerenity Foundation, St. Paul, MN; Cerenity-Humboldt Foundation, St. Paul, MN; Cerenity-Marian of St. Paul Foundation, St. Paul, MN; Cerenity-White Bear Lake Foundation, White Bear Lake, MN; Innsbruck Foundation, New Brighton, MN; Koda Living Community Foundation, Owatonna, MN; Living Community of St. Joseph Foundation, St. Joseph, MO; Madonna Living Community Foundation of Rochester, Rochester, MN; Nazareth Living Center Foundation, St. Louis, MO; Saint Anne Foundation, Winona, MN; St. Crispin Foundation, Red Wing, MN; St. Gertrude's Foundation, Shakopee, MN; St. Mary's of Winsted Foundation, Winsted, MN; St. Michael's Foundation, Virginia, MN; St. Raphael's Foundation, Eveleth, MN; Villa St. Benedict Foundation, Lisle, IL; Villa St. Vincent/The Summit Foundation, Crookston, MN.

Benedictine Health Center (Sub. of Benedictine Health System) 935 Kenwood Ave., 55811.
Tel: 218-723-6408; Fax: 218-723-6449; Email: brian.pattock@bhshealth.org. Brian Pattock, Admin.

Benedictine Living Communities Inc., 4560 Norway Pines Pl., Hermantown, 55811. Tel: 218-786-2370; Fax: 218-786-2373; Email: steve.przybilla@bhshealth.org. Steven Pryzbilla, COO. (Sub. of Benedictine Health System).

St. Mary's Medical Center, 407 E. Third St., 55805.
Tel: 218-786-4000; Fax: 218-786-4383. James Garvey, Admin.; Sr. Joan Marie Stelman, O.S.B., Prog. Dir., Mission Integration for Essentia Health; Rev. Thomas J. Foster, Chap.; Anne Stephen, Chief Medical Officer. Affiliate: St. Mary's Hospital of Superior, WI.

St. Joseph's Medical Center, Brainerd Affiliated with Essentia Health 523 N. Third St., Brainerd, 56401. Tel: 218-829-2861; Fax: 218-828-3103. Adam Rees, Pres. & CEO.

Polinsky Medical Rehabilitation Center, 530 E. Second St., 55805. Tel: 218-786-5360;
Fax: 218-786-5340. Joan Jeanetta, Dir. (Sub. of St. Mary's Medical Center).

The Blessed Nuno Society, P.O. Box 3484, 55803.
Tel: 218-310-5110; Email: blessednunosociety@gmail.com; Web: www.blessednuno.org. Carl Sylvester, Exec. Dir.

Holy Rosary Parish Endowment Fund, 2801 E. Fourth St., 55812. Tel: 218-728-3646; Email: business@duluthcathedral.com. Rev. Peter Muhich, Rector.

The Human Life and Development Fund of the Diocese of Duluth, 2830 E. Fourth St., 55812.
Tel: 218-724-9111; Fax: 218-724-1056; Email: fhoefferle@dioceseduluth.org. Mr. Franz Hoefferle, Dir., Fin.

The Seminary Endowment Fund of the Diocese of Duluth, 2830 E. 4th St., 55812. Tel: 218-724-9111;
Fax: 218-724-1056; Email: fhoefferle@dioceseduluth.org. Mr. Franz Hoefferle, Sec./Treas.

The Catholic Religious Education Endowment Fund of the Diocese of Duluth, 2830 E. 4th St., 55812.
Tel: 218-724-9111; Fax: 218-724-1056; Email: fhoefferle@dioceseduluth.org. Mr. Franz Hoefferle, Fin. Dir.

CLOQUET. *Educational Endowment Trust, Queen of Peace Church*, 102 4th St., Cloquet, 55720.
Tel: 218-879-6793; Email: qopoffice@gmail.com. Rev. Justin Fish.

DEER RIVER. **Our Lady of the Holy Trinity Magnificat Chapter*, 33350 State Hwy. 46, Deer River, 56636.
Tel: 218-251-6556; Email: rtnorris7@gmail.com. Teresa Norris, Coordinator. (Sub-chapter of S.W. Deanery Chapter of the Magnificat-Our Lady of the Lakes).

HACKENSACK. *S.W. Deanery Chapter of Magnificat of the Diocese of Duluth*, 3989 Bayview Dr., N.W., Hackensack, 56452. Tel: 218-675-6180; Email: garoutte@tds.net. Betty Garoutte.

HERMANTOWN. **Sister Thea Bowman Black Catholic Educational Foundation*, 4870 Woodridge Dr., Hermantown, 55811. Tel: 218-969-6227; Email: maryloujll@aol.com. Mrs. Mary Lou Jennings, Exec. Dir.

HIBBING. *Hibbing Catholic Schools Endowment Fund*, 2310 7th Ave. E., Hibbing, 55746.
Tel: 218-262-5541; Fax: 218-263-3682; Email: parish@blsachibbing.org. Rev. Gabriel Waweru, Contact Person.

PROCTOR. *Christ Child Society of Duluth, Inc.*, 5566 Halie Rd., Proctor, 55810. Email: kathfors@hotmail. Rev. Pio Antonio, Spiritual Adv./Care Svcs.

TWO HARBORS. *Saint Raphaels Guild A Chartered Guild of the Catholic Medical Association*, 398 Scenic Dr., Two Harbors, 55616. Cell: 218-349-9175. Timothy J. Egan, M.D., Pres.

RELIGIOUS INSTITUTES OF MEN REPRESENTED IN THE DIOCESE

For further details refer to the corresponding bracketed number in the Religious Institutes of Men or Women section.

[0630]—*Missionaries of the Holy Family*—M.S.F.

RELIGIOUS INSTITUTES OF WOMEN REPRESENTED IN THE DIOCESE

[0230]—*Benedictine Sisters of Pontifical Jurisdiction* (St. Joseph, MN; Watertown, SD; St. Paul, MN; Duluth, MN)—O.S.B.

[1000]—*Congregation of Divine Providence of Kentucky*—C.D.P.

[1870]—*Handmaids of the Heart of Jesus*—A.C.J.

DIOCESAN CEMETERIES

DULUTH. *Calvary Cemetery*, 4820 Howard Gnesen Rd., 55803. Tel: 218-724-3376; Fax: 218-724-9700; Email: tsail.calvaryduluth@gmail.com; Email: calvaryduluth@gmail.com; Web: www.calvarycemeteryduluth.com. Mr. Tim Sailstad, Supt. & Sexton

NECROLOGY

† Moran, Patrick, (Retired), Died Mar. 11, 2018
† Perkovich, Frank, (Retired), Died Jul. 16, 2018

An asterisk (*) denotes an organization that has established tax-exempt status directly with the IRS and is not covered by the USCCB Group Ruling.

Diocese of El Paso

(Dioecesis Elpasensis)

Most Reverend

MARK J. SEITZ

Bishop of El Paso; ordained May 17, 1980; appointed Titular Bishop of Cozyla and Auxiliary Bishop of Dallas March 11, 2010; ordained April 27, 2010; appointed Bishop of El Paso May 6, 2013; installed July 9, 2013. *Office: 499 St. Matthews St., El Paso, TX 79907.*

Chancery Office: 499 St. Matthews St., El Paso, TX 79907. Tel: 915-872-8407; Fax: 915-872-8413.

Web: www.elpasodiocese.org

ERECTED MARCH 3, 1914.

Square Miles 26,686.

Comprises in Texas, the Counties of El Paso, Brewster, Culberson, Hudspeth, Jeff Davis, Loving, Presidio, Reeves, Ward and Winkler.

For legal titles of parishes and diocesan institutions, consult the Chancery Office.

STATISTICAL OVERVIEW

Personnel	
Bishop	1
Priests: Diocesan Active in Diocese	50
Priests: Diocesan Active Outside Diocese	2
Priests: Retired, Sick or Absent	33
Number of Diocesan Priests	85
Religious Priests in Diocese	48
Total Priests in Diocese	133
Extern Priests in Diocese	8
Ordinations:	
Diocesan Priests	2
Religious Priests	1
Transitional Deacons	3
Permanent Deacons in Diocese	33
Total Brothers	5
Total Sisters	100
Parishes	
Parishes	59
With Resident Pastor:	
Resident Diocesan Priests	35
Resident Religious Priests	19
Without Resident Pastor:	
Administered by Deacons	1
Administered by Religious Women	1
Administered by Lay People	1
Missions	19
Professional Ministry Personnel:	
Brothers	5
Sisters	100
Lay Ministers	1
Welfare	
Health Care Centers	1
Special Centers for Social Services	1
Educational	
Seminaries, Diocesan	1
Students from This Diocese	4
Diocesan Students in Other Seminaries	24
Total Seminarians	28
High Schools, Private	3
Total Students	922
Elementary Schools, Diocesan and Parish	6
Total Students	1,445
Elementary Schools, Private	2
Total Students	393
Catechesis/Religious Education:	
High School Students	5,159
Elementary Students	9,436
Total Students under Catholic Instruction	17,383
Teachers in the Diocese:	
Brothers	5
Sisters	10
Lay Teachers	214
Vital Statistics	
Receptions into the Church:	
Infant Baptism Totals	3,090
Minor Baptism Totals	395
Adult Baptism Totals	167
Received into Full Communion	410
First Communions	3,105
Confirmations	3,386
Marriages:	
Catholic	638
Interfaith	84
Total Marriages	722
Deaths	2,257
Total Catholic Population	720,226
Total Population	900,283

Former Bishops—Most Revs. JOHN J. BROWN, S.J., preconized Bishop of El Paso, Jan. 22, 1915; resigned June 16, 1915; ANTHONY J. SCHULER, S.J., D.D., cons. Oct. 28, 1915; died June 3, 1944; SIDNEY M. METZGER, S.T.D., J.C.D., cons. April 10, 1940; succeeded to See, Nov. 29, 1942; retired May 29, 1978; died April 12, 1986; PATRICK F. FLORES, D.D., cons. May 5, 1970; installed Bishop of El Paso, May 29, 1978; appt. Archbishop of San Antonio, Aug. 28, 1979; RAYMUNDO J. PENA, D.D., cons. Dec. 13, 1976; appt. Bishop of El Paso, April 29, 1980; appt. Bishop of Brownsville, May 23, 1995; ARMANDO X. OCHOA, D.D., ord. May 23, 1970; appt. Titular Bishop of Sitifi and Auxiliary of the Archdiocese of Los Angeles Dec. 29, 1986; ord. Bishop Feb. 23, 1987; appt. Bishop of El Paso April 1, 1996; installed June 26, 1996; appt. Bishop of Fresno Dec. 1, 2011; retired March 5, 2019.

Vicar General and Moderator of the Curia—Very Rev. BENJAMIN FLORES, V.G.

Vicar for Clergy—Rev. MIGUEL BRISENO, O.F.M.Conv.

Chancellor—MS. PATRICIA L. FIERRO.

Liaison for Women Religious—Sr. JANET GILDEA, S.C., M.D., 499 St. Matthews St., El Paso, 79907. Tel: 915-872-8407.

Diocesan Pastoral Center—499 St. Matthews St., El Paso, 79907. Tel: 915-872-8400; Fax: 915-872-8423. Refer all official business to this address.

Presbyteral Council—Most Rev. MARK J. SEITZ; Very Rev. BENJAMIN FLORES, V.G.; Revs. SAUL PACHECO; MARIANO H. LOPEZ; FRANCISCO HERNANDEZ; ALLAN OLUOCH ALAKA; MIGUEL BRISENO, O.F.M.Conv.; EDWARD C. CARPENTER; PABLO MATTA; Very Rev. ANTHONY C. CELINO, J.C.L., V.F.; Revs. WILSON CUEVAS; MIGUEL ANGEL SANCHEZ; KENNON Y. DUCRE, S.T.L.; MIGUEL ALCUINO; Rev. Msgr. DAVID G. FIERRO.

Ex Officio—Revs. ROBERT S. KOBE; JOE MOLINA; TRINIDAD FUENTEZ; FRANK LOPEZ; MIGUEL BRISENO, O.F.M.Conv.; Very Rev. ANTHONY C. CELINO, J.C.L., V.F.

Diocesan Tribunal—499 St. Matthews St., El Paso, 79907. Tel: 915-872-8402. Very Rev. ANTHONY C. CELINO, J.C.L., V.F. Adjutant Vicars: Revs. STEPHEN PETERS, (Retired); ROBERT S. KOBE.

Judges—Very Rev. ANTHONY C. CELINO, J.C.L., V.F.; Revs. STEPHEN PETERS, (Retired); ROBERT S. KOBE; JAMES W. HALL, (Retired).

Defenders of the Bond—Rev. Msgr. DAVID G. FIERRO; Rev. TRINIDAD FUENTEZ; Sr. DIANE MASSON, C.S.S.F., J.C.L.; MS. ANNE BRYANT, J.C.L.

Advocates—Rev. Msgr. FRANCIS J. SMITH, P.A., (Retired); Revs. ROLANDO FONSECA; EDWARD C. CARPENTER; SAUL PACHECO; Deacon JOSE LUIS SANCHEZ, J.D.

Lay Advocates—MRS. CARMEN RODRIGUEZ; Judge SUE KURITA, J.D.; MS. KARLA MORENO; RALPH CHIOCCO.

Tribunal Ecclesiastical Notary—MS. YOLANDA RUIZ.

Peritus—VACANT.

Promoter of Justice—VACANT.

Vicariates—St. Peter: Rev. MIGUEL ANGEL SANCHEZ, Vicar Forane, San Judas Tadeo Parish, 4006 Hidden Way, El Paso, 79922. Tel: 915-584-1095; Fax: 915-581-6785. St. Paul: Rev. WILSON CUEVAS, Vicar Forane, St. Pius X, 1050 N. Clark St., El Paso, 79905. Tel: 915-772-3226; Fax: 915-771-6665. St. John: Rev. EDWARD C. CARPENTER, Vicar Forane, St. Joseph, 1315 Travis St., El Paso, 79903. Tel: 915-566-9396. St. Mark and St. Luke: Rev. MIGUEL ALCUINO, Vicar Forane, Santa Teresa De Jesus, 1101 W. O'Reilly, Presidio, 79845. Tel: 432-229-3235; Fax: 432-229-3953. St. Matthew: Rev. MIGUEL BRISENO, O.F.M.Conv., Vicar Forane, Our Lady of Mt. Carmel Parish, 131 S. Zaragoza Rd., El Paso, 79907. Tel: 915-859-9848; Fax: 915-859-9340. Our Lady of Guadalupe: Very Rev. ANTHONY C. CELINO, J.C.L., V.F., Vicar Forane, St. Raphael Parsh, 2301 Zanzibar, El Paso, 79925. Tel: 915-598-3431; Fax: 915-598-0944.

Diocesan Master of Ceremonies—Rev. MARCUS MCFADIN, D.Min., 499 St. Matthews St., El Paso, 79907. Tel: 915-872-8400.

Peace & Justice Office—MR. MARCO RAPOSO, Dir., 499 St. Matthews, El Paso, 79907. Tel: 915-872-8422.

Finance Council—Most Rev. MARK J. SEITZ; Very Rev. BENJAMIN FLORES, V.G.; Rev. Msgr. FRANCIS J. SMITH, P.A., (Retired); Rev. LEONIDES RIVERO; Deacon ROBERT GUERRA; MR. CHRIS ANTCLIFF; MR. PHILLIP MULLIN; MR. JOSE VILLA, CPA.

Diocesan Building Committee—Most Rev. MARK J. SEITZ; Very Rev. BENJAMIN FLORES, V.G.; Revs. MARCUS MCFADIN, D.Min.; FRANK LOPEZ; MR. CRUZ GARCIA; MR. JORGE VERGEN; MR. ALLAN SIMPSON; MR. THOMAS EYEINGTON, A.I.A.; MR. SERGIO ORNELAS; MR. LUIS B. MORALES JR.

College of Consultors—Revs. ANTONIO LASHERAS, O.A.R.; FRANK LOPEZ; TRINIDAD FUENTEZ; ROBERT S. KOBE; MIGUEL BRISENO, O.F.M.Conv.; JOE MOLINA.

Diocesan Review Board—MAUREEN DE LA ROSA, M.S.; MR. ENRIQUE MORENO, J.D.; Sr. ELIZABETH ANNE SWARTZ, S.S.N.D.; MR. MICHAEL BULKO; MR. JOSE CASTRELLON, L.C.S.W.; MR. WALTER DEINES, L.C.S.W.; MRS. SUSAN MARTINEZ, L.C.S.W.; Rev. JOE MOLINA; DR. ROBERT RANKIN, Ph.D.

Pastoral Review Board—MAUREEN DE LA ROSA, M.S.; MR. ENRIQUE MORENO, J.D.; Sr. ELIZABETH ANNE SWARTZ, S.S.N.D.; MR. MICHAEL BULKO; MR. JOSE CASTRELLON, L.C.S.W.; MRS. SUSAN MARTINEZ, L.C.S.W.; MR. WALTER DEINES, L.C.S.W.; Rev. JOE MOLINA; DR. ROBERT RANKIN, Ph.D.; Rev. STEPHEN PETERS, (Retired).

Diocesan Pastoral Council—Most Rev. MARK J. SEITZ; ANA ELENA ALLEN; ROMAN BUSTILLOS; Deacon JESUS A. CARDENAS; BRIAN DAW; DOLORES DE AVILA; Sr. MARIA ISABEL DOMINGUEZ; MS. PATRICIA L. FIERRO; Very Rev. BENJAMIN FLORES, V.G.; DANIEL FLORES; AL MELERO; DR. VERONICA RAYAS; MARTIN RUBIO; YOLANDA SUSTAITA; ESMERALDA VALDEZ.

Natural Family Planning—499 St. Matthews St., El Paso, 79907. Tel: 915-872-8401. GRACE AKERS.

Youth and Young Adult Ministry—Rev. FABIAN MARQUEZ, 499 St. Matthews St., El Paso, 79907. Tel: 915-872-8438.

Catholic Communications Ministry—499 St. Matthews St., El Paso, 79907. Tel: 915-872-8414. VACANT.

Diocesan Newspaper—Rio Grande Catholic *Rio Grande Catholic, 499 St. Matthews St., El Paso, 79907*. Tel: 915-872-8414. VACANT, Editor.

Campaign for Human Development—MR. MARCO RAPOSO, 499 St. Matthews St., El Paso, 79907. Tel: 915-872-8422.

Office of Marriage and Family Life—Deacon FRANCISCO R. SEGURA, 499 St. Matthews St., El Paso, 79907. Tel: 915-872-8401.

Permanent Diaconate Office—Deacon JESUS A. CARDENAS, Dir., 499 St. Matthews, El Paso, 79907. Tel: 915-872-8420.

Priests' Retirement and Disability Plan—Rev. Msgr. FRANCIS J. SMITH, P.A., Pres., (Retired); Revs. EDILBERTO (BETO) LOPEZ; LEONIDES RIVERO; Very Rev. BENJAMIN FLORES, V.G.; MS. CAROLYN MORA, CPA.

Missions Office/Propagation of the Faith/Catholic Relief Services499 St. Matthews St., El Paso, 79907. Tel: 915-872-8407. Very Rev. BENJAMIN FLORES, V.G.

Office of Education—499 St. Matthews St., El Paso, 79907. Tel: 915-872-8426. MR. STEVE SANCHEZ, Interim Dir.

Tepeyac Institute—Deacon JESUS A. CARDENAS, Dir., 499 St. Matthews St., El Paso, 79907. Tel: 915-872-8420.

Reverence for Life Ministry—GABRIELA AVILA, 499 St. Matthews St., El Paso, 79907. Tel: 915-872-8401.

Vocations & Seminarians—Rev. MARIANO H. LOPEZ, Rector, 499 St. Matthews, El Paso, 79907. Tel: 915-872-8403. 8330 Park Haven, El Paso, 79907. Tel: 915-872-8460.

Religious Formation—DR. VERONICA RAYAS, Dir., 901 W. Main Dr., El Paso, 79902. Tel: 915-262-4700.

Native American (Tigua) Ministry—MIKE LARA, 131 S. Zaragosa, El Paso, 79907. Tel: 915-859-9848.

Victim Assistance Coordinator—MRS. SUSAN MARTINEZ, L.C.S.W., 499 St. Matthews, El Paso, 79907. Tel: 915-872-8424; Email: smartinez@elpasodiocese.org.

Catholic Campus Ministry—2230 N. Oregon, El Paso, 79902. Tel: 915-838-0300. Rev. MARIO SERRANO, O.F.M. Conv., Dir.

Finance Office—GREGORY WATTERS, Dir., 499 St. Matthews, El Paso, 79907. Tel: 915-872-8404.

Human Resources—MS. PATRICIA L. FIERRO, Dir., 499 St. Matthews, El Paso, 79907. Tel: 915-872-8407.

Office of Worship—Rev. MARCUS MCFADIN, D.Min., 499 St. Matthews, El Paso, 79907. Tel: 915-872-8400.

Office of Safe Environment—MRS. DIANA BULKO, Coord., 499 St. Matthews, El Paso, 79907. Tel: 915-872-8427.

CLERGY, PARISHES, MISSIONS AND PAROCHIAL SCHOOLS

CITY OF EL PASO

(EL PASO COUNTY)

1—ST. PATRICK CATHEDRAL
1118 N. Mesa St., 79902. Tel: 915-533-4451; Email: stpatrickclerks@yahoo.com; Email: enrocha2111@aol.com. Rev. Trinidad Fuentez, Rector; Deacons Ernesto Rodriguez; Roberto (Bob) Guerra.
School—St. Patrick Cathedral School, (Grades K-8), 1111 N. Stanton St., 79902. Tel: 915-532-4142; Fax: 915-532-2897; Email: stpat1111@netzero.net. Liliana Esparza, Prin. Lay Teachers 16; Students 185; Clergy / Religious Teachers 1.
Catechesis Religious Program—Rosa M. Thorpe, P.C.L. Students 381.

2—ALL SAINTS (1967)
1415 Dakota St., 79930. Tel: 915-566-9711; Email: allsaintselptx@aol.com. Rev. Andrés Sosa Medellin.
Catechesis Religious Program—Email: pfavela@aol.com. Paula Favela, D.R.E. Students 27.

3—BLESSED SACRAMENT
9025 Diana Dr., 79904. Tel: 915-755-7658; Email: office@epblessedsacrament.org. Very Rev. Benjamin Flores, V.G.; Rev. Mount Joseph Durai Raj Selvan, Parochial Vicar; Deacon Ignacio M. Bustillos.
Catechesis Religious Program—Tel: 915-755-7658. Patricia Hernandez, P.C.L. Students 298.

4—CHRIST THE SAVIOR (1982)
5301 Wadsworth Ave., 79924. Tel: 915-821-3766; Email: ctselpasotx@gmail.com. Revs. Kennon Y. Ducre, S.T.L.; Peter Koo IL-MO, Korean Comm.
Catechesis Religious Program—Email: eileen.kuns@christthesaviorep.org. Eileen Kuns, D.R.E. Students 50.

5—CORPUS CHRISTI
9205 North Loop Dr., 79907. Tel: 915-858-0488; Email: corpuschristidesk@gmail.com; Web: www.corpuschristicc.com. Revs. Antonio Mena; Roberto Alvarado, Parochial Vicar; Deacon Juan M. Alvarez.

6—CRISTO REY CHURCH
8011 Williamette, 79907. Tel: 915-591-0688; Email: cristorey8011@sbcglobal.net. Mr. Jose Manny Barrios Jr., Parish Life Coord.; Rev. Esteban Sescon, Sacramental Min.; Deacons Antonio Mascorro; Jose Zaragoza.
Catechesis Religious Program—Gloria Ibarra, P.C.L. Students 323.

7—EL BUEN PASTOR MISSION
311 Peyton, 79928. Tel: 915-852-4010; Email: elbuencatholic@sbcgloba.net. Rev. Fabian Marquez, Admin.
Mission—La Resurreccion Mission, 1140 Timothy, El Paso Co. 79928.
Catechesis Religious Program—Francisca Renteria, P.C.L. Students 192.

8—ST. FRANCES XAVIER CABRINI PARISH (1993)
12200 Vista del Sol, 79936. Tel: 915-857-1263; Email: aacalderon24@email.com. Rev. Msgr. David G. Fierro; Deacon James T. Szostek.
Catechesis Religious Program—Ms. Rosie Torres, P.C.L. Students 394.

9—ST. FRANCIS OF ASSISI
5750 Doniphan, 79913. Tel: 915-584-7130; Email: info@stfrancisofelpaso.org. Mailing Address: P.O. Box 220034, 79932. Revs. Jose Alfredo Ramirez, O.F.M.; Juan Francisco Figueroa Moran, Parochial Vicar.
Catechesis Religious Program—Maria Guzman, P.C.L. Students 295.

10—ST. FRANCIS XAVIER (1932)
519 S. Latta St., 79905. Tel: 915-532-2761; Email: sfxcc519@yahoo.com. Rev. Jose Vera-Perez, O.F.M.
Catechesis Religious Program—Felipe Salinas, D.R.E. Students 83.

11—GUARDIAN ANGEL (1908)
3021 Frutas Ave., 79905. Tel: 915-533-2077; Email: santoangelusa@gmail.com. Revs. Humberto Cruz, O.A.R.; Andres Alava, Parochial Vicar.
Catechesis Religious Program—Salvador Vargas, P.C.L. Students 122; RCIA 12.

12—HOLY FAMILY (1916) (Hispanic)
104 Fewel St., 79902. Tel: 915-532-8462; Email: holyfamily@elp.rr.com; Email: hfsecretary@elp.rr.com. Rev. Ronald Eid, Parish Life Coord.; Deacon Roberto E. Saucedo, Parish Life Coord.
Catechesis Religious Program—Email: hfsecretary@elp.rr.com. Suzanne Brown, P.C.L. Students 27.

13—ST. IGNATIUS OF LOYOLA
408 Park St., 79901. Tel: 615-532-9534; Email: sanignaciochurch@gmail.com. Revs. Tobias Macias, O.S.M.; Jorge M. Palacio, O.S.M., Parochial Vicar.
Catechesis Religious Program—Robert Hernandez, P.C.L. Students 122.

14—IMMACULATE CONCEPTION
118 N. Campbell St., 79901-2404. Tel: 915-533-3427; Email: ic.ecclesia@gmail.com; Email: iscorchado@gmail.com. Revs. Kevin O'Neill, F.S.S.P.; Joshua Houch, Parochial Vicar.

15—ST. JOSEPH'S
1315 Travis St., 79903. Tel: 915-566-9396; Email: sjosephschurch@aol.com. Rev. Edward C. Carpenter.
School—St. Joseph's School, (Grades K-8), Tel: 915-566-1661; Fax: 915-566-1664; Email: stjosephs@aol.com. Ms. Edna Ramos, Admin.; Marcela Hernandez, Prin.; Cristina Gomez Landero, Librarian. Lay Teachers 22; Students 249.
Catechesis Religious Program—Email: mdsianez@gmail.com. Dolores Sianez, P.C.L. Students 55.

16—ST. LUKE (1992)
930 E. Redd Rd., 79912. Tel: 915-585-0255; Fax: 915-585-6355; Email: stlukeparish@att.net; Web: www.stlukeelpaso.org. Rev. Marcus McFadin, D.Min.; Deacons John Farley; Guillermo Jiron.
Catechesis Religious Program—Email: maryhrndz2@ymail.com. Mary L. Hernandez, P.C.L. Students 834.

17—ST. MARK (1992)
11700 Pebble Hills, 79936. Tel: 915-300-2800; Email: stmarkcatholic14@gmail.com; Web: home.catholicweb.com/StMarkCatholic/. Rev. Msgr. Arturo Banuelas; Rev. Francisco Hernandez, Parochial Vicar; Deacon Jesus A. Cardenas.
Catechesis Religious Program—Students 1,419.

18—ST. MATTHEW
400 W. Sunset Rd., 79922. Tel: 915-584-3461; Email: stmatthewcatholic@sbcglobal.net. Revs. Frank Lopez; Alfonso Bonilla, Parochial Vicar.
School—St. Matthew Catholic School, (Grades K-8), Tel: 915-581-8801; Email: vdelacruz@stmatthewelpaso.org; Web: www.stmatthewelpaso.org. Veronica De La Cruz, Prin. Lay Teachers 22; Students 309.
Catechesis Religious Program—Mrs. Jane Snyder, P.C.L. Students 700.

19—MOST HOLY TRINITY (1967)
10000 Pheasant Rd., 79924. Tel: 915-751-6416; Email: mostholytrinity@gmail.com. Rev. Antonio De Guzman Jr., Admin.
School—Most Holy Trinity School, (Grades K-8), Tel: 915-751-2566; Fax: 915-751-2596. James Horan, Prin. Lay Teachers 12; Students 145.
Catechesis Religious Program—Students 297.

20—OUR LADY OF ASSUMPTION
4800 Byron St., 79930. Tel: 915-566-4040; Email: pservian68@gmail.com. 4805 Byron St., 79930. Rev. Mark N.P. Salas; Deacon Francisco R. Segura.
Catechesis Religious Program—Email: rmedina024.rm@gmail.com. Students 23.

21—OUR LADY OF GUADALUPE (1929)
2709 Alabama St., 79930. Tel: 915-562-4304; Email: ourladyofguadalupeparishelpaso@gmail.com. Revs. Juan Antonio Gutierrez, O.F.M.; Roberto Hernandez, O.F.M., Parochial Vicar; Deacon Jesus Carlos Cortinas.
Catechesis Religious Program—Fax: 915-566-3307. Students 241.

22—OUR LADY OF MT. CARMEL
131 S. Zaragoza, 79907. Tel: 915-859-9848; Email: olmcsecretary@yahoo.com; Web: ysletamission.org. Revs. Miguel Briseno, O.F.M.Conv.; Mario Serrano, O.F.M. Conv., Campus Min.; Deacon Hector Melendez.
Catechesis Religious Program—Email: mlara@ysletamission.org. Mike Lara, P.C.L. Students 248.

23—OUR LADY OF SORROWS
7712 Rosedale St., 79915. Tel: 915-433-8694; Email: olsorrows1977@gmail.com. Revs. Arturo M. Gonzalez, O.S.M.; Rogelio M. Rayas, Parochial Vicar; Fr. Mateus Pol, Vicar.
Catechesis Religious Program—Gloria Moreno, P.C.L. Students 121.

24—OUR LADY OF THE LIGHT
4700 Delta Dr., 79905. Tel: 915-532-1757; Email: olol4700@yahoo.com. Rev. Antonio Lasheras, O.A.R.
Catechesis Religious Program—Tel: 915-772-1113; Email: valdiviezcookie@yahoo.com. Cookie Valdiviez, P.C.L. Students 325.

25—OUR LADY OF THE VALLEY (1945)
8600 Winchester, 79907. Tel: 915-853-7939; Email: olvchurch@elp.rr.com. Rev. Donald Adamski, O.F.M.Conv.; Deacon Ray H. Niblett.
Catechesis Religious Program—David Perez, P.C.L. Students 182.

26—ST. PAUL THE APOSTLE (1963)
7424 Mimosa Ave., 79915. Tel: 915-778-5304; Email: pastor@stplap.com. Rev. Pablo Matta; Deacons Vicente G. Aguirre; Gus J. Rodriguez Sr.
Catechesis Religious Program—Danny Campos, P.C.L. Students 140.

27—STS. PETER AND PAUL (1972)
673 Old Hueco Tanks Rd., 79927. Tel: 915-859-3758; Email: stspeterandpaulelp@yahoo.com. Rev. Raul Trigueros.
Catechesis Religious Program—Email: stspeterandpaulccd@gmail.com. Elena Velasco, P.C.L.; Mrs. Marisol Anchondo, P.C.L. Students 404.

28—ST. PIUS X
1050 N. Clark Rd., 79905. Tel: 915-772-3226; Email: stpiusxparish@sbcglobal.net; Email: stpiusparish123@gmail.com. Revs. Wilson Cuevas; Cong Vo, Parochial Vicar; Deacon Rolando Lujan.
School—St. Pius X School, (Grades PreK-8), 1007 Geronimo, 79905. Tel: 915-262-4846; Fax: 915-262-0176; Email: asilva@elpasostpiusx.org. Ana Silva, Prin. Lay Teachers 17; Students 248; Clergy / Religious Teachers 1.
Catechesis Religious Program—Tel: 915-772-0224; Email: stpiusrelfor@gmail.com. Sr. Olivia Gutierrez, O.P., P.C.L. Students 411.

29—QUEEN OF PEACE
1551 Belvidere, 79912. Tel: 915-584-5817; Email: 1983@qpelp.com. Rev. Emanuel Alcazar; Deacons Orlando Sanchez; Roberto Diaz.
Catechesis Religious Program—Elizabeth Mata, P.C.L. Students 569.

30—St. Raphael (1967)
2301 Zanzibar Rd., 79925. Tel: 915-598-3431; Email: straphaelparishep@sbcglobal.net; Email: rebecca_aguilera@sbcglobal.net. Very Rev. Anthony C. Celino, J.C.L., V.F.; Rev. Victorino Lorezca, Parochial Vicar; Deacon Victor Acosta.
School—St. Raphael School, (Grades K-8), 2310 Woodside, 79925. Tel: 915-598-2241;
Fax: 915-598-3002; Email: info@straphaelelpaso.org. Ms. Ana O'Neill, Prin.; Rachel Banales, Librarian. Lay Teachers 18; Students 268; Part Time Teachers 4.
Catechesis Religious Program—Guillermo Tajonar, P.C.L. Students 622.

31—Sacred Heart
602 S. Oregon St., 79901. Tel: 915-532-5447; Email: reception@sacredheartelpaso.org. Revs. Ronald D. Gonzales, S.J.; Michael E. Chesney, S.J.; Rafael Garcia, S.J., Parochial Vicar; Samuel Rosales, S.J., In Res.
Catechesis Religious Program—Sr. Soledad Garcia, O.P., P.L.C. Students 64.

32—San Antonio (1917) (Mexican—American)
Mailing Address: 503 Hunter Dr., 79915.
Tel: 915-598-1457; Fax: 915-590-1312; Email: sanantoniocc@sbcglobal.net; Web: www.paduaofelpaso.org. Rev. Leonides Rivero; Deacon Samuel Bernal.
Res.: 7420 North Loop, 79915.
Catechesis Religious Program—Yolanda Valdez, D.R.E.; Amelia Gonzalez, D.R.E.; Martina Gomez, Admin.; Rebecca Lopez, Sec. Students 127.

33—San Jose
8100 San Jose Rd., 79907. Tel: 915-598-6285; Email: sanjosechurchelpaso@gmail.com. Rev. Frederico Franco; Deacon Aurelio Melucci.
Catechesis Religious Program—Rosa Aguon, P.C.L.

34—San Juan Bautista (1923)
5649 Dailey Street, 79905. Revs. Wilson Cuevas; Cong Vo, Parochial Vicar; Deacons Rolando Lujan; Juan M. Alvarez.
Res.: 1050 N. Clark, 79905.

35—San Juan Diego Parish (1992)
14520 E. Montana Ave., 79938. Tel: 915-855-2217; Email: soyuncordel@gmail.com. Rev. Rolando Fonseca.
Catechesis Religious Program—6148 Westside Rd., Dell City, 79837. Tel: 915-964-2601. Michael Dorosin, P.L.C. Students 200.
Mission—San Isidro Mission, 6148 Westside Rd., Dell City, 79837. Tel: 915-964-2601.

36—San Judas Tadeo (1982)
4006 Hidden Way, 79922. Tel: 915-584-1095; Email: stjudeep@gmail.com; Web: www.santuariosanjudastadeo.com. Revs. Miguel Angel Sanchez; Antonio Martinez, Parochial Vicar.
Catechesis Religious Program—Rudy Gonzales, P.C.L. Students 417.
Mission—Santa Teresita, 3400 Zapal St., El Paso Co. 79922.

37—Santa Lucia
518 Gallagher St., 79915. Tel: 915-592-5245; Email: santaluciachurch@sbcglobal.net. Rev. Federico M. Franco, O.S.M.; Deacon Aurelio Melucci.
Catechesis Religious Program—Becky Gomez, Confirmation Coord. Students 68.

38—Santo Nino De Atocha
210 S. Clark, 79905. Tel: 915-779-3164. Rev. John Telles.
Catechesis Religious Program—Rebeca Rodela, P.C.L.; Cindy Luna, Confirmation Coord. Students 156.

39—St. Stephen, Deacon and Martyr
1700 George Dieter, 79936. Tel: 915-855-1661; Email: receptionist@ststephendeaconandmartyr.org; Web: www.ststephendeaconandmartyr.org. Rev. Joe Molina; Deacon Hector E. Grijalva.
Catechesis Religious Program—Deborah Montoya, P.C.L. Students 452.

40—Saint Therese of the Little Flower Parish
171 Polo Inn Rd., 79915. Tel: 915-772-1285; Email: littleflowerchurch@outlook.com. Rev. Jose Luis Garayoa, O.A.R.
Catechesis Religious Program—Email: alblara4@gmail.com. Blanca Lara, P.C.L. Students 66.

41—St. Thomas Aquinas (1981)
10970 Bywood, 79936. Tel: 915-592-1333; Email: saintthomasa@sbcglobal.net; Email: sta.records@icloud.com; Web: www.stthomas-elpaso.com. Rev. Ed Roden-Lucero, D.Min., J.C.L., D.Min.; Deacons Jose E. Soto; Ricardo Corella.
Catechesis Religious Program—Email: chromero3@gmail.com. Mr. Christopher Romero, P.C.L. Students 230.

OUTSIDE THE CITY OF EL PASO

Alpine, Brewster Co., Our Lady of Peace, [CEM]
Mailing Address: 406 S. Sixth, Alpine, 79830.
Tel: 432-837-3304; Email: olpalpine@gmail.com. Revs. Edilberto (Beto) Lopez; Hector Chicas, Parochial Vicar; Deacon Paul A. Lister.
Catechesis Religious Program—Ritchie Skelton, P.C.L.; Rebecca Ramos, D.R.E.; Kristin Rosas, D.R.E. Students 149.
Missions—St. Mary—203 NW 3rd St., Marathon, 79842. P.O. Box 268, Marathon, Brewster Co. 79842.
Catechesis Religious Program—Carmen Santa Maria, P.C.L. Students 5.
St. Joseph Mission, 800 N. State St. (Hwy. 171), Fort Davis, 79734.

Balmorhea, Reeves Co., Christ the King, Under pastoral care of Santa Rosa, Pecos. Rev. Jose Delacruz Longoria, M.N.M.
Res.: Rte. 1, #3, P.O. Box 686, Balmorhea, 79718.
Tel: 432-445-2309.
Catechesis Religious Program—Email: wtccre@yahoo.com. Sonia Urias, D.R.E. Students 38.
Mission—Our Lady of Guadalupe, Saragosa, Reeves Co.

Canutillo, El Paso Co., St. Patrick (1912) [CEM]
7065 Second St., Canutillo, 79835. Tel: 915-877-3997; Email: canutillostpatrick@att.net. Mailing Address: P.O. Box 10, Canutillo, 79835. Revs. William Donnelly, Admin.; Michael Gould, Admin.
Catechesis Religious Program—Oscar Rodriguez, P.C.L. Students 193.

Clint, El Paso Co., San Lorenzo (1914)
13021 Center St., Clint, 79836. Tel: 915-851-2255; Email: sanlorenzo1914@sbcglobal.net. Mailing Address: P.O. Box 215, Clint, 79836. Rev. Faustino Ortiz, M.N.M.
Res.: 611 Avenida de San Lorenzo, Clint, 79836.
Catechesis Religious Program—Yolanda Valdez, P.C.L. Students 245.

Fabens, El Paso Co., Our Lady of Guadalupe, [CEM]
127 W. Main, 79838. Tel: 915-764-3942; Email: officeofolg@gmail.com. Mailing Address: P.O. Box 356, Fabens, 79838. Rev. Celimo Osorio; Deacon Robert Garcia.
Catechesis Religious Program—Tel: 915-525-4884. Terry Avila, P.C.L. Students 309.
Missions—San Jose—Cuadrilla, El Paso Co.
Santa Rita, 19235 Cobb St., Tornillo, El Paso Co. 79853.
San Luis, La Isla, El Paso Co.

Fort Davis, Jeff Davis Co., St. Joseph, [CEM]
800 N. State St. (HWY 171), P.O. Box 787, Fort Davis, 79734. Tel: 432-837-3304; Email: olpalpine@gmail.com. Rev. Edilberto (Beto) Lopez.
Catechesis Religious Program—Saundra Lee, P.C.L. Students 16.

Fort Hancock, Hudspeth Co., Santa Teresa (1920)
1042 N. Knox, Fort Hancock, 79839.
Tel: 915-769-3771; Fax: 915-769-3771; Email: santa_teresa215@windstream.net. Mailing Address: P.O. Box 215, Fort Hancock, 79839. Sr. Silvia Chacon, A.S.C., Pastoral Life Coord.
Catechesis Religious Program—Students 14.

Horizon City, El Paso Co., Holy Spirit (1975)
14132 McMahon, Horizon City, 79928.
Tel: 915-852-3582; Email: office@hscc4u.org. Rev. Jose A. Morales.
Church: 14100 Horizon Blvd., Horizon City, 79928.
Catechesis Religious Program—Email: faithformation@hscc4u.org. Students 240.

Kermit, Winkler Co.
1—St. Joseph the Worker, Merged with St. Thomas in 1990 to form St. Thomas & St. Joseph.
2—St. Thomas & St. Joseph
838 Bellaire St., Kermit, 79745. Tel: 432-586-3922; Email: stthomas2100@att.net. Rev. Gleen Carpe, Admin.
Catechesis Religious Program—Kathy Barriga, P.C.L. Students 145.

Marfa, Presidio Co., St. Mary's, [CEM]
217 W. San Antonio, Marfa, 79843.
Tel: 432-729-4694; Email: church.marfa@gmail.com. Mailing Address: P.O. Box 356, Marfa, 79843. Rev. John Paul Madanu, Parochial Vicar.
Catechesis Religious Program—Students 65.
Mission—Sacred Heart Mission, Rev. Edilberto (Beto) Lopez.

Monahans, Ward Co., St. John the Apostle and Evangelist, [JC]
Mailing Address: 5th & S. Ike St., Monahans, 79756.
Tel: 432-943-5114; Email: stjohnchurchmonahans@gmail.com. Rev. Allan Oluoch Alaka, Admin.
Res.: 500 S. Ike St., Monahans, 79756.
Catechesis Religious Program—Cyndi Ortega, P.C.L.; Eloiza Collazo, P.C.L. Students 269.
Mission—St. Gertrude, P.O. Box 181, Grandfalls, Ward Co. 79742.

Pecos, Reeves Co.
1—St. Catherine
1201 S. Plum, Pecos, 79772. Tel: 432-445-2309; Email: wtcc@classicnet.net. Mailing Address: P.O. Box 686, Pecos, 79772. Rev. Jose Delacruz Longoria, M.N.M.
2—Santa Rosa de Lima, [CEM]
620 E. 4th St., Pecos, 79772. Tel: 432-445-2309; Email: wtcc@classicnet.net. Mailing Address: P.O. Box 686, Pecos, 79772. Revs. Jose Delacruz Longoria, M.N.M.; Valentin Cota, Parochial Vicar.
Catechesis Religious Program—Email: wtccre@yahoo.com. Sonia Urias, P.C.L. Students 465.
Missions—Our Lady of Refuge—
Christ the King, See separate listing under Balmorhea.
Shrine—Our Lady of Guadalupe, See listing under Christ the King, Balmorhea.
Mission—St. Emily, Toyah, Reeves Co.

Presidio, Presidio Co., Santa Teresa de Jesus, [CEM]
1101 W. O'Reilly, Presidio, 79845. Tel: 432-229-3235; Email: santateresachurch.2014@gmail.com. Mailing Address: P.O. Box 2049, Presidio, 79845. Rev. Miguel Alcuino.
Catechesis Religious Program—Students 112.
Missions—Sgdo. Corazon de Jesus—Shafter, Presidio Co.
San Jose, San Jose Mission is in Redford, TX and served by Santa Teresa de Jesus in Presidio, TX.
Our Lady of Peace, Candelaria, Presidio Co.
Lajitas Mission, Lajitas, Brewster Co.

San Elizario, El Paso Co., San Elceario, [JC]
1556 San Elizario Rd., San Elizario, 79849.
Tel: 915-851-2333; Email: esheramparansecc@gmail.com. P.O. Box 910, San Elizario, 79849. Rev. Juan Victor Gamino, M.N.M.
Catechesis Religious Program—Students 148.

Socorro, El Paso Co.
1—La Purisima (1863)
328 S. Nevarez St., Socorro, 79927.
Tel: 915-307-4349; Email: lapurisima@earthlink.net. Rev. Angel M. Maldonado, O.S.M., Admin.
Catechesis Religious Program—Eloy Carmona, P.C.L. Students 92.
2—San Felipe de Jesus
401 Passmore, Socorro, 79927. Tel: 915-851-3039; Email: sanfelipedejusus401@outlook.com. Mailing Address: P.O. Box 1070, San Elizario, 79849. Rev. Ralph Solis Jr.; Deacon Pilar Grijalva Jr.
Catechesis Religious Program—David Solis, P.C.L. Students 132.

Van Horn, Culberson Co., Our Lady of Fatima
308 S. Almond St., Van Horn, 79855.
Tel: 432-283-1058; Email: ourladyoffatimac@gmail.com. P.O. Box 398, Van Horn, 79855. Rev. Apolinar Samboni, Admin.
Catechesis Religious Program—Carmen Garibay, P.C.L. Students 109.
Missions—Our Lady of Miracles—556 E. Cavender, Sierra Blanca, Hudspeth Co. 79851.
Catechesis Religious Program—Students 17.
San Isidro, P.O. Box 65, Dell City, Hudspeth Co. 79837.

Chaplains of Public Institutions

El Paso. *El Paso County Jail*. Vacant.
El Paso Juvenile Detention Center. Vacant.
Anthony. *La Tuna Federal*. Vacant.

On Duty Outside of Diocese:
Revs.—
Aguilera, Salvador, U.S. Naval Academy, Annapolis, MD 21402. U.S. Navy
Kim, Nam Joseph, (Society of St. Sulpice).

Graduate Studies:
Rev.—
Alzate Agudelo, German, Mundelein Seminary.

Absent on Leave:
Revs.—
Bengert, Tony
Knopp, John
Maraya, Felipe
Marin, Miguel
Munoz, Manuel
Narez, Juan
Olivas, J. Alfredo
Ponce, Demetrio
Ramirez, Jose Nieves
Ruiz, Rick
Zamorano, Richard.

Retired:
Rev. Msgrs.—
Calles, Robert S., (Retired)
Smith, Francis J., P.A., (Retired)
Revs.—
Alcocer, Jose, (Retired)
Cervantes, Fidel, (Retired)
Fry, Wallace Blake, (Retired)
Hall, James W., (Retired)
Herrera, Francisco, (Retired)

Lacerna, Rodolfo, (Retired)
Meneses, Miguel, (Retired)
Peters, Stephen, (Retired)
Rini, John, (Retired)
Rizzo, Mark, (Retired)
Uribe, Saul de Jesus, (Retired)
Waiwood, Richard, (Retired)
Weiss, Richard, (Retired).

Permanent Deacons:
Acosta, Victor, St. Raphael, El Paso
Aguirre, Vicente G., St. Paul the Apostle, El Paso
Alvarez, Juan M., Corpus Christi, El Paso
Araiza, Arturo, San Juan Diego, El Paso
Bernal, Samuel, San Antonio de Padua, El Paso
Bustillos, Ignacio M., Blessed Sacrament, El Paso
Cardenas, Jesus A., St. Mark, El Paso
Corella, Ricardo, St. Thomas Aquinas, El Paso
Cortinas, Jesus Carlos, Our Lady of Guadalupe, El Paso
Diaz, Roberto, Queen of Peace, El Paso
Elsey, Ken, Holy Spirit, Horizon City
Farley, John, St. Luke, El Paso
Garcia, Robert, Our Lady of Guadalupe, Fabens
Grijalva, Hector E., St. Stephen, El Paso
Grijalva, Pilar Jr., San Felipe de Jesus, El Paso
Guerra, Roberto (Bob), St. Patrick Cathedral, El Paso
Jiron, Guillermo, St. Luke, El Paso
Lister, Paul A., Our Lady of Peace, Alpine
Lujan, Rolando, St. Pius X, El Paso
Mascorro, Antonio, Cristo Rey, El Paso
Melendez, Hector, Our Lady of Mt. Carmel, El Paso
Melucci, Aurelio, San Jose, El Paso
Niblett, Ray H., Our Lady of the Valley, El Paso
Reyes, William, El Paso
Rodriguez, Ernesto, St. Patrick Cathedral, El Paso
Rodriguez, Gus J. Sr., St. Paul the Apostle, El Paso
Sanchez, Orlando, Queen of Peace, El Paso
Saucedo, Roberto E., Holy Family, El Paso
Segura, Francisco R., Our Lady of Assumption, El Paso
Solis, Ralph, (Retired)
Soltero, Martin, Most Holy Trinity, El Paso
Soto, Jose E., St. Thomas Aquinas, El Paso
Szostek, James T., St. Francis X. Cabrini, El Paso
Torres, Ignacio J., Most Holy Trinity, El Paso
Vasquez, George, (Retired)
Zaragoza, Jose, Cristo Rey, El Paso.

INSTITUTIONS LOCATED IN DIOCESE

[A] SEMINARIES, DIOCESAN

EL PASO. *St. Charles Seminary* (1961) 8330 Park Haven, 79907. Tel: 915-872-8460; Fax: 915-872-8468; Email: dstoecklein@elpasodiocese.org; Email: lleos@elpasodiocese.org. Rev. Mariano H. Lopez, Rector; Sr. Darlene Stoecklein, A.S.C., Librarian/ Formation Staff. Seminarians 28; Students 28.

[B] SEMINARIES, RELIGIOUS OR SCHOLASTICATES

EL PASO. *St. Anthony's School of Theology* (1935) 4601 Hastings Dr., 79903. Tel: 915-566-2261; Fax: 915-566-8851; Email: stanthonysseminary@hotmail.com. 2310 Woodside, 79903. Revs. Alfredo Ramirez, O.F.M., Dean; Emilio Flores, O.F.M., Rector; Francisco Javier Rodriguez, Parochial Vicar; Gerardo Francisco Salgado, O.F.M., Parochial Vicar. Franciscan Fathers of St. Peter and St. Paul Province, Michoacan, Mexico. Clergy 5; Priests 5; Students 21; Clergy / Religious Teachers 5.

Roger Bacon College (1940) 2400 Marr St., 79903. Tel: 915-565-2921; Fax: 915-562-4756; Email: rogerbaconcollege@huno.com. Revs. Flavio Alberto Hernandez, O.F.M., Rector; Lazaro Gonzalez, O.F.M., Vicar. Minor Seminary of the Franciscan Fathers, Province of the Holy Gospel. Brothers 1; Clergy 2; Priests 2; Students 25; Clergy / Religious Teachers 2.

[C] HIGH SCHOOLS, PRIVATE

EL PASO. *Cathedral High School, Inc.* (Boys) 1309 N. Stanton St., 79902. Tel: 915-532-3238; Fax: 915-533-8248; Email: ngonzalez80@cathedral-elpaso.org; Web: cathedral-elpaso.org. Bro. Nick Gonzalez, F.S.C., Interim Prin.; Mr. Pedro Espinoza, Vice Prin.; Mr. Adolfo Sanchez, Asst. Brothers 4; Lay Teachers 26; Students 441; Clergy / Religious Teachers 5; Part Time Teachers 8.

Father Yermo Schools, (Grades PreK-12), High School/Elementary/Learning Center. 220 Washington St., 79905. Tel: 915-532-6875; Fax: 915-532-2827; Web: fatheryermoschools.com. 250 Washington St., 79905. Sisters Maria Jesus Munguia, S.S.H.J.P., Pres. & Admin.; Margarita Sanchez de la Vega, S.S.H.J.P., Prin.; Yamila Trejo, S.S.H.J.P., Prin.; Robert Larios, Librarian. Servants of the Sacred Heart of Jesus and of the Poor. Lay Teachers 27; Sisters 6; Students 255.

Loretto Academy, (Grades PreK-12), 1300 Hardaway, 79903. Tel: 915-566-8400; Fax: 915-564-0563; Email: hsilva@loretto.org; Web: www.loretto.org. Sr. Mary Beth Buffy Boesen, S.L., Pres.; Ms. Jane German, Dir.; Mr. Homero Silva, Dir. Sisters of Loretto at the Foot of the Cross. Lay Teachers 34; Students 346; Clergy / Religious Teachers 1.

[D] CLINICS

EL PASO. *Centro San Vicente* (1988) 8061 Alameda, 79915. Tel: 915-859-7545; Fax: 915-859-9862; Email: jlunamd@csv.tachc.org; Web: www.sanvicente.org. Jose Luna, M.D., CEO, Email: jlunamd@csv.tachc.org

Centro San Vicente Bed Capacity 12; Tot Asst. Annually 15,600; Total Staff 188; Total Assisted 15,600.

[E] MONASTERIES & RESIDENCES FOR PRIESTS & BROTHERS

EL PASO. *Christian Brothers*, 1204 N. Mesa, 79902-4012. Tel: 915-532-9314; Email: info@cathedral-elpaso.org. Bro. Nick Gonzalez, F.S.C., Contact Person.

[F] CONVENTS AND RESIDENCES FOR WOMEN

EL PASO. *Adorers of the Blood of Christ (A.S.C.)* (1834) 199 Pendale Rd., 79907. Tel: 915-566-5855; Email: micasa2chante@msn.com. Sisters Silvia Chacon, A.S.C., Parish Life Coord.; Razura Esperanza, Pastoral Assoc.; Darlene Stoecklein, A.S.C., Contact Person. Sisters 3.

Daughters of Charity of St. Vincent De Paul (D.C.), 3014 Moye, 79930. Tel: 915-564-5921; Email: isabel.fierro@yahoo.com; Email: doris.clippard@doc.org. Sisters Isabel Fierro, D.C., Contact Person; Emile Morgan, Reynold's Home; Doris Clippard, Nurse Practricioner, Centro San Vicente; Migdalia "Meggie" Flores, Opportunity Center. Sisters 8.

Daughters of Charity of St. Vincent de Paul (DC), 9213 Moye Dr., 79925. Tel: 915-401-4272; Email: isabel.fierro@yahoo.com. Sr. Isabel Fierro, D.C., Supr. Sisters 5.

Hermanas Contemplativas del Buen Pastor (H.C.B.P.) (1835) (Cloistered) Good Shepherd Convent, 8824 Old County Rd., P.O. Box 17254, 79917. Tel: 915-859-3683; Fax: 915-872-0698; Email: jgildea@elpasodiocese.org. Sr. Ernestina Estrada, Supr. Sisters 4.

Hermanas del Servicio Social (1945) 4614 Trowbridge, Nazareth Hall, 79903. Tel: 915-781-3215; Email: hsscarmena@yahoo.com. Sr. Caramen Aurora Gomez, H.S.S., Contact Person. Sisters 2.

Hermanas Dominicas de la Doctrina Cristiana (O.P.) (1948) San Alberto Magno Provincial Convent, 634 Hampton Rd., 79907. Tel: 915-590-3107; Email: MNC_terrazas79@yahoo.com. Sisters Monica P. Terrazas, Dir. of Novices; Gloria Gil, Supr.; Maria Garcia, Local Vicar, Convent, Hermans Dominicas; Karina Alvarez, D.R.E./Parish Life Coord.; Sara Cisneros, Mistress of Postulants; Soledad Corona, Parish Life Coord.; Maria Luisa Molina, Convent, Hermanas Dominicas; Leticia Olivas, Spiritual Advisor/Care Svcs.; Catalina Leon, Pastoral Min./ Coord. Sisters 8.

Missionary Sisters of Jesus, Mary & Joseph (M.J.M.J.), 7681 Barton Dr., 79915. Tel: 915-779-6943; Email: sistertnt@gmail.com. Sisters Rachel Vallarta, M.J.M.J., Dir. of min. at Blessed Sacrament Parish; Margie Silguero, M.J.M.J., Min. Coord. at St. Patrick Cathedral; Julia Doñez, Supr., (Retired); Margarita Cervera, (Retired). Sisters 3.

Servants of the Sacred Heart of Jesus and of the Poor (S.S.H.J.P.), Father Yermo Convent, 237 Tobin Pl., 79905. Tel: 915-777-1385; Email: sryolandaf@gmail.com. Sr. Maria Yolanda Fernandez, S.S.H.J.P., Supr. Sisters 11.

Queen of Peace Convent, 3119 Pera Ave., 79905. Tel: 915-533-0590; Email: queenofpeaceconvent@gmail.com. Magdalena Sofia Juarez, Supr. Sisters 7.

Sisters of Loretto at the Foot of the Cross (S.L.), 1300 Hardaway St., 79903. Tel: 915-566-8400; Fax: 915-566-0636; Email: bboesen@loretto.org; Web: www.lorettocommunity.org. Sisters Mary Beth Buffy Boesen, S.L., Supr.; Elisa Rodriguez, Chap.; Helen Santamaria, S.L., Spiritual Advisor/ Care Svcs.; Mary Margaret Murphy, S.L., Case Mgr., Villa Maria; Deines Elizabeth, Teacher at Loretto Academy. Sisters 5.

Sisters of Our Lady of Charity of the Good Shepherd - El Paso, Inc. (1931) 415 N. Glenwood Dr., 79905. Tel: 915-772-0737; Fax: 915-779-2664; Email: marthahmolc@aol.com. P.O. Box 340, Carrollton, OH 44615. Sisters Martha Hernandez, R.G.S., Supr.; Maria del Rocio Hernandez, D.R.E.; Rebecca Ortega, D.R.E.; Clementina Sanchez, D.R.E.; Maria Yañez, House Sister; Teresa Gomez Ramirez; Maria Andujo; Angelica de Alba; Susana Cervantes; Angelina Tovar. Sisters 6.

Sisters of Our Lady of Charity of the Good Shepherd (R.G.S.) (1835) Good Shepherd Convent, 8824 Old County Rd., P.O. Box 17635, 79917. Tel: 915-858-0692; Email: Chiobuenpastor1@aol.com. Sisters Maria del Rocio Hernandez, Supr.; Rebecca Ortega, Catechesis-Anunciation House; Clementina Sanchez, Catechesis-Anunciation House. Sisters 3.

Sisters of Perpetual Adoration (A.P.) (1937) Corpus Christi Monastery, 451 Mockingbird Ln., 79907. Tel: 915-591-5662; Fax: 915-598-6203; Email: ccmonast@aol.com. Sr. Maria Gema del Santisimo Sacramento, A.P., Supr. (Cloistered) Sisters 9.

Sisters of Perpetual Adoration (A.P.) (1979) Cristo Rey Monastery, 145 N. Cotton St., 79901. Tel: 915-533-5323; Email: mary.guadalupe@att.net; Web: www.christthekingmonastery.org. Sr. Ma Zoial Flores, Supr.

Monastery of Perpetual Adoration Sisters 11.

MARFA. *Missionary Sisters of Jesus, Mary & Joseph*, P.O. Box 1118, Marfa, 79843. Tel: 432-729-3385; Email: sistertnt@gmail.com. Sisters Rachel Vallarta, M.J.M.J., Dir. of Min. at Blessed Sacrament Parish; Margie Silguero, M.J.M.J., Min. Coord. St. Patrick Cathedral; Julia Donez, Supr.; Margarita Cervera, (Retired). Sisters 4.

[G] NEWMAN CENTERS

EL PASO. *Catholic Campus Ministry at University of Texas at El Paso*, 2230 N. Oregon, 79902. Tel: 915-838-0300; Fax: 915-838-0300. Rev. Mario Serrano, O.F.M. Conv., Campus Min. Administrators 1.

ALPINE. *Sul Ross State University Newman Center*, Hwy. 90 East, P.O. Box C 78, Alpine, 79832. Tel: 432-837-8790; Fax: 915-837-8714; Email: joecal3ramirez@sbcglobal.net. Joe Ray Ramirez, Campus Min. Administrators 1.

[H] MISCELLANEOUS LISTINGS

EL PASO. *Adoracion Nocturna (Nocturnal Adoration)*, 499 St. Matthews, c/o Liaison for Women Religious, 79907. Tel: 915-820-8567; Email: marriaga@elpasodiocese.org. Jorge Maldonado, Pres.

Annunciation House (1978) 1003 E. San Antonio, 79901. Tel: 915-533-4675; Fax: 915-351-1343; Email: rubengarcia@annunciationhouse.org; Web: www.annunciationhouse.org. c/o 499 St. Matthews St., 79901. Mr. Ruben Garcia, Dir. Administrators 1.

Apostolado de la Cruz (Apostolate of the Cross), Our Lady of Mt. Carmel, 131 S. Zaragoza, 79907. Tel: 915-859-9848; Email: olmcsecretary@yahoo.com. Fr. Miguel Briseño.

Casa Vides (Shelter for displaced families) 325 Leon St., 79901. Tel: 915-533-4675; Email: rubengarcia@annunciationhouse.org. Mr. Ruben Garcia, Dir.

Catholic Counseling Services, Inc., 499 St. Matthews St., 79907. Tel: 915-872-8424; Fax: 915-872-8425; Email: jcastrellon@elpasodiocese.org; Email: ccs@elpasodiocese.org. Mr. Jose Castrellon, L.C.S.W., Exec. Dir. Tot Asst. Annually 339; Total Staff 3.

Catholic Properties of El Paso, Inc., 499 St. Matthews St., 79907. Tel: 915-872-8406; Email: jvergen@elpasodioces.org. Mr. Jorge Vergen, Exec. Dir.

Christ Child Society, Katherine Haninger Chapter, 3220 Shetland Rd., 79925. Tel: 915-592-3032; Email: marymel1@att.net. Maria Elena Schuerman, Member.

Cursillos de Cristianidad, 499 St. Matthews, Bldg. F - Deacons Director, 79907. Tel: 915-613-6785; Email: aureliomelucci@hotmail.com. Rev. Pablo Matta, Diocesan Dir.

Diocesan Migrant and Refugee Services, Inc. (1987) 2400-A E. Yandell, 79903. Tel: 915-532-3975; Fax: 915-532-4071; Web: www.dmrs-ep.org. Ms. Melissa M. Lopez, Exec. Dir. & Attorney at Law.

Diocese of El Paso Charity Trust, 499 St. Matthews St., 79907. Tel: 915-872-8400; Email: lcaro@elpasodiocese.org. Ms. Linda Caro, Interim Dir.

Diocese of El Paso Clergy Continuing Education

Trust, 499 St. Matthews St., 79907. Tel: 915-872-8412. Ms. Linda Caro, Interim Dir.

Diocese of El Paso Education Assistance Fund, Inc., c/o 499 St. Matthews, 79907. Tel: 915-872-8426; Fax: 915-872-8464; Email: elpasocs@elpasodiocese.org. Ms. Linda Caro, Interim Dir.

Diocese of El Paso Historic Missions Restoration Trust, 499 St. Matthews St., Bldg. G, 79907. Tel: 915-872-8412; Email: jyoung@elpasodiocese.org. Ms. Linda Caro, Dir.

Diocese of El Paso Insurance Trust, 499 St. Matthews St., 79907. Tel: 915-872-8412. Ms. Linda Caro, Interim Dir.

Diocese of El Paso Investment Trust, 499 St. Matthews St., 79907. Tel: 915-872-8412. Ms. Linda Caro, Interim Dir.

Diocese of El Paso Seminarian Education Trust, 499 St. Matthews St., 79907. Tel: 915-872-8412. Ms. Linda Caro, Interim Dir.

El Paso Villa Maria, 920 S. Oregon, 79901. Tel: 915-544-5500; Fax: 915-544-5502; Email: villamaria_elp@sbcglobal.net. Linda Velarde, Exec. Dir., Email: l_velarde@sbcglobal.net; Sr. Mary Margaret Murphy, S.L., Case Mgr.

Foundation for the Diocese of El Paso (2001) 499 St. Matthews, 79907. Tel: 915-872-8412; Fax: 915-872-8411; Web: www.elpasodiocesefoundation.org. Ms. Linda Caro, CEO.

Franciscans, Secular Order of Franciscans, Our Lady of Mt. Carmel, 131 Zaragoza, 79907. Tel: 915-859-9848; Email: frbriseno@ysletamission.org. Rev. Miguel Briseno, O.F.M.Conv.

Historic Missions Restoration, Inc., 499 St. Matthews St., 79907. Tel: 915-872-8412. Ms. Linda Caro, Interim Dir.

Legion of Mary, c/o 499 St. Matthews St., 79907. Tel: 915-872-8401. Deacon Francisco R. Segura, Pastoral Min./Coord.

Mount Carmel Cemetery Perpetual Care Trust, 401 S. Zaragoza, 79907. P.O.Box 17655, 79917. Tel: 915-860-0606; Email: jvergen@elpasodiocese.org. Rudy Rios, Admin.

Open Arms Community, Centro Santa Fe (1972) 8210 N. Loop Dr., 79907. Tel: 915-595-0589; Fax: 915-851-2251; Email: openarmselpaso@gmail.com; Web: openarmscommunity.org. Joanne D. Ivey, Dir.

Our Lady's Youth Center (1953) 501 E. Paisano, 79901. Tel: 915-533-9122; Fax: 575-233-3829; Email: olyc77@gmail.com. P.O. Box 1371, 79948. Ellen Hogarty, Pres.

World Apostolate of Fatima, 499 St. Matthews St., Bldg. A - Bishop's Office, 79907. Tel: 915-217-9615; Email: lily@reedcommunicatios.com. Mr. Bruce Reed, Chm.

Zaragosa, Texas Catholic Relief Trust, 499 St. Matthews St., 79907. Tel: 915-872-8407. Ms. Linda Caro, Interim Dir.

RELIGIOUS INSTITUTES OF MEN REPRESENTED IN THE DIOCESE

For further details refer to the corresponding bracketed number in the Religious Institutes of Men or Women section.

[0330]—*Brothers of the Christian Schools* (New Orleans and Santa Fe Provs.)—F.S.C.

[]—*Catholic Foreign Mission Society of America, Inc.*—M.M.

[0480]—*Conventual Franciscan Friars* (Province of Our Lady of Consolation)—O.F.M.Conv.

[0520]—*Franciscan Friars* (Holy Gospel Prov. and St. Peter & Paul Prov., Mexico)—O.F.M.

[0690]—*Jesuit Fathers and Brothers* (Prov. of New Orleans)—S.J.

[]—*Misioneros de la Natividad de Maria*—M.N.M.

[0370]—*Missionary Society of Saint Columban*—S.S.C.

[]—*Order of Augustinian* (Province of Our Mother of Good Counsel)—O.S.A.

[]—*Priestly Fraternity of St. Peter*—F.S.S.P.

[1240]—*Servites* (Province of Mexico)—O.S.M.

RELIGIOUS INSTITUTES OF WOMEN REPRESENTED IN THE DIOCESE

[3190]—*Adoratrices del Santisimo Sacramento*—A.P.

[0100]—*Adorers of the Blood of Christ*—A.S.C.

[]—*Adrian Dominican Sisters*—O.P.

[0760]—*Daughters of Charity of St. Vincent de Paul*—D.C.

[1370]—*Franciscan Missionaries of Mary*—F.M.M.

[]—*Hermanas Contemplativas del Buen Pastor*—H.C.B.P.

[]—*Hermanas de San Jose de Lyon* (Prov. Mex.).

[]—*Hermanas del Servicio Social*—H.S.S.

[]—*Hermanas Dominicas de la Doctrina Cristiana*—O.P.

[]—*Hermanas Franciscanas de San Jose*—H.F.S.J.

[]—*Maryknoll Sisters of St. Dominic*—M.M.

[2770]—*Missionary Sisters of Jesus, Mary and Joseph*—M.J.M.J.

[2970]—*School Sisters of Notre Dame*—S.S.N.D.

[1680]—*School Sisters of St. Francis*—S.S.S.F.

[3660]—*Servants of the Sacred Heart of Jesus and of the Poor*—S.S.H.J.P.

[]—*Sisters of Charity of Cincinnati*—S.C.

[0460]—*Sisters of Charity of the Incarnate Word*—C.C.V.I.

[]—*Sisters for Christian Community*—S.F.C.C.

[]—*Sisters of Jesus and Mary.*

[2360]—*Sisters of Loretto at the Foot of the Cross*—S.L.

[]—*Sisters of Our Lady of Charity of the Good Shepherd*—R.G.S.

[1630]—*Sisters of St. Francis of Penance and Christian Charity*—O.S.F.

[]—*Sisters of St. Francis of Neumann*—O.S.F.

[]—*Sisters of St. Francis of Our Lady of Lourdes*—O.S.F.

[]—*Sisters of St. Francis of the Holy Family*—O.S.F.

[]—*Sisters of St. Joseph of Concordia, Kansas*—C.S.J.

[]—*Sisters of the Holy Spirit and Immaculate Mary*—S.J.Sp.

DIOCESAN CEMETERY

El Paso. *Mount Carmel*, 401 S. Zaragoza Rd., Box 17655, 79917. Tel: 915-860-0606; Email: rrios@mtcarmelep.org. Rudy Rios, Admin. Plots Available 10,000; Total Plots 60,000.

An asterisk (*) denotes an organization that has established tax-exempt status directly with the IRS and is not covered by the USCCB Group Ruling.

Diocese of Erie

(Dioecesis Eriensis)

Most Reverend

LAWRENCE T. PERSICO, J.C.L.

Bishop of Erie; ordained April 30, 1977; appointed Bishop of Erie July 31, 2012; installed October 1, 2012.

Most Reverend

DONALD W. TRAUTMAN, S.T.D., S.S.L.

Bishop Emeritus of Erie; ordained April 7, 1962; appointed Titular Bishop of Sassura and Auxiliary Bishop of Buffalo February 27, 1985; consecrated April 16, 1985; appointed to Erie June 12, 1990; installed July 16, 1990; retired July 31, 2012. *Res.: St. Mark Catholic Ctr., P.O. Box 10397, Erie, PA 16514.* Tel: 814-824-1120; Fax: 814-824-1124.

ESTABLISHED 1853.

Square Miles 10,167.

Comprises the following Counties in Northwestern Pennsylvania: Erie, Crawford, Mercer, Venango, Forest, Clarion, Jefferson, Clearfield, Cameron, Elk, McKean, Potter and Warren.

For legal titles of parishes and diocesan institutions, consult the Chancery.

Chancery: St. Mark Catholic Center, P.O. Box 10397, Erie, PA 16514. Tel: 814-824-1111; Fax: 814-824-1128.

Web: www.eriercd.org

STATISTICAL OVERVIEW

Personnel	
Bishop	1
Retired Bishops	1
Priests: Diocesan Active in Diocese	104
Priests: Diocesan Active Outside Diocese	6
Priests: Retired, Sick or Absent	56
Number of Diocesan Priests	166
Religious Priests in Diocese	4
Total Priests in Diocese	170
Extern Priests in Diocese	5
Ordinations:	
Diocesan Priests	2
Permanent Deacons in Diocese	75
Total Sisters	237
Parishes	
Parishes	97
With Resident Pastor:	
Resident Diocesan Priests	72
Resident Religious Priests	2
Without Resident Pastor:	
Administered by Priests	23
Missions	24
Professional Ministry Personnel:	
Sisters	12
Lay Ministers	45
Welfare	
Health Care Centers	1
Total Assisted	300
Homes for the Aged	7
Total Assisted	2,278
Day Care Centers	3
Total Assisted	209
Specialized Homes	5
Total Assisted	5,552
Special Centers for Social Services	6
Total Assisted	16,748
Residential Care of Disabled	1
Total Assisted	33
Other Institutions	5
Total Assisted	9,214
Educational	
Seminaries, Diocesan	1
Students from This Diocese	7
Students from Other Diocese	6
Diocesan Students in Other Seminaries	7
Total Seminarians	14
Colleges and Universities	2
Total Students	7,187
High Schools, Diocesan and Parish	6
Total Students	1,376
High Schools, Private	1
Total Students	506
Elementary Schools, Diocesan and Parish	26
Total Students	3,594
Catechesis/Religious Education:	
High School Students	3,670
Elementary Students	4,100
Total Students under Catholic Instruction	20,447
Teachers in the Diocese:	
Priests	8
Sisters	3
Lay Teachers	816
Vital Statistics	
Receptions into the Church:	
Infant Baptism Totals	959
Minor Baptism Totals	46
Adult Baptism Totals	86
Received into Full Communion	103
First Communions	1,203
Confirmations	1,305
Marriages:	
Catholic	246
Interfaith	145
Total Marriages	391
Deaths	2,083
Total Catholic Population	198,249
Total Population	826,036

Former Bishops—Most Revs. MICHAEL O'CONNOR, D.D., ord. June 1, 1833; appt. Bishop of Pittsburgh Aug. 11, 1843; cons. Aug. 15, 1843; appt. Bishop of Erie July 29, 1853; reappt. Bishop of Pittsburgh Dec. 20, 1853; cons. Feb. 18, 1854; resigned May 20, 1860; entered Society of Jesus Dec. 22, 1860; died Oct. 18, 1872.; JOSUE M. YOUNG, D.D., ord. April 1, 1838; appt. Bishop of Erie Dec. 20, 1853; cons. April 23, 1854; died Sept. 18, 1866; TOBIAS MULLEN, D.D., ord. Sept. 1, 1844; appt. Bishop of Erie March 3, 1868; cons. Aug. 2, 1868; resigned Aug. 10, 1899; appt. Titular See of Germanicopolis; died April 22, 1900; JOHN E. FITZMAURICE, D.D., ord. Dec. 21, 1862; appt. Coadjutor Bishop of Erie Dec. 14, 1897; cons. Feb. 24, 1898; succeeded to See Sept. 15, 1899; died June 18, 1920; EDWARD P. MCMANAMAN, S.T.D., Titular Bishop of Floriana and Auxiliary Bishop of Erie; cons. Oct. 28, 1948; died July 18, 1964; JOHN MARK GANNON, D.D., Archbishop-Bishop of Erie; ord. Dec. 21, 1901; appt. Titular Bishop of Nilopolis, Nov. 13, 1917; cons. Feb. 6, 1920; appt. Bishop of Erie, Aug. 16, 1920; installed Dec. 16, 1920; appt. Assistant at the Pontifical Throne Nov. 4, 1944; appt. Archbishop "ad personam" Nov. 25, 1953; resigned Sept. 21, 1966 and transferred to Titular See of Tacarata, Dec. 14, 1966; died Sept. 5, 1968; JOHN F. WHEALON, S.T.L., S.S.L., appt. Titular Bishop of Andrapa and Auxiliary Bishop of Cleveland, June 2, 1961; cons. July 6, 1961; appt. Bishop of Erie Nov. 30, 1966; appt. Archbishop of Hartford Dec. 28, 1968; died Aug. 2, 1991; ALFRED M. WATSON, D.D., Bishop of Erie; ord. May 10, 1934; Titular Bishop of Nationa and Auxiliary Bishop of Erie; appt. May 17, 1965; cons. June 29, 1965; succeeded to See, March 19, 1969; retired July 16, 1982; died Jan. 4, 1990; MICHAEL J. MURPHY, D.D., S.T.L., Titular Bishop of Arindola and Auxiliary Bishop of Cleveland; appt. April 20, 1976; cons. June 11, 1976; Coadjutor Bishop of Erie; appt. Nov. 28, 1978; succeeded to See, July 16, 1982; retired July 1, 1990; died April 2, 2007.; DONALD W. TRAUTMAN, S.T.D., S.S.L., (Retired), ord. April 7, 1962; appt. Titular Bishop of Sassura and Auxiliary Bishop of Buffalo Feb. 27, 1985; cons. April 16, 1985; appt. to Erie June 12, 1990; installed July 16, 1990; retired July 31, 2012.

Office of the Bishop—ROBERTA PALMISANO, Sec. to the Bishop, Mailing Address: St. Mark Catholic Center, P.O. Box 10397, Erie, 16514. Tel: 814-824-1120; Fax: 814-824-1124.

Vicar General—Mailing Address: St. Mark Catholic Center, P.O. Box 10397, Erie, 16514-0397. Tel: 814-824-1130; Fax: 814-824-1124.

Vicar General/Moderator of the Curia—Rev. Msgr. EDWARD M. LOHSE, J.C.D., V.G.

Human Resources—JAMES TOMETSKO, Dir.

Chancery—Mailing Address: St. Mark Catholic Center, P.O. Box 10397, Erie, 16514. Tel: 814-824-1135; Fax: 814-824-1124.

All requests for marriage dispensations, permissions, and rogatory commissions should be sent to this office.

Chancellor—Rev. CHRISTOPHER J. SINGER, J.C.L.

Vice Chancellor—Sr. KATHLEEN DIETZ, F.S.O., S.T.D.

Diocesan Archivist—Rev. JUSTIN P. PINO, St. Mark Catholic Center, P.O. Box 10397, Erie, 16514. Tel: 814-824-1135.

Episcopal Vicars—

Northern Vicariate—(See Vicar General).

Eastern Vicariate—116 S. State St., DuBois, 15801. Tel: 814-371-8556. Rev. Msgr. RICHARD R. SIEFER, E.V.

Western Vicariate—2325 Highland Rd., Hermitage, 16148. Tel: 724-981-5566. Very Rev. RICHARD J. ALLEN, E.V.

Director of the Office for Religious—Sr. NANCY FISCHER, S.S.J., Mailing Address: St. Mark Catholic Center, P.O. Box 10397, Erie, 16514-0397. Tel: 814-824-1125.

Office for the Protection of Children and Youth—Rev. Msgr. EDWARD M. LOHSE, J.C.D., V.G., Dir.; CYNTHIA ZEMCIK, Coord., Mailing Address: St. Mark Catholic Center, P.O. Box 10397, Erie, 16514-0397. Tel: 814-824-1222; DR. ROBERT NELSEN, Victim Assistance Coord., Tel: 814-451-1521.

Advisory To Bishop

Administrative Cabinet—Rev. Msgrs. EDWARD M. LOHSE, J.C.D., V.G.; RICHARD R. SIEFER, E.V.; ROBERT J. SMITH, J.C.L., M.Div., P.A.; Very Rev. RICHARD J. ALLEN, E.V.; Revs. NICHOLAS J. ROUCH, S.T.D.; CHRISTOPHER J. SINGER, J.C.L.; MARC A. STOCKTON, J.C.L.; Sr. NANCY FISCHER, S.S.J.; ANN BADACH, M.A.; JOHN DEY, CPA; LISA LOUIS; ANNE-MARIE WELSH.

College of Consultors—Rev. Msgrs. EDWARD M. LOHSE, J.C.D., V.G.; CHARLES A. KAZA; ROBERT J. SMITH, J.C.L., M.Div., P.A.; JOSEPH J. RICCARDO, V.F.; Revs. MATTHEW J. RUYECHAN; CHRISTOPHER J. SINGER, J.C.L.; RICHARD J. TOOHEY; GLENN R. WHITMAN.

Finance Council—Most Rev. LAWRENCE T. PERSICO, J.C.L.; Very Rev. PHILLIP A. PINCZEWSKI; MS. MAUREEN BARBER-CAREY, Ed.D.; THOMAS C. GUELCHER; JOSEPH M. HILBERT; AL LANDER, Esq.; JAMES E. MARTIN; LISA SLOMSKI; PETER C. VARISCHETTI. Ex Officios: Rev. Msgr. EDWARD M. LOHSE, J.C.D., V.G.; JOHN DEY, CPA.

Deans—Very Revs. JOHN P. MALTHANER, V.F., Erie East; MICHAEL P. FERRICK, V.F., Erie West; JOSEPH C. GREGOREK, Ph.D., V.F., Gannon University, (Retired); MATTHEW J. KUJAWINSKI, V.F., Sharon; JOSEPH R. CZARKOWSKI, V.F., Oil City; RAYMOND C. GRAMATA, V.F., Bradford; ZAB AMAR, V.F., Clearfield; JEFFERY J. LUCAS, V.F., Meadville; Rev. Msgr. JOSEPH J. RICCARDO, V.F., DuBois; Very Revs. JEFFREY J. NOBLE, V.F., St. Marys; JAMES G. GUTTING, V.F., Warren.

Presbyteral Council—Most Rev. LAWRENCE T. PERSICO, J.C.L.; Rev. Msgrs. CHARLES A. KAZA; EDWARD M. LOHSE, J.C.D., V.G.; JOSEPH J. RICCARDO, V.F.; RICHARD R. SIEFER, E.V.; ROBERT J. SMITH, J.C.L., M.Div., P.A.; Very Revs. RICHARD J. ALLEN, E.V.; ZAB AMAR, V.F.; JOSEPH R. CZARKOWSKI, V.F.; MICHAEL P. FERRICK, V.F.; RAYMOND C. GRAMATA, V.F.; JOSEPH C. GREGOREK, Ph.D., V.F., (Retired); JAMES G. GUTTING, V.F.; MATTHEW J. KUJAWINSKI, V.F.; JEFFERY J. LUCAS, V.F.; JOHN P. MALTHANER, V.F.; JEFFERY J. NOBLE, V.F.; PHILLIP A. PINCZEWSKI; Revs. BRANDON M. KLECKNER; NICHOLAS J. ROUCH, S.T.D.; MATTHEW J. RUYECHAN; CHRISTOPHER J. SINGER, J.C.L.; RICHARD J. TOOHEY; GLENN R. WHITMAN.

Priest Personnel Board—Most Rev. LAWRENCE T. PERSICO, J.C.L.; Rev. Msgrs. ROBERT J. SMITH, J.C.L., M.Div., P.A.; EDWARD M. LOHSE, J.C.D., V.G., Chm.; Very Revs. MICHAEL P. FERRICK, V.F.; JEFFREY J. NOBLE, V.F.; PHILLIP A. PINCZEWSKI; Revs. MICHAEL C. POLINEK; BRIAN E. VOSSLER.

Priest Retirement Board—Most Rev. LAWRENCE T. PERSICO, J.C.L.; Rev. Msgrs. ROBERT J. SMITH, J.C.L., M.Div., P.A.; EDWARD M. LOHSE, J.C.D., V.G.; DANIEL E. MAGRAW; Rev. CHRISTOPHER J. SINGER, J.C.L.; SAMUEL ZAFFUTO; THOMAS C. GUELCHER. Staff: JOHN DEY, CPA, CFO.

Episcopal Delegate for Retired Priests—VACANT.

Pennsylvania Catholic Conference—Rev. NICHOLAS J. ROUCH, S.T.D., Personal Rep. of the Bishop, Mailing Address: St. Mark Catholic Center, P.O. Box 10397, Erie, 16514. Tel: 814-824-1220.

The Bishop's Medical/Moral Advisory Committee—Very Rev. JOSEPH C. GREGOREK, Ph.D., V.F., (Retired); Revs. JASON A. GLOVER, S.T.L.; JASON MITCHELL; CHRISTOPHER J. SINGER, J.C.L.; Sisters KATHLEEN DIETZ, F.S.O., S.T.D.; KAREN WILLENBRING, C.A., M.D.; GARY SILKO, M.D.

Matrimonial Concerns

Diocesan Tribunal—Mailing Address: St. Mark Catholic Center, P.O. Box 10397, Erie, 16514. Tel: 814-824-1140; Fax: 814-824-1149.

Judicial Vicar—Rev. MARC A. STOCKTON, J.C.L.

Coordinator of the Office of Matrimonial Concerns and Tribunal—Sr. SYLVIA BURNETT, O.S.B.M.

Promoter of Justice—Rev. CHRISTOPHER J. SINGER, J.C.L.; Rev. Msgr. DANIEL E. MAGRAW, Bishop's Delegate for Dispensation & Permissions.

Defender of the Bond—MS. DANIELA KNEPPER, J.C.L., Email: d.knepper@earthlink.net.

Matrimonial Judges—Revs. MARC A. STOCKTON, J.C.L.; DANIEL R. HOFFMAN, J.C.L.; Deacon RICHARD D. SHEWMAN, D.Min., J.C.L.

Auditor—Sr. SYLVIA BURNETT, O.S.B.M.

Secretaries/Notaries—CINDY MANGIARACINA; PATRICIA WIERBINSKI.

Catholic Education

Unless otherwise indicated, all correspondence for Catholic Education should be directed to St. Mark Catholic Center, P.O. Box 10397, Erie, PA 16514-0397.

Vicar for Catholic Education—Rev. NICHOLAS J. ROUCH, S.T.D., Tel: 814-824-1220.

Superintendent of Catholic Schools—JAMES GALLAGHER, Tel: 814-824-1243.

Curriculum—KIMBERLY LYTLE, Dir., Tel: 814-824-1248.

Chastity Education—Tel: 814-824-1259. KATE WHITEFORD, Dir.; CATHY DORNISCH, NFP Coord.

Government Programs—ROBERTA BUCCI, Dir., Tel: 814-824-1238.

Catholic Schools and School Personnel—DR. SAMUEL SIGNORINO, Dir., Tel: 814-824-1247.

Athletics—DOUGLAS CHUZIE, Dir., Tel: 814-824-1245.

Faith Formation

All Communication for Faith Formation should be directed to St. Mark Catholic Center, P.O. Box 10397, Erie, PA 16514-0397. Tel: 814-824-1215.

Executive Director—Deacon STEPHEN J. WASHEK.

Campus Ministry—Deacon STEPHEN J. WASHEK, Diocesan Dir. Campus Min. See Separate listing in the Institution Section for details on Campus Ministry and Newman Centers.

Community Formation & Lay Ministry Training—Sr. NANCY FISCHER, S.S.J., Dir., Tel: 814-824-1210. Interim Dir. Office of Youth & Young Adults. Tel: 814-824-1217.

Family Life Office—CHRISTINE HESS, Dir., Tel: 814-824-1263. Office includes Marriage Preparation and Enrichment Programs, Family Ministry, Retrouvaille.

Office of Youth & Young Adults—JENNIFER DURNEY, Tel: 814-824-1217.

RCIA—Sr. NANCY FISCHER, S.S.J., Dir., Tel: 814-824-1210.

Catholic Charities

All communication for the Catholic Charities Central Administration should be directed to St. Mark Catholic Center, P.O. Box 10397, Erie, PA 16514-0397. Tel: 814-824-1251.

Office of Catholic Charities—ANN BADACH, M.A., Exec. Dir.

Office of Diocesan and International Missions—INDIRA SUAREZ, Dir.

Office of Social Justice and Life—PATRICE SWICK, Dir.

Office of Ministry for Persons with Disabilities and the Deaf/Hard of Hearing—MICHELLE INTER, M.Ed., Dir.

Affiliated Offices, Agencies and Institutions

Catholic Charities of the Diocese of Erie, Inc.—ANN BADACH, M.A., Contact, Devel. & Funding for Charitable Activities.

Refugee Ministry—JOSEPH J. HAAS, L.P.C., Dir., Tel: 800-673-2535; Email: jhcccas@verizon.net.

Catholic Rural Ministry - Bradford Deanery—Co Directors: Sisters PHYLLIS SCHLEICHER, O.S.B.; MARY HOFFMAN, O.S.B., 472 Sartwell Creek Rd., Port Allegany, 16743. Tel: 814-544-8017.

Catholic Rural Ministry - Oil City Deanery—Sisters MARIAN WEHLER, O.S.B., Co Dir., Email: marianwehler@yahoo.com; TINA GEIGER, R.S.M., Co Dir., Mailing Address: 7 Pulaski St., Oil City, 16301. Tel: 814-677-2032; Email: srtinag@gmail.com.

Community Counseling Services

Catholic Charities Counseling and Adoption Services—JOSEPH J. HAAS, L.P.C., Agency Dir., Tel: 814-456-2091.

Northern Vicariate - Erie Office—JOSEPH J. HAAS, L.P.C., 329 W. 10th St., Erie, 16502-1496.

Western Vicariate - Sharon Office—CONNIE MASIAN, L.S.W., Area Supvr., 995 Linden St., Sharon, 16146. Tel: 412-346-4142.

Eastern Vicariate - DuBois Office—90 Beaver Dr., Ste. 119 D, Box 2, DuBois, 15801. Tel: 814-371-4717. VACANT, Area Supvr.

Residential Services for Older Persons

Saint John XXIII Home—KIRK HAWTHORNE, Admin., 2250 Shenango Fwy., Hermitage, 16148. Tel: 814-981-3200.

Christ the King Manor—SAMUEL ZAFFUTO, Admin., 1100 W. Long Ave., Du Bois, 15801. Tel: 814-371-3180.

Community Social Services

**St. Martin Center*—MR. DAVID GONZALEZ, M.S., CEO, 1701 Parade St., Erie, 16503. Tel: 814-452-6113.

Harborcreek Youth Services—MR. JOHN D. PETULLA, A.C.S.W., M.S.W., 5712 Iroquois Ave., Harborcreek, 16421. Tel: 814-899-7664.

Prince of Peace Center—JOSEPH FLECHER, B.S., Dir., 502 Darr Ave., Box 89, Farrell, 16121. Tel: 412-346-5777.

Better Housing for Erie—226 F E. 17th St., Erie, 16503. Tel: 814-455-8379. BRADY MERKLE, Site Mgr.

Good Samaritan Center—11 N. Front St., Clearfield, 16830. Tel: 814-768-7229. DOUGLAS BLOOM.

St. Elizabeth Center—311 Emerald St., Oil City, 16301. Tel: 814-677-0203. DOUGLAS KENNEDY, Dir.

Parish Services

Unless otherwise noted, all communication for Parish Services should be directed to St. Mark Catholic Center, P.O. Box 10397, Erie, PA 16514-0397. Tel: 814-824-1274.

Office of Worship—MATTHEW CLARK, Admin.

Office of Communications—ANNE-MARIE WELSH, Dir.

Faith Magazine—The Magazine of the Catholic Diocese of Erie *429 E. Grandview Blvd., Erie, 16504.* Tel: 814-824-1167; Fax: 814-824-1128; Email: faith@eriercd.org. MARY SOLBERG, Exec. Editor.

Financial Services

Unless otherwise noted, all communication for Financial Services should be directed to St. Mark Catholic Center, P.O. Box 10397, Erie, PA 16514-0397. Tel: 814-824-1180.

Chief Financial Officer—JOHN DEY, CPA.

Financial Services Office—JOHN DEY, CPA, Dir.; JAMES L. BOGNIAK, Dir. Accounting; THOMAS E. BURIK, CPA, Dir. Parish Financial Svcs.; CHARLES BANDUCCI, Dir. School Financial Svcs.

Diocesan Attorney—JOHN B. FESSLER, Esq., Buseck, Leemhuis, Toohey & Kroto, Inc., 2222 W. Grandview Blvd., Erie, 16506. Tel: 814-833-2222.

Erie Diocesan Cemeteries—Directors: Most Rev. LAWRENCE T. PERSICO, J.C.L.; Rev. Msgr. EDWARD M. LOHSE, J.C.D., V.G.; Revs. CHRISTOPHER J. SINGER, J.C.L.; THOMAS M. FIALKOWSKI, Bishop's Liaison, (Retired); JOHN DEY, CPA; JOHN HROMYAK, Gen. Mgr., 3325 West Lake Rd., Erie, 16505. Tel: 814-838-7724.

Clergy Formation

Clergy Personnel—Rev. Msgr. ROBERT J. SMITH, J.C.L., M.Div., P.A., Dir., Mailing Address: St. Mark Catholic Center, P.O. Box 10397, Erie, 16514-0397. Tel: 814-824-1130; Fax: 814-824-1124.

Permanent Diaconate Program—Rev. MARK A. NOWAK, Dir.; Deacon RICHARD D. SHEWMAN, D.Min., J.C.L., Assoc. Dir.

Clergy Continuing Education and Formation—Rev. JUSTIN P. PINO, Coord., St. Leo Magnus Parish, 111 Depot St., Ridgway, 15853. Tel: 814-772-3135. Mailing Address: St. Mark Catholic Center, P.O. Box 10397, Erie, 16514-0397. Tel: 814-824-1130.

Vocation Office—Rev. MICHAEL C. POLINEK, Dir., Mailing Address: St. Mark Catholic Ctr., P.O. Box 10397, Erie, 16514-0397. Tel: 814-824-1200.

St. Mark Seminary—Very Rev. MICHAEL T. KESICKI, Rector & Dir. Seminarians; Revs. NICHOLAS J. ROUCH, S.T.D., Vice Rector & Assoc. Dir. Seminarians; STEPHEN J. SCHREIBER, Resident Spiritual Dir.; Sr. JOSEPHINE VUODI, F.S.O., Formation Asst.

Special Apostolates

Bishop's Delegate to the Hispanic Apostolate—Rev. CHRISTOPHER J. SINGER, J.C.L., P.O. Box 10397, Erie, 16514. Tel: 814-824-1135.

Apostleship of the Sea and Chaplain to the Port of Erie—VACANT, Tel: 814-824-1135.

World Apostolate of Fatima (Blue Army)—Rev. JERRY S. PRISCARO, Chap., 502 Peach St., Erie, 16501-1104. Tel: 814-454-6494.

Cursillo Movement—Rev. Msgr. DANIEL K. ARNOLD, Dir., Mailing Address: St. Mark Catholic Center, P.O. Box 10397, Erie, 16514. Tel: 814-824-1111.

Legion of Mary—Rev. JAMES T. O'HARA, Spiritual Dir., 913 Fulton St., Erie, 16503. Tel: 814-452-4832.

Charismatic Movement—Mailing Address: St. Mark Catholic Center, P.O. Box 10397, Erie, 16514-0397. Rev. JOHNATHAN P. SCHMOLT, Spiritual Dir.

Bread of Life Community—Rev. LAWRENCE R. RICHARDS, Moderator, St. Joseph Parish, 147 W. 24th St., Erie, 16502-2897. Tel: 814-452-2982.

Word of Life Charismatic Renewal—St. Mark Catholic Center, 429 E. Grandview Blvd., P.O. Box 10397, Erie, 16514-0397. Tel: 814-824-1286. DIANE WILER, Office Mgr.

Ecumenism

Pennsylvania Conference on Inter-Church Cooperation—Rev. CHRISTOPHER J. SINGER, J.C.L.

Ecumenical Officers—

Eastern Vicariate—VACANT.

Western Vicariate—VACANT.

Northern Vicariate—VACANT.

CLERGY, PARISHES, MISSIONS AND PAROCHIAL SCHOOLS

CITY OF ERIE

(ERIE COUNTY)

1—ST. PETER CATHEDRAL (1893)
230 W. 10th St., 16501. Tel: 814-453-6677; Email: finance@stpetercathedral.com. Very Rev. Michael P. Ferrick, V.F., Rector; Deacons Raymond Sobina; Jeffrey Swanson.
Church: 10th St. & Sassafras St., 16501.
Catechesis Religious Program—Margie Frezza, D.R.E. Students 56.

2—ST. ANDREW (1871)
1116 W. Seventh St., 16502. Tel: 814-454-2486; Email: saintandrewerie@gmail.com; Web: www.saintandrewerie.org. Rev. Mark O'Hern, V.F.; Rev. Msgr. Daniel K. Arnold, Sr. Assoc.; Rev. Daniel J. Prez, (In Res.); Deacon Ralph DeCecco. Partnered with Sacred Heart and St. Paul parishes
Catechesis Religious Program—Carol Hoffman, D.R.E. Students 55.

3—BLESSED SACRAMENT (1938)
1626 W. 26th St., 16508. Tel: 814-454-0171; Email: dfisher@bserie.org; Web: www.bsparisherie.org. Very Rev. Phillip Pinczewski, V.F.; Deacon Kevin Kunik.
Catechesis Religious Program—Jennifer Durney, D.R.E. Students 157.

4—ST. BONIFACE (1857) [CEM]
9367 Wattsburg Rd., 16509. Tel: 814-825-4439; Email: boniface@roadrunner.com. Rev. Marc A. Stockton, J.C.L.; Deacon Timothy Good.
Catechesis Religious Program—
Tel: 814-825-4439, Ext. 230. Sr. Rose Kuzma, O.S.F., D.R.E. Students 140.

5—ST. GEORGE (1922)
5145 Peach St., 16509. Tel: 814-866-0622;
Fax: 814-866-7532; Email: info@stgeorgeerie.org; Web: www.stgeorgeerie.org. Revs. Brian E. Vossler; James P. Power, Parochial Vicar; Deacons Robert Ball; Stephen Washek; Stephen Frezza.
Catechesis Religious Program—
Tel: 814-864-0622, Ext. 281. Mary Lou Pacoe, D.R.E. Students 243.

6—ST. HEDWIG (1910) Merged See St. Stanislaus, Erie.

7—HOLY ROSARY (1923)
2701 East Ave., 16504. Tel: 814-456-4254; Email: parish.secretary@holyrosaryerie.org. Rev. John B. Jacquel. In Res., Rev. Christopher J. Singer, J.C.L.
Catechesis Religious Program—Tel: 814-454-6322. Mary Hickin, D.R.E., Eastside Faith Formation. Students 23.

8—HOLY TRINITY (1903) (Polish)
2220 Reed St., 16503. Tel: 814-456-0671; Email: holytrinityrcc@neohio.twcbc.com. Rev. Msgrs. Bernard J. Urbaniak; Daniel E. Magraw.
Catechesis Religious Program—Mary Hickin, D.R.E., Eastside Faith Formation.

9—ST. JAMES (1921)
2635 Buffalo Rd., 16510. Tel: 814-899-6187; Email: rectory@saintjamesrcc.org; Web: www.saintjamesrcc.org. Revs. James P. McCormick; Scott W. Jabo, Sacramental Min.; Deacon Charles Adamczyk.
Catechesis Religious Program—Students 108.

10—ST. JOHN THE BAPTIST (1870)
509 E. 26th St., 16504. Tel: 814-454-2873; Email: secretary@sjberie.org; Web: www.sjberie.org. c/o Holy Rosary Parish, 2701 East Ave., 16504. Rev. John B. Jacquel; Deacon Denis Coan.
Catechesis Religious Program—Tel: 814-454-6322; Fax: 814-459-8082. Mary Hickin, D.R.E., Eastside Faith Formation. Part of the East Side Faith Formation Program. Students 8.

11—ST. JOSEPH aka St. Joseph Church - Bread of Life Community (1867)
147 W. 24th St., 16502. Tel: 814-452-2982; Web: www.stjoesbol.org. Rev. Lawrence R. Richards; Deacons Andrew Froberg; Douglas Konzel. In Res., Rev. Gerald Wright, O.M.V.
Catechesis Religious Program—Margie Frezza, D.R.E. Students 130.

12—ST. JUDE THE APOSTLE (1955)
2801 W. 6th St., 16505. Tel: 814-833-0927; Email: secretary@stjudeapos.org; Web: www.stjudeapos.org. Rev. John J. Detisch, V.P.; Deacon Richard Brogdon.
Catechesis Religious Program—Jesse Spanogle, C.R.E. & Youth Min. Students 233.

13—ST. JULIA (1938)
638 Roslyn Ave., 16505. Tel: 814-833-4347; Email: cjulia@roadrunner.com. Rev. Msgr. Bruce R. Allison; Deacon Jerome Peterson.
See Our Lady's Christian, Erie under St. Jude the Apostle, Erie for details.
Catechesis Religious Program—Cheryl Ann Morrison, D.R.E. Students 101.

14—ST. LUKE (1954)
421 E. 38th St., 16504. Tel: 814-825-6920; Email: stluke@slserie.org. Very Rev. John P. Malthaner, V.F.; Rev. John J. Murphy, (In Res.); Deacons Richard Shewman; Glenn Kuzma.
Catechesis Religious Program—Students 100.

15—ST. MARK THE EVANGELIST (Lawrence Park) (1938)
695 Smithson Ave., 16511. Tel: 814-899-3000;
Fax: 814-899-5212; Email: office@smmc.church; Web: www.StMarkMtCalvary.Church. Rev. Thomas Trocchio; Deacon James Moss.
Catechesis Religious Program—Email: pmarshall@smmc.church. Pat Marshall, B.A., D.R.E. (6-12); Geri Hadlock, D.R.E. (K-5) & Youth Min. Students 112.

16—MOUNT CALVARY (1951)
695 Smithson Ave., 16511. Rev. Thomas Trocchio; Deacon James Moss. Mt. Calvary Parish was partnered with St. Mark the Evangelist Parish, Erie PA, effective February 13, 2017. They share clergy, staff and joint office at 695 Smithson Avenue, Erie PA 16511.

17—OUR LADY OF MERCY (1946)
837 Bartlett Rd., Harborcreek, 16421.
Tel: 814-899-5342; Email: info@ourladyofmercychurch.org; Web: www.ourladyofmercychurch.org. Rev. Msgr. Gerald T. Ritchie; Brandon Vogt, Liturgy Dir.; Donna Clark, Pastoral Min.
Catechesis Religious Program—Irene Lucas, D.R.E. Students 185.

18—OUR LADY OF MT. CARMEL (1960)
1551 E. Grandview Blvd., 16510. Tel: 814-825-7313; Email: rectory@olmc-erie.org. Rev. Raymond W. Hahn; Deacon Frank Pregler.
Catechesis Religious Program—Sue Berdis, Rel. Educ. Facilitator. Students 116.

19—OUR LADY OF PEACE (1955)
2401 W. 38th St., 16506. Tel: 814-833-7701; Email: olp@olp.org; Web: olp.org. Revs. Richard J. Toohey; Kyle Seyler, Parochial Vicar; Deacons Joseph Yochim; John Mang; Rev. T. Shane Mathew, In Res.
Catechesis Religious Program—Tammie Mang, Dir. Faith Formation. Students 406.

20—OUR MOTHER OF SORROWS (2009)
913 Fulton St., 16503. Tel: 814-452-4832;
Fax: 814-453-2275; Email: hfc5103@yahoo.com; Web: www.motherofsorrowerie.org. Rev. James T. O'Hara; Deacon Jerome Sobrowski. In Res., Rev. Msgr. Gerald J. Koos, (Retired); Rev. Jerry S. Priscaro.
Worship Sites—
St. Ann Church—921 East Ave., 16503.
St. Casimir Church, 629 Hess Ave., 16503.
Holy Family Church.
Catechesis Religious Program—Patricia Devore, D.R.E. Students 9.

21—ST. PATRICK (1837)
130 E. 4th St., 16507. Tel: 814-454-8085; Email: stpats@neo.rr.com; Web: www.saintpatrickparisherie.org. Rev. Msgr. Henry A. Kriegel.

22—ST. PAUL (1891) (Italian)
Tel: 814-459-3173; Fax: 814-456-0105; Email: jeanking@neo.rr.com; Web: www.stpaulrcerie.org. Rev. Mark O'Hern, V.F.

23—SACRED HEART (1894) Partnered with St. Andrew and St. Paul parishes
816 W. 26th St., 16508. Tel: 814-456-6256; Email: sacredheart.secretary816@gmail.com; Web: sacredhearterie.org. Rev. Mark O'Hern, V.F. In Res., Rev. Jerome S. Simmons, (Retired).
Catechesis Religious Program—Carol Hoffman, D.R.E. Students 23.

24—ST. STANISLAUS (1885) (Polish)
516 E. 13th St., 16503. Tel: 814-452-6606; Email: ststaner@outlook.com; Web: www.ststanserie.org. Rev. Msgrs. Bernard J. Urbaniak; Daniel E. Magraw, Senior Assoc.; Deacon Robert L. Walker.
St. Hedwig, 521 E. 3rd St., 16507.
Catechesis Religious Program—East Side Catholic Faith Formation, Mary Hickin, D.R.E. Students 9.

25—ST. STEPHEN (1917) (Hungarian—Hispanic)
1237 W. 21 St., 16502. Tel: 814-459-0543; Email: padrejc@yahoo.com. Rev. Jorge C. Villegas; Deacon Miguel Alvarez.
Catechesis Religious Program—Sr. Severiana Morales, O.L.C., D.R.E. Students 36.

OUTSIDE THE CITY OF ERIE

ALBION, ERIE CO., ST. LAWRENCE THE MARTYR (1914)
180 E. State St., Albion, 16401. Tel: 814-756-3623; Email: stlawrencealbion@gmail.com. Rev. James J. Kennelley.
St. Lawrence Catechetical Center—129 E. Pearl St., Albion, 16401.
Catechesis Religious Program—Criss Rotko, C.R.E. Students 47.
Mission—St. Philip, 25797 State Hwy. 98, Edinboro, 16412.

BRADFORD, MCKEAN CO.

1—ST. BERNARD (1880)
P.O. Box 2394, Bradford, 16701. Tel: 814-362-6825; Email: sboffice@atlanticbb.net; Web: stbernardcatholic.org. 98 E. Corydon St., Bradford, 16701. Very Rev. Raymond C. Gramata, V.F.; Rev. Stanley J. Swacha.
School—St. Bernard School, (Grades PreK-8), 450 W. Washington St., Bradford, 16701.
Tel: 814-368-5302; Fax: 814-368-1464; Email: cecchetti@stbernardcatholic.org. Linda Cecchetti, Prin.; Lisa Webster, Librarian. Lay Teachers 9; Preschool 18; Students 55.

2—ST. FRANCIS OF ASSISI (1946) [JC]
15 St. Francis Dr., Bradford, 16701.
Tel: 814-362-6825; Email: sboffice@atlanticbb.net; Web: stbernardcatholic.org. 95 E. Corydon St., P.O. Box 2394, Bradford, 16701. Very Rev. Raymond C. Gramata, V.F.; Rev. Stanley J. Swacha.
Mission—Our Mother of Perpetual Help, 37 Lafayette Ave, Lewis Run, 16738.

BRANDY CAMP, ELK CO., HOLY CROSS (1908) [CEM] (Italian), Merged See St. Boniface, Kersey.

BROCKWAY, JEFFERSON CO., ST. TOBIAS (1898) [CEM]
1135 Hewitt St., Brockway, 15824. Tel: 814-268-3655 ; Fax: 814-268-1147; Email: tobias@brockwaytv.com; Web: www.sttobias.com. Rev. Msgr. Charles A. Kaza; Rev. David Whiteford, (In Res.); Deacon Robert P. DeNoon.
Catechesis Religious Program—Tara Starr, D.R.E. Students 142.

BROOKVILLE, JEFFERSON CO., IMMACULATE CONCEPTION (1852) [CEM]
129 Graham Ave., Brookville, 15825.
Tel: 814-849-8697; Email: icbrookville@windstream.net; Web: www.icbrookville.com. Rev. William M. Laska.
Catechesis Religious Program—Penny Rakovan, D.R.E. Students 81.
Mission—St. Dominic, [CEM] Catholic Church Rd., Sigel, Jefferson Co. 15860. Chris Koladish.

CAMBRIDGE SPRINGS, CRAWFORD CO., ST. ANTHONY OF PADUA (1894)
165 Beach Ave., Cambridge Springs, 16403.
Tel: 814-398-4234; Email: saint.anthony@verizon.net. P.O. Box 214, Cambridge Springs, 16403.
Catechesis Religious Program—Sue Parkin, C.R.E. Students 24.
Mission—St. Bernadette, 222 Renner Ln., Saegertown, Crawford Co. 16433. Josie Osiecki, Contact Person.

CLARION, CLARION CO., IMMACULATE CONCEPTION (1855) [CEM]
715 E. Main St., Clarion, 16214. Tel: 814-226-8433; Email: montysayers@hotmail.com; Web: www.icclarion.org. 720 Liberty St., Clarion, 16214. Rev. B. LaMounte Sayers.
School—Immaculate Conception School, (Grades PreK-6), 729 E. Main St., Clarion, 16214.
Tel: 814-226-8433; Email: lcratty@clarionichawks.net. Lori Cratty, Prin. Lay Teachers 9; Students 58; PreK Students 8.
Catechesis Religious Program—Students 136.

CLEARFIELD, CLEARFIELD CO., ST. FRANCIS (1830) [CEM]
212 S. Front St., Clearfield, 16830. Tel: 814-765-9671 ; Email: msgrglynn@atlanticbb.net. 211 S. Second St., Clearfield, 16830. Rev. Brandon M. Kleckner; Deacon Robert Wilson. In Res., Rev. Msgr. Henry L. Krebs, V.F.
School—St. Francis School, (Grades PreK-8), 230 S. Second St., Clearfield, 16830. Tel: 814-765-2618; Fax: 814-765-6704; Email: sfsoffice@atlanticbbn.net. Sheila Clancy, Prin.; Abigail Houston, Librarian. Lay Teachers 15; Preschool 36; Students 144.
Catechesis Religious Program—Tel: 814-765-2618; Email: nzupich@atlanticbbn.net. Nancy Zupich, D.R.E. Students 85.

COALPORT, CLEARFIELD CO., ST. BASIL THE GREAT (1887) [CEM]
183 Locust St., Coalport, 16627. Tel: 814-672-3561; Fax: 814-672-5954; Email: stbasiloffice@yahoo.com. Very Rev. Zab Amar, V.F.
Catechesis Religious Program—Annette Smith, Rel. Educ. Leader. Students 78.
Mission—Holy Trinity, 52 Parish St., Ramey, 16671.

CONNEAUT LAKE, CRAWFORD CO., OUR LADY QUEEN OF THE AMERICAS (1958) [CEM]
155 S. 9th St., Conneaut Lake, 16316.
Tel: 814-382-7252; Email: olqaoffice@zoominternet.net. Rev. David E. Carter.
Catechesis Religious Program—Tel: 814-382-7256. Denise Thomas, C.R.E.; Amanda Darke, C.R.E. Students 91.

CONNEAUTVILLE, CRAWFORD CO., ST. PETER (1853) [CEM] (Irish)
Mailing Address: 501 Washington St., Conneautville, 16406. Tel: 814-683-5313; Email: ss.ppmainffice@gmail.com; Web: stspeterphilip.com. 401 S. Mercer St., Linesville, 16424. Rev. Christopher M. Hamlett, M.S.
Catechesis Religious Program—Paula Vorisek, D.R.E. Students 21.

CORRY, ERIE CO.

1—ST. ELIZABETH (1876) [CEM] Merged See St. Thomas Parish, Corry.
2—ST. THOMAS THE APOSTLE (1862) [CEM]
203 W. Washington St., Corry, 16407. Rev. D.G. Davis III; Deacon William Saborsky.
St. Elizabeth, 26 W. Pleasant St., Corry, 16407.
Catechesis Religious Program—Marcus Johnson, C.R.E.; Vickie Stull, C.R.E.; James Erdman, RCIA Coord. Students 40.
COUDERSPORT, POTTER CO., ST. EULALIA (1891) [CEM]
203 E. Arnold Ave., Port Allegany, 16743.
Tel: 814-274-8646; Email: steulalia@zitomedia.net. 6 E. Maple St., Coudersport, 16915. Rev. James C. Campbell.
Catechesis Religious Program—Tel: 814-274-8552. Students 55.
CROSSINGSVILLE, CRAWFORD CO., ST. PHILIP (1840) [CEM] Merged Now a mission of St. Lawrence, Albion.
CROWN, CLARION CO., ST. MARY (1848) [CEM 2]
117 Lencer Dr., Crown, 16220. Tel: 814-744-9919; Email: samarch@zoominternet.net. Rev. Christopher M. Barnes; Deacon Michael Dittman.
Catechesis Religious Program—Sheila Martz, C.R.E. Students 36.
Mission—St. Ann, 101 Hemlock St., Marienville, Forest Co. 16239. Mildred Cussins, Contact Person.
CURWENSVILLE, CLEARFIELD CO., ST. TIMOTHY (1915) [CEM]
306 Walnut St., Curwensville, 16833.
Tel: 814-236-1845; Email: sttimothychurch@atlanticbb.net. Rev. Stephen L. Collins; Deacon Anthony Indelicato.
Catechesis Religious Program—Terri A. Clarkson, D.R.E. Students 49.
DU BOIS, CLEARFIELD CO.
1—ST. CATHERINE OF SIENA (1877) [CEM]
118 S. State St., Du Bois, 15801. 123 S. State St., Du Bois, 15801. Rev. Msgr. Richard R. Siefer, E.V.
Res.: 116 S. State St., Du Bois, 15801.
Tel: 814-371-8556; Fax: 814-371-0592; Email: sienadubois@stcatherine.comcastbiz.net; Web: www.stcathstmikedubois.org.
Catechesis Religious Program—Rita Smith, C.R.E. Students 71.
2—ST. JOSEPH (1893) [CEM] (Lithuanian), Merged See St. Michael, DuBois.
3—ST. MICHAEL (1912) [CEM] (Polish)
15 Robinson St., Du Bois, 15801. Tel: 814-371-8556; Fax: 814-371-0592; Email: stmichaeldubois@gmail.com; Web: www.stcathstmikedubois.org. c/o St. Catherine of Siena Parish, 118 S. State St, DuBois, 15801. Rev. Msgr. Richard R. Siefer, E.V.
St. Joseph, 301 S. State St., DuBois, 15801.
EAST BRADY, CLARION CO., ST. EUSEBIUS (1877) [CEM]
301 E. 2nd St., East Brady, 16028. Tel: 724-526-3366 ; Email: st.eusebius@yahoo.com. Rev. William M. Kuba, Admin., (Retired).
Catechesis Religious Program—Students 9.
Mission—St. Richard, Purity Ave., Rimersburg, Clarion Co. 16248. Mary Donaldson, Contact Person.
EDINBORO, ERIE CO., OUR LADY OF THE LAKE (1950)
128 Sunset Dr., Edinboro, 16412. Tel: 814-734-3113; Email: ololchurch.office@gmail.com; Web: ololake.com/. Rev. Daniel R. Hoffman, J.C.L.; Deacon David Romanowicz.
Catechesis Religious Program—Mary Rose Shinsky, D.R.E. Students 169.
ELDRED, MCKEAN CO., ST. RAPHAEL (1847) [CEM 2]
16 First St., Eldred, 16731. Tel: 814-225-4231; Fax: 814-225-3172; Email: trams3@hotmail.com. P.O. Box 252, Eldred, 16731. Rev. Thomas E. Brown, V.F.
Catechesis Religious Program—
Missions—St. Mary—[CEM] 630 Newell Creek Rd., Eldred, McKean Co. 16731.
St. Theresa, 111 S. Puritan St., Shinglehouse, 16748.
EMLENTON, VENANGO CO., ST. MICHAEL (1867) [CEM]
807 Chestnut St., Emlenton, 16373. P.O. Box 177, Emlenton, 16373. Rev. Johnathan P. Schmolt.
Res.: 809 Chestnut St., P.O. Box 177, Emlenton, 16373. Tel: 724-867-2422; Fax: 724-835-8536; Email: info@stmichaelrcchurch.org; Web: www.stmichaelrcchurch.com.
Catechesis Religious Program—Elisa Cirell, D.R.E. Students 51.
EMPORIUM, CAMERON CO., ST. MARK (1888) [CEM]
235 E. 4th St., Emporium, 15834. Tel: 814-486-0569; Email: stmarkemp@zitomedia.net; Web: stmarkemporium.org/. Rev. Paul S. Siebert.
Catechesis Religious Program—Jennifer Abriatis, Rel. Educ. Facilitator. Students 77.
Mission—St. James, 7305 3rd St., Driftwood, Cameron Co.. Kim Pennington, Contact Person.
FAIRVIEW, ERIE CO., HOLY CROSS (1963)
Mailing Address: P.O. Box 10, Fairview, 16415. 7100 W. Ridge Rd., Fairview, 16415. Rev. Thomas L. Tyler, V.F.
Res.: 7125 Old Ridge Rd., Fairview, 16415.
Tel: 814-474-2605; Fax: 814-474-1256; Email: res6mt29@verizon.net; Web: www.holycrossfairview.org.
Catechesis Religious Program—Kathleen Kutz, D.R.E. Students 130.
FALLS CREEK, JEFFERSON CO., ST. BERNARD (1952)
P.O. Box 362, Falls Creek, 15840. Tel: 814-371-0428; Email: stbernardrcc@yahoo.com. 205 Taylor Ave., Falls Creek, 15840. Rev. Edward J. Walk, Admin.
Catechesis Religious Program—Tel: 814-449-3624. Students 13.
FARRELL, MERCER CO.
1—ST. ADALBERT (1913) [CEM] (Polish), Merged See St. Anthony, Sharon.
2—OUR LADY OF FATIMA (1952) [CEM 3]
601 Roemer Blvd., Farrell, 16121. Tel: 724-346-3359; Email: olfrectory@yahoo.com. Rev. Matthew J. Ruyechan.
Catechesis Religious Program—Students 60.
FORCE, ELK CO., ST. JOSEPH (1906) [CEM]
17764 Bennetts Valley Hwy., Force, 15841. P.O. Box 124, Force, 15841. Rev. Mark J. Mastrian; Deacon Paul Bauman.
Res.: 17735 Bennetts Valley Hwy., Force, 15841.
Tel: 814-787-4151; Fax: 814-787-4478; Email: stjosephforce@windstream.net.
Catechesis Religious Program—Mary Stoker, Coord. Faith Formation. Students 61.
FRANKLIN, VENANGO CO., ST. PATRICK (1867) [CEM]
949 Liberty St., Franklin, 16323. Tel: 814-437-5763; Email: church@stpatrickfranklin.org. Rev. Msgr. John J. Herbein, V.F.; Deacons Walter Jones, (Retired); Richard Reed; Richard O'Polka.
School—St. Patrick School, (Grades PreK-8), 952 Buffalo St., Franklin, 16323. Tel: 814-432-8689; Fax: 814-437-6538; Email: clong@stpatrickfranklin.org. Carol Long, Prin.; Rev. Msgr. John J. Herbein, V.F., Admin. Lay Teachers 9; Preschool 16; Students 54.
Catechesis Religious Program—Email: tmarshall@stpatrickfranklin.org. Therese Marshall, C.R.E. Students 75.
FRENCHTOWN, CRAWFORD CO., ST. HIPPOLYTE (1838) [CEM]
25997 Hwy. 27, Guys Mills, 16327. Tel: 814-789-2022 ; Fax: 814-789-2025; Email: office@sainthippolytechurch.com; Web: www.sainthippolytechurch.com. 26012 N. Frenchtown Rd., Guys Mills, 16327. Rev. Daniel J. Prez.
Catechesis Religious Program—Joyce Tarr, D.R.E. Students 86.
Mission—Our Lady of Lourdes, 251 S. Franklin St., Cochranton, Crawford Co. 16314. Tel: 814-425-7550.
FRENCHVILLE, CLEARFIELD CO., ST. MARY OF THE ASSUMPTION (1840) [CEM]
P.O. Box 159, Frenchville, 16836. Tel: 814-263-4354; Email: rectory123@outlook.com. 64 St. Mary's Ln., Frenchville, 16836. Rev. David A. Perry; Deacon Robert Hoover.
Catechesis Religious Program—Sr. Suzanne, D.R.E. Students 50.
Missions—SS. Peter & Paul—[CEM] Grassflat Ave., Frenchville, Clearfield Co. 16836.
St. Severin, [CEM] 6789 Kylertown-Drifting Hwy, Drifting, Clearfield Co. 16834. Jessica Minor, Contact Person.
FRYBURG, CLARION CO., ST. MICHAEL (1846) [CEM]
P.O. Box 9, Lucinda, 16235. Tel: 814-226-7288; Email: marcia.ochs@stjosephlucinda.com. 18765 Rte. 208, Fryburg, 16326. Very Rev. Joseph R. Czarkowski, V.F.
84 Rectory Ln., Lucinda, 16235.
Catechesis Religious Program—Bernice Strauser, D.R.E. Students 67.
GALETON, POTTER CO., ST. BIBIANA (1888) [CEM] (Italian)
111 Germania, Galeton, 16922. Tel: 814-435-2303; Fax: 814-435-3453; Email: st.bibiana10@gmail.com. Rev. Joseph V. Dougherty.
Catechesis Religious Program—Students 13.
Missions—St. Augustine—[CEM] 33 Turner St., Austin, Potter Co. 16720.
Sacred Heart, 263 Main St., Genesee, Potter Co.. Renee Kratz, Contact Person.
GIRARD, ERIE CO., ST. JOHN THE EVANGELIST (1853) [CEM]
101 Olin Ave., Girard, 16417. P.O. Box 336, Girard, 16417. Rev. Scott P. Detisch, Ph.D., Admin.; Deacon Joseph Cicero.
Res.: 32 Penn Ave, Box 336, Girard, 16417.
Tel: 814-774-4108; Fax: 814-774-2097; Email: stjohnolin@gmail.com.
Catechesis Religious Program—Tel: 814-774-4061. Jennifer King, C.R.E. Students 109.
GRAMPIAN, CLEARFIELD CO., ST. BONAVENTURE (1833) [CEM]
c/o St. Timothy Parish, 306 Walnut St., Curwensville, 16833. Tel: 814-236-1845; Email: stbon@verizon.net. 461 Main St., Grampian, 16838. Rev. Stephen L. Collins; Deacon Anthony Indelicato Sr.
Catechesis Religious Program—Tel: 814-236-0366. Terri A. Clarkson, D.R.E. Students 35.
GREENVILLE, MERCER CO., ST. MICHAEL (1850) [CEM]
85 N. High St., Greenville, 16125. Tel: 724-588-9800; Fax: 724-588-7053; Email: st.michaelchurch@neohio.twcbc.com. Rev. V. David Foradori; Deacon Frank Luciani.
Res.: 81 N. 2nd St., Greenville, 16125.
School—St. Michael School, (Grades PreK-8), 80 N. High St., Greenville, 16125. Tel: 724-588-7050; Fax: 724-588-7056; Email: nancy.kremm@saintmichael1.org. Nancy Kremm, Prin. Lay Teachers 10; Preschool 10; Students 73.
Catechesis Religious Program—Teia Barger, Dir. Faith Formation. Students 166.
Mission—St. Margaret, 701 Denver St., Jamestown, Mercer Co. 16134. Roseanne McConnell, Contact Person.
GROVE CITY, MERCER CO., BELOVED DISCIPLE (1925) [CEM]
1310 S. Center St. Ext., Grove City, 16127.
Tel: 724-748-6700; Email: secretary@beloveddiscipleparish.org. Rev. Michael P. Allison; Deacon Owen Wagner.
Res.: 321 N. Broad St., Grove City, 16127.
Catechesis Religious Program—Angie Felicetty, Rel. Educ. Facilitator; Michelle Boarts, Rel. Educ. Facilitator. Students 173.
HERMITAGE, MERCER CO., NOTRE DAME (1960)
2325 Highland Rd., Hermitage, 16148.
Tel: 724-981-5566; Fax: 724-981-3215; Email: churchofnotredame@live.com. Very Rev. Richard J. Allen, E.V.
Catechesis Religious Program—Joe Ranelli, D.R.E. Students 259.
HOUTZDALE, CLEARFIELD CO., CHRIST THE KING (1970) [CEM]
123 Good St., Houtzdale, 16651. Tel: 814-378-7653; Fax: 814-378-8333; Email: christtheking.office@comcast.net. 100 Brisbin St., Houtzdale, 16651. Rev. Marc J. Solomon; Deacon Eugene Miller Jr.
Catechesis Religious Program—Tel: 814-378-7109. Nancy Yarger, D.R.E. Students 147.
JOHNSONBURG, ELK CO., HOLY ROSARY (1896) [CEM]
210 Bridge St., Johnsonburg, 15845. Rev. David J. Wilson.
Res.: 606 Penn St., Johnsonburg, 15845.
Tel: 814-965-2819; Fax: 814-965-3482; Email: holyrosary@ncentral.com.
Catechesis Religious Program—Tel: 814-965-2812. Margaret Griffin, D.R.E. Students 154.
Mission—St. Anne, 75 Buchanan St., Wilcox, 15870.
KANE, MCKEAN CO., ST. CALLISTUS (1866) [CEM]
342 Chase St., Kane, 16735. Tel: 814-837-6694; Email: secretary@stcallistuskane.org. Rev. William J. O'Brien.
Sts. John & Stephen, 178 Delaware Ave., James City, 16734. (Secondary Church).
Catechesis Religious Program—Michele Smith, F.R.E. Students 133.
KERSEY, ELK CO., ST. BONIFACE (1832) [CEM]
355 Main St., Kersey, 15846. Tel: 814-885-8941; Email: church.office@st-boniface.org; Web: www.st-boniface.org. Rev. Ross R. Miceli.
Holy Cross, 15822 US-219, Brandy Camp, 15822.
Catechesis Religious Program—Leslie Gahr, D.R.E. Students 99.
LEWIS RUN, MCKEAN CO., OUR MOTHER OF PERPETUAL HELP (1946) Merged Now a mission of St. Francis of Assisi Parish, Bradford.
LINESVILLE, CRAWFORD CO., ST. PHILIP (1959) [CEM]
401 S. Mercer St., Linesville, 16424.
Tel: 814-683-5313; Email: ss.ppmainoffice@gmail.com. Rev. Christopher M. Hamlett, M.S.
Catechesis Religious Program—Regina Pouliot, C.R.E. Students 8.
LUCINDA, CLARION CO., ST. JOSEPH (1840) [CEM]
112 Rectory Ln., Lucinda, 16235. Tel: 814-226-7288; Email: marcia.ochs@stjosephlucinda.com. P.O. Box 9, Lucinda, 16235. Very Rev. Joseph R. Czarkowski, V.F.
School—St. Joseph School, (Grades PreK-6), 72 Rectory Ln., Lucinda, 16235. Tel: 814-226-8018; Fax: 814-223-9620; Email: bochs.stjoseph@gmail.com. Betsy Ochs, Prin. Lay Teachers 8; Preschool 24; Students 38.
Catechesis Religious Program—Mr. Norm Wolbert, D.R.E.; Mrs. Judy Wolbert, D.R.E. Students 72.
MCKEAN, ERIE CO., ST. FRANCIS XAVIER (1838) [CEM]
8880 Main St., Mc Kean, 16426-0317.
Tel: 814-476-7657; Email: stfran317@neohio.twcbc.com; Web: www.stfrancisxaviermckean.org. P.O. Box 317, McKean, 16426. Rev. Jason R. Feigh; Deacon Ronald Fronzaglia, Deacon Asst.
Catechesis Religious Program—Cynthia Zemcik, C.R.E. Students 13.
MEADVILLE, CRAWFORD CO.
1—ST. AGATHA (1849) [CEM]
353 Pine St., Meadville, 16335. Tel: 814-336-1112; Fax: 814-240-5998; Email: contact@catholic-

meadville.org; Web: www.catholic-meadville.org. Very Rev. Jeffery J. Lucas, V.F.; Rev. Andrew M. Boyd, Parochial Vicar.
School—Seton School, (Grades PreK-8),
Tel: 814-336-2320; Email: lblake@seton-school.com. Laura Blake, Prin. Lay Teachers 13; Students 132; PreK Students 19.
Catechesis Religious Program—Tel: 814-336-2274. Marialyce Garvis, D.R.E. Twinned with St. Brigid Meadville Students 60.

2—ST. BRIGID (1865) [CEM] (Irish)
Mailing Address: c/o St. Agatha, 353 Pine St., Meadville, 16335. 383 Arch St., Meadville, 16335. Revs. Jeffrey Lucas; Andrew M. Boyd, Parochial Vicar; Deacons Kenneth Reisenweber; Todd Sommers.
Res.: 967 Chancery Ln., Meadville, 16335.
Tel: 814-336-4459; Email: contact@catholic-meadville.org; Fax: 814-240-5998; Web: www.stbrigidchurch.org.
Catechesis Religious Program—Marialyce Garvis, D.R.E. Students 186.

3—ST. MARY OF GRACE (1909) (Italian)
Mailing Address: c/o St. Agatha, 353 Pine St., Meadville, 16335. Tel: 814-333-6161;
Fax: 814-240-5998; Email: contact@catholic-meadville.org. 1085 Water St., Meadville, 16335. Very Rev. Jeffery J. Lucas, V.F.; Rev. Andrew M. Boyd, Parochial Vicar; Edward R. Horneman.
Catechesis Religious Program—
Tel: 814-333-6161, Ext. 5. Marialyce Garvis, D.R.E. Students 83.

MERCER, MERCER CO., IMMACULATE HEART OF MARY (1838) [CEM]
100 Penn Ave., Mercer, 16137. Tel: 724-662-2999; Fax: 724-662-5094; Email: ihm@zoominternet.net; Web: www.ihmcmercer.com/. Very Rev. Matthew J. Kujawinski, V.F.
Catechesis Religious Program—Barb Kehlbeck, C.R.E. Students 65.
St. Hermenegild, 28 Church Rd., Mercer, 16137. (Secondary Church).

MORRISDALE, CLEARFIELD CO., ST. AGNES (1891) [CEM]
Mailing Address: 22 St. Agnes Dr., Morrisdale, 16858. Tel: 814-342-2583; Email: stagnesrcc@gmail.com. 65 Deer Creek Rd., Morrisdale, 16858. Rev. Robert Horgas; Deacon Dennis Socash.
Catechesis Religious Program—Students 43.
Mission—SS. Peter & Paul, [CEM] Sixth St., Hawk Run, Clearfield Co. 16840. Carolann Socas.

MOUNT JEWETT, MCKEAN CO., ST. JOSEPH (1898) Merged Now a mission of St. Elizabeth of Hungary, Smethport.

NEW BETHLEHEM, CLARION CO., ST. CHARLES CHURCH (1872) [CEM]
201 Washington St., New Bethlehem, 16242.
Tel: 814-275-3446; Fax: 814-275-7550; Email: stcharles@dioceseoferie.org. Rev. Samuel Bungo.
Catechesis Religious Program—Kristen Landers, D.R.E. Students 70.
Mission—St. Nicholas, [CEM] 3028 Shannondale Rd., Mayport, 16240. Dan Landers, Contact Person.

NORTH EAST, ERIE CO., ST. GREGORY THAUMATURGUS (1875) [CEM]
136 W. Main St., North East, 16428.
Tel: 814-725-9691; Email: stgregs@roadrunner.com; Web: www.stgregoryparish.info. 48 S. Pearl St., North East, 16428. Rev. Thomas M. Brooks; Deacon Richard E. Winschel.
School—St. Gregory Thaumaturgus School, (Grades PreK-8), 140 W. Main St., North East, 16428.
Tel: 814-725-4571; Fax: 814-725-4572; Email: npierce@stgregs.net. Nancy Pierce, Prin.; Mrs. Lisa Braun, Librarian. Lay Teachers 12; Preschool 17; Students 76.
Catechesis Religious Program—Jennifer Humes, Dir. Faith Formation. Students 180.

OIL CITY, VENANGO CO.
1—ASSUMPTION OF THE BLESSED VIRGIN MARY (1899) (Polish), Merged See St. Joseph, Oil City.

2—ST. JOSEPH (1864) [CEM 2]
35 Pearl Ave., Oil City, 16301. Tel: 814-677-3020; Email: k.fornof@oilcitycatholic.com. c/o St. Stephen Parish, 210 Reed St., Oil City, 16301. Revs. John L. Miller III; Ian R. McElrath, Parochial Vicar.
Assumption of the Blessed Virgin Mary—7 Pulaski St., Oil City, 16301.
Our Lady Help of Christians, 564 Colbert Ave., Oil City, 16301.

3—OUR LADY HELP OF CHRISTIANS (1914) Merged See St. Joseph, Oil City.

4—ST. STEPHEN (1898)
210 Reed St., Oil City, 16301. Tel: 814-677-3020; Email: office@oilcitycatholic.com; Web: www.saintstephens.org. 21 State St., Oil City, 16301. Revs. John L. Miller III; Ian R. McElrath, Parochial Vicar; Deacon J. Timothy Wren.
St. Venantius, 403 Main St., Rouseville, 16344.
School—St. Stephen School, (Grades PreK-8), 214 Reed St., Oil City, 16301. Tel: 814-677-3035;
Fax: 814-677-2053; Email: mmhajduk3@ststephenschool.org. Marge Hajduk, Prin. Lay Teachers 10; Preschool 15; Students 111.
Catechesis Religious Program—Tel: 814-677-3078. Dianne Phillips, D.R.E. Twinned with Our Lady Help of Christians, Oil City. Students 56.

OSCEOLA MILLS, CLEARFIELD CO., IMMACULATE CONCEPTION PARISH (1866) [CEM 2]
408 Stone St., Osceola Mills, 16666.
Tel: 814-339-7321; Fax: 814-339-5026; Email: horgas@hotmail.com. c/o St. Agnes Parish, 22 St. Agnes Dr., Morrisdale, 16858. Rev. Robert Horgas.

PORT ALLEGANY, MCKEAN CO., ST. GABRIEL THE ARCHANGEL (1876) [CEM]
203 E. Arnold Ave., Port Allegany, 16743. Rev. James C. Campbell.
Res.: 6 E. Maple St., Coudersport, 16915.
Tel: 814-642-2847; Fax: 814-642-7990; Email: stgabriel@zitomedia.net.
Catechesis Religious Program—Students 22.

PUNXSUTAWNEY, JEFFERSON CO., SS. COSMAS AND DAMIAN (1885) [CEM]
616 W. Mahoning St., Punxsutawney, 15767.
Tel: 814-938-6540; Fax: 814-938-7439; Email: sscdofc@comcast.net; Web: www.sscdchurch.com. Rev. Msgr. Joseph J. Riccardo, V.F.
School—SS. Cosmas and Damian School, (Grades PreK-8), 205 N. Chestnut St., Punxsutawney, 15767.
Tel: 814-938-4224; Fax: 814-939-3759; Email: heather.kunselman@sscdschool.com. Heather Kunselman, Prin. Lay Teachers 6; Preschool 36; Students 49.
Catechesis Religious Program—Sue Dahrouge, C.R.E. Students 122.
Missions—St. Anthony of Padua—1 Church Rd., Walston, Jefferson Co. 15781.
St. Joseph, Husband of Mary, 197 Birch, Anita, Jefferson Co. 15711.
St. Adrian, 61 Church Ave., De Lancey, 15733.

RAMEY, CLEARFIELD CO., HOLY TRINITY (1937) [CEM] Merged See St. Basil the Great, Coalport.

REYNOLDSVILLE, JEFFERSON CO., ST. MARY (1872) [CEM]
607 E. Main St., Reynoldsville, 15851.
Tel: 814-653-8586; Email: stmaryschurch2@verizon.net. Rev. William R. Barron; Deacon Daniel F. Satterlee.
Catechesis Religious Program—Barb Murray, D.R.E. Students 56.

RIDGWAY, ELK CO., ST. LEO MAGNUS (1874) [CEM]
111 Depot St., Ridgway, 15853. Tel: 814-772-3135; Email: stleomagnus@comcast.net; Web: stleomagnus.org. Rev. Justin P. Pino.

ROUSEVILLE, VENANGO CO., ST. VENANTIUS (1872) Merged See St. Stephen, Oil City.

ST. MARYS, ELK CO.
1—ST. MARY (1842) [CEM] (German)
325 Church St., St. Marys, 15857. 315 Church St., St. Marys, 15857. Rev. Peter Augustine H. Pierjok, O.S.B.; Deacon Raymond Ehrensberger.
Res.: 144 Church St., St. Marys, 15857-7594.
Tel: 814-781-1019; Email: smchurchfrontoffice@gmail.com.
Catechesis Religious Program—

2—QUEEN OF THE WORLD (1954)
134 Queens Rd., St. Marys, 15857. Tel: 814-834-4701; Email: qwchurch@windstream.net. Rev. Jeffery J. Noble.
Catechesis Religious Program—325 Church St., St. Marys, 15857.

3—SACRED HEART (1876) [JC]
337 Center St., St. Marys, 15857. Rev. Michael Gabler; Deacon William Gibson.
Res.: 144 Church St., St. Marys, 15857.
Tel: 814-834-7861; Fax: 814-834-1376; Email: sacredheartparish@windstream.net.
Catechesis Religious Program—Janet VanEerden, Dir. Faith Formation; Meredith Bon, Youth & Young Adult Min. Inter-parish with St. Mary's Church and Queen of the World. Students 302.

SHARON, MERCER CO.
1—ST. ANTHONY (1924) [CEM] (Croatian)
804 Idaho St., Sharon, 16146. Tel: 724-342-7391; Email: themustardseed3@yahoo.com. Rev. Matthew J. Ruyechan.
St. Adalbert—1035 Fruit Ave., Farrell, 16121.
St. Stanislaus Kostka, 370 Spruce Ave., Sharon, 16146.

2—ST. JOSEPH (1860) [CEM] [JC]
79 Case Ave., Sharon, 16146. Tel: 724-981-3232; Email: office@stjosephs-sharon.org; Web: www.StJosephs-Sharon.org. Rev. Thomas J. Whitman.
Sacred Heart, 40 S. Irvine Ave., Sharon, 16146.
Catechesis Religious Program—Sr. Sandy Pedone, H.M., D.R.E. Students 242.

3—SACRED HEART (1864) [CEM] Merged See St. Joseph, Sharon.

4—ST. STANISLAUS KOSTKA-HOLY TRINITY (2009) [CEM 2] (Polish—Hungarian), Merged See St. Anthony, Sharon.

SHARPSVILLE, MERCER CO., ST. BARTHOLOMEW (1874)
311 W. Ridge Ave., Sharpsville, 16150.
Tel: 724-962-7130; Email: secretary@saintbartholomews.com; Web: www.saintbartholomews.com. Rev. Matthew J. Strickenberger.
Catechesis Religious Program—Students 161.

SHEFFIELD, WARREN CO., ST. ANTHONY (1878) Merged Now a mission of Holy Redeemer, Warren.

SHINGLEHOUSE, POTTER CO., ST. THERESA (1901) [CEM] Merged Now a mission of St. Raphael, Eldred.

SMETHPORT, MCKEAN CO., ST. ELIZABETH (1875) [CEM]
307 Franklin St., Smethport, 16749.
Tel: 814-887-9254; Email: stelizabethrcc@comcast.net; Web: saintelizabethofhungarychurch.weebly.com. Rev. Vincent P. Cieslewicz.
Catechesis Religious Program—Heather Ritts, D.R.E. Students 63.
Mission—St. Joseph, 20 Division St., Mount Jewett, 16740.

STONEBORO, MERCER CO., ST. COLUMBKILLE (1860) [CEM]
P.O. Box 206, Stoneboro, 16153. Tel: 724-376-3393; Email: stcolumbkillechurch@windstream.net. 70 Franklin St., Stoneboro, 16153. Rev. Robert A. Manning.
Catechesis Religious Program—Combined with Beloved Disciple, Grove City Students 5.

SYKESVILLE, JEFFERSON CO., ASSUMPTION OF BLESSED VIRGIN MARY (1923) [CEM]
P.O. Box J, Sykesville, 15865. Tel: 814-653-8586; Email: abvmchurch20@gmail.com. 20 Shaffer St., Sykesville, 15865. Rev. William R. Barron.

TIDIOUTE, WARREN CO., ST. JOHN (1866) [CEM]
25 First St., Tidioute, 16351. Tel: 814-484-7747;
Fax: 814-484-0275; Email: stjstaparish@zoominternet.net. Rev. Joseph Kalinowski.
Catechesis Religious Program—Frances O'Hosky, D.R.E. Students 9.
Mission—St. Anthony, 112 Bridge St., Tionesta, Forest Co. 16353. Jane Downey, Contact Person.

TITUSVILLE, CRAWFORD CO.
1—ST. TITUS (1862) [CEM] [JC]
513 W. Main St., Titusville, 16354. Tel: 814-827-4636; Email: titus@zoominternet.net; Web: www.sainttitus.com. Rev. Walter E. Packard; Deacon Kevin Harmon.
St. Walburga, 120 Brook St., Titusville, 16354.
Catechesis Religious Program—Melissa Singh, D.R.E. Students 66.
Mission—Immaculate Conception, 17932 Wright Rd., Centerville, Crawford Co. 16404.

2—ST. WALBURGA (1872) [CEM] (German), Merged See St. Titus Parish, Titusville.

UNION CITY, ERIE CO., ST. TERESA OF AVILA (1906) [CEM]
9 Third Ave., Union City, 16438. Tel: 814-438-3408; Email: stteresa@verizon.net; Web: www.st-teresa-unioncity.org. Revs. D.G. Davis III; F. Thomas Suppa, In Res.
Catechesis Religious Program—Tel: 814-438-3408. Cheryl Godak-Nothum, D.R.E. Students 127.
Mission—Our Lady of Fatima, 36198 Lake Rd., Union City, 16438. Jim Jackman, Contact Person.

WARREN, WARREN CO.
1—HOLY REDEEMER (1912)
11 Russell St., Warren, 16365. Tel: 814-723-4222; Email: hrparishoffice1@atlanticbbn.net. Very Rev. James G. Gutting, V.F.; Deacons Joseph Lucia Jr.; Raymond Wiehagen.
Catechesis Religious Program—
Tel: 814-723-1531 (Religious Ed.). Diana Lillard, C.R.E. Students 100.
Mission—St. Anthony, 7222 Rte. 6, Sheffield, 16347.

2—ST. JOSEPH (1858) [CEM] [JC]
600 Penna Ave., W., Warren, 16365.
Tel: 814-723-2090; Email: office.sjc@westpa.net; Web: stjosephwarrenpa.org. Rev. Richard C. Tomasone, V.F.
School—St. Joseph School, (Grades PreK-6),
Tel: 814-723-2030; Email: nwarner@sjcswarren.org. Nancy Warner, Prin. Lay Teachers 14; Students 160; PreK Students 24.
Catechesis Religious Program—Jennifer Wortman, D.R.E. Students 106.
Mission—St. Luke, 420 N. Main St., Youngsville, 16371.

WATERFORD, ERIE CO., ALL SAINTS (2005)
11264 Route 97 N., Waterford, 16441.
Tel: 814-796-3023; Fax: 814-796-3025; Email: allsaint@allsaintsrcc.org. Rev. Gregory P. Passauer; Deacons William C. Spinks; Thomas McAraw.
Catechesis Religious Program—Danielle Schoenfeldt, F.R.E. Students 119.

WEST MIDDLESEX, MERCER CO., GOOD SHEPHERD (1955) [JC]
Mailing Address: P.O. Box 226, West Middlesex, 16159. Tel: 724-528-3539; Fax: 724-528-2928; Email: goodshepherd55@roadrunner.com; Web: www.goodshepherdwm.org. 3613 Sharon Rd., West Middlesex, 16159. Rev. Glenn R. Whitman.

Catechesis Religious Program—Rose DeMarco, F.R.E. Students 116.

WILCOX, ELK CO., ST. ANNE (1890) Merged See Holy Rosary, Johnsonburg.

YOUNGSVILLE, WARREN CO., ST. LUKE (1957) Merged Now a mission of St. Joseph, Warren.

Chaplains of Public Institutions

ERIE. *Erie County Prison*. Rev. Gerald Wright, O.M.V., Deacon David Romanowicz.

Hamot Medical Center, 201 State St., 16550. Sr. Charlene Schaaf, C.D.P., Pastoral Care Coord.

Pleasant Ridge Manor West. Rev. Msgr. Robert J. Smith, J.C.L., M.Div., P.A.

Soldiers and Sailors Home. Rev. Jerry S. Priscaro, Deacon Andrew Froberg.

Veterans Affairs Medical Center. Rev. Thomas M. Aleksa, (Retired).

St. Vincent's Health Center, 232 W. 25th St., 16544. Tel: 814-452-5360; Email: damartin@eriercd.org. Rev. Dennis A. Martin, Chap.

ALBION. *Albion State Correctional Facility*. Deacons Ralph DeCecco, Facility Chap. Prog. Dir. & Diocesan Coord. Prison Ministry, Thomas McAraw.

BRADFORD. *Federal Correction Institution-McKean*, P.O. Box 5000, Bradford, 16701-0950. Rev. Vincent P. Cieslewicz.

CAMBRIDGE SPRINGS. *Cambridge Springs Correction Institution*.

DUBOIS. *DuBois Regional Hospital*, 100 Hospital Ave., Du Bois, 15801. Rev. Matias M. Quimno.

HOUTZDALE. *State Correctional Institution-Houtzdale*, P.O. Box 1000, Houtzdale, 16698. Rev. Marc J. Solomon, Deacon Robert Hoover.

MARIENVILLE. *State Correctional Institution-Forest County*, P.O. Box 307, Marienville, 16239. Rev. Christopher M. Barnes, Deacon Michael Dittman.

MERCER. *State Correctional Institution-Mercer*, 801 Butler Pike, Mercer, 16137. Very Rev. Matthew J. Kujawinski, V.F.

POLK. *Polk Center*, Box 94, Polk, 16342. Tel: 814-432-0262. Rev. Robert A. Manning, Chap., Deacon Richard Reed, Chap., Mary Ellen McNellie, Chap.

WARREN. *Warren State Hospital*. Very Rev. James G. Gutting, V.F.

On Duty Outside Diocese:
Revs.—
Beal, John P., J.C.D.
Campbell, Joseph C.
Gula, Richard, P.S.S.
Renne, David M.
Witherup, Ronald, P.S.S.

On Leave of Absence:
Revs.—
Faluszczak, James G.
Hoffman, Mark A.
Neff, John R.
Schultz, John M.
Walsh, John A.

Retired:
Most Rev.—
Trautman, Donald W., S.T.D., S.S.L., (Retired)
Rev. Msgrs.—
Appleyard, George, (Retired)
Bobal, Joseph K., V.F., (Retired)
Bogniak, Casimir A., (Retired)
Brugger, Robert L., (Retired)
Daley, Ernest J., (Retired)
Karg, Andrew H., (Retired)
Koos, Gerald J., (Retired)
Malene, Robert M., (Retired)
Mayer, Richard G., (Retired)
McGee, H. Desmond Jr., (Retired), Inactive, under investigation
McSweeney, Thomas J., (Retired)
Olowin, Jan C., (Retired), Inactive, under investigation
Orbanek, Gerald L., M.A., (Retired)
Sanner, James E., (Retired)
Schauerman, Henry J., (Retired)
Snyderwine, L. Thomas, (Retired), Inactive, under investigation
Swoger, John W., (Retired)
Wardanski, Joseph V., (Retired)
Revs.—
Aleksa, Thomas M., (Retired)
Amico, Alexander D., (Retired)
Andrae, Henry C., (Retired)
Barwin, John G., (Retired)
Bilotte, Philip, (Retired)
Chaplin, John G., (Retired)
Downs, James A., (Retired)
Fialkowski, Thomas M., (Retired)
Fischer, John M., (Retired)
Gallina, Leo J., (Retired)
Gregorek, Joseph C., (Retired)
King, Howard J., (Retired)
Kresinski, Daniel J., (Retired)
Kuba, William M., (Retired)
Oriole, Philip M., (Retired)
Rice, William A., (Retired), Inactive, under investigation
Santor, John E., (Retired)
Schill, Paul A., (Retired)
Schmitt, Charles R., (Retired), Inactive
Simmons, Jerome S., (Retired)
Staszewski, Joseph P., V.F., (Retired)
Strohmeyer, George E., M.A., (Retired)
Susa, Robert P., M.A., (Retired)
Tito, Rocco A., (Retired).

INSTITUTIONS LOCATED IN DIOCESE

[A] SEMINARIES, DIOCESAN

ERIE. *St. Mark's Seminary*, 429 E. Grandview Blvd., P.O. Box 10397, 16514. Tel: 814-824-1200; Fax: 814-824-1181; Email: seminary@eriercd.org; Web: www.erievocations.org. Very Rev. Michael T. Kesicki, Rector; Revs. Nicholas J. Rouch, S.T.D., Vice Rector; Michael C. Polinek, Vocation Dir.; Stephen J. Schreiber, Res. Spiritual Dir.; Sr. Josephine Vuodi, F.S.O., Formation Asst. Clergy 4; Religious Teachers 3; Students 14.

[B] COLLEGES AND UNIVERSITIES

ERIE. *Gannon University*, (Grades Associate-Doctorate), 109 University Square, 16541. Tel: 814-871-7000; Fax: 814-871-5372; Web: www.gannon.edu. Keith Taylor, Ph.D., Pres.; Very Rev. Joseph C. Gregorek, Ph.D., V.F., (Retired); Rev. Casimir Wozniak, Ph.D.; Very Rev. Michael T. Kesicki; Rev. Jason A. Glover, S.T.L.; Ken Brundage, Dir.; Rev. Jason Mitchell, Faculty. Religious Teachers 6; Lay Teachers 222; Priests 6; Sisters 1; Students 4,695.

Mercyhurst University, (Grades Associate-Masters), 501 E. 38th St., 16546. Tel: 814-824-2000; Email: president@mercyhurst.edu; Web: www.mercyhurst.edu. Dr. Michael T. Victor, Ph.D., Pres.; Rev. James Piszker, Chap.; Betsy Frank, Dir., Exec. Office Projects & Events; Darcy Jones, Librarian. Religious Teachers 2; Lay Teachers 158; Priests 2; Sisters 3; Students 2,812.

[C] SCHOOLS, PRIVATE

ERIE. *Mercyhurst Preparatory School*, 538 E. Grandview Blvd., 16504. Tel: 814-824-2210; Fax: 814-824-2116; Email: ecurtin@mpslakers.com. Mr. Edward Curtin, Pres.; Marcia DiTullio, Contact Person. Religious Teachers 6; Lay Teachers 45; Priests 1; Students 506.

[D] SCHOOLS, DIOCESAN

ERIE. *Erie Catholic Preparatory School*, 225 W. 9th St., 16501. Tel: 814-453-7737; Fax: 814-459-6188; Email: scott.jabo@prep-villa.com; Web: www.prep-villa.com. Rev. Scott W. Jabo, Pres. Religious Teachers 4; Lay Teachers 58; Students 822.

Cathedral Preparatory School, (Grades 9-12), 225 W. 9th St., 16501. Tel: 814-453-7737; Fax: 814-453-6180; Email: rick.herbstritt@prep-villa.com. Rev. Scott W. Jabo, Pres.; Rick Herbstritt, Vice Pres.; William Pituch, Vice Pres. Religious Teachers 4; Lay Teachers 35; Students 496.

Mother Teresa Academy, (Grades K-8), 160 W. 11th St., 16501. Tel: 814-455-0580; Email: jamie.brim@mtasaints.com. Jamie Brim, Prin. Lay Teachers 9; Students 194.

Villa Maria Academy, 2403 W. 8th St., 16505. Tel: 814-838-2061; Fax: 814-836-0881; Email: william.pituch@prep-villa.com; Web: www.prep-villa.com. 225 W. 9th St., 16501. Rev. Scott W. Jabo, Pres.; Veronica Connaroe, Vice Pres.; William Pituch, Vice Pres. Clergy 1; Lay Teachers 23; Sisters 1; Students 326.

Erie Catholic School System, Inc., 1531 E. Grandview Blvd., Ste. 100, 16510. Tel: 814-806-2423; Fax: 814-833-6132; Email: office@eriecatholic.org; Web: www.eriecatholic.org. Mr. Damon Finazzo, Pres.

Blessed Sacrament School, Erie, (Grades PreK-8), 2510 Greengarden Rd., 16502-2112. Tel: 814-455-1387; Fax: 814-461-0247; Email: jwagner@eriecatholic.org; Web: www.eriecatholic.org/bss/. Jane Wagner, Prin. Lay Teachers 26; Preschool 84; Religious Teachers 1; Students 305.

Our Lady of Peace School, (Grades PreK-8), 2401 W. 38th St., 16506. Tel: 814-838-3548; Fax: 814-838-9133; Email: lpanighetti@eriecatholic.org; Web: www.eriecatholic.org/olp. Lisa Panighetti, Prin. Clergy 1; Lay Teachers 33; Students 439; PreK Students 100.

St. George School, (Grades PreK-8), 1612 Bryant St., 16509. Tel: 814-864-4821; Fax: 814-866-8297; Email: alathan@eriecatholic.org; Web: www.eriecatholic.org/sgs. Ann Marie Lathan, Prin. Religious Teachers 1; Lay Teachers 34; Preschool 139; Students 427.

St. James School, (Grades PreK-8), 2602 Buffalo Rd., 16510. Tel: 814-899-3429; Fax: 814-898-8285; Email: lnorton@eriecatholic.org; Web: www.eriecatholic.org/sja. Lisa A. Norton, Prin. Lay Teachers 20; Preschool 54; Students 217.

St. Jude School, (Grades PreK-8), 606 Lowell Ave., 16505. Tel: 814-838-7676; Fax: 814-838-6860; Email: vkill@eriecatholic.org; Web: www.eriecatholic.org/sju. Violet Kill, Prin. Lay Teachers 28; Students 284; PreK Students 83.

St. Luke School, (Grades PreK-8), 425 E. 38th St., 16504. Tel: 814-825-7105; Fax: 814-825-7169; Email: acoletta@eriecatholic.org. Audry Coletta, Prin. Lay Teachers 25; Preschool 53; Students 346.

DU BOIS. *DuBois Area Catholic School System*, (Grades PreK-12), 200/210 Central Christian Rd., P.O. Box 567, Du Bois, 15801. Tel: 814-371-3060; Fax: 814-371-3215; Email: jtaylor@duboiscatholic.com; Email: gcaruso@duboiscatholic.com; Web: www.duboiscatholic.com. Rev. Msgr. Charles A. Kaza, Pres. Lay Teachers 54; Priests 1; Students 501.

DuBois Central Catholic High School, 200 Central Christian Road, P.O. Box 567, Du Bois, 15801. Tel: 814-371-3060; Fax: 814-371-3215; Email: dbressler@duboiscatholic.com. Rev. Msgr. Charles A. Kaza, Pres.; Mrs. Dawn Bressler, Prin.; Revs. Edward J. Walk, Teacher; David Whiteford, Teacher.

DuBois Central Catholic Middle School, (Grades 6-8), 200 Central Christian Rd., P.O. Box 567, Du Bois, 15801-5706. Tel: 814-371-3060; Fax: 814-371-3215; Email: dbressler@duboiscatholic.com. Rev. Msgr. Charles A. Kaza, Pres.; Mrs. Dawn Bressler, Prin.

DuBois Central Catholic Elementary School, (Grades PreK-5), 210 Central Christian Rd., P.O. Box 567, Du Bois, 15801-1698. Tel: 814-371-2570; Fax: 814-371-1551; Email: gcaruso@duboiscatholic.com. Gretchen Caruso, Prin.; Joe Lesnick, Librarian.

HERMITAGE. *Shenango Valley Catholic School System, Inc.*, (Grades PreK-12), 2120 Shenango Valley Freeway, Hermitage, 16148-3011. Tel: 724-346-5531; Fax: 724-346-3011; Email: kchs@kennedy-catholic.org; Web: kennedycatholicschools.org. Rev. Jason A. Glover, S.T.L., Pres. Lay Teachers 33; Students 347.

Kennedy Catholic High School, 2120 Shenango Valley Freeway, Hermitage, 16148-2563. Email: wlyon@kennedycatholicschools.org. Mr. William Lyon, Headmaster/Prin.; Rev. Jason A. Glover, S.T.L., Pres. Lay Teachers 13; Priests 1; Students 155.

Kennedy Catholic Middle School, (Grades 7-8), 2120 Shenango Valley Freeway, Hermitage, 16148-2563. Email: wlyon@kennedycatholicschools.org. Rev. Jason A. Glover, S.T.L., Pres.; Mr. William Lyon, Principal/Headmaster. Students 33.

Saint John Paul II Elementary School, (Grades PreK-6), 2335 Highland Rd., Hermitage, 16148-2820. Tel: 724-342-2205; Fax: 724-704-7397; Email: hpatterson@kennedycatholicschools.org. Rev. Jason A. Glover, S.T.L., Pres.; Mrs. Heidi Patterson, Prin. Lay Teachers 15; Students 119; PreK Students 39.

OIL CITY. *Venango Catholic High School*, 1505 W. 1st St., Oil City, 16301-3298. Tel: 814-677-3098; Fax: 814-676-4453; Email: info@venangocatholic.org; Web: www.venangocatholic.org. Brian Slider, Headmaster. Lay Teachers 11; Students 52.

SAINT MARYS. *Elk County Catholic School System, Inc.*, (Grades PreK-12), 600 Maurus St., St. Marys, 15857. Tel: 814-834-7800; Fax: 814-781-3441; Email: macdonalds@eccss.org; Web: www.eccss.org. Sam MacDonald, Pres. Clergy 1; Lay Teachers 70; Students 770.

Elk County Catholic High School, 600 Maurus St., St. Marys, 15857. Tel: 814-834-7800; Fax: 814-781-3441; Email: schneider@eccss.org. Sam MacDonald, Pres.; Mr. John Schneider, Prin.; Rev. Ross R. Miceli, Campus Min.; Mrs. Jen Meyer, Campus Min.; Mrs. Dana Gebauer, Librarian. Lay Teachers 25; Students 197.

St. Boniface Elementary School, (Grades PreK-5), 359 Main St., Kersey, 15846-9127.
Tel: 814-885-8093; Fax: 814-885-8611; Email: knightr@eccss.org. Monica Schloder, Prin. Lay Teachers 5; Preschool 12; Students 31.

St. Leo Elementary School, (Grades PreK-8), 125 Depot St., Ridgway, 15853-1304.
Tel: 814-772-9775; Fax: 814-772-9295; Email: schloderm@eccss.org. Monica Schloder, Prin.; Erica Brazinski, Librarian. Clergy 1; Lay Teachers 10; Preschool 33; Students 105.

St. Marys Catholic Middle School, (Grades 6-8), 600 Maurus St., St. Marys, 15857. Tel: 814-834-2665; Fax: 814-834-5339; Email: schneiderj@eccss.org. Sam MacDonald, Pres.; Mr. John Schneider, Prin.; Miss Mary Ann Rettger, Campus Min.; Mrs. Susan Bon, Librarian. Lay Teachers 14; Students 112.

St. Marys Catholic Elementary School, (Grades PreK-5), 114 Queens Rd., St. Marys, 15857.
Tel: 814-834-4169; Fax: 814-834-7830; Email: slayd@eccss.org. Sam MacDonald, Pres.; Mrs. Deborah Slay, Prin.; Mrs. Patricia Cotter, Campus Min. & Librarian. Lay Teachers 20; Students 199; PreK Students 82.

[E] SPECIAL MINISTRIES

ERIE. *St. Benedict Child Development Center*, 345 E. 9th St., 16503. Tel: 814-454-4514;
Fax: 814-452-1905; Email: admin@stbenedictctr.com. Sr. Diane Rabe, O.S.B., Admin. Religious Teachers 2; Lay Staff 22; Sisters 3; Students 110.

St. Benedict Education Center, 330 E. 10th St., 16503. Tel: 814-452-4072, Ext. 299;
Fax: 814-454-2686; Email: nsabol@stben.org; Web: www.sbec-erie.org. Ms. Nancy Sabol, Dir. Religious Teachers 4; Students 722; Personnel 22.

Erie East Coast Migrant Program, 345 E. 9th St., 16503. Tel: 814-454-4514; Fax: 814-452-1905; Email: admin@stbenedictctr.com. Sr. Diane Rabe, O.S.B., Dir. Benedictine Sisters of Erie. Students 35.

Inner-City Neighborhood Art House, 201 E. 10th St., 16503. Tel: 814-455-5508; Fax: 814-480-8942; Email: nah@neighborhoodarthouse.org. Sr. Annette Marshall, O.S.B., Exec. Dir.

L'Arche Erie, 3745 W. 12th St., 16505.
Tel: 814-452-2065; Fax: 814-452-4188; Email: office@larcheerie.org; Web: www.larcheerie.org. Vicki Washek, Dir. Tot Asst. Annually 33.

Mercy Center of the Arts, 444 E. Grandview Blvd., 16504. Tel: 814-824-2519; Email: abauschard@mercyhurst.edu; Web: www.mercycenterofthearts.com. Amy Bauschard, Admin. PreK Students 64.

Word of Life Catholic Charismatic Renewal, 429 E. Grandview Blvd., 16514-0397. Tel: 814-824-1286; Email: office@wordoflifeccrc.org; Web: www.wordoflifeccrc.org. Theresa Walkiewicz, Contact Person. Total Staff 1.

FAIRVIEW. *Camp Notre Dame*, 400 Eaton Rd., Fairview, 16415. Tel: 814-474-5001; Fax: 814-474-4818; Email: office@campnotredame.com; Web: www.campnotredame.com. P.O. Box 74, Fairview, 16415. William Hilbert Jr.; Eric S. Dart, Pres.; John Yonko, Exec. Dir.

[F] PROTECTIVE INSTITUTIONS

HARBORCREEK. *Harborcreek Youth Services*, 5712 Iroquois Ave., Harborcreek, 16421.
Tel: 814-899-7664; Fax: 814-899-3075; Email: jpetulla@hys-erie.org. Mr. John D. Petulla, A.C.S.W., M.S.W., CEO. Bed Capacity 72; Children 141; Tot Asst. Annually 186; Total Staff 145.

[G] APARTMENTS FOR SENIOR CITIZENS

ERIE. *Mercy Terrace Apartments*, 430 E. Grandview Blvd., 16504. Tel: 814-825-6791;
Fax: 814-825-6541; Email: mta430@verizon.net. Sr. Mary Felice Duska, R.S.M., Exec. Dir. Sponsored by Sisters of Mercy of the Americas - New York, Pennsylvania, Pacific West Community. Bed Capacity 64; Full-time Staff 1; Part-time Staff 3; Annually assisted 75.

HARBORCREEK. **Benetwood Apartments for Persons Elderly and Disabled*, 641 Troupe Rd., Harborcreek, 16421-1048. Tel: 814-899-0088;
Fax: 814-898-2513; Email: benetwood@neohio.twcbc.com. Sr. Patricia Hause, O.S.B., Admin. Benedictine Sisters of Erie. Residents 80; Total Staff 7.

[H] RESIDENCES FOR RETIRED PRIESTS

ERIE. *Bishop Michael J. Murphy Residence for Retired Priests*, 400 E. Gore Rd., 16509. Tel: 814-825-0680; Fax: 814-825-9761; Email: lfeikles@eriercd.org. Rev. Msgr. Robert J. Smith, J.C.L., M.Div., P.A., Dir. Residents 8.

[I] NURSING HOMES

ERIE. *Saint Mary's Home of Erie* dba Saint Mary's East and Saint Mary's at Asbury Ridge, Mailing Address: 607 E. 26th St., 16504. Tel: 814-459-0621; Fax: 814-454-0909; Email: pmccracken@stmaryshome.org; Web: www.stmaryshome.org. Sr. Phyllis McCracken, S.S.J., M.S., R.N., N.H.A., Pres., CEO & Contact Person. Bed Capacity 514; Total Staff 456.

Saint Mary's Home of Erie dba Saint Mary's East, 607 E. 26th St., 16504. Tel: 814-459-0621;
Fax: 814-454-0909; Email: pmccracken@stmaryshome.org; Web: www.stmaryshome.org. Sr. Phyllis McCracken, S.S.J., M.S., R.N., N.H.A., Pres., CEO & Contact Person; Cheryl Truett, Admin.; Rev. Msgr. William E. Sutherland, Chap. Residents 60; Sisters 4; Adult Day Services 51.

Saint Mary's Home of Erie dba Saint Mary's at Asbury Ridge, 4855 W. Ridge Rd., 16506.
Tel: 814-836-5300; Fax: 814-836-5326; Email: pmccracken@stmaryshome.org; Web: www.stmaryshome.org. Sr. Phyllis McCracken, S.S.J., M.S., R.N., N.H.A., Pres., CEO & Contact Person; Audrey Urban, Admin.; Rev. G. William Fischer, O.S.F.S., Chap. Residents 164; Sisters 2; Patients in Nursing Home 80; Carriage Homes Independent Living 80.

Saint Mary's Home of Erie dba Carleton Court, 2710 Carleton Ct., 16506. Tel: 814-452-3681; Email: pmccracken@stmaryshome.org. Sr. Phyllis McCracken, S.S.J., M.S., R.N., N.H.A., Pres. Tot Asst. Annually 60; Apartments (Independent Living) 60.

DU BOIS. *Christ the King Manor, Inc.*, 1100 W. Long Ave., Du Bois, 15801. Tel: 814-371-3180;
Fax: 814-371-4101; Email: info@christthekingmanor.org; Web: www.christthekingmanor.org. P.O. Box 448, DuBois, 15801. Samuel Zaffuto, Admin.; Rev. Matias M. Quimno, Chap. Residents 220.

HERMITAGE. *Saint John XXIII Home*, 2250 Shenango Fwy., Hermitage, 16148. Tel: 724-981-3200;
Fax: 724-981-1677; Email: klhawthorne@john23home.org; Web: www.johnxxiiihome.org. Kirk L. Hawthorne, Admin. Residents 288.

[J] SHELTERS FOR MEN AND WOMEN

ERIE. *St. Patrick Haven, Inc.*, 239 E. 12 St., 16503.
Tel: 814-454-7219; Tel: 814-836-4153; Email: betsy.wiest@ssjerie.org. 5031 W. Ridge Rd., 16506. Sr. Clare Marie Beichner, S.S.J., L.S.W., Contact Person. Bed Capacity 24; Tot Asst. Annually 202; Total Staff 3.

MEADVILLE. *St. James Haven*, 779 N. Main St., P.O. Box 15, Meadville, 16335. Tel: 814-337-6082; Email: samantha.stump@ssjerie.org. Samantha Stump, Contact Person. Bed Capacity 16; Tot Asst. Annually 2,441; Total Staff 3.

[K] CONVENTS AND RESIDENCES FOR SISTERS

ERIE. *Holy Family Monastery* aka Carmelite Monastery of Erie Pennsylvania, 510 E. Gore Rd., 16509-3799. Tel: 814-825-0846; Tel: 814-824-1200; Email: seminary@eriercd.org; Web: www.ErieRCD.org/carmelites/. Very Rev. Michael T. Kesicki, Chap.; Rev. Nicholas J. Rouch, S.T.D., Chap. Discalced Carmelite Nuns Sisters 4.

Julia House, 4415 Briggs Ave., 16504.
Tel: 814-520-8559; Email: erie@thework-fso.org; Web: www.thework-fso.org. Sr. Josephine Vuodi, F.S.O., Supr. The Spiritual Family The Work Sisters 4.

Mount Saint Benedict Monastery, 6101 E. Lake Rd., 16511. Tel: 814-899-0614; Fax: 814-898-4004; Email: prioress.mt@mtstbenedict.org; Web: www.eriebenedictines.org. Sisters Anne Wambach, O.S.B., Prioress; Susan Doubet, O.S.B., Sub-Prioress. Benedictine Sisters of Erie. Professed Sisters in Community 90.

Benedicta Riepp Priory, 3904 Tuttle Ave., 16504.
Tel: 814-825-2767. Benedictine Sisters of Erie 2.

Benet Priory, 346 E. 10th St., 16503.
Tel: 814-459-5103. Benedictine Sisters of Erie 2.

Pax Priory, 345 E. Ninth St., 16503.
Tel: 814-452-6318; Fax: 814-459-8066; Web: www.eriebenedictines.org. Sisters 5.

Saint Benedict Community Center, 320 E. 10th St., 16503. Tel: 814-459-2406; Email: iluv2kayak@earthlink.net. Sr. Dianne Sabol, O.S.B., Dir.

St. Scholastica Priory, 355 E. 9th St., 16503.
Tel: 814-454-4052; Fax: 814-459-8066; Email: sdoubet@mtstbenedict.org; Web: www.eriebenedictines.org. Sr. Anne Wambach, O.S.B., Prioress. Sisters 2.

St. Walburga Priory, 302 E. 10th St., 16503.
Tel: 814-454-4846; Email: bsisters@neo.rr.com; Web: www.eriebenedictines.org. Sr. Theresa Zoky, O.S.B., Contact Person. Sisters 2.

Sisters of Mercy of the Americas - New York, Pennsylvania, Pacific West Community, 444 E. Grandview Blvd., 16504. Tel: 814-824-2516; Fax: 814-824-2127; Email: nhoff@mercynyppaw.org; Web: www.sistersofmercy.org. Sr. Nancy Hoff, R.S.M., Leader. Sisters 302; Sisters in Diocese 31; Total in Community 303.

Sisters of Our Lady of Charity of the Good Shepherd - Erie, Inc., 416 Euclid Ave., 16511. Cell: 814-392-8554; Email: sseveriana@aol.com; Web: rgs.gssweb.org. Sr. Severiana Morales, O.L.C., Pastoral Assoc. Sisters 2.

Sisters of Saint Joseph of Northwestern Pennsylvania, 5031 W. Ridge Rd., 16506-1249.
Tel: 814-836-4100; Fax: 814-836-4278; Email: jennifer.woodard@ssjerie.org; Web: www.ssjerie.org. Sr. Mary Herrmann, S.S.J., Pres.; Rev. Jerome S. Simmons, Chap., (Retired). The Sisters of St. Joseph of Northwestern PA. Sisters 89.

[L] SOCIOLOGICAL

ERIE. *Emmaus Ministries, Inc.*, 345 E. 9th St., 16503.
Tel: 814-459-8349; Fax: 814-459-8066; Email: mkloecker@emmauserie.org; Web: www.emmauserie.org. Sr. Mary Miller, O.S.B., Dir. Tot Asst. Annually 2,900.

Erie DAWN, 2816 Elmwood Ave., 16508.
Tel: 814-453-5921; Fax: 814-453-5831; Email: maureen@eriedawn.org; Web: www.eriedawn.org. Maureen Dunn, Exec. Dir. Tot Asst. Annually 300.

Mercy Center for Women, 1039 E. 27th St., 16504.
Tel: 814-455-4577; Fax: 814-459-7012; Email: jhagerty@mcwerie.org; Web: www.mcwerie.org. Jennie Hagerty, Exec. Tot Asst. Annually 150.

Mercy Hilltop Center, Inc., 444 E. Grandview Blvd., 16504-2604. Tel: 814-824-2214; Fax: 814-824-2127; Email: jamiejohnson2205@gmail.com; Web: www.mercyhilltopcenter.com. James Johnson, Exec. Dir.

Partnership of Women Religious, 6101 E. Lake Rd., 16511. Tel: 814-899-0614; Email: prioress.mt@mtstbenedict.org. Sr. Anne Wambach, O.S.B., Prioress.

Sisters of St. Joseph Neighborhood Network, Inc., 425 W. 18th St., 16502. Tel: 814-454-7814;
Fax: 814-454-7915; Email: info@ssjnn.org; Web: www.ssjnn.org. Heather May Caspar, Exec. Dir. Tot Asst. Annually 1,200.

[M] RETREAT & RENEWAL CENTERS

ERIE. *Glinodo Center*, 6270 E. Lake Rd., 16511.
Tel: 814-899-0614; Fax: 814-898-4004; Email: sdoubet@mtstbenedict.org; Web: www.eriebenedictines.org. Sr. Dianne Sabol, O.S.B., Dir. Benedictine Sisters of Erie.

FRENCHVILLE. *Young People Who Care Inc.*, 1031 Germania Rd., P.O. Box 129, Frenchville, 16836.
Tel: 814-263-4855; Fax: 814-263-7106; Email: bethanyretreatcenter@gmail.com; Web: www.ypwcministries.org. Sr. Ruth Ann Madera, Gen. Dir.

[N] CAMPUS MINISTRY

ERIE. *Newman Centers and Campus Ministry*, 429 E. Grandview Blvd., P.O. Box 10397, 16514-0397.
Tel: 814-824-1220; Fax: 814-824-1239; Email: krobbinson@eriercd.org. Rev. Nicholas J. Rouch, S.T.D., Vicar; Deacon Stephen J. Washek, Dir.

Allegheny College, Catholic Campus Ministry, 520 N. Main St., P.O. Box 14, Meadville, 16335.
Tel: 814-336-1112; Fax: 814-240-5998; Email: krobbinson@eriercd.org. Rev. Jeffrey Lucas; Edward R. Horneman, Deacon.

University of Pittsburgh - Bradford Campus, St. Bernard Parish, 95 East Corydon St., P.O. Box 2394, Bradford, 16701. Tel: 814-362-6825;
Fax: 814-362-1497; Email: krobbinson@eriercd.org. Very Rev. Raymond C. Gramata, V.F., Pastor.

Clarion University of Pennsylvania, Immaculate Conception Parish, 720 Liberty St., Clarion, 16214. Tel: 814-226-8433; Fax: 814-226-1092; Email: krobbinson@eriercd.org. Rev. B. LaMounte Sayers.

Lock Haven University - Clearfield Campus, 212 S. Front St., Clearfield, 16830. Tel: 814-765-9671;
Fax: 814-765-9489; Email: krobbinson@eriercd.org. 212 S. Front St., Clearfield, 16830. Rev. Brandon M. Kleckner.

Penn State University - DuBois Campus, 123 S. State St., DuBois, 15801. Tel: 814-371-8556;
Fax: 814-371-0592; Email: krobbinson@eriercd.org. 118 S. State St., DuBois, 15801. Rev. Msgr. Richard Siefer, Pastor.

Edinboro University of Pennsylvania, Newman Center, 128 Sunset Dr., Edinboro, 16412.
Tel: 814-734-3113; Fax: 814-734-3085; Email: krobbinson@eriercd.org. Rev. Daniel R. Hoffman, J.C.L.; Christopher Beran, Campus Min.

Gannon University, 109 University Sq., 16541.
Tel: 814-871-7435; Fax: 814-871-5561; Email: krobbinson@eriercd.org. Brent Heckman, Dir. Campus Ministry; Very Rev. Michael T. Kesicki, Chap.

Grove City College, Beloved Disciple Parish, 321 N. Broad St., Grove City, 16127. Tel: 724-748-6700;

Fax: 724-748-6701; Email: krobbinson@eriercd.org. Rev. Michael P. Allison, Pastor.

Mercyhurst University, 501 E. 38th St., 16546. Tel: 814-824-2467; Email: krobbinson@eriercd.org. Rev. James Piszker, Chap. & Dir., Tel: 814-824-2467; Michelle Scully, Campus Min.

Mercyhurst University, North East, 16 W. Division St., North East, 16428. Tel: 814-725-6277; Email: krobbinson@eriercd.org. Patricia Sullivan, Campus Min.

Clarion State University of PA - Venango Campus, St. Stephen Parish, 210 Reed St., Oil City, 16301. Tel: 814-677-3020; Fax: 814-678-8841; Email: krobbinson@eriercd.org. St. Stephen Parish, 21 State St., Oil City, 16301. Rev. John L. Miller III, Pastor.

Penn State Erie, The Behrend College, 4701 College Dr., 16563-0906. Tel: 814-898-6245; Fax: 814-898-6608; Email: krobbinson@eriercd.org. Matthew Durney, Campus Min.

Indiana University of PA - Punxsutawney Campus, Ss. Cosmas & Damian Parish, 616 W. Mahoning St., Punxsutawney, 15767. Tel: 814-938-6540; Fax: 814-938-7439; Email: krobbinson@eriercd.org. Rev. Msgr. Joseph J. Riccardo, V.F., Pastor.

Penn State University - Shenango Valley Campus, St. Joseph Parish, 79 Case Ave., Sharon, 16146. Tel: 724-981-3232; Fax: 724-981-4174; Email: krobbinson@eriercd.org. Rev. Thomas J. Whitman, Pastor.

Thiel College, St. Michael Parish, 85 N. High St., Greenville, 16125. Tel: 724-588-9800; Fax: 724-588-7053; Email: krobbinson@eriercd.org. V. David Foradori, Pastor; Deacon Frank Luciani.

University of Pittsburgh - Titusville Campus, St. Titus Parish, 513 W. Main St., Titusville, 16354. Tel: 814-827-4636; Fax: 814-827-3958; Email: krobbinson@eriercd.org. Rev. Walter E. Packard, Pastor.

[O] MISCELLANEOUS

ERIE. *Alliance for International Monasticism (AIM)-USA Secretariat (AIM-USA)*, 345 E. 9th St., 16503-1107. Tel: 814-453-4724; Fax: 814-459-8066; Email: aim@aim-usa.org; Email: director@aim-usa.org; Web: www.aim-usa.org. Sr. Ann Hoffman, O.S.B., Exec. Dir. AIM is an organization founded to assist Benedictine and Cistercian monasteries in Africa, Asia and Latin America.

The Catholic Deposit and Loan Fund of Northwest Pennsylvania, 429 E. Grandview Blvd., 16504. Tel: 814-824-1180; Email: jdey@eriercd.org. P.O. Box 10397, 16514. John Dey, CPA, Exec.

The Catholic Foundation of the Roman Catholic Diocese of Erie, Inc. dba Catholic Foundation of Northwest Pennsylvania, Mailing Address: St. Mark Catholic Center, P.O. Box 10397, 16514-0397. Tel: 814-824-1253; Fax: 814-824-1128; Email: info@cfnwpa.org; Web: www.mycatholicfoundation.org. 429 E. Grandview Blvd., 16504. Lisa Louis, Exec.

Sisters of St. Joseph Mission & Ministries Foundation, 5031 W. Ridge Rd., 16506. Tel: 814-836-4202; Email: dhanna@ssjerie.org; Web: www.ssjerie.org. Sr. Mary Herrmann, S.S.J., Trustee.

Star Foundation, c/o St. Mark Catholic Center, 429 E. Grandview Blvd., P.O. Box 10397, 16514-0397. Tel: 814-824-1188; Fax: 814-824-1181; Email: cbanducci@eriercd.org. Charles Banducci, Contact Person.

St. Thomas More Society, 429 E. Grandview Blvd., P.O. Box 10397, 16514-0397. Tel: 814-824-1135; Fax: 814-824-1124; Email: csinger@eriercd.org. Rev. Christopher J. Singer, J.C.L., Admin.

FRENCHVILLE. *Anawim Community of Frenchville*, 1031 Germania Rd., P.O. Box 35, Frenchville, 16836. Tel: 814-263-4518; Fax: 814-263-7106; Email: anawimco@gmail.com; Web: www.anawimcommunity.org. P.O. Box 35, Frenchville, 53056. Sr. Karen Willenbring, C.A., M.D., Servant Leader.

RELIGIOUS INSTITUTES OF MEN REPRESENTED IN THE DIOCESE

For further details refer to the corresponding bracketed number in the Religious Institutes of Men or Women section.

[0200]—*Benedictine Monks* (St. Vincent Archabbey)—O.S.B.

[0290]—*Oblates of St. Francis de Sales*—O.S.F.S.

[0940]—*Oblates of the Virgin Mary*—O.M.V.

RELIGIOUS INSTITUTES OF WOMEN REPRESENTED IN THE DIOCESE

[0160]—*Benedictine Sisters of Erie*—O.S.B.

[]—*Community of Anawim (Private Association of the Christian Faithful)*—C.A.

[]—*Congregation of Divine Providence* (Pittsburgh)—C.D.P.

[]—*Congregation of Our Lady of the Charity of the Good Shepherd*—R.G.S.

[0420]—*Discalced Carmelite Nuns*—O.C.D.

[]—*Mission Helpers of the Sacred Heart*—M.H.S.H.

[2820]—*Missionary Sisters of Our Lady of Africa*—M.S.O.L.A.

[1690]—*School Sisters of the Third Order of St. Francis*—O.S.F.

[2570]—*Sisters of Mercy - New York, Pennsylvania West Community* (New York, PA, Pacific West Community)—R.S.M.

[]—*Sisters of Mercy - Northeast Community* (Northeast Community)—R.S.M.

[3830]—*Sisters of St. Joseph of Northwestern Pennsylvania*—S.S.J.

[2110]—*Sisters of the Humility of Mary*—H.M.

[]—*Sisters of the Order of St. Basil the Great*—O.S.B.M.

[]—*The Spiritual Family the Work*—F.S.O.

DIOCESAN CEMETERIES

ERIE. *Trinity, Calvary & Gate of Heaven*, 3325 W.Lake Rd., 16505. Tel: 814-838-7724; Email: john@eriedc.org. Rev. Thomas M. Fialkowski, (Retired).

Queen of Peace, 6000 Lake Pleasant Rd., 16509. Tel: 814-838-7724; Email: john@eriedc.org. 3325 W. Lake Rd., 16505. John Hromyak, Gen. Mgr.

NECROLOGY

† Karg, William C., (Retired), Died Mar. 15, 2018

† Murcko, Charles S., (Retired), Died Mar. 6, 2018

† Berdis, Donald E., (Retired), Died May. 27, 2018

An asterisk (*) denotes an organization that has established tax-exempt status directly with the IRS and is not covered by the USCCB Group Ruling.

Diocese of Evansville

(Dioecesis Evansvicensis)

Most Reverend

JOSEPH M. SIEGEL

Bishop of Evansville; ordained June 4, 1988; appointed Auxiliary Bishop of Joliet October 28, 2009; ordained January 19, 2010; appointed Bishop of Evansville October 18, 2017; installed December 15, 2017. *Mailing Address: Catholic Center, 4200 N. Kentucky Ave., P.O. Box 4169, Evansville, IN 47724-0169.*

Catholic Center: 4200 N. Kentucky Ave., P.O. Box 4169, Evansville, IN 47724-0169. Tel: 812-424-5536; Fax: 812-421-1334.

Web: www.evdio.org

Most Reverend

GERALD ANDREW GETTELFINGER

Bishop Emeritus of Evansville; ordained May 7, 1961; appointed Fourth Bishop of Evansville March 11, 1989; ordained and installed April 11, 1989; retired April 26, 2011. *Res.: 12222 St. Wendel Rd., Evansville, IN 47720.*

ESTABLISHED NOVEMBER 11, 1944.

Square Miles 5,010.

Comprises twelve Counties in the Southwestern part of Indiana: Daviess, Dubois, Gibson, Greene, Knox, Martin, Pike, Posey, Spencer (except township of Harrison), Sullivan, Vanderburgh, Warrick.

The Diocese of Evansville was established by decree of Pope Pius XII, November 11, 1944, and the See was fixed at Evansville.

For legal titles of parishes and diocesan institutions, consult the Chancery.

STATISTICAL OVERVIEW

Personnel	
Bishop	1
Retired Bishops	1
Priests: Diocesan Active in Diocese	38
Priests: Diocesan Active Outside Diocese	1
Priests: Retired, Sick or Absent	26
Number of Diocesan Priests	65
Religious Priests in Diocese	5
Total Priests in Diocese	70
Extern Priests in Diocese	3
Ordinations:	
Transitional Deacons	2
Permanent Deacons in Diocese	60
Total Sisters	207
Parishes	
Parishes	45
With Resident Pastor:	
Resident Diocesan Priests	26
Resident Religious Priests	1
Without Resident Pastor:	
Administered by Priests	18
Pastoral Centers	7
Professional Ministry Personnel:	
Sisters	1
Lay Ministers	66
Welfare	
Catholic Hospitals	2
Total Assisted	795,391
Homes for the Aged	2
Total Assisted	75
Day Care Centers	1
Total Assisted	165
Special Centers for Social Services	8
Total Assisted	125,000
Educational	
Diocesan Students in Other Seminaries	12
Total Seminarians	12
High Schools, Diocesan and Parish	4
Total Students	1,431
Elementary Schools, Diocesan and Parish	22
Total Students	5,641
Catechesis/Religious Education:	
High School Students	1,212
Elementary Students	3,353
Total Students under Catholic Instruction	11,649
Teachers in the Diocese:	
Sisters	5
Lay Teachers	475
Vital Statistics	
Receptions into the Church:	
Infant Baptism Totals	925
Adult Baptism Totals	67
Received into Full Communion	115
First Communions	1,015
Confirmations	889
Marriages:	
Catholic	219
Interfaith	128
Total Marriages	347
Deaths	848
Total Catholic Population	75,838
Total Population	512,393

Former Bishops—Most Revs. HENRY JOSEPH GRIMMELSMAN, D.D., appt. Nov. 11, 1944; cons. Dec. 21, 1944; retired and named Titular Bishop of Tabla Oct. 20, 1965; died June 26, 1972; PAUL F. LEIBOLD, D.D., J.C.D., appt. Titular Bishop of Trebenna and Auxiliary of Cincinnati April 10, 1958; cons. June 17, 1958; appt. to Evansville April 6, 1966; translated to Archbishop of Cincinnati July 23, 1969; died June 1, 1972; FRANCIS R. SHEA, appt. Dec. 10, 1969; ordained & installed Feb. 3, 1970; retired April 11, 1989; died Aug. 18, 1994; GERALD A. GETTELFINGER, ord. May 7, 1961; appt. Fourth Bishop of Evansville March 11, 1989; ord. and installed April 11, 1989; retired April 26, 2011.; CHARLES C. THOMPSON, ord. May 30, 1987; appt. Bishop of Evansville April 26, 2011; ord. June 29, 2011; appt. Archbishop of Indianapolis June 13, 2017; installed July 28, 2017.

Catholic Center—4200 N. Kentucky Ave., P.O. Box 4169, Evansville, 47724-0169. Tel: 812-424-5536; Fax: 812-421-1334. Office Hours: Mon.-Thurs. 8-5, Fri. 8-4:30.

Vicar General—Very Rev. BERNARD T. ETIENNE.

Chief Operating Officer/Chancellor—TIMOTHY J. MCGUIRE.

Vice Chancellor—DOMINIC E. FARAONE.

Secretary to the Bishop—RENEE WERNER.

Treasurer—ROBERT J. COX, CPA.

Associate Treasurers—SCOTT BRITT; KAREN CAIN.

Benefits Coordinator/Accounting Clerk—RHONDA WEIS.

Accounting Clerk—BARBARA LAMBLE.

Office of the Tribunal—Mailing Address: P.O. Box 4169, Evansville, 47724-0169.

Judicial Vicar—Very Rev. J. KENNETH WALKER, M.Div., M.C.L., J.C.L.; MARY GEN BLITTSCHAU, M.A., M.C.L., J.C.L., Judge.

Judge—Rev. STEPHEN P. LINTZENICH, (Retired).

Defender of the Bond—Rev. JOSEPH F. ERBACHER.

Court Psychological Expert—Deacon THOMAS E. HOLSWORTH, Ph.D., H.S.P.P.

Advocates—Revs. JOHN H. SCHIPP; MICHAEL MADDEN, (Retired).

Ecclesiastical Notaries—LINDA PAYNE; LEIGH ANNE COSTLOW.

Archivist—DOMINIC E. FARAONE.

Diocesan Consultors—Very Revs. J. KENNETH WALKER, M.Div., M.C.L., J.C.L.; BERNARD T. ETIENNE; DAVID G. FLECK; Revs. ALEX ZENTHOEFER; PAUL ANTHONY FERGUSON; JAMES KORESSEL.

Diocesan Council of Priests—Very Rev. J. KENNETH WALKER, M.Div., M.C.L., J.C.L.; Revs. WILLIAM TRAYLOR; PAUL ANTHONY FERGUSON; CLAUDE THOMAS BURNS; RYAN PAUL HILDERBRAND; JASON GRIES; BENNY ALIKANDAYIL CHACKO; JERRY PRATT; Very Revs. DAVID G. FLECK; BERNARD T. ETIENNE; Rev. Msgr. KENNETH R. KNAPP, A.C.S.W., M.S., (Retired).

Clergy Personnel Board—Most Rev. JOSEPH M. SIEGEL; Deacons DAVID RICE, Dir.; RICHARD LEIBUNDGUTH; Revs. DAVID H. NUNNING, (Retired); JAMES KORESSEL; JACK J. DURCHHOLZ; RONALD LEE KREILEIN; GARY EDWARD KAISER; Very Revs. J. KENNETH WALKER, M.Div., M.C.L., J.C.L.; BERNARD T. ETIENNE.

Deans—Very Revs. GODFREY MULLEN, O.S.B., South; RAYMOND BRENNER, East; ANTHONY ERNST, West; DAVID G. FLECK, North.

Vicar for Retired Priests—Very Rev. JOSEPH L. ZILIAK, S.T.L., (Retired).

Censor of Books—MARY GEN BLITTSCHAU, M.A., M.C.L., J.C.L.

Diocesan Offices And Directors

Catholic Committees for Boy Scouts and Girl Scouts—Deacon CHARLES KORESSEL, Chap.

Campus Ministry—CHRISTINE HOEHN, Coord.

Catholic Charities—SHARON A. BURNS, Exec. Dir., 610 E. Walnut St., Ste. 220A, Evansville, 47713. Tel: 812-423-5456.

Catholic Diocese of Evansville, Inc.—Most Rev. JOSEPH M. SIEGEL.

Catholic Education Endowment, Inc. (Washington)—LYNN WILLIAMS, Pres.

Catholic Education Foundation, Inc. (Evansville)—VACANT.

The Catholic Foundation of Southwestern Indiana, Inc.—TODD BROCK, Exec. Dir., Mailing Address: P.O. Box 4169, Evansville, 47724-0169.

Holy Trinity Endowment Committee—950 Church Ave., Jasper, 47546. BRIAN ECKMAN, Pres.

Catholic Education, Office of—DARYL HAGAN, Supt. Associate Superintendents: SALLY STERNBERG; MICHELLE PRIAR; RHONDA WEISSMANN, Sec.

Catholic Communication Office—TIMOTHY LILLEY, Dir., Mailing Address: P.O. Box 4169, Evansville, 47724-0169.

Catholic Hospitals, Diocesan Representative—VACANT.

Catholic Relief Services—SHARON A. BURNS, 610 E. Walnut St, Ste. 220A, Evansville, 47713. Tel: 812-423-5456.

Cemeteries—Rev. EUGENE A. SCHROEDER, Dir., 6202 W. St. Joseph Rd., Evansville, 47720. Tel: 812-963-3273.

Christian Educational Foundation of Vincennes, Inc.—VACANT.

Continuing Education of Clergy—4200 N. Kentucky Ave., Evansville, 47711. VACANT.

Cursillos in Christianity—PETE BERRY, Lay Dir.

Deaf Ministry—Rev. HENRY KUYKENDALL, (Retired). Diocesan Finance Council: Most Rev. JOSEPH M. SIEGEL; Very Rev. BERNARD T. ETIENNE; TIMOTHY J. MCGUIRE; ROBERT COX; GARY BECKMAN; STEVE WITTING; JEFF BONE; WILLIAM KAISER; RON POHL; JOHN PORTER; JEFF HENNING

Diocese of Evansville Retirement Trust Agreement and Plan for Priests—Office of the Bishop: 4200 N. Kentucky Ave., P.O. Box 4169, Evansville, 47724-0169. Tel: 812-424-5536.

Ecumenism—4200 N. Kentucky Ave., P.O. Box 4169, Evansville, 47724-0169. Tel: 812-424-5536.

Evangelization, Office of—4200 N. Kentucky Ave., P.O. Box 4169, Evansville, 47724-0169. Tel: 812-424-5536.

Office of Hispanic Ministry—Evansville Office: 610 E. Walnut St., Ste. 220A, Evansville, 47713. Tel: 812-683-5212. *Huntingburg Office: 317 N. Washington St., 2nd Fl., Huntingburg, 47542*. Tel: 812-683-5212. SHARON A. BURNS, Dir.

Propagation of the Faith and Holy Childhood Association4200 N. Kentucky Ave., P.O. Box 4169, Evansville, 47724-0169. Tel: 812-424-5536.

Justice and Peace—(Please refer to Catholic Charities for further information).

Legion of Mary—VACANT, Evansville; Deacon DONALD HAAG, Washington.

Message, The—Catholic Press of Evansville Most Rev. JOSEPH M. SIEGEL, Publisher; TIMOTHY LILLEY, Editor.

Newly Ordained and Missionary Priests—Very Rev. ANTHONY ERNST, Dir., 211 N. Vine St., Haubstadt, 47639.

Permanent Diaconate Program—Mailing Address: P.O. Box 4169, Evansville, 47724-0169. Deacon THOMAS EVANS, Dir.

Office of Catechesis—KATHY GALLO, Dir.; MARY KAYE FALCONY, Asst. Dir.; ANDREA GUNTER, Administrative Asst.

Rural Life Conference—Rev. JOHN BOEGLIN, Dir., Holy Family Church, 950 E. Church Ave., Jasper, 47546-3797.

Sarto Retreat House—MARGIE NORD, Coord.; ANDY RECKELHOFF, Dir. Maintenance.

Secretariat for Charismatic Renewal—JOHN BENNETT.

Stewardship / Development, Office of—VACANT, P.O. Box 4169, Evansville, 47724-0169. Tel: 812-424-5536.

Victim Assistance Coordinator—THOMAS WANNEMUEHLER, L.C.S.W., Tel: 812-490-9565 (local); Tel: 866-200-3004 (long distance).

Vocation Office—Mailing Address: P.O. Box 4169, Evansville, 47724-0169. Tel: 812-424-5536. Revs. ALEX ZENTHOEFER, Dir.; TYLER R. TENBARGE, Assoc. Dir.

Worship—MATTHEW MILLER, Dir., 4200 N. Kentucky, P.O. Box 4169, Evansville, 47724-0169. Tel: 812-424-5536.

Youth and Young Adult Ministry—4200 N. Kentucky, P.O. Box 4169, Evansville, IL 47724-0169. Tel: 812-424-5536. STEVEN DABROWSKI JR., Dir.

CLERGY, PARISHES, MISSIONS AND PAROCHIAL SCHOOLS

CITY OF EVANSVILLE

(VANDERBURGH COUNTY)

1—ST. BENEDICT CATHEDRAL
1328 Lincoln Ave., 47714-1516. Tel: 812-425-3369; Fax: 812-425-3378; Web: www.saintbenedictcathedral.org. Very Rev. Godfrey Mullen, O.S.B., Rector; Sr. Patricia McGuire, O.S.B., Pastoral Assoc.; Deacon David Rice.
Res.: 1312 Lincoln Ave., 47714.
School—St. Benedict Cathedral School, (Grades PreK-8), Tel: 812-425-4596; Email: admin@stbens.com; Web: www.saintbenedictcathedral.org/school. Kari Ford, Prin. Lay Teachers 24; Sisters of St. Benedict 1; Students 360.
Catechesis Religious Program—Bertha Melendres, CRE.

2—ALL SAINTS
704 1st Ave., 47710-1632. Tel: 812-423-5209; Fax: 812-424-5498; Web: allsaintsevansville.org. Rev. John Davidson, Admin.; Lisa Foster, Pastoral Assoc.
Catechesis Religious Program—Email: svogler@evdio.org. Sharon Vogler, D.R.E. Students 54.

3—ANNUNCIATION OF THE LORD
3010 E. Chandler Ave., 47714. Tel: 812-476-3061; Fax: 812-476-3062; Web: www.annunciationevv.org. Revs. Alex Zenthoefer; Pascal Nduka; Deacon John McMullen.
School—Annunciation of the Lord School, (Grades PreK-8), Tel: 812-476-1792; Tel: 812-477-9082; Email: mmoore@evdio.org; Email: dmemmer@evdio.org; Web: annunciationangels.org. Matthew Moore, Prin.; David Memmer, Prin. Lay Teachers 25; Students 311.
Catechesis Religious Program—Students 20.

4—ST. BONIFACE
1626 Glendale Ave., 47712. Tel: 812-423-1721; Email: spiper@evdio.org; Web: stbonifaceevansville.com. Rev. John Brosmer; Deacons Russell Maples; Robert Mattingly; Wayne Hoy.
School—Westside Catholic School, (Grades PreK-8), c/o St. Boniface Parish, 1626 Glendale Ave., 47712. Tel: 812-422-1014; Web: www.westsidecatholic.org. Kelsey Meier, Prin. Lay Teachers 18; Students 190.
Catechesis Religious Program—Email: jmayer@evdio.org. Jenny Mayer, D.R.E. Students 9.

5—CORPUS CHRISTI
5528 Hogue Rd., 47712. Tel: 812-422-2027; Fax: 812-421-8316; Web: www.corpuschristievansville.org. Revs. Claude Thomas Burns; Gordon Mann, Parochial Vicar; Deacon Tom Goebel.
School—Corpus Christi School, (Grades PreK-8), Tel: 812-422-1208; Email: mcraig@evdio.org; Web: corpuschristischoolevansville.org. Martha Craig, Prin. Lay Teachers 15; Students 252.
Catechesis Religious Program—Email: kcurtis@evdio.org. Kathryn Curtis, D.R.E. Students 36.

6—GOOD SHEPHERD
2301 N. Stockwell, 47715. Tel: 812-477-5405; Fax: 812-469-2907; Web: gsparish.org. Rev. Zachary J. Etienne; Deacon Dan DeCastra.
School—Good Shepherd School, (Grades PreK-8), Tel: 812-476-4477; Email: kgirten@evdio.org; Web: gsparish.org/good-shepherd-catholic-school. Kristen Girten, Prin. Lay Teachers 26; Students 358.
Catechesis Religious Program—Email: skroupa@evdio.org. Sue Kroupa, D.R.E. Students 36.

7—HOLY REDEEMER
918 W. Mill Rd., 47710. Tel: 812-424-8344; Fax: 812-424-7166; Web: www.holyredeemerchurch.org. Revs. Jason Gries; Sudhakar Bhastati, Parochial Vicar; Deacons Kevin Bach; Thomas Cervone.
School—Holy Redeemer School, (Grades PreK-8), Tel: 812-422-3688; Email: tmcintosh@evdio.org; Web: holyredeemercatholicschool.com. Tim McIntosh, Prin. Lay Teachers 16; Students 203.
Catechesis Religious Program—Email: drasler@evdio.org. Doug Rasler, D.R.E. Students 52.

8—HOLY ROSARY
1301 S. Green River Rd., 47715. Tel: 812-477-8923; Fax: 812-471-7226; Web: hrparish.org. Very Rev. Bernard T. Etienne; Rev. Homero Rodriguez; Sr. Mary Mundy, S.P., Pastoral Assoc.; Deacons Jose Garrido; Christian Borowiecki.
School—Holy Rosary School, (Grades PreK-8), Tel: 812-477-2271; Email: jfredrich@evdio.org; Web: holyrosaryrams.org. Joan Fredrich, Prin. Lay Teachers 24; Students 488.
Catechesis Religious Program—Email: cagaddis@evdio.org. Carol Ann Gaddis, D.R.E. Students 53.

9—ST. JOHN THE EVANGELIST, [CEM]
5301 Daylight Dr., 47725-7636. Tel: 812-867-3718; Web: www.catholicdaylight.org. Rev. Christopher Forler; Deacon Richard Leibundguth.
Catechesis Religious Program—Email: jpadgett@evdio.org. Joel Padgett, D.R.E. Students 137.

10—ST. JOSEPH, [CEM]
6202 W. St. Joseph Rd., 47720. Tel: 812-963-3273; Web: www.stjoeco.org. Rev. Eugene A. Schroeder.
School—St. Joseph School, (Grades PreK-8), Tel: 812-963-3335; Web: stjoeco.org/school. Nathan Winstead, Prin. Lay Teachers 9; Students 199; Clergy / Religious Teachers 1.
Catechesis Religious Program—Email: jreckelhoff@evdio.org. Jessica Reckelhoff, C.R.E. Students 26.

11—STS. MARY & JOHN
613 Cherry St., 47713. Tel: 812-425-1577; Fax: 812-426-1416; Web: stsmaryandjohnparish.org. Rev. Benny Alikandayil Chacko, Admin.; Deacons Dennis Russell; Thomas Kempf.
Res.: 609 Cherry St., 47713.
Catechesis Religious Program—

12—RESURRECTION
5301 New Harmony Rd., 47720. Tel: 812-963-3121; Fax: 812-963-1141; Web: www.resurrectionweb.org. Very Rev. Godfrey Mullen, O.S.B., Temporary Admin.
School—Resurrection School, (Grades PreK-8), Tel: 812-963-6148; Email: tberendes@evdio.org; Web: resurrectioncatholicschool.org. Theresa Berendes, Prin. Lay Teachers 24; Students 373.
Catechesis Religious Program—Email: jkeith@evdio.org. Joe Keith, D.R.E. Students 49.

13—ST. WENDEL, [CEM]
10542 W. Boonville-New Harmony Rd., 47720. Tel: 812-963-3733; Fax: 812-963-3061; Web: www.saintwendelparish.org. Rev. Edward Schnur; Deacon Mark McDonald.
School—St. Wendel School, (Grades PreK-8), Tel: 812-963-3958; Email: hscheu@evdio.org; Web: saintwendelschool.org. Hallie Scheu, Prin. Lay Teachers 11; Students 206.
Catechesis Religious Program— Twinned with St. Francis, Poseyville Email: scooley@evdio.org. Sherie Cooley, D.R.E.

OUTSIDE CITY OF EVANSVILLE

BICKNELL, KNOX CO., ST. PHILIP NERI
605 W. Fourth St., Bicknell, 47512. Tel: 812-735-4069. Revs. Donald Ackerman, Temporary Admin.; Simon Natha; Deacons Rey Carandang; Paul Vonderwell; Cletus Yochum Jr.
Catechesis Religious Program—Email: epepmeier@gmail.com. Elaine Pepmeier, C.R.E. Students 33.

BLOOMFIELD, GREENE CO., HOLY NAME, [CEM]
Mailing Address: 700 Lincoln Dr., Bloomfield, 47424. Tel: 812-847-7821. Rev. Biju Thomas, Admin.
Catechesis Religious Program—Linda Welch, C.R.E. Students 18.

BOONVILLE, WARRICK CO., ST. CLEMENT
422 E. Sycamore St., Boonville, 47601. Tel: 812-897-4653; Fax: 812-897-4692; Web: www.stclementparish.org. Rev. Jack Durchholz; Deacons David Seibert; Tom Lambert.
Catechesis Religious Program—Email: kvollmer@evdio.org. Katie Vollmer, D.R.E. Students 96.

CELESTINE, DUBOIS CO., ST. ISIDORE THE FARMER (2016) [CEM]
6864 E. State Rd. 164, P.O. Box 1, Celestine, 47521. Tel: 812-634-1875; Fax: 812-634-7255; Web: www.saintisidoreparish.com. Rev. Eugene R. Schmitt; Deacon Michael Seibert.
Catechesis Religious Program—Email: greckelhoff@evdio.org. Glenda Reckelhoff, C.R.E. Students 383.

CHRISNEY, SPENCER CO., ST. MARTIN, [CEM]
58 S. Church St., Chrisney, 47611. Tel: 812-649-4811 ; Fax: 812-649-4176; Web: www.stmartinchrisney.org. Rev. Ronald Kreilein; Deacon Michael Waninger.
Catechesis Religious Program—Carolyn Thorpe, D.R.E. Students 27.

DALE, SPENCER CO., ST. FRANCIS OF ASSISI
Mailing Address: 8 E. Maple St., P.O. Box 684, Dale, 47523. Tel: 812-937-2200; Fax: 812-937-4197; Web: www.saintfrancisofassisi.net. Rev. Crispine Adongo, Admin.; Deacons Paul Cox; James Woebkenberg.
Catechesis Religious Program—Email: mfischer@evdio.org. Michelle Fischer, C.R.E. Students 248.

FERDINAND, DUBOIS CO., CHRIST THE KING
341 E. 10th St., P.O. Box 156, Ferdinand, 47532. Tel: 812-367-1212; Fax: 812-367-1066; Web: christthekingdc.org. Rev. Anthony Govind, Admin.; Deacon James King.
Catechesis Religious Program—Kacie Klem, D.R.E.; Debbie Schmitt, D.R.E. Students 470.

FORT BRANCH, GIBSON CO.
1—ST. BERNARD, [CEM]
5342 E. State Rd., Fort Branch, 47648-8564.

Tel: 812-753-4568; Web: www.stbernardsnakerun.org. Rev. Brian Emmick.
Catechesis Religious Program—Email: robert@evdio.org. Rose Obert, C.R.E. Students 51.
2—HOLY CROSS, [CEM]
305 E. Walnut St., Fort Branch, 47648.
Tel: 812-753-3548; Web: www.holycrossparish.info. Very Rev. Anthony Ernst; Rev. Ambrose M. Wanyonyi; Deacons Joseph Siewers; William Brandle.
School—Holy Cross School, (Grades PreK-5),
Tel: 812-753-3280; Email: jhollis@evdio.org; Web: holycrossparish.info/holy-cross-school.html. John Hollis, Prin. Lay Teachers 8; Students 185.
Catechesis Religious Program—Email: lgoedde@evdio.org. Laura Goedde, C.R.E. Students 95.
HAUBSTADT, GIBSON CO.
1—ST. JAMES, [CEM]
12300 S. 50 W., Haubstadt, 47639. Tel: 812-867-5175 ; Fax: 812-867-5589; Web: www.stjameshaubstadt.com. Very Rev. Anthony Ernst; Revs. Kenneth Betz, Snr. Assoc. Pastor; Ambrose M. Wanyonyi; Deacons William Brandle; Joseph Siewers.
School—St. James School, (Grades PreK-8),
Tel: 812-867-2661; Email: ajohnson@evdio.org; Web: www.stjameshaubstadt.com. Angie Johnson, Prin. Lay Teachers 12; Students 211; Clergy / Religious Teachers 1.
Catechesis Religious Program—Email: cbaehl@evdio.org. Connie Baehl, D.R.E. Students 29.
2—SS. PETER AND PAUL, [CEM]
211 N. Vine St., Haubstadt, 47639.
Tel: 812-768-6457; Fax: 812-768-9371; Web: www.stsppchurch.com. Very Rev. Anthony Ernst; Rev. Ambrose M. Wanyonyi; Deacons William Brandle; Joseph Siewers.
School—SS. Peter and Paul School, (Grades PreK-5),
Tel: 812-768-6775; Email: kherrmann@evdio.org; Web: www.stsppchurch.com/school. Kalyn Herrmann, Prin. Lay Teachers 13; Students 195.
Catechesis Religious Program—Email: lgoedde@evdio.org. Laura Goedde, C.R.E. Students 162.
HUNTINGBURG, DUBOIS CO., VISITATION OF THE BLESSED VIRGIN MARY, [CEM]
313 Washington St., Huntingburg, 47542.
Tel: 812-683-2372; Fax: 812-683-2747; Web: www.stmaryshuntingburg.org. Rev. Ryan Paul Hilderbrand; Deacon Thomas E. Holsworth, Ph.D., H.S.P.P.
Catechesis Religious Program—Email: rwright@evdio.org. Rachel Wright, D.R.E. Students 271.
IRELAND, DUBOIS CO., ANNUNCIATION OF THE BLESSED VIRGIN MARY, [CEM] (St. Mary's)
P.O. Box 67, Ireland, 47545. Tel: 812-482-7041;
Fax: 812-482-3699; Web: stmary.irelandindiana.com. Rev. Joseph Erbacher; Deacon John Huether.
See Holy Trinity School, Jasper under Elementary Schools, Inter-Parochial in the Institutions section.
Catechesis Religious Program—Email: mjschmitt@evdio.org. Martha Schmitt, D.R.E. Students 425.
JASONVILLE, GREENE CO., ST. JOAN OF ARC, Attended by St. Mary, Sullivan, Tel: 812-268-4088.
c/o St. Mary, 105 E. Jackson St., P.O. Box 506, Sullivan, 47882. Tel: 812-268-4088;
Fax: 812-268-4980; Email: njenkins@evdio.org; Web: www.stmarys-sullivan.com. Rev. Jeff Read; Deacon Albert Frabutt.
Catechesis Religious Program—Email: ahitt@evdio.org. Ann Hitt, C.R.E.
JASPER, DUBOIS CO.
1—HOLY FAMILY, [JC]
950 E. Church Ave., Jasper, 47546.
Tel: 812-482-3076; Fax: 812-634-6998; Web: www.holyfamilyjasper.com. Rev. John Boeglin; Deacons Michael Helfter; David McDaniel.
See Holy Trinity School, Jasper under Elementary Schools, Inter-Parochial in the Institutions section.
Catechesis Religious Program—Email: jmunning@evdio.org. Joseph Munning IV, D.R.E. Students 29.
2—ST. JOSEPH, [JC]
1029 Kundek St., Jasper, 47546. Tel: 812-482-1805;
Fax: 812-482-1814; Web: www.saintjosephjasper.org. Very Rev. Raymond Brenner; Revs. William Traylor; Jerry Pratt; Deacon Levi Schnellenberger.
Catechesis Religious Program—Email: pfreyberger@evdio.org. Pam Freyberger, D.R.E. Students 346.
3—PRECIOUS BLOOD, [JC]
1385 W. 6th St., Jasper, 47546. Tel: 812-482-4461;
Fax: 812-482-7762; Email: bhopf@evdio.org; Web: www.preciousbloodjasperin.org. Rev. Gary Edward Kaiser; Deacons Michael Jones; Gerald Gagne.
Res.: 1458 Gregory Ln., Jasper, 47546.
See Holy Trinity School, Jasper under Elementary Schools, Inter-Parochial in the Institutions section.
Catechesis Religious Program—Email: bmeadows@evdio.org. Bonnie Meadows, C.R.E. Students 102.
LINTON, GREENE CO., ST. PETER, [CEM]
489 E St., N.E., Linton, 47441. Tel: 812-847-7821. Rev. Biju Thomas, Admin.
Catechesis Religious Program—Jerome Quigley, C.R.E. Students 23.
LOOGOOTEE, MARTIN CO., ST. JOHN, [CEM]
408 Church St., Loogootee, 47553. Tel: 812-295-2225;
Fax: 812-295-2031; Web: www.stjohnloogootee.com. Very Rev. J. Kenneth Walker, M.Div., M.C.L., J.C.L.; Deacon William Consley.
Catechesis Religious Program—Email: pringwald@evdio.org. Paula Ringwald, D.R.E. Students 168.
MONTGOMERY, DAVIESS CO., ST. PETER, [CEM]
305 N 2nd St., P.O. Box 10, Montgomery, 47558.
Tel: 812-486-3149; Fax: 812-486-2571; Web: www.stpetermont.org. Rev. James Koressel.
Catechesis Religious Program—Email: dmbradley@evdio.org. Donna Bradley, D.R.E. Students 98.
MOUNT VERNON, POSEY CO.
1—ST. MATTHEW, [CEM]
421 Mulberry St., Mount Vernon, 47620.
Tel: 812-838-2535; Fax: 812-838-0237; Web: www.stmatthewparish.us. Rev. James Sauer, Admin.; Deacon Thomas Evans.
School—St. Matthew School, (Grades PreK-5),
Tel: 812-838-3621; Email: vwannemuehler@evdio.org; Web: stmatthewmtvernon.org. Vickie Wannemuehler, Prin. Lay Teachers 7; Students 105.
Catechesis Religious Program—Email: mgondi@evdio.org. Michelle Gondi, D.R.E. Students 39.
2—ST. PHILIP, [CEM]
3500 St. Philip Rd. S., Mount Vernon, 47620.
Tel: 812-985-2275; Fax: 812-985-2590; Web: saintphilipchurch.net. Revs. Claude Thomas Burns; Gordon Mann, Parochial Vicar; Deacons Charles Koressel; Thomas Kirsch.
School—St. Philip School, (Grades PreK-8),
Tel: 812-985-2447; Email: mhowington@evdio.org; Web: stphilipschool.net. Megan Howington, Prin. Lay Teachers 13; Students 217.
Catechesis Religious Program—Students 51.
NEWBURGH, WARRICK CO., ST. JOHN THE BAPTIST, [CEM]
625 Frame Rd., Newburgh, 47630. Tel: 812-490-1000 ; Fax: 812-490-1010; Web: sjbnewburgh.org. Revs. Thomas Kessler; John Pfister; Deacons Joseph Seibert; Anthony Schapker; Jay VanHoosier.
School—St. John the Baptist School, (Grades PreK-8), Tel: 812-490-2000; Email: eflatt@evdio.org; Web: sjbschoolnewburgh.org. Elizabeth Flatt, Prin. Lay Teachers 27; Students 358.
Catechesis Religious Program—Email: jwvanhoosier@evdio.org. Deacon Jay VanHoosier, D.R.E. Students 224.
OAKLAND CITY, GIBSON CO., BLESSED SACRAMENT
11092 E. Lincoln Hgts Rd., Oakland City, 47660.
Tel: 812-749-4474. Rev. Frank G. Renner; Deacon Mark Wade.
Catechesis Religious Program—Lori Stolz, C.R.E. Students 14.
PETERSBURG, PIKE CO., SS. PETER AND PAUL
711 Walnut St., Petersburg, 47567.
Tel: 812-354-6942. Rev. Frank G. Renner; Deacon Mark Wade.
Catechesis Religious Program—Gary Keepes, C.R.E. Students 5.
POSEYVILLE, POSEY CO., ST. FRANCIS XAVIER, [CEM]
10 N. St. Francis Ave., P.O. Box 100, Poseyville, 47633. Tel: 812-874-2220; Fax: 812-963-3061; Web: www.saintwendelparish.org. Rev. Edward Schnur; Deacon Mark McDonald.
Catechesis Religious Program—Email: scooley@evdio.org. Sherie Cooley, D.R.E. Shared program with St. Wendel. Students 128.
PRINCETON, GIBSON CO., ST. JOSEPH, [CEM]
410 S. Race St., Princeton, 47670. Tel: 812-385-2617;
Fax: 812-648-0025; Web: stjosephprinceton.org. Rev. Brian Emmick.
School—St. Joseph School, (Grades PreK-5),
Tel: 812-385-2228; Email: dgilbert@evdio.org; Web: stjosephprinceton.com. Dan Gilbert, Prin. Lay Teachers 7; Students 167.
Catechesis Religious Program—Debbie Bateman, CRE. Students 42.
ROCKPORT, SPENCER CO., ST. BERNARD, [CEM]
547 Elm St., Rockport, 47635. Tel: 812-649-4811;
Fax: 812-649-4176; Web: www.stbernardrockport.org. Rev. Ronald Kreilein; Deacon Michael Waninger.
School—St. Bernard School, (Grades PreK-8),
Tel: 812-649-2501; Email: bstrodel@evdio.org; Web: stbernardschool.info. Beth Strodel, Prin. Lay Teachers 10; Students 117.
Catechesis Religious Program—Email: cthorpe@evdio.org. Carolyn Thorpe, C.R.E. Students 40.
ST. ANTHONY, DUBOIS CO., DIVINE MERCY (2016) [CEM]
4444 S. Ohio St., P.O. Box 98, St. Anthony, 47575-0098. Tel: 812-326-2777; Web: www.divinemercyduco.org. Rev. Christopher Lee Droste; Deacon Charles Johnson.
Catechesis Religious Program—Email: jakempf@evdio.org. Janie Kempf, Coord. of Rel. Ed. Students 296.
SULLIVAN, SULLIVAN CO., ST. MARY
105 E. Jackson St., P.O. Box 506, Sullivan, 47882.
Tel: 812-268-4088; Fax: 812-268-4980; Web: www.stmarys-sullivan.com. Rev. Jeff Read; Deacon Albert Frabutt.
Catechesis Religious Program—Email: ahitt@evdio.org. Ann Hitt, C.R.E. Students 25.
VINCENNES, KNOX CO., ST. FRANCIS XAVIER, [JC]
803 Main St., Vincennes, 47591. Tel: 812-882-5638;
Fax: 812-882-2478; Web: www.stfrancisxaviervincennes.com. Very Rev. David G. Fleck; Revs. Donald Ackerman, Temporary Admin.; Simon Natha; Deacons Cletus Yochum Jr.; Rey Carandang; Paul Vonderwell.
Church: 205 Church St., Vincennes, 47591. Email: klane@evdio.org.
School—Vincennes Schools Consolidated, (Grades PreK-5), Tel: 812-882-5460; Email: lwissel@evdio.org; Web: flagetces.org. Lori Wissel, Prin. Lay Teachers 15; Students 274.
Catechesis Religious Program—Tel: 812-882-5638. Students 91.
WASHINGTON, DAVIESS CO., OUR LADY OF HOPE, [JC]
315 N.E. Third St., Washington, 47501.
Tel: 812-254-2883; Fax: 812-254-2884; Email: dwichman@evdio.org; Web: www.ccwash.org. Rev. Paul Anthony Ferguson; Deacon Dennis Hilderbrand; Yvonne Evans, Pastoral Assoc.
School—Our Lady of Hope School, (Grades PreK-4), 310 N.E. Second St., Washington, 47501.
Tel: 812-254-3845; Email: acline@evdio.org; Web: wccardinals.org. Amy Cline, Prin. Washington Catholic Interparochial Schools Elementary. Lay Teachers 13; Students 318.
See High Schools, Inter-Parochial under Institutions Located in the Diocese for details.
Catechesis Religious Program—Email: kbatz@evdio.org. Maria Batz, D.R.E. Students 82.

CLOSED AND MERGED PARISHES

EVANSVILLE:
1—ST. AGNES, Merged (2014) with St. Boniface, where parish records are kept.
2—ST. ANTHONY, Merged (2015) with St. Joseph and renamed All Saints, where parish records are kept.
3—ASSUMPTION CATHEDRAL, Merged (1964) with Holy Trinity. For inquiries for parish records contact Sts. Mary and John.
4—CHRIST THE KING, Merged (2014) with Holy Spirit and renamed Annunciation of the Lord, where parish records are kept.
5—HOLY SPIRIT, Merged (2014) with Christ the King and renamed Annunciation of the Lord, where parish records are kept.
6—HOLY TRINITY, Merged (2015) with Sts. Mary and John where parish records are kept.
7—ST. JOHN THE APOSTLE, Merged (2014) with St. Mary and renamed Sts. Mary & John, where parish records are kept.
8—ST. JOSEPH, Merged (2015) with St. Anthony and renamed All Saints, where parish records are kept.
9—ST. MARY, Merged (2014) with St. John the Apostle and renamed Sts. Mary & John, where parish records are kept.
10—NATIVITY, Merged (2016) with Holy Rosary, where parish records are kept.
11—SACRED HEART, Merged (2014) with St. Boniface, where parish records are kept.
12—ST. THERESA, Merged (2016) with Good Shepherd, where parish records are kept.
CANNELBURG:, ALL SAINTS, Merged (2014) with St. Peter, Montgomery where parish records are kept.
CELESTINE:, ST. PETER CELESTINE, [CEM] Merged (2016) with St. Raphael, Dubois and renamed St. Isidore the Farmer, where records are kept.
CORNING:
ST. PATRICK'S, Merged (1997) with St. Peter, Montgomery where parish records are kept.
DALE:, ST. JOSEPH, Merged (2015) with Mary, Help of Christians, Mariah Hill and St. Nicholas, Santa Claus and renamed St. Francis of Assisi, where parish records are kept.
DUBOIS:, ST. RAPHAEL, Merged (2016) with St. Peter Celestine, Celestine and renamed St. Isidore the Farmer, where parish records are kept.
DUGGER:, OUR LADY OF PERPETUAL HELP, Merged (1982) with St. Mary, Sullivan, where parish records are kept.
FERDINAND
1—ST. FERDINAND, [CEM] Merged with St. Henry, Ferdinand to form Christ the King, Ferdinand.
2—ST. HENRY, [CEM] Merged with St. Ferdinand, Ferdinand to form Christ the King, Ferdinand.

LOOGOOTEE:
ASSUMPTION OF MARY, Merged (1997) with St. Joseph and church designated a chapel under the care of St. Joseph. Now under the care of St. John, where parish records are kept.
2—ST. JOSEPH, Merged (2014) with three neighboring parishes, including St. John, where parish records are kept.
3—ST. MARTIN, Merged (2014) with three neighboring parishes including St. John, Loogootee where parish records are kept.
MARIAH HILL:, MARY, HELP OF CHRISTIANS, [CEM] Merged (2015) with St. Joseph, Dale and St. Nicholas, Santa Claus and renamed St. Francis Assisi, where parish records are kept.
MONTGOMERY:, ST. MICHAEL, Merged (1997) with St. Peter, Montgomery, where parish records are kept.
NEW BOSTON:, ST. JOHN CHRYSOSTOM, Merged (2014) with St. Martin, Chrisney, where parish records are kept.
NEW HARMONY:, HOLY ANGELS, Merged (2014) with St. Francis Xavier, Poseyville, where parish records are kept.
RED BRUSH:, ST. RUPERT, Merged (2014) with St. Clement, Boonville, where parish records are kept.
ST. ANTHONY:, ST. ANTHONY, Merged (2016) with Sacred Heart, Schnellville and renamed Divine Mercy, where parish records are kept.
SANTA CLAUS:, ST. NICHOLAS, Merged (2015) with Mary, Help of Christians, Mariah Hill and St. Joseph, Dale and renamed St. Francis of Assisi, where parish records are kept.
SCHNELLVILLE:, SACRED HEART, Merged (2016) with St. Anthony, St. Anthony and renamed Divine Mercy, where parish records are kept.
SHELBURN:, ST. ANN, Merged (1978) with St. Mary, Sullivan, where parish records are kept.
SHOALS:, ST. MARYS, Merged (2014) with three neighboring parishes including St. John, Loogootee, where records are kept.
VINCENNES:
1—ST. JOHN THE BAPTIST, [JC] Merged (2016) with four neighboring parishes including St. Francis Xavier, where parish records are kept.
2—SACRED HEART, Merged (2016) with four neighboring parishes including St. Francis Xavier, where parish records are kept.
3—ST. THOMAS THE APOSTLE, Merged (2016) with four neighboring parishes including St. Francis Xavier, where parish records are kept.
4—ST. VINCENT DE PAUL, Merged (2016) with four neighboring parishes including St. Francis Xavier, where parish records are kept.
WASHINGTON:
1—IMMACULATE CONCEPTION, Merged (2008) with St. Simon and renamed Our Lady of Hope, where parish records are kept.
2—ST. SIMON, Merged (2008) with Immaculate Conception and renamed Our Lady of Hope, where parish records are kept.

Special Assignment:
Very Revs.—
Ernst, Anthony, 211 N. Vine St., Haubstadt, 47639
Etienne, Bernard T., Vicar Gen., 1301 S. Green River Rd., 47715-5617. P.O. Box 4169, 47724-0169
Walker, J. Kenneth, M.Div., M.C.L., J.C.L., Judicial Vicar, P.O. Box 4169, 47724-0169
Ziliak, Joseph L., S.T.L., (Retired), 100 W. Water St., #1, Newburgh, 47630
Revs.—
Tenbarge, Tyler R., 1626 Glendale Ave., 47712
Zenthoefer, Alex, 3010 E. Chandler Ave., 47714.

Absent on Medical Leave:
Revs.—
Breidenbach, John
Steckler, Kenneth.

Retired:
Rev. Msgr.—
Knapp, Kenneth, (Retired), 5312 Somerset Ave., 47715
Very Rev.—
Ziliak, Joseph L., S.T.L., (Retired), 100 W. Water St., #1, Newburgh, 47630
Revs.—
Dietsch, William, (Retired), 2562 E. County Rd. 850 S., 47648
Dilger, Donald, (Retired), 6621 Smith Diamond Rd., 47712
Endress, James, S.T.L., M.S., M.A., (Retired), 3001 Galaxy Dr., Rm. 308, 47715
Kane, Joseph, (Retired), 8427 Gannon, Saint Louis, MO 63132-4906
Kiesel, Leo C., (Retired), 315 Doyle Ave., Loogootee, 47553
Kissel, Anthony, (Retired), 14235 21st St., Dade City, FL 33523
Kuykendall, Henry, (Retired), 8105 Gateway Dr., 47715
Lintzenich, Stephen, (Retired), 704 N. First Ave., 47710
Lutz, Bernard A., (Retired), 24 Williams Ln., Newburgh, 47630
Madden, Michael, (Retired), 457 Rumbach Ave., Jasper, 47546
Martin, David, (Retired), 5371 W. 1200 S., Cynthiana, 47612
Nemergut, Robert S., (Retired), 100 W. Main St., Apt. 409, Bloomfield, 47424
Nunning, David, (Retired), P.O. Box 201, Poseyville, 47633
Rohleder, Earl, (Retired), 2540 Calle Rincon Bonito, Santa Fe, NM 87505
Schipp, John, (Retired), P.O. Box 283, Ferdinand, 47532
Schipp, Ralph, (Retired), 278 S. Tinsel Cir. E., Santa Claus, 47579
Tempel, Theodore, (Retired), 1236 Lincoln Ave., 47714
Tenbarge, Timothy, (Retired), 4113 E. State Rd. 164, Jasper, 47546
Vogler, Jean, (Retired), 83 E. Mistletoe Dr., Santa Claus, 47579
Will, Lowell C., (Retired), 418 N. Wabash Ave., 47712
Zgunda, Ronald S., (Retired), 7132 Arkansas Ave., Hammond, 46323.

Permanent Deacons:
Altmeyer, Emil, (Retired)
Bach, Kevin, Holy Redeemer, Evansville
Bernardin, Vincent, (Leave of Absence)
Borowiecki, Christian, Holy Rosary, Evansville
Brandle, William, Sts. Peter & Paul, Haubstadt; St. James, Haubstadt; Holy Cross, Fort Branch
Carandang, Reynaldo, St. Francis Xavier, Vincennes; St. Philip Neri, Bicknell
Cervone, Thomas, Holy Redeemer, Evansville
Consley, William, St. John, Loogootee
Cook, David, (Retired)
Cox, Paul, St. Francis of Assisi, Dale
DeCastra, Dan, Good Shepherd, Evansville
Evans, Thomas, St. Matthew, Mt. Vernon; Dir., Permanent Deacons
Flynn, James, (Retired)
Frabutt, Albert, St, Mary, Sullivan; St. Joan of Arc, Jasonville
Franklin, David, (Retired)
Gagne, Gerald, Precious Blood, Jasper
Garrido, Jose, Holy Rosary, Evansville
Goebel, Thomas, Corpus Christi, Evansville
Grannan, Richard, (Retired)
Haag, Donald, (Retired)
Helfter, Michael, Holy Family Parish, Jasper
Hilderbrand, Dennis, Our Lady of Hope, Washington
Holsworth, Thomas E., Ph.D., H.S.P.P., St. Mary, Huntingburg
Hoy, Wayne, St. Boniface, Evansville
Huether, John, St. Mary, Ireland
Johanning, Kenneth, (Leave of Absence)
Johnson, Charles, Divine Mercy, St. Anthony
Jones, Michael R., Precious Blood, Jasper
Keller, William, (Leave of Absence)
Kempf, Thomas, Sts. Mary and John, Evansville
King, James, Asst. Dir. Permanent Deacons, Christ the King, Ferdinand
Kirsch, Thomas, St. Philip, Mt. Vernon
Koressel, Charles, St. Philip, Mt. Vernon
Lambert, Thomas, St. Clement, Boonville
Leibundguth, Richard, St. John, Daylight
Maples, Russell, St. Boniface, Evansville
Mattingly, Robert, St. Boniface, Evansville
McDaniel, David, Holy Family, Jasper
McDonald, Mark, St. Wendel, St. Wendel; St. Francis Xavier, Poseyville
McMullen, John, Annunciation, Evansville
Morris, Michael, Prison Ministry
Preske, Richard, (Retired)
Rice, David, Clergy Personnel Dir., St Benedict, Evansville
Ruppel, Earl, (Retired)
Russell, Dennis, Sts. Mary and John, Evansville
Schapker, Anthony, St. John the Baptist, Newburgh
Schnellenberger, Levi, St. Joseph, Jasper
Seibert, David, St. Clement, Boonville
Seibert, Joseph S., St. John the Baptist, Newburgh
Seibert, Michael, St. Isodore, Celestine
Siewers, Joseph, Holy Cross, Fort Branch; St. James, Haubstadt; Sts. Peter & Paul, Haubstadt
VanHoosier, Jay, St. John the Baptist, Newburgh
Vonderwell, Paul, St. Francis Xavier, Vincennes; St. Philip Neri, Bicknell
Wade, Mark, Sts. Peter and Paul, Petersburg; Blessed Sacrament, Oakland City
Waninger, Michael, St. Martin, Chrisney; St. Bernard, Rockport
Wilkerson, Edward, (Retired)
Will, Cyril, (Retired)
Woebkenberg, James, St. Francis of Assisi, Dale
Yochum, Cletus Jr., St. Frances Xavier, Vincennes; St. Philip Neri, Bicknell
Yochum, Donald, (Retired).

INSTITUTIONS LOCATED IN DIOCESE

[A] HIGH SCHOOLS, INTER-PAROCHIAL

EVANSVILLE. *Mater Dei High School*, 1300 Harmony Way, 47712. Tel: 812-426-2258; Fax: 812-421-5717; Email: tdickel@evdio.org; Web: www.materdeiwildcats.com. Timothy Dickel, Pres.; Darin Knight, Prin.; Darlene Quinlin, Asst. Prin.; Melba Wilderman, Asst. Prin.; Rev. Pascal Nduka, Chap. Lay Teachers 40; Students 497.

Reitz Memorial High School, 1500 Lincoln Ave., 47714. Tel: 812-476-4973; Fax: 812-474-2942; Email: jbrowning@evdio.org; Web: www.reitzmemorial.org. John Browning, Pres.; Marie Williams, Prin.; Mr. Rick Wilgus, Asst. Prin., Student Svcs.; Mrs. Lisa Popham, Asst. Prin., Curriculum & Instruction; Rev. Zachary J. Etienne, Chap. Lay Teachers 51; Students 612; Clergy / Religious Teachers 1.

VINCENNES. *Jean Francois Rivet High School*, (Grades 6-12), 210 Barnett St., Vincennes, 47591. Tel: 812-882-6215; Fax: 812-886-1939; Email: rivet@evdio.org; Web: www.rivethighschool.com. Janice Jones, Prin. Lay Teachers 15; Students 159; Clergy / Religious Teachers 1.

WASHINGTON. *Washington Catholic Interparochial Schools*, (Grades 5-12), 201 N.E. Second St., Washington, 47501. Tel: 812-254-2050; Fax: 812-254-8745; Email: kcraney@evdio.org; Web: www.wccardinals.org. Karie Craney, Prin. Lay Teachers 17; Students 163.

[B] ELEMENTARY SCHOOLS, INTER-PAROCHIAL

JASPER. *Holy Trinity School*, (Grades PreK-8), 1385 W. 6th St., Jasper, 47546. Tel: 812-482-4461; Fax: 812-482-7762; Web: www.holytrinitysaints.com. Jonathan Temple, Prin.; Jenna Seng, Asst. Prin. Lay Teachers 35; Sisters 1; Students 554.

[C] DAY CARE CENTERS

EVANSVILLE. *St. Vincent Early Learning Center, Inc.*, 730 W. Delaware St., 47710. Tel: 812-424-4780; Fax: 812-425-2502; Email: kmulfinger@stvincentelc.org; Web: www.stvincentearlylearningcenter.org. Kim Mulfinger, Exec. Dir. Total Students 165.

[D] GENERAL HOSPITALS

EVANSVILLE. *St. Vincent Evansville*, 3700 Washington Ave., 47750. Tel: 812-485-4000; Fax: 812-485-7800; Web: www.stvincentswin.org. Dan Parod, Pres. (Includes St. Vincent, Warrick County) Bed Capacity 443; Patients Asst Anual. 487,391; Tot Asst. Annually 276,043; Total Staff 3,174; Daughters of Charity of St. Vincent de Paul 5.

JASPER. *Memorial Hospital and Health Care Center, Little Company of Mary Hospital of Indiana, Inc.*, 800 W. 9th St., Jasper, 47546. Tel: 812-996-2345, Ext. 0198; Fax: 812-996-0302; Email: dkempf@mhhcc.org; Web: www.mhhcc.org. Kyle Bennett, Pres. & CEO. Bed Capacity 137; Tot Asst. Annually 308,000; Total Staff 1,740; Little Company of Mary Sisters - USA 1; Palliative Care Patients 46.

Memorial Hospital Foundation, Inc., 800 W. 9th St., Jasper, 47546. Tel: 812-996-8426; Fax: 812-996-8427; Email: mjones@mhhcc.org. William A. Rubino, Chair Person; Michael A. Jones, Exec. Dir.

[E] HOMES FOR AGED

EVANSVILLE. *Seton Residence*, 9200 New Harmony Rd., 47720-8918. Tel: 812-963-7600; Fax: 812-963-7654; Email: marietherese.sedgwick@doc.org. 4330 Olive St., Saint Louis, MO 63108. Sr. Marie Therese Sedgwick, D.C., Admin. Home for the Senior Sisters of the Daughters of Charity of St. Vincent de Paul.

FERDINAND. *Hildegard Health Center, Inc.*, 802 E. 10th St., Ferdinand, 47532-9239. Tel: 812-367-2022; Fax: 812-367-1309; Email: kbilskie@good-sam.com; Web: www.thedome.org. Sr. Kathy Bilskie, O.S.B., Admin. Sisters on Staff 3; Sisters in Residence 17.

[F] RETREAT HOUSES

EVANSVILLE. *Sarto Retreat House*, 4200 N. Kentucky Ave., P.O. Box 4169, 47724-0169.
Tel: 812-424-5536; Fax: 812-421-1334; Email: mnord@evdio.org; Web: evdio.org. Margie Nord, Coord.

FERDINAND. *Benedictine Hospitality Center*, 802 E. 10th St., Ferdinand, 47532-9216.
Tel: 812-367-1411; Fax: 812-367-2313; Email: hospitality@thedome.org; Web: www.thedome.org/hospitality. Sisters Barbara Lynn Schmitz, O.S.B., Prioress; Jackie Kissel, O.S.B., Dir.

[G] CONVENTS AND RESIDENCES FOR SISTERS

EVANSVILLE. *Daughters of Charity of St. Vincent de Paul - Mater Dei Residence*, 9400 New Harmony Rd., 47720. Tel: 812-963-7517; Fax: 812-963-7589; Email: tom.beck@doc.org; Web: www.daughtersofcharity.org. 4330 Olive Street, Saint Louis, MO 63108. Sr. Virginia Ann Brooks, Local Supr. Sisters in Residence 12.

Monastery of St. Clare, Franciscan Monastery of St. Clare: 6825 Nurrenbern Rd., 47712.
Tel: 812-425-4396; Fax: 812-425-0089; Email: janemdelevin@gmail.com. Sr. Jane Marie DeLand, O.S.C., Abbess. Franciscan Poor Clare Nuns. Sisters 6; Solemnly Professed Cloistered Nuns 6.

FERDINAND. *Sisters of St. Benedict of Ferdinand, IN, Inc., Monastery Immaculate Conception*, 802 E. Tenth St., Ferdinand, 47532. Tel: 812-367-1411; Fax: 812-367-2313; Email: sisters@thedome.org; Web: www.thedome.org. Sr. Barbara Lynn Schmitz, O.S.B., Prioress; Rev. Pius Klein, O.S.B., Chap., St. Meinrad Chaplain Team Coord. Sisters of St. Benedict. Novices 1; Professed Sisters in Community 136; Temporary Commitment 4.

[H] NEWMAN CENTERS & CAMPUS MINISTRY

EVANSVILLE. *Newman Center for the University of Evansville*, 1901 Lincoln Ave., 47714.
Tel: 812-477-6446; Email: jkoch@evdio.org. Jenny Koch, Dir.

University of Southern Indiana Newman Center, 8113-A O'Daniel Ln., 47712. Tel: 812-465-7095; Email: choehn@evdio.org. Christine Hoehn, Dir.

OAKLAND CITY. *Oakland City College Newman Center*, R.R. 1, Box 72-A, Oakland City, 47660.
Tel: 812-749-4474; Email: sdabrowski@evdio.org. Steven Dabrowski Jr., Dir. Office of Youth and Young Adult Ministry.

VINCENNES. *Vincennes University-Newman Center*, c/o St. Francis Xavier Parish, 803 Main St., Vincennes, 47591. Tel: 812-882-1762; Email: sdabrowski@evdio.org. Steven Dabrowski Jr., Dir. Office of Youth and Young Adult Ministry.

[I] MISCELLANEOUS

EVANSVILLE. *Catholic Education Foundation, Inc.*, 520 S. Bennighof, 47714. Tel: 812-402-6700, Ext. 302; Email: rweissmann@evdio.org. John Browning, Interim Dir.

Evansville Catholic Interparochial High Schools, 4200 N. Kentucky Ave., 47711. Tel: 812-424-5536; Email: jbrowning@evdio.org. John Browning, Contact Person.

Marian Educational Outreach, 520 S. Bennighof, 47714. Tel: 812-402-6700, Ext. 312;
Fax: 812-474-2949; Web: www.meoforkids.org. Annie-Rose Keith, Dir.

Mission and Ministry, Inc., 9400 New Harmony Rd., 47720. Tel: 812-963-7569; Fax: 812-963-7526; Email: tom.beck@doc.org. Mary Wildeman, Exec. Dir.

LOOGOOTEE. *American-Innsbruck Alumni Association*, P.O. Box 4169, 47724-0169. Tel: 812-295-3214; Email: dfaraone@evdio.org. Rev. Michael Scheible, Contact Person, (Retired).

VINCENNES. *Old Cathedral Library & Museum, Inc.*, 205 Church St., Vincennes, 47591.
Tel: 812-882-7016; Web: evdio.org. Rev. Donald Ackerman, Temporary Admin.

RELIGIOUS INSTITUTES OF MEN REPRESENTED IN THE DIOCESE

For further details refer to the corresponding bracketed number in the Religious Institutes of Men or Women section.

[0200]—*Benedictine Monks*—O.S.B.

[1330]—*Congregation of the Mission Western Province*—C.M.

[0585]—*Heralds of Good News*—H.G.N.

RELIGIOUS INSTITUTES OF WOMEN REPRESENTED IN THE DIOCESE

[0230]—*Benedictine Sisters of Pontifical Jurisdiction*—O.S.B.

[1730]—*Congregation of the Third Order of St. Francis*—O.S.F.

[0760]—*Daughters of Charity of St. Vincent de Paul*—D.C.

[3760]—*Order of St. Clare*—O.S.C.

[3360]—*Sisters of Providence of Saint Mary-of-the-Woods, Indiana*—S.P.

[2270]—*Sisters of the Little Company of Mary*—L.C.M.

JOINT CEMETERIES

EVANSVILLE. *St. Joseph*, 2500 Mesker Park Dr., 47712. Tel: 812-423-1356; Email: jshake@evdio.org. Joe Shake, Contact Person

JASPER. *Fairview*, 1215 Newton St., Jasper, 47546.
Tel: 812-634-7525; Email: dfaraone@evdio.org. Brad Popp, Contact Person

VINCENNES. *Calvary*, P.O. Box 4, Vincennes, 47591.
Tel: 812-882-4691. Rev. Donald Ackerman, Contact Person

WASHINGTON. *St. John*, 101 N. Meridian St., Washington, 47501. Tel: 812-254-3612; Email: dfaraone@evdio.org. Ron Murphy, Contact Person

NECROLOGY

† Heerdink, Eugene, (Retired), Died Apr. 13, 2018
† Herr, Kenneth H., (Retired), Died Nov. 12, 2018
† Kreilein, Philip, Evansville, IN Resurrection Parish, Died Oct. 23, 2018

An asterisk (*) denotes an organization that has established tax-exempt status directly with the IRS and is not covered by the USCCB Group Ruling.

Diocese of Fairbanks

Most Reverend

CHAD W. ZIELINSKI

Bishop of Fairbanks; ordained June 8, 1996; appointed Bishop of Fairbanks November 8, 2014; ordained and installed December 15, 2014. *Chancery Office, 1316 Peger Rd., Fairbanks, AK 99709.*

Chancery Office: 1316 Peger Rd., Fairbanks, AK 99709. Tel: 907-374-9500; Fax: 907-374-9580.

Web: www.cbna.info

Email: info@cbna.org

Square Miles 409,849.

Corporate Title: "Catholic Bishop of Northern Alaska."

Established as the Prefecture Apostolic of Alaska, July 27, 1894.

Erected into the Vicariate of Alaska, Dec. 22, 1916; elevated to a Diocese, Aug. 8, 1962.

Comprises all of the State of Alaska, north of the old Territorial Third Judicial Division whose boundary extended in a northwesterly direction from the Canadian Border along the crest of the Alaska range to Mount McKinley, thence southwesterly to Cape Newenham and west along the 58 parallel north of the Pribilof Islands.

For legal titles of parishes and diocesan institutions, consult the Chancery Office.

STATISTICAL OVERVIEW

Personnel	
Bishop	1
Priests: Diocesan Active in Diocese	2
Priests: Diocesan Active Outside Diocese	1
Priests: Retired, Sick or Absent	6
Number of Diocesan Priests	9
Religious Priests in Diocese	6
Total Priests in Diocese	15
Extern Priests in Diocese	12
Permanent Deacons in Diocese	26
Total Brothers	2
Total Sisters	3
Parishes	
Parishes	46
With Resident Pastor:	
Resident Diocesan Priests	5
Without Resident Pastor:	
Administered by Priests	17
Administered by Deacons	1
Administered by Professed Religious Men	2
Administered by Lay People	18
Administered by Pastoral Teams, etc.	1
Completely Vacant	2
Missions	2
Pastoral Centers	2
Professional Ministry Personnel:	
Brothers	2
Educational	
Diocesan Students in Other Seminaries	4
Total Seminarians	4
High Schools, Diocesan and Parish	1
Total Students	173
Elementary Schools, Diocesan and Parish	1
Total Students	236
Catechesis/Religious Education:	
High School Students	201
Elementary Students	424
Total Students under Catholic Instruction	1,038
Teachers in the Diocese:	
Lay Teachers	40
Vital Statistics	
Receptions into the Church:	
Infant Baptism Totals	213
Minor Baptism Totals	30
Adult Baptism Totals	16
Received into Full Communion	69
First Communions	215
Confirmations	92
Marriages:	
Catholic	16
Interfaith	12
Total Marriages	28
Deaths	106
Total Catholic Population	9,880
Total Population	165,131

Former Bishops—Most Revs. JOSEPH RAPHAEL CRIMONT, S.J., D.D:, Vicar-Apostolic of Alaska; ord. Aug. 26, 1888; appt. Prefect-Apostolic March 28, 1904; appt. Vicar-Apostolic of Alaska Feb. 15, 1917; preconized Titular Bishop of Ammaedera, March 22, 1917; cons. July 25, 1917; died May 20, 1945; WALTER J. FITZGERALD, S.J., D.D., Vicar-Apostolic of Alaska; ord. May 16, 1918; appt. Coadjutor Vicar-Apostolic of Alaska cum jure successionis, Dec. 14, 1938; cons. Titular Bishop of Tymbrias, Feb. 24, 1939; succeeded to as Vicar-Apostolic of Alaska, May 20, 1945; died July 19, 1947; GEORGE T. BOILEAU, S.J., D.D., appt. Coadjutor Bishop cum jure successionis, April 21, 1964; cons. Titular Bishop of Ausuccura, July 31, 1964; died Feb. 25, 1965; FRANCIS D. GLEESON, S.J., D.D., ord. July 29, 1926; appt. Titular Bishop of Cotenna and Vicar-Apostolic of Alaska Jan. 8, 1948; cons. April 5, 1948; appt. First Bishop of Fairbanks Aug. 8, 1962; retired Nov. 30, 1968; transferred to Titular See of Cuicul in Numidia and Assistant at the Pontifical Throne by Pope Paul VI, Feb. 3, 1969; died April 30, 1983; ROBERT LOUIS WHELAN, S.J., D.D., retired Bishop of Fairbanks; ord. June 17, 1944; appt. Titular Bishop of Sicilibba and Coadjutor Bishop of Fairbanks, cum jure successionis Dec. 6, 1967; cons. Feb. 22, 1968; succeeded to Nov. 30, 1968; retired July 28, 1985; died Sept. 15, 2001; MICHAEL J. KANIECKI, S.J., D.D., ord. June 5, 1965; appt. Coadjutor Bishop cum jure successionis, March 8, 1984; cons. May 1, 1984; succeeded to July 28, 1985; died Aug. 6, 2000; DONALD J. KETTLER, ord. May 29, 1970; appt. Bishop of Fairbanks June 7, 2002; installed Aug. 22, 2002; appt. Bishop of St. Cloud Sept. 20, 2013; installed Nov. 7, 2013.

Vicar General—Rev. ROSS TOZZI, V.G.

Superior Regular—Mailing Address: Bro. Joe Prince House, P.O. Box 3064, Bethel, 99559. Rev. RICHARD P. MAGNER, S.J., Pastoral Ministry.

Chancery Office—1316 Peger Rd., Fairbanks, 99709. Tel: 907-374-9500; Fax: 907-374-9580; Email: info@cbna.org; Web: www.cbna.info.

Chancellor and Chief Operations Officer—LEIGH SCARBORO, 1316 Peger Rd., Fairbanks, 99709.

Chief Financial Officer—1316 Peger Rd., Fairbanks, 99709. SUSAN CLIFTON.

Diocesan Tribunal—

Tribunal Administrator—BARBARA THIEME TOLLIVER.

Judicial Vicar—Rev. PATRICK J. TRAVERS, J.C.L., J.D.

Defender of the Bond—Rev. SCOTT GARRETT, J.C.L.

Promoter of Justice—MARK L. RAPER, J.C.L.

Auditor—BARBARA THIEME TOLLIVER.

Notaries—Tribunal: BARBARA THIEME TOLLIVER; LEIGH SCARBORO.

Presbyteral Council—Revs. KASPARAJ MALLAVARAPU; MARK A. HOELSKEN, S.J.; ROBERT FATH; ROSS TOZZI, V.G.; THOMAS KUFFEL; A. KUMAR PASALA; Revs. RICHARD P. MAGNER, S.J.; THINH VAN TRAN; JONATHAN DELLINGER.

Consultors—Revs. KASPARAJ MALLAVARAPU; MARK A. HOELSKEN, S.J.; ROBERT FATH; ROSS TOZZI, V.G.; THOMAS KUFFEL; A. KUMAR PASALA; Revs. RICHARD P. MAGNER, S.J.; THINH VAN TRAN; JONATHAN DELLINGER.

Diocesan Archivist—DAVID SCHIENLE, Archives Coord.

Diocesan Offices and Directors

Alaskan Shepherd Office—PATTY WALTER, Editor & Dir. Direct Mail Fundraising, Tel: 907-374-9536; LIN CRAIG, Office Mgr., 1312 Peger Rd., Fairbanks, 99709. Tel: 907-374-9532.

Catholic Campaign for Human Development—TERESA CHEPODA USIBELLI.

Campus Ministry—MARY PAT BOGER, 514 Copper Ln. - UAF, P.O. Box 750166, Fairbanks, 99775-0166. Tel: 907-474-6776.

Construction Committee—CYNTHIA JACOBSON, Chm.; Rev. ROSS TOZZI, V.G.; BILL CHRISMAN; JAMES WALTER; LARRY KOLLMEYER; MARK MARTIN, P.E.

Engaged Encounter—Deacon SEAN STACK; JODI STACK.

Finance Advisory Board—CYNTHIA KLEPASKI; SUSAN MURPHY; Rev. ROSS TOZZI, V.G.; JEFFREY JOHNSON; JOSEPH PASKVAN; Sr. KATHLEEN RADICH, O.S.F.; JEFFREY BROOKS; JIM HASELBERGER; ROBERT HAJDUKOVICH.

Hispanic Ministry—LOURDES BERNAL.

Native Alaskan Ministries Coordinators—Sr. KATHLEEN RADICH, O.S.F., Mailing Address: St. Mary's Conf. Ctr., P.O. Box 29, St. Marys, 99658; Bro. ROBERT J. RUZICKA, O.F.M., Mailing Address: Our Lady of the Snows, P.O. Box 89, Nulato, 99765.

Ministry of Sick, Aged and Imprisoned—ANN NICKERSON, Dir. Stephen Ministry, Tel: 907-978-5281.

Office of Child Protection—BARBARA THIEME TOLLIVER, Dir., Tel: 907-374-9516.

Office of Faith & Family Formation—Rev. ROBERT FATH, Dir., 1316 Peger Rd., Fairbanks, 99709. Tel: 907-374-9500; Fax: 907-374-9580.

Office of Native Permanent Diaconate—Rev. MARK A. HOELSKEN, S.J., Dir., P.O. Box 3064, Bethel, 99559. Tel: 907-438-6136.

Pontifical Association of the Holy Childhood—Chancery Office.

Pontifical Society for Propagation of the FaithTERESA CHEPODA USIBELLI, Chancery Office.

Schools—615 Monroe St., Fairbanks, 99701. Tel: 907-456-7970. AMANDA ANGAIAK, Exec. Dir.

Victim Assistance Coordinator—BARBARA THIEME TOLLIVER.

Vocation Director—Rev. ROBERT FATH, 1316 Peger Rd., Fairbanks, 99709.

Retrouvaille—Deacon GEORGE W. BOWDER; WANDA BOWDER.

Catholic Relief Services—TERESA CHEPODA USIBELLI.

Catholic Trust of Northern Alaska—SUSAN CLIFTON, Exec. Officer.

Office of Stewardship and Development—MISTY MEALEY, Dir. Communications; DR. LESLIE T. MAIMAN JR., D.Min., Dir. Mission Outreach; TERESA CHEPODA USIBELLI, Stewardship & Devel. Officer.

CLERGY, PARISHES, MISSIONS AND PAROCHIAL SCHOOLS

CITY OF FAIRBANKS

NORTH STAR BOROUGH

1—SACRED HEART CATHEDRAL CATHOLIC CHURCH FAIRBANKS (1966)
1300 Peger Rd., 99709. Tel: 907-474-9032; Email: shcparishoffice@gmail.com; Web: www.sacredheartak.org. Most Rev. Chad W. Zielinski; Rev. Ross Tozzi, V.G., Rector.
Res.: 2890 N. Kobuk Ave., 99709.
Catechesis Religious Program—Michelle Seminario, Rel. Ed. Coord. Students 84.

2—IMMACULATE CONCEPTION CATHOLIC PARISH FAIRBANKS (1904) [JC]
2 Doyon Pl., 99701. Tel: 907-452-3533; Email: iccsecretary2@cbna.org; Web: www.iccfairbanks.org. Revs. Thomas Kuffel; Balaswamy Gangarapu, Parochial Vicar; Deacons Sean Stack; Robert P. Barnard.
Catechesis Religious Program—Cindy Fields, Community Svc. Dir.; Grayce Barnard, Rel. Ed. Facilitator. Students 13.

3—ST. MARK UNIVERSITY CATHOLIC PARISH FAIRBANKS (1977)
Mailing Address: P.O. Box 750166, 99775-0166. Tel: 907-474-6776; Email: uaf.stmark@gmail.com. Rev. Kasparaj Mallavarapu; Mary Pat Boger, Parish Admin.
CAMPUS MINISTRY, 517 Copper Ln.-UAF, 99775-0166.

4—ST. RAPHAEL CATHOLIC CHURCH FAIRBANKS (1991)
P.O. Box 10508, 99710. Tel: 907-457-6603; Fax: 907-457-4461; Email: straphaelcatholicparish@gmail.com; Web: www.straphaelfairbanks.org. 1125 Old Steese Hwy N, 99712. Rev. Kasparaj Mallavarapu; Deacon George Bowder; Camille Connelly-Terhune, Lay Min.; Marie Martin, Lay Min.
Catechesis Religious Program—Students 67.

OUTSIDE CITY OF FAIRBANKS

ALAKANUK, ST. IGNATIUS CATHOLIC CHURCH ALAKANUK (1954) [CEM] [JC] (Yup'ik)
P.O. Box 53, Alakanuk, 99554. Tel: 907-238-3914. Rev. Stanislaw Jaszek; Deacon Denis Shelden; Rev. Robert Fath, Diocesan D.R.E.
Catechesis Religious Program—
Mission—St. Peter Catholic Church Nunam Iqua.

ANIAK, ST. THERESA CATHOLIC CHURCH ANIAK (1935) [CEM] (Yup'ik)
P.O. Box 308, Aniak, 99557. Tel: 907-675-4448. Rev. Robert Fath, Diocesan D.R.E.; Sr. Marian Leaf, O.S.F., Parish Facilitator; Deacon Carl Morgan; Edith Morgan, Acting Parish Admin.; Angela Morgan, Acting Parish Life Coord.
Catechesis Religious Program—

BARROW, NORTH SLOPE BOROUGH, ST. PATRICK CATHOLIC CHURCH BARROW (1954) [JC] (Served out of Fairbanks, St. Raphael Church.)
Mailing Address: P.O. Box 389, Barrow, 99723. Tel: 907-852-3515; Email: barrowstpatrickchurch@gmail.com. Revs. Kasparaj Mallavarapu; Thomas Sagili, Parochial Vicar; Robert Fath, Diocesan D.R.E.; Peata Tuifua, Parish Admin.
Catechesis Religious Program—

BETHEL, IMMACULATE CONCEPTION CATHOLIC CHURCH BETHEL (1942)
P.O. Box 429, Bethel, 99559. Tel: 907-543-2464; Email: iccbct@gci.net; Web: www.bethelcatholic.org. Rev. Richard P. Magner, S.J.; Susan Murphy, Parish Admin.; Deacon Louie Andrew.
Res.: 775 2nd Ave., Bethel, 99559.
Catechesis Religious Program—Students 39.

CHEFORNAK, ST. CATHERINE OF SIENA CATHOLIC CHURCH CHEFORNAK (1937) [CEM] (Yup'ik)
P.O. Box 90, Chefornak, 99561. Tel: 907-374-9500; Email: cyf_st_catherine@yahoo.com. Agnes Kairaiuak, Acting Parish Admin.; Deacons Joe Avugiak; Jonathan Lewis; Cecelia Kinegak, Contact Person.
Catechesis Religious Program—Elizabeth Kusaiak, Head Catechist. Students 142.

CHEVAK, SACRED HEART CATHOLIC CHURCH CHEVAK (1952) [CEM] (Cup'ik)
P.O. Box 249, Chevak, 99563. Tel: 907-858-7826; Email: info@cbna.org. Rev. Gregg D. Wood, S.J.; Deacon Peter Boyscout; Rev. Robert Fath, Diocesan D.R.E.
Catechesis Religious Program—Students 6.

DELTA JUNCTION, OUR LADY OF SORROWS CATHOLIC CHURCH DELTA JUNCTION (1959)
2565 Deborah St., Delta Junction, 99737.
Tel: 907-895-5232; Email: olsdelta@wildak.net. P.O. Box 446, Delta Junction, 99737. Revs. Szymon Czuwara; Robert Fath, Diocesan D.R.E.
Catechesis Religious Program—Students 10.
Mission— aka St. Francis Xavier Catholic Church Eagle.

EMMONAK, SACRED HEART CATHOLIC CHURCH EMMONAK (1953) [JC] (Yup'ik)
P.O. Box 69, Emmonak, 99581. Tel: 907-949-1012. Rev. Stanislaw Jaszek; Lawrence Yupanik, Acting Parish Admin.; Deacons Raymond Waska; Philip Yupanik; Patrick Tam, Pastoral Facilitator.
Catechesis Religious Program—Patrick Tam, Dir. Adult Faith Formation, Yukon-Kuskokwin Region. Students 10.

GALENA, ST. JOHN BERCHMANS CATHOLIC CHURCH GALENA (1923) (Athabascan)
P.O. Box 131, Galena, 99741. Tel: 907-656-7449. Agnes Sweetsir, Admin.; Rev. Thinh Tran, Pastoral Min.; Bro. R Justin Huber, O.F.M., Pastoral Min.; Rev. Robert Fath, Diocesan D.R.E.
Catechesis Religious Program—Tel: 907-656-2777.

HEALY, DENALI BOROUGH, HOLY MARY OF GUADALUPE CATHOLIC CHURCH HEALY (1984) (Served out of Fairbanks, Immaculate Conception Church.)
P.O. Box 32, Healy, 99743. Tel: 907-683-2535; Email: holymaryofguadalupe@gmail.com. Revs. Thomas Kuffel; Balaswamy Gangarapu, Parochial Vicar.
Catechesis Religious Program—Clara Saxe, Head Catechist. Students 8.
Mission— aka Denali National Park Catholic Community, [JC] .

HOLY CROSS, HOLY FAMILY CATHOLIC CHURCH HOLY CROSS (1888)
P.O. Box 101, Holy Cross, 99602. Tel: 907-374-9500. Connie Werba, Parish Admin.; Sr. Marian Leaf, O.S.F., Parish Facilitator; Rev. Robert Fath, Diocesan D.R.E.
Catechesis Religious Program—

HOOPER BAY, LITTLE FLOWER OF JESUS CATHOLIC CHURCH HOOPER BAY (1928) [JC] (Yup'ik)
P.O. Box 9, Hooper Bay, 99604. Tel: 907-758-4620. Rev. Greg Wood.
Catechesis Religious Program—Dora Bell, Head Catechist. Students 9.

HUSLIA, ST. FRANCIS REGIS CATHOLIC CHURCH HUSLIA
P.O. Box 89, Huslia, 99746-0089. Tel: 907-829-2234; Email: info@cbna.org. Bro. R Justin Huber, O.F.M., Parish Min.

KALSKAG, IMMACULATE CONCEPTION CATHOLIC CHURCH KALSKAG
P.O. Box 11, Kalskag, 99607. Tel: 907-471-2298; Email: info@cbna.org. Sr. Marian Leaf, O.S.F., Parish Facilitator; Bonnie Perrson, Acting Parish Admin.; Marcus Dammeyer, Contact Person; Rev. Robert Fath, Diocesan D.R.E.
Catechesis Religious Program—

KALTAG, ST. TERESA CATHOLIC CHURCH, [JC] (Athabascan)
P.O. Box 69, Kaltag, 99748. Tel: 907-534-2218. Revs. Joseph Hemmer, O.F.M.; Robert Fath, Diocesan D.R.E.
Catechesis Religious Program—Students 8.

KOTLIK, ST. JOSEPH CATHOLIC CHURCH KOTLIK (1949) (Yup'ik)
P.O. Box 20228, Kotlik, 99620. Tel: 907-899-4715; Email: kotstjoseph4715@yahoo.com. Rev. Stanislaw Jaszek; Theresa George, Bookkeeper, Bookkeeper.
Catechesis Religious Program—Winnie Hunt, D.R.E. Students 26.

KOTZEBUE, NORTHWEST ARCTIC BOROUGH, ST. FRANCIS XAVIER CATHOLIC CHURCH KOTZEBUE (1929) [CEM] [JC] (Served out of Nome)
P.O. Box 358, Kotzebue, 99752. Tel: 907-442-3239; Email: stfrancisxavier@cbna.org; Web: www.walaskacatholic.org. 342 Second St., Kotzebue, 99752. Rev. Kumar Pasala, Parochial Admin.; Winifred Reeve, Parish Admin.
Catechesis Religious Program—Students 11.

KOYUKUK, ST. PATRICK CATHOLIC CHURCH GALENA, (Athabascan)
P.O. Box 54010, Koyukuk, 99754. Tel: 907-927-2240; Email: info@cbna.org. Bro. Bob Ruzicka, O.F.M., Pastoral Min. & Head Catechist; Eliza Jones, Acting Parish Admin. (Served out of Galena)
Catechesis Religious Program—Students 9.

MARSHALL, IMMACULATE HEART OF MARY CATHOLIC CHURCH MARSHALL (1930)
Mailing Address: P.O. Box 69, Marshall, 99585.
Tel: 907-679-6639; Email: info@cbna.org. Mrs. Clara Shorty, Parish Admin./Parish Life Coord.; Sr. Ellen Callaghan, O.S.F., Parish Facilitator.
Mission—Our Lady of Guadalupe Catholic Church Russian Mission, P.O. Box 56, Russian Mission, Wade Hampton Co. 99657. Tel: 907-374-9500. Theresa Vaska, Admin. Number of Minor Baptisms (ages 7 to 17) 3.

MCGRATH, ST. MICHAEL CATHOLIC CHURCH MCGRATH (1960)
P.O. Box 141, McGrath, 99627. Tel: 907-374-9500. Sharon R. Strick, Parish Admin.

MOUNTAIN VILLAGE, ST. LAWRENCE CATHOLIC CHURCH MOUNTAIN VILLAGE
P.O. Box 32205, Mountain Village, 99632.
Tel: 907-374-9500; Email: info@cbna.org. Rev. Yakubu Aiden; Deacon Elmer Beans; Ms. Karen Peterson, Parish Admin.

NENANA, ST. THERESA CATHOLIC CHURCH NENANA (1922) [JC2] (Served out of Fairbanks, Immaculate Conception Church.)
Mailing Address: P.O. Box 312, Nenana, 99760.
Tel: 907-832-5617. Revs. Thomas Kuffel; Balaswamy Gangarapu, Parochial Vicar; Penelope A. Forness, Acting Parish Admin.

NEWTOK, HOLY FAMILY CATHOLIC CHURCH NEWTOK (1950) [CEM] (Yup'ik)
P.O. Box 5569, Newtok, 99559. Tel: 907-237-2427. Rev. Thomas Provinsal, S.J., Head Catechist; Deacon John F. Andy; Ignatius Tommy, Contact Person.
Catechesis Religious Program—Students 5.

NIGHTMUTE, OUR LADY OF PERPETUAL HELP (1950) [CEM] (Yup'ik)
P.O. Box 90035, Nightmute, 99690.
Tel: 907-647-6428. Rev. Thomas G. Provinsal, S.J.; Deacons Ignatius Matthias; Christopher Tulik; Anna Tom, Contact Person; Rev. Robert Fath, Diocesan D.R.E.
Legal Name: Our Lady of Perpetual Help Catholic Church Nightmute
Catechesis Religious Program—Students 5.

NOME, ST. JOSEPH CATHOLIC CHURCH NOME (1901)
100 W. King Pl., Nome, 99762. Tel: 907-443-5527; Email: st.josephnome@live.com; Web: www.walaskacatholic.org. P.O. Box 1010, Nome, 99762. Rev. Kumar Pasala, Parochial Admin.
Church: 405 Steadman St., Nome, 99762.
Catechesis Religious Program—Caroline Proulx, D.R.E. Students 7.
Mission—St. Jude Catholic Church Little Diomede.

NORTH POLE, FAIRBANKS, NORTH STAR BOROUGH, ST. NICHOLAS CATHOLIC CHURCH NORTH POLE (1975)
707 St. Nicholas Dr., North Pole, 99705.
Tel: 907-488-2595; Email: stnicks@acsalaska.net; Web: www.stnicholasnp.org. Rev. Jonathan Dellinger; Deacons Chuck Bowman; Ronald Jones; Anne Armour, Parish Coord.
Catechesis Religious Program—Heather Pariera-Kimmerling, D.R.E.; Melody Doudna, Youth Min. Students 135.

NULATO, OUR LADY OF SNOWS CATHOLIC CHURCH NULATO (1877)
P.O. Box 98, Nulato, 99765. Tel: 907-898-2242. Bro. Robert J. Ruzicka, O.F.M., Pastoral Admin. & Head Catechist.
Catechesis Religious Program—Students 18.

PILOT STATION, ST. CHARLES SPINOLA CATHOLIC CHURCH PILOT STATION (1914) [JC] (Yup'ik)
Mailing Address: P.O. Box 5120, Pilot Station, 99650. Tel: 907-549-3231; Fax: 907-549-3231; Email: info@cbna.org. Rev. Yakubu Aiden; Sr. Ellen Callaghan, O.S.F., Pastoral Facilitator; Ms. Regina Mike, Acting Parish Admin.; Rev. Robert Fath, Diocesan D.R.E.
Catechesis Religious Program—Students 5.

RUBY, ST. PETER-IN-CHAINS CATHOLIC CHURCH GALENA (1912) [JC]
P.O. Box 68207, Ruby, 99768. Tel: 907-468-4413. Rev. Joseph Hemmer, O.F.M.

ST. MARYS, CHURCH OF THE NATIVITY CATHOLIC CHURCH ST. MARYS (1970)
Mailing Address: P.O. Box 109, St. Marys, 99658.
Tel: 907-438-2133. Rev. Yakubu Aiden; Michelle Thompson, Contact Person; Rev. Robert Fath, Diocesan D.R.E.
Catechesis Religious Program—Students 7.

ST. MICHAEL, ST. MICHAEL CATHOLIC CHURCH ST. MICHAEL (1895) [JC]
P.O. Box 29, St. Michael, 99659. Tel: 907-923-3151; Fax: 907-923-3151; Email: info@cbna.org. Rev. Alphonsus Afina, Parochial Vicar; Jessica Acomen, Acting Parish Admin.
Catechesis Religious Program—Jessica Marks, Head Catechist.

SCAMMON BAY, BLESSED SACRAMENT CATHOLIC CHURCH SCAMMON BAY (1968) [JC]
P.O. Box 170, Scammon Bay, 99662.
Tel: 907-558-5229. Rev. Gregg D. Wood, S.J.; Jason Akerelrea, Parish Admin.
Catechesis Religious Program—Caroline Ulak, D.R.E. & Catechetical Leader.

STEBBINS, ST. BERNARD CATHOLIC CHURCH STEBBINS (1908) [JC]
P.O. Box 71102, Stebbins, 99671. Tel: 907-934-3151. Rev. Alphonsus Afina; Deacon Francis Pete, Parish Admin.
Catechesis Religious Program—Anna Flynn, Head Catechist.

TANANA, ST. ALOYSIUS CATHOLIC CHURCH GALENA (1887) [JC]
P.O. Box 77006, Tanana, 99777. Tel: 907-366-7238. Lois Huntington, Parish Admin.
Legal Title: St. Aloysius Catholic Church Tanana.

TELLER, ST. ANN CATHOLIC CHURCH TELLER (1909) (Served out of Nome)
c/o St. Joseph Church: P.O. Box 1010, Nome, 99762.
Tel: 907-443-5527. Rev. Kumar Pasala, Parochial Admin.; Paula Alvanna, Parish Admin.

TOK, HOLY ROSARY CATHOLIC CHURCH TOK (1949)

P.O. Box 369, Tok, 99780. Tel: 907-883-4111. Rev. Szymon Czuwara. (Served out of Delta Junction, Our Lady of Sorrows Church.).

TOKSOOK BAY, ST. PETER THE FISHERMAN (1964) [CEM] Mailing Address: P.O. Box 37046, Toksook Bay, 99637. Tel: 907-427-7813; Fax: 907-427-7813; Email: stpeter@gci.net. Rev. Richard P. Magner, S.J.; Deacons James Charlie; Nick Therchik Sr.; Joe Asuluk; Maggie John, Parish Admin. & Parish Life Coord.
Legal Name: St. Peter the Fisherman Catholic Church Toksook Bay
Catechesis Religious Program—Tel: 907-427-7826; Email: info@cbna.org. Cathy John, Head Catechist. Students 198.

TUNUNAK, ST. JOSEPH CATHOLIC CHURCH TUNUNAK (1889) [CEM] (Yup'ik)
P.O. Box 9, Tununak, 99681. Tel: 907-652-6214; Email: info@cbna.org. Nellie Lincoln, Acting Co-Admin.; Josephine M. Link, Acting Co-Admin.
Catechesis Religious Program—Elsie Hooper, Head Catechist.

UNALAKLEET, CHURCH OF THE HOLY ANGELS CATHOLIC CHURCH UNALAKLEET (1952)
P.O. Box 358, Unalakleet, 99684. Tel: 907-624-3711. Rev. Alphonsus Afina; Mr. Patrick Cutler, Acting Parish Admin.
Catechesis Religious Program—

Leave of Absence:
Revs.—
Bayler, Frederick C.
Bergquist, Patrick
Wallner, Gerhard.

Retired:
Revs.—
de Verteuil, Jack, (Retired)
Hinsvark, John, (Retired), 200 W. 34th Ave., #545, Anchorage, 99503.

Permanent Deacons:
Andrew, Louie, Immaculate Conception, Bethel
Andy, John F., Holy Family, Newtok
Avugiak, Joe, St. Catherine, Chefornak
Barnard, Robert P., Immaculate Conception, Fairbanks
Beans, Elmer, Mountain Village
Bowder, George, St. Raphael, Fairbanks
Bowman, Chuck, St. Nicholas Church, North Pole
Boyscout, Peter, Sacred Heart, Chevak
Charlie, James, St. Peter the Fisherman, Toksook Bay
Froehle, Robert, St. Joseph Catholic Church, Nome
Gelinas, Walt, (Retired), St. Nicholas, North Pole
Gwizdak, Stan, Sacred Heart Cathedral; Fairbanks
Jones, Ronald, St. Nicholas, North Pole
Mantei, Robert, (Retired), Immaculate Conception, Fairbanks
Matthias, Ignatius, Our Lady of Perpetual Help, Nightmute
Morgan, Carl, St. Theresa, Aniak
Perreault, Paul, Sacred Heart Cathedral, Fairbanks
Pete, Francis, St. Bernard, Stebbins
Phillip, Joseph, (Retired), St. Ignatius, Alakanuk
Shelden, Denis, St. Ignatius, Alakanuk
Stack, Sean, Immaculate Conception, Fairbanks
Therchik, Nick, St. Peter the Fisherman, Toksook Bay
Tulik, Camillus, (Retired), Our Lady of Perpetual Help, Nightmute
Tulik, Christopher, Our Lady of Perpetual Help, Nightmute
Waska, Ray, Sacred Heart, Emmonak
Yupanick, Phillip, Sacred Heart, Emmonak.

INSTITUTIONS LOCATED IN DIOCESE

[A] HIGH SCHOOLS, DIOCESAN

FAIRBANKS. *Monroe Catholic Junior-Senior High School*, (Grades 7-12), 615 Monroe St., 99701. Tel: 907-202-9310; Fax: 907-452-5978; Email: monroeprincipal@catholic-schools.org; Web: www.catholic-schools.org. Patrick Riggs, Prin.; Kerry Halvarson, Librarian. Lay Teachers 23; Students 173.

[B] GRADE SCHOOLS, DIOCESAN

FAIRBANKS. *Immaculate Conception Grade School*, (Grades PreK-6), 615 Monroe St., 99701. Tel: 907-202-9310; Fax: 907-452-5978; Email: icsprincipal@catholic-schools.org; Web: www.catholic-schools.org. Amanda Angaiak, Prin.; Kerry Halvarson, Librarian. Lay Teachers 17; Students 236.

[C] RESIDENCES FOR PRIESTS AND BROTHERS

FAIRBANKS. *St. Ignatius Residence*, 2890 Kobuk Ave., 99709. 1316 Peger Rd., 99709. Tel: 907-374-9500; Email: info@cbna.org. Most Rev. Chad W. Zielinski, In Res.; Revs. Frederick C. Bayler, In Res.; Ross Tozzi, V.G., In Res.
Bl. Pier Giorgio Frassati House of Discernment, 1316 Peger Rd., 99709. Tel: 907-374-9500; Email: info@cbna.org. Rev. Robert Fath, Dir.

[D] MISCELLANEOUS LISTINGS

FAIRBANKS. *Catholic Trust of Northern Alaska*, 1316 Peger Rd., 99709. Tel: 907-374-9500; Email: accounting@cbna.org. Susan Clifton, Exec. Officer.
**Little Flower Ministries*, P.O. Box 81476, 99708. Tel: 907-451-4868; Email: info@kqhe.org; Web: kqhe.org. Steve Mullins, Pres.
St. Mary's of the Lake, c/o 1316 Peger Rd., 99709. Tel: 907-374-9500; Email: nhanson@catholic-schools.org. Nancy Hanson, Contact Person.
**Monroe Foundation, Inc.*, 718 Betty St., 99707. Tel: 907-456-7970; Fax: 907-456-7481; Email: director@catholic-schools.org; Web: www.catholic-schools.org. Nancy Hanson, Pres.

BETHEL. *Brother Joe Prince Jesuit Community*, P.O. Box 3064, Bethel, 99559. Tel: 907-438-6016. Revs. Richard P. Magner, S.J., Supr.; Gregg D. Wood, S.J., Pastoral Ministry, Hooper Bay, Scammon Bay & Chevak, AK & Villages of Nelson Island & SW Coast; Mark A. Hoelsken, S.J., Pastoral Ministry Newtok & Dir. Native Deacon Prog.; Thomas G. Provinsal, S.J., Pastoral Ministry, Villages of Nelson Island & SW Coast. Priests 4; Total Assisted 6,150.

NOME. **KNOM Radio Mission, Inc.*, Box 988, Nome, 99762. Tel: 907-443-5221. Lynette Schmidt, Gen. Mgr.

ST. MARYS. *Native Ministry Training Program*, P.O. Box 29, St. Marys, 99658-0029. Tel: 907-438-2832; Fax: 907-438-2823; Email: nmtp@juno.com. Sisters Ellen Callaghan, O.S.F., Dir.; Kathleen Radich, O.S.F. Total in Residence 2; Staff 2.

RELIGIOUS INSTITUTES OF MEN REPRESENTED IN THE DIOCESE

For further details refer to the corresponding bracketed number in the Religious Institutes of Men or Women section.

[0520]—*Franciscan Friars and Brothers*—O.F.M.
[0690]—*Jesuit Fathers and Brothers*—S.J.

RELIGIOUS INSTITUTES OF WOMEN REPRESENTED IN THE DIOCESE

[1650]—*The Sisters of St. Francis of Philadelphia*—O.S.F.

NECROLOGY

† Martinek, John, (Retired), Died Jul. 28, 2018

An asterisk (*) denotes an organization that has established tax-exempt status directly with the IRS and is not covered by the USCCB Group Ruling.

Diocese of Fall River

(Dioecesis Riverormensis)

Most Reverend

EDGAR M. DA CUNHA, S.D.V.

Bishop of Fall River; ordained March 27, 1982; appointed Titular Bishop of Ucres and Auxiliary Bishop of Newark June 27, 2003; Episcopal ordination September 3, 2003; appointed Bishop of Fall River July 3, 2014; installed September 24, 2014. *Office: P.O. Box 2577, Fall River, MA 02722.*

The Chancery: P.O. Box 2577, Fall River, MA 02722. Tel: 508-675-1311; Fax: 508-730-2447.

Email: chancery@dioc-fr.org

Most Reverend

GEORGE W. COLEMAN

Retired Bishop of Fall River; ordained December 16, 1964; appointed Bishop of Fall River April 30, 2003; consecrated July 22, 2003; retired July 3, 2014. *Office: P.O. Box 2577, Fall River, MA 02722.*

ESTABLISHED MARCH 12, 1904.

Square Miles 1,194.

Comprises Bristol, Barnstable, Dukes and Nantucket Counties, and the Towns of Marion, Mattapoisett and Wareham in Plymouth County, Massachusetts.

For legal titles of parishes and diocesan institutions, consult the Chancery Office.

STATISTICAL OVERVIEW

Personnel	
Bishop	1
Retired Bishops	1
Priests: Diocesan Active in Diocese	73
Priests: Diocesan Active Outside Diocese	7
Priests: Retired, Sick or Absent	53
Number of Diocesan Priests	133
Religious Priests in Diocese	58
Total Priests in Diocese	191
Extern Priests in Diocese	7
Ordinations:	
Diocesan Priests	3
Religious Priests	1
Transitional Deacons	1
Permanent Deacons in Diocese	87
Total Brothers	13
Total Sisters	112
Parishes	
Parishes	80
With Resident Pastor:	
Resident Diocesan Priests	59
Resident Religious Priests	12
Without Resident Pastor:	
Administered by Priests	9
Missions	11
Closed Parishes	2
Professional Ministry Personnel:	
Sisters	4
Lay Ministers	6
Welfare	
Homes for the Aged	5
Total Assisted	1,048
Residential Care of Children	1
Total Assisted	762
Day Care Centers	1
Total Assisted	40
Specialized Homes	5
Total Assisted	57
Special Centers for Social Services	5
Total Assisted	49,101
Residential Care of Disabled	3
Total Assisted	375
Other Institutions	145
Total Assisted	317
Educational	
Diocesan Students in Other Seminaries	14
Total Seminarians	14
Colleges and Universities	1
Total Students	2,401
High Schools, Diocesan and Parish	5
Total Students	2,790
Elementary Schools, Diocesan and Parish	17
Total Students	3,722
Catechesis/Religious Education:	
High School Students	2,405
Elementary Students	15,556
Total Students under Catholic Instruction	26,888
Teachers in the Diocese:	
Priests	11
Sisters	5
Lay Teachers	681
Vital Statistics	
Receptions into the Church:	
Infant Baptism Totals	2,057
Minor Baptism Totals	77
Adult Baptism Totals	49
Received into Full Communion	63
First Communions	2,506
Confirmations	2,559
Marriages:	
Catholic	570
Interfaith	91
Total Marriages	661
Deaths	3,158
Total Catholic Population	278,863
Total Population	836,255

Former Bishops—Most Revs. WILLIAM STANG, D.D., ord. June 15, 1878; appt. March 12, 1904; cons. May 1, 1904; died Feb. 2, 1907; DANIEL F. FEEHAN, D.D., ord. Dec. 20, 1879; appt. July 2, 1907; cons. Sept. 19, 1907; died July 19, 1934; JAMES E. CASSIDY, D.D., ord. Sept. 8, 1898; appt. Titular Bishop of Ibora and Auxiliary, March 21, 1930; cons. May 27, 1930; succeeded to the See, July 28, 1934; died May 17, 1951; JAMES L. CONNOLLY, D.D., D.Sc.H., ord. Dec. 21, 1923; appt. Titular Bishop of Mylasa and Coadjutor "cum jure successionis," April 18, 1945; cons. May 24, 1945; succeeded to See, May 17, 1951; retired Oct. 30, 1970; died Sept. 12, 1986; DANIEL A. CRONIN, D.D., S.T.D., ord. Dec. 20, 1952; appt. Titular Bishop of Egnatia and Auxiliary Bishop of Boston, June 10, 1968; cons. Sept. 12, 1968; transferred to Fall River, Oct. 30, 1970; installed Dec. 16, 1970; transferred to Hartford, Dec. 9, 1991; His Eminence SEAN CARDINAL O'MALLEY, O.F.M.Cap., Ph.D., ord. Aug. 29, 1970; appt. Coadjutor Bishop of St. Thomas, Virgin Islands May 30, 1984; ord. Aug. 2, 1984; succeeded to See Oct. 16, 1985; appt. Bishop of Fall River June 16, 1992; installed Aug. 11, 1992; transferred to Palm Beach Sept. 3, 2002; installed Oct. 19, 2002; transferred to Boston July 1, 2003; installed July 30, 2003; Named Cardinal Priest with the title of Santa Maria della Vittoria, in the consistory of March 24, 2006; installed October 1, 2006.; Most Rev. GEORGE W. COLEMAN, ord. Dec. 16, 1964; appt. Bishop of Fall River April 30, 2003; cons. July 22, 2003; retired July 3, 2014.

Vicar General—Very Rev. GREGORY A. MATHIAS, V.G., Mailing Address: P.O. Box 2577, Fall River, 02722.

Moderator of the Curia—Rev. JOHN M. MURRAY.

The Chancery—450 Highland Ave., Fall River, 02720. Mailing Address: P.O. Box 2577, Fall River, 02722-2577. Tel: 508-675-1311; Fax: 508-730-2447.

Chancellor and Chief Financial Officer—MR. KEVIN R. KILEY.

Diocesan Tribunal—887 Highland Ave., Fall River, 02720-3820. Tel: 508-675-7150; Fax: 508-675-7295.

Judicial Vicar—Very Rev. JEFFREY CABRAL, J.C.L.

Promotor Justitiae—Rev. RICHARD D. WILSON, J.C.L.

Judges—Revs. THOMAS L. RITA, (Retired); RODNEY E. THIBAULT, J.C.L.; Very Revs. JAY T. MADDOCK, J.C.L., V.F.; JEFFREY CABRAL, J.C.L.; Rev. THOMAS E. MCGLYNN, J.C.L.

Defenders of the Bond—Rev. Msgr. DANIEL F. HOYE, J.C.L., (Retired); Rev. GERARD A. HEBERT, J.C.L.

Procurator-Advocates—Revs. MARK R. HESSION, J.C.L.; BRUCE M. NEYLON.

Auditors—Very Rev. DANIEL W. LACROIX, V.F.; Revs. JOHN J. PERRY; DARIUSZ KALINOWSKI; MARK R. HESSION, J.C.L.; DAVID C. FREDERICI; THOMAS E. MCGLYNN, J.C.L.

Office Manager—MRS. DENISE D. BERUBE.

Notaries—MRS. DENISE D. BERUBE; MRS. CAROL A. ROCHEFORT.

Diocesan Consultors—Very Rev. GREGORY A. MATHIAS, V.G.; Rev. Msgr. STEPHEN J. AVILA, V.F.; Rev. JOHN J. OLIVEIRA; Very Rev. TIMOTHY P. REIS, V.F.; Revs. THOMAS C. LOPES, (Retired); ARNOLD R. MEDEIROS; JOHN M. MURRAY.

Deans—Fall River Deanery: Very Rev. JAY T. MADDOCK, J.C.L., V.F., Holy Name Rectory, 709 Hanover St., Fall River, 02720. Taunton Deanery: Very Rev. RICHARD E. DEGAGNE, V.F., Immaculate Conception Rectory, 193 Main St., Easton, 02356. Attleboro Deanery: Very Rev. TIMOTHY P. REIS, V.F., St. Mary Rectory, 1 Power St., Norton, 02766-3127. Cape Cod Deanery: Rev. Msgr. STEPHEN J. AVILA, V.F., St. Anthony Rectory, 167 E. Falmouth Hwy., East Falmouth, 02536. New Bedford Deanery: Very Rev. DANIEL W. LACROIX, V.F., St. Mary Rectory, 106 Illinois St., New Bedford, 02745.

Minister for Priests—Rev. EDWARD E. CORREIA, (Retired).

Diocesan Offices and Directors

Apostolate for Persons with Disabilities—MATTHEW DANSEREAU, Coord., 1600 Bay St., Fall River, 02724. Tel: 508-997-7337; Tel: 508-679-8373.

Campus Ministry—

Director—Rev. DAVID C. FREDERICI, Mailing address: Catholic Campus Ministry, P.O. Box 70737, Dartmouth, 02747. Tel: 774-202-3047; Email: frdavid@stgeorgecatholics.org; Web: www.fallrivercampusministry.com.

Newman House—359 Old Westport Rd., Dartmouth, 02747. Tel: 774-202-2274; Email: flucca@umassd.edu. Deacon FRANK R. LUCCA, Campus Min.

Bristol Community College—771 Elsbree St., Fall River, 02720. Tel: 508-678-2811, Ext. 2810; Email: frdavid@stgeorgecatholics.org; Web: www.bcccatholics.com. Rev. DAVID C. FREDERICI, Chap.

University of Massachusetts Dartmouth—Rev. DAVID C. FREDERICI, Chap.; Deacon FRANK R. LUCCA, Campus Min., 285 Old Westport Rd., Dartmouth, 02747. Tel: 508-999-8872; Email: flucca@umassd.edu.

Wheaton College—Rev. DAVID C. FREDERICI, Chap., Mailing Address: Catholic Campus Ministry, P.O. Box 70737, Dartmouth, 02747. Tel: 774-202-3047; Web: www.wheatoncatholics.com.

Cape Cod Community College/Massachusetts Maritime Academy—Rev. DAVID C. FREDERICI, Chap., c/o St. George, 12 Highland Ave., Westport, 02790. Tel: 774-319-5579; Fax: 774-319-5499; Email: frdavid@stgeorgecatholics.org.

Stonehill College—320 Washington St., Easton, 02357. Tel: 508-565-1487; Email: aszakaly@stonehill.edu. Rev. ANTHONY V. SZAKALY, C.S.C., Dir. Campus Ministry.

Catholic Youth Organization—709 Hanover St., Fall River, 02720. Tel: 508-679-6732; Fax: 508-675-4755; Email: office@holynamefr.com. Very Rev. JAY T. MADDOCK, J.C.L., V.F., Diocesan Dir.

The Catholic Foundation of Southeastern Massachusetts—450 Highland Ave., P.O. Box 1470, Fall River, 02722. Tel: 508-985-6510; Fax: 508-676-6591. MIRIAM FINN SHERMAN, CEO, Email: msherman@catholicfoundationsema.org.

Diocesan Apostolate to Hispanics—Rev. CRAIG A. PREGANA, Diocesan Dir., Mailing Address: 233 County St., New Bedford, 02740. Tel: 508-992-9408; Fax: 508-990-0575; Web: guadalupenewbedford@gmail.com. Area Communities: . Fall River: Very Rev. THOMAS WASHBURN, O.F.M., Rector; Rev. JUAN CARLOS MUNOZ, Parochial Vicar, St. Mary's Cathedral, 327 Second St., Fall River, 02721. Tel: 508-673-2833. Attleboro: Revs. CHRISTOPHER M. PESCHEL, Parochial Admin.; GERMAN CORREA AGUDELO, Parochial Vicar, St. Vincent de Paul Church, 71 Linden St., Attleboro, 02703. Tel: 508-226-1115; Fax: 888-239-9322. Taunton: Revs. JAMES J. DOHERTY, C.S.C, Pastor; RICHARD D. WILSON, J.C.L., Spanish Ministry, St. Mary's Church, 14 St. Mary's Square, Taunton, 02780. New Bedford: Revs. CRAIG A. PREGANA, Pastor, Our Lady of Guadalupe at St. James Church, 233 County St., New Bedford, 02740. Tel: 508-994-9408; Fax: 508-990-0575; OCTAVIO CORTEZ, I.V.E., Pastor, St. Anthony of Padua Church, 1359 Acushnet Ave., New Bedford, 02746. Tel: 508-993-1691; Fax: 508-999-4775. Nantucket: Revs. JOHN P. KELLEHER, O.S.B., Pastor; CARLOS PATINO VILLA, Parochial Vicar, Mailing Address: St. Mary/Our Lady of the Isle, P.O. Box 1168, Nantucket, 02554-1168. Tel: 508-228-0100; Fax: 508-325-7991. Cape Cod: Revs. MICHAEL J. FITZPATRICK, Pastor; MATTHEW GILL, Dir. Spanish Min., St. Francis Xavier Church, 261 South St., Hyannis, 02601. Tel: 508-771-2658.

Brazilian Apostolate—St. Mary's Cathedral Rectory, 327 Second St., Fall River, 02720. Tel: 508-673-2833; Fax: 508-672-0667. Rev. MESSIAS ALBUQUERQUE, Dir.

Portuguese Apostolate—Rev. JOHN J. OLIVEIRA, Coord., Our Lady of Mount Carmel Rectory, 230 Bonney St., New Bedford, 02744. Tel: 508-993-4704; Fax: 508-991-5536.

Diocesan Archives—Mailing Address: P.O. Box 2577, Fall River, 02722. Tel: 508-675-1311; Email: djaacks@dioc-fr.org. MR. KEVIN R. KILEY, Chancellor.

Diocesan Office of Communications—JOHN E. KEARNS JR., Dir., 450 Highland Ave., P.O. Box 2577, Fall River, 02722. Tel: 508-675-1311; Fax: 508-730-2447; Email: jkearns@dioc-fr.org; Web: www.fallriverdiocese.org.

Diocesan Director of Cemeteries—Rev. JOHN J. PERRY, 230 S. Main St., Centerville, 02632.

Diocesan Education Center—MR. STEPHEN A PERLA, Supt. Schools; MRS. SANDRA M. DRUMMEY, Asst. Supt., Academics & Personnel; MRS. DENISE M. PEIXOTO, Asst. Supt., Academics & Student Affairs; CLAIRE M. MCMANUS, S.T.L., Dir. Faith Formation; SARAH HEATON, Dir., Enrollment & Mktg.; Deacon BRUCE J. BONNEAU, Asst. Dir., Adult Evangelization & Spirituality; RCIA; WILLIAM MILOT, Dir., Educational Technology; DR. MARY PATRICIA TRANTER, Ph.D., Dir., Strategic Initiatives; SHARON SAMPSON, Exec. Asst. to Supt.; SUSAN GARMAN, Business Mgr.; ROSE MARY SARAIVA, Marriage & Family Ministry, Events Coord. & Bereavement Min., Catholic Education Center, 423 Highland Ave., Fall River, 02720. Tel: 508-678-2828; Fax: 508-674-4218.

Diocesan Department of Pastoral Care for the Sick—Rev. RODNEY E. THIBAULT, J.C.L., Dir., Office: St. Mary's Parish, 783 Dartmouth St., South Dartmouth, 02748. Tel: 508-992-7163; Fax: 508-992-5209.

St. Anne's Hospital—795 Middle St., Fall River, 02721. Tel: 508-674-5741, Ext. 2061. Rev. LEONARD KAYONDO; Sisters CAROLE V.M. MELLO, O.P.; MARIE THERESE DYER, F.C.J.; JUDITH COSTA, S.S.D.; MR. DANIEL SULLIVAN; MRS. MARIKA HULL; Sisters GLORIA JUGO, O.P.; LORNA RIORDAN, O.P.

Charlton Memorial Hospital—Highland Ave. at New Boston Rd., Fall River, 02720. Tel: 508-679-3131, Ext. 7114. Rev. DAVID C. DESTON; Sr. ROBERTA O'CONNELL, F.C.J.; MRS. JANICE M. HART.

Sturdy Memorial Hospital—211 Park St., P.O. Box 649, Attleboro, 02703. Tel: 508-236-8560. Rev. GERMAN CORREA AGUDELO; Deacons PAUL M. FOURNIER; ADELBERT F. MALLOY.

Cape Cod Hospital—27 Park St., Hyannis, 02601. Tel: 508-862-5286. Rev. RONNIE P. FLOYD; MRS. GRETCHEN MACKOUL.

St. Luke's Hospital—101 Page St., New Bedford, 02740. Tel: 508-997-1515. Sisters JUDITH COSTA, S.S.D.; FATIMA SIMAS, S.S.D.; MS. DENISE BENJAMIN; MS. KATHRYN MCGRATH.

Morton Hospital—88 Washington St., Taunton, 02780. Tel: 508-828-7000. Deacons ANTHONY A. CIPRIANO; PHILIP E. BEDARD.

Tobey Hospital—43 High St., Wareham, 02571. Tel: 508-273-4105. Deacon PAUL D. COUGHLIN.

Spaulding Rehabilitation Hospital of the Cape and Islands—311 Service Rd., East Sandwich, 02537. Tel: 508-833-4000. Deacon C. MICHAEL HICKEY.

Falmouth Hospital—100 Ter Heun Dr., Falmouth, 02540. Tel: 508-548-5300. Deacon BRUCE J. BAXTER; MR. RICHARD BISSON.

Diocesan Department of Catholic Social Services—1600 Bay St., Box M, S. Station, Fall River, 02724. Tel: 508-674-4681; Fax: 508-675-2224. MS. SUSAN MAZZARELLA, M.A., L.S.W., CEO.

Diocesan Finance Council—Members: Most Rev. EDGAR M. DA CUNHA, S.D.V., Bishop of Fall River; Very Rev. GREGORY A. MATHIAS, V.G.; Revs. MICHAEL K. MCMANUS; JOHN M. MURRAY; DAVID T. GAY, Esq.; MS. PAULA A. FREITAS; MR. E. DENNIS KELLY JR.; MR. RICHARD A. KELLEY; MR. DENNIS F. LEAHY; MS. SANDRA L. SEVIGNEY.

Finance Office—450 Highland Ave., P.O. Box 2577, Fall River, 02722. Tel: 508-675-1311; Fax: 508-730-2447. MR. STUART MACDONALD, Dir. Finance, Email: smacdonald@dioc-fr.org; MR. JOSEPH HARRINGTON, Dir., Financial Planning for Parishes & Schools, Email: jharrington@dioc-fr.org.

Diocesan Guild for the Blind—Rev. BRUCE M. NEYLON, Holy Trinity Parish, 951 Stafford Rd., Fall River, 02721. Tel: 508-672-3200; Fax: 508-673-5518.

Diocesan Health Facilities—Rev. Msgr. EDMUND J. FITZGERALD, Exec. Dir., Office, 368 N. Main St., Fall River, 02720. Tel: 508-679-8154; Fax: 508-679-1422.

Diocesan Insurance Department—JOSEPH A. FIGLOCK, Benefits Mgr. & Insurance Coord.; SHAUN P. KERRIGAN, Asst. Benefits Mgr., Mailing Address: P.O. Box 2577, Fall River, 02722. Tel: 508-675-1311; Fax: 508-672-3802.

Diocesan Newspaper—The Anchor *Office: 887 Highland Ave., Fall River, 02720.* Tel: 508-675-7151; Fax: 508-675-7048. Rev. RICHARD D. WILSON, J.C.L., Exec. Editor; MR. DAVID B. JOLIVET, Editor; MR. WAYNE R. POWERS, Advertising; MR. KENNETH J. SOUZA, Reporter.

Ecumenical and Inter-religious Affairs Office—Rev. EDWARD J. HEALEY, Mailing Address: Christ the King Rectory, The Commons, P.O. Box 1800, Mashpee, 02649. Tel: 508-477-7700, Ext. 12; Fax: 508-477-8158.

Episcopal Representative for Religious and Associate Director of Vocations—Sr. PAULINA HURTADO, O.P., Mailing Address: P.O. Box 2577, Fall River, 02722. Tel: 508-675-1311; Fax: 508-679-9220; Email: sr.paulina@dioc-fr.org.

Family Ministry—ROSE MARY SARAIVA, Email: rsaraiva@dfrcs.org.

Holy Childhood Association, The—Rev. Msgr. JOHN J. OLIVEIRA, P.A., Dir., 106 Illinois St., New Bedford, 02745. Tel: 508-995-6168; Fax: 508-995-2453.

Human Resources and Administration—Mailing Address: P.O. Box 2577, Fall River, 02722. MR. PETER J. POWERS, Exec. Dir., Tel: 508-985-6507; Fax: 508-689-7920; Email: ppowers@dioc-fr.org; MICHELLE R. BERTOLDI, Human Resources Mgr., Tel: 508-985-6515; Fax: 508-689-7920; Email: mbertoldi@dioc-fr.org.

Missionary Cooperative Plan—106 Illinois St., New Bedford, 02745. Tel: 508-995-6168; Fax: 508-995-2453. Rev. Msgr. JOHN J. OLIVEIRA, P.A., Dir., Email: propoffaithnb@verizon.net.

Office for Divine Worship—Rev. JON-PAUL GALLANT, S.L.L., Dir., 18 Baltic St., South Attleboro, 02703. Tel: 508-761-8111; Fax: 508-761-5475; Email: odwfr@aol.com.

Office of Pastoral Planning—Office of Most Rev. Edgar M. Da Cunha, S.D.V.: Bishop of Fall River, 47 Underwood St., P.O. Box 2577, Fall River, 02722. Tel: 508-675-1311; Fax: 508-672-3802; Email: bishop@dioc-fr.org.

Permanent Diaconate Program—Rev. ROBERT A. OLIVEIRA, Co Dir.; Deacon FRANK R. LUCCA, Co Dir.; JACKIE COLLINS, Admin. Asst., Holy Name of the Sacred Heart of Jesus Parish, 121 Mount Pleasant St., New Bedford, 02740. Tel: 508-990-0341; Fax: 508-984-3406; Email: office@frpermanentdiaconate.com.

Pro-Life Apostolate—450 Highland Ave., P.O. Box 2577, Fall River, 02722. Tel: 508-675-1311; Fax: 508-730-2447. MS. IRINA DE LUCCA, Acting Dir., Email: idelucca@dioc-fr.org.

Propagation of the FaithRev. Msgr. JOHN J. OLIVEIRA, P.A., Dir., Office, 106 Illinois St., New Bedford, 02745. Tel: 508-995-6168; Fax: 508-995-3800; Email: propoffaithnb@verizon.net.

St. Vincent De Paul Society—MR. STEPHEN MEANEY, Council Pres., 444 N. Washington St., North Attleboro, 02760. Tel: 508-699-4185.

Television Apostolate—Rev. Msgr. STEPHEN J. AVILA, V.F., Dir., 167 E. Falmouth Hwy., East Falmouth, 02536. Tel: 508-548-0108; Fax: 508-457-1723; Email: frsteveavila@gmail.com.

Victim Assistance Coordinator—Deacon JOSEPH E. REGALI, Tel: 508-675-1311; Fax: 508-672-3802; Email: jregali@dioc-fr.org.

Vocations—Revs. KEVIN A. COOK, Dir. Vocations & Seminarians, Email: frcook@fallrivervocations.org; JOHN M. SCHRADER, Assoc. Dir. Vocations & Seminarians; Sr. PAULINA HURTADO, O.P., Assoc. Dir. Vocations, Mailing Address: P.O. Box 519, Seekonk, 02771.

Commissions and Councils

Campaign for Human Development—Mailing Address: S. Station, P.O. Box M, Fall River, 02724. Tel: 508-674-4681; Fax: 508-675-2224. MS. SUSAN MAZZARELLA, M.A., L.S.W.

Catholic Scouting—Mailing Address: c/o Office for Campus Ministry, P.O. Box 70737, Dartmouth, 02747. Tel: 774-202-3047. Rev. DAVID C. FREDERICI, Chap., Email: frdavid@stgeorgecatholics.org; MR. MICHAEL MCCORMACK, Chm.

Continuing Education and Formation of the Clergy—Very Rev. RICHARD D. WILSON, J.C.L., V.F., Mailing Address: Holy Family Parish, P.O. Box 619, East Taunton, 02718. Tel: 508-824-5707; Fax: 508-824-5665.

Diocesan Council of Catholic Women—Rev. MICHAEL S. RACINE, Moderator, Mailing Address: St. Bernard Parish, P.O. Box 370, Assonet, 02702-0370. Tel: 508-644-5585.

Diocesan Liaison with Charismatic Groups—Rev. EDWARD A. MURPHY, Dir., St. Andrew the Apostle Parish, 19 Kilmer Ave., Taunton, 02780. Tel: 508-824-5577; Fax: 508-822-1401; Email: freamurphy1@verizon.net.

Diocesan Liaison with Portuguese Charismatic Groups—Rev. HENRY S. ARRUDA, (Retired), 375 Elsbree St., Fall River, 02720. Tel: 508-675-1050.

Diocesan Pastoral Council—Very Rev. GREGORY A. MATHIAS, V.G., Mailing Address: P.O. Box 2577, Fall River, 02722.

Legion of Mary—Mailing Address: Holy Family Parish, P.O. Box 619, East Taunton, 02718. Tel: 508-824-5707; Fax: 508-824-5665. Rev. RICHARD D. WILSON, J.C.L.

CLERGY, PARISHES, MISSIONS AND PAROCHIAL SCHOOLS

CITY OF FALL RIVER

(BRISTOL COUNTY)

1—CATHEDRAL OF ST. MARY OF THE ASSUMPTION (1838) 327 Second St., 02721. Tel: 508-673-2833; Fax: 508-672-0667; Email: frtomw@gmail.com; Web: cathedralfallriver.com. Very Rev. Thomas Washburn, O.F.M., Rector; Revs. Juan Carlos Munoz, Parochial Vicar; Messias Albuquerque, In Res.; Deacon Peter R. Cote.
Catechesis Religious Program—467 Spring St., 02721. Tel: 508-672-5531; Email: cathedralfr@aol.com.

2—ST. ANNE (1869) (French), Closed. For inquiries for parish records contact the chancery.

3—ST. ANTHONY OF PADUA (1911) (Portuguese) 48 Sixteenth St., 02723. Tel: 508-673-2402. Rev. Brian E. Albino.
Catechesis Religious Program—Tel: 508-674-1986. Ms. Judith DaCosta, D.R.E. Students 46.

4—SAINT BERNADETTE PARISH (2012) Closed. For inquiries for parish records contact the chancery.

5—BLESSED SACRAMENT (1902) (French), Merged with Our Lady of the Angels and St. Patrick's, Fall River to form the Parish of the Good Shepherd, Fall River.

6—ST. ELIZABETH'S (1915) Merged with St. Jean Baptiste and St. William to form Holy Trinity.

7—ESPIRITO SANTO (1904) (Portuguese) 311 Alden St., 02723. Tel: 508-672-3352; Fax: 508-646-1787; Email: esfallriver@yahoo.com. Revs. Maurice O. Gauvin; David C. Deston, In Res.; Deacon Gary M. John.
School—Espirito Santo School, (Grades PreK-8), 143 Everett St., 02723. Tel: 508-672-2229; Fax: 509-672-7724; Web: www.espiritosantoschool.org; Email: araposo@es.dfrcs.org. Mr. Andrew J. Raposo, Prin., Elementary Prin. Lay Teachers 25; Students 205.
Catechesis Religious Program—Tel: 508-673-1055. Students 239.

8—HOLY CROSS (1916) (Polish), Merged with SS. Peter & Paul, Fall River.

9—HOLY NAME (1923) 709 Hanover St., 02720. Tel: 508-679-6732; Email: office@holynamefr.com. Very Rev. Jay T. Maddock, J.C.L., V.F.; Rev. Daniel Nunes, Parochial Vicar.
School—Holy Name School, (Grades PreK-8), 850 Pearce St., 02720. Tel: 508-674-9131; Fax: 508-679-0571; Email: pwardell@hnsfr.org; Web: www.hnsfr.org. Dr. Patricia M. Wardell, Prin. - Elementary. Lay Teachers 16; Students 212.
Catechesis Religious Program—Tel: 508-678-7532; Email: faithformation@holynamefr.com. Mr. Patrick McNabb, D.R.E. Students 211.

10—HOLY TRINITY (2000) 951 Stafford Rd., 02721. Tel: 508-672-3200; Fax: 508-673-5518; Email: holytrinityparish@comcast.net; Web: www.holytrinityfallriver.com. Rev. Bruce M. Neylon.
School—Holy Trinity School, (Grades PreK-8), 64 Lamphor St., 02721. Tel: 508-673-6772; Fax: 508-730-1864; Email: bgagnon@htfr.dfrcs.org; Web: www.holytrinityfallriver.com. Mrs. Brenda Gagnon, Prin. - Elementary. Lay Teachers 15; Students 274.
Catechesis Religious Program—Carolyn Boff, D.R.E.; Dorothy Mahoney-Pacheco, D.R.E. Students 85.

11—ST. JEAN BAPTISTE (1901) Merged with St. Elizabeth and St. William to form Holy Trinity Parish.

12—ST. JOSEPH (1873) Rev. Jay Mello. Res.: 1335 N. Main St., 02720. Tel: 508-673-1123; Fax: 508-673-7230; Email: stjosephsfallriver@gmail.com; Web: www.stjosephachurchfr.com.
Catechesis Religious Program—Tel: 508-567-3638. Ms. Jean Revil, Catechetical Leader; Ms. Lisa Ouellette, Catechetical Leader; Mrs. Ana Mello, Catechetical Leader. Students 259.

13—ST. LOUIS (1885) Closed. Sacramental records can be found at St. Mary's Cathedral.

14—ST. MATHIEU (1887) Closed. For inquiries for parish records, please see St. Anne Parish, Fall River.

15—ST. MICHAEL (1902) (Portuguese) Rev. Jay Mello. Res.: 189 Essex St., 02720. Tel: 508-672-6713; Fax: 508-673-7230; Email: stmichaelsfallriver@gmail.com; Web: www.smpfr.org/.
School—St. Michael School, (Grades PreK-8), 209 Essex St., 02720. Tel: 508-678-0266; Fax: 508-324-4433; Email: pleary@smsfr.dfrcs.org. Pamela Leary, Elementary Prin. Lay Teachers 18; Students 184.
Catechesis Religious Program—Tel: 508-567-3638. Ms. Lisa Ouellette, Catechetical Leader; Ms. Jean Revil, Catechetical Leader; Mrs. Ana Mello, Catechetical Leader. Students 259.

16—NOTRE DAME DE LOURDES (1874) (French), Closed. For inquiries for parish records please contact Saint Bernadette Parish, Fall River.

17—OUR LADY OF HEALTH (1924) (Portuguese), Closed. For inquiries for parish records, please see Espirito Santo Parish, Fall River.

18—OUR LADY OF THE ANGELS (1915) (Portuguese), Merged with Blessed Sacrament and St. Patrick's, Fall River to form the Parish of the Good Shepherd, Fall River.

19—OUR LADY OF THE HOLY ROSARY (1904) (Italian), Closed. For inquiries for parish records contact Cathedral of St. Mary of the Assumption, Fall River.

20—OUR LADY OF THE IMMACULATE CONCEPTION (1882) Closed. For inquiries for parish records please contact Saint Bernadette Parish, Fall River.

21—PARISH OF THE GOOD SHEPHERD (2002) 1598 S. Main St., 02724-2586. Tel: 508-678-7412; Fax: 508-678-7405; Email: gsfallriver@gmail.com; Email: frtomw@gmail.com; Web: www.gsfallriver.com. Very Rev. Thomas Washburn, O.F.M., Admin.; Revs. Juan Carlos Munoz, Parochial Vicar; Leonard Kayondo, In Res.; Deacon Timothy E. Flaherty.
Catechesis Religious Program—Tel: 401-662-7694. Students 137.

22—ST. PATRICK'S (1873) Merged with Blessed Sacrament and Our Lady of the Angels, Fall River to form the Parish of the Good Shepherd, Fall River.

23—SS. PETER AND PAUL (1882) Closed. For inquiries for parish records, please contact Cathedral of St. Mary of the Assumption Parish, Fall River.

24—ST. ROCH (1899) Closed. For inquiries for parish records, please see St. Bernadette Parish, Fall River.

25—SACRED HEART (1872) Closed. For inquiries for parish records, please contact Cathedral of St. Mary of the Assumption, Fall River.

26—SANTO CHRISTO (1892) (Portuguese) Revs. Gastao A. Oliveira, (Retired); Thomas M. Kocik, Parochial Vicar; Jason Brilhante, In Res. Res.: 185 Canal St., 02721. Tel: 508-676-1184; Fax: 508-676-9701; Email: scp1892@yahoo.com; Web: www.santochristo.com.
Catechesis Religious Program—Tel: 508-675-3007. Mr. Osvaldo Pacheco, Catechetical Leader. Students 240.

27—ST. STANISLAUS (1898) (Polish) 36 Rockland St., P.O. Box 300, 02724. Tel: 508-678-7412; Fax: 508-678-7405; Email: frtomw@gmail.com; Web: saintstanislausfr.com. Very Rev. Thomas Washburn, O.F.M., Admin.; Rev. Juan Carlos Munoz, Parochial Vicar; Deacon Timothy E. Flaherty; Rev. Leonard Kayondo, In Res.
School—St. Stanislaus School, (Grades PreK-8), 37 Rockland St., P.O. Box 300, 02724. Tel: 508-674-6771 ; Fax: 508-677-1622; Email: jwillis@saintstanislaus.com; Web: www.saintstanislaus.com. Ms. Jean Willis, Prin. (Elementary). Lay Teachers 16; Students 185.
Catechesis Religious Program—Tel: 401-662-7694. Ms. Eileen Hadfield, Catechetical Leader; Mr. Daniel Seseske, Catechetical Leader. Students 27.

28—ST. WILLIAM'S (1905) Merged with St. Elizabeth and St. Jean Baptiste to form Holy Trinity Parish.

OUTSIDE THE CITY OF FALL RIVER

ACUSHNET, BRISTOL CO., ST. FRANCIS XAVIER'S (1915) 125 Main St., Acushnet, 02743. Tel: 508-995-7600; Email: info@sfxparish.com. Rev. Riley J. Williams, Admin.; Deacon David B. Pepin; Mr. Steven N. Guillotte, Pastoral Assoc.
School—St. Francis Xavier School, (Grades PreK-8), 223 Main St., Acushnet, 02743. Tel: 508-995-4313; Fax: 508-995-0456; Email: info@sfxacushnet.com; Web: www.sfxacushnet.com. Ms. Michelle Russo, Prin. (Elementary). Lay Teachers 14; Students 266.
Catechesis Religious Program—Janine Hammarquist, Catechetical Leader. Students 99.

ASSONET, BRISTOL CO., ST. BERNARD'S (1938) Rev. Michael S. Racine; Deacons Paul R. Levesque; Jesse L. Martins. Res.: 32 S. Main St., P.O. Box 370, Assonet, 02702. Tel: 508-644-5585; Fax: 508-644-2136; Email: stbernardassonetrectory@comcastbiz.net; Web: www.stbernardassonet.org.
Catechesis Religious Program—Tel: 508-644-2032. Ms. Marlene Correia, Catechetical Leader; Mr. Brian Correia, Catechetical Leader. Students 465.

ATTLEBORO, BRISTOL CO.

1—HOLY GHOST (1921) Closed. For inquiries for parish records, please contact Saint Vincent de Paul Parish, Attleboro.

2—ST. JOHN THE EVANGELIST (1883) 1 St. John Pl., Attleboro, 02703-2249. Tel: 508-222-1206; Fax: 508-226-6461; Email: office@sje-church.org; Web: www.sje-church.org. Revs. Christopher M. Peschel, Admin.; German Correa Agudelo, Parochial Vicar; Deacon Adelbert F. Malloy.
School—St. John the Evangelist School, (Grades PreK-8), 13 Hodges St., Attleboro, 02703. Tel: 508-222-5062; Fax: 508-223-1737; Email: mholden@sje-school.com; Web: www.sje-school.com. Sr. Mary Holden, C.P., Prin. (Elementary). Participating Parishes: O.L. Queen of Martyrs, Seekonk; St. Theresa's, South Attleboro; St. Mary's, Mansfield, Norton, Wrentham & North Attleboro; Sacred Heart, North Attleboro; St. Vincent de Paul, Attleboro Lay Teachers 23; Students 266; Religious Teachers 2.
Catechesis Religious Program—Tel: 508-222-0707; Fax: 508-222-0701. Margaret Keenan, Catechetical Leader. Students 613.

3—ST. JOSEPH'S (1905) Closed. For inquiries for parish records, please contact Saint Vincent de Paul Parish, Attleboro.

4—ST. STEPHEN'S (1875) [CEM] Closed. For inquiries for parish records contact Our Lady Queen of Martyrs Parish, Seekonk.

5—ST. THERESA OF THE CHILD JESUS (1925) Rev. Jon-Paul Gallant, S.L.L.; Deacon Wilfred R. Varieur; Mr. George Creighton, Music Director. Res.: 18 Baltic St., Attleboro, 02703. Tel: 508-761-8111; Fax: 508-761-5475; Email: sttcj@aol.com; Web: www.sainttheresaattleboro.org.
Catechesis Religious Program—Tel: 508-761-5367. Ms. Wendy Smith, Catechetical Leader. Students 199.

6—SAINT VINCENT DE PAUL PARISH 71 Linden St., Attleboro, 02703. Tel: 508-226-1115; Fax: 888-239-9322; Email: saintvincentdpattleboro@gmail.com; Web: www.stvincent-attleboro.org. Revs. Christopher M. Peschel, Admin.; German Correa Agudelo, Parochial Vicar; Deacons Paul M. Fournier; Anthony A. Cipriano.
Catechesis Religious Program—Tel: 508-222-6756. Charlotte Santos, D.R.E. Students 115.

ATTLEBORO FALLS, BRISTOL CO., ST. MARK'S (1967) 105 Stanley St., Attleboro Falls, 02763-0240. Tel: 508-695-6161; Fax: 508-695-5248; Email: stmaryna@noozi.com; Web: www.stmarks-attleborofalls.org. 14 Park St., North Attleboro, 02760. Revs. David A. Costa; John M. Schrader, Parochial Vicar; Sr. Kathleen Corrigan, S.U.S.C., Pastoral Assoc.; Deacon Joseph E. Regali.
Catechesis Religious Program—Tel: 508-695-7773. Ms. Elaine Corvese, Catechetical Leader. Students 452.

BREWSTER, BARNSTABLE CO., OUR LADY OF THE CAPE (1961) 468 Stony Brook Rd., Brewster, 02631-7799. Tel: 508-385-3252; Fax: 508-385-6864; Email: ourladyofthecapebrewster@gmail.com; Web: www.ourladyofthecape.org. P.O. Box 1799, Brewster, 02631. Revs. William Kaliyadan, M.S.; John R. Dolan, M.S., Parochial Vicar; Raymond Vaillancourt, M.S., In Res., (Retired).
Catechesis Religious Program—Mrs. Priscilla Silva, Catechetical Leader; Ms. Kathleen Russo, Catechetical Leader. Students 252.
Mission—Immaculate Conception, 2580 Main St., Rte. 6A, Brewster, Barnstable Co. 02631.

BUZZARDS BAY, BARNSTABLE CO., ST. MARGARET (1915) [JC] Very Rev. Thomas Washburn, O.F.M.; Deacon Ralph J. Guerra. Res.: 141 Main St., Buzzards Bay, 02532. Tel: 508-759-7777; Fax: 508-759-4797; Email: sacristy1@comcast.net; Web: www.stmargaretbbay.org.
School—St. Margaret Regional School, (Grades PreK-8), 143 Main St., Buzzards Bay, 02532. Tel: 508-759-2213; Fax: 508-759-8776; Email: gmilot@smrs.dfrcs.org; Web: www.smrsbb.org. Dr. George A. Milot, Prin. Lay Teachers 14; Students 135; Total Staff 14.
Catechesis Religious Program—Students 82.
Mission—St. Mary Star of the Sea, Onset Bay Ln., Onset, Plymouth Co. 02558.

CENTERVILLE, BARNSTABLE CO., OUR LADY OF VICTORY (1957) 230 S. Main St., Centerville, 02632. Tel: 508-775-5744; Fax: 508-771-1614; Web: www.olvparish.org. Revs. John J. Perry; Matthew Gill, Parochial Vicar; Deacons James M. Barrett; Theodore E. Lukac.
Catechesis Religious Program— Tel: 508-775-5744, Ext. 119; Web: www.olvgift.com. Mr. William Bussiere, Catechetical Leader. Students 416.
Mission—Our Lady of Hope.

CHATHAM, BARNSTABLE CO., HOLY REDEEMER (1955) [JC] 57 Highland Ave., Chatham, 02633. Tel: 508-945-0677; Fax: 508-945-3186; Email: parish@holyredeemerchatham.org. Rev. John M. Sullivan; Deacons Joseph F. Mador; Richard S. Stenberg.
Catechesis Religious Program—Ms. Bethel Norcross, D.R.E.; Mr. Howard Whelden, Business Mgr. Students 45.
Mission—Our Lady of Grace, 60 Meetinghouse Rd. Rte. 137, South Chatham, 02659.

DIGHTON, BRISTOL CO., ST. PETER'S (1904) Closed. For inquiries for parish records contact St. Nicholas of Myra Parish, North Dighton.

EAST FALMOUTH, BARNSTABLE CO., ST. ANTHONY'S (1923) [CEM] Rev. Msgr. Stephen J. Avila, V.F.
Res.: 167 E. Falmouth Hwy., East Falmouth, 02536.
Tel: 508-548-0108; Fax: 508-457-1723; Email: stanthony31@comcast.net; Web: www.stanthonyscapecod.org.
Catechesis Religious Program—Tel: 508-548-3515. Mr. Jonathan Galo, Catechetical Leader. Students 224.

EAST FREETOWN, BRISTOL CO., ST. JOHN NEUMANN (1984)
157 Middleboro Rd., East Freetown, 02717.
Tel: 508-763-2240; Email: contact@sjnfreetown.org; Web: www.sjnfreetown.org. P.O. Box 718, East Freetown, 02717. Very Rev. Gregory A. Mathias, V.G.; Deacon Bruce J. Bonneau.
Catechesis Religious Program—Tel: 508-763-8122. Michelle D'Ordine, D.R.E. Students 419.

EAST SANDWICH, BARNSTABLE CO., CORPUS CHRISTI (1830) [CEM]
324 Quaker Meetinghouse Rd., East Sandwich, 02537-1327. Revs. George E. Harrison; Andrew Johnson, Parochial Vicar; Deacons Arthur LaChance; Dennis O'Connell.
Catechesis Religious Program—George Hults, D.R.E.; Jennifer Cho, D.R.E. Students 537.
Mission—St. Theresa Chapel, Sagamore, Barnstable Co.. Closed.

EAST TAUNTON, BRISTOL CO., HOLY FAMILY (1900)
370 Middleboro Ave., P.O. Box 619, East Taunton, 02718. Tel: 508-824-5707; Fax: 508-822-2915; Email: secretary@holyfamilytaunton.org; Web: hfparish.net. Rev. Richard D. Wilson, J.C.L.; Deacons Robert M. Craig; John J. Fitzpatrick.
Catechesis Religious Program—Ms. Karen Coughlin, Catechetical Leader. Students 279.

EDGARTOWN, DUKES CO., ST. ELIZABETH (1925) Closed. For inquiries for parish records contact Good Shepherd Parish, Oak Bluffs.

FAIRHAVEN, BRISTOL CO.
1—ST. JOSEPH'S (1905)
74 Spring St., Fairhaven, 02719. Rev. Stephen Banjare, SS.CC.; Deacons Douglas Medeiros; Robert Lorenzo.
School—St. Joseph School, (Grades PreK-8), 100 Spring St., Fairhaven, 02719. Tel: 508-996-1983; Fax: 508-996-1998; Email: secretary@stjosephparish.comcastbiz.net; Web: www.saintjosephschool.org. Ms. Faith Piazza, Prin. Elementary. Lay Teachers 11; Students 180; Total Staff 11.
Catechesis Religious Program—Tel: 508-264-4145. Mrs. Cherilyn Courville, Catechetical Leader. Students 186.
2—ST. MARY'S (1933) Rev. David Lupo, SS.CC.
Res.: 41 Harding Rd., Fairhaven, 02719.
Tel: 508-992-0685; Fax: 508-992-0685; Email: stmarysfairhaven@comcast.net; Web: www.sscc.org/stmaryfhvn.
Catechesis Religious Program—Tel: 508-992-8721. Sr. Eleanor Marie Cyr, SS.CC., Catechetical Leader. Students 245.
3—SACRED HEARTS (1907) Closed. For inquiries for parish records, please see St. Mary Parish, Fairhaven.

FALMOUTH, BARNSTABLE CO., ST. PATRICK'S (1928) [CEM] Rev. Timothy J. Goldrick; Deacons John E. Simonis; William W. Hays.
Res.: 511 Main St., P.O. Box 569, Falmouth, 02541.
Tel: 508-548-1065; Fax: 508-495-0875; Email: stpatrick80@gmail.com; Web: www.stpatrickfalmouth.org.
Catechesis Religious Program—Students 96.
Chapel—St. Thomas, Falmouth Heights Rd., Falmouth, 02540.

HYANNIS, BARNSTABLE CO., ST. FRANCIS XAVIER'S (1904) [CEM 2] Revs. Michael J. Fitzpatrick, Parochial Admin.; Ronnie P. Floyd, In Res.; Edivar daSilva Ribeiro, In Res.; Deacons David Boucher; Bruce J. Baxter.
Res.: 21 Cross St., Hyannis, 02601.
Tel: 508-775-0818; Fax: 508-771-5940; Email: stfrancis@stfrancishyannis.org; Web: stfrancishyannis.org.
Church: 347 South St., Hyannis, 02601.
School—St. Francis Xavier Preparatory School, 120 High School Rd., Hyannis, 02601. Tel: 508-862-6336; Fax: 508-862-6339; Email: ckeavy@pjp2hs.org; Web: www.pjp2hs.org. Christopher W. Keavy, Headmaster; Mrs. Elizabeth Kelley, Prin. Elementary; Rev. Ronnie P. Floyd, Chap.
Catechesis Religious Program—Mrs. Mary Crofford, Catechetical Leader. Students 85.
Mission—Sacred Heart Chapel, 32 Summer St., Yarmouth Port, Barnstable Co. 02675.

MANSFIELD, BRISTOL CO., ST. MARY'S (1894) [CEM]
330 Pratt St., Mansfield, 02048-1581.
Tel: 508-339-2981; Fax: 508-339-0612; Email: office@stmarymansschool.org; Web: www.stmarymans.org. Rev. Michael K. McManus; Deacon Thomas P. Palanza.
School—St. Mary Catholic School, (Grades PreK-8), Tel: 508-339-4800; Fax: 508-337-2063; Email: info@stmarymansschool.org; Web: www.stmarymansschool.org. Mr. Matthew Bourque, Prin. Lay Teachers 17; Students 174; Religious Teachers 2.
Catechesis Religious Program—Tel: 508-339-4800. Kristin Kreckler, Catechetical Leader; Carole Rush, Catechetical Leader; Carleen Nathan, Catechetical Leader. Students 1,233.

MARION, PLYMOUTH CO., ST. RITA'S (1972)
113 Front St., P.O. Box 902, Marion, 02738.
Tel: 508-748-1497; Fax: 508-748-0604; Email: stritamarion@comcast.net. Rev. John C. Ozug.
Res.: 113 Front St., P.O. Box 902, Marion, 02738.
Tel: 508-748-1497; Fax: 508-748-0604; Email: stritamarion@comcast.net; Web: www.stanthonystrita.com.
Catechesis Religious Program—Students 133.

MASHPEE, BARNSTABLE CO., CHRIST THE KING (1984)
5 Jobs Fishing Rd., Mashpee, 02649.
Tel: 508-477-7700; Fax: 508-477-8158; Email: office@christthekingparish.com; Email: pastor@christthekingparish.com; Web: www.christthekingparish.com. P.O. Box 1800, Mashpee, 02649. Rev. Edward J. Healey; Deacons Frank D. Fantasia; Robert D. Lemay; David E. Pierce; Paul J. Harney.
Catechesis Religious Program—
Tel: 508-477-7700, Ext. 21. Ms. Kathleen Laird, Catechetical Leader. Students 210.

MATTAPOISETT, PLYMOUTH CO., ST. ANTHONY'S (1908) [CEM] Rev. John C. Ozug.
Res.: 22 Barstow St., Mattapoisett, 02739.
Tel: 508-758-3719; Fax: 508-758-3019; Email: office@stanthony.comcastbiz.net; Web: www.stanthonystrita.com.
Catechesis Religious Program—Ms. Mary Chaplain, Catechetical Leader. Students 248.

NANTUCKET, NANTUCKET CO., ST. MARY'S, OUR LADY OF THE ISLE (1903) [CEM]
3 Federal St., Nantucket, 02554-1168.
Tel: 508-228-0100; Email: stmarys@stmarysnantucket.org. P.O. Box 1168, Nantucket, 02554-1168. Rev. John P. Kelleher, O.S.B.; Mrs. Judy DeBaggis, Youth Min.
Catechesis Religious Program—Tel: 508-228-4852. Mrs. Heidi E. Meadows, D.R.E. Students 272.

NEW BEDFORD, BRISTOL CO.
1—ST. ANNE (1908) (French), Closed. For inquiries for parish records contact Our Lady of Guadalupe Parish, New Bedford.
2—ST. ANTHONY OF PADUA'S (1895) (French)
1359 Acushnet Ave., New Bedford, 02746.
Tel: 508-993-1691; Email: office@saintanthonynewbedford.com. Revs. Octavio Cortez, I.V.E.; Brendan A. O'Rourke, I.V.E.; Deacons Eduardo M. Borges; Leo W. Racine.
Catechesis Religious Program—Mrs. Monique Marshall, D.R.E. Students 178.
3—ST. BONIFACE (1906) Closed. For inquiries for parish records, please see Holy Name of the Sacred Heart of Jesus Parish, New Bedford.
4—ST. CASIMIR (1927) (Polish), Closed. For inquiries for parish records, please see Our Lady of Perpetual Help, New Bedford.
5—ST. FRANCIS OF ASSISI (1928) (Italian)
247 North St., New Bedford, 02740.
Tel: 508-997-7732; Fax: 508-991-6630; Email: sfanb247@gmail.com; Web: www.sfanb.org. Rev. Kevin J. Harrington.
Catechesis Religious Program—Mrs. Jackie Smith, Catechetical Leader.
6—ST. HEDWIG, Closed. For inquiries for Parish records, please contact Our Lady of Guadalupe, New Bedford.
7—HOLY NAME, Merged with Sacred Heart, New Bedford to form Holy Name of the Sacred Heart of Jesus, New Bedford.
8—HOLY NAME OF THE SACRED HEART OF JESUS (1999)
121 Mt. Pleasant St., New Bedford, 02740.
Tel: 508-992-3184; Fax: 508-984-3406; Email: holynamesacredheartparish@comcast.net. Rev. Robert A. Oliveira; Deacon Eugene E. Sasseville.
Catechesis Religious Program—Tel: 508-996-8654. Mr. Theodore Machado, Catechetical Leader. Students 89.
9—ST. HYACINTH (1890) Closed. For inquiries for parish records, please see Our Lady of Guadalupe Parish, New Bedford.
10—ST. JAMES (1888) Closed. For inquiries for parish records contact Our Lady of Guadalupe Parish, New Bedford.
11—ST. JOHN THE BAPTIST (1871) (Portuguese), Closed. For inquiries for parish records, please contact Our Lady of Mount Carmel, New Bedford.
12—ST. JOSEPH (1910) Merged with St. Theresa, New Bedford to form St. Joseph-St. Therese, New Bedford.
13—ST. JOSEPH-ST. THERESE (1999)
51 Duncan St., New Bedford, 02745-6108.
Tel: 508-995-5235; Fax: 508-995-7266; Email: stjosstthere se@aol.com; Web: www.stjosstthere se@aol.com. Rev. Philip N. Hamel.
Catechesis Religious Program—Students 100.
14—ST. KILIAN (1896) Closed. For inquiries for parish records, please contact St. Anthony of Padua Parish, New Bedford.
15—ST. LAWRENCE MARTYR (1821)
110 Summer St., New Bedford, 02740.
Tel: 508-997-7732; Fax: 508-991-6630; Email: sfanb247@gmail.com; Web: www.sfanb.org. Rev. Robert J. Powell, (Retired); Deacon Maurice A. Ouellette.
School—Holy Family-Holy Name School, (Grades PreK-8), Participating parishes: St. Lawrence, Holy Name of the Sacred Heart of Jesus, New Bedford 91 Summer St., New Bedford, 02740. Tel: 508-993-3547; Fax: 508-993-8277; Email: stloffice@saintlawrencemartyr.com; Web: www.hfhn.org. Ms. Cecilia M. Felix, Prin. - Elementary. Lay Teachers 13; Sisters 1; Students 279; Total Staff 14; Religious Teachers 1.
Catechesis Religious Program—Tel: 508-993-3547. Ms. Teresa Ouellette, Catechetical Leader. Students 64.
16—ST. MARY'S (1927)
343 Tarkiln Hill Rd., New Bedford, 02745.
Tel: 508-995-3593; Fax: 508-995-2453; Email: stmarysnb@stmarysnb.com; Web: stmarysnb.com. 106 Illinois St., New Bedford, 02745. Very Rev. Daniel W. Lacroix, V.F.
School—All Saints Catholic School, (Grades PreK-8), 115 Illinois St., New Bedford, 02745.
Tel: 508-995-3593; Fax: 508-995-0840; Web: www.ascsnb.org. Mrs. Susan Massoud, Prin. - Elementary. Lay Teachers 11; Students 300; Total Staff 11.
Catechesis Religious Program—David Beaulieu, Catechetical Leader. Students 154.
17—NUESTRA SENORA DE GUADALUPE (1993) (Hispanic), Closed. For inquiries for parish records contact Our Lady of Guadalupe Parish, New Bedford.
18—OUR LADY OF FATIMA (1966)
4256 Acushnet Ave., New Bedford, 02745.
Tel: 508-995-7351; Email: olofnb@comcast.net. Rev. John A. Raposo.
Catechesis Religious Program—Mrs. Pearl Enos, D.R.E. Students 165.
19—OUR LADY OF GUADALUPE (2004)
233 County St., New Bedford, 02740-4717.
Tel: 508-992-9408; Fax: 508-990-0575; Email: guadalupenewbedford@gmail.com; Web: www.GuadalulpeNewBedford.com. Rev. Craig A. Pregana.
School—St. James-St. John, (Grades PreK-8), 180 Orchard St., New Bedford, 02740. Tel: 508-996-0534; Fax: 508-717-6969; Email: principal@sjsjschool.com; Web: www.sjsjschool.com. Mrs. Cristina Raposo, Prin. Lay Teachers 11; Priests 2; Students 214; Total Staff 13; Religious Teachers 2.
20—OUR LADY OF MT. CARMEL (1902) (Portuguese)
230 Bonney St., New Bedford, 02744.
Tel: 508-993-4704; Email: olmcnb@comcast.net; Web: www.olmcnb.com. Rev. John J. Oliveira; Deacons Paul J. Macedo; Abilio Pires.
Catechesis Religious Program—Tel: 508-984-7097. Ms. Nancy Morin, Catechetical Leader. Students 388.
21—OUR LADY OF PERPETUAL HELP (1905) (Polish) Rev. Conrad Salach, O.F.M.Conv.
Res.: 235 N. Front St., New Bedford, 02746.
Tel: 508-992-9378; Fax: 508-993-4881; Email: olphrectorynb@gmail.com; Web: www.olphchurchnb.org.
Catechesis Religious Program—
22—OUR LADY OF THE ASSUMPTION (1905) (Cape Verdean)
Mailing Address: 47 S. 6th St., New Bedford, 02740.
Tel: 508-994-7602 Parish Center; Fax: 508-994-9461; Email: oloaoffice@verizon.net. Revs. Sudhir Christodas Nayak, SS.CC.; Alphonsus McHugh, SS.CC., In Res.
Res. & Parish Center: 54 S. 6th St., New Bedford, 02740.
Catechesis Religious Program—Maria Grace, D.R.E. Students 103.
23—OUR LADY OF THE HOLY ROSARY (1908) Closed. For inquiries for parish records, please see St. Anthony of Padua Parish, New Bedford.
24—OUR LADY OF THE IMMACULATE CONCEPTION (1909) (Portuguese)
136 Earle St., New Bedford, 02746.
Tel: 508-992-9892; Fax: 508-992-9907; Email: i.conception@comcast.net. Rev. Daniel O. Reis; Deacons Albertino F. Pires; Eduardo M. Borges. Portuguese Mass
Catechesis Religious Program—Tel: 508-990-0249. Delia Silva Guilherme, D.R.E.
25—SACRED HEART (1874) (French), Merged With Holy

Name, New Bedford to form Holy Name of the Sacred Heart of Jesus, New Bedford.
26—St. Theresa (1926) (French), Merged with St. Joseph's, New Bedford to form St. Joseph-St. Therese, New Bedford.
North Attleboro, Bristol Co.
1—St. Mary of the Immaculate Conception (1890) [CEM]
14 Park St., North Attleboro, 02760.
Tel: 508-695-6161; Fax: 508-695-5248; Email: stmaryna@noozi.com; Web: www.saintmaryna.com. Revs. David A. Costa; John M. Schrader, Parochial Vicar; Sr. Kathleen Corrigan, S.U.S.C., Pastoral Assoc.; Deacon Joseph E. Regali.
See St. Mary's-Sacred Heart Consolidated School, North Attleboro under Sacred Heart, North Attleboro details.
Catechesis Religious Program—Ms. Elaine Corvese, D.R.E.; Mrs. Linda Nolan, Confirmation. Students 388.
2—Sacred Heart (1904)
58 Church St., North Attleboro, 02760.
Tel: 508-695-6161; Email: stmaryna@noozi.com; Web: www.shna.org. 14 Park St., North Attleboro, 02760. Revs. David A. Costa; John M. Schrader, Parochial Vicar; Deacon Joseph E. Regali; Sr. Kathleen Corrigan, S.U.S.C., Pastoral Assoc.
School—St. Mary-Sacred Heart School, (Grades PreK-8), 57 Richards Ave., North Attleboro, 02760.
Tel: 508-695-3072; Fax: 508-695-9074; Email: smshna@smshna.dfr.org; Web: www.smshna.com. Mrs. Charlotte Lourenco, Prin. Participating parishes: St. Mary, North Attleboro; Sacred Heart, North Attleboro; St. Mark, Attleboro Falls Lay Teachers 21; Students 268; Total Staff 21.
Catechesis Religious Program—Ms. Elaine Corvese, D.R.E.; Mrs. Linda Nolan, Confirmation. Students 309.
North Dartmouth, Bristol Co., St. Julie Billiart (1969)
494 Slocum Rd., North Dartmouth, 02747.
Tel: 508-993-2351; Fax: 508-993-2437; Email: teri@saintjulies.org; Web: www.saintjulies.org. Rev. Richard M. Roy; Ms. Paula Raposo, Pastoral Assoc.
Catechesis Religious Program—Tel: 508-990-0287. Mr. Joseph Martino, Catechetical Leader; Ms. Kathy Kosinski, Catechetical Leader. Students 440.
North Dighton, Bristol Co.
1—St. Joseph's (1913) [JC2] Closed. For inquiries for parish records contact St. Nicholas of Myra Parish, North Dighton.
2—St. Nicholas of Myra Parish (2008)
Mailing Address: 499 Spring St., P.O. Box 564, North Dighton, 02764. Tel: 508-822-1425;
Fax: 508-822-3886; Email: st.nicholasofmyra@comcast.net; Web: saintnicholasofmyra.org. Rev. Paul C. Fedak.
Res.: 2039 County St., Dighton, 02715.
Catechesis Religious Program—Tel: 508-824-6581. Ms. Sandra Cabral, Catechetical Leader. Students 336.
North Easton, Bristol Co., Immaculate Conception (1871) [CEM]
193 Main St., North Easton, 02356.
Tel: 508-238-3232; Tel: 508-238-3230;
Fax: 508-238-7849; Email: rectory@icceaston.org; Email: music@icceaston.org; Email: pastor@icceaston.org; Web: www.icceaston.org. Very Rev. Richard E. Degagne, V.F.; Deacon Gary A. Porter.
Catechesis Religious Program—Email: religioused@icceaston.org. Ms. Elide Rodrigues, D.R.E. Students 399.
North Falmouth, Barnstable Co., St. Elizabeth Seton (1977)
481 Quaker Rd., P.O. Box 861, North Falmouth, 02556. Rev. Arnold R. Medeiros; Deacon Peter M. Guresh.
Catechesis Religious Program—Mrs. Lori Marquez, D.R.E.; Mr. Jack Goulet, Catechetical Leader. Students 96.
Chapel—Chapel of St. Joseph, 33 Millfield St., Woods Hole, 02543.
Norton, Bristol Co., St. Mary's (1925)
1 Power St., Norton, 02766-0430. Tel: 508-285-6642; Fax: 508-285-5589; Email: secretary@stmarysnorton.com; Web: www.stmarysnorton.com. Very Rev. Timothy P. Reis, V.F.; Deacon Alan J. Thadeu.
Res.: 133 S. Worcester St., Norton, 02766-0430.
Catechesis Religious Program—Ms. Laura Vergow, D.R.E.; Ms. Judy Burgess, Catechetical Leader. Students 609.
Oak Bluffs, Dukes Co., Sacred Heart (1880) [CEM] Closed. For inquiries for parish records contact Good Shepherd Parish, Oak Bluffs.
Orleans, Barnstable Co., St. Joan of Arc (1947)
61 Canal Rd., Orleans, 02653. Tel: 508-255-0170; Fax: 508-240-6741; Email: joanarc@c4.net; Web: www.joanarc.org. Rev. William M. Rodrigues; Deacons Norman McEnaney; John Twerago.
Catechesis Religious Program—Ms. Judy Burt-Walker, Catechetical Leader. Students 110.
Osterville, Barnstable Co., Our Lady of the Assumption (1928)
76 Wianno Ave., Osterville, 02655. Tel: 508-428-2011 ; Fax: 508-428-0154; Email: office@assumption-capecod.org; Web: www.assumption-capecod.org. Revs. John J. Perry; Matthew Gill, Parochial Vicar; Deacons James M. Barrett; Theodore E. Lukac.
Church: 86 Wianno Ave., P.O. Box E, Osterville, 02655.
Pocasset, Barnstable Co., St. John the Evangelist (1969)
841 Shore Dr., Pocasset, 02559. Tel: 508-563-5887; Fax: 508-445-6464; Email: patty@sjeparish.com; Web: www.stjohnspocasset.org. P.O. Box 1558, Pocasset, 02559. Rev. Thomas A. Frechette; Deacons Brendan W. Brides; John J. Burkly; John Brennan, Music Min.
Res.: 15 Virginia Rd., P.O. Box 1558, Pocasset, 02559.
Catechesis Religious Program—Mrs. Deborah Boucher, Catechetical Leader; Mrs. Crystal Rogerson, Catechetical Leader. Students 182.
Provincetown, Barnstable Co., St. Peter the Apostle (1874) [CEM] Rev. Hugh J. McCullough; Deacon Chester Cook.
Res.: 11 Prince St., Provincetown, 02657.
Tel: 508-487-0095; Fax: 508-487-2564; Email: stpeterspto wn@aol.com; Web: www.stpeters-ptown.org.
Catechesis Religious Program—Ms. Bethany Edwards, Catechetical Leader. Students 31.
Raynham Center, Bristol Co., St. Ann (1960)
660 N. Main St., Raynham, 02767. Tel: 508-823-9833 ; Fax: 508-824-1090; Email: office@stannsraynham.org; Web: www.stannsraynham.org. P.O. Box 247, Raynham Center, 02768. Rev. John M. Murray; Deacon Joseph A. McGinley.
Catechesis Religious Program—725 N. Main St., P.O. Box 247, Raynham Center, 02768. Tel: 508-824-9021; Email: religioused@stannsraynham.org. Mrs. Jennifer Murphy, D.R.E. Students 708.
Seekonk, Bristol Co.
1—St. Mary's (1906) Closed. For inquiries for parish records contact Our Lady Queen of Martyrs Parish, Seekonk.
2—Our Lady of Mt. Carmel (1922)
984 Taunton Ave., Seekonk, 02771.
Tel: 508-336-5549; Fax: 508-336-9010; Email: office@olmcseekonk.org. P.O. Box 519, Seekonk, 02771. Rev. Kevin A. Cook.
Catechesis Religious Program—1040 Taunton Ave., Seekonk, 2771. Tel: 508-336-9015; Email: m.brawley.olmc@gmail.com; Email: c.gregorek.olmc@gmail.com. Mrs. Christine Gregorek, Catechetical Leader; Mrs. Maureen Brawley, Catechetical Leader. Students 417.
3—Our Lady Queen of Martyrs, [JC]
385 Central Ave., Seekonk, 02771. Tel: 508-399-8440 ; Fax: 508-399-7398; Email: olqmseekonk@comcast.net; Web: www.olqmseekonk.org. Rev. Raymond Cambra Jr.; Deacon Thomas J. McMahon; Ms. Rose Parenteau, Pastoral Assoc.
Catechesis Religious Program—Tel: 508-399-7534. Cynthia Gamache, D.R.E.; Eric Queenan, D.R.E. Students 209.
Somerset, Bristol Co.
1—St. John of God (1928) [CEM] (Portuguese)
996 Brayton Ave., Somerset, 02726.
Tel: 508-678-5513; Fax: 508-678-6458; Email: office@sjogsomerset.org; Web: www.sjogsomerset.org. Rev. Jason Brilhante, Admin.; Deacon Robert A. Faria.
Catechesis Religious Program—1036 Brayton Ave., Somerset, 02726. Tel: 774-955-0586;
Fax: 508-978-6458. Ms. Deborah Jesak, Catechetical Leader; Debra Vieira, Catechetical Leader. Students 261.
2—St. Patrick's (1883) [CEM] Rev. Paul Bernier; Deacon Edward Hussey.
Res.: 306 South St., Somerset, 02726-5617.
Tel: 508-672-1523; Fax: 508-675-5787; Email: stpatparish@comcast.net; Web: www.stpatricksomerset.com.
Catechesis Religious Program—Tel: 508-675-1073. Ms. Christine Matton, Catechetical Leader; Michele Oehmen, Catechetical Leader. Students 183.
3—St. Thomas More (1949)
386 Luther Ave., Somerset, 02726. Tel: 508-673-7831 ; Fax: 508-567-5177; Email: office@stthomasmoresomerset.org; Web: www.stmsomerset.org. Rev. Msgr. Edmund J. Fitzgerald.
Catechesis Religious Program—Rev. Michael Joseph Fitzpatrick, D.R.E. Students 153.
South Dartmouth, Bristol Co., St. Mary's (1930) Rev. Rodney E. Thibault, J.C.L.
Res.: 783 Dartmouth St., South Dartmouth, 02748.
Tel: 508-992-7163; Fax: 508-992-5209; Email: info@stmarysdartmouth.org; Web: www.stmarysdartmouth.org.
Catechesis Religious Program—789 Dartmouth St., South Dartmouth, 02748. Tel: 508-992-7505. Ms. Beni Costa-Reedy, Catechetical Leader. Students 437.
South Easton, Bristol Co., Holy Cross (1967)
225 Purchase St., South Easton, 02375.
Tel: 508-238-2235; Fax: 508-238-0500; Email: info@holycrosseaston.org; Web: www.holycrosseaston.org. Revs. Bradley J. Metz, C.S.C.; James T. Preskenis, C.S.C., Parochial Vicar; Deacon George Zarella; Christopher Iannitelli, Music Min.
Catechesis Religious Program—Ms. Marie Chabot, Catechetical Leader. Students 704.
South Yarmouth, Barnstable Co., St. Pius Tenth (1954)
5 Barbara St., South Yarmouth, 02664.
Tel: 508-398-2248; Fax: 508-398-7233; Email: stpiusxoffice@comcast.net; Web: stpiusxsy.com. Very Rev. Paul A. Caron, V.F.; Rev. Christopher Stanibula, Parochial Vicar; Deacons C. Michael Hickey; William Gallerizzo; Thomas Bailey; David Akin; Richard C. Zeich; Anthony R. Surozenski.
School—St. Pius Tenth School, (Grades PreK-8), 321 Wood Rd., South Yarmouth, 02664.
Tel: 508-398-6112; Fax: 508-398-6113; Email: info@spxschool.org; Web: www.spxschool.org. Mrs. Anne Dailey, Prin. - Elementary. Lay Teachers 18; Students 224; Total Staff 18.
Catechesis Religious Program—Tel: 508-394-0709; Email: stpiusxreled@comcast.net. Ms. Rebecca Gallerizzo, Catechetical Leader. Students 223.
Chapel—Our Lady of the Highway, Rte. 28, South Yarmouth, 02664.
Swansea, Bristol Co.
1—St. Dominic's (1911)
1277 Grand Army Hwy., P.O. Box 205, Swansea, 02777. Tel: 508-675-7206; Fax: 508-672-4716; Email: saintdominicparish@comcast.net; Web: www.stdominicparish.org. Rev. Joseph F. Viveiros; Deacon Frank R. Lucca.
Catechesis Religious Program—Tel: 508-675-7002. Ms. Barbara Dominque, Catechetical Leader. Students 212.
2—Saint Francis of Assisi (1922)
270 Ocean Grove Ave., Swansea, 02777.
Tel: 508-673-2808; Fax: 508-672-6241; Email: stfrancisswansea@comcast.net; Web: www.stfrancisswansea.com. Rev. Michael A. Ciryak.
Church: 530 Gardner Neck Rd., Swansea, 02777.
Catechesis Religious Program—Tel: 508-674-0024. Mrs. Christine Gregorek, D.R.E.
3—St. Louis de France (1928) (French)
56 Buffington St., Swansea, 02777.
Tel: 508-674-1103; Fax: 508-672-8889; Email: sldfo@comcast.net; Web: stlouisdefrance.net. Mailing Address: P.O. Box 70, Somerset, 02726. Rev. James M. Fitzpatrick, Admin.
Catechesis Religious Program—Tel: 508-672-0615. Ms. Paulette J. Normandin, Catechetical Leader. Students 229.
4—St. Michael's, Closed. For inquiries for parish records please see Saint Francis of Assisi, Swansea.
5—Our Lady of Fatima (1958) Closed. For inquiries for parish records, please see Saint Francis of Assisi, Swansea.
Taunton, Bristol Co.
1—Saint Andrew the Apostle Parish (2008)
19 Kilmer Ave., Taunton, 02780. Tel: 508-824-5577;
Fax: 508-822-1401; Email: standrewtaunton@comcast.net; Web: www.standrewtaunton.org. Rev. Edward A. Murphy.
Catechesis Religious Program—Mr. Joseph Sollecito, Catechetical Leader; Mrs. Sally Medeiros, Catechetical Leader. Students 273.
2—Annunciation of the Lord (2001) Rev. Thomas E. Costa; Deacon Thomas J. Souza.
Res.: 31 First St., Taunton, 02780. Tel: 508-823-2521 ; Fax: 508-823-2522; Email: annol325@comcast.net; Web: www.annunciationtaunton.com.
Office: 311 Somerset St., Taunton, 02780.
School—Our Lady of Lourdes, (Grades PreK-5), 52 First St., Taunton, 02780. Tel: 508-822-3746;
Fax: 508-822-1450; Email: olol@tmlp.com; Web: www.oloItaunton.com. Maria J. Turner, Prin. Lay Teachers 16; Sisters 2; Students 146; Total Staff 18; Religious Teachers 2.
Catechesis Religious Program—Tel: 508-824-6791. Mr. Gualter Chaves, Catechetical Leader. Students 100.
3—St. Anthony's (1903) (Portuguese) Rev. William M. Rodrigues; Deacon Jose H. Medina.
Res.: 126 School St., Taunton, 02780.
Tel: 508-822-0714; Fax: 508-828-5844; Email: stanthony@comcast.net; Web: www.stanthonytaunton.org.
Catechesis Religious Program—Tel: 508-824-6241. Students 193.
4—St. James (1904) (French), Closed. For inquiries for parish records contact St. Jude the Apostle Parish, Taunton.
5—St. Joseph's (1896) Closed. For inquiries for parish

records contact St. Andrew the Apostle Parish, Taunton.
6—ST. JUDE THE APOSTLE (2007)
Mailing Address: 249 Whittenton St., Taunton, 02780. Tel: 508-824-3330; Fax: 508-880-3865; Email: stjudesecretary@verizon.net; Web: www. stjudetaunton.com. Rev. Gerard A. Hebert, J.C.L.; Deacons Philip E. Bedard; Joseph P. Medeiros.
Catechesis Religious Program—468 Bay St., Taunton, 02780. Tel: 508-824-4545. Miss Elizabeth Hoye, D.R.E. Students 134.
Convent—279 Whittenton St., Taunton, 02780.
Chapel—Chapel of Our Lady of the Holy Rosary, 80 Bay St., Taunton, 02780.
7—ST. MARY'S (1828)
14 St. Mary's Sq., Taunton, 02780. Tel: 508-822-7116 ; Email: stmarystaunton@verizon.net. Revs. James J. Doherty, C.S.C; Richard D. Wilson, J.C.L., Vicar.
Catechesis Religious Program—Tel: 508-822-3048. Mrs. Rosana Rosado-Ruiz, Catechetical Leader. Students 107.
Dolan Parish Center—
8—OUR LADY OF LOURDES (1905) (Portuguese), Merged with Sacred Heart, Taunton to form Annunciation of the Lord, Taunton.
9—OUR LADY OF THE HOLY ROSARY (1909) [JC] (Polish), Closed. For inquiries for parish records, please contact St. Jude the Apostle Parish, Taunton.
10—OUR LADY OF THE IMMACULATE CONCEPTION (1883) Closed. For inquiries for parish records contact St. Jude the Apostle Parish, Taunton.
11—ST. PAUL'S (1904) Closed. For inquiries for parish records contact St. Andrew the Apostle Parish, Taunton.
12—SACRED HEART (1873) Merged with Our Lady of Lourdes, Taunton to form Annunciation of the Lord, Taunton.
VINEYARD HAVEN, DUKES CO.
1—ST. AUGUSTINE (1962) Closed. For inquiries for parish records contact Good Shepherd Parish, Oak Bluffs.
2—GOOD SHEPHERD (2004) [JC]
55 School St., Oak Bluffs, 02557. Tel: 508-693-0342; Email: frnagle@goodshepherdmv.com; Web: www. goodshepherdmv.com. Mailing Address: P.O. Box 1058, Vineyard Haven, 02568. Revs. Michael R. Nagle, D.Min.; Edivar daSilva Ribeiro, Parochial Vicar; Deacon Karl G. Buder.
Worship Sites—
Our Lady Star of the Sea—22 Massasoit Ave., Oak Bluffs, 02557.
St. Elizabeth's Church, Church & Res.: 86 Main St., Edgartown, 02539.
St. Augustine's Church, 56 Franklin St., Vineyard Haven, 02568.
Catechesis Religious Program—Ms. Susan Pagliccia, Catechetical Leader. Students 94.
WAREHAM, PLYMOUTH CO., ST. PATRICK'S (1911) [CEM]
82 High St., Wareham, 02571-0271.
Tel: 508-295-2411; Fax: 508-295-2417; Email: info@stpatrickswareham.org; Web: www. stpatrickswareham.org. Revs. Antonio da Silva, S.D.V.; Cyril Offiong, S.D.V., Parochial Vicar; Rowland Onuegbu, S.D.V., In Res.; Deacon David C. Murphy.
Catechesis Religious Program—Students 201.
Mission—St. Anthony, Gault Rd., Wareham, Plymouth Co. 02571.
WELLFLEET, BARNSTABLE CO., OUR LADY OF LOURDES (1911) [CEM 2] Rev. Hugh J. McCullough; Vicky Anderson, Music Min.
Res.: 2282 Rt. 6, P.O. Box 1414, Wellfleet, 02667-1414. Tel: 508-487-0095; Fax: 508-349-9612; Email: olol2282@comcast.net; Web: www.olohwellfleet.org.
Catechesis Religious Program—Tel: 508-349-2222. Ms. Lisa Colley, Catechetical Leader. Students 9.
Mission—Visitation Church, 930 Massasoit Rd., North Eastham, Barnstable Co. 02651.
Fax: 508-349-9612.
WEST HARWICH, BARNSTABLE CO., HOLY TRINITY (1918) [CEM]
246 Main St., West Harwich, 02671.
Tel: 508-432-4000; Fax: 508-432-3494; Email: htchurch@comcast.net; Web: holytrinitycapecod.org. P.O. Box 428, West Harwich, 02671. Rev. Marc P. Tremblay; Deacons John W. Foley; Ralph F. Cox; Christian Devos.
Catechesis Religious Program—Davida Peninger, D.R.E. Students 144.
Mission—Our Lady of the Annunciation, [CEM] 187 Upper County Rd., Dennis Port, 02639.
WESTPORT, BRISTOL CO.
1—ST. GEORGE'S (1914)
12 Highland Ave., Westport, 02790.
Tel: 774-319-5579; Fax: 508-300-7968; Email: office@stgeorgecatholics.org; Web: www. stgeorgecatholics.org. Rev. David C. Frederici; Deacon Frank R. Lucca.
Catechesis Religious Program—Tel: 508-636-2941. Ms. Joy Viveiros, Catechetical Leader. Students 121.
2—ST. JOHN THE BAPTIST (1930)
945 Main Rd., Box 3328, Westport, 02790.
Tel: 508-636-2251; Fax: 508-636-8306; Email: stjb@sprintout.net; Web: www. stjohnthebaptistwestport.org. Rev. Leonard P. Hindsley.
3—OUR LADY OF GRACE (1954) Rev. Dariusz Kalinowski.
Res.: 569 Sanford Rd., Westport, 02790.
Tel: 508-674-6271; Fax: 508-675-4128; Email: ologwestportma@aol.com; Web: www.ologwestport. com.
Catechesis Religious Program—Tel: 508-675-5857. Ms. Jane Callahan, Catechetical Leader. Students 105.
WOODS HOLE, BARNSTABLE CO., ST. JOSEPH'S (1882) Closed. For inquiries for parish records, please contact St. Elizabeth Seton Parish, North Falmouth.

Chaplains of Public Institutions

BARNSTABLE. *Barnstable County House of Correction*. c/o St. Patrick's Parish, 82 High St., P.O. Box 271, Wareham, 02571. Deacon Daniel M. Donovan, Coord.
NEW BEDFORD. *Bristol Co. House of Correction & Eastern Massachusetts Correctional Alcohol Center*.
824 Tucker Rd., North Dartmouth, 02747.
Tel: 508-996-2413. Rev. Rowland Onuegbu, S.D.V.

Unassigned:
Revs.—
Bissinger, Karl C.
Blyskosz, Joseph J.
Fournier, Peter J.
Harrington, John P.
Kozanko, Andrzej J.
Kuhn, Michael F.
Scales, George
Swiercz, Pawel A.
Sylvia, William M.

On Duty Outside the Diocese:
Rev. Msgr.—
O'Connor, Gerard P., Office of Divine Worship, Archdiocese of Portland, c/o St. Rose of Lima Rectory, 2727 N.E. 54th Ave., Portland, OR 97213
Revs.—
Dominguez, Ramon, McLean, VA
Landry, Roger J., Permanent Observer Mission of the Holy See to the UN, New York, NY
Pacholczyk, Tadeusz, 6399 Drexel Rd., Philadelphia, PA 19151
Pignato, David A., S.T.L., 127 Lake St., Brighton, 02135
Sharland, David, McLean, VA.

Retired:
Rev. Msgrs.—
Hoye, Daniel F., J.C.L., (Retired), 783 Dartmouth St., Dartmouth, 02748
Oliveira, John J., P.A., (Retired), 23 Longwood Ave., New Bedford, 02740
Perry, John A., (Retired), 375 Elsbree St., 02720
Smith, John J., (Retired), 375 Elsbree St., 02720
Tosti, Ronald A., (Retired), P.O. Box 814, Cotuit, 02635-0814
Wall, Barry W., (Retired), 375 Elsbree St., 02720
Revs.—
Andrews, John F., (Retired)
Arruda, Henry S., (Retired), 375 Elsbree St., 02720
Barnwell, Gerald P., (Retired), 430 Eastern Ave., 02723
Bellenoit, George C., (Retired), 37 Carol Ann Dr., Brewster, 02631
Blottman, William P., (Retired), 375 Elsbree St., 02720
Bouchard, Marcel H., (Retired), 37 Carol Ann Dr., Brewster, 02631
Buckley, James F., (Retired), 209 Union St., Yarmouthport, 02675
Buote, Martin L., (Retired), 164 Marion Rd., Wareham, 02571-1450
Byington, Edward J., (Retired), P.O. Box 571, Taunton, 02780
Camara, Michael M., (Retired)
Campbell, William G., (Retired), 16 White Pine Ave., W., West Wareham, 02576
Canuel, Paul E., (Retired), 375 Elsbree St., 02720
Chretien, Richard L., (Retired), 375 Elsbree St., 02720
Correia, Edward E., (Retired), 375 Elsbree St., 02720
Dahl, Henry J., (Retired)
Davignon, Philip A., (Retired), 19 Carmen St., Attleboro, 02703
Driscoll, John P., (Retired), 2446 Highland Ave., 02720
Ferreira, Manuel P., (Retired), 2446 Highland Ave., 02720
Ferry, James, (Retired), 17295 East 520 Rd., Inola, OK 74036
Gomes, John A., (Retired), 375 Elsbree St., 02720
Graziano, Peter N., S.T.L., M.A., M.S.W., (Retired), 185 Woodside Ave., Winthrop, 02152
Harrington, Brian J., (Retired)
Kropiwnicki, Henry, (Retired), 375 Elsbree St., 02720
Lamb, Paul T., (Retired), 15 Toby Cir., Hyannis, 02601
LeDuc, Roger D., (Retired), P.O. Box 3734, Oakhurst, CA 93644
Lopes, Thomas C., (Retired), 375 Elsbree St., 02720
Mauritzen, Joseph H., (Retired)
McLellan, James R., (Retired), 375 Elsbree St., 02720
Morse, James H., (Retired), 385 Central Ave., Seekonk, 02771
Nichols, Herbert T., (Retired), 2402 Highland Ave., 02720
Oliveira, Gastao A., (Retired)
Pereira, Luciano J., (Retired)
Powell, Robert J., (Retired)
Rita, Thomas L., (Retired), 375 Elsbree St., 02720
Salvador, Stephen B., (Retired), 114 Rockland St., South Dartmouth, 02748
Shovelton, Gerald T., (Retired), 419 Chula Vista Ave., Lady Lake, FL 32159
Travassos, Horace J., (Retired), 345 Tower St., 02724
Vanasse, Bernard, (Retired), 2402 Highland Ave., 02720
Wingate, Arthur K., (Retired), 375 Elsbree St., 02720.

Permanent Deacons:
Akin, David P., (Retired), St. Pius X, South Yarmouth
Alence, Robert, (Retired), Corpus Christi, East Sandwich; Boston, MA
Bailey, Thomas C., (Retired), Hartford, CT (Unassigned)
Barrett, James M., (Retired), Our Lady of Victory, Centerville
Battiston, Donald L., (Retired), St. Mary, Our Lady of the Isle, Nantucket; Hartford, CT
Baxter, Bruce J., St. Francis Xavier, Hyannis
Bedard, Philip E., St. Jude the Apostle, Taunton
Biron, Donald R., (Retired), Our Lady of the Cape, Brewster; Boston, MA
Bonneau, Bruce J., St. John Neumann, East Freetown
Borges, Eduardo M., Our Lady of the Immaculate Conception & St. Anthony of Padua, New Bedford
Boucher, David R., St. Francis Xavier, Hyannis
Bousquet, Louis A., (Unassigned)
Branco, John F., (Retired), Good Shepherd & Holy Trinity, Fall River
Brides, Brendan W., St. John the Evangelist, Pocasset
Buder, Karl G., Good Shepherd, Martha's Vineyard
Burkly, John J., St. John the Evangelist, Pocasset, Boston, MA
Camacho, Francis, Florida
Cipriano, A. Anthony, St. Vincent de Paul, St. John the Evangelist, Attleboro
Coates, Vincent J. Jr., (Retired), Pocasset; Washington, DC (Unassigned)
Cote, Peter R., St. Mary's Cathedral, Fall River
Cox, Ralph F., (Retired), Holy Trinity, West Harwich; Galveston-Houston, TX
Craig, Robert M., Holy Family, East Taunton
De Vos, Christian, Holy Trinity, West Harwich; Chicago
Dexter, Leonard C. Jr., (Retired)
Donovan, Daniel M., (Retired), St. Patrick, Wareham
Emmert, John J., (Unassigned)
Fantasia, Frank D., (Retired), Christ the King, Mashpee
Faria, Robert A., (Retired), St. John of God, Somerset
Fitzpatrick, John J., (Retired), Holy Family, East Taunton
Flaherty, Timothy E., St. Stanislaus & Good Shepherd, Fall River
Foley, John W., Holy Trinity, West Harwich
Fournier, Paul M., St. Vincent de Paul, St. John the Evangelist, Attleboro
Gallerizzo, William, St. Pius X, South Yarmouth; Washington
Gardyna, Henry A., (Retired), St. Patrick, Wareham; Boston, MA
Gendron, Ernest J., (Retired), St. Margaret, Buzzards Bay
Grant, John D., (Unassigned)
Guerra, Ralph J., St. Margaret, Buzzards Bay
Gundlach, Richard J., (Retired), South Carolina

Guresh, Peter M., St. Elizabeth Seton, North Falmouth
Guy, Michael P., New Hampshire
Harney, Paul J., Christ the King, Mashpee
Hays, William W., St. Patrick's, Falmouth; Worcester, MA
Hickey, C. Michael, (Retired), St. Pius X, South Yarmouth; Boston, MA
Hill, Robert J., (Retired), Florida
Hussey, Edward J., (Retired), St. Patrick, Somerset
John, Gary M., Unassigned
Kane, Joseph K., Hartford, CT
LaChance, Arthur L. Jr., Corpus Christi, East Sandwich
LaPiana, Fred G. III, Florida
Lemay, Robert D., (Retired), Christ the King, Mashpee
Levesque, Paul R., St. Joseph/St. Michael, Fall River
Liegey, Gabriel J., (Retired), Vermont
Lorenzo, Robert G., (Retired), St. Joseph, Fairhaven; Camden, NJ
Lucca, Frank R., St. Dominic, Swansea; St. George, Westport
Lukac, Theodore E., Our Lady of Victory, Centerville; Our Lady of the Assumption, Osterville
Macedo, Paul J., Our Lady of Mt. Carmel, New Bedford
Mador, Joseph F., (Retired), Holy Redeemer, Chatham
Mahoney, Patrick J., (Retired), St. Patrick, Falmouth; Hartford, CT
Malloy, Adelbert F., St. John the Evangelist, St. Vincent de Paul, Attleboro
Martin, William A., (Retired), Florida
Martins, Jesse L., (Retired), St. Bernard, Assonet; Providence, RI
Massoud, Donald P., St. Anthony of the Desert, Fall River
Mattar, Jean E., Our Lady of Purgatory, New Bedford
McCarthy, Dana G., Florida
McEnaney, Norman F., (Retired), St. Joan of Arc, Orleans
McGinley, Joseph A., St. Ann, Raynham
McMahon, Thomas J., Our Lady Queen of Martyrs, Seekonk
Medeiros, Douglas R., St. Joseph, Fairhaven
Medeiros, Joseph P., St. Jude the Apostle, Taunton
Medina, Jose H., St. Anthony, Taunton
Messina, Dominic, (Retired), Christ the King, Mashpee; Newark, NJ
Metilly, Paul, Florida
Minninger, Steven M., St. Francis Xavier, Hyannis
Moniz, John de A., Florida
Murphy, David C., St. Patrick's, Wareham
Murphy, Richard J., (Retired), St. Francis Xavier, Hyannis
Nasser, Andre P., (Retired), St. Anthony of the Desert, Fall River
Nogueira, Benjamin, Diocese of Worcester
Normandin, Robert G., (Retired), St. Louis de France, Swansea
Norton, Victor K., Texas
O'Connell, Dennis G., Corpus Christi, East Sandwich
Ouellette, Maurice A., St. Lawrence, New Bedford
Pacheco, Eduardo M., (Retired), Our Lady of the Assumption, New Bedford
Palanza, Thomas P., St. Mary, Mansfield
Pepin, David B., St. Francis Xavier, Acushnet
Pierce, David E., Christ the King, Mashpee
Pires, Abilio dos A., (Retired), Our Lady of Mt. Carmel, New Bedford
Pires, Albertino F., Our Lady of the Immaculate Conception, New Bedford
Porter, Gary A., Immaculate Conception, Easton
Racine, Leo W., (Retired), St. Anthony of Padua, New Bedford
Regali, Joseph E., Sacred Heart, St. Mary, North Attleboro; St. Mark, Attleboro Falls
Roma, Paul K., (Retired), St. Anthony, E. Falmouth
Sasseville, Eugene E., (Retired), Holy Name of the Sacred Heart of Jesus, New Bedford
Simonis, John E., St. Patrick, Falmouth
Souza, Thomas J., (Retired), Annunciation of the Lord, Taunton
St. Onge, Lawrence A., (Retired), St. John Neumann, East Freetown
Stenberg, Richard S., (Retired), Holy Redeemer, Chatham; Bridgeport CT
Surozenski, Anthony R., St. Pius Tenth, South Yarmouth; Worcester, MA
Surprenant, Robert L., (Retired), St. John Neumann, East Freetown
Thadeu, Alan J., St. Mary, Norton
Thomas, Walter D., Florida
Twerago, John P., (Retired), St. Joan of Arc, Orleans; Hartford, CT
Varieur, Wilfred R., St. Theresa of the Child Jesus, South Attleboro
Wallace, Forrest, Cincinnati, Ohio
Welch, John, (Retired), St. Ann, Raynham
Zarella, George H., Holy Cross, Easton
Zeich, Richard C., (Retired), St. Pius X, South Yarmouth; Paterson, NJ
Zonghetti, Michael T., St. Mary, Norton.

INSTITUTIONS LOCATED IN DIOCESE

[A] COLLEGES AND UNIVERSITIES

NORTH EASTON. *Holy Cross Fathers Religious*, 480 Washington St., North Easton, 02356.
Tel: 508-238-8828; Fax: 508-238-1297; Email: aszakalycsc@gmail.com; Web: www.holycrosscsc.org. Revs. James T. Preskenis, C.S.C., Parochial Vicar; Anthony V. Szakaly, C.S.C., Supr.; Leo Polselli, C.S.C., Asst. Supr.; Matthew E Fase, Campus Min.; Marc F. Fallon, C.S.C., Chap.; Richard E. Gribble, C.S.C.; Joseph F. Callahan, C.S.C.; James W. Chichetto, C.S.C.; Michael B. Wurtz, C.S.C.; John F. Denning, C.S.C.; Thomas P. Gariepy, C.S.C.; Jeffrey L. Allison, C.S.C.; William H. Kelley, C.S.C.; Bradley J. Metz, C.S.C.; Pinto Paul, C.S.C.; George Piggford, C.S.C.; Charles L. Wallen, C.S.C., (Retired); Wilfred J. Raymond, C.S.C.; Kevin P. Spicer, C.S.C.; Thomas E. Gaughan, C.S.C.; Stephen S. Wilbricht, C.S.C.; Bro. Subal Rosario, C.S.C., (Bangladesh). Priests 24; Students 2,500; Clergy / Religious Teachers 24.
Stonehill College (1948) 320 Washington St., North Easton, 02356. Tel: 508-565-1301;
Fax: 508-565-1432; Email: president@stonehill.edu; Web: www.stonehill.edu. Revs. John F. Denning, C.S.C., Pres.; James W. Chichetto, C.S.C., Faculty; Thomas P. Gariepy, C.S.C., Faculty; Richard E. Gribble, C.S.C., Faculty; George Piggford, C.S.C., Faculty; Bro. Subal Rosario, C.S.C., (Bangladesh) Finance; Revs. Kevin P. Spicer, C.S.C., Faculty; Stephen S. Wilbricht, C.S.C., Faculty; Anthony V. Szakaly, C.S.C., Supr. (Easton Community), Alumni & Athletic Chap. & Dir., Campus Ministry (Stonehill); Cheryl E. McGrath, Dir., Library; Revs. Jeffrey L. Allison, C.S.C., Associate Registrar; Matthew E Fase, Admin. Lay Teachers 161; Students 2,401; Religious Teachers 6.

[B] HIGH SCHOOLS, DIOCESAN

FALL RIVER. *Bishop Connolly High School*, 373 Elsbree St., 02720. Tel: 508-676-1071; Fax: 508-676-8594; Email: cmyron@bchs.dfrcs.org; Web: www.bishopconnolly.com. Rev. David C. Deston, Chap.; E. Christopher Myron, Prin. Lay Teachers 22; Students 226; Clergy / Religious Teachers 1.
ATTLEBORO. *Bishop Feehan High School*, 70 Holcott Dr., Attleboro, 02703. Tel: 508-226-6223;
Fax: 508-226-7696; Email: webmaster@bfhs.dfrcs.org; Email: lcayer@bishopfeehan.com; Web: www.bishopfeehan.com. Mr. Timothy B. Sullivan, Pres.; Mr. Sean Kane, Prin.; Rev. David A. Costa, Chap. Lay Teachers 96; Students 1,083; Non-Teaching 25.
HYANNIS. *Saint John Paul II High School and St. Francis Xavier Preparatory School*, 120 High School Rd., Hyannis, 02601. Tel: 508-862-6336;
Fax: 508-862-6339; Email: ckeavy@jp.dfrcs.org; Email: mvalentino@jp.dfrcs.org; Web: www.sjp2hs.org. Christopher W. Keavy, Headmaster; Mrs. Elizabeth Kelley, Prin.; Mona Lisa Valentino, Prin.; Rev. Ronnie P. Floyd, Chap. Lay Teachers 40; Students 475.
NORTH DARTMOUTH. *Bishop Stang High School*, 500 Slocum Rd., North Dartmouth, 02747-2999.
Tel: 508-996-5602; Fax: 508-994-6756; Email: office@bishopstang.org; Web: www.bishopstang.org. Peter Shaughnessy, Pres. & Prin.; Mr. Michael P. O'Brien, Prin.; Rev. Richard M. Roy, Chap.; Kathleen Ruginis, Prin.; Nicole Dias, Dir. Guidance; Ann O'Leary, Librarian. Lay Teachers 49; Priests 1; Students 581; Support Staff 14.
TAUNTON. *Coyle and Cassidy High School & Middle School* (1971) 2 Hamilton St., Taunton, 02780.
Tel: 508-823-6164; Fax: 508-823-2530; Email: sfreitas@cc.dfrcs.org; Web: www.coylecassidy.com. Dr. Mary Patricia Tranter, Ph.D., Pres.; Kathleen St. Laurent, Prin.; Rev. William M. Rodrigues, Chap. Lay Teachers 44; Priests 1; Students 425.

[C] RESIDENTIAL CHILD CARE FACILITIES

FALL RIVER. *St. Vincent's Home Corp.*, 2425 Highland Ave., 02720. Tel: 508-679-8511; Fax: 508-672-2558; Email: jweldon@stvincentshome.org; Web: www.stvincentshome.org. Mr. John T. Weldon, CEO; Margaret Maiato, M.S., Spec. Educ. Admin. & Prin.; Kristen Dutra, M.A., Clinical Dir. Families 750; Lay Teachers 3; Sisters 4; Students 12; Total Staff 290; Religious Teachers 1.

[D] HOMES FOR AGED

FALL RIVER. *Catholic Memorial Home Inc.*, 2446 Highland Ave., 02720-4599. Tel: 508-679-0011;
Fax: 508-672-5858; Email: thealy@dhfo.org. Thomas F. Healy, Supr. & Admin.; Rev. Michael J. O'Hearn. Bed Capacity 272; Tot Asst. Annually 335; Total Staff 395.
FAIRHAVEN. *Our Lady's Haven of Fairhaven Inc.*, 71 Center St., Fairhaven, 02719. Tel: 508-999-4561;
Fax: 508-997-0254; Email: madasilva@dhfo.org; Web: www.dhfo.org. Lisa Cadime, Admin.; Rev. James E. McDonough, SS.CC., Chap. Bed Capacity 117; Residents 117; Tot Asst. Annually 152; Total Staff 172.
NEW BEDFORD. *Sacred Heart Home*, 359 Summer St., New Bedford, 02740. Tel: 508-996-6751;
Fax: 508-992-3145; Email: jdavis@dhfo.org; Web: www.dhfo.org. Jennifer Davis, Admin.; Rev. Alphonsus McHugh, SS.CC., Chap. Bed Capacity 217; Residents 192; Tot Asst. Annually 192; Total Staff 300.
NORTH ATTLEBORO. *Madonna Manor Inc.* (1966) 85 N. Washington St., North Attleboro, 02760.
Tel: 508-699-2740; Fax: 508-699-0481; Email: mmurpy@dhfo.org; Web: www.dhfo.org. Mary-Ellen Murphy, R.N., B.S.N., M.S., Admin.; Halina Malec, Dir. of Pastoral Care. Bed Capacity 129; Tot Asst. Annually 253; Total Staff 204.
TAUNTON. *Bethany House Adult Day Care*, 72 Church Green, Taunton, 02780. Tel: 508-822-9200; Email: pworcester@dhfo.org. Jessica L. Costa, Admin. Bed Capacity 41; Total Staff 10; Total Assisted 40.
Marian Manor Inc., 33 Summer St., Taunton, 02780.
Tel: 508-822-4885; Fax: 508-880-3386; Email: jcosta@dhfo.org. Jessica L. Costa, Admin.; Rev. Bernard Vanasse, Chap., (Retired). Bed Capacity 116; Tot Asst. Annually 116; Total Staff 165.

[E] MONASTERIES AND RESIDENCES OF PRIESTS AND BROTHERS

FALL RIVER. *Cardinal Medeiros Residence-Retirement Facility for Priests*, 375 Elsbree St., 02720-7211.
Tel: 508-675-1050; Fax: 508-675-2181; Email: jflanagan@dhfo.org. Joann Flanagan, Supervr.
Priests' Hostel, 2402 Highland Ave., 02720.
Tel: 508-672-1632; Email: ejfitzgerald@dhfo.org. Rev. Msgr. Edmund J. Fitzgerald, Dir. Diocesan Health Facilities Office. In Res. Revs. Joseph J. Blyskosz; Herbert T. Nichols, (Retired); Michael J. O'Hearn; Pawel A. Swiercz; Bernard Vanasse, (Retired).
ATTLEBORO. *La Salette Missionary Association*, 947 Park St., P.O. Box 2965, Attleboro, 02703.
Tel: 508-222-0027; Fax: 508-222-2504; Email: lsmajp@aol.com; Web: www.lasalettemissionary.org. Very Rev. Rene J. Butler, M.S., Prov.; Rev. Bernard B. Baris, M.S., Dir.
Missionaries of La Salette (MA), Inc.
La Salette Shrine & Retreat Center, 947 Park St., Attleboro, 02703. Tel: 508-222-5410;
Fax: 508-222-6770; Email: lasaletteshrinesecretary@gmail.com; Web: www.lasalette-shrine.org. Revs. Edward J. Brown, M.S., Dir.; Andre A. Patenaude, M.S., Supr.; Flavio Gillio, M.S., Contact Person. Brothers 7; Priests 11. In Res. Revs. Ronald G. Gagne, M.S., Prov. Communications Dir.; Donald P. Jeffrey, M.S.; Dennis J. Loomis, M.S.; Lamartine J. Eliscar, M.S.; Cyriac Mattathilanickal, M.S., Dir. Retreat House; Bros. Donald Wininski, M.S.; Paul Boucher, M.S.; Lucien Brodeur, M.S.; David L. Eubank, M.S.; Roger Moreau, M.S.; Rev. Manuel C. Pereira, M.S., (Retired); Bro. Roger St. Germain, M.S., (Retired); Rev. Edward J. Brown, M.S., Shrine Dir.; Bro. Ronald Taylor, M.S.; Rev. Ernest J. Corriseau, M.S., (Retired). *La Salette Communications Office*, 947 Park St., Attleboro, 02703. Tel: 508-838-0313; Email: rongagne@aol.com. Rev. Ronald G. Gagne, M.S., Dir. Communications.
FAIRHAVEN. *Sacred Hearts Provincial Administration Office*, 77 Adams St., P.O. Box 111, Fairhaven, 02719-0111. Tel: 508-993-2442; Fax: 508-996-5499; Email: usprovincial@sscc.org; Web: www.sscc.org. Very Rev. Herman Gomes, SS.CC., Prov.; Rev. Stephen Banjare, SS.CC.; Bro. Paul R. Alves, SS.CC. Congregation of the Sacred Hearts-United States Province. Brothers 1; Fathers 2. *National Center of the Enthronement*, P.O. Box 111, Fairhaven, 02719-0111. Tel: 508-999-2680; Fax: 508-993-8233; Email: necenter@juno.com; Web: www.sscc.org. Rev. Kevin (Columban) Crotty, SS.CC., Dir. Congregation of the Sacred Hearts-United States Province. Total Staff 2. *Damien Residence*, 73 Adams St., P.O. Box 111, Fairhaven, 02719-0111.
Tel: 508-990-0500; Fax: 508-990-7173; Email: usprovincial@sscc.org. Revs. James E. McDonough, SS.CC., House Dir.; Kevin (Columban)

Crotty, SS.CC.; Albert Dagnoli, SS.CC., (Retired); Martin T. Gomes, SS.CC.; Michael Kelly, SS.CC.; Brian Marggraf, SS.CC., (Retired); Michael Shanahan, SS.CC.; Matthias Shanley, SS.CC.; Desmond (Fintan) Sheeran, SS.CC.

Sacred Hearts Missions Fathers 9.

NEW BEDFORD. *Marian Friary of Our Lady, Queen of the Seraphic Order*, 600 Pleasant St., New Bedford, 02740-6299. Tel: 508-996-8274; Email: ffi@marymediatrix.com; Email: fr.maximilian@gmx.com; Web: www.marymediatrix.com. Revs. Matthias M. Sasko, F.I., Supr.; Maximilian M. Warnisher, F.I., Vicar; Friars John M. Risse, F.I., Sec.; Pedro Francisco M. Olhero, F.I.; Rev. Alan Bernardine Wharton, F.I. Brothers 2; Priests 3.

ONSET. *St. Joseph Friary-Franciscan Friars*, 46 Robinwood Rd., P.O. Box 63, Onset, 02558. Tel: 508-759-7280; Email: charles848@aol.com. Deacon Charles Gingerich, O.F.M., M.R.E., Guard. & Deacon. Total in Residence 1; Total Staff 1.

[F] CONVENTS AND RESIDENCES FOR SISTERS

DIGHTON. *Dominican Sisters of Charity of the Presentation of the Blessed Virgin*, 3012 Elm St., Dighton, 02715. Tel: 508-669-5425; Tel: 508-669-5023 (Novitiate); Fax: 508-669-6521; Email: domsrs@presentation-op-usa-org; Web: www.presentation-op-usa-.org. Sr. Vimala Vadakumpadan, O.P., Major Supr. Provincial House-Residence, Residence for Aged Sisters, Novitiate. Sisters 32.

FAIRHAVEN. *Sisters of the Sacred Hearts, Community Headquarters*, 35 Huttleston Ave., Fairhaven, 02719-3154. Tel: 508-994-9341; Email: cbouchard@sscc.org. Sisters Eleanor Marie Cyr, SS.CC., Supr.; Claire Bouchard, SS.CC.; Muriel Ann Lebeau, SS.CC.

Sisters of the Sacred Hearts of Jesus and Mary and of Perpetual Adoration, SS.CC. Sisters in Community 3.

SOUTH DARTMOUTH. *Dominican Sisters of Hope* (1995) Bethany Community, 51 Middle St., Dartmouth, 02748. Tel: 508-996-1305; Web: www.ophope.org. Sr. Lorelle Elcock, O.P., Prioress. Sisters 2.

TAUNTON. *Villa Fatima* (1934) 90 County St., Taunton, 02780. Tel: 508-822-6282; Fax: 508-823-0825; Email: roe23roe@aol.com; Web: www.sistersofsaintdorothy.org. Sr. Rosalie Patrello, S.S.D., Local Coord. Sisters of St. Dorothy. Professed Sisters 5.

[G] RETREAT HOUSES

ATTLEBORO. *La Salette Retreat and Conference Center*, 947 Park St., Attleboro, 02703-0965. Tel: 508-222-8530; Fax: 508-236-9089; Email: office@lasaletteretreatcenter.com; Web: www.lasaletteretreatcenter.com. Rev. Bernard B. Baris, M.S., Dir.; Bro. Donald Wininski, M.S., Hospitality; Justin Richardson, Youth Retreat Facilt.; Dorothy J. Levesque, Retreat Leader. Priests 1; Total Staff 10; Total Assisted 5,200.

EAST FREETOWN. *Cathedral Camp and Retreat Center* (1919) 167 Middleboro Rd., P.O. Box 428, East Freetown, 02717-0428. Tel: 508-763-8874; Fax: 508-763-2230; Email: rena@cathedralcamp.net; Web: www.cathedralcamp.net. Rena Lemieux, Dir. Total Staff 60.

Cathedral Camp Retreat Center, 167 Middleboro Rd., P.O. Box 428, East Freetown, 02717-0428. Tel: 508-763-8874; Fax: 508-763-2230; Email: rena@cathedralcamp.net; Web: www.cathedralcamp.net. Rena Lemieux, Asst. Dir. Total Staff 6.

NORTH EASTON. *Holy Cross Retreat House*, 490 Washington St., North Easton, 02356-1294. Tel: 508-238-2051; Fax: 508-238-0164; Email: jfcal44@hotmail.com; Web: www.retreathouse.org. Rev. Joseph F. Callahan, C.S.C., Spiritual Dir. Priests 1.

WAREHAM. *Sacred Hearts Retreat Center*, 226 Great Neck Rd., Wareham, 02571. Tel: 508-295-0100; Fax: 508-291-2624; Email: retreats@sscc.org; Web: www.sscc.org. Sr. Claire Bouchard, SS.CC., Admin. Congregation of the Sacred Hearts - United States Province.

Sacred Hearts Missions Sisters 1; Total Staff 3.

[H] DEPARTMENT OF CATHOLIC SOCIAL SERVICES AND SPECIAL APOSTOLATES

FALL RIVER. *Campaign For Human Development Apostolate*, 1600 Bay St., P.O. Box M, S. Sta., 02724. Tel: 508-674-4681; Fax: 508-675-2224; Email: SMazzarella@cssdioc.org; Email: DBerg@cssdioc.org. Ms. Susan Mazzarella, M.A., L.S.W., CEO; Debora Berg, Coord. Tot Asst. Annually 2; Total Staff 1.

Catholic Social Services of Fall River, 1600 Bay St., P.O. Box M, S. Sta., 02724. Tel: 508-674-4681; Fax: 508-675-2224; Email: SMazzarella@cssdioc.org. Ms. Susan Mazzarella, M.A., L.S.W., CEO; Mateus Barbosa, Vice Pres.; Martha Reed, Admin. Tot Asst. Annually 40,000; Total Staff 110.

Catholic Social Services of New Bedford, 238 Bonney St., New Bedford, 02744. Tel: 508-997-7337; Fax: 508-984-1667; Email: SMazzarella@cssdioc.org. Ms. Susan Mazzarella, M.A., L.S.W., CEO. Total Staff 38.

Catholic Social Services of Cape Cod, 261 South St., Hyannis, 02601. Tel: 508-771-6771; Fax: 508-771-4711; Email: SMazzarella@cssdioc.org. Ms. Susan Mazzarella, M.A., L.S.W., CEO. Tot Asst. Annually 1,290; Total Staff 14.

Adoption By Choice, 1600 Bay St., P.O. Box M S. Sta., 02724. 311 Hooper St., Tiverton, RI 02878. Tel: 401-624-9270; Fax: 508-675-2224; Email: SMazzarella@cssdioc.org. Ms. Susan Mazzarella, M.A., L.S.W., CEO. Tot Asst. Annually 18; Total Staff 2.

HYANNIS. *St. Clare's Residence for Women* Elaine Haley, Contact Person. Bed Capacity 5; Tot Asst. Annually 16; Total Staff 6.

[I] CAMPS AND COMMUNITY CENTERS

FALL RIVER. *Diocesan Catholic Youth Organization*, 709 Hanover St., 02720. Tel: 508-679-6732; Fax: 508-675-4755. Very Rev. Jay T. Maddock, J.C.L., V.F., Diocesan Dir.

Fall River Area Catholic Youth Organization, Sullivan-McCarrick CYO Center, 403 Anawan St., 02720. Tel: 508-672-9644; Fax: 508-675-4755; Email: office@holynamefr.com. Mr. Thomas Chippendale, Area Dir.

New Bedford Area Catholic Youth Organization, Kennedy Youth Center, 377 County St., New Bedford, 02740. Tel: 508-996-0536; Email: office@holynamefr.com. Mr. Gregory Parker, Dir.

Taunton Area Catholic Youth Organization, 61 Summer St., Taunton, 02780. Tel: 774-222-1834; Fax: 508-675-4755; Email: office@holynamefr.com. Mr. Donald Morrison, Area Dir.

[J] NEWMAN CENTERS AND CAMPUS MINISTRY

FALL RIVER. *Bristol Community College Campus Ministry*, 777 Elsbree St., 02720-7395. Tel: 508-678-2811, Ext. 2810; Fax: 508-730-3286; Email: father.frederici@bristolcc.edu; Web: www.bcccatholics.com. Rev. David C. Frederici, Chap. Total Staff 1.

Diocesan Education Center, 423 Highland Ave., 02720. Tel: 508-678-2828; Fax: 508-674-4218; Email: sperla@catholicsa.org; Web: www.catholicschoolsalliance.org. Mr. Stephen A Perla, Supt.; Sandra M. Drummey, Asst. Supt. for Academics and Personnel; Denise M. Peixoto, Asst. Supt. for Academics and Student Affairs; Claire M. McManus, S.T.L., Dir. Faith Formation.

NORTH DARTMOUTH. *UMass Dartmouth Campus Ministry*, 285 Old Westport Rd., North Dartmouth, 02747-2300. Tel: 508-999-8872; Email: dfrederici@umassd.edu; Web: www.umassdcatholics.com. Rev. David C. Frederici, Chap.; Deacon Frank R. Lucca, Campus Min. Total Staff 2.

Wheaton College Office for Campus Ministry, P.O. Box 70737, North Dartmouth, 02747. Fax: 774-202-3047. Rev. David C. Frederici, Dir.

WEST BARNSTABLE. *Cape Cod Campus Ministry*, P.O. Box 1558, Pocasset, 02559. Tel: 774-202-3047; Email: dfrederici@umass.edu; Web: www.capecatholics.com/. Rev. David C. Frederici, Chap.

[K] MISCELLANEOUS LISTINGS

FALL RIVER. *Assisi Housing Corporation*, 1600 Bay St., 02724. Tel: 508-997-0130; Fax: 774-425-3790; Email: nlawson@cafbh.org. 72 Eighth St., New Bedford, 02740. Arlene A. McNamee, L.C.S.W., CEO, Contact Person. Families 17; Lay Staff 2; Total Apartments 17.

Community Action for Better Housing, Inc., 72 Eighth St., New Bedford, 02740. Tel: 508-997-0130 ; Fax: 774-425-3790; Email: AMcNamee@cafbh.org. Debora Berg, CEO; Ed Allard, Prog. Coord.

Diocesan Facilities Self-Insurance Group, Inc., 450 Highland Ave., 02720. Tel: 508-675-1311; Email: shaunk@dioc-fr.org. P.O. Box 1110, 02722. Rev. John M. Murray, Clerk.

St. Dominic's Apartments, Inc., 72 Eighth St., New Bedford, 02740. Tel: 508-916-2434; Fax: 508-997-0130; Email: EAbdow@cafbh.org; Email: nlawson@cafbh.org. 818 Middle St., 02721. Arlene A. McNamee, L.C.S.W., CEO. Aged Residents 17; Total Apartments 17; Tot Asst. Annually 17; Total Staff 2.

Foundation to Advance Catholic Education, Inc., P.O. Box 2577, 02722. Email: sduxbury@dioc-fr.org. 450 Highland Ave., 02720. Tel: 508-675-1311; Fax: 508-676-6591; Web: www.face-dfr.org. Mrs. Sandi Duxbury, Exec. Dir.

Oscar Romero House, Inc., 8 Allen St., New Bedford, 02740. Tel: 774-202-6971; Tel: 508-997-0130; Email: sfyock@cafbh.org; Email: nlawson@cafbh.org. 72 Eighth St., New Bedford, 02740. Arlene A. McNamee, L.C.S.W., CEO, Contact Person. Employees 1; Families 4; Total Apartments 12; Total Assisted 16.

FAIRHAVEN. *Congregation of the Sacred Hearts - United States Province* aka Sacred Hearts Fathers; Sacred Hearts Missions, 77 Adams St., P.O. Box 111, Fairhaven, 02719. Tel: 508-993-2442; Fax: 508-996-5499; Email: usprovincial@sscc.org; Web: www.sscc.org. Rev. Richard McNally, SS.CC., Vicar; Very Rev. Herman Gomes, SS.CC., Prov.; Revs. Stephen Banjare, SS.CC., Dir.; Richard J. Danyluk, SS.CC., Dir.; Martin T. Gomes, SS.CC., Dir.

Sacred Hearts Missions.

NEW BEDFORD. *The Institute of the Incarnate Word, Inc.*, 1359 Acuschnet Ave., New Bedford, 02746. Tel: 508-993-1691; Fax: 508-999-4775; Email: octaviocortez@ive.org; Web: www.saintanthonynewbedford.com. Rev. Octavio Cortez, I.V.E. Priests 2; Total Staff 4; Total Assisted 150.

Missionaries of Charity, 556 County St., New Bedford, 02740. Tel: 508-997-7347; Email: srpaulina.hurtado@yahoo.com. Sr. Benedict Ann, Supr. Shelter for homeless women. Total in Residence 4; Total Assisted 228.

NORTH EASTON. *Holy Cross Family Ministries* (1942) 518 Washington St., North Easton, 02356-1200. Tel: 508-238-4095; Fax: 508-238-3953; Email: swallace@hcfm.org; Email: amcmenamy@hcfm.org; Web: www.hcfm.org. Rev. Wilfred Raymond, C.S.C., Pres.; Susan Wallace, Dir. External Rels.; Rev. David Guffey, C.S.C., Natl. Dir. of Family Theater Productions; Cynthia Slattery, CFO. Corporate Name: The Family Rosary, Inc.; Sponsored by Congregation of Holy Cross (U.S. Province).

RELIGIOUS INSTITUTES OF MEN REPRESENTED IN THE DIOCESE

For further details refer to the corresponding bracketed number in the Religious Institutes of Men or Women section.

[0600]—*Brothers of the Congregation of Holy Cross*—C.S.C.

[1140]—*Congregation of the Sacred Hearts of Jesus and Mary*—SS.CC.

[0480]—*Conventual Franciscans* (Buffalo, NY)—O.F.M.Conv.

[0520]—*Franciscan Friars* (Immaculate Conception Prov.)—O.F.M.

[0533]—*Franciscan Friars of the Immaculate*—F.I.

[]—*Franciscan of Our Lady of the Holy Family*—F.L.H.F.

[0685]—*Institute of the Incarnate Word*—I.V.E.

[0720]—*Missionaries of Our Lady of La Salette*—M.S.

[0610]—*Priests of the Congregation of Holy Cross* (Eastern Prov.)—C.S.C.

[1340]—*Vocationist Fathers.*

RELIGIOUS INSTITUTES OF WOMEN REPRESENTED IN THE DIOCESE

[]—*Congregation of the Sisters of Mercy of Ireland.*

[3815]—*Congregation of the Sisters of St. Joan of Arc*—S.J.A.

[]—*Consecrated Virgin.*

[0750]—*Daughters of the Charity of the Sacred Heart of Jesus* (Sacred Heart Prov.)—F.C.S.C.J.

[1100]—*Dominican Sisters of Charity of the Presentation of the Blessed Virgin*—O.P.

[1105]—*Dominican Sisters of Hope*—O.P.

[3790]—*Institute of the Sisters of St. Dorothy*—S.S.D.

[2710]—*Missionaries of Charity*—M.C.

[2790]—*Missionary Servants of the Most Blessed Trinity*—M.S.B.T.

[3450]—*Religious of Jesus and Mary*—R.J.M.

[2070]—*Religious of the Holy Union of the Sacred Hearts* (Immaculate Heart and Sacred Heart Provs.)—S.U.S.C.

[]—*Secular Institute of the Kingship of Christ*—S.I.M.

[]—*Sisters of Adoration of the Blessed Sacrament*—S.A.B.S.

[2575]—*Sisters of Mercy of the Americas*—R.S.M.

[]—*Sisters of Our Lady of La Salette*—S.N.D.S.

[3720]—*Sisters of Saint Anne*—S.S.A.

[3830-16]—*Sisters of St. Joseph* (Springfield, MA)—S.S.J.

[0150]—*Sisters of the Assumption*—S.A.S.V.

[3180]—*Sisters of the Cross and Passion*—C.P.

[1830]—*Sisters of the Good Shepherd (Contemplative/Religious)*—C.G.S./R.G.S.

[3690]—*Sisters of the Sacred Hearts of Perpetual Adoration*—SS.CC.

[4048]—*Society of the Sisters, Faithful Companions of Jesus*—F.C.J.

DIOCESAN CEMETERIES

FALL RIVER. *St. John*

St. Mary

Notre Dame

St. Patrick

ATTLEBORO. *St. John*

St. Stephen
EAST FALMOUTH. *St. Anthony*
HYANNIS. *St. Francis*
MANSFIELD. *St. Mary*, Towne Street, Attleboro Falls, 02763. Tel: 508-695-1173; Email: stmaryna@noozi.com. 14 Park St., North Attleboro, 02760. Rev. David A. Costa
MATTAPOISETT. *St. Anthony*
NANTUCKET. *St. Mary*
NEW BEDFORD. *St. John*
St. Mary
New Bedford Catholic Cemeteries, 1540 Stafford Rd., 02721. Tel: 508-998-1195; Email: cemetery2@verizon.net. Rev. John J. Perry, Dir.
Sacred Heart
NORTH ATTLEBORO. *St. Mary*
NORTH EASTON. *Immaculate Conception*
OAK BLUFFS. *Sacred Heart*
PROVINCETOWN. *St. Peter*
SANDWICH. *St. Peter*
SOMERSET. *St. Patrick*
TAUNTON. *St. Francis*
St. James
St. Joseph
St. Mary
TRURO. *Sacred Heart*
WAREHAM. *St. Patrick*
WELLFLEET. *Our Lady of Lourdes*
WEST HARWICH. *Holy Trinity*

NECROLOGY

† Moore, John F., (Retired), Died Aug. 12, 2018
† Costello, William M., (Retired), Died Aug. 1, 2018
† Levesque, Roger J., (Retired), Died Jul. 23, 2018

An asterisk (*) denotes an organization that has established tax-exempt status directly with the IRS and is not covered by the USCCB Group Ruling.

Diocese of Fargo

(Dioecesis Fargensis)

Most Reverend

JOHN T. FOLDA

Bishop of Fargo; ordained May 27, 1989; appointed Bishop of Fargo April 8, 2013; ordained June 19, 2013. *Chancery Office: 5201 Bishops Blvd., S., Ste. A, Fargo, ND 58104-7605.*

Chancery Office: 5201 Bishops Blvd., S., Ste. A, Fargo, ND 58104-7605. Tel: 701-356-7900; Fax: 701-356-7999.

Web: www.fargodiocese.org

Email: news@fargodiocese.org

Square Miles 35,351.

Corporate Title: The Diocese of Fargo.

Formerly Diocese of Jamestown.

Established November 12, 1889; Transferred to Fargo, April 6, 1897.

Comprises the Counties of Barnes, Benson, Bottineau east of U.S. Highway 83 and State Highway 256, Cass, Cavalier, Dickey, Eddy, Foster, Grand Forks, Griggs, Kidder, LaMoure, Logan, McHenry, McIntosh, Nelson, Pembina, Pierce, Ramsey, Ransom, Richland, Rolette, Sargent, Sheridan, Steele, Stutsman, Towner, Traill, Walsh and Wells in the State of North Dakota.

For legal titles of parishes and diocesan institutions, consult the Chancery Office.

STATISTICAL OVERVIEW

Personnel	
Bishop	1
Priests: Diocesan Active in Diocese	82
Priests: Diocesan Active Outside Diocese	3
Priests: Retired, Sick or Absent	42
Number of Diocesan Priests	127
Religious Priests in Diocese	6
Total Priests in Diocese	133
Extern Priests in Diocese	7
Ordinations:	
Transitional Deacons	2
Permanent Deacons in Diocese	42
Total Sisters	76
Parishes	
Parishes	131
With Resident Pastor:	
Resident Diocesan Priests	63
Resident Religious Priests	5
Without Resident Pastor:	
Administered by Priests	63
Professional Ministry Personnel:	
Sisters	4
Lay Ministers	67
Welfare	
Catholic Hospitals	8
Total Assisted	136,128
Homes for the Aged	12
Total Assisted	1,087
Specialized Homes	1
Total Assisted	75
Special Centers for Social Services	3
Total Assisted	15,575
Residential Care of Disabled	1
Total Assisted	225
Educational	
Diocesan Students in Other Seminaries	17
Total Seminarians	17
Colleges and Universities	1
Total Students	250
High Schools, Diocesan and Parish	1
Total Students	351
Elementary Schools, Diocesan and Parish	13
Total Students	1,835
Catechesis/Religious Education:	
High School Students	1,600
Elementary Students	4,514
Total Students under Catholic Instruction	8,567
Teachers in the Diocese:	
Priests	1
Sisters	2
Lay Teachers	42
Vital Statistics	
Receptions into the Church:	
Infant Baptism Totals	957
Minor Baptism Totals	80
Adult Baptism Totals	45
Received into Full Communion	121
First Communions	970
Confirmations	1,009
Marriages:	
Catholic	162
Interfaith	90
Total Marriages	252
Deaths	857
Total Catholic Population	73,434
Total Population	421,288

Former Bishops—Rt. Rev. JOHN SHANLEY, D.D., ord. May 30, 1874; cons. Dec. 27, 1889; died July 16, 1909; Most Rev. JAMES O'REILLY, D.D., ord. June 24, 1880; cons. May 19, 1910; installed June 1, 1910; died Dec. 19, 1934; His Eminence ALOISIUS CARDINAL MUENCH, ord. June 8, 1913; appt. Bishop of Fargo, Aug. 10, 1935; cons. Oct. 15, 1935; installed Nov. 6, 1935; appt. Apostolic Visitator for Germany, July 8, 1946; granted personal title of Archbishop, Nov. 1, 1950; appt. Papal Nuncio to Germany, March 10, 1951; created Cardinal Priest and elevated to the Roman Curia, Dec. 14, 1959; died Feb. 15, 1962; Most Revs. LEO F. DWORSCHAK, D.D., ord. May 29, 1926; appt. Coadjutor Bishop of Rapid City, June 23, 1946; cons. Aug. 22, 1946; appt. Auxiliary Bishop of Fargo, April 10, 1947; succeeded to See, May 10, 1960; retired Sept. 8, 1970; died Nov. 5, 1976; JUSTIN A. DRISCOLL, D.D., ord. July 28, 1945; appt. Bishop of Fargo, Sept. 8, 1970; cons. and installed Oct. 28, 1970; died Nov. 19, 1984; JAMES S. SULLIVAN, ord. June 4, 1955; cons. Auxiliary Bishop of Lansing Sept. 21, 1972; appt. Bishop of Fargo April 2, 1985; installed May 30, 1985; retired March 18, 2002; died June 12, 2006.; SAMUEL J. AQUILA, ord. June 5, 1976; appt. Coadjutor Bishop of Fargo June 12, 2001; ord. Aug. 24, 2001; appt. Bishop of Fargo March 18, 2002; appt. Archbishop of Denver May 29, 2012.

Chancery Office—5201 Bishops Blvd. S., Fargo, 58104. Tel: 701-356-7900; Fax: 701-356-7999.

Moderator of the Curia—Rev. Msgr. JOSEPH P. GOERING, V.G.

Vicar General—Rev. Msgr. JOSEPH P. GOERING, V.G.

Chancellor—Very Rev. ANDREW JASINSKI.

Vicar for Clergy—Rev. Msgr. JOSEPH P. GOERING, V.G.

Vice Chancellor—Rev. MATTHEW KRAEMER.

Archivist—Very Rev. ANDREW JASINSKI.

Chief Financial Officer—MR. SCOTT A. HOSELTON, CPA.

Diocesan Tribunal—5201 Bishops Blvd. S., Fargo, 58104. Tel: 701-356-7940.

Judicial Vicar—Very Rev. JAMES GOODWIN, J.C.L.

Promotor Justitiae—Rev. DANIEL GOOD, J.C.L.

Defensor Vinculi—MR. JAY COZEMIUS, J.C.L.; Rev. Msgr. DANIEL J. PILON, J.C.L., (Retired).

Judges—Rev. JARED KADLEC, J.C.L.; Very Rev. JAMES GOODWIN, J.C.L.; Rev. JASON ASSELIN, J.C.L.; MR. TIMOTHY OLSON, J.C.L.

Advocates—Rev. ROBERT IRWIN; MS. JONI TOLLEFSON; MS. ELLEN O'CONNOR; MS. JOAN HOUDEK; MR. EDWARD CONDON, J.C.D.; MR. STEVEN GARBITELLI, J.C.L.; MS. DANIELLA KNEPPER, J.C.L.; REV. SHANE KIRLY, J.C.L.; MS. ELIZABETH SOUDAG, J.C.L.

Auditors—Rev. ROBERT IRWIN; MR. TIMOTHY OLSON, J.C.L.

Notaries—Very Rev. ANDREW JASINSKI, Chancellor; Rev. Msgr. GREGORY J. SCHLESSELMANN; MR. SCOTT A. HOSELTON, CPA; MS. KRISTI BARTHOLOMEW.

Deans—Deanery 1: Very Rev. DALE LAGODINSKI, Wahpeton. Deanery 2: Very Rev. PAUL C. DUCHSCHERE, Fargo. Deanery 3: Rev. Msgr. BRIAN G. DONAHUE, Grand Forks. Deanery 4: Very Rev. PHILLIP ACKERMAN, Langdon. Deanery 5: Very Rev. CHAD F. WILHELM, Devils Lake. Deanery 6: Very Rev. FRANKLIN MILLER, Harvey. Deanery 7: Rev. Msgr. DENNIS A. SKONSENG, Valley City. Deanery 8: Very Rev. WENCESLAUS KATANGA, Wishek.

Diocesan Offices and Directors

Corporate Board—Rev. Msgr. JOSEPH P. GOERING, V.G.; Very Rev. ANDREW JASINSKI; MR. BOB WILMOT; MR. SCOTT A. HOSELTON, CPA.

Apostleship of Prayer—Very Rev. CHAD F. WILHELM, Dir.

Diocesan Finance Council—Rev. Msgr. JOSEPH P. GOERING, V.G.; Very Rev. ANDREW JASINSKI; MR. GRANT SHAFT; MR. RICHARD SCHLOSSER; MS. MARIANNE SEARS; MR. STEVEN SCHONS; MR. SCOTT A. HOSELTON, CPA; MS. LAURIE STRAUS; MS. LEONICE SPLICHAL; MR. BRIAN SCHANILEC; MR. BOB WILMOT; MR. RONALD J. VOLK; MR. ROB ASHEIM; MR. MIKE ST. ONGE.

Catholic Church Deposit & Loan Fund of Eastern North Dakota—Same as corporate board.

Pension Plan—MR. SCOTT A. HOSELTON, CPA.

Censor Librorum—Very Rev. ANDREW JASINSKI.

Liturgy Office—Rev. MATTHEW KRAEMER.

Continuing Education of Priests—Rev. KURTIS GUNWALL.

Arbitration & Conciliation Board—Rev. Msgr. JOSEPH P. GOERING, V.G.; MS. BARB AUGDAHL.

Ecumenical Commission—VACANT.

Director of Stewardship and Development—MR. STEVEN SCHONS.

Holy Childhood Association—Very Rev. ANDREW JASINSKI.

Communications—MR. PAUL BRAUN.

The "New Earth" (Diocesan Newspaper)—MR. PAUL BRAUN.

North Dakota Catholic Conference—MR. CHRISTOPHER DODSON, 103 S. 3rd St., Ste. 10, Bismarck, 58501-3800.

Permanent Diaconate—Rev. Msgr. GREGORY J. SCHLESSELMANN, Dir.; Rev. KYLE P. METZGER, Sec. Diaconate; Deacon JIM MCALLISTER, Dir. Formation.

Propagation of the FaithVery Rev. ANDREW JASINSKI.

Rural Life—Rev. THOMAS GRANER, Dir., Mailing Address: 218 3rd St., S.E., Rugby, 58368. Tel: 701-776-6388.
Technology / Computer Office—MR. LOREN LOH.
Catholic Education and Formation—Very Rev. ANDREW JASINSKI, Dir.
Catechesis—MS. MARY HANBURY.
Evangelization—MS. ASHLEY GRUNHOVD.
Marriage & Family Life—MR. BRAD GRAY.
Healthcare Director—Revs. DALE H. KINZLER; ROSS LAFRAMBOISE.
Youth / Young Adults—MS. KATHY LONEY.
Catholic Schools—MR. MICHAEL HAGSTROM.
Respect Life Office—MS. RACHELLE L. SAUVAGEAU.
Vocation Director—Rev. KYLE P. METZGER.
Catholic Cemeteries—MR. SCOTT A. HOSELTON, CPA.
Hispanic Ministry—Rev. TIMOTHY SCHROEDER, Mailing Address: St. John the Evangelist, 344 15th St. W., Grafton, 58237-2023.
Prison Apostolate—Rev. PAUL R. SCHUSTER.
Liaison with Charismatic Movement—Rev. NEIL J. PFEIFER.

CLERGY, PARISHES, MISSIONS AND PAROCHIAL SCHOOLS

CITY OF FARGO

(CASS COUNTY)

1—ST. MARY'S CATHEDRAL OF FARGO (1880) [JC]
604 Broadway, 58102. Tel: 701-235-4289; Email: cathedral@fargodiocese.org; Web: www.cathedralofstmary.com. 619 7th St. N., 58102. Rev. Msgr. Joseph P. Goering, V.G., Rector; Revs. Robert Smith, Parochial Vicar; Charles Fischer, In Res.; Deacons George Loegering; Raymond Desjarlais.
Catechesis Religious Program—Email: diane@cathedralofstmary.com. Diane Dahlin, D.R.E. Students 131.

2—STS. ANNE & JOACHIM CHURCH OF FARGO (1995) [JC]
5202 25th St. S., 58104. Tel: 701-235-5757; Fax: 701-235-0764; Email: stsaaj@stsaaj.org; Web: www.stsaaj.org. Very Rev. Paul C. Duchschere; Revs. Jayson Miller, Parochial Vicar; Robert Irwin, In Res.; Charles LaCroix, In Res.; Deacon Michael Dodge.
Catechesis Religious Program—Email: cdulany@stsaaj.org. Connie Dulany, D.R.E. Students 377.

3—ST. ANTHONY OF PADUA'S CHURCH OF FARGO (1917) [JC]
710 S. 10th St., 58103. Tel: 701-237-6063; Email: deidra@stanthonyfargo.org; Web: www.stanthonyfargo.org. Revs. Raymond P. Courtright; Scott Karnik, Parochial Vicar; Deacon Stuart Longtin.
Catechesis Religious Program—Mrs. Maria Giezen, D.R.E. Students 86.

4—HOLY SPIRIT CHURCH OF FARGO (1951) [JC]
1420 N. 7th St., 58102. Tel: 701-232-5900; Email: holyspirit1420@gmail.com; Web: www.holyspiritchurchfargo.com. Revs. Ross Laframboise; Petro Ndunguru.
Please see Holy Spirit Elementary School under Catholic Schools in the Institutions Located in the Diocese section.
Catechesis Religious Program—Students 139.

5—NATIVITY CHURCH OF FARGO (1960) [JC]
1825 11th St. S., 58103. Tel: 701-232-2414; Email: kevin.boucher@fargodiocese.org; Web: nativitycatholicchurch.net. Revs. Kevin Boucher; David Michael, Parochial Vicar.
Please see Nativity Elementary School under Catholic Schools in the Institutions Located in the Diocese section.
Catechesis Religious Program—Email: kathyb@nativitycatholicchurch.net. Kathy Bourdon, D.R.E. Students 134.

6—ST. PAUL'S NEWMAN CHURCH OF FARGO (1928) [JC]
1141 N. University Dr., 58102. Tel: 701-235-0142. Rev. James Cheney; Rev. Msgr. Gregory J. Schlesselmann, Spiritual Dir.
Catechesis Religious Program—Email: emma@bisoncatholic.org. Emma Hergenroeder, D.R.E. Students 38.

OUTSIDE THE CITY OF FARGO

ALICE, CASS CO., ST. HENRY (1902) Closed. For inquiries for parish records contact the Chancellor's Office. Sacramental records are at St. Patrick in Enderlin.

ANAMOOSE, MCHENRY CO., ST. FRANCIS XAVIER CHURCH OF ANAMOOSE (1899) [CEM] Also serving Drake.
605 1st St W, Anamoose, 58710-0049.
Tel: 701-465-3780; Email: stfx@gondtc.com. P.O. Box 49, Anamoose, 58710. Rev. Robert Wapenski.
Catechesis Religious Program—Students 7.

ANETA, NELSON CO., SACRED HEART CHURCH OF ANETA (1907) Served from Cooperstown.
Mailing Address: c/o St. George, P.O. Box 217, Cooperstown, 58425. Tel: 701-797-2624. 307 1st St. N., Aneta, 58212. Rev. Dale H. Kinzler.
Catechesis Religious Program—804 Foster Ave. NW, Cooperstown, 58425. Students 5.

ARDOCH, WALSH CO., ST. JOHN THE BAPTIST (1883) [CEM] Closed. For inquiries for parish records contact the chancery. Sacramental records are at Sacred Heart, Minto.

ARGUSVILLE, CASS CO., ST. WILLIAM'S CHURCH OF ARGUSVILLE (1942) [JC] Served from Hillsboro.
107 Drake Ave., Argusville, 58005. Tel: 701-484-5211 ; Email: stwilliamscc@live.com. Rev. K. S. Kopacz, J.C.L.
Catechesis Religious Program—Tel: 701-484-5211. Lacee Steinberger, D.R.E. Students 43.

ASHLEY, MCINTOSH CO., ST. DAVID'S CHURCH OF ASHLEY (1920) Served from Wishek.
Mailing Address: c/o St. Patrick, P.O. Box 293, Wishek, 58495. Tel: 701-423-5494. 601 2nd Ave. N.E., Ashley, 58413. Email: wenceslaus.katanga@fargodiocese.org. Very Rev. Wenceslaus Katanga.
Catechesis Religious Program—Tel: 701-452-2970. Students 15.

BALFOUR, MCHENRY CO., ST. JOSEPH (1906) Closed. For inquiries for parish records please contact the Chancellor's office. Sacramental records are at St. Margaret Mary, Drake.

BALTA, PIERCE CO., OUR LADY OF MT. CARMEL CHURCH OF BALTA (1902) [CEM] Served from Esmond.
301 Main St. N., Balta, 58313. Tel: 701-249-8360; Email: boniface@gondtc.com. 108 Alta Ave. N., P.O. Box 37, Esmond, 58332. Rev. Brian Bachmeier.
Religious Education Program—Students 40.

BATHGATE, PEMBINA CO., ST. ANTHONY (1883) Closed. For inquiries for parish records contact the Chancellor's Office. Sacramental records are at St. Brigid, Cavalier.

BECHYNE, WALSH CO.

BELCOURT, ROLETTE CO.

1—ST. ANN (1885) [CEM] Also serving St. Anthony.
1115 Louis Riel Dr., Belcourt, 58316.
Tel: 701-477-5601; Email: SAsecretary@utma.com. P.O. Box 2000, Belcourt, 58316. Revs. Dennis Mary Dugan, S.O.L.T.; James Mulligan, S.O.L.T., Parochial Vicar; Anthony Hession, Parochial Vicar; Deacon Francis Davis
Legal Titles: St. Ann's Church of Belcourt
School—*St. Ann*, (Grades PreK-6), Hwy 5, St. Ann's Rd., P.O. Box 2020, Belcourt, 58316-2020.
Tel: 701-477-2667; Email: sacsbelcourt@gmail.com. Allan Mehrer, Prin. Lay Teachers 7; Students 46; Religious Teachers 1.
Catechesis Religious Program—Michelle Martin, D.R.E. Students 76.

2—ST. ANTHONY CHURCH OF ALCIDE (1885) [CEM] Served from St. Ann, Belcourt.
5 miles west on Hwy #5, Alcide, 58316.
Tel: 701-477-5601; Email: dmdsolt@gmail.com. P.O. Box 2000, Belcourt, 58316. Rev. Dennis Mary Dugan, S.O.L.T.

3—ST. BENEDICT'S CHURCH OF BELCOURT (1940) Served from St. John.
Mailing Address: P.O. Box 170, St. John, 58369-0170. Tel: 701-477-3081; Email: saintjohnthebaptistnd@gmail.com. 3821 Bureau of Indian Affairs Rd. #6, Belcourt, 58316. Rev. Richard Fineo, Admin.
Catechesis Religious Program—Students 8.

BISBEE, TOWNER CO., HOLY ROSARY CHURCH OF BISBEE (1889) [CEM] Served from Rolette.
304 3rd Ave. W., Bisbee, 58317. Rev. Paulraj Thondappa.

BOTTINEAU, BOTTINEAU CO., ST. MARK'S CHURCH OF BOTTINEAU (1901) [CEM] Also serving Westhope.
322 Sinclair St., Bottineau, 58318-1024.
Tel: 701-228-3164; Tel: 701-228-5164; Email: stsmanda@utma.com; Web: www.stmark-standrew.org. Rev. Michael Hickin.
Catechesis Religious Program—Mary Gorder, D.R.E. Students 40.

BREMEN, WELLS CO., ST. JOSEPH (1896) [CEM] Closed. For inquiries for parish records contact the chancery. Sacramental records located at St. John, New Rockford.

BROCKET, RAMSEY CO., ST. JOSEPH (1910) Closed. For inquiries for parish records contact the Chancellor's Office. Sacramental records are at St. Mary, Lakota.

BUCHANAN, STUTSMAN CO., ST. MARGARET CHURCH OF BUCHANAN (1924) [CEM] Served from Jamestown.
410 Main St., Buchanan, 58420. Tel: 701-252-0119; Fax: 701-952-6992; Email: basilica@stjamesbasilica.org. 622 1st Ave. S., Jamestown, 58401. Rev. Msgr. Jeffrey Wald.
Catechesis Religious Program—Tel: 701-252-0478; Email: ffsecretary@stjamesbasilica.org. Claudia Sharp, Sec. Students 6.

BUFFALO, CASS CO., ST. THOMAS CHURCH OF BUFFALO (1900) [JC] Served from Casselton.
401 3rd St. N, Buffalo, 58011. Tel: 701-347-4609; Email: stleo@casselton.net. P.O. Box 340, Casselton, 58012. Rev. James Ermer.
Catechesis Religious Program—Tel: 701-347-4609. Sue Knoll, D.R.E. Students 27.

BURNSTAD, LOGAN CO., ST. CLARE OF ASSISI (1915) Closed. For inquiries for parish records contact the chancery. Sacramental records are at St. Philip Meri, Napoleon.

CANDO, TOWNER CO., SACRED HEART CHURCH OF CANDO (1893) [CEM] Also serving Leeds.
307 3rd St., Cando, 58324. Tel: 701-968-3830. Mailing Address: P.O. Box 399, Cando, 58324. Rev. Daniel Musgrave.
Catechesis Religious Program—Students 52.

CARRINGTON, FOSTER CO., SACRED HEART CHURCH OF CARRINGTON (1887) [CEM] Also serving Sykeston.
663 1st St. S., Carrington, 58421. Tel: 701-652-2519; Email: sacredheart@daktel.com; Web: sacredheartcarrington.blogspot.com. Mailing Address: P.O. Box 420, Carrington, 58421. Rev. Thomas E. Dodge Jr.
Catechesis Religious Program—Tel: 701-652-2072; Email: sacredheartccd@outlook.com. Susan Thompson, D.R.E. Students 96.

CASSELTON, CASS CO., ST. LEO'S CHURCH OF CASSELTON (1880) [CEM] Also serving Buffalo.
211 Langer Ave. N, Casselton, 58012.
Tel: 701-347-4609; Email: stleo@casselton.net. P.O. Box 340, Casselton, 58012. Rev. James Ermer.
Catechesis Religious Program—Sue Knoll, D.R.E. Students 149.

CAVALIER, PEMBINA CO., ST. BRIGID OF IRELAND CHURCH OF CAVALIER (1883) [CEM] Also serving Crystal.
107 W 1st Ave. S, Cavalier, 58220. Tel: 701-265-8877 ; Fax: 701-265-8848; Email: stbrigidm@polarcomm.com. P.O. Box 280, Cavalier, 58220. Rev. Robert Pecotte.
Catechesis Religious Program—Email: stbrigiddre@polarcomm.com. Cindy Miller, D.R.E. Students 35.

CAYUGA, SARGENT CO., STS. PETER & PAUL CHURCH OF CAYUGA (1916) Served from Lidgerwood.
229 Franklin Ave W, Cayuga, 58013.
Tel: 701-538-4604; Fax: 701-538-4600; Email: stboniface@rrt.net. 230 1st St. NW, Lidgerwood, 58053. Rev. Peter J. Anderl.

COGSWELL, SARGENT CO., OUR LADY OF MERCY (1903) [CEM] Closed. For inquiries for parish records contact the chancery. Sacramental records are at St. Mary, Forman.

CONWAY, WALSH CO., ST. MARK (1884) Closed. For inquiries for parish records contact the Chancellor's Office. Sacramental records are at St. John, Pisek.

COOPERSTOWN, GRIGGS CO., ST. GEORGE CHURCH OF COOPERSTOWN (1939) [CEM] Also serving Aneta, Jessie, Finley.
804 Foster Ave. NW, Cooperstown, 58425.
Tel: 701-797-2624; Email: stgeorge@mlgc.com; Web: www.stgeorgecooper.org. Mailing Address: P.O. Box 217, Cooperstown, 58425. Rev. Dale H. Kinzler; Deacon Wallace Dalman.
Catechesis Religious Program—Students 22.

COURTENAY, STUTSMAN CO., ST. MARY, [CEM] Closed. For inquiries for parish records contact the chancery. Sacramental records are at St. Boniface, Wimbledon.

CRARY, RAMSEY CO., ST. BENEDICT (1910) [CEM] Closed. For inquiries for parish records contact the chancery. Sacramental records are at St. Joseph, Devil Lake.

CROW HILL, BENSON CO., ST. JEROME'S CHURCH OF CROW HILL (1892) [CEM] (Native American) Served from Fort Totten.
Mailing Address: Box 299, Fort Totten, 58335.
Tel: 701-766-4314; Email: charles.leute@fargodiocese.org. 3971 69th Ave. N.E., Oberon, 583357. Rev. Charles J. Leute, O.P.
Catechesis Religious Program—Students 7.

CRYSTAL, PEMBINA CO., ST. PATRICK'S CHURCH OF CRYSTAL (1892) [CEM] Served from Cavalier.
4th & Garfield, Crystal, 58222. Mailing Address: P.O. Box 280, Cavalier, 58220. Tel: 701-265-8877; Fax: 701-265-8848; Email: stbrigidm@polarcomm.com. Rev. Robert Pecotte.
Catechesis Religious Program—Tel: 701-993-8434; Email: tanya@dakotadynamics.com. Tanya Wieler, D.R.E. Students 24.

DAZEY, BARNES CO., ST. MARY'S CHURCH OF DAZEY (1899) [CEM] Served from Wimbledon.
1606 116th St. SE, Dazey, 58429. Tel: 701-435-2310; Email: boniface@daktel.com. Mailing Address: P.O. Box 9, Wimbledon, 58492. Rev. Sean P. Mulligan.
Catechesis Religious Program—302 1st St. N.,

Wimbledon, 58492. Email: St.BonifaceND@gmail.com. Students 15.

DEVILS LAKE, RAMSEY CO., ST. JOSEPH CHURCH (1884)
501 4th St., N.E., Devils Lake, 58301.
Tel: 701-662-7558; Fax: 701-662-7559; Email: stjosephschurch@dvl.midco.net. P.O. Box 898, Devils Lake, 58301. Very Rev. Chad F. Wilhelm; Rev. Steven Wirth.
School—St. Joseph's Church of Devils Lake School, (Grades PreK-6), 824 10th Ave., N.E., Devils Lake, 58301. Tel: 701-662-5016; Fax: 701-662-5017; Email: michelle.clouse@stjosephschooldl.org. Mrs. Michelle Clouse, Prin. Lay Teachers 15; Students 194; Religious Teachers 3; Clergy / Religious Teachers 3.
Catechesis Religious Program—824 10th Ave. N.E., Devils Lake, 58301. Tel: 701-662-5071; Email: stjoesre@gmail.com. Joni Flaten, D.R.E. Students 150.

DICKEY, LAMOURE CO., ASSUMPTION CHURCH OF DICKEY (1909) [CEM] Served from LaMoure.
106 Main St., Dickey, 58458. Tel: 701-883-5987; Email: holyrosery.church@gmail.com; Web: www.holyrosarylamoure.com. Mailing Address: P.O. Box 217, Lamoure, 58458. Rev. Gregory Haman.
Catechesis Religious Program—209 1st St. S.E., LaMoure, 58458. Suzanne Lahlum, D.R.E. Students 2.

DRAKE, MCHENRY CO., ST. MARGARET MARY CHURCH OF DRAKE (1910) [CEM] Served by Anamoose.
605 Main St., Drake, 58736. Tel: 701-465-3780; Email: stfx@gondtc.com. P.O. Box 197, Drake, 58736. Rev. Robert Wapenski.
Catechesis Religious Program—Tel: 701-465-3284. Students 17.

DRAYTON, PEMBINA CO., ST. EDWARD'S CHURCH OF DRAYTON (1889) [CEM] Also serving Pembina.
102 E Wallace Ave., Drayton, 58225.
Tel: 701-454-6171; Fax: 701-454-6171; Email: stedward@polarcomm.com. Mailing Address: P.O. Box 215, Drayton, 58225. Rev. Joseph Okogba.
Catechesis Religious Program—102 E. Wallace Ave., Drayton, 58225. Tel: 701-520-9838. Margaret Pollestad, D.R.E. Students 7.

DUNSEITH, ROLETTE CO.

1—IMMACULATE HEART OF MARY (1948) [CEM] Closed. For inquiries for parish records please see St. Michael's Church, Dunseith.

2—ST. LOUIS KING OF FRANCE (1882) [CEM] Closed. For inquiries for parish records please St. Michael's Church, Dunseith.

3—ST. MICHAEL THE ARCHANGEL DUNSEITH (2007)
112 1st St. NW, Dunseith, 58329. Tel: 701-244-5738; Email: stmichaeldunseith@gmail.com; Web: stmichaeldunseith.com. P.O. Box 160, Dunseith, 58329. Rev. Michael Slovak.
Catechesis Religious Program—Shelly Azure, D.R.E. Students 59.

EDGELEY, LAMOURE CO., TRANSFIGURATION CHURCH OF EDGELEY (1889) [CEM] Also serving Nortonville.
205 Main St., Edgeley, 58433. Tel: 701-493-2387; Email: transholy@drtel.net. P.O. Box 347, Edgeley, 58433. Rev. Jake Miller.
Catechesis Religious Program—Students 58.

ELLENDALE, DICKEY CO., ST. HELENA'S CHURCH OF ELLENDALE (1888) [CEM] Also serving Fullerton.
Mailing Address: P.O. Box 796, Ellendale, 58436. Rev. Jason Asselin, J.C.L.
Catechesis Religious Program—Tel: 701-349-4128. Students 57.

ENDERLIN, RANSOM CO., ST. PATRICK'S CHURCH OF ENDERLIN (1901) [CEM] Also serving Sheldon and Fingal.
Mailing Address: 302 Bluff St., Enderlin, 58027.
Tel: 701-437-2791; Email: stpatrick@mlgc.com; Web: www.enderlinfingalsheldon.org. Rev. Christopher J. Markman.
Catechesis Religious Program—Students 14.

ESMOND, BENSON CO., ST. BONIFACE CHURCH OF ESMOND (1909) [CEM] Also serving Maddock and Balta.
108 Alta Ave. N., Esmond, 58332-3202.
Tel: 701-249-8360; Email: boniface@gondtc.com. Mailing Address: P.O. Box 37, Esmond, 58332-0037. Rev. Brian Bachmeier
Legal Title: Formerly St. Agnes Church of Esmond - parish name changed on April 6, 1938
Catechesis Religious Program—Religious Education, Students 6.

FAIRMOUNT, RICHLAND CO., ST. ANTHONY'S CHURCH OF FAIRMOUNT (1909) [CEM] Served from Hankinson.
204 2nd St. N, Fairmount, 58030. Tel: 701-474-5518; Email: saintphilip@fargodiocese.org. Mailing Address: P.O. Box 292, Fairmount, 58030. Rev. Scott Sautner.

FESSENDEN, WELLS CO., ST. AUGUSTINE'S CHURCH OF FESSENDEN (1896) Also serving Hurdsfield and McClusky.
105 7th Ave. S., Fessenden, 58438-7404.
Tel: 701-547-3430; Email: staugustineparish@outlook.com. Rev. Jeffrey Eppler, S.O.L.T., Admin.
Catechesis Religious Program—Students 10.

FINGAL, BARNES CO., HOLY TRINITY CHURCH OF FINGAL (1889) [CEM 2] Served by Enderlin.
419 1st Ave., Fingal, 58031. Mailing Address: 302 Bluff St., Enderlin, 58027. Tel: 701-437-2791; Email: stpatrick@mlgc.com; Web: www.enderlinfingalsheldon.org. Rev. Christopher J. Markman.
Catechesis Religious Program—Students 13.

FINLEY, STEELE CO., ST. OLAF CHURCH OF FINLEY (1948) [JC] Served from Cooperstown.
100 Taft St., Finley, 58230. Tel: 701-797-2624; Email: stgeorge@mlgc.com; Web: www.stgeorgecooper.org. Mailing Address: P.O. Box 217, Cooperstown, 58425. Rev. Dale H. Kinzler.
Catechesis Religious Program—Students 10.

FORMAN, SARGENT CO., ST. MARY CHURCH OF FORMAN (1913) [CEM] Served from Oakes.
Mailing Address: 484 4th St., S.W., Forman, 58032.
Tel: 701-724-3319; Email: 4steeples@drtel.net. Rev. William P. Gerlach.
Catechesis Religious Program—Dixie Bopp, D.R.E. Students 26.

FORT TOTTEN, BENSON CO., SEVEN DOLORS OF FORT TOTTEN (1875) [CEM] (Native American) Also serving Crow Hill, Tokio.
Mailing Address: P.O. Box 299, Fort Totten, 58335-0299. Tel: 701-766-4314; Email: charles.leute@fargodiocese.org. 213 Dakotah Rd., Fort Totten, 58335-0299. Rev. Charles J. Leute, O.P.; Deacon Anthony McDonald.
Catechesis Religious Program—Students 16.

FRIED, STUTSMAN CO., SACRED HEART (1888) Closed. For inquiries for parish records contact the Chancellor's Office. Sacramental records are at Basilica St. James, Jamestown.

FULDA, MCHENRY CO., ST. ANSELM (1901) [CEM] Closed. For inquiries for parish records contact the chancery. Sacramental records are at St. Therese, Rugby.

FULLERTON, DICKEY CO., ST. PATRICK CHURCH OF FULLERTON (1921) [CEM] Served from Ellendale.
207 Monroe St. N, Fullerton, 58441.
Tel: 701-349-3297; Email: jason.asselin@fargodiocese.org. Mailing Address: c/o St. Helena, P.O. Box 796, Ellendale, 58436. Rev. Jason Asselin, J.C.L.

GACKLE, LOGAN CO., ST. ANNE (1951) Closed. For inquiries for parish records contact the chancery. Sacramental records are at St. Philip Neri, Napoleon.

GENESEO, SARGENT CO., ST. MARTIN'S CHURCH OF GENESEO (1907) [CEM] Served from Lidgerwood.
413 Main St., Geneseo, 58053. Tel: 701-538-4604; Email: stboniface@rrt.net. c/o St. Boniface: 230 1st St. NW, Lidgerwood, 58053. Rev. Peter J. Anderl.

GRAFTON, WALSH CO., ST. JOHN THE EVANGELIST'S CHURCH OF GRAFTON (1881) [CEM] Also Serving Oakwood.
344 15th St. W., Grafton, 58237. Tel: 701-352-1648; Email: office.stjohns@midconetwork.com. Rev. Timothy Schroeder; Deacon Michael Grzadzielewski.
Catechesis Religious Program—1515 Western Ave., Grafton, 58237. Email: vicki.stjohns@midconetwork.com. Brent Hermans, D.R.E. Students 163.

GRAND FORKS, GRAND FORKS CO.

1—HOLY FAMILY CHURCH OF GRAND FORKS (1960) [JC]
1018 18th Ave. S., Grand Forks, 58201-6828.
Tel: 701-746-1454; Fax: 701-746-1456; Email: stacey@holyfamilygf.org; Web: www.holyfamilygf.org. Rev. Msgr. Brian G. Donahue; Deacon Paul Kuhn, Parochial Vicar.
School—Holy Family Church of Grand Forks School, (Grades K-5), Tel: 701-775-9886; Email: kmayer@hfsmschool.org; Web: www.hfsmschool.org. Katie Mayer, Prin. Lay Teachers 10; Students 94; Religious Teachers 3.
Catechesis Religious Program—Fax: 701-746-1456; Email: sharon@holyfamilygf.org. Students 120.

2—ST. MARY CHURCH OF GRAND FORKS (1915) [JC]
216 Belmont Rd., Grand Forks, 58201.
Tel: 701-775-9318; Fax: 701-775-7568; Email: stmarysgfnd@yahoo.com; Web: stmarysgfnd.com. Rev. James Gross.
Catechesis Religious Program—Tel: 701-775-2842; Email: stmarysdonp@yahoo.com. Donald Palmiscno, D.R.E. Students 100.

3—ST. MICHAEL'S CHURCH OF GRAND FORKS (1872) [JC]
Mailing Address: 418 N. 6th St., Grand Forks, 58203. Tel: 701-772-2624; Web: www.stmichaelschurchgf.com. 524 5th Ave. N., Grand Forks, 58203. Revs. H. Gerard Braun; Robert Keller.
School—St. Michael's Church of Grand Forks School, (Grades PreK-5), 504 5th Ave. N., Grand Forks, 58203. Tel: 701-772-1822; Fax: 701-772-0211; Email: sara.dudley@stmichaelsgf.com; Web: http://stmichaelsgf.com/school. Sara Dudley, Prin. Lay Teachers 16; Students 168; Religious Teachers 1.
Catechesis Religious Program—Tel: 701-772-2282; Email: jennifer.carlson@stmichaelsgf.com. Jennifer Carlson, D.R.E. Students 169.

4—ST. THOMAS AQUINAS NEWMAN CENTER OF GRAND FORKS (1951) [JC]
410 Cambridge St., Grand Forks, 58203.
Tel: 701-777-6850; Email: jessica.kuznia@undcatholic.org; Web: www.undcatholic.org. Rev. Luke D. Meyer.
Catechesis Religious Program—Students 6.

GRANVILLE, MCHENRY CO., OUR LADY OF PERPETUAL HELP (1933) Closed. For inquiries for parish records contact the chancery. Sacramental records are at St. Cecilia, Towner.

GWINNER, SARGENT CO., ST. VINCENT'S CHURCH OF GWINNER (1984) [CEM] Served from Lisbon.
701 Oak St., Lisbon, 58054. Tel: 701-683-4620; Fax: 701-683-5703; Email: staloysius@drtel.net. Rev. Jerald L.C. Finnestad.
Catechesis Religious Program—Tel: 701-678-2364. Christina Ferderer, D.R.E. Students 16.

HANKINSON, RICHLAND CO., ST. PHILIP'S CHURCH OF HANKINSON (1889) [CEM]
612 S. Main, Hankinson, 58041. Tel: 701-242-7327; Fax: 701-242-7773; Email: saintphilip@fargodiocese.org. P.O. Box 419, Hankinson, 58041. Rev. Scott Sautner.
Catechesis Religious Program—Students 81.

HANSBORO, TOWNER CO., SACRED HEART, Closed. For inquiries for parish records please contact the Chancellor's Office. Sacramental records are at St. Joachim, Rolla.

HARVEY, WELLS CO., ST. CECILIA'S CHURCH OF HARVEY (1895) [CEM] Also serving Selz.
413 E. Brewster St., Harvey, 58341.
Tel: 701-324-2144; Fax: 701-324-2637; Email: stcecilia@gondtc.com; Web: stceciliaharvey.org. Very Rev. Franklin Miller; Deacon Jeffrey M. Faul.
Catechesis Religious Program—Tel: 701-721-7483; Email: aziegler@gondtc.com. Amber Ziegler, D.R.E. Students 56.

HILLSBORO, TRAILL CO., ST. ROSE OF LIMA'S CHURCH OF HILLSBORO (1892) [CEM] Also serves Argusville.
503 3rd St. SE, Hillsboro, 58045. Mailing Address: P.O. Box 459, Hillsboro, 58045. Tel: 701-636-4541; Email: usml@aol.com. Rev. K. S. Kopacz, J.C.L.
Catechesis Religious Program—Tel: 701-636-5981. Carmen Henn, D.R.E. Students 114.

HOPE, STEELE CO., ST. AGATHA'S CHURCH OF HOPE (1907) Served from Oriska.
Mailing Address: c/o St. Bernard's Church of Oriska, 606 5th St., Oriska, 58063. Tel: 701-845-3713; Fax: 701-845-0172; Email: oriska_tri_parish@yahoo.com. 604 Steele Ave., Hope, 58046. Rev. Joseph Barrett.
Catechesis Religious Program—Amy Fugelstadt, D.R.E. Students 11.

HUNTER, CASS CO., ST. AGNES CHURCH OF HUNTER (1898) Served by Mayville.
102 1st St. E, Hunter, 58048. Tel: 701-788-3234; Email: catholic@gra.midco.net. 846 5th St., S.E., Mayville, 58257. Rev. Philip Chacko.
Catechesis Religious Program—Tel: 701-967-8970. Michelle Thompson, D.R.E. Students 22.

HURDSFIELD, WELLS CO., ST. PATRICK'S CHURCH OF HURDSFIELD (1907) Served from Fessenden.
c/o St. Augustine, 105 7th Ave. S., Fessenden, 58438.
Tel: 701-547-3430; Email: staugustineparish@outlook.com. Rev. Jeffrey Eppler, S.O.L.T., Admin.

JAMESTOWN, STUTSMAN CO., ST. JAMES BASILICA OF JAMESTOWN (1881) [CEM] Also Serving Buchanan, Windsor and Pingree.
622 1st Ave. S., Jamestown, 58401-4648.
Tel: 701-252-0119; Email: basilica@stjamesbasilica.org; Web: www.stjamesbasilica.org. Rev. Msgr. Jeffrey Wald; Revs. John F. Aerts; Patrick Parks; Deacons Thomas Geffre; Kenneth Votava.
School—St. John Academy, (Grades PreK-6), 215 5th St., S.E., Jamestown, 58401. Tel: 701-252-3397; Email: lawrie.paulson@k12.nd.us; Web: www.stjamesbasilica.org/stjohn. Lawrie Paulson, Prin. Lay Teachers 20; Students 196; Religious Teachers 1.
Catechesis Religious Program—Katie Webster, D.R.E.; Whitney Somsen, Youth Min.; Claudia Sharp, Sec. Students 133.

JESSIE, GRIGGS CO., ST. LAWRENCE CHURCH OF JESSIE (1888) [CEM] Served from Cooperstown.
105 Dewey St., Jessie, 58452. Tel: 701-797-2624; Email: stgeorge@mlgc.com. P.O. Box 217, Cooperstown, 58425. Rev. Dale H. Kinzler.
Catechesis Religious Program—804 Foster Ave. NW, Cooperstown, 58425. Students 12.

KARLSRUHE, MCHENRY CO., STS. PETER & PAUL CHURCH OF KARLSRUHE (1905) [CEM] Served from Velva.
401 Main Street, Karlsruhe, 58744.
Tel: 701-338-2663; Email: velvakarls@srt.com; Web: stceciliavelvand.org. Rev. Peter Sharpe.

KENSAL, STUTSMAN CO., ST. JOHN'S CHURCH OF KENSAL (1917) [CEM] Served from Wimbledon.
407 Pleasant Ave., Kensal, 58455. Tel: 701-435-2310.

P.O. Box 9, Wimbledon, 58492. Rev. Sean P. Mulligan.
Catechesis Religious Program—302 1st St. N., Wimbledon, 58492. Email: St.BonifaceND@gmail.com. Students 1.

KINDRED, CASS CO., ST. MAURICE CHURCH OF KINDRED (1965)
5313 165th Ave., S.E., Kindred, 58051. P.O. Box 272, Kindred, 58051. Tel: 701-428-3094; Web: www.stmaurices.org. Very Rev. James Goodwin, J.C.L.; Deacon Clarence Vetter; Beverly Lindsey, Sec.
Catechesis Religious Program—Bethany Johnson, D.R.E. Students 43.

KINTYRE, LOGAN CO., ST. BONIFACE (1905) [CEM] Closed. For inquiries for parish records contact the chancery. Sacramental records are at St. Philip Neri, Napoleon.

KNOX, BENSON CO., ST. MARY'S CHURCH OF KNOX (1936) [CEM] Served from Rugby.
129 Morgan St., Knox, 58343. c/o St. Therese the Little Flower, 218 3rd St., S.E., Rugby, 58368-1814. Tel: 701-776-6388; Tel: 701-776-5327; Email: lfparish@gondtc.com. Revs. Thomas Graner; Prahbakar Marneni, Parochial Vicar.
Catechesis Religious Program—129 Morgan St., Knox, 58343. Lisa Volk, D.R.E. Students 15.

LA MOURE, LA MOURE CO., HOLY ROSARY CHURCH OF LA MOURE (1890) [CEM] Also serving Dickey and Verona.
209 1st. SE, LaMoure, 58458. Tel: 701-883-5987; Email: holyrosery.church@gmail.com. Mailing Address: P.O. Box 217, La Moure, 58458. Rev. Gregory Haman.
Catechesis Religious Program—Email: nd.bisonfan@gmail.com. Suzanne Lahlum, D.R.E. Students 54.

LAKE WILLIAMS, KIDDER CO., OUR LADY OF THE LAKE (1946) Closed. For inquiries for parish records contact the Chancellor's Office. Sacramental records are at St. Francis de Sales, Steele.

LAKOTA, NELSON CO., ST. MARY'S CHURCH OF LAKOTA (1902) Also serving Tolna and Michigan.
109 East Ave. E, Lakota, 58344. Tel: 701-247-2584; Email: smcc@polarcomm.com. P.O. Box 509, Lakota, 58344. Rev. Steven Meyer.
Catechesis Religious Program—Tel: 701-247-3356; Email: laurieeidsness@hotmail.com. Laurie Eidsness, D.R.E. Students 26.

LANGDON, CAVALIER CO., ST. ALPHONSUS CHURCH OF LANGDON (1888) [CEM] Also serving Nekoma and Wales.
Mailing Address: 1010 3rd St., Langdon, 58249.
Tel: 701-256-5966; Fax: 701-256-2358; Email: phillip.ackerman@fargodiocese.org; Web: www.stalphonsuslangdon.com/. Very Rev. Phillip Ackerman; Rev. William Ovsak.
School—St. Alphonsus Church of Langdon School, (Grades PreK-8), 209 10th Ave., Langdon, 58249.
Tel: 701-256-2354; Email: saints@utma.com; Web: www.stalphonsuslangdon.com. Derek Simonsen, Prin.; Jackie Kram, Sec. Lay Teachers 9; Students 75; Clergy / Religious Teachers 2.
Catechesis Religious Program—Carla Horpestad, D.R.E. Students 73.

LANKIN, WALSH CO.
1—ST. JOSEPH'S CHURCH OF LANKIN (1906) [CEM] Served by Pisek.
506 4th Ave., Lankin, 58250. Tel: 701-284-6060; Email: stjohnne@polarcomm.com. P.O. Box 27, Pisek, 58273. Rev. Jason Lefor.
Catechesis Religious Program—Students 2.
2—STS. PETER & PAUL CHURCH OF BECHYNE (1886) [CEM] Served from Pisek.
11951 Cty. Rd. 19, Lankin, 58250. Mailing Address: P.O. Box 27, Pisek, 58273. Tel: 701-284-6060; Email: stjohnne@polarcomm.com. Rev. Jason Lefor.
Catechesis Religious Program—Students 2,321.

LARIMORE, GRAND FORKS CO., ST. STEPHEN'S CHURCH OF LARIMORE (1882)
311 W Front St., Larimore, 58251. Tel: 701-343-2377 ; Fax: 701-343-2316; Email: ststlarimore@msn.com. Mailing Address: P.O. Box 778, Larimore, 58251. Rev. William McDermott.
Catechesis Religious Program—Lori Larson, D.R.E. Students 51.

LEEDS, BENSON CO., ST. VINCENT DE PAUL CHURCH OF LEEDS (1897) [CEM] Served from Cando.
Central Ave., Leeds, 58346. Mailing Address: P.O. Box 399, Cando, 58324. Tel: 701-968-3830. Rev. Daniel Musgrave.
Catechesis Religious Program—Tel: 701-968-3830. Students 15.

LEROY, PEMBINA CO., ST. JOSEPH (1873) [CEM] Closed. For inquiries for parish records contact the chancery. Sacramental records are at St. Boniface, Walhalla.

LIDGERWOOD, RICHLAND CO., ST. BONIFACE CHURCH OF LIDGERWOOD (1887) [CEM] Also serving Geneseo and Cayuga.
Mailing Address: 230 1st St. NW, Lidgerwood, 58053. Tel: 701-538-4604; Fax: 701-538-4600; Email: stboniface@rrt.net; Web: www.stboniface.net. Rev. Peter J. Anderl.
Catechesis Religious Program—Email: stbonifacedre@rrt.net. Mrs. Melodi Novotny, D.R.E. Students 51.

LISBON, RANSOM CO., ST. ALOYSIUS CHURCH OF LISBON (1884) [CEM] Also serving Gwinner.
701 Oak St., Lisbon, 58054. Rev. Jerald L.C. Finnestad.
Catechesis Religious Program—Lynn Hansen, D.R.E. Students 58.

LOMICE, WALSH CO., ST. CATHERINE (1936) [CEM] Closed. For inquiries for parish records contact the chancery. Sacramental records are at St. Mary, Lakota.

MADDOCK, BENSON CO., ST. WILLIAM CHURCH OF MADDOCK (1954) Served from Esmond.
204 Roosevelt Ave., Maddock, 58348.
Tel: 701-249-8360; Email: boniface@gondtc.com. 108 Alta Ave. N., P.O. Box 37, Esmond, 58332. Rev. Brian Bachmeier.
Catechesis Religious Program—Religious Education Program, Students 19.

MANTADOR, RICHLAND CO., STS. PETER & PAUL CHURCH OF MANTADOR (1881) [CEM] Served from Mooreton.
609 Cty. Rd. 25, Mantador, 58058. Tel: 701-274-8259 ; Web: sts-peter-paul-catholic-church.business.site. Mailing Address: P.O. Box 39, Mantador, 58058. Rev. Kurtis Gunwall.

MANVEL, GRAND FORKS CO., ST. TIMOTHY'S CHURCH OF MANVEL (1882) [CEM]
Mailing Address: 1207 Oldham Ave., Manvel, 58256-4335. Tel: 701-696-2219; Email: sttimothys@invisimax.com. Rev. John Ejike.
Catechesis Religious Program—Bonnie Ferry, D.R.E. Students 66.

MARION, LA MOURE CO., ST. FRANCIS (1910) [CEM] Closed. For inquiries for parish records contact the chancery. Sacramental records are at Holy Rosary, La Moure.

MAYVILLE, TRAILL CO., OUR LADY OF PEACE CHURCH OF MAYVILLE (1945) Also serving Hunter.
846 5th St., S.E., Mayville, 58257. Tel: 701-788-3234; Email: catholic@gra.midco.net. Rev. Philip Chacko.
Catechesis Religious Program—Students 54.

MCCLUSKY, SHERIDAN CO., HOLY FAMILY CHURCH OF MCCLUSKY (1905) Served from Fessenden.
Mailing Address: c/o St. Augustine, 105 7th Ave. S., Fessenden, 58438. Tel: 701-547-3430; Email: staugustineparish@outlook.com. Rev. Jeffrey Eppler, S.O.L.T., Admin.

MCHENRY, FOSTER CO., STS. PETER & PAUL CHURCH OF MCHENRY (1912) [CEM] Served from New Rockford.
391 Conn St., McHenry, 58464. Tel: 701-947-5325; Email: reese.weber@fargodiocese.org; Web: www.newrockford.com. 116 1st Ave. N., New Rockford, 58356-1802. Rev. Reese Weber.
Catechesis Religious Program—Sharon Eversvik, D.R.E. Students 14.

MEDINA, STUTSMAN CO., ST. MARY'S CHURCH OF MEDINA (1905) [CEM] Served from Steele.
105 3rd Ave. SE, Medina, 58467. Mailing Address: P.O. Box 87, Steele, 58482. Tel: 701-475-2333; Email: jerome.hunkler@fargodiocese.org. Rev. Jerome Hunkler.
Catechesis Religious Program—Students 5.

MICHIGAN, NELSON CO., ST. LAWRENCE O'TOOLE'S CHURCH OF MICHIGAN (1883) Served from Lakota.
214 Broadway N, Lakota, 58344. Tel: 701-247-2594; Email: steven.meyer@fargodiocese.org. P.O. Box 509, Michigan, 58259. Rev. Steven Meyer.
Catechesis Religious Program—Tel: 701-247-2584. Students 13.

MILNOR, SARGENT CO., ST. ARNOLD'S CHURCH OF MILNOR (1905) [CEM] Served from Wyndmere.
107 3rd St., Milnor, 58060. Rev. Troy K. Simonsen.
Catechesis Religious Program—Tel: 701-427-5327. Betty Speich, D.R.E. Students 26.

MILTON, CAVALIER CO., ST. CLOTILDE (1893) Closed. For inquiries for parish records contact the Chancellor's Office. Sacramental records are at St. Alphonsus, Langdon.

MINNEWAUKAN, BENSON CO., ST. JAMES (1899) Closed. For inquiries for parish records, contact the Chancellor's Office. Sacramental records are at St. Joseph, Devil's Lake.

MINTO, WALSH CO., SACRED HEART CHURCH OF MINTO (1905) [CEM] Also serving Warsaw.
621 3rd St., Minto, 58261-0316. Tel: 701-248-3589; Email: sacredheartminto@hotmail.com; Web: www.sh-ss.org. Mailing Address: P.O. Box 316, Minto, 58261. Rev. Brian Moen.
Catechesis Religious Program—Students 62.

MOORETON, RICHLAND CO., ST. ANTHONY'S CHURCH OF MOORETON (1884) [CEM] Also serving Mantador.
204 Mooreton Ave. N., Mooreton, 58061.
Tel: 701-274-8259; Email: mooretonmantadorcatholic@gmail.com; Web: stanthony-catholic-church.business.site. Rev. Kurtis Gunwall.
Catechesis Religious Program—Anita Onchuck, D.R.E. Students 43.

MOUNT CARMEL, CAVALIER CO., OUR LADY OF MOUNT CARMEL (1888) [CEM] Closed. For inquiries for parish records contact the chancery. Sacramental records located at St. Alphonsus, Langdon.

MUNICH, CAVALIER CO., ST. MARY CHURCH OF MUNICH (1916) [CEM 3] Also serving Starkweather.
607 Main, Munich, 58352. Tel: 701-682-5178; Email: stmarys@utma.com. P.O. Box 159, Munich, 58352. Rev. Mathew V. Pamplaniyil.
Catechesis Religious Program—Email: fosterdanielle10@yahoo.com. Students 28.

NAPOLEON, LOGAN CO., ST. PHILIP'S CHURCH OF NAPOLEON aka St. Philip Neri Catholic Church (1906) [CEM]
401 Broadway, Napoleon, 58561-7013.
Tel: 701-754-2860; Email: stphilipneri@bektel.com; Web: stphilipnerinapoleon.org. Rev. Neil J. Pfeifer; Deacons Allen Baumgartner; Gary Schumacher.
Catechesis Religious Program—Email: allebek@bektel.com. Students 126.

NECHE, PEMBINA CO., STS. NEREUS & ACHILLEUS CHURCH OF NECHE (1887) [CEM] Served from Walhalla.
801 Central Ave., Walhalla, 58282. Mailing Address: c/o St. Boniface, P.O. Box 228, Walhalla, 58282.
Tel: 701-549-3256; Email: boniface@utma.com. Rev. John Fisher Kizito.
Catechesis Religious Program—Students 5.

NEKOMA, CAVALIER CO., ST. EDWARD CHURCH OF NEKOMA (1907) [CEM] Served from Langdon.
323 Main St, Nekoma, 58355. Tel: 701-256-5966; Fax: 701-256-2358; Email: phillip.ackerman@fargodiocese.org; Web: www.stalphonsuslangdon.com. 1010 3rd St., Langdon, 58249. Very Rev. Phillip Ackerman; Rev. William Ovsak.
Catechesis Religious Program—Students 2.

NEW ROCKFORD, EDDY CO., ST. JOHN'S CHURCH OF NEW ROCKFORD (1904) [CEM] Also serving McHenry.
116 1st Ave. N., New Rockford, 58356.
Tel: 701-947-5325; Email: stjohnsnr@outlook.com; Web: www.cityofnewrockford.com. Rev. Reese Weber.
Catechesis Religious Program—Sharon Eversvik, D.R.E. Students 50.

NORTONVILLE, LAMOURE CO., HOLY SPIRIT CHURCH OF NORTONVILLE (1912) [JC] Served from Edgeley.
201 5th Ave., Nortonville, 58454. Tel: 701-493-2387; Email: transholy@drtel.net. Mailing Address: P.O. Box 348, Edgeley, 58433. Rev. Jake Miller.
Catechesis Religious Program—Students 18.

OAKES, DICKEY CO., ST. CHARLES CHURCH OF OAKES (1905) [CEM] Also serving Forman.
410 Seventh St. N., Oakes, 58474. Tel: 701-742-2418; Email: st.charlesoakes@gmail.com. Rev. William P. Gerlach.
Catechesis Religious Program—Tel: 701-742-2911. Students 84.

OAKWOOD, WALSH CO., SACRED HEART CHURCH OF OAKWOOD (1881) [CEM] Served from Grafton.
344 W. 15th St., Grafton, 58237-8860.
Tel: 701-352-1648; Email: bev.stjohns@midconetwork.com. Rev. Timothy Schroeder.
Catechesis Religious Program—

OLGA, CAVALIER CO., OUR LADY OF THE SACRED HEART (1882) [CEM 2] Closed. For inquiries for parish records contact the chancery. Sacramental records are at St. Boniface, Walhalla.

ORISKA, BARNES CO., ST. BERNARD'S CHURCH OF ORISKA (1881) [CEM] Also serving Hope and Sanborn.
606 5th St., Oriska, 58063. Tel: 701-845-3713;
Fax: 701-845-0172; Email: oriska_tri_parish@yahoo.com. Rev. Joseph Barrett; Deacon Jim McAllister.
Catechesis Religious Program—Tel: 701-845-3713. Students 6.

ORRIN, PIERCE CO., SACRED HEART (1903) [CEM] Closed. For inquiries for parish records contact the chancery. Sacramental records located at St. Therese, Rugby.

OSNABROCK, CAVALIER CO., ST. JOSEPH (1909) Closed. For inquiries for parish records contact the Chancellor's Office. Sacramental records are at St. Alphonsus, Langdon.

PAGE, CASS CO., ST. JAMES (1909) [CEM] Closed. For inquiries for parish records contact the chancery. Sacramental records are at St. Bernard, Oriska.

PARK RIVER, WALSH CO., ST. MARY CHURCH OF PARK RIVER (1888) [CEM] Also serving Veseleyville.
505 Park St. E, Park River, 58270. P.O. Box 110, Park River, 58270-0110. Tel: 701-284-6165; Email: stmarys@polarcomm.com; Web: www.saintsml.org. Rev. Bert Miller.
Catechesis Religious Program—Email: cherylddre@polarcomm.com. Cheryl Daley, D.R.E. Students 81.

PEMBINA, PEMBINA CO., ASSUMPTION CHURCH OF PEMBINA (1818) [CEM] Served from Drayton.

143 Hayden St., Pembina, 58271. Tel: 701-825-6266. Rev. Joseph Okogba.
Catechesis Religious Program—Students 12.

PENN, RAMSEY CO., IMMACULATE CONCEPTION (1986) Closed. For inquiries for parish records contact the Chancellor's Office. Sacramental records are at St. Vincent de Paul, Leeds.

PINGREE, STUTSMAN CO., ST. MICHAEL CHURCH OF PINGREE (1905) [CEM] Served from Jamestown.
518 Bentley Ave., Pingree, 58476. Tel: 701-252-0119; Fax: 701-952-6992; Email: basilica@stjamesbasilica.org. Mailing Address: c/o St. James Basilica, 622 1st. Ave. S., Jamestown, 58401-4648. Rev. Msgr. Jeffrey Wald.
Catechesis Religious Program—Tel: 701-252-0478; Email: ffsecretary@stjamesbasilica.org. Claudia Sharp, Sec.

PISEK, WALSH CO., ST. JOHN NEPOMUCENE'S CHURCH OF PISEK (1886) [CEM] Also serving Lankin and Bechyne.
167 Newton Ave., Pisek, 58273. Tel: 701-284-6060; Email: stjohnne@polarcomm.com. P.O. Box 27, Pisek, 58273. Rev. Jason Lefor.
Catechesis Religious Program—Students 13.

REYNOLDS, GRAND FORKS CO., OUR LADY OF PERPETUAL HELP CHURCH OF REYNOLDS (1895) [CEM] Serves Thompson.
424 5th St., Reynolds, NE 58275-0068.
Tel: 701-847-3096; Email: john.cavanaugh@fargodiocese.org; Web: www.olphsj.org. P.O. Box 68, Reynolds, 58275-0068. Rev. John Cavanaugh.

ROCK LAKE, TOWNER CO., IMMACULATE HEART OF MARY CHURCH OF ROCK LAKE (1949) Served from Rolla.
Mailing Address: c/o St. Joachim, P.O. Box 788, Rolla, 58367. Tel: 701-477-3568; Email: stjpastor@utma.com. 54 Eller Ave., Rock Lake, 58365. Rev. Thaines Arulandu.
Catechesis Religious Program—Students 11.

ROLETTE, ROLETTE CO., SACRED HEART CHURCH OF ROLETTE (1918) [CEM 3] Also serving Willow City and Bisbee.
505 Main St., Rolette, 58366. Tel: 701-246-3449; Fax: 701-246-3449; Email: shrolette@fargodiocese.org. Mailing Address: P.O. Box 127, Rolette, 58366. Rev. Paulraj Thondappa.
Catechesis Religious Program—Mrs. Amy Jo Leonard, D.R.E. Students 14.

ROLLA, ROLETTE CO., ST. JOACHIM'S CHURCH OF ROLLA (1894) [CEM] Also serving Rock Lake.
210 2nd St. NE., Rolla, 58367. Tel: 701-477-3568; Email: stjpastor@utma.com; Email: stjhm@utma.com. Mailing Address: P.O. Box 788, Rolla, 58367-0788. Rev. Thaines Arulandu; Deacon Emery Mears.
Catechesis Religious Program—Students 72.

RUGBY, PIERCE CO., ST. THERESA, LITTLE FLOWER CHURCH OF RUGBY (1910) [CEM] Also serves Knox.
218 3rd St., S.E., Rugby, 58368-1814.
Tel: 701-776-6388; Tel: 701-776-5327; Email: lfparish@gondtc.com; Web: www.littleflowerrugby.org. Revs. Thomas Graner; Prahbakar Marneni, Parochial Vicar; Deacons Arlen Blessum; Richard Lagasse.
School—St. Theresa, Little Flower Church of Rugby School, (Grades PreK-6), 306 Third Ave., S.E., Rugby, 58368. Tel: 701-776-6258; Email: lfs@gondtc.com; Web: www.little-flower.k12.nd.us. Mrs. Kimberly Anderson, Prin.; Sr. Jean Louise Schafer, O.S.F., Librarian. Lay Teachers 6; Sisters of St. Francis of the Immaculate Heart of Mary (Hankinson, ND) 2; Students 53.
Catechesis Religious Program—Rebecca Leier, D.R.E. Students 140.

ST. JOHN, ROLETTE CO., ST. JOHN'S CHURCH OF ST. JOHN aka St. John the Baptist Catholic Church (1882) [CEM] Also serves St. Benedict, Belcourt.
107 Saint Ann St. SE, St. John, 58369.
Tel: 701-477-3081; Email: saintjohnthebaptistnd@gmail.com. Mailing Address: P.O. Box 170, St. John, 58369. Rev. Richard Fineo, Admin.
Catechesis Religious Program—Students 7.

ST. MICHAEL, BENSON CO., ST. MICHAEL'S CHURCH OF ST. MICHAEL (1874) [CEM] (Native American)
Mailing Address: P.O. Box 958, Devils Lake, 58301. Tel: 701-766-4151; Email: michaels@gondtc.com. 136 1st, St. Michael, 58370. Rev. Paul R. Schuster.
Catechesis Religious Program—Students 10.

ST. THOMAS, PEMBINA CO., ST. THOMAS CHURCH OF ST. THOMAS (1882) [CEM] Closed. For inquiries for parish records contact the Chancellor's Office. Sacramental records are at St. Johns, Grafton.

SANBORN, BARNES CO., SACRED HEART CHURCH OF SANBORN (1904) [CEM] Served from Oriska.
Mailing Address: c/o St. Bernard's Church of Oriska, 606 5th St., Oriska, 58063. Tel: 701-845-3713; Email: oriska_tri_parish@yahoo.com. 711 4th St., Sanborn, 58480. Rev. Joseph Barrett.

SELZ, PIERCE CO., ST. ANTHONY CHURCH OF SELZ (1916) [CEM] Served from Harvey.
Mailing Address: 29 Girard St., Selz, 58341. Tel: 701-324-4059; Fax: 701-324-2144; Email: stcecilia@gondtc.com. Very Rev. Franklin Miller.
Catechesis Religious Program—Twinned with St. Cecilia, Harvey. Students 5.

SHELDON, RANSOM CO., OUR LADY OF THE SCAPULAR CHURCH OF SHELDON (1883) [CEM] Served from Enderlin.
145 Crosswell St., Sheldon, 58068. Tel: 701-437-2791 ; Email: stpatrick@mlgc.com; Web: www.enderlinfingalsheldon.org. Our Lady of the Scapular: 302 Bluff St., Enderlin, 58027. Rev. Christopher J. Markman.
Catechesis Religious Program—Tel: 701-437-2791. Students 11.

STARKWEATHER, RAMSEY CO., ASSUMPTION CHURCH OF STARKWEATHER (1905) [CEM] Served from Munich.
502 Main St., Starkweather, 58377.
Tel: 701-682-5178; Email: mathew.pamplaniyil@fargodiocese.org. Mailing Address: P.O. Box 159, Munich, 58352-0159. Rev. Mathew V. Pamplaniyil.
Catechesis Religious Program—Charlotte Kitsch, D.R.E. Students 9.

STEELE, KIDDER CO., ST. FRANCIS DE SALES CHURCH OF STEELE (1958) [CEM] Also serves Tappen and Medina.
318 2nd St. SW, Steele, 58482. Tel: 701-475-2333; Fax: 701-475-2335; Email: jerome.hunkler@fargodiocese.org. Mailing Address: P.O. Box 87, Steele, 58482-0087. Rev. Jerome Hunkler.
Catechesis Religious Program—Nadine Hoffman, D.R.E. Students 58.

STIRUM, SARGENT CO., ST. VINCENT (1986) Closed. For inquiries for parish records contact the Chancellor's Office. Sacramental records are at St. Aloysius, Lisbon.

SYKESTON, WELLS CO., ST. ELIZABETH'S CHURCH OF SYKESTON (1906) [CEM] (German) Served from Carrington.
130 Anson Ave. NE, Sykeston, 58486.
Tel: 701-984-2266; Email: stelizabeth@daktel.com. Mailing Address: P.O. Box 312, Sykeston, 58486. Rev. Thomas E. Dodge Jr.
Catechesis Religious Program—Nikki Neumiller, D.R.E. Students 14.

TAPPEN, KIDDER CO., ST. PAUL OF TAPPEN (1924) Served from Steele.
218 1st St. NE, Tappen, 58487. Tel: 701-475-2333; Fax: 701-475-2335; Email: jerome.hunkler@fargodiocese.org. Mailing Address: c/o St. Francis, P.O. Box 87, Steele, 58482. Rev. Jerome Hunkler.
Catechesis Religious Program—Karen Dockter, D.R.E. Students 8.

THOMPSON, GRAND FORKS CO., ST. JUDE'S CHURCH OF THOMPSON (1895) [CEM] Served from Reynolds.
329 Broadway St., Thompson, 58278-0305.
Tel: 701-599-2574; Tel: 701-847-3096; Email: john.cavanaugh@fargodiocese.org; Web: www.olphsj.org. P.O. Box 305, Reynolds, 58278-0305. Rev. John Cavanaugh; Deacon Jim West.
Catechesis Religious Program—Tel: 701-599-9018; Email: kims4church@gmail.com. Kim Garman, D.R.E. Students 96.

TOKIO, BENSON CO., CHRIST THE KING CHURCH OF TOKIO (1938) (Native American) Served from Fort Totten.
134 2nd St., Fort Totten, 58335. Tel: 701-766-4314; Email: charles.leute@fargodiocese.org. Mailing Address: P.O. Box 299, Fort Totten, 58335. Rev. Charles J. Leute, O.P.

TOLNA, NELSON CO., ST. JOSEPH CHURCH OF TOLNA (1911) [CEM] Served from Lakota.
220 Main St., Tolna, 58380. Tel: 701-247-2584; Email: steven.meyer@fargodiocese.org. P.O. Box 509, Lakota, 58380. Rev. Steven Meyer.
Catechesis Religious Program—Tel: 701-247-2594. Leah Dahl, D.R.E. Students 5.

TOWNER, MCHENRY CO., ST. CECILIA'S CHURCH OF TOWNER (1903) [CEM]
503 1st St. SW, Towner, 58788. Tel: 701-537-5133; Email: stcs@srt.com. P.O. Box 267, Towner, 58788. Rev. Michael Schommer.
Catechesis Religious Program—Faye Jorde, D.R.E. Students 30.

VALLEY CITY, BARNES CO., ST. CATHERINE'S CHURCH OF VALLEY CITY (1882) [CEM]
540 Third Ave., N.E., Valley City, 58072-2628.
Tel: 701-845-0354; Fax: 701-845-0556; Email: chris_stkates@yahoo.com. Rev. Msgr. Dennis A. Skonseng; Deacons Arlie Braunberger; Raphael Grim; Edward Didier; Carl M. Orthman; Joseph Leitner; Eugene Klein.
School—St. Catherine's Church of Valley City School, (Grades K-6), Tel: 701-845-1453; Fax: 701-845-0556; Web: www.stcatherine.k12.nd.us. Dawn Ihry, Supt. Lay Teachers 7; Students 47.
Catechesis Religious Program—Nichole Haugen, D.R.E. Students 87.

VELVA, MCHENRY CO., ST. CECILIA'S CHURCH OF VELVA (1905) [CEM] Also serving Karlsruhe.
201 2nd Ave. W, Velva, 58790. Tel: 701-338-2663; Email: velvakarls@srt.com; Web: stceciliavelvand.org. P.O. Box K, Velva, 58790. Rev. Peter Sharpe.
Catechesis Religious Program—

VERONA, LAMOURE CO., ST. RAPHAEL'S CHURCH OF VERONA (1898) [CEM] Served from Lamoure.
205 1st St., Verona, 58490. Mailing Address: c/o Holy Rosary, P.O. Box 217, Lamoure, 58458.
Tel: 701-883-5987; Email: holyrosery.church@gmail.com; Web: www.holyrosarylamoure.org. Rev. Gregory Haman.
Catechesis Religious Program—Email: nd.bisonfan@gmail.com. Suzanne Lahlum, D.R.E. Students 2.

VESELEYVILLE, WALSH CO., ST. LUKE'S CHURCH OF VESELEYVILLE (1880) [CEM] Served from Park River.
14207 63rd St., N.E., Grafton, 58237.
Tel: 701-284-6165; Email: stmarys@polarcomm.com; Web: www.saintsml.org. Rev. Bert Miller.
Catechesis Religious Program—Students 2.

WAHPETON, RICHLAND CO., ST. JOHN'S CHURCH OF WAHPETON (1876) [CEM]
Office: 115 Second St. N., Wahpeton, 58075.
Tel: 701-642-6982; Email: betsy@702com.net; Web: www.stjohns-wahpeton.org. Very Rev. Dale Lagodinski; Rev. Anthony Welle, Parochial Vicar; Deacon Douglas Campbell.
School—St. John's Church of Wahpeton School;, (Grades PreK-6), 212 Dakota Ave., Wahpeton, 58075. Tel: 701-642-6116; Email: stjohnsschool@702com.net; Web: http://www.stjohns-wahpeton.org/school/. Renee Langenwalter, Prin. Lay Teachers 12; Students 122.
Catechesis Religious Program—Michelle Fehr, D.R.E. Students 197.

WALES, CAVALIER CO., ST. MICHAEL'S CHURCH OF WALES (1889) [CEM] Served from Langdon.
221 2nd Ave., Wales, 58281. Tel: 701-256-5966; Email: phillip.ackerman@fargodiocese.org; Web: www.stalphonsuslangdon.com. 1010 3rd St., Langdon, 58249. Very Rev. Phillip Ackerman; Rev. William Ovsak.
Catechesis Religious Program—Students 5.

WALHALLA, PEMBINA CO., ST. BONIFACE CHURCH OF WALHALLA (1848) [CEM] Also serving Neche.
801 Central Ave., Walhalla, 58282.
Tel: 701-549-2729; Email: boniface@utma.com. Mailing Address: P.O. Box 228, Walhalla, 58282. Rev. John Fisher Kizito; Deacon Stanley (Jim) Carpenter.
Catechesis Religious Program—Tel: 701-549-2750; Email: carignan@utma.com. Bonnie Carignan, D.R.E. Students 40.

WARSAW, WALSH CO., ST. STANISLAUS CHURCH OF WARSAW (1882) [CEM] Served from Minto.
6098 County Rd. 4, Warsaw, 58261-0316.
Tel: 701-248-3589; Email: sacredheartminto@hotmail.com. P.O. Box 316, Minto, 58261-0316. Rev. Brian Moen.
Catechesis Religious Program—Students 41.

WEST FARGO, CASS CO.

1—BLESSED SACRAMENT CHURCH OF WEST FARGO (1936) [CEM]
210 Fifth Ave. W., West Fargo, 58078-1747.
Tel: 701-282-3321; Web: www.bscwf.org. Rev. Gary Luiten; Very Rev. Andrew Jasinski, In Res.
Catechesis Religious Program—Ms. Lucy Elshaug, D.R.E. Students 195.

2—HOLY CROSS CHURCH OF WEST FARGO (1981) [CEM]
2711 7th St. E., West Fargo, 58078.
Tel: 701-282-7217; Fax: 701-282-2753; Email: holycrosscc@holycrosswestfargo.com; Web: www.holycrosswestfargo.com. Revs. James Meyer; Chinnaiah Konka, Parochial Vicar; William Slattery, Parochial Vicar; Deacon James Eggl.
Catechesis Religious Program—Email: bmears@holycrosswestfargo.com. Students 529.

WESTHOPE, BOTTINEAU CO., ST. ANDREW'S CHURCH OF WESTHOPE (1904) [CEM] Served from Bottineau.
260 1st Ave. E, Westhope, 58793-0365.
Tel: 701-245-6171; Tel: 701-228-3164; Email: stsmanda@utma.com; Web: www.stmark-standrew.org. P.O. Box 365, Westhope, 58793-0365. Rev. Michael Hickin.
Catechesis Religious Program—Valerie Heth, D.R.E. Students 56.

WILD RICE, CASS CO., ST. BENEDICT'S CHURCH OF WILD RICE (1870) [CEM]
Mailing Address: 11743 38th St. S., Horace, 58047-9512. Tel: 701-588-4288; Fax: 701-588-9290; Email: office@stbensnd.org; Web: www.stbensnd.org. Rev. Jared Kadlec, J.C.L.; Deacon Clarence Vetter.
Catechesis Religious Program—Email: dre@stbensnd.org. Linda Skjerseth, D.R.E. Students 83.

WILLOW CITY, BOTTINEAU CO., NOTRE DAME DE LA VICTOIRE CHURCH OF WILLOW CITY aka Religious Education Program (1895) [CEM 2] Served by Rolette.
215 1st St. N., Willow City, 58384. Tel: 701-246-3449 ; Fax: 701-246-3449; Email: shrolette@fargodiocese.

org. Mailing Address: P.O. Box 115, Willow City, 58384. Rev. Paulraj Thondappa.
Catechesis Religious Program—Mrs. Sharon Harold, D.R.E. Students 10.

WIMBLEDON, BARNES CO., ST. BONIFACE CHURCH OF WIMBLEDON (1886) [CEM] Also serving Kensal and Dazey.
302 1st St. N, Wimbledon, 58492. Tel: 701-435-2310; Email: boniface@daktel.com. P.O. Box 9, Wimbledon, 58492. Rev. Sean P. Mulligan.
Catechesis Religious Program—Students 18.

WINDSOR, STUTSMAN CO., ST. MATHIAS CHURCH OF WINDSOR (1910) [CEM] Served from Jamestown.
207 Washington Ave., Windsor, 58424.
Tel: 701-252-0119; Email: basilica@stjamesbasilica.org. 622 1st Ave. S., Jamestown, 58401. Rev. Msgr. Jeffrey Wald.
Catechesis Religious Program—Tel: 701-252-0478; Email: ffsecretary@stjamesbasilica.org. Claudia Sharp, Sec. Students 11.

WISHEK, MCINTOSH CO., ST. PATRICK CHURCH OF WISHEK (1925) [CEM] Also serving Zeeland and Ashley.
305 7th St. S, Wiskek, 58495. Tel: 701-452-2970; Email: wenceslaus.katanga@fargodiocese.org. Mailing Address: P.O. Box 293, Wishek, 58495. Very Rev. Wenceslaus Katanga.
Catechesis Religious Program—Students 51.

WYNDMERE, RICHLAND CO., ST. JOHN THE BAPTIST CHURCH OF WYNDMERE (1912) [CEM] Also serving Milnor.
630 6th St., Wyndmere, 58081. Tel: 701-439-2200; Email: johnthebaptist.arnolds@gmail.com. Rev. Troy K. Simonsen.
Catechesis Religious Program—John Manstrom, D.R.E. Students 77.

ZEELAND, MCINTOSH CO., ST. ANDREW'S CHURCH OF ZEELAND (1906) [CEM 2] Served from Wishek.
301 1st Ave. SE, Zeeland, 58581. Tel: 701-423-5494; Email: wenceslaus.katanga@fargodiocese.org. P.O. Box 293, Wishek, 58495. Very Rev. Wenceslaus Katanga.
Catechesis Religious Program—P.O. Box 1, Zeeland, 58581. Sharon Wold, D.R.E. Students 20.

INDIAN MISSIONS

FORT TOTTEN RESERVATION
1—CHRIST THE KING - TOKIO (1938)
c/o Seven Dolors, Box 299, Fort Totten, 58335-0299. Rev. Charles J. Leute, O.P.
2—ST. JEROME - CROW HILL (1892)
P.O. Box 299, Fort Totten, 58335. 3971 69th Ave. N.E., Oberon, 58335. Rev. Charles J. Leute, O.P. Served from Fort Totten.
3—SEVEN DOLORS INDIAN MISSION, [CEM]
Box 299, Fort Totten, 58335. Rev. Charles J. Leute, O.P. Also serving Crow Hill, Tokio.

ST. MICHAEL, ST. MICHAEL'S CHURCH OF ST. MICHAEL (1874)
136 1st St., St. Michael, 58370-0042.
Tel: 701-766-4151; Email: paul.schuster@fargodiocese.org. P.O. Box 958, Devils Lake, 58301. Rev. Paul Schuster.

TURTLE MOUNTAIN RESERVATION
1—ST. ANN
wy. 5 St. Ann's Rd., P.O. Box 2000, Belcourt, 58316. Tel: 701-477-5601; Email: dmdsolt@gmail.com. Rev. Dennis Mary Dugan, S.O.L.T.
2—ST. ANTHONY
Belcourt, Rolette Co. 58316. Tel: 701-477-5601; Email: dmdsolt@gmail.com. Rev. Dennis Mary Dugan, S.O.L.T. Served from St. Ann's Belcourt. St. Anthony's is in the Alcide part of rural Belcourt.
3—ST. BENEDICT, Served from Saint John.
3821 BIA Rd. 6, Belcourt, Rolette Co. 58316.
Tel: 701-477-3081. P.O. Box 170, St. John, 58369. Rev. Fred Alexander, S.O.L.T.

Chaplains of Public Institutions

GRAND FORKS. *Grand Forks Air Force Base*, Our Lady of the Snows, 319 ABW/HC Blvd., 345 Tuskegee Airman Blvd., Grand Forks AFB, 58205-6335.
Tel: 701-747-5673. Rev. Alex Labacevic, Chap.

Special Assignment:
Rev. Msgr.—
Schlesselmann, Gregory J., Dir. Perm. Diaconate
Very Revs.—
Goodwin, James, J.C.L., Judicial Vicar, 5201 Bishops Blvd., 58104
Jasinski, Andrew, Chancellor, 5201 Bishops Blvd. S., 58104
Revs.—
Brooks, Armand L., Hankinson, 58041
Christensen, Joseph, F.M.I., Franciscans of Mary Immaculate, Warsaw, ND
Feltman, Thomas
Fischer, Charles, Fargo
Fitzpatrick, Vincent, Fargo
Irwin, Robert, Marriage Tribunal
Johnson, Timothy, Fargo
Kraemer, Matthew, Liturgy Office & Priest Sec. to Bishop, 5201 Bishop Blvd. S., 58104
LaCroix, Charles, Chap., 5600 25th St. S., 58104
Metzger, Kyle P., Dir. Vocations
Tiu, Jim, Chap., Carmelites, Wahpeton.

On Duty Outside the Diocese:
Very Rev.—
Kleinschmidt, John, Wisconsin
Revs.—
D'Aco, Joseph, Bronx, NY
Mikes, Pavel, Austria
Schill, Damien, Chap., VA, Minneapolis, MN.

Absent on Leave:
Revs.—
Fallon, John P.
Vos, Jude.

Retired:
Rev. Msgrs.—
Gross, Val, (Retired), Napoleon
Laliberte, Robert, Ph.D., (Retired), Fargo, ND
Pilon, Daniel J., J.C.L., (Retired), Grand Forks, ND
Senger, Joseph, (Retired), Minot, ND
Revs.—
Bachmeier, A. Bernard, (Retired), San Diego, CA
Billman, George, (Retired), Traverse City, MI
Bitz, Longinus (Al) M., (Retired), Bismarck
Callery, William V., (Retired), Bismark
Cote, Duaine, (Retired), Fargo
Dr. Flisk, Louden-Hans W., (Retired), Nortonville
Goellen, Richard M., (Retired), Fargo
Haas, Lawrence W., (Retired), Carrington
Herron, Jack B., (Retired), Pensacola, FL
Kinney, Leo Clayton, (Retired), Minot, ND
Kupisz, Julian, (Retired), Poland
LaCorte, Richard, (Retired), Kiln, MS
Lauerman, James P., (Retired), West Fargo
Leiphon, Donald A., (Retired), Valley City
Lewandowski, John, (Retired), Bull Shoals, AR
McCarthy, Gerald A., (Retired), Hankinson
McGinnis, John Arthur, (Retired), Conshohocken, PA
Myers, Gerald, (Retired), Tucson, AZ
Parrotta, Michael, (Retired), West Palm Beach, FL
Pfau, Bernard, (Retired), Devils Lake
Ruge, Paul, (Retired), Washington, NJ
Schneider, Bernard R., (Retired), Grafton
Sherman, Edward, (Retired), Grand Forks
Sherman, William C., (Retired), Grand Forks
Snell, Roger K., (Retired), Cavalier
Tuchscherer, Vincent, (Retired), Fargo
Unger, Robert P., (Retired), Bradenton, FL.

Permanent Deacons:
Baumgartner, Allen, St. Phillip Neri, Napoleon
Blessum, Arlen, (Retired)
Braunberger, Arlie, St. Catherine, Valley City
Bredemeier, John, St. Michael, Grand Forks
Campbell, Douglas, St. John, Wahpeton
Carpenter, Stanley (Jim), St. Boniface, Walhalla
Dahl, Bruce, Nativity, Fargo
Dalman, Wallace, St. George, Cooperstown
Davis, Francis R., St. Ann, Belcourt
Desjarlais, Raymond, St. Mary's Cathedral, Fargo
Didier, Edward, St. Catherine, Valley City
Dodge, Michael, Sts. Anne & Joachim, Fargo
Eggl, James, Holy Cross, West Fargo
Faul, Jeffrey, St. Cecilia, Harvey
Geffre, Thomas, St. James Basilica, Jamestown
Grim, Raphael, St. Catherine, Valley City
Grzadzielewski, Michael, St John the Evangelist, Grafton
Haney, David, (Retired)
Hoefs, Gene, (Retired)
Hunt, James, St. Philip, Hankinson
Klein, Eugene, (Retired)
Lagasse, Richard, St. Therese, Rugby
Leitner, Joseph, St. Catherine, Valley City
Loegering, George, St. Mary Cathedral, Fargo
Longtin, Stuart, St. Anthony, Fargo
Marcy, Timothy, Greenville, TN
McAllister, James, St. Bernard, Oriska
McDonald, Anthony, Seven Dolors, Fort Totten
Mears, Emery, St. Joachim, Rolla
Noehre, Leslie, Holy Family, Grand Forks
Orthman, Carl M., St. Catherine, Valley City
Perius, James, (Retired)
Pupino, Samuel, St. Mary, Grand Forks
Schlosser, Neal, Transfiguration, Edgeley
Schneider, Paul, Holy Spirit, Fargo
Schumacher, Gary, St. Philip Neri, Napoleon
Severinson, Kenneth, St. Joseph, Devils Lake
Tinguely, Donald, (Retired)
Uline, James, (Retired)
Vanorny, Thomas, St. Charles, Oakes
Vetter, Clarence, St. Maurice, Kindred
Votava, Kenneth, St. James Basilica, Jamestown
West, James, St. Jude, Thompson.

INSTITUTIONS LOCATED IN DIOCESE

[A] CATHOLIC SCHOOLS

FARGO. *St. John Paul II Catholic Schools Network*, (Grades PreSchool-12), 5600 25th St., S.W., 58104. Tel: 701-893-3200; Fax: 701-893-3277; Email: mike.hagstrom@jp2schools.org; Web: www.jp2schools.org. Mr. Michael Hagstrom, Pres. Lay Teachers 87; Students 1,219; Clergy / Religious Teachers 2.
Holy Spirit Elementary School, (Grades PreSchool-5), 1441 8th St. N., 58102. Tel: 701-232-4087; Fax: 701-232-8240; Email: jason.kotrba@jp2schools.org; Web: www.jp2schools.org. Jason Kotrba, Prin. Clergy 3; Lay Teachers 13; Students 132.
Nativity Elementary School, (Grades K-5), 1825 11th St. S., 58103. Tel: 701-232-7461; Email: kimbra.amerman@jp2schools.org. Kimbra Amerman, Prin. Clergy 2; Lay Teachers 20; Students 240.
Shanley High School, (Grades 6-12), 5600 25th St., S.W., 58104. Tel: 701-893-3200; Fax: 701-893-3277 ; Web: www.jp2schools.org. Jon Spies, Prin.; Mary Beth Traynor, Vice Pres.; Rev. Charles LaCroix, Chap. Lay Teachers 27; Students 351; Clergy / Religious Teachers 1.
Sullivan Middle School, 5600 25th St. S., 58104. Tel: 701-893-3200; Email: leon.knodel@jp2schools.org. Leon Knodel, Prin.; Mary Beth Traynor, Vice Pres. Lay Teachers 18; Students 272; Clergy / Religious Teachers 2.
Trinity Elementary School, 2811 7th St. E., West Fargo, 58078. Tel: 701-356-0793. Karissa Flieth, Prin. Lay Teachers 27; Students 224; Clergy / Religious Teachers 5.

[B] PROTECTIVE INSTITUTIONS

FARGO. *Villa Nazareth* dba CHI Friendship, 801 Page Dr., 58103. Tel: 701-235-8217; Fax: 701-235-7538; Email: dorileslie@catholichealth.net; Email: kristinechristensen@catholichealth.net; Web: www.chifriendship.com. Dori Leslie, Pres. Presentation Sisters (P.B.V.M.). Catholic Health Initiatives.A community-based facility providing an array of residential, vocational, educational, social and clinical services for children and adults with intellectual/developmental disabilities.
Villa Nazareth dba CHI Friendship Tot Asst. Annually 300; Total Staff 400.

[C] GENERAL HOSPITALS

FARGO. *SMP Health System*, 1202 Page Dr., S.W., 58103. Tel: 701-237-9290; Email: aaron.alton@smphs.org. Aaron Alton, CEO. Total Staff 8.

BOTTINEAU. *St. Andrew's Health Center*, 316 Ohmer St., Bottineau, 58318. Tel: 701-228-9300; Fax: 701-228-9384; Email: sahc@utma.com; Web: www.standrewshealth.com. Alfred Sams, CEO. Bed Capacity 25; Tot Asst. Annually 13,200; Total Staff 110.

CARRINGTON. *Carrington Health Center* Catholic Health Initiatives. 800 N. 4 St., P.O. Box 461, Carrington, 58421. Tel: 701-652-3141; Fax: 701-652-2884; Email: beckypretzer@catholichealth.net; Web: www.carringtonhealthcenter.org. Ms. Mariann Doeling, Admin.
CHI St. Alexius Health Carrington Medical Center Bed Capacity 25; Tot Asst. Annually 20,876; Total Staff 125; Staff 125.

DEVILS LAKE. *CHI St. Alexius Health Devils Lake Hospital* dba CHI St. Alexius Health Devils Lake Hospital, 1031 7th St., N.E., Devils Lake, 58301-2798. Tel: 701-662-2131; Tel: 701-662-9710; Tel: 701-662-9711; Fax: 701-662-9651; Email: andrewlankowicz@catholichealth.net; Email: shannonlauinger@catholichealth.net; Web: www.chistalexiushealth.org/locations/devils-lake. Andrew Lankowicz, Pres.
Legal Title: Mercy Hosptial of Devils Lake. Bassinets 7; Bed Capacity 25; Tot Asst. Annually 23,000; Total Staff 151.

HARVEY. *St. Aloisius Medical Center* (1938) 325 E. Brewster St., Harvey, 58341. Tel: 701-324-4651; Fax: 701-324-4687; Email: mzwicker@staloisius.com; Web: www.staloisius.com. Mike Zwicker, Pres.; Sr. Mary Huber, Spiritual Advisor/Care Svcs. Sisters of Mary of the Presentation. Bed

Capacity 25; Tot Asst. Annually 41,325; Total Staff 240; Long Term Care 85.

LISBON. *Lisbon Area Health Services*, Catholic Health Initiatives, 905 Main St., Lisbon, 58054. Tel: 701-683-6400; Fax: 701-683-4345; Email: peggyareinke@catholichealth.net; Web: Lisbonhospital.com. P.O. Box 353, Lisbon, 58054. Sr. Donna Welder, O.S.F., Member, Hospital Bd. Bed Capacity 25; Tot Asst. Annually 5,000; Total Staff 80.

OAKES. *CHI Oakes Hospital*, 1200 N. 7th St., Oakes, 58474-2502. Tel: 701-742-3291; Fax: 701-742-3639. Rebecca Thompson, Pres. Bed Capacity 20; Tot Asst. Annually 7,815; Total Staff 95.

ROLLA. *Presentation Medical Center*, 213 Second Ave., N.E., P.O. Box 759, Rolla, 58367-0759. Tel: 701-477-3161; Fax: 701-477-5564; Email: chrisalbertson@pmc-rolla.com; Web: www.pmc-rolla.com. Chris Albertson, CEO. Bed Capacity 25; Tot Asst. Annually 12,616; Total Staff 82.

VALLEY CITY. *Mercy Hospital of Valley City* dba CHI Mercy Health (1928) Catholic Health Initiatives. 570 Chautauqua Blvd., Valley City, 58072. Tel: 701-845-6400; Fax: 701-845-6413; Email: lisaurbatsch@catholichealth.net; Web: www.mercyhospitalvalleycity.org. Mr. Keith Heuser, Pres. Bed Capacity 25; Tot Asst. Annually 12,296; Total Staff 96.

[D] HOMES FOR AGED

FARGO. *Riverview* dba CHI Riverview (1987) 5300 12th St. S., 58104. Tel: 701-237-4700; Fax: 701-235-5738; Email: kdew@chilivingcomm.org; Web: www.homeishere.org. Ms. Kari Dew, Admin.; Ms. Mary Jo Zacher, Spiritual Advisor/Care Svcs. CHI Living Communities, a subsidiary of Catholic Health Initiatives Residents 150; Staff 75; Total Assisted 54.

Rosewood on Broadway, SMP Health System, 1351 Broadway N., 58102. Tel: 701-277-7999; Fax: 701-277-7989; Email: tony.keelin@smphs.org; Web: rosewoodonbroadway.com. Tony Keelin, CEO. Bed Capacity 125; Total Staff 220; Resident Days 42,635.

Villa Maria, SMP Health System, 3102 University Dr. S., 58103. Tel: 701-293-7750; Fax: 701-293-5845; Email: tony.keelin@smphs.org; Web: www.villamariafargo.com. Tony Keelin, CEO. Bed Capacity 140; Total Staff 232; Resident Days 49,350.

EDGELEY. *Manor St. Joseph*, 404 Fourth Ave., P.O. Box 305, Edgeley, 58433. Tel: 701-493-2477; Fax: 701-493-2712; Email: stjoseph@drtel.net. Tammy Jangula, Admin. Bed Capacity 28; Tot Asst. Annually 21; Staff 30.

ELLENDALE. *Prince of Peace Care Center*, 201 8th St. N., Ellendale, 58436. Tel: 701-349-3312; Fax: 701-349-3944; Email: tony.hanson@bhshealth.org. Mr. Tony Hanson, Admin. Operated by Benedictine Living Communities, Inc. Bed Capacity 53; Tot Asst. Annually 71; Total Staff 89.

ENDERLIN. *Maryhill Manor*, SMP Health System, 110 Hillcrest Dr., Enderlin, 58027. Tel: 701-437-3544; Fax: 701-437-3816; Email: nancy.farnham@smphs.org; Web: www.maryhillmanor.net. Nancy Farnham, Admin. Bed Capacity 48; Tot Asst. Annually 98; Total Staff 84; Resident Days 16,043.

GRAND FORKS. *St. Anne's Guest Home*, 524 N. 17th St., Grand Forks, 58203. Tel: 701-746-9401; Fax: 701-795-7825; Email: stannes@midconetwork.com. Sr. Rebecca Metzger, O.S.F., Admin. Beds 77; Guests 77; Sisters of St. Francis of the Immaculate Heart of Mary (Hankinson, ND) 3; Tot Asst. Annually 106; Total Staff 35.

HANKINSON. *St. Gerard Community of Care*, 613 1st Ave., S.W., P.O. Box 448, Hankinson, 58041. Tel: 701-242-7891; Fax: 701-242-7896; Email: stgerard@rrt.net; Web: stgerards.org. Jill Foertsch, Admin.; Sr. Mary Louise, O.S.F., Asst. Admin. Bed Capacity 37; Franciscan Sisters of Dillingen (Hankinson, ND) 3; Tot Asst. Annually 80; Total Staff 95; Independent Living Unit Beds 12; Children in Daycare 18.

JAMESTOWN. *Ave Maria Village*, SMP Health System, 501 19th St., N.E., Jamestown, 58401. Tel: 701-252-5660; Fax: 701-251-2643; Email: tim.burchill@smphs.org; Web: www.avemariavillage.org. Timothy N. Burchill, Admin. Bed Capacity 100; Tot Asst. Annually 268; Total Staff 222; Resident Days 35,721.

LAMOURE. *St. Rose Care Center*, 315 1st St., S.E., LaMoure, 58458. Tel: 701-883-5363; Fax: 701-883-5711; Email: kelsey.peterson@bhshealth.org. Kelsey Peterson, Admin. Operated by Benedictine Living Communities, Inc. Bed Capacity 44; Total Staff 70; Total Assisted 81.

VALLEY CITY. *Sheyenne Center*, SMP Health System, 979 N. Central Ave., Valley City, 58072. Tel: 701-845-8222; Fax: 701-845-8270; Email: craig.christianson@smphs.org. Craig Christianson, CEO. A ministry of SMP Health System, sponsored by the Sister of Mary of the Presentation Health Ministry, a public Juridic Person. Bed Capacity 170; Tot Asst. Annually 243; Total Staff 265; Resident Days 61,512.

WAHPETON. *Benedictine Living Community of Wapheton*, 1307 N. 7th St., Wahpeton, 58075. Tel: 701-642-6667; Fax: 701-642-2485; Email: jim.cornelius@bhshealth.org; Web: www.blcwahpeton.org. Jim Cornelius, Admin. Bed Capacity 84; Tot Asst. Annually 200; Total Staff 118.

St. Catherine's Living Center, 1307 N. Seventh St., Wahpeton, 58075. Tel: 701-642-6667; Fax: 701-642-2485; Email: jim.cornelius@bhshealth.org. Jim Cornelius, Admin. Operated by Benedictine Living Communities, Inc. Total Staff 118; Long Term Care Beds 52; Basic Care Beds 16.

[E] CATHOLIC CHARITIES

FARGO. *Catholic Charities North Dakota - Fargo* (1923) 5201 Bishops Blvd., Ste. B, 58104. Tel: 701-235-4457; Fax: 701-356-7993; Email: info@catholiccharitiesnd.org; Web: www.catholiccharitiesnd.org. Dianne Nechiporenko, Exec. Dir. Statewide social service agency providing adoption services, guardianship services, pregnancy services, Adults Adopting Special Kids (AASK), and counseling services. Tot Asst. Annually 2,500; Total Staff 52.

GRAND FORKS. *St. Joseph's Social Care and Thrift Store*, 620 8th Ave. S., Grand Forks, 58201-4816. Tel: 701-795-8614; Fax: 701-746-6648; Email: jbrundin@yahoo.com. Jo Ann Brundin, Dir. Tot Asst. Annually 13,000; Total Staff 5.

WARSAW. *Saint Gianna's Home Inc.* Residence for pregnant women and their children. 15605 Country Rd. 15, Minto, 58261. Tel: 701-248-3077; Email: saintgiannahome@hotmail.com; Web: www.saintgiannahome.org. Mary Pat Jahner, Dir.; Rev. Joseph Christensen, F.M.I., Chap. Priests 1; Tot Asst. Annually 75; Total Staff 6.

[F] CONVENTS AND RESIDENCES FOR SISTERS

FARGO. *Presentation Center-Sacred Heart Convent*, 1101 32nd Ave. S., 58103. Tel: 701-237-4857; Fax: 701-237-9822; Email: SacredHeartConvent@pbvmunion.org; Web: www.pbvmunion.org. Sr. Stella Olson, P.B.V.M., Admin. Sisters 31.

HANKINSON. *Franciscan Sisters of Dillingen* Hankinson, ND, P.O. Box 447, Hankinson, 58041-0447. Tel: 701-242-7195; Fax: 701-242-7198; Email: dillingenfranciscansusa@rrt.net; Web: www.dillingenfranciscansusa.org. Rev. Armond Brooks, Chap.; Sr. Ann Marie Friederichs, O.S.F., Prov. Supr. Sisters 18.

VALLEY CITY. *Sisters of Mary of the Presentation*, 3150 116A Ave. SE, Valley City, 58072. Tel: 701-845-2864; Fax: 701-845-0805; Email: suzanne.stahl@smphs.org; Web: www.sistersofmaryofthepresentation.com. Sr. Suzanne Stahl, Supr.; Rev. Donald A. Leiphon, Chap., (Retired). Sisters 18.

WAHPETON. *Carmel of Mary* (1954) 17765 78th St., S.E., Wahpeton, 58075. Tel: 701-642-2360; Email: carmelofmary@carmelnet.org. Mother Madonna of the Assumption, O.Carm., Prioress; Rev. Jim Tiu, Chap. Carmelite Nuns of the Ancient Observance. Solemn Professed Nuns 9.

[G] RETREAT HOUSES

FARGO. *Presentation Prayer Center* (1981) 1101 32nd Ave., 58103. Tel: 701-237-4857; Fax: 701-237-9822; Email: presprayerctr@pbvmunion.org. Peter Edwards, Dir. Sisters 2.

[H] NEWMAN FOUNDATIONS

FARGO. *St. Paul's Newman Church of Fargo* (1928) 1141 N. University Dr., 58102. Tel: 701-235-0142; Email: pastor@bisoncatholic.org; Web: www.bisoncatholic.org. Rev. Msgr. Gregory J. Schlesselmann, Spiritual Advisor/Care Svcs.; Rev. James Cheney. Students 4,000; Total Staff 20.

GRAND FORKS. *St. Thomas Aquinas Newman Church of Grand Forks* (1951) 410 Cambridge St., Grand Forks, 58203. Tel: 701-777-6850; Email: jessica.kuznia@undcatholic.org; Web: www.undcatholic.org. Rev. Luke D. Meyer. Total Staff 12; Catholic Students 2,916.

WAHPETON. *State College of Science Newman Student Parish*, 115 N. 2nd St., Wahpeton, 58075. Tel: 701-642-6982; Email: betsy@702com.net. Very Rev. Dale Lagodinski. Religious Teachers 1.

[I] MISCELLANEOUS LISTINGS

FARGO. *Catholic Chaplains Association*, Diocese of Fargo, 5201 Bishops Blvd. S., Ste. A, 58104. Tel: 701-356-7900; Email: andrew.jasinski@fargodiocese.org. Very Rev. Andrew Jasinski.

Catholic Development Foundation (1989) 5201 Bishops Blvd. S., Ste A, 58104-7605. Tel: 701-356-7930; Fax: 701-356-7998; Email: steve.schons@fargodiocese.org; Web: www.cdfnd.org. Steve Schons, Dir. A nonprofit foundation for religious charitable and educational purposes.

Cursillo Movement of the Fargo Diocese, 5201 Bishops Blvd. S., Ste. A, 58104. Tel: 701-356-7900; Email: contact@fargodiocese.org; Web: www.natl-cursillo.org. Rev. Duaine Cote, Chap., (Retired).

Fargo Guild of Catholic Physicians, 5201 Bishops Blvd. S., 58104. Tel: 701-356-7900; Email: andrew.jasinski@fargodiocese.org. Very Rev. Andrew Jasinski, Contact Person.

Hughes, Inc., Union of Sisters of the Presentation of the Blessed Virgin Mary, 1101 32nd Ave. S., 58103. Tel: 701-237-4857; Fax: 701-237-9822; Email: kfennell@pbvmunion.org; Web: www.pbvmunion.org. Sr. Katherine Fennell, P.B.V.M., Treas. Assisting, providing and expanding low-cost housing (in part for senior citizens along with other groups). Administrators 1.

Marriage Encounter, 804 Foster Ave. N.W., P.O. Box 217, Cooperstown, 58425. Tel: 701-797-2624; Fax: 701-797-2632; Email: stgeorge@mlgc.com. Rev. Dale H. Kinzler.

The Presentation Foundation, Sacred Heart Convent, 1101 32nd Ave. S., 58103. Tel: 701-237-4857; Fax: 701-237-9822; Email: srjosephineb@gmail.com; Web: www.presentationsistersunion.org. Sr. Josephine Brennan, Dir. Administrators 1.

Presentation Partners in Housing, 1101 32nd Ave S., 58103. Tel: 701-235-6861; Fax: 701-237-9822; Email: presentationpartnersinhouseing@pbvmunion.org; Web: www.presentationsistersunion.org. Mrs. Cheri Gerken, Dir. Director 1.

BATHGATE. *Bethlehem Community*, 10194 Garfield St. S., Bathgate, 58216. Tel: 701-265-3717; Fax: 701-265-3716; Email: contact@bethlehembooks.com. Lydia Reynolds, Contact Person.

GRAND FORKS. *Grand Forks Catholic Schools Association*, Tel: 701-701-7001. A nonprofit organization developing curriculum study, scholarship, transportation, personnel and fund raising.

JAMESTOWN. *University of Jamestown*, 214 4th St., S.E., Jamestown, 58401. Tel: 701-252-0478; Email: youth@stjamesbasilica.org. Rev. Msgr. Jeffrey Wald. Students 200; Religious Teachers 3.

LANGDON. *St. Alphonsus School Foundation*, 908 3rd St., Langdon, 58249. Tel: 701-256-3717; Fax: 701-256-3720; Email: lyonsh@utma.com. Cameron Sillers, Pres.

MANVEL. *Beginning Experience Apostolate*, 5201 Bishops Blvd. S. Ste. A, 58104-7605. Tel: 701-356-7900; Email: bernard.schneider@fargodiocese.org. Rev. Bernard Schneider, Dir.

VALLEY CITY. *Valley City State University Newman Center*, c/o St. Catherine, 540 3rd Ave., N.E., Valley City, 58072. Tel: 701-845-0354; Fax: 701-845-0556; Email: dennis.skonseng@fargodiocese.org. Rev. Msgr. Dennis A. Skonseng. Students 8.

WARSAW. **Third Order Franciscans of Mary Immaculate*, 6098 County Rd. 4, Minto, 58261-9455. Tel: 701-248-3020; Email: fmi@fmifriars.com; Web: www.fmifriars.com. Rev. Joseph Christensen, F.M.I., Supr.; Bro. Francis Reineke. Religious 1; Seminarians 1.

RELIGIOUS INSTITUTES OF MEN REPRESENTED IN THE DIOCESE

For further details refer to the corresponding bracketed number in the Religious Institutes of Men or Women section.

[0585]—*Heralds of Good News*—H.G.N.
[0430]—*Order of Preachers-Dominicans*—O.P.
[0975]—*Society of Our Lady of the Most Holy Trinity*—S.O.L.T.

RELIGIOUS INSTITUTES OF WOMEN REPRESENTED IN THE DIOCESE

[0300]—*Calced Carmelites*—O.Carm.
[]—*Franciscan Sisters of Dillingen* (Hankinson, ND)—O.S.F.
[2450]—*Sisters of Mary of the Presentation* (Valley City, ND)—S.M.P.
[3320]—*Sisters of the Presentation of the B.V.M.* (Fargo, ND)—P.B.V.M.
[]—*Sisters of the Society of Our Lady of the Most Holy Trinity*—S.O.L.T.

DIOCESAN CEMETERIES

Calvary Cemetery Association, 216 Belmont Rd., Grand Forks, 58201. Tel: 701-772-7911; Email: calvarycemeterygfnd@yahoo.com. Rev. H. Gerard Braun, Vice Pres.; Darlyne Votava, Sec.

Holy Cross Cemeteries of Fargo, 1502 32nd Ave., N., 58102. Tel: 701-237-6671; Email: kevin.

boucher@fargodiocese.org. Rev. Kevin Boucher, Vice Pres.

NECROLOGY

† Nilles, Allan F., (Retired), Died Oct. 31, 2018

† Mrnarevic, Daniel, Died Sep. 23, 2018

† Stelten, Leo F., (Retired), Died Dec. 30, 2018

An asterisk (*) denotes an organization that has established tax-exempt status directly with the IRS and is not covered by the USCCB Group Ruling.

Diocese of Fort Wayne-South Bend

(Dioecesis Wayne Castrensis-South Bendensis)

Most Reverend

KEVIN C. RHOADES

Bishop of Fort Wayne-South Bend; ordained July 9, 1983; appointed Bishop of Harrisburg October 14, 2004; consecrated December 9, 2004; appointed Bishop of Fort Wayne-South Bend November 14, 2009; installed Bishop of Fort Wayne-South Bend January 13, 2010. *Mailing Address: P.O. Box 390, Fort Wayne, IN 46801.*

Archbishop Noll Catholic Center: 915 S. Clinton St., P.O. Box 390, Fort Wayne, IN 46801. Tel: 260-422-4611; Fax: 260-969-9145.

Web: www.diocesefwsb.org

Email: bishopsoffice@diocesefwsb.org

ESTABLISHED SEPTEMBER 22, 1857.

Square Miles 5,792.

Redesignated Diocese of Fort Wayne-South Bend on July 22, 1960.

Comprises the Counties of Adams, Allen, Dekalb, Elkhart, Huntington, Kosciusko, La Grange, Marshall, Noble, St. Joseph, Steuben, Wabash, Wells, Whitley in the State of Indiana.

For legal titles of parishes and diocesan institutions, consult the Chancery Office.

STATISTICAL OVERVIEW

Personnel	
Bishop	1
Priests: Diocesan Active in Diocese	64
Priests: Diocesan Active Outside Diocese	2
Priests: Retired, Sick or Absent	15
Number of Diocesan Priests	81
Religious Priests in Diocese	173
Total Priests in Diocese	254
Extern Priests in Diocese	30
Ordinations:	
Diocesan Priests	5
Religious Priests	3
Transitional Deacons	2
Permanent Deacons	11
Permanent Deacons in Diocese	30
Total Brothers	55
Total Sisters	376
Parishes	
Parishes	81
With Resident Pastor:	
Resident Diocesan Priests	59
Resident Religious Priests	22
Without Resident Pastor:	
Administered by Priests	4
Pastoral Centers	4
Professional Ministry Personnel:	
Brothers	3
Sisters	15
Lay Ministers	271
Welfare	
Catholic Hospitals	2
Total Assisted	468,440
Health Care Centers	6
Total Assisted	79,836
Homes for the Aged	7
Total Assisted	2,099
Specialized Homes	3
Total Assisted	41
Special Centers for Social Services	9
Total Assisted	219,492
Other Institutions	2
Total Assisted	7,579
Educational	
Diocesan Students in Other Seminaries	27
Seminaries, Religious	2
Students Religious	44
Total Seminarians	71
Colleges and Universities	5
Total Students	17,412
High Schools, Diocesan and Parish	4
Total Students	3,062
Elementary Schools, Diocesan and Parish	39
Total Students	9,339
Catechesis/Religious Education:	
High School Students	1,107
Elementary Students	6,254
Total Students under Catholic Instruction	37,245
Teachers in the Diocese:	
Brothers	1
Sisters	3
Lay Teachers	879
Vital Statistics	
Receptions into the Church:	
Infant Baptism Totals	1,975
Minor Baptism Totals	287
Received into Full Communion	438
First Communions	2,588
Confirmations	2,407
Marriages:	
Catholic	427
Interfaith	191
Total Marriages	618
Deaths	1,561
Total Catholic Population	156,576
Total Population	1,303,133

Former Bishops—Rt. Revs. JOHN HENRY LUERS, D.D., ord. Nov. 11, 1846; cons. Jan. 10, 1858; died June 29, 1871; JOSEPH DWENGER, C.PP.S., D.D., ord. Sept. 4, 1859; cons. April 14, 1872; died Jan. 27, 1893; JOSEPH RADEMACHER, D.D., ord. Aug. 2, 1863; cons. Bishop of Nashville, June 24, 1883; transferred to Fort Wayne, July 14, 1893; died Jan. 12, 1900; HERMAN JOSEPH ALERDING, D.D., cons. Nov. 30, 1900; died Dec. 6, 1924; Most Revs. JOHN FRANCIS NOLL, D.D., ord. June 4, 1898; cons. June 30, 1925; promoted to rank of Archbishop "ad personam," Sept. 2, 1953; died July 31, 1956; LEO A. PURSLEY, D.D., ord. June 11, 1927; cons. Sept. 19, 1950; retired Oct. 19, 1976; died Nov. 15, 1998; WILLIAM E. MCMANUS, D.D., ord. April 15, 1939; appt. Auxiliary Bishop of Chicago, June 21, 1967; appt. Bishop of Fort Wayne, Aug. 31, 1976; installed as 7th Bishop of Fort Wayne, Oct. 19, 1976; retired Feb. 25, 1985; died March 3, 1997; JOHN M. D'ARCY, ord. Feb. 2, 1957; appt. Auxiliary Bishop of Boston and Titular Bishop of Mediana Dec. 31, 1974; cons. Feb. 11, 1975; appt. Bishop of Fort Wayne-South Bend Feb. 26, 1985; installed May 1, 1985; retired Nov. 14, 2009; died Feb. 3, 2013.

Chancery Office—Archbishop Noll Catholic Center, 915 S. Clinton St., Fort Wayne, 46802. Mailing Address: P.O. Box 390, Fort Wayne, 46801. Tel: 260-422-4611; Fax: 260-969-9145. *St. John Paul II Center, 1328 W. Dragoon Tr., Mishawaka, 46544.* Tel: 574-234-0687; Fax: 574-252-0509. Office Hours: Mon.-Fri. 8:30-4:30. Other times by appointment.

Diocese of Fort Wayne-South Bend, Inc.—(Incorporated Aug. 29, 1955).Board of Directors: Most Rev. KEVIN C. RHOADES, D.D., S.T.L., J.C.L., Pres.; Very Rev. MARK ALLEN GURTNER, J.C.L., Vice Pres.; MR. JOSEPH RYAN, Sec. & Treas.

Diocese of Fort Wayne-South Bend Officials

Vicar General/Chancellor—Archbishop Noll Catholic Center, 915 S. Clinton St., Fort Wayne, 46802. Mailing Address: P.O. Box 390, Fort Wayne, 46801. Tel: 260-422-4611; Fax: 260-969-9145. Very Rev. MARK ALLEN GURTNER, J.C.L.

Moderator of the Curia—Archbishop Noll Catholic Center, 915 S. Clinton St., Fort Wayne, 46802. Mailing Address: P.O. Box 390, Fort Wayne, 46801. Tel: 260-422-4611; Fax: 260-969-9145. Very Rev. MARK ALLEN GURTNER, J.C.L.

Judicial Vicar—Archbishop Noll Catholic Center, 915 S. Clinton St., Fort Wayne, 46802. Mailing Address: P.O. Box 390, Fort Wayne, 46801. Tel: 260-422-4611; Fax: 260-969-9145. Very Rev. JACOB RUNYON, J.C.L.

Assistant to the Bishop in Pastoral Care—Archbishop Noll Catholic Center, 915 S. Clinton St., Fort Wayne, 46802. Mailing Address: P.O. Box 390, Fort Wayne, 46801. Tel: 260-422-4611; Fax: 260-483-1881. MARY L. GLOWASKI, L.S.W., M.A., Dir.

Secretary for Administrative Services—MR. JOSEPH RYAN, Dir. & CFO, Archbishop Noll Catholic Center, 915 S. Clinton St., Fort Wayne, 46802. Mailing Address: P.O. Box 390, Fort Wayne, 46801. Tel: 260-422-4611; Fax: 260-423-3382.

Secretary for Catholic Education—MR. CARL LOESCH, B.A., M.A., M.Ed., M.A. Educ. Admin., Dir., Archbishop Noll Catholic Center, 915 S. Clinton St., Fort Wayne, 46802. Mailing Address: P.O. Box 390, Fort Wayne, 46801. Tel: 260-422-4611; Fax: 260-426-3077.

Secretary for Communications—STEPHANIE PATKA, Dir., Archbishop Noll Catholic Center, 915 S. Calhoun St., Fort Wayne, 46802. Email: spatka@diocesefwsb.org. Mailing Address: P.O. Box 390, Fort Wayne, 46801. Tel: 260-456-2824; Fax: 260-744-1473.

Secretary for Evangelization and Discipleship—St. John Paul II Center, 1328 W. Dragoon Tr., Mishawaka, 46544. Tel: 574-234-0687; Fax: 574-252-0509. Deacon FREDERICK EVERETT, J.D., Dir.

Secretary for Stewardship and Development—St. John Paul II Center, 1328 W. Dragoon Tr., Mishawaka, 46544. Tel: 574-258-6571; Fax: 574-256-2709. *Archbishop Noll Catholic Center, 915 S. Clinton St., Fort Wayne, 46802. Mailing Address: P.O. Box 390, Fort Wayne, 46801.* Tel: 260-422-4611; Fax: 260-423-3382. JEFFERY BOETTICHER, Dir.

Diocesan Offices, Commissions, Boards and Programs

Adult Faith Formation and Catechesis—St. John Paul II Center, 1328 W. Dragoon Tr., Mishawaka, 46544. Tel: 574-234-0687. JOHN SIKORSKI, Dir.

Assistant to the Bishop in Pastoral Care—Archbishop Noll Catholic Center, 915 S. Clinton St., Fort Wayne, 46802. Mailing Address: P.O. Box 390, Fort Wayne, 46801. Tel: 260-422-4611; Fax: 260-483-1881. MARY L. GLOWASKI, L.S.W.,

M.A., Dir. Mediation of Pastoral Concerns; Victim Assistance; Disability and Deaf Ministry.

Black Catholic Ministry—Deacon MELVIN TARDY, Chair, Black Catholic Advisory Board: 2216 Oakwood Park Dr., South Bend, 46628. Tel: 574-707-1231; Email: mtardy@nd.edu.

Budget Committee—Rev. JASON EUGENE FREIBURGER; Very Rev. MARK A. GURTNER, J.C.L.; Revs. GLENN KOHRMAN; WILLIAM J. KUMMER; MR. JOSEPH RYAN; Revs. THOMAS SHOEMAKER; ANTHONY STEINACKER; Rev. Msgr. ROBERT C. SCHULTE.

Buildings and Improvements Advisory Board—BILL ARNOLD; JOHN BERGHOFF; JIM BRECKLER; MIKE HAMILTON; MR. JOSEPH RYAN; MARK SCHENKEL; Rev. JOHN DELANEY; Very Rev. MARK ALLEN GURTNER, J.C.L.; Revs. WILLIAM J. SULLIVAN; BENJAMIN J. MUHLENKAMP.

Business Administration Office—MR. JOSEPH RYAN, CFO, Archbishop Noll Catholic Center, 915 S. Clinton St., Fort Wayne, 46802. Mailing Address: P.O. Box 390, Fort Wayne, 46801. Tel: 260-422-4611; Fax: 260-423-3382.

Catechesis—Archbishop Noll Catholic Center: 915 S. Clinton St., Fort Wayne, 46802. Mailing Address: P.O. Box 390, Fort Wayne, 46801. Tel: 260-422-4611; Fax: 260-483-1881. JONATHAN KALTENBACH, Ph.D., Dir.

Catholic Campaign for Human Development—SHAWN STORER, Dir., St. John Paul II Center, 1328 W. Dragoon Tr., Mishawaka, 46544. Tel: 574-234-0687; Fax: 574-232-8483.

Catholic Cemetery—CASEY MILLER, Supt., Catholic Cemetery Assoc., 3500 Lake Ave., Fort Wayne, 46805. Tel: 260-426-2044; Fax: 260-422-7418.

Clergy Relief Services—SHAWN STORER, Dir., St. John Paul II Center, 1328 W. Dragoon Tr., Mishawaka, 46544. Tel: 574-234-0687; Fax: 574-232-8483.

Catholic Schools—MR. CARL LOESCH, B.A., M.A., M.Ed., M.A. Educ. Admin., Dir; MRS. MARSHA A. JORDAN, Supt., Archbishop Noll Catholic Center, 915 S. Clinton St., Fort Wayne, 46802. Mailing Address: P.O. Box 390, Fort Wayne, 46801. Tel: 260-422-4611; Fax: 260-426-3077.

Censor Librorum—Rev. Msgr. MICHAEL W. HEINTZ, Ph. D., (August 1 to May 1): Mount St. Mary's Seminary, 16300 Old Emmitsburg Rd., Emmitsburg, MD 21727. Summer Res.: St. Pius X Church, 52553 Fir Rd., Granger, 46530.

Clergy Retirement Board—Revs. ROBERT D'SOUZA; WILLIAM J. KUMMER; DAVID W. VOORS; PHILLIP A. WIDMANN; Rev. Msgrs. JOHN M. KUZMICH, (Retired); ROBERT C. SCHULTE.

College of Consultors—Rev. MATTHEW M. COONAN; Very Rev. MARK A. GURTNER, J.C.L.; Rev. GLENN KOHRMAN; Very Rev. JACOB RUNYON, J.C.L.; Rev. DANIEL SCHEIDT; Rev. Msgr. ROBERT C. SCHULTE; Revs. THOMAS SHOEMAKER; TIMOTHY A. WROZEK.

Communications/Today's Catholic Official Publication—Archbishop Noll Catholic Center, 915 S. Clinton St., Fort Wayne, 46802. Mailing Address: P.O. Box 390, Fort Wayne, 46801. Tel: 260-456-2824; Fax: 260-744-1473. STEPHANIE PATKA, Dir.; JODI MARLIN, Publication Mgr., Tel: 260-399-1453.

Continuing Formation of Priests and Deacons—Archbishop Noll Catholic Center, 915 S. Clinton St., Fort Wayne, 46802. Mailing Address: P.O. Box 390, Fort Wayne, 46801. Tel: 260-422-4611; Fax: 260-969-9145. Very Rev. MARK ALLEN GURTNER, J.C.L.

Courage/EnCourage—

Fort Wayne Chapter—Rev. FRANCIS CHUKWUMA, J.C.L., Tel: 260-693-9578.

South Bend Chapter—Rev. KEVIN M. RUSSEAU, C.S.C., Tel: 574-234-3134, Ext. 20.

Diocesan Archives—JANICE CANTRELL, Archivist, Archbishop Noll Catholic Center, 915 S. Clinton St., Fort Wayne, 46802. Mailing Address: P.O. Box 390, Fort Wayne, 46801. Tel: 260-422-4611; Fax: 260-420-6306; Email: jhackbush@diocesefwsb.org.

Diocesan Council of Catholic Women—Rev. BENJAMIN J. MUHLENKAMP, Chap., Tel: 260-749-4525; CAROL DOEHRMAN, Pres., Tel: 260-445-3888.

Diocesan Finance Council—Most Rev. KEVIN C. RHOADES, D.D., S.T.L., J.C.L.; Very Rev. MARK ALLEN GURTNER, J.C.L.; MR. JOSEPH RYAN, CFO; MEG DISTLER; ROBERT DOELLING JR.; TIMOTHY DOLEZAL; Deacon JAMES FITZPATRICK; MICHAEL HAMMES; JEROME KEARNS; Sr. JANE MARIE KLEIN, O.S.F.; CHRISTOPHER MURPHY; THOMAS SCHUERMAN; THOMAS SKIBA; LINDA TEETERS; GEORGE WITWER.

Diocesan Museum—1102 S. Calhoun St., Fort Wayne, 46802. Tel: 260-422-0812. *Mailing Address: P.O. Box 390, Fort Wayne, 46801.* Fax: 260-426-2029. Rev. PHILLIP A. WIDMANN, Dir.

Diocesan Purchasing Agency—CONNIE BRUNER, Purchasing Mgr., Archbishop Noll Catholic Center, 915 S. Clinton St., Fort Wayne, 46802. Mailing Address: P.O. Box 390, Fort Wayne, 46801. Tel: 260-422-4611; Fax: 260-420-6306; JOHN KLEIN, Opers. Mgr., Tel: 260-422-4611.

Ecumenical Ministry—Deacon FREDERICK EVERETT, J.D., Dir., St. John Paul II Center, 328 W. Dragoon Tr., Mishawaka, 46544. Tel: 574-234-0687; Fax: 574-252-0509; SHAWN STORER, Coord., 2501 Miami St., South Bend, 46614. Tel: 574-339-1100.

Good Shepherd Books & Gifts—Archbishop Noll Catholic Center, 915 S. Clinton St., Fort Wayne, 46802. Tel: 260-399-1442. KARA SLOCUM, Coord.

Hispanic Ministry—John Paul II Center, 1328 W. Dragoon Tr., Mishawaka, 46544. Tel: 574-234-0687. ESTHER TERRY, Mts, Dir., Email: eterry@diocesefwsb.org.

Marriage and Family Ministry—St. John Paul II Center, 1328 W. Dragoon Tr., Mishawaka, 46544. Tel: 574-234-0687; Fax: 574-252-0509. LISA EVERETT, Dir.

Marriage Encounter—GREG RICHARD; JENNIFER RICHARD, 1221 Kensington Blvd., Fort Wayne, 46805. Tel: 260-422-0803.

Permanent Diaconate—Archbishop Noll Catholic Center, 915 S. Clinton St., Fort Wayne, 46802. Mailing Address: P.O. Box 390, Fort Wayne, 46801. Tel: 260-422-4611; Fax: 260-969-9145. Very Rev. MARK ALLEN GURTNER, J.C.L., Dir. Deacon Personnel; Deacon STANLEY LEMIEUX, Dir. Formation.

Pontifical Mission Societies—DR. KATHLEEN SCHNEIDER, Dir., Archbishop Noll Catholic Center, 915 S. Clinton St., Fort Wayne, 46802. Tel: 260-396-2552; Fax: 260-396-2048. Mailing Address: P.O. Box 390, Fort Wayne, 46801.

Presbyteral Council—Most Rev. KEVIN C. RHOADES, D.D., S.T.L., J.C.L.; Very Rev. MARK A. GURTNER, J.C.L.; Revs. THADEUS BALINDA, (Uganda); KEVIN M. BAUMAN; MATTHEW M. COONAN; ANDREW CURRY; PHILIP DEVOLDER; GLENN KOHRMAN; Very Rev. JACOB RUNYON, J.C.L.; Revs. KEVIN M. RUSSEAU, C.S.C.; DANIEL SCHEIDT; Rev. Msgr. ROBERT C. SCHULTE; Revs. THOMAS SHOEMAKER; ANTHONY STEINACKER; TIMOTHY A. WROZEK.

Safe Environment/Youth Protection—CATHIE CICCHIELLO, Coord., Archbishop Noll Catholic Center, 915 S. Clinton St., Fort Wayne, 46802. Mailing Address: P.O. Box 390, Fort Wayne, 46801. Tel: 260-422-4611; Fax: 260-483-1881.

Scouting, Diocesan Catholic Committee—MR. CARL LOESCH, B.A., M.A., M.Ed., M.A. Educ. Admin., Chm., Archbishop Noll Catholic Center, 915 S. Clinton St., Fort Wayne, 46802. Mailing Address: P.O. Box 390, Fort Wayne, 46801. Tel: 260-422-4611; Fax: 260-426-3077; Rev. WILLIAM ANTHONY MEININGER, Chap., St. Mary of the Lake, 124 College Ave., Culver, 46511.

Stewardship and Development—St. John Paul II Center, 1328 W. Dragoon Tr., Mishawaka, 46544. Tel: 574-258-6751; Fax: 574-256-2709. *Archbishop Noll Catholic Center, 915 S. Clinton St., Fort Wayne, 46802. Mailing Address: P.O. Box 390, Fort Wayne, 46801.* Tel: 260-422-4611; Fax: 260-423-3382. JEFFERY BOETTICHER, Dir.

Today's Catholic Official Publication—Archbishop Noll Catholic Center, 915 S. Clinton St., Fort Wayne, 46802. Tel: 260-456-2824; Fax: 260-744-1473. *Mailing Address: P.O. Box 390, Fort Wayne, 46801.* JODI MARLIN, Publication Mgr.

Tribunal—Archbishop Noll Catholic Center, 915 S. Clinton St., Fort Wayne, 46802. Mailing Address: P.O. Box 390, Fort Wayne, 46801. Tel: 260-422-4611; Fax: 260-969-9140. Very Rev. JACOB RUNYON, J.C.L., Judicial Vicar; JANICE BRELL, Administrative Asst.

Advocate—VICKI FERRIER; ANNE THERESE STEPHENS.

Auditors—ELLEN BECKER; ISABELLA DURAN.

Promoter of Justice—Rev. Msgr. BRUCE PIECHOCKI, J.C.L.

First Court of Judges—Very Rev. JACOB RUNYON, J.C.L.; Rev. FRANCIS CHUKWUMA, J.C.L.

Pro-Synodal Judges—Very Rev. MARK A. GURTNER, J.C.L.; Rev. Msgrs. MICHAEL W. HEINTZ, Ph.D.; BRUCE PIECHOCKI, J.C.L.; WILLIAM C. SCHOOLER; Revs. JAMES SHAFER; THOMAS SHOEMAKER.

Vocation Office—Revs. ANDREW BUDZINSKI, Dir., Archbishop Noll Catholic Center, 915 S. Clinton St., Fort Wayne, 46802. Tel: 260-422-4611; Fax: 260-423-3382; TERRENCE COONAN JR., Asst. Vocation Dir., St. Therese, Little Flower, 54191 Ironwood Rd., South Bend, 46635. Tel: 574-272-7070.

Worship Office—BRIAN MACMICHAEL, Dir., Archbishop Noll Catholic Center, 915 S. Clinton St., Fort Wayne, 46802. Mailing Address: P.O. Box 390, Fort Wayne, 46801. Tel: 260-422-4611; Fax: 260-423-3382.

Liturgical Commission—Rev. Msgr. WILLIAM C. SCHOOLER, Chair; Rev. MICHAEL DRISCOLL, Ph.D.; DAVID FAGERBERG, Ph.D.; Deacon JAMES FITZPATRICK; Very Rev. MARK A. GURTNER, J.C.L.; Rev. Msgr. MICHAEL W. HEINTZ, Ph.D.; JEREMY HOY; Rev. PETER D. ROCCA, C.S.C.

Sacred Art and Architecture Committee—WILLIAM COLEMAN JR., A.I.A.; Very Rev. MARK A. GURTNER, J.C.L.; Rev. JACOB A. MEYER; Bro. DENNIS MEYERS, C.S.C.; ANDREW ROCHE, A.I.A.; Rev. DANIEL SCHEIDT; CHRISTOPHER SCHENKEL; DUNCAN STROIK, A.I.A.

Youth Organizations—

CYO—WENDY FLOTOW, Pres., Mailing Address: P.O. Box 445, Monroeville, 46733; Rev. JOSEPH GAUGHAN, Priest Mod.

Inter City Catholic League—TONY VIOLI, Pres., 225 Omer Ave., Mishawaka, 46545. Tel: 574-259-1638; Fax: 574-259-0995; Rev. TERRENCE COONAN JR., Moderator, Tel: 574-272-7070.

Young Adult and Campus Ministry—SEAN ALLEN, Dir., Saint John Paul II Center, 1328 W. Dragoon Tr., Mishawaka, 46544. Tel: 574-234-0687; Fax: 574-252-0509.

Youth Ministry—Archbishop Noll Catholic Center, 915 S. Clinton St., Fort Wayne, 46802. Tel: 260-422-4611; Fax: 260-483-1881. *Mailing Address: P.O. Box 390, Fort Wayne, 46801.* JOHN PRATT, Dir.

CLERGY, PARISHES, MISSIONS AND PAROCHIAL SCHOOLS

CITY OF FORT WAYNE

(ALLEN COUNTY)

1—CATHEDRAL OF THE IMMACULATE CONCEPTION (1836) (Calhoun, between Lewis and Jefferson Sts.).
1122 S. Clinton St., 46854. Tel: 260-424-1485; Email: jrunyon@cathedralfw.org; Web: www.cathedralfortwayne.org. Very Rev. Jacob Runyon, J.C.L., Rector; Revs. Peter Dee De, Parochial Vicar; Silvino Ndayambaje, (Uganda) Parochial Vicar.
Catechesis Religious Program—Fax: 260-424-7625; Email: sjordan@cathedralfw.org. Sue Jordan, D.R.E. Students 101.
Chapel—St. Mother Theodore Guerin Chapel, 1139 S. Calhoun St., 46802.

2—ST. ANDREW (1910) Closed. Parish closed June 28, 2003. Sacramental records are located in the Diocesan Archives Office, P.O. Box 390, Fort Wayne, IN. Tel: 260-422-4611.

3—ST. CHARLES BORROMEO (1957) [CEM]
4916 Trier Rd., 46815. Tel: 260-482-2186; Email: fathertom@scbfw.org; Web: stcharlesfortwayne.org. Revs. Thomas Shoemaker; Dennis DiBenedetto; James Kumbakkeel, O.S.B., (India) Parochial Vicar; Casey Ryan, Dir. Adult Formation; Mrs. Stacey Huneck, Youth Min.; Robert Carroll, Business Admin.; Mr. Timothy Robison, Liturgy Dir.; Ms. Karen Hope, Liturgy Dir.
School—St. Charles Borromeo School, (Grades PreK-8), 4910 Trier Rd., 46815. Tel: 260-484-3392; Fax: 260-482-2006; Email: schooloffice@stcharlesschoolfw.org; Email: schooladministration@stcharlesschoolfw.org; Web: www.stcharlesschoolfw.org. Robert Sordelet, Prin. Lay Teachers 40; Franciscan Sisters of the Sacred Heart 1; Students 696.
Catechesis Religious Program—Tel: 260-484-7322; Email: scbreligiouseducation@gmail.com. Amy Johns, D.R.E.; Lisa Schleinkofer, D.R.E. Students 82.

4—ST. ELIZABETH ANN SETON (1988)
10700 Aboite Center Rd., 46804. Tel: 260-432-0268; Email: parish@seasfw.org; Web: www.seasfw.org. Revs. David Voons; Augustine Mugarura; Thomas Zehr; Deacon James Kitchens.
School—St. Elizabeth Ann Seton School, (Grades PreK-8), 10650 Aboite Center School Rd., 46804. Tel: 260-432-4001; Fax: 260-432-6899; Email: lwidner@seascsfw.org; Web: www.seascsfw.org. Ms. Lois Widner, Prin.; Greg Slee, Admin. Lay Teachers 36; Students 535.
Catechesis Religious Program—Mrs. Kim Conte, D.R.E. Students 393.

5—ST. HENRY (1956)
2929 E. Paulding Rd., 46816. Tel: 260-447-4100; Email: revdandurkin@frontier.com. Rev. Daniel Durkin.
Catechesis Religious Program—Tel: 260-209-8359; Email: deetorrez41@gmail.com. Dolores Torrez, D.R.E.; Sonia Mares, Sec. Students 76.

6—ST. HYACINTH (1910) Closed. Parish closed

November 4, 1995. Sacramental records are located in the Diocesan Archives Office, P.O. Box 390, Fort Wayne, IN. Tel: 260-422-4611.

7—ST. JOHN THE BAPTIST (1929)
4500 Fairfield Ave., 46807. Tel: 260-744-4393. Mailing Address: 4525 Arlington Ave., 46807. Email: rnoll@stjohnsfw.org; Web: www.stjohnsfw.org. Rev. Andrew Budzinski.
School—St. John the Baptist School, (Grades PreK-8), Tel: 260-456-3321; Email: broyal@stjohnsfw.org; Web: www.stjohnsfw.org. Beatrice Royal, Prin. Lay Teachers 18; Students 234.
Catechesis Religious Program—Ed Fox, D.R.E. Students 28.

8—ST. JOSEPH (1914) (Italian)
2213 Brooklyn Ave., 46802. Tel: 260-432-5113; Fax: 260-432-4711; Email: psermersheim@saintjosephfw.org; Web: www.saintjosephfw.org. Rev. Evaristo R. Olivera, (Archdiocese: San Juan, Puerto Rico); Ken Jehle, Music Dir.
Res.: 1910 Hale Ave., 46802.
School—St. Joseph Catholic School, (Grades PreK-8), 2211 Brooklyn Ave., 46802. Tel: 260-432-4000; Fax: 260-432-8642; Email: cjordan@saintjosephfw.org; Web: www.saintjosephcatholicfw.org. Ms. Cristy Jordan, Prin., Email: cjordan@saintjoseph.org; Colleen Annis, Librarian. Lay Teachers 14; Students 180; Clergy / Religious Teachers 1.
Catechesis Religious Program—
Tel: 260-432-5113, Ext. 113; Email: aponce@saintjosephfw.org. Ana Ponce, D.R.E. Students 92.

9—ST. JOSEPH (1841) [CEM]
11337 Old U.S. 27 S., 46816. Tel: 260-639-3748; Fax: 260-639-3331; Email: st.josephhc@stjoehc.org; Web: www.stjoehc.org. Rev. William J. Kummer; Michelle Rupright, Business Mgr. & Sec.; Thomas Neuer, Music Min.
School—St. Joseph School, (Grades PreK-8), 11521 Old U.S. 27 S., 46816. Tel: 260-639-3580; Fax: 260-639-3675; Email: rbrown@stjoehc.org. Ms. Rachelle Brown, Prin.; Tammy Gladding, Librarian. Lay Teachers 13; Students 151; Pre K Enrollment 18; Elementary School Students 133.
Catechesis Religious Program—Email: gtmnschall@aol.com. Greta Schall, D.R.E. Students 10.

10—ST. JUDE (1929)
2130 Pemberton Dr., 46805. Tel: 260-484-6609; Email: info@stjudefw.org. Rev. Msgr. Robert C. Schulte; Revs. Robert D'Souza; David S. Huneck; Deacon James Tighe, RCIA Coord.; Ron Gage, Liturgy Dir.; John Offerle, Business Mgr.; Mary Pohlman, Pastoral Assoc.
Rectory—2101 Pemberton Dr., 46805.
School—St. Jude School, (Grades PreK-8), 2110 Pemberton Dr., 46805. Tel: 260-484-4611; Fax: 260-969-1607; Email: mobergfell@stjudefw.org; Web: www.stjudefw.org/school. Mike Obergfell, Prin.; Mr. Colin Wilkins, Vice Prin. Lay Teachers 26; Students 450; Clergy / Religious Teachers 1.
Catechesis Religious Program—Email: jschleitwiler@stjudefw.org. Julie Schleitwiler, D.R.E.; Vickie Lortie, Youth Min. Students 48.

11—ST. MARY'S CATHOLIC CHURCH (1848) [CEM] (German)
1101 S. Lafayette St., 46802-3202. Tel: 260-424-8231 ; Fax: 260-426-2029; Email: stmarysfw@stmarysfw.org; Web: www.stmaryfsw.org. Mailing Address: P.O. Box 11383, 46857-1383. Rev. Phillip A. Widmann.
Catechesis Religious Program—Students 21.

12—MOST PRECIOUS BLOOD (1897)
1515 Barthold St., 46808. Tel: 260-424-5535; Email: kroesler@preciousblood.org; Web: preciousblood.org. Rev. Joseph Gaughan.
School—Most Precious Blood School, (Grades PreK-8), 1529 Barthold St., 46808. Tel: 260-424-4832; Fax: 260-426-5904; Email: pbloodschool@preciousblood.org. Stanley Liponoga IV, Prin. Lay Teachers 15; Students 272; Clergy / Religious Teachers 1.
Catechesis Religious Program—Email: pbchurchfw@frontier.com. Students 272.

13—OUR LADY OF GOOD HOPE (1969)
7215 St. Joe Rd., 46835. Tel: 260-485-9615; Email: olgh.info@olghfw.com; Web: olghfw.com. Very Rev. Mark A. Gurtner, J.C.L.; Rev. Thomas Zehr, Pastoral Assoc.; Jeanne Kawiecki, Liturgy & Music Dir.; Jackie Oberhausen, Pastoral Assoc. & Youth Min.; Nicholas Oberhausen, Youth Min.; Donna Weldy, Admin.; Rev. Daniel Whelan, Parochial Vicar.
School—Our Lady School (2016) (Grades K-8), Tel: 260-485-5289; Email: admissions@ourladyfortwayne.org; Web: ourladyfortwayne.org. Ms. Samantha Smith, Prin. Aides 5; Lay Teachers 12; Students 136; Special Education Teachers 3.
Catechesis Religious Program—
Tel: 260-485-9615, Ext. 107; Email: olgh.dre@gmail.com; Web: olghfw.com/138. Kelly Ley, D.R.E. Students 86.

14—ST. PATRICK (1889) (Multicultural)
2120 S. Harrison St., 46802. Tel: 260-744-1450; Fax: 260-745-3645; Email: st.patrick.f.w@gmail.com; Web: saintpatrickfw.com. Revs. Dominic Nguyen, S.V.D.; Nam Vu, S.V.D.
Catechesis Religious Program—
Tel: 260-744-1450, Ext. 115; Email: drereligioused@gmail.com. Students 211.

15—ST. PAUL (1865) Closed. Parish closed June 28, 2003. Sacramental records are located at St. Patrick Catholic Church, 2120 Harrison St., Fort Wayne, IN 46802. Tel: 260-744-1450.

16—ST. PETER (1872) (German)
518 E. De Wald St., 46803. Tel: 260-744-2765; Email: stpeter1872@frontier.com. Rev. Tyrell J. Alles, O.S.B.

17—QUEEN OF ANGELS (1947) [CEM]
1500 W. State Blvd., 46808. Tel: 260-482-9411; Fax: 260-471-0005; Email: pastor@queenofangelsfw.org; Web: queenofangelsfw.org. Rev. Zachary Barry; Mr. Thomas Remenschneider, Liturgy Dir.
School—Queen of Angels School, (Grades PreK-8), 1600 W. State Blvd., 46808. Tel: 260-483-8214; Fax: 260-482-9412; Email: principal@queenofangelsschool.com. Lay Teachers 17; Students 185; Clergy / Religious Teachers 2.
Catechesis Religious Program—Email: religioused@queenofangelsfw.org. Michelle Meyer, D.R.E. Students 11.

18—SACRED HEART (1947)
4643 Gaywood Dr., 46806. Rev. Mark Wojdelski, F.S.S.P.

19—ST. THERESE (1947)
2304 Lower Huntington Rd., 46819.
Tel: 260-747-9139; Email: father@sttheresefw.org; Web: www.sttheresefw.org. Rev. Lawrence Teteh, C.S.Sp., (Nigeria).
School—St. Therese School, (Grades PreK-8), 2222 Lower Huntington Rd., 46819. Tel: 260-747-2343; Fax: 260-747-4767; Email: nbobay@sttheresefw.org. Nick Bobay, Prin. Lay Teachers 15; Preschool 8; Students 213.
Catechesis Religious Program—Email: lthomas@sttheresefw.org. Linda Thomas, D.R.E. Students 21.

20—ST. VINCENT DE PAUL (1846) [CEM]
1502 E. Wallen Rd., 46825. Tel: 260-489-3537; Email: church@saintv.org; Web: www.saintv.org. Revs. Daniel Scheidt; Polycarp Fernando, Parochial Vicar; Jay Horning, Parochial Vicar; Dorothy Schuerman, Pastoral Assoc.; Julia Thill, Pastoral Assoc.; Thomas Schuerman, Admin.
School—St. Vincent de Paul School, (Grades K-8), 1720 E. Wallen Rd., 46825.
Tel: 260-489-3537, Ext. 213; Fax: 260-489-5318; Email: school@saintv.org; Web: www.saintv.org/school. Cheryl Klinker, Prin. Lay Teachers 45; Students 745.
Catechesis Religious Program—
Tel: 260-489-3537, Ext. 204. Debbie Blackburn, D.R.E.; Mr. Stephen Jagla, Youth Min.; Ms. Lindsay Klinker, Youth Min. Students 457.

CITY OF SOUTH BEND

(ST. JOSEPH COUNTY)

1—ST. ADALBERT (1910)
2505 W. Grace St., South Bend, 46619.
Tel: 574-188-5708; Email: stadal139@diocesefwsb.org; Web: stadalbertparish.org. Revs. Paul Ybarra, C.S.C.; Ryan Pietrocarlo, C.S.C.
Res.: 2420 W. Huron St., South Bend, 46619.
School—St. Adalbert School, (Grades PreK-8), 519 S. Olive St., South Bend, 46619. Tel: 574-288-6645; Fax: 574-251-2788; Email: bzielinski@stadalbertschool.org. Joseph Miller, Prin. Lay Teachers 17; Students 235.
Catechesis Religious Program—
Tel: 574-288-5708, Ext. 218; Email: franciscaf2006@yahoo.com. Francisca Flores, D.R.E. Students 225.

2—ST. ANTHONY DE PADUA (1949)
2120 E. Jefferson Blvd., South Bend, 46617.
Tel: 574-282-2308; Fax: 574-288-8877; Email: church@stasb.org; Web: www.stasb.org. Rev. Robert Garrow; Deacon Brian L. Miller.
School—St. Anthony de Padua School, (Grades PreK-8), 2310 E. Jefferson Blvd., South Bend, 46615.
Tel: 574-233-7169; Fax: 574-233-7290; Email: kbogol@stasb.org; Web: www.school.stasb.org. Karen Bogol, Prin. Lay Teachers 24; Students 291.

3—ST. AUGUSTINE (1928) (African American)
P.O. Box 3198, South Bend, 46619-0198.
Tel: 574-234-7082; Email: leonardcollins@att.net; Web: www.SaintAugustineParish.org. Rev. Leonard J. Collins, C.S.C.; Deacon Melvin Tardy.
Res.: P.O. Box 929, Notre Dame, 46556.

4—ST. CASIMIR (1899)
1308 Dunham St., South Bend, 46619. Mailing Address: 2505 W. Grace St., South Bend, 46619.
Tel: 574-288-5708; Email: stadal139@diocesefwsb.org. Revs. Paul Ybarra, C.S.C.; Ryan Pietrocarlo, C.S.C.
Res.: 2420 W. Huron St., South Bend, 46619.

5—CHRIST THE KING (1933)
52473 Indiana State Rte. 933, South Bend, 46637.
Tel: 574-272-3113; Email: lfitzpatrick@christthekingonline.org; Web: christthekingonline.org. Revs. Stephen A. Lacroix, C.S.C.; Michael Belinsky, C.S.C., Parochial Vicar; Michael Palmer, C.S.C.
School—Christ the King School, (Grades PreK-8), Tel: 574-272-3922; Email: shoffman@christthekingonline.org. Lay Teachers 29; Students 475; Religious Teachers 4.
Catechesis Religious Program—Students 469.

6—CORPUS CHRISTI (1961)
2822 Corpus Christi Dr., South Bend, 46628.
Tel: 574-272-9982; Fax: 574-272-2545; Email: corpuschristi2005@sbcglobal.net; Web: www.corpuschristisb.org. Rev. Daryl Rybicki; Sr. M. Carmella Chojnacki, F.D.C., Pastoral Assoc.
School—Corpus Christi School, (Grades PreK-8), 2817 Corpus Christi Dr., South Bend, 46628.
Tel: 574-272-9868; Fax: 574-272-9894; Email: m.mackowiak@corpuschristisb.org; Web: www.corpuschristisb.org. Maggie Mackowiak, Prin.; Joan Kreskai, Librarian. Lay Teachers 17; Students 206.
Catechesis Religious Program—Michael Rafinski, D.R.E. Students 17.

7—ST. HEDWIG (1877) (Polish)
331 S. Scott St., South Bend, 46601. Revs. Cyril Fernandes; David Kashangaki, C.S.C., Parochial Vicar; Camillo Tirabassi, In Res., (Retired).

8—HOLY CROSS (1929)
920 Wilber St., South Bend, 46628.
Tel: 574-233-2179; Email: parish@hcssparish.org; Web: www.hcssparish.org. Revs. James E. Fenstermaker, C.S.C.; John M. Santone, C.S.C., J.C.L., Parochial Vicar; Edmund J. Sylvia, C.S.C., In Res.
Res.: 1520 Vassar Ave., South Bend, 46628-2748.
School—Holy Cross School, (Grades PreK-8), 1020 Wilber St., South Bend, 46628-2637.
Tel: 574-234-3422; Fax: 574-237-6725; Email: info@holycrosscrusaders.org; Web: www.holycrosscrusaders.org. Mrs. Angela Budzinski, Prin. Lay Teachers 19; Students 275; Clergy / Religious Teachers 4.
Catechesis Religious Program—Mrs. Kristen Hempstead McGann, D.R.E. Students 275.

9—HOLY FAMILY (1945) [JC]
56405 Mayflower Rd., South Bend, 46619-1517.
Tel: 574-282-2317; Fax: 574-282-2318; Email: hfamily135@diocesefwsb.org. Revs. Glenn Kohrman; Nathan Maskal.
School—Holy Family School, (Grades PreK-8), 56407 Mayflower Rd., South Bend, 46619.
Tel: 574-289-7375; Fax: 574-289-7386; Email: jveldman@hfssb.org. Mrs. Jennifer Veldman, Prin.; Reyna VanOverberge, Librarian. Lay Teachers 21; Students 256.
Catechesis Religious Program—Email: llagodney@hfssb.org. Linda Lagodney, D.R.E. Students 70.

10—ST. JOHN THE BAPTIST (1956)
3526 St. Johns Way, South Bend, 46628.
Tel: 574-233-5414; Email: johnthebaptistcc@aol.com; Web: stjohnsb.com. Revs. Glenn Kohrman; Nathan Maskal.
School—St. John the Baptist School, (Grades PreK-8), 3616 St. Johns Way, South Bend, 46628.
Tel: 574-232-9849; Fax: 574-232-9855; Email: office@stjohnsb.com; Web: www.stjohnsb.com. Mr. Brian Carver, Prin. Lay Teachers 8; Students 71.
Catechesis Religious Program— Religious program merged with Holy Family, South Bend.

11—ST. JOSEPH (1853)
226 N. Hill St., South Bend, 46617.
Tel: 574-234-3134; Email: secretary@stjoeparish.com. Revs. Kevin M. Russeau, C.S.C.; Daniel Ponisciak, C.S.C., Parochial Vicar.
School—St. Joseph School, (Grades K-8), 216 N. Hill St., South Bend, 46617. Tel: 574-234-0451; Fax: 574-234-2822; Email: gazar@stjosephgradeschool.com; Web: www.stjosephgradeschool.com. George Azar, Prin. Lay Teachers 35; Students 420.
Catechesis Religious Program—Students 141.

12—ST. JUDE CHURCH (1948)
Tel: 574-291-0570; Email: office@stjudeparish.net; Email: business@stjudeparish.net; Web: www.stjudeparish.net. Revs. John Delaney; Julius Okojie, (Nigeria) Parochial Vicar.
School—St. Jude Catholic School, (Grades PreK-8), 19657 Hildebrand St., South Bend, 46614.
Tel: 574-291-3820; Email: principal@stjudeschool.net; Web: www.stjudeschool.net. Mr. Stephen Donndelinger, Prin. Lay Teachers 18; Students 201.
Catechesis Religious Program—Email: faith@stjudeparish.net. Heather Buison, D.R.E. Students 45.

13—ST. MARY OF THE ASSUMPTION (1882) (German), Closed. For inquiries for parish records see St. Jude, South Bend.
14—ST. MATTHEW CATHEDRAL (1921)
1701 Miami St., South Bend, 46613.
Tel: 574-289-5539; Email: info@stmatthewcathedral.org; Web: stmatthewcathedral.org. Rev. Terry Fisher, Rector; Mrs. Cassandra Horner, Admin.; Trina Koldyke, Business Mgr.
School—St. Matthew Cathedral School, (Grades PreK-8), 1015 E. Dayton, South Bend, 46613.
Tel: 574-289-4535; Fax: 574-289-5439; Email: sistergiannamarie@stmatthewcathedral.org; Email: lrichardson@stmatthewcathedral.org; Email: dresbensen@stmatthewcathedral.org; Web: www.stmatthewcathedral.org. Sr. Gianna Marie Webber, Prin.; Mrs. JoAnn Palmer, Librarian. Lay Teachers 24; Students 370.
Catechesis Religious Program—1721 Miami St., South Bend, 46613. Tel: 574-289-4535; Email: jschwab@stmatthewcathedral.org. Jennifer Schwab, D.R.E. Students 85.
15—OUR LADY OF HUNGARY (1921) [CEM]
731 W. Calvert. St., South Bend, 46613.
Tel: 574-287-1700; Tel: 574-289-3272; Email: olhp@sbcglobal.net; Web: www.ourladyofhungary.org. Rev. Kevin M. Bauman.
Res.: 829 W. Calvert St., South Bend, 46613.
School—Our Lady of Hungary School, (Grades PreK-8), 735 W. Calvert St., South Bend, 46613.
Tel: 574-289-3272; Fax: 574-289-3272; Email: olhsec@olhsb.org. Kevin Goralczyk, Prin. Lay Teachers 13; Students 203; Clergy / Religious Teachers 8.
Catechesis Religious Program—Email: rectoryourladyofhungary@gmail.com. Valentina Guiterrez, D.R.E. Students 90.
16—ST. PATRICK (1858)
309 S. Taylor St., South Bend, 46625. Web: www.stpatricksb.org; Tel: 574-287-8932; Email: stspatrick-hedwig@att.net. Mailing Address: 331 S. Scott St., South Bend, 46601. Revs. Cyril Fernandes; David Kashangaki, C.S.C., Parochial Vicar.
Catechesis Religious Program—Rev. Mary Nyers, D.R.E. Students 5.
17—SACRED HEART OF JESUS (LAKEVILLE) (1932) [CEM] [JC]
63568 Old U.S. 31 S., South Bend, 46614.
Tel: 574-291-3775; Email: sacredheart11@juno.com; Web: www.sacredheartlakeville.org. Mailing Address: P.O. Box 2528, South Bend, 46680-2528. Revs. John Delaney; Julius Okojie, (Nigeria) Parochial Vicar.
Catechesis Religious Program— Twinned with St. Jude. 19704 Johnson Rd., South Bend, 46614. Email: faith@stjudeparish.net. Students 7.
18—ST. STANISLAUS BISHOP AND MARTYR (1899) (Polish)
415 N. Brookfield St., South Bend, 46628.
Tel: 574-223-1217; Email: pastor@ststanparish.com; Web: www.ststanparish.com. Rev. Msgr. John Fritz, F.S.S.P.; Rev. Daniel Mould, F.S.S.P.
19—ST. STEPHEN (1909) (Hispanic—Hungarian), Closed. Parish closed May 31, 2003. Sacramental records are located at St. Adalbert Catholic Church, 2420 W. Huron St., South Bend, IN 46619. Tel: 574-288-5708.
20—ST. THERESE, LITTLE FLOWER dba Little Flower Catholic Church (1937)
54191 Ironwood Rd., South Bend, 46635.
Tel: 574-272-7070; Fax: 574-243-3434; Email: info@littleflowerchurch.org; Web: littleflowerchurch.org. Rev. Terrence Coonan Jr.; Deacon Gregory Gehred.
Res. & Rectory: 18160 Bailey, South Bend, 46637.
Tel: 574-243-5421.
Catechesis Religious Program—Tel: 574-243-3439; Email: alexis@littleflowerchurch.org. Alexis Duffy, D.R.E., (Retired). Students 93.

OUTSIDE THE CITIES OF FORT WAYNE AND SOUTH BEND

ALBION, NOBLE CO., BLESSED SACRAMENT (1875) [JC]
2290 N. State Rd. 9, Albion, 46701.
Tel: 260-636-2072; Email: blessedsacramentc@gmail.com. Rev. John Steele, C.S.C., Admin.
Catechesis Religious Program—Susan Curtis, D.R.E. Students 53.
ANGOLA, STEUBEN CO., ST. ANTHONY OF PADUA (1926)
700 W. Maumee St., Angola, 46703.
Tel: 260-665-2259; Email: office@stanthonyangola.com; Web: www.stanthonyangola.com. Revs. Robert G. Showers, O.F.M.Conv.; Bernard Zajdel, O.F.M.-Conv., Parochial Vicar; Joseph Kiene, O.F.M.Conv., In Res.; Wilfrid Logsdon, O.F.M.Conv., In Res.; Friar Ray Mallett, O.F.M.Conv., In Res.; Katie Waltke, Business Mgr.; Marilee Roederer, Music Min.; Patti Webster, Sec.
Catechesis Religious Program—Email: cathy@stanthonyangola.com; Email: rcia@stanthonyangola.com; Email: cara@stanthonyangola.com. Cathy Bryan, D.R.E.; Jan Swensen, RCIA Coord.; Cara Molyet, Youth Min. Students 294.
ARCOLA, ALLEN CO., ST. PATRICK (1862) [CEM]
12305 Arcola Rd., 46818. Tel: 260-625-4151; Email: stpatarcola@earthlink.net. Rev. Thadeus Balinda, (Uganda).
Catechesis Religious Program—Tel: 260-625-4104. Students 152.
AUBURN, DE KALB CO., IMMACULATE CONCEPTION (1872) [CEM]
500 E. 7th St., Auburn, 46706. Tel: 260-925-3930; Email: office@iccauburn.com; Web: www.iccauburn.com. Rev. Timothy A. Wrozek.
Res.: 204 N. McClellan St., Auburn, 46706.
Catechesis Religious Program—Email: reled@iccauburn.com. Gary Helmkamp, D.R.E. Students 79.
AVILLA, NOBLE CO., ST. MARY OF THE ASSUMPTION (1853) [CEM]
232 N. Main St., Box 109, Avilla, 46710-0109.
Tel: 260-897-3261; Email: stmaryassumption@embarqmail.com. Rev. Daniel Chukwuleta.
Res.: 228 N. Main St., Box 700, Avilla, 46710-0700.
School—St. Mary of the Assumption School, (Grades PreK-8), Tel: 260-897-3481; Fax: 260-897-3706; Email: aadams@stmaryavilla.org; Web: stmaryavilla.org. Andrew Adams, Prin. Lay Teachers 11; Students 119; Clergy / Religious Teachers 1.
Catechesis Religious Program—Barbara Braley, D.R.E. Students 22.
BESANCON, ALLEN CO., ST. LOUIS (1846) [CEM 2] (French)
15535 Lincoln Hwy. E., New Haven, 46774.
Tel: 260-749-4525; Email: secretary@stlouisb.org; Web: stlouisb.org. Rev. Benjamin J. Muhlenkamp.
School—St. Louis School, (Grades PreK-8), 15529 Lincoln Hwy. E., New Haven, 46774.
Tel: 260-749-5815; Email: vdiller@stlouisacademy.org; Web: www.stlouisacademy.org. Mrs. Vanessa Diller, Prin. Lay Teachers 15; Students 159.
Catechesis Religious Program—Email: josie.ball@stlouisb.org. Students 32.
BIG LONG LAKE, LAGRANGE CO., ST. MARY OF THE ANGELS (1937) Closed. Parish closed February 25, 2006. Sacramental records are located at St. Michael Catholic Church, 1098 County Rd. 39, Waterloo, IN. Tel: 260-837-7115.
BLUFFTON, WELLS CO., ST. JOSEPH (1875)
1300 N. Main St., Bluffton, 46714-1127.
Tel: 260-824-1380; Email: stjosephchurch@adamswells.com; Web: stjosephchurchbluffton.org. Rev. David Violi; Sr. Rose Ehrlich, Music Min.
Catechesis Religious Program—Michelle Paxton, D.R.E. Students 72.
BREMEN, MARSHALL CO., ST. DOMINIC (1947) [JC]
803 W. Bike St., Bremen, 46506. Rev. Fernando Jimenez.
Church: 214 N. Maryland St., Bremen, 46506.
Tel: 260-249-8088; Email: phersho@yahoo.om.
Catechesis Religious Program—Email: rita.jeffirs@gmail.com. Rita Jeffirs, D.R.E. Students 179.
BRISTOL, ELKHART CO., ST. MARY OF THE ANNUNCIATION (1942) [JC]
411 W. Vistula St., Bristol, 46507. P.O. Box 245, Bristol, 46507. Tel: 574-848-4305;
Tel: 574-622-0039 (Rectory); Fax: 574-622-0159; Email: annunciationchurch-bristol@hotmail.com; Web: www.stmaryoftheannunciation.org. Rev. Robert Van Kempen.
Catechesis Religious Program—Email: mstutzman.stmarys@gmail.com. Mary Stutzman, D.R.E. Students 210.
CHURUBUSCO, WHITLEY CO., ST. JOHN BOSCO (1971)
216 N. Main St., Churubusco, 46723.
Tel: 260-693-9578; Email: saintjohn.bosco@gmail.com. Rev. Francis Chukwuma, J.C.L.
Catechesis Religious Program—Tel: 260-693-3332. Students 52.
CLEAR LAKE, STEUBEN CO., ST. PAUL CHAPEL (1941)
8780 E. 700 N., Fremont, 46737. Tel: 260-665-2259; Email: stpaulchapel@stanthonyangola.com; Web: www.stpaulcatholicchapel.org. Revs. Robert G. Showers, O.F.M.Conv.; Wilfrid Logsdon, O.F.M.-Conv., Chap.
Rectory—St. Anthony Rectory, 700 W. Maumee, Angola, 46703.
Catechesis Religious Program—Email: dre@stpaulcatholicchapel.org. Patricia Long, D.R.E. Students 18.
COLUMBIA CITY, WHITLEY CO., ST. PAUL OF THE CROSS (1860) [JC]
315 S. Line St., Columbia City, 46725.
Tel: 260-244-5723; Email: saintpaulchurch@embarqmail.com; Web: saintpaulcc.org. Rev. Gary Sigler.
Res.: 308 S. Chauncey St., Columbia City, 46725.
CULVER, MARSHALL CO., ST. MARY OF THE LAKE (1948) [JC]
124 College Ave., Culver, 46511. Email: bmeininger@stmaryculver.org. Mailing Address: 605 N. Plymouth St., Culver, 46511. Tel: 574-842-3667; Tel: 574-842-2522; Web: www.stmaryculver.org. Rev. William Anthony Meininger.
Catechesis Religious Program—Tel: 574-842-3667; Fax: 574-842-2549; Email: dmckee@stmaryculver.org. Donna McKee, D.R.E. Students 52.
DECATUR, ADAMS CO., ST. MARY OF THE ASSUMPTION (1840) [CEM] (German)
414 W. Madison St., Decatur, 46733.
Tel: 260-724-9159, Ext. 101; Email: tdebolt@sjdecatur.org; Web: www.stmarysdecatur.org. Revs. David Ruppert; Jose Panamattathil, V.C., Parochial Vicar; Deacon Jerome Kohrman; Judith Converset, Business Mgr.; Parker Maas, Music Min.; Toni DeBolt, Sec.; Mrs. Stephanie Ortiz-Brite, D.R.E.
School—St. Joseph, (Grades PreK-8), 127 N. Fourth St., Decatur, 46733. Tel: 260-724-2765; Email: school@sjdecatur.org; Web: www.stjosephdecatur.org. Jeffry Kiefer, Prin.; Elizabeth Alberding, Librarian. Lay Teachers 24; Students 300.
Catechesis Religious Program—Mrs. Stephanie Ortiz-Brite, D.R.E.; Mrs. Karen Weber, Youth Min. Students 300.
EGE, NOBLE CO., IMMACULATE CONCEPTION (1876) [CEM]
7046 E. 400 S., Laotto, 46763. Mailing Address: 216 N. Main St., Churubusco, 46723. Tel: 260-693-9578; Fax: 260-693-1608; Email: saintjohn.bosco@gmail.com. Rev. Francis Chukwuma, J.C.L.
Catechesis Religious Program—Students 45.
ELKHART, ELKHART CO.
1—ST. THOMAS THE APOSTLE (1949) [JC]
1405 N. Main St., Elkhart, 46514. Tel: 574-262-1505; Email: frjason@stselkhart.com. Rev. Jason Freiburger.
School—St. Thomas the Apostle School, (Grades PreK-8), 1331 N. Main St., Elkhart, 46514.
Tel: 574-264-4855; Fax: 574-262-8477; Email: bmahaffa@stselkhart.com; Web: www.stselkhart.com. Christopher Adamo, Prin.; Elizabeth Baker, Librarian. Lay Teachers 18; Students 223; Clergy / Religious Teachers 1.
Catechesis Religious Program—Tel: 574-264-0491. Students 101.
2—ST. VINCENT DE PAUL (1868) [CEM]
1108 S. Main St., Elkhart, 46516. Tel: 574-293-8231; Email: r.campanello@svcelkhart.org; Web: www.svcelkhart.org. Revs. Matthew M. Coonan; Patrick Hake.
School—St. Vincent de Paul School, (Grades K-8), 1114 S. Main St., Elkhart, 46516. Tel: 574-293-8451; Fax: 574-295-9702; Email: t.lundy@svcelkhart.org. Mrs. Tara Lundy, Prin. Lay Teachers 12; Students 167.
Catechesis Religious Program—Tel: 574-293-8071; Email: h.palmer@svcelkhart.org. Harry Palmer, D.R.E. (K-12). Students 662.
GARRETT, DE KALB CO., ST. JOSEPH (1876) [CEM]
301 S. Ijams St., Garrett, 46738-1424.
Tel: 260-357-3122; Email: parish@stjosephgarrett.org; Web: stjosephgarrett.com. Mailing Address: 300 W. Houston, Garrett, 46738-1424. Rev. James A. Shafer; Mrs. Eileen Sarrazine, Pastoral Assoc.; Ms. Danielle Sarrazine, Admin.
Res.: 307 S. Ijams St., Garrett, 46738.
School—St. Joseph School, (Grades PreK-6), 301 W. Houston, Garrett, 46738. Tel: 260-357-5137;
Fax: 260-357-5138; Email: office@stjosephgarrett.org; Web: www.stjosephgarrett.org. Ms. Jennifer Enrietto, Prin.; Jody Prokupek, Librarian; Mrs. Alice York, Sec. Lay Teachers 11; Students 102; Clergy / Religious Teachers 1.
Catechesis Religious Program—Email: sarrazine@stjosephgarrett.org. Students 55.
GENEVA, ADAMS CO., ST. MARY OF THE PRESENTATION (1883) [CEM]
5790 E. 1100 S., Geneva, 46740-9132.
Tel: 260-997-6558; Email: jbmper@yahoo.com. Rev. J. Bosco Perera, O.M.I., (Sri Lanka).
Catechesis Religious Program—
GOSHEN, ELKHART CO., ST. JOHN THE EVANGELIST (1840) [CEM]
114 W. Monroe St., Goshen, 46526.
Tel: 574-533-3385; Fax: 574-533-1814; Email: parishoffice@stjohncatholic.com; Web: www.stjohncatholic.com. Revs. Royce Gregerson; Eloy Jimenez, (Mexico); Deacons David Elchert; Giovani Munoz; Christopher Nieves.
School—St. John the Evangelist School, (Grades PreSchool-5), 117 W. Monroe, Goshen, 46526.
Tel: 574-533-9480; Email: mwillerton@stjohncatholic.com. Mattie Willerton, Prin. Lay Teachers 11; Sisters 1; Students 166.
Catechesis Religious Program—109 W. Monroe St., Goshen, 46526. Email: vmunoz@stjohncatholic.com. Virginia Munoz, D.R.E. Students 458.
GRANGER, ST. JOSEPH CO., ST. PIUS X (1955)
52553 Fir Rd., Granger, 46530. Tel: 574-272-8462; Email: parishoffice@stpius.net; Web: www.stpius.

net. Rev. Msgr. William C. Schooler; Rev. Eric Burgener, Parochial Vicar.
Res.: 52515 Santa Monica Dr., Granger, 46530.
School—St. Pius X School, (Grades PreK-8), Tel: 574-272-4935; Email: skoloszar@stpius.net. Elaine Holmes, Prin. Lay Teachers 36; Students 630; Clergy / Religious Teachers 1.
Catechesis Religious Program—Tel: 574-277-5760; Email: rkiley@stpius.net. Robby Kiley, D.R.E. Students 540.

HUNTINGTON, HUNTINGTON CO.
1—ST. MARY (1896) [JC]
903 N. Jefferson St., Huntington, 46750.
Tel: 260-356-4398; Email: stmary083@gmail.com; Web: stmaryhuntington.org. Rev. Stephen E. Colchin.
School—Huntington Catholic School, (Grades PreK-8), 960 Warren St., Huntington, 46750.
Tel: 260-356-1926; Fax: 260-356-8419; Email: dboone@huntingtoncatholic.org; Web: www.huntingtoncatholic.org. Primary Building: 820 Cherry St., Huntington, 46750. Tel: 260-356-2320. Derek Boone, Prin. Lay Teachers 15; Priests 2; Students 138; Clergy / Religious Teachers 3.
Catechesis Religious Program—Email: ddelly46@cinergymetro.net. Daniel DeLaGrange, D.R.E. Students 67.
2—SS. PETER AND PAUL (1843) [JC]
Tel: 260-356-4798; Email: SSPPbulletinnews@comcast.net; Web: sspeterpaulparish.org. Revs. Anthony Steinacker; Maicaal Lobo.
See Huntington Catholic School, Huntington under St. Mary, Huntington for details.
Catechesis Religious Program—Email: dstuart.sspp@gmail.com. Sr. Miriam Gill, S.S.N.D., D.R.E. Students 253.

KENDALLVILLE, NOBLE CO., IMMACULATE CONCEPTION (1867) [CEM]
301 E. Diamond St., Kendallville, 46755. Mailing Address: 319 E. Diamond St., Kendallville, 46755.
Tel: 260-347-4045; Tel: 260-347-2522; Email: icckendallville@live.com. Rev. James Stoyle.
Catechesis Religious Program—Students 57.

LAGRANGE, LAGRANGE CO., ST. JOSEPH (1930) [JC]
050 N. 100 E., LaGrange, 46761. Tel: 260-463-3472; Email: stjosephlagrange@gmail.com. Rev. John Steele, C.S.C.
Catechesis Religious Program—Tel: 260-585-5891. Guadalupe Hurtado, D.R.E. Students 137.

LAGRO, WABASH CO., ST. PATRICK (1838) Closed. Parish closed February 1, 1997. Sacramental records are located at St. Bernard Catholic Church, 207 North Cass St., Wabash, IN 46992-2441. Tel: 260-563-4750.

LIGONIER, NOBLE CO., ST. PATRICK (1860) [JC]
300 Ravine Park Dr., Ligonier, 46767-1301.
Tel: 260-894-4946; Email: stpatlig@ligtel.com. Rev. Wilson O. Corzo, (Colombia); Deacon Stanley LeMieux.
Catechesis Religious Program—Students 258.

MISHAWAKA, ST. JOSEPH CO.
1—ST. BAVO (1903)
502 W. 7th St., Mishawaka, 46544.
Tel: 574-255-1437; Email: office@stbavochurch.com; Web: www.stbavochurch.com. Rev. Peter Pacini, C.S.C.; Deacon Kevin M. Ranaghan.
Res.: 511 W. 7th St., Mishawaka, 46544.
School—Mishawaka Catholic School, (Grades PreK-2), Consolidated with St. Joseph, St. Monica, and St. Bavo. St. Bavo Campus, 524 W. 8th St., Mishawaka, 46544. Tel: 574-259-4214; Fax: 574-255-6381; Email: info@mcmish.org; Web: www.mcmish.org. Mrs. Karen Salvador, Prin. Lay Teachers 22; Students 261; Religious Teachers 1.
Catechesis Religious Program—Gus Zuehlke, D.R.E. Students 35.
2—ST. JOSEPH (1848) [CEM]
225 S. Mill St., Mishawaka, 46544.
Tel: 574-255-6134; Fax: 574-255-6387; Email: parish@stjoemish.com; Web: stjoemish.com. Rev. Christopher Raymond Lapp.
School—Mishawaka Catholic School, (Grades 3-5), Consolidated with St. Bavo, St. Monica, and St. Joseph. St. Joseph Campus, 230 S. Spring St., Mishawaka, 46544. Tel: 574-255-5554;
Fax: 574-255-6381; Email: info@mcmish.org; Web: www.mcmish.org. Mrs. Karen Salvador, Prin. Lay Teachers 22; Students 261; Religious Teachers 1.
Catechesis Religious Program—Email: gwulle1@gmail.com. Greg Wulle, D.R.E. Students 85.
3—ST. MONICA (1915)
222 W. Mishawaka Ave., Mishawaka, 46545.
Tel: 574-255-2247; Fax: 574-255-8375; Email: frjmeyer@stmonicamish.org; Web: www.stmonicamish.org. Rev. Jacob A. Meyer; Victoria Zmirski, Business Mgr.
School—Mishawaka Catholic School, (Grades 6-8), Consolidated with St. Bavo, St. Joseph, and St. Monica. St. Monica Campus, 223 W. Grove St., Mishawaka, 46545. Tel: 574-255-0709;
Fax: 574-255-6381; Email: info@mcmish.org; Web: www.mcmish.org. Mrs. Karen Salvador, Prin.; Beth Whitfield, Vice Prin. Lay Teachers 17; Priests 3; Students 265.
Catechesis Religious Program—Jeanette Dripps, D.R.E. Students 32.
4—QUEEN OF PEACE (1957)
4508 Vistula Rd., Mishawaka, 46544.
Tel: 574-255-9674; Tel: 574-255-0392;
Fax: 574-255-1029; Email: lhaverty@queenofpeace.cc; Web: www.queenofpeace.cc. Rev. John Eze; Mrs. Laurie Haverty, Admin.
School—Queen of Peace School, (Grades PreSchool-8), Email: office@queenofpeace.cc; Web: www.queenofpeace.cc/school. Jill Miller, Prin. Lay Teachers 14; Students 250; Clergy / Religious Teachers 2.
Catechesis Religious Program—Kelly Pant, D.R.E. Students 210.

MONROEVILLE, ALLEN CO., ST. ROSE OF LIMA (1868) [CEM]
206 Summit St., P.O. Box 406, Monroeville, 46773.
Tel: 260-623-6437; Fax: 260-623-6439; Email: strose206@yahoo.com; Web: www.saintrosechurch.com. Rev. Lourdino Fernandes.
School—St. Rose of Lima, (Grades PreK-8), 401 Monroe St., Monroeville, 46773. Tel: 260-623-3447; Fax: 260-623-3447; Email: fernandeslourdino@ymail.com; Web: www.saintrosemonroeville.org. Gale Powelson, Prin.; Mary Jo Linder, Librarian. Lay Teachers 11; Students 96; Clergy / Religious Teachers 1.

NAPANEE, ELKHART CO., ST. ISIDORE, Closed. Parish closed August 1, 1995. Sacramental records are located at St. Dominic, 803 W. Bike St., Bremen, IN. Tel: 574-546-3601.

NEW CARLISLE, ST. JOSEPH CO., ST. STANISLAUS KOSTKA (1884) (Polish)
55756 Tulip Rd., New Carlisle, 46552.
Tel: 574-654-3781; Email: dianeststan@embarqmail.com. Rev. Paul McCarthy.
Catechesis Religious Program—Kathy Henderson, D.R.E. Students 44.

NEW HAVEN, ALLEN CO., ST. JOHN THE BAPTIST (1859) [CEM]
943 Powers St., New Haven, 46774.
Tel: 260-493-4553; Tel: 260-749-9903; Email: stjohn111@diocesefwsb.org; Web: www.sjnewhaven.org. Rev. William J. Sullivan.
School—St. John the Baptist School, (Grades PreK-8), 204 S. Rufus St., New Haven, 46774.
Tel: 260-749-9903; Fax: 260-749-6047; Email: info@sjnewhaven.org; Web: www.sjnewhaven.org. Zachary Coyle, Prin. Lay Teachers 19; Students 222.
Catechesis Religious Program—
Tel: 260-493-4553, Ext. 306; Email: deb.rhinock@sjnewhaven.org. Mrs. Deborah Rhinock, D.R.E. Students 32.

NIX SETTLEMENT, WHITLEY CO., ST. CATHERINE OF ALEXANDRIA (1850) [CEM]
9989 S. State Rte. 9, Columbia City, 46725. P.O. Box 250, Roanoke, 46783-0250. Tel: 260-672-2838; Email: sscatherineandjoseph@comcast.net. Rev. Dale A. Bauman.
Rectory—St. Joseph, 641 N. Main St., Roanoke, 46783-0250.
Catechesis Religious Program—Dr. Kathleen Schneider, D.R.E. Students 4.

NORTH MANCHESTER, WABASH CO., ST. ROBERT BELLARMINE (1963) [JC]
1203 State Rd., 114 E., North Manchester, 46962.
Tel: 260-982-4404; Email: strobertsnm@gmail.com; Web: www.strobertsnmanchester.org. Rev. Andrew Curry.
Catechesis Religious Program—Students 54.

NOTRE DAME, ST. JOSEPH CO., SACRED HEART (1842) [CEM] [JC]
104 Sacred Heart Parish Center, Notre Dame, 46556-5662. Tel: 574-631-7511; Email: sacheart@nd.edu; Web: sacredheartparish.nd.edu. Rev. David J. Scheidler, C.S.C.; Deacon William J. Gallagher.
Res.: 100 Sacred Heart Parish Center, Notre Dame, 46556-5662.
Catechesis Religious Program—Tel: 574-631-7508; Email: michelle.kriss.1@nd.edu. Sr. Elise Kriss, O.S.F., B.Ed., M.S., Ph.D., D.R.E. Students 20.

PIERCETON, KOSCIUSKO CO., ST. FRANCIS XAVIER (1864) [CEM]
408 W. Catholic St., Pierceton, 46562.
Tel: 574-594-5750; Fax: 574-594-2347; Email: sfxpierceton@aol.com; Web: www.sfxpierceton.org. Rev. Charles A. Herman.
Catechesis Religious Program—Students 20.

PLYMOUTH, MARSHALL CO., ST. MICHAEL (1862) [CEM]
612 N. Walnut St., Plymouth, 46563.
Tel: 574-936-4935; Fax: 574-936-9293; Email: jkorcsmar@gmail.com; Web: saintmichaelplymouth.org. Revs. John S. Korcsmar, C.S.C.; Craig Borchard, Parochial Vicar.
School—St. Michael School, (Grades K-8), 612 N. Center St., Plymouth, 46563. Tel: 574-936-4329;
Fax: 574-936-1151; Email: aweidner@saintmichaelschool.org; Web: www.saintmichaelschool.org. Mrs. Amy Weidner, Prin. Lay Teachers 15; Students 170.
Catechesis Religious Program—Tel: 574-780-8971; Email: figueroa.1989@yahoo.com. Carolina Sanchez, D.R.E. Students 170.

ROANOKE, HUNTINGTON CO., ST. JOSEPH (1867) [CEM]
641 N. Main St., Roanoke, 46783-0250. P.O. Box 250, Roanoke, 46783. Tel: 260-672-2838; Email: sscatherineandjoseph@comcast.net. Rev. Dale A. Bauman.
Catechesis Religious Program—Tel: 260-396-2552; Email: kayschneider@embarqmail.com. Dr. Kathleen Schneider, D.R.E. Students 23.

ROME CITY, NOBLE CO., ST. GASPAR DEL BUFALO (1957) [CEM]
10871 N. State Rd. 9, Rome City, 46784.
Tel: 260-854-3100; Email: stgaspar2018@gmail.com. Rev. Bernard Ramenaden, O.S.B., (Sri Lanka).

SYRACUSE, KOSCIUSKO CO., ST. MARTIN DE PORRES (1966)
6941 E. Waco Dr., Syracuse, 46567-9496.
Tel: 574-457-8176; Email: stmartinchurch@yahoo.com. Rev. Andrew Nazareth, (India).
Catechesis Religious Program—Christine Huffman, Sec. Students 12.

WABASH, WABASH CO., ST. BERNARD (1864)
207 N. Cass St., Wabash, 46992. Tel: 260-563-4750; Email: stbernard@cinergymetro.net. Rev. Levi UC Nkwocha.
School—St. Bernard School, (Grades PreK-6), 191 N. Cass St., Wabash, 46992. Tel: 260-563-5746;
Fax: 260-563-4898; Email: tcteacher28@gmail.com; Email: stb191@cinergymetro.net; Web: stbernardcatholicschool.org. Theresa Carroll, Prin. Lay Teachers 6; Students 79; Clergy / Religious Teachers 1.

WALKERTON, ST. JOSEPH CO., ST. PATRICK (1856)
807 Tyler St., Walkerton, 46574. Tel: 547-586-7152; Email: info@saintpatricks.church; Web: saintpatricks.church. Rev. Eric A. Zimmer, S.J.; Ms. Ellen Swan, Business Mgr.; Mrs. Anna Chaffee, Music Min.
Res.: 801 Tyler St., Walkerton, 46574.
Catechesis Religious Program—Email: dre@saintpatricks.church. Barbara Blad, D.R.E. Students 49.

WARSAW, KOSCIUSKO CO.
1—OUR LADY OF GUADALUPE (1972) [CEM] (Hispanic)
225 Gilliam Dr., Warsaw, 46581. Mailing Address: P.O. Box 1136, Warsaw, 46581-1136.
Tel: 574-267-5324; Fax: 574-267-1472; Email: ologchurch-warsaw@outlook.com. Rev. Constantino Rocha; Deacon Marco Castillo.
Catechesis Religious Program—Students 94.
2—SACRED HEART (1852) [JC]
125 N. Harrison St., Warsaw, 46580.
Tel: 574-267-5842; Email: shc@sacredheart-warsaw.org; Web: www.sacredheart-warsaw.org. Rev. Jonathan Blake Norton; Mrs. Susan Armacost, Pastoral Min./Coord.; Mrs. Karen Kelsheimer, Liturgy Dir.; Mrs. Laura Gillis, Business Mgr.; Mrs. Michelle Frazzetta, Sec.
School—Sacred Heart School, (Grades PreK-6), 135 N. Harrison, Warsaw, 46590. Tel: 574-267-5874; Fax: 574-267-5136; Email: shs@sacredheart-warsaw.org. Mr. James L. Faroh Sr., Prin. Lay Teachers 13; Students 200; Clergy / Religious Teachers 1.
Catechesis Religious Program—Email: cathy-smith@sacredheart-warsaw.org. Mrs. Cathy Smith, D.R.E.; Mrs. Ida List, Youth Min. Students 207.

WATERLOO, DEKALB CO., ST. MICHAEL THE ARCHANGEL (1880) [CEM]
1098 County Rd. 39, Waterloo, 46793-9779.
Tel: 260-837-7115; Email: secretary@stmichaelwaterloo.com; Web: stmichaelwaterloo.com. Rev. Vincent Joseph, V.C., (India).
Catechesis Religious Program—Email: dre@stmichaelwaterloo.com. Arica Swygart, D.R.E.; Jenny Buchs, Youth Min.; Bobbie Charleswood, RCIA Coord. Students 75.
ST. MARY OF THE ANGELS, 5965 S. 1025 E., Hudson, 46747-9605. Tel: 260-351-4792; Email: stmary.biglong@gmail.com. Mary Bartlett, Contact Person.

YODER, ALLEN CO., ST. ALOYSIUS (1859) [CEM]
14623 Bluffton Rd., Yoder, 46798-9741.
Tel: 260-622-4491; Email: parish@stalyoder.org; Web: stalyoder.org. Rev. Msgr. Bruce Piechocki, J.C.L.
School—St. Aloysius School, (Grades PreK-8), 14607 Bluffton Rd., Yoder, 46798-9741. Tel: 260-622-7151; Fax: 260-622-7961; Email: tvoors@saintaloysiusyoder.info; Web: www.saintaloysiusyoder.info/School. Tina Voors, Prin. Lay Teachers 9; Students 85.
Catechesis Religious Program—Mrs. Louisea Baker, D.R.E. Students 23.

Chaplains of Public Institutions

FORT WAYNE. *St. Joseph Hospital*, 700 Broadway, 46802-1402. Tel: 260-425-3000.

Lutheran Hospital, Tel: 260-435-7001. Roseann Bloomfield, Tel: 260-435-7722.

Parkview Hospital, Tel: 260-484-6636, Ext. 26311. Rev. Robert D'Souza, Chap.

Parkview Regional Medical Center, 11109 Parkview Plaza, 46845. Tel: 260-266-1000. Rev. James Bromwich, Chap.

Veterans Administration Hospital. Rev. Chijoke Alphonsus Chigbo, Chap.

SOUTH BEND. *Memorial Hospital of South Bend*, 615 N. Michigan St., South Bend, 46601-9986. Tel: 574-647-1000; Fax: 574-647-7827. Rev. Joseph Oforchukwu, Chap.

On Special Assignment:

Rev. Msgr.—

Heintz, Michael W., Ph.D., 16300 Old Emmitsburg Rd., Emmitsburg, MD 21727.

Retired:

Rev. Msgrs.—

Galic, Bernard J., (Retired), 403 Parent Dr., Ossian, 46777

Kuzmich, John M., (Retired), P.O. Box 023, Notre Dame, 46556

Revs.—

Bly, Walter J., (Retired), Holy Cross Village at Notre Dame, P.O. Box 303, Notre Dame, 46556

England, Barry C., (Retired), P.O. Box 023, Notre Dame, 46556

Erpelding, Edward, (Retired), 2128 Ransom Dr., 46845

Gall, Jacob M., (Retired), 51958 Fawn Meadow Dr., Elkhart, 46514. Tel: 574-264-1119

Pfister, John F., (Retired), 1900 Randallia Dr., #30, 46805

Ruetz, Edward J., (Retired), 815 Spruce Crt., Mishawaka, 46545. Tel: 574-234-5652

Schmitt, Adam, (Retired), 1900 Randallia Dr., #1022, 46805

Seculoff, James F., (Retired), c/o P.O. Box 390, 46801

Sneyd, Derrick, (Retired), 31 St. Gregory Dr., Bluffton, SC 29909

Tirabassi, Camillo, (Retired), 331 S. Scott St., South Bend, 46601.

Permanent Deacons:

Byrne, Robert, 16819 Colony Dr., South Bend, 46635

Campos, Juan, 201 Leclere St., South Bend, 46767

Castillo, Marco, 2699 N. 175 E. Lot 102, Warsaw, 46582

DeCelles, Paul, (Retired), 809 Angela Blvd., South Bend, 46614

Egendorfer, Eugene, (Retired), 184 Palm Blvd., Parrish, FL 34219

Elchert, David, 828 Wentworth Dr., Goshen, 46526

Everett, Frederick, J.D., 22160 White Spruce Ct., South Bend, 46682

Fitzpatrick, James, 202 Osprey Ct., Huntertown, 46748

Fuchs, James, 54686 Sagewood Dr., Mishawaka, 46545

Gallagher, William J., 552 East Angela, South Bend, 46617

Garcia, Ricardo, 605 Revere Dr., Goshen, 46528

Gehred, Greg, M.D., 2613 Corby Blvd., South Bend, 46615

Giovanni, Louis, 15230 Longford Dr., Granger, 46530

Kitchens, James, 9404 Fireside Ct., 46804

Kohrman, Jerry, 809 Perry Lake Dr., 46845

Kuspa, Ervin, (Retired), 434 S. Liberty, South Bend, 46619

LeMieux, Stanley, 67426 Kensington Dr., Goshen, 46526

Messina, Joseph, (Retired), 200 Butterfly Ln., Hermitage, PA 16148

Miller, Brian L., 1115 North St. Peter St., South Bend, 46617

Munoz, Giovani, 16006 S. 15th St., Goshen, 46528

Nieves, Christopher, 2720 Lismore Dr., Goshen, 46526

Olayo, Blas

Ranaghan, Kevin, 18166 Annetta's Ct., South Bend, 46617

Rauner, James, 880 N. Brainbridge Ctr. Rd., Watervliet, MI 49098

Ruvaclaba, Jose, 56689 Fairmont Ave., South Bend, 46619

Sandoval, Victor, 3636 Elmhurst Dr., 46809

Tardy, Melvin, 2216 Oakwood Park Dr., South Bend, 46628

Tighe, James, 2120 Springfield Ave., 46805

Vasquez, Huberto, 521 Edge Knoll Ln., 46816

Walsh, James M., (Retired), 2212 Broadmoor Dr., Elkhart, 46514.

INSTITUTIONS LOCATED IN DIOCESE

[A] SEMINARIES, RELIGIOUS, OR SCHOLASTICATES

NOTRE DAME. *Moreau Seminary*, P.O. Box 668, Notre Dame, 46556. Tel: 574-631-7735; Fax: 574-631-9233; Email: jherman@holycrossusa.org. Revs. Thomas C. Bertone, C.S.C., In Res.; Brian C. Ching, C.S.C., In Res.; Jeffrey Cooper, C.S.C., In Res.; Matthew Gummess, O.Carm., In Res.; John Herman, C.S.C., In Res.; Stephen J. Kempinger, C.S.C., In Res.; Charles W. Kohlerman, C.S.C., In Res.; Wilson D. Miscamble, C.S.C., In Res.; Robert H. Moss, C.S.C., In Res.; Francis J. Murphy, C.S.C., In Res.; Linus Nvirri, C.S.C., In Res.; Peter D. Rocca, C.S.C., In Res.; John Vickers, C.S.C., In Res.; Nathan D. Wills, C.S.C., In Res.; Bros. Donald Stabrowski, C.S.C., In Res.; J. Rodney Struble, C.S.C., In Res. This is a college level and Theological Seminary run by the Congregation of Holy Cross United States Province of Priests and Brothers for Religious Priesthood and Brotherhood candidates. Brothers 5; Priests 11; Seminarians 30; Students 33; Total Staff 8; Clergy / Religious Teachers 1.

Old College, 200 Old College, P.O. Box 638, Notre Dame, 46556-0638. Tel: 574-631-0778; Fax: 574-631-0111; Email: bching@nd.edu; Web: vocations.holycrossusa.org. Rev. Brian C. Ching, C.S.C., Dir.; Mr. Mark Pedersen, Dir.; Bro. Donald Stabrowski, C.S.C., Chap. College candidates study here for up to three years before entering Moreau Seminary. Priests 1; Students 10; Total Staff 3; Candidates for the Priesthood in the First Three Years of Undergraduate Formation 11.

[B] COLLEGES AND UNIVERSITIES

FORT WAYNE. *University of Saint Francis* (1890) 2701 Spring St., 46808-3994. Tel: 260-399-7700, Ext. 6910; Email: ekriss@sf.edu; Email: vjacobs@sf.edu; Web: www.sf.edu. Sr. Elise Kriss, O.S.F., B.Ed., M.S., Ph.D., Pres.; Maureen McMahon, Librarian. Conducted by Sisters of St. Francis of Perpetual Adoration. Lay Teachers 162; Priests 1; Sisters 9; Students 2,199; Total Staff 235; Clergy / Religious Teachers 4.

SOUTH BEND. **University of Notre Dame Du Lac* (1842) Provost Office, 300 Main Bldg., South Bend, 46556. Tel: 574-631-5000; Tel: 574-631-6631 (Provost); Fax: 574-631-6897; Email: cleichty@nd.edu; Web: www.nd.edu. John Affleck-Graves, Ph.D., Exec. Vice Pres.; Revs. J. Douglas Archer, Faculty; Nicholas R. Ayo, C.S.C., Faculty; David C. Bailey, M.B.A., Vice Pres., Strategic Planning & Institutional Rsch.; Thomas Bear, Sr. Dir. Enrollment Mgmt.; Rev. E. William Beauchamp, C.S.C., Chap.; Robert Bernhard, Ph.D., Vice Pres., Rsch.; Donald Bishop, Assoc. Vice Pres. Undergraduate Enrollment; Revs. Thomas E. Blantz, C.S.C., Faculty; James A. Bracke, C.S.C., Faculty; Dennis Brown, Asst. Vice Pres. News & Media Rels.; Paul J. Browne, M.A., Vice Pres. for Public Affairs & Communications; Rev. Richard S. Bullene, C.S.C., Faculty; Thomas G. Burish, Ph.D., Provost; Drew Buscareno, Assoc. Vice Pres., Devel.; Sr. Kathleen Cannon, O.P., Faculty; Rev. Joseph H. Carey, C.S.C., Faculty; Laura A. Carlson, Ph.D., Vice Pres., Assoc. Provost & Dean, Graduate School; Revs. Gary S. Chamberland, C.S.C., Faculty; Brian C. Ching, C.S.C., Faculty; Austin I. Collins, C.S.C., Supr.; John E. Conley, C.S.C., Faculty; Michael E. Connors, C.S.C., Faculty; Joseph V. Corpora, C.S.C., Faculty; Marianne Corr, J.D., Vice Pres. & Gen. Counsel; Brian Coughlin, Assoc. Vice Pres., Student Devel.; Shannon Cullinan, Vice Pres., Finance; John Curran, Assoc. Vice Pres., New Business Devel.; Revs. William R. Dailey, C.S.C., Faculty; Brian Daley, S.J., Faculty; Michael M. DeLaney, C.S.C., Faculty; Louis A. DelFra, C.S.C., Faculty; Sr. Mary Donnelly, O.P., Faculty; Revs. Robert A. Dowd, C.S.C., Faculty; Paul F. Doyle, C.S.C., Faculty; Dolly Duffy, Assoc. Vice Pres., Univ. Rels.; Greg Dugard, Assoc. Vice Pres., Univ. Rels. & Exec. Dir., Campaign Admin.; Revs. Terrence P. Ehrman, C.S.C., Faculty; David Eliaona, C.S.C., Faculty; Warren von Eschenbach, Assoc. Vice Pres. & Asst. Provost, Internationalization; Ann Firth, J.D., Chief of Staff; Timothy J. Flanagan, Assoc Gen. Counsel; Scott Ford, Assoc. Vice Pres., Econ. Devel.; Revs. James K. Foster, C.S.C., Faculty; Patrick D. Gaffney, C.S.C., Faculty; John Gohsman, Vice Pres., IT & Chief Information Officer; Revs. Gregory A. Green, C.S.C., Faculty; Edward J. Griswold, Faculty; Daniel G. Groody, C.S.C., Faculty; Kevin G. Grove, C.S.C., Faculty; Ralph L. Haag, C.S.C., Faculty; Gregory P. Haake, C.S.C., Faculty; Erin Hoffmann Harding, J.D., Vice Pres., Student Affairs; David Harr, Assoc. Vice Pres., Auxiliary Opers.; Rev. William R. Headley, Faculty; Sisters Mary Jane Herb, I.H.M., Faculty; Mary Catherine Hilkert, O.P., Faculty; Rev. Matthew E. Hovde, C.S.C., Faculty; Charles Hurley, Registrar; Revs. John I. Jenkins, C.S.C., Pres.; Maxwell E. Johnson, Faculty; Emmanuel Katongole, Faculty; Stephen J. Kempinger, C.S.C., Faculty; Micki Kidder, Assoc. Vice Pres. & Exec. Dir., Devel.; Revs. Paul V. Kollman, C.S.C., Faculty; Matthew C. Kuczora, C.S.C., Faculty; Matthew Lahey, Assoc. Gen. Counsel; Revs. Donald LaSalle, Faculty; James M. Lies, C.S.C., Faculty; Robert L. Loughery, C.S.C., Faculty; Edward A. Malloy, C.S.C., Pres. Emeritus; Scott C. Malpass, M.B.A., Vice Pres. & Chief Investment Officer; Douglas Marsh, Vice Pres., Facilities Design & Opers. & Univ. Architect; Sr. Gail A. Mayotte, S.A.S.V., Faculty; Christine M. Maziar, Ph.D., Vice Pres. & Sr. Assoc. Provost; Revs. Peter M. McCormick, C.S.C., Faculty; Russell K. McDougall, C.S.C., Faculty; Sr. Mary Catherine McNamara, S.I.W., Faculty; Robert K. McQuade, M.B.A., Vice Pres., HR; Rev. John P. Meier, Faculty; Karrah Miller, Dir., Inst. Equity; Rev. Wilson D. Miscamble, C.S.C., Faculty; Sarah Misener, Assoc. Vice Pres., Campus Svcs.; Revs. Timothy Mouton, C.S.C., Faculty; Francis J. Murphy, C.S.C., Faculty; Louis M. Nanni, M.A., Vice Pres., Univ. Rels.; Revs. Stephen P. Newton, C.S.C., Chap.; Martin L. Nguyen, C.S.C., Faculty; Timothy L. O'Connor, C.S.C., Faculty; Paulinus Odozor, C.S.Sp., (Canada) Faculty; Gerard I. Olinger, C.S.C., Vice Pres., Mission Engagement & Church Affairs; Hugh R. Page Jr., Vice Pres. & Assoc. Provost, Undergraduate Affairs; Andrew M. Paluf, Assoc. Vice Pres. & Controller; Rev. Robert S. Pelton, C.S.C., Faculty; Michael Pippenger, Ph. D., Vice Pres. & Assoc. Provost, Internationalization; Heather Rakoczy Russell, Assoc. Vice Pres., Residential Life; Rev. Christopher Rehagen, C.S.C., Faculty; Bryan Ritchie, Vice Pres. & Assoc. Provost, Innovation; Brandon Roach, Assoc. Gen. Counsel; Revs. Peter D. Rocca, C.S.C., Rector; George A. Rozum, C.S.C., Faculty; Maura A. Ryan, Vice Pres. & Assoc. Provost, Faculty Affairs; Revs. Kevin J. Sandberg, C.S.C., Faculty; John M. Santone, C.S.C., J.C.L., Faculty; David J. Scheidler, C.S.C., Faculty; Timothy R. Scully, C.S.C., Faculty; Michael Seamon, Vice Pres., Campus Safety & Event Mngmt.; Mr. Timothy Sexton, Assoc. Vice Pres., Public Affairs; Jim Small, Assoc. Vice Pres., Devel.; William Stackman, Assoc. Vice Pres., Student Svcs.; John Sturm, Assoc. Vice Pres., Federal & Washington Rels.; Revs. Michael B. Sullivan, C.S.C., Faculty; Robert E. Sullivan, Assoc. Vice Pres., Academic Mission Support; Jack Swarbrick, J.D., Vice Pres. & Dir., Athletics; Deacon Melvin Tardy, Faculty; Revs. Mark B. Thesing, C.S.C., Faculty; David T. Tyson, C.S.C., Faculty; Ms. Diane Parr Walker, Librarian; Rev. Richard S. Wilkinson, C.S.C., Chap.; Ryan Willerton, Assoc. Vice Pres., Career & Professional Devel.; Revs. Oliver F. Williams, C.S.C., Faculty; Nathan D. Wills, C.S.C., Faculty. Notre Dame is organized into four undergraduate colleges - Arts and Letters, Science, Engineering, and the Mendoza College of Business - the School or Architecture, the Keough School of Global Affairs, the Law School, 10 major research institutes, more than 40 centers and special programs, and the University library system. Priests 68; Sisters 5; Students 12,467; Total Faculty 1,348; C.S.C. 21; Other Catholic Clergy 4; Non-Catholic Clergy 6; Lay 1,162; Clergy / Religious Teachers 99; Staff 5,046.

DONALDSON. *Ancilla Domini College*, P.O. Box 1, Donaldson, 46513. Tel: 574-936-8898; Fax: 574-935-1773; Email: admissions@ancilla.edu; Web: www.ancilla.edu. Sr. Michele Dvorak, Pres.; Donald Holland, Vice Pres. Finance & CFO; Sam Soliman, Vice Pres. Academic Affairs; Kristy Banks, Vice Pres. Enrollment Management; Emily Hutsell, Devel. & Alumni Rels. Mgr.; Cassaundra Bash, Library Dir. Poor Handmaids of Jesus Christ (Ancilla Domini Sisters). Lay Teachers 51; Sisters 1; Students 368; Clergy / Religious Teachers 1.

NOTRE DAME. *Holy Cross College, Holy Cross College, Inc.* (1966) 54515 State Rd., 933 N., P.O. Box 308, Notre Dame, 46556-0308. Tel: 574-239-8402; Fax: 574-239-8323; Email: dtyson@hcc-nd.edu; Web: www.hcc-nd.edu. Rev. David T. Tyson, C.S.C., Pres.; Justin Watson, Ph.D., Provost; Monica Markovich, Vice Pres. Finance; Michael Griffin, Vice Pres.

Holy Cross College, Inc. Brothers 3; Lay Teachers 17; Priests 3; Students 445; Total Staff 64; Clergy / Religious Teachers 2.

Saint Mary's College (1844) Saint Mary's College, 156 LeMans Hall, Notre Dame, 46556.
Tel: 574-284-4556; Fax: 574-284-4707; Email: jhersche@saintmarys.edu; Web: www.saintmarys.edu. Nancy Nekvasil, Pres. Sisters of the Holy Cross.An institution of higher education for women. Students 1,602; Lay Professors 226; Clergy / Religious Teachers 3.

[C] HIGH SCHOOLS, DIOCESAN

FORT WAYNE. *Bishop Dwenger High School* (1963) 1300 E. Washington Center Rd., 46825.
Tel: 260-496-4700; Fax: 260-496-4702; Email: saints@bishopdwenger.com; Web: www.bishopdwenger.com. Mr. Jason Schiffli, Prin.; Mr. Chris Svarczkopf, Asst. Prin. & Dean Students; Katie Burns, Devel. Dir.; Jill Schriner, Librarian; Tiffany Albertson, Admin.; Rev. Benjamin J. Muhlenkamp. Lay Teachers 60; Priests 1; Students 1,075; Total Staff 68.

Bishop Luers High School (1959) 333 E. Paulding Rd., 46816. Tel: 260-456-1261; Fax: 260-456-1262; Email: jhuth@bishopluers.org; Web: www.bishopluers.org. James Huth, Prin.; Kevin Mann, Dean; Randy Hawkins, Vice Prin.; Mandy Allen, Librarian. Lay Teachers 31; Priests 2; Students 541; Clergy / Religious Teachers 4.

SOUTH BEND. *Saint Joseph High School* (1953) 453 N. Notre Dame Ave., South Bend, 46617.
Tel: 574-233-6137; Fax: 574-472-1245; Email: sbdstjoehs@saintjoehigh.com; Web: www.saintjoehigh.com. 914 E. Jefferson Blvd., South Bend, 46617. John Kennedy, Prin.; Mr. Bob Tull, Asst. Prin.; Mrs. Marilyn Gibbs, Asst. Prin.; Revs. Walter J. Bly, Chap., (Retired); Camillo Tirabassi, Chap., (Retired), Email: ctirabassi@saintjoehigh.com; Terrence Coonan Jr., Chap.; Leslie Brenner, Librarian. Lay Teachers 61; Priests 1; Students 859.

MISHAWAKA. *Marian High School* (1964) 1311 S. Logan St., Mishawaka, 46544. Tel: 574-259-5257;
Fax: 574-258-7668; Email: mhs@marianhs.org; Web: www.marianhs.org. Mark Kirzeder, B.S., M.A., M.Ed., Prin.; Anelia Babcock, Pastoral Min.; Mary Dlugosz, Librarian. Lay Teachers 48; Priests 1; Sisters 1; Students 648; Clergy / Religious Teachers 1.

[D] HOSPITALS AND HEALTHCARE FACILITIES

MISHAWAKA. *Saint Joseph Regional Medical Center*, 5215 Holy Cross Pkwy., Mishawaka, 46545.
Tel: 574-335-5000; Fax: 574-335-1002; Email: paintelm@sjrmc.com; Web: www.sjmed.com. Chad Towner, CEO; Sr. Laureen M. Painter, O.S.F., Regional Vice Pres., Mission Integration. Bed Capacity 304; Tot Asst. Annually 383,782; Total Staff 2,079.

PLYMOUTH. *Saint Joseph Regional Medical Center - Plymouth*, 1915 Lake Ave., P.O. Box 670, Plymouth, 46563. Tel: 574-948-5000;
Fax: 574-948-5478; Web: www.sjmed.com. Chad Towner, CEO; Mr. Christopher Karan, Pres.; Sr. Laureen M. Painter, O.S.F., Regional Vice Pres., Mission Integration. Bed Capacity 58; Tot Asst. Annually 84,658; Total Staff 289.

[E] SPECIAL HOSPITALS

FORT WAYNE. *Saint Anne Home & Retirement Community* dba Saint Anne Communities,
Tel: 260-484-5555; Email: homeoffice@sacfw.org; Web: sacfw.org. David Deffenbaugh, Admin. Bed Capacity 252; Skilled Nursing Beds 157; Total Apartments 95.

Saint Anne Home at Randallia Place, 1900 Randallia Dr., 46805. Tel: 260-484-5555;
Fax: 260-482-8929; Email: homeoffice@sacfw.org; Web: www.sacfw.org. Revs. John Overmyer, Chap.; John F. Pfister, In Res., (Retired); Adam Schmitt, In Res., (Retired); David Deffenbaugh, COO

Saint Anne Home of the Diocese of Fort Wayne-South Bend, Inc. Bed Capacity 248; Residents 233; Total Apartments 95; Tot Asst. Annually 580; Total Staff 353.

Saint Anne at Victory Noll, 25 Victory Noll Dr., Huntington, 46750. Tel: 260-224-6848; Email: homeoffice@sacfw.org; Web: www.sacfw.org. Anne Crawley, Admin.; Tony Steinacker, Chap.

Saint Anne Home of the Diocese of Fort Wayne-South Bend, Inc. Bed Capacity 40; Apartments 40; Staff 25.

NOTRE DAME. *University Health Services*, 201 St Liam Hall, Notre Dame, 46556-5693. Tel: 574-631-7103;
Fax: 574-631-6047; Email: nrodrig4@nd.edu; Web: www.nd.edu/~uhs. Rev. James A. Bracke, C.S.C., Chap. Tot Asst. Annually 30,000; Total Staff 25.

[F] HOMES FOR THE AGED

AVILLA. *Presence Sacred Heart Home* dba Presence Life Connections Incorporated, 515 N. Main St., Avilla, 46710-9602. Tel: 260-897-2841; Fax: 260-897-2001; Email: William.Rees@PresenceHealth.org; Web: www.presencehealth.org/sacredheart. Jay Kroft, Admin.; Tom Novy, Dir. Spiritual Care. Sacred Heart Home is an Ascension Living Senior Health organization.

Presence Life Connections Incorporated dba Presence Sacred Heart Home Bed Capacity 133; Skilled Nursing Beds 133; Total Apartments 93; Total Assisted 20.

Provena LaVerna Terrace aka LaVerna Terrace Housing Corporation, 517 N. Main St., Avilla, 46710. Tel: 260-897-3120; Fax: 260-897-2086; Email: Sheri.Gibson@PresenceHealth.org; Email: Tiffany.Fields@PresenceHealth.org. Jay Kroft, Admin.; Tom Novy, Spiritual Care Dir. Ascension Living Senior Care.

LaVerna Terrace Housing Corporion dba Presence LaVerna Terrace Total Apartments 51.

DONALDSON. *Catherine Kasper Life Center, Inc.*, 9601 Union Rd., P.O. Box 1, Donaldson, 46513.
Tel: 574-935-1742; Fax: 574-935-1760; Web: cklc.poorhandmaids.org. Sisters Judith Diltz, P.H.J.C., Prov.; Nora Hahn, P.H.J.C., Vice Pres. & Sec.; Patricia Peters, P.H.J.C., Treas.; Rev. Mattais Alonyenu, Chap.; Scott Piotrowicz, Interim Exec. Dir.; Becky Anspach, Maria Center Mgr. Sponsored by the Poor Handmaids of Jesus Christ. (The Ancilla Domini Sisters, Inc.)Purpose: To provide quality care and address the spiritual, emotional, and physical needs of the aged, sick and disabled. Catherine Kasper Home: 82 bed facility (long-term care and rehab) including early stage locked memory care unit; Maria Center: 28 independent senior living apartments (efficiency to two bedrooms) offering a variety of services and activities. Skilled Nursing Beds 82; Total Apartments 28; Total Assisted 250.

NOTRE DAME. *Holy Cross Village at Notre Dame*, 54515 State Rd. 933 N., P.O. Box 303, Notre Dame, 46556-0303. Tel: 574-245-7800; Fax: 574-232-7933; Email: dnull@holycrossvillage; Web: www.holycrossvillage.com. Thomas Veldman, Chm.; Mr. David Null, Pres. & CEO; Rev. Kenneth Grabner, C.S.C., Chap.; Bro. Carlos Parrilla, Dir. Rel.; Sr. Marilyn Zugish, C.S.C., Dir. Spiritual Care. Independent Apartments & Assisted Living. (Other) 140.

[G] PERSONAL PRELATURES

SOUTH BEND. *Prelature of the Holy Cross and Opus Dei*, Windmoor Center, 1121 N. Notre Dame Ave., South Bend, 46617. Tel: 574-232-0550;
Fax: 574-287-4798; Email: info@windmoor.org; Web: www.windmoor.org. Rev. Oscar Regojo, Chap. Total in Residence 14; Total Staff 4.

[H] MONASTERIES AND RESIDENCES OF PRIESTS AND BROTHERS

NOTRE DAME. *Congregation of Holy Cross, Midwest Province*, Provincial Admin., 54515 State Rd. 933 N., P.O. Box 460, Notre Dame, 46556-0460.
Tel: 574-631-4000; Fax: 574-631-2999; Web: www.brothersofholycross.com. Bros. Kenneth Haders, C.S.C., Prov. Supr.; Robert Lavelle, C.S.C., Asst. Prov. & Vicar; Thomas Cunningham, C.S.C., Prov. Sec.; Paul Kelly, C.S.C., Prov. Steward; Lewis Brazil, C.S.C., Dir., Healthcare and Aging; John Affum, C.S.C., Prov. Councilor; Christopher Torrijas, C.S.C., Prov. Councilor; James Van Dyke, C.S.C., Prov. Councilor

Legal Title: Brothers of Holy Cross, Inc. Brothers 138. *Columba Hall*, P.O. Box 776, Notre Dame, 46556. Tel: 574-631-6284; Fax: 574-631-9882; Email: cdreyer@brothersofholycross.com. Bros. Douglas Roach, C.S.C., Supr.; Christopher Dreyer, C.S.C., B.A., M.S., B.S.W., Asst. Supr.; Rev. William G. Blum, C.S.C., Chap. Total in Residence 36. *Dujarie House, Infirmary*, Dujarie House, Holy Cross Village, P.O. Box 706, Notre Dame, 46556-0706. Tel: 574-287-1838; Fax: 574-289-7277; Email: dnull@holycrossvillage.com. Ms. Linda Lewis, Admin. Total in Residence 48; Laity 42. *Helen D. Schubert Villa, Assisted Living*, Schubert Villa, Holy Cross Village, P.O. Box 706, Notre Dame, 46556-706. Tel: 574-287-1986;
Fax: 574-289-7277; Email: dnull@holycrossvillage.com. Ms. Linda Lewis, Admin. Total in Residence 48; Laity 43. *Holy Cross Village*, 54515 SR 933 N., P.O. Box 839, Notre Dame, 46556.
Tel: 574-287-1838; Fax: 574-232-7933; Email: dnull@holycrossvillage.com; Email: mpendl@holycrossvillage.com. Mr. David Null, Admin. & CEO; Rev. Kenneth E. Grabner, C.S.C., Chap. Religious 17; Laity 250.

Congregation of Holy Cross, United States Province of Priests and Brothers, Province Administration Center, 54515 State Rd. 933 N., Notre Dame, 46556. Tel: 574-631-6196; Fax: 574-631-5655; Email: ssimmonds@holycrossusa.org; Web: www.holycrossusa.org. P.O. Box 774, Notre Dame, 46556-0774. Revs. Robert J. Austgen, C.S.C.; Nicholas R. Ayo, C.S.C.; Ernest J. Bartell, C.S.C.; Thomas C. Bertone, C.S.C.; Thomas E. Blantz, C.S.C.; William G. Blum, C.S.C.; James A. Bracke, C.S.C.; Robert J. Brennan, C.S.C.; Foster J. Burbank, C.S.C.; David B. Burrell, C.S.C.; Lawrence E. Calhoun, C.S.C.; Thomas F. Carten, C.S.C.; LeRoy E. Clementich, C.S.C.; James T. Connelly, C.S.C.; John Connor, C.S.C.; Richard Conyers, C.S.C.; Jeffrey Cooper, C.S.C.; William Crumley, C.S.C.; James J. Denn, C.S.C.; John F. Dias, C.S.C.; Jerome C. Esper, C.S.C.; David E. Farrell, C.S.C.; James J. Ferguson, C.S.C.; James F. Flanigan, C.S.C.; Robert Gilmour, C.S.C.; Kenneth E. Grabner, C.S.C.; Donald F. Guertin, C.S.C.; Andrew R. Guljas, C.S.C.; Lawrence J. Henry, C.S.C.; Michael J. Heppen, C.S.C.; Peter A. Jarret, C.S.C., Vicar; Thomas J. Jones, C.S.C.; David Kashangaki, C.S.C.; Fulgentius Katende, C.S.C.; John P. Keefe, C.S.C.; Stephen J. Kempinger, C.S.C.; Jerome E. Knoll, C.S.C.; Charles W. Kohlerman, C.S.C.; Edward C. Krause, C.S.C.; Christopher A. Kuhn, C.S.C.; James Lackenmier, C.S.C.; Richard Laurick, C.S.C.; Charles J. Lavely, C.S.C.; Andre E. Leveille, C.S.C.; William M. Lies, C.S.C., Prov.; L. Peter Logsdon, C.S.C.; James P. Madden, C.S.C.; Patrick H. Maloney, C.S.C.; Jose M. Martelli, C.S.C.; Jerome F. Matthews, C.S.C.; Thomas F. McNally, C.S.C.; Wilson D. Miscamble, C.S.C.; Francis J. Murphy, C.S.C.; Robert H. Moss, C.S.C.; William Neidhart, C.S.C.; Robert J. Nogosek, C.S.C.; Linus Nvirri, C.S.C.; Edward D. O'Connor, C.S.C.; Peter Pacini, C.S.C.; Robert S. Pelton, C.S.C.; David J. Porterfield, C.S.C., (Retired); Peter D. Rocca, C.S.C.; Kenneth J. Silvia, C.S.C.; S. Douglas Smith, C.S.C.; Kevin P. Spicer, C.S.C.; John Steele, C.S.C.; Richard E. Stout, C.S.C.; Patrick J. Sullivan, C.S.C.; Edmund J. Sylvia, C.S.C.; Joseph H. Tate, C.S.C.; Richard Teall, C.S.C., (Retired); Mark B. Thesing, C.S.C., Steward; James R. Trepanier, C.S.C., (Retired); Charles Van Winkle, C.S.C.; Robert A. Vozzo, C.S.C.; Neil F. Wack, C.S.C., Sec.; Richard V. Warner, C.S.C.; John Wironen, C.S.C.; Michael B. Wurtz, C.S.C.; Herbert C. Yost, C.S.C.; Herman F. Zaccarelli, C.S.C.; Francis D. Zagorc, C.S.C.; Bros. Thomas J. Combs, C.S.C.; James Lakofka, C.S.C.; Edward C. Luther, C.S.C; James H. Miller, C.S.C.; Donald Stabrowski, C.S.C.; J. Rodney Struble, C.S.C.

Congregation of Holy Cross, United States Province, Inc.

Congregation of Holy Cross-Eastern Province, Inc., 54515 State Rd. 993 N., Notre Dame, 46556.
Tel: 574-631-3700; Email: ssimmonds@holycrossusa.org. P.O. Box 1064, Notre Dame, 46556-1064. Rev. Mark B. Thesing, C.S.C., Treas.

Congregation of Holy Cross, Southern Province, Inc., 54515 State Rd. 933 N, Notre Dame, 46556.
Tel: 574-631-6196.; Email: ssimmonds@holycrossusa.org. Mailing Address: P.O. Box 774, Notre Dame, 46556-0774. Rev. Mark B. Thesing, C.S.C., Treas.

Holy Cross Community, Corby Hall, University of Notre Dame, 124 Corby Hall, Notre Dame, 46556-5680. Tel: 574-631-7325; Fax: 574-631-6715; Email: jnash@holycrossusa.org. Revs. William Beauchamp, C.S.C.; James A. Bracke, C.S.C.; Richard S. Bullene, C.S.C.; Francis Cafarelli; Joseph H. Carey, C.S.C., Steward; Gary S. Chamberland, C.S.C.; Brian C. Ching, C.S.C.; Austin I. Collins, C.S.C., Holy Cross Supr.; John E. Conley, C.S.C.; Michael E. Connors, C.S.C.; Joseph V. Corpora, C.S.C.; William R. Dailey, C.S.C.; Michael M. DeLaney, C.S.C.; Louis A. DelFra, C.S.C.; Robert A. Dowd, C.S.C.; Paul F. Doyle, C.S.C.; Terrence P. Ehrman, C.S.C.; David Eliaona, C.S.C.; James K. Foster, C.S.C.; Patrick D. Gaffney, C.S.C.; Gregory A. Green, C.S.C.; Daniel G. Groody, C.S.C.; Kevin G. Grove, C.S.C.; Ralph L. Haag, C.S.C.; Gregory P. Haake, C.S.C.; Matthew E. Hovde, C.S.C.; John I. Jenkins, C.S.C., Pres., Univ. of Notre Dame; Paul V. Kollman, C.S.C.; Matthew C. Kuczora, C.S.C.; James M. Lies, C.S.C.; William M. Lies, C.S.C.; Robert L. Loughery, C.S.C.; Edward A. Malloy, C.S.C., Pres. Emeritus & Prof. Theology; Peter M. McCormick, C.S.C., Dir., Campus Ministry; Russell K. McDougall, C.S.C.; Wilson D. Miscamble, C.S.C.; Timothy Mouton, C.S.C.; Francis J. Murphy, C.S.C.; Stephen P. Newton, C.S.C.; Martin Lam Nguyen, C.S.C.; Timothy L. O'Connor, C.S.C.; Gerard I. Olinger, C.S.C.; Christopher Rehagen, C.S.C., Asst. Supr.; George A. Rozum, C.S.C.; Kevin J. Sandberg, C.S.C.; David J. Scheidler, C.S.C.; Timothy R. Scully, C.S.C.; S. Douglas Smith, C.S.C.; Thomas G. Streit, C.S.C.; Michael B. Sullivan, C.S.C., (Eastern Prov.); Mark B. Thesing, C.S.C.; David T. Tyson, C.S.C.; Richard S. Wilkinson, C.S.C.; Oliver F. Williams, C.S.C.; Nathan D. Wills, C.S.C.; Bro. Patrick J. Lynch, C.S.C.,

Asst. Supr.; Deacon Brogan C. Ryan, C.S.C.; Mr. Thomas Bodart; Mr. Felipe Campos; Mr. Vincent Nguyen; Mr. Mark Pedersen; Mr. Gilbrian Stoy.

Priests of Holy Cross, Indiana Province, Inc. (1841) 54515 State Rd. 933 N., Notre Dame, 46556. Email: ssimmonds@holycrossusa.org. Mailing Address: P.O. Box 1064, Notre Dame, 46556-1064. Tel: 574-631-6196; Fax: 574-631-5655. Rev. Mark B. Thesing, C.S.C., Treas.

[I] CONVENTS AND RESIDENCES OF SISTERS

FORT WAYNE. *Sisters of St. Joseph of the Third Order of St. Francis Residences S.S.J.-T.O.S.F.*, 1217 New England Dr., 46815. Tel: 260-515-9927; Email: mwhite@ssj-tosf.org. Sr. Marjorie White, S.S.J.-T.O.S.F., Pres. Sisters 1.

Sisters of St. Joseph of the Third Order of St. Francis Residences S.S.J.-T.O.S.F., 2222 Abbey Dr., 46835. Tel: 260-485-4616; Email: terriduclos@frontier.com. Sr. Therese Duclos, Contact Person. Sisters 1.

SOUTH BEND. *Handmaids of the Most Holy Trinity Monastery-Hermitage* (1968) 23089 Adams Rd., South Bend, 46628-9674. Sr. Mary Emmanuel Baggoo, H.T., Representative. Contemplative Community; Prayer Ministry; Prayer Witness which includes Retreats and Spiritual Direction. Sisters 1.

Sarah House (1996) 1213 E. Bronson, South Bend, 46615. Tel: 574-287-8342; Fax: 574-287-8342; Email: connie.ss@att.net; Web: www.poorhandmaids.org. Sr. Connie Bach, P.H.J.C., Dir. Owned by the Poor Handmaids of Jesus Christ. Sisters 2.

The Sisters of St. Joseph of the Third Order of St. Francis, S.S.J.-T.O.S.F. (1901) 1425 Clayton Dr., South Bend, 46614. Tel: 574-287-5435; Fax: 574-291-1555; Email: sis@chiarahomerespite.org. Sr. Gretchen Clark, S.S.J.-T.O.S.F., Contact Person. Sisters 1.

DONALDSON. *Convent Ancilla Domini* (1922) 9601 Union Rd., P.O. Box 1, Donaldson, 46513. Tel: 574-936-9936; Fax: 574-935-1785; Email: judith.diltz@poorhandmaids.org; Web: www.poorhandmaids.org. Sr. Judith Diltz, P.H.J.C., Prov. Provincialate, Poor Handmaids of Jesus Christ (The Ancilla Domini Sisters) Sisters 68; Professed Sisters 18.

Ancilla College, 20097 9B Rd., Plymouth, 46563. Tel: 574-936-8898; Fax: 574-935-1779; Email: admissions@ancilla.edu; Web: www.ancilla.edu. P.O. Box 1, Donaldson, 46513. Sr. Michele Dvorak, COO.

Catherine's Cottage, 9601 Union Rd., P.O. Box 1, Donaldson, 46513. Tel: 574-935-1703; Fax: 574-935-1785; Email: mlama@poorhandmaids.org; Web: www.poorhandmaids.org. Sr. Marlene Ann Lama, P.H.J.C., Contact Person. Professed Sisters 9.

Catherine Kasper Home, 20155 9B Rd., Plymouth, 46563. Tel: 574-935-1742; Fax: 574-935-1760; Email: spiotrowicz@poorhandmaids.org; Web: cklc.poorhandmaids.org. P.O. Box 1, Donaldson, 46513. Scott Piotrowicz, Interim Exec. Dir. Nursing home for retired sisters & laity. Rooms 82.

Catherine Kasper Life Center, Inc. (1970) Tel: 574-935-1742; Fax: 574-935-1755. Retired Sisters 13.

**Catherine Kasper Place, Inc.*, 347 W. Berry St., Suite 101, 46802. Tel: 260-969-2001; Fax: 260-969-2004; Email: mdistler@sjchf.org; Web: catherinekasperplace.org. Meg Distler, Exec.

Earthworks, Inc., 9601 Union Rd., Plymouth, 46563. Tel: 574-935-1746; Email: cringer@poorhandmaids.org; Web: www.earthworksonline.org. P.O. Box 1, Donaldson, 46513. Mrs. Cheri Ringer, Coord. Earthcare Educ.

Lindenwood, Retreat & Conference Center, 9601 Union Rd., Plymouth, 46563. Tel: 574-935-1780; Fax: 574-935-1728; Email: cthelen@poorhandmaids.org; Web: www.lindenwood.org. P.O. Box 1, Donaldson, 46513. Christopher Thelen, Dir. Bed Capacity 102.

Maria Center, 9601 Union Rd., Plymouth, 46563. Tel: 574-935-1784; Fax: 574-935-1790; Email: banspach@poorhandmaids.org; Web: cklc.poorhandmaids.org. P.O. Box 1, Donaldson, 46513. Becky Anspach, Bus. Mgr. Senior Apartments (Efficiency and Singles) Apartments 27.

Moontree Community, P.O. Box 1, Donaldson, 46513. Tel: 574-935-1712; Fax: 574-935-1701; Email: mcelmer@poorhandmaids.org; Web: www.moontreecomunity.org. Sr. Mary Baird, Dir. Guests 366.

Poor Handmaids of Jesus Christ Community Support Trust, 9601 Union Rd., Plymouth, 46563. Tel: 574-936-9936; Fax: 574-935-1785; Email: mhunt@poorhandmaids.org. P.O. Box 1, Donaldson, 46513. Mary Hunt, Treas.

St. Joseph Community Health Foundation, 347 W. Berry St., 46802. Tel: 260-969-2001; Fax: 260-969-2004; Email: mdistler@sjchf.org; Web: sjchf.org. Meg Distler, Dir.

St. Joseph Medical Center of Fort Wayne, Inc., Hobart. Tel: 219-947-8665; Fax: 219-947-3708.

HUNTINGTON. *Victory Noll - Motherhouse of Our Lady of Victory Missionary Sisters* (1922) 1900 W. Park Dr., Huntington, 46750. Tel: 260-356-0628; Fax: 260-358-1504; Email: victorynoll@olvm.org; Email: maryjo@olvm.org; Web: www.olvm.org. Sr. Mary Jo Nelson, O.L.V.M., Pres. Legal Holding: Victory Noll Sisters Community Support Trust. Sisters 57; Professed Sisters 54.

MISHAWAKA. *St. Francis Provincialate*, 1515 W. Dragoon Tr., P.O. Box 766, Mishawaka, 46546-0766. Tel: 574-259-5427; Fax: 574-256-0822; Email: sister.angela@franciscanalliance.org; Web: www.ssfpa.org. Sr. M. Angela Mellady, O.S.F., Prov. Supr. Sisters of St. Francis of Perpetual Adoration, Inc.St. Francis Convent and Novitiate of Immaculate Heart of Mary Province. Novices 6; Postulants 1; Sisters 100.

Our Lady of the Angels Convent, 1515 W. Dragoon Tr., P.O. Box 766, Mishawaka, 46546-0766. Tel: 574-259-5427; Fax: 574-256-0822; Email: sister.angela@franciscanalliance.org; Web: www.ssfpa.org. Sr. M. Madonna Rougeau, O.S.F., Supr.; Rev. Francis Affelt, O.F.M., Chap. Convent for retired and infirm sisters. Sisters 30.

NOTRE DAME. *Congregation of the Sisters of the Holy Cross*, Saint Mary's of the Immaculate Conception, 309 Bertrand Hall, Notre Dame, 46556-5000. Tel: 574-284-5550; Fax: 574-284-5779; Web: www.cscsisters.org. Sisters M. Veronique Wiedower, C.S.C., B.M., M.A., Pres.; Sharlet Ann Wagner, C.S.C., B.J., J.D., First Councilor; Suzanne Brennan, C.S.C., B.A., M.S.W., M.P.A., Gen. Treas.; Brenda Cousins, C.S.C., B.A., M.A., Gen. Sec.; Angela Golapi Palma, C.S.C., B.A., B.Ed., M.Ed., Councilor. Generalate, Candidate Program, Associate Program.

Sisters of the Holy Cross, Inc.; Sisters of the Holy Cross, Inc. dba CSC Consultation Services. Novices 28; Sisters 414; Professed Sisters in Congregation 338; Temporarily Incorporated 33; Candidates 15.

Sisters of the Holy Cross Other Residences and Programs:. 727 Forest Ave., South Bend, 46616-1310. Tel: 574-246-0673. Sisters 2. 1023 Portage Ave., South Bend, 46616. Tel: 574-234-3208. Sisters 2. 2121 E. Madison St., South Bend, 46617-2517. Tel: 574-287-6071. Sisters 1.

All Saints Convent, 100 Lourdes Hall-Saint Mary's, Notre Dame, 46556-5014. Tel: 574-284-5660; Email: sbrennan@cscsisters.org. Sr. Suzanne Brennan, C.S.C., B.A., M.S.W., M.P.A., Treas. Sisters 7. *Andre - East*, 100 Andre East-Saint Mary's, Notre Dame, 46556-5015. Tel: 574-284-5644; Email: sbrennan@cscsisters.org. Sr. Suzanne Brennan, C.S.C., B.A., M.S.W., M.P.A., Treas. Sisters 3. *Andre - West*, 100 Andre West-Saint Mary's, Notre Dame, 46556-5016. Tel: 574-284-5645; Email: sbrennan@cscsisters.org. Sr. Suzanne Brennan, C.S.C., B.A., M.S.W., M.P.A., Treas. *Bethany Convent*, 100 Bethany Convent, Saint Mary's, Notre Dame, 46556-5038. Tel: 574-284-5674; Email: sbrennan@cscsisters.org. Sr. Suzanne Brennan, C.S.C., B.A., M.S.W., M.P.A., Treas. Sisters 3.

The Corporation of Saint Mary's College Sponsored Ministry. St. Mary's of the Immaculate Conception, 309 Bertrand Hall, Notre Dame, 46556-5000. Tel: 574-284-4707; Email: jhersche@saintmarys.edu. *Guadalupe Convent*, 300 Augusta Hall-Saint Mary's, Notre Dame, 46556-5002. Tel: 574-284-5717; Email: sbrennan@cscsisters.org. Sr. Suzanne Brennan, C.S.C., B.A., M.S.W., M.P.A., Treas. Sisters 2. *Holy Spirit Convent*, 300 Augusta Hall-Saint Mary's, Notre Dame, 46556-5002. Tel: 574-284-5715; Email: sbrennan@cscsisters.org. Sr. Suzanne Brennan, C.S.C., B.A., M.S.W., M.P.A., Treas. Sisters 2. *House of Shalem*, 100 House of Shalem, Saint Mary's, Notre Dame, 46556-5025. Tel: 574-284-5740. Sr. Suzanne Brennan, C.S.C., B.A., M.S.W., M.P.A., Treas. Sisters 2. *Immaculata Convent*, 200 Augusta Hall-Saint Mary's, Notre Dame, 46556-5002. Tel: 574-284-5707; Email: sbrennan@cscsisters.org. Sr. Suzanne Brennan, C.S.C., B.A., M.S.W., M.P.A., Treas. Sisters 3. *International Novitiate at Saint John's*, 100 Solitude-Saint Mary's, Notre Dame, 46556-5020. Tel: 574-284-5695; Email: sbrennan@cscsisters.org. Sr. Suzanne Brennan, C.S.C., B.A., M.S.W., M.P.A., Treas. Novices 14; Sisters 1. *International Novitiate at the Solitude*, Saint Mary's, 100 Saint Mary's, Notre Dame, 46556-5020. Tel: 574-284-5120; Email: sbrennan@cscsisters.org. Sr. Suzanne Brennan, C.S.C., B.A., M.S.W., M.P.A., Treas. Novices 14; Sisters 1. *Kateri Convent*, 400 Augusta-Hall Saint Mary's, Notre Dame, 46556-5002. Tel: 574-284-5993; Email: sbrennan@cscsisters.org. Sr. Suzanne Brennan, C.S.C., B.A., M.S.W., M.P.A., Treas. Sisters 3. *Loretto Convent*, 100 Loretto Convent, Saint Mary's, Notre Dame, 46556-5039. Tel: 574-284-5667; Email: sbrennan@cscsisters.org. Sr. Suzanne Brennan, C.S.C., B.A., M.S.W., M.P.A., Treas. *Madonna Convent*, 400 Augusta Hall-Saint Mary's, Notre Dame, 46556-5002. Tel: 574-284-5890; Email: sbrennan@cscsisters.org. Sr. Suzanne Brennan, C.S.C., B.A., M.S.W., M.P.A., Treas. Sisters 5. *Marian Convent*, 300 Augusta Hall-Saint Mary's, Notre Dame, 46556-5002. Tel: 574-284-5710. Sr. Suzanne Brennan, C.S.C., B.A., M.S.W., M.P.A., Treas. Sisters 5. *Moreau Convent*, 100 Lourdes Hall-Saint Mary's, Notre Dame, 46556-5030. Tel: 574-284-5663; Email: sbrennan@cscsisters.org. Sr. Suzanne Brennan, C.S.C., B.A., M.S.W., M.P.A., Treas. Sisters 4. *Nazareth Convent*, 200 Augusta Hall-Saint Mary's, Notre Dame, 46556-5002. Tel: 574-284-5822; Email: sbrennan@cscsisters.org. Sr. Suzanne Brennan, C.S.C., B.A., M.S.W., M.P.A., Treas. Sisters 2. *New Life Community*, 500 Saint Mary's Convent, Notre Dame, 46556-5014. Tel: 574-284-5579; Email: sbrennan@cscsisters.org. Sr. Suzanne Brennan, C.S.C., B.A., M.S.W., M.P.A., Treas. *Saint Ann Convent*, 300 Augusta Hall-Saint Mary's, Notre Dame, 46556-5002. Tel: 574-284-5713; Email: sbrennan@cscsisters.org. Sr. Suzanne Brennan, C.S.C., B.A., M.S.W., M.P.A., Treas. Sisters 2. *Saint Bridget Convent*, 100 Saint Bridget's Convent, Saint Mary's, Notre Dame, 46556-5024. Tel: 574-284-5752. Sr. Suzanne Brennan, C.S.C., B.A., M.S.W., M.P.A., Treas. Sisters 2. *Saint Claire Convent*, 400 Augusta Hall-Saint Mary's, Notre Dame, 46556-5002. Tel: 574-284-5892; Email: sbrennan@cscsisters.org. Sr. Suzanne Brennan, C.S.C., B.A., M.S.W., M.P.A., Treas. Sisters 2. *Saint Mary Convent*, 100 Saint Mary's Convent, Notre Dame, 46556-5007. Tel: 574-284-5688; Fax: 574-284-5801. Sr. Suzanne Brennan, C.S.C., B.A., M.S.W., M.P.A., Treas. Sisters 58. *Saint Theresa Convent*, 400 Augusta Hall-Saint Mary's, Notre Dame, 46556-5002. Tel: 574-284-5995; Email: sbrennan@cscsisters.org. Sr. Suzanne Brennan, C.S.C., B.A., M.S.W., M.P.A., Treas. Sisters 3.

Sisters of the Holy Cross, 701 Marquette Ave., South Bend, 46617. Tel: 574-520-1447; Email: sbrennan@cscsisters.org. Sr. Suzanne Brennan, C.S.C., B.A., M.S.W., M.P.A., Treas. Sisters 3.

Sisters of the Holy Cross, Saint Mary's of the Immaculate Conception, 309 Bertrand Hall, Notre Dame, 46556-5000. Tel: 574-284-5550; Email: sbrennan@cscsisters.org. *Rosary Convent*, 100 Rosary Convent, Saint Mary's, Notre Dame, 46556-5013. Tel: 574-284-5841; Email: sbrennan@cscsisters.org. Sr. Suzanne Brennan, C.S.C., B.A., M.S.W., M.P.A., Treas. Sisters 33. *Visitation Convent*, 200 Augusta Hall-Saint Mary's, Notre Dame, 46556-5002. Tel: 574-284-5820; Email: sbrennan@cscsisters.org. Sr. Suzanne Brennan, C.S.C., B.A., M.S.W., M.P.A., Treas. Sisters 2.

[J] RETREAT HOUSES & EDUCATIONAL CENTERS

SOUTH BEND. *Forever Learning Institute, Inc.* (1974) 54191 Ironwood Rd., South Bend, 46635. Tel: 574-282-1901; Email: director@foreverlearninginstitute.org; Web: www.foreverlearninginstitute.org. Eve Finnessy, Dir. To improve the quality and dignity of senior adult life through continuing intellectual challenge, spiritual reflection and social interaction.

DONALDSON. *Lindenwood Retreat & Conference Center* (1986) The Center at Donaldson, 9601 Union Rd., P.O. Box 1, Donaldson, 46513-0001. Tel: 574-935-1780; Fax: 574-935-1728; Email: lindenwood@poorhandmaids.org; Web: www.lindenwood.org. Christopher Thelen, Dir. Overnight facilities for 100, Conference rooms for 250, Handicapped accessibility. Bed Capacity 100.

[K] MISCELLANEOUS

FORT WAYNE. *Cathedral Museum* (1980) 1102 S. Calhoun St., 46802. Tel: 260-710-5954; Tel: 260-422-4611, Ext. 3307; Fax: 260-426-2029; Email: pwidmann@stmarysfw.org. P.O. Box 390, 46801. Rev. Phillip A. Widmann, Dir.

Catholic Charities of the Diocese of Ft. Wayne-South Bend, Inc. (1922) 915 S. Clinton St., 46802. Tel: 260-422-5625; Fax: 260-420-7382; Email: ccoffice@ccfwsb.org; Web: www.ccfwsb.org. Mailing Address: P.O. Box 10630, 46853. Most Rev. Kevin C. Rhoades, D.D., S.T.L., J.C.L., Chm.; Gloria Whitcraft, CEO; Mr. Joseph Ryan; Very Rev. Mark Allen Gurtner, J.C.L., Chancellor. Tot Asst. Annually 17,801; Total Staff 40.

Catholic Charities Fort Wayne Office & Administrative Office, 915 S. Clinton St., 46802.

Mailing Address: P.O. Box 10630, 46853. Gloria Whitcraft, CEO; Roberta Golani, Senior Admin. Officer. Tot Asst. Annually 3,304; Total Staff 30.

Catholic Charities South Bend Office, 1817 Miami St., South Bend, 46613. Tel: 574-234-3111; Fax: 574-289-1034; Email: ccoffice@ccfwsb.org; Web: www.ccfwsb.org. Claire Coleman, Dir. Tot Asst. Annually 5,098; Total Staff 7.

Catholic Charities Auburn Office, 107 W. 5th St., Auburn, 46706. Tel: 260-925-0917; Fax: 260-925-1732; Email: ccoffice@ccfwsb.org; Web: www.ccfwsb.org. Patti Sheppard, Dir. Tot Asst. Annually 9,399; Total Staff 3.

**The Christ Child Society of Fort Wayne, Inc.* (1997) P.O. Box 12708, 46864. Tel: 260-637-4181; Email: dbezdon19@comcast.net; Web: www.christchildsocietyfw.org. Mrs. Dianne Bezdon, Pres. Tot Asst. Annually 6,000.

Diocese of Fort Wayne-South Bend Investment Trust, Inc., 915 S. Clinton St., P.O. Box 390, 46801. Tel: 260-422-4611; Fax: 260-423-3382; Email: jryan@diocesefwsb.org. Most Rev. Kevin C. Rhoades, D.D., S.T.L., J.C.L., Admin.; Joseph Ryan, Contact Person & Chief Fin. Officer. To invest money received from qualified 501(c)(3) organizations that buy shares offered by the organization. All investments of share purchase proceeds shall be directed and conducted consistent with the investment policies and objectives established by the organization that are applicable to the type of share(s) sold to the participating 501 (c) (3) entities. All gains and any losses on investments, after administrative and money management fees, shall be reflected in share values.

**Fort Wayne Catholic Radio Group, Inc.* (Redeemer Radio, 106.3 FM and 95.7 FM South Bend) 4618 E. State Blvd., Ste. 200, 46815. Tel: 260-436-9598; Fax: 260-432-6179; Email: info@redeemerradio.com; Web: www.redeemerradio.com. Cindy Black, CEO; Jill O'Sullivan, Business Mgr.

**The Fort Wayne-South Bend Diocesan Division: World Apostolate of Fatima, The Blue Army*, P.O. Box 10032, 46850. Tel: 574-376-0046; Email: waf.fwsb@gmail.com; Web: www.fatimafwsb.org. Mrs. Ida List, Pres.; Revs. Glenn Kohrman, Spiritual Advisor/Care Svcs.; Vincent Rathappillil, V.C., Spiritual Advisor/Care Svcs.

The St. Joseph Community Health Foundation, Inc. (1998) 347 W. Berry St., Ste. 101, 46802. Tel: 260-969-2001; Fax: 260-969-2004; Email: mdistler@sjchf.org; Email: mrust@sjchf.org; Web: www.sjchf.org. Meg Distler, Exec. Dir.; Ciera Moore, Finance Coord.; Laura Dwire, Community Progs. Mgr.; Marla Rust, Exec. Asst. & Grants Coord.; Mark Burkholder, Digital Content Specialist. Total Staff 5.

Scholarship Granting Organization of Northeast Indiana, Inc., 915 S. Clinton St., P.O. Box 390, 46801. Tel: 260-422-4611; Fax: 260-426-3077; Email: mgurtner@diocesefwsb.org. Very Rev. Mark A. Gurtner, J.C.L., Contact Person.

SOUTH BEND. *Chiara Home, Inc.* (1993) 1425 Clayton Dr., South Bend, 46614. Tel: 574-287-5435; Fax: 574-291-1555; Email: sis@chiarahomerespite.org; Web: www.chiarahomerespite.org. Sr. Gretchen Clark, S.S.J.-T.O.S.F., Pres. & Admin. Respite Care for people with special needs. Total Staff 1; Families Served 400.

Christ Child Society of South Bend, P.O. Box 1286, South Bend, 46624. Tel: 574-288-6028; Email: info@christchildsb.org; Web: www.christchildsb.org. 308 S. Scott St., South Bend, 46601. Debbie Spillman, Pres. Total Assisted 3,579.

The Foundation of Saint Joseph Health System, 707 E. Cedar St., Ste. 100, South Bend, 46617. Tel: 574-335-4540; Fax: 574-335-0712; Email: thefoundation@sjrmc.com; Web: www.sjmed.com. Chad Towner, CEO

The Foundation of Saint Joseph Regional Medical Center, Inc. Total Staff 5.

Jesuit Community, 1713 Burdette St., South Bend, 46637. Tel: 574-243-0601; Email: mimagree@jesuits.net. Revs. Brian Daley, S.J.; Michael Magree, S.J.; Nathan O'Halloran, S.J.; Joseph Riordan, S.J.; John Peck, S.J. Priests 5.

St. Joseph's Tower, Inc. dba Trinity Tower, Trinity Tower, 316 S. Martin Luther King, Jr. Blvd., South Bend, 46601. Tel: 574-335-1900; Email: milltram@trinity-health.org; Web: www.trinityhealthseniorcommunities.org/sanctuary-at-trinity-tower-south-bend. Ms. Tracy Miller, Admin., Tel: 574-335-1902

This organization does business as "Trinity Tower".

**Women's Care Center, Inc.*, 360 N. Notre Dame Ave., South Bend, 46617. Tel: 574-234-0363; Email: annmanion1@hotmail.com; Email: pmanion89@gmail.com; Web: www.womenscarecenterfoundation.org. Ann Manion, Pres.

DONALDSON. *Earthworks, Inc.*, The Center at Donaldson, 9601 Union Rd., P.O. Box 1, Donaldson, 46513. Tel: 574-935-1746; Email: cringer@poorhandmaids.org; Web: www.earthworksonline.org. Mrs. Cheri Ringer, Education Coord. An environmental education center; a sponsored entity of the Poor Handmaids of Jesus Christ (P.H.J.C.) affiliated with Convent Ancilla Domini, Donaldson, IN.

GRABILL. **A Mother's Hope, Inc.*, P.O Box 308, Grabill, 46741. Tel: 260-602-4822; Email: maria@amothershopefw.org; Web: www.amothershopefw.org. Ms. Maria Nancarrow, Contact Person. Total Assisted 27.

HUNTINGTON. *Our Sunday Visitor, Inc.* (1912) 200 Noll Plaza, Huntington, 46750. Tel: 260-356-8400; Fax: 260-355-2248; Email: bthompson@osv.com; Web: www.osv.com. Most Rev. Kevin C. Rhoades, D.D., S.T.L., J.C.L., Bd. Chm.; Kyle Hamilton, CEO; Joe Wikert, Publishing Pres. Publishers of Catholic Periodicals, Books, Religious Education Materials, Curriculum, Offering Envelope Services, Increased Offertory Program, Parish Capital Campaigns, Consulting Services.

MISHAWAKA. *Catholic Community Foundation of Northeast Indiana, Inc.*, 9025 Coldwater Rd., Ste 200, 46825. Tel: 260-422-4611; Tel: 260-399-1436; Email: mshade@ccfnei.org; Web: www.ccfnei.org. Mr. Michael Shade, CEO.

**Franciscan Heath Foundation, Inc.*, 3510 Park Pl. W., Ste. 200, Mishawaka, 46544. Tel: 574-273-3855; Email: foundation@franciscanalliance.org; Web: www.franciscanalliance.org/foundation. Caitlin A. Leahy, Corp. Exec. Dir.

Franciscan Alliance, Inc. (1974) P.O. Box 1290, Mishawaka, 46546-1290. Tel: 574-256-3935; Email: Sister.Lethia@franciscanalliance.org; Web: www.franciscanalliance.org. 1515 W. Dragoon Tr., Mishawaka, 46544. Kevin D. Leahy, CEO.

**Hannah's House, Inc.*, 518 W. 4th St., Mishawaka, 46544. Tel: 574-254-5309; Tel: 574-254-7271; Fax: 574-254-5310; Email: info@hannahshousemichiana.com; Email: john@hannahshousemichiana.org; Web: www.hannahshousemichiana.org. P.O. Box 1413, Mishawaka, 46546. John Meiser, Exec. Dir. Maternity Home offering a range of residential services and programming for pregnant and parenting women facing homelessness.

**Hills Insurance Company, Inc.*, 1515 W. Dragoon Tr., Mishawaka, 46544. P.O. Box 1290, Mishawaka, 46546-1290. Tel: 574-254-6278; Email: Dan.Conner@Franciscanalliance.org. Sr. Jane Marie Klein, O.S.F., Chairperson of Bd.

Saint Joseph PACE, Inc., 250 E. Day Rd., Mishawaka, 46545. Tel: 574-247-8700; Fax: 574-335-0674; Email: saintjosephpace@trinity-health.org. Mrs. Stacey Newton, Dir. Adult Enrollment 180.

Saint Joseph Regional Medical Center, Inc., 5215 Holy Cross Pkwy., Mishawaka, 46545. Tel: 574-335-5000; Fax: 574-335-1002; Email: chad.towner@sjrmc.com; Email: paintelm@sjrmc.com; Email: karamc@sjrmc.com; Web: www.sjmed.com. Chad Towner, CEO; Sr. Laureen M. Painter, O.S.F., Vice Pres. Mission Integration. Total Staff 597; Total Assisted 201,621.

Sisters of St. Francis of Perpetual Adoration, Inc., 1515 W. Dragoon Tr., P.O. Box 766, Mishawaka, 46546-0766. Tel: 574-259-5427; Fax: 574-256-0822; Email: sister.angela@franciscanalliance.org; Web: www.ssfpa.org. Sr. M. Angela Mellady, O.S.F., Prov.

Sisters of St. Francis of Perpetual Adoration, Inc., Medical Benefits Trust, 1515 W. Dragoon Trl., P.O. Box 766, Mishawaka, 46546-0766. Tel: 574-259-5427; Fax: 574-256-0822; Email: sister.angela@franciscanalliance.org.

Sisters of St. Francis of Perpetual Adoration, Inc Capital Improvements Trust, 1515 W. Dragoon Trl., P.O. Box 766, Mishawaka, 46546-0766. Tel: 574-259-5427; Fax: 574-256-0822; Email: sister.angela@franciscanalliance.org; Web: www.ssfpa.org.

Sisters of St. Francis Charitable Mission Trust, 1515 W. Dragoon Trl., P.O. Box 766, Mishawaka, 46546-0766. Tel: 574-259-5427; Fax: 574-256-0822; Email: sister.angela@franciscanalliance.org.

Sisters of St. Francis Retirement Fund, 1515 W. Dragoon Trl., P.O. Box 766, Mishawaka, 46546-0766. Tel: 574-259-5427; Fax: 574-256-0822; Email: sister.angela@franciscanalliance.org.

SSFPA Ministry Corporation, 1515 W. Dragoon Tr., P.O. Box 766, Mishawaka, 46546. Tel: 574-259-5427; Fax: 574-256-0822; Email: sister.angela@franciscanalliance.org; Web: www.ssfpa.org. Sr. M. Angela Mellady, O.S.F., Prov. Supr.

NOTRE DAME. *American Maritain Association*, Jacques Maritain Center, 430 Geddes Hall, Notre Dame, 46556. Tel: 310-671-4412; Email: jhanink70@gmail.com; Web: www.maritainassociation.com. Jim Hanink, Pres.; Heather Erb, Ph.D., Treas. Purpose: For the purpose of perpetuating the wisdom, influence and inspiration of Jacques Maritain as a Catholic intellectual, saintly Christian and classical creative exponent of the philosophia perennis. To promote research, study and critical interpretations of the life and work of Jacques Maritain especially as that work continues and expands into a broader area of the tradition of the thought of Saint Thomas, to develop social and formative cultural movement based on the results of this research and study, cooperation with the Institute International "Jacques Maritain and its national and regional branches, and the promotion of publications, lecturers, study groups and similar activities.".

Ave Maria Press, Inc. (1865) 1865 Moreau Dr., P.O. Box 428, Notre Dame, 46556. Tel: 574-287-2831; Email: avemariapress.1@nd.edu; Web: www.avemariapress.com. Thomas Grady, CEO & Publisher; Karey Circosta, Vice Pres.; Mark Witbeck, Vice Pres. Owned and operated by the Congregation of Holy Cross, United States Province.

Blessed Basil Moreau Endowment Trust, 54515 State Rd. 933 N., Notre Dame, 46556. Tel: 574-631-3700; Fax: 574-631-3444; Email: dlamberti@holycrossusa.org. P.O. Box 774, Notre Dame, 46556-0774. Rev. Kevin M. Russeau, C.S.C., Trustee.

Brothers of Holy Cross Life Development Trust, P.O. Box 460, Notre Dame, 46556. Tel: 574-631-4000; Fax: 574-631-2999. Bro. James Leik, C.S.C., Trustee; Fred G. Botek, Trustee; Bros. William Dygert, C.S.C., Trustee & Chairperson; Paul Kelly, C.S.C., Trustees; Robert Lavelle, C.S.C., Trustees; Mr. Matthew A. Shannon, Trustee; Bro. Lawrence Skitzki, C.S.C., Trustees.

Father Edward Sorin Trust, 54515 State Rd. 933 N., P.O. Box 774, Notre Dame, 46556-0774. Tel: 574-631-3700; Tel: 574-631-6337; Fax: 574-631-3444; Email: dlamberti@holycrossusa.org. Rev. Stephen A. Lacroix, C.S.C. Brothers 7; Priests 44.

Holy Cross House, 1842 Moreau Dr., Notre Dame, 46556-1048.

Holy Cross Foreign Mission Society, Inc. dba Holy Cross Mission Center, Moreau Seminary, 1837 Moreau Dr., Notre Dame, 46556. Tel: 574-631-5477; Email: hcmc@holycrossusa.org. P.O. Box 543, Notre Dame, 46556. Rev. Michael M. DeLaney, C.S.C., Exec. Dir.

Saint Andre Bessette Continuing Care Trust, 54515 State Rd. 933 N., Notre Dame, 46556. P.O. Box 774, Notre Dame, 46556-0774. Tel: 574-631-3700; Fax: 574-631-3444; Email: dlamberti@holycrossusa.org. Rev. James K. Foster, C.S.C., Trustee.

RELIGIOUS INSTITUTES OF MEN REPRESENTED IN THE DIOCESE

For further details refer to the corresponding bracketed number in the Religious Institutes of Men or Women section.

[]—*Congregation of Holy Cross United States Province of Priests and Brothers*—C.S.C.
[]—*Congregation of the Holy Spirit*—C.S.Sp.
[]—*Congregation of the Passion*—C.P.
[]—*Montfort Missionaries (The Company of Mary)*—S.M.M.
[]—*Oblates of Mary Immaculate*—O.M.I.
[]—*Order of Friars Minor*—O.F.M.
[]—*Order of Friars Minor Conventual*—O.F.M.Conv.
[]—*Order of Preachers*—O.P.
[]—*Order of Saint Benedict*—O.S.B.
[]—*Priestly Fraternity of Saint Peter*—F.S.S.P.
[]—*Society of Divine Word*—S.V.D.
[]—*Society of Jesus (Jesuits)*—S.J.
[]—*Vincentian Congregation*—V.C.

RELIGIOUS INSTITUTES OF WOMEN REPRESENTED IN THE DIOCESE

[]—*Daughters of Divine Charity*—F.D.C.
[]—*Daughters of Mary Mother of Mercy*—D.M.M.M.
[]—*Dominican Sisters of Peace*—O.P.
[]—*Franciscan Sisters of the Sacred Heart*—O.S.F.
[]—*Our Lady of Victory Missionary Sisters*—O.L.V.M.
[]—*Poor Handmaids of Jesus Christ*—P.H.J.C.
[]—*School Sisters of Notre Dame*—S.S.N.D.
[]—*Sisters of Notre Dame*—S.N.D.
[]—*Sisters of Saint Agnes*—C.S.A.
[]—*Sisters of Saint Francis of Our Lady of Lourdes*—O.S.F.
[]—*Sisters of Saint Francis of Perpetual Adoration*—O.S.F.
[]—*Sisters of St. Joseph of the Third Order of St. Francis*—S.S.J.-T.O.S.F.
[]—*Sisters of the Holy Cross*—C.S.C.

DIOCESAN CEMETERY

FORT WAYNE. *Catholic Cemetery Association of Fort Wayne, Inc.* Divine Mercy Funeral Home 3500 Lake Ave., 46805-5572. Tel: 260-426-2044; Fax: 260-422-7418; Email:

cmiller@divinemercyfuneralhome.com; Web: www.catholic-cemetery.org. Casey Miller, Dir.

Saint Leo Catholic Cemetery, 3500 Lake Ave., 46805. Tel: 260-426-2044; Email: cmiller@catholic-cemetery.org. Leo, IN 46765.

Saint Michael Catholic Cemetery at Pierre Settlement, 3500 Lake Ave., 46805. Fort Wayne, IN.

NECROLOGY

† Tippmann, Laurence, (Retired), Died Jan. 3, 2019

An asterisk (*) denotes an organization that has established tax-exempt status directly with the IRS and is not covered by the USCCB Group Ruling.

Diocese of Fort Worth

(Dioecesis Arcis-Vorthensis)

Most Reverend

MICHAEL F. OLSON, S.T.D.

Bishop of Fort Worth; ordained June 3, 1994; appointed Bishop of Fort Worth November 19, 2013; installed fourth Bishop of the Diocese of Fort Worth January 29, 2014.

The Catholic Center: 800 West Loop 820 S., Fort Worth, TX 76108. Tel: 817-560-3300; Fax: 817-244-8839.

Web: www.fwdioc.org

ESTABLISHED AUGUST 09, 1969.

Square Miles 23,950.

Comprises the following twenty-eight Counties in the State of Texas: Archer, Baylor, Bosque, Clay, Comanche, Cooke, Denton, Eastland, Erath, Foard, Hardeman, Hill, Hood, Jack, Johnson, Knox, Montague, Palo Pinto, Parker, Shackleford, Stephens, Somervell, Tarrant, Throckmorton, Wichita, Wilbarger, Wise and Young.

For legal titles of parishes and diocesan institutions, consult the Chancery.

STATISTICAL OVERVIEW

Personnel	
Bishop	1
Priests: Diocesan Active in Diocese	38
Priests: Diocesan Active Outside Diocese	3
Priests: Retired, Sick or Absent	33
Number of Diocesan Priests	74
Religious Priests in Diocese	51
Total Priests in Diocese	125
Extern Priests in Diocese	10
Ordinations:	
Diocesan Priests	2
Permanent Deacons in Diocese	77
Total Sisters	59
Parishes	
Parishes	90
With Resident Pastor:	
Resident Diocesan Priests	35
Resident Religious Priests	44
Without Resident Pastor:	
Administered by Deacons	1
Missions	1
Welfare	
Specialized Homes	1
Total Assisted	140
Special Centers for Social Services	4
Total Assisted	77,824
Educational	
Diocesan Students in Other Seminaries	26
Total Seminarians	26
High Schools, Diocesan and Parish	2
Total Students	973
Elementary Schools, Diocesan and Parish	17
Total Students	3,852
Catechesis/Religious Education:	
High School Students	6,717
Elementary Students	22,325
Total Students under Catholic Instruction	33,893
Teachers in the Diocese:	
Priests	2
Sisters	8
Lay Teachers	451
Vital Statistics	
Receptions into the Church:	
Infant Baptism Totals	4,754
Minor Baptism Totals	492
Adult Baptism Totals	263
Received into Full Communion	853
First Communions	6,595
Confirmations	3,946
Marriages:	
Catholic	778
Interfaith	152
Total Marriages	930
Deaths	1,203
Total Catholic Population	1,010,383
Total Population	3,677,046

Former Bishops—Most Revs. JOHN J. CASSATA, D.D., ord. Dec. 8, 1932; Titular Bishop of Bida and Auxiliary of Dallas-Fort Worth; appt. March 20, 1968; cons. June 5, 1968; first Bishop, Fort Worth; appt. Aug. 22, 1969; retired Sept. 16, 1980; died Sept. 8, 1989; JOSEPH P. DELANEY, ord. Dec. 18, 1960; appt. Bishop of Fort Worth July 10, 1981; ord. Bishop Sept. 13, 1981; died July 12, 2005.; KEVIN W. VANN, ord. May 30, 1981; appt. Coadjutor Bishop of Fort Worth May 17, 2005; succeeded July 12, 2005; ord. Bishop July 13, 2005; appt. Bishop of Orange Sept. 21, 2012; installed Dec. 10, 2012.

Vicar General—Rev. Msgr. JUAN RIVERO.

Chancellor/Moderator of the Curia—Rev. Msgr. E. JAMES HART.

Vicar for Priests—VACANT.

Deans—Very Rev. DANIEL P. KELLEY, Arlington Deanery; VACANT, North Deanery; Very Rev. RAYMOND MCDANIEL, Northeast Deanery; Rev. HOA NGUYEN, West Central Deanery; Very Rev. LUCAS ALEJANDRO OLIVERA, O.F.M.Cap., East Central Deanery; Rev. ALEXANDER AMBROSE, H.G.N., Northwest Deanery; VACANT, Southwest Deanery; Very Rev. FERNANDO PRECIADO, South Deanery.

College of Consultors—Rev. Msgrs. E. JAMES HART; JUAN RIVERO; Revs. RICHARD ELDREDGE, T.O.R.; JAMES FLYNN; Very Rev. RAYMOND MCDANIEL; Revs. HOA NGUYEN; GEORGE PULLAMBRAYIL; JONATHAN WALLIS.

Presbyteral Council—Rev. Msgrs. E. JAMES HART; JUAN RIVERO; RAYMUND A. MULLAN, (Retired); Rev. MEL BESSELLIEU; Very Rev. BALAJI BOYALLA, S.A.C.; Revs. STEPHEN HAUCK; CRUZ MANUEL HOLGUIN; Very Revs. DANIEL P. KELLEY; RAYMOND MCDANIEL; Rev. JOHN MCKONE.

BOARDS AND ASSOCIATIONS

Diocesan Finance Council—Most Rev. MICHAEL F. OLSON, S.T.D., Chm.; MR. DON CRAM; MR. DONALD L. WAGNER, M.B.A.; MR. PHILIP HERNANDEZ; MR. DENNIS MAUNDER; Very Rev. RAYMOND MCDANIEL; MR. WILLIAM P. QUINN; Rev. Msgr. E. JAMES HART; MR. GEORGE SHELTON; Rev. JOSEPH KEATING; MR. CHUCK BARTUSH JR.; MS. HOLLY TRINH.

Diocesan Building Commission—Rev. Msgr. E. JAMES HART; MR. STEPHEN BECHT; MR. DONALD L. WAGNER, M.B.A.; MR. ROBERT BARHAM; MR. GARY JONES; MR. BRAD RUPAY; MR. DAVID SHIPMAN.

Diocesan Pastoral Finance Committee—Rev. Msgr. E. JAMES HART, Chm.; MR. DONALD L. WAGNER, M.B.A.; MR. KEVIN O'BRIEN; MR. EDWARD DOSKOCIL; Very Rev. RAYMOND MCDANIEL; MR. DON PHIFER; MR. STEPHEN BECHT; MS. RENEE UNDERWOOD.

Priests' Pension Plan Board of Trustees—Rev. Msgr. JUAN RIVERO, Chm.; MS. BARBARA MAY; MR. FRANKLIN MOORE; Revs. THOMAS J. CRAIG; D. TIMOTHY THOMPSON, J.C.L.; Rev. Msgr. E. JAMES HART; MR. DONALD L. WAGNER, M.B.A.

Employee Benefits Advisory Committee—Rev. D. TIMOTHY THOMPSON, J.C.L.; MS. TRUDY MILLER; Rev. Msgr. E. JAMES HART; Rev. JOSEPH KEATING; MS. KATHY MCCOY; MR. GARY PATTON; MS. JENNIFER PELLETIER; MR. JAMES SUTER; MR. DONALD L. WAGNER, M.B.A.

Employee Pension Plan, Board of Trustees—MR. DAN SHINE; MR. GARY PATTON; MR. DONALD L. WAGNER, M.B.A.

DIOCESAN PROGRAMS

Seminarian Formation—Rev. JONATHAN WALLIS, Dir.

Vocations - Liaisons—Revs. CRUZ MANUEL HOLGUIN; MAURICE LAWRENCE MOON; NGHIA NGUYEN; MATTHEW TATYREK.

Permanent Deacon Formation Program—DR. JUAN RENDON, Dir. Formation; Deacon RIGOBERTO LEYVA, Coord. Pastoral Field Formation; Rev. JOSEPH KEATING, Dir. Spiritual Formation.

Deacons—Deacon DON WARNER, Dir.

Tribunal—Revs. D. TIMOTHY THOMPSON, J.C.L., Judicial Vicar; JOY JOSEPH, T.O.R., J.C.L., Judge; Rev. Msgr. JOSEPH S. SCANTLIN, J.C.L., Judge, (Retired); Rev. KARL W. SCHILKEN, J.C.L., Judge; DR. SARA PAGLIALUNGA, Judge/Assessor.

Finance & Administrative Services Department—MR. DONALD L. WAGNER, M.B.A.

Financial Services—MR. DONALD L. WAGNER, M.B.A.; MS. CHRISTINA YBARRA; MR. KEVIN O'BRIEN; MR. JORGE MONTENEGRO.

Property Management and Construction—MR. STEPHEN BECHT; MR. TOM ROSS.

Claims and Risk Management - Catholic Mutual—MS. CHRISTINA ABLORH.

Business Manager for Schools—MRS. NANCY BENSON.

Records Management & Archives Department—VACANT.

Cemeteries and Columbaria—MR. KEVIN O'BRIEN.

Evangelization and Catechesis Department—MR. MARLON DE LA TORRE, Dir.

Adult Catechesis & RCIA—MR. MARLON DE LA TORRE, Dir.

Faith Formation/Children's Catechesis—MR. JASON WHITEHEAD, Dir.

Hispanic Ministry—MR. FRANCISCO JOEL RODRIGUEZ, Dir.

St. Junipero Serra Institute—MISS PAOLA QUINTERO-ARAUJO, Dir.

Youth, Young Adult & Campus Ministry—MR. JASON SPOOLSTRA, Dir.

Marriage and Family Life—MR. CHRIS VAUGHAN, Dir.

Natural Family Planning—MR. ANTHONY ABADIE, Coord.

Respect Life—MS. THERESA SCHAUF; MR. JEFF HEDGLEN, Dir. & Campus Min., Univ. of Texas at Arlington, 1010 Benge Dr., Arlington, 76013-2643. Tel: 817-460-1155; Email: jhedglen@fwdioc.org; MR. MARLON DE LA TORRE; MR. JASON SPOOLSTRA, Interim Dir. Campus Ministry, TCU Student Catholic Community: Catholic Campus Ministry, 2704 W. Berry St., Fort Worth, 76109. Tel: 817-945-9355; Email: jspoolstra@fwdioc.org;

MS. DEBRA NEELY, Catholic Campus Center: Midwestern State Univ., Wichita Falls, 76308. 3410 W. Louis J. Rodriguez Dr., Wichita Falls, 76308. Tel: 940-692-9778; Email: dneely@fwdioc.org; MR. PAUL CALDWELL, Catholic Campus Center: Tarleton State Univ., Stephenville. Tel: 830-688-3191; Email: caldwell@tarleton.edu.

Catholic Schools Department—MS. JENNIFER PELLETIER, School Supt.

Catholic Schools—MS. JENNIFER PELLETIER, School Supt.; MS. MELISSA KASMEIER, Asst. Supt.

Schools Marketing—MS. ERIN VADER, Coord., Schools Advancement & Alumni Rels.

School Nurses Consultant—MRS. NANCY EDER, R.N.

School Athletics—MR. MICHAEL CARLSON, Athletic Dir.

Communications Department—MR. PAT SVACINA, Dir.

Communications—MR. PAT SVACINA, Dir.

Communications/Web Site Services—MR. CHRIS KASTNER, Coord.; MS. AMBIL PALATTY, Asst. Coord.

Communications/News Magazine—North Texas Catholic Newsmagazine MR. JUAN GUAJARDO, Editor; MS. SUSAN MOSES, Assoc. Editor; MS. ROSA ROSALES, Editorial Asst.

Human Resources Department—MR. GARY PATTON, Dir.

Chief Human Resources Officer—MR. GARY PATTON.

Senior Human Resources Business Partner—MS. LAURA TATUM.

Human Resources Business Partner—MS. SHANNON DZIVAK.

Benefits Business Partner—MS. CASSIE HERITAGE.

Office of Child & Youth Protection—MR. RICHARD MATHEWS, Dir.

Conduct Review Board—Rev. Msgr. E. JAMES HART; MR. RICHARD MATHEWS.

Victim Assistance Ministry—Catholic Charities Counseling Services.

Safe Environment Program—MR. RICHARD MATHEWS, Dir.

Safe Environment Advisory Committee—MR. RICHARD MATHEWS.

Liturgy and Chaplaincy Department—Deacon DON WARNER.

Deaf Ministry—MS. CONNIE MARTIN.

Hospital Chaplaincy—Deacon BRUCE CORBETT; Rev. GEORGE THENNATTIL, T.O.R.

Prison Ministry—Deacons DON WARNER; BRUCE CORBETT; Rev. RICHARD COLLINS.

Diocesan Office of Pontifical MissionsRev. THOMAS J. CRAIG, Dir.

Diocesan Mission Council—Rev. THOMAS J. CRAIG, Chm.; MS. COLLEEN CARGILE; Rev. JONATHAN MICHAEL DEMMA; MR. BOB EILENFELDT; Sr. ROBERTA HESSE, S.S.M.N.; Very Rev. THOMAS KENNEDY; MARK LUKOWIAK; MS. JEAN MEEHAN; Deacon MICHAEL MOCEK; MR. TOM SNODGRASS; MS. ANNETTE SNODGRASS; MIKE WULLER.

Scouting—Rev. ERIC MICHAEL GRONER, S.V.D.

Clergy Personnel Services—Rev. Msgr. JUAN RIVERO.

Priests' Care Fund—Rev. Msgr. JUAN RIVERO.

Continuing Pastoral Formation—

Catholic Women, Council of—Rev. Msgr. E. JAMES HART.

Delegate for Women Religious—Sr. DIANA RODRIGUEZ, H.C.G.

Campaign for Human Development—VACANT.

Missionary Childhood Association—Rev. THOMAS J. CRAIG.

CLERGY, PARISHES, MISSIONS AND PAROCHIAL SCHOOLS

CITY OF FORT WORTH

(TARRANT COUNTY)

1—ST. PATRICK CATHEDRAL
1206 Throckmorton St., 76102. Tel: 817-332-4915; Fax: 817-338-1988; Email: mschulz@stpatrickcathedral.org; Web: www.stpatrickcathedral.org. Rev. John Robert Skeldon; Most Reverend Michael F. Olson, S.T.D.; Rev. Sojan George, H.G.N., Rector; Rev. Msgr. John Robert Skeldon, Parochial Vicar; Rev. George Thennattil, T.O.R., In Res.; Deacons James Crites; Don Warner.
Catechesis Religious Program—Tel: 817-338-4441; Email: pbransford@stpatrickcathedral.org. Patty Bransford, D.R.E. Students 433.

2—ALL SAINTS (1902)
214 N.W. 20th St., 76104. Tel: 817-626-3055; Fax: 817-626-3050; Email: irma@allsaintscc.net. Revs. Stephen Jasso, T.O.R., Parochial Admin.; Angel Infante Hernandez, T.O.R.; Deacons Juan Escamilla; Martin Garcia.
School—All Saints School, (Grades PreK-8), 2006 N. Houston St., 76164. Tel: 817-624-2670; Fax: 817-624-1221; Email: aprado@ascsfw.org. Arica Prado, Prin. Clergy 1; Lay Teachers 11; Students 147.
Catechesis Religious Program—Tel: 817-740-9176. Students 1,235.

3—ST. ANDREW (1953)
3314 Dryden Rd., 76109. Revs. James Gigliotti, T.O.R.; John Mark Klaus, T.O.R.; Deacons Lynn Sowers; Kevin Bagley.
Res.: 46 Chelsea Dr., 76134.
Church: 3312 Dryden Rd., 76109. Tel: 817-927-5383; Email: sachurch@standrewcc.org; Web: www.standrewcc.org.
School—St. Andrew Catholic School, (Grades PreK-8), 3304 Dryden Rd., 76109-3799. Tel: 817-924-8917; Fax: 817-921-1490; Email: vtucker@standrewsch.org. Veronica Tucker, Prin. Lay Teachers 42; Students 632.
Catechesis Religious Program—Students 368.

4—ST. BARTHOLOMEW (1969) Rev. Karl W. Schilken, J.C.L.; Deacon Reyes Tello.
Res.: 3601 Altamesa Blvd., 76133. Tel: 817-292-7703; Fax: 817-292-2568; Email: stbarts@stbartsfw.org; Web: www.stbartsfw.org.
Catechesis Religious Program—Students 734.

5—ST. BENEDICT PARISH (2015)
c/o St. Thomas Parish, 2920 Azle Ave., 76106.
Tel: 817-439-9944; Cell: 817-962-7962; Email: pastor@stbensfw.org. Revs. Karl A. Pikus, F.S.S.P; J. Peter Byrne, F.S.S.P., Parochial Vicar.

6—CHRIST THE KING (1996)
1112 Eagle Dr., 76111. Tel: 817-386-5582; Email: mnguyen4032@gmail.com; Web: www.chuakitovua.org. Revs. Philip M. Binh Tran, C.M.C.; Alphonse Tri Vu, C.M.C.; Deacon Truat Van Nguyen.
Catechesis Religious Program—Tel: 817-937-6045; Email: peter_na@msn.com. Peter Nguyen, D.R.E. Students 343.

7—ST. GEORGE (1941)
825 Karnes St., 76111. Tel: 817-831-4404; Email: Fr.RMercado@sgcctx.org. Rev. Ronaldo Mercado.
School—St. George School, (Grades PreK-8), 824 Hudgins St., 76111-4799. Tel: 817-222-1221; Fax: 817-838-0424; Email: mlongoria@sgcsfwtx.org. Ms. Mary Longoria, Prin. Lay Teachers 13; Students 166.
Catechesis Religious Program—Students 283.

8—HOLY FAMILY (1942)
6150 Pershing Ave., 76107. Tel: 817-737-6768; Fax: 817-737-6876; Email: pastoraloffice@holyfamilyfw.org; Web: www.holyfamilyfw.org. Rev. Hoa Nguyen; Deacon Michael Mocek.
School—Holy Family School, (Grades PreK-8), 6146 Pershing Ave., 76107. Tel: 817-737-4201; Fax: 817-738-1542; Email: busmgr@hfsfw.org; Web: www.hfsfw.org. Dr. John P. Shreve, Ed.D., Prin. Lay Teachers 17; Students 151.
Catechesis Religious Program—
Tel: 817-737-6768, Ext. 104; Email: jrodriguez@holyfamilyfw.org. Mr. Joe Rodriguez, D.R.E. Students 261.

9—HOLY NAME OF JESUS (1952)
2635 Burchill Rd., 76105. Tel: 817-536-9604; Email: holyname2003@sbcglobal.net. Revs. Francisco Alanis Gonzalez; Jose Jimenez Medina, Parochial Vicar; Mrs. Carol McElvany, Business Mgr.
Catechesis Religious Program—Tel: 817-535-3068; Email: sisterevasanchez@yahoo.com. Sr. Eva Sanchez, M.C.S.H., D.R.E. Students 1,230.

10—IMMACULATE HEART OF MARY (1961)
201 Thornhill Dr., 76115. Tel: 817-923-6323, Ext. 0; Fax: 817-923-6523; Email: parishoffice@ihmfw.com; Web: www.ihmfw.com. Mailing Address: 108 E. Hammond St., 76115. Revs. Oscar Sanchez Olvera, C.O.R.C.; Alejandro Lopez Chavez, C.O.R.C.; Deacon Marcelino Carranza.
Catechesis Religious Program—Tel: 817-923-8582; Fax: 817-923-6523. Students 1,781.

11—ST. JOHN THE APOSTLE (1964)
7341 Glenview Dr., North Richland Hills, 76180.
Tel: 817-284-4811; Fax: 817-284-1729; Email: church@sjtanrh.com; Web: sjtanrh.com. Very Rev. Jack McKone; Rev. Jonathan Michael Demma, Parochial Vicar; Deacons Juan Reyes; Ruben Aguirre; Matias Lagunas.
School—St. John the Apostle School, (Grades PreK-8), Tel: 817-284-2228; Fax: 817-284-1800; Email: afelton@stjs.org; Web: www.stjs.org. Mrs. Amy Felton, Prin. Lay Teachers 22; Students 193; Religous Order Teacher 2.
Catechesis Religious Program—Students 1,100.

12—ST. MARY OF THE ASSUMPTION (1909)
509 W. Magnolia Ave., 76104. Tel: 817-923-1911; Fax: 817-923-0769; Email: Sylvia@stmarysftw.org; Email: Pastor@stmarysftw.org; Web: www.stmarysftw.org. Rev. Jaison Mangalath, S.V.D.
Catechesis Religious Program—Students 550.

13—OUR LADY OF FATIMA
Mailing Address: 5109 E. Lancaster Ave., 76112.
Tel: 817-446-4114; Email: ourladyoffatima@sbcglobal.net; Web: giaoxufatima.org. Rev. John Tinh Tran, C.M.C.; Deacon Michael Hoang.
Catechesis Religious Program—Deacon Michael Hoang, D.R.E. Students 250.

14—OUR LADY OF GUADALUPE (1977) (Hispanic)
4100 Blue Mound Rd., 76106. Tel: 817-626-7421; Fax: 817-626-4461; Email: churchoffice@fwolg.com. Very Rev. Lucas Alejandro Olivera, O.F.M.Cap.; Revs. Pedro Romero Gutierrez, O.F.M.Cap., Parochial Vicar; Jose Feliciano Torres, O.F.M.Cap., Parochial Vicar.
Catechesis Religious Program—Tel: 817-546-9097; Email: sisterpatricia@fwolg.com. Sr. Maria Patricia Gonzalez, D.R.E. Students 1,161.

15—OUR MOTHER OF MERCY (1929) (African American)
1001 E. Terrell Ave., 76104-3788. Tel: 817-335-1695; Email: ourmother@omomftworth.org; Web: www.omomftworth.org. Rev. Bartlomiej Jasilek, S.V.D.; Mrs. Jennifer Rattliff, Business Mgr.; Florena Wohlwend, RCIA Coord.; Mrs. Zenobia Collins, Music Min.; Lydia Martinez, Sec.

16—ST. PAUL THE APOSTLE (1952) Rev. Brendan Murphy; Deacon Pedro Garcia.
Church: 5508 Black Oak Ln., 76114.
Tel: 817-738-9925; Fax: 817-735-8579; Email: secretary@stpaulfw.org; Email: religioused@stpaulfw.org; Email: pastor@stpaulfw.org; Web: stpaulfw.org.
Catechesis Religious Program—Students 240.

17—ST. PETER THE APOSTLE (1952) Rev. Cruz Manuel Holguin; Deacons Rigoberto Leyva; Wendell Geiger.
Office: 1201 S. Cherry Ln., 76108.
Tel: 817-246-3622, Ext. 307; Email: mary@stpeterfw.com; Web: www.stpeterfw.com.
School—St. Peter the Apostle School, (Grades PreK-8), Tel: 817-246-2032; Email: lgiardino@spsfw.org; Web: www.spsfw.org. Mrs. Lisa Giardino, Prin. Lay Teachers 20; Students 121.
Catechesis Religious Program—Email: yasmin@stpeterfw.com. Yasmin Cuevas, D.R.E. Students 473.

18—ST. RITA (1910)
5550 E. Lancaster, 76112. Tel: 817-451-9395; Fax: 817-451-9421; Email: churchoffice@stritafw.com. Rev. Eric Michael Groner, S.V.D.
School—St. Rita School, (Grades PreK-8), 712 Weiler Blvd., 76112-6398. Tel: 817-451-9383; Fax: 817-446-4465; Email: mburns@saintritaschool.net; Web: www.saintritaschool.net. Mary Burns, Prin. Clergy 2; Lay Teachers 13; Students 148.
Catechesis Religious Program—Students 495.

19—ST. THOMAS THE APOSTLE (1937)
5953 Bowman Roberts Rd., 76179. Tel: 817-624-2184 ; Email: m.long@sttafw.org; Email: b.oberdorf@sttafw.org; Web: www.sttafw.org. Revs. Mathew Kavipurayidam, T.O.R.; Benjamin Hembrom, Parochial Vicar; Deacon Hector Salva; Beverly Oberdorf, Business Mgr.
Catechesis Religious Program—Students 300.
Mission—Holy Trinity, 800 High Crest Dr., Azle, Tarrant Co. 76020. Tel: 817-444-3063; Email: b.riley@sttafw.org. Brenda Riley, Contact Person.
Catechesis Religious Program—Students 93.

OUTSIDE THE CITY OF FORT WORTH

ABBOTT, HILL CO., IMMACULATE HEART OF MARY (1946) [CEM]
601 W. Houston St., Abbott, 76621.
Tel: 254-582-3092; Email: ihom@airmail.net. Rev. Joseph Keating; Deacon Denver Crawley.
Catechesis Religious Program—Students 85.

ALBANY, SHACKELFORD CO., JESUS OF NAZARETH (1970)
7950 W. US Hwy. 180, Albany, 76430.
Tel: 254-559-2860; Email: shofjcc@gmail.com. 208 S. Miller St., Breckenridge, 76424. Rev. Brijil Lawrence.
Catechesis Religious Program—Students 5.

ALEDO, PARKER CO., HOLY REDEEMER PARISH (2001)
Mailing Address: 16250 Old Weatherford Rd., Aledo, 76008. Tel: 817-441-3500; Email: office@holyredeemeraledo.org; Web: www.holyredeemeraledo.org. Rev. Msgr. Publius Xuereb; Deacon Scott France.
Catechesis Religious Program—Email: DRE@holyredemeraledo.org. Lisa Harbour, D.R.E. Students 221.

ARLINGTON, TARRANT CO.

1—CHURCH OF THE VIETNAMESE MARTYRS (2000)
801 E. Mayfield Rd., Arlington, 76014.
Tel: 817-466-0800; Fax: 817-472-8681; Email: vpgxtd@yahoo.com; Web: www.cttdvn.net. Revs. Vinh Van Vu, C.M.C.; Bonaventure Tuan Van Nguyen, C.M.C.; Lawrence M. Chau Van Nguyen,

C.M.C.; Deacons Dominic Thi Hoang; John Ban Nguyen.
Catechesis Religious Program—Hung Dao, D.R.E. Students 919.

2—ST. JOSEPH (1988) Very Revs. Daniel P. Kelley; Thomas Kennedy, Parochial Vicar; Rev. Peter Ware, Parochial Vicar; Deacons James Harvey; Jose Roman; Bill Johnson.
Office: 1927 S.W. Green Oaks Blvd., Arlington, 76017-2734. Tel: 817-472-5181; Fax: 817-467-9319; Email: info@stjoe88.org.
School—St. Joseph School, (Grades PreK-8), 2015 S.W. Green Oaks Blvd., Arlington, 76017-2399.
Tel: 817-419-6800; Fax: 817-419-7080; Email: info@stjosephtx.org; Web: www.stjosephtx.org. Dr. Chad Riley, Prin. Sisters 2; Students 369; Total Staff 38.
Catechesis Religious Program—Email: abanda@stjoe88.org; Email: dre@stjoe88.org. Ana Garza, D.R.E.; Alex Banda, Dir. of Youth Min. Students 1,250.

3—ST. MARIA GORETTI (1941)
Mailing Address: 1200 S. Davis Dr., Arlington, 76013-2399. Tel: 817-274-0643; Fax: 817-277-4193; Email: kmccoy@smgparish.org. Fr. James Angert; Rev. Michael Ciski, T.O.R., Parochial Vicar.
School—St. Maria Goretti School, (Grades PreK-8), Tel: 817-275-5081; Email: secretary@smgschool.org; Web: www.smgschool.org. Mrs. Kimberly Pierce, Prin. Lay Teachers 29; Students 340.
Catechesis Religious Program—
Tel: 817-274-0643, Ext. 226; Email: kparker@smgparish.org. Keith Parker, D.R.E. Students 294.

4—ST. MATTHEW (1964)
2021 New York Ave., Arlington, 76010-6097.
Tel: 817-860-0130; Fax: 817-277-7159; Email: stmattcc@sbcglobal.net; Web: www.stmattcc.org. Revs. Alejandro Hernandez Garcia, C.O.R.C.; Ariel Sanchez.
Catechesis Religious Program—Students 993.

5—MOST BLESSED SACRAMENT (1978)
2100 N. Davis Dr., Arlington, 76012.
Tel: 817-460-2751; Fax: 817-460-2761; Web: www.mbs.church. Rev. Msgrs. Joseph Pemberton; Joseph S. Scantlin, J.C.L., Pastor Emeritus, (Retired); Deacons Mike Krempp; William Montano.
Catechesis Religious Program—Students 275.

6—ST. VINCENT DE PAUL (1976)
5819 W. Pleasant Ridge Rd., Arlington, 76016.
Tel: 817-478-8206; Fax: 817-582-0273; Web: svdpcc.org. Rev. Philip Brembah; Deacon Bruce Corbett.
Catechesis Religious Program—Email: nsenz@svdpcc.org; Email: ngutierrez@svdpcc.org. Nicholas Senz, D.R.E. (Adult and Children's Formation); Nic Gutierrez, D.R.E. (Youth Formation). Students 59.

BEDFORD, TARRANT CO., ST. MICHAEL (1977)
3713 Harwood Rd., Bedford, 76021-4097.
Tel: 817-283-8746; Fax: 817-283-1908; Email: mallen@smcchurch.org; Web: www.smcchurch.org. Revs. Balaji Boyalla, S.A.C.; Mariya James; Deacons Harold Heinz; Sangote Ulupano.
Catechesis Religious Program—Tel: 817-510-2726; Email: rharris@smcchurch.org. Robin Harris, D.R.E. Students 484.

BOWIE, MONTAGUE CO., ST. JEROME (1986) Attended by St. Mary, Henrietta.
1200 N. Matthews, Bowie, 76230. Tel: 940-538-4214; Email: stmaryhenrietta@yahoo.com; Web: stmarycatholichenrietta.org. Mailing Address: 105 S. Barrett, Henrietta, 76365. Rev. Albert Francis Kanjirathumkal, H.G.N.
Catechesis Religious Program—Students 25.

BRECKENRIDGE, STEPHENS CO., SACRED HEART OF JESUS (1920)
208 S. Miller St., Breckenridge, 76424.
Tel: 254-559-2860; Email: shofjcc@gmail.com; Web: www.shojcc.org. Rev. Brijil Lawrence.
Catechesis Religious Program—Maria Guadalupe Ponce, D.R.E. Clergy 1; Students 113.

BRIDGEPORT, WISE CO., ST. JOHN THE BAPTIZER (1889)
1801 Irvin, Bridgeport, 76426. Tel: 940-683-2743; Fax: 940-683-5958; Email: main_office@jbdcatholics.org; Web: jbdcatholics.org. Revs. Reehan Soosai Antony, S.A.C.; Prakash Dias, Parochial Vicar; Deacons Myles Miller; Lauro Huerta; Eldon Gray; Mauricio Hernandez.
Catechesis Religious Program—Students 223.

BURKBURNETT, WICHITA CO., ST. JUDE THADDEUS (1965)
600 Davey Dr., Burkburnett, 76354.
Tel: 940-569-1222; Fax: 940-569-2714; Email: stjudeburkburnett@gmail.com; Web: stjudeburkburnett.org. Rev. Khoi Tran, Parochial Admin.
Catechesis Religious Program—Email: dpoole746@gmail.com. David Poole, D.R.E. Students 34.

BURLESON, TARRANT CO., ST. ANN (1971)
100 S.W. Alsbury Blvd., Burleson, 76028.
Tel: 817-295-5621; Fax: 817-295-5482; Email: office@mystann.com; Web: stanninburleson.com. Rev. Mel Bessellieu.
Catechesis Religious Program—Tel: 817-426-1101; Fax: 817-426-1106; Email: dre@mystann.com. Students 558.

CARROLLTON, DENTON CO., ST. CATHERINE OF SIENA (1981)
Mailing Address: 1705 Peters Colony, Carrollton, 75007-3704. Tel: 972-492-3237; Fax: 972-394-0676; Email: churchinfo@stcatherine.org; Web: www.stcatherine.org. Rev. Sushil William Tudu, T.O.R.; Deacons Walter Stone; Kurt Maskow.
Catechesis Religious Program—Students 313.

CISCO, EASTLAND CO., HOLY ROSARY (1920) Attended by St. Rita, Ranger.
1109 Blackwell St., Ranger, 76470.
Tel: 254-647-3167; Email: ritaoffice17@att.net; Web: ciscoholyrosary.com. Rev. Vijaya Mareedu.
Catechesis Religious Program—Tel: 254-595-1111; Email: loftinvp@aol.com. Val Loftin, D.R.E. Students 10.

CLEBURNE, JOHNSON CO., ST. JOSEPH (1888)
Mailing Address: 807 N. Anglin St., Cleburne, 76031.
Tel: 817-645-4478; Fax: 817-558-9938; Email: stjo123@sbcglobal.net. Rev. Sergio Rizo.
Catechesis Religious Program—Students 337.

CLIFTON, BOSQUE CO., HOLY ANGELS (1954)
1915 W. Fifth St., Clifton, 76634. Tel: 254-675-8877; Fax: 254-675-3165; Email: holyangels@holyangelstx.org; Web: holyangelstx.org. Rev. Xavier Silvadasan, H.G.N., Parochial Admin.; Martha Rivera, Sec.
Catechesis Religious Program—Virginia Villarreal, Rel. Edu. Coord. Students 56.

COLLEYVILLE, TARRANT CO., GOOD SHEPHERD (1992)
1000 Tinker Rd., Colleyville, 76034.
Tel: 817-421-1387; Fax: 817-421-4709. Revs. Richard Eldredge, T.O.R.; Ronald Mohnickey, T.O.R., Parochial Vicar; Jason Wooleyhan, Parochial Vicar; Deacons John Clark; Patrick Lavery; Klaus Gutbier; Richard Griego.
See Holy Trinity Catholic School, Grapevine under Elementary and Secondary Schools, Parochial located in the Institution section.
Catechesis Religious Program—Students 940.

COMANCHE, COMANCHE CO., SACRED HEART (1964) Attended by St. Brendan, Stephenville.
Mailing Address: 1444 W. Washington Ave., Stephenville, 76401. Tel: 254-965-5693; Email: catholic@embarqmail.com; Web: www.stbrendanscc.org. 1206 N. Pearl St., Comanche, 76442. Revs. Matthew Sanka, S.A.C., Parochial Admin.; James Amasi; Deacon Tomas Diaz.
Catechesis Religious Program—Tel: 325-356-2040. Students 98.

CROWELL, FOARD CO., ST. JOSEPH (1910) Attended by Holy Family, Vernon. Rev. Philip Brembah, Parochial Admin.; Cheyenne Marrinan, Youth Min. Res. & Mailing Address: 2200 Roberts, Vernon, 76384. Tel: 940-552-2895; Fax: 940-552-6084; Email: philip.brembah@att.net; Email: cheyenne.marrinan@att.net; Email: jjoseph@holyfamilyvernon.org; Web: holyfamilyccvernon.org.
Catechesis Religious Program—Tel: 940-655-4003; Email: rubygm_2006@yahoo.com. Ruby Manney, D.R.E. Students 15.

DE LEON, COMANCHE CO., OUR LADY OF GUADALUPE (1975) Attended by St. Brendan, Stephenville.
1444 W. Washington, Stephenville, 76401.
Tel: 254-965-5693; Email: catholic@embarqmail.com; Web: www.stbrendanscc.org. 6044 Hwy. 16, DeLeon, 76444. Revs. Matthew Sanka, S.A.C.; James Amasi; Deacon William Bolf.
Catechesis Religious Program—Students 17.

DECATUR, WISE CO., ASSUMPTION OF THE BLESSED VIRGIN MARY (1938) Attended by St. John the Baptizer, Bridgeport.
1305 Deer Park Rd., Decatur, 76234-9701.
Tel: 940-627-3307; Fax: 940-683-5958; Email: main_office@jbdcatholics.org; Web: jbdcatholics.org. Rev. Prakash Dias, Parochial Vicar; Deacons Eldon Gray; Myles Miller; Lauro Huerta; Mauricio Hernandez.
Church Rectory: 1801 Irvin St., Bridgeport, 76426.
Catechesis Religious Program—Tel: 940-683-2743. Anna Boyles, D.R.E. Students 276.

DENTON, DENTON CO.

1—IMMACULATE CONCEPTION (1894)
2255 N Bonnie Brae St., Denton, 76207.
Tel: 940-565-1770; Email: reception.desk@iccdenton.org; Web: www.iccdenton.org. Revs. D. Timothy Thompson, J.C.L.; Kheim Nguyen; Deacons Barry Sweeden; Alfonso Ramirez; Art Cassias.
School—Immaculate Conception School, (Grades PreK-8), 2301 N. Bonnie Brae St., Denton, 76207.
Tel: 940-381-1155. Mrs. Elaine Schad, Prin.; Mrs. Rebecca Bevilacqua, Librarian. Lay Teachers 22; Students 270.
Catechesis Religious Program—Deacon Art Cassias, Dir. Faith Formaton & Hispanic Liason. Students 1,162.

2—ST. JOHN PAUL II PARISH (2012)
1303 Eagle Dr., Denton, 76201. Tel: 940-566-0004; Email: juliegarrison54@gmail.com; Web: jp2denton.org. Rev. Kyle Walterscheid.
Catechesis Religious Program—Mary Rak, D.R.E.

3—ST. MARK (1995)
6500 Crawford Rd., Argyle, 76226. Tel: 940-387-6223; Fax: 940-382-1641; Email: jgodfrey@stmarkdenton.org; Email: evasquez@stmarkdenton.org; Web: www.stmarkdenton.org. Rev. Baby George; Deacons James Dale Galbraith; Victor Norton; Edward Posvar; William Miller.
Catechesis Religious Program—Tel: 940-220-7326. Deacon Joe Standridge Jr., D.R.E. Students 909.

DUBLIN, ERATH CO., ST. MARY (1916) Attended by St. Brendan, Stephenville.
12286 US Hwy. 377, Dublin, 76446.
Tel: 254-965-5693; Email: catholic@embarqmail.com; Web: www.stbrendanscc.org. 1444 W. Washington St., Stephenville, 76401-4141. Revs. Matthew Sanka, S.A.C., Parochial Admin.; James Amasi.
Catechesis Religious Program—Tel: 254-445-0237. Students 240.

EASTLAND, EASTLAND CO., ST. FRANCIS XAVIER (1920) Attended by St. Rita, Ranger.
1109 Blackwell St., Ranger, 76470.
Tel: 254-647-3163; Web: stfranciseastland.org. Rev. Vijaya Mareedu.
Catechesis Religious Program—400 E Foch, Eastland, 76448. Tel: 254-484-1111; Email: loftinvp@aol.com. Val Loftin, D.R.E. Students 93.

ELECTRA, WICHITA CO., ST. PAUL (1966) [JC] Attended by St. Jude Thaddeus, Burkburnett.
500 N. Bailey Ave., Electra, 76354.
Tel: 940-569-1222; Email: stjudeburkburnett@gmail.com. 600 Davey Dr., Burkburnett, 76354. Rev. Khoi Tran.

GAINESVILLE, COOKE CO., ST. MARY (1879)
805 N. Weaver St., Gainesville, 76240.
Tel: 940-665-5395; Email: pam.hoedebeck@stmaryscatholic.com; Web: www.stmarygainesvillecc.org. 825N. Weaver St., Gainesville, 76240. Rev. John Pacheco, Parochial Admin.; Deacons Gelasio Garcia; Jerome Caplinger; David Finch.
School—St. Mary School, (Grades PreK-8), 931 N. Weaver St., Gainesville, 76240-3299.
Tel: 940-665-5395, Ext. 113; Fax: 940-665-9538; Email: jbayer@smsmustangs.com; Email: klee@smsmustangs.com; Web: smsmustangs.com. Ms. Karen Lee, Prin. Lay Teachers 13; Students 148.
Catechesis Religious Program—Email: silvia.lesko@stmaryscatholic.com. Silvia Jo Lesko, M.T.S., D.R.E. Students 133.

GLEN ROSE, SOMERVELL CO., ST. ROSE OF LIMA (1969) [JC] Attended by St. Frances Cabrini.
P.O. Box 7324, Glen Rose, 76048. Tel: 254-897-9970; Email: st.roseoflima@valornet.com. Very Rev. Fernando Preciado.
Catechesis Religious Program—Students 111.

GRAFORD, PALO PINTO CO., ST. FRANCIS OF ASSISI (1949) Attended by Mission church of Our Lady of Lourdes, Mineral Wells.
P.O. Box 404, Graford, 76449. Rev. Thomas Dsouza.
14965 N. State Highway 16, Graford, 76449.
Tel: 940-325-4789; Email: pastoratoll@gmail.com.

GRAHAM, YOUNG CO., ST. MARY (1922) [JC]
P.O.Box 547, Graham, 76450. Rev. Eugene Nyong, Parochial Admin.; Deacon Adolfo Gonzalez.
Res.: 1209 St. Michael Ct., Graham, 76450.
Tel: 940-549-4314; Email: stmarygm@sbcglobal.net.
Catechesis Religious Program—Tel: 940-549-1058. Vickie Keller, Volunteer D.R.E. Students 213.

GRANBURY, HOOD CO., ST. FRANCES CABRINI (1976) [JC]
2301 Acton Hwy., Granbury, 76049.
Tel: 817-326-2131; Fax: 817-326-3211; Email: lgarcia@stfrances.net. Very Rev. Fernando Preciado; Deacons Craig McAlister; Rodney McGuire.
Catechesis Religious Program—Students 494.

GRAPEVINE, TARRANT CO., ST. FRANCIS OF ASSISI (1949)
861 Wildwood, Grapevine, 76051-3398.
Tel: 817-481-2685; Fax: 817-488-3169; Email: stfrancis@sfatx.org; Web: www.sfatx.org. Rev. James Flynn; Deacons M. C. Marquez; Tom Bates, Email: tbates@sfatx.org.
See Holy Trinity Catholic School, Grapevine under Elementary and Secondary Schools, Parochial located in the Institution section.
Catechesis Religious Program—Students 806.

HENRIETTA, CLAY CO., ST. MARY (1879) [CEM] Rev. Albert Francis Kanjirathumkal, H.G.N.
105 S. Barrett St., Henrietta, 76365.
Tel: 940-538-4214; Fax: 940-538-6638; Email: stmaryhenrietta@yahoo.com; Web: stmarycatholichenrietta.org.
Catechesis Religious Program—Students 17.

HILLSBORO, HILL CO., OUR LADY OF MERCY (1887)
Mailing Address: 107 Crestridge, Hillsboro, 76645.

Tel: 254-582-5640; Email: olm@hillsboro.net; Web: www.ourladyofmercyhillsboro.org. Rev. Ouseph I. Thekkumthala, Parochial Admin.
Catechesis Religious Program—Email: lupe.mancha@yahoo.com. Guadalupe Mancha, D.R.E. Students 240.

HURST, TARRANT CO., KOREAN MARTYRS (2003)
415 Brown Tr., Hurst, 76053. Tel: 817-788-5530; Email: jbenito@hanmail.net; Web: www.cafe.daum.net/fortworthkmcc. Rev. Woon Pil Jeong.
Catechesis Religious Program—Youngmi Park, D.R.E. Students 28.

IOWA PARK, WICHITA CO., CHRIST THE KING (1980)
1008 N. First St., Iowa Park, 76367.
Tel: 940-569-1222; Email: stjudeburkburnett@gmail.com. 600 Davey Dr., Burkburnett, 76354. Rev. Khoi Tran.
Catechesis Religious Program—Students 16.

JACKSBORO, JACK CO., ST. MARY (1911) Attended by St. John the Baptizer, 1801 Irvin St., Bridgeport, TX 76426. Tel: 940-683-2743; Fax: 940-683-5958; Email: main_office@jbdcatholics.org; Web: jbdcatholics.org. 1186 State Hwy 148, Jacksboro, 76458. Rev. Prakash Dias, Parochial Vicar; Deacons Lauro Huerta; Mauricio Hernandez; Eldon Gray; Myles Miller.
Catechesis Religious Program—Anna Boyles, D.R.E. Students 48.

KELLER, TARRANT CO., ST. ELIZABETH ANN SETON (1985) Revs. Gary Picou; Michael Greco; Deacons Jose Hernandez; Jerry Rustand; Nelson Petzold; Larry Sandoval; Guido Serrano.
Office: 2016 Willis Ln., Keller, 76248.
Tel: 817-431-3857; Email: lsoutherland@seascc.org; Email: Office@seascc.org.
School—St. Elizabeth Ann Seton School, (Grades PreK-8), Tel: 817-431-4845; Email: wperales@seascs.net; Email: school@seascs.net; Web: www.seascs.net. William Perales, Prin. Lay Teachers 43; Students 521.
Catechesis Religious Program—Email: kbless@seascc.org. Karen Bless, D.R.E. Students 1,374.

KNOX CITY, KNOX CO., SANTA ROSA (1948) [JC] Attended by St. Joseph, Rhineland.
210 North Ave. G., P.O. Box 428, Knox City, 79529.
Tel: 940-658-5062; Email: stjosephrhineland@gmail.com. Rev. John Perikomalayil, H.G.N., Parochial Admin.
Catechesis Religious Program—Mary Escamilla, D.R.E. Students 19.

LEWISVILLE, DENTON CO., ST. PHILIP THE APOSTLE (1976) Very Rev. Raymond McDaniel; Rev. Msgr. Francis Boachie Tawiah, Parochial Vicar; Deacons Joe Standridge Jr.; Ramiro Rodriguez; Jim Rodgers.
Office: 1897 W. Main St., Lewisville, 75067.
Tel: 972-436-9581; Fax: 972-436-5302; Email: office@stphilipcc.org; Web: www.stphilipcc.org.
Catechesis Religious Program—Tel: 972-219-5838. Students 829.

LINDSAY, COOKE CO., ST. PETER (1892) [CEM]
P.O. Box 148, Lindsay, 76250. Rev. Matthew Tatyrek.
Res.: 325 W. Main St., Lindsay, 76250.
Tel: 940-668-7609; Email: stpeterschurch@ntin.net; Web: www.stpeterlindsay.org.
Catechesis Religious Program—
Tel: 940-668-7609, Ext. 24. Students 260.

MANSFIELD, TARRANT CO., ST. JUDE (1898) [CEM]
500 E. Dallas St., Mansfield, 76063.
Tel: 817-473-6709; Fax: 682-518-6508; Email: v.pina@stjudecc.org; Web: www.stjudecc.org. Rev. Thu Nguyen, Parochial Admin.; Deacons Jose Aragon; Jimmy Garcia. In Res., Rev. Msgr. Raymund A. Mullan, (Retired).
Catechesis Religious Program—Tel: 817-473-0768. Students 1,298.

MEGARGEL, ARCHER CO., ST. MARY (1909) [CEM] Attended by Sacred Heart, Seymour.
13th St. & St. Mary St., Megargel, 76370.
Tel: 940-889-5252; Fax: 940-889-2136; Email: shseymour@srcaccess.net; Web: sacredheartseymour.org. 206 N Cedar St., Seymour, 76380. Deacon James Novak, Pastoral Admin.
Catechesis Religious Program—Students 8.

MINERAL WELLS, PALO PINTO CO., OUR LADY OF LOURDES (1960) Rev. Thomas Dsouza; Deacon Jesus Esteban Cardenas.
Res.: 108 N.W. 4th Ave., Mineral Wells, 76067.
Tel: 940-325-4789; Fax: 940-327-8170; Email: pastoratoll@gmail.com; Web: www.ollcatholicchurch.com.
Catechesis Religious Program—Students 191.

MONTAGUE, MONTAGUE CO., ST. WILLIAM (1899) [CEM] Attended by St. Mary.
311 S. Union St., Montague, 76251.
Tel: 940-538-4214; Fax: 940-538-6638; Email: stmaryhenrietta@yahoo.com; Web: stmarycatholichenrietta.org. 105 S. Barrett, Henrietta, 76365. Rev. Albert Francis Kanjirathumkal, H.G.N.
Catechesis Religious Program—Students 100.

MORGAN, BOSQUE CO., OUR LADY OF GUADALUPE (1962)
304 Charles St., Morgan, 76671. Tel: 254-635-7219; Email: rosafavela.olg@gmail.com; Email: 304olg@windstream.net. Rev. Xavier Silvadasan, H.G.N.
Catechesis Religious Program—Students 55.

MUENSTER, COOKE CO., SACRED HEART (1889) [CEM]
212 E. 6th St., Muenster, 76252. Tel: 940-759-2500; Fax: 940-759-4422; Email: krobinson@shcmuenster.com; Web: www.shcmuenster.com. 714 N. Main, Muenster, 76252. Rev. Kenneth Robinson.
Child Care—Preschool, Lay Teachers 1; Students 17.
School—Sacred Heart School, (Grades K-8), 153 E. 6th St., Muenster, 76252. Tel: 940-759-2511; Email: sforshee@shcmuenster.com. Lay Teachers 11; Students 119; Clergy / Religious Teachers 1.
High School—Sacred Heart High School,
Tel: 940-759-2500; Email: sforshee@shcmuenster.com. Lay Teachers 8; Students 82.
Catechesis Religious Program—Kami Creed, D.R.E.; Michelle Spaeth, Youth Min. Students 188.

NOCONA, MONTAGUE CO., ST. JOSEPH (1948) Attended by St. Mary.
109 Denison, Nocona, 76255. Tel: 940-538-4214;
Fax: 940-538-6638; Email: stmaryhenrietta@yahoo.com. 105 S. Barrett, Henrietta, 76365. Rev. Albert Francis Kanjirathumkal, H.G.N.
Catechesis Religious Program—Students 5.

OLNEY, YOUNG CO., ST. THERESA (1935) [JC] Attended by St. Mary, Graham.
P.O. Box 547, Graham, 76450. Tel: 940-549-4314; Email: stmarygm@sbcglobal.net. Rev. Eugene Nyong, Parochial Admin.
Church: Oak & Ave. E, Olney, 76374. Elena Garcia, D.R.E. Students 40.

PENELOPE, HILL CO., NATIVITY OF THE BLESSED VIRGIN MARY (1909) [CEM 2] Attended by Immaculate Heart of Mary, Abbot.
Mailing Address: 219 W. Magnolia St., P.O. Box 98, Penelope, 76676. Tel: 254-582-3092;
Tel: 254-533-2325; Email: penelopecatholicchurch@windstream.net; Web: nbvm.org. Rev. Joseph Keating; Deacon Denver Crawley.
Catechesis Religious Program—Email: cnowlin@fwdioc.org. Callie Nowlin, D.R.E. Students 23.

PILOT POINT, DENTON CO., ST. THOMAS AQUINAS (1891) [CEM]
400 St. Thomas Aquinas Ave., Pilot Point, 76258.
Tel: 940-686-2088; Fax: 360-925-2952; Email: office@stthomaspilotpoint.org; Web: www.stthomaspilotpoint.org. Rev. John Martin; Deacons Dave Garza; Moises Camargo.
Catechesis Religious Program—Students 405.

PROSPER, DENTON CO., ST. MARTIN DE PORRES PARISH (2015)
3990 W. University, Prosper, 75078.
Tel: 469-287-7624; Email: stmartindp.prosper@gmail.com; Web: www.saintmartindp.org. Rev. Stephen Hauck.
School—St. Martin de Porres Catholic School, (Grades PreK-8), Tel: 469-362-2400; Email: Pastor@saintmartindp.org; Web: smdpcatholic.org. Clergy 1; Lay Teachers 17; Students 201; Clergy / Religious Teachers 1.
Catechesis Religious Program—Email: Nicole@saintmartindp.org. Niki MacDougal, D.R.E. Students 86.

QUANAH, HARDEMAN CO., ST. MARY (1914) [JC] Attended by Holy Family, Vernon.
2200 Roberts, Vernon, 76384. Tel: 940-552-2895; Fax: 940-552-6084; Email: philip.brembah@att.net; Email: cheyenne.marrinan@att.net; Web: holyfamilyccvernon.org. 609 Mercer Street, Quanah, 79252. Rev. Philip Brembah, Parochial Admin.; Cheyenne Marrinan, Youth Min.
Catechesis Religious Program—Tel: 940-839-6287; Email: celetawalther@sbcglobal.net. Celeta Walther, D.R.E. Students 16.

RANGER, EASTLAND CO., ST. RITA (1919)
1109 Blackwell St., Ranger, 76470.
Tel: 254-647-3163; Email: ritaoffice17@att.net. Rev. Vijaya Mareedu; Deacon Edward Ferguson; Val Loftin, D.R.E.

RHINELAND, KNOX CO., ST. JOSEPH (1895) [CEM]
10180 CR 6010, Munday, 76371. Tel: 940-422-4270; Tel: 940-422-4994; Email: stjosephrhineland@gmail.com; Web: stjosephrhineland.org. Rev. John Perikomalayil, H.G.N.
Catechesis Religious Program—Tel: 940-782-6497; Email: msehernandez@yahoo.com. Magdaleno Hernandez, D.R.E. Students 160.

SCOTLAND, ARCHER CO., ST. BONIFACE (1911) [CEM] Attended by St. Mary, Windthorst.
Tel: 940-423-6687; Fax: 940-423-6657; Email: windscot@comcell.net; Web: www.stmarystboniface.org. Rev. Michael Moloney.

SEYMOUR, BAYLOR CO., SACRED HEART (1910) [CEM] Deacon Jim Novak, M.T.S., Parochial Admin.
Sacred Heart Pastoral Center—206 N. Cedar St., Seymour, 76380. Tel: 940-889-5252;
Fax: 940-889-2136; Email: shseymour@srcaccess.net; Web: sacredheartseymour.org.
Catechesis Religious Program—Students 65.

STEPHENVILLE, ERATH CO., ST. BRENDAN (1958)
1444 W. Washington Ave., Stephenville, 76401.
Tel: 254-965-5693; Email: catholic@embarqmail.com; Web: www.stbrendanscc.org. Revs. Matthew Sanka, S.A.C., Parochial Admin.; James Amasi.
Catechesis Religious Program—Students 193.

STRAWN, PALO PINTO CO., ST. JOHN (1912) Attended by St. Rita.
1109 Blackwell Rd., Ranger, 76470.
Tel: 254-647-3163; Email: ritaoffice17@att.net. Rev. Vijaya Mareedu.
Catechesis Religious Program—Tel: 254-595-1111; Email: loftinvp@aol.com. Val Loftin, D.R.E. Students 25.

THE COLONY, DENTON CO., HOLY CROSS (1981)
Tel: 972-625-5252, Ext. 301; Email: jjoseph@holycrosscc.org. Rev. Joy Joseph, T.O.R., J.C.L.
Church: 7000 Morning Star Dr., The Colony, 75056.
Tel: 972-652-5252; Fax: 972-370-5524.
Catechesis Religious Program—Students 277.

VERNON, WILBARGER CO., HOLY FAMILY OF NAZARETH (1891)
2200 Roberts St., Vernon, 76384. Tel: 940-552-2895; Fax: 940-552-6084; Email: philip.brembah@att.net; Email: cheyenne.marrinan@att.net; Web: holyfamilyccvernon.org. Rev. Philip Brembah, Parochial Admin.; Cheyenne Marrinan, Youth Min.
Catechesis Religious Program—Tel: 940-414-0426; Tel: 940-613-2239; Email: mchristy_salto@gmail.com; Email: littlejalisco@sbcglobal.net. Mary Christy Medina, D.R.E.; Salvador Perez, D.R.E. Students 142.

WEATHERFORD, PARKER CO., ST. STEPHEN (1882) Rev. Michael T. O'Sullivan, S.A.C., Parochial Admin.; Deacon Carlos Frias.
Tel: 817-596-9585; Fax: 817-613-0808; Email: office@saintstephenschurch.org; Email: frmike@saintstephencc.org; Web: www.saintstephencc.org.

WICHITA FALLS, WICHITA CO.
1—IMMACULATE CONCEPTION OF MARY (2005) [CEM] [JC]
2901 Barnett Rd., Wichita Falls, 76310.
Tel: 940-692-1825; Email: icmwf246@yahoo.com. Rev. Joseph M. Cao Xuan Thanh, C.M.C.
Catechesis Religious Program—Thanh Ton, D.R.E. Students 56.

2—OUR LADY OF GUADALUPE (1927) [JC]
421 Marconi, Wichita Falls, 76301.
Tel: 940-766-2735; Fax: 940-766-4052; Email: contact@guadalupewf.org; Web: www.guadalupewf.org. Rev. Raul Martinez Lopez; Deacon Anastasio Perez.
Catechesis Religious Program—Email: evelyn.stokes@guadalupewf.org; Email: rodriguezia85@gmail.com. Evelyn Stokes, D.R.E.; Artemia Rodriguez, RCIA Coord. Students 117.

3—OUR LADY QUEEN OF PEACE (1956) [JC]
2601 Lansing Blvd., Wichita Falls, 76309.
Tel: 940-696-1253; Fax: 940-696-1216; Email: info@olqpwf.org; Web: www.olqpwf.org. 4040 York, Wichita Falls, 76309. Rev. Alexander Ambrose, H.G.N.; Deacons James Bindel; Vincent Blake.
Catechesis Religious Program—
Tel: 940-696-1253, Ext. 12; Email: apoplin@olqpwf.org. Students 176.

4—SACRED HEART (1891) [JC]
Mailing Address: 1504 Tenth St., Wichita Falls, 76301. Tel: 940-723-5288; Fax: 940-767-0160; Email: sheart@sacredheartwf.org. 1501 Ninth St., Wichita Falls, 76301. Deacons Roland Benoit; Bill Archer.
Catechesis Religious Program—Lori Shidell, D.R.E. Students 259.

WINDTHORST, ARCHER CO., ST. MARY (1892) [CEM]
P.O. Box 230, Windthorst, 76389. Rev. Michael Moloney.
Res.: 101 Church St., Windthorst, 76389.
Tel: 940-423-6687; Email: windscot@comcell.net; Web: www.stmarysstboniface.org.
Catechesis Religious Program—Students 232.

Chaplains of Public Institutions

FORT WORTH. *Federal Medical Center*, 76199.
DENTON. *State School*, 1215 E. Elm St., Denton, 76201. Tel: 817-387-1755. Deacon Emilio Gonzalez, Chap.
GAINESVILLE. *Texas Youth Council Youth Facility*, 805 N. Weaver, Gainesville, 76240. Tel: 817-665-2413.
WICHITA FALLS. *State Hospital*, Wichita Falls. Tel: 817-723-4111.

Outside the Diocese:
Rev.—
Thames, Robert, (Retired), Casilla 25, Santa Cruz, Bolivia.

On Leave of Absence:
Very Rev.—
Poirot, Jeff
Revs.—
Barba, Alfredo
Gremmels, John
Kirkham, Richard
Orozco, Isaac
Picou, Gary
Serrano, Rodrigo
Vallejo Garcia, Amado
Wilcox, James.

Removed from Active Ministry:
Rev.—
Pansza, Gilbert, (Retired).

Retired:
Rev. Msgrs.—
Mullan, Raymund A., (Retired)
Rivero, Juan, (Retired)
Scantlin, Joseph S., J.C.L., (Retired)
Revs.—
Bristow, David L., (Retired)
Edwards, Dale, (Retired)
Foley, George, (Retired)
Geurtz, Gary, (Retired)
Hawkins, Allan R.G., (Retired)
Holmberg, Michael, (Retired)
Irwin, Michael, (Retired)
Medina, Hector, (Retired)
Meledom, Joseph, (Retired)
Miranda, Luke, (Retired)
O'Toole, James, (Retired)
Perez, Salvador, (Retired)
Smith, Dennis, (Retired)
Spong, William, (Retired)
Stasiowski, John, (Retired)
Strittmatter, Robert, (Retired)
Swistovich, John
Thames, Robert, (Retired)
Wigginton, Ellsworth T., (Retired).

Permanent Deacons:
Aguirre, Ruben
Aragon, Jose
Archer, William
Bagley, Kevin
Bates, Thomas
Benoit, Roland, (Retired)
Bills, Larry, (Retired)
Bindel, James
Blake, Vincent, (Retired)
Bolf, William
Bowden, Edgar, (Retired)
Brown, Donald, (Retired)
Burke, Patrick, (Retired)
Camargo, Moisés
Caplinger, Jerome
Cardenas, Jesus Esteban
Carranza, Marcelino
Casias, Arturo S.
Castaneda, Ruben L., (Retired)
Castleberry, Charles, (Retired)
Clark, John
Corbett, Bruce
Crawley, Denver
Crites, James
Diaz, Tommy
Escamilla, Juan
Eschbach, Franklin, (Retired)
Ferguson, Edward
Finch, David
France, Scott
Frias, Carlos
Galbraith, James Dale
Garcia, Eduardo, (Retired)
Garcia, Gelasio
Garcia, Jimmy
Garcia, Martin
Garcia, Pedro
Gardner, Jack
Garza, Dave
Geiger, Wendell
Giovannitti, Thomas, (Retired)
Gonzalez, Adolfo
Gonzalez, Emilio, (Retired)
Gray, Glen Eldon
Green, Clifford, (Retired)
Griego, Richard
Gutbier, Klaus
Guzman, John, (Retired)
Harvey, James, (Retired)
Heinz, Harold
Hernandez, Jose
Hernandez, Mauricio
Hoang, Dominic T.
Hoang, Michael
Howard, Terrance
Huerta, Lauro
Johnson, William
Kerrigan, John
Krempp, Michael
Kunath, Wolfgang
Lagunas, Matias
Laremore, Robert, (Retired)
Lauhoff, John, (Retired)
Lavery, Patrick
Leyva, Rigoberto
Marquez, Mario
Maskow, Kurt
McAlister, Craig
McGuire, Rodney
Miller, Myles
Miller, William
Milligan, Joseph, (Retired)
Mocek, Michael
Montano, William
Nguyen, John Ban
Nguyen, Truat
Norton, Victor
Novak, Jim, M.T.S.
Onofre, Jose, (Retired)
Pereda, Manuel
Perez, Anastasio
Perez, Julio, (Retired)
Petzold, Nelson
Poole, James, (Retired)
Poth, Louis J., (Retired)
Pozvar, Ed
Ramirez, Alfonso
Reyes, Juan
Rodgers, Jim
Rodriguez, Jose
Rustand, Gerald
Salva, Hector
Sandoval, Larry
Serenil, Benito, (Retired)
Serrano, Guido
Sowers, Lynn
Stadler, Richard
Standridge, Joe Jr.
Stone, Walter
Sweeden, Barry
Tello, Reyes Jr.
Torrez, Simon
Ulupano, Sangote
Warner, Don
Weaver, Lonnie Jr., (Retired)
Wuenschel, Doug, (Retired).

INSTITUTIONS LOCATED IN DIOCESE

[A] HIGH SCHOOLS, DIOCESAN

FORT WORTH. *Cassata Catholic High School* (Coed Secondary). 1400 Hemphill St., 76104-4796. Tel: 817-926-1745; Fax: 817-926-3132; Web: www.cassatahs.org. Dr. Maggie Harrison, Prin. Students 86; Teachers 8; Staff 7.

Nolan Catholic High School (Coed) 4501 Bridge St., 76103-1198. Tel: 817-457-2920; Fax: 817-496-9775; Email: office@nolancatholichs.org; Web: www.nolancatholichs.org. Leah Rios, Pres.; Rev. Maurice Lawrence Moon, Chap.; William Perales, Prin. Lay Teachers 64; Sisters 2; Students 760.

Nolan School Trust.

WICHITA FALLS. *Notre Dame Catholic School*, (Grades PreK-8), 2821 Lansing Blvd., Wichita Falls, 76309-4999. Tel: 940-692-6041; Fax: 940-692-2811; Email: michael.edghill@ndcswf.org; Web: www.notredamecatholic.org. Michael Edghill, Prin. (Consolidated) Lay Teachers 13; Students 95.

[B] HIGH SCHOOLS, PAROCHIAL

MUENSTER. *Sacred Heart School*, (Grades K-12), 153 E. 6th St., Muenster, 76252-0588. Tel: 940-759-2511. Rev. Kenneth Robinson. Lay Teachers 21; Students 216.

**Sacred Heart Teachers Trust Fund*, Muenster.

[C] ELEMENTARY AND SECONDARY SCHOOLS, PAROCHIAL

DENTON. *Immaculate Conception Catholic School*, (Grades PreK-8), 2301 N. Bonnie Brae St., Denton, 76207-1019. Tel: 940-381-1155; Fax: 940-381-1837; Email: iccoffice@gmail.com; Web: www.catholicschooldenton.org. Mrs. Elaine Schad, Prin. Lay Teachers 23; Students 226.

GRAPEVINE. *Holy Trinity Catholic School*, (Grades PreK-8), 3750 William D. Tate Ave., Grapevine, 76051. Tel: 817-421-8000; Fax: 817-421-4468; Email: school@holytcs.org; Web: www.holytcs.org. Deacon Jeffrey Heiple, Prin.; Ms. Marianne Lippert, Librarian. (Consolidated) Lay Teachers 30; Students 333.

WICHITA FALLS. *Notre Dame Catholic School*, 2821 Lansing Blvd., Wichita Falls, 76309. Tel: 940-692-6041; Fax: 940-692-2811; Email: michael.edghill@ndcswf.org; Web: www.notredamecatholic.org. Michael Edghill, Prin. Lay Teachers 35; Students 190.

[D] ELEMENTARY SCHOOLS, PRIVATE

FORT WORTH. *Our Lady of Victory Catholic School*, 3320 Hemphill St., 76110-4098. Tel: 817-924-5123; Fax: 817-923-9621; Email: principalpetrey@olvfw.com; Web: www.olvfw.com. Linda (Petrey) Kuntz, Prin. Clergy 1; Lay Teachers 23; Students 104.

[E] SOCIAL AGENCIES, CATHOLIC CHARITIES

FORT WORTH. *Catholic Charities Diocese of Fort Worth Endowment, Inc.*, 249 W. Thornhill Dr., 76115. Tel: 817-534-0814; Fax: 817-535-8779; Email: leigh@ccdofw.org. P.O. Box 15610, 76119. Heather Reynolds, Pres. & CEO. Total Staff 1.

Catholic Charities, Diocese of Fort Worth, Inc., 249 W. Thornhill Dr., 76115. Tel: 817-534-0814; Fax: 817-535-8779; Email: infoccdofw@ccdofw.org; Web: www.catholiccharitiesfortworth.org. Heather Reynolds, Pres. & CEO. An Independent Corporation Founded by the Diocese of Fort Worth. Tot Asst. Annually 80,000; Total Staff 390.

Assessment Center of Tarrant, 249 W. Thornhill Dr., 76115. Tel: 817-534-0814; Fax: 817-535-8779; Email: afox@ccdofw.org. Heather Reynolds, CEO. (Children's Shelter) Bed Capacity 40; Tot Asst. Annually 200; Total Staff 15.

Hope Center, 249 W. Thornhill Dr., 76115. Tel: 817-534-0814; Fax: 817-535-8779; Email: malfonzo@ccdofw.org. Heather Reynolds, CEO. Tot Asst. Annually 14,000; Total Staff 10.

Clinical Counseling Department, 249 W. Thornhill Dr., 76115. Tel: 817-534-0814; Fax: 817-535-8779; Email: counseling_referrals@ccdofw.org.

Dental Clinic, 249 W. Thornhill Dr., 76115. Tel: 817-534-0814; Fax: 817-535-8779; Email: pvela@ccdofw.org. Heather Reynolds, CEO. Tot Asst. Annually 1,700; Total Staff 15.

Disaster Response Service, 249 W. Thornhill Dr., 76115. Tel: 817-534-0814; Fax: 817-535-8779; Email: fspeer@ccdofw.org. Heather Reynolds, CEO. Tot Asst. Annually 870; Total Staff 1.

Families First, 249 W. Thornhill Dr., 76115. Tel: 817-534-0814; Fax: 817-535-8779.

Financial Stability, 249 W. Thornhill Dr., 76115. Tel: 817-534-0814; Fax: 817-535-8779; Email: danaspringer@ccdofw.org. Heather Reynolds, CEO. Tot Asst. Annually 700; Total Staff 15.

Immigration & Refugee Services, 249 W. Thornhill Dr., 76115. Tel: 817-534-0814; Fax: 817-535-8779; Email: xchacin@ccdofw.org. Heather Reynolds, CEO. Tot Asst. Annually 4,300; Total Staff 15.

International Foster Care Program, 249 W. Thornhill Dr., 76115. Tel: 817-534-0814; Fax: 817-535-8779; Email: afox@ccdofw.org. Heather Reynolds, CEO. Tot Asst. Annually 70; Total Staff 15.

Street Outreach Services, 249 W. Thornhill Dr., 76115. Tel: 817-534-0814; Fax: 817-535-8779; Email: jsemple@ccdofw.org. Heather Reynolds, CEO. Tot Asst. Annually 700; Total Staff 7.

Veterans Services, 249 W. Thornhill Dr., 76115. Tel: 817-534-0814; Fax: 817-535-8779; Email: mrankin@ccdofw.org. Heather Reynolds, CEO. Tot Asst. Annually 1,400; Total Staff 10.

Translation and Interpreter Network (TIN), 249 W. Thornhill Dr., 76115. Tel: 817-534-0814; Fax: 817-535-8779; Email: mdibra@ccdofw.org. Heather Reynolds, CEO. Tot Asst. Annually 17,000; Total Staff 10.

Transportation, 249 W. Thornhill Dr., 76115. Tel: 817-534-0814; Fax: 817-535-8779; Email: shurbough@ccdofw.org. Heather Reynolds, CEO. Tot Asst. Annually 19,000; Total Staff 20.

[F] RETIREMENT & DISABILITY HOUSING

CROWLEY. *St. Francis Village, Inc.*, 4070 St. Francis Village Rd., Crowley, 76036. Tel: 817-292-5786; Fax: 817-294-2989; Email: davidt@saintfrancisvillage.com; Web: www.saintfrancisvillage.com. David Tolson, Exec. Dir. Active Retirement village, on shores of Lake Benbrook near Fort Worth, for retirees and the elderly sponsored by Franciscan Tertiary Provinces Foundation. Residents 530.

Franciscan Tertiary Provinces Foundation, 4070 St. Francis Village Rd., Crowley, 76036. Tel: 817-292-5786; Email: davidt@saintfrancisvillage.com. David Tolson, Exec. Sponsor corporation of St. Francis Village (retirement village) in Crowley, TX. Total Staff 22.

San Damiano, Inc., 4070 St. Francis Village Rd., Crowley, 76036. Tel: 817-292-5786; Fax: 817-294-2989; Email: davidt@saintfrancisvillage.com. David Tolson, Exec.

[G] MONASTERIES AND RESIDENCES OF PRIESTS AND BROTHERS

FORT WORTH. **Third Order Regular of St. Francis, Province of St. Thomas*, 8324 Crosswind Dr., 76179. Tel: 817-984-3750; Fax: 817-624-2184. Rev. Joy Joseph, T.O.R., J.C.L., Treas.

CROWLEY. *St. Maximilian Kolbe Friary* (Closed) One Marquard Cir., St. Francis Village, Crowley, 76036. Tel: 314-655-0525; Email: finance@thefriars.org. Rev. Robert C. Sieg, O.F.M., Supr.

SEYMOUR. *Heralds of Good News Mother Theresa Province, Inc.* (2010) Sacred Heart Catholic Church, 10180 CR 6010, Rhineland, 76371.
Tel: 940-422-4990; Email: hgnmtpusa@gmail.com; Web: www.heraldsofgoodnews.org. Rev. John Perikomalayil, H.G.N., Pres.

[H] CONVENTS AND RESIDENCES FOR SISTERS

FORT WORTH. *Hermanas Catequistas Guadalupanas*, 1215 Norman Cir., Arlington, 76104.
Tel: 817-945-9317. Sr. Diana Rodriguez, H.C.G., Supr. Sisters 3.

Sisters of Saint Mary of Namur, Provincialate, Our Lady of Victory Center, 909 W. Shaw St., 76110.
Tel: 817-923-3091; Fax: 817-923-1511; Email: gabriela.martinez@charter.net; Web: www.ssmnwestern.com. Sr. Gabriela Martinez, S.S.M.N., Prov. Supr. Provincial House of the Western Province, Sisters of St. Mary of Namur. Sisters 25.

ARLINGTON. *Monastery of the Most Holy Trinity, Discalced Carmelites*, 5801 Mt. Carmel Dr., Arlington, 76017. Tel: 817-468-1781;
Fax: 817-468-1782; Email: supcarmel@aol.com; Web: www.carmelnuns.com. Mother Anne Teresa Kulinski, O.C.D., Prioress. Novices 2; Sisters 11; Simple Professed 1; Solemnly Professed 8.

WICHITA FALLS. *Sisters of St. Mary of Namur*, Mercy Convent, 3000 Lansing Blvd., Wichita Falls, 76309. Tel: 940-692-9770; Fax: 940-689-0139; Email: maryjwarm@aol.com; Web: www.ssmnwestern.com. Sr. Gabriela Martinez, S.S.M.N., Supr. Sisters 4.

[I] RETREAT HOUSES

LAKE DALLAS. *Montserrat Jesuit Retreat House*, 600 N. Shady Shores Dr., P.O. Box 1390, Lake Dallas, 75065. Tel: 940-321-6020; Fax: 940-321-6040; Email: director@montserratretreat.org; Web: www.montserratretreat.org. Revs. John Payne, S.J., Assoc. Dir.; Anthony R. Borrow, S.J., Assoc. Dir. Bed Capacity 99.

Montserrat Foundation, Inc., 600 N Shady Shores Dr., P.O. Box 1390, Lake Dallas, 75065.
Tel: 940-321-6020; Fax: 940-321-6040; Email: director@montserratretreat.org. Rev. Anthony R. Borrow, S.J., Chm.

[J] COLLEGE CAMPUS MINISTRIES

FORT WORTH. *Texas Christian University Catholic Community*, 2704 W. Berry St., 76109.
Tel: 817-945-9376; Fax: 817-257-7304; Web: www.tcucatholic.org. Mr. Ed Hopkins, Campus Min.

ARLINGTON. *University Catholic Community at UT Arlington*, 1010 Benge Dr., Arlington, 76013-2643.
Tel: 817-460-1155; Web: utacatholics.org. Mr. Jeff Hedglen, Campus Min.
University of Texas at Arlington University Catholic Community.

WICHITA FALLS. *Catholic Campus Ministry*, 3410 Louis J. Rodriguez Dr., Wichita Falls, 76308.
Tel: 940-692-9778; Email: msuccc@yahoo.com. Ms. Debra Neely.

[K] MISCELLANEOUS

FORT WORTH. *Catholic Diocese of Fort Worth Advancement Foundation*, 800 W. Loop 820 S., 76108-2919. Tel: 817-945-9440; Fax: 817-945-9441; Email: runderwood@advancementfoundation.org; Web: www.advancementfoundation.org. Most Rev. Michael F. Olson, S.T.D., Chm.; Mr. Donald L. Wagner, M.B.A., Pres. Board of Directors Most Rev. Michael F. Olson, S.T.D., Chair; Ms. Mary Goosens, CPA, Pres.; Mrs. Paula K. Parrish, CFRE, Exec. Dir.; Very Rev. E. James Hart; Ryan F. Kagay; Mr. David Kimbell, Jr.; Mr. William P. Quinn.

Magnificat, Grapevine Chapter, 425 Misty Ln., Lewisville, 75067. Tel: 214-587-3478. Gloria Salerno Keiderling, Coord.

North Texas San Benito, Inc., 800 W. Loop 820 S., 76108. Tel: 817-945-9400. Most Rev. Michael F. Olson, S.T.D.

RELIGIOUS INSTITUTES OF MEN REPRESENTED IN THE DIOCESE

For further details refer to the corresponding bracketed number in the Religious Institutes of Men or Women section.

[0470]—*The Capuchin Franciscan Fathers* (La Piedad Michoacan, Mexico)—O.F.M.Cap.

[]—*Confraternidad Operarios del Reino de Christo* (Mexico)—C.O.R.C.

[]—*Congregation of the Mother of the Redeemer* (Carthage, MO)—C.R.M.

[0520]—*Franciscan Fathers* (St. Louis, MO)—O.F.M.

[]—*Fraternitas Sacerdotalis Sanci Petri - The Priestly Fraternity of Saint Peter* (S. Abington Township, PA)—F.S.S.P.

[0585]—*Heralds of Good News, Mary Queen of Apostles Province* (India)—H.G.N.

[]—*Heralds of the Good News, Mother Theresa Province* (India)—H.G.N.

[]—*Society of Jesus, New Orleans Province* (St. Louis, MO)—S.J.

[]—*Society of the Catholic Apostolate, Assumption of the Blessed Virgin Mary Province* (Karnataka, India)—S.A.

[0990]—*Society of the Catholic Apostolate, Mother of Divine Love Providence* (Dublin, Ireland)—S.A.C.

[0420]—*Society of the Divine Word* (Bay St. Louis, MS)—S.V.D.

[]—*Third Order Regular of Saint Francis, Province of San Antonio de Padua, Paraguay.*

[]—*Third Order Regular of Saint Francis, Province of Santa Maria de Guadalupe* (Mexico)—T.O.R.

[]—*Third Order Regular of Saint Francis, Province of St. Thomas, Inc.* (India)—T.O.R.

[]—*Third Order Regular of Saint Francis, Province of the Most Sacred Heart of Jesus, Inc.* (Loretto, PA)—T.O.R.

RELIGIOUS INSTITUTES OF WOMEN REPRESENTED IN THE DIOCESE

[4060]—*Congregation of Sisters of Charity of the Incarnate Word* (San Antonio)—C.C.V.I.

[]—*Congregation of the Divine Providence* (San Antonio)—C.D.P.

[0420]—*Discalced Carmelite Nuns*—O.C.D.

[]—*Dominican Sisters of Mary Immaculate Prov.*—O.P.

[1900]—*Hermanas Catequistas Guadalupanas* (Saltillo, Coah., Mexico)—H.C.G.

[]—*Hermanas Franciscans de la Inmaculada Concepcion* (Mexico)—H.F.I.C.

[]—*The Lovers of the Holy Cross Vihn* (Diocese of Vinh, Vietnam)—L.H.C.

[]—*Missionary Catechists of the Divine Providence* (San Antonio)—M.C.D.P.

[]—*Missionary Catechists of the Sacred Hearts of Jesus and Mary* (Victoria, TX)—M.C.S.H.

[]—*Olivetan Benedictine Sisters*—O.S.B.

[]—*Schoenstatt Sisters of Mary* (Waukesha, WI)—S.S.M.

[3950]—*Sisters of Saint Mary of Namur*—S.S.M.N.

[2050]—*Sisters of the Holy Spirit and Mary Immaculate*—S.H.Sp.

NECROLOGY

† Schumacher, Joseph A., (Retired), Died Nov. 1, 2018

An asterisk (*) denotes an organization that has established tax-exempt status directly with the IRS and is not covered by the USCCB Group Ruling.

Diocese of Fresno

(Dioecesis Fresnensis)

Most Reverend

JOSEPH V. BRENNAN

Bishop of Fresno; ordained June 21, 1980; appointed Titular Bishop of Trofimiana and Auxiliary Bishop of Los Angeles July 21, 2015; ordained September 8, 2015; appointed Bishop of Fresno March 5, 2019; installed May 2, 2019.

Most Reverend

ARMANDO XAVIER OCHOA

Bishop Emeritus of Fresno; ordained May 23, 1970; appointed Titular Bishop of Sitifi and Auxiliary of the Archdiocese of Los Angeles December 29, 1986; ordained Bishop February 23, 1987; appointed Bishop of El Paso April 1, 1996; installed June 26, 1996; appointed Bishop of Fresno December 1, 2011; installed February 2, 2012; retired March 5, 2019. *Chancery Office: 1550 N. Fresno St., Fresno, CA 93703.*

Chancery Office: 1550 N. Fresno St., Fresno, CA 93703-3788. Tel: 559-488-7400; Fax: 559-488-7464.

ESTABLISHED DECEMBER 15, 1967.

Square Miles 36,072.

Formerly Diocese of Monterey-Fresno.

Comprises the Counties of Fresno, Inyo, Kern, Kings, Madera, Mariposa, Merced and Tulare in the State of California.

Diocesan Patroness: St. Therese of the Child Jesus.

Legal titles of parishes and institutions, the Roman Catholic Bishop of Fresno, a Corporation Sole, Diocese of Fresno Education Corporation (for schools).

STATISTICAL OVERVIEW

Personnel	
Bishop	1
Retired Bishops	1
Priests: Diocesan Active in Diocese	73
Priests: Diocesan Active Outside Diocese	1
Priests: Diocesan in Foreign Missions	1
Priests: Retired, Sick or Absent	36
Number of Diocesan Priests	111
Religious Priests in Diocese	34
Total Priests in Diocese	145
Extern Priests in Diocese	32
Permanent Deacons in Diocese	68
Total Brothers	1
Total Sisters	116
Parishes	
Parishes	87
With Resident Pastor:	
Resident Diocesan Priests	75
Resident Religious Priests	9
Without Resident Pastor:	
Administered by Priests	2
Administered by Deacons	1
Missions	44
Professional Ministry Personnel:	
Brothers	1
Sisters	34
Lay Ministers	102
Welfare	
Catholic Hospitals	3
Total Assisted	564,259
Homes for the Aged	2
Total Assisted	165
Special Centers for Social Services	5
Total Assisted	200,519
Educational	
Diocesan Students in Other Seminaries	25
Seminaries, Religious	1
Total Seminarians	25
High Schools, Diocesan and Parish	2
Total Students	1,036
Elementary Schools, Diocesan and Parish	19
Total Students	4,484
Catechesis/Religious Education:	
High School Students	11,692
Elementary Students	23,631
Total Students under Catholic Instruction	40,868
Teachers in the Diocese:	
Sisters	11
Lay Teachers	376
Vital Statistics	
Receptions into the Church:	
Infant Baptism Totals	12,452
Minor Baptism Totals	1,491
Adult Baptism Totals	402
Received into Full Communion	507
First Communions	14,412
Confirmations	7,957
Marriages:	
Catholic	1,729
Interfaith	181
Total Marriages	1,910
Deaths	3,919
Total Catholic Population	1,200,000
Total Population	2,852,718

Former Prelates of Diocese of Monterey-Fresno—Most Revs. JOHN B. MACGINLEY, D.D., ord. June 8, 1895; cons. May 10, 1910; First Bishop of Monterey-Fresno, July 31, 1924; PHILIP G. SCHER, ord. June 6, 1903; appt. April 28, 1933; cons. June 29, 1933; died Jan. 3, 1953; ALOYSIUS J. WILLINGER, C.Ss.R., ord. July 2, 1911; cons. Bishop of Ponce, Puerto Rico, Oct. 28, 1929; Coadjutor Bishop of Monterey/Fresno "cum jure successionis," Dec. 12, 1946; succeeded to the See, Jan. 3, 1953; resigned Oct. 25, 1967; died July 25, 1973; HARRY ANSELM CLINCH, D.D., ord. June 6, 1936; cons. Feb. 27, 1957; appt. Auxiliary to the Bishop of Monterey-Fresno, Dec. 5, 1956; transferred to the See of Monterey, Dec. 14, 1967; retired Jan. 19, 1982; died March 8, 2003.

Former Bishops of the Diocese of Fresno—His Eminence TIMOTHY CARDINAL MANNING, D.D., J.C.D., ord. June 16, 1934; appt. Titular Bishop of Lesvi and Auxiliary of Los Angeles, Aug. 3, 1946; consecrated Oct. 15, 1946; installed as First Bishop of Fresno, Dec. 15, 1967; elevated to Coadjutor Archbishop of Los Angeles "cum jure successionis," May 26, 1969; succeeded to the See, Jan. 21, 1970; created Cardinal, March 5, 1973; died June 23, 1989; Most Rev. HUGH A. DONOHOE, D.D., Ph.D., ord. June 14, 1930; appt. Auxiliary in San Francisco, Aug. 2, 1947; consecrated Oct. 7, 1947; appt. Bishop of Stockton, Feb. 21, 1962; appt. Second Bishop of Fresno, Aug. 28, 1969; resigned July 1, 1980; died Oct. 26, 1987; His Eminence ROGER CARDINAL MAHONY, D.D., ord. May 1, 1962; appt. Auxiliary Bishop of Fresno, Jan. 7, 1975; ord. Bishop, March 19, 1975; transferred to Diocese of Stockton, Feb. 26, 1980; installed April 17, 1980; appt. Archbishop of Los Angeles, July 16, 1985; installed Sept. 5, 1985; created Cardinal, June 28, 1991; Most Revs. JOSEPH J. MADERA, M.Sp.S., D.D., ord. June 15, 1957; consecrated March 4, 1980; succeeded to the See on July 1, 1980; transferred to Archdiocese for the Military Services, Washington, DC May 28, 1991; retired 2004; died Jan. 21, 2017.; JOHN T. STEINBOCK, ord. May 1, 1963; appt. Titular Bishop of Midila and Auxiliary Bishop of Orange May 29, 1984; cons. July 14, 1984; appt. Bishop of Santa Rosa Jan. 27, 1987; appt. Bishop of Fresno Oct. 15, 1991; died Dec. 5, 2010.; ARMANDO X. OCHOA, ord. May 23, 1970; appt. Titular Bishop of Sitifi and Auxiliary of the Archdiocese of Los Angeles Dec. 29, 1986; ord. Bishop Feb. 23, 1987; appt. Bishop of El Paso April 1, 1996; installed June 26, 1996; appt. Bishop of Fresno Dec. 1, 2011; installed Feb. 2, 2012; retired March 5, 2019.

Chancery Office—1550 N. Fresno St., Fresno, 93703-3788. Tel: 559-488-7400; Fax: 559-488-7464; Web: www.dioceseoffresno.org.

Office of the Bishop—Most Rev. JOSEPH V. BRENNAN.

Executive Assistant—MARY CARDONA, Email: mcardona@dioceseoffresno.org.

Vicar General/Moderator of the Curia—Rev. Msgr. RAYMOND C. DREILING, V.G., Email: rcdreiling@dioceseoffresno.org.

Executive Assistant—CHERYL SARKISIAN, Email: csarkisian@dioceseoffresno.org.

Chancellor—TERESA DOMINGUEZ, Email: tdominguez@dioceseoffresno.org.

Monsignor James Culleton Archives—Tel: 559-488-7499; Email: archives@dioceseoffresno.org. TERESA DOMINGUEZ, Archivist; KIM O'CONNOR, Co Archivist/Administrative Asst. Assistant Archivists: MR. SCOTT ALSTON; MRS. ADRIENNE ALSTON.

Office Assistants—ESTHER CANTU, Email: ecantu@dioceseoffresno.org; ELY GUILLERMO, Email: eguillermo@dioceseoffresno.org.

Office of the Vicar General—Rev. Msgr. RAYMOND C. DREILING, V.G.; CHERYL SARKISIAN, Exec. Asst.

Continuing Formation of Clergy—Rev. ROBERT B. BORGES, Coord.

Clergy and Religious Legal Immigration and Spanish Translations—YONI HEPINGER, Coord., Tel: 559-488-7413; Email: yhepinger@dioceseoffresno.org.

Pontifical Mission Societies - Mission Office—ANNA BOTELLO, Tel: 559-493-2855, Ext. 104; Email: abotello@dioceseoffresno.org.

Office of Canonical Services/Marriage Tribunal—Tel: 559-488-7490. Rev. JESUS DEL ANGEL, J.C.L., Adjutant Judicial Vicar.

Judicial Vicar—VACANT.

Promoter of Justice—Rev. JESUS DEL ANGEL, J.C.L.

Ecclesiastical Notaries—Rev. Msgr. PERRY KAVOOKJIAN, V.F.; HORTENSIA RUBIO; ESTELA MANZANO; SONJA OLGUIN; LORENA MAGDALENO.

Defenders of the Bond—Rev. Msgr. MICHAEL BRAUN; Rev. JESUS DEL ANGEL, J.C.L.; Rev. Msgr. PATRICK JOSEPH MCCORMICK, V.F.

Advocates—Rev. Msgrs. JOHN ESQUIVEL, V.F.; STEPHEN A. FROST, J.C.L.; JOHN GRIESBACH; PERRY KAVOOKJIAN, V.F.; ROBERT D. WENZINGER.

Office of Catholic Education—1550 N. Fresno St., Fresno, 93703-3711. Tel: 559-488-7420; Fax: 559-488-7422; Email: sfarley@dioceseoffresno.org.

Superintendent—MONA FAULKNER, Email: mfaulkner@dioceseoffresno.org.

Assistant Superintendent—DONNA SMITH, Tel: 661-332-6954; Email: dsmithocedof@gmail.com.

Office of Child and Youth Protection—Rev. Msgr. RAYMOND C. DREILING, V.G., Dir.

Safe Environment—BIANCA BLANCHETTE, Coord., Tel: 559-493-2882; Email: bblanchette@dioceseoffresno.org.

Victim Assistance—CHERYL SARKISIAN, Coord., Tel: 559-488-7409; Email: csarkisian@dioceseoffresno.org.

Office of Communications—TERESA DOMINGUEZ, Chancellor/Dir., Tel: 559-493-2850; Email: tdominguez@dioceseoffresno.org.

Central California Catholic Life (CCCL)—Tel: 559-488-7440; Fax: 559-488-7444. Editors: Sr. ROSALIE ROHRER, I.H.M.; RUDY LUNA.

Diocesan Television Station - KNXT 49.1—Tel: 559-488-7440; Fax: 559-488-7444.

Web Services—CLAUDE A. MUNCEY, Webmaster - Main Site; RUDY LUNA, Co Webmaster KNXT 49.1, WWW.KNXT.TV 24/7 Live Streaming.

Office of Finance and Administration—GARY BETHKE, CPA, Dir. & CFO, Tel: 559-488-7426; Fax: 559-488-7461; Email: gbethke@dioceseoffresno.org.

Accounting—Tel: 559-488-7431; Fax: 559-488-7461. CYNTHIA MARTIN, CPA, C.D.F.M., Controller, Email: cmartin@dioceseoffresno.org.

Employee Benefits—CHARLES DE LA CERDA, Mgr., Tel: 559-488-7428; Fax: 559-488-7463; Email: cdelacerda@dioceseoffresno.org.

Insurance and Risk Management—DENISE MCKENZIE, Mgr., Tel: 559-488-7473; Fax: 559-488-7479; Email: dmckenzie@dioceseoffresno.org.

Parish Financial Reporting—GERRIE LENN PIMENTEL, CPA, C.D.F.M., Dir., Tel: 559-488-7472; Fax: 559-493-2876; Email: gpimentel@dioceseoffresno.org.

Cemeteries—MR. CARLOS RASCON, Dir., Tel: 559-488-7459; Fax: 559-488-7485; Email: cemeteries@dioceseoffresno.org.

Property/Construction—DOUGLAS DURIVAGE, Mgr., Tel: 559-493-2872; Fax: 559-493-2875; Email: ddurivage@dioceseoffresno.org.

Pastoral Center Facilities—THOMAS FORSE, Mgr., Tel: 559-488-7471; Fax: 559-488-7479; Email: tforse@dioceseoffresno.org.

Office of Formation and Evangelization—ROSE M. HERNANDEZ, Dir., Tel: 559-488-7474; Fax: 559-493-2847; Email: rhernandez@dioceseoffresno.org.

Bilingual Media Center—GLORIA GARIBAY, Tel: 559-488-7474; Fax: 559-493-2847; Email: ggaribay@dioceseoffresno.org.

Catechetical Ministry—ROMAN FLORES, Coord., Email: rflores@dioceseoffresno.org.

Family Life Ministry—Sr. JOANNE BAUER, C.S.C., Coord., Email: jbauer@dioceseoffresno.org.

Hispanic Ministry—BENITO MEDRANO, Coord., Email: bmedrano@dioceseoffresno.org.

School of Ministry—LINDA RAM, Coord., Email: lram@dioceseoffresno.org.

Catholic Committee for Scouting—Tel: 559-897-5953; Fax: 559-897-8599. Rev. GREGORY J. BEAUMONT, Chair.

Youth & Young Adult Ministry—KATRINA FLORES, Coord., Email: kflores@dioceseoffresno.org.

Multicultural/Multilingual Collaborators—African-American Catholic Ministry Hmong Ministry Lahu Ministry - Visalia Lao/Kmhmu Ministry-Fresno Native American Ministry-Fresno

Italian Catholic Federation—ROBYN PIRO, Pres.

Office of Human Resources—RALPH S. JIMENEZ, Dir., Tel: 559-488-7488; Fax: 559-488-7461; Email: rjimenez@dioceseoffresno.org.

Office of Pastoral Services—Rev. Msgr. RAYMOND C. DREILING, V.G., Dir.

Hospital Chaplains—Rev. Msgr. RAYMOND C. DREILING, V.G., Dir. Fresno Area Coord. Chaplains: Revs. CHIKA KAMALU; ABRAHAM KOMBO; EMMANUEL OGBONNAYA.

Health Ministries and Faith Community Nursing—ROXANNA STEVENS, Coord.; PILAR DE LA CRUZ, R.N., Coord., Tel: 559-593-9757; Email: roxanna@dioceseoffresno.org.

Office of Social Justice Ministry/Restorative Justice—JIM GRANT, Dir., Tel: 559-488-7463; Email: jgrant@dioceseoffresno.org.

Office of Stewardship—Tel: 559-488-7414; Fax: 559-493-2880. DEBBIE JAMES, Administrative Asst., Email: djames@dioceseoffresno.org.

Office of Vocations and Consecrated Life—

Permanent Diaconate—Deacon JOHN SOUSA, Dir., Tel: 559-493-2840; Fax: 559-493-2886; Email: jsousa@dioceseoffresno.org.

Vocations to the Priesthood—Rev. DANIEL AVILA, Dir., Tel: 559-488-7424; Fax: 559-488-7475; Email: vocations@dioceseoffresno.org.

Women Religious—Sr. INVENCION CANAS, R.A.D., Liaison, Tel: 559-488-7400; Fax: 559-488-7464.

Office of Worship and Christian Initiation—Rev. Msgr. PATRICK JOSEPH MCCORMICK, V.F., Dir./Master of Ceremonies, Tel: 559-434-7701; Fax: 559-434-7734.

Diocesan Retreat Centers—

St. Anthony Retreat Center—Rev. Msgr. JOHN GRIESBACH, Dir., Tel: 559-561-4595; Fax: 559-561-4493; Email: fatherjohn@stanthonyretreat.org.

Santa Teresita Youth Conference Center—CRISTAL JUAREZ, Dir., Tel: 559-561-1038; Fax: 559-561-1039; Email: cristal@stteresitayycc.org.

ORGANIZATIONS AND MISCELLANEOUS

Catholic Charities—149 N. Fulton, Fresno, 93701.

Cursillo Movement - English—Deacon LEONARD RODRIGUEZ.

Fresno Traditional Latin Mass Society—Rev. JOSE ZEPEDA, F.S.S.P.

Legion of Mary—CARLOS DEL POZO, Pres.

Newman Apostolate—Deacon JOHN SUPINO, Parish Life Coord./Admin., St. Paul Catholic Newman Ctr.

Ecumenical and Inter-Religious Affairs—Rev. GREGORY J. BEAUMONT, Dir., Tel: 559-897-5953; Fax: 559-897-8599.

DIOCESAN COUNCILS, BOARDS AND COMMITTEES

College of Consultors—Most Rev. ARMANDO XAVIER OCHOA, D.D.; Rev. DANIEL AVILA; Rev. Msgr. RAYMOND C. DREILING, V.G.; Rev. ROBERT B. BORGES; Rev. Msgr. RONALD SWETT, (Retired); Rev. EFRAIN MARTINEZ; Rev. Msgr. RICHARD URIZALQUI, V.F.; Rev. IVAN HERNANDEZ.

Vicars Forane—Rev. JOHN BRUNO, R.C.J., V.F.; Rev. Msgrs. HARVEY FONSECA, V.F.; PATRICK JOSEPH MCCORMICK, V.F.; Revs. LOJI PILONES, V.F.; KRIS SORENSON, V.F.; Rev. Msgr. RICHARD URIZALQUI, V.F.; Revs. JOHN WARBURTON, O.S.J., V.F.; SALVADOR GONZALEZ JR., V.F.

Priests' Council—Most Rev. ARMANDO XAVIER OCHOA, D.D.; Rev. Msgr. RAYMOND C. DREILING, V.G.; Revs. DANIEL AVILA; ROBERT B. BORGES; JOHN BRUNO, R.C.J., V.F.; Rev. Msgrs. HARVEY FONSECA, V.F.; PERRY KAVOOKJIAN, V.F.; PATRICK JOSEPH MCCORMICK, V.F.; Rev. KRIS SORENSON, V.F.; Rev. Msgr. RICHARD URIZALQUI, V.F.; Rev. JOHN WARBURTON, O.S.J., V.F.; Rev. Msgr. JOHN COELHO-HARGUINDEGUY, (Retired); Rev. MICHAEL COX; Rev. Msgr. SCOTT DAUGHERTY; Revs. JOHN P. FLUETSCH; JEAN-MICHAEL LASTIRI; EFRAIN MARTINEZ; Deacon JOHN SOUSA; Revs. LOJI PILONES, V.F.; SALVADOR GONZALEZ JR., V.F.

Personnel Board—Most Rev. ARMANDO XAVIER OCHOA, D.D.; Revs. ALFREDO ARIAS, V.F.; JOHN BRUNO, R.C.J., V.F.; Rev. Msgrs. RAYMOND C. DREILING, V.G.; HARVEY FONSECA, V.F.; JOHN GRIESBACH; PATRICK JOSEPH MCCORMICK, V.F.; Revs. LOJI PILONES, V.F.; KRIS SORENSON, V.F.; Rev. Msgrs. RONALD SWETT, (Retired); RICHARD URIZALQUI, V.F.; Revs. JOHN WARBURTON, O.S.J., V.F.; SALVADOR GONZALEZ JR., V.F.; IVAN HERNANDEZ-MELCHOR.

Diocesan Finance Committee—Most Rev. ARMANDO XAVIER OCHOA, D.D.; Rev. Msgr. RAYMOND C. DREILING, V.G.; GARY BETHKE, CPA, CFO; Rev. ROBERT B. BORGES; Rev. Msgr. MICHAEL BRAUN; ROSEMARY MCCAVE; GARY RENNER; JOSEPH ZIEMANN.

Our Faith, Our Family, Our Future Foundation, Inc.—Most Rev. ARMANDO XAVIER OCHOA, D.D.; Rev. Msgr. RAYMOND C. DREILING, V.G., Pres.; GARY BETHKE, CPA, Treas. & CFO; Rev. ROBERT B. BORGES; Rev. Msgrs. MICHAEL BRAUN; PATRICK JOSEPH MCCORMICK, V.F.; EDWARD PAINE.

Diocesan Review Board—Rev. Msgr. RAYMOND C. DREILING, V.G.; BRENDA FEEHAN; ZETTA A. HADDEN, L.C.S.W.; RALPH S. JIMENEZ, Dir. , Human Resources; MICHAEL S. MOSIER; DAVID RODRIGUEZ; CHERYL SARKISIAN, Ex Officio.

Catholic Charities Board of Directors—Most Rev. ARMANDO XAVIER OCHOA, D.D., Pres.; Rev. Msgr. RAYMOND C. DREILING, V.G., Episcopal Delegate; MR. JEFF NEGRETE, Dir.; JOHN FERNANDII, Chair; BILL LAZZERINI JR., Vice Chair; SUSIE KUSZMAR, Sec.; FRANK HAMBALEK JR., Treas.; Rev. Msgr. PATRICK JOSEPH MCCORMICK, V.F.; MARTY B. OLLER IV; BRUCE BATTI; BREE COMSTOCK; RYAN DONAGHY; Rev. JOHN P. FLUETSCH; CHUCK KASSIS; STEVEN SPENCER.

CLERGY, PARISHES, MISSIONS AND PAROCHIAL SCHOOLS

CITY OF FRESNO

(FRESNO COUNTY)

1—ST. JOHN'S CATHEDRAL (1882)
2814 Mariposa St., 93721. Tel: 559-485-6210; Email: stjohnscathedral@sbcglobal.net; Web: www.stjohnsfresno.org. Revs. Alex Chavez, Rector; Gonzalo Ramirez, Parochial Vicar.
Catechesis Religious Program—2811 Mariposa Street, 93721. Tel: 559-485-0161. Arcelia Cisneros, D.R.E. Students 647.

2—ST. ALPHONSUS (1908)
351 E. Kearney Blvd., 93706. Tel: 559-233-8275; Fax: 559-233-9379; Email: stalphonsus_church@yahoo.com. Rev. Dominic Savio Rajappa.
Catechesis Religious Program—Students 64.

3—ST. ANTHONY CLARET (Calwa Area) (1952)
2494 S. Chestnut Ave., 93725. Tel: 559-255-4260; Fax: 559-255-4264; Email: Sacbulletin@yahoo.com; Web: stanthonyclaretchurch.org. Revs. Brian Culley, C.M.F.; Agustin Carrillo; Patrick Ekong; Mr. Salvador Macias, Youth Min.; Mrs. Fabiola Acosta, Business Mgr.
Catechesis Religious Program—Tel: 559-255-0223. Mr. Alberto Alvarez, D.R.E. Students 603.
Mission—Christ the King, 3565 Calvin St., Malaga, Fresno Co. 93725.

4—ST. ANTHONY OF PADUA (1953)
5770 N. Maroa Ave., 93704-2038. Tel: 559-439-0124; Email: fatherrob@stanthonyfresno.org. Rev. Msgr. Robert D. Wenzinger; Revs. Ferdinand Udeolisa, Parochial Vicar; Regino Quijano, Parochial Vicar; Deacon Edward C. Valdez.
School—St. Anthony of Padua School, (Grades K-8), 5680 N. Maroa Ave., 93704. Tel: 559-435-0700; Fax: 559-435-6749; Web: www.sasfresno.com. Mrs. Jeanette Suter, Prin. Lay Teachers 25; Students 594.
Catechesis Religious Program—Tel: 559-439-0124. Students 589.
Mission—St. Agnes, 111 W. Birch, Pinedale, Fresno Co. 93650-1111. Tel: 559-439-2100; Fax: 559-439-0248.
Holy Cross Chaplaincy—5693 N. Del Mar Ave., 93704.

5—ST. GENEVIEVE (1941) [CEM]
1127 Tulare St., 93706. Tel: 559-486-2988; Email: victordinh@yahoo.com. Rev. Victor T. Dinh.
Catechesis Religious Program—Tel: 559-486-2988; Email: victortoandinh@yahoo.com. Students 25.

6—ST. HELEN (1955)
4875 E. Grant, 93727. Tel: 559-255-3871; Email: office.sthelens@sbcglobal.net. Rev. Genaro C. Demecais.
School—St. Helen School, (Grades K-8), 4888 E. Belmont Ave., 93727. Tel: 559-251-5855; Fax: 559-251-5948; Email: ppeterson@sthelensschool.org; Web: www.sthelensschool.org. Lay Teachers 13; Students 185.
Child Care—Junior Kindergarten, Monica Kay, Dir.
Catechesis Religious Program—4875 E. Grant, 93727. Students 183.

7—HOLY SPIRIT (1981)
355 E. Champlain Dr., 93720-1273.
Tel: 559-434-7701; Fax: 559-434-7734; Email: holyspirit@holyspiritfresno.org; Web: www.holyspiritfresno.org. Rev. Msgr. Patrick Joseph McCormick, V.F.; Linda Fierro, Business Mgr.
Catechesis Religious Program—Tel: 559-434-3522; Email: tafolla4@holyspiritfresno.org. Kate Mallam, D.R.E. Students 528.
Life Teen—Tel: 559-434-7708; Email: mperry@holyspiritfresno.org. Martha Perry, Youth Min.

8—ST. MARY QUEEN OF APOSTLES CATHOLIC CHURCH (1967) [CEM]
4636 W. Dakota, 93722. Tel: 559-275-2022; Fax: 559-275-2040; Email: stmaryfresno@gmail.com. Rev. Timothy N. Cardoso.
Catechesis Religious Program—Mary Eagan, D.R.E. Students 543.

9—OUR LADY OF LA VANG (2009)
4144 N. Millbrook Ave., 73726. Tel: 559-485-9467; Email: victordinh03@netzero.net. Rev. Victor T. Dinh.
Catechesis Religious Program—Email: victortoadinh@yahoo.com. Students 73.

10—OUR LADY OF MT. CARMEL (1955)

816 Pottle Ave., 93707. Tel: 559-264-2587; Email: olmcfresno@gmail.com. Rev. Joaquin S. Arriaga.
Catechesis Religious Program—Students 192.

11—OUR LADY OF VICTORY (1950)
2850 N. Crystal Ave., 93705-3851. Tel: 559-226-1163; Email: office@olvchurch-fresno.com. Rev. Jesus Del Angel, J.C.L.; Deacons Kurt Neuhaus; Nai Her; Cheng Her; Kenny Figueroa, D.R.E.
Church: 2838 N. West Ave., 93705.
School—Our Lady of Victory School, (Grades PreK-8), 1626 W. Princeton Ave., 93705. Tel: 559-229-0205; Fax: 559-229-3230; Email: olvoffice@fresnoolv.org; Web: www.fresnoolv.org. Mrs. Deborah Nettell, Prin. Lay Teachers 9; Students 142.
Catechesis Religious Program—Students 547.

12—ST. PAUL CATHOLIC NEWMAN CENTER (1964)
1572 E. Barstow St., 93710. Tel: 559-436-3434; Fax: 559-436-3430; Email: info@csufnewman.com; Web: www.csufnewman.com. Rev. Paul Keller, Sacramental Min.; Deacons John Supino, Parish Life Coord. & Admin.; Bill Lucido, Pastoral Outreach.
Catechesis Religious Program—Email: skd@csufnewman.com. Sr. Kathleen Drilling, S.S.N.D., D.R.E. Students 316.

13—SACRED HEART (1947)
2140 N. Cedar Ave., 93703. Tel: 559-237-4121; Email: sacredheartfresno@att.net. Rev. Hilary Silva.
Catechesis Religious Program—Fax: 559-237-4121. Students 350.

14—SHRINE OF ST. THERESE (1925)
855 E. Floradora Ave., 93728. Tel: 559-268-6388; Email: info@shrineofsttherese.org. Rev. Msgr. Raymond C. Dreiling, V.G.; Revs. Joseph Govindu, Parochial Vicar; Flordito Redulla, S.V.D.
Catechesis Religious Program—Email: info@shrineofsttherese.org. Students 106.

OUTSIDE THE CITY OF FRESNO

ARVIN, KERN CO., ST. THOMAS THE APOSTLE (1941)
350 E. Bear Mountain Blvd., Arvin, 93203.
Tel: 661-854-6150; Email: dmstthomas@gmail.com; Email: revjuan.maldonado@gmail.com; Email: be1stthomas@gmail.com. Revs. John Schmoll, Obl. O.S.B. Cam., Admin.; Juan Maldonado, Parochial Vicar; Deacon Rogelio Hernandez.
Catechesis Religious Program—Students 555.

ATWATER, MERCED CO., ST. ANTHONY (1909)
1799 Winton Way, Atwater, 95301.
Tel: 209-358-5743; Fax: 209-358-2423; Email: church.office@stanthonyatwater.org. Rev. Paul Kado; Deacons Kelly Canelo; Tony Mendez; Jesus Cisneros.
Res.: 1999 Juniper Ave., Atwater, 95301.
School—St. Anthony School, (Grades PreK-8), 1801 Winton Way, Atwater, 95301. Tel: 209-358-3341; Fax: 209-357-0186; Email: office@stanthonyknights.org; Web: www.stanthonyknights.com. Marianne Flynn, Prin.; Dianne Silva, Librarian. Lay Teachers 10; Students 120.
Child Care—Preschool, Tel: 209-358-3341. Mary Hernandez, Dir.
Catechesis Religious Program—Tel: 209-357-3259. Gloria Torres, D.R.E. Students 880.
Mission—Immaculate Conception, 1799 Winton Way, Atwater, 95301.

AVENAL, KINGS CO., ST. JOSEPH (1941)
500 E. Kern St., Avenal, 93204. Tel: 559-386-9523; Fax: 559-386-1068; Email: st.josephchurchavenal@hotmail.com. 428 E. Kern St., Avenal, 93204. Rev. Santiago Iriarte.
Catechesis Religious Program—Email: cdelarosa59@yahoo.com. Carmen De La Rosa, D.R.E. Students 333.
Mission—St. Cecilia, 800 Milham Ave., Kettleman City, Kings Co. 93239.

BAKERSFIELD, KERN CO.

1—CHRIST THE KING (1952)
1800 Bedford Way, Bakersfield, 93308.
Tel: 661-391-4640; Email: CTK@christtheking.ws; Web: christtheking.ws. Rev. Msgr. Stephen A. Frost, J.C.L.; Deacons Daniel Rindge; Joe Parugrug.
Catechesis Religious Program—Tel: 661-399-1956. Students 105.

2—ST. ELIZABETH ANN SETON
12300 Reina Rd., Bakersfield, 93312-6799.
Tel: 661-587-3626. Rev. Msgr. Perry Kavookjian, V.F.; Deacons David Rodriguez; Michael Richard.
Catechesis Religious Program—Email: lizneuman@setoncatholicchurch.org; Email: mpruett@setoncatholicchurch.org; Email: deaconmike@setoncatholicchurch.org. Mrs. Elizabeth Neuman, D.R.E.; Mrs. Megan Pruett, Youth Min. Students 601.

3—ST. FRANCIS OF ASSISI (1881)
900 H St., Bakersfield, 93304. Tel: 661-327-4734; Email: jetcheverry@stfran.org. Rev. Msgr. Craig F. Harrison; Rev. Rodolfo Esmero-Carcueva, Parochial Vicar.
School—St. Francis Parish School, (Grades PreK-8), 2516 Palm St., Bakersfield, 93304. Tel: 661-326-7955; Fax: 661-327-0395; Email: info@stfrancisparishschool.com; Web: stfran.org. Kelli Gruszka, Prin.; Mary Samson, Librarian. Lay Teachers 33; Students 406.
Child Care—Day Care/Preschool, Tel: 661-326-7958. Kelly Baker, Dir. Students 95.
Catechesis Religious Program—2424 Palm St., Bakersfield, 93304. Tel: 661-323-8800; Fax: 661-323-1445. Students 709.

4—ST. JOSEPH (1907)
1515 Baker St, Bakersfield, 93305.
Tel: 661-327-2744; Email: saintjosephbakersfield@gmail; Web: stjosephbak.wixsite.com. Revs. Miguel Flores, J.C.L.; Joseph Baca, Vicar.
Catechesis Religious Program—Students 700.

5—OUR LADY OF PERPETUAL HELP (1948)
124 Columbus St., Bakersfield, 93305.
Tel: 661-323-3108; Fax: 661-325-7067; Email: office@olphbakersfield.org; Web: www.olphbakersfield.org. Rev. Hector Lopez.
School—Our Lady of Perpetual Help School, (Grades PreK-8), Tel: 661-327-7741; Email: kmichaudolph@gmail.com; Web: www.olph1.org. Kelli Michaud, Prin. Lay Teachers 25; Students 350.
Catechesis Religious Program—
Tel: 661-323-3108, Ext. 2. Alvaro Romero, D.R.E. Students 158.

6—ST. PHILIP THE APOSTLE (1968)
Mailing Address: 7100 Stockdale Hwy., Bakersfield, 93309-1399. Tel: 661-834-7483; Fax: 661-834-2214; Email: info@stphilipchurch.org; Web: stphilipchurch.org. Revs. Salvador Gonzalez Jr., V.F.; Ignacio Villafan, Parochial Vicar; Breana Benavidez, Youth Min.; Desiree Joseph, ERE Coord.; Barbara Lomas, Business Mgr.; Javier Valenzuela, Music Min.
Child Care—Preschool, Mrs. Karen Cerri, PreSchool Dir.
Catechesis Religious Program—Alvaro Romero, Dir. Formation & Liturgy. Students 771.

7—SACRED HEART (1952)
9915 Ramos St., Bakersfield, 93307.
Tel: 661-831-8905; Email: sacheartbks@gmail.com. Rev. David Enriquez, V.F.
Catechesis Religious Program—Tel: 661-831-6223; Fax: 661-837-8073. Students 220.

8—SAN CLEMENTE MISSION PARISH
1305 Water St., Bakersfield, Kern Co. 93305.
Tel: 661-871-9190; Fax: 661-873-7286; Email: sanclementemission@gmail.com. Rev. Joachim Cheon.
Catechesis Religious Program—Students 147.

9—SHRINE OF OUR LADY OF GUADALUPE, CO-PATRONESS OF THE UNBORN (1925)
601 E. California Ave., Bakersfield, 93307.
Tel: 661-323-3148, Ext. 202; Email: monica@guadalupebakersfield.org. Revs. Larry Toschi, O.S.J.; Chummar Chirayath, O.S.J.; Steve Peterson, O.S.J., Parochial Vicar; Carlos Esquivel, O.S.J., Parochial Vicar
Legal Name: Shrine of Our Lady of Guadalupe, Co-Patroness of the Unborn
Worship Site, 4600 E. Brundage Ln., Bakersfield, 93307.
School—Our Lady of Guadalupe School, (Grades PreK-8), 609 E. California Ave., Bakersfield, 93307.
Tel: 661-323-6059; Email: olgs@olgsjs.org; Web: www.olgsjs.org. Sr. Susana Del Toro, S.J.S., Prin. Clergy 4; Lay Teachers 12; Sisters 4; Students 184; Parish / Independent 1.
Catechesis Religious Program—Tel: 661-323-7642. Aida Nunez, D.R.E. Students 1,052.
Missions—Holy Spirit—720 E. Belle Terrace, Bakersfield, Kern Co. 93307.
St. Jude, 825 Chapman, Bakersfield, Kern Co. 93307.

BISHOP, INYO CO., OUR LADY OF PERPETUAL HELP (1947)
849 N. Home St., Bishop, 93514. Tel: 760-872-7231; Fax: 760-873-8862; Email: olphsec@suddenlinkmail.com. Rev. John Gracey.
Catechesis Religious Program—Tel: 760-873-8862; Email: mike.olph@suddenlinkmail.com. Students 120.
Mission—St. Stephen, 461 S. Main St., Big Pine, Inyo Co. 93513.

BUTTONWILLOW, KERN CO., ST. MARY (1941)
420 N. Main St., Buttonwillow, 93206.
Tel: 661-764-5486; Email: stmarybw@gmail.com. Rev. Carlos Serrano.
Catechesis Religious Program—Students 75.

CALIFORNIA CITY, KERN CO., OUR LADY OF LOURDES (1982)
Mailing Address: P.O. Box 2060, California City, 93504. Tel: 760-373-2256; Fax: 760-373-2206; Email: ollcalcity@verizon.net. 9970 California City Bvd, California City, 93505. Revs. Kris Sorenson, V.F.; Balaswamy Gangarapu, Sacramental Priest; Deacon Clyde Davis, Marriage Facilitator.
Catechesis Religious Program—Pam Jakobsen, D.R.E. Students 81.
Mission—St. Joseph (1969) 12430 Boron Ave., Boron, 93516.

CHOWCHILLA, MADERA CO., ST. COLUMBA (1921) [JC]
213 Orange Ave., Chowchilla, 93610.
Tel: 559-665-3376; Email: st_columba@sbcglobal.net. Rev. Angel Sotelo.
Catechesis Religious Program—Tel: 559-665-5104. Students 410.
Mission—St. George, 10760 South HWY 59, El Nido, 95317.

CLOVIS, FRESNO CO.

1—DIVINE MERCY CATHOLIC CHURCH (2016)
2525 Alluvial Ave. Ste. 271, Clovis, 93611.
Tel: 559-374-2242; Fax: 559-294-5906; Email: lquintana@divinemercyclovis.org; Web: www.divinemercyclovis.org. Rev. Craig Plunkett, Admin.; Lisa Quintana, Parish Operations.

2—OUR LADY OF PERPETUAL HELP (1929)
929 Harvard, Clovis, 93612. Tel: 559-299-4270; Fax: 559-299-7126; Email: office@olphclovis.org; Web: olphclovis.org. Revs. Robert B. Borges; Athanasius Okure, Parochial Vicar; Deacons Gary Stevens; Horacio Corchado; Ricardo DeLeon.
Church: Ninth & DeWitt, Clovis, 93612.
School—Our Lady of Perpetual Help School, (Grades PreSchool-8), 836 DeWitt, Clovis, 93612.
Tel: 559-299-7504; Fax: 559-299-4627; Email: pdodd@olphschool.net; Web: olphschool.net. Patrick Dodd, Prin. Lay Teachers 12; Students 322.
Catechesis Religious Program—(Grades K-8), Email: kmentlewski@hotmail.com. Karen Mentlewski, D.R.E. Students 690.

COALINGA, FRESNO CO., ST. PAUL THE APOSTLE (1907) [JC]
637 Sunset St., P.O. Box 812, Coalinga, 93210.
Tel: 559-935-1872; Fax: 559-935-3763; Email: st.paulcoalinga@att.net. Rev. Viktor Perez, O.F.M.-Conv.; Bro. Andres Amador, O.F.M.Conv.
Catechesis Religious Program—Students 112.

CORCORAN, KINGS CO., OUR LADY OF LOURDES (1939)
1404 Hanna Ave., Corcoran, 93212.
Tel: 559-992-4414; Email: ourladyoflourdescorcoran@comcast.net. Rev. Alfredo Arias, V.F.
Catechesis Religious Program—Students 504.
Mission—Sacred Heart, 3860 Ave. 54, Alpaugh, Tulare Co. 93201. Tel: 559-949-8352.

CUTLER, TULARE CO., ST. MARY aka Santa Maria (1953)
12588 Ave. 407, Cutler, 93615. Tel: 559-590-5552; Email: stmarycutler@att.net. Rev. Juan Garcia.
Catechesis Religious Program—Students 391.

DEL REY, FRESNO CO., ST. KATHERINE (1956) (Quasi-parish included with St. Mary, Sanger).
828 "O" St., P.O. Box 335, Sanger, 93657.
Tel: 559-875-2025; Email: stmarysanger@verizon.net. Revs. John Bruno, R.C.J., V.F.; Devassy Painlasigui.
Catechesis Religious Program—Students 27.

DELANO, KERN CO.

1—ST. MARY OF THE MIRACULOUS MEDAL (1920)
916 Lexington St., Delano, 93215. Tel: 661-725-8456; Email: st.marydelanochurch@gmail.com. Rev. Loji Pilones, V.F.
Catechesis Religious Program—Tel: 661-721-2921. Nellie Sierra, D.R.E. Students 425.
Mission—St. Vincent, 500 Richgrove Dr., Delano, 93215. Alicia Cantutay, Contact Person.

2—OUR LADY OF GUADALUPE (1954)
1015 Clinton St., Delano, 93215.
Tel: 661-725-9087, Ext. 101; Email: guadalupechurchdelano@yahoo.com. Revs. Marlon Gomez, Vicar; Miguel Campos.
Catechesis Religious Program—
Tel: 661-725-9087, Ext. 103; Tel: 661-725-2777. Mrs. Nicolasa Velasco, Sec. Students 609.

DINUBA, TULARE CO., ST. CATHERINE OF SIENA (1948)
356 N. Villa Ave., Dinuba, 93618. Tel: 559-591-0931; Email: stcatherine356@yahoo.com. Rev. Raul Diaz; Mrs. Olivia Aguirre, Business Mgr.
Catechesis Religious Program—Tel: 559-591-2988; Email: laurallrllk@gmail.com. Laura Rico, D.R.E. Students 778.

DOS PALOS, MERCED CO., SACRED HEART (1924)
1655 Lucerne Ave., Dos Palos, 93620.
Tel: 209-392-2724; Fax: 209-392-1037; Email: sacredheartchurch1655@comcast.net. Rev. Anthony Iromenu.
Res.: 1650 Lucerne, Dos Palos, 93620-2623.
Catechesis Religious Program—Students 400.

EARLIMART, TULARE CO., ST. JUDE THADDEUS (1968)
1270 E. Washington Ave., P.O. Box 12187, Earlimart, 93219. Tel: 661-849-3170;
Fax: 661-849-0704; Email: st.judescatholicchurch@yahoo.com. Rev. Raul Silva Arredondo, M.S.C.
Res.: 964 Dove St., Earlimart, 93219.
Catechesis Religious Program—Students 296.

EASTON, FRESNO CO., ST. JUDE AND OUR LADY OF THE ASSUMPTION (1967)
208 W. Jefferson, Easton, 93706. Tel: 559-485-3870;

Fax: 559-485-3880; Email: sjcc@stjude-easton.org; Web: www.stjude-easton.org. Rev. Daniel Avila
Legal Name: Catholic Community of St. Jude and Our Lady of the Assumption
Catechesis Religious Program—Email: eastonstjude@gmail.com. Joseph Hernandez, D.R.E. Students 150.
Mission—Our Lady of the Assumption, Mary Rossotti, Contact Person.
EXETER, TULARE CO., SACRED HEART (1950)
417 North E St., Exeter, 93221. Tel: 559-592-2465; Email: sacredheart.stanthony@gmail.com. Rev. Juan Manuel Flores.
Catechesis Religious Program—Email: SrRosalie@dioceseoffresno.org. Celia Sanchez, D.R.E.; Nora Cortez, Sec. Students 627.
Mission—St. Anthony of Egypt, 521 W. Visalia Rd., Farmersville, Tulare Co. 93223. Tel: 559-747-0234.
FIREBAUGH, FRESNO CO., ST. JOSEPH (1950)
1558 12th St., Firebaugh, 93622. Tel: 559-659-2225; Email: stjosephfirebaugh@gmail.com. Rev. Guillermo Preciado, Admin.
Catechesis Religious Program—Mayra Gauna, D.R.E. Students 272.
FOWLER, FRESNO CO., ST. LUCY (1st Church, 1943; 2nd Church, 1965)
512 S. 5th St., Fowler, 93625.
Tel: 559-834-2624, Ext. 10; Email: stlucy1965@gmail.com; Web: stlucysfowler.org. Rev. Adrian Kim, Admin.
Catechesis Religious Program—Students 504.
FRAZIER PARK, KERN CO., OUR LADY OF THE SNOWS (1968) (Quasi-parish)
7115 Lakewood Dr., Frazier Park, 93225.
Tel: 661-245-3741; Fax: 661-245-1680; Email: olsfrazierpark@gmail.com; Web: www.ourladyofthesnows.net. Rev. Msgr. Craig F. Harrison, Admin.; Rev. Julian Policetti, (India) In Res.
Catechesis Religious Program—Tel: 661-245-2276; Tel: 661-245-3741; Email: bernie@frazmtn.com; Email: olsfrazierpark@gmail.com. Bernice Trojahn, D.R.E. Students 43.
GUSTINE, MERCED CO., SHRINE OF OUR LADY OF MIRACLES (1919)
370 Linden Ave., Gustine, 95322. Tel: 209-854-6692; Email: manunes@prodigy.net. Rev. Leonard J. Trindade.
School—Our Lady of Miracles Catholic School, (Grades PreK-8), Tel: 209-854-3180; Email: office@olmiracles.com; Email: cbrace@olmiracles.com; Web: olmiracles.com. Chandra Brace, Prin. Lay Teachers 7; Students 130.
Child Care—Preschool, Joleen Gomes, Dir. Students 21.
Catechesis Religious Program—Tel: 209-854-2834. Theresa Drumonde, D.R.E. Students 339.
HANFORD, KINGS CO.
1—ST. BRIGID (1886) [CEM]
1001 N. Douty St., Hanford, 93230.
Tel: 559-582-2533; Email: stbrigid@sti.net; Web: www.stbrigid.org. 200 E. Florinda, Hanford, 93230. Revs. Denis Ssekannyo, Admin.; Charles Ugwu, In Res.; Deacon John Sousa.
School—St. Rose-McCarthy Catholic School, (Grades K-8), 1000 N. Harris St., Hanford, 93230.
Tel: 559-584-5218; Email: secretary@strosemccarthy.com; Web: www.strosemccarthy.com. Jamie Perkins, Prin. Clergy 1; Lay Teachers 10; Religious Teachers 1; Students 129.
Catechesis Religious Program—Tel: 559-583-6563; Email: esteladiazm@hotmail.com. Estela Diaz, D.R.E. Students 378.
2—IMMACULATE HEART OF MARY (1948)
10355 Hanford-Armona Rd., Hanford, 93230.
Tel: 559-584-8576; Email: admin@ihmhanford.org; Web: www.ihmhanford.org. 10435 Hanford-Armona Rd., Hanford, 93230. Rev. Jean-Michael Lastiri; Deacons Manuel Lababit; Leonard Rodriguez.
Catechesis Religious Program—Tel: 559-582-5688. Students 186.
HILMAR, MERCED CO., HOLY ROSARY (1948)
8471 Cypress St., P.O. Box 429, Hilmar, 95324.
Tel: 209-667-8961; Email: info@hilmarholyrosary.org. Rev. Michael Moore.
Catechesis Religious Program—Tel: 209-632-7163; Email: Farmboys67@aol.com. Dina Brindeiro, D.R.E. Students 273.
Mission—St. Mary, 2809 Railroad, Stevinson, Merced Co. 95374.
HURON, FRESNO CO., ST. FRANCES CABRINI (1961)
36986 Los Angeles St., P.O. Box 939, Huron, 93234.
Tel: 559-945-2507; Email: s.cabrini@att.net. Revs. Hector Lopez; Juan Antonio Garcia, F.M.M., Parochial Vicar.
Catechesis Religious Program—Students 210.
KERMAN, FRESNO CO., ST. PATRICK (1953)
15437 W. Kearney Blvd., 567 S. 6th St., Kerman, 93630. Tel: 559-846-8190; Fax: 559-846-7705. P.O. Box 375, Kerman, 93630. Revs. Marcelinus Ekenedo, Admin.; John Okeke Agwu, S.M.M.M.
Catechesis Religious Program—Rosa Parra, D.R.E. Students 451.
KINGSBURG, FRESNO CO., HOLY FAMILY (1950) [JC]
1301 Smith St., P.O. Box 798, Kingsburg, 93631-0798. Tel: 559-897-5953; Email: holyfamily.kingsburg@comcast.net. Rev. Gregory J. Beaumont. Church: 1700 Lewis St., Kingsburg, 93631.
Catechesis Religious Program—Tel: 559-897-1520. Yolanda Alvarez, D.R.E. Students 338.
Missions—Santa Cruz—5626 Ave. 378, London, Tulare Co. 93631.
St. John the Baptist Educational Center, 4204 Merritt Dr., Traver, Tulare Co. 93673.
LAMONT, KERN CO., ST. AUGUSTINE (1962)
10601 Myrtle Ave., Lamont, 93241-2111.
Tel: 661-845-0003; Email: fjohndp@att.net. Rev. John Schmoll, Obl. O.S.B. Cam.
Catechesis Religious Program—Tel: 661-845-3622. Students 756.
LATON, FRESNO CO., SHRINE OF OUR LADY OF FATIMA (1953)
20855 S. Fatima Ave., Laton, 93242.
Tel: 559-923-4935. P.O. Box 119, Laton, 93242. Rev. Richard Smith; Deacon Jesus Hernandez.
Catechesis Religious Program—Tel: 559-923-3715. Pat Duarte, D.R.E. Students 181.
LEMOORE, KINGS CO., ST. PETER PRINCE OF APOSTLES (1912)
870 N. Lemoore Ave., Lemoore, 93245.
Tel: 559-924-2562; Fax: 559-924-5727; Email: office@stpeterslemoore.org.
Res.: 951 Murphy Dr., Lemoore, 93245.
School—Mary Immaculate Queen School, (Grades PreK-8), 884 N. Lemoore Ave., Lemoore, 93245.
Tel: 559-924-3424; Fax: 559-924-7848; Web: miqschool.com. ms. Rachael Manzo, Prin. Lay Teachers 13; Students 157.
Catechesis Religious Program—Tel: 661-758-6467. Alicia Gonzalez, D.R.E.; Maggie Morales, D.R.E. Students 313.
Missions—St. Joseph—19300 Empire St., Stratford, 93266.
Santa Rosa, [CEM] 16111 Alkaki, Tache Indian Reservation, Kings Co. 93245.
LINDSAY, TULARE CO., SACRED HEART (1925)
217 Lindero Ave., Lindsay, 93247-2623.
Tel: 559-562-4008; Email: shlindsay1@gmail.com. Rev. Kenneth Bozzo.
Catechesis Religious Program—Students 520.
Missions—St. Anthony Church—21631 Brooks Ave., Tonyville, Tulare Co. 93247.
St. James Catholic Church, 19752 Guthrie Rd., P.O. Box 4010, Strathmore, Tulare Co. 93267.
Tel: 559-568-0435.
Station—Plainview, Santa Cruz, Plainview.
LIVINGSTON, MERCED CO., ST. JUDE THADDEUS (1937)
330 Franci St., Livingston, 95334. Tel: 209-394-7251; Email: stjudethaddeus@frontiernet.net. P.O. Box 77, Livingston, 95334. Rev. Msgr. Harvey Fonseca, V.F.
Catechesis Religious Program—Tel: 209-394-7516. Rosa Maria Mercado, D.R.E. Students 468.
Mission—Saint Teresa of Calcutta, P.O. Box 86, Delhi, Merced Co. 95315.
LONE PINE, INYO CO., SANTA ROSA (1919)
311 E. Locust, Lone Pine, 93545. Tel: 760-876-4350; Email: santarosalonepine@gmail.com. P.O. Box 246, Lone Pine, 93545. Revs. Douglas Walker; Joel Aquino, Parochial Vicar.
Catechesis Religious Program—Students 13.
Missions—St. John the Baptist—Shoshone, 92384.
St. Therese, Tecopa, 92389.
St. Vivian, Independence, Inyo Co.
Stations—Furnace Creek—Death Valley.
Olancha.
LOS BANOS, MERCED CO., ST. JOSEPH (1905)
1621 Center Ave., Los Banos, 93635.
Tel: 209-826-4246; Email: stjosephlb@sbcglobal.net. 1516 Center Ave., Los Banos, 93635. Rev. Efrain Martinez; Deacon Leon Miller.
School—Our Lady of Fatima, (Grades PreK-8), 1625 Center Ave., Los Banos, 93635. Tel: 209-826-2709; Fax: 209-826-7320; Email: kdarnell@olfdof.org; Web: olfdof.org. Mrs. Kendyl Darnell, Prin. Lay Teachers 11; Students 134.
Catechesis Religious Program—Tel: 209-826-1512. Hector Medina, D.R.E. Students 771.
MADERA, MADERA CO., ST. JOACHIM (1881)
401 W. Fifth St., Madera, 93637. Tel: 559-673-3290; Email: church@sjoachim.org; Web: www.sjoachim.org. Revs. John Warburton, O.S.J., V.F.; Gustavo Lopez, O.S.J.; Jacob Shaji Athipozhi, O.S.J., Parochial Vicar; James Catalano, O.S.J.
School—St. Joachim School, (Grades K-8), 310 N. I St., Madera, 93637. Tel: 559-674-7628; Email: school@sjoachim.org. Darlene Lopez, Prin. Clergy 1; Lay Teachers 11; Immaculate Conception Sisters 3; Students 240.
Catechesis Religious Program—Tel: 559-674-5871; Email: ccd@sjoachim.org. Diana Saenz, D.R.E. Students 1,440.
Convent—310 N. "J" St., Madera, 93637.
Tel: 559-674-4085. Sisters of the Immaculate Conception (RCM).
Missions—St. Agnes—7308 Hwy. 145, Madera, Madera Co. 93637.
St. Anne, Raymond-Knowles, Raymond, Madera Co. 93653.
MARIPOSA, MARIPOSA CO., ST. JOSEPH (1863) [CEM 3]
4985 Bullion St., Mariposa, 95338. Tel: 209-966-2522 ; Email: sjccoff@yahoo.com. Mailing Address: P.O. Box 215, Mariposa, 95338. Rev. Michael Cox, Admin.
Catechesis Religious Program—Ms. Diana Terra, D.R.E. Students 15.
Mission—St. Catherine of Siena, Hornitos, Mariposa Co.
MCFARLAND, KERN CO., ST. ELIZABETH (1966)
835 E. Perkins, McFarland, 93250.
Tel: 661-792-3225; Tel: 661-792-3429;
Fax: 661-792-5645; Email: sisabel@msn.com; Email: espi221@yahoo.com. Rev. Antero Sanchez, M.S.C.
Catechesis Religious Program—Tel: 661-792-3429; Email: espi221@yahoo.com. Esperanza Melendez, D.R.E. Students 458.
MENDOTA, FRESNO CO., OUR LADY OF GUADALUPE (1953)
484 Quince St., P.O. Box 248, Mendota, 93640.
Tel: 559-655-4237; Email: ourladyofguadalupe.mendota@gmail.com. Rev. Miguel A. Mancia Calderon.
Catechesis Religious Program—Students 500.
Mission—Our Lady of Lourdes, 16101 S. Derrick, Three Rocks, Fresno Co. 93608. Tel: 559-829-3358.
MERCED, MERCED CO.
1—OUR LADY OF MERCY/ST. PATRICK'S (1867) [JC]
671 E. Yosemite, Merced, 95340. Tel: 209-383-3924; Email: info@olmstpatrick.org. Revs. John P. Fluetsch; Thomas Thippabathini, Parochial Vicar; Deacons Joseph Smith; Charles Reyburn; Jose Morales; Rich Brown.
Res.: 627 West Donna Dr., Merced, 95340. Email: mark@olmstpatrick.org. Mark Lewis, Contact Person.
Our Lady of Mercy (1867) 459 W. 21st St., Merced, 95340.
School—Our Lady of Mercy Elementary, (Grades PreSchool-8), 1400 E. 27th St., Merced, 95340.
Tel: 209-722-7496; Fax: 209-722-7532; Email: info@olmlancers.com; Web: www.olmlancers.com. Mrs. Judy Blackburn, Prin. Lay Teachers 12; Preschool 76; Students 362; K-8 Students 286.
Child Care—Preschool, Tel: 209-722-6657. Mary Kravec, Vice Prin.
Catechesis Religious Program—Tel: 209-723-8888; Fax: 209-723-8888. Debbie Rosa, D.R.E. Students 226.
2—SACRED HEART (1945)
519 W. 12th St., Merced, 95341. Tel: 209-383-6604; Email: sacredheart1merced@sbcglobal.net. Rev. Jose de Jesus Reynaga.
Catechesis Religious Program—Tel: 209-383-1528; Fax: 209-383-0187. Ms. Rocio Maciel, D.R.E. Students 602.
OAKHURST, MADERA CO., OUR LADY OF THE SIERRA (1999)
40180 Indian Springs Rd., Oakhurst, 93644.
Tel: 559-642-3452; Web: olscatholic.org. P.O. Box 2499, Oakhurst, 93644. Rev. Patrick Joel Davadilla Jr.; Deacon Ernie Molloy.
Res.: 49552 Pierce Dr., Oakhurst, 93644.
Tel: 559-642-3452, Ext. 100; Email: monicaodols@gmail.com.
Missions—St. Joseph the Worker—56522 Rd. 200, North Fork, Madera Co. 93643.
St. Dominic Savio (1961) 40077 Rd. 222, Bass Lake, Madera Co. 93604.
ORANGE COVE, FRESNO CO., ST. ISIDORE THE FARMER (1978)
480 Adams Ave., Orange Cove, 93646.
Tel: 559-626-4943; Fax: 559-626-4648; Email: stisidore3802@sbcglobal.net; Web: stisidoreoc.com. Rev. Isaque Meneses.
Catechesis Religious Program—Tel: 559-393-6313. Students 333.
Mission—St. Rita, 30673 George Smith Rd., Squaw Valley, Fresno Co. 93675.
PARLIER, FRESNO CO., OUR LADY OF SORROWS aka Nuestra Señora de Los Dolores (1965)
830 Tulare St., Parlier, 93648. Tel: 559-646-2161; Email: ourladysorrows_church@yahoo.com. Rev. Jose Luis Rico.
Res.: 940 Redwood Ave., Parlier, 93648.
Catechesis Religious Program—Students 302.
PLANADA, MERCED CO., SACRED HEART (1966) [JC]
9317 Amistad St., Planada, 95365. Tel: 209-382-0459 ; Email: sacredheartplanada@sbcglobal.net. Rev. Msgr. Anthony Janelli, (Retired); Deacons Javier Higareda; Higinio Yanez.
Catechesis Religious Program—Students 152.
Mission—Our Lady of Lourdes, 13145 Le Grand Rd., LeGrand, Merced Co. 95333.
PORTERVILLE, TULARE CO., ST. ANNE'S PARISH (1896)
378 N. F St., Porterville, 93257. Tel: 559-784-2800;

Email: information@stannesparish.com; Web: www.stannesparish.com. Rev. Msgr. Scott Daugherty; Rev. Pedro Umana, O.F.M., Vicar; Deacons James Dieterle, RCIA Coord.; John X. Rees; Rev. Michael A. Avila; Deacon Gregorio Echeveste, Pastoral Assoc./ Confirmation Dir.

School—St. Anne School, (Grades PreK-8), 385 N. F St., Porterville, 93257. Tel: 559-784-4096; Fax: 559-784-4188; Email: kaylat@stannesporterville.org. Mrs. Kayla Trueblood, Prin. Clergy 1; Lay Teachers 9; Pre-K Students 34; Sisters of the Love of God 1; Students 183; K-8 Students 149.

Child Care—Preschool, 331 F St., Porterville, 93257. Tel: 559-781-8614. Rhonda Dotters, Dir.

Catechesis Religious Program—Email: stannes@ocsnet.net. Sr. Maria Eugenia Guzman, D.R.E. Students 1,199.

Missions—Mater Dolorosa—Tule Indian Reservation, Tulare Co.. Tel: 559-784-2800.

Blessed Miguel Agustin Pro, 9120 Rd. 236, Terra Bella, Tulare Co. 93270.

St. Maximillian Kolbe, 35725 Hwy. 190, Springville, 93265.

REEDLEY, FRESNO CO., ST. ANTHONY OF PADUA (1906)
1060 F. St., Reedley, 93654. Tel: 559-638-2012; Email: stanthonychurch_reedley@comcast.net; Web: stanthonychurch-reedley.org. P.O. Box 188, Reedley, 93654. Rev. Msgr. John Esquivel, V.F.; Rev. Edwin Pena.

School—St. La Salle Grammar School, (Grades PreK-8), 404 E. Manning Ave., Reedley, 93654. Tel: 559-638-2621; Tel: 559-637-1446; Email: hannibalmarylucy@yahoo.com. Sisters Lucy Cassarino, F.D.Z., Prin., Preschool & Grammar School; Mary Lilly, Librarian. Clergy 2; Lay Teachers 13; Sisters 3; Students 299.

Child Care—LaSalle Preschool / Child Care Center, Tel: 559-638-2621; Fax: 559-638-5542; Email: hannibalmarylucy@yahoo.com; Web: www.stlasalle.org.

Catechesis Religious Program—Tel: 559-638-5608; Email: karen@stanthonyreedley-religed.org. Students 786.

RIDGECREST, KERN CO., ST. ANN (1965) [JC]
446 W. Church Ave., Ridgecrest, 93555. Tel: 760-375-2110, Ext. 0; Email: office@parishofsaintann.org; Web: parishofsaintann.org. P.O. Box 127, Ridgecrest, 93556. Rev. Rayanna Pudota, Admin.

School—St. Ann School, (Grades K-8), Tel: 760-375-4713; Email: principal@parishofsaintann.org; Email: school@parishofsaintann.org; Web: www.school.parishofsaintann.org. Mrs. Alicia Conliffe, Prin. Lay Teachers 13; Students 136.

Catechesis Religious Program— Tel: 760-375-2110, Ext. 313 & 305; Email: ccd@parishofsaintann.org; Email: Youth@parishofsaintann.org. Jeannine McReynolds, D.R.E.; Mrs. Jessica Fine, Youth Min. Students 117.

Mission—Santa Barbara, 72 Lexington Ave., Randsburg, Kern Co. 93554.

RIVERDALE, FRESNO CO., ST. ANN (1928) [JC]
3047 W. Mt. Whitney, P.O. Box 335, Riverdale, 93656. Tel: 559-867-3035. Rev. Michael Andrade, Admin.

Catechesis Religious Program—Email: stannriverdale@yahoo.com. Students 196.

Mission—Holy Family Chapel, c/o St. Ann, Riverdale Ca. 93656, Diener Ranch At Five Points, Fresno Co.

ROSAMOND, KERN CO., ST. MARY OF THE DESERT (1999)
Mailing Address: 3100 Fifteenth St. W., P.O. Box 1359, Rosamond, 93560. Tel: 661-256-4505; Fax: 661-338-9673; Email: st.mary3100@att.net. Revs. Kris Sorenson, V.F., Admin.; Balaswamy Gangarapu, Sacramental Min.

Catechesis Religious Program—Students 103.

Mission—St. Francis of Assisi Church, 15382 Meyer Rd., Mojave, 93501.

SANGER, FRESNO CO., ST. MARY (1922) [JC]
828 O St., P.O. Box 335, Sanger, 93657. Tel: 559-875-2025; Email: stmarysanger@verizon.net. Revs. John Bruno, R.C.J., V.F.; Devassy Painadath, R.C.J.

Catechesis Religious Program—2590 North Ave., Sanger, 93657. Students 530.

SELMA, FRESNO CO., ST. JOSEPH (1913)
2441 Dockery Ave., Selma, 93662. Tel: 559-896-1052; Email: stjosephchurchsecretary@gmail.com. Rev. Guadalupe Rios; Deacon Ed Harmon III, (Retired).

Catechesis Religious Program—Tel: 559-896-2620. Students 621.

SHAFTER, KERN CO., ST. THERESE (1952)
300 W. Lerdo, Shafter, 93263. Tel: 661-746-4471; Fax: 661-746-0945; Email: sainttherese1952@yahoo.com. Rev. Walter Colocho.

Catechesis Religious Program—Students 240.

TAFT, KERN CO., ST. MARY (1918) (Hispanic)
110 E. Woodrow St., Taft, 93268. Tel: 661-765-4292; Email: stmarystaft@gmail.com. Rev. Carlos Serrano.

Catechesis Religious Program—Students 63.

TEHACHAPI, KERN CO., ST. MALACHY (1887)
407 W. "E" St., Tehachapi, 93561-1642. Tel: 661-822-3060; Email: mcastillo@saintmalachy.church; Web: www.saintmalachy.church. Rev. Mark Maxon.

Catechesis Religious Program—Email: jcorral@saintmalachy.church. Juana Corral, D.R.E. Students 193.

TIPTON, TULARE CO., ST. JOHN THE EVANGELIST (1945)
232 S. Adams Rd., Tipton, 93272. Tel: 559-752-4544; Email: stjohnevangelisttipton@gmail.com. Rev. Jorge Robles Cuevas.

Catechesis Religious Program—Patricia Palomera, D.R.E. Students 500.

Mission—St. Francis of Assisi, 16410 Ave. 168, Woodville, Tulare Co. 93258.

Station—Our Lady of the Assumption, Pixley.

TRANQUILLITY, FRESNO CO., ST. PAUL (1924)
Res.: P.O. Box 575, Tranquillity, 93668. Tel: 559-698-7429; Fax: 559-698-1059.

Catechesis Religious Program—Tel: 559-693-4320. Students 201.

Mission—St. Vincent de Paul, San Joaquin, Fresno Co.

TULARE, TULARE CO.

1—ST. ALOYSIUS (1905)
125 E. Pleasant Ave., Tulare, 93274. Tel: 559-688-1796; Email: dmgtrans@hotmail.com. Rev. Msgr. Richard Urizalqui, V.F.

School—St. Aloysius School, (Grades K-8), 627 Beatrice, Tulare, 93274. Tel: 559-686-6250; Email: lsozinho@sastulare.net. Mrs. Luan Sozinho, Prin. Lay Teachers 10; Students 205.

Catechesis Religious Program—Tel: 559-688-8644. Students 435.

2—ST. RITA (1967)
954 S. O St., Tulare, 93274. Tel: 559-686-3847; Email: Ivan@stritacatholicchurch.com; Web: www.stritacatholicchurch.com. Rev. Ivan Hernandez-Melchor.

Catechesis Religious Program—Tel: 559-686-0802; Email: Benita@stritacatholicchurch.com. Sr. Benita, D.R.E. Students 1,071.

VISALIA, TULARE CO.

1—GOOD SHEPHERD CATHOLIC PARISH (2016)
506 N. Garden St., Visalia, 93291. Tel: 559-734-9522; Email: rparlier@gscparish.org; Web: www.gscparish.com. Revs. Eric Swearingen, V.U.; Victor Hernando; Cesar Solorio, Parochial Vicar; Rev. Msgr. John Coelho-Harguindeguy, In Res., (Retired); Revs. Henry Aguwa, In Res.; Jose Luis Varo, In Res., (Retired).

Holy Family Church— (1950) 1908 N. Court St., Visalia, 93291.

St. Charles Borromeo (2011) 5049 W. Caldwell Ave., Visalia, 93277.

St. Thomas the Apostle (1963) 6735 Ave. 308, Goshen, 93227.

The Nativity of the Blessed Virgin Mary Church (1861) 608 N. Church St., Visalia, 93291. Consolidated under the parish name of Good Shepherd Catholic Parish, Visalia, CA.

Catechesis Religious Program—Email: mverduzco@gscparish.org. Marlon Verduzco, D.R.E. Students 1,442.

2—HOLY FAMILY (1950) Merged with St. Charles Borromeo, Visalia; St. Thomas the Apostle, Goshen & The Nativity of the Blessed Virgin Mary, Visalia to form Good Shepherd Catholic Parish, Visalia.

3—ST. MARY (1861)
608 N. Church St., Visalia, 93291. Tel: 559-734-9522; Fax: 559-734-3435; Web: tccov.org. Revs. Eric Swearingen, V.U.; Cesar Solorio; Victor Hernando; Deacons Ken Ramage; Rick Miller; Doug Pingel; Henry Medina; Paul Hernandez; Julian Ponce; James Rooney; Charles Culbreth, Dir., Music.
Res.: 1908 N. Court St., Visalia, 93291.

School—The Catholic School of Visalia, George McCann Memorial Campus, (Grades PreK-8), 200 E. Race St., Visalia, 93291. Tel: 559-732-5831; Fax: 559-741-1562; Email: srast@ccsvgmc.org. Sheila Rast, Prin. Lay Teachers 12; Students 197.

Catechesis Religious Program—

Bethlehem Center— (1968) 1638 N. Dinuba Blvd., Visalia, 93291. Tel: 559-734-1572; Fax: 559-734-4921. Benjamin Rodriguez, Dir.

WASCO, KERN CO., ST. JOHN THE EVANGELIST (1913)
1129 9th St., Wasco, 93280. Tel: 661-758-6688. Rev. Raul Sanchez-Flores.
Res.: 1300 Ninth Pl., Wasco, 93280.

Catechesis Religious Program— (Family Catechesis) Tel: 661-758-6467. Alicia Gonzalez, D.R.E.; Maggie Morales, D.R.E. Students 121.

Mission—Nuestra Senora de la Paz, Lost Hills. 14846 Hwy. 33, Blackwell's Corner, Kern Co. 93249.

WOFFORD HEIGHTS, KERN CO., ST. JUDE (1969)
86 Nellie Dent Dr., Wofford Heights, 93285. Tel: 760-376-2416; Email: ruthann.cookstj@gmail.com. Mailing Address: P.O. Box 1190, Wofford Heights, 93285. Rev. Showreddy Thirumalareddy, Admin.; Deacon James Dewey.

Catechesis Religious Program—Students 18.

Station—Wofford Heights.

WOODLAKE, TULARE CO., ST. FRANCES CABRINI (1963)
599 N. Valencia Blvd., P.O. Box 459, Woodlake, 93286. Tel: 559-564-2647; Email: scabrini@att.net. Rev. Jesse C. Venzor.

Catechesis Religious Program—Students 319.

Missions—St. Clair—Alta Acres Dr., Three Rivers, Tulare Co. 93271.

San Felipe de Jesus, 32809 Rd. 159, Ivanhoe, Tulare Co. 93235.

YOSEMITE NATIONAL PARK, MARIPOSA CO., OUR LADY OF THE SNOWS (1963) Under the administration of Our Lady of the Sierra, Oakhurst.
40180 Indian Springs Rd., P.O. Box 4299, Oakhurst, 93644. Tel: 559-342-3452, Ext. 100; Email: monicaodols@gmail.com. Rev. Joel Davadilla.

Catechesis Religious Program—Students 127.

United States Federal Prison, P.O. Box 019000, Atwater, 95301. Tel: 209-386-0257.

Chaplains of Public Institutions

Please see page 1773C for additional listings.

On Special Assignment:
Rev. Msgrs.—
Dreiling, Raymond C., V.G.
Griesbach, John, St. Anthony Retreat Center, Dir.
Revs.—
Avila, Dan, Vocation Dir.
Del Angel, Jesus, J.C.L., Adjutant Judicial Vicar.

On Duty Outside the Diocese:
Revs.—
de la Torre, Jorge, Archdiocese of Dhaka, Bangladesh
Okorie, Onyema, Military Chap.

Retired:
Rev. Msgrs.—
Bezunartea, Herman O., (Retired)
Braun, Michael R., (Retired)
Coelho-Harguindeguy, John, (Retired)
Herrero, Nicolas, (Retired)
Janelli, Anthony, (Retired)
Lopez, Daniel, (Retired)
Marta, Raul, (Retired)
Meyer, Gilbert, (Retired)
Minhoto, Walter F., (Retired)
Shenoy, Leslie, (Retired)
Swett, Ronald, (Retired)
Revs.—
Alvernaz, Dennis, (Retired)
Amerando, Gerald, (Retired)
Azpericueta, Lucas, (Retired)
Blessing, Loren, (Retired)
Bray, Kevin, (Retired)
Bulfer, Stephen, V.F., (Retired)
Burns, John P., (Retired)
Chavez, Gerald F., (Retired)
Congdon, John, Military Chap., (Retired)
Flickenger, Don D., (Retired)
Gonzalez, Angel, (Retired)
Heffernan, Joseph A., (Retired)
Ignacio, Alejandro, (Retired)
Kudilil, James, (Retired)
Montiel, Jose, (Retired)
Pascual, Manuel, (Retired)
Reed, David, (Retired)
Simeone, Francis, (Retired)
Varo, Jose Luis, (Retired)
Vega, Jose Luis, (Retired).

INSTITUTIONS LOCATED IN DIOCESE

[A] HIGH SCHOOLS, DIOCESAN

FRESNO. *San Joaquin Memorial High School* (1945) 1406 N. Fresno St., 93703-3789. Tel: 559-268-9251; Fax: 559-268-1351; Email: tspencer@sjmhs.org; Web: www.sjmhs.org. Tom Spencer, Prin.; Rev. Msgr. Robert D. Wenzinger, Rector. Lay Teachers 38; Students 534.

BAKERSFIELD. *Garces Memorial High School* (1947) 2800 Loma Linda Dr., Bakersfield, 93305. Tel: 661-327-2578; Fax: 661-327-5427; Email: mpeck@garces.org; Web: www.garces.org. Ashleigh Rossi, Contact Person; Ms. Myka Peck, Prin.; Rev. Msgr. Perry Kavookjian, V.F., Rector. Lay Teachers 33; Students 504.

[B] GENERAL HOSPITALS

FRESNO. **Saint Agnes Medical Center* (1929) 1303 E. Herndon Ave., 93720. Tel: 559-450-3301; Fax: 559-450-2143; Email: nancy.hollingsworth@samc.com; Web: www.samc.com. A. Thomas Ferdinandi, Chm., Bd. of Trustees. Trinity Health. Bed Capacity 436; Nurses 877; Patients Asst Anual. 308,468; Sisters 4; Tot Asst. Annually 308,468; Total Staff 2,796.

Saint Agnes Medical Foundation, 1303 E. Herndon Ave., 93720. Tel: 559-449-3000; Fax: 559-449-2143 ; Email: jarrell.williamson@samc.com. Michael Prusatis, Treas.

BAKERSFIELD. *Mercy Hospital* dba Dignity Health (1910) Mercy Southwest is a campus of Mercy Hospital. 2215 Truxtun Ave., Bakersfield, 93301. Tel: 661-632-5000; Fax: 661-327-2592; Email: Robert.Sahagian@DignityHealth.org; Web: www.dignityhealth.org/mercy-bakersfield. Bruce Peters, Pres. Sponsored by Sisters of Mercy of the Americas West Midwest Community Bed Capacity 226; Sisters 3; Tot Asst. Annually 136,073; Total Staff 1,562.

Mercy Southwest Hospital dba Dignity Health, 400 Old River Rd., Bakersfield, 93311. Tel: 661-663-6000; Fax: 661-663-6570; Email: Robert.Sahagian@DignityHealth.org; Web: www.dignityhealth.org/mercy-bakersfield. Bruce Peters, Pres. Bed Capacity 82.

Mercy Foundation, Bakersfield dba Friends of Mercy Foundation, 2215 Truxtun Ave., Bakersfield, 93302. Tel: 661-663-6700; Fax: 661-663-6755; Email: Robert.Sahagian@DignityHealth.org; Web: supportfriendsofmercy.org. Toni Dougherty, Vice Pres.

MERCED. *Mercy Medical Center* dba Dignity Health (1923) 333 Mercy Ave., Merced, 95340. Tel: 209-564-5000; Fax: 209-564-5096; Email: Robert.Sahagian@DignityHealth.org; Web: mercymercedcares.org. Chuck Kassis, Pres. Sponsored by the Dominican Sisters of St. Catherine of Siena of Kenosha, Wisconsin. Bed Capacity 186; Tot Asst. Annually 119,718; Staff 1,347.

[C] HOMES FOR INVALID AND AGED

FRESNO. *Nazareth House of Fresno*, 2121 N. First St., 93703. Tel: 559-237-2257; Fax: 559-237-1958; Email: Rosemary@nazarethfresno.org. Rosemary O'Neill, Admin. Sisters of Nazareth of Fresno, Inc. 3; Total Staff 82; Residential Care/Assisted Living 89.

LOS BANOS. *New Bethany Residential Care and Skilled Nursing Community*, 1441 Berkeley Dr., Los Banos, 93635. Tel: 209-827-8933; Fax: 209-827-8989; Email: lucif@newbethanyconfhic.org; Web: www.newbethanyfhic.org. Sisters Helen Petrovich, F.H.I.C., Pres.; Julia Fonseca, F.H.I.C., Dir., Residential Care; Lucinda Fonseca, F.H.I.C., Skilled Nursing Admin.; Rev. Jose Carlos Santos, O.F.M., Chap. Capacity 99; Franciscan Hospitaller Sisters of the Immaculate Conception 9; Total Staff 87; Residential Care 48; Skilled Nursing 28.

[D] CATHOLIC CHARITIES

FRESNO. *Catholic Charities of the Diocese of Fresno*, 149 N. Fulton St., 93701. Tel: 559-237-0851; Fax: 559-237-7050; Email: jnegrete@ccdof.org; Web: www.ccdof.org. Mr. Jeff Negrete, Exec. Tot Asst. Annually 71,253; Total Staff 36; Total Assisted in All Locations 71,253.

Catholic Charities Thrift Store, 149 N. Fulton St., 93701-1607. Tel: 559-237-0851; Fax: 559-237-7050; Email: jhudson@ccdof.org; Email: tjacobs@ccdof.org. Jody Hudson, Opers. and Mktg. Dir. Tot Asst. Annually 81,136; Total Staff 1.

Senior Companion Program, 149 N. Fulton St., 93701. Tel: 559-498-6377; Fax: 559-485-1591; Email: lvalencia@ccdof.org. Lorraine Valencia, Member. Tot Asst. Annually 183; Total Staff 3; Total Assisted 183.

BAKERSFIELD. *Catholic Charities, Diocese of Fresno*, Kern and Inyo County Resource Center, 825 Chester Ave., Bakersfield, 93301. Tel: 661-281-2130; Tel: 661-616-4036; Fax: 661-281-2139; Email: avorhees@ccdof.org; Web: www.ccdof.org. Mr. Jeff Negrete, Dir. Tot Asst. Annually 37,034; Total Staff 8.

MERCED. *Catholic Charities, Diocese of Fresno*, 336 W. Main #1, Merced, 95340. Tel: 209-383-2494; Fax: 209-383-3975; Email: jnegrete@ccdof.org; Web: www.ccdof.org. Kelly Lilles, Dir. Tot Asst. Annually 40,630; Total Staff 3.

[E] CONVENTS AND RESIDENCES FOR SISTERS

FRESNO. *St. Agnes Medical Center Convent* (1975) 1261 E. Los Altos Ave., 93710. Tel: 559-431-3376; Email: sbrennan@cscsisters.org. Sr. Suzanne Brennan, Treas. Congregation of the Sisters of the Holy Cross. Sisters of the Holy Cross 4.

Congregation of the Sisters of Nazareth, 2121 N. First St., 93703. Tel: 559-237-2257; Fax: 559-237-1958; Email: pmurphy@nazarethhousela.org. Sr. Philomena Murphy, S.N., Supr. Sisters 3.

Pious Disciples of the Divine Master, 3700 N. Cornelia Ave., 93722. Tel: 559-275-1656; Fax: 559-275-2725; Email: eugeniabpddm@aol.com. Sr. Eugenia Pia Bianco, P.D.D.M., Supr. Sisters 8.

BAKERSFIELD. *Sister Servants of the Blessed Sacrament (SJS)*, 1100 S. Kern St., Bakersfield, 93307. Tel: 661-869-1086 (Convent); Fax: 661-323-6058. Sisters 5.

LOS BANOS. *Franciscan Hospitallers of the Immaculate Conception (FHIC)*, 1441 Berkeley Dr., Los Banos, 93635-9599. Tel: 209-827-8933; Fax: 209-827-8989; Email: confhic@sbcglobal.net; Web: www.fhiccalp.org. Sisters 10.

MADERA. *Sisters of the Immaculate Conception (RCM)* (1892) 310 N. "J" St., Madera, 93637. Tel: 559-674-4085; Email: monikemsanz@hotmail.com; Web: www.concepcionistas.com; Web: www.concepcionistas.es. Sisters 4.

REEDLEY. *Daughters of Divine Zeal (FDZ)* (1897) 379 E. Manning Ave., Reedley, 93654. Tel: 559-638-1916; Fax: 559-638-5542; Email: hannibalmarylucy@yahoo.com; Web: www.figliedivinozelo.it. Sr. Lucy Cassarino, F.D.Z., Prin. Sisters 4.

TEHACHAPI. *Norbertine Canonesses of the Bethlehem Priory of St. Joseph*, 17831 Water Canyon Rd., Tehachapi, 93561. Tel: 661-823-1066; Fax: 661-823-1066; Email: mothermarya@aol.com; Email: norbertinecanonesses@gmail.com; Web: www.norbertinesisters.org. Mother Mary Augustine Petit, Prior. Sisters 45.

[F] RETREAT HOUSES

THREE RIVERS. *St. Anthony's Retreat Center*, 43816 Sierra Dr., Hwy. 198, Three Rivers, 93271. Tel: 559-561-4595; Fax: 559-561-4493; Email: mike@stanthonyretreat.org; Web: stanthonyretreat.org. Rev. Msgr. John Griesbach, Dir.; Rev. Rod L. Craig, Chap.; Sr. Danielle Witt, S.S.N.D., Co-Dir.; Mr. Mike Hand, Business Mgr. Priests 2; Religious 1.

Santa Teresita Youth Center, 43816 Sierra Dr., Hwy. 198, Three Rivers, 93271. Tel: 559-561-4595; Fax: 559-561-1039; Email: cristal@stteresitaycc.org; Web: www.stteresitaycc.org. Rev. Msgr. John Griesbach, Exec. Dir.; Rev. Roderick L. Craig, Youth Chap.; Mr. Mike Hand, Business Mgr.; Cristal Juarez, Youth Min.

[G] NEWMAN CENTERS

FRESNO. *St. Paul Catholic Newman Center* (1964) 1572 E. Barstow Ave., 93710. Tel: 559-436-3434; Fax: 559-436-3430; Email: info@csufnewman.com; Web: csufnewman.com. Deacon John Supino, Admin. Administrators 1; Clergy 1; Deacons 2; Employees 7; Sisters 1; Adult Enrollment 162; High School Students 173; Elementary School Students 166; Estimated Number of Catholics 2,646.

[H] MISCELLANEOUS & AGENCIES

FRESNO. *Catholic Professional and Business Club of Fresno*, c/o 1550 N. Fresno St., 93703-3788. Tel: 559-434-2722; Email: president@cpbcfresno.org.

Our Faith, Our Family, Our Future Foundation, Inc., 1550 N. Fresno St., 93703. Tel: 559-488-7426; Fax: 559-488-7461; Email: gbethke@dioceseoffresno.org. Gary Bethke, CPA, Contact Person.

MERCED. **Apostoles de la Palabra of California*, 168 Cone Ave., Merced, 95341. Tel: 209-385-0795; Email: SrRosalie@dioceseoffresno.org. Sr. Julia Valencia, Supr. Associates 2.

Catholic Professional & Business Club of the Fresno Diocese, c/o 1550 N. Fresno St., 93703-3788. Tel: 559-434-2722 Fresno County; Tel: 559-740-9599 Tulare / Kings County; Email: president@cpbcfresno.org Fresno County; Email: jjmartinusen@gmail.org Tulare & Kings County. Mr. Matt Seals, Pres.

SANGER. *Fr. Hannibal House Social Service Center*, 1401 14th St., P.O. Box 37, Sanger, 93657. Tel: 559-875-0564. Ed Cuadros, Exec. Dir. Tot Asst. Annually 7,500; Total Staff 2; Total Families Assisted: Food Distribution 7,500.

RELIGIOUS INSTITUTES OF MEN REPRESENTED IN THE DIOCESE

For further details refer to the corresponding bracketed number in the Religious Institutes of Men or Women section.

[0310]—*Christian Brothers*—C.F.C.
[0360]—*Claretian Missionaries* (Western Prov.)—C.M.F.
[]—*Congregation of the Mother Co-Redemptrix*—S.M.Q.A.
[0480]—*Conventual Franciscans* (St. Joseph Cupertino Prov.)—O.F.M.Conv.
[]—*Divine Word Missionaries.*
[0520]—*Franciscan Friars* (St. Barbara Prov.)—O.F.M.
[0855]—*Fraternidad Misionera de Maria*—F.M.M.
[]—*Missioneros del Sagrado Corazon y Santa Maria de Guadalupe*—M.S.C.
[0930]—*Oblates of St. Joseph* (Asti, Italy)—O.S.J.
[]—*Pacem Missionaries*—M.A.P.M.
[1065]—*Priestly Fraternity of St. Peter*—F.S.S.P.
[1070]—*Redemptorists*—C.Ss.R.
[1090]—*Rogationist Fathers*—R.C.J.
[]—*Salesians of Don Bosco.*
[0420]—*Society of the Divine Word* (Philippines)—S.V.D.
[]—*Sons of Mary Mother of Mercy* (Umvahia, Nigeria)—S.M.M.M.
[]—*Ukrainian Catholic of St. Nicholas* (Chicago, IL).

RELIGIOUS INSTITUTES OF WOMEN REPRESENTED IN THE DIOCESE

[]—*Association of the Faithful Instituto Misionero Apostoles de la Palabra*—I.M.A.P.
[0795]—*Daughters of Divine Zeal* (Rome, Italy)—F.D.Z.
[]—*Daughters of Holy Spirit*—D.H.S.
[1070-20]—*Dominican Sisters* (Congregation of St. Thomas Aquinas, Tacoma, WA)—O.P.
[]—*Eudist Servants of the 11th Hour*—E.S.E.H.
[1270]—*Franciscan Hospitaller Sisters of the Immaculate Conception* (San Jose, CA)—F.H.I.C.
[1190]—*Franciscan Sisters of the Atonement* (Garrison, NY)—S.A.
[2180]—*Immaculate Heart Community* (Los Angeles, CA)—I.H.M.
[]—*Misioneras Carmelitas de Santa Teresa del Nino Jesus* (Puebla, Puebla Mexico)—M.C.S.T.N.J.
[]—*Misioneras Eucaristicas de Maria Inmaculada* (Colima, Mexico)—M.E.M.I.
[]—*Norbertine Sisters of the Bethlehem Priory of St. Joseph*—O.Praem.
[0980]—*Pious Disciples of the Divine Master* (Staten Island, NY)—P.D.D.M.
[2970]—*School Sisters of Notre Dame* (St. Louis, MO)—S.S.N.D.
[]—*Secular Institute - Missionaries of the Kingship of Christ*—S.I.M.
[3499]—*Servants of the Blessed Sacrament* (El Segundo, CA)—S.J.S.
[2570]—*Sisters of Mercy of the Americas* (Silver Spring, MD)—R.S.M.
[3242]—*Sisters of Nazareth* (Los Angeles, CA)—S.N.
[]—*Sisters of Our Lady of Nazareth* (Fiji)—S.O.L.N.
[3830-13]—*Sisters of St. Joseph* (Baden, PA)—C.S.J.
[3840]—*Sisters of St. Joseph of Carondelet* (Los Angeles, CA)—C.S.J.
[1920]—*Sisters of the Holy Cross* (Notre Dame, IN)—C.S.C.
[1960]—*Sisters of the Holy Family* (Mission San Jose, CA)—S.H.F.
[2130]—*Sisters of the Immaculate Conception* (San Francisco, CA & Spain)—R.C.M.
[]—*Sisters of the Love of God* (La Puente, CA & Spain)—R.A.D.

DIOCESAN CEMETERIES

FRESNO. *Fresno Catholic Cemeteries*, 264 N. Blythe Ave., 93706. Tel: 559-488-7449; Fax: 559-488-7485; Email: cemeteries@dioceseoffresno.org; Web: www.dioceseoffresno.org/cemeteries. Mr. Carlos Rascon, Dir.; Ms. Maria Zavala, Office Mgr.

An asterisk (*) denotes an organization that has established tax-exempt status directly with the IRS and is not covered by the USCCB Group Ruling.

Diocese of Gallup

(Dioecesis Gallupiensis)

Most Reverend

JAMES S. WALL

Bishop of Gallup; ordained June 6, 1998; appointed Bishop of Gallup February 5, 2009; ordained and installed April 23, 2009. *Office: 503 W. Historic 66, Ste. B, P.O. Box 1338, Gallup, NM 87301.*

Chancery: 503 W. Historic 66, Ste. B, Gallup, NM 87301. Mailing Address: P.O. Box 1338, Gallup, NM 87305. Tel: 505-863-4406; Fax: 505-722-9131 (Bishop's Office); Fax: 505-863-2269.

ESTABLISHED DECEMBER 16, 1939.

Square Miles 55,468.

Comprises Apache, Navajo and those parts of the Navajo and Hopi Reservations in Coconino Counties in the State of Arizona; San Juan, McKinley, Catron, Cibola and those parts of Rio Arriba, Sandoval, Bernalillo and Valencia Counties lying west of 106, 52', 41" meridian in the State of New Mexico.

Legal Title: New Mexico: Roman Catholic Church of the Diocese of Gallup. Arizona: Bishop of the Roman Catholic Church of the Diocese of Gallup.
For legal titles of parishes and diocesan institutions, consult the Chancery Office.

STATISTICAL OVERVIEW

Personnel	
Bishop	1
Priests: Diocesan Active in Diocese	23
Priests: Diocesan Active Outside Diocese	2
Priests: Retired, Sick or Absent	12
Number of Diocesan Priests	37
Religious Priests in Diocese	12
Total Priests in Diocese	49
Extern Priests in Diocese	15
Ordinations:	
Diocesan Priests	1
Permanent Deacons in Diocese	22
Total Brothers	9
Total Sisters	61
Parishes	
Parishes	52
With Resident Pastor:	
Resident Diocesan Priests	21
Resident Religious Priests	12
Without Resident Pastor:	
Administered by Priests	14
Administered by Professed Religious Men	2
Administered by Religious Women	1
Administered by Lay People	2
Missions	22
Professional Ministry Personnel:	
Brothers	9
Sisters	61
Lay Ministers	11
Welfare	
Homes for the Aged	1
Total Assisted	50
Special Centers for Social Services	5
Educational	
Diocesan Students in Other Seminaries	3
Total Seminarians	3
High Schools, Private	1
Total Students	112
Elementary Schools, Diocesan and Parish	7
Total Students	541
Elementary Schools, Private	4
Total Students	639
Catechesis/Religious Education:	
High School Students	559
Elementary Students	1,207
Total Students under Catholic Instruction	3,061
Teachers in the Diocese:	
Priests	1
Brothers	2
Sisters	21
Lay Teachers	99
Vital Statistics	
Receptions into the Church:	
Infant Baptism Totals	361
Minor Baptism Totals	33
Adult Baptism Totals	63
Received into Full Communion	70
First Communions	480
Confirmations	342
Marriages:	
Catholic	93
Interfaith	30
Total Marriages	123
Deaths	722
Total Catholic Population	58,000
Total Population	490,000

Former Bishop—Most Revs. BERNARD T. ESPELAGE, O.F.M., D.D., ord. May 16, 1918; appt. Bishop of Gallup, July 20, 1940; cons. Oct. 9, 1940; resigned Sept. 3, 1969; died Feb. 19, 1971; JEROME J. HASTRICH, D.D., ord. Feb. 9, 1941; cons. Auxiliary Bishop of Madison and Titular Bishop of Gurza, July 31, 1963; transferred to the See of Gallup, Sept. 3, 1969; installed Dec. 3, 1969; retired March 20, 1990; died May 12, 1995; DONALD E. PELOTTE, S.S.S., D.D., Ph.D., ord. Sept. 2, 1972; appt. Coadjutor Bishop of Gallup Feb. 24, 1986; cons. May 6, 1986; succeeded to See, March 20, 1990; retired April 30, 2008; died Jan. 7, 2010.

Vicars General—Very Revs. MATTHEW A. KELLER; PETER M. SHORT.

Moderator of the Curia—Very Rev. MATTHEW A. KELLER.

Judicial Vicar—Very Rev. KEVIN H. FINNEGAN, J.C.L., (Retired).

Office of the Bishop—503 W. Historic 66, Ste. B, P.O. Box 1338, Gallup, 87305. Tel: 505-863-4406; Fax: 505-722-9131.

Chancery—503 W. Historic 66, Ste. B, P.O. Box 1338, Gallup, 87305. Tel: 505-863-4406; Fax: 505-863-2269. Office Hours: Mon.-Fri. 8:30-12 & 1-4:30.

Chancellor—Deacon RANDOLPH COPELAND, M.D., Chancellor; MRS. VERA PLACENCIO, Administrative Asst. to the Bishop.

Chief Financial Officer—BOB HORACEK.

Diocesan Tribunal (First Instance)—503 W. Historic Hwy. 66, Ste. B, P.O. Box 1338, Gallup, 87305. Tel: 505-863-4406; Fax: 505-722-9324.

Adjutant Judicial Vicar—VACANT.

Judge—VACANT.

Defenders of the Bond—Rev. THOMAS R. MAIKOWSKI, Ph.D., Ed.D.; Deacon TIMOTEO LUJAN.

Secretary / Notary—MRS. REBECCA BOUCHER.

Promoter of Justice—Very Rev. KEVIN H. FINNEGAN, J.C.L., (Retired).

Vicars Forane—Very Rev. DALE JAMISON, O.F.M., McKinley Vicariate; Revs. FLORECITO P.J. PABATAO, O.F.M., Apache Vicariate; RAJASEKHAR YERUVA, Navajo Vicariate; Very Revs. JOACHIM BLONSKI, White Mountain Vicariate; FRANK CHACON, San Juan Vicariate, (Retired); ALBERTO AVELLA, Cibola Vicariate, (Retired).

Bishop's Delegate for Religious—Sr. RENE BACKE, C.S.A.

Presbyteral Council—Most Rev. JAMES S. WALL; Very Revs. FRANK CHACON, (Retired), Mailing Address: P.O. Box 1338, Gallup, 87305; KEVIN H. FINNEGAN, J.C.L., (Retired); JOACHIM BLONSKI; DALE JAMISON, O.F.M., Moderator; MATTHEW A. KELLER; ALBERTO AVELLA, (Retired); PETER M. SHORT; Revs. JOSHUA MAYER, Vice Moderator; FLORECITO P.J. PABATAO, O.F.M.; RAJASEKHAR YERUVA; MRS. VERA PLACENCIO, Recording Sec.

Diocesan Consultors—Very Revs. JOACHIM BLONSKI; FRANK CHACON, (Retired); MATTHEW A. KELLER; KEVIN H. FINNEGAN, J.C.L., (Retired); DALE JAMISON, O.F.M.; ALBERTO AVELLA, (Retired); PETER M. SHORT; Revs. JOSHUA MAYER, Vice Moderator; FLORECITO P.J. PABATAO, O.F.M.; RAJASEKHAR YERUVA.

Vicar for Priests—Very Rev. JOACHIM BLONSKI.

Diocesan Offices and Directors

Archivist—MRS. CATHY MCCARTHY.

Catholic Committee on Scouting—DANIEL BURNHAM; CARLY BURNHAM.

Chief Financial Officer—BOB HORACEK.

Catholic Charities—MS. VICKI TRUJILLO, Exec. Dir., Main Office, Gallup: P.O. Box 3146, Gallup, 87305. 503 W. Hwy. 66 Ave., Gallup, 87301. Tel: 505-722-4407. Grants-Milan: 2595 W. Hwy. 66, Grants, 87020. Tel: 505-285-5451. Farmington: 119 W. Broadway, Farmington, 87401. Tel: 505-325-3734. Holbrook: P.O. Box 41, Holbrook, AZ 86025. Tel: 928-524-9720. White Mountain: 2190 E. White Mountain Blvd., Pinetop, AZ 85935. P.O. Box 552, McNary, AZ 85930. Tel: 928-334-2244.

Cursillos—Mailing Address: 314 N. 7th St., Bloomfield, 87413. Tel: 505-632-2672. LARRY REYES, Lay Dir.

Diocesan Superintendent of Catholic Schools—Rev. ISAAC OGBA.

Ecumenical Affairs in Arizona, Arizona Ecumenical Council—VACANT.

Ecumenical Affairs in New Mexico—VACANT.

Media Liaison—MS. SUZANNE HAMMONS.

Newspaper—Voice of the Southwest MS. SUZANNE HAMMONS, Coord. Web & Print Media Design, Mailing Address: P.O. Box 1338, Gallup, 87305. Tel: 505-863-4406; Email: designoffice@dioceseofgallup.org.

Diocesan Director of Religious Education—Deacon TODD CHURCH, P.O. Box 1338, Gallup, 87305. Tel: 505-863-4406, Ext. 32.

Priests' Retirement Board—Revs. TIMOTHY W. FARRELL, Chm.; DAN DAILY; THOMAS R. MAIKOWSKI, Ph.D., Ed.D., Chm.; NATHANAEL Z. BLOCK; ROBERT BADGER; DANIEL F. KASSIS.

Propagation of the FaithVery Rev. MATTHEW A. KELLER, Dir., Mailing Address: P.O. Box 1338, Gallup, 87305.

Radio—VACANT.

Search—Mailing Address: P.O. Box 5243, Farmington, 87499-5243. MARI ARREGUIN, Dir.
Spiritual Director—Rev. JOSHUA MAYER.

Life, Peace, Justice and Creation Stewardship—Sr. ROSE MARIE CECCHINI, M.M., Mailing Address:

P.O. Box 3146, Gallup, 87305. Tel: 505-722-4407, Ext. 103.

Vocations—For Priesthood: Mailing Address: 307 N. Church St., Bloomfield, 87413. Tel: 505-632-2014. Rev. JOSHUA MAYER, Dir. Deacon Vocations Co Directors: Deacons FRANK T. CHAVEZ, 5300 River Ridge Ave., N.W., Albuquerqe, 87114. Tel: 505-793-5735; TIMOTEO LUJAN, P.O. Box 2612, Milan, 87021. Bishop's Delegate for Religious: Sr. RENE BACKE, C.S.A., Mailing Address: P.O. Box 1338, Gallup, 87305.

Gallup. Cure of Ars House of Discernment—(2009) *300 Mount Carmel Ave., Gallup, 87301.* Tel: 505-863-4406; Fax: 505-722-9131; Email: chancellor@dioceseofgallup.org; Web: dioceseofgallup.org. Deacon RANDOLPH COPELAND, M.D., Chancellor.

Office of Youth Evangelization & Catechesis—Deacon TODD CHURCH.

Ministry Formation Program—Mailing Address: P.O. Box 1338, Gallup, 87305. Tel: 505-863-4406. Very Rev. DALE JAMISON, O.F.M., Dir. Native American Ministries, Builders of the New Earth & Native American Formation; Deacons FRANK T. CHAVEZ, Co Dir. Diaconate Formation, Email: ftchavez@mac.com; TIMOTEO LUJAN, Co Dir. Life & Ministry, Tel: 505-793-5735; Tel: 505-290-4836; Email: tlujan@tristategt.org; Sr. RENE BACKE, C.S.A., Academics, Diaconate Candidates: 8.

Diocesan Review Board for Sexual Abuse & Misconduct by Clergy, Religious and Other Church Personnel—Mailing Address: P.O. Box 1338, Gallup, 87305.

Victim Assistance Coordinator—Mailing Address: P.O. Box 1338, Gallup, 87301. Tel: 505-906-7357; Email: victimassistance@dioceseofgallup.org. ELIZABETH MASON TERRILL.

CLERGY, PARISHES, MISSIONS AND PAROCHIAL SCHOOLS

CITY OF GALLUP

(MCKINLEY COUNTY)

1—CATHEDRAL OF THE SACRED HEART (1939) (Dedicated June 19, 1955)
415 E. Green St., 87301. Tel: 505-722-6644; Fax: 505-722-6645; Email: shcathedralgallup@gmail.com. Very Rev. Matthew A. Keller, Rector; Revs. Thomas R. Walsh, Parochial Vicar; Anselm Amadi, Parochial Vicar; Deacon Randolph Copeland, M.D.
Catechesis Religious Program—Tel: 505-722-6644; Email: shcathedralgall@gmail.com. Debbie Trujillo, D.R.E. Students 127.

2—ST. FRANCIS OF ASSISI (1943) (Hispanic)
411 N. Second, 87301. Tel: 505-863-3033; Email: kathy@stfrancisgallup.org. 214 W. Wilson, 87301. Rev. Abel Olivas, O.F.M. In Res., Rev. Pio O'Connor, O.F.M.; Bro. Maynard Shirley, O.F.M.
Catechesis Religious Program—Email: kathy@stfrancisgallup.org. Sr. Eucharua Muobike, H.N.S.G., D.R.E. Students 132.

3—ST. JEROME, Closed. For inquiries for parish records contact Sacred Heart Cathedral.

4—ST. JOHN VIANNEY (1973)
3408 Zia Dr., 87301. Tel: 505-722-3361; Email: sjv@dioceseofgallup.org. Very Rev. Kevin H. Finnegan, J.C.L., (Retired); Deacon John Margis.
Catechesis Religious Program—Tel: 505-722-5085; Email: stjv@dioceseofgallup.org. JoNell Becenti, D.R.E. Students 59.

OUTSIDE THE CITY OF GALLUP, NEW MEXICO

ACOMA, CIBOLA CO., SAN ESTEBAN, ACOMA CATHOLIC INDIAN MISSION (1629) [CEM 3] (Native American)
P.O. Box 448, Pueblo of Acoma, 87034-0448.
Tel: 505-552-6403; Cell: 505-306-6562; Email: geraldsteinmetz@hotmail.com. 266 Pueblo Rd., Acoma, 87034. Revs. Gerald Steinmetz, O.F.M.; Christopher G. Kerstiens, O.F.M., Parochial Vicar.
Catechesis Religious Program—Mike Pino, D.R.E. Students 35.
Missions—St. Anne—Acomita, 87034.
Tel: 505-552-9403.
Santa Maria de Acoma, McCartys, 87034.

ARAGON, CATRON CO., SANTO NINO (1910) (Hispanic)
155 New Mexico Hwy. 435, Reserve, 87830.
Tel: 575-533-6719. P.O. Box 489, Reserve, 87830-0489. Rev. Anthony O. Dike, Parish Admin.; Deacons Edward Schaub; Juan Aragon.
Catechesis Religious Program—Students 12.
Missions—San Isidro—Lower San Francisco.
St. Francis, P.O. Box 489, Reserve, 87830. Email: dadandc@gilanet.com.
St. Anne, Horse Springs.
Santo Nino, Cat Walk Rd., P.O. Box 222, Glenwood, 88039.

AZTEC, SAN JUAN CO., ST. JOSEPH (1946) (Hispanic)
424 N. Mesa Verde Ave., Aztec, 87410. Rev. David Tate, Admin.; Deacon Matthew Lamoreux.
Catechesis Religious Program—Tel: 505-334-3542. Sr. Sara Marie Gomez, O.S.U., D.R.E. Students 168.

BLANCO, SAN JUAN CO., ST. ROSE OF LIMA (1900) [CEM]
Mailing Address: 307 N. Church St., Bloomfield, 87413. Tel: 505-632-2014; Fax: 505-634-0312; Email: stmarystrosestaff@gmail.com. 7378 U.S. Hwy. 64, Blanco, 87412. Revs. Joshua Mayer; Robert Badger, Parochial Vicar; Deacons Roger Garcia; Patrick R. Valdez.
Mission—Our Lady of Guadalupe, Los Martinez.

BLOOMFIELD, SAN JUAN CO., ST. MARY (1960) [CEM]
307 N. Church St., Bloomfield, 87413.
Tel: 505-632-2014; Fax: 505-634-0312; Email: stmarystrosestaff@gmail.com. Revs. Joshua Mayer; Robert Badger, Parochial Vicar; Deacons Roger Garcia; Patrick R. Valdez.
Catechesis Religious Program—Tel: 505-634-0312. Marilyn benedict, D.R.E. Students 260.

CHICHILTAH, MCKINLEY CO., ST. PATRICK (1965) (Native American)
P.O. Box 267, Vanderwagen, 87326.
Tel: 505-782-2014; Email: pastor@stanthonyzuni.org. 549 Cousins Rd., Vanderwagen, 87326. Revs. Patrick Nicholas McGuire, S.M.A., (Scotland); Francis Akano, Parochial Vicar. (Navajo Mission)
Catechesis Religious Program—Sr. M. Paulinetta, M.C., D.R.E. Students 13.

CHURCH ROCK, MCKINLEY CO., ST. PHILIP BENIZI, Closed. For inquiries for parish records please see Sacred Heart Cathedral, Gallup.
Station—Pindale.

CROWNPOINT, MCKINLEY CO., ST. PAUL (1961) [JC] (Native American)
268 Church Rd., Crownpoint, 87313.
Tel: 505-786-7110; Fax: 505-786-5376; Email: stpaulcrpt@yahoo.com. P.O. Box 268, Crownpoint, 87313. Rev. Gil Mangampo, Admin.; Deacon Sherman Manuelito.
Catechesis Religious Program—Sr. Michelle Woodruff, A,S,C,, D.R.E. Students 3.
Mission—Risen Savior, Thoreau.
Stations—Lake Valley.
St. Bonaventure.

CUBA, SANDOVAL CO., IMMACULATE CONCEPTION (Nacimiento) (1914) [CEM 4]
Mailing Address: P.O. Box 40, Cuba, 87013.
Tel: 575-289-3803; Email: icccuba@gmail.com. 6440 US-550, Cuba, 87013. Rev. Cornelius Onyigbuo, Admin.
Catechesis Religious Program—Email: lynettecrespin@yahoo.com. Lynette R. Crespin, D.R.E. Students 36.
Missions—Santo Nino—La Jara, Sandoval Co.
Saint Aloysius Gonzaga, San Luis, Sandoval Co.
San Jose, Cabezon, Sandoval Co.

FARMINGTON, SAN JUAN CO.

1—ST. MARY'S (1976) [CEM] (Hispanic)
2100 E. 20th St., Farmington, 87401.
Tel: 505-325-0287, Ext. 101; Fax: 505-564-8515; Email: stmarysfmt@msn.com. Very Rev. Frank Chacon, (Retired); Rev. Jeffrey King, Parochial Vicar; Deacon James Betts.
Catechesis Religious Program—
Tel: 505-325-0287, Ext. 101. Bonnie Gallegos, D.R.E. Students 304.

2—SACRED HEART (1929)
414 N. Allen Ave., Farmington, 87401.
Tel: 505-325-9743; Fax: 505-325-8860; Email: rectory@qwestoffice.net; Email: fathertim@qwestoffice.net; Web: sacredheartfarmington.weconnect.com/. Rev. Timothy W. Farrell.
Catechesis Religious Program—Tel: 505-564-8164; Email: aanecometothefeast@gmail.com. Anne Weigel, D.R.E. Students 360.

FLORA VISTA, SAN JUAN CO., HOLY TRINITY (1986)
42 Rd. 3520, Flora Vista, 87415. Tel: 505-334-6535;
Tel: 505-333-7366; Fax: 505-334-5902; Email: office@stjosephaztec.org; Web: www.stjosephaztec.org. 424 N. Mesa Verde Ave., Aztec, 87410. Rev. David Tate, Admin.; Deacon Matthew Lamoreux.
Catechesis Religious Program—

FORT WINGATE, MCKINLEY CO., ST. ELEANOR, Closed. For inquiries for parish records contact Sacred Heart Cathedral.
Station—Iyanbito.

GRANTS, CIBOLA CO., ST. TERESA OF AVILA (1942)
213 Smith St., P.O. Box 668, Grants, 87020.
Tel: 505-285-6645; Fax: 505-285-6646; Email: steresachurch@gmail.com; Web: cibolacatholiccommunity.com. Very Rev. Alberto Avella, (Retired); Revs. John Cormack, Parochial Vicar; Faustinus Ibebuike, Parochial Vicar; John Sauter, Parochial Vicar; Deacons Timoteo Lujan; Larry Chavez; Todd Church.
Catechesis Religious Program—Tel: 505-287-3549. Velma Dees, D.R.E. Students 149.

LAGUNA, CIBOLA CO., ST. JOSEPH (Laguna Indian Pueblo) (1699)
Mailing Address: 1 Friar Rd., Laguna, 87026.
Tel: 505-552-9330; Email: geraldsteinmetz@hotmail.com. P.O. Box 1000, Laguna, 87026. Revs. Gerald Steinmetz, O.F.M.; Christopher G. Kerstiens, O.F.M., Parochial Vicar.
Catechesis Religious Program—Tel: 505-552-7464; Email: gerasldsteinmetz@hotmail.com. Angela Riley, D.R.E. Students 32.
Missions—Nativity of the Blessed Virgin Mary—Encinal.
Sacred Heart, Mesita.
St. Elizabeth of Hungary, Paguate.
St. Margaret Mary, Paraje.
St. Anne, Seama.

LUMBERTON, RIO ARRIBA CO., ST. FRANCIS OF ASSISI (1910) (Hispanic—Native American)
3760 Sandhill Dr., P.O. Box 1147, Dulce, 87528.
Tel: 575-759-1307; Email: Francis.AnthonyofPadua@gmail.com. 21 County Rd. 356, Lumberton, 87528. Rev. Cornelius Onyigbuo, Admin.
Catechesis Religious Program—Email: valerielea711@gm.com. Valerie Gomez, D.R.E. Students 31.
Mission—St. Anthony, 3760 Sandhill, Dulce, 87528.

MILAN, CIBOLA CO., ST. VIVIAN (1969)
Mailing Address: 501 Sand St., P.O. Box 2938, Milan, 87201-2938. Tel: 505-287-9327; Email: stvivians@7cities.net; , Web: cibolacatholiccommunity.com. Very Rev. Alberto Avella, (Retired); Revs. John Cormack, Parochial Vicar; Faustinus Ibebuike, Parochial Vicar; John Sauter, Parochial Vicar.

NAVAJO, MCKINLEY CO., ST. BERARD (1963) [JC] (Native American)
P.O. Box 1284, Navajo, 87328. Tel: 928-729-5068; Email: stmikesofm@aol.com. P.O. Box 70, Fort Defiance, AZ 86504-0070. Revs. Jose Femilou Gutay, O.F.M.; Edgardo Diaz; Blane Grein, O.F.M.; Deacon Wilson Gorman.
Catechesis Religious Program—Tel: 505-777-2490. Students 22.
Mission—St. Francis Mission, P.O. Box 41, Sawmill, AZ 86549.
Station—Crystal.

PINEHAVEN, MCKINLEY CO., GOOD SHEPHERD CATHOLIC MISSION (1972) [CEM] (Native American)
P.O. Box 267, Vanderwagen, 87326.
Tel: pastor@stanthonyzuni.org. Revs. Patrick Nicholas McGuire, S.M.A., (Scotland); Francis Akano, Parochial Vicar.

QUEMADO, CATRON CO., SACRED HEART (1881) [CEM] (Hispanic)
3 Parish Ln., P.O. Box 339, Quemado, 87829-0339.
Tel: 575-773-4631; Email: sacredheart@gilanet.com. Revs. Edwin Bryan Diesen, Parish Admin.; Raymond F. Mahlmann, Parochial Vicar; Daniel P. Daley, Canonical Pastor, (Retired).
Catechesis Religious Program—
Mission—Nativity of the Blessed Virgin Mary, Old Hwy. 60, Datil, 87821.

SAN MATEO, CIBOLA AND MCKINLEY COS., SAN MATEO
Mailing Address: P.O. Box 668, Grants, 87020.
Tel: 505-285-6645; Email: steresachurch@gmail.com; Web: cibolacatholiccommunity.com. Very Rev. Alberto Avella, (Retired); Revs. John Cormack, Parochial Vicar; Faustinus Ibebuike, Parochial Vicar; John Sauter, Parochial Vicar; Deacons Larry Chavez; Timoteo Lujan; Todd Church.

SAN RAFAEL, CIBOLA CO., SAN RAFAEL
Mailing Address: P.O. Box 2938, Milan, 87201.
Tel: 505-287-9327; Email: stvivians@7cities.net. 100 Guadalupe Plaza, San Rafael, 87051. Very Rev. Alberto Avella, (Retired); Revs. John Cormack, Parochial Vicar; Faustinus Ibebuike, Parochial Vicar; John Sauter, Parochial Vicar; Deacons Larry Chavez; Todd Church; Timoteo Lujan.

SEBOYETA, CIBOLA CO., OUR LADY OF SORROWS (1774) [CEM] (Hispanic)
State Hwy 279, Seboyeta, 87014. Very Rev. Alberto Avella, (Retired); Revs. John Cormack, Parochial Vicar; Faustinus Ibebuike, Parochial Vicar; John Sauter, Parochial Vicar.
Missions—Our Lady of Light—P.O. Box 8098, Cubero, 87014. 17 Water Canyon Rd., Cubero, 87014.
Our Lady of Loretto, (Inactive) Bibo.
St. Joseph Mission, (Inactive) San Fidel, 87049.
Santa Rosalia, (Inactive) Moquino.
Station—Marquez.
Catechesis Religious Program—Daniel Gonzales, D.R.E. Students 15.

SHIPROCK, SAN JUAN CO., CHRIST THE KING (1924) [JC] (Native American)
Hwy. 564 W., P.O. Box 610, Shiprock, 87420.
Tel: 505-368-4532; Fax: 505-368-4532; Email: christkingparish@yahoo.com. Rev. Patrick Wedeking.

Catechesis Religious Program—Tel: 505-368-5845. Jerome Herbert, D.R.E. Students 10.

THOREAU, MCKINLEY CO., ST. BONAVENTURE
Mailing Address: P.O. Box 268, Crownpoint, 87313. Tel: 505-786-7110. Rev. Gil Mangampo, Chap.

TINAJA, CIBOLA CO., SAN LORENZO (1981) (Hispanic—Native American), Attended by St. Teresa, Grants, NM.
HCC 1, Box 47, Ramah, 87321. Tel: 505-782-2014; Email: pastor@stanthonyzuni.org. P.O. Box 486, Zuni, 87327. Revs. Patrick Nicholas McGuire, S.M.A., (Scotland); Francis Akano, Parochial Vicar.

TOHATCHI, MCKINLEY CO., ST. MARY CHURCH (1920) [CEM] (Native American)
Box 39, Tohatchi, 87325. Tel: 505-733-2243; Email: frdjamison@dioceseofgallup.org. Very Rev. Dale Jamison, O.F.M.
Catechesis Religious Program—Email: office@stmarytohatchi.org. Students 10.
Mission—St. Anthony, Naschitti.
Station—St. Joseph, Coyote Canyon, 87310.

WATERFLOW, SAN JUAN CO., SACRED HEART (1917) [CEM]
9 County Rd. 6820, Waterflow, 87421.
Tel: 505-598-5454; Email: patrickw515@earthlink.net. Rev. Patrick Wedeking.
Catechesis Religious Program—Tel: 505-598-9856; Email: patricia.b.paul@gmail.com. Patty Paul, D.R.E. Students 15.
Missions—San Juan Catholic Center—11 County Rd. 6446, P.O. Box 857, Kirtland, San Juan Co. 87417. Email: patrick515@earthlink.net.
Sacred Heart Missionary Cenacle, Fruitland. Sr. Ann Regis Barrett, M.S.B.T., Dir.

ZUNI, MCKINLEY CO., ST. ANTHONY (Zuni Indian Pueblo) (1923)
11 St. Anthony Dr., Zuni, 87327. Tel: 505-782-2014; Email: pastor@stanthonyzuni.org; Web: www.stanthonyzuni.org. P.O. Box 486, Zuni, 87327. Revs. Patrick Nicholas McGuire, S.M.A., (Scotland); Francis Akano, Parochial Vicar.
Catechesis Religious Program—Students 149.

ARIZONA

ALPINE, APACHE CO., ST. HELENA (1971)
42909 Hwy. 180, Alpine, AZ 85920.
Tel: 928-339-4363; Email: st.helena.alpine@gmail.com. P. O. Box 259, Alpine, AZ 85920-0259. Rev. Edwin Bryan Diesen, Admin.; Deacon Jorge Campos.
Catechesis Religious Program—

CHINLE, APACHE CO., OUR LADY OF FATIMA (1905) (Native American)
Navajo Rt. 7, P.O. Box 2119, Chinle, AZ 86503-2119. Tel: 928-674-5413; Email: ourladyoffatima_chinle@yahoo.com. Rev. Florecito P.J. Pabatao, O.F.M.
Mission—St. Anthony, P.O. Box 578, Many Farms, Apache Co. AZ 86538.
Catechesis Religious Program—Tel: 928-674-5254. Sr. Theresa Chato, S.B.S., D.R.E. Students 19.
Mission—St. Mary of the Rosary, P.O. Box 432, Pinon, Navajo Co. AZ 86510.
Catechesis Religious Program—Students 16.

CIBECUE, NAVAJO CO., ST. CATHERINE (1929) (Native American)
P.O. Box 80156, Cibecue, AZ 85911.
Tel: 928-338-4432; Email: stfranciswhiteriver@outlook.com. Mailing Address: P.O. Box 679, Whiteriver, AZ 85941. Rev. Larry Weidner, Sacramental Min., (Retired).
Catechesis Religious Program—
Mission—St. Anthony, Cedar Creek, AZ. (TUC).

CONCHO, APACHE CO., SAN RAFAEL (1977)
35411 US 180 A, P.O. Box 49, Concho, AZ 85936-0049. Tel: 928-337-4390; Email: santaritapadre@gmail.com. Very Rev. Joachim Blonski; Deacon Carl Sadlier.
Catechesis Religious Program— Combined with St. John the Baptist, St. Johns, AZ. Students 79.

FORT DEFIANCE, APACHE CO., OUR LADY OF BLESSED SACRAMENT (1915) [JC] (Native American)
P.O. Box 70, Fort Defiance, AZ 86504-0070.
Tel: 928-729-5068; Email: stmikesofm@aol.com. Revs. Jose Femilou Gutay, O.F.M.; Edgardo Diaz; Blane Grein, O.F.M., Parochial Vicar; Deacon Daniel Martin.
Catechesis Religious Program—173 Main St., Fort Defiance, AZ 86504-0070. Sr. Zoe Brenner, S.B.S., D.R.E. Students 27.

GANADO, APACHE CO., ALL SAINTS (1968) (Native American)
County Rd. 420, P.O. Box 119, Ganado, AZ 86505.
Tel: 928-755-3401; Email: paulobofm@yahoo.com. P.O. Box 119, Ganado, AZ 86505. Bro. Paul O'Brien, O.F.M., Admin.
Catechesis Religious Program—CRP: P.O. Box 209, Ganado, AZ 86505. Sr. Monica Dubois, O.P., D.R.E.; Teresa Gorman, D.R.E. Students 28.
Missions—St. Anne—P.O. Box 366, Chambers, AZ 86502-0366. Bro. Charles Schilling, S.C.
Our Lady of the Rosary, Box 119, Greasewood, Navajo Co. AZ 86505. Bro. Paul O'Brien, O.F.M.
Stations—Cornfields, AZ.
Wide Ruins, AZ.

HOLBROOK, NAVAJO CO., OUR LADY OF GUADALUPE (1923)
P.O. Box 849, Holbrook, AZ 86025. Tel: 928-524-3261 ; Email: olguadalupe@cableone.net. 212 E. Arizona St., Holbrook, AZ 86025-0849. Rev. Rajasekhar Yeruva, Admin.; Deacon Michael Ashenfelder.
Catechesis Religious Program—Email: mikew1949@hotmail.com. Students 38.

HOUCK, APACHE CO., ST. JOHN THE EVANGELIST (Tekakwitha Mission) (1927) [CEM] (Native American)
P.O. Box 48, Houck, AZ 86506. Tel: 505-934-5119; Email: srjmwilliams@doc1633.org. Very Rev. Matthew A. Keller, Canonical Pastor; Sr. Jean Marie Williams, Parish Life Coord.
Catechesis Religious Program—Students 2.
Mission—St. Rose, Pine Springs, AZ.

KAYENTA, NAVAJO CO., OUR LADY OF GUADALUPE (1967)
Hwy 163 MM195.4, P.O. Box 517, Kayenta, AZ 86033. Tel: 928-697-3429; Email: jjungcm@gmail.com. Rev. Jay Jung, C.M.

KEAMS CANYON, NAVAJO CO., ST. JOSEPH'S INDIAN MISSION (1920) (Hopi-Navajo-Tewa)
E. Main St., P.O. Box 128, Keams Canyon, AZ 86034. Tel: 928-738-2325; Email: peteshirley1214@gmail.com. Rev. Rajasekhar Yeruva, Admin.
Catechesis Religious Program—Students 6.
Station—Toyei, AZ.

LUKACHUKAI, APACHE CO., ST. ISABEL (1910) (Native American)
105 St. Isabel Ln., P.O. Box 128, Lukachukai, AZ 86507-0128. Tel: 928-787-2322; Email: pjey54@yahoo.com. Rev. Florecito P.J. Pabatao, O.F.M.
Catechesis Religious Program—Email: ourladyoffatima_chinle@yahoo.com. Students 47.
Missions—Our Lady of Guadalupe—Round Rock, AZ.
St. Ann, Tsaile, AZ.
Our Lady of the Lake, Wheatfields, AZ.

MCNARY, APACHE CO., ST. ANTHONY (1922) [CEM]
33 N. McQuatters Ave., P.O. Box 628, Mcnary, AZ 85930-0628. Tel: 520-373-8367; Email: officeofbishsop@dioceseofgallup.org. Rev. Robert A. Hyman.

OVERGAARD, NAVAJO CO., OUR LADY OF THE ASSUMPTION (1982)
P.O. Box 628, Overgaard, AZ 85933.
Tel: 928-535-5329;
Fax: ladyoftheassumption@frontiernet.net. 3048 Hwy. 277, Snowflake, AZ 85937. Jerry Thompson.
Catechesis Religious Program—Students 5.

PAGE, COCONINO CO., IMMACULATE HEART OF MARY (1958)
455 S. Lake Powell Blvd., Page, AZ 86040.
Tel: 928-645-2301; Email: ihmcatholic@cableone.net. P.O. Box 1387, Page, AZ 86040-1387. Rev. Thomas R. Maikowski, Ph.D., Ed.D., Admin.
Catechesis Religious Program—Students 75.

PINETOP, NAVAJO CO., ST. MARY OF THE ANGELS (1974)
1915 S. Penrod Ln., Box 819, Pinetop, AZ 85935.
Tel: 928-367-2080; Fax: 928-367-2085; Email: stmaryspinetop@frontiernet.net; Web: www.stmaryoftheangels.com. P.O. Box 819, Pinetop, AZ 85935. Rev. Daniel P. Daley, (Retired).
Catechesis Religious Program—Email: mikecaruth@yahoo.com. Michael Caruth, D.R.E. Students 70.

PINON, NAVAJO CO., ST. MARY OF THE ROSARY (1937) (Native American), Attended by and mission of Our Lady of Fatima, Chinle, AZ.
P.O. Box 2119, Pinon, AZ 86510. Tel: 928-674-5202; Email: pjey54@yahoo.com. Indian Rte. 8030, Chinle, AZ 86503. Rev. Florecito P.J. Pabatao, O.F.M.
Catechesis Religious Program—Students 6.
Stations—Tachee, AZ.
Blue Gap, AZ.
Forest Lake, AZ.
Whippoorwill Spring, AZ.
Hardrock, AZ.
Kits'iiLi, AZ.

ST. JOHNS, APACHE CO., ST. JOHN THE BAPTIST (1880)
203 E. Commercial St., St. Johns, AZ 85936-0309.
Tel: 928-337-4390; Cell: 928-892-9722;
Fax: 928-358-3901; Email: MariposaConcho@gmail.com. P.O. Box 309, St. Johns, AZ 85936. Very Rev. Joachim Blonski; Deacon Carl Sadlier.
Catechesis Religious Program—Email: csadlier@msn.com. Deacon Carl Sadlier, D.R.E. Students 68.

ST. MICHAELS, APACHE CO., ST. MICHAEL (1898) [JC] (Native American)
24 Mission Rd., P.O. Box 680, St. Michaels, AZ 86511-0680. Tel: 928-871-4171; Tel: 928-871-4172; Fax: 928-871-4186; Email: stmikesofm@aol.com. Revs. Jose Femilou Gutay, O.F.M.; Edgardo Diaz, In Res.
Catechesis Religious Program—Tel: 928-871-4186; Email: vmcardy@gmail.com. Ms. Verna Cardy, D.R.E. Students 8.
Mission—St. Michael's Mission for Navajo Indians, St. Michaels, AZ.

SHOW LOW, NAVAJO CO., ST. RITA (1962)
1400 E. Owens St., P.O. Box 1449, Show Low, AZ 85901. Tel: 928-537-2543; Fax: 928-532-8441; Email: stritacatholicchurch@cableone.net; Web: stritashowlow.com. Rev. Daniel F. Kassis; Deacon John Heal.
Catechesis Religious Program—Email: quintana.rebecca46@gmail.com. Rebecca Quintana, D.R.E. Students 88.

SNOWFLAKE, NAVAJO CO., OUR LADY OF THE SNOW (1963)
1655 S. Main St., Snowflake, AZ 85937.
Tel: 928-536-4559; Email: ols@citlink.net; Web: www.ourladyofthesnow.info. Rev. Maria Joseph Kodiganti; Deacon Raymond Melcher.
Catechesis Religious Program—Sally Rush, D.R.E.; Rev. Nathanael Z. Block, D.R.E. Students 47.

SPRINGERVILLE, APACHE CO., ST. PETER (1880) (Hispanic)
Mailing Address: 145 N. Papago St., Springerville, AZ 85938. Tel: 928-333-4423; Email: st.peterscatholicparish@yahoo.com; Web: www.stpeterchurch-az.com. P.O. Box 1566, Springerville, AZ 85938. Rev. Edwin Bryan Diesen, Admin.
Catechesis Religious Program—Tel: 928-333-4423; Email: winsen12@hotmail.cxom. Devin Ditmore, D.R.E. Students 50.

TUBA CITY, COCONINO CO., ST. JUDE (1956)
P.O. Box 248, Tuba City, AZ 86045.
Tel: 928-283-5391; Email: jjungcm@gmail.com. 100 Aspen Dr., Tuba City, AZ 86048. Rev. Jay Jung, C.M.
Catechesis Religious Program—Theresa Tsosie, D.R.E. Students 16.

WHITERIVER, NAVAJO CO., ST. FRANCIS (1921) (Native American)
9 W. Elm St., Whiteriver, AZ 85941.
Tel: 928-338-4432; Email: stfranciswhiteriver@outlook.com. P.O. Box 679, Whiteriver, AZ 85941. Revs. Larry Weidner, (Retired); Matthew Rydberg, Admin.
Catechesis Religious Program—Fax: 928-338-1568.

WINSLOW, NAVAJO CO.
1—ST. JOSEPH'S (1896)
300 W. Hillview St., Winslow, AZ 86047.
Tel: 928-289-2350; Email: sjschurch@yahoo.com; Web: catholiccommunityofwinslow.myfreesites.net. Very Rev. Peter M. Short; Deacon Greg Carlson. Catholic Community of Winslow
Catechesis Religious Program—Students 50.
2—MADRE DE DIOS (1950) (Hispanic)
300 W. Hillview St., Winslow, AZ 86047.
Tel: 928-289-2350; Email: sjschurch@yahoo.com. 1051 Central St., Winslow, AZ. Very Rev. Peter M. Short; Deacon Greg Carlson. Catholic Community of Winslow
Catechesis Religious Program—Combined with St. Joseph's, Winslow. Students 205.

Chaplains of Public Institutions

GALLUP. *Gallup Area Hospitals & Nursing Homes*, Tel: 505-722-0999. Rev. Pio O'Connor, O.F.M.

FARMINGTON. *Farmington Area Hospitals*, 414 N. Allen Ave., Farmington, 87401. Tel: 505-325-9743. Vacant.

On Duty Outside of Diocese:
Revs.—
Block, Nathanael Z.
Brown, Mitchell A.
Juric, Jakov, Gospinica 18, 21000 Split, Croatia
Pudota, Thomas.

On Leave of Absence:
Revs.—
McConvey, Michael
Obersteiner, Ernest.

Pastoral Leave:
Rev.—
Vigil, Michael A.

Retired:
Rev. Msgrs.—
Gomez, Leo, (Retired), 10098 Bridgepointe, N.E., Albuquerque, 87111
MacDonald, Arthur F., (Retired), P.O. Box 222, Glenwood, AZ 88039
Very Rev.—
O'Keefe, Lawrence, J.C.D., (Retired), P.O. Box 849, Holbrook, AZ 86025-0849
Revs.—

Day, William F., (Retired), 2828 Park Cir., Unit 3, Pinetop, AZ 85935
Downie, Arley T., (Retired), #15 Rd. 6015, Farmington, 87401
Mesley, Jerome T., (Retired), P.O. Box 1947, 87305
Morello, Peter, (Retired), P.O. Box 234, Hammondsport, NY 14840
O'Neill, Hugh, (Retired), 1900 Mark Ave., 87301
Richardson, Donald, (Retired), 205 E. Bik Diamond Canyon, 87301
Tachias, Alfred A., J.C.L., (Retired), 1900 Mark Ave., 87301
Universal, Patrick J., (Retired), 190 Highland Ave., Apt. 103, Somerville, MA 02143
Walker, James E., Ph.D., V.G., (Retired), 1900 Mark Ave., 87301.

Permanent Deacons:
Aragon, Juan, (Leave of Absence), HC62, Box 637, Aragon, 87820
Ashenfelder, Michael, P.O. Box 584, Joseph City, AZ 86032-0584
Betts, James, 2800 N. Dustin Ave.. Apt. 301, Farmington, 87401
Campos, Jorge, 639 South Ave., Springerville, AZ 85938
Carlson, Greg, 1014 Winslow Ave., Winslow, AZ 86049
Chavez, Frank T., 5300 River Ridge Ave. NW, Albuquerqe, 87114
Chavez, Larry, P.O. Box 1883, Grants, 87020
Church, Todd, 1625 Terrace Loop, Grants, 87020
Conn, Richard, 2466 S. Acanthus, Mesa, AZ 85216-6101. (Retired out of diocese)
Copeland, Randolph, M.D., 1609 Red Rock Dr., 87301
Didde, Joseph, (Retired), 12 CR 6427, Kirtland, 87417
Endter, Paul, (Retired), 3071 Red Bluff Ct., 87301
Fernandez-Rojo, Rogelio, 201 Jaffin Dr. SE, Rio Rancho, 87124. (Leave of absence)
Garcia, Roger, 14 CR 4989, Bloomfield, 87413
Gorman, Wilson C., P.O. Box 218, Fort Defiance, AZ 86504-0218
Heal, John, P.O. Box 2845, Snowflake, AZ 85937
Hoy, James, 4841 Deer Trial Rd., Silver City, 88061. (Ministry outside Diocese)
Kocjan, Gerald, P.O. Box 3748, Page, AZ 86040. (Leave of Absence)
Lamoreux, Matthew, 5700 Jackrabbit Jct., Farmington, 87401
Lente, Michael, 133 Camino del Pueblo, Bernalillo, 87004. (Outside of Diocese)
Lujan, Timoteo, P.O. Box 2612, Milan, 87021-2612
Manuelito, Sherman, P.O. Box 538, Crownpoint, 87313
Margis, John, P.O. Box 313, Prewitt, 87045
Martin, Daniel Nez, P.O. Box 724, Window Rock, AZ 86515
Melcher, Raymond, (Retired), P.O. Box 1266, Snowflake, AZ 85937-1226
Moffett, Stephen, 8401-226 Pan American, Albuquerque, 87115. (Ministry Outside of Diocese)
Schaub, Edward, P.O. Box 12, Buckhorn, 88025
Scott, James, 3509 Kayenta Dr., Farmington, 87402
Stando, Matthew, (Retired), 2446 Harlem Rd., Cheektowaga, NY 14225. (Outside Diocese)
Sullivan, Michael, (Retired), Villa Guadalupe, 1900 Mark Ave., 87301
Ulibarri, Fiomeno, (Retired), P.O. Box 453, Concho, AZ 85924
Valdez, Patrick R., P.O. Box 526, Blanco, 87412
Valdo, Larry, (Retired), P.O. Box 352, Pueblo Of Acoma, 87034
Valencia, Ernest, P.O. Box 461, Blanco, 87412. (On Leave of Absence).

INSTITUTIONS LOCATED IN DIOCESE

[A] ELEMENTARY SCHOOLS

GALLUP. *St. Francis of Assisi School* (PreK) 215 W. Wilson, P.O. Box 4060, 87301. Tel: 505-863-3145; Email: saintfrancisprincipal@gmail.com. P.O. Box 4060, 67305. Jodi Thomas, Dir. Religious Teachers 1; Lay Teachers 10; Sisters 2; Students 48.
Sacred Heart Catholic School, (Grades PreK-8), 515 Park Ave., 87301. Tel: 505-863-6652; Fax: 505-726-8142; Email: principal@gallupcatholicschool.org; Web: www.sacredheartschoolgallup.com. Linda Padilla, Prin.; Ann Sloan, Librarian. Lay Teachers 10; Sisters 1; Students 71.

CUBA. *Immaculate Conception School*, (Grades PreK-8), (Temporarily Closed) P.O. Box 218, Cuba, 87013. Tel: 575-289-3749; Fax: 575-289-0031; Email: catholicschools@dioceseofgallup.org. Mrs. Jeanette Suter, Supt.

FARMINGTON. *Sacred Heart Catholic School*, (Grades PreK-8), 404 N. Allen Ave., Farmington, 87401. Tel: 505-325-7152; Fax: 505-325-6157; Email: office@shcsfarmington.org; Web: www.shcsfarmington.org. Rosalia Beyhan, Prin. Lay Teachers 19; Students 122.

GRANTS. *St. Teresa of Avila School*, (Grades PreK-8), 402 E. High St., Grants, 87020. Tel: 505-287-2261; Email: info@stteresaschoolwarriors.com; Web: www.stteresaschoolwarriors.com. P.O. Box 729, Grants, 87020. Angela Brunson, Prin. Lay Teachers 8; Students 77.

LUMBERTON. *St. Francis School*, (Grades K-8), 21 County Rd. 356, Lumberton, 87528. Tel: 575-759-3252; Fax: 575-759-3844; Email: stfrancisoflumberton@gmail.com; Web: www.stfrancisoflumberton.org. Madeline Lyon, Prin.; Valerie Gomez, D.R.E. & Teacher, Grade 3. Lay Teachers 6; Students 76.

PAGE. *Immaculate Heart School*, P.O. Box 1387, Page, AZ 86040-1387.

ST. MICHAELS, AZ. *St. Michael Indian School*, (Grades PreK-12), 1 Lupton Rd., St. Michaels, AZ 86511. Tel: 505-979-5590; Fax: 505-979-5590; Email: tazbah.shortey@smischools.org; Web: www.stmichaelindianschool.org. P.O. Box 650, St. Michaels, AZ 86511. Dot Teso, Pres.; Tazbah Shortey, Prin. Lay Teachers 24; Priests 1; Sisters 2; Students 351.

SAN FIDEL. *St. Joseph School* aka St. Joseph Mission School, (Grades PreK-8), 26 School Rd., San Fidel, 87049. Tel: 505-552-6362; Fax: 505-552-0168; Email: esteele@stjosephmissionschool.org; Email: atrujillo@stjosephmissionschool.org; Web: www.stjosephmissionschool.com. P.O. Box 370, San Fidel, 87049-0370. Antonio Trujillo, Prin. Lay Teachers 6; Students 49.

SHOW LOW. *Saint Anthony School*, (Grades PreK-8), 1400 E. Owens, Show Low, AZ 85901. Tel: 928-537-4497; Fax: 928-537-4507; Email: admin@stantschool.org; Web: www.stantschool.org. P.O. Box 789, Show Low, AZ 85902. Bryan Yorksmith, Prin. Lay Teachers 16; Students 152.

THOREAU. *St. Bonaventure School*, (Grades PreK-8), 8 Lenore Ave., Thoreau, 87323. Tel: 505-862-7465; Fax: 505-862-7790; Email: tlee@sbms.k12.nm.us; Web: www.stbonaventuremission.org. P.O. Box 610, Thoreau, 87323. Mrs. Tracie Lee, Prin. Religious Teachers 1; Lay Teachers 11; Students 177.

ZUNI. *St. Anthony Indian Mission School*, (Grades PreK-8), 11 St. Anthony Dr., Zuni, 87327. Tel: 505-782-4596; Fax: 505-782-2013; Email: principal@stanthonyzuni.org; Web: www.stanthonyzuni.org. P.O. Box 486, Zuni, 87327. Sr. Marsha Moon, Prin.
St. Anthony Indian School Religious Teachers 3; Lay Teachers 11; Students 144.

[B] CONVENTS AND RESIDENCES FOR SISTERS

GALLUP. *Casa Reina*, 711 S. Puerco Dr., 87301. Tel: 505-722-5511; Email: sistershnsgj@gmail.com. P.O. Box 807, 87305. Mother Magda Garcia, H.N.S.G., Treas. Sisters of our Lady of Guadalupe and Saint JosephPerpetual Adoration Chapel. Immigration and Naturalization Services, Hispanic Ministry, Teaching. Sisters 10.

GOBERNADOR. *Monastery of Our Lady of the Desert*, 10258 Hwy. 64, Blanco, 87412. Tel: 505-419-2938; Fax: 505-212-0159; Email: kateriosb@ourladyofthedesert.org. P.O. Box 556, Blanco, 87412. Sr. Hilda Tuyuc, O.S.B., Prioress. Benedictine Nuns Subiaco-Cassinese Congregation Final Professed Nuns 12; Temporary Professed 9.

[C] HOMES FOR THE AGED

GALLUP. *Villa Guadalupe Home for the Aged*, 1900 Mark Ave., 87301. Tel: 505-863-6894; Fax: 505-722-4121; Email: adgallup@littlesistersofthepoor.org. Sr. Sarah Skelton, L.S.P., Supr. Little Sisters of the Poor 8; Total Assisted 50.

[D] MISCELLANEOUS LISTINGS

GALLUP. *Blue Army* (Fatima Apostolate) 711 S. Puerco Dr., 87301. Tel: 505-722-5511; Email: garciamagda1219@gmail.com. Sisters Magda Leticia Garcia, H.N.S.G., Spiritual Dir.; Zuniga Rosa, Contact Person.
Catholic Charities of Gallup, Inc., 503 W. Hwy. 66, Ste. C, 87301. Tel: 505-722-4407; Fax: 505-722-7512; Email: exectivedirector@catholiccharitiesgallup.org; Email: accountant@catholiccharitiesgallup.org; Web: www.catholiccharitiesgallup.org. P.O. Box 3146, 87305. Ms. Vicki Trujillo, Dir.
Catholic Peoples' Foundation, Inc., P.O. Box 369, 87305. Tel: 505-726-8295; Fax: 505-863-3309; Email: amanda@catholicpeoplesfoundation.com; Web: www.catholicpeoplesfoundation.com. 503 W. Historic Hwy. 66, Ste. A, 87301. Herbert B. Mosher, Exec. Dir.; Amanda Galaviz, Administrative Dir.
St. Joseph's Shelter and Soup Kitchen, 207 Black Diamond Canyon Dr., 87301. Tel: 505-722-5261 (Convent); Tel: 505-722-5156 (Soup Kitchen); Email: officeofbishop@dioceseofgalluo.org. Sr. Mariosa Soreng, M.C., Supr. Missionaries of Charity.Soup Kitchen & Shelter for Native American Clients. Missionaries of Charity 7; Total Assisted 24,623.
Sacred Heart Retreat, P.O. Box 1338, 87305. Tel: 505-722-6755; Email: shrc@dioceseofgallup.org; Web: Retreat.dioceseofgallup.org. Sr. Woohee Sofia Lee, S.F.M.A., Dir.
Southwest Indian Foundation, 100 W. Coal Ave., 87301. Tel: 505-863-2837; Fax: 505-863-2760; Email: bookkeeping@southwestindian.com; Web: www.southwestindian.com. P.O. Box 307, 87305. Mr. William McCarthy, Exec.
Board of Directors: Most Rev. James S. Wall; Mr. James Mason, Pres.; Mr. John Dowling, Vice Pres.; Victoria Begay, Sec.; Very Rev. Gilbert Schneider, O.F.M.; Cathy Gasparich; Gertrude Lee; Lyneve Garcia; Paula Mora; Matthew Blain.

PINETOP, AZ. *St. Vincent DePaul Society* (1990) P.O. Box 376, Pinetop, AZ 85935. Tel: 928-367-2029 (Thrift Shop); Tel: 928-367-3057 (Emergency Aid Office); Email: svdp.pinetop@gmail.com. 1525 S. Mccoy, Pinetop, AZ 85935. Mike Pimper, Pres.; Donald Lane, Thrift Store Mgr. Thrift Shop & Emergency Aid Office. Total Staff 4; Total Assisted 1,080.

THOREAU. *St. Bonaventure Indian Mission & School*, 25 Navarre Blvd. W., P.O. Box 610, Thoreau, 87323. Tel: 505-862-7847; Fax: 505-862-7029; Email: chaltar@stbonaventuremission.org; Web: www.stbonaventuremission.org. Chris Halter, Dir.

TUBA CITY. *Life Sharing Center, Inc., St. Jude Food Bank*, 100 Aspen Dr., Tuba City, AZ 86045. Tel: 928-283-6886; Email: lsc.sjfb@gmail.com; Web: stjudefoodbank.org. P.O. Box 1277, Tuba City, AZ 86045. Sr. Elizabeth Riddell, D.C., CEO.

WINSLOW, AZ. *La Casa de Nuestra Senora (Madonna House)* (1957) 213 Jefferson St., Winslow, AZ 86047. Tel: 928-289-9284; Email: mh.winslow@yahoo.com; Web: www.madonnahouse.org. Mary Lynn Murray, Dir.; Rev. Zachary Romanowsky. Mission of Madonna House Apostolate Combermere, Ontario, Canada; Prayer and Community Service Center; Catechesis of the Good Shepherd Program for 3 - 6 yr. olds.
Public Association of the Faithful Total in Residence 6.

RELIGIOUS INSTITUTES OF MEN REPRESENTED IN THE DIOCESE

For further details refer to the corresponding bracketed number in the Religious Institutes of Men or Women section.
[1100]—*Brothers of the Sacred Heart*—S.C.
[1330]—*Congregation of the Mission* (Western Prov.)—C.M.
[0490]—*Franciscan Brothers of Brooklyn, NY*—O.S.F.
[0520]—*Franciscan Friars* (Provs. of Our Lady of Guadalupe; St. John the Baptist)—O.F.M.

RELIGIOUS INSTITUTES OF WOMEN REPRESENTED IN THE DIOCESE

[0100]—*Adorers of the Blood of Christ*—A.S.C.
[]—*Benedictine Sisters*—O.S.B.
[]—*Congregation of Jesus Mary Joseph* (Shrin Zuni)—C.J.M.J.
[3710]—*Congregation of the Sisters of Saint Agnes*—C.S.A.
[1730]—*Congregation of the Sisters of the Third Order of St. Francis* (Oldenburg, Indiana)—O.S.F.
[0760]—*Daughters of Charity of St. Vincent de Paul*—D.C.
[1120]—*Dominican Sisters of Roman Congregation*—O.P.
[]—*Franciscan Immaculate Sisters*—S.F.I.
[]—*Franciscan Missionary Sisters of Assisi*.
[1780]—*Franciscan Sisters of Perpetual Adoration*—F.S.P.A.
[]—*Hermanas de Nuestra Senora de Guadalupe y San Jose*—H.N.S.G.
[2340]—*Little Sisters of the Poor*—L.S.P.
[2470]—*Maryknoll Sisters of St. Dominic*—M.M.
[2710]—*Missionaries of Charity*—M.C.
[]—*Religious Sisters of Charity*—R.S.C.
[0260]—*Sisters of the Blessed Sacrament for Indians and Colored People*—S.B.S.
[4120-05]—*Ursuline Sisters of Mount St. Joseph*—O.S.U.

NECROLOGY

† Mathieu, Robert E., Snowflake, AZ Our Lady of the Snows, Died Feb. 16, 2018

An asterisk (*) denotes an organization that has established tax-exempt status directly with the IRS and is not covered by the USCCB Group Ruling.

Archdiocese of Galveston-Houston

(Archidioecesis Galvestoniensis Houstoniensis)

His Eminence

DANIEL CARDINAL DINARDO

Archbishop of Galveston-Houston; ordained July 16, 1977; appointed Coadjutor Bishop of Sioux City August 19, 1997; consecrated October 7, 1997; appointed Bishop of Sioux City November 28, 1998; appointed Coadjutor Bishop of Galveston-Houston January 16, 2004; installed March 26, 2004; appointed Coadjutor Archbishop December 29, 2004; succeeded to the See February 28, 2006; elevated to Cardinal November 24, 2007. *Mailing Address: P.O. Box 907, Houston, TX 77001-0907.* Tel: 713-659-5461.

Chancery Office: P.O. Box 907, Houston, TX 77001-0907. Tel: 713-659-5461; Fax: 713-759-9151.

Most Reverend

JOSEPH A. FIORENZA, D.D.

Retired Archbishop of Galveston-Houston; ordained May 29, 1954; appointed Bishop of San Angelo September 4, 1979; consecrated and installed October 25, 1979; appointed Bishop of Galveston-Houston December 18, 1984; installed February 18, 1985; appointed Archbishop December 29, 2004; retired February 28, 2006. *Mailing Address: P.O. Box 907, Houston, TX 77001-0907.* Tel: 713-659-5461.

Most Reverend

GEORGE A. SHELTZ

Auxiliary Bishop of Galveston-Houston; ordained May 15, 1971; appointed Auxiliary Bishop of Galveston-Houston February 21, 2012; ordained May 2, 2012. *Mailing Address: P.O. Box 907, Houston, TX 77001-0907.* Tel: 713-659-5461.

Most Reverend

VINCENT M. RIZZOTTO, J.C.L.

Retired Auxiliary Bishop of Galveston-Houston; ordained May 26, 1956; appointed Auxiliary Bishop of Galveston-Houston June 22, 2001; ordained July 31, 2001; retired November 6, 2006.

ESTABLISHED IN 1847.

Square Miles 8,880.

Redesignated Diocese of Galveston-Houston on July 25, 1959; created Archdiocese December 29, 2004.

Comprises the Counties of Austin, Brazoria, Fort Bend, Galveston, Grimes, Harris, Montgomery, San Jacinto, Walker and Waller in the State of Texas.

For legal titles of parishes and archdiocesan institutions, consult the Chancery Office.

STATISTICAL OVERVIEW

Personnel	
Cardinals	1
Archbishops	1
Retired Archbishops	1
Bishop	2
Auxiliary Bishops	1
Retired Bishops	1
Priests: Diocesan Active in Diocese	145
Priests: Diocesan Active Outside Diocese	1
Priests: Diocesan in Foreign Missions	1
Priests: Retired, Sick or Absent	49
Number of Diocesan Priests	196
Religious Priests in Diocese	195
Total Priests in Diocese	391
Extern Priests in Diocese	33
Ordinations:	
Diocesan Priests	4
Transitional Deacons	8
Permanent Deacons in Diocese	376
Total Brothers	11
Total Sisters	395
Parishes	
Parishes	146
With Resident Pastor:	
Resident Diocesan Priests	100
Resident Religious Priests	42
Without Resident Pastor:	
Administered by Priests	3
Missions	7
Welfare	
Health Care Centers	8
Total Assisted	65,359
Homes for the Aged	4
Total Assisted	617
Residential Care of Children	4
Total Assisted	1,155
Specialized Homes	5
Total Assisted	9,821
Special Centers for Social Services	10
Total Assisted	378,477
Educational	
Seminaries, Diocesan	1
Students from This Diocese	22
Students from Other Diocese	48
Diocesan Students in Other Seminaries	16
Total Seminarians	38
Colleges and Universities	1
Total Students	3,314
High Schools, Private	10
Total Students	5,193
Elementary Schools, Diocesan and Parish	43
Total Students	10,855
Elementary Schools, Private	5
Total Students	2,212
Catechesis/Religious Education:	
High School Students	18,463
Elementary Students	56,540
Total Students under Catholic Instruction	96,615
Teachers in the Diocese:	
Priests	12
Brothers	2
Sisters	24
Lay Teachers	1,835
Vital Statistics	
Receptions into the Church:	
Infant Baptism Totals	9,315
Minor Baptism Totals	18,097
Adult Baptism Totals	2,296
Received into Full Communion	941
First Communions	19,123
Confirmations	13,300
Marriages:	
Catholic	2,623
Interfaith	700
Total Marriages	3,323
Deaths	3,918
Total Catholic Population	1,700,000
Total Population	7,086,708

Former Bishops—Rt. Revs. J. M. ODIN, C.M., D.D., ordained May 4, 1823; cons. Bishop of Claudiopolis and Vicar-Apostolic of Texas, March 6, 1842; transferred to Galveston 1847; promoted to New Orleans in 1861; died in Ambierle, France, May 25, 1870; C. M. DUBUIS, D.D., ordained June 1, 1844; cons. Nov. 23, 1862; resigned 1881; remained Titular Bishop of Galveston till 1892, when he was promoted to an Archbishopric i.p.i.; died May 21, 1895; at Vernaison, France; P. DUFAL, C.S.C., D.D., ordained Sept. 29, 1852; cons. Nov. 25, 1860; Bishop of Delcon, and Vicar-Apostolic of Eastern Bengal; transferred to Galveston; as Coadjutor of Rt. Rev. C. M. Dubuis, cum jure successionis, May 14, 1878; resigned 1880; died in Paris 1898; NICHOLAS A. GALLAGHER, D.D., ordained Dec. 25, 1868; consecrated Titular Bishop of Canopus, April 30, 1882; succeeded to Galveston, Dec. 16, 1892; died Jan. 21, 1918; Most Revs. CHRISTOPHER E. BYRNE, D.D., appt. July 18, 1918; cons. Nov. 10, 1918; made Assistant at the Pontifical Throne, May 8, 1941; died April 1, 1950; WENDELIN J. NOLD, S.T.D., appt. Nov. 29, 1947; consecrated Feb. 25, 1948; died Oct. 1, 1981; JOHN L. MORKOVSKY, S.T.D., ord. Dec. 5, 1933; Titular Bishop of Hieron and Auxiliary Bishop of Amarillo; appt. Dec. 22, 1955; cons. Feb. 22, 1956; succeeded to See Aug. 18, 1958; transferred to Galveston-Houston as Titular Bishop of Tigava and Coadjutor and Apostolic Administrator "cum jure successionis" April 1963; installed June 11, 1963; succeeded to the See of Galveston-Houston, April 22, 1975; retired Aug. 16, 1984; died March 24, 1990; JOSEPH A. FIORENZA, ord. May 29, 1954; appt. Bishop of San Angelo Sept. 4, 1979; cons. and installed Oct. 25, 1979; appt. Bishop of Galveston-Houston Dec. 18, 1984; installed Feb. 18, 1985; appt. Archbishop Dec. 29, 2004; retired Feb. 28, 2006.

Chancery Office—1700 San Jacinto St., Houston, 77002-8291. Mailing Address: P.O. Box 907, Houston, 77001-0907. Tel: 713-659-5461; Fax: 713-759-9151. Office Hours: Mon.-Fri. 8:30-4:30.

Chancellor and Moderator of the Curia—Most Rev. GEORGE A. SHELTZ, 1700 San Jacinto St., Houston, 77002-8291. Tel: 713-659-5461.

Vice Chancellor and Associate General Counsel—MS. CHRISTINA DEAJON, 1700 San Jacinto St., Houston, 77002-8291. Tel: 713-659-5461.

Vicar General—Most Rev. GEORGE A. SHELTZ.

Personal Secretary to the Office of the Cardinal—Rev. JEFFREY BAME.

Ethnic Vicars—Rev. REGINALD W. SAMUELS, Vicar, African American Catholics; VACANT, Vicar, Hispanic Catholics; Revs. THU NGOC NGUYEN, J.C.L.; EDMUND P. EDUARTE, Vicar of Filipino Catholics.

Vicar for Religious—2403 Holcombe, Houston, 77021. Tel: 713-741-8733. Sr. FRANCESCA KEARNS, C.C.V.I.

Deans and Vicariates—

Central Vicariate—Revs. ALBERT ZANATTA, C.R.S., Episcopal Vicar, Tel: 281-447-6381; PAUL G. FELIX, V.F., Central Dean, Tel: 713-695-0631; MIGUEL A. SOLORZANO, Northeast Dean; J. ABELARDO COBOS, Southeast Dean, Tel: 713-921-1261.

Northern Vicariate—Revs. NORBERT J. MADUZIA JR., D.Min., Tel: 281-370-3401; PHILIP A. WILHITE,

S.T.L., Northern Dean, Tel: 936-756-8186; TERENCE P. BRINKMAN, S.T.D., Eastern Dean; JOHN T. KELLER, San Jacinto Dean, Tel: 281-469-2686.

Southern Vicariate—Rev. Msgr. LEO WLECZYK, Episcopal Vicar, Tel: 979-297-3041; Revs. CHACKO PUTHUMAYIL, Galveston-Mainland Dean, Tel: 409-938-7000; WENCIL C. PAVLOVSKY, V.F., Bay Area Dean, Tel: 281-333-3891; JOHN KARE TAOSAN, C.I.M., V.F., Southern Dean, Tel: 281-331-3751.

Western Vicariate—Rev. Msgr. DANIEL L. SCHEEL, Episcopal Vicar, Tel: 713-468-9555; Rev. JOHN E. CAHOON, J.C.L., V.F., Western Dean, Tel: 281-778-0400; Rev. Msgr. BILL YOUNG, V.F., Southwest Dean, Tel: 713-729-0221; Revs. SEAN P. HORRIGAN, Northwest Dean; ERIC J. PITRE, M.Div., Bluebonnet Dean, Tel: 979-885-3868.

Secretariat Directors—

Secretariat For Administration—Most Rev. GEORGE A. SHELTZ, 1700 San Jacinto St., Houston, 77002-8291. Tel: 713-659-5461.

Secretariat For Clergy Formation and Chaplaincy Services—Rev. ITALO DELL'ORO, C.R.S., 1700 San Jacinto St., Houston, 77002-8291. Tel: 713-659-5461.

Secretariat For Communication—JONAH DYCUS, Dir., 1700 San Jacinto St., Houston, 77002-8291. Tel: 713-659-5461.

Secretariat For Finance—1700 San Jacinto St., Houston, 77002-8291. Tel: 713-659-5461. MR. AAD DE LANGE, Dir.

Secretariat For Pastoral and Educational Ministries—MR. JIM BARRETTE, Dir., 2403 Holcombe, Houston, 77021-2099. Tel: 713-741-8786.

Secretariat for Catholic Schools—DEBRA HANEY, Supt., 2403 Holcombe Blvd., Houston, 77021. Tel: 713-741-8704.

Secretariat for Social Concerns—VACANT, Dir., 2403 Holcombe, Houston, 77021-2099. Tel: 713-741-8769.

Tribunal Judicial—

Metropolitan Tribunal—Rev. R. LUCIEN (LUKE) MILLETTE, J.C.L., Judicial Vicar, Mailing Address: P.O. Box 907, Houston, 77001-0907. Tel: 713-807-9286; Fax: 713-807-9296; Email: tribunal@archgh.org.

Adjutant Judicial Vicar—Rev. RICHARD A. WAHL, C.S.B., J.C.L., Mailing Address: P.O. Box 907, Houston, 77001-0907. Tel: 713-807-9286; Fax: 713-807-9296; Email: tribunal@archgh.org.

Director of the Tribunal—MS. ANNE BRYANT, J.C.L.

Archdiocesan Judges—Revs. TRUNG V. NGUYEN, J.C.L.; ERIC J. PITRE, M.Div.; THU NGOC NGUYEN, J.C.L.

Promoter of Justice—Rev. JOHN E. CAHOON, J.C.L., V.F.

Defenders of the Bond—Rev. EDWIN A. COREAS, J.C.L.; MS. ANNE BRYANT, J.C.L.

Censor Librorum—Rev. TERENCE P. BRINKMAN, S.T.D., St John the Evangelist, Baytown, 77522.

Archdiocesan Councils, Commissions and Committees

Archdiocesan Presbyteral Council—1700 San Jacinto St., Houston, 77002-8291.

Presbyteral Council—His Eminence DANIEL CARDINAL DINARDO, D.D., S.T.L., Pres. Ex Officio Members: Most Rev. GEORGE A. SHELTZ, Vicar Gen.; Rev. ITALO DELL'ORO, C.R.S., Vicar for Clergy & Dir. Secretariat for Clergy. Appointees: Rev. Msgr. LEO WLECZYK; Rev. ALBERT ZANATTA, C.R.S.; Rev. Msgrs. DANIEL L. SCHEEL; CHESTER L. BORSKI; Rev. NORBERT J. MADUZIA JR., D.Min. Elected Members: Revs. JOHN ROONEY, Educational; THOMAS J. DOLCE, Spiritual/ Administrative, Mailing Address: P.O. Box 907, Houston, 77001. Chaplains: Rev. DOMINIC J. PISTONE, V.F. International Priest Representative: Rev. MICHAEL A. BARROSA, D.S. Area Representatives: Revs. WILLIAM ANDREW WOOD, Northern, Western and Bluebonnet; THOMAS V. PONZINI, Galveston-Mainland and Southern; REGINALD W. SAMUELS, Bay Area and Southeast; SEAN P. HORRIGAN, Southwest and Northwest; FELIX ILESANMI OSASONA, M.S.P., Eastern and San Jacinto; JOSE CARMEN HERNANDEZ-ANGULO, C.S., Central and Northeast.

College of Consultors—Rev. Msgrs. DANIEL L. SCHEEL; LEO WLECZYK; Most Rev. GEORGE A. SHELTZ; Rev. Msgr. CHESTER L. BORSKI; Revs. NORBERT J. MADUZIA JR., D.Min.; ALBERT ZANATTA, C.R.S.; HOWARD E. DRABEK.

Priests Personnel Committee—His Eminence DANIEL CARDINAL DINARDO, D.D., S.T.L.; Most Rev. GEORGE A. SHELTZ; Revs. ITALO DELL'ORO, C.R.S., Tel: 713-659-5461, Ext. 8241; FRANCIS M. MACATANGAY; THOMAS J. DOLCE; Rev. Msgr. CHESTER L. BORSKI; Revs. PHIL (SKIP) NEGLEY, M.S.; PHILIP A. WILHITE, S.T.L.; RICHARD R. HINKLEY.

Building and Planning Commission—Rev. NORBERT J. MADUZIA JR., D.Min.; Most Rev. GEORGE A. SHELTZ; MS. CHRISTINA DEAJON; Rev. Msgr. WILLIAM L. YOUNG; DEANNA ENNIS; MR. STEVE FAUGHT, Chm., 2403 Holcombe Blvd., Houston, 77021. Tel: 713-652-4456.

Ecumenism and Interreligious Affairs Commission—Rev. REGINALD W. SAMUELS, 1700 San Jacinto, Houston, 77002. Tel: 713-659-5461.

Liturgical Commission—Rev. JAMES M. BURKART, Chm., 11011 Hall Rd., Houston, 77089. Tel: 281-481-6816.

Secretariat for Administration—Most Rev. GEORGE A. SHELTZ, 1700 San Jacinto St., Houston, 77002-8291. Tel: 713-659-5461.

Archives and Current Records—MS. LISA MAY, Dir., 1700 San Jacinto St., Houston, 77002-8291. Tel: 713-659-5461.

Catholic Cemeteries—MS. STACY BATEY, Dir., Gulf Fwy. at Hughes Rd., P.O. Box 965, Dickinson, 77539. Tel: 281-337-1641; Tel: 409-948-1455.

Construction / Preventative Maintenance—MR. STEVE FAUGHT, Dir.; DEANNA ENNIS, Assoc. Dir. Preventive Maintenance, 2403 Holcombe Blvd., Houston, 77021. Tel: 713-652-4456.

Information Services—MR. RORY MURPHY, 1700 San Jacinto St., Houston, 77002-8921. Tel: 713-659-5461.

Internal Auditor—MS. MARGARET THOMPSON, 1700 San Jacinto St., Houston, 77002-8291. Tel: 713-659-5461.

Legal Services—MR. FRANK RYND, Dir., Gen. Counsel, 1700 San Jacinto St., Houston, 77002-8291. Tel: 713-659-5461.

Real Estate—MR. KEN SYKES, 1700 San Jacinto St., Houston, 77002-8291. Tel: 713-659-5461.

Human Resources—CHARLIE PAVLOVSKY, Dir., 1700 San Jacinto St., Houston, 77002. Tel: 713-659-5461.

Secretariat for Clergy Formation and Chaplaincy Services—Rev. ITALO DELL'ORO, C.R.S., 1700 San Jacinto St., Houston, 77002-8291. Mailing Address: P.O. Box 907, Houston, 77001-0907. Tel: 713-659-5461.

Apostleship of the Sea (Port Ministry)—Rev. CARLOS V. DE LA TORRE, Houston Dir., Mailing Address: Houston International Seaman's Center, P.O. Box 9506, Houston, 77261. Tel: 713-672-0511. Tel: 713-923-5843; MRS. KAREN PARSONS, Galveston, P.O. Box 2742, League City, 77574. Tel: 409-762-0021; Fax: 409-762-1436.

Catholic Chaplain Corps (Hospital Chaplains)—4206 MacGregor Way S., Houston, 77021-1598. Tel: 713-526-6438. DENICE FOOSE.

Catholic Relief Services—MRS. HILDA OCHOA, Dir., 1700 San Jacinto St., Houston, 77002-8921. Tel: 713-659-5461.

Correctional Ministries (Jail Chaplains)—Rev. RONALD F. CLOUTIER, Dir. (Chaplain Office at Harris County Jail), Office and Mailing Address, 2403 E. Holcombe, Houston, 77021-2098. Tel: 713-741-8745; Tel: 713-755-5326 (Jail).

Director of Ministry to Priests—Rev. PHIL (SKIP) NEGLEY, M.S., 1700 San Jacinto St., Houston, 77002-8921. Tel: 713-659-5461.

Diaconal Formation / Diaconal Ministry—Deacons PHILLIP JACKSON, Dir. Office of Diaconate, 9845 Memorial Dr., Houston, 77024. Tel: 713-686-4345, Ext. 268; DOMINIC ROMAGUERA, Dir. Diaconate Admission & Scrutinies, Tel: 713-686-4345, Ext. 419; ROBERT WARD, Dir. Diaconate Formation, 9845 Memorial Dr., Houston, 77024. Tel: 713-686-4345, Ext. 283.

Permanent Deacons—Deacon PHILLIP JACKSON, Dir. Permanent Diaconate, 9845 Memorial Dr., Houston, 77024. Tel: 713-686-4345, Ext. 268.

Mission Office—MS. HILDA OCHOA, Dir., 1700 San Jacinto St., Houston, 77002-8291. Tel: 713-659-5461. Holy Childhood, Propagation of the Faith.

Seminarian Support—1700 San Jacinto St., Houston, 77002-8291. Tel: 713-659-5461. Rev. RICHARD MCNEILLIE, Dir.

Vocations Office—1700 San Jacinto St., Houston, 77002-8291. Tel: 713-659-5461. Rev. RICHARD MCNEILLIE, Dir.

Secretariat for Communication—JONAH DYCUS, Dir., 1700 San Jacinto St., Houston, 77002-8291. Tel: 713-659-5461.

Radio—MRS. MADELINE JOHNSON, 1700 San Jacinto St., Houston, 77002-8291. Tel: 713-659-5461.

Texas Catholic Herald—REBECCA TORRELLAS, Editor, 1700 San Jacinto St., Houston, 77002-8291. Tel: 713-659-5461; Fax: 713-659-3444.

Secretariat for Finance—1700 San Jacinto St., Houston, 77002-8291. Tel: 713-659-5461. MR. AAD DE LANGE, Dir.

Accounting Department—ROSE MICHALEC, Controller, 1700 San Jacinto St., Houston, 77002-8291. Tel: 713-659-5461.

Development Office—1700 San Jacinto St., Houston, 77002-8291. Tel: 713-659-5461. MICHAEL SCHILLACI, Dir.

Insurance & Risk Manager—J. KIRK JENINGS, 1700 San Jacinto St., Houston, 77002-8291. Tel: 713-659-5461.

Claims Risk Manager—1700 San Jacinto St., Houston, 77002-8291. Tel: 713-652-4469; Tel: 800-856-4040; Fax: 713-739-0214. ANDREW RAUSCH, Dir.

Parish Accounting Services (PAS)—1700 San Jacinto St., Houston, 77002-8291. Tel: 713-659-5461. MRS. MARGARET WOODRUM, Dir.

Secretariat for Pastoral and Educational Ministries—MR. JIM BARRETTE, Dir., 2403 Holcombe, Houston, 77021-2099. Tel: 713-741-8786.

Aging Ministry—MRS. KATHY BINGHAM, Dir., 2403 Holcombe, Houston, 77021-2098. Tel: 713-741-8712.

Boy and Girl Scouts—Rev. PATRICK STUART GARRETT, 26777 Glen Loch Dr., The Woodlands, 77381-2921.

Campus Ministry and Young Adults—MS. GABRIELA KARASZEWSKI, Dir., 2403 Holcombe, Houston, 77021-2098. Tel: 713-741-8786.

Evangelization and Catechesis—JULIE BLEVINS, Dir., 2403 Holcombe, Houston, 77021-2099. Tel: 713-741-8730.

Circle Lake Retreat Center—MRS. GLORIA BUSTILLO, Dir., Mailing Address: P.O. Box 1410, Pinehurst, 77362-1410. Tel: 281-356-6764, Ext. 11; Fax: 281-356-6678; Email: circlelake@sbcglobal.net.

Deaf Apostolate—Rev. LEONARD R. BRONIAK, C.Ss.R., Dir., 2403 Holcombe Blvd., Houston, 77021-2099. Tel: 713-741-8721.

Family Life Ministry—2403 Holcombe, Houston, 77021-2099. Tel: 713-741-8710. VACANT, Dir.

Resource Center—Tel: 713-741-8781. VACANT.

Pro-Life Activities—JULIE FRITSCH, Dir., 2403 E. Holcombe Blvd., Houston, 77021-2099. Tel: 713-741-8728.

Worship—MRS. SANDRA HIGGINS, Dir., 2403 Holcombe, Houston, 77021-2099. Tel: 713-741-8760.

Adolescent Catechesis and Evangelization—2403 Holcombe, Houston, 77021-2099. Tel: 713-741-8723. TIM COLBERT, Dir.

Special Youth Services (Juvenile Detention Ministry)—MS. FRANCHELLE LEE STEWART, Dir., 2403 Holcombe, Houston, 77021-2099. Tel: 713-527-1894; Tel: 832-541-4718.

Secretariat for Catholic Schools—2403 Holcombe Blvd., Houston, 77021. Tel: 713-741-8704. DEBRA HANEY, Supt.

Catholic School Office—2403 Holcombe, Houston, 77021-2099. Tel: 713-741-8704. DEBRA HANEY, Supt.

School of Environmental Education - Camp Kappe—7738 Camp Kappe Rd., Navasota, 77363. Tel: 936-894-2141. RANDY ADAMS, Dir. Camp Kappe; MR. SHAYNE RODRIGUES, Dir. School Environmental Educ.

Secretariat for Social Concerns—VACANT, Dir., 2403 Holcombe, Houston, 77021-2099. Tel: 713-741-8769.

Campaign for Human Development—Deacon SAM DUNNING, Dir., 2403 Holcombe, Houston, 77021-2098. Tel: 713-741-8731.

Catholic Charities of the Archdiocese of Galveston-Houston—CYNTHIA NUNES COLBERT, M.S.W., Pres. & CEO, 2900 Louisiana St., Houston, 77006. Tel: 713-526-4611; Fax: 713-526-1546. Mailing Address: P.O. Box 66508, Houston, 77266.

Chief Financial Officer—Tel: 713-874-6713. BART FERRELL.

Chief Operating Officer—Tel: 713-874-6777. NYLA K. WOODS.

Vice President of Development & Stewardship—Tel: 713-874-6624. BRIAN GILLEN.

Communications—Tel: 713-874-6751. BETSY BALLARD.

St. Jerome Emiliani's Home for Children—Tel: 713-874-6301. CHANICA BROWN.

Senior Vice President of Programs—NATALIE WOOD, Tel: 713-874-6731.

Vice President of Case Management and Poverty Alleviation—Tel: 713-874-6772. SHANNON STROTHER.

Vice President, Disaster Recovery—Tel: 713-874-6745. BRIGID DELOACH.

St. Frances Cabrini Center for Immigrant Legal Assistance—Tel: 713-874-4145. ZENOBIA LAI.

Refugee Resettlement Services—ARDIANE ADEMI, Tel: 713-874-6516.

St. Michael's Homes for Children—Tel: 713-526-4611. SERGIO CRUZ.

Galveston County Center—Basic Needs Southern Region ELIZABETH KINARD, Dir. Galveston County - Bay Area; NORMA ROCHE, Coord. Galveston, Tel: 409-762-2064; ANNIE CAZARES, Coord. Texas City, Tel: 409-942-4267.
Mamie George Community Center/Fort Bend County—Tel: 281-202-6224. GLADYS BRUMFIELD JAMES, Dir.
Justice and Peace—Deacon SAM DUNNING, Dir., 2403 E. Holcombe, Houston, 77021-2099. Tel: 713-741-8730.
**St. Vincent de Paul Society*—MS. ANN SCHORNO, Exec. Dir., 2403 Holcombe, Houston, 77021-2099. Tel: 713-741-8783.
Council of Catholic Women—Rev. Msgr. DANIEL L. SCHEEL, Archdiocesan Moderator, 8825 Kempwood Dr., Houston, 77080. Tel: 713-468-9555.
Cursillos in Christianity—Deacon HECTOR MORALES, Admin.; Rev. EUGENE CANAS, O.M.I., Spiritual Dir., St. Paul Cursillo Center, 4000 Belk St., Houston, 77087. Tel: 713-643-7682.
Disaster Relief—J. KIRK JENINGS, 1700 San Jacinto, Houston, 77002. Tel: 713-659-5461.
Rural Life Bureau—VACANT, 1700 San Jacinto St., Houston, 77002-8291. Tel: 713-659-5461.
Victim Assistance Coordinator—
Tel: 713-659-5461, Ext. 499; Tel: 713-654-5799; Email: vac@archgh.org. DIANE VINES.

CLERGY, PARISHES, MISSIONS AND PAROCHIAL SCHOOLS

CITY OF GALVESTON

(GALVESTON COUNTY)

1—ST. MARY'S CATHEDRAL BASILICA (1840)
2011 Church St., Galveston, 77550-2091.
Tel: 409-762-9611; Fax: 406-765-8585.

2—HOLY FAMILY aka Holy Family Parish (2009)
1010 35th St., Galveston, 77550. Tel: 409-762-9646; Fax: 409-765-7636; Web: www.holyfamilygb.com. Revs. Jude E. Ezuma; Jorge Cabrera, Parochial Vicar; Stephen J. Payne, Parochial Vicar; Deacons Robert Standridge; John Pistone; Douglas Matthews; Sam Dell'Olio; Kimble Nobles; John Carrillo.
School—Holy Family School, 2601 Ursuline Ave., Galveston, 77550. Tel: 409-765-6607;
Fax: 409-765-5154; Email: rhesse@hfcsgalv.org. Rita Hesse, Prin. Lay Teachers 15; Sisters 1; Students 101.
Catechesis Religious Program—Mrs. Tammy Juarez, D.R.E. Students 375.

3—HOLY ROSARY (1888) Closed. For parish records contact the Archives of Galveston-Houston.

4—OUR LADY OF GUADALUPE, Closed. August 1992. Contact St Patrick, Galveston for further information.

5—ST. PATRICK (1870) Closed. For parish records contact the Archives of Galveston-Houston.

6—ST. PETER THE APOSTLE (1965) Closed. For parish records contact the Archives of Galveston-Houston.

7—SACRED HEART (1884) Closed. For parish records contact the Archives of Galveston-Houston.

CITY OF HOUSTON

(HARRIS COUNTY)

1—ST. ALBERT OF TRAPANI (1970)
11027 S. Gessner Dr., 77071-3599. Tel: 713-771-3596. Rev. Vincent Vu Tran; Deacons Pedro Salas; Alvaro Casas Jr.; Edwin F. Gosline.
Catechesis Religious Program—Peggy Popkey, D.R.E. Students 265.

2—ALL SAINTS (1908)
215 E. 10th St., 77008-7025. Tel: 713-864-2653;
Fax: 713-864-0761; Email: lupe.padilla@allsaints.us.com; Web: www.allsaintsheights.us.com. Revs. Williams A. Oliver; Ronald F. Cloutier, In Res.; Deacons Gary Hilbig; Rodolfo Cerda; Juan Pareja.
Catechesis Religious Program—John Guzman, D.R.E. Students 92.

3—ST. ALPHONSUS (1966)
9217 E. Ave. L, 77012-2727. Tel: 713-923-5843. Rev. Carlos V. de la Torre.
Catechesis Religious Program—Mrs. Mary Elizondo, C.R.E. Students 345.

4—ST. AMBROSE (1958)
4213 Mangum Rd., 77092-5599. Tel: 713-686-3497. Revs. Benjamin Smaistrla; Juan G. Pineda, (Colombia) Parochial Vicar.
School—St. Ambrose School, Tel: 713-686-6990;
Fax: 713-686-6902; Email: jfritsch@sashornets.org. Judy A. Fritsch, Prin. Lay Teachers 29; Students 284.
Catechesis Religious Program—Tel: 713-686-3497; Email: mthompson@stambrosehouston.org. Miguel Vences, D.R.E. Students 498.

5—ST. ANDREW KIM (1977) (Korean)
1706 Bingle Rd., 77055-2336. Tel: 713-465-2682; Email: standrewkimhouston@yahoo.com. Rev. Bong Ho Ko; Deacon Emmanuel Gwak.
Rectory—8557 Hiridge St., 77055. Tel: 713-465-2926.
Catechesis Religious Program—Tel: 281-889-9091. Mr. Dong Lee, D.R.E. Students 135.

6—ST. ANNE (1925)
2140 Westheimer, 77098-1419. Tel: 713-526-3276. Revs. Alvin A. Sinasac, C.S.B.; Jay Francis Walsh, C.S.B., Parochial Vicar; David J. Zapalac, C.S.B., Parochial Vicar; Deacon Jean-Paul Budinger.
School—St. Anne School, 2120 Westheimer, 77098.
Tel: 713-526-3279; Email: dmartinez@stannecs.org. Dawn Martinez, Prin. Lay Teachers 36; Students 513.
Catechesis Religious Program—Tel: 713-525-4273. Scott Harr, Dir. Catechesis, Children. Students 415.

7—ST. ANNE DE BEAUPRE (1948)
2810 Link Rd., 77009-1196. Tel: 713-869-1319. Rev. Felix Elosi, M.S.P.
Catechesis Religious Program—Pamela McCarthy, C.R.E. Students 14.

8—ANNUNCIATION (1869)
1618 Texas Ave., 77002. Tel: 713-222-2289;
Fax: 713-222-2280; Email: info@annunciationcc.org; Web: www.acchtx.org. P.O. Box 214, 77001-0214. Rev. Paul G. Felix, V.F.; Deacons Bart Hock; Robert George Alexander.
Catechesis Religious Program—Tel: 571-447-1734. Tammy Zanovello, D.R.E. Students 59.

9—ASCENSION CHINESE MISSION (1988) (Chinese)
4605 Jetty Ln., 77072-1222. Tel: 281-575-8855;
Fax: 281-575-6940. Deacons Patrick Cheung; Paul Kiang; Benny Chang.
Catechesis Religious Program—Tel: 832-275-8178. Bonnie Lee, D.R.E. Students 62.

10—ASSUMPTION (1948)
901 Rose Ln., 77037-4699. Tel: 281-447-6381;
Fax: 281-447-6382. Revs. Albert Zanatta, C.R.S.; Franco Cecchini, C.R.S., Parochial Vicar; Deacons Mario Ortega; Will Hunter.
School—Assumption School, 801 Rose Ln., 77037.
Tel: 281-447-2132; Email: dpalomino@houstonassumption.org; Email: jbates@houstonassumption.org. John William Bates, Prin. Lay Teachers 12; Sisters 1; Students 217.
Catechesis Religious Program—Tel: 281-445-1268. Deacon Mario Ortega, D.R.E. Students 1,105.

11—ST. AUGUSTINE (1955)
5560 Laurel Creek Way, 77017-6746.
Tel: 713-946-8968; Fax: 713-946-0080; Email: sacc@staugustinecc.com. Rev. Dwight M. Canizares; Deacon Benito Meza.
School—St. Augustine School, 5500 Laurel Creek Way, 77017. Tel: 713-946-9050; Fax: 713-943-3444; Email: drios@staugustinecs.org. Denise P. Rios, Prin. Lay Teachers 3; Students 361.
Catechesis Religious Program—Mary D. Silva, C.R.E. Students 159.

12—ST. BENEDICT THE ABBOT (1963)
4025 Grapevine, 77045-6320. Tel: 713-433-9836;
Fax: 713-433-3949. Revs. Clement N. Uchendu; Andy H. Do, C.S.Sp., Parochial Vicar.
Rectory—3931 Grapevine, 77045.
Catechesis Religious Program—Tel: 713-433-2436. Mrs. Alicia Bernal, D.R.E. Students 345.

13—ST. BERNADETTE SOUBIROUS (1977)
15500 El Camino Real, 77062-5793.
Tel: 281-486-0337; Fax: 281-218-9440. Rev. Robert S. Barras, V.F.; Deacon Bob Rumford.
Rectory—959 El Dorado Blvd., 77062.
Catechesis Religious Program—
Tel: 281-486-0337, Ext. 112. Barbara Aubuchon, D.R.E. (K-5). Students 553.

14—BLESSED SACRAMENT (1910)
4015 Sherman, 77003-2695. Tel: 713-224-5291;
Fax: 713-224-5292. Rev. Rudolfo Rudy Sanchez, Admin.
Catechesis Religious Program—Students 176.

15—ST. CATHERINE OF SIENA (1975)
10688 Shadow Wood Dr., 77043-2826.
Tel: 713-467-8170; Fax: 713-467-7149. Rev. Niall Nolan.
Rectory—1902 Stebbins Dr., 77043-2417.
Catechesis Religious Program—Robin Hayes, D.R.E. Students 76.

16—ST. CECILIA (1956)
11720 Joan of Arc Dr., 77024-2602.
Tel: 713-465-3414; Email: pastor@saintcecilia.org; Web: www.saintcecilia.org. Revs. Francis M. Macatangay; Paul A. Foltyn, Parochial Vicar; Deacons Gregory Evans; Sam Mancuso; Frank Davis.
Rectory—11701 Joan of Arc Dr., 77024.
School—St. Cecilia School, 11740 Joan of Arc Dr., 77024. Tel: 713-468-9515; Fax: 713-468-4698; Email: ceverling@saintcecilia.org; Web: www.saintceciliacatholicschool.org. Dr. Carol Ann Everling, Prin. Clergy 1; Lay Teachers 40; Sisters 1; Students 582; Clergy / Religious Teachers 2.
Catechesis Religious Program—Rosemary Munoz, Asst. D.R.E. Students 890.

17—ST. CHARLES BORROMEO (1962)
501 Tidwell, 77022-2121. Tel: 713-692-6303;
Fax: 713-692-6314. Revs. Miguel A. Solorzano; Michael McFall, Parochial Vicar; Deacons Charles R. Conant; Rodrigo Lozano; Thomas Gandara; Nwoko Kingsley.
Catechesis Religious Program—Tel: 832-297-1315. Sr. Esmeralda Alejo, D.J., D.R.E. Students 429.

18—CHRIST THE KING (1928)
4419 N. Main St., 77009-5199. Tel: 713-869-1449;
Fax: 713-869-1491. Revs. Julian Gerosa, C.R.S.; Varghese Arattukulam, Parochial Vicar; Italo Dell`Oro, C.R.S., In Res.
Catechesis Religious Program—Tel: 832-338-3867. Deacon Tomas Cano. Students 571.

19—CHRIST THE REDEEMER (1980)
11507 Huffmeister Rd., 77065-1051.
Tel: 281-469-5533; Email: office@ctrcc.com; Web: www.ctrcc.com. Revs. Sean P. Horrigan; Ralph O. Roberts, Parochial Vicar; Deacons Phillip Jackson; Lupe Trevino; Greg Hall; William Bradley; Kerry Bourque; Jack Alexander; Jay Gause; Stephen Moses; Jeff Speight; Jeffrey Willard.
School—Christ the Redeemer Catholic School, 11511 Huffmeister Rd., 77065. Tel: 281-469-8440;
Fax: 281-894-9669; Email: dan.courtney@ctrschool.com. Dan Courtney, Prin. Lay Teachers 27; Students 395.
Catechesis Religious Program—Ms. Kathy Kelley, D.R.E. Students 541.

20—CHRIST, THE INCARNATE WORD (1997) (Vietnamese)
8503 S. Kirkwood Rd., 77099-4056.
Tel: 281-495-8133; Fax: 281-568-1833. Revs. Thu Ngoc Nguyen, J.C.L.; Joseph T.P. Bui, Parochial Vicar; Deacons Cuong Nguyen; Joseph Si Bach Nguyen.
Catechesis Religious Program—Tel: 281-495-3741. Hien Le, D.R.E. Students 693.

21—ST. CHRISTOPHER (1924)
8150 Park Place Blvd., 77017-3033.
Tel: 713-645-6614; Fax: 713-640-1640. Revs. Joseph Thu Le; Hieu Nguyen; Deacons Allan Fredericksen; Benito Tristan; David D. Mitchell.
School—St. Christopher School, 8134 Park Place Blvd., 77017. Tel: 713-649-0009; Fax: 713-649-1104; Email: principal@sccs1939.org; Web: www.sccs1939.org. JoAnn Prater, Prin. Clergy 1; Lay Teachers 13; Sisters 1; Students 171; Clergy / Religious Teachers 2.
Catechesis Religious Program—Tel: 713-645-6142. Maria Fernandez, D.R.E. Students 210.

22—ST. CLARE OF ASSISI (1990)
3131 El Dorado Blvd., 77059-5100. Tel: 281-286-7729; Fax: 281-286-1256. Rev. Vincent Vuong-Quoc Nguyen; Deacons John H. Dean; Robert Hebert.
Rectory—15906 Laurelfield, 77059.
School—St. Clare of Assisi School, Tel: 281-286-3395; Email: al.varisco@stclarehouston.org. Dr. Al Varisco, Prin. Lay Teachers 23; Students 192.
Catechesis Religious Program—Tel: 281-486-0874. Sandra Trevino, Dir. Intergenerational Faith Formation. Students 332.

23—CO-CATHEDRAL OF THE SACRED HEART (1896)
1111 St. Joseph Pkwy., 77002-8127.
Tel: 713-659-1561; Fax: 713-651-1365. Very Rev. Lawrence W. Jozwiak, J.C.L.; Rev. Alfonso Tran; Deacons Daniel Addis; Johnny Salinas; Leonard P. Lockett; John Carrara.
Res.: 2016 Main St. #2603, 77002. Email: office@sacredhearthouston.org; Web: www.sacredhearthouston.org.
Catechesis Religious Program—Mrs. Selma DeMarco, Dir. Faith Formation. Students 209.

24—CORPUS CHRISTI (1956)
9900 Stella Link Rd., 77025-4718. Tel: 713-667-0497; Fax: 713-668-4742. Revs. Thomas Smithson, S.S.S.; RaviEarnest Sebastin, Parochial Vicar; Peter Tuong, Parochial Vicar.
School—Corpus Christi School, 4005 Cheena St., 77025. Tel: 713-664-3351; Fax: 713-664-6095; Web: www.corpuschristihouston.org. Dr. Mazie McCoy, Prin. Lay Teachers 16; Students 208.
Catechesis Religious Program—Claudia Sereno, D.R.E. Students 418.

25—ST. CYRIL OF ALEXANDRIA (1963)
10503 Westheimer Rd., 77042-3502.
Tel: 713-789-1250; Fax: 713-554-1555. Revs. Mario J. Arroyo; Jhon Jaime Florez, Parochial Vicar; Deacons Eduardo M. Dolpher; Arturo Mendoza.
Catechesis Religious Program—Tel: 713-554-1563. Aida Silva, D.R.E. Students 715.

26—ST. DOMINIC (1965)
8215 Reservoir St., 77049-1728. Tel: 281-458-2910;
Fax: 281-458-7114. Rev. Roger O. Estorque.
Catechesis Religious Program—Sr. Deandria Gonzalez, D.R.E. Students 465.

27—ST. ELIZABETH ANN SETON (1977)
6646 Addicks-Satsuma Rd., 77084-1599.

Tel: 281-463-7878; Email: office@seascatholic.org; Web: www.SeasCatholic.org. Revs. Stephen B. Reynolds; Gregory Tran, C.M.C., Parochial Vicar; Antonio Ortiz, Parochial Vicar; Preston Quintela, Parochial Vicar; Deacons German Godoy, Pastoral Assoc.; Charles G. Pennell; Gilbert R. Johnson; Alfonso Sosa; Peter Hoang; Tom Jeffers.
School—St. Elizabeth Ann Seton School, Tel: 281-463-1444; Fax: 281-463-8707; Email: iaguilera@seascs.org. Ignacio Aguilera, Prin. Lay Teachers 26; Students 310.
Catechesis Religious Program—Students 931.

28—ST. FRANCES CABRINI (1962)
10727 Hartsook St., 77034-3523. Tel: 713-946-5768; Fax: 713-946-3282. Rev. Frank T. Fabj; Deacons Robert Gregory Stevens; Freddy Ramirez; Daniel Lopez; Guadalupe Sanchez.
Rectory—10726 Bessemer St., 77034.
Catechesis Religious Program—Sr. Diane Perales, C.C.E. Coord. Students 967.

29—ST. FRANCIS DE SALES (1962)
8200 Roos Rd., 77036-6399. Tel: 713-774-7475; Fax: 713-774-6591. Revs. Joseph Son Thanh Phan; Enrique V. Salen, In Res.; Deacons Tony Flores; Alberto Ospina; Danilo Naranjo; Michael Quiray.
Res.: 8018 Roos Rd., 77036.
School—St. Francis de Sales School, 8100 Roos Rd., 77036. Tel: 713-774-4447; Fax: 713-271-6744; Email: wootend@sfdsschool.org. Diane Wooten, Prin. Lay Teachers 27; Sisters 1; Students 361; Clergy / Religious Teachers 1.
Catechesis Religious Program—Yolanda Salazar, D.R.E. Students 374.

30—ST. FRANCIS OF ASSISI (1950)
5102 Dabney St., 77026-3015. Tel: 713-672-7773; Fax: 713-673-1913. Deacons Ignatius Joseph; Michael St. Julian.
School—St. Francis of Assisi School, 5100 Dabney St., 77026. Tel: 713-674-1966; Fax: 713-674-9901; Email: ggomez@sfoacs.org. Gregory Gomez, Prin. Clergy 1; Lay Teachers 14; Sisters 1; Students 71; Clergy / Religious Teachers 2.
Catechesis Religious Program—
Tel: 713-672-7773, Ext. 106. Sr. Anthonia Osuesu, D.R.E./C.R.E. Students 27.

31—ST. FRANCIS XAVIER (1952)
4600 Reed Rd., 77051-2857. Tel: 713-738-2311. Rev. Michael Saah-Buckman, S.S.J.; Deacons Michael V. Jenkins; Darryl K. Drennon.
Catechesis Religious Program—Tel: 713-731-2775. Unella Baber, D.R.E. Students 90.

32—ST. GREGORY THE GREAT (1962)
10500 Nold Dr., 77016-2921. Tel: 713-631-3681; Fax: 713-631-6114. Rev. Francis Huan Ton Ngo, (Retired).
Catechesis Religious Program—Tel: 713-631-0058. Sr. Ann Theresa Nguyen, C.R.E. Students 160.

33—HOLY CROSS CHAPEL (Downtown) (1982)
905 Main St., 77002-6408. Tel: 713-650-1323. Rev. Francisco Vera.

34—HOLY GHOST (1946)
6921 Chetwood Dr., 77081-5697. Tel: 713-668-0463; Fax: 713-661-4645. Revs. William C. Bueche, C.Ss.R.; James C. Arrambide, C.Ss.R., Parochial Vicar; Andrew Meiners, C.Ss.R., Parochial Vicar; Peter H. Voelker, C.Ss.R., Parochial Vicar; Quy Duong, Parochial Vicar; Leonard R. Broniak, C.Ss.R., Parochial Vicar; Gan Nguyen, C.Ss.R., Parochial Vicar.
School—Holy Ghost School, 6920 Chimney Rock Rd., 77081. Tel: 713-668-5327; Fax: 713-667-4410; Email: mendez@holyghostschool.com. Christina Mendez, Prin. Lay Teachers 14; Students 85.
Catechesis Religious Program—Tel: 713-668-8001. Ms. Marilynn Wilson, D.R.E. (English); Norma Basurto, D.R.E. (Spanish). Students 483.

35—HOLY NAME (1920)
Mailing Address: 1920 Marion St., 77009-8497.
Tel: 713-222-1255; Fax: 713-222-1260. Rev. Anil Thomas, S.V.D.
Rectory—1917 Cochran St., 77009-8497. Email: holynamehouston@gmail.com; Web: holynamecatholic.org.
Catechesis Religious Program—Alicia Aviles, D.R.E. Students 253.

36—HOLY ROSARY (1913)
3601 Milam St., 77002-9591. Tel: 713-529-4854; Email: office@holyrosaryparish.org. Revs. Jorge Rativa; Peter Damian Harris, Parochial Vicar; Alberto Rodriguez Lopez, O.P., Parochial Vicar; Charles Johnson, Campus Min.; Martin Iott, O.P., In Res.; Juan M. Torres, O.P., In Res.; Anthony Hung N. Tran, O.P., In Res.
Rectory—3600 Travis St., 77002-9544.
Fax: 713-522-3967; Web: www.holyrosaryparish.org.
Catechesis Religious Program—Tel: 713-526-4389. Janet Hafernik, C.R.E. Students 234.

37—IMMACULATE CONCEPTION (1911)
7250 Harrisburg Blvd., 77011-4791.
Tel: 713-921-1261; Fax: 713-921-2304. Revs. Henry B. Walker, O.M.I.; Marco A. Ortiz, O.M.I., Parochial Vicar.
Catechesis Religious Program—Teresa Martinez, C.R.E. Students 494.

38—IMMACULATE HEART OF MARY (1926)
7539 Ave. K, 77012-1033. Tel: 713-923-2394; Fax: 713-923-6497. Revs. Timothy Paulsen, O.M.I.; Joseph B. Aluthwatte, O.M.I.; Eugene Canas, O.M.I., In Res.; Raymond Cook, O.M.I., In Res.
Catechesis Religious Program—Tel: 713-921-5431. Debra Cortez, D.R.E. Students 228.

39—ST. JEROME (1960)
8825 Kempwood, 77080-4199. Tel: 713-468-9555; Fax: 713-464-0325. Rev. Msgr. Daniel L. Scheel; Revs. David Angelino; Michael S. Van Cleve; Deacons Pedro Salas; Dan O'Dowd; Gil Vela.
Rectory—9011 Friendship, 77080.
School—St. Jerome School, Tel: 713-468-7946; Email: pjackson@stjeromecs.org. Patricia Jackson, Prin. Lay Teachers 19; Students 225; Clergy / Religious Teachers 1.
Catechesis Religious Program—Tel: 713-464-5029. Johana Gerro, D.R.E. Students 1,338.

40—ST. JOHN NEUMANN (1977)
2730 Nelwood Dr., 77038-1025. Tel: 281-931-0684; Fax: 281-931-5363. Rev. Msgr. Seth F. Hermoso, (Retired); Rev. Pierre Vertus, Parochial Vicar.
Rectory—2715 Nelwood Dr., 77038-1025.
Catechesis Religious Program—Tel: 281-931-1884. Blanca Dolpher, D.R.E. Students 578.

41—ST. JOHN VIANNEY (1966)
625 Nottingham Oaks Tr., 77079-6234.
Tel: 281-497-1500; Fax: 281-584-2024. Revs. R. Troy Gately; Clark Sample, Parochial Vicar; Charles J. Talar, In Res.; Deacons Dale W. Steffes; Albert E. Vacek Jr.; Frederick Kossegi; Gregory Stokes.
Catechesis Religious Program—Tel: 281-497-6665. Carolina Sayago, D.R.E. Students 1,265.

42—ST. JOSEPH-ST. STEPHEN (1880)
1505 Kane St., 77007-7711. Tel: 713-222-6193; Fax: 713-222-1729; Email: office@stjosephststephen.org; Web: www.stjosephststephen.org. Rev. Jorge Alvarado-Gonzalez, M.J.; Deacon Glen Pennell.
Catechesis Religious Program—Tel: 713-222-6579. Sr. Mary Esther Alonzo, D.R.E. Students 158.

43—ST. JUSTIN MARTYR (1982)
13350 Ashford Point Dr., 77082-5100.
Tel: 281-556-5116; Fax: 281-556-6932; Email: sjm@sjmtx.com; Web: www.sjmtx.org. Revs. Paul R. Chovanec; Peter Nguyen, Parochial Vicar; Deacons Garey Boyd; Cornelius C. Llorens; Nhat Tran.
Rectory—3142 W. Hampton, 77082.
Catechesis Religious Program—Students 432.

44—ST. LEO THE GREAT (1973)
2131 Lauder Rd., 77039-3199. Tel: 281-449-3664; Tel: 281-449-2344; Fax: 281-442-3156; Email: info@stleohouston.org; Web: www.stleohouston.org. Revs. Jose Carmen Hernandez-Angulo, C.S.; Juan Francisco Aguiar-Arce, Parochial Vicar; Vincenslaus Ino, C.S., Parochial Vicar.
Catechesis Religious Program—Nohemi Lara, C.M.S.T., D.R.E. Students 1,113.

45—ST. LUKE THE EVANGELIST (1975)
11011 Hall Rd., 77089-2999. Tel: 281-481-6816; Fax: 281-481-8780. Revs. Douglas J. Guthrie; Xavier Bilavendiran, Parochial Vicar; Deacons Jesse Tollett; Alvin Birsinger; Adolfo Mejia; John Rapacki.
Rectory: 8402 Kirkville, 77089.
Catechesis Religious Program—Ben Hernandez, D.R.E. Students 642.

46—ST. MARK THE EVANGELIST (1974)
5430 W. Ridgecreek Dr., 77053-3211.
Tel: 281-437-9114; Fax: 281-835-6303. Rev. Oscar M. Castro; Deacons Jorge Garcia; John Benoit.
Rectory—5302 Castlecreek Ln., 77053.
Tel: 281-437-9114; Fax: 281-835-6303.
Catechesis Religious Program—Tel: 281-416-0186; Email: elavorgna@stmarkshouston.org. Estela Lavorgna, D.R.E. Students 267.

47—ST. MARY OF THE PURIFICATION (1929)
3006 Rosedale, 77004-6128. Tel: 713-528-0571; Fax: 713-528-0572. Revs. Justin Arockiasamy; Paschal Chester, Parochial Vicar; Deacon Andrew B. Malveaux Sr.
School—St. Mary of the Purification School, 3002 Rosedale, 77004. Tel: 713-522-9276; Fax: 713-522-1879; Email: ostandford@stmaryshouston.org; Web: stmaryshouston.net/school. Natalie Garrett, Prin. Lay Teachers 6; Students 88.
Catechesis Religious Program—Dr. Evelyn Hunter, D.R.E. Students 113.

48—ST. MATTHEW THE EVANGELIST (1974)
9915 Hollister Dr., 77040-1702. Tel: 713-466-4030; Fax: 713-896-7235. Rev. Martial F. Oya; Deacons John W. Adams; Thomas Piotrowski; Thomas Whited; Carlos Porras; Juan Pareja.
Catechesis Religious Program—Tel: 713-466-0510. Silvia Nunez, D.R.E. Students 499.

49—ST. MAXIMILIAN KOLBE (1983)
10135 West Rd., 77064-5361. Tel: 281-955-7324; Fax: 281-955-7328. Revs. John Kha Tran; Michael Pham, Parochial Vicar; Deacons Dennis Hayes; Joseph Weir; Bob Henkel; John Naber; Joseph Steven Klak; Matthew Rust.
Rectory—9231 Chester Park, 77064.
Catechesis Religious Program—Mrs. Molly Smith, Dir. Students 533.

50—ST. MICHAEL (1925)
1801 Sage Rd., 77056-3502. Tel: 713-621-4370; Fax: 713-850-8341. Revs. Wayne W. Wilkerson; Michael Applegate, Parochial Vicar; Leon Strieder, In Res.; Deacons Thomas C. Newhouse; Robert J. Hesse.
Res., Church & Mailing Address: 5136 Delmonte, 77056-3502. Email: parishoffice@stmichaelchurch.net; Web: www.stmichaelchurch.net.
School—St. Michael School, 1833 Sage Rd., 77056-3502. Tel: 713-621-6847; Fax: 713-877-8812; Email: kcox@stmichaelcs.org. Dr. Kathleen Cox, Prin. Lay Teachers 41; Students 562.
Catechesis Religious Program—Tel: 713-403-4121. Mrs. Maria Reynolds, Dir. Students 738.

51—ST. MONICA (1960)
8421 W. Montgomery Rd., 77088-7116.
Tel: 281-447-5837; Cell: 281-447-8410. Revs. John M. Ayang, S.O.L.T.; Lauro Bejo, S.O.L.T.; Deacon Oscar Foster.
Catechesis Religious Program—Doris Barrow III, D.R.E. Students 158.

52—ST. NICHOLAS (1887)
2508 Clay St., 77003-4406. Tel: 713-223-5210; Fax: 713-222-0424. Rev. George Okeahialam, M.S.P.
Catechesis Religious Program—Clement Njowo, D.R.E. Students 30.

53—NOTRE DAME (1969)
7720 Boone Rd., 77072-3595. Tel: 281-498-4653; Fax: 281-879-1527. Rev. Msgr. Rolando V. Diokno; Rev. Lukose Manuel, O.S.H.; Deacons F.L. Ostrowski; Ernesto Abadejos; Elie P. Calonge; Anthony Olsovsky.
Rectory—11226 Pompano Ln., 77072-3595.
Catechesis Religious Program—Tel: 281-495-1256. Blanca Plasencia, D.R.E. Students 444.

54—OUR LADY OF CZESTOCHOWA (1982) (Polish)
1712 Oak Tree Dr., 77080. Rev. Waldemar Matusiak, S.Chr.
Church: 1731 Blalock Rd., 77080. Tel: 713-973-1081; Fax: 713-984-9501; Email: parish@parafiahouston.com; Web: www.parafiahouston.com.
Catechesis Religious Program—Students 36.

55—OUR LADY OF GUADALUPE (1912) [JC]
2405 Navigation Blvd., 77003-1599.
Tel: 713-222-0203; Fax: 713-636-9054. Revs. Duy Nguyen; Tim Gray, S.C.J., V.F.; Wojciech Adamczyk, Parochial Vicar; Deacon Manuel A. Laurel; Bro. Andy Gancarczyk.
School—Our Lady of Guadalupe School, Tel: 713-224-6904; Fax: 713-225-2122; Email: iortiz@olgschoolhouston.org. Irazema Ortiz, Prin. Lay Teachers 16; Students 200.
Catechesis Religious Program—Sandra Valles, D.R.E. Students 655.

56—OUR LADY OF LAVANG CHURCH (1985) (Vietnamese)
Mailing Address: 12311 Old Foltin Rd., 77086-3514.
Tel: 281-999-1672; Fax: 281-820-7095; Email: lavangchurch@yahoo.com; Web: www.lavangchurch.org. Revs. Thomas Thien-An Tran, O.P.; Dominic Huy Trinh, O.P., Parochial Vicar; Peter Khanh Pham, O.P., Parochial Vicar; Deacon Michael Kim Khanh Nguyen.
Catechesis Religious Program—Tel: 281-370-1338. Mr. Tai Nguyen, D.R.E. Students 855.

57—OUR LADY OF LOURDES (1994)
6550 Fairbanks N. Houston, 77040-4307.
Tel: 713-939-1906; Fax: 713-939-0771. Revs. Anthony Tien Dinh, O.P.; Joseph Nhan Cao Do, O.P., Parochial Vicar; Deacons Joseph Chuong Nguyen Do; J.B Dao; Vincent Nguyen.
Catechesis Religious Program—Deacon Andy Dao, D.R.E. Students 700.

58—OUR LADY OF MT. CARMEL (1952)
6723 Whitefriars Dr., 77087-6598. Tel: 713-645-6673; Fax: 713-645-6674. Rev. J. Abelardo Cobos; Deacon Juan Aguilar.
School—Our Lady of Mt. Carmel School, 6703 Whitefriars Dr., 77087. Tel: 713-643-0676; Fax: 713-649-1835; Email: mmendoza@olmchou.org. Maribel Mendoza, Prin. Lay Teachers 12; Students 166.
Catechesis Religious Program—Clara Cruz, D.R.E. Students 294.

59—OUR LADY OF SORROWS (1936)
3006 Kashmere St., 77026-5999. Tel: 713-673-5600. Rev. David Garnier.
Catechesis Religious Program—Tel: 832-858-9561. Oralia Guerrero, D.R.E. Students 112.

60—OUR LADY OF ST. JOHN (1947)
7500 Hirsch Rd., 77016-6215. Tel: 713-631-0810. Rev. Edwin A. Coreas, J.C.L.
Catechesis Religious Program—Rogelio Camacho, D.R.E. Students 224.

61—OUR LADY STAR OF THE SEA (1950)

1401 Fidelity St., 77029-4624. Tel: 713-674-9206. Rev. Stephen Sohe.
Catechesis Religious Program—Merrell Schalee, D.R.E. Students 26.
62—OUR MOTHER OF MERCY (1930)
4000 Sumpter St., 77020-2497. Rev. Rodney J. Armstrong, S.S.J.; Deacons Irvin Johnson Jr.; Rick L. Simon; Charles J. Allen Sr.
Catechesis Religious Program—Tel: 713-672-2037. Gerald Joseph, D.R.E. Students 112.
63—ST. PATRICK (1880)
4918 Cochran St., 77009-2117. Tel: 713-695-0631; Fax: 713-695-6255; Web: www.stpatrickhouston.com. Rev. Tom Hawxhurst; Deacon Reynaldo Torres.
Catechesis Religious Program—Tel: 713-697-4325. Ivana Meshell, D.R.E. Students 321.
64—ST. PAUL THE APOSTLE (1964)
18223 Point Lookout Dr., 77058-3594.
Tel: 281-333-3891; Fax: 281-333-3815. Rev. Wencil C. Pavlovsky, V.F.; Deacons Servando Rojas; Scott Bradley Daniel.
Rectory—18326 Point Lookout Dr., 77058.
Catechesis Religious Program—Tel: 281-957-7324. Heidi Clark, D.R.E. Students 581.
65—ST. PETER CLAVER (1964)
6005 N. Wayside Dr., 77028-4494. Tel: 713-674-3338; Fax: 713-674-6524. Rev. Kenneth J. Howard, S.S.J.
Catechesis Religious Program—Leticia De La Cruz, D.R.E. Students 71.
66—ST. PETER THE APOSTLE (1941)
6220 La Salette Dr., 77021-1323. Tel: 713-747-7800; Fax: 713-747-9671. Rev. Faustinus Okeyikam, M.S.P.; Deacon Dan Gilbert.
School—St. Peter the Apostle School,
Tel: 713-747-9484; Fax: 713-842-7055. Toni Marshall, Prin. Lay Teachers 8; Students 36.
Catechesis Religious Program—Stephanie Jackson, D.R.E. Students 48.
67—ST. PHILIP NERI (1961)
10960 Martin Luther King Jr. Blvd., 77048-1896.
Tel: 713-734-0320; Fax: 713-734-0331; Email: officespn@yahoo.com; Web: www.stphilipnerichurch.com. Rev. Christian Alimaji, M.S.P.; Deacons Ronald Simon; Orrin D. Burroughs.
Catechesis Religious Program—Tel: 713-733-8000. Angelia Linzy, D.R.E. Students 39.
68—ST. PHILIP OF JESUS (1958)
9700 Villita St., 77013-3851. Tel: 713-672-6141; Fax: 713-672-0223. Rev. Jesus E. Suarez; Deacon Roy Breaux.
Catechesis Religious Program—Nancy Mayorga, D.R.E. Students 811.
69—PRINCE OF PEACE (1971)
19222 Tomball Pkwy., 77070-3510.
Tel: 281-469-2686; Email: info@pophouston.org. Revs. John T. Keller; Biju Matthew; Alfonso Delgado, SS.CC.; Deacons Thomas Lattin; William Sheffield; William Barnes; Timothy Hartnett; Kenneth Stanley; Kenneth Henry; Kevin Cascarelli; Jeffrey Schmelter; Robert Trahan.
Catechesis Religious Program—Jill McAboy, Dir. Faith Formation. Students 1,835.
70—QUEEN OF PEACE (1942)
3011 Telephone Rd., 77023-5312. Tel: 713-921-6127; Fax: 713-921-6128. Revs. Michael J. Minifie, C.C.; John Paul Bolger, C.C., Parochial Vicar; Jorge Alvarado, C.C.; Ed Wade, C.C., In Res.; Deacons Jose L. Liendo; Jose M. Galvan.
School—Queen of Peace School, 2320 Oakcliff St., 77023. Tel: 713-921-1558; Fax: 713-921-0855; Email: principal@qophouston.com. Jan Krametbauer, Prin. Lay Teachers 6; Students 64.
Catechesis Religious Program—Tel: 713-926-4494. Students 247.
71—ST. RAPHAEL THE ARCHANGEL (1961)
3915 Ocee St., 77263-5417. Tel: 713-781-9511; Fax: 713-278-9705; Email: straphaelcc@comcast.net. Rev. Ramon J. Arechua.
Catechesis Religious Program—Mrs. Ired Franco, D.R.E. Students 487.
72—REGINA CAELI
8121 Breen Dr., 77064. Tel: 832-328-0876; Email: office@reginacaeliparish.org; Web: www.reginacaeliparish.org. Revs. Charles Van Vliet, F.S.S.P.; John Kodet.
Catechesis Religious Program—Mary Haddox, C.C.D. Coord. Students 93.
73—RESURRECTION (1920)
915 Zoe St., 77020-6898. Tel: 713-675-5333. Rev. Oscar H. Dubon.
School—Resurrection School, 916 Majestic St., 77020. Tel: 713-674-5545; Fax: 713-674-2151; Email: fnichols@rcchouston.org. Felicia Nichols, Prin. Lay Teachers 10; Students 117; Clergy / Religious Teachers 22.
Catechesis Religious Program—Tel: 713-675-0350. Carmen Valdez, Faith Formation Dir. Students 240.
Station—La Divina Providencia, Port Houston.
74—ST. ROSE OF LIMA (1946)
3600 Brinkman St., 77018-6329. Tel: 713-692-9123; Fax: 713-692-5638. Revs. Rafael Becerra, C.S., Admin.; Ruben C. Nwankwor, In Res.; Deacons Julio Suriano; Ed Herrera; John T. Murrell; Larry Hernandez.
Rectory—802 Judiway, 77018-6329.
School—St. Rose of Lima School, Tel: 713-691-0104; Fax: 713-692-8073; Email: bdrabek@stroselima.org. Bernadette Drabek, Prin. Lay Teachers 23; Students 347.
Catechesis Religious Program—Deacon John T. Murrell, D.R.E. Students 355.
75—ST. THERESA (1946)
6622 Haskell St., 77007-2097. Tel: 713-869-3783; Fax: 713-869-3784; Email: britishbulldog@sttheresa.cc; Web: www.sttheresa.cc. Rev. Philip P. Lloyd; Deacons Larry A. Vaclavik; William Wilson; Antonio Moya.
School—St. Theresa School, 6623 Rodrigo St., 77007. Tel: 713-864-4536; Fax: 713-869-5184; Email: Marcia.Mushinski@sttheresa.cc. Melissa Ilski, Prin. Clergy 1; Lay Teachers 27; Students 316.
Catechesis Religious Program—Janice Berger, D.R.E. Students 185.
76—ST. THOMAS MORE (1962)
10330 Hillcroft, 77096-4795. Tel: 713-729-0221; Fax: 713-729-3294; Email: rectory@stmhouston.org; Web: www.stmhouston.org. Revs. Hai Duc Dang; Joseph Methanath; John Samuel Puthenvila, In Res.; Deacons John Krugh; David Johnson.
School—St. Thomas More School, 5927 Wigton, 77096. Tel: 713-729-3434; Email: jgentempo@stmorenews.com. Kristin Thome, Prin. Lay Teachers 45; Students 517.
Catechesis Religious Program—Tel: 713-729-3435. Ana Luisa Garcia, D.R.E. Students 917.
77—VIETNAMESE MARTYRS (1986) (Vietnamese)
10610 Kingspoint Rd., 77075-4114.
Tel: 713-941-0521; Fax: 713-941-2464. Rev. Joseph Thanh Vu; Deacons Joseph Pham Nguyen; Joseph Ro Van Le.
Rectory—10614 Kingspoint Rd., 77075-4114.
Tel: 713-941-0521.
Catechesis Religious Program—Joseph Nguyen Pham, D.R.E. Students 700.
78—ST. VINCENT DE PAUL (1940)
6800 Buffalo Speedway, 77025-1405.
Tel: 713-667-9111; Fax: 713-667-3453; Email: info@svdp-houston.org. Rev. Msgr. William L. Young; Revs. J. Phong Nguyen, Parochial Vicar; David Hust, Parochial Vicar; Romanus O. Muoneke, In Res.; Deacons Daniel Pagnano, Business Mgr.; Gustavo Camacho del Rio.
School—St. Vincent de Paul School, 6802 Buffalo Speedway, 77025. Tel: 713-666-2345;
Fax: 713-663-3562; Email: csears@svdp-edu.org. Carolyn Sears, Prin. Lay Teachers 31; Students 504.
Catechesis Religious Program—Tel: 713-663-3565. Nick LaRocca, Dir. Faith Formation. Students 771.

OUTSIDE THE CITIES OF GALVESTON AND HOUSTON

ALVIN, BRAZORIA CO., ST. JOHN THE BAPTIST (1952)
110 E. South St., Alvin, 77511-3570.
Tel: 281-331-3751; Fax: 281-331-5430. Rev. John Kare Taosan, C.I.M., V.F.; Deacons David Bowman; Dale Hayden.
Catechesis Religious Program—Tel: 281-824-0877. Mrs. Mary Voight, D.R.E. Students 758.
ANDERSON, GRIMES CO., ST. STANISLAUS (1866) [CEM]
1511 Hwy. 90 S., Anderson, 77830-0210.
Tel: 936-873-2291; Fax: 936-873-3304; Email: ststan@embarqmail.com; Web: www.saintstans.org. Rev. Elias Lopez, Admin.
Catechesis Religious Program—Dana Wagner, C.R.E. Students 138.
ANGLETON, BRAZORIA CO., MOST HOLY TRINITY (1960)
1713 N. Tinsley St., Angleton, 77515-3551.
Tel: 979-849-2421; Fax: 979-849-2425. Rev. Victor C. Perez; Deacons Robert Ward; Luis G. Hernandez.
Res.: 740 N. Browning, Angleton, 77515.
Catechesis Religious Program—Cheryl Scott, D.R.E. Students 385.
BARRETT STATION, HARRIS CO., ST. MARTIN DE PORRES (1944) [JC]
12606 Crosby-Lynchburg Rd., Barrett Station, 77532-8628. Tel: 281-328-4451; Fax: 281-328-7306. Rev. Sebastian Umouyo, M.S.P.; Deacon Martin Lemond.
Catechesis Religious Program—Tel: 281-691-4424. Mary Ligons, D.R.E. Students 119.
BAYTOWN, HARRIS CO.
1—ST. JOHN THE EVANGELIST (1974)
800 W. Baker Rd., Baytown, 77521-2311.
Tel: 281-837-8180; Fax: 281-837-8181. Rev. Terence P. Brinkman, S.T.D.; Deacons Justin J. Wewer; John William Singer Jr.; Dan Foley.
Catechesis Religious Program—Tel: 281-837-0532; Email: a.medina@stjohnbaytown.org. Alison Medina, D.R.E. Students 276.
2—ST. JOSEPH (1924)
1907 Carolina St., Baytown, 77520-6098. Tel: 281-420-3588; Fax: 281-422-3044. Rev. Edmund P. Eduarte; Deacon George Silva.
School—St. Joseph School, 1811 Carolina St., Baytown, 77520-6099. Tel: 281-422-9749; Email: c.carrizales@sjsbaytown.org; Web: www.stjosephbaytown.com. Deborah Francis, Prin. Lay Teachers 12; Sisters 1; Students 117.
Catechesis Religious Program—Tel: 281-427-5920. Mrs. Jude Arceneaux, D.R.E. Students 141.
3—OUR LADY OF GUADALUPE (1958)
1124 Beech St., Baytown, 77520-4143.
Tel: 281-428-1507; Fax: 281-427-0595. Rev. Jesus Lizalde; Deacons Don Ramirez; Fernando Gonzalez Bangs; Rudy Venegas; George Rincon.
Catechesis Religious Program—Tel: 281-427-0810. Maria Ramirez, C.R.E. Students 338.
BEASLEY, FT. BEND CO., ST. WENCESLAUS MISSION (1923) [CEM] (Independent Mission)
Mailing Address: 1416 George St., Rosenberg, 77471-3198. Rev. William D. Bartniski.
Church: 407 S. 3rd St., Beasley, 77417.
Catechesis Religious Program—Tel: 979-387-2340. Angie Reid, D.R.E. Students 32.
BELLVILLE, AUSTIN CO., STS. PETER & PAUL (1860)
936 S. Front St., Bellville, 77418-0176.
Tel: 979-865-2368; Fax: 979-865-9929; Email: stspandp@sbcglobal.net. Rev. Timothy P. Bucek; Deacon Gerald W. DuPont.
Catechesis Religious Program—Tel: 315-281-4862. Kimberly Story, D.R.E. Students 191.
Mission—Immaculate Conception (1875) Industry, Austin Co.
BRAZORIA, BRAZORIA CO., ST. JOSEPH ON THE BRAZOS (1840)
219 Country Rd. 762, Brazoria, 77422-7621.
Tel: 979-798-2288; Fax: 979-798-2271. Rev. Tin Cosmas Kim Pham; Deacon Jimmy Smith.
Catechesis Religious Program—Tel: 979-798-4702. Deacon Jimmy T. Smith, C.R.E. Students 123.
CHANNELVIEW, HARRIS CO., ST. ANDREW (1970)
827 Sheldon Rd., Channelview, 77530-3511.
Tel: 281-452-9865; Fax: 281-452-2157; Email: standrew7067@comcast.net; Web: www.standrewchurch.net. Rev. Christopher Shackelford; Deacons Michael Muench; Javier Gomez.
Catechesis Religious Program—Ninfa Muench, D.R.E., Tel: 281-452-9865, Ext. 18. Students 654.
CLUTE, BRAZORIA CO., ST. JEROME (1969)
201 N. Lazy Ln., Clute, 77531-4001.
Tel: 979-265-5179; Fax: 979-265-4601. Rev. James F. Lynes Jr.; Deacon Agustin Cruz.
Church: 107 N. Lazy Ln., Clute, 77531-4001.
Tel: 979-265-5179; Fax: 979-265-4601; Email: jerome-clute@att.net; Web: www.stjeromeclute.org.
Catechesis Religious Program—Tel: 979-236-3927. Dina A. Tonche, D.R.E. Students 281.
CONROE, MONTGOMERY CO., SACRED HEART (1916)
109 N. Frazier St., Conroe, 77301-2802.
Tel: 936-756-8186; Email: parishoffice@shconroe.org; Web: www.shconroe.org. 704 Old Montgomery Rd., Conroe, 77301. Revs. Philip A. Wilhite, S.T.L.; Emmanuel Akpaidem, Parochial Vicar; Joseph Manapuram, Parochial Vicar; Deacons Bradley Hoover; Eddy Valbuena.
School—Sacred Heart School, 615 McDade St., Conroe, 77301-2758. Tel: 936-756-3848. Deborah Brown, Prin., Email: dbrown@shconroe.org. Lay Teachers 33; Students 288.
Catechesis Religious Program—Becki Lipari, D.R.E. Students 1,140.
CROSBY, HARRIS CO., SACRED HEART (1935)
915 Runneburg Rd., Crosby, 77532-5826.
Tel: 281-328-4871. Revs. Gary A. Rickles; Christian Unachukwu, In Res.; Deacons Archie Benham; Pete Melancon.
School—Sacred Heart School, 907 Runneberg Rd., Crosby, 77532. Tel: 281-328-6561; Fax: 281-462-0072; Email: sharris@sacredheartschoolcrosby.org. Susan Harris, Prin. Lay Teachers 14; Sisters 2; Students 220; Clergy / Religious Teachers 2.
Catechesis Religious Program—
Tel: 281-328-4871, Ext. 16. Mireya Torres, C.R.E. Students 288.
DAMON, BRAZORIA CO., STS. CYRIL AND METHODIUS (1925) [CEM]
603 Parrott Ave., Damon, 77430-0309.
Tel: 979-742-3383; Fax: 979-742-3395. Rev. Marty Pham.
Rectory—P.O. Box 95, Needville, 77461.
Catechesis Religious Program—Tel: 979-230-6928. Linda Pavlicek, D.R.E. Students 23.
DANBURY, BRAZORIA CO., ST. ANTHONY DE PADUA (1911) [CEM]
Mailing Address: P.O. Box 299, Danbury, 77534-0299. Tel: 979-922-1240; Fax: 979-922-8643. Rev. Joseph Phiet The Nguyen; Deacon Gerald Peltier.
Rectory—1603 Main St., Danbury, 77534.
Tel: 979-922-1253.
Church: 1523 Main St., Danbury, 77534-0299. Email: st1523@sbcglobal.net; Web: www.saopdtx.org.

Catechesis Religious Program—Tel: 979-922-1241. Mrs. Monica Sebesta, C.R.E. Students 92.
DEER PARK, HARRIS CO., ST. HYACINTH (1965)
2921 Center St., Deer Park, 77536-4997.
Tel: 281-479-4298; Email: info@sthyacinth.org; Web: sthyacinth.org. Rev. Reginald W. Samuels.
Catechesis Religious Program—
Tel: 281-479-8832, Ext. 22. Barbara Mackie, D.R.E. Students 700.
DICKINSON, GALVESTON CO., SHRINE OF THE TRUE CROSS (1909)
Mailing Address: P.O. Box 687, Dickinson, 77539-0687. Tel: 281-337-4112. Rev. Lawrence C. Wilson; Deacon Robert George Alexander.
Res.: 3720 Spruce, Dickinson, 77539.
Fax: 281-337-5779; Email: info@truecrosschurch.org; Web: www.truecrosschurch.org.
Church: 300 FM 517 E., Dickinson, 77539.
School—Shrine of the True Cross School, 400 FM 517 E., Dickinson, 77539. Tel: 281-337-5212; Email: yagrella@truecrosschurch.org. Yolanda Agrella, Prin. Lay Teachers 15; Students 129.
Catechesis Religious Program—Antonio Urbina, D.R.E. Students 263.
FREEPORT, BRAZORIA CO.
1—ST. HENRY (1932) Closed. For inquiries for parish records contact the chancery.
2—ST. MARY: STAR OF THE SEA (1926)
1019 W. 6th St., Freeport, 77541-5423.
Tel: 979-233-5271; Fax: 979-233-4418. Rev. Jesus (Jesse) Garcia; Deacons Wallace Shaw; Felipe Garza.
Catechesis Religious Program—Tel: 979-233-2771. Bro. William Hartnett, D.R.E. Students 130.
FRIENDSWOOD, GALVESTON CO., MARY, QUEEN (1965)
606 Cedarwood Dr., Friendswood, 77546-4551.
Tel: 281-482-1391; Fax: 281-482-4886; Web: www.maryqueencatholicchurch.org. Revs. James H. Kuczynski, M.S.; Sibi Kunninu, M.S., Parochial Vicar; Deacons Charles Turner; Paul Robinson; Darrell Moulton; Vince Eklund; Derick Soares.
Rectory—608 Cedarwood Dr., Friendswood, 77546.
Catechesis Religious Program—Students 1,007.
FULSHEAR, FORT BEND CO., ST. FAUSTINA CATHOLIC CHURCH (2014)
28102 FM 1093, Fulshear, 77441. Tel: 346-773-3500; Fax: 281-232-7450; Email: info@saintfaustinachurch.org. Revs. Dat Hoang; Simon Kipiti, Parochial Vicar; Deacons Ernesto Abadejos; Randy Graham.
Res.: 24435 Peroni Dr., Richmond, 77406.
Catechesis Religious Program—Tel: 346-773-3442. Brian Lennox, D.R.E. Students 1,249.
FRYDEK, AUSTIN CO., ST. MARY (1908) [CEM]
Mailing Address: 10471 Grotto Rd., Frydek, 77474-9055. Tel: 979-885-3131; Fax: 979-885-4555; Email: stmary@twlt.net. Rev. Thuy Quang Nguyen; Deacons Jerome D. Losack Sr.; Paul Franek.
Catechesis Religious Program—Tel: 979-885-3178. Sarah Blundell, D.R.E. Students 141.
GALENA PARK, HARRIS CO., OUR LADY OF FATIMA (1946)
1705 8th St., Galena Park, 77547-2924.
Tel: 713-675-0981; Fax: 713-675-0982. Rev. Angel Vincente Agila.
Res. & Church Address: 1801 8th St., Galena Park, 77547-2924. Tel: 713-675-0981; Fax: 713-675-0982; Email: info@olfparishgp.org; Web: www.olfparishgp.org.
School—Our Lady of Fatima School, (Grades PreSchool-7), 1702 Ninth St., Galena Park, 77547.
Tel: 713-674-5832; Fax: 713-674-3877; Email: kpham@olfatima-gp.org. Khanh Pham, Prin. Lay Teachers 8; Students 171.
Catechesis Religious Program—Elsy Montano, Coord.; Maria Velas, D.R.E. Students 445.
HEMPSTEAD, WALLER CO.
1—ST. KATHARINE DREXEL (2001)
800 F.M. 1488 Rd., Hempstead, 77445-1700.
Tel: 979-826-2275; Fax: 979-826-8057. Revs. David G. Harris; Jose L. Gutierrez, Parochial Vicar; Deacon John Pelletier.
Catechesis Religious Program—Rollins Brown, D.R.E. Students 399.
2—MARY, MOTHER OF GOD (1879) Merged with St. Martin de Porres, Prairie View to form St. Katherine Drexel, Hempstead.
HIGHLANDS, HARRIS CO., ST. JUDE THADDEUS (1946)
800 S. Main St., Highlands, 77562-4236.
Tel: 281-843-2422; Fax: 281-426-3671. Rev. Jose Mundadan, Admin.
Catechesis Religious Program—Maria Valle, D.R.E. Students 75.
HITCHCOCK, GALVESTON CO., OUR LADY OF LOURDES (1953)
10114 Hwy. 6, Hitchcock, 77563-4515.
Tel: 409-925-3579; Email: ppersad@ololchurch.org; Web: www.ololchurch.org. Rev. John H. Kappe.
School—Our Lady of Lourdes School, (Grades PreSchool-6), Tel: 409-925-3224; Fax: 409-925-9900; Email: mpriest@ololcs.org. Mr. Mark Priest, Prin. Lay Teachers 9; Students 64.

Catechesis Religious Program—Raquel Hinojosa, D.R.E. Students 200.
HUFFMAN, HARRIS CO., ST. PHILIP THE APOSTLE (1977)
2308 3rd St., Huffman, 77336. Tel: 281-324-1478; Fax: 281-715-5533. Rev. Richard E. Barker; Deacon John Sarabia.
Catechesis Religious Program—Tel: 713-516-7376. Becky Pursell, D.R.E. Students 142.
HUMBLE, HARRIS CO., ST. MARY MAGDALENE (1911)
527 S. Houston Ave., Humble, 77338-4763.
Tel: 281-446-8211; Fax: 281-446-8213. Revs. Felix Ilesanmi Osasona, M.S.P.; Anthony Udoh, M.S.P., Parochial Vicar.
Rectory—525 S. Houston Ave., Humble, 77338-4763.
School—St. Mary Magdalene School, 530 Ferguson, Humble, 77338. Tel: 281-446-8535;
Fax: 281-446-8527; Email: jraab@smmcs.org; Web: smmcs.org. Joshua A. Raab, Prin. Lay Teachers 21; Students 265.
Catechesis Religious Program—Tel: 281-446-2933. Mike Smith, D.R.E. Students 1,095.
HUNTSVILLE, WALKER CO., ST. THOMAS THE APOSTLE (1963)
1323 16th St., Huntsville, 77340-4431.
Tel: 936-295-8159; Email: stthomashuntsville@sbcglobal.net; Web: www.saintthomashuntsville.org. 1603 Ave. N, Huntsville, 77340. Rev. Fred W. Valone; Deacon Felix Ramos.
Rectory—1608 Ave. M, Huntsville, 77340-4431.
Catechesis Religious Program—Kathy Boscarino, D.R.E. Students 294.
KATY, HARRIS CO.
1—ST. BARTHOLOMEW THE APOSTLE (1965)
5356 11th St., Katy, 77493-1748. Tel: 281-391-4758; Fax: 713-554-1555. Revs. Christopher M. Plant; Nicolas Ramirez; Deacons William C. Wagner; Rolando Garcia; Gordon Robertson; Fred Dingas.
Rectory—5356-B 11th St., Katy, 77493-1748.
Catechesis Religious Program—Tel: 281-391-0839. Dan Guido, D.R.E. Students 1,610.
2—ST. EDITH STEIN (1999)
3311 N. Fry Rd., Katy, 77449-6235.
Tel: 281-492-7500; Email: jf@stedithstein.org. Rev. Ryszard Kulma; Deacons Leonard J. Broussard; Larry Biediger Jr.; Samuel Hull III; Ted F. Heap; Glenn Jackson.
Rectory—2903 Sinton Ct., Katy, 77449.
Catechesis Religious Program—Melissa Powell, D.R.E. Students 242.
3—EPIPHANY OF THE LORD (1981)
1530 Norwalk Dr., Katy, 77450-4918.
Tel: 281-578-0707; Fax: 281-578-9161. Rev. Tom Lam; Martins Emeh, Parochial Vicar; Deacons Don Kish; John Evanoff.
Catechesis Religious Program—Tel: 281-578-8271. Lou Ann Svoboda, D.R.E. Students 1,566.
KINGWOOD, HARRIS CO., ST. MARTHA (1979)
4301 Woodridge Pkwy., Porter, 77365-7709.
Tel: 281-358-6637; Fax: 281-358-7973; Email: indianaf@stmartha.com; Web: www.stmartha.com. Revs. Thomas J. Dolce; Jonathan Moré, Parochial Vicar; Deacons Alfred J. O'Brien; Robert MacFarlane; John Schuster; Guy Puglia; Anthony Cardella; Jonathan Barfield; Gary Yepsen.
Rectory—4343 Woodridge Pkwy., Porter, 77365-7709.
School—St. Martha School, 2411 Oakshores Dr., Kingwood, 77339. Tel: 281-358-5523;
Fax: 281-358-5526; Email: munscherj@stmarthacs.org; Web: stmarthacs.org. Jessica Munscher, Prin. Lay Teachers 27; Students 445.
Catechesis Religious Program—3702 Woodland Hills Dr., Kingwood, 77339. Tel: 281-358-1959, Ext. 212; Email: carlal@stmartha.com. Carla Lewton, D.R.E. Students 1,563.
LA MARQUE, GALVESTON CO., QUEEN OF PEACE (1951)
626 Laurel Ave., La Marque, 77568.
Tel: 409-938-7000. Rev. Chacko Puthumayil.
Church: 1200 Cedar Dr., La Marque, 77568.
Fax: 409-935-9791; Email: queenofpeacelm@sbcglobal.net; Web: www.queenofpeacelm.org.
Catechesis Religious Program—Tel: 409-935-3535. Sr. Esmeralda Alejo, D.J., Dir. Faith Formation. Students 132.
LA PORTE, HARRIS CO., ST. MARY (1951)
816 Park Dr., La Porte, 77571-5811.
Tel: 281-471-2000; Fax: 281-471-9365. Rev. Antonio A. Castro; Deacons Julio C. Matallana; Stan Avallone.
Catechesis Religious Program—Jessica Jaramillo, D.R.E. Students 235.
LAKE JACKSON, BRAZORIA CO., ST. MICHAEL (1966)
100 Oak Dr. S., Lake Jackson, 77566-5630.
Tel: 979-297-3041; Fax: 979-297-7895. Rev. Msgr. Leo Wleczyk; Rev. Loc D. Pham, Parochial Vicar; Deacon Gary Forse, D.R.E.
Catechesis Religious Program—Tel: 979-297-3043. Students 288.
LEAGUE CITY, GALVESTON CO., ST. MARY (1910)
1612 E. Walker St., League City, 77573-4137.

Tel: 281-332-3031; Fax: 281-332-8328. Rev. Howard E. Drabek; Deacons George Blanford Jr.; Sam Dell'Olio; Russell Carroll; Andrew DeYoung.
School—St. Mary School, Tel: 281-332-4014; Email: lnoonan@stmarylc.org. Laura Noonan, Prin. Lay Teachers 21; Students 248.
Catechesis Religious Program—Cindy Newman, D.R.E. Students 854.
MAGNOLIA, MONTGOMERY CO., ST. MATTHIAS THE APOSTLE (1978)
302 Magnolia Blvd., Magnolia, 77355-8535.
Tel: 281-356-2000. Rev. J. Christopher C. Nguyen.
Catechesis Religious Program—Marlene Grauvogl, D.R.E. Students 518.
MANVEL, BRAZORIA CO., SACRED HEART OF JESUS (1945)
6502 County Rd. 48, Manvel, 77578-4146.
Tel: 281-489-8720. Rev. Thomas V. Ponzini; Deacons Robert Reed Leicht Jr.; Ricardo Reyes.
Catechesis Religious Program—Camilla Chedester, Dir. Students 881.
MCNAIR, HARRIS CO., HOLY FAMILY (1945) [JC]
7122 Whiting Rock St., McNair, 77521-1124.
Tel: 281-426-8448; Fax: 281-426-8449. Rev. Nixon A. Mullah, S.J.J.; Deacon Steve Arceneaux Jr.
Catechesis Religious Program—Tel: 281-421-7042. Mrs. Vivian Randell-Alfred, D.R.E. Students 22.
MISSOURI CITY, FT. BEND CO.
1—ST. ANGELA MERICI (2007)
9009 Sienna Ranch Rd., Missouri City, 77549-3802.
Tel: 281-778-0400; Fax: 281-778-0401; Email: parishoffice@stamericigh.org; Web: www.stamericigh.org. Revs. John E. Cahoon, J.C.L.; Joy Thomas, M.S.F.S., Parochial Vicar; Deacon Jim Wright.
Rectory—3814 S. Barnett Way, Missouri City, 77459-6341.
Catechesis Religious Program—John Masterson, Dir. Faith Formation. Students 583.
2—HOLY FAMILY (1913)
1510 Fifth St., Missouri City, 77489-1298.
Tel: 281-499-9688; Fax: 281-499-9680. Revs. Sunny Joseph Plammoottil, O.S.H.; Joy James, O.S.H., Parochial Vicar; Deacons William E. Seifert Jr.; Jose Melendez; Lynn Carney.
Catechesis Religious Program—Tel: 281-499-4612. Yolanda Pena, D.R.E. Students 555.
NAVASOTA, GRIMES CO., CHRIST OUR LIGHT (1869)
9677 Hwy. 6, Navasota, 77868-3926.
Tel: 936-825-3920; Fax: 936-825-7612. Revs. Eli Lopez; Jorge Cabrera, Parochial Vicar; Deacon Grant E. Holt.
Rectory—9685 Hwy. 6, Navasota, 77868-3905.
Catechesis Religious Program—Tel: 832-696-6932. Mrs. Sasha Ramirez, D.R.E. Students 261.
NEEDVILLE, FORT BEND CO., ST. MICHAEL (1912) [CEM]
9214 Main St., Needville, 77461. Tel: 979-793-4477; Fax: 979-793-7456. Mailing Address: P.O. Box 95, Needville, 77461. Rev. Marty Pham.
Rectory—9202 Main St., Needville, 77461-0095.
Catechesis Religious Program—Jennifer Carlisle, Faith Formation Coord. Students 393.
NEW CANEY, MONTGOMERY CO., ST. JOHN OF THE CROSS (1989)
20000 Loop 494, New Caney, 77357-8213.
Tel: 281-399-9008; Fax: 281-399-1500. Rev. Linh N. Nguyen.
Catechesis Religious Program—Debbie Davis, D.R.E. Students 547.
NEW WAVERLY, WALKER CO., ST. JOSEPH (1869) [CEM 2]
101 Elmore, New Waverly, 77358-4105.
Tel: 936-344-6104; Fax: 936-344-2818. Rev. Daokim Nguyen; Deacon Klaus Petereit.
Catechesis Religious Program—Tel: 936-856-3713. Deacon Klaus Petereit, C.C.E. Coord. Students 140.
Mission—St. Stephen the Martyr, 101 Stagecoach, Pointblank, San Jacinto Co. 77364. Email: ststephenpb@gmail.com. Deacon Melvin Moulton.
PASADENA, HARRIS CO.
1—ST. JUAN DIEGO (1954) (Hispanic) (Formerly Guardian Angel)
3301 Pasadena Blvd., Pasadena, 77503-3201.
Tel: 713-477-6693; Fax: 713-477-0523. Revs. Gerald Goodrum; Jorge Rios, Parochial Vicar; Deacon Jose Jimenez.
Catechesis Religious Program—Tel: 713-628-0183. Gloria Raya, C.R.E. Students 1,681.
2—ST. PIUS V (1941)
824 S. Main St., Pasadena, 77506-3532.
Tel: 713-473-9484; Fax: 713-473-2731. Revs. Joseph A. Doran; Ricardo Lazo, Parochial Vicar; Jan Kubisa, In Res.; Deacons Celestino M. Perez; Daniel Seiler; Heath Hampton.
School—St. Pius V School, 812 Main St., Pasadena, 77506. Tel: 713-472-5172; Email: principal@spvpasadena.org. Felicia Nichols, Prin. Lay Teachers 4; Students 42.
Catechesis Religious Program—Mary Kay Wallace, D.R.E. Students 712.
PATTISON/BROOKSHIRE, WALLER CO., SACRED HEART (1915)

4445 F.M. 359 N., Pattison, 77466. Tel: 281-375-6799 . Rev. David J. DuBois.
Catechesis Religious Program—Tel: 281-579-9666. Carme de la Garza, D.R.E. Students 182.
PEARLAND, BRAZORIA CO., ST. HELEN (1952)
2209 Old Alvin Rd., Pearland, 77581-4499.
Tel: 281-485-2421; Fax: 281-485-6789; Email: shcc@sthelenchurch.org; Email: renee@sthelenchurch.org; Web: www.sthelenchurch.org. Revs. Carl James Courville; Richard R. Hinkley; Deacons J. Cruz Trujillo; Dale Almenario; Steven Griesmyer Sr.
School—St. Helen School, 2213 Old Alvin Rd., Pearland, 77581. Tel: 281-485-2845;
Fax: 281-485-7607; Email: pcoleman@sthelencatholicschool.org. Phyliss Coleman, Prin. Lay Teachers 24; Students 385.
Catechesis Religious Program—Tel: 281-485-5457. Julie Martinez, D.R.E. Students 1,834.
PLANTERSVILLE, GRIMES CO., ST. MARY (1894) [CEM]
8227 County Rd. 205, Plantersville, 77363.
Tel: 936-894-2223; Fax: 936-894-3613; Email: info@smsj.org; Web: www.smsj.org. Revs. Edward C. Kucera Jr.; William T. Kelly, In Res., (Retired).
Catechesis Religious Program—Cheryl Schratwieser, D.R.E. Students 260.
Mission—St. Joseph, Stoneham, Grimes Co. 11323 County Rd. 304, Plantersville, 77363-0388.
PORT BOLIVAR, GALVESTON CO., OUR MOTHER OF MERCY (1968) Closed. For parish records contact the Archives of Galveston-Houston.
PRAIRIE VIEW, WALLER CO., ST. MARTIN DE PORRES (1962) Merged with Mary, Mother of God, Hempstead to form St. Katherine Drexel, Hempstead.
RICHMOND, FORT BEND CO.
1—ST. JOHN FISHER (1952)
410 Clay St., Richmond, 77469-1708.
Tel: 281-342-5092; Fax: 281-633-9465. Rev. Jesse Jesse; Deacons Ruben Torres; Hector R. Rodriguez.
Rectory—406 Clay St., Richmond, 77469.
Catechesis Religious Program—Tel: 281-342-5092. Giovan Cuchapin, D.R.E. Students 644.
2—SACRED HEART (1935)
507 S. Fourth St., Richmond, 77469-3599.
Tel: 281-342-3609. Revs. Joseph Ho; Tokha Thomas Hoang, Parochial Vicar; Deacons Donald G. Ries; John Placette.
Rectory—303 Houston, Richmond, 77469.
Catechesis Religious Program—Tel: 281-342-8371. Ms. Theresa Morales, D.R.E. Students 508.
ROSENBERG, FORT BEND CO.
1—HOLY ROSARY (1911)
1416 George St., Rosenberg, 77471-3198.
Tel: 281-342-3089. Rev. Orrin Halepeska; Deacons Carlito Buhay; Billy Guerrero Jr.; Brick Hodge.
School—Holy Rosary School, 1426 George St., Rosenberg, 77471. Tel: 281-342-5813;
Fax: 281-344-1107; Email: lbradford@holyrosary-school.org. Linda Bradford, Prin. Lay Teachers 21; Students 169.
Catechesis Religious Program—Tina Hollopeter, D.R.E. Students 168.
2—OUR LADY OF GUADALUPE (1936) [CEM]
514 Carlisle St., Rosenberg, 77471.
Tel: 281-232-5113; Fax: 281-342-4008; Email: olgc.est1936@yahoo.com. 1600 Ave. D, Rosenberg, 77471. Rev. Lee A. Flores; Deacons Enrique G. Avila; Albert Yanez; Francisco Nunez.
Rectory—1601 Ave. E, Rosenberg, 77471-1822.
Catechesis Religious Program—Tel: 281-232-5113. Secundino Alameda, D.R.E. Students 484.
SEALY, AUSTIN CO., IMMACULATE CONCEPTION (1889) [CEM]
608 5th St., Sealy, 77474-0337. Tel: 979-885-3868;
Fax: 979-885-2246; Email: iccsealy@aol.com; Web: sealyicc.com. Rev. Eric J. Pitre, M.Div.; Deacons Frank Laredo; Robert Kent; Ben Munguia.
Rectory—525 5th St., Sealy, 77474. Web: www.iccsealy.com.
Church: 600 4th St., Sealy, 77474-2607.
Catechesis Religious Program—Tel: 979-885-0018. Carol Thormaehlen, D.R.E. Students 494.
SOUTH HOUSTON, HARRIS CO., OUR LADY OF GRACE (1971)
1211 Michigan St., South Houston, 77587-0164.
Tel: 713-946-6461; Fax: 713-378-9983. Rev. Maynard U. Parangan, Admin.
Res.: 1204 Michigan St., South Houston, 77587.
Catechesis Religious Program—Tel: 713-477-8883. Maria Rosario Flores, D.R.E. Students 291.
SPRING, HARRIS CO.
1—CHRIST THE GOOD SHEPHERD (1978)
18511 Klein Church Rd., Spring, 77379-4998.
Tel: 281-376-6831; Email: mstakes@cgscc.church; Web: cgscc.church. Revs. James Burkart; Innocent Okhifo, Parochial Vicar; Deacons Alberto J. Patetta; Luis G. Hernandez; Mark Clancy; James Gallagher; John Hagyari; Bob Hargraves.
Catechesis Religious Program—Email: jburkhart@cgscc.church. Alex Gotay, D.R.E. Students 927.
2—ST. EDWARD (1969)
2601 Spring Stuebner Rd., Spring, 77389-4824.
Tel: 281-353-9774; Fax: 281-353-9786. Revs. Christian Bui; Thomas Joseph, O.S.H., Parochial Vicar; Deacons Nicholas Thompson; Dominic Romaguera; Kenneth Martin; William Pitocco.
School—St. Edward School, Tel: 281-353-4570;
Fax: 281-353-8255; Email: tlewis@stedwardschool.org. Tina Lewis, Prin. Lay Teachers 28; Students 344.
Catechesis Religious Program—Amy Auzenne, D.R.E. Students 695.
3—ST. IGNATIUS OF LOYOLA (1985)
7810 Cypresswood Dr., Spring, 77379-7101.
Tel: 281-370-3401; Fax: 281-605-1640. Revs. Norbert J. Maduzia Jr., D.Min.; Augustin Khoi Le; Deacons Scott Glueck; Joseph Wright; Michael E. Higgins; Larry Vines; Mike Baker; Greg Mouton; Peter Olivier; Henry Vinklarek.
Catechesis Religious Program—Linda Krehmeier, Pastoral Assoc. Students 811.
4—ST. JAMES THE APOSTLE (1976)
22800 Aldine Westfield Rd., Spring, 77373-6565.
Tel: 281-353-5053; Fax: 281-355-8847; Email: saintjta@swbell.net; Web: www.stjta.org. Revs. Charles J. Samperi; Thomas Devasahayam, D.S., In Res.; Deacons Ray Oden, Business Mgr.; Alfonso Chicas; Paul Pinon; Arthur Zepeda.
Catechesis Religious Program—Students 297.
SUGAR LAND, FORT BEND CO.
1—ST. LAURENCE (1985)
3100 Sweetwater Blvd., Sugar Land, 77479-2630.
Tel: 281-980-9812; Fax: 281-980-0686; Email: toltremari@stlaurence.org; Web: www.stlaurence.org. Revs. William Andrew Wood; Jaison Thomas Pezhathinal, Parochial Vicar; Truong Nguyen, Parochial Vicar; Deacons Don Burns; Charles Plant; Albert G. Bothe; Renato Arellano; Dennis Henderson.
School—St. Laurence School, 2630 Austin Pkwy., Sugar Land, 77479-2630. Tel: 281-980-0500;
Fax: 281-980-0026; Email: sbarto@stlaurence.org; Web: stlaurenceschool.org. Suzanne Barto, Prin. Lay Teachers 49; Sisters 1; Students 701.
Catechesis Religious Program—Tel: 281-265-5774. Christine Dunn, D.R.E. Students 1,778.
2—ST. THERESA (1924)
Mailing Address: P.O. Box 968, Sugar Land, 77487-0968. Church: 705 St. Theresa Blvd., Sugar Land, 77498. Revs. Eurel Manzano; Jose J. Tharayil; Mathew Gilbert Suniga; Gregory Mirto, In Res.; Deacons John Kennedy; Gilbert Rodriguez; Glenn F. Haller; James Anderson.
Res. & Church Address: 116 Main St., Sugar Land, 77498-2622. Tel: 281-494-1156; Fax: 281-242-1393; Email: diane@sugarlandcatholic.com; Web: www.sugarlandcatholic.org.
School—St. Theresa, Tel: 281-494-1157;
Fax: 281-240-4870; Email: mnewcomb@sttheresacatholicschool.org. Mark Newcomb. Lay Teachers 17; Students 221.
Catechesis Religious Program—Students 816.
3—ST. THOMAS AQUINAS (1978)
12627 W. Bellfort Ave., Sugar Land, 77478-1844.
Tel: 281-240-6721; Fax: 281-240-6733; Email: contact@stasugarland.com; Web: www.stasugarland.com. Rev. Santy M. Kurian, M.S.F.S.; Deacon Robert Kirkpatrick.
Rectory—10415 Huntington Wood Dr., 77099-3721.
Catechesis Religious Program—Karina Wong, D.R.E. Students 226.
SWEENY, BRAZORIA CO., OUR LADY OF PERPETUAL HELP (1954)
310 N. McKinney St., Sweeny, 77480-2899.
Tel: 979-548-2020. Rev. Daniel S. Baguio.
Catechesis Religious Program—Tel: 979-548-6994. John Barber, D.R.E. Students 68.
Mission—St. John the Apostle, 807 Loggins, West Columbia, Brazoria Co. 77486-3843.
TEXAS CITY, GALVESTON CO., ST. MARY OF THE MIRACULOUS MEDAL (1911)
1620 Ninth Ave. N., Texas City, 77590-5708.
Tel: 409-948-8448; Fax: 409-945-8662. Rev. Clint C. Ressler; Deacons Joseph A. Hensley, D.R.E.; John Carrillo; Stephen A. Mistretta; Sid Cammeresi.
School—Our Lady of Fatima, 1600 Ninth Ave. N., Texas City, 77590. Tel: 409-945-3326;
Fax: 409-945-3389; Email: grodgers@fatimatc.org. Rev. Jennifer Lopez, Prin. Lay Teachers 12; Students 67.
Catechesis Religious Program—Tel: 409-948-1383. Students 365.
THE WOODLANDS, MONTGOMERY CO.
1—ST. ANTHONY OF PADUA (1997)
7801 Bay Branch Dr., The Woodlands, 77382-5359.
Tel: 281-419-8700; Email: communications@ap.church; Web: ap.church. Revs. Thomas F. Rafferty; Sebastine Okoye; Deacons Michael Mort, Dir.; Tom Vicknair; Ricardo Garcia; Ralph F. Risk; Richard Vogel.
Rectory—7979 Bay Branch Dr., The Woodlands, 77382-5312.
School—St. Anthony of Padua School, 7901 Bay Branch Dr., The Woodlands, 77382.
Tel: 281-296-0300; Email: Rnunez@staopcs.org. Renee Nunez, Prin. Lay Teachers 38; Students 491.
Catechesis Religious Program—Barbara Beale, D.R.E. Students 2,710.
2—STS. SIMON AND JUDE (1979)
26777 Glen Loch Dr., The Woodlands, 77381-2921.
Tel: 281-367-9885; Fax: 281-367-9888. Revs. Patrick Stuart Garrett; Kailas Hivale, M.S.F.S., Parochial Vicar; Deacons John E. Charnisky Jr.; Anthony G. Cantania; Joe Mignogna; Dennis Carazza.
Catechesis Religious Program—Katie Kozak, D.R.E. Students 545.
TOMBALL, HARRIS CO., ST. ANNE (1964)
1111 S. Cherry St., Tomball, 77375-6675.
Tel: 281-351-8106. Rev. Thomas W. Hopper; Deacons Thomas Davis; Pat Hancock; Garry Janota; Jose Gutierrez.
School—St. Anne School, Tel: 281-351-0093;
Fax: 281-357-1905; Email: jnoonan@stanneschool-tomball.org. Joseph Noonan, Prin. Lay Teachers 26; Students 259.
Catechesis Religious Program—Students 405.
WALLIS, AUSTIN CO., GUARDIAN ANGEL (1892) [CEM]
Mailing Address: P.O. Box 487, Wallis, 77485-0487.
Tel: 979-478-6532; Fax: 979-478-2735. Rev. Thuy Quang Nguyen, Admin.; Deacon Jerome D. Losack Sr.
Church & Res.: 5610 Demel St., Wallis, 77485-0487. Email: gacwallis@gmail.com.
Catechesis Religious Program—Students 139.

Chaplains of Public Institutions

HOUSTON. *Office of Correctional Ministries*, 2403 Holcombe Blvd., 77021-2098. Tel: 713-741-8732. Rev. Ronald F. Cloutier, Archdiocesan Dir.

Graduate Studies:
Rev.—
Angelino, David, Pontifical North American College.

Retired:
Rev. Msgrs.—
Francis, Eugene, (Retired), 6651 Camptown Cir., 77069-1214. Tel: 281-440-1303
Hermoso, Seth F., (Retired), Archbishop Fiorenza Residence, 2407 Holcombe Blvd., Galveston, 77021. Tel: 346-240-2869
Kleas, Milam, (Retired), 2401 Holcombe Blvd., #504, 77021-2023. Tel: 713-747-4853
O'Connor, Fred P., (Retired), Archbishop Fiorenza Residence, 2407 Holcombe Blvd., 77021. Tel: 713-741-7048
Randall, Edward, (Retired), 2409 Holcombe Blvd., #302, 77021-2023. Tel: 713-302-8285
Rossi, Frank H., S.T.L., (Retired), P.O. Box 2029, Woodville, 75979-2029. Tel: 409-283-5367
Wells, Patrick R., (Retired), Archbishop Fiorenza Residence, 2407 Holcombe Blvd., 77021. Tel: 346-240-2872
Zientek, Boleslaus, (Retired), 2409 Holcombe Blvd., #303, 77021-2023. Tel: 281-797-5916
Revs.—
Asenjo, Jose Maria, (Retired), 16807 Dale Oak Way, 77058. Tel: 832-428-8832
Chu, Peter Ngoc Thanh, (Retired), Archbishop Fiorenza Residence, 2407 Holcombe Blvd., 77021-2023. Tel: 346-240-2860
Connelly, Laurence D., (Retired), W. Holcombe, #225, 77025. Tel: 832-838-7693
Corrigan, Michael T., (Retired), Archbishop Fiorenza Residence, 2407 Holcombe Blvd., 77021-2023. Tel: 346-240-2865
Doroin, Elias E., (Retired), 2432 Sheridan St., 77030-1922
Ferguson, Peter A., (Retired), 5720 Jacaranda Ave., Lakeland, FL 33809-3337
Guenter, Frank, (Retired), 2126 Hoskins Dr., 7780-5422. Tel: 832-630-5177
Heberlein, Kenneth, (Retired), Archbishop Fiorenza Residence, 2407 Holcombe Blvd., 77021. Tel: 713-988-2468
Hoang, John Minh Toan, (Retired), Archbishop Fiorenza Residence, 2407 Holcombe Blvd., 77021-2023. Tel: 713-747-7707
Kelly, William T., (Retired), P.O. Box 388, Plantersville, 77363-0388. Tel: 936-894-2016
Martin, Roosevelt Jr., (Retired), (Contact Chancery)
Martinez, Jesus M., (Retired), Archbishop Fiorenza Residence, 2407 Holcombe Blvd., 77021. Tel: 346-240-2868
McGinnis, John P., (Retired), 43555 Deep Canyon Rd., Apt. 2B, Palm Desert, CA 92260-3124. Tel: 760-412-4837

Morfin, John N., (Retired), 8429 Sands Point Dr., Bldg. #18, 77036-2769. Tel: 281-650-7629
Ngo, Francis Huan Ton, (Retired), 10118 Willow Crossing Dr., 77064. Tel: 713-834-5878
Olsovsky, George J., (Retired), P.O. Box 292, Huffman, 77336-0292. Tel: 281-324-2873
Pasadilla, Nicolas O., (Retired), (Contact Chancery)
Sanchez, Jose M., (Retired), 2409 Holcombe Blvd., #308, 77021-2023
Sikorski, Louis S., (Retired), 2409 Holcombe Blvd., #311, 77021-2023. Tel: 713-907-0869
Tenhundfeld, Carl Anthony, (Retired), 11002 Hammerly #167, 77043. Tel: 713-854-4486
Warden, Daniel L., (Retired), Archbishop Fiorenza Residence, 2407 Holcombe Blvd., 77021. Tel: 281-974-0123.

Permanent Deacons:
Abadejos, Ernesto, (Retired)
Abram, Alfred Sr., (Retired)
Adams, John W., (Retired)
Addis, Daniel, Co-Cathedral of the Sacred Heart, Houston
Aguilar, Juan, Our Lady of Mount Carmel, Houston
Alessi, Tony, (Retired)
Alexander, Jack, (Retired)
Alexander, Robert George, Annunciation, Houston
Allen, Charles J. Sr., Our Mother of Mercy, Houston
Almenario, Adelfo, St. Helen, Pearland
Anderson, James, St. Theresa, Sugar Land
Arceneaux, Leon, (Retired)
Arceneaux, Steve Jr., (Retired)
Arellano, Renato, (Retired)
Ausmus, Sam III, Shrine of the True Cross, Dickinson
Avallone, Stan, St. Mary Church, La Porte
Avila, Enrique G., (Retired)
Baker, Theodore Otis, Tel: 89-695-9066. St. Matthias the Apostle, Magnolia
Barfield, Jonathan, St. Martha, Kingwood
Barnes, William, Prince of Peace
Barnett, James, Our Lady of Walsingham, Houston
Bart, James L., (Retired)
Bazan, Jeronimo, (Retired)
Benham, Archie, (Retired)
Benoit, John, (Retired)
Biediger, Larry Jr., Sr. Edith Stein, Katy
Birsinger, Alvin, (Retired)
Blanford, George Jr., (Retired)
Bothe, Albert G., (Retired)
Bottjer, Albert, (Retired)
Bourque, Kerry, Christ the Redeemer
Bowman, David
Boyd, Gary, St. Justin Martyr, Houston
Bradley, Donald V. Jr., (Retired)
Bradley, William, Christ the Redeemer, Houston
Branche, Olatunde Patrick Edward, St. Mary Magdalene, Humble
Breaux, Roy, St. Phillip of Jesus, Houston
Brinkman, Fred H., (Retired)
Broussard, Leonard J., (Retired)
Brown, Abner Sr., (Retired)
Brueggerhoff, Robert T., (Retired)
Budinger, Jean-Paul, (Retired)
Buhay, Carlito, Holy Rosary, Rosenberg
Burns, Don, (Retired)
Burroughs, Orrin D., St. Philip Neri, Houston
Busa, Walter, St. Stanislaus, Anderson
Calonge, Elie P., (Retired)
Calvillo, Pedro, (Retired)
Camacho-del Rio, Gustavo, St. Vincent de Paul, Houston
Camerino, Pat W., (Retired)
Cammeresi, Sidney, St. Mary, Texas City
Camunez, Richard F., (Retired)
Cano, Tomas, Christ the King, Houston
Cantu, Hector, (Retired)
Carazza, Dennis, Sts. Simon and Jude, The Woodlands
Cardella, Anthony, St. Martha, Kingwood
Carney, Lynn, Sacred Heart, Conroe
Carrara, John, (Retired)
Carrasco, Humberto, St. Bartholomew, Houston
Carrillo, John, St. Mary, Texas City
Carroll, Russell, St. Mary, League City
Caruso, James N.
Casas, Alvaro Jr., St. Albert, Houston
Cascarelli, Kevin, Prince of Peace
Castillo, Raul A., (Retired)
Catania, Anthony, (Retired)
Cerda, Rodolfo, (Retired)
Charnisky, John E. Jr., (Retired)
Cheung, Patrick, Ascension, Chinese Mission
Chicas, Alfonso, St. James the Apostle, Spring
Clancy, Mark, Christ the Good Shepherd, Spring
Coenen, Jerry, (Retired)
Coles, Dwight, St. Theresa, Houston
Conant, Charles, (Retired)
Contla, Juan M., St. John Neumann, Houston
Cox, Ralph, (Retired)
Cruz, Agustin, St. Jerome, Clute
Cruz, Michael, St. Leo the Great, Houston
Daniel, Scott Bradley, St. Paul the Apostle
Dao, Andy, Our Lady of Lourdes, Houston
Davis, Frank, (Retired)
Dean, John H., St. Clare of Assisi, Houston
Dell'Olio, L. S., (Retired)
DeYoung, Andrew, St. Mary, League City
Dinges, Adrian F. Jr., (Retired)
Do, Joseph Chuong Nguyen, (Retired)
Dolpher, Eduardo M., St. Cyril of Alexandria, Houston
Drenon, Darryl, St. Francis Xavier
Dunham, Robert, (Retired)
Dunning, Sam, St. Thomas Aquinas, Sugar Land
Dupont, Gerald W., (Retired)
Durden, Donathan, (Retired)
Evanoff, John, Epiphany of the Lord, Katy
Evans, Gregory, St. Cecilia, Houston
Fikac, Marvin R., (Retired)
Flores, Tony, (Retired)
Flynn, Robert E. Sr., (Retired)
Foley, Dan, (Retired)
Forse, Gary, St. Michael, Lake Jackson
Foster, Oscar, St. Monica, Houston
Franek, Paul, St. Mary, Frydek
Frederiksen, Allan, (Retired)
Froning, John Paul, (Retired)
Gallagher, James, (Retired)
Galvan, Jose M., Queen of Peace, Houston
Gandara, Thomas, St. Charles Borromeo, Houston
Garcia, Jorge, St. Mark the Evangelist, Houston
Garcia, Julio T., (Retired)
Garcia, Michael, Catholic Charismatic Center, Houston
Garcia, Ricardo, St. Anthony of Padua, The Woodlands
Garcia, Rolando, (Retired)
Garrett, William, (Retired)
Garvis, David, (Retired)
Garza, Felipe, St. Joseph on the Brazos, Brazoria
Gause, James, Christ the Redeemer
Gilbert, Daniel W., St. Peter the Apostle, Houston
Glueck, Scott, St. Ignatius, Spring
Godoy, German, (Retired)
Gomez, Javier, St. Andrew, Channelview
Gonzalez Bangs, Fernando, (Retired)
Gonzalez, Enrique, (Retired)
Gosline, Edwin F., (Retired)
Graham, Randy, St. Faustina, Fulshear
Griesmyer, Steven Sr., (Retired)
Guajardo, Fedrico, (Retired)
Guerra, Daniel Sr.
Guerrero, Billy Jr., Holy Rosary, Rosenberg
Gutierrez-Ayala, Jose, (Retired)
Gwak, Emmanuel, St. Andrew Kim, Houston
Hall, Greg, Christ the Redeemer, Houston
Haller, Glenn F., (Retired)
Hampton, Heath, St. Pius V, Pasadena
Hancock, James, St. Anne, Tomball
Hargraves, Wilfred, Christ the Good Shepherd, Spring
Hartnett, Timothy, Prince of Peace, Houston
Hayden, Dale, St. John the Baptist, Alvin
Hayes, Dennis, St. Maximilian Kolbe, Houston
Heap, Theodore Jr., St. Edith Stein, Katy
Hebert, Robert, St. Clare of Assisi, Houston
Henkel, Robert Sr., St. Maximilian Kolbe, Houston
Hennessy, Robert, (Retired)
Henry, Kenneth, (Retired)
Hensley, Joseph Jr., St. Mary of the Miraculous Medal, Texas City
Hernandez, Larry, St. Rose of Lima, Houston
Hernandez, Luis, Christ the Good Shepherd, Spring
Hernandez, Luis G., Most Holy Trinity, Angleton
Hernandez, Miguel, St. Mary of the Miraculous Medal, Texas City
Herrera, Edward, St. Rose of Lima, Houston
Hesse, Robert J., (Retired)
Hickey, Dennis, (Retired)
Higgins, Michael E., St. Ignatius, Spring
Hilbig, Gerard, All Saints, Houston
Hoang, Tuu, St. Elizabeth Ann Seton, Houston
Hodge, Brick, (Retired)
Holt, Grant E., Christ Our Light, Navasota
Hoover, Bradley, Sacred Heart, Conroe
Horr, Louis, (Retired)
Hull, Samuel III, (Retired)
Hunsucker, Paul, (Retired)
Hunter, Will, Assumption, Houston
Jackson, Phillip, Christ the Redeemer, Houston
Jackson, Raymond, St. Edith Stein, Katy
Janota, Garry, St. Anne, Tomball
Jelinek, Gregory N., M.D., (Retired)
Jenkins, Michael V., St. Francis Xavier, Houston
Jimenez, Jose, (Retired)
Johnson, David, St. Thomas More, Houston
Johnson, Gilbert R., St. Elizabeth Ann Seton, Houston
Johnson, Irvin Jr., Our Mother of Mercy, Houston
Joseph, Ignatius, (Retired)
Kelly, Joseph R. Sr., (Retired)
Kennedy, John, St. Theresa, Sugar Land
Kent, Robert, Immaculate Conception, Sealy
Kiang, Paul, Ascension Chinese Mission, Houston
Kish, Don, (Retired)
Klak, Joseph Steven, St. Maximilian Kolbe, Houston
Kossegi, Frederick, (Retired)
Krugh, John, St. Thomas More, Houston
Kulhanek, Jerry Peter Sr., Our Lady of Fatima, Galena Park
Labrecque, Richard, (Retired)
Landry, Burke J., (Retired)
Lane, John, St. Monica, Houston
Laredo, Frank, (Retired)
Lattin, Thomas, Prince of Peace, Houston
Laugermann, Frank J. Jr., (Retired)
Laurel, Manuel A., Our Lady of Guadalupe, Houston
Le, Ro, Vietnamese Martyrs, Houston
Leal, Merce C. Jr., (Retired)
Leicht, Robert Reed Jr., (Retired)
Lemond, Martin, St. Martin de Porres, Barrett Station
Lewis, Edward Thomas, (Retired)
Lewis, George, (Retired)
Liendo, Jose L., (Retired)
Llorens, Cornelius C., St. Justin Martyr, Houston
Lockett, Leonard P., Co-Cathedral of the Sacred Heart, Houston
Lockwood, James A.
Lopez, Daniel, St. Frances, Cabrini
Lopez, Richard, Sacred Heart, Conroe
Lorino, Joseph E., (Retired)
Losack, Jerome D. Sr., (Retired)
Lovelady, Alvin, Our Lady of Lourdes, Hitchcock
Malveaux, Andrew B. Sr., (Retired), St. Mary of the Purification, Houston
Mancuso, Salvatore, St. Cecilia, Houston
Martin, Henry Woods, (Retired)
Martin, Kenneth, (Retired)
Matallana, Julio C., (Retired)
Matthews, Douglas, Holy Family, Galveston
Matz, Winfield S., (Retired)
McAllister, Jerome, (Retired)
Mejia Parada, Adolfo, (Retired)
Melancon, Mervin, Sacred Heart, Crosby
Melchior, Daniel, St. Edith Stein
Melendez, Jose, Holy Family, Missouri City
Mendoza, Arturo, St. Cyril of Alexandria
Meshell, James, (Retired)
Meza, Benito, St. Augustine, Houston
Mignogna, Joseph, SS. Simon & Jude, The Woodlands
Miller, Steve, (Retired)
Millet, Rafael, St. Matthias the Apostle, Magnolia
Mistretta, Stephen A., St. Mary of the Miraculous Medal, Texas City
Monterrubio, Arturo, St. Paul the Apostle, Houston
Morales, Hector Hernando, (Retired)
Mort, Michael, St. Anthony of Padua, The Woodlands
Moses, Stephen, Christ the Redeemer, Houston
Moulton, Darrell, (Retired)
Moulton, Melvin, St. Stephen the Martyr Mission, Point Blank
Mouton, Gregory, St. Ignatius, Spring
Mouton, Melvin, (Retired)
Moya, Antonio, (Retired)
Muench, Michael, St. Andrew, Channelview
Munguia, Ben, Immaculate Conception, Sealy
Murrell, John T., St. Rose of Lima, Houston
Murrile, Donald, (Retired)
Naber, John, (Retired)
Naranjo, Danilo, St. Frances de Sales, Houston
Navarro, Raul G., (Retired)
Nelson, Gary, (Retired)
Newhouse, Thomas C., (Retired)
Nguyen, Cuong, Christ the Incarnate Word, Houston
Nguyen, Dinh Van, (Retired), Christ the Incarnate Word, Houston
Nguyen Kim Khanh, Michael, (Retired)
Nguyen Pham, Joseph, Vietnamese Martyrs, Houston
Nguyen Si Bach, Joseph, (Retired)
Nobles, Kimble, Holy Family, Galveston
O'Brien, Alfred J., (Retired)
O'Dowd, Daniel, St. Jerome, Houston
Oden, Edgar, St. James the Apostle, Spring
Olivier, Peter, St. Ignatius, Spring
Olsovsky, Anthony, (Retired)
Ortega, Mario, Assumption, Houston
Ortego, Frank P., (Retired)
Ospina, Alberto, (Retired)
Osterhaus, James H., (Retired)
Ostrowski, Francis L., (Retired)
Pagnano, Daniel, St. Vincent de Paul, Houston
Pareja, Juan Francisco, (Retired)
Patetta, Alberto J., Christ the Good Shepherd, Spring

Pelletier, John, St. Katherine Drexel, Hempstead
Peltier, Gerald, (Retired)
Pena, Eddy Valbuena, Sacred Heart, Conroe
Pennell, Charles G., St. Elizabeth Ann Seton, Houston
Pennell, Glen, St. Joseph, St. Stephen, Houston
Perez, Celestino M., (Retired)
Perez, Juan de Dios, St. Theresa, Houston
Petereit, Klaus, (Retired)
Pinon, Paul, St. James the Apostle, Spring
Piotrowski, Thomas, St. Matthew the Evangelist, Houston
Pistone, John Salvadore, (Retired)
Pitocco, William, St. Edward, Spring
Placette, John, Sacred Heart, Richmond
Plant, Charles, St. Laurence, Sugar Land
Porras, Carlos, (Retired)
Prescott, Allen W., (Retired)
Prewitt, Sidney, St. Mattias the Apostle, Magnolia
Puglia, Guy, St. Martha, Kingwood
Quiray, Michael, St. Francis de Sales, Houston
Quiroga, Gabriel Z., Our Lady of Guadalupe, Houston
Ramirez, Fernando, St. Frances Cabrini, Houston
Ramirez, Julio M., (Retired)
Ramirez, Octaviano, Our Lady of Guadalupe, Baytown
Ramon, Rene, St. Mary Magdalene, Humble
Ramos, Felix, St. Thomas the Apostle, Huntsville
Reyes, Ricardo, Sacred Heart Jesus, Manvel
Reynolds, Joseph, (Outside Diocese)
Richards, Thomas Edward, (Retired)
Ries, Donald G., (Retired)
Rincon, George, (Retired)
Risk, Ralph F., (Retired)
Robertson, Gordon, St. Bartholomew the Apostle, Katy
Robison, Paul L. Jr., (Retired)
Rodriguez, Gilbert, St. Theresa, Sugar Land
Rodriguez, Hector R., (Retired)
Rodriguez, Luis, St. Thomas More, Houston
Rojas, Servando, St. Frances Cabrini, Houston
Romaguera, Dominic, St. Edward, Spring
Romeu, Hector J., (Retired)
Rumford, Robert, St. Bernadette, Houston
Rust, Matthew, St. Maximilian Kolbe
Salas, Pedro, St. Jerome, Houston
Sanchez, Guadalupe, St. Frances Cabrini, Houston
Sandiford, Sid, (Retired)
Santos, John, (Retired)
Sarabia, John, St. Philip, Huffman
Schmelter, Jeffrey, Prince of Peace, Houston
Schuster, John, (Retired)
Seifert, William E. Jr., Holy Family, Missouri City
Seiler, Daniel, (Retired)
Shaw, Wallace, (Retired)
Sheffield, William L., Prince of Peace, Houston
Silva, George, St. Joseph, Baytown
Simon, Rick L., St. Mary Magdalene, Humble
Simon, Ronald, St. Philip Neri, Houston
Singer, John William Jr., (Retired)
Smaistrla, Denis J., (Retired)
Smith, Jimmy, (Retired)
Sosa, Alfonso, St. Elizabeth Ann Seton, Houston
Soto, Alfredo, (Retired)
Speight, Jeffery Allan, Christ The Redeemer, Houston
St. Julian, Michael, St. Francis of Assisi, Houston
Standridge, Robert, Holy Family, Galveston
Stanley, Kenneth, Prince of Peace, Houston
Steffes, Dale W., (Retired)
Stevens, Robert Gregory, St. Frances Cabrini, Houston
Stoessel, Edward T., (Retired)
Suriano, Julio S., (Retired)
Thompson, Nicholas, St. Edwards, Spring
Tollett, Jesse, (Retired)
Torres, Reynaldo, St. Patrick, Houston
Torres, Ruben, St. John Fisher, Richmond
Tran, Ky, St. Frances de Sales
Tran, Nhat, St. Justin Martyr, Houston
Trevino, Jose, Christ the Redeemer, Houston
Tristan, Benito, St. Christopher, Houston
Trosclair, George, (Retired)
Trujillo, J. Cruz, (Retired)
Turner, Charles, Mary Queen, Friendswood
Vacek, Albert E. Jr., (Retired)
Vaclavik, Larry A., St. Theresa, Houston
Vences, Carlos, (Retired)
Venegas, Rudy, (Retired)
Vicknair, Tom Jude, (Retired)
Villareal, Marcelino, (Retired), St. Mark the Evangelist, Houston
Vines, Larry, (Retired)
Vogel, Richard, St. Anthony of Padua, The Woodlands
Wagner, William C., (Retired)
Ward, Robert, Most Holy Trinity, Angleton
Weaver, Lonnie Lester Jr., (Retired)
Weir, Joseph, St. Maximilian Kolbe, Houston
Welsh, James, (Outside Diocese)
Werner, Robert Martin, (Retired)
Wewer, Justin J., (Retired)
Whited, Thomas, St. Matthew the Evangelist, Houston
Wiles, Philip Arlen, (Retired)
Willard, Jeffrey, Christ the Redeemer, Houston
Wilson, William, St. Theresa, Houston
Woodvine, Kevin, St. Bernadette, Houston
Wright, Jim, St. Angela Merici, Missouri City
Wright, Joseph, St. Ignatius, Spring
Yanez, Albert, Our Lady of Guadalupe, Rosenberg
Yepsen, Gary, St. Martha, Kingwood
Zepeda, Arthur, St. James the Apostle, Spring.

INSTITUTIONS LOCATED IN ARCHDIOCESE

[A] SEMINARIES, ARCHDIOCESAN

HOUSTON. *St. Mary's Seminary* (1901) 9845 Memorial Dr., 77024-3498. Tel: 713-686-4345; Fax: 713-681-7550; Email: sms@smseminary.com; Web: smseminary.com. Revs. Trung V. Nguyen, J.C.L., Rector; Dominic Anaeto, Formation Dir.; Vincent Anyama, Dir.; Manuel Razo, Dir.; Rev. Msgr. Chester L. Borski, Spiritual Advisor/Care Svcs.; Revs. John Rooney, M.R.E., Spiritual Advisor/Care Svcs.; Rafael R. Davila, M.M., Spiritual Advisor/Care Svcs.; Sandra Magie, S.T.D., Dean School of Theology; Revs. Paul E. Lockey, M.A., S.T.L., Ph.D., Prof.; Lawrence W. Jozwiak, J.C.L., Prof.; Richard Wahl, J.C.L., Prof.; Rev. Msgr. James B. Anderson, Prof.; Revs. Leon Strieder, Prof.; Charles J. Talar, Prof.; Francis M. Macatangay, Prof.; Dr. Laura Manzo, Prof.; Dr. Steven Meyer, Prof.; Mr. Richard McCarren, Business Mgr.; Dr. Mary Kelleher, Librarian. Lay Teachers 3; Priests 15; Students 88; Total Enrollment 88; Diocesan Seminarians 73; Religious Seminarians 15; Clergy / Religious Teachers 10.

[B] COLLEGES AND UNIVERSITIES

HOUSTON. **University of St. Thomas* (1947) 3800 Montrose Blvd., 77006-4696. Tel: 713-522-7911; Fax: 713-525-2125; Email: president@stthom.edu; Email: admissions@stthom.edu; Web: www.stthom.edu. Richard Ludwick, Pres.; Arthur Ortiz, Vice Pres.; Spencer Conroy, Vice Pres.; Jeff Olsen, Vice Pres.; Chris Evans, Vice Pres.; Rev. Christopher Valka, Chap.; Michelle Williams, Registrar; Mr. James Piccininni, Dean, Libraries; Dr. Sandra C. Magie, Dean School of Theology; Dr. Beena George, Dean Cameron School of Business; Dr. Paul Paese, Dean, School Educ.; Ms. Lynda McKendree, Dean Scholarships & Fin. Aid; Ms. Joanna Palasota, Asst. Vice Pres., Admin. Computing Svcs. & Inst. Research; Dr. Rose Signorello, Exec. Dir. Counseling, Disability Svcs.; Mr. Gary McCormack, Vice Pres. Planning & Technology; Special Assistant to Pres.; Mr. Howard Rose, Assoc. Vice Pres.; Ms. Patricia McKinley, Vice Pres. Student Affairs; Ms. Marionette Mitchell, Dir. Creative Svcs.; Dr. Mary Kelleher, Dir. Cardinal Beran Library; Ana Lopez, Dir. Res. Life & Conference Housing; Lee Holm, Dir., Academic Advising; Dr. Ulyses Balderas, Dir. Study Abroad; Ms. Lori Gallagher, Dir., William J. Flynn Center for Irish Studies; Mr. Todd Smith, Dir. Athletics; H. E. Jenkins, Chief, Univ. Police; Ms. Elsie Biron, Dir. Catholic Outreach; Dr. Poldi Tschirsch, Dean, School of Nursing; Sandra Soliz, Dir., Communications; Lindsey McPherson, Asst. Vice Pres., Student Svcs. & Dean, Students; Dr. Hans Stockton, Dir. Center for Intl. Studies; Assoc. Dean, School of Arts & Sciences; Lily Swan, Dir., Intl. Student & Scholar Svcs.; Rick Young, Dir., Pre-Law Prog.; Dr. Siobhan Fleming, Assoc. Vice Pres., Institutional Assessment & Effectiveness; Deacon Randy Graham, Assoc. Vice Pres., Human Resources, St. Faustina Fulshear - Active; David Carl Schaider, Dir., Campus Choir. Founded in 1947, Graduate Division (Five Schools). Undergraduate Division (Five Schools). Center for Thomistic Studies. Center for International Studies. Center for Ethical Leadership. William J. Flynn Center for Irish Studies. Center for Faith & Culture, Liberal Arts University. Students 3,237; Total Staff 244; Clergy / Religious Teachers 11; Lay Professors 168.

[C] JUNIOR HIGH SCHOOLS, ARCHDIOCESAN

HOUSTON. *Assumption Catholic School*, 801 Roselane St., 77037-4696. Tel: 281-447-2132; Fax: 281-447-1825; Email: jbates@houstonassumption.org; Web: www.houstonassumption.org. John William Bates, Prin.; Sr. Francis Marie Bordages, Librarian. Lay Teachers 12; Students 217.

[D] HIGH SCHOOLS, PRIVATE

GALVESTON. *O'Connell College Preparatory School*, 1320 Tremont St., Galveston, 77550-4513. Tel: 409-765-5534; Fax: 409-765-5536; Email: info@oconnellprep.com; Web: www.oconnellprep.com. Patti Abbott, Prin.; Barbara Alcala, Librarian. Lay Teachers 12; Students 105; Total Staff 6.

HOUSTON. *St. Agnes Academy* (1906) 9000 Bellaire Blvd., 77036-4683. Tel: 713-219-5400; Fax: 713-219-5499; Email: jane.meyer@st-agnes.org; Web: www.st-agnes.org. Sr. Jane Meyer, O.P., Head of School, Tel: 713-219-5400; Fax: 713-219-5499; Deborah Whalen, Prin. Girls 916; Lay Teachers 85; Dominican Sisters 2; Students 916; Full-time Faculty 94.

Duchesne Academy of the Sacred Heart (1960) (Girls) 10202 Memorial Dr., 77024-3299. Tel: 713-468-8211; Fax: 713-465-9809; Email: administration@duchesne.org; Email: admissions@duchesne.org; Web: www.duchesne.org. Patricia Swenson, Head of School; Donald Cramp, Prin. (Upper School); Tony Houle, Prin. (Middle School); Ginger Montalbano, Prin. (Lower School). Religious of the Sacred Heart. Lay Teachers 77; Sisters 2; Total Enrollment (PreK-12) 702.

Incarnate Word Academy (1873) 609 Crawford St., 77002-3668. Tel: 713-227-3637; Fax: 713-227-1014; Email: maamodt@incarnateword.org; Web: www.incarnateword.org. Sr. Lauren Beck, C.V.I., Pres.; Mary Aamodt, Prin. Sisters of the Incarnate Word and Blessed Sacrament. Girls 354; Lay Teachers 39; Students 354.

Jesuit Cristo Rey High School of Houston, Inc. dba Cristo Rey Jesuit College Preparatory School of Houston, Inc. (Co-Ed) 6700 Mt. Carmel St., 77087. Tel: 281-501-1298; Fax: 281-501-3485; Email: nkean@cristoreyjesuit.org; Web: www.cristoreyjesuit.org. Paul Posoli, Pres.; David Garcia-Prats, Prin. Lay Teachers 41; Priests 2; Total Enrollment 540.

St. Pius X High School, Inc. (1956) 811 W. Donovan, 77091-5699. Tel: 713-692-3581; Fax: 713-692-5725; Email: armisteadc@stpiusx.org; Web: www.stpiusx.org. Carmen G. Armistead, Headmaster; Diane Larsen, Prin. Lay Teachers 60; Dominican Sisters 3; Students 575; Total Staff 26; Clergy / Religious Teachers 1.

Strake Jesuit College Preparatory Inc., 8900 Bellaire Blvd., 77036-4699. Tel: 713-774-7651; Fax: 713-774-6427; Email: sjcom@strakejesuit.org; Web: www.strakejesuit.org. Mr. Ken Lojo, Prin.; Revs. Anthony Rauschuber, S.J., Pastoral Ministry; Jeffrey C. Johnson, S.J., Pres.; Douglas J. Hypolite, S.J., Teacher; Lourdu Marianna Pasala, S.J. Boys 1,075; Brothers 1; Lay Teachers 105; Priests 3.

St. Thomas High School (1900) 4500 Memorial Dr., 77007-7332. Tel: 713-864-6348 (School); Tel: 713-868-9209 (Residence); Fax: 713-864-5750; Web: www.sths.org. Revs. Kevin J. Storey, C.S.B., Pres.; James F. Murphy, C.S.B., Supr.; Mitch Dowalgo, C.S.B.; Joanie South-Shelley, Librarian. Basilian Residence, Basilian Fathers. Lay Teachers 57; Priests 3; Total Enrollment 700; Total Staff 103.

KATY. *St. John XXIII College Preparatory* (2004) 1800 W. Grand Pkwy. N., Katy, 77449. Tel: 281-693-1000; Fax: 281-693-1001; Email: news@sj23lions.org; Web: www.sj23lions.org. Rev. Steve Sellers, Pres.; Timothy Gallic, Prin.; Lynsey Hepburn, Admissions; Rev. Msgr. Bill Young, V.F., Bd. Pres.; Elizabeth Dronet, Librarian. Priests 2; Teachers 37; Total Enrollment 427; Total Staff 58.

SPRING. **Frassati Catholic High School (North Houston Catholic High School)* aka Frassati Catholic High School (North Houston Catholic High School), 22151 Frassati Way, Spring, 77389. Tel: 832-616-3217; Fax: 281-907-0675; Web: www.frassaticatholic.org. Sr. John Paul, O.P., Prin. Lay Teachers 25; Sisters 4; Students 281; Clergy / Religious Teachers 4.

[E] ELEMENTARY SCHOOLS, PRIVATE

HOUSTON. *St. Catherine's Montessori* (1966) 9821 Timberside, 77025. Tel: 713-665-2195; Fax: 713-665-1478; Email: stracy@stcathmont.org. Susan Tracy, Prin.; Sarah Lewis, Librarian. Lay Teachers 18; Students 304; Total Staff 55; Clergy / Religious Teachers 2.

St. John Paul II Catholic School (1988) (Grades PreK-8), 1400 Parkway Plaza Dr., 77077-1503. Tel: 281-496-1500; Fax: 281-496-2943; Email: principal@jp2.org; Email: communications@jp2.org; Web: www.jp2.org. Rebecca Bogard, Prin. Lay Teachers 43; Students 685; Total Staff 78.

The Regis School, 7330 Westview Dr., 77055-5122. Tel: 713-682-8383; Fax: 713-682-8388; Email: dphillips@theregisschool.org; Web: www.theregisschool.org. Mr. Dennis Phillips, Head of School; Mrs. Janna Roberson, Asst. Head of School; Ms. Laura Dozier, Dir.; Ms. Beth Schneider, Dir.

Catholic School for Boys. Lay Teachers 35; Students 275; Total Staff 55.

[F] ELEMENTARY SCHOOLS, CONSOLIDATED

GALVESTON. *Holy Family Catholic School* (1986) 2601 Ursuline Ave., Galveston, 77550-4398.
Tel: 409-765-6607; Fax: 409-765-5154; Email: rhesse@hfcsgalv.org; Web: hfcsgalv.org. Rita Hesse, Prin.; Dawn Cromie, Librarian & Mgr. Lay Teachers 15; Sisters 1; Students 112; Total Staff 18.

GALVESTON/HOUSTON. *School of Environmental Education - Camp Kappe* (1982) 7738 Camp Kappe Rd., Plantersville, 77363. Tel: 936-894-2141;
Fax: 936-894-2198; Email: mrichmond@archgh.org. Michael Richmond, Dir., S.E.E. Lay Teachers 4; Total Enrollment 1,200; Total Staff 4.

RICHWOOD. *Our Lady Queen of Peace Catholic School*, (Grades PreK-8), 1600 Hwy. 2004, Richwood, 77531. Tel: 979-265-3909; Fax: 979-265-9780; Email: kwilson@olqpschool.org; Web: www.olqpschool.org. Marianne Mechura, M.Ed., Prin. Serving the parishes of Holy Trinity, Angleton; St. Jerome, Clute; St. Anthony, Danbury; St. Mary Star of the Sea, Freeport; Lady of Perpetual Help, Sweeny; St. John the Apostle Mission, West Columbia; St. Joseph's, Brazoria, TX; St. Michaels, Lake Jackson. Lay Teachers 19; Students 196; Clergy / Religious Teachers 2.

[G] SOCIAL AGENCIES CATHOLIC CHARITIES

HOUSTON. *Catholic Charities of the Archdiocese of Galveston-Houston* (1943) 2900 Louisiana St., 77006. Tel: 713-526-4611; Fax: 713-526-1546; Email: hope@catholiccharities.org; Email: cjohns@catholiccharities.org; Web: www.catholiccharities.org. Cynthia Nunes Colbert, M.S.W., Pres.; Natalie Wood, Senior Vice Pres. of Programs, Tel: 713-874-6731; Brian Gillen, Vice Pres.; Nyla K. Woods, Vice Pres. Tot Asst. Annually 85,000; Total Staff 300.

Care for Children:

Pregnancy Services - Blessed Beginnings,
Tel: 713-874-6632.

St. Jerome Emiliani Home for Children - International Foster Care Program,
Tel: 281-202-6315.

St. Michael's Homes for Children, Tel: 713-526-4611
.

Strengthening Families:

Central, Tel: 713-526-4611.

Counseling Services, Tel: 713-526-4611.

Family Assistance Basic Needs, Tel: 713-227-9981.

Parish Social Ministry, Tel: 713-874-6659.

Texas City / Galveston / Bay Area, Tel: 409-948-0405.

Support for Refugees & Immigrants:

Refugee Resettlement, Tel: 713-874-6516.

St. Frances Cabrini Center for Immigrant Legal Assistance, Tel: 713-874-6570.

HIV / AIDS Ministry, Tel: 713-874-6724.

St. Frances Cabrini at Mamie George Community Center, Tel: 281-202-6200.

Senior Services and Special Needs,
Tel: 713-526-4611. Promoting independence for seniors, veterans and others.

Locations:

Central Office, 2900 Louisiana St., 77006.
Tel: 713-526-4611; Email: hope@catholiccharities.org; Web: www.CatholicCharities.org.

Guadalupe Center, 326 S. Jensen Dr., 77003.
Tel: 713-227-9981; Tel: 713-526-4611; Email: hope@catholiccharities.org; Web: www.CatholicCharities.org/basicneeds. 2900 Lousiana St., 77006. Greta Langley, Dir.

Maime George Community Center, 1111 Collins Rd., Richmond, 77469. Tel: 231-202-6200; Email: hope@catholiccharities.org; Web: www.CatholicCharities.org/mamiegeorge. Gladys Brumfield James, Exec.

Counseling Services:

Moran Health Center, 2615 Fannin, 77002.
Tel: 231-202-3100.

St. John Vianney Catholic Community, Social Ministry Office, 625 Nottingham Oaks Trl., 77079.
Tel: 281-497-1500.

St. Ignatius Loyola Catholic Church, 7810 Cypresswood, Spring, 77379. Tel: 281-370-3401;
Fax: 281-605-1640. Revs. Norbert J. Maduzia Jr., D.Min.; Khoi Le, Parochial Vicar; Deacons Mike Baker; Michael E. Higgins; Gregory Mouton; Larry Vines; Scott Glueck; Joseph Wright; Peter Olivier; Henry Vinklanek.

[H] HEALTH AND HOSPITALS

HOUSTON. **CHI St. Luke's Health (System)*, 6624 Fannin St., 77030. Tel: 832-355-1000; Web: www.chistlukeshealth.org. T. Douglas Lawson, CEO. Total Staff 8,000.

**CHI St. Luke's Health - Baylor St. Luke's Medical Center*, 6720 Bertner Ave., 77030.
Tel: 832-355-1000; Web: www.chistlukeshealth.org/baylorstlukes. Gay Nord, Pres. Bed Capacity 850; Tot Asst. Annually 100,000; Total Staff 3,919.

**CHI St. Luke's Health - Sugar Land Hospital*, 1317 Lake Point Pkwy., Sugar Land, 77478.
Tel: 281-637-7000; Web: www.chistlukeshealth.org/sugarlandhospital. Rob Heifner, Pres. Bed Capacity 100; Tot Asst. Annually 21,000; Total Staff 400.

**CHI St. Luke's Health - The Vintage Hospital*, 20171 Chasewood Park Dr., 77070.
Tel: 832-534-5000; Web: www.chistlukeshealth.org/thevintagehospital. Rob Heifner, Pres. Bed Capacity 106; Tot Asst. Annually 21,000; Total Staff 511.

CHRISTUS Literacy Center, 2420 Winnie St., Galveston, 77550. Tel: 409-765-6971; Email: angela.joseph@christushealth.org; Web: christusfoundation.org. Angela Joseph, Dir. Personnel 3.

CHRISTUS Our Daily Bread (1985) 2420 Winnie St., Galveston, 77550. Tel: 409-765-6971;
Fax: 409-765-8547; Web: christusfoundation.org. Tot Asst. Annually 2,500; Total Staff 7.

Sisters of Charity of the Incarnate Word, Houston, Texas (SCH), 6510 Lawndale St., 77023.
Tel: 713-928-6053; Fax: 713-928-8148. Sr. Mary Driscoll, Sec. Bed Capacity 112; Tot Asst. Annually 229; Total Staff 135.

KATY. *CHRISTUS St. Catherine Hospital*, 701 S. Fry Rd., Katy, 77450. Tel: 281-599-5700;
Fax: 281-398-2265. Bed Capacity 102; Patients Asst Anual. 72,229.

[I] CLINICS

HOUSTON. *San Jose Clinic* (1922) 2615 Fannin, P.O. Box 2808, 77252-2808. Tel: 713-490-2601;
Fax: 713-490-2641; Email: connect@sanjoseclinic.org; Web: www.sanjoseclinic.org. Paule Anne Lewis, Pres. & CEO. Lay Staff 45; Tot Asst. Annually 4,719; Total Staff 60; Volunteers 967.

[J] PROTECTIVE INSTITUTIONS

HOUSTON. *Casa de Esperanza De Los Ninos, Inc.* (1982) P.O. Box 66581, 77266-6581. Tel: 713-529-0639;
Fax: 713-529-9179; Email: casa@casahope.org; Web: www.casahope.org. Kathleen Foster, Dir. Homes for children in crisis situations, foster care, adoption.

Casa Juan Diego (1980) P.O. Box 70113, 77270.
Tel: 713-869-7376; Fax: 713-864-7295; Email: info@cjd.org; Web: www.cjd.org. Mrs. Louise Zwick, Dir. Bed Capacity 100; Tot Asst. Annually 50,425; Personnel 18; Houses 8.

Casa Maria de Guadalupe Medical Clinic and Social Service Center, 6101 Edgemoor, P. O. Box 70113, 77270. Tel: 713-869-7376;
Fax: 713-864-7295; Email: info@cjd.org; Web: www.cjd.org. Mrs. Louise Zwick, Dir. (Catholic Worker) Tot Asst. Annually 10,910; Total Staff 15.

Covenant House Texas, 1111 Lovett Blvd., 77006.
Tel: 713-523-2231; Fax: 713-523-6904; Email: Rgrobinson@covenanthouse.org; Web: www.covenanthousetx.org. Ronda G. Robinson, Exec. Dir. & CEO. Bed Capacity 70; Tot Asst. Annually 5,302; Total Staff 76.

Magnificat Houses Inc. (1968) 3300 Caroline St., P.O. Box 8486, 77288. Tel: 713-529-4231;
Tel: 713-520-0461; Email: mhlemond@gmail.com; Web: magnificathousesinc.org. Deacon Martin Lemond, Contact Person. Bed Capacity 178; Tot Asst. Annually 228,351; Total Staff 30; Resident Staff 25; Total Assisted Annually (Houses) 1,686; Meals Served Annually (Soup Kitchen) 88,623; Meals Served Annually (Houses) 137,800; Contract Staff 9.

Santa Maria Hostel, 2605 Parker Rd., 77093.
Tel: 713-691-0900; Fax: 713-691-0910; Email: nscamp@santamariahostel.org; Web: www.santamariahostel.org. 2005 Jacquelyn Rd., 77055.
Tel: 713-957-2413. 807 Paschall, 77009.
Tel: 713-691-0900. Nadine Scamp, CEO. Intensive and supportive residential treatment; housing, outpatient services (substance abuse) for women ages 18 and above and women with their children. Housing and substance abuse treatment for female veterans. Sober housing for pregnant & parenting women with children. Treatment for co-occurring disorders is also provided. Bed Capacity 231; Residents 399; Tot Asst. Annually 5,400; Total Staff 165.

[K] HOMES FOR THE AGED

HOUSTON. *St. Dominic Village* (1998) 2401 Holcombe Blvd., 77021. Tel: 713-741-8701;
Fax: 713-741-9811; Email: ashields@stdominicvillage.org; Web: www.stdominicvillage.org. Amy Shields, CEO. Bed Capacity 331; Total Staff 185.

Archbishop Joseph A. Fiorenza Priest Retirement Residence (1981) 2407 Holcombe Blvd., 77021-2023. Tel: 713-440-3437; Fax: 713-748-4608; Email: ghilbig@archgh.org. Deacon Gary Hilbig, Clergy Pastoral Outreach Min. Total Staff 3.

St. Dominic Village Rehabilitation and Nursing Center (1981) 2409 Holcombe Blvd., 77021.
Tel: 713-741-8701; Fax: 713-741-9811; Web: www.stdominicvillage.org; Email: ashields@stdominicvillage.org. Amy Shields, CEO. Bed Capacity 158; Total Staff 140; Total Served 262.

St. Dominic Village Independent & Assisted Living (1975) 2401A Holcombe Blvd., 77021.
Tel: 713-741-8700; Fax: 713-748-8305; Email: lgillespie@stdominicvillage.org. Amy Shields, CEO. Independent Living and Assisted Living. Bed Capacity 173; Total Staff 32; Total Served 94.

[L] RESIDENTIAL TREATMENT AND RENEWAL CENTERS

SPLENDORA. *Shalom Center, Inc.* (1980) 13516 Morgan Dr., Splendora, 77372-3121. Tel: 281-399-0520;
Fax: 281-399-3366; Email: info@shalomcenterinc.org; Web: www.shalomcenterinc.org. Daniel A. Kidd, Exec. Dir.; Dr. Patricia Reed, Dir. A residential treatment center for priests, brothers and sisters. Also offers sabbatical and retreats. Bed Capacity 20; Tot Asst. Annually 280; Total Staff 24.

[M] PERSONAL PRELATURES

HOUSTON. *Opus Dei*, 5505 Chaucer Dr., 77005.
Tel: 713-523-4351; Fax: 713-523-6829; Email: pparriagadai@gmail.com; Web: www.opusdei.org. Very Rev. Paul D. Kais, B.A., M.A., Ph.D., Vicar Opus Dei in Texas; Revs. Francisco Vera, Chap.; Christopher Schmitt; Pedro Arriagada. Prelature of the Holy Cross and Opus Dei.

[N] MONASTERIES AND RESIDENCES OF PRIESTS AND BROTHERS

HOUSTON. *The Basilian Fathers of Dillon House*, 1302 Kipling, 77006-4212. Tel: 713-204-7383;
Fax: 713-204-7383; Email: paulofchap@gmail.com. Revs. Paul F. O'Connor, C.S.B., Supr., (Retired); Philip Anthony Acquaro, C.S.B., (Retired); Wilfred S. Canning, C.S.B., (Retired); Carl L. Belisch, C.S.B., Acting Supr., (Retired); James Joseph Gaunt, C.S.B., (Retired); Robert James Klem, C.S.B., (Retired); Roy Joseph Oggero, C.S.B., (Retired); William Joseph Frankenberger, C.S.B., (Retired); James Francis Blocher, C.S.B., (Retired); Jamie M. Abercrombie, C.S.B., (Retired); John L. Boscoe, C.S.B.; Robert H. Glass, C.S.B. Basilian Fathers.

The Companions of The Cross, Companions of the Cross, 1949 Cullen Blvd., 77023. Tel: 866-885-8824
; Fax: 613-725-1590; Email: info@companionscross.org; Web: www.companionscross.org. Rev. Galen Bank, Treas.

Congregation of the Passion, Holy Name Passionist Community and Retreat Center, 430 Bunker Hill Rd., 77024. Tel: 713-464-4932; Fax: 713-932-7303; Email: kennethomalleycp@gmail.com; Web: www.passionist.org. Very Rev. Kenneth O'Malley, C.P., Local Supr. & Formation Dir.; Revs. Giuseppe Barbieri, C.P., Retreat Center Dir.; Cedric Pisegna, C.P.; Ronan Newbold, C.P.; George Stanfield; Antonio Curto, C.P.

Disciples of Hope (Texas) (1995) 15403 Palmway St., 77071. Tel: 713-721-2894; Web: www.thedisciplesofhope.org. Rev. Thomas Devasahayam, D.S., Hospital Chap.

Maryknoll Fathers and Brothers, 2360 Rice Blvd., 77005-2652. Tel: 713-529-1912; Fax: 713-529-0372; Email: gekelly@maryknoll.org; Web: www.maryknoll.org. Rev. Gerald E. Kelly, M.M., Dir.

Priests Residing Elsewhere: Revs. Rafael R. Davila, M.M., St. Mary Seminary, 9845 Memorial Dr., 77024-3498. Tel: 713-686-4345; Fax: 713-681-7550; Richard E. Paulissen, M.M., P.O. Box 9592, 77261. Tel: 713-921-2736.

Keon House (1947) 4019 Yoakum Blvd., 77006-4833. Cell: 281-702-1201; Cell: 713-823-8699; Email: kstorey@basilian.org. Revs. Kevin Story, Pres.; David Bittner, Supr.; Edward J. Baenziger, C.S.B.; Janusz Ihnatowicz, (Poland); Joseph E. Pilsner, C.S.B.; Mitch Dowalgo, C.S.B.; Ronald G. Schwenzer, C.S.B.; Christopher Valka; Richard A. Wahl, C.S.B., J.C.L.; Eduardo Rivera; Steven Huber; Oscar Carbajal.

US Foundation for the Congregation of the Holy Ghost and the Immaculate Heart of Mary, Inc. (1964) (Sharelink - Spiritan Worldwide Aid Foundation) 1700 W. Alabama St., 77098-2808.
Tel: 713-522-2882; Cell: 412-292-0807; Email: somacssptx@gmaill.com; Email: dtc79@hotmail.com; Web: www.spiritans.org. Very Rev. Michael T. Grey, C.S.Sp., Dir.; Rev. David Cottingham, C.S.Sp., Assoc. Dir. Total in Residence 2.

Vietnamese Dominican Vicariate of St. Vincent Liem, 12314 Old Foltin Rd., 77086. Tel: 281-999-4928;
Fax: 281-820-7095. Very Rev. Huong Pham, O.P.,

Reg. Supr. In Res. Rev. Martin Philip Nhan Thai Bui, O.P.

MISSOURI CITY. *The Society of the Oblates of Sacred Heart*, 1510 Fifth St., Missouri City, 77489-1298. Tel: 832-798-8579; Fax: 281-499-9680; Email: oblates.us@gmail.com; Web: www.oshsociety.org. Revs. Lukose Manuel, O.S.H., Supr.; Sunny Joseph Plammoottil, O.S.H.; Joy James, O.S.H.; Thomas Joseph, O.S.H.

SUGAR LAND. *Basilian Fathers Missions* (1936) 414 Main St., P.O. Box 708, Sugar Land, 77487-0708. Tel: 281-201-8690; Fax: 832-201-0593; Email: central@basilianfathersmissions.com; Web: www.basilianfathersmissions.org. Rev. Vincent J. Dulock, C.S.B., Dir.; Aron Fernandez, Admin.; Rev. Jack H. Hanna, C.S.B., Treas. Deacons 1; Novices 2; Priests 13; Scholastics 12.

Priests Serving in Foreign Missions: Revs. Francis A. Amico, C.S.B.; Robert J. Barringer, C.S.B., Mailing Address: c/o Basilian Fathers Mission Center, P.O. Box 708, Sugar Land, 77487-0708. (Supr. of Colombia); Alberto A. Ferrara, C.S.B.; Rafael I. Lopera, C.S.B., (Supr. of Colombia); Pedro M. Mora, C.S.B.; Bernard C. Owens, C.S.B.; Roberto Rojas, C.S.B.; Juan Carlos Rojas Ramos, C.S.B.; Robert J. Seguin, C.S.B.; Charles Daniel Porter, C.S.B.; Oscar Fernando Gomez Soto, C.S.B.; Paul F. Walsh, C.S.B.

Franciscan Missionary Brothers of North America, New York, St. Francis Friary, 11710 Cobblestone Point Dr., Sugar Land, 77498. Tel: 281-495-1558; Email: cmsfsugarland@gmail.com; Web: www.cmsfglobal.com. Bros. Jaison Augustine, C.M.S.F., Supr.; Joseph Chacko, Sec.; Roji Ignatius Devakulam, C.M.S.F. Brothers 3.

[O] CONVENTS AND RESIDENCES FOR SISTERS

HOUSTON. *Carmelite Sisters of the Sacred Heart (C.S.H.)* (1904) 22 Farrell, 77022-2609. Tel: 713-697-6020; Fax: 713-697-6020; Email: Carmelitas200@hotmail.com. Sr. Antonia Albarran, Supr. Sisters 4.

Casa Providencia, 3907 Rotman, 77003. Tel: 713-227-2555; Fax: 713-923-5866.

Congregation of Divine Providence (1762) (France) Providence House, 709 W. 34th St., 77018. Cell: 713-679-8820; Email: rakcdp@gmail.com. Sisters Rosalie Karstedt, C.D.P., Pastoral Formation, St. Mary's Seminary; Megan Grewing, Mental Health Counselor. Sisters 2.

Congregation of Our Lady of the Retreat in the Cenacle (R.C.), Cenacle Retreat House, 420 N. Kirkwood, 77079. Tel: 281-497-3131; Fax: 281-497-7632; Email: ministry@cenacleretreathouse.org; Web: www.cenacleretreathouse.org. Sisters 7.

Congregation of the Incarnate Word & Blessed Sacrament (C.V.I.) (Houston) (1873) Incarnate Word Convent, 3400 Bradford Pl., 77025-1398. Tel: 713-668-0423; Fax: 713-668-1857; Email: lbeck@incarnateword.org; Web: www.incarnatewordsistershouston.org. Sr. Lauren Beck, C.V.I., Supr. Sisters 26. *Casa Pacis Convent*, 3428 Bradford Pl., 77025. Tel: 713-661-3785. Sisters 2. *Incarnate Word Convent*, 1217 Hogan St., 77009. Tel: 713-223-4143. Sisters 2. *Visitation Convent*, 3418A Bradford Pl., 77025-1328. Tel: 713-664-8370 . Sisters 2. *Hidden Park Apartment*, 4225 Magnum Rd. #44, 77092. Tel: 713-682-2242. Sisters 1.

Marian Convent, Marian Convent, 3719 Glen Haven, 77025-1204. Tel: 713-667-2238; Email: lbeck@incarnateword.org. 3400 Bradford Pl., 77025. Sr. Lauren Beck, C.V.I., Pres. Sisters 2.

Congregation of the Sisters of Charity of the Incarnate Word, Houston, Texas (CCVI) (1866) 6510 Lawndale St., 77023-3913. Tel: 713-928-6053; Fax: 713-928-8148; Email: keating@ccvi-vdm.org; Web: www.sistersofcharity.org. P.O. Box 230969, 77223-0969. Sr. Rose Scanlan, C.C.V.I., Congregational Gen. Sec. Total Sisters in Congregation (Professed) 137. *St. Anne Community*, Tel: 713-928-6053; Fax: 713-928-8148. Sisters 6. *Annunciation Community*, Tel: 713-928-6053; Fax: 713-928-9962. Sisters 5.

Bernice Place Community, Tel: 713-928-6053; Fax: 713-928-9962; Web: www.sistersofcharity.org. Sisters 1.

Casa de la Paz Community, 6641 Wildwood Way, 77023-4021. Tel: 713-921-4878; Fax: 713-926-1697 ; Email: rscanlan@ccvi-vdm.org; Web: www.sistersofcharity.org. Sr. Rose Scanlan, C.C.V.I., Congregational Gen. Secy. Sisters 3. *De Matel Community*, Tel: 713-928-6053; Fax: 713-928-8148 . Sisters 6.

Dubuis Community, Tel: 713-928-6053; Fax: 713-218-7339. Sisters 1. *Edith Stein Community*, 6405 Pinehurst, 77023-3329. Tel: 713-926-6024; Email: rscanlan@ccvi-vdm.org; Web: www.sistersofcharity.org. Sr. Rose Scanlan, C.C.V.I., Congregational Gen. Sec. Sisters 2.

St. Jeanne Community, Tel: 713-928-6053; Fax: 713-928-8148. Sisters 2.

St. John Community, 2566 Costa Mesa, League City, 77573-6338. Tel: 281-678-8496; Email: rscanlan@ccvi-vdm.org; Web: www.sistersofcharity.org. Sr. Rose Scanlan, C.C.V.I., Congregational Gen. Sec. Sisters 1.

Marian Community, Tel: 713-928-6053; Fax: 713-928-8148. Sisters 17.

Placidus Place Community, Tel: 713-928-6053; Fax: 713-928-8148. Sisters 9.

St. Placidus Community, Tel: 713-928-6053; Fax: 713-928-8148. Sisters 15.

Shalom Community, Tel: 713-341-2723. Sisters 1.

Discipulas de Jesus, 9601 McGallion Rd., 77076. Tel: 713-691-3960; Email: discipulasdj_tx@outlook.com; Web: www.discipulasdejesus.org. Sr. Maria Rosalinda Navarro, D.J., Local Supr. Sisters 2.

Dominican Sisters of Houston (1882) Motherhouse Complex & Admin. Offices, 6501 Almeda Rd., 77021-2095. Tel: 713-747-3310; Fax: 713-747-4707; Email: bperez@domhou.org; Web: www.domhou.org. Sr. Donna M. Pollard, O.P., B.S., M.A., M.Ed., Prioress. The Sacred Heart Convent Retirement Trust.; St. Agnes Academy, Inc.; St. Agnes Academy Foundation, Inc.; St. Pius X High School, Inc.; St. Pius X High School Foundation, Inc.; The Sacred Heart Convent Retirement Trust.

Dominican Sisters of Houston, Texas Inc. (O.P.).

Dominican Sisters of Mary Immaculate Province (1978) Provincial House, 5250 Gasmer Dr., 77035. Tel: 713-723-8250; Fax: 713-723-8229; Email: maryimmaculate@dsmip.org; Web: www.houstondominicans.org. Sr. Angela Pham, Prov. Professed in Province 93. *Dominican Sisters of Mary Immaculate Province (St. Catherine Convent)*, Provincial House, 5250 Gasmer Dr., 77035. Tel: 713-723-8250; Fax: 713-723-8229; Email: srhuong@hotmail.com. Sr. Angela Pham, Prioress. Sisters 36. *Mary Immaculate Convent*, 5900 Chippewa Blvd., 77086. Tel: 281-445-9574; Tel: 281-591-6081; Fax: 281-445-6716. Sisters 14. *Our Lady of the Holy Rosary Convent (Novitiate)*, 1602 Adams St., Missouri City, 77489. Tel: 281-403-9300; Fax: 281-403-9300. Sisters 13.

Sacred Heart Convent, 911 Runneburg, Crosby, 77532. Tel: 281-328-4073; Email: shc.chithu@gmail.com. Sisters 4.

Marian Convent, 3719 Glenhaven Blvd., 77025-1204. Tel: 713-667-2238; Email: lbeck@incarnateword.org. 3400 Bradford Pl., 77025. Sisters Lauren Beck, C.V.I., Pres., Incarnate Word Academy; Carmel O'Malley, C.V.I. Sisters 30.

Missionary Carmelites of St. Teresa (C.M.S.T.) (1903) Holy Family Provincial House, 9548 Deer Trail Dr., 77038. Tel: 281-445-5520; Fax: 281-445-5748; Email: hfamprovcmst@yahoo.com. Sisters 4.

Divine Providence Convent, 9600 Deer Trail Dr., 77038. Tel: 281-847-3328. Sisters 5.

Infant Jesus of Prague Convent, 9600 Deer Trail Dr., 77038. Tel: 281-445-8830. Sisters 10.

St. Joseph Convent, 9815 Marek Rd., 77038. Tel: 281-445-0056. Sisters 10.

Novitiate of St. Theresa of Lisieux, 9608 Deer Trail Dr., 77038. Tel: 281-999-4435. Novices 2; Sisters 3.

Missionary Catechists of Divine Providence (M.C.D.P.), 704 Old Montgomery Rd., Conroe, 77301. Tel: 936-756-8186; Fax: 936-756-8105. *Sacred Heart Convent*, 105 N. Frazier St., Conroe, 77301. Tel: 713-659-5461 Chancery.

Missionary Sisters of the Eucharist, 3301 San Jacinto St., P.O.Box 88147, 77288-0147. Tel: 713-523-8831; Email: mseucharist@yahoo.com. Sr. Gabina Colo, M.S.E., Contact Person. Sisters 5.

Religious of the Sacred Heart (R.S.C.J.) (1960) Duchesne Community, 10204 Memorial Dr., 77024. Tel: 713-467-5312; Fax: 713-465-9809; Email: acaire@rscj.org; Web: www.rscj.org. Sr. Ann Caire, Contact Person. Sisters 2. 2424 ETC Jester Blvd., Apt. 6102, 77008. Tel: 281-381-0467. Sisters 1.

Sisters of the Incarnate Word and Blessed Sacrament (C.V.I.), Marian Convent, 3719 Glen Haven, 77025-1204. Tel: 713-667-2738.

MANVEL. **Sisters of St. Michael the Archangel (S.S.M.A.)*, 35 San Simeon Dr., Manvel, 77578. Tel: 281-692-1460; Cell: 832-259-3844; Email: ssmahouston@aol.com; Email: kejifash@yahoo.com; Web: www.sistersofstmichaelthearchangel.org. Sisters Morenikeji Francisca Faseemo, S.S.M.A., Mission Supr.; Adenike Oke, Rel. Order Leader. Sisters 5.

NEW CANEY. *Discalced Carmelite Nuns of New Caney, Texas* (1958) 1100 Parthenon Pl., New Caney, 77357-3276. Tel: 281-399-0270, Ext. 4; Fax: 832-543-5338; Email: carmelnewcaney.office@gmail.com; Email: carmelnewcaney@gmail.com; Web: www.newcaneycarmel.com. Sr. Angel Sweeney, Prioress. Sisters 8.

PEARLAND. *Handmaids of the Holy Child Jesus* (1931) 3614 Englewood Dr., Pearland, 77584. Tel: 281-692-0098; Fax: 281-692-0049; Email: usa@hhcj.org; Web: www.hhcj.org. Sisters Germaine Ocansey, Mission Supr., 3614 Englewood Dr., Pearland, 77584; Leonie-Martha O'Karaga, H.H.C.J., Supr. Gen., Generalate H.H.C.J., P.O. Box 155, Ifuho-Ikot Ekpene, Akwa Ibom Nigeria. Sisters 894.

Mission Development Office, Office: P.O. Box 740099, 77274. Tel: 281-914-4664; Email: missiondev@hhcjsisters.org; Web: www.hhcjsisters.org. Sr. Felicia Agibi, H.H.C.J., Dir. Devel., 7915 El Pico Dr., 77083. Tel: 281-914-4664.

STAFFORD. *Missionary Sisters of Mary Immaculate*, 630 Easy Jet Dr., Stafford, 77477-6358. Tel: 281-499-0030; Email: msmisisters@hotmail.com. Sisters Reena Thonippara, Supr.; Emiline Tharappel, Tel: 281-499-0030. Sisters 3.

[P] RETREAT HOUSES

HOUSTON. *Cenacle Retreat House*, 420 N. Kirkwood Rd., 77079. Tel: 281-497-3131; Fax: 281-497-7632; Email: ministry@cenacleretreathouse.org; Web: www.cenacleretreathouse.org. Sr. Pamela Falkowski, Supr.; Jennifer Walthall, Admin.; Julia Smelley, Devel. Coord.; Sisters Ann Goggin, R.C., Dir., Spiritual Direction Institute; Mary Peters, R.C., Dir., Ministry; Lois Dideon, R.C.; Mary Dennison, R.C.; Roselle Haas, R.C.; Barbara Regan. Sisters 7.

Holy Name Retreat Center, 430 Bunker Hill Rd., 77024-6399. Tel: 713-464-0211; Fax: 713-464-0671; Email: holyname@passionist.org; Web: passionist.org/holyname. Rev. Joseph Barbieri, C.P., Dir.; Deacon James Anderson, Admin.; Revs. Ronan Newbold, C.P., Assoc. Dir.; Antonio Curto, C.P., Assoc. Dir. Total in Residence 8; Total Staff 12.

DICKINSON. *Christian Renewal Center* aka CRC Retreat Partners, Inc, 1515 Hughes Rd., P.O. Box 699, Dickinson, 77539-0699. Tel: 281-337-1312 (Center); Fax: 281-337-2615; Email: kbrown@retreatcentercrc.org; Web: www.retreatcentercrc.org. Ms. Kim Brown, Dir. Total Staff 14.

[Q] NEWMAN CENTERS

GALVESTON. *Galveston Newman Center*, 602 Seawolf Pkwy., Ste. B (Pelican Island #5), Galveston, 77550. Tel: 409-740-3797; Fax: 409-740-3798; Email: gal.newmancenterum@gmail.com. Carl Erickson, Dir. Texas A&M University at Galveston; University of Texas Medical Branch; Galveston College; College of the Mainland.

HOUSTON. *Catholic Newman Association at the University of Houston Central Campus* (1968) 4805 Calhoun Rd., 77004. Tel: 713-748-2529; Fax: 713-748-8412; Email: catholic@uh.edu; Web: www.uhcatholic.org. Rev. Galen Bank, Dir.; Pita Escoto, Admin.; Claire McMullin, Campus Min. Priests 1; Total Staff 3; Total Assisted 10,000.

Catholic Student Center and St. Mary Chapel, 1703 Bolsover Rd., 77005. Tel: 713-526-3809; Fax: 713-526-6010; Email: rcook@rice.edu; Web: catholics.rice.edu. Rev. Raymond Cook, O.M.I., Dir., Campus Min. & Chap.; Rita M. Seng, Sec. & Ministry Asst. Total Staff 2.

Texas Southern University Catholic Newman Center, 3535 Wheeler Ave., 77004. Tel: 713-747-7595; Fax: 713-747-9595; Email: tsunewman@gmail.com. Deacon John Lane, Dir. Total Staff 1; Total Assisted 150.

University of St. Thomas Campus Ministry, 3800 Montrose Blvd., P.O. Box 27, 77006. Tel: 713-525-3589; Fax: 713-525-6943; Email: campusministry@stthom.edu; Web: www.stthom.edu. Revs. Christopher Valka, Dir.; David Bittner, Chap.; Nicole Driscoll, Campus Min.

HUNTSVILLE. *Catholic Student Center, S.H.S.U.*, 1310 17th St., Huntsville, 77340-4415. Tel: 936-291-2620; Email: info.shsucatholic@gmail.com; Web: www.shsu-catholic.org. Joseph Magee, Ph.D., Dir. Total Staff 3; Total Assisted 350.

PRAIRIE VIEW. *Prairie View A&M University Catholic Center*, 2403 Holcombe Blvd., 77021. Fax: 713-741-8780. Rev. Eliseus Ibeh, M.S.P., Dir.; Fabian Yanez, Campus Min. Total Staff 2.

[R] MISCELLANEOUS

HOUSTON. *Angela House*, 6725 Reed Rd., 77087. Tel: 281-445-9696; Fax: 281-501-2723; Email: mhittinger@angelahouse.org; Web: www.angelahouse.org. Sr. Maureen O'Connell, O.P., Trustee.

The Catholic Chaplain Corps (1967) 4206 S. MacGregor Way, 77021. Tel: 713-747-8445; Fax: 713-747-3642; Email: avacek@archgh.org. Revs. Dominic J. Pistone, V.F.; Teodoro Tim Y. Prado; Enrique V. Salen, Cell: 713-922-0700; Michael S. Van Cleve; Arnel B. Barrameda; Ronnie De La Cruz, D.S.; Ian Chris Balisnomo, F.L.P.; Michael A. Barrosa, D.S.; Rodolfo L. Cal-Ortiz Jr. Houston Hospitals: Baylor St. Luke's Medical Center, Texas Children's Hospital, Methodist, M. D. Anderson Cancer Center, The Institute of Rehabilitation and Research, Ben Taub General Hospital, Kindred Hospital, LBJ General Hospital, Memorial Hermann Medical Center, Memorial Hermann Southwest, Memorial Hermann Memorial City.

Catholic Charismatic Center (1972) 1949 Cullen Blvd., P.O. Box 230287, 77023-0287.
Tel: 713-236-9977; Fax: 713-236-0073; Email: cccDirector@cccgh.com; Web: www.cccgh.com. Revs. Mark J. Goring, Dir.; Francis A. Frankovich, C.C., Assoc. Dir.; David Bergeron, C.C., Assoc. Dir.; Jorge Alvarado, C.C.

Catholic Clerical Student Fund (1933) 4853 Hummingbird, 77035. Tel: 713-723-0118;
Fax: 713-433-8282. Marie A. Novak, Pres. Higher learning for the priesthood.

The Catholic Endowment Foundation of Galveston-Houston, 5701 Woodway, Ste. 320, 77057. Cell: 713-857-3964; Web: archgh.org. Boone Schwartzel, Sec.

Charity Guild of Catholic Women (1922) 1203 Lovett Blvd., 77006-3857. Tel: 713-529-0995;
Fax: 713-529-9263; Email: president@charityguildshop.org; Web: www.charityguildshop.org. Mrs. Susan Stromatt, Pres.

Charity Guild of St. Joseph (1988) 2132 Branard, 77098. Tel: 713-526-4239. Geralena Barone, Pres.

The Claude Marie Dubuis Religious and Charitable Trust, 6510 Lawndale St., 77023-3913.
Tel: 713-928-6053; Fax: 713-928-8148. Sr. Joyce Susan Njeri Mbataru, Trustee.

St. Dominic Center, Inc., 2403 Holcombe, 77021.
Tel: 713-741-8743; Fax: 713-741-8705; Email: wknight@archgh.org. Wayne Knight, Archdiocesan Facility Mgr.

Equestrian Order of the Holy Sepulchre of Jerusalem, Southwestern USA Lieutenancy, 2001 Kirby Dr., Ste. 902, 77019-1402. Tel: 713-524-5444;
Fax: 713-524-5333; Email: Lieutenant@EOHSsouthwest.com; Web: eohssouthwest.com. Thomas R. Standish, KGCHS, Lieutenant.

Incarnate Word Religious and Charitable Trust, 6510 Lawndale St., 77023-3913. Tel: 713-928-6053; Fax: 713-926-3085; Email: rscanlan@ccvi-vdi.org.

Martha's Kitchen Food Services (1992) 322 S. Jensen Dr., 77003. Tel: 713-224-2522; Fax: 713-224-7814;
Tel: 281-358-6637; Email: marthakitchen@stmartha.com. Rev. Msgr. Chester L. Borski. Sisters 2.

The St. Mary's Children's Relief Fund, Inc., NonProfit Corporation, 1700 San Jacinto, P.O. Box 907, 77001-0907. Tel: 713-659-5461;
Fax: 713-759-9151; Web: archgh.org. His Eminence Daniel Cardinal DiNardo, D.D., S.T.L., Pres. & Treas.

St. Pius X High School Foundation, Inc., 811 W. Donovan, 77091-5699. Tel: 713-692-3581;
Fax: 713-692-5725; Email: armisteadc@stpiusx.org; Web: www.stpiusx.org. James Black, Pres.; Ms. Carmen G. Armistead, B.S., M.Ed., Head of School; Sr. Lavergne Schwender, O.P., Sec.

The Society of the Holy Spirit, 1700 W. Alabama, 77098-2808. Tel: 713-522-2882; Cell: 412-292-0807;
Email: somacssptx@gmail.com. John Boyles, Pres.; Rev. David Cottingham, C.S.Sp., Board Member; Very Rev. Michael T. Grey, C.S.Sp., Board Member; Cynthia Sapio, Sec.

The St. Thomas More Parish School Endowment Foundation, 10330 Hillcroft St., 77096.
Tel: 713-729-0221; Fax: 713-729-3294; Web: www.stmhouston.org. Rev. Hai Duc Dang, Admin.

UST Chapelle, 3034 Quenby Ave., 77005.
Tel: 713-349-0921; Fax: 832-201-7556; Web: ustchapelle.org. Alain Maury, Contact Person.

RELIGIOUS INSTITUTES OF MEN REPRESENTED IN THE ARCHDIOCESE

For further details refer to the corresponding bracketed number in the Religious Institutes of Men or Women section.

[0170]—*Basilian Fathers* (Toronto, Canada)—C.S.B.
[0275]—*Carmelites of Mary Immaculate*—C.M.I.
[]—*Companions of the Cross* (Ottawa, Canada)—C.C.
[0220]—*Congregation of the Blessed Sacrament*—S.S.S.
[]—*Congregation of the Holy Spirit (Spiritans)*—C.S.Sp.
[]—*Congregation of the Mother Coredemptrix*—C.M.C.
[1130]—*Congregation of the Priests of the Sacred Heart*—S.C.J.
[]—*Disciples of Hope* (Careres, Philippines)—D.S.
[]—*Disciples of Jesus* (San Juan Diego, Pasadena)—D.J.
[0420]—*Divine Word Fathers*—S.V.D.
[0520]—*Franciscan Friars*—O.F.M.
[]—*Franciscan Missionary Brothers*—C.M.S.F.
[]—*Heralds of the Gospel*—E.P.
[0650]—*Holy Ghost Fathers* (Western Prov.)—C.S.Sp.
[]—*Incarnation Consecration Mission*—I.C.M.
[0690]—*Jesuit Fathers and Brothers* (New Orleans Prov.)—S.J.
[]—*Legionaries of Christ*—L.C.
[0800]—*Maryknoll*—M.M.
[0720]—*The Missionaries of Our Lady of La Salette* (Prov. of Mary Queen)—M.S.
[0920]—*Missionaries of St. Francis de Sales*—M.S.F.S.
[]—*Missionaries of St. Joseph* (Mexico)—M.J.
[]—*Missionaries of St. Paul*—M.S.P.
[0910]—*Oblates of Mary Immaculate*—O.M.I.
[1110]—*Oblates of the Sacred Heart*—O.S.H.
[0430]—*Order of Preachers-Dominicans* (Prov. of St. Albert the Great)—O.P.
[]—*Passionist Fathers*—C.P.
[1070]—*Redemptorist Fathers* (New Orleans Vice Prov.)—C.SS.R.
[]—*Scalabrinians*—C.S.
[1260]—*Society of Christ*—S.Ch.
[0975]—*Society of Our Lady of the Most Holy Trinity*—S.O.L.T.
[]—*Society of St. Joseph (Josephites)*—S.S.J.
[1250]—*Somascan Fathers*—C.R.S.

RELIGIOUS INSTITUTES OF WOMEN REPRESENTED IN THE ARCHDIOCESE

[0230]—*Benedictine Sisters of the Sacred Heart*—O.S.B.
[]—*Brothers and Sisters of Charity*—B.S.C.
[0390]—*Carmelite Missionaries of St. Teresa*—C.M.S.T.
[]—*Carmelite Sisters of the Sacred Heart*—C.S.C.
[]—*Comunidad Apostolica de Maria Siempre Virgen*—C.A.M.S.V.
[1010]—*Congregation of Divine Providence*—C.D.P.
[3110]—*Congregation of Our Lady of the Retreat in the Cenacle*—R.C.
[1070-07]—*Congregation of St. Cecilia* (Nashville, TN)—O.P.
[3830-01]—*Congregation of St. Joseph* (Boston, MA)—C.S.J.
[]—*Congregation of the Lovers of the Cross* (N. Vietnam)—H.C.L.
[0470]—*Congregation of the Sisters of Charity of the Incarnate Word, Houston, Texas*—CCVI.
[]—*Daughters of Divine Love* (Nigeria)—D.D.L.
[]—*Daughters of Mary Mother of Mercy*—D.M.M.M.
[0420]—*Discalced Carmelite Nuns of New Caney, Texas*—O.C.D.
[]—*Discipulas de Jesus*—D.J.
[1070-13]—*Dominican Sisters* (Adrian, MI)—O.P.
[1070-19]—*Dominican Sisters, Congregation of the Sacred Heart* (Houston)—O.P.
[]—*Dominican Sisters of Mary, Mother of the Eucharist*—O.P.
[]—*Eucharistic Missionaries of St. Theresa* (Mexico)—M.E.S.T.
[]—*Family of the Visitation of Mary*—F.M.V.
[]—*Handmaids of the Holy Child Jesus* (Nigeria)—H.H.C.J.
[]—*La Salle Sisters*—L.S.S.
[]—*Lay Consecrated Virgins Order of Virgins.*
[]—*Missionaries of Charity*—M.C.
[2690]—*Missionary Catechists of Divine Providence*—M.C.D.P.
[]—*Missionary Sisters of Mary Immaculate*—M.S.M.I.
[2725]—*Missionary Sisters of the Eucharist*—M.S.E.
[]—*Missionary Sisters of the Sacred Heart of Jesus*—M.S.C.
[]—*Regnum Christi*—R.C.
[4070]—*Religious of the Sacred Heart*—R.S.C.J.
[]—*School Sisters of Notre Dame*—S.S.N.D.
[]—*Sisters for Christian Community*—S.F.C.C.
[2245]—*Sisters of Jesus the Saviour*—S.J.S.
[]—*Sisters of Loretto*—S.L.
[1730]—*Sisters of St. Francis of Oldenburg, Indiana*—O.S.F.
[]—*Sisters of St. Michael the Archangel*—S.S.M.A.
[2190]—*Sisters of the Incarnate Word and Blessed Sacrament* (Houston)—C.V.I.
[3670]—*Sisters of the Sacred Heart of Jesus*—S.S.C.J.
[]—*Vietnamese Dominican Sisters*—O.P.

ARCHDIOCESAN CEMETERIES

GALVESTON. *Old Catholic, Calvary*
HOUSTON. *Holy Cross*
St. Vincent
DICKINSON. *Mount Olivet*

NECROLOGY

† Cejudo, Serafin, (Retired), Died Jan. 1, 2019
† Kellick, John W., (Retired), Died Sep. 12, 2018
† Solarski, John, (Retired), Opus Dei, Died Sep. 4, 2018
† Stredny, Anthony, (Retired), Died Nov. 26, 2018

An asterisk (*) denotes an organization that has established tax-exempt status directly with the IRS and is not covered by the USCCB Group Ruling.

Diocese of Gary

(Dioecesis Gariensis)

Most Reverend

DALE J. MELCZEK, D.D.

Retired Bishop of Gary; ordained June 6, 1964; appointed Auxiliary Bishop of Detroit and Titular Bishop of Trau December 3, 1982; consecrated January 27, 1983; appointed Apostolic Administrator of Gary August 19, 1992; appointed Coadjutor Bishop of Gary October 20, 1995; succeeded to the See of Gary June 1, 1996; retired November 24, 2014. *Office: 9292 Broadway, Merrillville, IN 46410.* Tel: 219-769-9292; Fax: 219-769-2066.

(VACANT SEE)

Chancery: 9292 Broadway, Merrillville, IN 46410. Tel: 219-769-9292; Fax: 219-738-9034.

Web: www.dcgary.org

ESTABLISHED DECEMBER 17, 1956.

Square Miles 1,807.

Comprises the Counties of Lake, LaPorte, Porter and Starke in the State of Indiana.

For legal titles of parishes and diocesan institutions, consult the Chancery.

STATISTICAL OVERVIEW

Personnel	
Retired Bishops	1
Priests: Diocesan Active in Diocese	53
Priests: Diocesan Active Outside Diocese	5
Priests: Retired, Sick or Absent	31
Number of Diocesan Priests	89
Religious Priests in Diocese	47
Total Priests in Diocese	136
Extern Priests in Diocese	5
Ordinations:	
Diocesan Priests	1
Transitional Deacons	1
Permanent Deacons in Diocese	68
Total Brothers	21
Total Sisters	53
Parishes	
Parishes	64
With Resident Pastor:	
Resident Diocesan Priests	43
Resident Religious Priests	4
Without Resident Pastor:	
Administered by Priests	17
Missions	2
Pastoral Centers	6
Closed Parishes	1
Professional Ministry Personnel:	
Brothers	1
Lay Ministers	14
Welfare	
Catholic Hospitals	7
Total Assisted	1,641,919
Homes for the Aged	2
Total Assisted	222
Residential Care of Children	2
Total Assisted	150
Day Care Centers	2
Total Assisted	495
Specialized Homes	2
Total Assisted	1,550
Special Centers for Social Services	7
Total Assisted	10,153
Residential Care of Disabled	1
Total Assisted	100
Educational	
Diocesan Students in Other Seminaries	13
Total Seminarians	13
Colleges and Universities	1
Total Students	551
High Schools, Diocesan and Parish	3
Total Students	1,140
High Schools, Private	1
Total Students	27
Elementary Schools, Diocesan and Parish	14
Total Students	4,533
Catechesis/Religious Education:	
High School Students	700
Elementary Students	6,065
Total Students under Catholic Instruction	13,029
Teachers in the Diocese:	
Priests	19
Brothers	1
Sisters	3
Lay Teachers	375
Vital Statistics	
Receptions into the Church:	
Infant Baptism Totals	1,134
Minor Baptism Totals	60
Adult Baptism Totals	73
Received into Full Communion	101
First Communions	1,548
Confirmations	1,497
Marriages:	
Catholic	325
Interfaith	53
Total Marriages	378
Deaths	1,374
Total Catholic Population	168,500
Total Population	786,966

Former Bishops—Most Revs. ANDREW GREGORY GRUTKA, D.D., ord. Dec. 5, 1933; appt. Bishop of Gary Dec. 29, 1956; cons. Feb. 25, 1957; retired July 9, 1984; died Nov. 11, 1993; NORBERT F. GAUGHAN, D.D., Ph.D., ord. Nov. 4, 1945; appt. Auxiliary Bishop of Greensburg April 2, 1975; cons. June 26, 1975; appt. Bishop of Gary July 9, 1984; retired June 1, 1996; died Oct. 1, 1999; DALE J. MELCZEK, ord. June 6, 1964; appt. Auxiliary Bishop of Detroit and Titular Bishop of Trau Dec. 3, 1982; cons. Jan. 27, 1983; appt. Apostolic Administrator of Gary Aug. 19, 1992; appt. Coadjutor Bishop of Gary Oct. 20, 1995; succeeded to the See of Gary June 1, 1996; retired Nov. 24, 2014.; DONALD J. HYING, ord. May 20, 1989; appt. Auxiliary Bishop of Milwaukee and Titular Bishop of Regiae May 26, 2011; installed July 20, 2011; appt. Bishop of Gary Nov. 24, 2014; installed Jan. 6, 2015; appt. Bishop of Madison April 25, 2019.

Vicar General—Rev. BRIAN D. CHADWICK, J.C.L.

Deans—Revs. CHARLES A. MOSLEY, Gary/North Lake Deanery; MICHAEL J. YADRON, South Lake Deanery; DOUGLAS J. MAYER, Porter Deanery; IAN J. WILLIAMS, LaPorte/Starke Deanery.

Chancery—9292 Broadway, Merrillville, 46410. Tel: 219-769-9292; Fax: 219-738-9034.

Executive Assistant to the Bishop—VALERIE D. MCMANUS, Tel: 219-769-9181; Fax: 219-769-2066.

Chief of Staff—MR. MICHAEL WICK.

Director of Strategic Planning and Pastoral Ministry—Deacon DANIEL L. LOWERY, Ph.D.

Bishop's Delegate for Sexual Misconduct Matters—KELLY VENEGAS, SPHR.

Chief Financial Officer—MS. KATHY TOMASIK.

Diocesan Tribunal—9292 Broadway, Merrillville, 46410. Tel: 219-769-9292.

Judicial Vicar—Rev. JAMES W. MEADE, J.D., S.T.L., J.C.L.

Director of the Tribunal—Rev. JAMES W. MEADE, J.D., S.T.L., J.C.L.

Judge—Rev. JAMES W. MEADE, J.D., S.T.L., J.C.L.

Promoter of Justice—Rev. Msgr. JOHN J. SIEKIERSKI, J.C.L.

Defender of the Bond—Rev. BRIAN D. CHADWICK, J.C.L.

Auditor—TERI KOPIL.

Notaries—VALERIE MCMANUS; MILDRED VIRUS.

Bishop's Council of Priests—Revs. JON J. PLAVCAN; RICHARD C. HOLY; MICHAEL J. YADRON; IAN J. WILLIAMS; ROBERT P. GEHRING, (Retired); DOUGLAS J. MAYER; BRIAN D. CHADWICK, J.C.L.; EDUARDO MALAGON; KEITH J. MCCLELLAN; THOMAS E. MISCHLER; CHARLES A. MOSLEY; Rev. Msgr. JOHN J. SIEKIERSKI, J.C.L.; Revs. JAMES E. WOZNIAK; EDWARD J. MOSZUR; JAMES W. MEADE, J.D., S.T.L., J.C.L.; TED J. MAUCH; PATRICK GAZA; PETER J. MUHA.

Consultors—Revs. DOUGLAS J. MAYER; BRIAN D. CHADWICK, J.C.L.; MICHAEL J. YADRON; IAN J. WILLIAMS; JON J. PLAVCAN; CHARLES A. MOSLEY.

Priests' Personnel Board—Revs. IAN J. WILLIAMS; BRIAN D. CHADWICK, J.C.L.; JON J. PLAVCAN; RICHARD C. HOLY; MICHAEL J. YADRON; DAVID W. KIME; MARTIN J. DOBRZYNSKI; DOUGLAS J. MAYER; KEITH J. MCCLELLAN; JAMES E. WOZNIAK.

Diocesan Offices and Directors

Boy Scouts Liaison—Rev. BENJAMIN J. ROSS, Chap., 107 Main St., P.O. Box 408, Hobart, 46342; SUSAN KRESICH, Chm., 3117 Maple Dr., Highland, 46322.

Campus Ministry—St. Teresa of Avila Catholic Student Center (Valparaiso University) Rev. CHRISTOPHER M. STANISH, Chap., 1511 LaPorte St., Valparaiso, 46383. Tel: 219-464-4042; Fax: 219-462-2711.

Catholic Relief Services—Operation Rice Bowl, annual Lenten collection, and disaster relief collections. *Catholic Charities, 940 Broadway, Gary, 46402.* Tel: 219-886-3549; Fax: 219-886-2428.

Catholic Foundation for Northwest Indiana—LIZ METTS, Dir., 9292 Broadway, Merrillville, 46410. Tel: 219-769-9292; Fax: 219-738-9034.

Catholic Services Appeal—9292 Broadway, Merrillville, 46410. Tel: 219-769-9292; Fax: 219-738-9034. LIZ METTS.

Catholic Youth Organization (CYO) Office—PAUL WENGEL, 7725 Broadway, Ste. C, Merrillville, 46410. Tel: 219-736-8931; Fax: 219-736-9457.

Cemeteries—Rev. ROY T. BEECHING, Dir., (Retired); MICHAEL P. WELSH, 1547 167th St., Hammond, 46324. Tel: 219-844-9475.

Catholic Charities—940 Broadway, Gary, 46402. Tel: 219-886-3549; Fax: 219-886-2428. Rev. MARK PRANAITIS, C.M., Exec. Dir.

Communications Office—DEBBIE BOSAK, Dir., 9292 Broadway, Merrillville, 46410. Tel: 219-769-9292, Ext. 286; Fax: 219-738-9034.

Council of Catholic Women—Rev. ROY T. BEECHING, Diocesan Moderator, (Retired), Mailing Address: P.O. Box 703, Crown Point, 46307.

Cursillos in Christianity—Revs. EDUARDO MALAGON, Chap. (Spanish), 4340 Johnson Ave., Hammond, 46327. Tel: 219-931-2589; THOMAS E. MISCHLER,

(English), 7667 E. 109th St., Crown Point, 46307. Tel: 219-661-0644.

Diaconate—Deacons BRIAN NOSBUSCH, Dir. Diaconate Formation, 2651 High Sierra Dr., Valparaiso, 46385. Tel: 219-465-6912; THOMAS GRYZBEK, Diaconate Dir. - Post Ordination, 1335 Capri Lane, Dyer, 46311. Tel: 219-865-2440.

Ecumenical Officer—JOAN CRIST, 7 Detroit St., Hammond, 46320. Tel: 219-932-2706.

Employee Benefits—CHERYL GRANDYS, Coord., 9292 Broadway, Merrillville, 46410. Tel: 219-769-9292; Fax: 219-738-9034.

Finance Council—Rev. BRIAN D. CHADWICK, J.C.L.; CALVIN E. BELLAMY; MR. MICHAEL WICK; MITCH GAFFIGAN; KATHY TOMASIK; JOHN J. DIEDERICH; DONNA SMITH; ANA GRANDFIELD; LOUIS GONZALEZ; SANDI SNEARLY VOSBERG.

Girl Scout Liaison—Rev. THEODORE A. NORDQUIST; JACKIE KRILICH, Chm., 10621 State Line Rd., Dyer, 46311. Tel: 219-365-5217.

Human Resources—KELLY VENEGAS, SPHR, Mgr., 9292 Broadway, Merrillville, 46410. Tel: 219-769-9292; Fax: 219-769-7597.

Indiana Catholic Conference—GREGORY SOBKOWSKI, 9292 Broadway, Merrillville, 46410. Tel: 219-769-9292; Fax: 219-769-7034.

Intercultural Ministry—ADELINE TORRES, 3814 Grand Blvd., East Chicago, 46312. Tel: 219-397-2125.

Lay Ministry Formation Office—9292 Broadway, Merrillville, 46410. Tel: 219-769-9292; Fax: 219-738-9034. Deacon DANIEL L. LOWERY, Ph. D., Dir.

Legal Counsel—ROBERT M. SCHWERD, 825 E. Lincolnway, Valparaiso, 46385. Tel: 219-841-5683; Fax: 219-841-5684.

Marriage Dispensations—Rev. BRIAN D. CHADWICK, J.C.L., 9292 Broadway, Merrillville, 46410. Tel: 219-769-9292, Ext. 222; Fax: 219-738-9034.

Marriage and Family Ministries—SEAN MARTIN, Dir., 9292 Broadway, Merrillville, 46410. Tel: 219-769-9292; Fax: 219-738-9034.

Marriage Encounter—JIM MCCULLOCH; KRIS MCCULLOCH, Tel: 800-442-3553.

Mission OfficeRev. JOHN J. ZEMELKO, Dir., 9601 Union Rd., P.O. Box 1, Donaldson, 46513. Tel: 574-935-1780.

Newspaper—Northwest Indiana Catholic *9292 Broadway, Merrillville, 46410.* Tel: 219-769-9292; Fax: 219-738-9034. DEBBIE BOSAK, Editor.

Persons with Disabilities—ADELINE TORRES, 3814 Grand Blvd., East Chicago, 46312. Tel: 219-397-2125; Fax: 219-738-9034.

Priestly Life Coordinator—Rev. RICHARD C. HOLY, 9292 Broadway, Merrillville, 46410. Tel: 219-769-9292; Fax: 219-738-9034.

Pro-Life Activities—Rev. THEODORE J. MENS, Dir., 525 N. Broad St., Griffith, 46319. Tel: 219-924-4163.

Religious Education and Evangelization Office—SEAN MARTIN, 9292 Broadway, Merrillville, 46410. Tel: 219-769-9292; Fax: 219-738-9034.

Religious, Liaison for Women—VACANT.

Retirement Plan of the Diocese of Gary, Indiana—KELLY VENEGAS, SPHR, Plan Admin., 9292 Broadway, Merrillville, 46410. Tel: 219-769-9292; Fax: 219-769-7597.

Safe Environment Program—KELLY VENEGAS, SPHR, Bishop's Delegate for Sexual Misconduct Cases, 9292 Broadway, Merrillville, 46410. Tel: 219-769-9292; Fax: 219-769-7597.

Victim Assistance Coordinator—STEVEN J. BUTERA, M.S., 9008 Cline Ave., Highland, 46322. Tel: 219-838-8001; Fax: 219-838-8020.

St. Vincent de Paul Society—DIANE MCKERN, Pres., 7132 Arizona Ave., Hammond, 46324. Tel: 219-845-7531.

Schools Office—JOSEPH MAJCHROWICZ, Ph.D., Dir. Catholic Schools, 9292 Broadway, Merrillville, 46410. Tel: 219-769-9292; Fax: 219-738-9034.

Stewardship and Development Office—9292 Broadway, Merrillville, 46410. Tel: 219-769-9292; Fax: 219-738-9034. LIZ METTS, Dir.

Vicar for Clergy—Rev. JON J. PLAVCAN, 638 N. Calumet Rd., Chesterton, 46304. Tel: 219-926-1282.

Vocations—Revs. DAVID W. KIME, Dir. Vocations; KEVIN R. HUBER, D.Min., Diocesan Liaison for Seminarians; CHRISTOPHER M. STANISH, Asst. Dir. Vocations, 9292 Broadway, Merrillville, 46410. Tel: 219-769-9292; Fax: 219-738-9034.

Worship and Spirituality, Office of—9292 Broadway, Merrillville, 46410. Tel: 219-769-9292; Fax: 219-738-9034. Rev. MARTIN J. DOBRZYNSKI, Dir.

Youth and Young Adult Ministry—KEVIN DRISCOLL, Dir., 9292 Broadway, Merrillville, 46410. Tel: 219-769-9292; Fax: 219-738-9034.

CLERGY, PARISHES, MISSIONS AND PAROCHIAL SCHOOLS

CITY OF GARY

(LAKE COUNTY)

1—CATHEDRAL OF THE HOLY ANGELS (1906)
640 Tyler St., Gary, 46402-2299. Tel: 219-882-6079; Email: cathedralholyangels@yahoo.com. Most Rev. Donald J. Hying; Deacon Jose A. Serrano.
Catechesis Religious Program—Students 6.

2—ST. ANN (1942)
Mailing Address: 525 N. Broad St., Griffith, 46319. 6025 W. 25th Ave., Gary, 46406. Rev. Theodore J. Mens, Admin.
Catechesis Religious Program—Paula Hammersley, D.R.E. Students 34.

3—ST. ANTHONY (1918) Closed. For inquiries for parish records contact Cathedral of Holy Angels, Gary.

4—BLESSED SACRAMENT (1947) Closed. For inquiries for parish records, contact Ss. Peter and Paul, Merrillville.

5—ST. CASIMIR (1916) (Lithuanian), Closed. For inquiries for parish records contact Holy Angels Cathedral.

6—ST. EMERIC (1911) Closed. For inquiries for parish records contact Holy Trinity (Hungarian), East Chicago.

7—ST. HEDWIG MISSION (1908) [JC] (Polish), Closed. For inquiries for parish records contact Gary Pastoral Center, Merrillville.

8—HOLY FAMILY (1926) (Polish), Closed. For inquiries for parish records, contact St. Bridget, Hobart.

9—HOLY ROSARY (1931) Closed. For inquiries for parish records contact Cathedrals of the Holy Angels, Gary.

10—HOLY TRINITY (1911) (African American), Closed. For inquiries for parish records contact Cathedral of Holy Angels, Gary.

11—ST. JOSEPH THE WORKER (1912) (Croatian)
330 E. 45th Ave., Gary, 46409. Tel: 219-980-1846; Email: stjosephgary@gmail.com. Revs. Kevin P. McCarthy; Roque Meraz; Deacon Christopher McIntire; Rosa Jimenez.
Catechesis Religious Program—Mildred Santos, D.R.E., Tel: 219-513-6065; Email: mildredsantos@sbcglobal.net. Students 6.

12—ST. LUKE (1917) Merged See Sts. Monica-Luke, Gary.

13—ST. MARK (1921) Closed. For inquiries for parish records contact St. Joseph the Worker, Gary.

14—ST. MARY OF THE LAKE (1929)
6060 Miller Ave., Gary, 46403. Tel: 219-938-1373; Email: stmary_garyin@comcast.net; Web: wwwgarycluster.org. Most Rev. Dale J. Melczek, Admin.; Judith Siroky, Parish Life Coord.
Catechesis Religious Program—Judith Siroky, Coord. Students 5.

15—SS. MONICA-ST. LUKE (1927; 1917)
Mailing Address: 645 Rhode Island, Gary, 46402. Tel: 219-883-1861; Email: monicaluke@comcast.net; Web: www.ssmonicaluke.org. Most Rev. Donald J. Hying, Admin.; Michael Cummings, Parish Life Dir.
Catechesis Religious Program—Tel: 219-887-5756; Email: anitamiller65@comcast.net. Anita Miller, D.R.E. Students 3.

16—SACRED HEART (1918) (Polish), Closed. For inquiries for parish records contact Cathedral of Holy Angels, Gary.

OUTSIDE THE CITY OF GARY

BEVERLY SHORES, PORTER CO., ST. ANN (1950) (Lithuanian)
433 E. Golfwood Rd., P.O. Box 727, Beverly Shores, 46301. Tel: 219-879-7565; Fax: 219-879-8893; Email: stannesdunnes@comcast.net; Web: www.st-ann-of-the-dunes.org. Revs. John B. Barasinski; Gediminas Kersys, (Pastoral Care for the Lithuanian Community).
Catechesis Religious Program—Students 70.

CEDAR LAKE, LAKE CO., HOLY NAME (1859) [CEM]
11000 W. 133rd Ave., Cedar Lake, 46303. Tel: 219-374-7160; Email: office@holynamecedarlake.com. Rev. Michael Surufka, O.F.M.; Deacons John Bacon; Thomas R. Kubik.
Parish Center—13209 Schneider St., Cedar Lake, 46303. Tel: 219-374-8798.
Catechesis Religious Program—Generations of Faith, Tel: 219-374-8798. Mercedes Austgen, D.R.E., Email: . Students 205.

CHESTERTON, PORTER CO., ST. PATRICK (1858) [CEM]
638 N. Calumet Rd., Chesterton, 46304-1502. Tel: 219-926-1282; Email: churchoffice@stpatsparish.org. Revs. Jon J. Plavcan; Nathaniel Edquist.
Rectory—642 N. Calumet Rd., Chesterton, 46304-1502. Tel: 219-926-9633.
School—St. Patrick School, 640 N. Calumet Rd., Chesterton, 46304-1502. Tel: 219-926-1707; Fax: 219-921-1922; Email: schooloffice@stpatsparish.org. Richard Rupcich, Prin. Lay Teachers 12; Students 230.
Catechesis Religious Program—Students 291.

CROWN POINT, LAKE CO.

1—ST. MARY (1865) [CEM] (German)
321 E. Joliet St., Crown Point, 46307. Tel: 219-663-0044; Fax: 219-663-1027; Email: stmarycp2004@yahoo.com; Web: www.stmarycrownpoint.org. Rev. Patrick J. Kalich.
School—St. Mary School, 405 E. Joliet St., Crown Point, 46307. Tel: 219-663-0676; Fax: 219-663-1347. L. Thomas Ruiz, Prin. Lay Teachers 31; Students 508.
Catechesis Religious Program—Marian Weeks, D.R.E. Students 983.

2—ST. MATTHIAS (1967)
Mailing Address: 101 W. Burrell Dr., Crown Point, 46307. Revs. James E. Wozniak; Joseph E. Vamos, Sr. Priest, (Retired); Deacon Gregory Fabian.
Catechesis Religious Program—Tel: 219-663-4281; Email: jackiemgentry@yahoo.com. Students 390.

DYER, LAKE CO.

1—ST. JOSEPH (1867) [CEM]
Tel: 219-865-2271; Email: office@stjosephdyer.org; Web: www.stjosephdyer.org. Rev. Ted J. Mauch; Deacon Gary Blue.
Catechesis Religious Program—430 Joliet St., Dyer, 46311. Email: dre@stjosephdyer.org. Yvonne Weaver, D.R.E. Students 85.

2—ST. MARIA GORETTI (1977)
500 Northgate Dr., Dyer, 46311. Tel: 219-865-8956; Email: goretti@stmariagorettichurch.org. Rev. Charles W. Niblick; Deacons Phillip L. Muvich; Daniel Ratliff.
Catechesis Religious Program—Tel: 219-322-6124; Email: smg.religed@yahoo.com; Web: www.stmariagorettichurch.org. Kimberly Hoogeveen, D.R.E. Students 310.

EAST CHICAGO, LAKE CO.

1—ASSUMPTION (1915) (Slovak), Closed. For inquiries for parish records contact St. Patrick, East Chicago.

2—ST. FRANCIS (1913) (Lithuanian), Closed. For inquiries for parish records contact St. John Cantius, East Chicago.

3—HOLY TRINITY (1916) (Croatian)
4754 Carey St., East Chicago, 46312. Tel: 219-398-3061. Rev. Terrence J. Steffens, Admin.
Catechesis Religious Program—Mrs. Cynthia Rivas, D.R.E.; Carmen Vasquez, D.R.E. Students 12.

4—IMMACULATE CONCEPTION (1933) (Italian), Closed. For inquiries for parish records contact St. Stanislaus, East Chicago.

5—ST. JOHN CANTIUS (1905) (Polish), Closed. For inquiries for parish records, contact St. Stanislaus, East Chicago.

6—ST. JOSEPH (1916) (Polish), Closed. For inquiries for parish records contact St. John Cantius, East Chicago.

7—ST. JUDE (1933) Closed. For inquiries for parish records contact Our Lady of Guadalupe, East Chicago.

8—ST. MARY (1890)
4316 Indianapolis Blvd., East Chicago, 46312. Tel: 219-398-2409; Fax: 219-391-8999; Email: office@stmaryec.com. Rev. Nestor A. Varon, A.I.C., (Colombia); Deacon Felipe Maldonado.
Catechesis Religious Program—Claudia Fierros, D.R.E. Students 531.

9—OUR LADY OF GUADALUPE (1927) (Hispanic)
Email: olguadalupe@hotmail.com. Rev. Carlos Martinez, A.I.C.
Res.: 3526 Deodar St., East Chicago, 46312. Tel: 219-398-0253; Fax: 219-398-0257; Email: olguadalupe@hotmail.com.
Catechesis Religious Program—Erica Jimenez, D.R.E. Students 132.

10—ST. PATRICK ROMAN CATHOLIC CHURCH (1902) (Hispanic)
Mailing Address: 3814 Grand Blvd., East Chicago, 46312. Rev. David G. Nowak, Admin.; Deacon Raymond E. Helfen, Sr. Deacon. In Res., Rev. David G. Nowak.
Res.: 3810 Grand Blvd., East Chicago, 46312. Tel: 219-398-1036; Email: co.spc@live.com.
Catechesis Religious Program—3510 Deodar St., East Chicago, 46312. Tel: 219-398-0253; Fax: 219-398-0257. Students 25.

11—SACRED HEART (1926) (Slovak), Closed. For inquiries for parish records, contact St. Stanislaus, East Chicago.

12—ST. STANISLAUS ROMAN CATHOLIC CHURCH (1900) (Polish)

808 W. 150th St., East Chicago, 46312.
Tel: 219-398-2341; Email: john_s96@yahoo.com. Rev. Msgr. John J. Siekierski, J.C.L.
School—St. Stanislaus School, 4930 Indianapolis Blvd., East Chicago, 46312. Tel: 219-398-1316; Fax: 219-398-9080. Anne Jackie Ruiz, Prin. Lay Teachers 14; Students 215.
Catechesis Religious Program—Sr. Gloria Jean Kozlowski, D.R.E. Students 6.
Convent—4914 Magoun Ave., East Chicago, 46312. Tel: 219-397-7059.

FISH LAKE, LA PORTE CO., ST. ANTHONY OF PADUA (1948)
7732 E. State Rd. 4, Walkerton, 46574.
Tel: 219-269-9500; Email: stanthony.kanty@frontier.com. Rev. Michael G. Heimer.
Catechesis Religious Program—7012 N. 600 E., Rolling Prairie, 46371. Email: rljchan@msn.com. Robert Chance, D.R.E. Students 6.

GRIFFITH, LAKE CO., ST. MARY (1928)
525 N. Broad St., Griffith, 46319-2225.
Tel: 219-924-4163; Email: stmarygriffith@comcast.net; Web: www.smgriffith.org. Rev. Theodore J. Mens.
School—St. Mary School, (Grades PreK-8), Tel: 219-924-8633; Fax: 219-922-2279. Mrs. Rebecca Maskovich, Prin. Lay Teachers 15; Students 258.
Catechesis Religious Program—Tel: 219-922-2277; Fax: 219-922-2291. Students 151.
Convent—508 N. Lafayette St., Griffith, 46319. Tel: 219-922-2278.

HAMLET, STARKE CO., HOLY CROSS (1888) [CEM]
6 W. Pearl St., P.O. Box 234, Hamlet, 46532.
Tel: 574-867-2461; Email: spanleyhcsd@gmail.com. Rev. Anthony L. Spanley.
Catechesis Religious Program—Students 5.
Mission—St. Dominic (1981) 10440 E. SR 23, P.O. Box 234, Hamlet, 46532.

HAMMOND, LAKE CO.
1—ALL SAINTS (1896) Rev. Eduardo Malagon.
Res.: 570 Sibley St., P.O. Box 836, Hammond, 46325-0836. Tel: 219-932-0204; Fax: 219-932-4507; Email: allsaint@comcast.net.
Catechesis Religious Program—Naomi Gomez, D.R.E. Students 43.

2—ST. CASIMIR (1890) [JC] (Polish)
4340 Johnson St., Hammond, 46327.
Tel: 219-931-2589; Email: saintcasimirchurch@comcast.net; Web: www.stcasschool.org. Revs. Eduardo Malagon; Stephen Gibson; Vladimir Janeczek, Sacramental Min., (Retired); Deacon Martin J. Brown.
School—St. Casimir School, 4329 Cameron St., Hammond, 46327. Tel: 219-932-2686; Fax: 219-932-4458. Renata Gajardo, Prin. Lay Teachers 24; Students 470.
Catechesis Religious Program—Elena Magallanes, D.R.E., Tel: 219-932-2686, Ext. 7005. Students 82.

3—ST. CATHERINE OF SIENA (1956)
3428 165th St., Hammond, 46323. Tel: 219-845-1939; Email: frmosley@sbcglobal.net; Web: scsparishfamily.wix.com/scos. Rev. Charles A. Mosley.
Catechesis Religious Program—Students 2.

4—ST. JOHN BOSCO (1934)
7113 Columbia Ave., Hammond, 46324.
Tel: 219-844-9027; Email: sjboffice@comcast.net; Web: www.sjbhammond.org. Rev. Richard A. Orlinski. In Res., Rev. Stanley Dominik.
Pastoral Center—1247 171st Pl., Hammond, 46324. Fax: 219-989-7947.
School—St. John Bosco, (Grades PreSchool-8), 1231 171st Pl., Hammond, 46324. Tel: 219-845-6226; Fax: 219-989-7946; Email: sjbprincipalmk@gmail.com. Mark Kielbania, Prin.; Polly Lopez, Librarian. Lay Teachers 14; Students 213.
Catechesis Religious Program—
Tel: 219-844-9027, Ext. 310. Mrs. Vickie Blackwood, D.R.E./Pastoral Assoc. Students 129.

5—ST. JOSEPH (1879)
5304 Hohman Ave., Hammond, 46320-1808.
Tel: 219-932-0702; Email: saintjosephhammon@comcast.net; Web: www.oursaintjoseph.org. Rev. Richard A. Orlinski.
Catechesis Religious Program—5314 Hohman Ave., Hammond, 46320. Tel: 219-932-7294. Students 43.

6—ST. MARGARET MARY (1947) [CEM]
1445 Hoffman St., Hammond, 46327.
Tel: 219-931-5229; Email: stmargaretmary149@gmail.com. Rev. Luis Ferneidy Cardona, A.I.C., Admin..
Catechesis Religious Program—Students 255.

7—ST. MARY (1912) Closed. For inquiries for parish records, contact St. John Bosco, Hammond.

8—OUR LADY OF PERPETUAL HELP (1937)
7132 Arizona St., Hammond, 46323.
Tel: 219-844-3438; Email: frmosley@sbcglobal.net; Web: olphparish.net. Rev. Charles A. Mosley.
Catechesis Religious Program—7128 Arizona St., Hammond, 46323. Robert Meaney, D.R.E. Students 179.

HEBRON, PORTER CO., ST. HELEN (1946)
302 N. Madison St., Hebron, 46341.
Tel: 219-996-4611; Email: sthelenchurch@comcast.net. Revs. Thomas E. Mischler; Frank D. Torres.
Catechesis Religious Program—Tel: 219-707-1640; Email: karenyankauskas@gmail.com. Karen Yankauskas, D.R.E. Students 46.

HIGHLAND, LAKE CO.
1—ST. JAMES THE LESS (1967)
Mailing Address: 9640 Kennedy Ave., Highland, 46322. Rev. Keith M. Virus; Deacons Martin Denkhoff; Raymond Dec; Michael W. Halas; Matthew Virus.
Res.: 2703 45th St., Highland, 46322.
Tel: 219-924-4220; Fax: 219-924-4295; Email: stjames4220@sbcglobal.net; Web: www.stjameshighland.org.
Catechesis Religious Program—Tel: 219-924-4222; Email: dre@stjameshighland.org. Emily Watroba, D.R.E. Students 222.

2—OUR LADY OF GRACE (1949)
3005 Condit St., Highland, 46322. Tel: 219-838-0395; Fax: 219-972-6372; Email: ourladygrace@sbcglobal.net; Web: olgcatholicchurchhighland.org. 3052 Hwy. Ave., Highland, 46322. Rev. Edward J. Moszur.
School—Our Lady of Grace School, (Grades K-8), 3025 Highway Ave., Highland, 46322.
Tel: 219-838-2901; Fax: 219-972-6389; Email: olgsecretary@yahoo.com; Web: www.olgraceschool.org. Mark Topp, Prin., Tel: 219-838-2901. Lay Teachers 13; Students 145.
Catechesis Religious Program—Tel: 219-838-6790; Email: olgdre1@yahoo.com. Donna Velez, D.R.E. Preschool 2; Students 143.

HOBART, LAKE CO., ST. BRIDGET (1873)
P.O. Box 408, Hobart, 46342-0408. 107 Main St., Hobart, 46342. Rev. Benjamin J. Ross.
Res.: 568 E. Second St., Hobart, 46342.
Tel: 219-942-6441; Email: dwilliams@stbridgethobart.org.
Catechesis Religious Program—
Tel: 219-942-6441, Ext. 121. Students 160.

KINGSFORD HEIGHTS, LA PORTE CO., IMMACULATE HEART OF MARY (1953) Closed. For inquiries for parish records contact St. Anthony, Fish Lake.

KNOX, STARKE CO., ST. THOMAS AQUINAS (1923)
406 E. Washington St., Knox, 46534.
Tel: 574-772-4134; Email: frloncars@gmail.com; Web: www.saintttthomasaquinas.net. Rev. Stephen Loncar, O.F.M.Conv.
Catechesis Religious Program—Tel: 574-806-0001; Email: ldk85@hotmail.com. Mrs. Linda Kelly, D.R.E. Students 51.

KOUTS, PORTER CO., ST. MARY (1884) [CEM]
P.O. Box 663, Kouts, 46347. Tel: 219-766-3680; Email: stmarykouts@frontier.com. Rev. Thomas T. Tibbs; Deacon Jim F. Knopf.
Catechesis Religious Program—(Grades K-8), Students 32.

LA PORTE, LA PORTE CO.
1—ST. JOSEPH (1858) [CEM]
Tel: 219-362-9595; Email: stjoseph@catholiclaporte.org; Web: www.catholiclaporte.org. Rev. Ian J. Williams; Deacons Robert Bucheit; Michael J. Green, Business Mgr.
Catechesis Religious Program—101 C St., La Porte, 46350. Students 201.

2—ST. PETER (1853)
1104 Monroe St., La Porte, 46350. Tel: 219-362-2509; Email: stpeter@catholiclaporte.org; Web: members.csinet.net/stpeterschurch. Rev. Ian J. Williams; Deacons Christopher Hawkins; Michael J. Green, Business Mgr.
Catechesis Religious Program—Tel: 219-362-2509; Fax: 219-362-2748. Christine Kusiac, D.R.E. Students 56.

3—SACRED HEART (1912) (Polish)
Mailing Address: 201 Bach St., La Porte, 46350. Rev. Ian J. Williams; Deacons Michael J. Green, Business Mgr.; Frank J. Zolvinski.
Res.: 130 Bach St., La Porte, 46350.
Tel: 219-362-2815; Email: pastor@catholiclaporte.org; Web: www.catholiclaporte.org.
Catechesis Religious Program—Tel: 219-362-4822. Students 120.

LAKE STATION, LAKE CO., ST. FRANCIS XAVIER (1930) [CEM]
2447 Putnam St., Lake Station, 46405.
Tel: 219-962-8626; Email: st.francis@frontier.com; Web: www.francis-xavier-ls.net. Revs. Nestor A. Varon, A.I.C., (Colombia); Roque Meraz.
Catechesis Religious Program—Tel: 219-962-4507; Email: lvbimmerle@gmail.com. L. Bim-Merle, D.R.E. Students 265.

LOWELL, LAKE CO., ST. EDWARD (1870) [CEM]
216 S. Nichols St., Lowell, 46356. Tel: 219-696-7307; Email: stedwardchurch@sbcglobal.net; Web: stedlowell.com. Rev. Richard C. Holy; Deacons William Hathaway; Roberto Mendoza.
Catechesis Religious Program—Tel: 219-696-4282. Students 122.

MERRILLVILLE, LAKE CO.
1—ST. ANDREW (1965)
801 W. 73rd Ave., 46410. Tel: 219-769-8534; Fax: 219-769-8543; Email: standrew73rd@gmail.com. Rev. Brian D. Chadwick, J.C.L.; Deacon Thomas Gryzbek.
School—St. Andrew School aka Aquinas Catholic Community School, (Grades PreK-8),
Tel: 219-769-2049. Lisa Gutierrez, Prin. Lay Teachers 10; Preschool 2; Students 181.
Catechesis Religious Program—Tel: 219-769-2049. Students 46.

2—ST. JOAN OF ARC (1968)
Mailing Address: 200 E. 78th Ave., 46410.
Tel: 219-769-1973; Email: StJoanMerr@comcast.net; Web: www.stjoanmerr.org. Rev. James W. Meade, J.D., S.T.L., J.C.L.; Deacon Steven Zubel.
Catechesis Religious Program—Mrs. Beth Lasky, D.R.E. Students 10.
St. Joan of Arc Center—

3—OUR LADY OF CONSOLATION (1947)
8303 Taft St., 46410. Tel: 219-769-1755;
Tel: 219-769-2785; Fax: 219-769-2177; Email: church@olcweb.org; Email: sacristan@olcweb.org; Web: www.olcweb.org. Rev. Peter J. Muha; Deacons Robert E. Gill; Ralph J. Huber Jr.; Thomas Maicher, R.C.I.A. Coord.
Catechesis Religious Program—Tel: 219-769-2295; Email: ffp@olcweb.org. Bonnie Hall, D.R.E. Students 83.

4—SS. PETER AND PAUL (1841)
5885 Harrison St., 46410. Tel: 219-980-2693;
Fax: 219-980-2851; Email: ssppchurch@msn.com. Rev. James W. Meade, J.D., S.T.L., J.C.L.

5—ST. STEPHEN, MARTYR (1968)
5920 Waite St., 46410. Tel: 219-980-9348; Email: ststephenmartyr@att.net. Rev. Michael L. Maginot, S.T.L., J.C.L.

MICHIGAN CITY, LA PORTE CO.
1—ST. MARY OF THE IMMACULATE CONCEPTION (1867)
411 W. 11th St., Michigan City, 46360.
Tel: 219-872-9196; Email: stmary.school@comcast.net. Rev. Kevin R. Huber, D.Min.; Deacon Michael J. Green, Email: stmarydeacon@comcast.net.
Catechesis Religious Program—Students 35.
Mission—Sacred Heart, 1001 W. Eighth St., Michigan City, 46360.

2—NOTRE DAME (1953)
1010 Moore Rd., Michigan City, 46360.
Tel: 219-872-4844; Email: kcate@notredameparish.net; Web: notredameparish.net. Rev. Keith J. McClellan.
School—Notre Dame School, (Grades PreK-8),
Tel: 219-872-6216; Email: nmagnusen@notredameparish.net. Lay Teachers 11; Students 206.

3—QUEEN OF ALL SAINTS (1950)
606 S. Woodland Ave., Michigan City, 46360.
Tel: 219-872-9196; Email: parishoffice@qas.org; Web: qas.org. Rev. Kevin R. Huber, D.Min.
School—Queen of All Saints School, (Grades PreSchool-8), 1715 E. Barker Ave., Michigan City, 46360. Tel: 219-872-4420; Fax: 219-872-1943; Email: susanh@qas.org. Marie Arter, Prin.; Kim Gondeck, Vice-Prin. Lay Teachers 14; Students 185.
Catechesis Religious Program—Tel: 219-878-9348. Kathy Moskovich, D.R.E. Students 127.

4—SACRED HEART MISSION (1915) (Lebanese), Closed. For inquiries for parish records contact the chancery.

5—ST. STANISLAUS KOSTKA (1891) (Polish)
Mailing Address: 1506 Washington St., Michigan City, 46360. Rev. Walter M. Ciesla; Bro. Shaun Gray.
Res.: 109 Ann St., Michigan City, 46360.
Tel: 219-879-9281; Email: ststanskostka@yahoo.com; Web: www.sanctusstanislaus.com.
School—St. Stanislaus Kostka School,
Tel: 219-872-2258; Fax: 219-872-2295. Lay Teachers 16; Students 160.
Catechesis Religious Program—Students 32.

MUNSTER, LAKE CO., ST. THOMAS MORE (1945)
8501 Calumet Ave., Munster, 46321.
Tel: 219-836-8610; Email: parish.office@stm-church.com; Web: www.stm-church.com. Revs. Michael J. Yadron; Jordan C. Fetcko; Deacons David J. Kapala; Joseph Stodola; Napoleon Tabion; Daniel W. Zurawski.
School—St. Thomas More School, 8435 Calumet Ave., Munster, 46321. Tel: 219-836-9151; Fax: 219-836-0982; Web: www.stm-school.com. Jay Harker, Prin. Lay Teachers 27; Students 486.
Catechesis Religious Program—Email: ehackett@stm-church.com. Miss Emily Hackett, D.R.E.; Angie Lorandos, Music Min. Students 512.

NEW CHICAGO, LAKE CO., ASSUMPTION OF THE BLESSED VIRGIN MARY (P.O. Hobart) (1917) (Polish)
3530 Illinois St., Hobart, 46342. Tel: 219-962-1073; Email: lourdupasala@yahoo.com. Rev. Lourdu Pasala, J.C.L.
Catechesis Religious Program—Tel: 219-962-6678. Students 32.

NORTH JUDSON, STARKE CO., SS. CYRIL AND METHODIUS (1881) [CEM]

303 Keller Ave., North Judson, 46366.
Tel: 574-896-2195; Email: sscyrilandmethodius@hotmail.com. Rev. Terrence W. Bennis; Peggy Okeley, Pastoral Assoc.
Catechesis Religious Program—Students 23.

OTIS, LA PORTE CO., ST. MARY (1873) [CEM] (Polish)
P.O. Box 386, Wanatah, 46390. Tel: 219-733-2955; Email: cberger@thecatholiccommunities.org; Web: thecatholiccommunities.org. 101 N. Church St., Otis, 46391. Rev. Paul E. Quanz, Admin.; Deacons Dale Walsh; Sherman Brown; Jeffery L. Newburn; Rev. John J. Zemelko, In Res.
Catechesis Religious Program—Email: mtgroszek@gmail.com. Mary Ann Groszek, Tel: 219-926-1639. Students 50.

PORTAGE, PORTER CO., NATIVITY OF OUR SAVIOR (1964)
2949 Willowcreek Rd., Portage, 46368.
Tel: 219-762-4858; Email: guernsey@nativityofoursavior.net. Rev. Kevin P. McCarthy, Admin.; Deacons Robert J. Bonta; Richard Huber; Dr. Stephen K. Grandfield; Dennis M. Guernsey.
School—Nativity of Our Savior School, (Grades PreK-8), 2929 Willowcreek Rd., Portage, 46368.
Tel: 219-763-2400; Fax: 219-764-3225; Email: principal@nativityofoursavior.net; Web: www.nativityofoursavior.net. Sally Skowronski, Prin. Lay Teachers 13; Students 178.
Catechesis Religious Program—Tel: 219-764-3143; Email: nativityfaithformation@yahoo.com. Janet Marie Guernsey, D.R.E. Students 181.

ROLLING PRAIRIE, LAPORTE CO., ST. JOHN KANTY (1888) [CEM] (Polish)
7732 E. State Rd. 4, Walkerton, 46574.
Tel: 219-369-9500; Email: stanthony.kanty@frontier.com; Web: www.stjohnkanty.com/church/. Rev. Michael G. Heimer, Admin.
Catechesis Religious Program—7012 N 600 E., Rolling Prairie, 46371. Robert Chance, D.R.E., Email: rljchan@msn.com. Students 40.

ST. JOHN, LAKE CO., ST. JOHN THE EVANGELIST (1839) [CEM]
11301 W. 93rd. Ave., St. John, 46373-9715.
Tel: 219-365-5678; Email: tplikuhn@stjohnparish.org; Web: www.stjohnparish.org. 10701 Olcott Ave., St. John, 46373. Rev. Sammie L. Maletta; Deacons Edwin J. Bodley; Joseph Codespoti; Khalil Hattar; Deacons Philip Coduti; Paul M. Krilich; James McFarland; William P. Sayre; Edward J. Shultz; Robert L. Viviano.
School—St. John the Evangelist School, (Grades PreK-8), 9400 Wicker Ave., St. John, 46373.
Tel: 219-365-5451; Fax: 219-365-6173; Email: boliver@stjohnparish.org; Web: www.sjeschool.org. Mrs. Brianne Oliver, Prin. Lay Teachers 25; Students 425.
Catechesis Religious Program—Sheila Lachcik, D.R.E. Students 178.

SAN PIERRE, STARKE CO., ALL SAINTS (1858) [CEM]
303 Keller Ave., North Judson, 46366.
Tel: 574-896-2195; Email: sscyrilandmethodius@hotmail.com. Rev. Terrence W. Bennis.
Catechesis Religious Program—

SCHERERVILLE, LAKE CO., ST. MICHAEL (1874) [CEM]
1 Wilhelm St., Schererville, 46375. Tel: 219-322-4505; Email: mike@stmichaelparish.life; Web: www.stmichaelparish.life. Revs. Martin J. Dobrzynski; Gregory Bim-Merle; Deacon Ronald L. Pyle.
Child Care—Preschool, Tel: 219-322-3077. (Good Shepherd Program) Students 29.
School—St. Michael School, 16 W. Wilhelm St., Schererville, 46375. Tel: 219-322-4531;
Fax: 219-322-1710; Email: ckennedy@stmichaelparish.life; Web: stmichaelparish.life/school. Colleen Kennedy, Prin. Lay Teachers 27; Students 201.
Catechesis Religious Program—Email: mswanson@stmichaelparish.life. Marge Swanson, D.R.E. Students 485.

SHELBY, LAKE CO., ST. THERESA (1939) Closed. Records kept at St. Edward, Lowell.

VALPARAISO, PORTER CO.
1—ST. ELIZABETH SETON (1978)
509 W. Division Rd., Valparaiso, 46385.
Tel: 219-464-1624; Email: parishoffice@seseton.com; Web: www.seton.com. Rev. Douglas J. Mayer; Deacons Michael Prendergast; Brian Nosbusch; Kim E. Eaton Sr.
Catechesis Religious Program—Tel: 219-462-2202. Deborah Poturalski, D.R.E., Email: ffdirector@seseton.com. Students 191.
2—OUR LADY OF SORROWS (South Haven) (1967)
356 W. 700 N., Valparaiso, 46385. Tel: 219-759-2400; Email: ols.parish356@gmail.com; Email: admsorrows@gmail.com; Web: www.ols-parish.org. Rev. Paul E. Quanz.
Catechesis Religious Program—Tel: 219-299-3426; Email: sorrows.faith.formation@gmail.com. Students 77.
3—ST. PAUL (1858) [CEM]
Mailing Address: P.O. Box 1475, Valparaiso, 46384-1475. Tel: 219-464-4831; Fax: 219-464-4833; Email: stpaulcathvalpo@netnitco.net; Web: www.saintpaulvalpo.org. 1855 W. Harrison Blvd., Valparaiso. Revs. Douglas J. Mayer, Admin.; Jeffery D. Burton; Deacons Michael Foster; James Caristi; David A. Bergstedt; Kenneth Klawitter; Rev. Nathaniel Edquist, Hispanic Ministry Asst.
Res.: 1955 W Harrison Blvd., Valparaiso, 46385.
Tel: 219-465-3723.
School—St. Paul School, 1755 W. Harrison Blvd., Valparaiso, 46385. Tel: 219-462-3374;
Fax: 219-477-1763; Email: principal@stpaulvalpo.org; Web: www.stpaulvalpo.org. Jane Scupham, Prin. Students 280; Full-time Lay Teachers 14; Part-time Lay Teachers 3.
Catechesis Religious Program—Tel: 219-464-8502; Fax: 219-531-6854; Email: stpaulre1755@gmail.com; Web: www.stpaulre.org. Diane Matthys, D.R.E.; Matt Pysh, Youth Min.; Catherine Dull, Middle School Youth Min. Students 220.
Child Care—Tiny Tim's Child Development Center, 1857 W. Harrison Blvd., Valparaiso, 46385.
Tel: 219-465-0882; Fax: 219-531-2047; Email: sptinytim@aol.com. Janet McCorkle, Dir.
St. Agnes Adult Day Service Center—1859 W. Harrison Blvd., Valparaiso, 46385. Tel: 219-477-5433; Fax: 219-462-9553. Barbara Kubiszak, Dir.

WANATAH, LA PORTE CO., SACRED HEART (1887) [CEM]
202 N. Ohio St, Wanatah, 46390. Tel: 219-733-2955; Email: cberger@thecatholiccommunities.org. P.O. Box 386, Wanatah, 46390. Rev. Paul E. Quanz, Admin.; Deacons Dale Walsh; Sherman Brown; Jeffery L. Newburn; Rev. John J. Zemelko, In Res.
Catechesis Religious Program—Tel: 219-733-2315; Email: shreligiousεd@thecatholiccommunities.org. Staci Bolakowski, D.R.E., Tel: 219-363-8216; Email: queenbski1@gmail.com. Students 70.
Mission—St. Martin (1860) 118 Lowell St., LaCrosse, LaPorte Co. 46348.

WHITING, LAKE CO.
1—ST. ADALBERT (1902) (Polish)
1849 Lincoln Ave., Whiting, 46394.
Tel: 219-659-0023; Email: chuchparishoffice@yahoo.com. 1340 121st St., Whiting, 46394. Rev. Mark R. Peres, C.PP.S.
Catechesis Religious Program—Jamie Sandona, D.R.E.
2—IMMACULATE CONCEPTION (1922) (Slovak), Closed. For inquiries for parish records contact St. John the Baptist, Whiting Rev. Jerome Stack, C.PP.S.
3—ST. JOHN THE BAPTIST St. John-St. Joseph (1897)
1849 Lincoln Ave., Whiting, 46394.
Tel: 219-659-0023; Email: churchparishoffice@yahoo.com; Web: mysjb.org. Rev. Mark R. Peres, C.PP.S.; Deacons Joseph Manchak; Leo V. Barron Jr.; Jon Gerba, Business Mgr.; Rebecca Flores, Sec.
School—St. John the Baptist School, (Grades PreK-8), 1844 Lincoln Ave., Whiting, 46394.
Tel: 219-659-3042; Fax: 219-473-7553; Email: jjones@stjohnbap.org. Scott Tabernacki, Prin.; Jeanine Jones, Sec. Lay Teachers 23; Students 354.
Catechesis Religious Program—Tel: 219-473-7557; Fax: 219-473-7553. Jamie Sandona, D.R.E. (Includes all Whiting Catholic Parishes in Program) Students 154.
4—STS. PETER AND PAUL (1910) Closed. For inquiries of parish records, contact Sacred Heart, Whiting.
5—SACRED HEART (1889)
1849 Lincoln Ave, Whiting, 46394. Tel: 219-659-0023; Email: churchparishoffice@yahoo.com. Rev. Mark R. Peres, C.PP.S.
Catechesis Religious Program—Tel: 219-473-7557; Fax: 219-473-7551. (Included with St. John the Baptist).

WINFIELD TOWNSHIP, LAKE CO., HOLY SPIRIT (1998)
7667 E. 109th Ave., Crown Point, 46307.
Tel: 219-661-0644; Fax: 219-662-2611; Email: holyspiritfrtom@gmail.com; Email: holyspirit.winfield@gmail.com; Web: catholicfamilyhs.org. Rev. Thomas E. Mischler; Deacon Thomas Maicher; Suzanne Mycka, Business Mgr.
Catechesis Religious Program—Email: formationmcnamara@gmail.com. Rochelle McNamara, D.R.E. Students 260.

Chaplains of Public Institutions

MICHIGAN CITY. *Indiana State Prison*. Deacon Michael Prendergast
123 Shorewood Dr., Valparaiso, 46385.

ROLLING PRAIRIE. *Sharing Meadows*. Rev. Dennis J. Blaney, (Retired)
P.O. Box 400, Rolling Prairie, 46371.
Tel: 219-778-9130.

WESTVILLE. *Westville Correctional Center*. Deacon Michael Prendergast
P.O. Box 473, Westville, 46391. Tel: 219-785-2511.

On Duty Outside the Diocese:
Rev.—
Gajardo, Leonardo J., P.S.S., S.T.L., J.C.L., S.T.B., Theological College of the National Seminary of the Catholic University of America, 401 Michigan Ave. NE, Washington, DC 20017.

Retired:
Rev. Msgrs.—
Morales, John F., (Retired), 333 N. Palm Dr., #305, Beverly Hills, CA 90210
Semancik, Joseph F., (Retired), 1919 Lake Ave, Whiting, 46394
Zollinger, Richard, (Retired), 301 S. Main St., Knox, 46534
Revs.—
Beeching, Roy T., (Retired), 1345 Wright St., Crown Point, 46307
Bertino, Dominic V., (Retired), P.O. Box 403, Hobart, 46342
Blaney, Dennis J., (Retired), P.O. Box 400, Rolling Prairie, 46371
Coriden, James A., (Retired), 4004 7th St., N.E., Washington, DC 20012
de Cristobal, Fernando, (Retired), Calle Carros, 1, 31330, Villafranca de Navarro, Spain
Dominik, Stanley J., (Retired), 7113 Columbia Ave., Hammond, 46324
Gaza, J. Patrick, (Retired), P.O. Box 11213, 46411
Gehring, Robert P., (Retired), 419 Autumn Tr. S., Michigan City, 46360
Gosnell, David H., (Retired), 917 Beechnut Blvd., Westville, 46391
Hand, Dennis M., (Retired), Pje. 6, Poligno E-Casa #101, Col. San Luis, San Martin, El Salvador
Hendricks, Clare, (Retired), 1428 Lyon St., Columbia, TN 38401
Holicky, Gregory P., (Retired), 5304 Hohman Ave., Hammond, 46320
Janeczek, Vladimir, (Retired), 211 Autumn Tr., Michigan City, 46360
Kashmer, George B., (Retired), 9292 Broadway, 46410
Kew, Lawrence J., (Retired), 606 E. 92nd Pl., 46410
Link, David T., (Retired), Holy Cross Village, P.O. Box 23, South Bend, 46556
Schweitzer, Gerald H., (Retired), P.O. Box 924, Chesterton, 46304
Scott, John V., (Retired), P.O. Box 8972, Michigan City, 46361
Skerl, Alphonse, (Retired), 2137 Lincoln Ave., Whiting, 46394
Sroka, Gerald A., (Retired), 209 Autumn Tr., Michigan City, 46360
Vamos, Joseph E., (Retired), 10789 Pike St., Crown Point, 46307.

Permanent Deacons:
Angelich, Robert
Bacon, John
Barron, Leo V. Jr.
Bergstedt, David A.
Blue, Gary
Bodley, Edwin J.
Bonta, Robert J., Senior Deacon
Brown, Martin J.
Brown, Sherman, Senior Deacon
Bucheit, Robert J.
Caristi, James
Codespoti, Joseph, Senior Deacon
Coduti, Philip
Dec, Raymond, Senior Deacon
Dedelow, Duane W.
Denkhoff, Martin J., Senior Deacon
Eaton, Kim E. Sr.
Fabian, Gregory G.
Foster, Michael
Gill, Robert E., Senior Deacon
Dr. Grandfield, Stephen K.
Green, Michael J.
Gryzbek, Thomas
Guernsey, Dennis M.
Halas, Michael W.
Hathaway, William R.
Hawkins, Christopher
Helfen, Raymond E.
Hilbrich, Richard F.
Hogan, Michael L.
Huber, Ralph J. Jr.
Huber, Richard
Jones, William E. Jr., Senior Deacon
Jurasevich, Nicholas J.
Kapala, David J.
Klawitter, Kenneth
Knopf, Jim F.
Kozub, Edward, Senior Deacon
Krilich, Paul M.
Kubik, Thomas R.
Litavecz, Robert J.
Lowery, Daniel L., Ph.D.
Lunsford, Malcolm, Senior Deacon

Maicher, Thomas
Maldonado, Felipe
Manchak, Joseph C.
Marben, Robert W.
McFarland, James
McIntire, Christopher
Mendoza, Roberto
Muvich, Phillip L.
Newburn, Jeffery L.
Nosbusch, Brian
Prendergast, Michael
Pyle, Ronald L.
Ratliff, Daniel
Rodriguez, Juan
Sayre, William P.
Serrano, Jose A.
Shultz, Edward J.
Stodola, Joseph
Tabion, Napoleon, Senior Deacon
Virus, Matthew
Viviano, Robert L., Senior Deacon
Walsh, Dale
Webdell, Dale P.
Zolvinski, Frank J.
Zubel, Steven
Zurawski, Daniel W.

INSTITUTIONS LOCATED IN DIOCESE

[A] COLLEGES AND UNIVERSITIES

WHITING. *Calumet College of St. Joseph*, 2400 New York Ave., Whiting, 46394. Tel: 219-473-7770; Fax: 219-473-4259; Email: kscalf@ccsj.edu; Web: www.ccsj.edu. Diana Francis, Registrar; Dionne Jones-Malone, Dean; Amy McCormack, Pres.; Lynn Miskus, Bus. Mgr.; Ginger Rodriguez, Dean; Rev. Kevin Scalf, C.PP.S., Exec. Calumet College of St. Joseph is a four year Catholic liberal arts college sponsored by the Missionaries of the Precious Blood. It is the only Catholic college in northwest Indiana. Brothers 2; Lay Teachers 30; Priests 1; Students 748; Religious Teachers 1.

[B] HIGH SCHOOLS, DIOCESAN

HAMMOND. *Bishop Noll Institute* (1921) 1519 Hoffman St., Hammond, 46327. Tel: 219-932-9058; Fax: 219-853-1736; Email: lpastrick@bishopnoll.org; Web: www.bishopnoll.org. Mr. Paul Mullaney, Pres.; Mrs. Lorenza Jara Pastrick, Prin.; Elizabeth Cotey, Librarian. Lay Teachers 40; Students 530; Total Enrollment 530; Total Staff 32; Priests Part Time 1.

MERRILLVILLE. *Andrean High School*, 5959 Broadway, 46410. Tel: 219-887-5959; Fax: 219-981-5072; Email: tbonta@andreanhs.org; Web: www.andreanhs.org. Dr. Anthony Bonta, Ph.D., Acting Admin.; Heather Lytton, Asst. Prin. - Academics; Scott Henwood, Asst. Prin. - Student Life; William Mueller, Dir., Athletics; Mrs. Darlene Talian, Librarian. Administrators 3; Lay Teachers 40; Students 418.

MICHIGAN CITY. *Marquette Catholic High School*, 306 W. Tenth St., Michigan City, 46360. Tel: 219-873-1325; Fax: 219-873-1327; Email: jquinlan@marquette-hs.org; Web: www.marquette-hs.org. James G. White, Pres.; Allyson Head, Prin. Lay Teachers 23; Students 290; Total Staff 35.

[C] ELEMENTARY SCHOOLS, INTERPAROCHIAL

ROLLING PRAIRIE. *Sacred Heart Apostolic School, Inc.*, (Grades 8-12), 5901 N. 500 E., Rolling Prairie, 46371. Tel: 219-778-4596; Fax: 219-778-9018; Email: bmrprairie@arcol.org. P.O. Box 7, Rolling Prairie, 46371. Bro. Andre Blanchette, L.C., Asst. Dean, Students; Rev. Ronald Conklin, L.C., Admissions Dir.; Christopher Daniels, Dean; Revs. Robert DeCesare, Asst. Admissions Dir.; Andrew Kolenda, L.C., Admin.; Steven Liscinsky, L.C., Dean; Bro. David Reising, L.C., Asst. Dean, Students; Revs. Paul Silva, L.C., Prof.; Timothy Walsh, Rector. Brothers 2; Religious Teachers 2; Lay Teachers 2; Priests 9; Students 29.

[D] GENERAL HOSPITALS

CROWN POINT. *Franciscan Health Crown Point* (1974) 1201 S. Main St., Crown Point, 46307-8483. Tel: 219-738-2100; Fax: 219-757-6242; Email: daniel.McCormick@franciscanalliance.org; Web: www.franciscanalliance.org/hospitals/crownpoint. Dr. Daniel McCormick, Pres.; Revs. Anthony F. Janik, O.F.M., Dir.; David Kelly, O.F.M., Chap.; Sr. Marlene Shapley, O.F.M., Vice Pres. Franciscan Alliance, Inc. Bassinets 30; Bed Capacity 263; Licensed Beds 411; Sisters 1; Tot Asst. Annually 407,913; Total Staff 1,164.

DYER. *Franciscan Health Dyer*, 24 Joliet, Dyer, 46311. Tel: 219-865-2141; Fax: 219-933-2585; Email: Patrick.Maloney@franciscanalliance.org; Web: www.franciscanhealth.org. Patrick Maloney, CEO; Rev. Henry Sequeira, Chap. Franciscan Alliance, Inc. Bassinets 16; Licensed 198; Licensed Beds 305; Sisters 1; Tot Asst. Annually 143,241; Total Staff 1,179.

EAST CHICAGO. *St. Catherine Hospital* (1928) 4321 Fir St., East Chicago, 46312. Tel: 219-392-1700; Fax: 219-392-7002; Email: tpedroza@comhs.org; Web: www.comhs.org. Leo Correa, CEO; Teresa Pedroza, Dir., Mission Integration; Lauren Trumbo, Finance Dir. Bassinets 9; Bed Capacity 211; Tot Asst. Annually 102,866; Total Staff 1,005.

HAMMOND. *Franciscan Health Hammond*, 5454 Hohman Ave., Hammond, 46320. Tel: 219-932-2300; Fax: 219-933-2585; Email: Patrick.Maloney@franciscanalliance.org; Web: www.franciscanhealth.org. Patrick Maloney, CEO; Revs. Gregory Holicky, Chap.; Theodore A. Nordquist, Chap. Franciscan Alliance, Inc. Licensed 46; Licensed Beds 477; Bed Capacity 221; Sisters 1; Tot Asst. Annually 172,877; Total Staff 1,302.

HOBART. *St. Mary Medical Center*, 1500 S. Lake Park Ave., Hobart, 46342. Tel: 219-942-0551; Fax: 219-947-6037; Email: tpedroza@comhs.org; Web: www.comhs.org. Teresa Pedroza, Dir., Mission Integration; Janice Ryba, CEO; Mary Sudicky, CFO. Bassinets 18; Bed Capacity 200; Tot Asst. Annually 257,545; Total Staff 1,133.

MICHIGAN CITY. *Franciscan Health Michigan City* (1904) 3500 Franciscan Way, Michigan City, 46360. Tel: 219-879-8511; Fax: 219-877-1409; Email: dean.mazzoni@franciscanalliance.org; Web: www.franciscanhealth.org. Dean Mazzoni, Pres. and CEO; Sr. M. Petra Nielsen, Vice Pres.; Barbara Rice-Wisthoff, Dir.; Rev. William F. O'Toole, Chap. Franciscan Alliance, Inc. Bassinets 15; Bed Capacity 123; Sisters 5; Tot Asst. Annually 418,793; Total Staff 1,080; Licensed Beds 310.

MUNSTER. *Franciscan Health Munster*, 701 Superior Ave., Munster, 46321. Tel: 219-922-4200; Fax: 219-924-7347; Email: Patrick.Maloney@franciscanalliance.org; Web: www.franciscanhealth.org. Patrick Maloney, CEO; Rev. Francis Tebbe, O.F.M., Dir. Bed Capacity 63; Sisters 1; Tot Asst. Annually 138,684; Total Staff 557.

[E] PROTECTIVE INSTITUTIONS

EAST CHICAGO. *Carmelite Home for Girls/Holy Innocents Shelter* (1913) 4840 Grasselli Ave., East Chicago, 46312. Tel: 219-397-1085; Fax: 219-392-3574; Email: srmgiuseppe.carmelite@gmail.com; Web: www.carmelitedcjnorth.org. Sr. Maria Giuseppe Moxley, Supr. & Admin. Tot Asst. Annually 264; Total Staff 140; Carmelite Sisters of the Divine Heart of Jesus 6.

[F] HOMES FOR THE AGED

CROWN POINT. *Franciscan Communities at St. Anthony Campus*, 203 Franciscan Dr., Crown Point, 46307-4824. Tel: 219-661-5100; Fax: 219-661-5102; Email: bmagerl@franciscancommunities.com; Web: www.stanthonyhome.com; www.franciscancommunities.com. Barbara Mageri, Admin.; Deacon Brian Nosbusch, Dir., Mission Integration & Pastoral Care; Rev. Mike Slattery. Deacons 2; Priests 1; Total Staff 500; Franciscan Sisters of Chicago 2.

St. Anthony Home, Tel: 219-661-5100; Fax: 219-661-5102; Email: bnosbusch@franciscancommunities.org; Web: www.stanthonyhome.com. Deacons Brian Nosbusch; Steven Zubel. Capacity 190.

St. Anthony Assisted Living Apartments, Tel: 219-661-5150; Fax: 219-661-5205; Web: www.stanthonyhome.com. Capacity 60.

Hospice Franciscan Communities, Tel: 219-661-5306; Fax: 219-661-5305; Web: www.stanthonyhome.com.

Franciscan Adult Day Services, Tel: 219-661-5200; Web: www.stanthonyhome.com. Capacity 25.

Holy Family Child Care, Tel: 219-661-5250. Children 175.

HAMMOND. *Albertine Home*, 1501 Hoffman St., Hammond, 46327. Tel: 219-937-0575; Fax: 219-937-0575; Email: albertineusa@att.net. Sr. Loretta Soja, Dir. Guests 32; Albertine Sisters 9.

[G] PERSONAL PRELATURES

VALPARAISO. *Opus Dei*, 359 West 200 N., Valparaiso, 46385. Tel: 219-462-0931; Tel: 219-462-6594; Fax: 219-465-6241; Email: shellbourne2@aol.com; Web: www.shellbourne.org. Ashley Petros, Dir. Prelature of the Holy Cross and Opus Dei, Shellbourne Conference Center.

[H] MONASTERIES AND RESIDENCES OF PRIESTS AND BROTHERS

CEDAR LAKE. *Our Lady of Lourdes Friary*, 12921 Parrish Ave., P.O. Box 156/500, Cedar Lake, 46303. Tel: 219-374-5931; Email: afjanik@yahoo.com. Revs. Francis Affelt, O.F.M., Chap., Franciscan Sisters, Mishawaka, IN; Anthony Chojnacki, O.F.M.; Anthony F. Janik, O.F.M., Vicar, St. Anthony Health, Crown Point, IN; David Kelly, O.F.M., Chap.; Bert Pepowski, O.F.M.; Michael Surufka, O.F.M., Guardian; Bros. Reynold Lesnar, O.F.M.; James Wisnewski, O.F.M. Franciscan Friars of the Assumption of the Blessed Virgin Mary Province (Order of Friars Minor, O.F.M.), Franklin, Wisconsin. Brothers 2; Deacons 1; Priests 5.

MERRILLVILLE. *Salvatorian Fathers (Society of the Divine Savior)* (1954) 5755 Pennsylvania St., 46410. Tel: 219-884-0714; Fax: 219-981-9224; Email: info@salwatorianie.us; Web: www.salwatorianie.us. Revs. Łukasz Kleczka, S.D.S., Supr.; Joseph R. Zuziak, S.D.S.; Stanislaw Pieczark, S.O.S., Chap.; Mikolaj Markiewicz, Treas.; Bronislaw Jakubiec, S.D.S.; Bro. Piotr Bogawski, S.D.S. Mission House for Polish Priests and Brothers. Our Lady of Czestochowa Diocesan Marian Shrine. Brothers 1; Priests 5.

MUNSTER. *Discalced Carmelite Fathers Monastery*, 1628 Ridge Rd., Munster, 46321. Tel: 219-838-7111; Fax: 219-838-7214; Email: carmelmunster@yahoo.com; Web: www.carmelitefathers.com. Revs. Jacek Palica, O.C.D.; Waclaw L. Lech, O.C.D.; Bronislaw F. Socha, O.C.D.; Bartlomiej Stanowski, O.C.D., First Counselor; Jacek Chodzynski, O.C.D.; Franciszek Czaicki, O.C.D., Prior; Pawel Furdzik, O.C.D.; Andrzej Gbur, O.C.D., Second Counselor; Bros. Marian Leszewicz, O.C.D., Rel. Bro.; Tomasz S. Paczek, O.C.D., Rel. Bro. Brothers 2; Priests 8.

[I] CONVENTS AND RESIDENCES OF SISTERS

GARY. *Missionaries of Charity* (1999) 509 W. Ridge Rd., Gary, 46408. Tel: 219-884-2140. Sisters M. Jonathan, M.C., Regl. Supr.; M. Coleta, M.C., Supr. Convent and emergency night shelter for women Sisters 4.

EAST CHICAGO. *St. Catherine Convent*, 4325 Elm St., East Chicago, 46312. Tel: 219-398-0403; Email: mdvorak@poorhandmaids.org; Web: www.poorhandmaids.org. Sisters Pamela Tholkes, P.H.J.C.; Barbara Kuper, P.H.J.C.; Kathlee Quinn, P.H.J.C.; Michele Dvorak, P.H.J.C., Visitation Convent, 4321 Elm St., East Chicago, 46312; Hoa Thi Pham, I.C.M.; Bich Vu Thi Ngac, I.C.M. Poor Handmaids of Jesus Christ 4.

HAMMOND. *Albertine Sisters (Prov. of Krakow, Poland)*, 1501 Hoffman St., Hammond, 46327. Tel: 219-937-0575; Fax: 219-937-0575; Email: albertineusa@att.net. Sr. Symforoza Anna Kicka, Supr. Sisters 9.

[J] DIOCESAN CHARITIES

GARY. *Catholic Charities, Diocese of Gary, Inc.* (1937) 940 Broadway, Gary, 46402. Tel: 219-886-3549; Fax: 219-886-2428; Email: mpranaitis@catholic-charities.org; Web: www.catholic-charities.org. Rev. Mark Pranaitis, C.M., Exec. Tot Asst. Annually 7,728; Total Staff 28.

Catholic Charities, 940 Broadway, Gary, 46402. Tel: 219-886-3549; Fax: 219-886-2428; Email: mpranaitis@catholic-charities.org. Rev. Mark Pranaitis, C.M., Dir.

Catholic Charity, 3901 Fir St., East Chicago, 46312. Tel: 219-397-5803; Fax: 219-397-5804; Email: mpranaitis@catholic-charities.org. Rev. Mark Pranaitis, C.M., Dir.

Foster Grandparent Program, 6919 Indianapolis Blvd., Hammond, 46324. Tel: 219-844-4883; Fax: 219-844-4885.

LaPorte & Starke Co., 321 W. 11th St., Michigan City, 46360. Tel: 219-874-8195; Fax: 219-879-9073.

Senior Companion Program, 6919 Indianapolis Blvd., Hammond, 46324. Tel: 219-844-4883; Fax: 219-844-4885.

[K] NEWMAN APOSTOLATES

VALPARAISO. *St. Teresa of Avila Catholic Student Center* (1974) 1511 La Porte Ave., Valparaiso, 46383-5818. Tel: 219-464-4042; Fax: 219-462-2711; Email: saintt.office@gmail.com. Rev. Christopher M. Stanish, Chap. Chapel and Center for Students attending Valparaiso University. Families 450; Students 200.

[L] MISCELLANEOUS

GARY. *Sojourner Truth House, Inc.*, 410 W. 13th Ave., Gary, 46407. Tel: 219-885-2282; Fax: 219-885-1984; Email: pspindler@sojournertruthhouse.org; Web: www.sojournertruthhouse.org. Sr. Peg Spindler, C.S.A., Exec. Dir.

CROWN POINT. *Franciscan Health Foundation - Northern Indiana*, 2050 N. Main St., Ste. A, Crown Point, 46307. Tel: 219-661-3401; Fax: 219-663-2548; Email: NIFoundation@franciscanalliance.org; Web: www.franciscanalliance.org/foundation. Richard Peltier, Exec.

EAST CHICAGO. *Office of Intercultural Ministry* (1983) 3814 Grand Blvd., East Chicago, 46312. Tel: 219-397-2125; Fax: 219-397-2168; Email: atorres@dcgary.org; Web: www.dcgary.org. Adeline Torres, Coord. Total Staff 3.

HAMMOND. **Alverno Provena Hospital Laboratories, Inc.*, 2434 Interstate Plaza Dr., Hammond, 46324. Tel: 219-989-3814; Fax: 219-845-2027; Email: sam.terese@franciscanalliance.org. Sam Terese, Pres.

HealthVisions Midwest, 3700 179th St., Hammond, 46323. Tel: 219-844-2698; Fax: 219-844-2702; Email: pwills@hvusa.org; Web: www.hvusa.org. Paula Willis, Exec. Dir.

HOBART. *Ancilla Systems Incorporated* (1967) 1419 S. Lake Park Ave., Hobart, 46342. Tel: 219-947-8500; Fax: 219-947-3708; Email: mgoeller@ancilla.org; Web: www.ancilla.org. Sisters Mary Ellen Goeller, P.H.J.C., Exec.; Judith Diltz, P.H.J.C., Chairperson.

Nazareth Home, P.O. Box 3067, East Chicago, 46312. Tel: 219-616-6090; Tel: 219-397-2021; Email: jbowman@nazarethhome.com; Web: www.nazarethhome.com. Jean Bowman, Dir.

**Poor Handmaids of Jesus Christ Foundation, Inc.*, 1419 S. Lake Park Ave., Hobart, 46342. Tel: 219-947-8565; Fax: 219-947-4037; Email: mgoeller@ancilla.org; Email: amaynard@ancilla.org. Sr. Michele Dvorak, P.H.J.C., Chm.; Amanda Maynard, Dir.

VALPARAISO. *Camp Lawrence* Diocesan Spiritual Center and Youth Camp. 68 E. 700 N., Valparaiso, 46383. Tel: 219-462-5261; Tel: 219-769-9292; Email: mwick@dcgary.org. 9292 Broadway, 46410. Mr. Michael Wick, Contact Person.

Catholic Youth Organization, 77725 Broadway, Ste. C, 46410. Tel: 219-736-8931; Fax: 219-736-9457; Email: nwicyo@comcast.net. Paul Wengel, Dir.

RELIGIOUS INSTITUTES OF MEN REPRESENTED IN THE DIOCESE

For further details refer to the corresponding bracketed number in the Religious Institutes of Men or Women section.

[]—*Association of the Immaculate Conception.*
[0170]—*Basilian Fathers* (Toronto)—C.S.B.
[0600]—*Brothers of the Congregation of Holy Cross*—C.S.C.
[0260]—*Discalced Carmelite Friars* (Holy Ghost Prov., Poland)—O.C.D.
[0520]—*Franciscan Friars* (Prov. of Assumption of B.V.M.; Prov. of St. John the Baptist; Prov. of the Sacred Heart)—O.F.M.
[]—*Institute of Christ the King Sovereign Priests.*
[]—*Legionaries of Christ.*
[1200]—*Society of the Divine Savior*—S.D.S.
[1060]—*Society of the Precious Blood*—C.PP.S.

RELIGIOUS INSTITUTES OF WOMEN REPRESENTED IN THE DIOCESE

[]—*Albertine Sisters* (Prov. of Krakow, Poland)—C.S.A.P.U.
[]—*Congregation of Mother of Carmel*—CMC.
[3710]—*Congregation of the Sisters of Saint Agnes*—C.S.A.
[]—*Dominican Sisters* (Vietnam)—O.P.
[1210]—*Franciscan Sisters of Chicago*—O.S.F.
[1450]—*Franciscan Sisters of the Sacred Heart*—O.S.F.
[]—*Lovers of the Holy Cross*—L.H.C.
[2710]—*Missionaries of Charity*—M.C.
[3230]—*Poor Handmaids of Jesus Christ*—P.H.J.C.
[]—*Sisters of Christian Community*—S.F.C.C.
[3780]—*Sisters of Saints Cyril and Methodius*—SS.C.M.
[1640]—*Sisters of St. Francis of Perpetual Adoration*—O.S.F.
[3930]—*Sisters of St. Joseph of the Third Order of St. Francis* (Immaculate Conception Prov.)—S.S.J.-T.O.S.F.

DIOCESAN CEMETERIES

HAMMOND. *Saint John-Saint Joseph*, 1547 167th St., Hammond, 46320. Tel: 219-844-9475; Fax: 219-844-3770; Email: mwelsh@garycathcems.org; Web: www.garycathcems.org. Rev. Roy T. Beeching, Dir. of Cemeteries, (Retired); Michael P. Welsh, COO. Employees 10

Saint Stanislaus, 1015 Greenwood Ave., Michigan City, 46360. Tel: 219-874-4310; Fax: 219-874-4310; Email: mwelsh@garycems.org. Michael P. Welsh, CEO

NECROLOGY

† Litot, Edward F., (Retired), Died May. 9, 2018

An asterisk (*) denotes an organization that has established tax-exempt status directly with the IRS and is not covered by the USCCB Group Ruling.

Diocese of Gaylord

(Dioecesis Gaylordensis)

Most Reverend

STEVEN J. RAICA, J.C.L., J.C.D.

Bishop of Gaylord; ordained October 14, 1978; appointed Bishop of Gaylord June 27, 2014; Episcopal ordination and installation August 28, 2014. *Diocesan Pastoral Center: 611 W. North St., Gaylord, MI 49735-8349.*

Diocesan Pastoral Center: 611 W. North St., Gaylord, MI 49735-8349. Tel: 989-732-5147; Fax: 989-705-3589.

Web: www.dioceseofgaylord.org

Email: ksmith@dioceseofgaylord.org

ESTABLISHED JULY 20, 1971.

Square Miles 11,171.

Comprises the following 21 Counties in the State of Michigan: Alcona, Alpena, Antrim, Benzie, Charlevoix, Cheboygan, Crawford, Emmet, Grand Traverse, Iosco, Kalkaska, Leelanau, Manistee, Missaukee, Montmorency, Ogemaw, Oscoda, Otsego, Presque Isle, Roscommon and Wexford.

For legal titles of parishes and diocesan institutions, consult the Chancery Office.

STATISTICAL OVERVIEW

Personnel	
Bishop	1
Priests: Diocesan Active in Diocese	41
Priests: Diocesan Active Outside Diocese	2
Priests: Retired, Sick or Absent	15
Number of Diocesan Priests	58
Religious Priests in Diocese	4
Total Priests in Diocese	62
Extern Priests in Diocese	15
Permanent Deacons in Diocese	18
Total Sisters	18
Parishes	
Parishes	75
With Resident Pastor:	
Resident Diocesan Priests	37
Resident Religious Priests	2
Without Resident Pastor:	
Administered by Priests	28
Administered by Deacons	1
Administered by Religious Women	3
Administered by Lay People	4
Professional Ministry Personnel:	
Sisters	5
Lay Ministers	52
Welfare	
Catholic Hospitals	1
Total Assisted	116,403
Residential Care of Children	2
Total Assisted	80
Day Care Centers	13
Total Assisted	484
Special Centers for Social Services	20
Total Assisted	35,478
Educational	
Diocesan Students in Other Seminaries	10
Total Seminarians	10
High Schools, Diocesan and Parish	4
Total Students	533
High Schools, Private	1
Total Students	21
Elementary Schools, Diocesan and Parish	15
Total Students	1,667
Catechesis/Religious Education:	
High School Students	650
Elementary Students	1,510
Total Students under Catholic Instruction	4,391
Teachers in the Diocese:	
Lay Teachers	270
Vital Statistics	
Receptions into the Church:	
Infant Baptism Totals	403
Minor Baptism Totals	60
Adult Baptism Totals	44
Received into Full Communion	71
First Communions	476
Confirmations	493
Marriages:	
Catholic	165
Interfaith	74
Total Marriages	239
Deaths	818
Total Catholic Population	47,870
Total Population	506,623

Former Bishops—Most Revs. EDMUND C. SZOKA, J.C.L., D.D., First Bishop of Gaylord; ord. June 5, 1954; cons. July 20, 1971; installed July 20, 1971; appt. Archbishop of Detroit March 28, 1981; installed May 17, 1981; named Cardinal Priest May 29, 1988; elevated June 28, 1988; Assigned to the Vatican, 1990; died Aug. 20, 2014; ROBERT J. ROSE, S.T.L., D.D., ord. Dec. 21, 1955; appt. Bishop of Gaylord Oct. 13, 1981; installed Dec. 6, 1981; transferred to Diocese of Grand Rapids July 11, 1989; installed Aug. 30, 1989; PATRICK R. COONEY, S.T.B., S.T.L., ord. Dec. 20, 1959; appt. Titular Bishop of Hodelm and Auxiliary Bishop of Detroit Dec. 3, 1982; cons. Jan. 27, 1983; appt. Bishop of Gaylord Nov. 21, 1989; installed Jan. 28, 1990; retired Oct. 7, 2009; died Oct. 15, 2012.; BERNARD A. HEBDA, J.C.L., J.D., ord. July 1, 1989; appt. Bishop of Gaylord Oct. 7, 2009; ord. Dec. 1, 2009; appt. Coadjutor Archbishop of Newark Sept. 24, 2013; installed Nov. 5, 2013; appt. Archbishop of St. Paul and Minneapolis March 24, 2016; installed May 13, 2016.

Diocesan Offices and Departments

Diocesan Pastoral Center—611 W. North St., Gaylord, 49735-8349. Tel: 989-732-5147; Fax: 989-705-3589. Office Hours: Mon.-Fri. 8-4:30All business should be directed to this office.

Members of the College of Consultors—Revs. CHARLES G. DONAJKOWSKI; ANTHONY M. CITRO; DONALD R. GEYMAN; MICHAEL S. JANOWSKI; Rev. Msgr. FRANCIS J. MURPHY, (Retired); Revs. JOSEPH MUSZKIEWICZ; DENNIS R. STILWELL; MATTHEW A. WIGTON.

Administrative Services, Secretariat for—KIM A. SMITH, Dir., 611 W. North St., Gaylord, 49735. Tel: 989-732-5147.

Audiovisual Resource Center—CANDACE NEFF, 611 W. North St., Gaylord, 49735. Tel: 989-732-5147.

Archivist—Rev. JOSEPH A. BLASKO, 611 W. North St., Gaylord, 49735. Tel: 989-732-5147.

Catholic Schools, Office of—611 W. North St., Gaylord, 49735. Tel: 989-732-5147. FRANK SANDER, Supt.

Communications, Secretariat for—CANDACE NEFF, Dir., 611 W. North St., Gaylord, 49735. Tel: 989-732-5147.

Council of Catholic Women, Diocesan—ANGELINE YARCH, Pres., 5848 M65 Hwy., Posen, 49776.

Cursillo—Rev. RAYMOND C. COTTER, Mailing Address: P.O. Box 95, Acme, 49610-0095.

Faith Development and Evangelization, Secretariat for—WAYNE WINTER, M.A., Dir., 611 W. North St., Gaylord, 49735-8349. Tel: 989-732-5147.

Finance Council, Diocesan—Most Rev. STEVEN J. RAICA, Bishop; Rev. DENNIS R. STILWELL; DONALD BARTOSH; Rev. MATTHEW A. WIGTON; STEPHEN BIEGEL; MARK ECKHOFF; STEVE HAJEK; Deacon BRENT H. HEMKER; JOEL KENDZORSKI; BRET KEEFE; KIM A. SMITH, Dir. Secretariat for Administrative Svcs.; RHONDA REYNOLDS, Parish Bookkeeping Specialist; TINA MAKAREWICZ, Stewardship Specialist.

Native American Apostolate—Sr. SUSAN GARDNER, O.P., Coord., St. Kateri Tekakwitha Parish, P.O. Box 369, Suttons Bay, 49682. Tel: 231-271-6651.

Knights of Columbus—JOEL KENDZORSKI, Diocesan Prog. Dir., 10425 County Rd. 451, P.O. Box 132, Hawks, 49743-0132. Tel: 989-766-2124.

Worship and Liturgical Formation, Secretariat for—BETH HICKS, Dir., 611 W. North St., Gaylord, 49735. Tel: 989-732-5147.

Marriage, Family Life and Respect Life—MARIE HAHNENBERG, Coord.; SETH PETERS, Coord., 611 W. North St., Gaylord, 49735. Tel: 517-732-5147.

Hispanic Apostolate—SILVIA CORTES-LOPEZ, 1026 Hannah, Ste. A, Traverse City, 49686. Tel: 231-929-4738.

Justice and Peace—Rev. WAYNE H. DZIEKAN, 611 W. North St., Gaylord, 49735. Tel: 989-732-5147.

Vicar for Clergy—Rev. DONALD R. GEYMAN, 611 W. North St., Gaylord, 49735. Tel: 989-732-5147.

Priests' Retirement Fund Board—Ex Officio Members: Most Rev. STEVEN J. RAICA, Bishop; Rev. DONALD R. GEYMAN; KIM A. SMITH; ROBERT T. WESTERMAN; TIMOTHY SCHAB; BRIAN BUCKINGHAM. Elected Members: Revs. ANTHONY M. CITRO; JAMES P. HAYDEN, (Retired); JOSEPH MUSZKIEWICZ; DUANE A. WACHOWIAK JR. Appointed Members: DONALD BARTOSH, Chm.; CAROL MROZEK.

Director of Vocations—Rev. MATTHEW A. WIGTON, Diocese of Gaylord, 611 W. North St., Gaylord, 49735. Tel: 989-732-5147.

Spiritual Formation for Deacons—Rev. JOSEPH P. GRAFF, Dir., 611 W. North St., Gaylord, 49735. Tel: 989-732-5147.

Tribunal Diocesan—Rev. DANIEL SMILANIC, Judicial Vicar; DR. JOHN AMOS, J.C.D., Dir. Tribunal Svcs. Defenders of the Bond: Revs. BENEDETTO J. PARIS; JOHN WILLIAM.

Judges—Revs. PETER O. EKE; MATTHEW A. FURGIUELE. Procurator-Advocate: MIRIAM STOLOQUE-HANDRICH, Notary, Inquiries may be made through the local pastors or directed to this office:, 611 W. North St., Gaylord, 49735. Tel: 989-732-5147.

Victim Assistance Coordinator—LARRY LACROSS, Tel: 989-705-9010.

CLERGY, PARISHES, MISSIONS AND PAROCHIAL SCHOOLS

CITY OF GAYLORD

(OTSEGO COUNTY), ST. MARY CATHEDRAL, [CEM]
606 N. Ohio Ave., 49735-1999. Tel: 989-732-5448; Email: parishoffice@stmarycathedral.org; Web: www.stmarycathedral.org. Revs. Matthew A. Wigton, Rector; Nicholas Cooper, Parochial Vicar; John William, Parochial Vicar.
Catechesis Religious Program—Students 267.

OUTSIDE THE CITY OF GAYLORD

ACME, GRAND TRAVERSE CO., CHRIST THE KING
3801 Shore Rd., Williamsburg, 49690.
Tel: 231-938-9214; Email: generalmail@christkingchurch.org. P.O. Box 95, Acme, 49610. Rev. Raymond C. Cotter.
See Grand Traverse Area Catholic School, Traverse City, under Interparochial Parish Schools located in the Institution section.
Catechesis Religious Program—Susan Noble, Dir. Faith Formation. Students 62.

AFTON, CHEBOYGAN CO., ST. MONICA, [CEM]
M-68 Hwy., Afton, 49705. P.O. Box 130, Onaway, 49765-0130. Tel: 989-733-6053; Email: parishoffice@stpaul-onaway.com. Rev. T. Patrick Maher.
Res.: 3856 Oak St., P.O. Box 130, Onaway, 49765.
Catechesis Religious Program—Pam Willey, D.R.E.

ALPENA, ALPENA CO.
1—ALL SAINTS, [JC]
817 Sable St., Alpena, 49707. Tel: 989-354-3019; Email: mkraft@alpenacatholics.org; Web: www.alpenacatholics.org. Revs. Joseph Muszkiewicz; Scott J. Lawler
Legal Title: Catholic Community of Alpena, St. Anne Catholic Parish, St. Bernard Catholic Parish, St. John the Baptist Catholic Parish, St. Mary Catholic Parish.
Catechesis Religious Program—Email: jbenson@alpenacatholics.org. Jacqueline Benson, D.R.E. Students 88.
2—ST. ANNE, Merged with St. Bernard, Alpena; St. Mary, Alpena & St. John the Baptist, Alpena to form All Saints, Alpena.
3—ST. BERNARD, [JC] Merged with St. John the Baptist, Alpena; St. Anne, Alpena & St. Mary, Alpena to form All Saints, Alpena.
4—ST. JOHN THE BAPTIST, Merged with St. Bernard, Alpena; St. Anne, Alpena & St. Mary, Alpena to form All Saints, Alpena.
5—ST. MARY, [JC] Merged with St. Bernard, Alpena; St. Anne, Alpena & St. John the Baptist, Alpena to form All Saints, Alpena.

ALVERNO, CHEBOYGAN CO., ST. FRANCIS OF ASSISI, Closed. For sacramental records contact St. Mary-St. Charles Parish, Cheboygan.

ATLANTA, MONTMORENCY CO., JESUS THE GOOD SHEPHERD
11483 County Rd. 487, Atlanta, 49709.
Tel: 989-742-4542; Email: staug.jtgs@src-milp.com. P.O. Box 216, Hillman, 49746. Rev. Michael P. Conner.
Church: 4521 County Rd. 491, Atlanta, 49709.
Catechesis Religious Program—Karen Landane, D.R.E.

BAY SHORE, EMMET CO., ST. FRANCIS SOLANUS, Closed. For inquiries for parish records contact the chancery.

BEAVER ISLAND, CHARLEVOIX CO., HOLY CROSS aka Holy Cross Catholic Church, [CEM]
37860 Kings Hwy., P.O. Box 145, Beaver Island, 49782. Tel: 231-448-2230; Email: jsiler1@mac.com. Revs. Dennis R. Stilwell, Admin.; James Siler, Parochial Vicar.
Catechesis Religious Program—Students 13.

BELLAIRE, ANTRIM CO., ST. LUKE
3088 M-88, Bellaire, 49615-0799. Tel: 231-533-8121; Email: stluke49615@gmail.com; Web: www.dioceseofgaylord.org/member-804/st.-luke-the-evangelist-157.html. P.O. Box 799, Bellaire, 49615-0799. Rev. Chester L. Collins.
Res.: 3078 S. M-88, P.O. Box 799, Bellaire, 49615-0799.
Catechesis Religious Program—Deb Haydell, D.R.E. Students 14.

BLACK RIVER, ALCONA CO., ST. GABRIEL, [CEM]
5570 N. Lake Shore Dr., Black River, 48721.
Tel: 989-471-5121; Email: stc-stg@stc-stg.org. 2188 W. Nicholson Hill Rd., Ossineke, 49766-9736. Rev. Robert H. Bissot, (Retired).
Catechesis Religious Program—Tel: 989-464-1959. Cathy MacFalda, D.R.E. Joined with St. Catherine, Ossineke. Students 0.

BOYNE CITY, CHARLEVOIX CO., ST. MATTHEW, [JC]
1303 Boyne Ave., Boyne City, 49712.
Tel: 231-582-7718; Email: parishoffice@jamcc.org; Web: jamcc.org. Patricia A. Furtaw, Pastoral Admin.
Catechesis Religious Program—Suzanne Dzwik, D.R.E. Students 15.

BOYNE FALLS, CHARLEVOIX CO., ST. AUGUSTINE, [CEM]
2347 Grove St., Boyne Falls, 49713.
Tel: 231-582-7718; Email: parishoffice@jamcc.org. 1303 Boyne Ave., Boyne City, 49712. Patricia A. Furtaw, Pastoral Admin.
Catechesis Religious Program—Students 15.

BURT LAKE, CHEBOYGAN CO., ASSUMPTION OF ST. MARY
3192 Indian Rd., Brutus, 49716. Tel: 231-627-2105; Email: monical@cprparishes.org. P.O. Box 40, Cheboygan, 49721. Rev. Duane A. Wachowiak Jr.
Res.: 118 N. D St., Cheboygan, 49721.

CADILLAC, WEXFORD CO., ST. ANN, [CEM]
800 W. 13th St., Cadillac, 49601-9281.
Tel: 231-775-2471; Email: ellenhovey@yahoo.com. Revs. Michael S. Janowski; Matthew John Cowan, Parochial Vicar.
Catechesis Religious Program—
Tel: 231-775-2471, Ext. 231; Email: geigerj@stanncadillac.org. Jennifer Geiger, D.R.E. Students 86.

CEDAR, LEELANAU CO., HOLY ROSARY, [CEM]
6982 S. Schomberg Rd., Cedar, 49621.
Tel: 231-228-5429; Email: holyrosarycedar@gmail.com. Revs. Donald L. Libby; Bradley Nursey, Parochial Vicar.
Catechesis Religious Program—Emily Hollabaugh, D.R.E. Students 93.

CHARLEVOIX, CHARLEVOIX CO., ST. MARY
1003 Bridge St., Charlevoix, 49720.
Fax: 231-547-6652; Email: mplude@stmaryschoolchx.com; Email: mjoy@stmaryschoolchx.com; Web: stmarycharlevoix.com. Rev. Peter T. Wigton.
Catechesis Religious Program—Mrs. Mary Plude, D.R.E. Students 58.

CHEBOYGAN, CHEBOYGAN CO., ST. MARY-ST. CHARLES, [JC]
120 N. D St., Cheboygan, 49721. Tel: 231-627-2105; Fax: 231-627-5362; Email: monical@cprparishes.org. P.O. Box 40, Cheboygan, 49721-0040. Rev. Duane A. Wachowiak Jr.
Catechesis Religious Program—Karen Derris, Dir. Ministries & Faith Formation. Students 58.

COPEMISH, MANISTEE CO., ST. RAPHAEL, [CEM]
18440 Cadillac Hwy., Copemish, 49625.
Tel: 231-889-4254; Email: stjosephonekama@gmail.com. P.O. Box 150, Onekama, 49675-0150. Rev. Ruben D. Munoz.
Church: M-115, Copemish, 49625.
Catechesis Religious Program—8380 Fifth St., Onekama, 49675. Tel: 231-590-3156. Sophie Engstrom, D.R.E.

CROSS VILLAGE, EMMET CO., HOLY CROSS, [CEM]
6624 N. Lake Shore Dr., Cross Village, 49723.
Tel: 231-526-2017; Email: office@holychildhoodchurch.org; Web: cclcparishes.org. Mailing Address & Res.: 150 W. Main St., Harbor Springs, 49740. Revs. James K. Gardiner, Admin., (Retired); Joseph A. Blasko, Parochial Vicar.

EAST JORDAN, CHARLEVOIX CO., ST. JOSEPH, [CEM]
207 Nichols, East Jordan, 49727. Tel: 231-536-2934; Email: stjoeschurch@att.net. P.O. Box 379, East Jordan, 49727-0379. Rev. Chester L. Collins.
Catechesis Religious Program—Barbara Kowal, D.R.E. Students 30.

EAST TAWAS, IOSCO CO.
1—HOLY FAMILY
516 W. Lincoln St., East Tawas, 48730.
Tel: 989-362-3162; Email: holyfamily@hf-sh.org; Web: hf-sh.org/holyfamily. Revs. Charles G. Donajkowski; Tyler A. Bischoff, Parochial Vicar.
Catechesis Religious Program—Tel: 989-739-9511; Email: rcopland@hf-sh.org. Richard J. Copland, D.R.E. Students 45.
2—ST. JOSEPH, Merged with Immaculate Heart of Mary, Tawas City to form Holy Family, East Tawas.

ELK RAPIDS, ANTRIM CO., SACRED HEART, [CEM]
143 Charles St., Elk Rapids, 49629.
Tel: 231-264-8087; Email: sacredheart@sacredheartelkrapids.org. Rev. Robert J. Zuchowski.
Catechesis Religious Program—Email: bbaldwin@sacredheartelkrapids.org. Brett Baldwin, Coord. Faith Formation/RCIA. Students 0.

ELMIRA, ANTRIM CO., ST. THOMAS AQUINAS, [CEM]
2567 Buell Rd., Elmira, 49730. 606 N. Ohio Ave., 49735. Tel: 989-732-5448; Email: jreynolds@stmarycathedral.org. Revs. Matthew A. Wigton; Nicholas Cooper, Parochial Vicar; John William, Parochial Vicar.
Res.: P.O. Box 128, Elmira, 49730.
Catechesis Religious Program—Students 3.

EMPIRE, LEELANAU CO., ST. PHILIP NERI, [CEM]
11411 LaCore, Empire, 49630. Tel: 231-326-5255; Email: stphilipneriempire@gmail.com; Web: www.stphilipneriempire.net. P.O. Box 257, Empire, 49630-0257. Rev. Zeljko J. Guberovic, Admin.
Catechesis Religious Program—Carolyn Ballmer, D.R.E. Students 35.

FIFE LAKE, GRAND TRAVERSE CO., ST. ALOYSIUS, [CEM]
403 E. Merritt St., Fife Lake, 49633.
Tel: 231-258-5021; Email: stmaryofthewoods@yahoo.com. 0438 County Rd. 612 N.E., Kalkaska, 49646. Rev. Norman Dickson, S.J., Admin.
Catechesis Religious Program—Robert Bowersox, O.F.S., D.R.E. Students 13.

FRANKFORT, BENZIE CO., ST. ANN aka St. Ann Catholic Church
508 Crystal Ave., Frankfort, 49635.
Tel: 231-352-4421; Email: stannoffice1@gmail.com; Web: saintanninfrankfort.org. P.O. Box 1168, Frankfort, 49635. Rev. Msgr. John F. Porter, Admin., (Retired).
Catechesis Religious Program—
Tel: 231-352-4421, Ext. 11; Email: stanneducation@gmail.com. Students 16.

GILLS PIER, LEELANAU CO., ST. WENCESLAUS, [CEM]
8500 E. Kolarik Rd., Suttons Bay, 49682.
Tel: 231-271-3574; Email: stwenceslausgp@gmail.com. Rev. Emmanuel Tizhe, Sacramental Min.; Deacon Martin Korson, Pastoral Admin.

GLENNIE, ALCONA CO., ST. FRANCIS OF ASSISI, Closed. For inquiries for parish records contact the chancery.

GOOD HART, EMMET CO., ST. IGNATIUS, [CEM]
101 N. Lamkin Rd., Good Hart, 49737. Mailing Address & Res.: 150 W. Main St., Harbor Springs, 49740. Tel: 231-526-2017; Fax: 231-526-9299; Email: office@holychildhoodchurch.org; Web: cclcparishes.org. Rev. James K. Gardiner, Admin., (Retired).

GRAYLING, CRAWFORD CO., ST. MARY
708 Peninsular Ave., Grayling, 49738.
Tel: 989-348-7657; Email: office@graylingstmary.org. 707 Spruce St., Grayling, 49738-1259. Rev. Gerard A. Hunko.
Catechesis Religious Program—Students 36.

HALE, IOSCO CO., ST. PIUS X
3901 N. M-65, Hale, 48739. Tel: 989-728-2278; Email: spxhale@gmail.com. P.O. Box 428, Hale, 48739-0428. Rev. Elias Chinzara, Admin.
Res.: P.O. Box 206, Whittemore, 48770.
Church: 3900 M-65, Hale, 48739.
Catechesis Religious Program—Deacon Brent Hemker, Dir. Ministry.

HANNAH, GRAND TRAVERSE CO., ST. MARY, [CEM]
2912 W. M 113, Kingsley, 49649. Tel: 231-263-5640; Email: jnewton@stmaryhannah.org; Web: www.stmaryhannah.org. Rev. Gerald C. Okoli, Admin.
Res.: 6955 Hannah Rd., Kingsley, 49649.
Tel: 231-263-2430; Email: frgokoli@gmail.com.
Catechesis Religious Program—Tel: 231-357-0105; Email: lm12weber@gmail.com. Liza Weber, D.R.E. Students 0.

HARBOR SPRINGS, EMMET CO., HOLY CHILDHOOD OF JESUS, [CEM]
150 W. Main St., Harbor Springs, 49740.
Tel: 231-526-2017; Email: office@holychildhoodchurch.org; Web: cclcparishes.org. Rev. James K. Gardiner, Admin., (Retired).
Catechesis Religious Program—Hope Evans, D.R.E. Students 56.

HARRIETTA, WEXFORD CO., ST. EDWARD
207 W. Gaston, Harrietta, 49638. Tel: 231-775-2471; Email: ellenhovey@yahoo.com. 800 W. 13th St., Cadillac, 49601. Revs. Michael S. Janowski; Matthew John Cowan, Parochial Vicar.
Catechesis Religious Program—Email: geigerj@stanncadillac.org. Jennifer Geiger, D.R.E.

HARRISVILLE, ALCONA CO., ST. ANNE, [CEM]
110 S. State St., Harrisville, 48740.
Tel: 989-724-6713; Fax: 989-724-5210; Email: stannechurch@sta-str.org. P.O. Box 345, Harrisville, 48740-0345. Rev. Robert H. Bissot, (Retired).
Catechesis Religious Program—Veronica Brown, D.R.E. Students 16.

HERRON, ALPENA CO., ST. ROSE OF LIMA
3433 Herron Rd., Herron, 49744. Tel: 989-379-4316; Email: strose@speedconnect.com. Revs. Joseph Muszkiewicz; Michael P. Conner, Sacramental Min.; Theresa M. Zbytowski, Lay Admin.
Catechesis Religious Program—Dianne Blissland, D.R.E. Students 6.

HIGGINS LAKE, ROSCOMMON CO., ST. HUBERT
7612 W. Higgins Lake Dr., Higgins Lake, 48627.
Tel: 989-821-5591; Email: jambert2012@gmail.com. P.O. Box 75, Higgins Lake, 48627-0075. Revs. Peter O. Eke; Bernard L. Tyler, Admin., (Retired).
Catechesis Religious Program—

HILLMAN, MONTMORENCY CO., ST. AUGUSTINE, [CEM]
24138 Veteran's Memorial Hwy., Hillman, 49746.
Tel: 989-742-4542; Email: staug.jtgs@src-milp.com. P.O. Box 216, Hillman, 49746-0216. Rev. Michael P. Conner.
Catechesis Religious Program—Karen Landane, D.R.E.

HOUGHTON LAKE, ROSCOMMON CO., ST. JAMES
7612 W. Higgins Lake Dr., P.O. Box 75, Higgins Lake, 48627-0075. Tel: 989-821-5591; Email: jambert2012@gmail.com. Revs. Peter O. Eke; Bernard L. Tyler, Admin., (Retired).

INDIAN RIVER, CHEBOYGAN CO., CROSS IN THE WOODS

CATHOLIC SHRINE, [CEM]
7078 M-68 Hwy., Indian River, 49749.
Tel: 231-238-8973; Email: nationalshrine@crossinthewoods.com; Web: www.crossinthewoods.com. Revs. Michael Haney, O.F.M.; Vernon Olmer, O.F.M., Parochial Vicar.
Catechesis Religious Program—Indian River, 49749. Students 30.

KALKASKA, KALKASKA CO., ST. MARY OF THE WOODS, [CEM]
0438 County Rd. 612, Kalkaska, 49646.
Tel: 231-258-5021; Email: stmaryofthewoods@yahoo.com. Rev. Norman Dickson, S.J., Admin.
Catechesis Religious Program—Robert Bowersox, O.F.S., D.R.E. Students 51.

KLACKING CREEK, HOLY FAMILY, [CEM]
402 W. Peters Rd., West Branch, 48661.
Tel: 989-345-0064, Ext. 302; Email: holyfamily.klackingcreek@gmail.com. 961 W. Houghton Ave., West Branch, 48661. Rev. Emmanual Finbarr, Admin.
Catechesis Religious Program—Email: denemyjma@gmail.com. Joan Denemy, D.R.E. Joined with St. Joseph, West Branch. Students 0.

LAKE CITY, MISSAUKEE CO., ST. STEPHEN
506 W. Union St., Lake City, 49651.
Tel: 231-839-2121; Email: ststephenlakecity@gmail; Web: ststephenlake.com. P.O. Box 379, Lake City, 49651-0379. Revs. Michael S. Janowski; Matthew John Cowan, Parochial Vicar.
Catechesis Religious Program—Patricia Crane, Dir. Adult Ed.; Trina Scott, Faith Formation Dir. Students 34.

LAKE LEELANAU, LEELANAU CO., ST. MARY, [CEM]
307 S. St. Mary St., P.O. Box 340, Lake Leelanau, 49653. Tel: 231-256-9676; Fax: 231-256-7812; Email: mkuznicki@stmarysll.org; Web: www.stmaryparishll.org. Rev. Bryan W. Medlin, Admin.
Church: 403 S. St. Mary St., Lake Leelanau, 49653.
Catechesis Religious Program—303 S. St. Mary St., P.O. Box 340, Lake Leelanau, 49653. Email: jthompson@stmarysll.org. Jude Thompson, D.R.E. Students 22.

LARKS LAKE, EMMET CO., ST. NICHOLAS, [CEM]
1987 Zulski Rd., Pellston, 49769. Tel: 231-526-2017; Email: office@holychildhoodchurch.org; Web: cclcparishes.org. 150 W. Main St., Harbor Springs, 49740. Rev. James K. Gardiner, Admin., (Retired).
Catechesis Religious Program—

LEWISTON, MONTMORENCY CO., ST. FRANCIS OF ASSISI, [CEM]
4086 Salling Ave., Lewiston, 49756.
Tel: 989-786-2235; Email: stfrancisassisi@frontier.com; Web: stfrancislewiston.org. P.O. Box 182, Lewiston, 49756-0182. Rev. Alfred M. Pillarelli, Admin.; Deacon Arthur LoVetere; Cathy Grachal, Music Min.
Church: 3060 Casey St., Lewiston, 49756.
Catechesis Religious Program—
Tel: 989-786-2235, Ext. 207; Email: stfrancismklein@gmail.com. Megan Klein, D.R.E. St. Francis Faith Formation (K-5) and St. Francis Youth Group (6-12th). Students 35.

MACKINAW CITY, EMMET CO., ST. ANTHONY OF PADUA, [CEM]
600 W. Central Ave., Mackinaw City, 49701.
Tel: 231-436-5561; Email: chrisop@sbcglobal.net. P.O. Box 460, Mackinaw City, 49701-0460. Sr. Chris Herald, O.P., Pastoral Admin.
Catechesis Religious Program—Students 4.

MANCELONA, ANTRIM CO., ST. ANTHONY OF PADUA, [CEM]
209 N. Jefferson St., Mancelona, 49659-0677.
Tel: 231-587-8401; Email: st.anthony1@charter.net. P.O. Box 677, Mancelona, 49659-0677. Rev. Chester L. Collins.

MANISTEE, MANISTEE CO.
1—DIVINE MERCY PARISH, [JC]
254 Sixth St., Manistee, 49660. Tel: 231-723-2619; Fax: 231-723-6827; Email: parish.office@divinemercymanistee.org; Web: www.divinemercymanistee.org. Revs. Zeljko J. Guberovic; Pablo Martinez, Parochial Vicar; Lawrence J. Sergott, Parochial Vicar.
Catechesis Religious Program—Email: danielat@divinemercymanistee.org. Daniela Thomas, D.R.E. Students 51.
2—GUARDIAN ANGELS, Merged with St. Joseph, Manistee & St. Mary of Mt. Carmel Shrine, Manistee to form Divine Mercy Parish, Manistee.
3—ST. JOSEPH, [JC] Merged with Guardian Angels, Manistee & St. Mary of Mt. Carmel Shrine, Manistee to form Divine Mercy Parish, Manistee.
4—ST. MARY OF MT. CARMEL SHRINE, [JC] Merged with Guardian Angels, Manistee & St. Joseph, Manistee to form Divine Mercy Parish, Manistee.

MANTON, WEXFORD CO., ST. THERESA
9475 14 & 1/4 Rd., Manton, 49663. P.O. Box 379, Lake City, 49651-0379. Tel: 231-839-2121; Email: ststephenlakecity@gmail.com; Web: www.ststephenlakecity.com. Revs. Michael S. Janowski; Matthew John Cowan, Parochial Vicar.

MAPLE CITY, LEELANAU CO., ST. RITA-ST. JOSEPH
8707 Hill St., Maple City, 49664. Tel: 231-326-5255; Fax: 231-326-5839; Email: stphilipneriempire@gmail.com. P.O. Box 75, Maple City, 49664-0075. Rev. Zeljko J. Guberovic, Admin.

MAPLETON, GRAND TRAVERSE CO., ST. JOSEPH, [CEM]
Mailing Address: 12675 Center Rd., Traverse City, 49686. Tel: 231-421-7310; Email: pastor@stjosephtc.org; Email: businessmanager@stjosephtc.org; Web: stjosephtc.org. Rev. James M. Bearss.
Catechesis Religious Program—Mary P. Mulvany, D.R.E. Students 50.

MCBAIN, MISSAUKEE CO., ST. RITA, Closed. For inquiries for parish records contact the chancery.

METZ, PRESQUE ISLE CO., ST. DOMINIC, [CEM]
9269 County Rd. 441, Posen, 49776.
Tel: 989-766-2694; Email: st_dominic_metz@i2k.com. Rev. Arthur F. Duchnowicz.
Catechesis Religious Program—Students 2.

MIKADO, ALOCONA CO., ST. RAPHAEL, [CEM]
2531 E. F-30, Mikado, 48740. P.O. Box 345, Harrisville, 48740-0345. Tel: 989-724-6713; Fax: 989-724-5210; Email: stannechurch@sta-str.org. Rev. Robert H. Bissot, (Retired).
Catechesis Religious Program—Ruth Johnson, D.R.E. Students 1.

MIO, OSCODA CO., ST. MARY
100 Deyarmond St., Mio, 48647. Tel: 989-826-5509; Email: stmarymio@m33access.com. P.O. Box 189, Mio, 48647-0189. Rev. Santiago M. Hoyumpa.
Catechesis Religious Program—Students 20.

NORTHPORT, LEELANAU CO., ST. GERTRUDE
701 Warren, Northport, 49670. Tel: 231-271-3744; Email: mary@stmichaelsb.com. P.O. Box 9, Suttons Bay, 49682-0009. Rev. Leonard Paul, Admin., (Retired).
Catechesis Religious Program— (Combined with St. Michael, Suttons Bay) 315 Broadway, Suttons Bay, 49682.

ONAWAY, PRESQUE ISLE CO., ST. PAUL, [CEM]
28011 Washington Ave., Onaway, 49765.
Tel: 989-733-6053; Fax: 989-733-2848; Email: parishoffice@stpaul-onaway.com; Web: stpaul-onaway.com. P.O. Box 130, Onaway, 49765-0130. Rev. T. Patrick Maher.
Office, Res. & Church: 3856 Oak St., P.O. Box 130, Onaway, 49765.
Catechesis Religious Program—Students 19.

ONEKAMA, MANISTEE CO., ST. JOSEPH, [CEM]
8380 Fifth St., Onekama, 49675. Tel: 231-889-4254; Email: stjosephonekama@gmail.com. P.O. Box 150, Onekama, 49675-0150. Rev. Ruben D. Munoz.
Catechesis Religious Program—Tel: 231-590-3156. Sophie Engstrom, D.R.E. Students 15.

OSCODA, IOSCO CO., SACRED HEART, [CEM]
5300 N. U.S.-23, Oscoda, 48750. Tel: 989-739-9511; Email: sacredheart@hf-sh.org; Web: www.hf-sh.org. Revs. Charles G. Donajkowski; Tyler A. Bischoff, Parochial Vicar.
Catechesis Religious Program—Email: rcopland@hf-sh.org. Richard J. Copland, D.R.E. Students 10.

OSSINEKE, ALPENA CO., ST. CATHERINE, [CEM]
2188 W. Nicholson Hill Rd., Ossineke, 49766-9736. Tel: 989-471-5121; Email: stc-stg@stc-stg.org. Rev. Robert H. Bissot, (Retired).
Catechesis Religious Program—Tel: 989-464-1959. Cathy MacFalda, D.R.E. Students 30.

PELLSTON, EMMET CO., ST. CLEMENT, [CEM]
202 N. Maple, Pellston, 49769. Tel: 231-627-2105; Email: monical@cprparishes.org. P.O. Box 40, Cheboygan, 49721-0040. Rev. Duane A. Wachowiak Jr.
Res.: 118 N. D St., Cheboygan, 49721.
Catechesis Religious Program—Students 3.

PESHAWBESTOWN, LEELANAU CO., SAINT KATERI TEKAKWITHA
2753 N. West Bay Shore Dr., Suttons Bay, 49682.
Tel: 231-271-6651, Ext. 0; Email: slg55us25@yahoo.com. P.O. Box 369, Suttons Bay, 49682-0369. Sr. Susan Gardner, O.P., Pastoral Admin.
2690 N. West Bay Shore Dr., Suttons Bay, 49682.

PETOSKEY, EMMET CO., ST. FRANCIS XAVIER, [CEM]
513 Howard St., Petoskey, 49770.
Tel: 231-347-4133, Ext. 410; Email: judymkrussell@gmail.com. Rev. Dennis R. Stilwell.
School—St. Francis Xavier School, (Grades K-8), 414 Michigan St., Petoskey, 49770. Tel: 231-347-3651; Fax: 231-348-6475; Email: adobrowolski@petoskeysfx.org. Mr. Adam Dobrowolski, Prin. Lay Teachers 18; Students 215.
Catechesis Religious Program—Tel: 231-347-2681; Email: petoskeysfx@gmail.com. Students 85.

POSEN, PRESQUE ISLE CO., ST. CASIMIR, [CEM]
10075 M-65 N., Posen, 49776. Tel: 989-766-2660; Email: stcasimir10075@gmail.com. P.O. Box 217, Posen, 49776-0217. Rev. Arthur F. Duchnowicz.
Catechesis Religious Program—Mary Hentkowski, D.R.E. Students 70.

PRAGA, ANTRIM CO., ST. JOHN NEPOMUCENE, [CEM]
3804 St. John's Rd., East Jordan, 49727.
Tel: 231-582-7718; Email: parishoffice@jamcc.org; Web: www.jamcc.org. 1303 Boyne Ave., Boyne City, 49712-8920. Patricia A. Furtaw, Pastoral Admin.
Catechesis Religious Program—

PRUDENVILLE, ROSCOMMON CO., OUR LADY OF THE LAKE
1037 W. Houghton Lake Dr., Prudenville, 48651.
Tel: 989-366-5533; Tel: 989-366-5592; Email: ollsc@ollrcs.org; Web: ollrcs.org. P.O. Box 800, Prudenville, 48651-0800. Rev. Peter O. Eke.
Catechesis Religious Program—Email: ollsc@ollrcs.org. Tracey Haggart, D.R.E. Students 51.

RIGGSVILLE, CHEBOYGAN CO., SACRED HEART
4989 Polish Line Rd., Cheboygan, 49721.
Tel: 231-627-2105; Email: monical@cprparishes.org. P.O. Box 40, Cheboygan, 49721-0040. Rev. Duane A. Wachowiak Jr.
Catechesis Religious Program— (Joined with St. Mary - St. Charles, Cheboygan) Karen Derris, D.R.E.

ROGERS CITY, PRESQUE ISLE CO., ST. IGNATIUS, [CEM]
585 S. Third St., Rogers City, 49779.
Tel: 989-734-2753; Email: parishoffice@stignatiuscs.org; Web: www.stignatiusrc.org. Rev. Rolando Silva.
Catechesis Religious Program—Tel: 989-734-3443. Students 21.

ROSCOMMON, ROSCOMMON CO., ST. MICHAEL
104 N. 6th St., Roscommon, 48653.
Tel: 989-275-5212; Fax: 989-275-9020; Email: smcc@stmichaelsrosco.org. P.O. Box 9, Roscommon, 48653-0009. Rev. Gerard A. Hunko.
Catechesis Religious Program—Email: smym@stmichaelrosco.org. Deborah Harris, D.R.E. Students 60.

ST. HELEN, ROSCOMMON CO., ST. HELEN
737 N. St. Helen Rd., St. Helen, 48656.
Tel: 989-389-4959; Email: St.helen@sbcglobal.net. P.O. Box 318, Saint Helen, 48656-0318. Rev. Wayne H. Dziekan, Canonical Pastor; Sr. Barbara Matievich, O.P., Pastoral Admin.

SKIDWAY LAKE, OGEMAW CO., ST. STEPHEN KING OF HUNGARY
2811 E. Greenwood Rd., Prescott, 48756.
Tel: 989-873-3340; Email: office@ststephenofhungary.org. Rev. Elias Chinzara, Admin.
Catechesis Religious Program—

SUTTONS BAY, LEELANAU CO., ST. MICHAEL THE ARCHANGEL, [CEM]
104 S. Elm St., Suttons Bay, 49682.
Tel: 231-271-3744; Email: mary@stmichaelsb.com. P.O. Box 9, Suttons Bay, 49682-0009. Rev. Leonard Paul, Admin., (Retired).
Catechesis Religious Program—Mary Mills, D.R.E. Students 6.

TAWAS CITY, IOSCO CO., IMMACULATE HEART OF MARY, Merged with St. Joseph, East Tawas to form Holy Family, East Tawas.

TRAVERSE CITY, GRAND TRAVERSE CO.
1—ST. FRANCIS OF ASSISI
1025 S. Union St., Traverse City, 49684.
Tel: 231-947-4620; Email: jim@sfparish.org. Revs. Donald R. Geyman; Benjamin Rexroat, Parochial Vicar.
Catechesis Religious Program—Email: cheryl@sfparish.org; Email: jim@sfparish.org. Cheryl A. Lee, RCIA Coord. & Youth Min.; Jim Belden, K-5 Faith Formation. Students 115.
2—IMMACULATE CONCEPTION
308 N. Cedar St., Traverse City, 49684.
Tel: 231-946-4211; Email: office@immaculatetc.org. Revs. Anthony M. Citro; James P. Hayden, Sacramental Min., (Retired); Christopher A. Jarvis, Parochial Vicar; Deacon Jude F. Younker.
Res.: 720 W. Second, Traverse City, 49684.
Catechesis Religious Program—Kammie Richardson, D.R.E. Students 89.
3—ST. PATRICK
630 W. Silver Lake Rd. S., Traverse City, 49685.
Tel: 231-913-4633; Email: stpattc@stpatricktc.org. Rev. Gregory P. McCallum.
Catechesis Religious Program—Students 81.

VANDERBILT, OTSEGO CO., HOLY REDEEMER
8075 Lincoln St., Vanderbilt, 49795.
Tel: 989-732-5448; Email: parishoffice@stmarycathedral.org. Revs. Matthew A. Wigton; Nicholas Cooper, Parochial Vicar; John William, Parochial Vicar.
Res. & Mailing: 606 N. Ohio Ave., 49735-1999. Email: jreynolds@stmarycathedral.org.
Catechesis Religious Program—Students 26.

WEST BRANCH, OGEMAW CO., ST. JOSEPH, [CEM]
907 W. Houghton Ave., West Branch, 48661.
Tel: 989-345-0064; Fax: 989-345-8757; Email: pc.stjoseph@gmail.com. Mailing Address: 961 W. Houghton Ave., West Branch, 48661. Rev. Emmanual Finbarr, Admin.
School—St. Joseph School, (Grades PreSchool-8), 935 W. Houghton Ave., West Branch, 48661.
Tel: 989-345-0220; Fax: 989-345-3030; Email: dwalby@wbstjoseph.com. David Walby, Prin.; Traci

Hintz, Librarian. Clergy 1; Lay Teachers 6; Students 91.

Catechesis Religious Program—Email: denemyjma@gmail.com. Joan Denemy, D.R.E. Students 26.

WHITTEMORE, IOSCO CO., ST. JAMES aka St. James Catholic Church, [CEM]
202 E. Sherman St., Whittemore, 48770.
Tel: 989-756-2591; Fax: 989-756-3255; Email: stjames206@yahoo.com. P.O. Box 206, Whittemore, 48770-0206. Rev. Elias Chinzara, Admin.
Church: 208 E. Sherman, Whittemore, 48770.

Retired:
Rev. Msgrs.—
Brucksch, James L., (Retired), 10208 Tennessee St., Oscoda, 48750
Murphy, Francis J., (Retired), 712 Pheasant Blvd., Cadillac, 49601
Revs.—
Bereda, Stanislaw J., (Retired), 1180 Barepoint Rd., Alpena, 49707
Bissot, Robert H., (Retired), 2188 Nicholson Hill Rd., Ossineke, 49766
Boks, Lawrence E., (Retired), 5853 Nancy Ct., Tawas City, 48763
Doherty, James M., (Retired), Hillside Village, 305 W. Main St. #214, Harbor Springs, 49740
Gardiner, James K., (Retired), P.O. Box 911, Indian River, 49749-0911
Greene, John C., (Retired)
Hayden, James P., (Retired), 13071 Beechwood Dr., Charlevoix, 49720
Ladd, John O., (Retired), 3069 E. Snover Rd., Mayville, 48744
Lipscomb, William W., (Retired), 6073 Dover Ln., Traverse City, 49684
McCracken, John E., (Retired), 1003 Bowersox Dr., Lady Lake, FL 32159
Megge, Paul, (Retired), 220 Clay St., Cheboygan, 49721
Nalley, Robert W., (Retired), 11749 Harbor Ln., Belleville, 48111
Reitz, Joseph A., (Retired), St. Ann's Home, 2161 Leonard St. NW, Grand Rapids, 449504.

Permanent Deacons:
Bousamra, Thomas, (Retired)
Duggan, Dennis, (Retired), (Outside of Diocese)
Endres, Kevin L., Christ the King, Acme; Grand Traverse Area Catholic Schools
Falicki, John, (Outside of Diocese)
Fifer, Paul, St. Francis Xavier, Petoskey
Friend, Harry, St. Philip, Empire
Hemker, Brent H., St. Pius X, Hale; St. Stephen, Skidway Lake; St. James, Whittemore
Hoenscheid, Rene, St. Patrick, Traverse City
Kopasz, Frank P., St. Ann, Cadillac; St. Stephen, Lake City; St. Theresa, Manton; St. Edward, Harrietta
Korson, Martin P., St. Wenceslaus, Gills Pier
Krupka, Jim, Immaculate Conception, Traverse City
Landane, Scott J., St. Ignatius, Rogers City
LoVetere, Arthur, Jesus the Good Shepherd, Atlanta
Painter, Glen, Holy Family, Klacking Creek
Riley, Charles, St. Francis of Assisi, Traverse City
Rowe, Ronald, St. Anthony of Padua, Mancelona
Wendell, Max, St. Philip Neri, Empire
Wigton, Douglas, Holy Rosary, Cedar
Younker, Jude F., Immaculate Conception, Traverse City.

INSTITUTIONS LOCATED IN DIOCESE

[A] INTERPAROCHIAL SCHOOLS

MANISTEE. *Manistee Catholic Central School*, (Grades PreK-12), 1200 U.S. 31 S., Manistee, 49660.
Tel: 231-723-2529; Fax: 231-723-0669; Email: jallen@sabers.org; Web: www.sabers.org. Jason Allen, Prin.; Mrs. Rachel Henderson, Academic Counselor. Clergy 3; Lay Teachers 12; Students 173; Clergy / Religious Teachers 1.

TRAVERSE CITY. *St. Elizabeth Ann Seton Middle School*, (Grades 6-8), 1601 Three Mile Rd. N., Traverse City, 49696. Tel: 231-932-4810;
Fax: 231-932-4814; Email: mlundberg@gtacs.org; Web: www.gtacs.org. Carl Scholten, Prin.; Molly Jarema, Librarian. Lay Teachers 19; Students 247.

St. Francis High School, 123 E. 11th St., Traverse City, 49684. Tel: 231-946-8038; Fax: 231-946-1878; Email: echittle@gtacs.org; Web: www.gtacs.org. Erick Chittle, Prin.; Vanessa Tucker, Librarian. Lay Teachers 22; Students 357.

Grand Traverse Area Catholic Schools, (Grades PreK-12), 123 E. 11th St., Traverse City, 49684.
Tel: 231-946-8100; Fax: 231-946-1878; Email: emulvany@gtacs.org; Web: www.gtacs.org. Michael R. Buell, Supt.; Erick Chittle, Prin.; Vanessa Tucker, Librarian. Clergy 2; Lay Teachers 70; Students 1,003; Clergy / Religious Teachers 1.

Holy Angels Elementary, (Grades PreSchool-5), 130 E. 10th St., Traverse City, 49684.
Tel: 231-946-5961; Fax: 231-946-1878; Email: emulvany@gtacs.org; Web: www.gtacs.org. Jessica Lesinski, Prin.; Mrs. Maureen DeYoung, Vice Prin.; Kathy Hiatt, Librarian; Margaret Wilson, Librarian. Clergy 1; Lay Teachers 26; Students 547; Clergy / Religious Teachers 1.

Immaculate Conception Elementary School, (Grades 4-5), Merged with Holy Angels Elementary School temporarily while the new Immaculate Conception Elementary school is being built.

[B] PAROCHIAL SCHOOLS

GAYLORD. *St. Mary Cathedral School*, (Grades PreSchool-12), 321 N. Otsego Ave., 49735.
Tel: 989-732-5801; Fax: 989-732-2085; Email: nhatch@gaylordstmary.org. Nicole M. Hatch, Prin., Email: nhatch@gaylordstmary.org. Lay Teachers 22; Students 310.

ALPENA. *All Saints Catholic School*, (Grades PreK-7), 500 N. Second Ave., Alpena, 49707.
Tel: 989-354-4911; Fax: 989-354-3752; Email: adietz@alpenaallsaints.org; Web: alpenaallsaints.org. Alecia Dietz, Prin. Lay Teachers 9; Preschool 47; Students 124; Clergy / Religious Teachers 1.

CADILLAC. *St. Ann Elementary*, (Grades PreK-6), 800 W. 13th, Cadillac, 49601. Tel: 231-775-1301;
Fax: 231-775-5433; Web: www.stanncadillac.org. Robert Kellogg, Prin. Lay Teachers 8; Preschool 38; Students 163.

CHARLEVOIX. *St. Mary Elementary*, (Grades PreK-8), 1005 Bridge St., Charlevoix, 49720.
Tel: 231-547-9441; Fax: 231-547-6658; Email: mjoy@stmaryschoolchx.com; Email: kdvoracek@stmaryschoolchx.com; Web: www.stmaryschoolcharlevoix.com. Kathleen Dvoracek, Prin.; Monica Mailloux, Librarian. Lay Teachers 8; Preschool 21; Students 63.

CHEBOYGAN. *Bishop Baraga Catholic School*, (Grades PreK-7), 623 W. Lincoln Ave., Cheboygan, 49721.
Tel: 231-627-5608; Fax: 231-627-6048; Email: klablance@bishopbaraga.com; Web: www.bishopbaraga.com. Kitty LaBlance, Prin.; Marian North, Librarian. Clergy 1; Lay Teachers 10; Students 156.

EAST TAWAS. *Holy Family Elementary School*, (Grades K-7), 411 N. Wilkinson, East Tawas, 48730.
Tel: 989-362-5651; Fax: 989-362-6916; Email: principal@hfs-tawas.org. Tim St. Aubin, Prin. Lay Teachers 6; Students 74.

KINGSLEY. *St. Mary - Hannah School*, (Grades PreK-8), 2912 W. M-113, Kingsley, 49649.
Tel: 231-263-5288; Fax: 231-263-5288; Email: rgebhard@stmaryhannah.org; Web: www.stmaryhannah.org. Richard Gebhard, Prin. Lay Teachers 4; Students 20.

LAKE LEELANAU. *St. Mary School*, (Grades PreK-12), 303 S. St. Mary St., Lake Leelanau, 49653.
Tel: 231-256-9636; Fax: 231-256-7239; Email: info@stmarysll.org; Web: www.stmarysll.org. P.O. Box 340, Lake Leelanau, 49653. Megan Glynn, Prin.; Donna Allington, Librarian. Lay Teachers 19; Preschool 15; Students 208.

PRUDENVILLE. *Our Lady of the Lake*, (Grades PreK-8), 1039 W. Houghton Lake Dr., Prudenville, 48651.
Tel: 989-366-5592; Fax: 989-366-1348; Email: ollsc@ollccs.org; Web: www.ollrcs.org. P.O. Box 800, Prudenville, 48651. Elizabeth Kindermann, Prin. Lay Teachers 6; Students 63.

ROGERS CITY. *St. Ignatius*, (Grades K-8), 545 S. Third St., Rogers City, 49779. Tel: 989-734-3443;
Fax: 989-734-3443; Email: arabeau@stignatiuscs.org; Web: www.stignatiusparishschool.com. Amy Rabeau, Prin. Lay Teachers 6; Students 69.

[C] CHILD CARE FACILITIES

TRAVERSE CITY. *Holy Cross Services - Northern Michigan CB*, 1305 E. 8th St., Ste. B, Traverse City, 49686. Tel: 231-922-9664; Tel: 989-596-3557; Fax: 231-922-9675; Email: cdevaux@hccsnet.org; Web: www.HolyCrossServices.org. 1013 N. River Rd., Saginaw, 48609. Sharon Berkobien, CEO. (Part of HCS, Diocese of Lansing) This program provides Specialized Foster Care Services for boys and girls. Alpena falls under Traverse City Contract. Clergy 3; Students 80; Youths - Traverse City 61; Youths - Alpena 19.

[D] GENERAL HOSPITALS

TAWAS CITY. *Ascension St. Joseph Hospital*, 200 Hemlock Rd., Tawas City, 48764-0659.
Tel: 989-362-9301; Fax: 989-362-7277; Web: healthcare.ascension.org/locations/michigan/tawas-city-saint-joseph-health-system. P.O. Box 659, Tawas City, 48764-0659. Christopher Palazzolo, CEO; Ann M. Balfour, Chief Admin. Officer; Andy Kruse, Regl. Lead; Thomas Anderson, Chap. Associated with Ascension Health, St. Louis, MO. Bed Capacity 47; Tot Asst. Annually 116,403; Total Staff 329.

[E] CONVENTS AND RESIDENCES FOR SISTERS

CONWAY. *Sacramentine Monastery of Perpetual Adoration*, 2798 U.S. 31 N., Conway, 49722.
Tel: 231-347-0447; Email: augustinecenter@gmail.com. P.O. Box 86, Conway, 49722-0086. Sr. Mary Rosalie Smith, O.S.S., Prioress. Sacramentine Sisters 1.

TRAVERSE CITY. *Infant Jesus of Prague Monastery* aka Carmelite Monastery, 3501 Silver Lake Rd., Traverse City, 49684-8949. Tel: 231-946-4960;
Fax: 231-947-7729; Email: tccarmel@charter.net; Web: www.carmeloftraversecity.org. Mother Mary of Jesus Markey, O.C.D., Prioress. Carmelite Nuns 4.

[F] RETREAT CENTERS AND CAMPS

GAYLORD. *Camp Sancta Maria*, 5361 W. M-32, 49735.
Tel: 231-546-3878; Tel: 248-822-8199;
Fax: 866-875-1933; Email: office@campsanctamaria.org; Web: www.campsanctamaria.org. P.O. Box 338, 49734. Mr. John David Kuhar, Exec. Residential summer camp for kids age 8-17, single gender. Total Staff 59; Campers 614.

CONWAY. *Augustine Center*, 2798 U.S. 31 N., Conway, 49722. Tel: 231-347-3657; Fax: 231-347-9502; Email: augustinecenter@gmail.com. P.O. Box 84, Conway, 49722-0084. Adam Chittle, Dir.

[G] CATHOLIC SOCIAL SERVICE AGENCIES

GAYLORD. *Catholic Human Services*, 1000 Hastings St., Traverse City, 49686. Tel: 231-947-8110; Email: chstraverse@catholichumanservices.org; Web: www.catholichumanservices.org. Edward Cieslinski, Pres. Tot Asst. Annually 35,650; Total Staff 80.
Area Offices:
154 S. Ripley Blvd., Alpena, 49707.
Tel: 989-356-6385; Fax: 989-356-4909; Email: chsalpena@catholichumanservices.org; Web: www.catholichumanservices.org. Kara Steinke, Admin.
421 S. Mitchell, Cadillac, 49601. Tel: 231-775-6581;
Fax: 231-775-5421; Email: chscadillac@catholichumanservices.org; Web: www.catholichumanservices.org. Edward Cieslinski, Admin.
829 W. Main St., Ste. C-5, 49735. Tel: 989-732-6761;
Fax: 989-732-6763; Email: chsgaylord@catholichumanservices.org; Web: www.catholichumanservices.org. Kara Steinke, Admin.
1000 Hastings St., Traverse City, 49686.
Tel: 231-947-8110; Fax: 231-947-3522; Email: chstraverse@catholichumanservices.org; Web: www.catholichumanservices.org. Edward Cieslinski, Admin.

[H] MISCELLANEOUS

GAYLORD. *Northern Michigan Catholic Foundation, Inc.*, 311 E. Front St., Traverse City, 49686.
Tel: 231-922-9070; Email: christie@nmcatholicfoundation.org; Web: nmcatholicfoundation.org. Joel Myler, Chm.; Tim Clulo, Dir.; John Puetz, Treas.; Stefan Scholl.

ALPENA. *Madonna House Apostolate*, Madonna House, 114 S. 5th Ave., Alpena, 49707-2511.
Tel: 989-354-4073; Email: rhoran@hotmail.com. Rosemary Horan, Dir.

HARBOR SPRINGS. *Christ Child Society of Northern Michigan, Inc.*, 192 W. Third Street, Harbor Springs, 49740. Tel: 231-526-7271; Email: dknachtrab@christchildsocietynorthernmichigan.org. P.O. Box 132, Harbor Springs, 49740-0132. Kim Jones, Pres.

JOHANNESBURG. *Stella Maris Hermitage*, 19466 Black River Rd., Johannesburg, 49751. Tel: 989-350-5495; Email: rwkropf@gmail.com; Web: www.stellamar.net. P.O. Box 315, Johannesburg, 49751-0315. Rev. Richard Kropf.

TRAVERSE CITY. **Baraga Broadcasting, Inc.* aka Baraga Radio, 1020 Hastings St., Ste. 101, Traverse City, 49686-3457. Tel: 844-238-8508;
Fax: 231-238-8500; Email: steve@baragaradio.com; Email: kay@baragaradio.com; Email: nick@baragaradio.com; Web: www.baragaradio.com. Mr. Steve Gregosky, Exec. Baraga Radio Network.

**Northern Michigan Catholic Foundation*, 311 E. Front St., Traverse City, 49684.

Respect Life of the Diocese of Gaylord, Michigan, 4020 Copper View, Ste. 129, Traverse City, 49684. Tel: 231-944-6937; Email: respectlifegaylord@gmail.com; Web: www.respectlifegaylord.com. Doug Wigton, Registered Agent, Tel: 231-946-7360.

RELIGIOUS INSTITUTES OF MEN REPRESENTED IN THE DIOCESE

For further details refer to the corresponding bracketed number in the Religious Institutes of Men or Women section.

[0520]—*Franciscan Friars* (Assumption, Sacred Heart Provs.)—O.F.M.

[0690]—*Jesuit Fathers & Brothers* (Detroit Prov.)—S.J.

RELIGIOUS INSTITUTES OF WOMEN REPRESENTED IN THE DIOCESE

[0420]—*Discalced Carmelite Nuns*—O.C.D.

[1070]—*Dominican Sisters*—O.P.

[2580]—*Institute of the Sisters of Mercy of the Americas*—R.S.M.

[3490]—*Sacramentine Nuns*—O.S.S.

[3560]—*Servants of Jesus*—S.J.

[3590]—*Servants of Mary*—O.S.M.

[]—*Sisters for Christian Community*—S.F.C.C.

[3830]—*Sisters of St. Joseph*—S.S.J.

[]—*Sisters of St. Francis*—O.S.F.

NECROLOGY

† Kendziorski, James T., (Retired), Died Jan. 6, 2018

† Magoon, R. Dale, (Retired), Died Apr. 12, 2018

An asterisk (*) denotes an organization that has established tax-exempt status directly with the IRS and is not covered by the USCCB Group Ruling.

Diocese of Grand Island

(Dioecesis Insulae Grandis)

Most Reverend

JOSEPH G. HANEFELDT

Bishop of Grand Island; ordained July 14, 1984; appointed Bishop of Grand Island January 14, 2015; ordained March 19, 2015. *Office: 2708 Old Fair Rd., Grand Island, NE 68803.*

Chancery Office: 2708 Old Fair Rd., Grand Island, NE 68803. Tel: 308-382-6565; Fax: 308-382-6569.

Most Reverend

WILLIAM J. DENDINGER, D.D., M.A.

Retired Bishop of Grand Island; ordained May 29, 1965; appointed Bishop of Grand Island October 14, 2004; ordained December 13, 2004; retired January 14, 2015. *Mailing Address: 2708 Old Fair Rd., Grand Island, NE 68803.* Tel: 308-382-6565; Fax: 308-382-6569.

Square Miles 40,000.

Erected at Kearney, March 8, 1912; See Transferred to Grand Island, April 11, 1917.

Comprises the Counties of Arthur, Banner, Blaine, Box Butte, Brown, Buffalo, Cherry, Cheyenne, Custer, Dawes, Deuel, Garden, Garfield, Grant, Greeley, Hooker, Howard Keyapaha, Kimball, Logan, Loup, McPherson, Morrill, Rock, Scotts Bluff, Sheridan, Sherman, Wheeler, Sioux, Thomas, Valley, and those portions of Dawson, Hall, Lincoln and Keith lying north of the South Platte River in the State of Nebraska.

For legal titles of parishes and diocesan institutions, consult the Chancery Office.

STATISTICAL OVERVIEW

Personnel	
Bishop	1
Retired Bishops	1
Priests: Diocesan Active in Diocese	34
Priests: Retired, Sick or Absent	27
Number of Diocesan Priests	61
Total Priests in Diocese	61
Extern Priests in Diocese	7
Ordinations:	
Permanent Deacons	2
Permanent Deacons in Diocese	15
Total Sisters	32
Parishes	
Parishes	35
With Resident Pastor:	
Resident Diocesan Priests	33
Resident Religious Priests	1
Without Resident Pastor:	
Administered by Priests	1
Missions	33
Professional Ministry Personnel:	
Sisters	11
Lay Ministers	30
Welfare	
Catholic Hospitals	2
Total Assisted	52,390
Homes for the Aged	1
Total Assisted	75
Educational	
Diocesan Students in Other Seminaries	5
Total Seminarians	5
High Schools, Diocesan and Parish	4
Total Students	472
Elementary Schools, Diocesan and Parish	6
Total Students	956
Catechesis/Religious Education:	
High School Students	2,200
Elementary Students	3,100
Total Students under Catholic Instruction	6,733
Teachers in the Diocese:	
Sisters	1
Lay Teachers	114
Vital Statistics	
Receptions into the Church:	
Infant Baptism Totals	647
Minor Baptism Totals	63
Adult Baptism Totals	63
Received into Full Communion	142
First Communions	822
Confirmations	650
Marriages:	
Catholic	129
Interfaith	74
Total Marriages	203
Deaths	483
Total Catholic Population	48,515
Total Population	309,366

Former Bishops—Most Revs. JAMES ALBERT DUFFY, D.D., cons. April 16, 1913; resigned See, May 7, 1931; appt. Titular Bishop of Silando; died Feb. 12, 1968; STANISLAUS V. BONA, D.D., appt. Bishop of Grand Island, Dec. 18, 1931; cons. Feb. 25, 1932; appt. Coadjutor Bishop of Green Bay and Titular Bishop of Mela, Dec. 2, 1944; succeeded to See, March 3, 1945; died Dec. 1, 1967; EDWARD J. HUNKELER, D.D., ord. June 14, 1919; appt. March 10, 1945; cons. May 1, 1945; transferred to Kansas City in Kansas, March 31, 1951; died Oct. 1, 1970; JOHN L. PASCHANG, D.D., Ph.D., J.C.D., ord. June 12, 1921; appt. July 28, 1951; cons. Oct. 9, 1951; resigned July 25, 1972; died March 21, 1999; JOHN J. SULLIVAN, D.D., ord. Sept. 23, 1944; appt. July 25, 1972; cons. Sept. 19, 1972; transferred to Kansas City-St. Joseph in Missouri, Aug. 17, 1977; died Feb. 11, 2001; LAWRENCE J. MCNAMARA, D.D., S.T.L., ord. May 30, 1953; appt. Jan. 10, 1978; cons. March 28, 1978; retired Oct. 14, 2004; died Dec. 17, 2004; WILLIAM J. DENDINGER, ord. May 29, 1965; appt. Bishop of Grand Island Oct. 14, 2004; ord. Dec. 13, 2004; retired Jan. 14, 2015.

Vicar General—Rev. JAMES R. GOLKA, 2708 Old Fair Rd., Grand Island, 68803. Email: jgolka@gidiocese.org.

Chancery Office—2708 Old Fair Rd., Grand Island, 68803. Tel: 308-382-6565; Fax: 308-382-6569. Office Hours: 8-4:30.

Chancellor—KATHLEEN M. HAHN, J.C.L.

Diocesan Tribunal—Mailing Address: 2708 Old Fair Rd., Grand Island, 68803. Tel: 308-382-6364.

Vicar-Judicial—Rev. MICHAEL F. MCDERMOTT, J.C.L.

Adjutant Vicar-Judicial—Rev. RICHARD L. PIONTKOWSKI JR., S.T.L., J.C.D.

Defenders of the Bond—Revs. RICHARD L. PIONTKOWSKI JR., S.T.L., J.C.D.; THOMAS A. RYAN, (Retired).

Judges—Revs. CHARLES L. TORPEY, S.T.L., J.C.L., (Retired); MICHAEL F. MCDERMOTT, J.C.L.

Procurator—Rev. DONALD A. BUHRMAN.

Advocates—Rev. DONALD A. BUHRMAN; RINA HUNTWORK; KATHLEEN M. HAHN, J.C.L.

Associate Director-Notary—MARIE RYAN.

Diocesan Consultors—Revs. DONALD A. BUHRMAN; JOSHUA S. BROWN; PAUL J. COLLING; BRYAN D. ERNEST; JAMES R. GOLKA; ANTONY THEKKEKARA; MICHAEL F. MCDERMOTT, J.C.L.

Vicar for Religious Communities of Women—VACANT.

Diocesan Offices and Directors

Charities—Rev. CHRISTOPHER KUBAT, Dir., Catholic Social Svcs., 515 W. 3rd St., Hastings, 68901. Tel: 402-463-2112.

Communications—ANGIE FISHER, Dir.

Operations and Human Resources—GREG FISHER.

Ongoing Formation for Clergy and Liturgy—Revs. JOSHUA S. BROWN, Mailing Address: 415 N. Chestnut, North Platte, 69101. Tel: 308-532-0942; PAUL J. COLLING, 2407 W. 56th St., Kearney, 68845. Tel: 308-236-9171.

Council of Catholic Women, Diocesan—Rev. STEPHEN F. DEAVER, Diocesan Moderator, (Retired).

Faith Formation & Evangelization—2708 Old Fair Rd., Grand Island, 68803. Tel: 308-382-6565; Fax: 308-382-6569. ARMANDO CHAVARRIA.

Episcopal Vicar for Hispanic Issues—Rev. JOSE M. CHAVEZ, Dir., Mailing Address: P.O. Box 578, Lexington, 68850. Tel: 308-324-2616.

Newspaper—The West Nebraska Register MARY PARLIN, Editor; COLLEEN GALLION, Assoc. Editor, Address all correspondence to: P.O. Box 608, Grand Island, 68802. Tel: 308-382-4660; Fax: 308-382-6569.

Personnel Board—Revs. JOSE M. CHAVEZ; JOSEPH A. HANNAPPEL; JAMES R. GOLKA; NEAL J. HOCK; SIDNEY B. BRUGGEMAN; JAMES E. NOVAKOWSKI, Died Apr. 25, 2018; Revs. BRYAN D. ERNEST; MATTHEW J. KOPERSKI.

Priests' Advisory Board (Presbyteral Council)—Revs. SCOTT M. HARTER; MICHAEL F. MCDERMOTT, J.C.L.; TIMOTHY L. STONER; BRYAN D. ERNEST; JONATHAN D. SORENSEN; JORGE CANELA; JAMES M. HUNT; PAUL J. COLLING; DONALD A. BUHRMAN; JAMES R. GOLKA; ANTONY THEKKEKARA; JOSEPH K. JOSEPH.

Catholic Relief Services—Most Rev. JOSEPH G. HANEFELDT, Dir.

Priests' Pension and Welfare Board—Address all mail to: Rev. JAMES M. HUNT, Mailing Address: P.O. Box 405, Broken Bow, 68822-0405.

Propagation of the FaithRev. MICHAEL D. MCDONALD, Dir., Mailing Address: P.O. Box 33, Gering, 69341. Tel: 308-436-2290.

Pro Life—2212 W. Louise, Grand Island, 68803. Tel: 308-390-1605. MICHAEL KUBE, Dir.

Religious Education—ARMANDO CHAVARRIA, Dir., 2708 Old Fair Rd., Grand Island, 68803. Tel: 308-382-6565; Fax: 308-382-6569.

Rural Life Conference—Rev. BRYAN D. ERNEST, Dir., 417 E. 3rd St., Ogallala, 69153.

Schools—GREGORY LOGSDON, Diocesan Supt. of Schools, 2708 Old Fair Rd., Grand Island, 68803. Tel: 308-682-6565; Fax: 308-382-6569.

Stewardship and Development—2708 Old Fair Rd., Grand Island, 68803. Tel: 308-382-6565; Fax: 308-382-6569. KORY KORALEWSKI, Dir.

Vocations—Rev. NEAL J. HOCK, Dir., P.O. Box 1024, Kearney, 68848. Tel: 308-234-1539.

Youth & Young Adult—2708 Old Fair Rd., Grand Island, 68803. Tel: 308-382-6565; Fax: 308-382-6569. L. ERIC HECKMAN, Dir.

CEC (Catholics Encounter Christ)—Rev. LOUIS A. NOLLETTE, Spiritual Dir., (Retired).

Community Mental Health—Rev. MICHAEL F. MCDERMOTT, J.C.L., Mailing Address: Box 99, Sidney, 69162.

Victim Assistance Coordinators—Grand Island: Victim Assistance Line: 800-652-2229 ELIZABETH HEIDT, Ph.D., Tel: 308-379-1949; Email: cpo@gidiocese.org. Ravenna: CHERYL ALBRIGHT, M.S., Tel: 308-440-7644; Email: calbright@gidiocese.org. en Espanol: Tel: 800-652-2229. Rev. JOSE M. CHAVEZ.

Office of Child Protection—ELIZABETH HEIDT, Ph.D., Dir.; CHERYL ALBRIGHT, M.S., Outreach Coord., Mailing Address: 2708 Old Fair Rd., Grand Island, 68803. Tel: 308-382-6565; Fax: 308-382-6569; Email: cpo@gidiocese.org.

CLERGY, PARISHES, MISSIONS AND PAROCHIAL SCHOOLS

CITY OF GRAND ISLAND

(HALL COUNTY)

1—CATHEDRAL OF THE NATIVITY OF THE BLESSED VIRGIN MARY (1864)
204 S. Cedar St., 68801. Tel: 308-384-2523; Email: office@stmarysgi.com. 112 S. Cedar St., 68801. Revs. James R. Golka; Scott M. Harter; Deacons John Farlee; Randy Lewandowski; Frank Moreno; Robert Puhalla.
Res.: 207 S. Elm St., 68801.
Catechesis Religious Program—112 S. Cedar, 68801. Tel: 308-382-1198. Sr. Isabel Sandino, O.Carm., Youth 6-12; De Tenski, D.R.E. K-5. Students 270.

2—BLESSED SACRAMENT (1949)
518 W. State St., 68801. Tel: 308-384-0532. Rev. Martin L. Egging; Sr. Bernadette Engelhaupt, O.S.F., Pastoral Assoc.
Res.: 1724 N. Walnut, 68801.
Catechesis Religious Program—Tel: 308-395-8521; Email: debwetzel@hotmail.com; Web: blsachurch.net. Ms. Debra Wetzel, D.R.E. Students 240.

3—ST. LEO (1972)
2410 S. Blaine, 68801. Tel: 308-382-4753; Email: office@saintleos.org; Web: www.saintleos.weebly.com. Revs. Donald A. Buhrman; Mark Maresh; Deacon William Buchta.
Catechesis Religious Program—Jodi Stauffer, D.R.E. Children; Rita Hemmer, Youth & Young Adult Ministry. Students 33.

4—RESURRECTION aka Church of the Resurrection (1973)
4130 Cannon Rd., 68803. Tel: 308-382-8644; Email: patj@giresurrection.com; Web: www.giresurrection.com. Rev. Joseph Kadaprayil, S.D.B.; Deacon John Willmes.
Res.: 4110 Cannon Rd., 68803.
Catechesis Religious Program—Tel: 308-382-0976. Therese Stump, D.R.E.; Michalene Iverson, Youth Dir. Students 177.

OUTSIDE THE CITY OF GRAND ISLAND

AINSWORTH, BROWN CO., ST. PIUS X (1955)
P.O. Box 7, Ainsworth, 69210. Tel: 402-387-1275; Email: stpiusxne@msn.com. Rev. Phil Flott.
Catechesis Religious Program—Tel: 402-387-2260. Jessica Pozehl, D.R.E. Students 75.
Mission—Holy Cross, Bassett, Rock Co.

ALLIANCE, BOX BUTTE CO., HOLY ROSARY (1894) [CEM]
1104 Cheyenne Ave., Alliance, 69301.
Tel: 308-762-2009; Email: tstonertls@hotmail.com. Rev. Timothy L. Stoner; Theresa Dykes, Pastoral Min.
Res.: 916 Cheyenne Ave., Alliance, 69301.
School—St. Agnes Academy, (Grades PreSchool-8), Tel: 308-762-2315; Email: rwilhelm@stagnesacademy.com; Web: www.stagnesacademy.com. Mr. Rodney Wilhelm, Prin. Lay Teachers 14; Students 126.
Catechesis Religious Program—Tel: 308-762-2830; Email: faithformation@bbc.net; Web: holyrosaryalliance.weebly.com. Noreen Placek, D.R.E. Students 109.
Mission—St. Bridget (1888) 801 Niobrara Ave., P.O. Box 67, Hemingford, Box Butte Co. 69348.
Tel: 308-487-3617; Fax: 308-487-3608; Email: stbridget@bbc.net.
Catechesis Religious Program—Students 47.

BRIDGEPORT, MORRILL CO., ALL SOULS (1919) [CEM]
701 P St., Bridgeport, 69336. Tel: 308-262-0709; Email: cpvsdb@gmail.com. Rev. C. P. Varghese, S.D.B.
Catechesis Religious Program—Jennifer Eckhardt, D.R.E.; Zel Christensen, D.R.E.; James Cawley, D.R.E. Students 102.
Missions—St. Mary—East Francis St., Dalton, 69131.
Sacred Heart, P.O. Box 190, Bayard, 69334-0190.

BROKEN BOW, CUSTER CO., ST. JOSEPH'S (1888) [CEM]
1407 S. E St., P.O. Box 405, Broken Bow, 68822.
Tel: 308-872-5809 (Office); Fax: 308-872-5809; Email: stjoescatholic@msn.com. Rev. James M. Hunt.
Catechesis Religious Program—Rashelle Ryan, D.R.E. Students 122.
Missions—St. Anselm's—[CEM 2] Anselmo, Custer Co..
Catechesis Religious Program—Jessica Burnett, D.R.E. (Grades P-12). Students 35.
Assumption of the Blessed Virgin Mary, Sargent, Cluster Co..

Catechesis Religious Program—Laura Kipp, D.R.E. Students 42.

CHADRON, DAWES CO., ST. PATRICK'S (1886) [CEM]
340 Cedar St., P.O. Box 231, Chadron, 69337.
Tel: 308-432-2626; Email: stpats@chadronstpatricks.org. Rev. Todd K. Philipsen.
Catechesis Religious Program—Tel: 308-432-2161. Sandi Schiaffo, D.R.E. Students 110.

CHAPPELL, DEUEL CO., ST. JOSEPH'S (1909) [CEM] Rev. Rayappa Pasala.
Res.: 1049 2nd St., P.O. Box 586, Chappell, 69129.
Tel: 308-772-3221; Email: stjosephchappell@yahoo.com.
Catechesis Religious Program—Students 25.
Missions—St. Elizabeth—300 W. 4th, P.O. Box 586, Oshkosh, Garden Co. 69154.
Catechesis Religious Program—Students 13.
St. Gall, 307 1st St., Lisco, Garden Co. 69148.

COZAD, DAWSON CO., CHRIST THE KING (1951) (Irish)
613 W. 13th St., Cozad, 69130. Tel: 308-784-4161; Email: pamparasdb@gmail.com. Rev. Michael Pampara.
Res.: 1220 Ave. M, Cozad, 69130.
Catechesis Religious Program—512 E. 19th.
Tel: 308-784-2696. Julie Linn, D.R.E. Students 141.
Mission—Our Lady of Good Counsel, 1915 Ave. J, Gothenburg, Dawson Co. 69138.
Catechesis Religious Program—Mary Meisinger, Dir. Students 73.

CRAWFORD, DAWES CO., ST. JOHN THE BAPTIST (1896) [CEM 2] (German—Irish)
808 4th St., Crawford, 69339. Tel: 308-665-1584; Email: stjohncrawford@bbc.net. Rev. Arul Raj Innaiah.
Catechesis Religious Program—Tel: 308-665-2240; Email: mhughes@bbc.net. Melany Hughes, D.R.E. Students 25.
Mission—Church of the Nativity of the Blessed Virgin Mary, 280 Kate St., Harrison, Sioux Co. 69339.
Catechesis Religious Program—Students 17.

ELM CREEK, BUFFALO CO., IMMACULATE CONCEPTION (1879) [CEM]
310 N. Church St., Elm Creek, 68836.
Tel: 308-856-4375; Email: immaculate.holyrosary.stjohn@gmail.com. P.O. Box 530, Elm Creek, 68836. Rev. Alexander J. Borzych; Deacon William O'Donnell; Helen Glatter, Office Mgr.
Res.: 314 N. Church St., Elm Creek, 68836.
Catechesis Religious Program—Cheska Hubbard, D.R.E. Students 42.
Missions—Holy Rosary—503 D St., Overton, Dawson Co. 68863.
Catechesis Religious Program—Sue Kizer, D.R.E. Students 37.
St. John Capistran, 118 N. Ash, Amherst, Buffalo Co. 68812.
Catechesis Religious Program—Annette Line, D.R.E. Students 48.

GERING, SCOTTS BLUFF CO., CHRIST THE KING (1958)
1345 18th St., P.O. Box 33, Gering, 69341.
Tel: 308-436-2290; Email: christking@allophone.com. Rev. Michael D. McDonald.
Res.: 1730 'N' St., P.O. Box 33, Gering, 69341.
Catechesis Religious Program—P.O. Box 33, Gering, 69341. Tel: 308-436-2290. Micki Walker, D.R.E. & Dir. Youth Ministry. Students 270.

GORDON, SHERIDAN CO., ST. LEO'S (1887) [JC]
228 N. Maverick, Gordon, 69343. Tel: 308-282-0427; Email: stleosgordon@gmail.com. Rev. Joseph K. Joseph.
Catechesis Religious Program—Mary Thies, D.R.E. Students 27.
Missions—Immaculate Conception—606 Church St., P.O. Box 279, Rushville, Sheridan Co. 69360.
Catechesis Religious Program—Michelle Heck, D.R.E.; Vicki Wellnitz, D.R.E. Students 31.
St. Columbkille, 545 N. Main, Hay Springs, Sheridan Co. 69347.
Catechesis Religious Program—Miriam Kearns, D.R.E. Students 33.

KEARNEY, BUFFALO CO.

1—ST. JAMES (1881)
Church Office: 3801 A Ave., Kearney, 68847.
Tel: 308-234-5536; Email: frjoe@stjameschurchkearney.org; Web: www.stjameschurchkearney.org. Revs. Joseph A. Hannappel; Arthur A. Faesser; Sr. Catherine Bones, S.C.L., Pastoral Min.; Ron Dobesh, Admin.; Mary Bowman, Adult Faith Formation.
Res.: 7 Sioux Ln., Kearney, 68847.
High School—Kearney Catholic, (Grades 6-12), 110 E. 35th St., Kearney, 68847. Tel: 308-234-2610; Fax: 308-234-4986; Email: terry.torson@kearneycatholic.org; Web: www.kearneycatholic.org. P.O. Box 1866, Kearney, 68848-1866. Mr. Terrence Torson, Admin.; Janet Anderson, Librarian. Lay Teachers 29; Students 345.
Catechesis Religious Program—Tel: 308-234-9695; Fax: 308-234-9818. Deb Kratochvil, D.R.E. Students 380.

2—PRINCE OF PEACE (1986)
2407 W. 56th St., Kearney, 68845-4113.
Tel: 308-236-9171; Email: deann@kearneyprinceofpeace.org; Web: www.princeofpeacekearney.com. Rev. Paul J. Colling; Deacon Thomas Martin; Sr. Jan Ludvik, N.D., Pastoral Min./Coord.; Stephen Friesell, Youth Min.; JoAnn Hoffman, Business Mgr.; Ms. DeAnn Nickol, Contact Person; Katie Ridder, Sec.
Catechesis Religious Program—Lynn Cooper, D.R.E. Students 281.

KIMBALL, KIMBALL CO., ST. JOSEPH'S (1921) Closed. Now a mission of St. Patrick's, Sidney.

LEXINGTON, DAWSON CO., ST. ANN'S (1883) [CEM]
303 E. 6th St., Lexington, 68850. Tel: 308-324-4647; Email: stannscatholic@gmail.com; Web: www.lexstanns.com. P.O. Box 578, Lexington, 68850-0578. Revs. Matthew J. Koperski; Jose M. Chavez; Sr. Mary Ann Flax, C.S.J., Pastoral Min.
Catechesis Religious Program—St. Ann's Parish Center, 1003 Taft St., Lexington, 68850. Linda Saiz, D.R.E. Students 450.

LOUP CITY, SHERMAN CO., ST. JOSAPHAT'S (1882) (Polish)
704 N. 9th St., P.O. Box 626, Loup City, 68853.
Tel: 308-745-0315; Email: josaphatsaint@yahoo.com; Email: piontkow@nponline.net. Rev. Richard L. Piontkowski Jr., S.T.L., J.C.L.
Catechesis Religious Program—Tel: 308-745-1235. Lorraine Panowicz, D.R.E. (7-12). Students 91.
Missions—St. Francis—[CEM] Ashton, Sherman Co. 68817.
Catechesis Religious Program—Marie Curlo, D.R.E. Students 25.
St. Gabriel, Hazard, Sherman Co. 68844.
Catechesis Religious Program—Jason Gross, D.R.E. Students 34.

MITCHELL, SCOTTS BLUFF CO., ST. THERESA'S (1930)
1715 17th St., Mitchell, 69357. Tel: 308-623-2245; Email: office@sttheresas.org. Revs. Michael D. McDonald; Michael E. Wetovick.
Catechesis Religious Program—Tel: 308-623-2245. Students 29.
Missions—St. Ann—Hwy. 26 & Walsh, Morrill, Scotts Bluff Co. 69358.
Sacred Heart, 203 E. "O" St., Lyman, Scotts Bluff Co. 69352.

MULLEN, HOOKER CO., ST. MARY'S (1910)
304 S. Blaine, P.O. Box 191, Mullen, 69152.
Tel: 308-546-2250; Email: stmarysmullen@nebsandhills.net. Rev. Louis A. Nollette, Admin., (Retired).
Catechesis Religious Program—Students 74.
Missions—All Saint's—201 S Manderson, Hyannis, Grant Co. 69152.
St. Thomas of Canterbury, Thedford, Thomas Co. 69152.

NORTH PLATTE, LINCOLN CO.

1—HOLY SPIRIT (1973)
2801 W. E St., North Platte, 69101.
Tel: 308-534-6623; Email: holy1spirit@allphone.com; Web: www.holyspiritcatholicchurch.com. Rev. Vidya S. Arikotla, S.D.B.
Res.: 1920 Kristen Ct., North Platte, 69103.
Catechesis Religious Program—Tel: 308-534-7906; Fax: 308-534-6525. Students 70.
Mission—Sacred Heart, P.O. Box 398, Sutherland, Lincoln Co. 69165. Tel: 308-386-4300.
Catechesis Religious Program—Kyleen Stokey, D.R.E. Students 96.

2—ST. PATRICK (1875) [CEM]
415 N. Chestnut, North Platte, 69101.
Tel: 308-532-0942; Email: office@st-pats-online.org. Revs. Joshua S. Brown; Matthew Nash.
School—McDaid Elementary, (Grades K-6), Tel: 308-532-1874; Fax: 308-532-8015; Email: p.

wood@npcschools.org; Web: www.npcschools.org. Mary Ellis, Librarian; Pam Wood, Prin. Lay Teachers 21; Students 324.

High School—St. Patrick High School, (Grades 7-12), 500 S. Silber, North Platte, 69101. Tel: 308-532-1874 ; Fax: 308-532-8015; Email: k.dodson@npcschools. org. c/o North Platte Catholic Schools, P.O. Box 970, North Platte, 69101. Mr. Kevin Dodson, Supt.; Mark Skillstad, Prin. Lay Teachers 16; Students 88.

Catechesis Religious Program—

Tel: 308-532-6388, Ext. 203; Email: formation@st-pats-online.org; Email: religioused@st-pats-online. org; Web: www.st-pats-online.org. Mary Wyatt, Dir. Faith Formation; Jennifer Prince, D.R.E. Students 121.

OGALLALA, KEITH CO., ST. LUKE'S (1887) [JC]

417 E. Third, Ogallala, 69153. Tel: 308-284-3196; Email: FrB@kccatholics.com; Web: www.kccatholics. com. Revs. Bryan D. Ernest; Loren G. Pohlmeier, In Res., (Retired).

School—St. Luke's School, (Grades PreSchool-5), Tel: 308-284-4841; Email: stlukesschool@saintlukesschool.com. Sr. Loretta Krajewski, O.S.U., Prin. Clergy 1; Lay Teachers 5; Students 73; Clergy / Religious Teachers 1.

St. Luke Catholic School Endowment—

Catechesis Religious Program—Lori Beckius, Faith Formation. Students 125.

Mission—St. Patrick's Church, 301 E. 4th St., Paxton, Keith Co. 69155. Tel: 308-386-4300; Email: sacredheart@gpcom.net; Web: www.kccatholics.com.

ORD, VALLEY CO., OUR LADY OF PERPETUAL HELP (1908) [CEM]

527 N. 19th St., P.O. Box 123, Ord, 68862.

Tel: 308-728-3351; Web: www.orcatholicchurch.org. Laura Porkorny, Business Mgr.

School—Our Lady of Perpetual Help School, (Grades K-6), 527 N. 20th St., Ord, 68862. Tel: 308-728-5389; Email: pvalasek@esu10.org. Patricia Valasek, Prin. Clergy 1; Lay Teachers 5; Students 45; Clergy / Religious Teachers 1.

Catechesis Religious Program—Sr. Lee Anne Danczak, S.J., D.R.E. Elem.; Laura Pokorny, D.R.E. High School. Students 112.

Mission—Sacred Heart, Burwell, Garfield Co. 68823. Tel: 308-346-4190; Email: shcburwell@gmail.com.

Catechesis Religious Program—Kevin Carson, D.R.E.; Kathy Carson, D.R.E. Students 55.

RAVENNA, BUFFALO CO., OUR LADY OF LOURDES (1887) (German)

515 Sicily Ave., Box 90, Ravenna, 68869.

Tel: 308-452-3109; Email: piontkow@nponline.net. Rev. Richard L. Piontkowski Jr., S.T.L., J.C.D.; Sr. Paulette Kuta, Pastoral Min.

Catechesis Religious Program—Joan Clifton, D.R.E. & Youth Min. Students 108.

Mission—St. Mary's (1909) [CEM] [JC] 504 N. Syracuse St., Box 134, Pleasanton, Buffalo Co. 68866.

ST. LIBORY, HOWARD CO., ST. LIBORY'S (1884) [CEM]

505 Spruce St., St. Libory, 68872. Tel: 308-687-6276; Email: sbruggeman@gidiocese.org; Web: www. stliborycatholic.com. Rev. Sidney B. Bruggeman.

Catechesis Religious Program—Tel: 308-687-6273. Donna Placke, D.R.E. Students 83.

ST. PAUL, HOWARD CO., SS. PETER AND PAUL (1878) [JC]

713 Elm St., St. Paul, 68873. Tel: 308-754-4649; Email: spandp@spandp.com. Rev. Rayappa Konka.

Res.: 1405 Custer St., St. Paul, 68873.

Catechesis Religious Program—Tel: 308-754-4002. Becky Knox, Youth Min.; Judi Baker, D.R.E. (PK-4). Students 177.

Missions—St. Joseph—1803 Hwy. 11, Elba, Howard Co. 68838.

Catechesis Religious Program—Cynthia Paczosa, D.R.E. Students 18.

St. Anthony of Padua (1877) [CEM 3] 103 Kearns Ave., Box 156, Farwell, Howard Co. 68838.

Catechesis Religious Program—

Tel: 308-754-3351. Kathy Gorecki, D.R.E., Tel: 308-336-3351; Cynthia Paczosa, D.R.E. Students 26.

SCOTTSBLUFF, SCOTTS BLUFF CO.

1—ST. AGNES (1912)

2314 3rd Ave., P.O. Box 349, Scottsbluff, 69363.

Tel: 308-632-2541; Email: office@st-agnes-church. com; Web: www.st-agnes-church.com. Rev. Vincent L. Parsons; Sr. Vera Meis, C.S.J.

School—St. Agnes School, (Grades PreK-5),

Tel: 308-632-6918; Email: office@stagnesonline.org. Julie Brown, Headmaster. Lay Teachers 9; Students 119.

Catechesis Religious Program—Email: dre@st-agnes-church.com. Terri Calvert, D.R.E. Students 187.

2—OUR LADY OF GUADALUPE (1948) (Hispanic)

1102 12th Ave., Scottsbluff, 69361. Tel: 308-632-2845 ; Fax: 308-632-7356; Email: office@guadalupescottsbluff.com. P.O. Box 2485, Scottsbluff, 69363-2485. Rev. Jonathan D. Sorensen.

Catechesis Religious Program—Laura Lopez, D.R.E. Students 142.

SIDNEY, CHEYENNE CO., ST. PATRICK'S (1878) [JC]

1039 14th Ave., P.O. Box 99, Sidney, 69162.

Tel: 308-254-2828; Email: parish@sidneystpats.com; Web: www.sidneystpats.com. Rev. Michael F. McDermott, J.C.L.; Patricia Mertz, Pastoral Assoc.

Res.: 442 College Dr., P.O. Box 99, Sidney, 69162.

Catechesis Religious Program—Joan Falcon, D.R.E. Students 164.

Mission—St. Joseph's, 511 S. Howard St., P.O. Box 576, Kimball, 69145. Tel: 308-235-2162. Rev. Vidya S. Arikotla, S.D.B.

SPALDING, GREELEY CO., ST. MICHAEL'S (1887) [CEM 2]

150 E. Marguerite, P.O. Box 310, Spalding, 68665.

Tel: 308-497-2662; Email: frantony@families-infaith. com. Rev. Antony Thekkekara.

School—Spalding Academy, (Grades K-12),

Tel: 308-497-2103; Email: amy. cmkay@spaldingacademy.org. Amy McKay, Prin. Lay Teachers 20; Students 81.

Catechesis Religious Program—Holly Carraher, D.R.E. Students 85.

Missions—St. Theresa of the Child Jesus—

Catechesis Religious Program—Students 16.

Sacred Heart, P.O. Box 99, Greeley, Greeley Co. 68842. Tel: 308-428-2855.

Catechesis Religious Program—Students 59.

STAPLETON, LOGAN CO., ST. JOHN THE EVANGELIST (1913) [CEM] (German)

301 H St., P.O. Box 309, Stapleton, 69163.

Tel: 308-636-2421; Email: stjohnscatholic@hotmail. com; Web: www.abjcatholic.org. Rev. Thomas Gudipalli.

Catechesis Religious Program—Nancy Lashley, D.R.E. Students 15.

Missions—St. Agnes—503 N. Carroll, Arnold, Custer Co. 69163. Tel: 308-848-2442.

Catechesis Religious Program—Aleta Ambler, D.R.E. Students 21.

St. Boniface, 204 S. Morgan Ave., Callaway, Logan Co. 68825. Tel: 308-836-2606.

Catechesis Religious Program—Mary Riddler, D.R.E. Students 25.

VALENTINE, CHERRY CO., ST. NICHOLAS (1893) [JC]

400 W. 5th St., P.O. Box 510, Valentine, 69201.

Tel: 402-376-1672; Email: stnicholas. valentine@gmail.com. Rev. Abraham Kaduthodiyil.

Catechesis Religious Program—Wanda Nielson, D.R.E.; Jessica McGinley, D.R.E. Students 109.

Mission—St. Mary, [CEM] Nenzel, Cherry Co. 69219.

WOOD RIVER, HALL CO., ST. MARY'S (1884) [CEM]

1108 Dodd St., Wood River, 68883. Tel: 308-583-2464 ; Email: stmary_sheart@hotmail.com. P.O. Box 37, Wood River, 68883. Rev. Jorge Canela.

Catechesis Religious Program—Lisa Hermann, D.R.E. Students 79.

Mission—Sacred Heart, 508 B Street, P.O. Box 190, Shelton, Buffalo Co. 68876.

Catechesis Religious Program—Rhonda O'Brien, D.R.E. Students 61.

Chaplains of Public Institutions

GRAND ISLAND. *Nebraska Veterans Home*. Vacant.

U.S. Veterans' Hospital. Rev. Sidney B. Bruggeman.

Administrative Leave:

Rev.—

Kakkuzhiyil, John, S.D.B.

Retired:

Revs.—

Chamberlain, Robert F., (Retired), 910 Parkview Ct., North Platte, 69101

Curran, Francis T., (Retired), 4000 S. 56th St., Unit 105A, Lincoln, 68506

Deaver, Stephen F., (Retired), 615 W. 42nd St., Scottsbluff, 69361

Harr, Gerald J., (Retired), 2350 Five Rocks Rd., #111, Gering, 69341

Heithoff, James H., (Retired), 3266 29th Ave., Columbus, 68601

Janovec, James J., (Retired), 2932 Pinnacle Pointe Dr., 68803

Karnish, Robert, (Retired), 513 S. Chestnut, Kimball, 69145

Kosmicki, Raymond M., (Retired), 404 Woodland Dr, Rm. 56, 68801

Larmore, Donald E., J.C.D., (Retired), 1300 W. Warner Rd., Apt. 1026, Gilbert, AZ 85233

Mullowney, Thomas E., (Retired), 417 W. 17th St., Apt. A, Kearney, 68845

Murphy, James E., (Retired), 211 S. Cedar, Apt. 3, Spalding, 68665

Nollette, Louis A., (Retired), 201 S. Main St., Nenzel, 69219

Nollette, Neal P., (Retired), 105 W. Front St., Nenzel, 69219

O'Brien, Donald J., (Retired), 4106 H Ave., Kearney, 68847

O'Kane, James D., (Retired), 105 S. 9th St., #702, Omaha, 68102

Pohlmeier, Loren G., (Retired), 417 E. Third, Ogallala, 69153

Pruss, Rodney Lee A., (Retired), 15723 W. Amelia Dr., Goodyear, AZ 85338

Rademacher, John R., (Retired), 2497 Marston Hts., Colorado Springs, CO 80920

Rooney, Robert B., (Retired), 5401 South St., Rm. 418, Lincoln, 68506

Ryan, Thomas A., (Retired), 3236 Westside St., 68803

Rykwalder, David L., (Retired), 2921 Bearing Pointe Dr., 68803

Schmitt, James C., (Retired), 23 Chantilly, 68803

Spanel, Hubert J., (Retired), 145 Memorial Dr., #518, Broken Bow, 68822

Torpey, Charles L., S.T.L., J.C.L., (Retired), 2635 Brennen Ln., 68803

Warner, James P., (Retired), 726 E. Carrol, Harlingen, TX 78552

Wetovick, Jerry P., (Retired), 2300 Ave. O, #118, Cozad, 69130.

Permanent Deacons.

Deacons—

Neil Baquet, Sts. Peter and Paul, St. Paul

William Buchta, St. Leo, Grand Island

Michael Davis, Holy Spirit, North Platte

John Farlee, Cathedral of the Nativity of the Blessed Virgin Mary, Grand Island

Matthew Irish, St. Patrick, North Platte

Randy Lewandowski, Cathedral of the Nativity of the Blessed Virgin Mary, Grand Island

Mark Lister, St. Patrick, North Platte

Thomas Martin, Prince of Peace, Kearney

Frank Moreno, Cathedral of the Nativity of the Blessed Virgin Mary

William O'Donnell, Immaculate Conception, Elm Creek

Eric Parker, St. Patrick, North Platte

Dixon Powers, St. Patrick, North Platte

Robert Puhalla, Cathedral of the Nativity of the Blessed Virgin Mary, Grand Island

Mark Stadler, Holy Spirit, North Platte

John Willmes, Resurrection, Grand Island.

INSTITUTIONS LOCATED IN DIOCESE

[A] HIGH SCHOOLS, DIOCESAN

GRAND ISLAND. *Central Catholic Schools*, (Grades 6-12), 1200 Ruby Ave., 68803. Tel: 308-384-2440; Fax: 308-389-3274; Email: jengle@gicc.org. Mr. Jordan Engle, Prin.; Mr. Phou Manivong, Asst. Prin. Lay Teachers 28; Students 273; Clergy / Religious Teachers 2.

[B] GENERAL HOSPITALS

GRAND ISLAND. *Saint Francis Medical Center*, 2620 W. Faidley Ave., P.O. Box 9804, 68802.

Tel: 308-384-4600; Email: info@alegent.org; Web: www.chihealth.com/st-francis. Edward Hannon, Pres.; Colleen Leise, Div. Mgr., Pastoral Care; Shirley Murphy, Chap. Bed Capacity 159; Tot Asst. Annually 29,412; Total Staff 659.

KEARNEY. *Good Samaritan Hospital*, 10 E. 31st St., P.O. Box 1990, Kearney, 68848-1990.

Tel: 308-865-7100; Email: info@alegent.org; Web: www.chihealth.com/good-samaritan. Michael H. Schnieders, Pres.; Sr. Rose Donnelly, Chap.; Erica Klaich, Pastoral Assoc.; Frank Parrington, Pastoral Assoc. Bed Capacity 172; Tot Asst. Annually 22,979; Total Staff 896.

Richard H. Young Hospital, 4600 17th Ave., Kearney, 68847. Tel: 308-865-2000; Email: Info@alegent.org.

[C] HOMES FOR THE AGED

KEARNEY. *Mount Carmel Home-Keens' Memorial*, 412 W. 18th St., Kearney, 68847. Tel: 308-338-1263; Fax: 308-236-9380; Email: marycarmelite@hotmail.com; Web: www. corpuschristicarmelites.org. Sr. Mary Florence Blavet, O.Carm., Supr. Residents 74; (Carmelites) 5; Total Staff 120.

[D] NEWMAN CENTERS

CHADRON. *Chadron State College-Newman House*, 907 Main St., Chadron, 69337. Tel: 308-432-3673; Email: newmanhouse@yahoo.com. Amy Graham, Campus Min.

KEARNEY. *University of Nebraska at Kearney Newman*

Apostolate, 821 W. 27th St., Kearney, 68845. Tel: 308-234-1539; Fax: 308-233-5718; Email: newmancenterunk@gmail.com; Web: www.lopercatholic.org. Pam Cimfel, Admin.; Rev. Neal J. Hock, Chap. Total in Residence 10; Total Staff 3.

[E] MISCELLANEOUS

GRAND ISLAND. **The Family of the Good Shepherd, Inc.*, 611 S Broadwell, 68803. Tel: 308-675-3002; Cell: 402-206-8088; Email: catherine.nagl@gmail.com; Web: www.thefamilyofthegoodshepherd.org. P.O. Box 911, Ravenna, 68803. Catherine Nagle, Dir.

ALLIANCE. *Magnificat Alliance, NE Chapter*, 1104 Cheyenne Ave., Alliance, 69301. Tel: 308-762-2009; Email: zumbahlen@bbc.net. Deb Zumbahlen, Contact Person.

KEARNEY. *Magnificat - Mary Full of Grace, Inc.*, 2811 W. 24th St., Kearney, 68845. Tel: 308-234-1661; Email: tsorensen55@yahoo.com. Teresa Sorensen, Contact Person.

OGALLALA. *Magnificat - Our Lady of the Harvest Chapter - Ogallala*, 1051 Rd. East L North, Paxton, 69155. Email: conniefrosh@opsd.org. Mrs. Connie Frosh, Contact Person.

RELIGIOUS INSTITUTES OF WOMEN REPRESENTED IN THE DIOCESE

For further details refer to the corresponding bracketed number in the Religious Institutes of Men or Women section.

[0350]—*Carmelite Sisters (Corpus Christi)*—O.Carm.

[3830-18]—*Congregation of St. Joseph* Cleveland—C.S.J.

[3832]—*Congregation of the Sisters of St. Joseph* (Concordia, KS)—C.S.J.

[2960]—*Notre Dame Sisters*—N.D.

[1680]—*School Sisters of St. Francis, WI.*

[3580]—*Servants of Mary* (Omaha, NE)—O.S.M.

[]—*Servants of the Risen Christ* (Santiago, Dominican Republic).

[0480]—*Sisters of Charity of Leavenworth.*

[1630]—*Sisters of St. Francis of Penance and Christian Charity*—O.S.F.

[3930]—*Sisters of St. Joseph of the Third Order of St. Francis P*—S.S.J.-T.O.S.F.

[2110]—*Sisters of the Humility of Mary*—H.M.

[4120-03]—*Ursuline Nuns of the Congregation of Paris* (Louisville, KY)—O.S.U.

NECROLOGY

† Berger, Bernard M., (Retired), Died Aug. 15, 2018

† Coulter, Lawrence W., (Retired), Died Nov. 21, 2018

† Novakowski, James E., North Platte, NE Holy Spirit, Died Apr. 25, 2018

† Schlaf, John E., (Retired), Died Feb. 16, 2018

An asterisk (*) denotes an organization that has established tax-exempt status directly with the IRS and is not covered by the USCCB Group Ruling.

Diocese of Grand Rapids

(Dioecesis Grandormensis)

Most Reverend

DAVID J. WALKOWIAK, J.C.D.

Bishop of Grand Rapids; ordained June 9, 1979; appointed Bishop of Grand Rapids April 18, 2013; consecrated June 18, 2013. *Office: Cathedral Square Center, 360 Division Ave. S., Grand Rapids, MI 49503.*

Most Reverend

WALTER A. HURLEY, J.C.L.

Retired Bishop of Grand Rapids; ordained June 5, 1965; appointed Titular Bishop of Chunavia and Auxiliary Bishop of Detroit July 7, 2003; consecrated August 12, 2003; appointed Bishop of Grand Rapids June 21, 2005; installed August 4, 2005; retired April 18, 2013. *Office: Cathedral Square Center, 360 Division Ave., S., Grand Rapids, MI 49503.* Tel: 616-243-0491.

Most Reverend

ROBERT J. ROSE, S.T.L., D.D.

Retired Bishop of Grand Rapids; ordained December 21, 1955; appointed Bishop of Gaylord October 13, 1981; consecrated December 6, 1981; appointed Bishop of Grand Rapids July 11, 1989; installed August 30, 1989; retired October 13, 2003. *Res.: 1200 104th, Apt. A, Byron Center, MI 49315.* Tel: 616-583-1260.

ESTABLISHED MAY 19, 1882.

Square Miles 6,795.

Comprises the following Counties of the Lower Peninsula of the State of Michigan: Ionia, Kent, Lake, Mason, Mecosta, Montcalm, Muskegon, Newaygo, Oceana, Osceola, Ottawa.

For legal titles of parishes and diocesan institutions, consult the Chancery Office.

Administrative Offices of the Diocese of Grand Rapids: Cathedral Square Center, 360 Division Ave., S., Grand Rapids, MI 49503. Tel: 616-243-0491; Fax: 616-243-4910.

Web: www.grdiocese.org

STATISTICAL OVERVIEW

Personnel	
Bishop	1
Retired Bishops	2
Priests: Diocesan Active in Diocese	66
Priests: Retired, Sick or Absent	39
Number of Diocesan Priests	105
Religious Priests in Diocese	16
Total Priests in Diocese	121
Extern Priests in Diocese	9
Ordinations:	
Diocesan Priests	1
Transitional Deacons	3
Permanent Deacons	3
Permanent Deacons in Diocese	33
Total Brothers	1
Total Sisters	225
Parishes	
Parishes	80
With Resident Pastor:	
Resident Diocesan Priests	57
Resident Religious Priests	2
Without Resident Pastor:	
Administered by Priests	16
Administered by Lay People	2
Missions	3
Closed Parishes	1
Professional Ministry Personnel:	
Sisters	7
Welfare	
Catholic Hospitals	2
Total Assisted	2,404,827
Homes for the Aged	1
Total Assisted	150
Residential Care of Children	160
Total Assisted	400
Specialized Homes	1
Total Assisted	50
Special Centers for Social Services	11
Total Assisted	31,396
Educational	
Diocesan Students in Other Seminaries	28
Total Seminarians	28
Colleges and Universities	1
Total Students	1,619
High Schools, Diocesan and Parish	4
Total Students	1,310
High Schools, Private	1
Total Students	123
Elementary Schools, Diocesan and Parish	24
Total Students	4,815
Elementary Schools, Private	2
Total Students	307
Catechesis/Religious Education:	
High School Students	1,823
Elementary Students	7,468
Total Students under Catholic Instruction	17,493
Teachers in the Diocese:	
Sisters	3
Lay Teachers	454
Vital Statistics	
Receptions into the Church:	
Infant Baptism Totals	1,857
Minor Baptism Totals	140
Adult Baptism Totals	227
Received into Full Communion	310
First Communions	1,955
Confirmations	1,820
Marriages:	
Catholic	391
Interfaith	202
Total Marriages	593
Deaths	1,288
Total Catholic Population	191,000
Total Population	1,418,932

Former Bishops—Most Revs. HENRY JOSEPH RICHTER, D.D., ord. June 10, 1865; cons. April 22, 1883; died Dec. 26, 1916; MICHAEL JAMES GALLAGHER, D.D., ord. March 19, 1893; appt. titular Bishop of Tipasa and Coadjutor Bishop of Grand Rapids July 5, 1915; cons. Sept. 8, 1915; succeeded to the Diocese of Grand Rapids, Dec. 26, 1916; transferred to the See of Detroit, July 18, 1918; died Jan. 20, 1937; EDWARD DENIS KELLY, ord. June 16, 1886; cons. Auxiliary Bishop of Detroit, Jan. 26, 1911; transferred to the See of Grand Rapids, Jan. 16, 1919; died March 26, 1926; JOSEPH GABRIEL PINTEN, D.D., ord. Nov. 1, 1890; cons. Bishop of Superior May 3, 1922; transferred to See of Grand Rapids June 25, 1926; resigned and appt. Titular Bishop of Sela Nov. 1, 1940; died Nov. 6, 1945; JOSEPH CASIMIR PLAGENS, ord. July 5, 1903; cons. Sept. 30, 1924, Auxiliary Bishop of Detroit and Titular Bishop of Rhodiopolis; transferred to See of Marquette Nov. 16, 1935; transferred to See of Grand Rapids Dec. 16, 1940; installed as Bishop of Grand Rapids Feb. 18, 1941; died March 31, 1943; FRANCIS JOSEPH HAAS, D.D., ord. June 11, 1913; appt. Sept. 26, 1943; cons. and installed as Bishop of Grand Rapids, Nov. 18, 1943; died Aug. 29, 1953; ALLEN JAMES BABCOCK, D.D., ord. March 7, 1925; appt. Titular Bishop of Irenopolis and Auxiliary of Detroit Feb. 15, 1947; cons. March 25, 1947; appt. to Grand Rapids March 23, 1954; died June 27, 1969; JOSEPH MATTHEW BREITENBECK, D.D., ord. May 30, 1942; appt. Titular Bishop of Tepelta and Auxiliary of Detroit Oct. 18, 1965; cons. Dec. 20, 1965; appt. Bishop of Grand Rapids Oct. 15, 1969; installed Dec. 2, 1969; retired Aug. 3, 1989; died March 12, 2005; ROBERT JOHN ROSE, D.D., S.T.L., (Retired), ord. Dec. 21, 1955; appt. Bishop of Gaylord Oct. 13, 1981; cons. Dec. 6, 1981; appt. Bishop of Grand Rapids July 11, 1989; installed Aug. 30, 1989; retired Oct. 13, 2003; KEVIN MICHAEL BRITT, ord. June 28, 1970; appt. Auxiliary Bishop of Detroit, Titular Bishop of Esco Nov. 23, 1993; cons. Jan. 6, 1994; appt. Coadjutor Bishop of Grand Rapids Dec. 10, 2002; Succeeded to See Oct. 13, 2003; died May 15, 2004; WALTER ALLISON HURLEY, J.C.L., ord. June 5, 1965; appt. Titular Bishop of Chunavia and Auxiliary Bishop of Detroit July 7, 2003; cons. Aug. 12, 2003; appt. Bishop of Grand Rapids June 21, 2005; installed Aug. 4, 2005; retired April 18, 2013.

Vicar General/Moderator of the Curia—Rev. Msgr. WILLIAM H. DUNCAN, J.C.L., Tel: 616-514-6050.

Secretary to the Bishop—Tel: 616-514-6050. GAIL A. WELSH.

Vicar for Clergy—Rev. THOMAS P. PAGE, Tel: 616-243-0491.

Chancellor—MICHAEL A. LOWN, Tel: 616-475-1247.

Tribunal—360 Division Ave., S., Grand Rapids, 49503. Tel: 616-459-4509.

Judicial Vicar—Tel: 616-459-4509. Rev. Msgr. EDWARD A. HANKIEWICZ, J.C.L.

Marriage Dispensations/Permissions—
Tel: 616-514-6050. Rev. Msgr. WILLIAM DUNCAN.

College of Consultors—Rev. THOMAS J. BROWN; Rev. Msgr. WILLIAM H. DUNCAN, J.C.L.; Revs. STEPHEN S. DUDEK; DAVID C. GROSS; JOHN F. VALLIER; THOMAS P. PAGE.

Presbyteral Council—Deans: Revs. CHRIS W. ROUECH; MICHAEL G. HODGES; WAYNE B. WHEELER JR.; ANTHONY S. RUSSO; CHARLES D. BROWN. Elected Members: Revs. MICHAEL E. BURT; STEPHEN S. DUDEK; DAVID C. GROSS; THOMAS P. PAGE; PHILLIP A. SLIWINSKI; THOMAS J. BROWN; DARREL CALVIN KEMPF. Senior Priest Representative: Rev. WILLIAM F. ZINK, (Retired). Appointed: Rev. DANIEL P. SCHUMAKER. Ex Officio: Rev. Msgr. WILLIAM H. DUNCAN, J.C.L.

Deans—Revs. CHRIS W. ROUECH, South Deanery; THOMAS J. BROWN, East Deanery; CHARLES D. BROWN, West Deanery; ANTHONY S. RUSSO, North

Deanery; MICHAEL G. HODGES, Northest Deanery; WAYNE B. WHEELER JR., Northwest Deanery.
Diocesan Finance Council—Sr. AQUINAS WEBER, O.P.; Rev. LEONARD A. SUDLIK; RICHARD A. WENDT; THOMAS J. WESHOLSKI; TODD HARVEY, C.F.P.; JOHN NOWAK.

Diocesan Offices and Ministries
Chief Financial Officer—Tel: 616-475-1247. MICHAEL A. LOWN.
Comptroller—KEVIN SIMON.
Black Catholic Ministry—Rev. GODFREY C. ONYEKWERE, Office for Black Catholic Ministry, Tel: 616-243-0491.
Catechesis—TAMARA GRAVES, Tel: 616-288-0912.
The Catholic Foundation of West Michigan—MARK MORROW, Dir., Tel: 616-475-1251.
Catholic Services Appeal—Tel: 616-243-0491. KATIE OLDING.
Communications—Tel: 616-475-1240. ANNALISE LAUMEYER.
Cursillo Movement—Tel: 616-243-0491. Rev. JOSE LUIS QUINTANA.
Courage International—Tel: 616-288-0914. Rev. WILLIAM R. VANDER WERFF.
Diocesan Council of Catholic Women—BARB VESNO, Tel: 616-481-2529.
Ecumenical Affairs—Tel: 616-456-1454. Very Rev. RENE CONSTANZA, C.S.P.
EnCourage Ministries—Tel: 616-288-0918. Rev. THOMAS J. CAVERA.
Faith Formation—Sr. BARBARA CLINE, F.S.E., Tel: 616-551-4743.
Family and Youth—MARK MANN, Tel: 616-475-1243.
Hispanic Ministry—JUAN CARLOS FARIAS GONZALEZ, Tel: 616-246-0598.
Immigration Legal Services—Tel: 616-551-4746. REBECCA LAIR-YBANEZ.
Liturgical Music—Deacon DENNIS RYBICKI, Tel: 616-243-5590.
Missions Office—Tel: 616-243-0491. Rev. STEPHEN S. DUDEK.
Native American Ministry—DEBRA GUTOWSKI, Tel: 616-514-6065.
Pastoral Services—D.J. FLORIAN, Tel: 616-551-4748.
Prison/Jail Ministry—TRICIA WORRELL, Tel: 616-475-1255.
Pro-Life Ministry—Tel: 616-551-4748. D.J. FLORIAN.
Safe Environment—Tel: 616-475-1246. CHRIS CASTANO.
Stewardship & Development; Catholic Relief Services—Tel: 616-475-1251. MARK MORROW.
Victim Assistance Coordinator—Tel: 616-514-6050. ALLISON BUSH.
Vietnamese Ministry—Rev. VICTOR KYNAM, Tel: 616-243-0491.
Worship—AARON SANDERS, Tel: 616-475-1241.

Clergy and Religious Services Division

Office of Priestly Vocations and Continuing Formation for Clergy—Tel: 616-475-1254. Revs. RONALD D. HUTCHINSON; STEPHEN J. DURKEE.
Diaconate Formation—Deacon JAMES HESSLER, Tel: 616-288-0913.
Permanent Diaconate—Rev. MARK C. PRZYBYSZ, Tel: 616-288-0910.
Priest Retirement Fund—Tel: 616-243-0491. Rev. STEVEN D. CRON.

Administration Division

Archives—Rev. DENNIS W. MORROW, Tel: 616-243-0491.
Building and Planning—MICHAEL A. LOWN, Tel: 616-475-1247.
Cemeteries—JAMES ARSULOWICZ, Tel: 616-453-1636. Grand Rapids: Mt. Calvary Cemetery; St. Andrew Cemetery; Holy Cross Cemetery; SS Peter & Paul Cemetery. Wyoming: Resurrection Cemetery.
Deposit and Loan Program—KEVIN SIMON, Tel: 616-475-1253.
Facilities/Real Estate—MICHAEL A. LOWN, Tel: 616-475-1247.
Human Resources—TRACI DOUGLAS, Tel: 616-475-1242.
Parish Review Services—Tel: 616-288-0909. Sr. MARIA SERRA GARCIA, F.S.E.
Self-Insurance Program—MICHAEL A. LOWN, Tel: 616-475-1247.
Technology—ALEC SATURLEY, Tel: 616-246-0593.

Education Division

Superintendent of Catholic Schools—DAVID A. FABER, Tel: 616-233-5975.
Assistant Superintendent of Catholic Schools—JILL ANNABLE, Tel: 616-551-5633.
Catholic Information Center—Tel: 616-459-7267. Very Rev. RENE CONSTANZA, C.S.P., Dir.

Institutions Located in the Diocese

Catholic Charities West Michigan—40 Jefferson Ave., S.E., Grand Rapids, 49503. CHRISTOPHER SLATER, CEO, Tel: 616-456-1443.
Service Locations—Cathedral Square Center, 360 Division Ave. S., Grand Rapids, 49503. Big Rapids: *605 S. Third Ave., Ste. AA, Big Rapids, 49307.* Grand Rapids: *CASA Visit House, 1935 Plainfield Ave., Grand Rapids, 49505. God's Kitchen, 303 Division Ave. S., Grand Rapids, 49503.* Tel: 616-454-4110. Holland: *456 Century Ln., Holland, 49423.* Tel: 616-796-9595. Ionia: *601 E. Washington St., Ste. A, Ionia, 48846.* Tel: 616-522-0836. Kalamazoo: *1441 S. Westnedge Ave., Kalamazoo, 49008.* Tel: 269-381-1234. Ludington: *5868 W. US 10, Ludington, 49431.* Tel: 231-843-4899. Muskegon: *1095 3rd St., #125, Muskegon, 49441.* Tel: 231-726-4735. Stanton: *406 N. State St., Ste. D, P.O. Box 480, Stanton, 48888.* Tel: 616-855-5923. Traverse City: *806 Hastings St., Ste. R, Traverse City, 49686.* Tel: 231-346-5250. White Cloud: *1195 E. Wilcox, P.O. Box 912, White Cloud, 49349.* Tel: 231-689-6701.

CLERGY, PARISHES, MISSIONS AND PAROCHIAL SCHOOLS

CITY OF GRAND RAPIDS

(KENT COUNTY)

1—CATHEDRAL OF ST. ANDREW (1833) [CEM]
301 Sheldon Blvd. S.E., 49503. Tel: 616-456-1454; Email: barb@cathedralofsaintandrew.org; Web: www.cathedralofsaintandrew.org. 215 Sheldon Blvd. S.E., 49503. Revs. William Edens, C.S.P., Parochial Vicar; Michael Hennessy, Parochial Vicar.
See San Juan Diego Academy under Inter Parochial Elementary Schools located in the Institution section.
Catechesis Religious Program—
Tel: 616-456-1454, Ext. 1913; Email: sdonovan@cathedralofsaintandrew.org. Mr. Sean Donovan, D.R.E. Students 100.

2—ST. ALPHONSUS (1888) [JC]
224 Carrier St., N.E., 49505. Tel: 616-451-3043; Email: stalphonsusgr@catholicweb.com; Web: stalphonsusgr.org. Revs. Patrick Grile, C.Ss.R.; Bernard Carlin, C.Ss.R.; Brian Johnson, C.Ss.R.; Tuan Anh Nguyen, C.Ss.R.; Thomas Danielsen, C.Ss.R., In Res.; Bro. Andrew Patin, C.Ss.R., In Res.
See All Saints Academy under Diocesan Elementary Schools, located in the Institution section.
Catechesis Religious Program—Tel: 616-459-5472. Maggie Vugteveen, D.R.E. Students 106.

3—ST. ANTHONY OF PADUA (1906)
2510 Richmond St., N.W., 49504.
Tel: 616-453-8229, Ext. 100; Email: parishoffice@saparish.com; Web: www.saparish.com. Revs. Mark C. Przybysz; Luis F. Garcia; Deacon Leo Ferguson.
School—St. Anthony of Padua School, (Grades PreK-8), Email: dhillary@saparish.com. Ms. Jenny Pudelko, Prin. Lay Teachers 28; Students 274.
Catechesis Religious Program—Email: lhaley@saparish.com. Lynne Haley, D.R.E. Students 242.

4—BASILICA OF ST. ADALBERT (1881) [JC] (Polish)
654 Davis N.W., Fl. #2, 49504-5199.
Tel: 616-458-3065; Email: jmitus@basilicagr.org; Web: www.basilicagr.org. Revs. Ronald D. Hutchinson; Daniel P. Schumaker, Parochial Vicar; Deacon Stanley Lechtanski, Pastoral Assoc.
Church: 4th and Davis, N.W., 49504. Email: parishoffices@basillicagr.org.
St. James, 733 Bridge St., 49504.
Catechesis Religious Program—Email: dre@basilicagr.org. Margaret Downer, C.R.E. Students 37.

5—BLESSED SACRAMENT (1946) [JC]
2275 Diamond Ave., N.E., 49505. Tel: 616-361-7339; Email: church@bsacrament.net; Email: father@bsacrament.net; Web: www.bsacrament.net. Rev. George E. Darling.
See All Saints Academy under Diocesan Elementary Schools, located in the Institution section.
Catechesis Religious Program—
Tel: 616-361-7339, Ext. 1253; Email: jdegraw@bsacrament.net. Jody DeGraw, D.R.E. Students 46.

6—ST. DOMINIC (1974) Closed.
50 Bellevue, S.W., 49548. Tel: 616-241-2485; Email: sfxolgoffice@sbcglobal.net. 245 Griggs St. S.E., 49507. For inquiries for parish records see Shrine of St. Francis Xavier and Our Lady of Guadalupe, Grand Rapids.

7—HOLY SPIRIT (1952)
2230 Lake Michigan Dr., N.W., 49504.
Tel: 616-453-6369; Email: office@hsparish.org; Web: www.hsparish.org. Revs. Mark E. Peacock; Michael Steffes, Parochial Vicar.
School—Holy Spirit School, (Grades PreK-8), 2222 Lake Michigan Dr., N.W., 49504. Tel: 616-453-2772; Fax: 616-453-0018; Email: pkalahar@hsparish.org; Web: www.holyspiritschool.org. Patrick Kalahar, Prin. Clergy 1; Lay Teachers 16; Students 287.
Catechesis Religious Program—Tel: 616-453-1591; Email: dschoof@hsparish.org. Mrs. Diane Schoof, D.R.E. Students 136.

8—IMMACULATE HEART OF MARY
1935 Plymouth Ave. S.E., 49506. Tel: 616-241-4477; Email: parish@ihmparish.com. Rev. Troy Nevins.
School—Immaculate Heart of Mary School, (Grades PreK-8), 1951 Plymouth, S.E., 49506.
Tel: 616-241-4633; Fax: 616-241-4418; Email: principal@ihmschoolgr.com; Web: ihmparish.com/school/. Michael Thomasma, Prin. Lay Teachers 26; Students 306.
Catechesis Religious Program—
Tel: 616-241-4477, Ext. 105; Email: pa@ihmparish.com. Students 90.

9—ST. ISIDORE (1897) [JC] (Polish)
628 Diamond Ave., N.E., 49503. Tel: 616-459-4731; Email: dianeschmidt@saintisidorechurch.org; Web: www.saintisidorechurch.org. Rev. Msgr. Edward A. Hankiewicz, J.C.L.
See All Saints Academy under Diocesan Elementary Schools, located in the Institution section.
Catechesis Religious Program—625 Spring Ave. N.E., 49503. Tel: 616-459-4731, Ext. 33; Email: sisterzelita@saintisidorechurch.org. Sr. Zelita M. Bragagnolo, M.C., D.R.E. Students 61.

10—ST. JAMES (1870) Merged with Basilica of St. Adalbert, Grand Rapids. For inquiries for parish records contact the Basilica of St. Adalbert, Grand Rapids.

11—ST. JOHN VIANNEY, [JC]
4101 Clyde Park, S.W., Wyoming, 49509.
Tel: 616-534-5449; Email: hcoppock@stjohnvianney.net. Rev. John F. Vallier.
School—St. John Vianney School, (Grades K-8),
Tel: 616-532-7001; Fax: 616-532-1884; Email: gbruno@stjohnvianney.net. Mr. Gregg Bruno, Prin. Lay Teachers 16; Students 226; Religious Teachers 2.
Catechesis Religious Program—Tel: 616-724-3123; Email: jhurst@stjohnvianney.net. Marty Best, D.R.E. Students 43.

12—ST. JUDE (1946)
1120 Four Mile, N.E., 49525.
Tel: 616-363-6885, Ext. 1150; Email: lparks@stjudes.net. Rev. Thomas P. Page; Deacon Larry Hoogeboom.
See All Saints Academy under Diocesan Elementary Schools, located in the Institution section.
Catechesis Religious Program—Email: cschwartz@stjudes.net. Students 62.

13—ST. MARY (1857)
423 1st St. N.W., 49504. Tel: 616-459-7390; Email: parish@stmarygr.org; Email: wanda@stmarygr.org. Revs. Ronald D. Hutchinson, Admin.; Daniel P. Schumaker, Parochial Vicar.
Catechesis Religious Program—Students 58.

14—ST. MARY MAGDALEN (1956)
1253 52nd St., S.E., Kentwood, 49508.
Tel: 616-455-9310; Email: jhakeem@stmmagdalen.org. Rev. Peter G. Vu.
Catechesis Religious Program—Ms. Molly Wisdom, D.R.E. Students 185.

15—OUR LADY OF SORROWS (1908) (Italian)
101 Hall St., S.E., 49507. Tel: 616-243-0222; Email: office@ourladyofsorrows-gr.org. 116 Green St., S.E., 49507. Rev. Theodore Kozlowski.
See San Juan Diego Academy under Inter Parochial Elementary Schools located in the Institution section.
Catechesis Religious Program—1159 Sheldon Ave., S.E., 49507. Ms. Mary Lou Pacensia-Lopez, D.R.E. Students 44.

16—ST. PAUL THE APOSTLE (1965)
2750 Burton St., S.E., 49546. Tel: 616-949-4170; Fax: 616-949-5295; Email: pmarshall@stpaulapostle.com; Web: www.stpaulapostle.com. Rev. Peter Damian.
School—St. Paul the Apostle School, (Grades PreK-8), Tel: 616-949-1690; Email: bbissell@stpaul-school.org; Web: www.stpaul-school.org. Mrs. Michelle Morrow, Prin. Lay Teachers 18; Students 191.
Catechesis Religious Program—Mrs. Jeanne Winkelmann, D.R.E. Students 142.

17—SS. PETER AND PAUL (1904) [CEM] (Lithuanian)

520 Myrtle St., N.W., 49504-3277. Tel: 616-454-6000; Tel: 616-454-5611; Fax: 616-454-4532; Web: www.ssppgr.com. Rev. Dennis W. Morrow.
Catechesis Religious Program—1433 Hamilton Ave. N.W., 49504. Mrs. Sally Augdahl, D.R.E. Students 33.

18—SACRED HEART OF JESUS (1904) [JC]
156 Valley Ave SW, 49504. Tel: 616-459-8362; Email: parishoffice@sacredheartgr.org; Web: sacredheartgr.com. Rev. Robert A. Sirico.
School—Sacred Heart Academy, (Grades PreK-12), 1200 Dayton S.W., 49504. Tel: 616-459-0948; Email: headmaster@sacredheartgr.org; Email: ssurrell@sacredheartgr.org; Web: sacredheartacademygr.org. Mr. Sean Maltbie, Headmaster. Lay Teachers 31; Students 315; Clergy / Religious Teachers 2.
Catechesis Religious Program—Email: dre@sacredheartgr.org. Michael Tober, D.R.E. Students 42.

19—SHRINE OF ST. FRANCIS XAVIER AND OUR LADY OF GUADALUPE (1914) [JC]
250 Brown St., S.E., 49507.
Tel: 616-241-2485, Ext. 10; Email: sfxolgoffice@sbcglobal.net; Web: sfxolg.org. 245 Griggs St. S.E., 49507. Rev. Jose Luis Quintana; Laura Brizio-Blas, Admin.; Fernando I. Gutierrez-Perez, Pastoral Assoc.
See San Juan Diego Academy under Inter Parochial Elementary Schools located in the Institution section.
Catechesis Religious Program—Tel: 616-202-8262; Tel: 616-432-4663; Email: jcpaiz96@gmail.com. Colleen Paiz, Faith Formation; Elidia Buitron, Faith Formation, Hispanic; Mr. Steve VanderLaan, Adult Rel. Educ. Students 140.

20—ST. STEPHEN CATHOLIC CHURCH (1925) [JC]
750 Gladstone Ave. S.E., East Grand Rapids, 49506-2821. Tel: 616-243-8998; Fax: 616-245-7360; Email: parishoffice@ststephenparish.com; Web: www.ststephenparish.com. 723 Rosewood Ave. S.E., East Grand Rapids, 49506. Rev. Scott T. Nolan.
School—St. Stephen Catholic Church School, (Grades PreK-8), 740 Gladstone Ave., S.E., East Grand Rapids, 49506. Tel: 616-243-8998, Ext. 206; Email: schooloffice@ststephenparish.com; Web: ststephenschoolgr.com. Cindy Thomas, Prin. Lay Teachers 22; Students 200; Clergy / Religious Teachers 1.
Catechesis Religious Program—Email: brenne@ststephenparish.com. Brittany Renne, D.R.E. Students 97.

21—ST. THOMAS THE APOSTLE (1924) [JC]
1449 Wilcox Park Dr., S.E., 49506.
Tel: 616-459-4662, Ext. 1202; Email: margodean@stthomasgr.org; Web: www.stthomasapostlegr.org. Rev. James A. Chelich; Deacons James Thorndill; Dennis Williams; Dean Vernon
Legal Title: St. Thomas the Apostle Parish
School—St. Thomas the Apostle School, (Grades PreK-8), 1429 Wilcox Park Dr., S.E., 49506. Tel: 616-458-4228; Fax: 616-458-4583; Web: www.stthomasapostle.catholicweb.com. Tim Gibson, Dean; Suzi Furtwangler, Prin. Lay Teachers 19; Students 334.
Catechesis Religious Program—
Tel: 616-459-4662, Ext. 1209; Email: pattireynolds@stthomasgr.org. Patti Reynolds, D.R.E. Students 116.

OUTSIDE THE CITY OF GRAND RAPIDS

ADA, KENT CO., ST. ROBERT OF NEWMINSTER (1951)
6477 Ada Dr. S.E., Ada, 49301. Tel: 616-676-9111; Email: parishmail@strobertchurch.org; Web: strobertchurch.org. Revs. Leonard A. Sudlik; Colin J. Mulhall, Parochial Vicar; Sr. Darlene Wessling, Pastoral Min./Coord.
Catechesis Religious Program—
Tel: 616-676-9111, Ext. 114; Email: tburns@strobertchurch.org. Teri Burns, D.R.E. Students 707.

ALLENDALE, OTTOWA CO., ST. LUKE UNIVERSITY PARISH (2007)
10144 42nd Ave., Jenison, 49428. Tel: 616-895-2247; Fax: 616-895-2249; Email: frbill@lukespot.com; Web: www.lukespot.com. Rev. William R. Vander Werff.
Catechesis Religious Program—Email: faithformation@lukespot.com. Mr. John Graveline, D.R.E. Students 97.
Mission—Grand Valley State University - Catholic Campus Ministry.

ALPINE, KENT CO., HOLY TRINITY (1848) [CEM]
1200 Alpine Church Rd., N.W., Comstock Park, 49321. Tel: 616-784-0677; Fax: 616-784-0678; Email: parishoffice@holytrinitycp.org; Web: www.holytrinitycp.org. Rev. Thomas G. Simons; Deacon Gerald Roersma.
School—Holy Trinity School, (Grades PreK-8), 1304 Alpine Church Rd., Comstock Park, 49321.
Tel: 616-784-0696; Fax: 616-988-9415; Email: krand@holytrinitycp.org; Web: holytrinityschool.catholicweb.com. Kathy Rand, Prin. Lay Teachers 9; Students 164; Religious Teachers 2.
Catechesis Religious Program—Email: bdunneback@holytrinitycp.org. Rebbeca Dunneback, D.R.E. Students 83.

BALDWIN, LAKE CO., ST. ANN - ST. IGNATIUS (1912)
740 E. Ninth St., Baldwin, 49304. Tel: 231-745-7997; Fax: 231-745-9844; Email: annigna@sbcglobal.net. P.O. Box 729, Baldwin, 49304. Rev. Ronald F. Schneider.
St. Ignatius: 701 State St., Luther, 49656.
Catechesis Religious Program—Tel: 231-580-9281; Email: burtonamanda18@yahoo.com. Amanda Burton, D.R.E. Students 10.

BELDING, IONIA CO.
1—ST. JOSEPH (1894) [CEM] Merged with St. Mary's, Miriam to form St. Joseph-St. Mary, Belding.
2—ST. JOSEPH-ST. MARY
409 S. Bridge St., Belding, 48809. Tel: 616-754-4194. 505 S. Lafayette St., Greenville, 48838. Revs. James B. Wyse; Mark F. Bauer; Deacon Daniel Schneider.
Catechesis Religious Program—Tel: 616-754-3196; Fax: 616-754-2357. Tessa Hoffman, Rel. Ed. Coord. Students 55.
Chapel—St. Mary Chapel / Oratory, 9041 Krupp Rd., Belding, 48809.

BELMONT, KENT CO., ASSUMPTION OF THE BLESSED VIRGIN MARY (1913) [CEM]
6369 Belmont Ave. NE, Belmont, 49306.
Tel: 616-361-5126; Web: www.assumptionbvm.com. Rev. Anthony M. Pelak; Deacons Peter P. Conigliaro; Michael J. Mauer.
School—Assumption of the Blessed Virgin Mary School, (Grades PreK-8), 6393 Belmont Ave., Belmont, 49306. Tel: 616-361-5483;
Fax: 616-361-2553; Email: schoolsecretary@abvmschool1.org; Web: www.schoolassumptionbvm.com. Mr. Domenic Franconi, Prin. Lay Teachers 10; Students 208.
Catechesis Religious Program—6391 Belmont Ave., Belmont, 49306. Tel: 616-361-5126, Ext. 257; Email: religiouseddirector@assumptionbvm.com. Ms. Cheryl Sokolowski, D.R.E. Students 201.

BIG RAPIDS, MECOSTA CO.
1—ST. MARY (1873) [CEM] Merged with St. Paul's Campus Parish, Big Rapids to form St. Mary-St. Paul Parish, Big Rapids.
2—ST. MARY-ST. PAUL PARISH (1873)
1009 Marion Ave., Big Rapids, 49307.
Tel: 231-796-5202; Email: nspedowski@stmarystpaulbr.org. Revs. Michael E. Burt; Patrick Fickel, Rev. Patrick Fickel.
Church: St. Paul, One Damascus Rd., Big Rapids, 49307. Tel: 231-598-9445.
School—St. Mary Catholic School, (Grades PreSchool-8), 927 Marion Ave., Big Rapids, 49307.
Tel: 231-796-6731; Fax: 231-976-9293; Email: jbwatters@stmarybr.org. J.B. Watters, Prin. Lay Teachers 6; Students 101; Religious Teachers 6.
Catechesis Religious Program—Email: lshields@stmarystpaulbr.org; Email: nancyjoe@netonecom.net. Linda Shields, Faith Formation, Evening; Joe Spedowski, RCIA Coord. Students 46.
3—ST. PAUL CAMPUS PARISH (1958) Merged with St. Mary's, Big Rapids to form St. Mary-St. Paul Parish, Big Rapids.

BRUNSWICK, NEWAYGO CO., ST. MICHAEL (1886) [CEM]
6382 S. Maple Island Rd., Fremont, 49412.
Tel: 231-924-3389; Fax: 231-924-0402. Rev. Peter C. Schafer.
Catechesis Religious Program—Students 39.
Chapel—Chapel / Oratory Christ the King, Hesperia.

BYRON CENTER, KENT CO., ST. SEBASTIAN (1852) [CEM]
9408 Wilson Ave., S.W., Byron Center, 49315.
Tel: 616-878-1619; Email: sue@stsebastianmi.org; Web: www.stsebastianmi.org. Rev. Msgr. William H. Duncan, J.C.L.
Catechesis Religious Program—
Tel: 616-787-1619, Ext. 102; Email: parishoffice@stsebastianmi.org. Debbie Mayer, D.R.E.; Rodney Wood, Youth Min. Students 336.

CALEDONIA, KENT CO., HOLY FAMILY (1970) [CEM 3]
9669 Kraft Ave., S.E., Caledonia, 49316.
Tel: 616-891-9259; Fax: 616-891-1346; Email: parishoffice@holyfamilycaledonia.org; Web: www.holyfamilycaledonia.org. Rev. Loc Q. Trinh.
Catechesis Religious Program—Tel: 616-891-8867. Christine Shafer, D.R.E. Students 284.

CARSON CITY, MONTCALM CO., ST. MARY (1896) [CEM]
Clustered with St. John the Baptist Parish, Hubbardston.
404 N. Division St., Carson City, 48811.
Tel: 989-584-6044; Email: nwoodcock@cmsinter.net; Web: stmarystjohn.net. Nancy Woodcock, Parish Life Coord.
Catechesis Religious Program—Nancy Woodcock, D.R.E. Students 47.

CEDAR SPRINGS, KENT CO., SAINT JOHN PAUL II (2013)
Clustered with Mary Queen of Apostles, Sand Lake and Merged with St. Margaret Chapel, Harvard/Cedar Springs.
3110 17 Mile Rd., N.E., Cedar Springs, 49319.
Tel: 616-696-3904; Fax: 616-696-2168; Email: akogut@jp2-mqa.org; Email: kmendenhall@jp2-mqa.org; Web: jp2-mqa.org. Rev. Lam T. Le.
Catechesis Religious Program—Ms. Katie Mendenhall, D.R.E. Students 150.

CONKLIN, OTTAWA CO., ST. FRANCIS XAVIER (1892) [CEM] Clustered with St. Catherine, Ravenna and St. Joseph, Wright.
2034 Gooding Rd., Conklin, 49403. Tel: 231-853-6222; Fax: 231-853-2664; Email: stfrancisconklin@ourcluster.org; Web: ourcluster.org. 3376 Thomas St., P.O. Box 216, Ravenna, 49451. Rev. G. Fredrick Brucker, S.T.L., J.C.L.
Catechesis Religious Program—Email: dre@ourcluster.org. Diane Beckwith, D.R.E. Students 10.

COOPERSVILLE, OTTAWA CO., ST. MICHAEL (1950) [CEM] [JC]
17150 88th Ave., Coopersville, 49404.
Tel: 616-384-4026; Fax: 616-837-7893; Email: secretary@saintmichaels.us; Web: www.saintmichaels.us. Rev. Ayub Nasar. Clustered with St. Mary, Marne.
School—St. Michael School, (PreK) Email: preschool@saintmichaels.us. Annette Lown, Dir. & Teacher. Lay Teachers 1; Students 12.
Catechesis Religious Program—Email: childrensministry@saintmichaels.us. Students 87.

CUSTER, MASON CO.
1—ST. MARY (1933) [CEM] [JC] Merged with St. Jerome, Scottville to form St. Mary-St. Jerome Parish, Custer.
2—ST. MARY-ST. JEROME PARISH, [CEM] [JC]
85 S. Madison Ave., P.O. Box 68, Custer, 49405.
Tel: 231-757-4709; Tel: 231-757-3709;
Fax: 231-757-4709; Email: stjeromesc@sbcglobal.net; Web: stmarycuster.org. Rev. Daniel R. DePew.
Catechesis Religious Program—Tel: 231-464-5567; Email: marykovalcik@gmail.com. Mary Kovalcik, D.R.E. Students 32.

EDMORE, MONTCALM CO., ST. MARGARET MARY (1963) Merged with St. Bernadette of Lourdes, Stanton to form St. Bernadette of Lourdes-St. Margaret Mary Alacoque, Stanton.

EVART, OSCEOLA CO., SACRED HEART (1874)
9878 E. US 10, P.O. Box 778, Evart, 49631.
Tel: 231-734-3171; Fax: 231-734-6880; Email: sacred@netonecom.net. Rev. Joseph J. Fix.
Catechesis Religious Program—Tel: 231-872-5754. Ann Johnson, D.R.E. Students 25.

FREE SOIL, MASON CO., ST. JOHN CANTIUS (1906) [CEM]
2845 E. Michigan, Free Soil, 49411.
Tel: 231-464-5672; Tel: 231-266-5155; Email: saintbernardchurch@hotmail.com. P.O. Box 155, Irons, 49644. Rev. Dennis O'Donnell.

FREMONT, NEWAYGO CO., ALL SAINTS (1901) [CEM]
500 Iroquois Dr., Fremont, 49412. Tel: 231-924-7705; Fax: 231-924-7708; Email: office@allsaintsfremont.org; Web: www.allsaintsfremont.org. Rev. Peter C. Schafer.
Catechesis Religious Program—Tel: 231-924-7571; Email: dre@allsaintsfremont.org. Denise Hudson, D.R.E. Students 63.

GRAND HAVEN, OTTAWA CO., ST. PATRICK - ST. ANTHONY (1857)
920 Fulton Ave., Grand Haven, 49417.
Tel: 616-842-0001; Email: parishoffice@stpatsgh.org; Web: www.stpatsgh.org. Rev. Charles J. Schwartz.
Catechesis Religious Program—Jimmy Beauchamp, Admin. Students 254.
Mission—St. Anthony Chapel, Contact St. Patrick Church, Grand Haven with inquiries and parish records of the Mission of St. Anthony, Robinson Township.

GRANDVILLE, KENT CO., ST. PIUS X (1953)
3937 Wilson Ave., S.W., Grandville, 49418.
Tel: 616-532-9344; Email: parishoffice@spxcatholic.org; Web: spxcatholic.org. Rev. Chris W. Rouech.
Catechesis Religious Program—Tel: 616-538-2600; Email: formation@spxcatholic.org. Ms. Elizabeth Post, D.R.E. Students 308.

GREENVILLE, MONTCALM CO., ST. CHARLES BORROMEO (1849) [CEM]
505 S. Lafayette, Greenville, 48838.
Tel: 616-754-4194; Email: bulletin@saintscjm.com; Web: saintscjm.com. Revs. James B. Wyse; Mark F. Bauer.
School—St. Charles Borromeo School, (Grades PreK-8), 502 S. Franklin St., Greenville, 48838.
Tel: 616-754-3416; Fax: 616-754-9262; Email: principal@saintscjm.com; Web: www.saintscjm.com/school. Margaret Karpus, Prin. Lay Teachers 6; Students 96.
Catechesis Religious Program—Email: thoffman@saintscjm.com. Molly Scoby, Adult Faith Formation, Tel: 616-754-4194; Natalie Klackle,

Youth Min. Coord.; Tessa Hoffman, Rel. Ed. Coord. Students 56.

HART, OCEANA CO.

1—ST. GREGORY (1908) Merged with Our Lady of Fatima, Shelby to form St. Gregory-Our Lady of Fatima, Hart.

2—ST. GREGORY-OUR LADY OF FATIMA
316 S. Peach Ave., Hart, 49420. Tel: 231-873-2660; Email: parish@stgregoryathart.org; Web: www.stgregoryathart.org. Rev. Thomas Bolster.
Church & Office: 1372 S. Oceana Dr., Shelby, 49455.
Catechesis Religious Program—Email: reled@stgregoryathart.org. Linda Foster, D.R.E. Students 227.

HOLLAND, OTTAWA CO.

1—ST. FRANCIS DE SALES (1903)
171 W. 13th St., Holland, 49423. Tel: 616-392-6700; Web: www.stfrancisholland.org. 195 W. 13th St., Holland, 49423. Revs. Charles D. Brown; Kyle Kilpatrick.
Catechesis Religious Program—Email: rvaldez@stfrancisholland.org. Students 350.

2—OUR LADY OF THE LAKE (1979)
480 152nd Ave., Holland, 49424. Tel: 616-399-1062; Fax: 616-399-5766; Email: office@oll.org; Web: www.oll.org. Rev. Michael Cilibraise.
Catechesis Religious Program—Ms. Carla Niziolek, Dir. of Discipleship. Students 236.

HOWARD CITY, MONTCALM CO., CHRIST THE KING-ST. FRANCIS DE SALES (1975) [CEM] with St. Francis de Sales, Lakeview to form Christ the King-St. Francis de Sales, Howard City.
9596 N. Reed Rd., Howard City, 49329.
Tel: 231-937-5757; Email: king-francis@ctknsf.org; Web: www.ctknsf.org. Rev. James R. Vander Laan; Deacon Richard Dubridge.
Catechesis Religious Program—Email: faithformation@ctknsf.org. Julie Gould, D.R.E. Students 35.

HUBBARDSTON, IONIA CO., ST. JOHN THE BAPTIST (1853) [CEM] Clustered with St. Mary, Carson City.
413 River St., Hubbardston, 48845.
Tel: 989-584-6044; Email: nwoodcock@cmsinter.net; Web: stmarystjohn.net. Mailing Address: 404 N. Division St., Carson City, 48811. Nancy Woodcock, Parish Life Coord.
Catechesis Religious Program—Nancy Woodcock, D.R.E. Clustered with St. Mary Parish - Carson City - Joint Religious Education Program. Students 29.

IONIA, IONIA CO., SS. PETER AND PAUL (1861) [CEM]
434 High St., Ionia, 48846. Tel: 616-527-3610; Fax: 616-527-3697; Email: parishoffice@ssppcatholic.com; Web: www.saintspeterandpaulionia.org. Revs. Thomas J. Brown; Oscar Londono Builes; Deacon Zenon Cardenas Sr.
School—SS. Peter and Paul School, (Grades K-8), 317 Baldie St., Ionia, 48846. Tel: 616-527-3561; Fax: 616-527-3562; Email: jleik@ssppcatholic.com; Web: www.ssppcatholic.com. Mrs. Jennifer Leik, Prin. Lay Teachers 6; Students 79.
Catechesis Religious Program—
Tel: 616-527-3610, Ext. 21; Email: vbooth@ssppcatholic.com. Vanessa Booth, D.R.E.; Mrs. Sandra Thelen, Contact Person. Students 66.

IRONS, LAKE CO., ST. BERNARD
5734 W. 10 1/2 Mile Rd., P.O. Box 155, Irons, 49644.
Tel: 231-266-5155; Email: saintbernardchurch@hotmail.com. Rev. Dennis O'Donnell.

JENISON, OTTAWA CO., HOLY REDEEMER (1975)
2700 Baldwin Dr., Jenison, 49428.
Tel: 616-669-9220, Ext. 1100; Email: hrpsecr@holyredeemerparish.org. Rev. Donald E. Weber, Admin., (Retired).
Catechesis Religious Program—Tel: 616-669-0820; Email: cbaker@holyredeemerparish.org. Christopher Baker, D.R.E.; Mr. Michael Hurst, Youth Min. Students 333.

LAKE ODESSA, IONIA CO., ST. EDWARD (1945)
531 Jordan Lake St., Lake Odessa, 48849.
Tel: 616-374-7253; Email: stedwards@wowway.biz. Rev. Thomas J. Brown.
Catechesis Religious Program—Vanessa Booth, D.R.E. Students 33.

LAKEVIEW, MONTCALM CO., ST. FRANCIS DE SALES (1943) Merged with Christ the King, Howard City to form Christ the King-St. Francis de Sales, Howard City.

LAKEWOOD CLUB, MUSKEGON CO., ST. MARY OF THE WOODS (1916) Merged with Prince of Peace, Muskegon.

LOWELL, KENT CO., ST. MARY aka St. Mary Great Mother of God Catholic Church (1879) [CEM]
402 Amity St., Lowell, 49331. Tel: 616-897-9820; Email: stmarylowell@att.net. Rev. Aaron R. Ferris.
Catechesis Religious Program—Email: stmarylowelldre@att.net. Jennie Forney, D.R.E. Students 76.

LUDINGTON, MASON CO.

1—ST. SIMON (1876) [CEM]
702 E. Bryant Rd., Ludington, 49431.
Tel: 231-843-8606; Email: stsimon@stsimonchurch.com. Rev. Wayne B. Wheeler Jr.
School—St. Simon School aka Ludington Area Catholic School, (Grades PreK-8), 700 E. Bryant Rd., Ludington, 49431. Tel: 231-843-3188; Email: cthompson@lacschool.com. Collin Thompson, Prin. Lay Teachers 7; Students 119; Clergy / Religious Teachers 2.
Catechesis Religious Program—Tel: 231-843-3497; Email: ekokx@stsimonchurch.net. Ms. Emily Kokx, D.R.E. Students 138.

2—ST. STANISLAUS, [JC] Closed. For inquiries for parish records see St. Simon's Ludington.

MARION, OSCEOLA CO., ST. AGNES (1888)
603 E. Main St., Marion, 49665. Tel: 231-734-3171; Email: sacred@netonecom.net. P.O. Box 778, Evart, 49631. Rev. Joseph J. Fix.
Catechesis Religious Program—Tel: 231-734-6845; Email: marciebennett999@gmail.com. Marcella Bennett, D.R.E. Students 40.

MARNE, OTTAWA CO., ST. MARY (1852) [CEM]
15164 Juniper Dr., Marne, 49435. Tel: 616-677-3934; Fax: 616-677-5866; Email: secretary@saintmarysmarne.org; Web: www.saintmarysmarne.org. Rev. Ayub Nasar.
Catechesis Religious Program—Tel: 616-677-5065; Email: dre@saintmarysmarne.org. Theresa Steffes, D.R.E. Students 129.

MIRIAM, IONIA CO., ST. MARY (1871) [CEM] Merged with St. Joseph, Belding to form St. Joseph-St. Mary Parish, Belding. For inquiries for parish records see St. Joseph-St. Mary Parish, Belding.

MONTAGUE, MUSKEGON CO., ST. JAMES (1876) [CEM]
5149 Dowling St., Montague, 49437.
Tel: 231-893-3085; Email: office.manger@stjamescatholicparish.org; Web: stjamescatholicparish.org. Rev. Peter O. Omogo; Deacon Gregory Anderson.
Catechesis Religious Program—
Tel: 231-893-3085, Ext. 3103; Email: faithformation@stjamescatholicparish.org. Mitzi Luttrul, D.R.E.; Kristin Schaub, D.R.E. Students 84.

MUSKEGON, MUSKEGON CO.

1—ST. FRANCIS DE SALES (1948) [JC]
2929 McCracken St., Norton Shores, 49441.
Tel: 231-755-1953, Ext. 200; Fax: 231-759-7074; Email: parish@stfrancisns.org;
Tel: www.stfrancisns.org. Rev. Charles D. Hall.
Catechesis Religious Program—
Tel: 231-755-1953, Ext. 225; Email: s_siuda@stfrancisns.org. Students 160.

2—ST. JEAN BAPTISTE (1883) [JC] Closed. for inquiries for parish records contact St. Mary of the Immaculate Conception, Muskegon.

3—ST. JOSEPH, Closed. For inquiries for parish records please see Our Lady of Grace, 451 S. Getty St., Muskegon, MI 49442.

4—ST. MARY (1856) [JC] Merged with St. Jean Baptiste, Muskegon to form St. Mary of the Immaculate Conception, Muskegon. For inquiries for parish records contact St. Mary of the Immaculate Conception, Muskegon.

5—ST. MARY OF THE IMMACULATE CONCEPTION 1856 [CEM]
196 W. Webster Ave., Muskegon, 49440-1213.
Tel: 231-722-2803; Web: stmarysmuskegon.org. 451 S. Getty St., Muskegon, 49442. Revs. Matthew J. Barnum; Edwin Carreno, Parochial Vicar; Deacon William Cook.
Catechesis Religious Program—Students 128.
Our Lady of Grace, Tel: 231-722-2803; Web: stmarysmuskegon.org.

6—ST. MICHAEL (1909) [JC]
1716 Sixth St., Muskegon, 49441. Tel: 231-722-3071; Email: stmichaelmusk@aol.com; Web: saintmichaelsmuskegon.com. Rev. Charles D. Hall.
Catechesis Religious Program— Religious Programs held at St. Francis De Sales, Norton Shores. Sr. Agnes Mary Wojtkowiak, O.P., D.R.E. Students 0.

7—OUR LADY OF GRACE (1923) [JC] Merged with St. Mary of the Immaculate Conception to form St. Mary of the Immaculate Conception, Muskegon.

8—ST. THOMAS THE APOSTLE (1948)
3252 Apple Ave., Muskegon, 49442.
Tel: 231-773-3160; Fax: 231-777-7866; Email: saint_thomas@frontier.com; Web: stthomasmuskegon.org. Rev. Philip A. Shangraw, Admin.
Catechesis Religious Program—Mrs. Sue Peterson, Rel. Ed. Dir. Students 21.

MUSKEGON HEIGHTS, MUSKEGON CO., SACRED HEART (1919) [JC]
150 E. Summit Ave., Muskegon Heights, 49444.
Tel: 231-733-2440; Email: sacred_heart1@frontier.com; Web: sacredheartmuskegon.org. Rev. Philip A. Shangraw, Admin.
Catechesis Religious Program—Karen Edens, D.R.E. Students 20.

NEWAYGO, NEWAYGO CO., ST. BARTHOLOMEW (1885) [CEM]
599 W. Brooks St., Newaygo, 49337.
Tel: 231-652-1286; Email: parishoffice@stbart-stjoe.org. Rev. Steven Geerling, Admin.
Catechesis Religious Program—
Tel: 231-652-1286, Ext. 22; Email: lkoester@stbart-stjoe.org. Students 124.

NORTH MUSKEGON, MUSKEGON CO., PRINCE OF PEACE (1975)
1110 Dykstra Rd., North Muskegon, 49445-2014.
Tel: 231-744-3321; Email: office@princeofpeacenm.org; Email: ganderson@princeofpeacenm.org; Email: tsteward@princeofpeacenm.org; Web: princeofpeacenm.org. Rev. Godfrey C. Onyekwere; Deacons Gregory Anderson, Business Mgr.; James J. Schiltz.
Catechesis Religious Program—
Tel: 231-744-3321, Ext. 128; Email: dphillips@princeofpeacenm.org; Email: bperri@princeofpeacenm.org. Walter Elliott, Youth Min.; Donna Phillips, Children's Faith Formation. Students 95.

PARNELL, KENT CO., ST. PATRICK (1844) [CEM]
4351 Parnell Ave. N.E., Ada, 49301.
Tel: 616-691-8541; Fax: 616-691-6309; Email: secretary@stpatrickparnell.org; Web: stpatrickparnell.org. Rev. Thomas J. Cavera, Admin.
School—St. Patrick School, (Grades PreK-8), 4333 Parnell Ave., N.E., Ada, 49301. Tel: 616-691-8833; Email: assistants@stpatrickparnellschool.org; Email: principal@stpatrickparnellschool.org; Web: www.stpatrickparnellschool.org. Scott Czarnopys, Prin. Lay Teachers 11; Students 214.
Catechesis Religious Program—
Tel: 616-691-8541, Ext. 41; Email: faithformation@stpatrickparnell.org. Kristin Wahmoff, Coord. of Faith Formation & Middle School Youth Ministry. Students 202.

PEWAMO, IONIA CO., ST. JOSEPH (1903) [CEM]
126 East St., P.O. Box 37, Pewamo, 48873.
Tel: 989-593-3440; Tel: 989-593-3400; Email: parishoffice@stjosephpewamo.org; Email: principal@stjosephpewamo.org; Web: www.stjosephpewamo.org. Rev. Darrel Calvin Kempf.
School—St. Joseph School, (Grades 1-8), 160 East St., P.O. Box 38, Pewamo, 48873. Email: principal@stjosephpewamo.org. Patricia O'Mara, Prin. Lay Teachers 7; Students 94; Religious Teachers 1.
Catechesis Religious Program—Email: downes@stjosephpewamo.org. Daniel Downes, D.R.E. Students 192.

PORTLAND, IONIA CO., ST. PATRICK (1878)
140 Church St., Portland, 48875. Tel: 517-647-6505; Email: parishoffice@portlandstpats.com; Web: stpatrickportland.com. Rev. Michael J. Alber.
School—St. Patrick School, (Grades PreK-8), 122 West St., Portland, 48875. Tel: 517-647-7551; Fax: 517-647-4545; Email: office@portlandstpats.com; Web: portlandstpats.com. Randy Hodge, Prin. Lay Teachers 12; Students 227; Clergy / Religious Teachers 1.
Catechesis Religious Program—Lori Thelen, Children's Faith Formation; Carolyn Kwiecinski, RCIA Coord.; George Rutherford, Youth Min. Students 220.

RAVENNA, MUSKEGON CO., ST. CATHERINE (1908) [CEM] Clustered with St. Joseph, Wright and St. Francis Xavier, Conklin.
3376 Thomas St., P.O. Box 216, Ravenna, 49451.
Tel: 231-853-6222; Email: stcatherinealex@ourcluster.org; Web: ourcluster.org. Rev. G. Fredrick Brucker, S.T.L., J.C.L.
Catechesis Religious Program—Email: dre@ourcluster.org. Diane Beckwith, D.R.E. Students 81.

REED CITY, OSCEOLA CO., ST. PHILIP NERI, [CEM]
831 S. Chestnut, Reed City, 49677.
Tel: 231-832-5544; Email: pneri831@stphilipanne.org. Rev. Michael G. Hodges.
Catechesis Religious Program—Elizabeth Dake, Dir. Faith Formation. Students 39.
Mission—St. Anne, 23949 22 Mile Rd., Paris, 49338.

REMUS, MECOSTA CO., ST. MICHAEL THE ARCHANGEL (1888) [CEM]
8929 50th Ave., Remus, 49340. Tel: 989-967-3520; Email: parishoffice@stmikes.us. Rev. Thomas F. Boufford.
School—St. Michael the Archangel School, (Grades PreK-6), 8944 50th Ave., Remus, 49340.
Tel: 989-967-3681; Fax: 989-967-3061; Email: jerryward1@stmikes.us; Web: www.stmikes.us. Jerry Ward, Prin. Lay Teachers 5; Students 84.
Catechesis Religious Program—
Tel: 989-967-3520, Ext. 204; Email: faithformation@stmikes.us. Kristina Beers, D.R.E. Students 14.

ROCKFORD, KENT CO., OUR LADY OF CONSOLATION (1972)
4865 Eleven Mile Rd., Rockford, 49341.
Tel: 616-866-0931; Email: trusso@olcparish.net; Email: nwentworth@olcparish.net; Web: www.olcparishrockford.com. Rev. Anthony S. Russo.

School—Our Lady of Consolation School, (Grades PreK-8), Tel: 616-866-2427; Email: kvarner@olcparish.net. Kevin Varner, Prin. Lay Teachers 13; Students 325; Clergy / Religious Teachers 3.
Catechesis Religious Program—Tel: 616-866-2577; Email: adesantis@olcparish.net. Anne Marie DeSantis, D.R.E. Students 445.

ROTHBURY, OCEANA CO., OUR LADY OF THE ASSUMPTION (1923) [CEM]
3000 W. Winston Rd., Rothbury, 49452.
Tel: 231-893-3085; Email: office.manager@stjamescatholicparish.org. 5149 Dowling St., Montague, 49437. Rev. Peter O. Omogo; Deacon Gregory Anderson.

SAND LAKE, KENT CO., MARY, QUEEN OF APOSTLES, [CEM 2]
1 Maple St., P.O. Box 140, Sand Lake, 49343-0140.
Tel: 616-636-5671; Fax: 616-636-4570; Email: sbrewster@jp2-mqa.org; Web: jp2-mqa.org. Rev. Lam T. Le.
Catechesis Religious Program—Email: info@jp2mqa.org. Students 15.
Chapel—St. Clara, 4584 N. Bailey Rd., Coral, 49322.

SARANAC, IONIA CO., ST. ANTHONY (1951)
6070 David Hwy., Saranac, 48881. Tel: 616-642-6119; Email: stanthonysar@att.net; Web: StAnthonyofSaranac.org. 3936 Jackson Rd., Saranac, 48881. Rev. Aaron R. Ferris.
Catechesis Religious Program—Mrs. Susan Lauer, D.R.E. Students 25.

SCOTTVILLE, MASON CO., ST. JEROME (1912) [CEM] Merged with St. Mary, Custer to form St. Mary-St. Jerome Parish, Custer. For inquiries for parish records contact St. Mary-St. Jerome Parish, Custer.

SHELBY, OCEANA CO., OUR LADY OF FATIMA, Merged with St. Gregory, Hart to become St. Gregory-Our Lady of Fatima.

SPARTA, KENT CO., HOLY FAMILY (1947)
425 S. State St., Sparta, 49345. Tel: 616-887-8222; Email: parishoffice@holyfamilysparta.org; Web: holyfamilysparta.org. Rev. Msgr. Terrence L. Stewart.
Catechesis Religious Program—Tel: 616-887-8857; Email: srbgazda@holyfamilysparta.org. Sr. Bernadine Gazda, O.S.J., D.R.E. Students 82.

SPRING LAKE, OTTAWA CO., ST. MARY (1863)
406 E. Savidge, Spring Lake, 49456.
Tel: 616-842-1702; Email: parishoffice@stmarysl.org; Web: www.stmarysl.org. Rev. David C. Gross; Deacon William Charron.
School—St. Mary School, (Grades PreSchool-8), 430 E. Savidge St., Spring Lake, 49456.
Tel: 616-842-1282; Fax: 616-842-8048; Email: schooloffice@stmarysl.org. Steve Van Hammen, Prin. Lay Teachers 12; Students 190; Religious Teachers 1.
Catechesis Religious Program—Tel: 616-842-2840. Mrs. Cathy Pearce, D.R.E.; Mr. David Heinert, Adult Faith Formation Coord.; Mr. Chris Iwan, Youth Min. Students 286.

STANTON, MONTCALM CO.
1—ST. BERNADETTE OF LOURDES (1963) Merged with St. St. Margaret Mary, Edmore to form St. Bernadette of Lourdes-St. Margaret Mary Alacoque, Stanton.
2—ST. BERNADETTE OF LOURDES-ST. MARGARET MARY ALACOQUE (1963)
991 E. Main St., Stanton, 48888. Tel: 989-831-5914; Email: sbl.smm.church@frontier.com. Rev. Dominic Tirkey.
Catechesis Religious Program—Tel: 989-291-0825; Email: ssines@charter.com. Stephanie Sines, D.R.E. Students 17.

WEARE TWP., OCEANA CO., ST. JOSEPH (1884) [CEM]
2380 W. Jackson Rd., Hart, 49420. Tel: 231-873-5776; Tel: 231-869-2601; Email: StJosephWeare@comcast.net; Web: www.stjosephweare.org. Rev. Philip Sliwinski.
Catechesis Religious Program—Tel: 231-329-1244. Renee Dennert, D.R.E. Students 53.
Mission—St. Vincent, 637 E. Sixth, Pentwater, 49449.

WHITE CLOUD, NEWAYGO CO., ST. JOSEPH, [CEM]
965 Newell St., White Cloud, 49349.
Tel: 231-652-1286; Email: parishoffice@stbart-stjoe.org. 599 W. Brooks St., Newaygo, 49337. Rev. Steven Geerling, Admin.
Catechesis Religious Program—Students 20.

WRIGHT TOWNSHIP, OTTAWA CO., ST. JOSEPH WRIGHT (1853) [CEM] Clustered with St. Catherine-Ravenna and St. Francis Xavier-Conklin.
18784 Eighth Ave., Conklin, 49403-9718.
Tel: 616-899-2286; Email: stjosephwright@ourcluster.org. Rev. G. Fredrick Brucker, S.T.L., J.C.L.
School—Divine Providence Academy of St. Joseph, (Grades PreK-8), 18768 Eighth Ave., Conklin, 49403.
Tel: 616-899-5300; Fax: 616-899-5491; Email: wings@wingsdpa.org; Web: www.wingsdpa.org. Kate Beuschel, Prin. Lay Teachers 6; Students 102; Clergy / Religious Teachers 1.
Catechesis Religious Program—Tel: 231-853-6222; Email: dre@ourcluster.org. Diane Beckwith, D.R.E. Students 57.

WYOMING, KENT CO.
1—HOLY NAME OF JESUS (1908) [JC]
1630 Godfrey Ave., S.W., Wyoming, 49509.
Tel: 616-241-6489; Email: hnjbookkeeper@gmail.com. Rev. Stephen S. Dudek; Deacon Carlos Gutierrez.
See San Juan Diego Academy under Inter Parochial Elementary Schools located in the Institution section.
Catechesis Religious Program—Email: releducma@gmail.com. Luz Margarita Aguirre, D.R.E. Students 163.
2—ST. JOSEPH THE WORKER (1887)
225 32nd St., S.W., Wyoming, 49548.
Tel: 616-456-7982, Ext. 0; Email: stevencron@sanjoseobrero.net; Email: secretaria@sanjoseobrero.net; Web: sanjoseobrero.net. 3138 Birchwood Ave., S.W., Wyoming, 49548. Rev. Steven D. Cron; Deacons Martin Zapata, Pastoral Assoc.; Carlos Gutierrez, Pastoral Assoc.
See San Juan Diego Academy under Inter Parochial Elementary Schools located in the Institution section.
Catechesis Religious Program—St. John Vianney School: 4101 Clyde Park Ave. S.W., Wyoming, 49509. Ms. Teresa Cruz-Vega, D.R.E. Students 105.
3—OUR LADY OF LAVANG (1999) [JC]
2019 Porter St. S.W., Wyoming, 49519.
Tel: 616-531-5213; Fax: 616-531-1948; Email: victorkynam@gmail.com. Rev. Victor Kynam; Deacon Thanh Van Nguyen, Our Lady of La-Vang, Wyoming.
Catechesis Religious Program—Cell: 616-307-9735. Students 228.

CHAPELS

GRAND RAPIDS
1—CHAPEL OF OUR LADY OF AGLONA, LATVIAN APOSTOLATE
Latvian Community Center, 504 Grand Ave., N.E., 49503. Tel: 616-363-4997; Email: marybrons@comcast.net. Zifrieds Zadvinskis, Admin.
2—GRAND RAPIDS HOME FOR VETERANS CATHOLIC CHAPEL
3000 Monroe Ave., N.E., 49505. Tel: 616-364-5323; Email: mlown@dioceseofgrandrapids.org. Michael A. Lown, Chancellor/CFO.

Leave of Absence:
Rev.—
Tran, Dung Anton.

Unassigned:
Rev.—
Badgerow, Rock J.

Graduate Studies:
Rev.—
Braun, Douglas A., Catholic University of America, Washington, DC.

Retired:
Rev. Msgrs.—
Ancona, Gaspar F., (Retired)
Porter, John F., (Retired)
Schneider, Ernest P., (Retired)
Revs.—
Anderson, Louis L., (Retired)
Antekeier, Charles R., (Retired)
Bernott, Ernest J., (Retired)
Bozung, James M., (Retired)
Cawley, Patrick T., (Retired)
Danner, Michael A., (Retired)
DeYoung, Thomas J., (Retired)
Droski, Norman P., (Retired)
Fekete, George J., (Retired)
Fox, Melvin E., (Retired)
Garcia, Pedro V., (Retired)
Golas, Eugene S., (Retired)
Hack, Thomas J., (Retired)
Host, Richard J., (Retired)
Kenshol, Joseph W., (Retired)
King, Lawrence J., (Retired)
La Goe, John P., (Retired)
Langlois, William A., (Retired)
Leyrita, Norbert L., (Retired)
Lomasiewicz, Donald E., (Retired)
Lowie, Richard J., (Retired)
Mason, Charlon O., (Retired)
McKinney, Thomas A., (Retired)
Milanowski, Paul A., (Retired)
Mitchell, Mark E., (Retired)
Nghiem, Peter Hoang-Xuan, (Retired)
Olson, Michael P., (Retired)
Reginato, Julian, (Retired)
Schichtel, Kenneth H., (Retired)
Vainavicz, Anthony C., (Retired)
VanLente, Richard J., (Retired)
Vesbit, Thomas S., (Retired)
Weber, Donald E., (Retired)
Witkowski, Phillip J., (Retired)
Zink, William F., (Retired).

Permanent Deacons:
Anderson, Gregory
Ashmore, John
Burns, Jeffrey
Cardenas, Zenon Sr.
Charron, William
Conigliaro, Pietro
Cook, William
Dordan, Michael, (Retired)
Dubridge, Richard
Falicki, John
Ferguson, Leo, (Retired)
Fett, Richard, (Retired)
Gonzalez, Edwin
Gutierrez, Carlos
Harwood, Edward
Hessler, James
Hoogeboom, Larry
Jurek, Thomas, (Retired)
Kaspryzk, David
Lechtanski, Stanley
Luscomb, Leonard C.
Mauer, Michael J.
McClintic, Robert
Nguyen, Thanh Van
Pitt, Richard, (Retired)
Riksen, Norman, (Retired)
Roersma, Gerald
Rybicki, Dennis
Schlitz, James
Schneider, Daniel
Sobolewski, Donald F.
Thorndill, James
Vande Voren, Lawrence, (Retired)
Vernon, Dean
Walters, Lance
Williams, Dennis
Wood, Michael
Zapata, Martin.

INSTITUTIONS LOCATED IN DIOCESE

[A] COLLEGES AND UNIVERSITIES

GRAND RAPIDS. *Aquinas College*, 1700 Fulton St. E., 49506. Tel: 616-632-8900; Tel: 616-632-2885; Fax: 616-732-4589; Web: www.aquinas.edu. Stephen P. Barrows, Exec. Vice Pres.; Eric Bridge, Service Learning Coord.; Nicholas Davidson, Dir. Athletics; Rev. Stanley Drongowski, Chap.; Shellie Jeffries, Co-Dir. Library; Darcy Kampfschulte, Dir. Financial Aid; Terry Marshall, Liturgist; Brian Matzke, M.M., Assoc. Vice Pres., Student Affairs; Cecelia Mesler, B.A., Registrar; Francine Paolini, Co-Dir. Library; Kevin G. Quinn, Pres.; Lisa H. VanDeWeert, Vice Pres.; Frank Doria, Vice Pres. Lay Teachers 90; Priests 1; Students 1,619; Religious Teachers 1; Clergy / Religious Teachers 1.

[B] HIGH SCHOOLS, DIOCESAN

GRAND RAPIDS. *Catholic Central High School*, 319 Sheldon Ave., S.E., 49503. Tel: 616-233-5803; Fax: 616-459-0257; Email: gregdeja@grcatholiccentral.org; Web: www.grcatholiccentral.com. Greg Deja, Prin. Lay Teachers 40; Students 625; Clergy / Religious Teachers 1.
West Catholic High School, 1801 Bristol, N.W., 49504. Tel: 616-233-5900; Fax: 616-453-4320; Email: cynthiakneibel@grwestcatholic.org; Email: meganpittman@grwestcatholic.org. Mrs. Cindy Kneibel, Prin. Lay Teachers 33; Students 520.

[C] HIGH SCHOOLS, PARISH

GRAND RAPIDS. *Sacred Heart Academy*, 1200 Dayton St., S.W., 49504. Tel: 616-459-0948; Email: smaltbie@sacredheartgr.org; Email: ssurrell@sacredheartgr.org; Web: www.sacredheartacademygr.org. Mr. Sean Maltbie, Headmaster. Lay Teachers 15; Students 316; Religious Teachers 1; Clergy / Religious Teachers 2.

PORTLAND. *St. Patrick High School*, 122 West St., Portland, 48875. Tel: 517-647-7551; Fax: 517-647-4545; Email: office@portlandstpats.com; Web: www.portlandstpats.com. Randy Hodge, Prin.; Rev. Michael J. Alber. Lay Teachers 11; Students 98.

[D] HIGH SCHOOLS, PRIVATE

MUSKEGON. *Muskegon Catholic Central*, 1145 W. Laketon Ave., Muskegon, 49441. Tel: 231-755-2201 ; Fax: 231-755-2415; Email: krasp@muskegoncatholic.org; Web: www.muskegoncatholic.org. Allison Aldrich, Prin.; Ken R. Rasp, Pres. Lay Teachers 21; Students 176.

[E] INTERPAROCHIAL ELEMENTARY SCHOOLS

HOLLAND. *Corpus Christi School*, (Grades PreK-8), 12100 Quincy St., Holland, 49424.
Tel: 616-994-9864; Fax: 616-994-9870; Email: joanneswan-jones@dogrschools.org; Web: www.corpuschristischool.us. Joanne Swan Jones, Prin.; Amy Supple, Academic Dean. Lay Teachers 20; Students 142.

WYOMING. *San Juan Diego Academy*, (Grades K-8), 1650 Godfrey Ave., S.W., Wyoming, 49509.
Tel: 616-243-1126; Email: rmuniz@sanjuandiegoacademy.com; Web: www.sanjuandiegoacademy.com. Rick Muniz, Prin.; Rev. Stephen S. Dudek, Pastoral Min./Coord. Administrators 1; Lay Teachers 9; Students 200; Estimated Number of Catholics 235.

[F] DIOCESAN ELEMENTARY SCHOOLS

GRAND RAPIDS. *All Saints Academy*, (Grades PreK-8), PK-3 Campus: 2233 Diamond Ave., N.E., 49505.
Tel: 616-364-9453; Tel: 616-363-7725;
Fax: 616-361-6991; Fax: 616-363-3086; Email: mdebri@asagr.org; Web: www.asagr.org. Michael Debri, Prin. Lay Teachers 19; Students 315.

[G] GRADE SCHOOLS, PRIVATE

ADA. *St. Robert Catholic School*, 6477 Ada Dr., S.E., Ada, 49301. Email: lpeters@strobertschoolada.org. Liz Peters, Prin.

MUSKEGON. *Muskegon Catholic Central Elementary School*, (Grades PreK-6), 1145 Laketon Ave., Muskegon, 49441. Tel: 231-755-2201;
Fax: 231-755-2744; Email: krasp@muskegoncatholic.org; Web: www.muskegoncatholic.org. Marie Jones, Prin.; Ken R. Rasp, Pres. Lay Teachers 10; Students 209.

[H] GENERAL HOSPITALS

GRAND RAPIDS. *Mercy Health Saint Mary's*, 200 Jefferson, S.E., 49503. Tel: 616-685-6567;
Tel: 616-685-6580; Email: bergmanm@mercyhealth.com; Web: www.mercyhealth.com. Rev. Joachim Adione, Chap.
Legal Title: Sponsored by Trinity Health Bed Capacity 374; Tot Asst. Annually 1,224,665; Total Staff 3,117.

MUSKEGON. *Mercy Health*, 1500 E. Sherman Blvd., Muskegon, 49444. Tel: 231-672-2000; Email: tricia.karnes@mercyhealth.com; Web: www.mercyhealth.com. Mr. Gary Allore, Pres. Sponsored by Trinity Health. Bed Capacity 409; Tot Asst. Annually 548,125; Total Staff 4,178.
Mercy Health Hackley Campus, 1700 Clinton Ave., Muskegon, 49442. Tel: 231-672-2000; Email: tricia.karnes@mercyhealth.com. Mr. Gary Allore, Pres.
Mercy Health Lakeshore Campus, 72 S. State St., Shelby, 49455. Tel: 231-861-2156; Email: cholkad@mercyhealth.com. Jay Bryan, Pres.

[I] HOMES FOR THE AGED

GRAND RAPIDS. *St. Ann's Home* (1951) 2161 Leonard St., N.W., 49504. Tel: 616-453-7715;
Fax: 616-453-7359; Email: info@stannshome.com; Web: stannshome.com. Sr. M. Gabriela Hilke, D.C.J., Dir.; Mrs. Dana Prince, Dir. Carmelite Sisters of the Divine Heart of Jesus. Priests 3; Residents 150; Sisters 6; Total Staff 225; Total Assisted 150.

[J] CONVENTS AND RESIDENCES FOR SISTERS

GRAND RAPIDS. *Motherhouse of the Dominican Sisters*, Marywood, 2025 E. Fulton St., 49503-3895.
Tel: 616-459-2910; Fax: 616-454-6105; Web: www.grdominicans.org. Sisters Janet Brown, O.P., Dir. Pastoral Life; Sandra Delgado, O.P., Treas.; Maureen Geary, O.P., Treas. Motherhouse and Novitiate for the Sisters of the Order of St. Dominic of the Congregation of Our Lady of the Sacred Heart.
Sisters of St. Dominic of the Congregation of Our Lady of the Sacred Heart (The Religious Institute)
Sisters of the Order of St. Dominic of Grand Rapids, Michigan (The Corporation). Sisters 179.
Dominican Center at Marywood A ministry of the Dominican Sisters at the Motherhouse. 2025 E. Fulton St., 49503-3895. Tel: 616-454-1241;
Fax: 616-454-2861; Email: sdelgado@grdominicans.org; Web: www.dominicancenter.com. Sr. Sandra Delgado, O.P., Treas. Sisters 192.

ADA. *Discalced Carmelite Nuns, Monastery of Our Lady of Guadalupe* (1916) 4300 Mount Carmel Dr., N.E., Ada (Parnell), 49301-9784. Tel: 616-691-7764 ; Email: carmelparnell@mymailstation.com; Web: carmelitenuns.org. Mother Mary Angela, O.C.D., Prioress. Sisters 9.

BELMONT. *Consolata Missionary Sisters* (1954) 6801 Belmont Rd., P.O. Box 371, Belmont, 49306.
Tel: 616-361-2072; Fax: 616-361-2072; Email: reusamc@consolatasisters.org; Web: www.consolatasisters.org. Sr. Riccardina Silvestri, M.C., Supr. Sisters 600; Consolata Sisters 23.

LOWELL. *Franciscan Sisters of the Eucharist*, 11600 Downes St. NE, Lowell, 49331. Tel: 616-897-5590;
Fax: 616-897-5088; Email: smaschmitz@fsecommunity.org. Sr. Margaret Dahl, F.S.E., Supr. Sisters 14.

[K] NEWMAN CENTERS

ALLENDALE. *St. Luke University Parish and Catholic Campus Ministry*, 10144 42nd Ave., Jenison, 49428. Tel: 616-895-2247; Fax: 616-895-2249; Email: frbill@lukespot.com; Web: www.gvsucatholic.org. Rev. William R. Vander Werff, Campus Min.

[L] MISCELLANEOUS LISTINGS

GRAND RAPIDS. *Basilica of St. Adalbert Education Foundation* (1985) 654 Davis N.W., 49504.
Tel: 616-458-3065; Fax: 616-458-0563; Web: basilicagr.org. Rev. Ronald D. Hutchinson.
Cathedral Square, Inc., Cathedral Square Center, 360 Division Ave., S., 49503. Tel: 616-514-6059;
Fax: 616-243-4910; Email: mlown@dioceseofgrandrapids.org. Michael A. Lown, Chancellor/CFO.
Catholic Charities West Michigan, Catholic Charities West Michigan, 360 Division Ave. S., Ste. 3A, 49503. Tel: 616-475-1252; Fax: 616-551-5677; Web: www.ccwestmi.org. Mr. Christopher Slater, CEO. ; Licensed Foster Homes 160; Relationship 100; Shelter 2; Absent without Leave 3; Independent Living 13; Parental Home 20, Specialized Sites: Substance Abuse; Halfway Homes; Physically abused children or adults; AIDS/ARC; Ex-Offenders; Pregnant Women; Adjudicated Delinquents 2; Runaway Youths., Site Programs: Foster Care; Adoption Licensing; Pregnancy Counseling 86; Infant Adoptions 6; Number assisted annually 350., Residential care of persons with physical and/ or mental disability: Number assisted annually 28 (mental disability)., Behavioral Health: Number of Clients 5380; Service Visits 65,241., Other Institutions CASA Visit House. Number assisted annually 400 children and families.
The Catholic Foundation of West Michigan, 360 Division Ave. S., 49503. Tel: 616-475-1247;
Fax: 616-243-4910; Email: mlown@dioceseofgrandrapids.org. Michael A. Lown, Chancellor/CFO.
Catholic Information Center, Cathedral Square Center, 360 Division Ave. S., Suite 2A, 49503.
Tel: 616-459-7267; Fax: 616-459-4645; Email: istrom@catholicinformationcenter.org. Very Rev. Rene Constanza, C.S.P., Exec. Dir.
Christopher House, Cathedral Square Center, 360 Division Ave., S., 49503. Tel: 616-475-1247;
Fax: 616-243-4910; Email: mlown@dioceseofgrandrapids.org. Michael A. Lown, Chancellor/CFO.
The Foundation for Catholic Secondary Education of Greater Grand Rapids, Inc., Cathedral Square Center, 360 Division Ave., S., 49503.
Tel: 616-458-1247; Fax: 616-458-7740; Email: mlown@dioceseofgrandrapids.org. Michael A. Lown, Chancellor/CFO.
Marywood Academy, 2025 E. Fulton St., 49503.
Tel: 616-459-2910; Fax: 616-454-6105; Web: www.grdominicans.org. Sr. Maureen Geary, O.P., Treas.
Ministry Ventures, 2025 Fulton St. E., 49503.
Tel: 616-514-3102; Fax: 616-454-6105; Web: www.grdominicans.org. Greg Jaroch, CFO; Sr. Maureen Geary, O.P., Treas.
Sisters of St. Dominic Charitable Trust, 2025 E. Fulton St., 49503. Tel: 616-459-2910;
Fax: 616-454-6105; Web: www.grdominicans.org. Sr. Sandra Delgado, O.P., Prioress
Sisters of St. Dominic of the Congregation of Our Lady of the Sacred Heart Charitable Trust (The Trust).
The Society of the Redemptorists of the City of Grand Rapids, 224 Carrier St., N.E., 49505.
Tel: 616-451-3043; Fax: 616-458-5667; Email: stalphonsusgr@catholicweb.com; Web: stalphonsusgr.com. Revs. Francis Thomas Danielsen, C.Ss.R., Supr.; Patrick Grile, C.Ss.R., Pastor; Bernard Carlin, C.Ss.R., Pastoral Assoc.; Brian Johnson, C.Ss.R., Pastoral Assoc.; Tuan Anh Nguyen, C.Ss.R., Pastoral Assoc.; Bro. Andrew Patin, C.Ss.R., Bus. Mgr. Represented in the Diocese.In Res. Rev. Robert Balser, C.Ss.R.; Bro. Andrew Patin, C.Ss.R.
Steepletown Neighborhood Services, Inc. (1994) 671 Davis, N.W., Steepletown Center, 49504.
Tel: 616-451-4215; Fax: 616-451-0557; Email: dick@steepletown.org. Richard Bulkowski, Exec. Neighborhood Center for Social Service and Assistance.
The Society For The Propagation Of The Faith, Cathedral Square Center, 360 Division Ave., S., 49503. Tel: 616-243-0491; Fax: 616-243-4910; Email: gwelsh@dioceseofgrandrapids.org. Rev. Stephen S. Dudek, Dir.

BELMONT. *Grand Rapids Catholic Committee on Scouting*, 9380 Grange Ave. N.E., Rockford, 49341.
Tel: 616-780-9088; Tel: 616-866-2767; Email: scottharvey@prodigy.net; Web: www.grccscouting.org. Scott Harvey, Chm.

LOWELL. *Franciscan Life Process Center* aka Franciscan Life Center Network, Inc., dba, Franciscan Life Process Center (1999) 11650 Downes St., Lowell, 49331. Tel: 616-897-7842;
Fax: 616-897-7054; Email: scanagle@lifeprocesscenter.org; Web: www.lifeprocesscenter.org. Sr. Colleen Ann Nagle, F.S.E., Dir.

MUSKEGON. *The English Cursillo Movement of the Diocese of Grand Rapids, MI, Inc.*, 1920 Whitehall Rd., Muskegon, 49445. Cell: 231-638-0857;
Tel: 616-824-0701. Rev. Mark E. Mitchell, (Retired).

PORTLAND. *The Father Flohe Foundation*, 140 Church St., Portland, 48875. Tel: 517-647-6505;
Fax: 517-647-7807; Email: parishoffice@portlandstpats.com; Web: http://www.portlandstpats.com/fatherflohefoundation.htm. Rev. Michael J. Alber.

WYOMING. *Catholic Cemeteries Extended Care Fund* aka Diocese of Grand Rapids Catholic Cemeteries,
Tel: 616-453-1636; Tel: 616-531-9320; Email: jima@grcathcem.org; Email: connies@grcathcem.org. James Arsulowicz, Dir. & Mgr.

RELIGIOUS INSTITUTES OF MEN REPRESENTED IN THE DIOCESE

For further details refer to the corresponding bracketed number in the Religious Institutes of Men or Women section.

[0520]—*Franciscan Friars*—O.F.M.
[0430]—*Order of Preachers (Dominicans)*—O.P.
[1030]—*Paulist Fathers*—C.S.P.
[1070]—*Redemptorist Fathers* (Denver Prov.)—C.Ss.R.

RELIGIOUS INSTITUTES OF WOMEN REPRESENTED IN THE DIOCESE

[0360]—*Carmelite Sisters of the Divine Heart of Jesus Carmel*—C.D.C.J.
[0720]—*Consolata Missionary Sisters*—M.C.
[0420]—*Discalced Carmelite Nuns*—O.C.D.
[1070-14]—*Dominican Sisters Congregation of Our Lady of the Sacred Heart*—O.P.
[2575]—*Institute of the Sisters of Mercy of the Americas*—R.S.M.
[3560]—*Servants of Jesus*—S.J.
[3670]—*Sister Servants of the Most Sacred Heart of Jesus*—S.S.C.J.
[0460]—*Sisters of Charity of Incarnate Word*—C.C.V.I.
[3980]—*Sisters of St. Paul de Chartres*—S.P.C.
[1250]—*The Institute for the Franciscan Sisters of the Eucharist*—F.S.E.
[]—*Trinitarian Sisters of Mary*—T.M.

NECROLOGY

† Dautremont, Charles R., (Retired), Died Aug. 28, 2018

Diocese of Great Falls - Billings

(Dioecesis Magnocataractensis-Billingensis)

ALWAYS TO WALK IN CHRIST

Most Reverend

MICHAEL W. WARFEL

Bishop of Great Falls-Billings; ordained April 26, 1980; appointed Bishop of Juneau November 19, 1996; ordained December 17, 1996; appointed Apostolic Administrator of Fairbanks October 23, 2001; resigned June 7, 2002; appointed Bishop of Great Falls-Billings November 20, 2007; installed January 16, 2008. *121 23rd St. S., Great Falls, MT 59401-3939.* Tel: 406-727-6683.

Pastoral Office: 121 23rd St. S., Great Falls, MT 59401-3939. Mailing Address: P.O. Box 1399, Great Falls, MT 59403-1399. Tel: 406-727-6683; Tel: 800-332-9998 (Toll Free); Fax: 406-454-3480.

Web: www.diocesegfb.org

Email: chancery@diocesegfb.org

ERECTED MAY 18, 1904.

Square Miles 94,158.

Corporation Title: "Roman Catholic Bishop of Great Falls, Montana, a corporation sole."

Comprises the eastern part of the State of Montana and is made up of the following Counties: Big Horn, Blaine, Carbon, Carter, Cascade, Chouteau, Custer, Daniels, Dawson, Fallon, Fergus, Garfield, Golden Valley, Hill, Judith Basin, Liberty, McCone, Musselshell, Park, Petroleum, Phillips, Powder River, Prairie, Richland, Roosevelt, Rosebud, Sheridan, Stillwater, Sweet Grass, Treasure, Valley, Wibaux, Yellowstone and parts of Toole.

For legal titles of parishes and diocesan institutions, consult the Pastoral Office.

STATISTICAL OVERVIEW

Personnel	
Bishop	1
Priests: Diocesan Active in Diocese	25
Priests: Diocesan Active Outside Diocese	1
Priests: Retired, Sick or Absent	25
Number of Diocesan Priests	51
Religious Priests in Diocese	19
Total Priests in Diocese	70
Extern Priests in Diocese	6
Permanent Deacons in Diocese	13
Total Brothers	2
Total Sisters	39
Parishes	
Parishes	50
With Resident Pastor:	
Resident Diocesan Priests	21
Resident Religious Priests	12
Without Resident Pastor:	
Administered by Deacons	1
Completely Vacant	11
Missions	52
Professional Ministry Personnel:	
Brothers	2
Sisters	22
Lay Ministers	48
Welfare	
Catholic Hospitals	2
Total Assisted	211,804
Homes for the Aged	1
Total Assisted	84
Day Care Centers	2
Total Assisted	241
Specialized Homes	1
Total Assisted	8
Educational	
Diocesan Students in Other Seminaries	3
Total Seminarians	3
Colleges and Universities	1
Total Students	950
High Schools, Diocesan and Parish	2
Total Students	450
High Schools, Private	1
Total Students	163
Elementary Schools, Diocesan and Parish	7
Total Students	1,536
Elementary Schools, Private	3
Total Students	435
Catechesis/Religious Education:	
High School Students	584
Elementary Students	1,894
Total Students under Catholic Instruction	6,015
Teachers in the Diocese:	
Priests	3
Brothers	2
Sisters	6
Lay Teachers	289
Vital Statistics	
Receptions into the Church:	
Infant Baptism Totals	484
Minor Baptism Totals	86
Adult Baptism Totals	37
First Communions	533
Confirmations	551
Marriages:	
Catholic	55
Interfaith	21
Total Marriages	76
Deaths	630
Total Catholic Population	26,396
Total Population	425,368

Former Bishops—Most Revs. MATHIAS C. LENIHAN, D.D., ord. Dec. 20, 1879; cons. First Bishop of Great Falls, Sept. 21, 1904; resigned Jan. 18, 1930; created Titular Archbishop of Preslavo, Feb. 14, 1930; died Aug. 19, 1943; EDWIN V. O'HARA, D.D., ord. June 10, 1905; appt. Aug. 1, 1930; cons. Oct. 28, 1930; appt. Bishop of Kansas City April 15, 1939; made asst. at the Pontifical Throne Jan. 5, 1949; appt. Archbishop "Ad Personam" June 29, 1954; died Sept. 11, 1956, Milan, Italy; WILLIAM J. CONDON, D.D., ord. Oct. 14, 1917; appt. Aug. 5, 1939; cons. Oct. 18, 1939; asst. at the Pontifical Throne Dec. 9, 1964; died Aug. 17, 1967; ELDON BERNARD SCHUSTER, D.D., ord. May 27, 1937; appt. Titular Bishop of Amblada; cons. Dec. 21, 1961; appt. Bishop of Great Falls Dec. 2, 1967; resigned Dec. 27, 1977; died Sept. 4, 1998; THOMAS JOSEPH MURPHY, D.D., S.T.D., ord. April 12, 1958; appt. Bishop of Great Falls July 5, 1978; Episcopal ordination and installation Aug. 21, 1978; appt. Coadjutor Archbishop of Seattle May 26, 1987; died June 26, 1997; ANTHONY M. MILONE, D.D., ord. Dec. 15, 1957; appt. Titular Bishop Plestia and Auxiliary of Omaha Nov. 10, 1981; Episcopal ord. Jan. 6, 1982; appt. Bishop of Great Falls-Billings Dec. 14, 1987; installed Feb. 23, 1988; resigned July 12, 2006; died May 17, 2018.

Vicar General—Very Rev. JAY H. PETERSON, V.G., (Retired), Email: vicargeneral@diocesegfb.org.

Pastoral Office—121 23rd St. S., P.O. Box 1399, Great Falls, 59403. Tel: 406-727-6683;
Tel: 800-332-9998 (Toll Free Number);
Fax: 406-454-3480. All applications for dispensations and official communications should be addressed to this office.

Chancellor—MR. DARREN EULTGEN, Email: chancellor@diocesegfb.org. Send all Marriage Correspondence to the Director of the Tribunal.

Moderator of the Curia—VACANT.

Interim Fiscal Officer—MRS. SHANNY MURPHY.

Diocesan Tribunal—121 23rd St. S., P.O. Box 1399, Great Falls, 59403. Tel: 406-727-6683;
Tel: 800-332-9998 (Toll Free Number); Email: tribunal@diocesegfb.org.

Judicial Vicar—Rev. ROBERT D. GROSCH, J.C.L.

Promoter of Justice—Rev. JOHN W. ROBERTSON, J.C.L.

Defenders of the Bond—Rev. SAMUEL SPIERING, J.C.L.; Sr. LUCY VADAKKETHALA, S.J., J.C.L.

Director of the Tribunal—TERRYAL ANN REAVLEY.

Notary—TERRYAL ANN REAVLEY.

Diocesan Consultors—Revs. RYAN ERLENBUSH; ROBERT GROSCH; GARRETT J. NELSON; Very Rev. JAY H. PETERSON, V.G., (Retired); Revs. NAVIL RODRIGUES; FRANCIS SCHREIBER; SAMUEL SPIERING, J.C.L.; CORY D. STICHA.

Personnel Board—Revs. DANIEL WATHEN; ROBERT D. GROSCH, J.C.L.; DAVID PAUL WILKINS; FRANCIS ANTON SCHREIBER; PATRICK R. ZABROCKI; Deacon TIMOTHY MARONEY; Very Rev. JAY H. PETERSON, V.G., (Retired).

Vicars Forane—Revs. STEPHEN J. ZABROCKI, Billings; ALPHONSUS ENELICHI, M.S.P., Great Falls; DANIEL WATHEN, Havre; FRANCIS SCHREIBER, Miles City; JAMES O'NEIL, Wolf Point.

Cemetery Board—Mount Olivet Cemetery (Great Falls): Most Rev. MICHAEL W. WARFEL. Holy Cross Cemetery (Billings): Rev. BARTON K. STEVENS.

Cum Christo/Cursillo—BOB MEYERS, Tel: 406-788-3519; Web: www.bigskycumchristo.org; RENE STEINBERGER, Forsyth, Email: rsteinberger@hotmail.com; MARK BRODHEAD, Sidney, Email: bbtrailcrs@midrivers.com; ROSIE REYNOLDS, Absarokee, Email: rreynoldsool@gmail.com.

Diocesan Offices and Directors

Boy Scouts—Rev. LEO G. MCDOWELL, Chap., Mailing Address: P.O. Box 646, Livingston, 59047. Tel: 406-222-1393; Email: frleo@frleo.org.

Catholic Campaign for Human Development—MR. DARREN EULTGEN, Diocesan Dir., 121 23rd St. S., Great Falls, 59401. Mailing Address: P.O. Box 1399, Great Falls, 59403. Tel: 406-727-6683; Fax: 406-454-3480.

Catechesis—VACANT, P.O. Box 1399, Great Falls, 59403. Tel: 406-727-6683.

Catholic Relief Services—MR. DARREN EULTGEN.

Clerical Benefit Association—Most Rev. MICHAEL W. WARFEL; Rev. J. DOUGLAS KRINGS; MR. RICK MCCANN; MR. CHUCK PAUL; Revs. PATRICK R. ZABROCKI; STEPHEN J. ZABROCKI.

Continuing Formation of Clergy—Rev. RICHARD SCHLOSSER, (Retired).

Diocesan Pastoral Council—Mailing Address: 121 23rd St. S., P.O. Box 1399, Great Falls, 59403-1399. Tel: 406-727-6683. MR. DARREN EULTGEN, Exec. Coord.; Most Rev. MICHAEL W. WARFEL.

Membership—DAWN CLUTTER, Great Falls; MARY JO STEBBINS, Great Falls; HARRY MERCHANT, Billings; RICHARD HALL, Billings; BRENDA RUMMEL, Havre; TONY SANDAU, Miles City; JENNIFER VAIRA, Wolf Point; KATHY BIDEGARAY,

Wolf Point; Revs. RYAN ERLENBUSH, Priest Rep.; SAMUEL SPIERING, J.C.L., Priest Council Rep.; CORY D. STICHA, Priest Rep.; Sisters EILEEN HURLEY, S.C.L., Rel. Sisters Rep.; MARY DOSTAL, Chair Rel. Sisters Rep.; Deacon PETER WOELKERS, Deacon Rep.; RENE RIEHL, Stewardship Council Rep.; NICOLAS ESTRADA, Univ. Providence; KELLY IHDE, Catholic Daughters Rep.; BETTY KOCH, CCW Rep.; STEVE ZACHMAN, KC Rep.; LEE WEGMANN, Cum Christo Rep.; DR. TIMOTHY UHL, Supt.; Rev. GARRETT J. NELSON, Vocations.

D.C.C.W.—SUSAN FOX, Pres.; Rev. CORY D. STICHA.

Education—DR. TIMOTHY UHL, Supt. Catholic Schools, Mailing Address: P.O. Box 1399, Great Falls, 59403-1399. Tel: 406-727-6683; Tel: 800-332-9998; Fax: 406-454-3480; Email: superintendent@montanaacc.org.

Finance Council—Most Rev. MICHAEL W. WARFEL; Very Rev. JAY H. PETERSON, V.G., Ex Officio, (Retired); Rev. PATRICK ZABROCKI; MR. DARREN EULTGEN, Chancellor & Ex Officio; MARIA CHRISTIAENS; RANDALL HOLOM; ALBERT MARTENS; ROBBIN MAKELKY; ARTHUR MALISANI; Rev. LEO G. MCDOWELL; PATRICK O'LEARY; ZAC ROHRER; MRS. AMY SEYMOUR; MRS. SHANNY MURPHY, Diocesan Consultant; MR. KURT DEPNER; JODY HELLEGAARD; TAMI MALTESE; Rev. SAMUEL SPIERING, J.C.L.; JERRY HORTON, Property Mgr.

Fiscal Officer—MRS. SHANNY MURPHY, Interim Fiscal Officer.

Office of Vocations & Ministry Formation—Rev. GARRETT J. NELSON.

Office of Worship—VACANT, Dir.

Newspaper—The Harvest Deacon PETER WOELKERS.

Pastoral Outreach—MR. DARREN EULTGEN, Chancellor, Diocesan Pastoral Council & Liaison for Planning; DR. TIMOTHY UHL, Supt. Catholic Schools; TERRYAL ANN REAVLEY, Dir. Tribunal; JUDY HELD, Pres., Catholic Foundation of Eastern Mt.; Deacon PETER WOELKERS; LAURIE HORTON; MR. MATTHEW BROWER, Mt. Catholic Conference.

Priests' Council—Most Rev. MICHAEL W. WARFEL; Revs. FRANCIS SCHREIBER; SAMUEL SPIERING, J.C.L.; RYAN ERLENBUSH; CORY D. STICHA; Very Rev. JAY H. PETERSON, V.G., Ex Officio, (Retired); Revs. J. DOUGLAS KRINGS; MARTIN EZEIHUAKU, M.S.P.; RANDOLPH GRACZYK, O.F.M.Cap.; GARRETT J. NELSON; NAVIL RODRIGUES.

Sister's Council—MR. DARREN EULTGEN, Rep.

Inter-Diocesan Organizations

Montana Catholic Conference—MR. MATTHEW BROWER, Mailing Address: P.O. Box 1708, Helena, 59624. Tel: 406-442-5761; Fax: 406-442-9047; Email: director@montanaacc.org; Web: www.montanacc.org.

Catholic Social Services of Montana—Mailing Address: P.O. Box 907, Helena, 59624-0907. Tel: 406-442-4130; Fax: 406-442-4192; Web: www.cssmt.org; Email: twila@cssmt.org. *1301 11th Ave., Helena, 59601.* TWILA COSTIGAN, Dir. Provides adoption and counseling services for families, children and infants.

Billings Office—Social Worker: MICHELLE PERLICK.

Great Falls Office—JANN PETEK.

Havre Office—JANN PETEK.

Missoula Office—JENNY GREENWOOD, 420 W. Pine St., Missoula, 59802. Tel: 406-728-5429; Fax: 406-327-8537; Email: missoula@cssmt.org.

Victim Assistance Coordinator—TERESA SCHMIT, Tel: 406-750-2373.

Safe Environment Coordinator—LAURIE HORTON.

CLERGY, PARISHES, MISSIONS AND PAROCHIAL SCHOOLS

CITY OF GREAT FALLS

(CASCADE COUNTY)

1—ST. ANN'S CATHEDRAL
715 Third Ave. N., 59401. Tel: 406-761-5456; Email: office@stannscathedral.org; Web: www.stannscathedral.org. P.O. Box 1708, 59403. Revs. Oliver Doyle; John Osom, M.S.P.
Catechesis Religious Program—Email: blessingsflow@mt.net. Georgia Miller, Youth Min. Students 65.

2—CORPUS CHRISTI (2012)
410 22nd Ave., N.E., 59404. Tel: 406-453-6546; Email: corpuschristigreatfalls@gmail.com. Rev. Ryan Erlenbush.
Res.: 422 22nd Ave., N.E., 59404. Tel: 406-453-6545; Web: corpuschristigreatfalls.blogspot.com.
Catechesis Religious Program—Students 58.

3—ST. GERARD MAJELLA, Closed. For inquiries for parish records contact the chancery.

4—HOLY FAMILY, Closed. See Holy Spirit.

5—HOLY SPIRIT (1998)
201 44th St. S., 59405. Tel: 406-452-6491. Rev. Doug Krings; Deacons William Medved; Peter Woelkers; Mark Meyer, Parish Admin.
Sts. Peter & Paul Education Center—200 44th St. S., 59405.
School—Holy Spirit School, (Grades K-8), 2820 Central Ave., 59401. Tel: 406-761-5775;
Fax: 406-761-5887; Web: www.holyspiritcs.org. Jim Wichman, Prin. Lay Teachers 20; Students 197.
Catechesis Religious Program—Tel: 406-452-6491; Email: aubrey@holyspiritgf.org. Aubrey Rearden, D.R.E. Students 200.
Chapel—Holy Family, 2800 Central Ave., 59401.

6—ST. LUKE THE EVANGELIST (1967) Merged with St. Joseph and Most Blessed Sacrament to form Corpus Christi, Great Falls. Contact Corpus Christi for sacramental records.

7—OUR LADY OF LOURDES
409 13th St. S., 59405. Tel: 406-452-6464. Rev. Alphonsus Enelichi, M.S.P.; Ms. Alicia Davis, Pastoral Assoc.; Mrs. Mary Stebbins, Youth Min.
School—Our Lady of Lourdes School, (Grades PreK-8), 1305 5th Ave. S., 59405. Tel: 406-452-0551;
Fax: 406-761-7180; Web: www.ollschoolgfmt.org. Mrs. Sherri Schmitz, Prin. Lay Teachers 15; Students 186; Religious Teachers 1.
Catechesis Religious Program—Barbara Brown, D.R.E. & Youth Min. Students 18.

8—STS. PETER & PAUL, Closed. See Holy Spirit.

CITY OF BILLINGS

(YELLOWSTONE COUNTY)

1—ST. BERNARD (1971)
226 Wicks Ln., Billings, 59105. Tel: 406-259-4350. Rev. David Reichling, O.F.M.Cap.
Catechesis Religious Program—Email: brians@stbernardblgs.org. Brian Shea, D.R.E. Students 287.
Mission—Sts. Cyril & Methodius, 16 S. Corner Rd., Ballantine, 59006.

2—HOLY ROSARY (1951) Merged with Little Flower & Our Lady of Guadalupe to form Mary Queen of Peace, Billings. Contact Mary Queen of Peace for sacramental records.

3—LITTLE FLOWER (1931) Merged with Holy Rosary & Our Lady of Guadalupe to form Mary Queen of Peace, Billings. Contact Mary Queen of Peace for sacramental records.

4—MARY QUEEN OF PEACE (2012)
210 S. 34th St., Billings, 59101. Tel: 406-259-7611; Fax: 406-248-8921; Email: info@maryqueenofpeacebillings.org. Rev. Jose Marquez.
Catechesis Religious Program—Bill Kuzma, D.R.E. Students 78.

5—OUR LADY OF GUADALUPE (1953) Merged with Little Flower & Holy Rosary to form Mary Queen of Peace, Billings. Contact Mary Queen of Peace for sacramental records.

6—ST. PATRICK CO-CATHEDRAL (1906)
215 N. 31st St., Billings, 59101. Tel: 406-259-3389; Email: rdjgrosch@gmail.com; Web: www.stpatrickcocathedral.org. Rev. Robert D. Grosch, J.C.L.
Rectory—1989 Weston Dr., Billings, 59102.
Catechesis Religious Program—Email: stpatricksyouthministrydre@gmail.com. Sr. Jeanne Tranel, O.P., RCIA Coord.; Mary Gilluly, D.R.E. Students 73.

7—ST. PIUS X (1958)
717 18th St. W., Billings, 59102. Tel: 406-656-2522; Email: rb@stpiusxblgs.org; Web: www.stpiusxblgs.org. Rev. Gregory Staudinger; Deacon Tom Landry; Karyn Haider, Business Mgr.
Catechesis Religious Program—Jessica Rohrer, Children's Min. Coord. Students 193.

8—ST. THOMAS THE APOSTLE (1965)
2055 Woody Dr., Billings, 59102. Tel: 406-656-5800; Email: church@stthomasbillings.org; Web: www.stthomasbillings.org. Rev. Stephen J. Zabrocki.
Res.: 2101 24th St. W., Billings, 59102.
Catechesis Religious Program—Joyce Hollowell, D.R.E.; Cathy Day, Youth Min. Students 213.

OUTSIDE THE CITIES OF GREAT FALLS AND BILLINGS

ASHLAND, ROSEBUD CO., ST. LABRE (1884)
1000 Tongue River Rd., Ashland, 59003.
Tel: 406-784-4516; Email: lwebber@stlabre.org; Web: sites.google.com/stlabre.org/st-labre-parish/home.
P.O. Box 228, Ashland, 59003. Revs. Lawrence Webber, O.F.M.Cap., Admin.; Gebreysus Boyine.

BAKER, FALLON CO., ST. JOHN THE EVANGELIST
210 W. Center Ave., Baker, 59313. Tel: 406-778-2297. P.O. Box 1519, Baker, 59313. Rev. Philip Chinnappan.
Catechesis Religious Program—Rita Breitbach, D.R.E. Students 61.
Missions—St. Joan of Arc—100 Church Ave., Ekalaka, 59324. Tel: 406-775-6310.
St. Anthony, [CEM] 201 W. Conser Ave., Plevna, 59344.

BELT, CASCADE CO., ST. MARK THE EVANGELIST
128 Castner St., Belt, 59412. Tel: 406-277-3539. P.O. Box 213, Belt, 59412. Rev. Rodrigo Mingollo, Admin.
Catechesis Religious Program—Tel: 406-277-3366. Katrina Paulson, D.R.E. Students 37.
Missions—St. Mary—100 Main St., Raynesford, 59469.
Holy Trinity, 692 Stockett Rd., Centerville, 59480.
Chapel—St. Clement, 62 Cascade Ave., Monarch, 59463. Tel: 406-727-6683. Mr. James Hoxter, Contact Person.

BIG SANDY, CHOUTEAU CO., ST. MARGARET MARY (1910)
364 Johannes, Big Sandy, 59520. Tel: 406-395-4380. P.O. Box 3009, Box Elder, 59521. Rev. Joseph Tran; Sisters Margaret Mary O'Doherty, O.P., Pastoral Assoc. & D.R.E.; Kathleen Kane, O.P., Pastoral Assoc.
Catechesis Religious Program—St. Margaret Mary, Tel: 406-378-2369. Students 90.
Missions—St. Anthony—235 E. Main, Box Elder, 59521.
St. Mary, 88 Church Hill Rd., Box Elder, 59521.

BIG TIMBER, SWEET GRASS CO., ST. JOSEPH
910 McLeod St., Big Timber, 59011.
Tel: 406-932-4728. P.O. Box 871, Big Timber, 59011. Revs. Leo G. McDowell; Amulraj Yedanapalli.
Catechesis Religious Program—Doug Lair, D.R.E. Students 8.

BLACK EAGLE, CASCADE CO., MOST BLESSED SACRAMENT, Merged with St. Joseph, Great Falls and St. Luke the Evangelist, Great Falls to form Corpus Christi, Great Falls. Contact Corpus Christi for sacramental records.

BRIDGER, CARBON CO., SACRED HEART
209 S. 4th St., Bridger, 59014. Tel: 406-662-3550. P.O. Box 309, Bridger, 59014. Rev. Masilamani Suvakkin.
Catechesis Religious Program—404 W. Central St., Joliet, 59041. Mrs. Amy Seymour, D.R.E. Students 17.
Missions—St. Joseph—202 N. Montana St., Fromberg, 59029.
St. John, 404 W. Central, Joliet, 59041.

BROADUS, POWDER RIVER CO., ST. DAVID (1931)
225 N. Wilbur, Broadus, 59317. Tel: 406-436-2430; Email: shchurch@midrivers.com. Rev. Robert Oswald.
Catechesis Religious Program—Students 12.

CHESTER, LIBERTY CO., ST. MARY (1950)
11 W. Quincy Ave., Chester, 59522.
Tel: 406-759-5377. P.O. Box 647, Chester, 59522. Rev. Herbert Magaso, Admin.; Natalie Ghekiere, Pastoral Assoc.
Res.: 504 Main, Chester, 59522. Tel: 406-759-5377; Email: stmolrsh@itstriangle.com.
Catechesis Religious Program—504 Main, Chester, 59522. Tel: 406-759-5389. Natalie Ghekiere, D.R.E. Students 30.
Mission—Sacred Heart, 630 Main, Inverness, Hill Co. 59530.

CHINOOK, BLAINE CO., ST. GABRIEL (1896)
404 8th St. W., Chinook, 59523. Tel: 406-357-2073; Email: stgabriel@itstriangle.com. P.O. Box 1089, Chinook, 59523. Rev. Michael Schneider, J.C.L. (Cand.).
Rectory—Tel: 406-357-3189.
Catechesis Religious Program—Tami Schoen, D.R.E. Students 36.
Missions—St. Thomas the Apostle—P.O. Box 1125, Harlem, 59526. 210 1st Ave., S.E., Harlem, Blaine Co. 59526.
St. Thomas Aquinas, Mailing Address: P.O. Box 1089, Chinook, 59523. 10610 Wing Rd., Hogeland, Blaine Co. 59529.

CIRCLE, MCCONE CO., ST. FRANCIS XAVIER
1102 C Ave., Circle, 59215-0160. Tel: 406-485-3520; Email: stx@midrivers.com. P.O. Box 160, Circle, 59215. Rev. Joseph Ponessa.
Church: 1100 C Ave., Circle, 59215.
Catechesis Religious Program—Shanna Murnion, D.R.E. Students 5.
Missions—St. Francis de Sales—301 S. Main St., Richey, Dawson Co. 59259.
St. John the Baptist, 412 Leavitt Ave., Jordan, Garfield Co. 59337.

COLSTRIP, ROSEBUD CO., ST. MARGARET MARY (1924)
320 Water Ave., Colstrip, 59323. Tel: 406-748-2234; Email: stmargaretmary1@gmail.com. P.O. Box 305, Colstrip, 59323. Rev. Anthony Raj Kumar, H.G.N.
Catechesis Religious Program—Mrs. Susan McKamey, D.R.E. Students 16.

COLUMBUS, STILLWATER CO., ST. MARY (1913)
240 4th Ave N, Columbus, 59019. Tel: 406-322-5541; Email: secretary@stmarycolumbus.org; Web:

mystmary.com. P.O. Box 956, Columbus, 59019. Rev. Navil Rodrigues.
Rectory—243 5th St. N., Columbus, 59019.
Catechesis Religious Program—Mrs. Mandy O'Connor, D.R.E. Students 19.
Mission—*St. Michael*, 307 S. Woodard St., Absarokee, 59001.

CROW AGENCY, BIG HORN CO., ST. DENNIS (1892)
76 Hwy. 1, Crow Agency, 59022. Tel: 406-620-7500. P.O. Box 57, Crow Agency, 59022. Rev. Mark Joseph Costello, O.F.M.Cap.; Bro. Jerry Cornish, O.F.M.-Cap., In Res.; Revs. Tien Dinh, O.F.M.Cap., In Res.; William Frigo, O.F.M.Cap., In Res.
St. Katharine Friary, St. Katherine Friary, 96 Highway 1, Crow Agency, 59022. Tel: 406-620-7500; Email: mjcoste@yahoo.com.
Church: 2116 Mission Loop, Crow Agency, 59022.
Catechesis Religious Program—Email: mjcoste@yahoo.com. Students 21.
Mission—*St. Francis Xavier*, 5936 W. 18300 S., St. Xavier, Big Horn Co. 59075. P.O. Box 138, St. Xavier, 59075.

CULBERTSON, ROOSEVELT CO., ST. ANTHONY, Closed. Now a mission of Our Lady of Lourdes, Poplar.

FORSYTH, ROSEBUD CO., IMMACULATE CONCEPTION
521 N. 12th Ave. N., Forsyth, 59327.
Tel: 406-346-9239; Email: immaculateconceptionforsyth@gmail.com. P.O. Box 166, Forsyth, 59327. Rev. Anthony Raj Kumar, H.G.N.
Church: 509 N. 12th Ave., Forsyth, 59327.
Catechesis Religious Program—Mrs. Diane Wyrick, D.R.E. Students 6.
Mission—*St. Joseph*, 206 Orchard Ave., Hysham, Treasure Co. 59038.

FORT BENTON, CHOUTEAU CO., IMMACULATE CONCEPTION aka Fort Benton (1846)
1223 16th St. S, Fort Benton, 59442.
Tel: 406-622-3726; Email: fralby1983@gmail.com. P.O. Box 849, Fort Benton, 59442. Rev. Mohan Raj
Legal Title: ICC
Catechesis Religious Program—Mrs. Debbie Kittredge, D.R.E. Students 18.
Mission—*St. Margaret*, 700 Brewster St., Geraldine, Chouteau Co. 59446-0050. Tel: 406-737-4573; Email: 7jeklund@itstriangle.com. P.O. Box 50, Geraldine, 59446. Trish Eklund, Contact Person.

FORT SHAW, CASCADE CO., ST. ANN
13327 MT. Hwy 200, Fort Shaw, 59443.
Tel: 406-264-5554. Rev. David Paul Wilkins.
Catechesis Religious Program—Students 12.
Mission—*Sacred Heart*, 22 2nd St., N.W., Cascade, Cascade Co. 59421. Email: dpwilkins40@gmail.com.

GLASGOW, VALLEY CO., ST. RAPHAEL
412 3rd Ave. N., Glasgow, 59230. Tel: 406-228-9800. P.O. Box 471, Glasgow, 59230. Rev. Jose Valliparambil; Deacon Eddie Malone.
Church: 402 3rd Ave. N., Glasgow, 59230.
Catechesis Religious Program—Email: dffym@nemont.net. Jewel Etherington, D.R.E. Students 62.
Missions—*Holy Family*—116 1st Ave., N., Glentana, 59240.
St. Albert, 304 Minnesota, Hinsdale, 59241.
Queen of the Angels, 206 Hobart, Nashua, 59248.

GLENDIVE, DAWSON CO., SACRED HEART (1907)
320 W. Benham St., Glendive, 59330.
Tel: 406-377-2585. P.O. Box 36, Glendive, 59330. Rev. Francis Schreiber.
Mission—*Sacred Heart*, 302 S. McDonald Ave., Terry, Prairie Co. 59349. Tel: 406-635-5569. P.O. Box 526, Terry, 59349.
Catechesis Religious Program—Tel: 406-377-4569.

HARDIN, BIG HORN CO., ST. JOSEPH
710 N. Custer, Hardin, 59034. Tel: 406-665-1432. P.O. Box 510, Hardin, 59034. Rev. Thomas Selvaraj.
Catechesis Religious Program—Students 19.
Mission—*St. Mary*, 214 4th Ave., Custer, Yellowstone Co. 59024. P.O. Box 223, Custer, 59024.

HAVRE, HILL CO., ST. JUDE THADDEUS (1904)
624 4th St, Havre, 59501. Tel: 406-265-4261; Email: stjudehavre@gmail.com; Web: stjudehavre.org. P.O. Box 407, Havre, 59501. Rev. Daniel Wathen; Deacon Timothy Maroney, Pastoral Min./D.R.E.
Res.: 617 4th St, Havre, 59501.
School—*St. Jude Thaddeus School*, (Grades PreK-8), 430 7th Ave., Havre, 59501. Tel: 406-265-4613; Fax: 406-265-1315; Email: mhaugen@stjudeschoolmt.org; Web: stjudeschoolmt.org. Michael Haugen, Prin. Lay Teachers 10; Students 146.
Catechesis Religious Program—Students 65.
Chapel—*St. John the Baptist*, P.O. Box 407, Havre, 59501.

HAYS, BLAINE CO., ST. PAUL'S INDIAN MISSION (1886)
301 Mission St., Hays, 59527. Tel: 406-673-3300. P.O. Box 40, Hays, 59527. Rev. Jose Panickomveli, Admin.
School—*St. Paul's Indian Mission School*, (Grades K-6), 761 Hays Rd., Hays, 59527. Tel: 406-673-3123; Email: mgs@itstriangle.com. Sr. Christine Ferrar, O.P., Prin. Lay Teachers 8; Students 82; Clergy / Religious Teachers 3.
Missions—*St. Joseph*—300 Azure Ave., Zortman, 59546.
St. Thomas, 8893 Lodgepole Rd., Lodgepole, Blaine Co. 59524.
Sacred Heart, Fort Belknap, 210 Chipewa Ln., Harlem, Blaine Co. 59526. Tel: 406-353-2257. P.O. Box 236, Fort Belknap, 59526.

HINGHAM, HILL CO., OUR LADY OF RANSOM (1910)
201 2nd St., Hingham, 59528. Tel: 406-759-5377. St. Mary Church: P.O. Box 647, Chester, 59522. Rev. Herbert Magaso, Admin.
Catechesis Religious Program—Dianne Folk, D.R.E. Students 26.

LAME DEER, ROSEBUD CO., BLESSED SACRAMENT
630 Cheyenne Ave., Lame Deer, 59043.
Tel: 406-477-6384; Email: dj@rangeweb.net. P.O. Box 100, Lame Deer, 59043. Deacon Joseph Kristufek, Pastoral Admin.; Sr. LeAnn Probst, O.P., Pastoral Assoc.
Catechesis Religious Program—Students 20.
Mission—*Christ the King*, P.O. Box 315, Busby, Big Horn Co. 59016. Tel: 406-592-3568. Church: 13268 S. 5th St., Busby, 59016. Lenora Wolfname, Contact Person.

LAUREL, YELLOWSTONE CO., ST. ANTHONY (1907) [CEM]
715 4th Ave., Laurel, 59044. Tel: 406-628-7484;
Tel: 406-628-7182; Email: paduaoffice@gmail.com; Web: www.saintanthonycatholicchurch.org; Web: www.facebook.com/saintanthonycatholicchurchmontanalaurel.com. 317 W. 7th St., Laurel, 59044. Rev. Barton K. Stevens.
Catechesis Religious Program—Tel: 406-628-7484. Students 78.

LEWISTOWN, FERGUS CO., ST. LEO (1888) [CEM]
102 W. Broadway, Lewistown, 59457.
Tel: 406-538-9306; Email: saintleoscatholicchurch@gmail.com; Web: www.stleoscatholicchurch.org. P.O. Box 421, Lewistown, 59457. Rev. Samuel Spiering, J.C.L., Admin.
Catechesis Religious Program—Shawna Sandau, Youth Min. Students 105.
Mission—*Holy Family*, 530 Main St., Winifred, Fergus Co. 59489.

LIVINGSTON, PARK CO., ST. MARY, [CEM]
41 View Vista Dr., Livingston, 59047-0646.
Tel: 406-222-1393; Email: secretary@stmaryscommunity.org. P.O. Box 646, Livingston, 59047. Revs. Leo G. McDowell; Amulraj Anathiya.
Res.: 39 View Vista Dr., Livingston, 59047-0646.
Tel: 406-222-1393; Email: secretary@stmaryscommunity.org; Web: stmaryscommunity.org.
School—*St. Mary's School*, (Grades PreK-8), P.O. Box 646, Livingston, 59047. Catherine Kirchner, Prin. Lay Teachers 5; Students 74.
Catechesis Religious Program—Bridget Yuvan, D.R.E. Students 22.
Missions—*St. Margaret*—206 1st. Ave. N., Clyde Park, Park Co. 59018.
St. William, 705 Scott St., W., Gardiner, Park Co. 59030.

LODGE GRASS, BIG HORN CO., OUR LADY OF LORETTO (1909)
11723 E. Helen St., Lodge Grass, 59050.
Tel: 406-639-2254. P.O. Box 509, Lodge Grass, 59050. Rev. Tien Dinh, O.F.M.Cap.
Catechesis Religious Program—Students 10.
Mission—*Blessed Kateri Tekakwitha*, 309 S. Mondel Ave., Wyola, 59089.

MALTA, PHILLIPS CO., ST. MARY
27 S. 7th St. W., Malta, 59538. Tel: 406-654-1446;
Fax: 406-654-1467; Web: www.SaintMarysMalta.org. P.O. Box 70, Malta, 59538. Rev. Cory D. Sticha.
Catechesis Religious Program—Email: brenda@saintmarysmalta.org. Brenda Rummel, D.R.E. Students 44.
Missions—*Sacred Heart*—225 2nd St., E., Dodson, 59524.
St. Francis of Assisi, 500 Wilson Ave., Saco, 59261.
Chapel—*St. John*, 230 1st Ave. E., Whitewater, 59544.

MILES CITY, CUSTER CO., SACRED HEART (1881)
120 N. Montana Ave., Miles City, 59301.
Tel: 406-234-1691; Fax: 406-234-9233; Email: shchurch@midrivers.com; Web: sacredheart.weconnect.com. Mailing Address: P.O. Box 1016, Miles City, 59301. Rev. Robert Oswald.
Res.: 1515 Palmer St., Miles City, 59301.
School—*Sacred Heart School*, (Grades PreSchool-8), 519 N. Center Ave., Miles City, 59301.
Tel: 406-234-3850; Email: shschool@midrivers.com; Web: www.midrivers.com/~shschool. Bart Freese, Prin. Lay Teachers 10; Sisters 1; Students 158.
Catechesis Religious Program—Mrs. Tammy Herzog, Contact Person. Students 46.
Mission—*St. David*, 217 N. Wilbur, Broadus, Powder River Co. 59317. Tel: 406-436-2430. P.O. Box 52, Broadus, 59317.

PLENTYWOOD, SHERIDAN CO., ST. JOSEPH
309 N. Main, Plentywood, 59254. Tel: 406-765-2250; Email: stjoe@nemont.net. P.O. Box 167, Plentywood, 59254-0167. Rev. Patrick Zabrocki.
Church: 301 N. Main St., P.O. Box 167, Plentywood, 59254.
Catechesis Religious Program—
Mission—*St. Patrick*, 401 Main St., Medicine Lake, 59247.

POPLAR, ROOSEVELT CO., OUR LADY OF LOURDES
105 F St. W., Poplar, 59255. Tel: 406-768-3305. P.O. Box 187, Poplar, 59255. Rev. Jude Alih, M.S.P.
Catechesis Religious Program—Mrs. Val Gorder, D.R.E. Students 44.
Mission—*St. Anthony*, 413 3rd St., W., Culbertson, Roosevelt Co. 59218. Tel: 406-787-6685. Mrs. Lynn Finnicum, Contact Person.
Chapels—*Fort Kipp, St. Anthony*—
Sacred Heart, 314 Clinton St., Bainville, Roosevelt Co. 59212.
St. Thomas, 3022 BIA Rd. 173, Brockton, Roosevelt Co. 59213.

PRYOR, BIG HORN CO., ST. CHARLES BORROMEO CHURCH (1891)
21228 S. Pryor Gap Rd., Pryor, 59066.
Tel: 406-259-9747. P.O. Box 29, Pryor, 59066. Rev. Randolph Graczyk, O.F.M.Cap.
Catechesis Religious Program—

RED LODGE, CARBON CO., ST. AGNES (1889)
1 N. Word Ave., Red Lodge, 59068. Tel: 406-322-5541 ; Email: stagnesrl@gmail.com; Web: www.stagnesrl.com. P.O. Box 1067, Red Lodge, 59068. Rev. Navil Rodrigues. Administered from St. Mary, Columbus.
Catechesis Religious Program—Students 45.

ROUNDUP, MUSSELSHELL CO., ST. BENEDICT (1908)
503 Main St., Roundup, 59072. Tel: 406-323-1019. Rev. Julian Nix, O.S.B.
Catechesis Religious Program—Students 27.
Missions—*Our Lady of Mercy*—121 6th Ave., Melstone, Musselshell Co. 59054.
St. Aloysius, 112 W. Main St., Winnett, Petroleum Co. 59087.
St. Theresa the Little Flower, 16638 Iowa, Broadview, Yellowstone Co.
St. Mathias, 305 Kemp St., Ryegate, Golden Valley Co. 59074.
Chapels—*St. Honorata*—22 3rd Ave., Musselshell, 59059.
Our Lady of the Assumption, Broadview, 59015.

SCOBEY, DANIELS CO., ST. PHILIP BONITUS
404 Timmons St., Scobey, 59263-0827.
Tel: 406-487-5525; Email: stphilip@nemont.net. P.O. Box 827, Scobey, 59263-0827. Rev. Patrick Zabrocki.
Res.: 400 Timmons St., Scobey, 59263.
Tel: 406-487-5525; Email: stphilip@nemont.net.
Catechesis Religious Program—Matt Goettle, D.R.E. Students 30.

SIDNEY, RICHLAND CO., ST. MATTHEW
219 Seventh St., S.E., Sidney, 59270.
Tel: 406-433-1068; Tel: 406-433-2510;
Fax: 406-433-2509; Email: stmatt@midrivers.com; Web: www.stmattsidney.com. Revs. Jim O'Neil; Callistus Igwenagu; Stacie Olson, Office Mgr.
Catechesis Religious Program—Tel: 406-433-2510; Email: stmattdre@midrivers.com. Mary Quiroz, D.R.E. Students 71.
Missions—*St. Catherine*—317 7th St., W., P.O. Box 494, Fairview, Richland Co. 59221. Harriet Carico, Contact Person.
St. Theresa, 212 N. Main St., P.O. Box 153, Lambert, Richland Co. 59243.
St. Bernard, 301 Rd. 148, Charlie Creek, Richland Co. 59270. Mailing Address: 31789 CR148, Box 409, Brockton, 59213.
St. Michael, 120 2nd Ave., P.O. Box 95, Savage, Richland Co. 59262.

STANFORD, JUDITH BASIN CO., ST. ROSE OF LIMA (1908)
101 4th St. W., Stanford, 59479. Tel: 406-566-2531; Email: fr.dom@live.com. P.O. Box 250, Stanford, 59479. Rev. Domenico Pizzonia.
Res.: 305 2nd St. S., Stanford, 59479.
Missions—*St. Anthony*—1100 Main Ave., Denton, Fergus Co. 59430. Tel: 406-567-2438. P.O. Box 384, Denton, 59430.
St. Cyril, 100 Hill Ave., Geyser, Judith Basin Co. 59447. R.R. 1 Box 50A, Geyser, 59447.
St. Mathias, 310 2nd St., N.E., Moore, Fergus Co. 59464. P.O. Box 104, Moore, 59464.
Sacred Heart, 100 2nd Ave. E., Hobson, Judith Basin Co. 59452.

WIBAUX, WIBAUX CO., ST. PETER
312 W. 1st Ave. S., Wibaux, 59353. Tel: 406-769-2215 ; Email: apxavi@gmail.com. P.O. Box 217, Wibaux, 59353. Rev. Xavier Arimboor; Deacon Richard Miske.
Catechesis Religious Program—Students 33.
Mission—*St. Philip*, 61 Lamesteer Rd, Wibaux, 59353. Tel: 406-796-8188.

WOLF POINT, ROOSEVELT CO., IMMACULATE CONCEPTION, [CEM]
513 Dawson St., Wolf Point, 59201.

Tel: 406-653-2610. P.O. Box 789, Wolf Point, 59201.
Rev. Martin Ezeihuaku, M.S.P., Admin.
Res.: 500 Fifth Ave. S., Wolf Point, 59201.
Tel: 406-653-2610.
Catechesis Religious Program—Email: iccreann@gmail.com. Ann Wienke, D.R.E. Students 90.
Mission—St. Ann, 102 Shell St., Vida, 59274.
Chapels—Sacred Heart—1022 Hwy. 201, Riverside, 59201.
St. Joseph, 331 Moccasin, Frazer, Valley Co. 59225.

Special Assignment:
Revs.—
Alih, Jude, M.S.P., Our Lady of Lourdes Church, P.O. Box 187, Poplar, 59255
Anthonysamy, Silvester, H.G.N., St. Ann Cathedral, P.O. Box 1708, 59403
Arimboor, Xavier, P.O. Box 217, Wibaux, 59353
Arockiasamy, Mohanraj, H.G.N., Immaculate Conception Church, P.O. Box 849, Fort Benton, 59442
Chiaka, Ralph, 2816 Central Ave., 59401
Chinnappon, Philip, H.G.N., St. John the Evangelist Church, P.O. Box 1519, Baker, 59313
Enelichi, Alphonsus, M.S.P., Our Lady of Lourdes, 409 13th St. S., 59405
Ezeihuaku, Martin, M.S.P., Immaculate Conception, P.O. Box 789, Wolf Point, 59201
Igwenagu, Callistus, St. Matthew, 219 7th St. SE, 59270
Kumar, Arumugan, H.G.N., Immaculate Conception Church, P.O. Box 166, Forsyth, 59327
Magaso, Herbert, St. Mary Church, P.O. Box 647, Chester, 59522
Marquez, Jose, Mary Queen of Peace, 210 S. 34th St., Billings, 59101
Mwampela, Ayub, St. Vincent Healthcare, 1233 N. 30th St., Billings, 59101
Nix, Julian, O.S.B., St. Benedict, 503 Main St., Roundup, 59072
Panickomveli, Jose, St. Paul Mission, P.O. Box 40, Hays, 59527
Rodrigues, Navil, P.O. Box 160, Circle, 59215
Selvvaraj, Thomas, H.G.N., St. Joseph, P.O. Box 510, Hardin, 59034
Tran, Hilary Nhuan, P.O. Box 3009, Box Elder, 59521
Yedanapalli, Amulraj, St. Mary, P.O. Box 646, Livingston, 59047.

Retired:
Very Rev.—
Peterson, Jay H., V.G., (Retired), 1701 26th St. S, Apt. 1, 59405
Revs.—
Beggin, Thomas M., (Retired), 1631-41st St. W., Billings, 59106-1742
Birkmaier, James, (Retired), 1801 9th St. S., Apt. 225, 59405-5173
Cawley, William M., (Retired), 1701 26th St. S., Apt. 4, 59405
Connolly, Jerry, (Retired), 3940 Rimrock Rd., Billings, 59102
D'Souza, William, (Retired), Vianney Bhavan, St. Jude's Hospital Campus, Sipri Post, Jhansik, India. Vianney Bhavan, St. Jude's Hospital Campus, Sipri Post, Jhansik, India
Diekhans, Joseph, (Retired), 909 W. Central Ave., Missoula, 59801
Frazer, Edward J., S.S., (Retired), 603 Maiden Choice Ln., Baltimore, MD 21228-3697
Gorman, Charles, (Retired), 2351 Solomon Ave., Apt. 157, Billings, 59102
Guthneck, Peter E., (Retired), P.O. Box 269, Box Elder, 59521
Harney, Thomas C., (Retired), 1440 Granite Ave., Apt. B, Billings, 59102
Hogan, William A., (Retired), 1801 9th St. S., Apt. 105, 59405
Houlihan, John J., (Retired), 2003 Woody Dr., Apt. 4, Billings, 59102
Krauth, Lothar, (Retired), 3724 8th Ave. N., 59401
Krier, John P., (Retired), P.O. Box 449, Airway Heights, WA 99001
O'Hanlon, Michael A., (Retired), Danesfort, Dromahane Mallow, County Cork Ireland 022-50140
O'Rourke, Daniel, (Retired), 1701 26th St. S., Apt. 2, 59405
Osterman, Richard, (Retired), P.O. Box 1093, Red Lodge, 59068-1093
Pittard, Wayne M., (Retired), 2003 Woody Dr., Apt. 3, Billings, 59102
Regan, Terrence P., (Retired), 2805 3rd Ave. N., 59401
Schlosser, Richard, (Retired), 4240 Clark Ave., 59405
Sikora, James, (Retired), 1915 13th Ave. S., 59405
Szudera, Theodore, (Retired), P.O. Box 6507, 59403
Tobin, Thomas, (Retired), P.O. Box 407, Ekalaka, 59324
Vogel, Marcel, (Retired), 1701 26th St. S., Apt. 3, 59405.

Permanent Deacons:
Ackerman, Robert, 1615 E. Ames Wye, Glendive, 59330
Birkle, Timothy J., (Retired), 3820 Towhee Ln., Billings, 59102-7723
Daem, Robert W., (Retired), 220 34th St. W., Billings, 59102-4473
Ferguson, Robert, 3847 4th Ave. S., 59405
Kristufek, Joseph M., P.O. Box 100, Lame Deer, 59043-0100
Landry, Thomas, 3722 San Juan Dr., Billings, 59102
Malone, Eddie, P.O. Box 46, Nashua, 59248
Maroney, Timothy, P.O. Box 252, Havre, 59501
Medved, William, 120 Riverview Dr. E., 59404
Melius, Melvin A., (Retired), 1437 Ave. D, Billings, 59102-3124
Miske, Richard, 261 Red Top Rd., Wibaux, 59353
Quintus, Terry, P.O. Box 405, Wibaux, 59353
Rodgers, James, 41 Eagle Point Ln., Bridger, 59014
Woelkers, Peter, 205 Riverfront Ln., 59404.

INSTITUTIONS LOCATED IN DIOCESE

[A] COLLEGES AND UNIVERSITIES

GREAT FALLS. *University of Great Falls* (1932) 1301 20th St. S., 59405. Tel: 406-791-5300; Fax: 406-791-5391; Email: trudi.cole@uprovidence.edu; Web: www.uprovidence.edu. Dr. Anthony Aertz, Pres.; Revs. Oliver Doyle, Vice Pres.; Silyester Anthonysamy, H.G.N., Chap.; Dan McGuire, Prof. Providence Ministries. Lay Teachers 49; Sisters 1; Students 950; Religious Teachers 1; Clergy / Religious Teachers 1.

[B] HIGH SCHOOLS, DIOCESAN

GREAT FALLS. *Great Falls Central Catholic High School*, 2800 18th Ave. S., 59405.
Tel: 406-216-3344; Fax: 406-216-3343; Email: mwoelkers@greatfallscentral.org; Web: greatfallscentral.org. Mr. Phillip VanDenBrink, Prin.; Mrs. Monica Woelkers, Admin. Deacons 1; Lay Teachers 18; Students 125; Clergy / Religious Teachers 2.

BILLINGS. *Central Catholic High School*, 3 Broadwater Ave., Billings, 59101. Tel: 406-245-6651;
Fax: 406-259-3124; Email: shanser@billingscatholicschools.org; Email: jhawbaker@billingscatholicschools.org; Web: www.billingscatholicschools.org. Sheldon Hanser, Prin.; Jim Hawbaker, Assoc. Prin. Lay Teachers 25; Students 325.

[C] HIGH SCHOOLS, PRIVATE

ASHLAND. *St. Labre Indian Catholic High School*, P.O. Box 216, Ashland, 59003. Tel: 406-784-4561;
Fax: 406-784-4565; Web: stlabreindianschool.org. 1000 Tongue River Rd., Ashland, 59003. Crystal Redgrave, Dir.; Trivian Rides The Bear, Prin.; Dan Burke, Librarian. Lay Teachers 28; Students 163.

[D] ELEMENTARY SCHOOLS, DIOCESAN

BILLINGS. *St. Francis School*, (Grades 3-5), 2202 Colton Blvd., Billings, 59102. Tel: 406-259-5037;
Fax: 406-259-9119; Email: dhayes@billingscatholicschools.org; Web: billingscatholicschools.org. Debra Hayes, Prin.; Jim Stanton, Prin.; Donna Petriccione, Librarian. Lay Teachers 47; Students 693.

[E] ELEMENTARY SCHOOLS, PRIVATE

ASHLAND. *St. Labre Indian Catholic Elementary School*, (Grades PreK-5), P.O. Box 216, Ashland, 59003. Tel: 406-784-4550; Fax: 406-784-4565. 1000 Tongue River Rd., Ashland, 59003. Crystal Redgrave, Dir.; Holly Bailey, Prin. Lay Teachers 14; Students 145.
St. Labre Academy, (Grades 5-8), Tel: 406-784-4550; Email: hbailey@stlabre.org. Holly Bailey, Prin. Lay Teachers 14; Students 94.

PRYOR. *St. Charles Mission School*, (Grades PreK-8), 21228 Pryor Gap Rd., Pryor, 59066.
Tel: 406-259-9976; Fax: 406-259-7092; Email: bvandyke@stlabre.org; Web: www.stlabre.org. P.O. Box 29, Pryor, 59066. Bambi Van Dyke, Prin.; Jane Giard, Librarian. Lay Teachers 17; Students 133; Religious Teachers 1.

ST. XAVIER. *Pretty Eagle Catholic Academy*, (Grades PreK-8), P.O. Box 257, St. Xavier, 59075.
Tel: 406-666-2215; Fax: 406-666-2245; Email: gwilliamson@stlabre.org; Web: www.stlabre.org. 5936 W. 18300 S., St. Xavier, 59075. Garla Williamson, Prin.; Molly Joyce, Librarian. Lay Teachers 12; Students 157; Religious Teachers 1.

[F] CHILD CARE & YOUTH SERVICES

GREAT FALLS. *St. Thomas Child and Family Center*, 1710 Benefis Ct., 59405. Tel: 406-761-6538;
Fax: 406-727-0670; Email: carrie@stthomaskids.org; Web: www2.providence.org/stthomas. Carrie Sammons, Exec. Dir.; Melissa Kingsland, Pres.; Tessa Donahue, Sec. Providence Ministries. Bed Capacity 120; Lay Staff 30; Tot Asst. Annually 120; Total Staff 30; Child Care & Pre-School Children 106.

BILLINGS. *Billings Catholic Schools Early Education Center*, 1734 Yellowstone Ave, Billings, 59102.
Tel: 406-656-2300; Email: mtrafton@billingscatholicschools.org; Email: ssaks@billingscatholicschools.org. Sue Saks, Dir.; Michelle Trafton, Dir. Lay Teachers 11; Preschool 101; Students 121; Pre K Enrollment 20.

[G] GENERAL HOSPITALS

BILLINGS. *St. Vincent Healthcare*, 1233 N. 30th St., Billings, 59101. Tel: 406-237-7000;
Fax: 406-237-3078; Web: svh-mt.org. P.O. Box 35200, Billings, 59107-5200. Steve Loveless, Pres. & CEO. Sisters of Charity of Leavenworth, Kansas. Bed Capacity 286; Tot Asst. Annually 187,129; Total Staff 2,100.

MILES CITY. *Holy Rosary Healthcare*, 2600 Wilson St., Miles City, 59301. Tel: 406-233-2600;
Tel: 800-843-3820; Fax: 406-233-2611; Web: www.sclhealth.org; Email: jackie.muri@sclhs.net. Paul Lewis, CEO. Charity of LeavenworthCritical Access Hospital. Bed Capacity 109; Tot Asst. Annually 24,675; Total Staff 330; Beds: Acute Care 25; Extended Care 84.

[H] CONVENTS AND RESIDENCES FOR SISTERS

GREAT FALLS. *Poor Clares of Montana, Inc.*, 3020 18th Ave. S., 59405. Tel: 406-453-7891; Email: sisters@poorclaresmt.org; Web: www.poorclaresmt.org. Sr. Judith Ann Crosby, Abbess. Sisters 7.

BILLINGS. *Sisters of Charity of Leavenworth*, 1114 N. 30th St., Billings, 59101. Tel: 913-702-2049. Sr. Eileen Hurley, S.C.L., Contact Person. Sisters 2.

[I] MISCELLANEOUS LISTINGS

GREAT FALLS. Rev. Oliver Doyle. *Big Sky Cum Christo / Cursillo*, 121 23rd St. S., 59403-1399.
Tel: 406-788-3519; Email: bigskybrooklynbob@yahoo.com; Web: www.bigskycumchristo.org. c/o Bob Meyers, P.O. Box 1399, 59403-1399. Mark Broadhead, (Sidney); Bob Meyers, (Great Falls); Rosie Reynolds, (Absarokee); Rene Steinberger, (Fursyth); Carmen Thorsen, Treas., (Great Falls).
World Wide Marriage Encounter, 11739 EW Tenny Rd., Shepherd, 59079. Tel: 406-794-1582; Email: dcsprojim@gmail.com; Web: www.agme.org. Greg Ledgerwood; D'awn Ledgerwood, Tel: 406-480-9162.
**Cascade County Council of the St. Vincent de Paul Society*, 426 Central Ave. W., 59403.
Tel: 406-761-0870; Email: administrator@svdpncmt.org; Fax: 406-761-0996; Web: www.svdpncmt.org. Doborah Kottel, Dir.
Catholic Foundation of Eastern Montana, Inc., 121 23rd St., S., 59405. Tel: 406-315-1765;
Fax: 406-454-3480; Email: info@catholicfoundationmt.org; Web: www.catholicfoundationmt.org. P.O. Box 1345, 59403-1345. Judy Held, Pres.
Diocese of Great Falls-Billings Juridic Persons Capital Assets Support, 121 23rd St., S., 59403-1399. Tel: 406-727-6683. P.O. Box 1399, 59403. Mrs. Shanny Murphy, C.E.O.
Diocese of Great Falls-Billings Juridic Persons Real Property Support, 121 23rd St., S., 59403-1399.
Tel: 406-727-6683. P.O. Box 1399, 59403. Mrs. Shanny Murphy, C.E.O.
Engaged Encounter, 3633 6th Ave. S., 59405-3503. Email: greatfallsee@gmail.com. Bill Chafin; Brenda Chafin; Dave Stukey; Terry Stukey.
Frank & Isabell Stites Memorial Center (Retired Priests & Lay People Living) Pastoral Center, 1701 26th St., S., 59403. Tel: 406-727-6683;
Fax: 406-454-3480; Email: business@diocesegfb.org; Web: www.diocesegfb.org. P.O. Box 1399, 59403. Mrs. Shanny Murphy, C.E.O. Aged Residents 9; Priests 4; Total Apartments 13.
1701 26th St. S., 59403.
Heisey Community Center at St. Ann's, 313 7th St. N., 59401. Tel: 406-453-1211; Email:

office@stannscathedral.org. Rev. Oliver Doyle. Recreation center serving the adults and youth of the community.

Holy Spirit Catholic School Endowment Trust, 2820 Central Ave., 59401-3412. Tel: 406-761-5775; Fax: 406-761-5887; Email: clongin@holyspiritgf.org. Tom Hayes, Contact Person.

St. Joseph's Education Trust, 410 22nd Ave., N.E., 59404. Tel: 406-453-6546; Email: corpuschristigreatfalls@gmail.com. Rev. Ryan Erlenbush.

**St. Martin De Porres Mission of Great Falls*, 1920 10th Ave., S., 59405. Tel: 406-771-6695. Mr. Jim Delaney, Contact Person. Tot Asst. Annually 185.

Retrouvaille of Montana, 121 23rd St., S., 59403-0004. Tel: 800-470-2330; Tel: 406-761-4830; Email: retromt14@gmail.com. P.O. Box 4, 59403. Rev. Joseph Fleming; Terryal Ann Reavley, Co-Coord.

BILLINGS. *Billings Area Catholic Education Trust* (BACET) 215 N. 31st St., Billings, 59101. Tel: 406-252-0252; Fax: 406-252-5731; Email: jhaider@billingscatholicschools.org; Web: billingscatholicschoolsfoundation.org. P.O. Box 31158, Billings, 59107-1908. Janyce Haider, Pres.

Billings Catholic Schools Foundation, 215 N. 31st St., Billings, 59101. Tel: 406-252-0252; Fax: 406-252-5731; Email: jhaider@billingscatholicschools.org; Web: billingscatholicschoolsfoundation.org. P.O. Box 31158, Billings, 59107-1158. Janyce Haider, Pres.

Regina Cleri, Pastoral Center: 121 23rd St., S., P.O. Box 1399, 59403. Tel: 406-727-6683; Fax: 406-454-3480; Email: business@diocesegfb.org; Web: www.diocesegfb.org. Mrs. Shanny Murphy, Business Mgr. Retired Priests Living. Total Apartments 4.

St. Vincent Healthcare Foundation, 1106 N. 30th St., Billings, 59101. Tel: 406-237-3600; Fax: 406-237-3619; Email: dennis.sulser@sclhs.net; Web: www.svfoundation.org. Dennis Sulser, Pres. & CEO.

ASHLAND. *St. Labre Indian School Educational Association* A Nonprofit Corporation. P.O. Box 77, Ashland, 59003. Tel: 406-784-4500; Fax: 406-784-4512; Email: cyarlott@stlabre.org; Web: www.stlabre.org. 1000 Tongue River Rd., Ashland, 59003. Curtis Yarlott, Pres. & Exec. Dir. Four Catholic schools for Native Americans: St. Labre Indian School at Ashland; Pretty Eagle Catholic Academy, St. Xavier; St. Charles Mission School, Pryor.

St. Labre Youth & Family Services, 1000 Tongue River Rd., Ashland, 59003. Tel: 406-784-4521; Tel: 877-785-4457; Fax: 406-784-4527; Web: www.stlabre.org. P.O. Box 458, Ashland, 59003. Vicki Anderson, Dir. Residential Group Home: Shilo Home for Native American Children (licensed for 8 children). Other Services: St. Labre Clothes Room Thrift Store; St. Labre Daycare Center; St. Labre Outreach Services (food, gas, heating, medical, funeral). Capacity 8.

LEWISTOWN. *St. Leo's Catholic Education Trust*, 102 W. Broadway St., Lewistown, 59457. Tel: 406-538-9306; Fax: 406-538-7624. P.O. Box 421, Lewistown, 59457. Rev. Samuel Spiering, J.C.L.

MALTA. *St. Mary's Catholic Education Trust*, 27 S. 7th St. W., Malta, 59538. Tel: 406-654-1446; Fax: 406-654-1467; Email: office@saintmarysmalta.org; Web: www.saintmarysmalta.org. P.O. Box 70, Malta, 59538. Rev. Cory D. Sticha.

MILES CITY. **Custer County Conference of the Society of Saint Vincent de Paul and Thrift Store*, 407 Main St., Miles City, 59301. Tel: 406-234-3011; Email: info@stvincentsmilescity.com. Charlie Carranco, Dir.

Holy Rosary Healthcare Foundation aka Holy Rosary Foundation, 2600 Wilson St., Miles City, 59301. Tel: 406-233-2604; Email: erika.swanson@sclhealth.org; Web: www.supportholyrosary.com. Erika Swanson, Dir. The Holy Rosary Healthcare Foundation is a charitable entity that supports Holy Rosary Healthcare in Miles City, MT. Holy Rosary Healthcare is a part of the SCL Health system and supports residents in eastern Montana. Donations commonly support Hospice, Residential Living, Greatest Need, Staff Education, Nurses, Mom & Baby, Oncology, Men's Health, Patient's Assistance, Associate Loans, Pediatrics, and Behavioral Health.

MONARCH. *Thieltges-St. Thomas Camp*, P.O. Box 1399, 59403. Tel: 406-727-6683; Email: business@diocesegfb.org. 121 23rd St., S., 59401. Mrs. Shanny Murphy, C.E.O. Students 120; Religious Teachers 4; Clergy / Religious Teachers 4.

RELIGIOUS INSTITUTES OF MEN REPRESENTED IN THE DIOCESE

For further details refer to the corresponding bracketed number in the Religious Institutes of Men or Women section.

[0200]—*Benedictine Monks* (Assumption Abbey, Richardton, ND; Cleveland, OH)—O.S.B.

[0200]—*Benedictine Monks* (St. Anselm's Abbey, Washington, DC)—O.S.B.

[0470]—*The Capuchin Friars* (Prov. of St. Joseph, Detroit)—O.F.M.Cap.

[0585]—*Heralds of the Good News* (Middlesboro, KY)—H.G.N.

[0854]—*Missionary Society of St. Paul of Nigeria* (Houston, TX)—M.S.P.

RELIGIOUS INSTITUTES OF WOMEN REPRESENTED IN THE DIOCESE

[0220]—*Congregation of the Benedictine Sisters of Perpetual Adoration of Pontifical Jurisdiction* (Dayton, WY)—O.S.B.

[2100]—*Congregation of the Humility of Mary* (Davenport, IA)—C.H.M.

[1115]—*Dominican Sisters of Peace* (Columbus, OH)—O.P.

[1070-11]—*Dominican Sisters, Congregation of Our Lady of the Rosary* (Sparkill, NY)—O.P.

[3040]—*Oblate Sisters of Divine Providence/ Missionary Sisters of Divine Providence* Nigeria—M.S.D.P.

[3760]—*Order of St. Clare, Holy Name Federation* (Great Falls, MT)—O.S.C.

[2970]—*School Sisters of Notre Dame, Central Pacific Province* (St. Louis, MO)—S.S.N.D.

[1070-03]—*Sinsinawa Dominican Congregation of the Most Holy Rosary* (Sinsinawa, WI)—O.P.

[0480]—*Sisters of Charity of Leavenworth, Kansas*—S.C.L.

[]—*Sisters of Jesus* Sagar, India.

[1720]—*Sisters of the Third Order Regular of St. Francis of the Congregation of Our Lady of Lourdes* (Rochester, MN)—O.S.F.

[4110]—*Ursuline Nuns* (Santa Rosa, CA)—O.S.U.

DIOCESAN CEMETERIES

BILLINGS. *Holy Cross*, 1601 Mullowney Ln., Billings, 59101. Cell: 406-839-8387. Laurie Kops, Dir.

GREAT FALLS. *Calvary*, Gibson Flats, 59405. Tel: 406-727-6683. P.O. Box 1399, 59403. Laurie Kops, Dir.

Mount Olivet, 2101 26th St. S., 59405. Tel: 406-453-8251. P.O. Box 1399, 59403. Mr. Eric Spragg, Family Svcs. Advisor

NECROLOGY

† Crowley, Cale John, (Retired), Died Oct. 7, 2018

† Maloney, Anthony Michael, (Retired), Died May. 17, 2018

† Schuster, Anthony Jerome, (Retired), Died Apr. 7, 2018

An asterisk (*) denotes an organization that has established tax-exempt status directly with the IRS and is not covered by the USCCB Group Ruling.

Diocese of Green Bay

(Dioecesis Sinus Viridis)

Most Reverend

DAVID LAURIN RICKEN, D.D., J.C.L.

Bishop of Green Bay; ordained September 12, 1980; appointed Coadjutor Bishop of Cheyenne December 14, 1999; Episcopal Ordination January 6, 2000; succeeded to See September 26, 2001; appointed Bishop of Green Bay July 9, 2008; installed August 28, 2008. *Office: 1825 Riverside Dr., Green Bay, WI 54301. Mailing Address: P.O. Box 23825, Green Bay, WI 54305-3825.*

Chancery: 1825 Riverside Dr., Green Bay, WI 54301. Tel: 920-437-7531; Fax: 920-435-1330. . *Mailing Address: P.O. Box 23825, Green Bay, WI 54305-3825.*

Web: www.gbdioc.org

Most Reverend

ROBERT J. BANKS, D.D.

Bishop Emeritus of Green Bay; ordained December 20, 1952; consecrated September 19, 1985; appointed Auxiliary Bishop to the Archbishop of Boston and Titular Bishop of Taraqua on June 26, 1985; appointed to Green Bay October 16, 1990; installed December 5, 1990; retired December 12, 2003. *Office: 1825 Riverside Dr., Green Bay, WI 54301. Mailing Address: P.O. Box 23825, Green Bay, WI 54305-3825.*

Most Reverend

ROBERT F. MORNEAU, D.D.

Auxiliary Bishop Emeritus of Green Bay; ordained May 28, 1966; appointed Auxiliary Bishop of Green Bay and Titular Bishop of Massa Lubrense December 19, 1978; consecrated February 22, 1979; retired October 7, 2013. *Res.: 333 Hilltop Dr., Green Bay, WI 54301-2713. Office: 1825 Riverside Dr., Green Bay, WI 54301.* Tel: 920-437-7531. *Mailing Address: P.O. Box 23825, Green Bay, WI 54305-3825.*

ESTABLISHED MARCH 3, 1868.

Square Miles 10,728.

Incorporated January 16, 1907.

Comprises these 16 Counties: Brown, Calumet, Door, Florence, Forest, Kewaunee, Langlade, Manitowoc, Marinette, Menominee, Oconto, Outagamie, Shawano, Waupaca, Waushara and Winnebago in the State of Wisconsin.

Legal Title: Catholic Diocese of Green Bay, Inc.
For legal titles of parishes and diocesan institutions, consult the Chancery Office.

STATISTICAL OVERVIEW

Personnel	
Bishop	1
Retired Bishops	2
Abbots	1
Retired Abbots	2
Priests: Diocesan Active in Diocese	72
Priests: Diocesan Active Outside Diocese	2
Priests: Retired, Sick or Absent	79
Number of Diocesan Priests	153
Religious Priests in Diocese	93
Total Priests in Diocese	246
Extern Priests in Diocese	27
Ordinations:	
Diocesan Priests	3
Religious Priests	1
Transitional Deacons	2
Permanent Deacons	6
Permanent Deacons in Diocese	151
Total Brothers	20
Total Sisters	359
Parishes	
Parishes	156
With Resident Pastor:	
Resident Diocesan Priests	69
Resident Religious Priests	9
Without Resident Pastor:	
Administered by Priests	54
Administered by Deacons	12
Administered by Religious Women	6
Administered by Lay People	6
Missions	2
Pastoral Centers	44
Professional Ministry Personnel:	
Brothers	2
Sisters	17
Lay Ministers	154
Welfare	
Catholic Hospitals	9
Total Assisted	958,063
Health Care Centers	1
Total Assisted	163,132
Homes for the Aged	6
Total Assisted	2,526
Day Care Centers	3
Total Assisted	195
Special Centers for Social Services	2
Total Assisted	5,200
Educational	
Diocesan Students in Other Seminaries	14
Students Religious	3
Total Seminarians	17
Colleges and Universities	2
Total Students	2,624
High Schools, Diocesan and Parish	5
Total Students	1,240
High Schools, Private	1
Total Students	777
Elementary Schools, Diocesan and Parish	47
Total Students	7,158
Catechesis/Religious Education:	
High School Students	5,851
Elementary Students	11,855
Total Students under Catholic Instruction	29,522
Teachers in the Diocese:	
Priests	2
Brothers	1
Sisters	1
Lay Teachers	675
Vital Statistics	
Receptions into the Church:	
Infant Baptism Totals	2,538
Adult Baptism Totals	74
Received into Full Communion	101
First Communions	2,621
Confirmations	2,444
Marriages:	
Catholic	609
Interfaith	176
Total Marriages	785
Deaths	2,931
Total Catholic Population	295,377
Total Population	1,029,453

Former Bishops—Rt. Revs. JOSEPH MELCHER, D.D., ord. March 27, 1830; cons. July 12, 1868; died Dec. 20, 1873; FRANCIS XAVIER KRAUTBAUER, D.D., ord. July 16, 1850; cons. June 29, 1875; died Dec. 17, 1885; FREDERICK XAVIER KATZER, D.D., ord. Dec. 21, 1866; appt. July 13, 1886; cons. Sept. 21, 1886; appt. Archbishop of Milwaukee, Jan. 30, 1891; died July 20, 1903; SEBASTIAN GEBHARD MESSMER, D.D., ord. July 23, 1871; cons. Bishop of Green Bay, March 27, 1892; appt. Archbishop of Milwaukee, Nov. 28, 1903; died Aug. 4, 1930; JOSEPH J. FOX, D.D., ord. June 7, 1879; cons. Bishop of Green Bay, July 25, 1904; resigned Dec. 4, 1914; appt. Titular Bishop of Ionopolis; died March 14, 1915; Most Revs. PAUL P. RHODE, D.D., ord. June 17, 1894; cons. Titular Bishop of Barca and Auxiliary to the Archbishop of Chicago, July 29, 1908; transferred to the See of Green Bay, July 5, 1915; died March 3, 1945; STANISLAUS V. BONA, D.D., ord. Nov. 1, 1912; appt. Bishop of Grand Island, NE Dec. 18, 1931; cons. Feb. 25, 1932; appt. Coadjutor Bishop of Green Bay, Dec. 2, 1944; succeeded to See, March 3, 1945; died Dec. 1, 1967; ALOYSIUS J. WYCISLO, D.D., ord. April 7, 1934; appt. Titular Bishop of Stadia and Auxiliary Bishop of Chicago Oct. 17, 1960; cons. Dec. 21, 1960; appt. to Green Bay, March 8, 1968; retired May 10, 1983; died Oct. 11, 2005; ADAM J. MAIDA, J.C.L., J.D., S.T.L., ord. May 26, 1956; appt. to Green Bay, Nov. 8, 1983; cons. Jan. 25, 1984; installed as Archbishop of Detroit, June 12, 1990; created Cardinal on Nov. 26, 1994; ROBERT J. BANKS, D.D., ord. Dec. 20, 1952; cons. Sept. 19, 1985; appt. Auxiliary Bishop to the Archbishop of Boston and Titular Bishop of Taraqua on June 26, 1985; appt. to Green Bay Oct. 16, 1990; installed Dec. 5, 1990; retired Dec. 12, 2003; DAVID A. ZUBIK, ord. May 3, 1975; appt. Auxiliary Bishop of Pittsburgh and Titular Bishop of Jamestown Feb. 18, 1997; cons. April 6, 1997; appt. Bishop of Green Bay Oct. 10, 2003; installed Dec. 12, 2003; appt. Bishop of Pittsburgh July 18, 2007.

Vicar General—Very Rev. DANIEL J. FELTON, Tel: 920-272-8180.

Chancery—1825 Riverside Dr., Green Bay, 54301. Tel: 920-437-7531; Fax: 920-435-1330. *Mailing Address: P.O. Box 23825, Green Bay, 54305-3825.*

Vicar of Canonical Services/Associate Moderator of the Curia—Very Rev. JOHN W. GIROTTI, J.C.L., Tel: 920-272-8124.

Chancellor—MRS. TAMMY BASTEN, Tel: 920-272-8175.

Vicar General/Moderator of the Curia—Very Rev. DANIEL J. FELTON.

Archivist—MS. OLIVIA WENDT, Tel: 920-272-8195.

Executive Assistants to Bishop—MRS. TANIA LEFEVRE, Tel: 920-272-8194; MRS. DEBRA ADAMS, Tel: 920-272-8183.

Executive Assistant to Vicar General/Moderator of the Curia—MRS. JAMI DUVALL, Tel: 920-272-8189.

Executive Assistant to Chancellor and to the Vicar of Canonical Services/Associate, Moderator of the Curia—MS. PATRICIA VONHADEN, Tel: 920-272-8188.

Diocesan Tribunal—1825 Riverside Dr., Green Bay, 54301. Tel: 920-437-7531. *Mailing Address: P.O. Box 23825, Green Bay, 54305-3825.*

Judicial Vicar—Very Rev. BRIAN S. BELONGIA, J.C.L.

Adjutant Judicial Vicars—Very Revs. JOHN W. GIROTTI, J.C.L.; RICHARD GETCHEL, J.C.L.

Judges—Sr. ANN F. REHRAUER, J.C.L., M.A.; Very Revs. RICHARD GETCHEL, J.C.L.; JOHN W. GIROTTI, J.C.L.

Promoter of Justice—Sr. ANN F. REHRAUER, J.C.L., M.A.

Defenders of the Bond—MS. DANIELA KNEPPER, J.C.L.; Sr. ANN F. REHRAUER, J.C.L., M.A.

Diocesan Healthcare Services—Very Rev. RICHARD H. KLINGEISEN, Coord., 19 S. County Rd. J, Cato, 54230-8329. Tel: 920-684-3718.

College of Consultors—Most Rev. DAVID L. RICKEN, D.D., J.C.L.; Rev. Msgr. JAMES DILLENBURG; Revs. ROBERT KOLLATH; JOEL A. SEMBER; Very Rev. DANIEL J. FELTON; Revs. ROBERT J. KABAT, J.C.L.; TIMOTHY D. SHILLCOX, O.Praem. Resource: BARBARA WIEGAND.

Regional Vicars—Very Revs. THOMAS J. FARRELL, Vicariate I - North; PHILIP DINH-VAN-THIEP, Asst. Vicar, Vicariate I - North; MICHAEL L. INGOLD, Vicariate II - Mid-North; JEROME P. PASTORS, Vicariate III - Southwest; Rev. JAMES W. LUCAS, Vicariate IV - Mid-South; Very Revs. RYAN E. KRUEGER, Vicariate V - Southeast; RICHARD GETCHEL, J.C.L., Vicariate VI - Mid-East; Rev. WILLIAM O'BRIEN, Vicariate VII - Peninsula, (Retired).

Diocesan Pastoral Council—Most Rev. DAVID L. RICKEN, D.D., J.C.L., Chm.

Vicariate Representatives—

Vicariate I—MS. PAT KOSUTH, (Marinette); VACANT, (Wausaukee).

Vicariate II—MR. JEFF TAYLOR, (Green Bay); MR. MICHAEL WITTE, (Green Bay).

Vicariate III—JAMES FAY, (Oshkosh); JOHN FOLK, (Fremont).

Vicariate IV—VACANT, (Appleton); WALTER THOMSON, (Neenah).

Vicariate V—BETTY HOVE, (Valders); JOYCE ROLLAND, (Manitowoc).

Vicariate VI—MR. DAVID WHEELER, (De Pere); MR. STEVE PARENT, (New Franken).

Vicariate VII—MR. WILLIAM GRAF, (Sturgeon Bay); MR. MARK MERKATORIS, (Sturgeon Bay).

Appointed Representatives—MS. PAULA FREIMUTH, (DCCW Rep.) (Plainfield); Deacons DAVID J. SCHEUER, (Maribel); CHARLES R. SCHUMACHER, (Peshtigo); ELIZABETH KOSTICHKA, (Green Bay); MRS. PATRICIA RATAJCZAK, (Dyckesville).

Appointed Religious Representatives—Sr. NATALIE BINVERSIE, O.S.F., (Manitowoc); Very Rev. JAMES T. BARANIAK, O.Praem., (De Pere).

Ex Officio Members—Most Rev. DAVID L. RICKEN, D.D., J.C.L.; Very Rev. DANIEL FELTON, Vicar Gen. & Moderator of the Curia.

Presbyteral Council Membership—

President—Most Rev. DAVID L. RICKEN, D.D., J.C.L.

Chairman—Rev. JOEL A. SEMBER.

Vice Chairman—Very Rev. PHILIP DINH-VAN-THIEP.

Ex Officio, Vicar General / Moderator of Curia—Very Rev. DANIEL J. FELTON.

Appointed Members—Revs. ADAM BRADLEY; CARL E. SCHMITT; JAMES P. LEARY, O.F.M.Cap.; TIMOTHY D. SHILLCOX, O.Praem.; JOEL A. SEMBER.

Elected Members—Vicariate: Very Rev. PHILIP DINH-VAN-THIEP, I - North; Revs. DAVID J. HOFFMAN, II - Mid-North; JASON J. BLAHNIK, III - Southwest; RICHARD L. ALLEN, IV - Mid-South, (Retired); DOUGLAS E. LECAPTAIN, V - Southeast; WILLIAM A. HOFFMAN, VI - Mideast; Rev. Msgr. JAMES DILLENBURG, VII - Peninsula.

Ex Officio—Very Revs. LUKE A. FERRIS; DANIEL J. FELTON.

Bishop's Finance Council—

Diocesan Members—Most Rev. DAVID L. RICKEN, D.D., J.C.L., Bishop of Green Bay; Very Rev. DANIEL J. FELTON, Vicar General/Moderator of the Curia; PAUL KOLBACH, Finance Officer.

Appointed Members—MR. DANIEL ARIENS, Administrative Committee; MRS. JOANN COTTER, CPA, Administrative Committee; Rev. ROBERT K. FINNEGAN, O.Praem., Investment Advisory Committee; MR. ROBERT C. GALLAGHER, Investment Advisory Committee; MR. PAUL GEHL, Administrative Committee; MR. JOSEPH VARKOLY, Administrative Committee; MR. THOMAS VORPAHL, Investment Advisory Committee.

Vicar of Canonical Services and Associate Moderator of the Curia—Very Rev. JOHN W. GIROTTI, J.C.L.

Censores Librorum—Very Rev. JOHN W. GIROTTI, J.C.L.

Discipleship & Leadership Development Mission Team

Mission Team Co-Leaders—MS. JULIANNE STANZ, Tel: 920-272-8270; Very Rev. LUKE A. FERRIS, Tel: 920-272-8165.

Office of Discipleship Formation—MS. JULIANNE STANZ, Dir., Discipleship & Leadership Formation, Tel: 920-272-8270; VACANT, Dir. Discipleship Formation; HEIDI ROSENTHAL, Discipleship Support Coord., Tel: 920-272-8329; MR. JAMIE WHALEN, Dir. Lay Leader Formation, Tel: 920-272-8268; Sr. JANE A. RIHA, O.S.F., Hispanic Ministry Formation Coord., Tel: 920-272-8331; VERONICA CORTES, Administrative Asst., Tel: 920-272-8289.

Office of Priest & Pastoral Leader Formation—Very Rev. LUKE A. FERRIS, Vicar for Clergy & Pastoral Leaders, Tel: 920-272-8165; GLORIA KOTH, Priest Nurse & Health Care Advocate, Tel: 920-272-8207; JENNIE HUETTL, Administrative Asst., Tel: 920-272-8316.

Representative for Religious—Sr. LOUISE HEMBRECHT, O.S.F., Tel: 920-272-8316.

Office of Diaconate Formation—Deacons ANTHONY J. ABTS, Dir. Diaconate, Tel: 920-272-8290; PETER J. GARD, Assoc. Dir., Diaconate & Intl. Priest Coord., Tel: 920-272-8325; VERONICA CORTES, Administrative Asst., Tel: 920-272-8289.

Office of Vocations—Revs. MARK MLEZIVA, Dir., Tel: 920-272-8293; DANIEL J. SCHUSTER, Dir., Tel: 920-272-8293; QUENTIN A. MANN, C.D.L., Assoc. Dir., Tel: 920-312-0070; JENNIE HUETTL, Administrative Asst., Tel: 920-272-8316.

Chancery Mission Team

Mission Team Leader—Very Rev. DANIEL J. FELTON, Tel: 920-272-8180.

Office of Administration—Very Rev. DANIEL J. FELTON, Vicar Gen. & Moderator of the Curia, Tel: 920-272-8180; MRS. JAMI DUVALL, Exec. Asst., Tel: 920-272-8189; Very Rev. JOHN W. GIROTTI, J.C.L., Assoc. Moderator of the Curia, Tel: 920-272-8124; MS. PATRICIA VONHADEN, Exec. Asst., Tel: 920-272-8188.

Office of Canonical Services—Very Rev. JOHN W. GIROTTI, J.C.L., Vicar for Canonical Svcs., Tel: 920-272-8124; MS. PATRICIA VONHADEN, Exec. Asst., Tel: 920-272-8188; JOHN FLANNERY, Victim Assistance Coord., Tel: 920-272-8171; Very Rev. RICHARD H. KLINGEISEN, Coord., Diocesan Healthcare Svcs., Tel: 920-775-4365.

Office of the Chancellor—MRS. TAMMY BASTEN, Chancellor, Tel: 920-272-8175; MS. PATRICIA VONHADEN, Exec. Asst., Tel: 920-272-8188.

Archives—MS. OLIVIA WENDT, Archivist, Tel: 920-272-8195; Bro. STEVEN J. HERRO, O.Praem., Asst. Archivist, Tel: 920-272-8187; BETTY ALLEN, Archives Administrative Asst., Tel: 920-272-8186.

Safe Environment—Deacon DANIEL WAGNITZ, Coord., Tel: 920-272-8174; MS. DEBRA KNAUS, Asst., Tel: 920-272-8198.

Office of Marriage Tribunal—Very Rev. BRIAN S. BELONGIA, J.C.L., Judicial Vicar, Tel: 920-272-8172; CINDY KAPLA, Tribunal Asst., Tel: 920-272-8169; KERRY ADAM, Tribunal Admin. Asst., Tel: 920-272-8167.

Family & Schools of Discipleship Mission Team

Mission Team Leader—DR. PETER MURPHY, Tel: 920-272-8178.

Office of Catholic Schools—Fax: 920-272-8430. TODD BLAHNIK, Supt. Catholic Schools, Tel: 920-272-8273; JANE SCHUELLER, Asst. Supt. Instruction & Academic Accountability, Tel: 920-272-8284; DEBBIE LINNANE, Office Mgr./Administrative Asst., Tel: 920-272-8303; LISA FRANCL, Administrative Asst., Tel: 920-272-8279; VACANT, Assoc. Supt., Mission Effectiveness & Leadership Formation; LORI PAUL, Advancement Dir. for Catholic Schools, Tel: 920-272-8163; DEAN GERONDALE, Financial Planning Dir. for Catholic Schools, Tel: 920-272-8122.

Office of Children & Youth Faith Formation—MAXIMUS CABEY, Dir., Tel: 920-272-8288; CALLIE KOWALSKI, Asst. Dir., Tel: 920-272-8285; CAROL FOUNTAIN, Administrative Asst., Tel: 920-272-8309; SHEILA RE, Administrative Asst., Tel: 920-272-8283.

Office of Marriage and Family Ministries—Fax: 920-272-8430. MS. ELISA TREMBLAY, Dir., Tel: 920-272-8315; TODD PHILLIPS, Assoc. Coord., Tel: 920-272-8317.

Office of Campus Ministry—

UWGB Catholic Campus Ministry—Tel: 920-288-0237. Sr. LAURA ZELTEN, O.S.F., Dir.; Revs. SCOTT VALENTYN, Priest Celebrant; MICHAEL THIEL, Priest Celebrant.

UWO Catholic Campus Ministry - Newman Center—Tel: 920-233-5555. Rev. JASON J. BLAHNIK, Dir.; SARA SCHUENEMANN, Administrative Asst.; MARIE VANDEHEY, Music Ministry.

Office of Camp Tekakwitha—Tel: 715-526-2316. REBECCA SIEVERS, Dir., Tel: 920-272-8162; MCKENNA ROHAN, Assoc. Dir., Tel: 715-526-2316.

Parish Life Mission Team

Mission Team Leader—BARRY METZENTINE, Tel: 920-272-8297.

Office of Parish Mission Planning—DR. JOSEPH BOUND, Dir., Tel: 920-272-8179; GABRIELA CHAVEZ, Coord. (Bilingual), Tel: 920-272-8286; PATTY YOUNG, Mgmt. Support Coord., Tel: 920-272-8295; TRACY GRANIUS, Administrative Asst., Tel: 920-272-8312.

Office of Divine Worship—Fax: 920-272-8441. MICHAEL PORADEK, Dir., Tel: 920-272-8342; CLARE STURM, Coord., Tel: 920-272-8311; ARVILLA RUSNAK, Tel: 920-272-8341.

Office of Parish Evangelization—JOE TREMBLAY, Coord., Tel: 920-272-8313; MARIA GARCIA, Administrative Asst., Tel: 920-272-8276.

Office of Hispanic & Multi-Cultural Ministry—VACANT, Dir.

Office of Young Adult Ministry—JANE ANGHA, Coord., Tel: 920-272-8304.

Catholic Charities & Living Justice Mission Team

Mission Team Leader—Very Rev. JOHN W. GIROTTI, J.C.L., Tel: 920-272-8124.

Catholic Charities—Tel: 920-272-8234; Fax: 920-437-4067. TED PHERNETTON, Dir., Tel: 920-272-8226; THERESA MCKENNA, Administrative Asst., Tel: 920-272-8291.

Office of Living Justice—PETER WEISS, Living Justice Advocate/Prog. Mgr., Tel: 920-272-8321; ERIC WEYDT, Coord. Catholic Social Justice, Tel: 920-272-8344.

Administrative Support Services—JESSE BRUNETTE, Administrative Svcs. Mgr., Tel: 920-272-8233. Administrative Assistants: MARY ANN DENSING; JOAN KLOSTER; ERIN GUERRERO, Tel: 920-272-8234.

Child and Family Services—TARA DEGRAVE, Prog. Mgr., Tel: 920-272-8246; CHELSEA BAUCOM-YOUNG, Adoption Specialist/Social Worker, Tel: 920-272-8247; EMILY ANNOYE, Case Mgr., Tel: 920-272-8330; CASSANDRA KRUEGER, Case Mgr., Tel: 920-272-8227; BREANA PICKARD, Case Mgr., Tel: 920-272-8237; RICCI VAN HANDEL, Adoption Case Mgr., Tel: 920-272-8237; ALYSSA ALBIZU, Agency Intake/Case Mgmt. Specialist, Tel: 920-272-8323; ALNILDA ALBIZU, Agency Intake/Case Mgmt. Specialist, Tel: 920-272-8323.

Financial Health Services—BOBBIE LISON, Opers. Mgr., Tel: 920-272-8252. Budget Counselors: RUTH AROCA, Tel: 920-272-8250; MEGAN SANTKUYL, Tel: 920-272-8234; KELLY DEKARSKE, Debt Mgmt. Prog./Representative Payee Specialist, Tel: 920-272-8249.

Counseling and Treatment Services—CELIA GARDNER, Mgr. Counseling & Treatment Svcs., Tel: 920-272-8231. Mental Health Counselors: ELAINE CONWAY, Tel: 920-272-8235; CLAUDIA "JEANNIE" CHASE, Tel: 920-272-8234; MARION JIMOS, Tel: 920-272-8234; JANICE PROSKI, Therapist in Training, Tel: 920-272-8228. Domestic Violence Group Facilitators: REGINA CUELLAR-PROCTOR; ROBERTO TORREZ; PAMELA NIKODEM, Tel: 920-272-8234.

Refugee, Immigrant and Family Strengthening Services—ANA RODRIGUEZ, Immigration Counselor, Tel: 920-272-8241; LAURIE MARTINEZ, Family Strengthening Supvr./Immigration Counselor, Tel: 920-272-8232; SO THAO, Refugee Resettlement Svcs. Coord., Tel: 920-272-8242; Sr. GUADALUPE MUNOZ, Hispanic Outreach Case Mgr., Tel: 920-272-8277; Rev. WILLIAM H. RIBBENS, O.Praem., Volunteer, Tel: 920-272-8230; NENGLEE VANG, Refugee Family Strengthening Coord., Tel: 920-272-8234; NICOLE SENGKHAMMEE, Case Mgr., Tel: 920-272-8318.

Pastoral Care—MARY ARMBRUST, Pastoral Care & Ministry Coord., Tel: 920-272-8300.

Catholic Charities - Menasha—Mental Health Counselors: MARION JIMOS; MELANIE CREGER; CLAUDIA "JEANNIE" CHASE; KARI MEYER, Therapist in Training; CASSANDRA KRUEGER, Case Mgr.; CHAMAO XIONG, Case Mgr., Refugee Family Strengthening; CAROLYN SALSIEDER, Administrative Asst.

Catholic Charities - Manitowoc—206 N. 8th St., Manitowoc, 54220. Tel: 920-684-6651; Fax: 920-684-6652. *Mailing Address: P.O. Box 1312, Manitowoc, 54221-1312.* NENGLEE VANG, Refugee Family Strengthening Coord.; BETH SNYDER, Budget Counselor; JESSICA LOPEZ DIAZ, Administrative Asst.

Catholic Charities - Marinette—1712 Dunlap Ave., Ste. 5, Marinette, 54143. Tel: 715-735-7802; Fax: 715-735-5794. DEBRA MULLEN, Mental Health Counselor; LINDA STOFFLE, Domestic Violence Group Facilitator; BROOKE MULLINS, Administrative Asst.

Catholic Charities - Oshkosh—36 Broad St., Oshkosh,

54901. Tel: 920-235-6002; Fax: 920-303-9287. MARION JIMOS, Mental Health Counselor; KARI MEYER, Therapist in Training; TERRI REYNEBEAU, Administrative Asst.

Catholic Charities - Waupaca—N2845 Shadow Rd., Waupaca, 54981. Tel: 920-734-2601. MELANIE CREGER, Mental Health Counselor.

Catholic Charities - Wautoma—364 S. Cambridge St., Wautoma, 54982. Tel: 920-734-2601. MELANIE CREGER, Mental Health Counselor.

Resource & Support Mission Team

Mission Team Leader—MRS. TAMMY BASTEN, Tel: 920-272-8175.

Office of Communications—Fax: 920-437-9356. MRS. JUSTINE LODL, Dir., Tel: 920-272-8213; SARAH BRADFORD, Communications Coord., Tel: 920-272-8209; MATTHEW LIVINGSTONE, Dir. Social Communications, Tel: 920-272-8214; JESSICA JACQUES, Digital Media Content Specialist, Tel: 920-272-8224.

The Compass—SAM LUCERO, News & Information Mgr., Tel: 920-272-8210; PAT KASTEN, Assoc. Editor, Tel: 920-272-8203; JEFF KUROWSKI, Assoc. Editor, Tel: 920-272-8204; AMY KAWULA, Advertising & Mktg. Mgr., Tel: 920-272-8212; SUE SIMOENS, Graphic Design & Sales Specialist, Tel: 920-272-8215; BARB GAUTHIER, Administrative Asst., Tel: 920-272-8208.

Office of Facilities & Properties—Fax: 920-272-8435. BARBARA WIEGAND, Dir., Tel: 920-272-8260; MIKE GERRITS, Mgr. Bldgs. & Grounds, Tel: 920-272-8335; KAYLA SWENTY, Administrative Asst., Tel: 920-272-8314; LAURA KELLY, Mail Clerk/Purchasing Coord., Tel: 920-272-8320.

Allouez Catholic Cemetery and Chapel Mausoleum—2121 Riverside Dr., Green Bay, 54301-2397. Tel: 920-432-7585; Fax: 920-432-0425. MARY BREIVOGEL, Admin., Tel: 920-272-8352; TRACY MULKEY, Administrative Asst., Tel: 920-272-8353; MS. KAREN R. BASS, Family Svcs. Counselor, Tel: 920-272-8354; LYNN RASMUSSEN, Family Svcs. Counselor, Tel: 920-272-8355.

Office of Finance & Accounting—PAUL KOLBACH, CFO, Tel: 920-272-8206; MARY REYNEBEAU, Finance Asst., Tel: 920-272-8223; MIKE SPEEL, Controller, Tel: 920-272-8259; KAREN ROTTIER, Project Accountant, Tel: 920-272-8298; NICK SPEEL, Accounting Mgr., Tel: 920-272-8267; JESSIE CLARK, Accounting Supvr., Tel: 920-272-8264; JACKIE JOCEWICZ, Accounting Specialist, Tel: 920-272-8258. Accounting Coordinators: LUANN NELSON, Tel: 920-272-8275; ALYCE SAUER, Tel: 920-272-8272. Bookkeepers: SUE DE WANE, Tel: 920-272-8262; KATHY NOHR, Tel: 920-272-8265; LAURA PAIDER, Tel: 920-272-8256.

Office of Human Resources—Fax: 920-437-9296. JENNIFER BUECHEL, Dir., Tel: 920-272-8343; PAUL DOELL, Staffing Mgr., Tel: 920-272-8218; MARY SUMMERS, Administrative Asst., Tel: 920-272-8200.

Benefits/Insurance—BONNIE CLANCY, Benefits Mgr., Tel: 920-272-8201; DAWN NELSON, Sr. HR Generalist - Benefits, Tel: 920-272-8348; JENNY WALSKE, Benefits Asst., Tel: 920-272-8202.

Employee Relations—JENNIFER ARNOLD, Coord., Tel: 920-272-8216.

Office of Information Technology—Email: gbdhelpdesk@gbdioc.org. Deacon CONRAD J. KIELTYKA, IT Dir., Tel: 920-272-8116; TIM ROHLOFF, IT Mgr., Tel: 920-272-8253; NICK GRIFFIE, Systems Admin. - Software, Tel: 920-272-8245; ROY VERSTEGEN, Systems Admin. - Hardware, Tel: 920-272-8251; KAREN SZCZEPANSKI, IT Support Specialist, Tel: 920-272-8254; BECKY KRAHN, Power School Support Specialist, Tel: 920-272-8113; ROBERT WEYDT, Systems Admin. - Network, Tel: 920-272-8114.

Catholic Foundation—Mailing Address: P.O. Box 22128, Green Bay, 54305-2128. Fax: 920-272-8435; Email: catholicfoundation@gbdioc.org; Web: www.catholicfoundationgb.org. JOSH DIEDRICH, Exec. Dir., Tel: 920-272-8197.

Office of Bishop's Appeal—TAMMY DANZ, Dir. Bishop's Appeal, Tel: 920-272-8123; AMY MACKENZIE, Mktg. Specialist, Tel: 920-272-8185; DEBBIE DEGRAVE, Database Admin., Tel: 920-272-8184; MARY JANE HEIM, Data Entry Specialist, Tel: 920-272-8243; KENDRA RIOS, Senior Data Entry Specialist, Tel: 920-272-8121.

Office of Planned Giving—JANET WAGNER, Dir. Devel., Tel: 920-272-8199; CINDI BRAWNER, Senior Relationship Mgr., Tel: 920-272-8173; REBECCA HAENY, Administrative Support Specialist, Tel: 920-272-8181; TERESA ADLER, Campaign Specialist, Tel: 920-272-8211; BOBBI JO SMIDEL, Administrative Asst., Tel: 920-272-8166; ADAM WITHBROE, Parish Campaign Dir., Tel: 920-272-8156; EMILY KAISER, Parish Campaign Dir., Tel: 920-272-8155; VACANT, Grant Coord., Tel: 920-272-8182.

Office of World Missions—CYNTHIA ST. AUBIN, Dir., Tel: 920-272-8192.

Priests' Personnel Board—Mailing Address: P.O. Box 23825, Green Bay, 54305-3825. Tel: 920-437-7531. Most Rev. DAVID L. RICKEN, D.D., J.C.L.; Very Rev. LUKE A. FERRIS, Chm.; Rev. WALTER P. STUMPF; Very Rev. DANIEL J. FELTON; Rev. DONALD E. EVERTS; Very Rev. RYAN E. KRUEGER; BARRY METZENTINE; Revs. DENNIS M. RYAN, (Retired); DAVID R. SCHMIDT; Sr. MARLA J. CLERCX, A.N.G.; Deacon PETER J. GARD.

Leo Benevolent Association—Mailing Address: P.O. Box 23825, Green Bay, 54305-3825. Rev. MICHAEL E. BETLEY, Pres., N369 Military Rd., Sherwood, 54169. Tel: 920-989-1515.

CLERGY, PARISHES, MISSIONS AND PAROCHIAL SCHOOLS

CITY OF GREEN BAY

(BROWN COUNTY)

1—ST. FRANCIS XAVIER CATHEDRAL (1851) Also serves St. John, Green Bay.
139 S. Madison St., 54301-4501. Tel: 920-432-4348; Fax: 920-435-5068; Email: cathedral.sfx@gmail.com; Web: www.sfxcathedralgb.org. Rev. Joseph E. Dorner; Deacons Thomas J. Mahoney; Conrad J. Kieltyka.
School: See St. Thomas More School, Green Bay (part of the GRACE, Inc. System), located under Consolidated Schools in the Institutions section.
Catechesis Religious Program—Tel: 920-432-0820. Mrs. Connie Demeuse, D.R.E.

2—ST. AGNES (1953)
1484 9th St., 54304-3061. Tel: 920-494-2534; Email: stagnesparishoffice@netnet.net; Web: www.stagnesgreenbay.org. Rev. Patrick C. Beno; Deacon Greg Rotherham.
School—Holy Family School, (Part of the GRACE, Inc. System) 1204 S. Fisk St., 54304-2299.
Tel: 920-494-1931; Fax: 920-494-4942; Email: hfsoffice@gracesystem.org; Web: www.holyfamilygreenbay.com. Allison Moseng, Prin. Students 229.
Catechesis Religious Program—Tel: 920-494-6450. Deborah Gretzinger, D.R.E. Students 190.

3—ANNUNCIATION OF THE BLESSED VIRGIN MARY (1932) Also serves St. Joseph, Green Bay; St. Jude, Green Bay; St. Patrick, Green Bay.
Mailing Address: 1087 Kellogg St., 54303-3058.
Tel: 920-496-2160; Fax: 920-496-2167; Email: lverheyden@quad-parish.org; Web: www.quad-parish.org. Revs. David R. Schmidt; Gregory Parent, Parochial Vicar; Deacons Michael J. Mervilde; Daniel Wagnitz.
Church: 401 Gray St., 54303.
Catechesis Religious Program— Combined with St. Joseph, Green Bay, St. Jude, Green Bay and St. Patrick, Green Bay. Becky Van Kauwenberg, D.R.E.

4—ST. BERNARD (1956)
2040 Hillside Ln., 54302-4098. Tel: 920-468-4811; Email: office@stbernardcong.org; Web: www.stbernardgb.org. Rev. Mark P. Vander Steeg; Deacons Keith P. Holschbach; Bernard Terrien; Larry V. Mastalish.
School—St. Bernard School, (Part of the GRACE, Inc. System) 2020 Hillside Ln., 54302-4099.
Tel: 920-468-5026; Fax: 920-468-3478; Email: cblahnik@gracesystem.org; Web: www.stbernardgb.org. Crystal Blahnik, Prin. Students 462.
Catechesis Religious Program—Email: adam@stbernardcong.org. Mr. Adam Horn, D.R.E.

5—ST. ELIZABETH ANN SETON (1978)
2771 Oakwood Dr., 54304-1699. Tel: 920-499-1546; Fax: 920-499-2207; Email: seas@seasgb.org; Web: seasgb.org. Sr. Marla J. Clercx, A.N.G., Pastoral Leader; Deacon Steven J. Meyer.
School: See Holy Family School, Green Bay, (part of the GRACE, Inc. System) located under Consolidated Schools in the Institutions section.
Catechesis Religious Program—Email: jbrown@seasgb.org. Ms. Carrie Lundy, D.R.E.

6—HOLY MARTYRS OF GORCUM, [CEM] Merged with Holy Trinity, Pine Grove to form Prince of Peace, Green Bay.

7—ST. JOHN THE EVANGELIST (1831) Served from St. Francis Xavier Cathedral, Green Bay.
413 St. John St., 54301-4116. Tel: 920-436-6380; Email: sjeoffice@sbcglobal.net; Web: stjohngb.org. Rev. Joseph E. Dorner; Deacons Thomas J. Mahoney; Conrad J. Kieltyka.
Catechesis Religious Program—139 S. Madison St., 54301. Tel: 920-609-1826; Email: faithformation.sfx.sje@gmail.com. Mrs. Connie Demeuse, D.R.E.

8—ST. JOSEPH (1914) Served from Annunciation of BVM, Green Bay.
1087 Kellogg St., 54303. Tel: 920-496-2160; Email: ckittell@quad-parish.org; Web: www.quad-parish.org. 936 Ninth St., 54304. Revs. David R. Schmidt; Gregory Parent, Parochial Vicar; Deacons Michael J. Mervilde; Daniel Wagnitz.
Church: 936 9th St., 54304.
Catechesis Religious Program— Combined with Annunciation of the Blessed Virgin Mary, Green Bay, St. Jude, Green Bay and St. Patrick, Green Bay. Tel: 920-497-7042; Fax: 920-491-0121. Becky Van Kauwenberg, D.R.E.

9—ST. JUDE, Served from Annunciation of the BVM, Green Bay.
1420 Division St., 54303. 1087 Kellogg St., 54303.
Tel: 920-496-2160; Fax: 920-496-2167; Email: ckittell@quad-parish.org. Revs. David R. Schmidt; Gregory Parent, Parochial Vicar; Deacons Michael J. Mervilde; Daniel Wagnitz.
Catechesis Religious Program— Combined with Annunciation of the Blessed Virgin Mary, Green Bay, St. Joseph, Green Bay and St. Patrick, Green Bay. 936 9th St., 54304-3439. Tel: 920-497-7042; Fax: 920-491-0121; Email: tmeyer@allofuswestgb.org. Becky Van Kauwenberg, D.R.E.

10—ST. MARY OF THE ANGELS (1898)
650 S. Irwin Ave., 54301-3303. Tel: 920-437-1979; Tel: 920-432-2747. Rev. Anthony Cirignani, O.F.M.; Deacon Paul P. Umentum.
School—St. Thomas More School, (Part of the GRACE, Inc. System) 1420 Harvey St., 54302.
Tel: 920-432-8242; Email: oamor@gracesystem.org; Web: www.stmoregb.org. Olgamar Amor, Prin. Students 145.
Catechesis Religious Program—Tel: 920-432-2747; Email: saintmaryfaith@gmail.com. Beth Gajeski, D.R.E.

11—ST. MATTHEW (1922)
130 St. Matthews St., 54301-2910. Email: pfdart91@gmail.com. Rev. Robert J. Kabat, J.C.L.; Deacon Robert Hornacek.
Res.: 2311 Nelson Ct., 54301-2910. Tel: 920-435-6811; Email: parishoffice@stmattsgb.org.
School—Father Allouez Catholic School, St. Matthew Campus, (Part of the GRACE, Inc. System) 2575 S. Webster Ave., 54301-2998. Tel: 920-432-5223; Email: smsoffice@gracesystem.org; Web: www.fatherallouezschool.org. Kay L. Franz, Prin. Students 185.
Catechesis Religious Program—Email: mwestenberg@stmattsgb.org. Michael Westenberg, D.R.E.

12—NATIVITY OF OUR LORD (1964)
2270 S. Oneida St., 54304-4712. Tel: 920-499-5156; Fax: 920-429-9285; Email: natscene@nativityparish.com; Web: www.nativityparish.com. Very Rev. Michael L. Ingold; Deacons John J. Bundra; Michael W. Dabeck.
Catechesis Religious Program—Tel: 920-499-6012; Email: natmc@nativityparish.com. Mrs. Mary P. Carter, D.R.E.

13—ST. PATRICK (1864) Served from Annunciation of BVM, Green Bay.
1087 Kellogg St., 54303-3058. Tel: 920-496-2160; Fax: 920-496-2167; Email: lverheyden@quad-parish.org; Web: www.quad-parish.org. 211 N. Maple Ave., 54303. Revs. David R. Schmidt; Gregory Parent, Parochial Vicar; Deacons Michael J. Mervilde; Daniel Wagnitz.
Catechesis Religious Program— Combined with Annunciation of the Blessed Virgin Mary, Green Bay, St. Joseph, Green Bay and St. Jude, Green Bay. 936 9th St., 54304-3439. Tel: 920-497-7042; Fax: 920-491-0121; Email: tmeyer@allofuswestgb.org. Becky Van Kauwenberg, D.R.E.; Ms. Mindy Wegner, D.R.E.

14—SS. PETER AND PAUL CATHOLIC CONGREGATION (1875)
720 N. Baird St., 54302-1902. Tel: 920-435-7548; Fax: 920-432-1321; Email: sspeterpaulgb@gmail.com; Web: sspeterpaulgb.org. Rev. Anthony Cirignani, O.F.M.
School: See St. Thomas More School, Green Bay (part of the GRACE, Inc. System), located under Consolidated Schools in the Institutions section.
Catechesis Religious Program—Michael F. Lee, D.R.E., Tel: 920-437-0651; Email: mikeleegbw@gmail.com. Students 75.

15—ST. PHILIP THE APOSTLE (1938)
312 Victoria St., 54302-2818. Tel: 920-468-7848; Fax: 920-468-1025; Email: bnoel@stphilipcong.org; Email: lcorroy@stphilipcong.org. Rev. William A. Hoffman, Priest Mod.; Juanita Fiscal, Hispanic Ministry, Email: jfiscal@stphilipcong.org.

Catechesis Religious Program—Email: mvazquez@stphilipcong.org. Maura Vazquez, D.R.E. Students 435.

16—PRINCE OF PEACE (2005)
3425 Willow Rd., 54311-8232. Tel: 920-468-5718; Fax: 920-468-5713; Email: parish@popgb.org; Web: www.popgb.org. Rev. Daniel Viertel; Deacon William J. Burkel.
School: See Green Bay Area Catholic Education, Inc. (GRACE), Green Bay located under Consolidated Schools in the Institutions section.
Catechesis Religious Program—Email: cwhitcomb@princeofpeaceparish.com. Nancy Baldschun, D.R.E.

17—RESURRECTION (1963)
333 Hilltop Dr., 54301-2799. Tel: 920-336-7768; Fax: 920-336-1949; Email: ResurrectionParish@gbres.org; Web: www.gbres.org. Rev. Timothy D. Shillcox, O.Praem.; Deacon Donald J. Ropson.
School—Father Allouez Catholic School, Resurrection Campus, (Part of the GRACE, Inc. System) Tel: 920-336-3230; Email: resoffice@gracesystem.org. Kay L. Franz, Prin. Students 118.
Catechesis Religious Program—Email: rabaloun@gbres.org. Rosemary A. Baloun, D.R.E.

18—ST. WILLEBRORD (1864)
209 S. Adams St., 54301-4584. Tel: 920-435-2016; Fax: 920-435-2039; Email: frandy@stwillys.org. Revs. Andrew G. Cribben, O.Praem.; John P. MacCarthy, O.Praem., Parochial Vicar; Deacon Luis Sanchez.
Catechesis Religious Program—Ms. Susan K. Perrault, D.R.E., English; Ms. Alma Vazquez, D.R.E., Spanish.

OUTSIDE THE CITY OF GREEN BAY

ABRAMS, OCONTO CO., ST. LOUIS, [JC] Merged with St. Joseph, Chase and St. John Cantius, Sobieski to form St. Maximilian Kolbe, Sobieski.

ALGOMA, KEWAUNEE CO., ST. MARY (1860) [CEM]
Mailing Address: 214 Church St., Algoma, 54201-1035. Tel: 920-487-5005; Email: pkubetz@smsalgoma.com. Rev. Alvan Amadi, Admin.
School—St. Mary School, Tel: 920-487-5004; Email: mhall@smsalgoma.com. Margaret Hall, Prin. Lay Teachers 5; Students 32.
Catechesis Religious Program—Barb Heiges, D.R.E., Tel: 920-487-5005, Ext. 112.

ALVERNO, MANITOWOC CO., ST. JOSEPH, Merged with St. Casimir, Northeim; St. Isidore, Osman; and St. Wendel, Cleveland to form St. Thomas the Apostle, Northeim.

AMBERG, MARINETTE CO., ST. AGNES (1890) Served from St. Augustine, Wausaukee.
Mailing Address: 507 Church St., Wausaukee, 54177-9749. Tel: 715-856-5276; Email: staugustine@centurytel.net. W8031 Wright Ave., Amberg, 54102. Revs. Frederick Sserugga, Admin.; Donald R. Burkart, Priest Celebrant, (Retired); John J. Hephner, Priest Celebrant, (Retired); Deacon Richard F. Elfering.
Catechesis Religious Program—

ANIWA, SHAWANO CO., ST. BONIFACE, [CEM] Served from St. Philomena, Birnamwood. Rev. Vicente Llagas, Admin.
Res.: P.O. Box K, Birnamwood, 54414-0911.
Tel: 715-449-0050; Email: philboniface@charter.net.
Church: W19104 Church St., Aniwa, 54408.
Catechesis Religious Program—

ANTIGO, LANGLADE CO.

1—ST. HYACINTH, Merged with St. Mary, Antigo to form SS. Mary & Hyacinth, Antigo.

2—ST. JOHN (1880) [JC]
415 6th Ave., Antigo, 54409-2104. Very Rev. Mathew J. Simonar; Rev. Zachary Weber, Parochial Vicar; Deacon Andrew P. Bures. Also serves St. Mary & Hyacinth, Antigo, St. Wenceslaus, Neva and SS. James & Stanislaus, White Lake/Langlade.
School: See All Saints Catholic Schools, Inc., Antigo, located under Consolidated Schools in the Institution Section.
Catechesis Religious Program—Fax: 715-623-2024; Email: antigo_re@granitewave.com. Pete Schlegel, D.R.E.; Tracey Minish, D.R.E.

3—ST. MARY, Merged with St. Hyacinth, Antigo to form SS. Mary & Hyacinth, Antigo.

4—SS. MARY & HYACINTH (2001) [JC] Served from St. John, Antigo. Has records for St. Mary & St. Hyacinth, Antigo.
819 3rd Ave., Antigo, 54409-1930. Very Rev. Mathew J. Simonar; Rev. Zachary Weber, Parochial Vicar; Deacon Andrew P. Bures.
Church: 829 3rd Ave., Antigo, 54409.
School: See All Saints Catholic Schools, Inc., Antigo, located under Consolidated Schools in the Institution Section.
Catechesis Religious Program—Inter-Parish Faith Formation Center, Joint program with St. John the Evangelist, Antigo & St. Wenceslaus, Neva. Tel: 715-623-5255; Email: antigo_re@granitewave.com. Pete Schlegel, D.R.E.; Tracey Minish, C.R.E.

APPLETON, OUTAGAMIE CO.

1—ST. BERNADETTE (1960)
2331 E. Lourdes Dr., Appleton, 54915-3698. Tel: 920-739-4157; Fax: 920-739-2795; Email: jlueck@saint-bernadette.org; Web: www.saint-bernadette.org/. Rev. Jon Thorsen, Parochial Vicar; Very Rev. Donald M. Zuleger; Deacon Gilbert F. Schmidt. Also serves Sacred Heart, Appleton
School—St. Francis Xavier Catholic School System, Inc., 101 E. Northland Ave., Appleton, 54911. Tel: 920-735-9380; Fax: 920-735-1787; Email: rduboise@xaviercatholicschools.org; Web: www.xaviercatholicschools.org. Deacon Ray DuBois, Pres. Lay Teachers 133; Students 1,502.
Catechesis Religious Program—Tel: 920-739-4157; Email: asirianni@saint-bernadette.org. Ann Sirianne, D.R.E.

2—ST. BERNARD CONGREGATION OF APPLETON (1966)
1617 W. Pine St., Appleton, 54914-5118. Tel: 920-739-0331; Fax: 920-749-9771; Email: stbernard@stbernardappleton.org; Web: stbernardappleton.org. Rev. Amal Raj Roche, Admin.; Deacon Michael J. Eash; Dr. Colleen Sargent-Day, Business Mgr.
School—St. Francis Xavier Catholic School System, Inc., 101 E. Northland Ave., Appleton, 54911-2104. Tel: 920-735-9380; Fax: 920-735-1787; Email: rdubois@xaviercatholicschools.org. Deacon Ray DuBois, Pres. Lay Teachers 133; Students 1,502.
Catechesis Religious Program—Tel: 920-739-8912; Email: moveresch@stbernardappleton.org. Maurine Overesch, D.R.E.

3—ST. JOSEPH (1868)
404 W. Lawrence St., Appleton, 54911-5855. Tel: 920-734-7195; Email: frjim@saintjosephparish.org. Rev. James P. Leary, O.F.M.Cap.; Deacons Clarence F. Dedman; Mark J. Farrell.
School—St. Francis Xavier Middle School, (Grades 5-8), (Part of the St. Francis Xavier Catholic School System, Inc.) 2626 N. Oneida St., Appleton, 54911-2099. Tel: 920-730-8849; Fax: 920-703-4147; Email: rbires@xaviercatholicschools.org. 101 E. Northland Ave., Appleton, 54911. Deacon Ray DuBois, Pres.; Robert Bires, Prin. Lay Teachers 40; Students 418.
Catechesis Religious Program—Tel: 920-738-7413; Email: iprf@inter-parish.org. Andrew J. Russell, D.R.E. Associated with St. Mary's, Appleton.

4—ST. MARY (1859) [CEM]
312 S. State St., Appleton, 54911-5926. Tel: 920-739-5119; Email: stmary@stmaryparish.org; Web: stmaryparish.org. Rev. William Swictenberg; Deacons Gerard J. Schraufnagel, Min., Parish Vitality; Jeffrey M. Prickette, Pastoral Min.
School—St. Francis Xavier Catholic School System, Inc., 101 E. Northland Ave., Appleton, 54911-5929. Tel: 920-733-3709; Fax: 920-735-1787; Email: rdubois@xaviercatholicschools.org; Web: www.xaviercatholicschools.org. Deacon Ray DuBois, Pres. Lay Teachers 133; Students 1,502.
Catechesis Religious Program—404 W. Lawrence St., Appleton, 54911-5817. Tel: 920-738-7413; Email: iprf@inter-parish.org. Andrew J. Russell, D.R.E. Associated with St. Joseph-St. Mary Interparish.

5—ST. PIUS X (1957)
500 W. Marquette St., Appleton, 54911-1996. Tel: 920-733-0575; Email: secretary@stpiusxappleton.com; Web: www.stpiusappleton.org. Revs. James R. Jugenheimer; Adam Bradley, Parochial Vicar; Deacons Richard S. Simon; Robert Seymour; Daniel W. Zajicek.
School—St. Francis Xavier Catholic School - Marquette, (Grades PreK-4), (Part of the St. Francis Xavier Catholic School System, Inc.) 500 W. Marquette St., Appleton, 54911-1996. Tel: 920-733-4918; Email: lbarnett@xaviercatholicschools.org; Web: www.xaviercatholicschools.org. 101 E. Northland Ave., Appleton, 54911-2104. Deacon Ray DuBois, Pres.; Laura Barnett, Prin. Lay Teachers 24; Students 285.
Catechesis Religious Program—Tel: 920-733-4919; Email: kathleenschommer@stpiusxappleton.com. Erin K. Riley, D.R.E. (Grades 1-4); Kathy Schommer, D.R.E. (Grades 8-10).

6—SACRED HEART (1898) Very Rev. Donald M. Zuleger; Rev. Jon Thorsen, Parochial Vicar; Deacons Daniel T. Koszalinski; Gilbert F. Schmidt. Served from St. Bernadette, Appleton.
Res.: 222 E. Fremont St., Appleton, 54915-1890. Tel: 920-739-3196; Fax: 920-739-4062; Email: office@sacredheartappleton.com.
Catechesis Religious Program—Email: faith@sacredheartappleton.com. Mrs. Kelly Koszalinski, D.R.E.

7—ST. THERESE (1926)
213 E. Wisconsin Ave., Appleton, 54911-4875. Rev. Ryan Starks; Deacons Anthony J. Abts; Ernesto L. Gonzalez Jr.
School—St. Francis Xavier Catholic School System, Inc., 101 E. Northland Ave., Appleton, 54911-2104. Tel: 920-735-9380; Fax: 920-735-1787; Email: rdubois@xaviercatholicschools.org; Web: www.xaviercatholicschools.org. Deacon Ray DuBois, Pres. Lay Teachers 133; Students 1,502.
Catechesis Religious Program—Mrs. Margaret A. Jensen, D.R.E.

8—ST. THOMAS MORE (1963) Revs. James W. Lucas; Gerald R. Falk, Pastor Emeritus, (Retired); Deacons Donald J. Wetzel; Timothy E. Downey; Ray DuBois.
Res.: 1810B N. McDonald St., Appleton, 54911-3450. Tel: 920-739-7758; Email: stmparish@stmcath.org.
School—St. Francis Xavier Catholic School System, (Grades PreSchool-4), (Part of the St. Francis Xavier Catholic School System, Inc.) McDonald St. Campus, 1810 N. McDonald St., Appleton, 54911-3498. Tel: 920-739-2376; Fax: 920-739-2376; Email: creuter@xaviercatholicschools.org; Web: www.xaviercatholicschools.org. 101 E. Northland Ave., Appleton, 54911. Deacon Ray DuBois, Pres.; Mrs. Carolyn Reuter, Prin. Lay Teachers 24; Students 261.
Catechesis Religious Program—Tel: 920-739-8172; Email: anita@stmcath.org. Mrs. Anita Revord, D.R.E.

ARGONNE, FOREST CO., ST. MARY, Merged with St. Joseph, Crandon.

ARMSTRONG CREEK, FOREST CO., ST. STANISLAUS KOSTKA (1911) Also serves St. Joan of Arc, Goodman.
Mailing Address: 521 U.S. Hwy. 8, P.O. Box 39, Armstrong Creek, 54103-2334. Tel: 715-336-2334; Email: ststanislausarmstrong@gmail.com. Rev. Timothy Brandt.

AURORA, FLORENCE CO., SACRED HEART, Served from St. Anthony, Niagara.
Mailing Address: 1432 River St., Niagara, 54151. Tel: 715-251-3879; Email: office@stanthonyniagara.org. W782 County Hwy. N., Aurora. Rev. Michael Lightner.

BAILEYS HARBOR, DOOR CO., ST. MARY OF THE LAKE, Merged with St. John the Baptist, Egg Harbor; St. Paul, Fish Creek; St. Michael, Jacksonport and St. Rosalia, Sister Bay to form Stella Maris, Egg Harbor.

BAY SETTLEMENT, BROWN CO., HOLY CROSS (1852) [CEM]
3009 Bay Settlement Rd., 54311-7301. Tel: 920-468-0595; Email: blsholycross@gmail.com; Web: holycrossfamily.blogspot.com. Rt. Rev. Gary J. Neville, O.Praem., J.C.D.
School—Holy Cross School, (Part of the GRACE, Inc. System) 3002 Bay Settlement Rd., 54311-7302. Tel: 920-866-4000; Fax: 920-468-0625; Email: sgast@gracesystem.org; Web: www.holycrossfamily.org. Sharon Gast, Prin. Students 114.
Catechesis Religious Program—Tel: 920-468-6554; Email: holycrossff@hotmail.com. Mrs. Tina Reignier, D.R.E.

BEAR CREEK, OUTAGAMIE CO., ST. MARY (1867) [CEM] Served from St. Rose, Clintonville.
Mailing Address: 140 Auto St., Clintonville, 54929-1712. Tel: 715-201-9913; Email: sborlen@ssrmparishes.org. Revs. Joseph Dorner, Sacramental Min.; John T. Mullarkey, Priest Celebrant, (Retired); Deacons Paul J. Brulla; Lincoln Wood.
Catechesis Religious Program—Email: mscherer@ssrmparishes.org. Maria Scherer, C.R.E. Associated with St. Rose, Clintonville.

BIRNAMWOOD, SHAWANO CO., ST. PHILOMENA (1903) [CEM] Also serves St. Boniface, Aniwa.
P.O. Box K, Birnamwood, 54414-0911. Tel: .715-449-0050; Fax: 715-449-0029; Email: philboniface@charter.net. Rev. Anthony Ibekwe, Admin.
Church: 434 State Rd., Birnamwood, 54414.
Catechesis Religious Program—Jennifer Duranceau, D.R.E.

BLACK CREEK, OUTAGAMIE CO., ST. MARY (1895) [CEM]
P.O. Box 217, Black Creek, 54106-0217. Tel: 920-984-3319; Email: tobac_99@yahoo.com. Rev. Theodore J. Hendricks.

BRILLION, CALUMET CO.

1—HOLY FAMILY (2001) [JC] Formerly St. Mary, Brillion & St. Mary-St. Patrick, Reedsville/Maple Grove.
1100 W. Ryan St., Brillion, 54110-1074. Tel: 920-756-2535; Fax: 920-756-9802; Email: office@holyfamily-parish.org; Web: www.holyfamilybrillion.org. Rev. Thomas Pomeroy.
School—Holy Family School, 209 N. Custer St., Brillion, 54110-1236. Tel: 920-756-2502; Fax: 920-756-9702; Email: hfsc@holyfamily-parish.org; Web: www.hfcsbrillion.org. Scott Smith, Prin. Lay Teachers 8; Students 65.
Catechesis Religious Program—Email: deb@holyfamily-parish.org. Debra Braden, D.R.E. Students 252.

2—ST. MARY, Merged with St. Mary-St. Patrick, Reedsville to form Holy Family, Brillion.

BRUSSELS, DOOR CO.

1—ST. FRANCIS & ST. MARY PARISH (1993) [CEM 3] Formerly St. Francis Xavier, Brussels & St. Mary,

Namur.
9716 Cemetery Rd., Brussels, 54204-9749.
Tel: 920-825-7555; Email: stfrancis@centurytel.net; Web: brusselscatholicchurch.com. Rev. Edward L. Looney, Admin.
Catechesis Religious Program—Laura Hoffman, D.R.E.

2—ST. FRANCIS XAVIER, Merged with St. Mary, Namur to form St. Francis-St. Mary, Brussels.

CASCO/SLOVAN, KEWAUNEE CO., HOLY TRINITY (1856) [CEM]
510 Church Ave., Casco, 54205-9712.
Tel: 920-837-7531; Fax: 920-837-2361; Email: office@holytrinitycasco.com; Web: www.holytrinitycasco.com. Rev. Daniel J. Schuster, Admin.; Deacon Robert J. Miller. Formerly Holy Trinity, Casco & Mission of St. Adalbert, Slovan.
School—Holy Trinity School, (Grades PreK-6), Tel: 920-837-7531; Fax: 920-837-2361; Email: holytrinitycasco@hotmail.com; Web: www.holytrinitycasco.com. Gail Waterstreet, Prin. Clergy 1; Lay Teachers 5; Students 26.
Catechesis Religious Program—Email: millerrobert07@aol.com. Mary Voyles, D.R.E.

CECIL, SHAWANO CO., ST. MARTIN OF TOURS CATHOLIC PARISH (1889) [CEM]
407 S. Warrington Ave., Cecil, 54111-9279.
Tel: 715-745-6681; Email: stmartin_cecil@frontiernet.net; Web: www.stmartin-cecil.org. Deacon Michael G. Grzeca, Pastoral Leader; Very Rev. Thomas J. Farrell, Moderator; Deacon Kenneth J. Banker.
Catechesis Religious Program—

CHAMPION, BROWN CO., ST. JOSEPH (1862) [CEM]
Mailing Address: 5930 Humboldt Rd., Luxemburg, 54217-9325. Tel: 920-863-6113; Email: parishoffice@baycomwi.com; Fax: 920-845-5180. Rev. Carlo Villaluz, Admin. Served from St. Thomas the Apostle, Humboldt.
Catechesis Religious Program—5996 County Rd. K, New Franken, 54229-9456. Ms. Lisa Laurent, C.R.E.

CHARLESBURG, CALUMET CO., ST. CHARLES BORROMEO, Merged with St. Augustine, Chilton; St. Mary, Chilton; St. Martin, Charlestown; Holy Trinity, Jericho and St. Elizabeth, Kloten to form Good Shepherd, Chilton.

CHARLESTOWN, CALUMET CO., ST. MARTIN, Merged with St. Augustine, Chilton; St. Mary, Chilton; St. Charles Borromeo, Charlesburg; Holy Trinity, Jericho and St. Elizabeth, Kloten to form Good Shepherd, Chilton.

CHASE, OCONTO CO., ST. JOSEPH, [CEM] Merged with St. Louis, Abrams and St. John Cantius, Sobieski to form St. Maximilian Kolbe, Sobieski.

CHILTON, CALUMET CO.

1—ST. AUGUSTINE, Merged with St. Mary, Chilton; St. Charles Borromeo, Charlesburg; St. Martin, Charlestown; Holy Trinity, Jericho and St. Elizabeth, Kloten to form Good Shepherd, Chilton.

2—GOOD SHEPHERD (2005) [CEM]
62 E. Main St., Chilton, 53014-1428.
Tel: 920-849-9363; Email: goodshepherdbusinessmanager@gmail.com; Web: www.goodshepherdchilton.org. Very Rev. Ryan E. Krueger; Deacon Dennis G. Bennin. Formerly St. Augustine, Chilton; St. Mary, Chilton; St. Charles Borromeo, Charlesburg; St. Martin, Charlestown; Holy Trinity, Jericho & St. Elizabeth, Kloten
School—Chilton Area Catholic School, (Grades PreK-8), 60 E. Washington St., Chilton, 53014-1297. Tel: 920-849-4141; Email: lrollmann@chiltonareacatholic.org; Web: chiltonareacatholic.org. Mrs. Elisabeth Rollmann, Prin. Clergy 1; Lay Teachers 14; Students 94.
Catechesis Religious Program—Angeline Heiberger, C.R.E.

3—ST. MARY, Merged with St. Augustine, Chilton; St. Charles Borromeo, Charlesburg; St. Martin, Charlestown; Holy Trinity, Jericho and St. Elizabeth, Kloten to form Good Shepherd, Chilton.

CLARKS MILLS, MANITOWOC CO., IMMACULATE CONCEPTION (1865) [CEM] Also serves St. Michael, Whitelaw. Very Rev. Richard H. Klingeisen.
Res.: 15 S. County Rd. J, Cato, 54230-8329.
Tel: 920-775-4365; Fax: 920-775-4365; Email: stmarycm@tds.net.
School: See St. Mary/St. Michael School, Cato under Consolidated Schools located in the Institution section.
Catechesis Religious Program—Tel: 920-775-4876; Email: stmarycm@tds.net. Mrs. Teresa Pederson, D.R.E. Students 72.

CLEVELAND, MANITOWOC CO., ST. WENDEL, Merged with St. Isidore, Osman; St. Joseph, Alverno; and St. Casimir, Northeim to form St. Thomas the Apostle, Northeim.

CLINTONVILLE, WAUPACA CO., ST. ROSE (1881) [CEM] Also serves St. Mary, Bear Creek.
140 Auto St., Clintonville, 54929-1712.
Tel: 715-201-9913; Email: sborlen@ssrmparishes.org; Web: ssrmparishes.org. Revs. Joseph Dorner, Sacramental Min.; John T. Mullarkey, (Retired); Deacon Lincoln Wood; Senior Deacon Thomas V. Jozwiak; Deacon Paul J. Brulla.
School—St. Rose/St. Mary School, Tel: 715-201-9913; Tel: sborlen@ssrmparishes.org; Web: www.ssrmschool.org. Michelle Vosters, Prin. Lay Teachers 6; Students 60.
Catechesis Religious Program—Tel: 715-823-5266. Maria Scherer, D.R.E.

COLEMAN, MARINETTE CO.

1—ST. ANNE PARISH (2009)
P.O. Box 30, Lena, 54139-0030. Tel: 920-829-5222; Fax: 920-829-6027; Email: stanne1@centurytel.net; Web: www.saintannesparish.com. Rev. Nonito Jesus Barra, Admin.; Deacon Peter J. Gard.
Church: 221 E. Main St., Lena, 54139.
Church: 228 E. Main St., Coleman, 54112.
Catechesis Religious Program—Email: maggie@saintannesparish.com. Maggie Cook, D.R.E. Students 139.

2—ST. FRANCIS OF ASSISI, Merged with St. Wenceslaus, Klondike to form SS. Francis-Wenceslaus, Coleman.

COMBINED LOCKS, OUTAGAMIE CO., ST. PAUL (1923) [CEM]
410 Wallace St., Combined Locks, 54113-1128.
Tel: 920-788-4553; Email: stpaulcl@newbc.rr.com; Web: stpaulcl.org. Rev. Andrew T. Kysely
Saint Paul's Congregation of the Village of Combined Locks
Catechesis Religious Program—Tel: 920-788-5711; Email: maggie@newbc.rr.com. Ms. Maggie Melchior, D.R.E. Students 230.

COOPERSTOWN, MANITOWOC CO., ST. JAMES (1850) [CEM] Linked with St. Joseph, Kellnersville. Sr. Geraldine Krautkramer, O.S.F., Pastoral Leader; Rev. Dennis M. Ryan, Sacramental Min., (Retired); Deacon Clarence Naidl.
Res.: 18228 County Rd. R, Denmark, 54208-9554.
Tel: 920-863-2585; Fax: 920-863-5445; Email: stjamescoop@tm.net.
Catechesis Religious Program—Email: recoordinator@tm.net. Mrs. Katherine A. Styer, D.R.E. Students 170.

CRANDON, FOREST CO., ST. JOSEPH (1886) (Has records for St. Mary, Argonne & St. Michael Station, Hiles.)
208 N. Park Ave., Crandon, 54520-1351.
Tel: 715-478-3396; Email: stjosephcrandon@gmail.com. Rev. Callistus I. Elue, Admin.
Catechesis Religious Program—

CRIVITZ, MARINETTE CO., ST. MARY (1903) [CEM] Also serves Station at Caldron Falls.
Mailing Address: P.O. Box 159, Crivitz, 54114-0159. Tel: 715-854-2501; Email: stmarycrivitz@centurytel.net; Web: www.stmarycrivitz.net. 808 Henriette Ave., Crivitz, 54114. Rev. Frederick Sserugga, Admin.; Deacon Richard F. Elfering.
Catechesis Religious Program—Cassandra Kowalski, C.R.E.

DARBOY, OUTAGAMIE CO. (APPLETON P.O.), HOLY ANGELS, [CEM] Merged with Holy Name of Jesus, Kimberly to form Holy Spirit, Kimberly/Darboy.

DE PERE, BROWN CO.

1—ST. BONIFACE, Merged with St. Joseph, De Pere to form Our Lady of Lourdes, De Pere.

2—ST. FRANCIS XAVIER (1864) [JC] Served from St. Mary, De Pere.
220 S. Michigan St., De Pere, 54115-2794.
Tel: 920-336-1813; Fax: 920-336-1814; Email: office@stfrancisdepere.org; Web: www.stfrancisdepere.org. Very Rev. Richard Getchel, J.C.L.; Rev. Michael Thiel, Parochial Vicar; Deacons James R. Gauthier; Mark G. Mullins.
School—Notre Dame School, (Part of the GRACE, Inc. System) 221 S Wisconsin St., De Pere, 54115-2797. Tel: 920-337-1115; Email: gbalza@gracesystem.org. Mr. Gregory Balza, Prin. Students 100.

3—ST. JOSEPH, Merged with St. Boniface, De Pere to form Our Lady of Lourdes, De Pere.

4—ST. MARY (1869) [JC] Also serves St. Francis Xavier, De Pere.
Mailing Address: P.O. Box 70, De Pere, 54115-0070. Tel: 920-337-2330; Fax: 920-337-2332; Email: office@stmarydepere.org; Web: www.stmarydepere.org. 4805 Sportsman Dr., De Pere, 54115. Very Rev. Richard Getchel, J.C.L.; Rev. Michael Thiel, Parochial Vicar; Deacons James R. Gauthier; Mark G. Mullins.
School—Notre Dame School, (Part of the GRACE, Inc. System) 221 S. Wisconsin St., De Pere, 54115-2797. Tel: 920-337-1115; Email: gbalza@gracesystem.org; Web: www.notredameofdepere.com. Mr. Gregory Balza, Prin. Students 100.
Catechesis Religious Program—Email: mlotto@stmarydepere.org. Mr. Michael Lotto, D.R.E.

5—ST. NORBERT COLLEGE (1976)
Mailing Address: 100 Grant St., 15-MB, De Pere, 54115-2002. Tel: 920-403-3010; Fax: 920-403-4432; Email: parish@snc.edu; Web: www.snc.edu/parish. 123 Grant St., De Pere, 54115. Revs. Peter Ambting, Chap.; Michael Brennan, Chap.; Jay J. Fostner, O.-Praem., Ph.D., Chap.; Michael J. Weber, O.Praem., Chap.; Deacon Kevin DeCleene, Pastoral Min.
Catechesis Religious Program—Tel: 920-403-3474.

6—OUR LADY OF LOURDES (1996) [CEM] (Has records for St. Joseph, De Pere & St. Boniface, De Pere.)
1307 Lourdes Ave., De Pere, 54115-1018.
Tel: 920-336-4033; Email: parish@lourdesdepere.org; Web: www.lourdesdepere.org. Rev. Benny Jacob, O.-Praem.; Deacon Michael D. Vander Bloomen.
School—Our Lady of Lourdes School, (Part of the GRACE, Inc. System) 1305 Lourdes Ave., De Pere, 54115-1018. Tel: 920-336-3091; Fax: 920-337-6806; Email: csmits@gracesystem.org. Mr. Jeffrey S. Young, Prin. Lay Teachers 19; Students 183.
Catechesis Religious Program—Tel: 920-337-0443; Email: abieda@lourdesdepere.org. Mrs. Traci La-Crosse, D.R.E.; Mrs. Angela R. Bieda, D.R.E.

DENMARK, BROWN CO., ALL SAINTS (1911) [CEM] Also serves Holy Trinity Mission, New Denmark, St. Mary Parish, Glenmore/Stark.
P.O. Box 787, Denmark, 54208-0787.
Tel: 920-863-5256; Email: asden_parish@allsaintsschool.net. Very Rev. Paul E. Demuth, Mod.; Deacons James Trzinski, Pastoral Min.; David J. Scheuer.
Church: 125 Saint Claude St., Denmark, 54208.
School—All Saints School, (Grades PreK-8), Tel: 920-863-2449; Email: asden_office@allsaintsschool.net. Clergy 1; Lay Teachers 6; Students 46.
Catechesis Religious Program—Jessica Phillips, D.R.E., Tel: 920-883-7357; Email: odyfaithenergy@gmail.com. Associated with Holy Trinity, New Denmark. Students 214.

DYCKESVILLE, KEWAUNEE CO., ST. LOUIS (1863) [CEM 2]
N8726 County Line Rd., Luxemburg, 54217-8629.
Tel: 920-866-2410; Fax: 920-866-3591; Email: patr@stlouisdyckesville.com; Web: www.stlouisdyckesville.com. Mrs. Patricia Ratajczak, Pastoral Leader; Rev. John H. Van Deuren, Sacramental Min., (Retired).
Catechesis Religious Program—N8710 County Line Rd., Luxemburg, 54217-8629. Tel: 920-866-2842; Fax: 920-866-2611; Email: Kathyc@stlouisdyckesville.com. Mrs. Kathleen Cornette, D.R.E.

EATON, BROWN CO., SS. CYRIL AND METHODIUS, Merged with Our Lady Queen of Peace, Humboldt to form St. Thomas the Apostle, Humboldt.

EGG HARBOR, DOOR CO.

1—ST. JOHN THE BAPTIST, Merged with St. Mary of the Lake, Baileys Harbor; St. Paul, Fish Creek; St. Michael, Jacksonport and St. Rosalia to form Stella Maris, Egg Harbor.

2—STELLA MARIS (2005) Merger of St. John the Baptist, Egg Harbor; St. Mary of the Lake, Baileys Harbor; St. Paul, Fish Creek; St. Michael, Jacksonport; St. Rosalia, Sister Bay & the Station at Washington Island. (Has records for all 5 parishes)
Mailing Address: P.O. Box 49, Egg Harbor, 54209-0049. Tel: 920-868-3241; Fax: 920-868-1481; Email: churchoffice@dcwis.com; Web: www.stellamarisparish.com. 7710 Hwy. 42, Egg Harbor, 54209. Rev. David C. Ruby; Deacon David J. Kowalski.
Catechesis Religious Program—Tel: 920-421-2195; Email: faithchurch@dcwis.com. Linda Cummer, D.R.E.

ELAND, SHAWANO CO., ST. WILLIAM, Merged with Holy Family, Wittenberg to form Holy Family-St. William, Wittenberg.

ELCHO, LANGLADE CO., HOLY FAMILY (1905) [CEM] Also serves St. Mary Parish, Pickerel.
Mailing Address: P.O. Box 128, Elcho, 54428-0128.
Tel: 715-275-3750; Email: holyfamilyelcho@frontiernet.net. Rev. David M. Zimmerman.
Church: W10524 Cole St., Elcho, 54428.

FISH CREEK, DOOR CO., ST. PAUL, Merged with St. John the Baptist, Egg Harbor; St. Mary of the Lake, Baileys Harbor; St. Michael, Jacksonport and St. Rosalia, Sister Bay to form Stella Maris, Egg Harbor.

FLINTVILLE, BROWN CO., SS. EDWARD AND ISIDORE (1883) [CEM]
Mailing Address: 3667 Flintville Rd., 54313-8330.
Tel: 920-865-7844; Fax: 920-865-4375; Email: kburkel@stedwardisidore.org; Web: www.stedwardisidore.org. Rev. David J. Hoffman; Deacon Gregory J. Humpal.
Catechesis Religious Program—Tel: 920-865-7677; Email: phendricks@stedwardisidore.org. Ms. Phyllis Hendricks, D.R.E.

FLORENCE, FLORENCE CO., IMMACULATE CONCEPTION (1881) [CEM]
P.O. Box 166, Florence, 54121-0166.
Tel: 715-528-3310; Email: stmary@borderlandnet.net; Web: www.stmaryflorence.org. 308 Florence Ave., Florence, 54121. Rev. Timothy Brandt.
Catechesis Religious Program—Email:

lemanski_mom@hotmail.com. Carolyn Lemanski, D.R.E. Students 40.

FRANCIS CREEK, MANITOWOC CO., ST. ANNE (1848) [CEM] Served from Holy Cross, Mishicot.
P.O. Box 218, Francis Creek, 54214-0218.
Tel: 920-755-2550. Rev. Jeffrey Briones.
Church: 423 S. Main St., Mishicot, 54228.
Tel: 920-682-6640; Email: holycrossparish@holycrossmishicot.com.
Catechesis Religious Program—Ms. Eileen Gale, D.R.E.

FREEDOM, OUTAGAMIE CO., ST. NICHOLAS (1860) [CEM] Also serves St. Edward, Mackville.
W2037 County Rd. S., Freedom, 54130-7565.
Tel: 920-788-1492; Fax: 920-788-0728; Email: parish@stnicholasfreedom.org; Web: www.stnicholasfreedom.org. Rev. Walter P. Stumpf; Deacons Jeffrey J. Hofacker; Gary Vanness; Raymond G. Ambrosius Jr.
School—St. Nicholas School, W2035 County Rd. S., Freedom, 54130-7565. Tel: 920-788-9371; Email: tgerritts@stnicholasfreedom.org; Web: www.stnicholasfreedom.org/school. Travis Gerritts, Prin. Lay Teachers 14; Students 119.
Catechesis Religious Program—St. Nicholas New Evangelization, Tel: 920-788-1451; Email: kbrennan@stnicholasfreedom.org. Kathy Brennan, C.R.E.

GILLETT, OCONTO CO., ST. JOHN (1872) [CEM] Also serves St. Michael, Suring & Chute Pond Station.
127 Garden St., Gillett, 54124-9413.
Tel: 920-855-2542; Fax: 920-855-1449; Email: stjohnsec@centurytel.net; Web: stjohnstmichael.com. Rev. Robert Ni Ni, Admin.
Catechesis Religious Program—Email: bigdogpromo@gmail.com. Sheelagh School, D.R.E.

GLENMORE, BROWN CO., IMMACULATE CONCEPTION, Merged with St. Mary, Stark to form St. Mary, Glenmore/Stark.

GLENMORE/STARK, BROWN CO., ST. MARY (1998) [CEM 2]
Mailing Address: 5840 Big Apple Rd., De Pere, 54115-9766. Tel: 920-864-7641; Email: secretarystmarysparish@gmail.com. Deacons James Trzinski, Admin.; David J. Scheuer.
Catechesis Religious Program—Tel: 920-863-8307; Email: bigdgl@peoplepc.com. Denis Lotto, D.R.E.

GOODMAN, MARINETTE CO., ST. JOAN OF ARC (1909) Served from St. Stanislaus Kostka, Armstrong Creek.
Mailing Address: P.O. Box 218, Goodman, 54125-0218. Tel: 715-336-2334. 602 Main St., Goodman, 54125. Rev. Timothy Brandt.

GREENLEAF, BROWN CO., ST. CLARE CORP. (2009)
2218 Day St., Greenleaf, 54126-9200.
Tel: 920-864-2550; Email: office@stclareagw.org; Web: stclareagw.org. Rev. Brian Wideman; Deacons Kenneth J. Kabat; Michael R. Zebroski; Michael Madden; Kay Arndt, Business Mgr.; Theresa Reynders, Music Min.
St Clare Parish Corporation
School—St. Clare School, 425 Main St., Wrightstown, 54180-1057. Tel: 920-532-4833; Email: stclareschool@stclareagw.org. Lisa Gruber, Prin. Lay Teachers 12; Students 113.
Catechesis Religious Program—Tel: 920-864-2585; Email: stclarefaith@stclareagw.org. Ms. Anne P. Stemper, D.R.E. Students 300.

GREENVILLE, OUTAGAMIE CO., ST. MARY (1855) [CEM]
Mailing Address: N2385 Municipal Dr., Greenville, 54942-9713. Tel: 920-757-6555; Email: parish@stmarygreenville.org. Rev. Michael J. Warden, Admin.; Deacon David L. DeYoung.
School—St. Mary School, (Grades PreK-8), N2387 Municipal Dr., Greenville, 54942-9713.
Tel: 920-757-6555, Ext. 233; Email: dfuller@stmarygreenville.org. Mrs. Debra Fuller, Prin. Lay Teachers 13; Students 149.
Catechesis Religious Program—Email: lgietman@stmarygreenville.org. Luke Gietman, Contact Person.

GRESHAM, SHAWANO CO., ST. FRANCIS SOLANUS (1882) [CEM] Served from St. Michael, Keshena.
Mailing Address: P.O. Box 177, Gresham, 54128.
Tel: 715-787-3250; Email: sfrancis@livingwaterslivingfaith.org. 1050 Main St., Gresham, 54128-0177. Revs. Nonito Jesus Barra, Admin.; Joel Jores, M.F., Parochial Vicar.
Catechesis Religious Program—Tel: 715-787-3250. Michelle Martinez, D.R.E. Students 22.

HILBERT, CALUMET CO., ST. MARY (1890) [CEM] Served from St. John-Sacred Heart, Sherwood.
P.O. Box 386, Hilbert, 54129-0386. Email: stmary_hilbert@new.rr.com. 108 S. 6th St., Hilbert, 54129. Rev. Michael E. Betley.
School—St. Mary School, 154 S. 6th St., P.O. Box 249, Hilbert, 54129-0249. Tel: 920-853-3216; Web: www.stmaryhilbert.com; Email: chasro@stmaryhilbert.com. Chandra L. Sromek, Prin. Clergy 1; Lay Teachers 5; Students 41.
Catechesis Religious Program—N369 Military Rd., Sherwood, 54169-9661. Tel: 920-989-2400; Email: triparishre@gmail.com. Students 68.

HOFA PARK, SHAWANO CO., ST. STANISLAUS (1883) [CEM] Served from Assumption BVM, Pulaski.
P.O. Box 379, Pulaski, 54162. Rev. Patrick M. Gawrylewski, O.F.M.; Deacons Dennis Majewski; David J. Parker; Janet Maroszek.
Res.: 124 E. Pulaski St., Pulaski, 54162.
Tel: 920-822-3279; Fax: 920-822-8030; Email: parishoffice@abvm.org; Web: www.abvmcast.org.
Catechesis Religious Program—109 E. Pulaski St., Pulaski, 54162-9287. Tel: 920-822-5650;
Fax: 920-822-8003; Email: deanne.wilinski@abvm.org. Deanne Wilinski, Contact Person.

HOLLANDTOWN, BROWN CO., ST. FRANCIS, [CEM] Merged with St. Mary of the Annunciation, Kaukauna and St. Aloysius, Kaukauna to form St. Katharine Drexel, Kaukauna.

HORTONVILLE, OUTAGAMIE CO., SS. PETER AND PAUL (1861) [CEM]
107 N. Olk St., Hortonville, 54944. Rev. James R. Jugenheimer, Mod.-Elect; Mr. Greg Layton, Pastoral Leader.
Res.: 105 N. Olk St., P.O. Box 238, Hortonville, 54944-0238. Tel: 920-779-6133; Fax: 920-779-0166; Email: sspeterandpaul@sbcglobal.net; Web: ssppp.org/.
Church: 109 N. Olk St., Hortonville, 54944.
School—St. Mary School, N2387 Municipal Dr., Greenville, 54942-7801. Tel: 920-757-6555;
Fax: 920-757-6560; Email: dfuller@stmarygreenville.org. Mrs. Debra Fuller, Prin. Students 149.
Catechesis Religious Program—Tel: 920-779-0551. Lori Pugliese, Tel: 920-779-0551. Students 223.

HOWARD, BROWN CO., ST. JOHN THE BAPTIST (1849) [CEM]
2597 Glendale Ave., 54313-6899. Tel: 920-434-2145; Fax: 920-434-5015; Email: mtorres@sjbh.org; Web: www.sjbh.org. Very Rev. John P. Bergstadt; Rev. Scott Valentyn, Parochial Vicar; Deacons Manuel Torres; Nicholas J. Williams.
School—St. John the Baptist School, (Part of the GRACE, Inc. System) 2561 Glendale Ave., 54313-6898. Tel: 920-434-3822; Fax: 920-434-5016; Email: amulloy@gracesystem.org; Web: www.sjbhschool.org. Andrew Mulloy, Prin. Lay Teachers 24; Students 272.
Catechesis Religious Program—Tel: 920-434-2145; Email: amott@sjbh.org. Amy Mott, D.R.E.

HUMBOLDT, BROWN CO.
1—OUR LADY QUEEN OF PEACE, Merged with SS. Cyril & Methodius, Eaton to form St. Thomas the Apostle, Humbolt.
2—ST. THOMAS THE APOSTLE (1999) [JC4] Also serves St. Kilian, New Franken & St. Joseph, Champion.
5930 Humboldt Rd., Luxemburg, 54217-9325.
Tel: 920-863-6113; Fax: 920-845-5180; Email: parish.office@threecatholicchurches.com. Rev. Carlo Villaluz, Admin.
Catechesis Religious Program—3041 S. County Rd. T, 54311-9429. Tel: 920-863-5297. Karley Prue, D.R.E.

INSTITUTE, DOOR CO., SS. PETER AND PAUL (1884) [CEM] Served from St. Joseph, Sturgeon Bay.
4767 E. Dunn Rd., Sturgeon Bay, 54235-8822.
Tel: 920-743-4842; Email: ssppchurch@charter.net. Rev. Robert Stegmann; Deacon Kenneth D. Kopydlowski.
See St. John Bosco Catholic School, Inc., Sturgeon Bay under Elementary Schools, Diocesan in the Institution Section.

ISAAR, OUTAGAMIE CO., ST. SEBASTIAN (1893) [CEM] Served from St. John, Seymour.
N9269 Isaar Rd., Seymour, 54165-9428.
Tel: 920-833-2558; Email: stseb2010@centurylink.net; Web: stsebastianseymour.weconnect.com. Very Rev. Brian S. Belongia, J.C.L.; Deacon Richard J. Matuszak, Admin.
Catechesis Religious Program—

JACKSONPORT, DOOR CO., ST. MICHAEL, Merged with St. John the Baptist, Egg Harbor; St. Mary of the Lake, Baileys Harbor; St. Paul, Fish Creek and St. Rosalia, Sister Bay to form Stella Maris, Egg Harbor.

JERICHO, CALUMET CO., HOLY TRINITY, Merged with St. Augustine, Chilton; St. Mary, Chilton; St. Charles Borromeo, Charlesburg; St. Martin, Charlestown and St. Elizabeth, Kloten to form Good Shepherd, Chilton.

KAUKAUNA, OUTAGAMIE CO.
1—ST. ALOYSIUS, Merged with St. Mary of the Annunciation, Kaukauna and St. Francis, Hollandtown to form St. Katharine Drexel, Kaukauna.
2—HOLY CROSS (1873) [CEM]
309 Desnoyer St., Kaukauna, 54130-2187.
Tel: 920-766-1445; Fax: 920-766-3774; Email: KaukaunaCatholicParishes@kaucp.org. 119 W. 7th St., Kaukauna, 54130. Revs. Donald E. Everts; Kyle T. Sladek, Parochial Vicar; Deacons Bruce H. Corey, Pastoral Assoc.; Mark A. Ebben; Randall A. Haak; Steven VandeHey.
School—St. Ignatius of Loyola Catholic School, Holy Cross Campus, 220 Doty St., Kaukauna, 54130-2188. Tel: 920-766-0186; Fax: 920-759-2428; Email: headmaster@stignatiuskaukauna.org. Mr. Lawrence Konetzke, Prin. Clergy 1; Lay Teachers 16; Students 155.
Catechesis Religious Program—212 Doty St., Kaukauna, 54130-2108. Tel: 920-766-3510;
Tel: 920-766-7887; Email: jwallace@holycrosskaukauna.org; Email: gackerman@holycrosskaukauna.org. Ms. Mrs. Gloria Ackerman, D.R.E.; Mrs. Jacqueline Wallace, D.R.E. Students 370.
3—ST. KATHARINE DREXEL (2007)
119 W. 7th St., Kaukauna, 54130-2356.
Tel: 920-766-1445; Fax: 920-766-1476; Email: KaukaunaCatholicParishes@kaucp.org. Revs. Donald E. Everts; Kyle T. Sladek, Parochial Vicar; Deacons Bruce H. Corey; Randall A. Haak; Steven VandeHey, Pastoral Min./Coord.; Mark A. Ebben. Merger of St. Aloysius, Kaukauna, St. Mary of the Annunciation, Kaukauna & St. Francis, Hollandtown. Has records for all 3 parishes.
School—St. Ignatius Catholic School, (Joint school system with Holy Cross, Kaukauna) 220 Doty St., Kaukauna, 54130. Tel: 920-766-0186;
Fax: 920-766-5229; Email: headmaster@stignatiuskaukauna.org. Mr. Lawrence Konetzke, Prin.
Catechesis Religious Program— St. Katharine Drexel G.I.F.T. (Growing in Faith Together)
Tel: 920-766-5977; Email: everges@skdchurch.org. Elizabeth Verges, D.R.E.
4—ST. MARY OF THE ANNUNCIATION, [JC] Merged with St. Aloysius, Kaukauna, and St. Francis, Hollandtown to form St. Katharine Drexel, Kaukauna.

KELLNERSVILLE, MANITOWOC CO., ST. JOSEPH (1859) [CEM 2] Linked with St James Parish, Cooperstown.
P.O. Box 27, Kellnersville, 54215-0027.
Tel: 920-732-3770; Web: www.Circle-of-Faith.org. Sr. Geraldine Krautkramer, O.S.F., Pastoral Leader; Rev. Dennis M. Ryan, Sacramental Min., (Retired); Deacon Clarence Naidl.
Catechesis Religious Program—Lisa Vander Kelen, D.R.E.

KESHENA, MENOMINEE CO., ST. MICHAEL (1873) [CEM] (Native American) Also serves St. Mary, Leopolis, St. Francis Solanus, Gresham & St. Anthony, Neopit.
Mailing Address: P.O. Box 610, Keshena, 54135-0610. Tel: 715-799-3811; Email: stmichaels@livingwaterslivingfaith.org; Web: www.stmichaelkeshena.org. N816 State Hwy. 47-55, Keshena, 54135. Revs. Nonito Jesus Barra, Admin.; Joel Jores, M.F., Parochial Vicar.
Catechesis Religious Program—Tel: 715-799-3234. Lois Maczuzak, D.R.E.

KEWAUNEE, KEWAUNEE CO., HOLY ROSARY (1856) [CEM] Served from St. Mary, Algoma.
Tel: 920-388-2285; Email: hrparish521@yahoo.com; Web: www.holyrosarykewaunee.com. Rev. Alvan Amadi, Priest Celebrant; Deacon Thomas C. Agnew.
School—Holy Rosary School, (Grades PreK-8), 519 Kilbourn St., Kewaunee, 54216-1343.
Tel: 920-388-2431; Email: kstollberg@holyrosarykewaunee.com; Web: www.holyrosarykewaunee.com/school. Kris Stollberg, Prin. Lay Teachers 7; Students 70.
Catechesis Religious Program—Janet Fisher, D.R.E. Students 132.

KIEL, MANITOWOC CO., SS. PETER & PAUL CONGREGATION (1859) [CEM] Also serves Holy Rosary, New Holstein & St. Ann, St. Anna.
413 Fremont St., Kiel, 53042-1398.
Tel: 920-894-3553; Email: secretary@sspeternpaul.org. Revs. Anthony Ibekwe, Mod.; Carl Diederichs, Sacramental Min.; Deacon Bernard (Pat) P. Knier; Mr. Joseph Zenk, Pastoral Leader.
School—Divine Savior Catholic School, 423 Fremont St., Kiel, 53042-1316. Tel: 920-894-3533; Email: dsprincipalsievert@gmail.com. Mr. Kerry Sievert, Prin.
Catechesis Religious Program—409 Fremont St., Kiel, 53042-1316. Email: daniellefaithformation@gmail.com. Mrs. Danielle Ehlenbeck, Contact Person, Email: faithformation@gmail.com.

KIMBERLY, OUTAGAMIE CO.
1—HOLY NAME OF JESUS, [CEM] Merged with Holy Angels, Darboy to form Holy Spirit, Kimberly/Darboy.
2—HOLY SPIRIT (2005) [CEM] Merger of Holy Name of Jesus, Kimberly & Holy Angels, Darboy.
620 E. Kimberly Ave., Kimberly, 54136-1513.
Tel: 920-788-7640; Fax: 920-788-7658; Email: vanheuklons@holyspirit-parish.org; Web: holyspirit-parish.org. Rev. Robert Kollath; Deacons Cyril J. Klister; Dennis G. Bennin; Leah Ackley, Pastoral Coord.; Margaret Franz, Liturgy Dir.; Patricia Vande Voort, Business Mgr.; Mary Zuleger, Music Min.
School—Holy Spirit School, W2796 County Rd. KK,

Appleton, 54915-9407. Tel: 920-733-2651; Email: mike.zuleger@holyspiritknights.org; Web: www.holyspiritknights.org. Mr. Michael Zuleger, Prin. Religious Teachers 10; Lay Teachers 16; Students 224.
Catechesis Religious Program—Tel: 920-788-7655. Tim Singler, D.R.E.

KING, WAUPACA CO., ST. GEORGE, Closed. For inquiries for parish records, please see St. Mary Magdalene, Waupaca.

KLONDIKE, OCONTO CO., ST. WENCESLAUS, Merged with St. Francis of Assisi, Coleman, to form SS. Francis-Wenceslaus, Coleman.

KLOTEN, CALUMET CO., ST. ELIZABETH, Merged with St. Augustine, Chilton; St. Mary, Chilton; St. Charles Borromeo, Charlesburg; St. Martin, Charlestown and Holy Trinity, Jericho to form Good Shepherd, Chilton.

KOSSUTH, MANITOWOC CO., ST. AUGUSTINE (1864) [CEM] Served from Holy Cross, Mishicot.
Mailing Address: P.O. Box 218, Francis Creek, 54214-0218. Tel: 920-755-2550; Email: holycrossparish@hoycrossmishicot.com. Rev. Jeffrey Briones, Admin.
Church: 423 S. Main St., Mishicot, 54228.
Catechesis Religious Program—Tel: 920-682-1454. Ms. Eileen Gale, D.R.E. Associated with St. Anne, Francis Creek.

KRAKOW, SHAWANO CO., ST. CASIMIR (1898) [CEM] Served from Assumption of BVM, Pulaski.
Mailing Address: P.O. Box 379, Pulaski, 54162.
Tel: 920-822-3279; Fax: 920-822-8030; Email: parishoffice@abvm.org; Web: www.abvmcast.org. W146 Park St., Krakow, 54137. Rev. Patrick M. Gawrylewski, O.F.M.; Deacons Dennis Majewski; David J. Parker; Janet Maroszek.

KROK, KEWAUNEE CO., ST. JOHN, Merged with St. Joseph, Montpelier to form St. Joseph-St. John, Montpelier.

LAKEWOOD, OCONTO CO., ST. MARY OF THE LAKE (1905) [CEM] Also serves St. Ambrose, Wabeno & stations at Crooked Lake and Silver Cliff.
P.O. Box 219, Lakewood, 54138-0219.
Tel: 715-276-7364; Email: stmary01@centurytel.net. Very Rev. Philip Dinh-Van-Thiep; Deacon William V. Doran.
Church: 15232 County Rd. F, Lakewood, 54138.
Catechesis Religious Program—Ms. Kendra Yingling, D.R.E.
Stations—Crooked Lake, Crooked Lake Station—Silver Cliff, Silver Cliff Station.

LANGLADE, LANGLADE CO., ST. STANISLAUS KOSTKA, Merged with St. James, White Lake to form SS. James-Stanislaus, White Lake.

LAONA, FOREST CO., ST. LEONARD (1900) [JC] Also serves St. Norbert, Long Lake & St. Hubert Mission, Newald.
5330 Beech St., Laona, 54541-9340.
Tel: 715-674-3241; Email: stleonardlaona@gmail.com. Rev. Felix Martin Penetrante, Admin.
Catechesis Religious Program—Tel: 715-674-3862; Email: cbeairl@centurytel.net. Ms. Cynthia Beairl, D.R.E.

LEBANON, WAUPACA CO., ST. PATRICK (1856) [CEM]
N5705 County Rd. T, New London, 54961-8464.
Tel: 920-982-5475; Web: www.stpatrickslebanon.com. Rev. John Kleinschmidt, Admin.
Catechesis Religious Program—Email: btate41@charter.net. Ms. Barbara Tate, D.R.E.

LENA, OCONTO CO., ST. CHARLES BORROMEO, Merged with Sacred Heart, Spruce to form Holy Cross, Lena.

LEOPOLIS, SHAWANO CO., ST. MARY (1883) [CEM] Served from St. Michael, Keshena.
Mailing Address: P.O. Box 177, Gresham, 54128.
Tel: 715-787-3250; Email: stfrancis@livingwaterslivingfaith.org. W11842 3rd St., Leopolis, 54128. Revs. Nonito Jesus Barra, Admin.; Joel Jores, M.F., Parochial Vicar; Deacon Howard R. Bricco.
Catechesis Religious Program—Michelle Martinez, D.R.E. Students 37.

LINCOLN, KEWAUNEE CO., ST. PETER, Merged Merged with St. Hubert, Rosiere to become St. Peter and St. Hubert, Rosiere/Lincoln.

LITTLE CHUTE, OUTAGAMIE CO., ST. JOHN NEPOMUCENE (1836) [CEM]
323 Pine St., Little Chute, 54140-1854.
Tel: 920-788-9061; Fax: 920-687-0851; Email: parishoffice@sjslc.net; Web: www.stjn.org. Rev. Ronald C. Belitz; Deacons David G. Van Eperen, Business Mgr.; George J. Schraufnagel, Pastoral Assoc.
School—St. John Nepomucene School, 328 Grand Ave., Little Chute, 54140-1704. Tel: 920-788-9082; Email: davidvaneperen@sjslc.net. Kevin Flottmeyer, Prin. Lay Teachers 24; Students 230.
Catechesis Religious Program—325 Pine St., Little Chute, 54140-1854. Tel: 920-788-9033; Email: faithdevelopment@sjslc.net. Mrs. Charlene A. Kilsdonk, D.R.E.

LITTLE SUAMICO, OCONTO CO., ST. PIUS (1893) Served from St. Benedict Parish, Suamico.
Mailing Address: P.O. Box 66, Suamico, 54173-0066. Tel: 920-434-2024; Email: sbsp@wi.twcbc.com; Web: www.St.PiusLittleSuamico.com. Rev. Judah Ben-Hur S. Pigon, M.F., Admin.
Church: 1211 County Rd. J, Little Suamico, 54141.
Catechesis Religious Program—Tel: 920-434-1219. Ms. Tammi LaLuzerne, D.R.E.

LONG LAKE, FLORENCE CO., ST. NORBERT (1908) Served from St. Leonard, Laona (Laona also serves St. Hubert Mission, Newald).
P.O. Box 101, Long Lake, 54542-0101.
Tel: 715-674-3241; Email: stnorbertlonglake@yahoo.com. Rev. Felix Martin Penetrante, Admin.

LUXEMBURG, KEWAUNEE CO., IMMACULATE CONCEPTION (1864) [CEM]
1412 Main St., Luxemburg, 54217-1308.
Tel: 920-845-2056; Email: parishoffice@stmarysluxemburg.org; Web: stmarysluxemburg.org. Revs. Daniel J. Schuster; Milton M. Suess, Pastor Emeritus, (Retired); Deacon Robert J. Miller.
School—Immaculate Conception, (Grades PreK-6), 1406 Main St., Luxemburg, 54217-1308.
Tel: 920-845-2224; Email: mvandenhouten@stmarysluxemburg.org. Clergy 2; Lay Teachers 12; Students 96.
Catechesis Religious Program—Mr. Lee Treml, D.R.E. Students 235.

MACKVILLE, OUTAGAMIE CO., ST. EDWARD (1849) [CEM] Served from St. Nicholas, Freedom.
N2926 State Rd. 47, Appleton, 54913-9564.
Tel: 920-733-9266; Fax: 920-733-7964; Email: parish@stedwardmackville.org; Web: www.stedwardmackville.org. Rev. Walter P. Stumpf; Deacons Jeffrey J. Hofacker; Gary Vanness; Raymond G. Ambrosius Jr.
School—St. Edward School, (Grades PreSchool-5), N2944 State Rd. 47, Appleton, 54913-9564.
Tel: 920-733-6276; Email: saintedward@catholicweb.com; Web: www.stedwardk5.org. Renee Cowart, Prin. Lay Teachers 11; Students 71.
Catechesis Religious Program—Tel: 920-733-6070; Email: cmckee@stedwardmackville.org.. Celia J. McKee, D.R.E. Students 103.

MANAWA, WAUPACA CO., SACRED HEART (1874) [JC]
P.O. Box 10, Manawa, 54949-0010.
Tel: 920-596-3323; Fax: 920-596-3323; Email: shmanawa@wolfnet.net. 614 S. Bridge St., Manawa, 54949. Rev. Xavier Santiago, Admin.
Catechesis Religious Program—Email: shmanawa@wolfnet.net. Ms. JoAnn Schuelke, Contact Person.

MANITOWOC, MANITOWOC CO.
1—ST. ANDREW, Merged with St. Boniface, Manitowoc; Holy Innocents, Manitowoc; St. Mary, Manitowoc; St. Paul, Manitowoc and Sacred Heart, Manitowoc to form St. Francis of Assisi, Manitowoc.
2—ST. BONIFACE, Merged with St. Andrew, Manitowoc; Holy Innocents, Manitowoc; St. Mary, Manitowoc; St. Paul, Manitowoc and Sacred Heart, Manitowoc to form St. Francis of Assisi, Manitowoc.
3—ST. FRANCIS OF ASSISI (2005) [CEM]
Mailing Address: 601 N. 8th St., Manitowoc, 54220-3919. Tel: 920-684-3718; Fax: 920-682-1096; Email: doug.lecaptain@sfamanitowoc.org; Email: info@sfamanitowoc.org; Web: www.sfamanitowoc.org. Revs. Douglas E. LeCaptain; Jose Lopez Vargas, Parochial Vicar; David J. Pleier; Mark Knipp, Dir.; Deacons Michael Dolezal; Richard D. Bahnaman; Alan L. Boeldt; Robert Beehner; Mark V. LeGreve.
4—HOLY INNOCENTS, Merged with St. Andrew, Manitowoc; St. Boniface, Manitowoc; St. Mary, Manitowoc; St. Paul, Manitowoc and Sacred Heart, Manitowoc to form St. Francis of Assisi, Manitowoc.
5—ST. MARY, Merged with St. Andrew, Manitowoc; St. Boniface, Manitowoc; Holy Innocents, Manitowoc; St. Paul, Manitowoc and Sacred Heart, Manitowoc to form St. Francis of Assisi, Manitowoc.
6—ST. PAUL, Merged with St. Andrew, Manitowoc; St. Boniface, Manitowoc; Holy Innocents, Manitowoc; St. Mary, Manitowoc and Sacred Heart, Manitowoc to form, St. Francis of Assisi, Manitowoc.
7—SACRED HEART, Merged with St. Andrew, Manitowoc; St. Boniface, Manitowoc; Holy Innocents, Manitowoc; St. Mary, Manitowoc and St. Paul, Manitowoc to form St. Francis of Assisi, Manitowoc.

MAPLE GROVE, MANITOWOC CO., ST. PATRICK, Merged with St. Mary, Reedsville to form St. Mary-St. Patrick, Reedsville.

MAPLEWOOD, DOOR CO., ST. MARY (1871) [CEM 2]
Mailing Address: 7491 County Rd. H, Sturgeon Bay, 54235-8757. Tel: 920-856-6440; Email: office@holynameofmary.church. Rev. Carl E. Schmitt; Deacon Mark R. Hibbs. Served from Corpus Christi, Sturgeon Bay.
Catechesis Religious Program—June Gordon, D.R.E. Students 15.

MARCHAND, DOOR CO., ST. FRANCIS DE PAUL (Duvall) Closed. For inquiries for parish records contact St. Louis, Dyckesville.

MARINETTE, MARINETTE CO.
1—ST. ANTHONY, Merged with St. Joseph, Sacred Heart, and Our Lady of Lourdes, Marinette to form Holy Family, Marinette.
2—HOLY FAMILY (1989) [CEM 2] Has records for St. Anthony, St. Joseph, Our Lady of Lourdes & Sacred Heart, Marinette.
2715 Taylor St., Marinette, 54143-1537.
Tel: 715-735-9100; Fax: 715-735-9650; Email: holyfamily@holyfamparish.com; Web: www.holyfamparish.com. Very Rev. Celestine Byekwaso; Deacon Jerome E. Thetreau.
School—St. Thomas Aquinas Academy, 1200 Main St., Marinette, 54143. Tel: 715-735-7481;
Fax: 715-735-3375; Email: principal.staa@gmail.com; Web: www.thomas-aquinas.org. Mr. Michael Cattani, Prin. Clergy 2; Lay Teachers 19; Students 100.
Catechesis Religious Program—Email: faithform@hotmail.com. Debra Meunier, D.R.E.
3—ST. JOSEPH, Merged with St. Anthony, Our Lady of Lourdes & Sacred Heart, Marinette to become Holy Family Parish.
4—OUR LADY OF LOURDES, Closed. For inquiries for parish records please see Holy Family, Marinette.
5—SACRED HEART CONGREGATION, Merged with St. Anthony, St. Joseph, and Our Lady of Lourdes, Marinette to form Holy Family, Marinette.

MARION, WAUPACA CO., ST. MARY (1889) [CEM] Served from St. Anthony, Tigerton.
Mailing Address: P.O. Box 106, Tigerton, 54486-0106. Tel: 715-535-2571; Fax: 715-535-2953; Email: office@catholicsupnorth.org. 725 NE 7th St., Marion, 54950. Rev. Matthew W. Settle, Admin.; Deacons Patrick G. Berg; Howard R. Bricco; Michael J. Brandt.
Catechesis Religious Program—Tammy Wendler, C.R.E. Associated with St. Anthony, Tigerton. Students 21.

MATTOON, SHAWANO CO., HOLY FAMILY, [CEM] Merged with St. Joseph, Phlox, to form St. Joseph-Holy Family Parish, Phlox. Served from St. Anthony, Neopit.

MENASHA, WINNEBAGO CO.
1—ST. JOHN THE BAPTIST (1888) [CEM] Served from St. Mary, Menasha.
528 2nd St., Menasha, 54952-3112.
Tel: 920-725-7714; Email: smsjparishes528@gmail.com. 516 Depere St., Menasha, 54952-3112. Rev. Paul J. Paider; Deacons Richard B. Dvorak; Donald E. Schultz.
School: See St. Mary Catholic Schools, Inc., Neenah/Menasha, under Consolidated Schools located in the Institutions Section.
2—ST. MARY (1867) [CEM] Also serves St. John, Menasha.
528 2nd St., Menasha, 54952-3112.
Tel: 920-725-7714; Email: smsjparishes528@gmail.com; Web: menashacatholicparishes.org/. Rev. Paul J. Paider; Deacons Richard B. Dvorak; Donald E. Schultz.
School: See St. Mary Catholic Schools, Inc., Neenah/Menasha, under Consolidated Schools located in the Institutions Section.
Catechesis Religious Program—Email: smichalkiewicz@smcatholicschools.org. Mrs. Sally Michalkiewicz, D.R.E.
3—ST. PATRICK (1848) [JC]
324 Nicolet Blvd., Menasha, 54952-3334.
Tel: 920-725-8381; Fax: 920-725-5544; Email: stpatmen@gmail.com; Web: stpatricksnm.org. Revs. Larry J. Seidl; James A. Hablewitz, Sacramental Min., (Retired); Mary F. Krueger, Pastoral Leader; Deacon Kurt L. Grube
St. Patrick's Congregation
School: See St. Mary Catholic Schools, Inc., Neenah/Menasha, under Consolidated Schools located in the Institutions Section.
Catechesis Religious Program—Email: cstinski@stpatrickmenasha.org. Mrs. Cheryl Stinski, Contact Person.

MISHICOT, MANITOWOC CO., HOLY CROSS (1861) [JC] Also serves St. Anne, Francis Creek & St. Augustine, Kossuth.
423 S. Main St., Mishicot, 54228-9777.
Tel: 920-755-2550; Email: holycrossparish@holycrossmishicot.com. Rev. Jeffrey Briones.
Catechesis Religious Program—423 E. Church St., Mishicot, 54228-9688. Tel: 920-755-2487; Email: egale@holycrossmishicot.com. Ms. Eileen Gale, D.R.E.

MONTPELIER, KEWAUNEE CO.
1—ST. JOSEPH, Merged with St. John, Krok to form St. Joseph-St. John, Montpelier.
2—ST. JOSEPH-ST. JOHN, Merged with St. Lawrence, Stangelville and St. Hedwig, West Kewaunee to form St. Therese de Lisieux, Stangelville.

NAMUR, DOOR CO., ST. MARY, Merged with St. Francis Xavier, Brussels to form St. Francis-St. Mary, Brussels.

NAVARINO, SHAWANO CO., ST. LAWRENCE (1920) [CEM]

W5125 State Hwy. 156, Bonduel, 54107-8614.
Tel: 715-758-8161; Email: stlawrence@granitewave.com. Rev. Theodore J. Hendricks, Admin.
Catechesis Religious Program—Karly Pennings, D.R.E.

NEENAH, WINNEBAGO CO.

1—ST. GABRIEL THE ARCHANGEL (1959) [JC]
900 Geiger St., Neenah, 54956-2302.
Tel: 920-722-4914; Fax: 920-722-2566; Email: stgabriel@smcatholicschools.org. Rev. Larry J. Seidl.
School—St. Mary Catholic Schools, Includes: St. Mary Elementary; St. Margaret Mary Elementary; St. Mary Catholic Middle School; St. Mary Catholic High School. Tel: 920-725-4161; Email: henglebert@smcatholicschools.org. Helen Englebert, Prin.
Catechesis Religious Program—Tel: 920-725-0660. Jenny Schneider, D.R.E. Students 296.

2—ST. MARGARET MARY (1932) [JC]
Mailing Address: 439 Washington Ave., Neenah, 54956-3398. Tel: 920-729-4560; Email: bmathews@smcatholicschools.org; Web: www.smmneenah.org. 620 Division St., Neenah, 54956. Rev. Dennis L. Bergsbaken; Deacon Daniel Laurent.
School—St. Mary Catholic Schools, Inc., St. Margaret Mary School, 610 Division St., Neenah, 54956-3094. Tel: 920-729-4565. Eleanor Healy, Prin.
Catechesis Religious Program—Amy M. Matz, D.R.E.

NEOPIT, MENOMINEE CO., ST. ANTHONY (1909) [CEM] Served from St. Michael, Keshena.
Mailing Address: P.O. Box 241, Neopit, 54150-0241.
Tel: 715-756-2361; Email: stanthony@livingwaterslivingfaith.org. Revs. Nonito Jesus Barra, Admin.; Joel Jores, M.F., Parochial Vicar.

NEVA, LANGLADE CO., ST. WENCESLAUS (1897) [CEM] Served from St. John, Antigo.
Mailing Address: P.O. Box 50, Deerbrook, 54424-0050. Tel: 715-627-2126; Fax: 715-627-2126; Email: stwencelneva@yahoo.com. Very Rev. Mathew J. Simonar; Rev. Zachary Weber; Deacon Andrew P. Bures.
Res.: N5340 Church Rd., Deerbrook, 54424-9413.
Tel: 715-623-7019.
School—All Saints Catholic School, Inc., 419 6th Ave., Antigo, 54409-2104. Tel: 715-623-4835;
Fax: 715-623-3202; Email: pgaluska@ascscrusaders.org. Mr. Paul Galuska, Prin. Lay Teachers 14; Students 194.
Catechesis Religious Program—Tel: 715-623-5255; Email: brettingensusan@gmail.com. Mrs. Susan Brettingen, D.R.E.

NEW DENMARK, BROWN CO., HOLY TRINITY MISSION (1866) [CEM] Served from All Saints, Denmark.
P.O. Box 787, Denmark, 54208-0787.
Tel: 920-863-5256; Email: asden_parish@allsaintsschool.net. Very Rev. Paul E. Demuth, Mod.; Deacons James Trzinski, Pastoral Min.; David J. Scheuer.
Church: 6397 County Rd. NN, Denmark, 54208.
Catechesis Religious Program—Jessica Phillips, D.R.E., Tel: 920-883-7357; Email: odyfaithenergy@gmail.com.

NEW FRANKEN, BROWN CO., ST. KILIAN (1849) [CEM] Served from St. Thomas the Apostle, Humboldt.
5930 Humboldt Rd., Luxemburg, 54217-9325.
Tel: 920-863-6113; Email: parish.office@threecatholicchurches.com. Rev. Carlo Villaluz, Admin.
Church: 2508 Saint Kilian Rd., New Franken, 54229.
Catechesis Religious Program—3041 County Rd. T, 54311-9429. Tel: 920-863-5297; Email: ministry4kjtyouth@gmail.com. Karley Prue, D.R.E. Students 122.

NEW HOLSTEIN, CALUMET CO., HOLY ROSARY (1910) [CEM]
1724 Madison St., New Holstein, 53061-1389.
Tel: 920-898-4884; Fax: 920-898-4884; Email: hrparish_1@charter.net; Web: holyrosarynewholstein.org. Rev. Anthony Ibekwe, Mod.; Mr. Joseph Zenk, Pastoral Leader; Very Rev. John W. Girotti, J.C.L., Priest Celebrant; Deacons Bernard (Pat) P. Knier, Pastoral Assoc.; Randy Jaeckels.
School—Divine Savior Catholic School, 423 Fremont St., Kiel, 53042-1316. Tel: 920-894-3533; Email: dsprincipalsievert@gmail.com; Email: divinesaviorcatholicschool@gmail.com. Mr. Kerry Sievert, Prin. Clergy 1; Lay Teachers 14; Students 90.
Catechesis Religious Program—1814 Madison St., New Holstein, 53061-1647. Tel: 920-898-9248; Email: holyrosaryreled@gmail.com. Susan Philippi, D.R.E.

NEW LONDON, WAUPACA CO., MOST PRECIOUS BLOOD (1855) [CEM]
712 S. Pearl St., New London, 54961-1861.
Tel: 920-982-2346. Rev. John Kleinschmidt, Admin.
Church: 808 S. Pearl St., New London, 54961.
School—Most Precious Blood School, (Grades PreSchool-4), 120 E. Washington St., New London, 54961-1891. Tel: 920-982-2134; Fax: 920-982-1572; Email: mpbcs@mpbparishnl.org. Sandra Piotrowski, Prin. Lay Teachers 4; Students 38.
Catechesis Religious Program—Tel: 920-982-9025; Email: eclarke@mpbnewlondon.org. Joan Stemler, D.R.E., Tel: 920-982-9025; Email: jstemler@mpbparishnl.org.

NEWALD, ARGONNE CO., ST. HUBERT MISSION (1929) Served from St. Leonard, Laona.
5330 Beech St., Laona, 54541-9340.
Tel: 715-674-3241; Fax: 715-674-3241; Email: stleonardlaona@gmail.com. Rev. Felix Martin Penetrante.
Catechesis Religious Program—Tel: 715-674-3862; Email: cbeairl@centurytel.net. Ms. Cynthia Beairl, D.R.E.

NEWTON, MANITOWO CO., ST. THOMAS THE APOSTLE (2000) [CEM] Merger of St. Joseph, Alverno; St. Wendel, Cleveland; St. Isidore, Osman & St. Casimir, Northeim. Also, has records for all St. George, Hika & St. Fidelis, Meeme.
8100 Brunner Rd., Newton, 53063-9607.
Tel: 920-726-4228; Fax: 920-726-4229; Email: marlitah812@gmail.com; Web: stthomasnewton.org. Sr. Marlita Henseler, O.S.F., Pastoral Leader; Rev. David B. Beaudry, Sacramental Min.
Catechesis Religious Program—Email: pfischer7662@gmail.com. Mrs. Pamela Fischer, D.R.E. Students 15,074.

NIAGARA, MARINETTE CO., ST. ANTHONY (1902) Also serves St. Margaret, Pembine & Sacred Heart, Aurora.
1432 River St., Niagara, 54151-1599.
Tel: 715-251-3879; Email: office@stanthonyniagara.org; Web: stanthonyniagara.org. Rev. Michael Lightner.
Catechesis Religious Program—Email: office@stanthonyniagara.org. Ms. Dawn L. Johnson, D.R.E. Students 59.

NORMAN, KEWAUNEE CO., ST. JOSEPH, Merged with Nativity of the Blessed Virgin Mary, Tisch Mills to form St. Isidore the Farmer, Tisch Mills.

NORTHEIM, MANITOWOC CO., ST. CASIMIR, Merged with St. Joseph, Alverno; St. Wendel, Cleveland; and St. Isidore, Osman to form St. Thomas the Apostle, Northeim.

OCONTO, OCONTO CO.

1—HOLY TRINITY (1996) [CEM] Also serves Oconto Falls and Stiles.
716 Madison St., Oconto, 54153-1668.
Tel: 920-835-5900; Fax: 920-835-5907; Email: holytrinity@holy3.org; Web: www.holytrinityoconto.org. Rev. Joel A. Sember.
Catechesis Religious Program—Kevin Smits, D.R.E., Email: ksmits@holy3.org.

2—ST. JOSEPH, Merged with St. Peter, Oconto to form Holy Trinity, Oconto.

3—ST. PETER, Merged with St. Joseph, Oconto to form Holy Trinity, Oconto.

OCONTO FALLS, OCONTO CO., ST. ANTHONY (1896) [CEM] Served from Holy Trinity, Oconto. Rev. Joel A. Sember.
Church: 253 N. Franklin St., Oconto Falls, 54154-1042. Tel: 920-846-2276; Fax: 920-846-2180; Email: lscanlan@holy3.org.
School—St. Anthony School, Tel: 920-846-2276; Email: lscanlan@holy3.org. Lay Teachers 5; Students 55.
Catechesis Religious Program—Email: lbeaumier@holy3.org. Ms. Lynn Beaumier, D.R.E. Associated with St. Patrick, Stiles.

OMRO, WINNEBAGO CO., ST. MARY (1893)
730 Madison Ave., Omro, 54963-1630.
Tel: 920-685-2258; Web: www.stmarychurches.org. Sisters Pamela A. Biehl, O.S.F., Pastoral Leader; Patrick Flanigan, Hispanic Min.; Very Rev. W. Thomas Long, Priest Moderator/Priest Celebrant; Rev. Matthew Rappl, Priest Celebrant; Rose Unser, Faith Formation Coord.
Catechesis Religious Program—Sr. Regina Rose Pearson, O.S.F., D.R.E.

ONEIDA, BROWN CO., ST. JOSEPH (1876) [CEM] Also serves Immaculate Conception, Oneida.
145 Saint Joseph Dr., Oneida, 54155-8914.
Tel: 920-869-2244; Email: parishsecsjic@gmail.com. Rev. John C. Katamba, Admin.; Deacon James P. Heider.
Catechesis Religious Program—Email: mvanreoffice.@aol.com. Mrs. Mary Van Schyndel, D.R.E.

ONEIDA TOWNSHIP, OUTAGAMIE CO., IMMACULATE CONCEPTION (1889) [CEM] Served from St. Joseph, Oneida.
Mailing Address: 145 Saint Joseph Dr., Oneida, 54155-8914. Tel: 920-869-2244; Tel: 920-869-2244; Email: parishsecsjic@gmail.com. Rev. John C. Katamba, Admin.; Senior Deacon Everett L. Doxtator; Deacon James P. Heider.
Res.: N5589 County Rd. E., De Pere, 54115-8529.
Tel: 920-869-2626; Email: parishsecretarysjic@gmail.com.
Catechesis Religious Program—Sue Meyer, D.R.E.

OSHKOSH, WINNEBAGO CO.

1—ST. JOHN, [JC] Merged with Sacred Heart, Oshkosh and St. Vincent de Paul, Oshkosh to form St. Jude the Apostle, Oshkosh.

2—ST. JOSAPHAT, Merged with St. Mary, Oshkosh and St. Peter, Oshkosh to form Most Blessed Sacrament, Oshkosh.

3—ST. JUDE THE APOSTLE
1025 W. 5th Ave., Oshkosh, 54902-5725.
Tel: 920-235-7412; Fax: 920-651-9826; Email: office@stjudeoshkosh.org. Rev. Louis R. Golamari, Admin.; Deacon G. Patrick Gelhar. Merger of St. John, Oshkosh, St. Vincent de Paul, Oshkosh & Sacred Heart, Oshkosh. Has records for all 3 parishes.
See Lourdes Academy, Oshkosh under Consolidated Schools located in the Institution section.
Catechesis Religious Program—Email: mzspan2@aol.com. Ms. Michele Spanbauer, Contact Person.

4—ST. MARY, Merged with St. Josaphat, Oshkosh and St. Peter, Oshkosh to form Most Blessed Sacrament, Oshkosh.

5—MOST BLESSED SACRAMENT (2007)
449 High Ave., Oshkosh, 54901-4708.
Tel: 920-231-9782; Email: mbslpollack@gmail.com; Web: mbsoshkosh.com. Very Rev. Jerome P. Pastors; Senior Deacon Peter A. Cheskie; Deacon Richard A. Hocking, Email: rickhocking@gmail.com. Merger of St. Josaphat, Oshkosh, St. Mary, Oshkosh & St. Peter, Oshkosh. Has records for all 3 parishes.
See Lourdes Academy, Oshkosh under Consolidated Schools located in the Institution section.
Catechesis Religious Program—Email: mwichmann@mbsoshkosh.org. Mrs. Mary Wichmann, D.R.E. - PreK-8; Mrs. Kathleen Geffers, D.R.E. - 9-12.

6—ST. PETER, [JC] Merged with St. Josaphat, Oshkosh and St. Mary, Oshkosh to form Most Blessed Sacrament, Oshkosh.

7—ST. RAPHAEL THE ARCHANGEL (1978) [JC]
830 S Westhaven Dr., Oshkosh, 54904-7977.
Tel: 920-233-8044; Fax: 920-233-2360; Email: parish.office@raphael.org; Web: www.raphael.org. Very Rev. W. Thomas Long, Email: tom.long@raphael.org; Rev. Matthew Rappl, Parochial Vicar; Deacons Gregory A. Grey; John Ingala; Paul Vidmar.
See Lourdes Academy, Oshkosh under Consolidated Schools located in the Institution section.
Catechesis Religious Program—Email: jessie.adrians@raphael.org. Jessica Adrians, D.R.E.

8—SACRED HEART, [CEM] Merged with St. John, Oshkosh and St. Vincent de Paul, Oshkosh to form St. Jude the Apostle, Oshkosh.

9—ST. VINCENT DE PAUL, [JC] Merged with St. John, Oshkosh and Sacred Heart, Oshkosh to form St. Jude the Apostle, Oshkosh.

OSMAN, MANITOWOC CO., ST. ISIDORE, Merged with St. Wendel, Cleveland, St. Joseph, Alverno; and St. Casimir, Northeim to form St. Thomas the Apostle, Northeim.

PEMBINE, MARINETTE CO., ST. MARGARET (1926) Served from St. Anthony, Niagara.
Mailing Address: P.O. Box 235, Pembine, 54156-0235. Tel: 715-324-5849; Email: stmargaretpembine@gmail.com; Web: www.stanthonyniagara.org. N18844 Hwy. 141 & 8, Pembine, 54156. Rev. Michael Lightner, Admin.

PESHTIGO, MARINETTE CO., ST. MARY (1865) Also serves SS. Joseph & Edward, Walsh.
171 S. Wood Ave., Peshtigo, 54157-1426.
Tel: 715-582-3876; Email: st.marypeshtigo@gmail.com; Web: www.stmaryjosephedwardparish.org. Rev. Jesus Berdol, Admin.; Deacon Charles R. Schumacher.
School—St. Thomas Aquinas Academy, (Grades 7-12), 1200 Main St., Marinette, 54143.
Tel: 715-735-7481; Fax: 715-735-3375; Email: principal.staa@gmail.com. Mr. Michael Cattani, Prin. Clergy 1; Lay Teachers 12; Students 48.
Catechesis Religious Program—Tel: 715-582-4897. Email: duranchar33@gmail.com. Charlotte Duran, D.R.E.

PHLOX, LANGLADE CO.

1—ST. JOSEPH, [CEM] Merged with Holy Family, Mattoon to form St. Joseph-Holy Family Parish, Phlox. Served from St. Anthony, Neopit.

2—ST. JOSEPH-HOLY FAMILY PARISH (2006) Merger of St. Joseph, Phlox & Holy Family, Mattoon. Has records for both parishes.
Mailing Address: P.O. Box 73, Phlox, 54464-0073.
Tel: 715-489-3330; Email: sjhfphlox@granitewave.com. Deacon Thomas W. Hartman, Pastoral Coord.; Rev. David R. Schmidt, Priest Mod.
Church: W7365 State Hwy. 47, Phlox, 54464.
Catechesis Religious Program—Casey Meidl, D.R.E.

PICKEREL, LANGLADE CO., ST. MARY (1914) [CEM] Served from Holy Family, Elcho.
Mailing Address: P.O. Box 77, Pickerel, 54465-0077.
Tel: 715-484-4300; Email:

holyfamilyelcho@frontiernet.net. Rev. David M. Zimmerman.
Church: N9155 State Hwy. 55, Pickerel, 54465.
Catechesis Religious Program—Students 11.

PINE GROVE, BROWN CO., HOLY TRINITY, [CEM] Merged with Holy Martyrs of Gorcum, Green Bay to form Prince of Peace, Green Bay.

PLAINFIELD, WAUSHARA CO., ST. PAUL (1898) [CEM] (Served from St. Joseph, Wautoma)
622 S. Beach St., Plainfield, 54966-9637.
Tel: 715-335-4314; Email: stpaul@uniontel.net. Rev. Andrew J. Kurz, Admin.
Catechesis Religious Program—Carla Murray, Contact Person.

POY SIPPI, WAUSHARA CO., SACRED HEART OF JESUS (1920) Served from St. Mark, Redgranite.
Mailing Address: P.O. Box 273, Redgranite, 54970-0273. Tel: 920-566-4442; Email: sacredheartps@centurytel.net. 2304 Liberty St., Poy Sippi, 54967. Very Rev. Jerome P. Pastors; Deacon Robert L. Precourt, Parish Life Coord.; Rev. Jason J. Blahnik, Priest Celebrant.

PULASKI, BROWN CO., ASSUMPTION OF THE BLESSED VIRGIN MARY (1887) [CEM] Also serves St. Stanislaus, Hofa Park and St. Casimir, Krakow.
P.O. Box 379, Pulaski, 54162-0379.
Tel: 920-822-3279; Email: parishoffice@abvm.org; Web: www.abvmcast.org. 119 E. Pulaski St, Pulaski, 54162. Rev. Patrick M. Gawrylewski, O.F.M.; Deacons Dennis G. Majewski; David J. Parker; Janet Maroszek, Pastoral Assoc.; Pamela A. Janseh, RCIA Coord.; Diane Peters, Music Min.
Res.: 124 E. Pulaski St., Pulaski, 54162-0379.
School—Assumption of the Blessed Virgin Mary School, (Grades 1-5), 109 E. Pulaski St., Pulaski, 54162-9287. Tel: 920-822-5650; Email: deanne.wilinski@abvm.org; Web: www.abvmeducation.org. Deanne Wilinski, Prin. & D.R.E. Lay Teachers 12; Students 75.
Catechesis Religious Program—Deanne Wilinski, D.R.E., Tel: 920-822-5650; Email: deanne.wilinski@abvm.org; Todd Skinkis, Youth Min.; Staci Karcz, C.R.E. (Grades 1-6). Students 95.

REDGRANITE, WAUSHARA CO., ST. MARK (1906) [CEM] Also serves Sacred Heart of Jesus, Poy Sippi.
Mailing Address: P.O. Box 273, Redgranite, 54970-0273. Tel: 920-566-4442; Email: stmarkredgranite@centurytel.net. Deacon Robert L. Precourt, Pastoral Leader; Very Rev. Jerome P. Pastors, Moderator; Rev. Jason J. Blahnik, Priest Celebrant.

REEDSVILLE, MANITOWOC CO.
1—ST. MARY, Merged with St. Patrick's, Maple Grove to form St. Mary-St. Patrick, Reedsville.
2—ST. MARY-ST. PATRICK, Merged with St. Mary, Brillion to form Holy Family, Brillion.

ROSIERE, KEWAUNEE CO., ST. HUBERT, Merged with St. Peter, Lincoln to form St. Peter & St. Hubert, Rosiere/Lincoln.

ROSIERE/LINCOLN, KEWAUNEE CO., ST. PETER AND ST. HUBERT (1994) [JC4] Rev. Edward L. Looney, Admin.
Res.: E3085 County Rd. X, Casco, 54205-9787.
Tel: 920-837-2852; Email: stpnh@centurytel.net; Web: www.stpeterandsthubert.com.
Catechesis Religious Program—Tel: 920-493-2333; Email: renewenergies@itol.com. Bill Lohrey, D.R.E.; Sue Lohrey, D.R.E.

SAINT ANNA, CALUMET CO., ST. ANN (1851) [CEM] Served from Ss. Peter & Paul, Kiel.
N188 School St., New Holstein, 53061-9776.
Tel: 920-894-3147; Fax: 920-894-3147; Email: stann1851@gmail.com; Web: stannwi.org. Rev. Anthony Ibekwe, Mod.; Mr. Joseph Zenk, Pastoral Leader; Deacons Bernard (Pat) P. Knier; Randy Jaeckels.
Catechesis Religious Program—Email: wisco_02@hotmail.com. Mrs. Laura Winkel, D.R.E. Students 30.

SAINT JOHN, CALUMET CO., ST. JOHN THE BAPTIST, Merged with Sacred Heart, Sherwood, to form St. John-Sacred Heart, Sherwood.

SAINT NAZIANZ, MANITOWOC CO., ST. GREGORY (1854) [CEM] Also serves Holy Trinity, School Hill.
Mailing Address: P.O. Box 199, St. Nazianz, 54232-0199. Tel: 920-773-2511; Fax: 920-773-3086; Email: stgregory100@tds.net. 214 Church, St. Nazianz, 54232. Rev. Anthony Ibekwe, Admin.; Deacon Gary Wilhelm.
Catechesis Religious Program—212 Church St., St. Nazianz, 54232. Patty Wilhelm, D.R.E.

SCHOOL HILL, MANITOWOC CO., HOLY TRINITY (1869) [CEM] Served from St. Gregory, St. Nazianz.
11928 Marken Rd., Kiel, 53042-9750.
Tel: 920-773-2380; Email: holytrinityparish@tds.net; Web: holytrinityschoolhill.org. Rev. Anthony Ibekwe, Admin.; Deacon Gary Wilhelm.
Catechesis Religious Program—Patty Wilhelm, D.R.E.

SEYMOUR, OUTAGAMIE CO., ST. JOHN (1873) [CEM]
Mailing Address: 915 Ivory St., Seymour, 54165-1629. Tel: 920-833-6140; Email: office@stjohnseymour.com. Very Rev. Brian S. Belongia, J.C.L.; Deacon Richard J. Matuszak.
Catechesis Religious Program—Tel: 920-833-2122; Email: mcarter@stjohnseymour.com. Mrs. Mary P. Carter, D.R.E.

SHAWANO, SHAWANO CO., SACRED HEART (1867) [CEM 2]
321 S. Sawyer St., Shawano, 54166-2437.
Tel: 715-526-2023; Email: lmathieu@sacredheartshawano.org; Web: www.sacredheartshawano.org. Very Rev. Thomas J. Farrell; Deacons James Lonick; Todd Raether.
Church: 302 S. Main St., Shawano, 54166.
School—Sacred Heart School, 124 E. Center St., Shawano, 54166-2499. Tel: 715-526-5328; Email: ayoung@sacredheartshawano.org; Email: lmeisner@sacredheartshawano.org. Aleta Young, Prin. Lay Teachers 14; Students 98.
Catechesis Religious Program—Email: shinfo@sacredheartofshawano.org. Lori Mathwich, D.R.E., Tel: 715-526-4104; Email: lmathwich@sacredheartshawano.org. Students 126.

SHERWOOD, CALUMET CO.
1—ST. JOHN-SACRED HEART (1995)
N369 Military Rd., Sherwood, 54169-9661.
Tel: 920-989-1515; Fax: 920-989-8585; Email: triparish369@gmail.com; Web: www.stjohnsacredheart.org. Rev. Michael E. Betley, Email: michaelbetley@gmail.com.
School—St. John-Sacred Heart School, (Grades PreK-8), N361 Military Rd., Sherwood, 54169-9661. Tel: 920-989-1373; Fax: 920-989-1689; Email: sjshprincipal@gmail.com. P.O. Box 78, Sherwood, 54169. Jacklyn Behnke, Prin. Students 84.
Catechesis Religious Program—Tel: 920-989-2400; Email: triparishre@gmail.com. Mrs. Debbie Peters, Contact Person.
2—SACRED HEART, Merged with St. John the Baptist, St. John to form St. John-Sacred Heart, Sherwood.

SHIOCTON, OUTAGAMIE CO., ST. DENIS (1898) [CEM] Served from St. Patrick, Stephensville.
Mailing Address: N3686 State Rd. 76, Hortonville, 54944-8320. Tel: 920-757-5090; Email: stpatdenis@new.rr.com; Web: www.stdenis-shiocton.org. Rev. Donald E. Everts, Admin.; Deacon Kenneth D. Bilgrien, Pastoral Coord.
Catechesis Religious Program—N5591 Second St., Shiocton, 54170. Ben Wolf, D.R.E. Students 96.

SISTER BAY, DOOR CO., ST. ROSALIA, Merged with St. John the Baptist, Egg Harbor; St. Mary of the Lake, Baileys Harbor; St. Paul, Fish Creek and St. Michael, Jacksonport to form Stella Maris, Egg Harbor.

SLOVAN, KEWAUNEE CO., ST. ADALBERT, Merged with Holy Trinity, Casco.

SOBIESKI, OCONTO CO.
1—ST. JOHN CANTIUS, [CEM] Merged with St. Louis, Abrams and St. Joseph, Chase to form St. Maximilian Kolbe, Sobieski.
2—ST. MAXIMILIAN KOLBE (2007)
6051 Noble St., Sobieski, 54171-9724.
Tel: 920-822-5255; Fax: 920-822-5255; Email: stmaxkolbeparish@gmail.com; Web: www.stmaximiliankolbe.com/. Rev. Antonio de los Santos, Admin.
Catechesis Religious Program—Tel: 920-822-8795. Michelle Bukowiec, D.R.E.

SOUTH BRANCH, MENOMINEE RESERVATION, ST. JOSEPH OF THE LAKE, Closed. For inquiries for parish records contact the chancery.

SPRUCE, OCONTO CO., SACRED HEART OF JESUS, Merged with St. Charles Borromeo, Lena to form Holy Cross, Lena.

STANGELVILLE, KEWAUNEE CO.
1—ST. LAWRENCE, Merged with St. Joseph-St. John, Montpelier and St. Hedwig, West Kewaunee to form St. Therese de Lisieux, Stangelville.
2—ST. THERESE DE LISIEUX (2000) [JC] Also serves St. Isidore the Farmer, Tisch Mills.
Mailing Address: N2085 County Rd. AB, Denmark, 54208-7705. Tel: 920-863-8747; Fax: 920-863-5768; Email: stherese@netnet.net. Rev. Dennis G. Drury.
Catechesis Religious Program—Mrs. Sandy Salentine, D.R.E.

STEPHENSVILLE, OUTAGAMIE CO., ST. PATRICK (1867) [CEM] Also serves St. Denis, Shiocton.
N3686 State Rd. 76, Hortonville, 54944-8320.
Tel: 920-757-5090; Email: stpatdenis@new.rr.com; Web: www.stpatrick-stephensville.org. Rev. Donald E. Everts, Admin.; Deacon Kenneth D. Bilgrien, Pastoral Coord.
Catechesis Religious Program—Students 3.

STILES, OCONTO CO., ST. PATRICK (1870) [JC] Served from Holy Trinity, Oconto.
Mailing Address: 253 N. Franklin St., Oconto Falls, 54154-1042. Rev. Joel A. Sember.
Res.: 5246 St. Patrick's Rd., Lena, 54139-9105.
Tel: 920-846-2276; Email: lscanlan@holy3.org.
Catechesis Religious Program—Kathleen Sayers, D.R.E. Associated with St. Anthony, Oconto Falls.

STOCKBRIDGE, CALUMET CO., ST. MARY (1882) [CEM] Served From St. John-Sacred Heart Sherwood, Saint John.
P.O. Box 8, Stockbridge, 53088-0008.
Tel: 920-439-1515; Email: stmarystockbridge@tds.net. Rev. Michael E. Betley.
Catechesis Religious Program—N369 Military Rd., Sherwood, 54169-9661. Tel: 920-898-2400; Email: re@tds.net. Mrs. Debbie Peters, Contact Person.

STURGEON BAY, DOOR CO.
1—CORPUS CHRISTI (1904) [JC]
Mailing Address: 25 N. Elgin Ave., Sturgeon Bay, 54235-2963. Email: office@ccparish.net. Rev. Carl E. Schmitt; Deacon Mark R. Hibbs.
Res.: 722 W. Maple St., Sturgeon Bay, 54235.
School—St. John Bosco School, 730 W. Maple, Sturgeon Bay, 54235-2995. Tel: 920-743-4144; Email: vickie.dassler@johnboscoschool.org; Web: www.johnboscoschool.org. Vickie Dassler, Prin. Lay Teachers 20; Students 123.
Catechesis Religious Program—Email: office@ccparish.net. Debby Brauer, D.R.E.; Ms. Penny Biwer, D.R.E.
Oratory, [JC] Tel: 920-743-4716; Fax: 920-743-3711; Email: christiparish@corpuschristiparish.us.
2—ST. JOSEPH (1865) Serves Ss. Peter & Paul Parish, Institute.
526 Louisiana St., Sturgeon Bay, 54235-1796.
Tel: 920-743-2062; Fax: 920-743-6786; Email: bwagner@stjosephsb.com; Web: www.stjosephsb.com. Rev. Robert Stegmann; Deacon Kenneth D. Kopydlowski.
Church: 110 N. 5th Ave., Sturgeon Bay, 54235.
School: See St. John Bosco Catholic School, Inc., Sturgeon Bay under Elementary Schools, Diocesan in the Institution Section.
Catechesis Religious Program—Email: pbiwer@hotmail.com. Ms. Penny Biwer, D.R.E.; Sarah Gavin, D.R.E.

SUAMICO, BROWN CO., ST. BENEDICT (1917) [CEM] Also serves St. Pius, Little Suamico.
Mailing Address: 3370 Deerfield W., P.O. Box 66, Suamico, 54173-0066. Tel: 920-434-2024; Email: sbsp@wi.twcbc.com; Web: St.BenedictSuamico.com. Rev. Judah Ben-Hur S. Pigon, M.F., Admin.
Catechesis Religious Program—Tel: 920-434-1219. Ms. Dyan Devroy, D.R.E.

SURING, OCONTO CO., ST. MICHAEL (1906) [CEM] Served from St. John, Gillett, with Station at Chute Pond.
Mailing Address: P.O. Box 248, Suring, 54174-0248.
Tel: 920-842-2580; Fax: 920-842-9825; Email: stmikesuring@centurytel.net. 210 S Krueger St., Suring, 54174. Rev. Robert Ni Ni.
Catechesis Religious Program—Sheelagh School, D.R.E. Students 25.

THIRY DAEMS, KEWAUNEE CO., ST. ODILE, Closed. For inquiries for parish records, please see St. Joseph, Champion.

TIGERTON, SHAWANO CO., ST. ANTHONY (1881) Also serves St. Mary, Marion & Holy Family-St. William, Wittenberg.
Mailing Address: P.O. Box 106, Tigerton, 54486-0106. Tel: 715-535-2571; Fax: 715-535-2953; Email: office@catholicsupnorth.org. 430 Swanke St., Tigerton, 54486. Rev. Matthew W. Settle, Admin.; Deacons Patrick G. Berg; Howard Bricco; Michael J. Brandt.
Catechesis Religious Program—Email: re@catholicsupnorth.org. Tammy Wendler, D.R.E. Students 19.

TISCH MILLS, MANITOWOC CO.
1—ST. ISIDORE THE FARMER (2002) Merger of Nativity of the Blessed Virgin Mary & St. Joseph, Norman. Has records for both parishes. Served from St. Therese de Lisieux Parish, Stangelville.
Mailing Address: 18424 Tisch Mills Rd., Denmark, 54208-9508. Tel: 920-776-1555; Fax: 920-776-1814; Email: st.isidore@tm.net. Rev. Dennis G. Drury.
Catechesis Religious Program—Email: bzipperer@hughes.net. Barbara Zipperer, D.R.E.; Christal Wavrunek, D.R.E.
2—NATIVITY OF THE BLESSED VIRGIN MARY, Merged with St. Joseph, Norman to form St. Isidore the Farmer, Tisch Mills.

TONET, KEWAUNEE CO., ST. MARTIN, Closed. For inquiries for parish records, please see St. Joseph, Champion.

TWO RIVERS, MANITOWOC CO.
1—HOLY REDEEMER - SACRED HEART (2000) Merged with St. Luke and St. Mark, Two Rivers to form St. Peter the Fisherman, Two Rivers.
2—ST. LUKE, Merged with St. Mark and Holy Redeemer-Sacred Heart, Two Rivers to form St. Peter the Fisherman, Two Rivers.
3—ST. MARK, Merged with St. Luke and Holy Redeemer-Sacred Heart, Two Rivers to form St. Peter the Fisherman, Two Rivers.
4—MOST HOLY REDEEMER, Merged with Sacred Heart, Two Rivers to form Holy Redeemer-Sacred Heart, Two Rivers.
5—ST. PETER THE FISHERMAN (2002) [CEM] Merger of

St. Luke, St. Mark & Holy Redeemer-Sacred Heart, Two Rivers. Holds records for St. Luke, St. Mark & Most Holy Redeemer-Sacred Heart.
Mailing Address: 3201 Mishicot Rd., Two Rivers, 54241-1501. Tel: 920-793-4531; Fax: 920-793-8067; Email: parish@spfcp.org. Rev. Thomas J. Reynebeau; Deacons Paul J. Gleichner; Frank Birr; Thomas Tomaszewski.
Catechesis Religious Program—3218 Tannery Rd., Two Rivers, 54241-1648. Email: bhuettl@spfcp.org. Bernie Huettl, D.R.E.

6—SACRED HEART, Merged with Most Holy Redeemer, Two Rivers to form Holy Redeemer-Sacred Heart, Two Rivers.

WABENO, FOREST CO., ST. AMBROSE (1905) [CEM] Served from St. Mary of the Lake, Lakewood.
Mailing Address: P.O. Box 280, Wabeno, 54566-0280. Tel: 715-473-2511; Email: stambrose@centurylink.net; Web: wabenocatholic.com. 4265 N. Branch Ave., Wabeno, 54566. Very Rev. Philip Dinh-Van-Thiep.
Catechesis Religious Program—Ann Barfknecht, D.R.E.

WAGNER, MARINETTE CO., ST. EDWARD, [CEM] Merged with St. Joseph, Walsh to form SS. Joseph & Edward, Walsh. For inquiries for parish records contact St. Joseph & Edward, Walsh.

WALHAIN, KEWAUNEE CO., ST. AMAND, Closed. For inquiries for parish records, please see St. Joseph, Champion.

WALSH, MARINETTE CO.

1—ST. JOSEPH, Merged with St. Edward, Wagner to form SS. Joseph & Edward, Walsh. For inquiries for parish records contact St. Joseph & Edward, Walsh.

2—SS. JOSEPH & EDWARD (1894) Served from St. Mary, Peshtigo. (Has records for St. Edward, Wagner & St. Joseph, Walsh.)
Mailing Address: W3308 County Road G, Porterfield, 54159-9736. Tel: 715-789-2254; Fax: 715-789-2293; Email: stsjosed@centurytel.net; Web: www.stmaryjosephedwardparish.org. Rev. Jesus Berdol, Admin.; Deacon Charles R. Schumacher.
Catechesis Religious Program—Tel: 715-582-4897; Email: duranchar33@gmail.com. Charlotte Duran, D.R.E.

WAUPACA, WAUPACA CO., ST. MARY MAGDALENE (1890) [CEM] Also serves Sacred Heart, Manawa & Ss. Peter & Paul, Weyauwega. Has records for St. George, King.
PO Box 409, Waupaca, 54981-0409.
Tel: 715-258-2088; Email: info@smm-waupaca.org. Rev. Xavier Santiago, Admin.
Church: N2845 Shadow Rd., Waupaca, 54981.
Catechesis Religious Program—Email: bettymanion@yahoo.com. Mrs. Elizabeth Manion, D.R.E.; Mrs. Catherine Miller, D.R.E.

WAUSAUKEE, MARINETTE CO., ST. AUGUSTINE (1889) Also serves St. Agnes, Amberg.
Mailing Address: 507 Church St., Wausaukee, 54177-9749. Tel: 715-856-5276; Email: staugustine@centurytel.net. Revs. Frederick Sserugga, Admin.; John J. Hephner, Priest Celebrant, (Retired); Donald R. Burkart, Priest Celebrant, (Retired); Deacon Richard F. Elfering.
Catechesis Religious Program—Sherri L. Schlies, D.R.E.

WAUTOMA, WAUSHARA CO., ST. JOSEPH (1885) [CEM] (Also serves St. Paul, Plainfield)
364 S. Cambridge St., Wautoma, 54982-8101.
Tel: 920-787-3848; Fax: 920-787-4781; Email: office@stjosephwautoma.com; Web: stjosephwautoma.weconnect.com. Rev. Andrew J. Kurz, Admin.; Deacon Paul K. Grimm.
Catechesis Religious Program—Therese Kasuboski, D.R.E. (Grades PreK-5); Paula Caswell, D.R.E. (Grades 6-11).

WEST KEWAUNEE, KEWAUNEE CO., ST. HEDWIG, Merged with St. Joseph-St. John, Montpelier and St. Lawrence, Stangelville to form St. Therese de Lisieux, Stangelville.

WEYAUWEGA, WAUPACA CO., SS. PETER AND PAUL (1890) [CEM]
P.O. Box 548, Weyauwega, 54983-0548.
Tel: 920-867-2179; Email: sspeterpaul@charter.net; Web: www.sspeterpaulchurch.org. 608 E. Main St., Weyauwega, 54983. Rev. Xavier Santiago, Admin.
Catechesis Religious Program—Tel: 920-867-2170; Email: peterpauled@charter.net. Stephanie A. Hansen, D.R.E.

WHITE LAKE, LANGLADE CO.

1—ST. JAMES, Merged with St. Stanislaus Kostka, Langlade to become SS. James & Stanislaus, White Lake/Langlade.

2—SS. JAMES-STANISLAUS (1992) [CEM 2]
Mailing Address: P.O. Box 36, White Lake, 54491-0036. Tel: 715-882-2551; Email: stjames2551@frontier.com. 235 Bissell St., White Lake, 54491. Rev. Edmundo Nachor Siguenza.
Res.: 252 Bissell St., White Lake, 54491.
Catechesis Religious Program—

WHITELAW, MANITOWOC CO., ST. MICHAEL (1872) [CEM] Served from Immaculate Conception, Clarks Mills.
Mailing Address: P.O. Box 206, Whitelaw, 54247-0206. Tel: 920-732-3901; Email: stmichael3901@comcast.net. Very Rev. Richard H. Klingeisen; Deacon Randy Meidl.
Church: 110 W. Menasha Ave., Whitelaw, 54247.
School—St. Mary/St. Michael School, 19 S. County Rd., Reedsville, 54230-8329. Tel: 920-775-4366; Email: rhamcher@stmarystmichael.com. Rick Hamacher, Prin.
Catechesis Religious Program—15 S. County Rd. J, Cato, 54230-8329. Tel: 920-775-4876; Fax: 820-775-4365. Mrs. Teresa Pederson, D.R.E.

WINNECONNE, WINNEBAGO CO., ST. MARY (1884) [JC] Also serves St. Mary Omro.
P.O. Box 487, Winneconne, 54986-0487.
Tel: 920-582-7712; Fax: 920-582-0181; Email: stmarywinn@stmarychurches.org. Sr. Pamela A. Biehl, O.S.F., Pastoral Leader; Very Rev. W. Thomas Long, Priest Moderator/Priest Celebrant; Rev. Matthew Rappl, Priest Celebrant; Rose Unser; Ms. Andrea Krueger, Faith Formation Coord.
Catechesis Religious Program—Email: andystmary@sbcglobal.net. Ms. Andrea Krueger, Contact Person.

WITTENBERG, SHAWANO CO.

1—HOLY FAMILY, Merged with St. William, Eland to form Holy Family & St. William, Wittenberg/Eland. Has records for both parishes.

2—HOLY FAMILY-ST. WILLIAM (2000) [CEM] Merger of Holy Family, Wittenberg & St. William, Eland. Has records for both parishes.
106 N. Ellms St., Wittenberg, 54499-9099. Mailing Address: P.O. Box 106, Tigerton, 54486-0106.
Tel: 715-535-2571; Fax: 715-535-2953; Email: office@catholicsupnorth.org. Rev. Matthew W. Settle, Admin.; Deacons Patrick G. Berg; Howard R. Bricco; Michael J. Brandt.
Church: 202 N. Ellms St., Wittenberg, 54499.
Catechesis Religious Program—Email: re@catholicsupnorth.org. Tammy Wendler, D.R.E.

Special Assignment:
Very Revs.—
Felton, Daniel J., Vicar General & Mod. Curia, P.O. Box 23825, 54305-3825
Ferris, Luke A., Vicar for Clergy and Pastoral Leaders, P.O. Box 23825, 54305-3825
Girotti, John W., J.C.L., Vicar for Canonical Svcs. & Assoc. Mod. for Curia, 6100 Pepper Rd., Denmark, 54208-9473
Revs.—
Blahnik, Jason, Dir. Newman Center, 800 Elmwood Ave., Oshkosh, 54901-3518
Mann, Quentin A., C.D.L., Assoc. Vocation Dir., 3035 O'Brien Rd., Baileys Harbor, 54202-9132
Mleziva, Mark, Dir., Vocation, P.O. Box 23825, 54305-3825.

Military Chaplains:
Revs.—
Brunner, William J. III, Our Lady of Grace Parish, 2766 Navajo Rd., El Cajon, CA 92020
Dory, Michael, Lt. Cmdr., 16113 W. Quail Creek Ln., Surprise, AZ 85374-4910.

Absent on Leave, Sick, Disabled or Inactive:
Rev. Msgr.—
Rose, Donald, (Retired)
Revs.—
Duffeck, David A., Place 2B Community Center, 1062 N. Koeller St., Oshkosh, 54902
Heymen, Richard, (Retired)
Hoffman, Philip, (Retired)
Schneider, Ronald
Somers, Michael
Van Dynhoven, William J.

Retired:
Most Rev.—
Banks, Robert J., D.D., J.C.D., (Retired), P.O. Box 23825, 54305-3825
Rev. Msgrs.—
Dewane, John B., M.A., S.T.L., D.Min., (Retired), 1435 N. McCarthy Rd., Apt. 3, Appleton, 54913-8285
Dillenburg, James E., (Retired), 704 Baumeister Rd., Kewaunee, 54216
Feely, James B., (Retired), 2785 Taurus Rd., 54311
Koszarek, Paul P., (Retired), 2788 W. Shore Ln., Crandon, 54520
Schuh, John H., (Retired), 226 S. Walnut St., Kimberly, 54136
Vanden Hogen, James, (Retired), 925 Wilson St., Little Chute, 54140
Revs.—
Allen, Richard L., (Retired), 3220 E. Parkside Blvd., Apt. 82, Appleton, 54915. Tel: 920-213-0985
Ashbeck, David K., (Retired), 18035 W. Tierra Del Sol Dr., Surprise, AZ 85387
Barrett, David S., (Retired), N6772 Black Oak Cir., Shawano, 54166
Barwig, Regis, (Retired), 2804 Oakwood Ln., Oshkosh, 54904-8406
Becker, John J., (Retired), W6395 Sonny Dr., Apt. 7, Menasha, 54952
Berryman, Harold L., (Retired), 2514 Wisconsin Ave., New Holstein, 53061
Birdsall, Anthony J., (Retired), 2105 Shiloh Rd., Sturgeon Bay, 54235
Brooks, Charles R., (Retired), 825 Cobblestone Ln. #233, Kimberly, 54136
Buhl, Wilbert L., (Retired), 224 Iroquois Ave., #1, 54301
Burkart, Donald R., (Retired), N7374 Birchwood Rd., Crivitz, 54114
Canavera, Lawrence J., (Retired), 1030 F. West Elm Dr., Apt. 10, Little Chute, 54140-1098
Cerkas, John W., (Retired), 4308 River Trail Rd., Cavour, 54511
Colombo, Ronald A., (Retired), 1010 Oxford Ave., Sturgeon Bay, 54235-2070
Dantinne, Gary J., (Retired), 400 Angels Touch Pass #9, De Pere, 54115
Demuth, Paul E., (Retired), 413 St. John St., 54301-4116
Dombroski, Dean W., (Retired), 1878 Guns St., 54311
Dowling, Raymond, (Retired), 7230 Wyoming Spring Dr., Rm. 110, Round Rock, TX 78681-4320
DuCharme, Paul, (Retired), 224 Iroquois Ave., #8, 54301-1998
Evers, Leonard M., (Retired), P.O. Box 23825, 54305
Falk, Gerald R., (Retired), 316 E. 14th St., Apt. 302, Kaukauna, 54130-3304
Foley, Gerald J., (Retired), 1700 S. 18th St., #214, Manitowoc, 54220
Fox, Martin F., (Retired), 4287 Bay View Dr., Sturgeon Bay, 54235
Frozena, Kenneth R., (Retired), W5045 Golf Course Rd., Sherwood, 54169
Gallagher, John M., (Retired), 310 1A Yorkshire Ln., Manitowoc, 54220
Geiser, Allen A., (Retired), 224 Iroquois Ave., #4, 54301
Gerend, Lawrence, (Retired), 1590 Polo Run Terr., 54313
Groher, Robert C., (Retired), 5082 Lucas Rd., Oconto, 54153-9408
Hablewitz, James A., (Retired), 635 Ridgeview Cir., Apt. 226, Appleton, 54911-1189
Hafeman, Harry G., (Retired), 528 Challenger Dr., 54311
Harper, John H., (Retired), c/o Nativity of Our Lord Parish, 2270 S. Oneida St., 54304
Hephner, John J., (Retired), N15211 Beazley Rd., Amberg, 54102-9177
Hoffmann, Charles, (Retired), 512 Brian Dr., Antigo, 54409
Karuhn, Robert J., (Retired), 1518 Redstone Trl., #6, 54313
Kelley, Omer C., (Retired), 918 Elm St., Antigo, 54409-1525
Koch, David J., (Retired), 26014 S. Howard Dr., Sun Lakes, AZ 85248
Krutzik, Norman, (Retired), 5800 Pennsylvania Ave., #116, Appleton, 54914
Kuhr, William, (Retired), 631 Haylett St., Neenah, 54956
Kutiuk, Casimir, (Retired), 3170 Eden Ln., Rm. 209, Oshkosh, 54904
LaCombe, C. Terrence, (Retired), 20044 N. Siesta Rock Dr., Surprise, AZ 85374-4532
Lenzner, George, (Retired), 2582 Trojan Dr., Apt. 2, 54304-1469
Lexa, Robert, (Retired), 232 S. Pleasant Dr., Appleton, 54914-4205
Massart, James P., (Retired), 625 N. Broadway, De Pere, 54115
Mattern, Joseph A., (Retired), 320 N. Webster Ave., Omro, 54963
Mayefske, Thomas J., (Retired), 1017 Florida St., S.E., Albuquerqe, NM 87108-4823
Mullarkey, John T., (Retired), 1409 Alcan Dr., Menasha, 54952
Nickel, Leander, (Retired), 600 S. Webster Ave., 54301
O'Brien, John, (Retired), 502 N. Front St., Apt. 4, De Pere, 54115-2546
O'Brien, William, (Retired), E490 County Road KB, Denmark, 54208-9332
Radetski, Paul J., (Retired), 200 DeLeers St., Apt. 7, 54302
Rank, Robert F., (Retired), TX. Tel: . 772 W. Rio San Pedro, Green Valley, AZ 85614
Reuter, John F., (Retired), Apartado 46, Tlaxiaco, Oaxca Mexico 69800
Rhyner, Robert E., (Retired), 340 W. St. Joseph St., #5, 54301
Ryan, Dennis M., (Retired), 139 S. Madison St., 54301

Schiavone, Robert W., (Retired), 4515 W. Clayton Crest Ave., Greenfield, 53220
Serafini, Augustine, (Retired), 2804 Oakwood Ln., Oshkosh, 54904-8406
Smet, Leroy R., (Retired), N3640 Rocky Mountain Dr., New London, 54961
Stengel, William J., (Retired), W8445 Germantown Rd., Crivitz, 54114
Strebel, Roger W., (Retired), 17444 Riggin St., Townsend, 54175
Suess, Milton M., (Retired), 1722 Alfred Dr., Apt. C3, Luxemburg, 54217-1371
Taddy, Jerome J., (Retired), WI Veterans Home, 600 Mitchell Ave., HO511, King, 54946
Taylor, Peter, (Retired), 1339 Nelson St., 54304
Van De Kreeke, William L., J.C.L., (Retired), 376-A Wyldewood Dr., Oshkosh, 54904
Van De Loo, Willard J., (Retired), 825 E. River Dr., #4, De Pere, 54115
Van Deuren, John H., (Retired), 1490 Capitol Dr., #12, 54303
Vanden Hogen, Paul, (Retired), 224 Iroquois Ave, Unit 2, 54301-1994
Vander Heyden, William F., (Retired), 2062 Wasatch Dr., Sarasota, FL 34235-9173
Vennix, James J., (Retired), 28 Shadow Woods Ln., Waupaca, 54981
Weber, Frank N., (Retired), 2301 Mary Ave., New Holstein, 53061-1242
Werner, Justin, (Retired), N1682 Ridgeway Dr., Greenville, 54942.

Permanent Deacons:
Abts, Anthony J., St. Therese, Appleton
Agnew, Thomas C., Holy Rosary, Kewaunee
Ambrosius, Raymond G. Jr., St. Edward, Mackville; St. Nicholas, Freedom
Bahnaman, Richard D., St. Francis of Assisi Church, Manitowoc
Banker, Kenneth J., St. Martin Church, Cecil
Beehner, Robert, St. Francis of Assisi Church, Manitowoc
Bennin, Dennis G., Holy Spirit, Kimberly
Berg, Patrick G., St. Anthony, Tigerton; St. Mary, Marion; Holy Family-St. William, Wittenberg; St. Mary, Leopolis
Bilgrien, Kenneth, Pastoral Coord., St. Denis, Shiocton; St. Patrick, Stephensville
Birr, Frank, St. Peter the Fisherman, Two Rivers
Boeldt, Alan L., St. Francis of Assisi Church, Manitowoc
Boucher, Paul, (Retired), Gresham
Brandt, Michael J., St. Anthony, Tigerton; St. Mary, Marion; Holy Family - St. William, Wittenberg
Bricco, Howard, St. Anthony, Tigerton; St. Mary, Marion; Holy Family-St. William, Wittenberg; St. Mary, Leopolis
Brulla, Paul J., St. Rose, Clintonville; St. Mary, Bear Creek
Bundra, John J., Nativity of Our Lord, Green Bay
Bures, Andrew P., St. Wenceslaus, Neva; St. John, Antigo; Ss. Mary & Hyacinth, Antigo
Burkel, William J., Prince of Peace Church, Green Bay
Cibula, Paul J., St. Matthew, Green Bay
Coenen, Donald F., (Retired), De Pere
Corey, Bruce H., Holy Cross, Kaukauna
Cross, Gerald H., St. Leonard, Laona; St. Huber Mission, Newald
Dabeck, Michael W., Nativity of Our Lord, Green Bay
De Groot, Vincent M., (Retired), Little Chute
Debroux, Anthony J., St. Joseph/Holy Family, Phlox
DeCleene, Kevin, St. Norbert College Parish, De Pere
Dedman, Clarence F., St. Joseph, Appleton
DeYoung, David L., St. Mary Church, Greenville
Dolezal, Michael, St. Francis of Assisi, Manitowoc
Doran, William V., St. Mary of the Lake, Lakewood
Downey, Timothy E., St. Thomas More, Appleton
DuBois, Ray, St. Thomas More, Appleton
Dvorak, Richard B., St. Mary Church, Menasha; St. John Church, Menasha
Eash, Michael J., St. Bernard, Appleton
Ebben, Mark A., Holy Cross, Kaukauna
Elfering, Richard F., St. Mary, Crivitz; St. Agnes Parish, Amberg; St. Augustine, Parish, Wausaukee
Farrell, Mark J., St. Joseph Church, Appleton
Fuller, Mark, St. Michael Parish, Keshena; St. Francis Solanus Parish, Gresham; St. Anthony Parish, Neopit
Gard, Peter J., St. Anne, Coleman/Lena
Gauthier, James R., St. Mary, De Pere; St. Francis Xavier, De Pere
Gelhar, G. Patrick, St. Jude the Apostle Church, Oshkosh
Gigure, Donald J., (Retired), Appleton
Gleichner, Paul J., St. Peter the Fisherman Church, Two Rivers
Gonzalez, Ernesto L. Jr., St. Therese, Appleton
Grey, Gregory A., St. Raphael the Archangel, Oshkosh
Grimm, Paul K., St. Joseph, Wautoma
Gritton, Thomas, St. Gabriel the Archangel, Neenah
Grube, Kurt L., St. Patrick, Menasha
Grzeca, Michael G., Pastoral Leader, St. Martin, Cecil
Haak, Randall A., St. Katharine Drexel Church, Kaukauna
Hanley, Thomas J., (Retired), Antigo
Hartman, Thomas W., (Retired), Phlox
Heider, James P., St. Joseph and Immaculate Conception, Oneida
Hibbs, Mark R., St. Mary, Maplewood; Corpus Christi, Sturgeon Bay
Hocking, Richard A., Most Blessed Sacrament, Oshkosh
Hofacker, Jeffrey J., St. Edward, Mackville; St. Nicholas, Freedom; St. Mary, Greenville
Holschbach, Keith, St. Bernard Church, Green Bay
Hornacek, Robert, St. Matthew, Green Bay
Humpal, Gregory J., St. Edward and Isidore, Flintville
Ingala, John, St. Raphael the Archangel, Oshkosh
Jaeckels, Randy, Holy Rosary, New Holstein; Sts. Peter and Paul, Kiel; St. Ann, Saint Anna
Kabat, Kenneth, St. Clare Church, Greenleaf/Askeaton/Wrightstown
Kaszynski, Walter, (Retired), Oconto
Kieltyka, Conrad J., St. Francis Xavier Cathedral, Green Bay; St. John the Evangelist, Green Bay
Klister, Cyril, Holy Spirit Church, Kimberly/Darboy
Knier, Bernard (Pat) P., SS. Peter & Paul Church, Kiel; Holy Rosary, New Holstein & St. Ann, St. Anna
Kopydlowski, Kenneth D., St. Joseph, Sturgeon Bay; SS. Peter & Paul, Institute
Koszalinski, Daniel T., Sacred Heart Church, Appleton
Kowalski, David J., (Retired), Baileys Harbor
Kuborn, Gerald G., (Retired), Little Chute
Laurent, Daniel, St. Margaret Mary, Neenah
Le Mere, David, Green Bay
LeGreve, Mark V., St. Peter the Fisherman, Two Rivers
Lehman, Joseph M., St. Edward, Mackville; St. Nicholas, Freedom
Lonick, James, Sacred Heart, Shawano
Madden, Michael, St. Clare, Wrightstown/Greenleaf/Askeaton
Mahoney, Thomas J., St. Francis Xavier Cathedral & St. John, Green Bay
Majewski, Dennis, Assumption of the Blessed Virgin Mary Church, Pulaski; St. Stanislaus Parish, Hofa Park; St. Casimir Park, Krakow
Maloney, John R., (Retired), Suamico
Mastalish, Larry V., St. Bernard Church, Green Bay
Matuszak, Richard J., St. John, Seymour; St. Sebastian, Isaar
Meidl, Richard, Peoria, AZ
Merrick, Craig, St. Thomas More Church, Appleton
Mervilde, Michael J., St. Joseph, St. Jude, Annunciation & St. Patrick, Green Bay
Meyer, Steven J., St. Elizabeth Ann Seton, Green Bay
Miech, Richard M., St. Germaine, WI
Miller, Robert J., Immaculate Conception, Luxemburg; Holy Trinity, Casco/Slovan
Mullins, Mark G., St. Elizabeth Ann Seton, Green Bay
Naidl, Clarence, St. James, Cooperstown; St. Joseph, Kellnersville
Nardi, Gerald A., (Retired), Niagara
Nass, Donald, (Retired), Appleton
Nelesen, Kenneth R., (Retired), Manitowoc
Newhouse, Don, (Retired), Kaukauna
Otradovec, Byron A., (Retired), Florida
Parker, David J., Assumption of the Blessed Virgin Mary Parish, Pulaski; St. Stanislaus Parish, Hofa Park; St. Casimir Parish, Krakow
Penzenstadler, Robert, (Retired), Arizona
Precourt, Robert L., Pastoral Leader - St. Mark, Redgranite; Sacred Heart of Jesus, Poy Sippi
Prickette, Jeffrey M., St. Paul, Combined Locks
Quinette, Harvey J., (Retired), De Pere
Reed, Maurice F., (Retired)
Reilly, Timothy G., General Dir., Diocesan Curia & Resurrection Church, Green Bay; Resurrection, Green Bay
Rocchi, Steven, (Retired), Wild Rose
Ropson, Donald J., Resurrection Church, Green Bay
Sambs, Kenneth F., (Retired), Tigerton
Sanchez, Luis, St. Willebrord Church, Green Bay
Scheuer, David J., All Saints, Denmark; Holy Trinity, New Denmark; St. Mary, Glenmore/Stark
Schmidt, Gilbert F., St. Bernadette, Appleton; Sacred Heart, Appleton
Schmidt, Michael, (Retired)
Schraufnagel, George J., St. John Nepomucene Parish, Little Chute
Schraufnagel, Gerard J., St. Mary, Appleton
Schultz, Donald E., St. John and St. Parish, Menasha
Schumacher, Charles R., St. Mary Church, Peshtigo; SS. Joseph & Edward, Walsh
Seymour, Robert, St. Pius X Parish, Appleton
Simon, Richard S., St. Pius X, Appleton
Steffen, James E., (Retired)
Terrien, Bernard, St. Bernard Parish, Green Bay
Teske, Glenn, (Retired), Green Bay
Thetreau, Jerome E., Holy Family Church, Marinette
Tomaszewski, Thomas, St. Francis of Assisi, Manitowoc
Torres, Manuel, St. John the Baptist, Howard
Umentum, Paul, St. Mary of the Angels Church, Green Bay; St. Peter & Paul, Green Bay; Asst. Episcopal & Diocesan Master of Ceremonies
Van Eperen, David G., St. John Nepomucene, Little Chute
VandeHey, Steven, St. Katharine Drexler, Kaukauna
Vander Bloomen, Michael D., Our Lady of Lourdes Church, DePere
Vang, Shuying (Joe), St. Bernard, Appleton
Vanness, Gary, St. Edward, Mackville; St. Nicholas, Freedom
Vincent, John, Holy Family Memorial Hospital, Manitowoc
Vincent, Robert H., (Retired), Appleton
Wagnitz, Daniel, Annunciation of the BVM, St. Joseph, St. Jude & St. Patrick, Green Bay
Wetzel, Donald J., (Retired), Appleton
Whitcomb, Patrick, (Retired), Green Bay
Wilhelm, Gary, St. Gregory, Saint Nazianz; Holy Trinity, School Hill
Williams, Nicholas J., St. John the Baptist Church, Howard
Wood, Lincoln, Pastoral Leader, St. Rose, Clintonville; St. Mary, Bear Creek
Zajicek, Daniel W., St. Pius X Parish, Appleton
Zebroski, Michael R., St. Clare, Greenleaf/Askeaton/Wrightstown
Zimmer, Steven, St. Thomas the Apostle, Newton
Cheskie, Peter A., Most Blessed Sacrament, Oshkosh
Coenen, Jerry H., Green Bay
Doxtator, Everett L., (Retired), Oneida
Ellis, Robert F., St. Peter and Paul, Green Bay
Jozwiak, Thomas V., (Retired), Tigerton
Laurant, John H., (Retired), Green Bay
Letourneaux, Stephen T., (Retired), Portage.

INSTITUTIONS LOCATED IN DIOCESE

[A] SEMINARIES, RELIGIOUS OR SCHOLASTICATES

DE PERE. *St. Norbert Abbey*, 1016 N. Broadway, De Pere, 54115-2697. Tel: 920-337-4300; Fax: 920-337-4328; Email: prior@norbertines.org; Web: www.norbertines.org. Rev. Bradley R. Vanden Branden, O.Praem., Prior; Rt. Rev. Gary J. Neville, O.Praem., J.C.D., Abbot; Revs. Dane J. Radecki, O.Praem., Abbot; John P. Kastenholz, O.-Praem., Sec. & Treas.; Rt. Revs. E. Thomas De Wane, O.Praem., Abbot; Jerome G. Tremel, O.-Praem., Abbot; Very Rev. James T. Baraniak, O.-Praem., Asst. Dir., Formation - Master Professed; Revs. David M. Komatz, O.Praem., Dir., Formation - Novice Master; Bartholomew A. Agar, O.Praem.; Peter Ambting; Sengole Arockia Dass; Michael Brennan; Richard Chiles; Andrew G. Cribben, O.-Praem.; Kenneth J. De Groot, O.Praem., (Retired); Vincent De Leers; Rowland C. De Peaux, O.-Praem.; Matthew Dougherty, O.Praem.; Mark D. Falcone, O.Praem; Angelo J. Feldkamp, O.Praem.; Roderick R. Fenzl, O.Praem.; Robert K. Finnegan, O.Praem.; Jay J. Fostner, O.Praem., Ph.D.; Michael F. Frisch, O.Praem.; Bro. Steven J. Herro, O.-Praem.; Revs. Benny Jacob, O.Praem.; Samuel D. Jadin, O.Praem.; Bro. Terrence R. Lauerman, O.-Praem.; Revs. John P. MacCarthy, O.Praem.; Alfred A. McBride, O.Praem.; David R. McElroy, O.Praem.; Brendan J. McKeough, O.Praem.; Conan P. Mulrooney, O.Praem.; James P. Neilson, O.Praem.; Brian J. Prunty, O.Praem.; Christin Raj; Peter J. Renard, O. Praem.; William H. Ribbens, O.Praem.; Stephen J. Rossey, O.Praem.; Sebastian Schalk, O.Praem.; Timothy D. Shillcox, O.Praem.; Bro. Jacob Sircy; Revs. John M. Tourangeau, O.Praem.; Steven J. Vanden Boogard, O.-

Praem., (Retired); Michael J. Weber, O.Praem. Brothers 3; Priests 48; Seminarians 3; Total Staff 54.

[B] COLLEGES AND UNIVERSITIES

DE PERE. *St. Norbert College*, 100 Grant St., De Pere, 54115. Tel: 920-403-3238; Email: joanne.blascak@snc.edu; Email: oie@snc.edu; Web: www.snc.edu. Joanne Blascak, Admin. Religious Teachers 2; Students 2,228.

MANITOWOC. *Silver Lake College of the Holy Family* (1935) 2406 S. Alverno Rd., Manitowoc, 54220-9319. Tel: 920-684-6691; Fax: 920-684-7082; Email: janeen.meifert@sl.edu; Web: www.sl.edu. Robert Callahan, Pres.; Sr. Louise Hembrecht, O.S.F., Vice Pres. Sponsored by the Franciscan Sisters of Christian Charity. Sisters 8; Students 444; Lay Faculty 44.

[C] HIGH SCHOOLS, DIOCESAN

MANITOWOC. *Roncalli High School* (1965) 2000 Mirro Dr., Manitowoc, 54220-6799. Tel: 920-682-8801; Fax: 920-686-8110; Email: canhalt@roncallijets.net; Web: www.roncallijets.net. Mr. John Stelzer, Pres.; Mr. Tim Olson, Prin.; Mr. Taylor Geiger, Campus Min.; Mrs. Sue Rohrer, Librarian. Diocese of Green Bay. Religious Teachers 2; Lay Teachers 30; Sisters 2; Students 247.

MARINETTE. *St. Thomas Aquinas Academy - Secondary Campus*, 1200 Main St., Marinette, 54143-2594. Tel: 715-735-7481; Fax: 715-735-3375; Email: principal.staa@gmail.com; Web: www.thomas-aquinas.org. Mr. Michael Cattani, Prin. Lay Teachers 12; Students 48.

[D] HIGH SCHOOLS, PRIVATE

GREEN BAY. *Notre Dame de la Baie Academy*, 610 Maryhill Dr., 54303-2092. Tel: 920-429-6100; Fax: 920-429-6168; Email: kshaw@notredameacademy.com; Email: cdunlap@notredameacademy.com; Web: www.notredameacademy.com. Kevin Shaw, Pres.; Mr. Patrick Browne, Prin.; Mr. Greg Masarik, Assoc. Prin.; Mr. Ken Flaten, Vice Pres. Business Opers.; Katie Gelb, Librarian; Rev. Brad Vanden Branden, O.Praem., Chap. Religious Teachers 1; Lay Teachers 52; Students 774.

[E] ELEMENTARY SCHOOLS, DIOCESAN

KIEL. *Divine Savior Catholic Elementary School, Inc.*, 423 Fremont St., Kiel, 53042. Tel: 920-894-3533; Email: divinesaviorcatholicschool@gmail.com; Web: www.divinesaviorschool.org. Mr. Kerry Sievert, Prin.; Mr. Joseph Zenk, Pastoral Leader. Clergy 1; Lay Teachers 13; Students 82.

STURGEON BAY. *St. John Bosco Catholic School, Inc.*, (Grades PreK-8), 730 W. Maple St., Sturgeon Bay, 54235. Tel: 920-743-4144; Fax: 920-743-4106; Email: vickie.dassler@johnboscoschool.org. Vickie Dassler, Prin. Lay Teachers 13; Priests 2; Students 123.

[F] CONSOLIDATED SCHOOLS

GREEN BAY. *Green Bay Area Catholic Education, Inc. (GRACE)*, 1087 Kellogg St., 54303. Tel: 920-499-7330; Fax: 920-272-6564; Email: graceoffice@gracesystem.org; Web: www.gracesystem.org. Kimberly Desotell, Pres. GRACE is a 9-school system: Father Allouez Catholic School, Holy Cross Catholic School, Holy Family School, Notre Dame School of De Pere, Our Lady of Lourdes Catholic School, St. Bernard Catholic School, St. John the Baptist School, St. John Paul II Classical School, and St. Thomas More Catholic School.

GRACE Holy Family School, 1204 S. Fisk St., 54303-2299. Tel: 920-494-1931; Fax: 920-494-4942; Email: hfsoffice@gracesystem.org. Steve Gromala, Prin. Students 229.

GRACE Father Allouez Catholic School, Resurrection Campus, 333 Hilltop Dr., 54301-2799. Tel: 920-336-3230; Email: resoffice@gracesystem.org; Web: www.fatherallouezschool.org. Kay L. Franz, Prin. Students 99.

GRACE Father Allouez Catholic School, St. Matthew Campus, 2575 S. Webster Ave., 54301-2998. Tel: 920-432-5223; Email: smsoffice@gracesystem.org; Web: www.fatherallouezschool.org. Kay L. Franz, Prin. Students 185.

GRACE St. Bernard Catholic School, 2020 Hillside Ln., 54302-4099. Tel: 920-468-5026; Fax: 920-468-3478; Email: cblahnik@gracesystem.org; Web: www.stbernardgb.org. Crystal Blahnik, Prin. Students 462.

GRACE Holy Cross School, Bay Settlement, 3002 Bay Settlement Rd., 54311-7302. Tel: 920-468-0625; Fax: 920-866-4000; Email: sgast@gracesystem.org; Web: www.holycrossfamily.org. Sharon Gast, Prin. Students 121.

GRACE Notre Dame Elementary & Middle School, De Pere, Elementary School, 100 S. Huron St., De Pere, 54115-2819. Tel: 920-337-1103; Email: mmares@gracesystem.org; Web: notredameofdepere.com. Molly Mares, Prin. Clergy 2; Lay Teachers 40; Students 350.

GRACE Our Lady of Lourdes School, De Pere, 1305 Lourdes Ave., De Pere, 54115-1018. Tel: 920-336-3091; Email: jyoung@gracesystem.org; Web: www.lourdesschooldepere.org. Jeff Young, Prin. Students 180.

GRACE St. John the Baptist School, 2561 Glendale Ave., 54313-6821. Tel: 920-434-3822; Fax: 920-434-5016; Email: amulloy@gracesystem.org. Andrew Mulloy, Prin. Students 273.

GRACE St. Thomas More School, 1420 Harvey St., 54302. Tel: 920-432-8242; Email: oamor@gracesystem.org; Web: www.stmoregb.org. Olgamar Amor, Prin. Students 145.

GRACE St. John Paul II Classical School, 1204 Fisk St., 54304. Tel: 920-494-1931; Email: sjpiioffice@gracesystem.org. Frank Nicely, Headmaster. Students 53.

ANTIGO. *All Saints Catholic Schools, Inc.* (1998) (Grades PreK-8), 419 6th Ave., Antigo, 54409. Tel: 715-623-4835; Tel: 715-623-2211; Fax: 715-623-3202; Email: pgaluska@ascscrusaders.org; Web: www.ascscrusaders.org. Mr. Paul Galuska, Admin. & Prin.; Jenny Thom, Librarian. Religious Teachers 1; Lay Teachers 14; Priests 2; Students 200.

APPLETON. *St. Francis Xavier Catholic School System, Inc.*, 101 E. Northland Ave., Appleton, 54911. Tel: 920-735-9380; Fax: 920-735-1787; Email: rdubois@xaviercatholicschools.org; Web: www.xaviercatholicschools.org. Deacon Ray DuBois, Pres.; Dr. John Ravizza, Superintendent. 4-school system: of St. Francis Xavier High School, St. Francis Xavier Middle School, St. Francis Xavier Elementary-Marquette & St. Francis Xavier Elementary-McDonald, Appleton. Lay Teachers 121; Students 1,500.

St. Francis Xavier High School Coed 1600 W. Prospect Ave., Appleton, 54914. Tel: 920-733-6632; Email: mmauthe@xaviercatholicschools.org; Web: www.xaviercatholicschools.org. Deacon Ray DuBois, Pres.; Mr. Mike Mauthe, Prin. Lay Teachers 44; Students 520.

St. Francis Xavier Middle School, (Grades 5-8), 2626 N. Oneida St., Appleton, 54911. Tel: 920-730-8849; Fax: 920-730-4147; Email: rbires@xaviercatholicschools.org; Web: www.xaviercatholicschools.org. 101 E. Northland Ave., Appleton, 54911. Deacon Ray DuBois, Pres.; Robert Bires, Prin. Lay Teachers 39; Students 427.

St. Francis Xavier Elementary - Marquette, (Grades PreK-4), 500 W. Marquette St., Appleton, 54911. Tel: 920-733-4918; Fax: 920-733-7269; Email: lbarnett@xaviercatholicschools.org; Web: www.xaviercatholicschools.org. 101 E. Northland Ave., Appleton, 54911. Deacon Ray DuBois, Pres.; Laura Barnett, Prin. Lay Teachers 17; Students 274.

St. Francis Xavier Elementary - McDonald, (Grades PreK-4), 1810 N. McDonald St., Appleton, 54911. Tel: 920-739-7826; Fax: 920-739-2376; Email: atapelt@xaviercatholicschools.org; Web: www.xaviercatholicschools.org. 101 E. Northland Ave., Appleton, 54911. Deacon Ray DuBois, Pres.; Alena Tapelt, Prin. Lay Teachers 21; Students 268.

CATO. *St. Mary/St. Michael School*, (Grades PreSchool-8), 19 S. County Rd. J, Cato, 54230-8329. Tel: 920-775-4366; Fax: 920-775-4365; Email: rhamacher@stmarystmichael.com. Rick Hamacher, Prin. Lay Staff 10; Priests 1.

KAUKAUNA. *St. Ignatius of Loyola Catholic School*, 220 Doty St., Kaukauna, 54130-2108. Tel: 920-766-0186; Fax: 920-759-2428; Email: headmaster@stignatiuskaukauna.org; Web: www.stignatiuskaukauna.org. Mr. Lawrence Konetzke, Headmaster & Admin. Lay Teachers 16; Students 158.

Holy Cross Campus, 220 Doty St., Kaukauna, 54130-2188. Tel: 920-766-0186. Mr. Lawrence Konetzke, Prin.

MANITOWOC. *St. Francis of Assisi School*, 1408 Waldo Blvd., Manitowoc, 54220. Tel: 920-683-6892; Email: kyle.kapinos@sfamanitowoc.com. Mr. Steve Thiele, Middle School Prin.; Kyle Kapinos, Elementary Schl. Prin. Religious Teachers 70; Lay Teachers 28; Total Enrollment 440.

MARINETTE. *St. Thomas Aquinas Academy*, (Grades PreK-12), 1200 Main St., Marinette, 54143. Tel: 715-735-7481; Fax: 715-735-3375; Email: accounting.staa@gmail.com; Email: principal.staa@gmail.com; Web: www.thomas-aquinas.org. Mr. Michael Cattani, Prin. Lay Teachers 16; Students 110.

NEENAH/MENASHA. *St. Mary Catholic Schools, Inc.*, 1050 Zephyr Dr., Neenah, 54956. Tel: 920-722-7796; Tel: 920-215-7442; Fax: 920-722-5940; Email: henglebert@smcatholicschools.org; Email: lmichalkiewicz@smcatholicschools.org; Email: jlee@smcatholicschools.org; Web: www.smcatholicschools.org. Helen Englebert, Pres. 5-school system: St. Gabriel School, St. Margaret Mary School & St. Mary Catholic High School, Neenah and St. Mary Elementary School & St. Mary Catholic Middle School, Neenah.

St. Mary Catholic High School, 1050 Zephyr Dr., Neenah, 54956-1389. Tel: 920-722-7796; Fax: 920-722-5940; Email: lmichalkiewicz@smcatholicschools.org. Helen Englebert, Pres.

St. Mary Catholic Middle School, (Grades 6-8), 1000 Zephyr Dr., Neenah, 54956. Tel: 920-722-7796; Email: lmichalkiewicz@smcatholicschools.org. Lay Teachers 15; Students 156.

St. Gabriel Elementary, (Grades PreSchool-5), 900 Geiger St., Neenah, 54956. Tel: 920-722-7796; Email: lmichalkiewicz@smcatholicschools.org. Helen Englebert, Pres. Lay Teachers 10; Students 125.

St. Margaret Mary Elementary, (Grades PreSchool-5), 610 Division St., Neenah, 54956. Tel: 920-722-7796; Email: lmichalkiewicz@smcatholicschools.org. 1050 Zephyr Dr., Neenah, 54956. Helen Englebert, Pres. Lay Teachers 20; Students 250.

St. Mary Elementary, (Grades PreSchool-5), 540 Second St., Menasha, 54952. Tel: 920-722-7796; Email: lmichalkiewicz@smcatholicschools.org. Helen Englebert, Pres. Lay Teachers 8; Students 98.

OSHKOSH. *Lourdes Academy of Oshkosh, Wisconsin, Inc.*, (Grades PreK-12), 250 N. Sawyer St., Oshkosh, 54902. Tel: 920-426-3626; Fax: 920-230-2366; Email: jdinegan@lourdes.today; Web: www.lourdes.today. John Dinegan, Pres.

Unified Catholic Schools, Oshkosh Area Catholic Education System Lay Teachers 70; Students 631.

Lourdes Academy Middle & High School (1959) (Grades 5-12), Coed 110 N. Sawyer St., Oshkosh, 54902. Tel: 920-235-5670; Fax: 920-235-7453; Email: info@lourdes.today; Web: www.lourdes.today. David Mikesell, Prin. Lay Teachers 29; Students 325.

Lourdes Academy Elementary School, (Grades PreK-4), 1207 Oregon St., Oshkosh, 54902. Tel: 920-235-4060; Fax: 920-426-6430; Email: info@lourdes.today; Web: www.lourdes.today. Mrs. Amy Geffers, Prin. Lay Teachers 21; Students 300.

PESHTIGO. *St. Thomas Aquinas - Elementary*, (Grades PreK-5), 171 S. Wood Ave., Peshtigo, 54157. Tel: 715-582-4041; Fax: 715-582-1165; Email: principal.staa@gmail.com. Mr. Michael Cattani, Prin. Religious Teachers 1; Lay Teachers 5; Students 66.

[G] GENERAL HOSPITALS

GREEN BAY. *St. Mary's Hospital Medical Center*, 1726 Shawano Ave., 54303-3282. Tel: 920-498-4200; Fax: 920-497-3707; Email: mary.salm@hshs.org; Email: Mark.Repenshek@hshs.org; Web: www.stmgb.org. Therese Pandl, Pres.; Brian Charlier, COO; Mark Repenshek, Exec. Hospital Sisters of Third Order of St. Francis. Bassinets 12; Bed Capacity 158; Tot Asst. Annually 102,803; Total Staff 607.

HSHS St. Vincent Hospital (1888) P.O. Box 13508, 54307-3508. Tel: 920-433-0111; Tel: 920-433-8163; Fax: 920-431-3275; Email: Amy.Bulpitt@hshs.org; Web: www.stvincenthospital.org. Therese Pandl, CEO. Hospital Sisters of the Third Order of St. Francis. Bed Capacity 277; Tot Asst. Annually 204,241; Total Staff 2,072.

ANTIGO. *Langlade Hospital - Hotel Dieu of St. Joseph of Antigo Wisconsin* dba Aspirus Langlade Hospital, 112 E. 5th Ave., Antigo, 54409. Tel: 715-623-2331; Fax: 715-623-9440; Email: andy.barth@aspirus.org; Email: meghan.mattek@aspirus.org; Web: www.aspirus.org. Andrew Barth, CEO; Sisters Dolores Demulling, Mission & Values Coord.; Adele Demulling, R.H.S.J., Pastoral Care Chap.; Rev. Hillary Andebo, Chap. Religious Hospitallers of St. Joseph. Bed Capacity 23; Tot Asst. Annually 19,070; Total Staff 513.

Religious Hospitalliers of St. Joseph (1636) Sisters Res.: 650 Langlade Rd., Antigo, 55409. Tel: 715-623-4615; Fax: 715-623-4615; Email: dolores.demulling@aspirus.org; Web: www.rhsj.org/. Sr. Dolores Demulling, Contact Person. Sisters 2.

APPLETON. *Ascension NE Wisconsin, Inc.* dba Ascension NE Wisconsin - St. Elizabeth Campus, 1506 S. Oneida St., Appleton, 54915-1305. Tel: 920-738-2000; Email: timothy.waldoch@ascension.org; Web: healthcare.ascension.org. Travis Andersen, Regl. Pres.; Timothy Waldoch, Chief Mission Integration Officer; Antonina Olszewski, Dir., Spiritual Svcs. Sponsored by Ascension Health Ministries (Ascension Sponsor), a public juridic person.

St. Elizabeth Hospital, Inc. Bed Capacity 190; Tot Asst. Annually 21,526; Total Staff 878.

CHILTON. *Ascension Calumet Hospital, Inc.*, 614 Memorial Dr., Chilton, 53014-1568.
Tel: 920-849-2386; Fax: 920-849-7510; Email: timothy.waldoch@ascension.org; Web: healthcare.ascension.org. Travis Andersen, Regl. Pres.; Timothy Waldoch, Chief Mission Integration Officer; Antonina Olszewski, Dir., Spiritual Care. Sponsored by Ascension Health Ministries (Ascension Sponsor), a public juridic person. Bed Capacity 25; Tot Asst. Annually 2,702; Total Staff 108.

MANITOWOC. *Holy Family Memorial, Inc.* (1898) 2300 Western Ave., P.O. Box 1450, Manitowoc, 54221-1450. Tel: 920-320-2011;
Tel: 800-994-3662 (Toll free); Fax: 920-320-5110; Email: services@hfmhealth.org; Web: www.hfmhealth.org. Brett Norell, Pres.; Sr. Kay Klackner, O.S.F., Dir. Bed Capacity 87; Franciscan Sisters of Christian Charity 1; Tot Asst. Annually 431,000; Total Staff 1,122; Licensed Beds 167; Maternity Rooms 15; Patient Rooms 72.

OCONTO FALLS. **St. Clare Memorial Hospital, Inc.*, 855 S. Main St., Oconto Falls, 54154. Tel: 920-846-3444 ; Email: mark.repenshek@hshs.org; Email: mary.salm@hshs.org; Web: www.stclarememorial.org. Therese Pandl, Pres. & Dir.; Mark Repenshek, Exec.; Christopher Brabant, Exec. Bed Capacity 25; Tot Asst. Annually 18,504; Total Staff 143.

OSHKOSH. *Mercy Medical Center of Oshkosh, Inc.* dba Ascension NE Wisconsin - Mercy Campus, 500 S. Oakwood Rd., P.O. Box 3370, Oshkosh, 54904.
Tel: 920-223-0120; Email: Timothy.Waldoch@ascension.org; Web: healthcare.ascension.org. Travis Andersen, Regl. Pres.; Timothy Waldoch, Chief Mission Integration Officer; Antonina Olszewski, Dir., Spiritual Svcs. Sponsored by Ascension Health Ministries (Ascension Sponsor), a public juridic person; Merged into St. Elizabeth Hospital, Inc. n.k.a. Ascension NE Wisconsin, Inc. Bed Capacity 110; Patients Asst Anual. 11,333; Total Staff 407.

STURGEON BAY. **Door County Memorial Hospital* dba Door County Medical Center (1943) 323 S. 18th Ave., Sturgeon Bay, 54235-1401. Tel: 920-743-5566 ; Email: Mark.Repenshek@hshs.org; Email: Mary.Salm@hshs.org; Email: Brian.Stephens@dcmedical.org; Web: www.dcmedical.org. Brian Stephens, Pres.; Therese Pandl, Dir.; Mark Repenshek, Exec. In partnership with Hospital Sisters Health System. Bassinets 4; Bed Capacity, Critical Access Hospital 25; Tot Asst. Annually 146,884; Total Staff 681.

[H] PROTECTIVE INSTITUTIONS

GREEN BAY. *St. Vincent Hospital* dba Libertas, 835 South Van Buren, 54301. Tel: 920-433-0111; Email: Mark.Repenshek@hshs.org; Email: Mary.Salm@hshs.org; Web: www.stvincenthospital.org. Therese Pandl, Pres. & Dir.; Brian Charlier, COO; Mark Repenshek, Exec. St. Vincent Hospital of the Hospital Sisters of the Third Order of St. Francis; St. Vincent Hospital of the Hospital Sisters of the Third Order of St. Francis d/b/a Libertas Treatment Center; St. Vincent Hospital d/b/a Prevea Health. Bassinets 24; Bed Capacity 517; Tot Asst. Annually 163,132; Total Staff 2,055.

[I] HOMES FOR AGED

GREEN BAY. *St. Paul Elder Services, Inc.* dba McCormick Assisted Living (1921) 212 Iroquois Ave., 54301-1918. Tel: 920-437-0883;
Fax: 920-437-2696; Email: sondran@stpaulelders.org; Web: www.mccormickassistedliving.com. 316 E. 14th St., Kaukauna, 54130. Sondra Norder, CEO; Rev. Allen A. Geiser, Chap., (Retired). Bed Capacity 69; Residents 50; Tot Asst. Annually 80; Total Staff 33; Nursing Staff 9.

KAUKAUNA. *St. Paul Elder Services, Inc.*, 316 E. 14th St., Kaukauna, 54130. Tel: 920-766-6020;
Fax: 920-766-7945; Email: sondran@stpaulelders.org; Web: stpaulelders.org. Sondra Norder, Pres. & CEO; Becky Reichelt, COO & Admin. Bed Capacity 242; Tot Asst. Annually 1,500; Total Staff 400.

St. Paul Home, 316 E. 14th St., Kaukauna, 54130.
Tel: 920-766-6020; Fax: 920-766-9161. Bed Capacity 129.

St. Paul Manor, 224 E. 14th St., Kaukauna, 54130.
Tel: 920-766-6020; Fax: 920-462-5912. Total Apartments 24.

St. Paul Villa, 312 E. 14th St., Kaukauna, 54130.
Tel: 920-766-6020; Fax: 920-766-7945. Total Apartments 89.

MANITOWOC. *Felician Village*, 1635 S. 21st St., Manitowoc, 54220-5652. Tel: 920-684-7171;
Fax: 920-684-0240; Email: bfricke@felicianvillage.org; Web: www.felicianvillage.org. Frank Soltys, Pres. Bed Capacity 284; Tot Asst. Annually 636; Total Staff 280.

Felician Village Inc. dba The Gardens at Felician Village, 1635 S. 21st St., Manitowoc, 54220-5652.
Tel: 920-684-7171; Fax: 920-684-0240; Email: bfricke@felicianvillage.org; Web: felicianvillage.org. Roselle Holschbach, Mgr. Independent Living. Apartments 122.

St. Mary's Home for the Aged, Inc. dba St. Mary's at Felician Village, 1635 S. 21st St., Manitowoc, 54220-5652. Tel: 920-684-7171; Fax: 920-684-0240 ; Web: felicianvillage.org. Aged Residents 84; Sisters 4.

St. Mary's Home for the Aged, Inc. dba The Court at Felician Village, 1635 S. 21st St., Manitowoc, 54220-5652. Tel: 920-684-7171; Fax: 920-684-0240 ; Email: lvoda@felicianvillage.org; Web: felicianvillage.org. Total Apartments 48.

St. Mary's Home for the Aged, Inc. dba The Villa at Felician Village, 1635 S. 21st St., Manitowoc, 54220-5652. Tel: 920-684-7171; Fax: 920-684-0240 ; Email: lvoda@felicianvillage.org; Web: felicianvillage.org. Frank Soltys, CEO. Beds 32.

NEENAH. *Assisi Homes of Neenah, Inc.* (1989) 210 Byrd Ave., Neenah, 54956. Tel: 920-729-1771;
Fax: 920-729-1797; Tel: 303-830-3300; Email: mrankin@mercyhousing.org; Web: www.mercyhousing.org. Melissa Clayton, Contact Person. (An independent living community for Seniors.) Total in Residence 40; Total Staff 3; Housing Units 40.

NEW LONDON. *St. Joseph Residence, Inc., New London*, 107 E. Beckert Rd., New London, 54961.
Tel: 920-982-5354; Fax: 920-982-5420; Email: gblank@sjrcares.org; Web: www.stjosephresidence.com. Gidget Blank, CEO. Bed Capacity 134; Total Staff 135.

Trinity Terrace, 1835 Division St., New London, 54961. Tel: 920-982-5354; Email: gblank@sjrcares.org; Web: www.stjosephresidence.com. 107 E. Beckert Rd., New London, 54961. Gidget Blank, CEO. Total in Residence 28.

Marion Heights Apartments, 101 E. Beckert Rd., New London, 54961. Tel: 920-982-5354; Email: gblank@sjrcares.org; Web: www.stjosephresidence.com. 107 E. Beckert Rd., New London, 54961. Gidget Blank, CEO. An independent apartment owned and operated by St. Joseph Residence. Residents 26.

St. Joseph Residence - The Washington Center, Inc., 500 Washington St., New London, 54961.
Tel: 920-982-9200; Email: gblank@sjrcares.org; Web: www.stjosephresidence.com. 107 E. Beckert Rd., New London, 54961. Gidget Blank, CEO. Apartments 33.

NIAGARA. *Maryhill Manor (SNF)*, 501 Madison Ave., Niagara, 54151. Tel: 715-251-3172;
Fax: 715-251-1193; Email: maryhill@borderlandnet.net; Web: www.maryhillmanor.org. Michelle Grailer, Admin. Sponsored by School Sisters of St. Francis, Milwaukee. Tot Asst. Annually 136; Total Staff 103; Capacity 71; Nursing Care Residents 71.

[J] MONASTERIES AND RESIDENCES OF PRIESTS AND BROTHERS

GREEN BAY. *St. Mary of the Angels Friary*, 645 S. Irwin Ave., 54301-3303. Tel: 920-437-1979 (Res.); Email: stmarygb@gmail.com. Rev. Anthony Cirignani, O.F.M., Contact Person. Franciscan Friars, Assumption of the Blessed Virgin Mary Province (Order of Friars Minor).

APPLETON. *St. Fidelis Friary*, 1100 N. Ballard Rd., Appleton, 54911-5100. Tel: 920-954-8954;
Fax: 920-954-1095; Email: smaas@thecapuchins.org; Web: www.thecapuchins.org. Revs. Ralph Fellenz, O.F.M.Cap., (Retired); David J. Funk, O.F.M.-Cap.; Werner Wolf, O.F.M.Cap.; Jerome Schroeder, O.F.M.Cap.; Reynold Rynda, O.F.M.Cap., (Retired); Mel Hermann, O.F.M.Cap.; Bernie Wagner; Paschal Siler, O.F.M.Cap., (Retired); Alexis Luzi, O.F.M.Cap., (Retired); Timon Costello, O.F.-M.Cap., (Retired); Bros. John Gau, O.F.M.Cap.; Lawrence Groeschel, O.F.M.Cap., (Retired); August Seubert, O.F.M.Cap., (Retired); Revs. James Zelinsk, O.F.M.Cap.; Wilbert Lanser, (Retired); Martin Pable; Ronald Rieder, (Retired); Ronald Smith. Order of Friars Minor Capuchin. Brothers 2; Priests 16; Total Staff 9.

St. Joseph Church, 404 W. Lawrence St., Appleton, 54911-5855. Tel: 920-734-7195; Fax: 920-734-0227; Email: frjim@saintjosephparish.org; Web: www.saintjosephparish.org. Rev. James P. Leary, O.F.-M.Cap., Pastor. Order of Friars Minor Capuchin.

DE PERE. *St. Norbert Abbey* (1898) 1016 N. Broadway, De Pere, 54115-2610. Tel: 920-337-4300;
Fax: 920-337-4328; Email: prior@norbertines.org; Web: www.norbertines.org. Rt. Revs. Gary J. Neville, O.Praem., J.C.D., Abbot; Jerome G. Tremel, O.Praem., Abbot Emeritus; Revs. Peter Ambting; Bartholomew A. Agar, O.Praem.; Very Rev. James T. Baraniak, O.Praem., Prior; Revs. John L. Bostwick, O.Praem.; Andrew Ciferni, O.-Praem.; Michael Brennan, Vocations; Xavier G. Colavechio, O.Praem.; Richard Chiles; Kenneth DeGroot, O.Praem.; Vincent J. DeLeers, O.Praem.; Rowland C. DePeaux, O.Praem.; Mark D. Falcone, O.Praem; Angelo J. Feldkamp, O.Praem.; Roderick R. Fenzl, O.Praem.; Robert K. Finnegan, O.Praem.; Jay J. Fostner, O.Praem., Ph.D.; Michael F. Frisch, O.Praem.; Samuel D. Jadin, O.Praem.; John P. Kastenholz, O.Praem., Treas.; David M. Komatz, O.Praem.; John P. MacCarthy, O.Praem.; Alfred A. McBride, O.Praem., Weston, MA; David R. McElroy, O.Praem.; Brendan J. McKeough, O.Praem.; Conan P. Mulrooney, O.Praem.; James P. Neilson, O.Praem.; Brian J. Prunty, O.Praem.; Dane J. Radecki, O.Praem.; Peter J. Renard, O. Praem.; William H. Ribbens, O.Praem.; Stephen J. Rossey, O.Praem.; Sebastian Schalk, O.Praem.; Timothy D. Shillcox, O.Praem.; John M. Tourangeau, O.-Praem.; Steven J. Vanden Boogard, O.Praem., (Retired); Binu Varghese, O.Praem.; Matthew Dougherty, O.Praem.; Bro. Steven J. Herro, O.-Praem.; Revs. Benny Jacob, O.Praem.; Bradley R. Vanden Branden, O.Praem.; Bro. Terrence R. Lauerman, O.Praem.; Rev. Jude Lucier; Bro. Jacob Sircy; Rev. Michael J. Weber, O.Praem. Canons Regular of Premontre.

The Premonstratensian Fathers
NORBERT & CO., a nominee of The Premonstratensian Fathers, Norbertine Fathers
St. Norbert Abbey, Inc.
Augustine Stewardship Fund Trust
Norbertine Retirement Fund Trust
St. Norbert Abbey Seminary and Education Fund Trust
The Walnut Markets, Inc.
Los Amigos del Peru, Inc. Brothers 3; Priests 51; Seminarians 4.

MANITOWOC. *Blessed Giles Friary*, 1820 Grand Ave., Manitowoc, 54220. Tel: 920-684-5201; Email: friarski@gmail.com. Revs. John Dombrowski, Supr.; Andrew Buvala; Richard Duffy; Peter Fritz; Jonathan Foster, O.F.M.; Lester Kochlin; Lambert Leykam; Paul Pare, O.F.M., (Retired); John Rausch, O.F.M., (Retired); Ildephonse Skorup; Harry Speckman; Jose Valenzuela; Bros. Earl Benz, O.F.M., (Retired); Pauli Johnson; Donald Lachowicz, O.FM.; Daniel Piasecki; Herbert Rempe. (Franciscan Friars, Sacred Heart Province) Religious 17.

OSHKOSH. *Community of Our Lady* (1968) (Diocesan Pious Union) 2804 Oakwood Ln., Oshkosh, 54904-8406. Tel: 920-233-5633; Fax: 920-233-5604; Email: noemail@noemail.com. Very Rev. Regis N. Barwig, Prior; Rev. Augustine Serafini, (Retired); Bro. Joseph G. Le Sanche. Brothers 1; Priests 2.

PULASKI. *Assumption of B.V.M. Friary* (1887) 143 E. Pulaski St., P.O. Box 100, Pulaski, 54162-0100.
Tel: 920-822-8125; Fax: 920-822-5423; Email: frpatrick@abvm.org; Email: janet.maroszek@abvm.org; Web: www.franciscan-friars.org. Rev. Patrick M. Gawrylewski, O.F.M., Supr.; Bro. Paul Belco, O.F.M.; Revs. Hilary J. Brzezinski, O.F.M.; Anthony Cirignani, O.F.M.; James Esser, O.F.M.; Bros. Anthony Gancarz, O.F.M.; Andrew Giba, O.F.M.; Austin Mysliwiec, O.F.M.; Rev. Gerald A. Prusakowski, O.F.M.; Bro. Peter Rydza, O.F.M.; Rev. Everard Scesney, O.F.M.; Bro. Robert Sembrat, O.F.M.; Rev. Placid Stroik, O.F.M.; Bro. Gerald Tokarz, O.F.M.; Rev. Brendan Wroblewski, O.F.M. (Order of Friars Minor).

[K] CONVENTS AND RESIDENCES FOR SISTERS

GREEN BAY. *Sisters of Our Lady of Charity of the Good Shepherd - Green Bay, Inc.* (1882) 2560 Shawano Ave., P.O. Box 10357, 54307-0357.
Tel: 920-434-8208; Fax: 920-662-0047; Email: sisterpat1165@gmail.com. Sr. Patrick Dolan, Supr. Sisters 8.

The Sisters of St. Francis of the Holy Cross, Inc. (1881) 3110 Nicolet Dr., 54311-7212.
Tel: 920-468-1828; Fax: 920-468-1207; Email: sr.ann@gbfranciscans.org; Web: www.gbfranciscans.org. Sr. Ann Rehrauer, Pres. Sisters 53; In Diocese 53.

DENMARK. *Monastery of the Holy Name of Jesus, Ltd.* (1992) Discalced Carmelite Nuns Monastery of the Holy Name of Jesus, Ltd., 6100 Pepper Rd., Denmark, 54208. Tel: 920-863-5055; Email: mttabor@holynamecarmel.org. Mother Christine Marie, O.C.D., Prioress; Very Rev. John W. Girotti, J.C.L., Chap. Sisters 15; Total in Residence 16.

MANITOWOC. *St. Francis Convent* (1869) 6835 Calumet Ave., Manitowoc, 54220-9700. Tel: 920-684-7884; Email: smaryannt@sfcc-calledtobe.org. Sr. Natalie Binversie, O.S.F., Prioress. Franciscan Sisters of Christian Charity. Sisters 37.

Holy Family Convent of Franciscan Sisters of Christian Charity (1869) Motherhouse and Novitiate dedicated to the Holy Family 2409 S.

Alverno Rd., Manitowoc, 54220-9320.
Tel: 920-682-7728; Fax: 920-682-4195; Email: snatalie@fscc-calledtobe.org; Web: fscc-calledtobe.org. Sr. Natalie Binversie, O.S.F., Community Dir.; Revs. Hilary J. Brzezinski, O.F.M., Chap., Silver Lake College of the Holy Family, Holy Family Convent Rectory, 2411 S. Alverno Rd., Manitowoc, 54220; Placid Stroik, O.F.M., Chap. Sisters 223; Total in Residence 125; In Diocese 47.

OSHKOSH. *SSM Franciscan Courts*, 815 S. Westhaven Dr., Ste. 100, Oshkosh, 54904-7978.
Tel: 920-426-2440; Fax: 920-426-3196; Email: jfuller@affinityhealth.org; Web: www.FranciscanCourts.org. Sr. Lois Bush, Contact Person. Sisters of the Sorrowful Mother. Sisters 29.

Sisters of the Sorrowful Mother St. Clare of Assisi Region, 815 S. Westhaven Dr., Ste. 100, Oshkosh, 54904. Tel: 920-230-2040; Fax: 920-230-2041; Email: lois.bush@ssm-courts.org. Sr. Lois Bush, Supr. Sisters 71.

Sisters of the Sorrowful Mother, 2185 Abbey Ave., Oshkosh, 54904. Tel: 920-230-2040; Email: pegg@ssmfinance.org. 815 S. Westhaven Dr., Ste. 100, Oshkosh, 54904-7978. Sr. Lois Bush, Contact Person. Sisters 3.

Sisters of the Sorrowful Mother, 2485 Arcadia Ave., Oshkosh, 54904. Tel: 920-230-2040; Email: pegg@ssmfinance.org. Sr. Lois Bush, Contact Person. Sisters 2.

Sisters of the Sorrowful Mother, 1145 Devonshire Dr., Oshkosh, 54904. Tel: 920-230-2040; Email: pegg@ssmfinance.org. 815 S. Westhaven Dr., Ste 100, Oshkosh, 54904-7978. Sr. Lois Bush, Contact Person. Sisters 4.

[L] SHRINES

NEW FRANKEN. *The National Shrine of Our Lady of Good Help, Inc.*, 4047 Chapel Dr., New Franken, 54229. Tel: 920-866-2571; Email: info@shrineofourladyofgoodhelp.com; Web: www.shrineofourladyofgoodhelp.com. Rev. John Broussard, C.P.M., Rector; Don Warden, Dir.; Revs. George McInnis, Chap.; Thomas Reagan, Chap.
The National Shrine of Our Lady of Good Help.

[M] RETREAT HOUSES

DE PERE. *Norbertine Center for Spirituality* (1979) (An Apostolate of the Norbertine Fathers) St. Norbert Abbey, 1016 N. Broadway, De Pere, 54115-2697.
Tel: 920-337-4315; Fax: 920-337-4385; Email: norbertinecenter@yahoo.com; Web: www.norbertines.org. Tony Pichler, Dir. Total Staff 6.

MENASHA. *Mount Tabor Center* aka SPIRITUS Ministries (1983) 522 2nd St., Menasha, 54952-3112. Tel: 920-722-8918; Fax: 920-722-8918; Email: annettehovie@spiritusministries.org; Email: edenfoord@spiritusministries.org; Web: spiritusministries.org. Eden Foord, Dir.; Katherine Foord, Asst. Dir. Total Staff 28.

OSHKOSH. *Jesuit Retreat House* (1961) 4800 Fahrnwald Rd., Oshkosh, 54902-7598. Tel: 920-231-9060; Email: office@jesuitretreathouse.org; Email: cmanahan@jesuitretreathouse.org; Web: www.jesuitretreathouse.org. Revs. Eugene L. Donahue, S.J., Retreat Dir.; John L. Treloar, S.J., Retreat Dir.; Christopher J. Manahan, S.J., Dir. Society of Jesus.

SHAWANO. *Camp Tekakwitha Retreat and Conference Center, Inc.*, W5248 Lake Dr., Shawano, 54166.
Tel: 920-272-8162; Email: camptekakwitha@gbdioc.org; Web: www.camptekakwitha.org. Dr. Joseph Bound, Pres.; Rebecca Sievers, Dir.

[N] NEWMAN CENTERS

GREEN BAY. *Catholic Campus Ministry, U.W.G.B.*, 1825 Riverside Dr., P.O. Box 23825, 54305-3825.
Tel: 920-288-0237; Tel: 920-272-8394; Email: lzelten@gbdioc.org; Web: www.phoenixcatholic.org. Sr. Laura Zelten, O.S.F., Campus Min.

Lawrence University Newman Center, Appleton, 54911.

Newman Center of Oshkosh, Inc., 800 Elmwood Ave., Oshkosh, 54901-3518. Tel: 920-233-5555; Email: titancatholics@gbdioc.org; Web: titancatholics.org. Rev. Jason J. Blahnik, Dir. Newman Center.

[O] MISCELLANEOUS LISTINGS

GREEN BAY. *Catholic Charities of the Diocese of Green Bay, Inc.*, 1825 Riverside Dr., P.O. Box 23825, 54305-3825. Tel: 920-272-8234; Fax: 920-437-0694; Email: tphernetton@gbdioc.org. Ted Phernetton, Dir.

The Catholic Foundation for the Diocese of Green Bay, Inc. (1998) Mailing Address: 1825 Riverside Dr., P.O. Box 22128, 54305-2128.
Tel: 920-272-8173; Fax: 920-272-8435; Email: catholicfoundation@gbdioc.org; Web: www.catholicfoundationgb.org. Josh Diedrich, Exec.

Catholic High School Foundation, L.T.D., P.O. Box 1117, 54305-1117. Tel: 920-337-4321;
Fax: 920-337-4357; Email: jglover@netnet.net; Email: cdunlap@notredameacademy.com. Mr. Thomas Konop, Pres.; William Micksch, Vice Pres.

The Diocesan Charismatic Renewal Center, 650 S. Irwin St., 54302. Tel: 920-405-1960; Email: dcrcgb@gmail.com; Web: charismaticrenewal.org. Judy Goolsbey, Office Mgr.; Rev. Callistus Elue, Liaison to the Bishop, 208 N. Park Ave., Crandon, 54520. Tel: 920-606-6839.

St. Francis Xavier Investment Corp. (1998) 1825 Riverside Dr., P.O. Box 23825, 54305-3825.
Tel: 920-437-7531, Ext. 8206; Fax: 920-272-8257; Email: pkolbach@gbdioc.org; Tel: 920-272-8206; Web: gbdioc.org. Paul Kolbach, Dir.

St. Gianna Molla Guild of Northeast Wisconsin, Inc., C/O Hjortness and Associates, 851 Racine St., Ste. B, Menasha, 54952. Tel: 920-725-1040; Email: gail@hjortnesscpa.com; Web: sgmgnew.com. Dr. Susan Allen, Pres.

St. Gianna Clinic, 1727 Shawano Ave., 54303.
Tel: 920-884-3590; Email: Mark.Repenshek@hshs.org; Email: Mary.Salm@hshs.org; Web: www.stmgb.org/Medical-Services/St-Gianna-Clinic.aspx. Mark Repenshek, Exec.; Greg Simia, Exec.; Amber Chibuk, Dir.; Therese Pandl, Dir. Medical clinic.
St. Mary's Hospital Medical Center d.b.a. St. Gianna Clinic.
St. Mary's Hospital Medical Center d.b.a. St. Gianna Molla Clinic. Staff 6.

The Green Bay Catholic Compass, Inc., 1825 Riverside Dr., P.O. Box 23825, 54305-3825.
Tel: 920-437-7531;
Tel: 920-233-5555 (Appleton Area); Email: jlodl@gbdioc.org. Sam Lucero, Editor, Tel: 920-272-8210; Amy Kawula, Advertising & Mktg. Mgr.; Pat Kasten, Assoc. Editor, Tel: 920-272-8203; Jeff Kurowski, Assoc. Editor, Tel: 920-272-8204.

St. John the Evangelist Homeless Shelter, Inc., 411 St. John St., P.O. Box 1743, 54305.
Tel: 920-436-9344; Fax: 920-436-9765; Email: awood@sjehs.org. Alexia Wood, Exec. Dir.

The Micah Center, 700 E. Walnut St., 54301.
Tel: (920) 617-8700; Email: awood@sjehs.org; Web: www.stjohnhomelessshelter.org. Alexia Wood, Exec. Resource center for the homeless.

St. Joseph Real Estate Services Corporation, Diocesan Central Offices, 1825 Riverside Dr., P.O. Box 23825, 54305-3825. Tel: 920-272-8260;
Tel: 920-272-8314; Email: bwiegand@gbdioc.org; Web: www.gbdioc.org. Barbara Wiegand, Dir., Facilities & Properties.

St. Luke Benefit & Insurance Services Corp., 1825 Riverside Dr., P.O. Box 23825, 54305-3825.
Tel: 920-272-8343; Fax: 920-437-9296; Email: jbuechel@gbdioc.org; Web: www.gbdioc.org. Jennifer Buechel, Contact Person.

A New Genesis Community, Inc. A Public Association of the Faithful P.O. Box 8642, 54308.
Tel: 920-989-3902; Email: maryloislqpeace@yahoo.com; Email: smgils@new.rr.com. Sr. Marita Gilsdort, Admin. Total Members 27; Vowed in Diocese 23.

Notre Dame de la Baie Foundation, Inc., 610 Maryhill Dr., 54303. Tel: 920-429-6110;
Fax: 920-429-6140; Email: cdunlap@notredameacademy.com; Email: deanjre6388@gmail.com. Dean Re, Chm.; Kevin Shaw, Pres.

Oratory of St. Patrick Institute of Christ the King Sovereign King 211 N. Maple Ave., 54303.
Tel: 920-437-9660; Fax: 920-437-5154; Email: stjoseph@institute-christ-king.org; Web: institute-christ-king.org/greenbay/. Antoine M. Boucheron, Rector.

Society for Faith and Children's Education, Inc., 423 Woodfield Dr., 54313. Tel: 920-434-2420; Email: sfacegreenbay@yahoo.com; Web: www.sfacemission.org. June L. Ingold, Pres. & Contact Person; Rev. Savio J. Samala, Sec. & Treas.

**Immaculate Heart Media, Inc.* dba Relevant Radio, 1496 Bellevue St., Ste. 202, 54311.
Tel: 877-291-0123; Fax: 920-465-9986; Email: jlee@relevantradio.com; Web: www.relevantradio.com. Jennifer Lee, Exec. Asst.; Rev. Francis J. Hoffman, J.C.D., Exec. Dir. Total Staff 100.

Teens Encounter Christ (TEC), Green Bay Chapter, Anchor of Hope TEC, P.O. Box 5715, De Pere, 54115-5715. Tel: 920-445-6121; Email: tecgreenbay@gmail.com; Web: www.anchorofhopetec.org. St. Joseph Church, 936 Ninth St, 54304. Rev. Joel A. Sember, Spiritual Dir. Clergy 20; Students 1,562.

St. Therese of the Little Flower, Inc., 1825 Riverside Dr., 54305-3825. Tel: 920-272-8206;
Fax: 920-272-8257; Email: pkolbach@gbdioc.org; Web: gbdioc.org. Paul Kolbach, Dir.

St. Thomas More Society of the Roman Catholic Diocese of Green Bay, Inc., P.O. Box 22336, 54305-2336. Email: tbasten@gbdioc.org; Web: www.stmsgb.com. Corey Kimps, Contact Person.

ANTIGO. *Religious Hospitallers of St. Joseph Health Corporation "RHSJ Health Corporation"*, 650 Langlade Rd., Antigo, 54409. Tel: 715-623-2331;
Fax: 715-623-9440; Email: dlaporte@rhsj.org. Sr. Dolores Demulling, Contact Person.

APPLETON. **Affinity Health System*, 1506 S. Oneida St., Appleton, 54915. Tel: 920-831-8912;
Fax: 920-831-8916; Email: timothy.waldoch@ascension.org; Web: healthcare.ascension.org. Travis Andersen, Regl. Pres.; Timothy Waldoch, Chief Mission Integration Officer. Sponsored by Ascension Health Ministries (Ascension Sponsor), a public juridic person.

St. Elizabeth Hospital Foundation, Inc., 1506 S. Oneida St., Appleton, 54915-1397.
Tel: 920-831-1475; Fax: 920-738-2061; Email: timothy.waldoch@ascension.org; Web: healthcare.ascension.org/Donate. Tonya L. Dedering, Regl. Dir., Affinity Health Systems Foundations; Lisa Froemming, Vice Pres., Philanthropy. Sponsored by Ascension Health Ministries (Ascension Sponsor), a public juridic person.

Global Outreach, Inc. (1994) 4815 Whitetail Way, Appleton, 54914. Tel: 920-540-3085; Email: barbara.tota-boryczka@globaloutreachprogram.com; Web: www.globaloutreachprogram.com. Barbara Tota-Boryczka, Exec. Dir.; Pam Mullins, Pres.; Tom Kropidlowski, Vice Pres.; Gary Elmer, Treas. Tot Asst. Annually 25; Total Staff 3.

**Ascension Medical Group - Fox Valley Wisconsin, Inc.*, 1506 S. Oneida St., Appleton, 54915.
Tel: 920-738-2000; Email: timothy.waldoch@ascension.org; Web: healthcare.ascension.org. Mary Beth McDonald, Pres.; Timothy Waldoch, Chief Mission Integration Officer; Antonina Olszewski, Spiritual Care Dir. Sponsored by Ascension Health Ministries (Ascension Sponsor), a public juridic person Tot Asst. Annually 669,905; Total Staff 818.

**Widows of Prayer, Inc.*, 1600 S. Rebecca Ln., Appleton, 54915. Tel: 920-734-8308; Email: widowsofprayer@yahoo.com. Carlotta Stricken, Pres.

BAILEYS HARBOR. *Catholic Youth Expeditions, Inc.*, 3035 O'Brien Rd., Baileys Harbor, 54202.
Tel: 920-574-0290; Email: gmann@cyexpeditions.org; Web: www.cyexpeditions.org. Rev. Quentin A. Mann, C.D.L., Exec. Dir. & Founder. To encounter Jesus Christ and foster Catholic Christian community through expedition retreats of prayer, proclamation of the Gospel and outdoor adventure.

Missionaries of the Word, Inc (2013) 3035 O'Brien Rd., Baileys Harbor, 54202-9132.
Tel: 920-915-6592; Email: mothermarycatherinemw@gmail.com; Email: missionariesoftheword@gmail.com. Mother Mary Catherine, M.W., Sister Supr.

DE PERE. *Augustine Stewardship Fund Trust* (1986) 1016 N. Broadway, De Pere, 54115-2697.
Tel: 920-337-4300; Fax: 920-337-4328; Email: john.kastenholz@snc.edu; Web: www.norbertines.org. Rev. John P. Kastenholz, O.Praem., Sec.

Los Amigos del Peru, Inc. (1991) 1016 N. Broadway St., De Pere, 54115-2697. Tel: 920-337-4300;
Fax: 920-337-4328; Email: john.kastenholz@snc.edu; Web: www.norbertines.org. Rev. John P. Kastenholz, O.Praem., Sec.

NORBERT & CO. (1978) A nominee of The Premonstratensian Fathers 1016 N. Broadway, De Pere, 54115-2697. Tel: 920-337-4300;
Fax: 920-337-4328; Email: john.kastenholz@snc.edu; Web: www.norbertines.org. Revs. Dane J. Radecki, O.Praem., Abbot; Bradley R. Vanden Branden, O.Praem., Prior; John P. Kastenholz, O.Praem., Sec. & Treas.

St. Norbert Abbey Seminary and Education Fund Trust (1989) 1016 N. Broadway, De Pere, 54115-2697. Tel: 920-337-4300; Fax: 920-337-4328; Email: john.kastenholz@snc.edu; Web: www.norbertines.org. Rev. John P. Kastenholz, O.Praem., Sec.

Norbertine Generalate, Inc. (1989) 1016 N. Broadway, De Pere, 54115-2697. Tel: 920-337-4300; Fax: 920-337-4328; Email: rkfinn@netnet.net; Email: lynne.smet@snc.edu; Web: www.premontre.org. Revs. Jos Wouters, O.Praem., Pres.; Dane J. Radecki, O.Praem., Vice Pres.; Robert K. Finnegan, O.Praem., Sec. & Treas.

Norbertine Retirement Fund Trust (1986) 1016 N. Broadway, De Pere, 54115-2697. Tel: 920-337-4300; Fax: 920-337-4328; Email: john.kastenholz@snc.edu; Web: www.norbertines.org. Rev. John P. Kastenholz, O.Praem., Sec.

DEERBROOK. **Living Waters International, Inc.* (1996) N7544 County Rd. S., Deerbrook, 54424.
Tel: 715-627-4782; Fax: 715-627-4782; Email: livingh2o@livingwatersinternational.org; Web: www.livingwatersinternational.org. Dr. Stephen L. Zimmerman, Ph.D., Exec. Dir.

MANITOWOC. *Franciscan Sisters of Christian Charity Sponsored Ministries, Inc.* (1985) 1415 S. Rapids Rd., Manitowoc, 54220-9302. Tel: 920-684-7071; Fax: 920-684-6417; Email: bkane@fsccm.org; Email: mziarnik@fsccm.org; Web: www.fsccm.org. Scott McConnaha, Pres.

NEENAH. *St. Mary's Catholic Schools Foundation, Inc.*, 1050 Zephyr Dr., Neenah, 54956-1389.
Tel: 920-722-7796; Fax: 920-722-5940; Email: jlee@smcatholicschools.org; Web: www.smcatholicschools.org. Helen Englebert, Pres.

NEW HOLSTEIN. *Salvatorian Mission Warehouse*, 1303 Milwaukee Dr., New Holstein, 53061.
Tel: 920-898-5898; Email: dholton@salvatorians.com. Dave Holton, Dir. Relief goods sent to missionary countries.

OSHKOSH. *Christ Child Society, Oshkosh Chapter*, P.O. Box 2201, Oshkosh, 54903. Tel: 920-232-0962; Email: ltkroening@gmail.com. Lori Kroening, Pres.
Sisters of the Sorrowful Mother U.S. Region, Inc., 815 S. Westhaven Dr., Ste. 100, Oshkosh, 54904-7978. Tel: 920-230-2040; Fax: 920-230-2041; Email: lois.bush@ssm-courts.org; Web: www.sistersofthesorrowfulmother.org. Sr. Lois Bush, Supr.

STURGEON BAY. *Christ Child Society of Door County* (1996) St. Peter and Paul School, 4767 Dunn Rd., P.O.Box 572, Sturgeon Bay, 54235-0572.
Tel: 920-495-5857; Email: kathy.markdc@live.com. Kathleen Kunstman, Pres.

[P] CLOSED AND MERGED PARISHES

GREEN BAY. *Green Bay Diocesan Archives*, 1825 Riverside Dr., P.O. Box 23825, 54305-3825.
Tel: 920-272-8186; Web: www.gbdioc.org. Ms. Olivia Wendt, Archivist. Parish sacramental records for parishes that have closed or merged can be found at the locations listed below. As the location of sacramental records can change periodically, inquiries for records of parishes on this list should be directed to the above address.

St. Louis, Abrams Please see St. Maximilian Kolbe, Sobieski.
St. Joseph, Alverno, Tel: 920-726-4228; Fax: 920-726-4229. Please see St. Thomas the Apostle, Newton.
St. Hyacinth, Antigo Please see SS. Mary & Hyacinth, Antigo.
St. Mary, Antigo Please see SS. Mary & Hyacinth, Antigo.
St. Mary, Argonne, Tel: 715-478-3396. Please see St. Joseph, Crandon.
St. Patrick, Askeaton Please see St. Clare Corp., Greenleaf.
St. Mary of the Lake, Baileys Harbor Please see Stella Maris, Egg Harbor.
St. Mary, Brillion, Tel: 920-753-2535; Fax: 920-753-9802. Please see Holy Family, Brillion.
St. Charles Borromeo, Charlesburg Please see Good Shepherd, Chilton.
St. Martin, Charlestown Please see Good Shepherd, Chilton.
St. Joseph, Chase Please see St. Maximilian Kolbe, Sobieski.
St. Augustine, Chilton Please see Good Shepherd, Chilton.
St. Mary, Chilton Please see Good Shepherd, Chilton.
St Wendel, Cleveland, Tel: 920-726-4228; Fax: 920-726-4229. Please see St. Thomas the Apostle, Newton.
St. John the Baptist, Coleman, Tel: 920-897-3226; Fax: 920-897-4677. Please see St. Anne Parish, Corp., Coleman.
St. Francis of Assisi, Coleman, Tel: 920-897-3226; Fax: 920-897-4677. Please see St. Anne Parish, Corp., Coleman.
SS. Francis-Wenceslaus, Coleman Please see St. Anne Parish Corp., Coleman.
Holy Angels, Darboy, Tel: 920-788-7640; Fax: 920-788-7658. Please see Holy Spirit, Kimberly.
St. Boniface, De Pere, Tel: 920-336-4033; Fax: 920-336-3910. Please see Our Lady of Lourdes, De Pere.
St. Joseph, De Pere, Tel: 920-336-4033; Fax: 920-336-3910. Please see Our Lady of Lourdes, De Pere.
SS. Cyril and Methodius, Eaton, Tel: 920-863-2593; Fax: 920-845-5180. Please see St. Thomas the Apostle, Humboldt.
St. John the Baptist, Egg Harbor
Please see Stella Maris, Egg Harbor.
St. William, Eland, Tel: 715-253-2050; Fax: 715-253-3020. Please see Holy Family-St. William, Wittenberg.
St. Paul, Fish Creek
Please see Stella Maris, Egg Harbor.
Holy Marytrs of Gorcum, Green Bay See Prince of Peace, Green Bay.
St. Mary, Greenleaf Please see St. Clare Corp., Greenleaf.
St. Michael, Hiles, Tel: 715-478-3396. Please see St Joseph, Crandon.
St. Francis, Hollandtown Please see St. Katharine Drexel, Kaukauna.
Our Lady Queen of Peace, Humboldt, Tel: 920-863-2593; Fax: 920-845-5180. Please see St. Thomas the Apostle, Humboldt.
St. Michael, Jacksonport Please see Stella Maris, Egg Harbor.
Holy Trinity, Jericho Please see Good Shepherd, Chilton.
Holy Trinity, Kasson Please see Holy Family, Brillion.
St. Aloysius, Kaukauna Please see St. Katharine Drexel, Kaukauna.
St. Mary of the Annunciation, Kaukauna Please see St. Katharine Drexel, Kaukauna.
Holy Name of Jesus, Kimberly Please see Holy Spirit, Kimberly.
St. George, King, Tel: 715-258-3000; Fax: 715-258-5708. Please see St. Mary Magdalene, Waupaca.
St. Wenceslaus, Klondike, Tel: 920-897-3226; Fax: 920-897-4677. Please see St. Anne Parish, Corp., Coleman.
St. Elizabeth, Kloten Please see Good Shepherd, Chilton.
St. John, Krok, Tel: 920-863-8747; Fax: 920-863-5768. Please see St. Therese de Lisieux, Stangelville.
St. Stanislaus Kostka, Langlade, Tel: 715-882-2551. Please see SS. James and Stanislaus, White Lake.
St. Charles Borromeo, Lena, Tel: 920-829-5222. Please see Holy Cross, Lena.
Holy Cross, Lena Please see St. Anne Parish Corp., Coleman.
St. Peter, Lincoln, Tel: 920-837-2852. Please see St. Peter and St. Hubert, Rosiere.
St. Andrew, Manitowoc Please see St. Francis of Assisi, Manitowoc.
St. Boniface, Manitowoc Please see St. Francis of Assisi, Manitowoc.
Holy Innocents, Manitowoc Please see St. Francis of Assisi, Manitowoc.
St. Mary, Manitowoc Please see St. Francis of Assisi, Manitowoc.
St. Paul, Manitowoc Please see St. Francis of Assisi, Manitowoc.
Sacred Heart, Manitowoc Please see St. Francis of Assisi, Manitowoc.
St. Patrick, Maple Grove, Tel: 920-756-2535; Fax: 920-756-9802. Please see Holy Family, Brillion/Reedsville.
St. Francis De Paul, Marchand (Duvall), Tel: 920-866-2410; Fax: 920-866-3591. Please see St. Louis, Dyckesville.
Our Lady of Lourdes, Marinette, Tel: 715-735-9100; Fax: 715-735-9650. Please see Holy Family, Marinette.
Sacred Heart of Jesus, Marinette, Tel: 715-735-9100 ; Fax: 715-735-9650. Please see Holy Family, Marinette.
St. Anthony, Marinette, Tel: 715-735-9100; Fax: 715-735-9650. Please see Holy Family, Marinette.
St. Joseph, Marinette, Tel: 715-735-9100; Fax: 715-735-9650. Please see Holy Family, Marinette.
Holy Family Church, Mattoon Please see St. Joseph-Holy Family, Phlox.
St. Joseph, Montpelier, Tel: 920-863-8747; Fax: 920-863-5768. Please see St. Therese de Lisieux, Stangelville.
St. Joseph-St. John, Montpelier, Tel: 920-863-8747; Fax: 920-863-5768. Please see St. Therese de Lisieux, Stangelville.
St. Mary, Namur, Tel: 920-825-7555; Fax: 920-825-1492. Please see St. Francis and St. Mary, Brussels.
St, Joseph, Norman, Tel: 920-776-1555; Fax: 920-776-1555. Please see St. Isidore the Farmer, Tisch Mills.
St. Casimir, Northeim, Tel: 920-726-4228; Fax: 920-726-4229. Please see St. Thomas the Apostle, Newton.
St. Joseph, Oconto, Tel: 920-835-5900; Fax: 920-835-5907. Please see Holy Trinity, Oconto.
St. Peter, Oconto, Tel: 920-835-5900; Fax: 920-835-5907. Please see Holy Trinity, Oconto.
St. John, Oshkosh Please see St. Jude the Apostle, Oshkosh.
St. Josaphat, Oshkosh Please see Most Blessed Sacrament, Oshkosh.
St. Mary, Oshkosh Please see Most Blessed Sacrament, Oshkosh.
St. Peter, Oshkosh Please see Most Blessed Sacrament, Oshkosh.
Sacred Heart, Oshkosh Please see St. Jude the Apostle, Oshkosh.
St. Vincent De Paul, Oshkosh Please see St. Jude the Apostle, Oshkosh.
St. Isidore, Osman, Tel: 920-726-4228; Fax: 920-726-4229. Please see St. Thomas the Apostle, Newton.
Holy Trinity, Pine Grove See Prince of Peace, Green Bay.
St. Leo, Pound, Tel: 920-897-3226; Fax: 920-897-4677. Please see St. Anne Parish, Corp., Coleman.
St. Mary, Reedsville, Tel: 920-756-2535; Fax: 920-756-9802. Please see Holy Family, Brillion.
St. Mary-St. Patrick, Reedsville / Maple Grove, Tel: 920-756-2535; Fax: 920-756-9802. Please see Holy Family, Brillion.
St. Rosalia, Sister Bay Please see Stella Maris, Egg Harbor.
St. Adalbert, Slovan, Tel: 920-837-7234; Fax: 920-837-2361. Please see Holy Trinity, Casco.
St. John Cantius, Sobieski Please see St. Maximilian Kolbe, Sobieski.
St. Joseph of the Lake, South Branch, Tel: 715-799-3811; Fax: 715-799-5092. Please see St. Michael, Keshena.
Sacred Heart, Spruce, Tel: 920-829-5222. Please see Holy Cross, Lena.
St. John the Baptist, St. John, Tel: 920-989-1515; Fax: 920-989-8585. Please see St. John-Sacred Heart, Sherwood.
St. Lawrence, Stangelville, Tel: 920-863-8747; Fax: 920-863-5768. Please see St. Therese de Lisieux, Stangelville.
St. Mary, Stark, Tel: 920-864-7641. Please see St. Mary, Glenmore.
St. Odile, Thiry Daems, Tel: 920-866-9961. Please see St. Joseph, Champion.
Nativity of the BVM, Tisch Mills, Tel: 920-776-1555; Fax: 920-776-1555. Please see St. Isidore the Farmer, Tisch Mills.
St. Martin, Tonet, Tel: 920-866-9961. Please see St. Joseph, Champion.
Holy Redeemer-Sacred Heart, Two Rivers, Tel: 920-793-4531; Fax: 920-793-8067. Please see St. Peter the Fisherman, Two Rivers.
Sacred Heart, Two Rivers, Tel: 920-793-4531; Fax: 920-793-8067. Please see St. Peter the Fisherman, Two Rivers.
St. Luke, Two Rivers, Tel: 920-793-4531; Fax: 920-793-8067. Please see St. Peter the Fisherman, Two Rivers.
St. Mark, Two Rivers, Tel: 920-793-4531; Fax: 920-793-8067. Please see St. Peter the Fisherman, Two Rivers.
St. Edward, Wagner See St. Joseph & Edwards, Walsh.
St. Amand, Walhain, Tel: 920-866-9961. Please see St. Joseph, Champion.
St. Joseph, Walsh Please see SS. Joseph & Edward, Walsh.
St. Hedwig, West Kewaunee, Tel: 920-863-8747; Fax: 920-863-5768. Please see St. Therese de Lisieux, Stangelville.
St. James, White Lake Please see SS. James & Stanislaus, White Lake/Langlade.
St. Paul, Wrightstown Please see St. Clare Corp., Greenleaf.

RELIGIOUS INSTITUTES OF MEN REPRESENTED IN THE DIOCESE

For further details refer to the corresponding bracketed number in the Religious Institutes of Men or Women section.

[0900]—*Canons Regular of Premontre*—O.Praem.
[0470]—*The Capuchin Friars* (Province of St. Joseph)—O.F.M.Cap.
[0820]—*Congregation of the Fathers of Mercy*—C.P.M.
[0690]—*Franciscan Friars* Assumption of the Blessed Virgin, Franklin, WI—O.F.M.
[0520]—*Franciscan Friars* Sacred Heart, St. Louis, MO—OFM.
[0305]—*Institute of Christ the King*—I.C.
[0690]—*Jesuit Fathers and Brothers* (Wisconsin Province)—S.J.
[0800]—*Maryknoll Fathers*—M.M.
[]—*Missionaries of Faith*—M.F.

RELIGIOUS INSTITUTES OF WOMEN REPRESENTED IN THE DIOCESE

[]—*Ancilae Mariae Reginae*—A.M.R.
[]—*Daughters of Mary (Bannabikiria)*—D.M.
[0420]—*Discalced Carmelite Nuns*—O.C.D.
[1070-03]—*Dominican Sisters* Adrian, MI—O.P.
[1070-09]—*Dominican Sisters* Racine, WI—O.P.
[1070-14]—*Dominican Sisters* Sinsinawa, WI—O.P.
[1115]—*Dominican Sisters of Peace*—O.P.
[1170]—*Felician Sisters* (Our Lady of Hope Province)—C.S.S.F.
[1230]—*Franciscan Sisters of Christian Charity*—O.S.F.

[]—*Handmaids of the Divine Redeemer* Ghana—H.D.R.
[1820]—*Hospital Sisters of the Third Order of St. Francis*—O.S.F.
[]—*Little Sisters of St. Francis*—L.S.O.S.F.
[]—*Missionaries of the Word*—M.W.
[3440]—*Religious Hospitallers of Saint Joseph*—R.H.S.J.
[2970]—*School Sisters of Notre Dame*—S.S.N.D.
[]—*School Sisters of St. Francis*—S.S.S.F.
[]—*Sisters of Mercy of the Holy Cross*—S.C.S.C.
[3070]—*Sisters of Our Lady of Charity of the Good Shepherd*—R.G.S.
[]—*Sisters of St. Elizabeth* Chicago, Il—S.S.E.
[1550]—*Sisters of St. Francis of the Holy Cross*—O.S.F.
[3840]—*Sisters of St. Joseph of Carondelet* (Prov. of St. Louis)—C.S.J.
[3930]—*Sisters of St. Joseph of the Third Order of St. Francis*—S.S.J.-T.O.S.F.
[1030]—*Sisters of the Divine Savior*—S.D.S.
[4100]—*Sisters of the Sorrowful Mother (Third Order of St. Francis)*—S.S.M.
[]—*Society of Sisters for the Church* Green Bay, WI—S.S.C.

DIOCESAN CEMETERIES

GREEN BAY. *Diocesan Cemeteries*, P.O. Box 23825, 54305-3825. Tel: 920-435-6850; Email: mbreivogel@gbdioc.org. Mary Breivogel, Admin. Total Plots 27,000; Plots Available 50,000.

Allouez Catholic Cemetery and Mausoleum, 2121 Riverside Dr., 54301. Tel: 920-432-7585; Fax: 920-432-0425; Email: mbreivogel@gbdioc.org; Web: allouezcatholiccemetery.com. Mary Breivogel, Admin.

Calvary Cemetery of Manitowoc, Inc., 2601 S. 14th St., Manitowoc, 54220-6467. Tel: 920-684-3646; Email: calvarymausoleum@yahoo.com. Jerry Schermetzler, Admin.

NECROLOGY

† Browne, Stanley T., (Retired), Died Oct. 5, 2018
† Lessard, Leo R., (Retired), Died Mar. 1, 2018
† Schuetze, John W., Died Aug. 27, 2018
† Stencil, Rallen H., (Retired), Died Apr. 15, 2018
† Worman, Jeremiah F., (Retired), Died Oct. 27, 2018

An asterisk (*) denotes an organization that has established tax-exempt status directly with the IRS and is not covered by the USCCB Group Ruling.

Diocese of Greensburg

(Dioecesis Greensburgensis)

Most Reverend

EDWARD C. MALESIC, J.C.L.

Bishop of Greensburg; ordained May 30, 1987; appointed Bishop of Greensburg April 24, 2015; installed July 13, 2015. *Office: 723 E. Pittsburgh St., Greensburg, PA 15601.*

Most Reverend

LAWRENCE E. BRANDT, J.C.D., PH.D.

Retired Bishop of Greensburg; ordained December 19, 1969; appointed Bishop of Greensburg January 2, 2004; installed March 4, 2004; retired July 13, 2015. *Office: 723 E. Pittsburgh St., Greensburg, PA 15601.*

Pastoral Center: 723 E. Pittsburgh St., Greensburg, PA 15601. Tel: 724-837-0901; Fax: 724-837-0857.

Web: www.catholicgbg.org

ESTABLISHED MARCH 10, 1951.

Square Miles 3,334.

Comprises the Counties of Armstrong, Fayette, Indiana and Westmoreland in the State of Pennsylvania.

For legal titles of parishes and diocesan institutions, consult the Chancery Office.

STATISTICAL OVERVIEW

Personnel	
Bishop	1
Retired Bishops	1
Abbots	1
Priests: Diocesan Active in Diocese	50
Priests: Diocesan Active Outside Diocese	1
Priests: Retired, Sick or Absent	43
Number of Diocesan Priests	94
Religious Priests in Diocese	169
Total Priests in Diocese	263
Extern Priests in Diocese	17
Ordinations:	
Diocesan Priests	1
Religious Priests	1
Permanent Deacons	1
Permanent Deacons in Diocese	7
Total Brothers	38
Total Sisters	206
Parishes	
Parishes	78
With Resident Pastor:	
Resident Diocesan Priests	45
Resident Religious Priests	5
Without Resident Pastor:	
Administered by Priests	28
Professional Ministry Personnel:	
Sisters	11
Lay Ministers	129
Welfare	
Homes for the Aged	2
Total Assisted	465
Special Centers for Social Services	6
Total Assisted	1,876
Residential Care of Disabled	1
Total Assisted	65
Educational	
Diocesan Students in Other Seminaries	5
Seminaries, Religious	1
Students Religious	18
Total Seminarians	23
Colleges and Universities	2
Total Students	3,618
High Schools, Diocesan and Parish	2
Total Students	570
Elementary Schools, Diocesan and Parish	11
Total Students	1,935
Elementary Schools, Private	3
Total Students	150
Catechesis/Religious Education:	
High School Students	1,431
Elementary Students	5,930
Total Students under Catholic Instruction	13,657
Teachers in the Diocese:	
Priests	13
Brothers	4
Sisters	12
Lay Teachers	461
Vital Statistics	
Receptions into the Church:	
Infant Baptism Totals	870
Minor Baptism Totals	43
Adult Baptism Totals	33
Received into Full Communion	199
First Communions	1,036
Confirmations	529
Marriages:	
Catholic	411
Interfaith	146
Total Marriages	557
Deaths	2,062
Total Catholic Population	133,734
Total Population	659,596

Former Bishops—Most Revs. HUGH L. LAMB, S.T.D., First Bishop of Greensburg; ord. May 29, 1915; appt. Titular Bishop of Helos and Auxiliary of Philadelphia Dec. 19, 1935; cons. March 19, 1936; promoted to Greensburg May 28, 1951; installed Jan. 16, 1952; died Dec. 8, 1959; WILLIAM G. CONNARE, D.D., ord. June 14, 1936; appt. Feb. 23, 1960; cons. May 4, 1960; retired Jan. 20, 1987; died June 12, 1995; ANTHONY G. BOSCO, D.D., J.C.L., ord. June 7, 1952; appt. Auxiliary Bishop of Pittsburgh and Titular Bishop of Labico May 14, 1970; cons. June 30, 1970; appt. Bishop of Greensburg April 14, 1987; installed June 30, 1987; retired Jan. 2, 2004; died July 2, 2013.; LAWRENCE E. BRANDT, ord. Dec. 19, 1969; appt. Bishop of Greensburg Jan. 2, 2004; installed March 4, 2004; retired July 13, 2015.

Pastoral Center—723 E. Pittsburgh St., Greensburg, 15601-2697. Tel: 724-837-0901; Fax: 724-837-0857. Office Hours: Mon.-Fri. 8:45-5.

Vicar General—Rev. Msgr. LARRY J. KULICK, J.C.L., Tel: 724-837-0901.

Chancellor—MS. MARGARET DIVIRGILIO.

Chief Financial Officer—MRS. SHEILA R. MURRAY, CPA, M.B.A.

Deaneries—Very Revs. KENNETH G. ZACCAGNINI, V.F., Deanery 1; THOMAS A. FEDERLINE, V.F., Deanery 2; Rev. Msgr. JAMES T. GASTON, V.F., Deanery 3; Very Rev. DANIEL C. MAHONEY, V.F., Deanery 4; Rev. Msgr. MICHAEL W. MATUSAK, V.F., Deanery 5.

Vicar for Clergy—723 E. Pittsburgh St., Greensburg, 15601-2697. Tel: 724-837-0901; Fax: 724-837-0857. Rev. Msgr. LARRY J. KULICK, J.C.L.

Bishop's Liaison for Consecrated Life—723 E. Pittsburgh St., Greensburg, 15601. Tel: 724-837-0901. Rev. ANTHONY J. CARBONE, J.C.L.

Tribunal—Address all correspondence to *723 E. Pittsburgh St., Greensburg, 15601-2697.* Tel: 724-837-0901.

Judicial Vicar—Rev. Msgr. WILLIAM R. RATHGEB, J.C.L.

Defenders of Bond—Rev. Msgr. LARRY J. KULICK, J.C.L.; Rev. RICHARD J. KOSISKO, J.C.L.

Judges—Rev. Msgr. LARRY J. KULICK, J.C.L.; Revs. RICHARD J. KOSISKO, J.C.L.; ANTHONY J. CARBONE, J.C.L.

Advocate—Rev. Msgr. LARRY J. KULICK, J.C.L.

Notaries—MRS. CINDY J. OZZELLO; MS. KATHLEEN POLOSKY.

Tribunal Coordinator and Auditor—MS. KATHLEEN POLOSKY.

Advisory Bodies

College of Consultors—Most Rev. EDWARD C. MALESIC, J.C.L.; Rev. Msgr. LARRY J. KULICK, J.C.L.; Very Rev. KENNETH G. ZACCAGNINI, V.F.; Rev. Msgr. MICHAEL W. MATUSAK, V.F.; Revs. JOHN A. MOINEAU; LAWRENCE L. MANCHAS; Rev. Msgr. JAMES T. GASTON, V.F.; Revs. DANIEL L. BLOUT; JOHN M. FORISKA.

Diocesan Pastoral Council—VACANT.

Bishop's Priests Council—Rev. Msgr. LARRY J. KULICK, J.C.L.; Very Rev. THOMAS A. FEDERLINE, V.F.; Rev. Msgr. JAMES T. GASTON, V.F.; Very Revs. DANIEL C. MAHONEY, V.F.; KENNETH G. ZACCAGNINI, V.F.; Rev. Msgr. MICHAEL W. MATUSAK, V.F.; Revs. JOHN A. MOINEAU; JOHN M. FORISKA; DANIEL L. BLOUT; Rev. Msgr. RICHARD G. CURCI; Revs. DOUGLAS E. DORULA; WILLIAM G. BERKEY; LAWRENCE L. MANCHAS; FRANCISCO ROBLES GAN JR.; ALEXANDER L. PLEBAN, S.T.L., (Retired).

Finance Council—Most Rev. EDWARD C. MALESIC, J.C.L.; Rev. Msgrs. LARRY J. KULICK, J.C.L.; JAMES T. GASTON, V.F.; MR. MICHAEL WALKER; MR. DICK BARTON; MS. MARGARET DIVIRGILIO; MRS. RUTH GRANT; MR. WILLIAM THALMAN.

Diocesan Representatives—Rev. Msgr. RAYMOND E. RIFFLE, M.S.W., M.P.A.; MRS. SHEILA R. MURRAY, CPA, M.B.A.; MS. JENNIFER MIELIE; DR. MAUREEN MARSTELLER; MR. JEROME ZUFELT.

Diocesan Offices, Commissions and Special Programs

The Catholic Foundation for the Diocese of Greensburg—The Catholic Foundation for the Diocese of Greensburg (the Foundation) is a not-for-profit, tax-exempt corporation established by the Diocese of Greensburg (diocese) in 1986. Effective July 1, 2009, Bishop Lawrence E. Brandt announced the restructuring of The Catholic Foundation and new by-laws were adopted for the Foundation. These by-laws provide for a three-tier management structure designed to enhance monitoring of policies and procedures, and ensure effective accomplishment of the Foundation's mission. As the philanthropic arm of the Diocese, the Foundation exists to support the pastoral, educational, and social service ministries of the Diocese of Greensburg. This includes, but is not exclusive to parishes, Catholic schools, Catholic Charities, Catholic Cemeteries, and other Diocesan ministries. *723 E. Pittsburgh St., Greensburg, 15601.*

Members of the Corporation—Most Rev. EDWARD C. MALESIC, J.C.L., Chm.; Rev. Msgr. LARRY J. KULICK, J.C.L., Vice Chm.

Board of Trustees—MR. RAYMOND J. HANLEY, Pres.; MR. LEO N. HITT, Vice Pres.; MS. SHIRLEY A. MAKUTA; MR. JOHN J. TURCIK; MR. PAUL MONGELL; MR. PAUL A. ROCKER JR.; MR. STEPHEN A. PETERS.

Ex-Officio Trustees—Very Revs. KENNETH G. ZACCAGNINI, V.F.; THOMAS A. FEDERLINE, V.F.; Rev. Msgr. JAMES T. GASTON, V.F.; Very Rev. DANIEL C. MAHONEY, V.F.; Rev. Msgr. MICHAEL W. MATUSAK, V.F.

College of Deans—Very Revs. KENNETH G. ZACCAGNINI, V.F., Deanery I; THOMAS A. FEDERLINE, V.F., Deanery II; Rev. Msgr. JAMES T. GASTON, V.F., Deanery III; Very Rev. DANIEL C. MAHONEY, V.F., Deanery IV; Rev. Msgr. MICHAEL W. MATUSAK, V.F., Deanery V.

Diocese of Greensburg - Managing Directors—MRS. SHEILA R. MURRAY, CPA, M.B.A., CFO; DR. MAUREEN MARSTELLER, Supt. Catholic Schools; Rev. Msgrs. RAYMOND E. RIFFLE, M.S.W., M.P.A., Catholic Charities; WILLIAM R. RATHGEB, J.C.L., Judicial Vicar; Ms. MARGARET DIVIRGILIO; MS. JENNIFER MIELIE.

The Catholic Institute of Greensburg—A Corporation, not-for-profit, incorporated under the law of the Commonwealth of Pennsylvania on the 4th day of June, 1954, and effective July 1, 1998, revised by-laws were adopted that provide for a three-tier management structure having as its purpose to operate as a lending and savings program for the mutual benefit of the parishes and other related entities.

Board of Members of the Corporation—Most Rev. EDWARD C. MALESIC, J.C.L.; Rev. Msgr. LARRY J. KULICK, J.C.L.

Board of Trustees—MR. JOHN N. STEVENS, Pres.; MR. JOHN J. DOLAN; MR. MARK E. LOPUSHANSKY; Rev. JOHN A. MOINEAU; MRS. SHEILA R. MURRAY, CPA, M.B.A., CFO. Staff: MS. MARA BRADFORD, CPA, Dir. Fin. Oper.; MS. SARA DUCAR, Catholic Inst./ Accounts Receivable Accountant.

Greensburg Catholic Accent and Communications, Inc.—A corporation, not-for-profit, under the laws of the Commonwealth of Pennsylvania having as its purpose the support of any Roman Catholic benevolent, charitable, educational or missionary undertaking. Most Rev. EDWARD C. MALESIC, J.C.L.; Rev. Msgr. LARRY J. KULICK, J.C.L.; VACANT, Treas., 723 E. Pittsburgh St., Greensburg, 15601-2697. Tel: 724-837-0901; Fax: 724-837-0857.

Catholic Charities of the Diocese of Greensburg, PA, Inc.—A corporation not-for-profit incorporated under the law of the Commonwealth of Pennsylvania on the 27th day of August, 1954, having as its purpose, the support of any Roman Catholic benevolent, charitable, educational or missionary undertaking. Most Rev. EDWARD C. MALESIC, J.C.L., Chm. Bd. Members of the Corp.; GEORGE BUTLER, Pres. Bd. of Trustees; Rev. Msgr. RAYMOND E. RIFFLE, M.S.W., M.P.A., Mng. Dir., 711 E. Pittsburgh St., Greensburg, 15601-2636. Tel: 724-837-1840; Fax: 724-837-4077.

Archives—723 E. Pittsburgh St., Greensburg, 15601. Tel: 724-837-0901. VACANT, Archivist.

Catholic Charities—Rev. Msgr. RAYMOND E. RIFFLE, M.S.W., M.P.A., Mng. Dir.; MS. HEATHER P. RADY, M.B.A., Dir. Community Rels. & Special Events, 711 E. Pittsburgh St., Greensburg, 15601-2636. Tel: 724-837-1840; Fax: 724-837-4077.

Catholic Relief Services Representative—Rev. ANTHONY J. CARBONE, J.C.L.; MS. MARY ELLEN PELLEGRINO, 723 E. Pittsburgh St., Greensburg, 15601-2697. Tel: 724-837-0901.

The Office of Communications and Evangelization—MS. JENNIFER MIELIE, Chief Communications Officer & Mng. Dir. Evangelization; JOHN ZYLKA, Dir. Visual Communications; ROBIN MULL, Dir. Mktg.; MR. JERRY ZUFELT, Sr. Writer; MARY SEAMENS, Multimedia Coord.

Diocesan Ecumenical Office—Sacred Heart Church, 421 Main St., P.O. Box 328, Youngstown, 15696. Tel: 724-537-7358; Fax: 724-537-6988. Rev. JAMES F. PODLESNY, O.S.B.

Office of Information Technology—MS. KAREN CORNELL, Dir.; MR. BRIAN LOOSZ, Network Analyst; MR. ANDREW ROSS, IT Support Specialist; MR. DARREN DORN, Client Technology Specialist; MR. JORDAN GOVI, Database & System Admin.; MR. JACOB GLESSNER, IT Support Specialist; MRS. CINDY STICKLE, IT Asset Management & Contract Admin.

Youth & Young Adult Ministry and Adult Initiation—CHRISTINA M. SMITH.

Marriage Preparation and Enrichment Trainers—Coordinators: RICHARD RYBA; LEEANNA RYBA.

Diocesan Catholic Scoutmaster—Rev. E. GEORGE SALETRIK, 723 E. Pittsburgh St., Greensburg, 15601-2697. Tel: 724-837-0901; Fax: 724-837-0857.

Office of Catholic Schools—DR. MAUREEN MARSTELLER, Supt. Schools; MRS. BARBARA SABO, Dir.; MS. SHARYN ZALNO, Dir. Curriculum & Instruction; MRS. AMANDA IWINSKI, Coord. Office of Cathlic Schools & CYO Athletic Coord.

Athletics—MRS. AMANDA IWINSKI, CYO Athletic Dir.

Office for Worship—Rev. MICHAEL P. SIKON, Dir.

Office for Priestly Vocations—Tel: 724-837-0901; Fax: 724-837-0857. Rev. TYLER J. BANDURA, Dir.

Office for the Permanent Diaconate—723 E. Pittsburgh St., Greensburg, 15601. Tel: 724-837-0901; Fax: 724-837-0857. Deacon WILLIAM J. HISKER, Dir.

MissionsSociety for the Propagation of the Faith and Holy Childhood, Rev. ANTHONY J. CARBONE, J.C.L., Dir., 723 E. Pittsburgh St., Greensburg, 15601-2697. Tel: 724-837-0901; Fax: 724-837-0857.

Engineering and Facility Management Office—723 E. Pittsburgh St., Greensburg, 15601-2697. Tel: 724-837-0901; Tel: 724-552-2570; Fax: 724-836-5592. MR. JAMES GAVIN, Dir.

SPECIAL PROGRAMS

Apostleship of Prayer—VACANT, 723 E. Pittsburgh St., Greensburg, 15601. Tel: 724-837-0901; Fax: 724-837-0857.

Apostolate for the Deaf—VACANT, 723 E. Pittsburgh St., Greensburg, 15601. Tel: 724-837-0901.

Catholic Business and Professional Women's Association—Rev. Msgr. LARRY J. KULICK, J.C.L., Spiritual Moderator, 723 E. Pittsburgh St., Greensburg, 15601-2697. Tel: 724-837-0901; Fax: 724-837-0857.

Catholic Daughters of America—Rev. DANIEL L. BLOUT, Chap., Our Lady of Grace Church, 1011 Mt. Pleasant Rd., Greensburg, 15601. Tel: 724-838-9480; Fax: 724-838-1842.

Cemeteries—723 E. Pittsburgh St., Greensburg, 15601-2697. Tel: 724-837-0901.

Charismatic—JOHN HUTCHINS; KIM HUTCHINS, 917 Clayton St., Greensburg, 15601. Tel: 724-837-7129; Tel: 412-817-5465; Email: hutchins@hssop.org.

Cursillo—c/o Diocese of Greensburg, 723 E. Pittsburgh St., Greensburg, 15601. Tel: 724-837-0901; Fax: 724-837-0857.

Diocesan Council of Catholic Women—Rev. Msgr. LARRY J. KULICK, J.C.L., Dir., 723 E. Pittsburgh St., Greensburg, 15601. Tel: 724-837-0901, Ext. 1220.

Holy Childhood Association—Rev. ANTHONY J. CARBONE, J.C.L., Dir., 723 E. Pittsburgh St., Greensburg, 15601-2697. Tel: 724-837-0901; Fax: 724-837-0857.

Holy Name Society—Rev. JOHN S. SZCZESNY, St. Joseph Church, 1125 Leishman Ave., New Kensington, 15068. Tel: 724-337-6412.

Legion of Mary—Rev. ALAN W. GROTE, St. Lawrence Church, P.O. Box 114, Cadogan, 16212. Tel: 724-763-1089; Fax: 724-763-8100.

Pilgrimages—Rev. WILLIAM J. LECHNAR, Dir., Diocese of Greensburg, 723 E. Pittsburgh St., Greensburg, 15601. Tel: 724-837-0901; Fax: 724-837-0857.

Priests' Eucharistic League—VACANT, 723 E. Pittsburgh St., Greensburg, 15601. Tel: 724-837-0901; Tel: 724-837-0901; Fax: 724-837-0857.

St. Luke Society for Health Care Professionals—Deacon WILLIAM J. HISKER, Chap., Blessed Sacrament Cathedral, 300 N. Main St., Greensburg, 15601. Tel: 724-834-3710; Fax: 724-834-1518.

St. Thomas More Society for Lawyers—Rev. TIMOTHY J. KRUTHAUPT, Chap., 118 Church St., Brownsville, 15417. Tel: 724-785-7781; Fax: 724-785-0844.

St. Vincent de Paul Society—Rev. JOHN A. SEDLAK, Spiritual Dir., P.O. Box 187, United, 15689. Tel: 724-423-4431; Fax: 724-423-4438.

Bishop's Delegate—Rev. Msgr. RAYMOND E. RIFFLE, M.S.W., M.P.A., Tel: 724-837-0901, Ext. 1221; Email: rriffle@dioceseofgreensburg.org.

Victim Assistance Coordinator—DR. PAUL NIEMIEC, Tel: 724-837-1840; Email: pniemiec@dioceseofgreensburg.org.

CLERGY, PARISHES, MISSIONS AND PAROCHIAL SCHOOLS

CITY OF GREENSBURG

(WESTMORELAND COUNTY)

1—BLESSED SACRAMENT CATHEDRAL (1846) [CEM]
300 N. Main St., 15601. Tel: 724-834-3710; Fax: 724-834-1518; Email: rriffle@dioceseofgreensburg.org; Web: www.blessedsacramentcathedral.org. Rev. Msgr. Raymond E. Riffle, M.S.W., M.P.A., Rector; Rev. Matthew J. Morelli; Deacon William J. Hisker; Sr. Jeanne Marie Vonder Haar, Pastoral Assoc./Diocesan D.R.E.; Christopher Pardini, Dir. Liturgy & Music.
See Aquinas Academy, Greensburg under Elementary Schools, Inter-Parochial located in the Institution section.
Catechesis Religious Program—Students 160.

2—ST. BRUNO (1919)
1715 Poplar St., 15601. Tel: 724-836-0690; Email: Afiaschetti@dioceseofgreensburg.org; Web: www.stbrunodioceseofgreensburg.org. Revs. Lawrence L. Manchas, Admin.; James B. Morley.
See Aquinas Academy, Greensburg under Elementary Schools, Inter-Parochial located in the Institution section.
Catechesis Religious Program—
Tel: 724-836-0690, Ext. 11. Christine Gannon, C.R.E. Students 60.

3—OUR LADY OF GRACE (1910)
1011 Mount Pleasant Rd., 15601. Tel: 724-838-9480; Email: dblout@dioceseofgreensburg.org. Revs. Daniel L. Blout; Marlon Pates; Marisa Cazden, Music Min.
See Aquinas Academy, Greensburg under Elementary Schools, Inter-Parochial located in the Institution section.
Catechesis Religious Program—Tel: 724-832-6730. Katrina Coleman, Dir. Parish Formation & Evangelization. Students 226.

4—ST. PAUL (1955)
824 Carbon Rd., 15601. Tel: 724-834-6880; Email: jmosser@dioceseofgreensburg.org; Web: stpauldioceseofgreensburg.org. Revs. Lawrence L. Manchas; James B. Morley.
See Aquinas Academy, Greensburg under Elementary Schools, Inter-Parochial located in the Institution section.
Catechesis Religious Program—Students 82.

OUTSIDE THE CITY OF GREENSBURG

APOLLO, ARMSTRONG CO., ST. JAMES THE GREATER
109 Owens View Ave., Apollo, 15613.
Tel: 724-478-4958; Fax: 724-478-3551; Email: dsummerhill@dioceseofgreensburg.org. Rev. Vincent E. Zidek, O.S.B.
Catechesis Religious Program—Megan Krachanko, Rel. Educ. Coord. Students 97.

ARNOLD, WESTMORELAND CO., ALL SAINTS, (Slovak), Closed. For inquiries for parish records, see St. Joseph, New Kensington.

AVONMORE, WESTMORELAND CO., ST. AMBROSE
505 Cambria Ave., P.O. Box 617, Avonmore, 15618.
Tel: 724-697-4129; Email: jharrold@dioceseofgreensburg.org; Web: www.partnerparishesmas.org. Rev. John J. Harrold; Deacon F. William Frescura.
Catechesis Religious Program—Grace Sikora, D.R.E. Students 36.

BELLE VERNON, WESTMORELAND CO., ST. SEBASTIAN
801 Broad Ave., Belle Vernon, 15012.
Tel: 724-929-9300; Email: stsebastian@dioceseofgreensburg.org. Rev. Francisco Robles Gan Jr.
Catechesis Religious Program—Mrs. Christy Cabaniss, Parish Min. Students 98.

BLAIRSVILLE, INDIANA CO., SS. SIMON AND JUDE (1830) [CEM]
155 N. Brady St., Blairsville, 15717.
Tel: 724-459-7103. Rev. Stephen R. Bugay; Elaine Scherer, Pastoral Assoc.

BOVARD, WESTMORELAND CO., ST. BEDE, Closed. For inquiries for parish records, see Blessed Sacrament Cathedral, Greensburg.

BRADY'S BEND, ARMSTRONG CO., ST. PATRICK 1806 [CEM 2]
915 State Rte. 68, East Brady, 16028.

Tel: 724-526-5079; Fax: 724-526-3028; Email: stpatrick@dioceseofgreensburg.org; Web: www.stpatrickbradysbend.org. Rev. John M. Butler.
Catechesis Religious Program—Email: mseybert@dioceseofgreensburg.org. Mrs. Mary Anne Seybert, D.R.E. Students 72.

BROWNSVILLE, FAYETTE CO.
1—ST. MARY, [CEM] (Slovak), Closed. For inquiries for parish records please see St. Peter Parish.
2—ST. PETER aka The Historic Church of St. Peter, [CEM 2]
300 Shaffner Ave., Brownsville, 15417.
Tel: 724-785-7781; Email: tkruthaupt@dioceseofgreensburg.org; Web: www.historicchurchofstpeter.org. 118 Church St., Brownsville, 15417. Revs. Timothy J. Kruthaupt; Thumma Fathimareddy, Parochial Vicar.
Res.: 304 Shaffner Ave., Brownsville, 15417.
Catechesis Religious Program—Patty Craig, D.R.E. Students 130.

CADOGAN, ARMSTRONG CO., ST. LAWRENCE, [CEM]
c/o 718 Fourth Ave., Ford City, 16226.
Tel: 724-763-9141; Email: sgallovich@dioceseofgreensburg.org. Revs. Ricky Cortez, Admin.; Alan W. Grote, In Res.
Catechesis Religious Program—Tel: 724-763-7973. Paula Sypulski, D.R.E. Students 6.
Chapel—Nicholson Run, Guardian Angel Cemetery and Chapel, Cadogan-Slatelick Rd., Kittanning, 16201.

CALUMET, WESTMORELAND CO., ST. STANISLAUS, [CEM] (Polish), Closed. For inquiries for parish records please see Saint Florian, United.

CARDALE, FAYETTE CO., MADONNA OF CZESTOCHOWA, [CEM] (Polish), Closed. For inquiries for parish records please see St. Francis of Assisi, Masontown.

CLYMER, INDIANA CO., CHURCH OF THE RESURRECTION (1995) [CEM]
349 Morris St., Clymer, 15728-1266.
Tel: 724-254-3041; Email: cor@dioceseofgreensburg.org; Web: www.churchresurrection.org. Revs. E. George Saletrik; Gregorio Soldevilla Jr., Parochial Vicar; Deacon Stephen Black.
Catechesis Religious Program—Students 138.
Chapel—Cameron's Bottom, Chapel of Church of the Resurrection, Clymer, Suppressed June 21, 1995.

CONNELLSVILLE, FAYETTE CO.
1—HOLY TRINITY, [CEM] (Polish), Closed. For inquiries for parish records, see Immaculate Conception, Connellsville.
2—IMMACULATE CONCEPTION (1870) [CEM 5]
Mailing Address: c/o 116 S. Second St., Connellsville, 15425. Revs. Robert T. Lubic; Daniel J. Ulishney; Julius Capongpongan.
Res.: 148 E. Crawford Ave., Connellsville, 15425.
Fax: 724-628-0838.
See Conn-Area Catholic School, Connellsville under Elementary Schools, Inter-Parochial located in the Institution section.
Catechesis Religious Program—Mary Sampey, Faith Formation. Students 101.
Chapel—Dawson, Sacred Heart Chapel, Suppressed April 16, 2007.
3—ST. JOHN THE EVANGELIST (1895) [CEM] (Slovak)
c/o 116 S. Second St., Connellsville, 15425.
Tel: 724-628-6840; Email: rlubic@dioceseofgreensburg.org; Web: www.connellsvillecatholicchurches.org. Revs. Robert T. Lubic, Admin.; Daniel J. Ulishney; Julius Capongpongan.
Res.: 908 W. Crawford Ave., Connellsville, 15425.
Fax: 724-628-0838.
See Conn-Area Catholic School, Connellsville under Elementary Schools, Inter-Parochial located in the Institution section.
Catechesis Religious Program—Students 63.
4—ST. RITA (1915) [CEM] (Italian)
116 S. Second St., Connellsville, 15425.
Tel: 724-628-6840; Fax: 724-628-0838. Revs. Robert T. Lubic; Daniel J. Ulishney; Julius Capongpongan.
See Conn-Area Catholic School, Connellsville under Elementary Schools, Inter-Parochial located in the Institution section.
Catechesis Religious Program—Students 80.

CORAL, INDIANA CO.
1—ST. FRANCIS, [CEM] Merged with St. Louis, Lucernemines to form Our Lady of the Assumption, Coral.
2—OUR LADY OF THE ASSUMPTION
2434 Neal Rd., P.O. Box G, Coral, 15731.
Tel: 724-479-9542. Revs. Alan N. Polczynski; Andres Gumangan, Parochial Vicar.
Res.: 403 Lucerne Rd., P.O. Box 197, Lucernemines, 15754.
Catechesis Religious Program—Email: mdodge@dioceseofgreensburg.org. Michelle Dodge, D.R.E. Students 91.

CRABTREE, WESTMORELAND CO., ST. BARTHOLOMEW (1889) [CEM]
2538 State Rte. 119, P.O. Box A, Crabtree, 15624.
Tel: 724-834-0709; Email: jmatro@dioceseofgreensburg.org; Web: www.stbart@dioceseofgreensburg.org. Revs. Justin M. Matro, O.S.B.; Thomas Acklin, O.S.B., In Res.
Catechesis Religious Program—Eric Kocian, D.R.E. Students 66.

DELMONT, WESTMORELAND CO., ST. JOHN BAPTIST DE LA SALLE
c/o 5900 Kennedy Ave., Export, 15632.
Tel: 724-327-0647; Email: eambre@doiceseofgreensburg.org. Rev. Efren C. Ambre; Deacon Jeffrey Cieslewicz.
Res.: 497 Athena Dr., Delmont, 15626.
Fax: 724-325-3784.
Catechesis Religious Program—Students 57.

DERRY, WESTMORELAND CO., ST. JOSEPH, [CEM]
117 S. Ligonier St., Derry, 15627. Tel: 724-694-5359; Email: slamendola@dioceseofgreensburg.org. Rev. Salvatore R. Lamendola, M.Div.
Catechesis Religious Program—Betty Wechtenhiser, D.R.E. Students 100.

DONEGAL, WESTMORELAND CO., ST. RAYMOND OF THE MOUNTAINS (1919) [CEM]
170 School House Ln., P.O. Box 330, Donegal, 15628.
Tel: 724-593-7479; Email: rkosisko@dioceseofgreensburg.org; Web: www.straymondchurch.org. Revs. Richard J. Kosisko, J.C.L.; Teodoro Cortezano.
Catechesis Religious Program—Bill Pospisil, D.R.E. Students 51.

DUNBAR, FAYETTE CO., ST. ALOYSIUS, [CEM]
459 Ranch Rd., Dunbar, 15431. Tel: 724-277-4236; Email: blubic@dioceseofgreensburg.org. Rev. Robert T. Lubic.

EAST VANDERGRIFT, WESTMORELAND CO., OUR LADY, QUEEN OF PEACE
400 Kennedy Ave., P.O. Box 429, East Vandergrift, 15629. Tel: 724-567-7603; Email: vzidek@dioceseofgreensburg.org. Revs. Thomas Sikora, O.S.B.; Michael J. Sciberras, In Res.
Catechesis Religious Program—Megan Krachanko, Coord.; Beth Kindall, Coord. Students 17.

ERNEST, INDIANA CO., CHURCH OF THE ASSUMPTION, Closed. For inquiries for parish records contact Church of the Resurrection, Clymer.

EVERSON, FAYETTE CO., ST. JOSEPH, [CEM] (Polish)
Mailing Address: c/o 416 S. Broadway, Scottdale, 15683. Tel: 724-887-6321; Email: akawecki@dioceseofgreensburg.org; Web: www.stjohnsandstjosephs.org. Rev. Andrew M. Kawecki, Admin.
Res.: 201 Painter St., Everson, 15631.
Tel: 724-887-6321; Fax: 724-887-6324.
Catechesis Religious Program—Students 15.

EXPORT, WESTMORELAND CO., ST. MARY
Mailing Address: 5900 Kennedy Ave., Export, 15632.
Tel: 724-327-0647; Email: eambre@dioceseofgreensburg.org; Web: www.stjohnstmary.org. Rev. Efren C. Ambre, Admin.; Susan Wagner, Business Mgr.; Marybelle Weber, Coord. Music Ministry.
Res.: 497 Athena Dr., Delmont, 15626.
Fax: 724-325-3784.
Catechesis Religious Program—Julie Ebersole, C.R.E. Students 57.

FAIRCHANCE, FAYETTE CO., SS. CYRIL AND METHODIUS, [CEM]
50 Morgantown St., Fairchance, 15436.
Tel: 724-564-7436; Email: greddy@dioceseofgreensburg.org. Rev. Gade Show Reddy.
Catechesis Religious Program—Tel: 724-438-5271. Rita Kennison, C.R.E. Students 23.
Chapel—Shoaf, Chapel of SS. Cyril & Methodius, Fairchance, Suppressed Oct. 1, 2007.

FARMINGTON, FAYETTE CO., ST. JOAN OF ARC, [CEM]
3523 National Pike, P.O. Box 92, Farmington, 15437.
Tel: 724-329-4522; Email: dmurren@dioceseofgreensburg.org. Rev. James F. Petrovsky.
Catechesis Religious Program—Mary Judd, D.R.E. Students 20.

FAYETTE CITY, FAYETTE CO., HOLY SPIRIT, Closed. For inquiries for parish records, see Saint Sebastian, Belle Vernon.

FOOTEDALE, FAYETTE CO., ST. THOMAS, [CEM] (Polish), Closed. For inquiries for parish records please see St. Francis of Assisi, Masontown.

FORBES ROAD, WESTMORELAND CO., ST. MARY, Closed. For inquiries for parish records, see St. Bartholomew, Crabtree.

FORD CITY, ARMSTRONG CO.
1—CHRIST, PRINCE OF PEACE PARISH
718 Fourth Ave., Ford City, 16226. Tel: 724-763-9141; Email: sgallovich@dioceseofgreensburg.org. Revs. Ricky Cortez; Alan W. Grote, Parochial Vicar.
Res.: 736 Fifth Ave., Ford City, 16226.
Fax: 724-763-9142.
Catechesis Religious Program—Tel: 724-763-2521. Darlene Scopel, D.R.E. Students 61.
2—ST. FRANCIS OF PAOLA, (Polish), Merged with St. Mary and Holy Trinity, Ford City to form Christ, Prince of Peace Parish, Ford City.
3—HOLY TRINITY, (Slovak), Merged St. Mary and St. Francis of Paola, Ford City to form Christ, Prince of Peace Parish, Ford City.
4—ST. MARY, Merged with St. Francis of Paola and Holy Trinity, Ford City to form Christ, Prince of Peace Parish, Ford City.

FREEPORT, ARMSTRONG CO., ST. MARY (1826) [CEM]
608 High St., Freeport, 16229. Tel: 724-295-2281; Email: rmaqinana@dioceseofgreensburg.org. Rev. Ronald Maquinana.
Catechesis Religious Program—610 High St., Freeport, 16229. Students 140.

GLEN CAMPBELL, INDIANA CO., ST. MICHAEL, Closed. For inquiries for parish records contact Church of the Resurrection, Clymer.

GRINDSTONE, FAYETTE CO., ST. CECILIA, (Slovak)
c/o 118 Church St., Brownsville, 15417.
Tel: 724-785-7781; Fax: 724-785-0844; Email: ssealy@dioceseofgreensburg.org. Revs. Timothy J. Kruthaupt, Admin.; Alvin E. Cabungcal.
Catechesis Religious Program—Patty Craig, D.R.E. Students 130.

HARRISON CITY, WESTMORELAND CO., ST. BARBARA, [CEM]
111 Raymaley Rd., Harrison City, 15636.
Tel: 724-744-7474; Fax: 724-744-3056; Email: jshepherd@dioceseofgreensburg.org; Web: www.stbarbara.org. Rev. Michael P. Sikon.
Res.: 91 Raymaley Rd., Harrison City, 15636.
Tel: 724-392-4600.
Catechesis Religious Program—Joan Duncan, D.R.E. Students 245.

HEILWOOD, INDIANA CO., ST. JOHN THE BAPTIST, Closed. For inquiries for parish records contact Church of the Resurrection, Clymer.

HERMINIE, WESTMORELAND CO., ST. EDWARD (1920)
120 St. Edward Ln., Herminie, 15637. Rev. Joseph E. Bonafed; Deacon John Zombar.
Catechesis Religious Program—Mrs. Kathleen Topolosky, D.R.E. Students 98.

INDIANA, INDIANA CO.
1—ST. BERNARD OF CLAIRVAUX, [CEM]
200 Clairvaux Dr., Indiana, 15701.
Tel: 724-465-2210; Fax: 724-465-0422; Email: info@saintbernardparish.org. Very Rev. Thomas A. Federline, V.F.
Catechesis Religious Program—
Tel: 724-465-2210, Ext. 114. Students 157.
2—ST. THOMAS MORE UNIVERSITY PARISH, (Newman Center)
1200 Oakland Ave., Indiana, 15701.
Tel: 724-463-2277; Email: dcawley@dioceseofgreensburg.org; Web: www.stmup.org. Revs. Alan N. Polczynski; Andres Gumangan, Parochial Vicar; Diane Cawley, Parish & Fin. Sec.; Cindy Schillinger, Pastoral Assoc. & Dir. Campus Min.; Alexandra Stossel, Music Min.
Catechesis Religious Program—Mary Beth Palko, Coord., Catechesis of the Good Shepard & Youth Min. Students 109.

IRWIN, WESTMORELAND CO., IMMACULATE CONCEPTION (1868) [CEM]
308 Second St., Irwin, 15642. Tel: 724-863-9550; Email: jmoineau@dioceseofgreensburg.org. Revs. John A. Moineau; Roniel Duenas.
See Queen of Angels Regional Catholic School, under Elementary Schools, Inter-Parochial located in the Institution section.
Catechesis Religious Program—Ginny McConnell, D.R.E. Students 475.

ISELIN, INDIANA CO., HOLY CROSS, Closed. For inquiries for parish records contact Church of the Good Shepherd, Kent.

JEANNETTE, WESTMORELAND CO.
1—ASCENSION (1918) (Italian)
615 Division St., Jeannette, 15644.
Tel: 724-523-2560; Email: plisik@dioceseofgreensburg.org; Web: www.ascensionsacredheartchurches.org. c/o 504 Cowan Ave., Jeannette, 15644. Rev. Paul A. Lisik, Admin.; Deacon William M. Newhouse.
Catechesis Religious Program—John Ridilla, D.R.E. Students 68.
2—SACRED HEART (1889) [CEM]
504 Cowan Ave., Jeannette, 15644.
Tel: 724-523-2560; Email: shjeannette@dioceseofgreensburg.org. Rev. Paul A. Lisik; Deacon William M. Newhouse, In Res.
Catechesis Religious Program—Students 68.

KENT, INDIANA CO., CHURCH OF THE GOOD SHEPHERD (1989)
100 Good Shepherd Dr., P.O. Box 99, Kent, 15752.
Tel: 724-479-3881; Email: wlechnar@dioceseofgreensburg.org. Rev. William J. Lechnar.
Catechesis Religious Program—Danielle Cribbs, Asst. Coord., Faith Formation; Carolyn Davis, Asst. Coord., Faith Formation. Students 64.

KITTANNING, ARMSTRONG CO., ST. MARY, OUR LADY OF

GUADALUPE (1854) [CEM]
101 W. High St., Kittanning, 16201.
Tel: 724-548-7649. Revs. Douglas E. Dorula; Victor Baguna, Parochial Vicar.
Office: 348 N. Water St., Kittanning, 16201. Email: ddorula@dioceseofgreensburg.org; Web: www.stmarykittanning.org.
Catechesis Religious Program—Joseph Kacprowski, Faith Formation Coord. Students 84.

LATROBE, WESTMORELAND CO.
1—ST. BONIFACE, Closed. For inquiries for parish records please see St. Raymond of the Mountains, Donegal.
2—HOLY FAMILY, [CEM]
1200 Ligonier St., Latrobe, 15650. Tel: 724-539-9751; Email: ssutton@dioceseofgreensburg.org. Very Rev. Daniel C. Mahoney, V.F.; Deacon Michael J. Orange.
See Christ the Divine Teacher School, Latrobe under Elementary Schools, Inter-Parochial located in the Institution section.
Catechesis Religious Program—Tel: 724-539-3638. Marlene Rafferty, Coord.Faith Formation. Students 117.
3—ST. JOHN THE EVANGELIST (1901)
306 St. John Dr., Latrobe, 15650. Tel: 724-537-8909; Email: acarbone@dioceseofgreensburg.org. Revs. Anthony J. Carbone, J.C.L.; Rogelio Rodriguez.
See Christ the Divine Teacher School, Latrobe under Elementary Schools, Inter-Parochial located in the Institution section.
Catechesis Religious Program—Eva Japalucci, Faith Formation Facilitator. Students 18.
4—ST. ROSE (1893) [CEM]
4969 Rte. 982, Latrobe, 15650. Tel: 724-537-3709; Email: acarbone@dioceseofgreensburg.org. Revs. Anthony J. Carbone, J.C.L., Admin.; Rogelio Rodriguez, In Res.
See Christ the Divine Teacher School, Latrobe under Elementary Schools, Inter-Parochial located in the Institution section.
Catechesis Religious Program—Eva Japalucci, D.R.E. Students 40.
5—ST. VINCENT BASILICA, [CEM]
300 Fraser Purchase Rd., Latrobe, 15650.
Tel: 724-539-8629; Email: tcurry@dioceseofgreensburg.org. Revs. Thomas P. Curry, O.S.B.; Daniel Paul O'Keefe, O.S.B.; Kristina Antolin Davies, Pastoral Assoc.
See Christ the Divine Teacher School, Latrobe under Elementary Schools, Inter-Parochial located in the Institution section.
Catechesis Religious Program—
Tel: 724-539-8629, Ext. 16. Students 246.

LECKRONE, FAYETTE CO., OUR LADY OF PERPETUAL HELP (ST. MARY) (1902) [CEM] Closed. For inquiries for parish records please see St. Francis of Assisi, Masontown.

LEECHBURG, ARMSTRONG CO.
1—ST. CATHERINE OF ALEXANDRIA, Closed. For inquiries for parish records contact Christ the King, Leechburg.
2—CHRIST THE KING, [CEM]
Tel: 724-845-8191; Web: www.ctkleechburg.org. Rev. James H. Loew, O.S.B., Admin.
3—CHURCH OF THE ASSUMPTION, Closed. For inquiries for parish records contact Christ the King, Leechburg.
4—ST. MARTHA, (Slovak), Closed. For inquiries for parish records contact Christ the King, Leechburg.

LEISENRING, FAYETTE CO., ST. VINCENT DE PAUL, [CEM] Closed. For inquiries for parish records, see Saint Aloysius, Dunbar.

LIGONIER, WESTMORELAND CO., HOLY TRINITY, [CEM]
342 W. Main St., Ligonier, 15658. Tel: 724-238-6434; Email: aevangeliste@dioceseofgreensburg.org. Rev. John M. Foriska.
Catechesis Religious Program—Tel: 724-238-6341. Students 84.

LOWER BURRELL, WESTMORELAND CO., ST. MARGARET MARY
3055 Leechburg Rd., Lower Burrell, 15068. Very Rev. Kenneth G. Zaccagnini, V.F.
Res.: 231 Park Dr., Lower Burrell, 15068.
Fax: 724-335-1945.
Catechesis Religious Program—Donna Misak, Regl. Pastoral Assoc. Faith Formation. Students 174.

LUCERNEMINES, INDIANA CO., ST. LOUIS, [CEM] Merged with St. Francis, Coral to form Our Lady of the Assumption, Coral.

MARGUERITE, WESTMORELAND CO., ST. BENEDICT (1901)
260 Bruno Rd., 15601. Tel: 724-838-9480;
Fax: 724-834-1880; Email: dblout@dioceseofgreensburg.org. Rev. Daniel L. Blout.
Catechesis Religious Program—Paula Aiello, Coord. (PreK-5th); Renie Prengaman, Coord. (Middle School Youth Min.); Michele Ruby, H.S. Youth Min. Students 138.

MASONTOWN, FAYETTE CO.
1—ALL SAINTS, [CEM] Closed. For inquiries for parish records please see St. Francis of Assisi, Masontown.
2—SAINT FRANCIS OF ASSISI (2013) [CEM]
101 W. Church Ave., Masontown, 15461.
Tel: 724-583-7866; Email: wberkey@dioceseofgreensburg.org. Revs. William G. Berkey; Thumma Fathimareddy.
Catechesis Religious Program—Ms. Wanda Wokulich, D.R.E. Students 84.
Chapel—McClellandtown, Chapel of All Saints, Masontown.

MAXWELL, FAYETTE CO., ST. JAMES, Closed. For inquiries for parish records, see Saint Peter, Brownsville.

MONESSEN, WESTMORELAND CO., THE EPIPHANY OF OUR LORD, [CEM 2]
44 Pennsylvania Blvd., Monessen, 15062.
Tel: 724-684-7661; Fax: 724-684-8981; Email: mcrookston@dioceseofgreensburg.org; Web: www.eolparish.com. Rev. Michael J. Crookston.
Catechesis Religious Program—Students 14.

MOUNT PLEASANT, WESTMORELAND CO.
1—ST. PIUS X (1972) [CEM]
740 W Walnut St, Mount Pleasant, 15666. Revs. Richard J. Kosisko, J.C.L.; Teodoro Cortezano; Sr. Edith Strong, S.C., Pastoral Assoc.; Mr. Joseph G. Klocek, Business Mgr.
Res.: 216 Spruce St., Mount Pleasant, 15666.
Tel: 724-547-1911; Web: www.mpcatholicchurches.org.
Catechesis Religious Program—Students 89.
2—TRANSFIGURATION, [CEM] (Polish), Closed. For inquiries for parish records contact the chancery.
3—VISITATION OF THE BLESSED VIRGIN MARY (1893) [CEM] (Slovak)
740 W Walnut St., Mount Pleasant, 15666.
Tel: 724-547-1911; Fax: 724-547-2630; Email: rkosisko@dioceseofgreensburg.org. Revs. Richard J. Kosisko, J.C.L., Admin.; Teodoro Cortezano; Sr. Edith Strong, S.C.; Mr. Joseph G. Klocek, Business Mgr.
Res.: 216 Spruce St., Mount Pleasant, 15666.
Catechesis Religious Program—Students 57.

MURRYSVILLE, WESTMORELAND CO., MOTHER OF SORROWS (1939)
4202 Old William Penn Hwy., Murrysville, 15668.
Tel: 724-733-8870; Fax: 724-733-8108; Web: www.motherofsorrowschurch.org. Rev. Msgr. James T. Gaston, V.F.; Rev. Eric J. Dinga.
Catechesis Religious Program—Erin Colcombe, Dir. Faith Formation. Students 332.

NEW ALEXANDRIA, WESTMORELAND CO., ST. JAMES
306 Saint James Ln., New Alexandria, 15670.
Tel: 724-668-2829; Fax: 724-668-7327; Email: lkulick@dioceseofgreensburg.org; Web: www.stjamesnewalexandria.org. Rev. Msgr. Larry J. Kulick, J.C.L.
Catechesis Religious Program—William J. D'Angelo, D.R.E. Students 27.

NEW DERRY, WESTMORELAND CO., ST. MARTIN, [CEM]
c/o 117 S. Ligonier St., Derry, 15627.
Tel: 724-694-5359; Fax: 724-694-5716; Email: slamendola@dioceseofgreensburg.org. Rev. Salvatore R. Lamendola, M.Div., Admin.
Catechesis Religious Program—Betty Wechtenhiser, D.R.E. Students 50.

NEW KENSINGTON, WESTMORELAND CO.
1—ST. JOSEPH (1891)
1125 Leishman Ave., New Kensington, 15068.
Tel: 724-337-6412; Email: jszczesny@dioceseofgreensburg.org. Revs. John S. Szczesny; Rodel Molina.
See Mary Queen of Apostles, New Kensington, located under Inter-Parochial Schools in the Institution Section.
Catechesis Religious Program—Students 63.
2—ST. MARY OF CZESTOCHOWA (1893) [CEM] (Polish)
857 Kenneth Ave., New Kensington, 15068.
Tel: 724-335-8212; Email: jszczesny@dioceseofgreensburg.org. Revs. John S. Szczesny, Admin.; Rodel Molina; Sr. Mary Carol Kardell, C.S.S.F., Pastoral Min.
Catechesis Religious Program—Deborah Discello, D.R.E. Students 65.
3—MT. ST. PETER, (Italian)
100 Freeport Rd., New Kensington, 15068.
Tel: 724-335-9877; Email: mbegolly@dioceseofgreensburg.org. Rev. Msgr. Michael J. Begolly, D.Min., M.A.; Rev. Rodel Molina.
Catechesis Religious Program—Students 193.

NEW SALEM, FAYETTE CO., ST. PROCOPIUS, [CEM] Closed. For inquiries for parish records please see St. Francis of Assisi, Masontown.

NORTH HUNTINGDON, WESTMORELAND CO.
1—ST. AGNES
11400 St. Agnes Ln., North Huntingdon, 15642.
Tel: 724-863-2626. Rev. Msgr. V. Paul Fitzmaurice.
See Queen of Angels Regional Catholic School, North Huntingdon under Elementary Schools, Inter-Parochial located in the Institution section.
Catechesis Religious Program—Tel: 724-864-5393. Mary Blythe, D.R.E. Students 217.
2—ST. ELIZABETH ANN SETON (1978)
200 Leger Rd., North Huntingdon, 15642.
Tel: 724-864-6364; Web: www.seasnh.org. Revs. John A. Moineau; Roniel Duenas, Parochial Vicar; Deacon Jeffrey Cieslewicz.
Res.: 119 Katherine Dr., North Huntingdon, 15642.
Catechesis Religious Program—Sr. Charlene Ozanick, C.S.S.F., D.R.E. Students 194.

PALMER, FAYETTE CO., ST. ALBERT, Closed. For inquiries for parish records, see St. Mary, Our Lady of Perpetual Help, Leckrone.

PARKER, ARMSTRONG CO., ST. MARY, OUR LADY OF THE SNOWS, Closed. For inquiries for parish records, see Saint Patrick, Brady's Bend.

PENN, WESTMORELAND CO., ST. BONIFACE, [CEM] Closed. For inquiries for parish records, see Sacred Heart, Jeannette.

PERRYOPOLIS, FAYETTE CO., ST. JOHN THE BAPTIST (1904) [CEM]
3332 Pittsburgh Rd., Perryopolis, 15473.
Tel: 724-736-4442; Email: sjbperry@dioceseofgreensburg.org. Rev. Alvin E. Cabungcal.
Catechesis Religious Program—Tel: 724-736-0158; Email: chall@dioceseofgreensburg.org. Cheryl Hall, D.R.E. Students 78.

POINT MARION, FAYETTE CO., ST. HUBERT
c/o 50 N. Morgantown St., Fairchance, 15436.
Tel: 724-564-7436; Email: greddy@dioceseofgreensburg.org; Web: www.sthubertpointmarion.org. Rev. Gade Show Reddy.
Catechesis Religious Program—Students 1.

REPUBLIC, FAYETTE CO., HOLY ROSARY (1916) [CEM] Closed. For inquiries for parish records please see St. Francis of Assisi, Masontown.

ROSSITER, INDIANA CO., ST. FRANCIS OF ASSISI, Closed. For inquiries for parish records contact the Church of the Resurrection, Clymer.

ROSTRAVER TOWNSHIP, WESTMORELAND CO., ST. ANNE (1957)
1870 Rostraver Rd., Rostraver Township, 15012.
Tel: 724-842-3555; Fax: 724-872-3373; Email: stanne@dioceseofgreensburg.org; Web: www.stannerostraver.org. Rev. Vincent J. Gigliotti.
Catechesis Religious Program—Tel: 724-872-3486. Barbara Zucconi, D.R.E. Students 200.

SAGAMORE, ARMSTRONG CO., SACRED HEART, [CEM] Closed. Parish closed Oct. 1, 2007. For inquiries for parish records, see St. Mary, Yatesboro.

SALTSBURG, INDIANA CO., ST. MATTHEW, [CEM] (Italian)
505 Cambria Ave., P.O. Box 617, Avonmore, 15618.
Tel: 724-697-4129; Email: jharrold@dioceseofgreensburg.org. Rev. John J. Harrold, Admin.; Deacon Daniel Frescura.
Catechesis Religious Program—703 Indiana Ave., Saltsburg, 15681. Students 48.

SCOTTDALE, WESTMORELAND CO., ST. JOHN THE BAPTIST (1878) [CEM]
416 S. Broadway, Scottdale, 15683.
Tel: 724-887-6321; Email: akawecki@dioceseofgreensburg.org; Web: stjosephsandstjohns.org/Pages/default.aspx. Rev. Andrew M. Kawecki.
Catechesis Religious Program—Linda Benko, Coord. Faith Formation/RCIA. Students 74.

SEWARD, WESTMORELAND CO., HOLY FAMILY (1907) [CEM 3]
425 Bridge St., Seward, 15954. Tel: 814-446-5759; Email: rwashko@dioceseofgreensburg.org. Rev. Robert M. Washko.
Catechesis Religious Program—Gail Smyder, D.R.E. Students 107.

SLICKVILLE, WESTMORELAND CO., ST. SYLVESTER
3028 Rt. 819, Box 307, Slickville, 15684.
Tel: 724-468-5794; Email: jharrold@dioceseofgreensburg.org. Rev. John J. Harrold, Admin.; Deacon F. Daniel Frescura.
Catechesis Religious Program—Students 6.

SMITHTON, WESTMORELAND CO., ST. TIMOTHY, [CEM] Closed. For inquiries for parish records, see St. Ann, Rostraver.

SMOCK, FAYETTE CO., ST. HEDWIG, [CEM 2] (Slovak), Closed. For inquiries for parish records please see St. John the Baptist, Perryopolis.

STARFORD, INDIANA CO., ST. ELIZABETH, Closed. For inquiries for parish records contact Church of the Resurrection, Clymer.

SUTERSVILLE, WESTMORELAND CO., ST. CHARLES BORROMEO, Closed. For inquiries for parish records, see Holy Family, West Newton.

TRAFFORD, WESTMORELAND CO., ST. REGIS
517 Homewood Ave., Trafford, 15085.
Tel: 412-372-4577; Fax: 412-373-5979; Email: dnazimek@dioceseofgreensburg.org; Email: fgradisek@dioceseofgreensburg.org; Email: kmcdade@dioceseofgreensburg.org; Email: mdaversa@dioceseofgreensburg.org; Email: jmiller@dioceseofgreensburg.org; Web: www.

stregistrafford.org. Rev. David Nazimek; Ms. Florence Gradisek, Liturgy Dir.; Mr. Michael Daversa, Business Mgr.; Mrs. Karen McDade, D.R.E.; Ms. Joyce Miller, Sec.

TRAUGER, WESTMORELAND CO., FORTY MARTYRS, [CEM] (Hungarian), Closed. For inquiries for parish records, see St. Florian, United.

UNIONTOWN, FAYETTE CO.

1—ST. JOHN THE EVANGELIST
88 S. Pennsylvania Ave., Uniontown, 15401.
Tel: 724-437-7569; Fax: 724-437-6277; Email: aklimko@dioceseofgreensburg.org. Rev. Msgr. Michael W. Matusak, V.F.; Revs. Anthony J. Klimko, Admin.; Vincent Concepcion.
Res.: 50 Jefferson St., Uniontown, 15401.
Catechesis Religious Program—Students 72.

2—ST. JOSEPH, [CEM] (Polish)
180 Old Walnut Hill Rd., Uniontown, 15401.
Tel: 724-437-3927; Email: aklimko@dioceseofgreensburg.org. Rev. Msgr. Michael W. Matusak, V.F., Admin.; Revs. Anthony J. Klimko, Admin.; Vincent Concepcion.
Catechesis Religious Program—Tel: 724-438-2341. Marlene Bandzuch, D.R.E. Students 43.

3—NATIVITY OF THE BLESSED VIRGIN MARY (1903) [CEM] (Slovak)
61 N. Mount Vernon Ave., Uniontown, 15401.
Tel: 724-437-1512; Email: aklimko@dioceseofgreensburg.org. Rev. Msgr. Michael W. Matusak, V.F.; Revs. Anthony J. Klimko, Admin.; Vincent Concepcion.
Catechesis Religious Program—Students 67.

4—ST. THERESE, THE LITTLE FLOWER OF JESUS, (Italian)
61 Mill St., Uniontown, 15401. Tel: 724-438-2341; Fax: 724-437-0622. Rev. Msgr. Michael W. Matusak, V.F.; Revs. Anthony J. Klimko, Admin.; Vincent Concepcion.
Catechesis Religious Program—Marlene Bandzuch, D.R.E. Students 177.

UNITED, WESTMORELAND CO., ST. FLORIAN, [CEM]
4261 Rt. 981, P.O. Box 187, United, 15689.
Tel: 724-423-4431; Email: jsedlak@dioceseofgreensburg.org; Web: www.saintflorian.org. Rev. John A. Sedlak.
School—St. Florian School, 4257 Rt. 981, Mount Pleasant, 15666. Tel: 724-423-4437. Lay Teachers 2; Students 30.
Catechesis Religious Program—Joseph Dreliszak, D.Ed., Dir. Catechesis, Faith Formation & Evangelization; Angela Reese, Office Asst. Students 59.

VANDERGRIFT, WESTMORELAND CO., ST. GERTRUDE, [CEM]
303 Franklin Ave., Vandergrift, 15690.
Tel: 724-568-2331; Email: jloew@dioceseofgreensburg.org. Rev. James H. Loew, O.S.B.
Catechesis Religious Program—James Peterman, D.R.E. Students 61.

WEST NEWTON, WESTMORELAND CO., HOLY FAMILY
225 N. Second St., West Newton, 15089.
Tel: 724-872-6123; Email: pdeclaudio@dioceseofgreensburg.org. Rev. Joseph E. Bonafed; Deacon John Zombar.
Catechesis Religious Program—Tel: 724-872-2106. Michalene Lovato, D.R.E. Students 50.

WHITNEY, WESTMORELAND CO., ST. CECILIA
218 St. Cecilia Rd., P.O. Box 80, Whitney, 15693.
Tel: 724-423-3777; Email: swagner@dioceseofgreensburg.org. Rev. James F. Podlesny, O.S.B., Admin.
Catechesis Religious Program—William Smith, C.R.E. Students 28.

YATESBORO, ARMSTRONG CO., ST. MARY (1903) [CEM]
111 Second St., Yatesboro, 16263. Tel: 724-783-7191; Email: sacredmary@dioceseofgreensburg.org; Web: www.stmaryyatesboro.org. P.O. Box 327, Yatesboro, 16263. Revs. Douglas E. Dorula, Admin.; Victor Baguna, Parochial Vicar.
Res.: 109 Second St., P.O. Box 327, Yatesboro, 16263.
Fax: 724-783-7783; Email: bboltz@dioceseofgreensburg.org; Web: www.saintmaryyatesboro.org.
Catechesis Religious Program—Email: bfrailey@dioceseofgreensburg.org. Bonnie Frailey, D.R.E. Students 48.

YOUNGSTOWN, WESTMORELAND CO., SACRED HEART (1875)
421 Main St, P.O. Box 328, Youngstown, 15696.
Tel: 724-537-7358. c/o 218 St. Cecilia Rd., P.O. Box 80, Whitney, 15693. Rev. James F. Podlesny, O.S.B.
Catechesis Religious Program—William Smith, C.R.E. Students 31.

YOUNGWOOD, WESTMORELAND CO., HOLY CROSS
711 Depot St., Youngwood, 15697. Tel: 724-925-7811; Email: mbrinza@dioceseofgreensburg.org. Rev. William C. McGuirk.
Catechesis Religious Program—Brian Lohr, Faith Formation Coord. Students 277.

YUKON, WESTMORELAND CO., SEVEN DOLORS (1909) [CEM]
102 Center St., P.O. Box 308, Yukon, 15698.
Tel: 724-722-3141; Email: rulam@dioceseofgreensburg.org. Rev. Richard Ulam, O.S.B., Admin.
Catechesis Religious Program—Lauretta B. Stanley, D.R.E. Seven Dolors Church. Students 45.

Chaplains of Public Institutions

GREENSBURG. *Excela Health - Westmoreland Hospital*, Tel: 724-832-4000;
Tel: 724-832-4447 (Chaplain's Office). Revs. Richard Chirichiello, O.S.B., Assoc. Chap., Chad Ficorilli, O.S.B., Assoc. Chap., Robert Keffer, O.S.B., Assoc. Chap.

BROWNSVILLE. *Brownsville General Hospital*. Attended by St. Peter, Brownsville, Tel: 724-785-7200; 724-785-7781 (Res.).

CONNELLSVILLE. *Highlands Hospital & Health Center*, Connellsville. Tel: 724-628-1500. Attended by Partner Parishes of St. Rita, Immaculate Conception & Saint Rita, Connellsville, Tel: 724-628-6840.

INDIANA. *Indiana Hospital*, Indiana. Tel: 724-357-7000. Attended by Church of Resurrection, Clymer, Tel: 724-465-3900 (Indiana County Home); 724-465-5840 (Res.).

KITTANNING. *Armstrong County Hospital*, Kittanning. Tel: 724-543-8500. Rev. Alan W. Grote, Tel: 724-763-1089 (Res.).

LATROBE. *Excela Health - Latrobe Area Hospital*, Latrobe. Tel: 724-537-1000. Revs. Robert Keffer, O.S.B., Assoc. Chap., Jeremiah Lange, O.S.B., Ph. D., Assoc. Chap., Dominic J. Petroy, O.S.B., Assoc. Chap., John Mary Tompkins, O.S.B., Assoc. Chap., Tel: 724-539-9761.

MOUNT PLEASANT. *Excela Health Frick Hospital*, Mount Pleasant. Tel: 724-547-1500 (Hospital). Attended by Partner Parishes of St. Rita, Immaculate Conception & Saint Rita, Connellsville, Tel: 724-628-6840.

NEW KENSINGTON. *Citizens General Hospital*, New Kensington. Tel: 724-337-3541. Attended by St. Mary, New Kensington, Tel: 724-335-8212 (Res.); St. Joseph, New Kensington, Tel: 724-337-6412 (Res.); Mount St. Peter, New Kensington, Tel: 724-335-9877 (Res.).

TORRANCE. *Torrance State Hospital*, Torrance. Tel: 724-459-8000.

UNIONTOWN. *Uniontown Hospital*, Uniontown. Tel: 724-430-5000 (Res.); Tel: 724-246-9657. Rev. James W. Clark, Chap.

Graduate Studies:
Rev.—
Carr, Daniel E., Pontifical North American College, Vatican City State 00120.

Priests On Leave:
Rev.—
Trupkovich, Thomas S.

Retired:
Rev. Msgrs.—
Conway, John L., V.F., (Retired), Saint Anne Home, 685 Angela Dr., 15601
McCullough, J. Edward, (Retired), Saint Ann Home, 685 Angela Dr., 15601
Revs.—
Kacinko, Elmer A., (Retired), 1987 Centurion Dr., Apt. 601, Pittsburgh, 15221
Kiel, William J., (Retired), 47 Barbara Ln., Uniontown, 15401
Lukac, Thomas M., (Retired), Saint Anne Home, 685 Angela Dr., 15601
Mandock, Patrick H., (Retired), P.O. Box 497, Elephant Butte, NM 87935
Rutkowski, Ronald J., (Retired), Avalon Springs Nursing Center, 745 Greenville Rd., Mercer, 16137.

INSTITUTIONS LOCATED IN DIOCESE

[A] SEMINARIES, RELIGIOUS OR SCHOLASTICATES

LATROBE. *St. Vincent Seminary*, 300 Fraser Purchase Rd., Latrobe, 15650. Tel: 724-805-2592;
Tel: 724-805-2845; Fax: 724-532-5052; Email: edward.mazich@stvincent.edu; Web: www.saintvincentseminary.edu. Revs. Edward M. Mazich, O.S.B., S.T.D., Rector; Emmanuel Afunugo, Dean of Students; Boniface Hicks, O.S.B., Dir. Spiritual Formation; Cyprian G. Constantine, O.S.B., Dir., Liturgy; John Mary Tompkins, O.S.B., Vice Rector & Dir. of Human Formation; Nathan J. Munsch, O.S.B., Dir. Pastoral Formation; Patrick T. Cronauer, O.S.B., Academic Dean; Deacon Lawrence Sutton, Dir. Pre-Theology Formation; Bro. David Kelly, O.S.B., Dir. Library. Clergy 15; Professors 14; Lay Students 4; Benedictine Seminarians 18; Diocesan Seminarians 32; ESL 3; Clergy / Religious Teachers 15.

[B] COLLEGES AND UNIVERSITIES

GREENSBURG. *Seton Hill University*, 1 Seton Hill Dr., 15601. Tel: 724-834-2200; Fax: 724-830-4611; Email: admit@setonhill.edu; Web: www.setonhill.edu. Mary C. Finger, Ed.D., Pres.; Sisters Susan Yochum, S.C., Acting Provost; Maureen O'Brien, S.C., Dir., Campus Min.; Mr. David Stanely, Dir. Reeves Library. Sisters of Charity of Seton Hill. Lay Teachers 103; Sisters 2; Students 1,942.

LATROBE. *Saint Vincent College*, 300 Fraser Purchase Rd., Latrobe, 15650-2690. Tel: 724-805-2271;
Fax: 724-532-5065; Email: president@stvincent.edu; Web: www.stvincent.edu. Rt. Rev. Douglas R. Nowicki, O.S.B., Chancellor; Bros. Norman W. Hipps, O.S.B., Pres.; David Kelly, O.S.B., Dir. Libraries
Saint Vincent College Corporation Brothers 4; Lay Teachers 100; Priests 12; Students 1,676; Clergy / Religious Teachers 15.

[C] HIGH SCHOOLS, DIOCESAN

GREENSBURG. *Greensburg Central Catholic High School Jr./Sr. High School*, (Grades 7-12), 911 Armory Dr., 15601. Tel: 724-834-0310;
Fax: 724-834-2472; Email: info@gcchs.org; Web: www.gcchs.org. Rev. Tyler J. Bandura, Chap. & Rel. Instructor; Benjamin Althof, Prin., Email: balthof@gcchs.org; Carol Whalen, Librarian. Lay Teachers 29; Priests 2; Sisters 1; Students 394.

CONNELLSVILLE. *Geibel Catholic Junior-Senior High School*, (Grades 7-12), 611 E. Crawford Ave., Connellsville, 15425. Tel: 724-628-5600;
Fax: 724-626-5700; Email: geibelinfo@geibelcatholic.org; Web: www.geibelcatholic.org. Revs. Robert T. Lubic, Chap. & Rel. Instructor; Daniel J. Ulishney, Chap.; Sr. Christine Kiley, A.S.C.J., Dir. Campus Ministry; Patricia L. Nickler, Prin., Email: pnickler@geibelcatholic.org. Lay Teachers 14; Priests 1; Students 176.

[D] ELEMENTARY SCHOOLS, INTER-PAROCHIAL

CONNELLSVILLE. *Conn-Area Catholic School*, 613 E. Crawford Ave., Connellsville, 15425.
Tel: 724-628-5090; Fax: 724-628-1745; Email: csolan@connareacatholic.org; Web: www.connareacatholic.org. Mrs. Cecilia Solan, Prin. Lay Teachers 14; Students 154; Clergy / Religious Teachers 1.

NEW KENSINGTON. *Mary Queen of Apostles*, (Grades PreK-8), (Regional School) 110 Elmtree Rd., New Kensington, 15068. Tel: 724-339-4411;
Fax: 724-337-6457; Email: mqa@mqaschool.org; Web: www.mqaschool.org. Catherine M. Collett, Prin. Lay Teachers 22; Students 206.

[E] ELEMENTARY SCHOOLS - REGIONAL

GREENSBURG. *Aquinas Academy*, (Grades PreK-6), 340 N. Main St., 15601. Tel: 724-834-7940;
Fax: 724-836-0497; Email: info@aquinasacademy.org. Joseph J. Rice, Prin., Email: kpoole@aquinasacademy.org; Mrs. Michelle Finoli, Librarian. Lay Teachers 13; Students 160.

BELLE VERNON. *St. Sebastian Regional School*, 815 Broad Ave., Belle Vernon, 15012.
Tel: 724-929-5143; Fax: 724-929-3038. Dr. Nina Zetty, Prin., Email: nzetty@sssbv.org. Lay Teachers 15; Students 159.

FORD CITY. *Divine Redeemer School*, (Grades PreSchool-6), 726 Fourth Ave., Ford City, 16226.
Tel: 724-763-3761; Fax: 724-763-4112; Email: ncarlesi@dioceseofgreensburg.org. Nicalena Carlesi, Prin. Lay Teachers 12; Students 142.

INDIANA. *St. Bernard Regional School*, 300 Clairvaux Dr., Indiana, 15701. Tel: 724-465-7139;
Fax: 724-465-0803; Email: dswope@dioceseofgreensburg.org. Denise Swope, Prin. Lay Teachers 13; Students 124.

LATROBE. *Christ the Divine Teacher School*, (Grades PreK-6), 323 Chestnut St., Latrobe, 15650.
Tel: 724-539-1561; Fax: 724-532-3873; Email: cdt@cdtschool.org; Web: www.cdtschool.org. J. Kevin Frye, Prin. Lay Teachers 14; Students 161.

MURRYSVILLE. *Mother of Sorrows School*, 3264 Evergreen Dr., Murrysville, 15668.
Tel: 724-733-8840; Fax: 724-325-1144; Email: tszmed@mosschool.org; Web: www.mosschool.org.

Theresa A. Szmed, Prin., Email: tszmed@dioceseofgreensburg.org. Lay Teachers 26; Students 250.

NORTH HUNTINGDON. *Queen of Angels School/The Bishop Anthony G. Bosco Center*, One Main St., North Huntingdon, 15642. Tel: 724-978-0144; Fax: 724-978-0171; Email: info@queenofangelssch.org; Web: www.queenofangelssch.org. Sandra Stonebraker, Prin. Lay Teachers 19; Students 200.

UNIONTOWN. *St. John the Evangelist Regional Catholic School*, (Grades PreK-8), 52 Jefferson St., Uniontown, 15401. Tel: 724-438-8598; Fax: 724-438-8585; Email: croskovensky@dioceseofgreensburg.org. Christine Roskovensky, Prin. Lay Teachers 12; Students 200.

VANDERGRIFT. *The Cardinal Maida Academy*, (Grades PreSchool-6), 315 Franklin Ave., Vandergrift, 15690. Tel: 724-568-3304; Fax: 724-567-1900. Mark Talarico, Prin. Lay Teachers 9; Students 84.

[F] SPECIAL EDUCATION

GREENSBURG. *Clelian Heights School for Exceptional Children*, (Grades K-12), 135 Clelian Heights Ln., 15601. Tel: 724-837-8120; Fax: 724-837-6480; Email: clelian@aol.com; Web: www.clelianheights.org. Sisters Deborah Lopez, A.S.C..J., Pres.; Charlene Celli, A.S.C.J., Prin.; Rev. James B. Morley, Chap. Apostles of the Sacred Heart of Jesus. *Corporation Name: Clelian Heights, Inc.* Lay Staff 118; Sisters 9; Students 65; Adult Clients 92.

Elizabeth Seton Montessori School of Westmoreland County, Inc., 294 Frye Farm Rd., P.O. Box 268, 15601. Tel: 724-837-8500; Fax: 724-836-0772; Email: esmontessori@comcast.net. Sr. Anita Schulte, S.C., Admin. & Pres. Bd. of Dirs.; Mrs. Linda M. Fidazzo, Prin. Sisters of Charity. Lay Teachers 3; Sisters 2; Students 35.

MOUNT PLEASANT. *Verna Montessori School*, 268 Prittstown Rd., Mount Pleasant, 15666. Tel: 724-887-8810; Fax: 724-887-2977; Email: vmsami@zoominternet.net. Sisters M. Letizia Tribuzio, S.C.I.C., Prin.; Juliana Tengia; Kristin Malone-Bodair, Asst. Prin.; Debora Witt, Librarian. Ivrea Sisters of Charity of the Immaculate Conception of Ivrea Lay Teachers 10; Sisters 2; Students 115.

[G] HOMES FOR AGED

GREENSBURG. *St. Anne Home*, 685 Angela Dr., 15601. Tel: 724-837-6070; Fax: 724-837-6099; Email: jlong@stannehome.org; Web: www.stannehome.org. Rev. Dennis A. Bogusz, Chap.; Rev. Msgr. John L. Conway, V.F., In Res., (Retired); Revs. Lawrence Hoppe, In Res., (Retired); Thomas M. Lukac, In Res., (Retired); Rev. Msgrs. J. Edward McCullough, In Res., (Retired); Donald J. Mondello, In Res.; Rev. Henry S. Preneta, In Res., (Retired). Capacity for Intermediate Skilled Care 125; Felician Sisters 5; Personal Care 54; Independent Living 7.

Neumann House, 2900 Seminary Dr., 15601. Tel: 724-834-7350; Fax: 724-834-7351; Email: jbertig@dioceseofgreensburg.org. Revs. Robert R. Byrnes, In Res., (Retired); James M. Goldberg, In Res., (Retired); Thaddeus J. Kaczmarek, In Res., (Retired); Rev. Msgr. Lawrence R. Kiniry, In Res., (Retired); Revs. Emil S. Payer, In Res., (Retired); Peter L. Peretti, In Res.; Alexander L. Pleban, S.T.L., In Res., (Retired); Rev. Msgr. John A. Regoli, In Res., (Retired); Revs. Leonard W. Stoviak, In Res.; Donald P. Trexler, In Res., (Retired); Anthony A. Wozniak, In Res., (Retired). Residence for retired Priests.

[H] MONASTERIES AND RESIDENCES OF PRIESTS AND BROTHERS

BOLIVAR. *Mount Carmel Hermitage*, 244 Baileys Rd., Bolivar, 15923. Tel: 724-238-0423; Fax: 724-238-0423; Email: smarr@windbeam.com. Revs. Bede J.K. Mulligan, O.Carm., Prior; Simeon D. Marro, O.Carm., Procurator; Bro. Robert Ryba, O.Carm. Brothers 1; Priests 2.

KITTANNING. *Pauline Fathers Monastery*, 543 Bunker Hill Rd., P.O. Box 66, Kittanning, 16201. Tel: 724-763-1375; Fax: 724-763-8100; Email: paulinefathers@comncast.net. Revs. Sebastian J. Hanks, O.S.P.P.E., Supr.; Raphael K. Glinkowski, O.S.P.P.E., In Res. Priests 2.

LATROBE. *Saint Vincent Archabbey*, 300 Fraser Purchase Rd., Latrobe, 15650-2690. Tel: 724-532-6600; Fax: 724-539-2110; Email: archabbot@stvincent.edu; Web: www.saintvincentarchabbey.org. Rt. Rev. Douglas R. Nowicki, O.S.B., Archabbot; Most Rev. Rembert G. Weakland, O.S.B., (Retired); Very Rev. Earl J. Henry, O.S.B., Prior; Bro. Anthony Kirsch, O.S.B., Subprior; Revs. Warren D. Murrman, O.S.B., Master of Novices; Philip M. Kanfush, O.S.B., Procurator; Thomas Acklin, O.S.B.; Joseph M. Adams, O.S.B.; Benoit Alloggia, O.S.B.; Shawn Matthew Anderson, O.S.B.; Michael Antonacci, O.S.B.; Martin R. Bartel, O.S.B.; Kurt J. Belsole, O.S.B.; Brian D. Boosel, O.S.B.; Jude Brady, O.S.B.; Cristiano E. Brito, O.S.B.; Ananias G. Buccicone, O.S.B.; Aaron N. Buzzelli, O.S.B.; Frederick Byrne, O.S.B.; Andrew S. Campbell, O.S.B.; Cornelius P. Chang, O.S.B.; Athanasius C. Cherry, O.S.B.; Richard Chirichiello, O.S.B.; Wulfstan F. Clough, O.S.B.; Stephen P. Concordia, O.S.B.; Cyprian G. Constantine, O.S.B.; Lucas Torrell deAlmeida Costa, O.S.B.; Patrick T. Cronauer, O.S.B., Master of Juniors, St. Vincent Archabbey; Vincent R. Crosby, O.S.B.; Thomas P. Curry, O.S.B.; Bonaventure J. Curtis, O.S.B.; Mauro N. de Souza Fernandes, O.S.B.; Chad R. Ficorilli, O.S.B.; Augustine A. Flood, O.S.B.; Job J. Foote, O.S.B.; Mario A. Fulgenzi, O.S.B.; Michael J. Gabler, O.S.B.; Ronald Gatman, O.S.B.; Campion P. Gavaler, O.S.B.; Joseph U. Gerg, O.S.B.; David R. Griffin, O.S.B.; Anthony J. Grossi, O.S.B.; Thomas M. Hart, O.S.B.; Bede J. Hasso, O.S.B.; Isaac (Paul) Haywiser, O.S.B.; John Paul (Ryan) Heiser, O.S.B.; Boniface Hicks, O.S.B.; David Liang Ho, O.S.B.; Vernon A. Holtz, O.S.B.; Stephen Honeygoskey, O.S.B.; Leon Hont, O.S.B.; Myron M. Kirsch, O.S.B.; Rene M. Kollar, O.S.B.; Matthew T. Laffey, O.S.B.; Jeremiah (George) Lange, O.S.B.; Meinrad J. Lawson, O.S.B., Pastor, St. Vincent Basilica, Latrobe; Killian (Richard) Loch, O.S.B.; James H. Loew, O.S.B.; Stanley T. Markiewicz, O.S.B.; Matthias Martinez, O.S.B.; Matthew Lambert, O.S.B.; Justin M. Matro, O.S.B.; Maximillian (Mark) Maxwell, O.S.B.; Edward M. Mazich, O.S.B., S.T.D.; Paschal A. Morlino, O.S.B.; Maurus B. Mount, O.S.B.; Nathan J. Munsch, O.S.B.; Jonathan J. Murrman, O.S.B.; Justin Nolan, O.S.B.; Jeffrey Nyardy, O.S.B.; Daniel Paul O'Keefe, O.S.B.; Very Rev. Paulo Sergio Panza, O.S.B.; Revs. Alfred Patterson, O.S.B.; John Peck, O.S.B.; Dominic J. Petroy, O.S.B.; James F. Podlesny, O.S.B.; Luke E. Policicchio, O.S.B.; Nathanael R. Polinski, O.S.B.; Jerome J. Purta, O.S.B.; Donald Raila, O.S.B.; Thaddeus E. Rettger, O.S.B.; Noel H. Rothrauff, O.S.B., Dir. of Foreign Missions; Paul E. Rubadue, O.S.B.; Chrysostom V. Schlimm, O.S.B.; Paul-Alexander Shutt, O.S.B.; Thomas More Sikora, O.S.B.; Ralph Tajak, O.S.B.; Paul R. Taylor, O.S.B.; John Mary Tompkins, O.S.B.; Richard Ulam, O.S.B.; Eric Vogt, O.S.B.; Damian J. Warnock, O.S.B.; Mark Edward Wenzinger, O.S.B.; Anthony Wesolowski, O.S.B.; Daniel C. Wolfel, O.S.B.; Lee R. Yoakam, O.S.B., US Army: Active Duty-Hunter Army Airfield, Savannah, GA; Jean-Luc C. Zadroga, O.S.B.; Vincent E. Zidek, O.S.B.; Frank Ziemkiewicz, O.S.B.; Peter Adamonis, O.S.B.
The Benedictine Society of Westmoreland County
Saint Vincent College Corporation
The Wimmer Corporation
The Saint Vincent Cemetery Corporation Brothers 33; Deacons 3; Priests in Archabbey 105; Junior Professed Monks 16; Choir Novices 7.

[I] CONVENTS AND RESIDENCES FOR SISTERS

GREENSBURG. *Apostles of the Sacred Heart of Jesus*, Clelian Heights Convent, 135 Clelian Heights Ln., 15601-6665. Tel: 724-837-8120; Fax: 724-837-6480; Email: clelian@aol.com; Web: www.clelianheights.org. Revs. Anthony W. Ditto, Chap.; James B. Morley, Chap.; Sr. Deborah Lopez, A.S.C..J., Local Supr. Sisters 10.

Benedictine Nuns, St. Emma Monastery, 1001 Harvey Ave., 15601-1494. Tel: 724-834-3060; Fax: 724-834-5772; Email: benedictinenuns@stemma.org; Web: www.stemma.org. Mother Mary Anne Noll, O.S.B., Prioress; Rev. Thomas Acklin, O.S.B., Chap. Sisters 7.

Sisters of Charity, 144 DePaul Center Rd., 15601. Tel: 724-836-0406; Fax: 724-836-8280; Email: cmeinert@scsh.org; Web: www.scsh.org. Sr. Catherine Meinert, S.C., Pres.

Sisters of Charity of Seton Hill, United States Province Greensburg, Pennsylvania (DePaul Center), 144 DePaul Center Rd., 15601. Tel: 724-836-0406; Fax: 724-836-8280; Email: sjenny@scsh.org; Web: www.scsh.org. Sr. Catherine Meinert, S.C., Supr. Sisters 165.

Sisters of Charity of Seton Hill, Caritas Christi Motherhouse, 129 DePaul Center Rd., 15601. Tel: 724-853-7948; Fax: 724-838-1512; Web: www.scsh.org. Sisters 84.

Sisters of Charity of Seton Hill, United States Province, Marian Hall, 449 Mt. Thor Rd., 15601. Tel: 724-837-5863; Web: www.scsh.org. Sisters 2.

Sisters of Charity of Seton Hill, United States Province, Bayley House, Tel: 724-836-6398. Sisters 3.

Sisters of Charity of Seton Hill, United States Province, Doran Hall, Tel: 724-837-8645. Sisters 12.

Sisters of Charity of Seton Hill, United States Province, Ennis Hall, Tel: 724-836-7940. Sisters 10.

Sisters of Charity of Seton Hill, United States Province, Regina House, Regina House, 469 Mt. Thor Rd., 15601. Tel: 724-836-0406; Fax: 724-836-8280. Sisters 4.

LATROBE. *Discalced Carmelite Nuns*, Carmel of the Assumption, 5206 Center Dr., Latrobe, 15650-5204. Tel: 724-539-1056; Email: contact@latrobecarmel.org; Web: www.latrobecarmel.org. Sr. Mary Wild, O.C.D., Prioress. Sisters 11.

LEECHBURG. *Catechist Sisters of Mary Immaculate Help of Christians*, 118 Park Rd., Leechburg, 15656. Tel: 724-845-2828; Fax: 724-845-1658; Email: lbgsmi@gmail.com. Sr. Jossy Jacob, Admin. & Pres. Sisters 5.

MOUNT PLEASANT. *Sisters of Charity of the Immaculate Conception of Ivrea*, Immaculate Virgin of Miracles Convent, 268 Prittstown Rd., Mount Pleasant, 15666. Tel: 724-887-6753; Fax: 724-887-2977; Email: sr.letizia@vernamontessorischool.org. Sr. Angelina Grimoldi, S.C.I.C., Local Supr. Sisters 8.

[J] RETREAT HOUSES

GREENSBURG. *St. Emma Retreat House*, 1001 Harvey Ave., 15601. Tel: 724-834-3060; Fax: 724-834-5772; Email: benedictinenuns@stemma.org; Web: www.stemma.org. Mother Mary Anne Noll, O.S.B., Prioress. Benedictine Nuns.

[K] MISCELLANEOUS LISTINGS

GREENSBURG. *Christ Our Shepherd Center*, 2900 Seminary Dr., 15601. Tel: 724-834-7350; Fax: 724-834-7351; Email: jbertig@dioceseofgreensburg.org; Web: www.bishopconnarecenter.org. Mr. Gerald R. Bertig, Dir. Facilities Mgmt. In Res. Rev. Msgr. Richard G. Curci.

Elizabeth Seton Care Center, 129 DePaul Center Rd., 15601. Tel: 724-853-7948; Email: rberlingo@scsh.org. Sr. Catherine Meinert, S.C., Prov.

Gilbert Straub Plaza, 620 Reamer Ave., 15601. Tel: 724-832-2280; Fax: 724-832-9511; Email: jgrindle@scsh.org. Sr. Mary Janice Grindle, S.C., Mgr. Sisters of Charity. Sisters 1.

Magnificat - Greensburg, PA, 931 Mace St., 15601. Email: plholtzer@gmail.com. Patricia Holtzer, Coord.

Sisters of Charity of Seton Hill, United States Province Charitable Trust for the Aged, Infirmed and Disabled Vowed Members, 144 DePaul Center Rd., 15601. Tel: 724-836-0406; Email: sjenny@scsh.org.

DUNBAR. *Rendu Services, Inc.*, 453 Pechin Rd., Dunbar, 15431. Tel: 724-277-8680; Fax: 724-277-8681; Email: sncdc449@yahoo.com; Email: ddolan@scsh.org; Web: www.renduservices.org. Sr. Nancy Cassidy, D.C., Exec. Dir.

INDIANA. *Clairvaux Commons*, 100 Clairvaux Dr., Indiana, 15701. Tel: 724-349-2920; Fax: 724-349-1355; Email: clairvau@verizon.net. Very Rev. Thomas A. Federline, V.F., Dean. Christian Housing.

LEECHBURG. *Bishop Morrow Personal Care Home, Inc.*, 118 Park Rd., Leechburg, 15656. Tel: 724-845-2828 ; Fax: 724-845-1658; Email: lbgsmi@comcast.net. Sr. Jossy Jacob, Local Supr. Sisters of Mary Immaculate.

UNITED. *Ladies of Charity*, c/o St. Florian Church, P.O. Box 187, United, 15689. Tel: 724-423-4431; Fax: 724-423-4438; Email: jsedlak@dioceseofgreensburg.org. Rev. John A. Sedlak, Spiritual Advisor.

RELIGIOUS INSTITUTES OF MEN REPRESENTED IN THE DIOCESE

For further details refer to the corresponding bracketed number in the Religious Institutes of Men or Women section.

[0200]—*Benedictine Monks* (St. Vincent Archabbey)—O.S.B.
[0270]—*Carmelite Fathers and Brothers*—O.Carm.
[1010]—*Pauline Fathers*—O.S.P.P.E.

RELIGIOUS INSTITUTES OF WOMEN REPRESENTED IN THE DIOCESE

[0130]—*Apostles of the Sacred Heart of Jesus*—A.S.C.J.
[0190]—*Benedictine Sisters*—O.S.B.
[0230]—*Benedictine Sisters of Pontifical Jurisdiction*—O.S.B.
[0420]—*Discalced Carmelite Nuns*—O.C.D.
[1170]—*Felician Sisters*—C.S.S.F.
[2575]—*Institute of the Sisters of Mercy of the Americas* (Pittsburgh, PA)—R.S.M.
[1690]—*School Sisters of the Third Order of St. Francis*—O.S.F.
[0570]—*Sisters of Charity of Seton Hill, Greensburg, Pennsylvania*—S.C.
[0450]—*Sisters of Charity of the Immaculate Conception of Ivrea*—S.C.I.C.
[0990]—*Sisters of Divine Providence* (St. Peter Prov.)—C.D.P.
[2440]—*Sisters of Mary Immaculate*—S.M.I.

[1660]—*Sisters of Saint Francis of the Providence of God*—O.S.F.
[1620]—*Sisters of Saint Francis, Millvale, Pennsylvania*—O.S.F.
[3830-13]—*Sisters of St. Joseph*—C.S.J.
[2040]—*Sisters of the Holy Spirit*—S.H.S.
[3730]—*Sisters of the Order of St. Basil the Great*—O.S.B.M.
[4160]—*Vincentian Sisters of Charity*—V.S.C.

NECROLOGY

† Dylag, Michael R., (Retired), Died Dec. 1, 2018
† Kozoil, Micah E., (Retired), Died Nov. 13, 2018
† Raimer, Chester J., (Retired), Died Jul. 11, 2018

An asterisk (*) denotes an organization that has established tax-exempt status directly with the IRS and is not covered by the USCCB Group Ruling.

Diocese of Harrisburg

(Dioecesis Harrisburgensis)

EX DE PLENITUDINE - GRATIAM PRO GRATIA

Most Reverend

RONALD W. GAINER

Bishop of Harrisburg; ordained May 19, 1973; appointed Bishop of Lexington December 13, 2002; consecrated February 22, 2003; appointed Bishop of Harrisburg January 24, 2014; installed March 19, 2014. *Office: 4800 Union Deposit Rd., Harrisburg, PA 17111-3710.*

Diocesan Center: 4800 Union Deposit Rd., Harrisburg, PA 17111-3710. Tel: 717-657-4804; Fax: 717-657-2453.

Web: www.hbgdiocese.org

Email: vicargeneraloffice@hbgdiocese.org

ESTABLISHED MARCH 3, 1868.

Square Miles 7,660.

Comprises the Counties of Dauphin, Lebanon, Lancaster, York, Adams, Franklin, Cumberland, Perry, Juniata, Mifflin, Snyder, Northumberland, Union, Montour and Columbia in the State of Pennsylvania.

Patron of Diocese: St. Patrick, Bishop and Confessor.

Legal Title: The Diocese of Harrisburg and each parish in the diocese are organized as separate Pennsylvania Charitable Trusts. For further information, consult the Office of the Vicar General.

STATISTICAL OVERVIEW

Personnel	
Bishop	1
Priests: Diocesan Active in Diocese	89
Priests: Diocesan Active Outside Diocese	5
Priests: Retired, Sick or Absent	33
Number of Diocesan Priests	127
Religious Priests in Diocese	31
Total Priests in Diocese	158
Extern Priests in Diocese	5
Ordinations:	
Diocesan Priests	6
Transitional Deacons	4
Permanent Deacons in Diocese	59
Total Brothers	1
Total Sisters	174
Parishes	
Parishes	89
With Resident Pastor:	
Resident Diocesan Priests	72
Resident Religious Priests	13
Without Resident Pastor:	
Administered by Priests	4
Missions	7
Professional Ministry Personnel:	
Brothers	1
Sisters	15
Lay Ministers	77
Welfare	
Catholic Hospitals	1
Total Assisted	272,739
Homes for the Aged	5
Total Assisted	729
Specialized Homes	5
Total Assisted	227
Special Centers for Social Services	9
Total Assisted	2,386
Educational	
Diocesan Students in Other Seminaries	26
Total Seminarians	26
High Schools, Diocesan and Parish	7
Total Students	3,009
Elementary Schools, Diocesan and Parish	33
Total Students	7,204
Elementary Schools, Private	2
Total Students	74
Catechesis/Religious Education:	
High School Students	898
Elementary Students	11,140
Total Students under Catholic Instruction	22,351
Teachers in the Diocese:	
Brothers	1
Sisters	12
Lay Teachers	709
Vital Statistics	
Receptions into the Church:	
Infant Baptism Totals	1,411
Minor Baptism Totals	447
Adult Baptism Totals	257
Received into Full Communion	270
First Communions	2,030
Confirmations	2,174
Marriages:	
Catholic	323
Interfaith	305
Total Marriages	628
Deaths	2,081
Total Catholic Population	226,298
Total Population	2,243,297

Former Bishops—Rt. Revs. JEREMIAH F. SHANAHAN, D.D., ord. July 3, 1859; cons. July 12, 1868; died Sept. 24, 1886; THOMAS MCGOVERN, D.D., ord. Dec. 27, 1861; cons. March 11, 1888; died July 25, 1898; JOHN W. SHANAHAN, D.D., ord. Jan. 2, 1869; cons. May 1, 1899; died Feb. 19, 1916; Most Revs. PHILIP R. MCDEVITT, D.D., cons. Sept. 21, 1916; died Nov. 11, 1935; GEORGE L. LEECH, D.D., J.C.D., appt. Auxiliary of Harrisburg July 6, 1935; cons. Oct. 17, 1935; succeeded to See Dec. 19, 1935; retired Oct. 19, 1971; died March 12, 1985; JOSEPH T. DALEY, D.D., cons. Jan. 7, 1964; appt. Coadjutor Bishop July 31, 1967; succeeded to See Oct. 19, 1971; died Sept. 2, 1983; WILLIAM H. KEELER, ord. July 17, 1955; cons. Sept. 21, 1979; appt. Bishop of Harrisburg, Nov. 10, 1983; succeeded to See Jan. 4, 1984; transferred to Baltimore May 23, 1989; NICHOLAS C. DATTILO, D.D., ord. May 31, 1958; appt. Eighth Bishop of Harrisburg Nov. 21, 1989; cons. Jan. 26, 1990; died March 5, 2004; KEVIN C. RHOADES, ord. July 9, 1983; appt. Ninth Bishop of Harrisburg Oct. 14, 2004; cons. Dec. 9, 2004; appt. Bishop of Fort Wayne-South Bend Nov. 14, 2009; installed Jan. 13, 2010.; JOSEPH P. MCFADDEN, ord. May 16, 1981; appt. Auxiliary Bishop of Philadelphia and Titular Bishop of Horreomargum June 8, 2004; cons. July 28, 2004; appt. Bishop of Harrisburg June 22, 2010; installed Aug. 18, 2010; died May 2, 2013.

Diocese of Harrisburg Officials

Vicar General—Very Rev. DAVID L. DANNEKER, Ph.D., Mailing Address: 4800 Union Deposit Rd., Harrisburg, 17111-3710. Tel: 717-657-4804; Fax: 717-657-2453; Email: vicargeneraloffice@hbgdiocese.org.

Director of the Office for Divine Worship—Rev. JOSHUA R. BROMMER, Mailing Address: 4800 Union Deposit Rd., Harrisburg, 17111-3710. Tel: 717-657-4804; Fax: 717-657-2453.

Moderator of the Curia—Very Rev. DAVID L. DANNEKER, Ph.D., Mailing Address: 4800 Union Deposit Rd., Harrisburg, 17111-3710.

Secretary for Catholic Charities—MARK A. TOTARO, Ph. D., MBA, Mailing Address: 4800 Union Deposit Rd., Harrisburg, 17111-3710. Tel: 717-657-4804; Fax: 717-657-8683.

Secretary for Administrative Services—MR. DONALD J. KAERCHER, CPA, CFO, Mailing Address: 4800 Union Deposit Rd., Harrisburg, 17111-3710. Tel: 717-657-4804; Fax: 717-671-7021.

Secretary for Clergy and Consecrated Life—4800 Union Deposit Rd., Harrisburg, 17111-3710. Tel: 717-657-4804; Fax: 717-657-2453. Very Rev. WILLIAM C. FORREY, V.F.

Secretariat for Public Relations—Mailing Address: 4800 Union Deposit Rd., Harrisburg, 17111-3710. Tel: 717-657-4804; Fax: 717-657-7673. MS. RACHEL BRYSON, Exec. Dir.

Secretary for Education—Very Rev. EDWARD J. QUINLAN, M.Div., M.A., M.S., Mailing Address: 4800 Union Deposit Rd., Harrisburg, 17111-3710. Tel: 717-657-4804; Fax: 717-657-3790.

Secretary for Catholic Life and Evangelization—Mailing Address: 4800 Union Deposit Rd., Harrisburg, 17111-3710. Tel: 717-657-4804; Fax: 717-657-4041. VACANT.

Judicial Vicar—Very Rev. PAUL M. CLARK, J.C.L., Mailing Address: 4800 Union Deposit Rd., Harrisburg, 17111-3710. Tel: 717-657-4804; Fax: 717-657-1573.

Chancellor—DR. CAROL L. HOUGHTON, S.T.D., J.C.D., Mailing Address: 4800 Union Deposit Rd, Harrisburg, 17111-3710. Tel: 717-657-4804; Fax: 717-657-1573.

Vice Chancellor—Rev. ANTHONY R. DILL, J.C.L.

Diocesan Offices, Commissions, Boards and Programs

Adult Education and Catechist Formation, Office of—MR. RYAN BOLSTER, Dir., Mailing Address: 4800 Union Deposit Rd., Harrisburg, 17111-3710. Tel: 717-657-4804, Ext. 225; Fax: 717-657-3790.

Catholic History and Archives, Office of—DR. CAROL L. HOUGHTON, S.T.D., J.C.D., Chancellor; MR. MICHAEL YURICH, Archivist & Vice Chancellor Archives, 4800 Union Deposit Rd., Harrisburg, 17111-3710. Tel: 717-657-4804.

Black Catholic Apostolate—4800 Union Deposit Rd., Harrisburg, 17111-3710. Tel: 717-657-4804. MRS. JACLYN CURRAN.

Buildings and Properties—4800 Union Deposit Rd., Harrisburg, 17111-3710. Tel: 717-657-4804; Fax: 717-657-6208. TERRY CONNER, Dir.

Campus Ministry—MR. ROBERT J. WILLIAMS, Dir., Mailing Address: 4800 Union Deposit Rd., Harrisburg, 17111-3710. Tel: 717-657-4804.

Catholic Charities Administration, Department for—MARK A. TOTARO, Ph.D., MBA, Exec. Dir. & CEO; PETER A. BIASUCCI, L.S.W., Asst. Exec. Dir.; CAROLE A. KLINGER, M.B.A., Dir. Admin.; CHRISTOPHER MEEHAN, M.B.A., Dir. Devel., Mailing Address: 4800 Union Deposit Rd., Harrisburg, 17111-3710.

Catholic Charities Counseling/Field Services, Department for—Associate Executive Directors: ANNETTE MARTIN, M.H.S.; KATE DOWNES, M.S.W., M.B.A.; CHRISTOPHER VANDENBERG, M.H.S.

Catholic Physicians League—Very Rev. DAVID L. DANNEKER, Ph.D., Liaison, 4800 Union Deposit Rd., Harrisburg, 17111-3710.

Catholic Schools, Department for—MRS. LIVIA ANN RILEY, Supt., Mailing Address: 4800 Union Deposit Rd., Harrisburg, 17111-3710. Tel: 717-657-4804; Fax: 717-657-3790.

The "Catholic Witness"—MS. JENNIFER REED, Mng. Editor, 4800 Union Deposit Rd., Harrisburg, 17111-3710. Tel: 717-657-4804; Fax: 717-657-7673.

Catholic Women, Diocesan Council of—JEANNE WARREN, 965 Hedgewyck Ln., Elizabethtown, 17022. Tel: 717-367-9306.

Cemeteries—MR. DONALD J. KAERCHER, CPA, Diocesan Finance Officer & Sec. for Admin. Svcs., 4800 Union Deposit Rd., Harrisburg, 17111-3710. Tel: 717-657-4804.

Charismatic Renewal—Rev. FRANCIS J. KARWACKI, Liaison, 47 S. Market St., Mount Carmel, 17851. Tel: 570-339-1036.

Consultors, College—Rev. Msgr. WILLIAM J. KING, J.C.D.; Rev. JOSHUA R. BROMMER, S.T.L.; Rev. Msgr. ROBERT E. LAWRENCE; Revs. DANIEL C. MITZEL; CHARLES L. PERSING; Very Rev. THOMAS J. ROZMAN, V.F.; Rev. ALFRED P. SCESKI; Very Rev. NEIL S. SULLIVAN, V.F.

Continuing Formation of Priests, Office of—Tel: 717-657-4804; Fax: 717-657-2453. Very Rev. WILLIAM C. FORREY, V.F.

Continuing Formation of Deacons, Office of—Rev. PAUL C.B. SCHENCK.

Cursillo Movement—Rev. WILLIAM M. WEARY, V.F.

Deans—Rev. Msgr. JAMES M. LYONS, M.Div., M.Ed., V.F., Adams Deanery; Very Revs. THOMAS J. ROZMAN, V.F., Cumberland/Perry Deanery; NEIL S. SULLIVAN, V.F., Dauphin Deanery; LUIS R. RODRIGUEZ, V.F., Franklin Deanery; STEVEN W. FAUSER, V.F., North Lancaster Deanery; PETER I. HAHN, V.F., South Lancaster Deanery; Rev. Msgr. WILLIAM M. RICHARDSON, V.F., Lebanon Deanery; Very Rev. FRANCIS J. TAMBURRO, V.F., Northern Deanery; Rev. MARTIN KOBOS, O.F.M.Conv., V.F., Northumberland Deanery; Very Rev. JONATHAN P. SAWICKI, V.F., York Deanery.

Diocesan Center—MRS. DONNAJOAN MATTIS, Coord., 4800 Union Deposit Rd., Harrisburg, 17111-3710. Tel: 717-657-4804; Fax: 717-671-7146.

Development, Office of—4800 Union Deposit Rd., Harrisburg, 17111-3710. Tel: 717-657-4804; Fax: 717-657-8757. MRS. KIM ROCHE, Dir.

Ecumenical and Interreligious Affairs, Office for—Rev. JAMES E. LEASE, Dir., 4800 Union Deposit Rd., Harrisburg, 17111-3710. Tel: 717-657-4804; Fax: 717-657-4041.

Evangelization, Catechesis and Sports Ministry, Office of—4800 Union Deposit Rd., Harrisburg, 17111-3710. Tel: 717-657-4804. MR. JAMES GONTIS, Dir.

Family Life, Office of—THOMAS P. O'NEILL, Dir., 4800 Union Deposit Rd., Harrisburg, 17111-3710. Tel: 717-657-4804; Fax: 717-657-4041.

Finance Council—

Harrisburg Catholic Administrative Services, Inc.—MR. DONALD J. KAERCHER, CPA, Diocesan Finance Officer & Sec. for Admin., 4800 Union Deposit Rd., Harrisburg, 17111-3710. Tel: 717-657-4804; Fax: 717-671-7021.

Health Care Ministry—4800 Union Deposit Rd., Harrisburg, 17111-3710. Tel: 717-657-4804; Fax: 717-657-4041. MRS. JACLYN CURRAN, Dir.

Holy Name Societies—Deacon THOMAS AUMEN, Liaison, 15 Oak Hill Dr., Hanover, 17331. Tel: 717-637-6491.

Knights of Columbus—MR. BERT LANGENDIJK, 34 Riverview Dr., Enola, 17025. Tel: 717-732-4086.

Human Resources, Department for—MRS. JANET E. JACKSON, M.C.I.P.D., 4800 Union Deposit Rd., Harrisburg, 17111-3710. Tel: 717-657-4804.

Legion of Mary—Rev. PAUL R. SHUDA, Moderator, (Retired), 675 Rutherford Rd., Harrisburg, 17109. Tel: 717-657-3147.

Mater Dei Community—(Traditional Latin Mass Community) *110 State St., Harrisburg, 17101.* Tel: 717-889-4217. Rev. GREGORY EICHMANN, F.S.S.P., Chap.

Mediation Services, Office of—MRS. BARBARA A. ROTH, Clerk, 4800 Union Deposit Rd., Harrisburg, 17111-3710. Tel: 717-657-4804.

Missions, Office of PontificalRev. ROBERT F. SHARMAN, S.T.L., Dir., 4800 Union Deposit Rd., Harrisburg, 17111-3710. Tel: 717-657-4804; Fax: 717-657-4042.

Ministry with People with Disabilities, Office for—LARRY KILEY, Dir., 4800 Union Deposit Rd., Harrisburg, 17111-3710. Tel: 717-657-4804; Fax: 717-657-4041.

Multicultural Ministries, Office for—4800 Union Deposit Rd., Harrisburg, 17111-3710. Tel: 717-657-4804; Fax: 717-657-4041. MRS. JACLYN CURRAN, Coord. Hispanic Apostolate, Korean Apostolate, Vietnamese Apostolate.

Natural Family Planning, Office of—4800 Union Deposit Rd., Harrisburg, 17111-3710. Tel: 717-657-4804; Fax: 717-657-4041. THOMAS P. O'NEILL, Dir.

Permanent Diaconate, Office for—Tel: 717-657-4804; Fax: 717-657-2453. Very Rev. WILLIAM C. FORREY, V.F.

Presbyteral Council—Revs. TIMOTHY D. MARCOE, Adams; PHILIP G. BURGER, Cumberland/Perry; Very Revs. NEIL S. SULLIVAN, V.F., Dauphin; LUIS R. RODRIGUEZ, V.F., Franklin; Revs. PANG S. TCHEOU, North Lancaster; LEO M. GOODMAN, South Lancaster; Very Rev. ROBERT M. GILLELAN JR., Lebanon; Rev. Msgr. ROBERT E. LAWRENCE, Northern; Revs. MARTIN KOBOS, O.F.M.Conv., V.F., Northumberland; DANIEL K. RICHARDS, York.

Appointed—Rev. JOSHUA R. BROMMER; Rev. Msgrs. WILLIAM J. KING, J.C.D.; JAMES M. LYONS, M.Div., M.Ed., V.F.; Revs. J. MICHAEL MCFADDEN, M.Div.; DANIEL C. MITZEL; CHARLES L. PERSING; Very Rev. THOMAS J. ROZMAN, V.F.; Revs. ALFRED P. SCESKI; ALLAN F. WOLFE.

Prison Ministry—4800 Union Deposit Rd., Harrisburg, 17111-3710. Tel: 717-657-4804; Fax: 717-657-4041. MRS. JACLYN CURRAN, Coord.

Respect Life, Office for—4800 Union Deposit Rd., Harrisburg, 17111-3710. Tel: 717-657-4804; Fax: 717-657-2453. THOMAS P. O'NEILL, Dir.

Consecrated Life, Office of—4800 Union Deposit Rd., Harrisburg, 17111-3710. Tel: 717-657-4804; Fax: 717-657-2453.

Saint Thomas More Society—MICHAEL KRIMMEL, Esq., Pres., 4800 Union Deposit Rd., Harrisburg, 17111-3710. Tel: 717-657-4804, Ext. 305.

Saint Vincent de Paul Society—VACANT.

Scout Chaplain—Rev. KEITH M. CARROLL.

Tribunal—4800 Union Deposit Rd., Harrisburg, 17111-3710. Tel: 717-657-4804; Fax: 717-657-1573.

Judicial Vicar—Very Rev. PAUL M. CLARK, J.C.L.

Case Services Administrator—MRS. BARBARA A. ROTH.

Diocesan Judges—Rev. Msgrs. RICHARD A. YOUTZ, J.C.L., (Retired); WILLIAM J. KING, J.C.D.; Rev. JORDAN HITE, T.O.R.; MS. BARBARA A. BETTWY, J.C.L.

Defenders of the Bond—Rev. EDWARD R. LAVELLE, (Retired); DR. CAROL L. HOUGHTON, S.T.D., J.C.D.

Promoter of Justice—DR. CAROL L. HOUGHTON, S.T.D., J.C.D.

Canonical Consultants—Rev. Msgr. HUGH A. OVERBAUGH, (Retired); Rev. ANTHONY R. DILL, J.C.L.

Auditor—Rev. ANTHONY R. DILL, J.C.L.

Advocates—MR. ROBERT F. O'DONNELL; MRS. BARBARA A. ROTH; MRS. ANITA M. PAYNTER.

Notary—MRS. MARLENE M. RAUDENSKY.

Victim Assistance Coordinator—MARK A. TOTARO, Ph. D., MBA, Tel: 717-657-4804; Email: mtotaro@hbgdiocese.org.

Vocations, Office for—Rev. BRIAN J. WAYNE, Dir., 4800 Union Deposit Rd., Harrisburg, 17111-3710. Tel: 717-657-4804; Fax: 717-657-4042.

World Apostolate of Fatima—Rev. JOHN A. SZADA JR., Spiritual Moderator, Carmel of Jesus, Mary and Joseph, 430 Monastery Rd., Elysburg, 17824. Tel: 570-672-2122.

Youth and Young Adult Ministry, Office for—MR. ROBERT J. WILLIAMS, Dir., 4800 Union Deposit Rd., Harrisburg, 17111-3710. Tel: 717-657-4804; Fax: 717-657-4041.

Youth Protection Program—Very Rev. DAVID L. DANNEKER, Ph.D.; MRS. JANET E. JACKSON, M.C.I.P.D., Compliance Coord., 4800 Union Deposit Rd., Harrisburg, 17111-3710. Tel: 717-657-4804; Fax: 717-657-2453.

CLERGY, PARISHES, MISSIONS AND PAROCHIAL SCHOOLS

CITY OF HARRISBURG

(DAUPHIN COUNTY)

1—CATHEDRAL PARISH OF ST. PATRICK (1995)
212 State St., 17101. Tel: 717-232-2169, Ext. 223; Email: cathedralsecretary@hbgdiocese.org; Email: cathedralparish@comcast.net; Web: www.stpatrickcathedral.com. Rev. Joshua R. Brommer, S.T.L., Rector; Deacons Lawrence R. Crudup, Pastoral Assoc.; Thomas A. Lang, Pastoral Assoc.
Catechesis Religious Program—Students 28.

2—ST. CATHERINE LABOURE (1948) (Shrine of the Miraculous Medal)
4000 Derry St., 17111. Tel: 717-564-1321; Email: frnsullivan@sclhbg.org. Very Rev. Neil S. Sullivan, V.F., Email: frnsullivan@sclhbg.org; Revs. Kevin Coyle, Parochial Vicar; Jordan Hite, T.O.R., In Res.; Deacon Thomas A. Fedor.
School—St. Catherine Laboure School, 4020 Derry St., 17111. Tel: 717-564-1760; Fax: 717-564-3010. Sr. Mary Anne Sweeney, I.H.M., Prin.; Kelly Rogers, Dir. Advancement. Lay Teachers 30; Sisters 2; Students 418.
Catechesis Religious Program—Joan Ellen Frist, D.R.E., Email: jfrist@sclhbg.org. Students 239.
Convent—4010 Derry St., 17111. Tel: 717-745-4134; Email: ihmsisters@sclhbg.org; Web: www.ihmimmaculata.org. Sr. Bernard Agnes Smith, I.H.M., Supr. Sisters, Servants of the Immaculate Heart of Mary.

3—ST. FRANCIS OF ASSISI (1901)
1439 Market St., 17103. Tel: 717-232-1003; Fax: 717-236-4536; Email: cfagan@hbgdiocese.org; Web: stfrancishbgpa.wordpress.com. Revs. Orlando Reyes, O.F.M.Cap.; Juan Antonio Ortiz, O.F.M.Cap., Parochial Vicar; Javed Kashif, O.F.M.Cap., Chap.; Bro. Michael Rubus, O.F.M.Cap., Chap.; Deacon Miguel Marroquin.
Catechesis Religious Program—Tel: 717-233-7912. Students 202.

4—HOLY FAMILY (1958)
555 S. 25th St., 17104. Tel: 717-232-4237; Email: froreyes@hbgdiocese.org. Revs. Orlando Reyes, O.F.-M.Cap.; Juan Antonio Ortiz, O.F.M.Cap., Parochial Vicar.
School—Harrisburg Catholic Elementary School, Mr. David Rushinski, Prin. Lay Teachers 9; Students 130.
Catechesis Religious Program—Students 14.

5—HOLY NAME OF JESUS (Lower Paxton Twp.) (1960)
6150 Allentown Blvd., 17112-2603.
Tel: 717-652-4211; Fax: 717-652-2033; Email: holynameofjesusparishharrisburg@hbgdiocese.org; Web: www.holynameofjesus.com. Very Rev. Edward J. Quinlan, M.Div., M.A., M.S.; Rev. Michael Metzgar; Deacons Jerome T. Foerster; Joseph J. Wrabel.
School—Holy Name of Jesus School, (Grades PreK-8), 6190 Allentown Blvd., 17112-2603.
Tel: 717-657-1704; Fax: 717-657-9135; Email: holynameofjesusschoolharrisburg@hbgdiocese.org. Sr. Rita Smith, S.S.J., Prin.; Mrs. Elaine Tomeck, Librarian. (Lower Paxton Twp.) Lay Teachers 24; Sisters of St. Joseph 1; Students 363.
Catechesis Religious Program—6190 Allentown Blvd., 17112. Sr. Rita Smith, S.S.J., D.R.E. Students 483.
Convent—Tel: 717-545-4357; Email: ssjhnj@ezonline.net. Sisters 1.

6—ST. LAWRENCE (1859) (German), Closed. See St. Patrick Cathedral, Harrisburg.

7—ST. MARGARET MARY ALACOQUE (Penbrook) (1948)
2800 Paxton Church Rd., 17110. Tel: 717-233-3062; Email: parishoffice@stmmparish.org. 2848 Herr St., 17103. Rev. Chester P. Snyder, Admin.
School—St. Margaret Mary Alacoque School, 2826 Herr St., 17103. Tel: 717-232-3771;
Fax: 717-232-0776; Web: school.stmmparish.org. Mrs. Jean Fennessy, Prin. Aides 2; Students 377; Full Time Lay Teachers 26; Part Time Lay Teachers 3.
Catechesis Religious Program—Email: prep@stmmparish.org. Elizabeth Emery, D.R.E. Students 85.

8—OUR LADY OF THE BLESSED SACRAMENT (1906)
2121 N. Third St., 17110-1812. Tel: 717-233-1014; Fax: 717-234-5652; Email: OurLadyoftheBlessedSacramentParishHarrisburg@hbgdiocese.org; Web: www.olbsharrisburg.org. Rev. Bernard Wamayose, A.J.; Joseph Tran; Deacon James B. Doyle. Vietnamese Masses
Catechesis Religious Program—Students 33.

9—SACRED HEART OF JESUS (1901) Closed. See St. Patrick Cathedral, Harrisburg.

OUTSIDE THE CITY OF HARRISBURG

ABBOTTSTOWN, YORK CO., IMMACULATE HEART OF MARY (1809) [CEM]
6084 W. Canal Rd., Abbottstown, 17301.
Tel: 717-259-0611; Email: P001ImmaculateHeart@HBGDiocese.org. Rev. Timothy D. Marcoe.
Catechesis Religious Program—Students 109.

ANNVILLE, LEBANON CO., ST. PAUL THE APOSTLE (1928)
125 S. Spruce St., Annville, 17003. Tel: 717-867-1525; Email: stpaultheapostlechurchannville@gmail.com. Revs. Job J. Foote, O.S.B.; Augustine Obasi, In Res.; Mary Beazley, Music Min.; Mary Langan, Sec.
Catechesis Religious Program—Tel: 717-867-7471;

Email: anna.mattern.cre@gmail.com. Anna Mattern, D.R.E. Students 183.
Station—Lebanon Valley College, Miller Chapel, Annville. Tel: 717-867-6135.
BERWICK, COLUMBIA CO.
1—IMMACULATE CONCEPTION OF THE BLESSED VIRGIN MARY (1906) [CEM]
1730 Fowler Ave., Berwick, 18603-1462.
Tel: 570-759-8113; Fax: 570-759-6637; Email: stmarys@pa.metrocast.net. Very Rev. Francis J. Tamburro, V.F.
See Holy Family Consolidated School, Berwick under Consolidated Elementary Schools located in the Institution section.
Catechesis Religious Program—Tel: 570-759-9225. Students 140.
2—ST. JOSEPH'S aka Saint Joseph Parish (1928)
721 Monroe St., Berwick, 18603. Tel: 570-752-7000; Web: www.stjosephberwick.com. Mailing Address: 730 Washington St., Berwick, 18603. Rev. Matthew Larllick.
See Holy Family Consolidated School, Berwick under Consolidated Elementary Schools located in the Institution section.
Catechesis Religious Program—Diane Kowalski, C.R.E. Students 51.
BLOOMSBURG, COLUMBIA CO., ST. COLUMBA (1882) [CEM] (Irish)
342 Iron St., Bloomsburg, 17815-1824.
Tel: 570-784-0801; Fax: 570-387-2604; Email: stcolumbaparishbloomsburg@hbgdiocese.org; Web: www.saintcolumbachurch.org. Rev. Msgr. Robert E. Lawrence; Rev. Richard Mowery, Campus Min.
School—St. Columba School, (Grades PreK-8), 40 E. Third St., Bloomsburg, 17815. Tel: 570-784-5932; Fax: 570-387-1257; Email: scsprincipal@saintcolumbaschool.org. Dr. Robert Marande, Prin.; Mrs. Helen McMenamin, Librarian. Lay Teachers 13; Sisters 2; Students 105.
Catechesis Religious Program—Tel: 570-784-0801. Students 168.
Mission—Christ the King, P.O. Box 297, Benton, 17814. Tel: 570-925-6969.
BLUE RIDGE SUMMIT, FRANKLIN CO., ST. RITA (1919) [JC]
256 Tract Rd., Fairfield, 17320. Tel: 717-642-8815; Fax: 717-642-9616; Email: bsites@hbgdiocese.org. 13219 Monterey Ln., Blue Ridge Summit, 17214. Revs. Peter DiTomasso, M.SS.CC.; Christopher Onyeneke, M.SS.CC.
Catechesis Religious Program—Tel: 717-794-2067. Students 52.
BONNEAUVILLE, ADAM CO., ST. JOSEPH THE WORKER (1859) [CEM]
12 E. Hanover St., Gettysburg, 17325-7750.
Tel: 717-334-2510; Email: stjosephget@comcast.net; Web: stjosephtheworkerpa.org. Rev. Benny Jose, M.SS.CC.; Deacon Richard J. Weaver.
Catechesis Religious Program—Students 31.
BUCHANAN VALLEY, ADAMS CO., ST. IGNATIUS LOYOLA (Orrtanna) (1817) [CEM]
1095 Church Rd., Orrtanna, 17353.
Tel: 717-677-8012; Fax: 717-677-6350; Email: stignatiusofloyola@hbgdiocese.org; Web: stignatiusofloyola.org. Rev. Dominic M. DiBiccaro; Deacon Stephen M. Huete, Pastoral Assoc.
Catechesis Religious Program—Students 32.
CAMP HILL, CUMBERLAND CO., GOOD SHEPHERD (1951)
3435 Trindle Rd., Camp Hill, 17011-4489.
Tel: 717-761-1167; Fax: 717-761-5313; Email: frpburger@hbgdiocese.org; Web: www.goodshepherdparish.com. Revs. Philip G. Burger; Bernard Oniwe, O.P., Parochial Vicar; James M. Sterner, In Res.; Deacons Francis C. Gorman; Patrick M. Kiley; Derrick Rosenstein, Parish Mgr.
School—Good Shepherd School, Elementary 3400 Market St., Camp Hill, 17011. Tel: 717-737-7261; Fax: 717-761-4673; Email: hkantes@gsschpa.org; Web: www.gsschpa.org. Dr. Stephen M. Fry, Prin. Clergy 3; Lay Teachers 22; Students 246.
Catechesis Religious Program—Amanda Spahr, D.R.E. Students 358.
CARLISLE, CUMBERLAND CO., SAINT PATRICK (1779) [CEM 2]
152 E. Pomfret St., Carlisle, 17013.
Tel: 717-243-4411; Email: po12stpatrickparishcarlisle@hbgdiocese.org; Web: www.saintpatrickchurch.org. Very Rev. Martin O. Moran III, V.F.; Revs. Joshua Cavender, Parochial Vicar; Gregory J. D'Emma, Parochial Vicar, (Retired).
School—Saint Patrick School, 87 Marsh Dr., Carlisle, 17015. Tel: 717-249-4826; Fax: 717-245-0522; Email: office@spscarlisle.org; Web: www.spscarlisle.org. Clergy 2; Lay Teachers 26; Students 272.
Catechesis Religious Program—Tel: 717-243-4891. Heather Ann Howie, C.R.E.; Mr. Joseph Goodman, Dir. Life Teen & Youth Min. Students 258.
Chapels—Pine Grove Furnace, St. Eleanor Regina—St. Katherine Drexel Chapel - Perpetual Adoration.
CENTRALIA, COLUMBIA CO., ST. IGNATIUS (1869) Closed. See Our Lady of Mount Carmel, Mount Carmel.
CHAMBERSBURG, FRANKLIN CO., CORPUS CHRISTI (1792) [CEM]
320 Philadelphia Ave., Chambersburg, 17201.
Tel: 717-264-6317; Email: dmccarty@corpuschristichbg.org. Very Rev. Luis R. Rodriguez, V.F.; Rev. Richard J. Lyons; Deacon Richard W. Ramsey.
School—Corpus Christi School, 305 N. Second St., Chambersburg, 17201. Tel: 717-263-5036; Fax: 717-263-6079; Email: tflohr@ccschambersburg.org; Web: www.cccschambersburg.org. Mrs. Mary A. Geesaman, Prin. Lay Teachers 20; Students 190.
Catechesis Religious Program—Tel: 717-263-9541. Students 210.
Mission—Our Lady of Refuge, 21169 Cross Rd., Doylesburg, Franklin Co. 17219. Tel: 717-349-7953.
COAL TOWNSHIP, NORTHUMBERLAND CO.
1—OUR LADY OF HOPE (1995)
863 W. Chestnut St., Coal Township, 17866-1995.
Tel: 570-648-4432; Email: p130ourladyhope2@hbgdiocese.org. Rev. Steven G. Frenier, O.F.M.Conv.
Catechesis Religious Program—Students 58.
2—ST. STEPHEN PROTOMARTYR (1898) (Polish), Closed. See Our Lady of Hope, Coal Township.
COLUMBIA, LANCASTER CO.
1—HOLY TRINITY (1860) [CEM]
409 Cherry St., Columbia, 17512. Tel: 717-684-2711; Email: frskelley@hbgdiocese.org. Rev. Stephen P. Kelley; Sr. Anna Cosgrave, O.S.F., Pastoral Assoc.
School—Holy Trinity School, (Consolidated) 404 Cherry St., Columbia, 17512. Tel: 717-684-2664; Fax: 717-684-5039. Mrs. Kimberly S. Winters, Prin. Lay Teachers 11; Students 182.
Catechesis Religious Program—Students 108.
Convent—Sisters of St. Francis of Philadelphia, 548 Cherry St., Columbia, 17512. Tel: 717-684-2232.
2—ST. PETER (1828) [CEM 2]
121 S. Second St., Columbia, 17512.
Tel: 717-684-7070; Email: dwickenheiser@hbgdiocese.org. Rev. Anthony Swamy Anthappa, M.S.F.S.
See Our Lady of Angels, Columbia under Consolidated Elementary Schools located in the Institution section.
Catechesis Religious Program—Corrinne Eck, D.R.E. Students 40.
Mission—Mother of Holy Purity Chapel, 217 Maple St., Wrightsville, 17368.
CONEWAGO TOWNSHIP, ADAMS CO., BASILICA OF THE SACRED HEART OF JESUS (1730) [CEM]
30 Basilica Dr., Hanover, 17331-8924.
Tel: 717-637-2721; Email: jleonard@hbgdiocese.org; Web: www.sacredheartbasilica.org. Rev. Joseph R. Howard.
School—Basilica of the Sacred Heart of Jesus School, 50 Basilica Dr., Hanover, 17331. Tel: 717-632-8715; Fax: 717-632-6596. Dianne Giampietro, Prin. Lay Teachers 11.
Catechesis Religious Program—Students 70.
Convent—Sisters of St. Joseph, 55 Basilica Dr., Hanover, 17331. Tel: 717-637-3370. Sisters 4.
CORNWALL, LEBANON CO., SACRED HEART OF JESUS (1886) [CEM]
2596 Cornwall Rd., P.O. Box 136, Cornwall, 17016-0136. Tel: 717-273-1574; Email: phall@hbgdiocese.org. Rev. Rodrigo A. Arrazola.
Catechesis Religious Program—Tel: 717-273-2160.
DALLASTOWN, YORK CO., ST. JOSEPH (1850) [CEM]
251 E. Main St., Dallastown, 17313.
Tel: 717-246-3007; Email: frmweiss@hbgdiocese.org; Web: sjdrcc.org. Rev. Mark E. Weiss; Deacon Daniel L. Bernardy.
School—St. Joseph School, (Grades PreK-6), 271 E. Main St., Dallastown, 17313. Tel: 717-244-9386; Fax: 717-244-9478. Margaret Snyder, Prin.; Kelli Tuffy, Librarian. Lay Teachers 12; Students 120.
Catechesis Religious Program—Tel: 717-246-9959; Email: ttracey@sjdrcc.org. Timothy Tracey, D.R.E. Students 120.
DANVILLE, MONTOUR CO., ST. JOSEPH (1848) [CEM 3]
68 Center St., Danville, 17821. Tel: 570-275-2512; Email: sjcd@verizon.net; Web: stjosephdanville.org. Revs. James E. Lease; Augustine Joseph, M.S.F.S., Parochial Vicar; Deacon Thomas J. Conlin, C.R.E.; John Novak, Business Mgr.; Dennis Bobber, Music Min.
School—St. Joseph School, (Grades K-8), 1027 Ferry St., Danville, 17821. Tel: 570-275-2435; Fax: 570-275-3947; Email: kwinters@stjosephdanville.com; Email: office@stjosephdanville.com; Web: www.stjosephdanville.com. Mrs. Kimberly S. Winters, Prin. Lay Teachers 13; Students 79.
Catechesis Religious Program—Email: DTConlin@hbgdiocese.org. Students 131.
DAUPHIN, DAUPHIN CO., ST. MATTHEW, APOSTLE AND EVANGELIST (1976)
607 Stoney Creek Dr., Dauphin, 17018.
Tel: 717-921-2363; Email: p021stmatthew@hbgdiocese.org. Very Rev. Paul M. Clark, J.C.L.; Deacon Richard Aull.
Res.: 420 Stony Creek Rd., Dauphin, 17018.
Catechesis Religious Program—Students 57.
DOYLESBURG, FRANKLIN CO., OUR LADY OF REFUGE MISSION (1802) [CEM]
21169 Cross Rd., Doylesburg, 17219-9707.
Tel: 717-349-7953; Email: frlrodriguez@hbgdiocese.org. Very Rev. Luis R. Rodriguez, V.F.
Catechesis Religious Program—Students 3.
ELIZABETHTOWN, LANCASTER CO., ST. PETER (1752) [CEM]
1840 Marshall Dr., Elizabethtown, 17022.
Tel: 717-367-1255; Fax: 717-367-1270; Email: secretary@stpeteretown.org; Web: www.stpeteretown.org. Very Rev. Steven W. Fauser, V.F.
Res.: 1 Saint Peter's Pl., Elizabethtown, 17022-1956.
Catechesis Religious Program—Email: cre@stpeteretown.org; Web: www.stpeteretown.org. Students 173.
ELYSBURG, NORTHUMBERLAND CO., QUEEN OF THE MOST HOLY ROSARY (1950)
599 W. Center St., Elysburg, 17824.
Tel: 570-672-2302; Email: frjscanlin@hbgdiocese.org; Web: www.qmhr.net. Very Rev. Joseph T. Scanlin, V.F.
Catechesis Religious Program—Students 136.
ENHAUT, DAUPHIN CO., ST. JOHN THE EVANGELIST (1902) Closed. See Prince of Peace, Steelton.
ENOLA, CUMBERLAND CO., OUR LADY OF LOURDES (1926)
225 Salt Rd., Enola, 17025. Tel: 717-732-9642; Email: frdbender@hbgdiocese.org. Rev. Donald H. Bender.
Catechesis Religious Program—Students 123.
EPHRATA, LANCASTER CO., OUR MOTHER OF PERPETUAL HELP (1914) [JC]
320 Church Ave., Ephrata, 17522. Tel: 717-733-9641; Email: perpetualhelp@dejazzd.com; Web: omph.org. Revs. John McLoughlin, C.Ss.R.; Gordon Cannoles, C.Ss.R.; Thomas Siconolfi, C.Ss.R.
Res.: 300 W. Pine St., Ephrata, 17522.
Tel: 717-733-6596; Fax: 717-733-0502; Email: ledger@ptd.net.
School—Our Mother of Perpetual Help School, 330 Church Ave., Ephrata, 17522. Tel: 717-738-2414; Fax: 717-738-3280; Email: office@omph.org; Web: www.omph.org. Dr. Thomas Castner, Prin. Clergy 1; Lay Teachers 12; Students 132.
Catechesis Religious Program—Tel: 717-738-4517; Email: omphreled@dejazzd.com. Kelly Lawerence, D.R.E. Students 150.
Convent—310 Church Ave., Ephrata, 17522. Tel: 717-733-1291.
FAIRFIELD, ADAMS CO., IMMACULATE CONCEPTION OF THE BLESSED VIRGIN MARY (1823) [CEM] [JC]
256 Tract Rd., Fairfield, 17320. Tel: 717-642-8815; Fax: 717-642-9616; Email: bsites@hbgdiocese.org. Revs. Peter DiTomasso, M.SS.CC.; Christopher Onyeneke, M.SS.CC.
Catechesis Religious Program—Students 53.
GETTYSBURG, ADAMS CO., ST. FRANCIS XAVIER (1831) [CEM]
455 Table Rock Rd., Gettysburg, 17325.
Tel: 717-334-3919. Revs. Daniel C. Mitzel; John Kuchinski.
Church: 25 W. High St., Gettysburg, 17325.
School—St. Francis Xavier School, 465 Table Rock Rd., Gettysburg, 17325. Tel: 717-334-4221; Email: bsieg@sfxcs-pa.org; Web: www.sfxcs-pa.org. Rebecca Sieg, Prin. Lay Teachers 14; Students 202.
Catechesis Religious Program—Tel: 717-334-1221. Students 274.
GREENCASTLE, FRANKLIN CO., ST. MARK THE EVANGELIST (1965) [JC]
395 S. Ridge Ave., Greencastle, 17225.
Tel: 717-597-2705; Email: stmkstlk@comcast.net. Rev. Kyle S. Sahd.
Catechesis Religious Program—Lucy Schemel, D.R.E. Students 140.
Mission—St. Luke the Evangelist, Overhill Dr. & Black Rd., Mercersburg, Franklin Co. 17236.
HANOVER, YORK CO.
1—ST. JOSEPH (1864) [CEM]
5125 Grandview Rd., Hanover, 17331.
Tel: 717-637-5236; Email: gernst@hbgdiocese.org. 5055 Grandview Rd., Hanover, 17331. Rev. Msgr. James M. Lyons, M.Div., M.Ed., V.F.; Revs. Matthew C. Morelli; Lawrence J. McNeil, D.Min., M.Div., In Res., (Retired); Deacons Thomas M. Aumen; Timothy J. Shultis.
School—Saint Joseph Catholic School, Tel: 717-632-0118; Fax: 717-632-0566; Email: office@sjshanover.org; Web: www.sjshanover.org. Mr. Terrance Golden, Prin. Clergy 2; Students 189; Full Time Lay Teachers 10; Part Time Lay Teachers 7.
Catechesis Religious Program—Students 415.
2—ST. VINCENT DE PAUL (1904) [CEM]
220 Third St., Hanover, 17331. Tel: 717-637-4625;

Email: bmiller@hbgdiocese.org. Revs. Michael P. Reid II; Joseph F. Gotwalt, In Res., (Retired); Ignacio Palomino, In Res.
Catechesis Religious Program—Students 40.
HERSHEY, DAUPHIN CO., ST. JOAN OF ARC (1920)
359 W. Areba Ave., Hershey, 17033-1602.
Tel: 717-533-7168, Ext. 100; Email: srobison@stjoanhershey.org. Revs. Alfred P. Sceski; Kenneth C. Roth, Parochial Vicar; Modestus Ngwu, O.P., Chap.; Michael Opoki, A.J., In Res.
School—St. Joan of Arc School, (Grades PreSchool-8), 329 W. Areba Ave., Hershey, 17033.
Tel: 717-533-2854; Fax: 717-534-0755; Email: sreileen@stjoanhershey.org. Sr. Eileen M. McGowan, Prin. Lay Teachers 18; Daughters of Our Lady of Mercy 3; Students 345; Librarian 1.
Catechesis Religious Program—Email: mwarner@stjoanhershey.org; Email: etropp@stjoanhershey.org. Marcie Warner, D.R.E.; Earl Tropp, D.R.E. Students 440.
Convent—Sisters 3.
KULPMONT, NORTHUMBERLAND CO.
1—ASSUMPTION OF THE BLESSED VIRGIN MARY (1909) Closed. See Holy Angels, Kulpmont.
2—ST. CASIMIR (1915) Closed. See Holy Angels, Kulpmont.
3—HOLY ANGELS (1995) [CEM 3]
855 Scott St., Kulpmont, 17834. Tel: 570-373-1221; Email: oneangel@ptd.net. Rev. Andrew J. Stahmer.
Catechesis Religious Program—863 Scott St., Kulpmont, 17834. Students 61.
LANCASTER, LANCASTER CO.
1—ST. ANNE (1923)
929 N. Duke St., Lancaster, 17602.
Tel: 717-392-2225; Email: StAnneParishLancaster@hbgdiocese.org. Rev. Tri M. Luong.
School—St. Anne School, (Grades PreK-8), 108 E. Liberty St., Lancaster, 17602. Tel: 717-394-6711; Fax: 717-394-8628; Email: woodsuzanne@stannelancaster.org; Email: woodsu@stannelancasterpa.org; Web: www.stannelancaster.org. Mrs. Suzanne Wood, Prin. Lay Teachers 16; Students 160; Students (Includes Pre-K at other location) 160.
Catechesis Religious Program—Caitlyn Dusablon, D.R.E. Students 24.
2—ST. ANTHONY OF PADUA (1870) [CEM]
501 E. Orange St., Lancaster, 17602.
Tel: 717-394-0669; Email: sickes@hbgdiocese.org. Rev. Daniel P. O'Brien.
See Resurrection, Lancaster under Consolidated Elementary Schools located in the Institution section.
Catechesis Religious Program—Tel: 717-392-2930. Patricia Meyer, D.R.E. Students 79.
Stations—Lancaster County Prison—Lancaster.
Tel: 717-299-7800.
Conestoga View Nursing Home, Lancaster.
Tel: 717-299-7850.
3—ASSUMPTION OF THE BLESSED VIRGIN MARY (1741)
119 S. Prince St., Lancaster, 17603.
Tel: 717-392-2578; Email: info@stmaryslancaster.org; Web: www.stmaryslancaster.org. Rev. Leo M. Goodman; Deacon Manuel Velazquez.
Catechesis Religious Program—Email: alan@stmaryslancaster.org. Mr. Alan H. Schwartz, D.R.E. Students 147.
4—IGLESIA CATOLICA SAN JUAN BAUTISTA (1972)
425 S. Duke St., Lancaster, 17602. Tel: 717-392-4118 ; Fax: 717-392-4789; Email: p127sanjuan@hbgdiocese.org. Rev. Allan F. Wolfe; Deacons Jose A. Lopez; Felix Ramos; Expedito Santos-Santiago; Manuel Velazquez.
Catechesis Religious Program—Armando Torres, D.R.E. Students 263.
5—ST. JOHN NEUMANN (1978)
601 E. Delp Rd., Lancaster, 17601. Tel: 717-569-8531 ; Email: info@sjnlancaster.org; Web: www.sjnlancaster.org. Very Rev. Daniel F.X. Powell, V.F.; Rev. Steven Arena, Parochial Vicar; Deacons Peter J. Jupin; Michael Oles; Thomas Conner, Parish Mgr.
Catechesis Religious Program—Coleen Kibler, D.R.E. (PreK-9th Grade). Students 476.
6—ST. JOSEPH CHURCH (1849) [CEM]
440 St. Joseph St., Lancaster, 17603-5298.
Tel: 717-397-6921; Web: www.stjosephslanc.com. Revs. Allan F. Wolfe; Brian Olkowski; Deogratias Rwegasira, A.J., In Res.; Deacon Martin C. Light Sr.
See Resurrection, Lancaster under Consolidated Elementary Schools located in the Institution section.
Catechesis Religious Program—Students 134.
7—SACRED HEART OF JESUS (1900)
558 W. Walnut St., Lancaster, 17603.
Tel: 717-394-0757; Email: shparish@sacredheartsch.org; Web: www.sacredheartlanc.org. Revs. Michael E. Messner; Sebastian Thekkedath, C.M.I., Parochial Vicar; Rev. Msgr. Richard A. Youtz, J.C.L., In Res., (Retired).
School—Sacred Heart of Jesus School, (Grades PreK-8), 235 Nevin St., Lancaster, 17603.
Tel: 717-393-8433; Fax: 717-393-1028; Email: shschool@sacredheartsch.org; Web: www.sacredheartschlanc.org. Sr. Danielle Truex, Prin. Lay Teachers 21; Students 240; Sisters (Servants of the Immaculate Heart of Mary) 6; Clergy / Religious Teachers 5.
Catechesis Religious Program—Kathy Hauk, D.R.E. Students 49.
Convent—565 W. Walnut St., Lancaster, 17603.
Tel: 717-392-4522. Sisters 6.
LEBANON, LEBANON CO.
1—ASSUMPTION OF THE BLESSED VIRGIN MARY (1812) [CEM]
2 N. Eighth St., Lebanon, 17046. Tel: 717-272-5674; Email: stm@abvmlebpa.org. Very Rev. Robert M. Gillelan Jr.; Deacon Richard Wentzel, Pastoral Assoc.; Rev. Harold F. Dagle, M.A., In Res., (Retired); Joseph M. Olikkara, M.S.T., (India) In Res.
Catechesis Religious Program—Email: aboltz@abvmlebpa.org. AnneMarie Boltz, D.R.E.
Mission—Our Lady of Fatima, US 22 & N. Mill St., Jonestown, Lebanon Co. 17038. Tel: 717-865-7439. Very Rev. Michael W. Rothan, V.F.
Catechesis Religious Program—Students 36.
2—ST. BENEDICT THE ABBOT (1995)
1300 Lehman St., Lebanon, 17046-3331.
Tel: 717-450-4506; Fax: 717-450-5623; Email: stbenedictlebanon@hbgdiocese.org; Web: stbenedictlebanon.org. Rev. Jose E. Mera-Vallejos, Parochial Admin.
Catechesis Religious Program—Students 48.
3—ST. CECILIA (1995) [CEM]
120 E. Lehman St., Lebanon, 17046.
Tel: 717-272-4412, Ext. 1; Email: stcecilia120@gmail.com. Rev. Michael Laicha.
Res.: 196 E. Lehman St., Lebanon, 17046.
Catechesis Religious Program—Tel: 717-272-4352; Email: mbender@osfphila.org. Sr. Margaret Bender, O.S.F., D.R.E. Students 181.
Convent—200 E. Lehman St., Lebanon, 17046.
4—SS. CYRIL AND METHODIUS (1905) (Slovak), Closed. See St. Benedict the Abbot, Lebanon.
5—ST. GERTRUDE (1906) Closed. See St. Cecilia, Lebanon.
6—ST. GREGORY THE GREAT (1965) Closed. See St. Cecilia, Lebanon.
LEWISBURG, UNION CO., SACRED HEART OF JESUS (1935)
814 St. Louis St., Lewisburg, 17837.
Tel: 570-523-3104; Email: FrMWilke@hbgdiocese.org; Email: sacredheart814@gmail.com; Email: pkeller@hbgdiocese.org; Web: sacredheartofjesus.org. Rev. Mark T. Wilke; Deacon Richard D. Owen.
Catechesis Religious Program—Sr. Thomas More Dzurnak, SS.C.M., D.R.E., Pastoral Asst. Students 185.
Mission—Saint George Church, 775 Forest Hill Rd., Mifflinburg, Union Co. 17844. Tel: 570-966-3088.
LEWISTOWN, MIFFLIN CO., SACRED HEART OF JESUS (1830) [CEM]
9 N. Brown St., Lewistown, 17044. Tel: 717-242-2781 ; Email: shparishoffice@sacredheartlewistown.com; Email: office@sacredheartschool.com; Web: www.sacredheartschool.com. Revs. William M. Weary, V.F.; Jayaseelan Amalanathan, Parochial Vicar.
Res.: 106 N. Dorcas St., Lewistown, 17044.
Tel: 717-242-1208.
School—Sacred Heart of Jesus School, 110 N. Dorcas St., Lewistown, 17044. Tel: 717-248-5351;
Fax: 717-248-1516; Email: office@sacredheartschool.com; Web: www.sacredheartschool.com. Dr. Joseph Maginnis, Prin. Lay Teachers 10; Students 65.
Catechesis Religious Program—Email: shparishoffice@sacredheartlewistown.com. Students 73.
LITITZ, LANCASTER CO., ST. JAMES (1977) [CEM 3]
505 Woodcrest Ave., Lititz, 17543. Tel: 717-626-5580; Email: p060stjames@hbgdiocese.org; Web: www.stjameslititz.org. Rev. James O'Blaney, C.Ss.R.
Catechesis Religious Program—Tel: 717-626-0244; Email: re060@hbgdiocese.org. Rose Barnas, D.R.E. Students 280.
LITTLESTOWN, ADAMS CO., ST. ALOYSIUS (1884) [CEM]
29 S. Queen St., Littlestown, 17340.
Tel: 717-359-4513; Email: frcmiller@hbgdiocese.org. Rev. Charles Anthony Miller.
Catechesis Religious Program—Cynthia Baughman, C.R.E. Students 37.
LOCUST GAP, NORTHUMBERLAND CO., ST. JOSEPH (1870) Closed. See Our Lady of Mount Carmel, Mount Carmel.
LOCUSTDALE, COLUMBIA CO., ST. JOSEPH (1913) Closed. See Our Lady of Mount Carmel, Mount Carmel.
LYKENS, DAUPHIN CO., OUR LADY HELP OF CHRISTIANS (1853) [CEM 2] [JC3]
732 E. Main St., Lykens, 17048. Tel: 717-453-7895; Email: OurLadyHelpofChristiansParishLykens@hbgdiocese.org. Rev. Michael Opoki, A.J.
Catechesis Religious Program—Students 71.
Mission—Sacred Heart of Jesus, 140 E. Market St., Williamstown, Dauphin Co. 17098.
MANCHESTER, YORK CO., HOLY INFANT (1972)
535 Conewago Creek Rd., Manchester, 17345.
Tel: 717-266-5286; Email: holyinfantparish@gmail.com; Web: www.holyinfantparish.com. Very Rev. William C. Forrey, V.F.; Rebecca Papa, Pastoral Asst.; Deacon Joseph J. Kramer.
Catechesis Religious Program—Students 126.
MANHEIM, LANCASTER CO., ST. RICHARD (1957) [JC]
201 Adele Ave., Manheim, 17545. Tel: 717-665-2465; Email: rminieri@hbgdiocese.org. Rev. Stephen D. Weitzel; Deacon William J. Jordan.
Catechesis Religious Program—Students 80.
MARIETTA, LANCASTER CO., PRESENTATION OF THE BLESSED VIRGIN MARY (1869) Closed. See Mary, Mother of the Church, Mount Joy.
MARION HEIGHTS, NORTHUMBERLAND CO., OUR LADY OF PERPETUAL HELP (1905) Closed. See Holy Angels, Kulpmont.
MARYSVILLE, PERRY CO., OUR LADY OF GOOD COUNSEL (1956)
121 Chestnut St., Marysville, 17053.
Tel: 717-957-2662. 121 William St., Marysville, 17053-1434. Rev. Dijo Thomas, M.S.F.S.; Deacon John C. Heil.
Mission—St. Bernadette (1954) 901 N. High St., Duncannon, Perry Co. 17020.
MCSHERRYSTOWN, ADAMS CO., ANNUNCIATION OF THE BLESSED VIRGIN MARY (1899) [CEM]
26 N. Third St., McSherrystown, 17344.
Tel: 717-637-1191; Email: parishoffice@abvmchurch.org; Web: www.abvmchurch.org. Rev. Charles L. Persing; Sr. Ann Marie Wierman, S.S.J., Pastoral Assoc.
School—St. Teresa of Calcutta Catholic School, 316 North St., McSherrystown, 17344. Tel: 717-637-3135 ; Fax: 717-637-1715; Email: abvmbusoff@abvmschool.org; Web: www.abvmschool.org. Mrs. Patricia Foltz, Prin. Lay Teachers 17; Students 196.
Catechesis Religious Program—Students 42.
MECHANICSBURG, CUMBERLAND CO.
1—ST. ELIZABETH ANN SETON (1977)
310 Hertzler Rd., Mechanicsburg, 17055.
Tel: 717-697-2614; Email: frwking@hbgdiocese.org; Web: www.steas.net. Rev. Msgr. William J. King, J.C.D.; Revs. Paul C.B. Schenck, Parochial Vicar; Anthony Eseke, Ph.D., In Res.; Deacon David L. Hall, Pastoral Assoc.
Catechesis Religious Program—Tel: 717-697-3545. Stephanie D. Tanguay, Life Teen Coord.; Judy Olinger, C.R.E.; LaDawnna Clancy, C.R.E. Students 347.
2—SAINT JOSEPH CATHOLIC CHURCH (1950)
410 E. Simpson St., Mechanicsburg, 17055-6507.
Tel: 717-766-9433; Email: officemanager@stjosephmech.org; Web: www.stjosephmech.org. Very Rev. Thomas J. Rozman, V.F.; Rev. Timothy J. Sahd, Parochial Vicar; Deacon Jack Paruso; John B. Durle, Business Mgr.; Justin Myers, Music Min.
Church: 400 E. Simpson St., Mechanicsburg, 17055.
School—Saint Joseph Catholic Church School, 420 E. Simpson St., Mechanicsburg, 17055.
Tel: 717-766-2564; Fax: 717-766-1226; Email: rbamberger@sjsmch.org. Rebecca Bamberger, Prin.; Mary Earnest, Asst. Prin. Lay Teachers 29; Students 426.
Catechesis Religious Program—Tel: 717-766-2472. Richard Groff, D.R.E. Students 843.
3—SAINT KATHARINE DREXEL (1988)
Mailing Address: One Peter Dr., Mechanicsburg, 17050. Tel: 717-697-8716; Email: KSmith@skdparish.com; Web: skdparish.com. Rev. Kenneth G. Smith; Jodi M. Bova, Business Mgr.; Rebecca Davis, Pastoral Assoc.; Natalie Pronio, Youth Min.; Scott Root, C.R.E. - Middle/Secondary; Mary Ann Schleihauf, C.R.E. - Primary/Elementary; Shannon Root, Music Min.
Res.: 87 Skyline Dr., Mechanicsburg, 17050.
Catechesis Religious Program—(Grades K-8),
Tel: 717-795-8572. Julie A. Worhach, D.R.E.; Suzanne Bruzga, Pastoral Assoc. Students 323.
MIDDLETOWN, DAUPHIN CO., SEVEN SORROWS OF THE BLESSED VIRGIN MARY (1855) [CEM]
280 N. Race St., Middletown, 17057.
Tel: 717-944-3133; Fax: 717-944-1170; Email: rkeating@ssbvm.org; Web: www.ssbvm.org. Rev. Edward J. Keating Jr.
School—Seven Sorrows of the Blessed Virgin Mary School, (Grades PreK-8), 360 E. Water St., Middletown, 17057. Tel: 717-944-5371;
Fax: 717-944-5419; Email: pbyrnes@ssbvm.org; Web: www.ssbvm.org. Mrs. Patricia A. Byrnes, Prin. Clergy 1; Students 200; Full Time Lay Teachers 16; Part Time Lay Teachers 5.
Catechesis Religious Program—Ray Kerwin, D.R.E. Students 150.
MIFFLINTOWN, JUNIATA CO., ST. JUDE (1959)
3918 William Penn Hwy., P.O. Box 187, Mifflintown, 17059. Tel: 717-436-6722; Email: gtreaster@hbgdiocese.org. Rev. William M. Weary, V.F.

Res.: 106 N. Dorcas St., Lewistown, 17044.
Tel: 717-242-2781.
Catechesis Religious Program—Students 37.
Mission—St. Jude Thaddeus, 3918 William Penn Hwy., P.O. Box 187, Mifflintown, 17059.
Tel: 717-436-6722.

MILLERSBURG, DAUPHIN CO., QUEEN OF PEACE (1952)
202 Zimmerman Rd., Millersburg, 17061.
Tel: 717-692-3504; Email: frdmoss@hbgdiocese.org. Rev. Darius G. C. Moss.
Catechesis Religious Program—Mrs. J. Roadcap, C.R.E. Students 26.

MILLERSVILLE, LANCASTER CO., ST. PHILIP THE APOSTLE (1965)
2111 Millersville Pike, Lancaster, 17603.
Tel: 717-872-2166; Fax: 717-872-2587; Email: lneff@hbgdiocese.org. Rev. Lawrence W. Sherdel; Ms. Linda Neff, Contact Person.
Catechesis Religious Program—
Tel: 717-872-5653 (Sundays only). Miss Christine M. Miller, D.R.E.; Stephen Sauer, Dir. Music. Students 260.

MILTON, NORTHUMBERLAND CO., ST. JOSEPH (1805) [CEM]
109 Broadway, Milton, 17847. Tel: 570-742-4356; Fax: 570-742-3475; Email: bgeiswite@hbgdiocese.org. Rev. John D. Hoke, V.F.
Catechesis Religious Program—854 Cemetery Rd., Milton, 17847. Tel: 570-724-4302. Harold Prentiss, C.R.E. Students 34.

MOUNT CARMEL, NORTHUMBERLAND CO.
1—DIVINE REDEEMER (1995) [CEM 4]
300 West Ave., Mount Carmel, 17851.
Tel: 570-339-3450; Fax: 570-339-5759; Email: parishdrc@ptd.net; Web: www.divineredeemerpa.weconnect.com. 438 West Ave., Mount Carmel, 17851. Rev. Ryan M. Fischer.
Catechesis Religious Program—Betty Ann Corrigan, C.R.E. Students 130.
2—HOLY CROSS (1892) (Lithuanian), Closed. See Divine Redeemer, Mount Carmel.
3—ST. JOHN THE BAPTIST (1892) (Slovak), Closed. See Divine Redeemer, Mount Carmel.
4—ST. JOSEPH (1875) (Polish), Closed. See Our Lady of Mount Carmel, Mount Carmel.
5—OUR LADY OF MOUNT CARMEL (1886) [JC4]
Our Lady of Mount Carmel Parish: 47 S. Market St., Mount Carmel, 17851. Tel: 717-339-1031;
Fax: 717-339-4814; Email: frankkarwacki@yahoo.com; Web: revfrankkarwacki.net. Rev. Francis J. Karwacki; Deacon Martin P. McCarthy.
Catechesis Religious Program—Tel: 570-339-5091; Email: hooperjudi@gmail.com. Judith Hooper, C.R.E. Students 111.
6—OUR MOTHER OF CONSOLATION (1895) (Polish), Closed. See Divine Redeemer, Mount Carmel.
7—ST. PETER (1905) (Italian), Closed. See Divine Redeemer, Mount Carmel.

MOUNT JOY, LANCASTER CO.
1—ASSUMPTION OF B.V.M. (1979) Closed. See Mary, Mother of the Church, Mount Joy.
2—MARY, MOTHER OF THE CHURCH (1995)
625 Union School Rd., Mount Joy, 17552-9712.
Tel: 717-653-4903; Email: p138marymother@hbgdiocese.org; Web: www.marymotherparish.org/home. Rev. Pang S. Tcheou.
Res.: 530 St. Mary Dr., Mount Joy, 17552-9712.
Catechesis Religious Program—Students 183.

MYERSTOWN, LEBANON COUNTY, MARY, GATE OF HEAVEN (1926)
188 W. McKinley Ave., Myerstown, 17067.
Tel: 717-866-5640; Email: frwrichardson@hbgdiocese.org. Rev. Msgr. William M. Richardson, V.F.
Catechesis Religious Program—Students 112.

NEW BLOOMFIELD, PERRY CO., ST. BERNARD (1942)
811 Shermans Valley Rd., P.O. Box 25, New Bloomfield, 17068. Tel: 717-582-4113; Email: stbernardcatholicchurch@embarqmail.com. Rev. Robert F. Sharman, S.T.L.
Catechesis Religious Program—Email: stbernardcatholicchurch@embargmail.com. Alice Vilk, D.R.E. Students 100.

NEW CUMBERLAND, CUMBERLAND CO., ST. THERESA OF THE INFANT JESUS (1928)
1300 Bridge St., New Cumberland, 17070.
Tel: 717-774-5918; Fax: 717-774-5915; Email: eherald@sainttheresaparish.org. Revs. J. Michael McFadden, M.Div.; Samuel Dubois.
School—St. Theresa of the Infant Jesus School, 1200 Bridge St., New Cumberland, 17070.
Tel: 717-774-7464; Fax: 717-774-3154. Matthew Shore, Prin. (Elementary). Lay Teachers 35; Students 390.
Catechesis Religious Program—Tel: 717-774-7296; Email: jmonaghan@sainttheresaparish.org. Jane Monaghan, D.R.E. Students 306.

NEW FREEDOM, YORK CO., ST. JOHN THE BAPTIST (1841) [CEM]
315 N. Constitution Ave., New Freedom, 17349.
Tel: 717-235-2156; Fax: 717-235-8595; Email: parish@sjbnf.org; Web: www.sjbnf.org. Revs. Robert A. Yohe Jr.; Benjamin J. Dunkelberger, Parochial Vicar; Deacon Frederick C. Horn, Pastoral Assoc.
School—St. John the Baptist School, (Grades PreK-6), Tel: 717-235-3525; Email: smareck@sjbnf.org; Web: stjnschool.org. Sue Mareck, Prin.
Catechesis Religious Program—Tel: 717-235-2439; Email: reled@sjbnf.org. Students 280.

NEW HOLLAND, LANCASTER CO., OUR LADY OF LOURDES (1972)
Mailing Address: 150 Water St., New Holland, 17557. Tel: 717-354-4686; Fax: 717-351-4936; Email: aoshea@hbgdiocese.org; Web: ourladyoflourdesnh.com. Rev. Walter F. Guzman-Alvarez.
Res.: 737 Walnut St., New Holland, 17557.
Tel: 717-354-2540; Fax: 717-354-4170.
Catechesis Religious Program—Tel: 717-354-3338. Students 142.

NEW OXFORD, ADAMS CO., IMMACULATE CONCEPTION OF THE BLESSED VIRGIN MARY (1852) [CEM]
106 Carlisle St., New Oxford, 17350.
Tel: 717-624-4121; Fax: 717-624-4221; Email: frmletteer@hbgdiocese.org. Rev. Michael C. Letteer.
School—Immaculate Conception of the Blessed Virgin Mary School, 101 N. Peter St., New Oxford, 17350. Tel: 717-624-2061; Fax: 717-624-9711. Mrs. Donna Hoffman, Prin. Lay Teachers 13; Students 108.
Catechesis Religious Program—Tel: 717-887-5646. Joanne Lauchman, D.R.E. Students 50.

NORTHUMBERLAND, NORTHUMBERLAND CO., ST. THOMAS MORE (1955) Closed. See St. Monica, Sunbury.

PALMYRA, LEBANON CO., CHURCH OF THE HOLY SPIRIT (1955)
300 W. Pine St., Palmyra, 17078. Tel: 717-838-3369;
Fax: 717-838-3065; Email: church@holyspiritpalmyra.com; Web: www.holyspiritpalmyra.com. Rev. Anthony R. Dill, J.C.L.
Res.: 245 W. Pine St., Palmyra, 17078.
Catechesis Religious Program—Daniel Colon, C.R.E. Students 273.

QUARRYVILLE, LANCASTER CO., ST. CATHERINE OF SIENA (1843) [CEM]
955 Robert Fulton Hwy., Quarryville, 17566-9543.
Tel: 717-786-2695; Email: stcatherinesiena@hbgdiocese.org; Web: stcatherineqville.com. Rev. Mark M. Speitel.
Catechesis Religious Program—Mrs. Diane Dalgaard, D.R.E. Students 70.

RANSHAW, NORTHUMBERLAND CO., ST. ANTHONY OF PADUA (1919) Closed. See Mother Cabrini, Shamokin.

ROARING CREEK, COLUMBIA CO., OUR LADY OF MERCY (1923) [CEM]
304 Slabtown Rd., Catawissa, 17820.
Tel: 717-799-5642; Email: frddalesandro@hbgdiocese.org. Rev. Dennis G. Dalessandro.
Catechesis Religious Program—Mrs. Margaret Jessick, D.R.E. Students 28.

ROHRERSTOWN, LANCASTER CO., ST. LEO THE GREAT (1964)
2427 Marietta Ave., Lancaster, 17601-1942.
Tel: 717-394-1742; Fax: 717-394-1779; Email: secretary@stleos.org. Rev. Benardo Pistone, In Res., (Retired); Very Rev. Peter I. Hahn, V.F.; Deacon Eugene Vannucci.
School—St. Leo the Great School, (Grades PreK-8), Fax: 717-392-4080; Email: secretary@stleoschool.org; Web: www.stleoschool.org. Christine Sieg, Prin. Students 370; Full-time Lay Teachers 16; Part-time Lay Teachers 10; Librarians 1.
Catechesis Religious Program—Email: dre@stleos.org. Sr. Dorothy Wilkinson, S.S.C., D.R.E. Students 390.

SELINSGROVE, SNYDER CO., ST. PIUS X (1964)
112 Fairview Dr., Selinsgrove, 17870-9406.
Tel: 570-374-4113; Fax: 570-374-0156; Email: spxc@ptd.net; Web: StPiusXParish.net. Rev. Tukura Pius Michael, O.P.
Catechesis Religious Program—Students 167.
Missions—Susquehanna University—Selinsgrove, Snyder Co. 17870.
Selinsgrove Center, Selinsgrove, Snyder Co. 17870.
Snyder County Prison, Selinsgrove, Snyder Co.

SHAMOKIN, NORTHUMBERLAND CO.
1—ASSUMPTION OF THE BLESSED VIRGIN MARY (1892) (Slovak), Closed. See Mother Cabrini, Shamokin.
2—ST. EDWARD (1866) Closed. See Mother Cabrini, Shamokin.
3—ST. JOSEPH (1913) Closed. See Our Lady of Hope, Coal Township.
4—ST. MICHAEL ARCHANGEL (1894) (Lithuanian), Closed. See Mother Cabrini, Shamokin.
5—MOTHER CABRINI (1995) [JC4]
Mailing Address: 214 N. Shamokin St., Shamokin, 17872. Tel: 570-648-4512, Ext. 210; Email: cabrini@ptd.net; Web: www.mothercabrini.net. Revs. Martin Kobos, O.F.M.Conv., V.F.; Adam Ziolkowski, O.F.M.Conv., Parochial Vicar; Edward Costello, O.F.M.Conv., In Res.
Res.: 106 N. Cherry St., Shamokin, 17872.
Tel: 570-644-0335; Fax: 570-644-0806.
Catechesis Religious Program—Email: judysurak@ptd.net. Judy Surak, C.R.E. Students 31.
6—ST. STANISLAUS KOSTKA (1874) (Polish), Closed. See Mother Cabrini, Shamokin.

SHIPPENSBURG, CUMBERLAND CO., OUR LADY OF THE VISITATION (1950)
305 N. Prince St., Shippensburg, 17257.
Tel: 717-532-2912; Fax: 717-532-3905; Email: ourlady106@yahoo.com; Web: www.olvshippensburg.org. Rev. Dwight D. Schlaline.
Catechesis Religious Program—Students 98.

SOUTH MOUNTAIN, FRANKLIN CO., MOST HOLY ROSARY, Closed. See St. Ignatius, Buchanan Valley.

SPRING GROVE, YORK CO., SACRED HEART OF JESUS (1976)
146 N. Main St., Spring Grove, 17362.
Tel: 717-225-1704; Email: SHJSG@hbgdiocese.org; Web: www.sacredheartsg.com. 1031 Sprenkle Rd., Spring Grove, 17362. Rev. Thomas R. Hoke.
Res.: 152 N. Main St., Spring Grove, 17362.
Catechesis Religious Program—Heather-Marie Merrill, C.R.E. & Head Faith Formation, Tel: 717-229-9444 (Home). Students 61.

STEELTON, DAUPHIN CO.
1—ST. ANN (1901) (Italian), Closed. See Prince of Peace, Steelton.
2—ASSUMPTION OF THE BLESSED VIRGIN MARY (1898) (Croatian), Closed. See Prince of Peace, Steelton.
3—ST. JAMES (1878) Closed. See Prince of Peace, Steelton.
4—ST. PETER (1909) (Slovenian), Closed. See Prince of Peace, Steelton.
5—PRINCE OF PEACE (1995)
815 S. Second St., Steelton, 17113. Tel: 717-985-1330; Fax: 717-985-1333; Email: pop.parish@comcast.net; Web: popsteelton.org. Very Rev. David L. Danneker, Ph.D.; Deacon Michael Grella.

SUNBURY, NORTHUMBERLAND CO.
1—ST. MICHAEL ARCHANGEL (1863) Closed. See St. Monica, Sunbury.
2—SAINT MONICA CHURCH (1995)
109 Market St., Sunbury, 17801. Tel: 570-286-1435; Email: stmonicaparishsunbury@hbgdiocese.org; Web: stmonicasunbury.wix.com/stmonicasunbury. Rev. Fred Wangwe, A.J., (Africa) Email: wangwe2@hbgdiocese.org; Mrs. Monica Shovlin, Business Mgr.; Mrs. Diane Bramhall, Sec.; Mr. Alan Reichenbach, Maintenance/Custodian.
Res.: 36 S. Front St., Sunbury, 17801.
Tel: 570-286-1435, Ext. 113.
Catechesis Religious Program—Mrs. Linda Walborn, D.R.E.; Mrs. Susan Bickhart, C.R.E. Students 39.

TREVORTON, NORTHUMBERLAND CO., ST. PATRICK (1850) [CEM]
331 W. Shamokin St., Trevorton, 17881-1523.
Tel: 570-797-8251; Fax: 570-797-3990; Email: stpats@ptd.net. Rev. Steven G. Frenier, O.F.M.Conv.
Catechesis Religious Program—863 W. Chestnut St., Coal Township, 17866. Tel: 570-648-4432; Email: SrEVincent@hbgdiocese.org. Sr. M. Emily Vincent, I.H.M., D.R.E. Shared with Our Lady of Hope Church, Coal Township. Students 16.

WAYNESBORO, FRANKLIN CO., ST. ANDREW (1893) [CEM]
12 N. Broad St., Waynesboro, 17268.
Tel: 717-762-1914; Fax: 717-762-8474; Email: office@standrewwbo.org; Web: www.standrewwbo.org. Very Rev. Robert P. Malagesi, M.SS.CC.
School—St. Andrew School, 213 E. Main St., Waynesboro, 17268. Tel: 717-762-3221;
Fax: 717-762-8474; Email: nmiller@saintandrewschool.org; Web: www.saintandrewschool.org. Mr. Lindsay Salmon, Prin. Lay Teachers 13; Students 120.
Catechesis Religious Program—(Grades PreSchool-9), Email: dre@standrewwbo.org. Margaret E. Wagaman, D.R.E. Students 103.

WILLIAMSTOWN, DAUPHIN CO., SACRED HEART OF JESUS (1875) [CEM] [JC]
E. Market St., Williamstown, 17098.
Tel: 717-453-7895; Fax: 717-453-9426; Email: OurLadyHelpofChristiansParishLykens@hbgdiocese.org. 732 Main St., Lykens, 17048. Rev. Michael Opoki, A.J.
Catechesis Religious Program—Tel: 717-647-2645. Nora Valovage, D.R.E. Students 19.

YORK, YORK CO.
1—IMMACULATE CONCEPTION OF THE BLESSED VIRGIN MARY (1852) [CEM] [JC]
309 S. George St., York, 17401. Tel: 717-845-7629; Web: www.stmarysyork.org. Very Rev. Jonathan P. Sawicki, V.F.; Rev. Charles Ocul, A.J., Chap.; Deacon Catalino Gonzalez, Pastoral Assoc.
Catechesis Religious Program—Tel: 717-846-6001; Email: mstarceski@stmarysyork.org. Mrs. Marisa Starceski, D.R.E. Students 221.
2—ST. JOSEPH (1913) [JC]

2935 Kingston Rd., York, 17402-4003.
Tel: 717-755-7503; Fax: 717-757-1900; Email: SJC@sjy.org. Revs. Stephen Fernandes, O.F.M.Cap.; James Menkhus, O.F.M.Cap., Snr. Priest; Jonathan Ulrick, O.F.M.Cap., Parochial Vicar; Deacons Neil A. Crispo; Joe Shriver.
School—St. Joseph School, (Grades PreK-6), 2945 Kingston Rd., York, 17402. Tel: 717-755-1797;
Fax: 717-751-0136; Email: gaito@sjy.org. Mrs. Patricia A. Byrnes, Prin. Lay Teachers 21; Students 336.

3—ST. PATRICK CHURCH (1776) [CEM]
219 S. Beaver St., York, 17401. Tel: 717-848-2007; Email: frkcarroll@stpatrickyork.net; Web: www.stpatrickyork.org. Revs. Keith M. Carroll; Hoa Van Nguyen, In Res.; Deacon Michael V. DeVivo; Sr. Monica Imgrund, R.S.M., Pastoral Assoc.
Res.: 231 S. Beaver St., York, 17401.
School—St. Patrick School, 235 S. Beaver St., York, 17401. Tel: 717-854-8263; Fax: 717-846-6049; Email: spcsoffice@stpatrickyork.net; Web: stpatrickyork.org. Ms. Kathleen Smith, Prin. Lay Teachers 13; Students 116.
Catechesis Religious Program—Tel: 717-854-6653; Email: reled@stpatrickyork.net. Lynda Starceski, D.R.E. Students 150.

4—ST. ROSE OF LIMA (1907) [JC]
950 W. Market St., York, 17401. Tel: 717-846-4935; Email: StRoseofLimaParishYork@hbgdiocese.org; Web: www.saintroseoflimayork.org. Rev. Daniel K. Richards.
School—St. Rose of Lima School, 115 N. Biesecker Rd., Thomasville, 17364. Tel: 717-792-0889;
Fax: 717-792-3959. Peggy Rizzuto, Prin. Lay Teachers 9; Students 79.
Catechesis Religious Program—Tel: 717-843-3043. Mrs. Sharon Egan, D.R.E. Students 111.

Chaplains of Public Institutions

HARRISBURG. *Community General Pinnacle Health Hospital*, 4300 Londonderry Rd., 17109.
Tel: 717-652-3000. Rev. Javed Kashif, O.F.M.Cap.
Pinnacle Health Harrisburg Hospital, 111 South Front St., 17101. Tel: 717-782-5208. Rev. Javed Kashif, O.F.M.Cap.

CAMP HILL. *State Correctional Institution*, 2500 Lisburn Rd., Camp Hill, 17001.
Tel: 717-737-4531, Ext. 4439. Deacon Jorge Vera, Chap.

DANVILLE. *Geisinger Medical Center*, 100 North Academy Dr., Danville, 17822. Tel: 717-275-2512. Rev. John Cyriac, M.S.F.S., Chap.
State Hospital, P.O. Box 219, Danville, 17821.
Tel: 717-275-7011. Rev. Augustine Joseph, A.J., Chap.

HERSHEY. *Penn State Milton S. Hershey Medical Center*, 500 University Blvd., Hershey, 17033.
Tel: 717-531-8659. Revs. Modestus Ngwu, O.P., Chap., Paul Bola Oye, O.P., Chap.

LANCASTER. *Lancaster County Prison*, 625 E. King St., Lancaster, 17602. Tel: 717-299-7800. Rev. Allan F. Wolfe.
Lancaster General Hospital, 555 North Duke St., Lancaster, 17602. Tel: 717-544-5511. Revs. Deogratias Rwegasira, A.J., Sebastian Thekkedath, C.M.I.

LEBANON. *Veterans Administration Medical Center*, 1700 S. Lincoln Ave., Lebanon, 17042.
Tel: 717-228-6021. Joseph M. Olikkara, M.S.T., (India).

LEWISBURG. *U.S. Penitentiary*, Lewisburg.
Tel: 570-523-1251. Vacant.

SELINSGROVE. *Selinsgrove Center*, 1000 Rte. 522, Selinsgrove, 17870. Tel: 717-374-2911, Ext. 425. Rev. Tukura Pius Michael, O.P.

SOUTH MOUNTAIN. *South Mountain Restoration Center*, 10058 S. Mountain Rd., South Mountain, 17261.
Tel: 717-749-3121, Ext. 3341. Rev. Joseph C. Carolin.

YORK. *York Hospital*, 1001 S. George St., York, 17405.
Tel: 717-771-2345. Rev. Charles Ocul, A.J.

Graduate Studies:
Rev.—
Logue, Stephen J., Pontifical North American College, 00120 Vatican City State.

On Duty Outside the Diocese:
Revs.—
Bateman, John B., Rome
Blackwell, Edward A., 2373 Montpelier Rd., Punta Gorda, FL 33983
Kemper, John C., S.S., Provincial House, 5408 Roland Ave., Baltimore, MD 21210-1988
LaVoie, Raymond J., U.S. Army.

Retired:
Rev. Msgrs.—
Overbaugh, Hugh A., (Retired)
Smith, Vincent J., (Retired)
Youtz, Richard A., J.C.L., (Retired)
Revs.—
Acri, John A., (Retired)
Bennett, Michael X., (Retired)
Capitani, Sylvan P., D.Min., (Retired)
Devine, Patrick A., (Retired)
Gotwalt, Joseph F., (Retired)
Heintzelman, Gerard T., (Retired)
Houser, Samuel E, (Retired)
Lavelle, Edward R., (Retired)
Mammarella, Dominick, (Retired)
Marickovic, Thomas C., (Retired)
Marinak, Andrew P., (Retired)
McGinley, Bernard P., M.A., (Retired)
McNeil, Lawrence J., D.Min., M.Div., (Retired)
Menei, Francis T., (Retired)
Moratelli, Ronald J., (Retired)
O'Brien, James R., (Retired)
Olszewski, Clarence A., (Retired)
Pistone, Benardo, (Retired)
Schmalhofer, John D., (Retired)
Shuda, Paul R., (Retired)
Snyder, Chester P., (Retired)
Stahura, Joseph L., (Retired)
Sullivan, William J., (Retired), St. Joseph, Mechanicsburg
Tancredi, Carl T., (Retired)
Topper, Charles J., (Retired).

Permanent Deacons:
Amarante, Gregory M., Sacred Heart of Jesus, Lewisburg
Anders, Joseph L., (Retired)
Aull, Richard H., St. Matthew, Dauphin
Aumen, Thomas M., St. Joseph, Hanover
Bahn, Michael P., St. Patrick, York
Baylor, Jeffrey A., St. Peter, Columbia
Bernardy, Daniel L., St. Joseph, Dallastown
Bertollo, Edward L. Jr., (Retired)
Conlin, Thomas J., St. Joseph, Danville
Crispo, Neil A., St. Joseph, York
Crudup, Lawrence R., St. Patrick Cathedral, Harrisburg
DeVivo, Michael V., St. Patrick, York
Doyle, James B., Our Lady of the Blessed Sacrament, Harrisburg
Enderle, Frank X., (Retired)
Fedor, Thomas A., St. Catherine Laboure, Harrisburg
Foerster, Jerome T., Holy Name of Jesus, Harrisburg
Garber, George M., Our Lady Help of Christians, Lykens; Sacred Heart, Williamstown
Gonzales, Catalino, Immaculate Conception BVM, York
Gorman, Francis C., Good Shepherd, Camp Hill
Grella, Michael A., Ed.D., Prince of Peace, Steelton
Hall, David L., St. Elizabeth Ann Seton, Mechanicsburg
Heil, John C., Our Lady of Good Counsel, Marysville
Horn, Frederick C., St. John the Baptist, New Freedom
Huete, Stephen M., St. Ignatius Loyola, Orrtanna
Jordan, William J., St. Richard, Manheim
Jupin, Peter J., St. John Neumann, Lancaster
Kearney, Anthony A., St. Paul the Apostle, Annville
Kenski, Francis G., (Retired)
Kiley, Patrick M., Good Shepherd, Camp Hill
Kramer, Joseph J., Holy Infant, York Haven
Ladouceur, Philip J., Holy Family, Harrisburg
Lang, Thomas A., Cathedral Parish of St. Patrick, Harrisburg
Lawrence, Joseph F., Annunciation BVM, McSherrystown
Light, Martin C. Sr., St. Joseph, Lancaster
Lopez, Jose A., San Juan Bautista, Lancaster
Mann, Donovan A., St. Richard, Manheim
Marroquin, Miguel, St. Francis of Assisi, Harrisburg
McCarthy, Martin P., Our Lady of Mt. Carmel, Mount Carmel
Miller, Gene R., (Retired)
Mortel, Rodrigue, St. Joan of Arc, Hershey
Mowery, John A., (Retired)
Oles, Michael, (Retired)
Owen, Richard D., Sacred Heart of Jesus, Lewisburg
Parr, Frank J., (Retired)
Paruso, John L., St. Joseph, Mechanicsburg
Ramos, Felix, San Juan Bautista, Lancaster
Ramsey, Richard W., Corpus Christi, Chambersburg
Robinson, Gerald P., St. Bernard, New Bloomfield
Ryan, Richard A., (Retired)
Santos-Santiago, Expidito, San Juan Bautista, Lancaster
Sferrella, Joseph, (Retired)
Shultis, Timothy J., St. Vincent de Paul, Hanover
Smith, Raymond, (Retired)
Solomon, Michael, St. John the Baptist, New Freedom
Vannucci, Eugene D., St. Leo the Great, Rohrerstown
Velazquez, Manuel, Assumption BVM & San Juan Bautista, Lancaster
Vera, Jorge, Chap., SCI Camp Hill
Weaver, Richard J., St. Joseph, Bonneauville
Wentzel, Richard W., Assumption BVM, Lebanon; Our Lady of Fatima Mission, Jonestown
Whale, William E., Our Lady of Lourdes, Daytona Beach, FL
Wrabel, Joseph J., Holy Name of Jesus, Harrisburg.

INSTITUTIONS LOCATED IN DIOCESE

[A] HIGH SCHOOLS

HARRISBURG. *Bishop McDevitt High School of Harrisburg*, 1 Crusader Way, 17111.
Tel: 717-236-7973; Fax: 717-234-1270; Email: cpagliaro@bishopmcdevitt.org; Web: www.bishopmcdevitt.org. Ms. Catherine Pagliaro, Prin.; Rev. Kevin Coyle, Chap. Lay Teachers 54; Sisters 4; Students 740; Clergy / Religious Teachers 4.

CAMP HILL. *Trinity High School*, 3601 Simpson Ferry Rd., Camp Hill, 17011. Tel: 717-761-1116;
Fax: 717-761-7309; Email: jcominsky@thsrocks.us; Web: www.thsrocks.us. John Cominsky, Prin.; Rev. Mark E. Weiss, Chap. Full-time Lay Teachers 44; Priests 1; Sisters 2; Students 522.

COAL TOWNSHIP. *Our Lady of Lourdes Regional School*, (Grades PreK-12), 2001 Clinton Ave., Coal Township, 17866-1699. Tel: 570-644-0375;
Fax: 570-644-7655; Email: lourdes@ptd.net; Web: www.lourdes.k12.pa.us. Deacon Martin P. McCarthy, Admin. & Prin., High School; Rev. Andrew J. Stahmer, Chap. Lay Teachers 35; Sisters 2; Students 524.

LANCASTER. *Lancaster Catholic High School*, 650 Juliette Ave., Lancaster, 17601. Tel: 717-509-0315;
Fax: 717-509-0312; Web: lchsyes.org. Tim Hamer, Pres.; Terry Klugh, Prin.; Rev. Steven Arena, Chap. Lay Teachers 42; Students 600.

LEBANON. *Lebanon Catholic School* (1859) (Grades PreK-12), 1400 Chestnut St., Lebanon, 17042.
Tel: 717-273-3731; Fax: 717-274-5167; Email: rosekury@lebanoncatholicschool.org; Email: lebanoncatholic@hbgdiocese.org; Web: www.lebanoncatholicschool.org. Rose Kury, Prin.; Mrs. Cynthia Williams, Elementary Dir.; Very Rev. Michael W. Rothan, V.F., Chap.; Mrs. Megan Sanchez, Secondary Dir. Lay Teachers 37; Students 380.

MCSHERRYSTOWN. *Delone Catholic High School*, 140 S. Oxford Ave., McSherrystown, 17344.
Tel: 717-637-5969; Fax: 717-637-0442; Email: information@delonecatholic.org; Web: www.delonecatholic.org. Richard La Rocca, Prin.; Mr. John Fournie, Librarian; Rev. Charles L. Persing, Chap. Lay Teachers 29; Students 402.

YORK. *York Catholic High School*, 601 E. Springettsbury Ave., York, 17403.
Tel: 717-846-8871; Fax: 717-843-4588; Email: info@yorkcatholic.org; Web: www.yorkcatholic.org. Katie Seufert, Prin.; Very Rev. Jonathan P. Sawicki, V.F., Chap.; Marie Murphy, Librarian. Lay Teachers 46; Students 615; Total Staff 73; Clergy / Religious Teachers 1.

[B] CONSOLIDATED ELEMENTARY SCHOOLS

HARRISBURG. *Harrisburg Catholic Elementary School* (1873) (Grades PreK-8), 555 S. 25th St., 17104.
Tel: 717-232-2551; Tel: 717-234-3797;
Fax: 717-213-2000; Email: drushinski@hbgcathelem.org; Web: www.hbgcathelem.org. Mr. David Rushinski, Prin. Lay Teachers 14; Students 202; Students 208; Clergy / Religious Teachers 1.
Middle School, (Grades PreK-8), Cathedral Campus:Tel: 717-234-3797; Fax: 717-213-2000. Lay Teachers 7.
Harrisburg Catholic Elementary School, (Grades K-4), Holy Family Campus:Tel: 717-232-2551. Mr. David Rushinski, Prin. Lay Teachers 7; Sisters 1.

BERWICK. *Holy Family Consolidated School*, 728 Washington St., Berwick, 18603. Tel: 570-752-2021 ; Fax: 570-752-2914. Laura Knorr, Librarian;

David Brown, Prin. Lay Teachers 6; Sisters 1; Students 90.

COLUMBIA. *Our Lady of the Angels School* (1998) 404 Cherry St., Columbia, 17512. Tel: 717-684-2433; Tel: 717-684-2664; Fax: 717-684-5039; Email: ayoung@ourladyoftheangels.org. Mrs. Amanda Young, Prin. Lay Teachers 15; Sisters 1; Students 194.

LANCASTER. *Resurrection Catholic School*, 521 E. Orange St., Lancaster, 17602. Tel: 717-392-3083; Fax: 717-735-7793; Email: bweaver@resurrectioncatholicschool.net. Miss Brenda Weaver, Prin.; Robin Beutler, Librarian. Lay Teachers 9; Students 113.

[C] PRESCHOOLS AND DAY NURSERIES

MCSHERRYSTOWN. *St. Joseph Academy Preschool*, 90 Main St., McSherrystown, 17344.
Tel: 717-630-9990; Email: sjaprek@gmail.com. Christina Donahue, Dir. Sisters of St. Joseph. Lay Teachers 2; Sisters 2; Students 25.

[D] CATHOLIC CHARITIES COUNSELING & FIELD SERVICES

HARRISBURG. *Department for Catholic Charities Administrative Office*, 4800 Union Deposit Rd., 17111-3710. Tel: 717-657-4804; Fax: 717-657-8683; Email: cklinger@hbgdiocese.org; Web: www.cchbg.org. Mark A. Totaro, Ph.D., MBA, Exec. Dir. & CEO; Peter A. Biasucci, L.S.W., Asst. Exec. Dir. Tot Asst. Annually 2,542; Total Staff 7.

Adoption Services, 939 E. Park Dr., Ste. 103, 17111. Tel: 717-564-7115; Email: kbolton@cchbg.org; Fax: 717-564-7180; Web: www.cchbg.org. Kelly M. Bolton, M.S.W., L.S.W., Dir. Adoption & Specialized Foster Care. Tot Asst. Annually 67; Total Staff 3.

Capital Region Office, 939 E. Park Dr., Ste. 101, 17111. Tel: 717-233-7978; Fax: 717-233-4194; Email: kdownes@cchbg.org; Web: www.cchbg.org. Kate Downes, M.S.W., M.B.A., Assoc. Exec. Dir. of Behavioral Health Svcs. Tot Asst. Annually 269; Total Staff 5.

Evergreen House Program, 120 Willow Rd., Ste. B, 17109. Tel: 717-412-4594; Fax: 717-972-0925; Email: lthomas@cchbg.org; Web: www.cchbg.org. Lydia Thomas, M.S., CCDP-DIP, Prog. Dir. Tot Asst. Annually 101; Total Staff 15.

Specialized Foster Care, 939 E. Park Dr., Ste. 103, 17111. Tel: 717-654-7115; Fax: 717-564-7180; Email: kbolton@cchbg.org. Kelly M. Bolton, M.S.W., L.S.W., Prog. Mgr.

Immigration and Refugee Services, 939 E. Park Dr., Ste. 102, 17111. Tel: 717-232-0568; Fax: 717-234-1742; Email: ahabeeb@cchbg.org; Web: www.cchbg.org. Annette Martin, M.H.S., Assoc. Exec. Residential Svcs. Tot Asst. Annually 324; Total Staff 4.5.

English As A Second Language, Tel: 717-232-0568; Fax: 717-234-7142. Sara Beck, B.A., Mgr.

Employment Services, Tel: 717-232-0568; Fax: 717-234-7142. Sinisa Jovic.

Resettlement Services, Tel: 717-232-0568; Fax: 717-909-0968. Annette Martin, M.H.S., Assoc. Exec. Residential Svcs.

Interfaith Shelter for Homeless Families, 120 Willow Rd., Ste. C, 17109. Tel: 717-652-8740; Fax: 717-545-0185; Email: lpeck@cchbg.org. Lisa Peck, M.S.Ed., Prog. Dir. Tot Asst. Annually 304; Total Staff 15.5.

Lourdeshouse Maternity Services, 120 Willow Rd., Ste. A, 17109. Tel: 717-412-4865; Fax: 717-412-4943; Email: amartin@cchbg.org. Annette Martin, M.H.S., Assoc. Exec. Residential Svcs.

Paradise School, 6156 West Canal Rd., Abbottstown, 17301-8982. Tel: 717-259-9537; Fax: 717-259-9262; Email: dlangeheine@cchbg.org. Dustin Langeheine, B.S., Prog. Dir. Tot Asst. Annually 356; Total Staff 9.

Lancaster Office, 925 N. Duke St., Lancaster, 17602. Tel: 717-299-3659; Tel: 717-392-2113 (Spanish); Fax: 717-299-1328; Email: kdownes@cchbg.org. Kate Downes, M.S.W., M.B.A., Prog. Dir. Tot Asst. Annually 188; Total Staff 2.75.

Intensive Day Treatment, 47 S. Mulberry St., Lancaster, 17603. Tel: 717-295-9630; Fax: 717-295-9525; Email: rdiamondstone@cchbg.org. Rebecca Diamondstone, M.S., Prog. Dir. Tot Asst. Annually 142; Total Staff 15.

York Office, 253 E. Market St., York, 17403. Tel: 717-845-2696; Fax: 717-843-3941; Email: kdownes@cchbg.org; Web: www.cchbg.org. Kate Downes, M.S.W., M.B.A., Assoc. Exec. Dir. Behavioral Health Svcs. Tot Asst. Annually 163; Total Staff 3.5.

York/Adams Family Based Program, c/o Paradise School, 6156 W. Canal Rd., Abbottstown, 17301-8982. Tel: 717-845-3373; Fax: 717-845-4101. Rebecca Jacoby, M.S., Prog. Dir. Total Staff 4.25; Total Assisted 105.

York Intensive Family Services, 253 E. Market St., York, 17401. Tel: 717-843-7986; Fax: 717-699-0020; Email: kballantine@cchbg.org. Karrie Ballantine, M.S., Prog. Dir. Tot Asst. Annually 471; Total Staff 9.

[E] GENERAL HOSPITALS

CAMP HILL. **Holy Spirit Corporation*, 503 N. 21st St., Camp Hill, 17011. Tel: 717-763-2100.

**Holy Spirit Health System*, 503 N. 21st St., Camp Hill, 17011-2288. Tel: 717-763-2100; Fax: 717-763-2183; Email: jmfegan@geisinger.edu; Web: www.hsh.org. Kyle C. Snyder, Chief Accounting Officer. Sisters of Christian Charity.
Holy Spirit Corporation.
Holy Spirit Hospital of the Sisters of the Christian Charity.
Spirit Physician Services, Inc.
West Shore ALS, Inc. Bassinets 15; Bed Capacity 307; Sisters 19; Total Staff 1,843; Inpatient Admissions 11,474; Outpatient Visits 243,418.

**Holy Spirit Hospital of the Sisters of Christian Charity*, 503 N. 21st St., Camp Hill, 17011.

**Spirit Physician Services, Inc.*, 503 N. 21st St., Camp Hill, 17011.

**West Shore ALS, Inc.*, 503 N. 21st St., Camp Hill, 17011.

[F] CONVALESCENT & RETIREMENT HOMES

HARRISBURG. *Bishop Dattilo Retirement Residence for Priests* (2001) 675 Rutherford Rd., 17109.
Tel: 717-657-3147; Fax: 717-657-3167; Email: retirementresidence@hbgdiocese.org. Mark A. Totaro, Ph.D., MBA, Exec. Tot Asst. Annually 12; Total Staff 4; Suites 15.

COLUMBIA. *St. Anne's Retirement Community* (1954) 3952 Columbia Ave., Columbia, 17512-9715.
Tel: 717-285-5443; Fax: 717-285-5950; Email: mturnbaugh@stannesrc.org. Mary Turnbaugh, Pres.; Rev. Norman C. Hohenwarter Jr., Chap. Adorers of the Blood of Christ. Bed Capacity 241; Residents 119; Tot Asst. Annually 63; Total Staff 275; Personal Care Staff 20; Cottages 37; Apartments 34; Residents in Retirement Village 34; Residents in Apartments 34; Personal Care 50.

DANVILLE. *Maria Hall, Inc.*, 190 Maria Hall Dr., Danville, 17821. Tel: 570-275-1120;
Fax: 570-275-1134; Email: mhpcadm@yahoo.com. Sr. M. Philothea Fabian, S.S.C.M., Admin.; Rev. Gerard T. Heintzelman, (Retired). Personal Care Home and Convent (Sisters of SS. Cyril & Methodius) and Carmelites of Danville. Sisters 39; Total Staff 19; Total Assisted 18.

Maria Joseph Manor, 1707 Montour Blvd., Danville, 17821. Tel: 570-275-4221; Fax: 570-275-4711; Email: rurick@mariajosephccc.org; Web: www.mariajosephccc.org. Sr. Sara Swayze, Treas. Bed Capacity 190; Religious 7; Sisters 6; Tot Asst. Annually 455; Total Staff 220.

The Meadows at Maria Joseph Manor, 1707 Montour Blvd., Danville, 17821. Tel: 570-271-1000; Email: rurick@mariajosephccc.org. Sr. M. Christopher Godlewski, Dir. Residents 151; Total Staff 6; Independent Living Units 112.

YORK. *Misericordia Nursing & Rehabilitation Center* (1943) 998 S. Russell St., York, 17402.
Tel: 717-755-1964; Fax: 717-840-0010; Email: mbittner@mn-rc.org. Marion Bittner, N.H.A., B.S., Admin. Daughters of Our Lady of Mercy. Bed Capacity 50; Sisters 3; Total Staff 92; Total Assisted 106.

[G] MONASTERIES AND RESIDENCES OF PRIESTS AND BROTHERS

EPHRATA. *St. Clement's Mission House*, 300 W. Pine St., Ephrata, 17522-2072. Tel: 717-733-6596; Fax: 717-733-0502; Email: ledger@ptd.net. Revs. Charles J. Brinkmann; Gordon Cannoles, C.Ss.R.; Richard Knappik, C.S.s.R., In Res.; Patrick McGarrity, C.Ss.R.; John McLoughlin, C.Ss.R.; James O'Blaney, C.Ss.R.; Thomas Siconolfi, C.Ss.R.; Gerard J. Szymkowiak, C.Ss.R., In Res.; Bro. Bosco Hammond, In Res. Redemptorist Fathers and Brothers. Total in Residence 12.
Mission Preaching Band: Rev. Paul Bryan, C.Ss.R.

[H] CONVENTS AND RESIDENCES FOR SISTERS

HARRISBURG. *Sisters of IHM Saint Catherine Laboure Convent*, 4010 Derry St., 17111. Tel: 717-745-4134; Email: ihm4010@comcast.net. Sr. Bernard Agnes, I.H.M., Supr. Sisters, Servants of the Immaculate Heart of Mary 8.

COLUMBIA. *Adorers of the Blood of Christ* (1834) Columbia Center of the Adorers of the Blood of Christ, 3954 Columbia Ave., Columbia, 17512-9714. Tel: 717-285-4536; Web: www.adorers.org. Bernice Klosterman, Contact Person. Sisters 5.

DANVILLE. *Discalced Carmelite Nuns of Danville, PA* (1953) 190 Maria Hall Dr., Danville, 17821-1237. Tel: 570-275-4682; Email: carmelmariahall@gmail.com; Fax: 570-275-4684. Sr. Angela Pikus, O.C.D., Prioress. Discalced Carmelite Nuns. Nuns in Solemn Vows 8.

Sisters of Saints Cyril and Methodius (1909) Villa Sacred Heart, 1002 Railroad St., Danville, 17821-1698. Tel: 570-275-3581, Ext. 300; Fax: 570-275-4037; Email: jambresscm@hotmail.com; Web: www.sscm.org. Sr. M. Michael Ann Orlik, SS.C.M., Gen. Supr. Motherhouse of the Sisters of Saints Cyril and Methodius. Sisters 69.

St. Cyril Academy Preschool and Kindergarten, Danville, 17821-1698. Tel: 570-275-3581, Ext. 160; Fax: 570-275-5997; Email: scpandk@hotmail.com; Web: www.stcyril1.vpweb.com. Sr. Donna Marie, SS.C.M., Dir.

St. Cyril Academy Spiritual Center, Danville, 17821-1698. Tel: 570-275-3581, Ext. 320; Fax: 570-275-5997; Email: jeanholupsscm@yahoo.com; Web: www.sscm.org. Sr. Jean Marie Holup, SS.C.M., Dir.

ELYSBURG. *Carmel of Jesus, Mary and Joseph in Elysburg, PA, Inc.*, 430 Monastery Rd., Elysburg, 17824. Tel: 570-672-2122; Fax: 570-672-2192; Email: elysburgcarmlites@gmail.com. Rev. John A. Szada Jr., Chap.

LANCASTER. *Dominican Nuns of the Perpetual Rosary, Incorporated* (1927) 1834 Lititz Pike, Lancaster, 17601-6585. Tel: 717-569-2104; Fax: 717-569-1598; Email: monlanc@aol.com; Web: www.opnunslancaster.org. Sr. Mary Veronica, O.P., Prioress; Rev. Joseph Ambrose Eckinger, O.P., S.T.B., Chap. Solemnly Professed Nuns 8.

[I] NEWMAN CENTERS

HARRISBURG. *Catholic Campus Ministry*, 4800 Union Deposit Rd., 17111-3710. Tel: 717-657-4804; Fax: 717-657-4041; Web: www.hbgdiocese.org. Mr. Robert J. Williams, Dir., Office for Youth & Young Adult Min., Tel: 717-657-4804.

Bloomsburg University of Pennsylvania, 353 E. Second St., Bloomsburg, 17815. Tel: 570-784-3123; Fax: 570-784-3583. Rev. Richard Mowery, Campus Min.; Ms. Nina Camaioni, Assoc. Dir.; Rev. David M. Hereshko, Campus Min.

Bucknell University, Newman Center, 610 St. George St., Lewisburg, 17837. Tel: 570-577-3766; Fax: 570-577-2760. Very Rev. Michael W. Rothan, V.F., Campus Min.

Dickinson College, 152 E. Pomfret St., Carlisle, 17013. Tel: 717-243-4411; Fax: 717-258-9281. Rev. Joshua Cavender, Campus Min.

Elizabethtown College, 1840 Marshall Dr., Elizabethtown, 17022. Tel: 717-367-1255. Very Rev. Steven W. Fauser, V.F.; Karen Bruskewicz, Assoc. Dir. of Catholic Campus Ministry; Ms. Ann Schwartz, Campus Min.

Franklin and Marshall College, Lancaster, 558 W. Walnut St., Lancaster, 17603. Tel: 717-394-0757. Rev. Michael E. Messner, Pastor, Sacred Heart Parish, Lancaster.

Gettysburg College, 300 N. Washington St., Box 427, Gettysburg, 17325-0136. Tel: 717-337-6284; Fax: 717-337-6284. Elizabeth Smith, Assoc. Dir., Campus Min.; Rev. John Kuchinski, Parochial Vicar St. Francis Xavier.

Lebanon Valley College, 125 S. Spruce St., Annville, 17003. Tel: 717-867-1525. Rev. Job J. Foote, O.S.B., Pastor, St. Paul's Church, Annville.

Messiah College, 310 Hertzler Rd., Mechanicsburg, 17055. Tel: 717-766-2511, Ext. 7192; Fax: 717-796-2349. Renee Thomas, Newman Club Coord.

Millersville University, Newman Center, 227 N. George St., Millersville, 17551. Tel: 717-872-3350; Fax: 717-872-3668. Rev. Brian J. Wayne, Campus Min.; Alicia Q. Spelfogel, Dir., Campus Min.

Penn State University, Mont Alto Campus, South Mountain, 12 N. Broad St., Waynesboro, 17268. Tel: 717-762-1914. Very Rev. Robert P. Malagesi, M.SS.CC., Pastor.

**Shippensburg University*, Cora I Grove Spiritual Center, 1871 Old Main Dr., Rm. 215, Shippensburg, 17257. Tel: 717-477-1244; Email: catholic@ship.edu. Rev. Dwight D. Schlaline, Campus Min.; Nichole Schneider, Campus Min.

Susquehanna University Catholic Campus Ministry, 112 Fairview Dr., Selinsgrove, 17870. Tel: 570-374-4113; Email: FrPius@ptd.net. Rev. Tukura Pius Michael, O.P., Pastor, St. Pius X Church, Selinsgrove.

York College, Catholic Campus Ministry: c/o Office of Spiritual Life, 441 Country Club Rd., York, 17403. Tel: 717-815-6524. Rev. Benjamin J. Dunkelberger, Campus Min.

[J] MISCELLANEOUS LISTINGS

HARRISBURG. *Harrisburg Catholic Administrative Services, Inc.*, 4800 Union Deposit Rd., 17111. Tel: 717-657-4804; Fax: 717-671-7021; Email:

hkline@hbgdiocese.org. Mr. Donald J. Kaercher, CPA, Exec.

Kolbe Catholic Publishing, Inc., 4800 Union Deposit Rd., 17111-3710. Tel: 717-657-4804, Ext. 387; Fax: 717-657-6208; Email: kolbepublishing@hbgdiocese.org. Mr. Patrick Kielwein, Print Broker.

The Neumann Scholarship Foundation, 4800 Union Deposit Rd., 17111-3710. Tel: 717-657-4804; Fax: 717-657-3790; Email: frequinlan@hbgdiocese.org. Very Rev. Edward J. Quinlan, M.Div., M.A., M.S., Dir.

Pennsylvania Catholic Conference, 223 North St., P.O. Box 2835, 17105. Tel: 717-238-9613; Fax: 717-238-1473; Email: info@pacatholic.org; Web: www.pacatholic.org. Eric Failing, Exec.

Pennsylvania Catholic Health Association (1963) 223 North St., P.O. Box 2835, 17105. Tel: 717-238-9613 ; Fax: 717-238-1473; Email: srccs@pacatholic.org; Web: www.pacatholic.org/pcha. Sr. Clare Christi Schiefer, O.S.F., Pres.

Roman Catholic Diocese of Harrisburg Charitable Trust, 4800 Union Deposit Rd., 17111. Tel: 717-657-4804; Fax: 717-657-2453. Very Rev. David L. Danneker, Ph.D., Contact Person.

Roman Catholic Diocese of Harrisburg Real Estate Trust, 4800 Union Deposit Rd., 17111. Tel: 717-657-4804; Fax: 717-657-2453. Very Rev. David L. Danneker, Ph.D., Contact Person.

ELIZABETHTOWN. **Stewardship: A Mission of Faith*, 48 Industrial Rd., Elizabethtown, 17022. Tel: 717-367-0100; Fax: 717-367-0103; Email: info@stewardshipmission.org. Rob Longo, Pres.

FAIRFIELD. *Missionaries of the Sacred Hearts of Jesus & Mary House of Studies*, 350 Tract Rd., Fairfield, 17320. Tel: 717-457-0114; Fax: 717-457-0094; Email: msscc5@yahoo.com. Rev. Peter DiTomasso, M.SS.CC., Delegate, USA Supr. Gen.

LANCASTER. *CHI St. Joseph Children's Health*, CHI St. Joseph Children's Health, 1929 Lincoln Hwy. E., Ste. 150, Lancaster, 17602. Tel: 717-397-7625; Fax: 717-397-6057; Email: ruthfellabaum@catholichealth.net; Web: www.chistjosephchildrenshealth.org. Ruth Fellabaum, Sec. (An affiliate of Catholic Health Initiatives.).

MCSHERRYSTOWN. *St. Joseph Village Corporation*, Tel: 215-248-7200; Fax: 215-248-7277; Email: msjc@ssjphila.org; Web: www.ssjphila.org. Susan Wagaman, Supr. Sisters of St. Joseph.Residence for Senior Citizens

Village Location (1995) 50 Academy St., McSherrystown, 17344. Tel: 717-637-4441; Fax: 717-637-2441. Sr. Joanne Fehrenbach, S.S.J., Gen. Sec. Total in Residence 40; Total Staff 3.

RELIGIOUS INSTITUTES OF MEN REPRESENTED IN THE DIOCESE

For further details refer to the corresponding bracketed number in the Religious Institutes of Men or Women section.

[]—*Apostles of Jesus*—A.J.
[]—*Benedictine Monks of Saint Vincent Archabbey, Latrobe*—O.S.B.
[]—*Capuchin Franciscan Fathers* (Prov. of Saint Augustine)—O.F.M. Cap.
[]—*Carmelites of Mary Immaculate*—C.M.I.
[]—*Conventual Franciscans* (Prov. of Saint Anthony of Padua)—O.F.M. Conv.
[]—*Missionaries of St. Francis de Sales*—M.S.F.S.
[1120]—*Missionaries of the Sacred Hearts of Jesus and Mary*—M.SS.CC.
[]—*Order of Preachers* (Prov. of Nigeria)—O.P.
[]—*Order of Preachers* (Prov. of Saint Joseph)—O.P.
[]—*Priestly Fraternity of Saint Peter*—F.S.S.P.
[1070]—*Redemptorist Fathers* (Baltimore Prov.)—C.SS.R.
[1060]—*Society of the Precious Blood* (Cincinnati Prov.)—C.PP.S.
[0560]—*Third Order Regular of Saint Francis* (Prov. of the Most Sacred Heart of Jesus)—T.O.R.

RELIGIOUS INSTITUTES OF WOMEN REPRESENTED IN THE DIOCESE

[0100]—*Adorers of the Blood of Christ*—A.S.C.
[]—*Carmel of Jesus, Mary and Joseph* (Elysburg)—O.C.D.
[0890]—*Daughters of Our Lady of Mercy*—D.M.
[]—*Discalced Carmelite Nuns of Danville*—O.C.D.
[]—*Dominican Nuns of the Perpetual Rosary*—O.P.
[]—*Holy Union Sisters*—S.U.S.C.
[]—*Missionary Sisters of Saint Benedict*—O.S.B.
[0660]—*Sisters of Christian Charity*—S.C.C.
[3630]—*Servants of the Most Sacred Heart of Jesus.*
[2575]—*Sisters of Mercy of the Americas*—R.S.M.
[]—*Sisters of Saint Joseph of Chestnut Hill*—S.S.J.
[3780]—*Sisters of Saints Cyril and Methodius*—SS.C.M.
[1650]—*The Sisters of St. Francis of Philadelphia*—O.S.F.
[]—*Sisters, Servants of the Immaculate Heart of Mary* (Philadelphia)—I.H.M.
[]—*Sisters, Servants of the Immaculate Heart of Mary* (Scranton)—I.H.M.
[]—*Society of the Sisters of the Church*—S.S.C.

NECROLOGY

† Farace, Frederick A., (Retired), Died Jul. 17, 2018
† Mannion, Thomas Ignatius, (Retired), Died Nov. 25, 2018
† McAndrew, David T., (Retired), Died Mar. 7, 2018
† Scala, Thomas A., (Leave of Absence), Died Oct. 15, 2018

An asterisk (*) denotes an organization that has established tax-exempt status directly with the IRS and is not covered by the USCCB Group Ruling.

Archdiocese of Hartford

(Archidioecesis Hartfortiensis)

Most Reverend

HENRY J. MANSELL, D.D.

Archbishop Emeritus of Hartford; ordained December 19, 1962; appointed Titular Bishop of Marazane and Auxiliary of New York November 24, 1992; ordained January 6, 1993; appointed Bishop of Buffalo April 18, 1995; installed June 12, 1995; appointed Archbishop of Hartford October 20, 2003; installed December 18, 2003; retired December 16, 2013. *Office & Res.: St. Augustine Rectory, 55 Hopewell Rd., P.O. Box 175, South Glastonbury, CT 06073-0175.* Tel: 860-633-9505; Fax: 860-633-1341.

Most Reverend

DANIEL A. CRONIN, D.D., S.T.D.

Archbishop Emeritus of Hartford; ordained December 20, 1952; appointed Titular Bishop of Egnatia and Auxiliary Bishop of Boston June 10, 1968; ordained Bishop September 12, 1968; appointed Bishop of Fall River October 30, 1970; installed December 16, 1970; appointed Archbishop of Hartford December 10, 1991; installed January 28, 1992; retired October 20, 2003. *Office: 469 Bloomfield Ave., Bloomfield, CT 06002.* Tel: 860-242-5628.

Most Reverend

CHRISTIE ALBERT MACALUSO, D.D., V.G.

Auxiliary Bishop Emeritus of Hartford; ordained May 22, 1971; appointed Auxiliary Bishop of Hartford and Titular Bishop of Grass Valley March 18, 1997; ordained Bishop June 10, 1997; retired December 15, 2017. *Office: 134 Farmington Ave., Hartford, CT 06105-3784.* Tel: 860-541-6491; Fax: 860-541-6293.

Most Reverend

LEONARD P. BLAIR, S.T.D., D.D.

Archbishop of Hartford; ordained June 26, 1976; appointed Titular Bishop of Voncariana and Auxiliary Bishop of Detroit July 9, 1999; ordained August 24, 1999; appointed Bishop of Toledo October 7, 2003; installed December 4, 2003; appointed Archbishop of Hartford October 29, 2013; installed December 16, 2013. *Office: 134 Farmington Ave., Hartford, CT 06105-3784.* Tel: 860-541-6491; Fax: 860-541-6293. *Res.: 1109 Prospect Ave., West Hartford, CT 06105.*

Chancery Office: The Hartford Roman Catholic Diocesan Corporation, 134 Farmington Ave., Hartford, CT 06105-3784. Tel: 860-541-6491; Fax: 860-541-6309.

Web: www.archdioceseofhartford.org

Most Reverend

PETER A. ROSAZZA, D.D.

Auxiliary Bishop Emeritus of Hartford; ordained June 29, 1961; appointed Auxiliary Bishop of Hartford and Titular Bishop of Oppido Nuovo February 28, 1978; ordained Bishop June 24, 1978; retired June 30, 2010. *Office: 467 Bloomfield Ave., Bloomfield, CT 06002-2999.* Tel: 860-761-7430; Fax: 860-242-4886; Email: prosazza@aol.com.

Most Reverend

JUAN MIGUEL BETANCOURT TORRES, S.E.M.V., S.S.L., M.DIV.

Auxiliary Bishop of Hartford; ordained April 21, 2001; appointed Auxiliary Bishop of Hartford and Titular See of Curzola September 18, 2018; ordained Bishop October 18, 2018. *Office: 134 Farmington Ave., Hartford, CT 06105-3784.* Tel: 860-541-6491; Fax: 860-541-6293.

Square Miles 2,288.

Established November 28, 1843; created Archdiocese August 6, 1953.

Corporate Title: "The Hartford Roman Catholic Diocesan Corporation."

Comprises the Counties of Hartford, Litchfield and New Haven in the State of Connecticut.

For legal titles of parishes and archdiocesan institutions, consult the Chancery Office.

STATISTICAL OVERVIEW

Personnel	
Archbishops	1
Retired Archbishops	2
Auxiliary Bishops	1
Retired Bishops	2
Priests: Diocesan Active in Diocese	153
Priests: Diocesan Active Outside Diocese	8
Priests: Retired, Sick or Absent	107
Number of Diocesan Priests	268
Religious Priests in Diocese	79
Total Priests in Diocese	347
Extern Priests in Diocese	39
Ordinations:	
Diocesan Priests	2
Transitional Deacons	2
Permanent Deacons	8
Permanent Deacons in Diocese	214
Total Brothers	139
Total Sisters	440
Parishes	
Parishes	131
With Resident Pastor:	
Resident Diocesan Priests	120
Resident Religious Priests	11
New Parishes Created	3
Professional Ministry Personnel:	
Brothers	1
Sisters	31
Lay Ministers	115
Welfare	
Catholic Hospitals	2
Total Assisted	560,149
Health Care Centers	3
Total Assisted	7,489
Homes for the Aged	6
Total Assisted	1,976
Day Care Centers	8
Total Assisted	587
Special Centers for Social Services	16
Total Assisted	21,000
Residential Care of Disabled	10
Total Assisted	42
Other Institutions	3
Total Assisted	17,000
Educational	
Diocesan Students in Other Seminaries	12
Seminaries, Religious	1
Students Religious	68
Total Seminarians	80
Colleges and Universities	2
Total Students	7,776
High Schools, Diocesan and Parish	4
Total Students	1,911
High Schools, Private	5
Total Students	2,102
Elementary Schools, Diocesan and Parish	35
Total Students	7,027
Elementary Schools, Private	2
Total Students	236
Catechesis/Religious Education:	
High School Students	7,293
Elementary Students	23,081
Total Students under Catholic Instruction	49,506
Teachers in the Diocese:	
Brothers	2
Sisters	24
Lay Teachers	678
Vital Statistics	
Receptions into the Church:	
Infant Baptism Totals	3,970
Minor Baptism Totals	318
Adult Baptism Totals	152
Received into Full Communion	228
First Communions	4,784
Confirmations	4,878
Marriages:	
Catholic	875
Interfaith	110
Total Marriages	985
Deaths	6,582
Total Catholic Population	469,061
Total Population	1,938,000

Former Bishops—Rt. Revs. WILLIAM TYLER, D.D., ord. June 3, 1829; first Bishop; cons. March 17, 1844; died June 18, 1849; BERNARD O'REILLY, D.D., ord. Oct. 13, 1831; second Bishop; cons. Nov. 10, 1850; perished at sea, Jan., 1856.; FRANCIS P. MCFARLAND, D.D., ord. May 18, 1845; third Bishop; cons. March 14, 1858; died Oct. 12, 1874; THOMAS GALBERRY, D.D., ord. Dec. 20, 1856; fourth Bishop; cons. March 19, 1876; died Oct. 10, 1878; LAWRENCE S. MCMAHON, D.D., ord. March 24, 1860; fifth Bishop; cons. Aug. 10, 1879; died Aug. 21, 1893; MICHAEL TIERNEY, D.D., ord. May 26, 1866; sixth Bishop; cons. Feb. 22, 1894; died Oct. 5, 1908; Most Revs. JOHN J. NILAN, D.D., ord. Dec. 2, 1878; seventh Bishop; cons. April 28, 1910; died April 13, 1934; MAURICE F. MCAULIFFE, D.D., eighth Bishop; ord. July 29, 1900; appt. Auxiliary to the Bishop of Hartford, Dec. 17, 1925; cons. April 28, 1926; appt. Bishop of Hartford, April 25, 1934; installed May 29, 1934; died Dec. 15, 1944; HENRY J. O'BRIEN, D.D., ninth Bishop, first Archbishop; ord. July 8, 1923; appt. Titular Bishop of Sita and Auxiliary to Bishop of Hartford, March 19, 1940; cons. May 14, 1940; appt. Bishop of Hartford, April 7, 1945; appt. Archbishop of Hartford, Aug. 6, 1953; appt. at Pontifical Throne, April 29, 1955; resigned and appt. Titular Archbishop of Utina, Nov. 20, 1968; Given title "Former Archbishop of Hartford", Nov. 14, 1970; died July 23, 1976; JOHN F. WHEALON, D.D., S.T.L., S.S.L., tenth Bishop, second Archbishop; ord. May 26, 1945; appt. Titular Bishop of Andrapa and Auxiliary of Cleveland, June 2, 1961; consecrated July 6, 1961; appt. Bishop of Erie, Nov. 30, 1966; installed March 7, 1967; appt. Archbishop of Hartford, Dec. 28, 1968; installed March 19, 1969; died Aug. 2, 1991; DANIEL A. CRONIN, D.D., S.T.D., ord. Dec. 20, 1952; appt. Titular Bishop of Egnatia and Auxiliary Bishop of Boston June 10, 1968; ord. Bishop Sept. 12, 1968; appt. Bishop of Fall River Oct. 30, 1970; installed Dec. 16, 1970; appt. Archbishop of Hartford Dec. 10, 1991; installed Jan. 28, 1992; retired Oct. 20, 2003.; HENRY J. MANSELL, D.D., ord. Dec. 19, 1962; appt. Titular Bishop of Marazane and Auxiliary of New York Nov. 24, 1992; ord. Bishop Jan. 6, 1993; appt. Bishop of Buffalo April 18, 1995; installed June 12, 1995; appt. Archbishop of Hartford Oct. 20, 2003; installed Dec. 18, 2003; retired Dec. 16, 2013.

Vicar General—Very Rev. STEVEN C. BOGUSLAWSKI, O.P., V.G.

Episcopal Vicars—Very Revs. JOHN J. GEORGIA, Southern Vicariate; CHRISTOPHER M. FORD, J.C.L., Western Vicariate; JAMES A. SHANLEY, Northern Vicariate.

Chancery Office—134 Farmington Ave., Hartford, 06105-3784. Tel: 860-541-6491;
Fax: 860-541-6293 (Archbishop's Office);
Fax: 860-541-6309 (Chancery). MRS. BERNADETTE FOLEY, Exec. Asst. All applications for dispensations and correspondence on diocesan business should be sent to this address. Office Hours: Mon.-Fri. 8:30-4:30.

Moderator of the Curia and Secretariat for

Administration—Very Rev. STEVEN C. BOGUSLAWSKI, O.P., V.G.; MRS. KATHLEEN CHRIST, Sec.

Chancellor and Secretary to the Archbishop—Fax: 860-578-1444. Rev. RYAN M. LERNER; DIANA TIERINNI, Sec.; LAURIE R. DELUCA, Sec.

Archivist—BRIDGETTE A. WOODALL, M.Div., M.L.I.S.

Vicar for Clergy—Very Rev. ROBERT B. VARGO, J.C.L.; MRS. GAYLE BRICK, Sec.

Secretariat for Communications and Public Relations—Very Rev. JAMES A. SHANLEY, Exec. Dir.

Office of Communications—MARIA ZONE, Dir., Email: mzone@aohct.org.

Office of Radio and Television—Rev. JOHN P. GATZAK, Exec. Dir., 15 Peach Orchard Rd., Prospect, 06712-1052. Tel: 203-758-7367; Fax: 203-758-7371; Web: www.ortv.org; Email: ortv@ortv-hartford.org. Radio Stations: WJMJ-FM 88.9 Hartford, 93.1 Hamden, 107.1 New Haven. Tel.: 860-242-8800. Licensed by St. Thomas Seminary, Bloomfield (Hartford), ORTV, Inc., 15 Peach Orchard, CT 06712.

Office of WJMJ-FM—Rev. JOHN P. GATZAK, Gen. Mgr., Fax: 203-758-7371; Web: www.wjmj.org; Email: wjmj@ortv-hartford.org.

Magazine - Catholic Transcript—The Catholic Transcript Incorporated, 467 Bloomfield Ave., Bloomfield, 06002-2999. Email: info@catholictranscript.org. Most Rev. LEONARD P. BLAIR, Pres. & Publisher; Very Rev. JAMES A. SHANLEY, Editor, Exec. Dir. Communications & Public Rels. Staff Reporters: SHELLEY WOLF; MARY CHALUPSKY; LESLIE DIVENERE, Graphics Editor.

Finance Department—

Chief Financial Officer—MATTHEW A. BYRNE, CPA, M.B.A.; LINDA A. CARROLL, Administrative Asst.

Treasury and Budget Manager—THERESA MROCZKOWSKI.

Director of Accounting for Offices and Corporations—JOHN MAJKOWSKI, CPA.

Director of School Finances—MRS. KATE K. RUNDLES, CPA.

Accounting Manager—DANIEL A. DUNPHY.

Budgets and Financial Reporting Analyst—GENE A. MUNSON.

General Insurance Coordinator—BRENDA ROCK.

Accounts Payable Coordinator—ARLYN PAGE.

Accounts Receivable Coordinator—CHERYL A. ROAIX.

Corporate and Offices Staff Accountant—KETU SHAH.

Parish Financial Manager—DEAN W. WALFORD.

Parish Project Manager—PATRICK EGAN.

Parish Review Manager—VEENA GOWDA, CPA.

Assurance Review Coordinator—MARYLEE RICCIO.

Director of Property and Assets—PAUL CONNERY; JO-ANN REILLY, Asst.

Development Office—Development Officers: SUSAN FEOLA; ELIZABETH WADE; AMANDA MARTINELLI.

Director of Development—WILLIAM MCLEAN.

Database Administrator for Archbishop's Annual Appeal—ANA ALEMAN.

Hartford's Bishop's Foundation—Development Officers: LISA OWENS; SJUAN ANDERSON.

Human Resources—

Director—KAREN A. KEAN.

Employee and Priest Benefits, Pension, and Payroll—LESLI ANDERSON.

Metropolitan Tribunal—467 Bloomfield Ave., Bloomfield, 06002-2999. Tel: 860-541-6491.

Judicial Vicar (Officialis)—Very Rev. GEORGE S. MUKUKA, J.C.L., Ph.D.

Promoter of Justice—Rev. Msgr. JOHN J. MCCARTHY, J.C.D., J.D.

Defender of the Bond—Rev. JAMES F. KINNANE, J.C.L.

Judges—Very Rev. ROBERT B. VARGO, J.C.L.; MR. CHRISTOPHER BRUST, J.C.L.; Very Rev. JUAN-DIEGO BRUNETTA, O.P., J.C.D.

Assessor—Very Rev. STEVEN C. BOGUSLAWSKI, O.P., V.G.

Auditor—Rev. DAIRO E. DIAZ.

Moderator—CAROL M. HATTEN.

Secretaries—LINDA WARKS; SHANNON LENER.

Expert—ROBERT SWORDS, M.D.

College of Consultors—Very Revs. STEVEN C. BOGUSLAWSKI, O.P., V.G.; JAMES A. SHANLEY; CHRISTOPHER M. FORD, J.C.L.; JOHN J. GEORGIA; GEORGE S. MUKUKA, J.C.L., Ph.D.; Revs. FREDERICK M. ANIELLO; RYAN M. LERNER; MICHAEL G. WHYTE; DARIUSZ GOSCINIAK; JAMES M. SULLIVAN.

Consultors - Canon 1742—Rev. Msgrs. JAMES G. COLEMAN, (Senior), (Retired); JOHN P. CONTE, (Senior), (Retired); GERARD G. SCHMITZ, (Senior), (Retired); Rev. LAWRENCE R. BOCK, (Senior), (Retired); Very Rev. JOHN J. GEORGIA; Revs. GENE E. GIANELLI; JOHN S. GOLAS; THOMAS R. MITCHELL; LAWRENCE S. SYMOLON.

Deans—Northern Vicariate: Revs. MARCIN P. PLUCIENNIK, Deanery 2; ROBERT M. KWIATKOWSKI, Deanery 3; DARIUSZ GOSCINIAK, Deanery 4. Southern Vicariate: Revs. MICHAEL J. DOLAN, Deanery 6; ROBERT L. TURNER, Deanery 7. Western Vicariate: Revs. PHILIP R. SCHULZE, Deanery 1; JAMES M. SULLIVAN, Deanery 5.

Presbyteral Council—

Ex Officio Members—Most Rev. JUAN M. BETANCOURT, S.E.M.V., Auxiliary Bishop; Very Revs. STEVEN C. BOGUSLAWSKI, O.P., V.G.; CHRISTOPHER M. FORD, J.C.L., Vicar for Western; JAMES A. SHANLEY, Vicar for Northern; JOHN J. GEORGIA, Vicar for Southern; Rev. RYAN M. LERNER, Chancellor.

Peritus Member—Very Rev. GEORGE S. MUKUKA, J.C.L., Ph.D.

Elected Members—

Deanery 1—Revs. GERALD H. DZIEDZIC; PHILIP R. SCHULZE; CARLOS ZAPATA.

Deanery 2—Revs. JOHN P. MELNICK; JOHN S. GOLAS.

Deanery 3—Revs. THOMAS J. WALSH; LAWRENCE R. BOCK, (Retired).

Deanery 4—Rev. DARIUSZ GOSCINIAK.

Deanery 5—Revs. JOHN L. LAVORGNA; CHRISTOPHER M. TIANO.

Deanery 6—Revs. JEFFREY V. ROMANS; MICHAEL J. DOLAN; JORGE E. CASTRO.

Deanery 7—Revs. ROBERT L. TURNER; JOHN PAUL WALKER, O.P.

Appointed Members—Revs. JEFFREY A. GUBBIOTTI; ALEXANDER AVENDANO; Rev. Msgr. DOUGLAS P. CLANCY; Revs. ISRAEL RIVERA; ROBERT M. KWIATKOWSKI; MARCIN P. PLUCIENNIK; JAMES M. SULLIVAN.

Ecumenical Affairs, Commission for—70 Gulf St., Milford, 06460. Tel: 203-878-3571. Rev. AIDAN N. DONAHUE, Ecumenical Officer.

Interreligious Affairs—2819 Whitney Ave., Hamden, 06518-2598. Tel: 203-248-0141. Rev. MICHAEL J. DOLAN, Dir.

Secretariat for Pastoral Services—134 Farmington Ave., Hartford, 06105-3784. Tel: 860-541-6491. Deacon ERNEST SCRIVANI, T.O.C., Exec. Dir.; MRS. GAIL BELLUCCI, Asst. Dir.

Office of Pastoral Planning—Office of Family Life, Marriage and Family Apostolate, Engaged Couples Conference. Pastoral Center, 467 Bloomfield Ave. Bloomfield, CT 06002-2999. www.hartfordmarriage.com.

Archbishop's Annual Appeal—Mailing Address: P.O. Box 28, Hartford, 06141. Tel: 860-541-6491; Fax: 860-541-6309. Rev. GARY F. SIMEONE, Chm.; TINA POET, Appeal Coord.

Secretariat for Education Evangelization and Catechesis—Pastoral Center: 467 Bloomfield Ave., Bloomfield, 06002-2999. Tel: 860-242-5573; Fax: 860-243-9690; Web: www.catholicedaohct.org. Sr. MARY GRACE WALSH, A.S.C.J., Ph.D., Provost; MICHAEL S. GRIFFIN, Ph.D., Supt. Schools; MRS. MARIA T. MAYNARD, Deputy Supt.; MRS. VALERIE MARA, Asst. Supt., Academics; MRS. ANNE CLUBB, Dir. Enrollment Mgmt. & Mktg.; MRS. LAURA MCCAFFERY, Dir. School Support & Academic Svcs.; MRS. KATE K. RUNDLES, CPA, Dir. School Finance.

Catholic Biblical School—MRS. BARBARA JEAN DALY HORELL, Dir.

Catechetical Education—MRS. KELLY HENDERSCHEDT, Dir.

Catechesis for Hispanics—MRS. ANA MARIA ALSTRUM, Dir.

Adult Faith Formation—MISS NICOLE PERONE, Dir.

Youth and Young Adult Ministry—MR. MICHAEL WELLINGTON, Dir.

Catechetical Initiatives—MRS. LISA ORCHEN, Dir.

Catholic Scouting—MRS. JENNIFER MCCLINTOCK, Coord.

Office of Safe Environment—KATHLEEN NOWOSADKO, Dir.; GINA MARIE GARABEDIAN, Coord.; RACHEL ZARRILLI, Coord.; THERESA HATFIELD, Background Check Coord.; TRACEY MILLER, Administrative Asst.

Victim Assistance Coordinator—KATHLEEN NOWOSADKO, Tel: 860-541-6475.

Retirement Plan for Secular Priests of the Archdiocese of Hartford—The Secular Priests of the Archdiocese of Hartford Retirement Trust. 134 Farmington Ave., Hartford, 06105-3784. Tel: 860-541-6491. Ex Officio: Very Rev. ROBERT B. VARGO, J.C.L.; Rev. SHAWN T. DALY; MATTHEW A. BYRNE, CPA, M.B.A. Appointed: Rev. Msgrs. GERARD G. SCHMITZ, (Senior), (Retired); DOUGLAS P. CLANCY; Revs. JOHN S. GOLAS; JOHN P. MELNICK; MICHAEL A. RUMINSKI; MICHAEL A. SANTIAGO.

Pro-Life Activities—Sr. SUZANNE GROSS, F.S.E., Prog. Coord., 271 Finch Ave., Meriden, 06451-2715. Tel: 203-639-0833; Email: prolife@flcenter.org; Web: www.prolifeministry.org.

Mission Office, The(Catholic Mission Aid Society of Hartford, Inc., Missionary Childhood Assoc., Mission Cooperative Planning Office, Propagation of the Faith) 467 Bloomfield Ave., Bloomfield, 06002-2999. Tel: 860-761-7440; Fax: 860-243-0661. Very Rev. ROBERT B. VARGO, J.C.L., Dir.; MRS. GAYLE BRICK, Assoc. Dir.

Social Service—MAREK K. KULKUKA, L.M.F.T., CEO, Catholic Charities, 839-841 Asylum Ave., Hartford, 06105. Tel: 860-493-1841; Fax: 860-548-1930.

Vocations—Rev. MICHAEL T. CASEY, Dir., Vicar of Seminarians; Very Rev. STEVEN C. BOGUSLAWSKI, O.P., V.G., Dir.; ELLEN TANGUAY, Administrative Asst., Pastoral Center, 467 Bloomfield Ave., Bloomfield, 06002-2999. Tel: 860-761-7456; Fax: 860-243-0661; Email: vocations@aohct.org.

Office of the Permanent Diaconate—467 Bloomfield Ave., Bloomfield, 06002-2999. Tel: 860-761-7445; Fax: 860-243-0661. Deacon ROBERT M. PALLOTTI, Dir., Email: dcn.pallotti@aohct.org.

Office for Religious—Sr. MARIETTE MOAN, A.S.C.J., Vicar, 467 Bloomfield Ave., Bloomfield, 06002-2999. Tel: 860-242-5573, Ext. 7492; Email: mmoan@aohct.org.

Office of Vicar For Clergy—Tel: 860-541-6491; Fax: 860-541-6493. Very Rev. ROBERT B. VARGO, J.C.L., Email: fr.vargo@aohct.org; MRS. GAYLE BRICK, Sec.

Office of Continuing Formation for Priests—St. Catherine of Siena Church, 265 Stratton Brook Rd., P.O. Box 184, West Simsbury, 06092-0184. Tel: 860-658-1642. Rev. MICHAEL G. WHYTE.

Archbishop Daniel A. Cronin Residence—Residence for Senior Priests Rev. RYAN M. LERNER, Dir.

Minister for Priests—Annunciation Parish, 626 Willard Ave., Newington, 06111. Tel: 860-666-1591 . Rev. SHAWN T. DALY.

Censor Librorum—VACANT.

Archdiocesan Offices and Directors

Archdiocesan Dispute Resolution Office—Very Rev. STEVEN C. BOGUSLAWSKI, O.P., V.G., Vicar Gen., 134 Farmington Ave., Hartford, 06105-3784. Tel: 860-541-6491.

Office for Catholic Social Justice Ministry—467 Bloomfield Ave., Bloomfield, 06002-2999. Tel: 860-242-5573; Email: ocsjm@catholicsocialjustice.org; Web: www.catholicsocialjustice.org. LYNN M. CAMPBELL, Exec. Dir.

Catholic Cemeteries Association—JOHN PINONE, Exec. Dir., 700 Middletown Ave., P.O. Box 517, North Haven, 06473-0517. Tel: 203-239-2557; Fax: 203-239-5035.

Catholic Deaf Apostolate—Deacon DENNIS R. FERGUSON, Dir., Tel: 860-233-5131.

Connecticut Catholic Conference—Deacon DAVID REYNOLDS, Legislative Liaison; LORI STEWART, Administrative Asst., 134 Farmington Ave., Hartford, 06105-3784. Tel: 860-524-7882; Fax: 860-525-0750; Email: ccc@ctcatholic.org.

Office for People with Disabilities—VACANT.

Office for Faith and Culture—134 Farmington Ave., Hartford, 06105. Sr. CLARE MILLEA, A.S.C.J., Dir.

Cursillo Movement, Archdiocesan Spiritual Advisor for English and Portuguese Language—Rev. CARLOS ZAPATA, Tel: 860-482-4433; Email: fr.zapata@aohct.org. Spiritual Advisor for Spanish Language: Rev. DIEGO A. JIMENEZ, Tel: 203-756-4439; Email: fr.jimenez@aohct.org.

CLERGY, PARISHES, MISSIONS AND PAROCHIAL SCHOOLS

CITY OF HARTFORD

(HARTFORD COUNTY)

1—CATHEDRAL OF ST. JOSEPH (1872)

140 Farmington Ave., 06105-3708. Tel: 860-249-8431 ; Fax: 860-249-5910; Email: cathedralofstjoseph@aohct.org. Rev. Msgr. Thomas M. Ginty, Rector; Most Rev. Daniel A. Cronin, In Res.; Sr. Ann Marie Strileckis, C.N.D., Pastoral Assoc.; Deacon Norris Taylor

Legal Title: St. Joseph's Cathedral, Hartford, Connecticut

Catechesis Religious Program—Students 101.

2—ST. ANNE (1889) (French), Closed. For inquiries for

sacramental records contact St. Anne-Immaculate Conception, Hartford.

3—ST. ANNE-IMMACULATE CONCEPTION (2000) (French—Spanish), Closed. For Inquiries or Sacramental Records, please see St. Augustine Parish, Hartford.

4—SAINT AUGUSTINE PARISH CORPORATION (1902)
10 Campfield Ave., 1st Fl., 06114-1832.
Tel: 860-522-7128; Fax: 860-246-1753; Email: staugustine@aohct.org; Web: www.staugustinehtfd.org. Revs. Thomas J. Walsh; Jose R. Linares, Parochial Vicar; Deacon Carmelo Hernandez.
School—St. Brigid - St. Augustine: A Partnership School, (Grades PreK-8), 100 Mayflower St., West Hartford, 06110-1420. Tel: 860-561-2130; Fax: 860-561-0011; Email: jmirabito@stbstapartnership.eduk12.net; Web: www.saintbrigidschool.org. John Mirabito, Prin.; Rev. Salvatore D. Altavista, M.S., Librarian. Lay Teachers 17; Students 156.
Catechesis Religious Program—Tel: 860-249-3430; Email: payala159@gmail.com. Mayra Ayala, D.R.E. Students 56.

5—SS. CYRIL AND METHODIUS (1902) (Polish)
55 Charter Oak Ave., 06106-1902. Tel: 860-522-9157; Fax: 860-524-9433; Email: sscyrilandmethodius@aohct.org. Revs. Adam Hurbanczuk, (Poland); Andrzej Pogorzelski, In Res.
Legal Title: The Church of S.S. Cyril & Methodius of Hartford, Connecticut
Catechesis Religious Program—35 Groton St., 06106. Tel: 860-522-9157. Cheryl Pietrycha, D.R.E. Students 95.
Convent— (Closed) 45 Groton St., 06106-2798.

6—HOLY TRINITY MISSION (1900) (Lithuanian)
53 Capitol Ave., 06106-1798. Tel: 860-246-4162; Fax: 860-246-4162; Email: fr.jacobs@aohct.org. Rev. Charles E. Jacobs, Admin.
Catechesis Religious Program—Mary Beth Murphy, D.R.E. Students 4.

7—IMMACULATE CONCEPTION (1899) Closed. For inquiries for sacramental records contact St. Anne-Immaculate Conception, Hartford.

8—SAINT JUSTIN - SAINT MICHAEL PARISH CORPORATION (1924) (African American—West Indian)
230 Blue Hills Ave., 06112-1836. Tel: 860-246-6897; Fax: 860-246-6898; Email: stjustinstmichael@aohct.org. Rev. Kingsley C. Ihejirika; Deacon Roman Rosado.
Catechesis Religious Program—Tel: 860-522-6184. Students 11.

9—MARIA, REINA DE LA PAZ PARISH CORPORATION (1885)
480 New Britain Ave., 06106-3797.
Tel: 860-522-1129; Fax: 860-549-4261; Email: mariareinadelapaz@aohct.org. 494 New Britain Ave., 06106-3797. Rev. Henry Avendano; Sr. Andrea Gil, Pastoral Assoc.; Paul Ravita, Business Mgr.; Mr. Carlos Vega, Comm. & Planning Coord.
Catechesis Religious Program—Tel: 860-543-9368. Saundra Liuzzo, D.R.E.; Mrs. Rosa Vazquez-Bilbraut, D.R.E. Students 185.

10—ST. LUKE (1930) Closed. For inquiries or Sacramental Records, please contact Christ the King Parish., Wethersfield.

11—ST. MICHAEL (1900) (African American—Hispanic), Closed. For Inquiries or Sacramental Records, please see St. Justin - St. Michael Parish, Hartford.

12—OUR LADY OF FATIMA (1958) (Portuguese)
50 Kane St.- Fatima Sq., 06106. Tel: 860-236-1443; Fax: 860-232-4455; Email: ourladyoffatimahartford@aohct.org. Rev. Antonio Jorge Tchingui, (Angola)
Legal Title: The Our Lady of Fatima Roman Catholic Church Corporation of Hartford
Res.: 22 Madison Ave., 06106.
Catechesis Religious Program—Tel: 860-236-1443; Fax: 860-232-4455; Email: olfcatequese@yahoo.com. Students 268.

13—OUR LADY OF SORROWS (1895)
16 Greenwood St., 06106-2109. Tel: 860-233-4424; Fax: 860-236-0149; Email: ourladyofsorrows@aohct.org; Web: fr.aherne@aohct.org. Rev. James J. Aherne, M.S.; Deacons Victor Bilbraut; Valentin Perez; Rosa Marcano, Sec.
Legal Title: Our Lady of Sorrows Church Corporation of Parkville, Hartford
Church: 79 New Park Ave., 06106-2177.
Catechesis Religious Program—Students 141.

14—ST. PATRICK-ST. ANTHONY (1829)
285 Church St., 06103. Tel: 860-756-4034; Email: stpatrickstanthony@aohct.org; Web: www.spsact.org. Revs. Thomas M. Gallagher, O.F.M.; Cidouane C. Joseph, O.F.M., Parochial Vicar; John J. Leonard, O.F.M., Parochial Vicar; James P. Kelly, O.F.M., Parochial Vicar; A. Francis Soucy, Parochial Vicar; Pamela Johnson, Business Mgr.; Gabriel Lofvall, Dir. of Music Ministry; Gertrude White Campbell, Dir. of Volunteer Ministry
Legal Title: St. Patrick and St. Anthony Roman Catholic Church Corporation
FRANCISCAN CENTER FOR URBAN MINISTRY.
Catechesis Religious Program—Deborah Pelletier, C.R.E.; Faith VosWinkel, Confirmation Coord. Students 368.

15—ST. PETER PARISH CORPORATION (1859) (Irish), Closed. For Inquiries or Sacramental Records, please see Maria, Reina de la Paz Parish, Hartford.

16—SACRED HEART (1872) (Spanish), Closed. For Inquiries or Sacramental Records, please see Maria, Reina de la Paz Parish, Hartford.

OUTSIDE THE CITY OF HARTFORD

ANSONIA, NEW HAVEN CO.

1—ST. ANTHONY (1915) (Lithuanian), Closed. For inquiries for sacramental records, contact Holy Rosary, Ansonia.

2—THE CHURCH OF THE ASSUMPTION OF THE B.V. aka Assumption (1870)
35 N. Cliff St., Ansonia, 06401-1698.
Tel: 203-735-7857; Fax: 203-734-5521; Email: welcome@assumptionansonia.church; Web: assumptionansonia.church. 61 N. Cliff St., Ansonia, 06401. Rev. James M. Sullivan; Deacon Laurent Yergeau.
School—Assumption School, (Grades K-8), 51 N. Cliff St., Ansonia, 06401-1698. Tel: 203-734-0855; Fax: 203-734-5521; Email: kmolner@assumptionschool.net; Web: assumption.eduk12.net. Mrs. Kathleen Molner, Prin.; Monica Masiero, Librarian. Lay Teachers 12; Students 185.

3—HOLY ROSARY CHURCH CORPORATION OF ANSONIA, CONNECTICUT (1908) (Italian)
10 Fr. Salemi Dr., Ansonia, 06401-2396.
Tel: 203-735-7874; Fax: 203-735-7874; Email: holyrosary@aohct.org; Email: fr.sullivan.jm@aohct.org; Web: www.holyrosaryansonia.org. Rev. Jeffrey A. Gubbiotti; Deacons Richard W. Renker; Michael Lynch.
Catechesis Religious Program—Tel: 203-736-0242; Email: reled@holyrosaryansonia.org. Sr. Karen Skurat, Dir. Faith Formation & Pastoral Assoc. Students 98.

4—THE ST. JOSEPH CHURCH CORPORATION OF ANSONIA (1925) (Polish)
32 Jewett St., Ansonia, 06401-2499.
Tel: 203-734-0402; Email: stjosephansonia@aohct.org. Revs. Mitchell Wanat, C.M.; Waclaw Hlond, C.M., In Res., (Retired).
Catechesis Religious Program—Students 38.

AVON, HARTFORD CO., ST. ANN'S CHURCH OF AVON (1917) [CEM]
289 Arch Rd., Avon, 06001-4209. Tel: 860-673-9858; Fax: 860-675-4350; Email: stann@aohct.org. Revs. John W. McHugh; Joseph Cheah, O.S.M., In Res.; Deacons Jeffrey B. Sutherland; Timothy Healy.
Catechesis Religious Program—Tel: 860-673-2137. Valerie St. Jean, D.R.E.; Rosemary Neamtz, Dir. Confirmation, Youth Ministry. Students 639.

BANTAM, LITCHFIELD CO., OUR LADY OF GRACE (1970) [CEM] Merged with Saint Anthony of Padua, Litchfield and Saint Thomas of Villanova, Goshen to form Saint Louis de Montfort Parish, Litchfield.

BEACON FALLS, NEW HAVEN CO., ST. MICHAEL (1899)
25 Maple Ave., Beacon Falls, 06403-1145.
Tel: 203-729-2504; Email: stmichaelbeaconfalls@aohct.org; Web: saintmichaelsonline.org. Rev. Mathai Vellappallil, S.D.B.; Deacon Victor M. Lembo
Legal Title: The St. Michael's Church Corporation, Beacon Falls, Connecticut
Catechesis Religious Program—Students 271.

BETHLEHEM, LITCHFIELD CO., CHURCH OF THE NATIVITY (1921) Merged with Saint Teresa of Avila, Woodbury to form Prince of Peace Parish, Woodbury.

BLOOMFIELD, HARTFORD CO.

1—CHRIST THE KING (1936) Closed. For inquiries for sacramental records contact Sacred Heart, Bloomfield.

2—SACRED HEART (1878)
26 Wintonbury Ave., Bloomfield, 06002.
Tel: 860-242-4142; Email: sacredheartbloomfield@aohct.org; Web: sacredheartbloomfieldct.com. Rev. Msgr. Douglas P. Clancy; Deacons Anthony Nwankwo; Richard D. Santos.
Rectory—35 Cold Spring Dr., Bloomfield, 06002. Tel: 860-242-1942.
Catechesis Religious Program—Students 44.

BRANFORD, NEW HAVEN CO.

1—ST. ELIZABETH (1966) Closed. For Inquiries or Sacramental Records, please see Saint John Bosco Parish, Branford.

2—SAINT JOHN BOSCO PARISH CORPORATION (1868) [CEM 2]
731 Main St., Branford, 06405-3693.
Tel: 203-488-1607; Tel: 203-488-2998;
Fax: 203-488-9208; Email: stjohnbosco@aohct.org; Web: www.saintjohnboscobranford.org. Revs. Daniel G. Keefe; Glen Dmytryszyn, Parochial Vicar; Rev. Msgr. David M. Walker, Snr. Status, (Retired); Deacon Robert J. Macaluso
Legal Title: Saint John Bosco Parish Corporation
School—East Shoreline Catholic Academy, (Grades PreK-8), 62 Cedar St., Branford, 06405-3646.
Tel: 203-488-8386; Fax: 203-488-2347; Email: srannette@esca.eduk12.net; Web: www.eastshorelinecatholicacademy.org. Mrs. Cheryl Panzo, Prin.; Sr. Annette D'Antonio, M.P.F., Vice Prin. Separate legal entity; co-sponsored by St. John Bosco Parish (Branford), St. George Parish (Guilford), and St. Margaret Parish (Madison) Lay Teachers 17; Students 165.
Catechesis Religious Program—105 Leetes Island Rd., Branford, 06405. Tel: 203-488-2998; Web: www.saintjohnboscobranford.org/faithformation. Mrs. Jennifer Canell, D.R.E. Students 480.

3—ST. THERESE (1947) Merged with St. Mary & St. Elizabeth, Branford to form Saint John Bosco Parish, Branford.

BRISTOL, HARTFORD CO.

1—ST. ANN (1908) (French), Merged with St. Anthony, Bristol to form Saint Francis de Sales Parish, Bristol.

2—ST. ANTHONY (1920) (Italian), Merged with St. Ann, Bristol to Form Saint Francis de Sales Parish, Bristol.

3—SAINT FRANCIS DE SALES PARISH CORPORATION (2017)
180 Laurel St., Bristol, 06010-8078.
Tel: 860-582-8169; Fax: 860-585-7139; Email: stfrancisdesales@aohct.org; Web: www.stfrancisdesalesbristolct.org. Rev. Alphonso R. Fontana.

4—ST. GREGORY THE GREAT (1957)
235 Maltby St., Bristol, 06010-3892.
Tel: 860-589-2295; Fax: 860-589-6692; Email: stgregorythegreat@aohct.org. Revs. Gary F. Simeone; Hector G. Rangel, Parochial Vicar; Deacon Stanley J. Piotrowski Jr.
Legal Title: The Saint Gregory Roman Catholic Church Corporation of Bristol, Connecticut
Catechesis Religious Program—1043 Stafford Ave., Bristol, 06010. Tel: 860-589-4232; Email: stgregory.ccd@comcast.net. Claudia Larson, D.R.E. Students 563.

5—ST. JOSEPH (1864) [CEM]
33 Queen St., Bristol, 06010-5115. Tel: 860-583-1369 ; Fax: 860-589-5374; Email: stjosephbristol@aohct.org; Web: stjosephbristol.org. 149 Goodwin St., Bristol, 06010-5115. Rev. Ivan D. Ramirez; Deacon Neil B. Richter
Legal Title: St. Joseph Church, Bristol, Connecticut
School—St. Joseph School, (Grades PreK-8), 335 Center St., Bristol, 06010. Tel: 860-582-8696; Fax: 860-584-9907; Email: schooloffice@stjosephbristol.org; Email: frenette@stjosephbristol.org; Web: www.schoolstjosephbristol.org. Eric C. Frenette, Prin. Lay Teachers 11; Students 175.
Catechesis Religious Program—Tel: 860-582-2888; Web: ore_stjosephbristol@hotmail.com. Kimberlee Donahue, D.R.E. Students 383.

6—ST. STANISLAUS PARISH (1919) (Polish)
510 West St., Bristol, 06011-1860. Tel: 860-583-4242; Fax: 860-583-9464; Email: ststanislausbristol@aohct.org. Rev. Tomasz Sztuber; Deacon Richard J. Wisniewski
Legal Title: The St. Stanislaus Church Corporation of Bristol
Catechesis Religious Program—Tel: 860-584-5378; Email: asiagrabowski@sbcglobal.net. Joanna Grabowski, D.R.E. Students 295.

BROAD BROOK, HARTFORD CO.

1—ST. CATHERINE (1886) [CEM] Merged with St. Philip, East Windsor to form Saint Marianne Cope Parish, Broad Brook.

2—SAINT MARIANNE COPE PARISH CORPORATION (2017)
6 Windsorville Rd., Broad Brook, 06016.
Tel: 860-623-4636; Email: stmariannecope@aohct.org; Web: smceastwindsor.org. Rev. Stuart H. Pinette, Admin.

CANAAN, LITCHFIELD CO.

1—ST. JOSEPH (1920) [CEM] [JC] Merged with St. Mary, Lakeville and Immaculate Conception, Norfolk to form Saint Martin of Tours Parish, Canaan.

2—SAINT MARTIN OF TOURS PARISH CORPORATION
4 Main St., P.O. Box 897, Canaan, 06018-0897.
Tel: 860-824-7078; Fax: 860-824-4925; Email: stmartinoftours@aohct.org; Web: www.stmartinoftoursct.org. Rev. M. David Dawson Jr.; Deacon Stephen Beecher.
Catechesis Religious Program—Email: spbeecher1960@gmail.com; Email: nch1622@hotmail.com. Mrs. Pat Beecher, D.R.E.; Nancy Hodgkins, D.R.E. Students 39.

CHESHIRE, NEW HAVEN CO.

1—SAINT BRIDGET OF SWEDEN PARISH CORPORATION (1871) [CEM]
175 Main St., Cheshire, 06410-2446.
Tel: 203-272-3531; Fax: 203-271-3356; Email:

rectory@stbridgetcheshire.org; Web: www.stbridgetcheshire.org. Revs. Jeffrey V. Romans; Philip T. O'Neill, P.V., Parochial Vicar; Deacons Richard Wilber; Paul P. Iadarola.
School—St. Bridget's School, (Grades PreK-8), 171 Main St., Cheshire, 06410. Tel: 203-272-5860; Fax: 203-271-7031; Email: jfurlong@stbridgetschool.org; Web: www.stbridgetschool.org. Jennifer Furlong, Prin.; Angela Badore, Librarian. Lay Teachers 33; Students 354.
Catechesis Religious Program—Tel: 203-272-6504; Email: dyatcko@stbridgetschool.org. Mrs. Donna Yatcko, D.R.E. Students 984.
2—CHURCH OF THE EPIPHANY (1967) Closed. For Inquiries or Sacramental Records, please see Saint Bridget of Sweden Parish, Cheshire.
3—ST. THOMAS BECKET (1971) Merged with St. Bridget and Epiphany, Cheshire to form Saint Bridget of Sweden Parish, Cheshire.
COLLINSVILLE, HARTFORD CO., ST. PATRICK (1856) [CEM] [JC2]
50 Church St., Collinsville, 06019-3309.
Tel: 860-693-8727; Email: stpatrickcollinsville@aohct.org. Rev. Collins I. Anaeche; Deacon Kenneth Bangs
Legal Title: St. Patrick's Church Corporation Collinsville, Connecticut
Catechesis Religious Program—Jessica Mulligan, D.R.E. Students 154.
CORNWALL BRIDGE, LITCHFIELD CO., ST. BRIDGET (1883) [CEM] Merged with St. Bernard, Sharon, and Sacred Heart, Kent to form Saint Kateri Tekakwitha Parish, Kent.
DERBY, NEW HAVEN CO.
1—ST. JUDE (1961) Merged with St. Mary the Immaculate Conception, Derby to form Our Lady, Queen of the Apostles, Meriden.
2—ST. MARY THE IMMACULATE CONCEPTION (1851) Merged with Saint Jude to become Our Lady, Queen of the Apostles, Derby.
3—ST. MICHAEL THE ARCHANGEL (1905) [CEM] (Polish)
75 Derby Ave., Derby, 06418-2098. Tel: 203-734-0005 ; Email: stmichaelthearchangel@aohct.org. Revs. A. Rafal Kopystynski, C.M.; Jan Szylar, C.M., Parochial Vicar
Legal Title: The St. Michael's Church of Derby
School—St. Mary-St. Michael, (Grades PreK-8), 14 Seymour Ave., Derby, 06418-1491. Tel: 203-735-6471 ; Fax: 203-732-9099; Email: gtorres@stmarystmichael.org; Web: www.stmarystmichaelct.eduk12.net. Grace Torres, Prin. Clergy 2; Lay Teachers 10; Students 140.
Catechesis Religious Program—Email: stmichaelsderby@sbcglobal.net. Students 74.
4—OUR LADY, QUEEN OF THE APOSTLES PARISH CORPORATION
212 Elizabeth St., Derby, 06418-1615.
Tel: 203-735-3341; Email: fr.tiano@aohct.org; Email: ourladyqueenoftheapostles@aohct.org; Web: queenoftheapostlesderby.org. Revs. Christopher M. Tiano; Vincent J. Curran, Parochial Vicar; Deacons Anthony Caraluzzi; Robert C. Johnson
Legal Title: Our Lady, Queen of the Apostles Corporation
School—St. Mary-St. Michael, (Grades PreK-8), 14 Seymour Ave., Derby, 06418. Tel: 203-735-6471; Email: gtorres@stmarystmichael.org. Grace Torres, Prin.
Catechesis Religious Program—Email: stmarycre@sbcglobal.net. Kathleen Brouillette, D.R.E. Students 150.
EAST BERLIN, HARTFORD CO., SACRED HEART (1896) Merged with Saint Paul, Kensington.
EAST HARTFORD, HARTFORD CO.
1—BLESSED SACRAMENT (1948) Closed. For Inquiries or Sacramental Records. please see Saint Edmund of Campion Parish, East Hartford.
2—ST. CHRISTOPHER (1965) Merged with Our Lady of Peace, East Hartford to form Saint Edmund Campion Parish, East Hartford.
3—SAINT EDMUND CAMPION PARISH CORPORATION
538 Brewer St., East Hartford, 06118-2305.
Tel: 860-568-5240; Fax: 860-568-0673; Web: stchriseh.org. Revs. John P. Gwozdz; Joseph Moonnanappallil, (India); Deacons Philip Gosselin; William Bartlett Jr.
School—St. Christopher School, (Grades PreK-8), 570 Brewer St., East Hartford, 06118-2305.
Tel: 860-568-4100; Fax: 860-568-1070; Email: welchk@saintchristopherschool.org; Web: saintchristopherschool.org. Kathleen Welch, Prin. Lay Teachers 18; Students 159.
Catechesis Religious Program—580 Brewer St., East Hartford, 06118-2305. Tel: 860-895-8692;
Fax: 860-568-0242. Mrs. Maria Sousa, D.R.E., Grades K-8; Kristina Gillespie, Confirmation & Youth Min., Grades 9-12. Students 116.
4—ST. ISAAC JOGUES (1964) Merged with St. Mary and St. Rose, East Hartford to form North American Martyrs Parish.
5—SAINT ISAAC JOGUES GHANAIAN CATHOLIC PARISH CORPORATION
1 Community St., East Hartford, 06108.
Tel: 860-290-1880; Email: fr.baffuor-awuah@aohct.org. Rev. Paul Baffuor-Awuah.
6—ST. MARY (1873) Merged with St. Rose and St. Isaac Jogues to form North American Martyrs Parish, East Hartford.
7—NORTH AMERICAN MARTYRS PARISH CORPORATION (2017)
15 Maplewood Ave., East Hartford, 06108.
Tel: 860-289-7916; Fax: 860-289-3224; Email: northamericanmartyrs@aohct.org; Web: www.namct.org. Rev. Timothy E. Ryan, Admin.
St. Mary's—1588 Main St., East Hartford, 06108.
St. Rose, 33 Church St., East Hartford, 06108.
St. Isaac Jogues, 1 Community St., East Hartford, 06108.
8—OUR LADY OF PEACE (1971) Merged with Saint Christopher, East Hartford to form Saint Edmund Campion Parish, East Hartford.
9—ST. ROSE (1920) Merged with St. Mary and St. Isaac Jogues to form North American Martyrs Parish, East Hartford.
EAST HAVEN, NEW HAVEN CO.
1—ST. CLARE (1947) Closed. For Inquiries or Sacramental Records, please see St. Pio of Pietrelcina Parish, East Haven.
2—SAINT PIO OF PIETRELCINA CHURCH CORPORATION (1947)
355 Foxon Rd., East Haven, 06513.
Tel: 203-469-0764; Fax: 203-469-3645; Email: stpioofpietrelcina@aohct.org. Rev. Jeremiah N. Murasso, Ph.D.
3—ST. VINCENT DE PAUL (1915) Merged with Our Lady of Pompeii, East Haven to form Saint Pio of Pietrelcina Parish, East Haven.
EAST WINDSOR, HARTFORD CO., ST. PHILIP THE APOSTLE (1959) [CEM] Merged with St. Catherine, Broad Brook to form Saint Marianne Cope Parish, Broad Brook.
ENFIELD, HARTFORD CO.
1—ST. ADALBERT'S (1915) [CEM] (Polish), Merged with St. Patrick, Enfield, to form Saint Raymond of Penafort, Enfield.
2—ST. BERNARD (1870) Merged with Holy Family, Enfield to form Saint Jeanne Jugan Parish, Enfield.
3—HOLY FAMILY (1965) Merged with Saint Bernard, Enfield to form Saint Jeanne Jugan, Enfield.
4—SAINT JEANNE JUGAN PARISH CORPORATION
23 Simon Rd., Enfield, 06082. Tel: 860-741-2101; Email: stjeannejugan@aohct.org; Web: sjjenfield.org. Rev. John S. Golas.
Schools—St. Bernard School—(Grades K-8), 232 Pearl St., Enfield, 06082-4399. Tel: 860-745-5275; Email: principal@sbsenfield.org; Fax: 860-741-7358; Web: www.sbsenfield.org. Charlene Mongillo, Prin. Lay Teachers 18; Sisters 1; Students 137.
Little Angels Catholic Preschool, 424 Hazard Ave., Enfield, 06082. Tel: 860-745-6135; Email: stbernardccd@yahoo.com. Charlene Mongillo, Prin. Lay Teachers 3; Students 66.
5—SAINT MARTHA PARISH CORPORATION (1961)
214 Brainard Rd., Enfield, 06082-2609.
Tel: 860-746-5616; Fax: 860-741-6731; Email: stmartha@aohct.org. Rev. Robert Villa; Deacons Robert E. Bernd; Michael Torres.
School—St. Martha School, (Grades K-8),
Tel: 860-745-3833; Fax: 860-745-3329; Email: saintmartha.school@snet.net; Web: stmarthaschool-ct.org. Dr. Ann Soutaworta, Prin. Lay Teachers 9; Students 140.
Catechesis Religious Program—Tel: 860-749-8457. Brian LeMay, D.R.E.; Lori Kedzior, Confirmation Dir. Students 89.
6—SAINT RAYMOND OF PENAFORT PARISH CORPORATION (1866) [CEM]
64 Pearl St., Enfield, 06082-3594. Tel: 860-745-2411; Fax: 860-253-9483; Email: straymondofpenafort@aohct.org. Rev. John G. Weaver, Admin.; Deacon Paul Robert.
Catechesis Religious Program—Tel: 860-741-0572. Carolyn Dague, D.R.E. Students 200.
FARMINGTON, HARTFORD CO., ST. PATRICK (1871)
110 Main St., P.O. Box 523, Farmington, 06032-2236. Tel: 860-677-2639; Fax: 860-677-2672; Email: stpatrickfarmington@aohct.org. Rev. Thomas J. Barry, J.C.L.; Deacons William A. Farrell; Robert J. Barry
Legal Title: St. Patricks Church Society of Farmington, Connecticut
Catechesis Religious Program—Tel: 860-676-0253; Email: religioused@stpatsfarm.com. Eileen Dignazio, D.R.E. Students 365.
FORESTVILLE, HARTFORD CO., ST. MATTHEW (1891)
120 Church Ave., Box 9216, Forestville, 06011-9216.
Tel: 860-583-1833; Fax: 860-582-6152; Email: stmatthew@aohct.org. Rev. John J. Dietrich; Deacons Brian Armstrong; James P. McCluskey
Legal Title: The St. Matthew's Church Corporation of Forestville, Connecticut
School—St. Matthew School, (Grades PreK-8), 33 Welch Dr., Forestville, 06010-6790.
Tel: 860-583-5214; Fax: 860-314-1541; Web: stmatthewschool.com. Helen L. Treacy, Prin.; Mr. Brett Bisson, Librarian. Lay Teachers 17; Students 268.
Parish Center—119 Church Ave., Forestville, 06010.
GLASTONBURY, HARTFORD CO.
1—SAINT DUNSTAN PARISH (1971)
Mailing Address: 1345 Manchester Rd., Glastonbury, 06033. Tel: 860-633-3317; Fax: 860-659-8611; Email: stdunstan@aohct.org; Web: www.stdunstanchurch.org. Rev. Msgr. John J. McCarthy, J.C.D., J.D.; Deacon Henry J. Szumowski
Legal Title: The Church of St. Dunstan of Glastonbury Corporation
Res.: 1150 Neipisc Rd., Glastonbury, 06033.
Tel: 860-633-3317; Fax: 860-659-8611; Email: stdunstanchurch@aol.com.
Catechesis Religious Program—Tel: 860-633-6876. Patricia Kearney, C.R.E.; Sharon Champagne, C.R.E. (K-8); Gina Raymond, C.R.E. (9-10) & Youth Min. Students 688.
2—ST. PAUL (1954)
2577 Main St., Glastonbury, 06033-2023.
Tel: 860-633-9419; Fax: 860-633-0040; Email: fr.suslenko@aohct.org; Email: ssisidoreandmaria@aohct.org. Rev. Mark S. Suslenko; Deacons Stephen L. Weaver; William Dziatko.
Catechesis Religious Program—Tel: 860-659-3029; Email: jon@isidoreandmaria.org. Dr. Jon Sozek, D.R.E. Students 600.
GOSHEN, LITCHFIELD CO., ST. THOMAS OF VILLANOVA (1877) [CEM] Merged with St. Anthony of Padua, Litchfield and Our Lady of Grace, Bantam to form Saint Louis de Montfort Parish, Litchfield.
GRANBY, HARTFORD CO., SAINT THERESE PARISH CORPORATION (1958)
120 W. Granby Rd., Granby, 06035-2907.
Tel: 860-653-3371; Fax: 860-653-5780; Email: sttherese@aohct.org; Web: www.StThereseGranby.com. Rev. Thomas E. Ptaszynski.
Catechesis Religious Program—Maura L. Fleming, D.R.E. Students 340.
GUILFORD, NEW HAVEN CO., ST. GEORGE (1870) [CEM]
33 Whitfield St., Guilford, 06437-2698.
Tel: 203-453-2788; Fax: 203-453-1707; Email: stgeorge@aohct.org; Web: www.stgeorgeguilford.org. Revs. Stephen M. Sledesky; Ricardo Emilio Borja, Parochial Vicar
Legal Title: St. George's Church
Catechesis Religious Program—Tel: 203-453-3496. Students 1,059.
HAMDEN, NEW HAVEN CO.
1—ST. ANN (1919) (Italian), Closed. For inquiries for Sacramental Records, please see Christ the Bread of Life Parish, Hamden.
2—ASCENSION (1964) Merged with Blessed Sacrament, Hamden, to form Christ the Bread of Life Parish, Hamden.
3—CHRIST THE BREAD OF LIFE PARISH CORPORATION (1939)
322 Circular Ave., Hamden, 06514.
Tel: 203-288-1652; Fax: 203-248-0873; Email: christthebreadoflife@aohct.org; Web: www.christthebreadoflife.org. Rev. Cornelius Kelechi Anyanwu.
Res.: 321 Circular Ave., Hamden, 06514-3428.
Catechesis Religious Program—306 Circular Ave., Hamden, 06514. Tel: 203-288-5228. Dominic Lonardo, D.R.E. Students 30.
4—ST. JOAN OF ARC (1971) Closed. For inquiries or Sacramental Records, please see Our Lady Mt. Carmel Parish, Hamden.
5—DIVINE MERCY PARISH CORPORATION
1620 Whitney Ave., Hamden, 06517-2024.
Tel: 203-248-5513; Tel: 203-288-6439;
Fax: 203-248-2684; Email: divinemercy@aohct.org. Revs. Joseph V. DiSciacca; Thomas Griffin-Smolenski, S.J., Parochial Vicar; Patrick M. Kane, In Res.; Deacon Joseph R. Ryzewski
Legal Title: Divine Mercy Parish Corporation
School—St. Rita School, (Grades PreK-8), 1601 Whitney Ave., Hamden, 06517. Tel: 203-248-3114; Fax: 203-248-1016; Email: ptiezzi.stritaschool@gmail.com; Web: stritaschool.org. Mrs. Patricia Tiezzi, Prin. Lay Teachers 39; Priests 1; Students 385; Apostles of the Sacred Heart 1.
Catechesis Religious Program—400 Ridge Rd., Hamden, 06517. Tel: 203-281-7522. Mrs. Megan Zinn, C.R.E.; Eleanor Shaw, D.R.E. Students 308.
6—OUR LADY OF MT. CARMEL PARISH CORPORATION (1869) [CEM]
2819 Whitney Ave., Hamden, 06518-2598.
Tel: 203-248-0141; Email: ourladyofmtcarmelhamden@aohct.org; Web: olomc.org. Revs. Michael J. Dolan; Jorge E. Castro, Parochial Vicar; Matthew G. Gworek, P.V., Parochial Vicar; Deacons Stephen Yatcko; John C. O'Donovan; Anthony P. Solli; Sr. Ann O'Neill, R.S.M., Pastoral Assoc.
Catechesis Religious Program—54 South New Rd.,

Hamden, 06518. Email: olomcreled1@gmail.com. Students 500.

7—St. Rita (1928) Merged with St. Stephen, Hamden, to form Divine Mercy Parish, Hamden.

8—St. Stephen (1953) Merged with St. Rita, Hamden, to form Divine Mercy Parish, Hamden.
School—St. Stephen School, (Grades PreK-8), Merged with St. Rita School, Hamden.

Harwinton, Litchfield Co., Immaculate Heart of Mary (1956) Merged with Immaculate Conception, New Hartford to form Our Lady of Hope, New Hartford.

Kensington, Hartford Co., Saint Paul Parish Corporation (1878)
485 Alling St., Kensington, 06037-2170.
Tel: 860-828-0331; Email: stpaul@aohct.org; Web: stpaulkensington.org. 467 Alling St., Kensington, 06037. Revs. Joseph Benicewicz; Raymond Borkowski, O.F.M. Conv., Parochial Vicar; Michael Englert, O.F.M.Conv., Parochial Vicar; Peter Tymko, Parochial Vicar; Deacon Carmen Guzzardi; Rev. John Imbimbo, Youth Min.
Res.: 479 Alling St., Kensington, 06037-2170.
School—(Grades PreK-8), 461 Alling St., Kensington, 06037-2170. Tel: 860-828-4343; Fax: 860-828-1226; Email: ourschool@stpaulkensington.org; Web: ourschool.stpaulkensington.org. Fayne Molloy, Prin.; Annalee McGuire, Librarian. Lay Teachers 24; Students 259.
Catechesis Religious Program—Tel: 860-828-1934; Email: r.veronesi@stpaulkensington.org. Robin Veronesi, D.R.E. Students 796.

Kent, Litchfield Co.

1—Saint Kateri Tekakwitha Parish Corporation
90 Cobble Rd., Kent, 06757-0186. Tel: 860-927-3003; Email: stkateritekakwitha@aohct.org; Web: saintkaterict.org. P.O. Box 186, Kent, 06757. Rev. Msgr. Vittorio Guerrera.

2—Sacred Heart (1970) [CEM] Merged with Saint Bernard, Sharon & Saint Bridget, Cornwall Bridge to form Saint Kateri Tekakwitha, Kent.

Lakeville, Litchfield Co., St. Mary (1874) [CEM] Merged with St. Joseph, Canaan and Immaculate Conception, Norfolk to form Saint Martin of Tours Parish, Canaan.

Litchfield, Litchfield Co.

1—St. Anthony of Padua (1882) [CEM] Merged with St. Thomas of Villanova, Goshen and Our Lady of Grace, Bantam, to form Saint Louis de Montfort Parish, Litchfield.

2—Saint Louis de Montfort Parish Corporation
49 South St., Litchfield, 06759-0097.
Tel: 860-567-5209; Email: stlouisdemontfort@aohct.org. P.O. Box 97, Litchfield, 06759-0097. Rev. Robert F. Tucker.

Madison, New Haven Co., St. Margaret (1937)
24 Academy St., Madison, 06443-0814.
Tel: 203-245-7301; Email: stmargaret@aohct.org; Web: www.stmargaretchurch.com. Rev. Daniel J. McLearen; Deacon Adam J. Michaele
Legal Title: The St. Margaret's Church Corporation of Madison, Connecticut
School—Our Lady of Mercy, (Grades PreK-8), 149 Neck Rd., Madison, 06443-2728. Tel: 203-245-4393; Fax: 203-245-3498; Email: cpanzo@olmschool.com; Web: olmschool.com. Mrs. Cheryl Panzo, Prin. Faculty 26; Lay Teachers 14; Students 167.
Catechesis Religious Program—Email: lauri.sturwold@stmargaretchurch.com. Lauri Sturwold, D.R.E., Tel: 203-245-7301, Ext. 107. Students 650.

Manchester, Hartford Co.

1—Assumption (1955) Closed. For Inquiries or Sacramental Records, please see St. James Parish, Manchester.

2—St. Bartholomew (1958) Merged with St. Bridget, Manchester to form Saint Teresa of Calcutta Parish, Manchester.

3—St. Bridget (1870) Merged with St. Bartholomew, Manchester, to form Saint Teresa of Calcutta Parish, Manchester.

4—Saint James Parish Corporation (1874)
896 Main St., Manchester, 06040-6079.
Tel: 860-643-4129; Email: stjames@aohct.org. Revs. Kevin P. Cavanaugh; Janusz Kukulka, M.A., S.T.L., Parochial Vicar.
School—St. James School, (Grades PreK-8), 73 Park St., Manchester, 06040. Tel: 860-643-5088; Fax: 860-649-6462; Email: bzorger@saintjamesschool.net. Mrs. Patricia Kanute, Prin.; Linda Carpenter, Librarian. Lay Teachers 29; Students 404.
Catechesis Religious Program—Macy Jordan, C.R.E. Students 161.

5—Saint Teresa of Calcutta Parish
80 Main St., Manchester, 06042.
Tel: 860-643-2403, Ext. 100; Email: stteresaofcalcutta@aohct.org; Web: manchestercatholic.org. Revs. Marcin P. Pluciennik; Sebastian K. Kos, Parochial Vicar; Nancy Lastrina, Business Mgr.; Steve DiMotta, Youth Min.; Mr. John Ryan, Pastoral Assoc.; Mrs. Mary Fitzpatrick, Contact Person.
School—St. Bridget School, (Grades PreK-8), 74 Main St., Manchester, 06042-3140.
Tel: 860-649-7731; Fax: 860-646-6936; Email: principal@saintbridget-school.com; Web: saintbridget-school.com. Mary Alice Nadaskay, Prin. Lay Teachers 16; Students 185.

Marlborough, Hartford Co., St. John Fisher (1972)
30 Jones Hollow Rd., Marlborough, 06447.
Tel: 860-295-0001; Email: stjohnfisher@aohct.org. Rev. Thomas J. Sas; Deacon John W. McKaig, Email: dcn.john@yahoo.com
Legal Title: The Church of St. John Fisher of Marlborough Corporation
Res.: 24 Cheney Rd., Marlborough, 06447-1327.
Catechesis Religious Program—Email: tbrysgel@stjfchurch.org. Theresa Brysgel, D.R.E. Students 271.

Meriden, New Haven Co.

1—The Corporation of the Church of the Holy Angels (1887) Merged with Our Lady of Mount Carmel and St. Joseph, Meriden to form Our Lady Queen of Angels, Meriden.

2—Saint Faustina Parish Corporation (2017) (Polish)
82 Akron St., Meriden, 06450. Tel: 203-235-6341; Email: stfaustina@aohct.org. Rev. Edward Ziemnicki.

3—St. Joseph (1900) Merged with Our Lady of Mount Carmel and Holy Angels, Meriden to form Our Lady Queen of Angels, Meriden.

4—St. Laurent (1880) (French), Closed. For Inquiries or Sacramental Records, please see Our Lady Queen of Angels Parish, Meriden.

5—St. Mary (1890) [CEM] (German), Closed. For Inquiries or Sacramental Records, please see Our Lady Queen of Angels Parish, Meriden.

6—Our Lady Queen of Angels Parish Corporation (1894) (Italian)
Parish: 109 Goodwill Ave., Meriden, 06451-3000.
Tel: 203-235-6381; Fax: 203-238-3629; Email: fr.sievel@aohct.org; Email: ourladyqueenofangels@aohct.org. Revs. Thomas A. Sievel; Lee W. Hellwig, Parochial Vicar; Deacons George W. Frederick; Jose Robles; Donald H. Smith Jr.
Res.: 17 North St., Meriden, 06451.
School—Our Lady of Mount Carmel School, (Grades PreK-8), 115 Lewis Ave., Meriden, 06451.
Tel: 203-235-2959; Email: christa.chodkowski@olmcmeridan.com. Christa Chodkowski, Prin. Lay Teachers 18; Students 250.
Catechesis Religious Program—Theresa Gannon, D.R.E. Students 109.

7—St. Rose of Lima (1848)
35 Center St., Meriden, 06450-5685.
Tel: 203-235-1644; Email: stroseoflima@aohct.org. Revs. James C. Manship; James W. Richardson, S.C., Parochial Vicar
Legal Title: Trustees of St. Roses Ch. Meriden, Connecticut
Catechesis Religious Program—Tel: 203-235-6887. Students 232.

8—St. Stanislaus (1891) [CEM] (Polish), Merged with SS. Peter and Paul, Wallingford to form Saint Faustina Parish, Meriden.

Middlebury, New Haven Co., St. John of the Cross Parish (1904)
1263 West St., Middlebury, 06762. Tel: 203-758-2659; Email: stjohnofthecross@aohct.org; Web: www.stjohnofthecrosschurch.org. P.O. Box 361, Middlebury, 06762-0361. Rev. Lawrence S. Symolon; Deacons Michael J. Walsh; Stephen L. Savarese
Legal Title: Roman Catholic Church of St. John of The Cross
Res.: 1321 Whittemore Rd., Middlebury, 06762-0361.
Tel: 203-758-2659; Fax: 203-577-6464; Email: st.john@snet.net.
Catechesis Religious Program—Mrs. Annette Williams, D.R.E.; Mrs. Jackie Beauvais, Coord. Youth Ministry. Students 254.

Milford, New Haven Co.

1—St. Agnes (1906) Merged with St. Mary, Milford to form Precious Blood Parish, Milford.

2—St. Ann (1924) Merged with St. Gabriel to form Saint Raphael Parish, Milford.

3—Christ the Redeemer (1966)
325 Oronoque Rd., Milford, 06461-1798.
Tel: 203-878-7431, Ext. 0; Fax: 203-878-0677; Email: fr.maliekal@aohct.org; Web: ctrmilford.net. Rev. Cyriac Maliekal; Deacon William J. Sayles
Legal Title: Christ the Redeemer Church Corporation of Milford
Catechesis Religious Program—Students 138.

4—St. Gabriel (Wildemere Beach) (1946) Merged with St. Ann, Milford to form Saint Raphael Parish, Milford.

5—St. Mary (1874) [CEM] Merged with St. Agnes, Milford to form Precious Blood Parish, Milford.

6—Precious Blood Parish Corporation (2017)
70 Gulf St., Milford, 06460. Tel: 203-878-3571. Revs. Aidan Donahue, S.T.M., S.T.L.; Sam John, Parochial Vicar; Deny Varghese, Parochial Vicar; Deacon Harold J. Hoffman Jr., Pastoral Assoc.
Legal Title: Precious Blood Parish Corporation
School—St. Mary School, (Grades PreK-8), 72 Gulf St., Milford, 06460. Tel: 203-878-6539.

7—Saint Raphael Parish Corporation (2017)
501 Naugatuck Ave., Milford, 06460.
Tel: 203-874-0634; Email: straphael@aohct.org; Web: saintraphaelmilford.org. Rev. John F. Brinsmade.

Naugatuck, New Haven Co.

1—Saint Francis of Assisi Parish Corporation (1866)
318 Church St., Naugatuck, 06770.
Tel: 203-729-4543; Email: stfrancisofassisinaugatuck@aohct.org; Web: stfrancisnaugatuck.org. Rev. John Kuzhikottayil, S.D.B.; Deacon Thomas J. Clifford.
Catechesis Religious Program—Mr. Leonard Tiscia, D.R.E.; Mrs. Christine Warren, D.R.E. Students 238.

2—St. Vincent Ferrer (1975)
1006 New Haven Rd., Naugatuck, 06770-4731.
Tel: 203-723-7497; Email: stvincentferrer@aohct.org. Rev. George Varkey, S.B.D.
Legal Title: The Church of St. Vincent Ferrer of Naugatuck Corporation
Catechesis Religious Program—Tel: 203-723-0782. Jessica Mulligan, D.R.E. Students 138.

New Britain, Hartford Co.

1—All Saints (1918) (Slovak), Closed. For inquiries for sacramental records, contact St. Ann, New Britain.

2—St. Andrew (1895) (Lithuanian), Merged with St. John the Evangelist Parish, New Britain to form Holy Apostles, New Britain.

3—St. Ann (1938) (Italian), Merged with St. Mary, New Britain to form Saint Joachim Parish, New Britain.

4—Divine Providence Parish Corporation aka St. Joseph Church St. Peter Church
195 S. Main St., New Britain, 06051.
Tel: 860-229-4851; Email: divineprovidence@aohct.org. Rev. Joseph F. Keough.

5—St. Francis of Assisi (1941)
1755 Stanley St., New Britain, 06053-2099.
Tel: 860-225-6449; Email: stfrancisofassisinewbritain@aohct.org; Web: stfranciscatholic.org. Rev. Michael T. Casey; Deacon Wayne F. Griffin
Legal Title: St. Francis of Assisi Church Corporation of New Britain.

6—Holy Apostles Parish Corporation (2017)
655 East St., New Britain, 06050-0515.
Tel: 860-223-3667; Email: fr.smith@aohct.org. Rev. Ronald T. Smith.

7—Holy Cross (1927) (Polish)
31 Biruta St., New Britain, 06053-2899.
Tel: 860-229-2011; Email: holycross@aohct.org. Revs. Dariusz Gosciniak; Daniel T. Wojtun, Parochial Vicar; Deacon Michael Rubitz
Legal Title: The Church of the Holy Cross, New Britain
Church: 220 Farmington Ave., New Britain, 06053.
Catechesis Religious Program—Pope John Paul II School of Religion, Tel: 860-839-2040. Eva Fadgyas, D.R.E. Students 236.

8—Saint Katharine Drexel Parish Corporation
1010 Slater Rd., New Britain, 06053.
Tel: 860-224-2411; Email: stkatharinedrexel@aohct.org; Web: www.stkdrexelct.org. Rev. John Granato.

9—St. Jerome (1958) Merged with St. Maurice, New Britain to form Saint Katharine Drexel Parish, New Britain.

10—Saint Joachim Parish Corporation (2017)
544 Main St., New Britain, 06051-1812.
Tel: 860-229-4894; Email: stjoachim@aohct.org; Web: www.stjoachimct.org. Rev. Israel Rivera.

11—St. John the Evangelist (1916) Merged with St. Andrew, New Britain to form Holy Apostles Parish, New Britain.

12—St. Joseph's (1896) Merged with St. Peter, New Britain to form Divine Providence Parish, New Britain.

13—St. Mary's (1848) Merged with Saint Ann, New Britain to form Saint Joachim Parish, New Britain.

14—St. Maurice (1946) Merged with St. Jerome Parish, New Britain to form Saint Katharine Drexel Parish, New Britain.

15—St. Peter (1873) (German—French), Merged with St. Joseph, New Britain to form Divine Providence Parish, New Britain.

16—Sacred Heart of Jesus (1894) [CEM] (Polish)
158 Broad St., New Britain, 06053-4195.
Tel: 860-229-0081; Email: sacredheartnewbritain@aohct.org. Rev. Msgr. Daniel J. Plocharczyk; Revs. Stanislaus Dudek, O.F.M. Conv., (Poland); William Baldyga, In Res.; Deacon Jacek Muszynski
Legal Title: Church Corporation of the Sacred Heart of Jesus of New Britain
School—Sacred Heart of Jesus School, (Grades PreK-8), 35 Orange St., New Britain, 06053.

Tel: 860-229-7663; Fax: 860-832-6098; Email: kmuller@sacredheartnb.eduk12.net. Katherine Muller, Prin. Lay Teachers 15; Daughters of Mary of the Immaculate Conception 2; Students 126.
Catechesis Religious Program—Tel: 860-225-3989. Sr. Mary Alma, D.R.E. Students 366.

NEW HARTFORD, LITCHFIELD CO.
1—IMMACULATE CONCEPTION (1869) [CEM] Merged with Immaculate Heart of Mary, Harwinton to form Our Lady of Hope Parish Corporation, New Hartford.
2—OUR LADY OF HOPE PARISH CORPORATION (2016)
60 Town Hill Rd., P.O. Box 285, New Hartford, 06057-0285. Tel: 860-379-5215; Email: ourladyofhope@aohct.org; Web: www.ourladyofhopeparish.com. Rev. Michael A. Ruminski; Deacon David Reynolds.

NEW HAVEN, NEW HAVEN CO.
1—SAINTS AEDAN AND BRENDAN PARISH CORPORATION (1900)
112 Fountain St., New Haven, 06515-0156. Tel: 203-389-2619; Email: ssaedanandbrendan@aohct.org. Rev. Robert A. Morgewicz II.
School—St. Aedan-St. Brendan Catholic School, (Grades PreK-8), 351 McKinley Ave., New Haven, 06515. Tel: 203-387-5693; Fax: 203-387-1609; Email: tduncan@catholicacademy.org. Mrs. Taryn Duncan, Prin.
Legal Title: Catholic Academy of New Haven Lay Teachers 10; Students 172.
Catechesis Religious Program—(see St. Brendan).
2—SAINT ANTHONY PARISH CORPORATION (1904) (Italian)
25 Gold St., New Haven, 06519. Tel: 203-624-1418; Email: stanthonynewhaven@aohct.org; Web: www.stanthony-church.org. Rev. Francis Snell.
Catechesis Religious Program—Students 15.
3—ST. BERNADETTE (1938)
385 Townsend Ave., New Haven, 06512-3998. Tel: 203-467-1007; Email: stberndtchurch@sbcglobal.net. Revs. Francis T. Carter; Timothy A. Meehan, In Res., (Retired); Deacon William H. Parkinson
Legal Title: The St. Bernadette's Church Corporation
School—St. Bernadette School, (Grades PreK-8), 20 Burr St., New Haven, 06512. Tel: 203-469-2271; Fax: 203-469-4615; Email: principal@sbcglobal.net. Edward Goad, Prin. Lay Teachers 18; Students 129.
Catechesis Religious Program—Tel: 203-467-8763; Fax: 203-467-3719. Lisa Furino, C.R.E. Students 179.
4—ST. BONIFACE (1868) (German), Closed. For inquiries for sacramental records contact St. Bernadette Parish, New Haven.
5—ST. BRENDAN (1913) Closed. For Inquiries or Sacramental Records, please see Saints Aedan and Brendan Parish, New Haven.
6—ST. CASIMIR (1912) (Lithuanian), Closed. For inquiries for sacramental records, contact St. Bernadette, New Haven.
7—ST. DONATO (1915) (Italian), Closed. For inquiries for sacramental records, contact St. Francis Parish, New Haven.
8—ST. FRANCIS (1868) Merged with Saint Rose of Lima, New Haven to form Our Lady of Guadalupe Parish, New Haven.
9—ST. JOHN THE BAPTIST (1893) Closed. For inquiries for Sacramental Records, please see Christ the Bread of Life Parish, Hamden.
10—ST. JOHN THE EVANGELIST, Closed. For inquiries for sacramental records contact Sacred Heart, New Haven.
11—ST. JOSEPH'S (1900) Merged with Saint Mary Parish, please see Saint Mary Parish, New Haven.
12—SAINT MARTIN DE PORRES (1942) (African American)
136 Dixwell Ave., New Haven, 06511-3400. Tel: 203-624-9944; Email: stmartindeporres@aohct.org. Rev. Joseph M. Elko
Legal Title: Saint Martin de Porres Church Corporation
Catechesis Religious Program—Students 13.
13—SAINT MARY PARISH CORPORATION (1832, 2017)
5 Hillhouse Ave., New Haven, 06511. Tel: 203-562-6193; Fax: 203-562-1273; Email: stmarynewhaven@aohct.org; Web: www.stmarysnewhaven.org. Revs. John Paul Walker, O.P.; Elias Alan Henritzy, O.P., Parochial Vicar; Joachim Kenney, Parochial Vicar; Henry A. Camacho, O.P., In Res.; Jonathan Kalisch, O.P., In Res.; James Lenaghan, O.P., In Res.
Catechesis Religious Program—Allyson Long, D.R.E. Students 51.
Shrine—The Shrine of the Infant Prague (Inc.), Tel: 203-562-9326; Tel: 203-562-6193, Ext. 116.
14—ST. MICHAEL PARISH aka St. Michael Church (1889) (Italian)
29 Wooster Pl., New Haven, 06511. Tel: 203-562-7178; Fax: 203-752-0157; Email: stmichaelnewhaven@aohct.org. Rev. Robert P. Roy
Legal Title: The St. Michael's Church Corporation, N. Haven, Connecticut
Catechesis Religious Program—Students 12.
15—OUR LADY OF GUADALUPE PARISH CORPORATION (2017)
397 Ferry St., New Haven, 06513-3698. Tel: 203-865-6149; Email: ourladyofguadalupe@aohct.org. Revs. Jose R. Linares; Carlos Zapata, Parochial Vicar; Deacon Tullio V. Ossa.
School—St. Francis/St. Rose of Lima School, (Grades PreK-8), Tel: 203-777-5352; Email: tduncan@stfrancis.eduk12.net. Mrs. Taryn Duncan, Prin. Lay Teachers 14; Students 255.
16—ST. PATRICK (1851) Closed. For inquiries for sacramental records, contact St. Michael, New Haven.
17—ST. PETER (1902) Closed. For inquiries for sacramental records contact Sacred Heart, New Haven.
18—ST. ROSE OF LIMA (1907) Merged with St. Francis, New Haven to form Our Lady of Guadalupe Parish, New Haven.
19—SACRED HEART (1876) Closed. For Inquiries or Sacramental Records, please see Saint Anthony Parish, New Haven.
20—ST. STANISLAUS PARISH (1901) (Polish)
9 Eld St., New Haven, 06511-3815. Tel: 203-562-2828; Tel: 203-624-0850; Email: ststanislausnewhaven@aohct.org; Web: www.ststanislaus-newhaven.com. Revs. Tadeusz Maciejewski, C.M.; Anthony F. Kuzia, C.M., Parochial Vicar; Stanley Miekina, C.M., In Res.
Legal Title: St. Stanislaus' Church of New Haven Connecticut
Catechesis Religious Program—Students 44.
St. Gregory Society (Latin Mass Association)—
St. Stanislaus Fraternity, Secular Franciscan Order—

NEW MILFORD, LITCHFIELD CO.
1—ST. FRANCIS XAVIER (1871) [CEM]
26 Chestnut Land Rd., New Milford, 06776. Tel: 860-354-2202; Fax: 860-355-9485; Email: stfrancisxaviernewmilford@aohct.org; Web: www.sfxnewmilford.org. Mailing Address: 1 Elm St., New Milford, 06776. Revs. Gerald H. Dziedzic; Chacko K. Kumplam, (India) Parochial Vicar; Deacons Alfred Gambone; Roland G. Miller
Legal Title: St. Francis Xavier New Milford Connecticut
Res.: 48 Old Park Lane Rd., New Milford, 06776-2508.
Catechesis Religious Program—Tel: 860-354-5372. Jessica Higgins, C.R.E. (K-5); Susan Pullen, Youth Min. (6-12). Students 580.
2—OUR LADY OF THE LAKES (1990)
3 Old Town Park Rd., New Milford, 06776-4212. Tel: 860-354-5239; Tel: 860-799-7449; Fax: 860-354-2968; Web: ourladyofthelakes@aohct.org. Rev. Gerald H. Dziedzic
Legal Title: Our Lady of the Lakes Corporation
Catechesis Religious Program—Tel: 860-355-5365. Karen O'Donnell, D.R.E. Students 140.

NEWINGTON, HARTFORD CO.
1—ANNUNCIATION PARISH CORPORATION (2017)
626 Willard Ave., Newington, 06111-2614. Tel: 860-666-1591; Email: annunciation@aohct.org. Revs. Shawn T. Daly; Joshua Wilbur, Parochial Vicar; Lawrence R. Bock, Pastor Emeritus, (Retired); James R. Kinnane, In Res., (Retired).
2—CHURCH OF THE HOLY SPIRIT (1964) Merged with Saint Mary to form Annunciation Parish, Newington.
3—ST. MARY (1924) Merged with Holy Spirit, Newington to form Annunciation Parish, Newington.

NORFOLK, LITCHFIELD CO., IMMACULATE CONCEPTION (1889) [CEM] Merged with St. Joseph, Canaan and St. Mary, Lakeville to form Saint Martin of Tours, Canaan.

NORTH BRANFORD, NEW HAVEN CO., SAINT AMBROSE PARISH CORPORATION (2016)
30 Caputo Rd., North Branford, 06471. Tel: 203-484-0403; Email: stambrose@aohct.org. Rev. Robert L. Turner; Deacon Joseph P. Marenna.
Catechesis Religious Program—Students 418.

NORTH HAVEN, NEW HAVEN CO.
1—ST. BARNABAS (1922) Merged with St. Therese and St. Frances Cabrini to form Saint Elizabeth of the Trinity Parish, North Haven.
2—SAINT ELIZABETH OF THE TRINITY PARISH CORPORATION (2017)
44 Washington Ave., North Haven, 06473. Tel: 203-239-5378; Email: stelizabethofthetrinity@aohct.org. Rev. Michael A. Santiago.
St. Barnabas Church—
St. Frances Cabrini Church, 57 Pond Hill Rd., North Haven, 06473.
St. Therese Church, 555 Middletown Ave., North Haven, 06473.
School—St. Therese Nursery School, 555 Middletown Ave., North Haven, 06473. Tel: 203-239-8012. Michele Adinolfi-Lucibello, Nursery School Dir. Students 72.
3—ST. FRANCES CABRINI (1967) Merged with St. Barnabas and St. Therese, North Haven to form Saint Elizabeth of the Trinity Parish, North Haven.
4—ST. THERESE (1925) Merged with St. Barnabas and St. Frances, North Haven to form Saint Elizabeth of the Trinity Parish, North Haven.

NORTHFORD, NEW HAVEN CO., ST. MONICA (1964) Closed. For Inquiries or Sacramental records, please contact the Chancery, Hartford.

OAKVILLE, LITCHFIELD CO., SAINT MARY MAGDALEN PARISH (1900)
16 Buckingham St., Oakville, 06779. Tel: 860-274-9273; Email: stmarymagdalen@aohct.org; Web: www.stmmagdalen-oakville.org. 145 Buckingham St., Oakville, 06779-1797. Rev. Thomas W. Hickey; Deacons George Malfitano; George M. Pettinico
Legal Title: Roman Catholic Church of St. Mary Magdalen
School—St. Mary Magdalen School, (Grades PreK-8), 140 Buckingham St., Oakville, 06779. Tel: 860-945-0621; Fax: 860-945-6162; Email: principal.smms@smmsoakville.org; Web: www.smmsoakville.org. Deborah Mulhall, Prin. Lay Teachers 20; Students 288; Clergy/Religious Teachers 23.
Catechesis Religious Program—Tel: 860-274-1955; Email: kshamanksy@gmail.com. Kelly A. Shamansky, Coord. Faith Formation. Students 204.

ORANGE, NEW HAVEN CO., HOLY INFANT (1952)
450 Racebrook Rd., Orange, 06477. Tel: 203-799-2379; Email: holyinfant@aohct.org. Rev. Norman L. Brockett; Deacon Joseph D. Sullivan
Legal Title: The Church of the Holy Infant
Catechesis Religious Program—Tel: 203-799-2417. Sheila Fremont, D.R.E. Students 626.

OXFORD, NEW HAVEN CO., ST. THOMAS THE APOSTLE (1966)
733 Oxford Rd., Oxford, 06478. Tel: 203-888-2382; Email: stthomastheapostleoxford@aohct.org; Web: stthomastheapostleoxford.org. Rev. Thomas B. Shepard
Legal Title: The Church of St. Thomas the Apostle of Oxford
Catechesis Religious Program—Angela Petrowski Arpino, Dir. Faith Formation. Students 598.

PLAINVILLE, HARTFORD CO., OUR LADY OF MERCY (1881) [CEM]
19 S. Canal St., Plainville, 06062-2756. Tel: 860-747-6825; Fax: 860-747-5407; Email: olmct@sbcglobal.net; Web: www.olmct.org. Rev. Raymond S. Smialowski; Deacon Robert A. Berube
Legal Title: Our Lady of Mercy Corporation
Res.: 15 S. Canal St., Plainville, 06062-2756. Email: fr.smialowski@aohct.org.
Catechesis Religious Program—Jeanne Gionfriddo, D.R.E. Students 117.

PLANTSVILLE, HARTFORD CO.
1—ST. ALOYSIUS (1961) [JC]
254 Burritt St., Plantsville, 06479-1426. Tel: 860-276-9208; Email: staloysius@aohct.org; Web: www.staloysiusplantsville.org. Rev. Ronald P. Zepecki; Deacon James V. Arena
Legal Title: The St. Aloysius Roman Catholic Church Corporation of Southington, Connecticut
Catechesis Religious Program—Students 550.
2—MARY OUR QUEEN (1961)
248 Savage St., Plantsville, 06479-1939. Tel: 860-628-4901; Email: fr.kargul@aohct.org; Email: maryourqueen@aohct.org. Rev. A. Waine Kargul
Legal Title: The Mary Our Queen Roman Catholic Church Corporation of Southington, Connecticut
Catechesis Religious Program—Tel: 860-628-0437; Email: moqfuscodre@aol.com. Annelise Fusco, D.R.E. Students 320.

POQUONOCK, HARTFORD CO., ST. JOSEPH'S (1874) [CEM] Merged with St. Gabriel, Windsor to form Saint Damien of Molokai Parish, Windsor.

PROSPECT, NEW HAVEN CO., ST. ANTHONY (1939)
4 Union City Rd., Prospect, 06712-0117. Tel: 203-758-4056; Email: stanthonyprospect@aohct.org; Web: stanthonyprospect.org. Rev. Grzegorz Jaworowski, (Poland); Deacon Domenic N. Stolfi
Legal Title: The St. Anthony's Church Corporation of Prospect
Catechesis Religious Program—Tel: 203-758-4848. Students 284.

ROCKY HILL, HARTFORD CO.
1—ST. ELIZABETH SETON (1985) Merged with St. James, Rocky Hill to form Saint Josephine Bakhita Parish, Rocky Hill.
2—ST. JAMES (1880) Merged with St. Elizabeth Seton, Rocky Hill to form Saint Josephine Bakhita Parish, Rocky Hill.
3—SAINT JOSEPHINE BAKHITA PARISH CORPORATION (2017)
767 Elm St., Rocky Hill, 06067-1902. Tel: 860-529-8655; Email: stjosephinebakhita@aohct.

org. Rev. George M. Couturier; Deacons Michael A. Shelto; Michael J. Ward.

SEYMOUR, NEW HAVEN CO.

1—ST. AUGUSTINE (1866) [CEM] Merged with Good Shepherd, Seymour to form Saint Nicholas Parish, Seymour.

2—GOOD SHEPHERD (1967) Merged with Saint Augustine, Seymour to form Saint Nicholas Parish, Seymour.

3—SAINT NICHOLAS PARISH CORPORATION (2018)
135 Mountain Ave., Seymour, 06483-2038.
Tel: 203-888-9243; Email: stnicholas@aohct.org. Rev. Thomas J. Cieslikowski.

SHARON, LITCHFIELD CO., ST. BERNARD (1885) [CEM] Merged with St. Bridget, Cornwall Bridge and Sacred Heart, Kent, to form Saint Kateri Tekakwitha Parish, Kent.

SIMSBURY, HARTFORD CO., THE ST. MARY'S CHURCH CORPORATION OF SIMSBURY (1921)
942 Hopmeadow St., Simsbury, 06070-0575.
Tel: 860-658-7627; Email: stmarysimsbury@aohct.org; Web: www.StMarySimsbury.org. P.O. Box 575, Simsbury, 06070. Rev. Frank J. Matera, M.A., Ph.D.; Deacon Arthur L. Miller.
Res.: 940 Hopmeadow St., P.O. Box 575, Simsbury, 06070-0575.
Parish Office—3 Massaco St., Simsbury, 06070-0575. Email: ParishOffice@StMarySimsbury.org.
School—St. Mary School, (Grades PreK-8), 946 Hopmeadow St., Simsbury, 06070. Tel: 860-658-9412 ; Fax: 860-658-1737; Email: smsoffice@stmarysimsbury.eduk12.net; Web: stmarysschoolsimsbury.org. Mrs. Margaret R. Williamson, Prin. Lay Teachers 16; Religious 1; Students 180.
Catechesis Religious Program—Tel: 860-658-5919. Lori Oleaz, Grades 1-6 Rel. Ed.; Kathleen Keating, High School Rel. Ed. Students 542.

SOUTH GLASTONBURY, HARTFORD CO., ST. AUGUSTINE (1877) [CEM]
2577 Main St., Glastonbury, 06033.
Tel: 860-633-9419; Email: fr.suslenko@aohct.org. Rev. Mark S. Suslenko; Most Rev. Henry J. Mansell, D.D., In Res.; Deacons William Dziatko; Stephen L. Weaver.
Res.: 55 Hopewell Rd., P.O. Box 175, South Glastonbury, 06073-0175. Tel: 860-633-9419; Fax: melissa@isidoreandmaria.org.
Catechesis Religious Program—Tel: 860-659-3029; Fax: 860-633-0040. Students 282.

SOUTH WINDSOR, HARTFORD CO.

1—ST. FRANCIS OF ASSISI (1941) Merged with Saint Margaret Mary, South Windsor to form the new Saint Junipero Serra Parish, South Windsor.

2—SAINT JUNIPERO SERRA PARISH (2017)
80 Hayes Rd., South Windsor, 06074.
Tel: 860-644-2411; Tel: 860-644-2549;
Fax: 860-644-5765; Email: fr.baranowski@aohct.org; Web: www.saintjuniperoserra.org. Revs. David J. Baranowski; Carlos Castrillon, Parochial Vicar; Mrs. Valeria Florez, Business Mgr.; Mark F. Cerrato, D.R.E.

3—ST. MARGARET MARY (1961) Merged with St. Francis of Assisi, South Windsor to form Saint Junipero Serra Parish, South Windsor.

SOUTHBURY, NEW HAVEN CO., SACRED HEART (1884) [CEM]
910 Main St., S., Southbury, 06488.
Tel: 203-264-5071; Email: sacredheartsouthbury@aohct.org; Email: mkorsu@shcsby.org. Rev. Joseph T. Donnelly; Sr. Patricia Torre, D.W., Pastoral Assoc.; Ami Conlan, Pastoral Assoc.
Legal Title: Church of the Sacred Heart, Southbury, Connecticut
Res.: 91 Old Waterbury Rd., Southbury, 06488.
Catechesis Religious Program—Tel: 203-264-5065; Fax: 203-264-4271. Students 524.

SOUTHINGTON, HARTFORD CO.

1—ST. DOMINIC (1971)
1050 Flanders Rd., Southington, 06489-1344.
Tel: 860-628-0349; Email: stdominic@aohct.org. Rev. Ronald P. May; Deacons Paul J. Kulas; John Thorpe
Legal Title: The Church of St. Dominic of Southington Corporation
School—Southington Catholic, (Grades PreK-5), 133 Bristol St., Southington, 06489. Tel: 860-628-2485; Email: esampiere@southingtoncatholicschool.org. Mrs. Eileen Sampiere, Prin. Lay Teachers 14; Religious 2; Students 147.
Catechesis Religious Program—Tel: 860-628-5159; Email: RelEd@saintdominicchurch.com. Theresa Kamradt, D.R.E. Students 654.

2—IMMACULATE CONCEPTION PARISH CORPORATION (1915) [CEM] (Polish)
130 Summer St., Southington, 06489.
Tel: 860-628-2181; Fax: 860-628-0341; Email: immaculateconceptionsouthington@aohct.org. Rev. Adam C. Subocz
Legal Title: The Immaculate Conception Church Corporation of Southington
Father Kolbe Catechetical Center—152 Summer St., Plantsville, 06479. Tel: 860-628-2181; Email: immaculateconception06489@gmail.com.

3—ST. THOMAS (1860) [CEM]
99 Bristol St., Southington, 06489-4599.
Tel: 860-628-4713; Email: stthomassouthington@aohct.org; Web: www.stthomassouthington.org. Rev. Joseph R. Cronin; Deacons Angelo J. Coppola; Vincent Raby
Legal Title: St. Thomas' Catholic Church Corporation
School—Southington Catholic, (Grades PreK-8), Southington Catholic School, 133 Bristol St., Southington, 06489. Tel: 860-628-2485; Email: esampiere@southingtoncatholicschool.org. Mrs. Eileen Sampiere, Prin. Lay Teachers 15; Religious 2; Students 147.
Catechesis Religious Program—Tel: 860-628-9679. Sr. Marie Roccapriore, M.P.F., D.R.E. Students 175.
Convent—Religious Sisters Filippini, 20 Eden Pl., Southington, 06489-4599. Tel: 860-621-1904.

SUFFIELD, HARTFORD CO.

1—ST. JOSEPH (1916) [CEM] (Polish), Closed. For Inquiries or Sacramental Records, please contact Sacred Heart Parish, Suffield.

2—SACRED HEART PARISH CORPORATION (1884) [JC]
446 Mountain Rd., P.O. Box 626, Suffield, 06078-0626. Tel: 860-668-4246; Fax: 860-668-1337; Email: sacredheartsuffield@aohct.org; Web: www.sacredheartct.com. Rev. Mark R. Jette.
Catechesis Religious Program—Tel: 860-668-7766; Fax: 860-370-5164; Email: shc_dre@sbcglobal.net. Donna Swols, D.R.E. Students 185.

TARIFFVILLE, HARTFORD CO., ST. BERNARD (1878) [CEM] Closed. For Inquiries or Sacramental Records, please see Saint Therese Parish, Granby.

TERRYVILLE, LITCHFIELD CO.

1—THE CHURCH OF ST. CASIMIR (1906) (Polish), Merged with Immaculate Conception, Terryville and St. Thomas, Thomaston to form Saint Maximilian Kolbe Parish, Thomaston.

2—THE IMMACULATE CONCEPTION OF TERRYVILLE (1882) [CEM 2] Merged with St. Thomas, Thomaston and St. Casimir, Terryville to form Saint Maximilian Kolbe, Thomaston.

THOMASTON, LITCHFIELD CO.

1—SAINT MAXIMILLIAN KOLBE PARISH CORPORATION (2017)
19 Electric Ave., Thomaston, 06787-1852.
Tel: 860-283-5817; Email: Stmaximiliankolbe@aohct.org. Rev. Joseph P. Crowley.

2—ST. THOMAS (1869) [CEM] Merged with Immaculate Conception and St. Casimir, Terryville to form Saint Maximilian Kolbe Parish, Thomaston.

TORRINGTON, LITCHFIELD CO.

1—SAINT JOHN PAUL THE GREAT PARISH CORPORATION (1877)
160 Main St., Torrington, 06790-5201.
Tel: 860-482-4433; Email: stjohnpaulthegreat@aohct.org; Web: JohnPaulGreatParish.com. Revs. Emmanuel I. Ihemedu; Elkin Mauricio Galvis, Parochial Vicar; Deacons Roy C. Dungan; Richard H. Hamel; Peter R. Hyde.
St. Francis of Assisi Church.
School—St. Peter / St. Francis School, (Grades PreK-8), 360 Prospect St., Torrington, 06790.
Tel: 860-489-4177; Fax: 860-489-1590; Email: principal@sfsfschool.org. Mrs. Jo-Anne Gauger, Prin. Lay Teachers 10; Students 93.
Catechesis Religious Programs—
Tel: 860-307-2291; Email: JohnPaulGreatReligiousEd@gmail.com. Jen Owens, D.R.E.; Jared Howe, RCIA; Lourdes Rodriguez, RCIA (Spanish).
Catholic Youth Ministry of Torrington—
Tel: 860-309-1900; Email: JohnPaulGreatYouth@gmail.com; Email: JohnPaulGreatConfirmation@gmail.com. Marlene Carrier, Middle School EDGE/Youth Group; Donna Puzacke, High School Confirmation Prog.

2—ST. MARY (1919) (Polish), Closed. For Inquiries or Sacramental Records, please contact St. John Paul the Great Parish, Torrington.

3—ST. PETER (1910) (Italian), Merged with Saint Francis of Assisi to form Saint John Paul the Great Parish, Torrington.

4—SACRED HEART (1910) (Slovak), Closed. For Inquiries or Sacramental Records, please contact St. John Paul the Great Parish, Torrington. Revs. John Granato; William Agyemang, Parochial Vicar; Deacons Roy C. Dungan; Richard H. Hamel; Peter R. Hyde; Beverly Sesko, Pastoral Min.

UNION CITY, NEW HAVEN CO.

1—ST. HEDWIG (Naugatuck) (1906) (Polish), Closed. For Inquiries or Sacramental Records, please see Saint Francis of Assisi Parish, Naugatuck.

2—ST. MARY (Naugatuck) (1907) Closed. For Inquiries or Sacramental Records, please see Saint Francis of Assisi Parish, Naugatuck.

UNIONVILLE, HARTFORD CO., ST. MARY STAR OF THE SEA (1874) [CEM]
16 Bidwell Sq., Unionville, 06085-1116.
Tel: 860-673-2422; Email: stmarystarofthesea@aohct.org. Rev. Msgr. Michael J. Motta; Deacon Thomas S. Sutak
Legal Title: The Star of the Sea Church Corporation of Unionville, Connecticut
Catechesis Religious Program—Tel: 860-675-8522; Email: st.mary.re@sbcglobal.net. Students 399.

WALLINGFORD, NEW HAVEN CO.

1—MOST HOLY TRINITY PARISH (1869)
68 N. Colony St., Wallingford, 06492.
Tel: 203-269-8791; Email: mostholytrinity@aohct.org. Revs. Andres Mendoza Floyd; Eduar Gutierrez, Parochial Vicar; Deacons Dominic Corraro; Eugene C. Riotte; Joseph S. Mazurek
Legal Title: Holy Trinity Roman Catholic Church, Wallingford
School—Holy Trinity School, (Grades 1-8), 11 N. Whittlesey Ave., Wallingford, 06492.
Tel: 203-269-4476; Fax: 203-294-4983; Email: school@myhts-wallingford.org. Deacon Dominic Corraro, Prin. Lay Teachers 9; Students 148.
Catechesis Religious Program—Tel: 203-265-6300. Frances Selmecki, D.R.E. Students 625.

2—SS. PETER AND PAUL (1924) [CEM] (Polish), Merged with Saint Stanislaus, Meriden to form Saint Faustina Parish, Meriden.

3—RESURRECTION (1963)
115 Pond Hill Rd., Wallingford, 06492-4836.
Tel: 203-265-1694; Email: resurrection@aohct.org. Very Rev. John J. Georgia; Rev. Hugh J. MacDonald, In Res., (Retired); Mr. Joseph R. Tatta, M.Div., Pastoral Assoc.
Legal Title: The Church of the Resurrection
Catechesis Religious Program—Tel: 203-269-4683; Fax: 203-269-4683. Mrs. Mary Ann Marchitto, D.R.E. Students 277.

WASHINGTON DEPOT, LITCHFIELD CO., OUR LADY OF PERPETUAL HELP PARISH CORPORATION (1893, 2017) [CEM]
34 Green Hill Rd., Washington Depot, 06794-0303.
Tel: 860-868-2600; Email: ourladyofperpetualhelp@aohct.org; Web: www.ourlady-stpatrick.org. P.O. Box 303, Washington Depot, 06794-0303. Rev. Philip R. Schulze; Deacon George H. Streib
Legal Title: Our Lady of Perpetual Help Parish Corporation
Catechesis Religious Program—Tel: 914-523-2981. Students 26.
Mission—St. Patrick's, Merged with Our Lady of Perpetual Help, Washington Depot.

WATERBURY, NEW HAVEN CO.

1—BASILICA OF THE IMMACULATE CONCEPTION (1847)
74 W. Main St., Waterbury, 06721-1670.
Tel: 203-574-0017; Fax: 203-756-8748; Email: basilicaoftheimmaculateconception@aohct.org. Very Rev. Christopher M. Ford, J.C.L., Rector; Revs. Joseph Karikunnel, C.S.T., Parochial Vicar; William Agyemang, Parochial Vicar; Deacon James F. Papillo
Legal Title: Corporation of the Church of the Immaculate Conception, Waterbury, Connecticut
Catechesis Religious Program—Students 174.

2—ALL SAINTS PARISH CORPORATION (1886) (French)
515 S. Main St., Waterbury, 06706-1089.
Tel: 203-756-4439; Fax: 203-754-3244; Email: allsaints@aohct.org. Revs. Diego A. Jimenez; John R. Mariano, Parochial Vicar; Hector G. Rangel, Parochial Vicar
Legal Title: All Saints Parish Corporation
Res.: 309 S. Main St., Waterbury, 06702.
Tel: 203-574-0017; Fax: 203-756-8748.
Catechesis Religious Program—Nidia Estrada, D.R.E.; Raul Santiago, Confirmation Prog.; Dino Pantoni, RCIA.

3—SAINT BLAISE PARISH CORPORATION
50 Charles St., Waterbury, 06708. Tel: 203-756-8837; Email: stblaise@aohct.org. Rev. Frederick M. Aniello.

4—BLESSED SACRAMENT (1911)
182 Robbins St., Waterbury, 06708.
Tel: 203-753-3149; Fax: 203-596-0740; Email: blessedsacrament@aohct.org. Rev. Roberto D. McCarthy, Admin.
Legal Title: The Corporation of the Church of the Blessed Sacrament in Waterbury
School—Catholic Academy of Waterbury, (Grades K-8), 386 Robinwood Rd., Waterbury, 06708-2750.
Tel: 203-756-5313; Fax: 203-756-5313; Email: mrsmbanachbssprincipal@gmail.com. Michele Banach, Prin.; Mary Rice, Prin. Lay Teachers 10; Students 156.
Catechesis Religious Program—Barbara Mule, C.R.E. Students 118.

5—ST. CECILIA (1893) (German), Closed. For inquiries for sacramental records, contact Sacred Heart-Sagrado Corazon, Waterbury.

6—ST. FRANCIS XAVIER (1896)
625 Baldwin St., Waterbury, 06706-1597.
Tel: 203-756-7804; Email: stfrancisxavierwaterbury@aohct.org. Rev. Paul J. Pace
Legal Title: St. Francis Xavier's Church Corporation of Waterbury, Connecticut
Catechesis Religious Program—St. Francis Xavier

Religious Ed.: 587 Baldwin St., Waterbury, 06706. Tel: 203-754-6996; Email: st.fxlciarello@yahoo.com. Mrs. Laurie Ciarello, D.R.E. Students 85.

7—ST. JOSEPH (1894) (Lithuanian), Merged with St. Patrick, Waterbury to form Saint Blaise Parish, Waterbury.

8—ST. LEO THE GREAT (1974) Merged with SS. Peter and Paul Parish, Waterbury to form Mary Mother of the Church Parish, Waterbury.

9—ST. LUCY (1926) (Italian), Closed. For Inquiries or Sacramental Records, please contact All Saints Parish, Waterbury.

10—MARY, MOTHER OF THE CHURCH PARISH CORPORATION (2017)
67 Southmayd Rd., Waterbury, 06705.
Tel: 203-756-7919; Email: mmcwaterbury@gmail.com; Web: mmcparish.com. Rev. John L. Lavorgna
Legal Titles: SS. Peter and Paul School
School—SS. Peter and Paul School, (Grades PreK-8), 116 Beecher Ave., Waterbury, 06705.
Tel: 203-755-0881; Email: ssppoffice@comcast.net. James Gambardella, Prin. Lay Teachers 12; Students 144.

11—ST. MARGARET (1910) (Hispanic), Closed. For sacramental records see All Saints Parish, Waterbury.

12—ST. MICHAEL (1902)
62 St. Michael Dr., Waterbury, 06704-1295.
Tel: 203-753-0689; Fax: 203-573-9101; Email: stmichaelwaterbury@aohct.org. Rev. Nathaniel C. Labarda
Legal Title: St. Michael's Church of Waterville, Connecticut
Catechesis Religious Program—Students 69.

13—OUR LADY OF FATIMA (1971) (Portuguese)
2071 Baldwin St., P.O. Box 1787, Waterbury, 06721.
Tel: 203-753-1424; Fax: 203-753-1424; Email: fr.eurico@aohct.org. Rev. Francisco Eurico
Legal Title: The Church of Our Lady of Fatima Corporation
Catechesis Religious Program—

14—OUR LADY OF LORETO (1971)
12 Ardsley Rd., Waterbury, 06708-1825.
Tel: 203-757-6112; Fax: 203-756-9656; Email: ourladyofloreto@aohct.org; Web: ourladyofloretowtby.org. Rev. Allan J. Hill
Legal Title: The Church of Our Lady of Loreto of Waterbury Corporation
Catechesis Religious Program—Tel: 203-510-4263; Email: StephenDRE1@gmail.com. Stephen Derasmo, D.R.E. Students 41.

15—OUR LADY OF LOURDES (1899) (Italian), Merged with St. Anne Shrine for Mothers to form All Saints Parish, Waterbury.

16—OUR LADY OF MT. CARMEL (1923) (Italian)
785 Highland Ave., Waterbury, 06708-4199.
Tel: 203-756-8981; Fax: 203-756-2074; Email: ourladyofmtcarmelwaterbury@aohct.org; Email: fr.aniello@aohct.org; Web: olmcwtby.com. Revs. Frederick M. Aniello; David Madejski, Parochial Vicar; Deacon Ernest H. Pagliaro Jr.
Legal Title: The Church of Our Lady of Mount Carmel
School—Our Lady of Mt. Carmel School, (Grades PreK-8), 645 Congress Ave., Waterbury, 06708-4198. Tel: 203-755-6809; Fax: 203-755-5850; Email: jack.tavares@mtcarmelschool.net. Joaquim (Jack) Tavares, Prin.; Karen Kleinschmidt, Librarian. Lay Teachers 18; Students 242.
Catechesis Religious Program—Virginia Ciochetti, D.R.E. Students 285.

17—ST. PATRICK (1880) (Irish), Merged with St. Joseph, Waterbury to form Saint Blaise Parish, Waterbury.

18—SS. PETER AND PAUL (1920) Merged with Saint Leo the Great, Waterbury, to form Mary Mother of the Church, Waterbury.

19—SACRED HEART-SAGRADO CORAZON (1885) Closed. For Inquiries or Sacramental Records, please contact All Saints Parish, Waterbury.

20—ST. STANISLAUS KOSTKA (1913) (Polish), Closed. For Inquiries or Sacramental Records, please contact All Saints Parish, Waterbury.

21—ST. THOMAS (1898) Closed. For inquiries for sacramental records contact St. Michael, Waterbury.

WATERTOWN, LITCHFIELD CO., ST. JOHN THE EVANGELIST (1878) [CEM]
574 Main St., Watertown, 06795. Tel: 860-274-8836; Fax: 860-274-0667; Web: stjohn.weconnect.com. 21 Academy Hill, Watertown, 06795-2101. Revs. Anthony J. Smith; David C. Carey, Parochial Vicar; Deacons Robert D. Gordon; Daniel Camerota; Victor C. Mitchell Jr.
Legal Title: The Corporation of St. John's Church of Watertown, Connecticut
School—St. John the Evangelist School, (Grades PreK-8), 760 Main St., Watertown, 06795.
Tel: 860-274-9208; Fax: 860-945-1082; Email: miannone@stjohnwtn.org; Email: bpiccolo@stjohnwtn.org; Web: www.stjohnwtn.org. Mrs. Marylou Iannone, Prin. Lay Teachers 15; Students 162.
Catechesis Religious Program—9 Academy Hill, Watertown, 06795. Tel: 860-274-4123; Email: stjohndre@optonline.net. Carmelina Calabrese, D.R.E. Students 291.

WEST HARTFORD, HARTFORD CO.

1—SAINT ANDREW DUNG-LAC PARISH CORPORATION
467 S. Quaker Ln., West Hartford, 06110.
Tel: 860-236-5965; Email: fr.mai@aohct.org. Rev. Tuan Anh Dinh Mai.

2—THE ST. BRIGID CHURCH CORPORATION OF WEST HARTFORD (1919) Merged with St. Mark the Evangelist and St. Helena, West Hartford to form Saint Gianna (Beretta Molla) Parish, West Hartford.

3—THE CHURCH OF ST. TIMOTHY (1958)
225 King Philip Dr., West Hartford, 06117-1209.
Tel: 860-233-5131; Fax: 860-232-2189; Email: sttimothy@aohct.org. 1116 N. Main St., West Hartford, 06117-1209. Rev. Alvin J. LeBlanc; Deacons Dennis R. Ferguson; C. Eric Thermer; Patricia A. Piano, Pastoral Assoc., Tel: 860-232-8594
Legal Title: The St. Timothy Roman Catholic Church Corporation of West Hartford
School—St. Timothy Middle School, (Grades 6-8), 225 King Philip Dr., West Hartford, 06117-1497.
Tel: 860-236-0614; Fax: 860-920-0293; Email: tbellefleur@stmswh.org; Web: stmswh.org. Tara Bellefleur, Prin. Lay Teachers 10; Students 110.
Catechesis Religious Program—Stephanie Barnes, C.R.E. (Grades PreK-5); Diane Whittemore, C.R.E. (Grade 9-10). Students 270.

4—SAINT GIANNA (BERETTA MOLLA) PARISH CORPORATION
1088 New Britain Ave., West Hartford, 06110.
Tel: 860-236-5965; Email: stgianna@aohct.org; Web: saintgiannaparish.org. Revs. Joseph T. Devine; Tuan Anh Dinh Mai, Parochial Vicar; Joseph Pullikattil, Parochial Vicar; Deacons Raymond J. Fugere Jr.; Robert J. Hilliard; James J. McCormack
Legal Title: Saint Gianna (Beretta Molla) Parish Corporation.

5—ST. HELENA (1966) Merged with St. Mark the Evangelist and St. Brigid, West Hartford to form Saint Gianna (Beretta Molla) Parish, West Hartford.

6—ST. JOHN THE EVANGELIST (1942) Closed. For inquiries for sacramental records contact St. Lawrence O'Toole, Hartford.

7—ST. MARK THE EVANGELIST (1942) Merged with St. Brigid and St. Helena, West Hartford to form Saint Gianna (Beretta Molla) Parish, West Hartford.

8—ST. PETER CLAVER (1966)
47 Pleasant St., West Hartford, 06107-1600.
Tel: 860-561-4235; Fax: 860-561-0552; Email: stpeterclaver@aohct.org. Rev. Robert M. Kwiatkowski, Tel: 860-561-0552; Deacons Robert M. Pallotti; James E. Hickey Jr.; Kiley Robert; Mrs. Gigi Frailey, Pastoral Assoc.; Mrs. Debbie Walgren, Business Mgr.
Legal Title: The St. Peter Claver Church Corporation of West Hartford
Catechesis Religious Program—Tel: 860-521-2904; Email: lauriejaneckospc@gmail.com. Laurie Janecko, D.R.E. Students 461.

9—ST. THOMAS THE APOSTLE (1921)
872 Farmington Ave., West Hartford, 06119-1499.
Tel: 860-233-8269; Fax: 860-523-8794; Email: stthomastheapostlewesthartford@aohct.org; Web: www.stawh.org. Rev. Edward M. Moran
Legal Title: The Church of St. Thomas the Apostle Corporation, West Hartford
School—St. Thomas the Apostle School, (Grades PreK-5), 25 Dover Rd., West Hartford, 06119-1298.
Tel: 860-236-6257; Fax: 860-236-8865; Email: cdisanto@stthomasapostlewh.org. Mrs. Colleen DiSanto, Prin.; Janet Cashman, Librarian. Lay Teachers 16; Students 226.
Catechesis Religious Program—Tel: 860-523-4209; Fax: 860-523-0273. Mrs. Elizabeth B. Kiselica, D.R.E. Students 255.

WEST HAVEN, NEW HAVEN CO.

1—ST. JOHN VIANNEY (1965) Closed. For sacramental records see Our Lady of Victory Parish, West Haven.

2—ST. LAWRENCE (1886) Merged with Saint Louis to form Saint John XXIII Parish, West Haven.

3—SAINT JOHN XXIII PARISH CORPORATION (1886) (French Territorial)
89 Bull Hill Ln., West Haven, 06516-3925.
Tel: 203-934-5249; Fax: 203-934-1055; Email: stjohnxxiii@aohct.org. Revs. Jose Angel Mercado Jr.; Eric Zuniga, Parochial Vicar.
School—St. Lawrence School, (Grades PreK-8), 231 Main St., West Haven, 06516. Tel: 203-933-2518; Fax: 203-932-2058; Email: pdefonzo@stlaw.eduk12.net; Web: www.stlaw.eduk12.net. Mr. Paul De Fronzo, Prin. Lay Teachers 11; Students 148.
Catechesis Religious Program—Students 376.

4—OUR LADY OF VICTORY PARISH CORPORATION (1935)
600 Jones Hill Rd., West Haven, 06516-6399.
Tel: 203-934-6357; Fax: 203-932-3315; Email: ourladyofvictory@aohct.org; Web: www.olov.org. Rev. Kevin M. Dillon; Deacons Paul E. Sabo; Dean A. Macchio; Frank J. Bevvino.
Catechesis Religious Program— Twinned with St. John Vianney Parish. Tel: 203-933-0044; Email: olovore@sbcglobal.net. Loriann Ruiz, D.R.E.
Convent—Ursuline Sisters of Tildonk, 634 Jones Hill Rd., West Haven, 06516-6398. Tel: 203-934-8601.

5—ST. PAUL'S (1916) (Italian), Closed. For Inquiries or Sacramental Records, please contact St. John XXIII Parish, West Haven.

WEST SIMSBURY, HARTFORD CO., ST. CATHERINE OF SIENA (1971)
265 Stratton Brook Rd., Box 184, West Simsbury, 06092. Tel: 860-658-1642; Email: stcatherineofsiena@aohct.org. Rev. Michael G. Whyte
Legal Title: The Church of St. Catherine of Siena of Simsbury Corporation
Catechesis Religious Program—Tel: 860-658-4737. Mrs. Kathi Bonner, D.R.E. Students 725.

WETHERSFIELD, HARTFORD CO.

1—CHRIST THE KING PARISH CORPORATION (1941)
Mailing Address: 84 Somerset St., Wethersfield, 06109. Tel: 860-529-2545; Fax: 860-529-5861; Email: christtheking@aohct.org. Revs. Nicholas P. Melo; George Vellaplackil, (India) Parochial Vicar.
Church: 601 Silas Deane Hwy., Wethersfield, 06109.
School—Corpus Christi School, (Grades PreK-8), 581 Silas Deane Hwy., Wethersfield, 06109.
Tel: 860-529-5487; Fax: 860-257-9106; Email: schoolmail@corpuschristict.eduk12.net; Web: corpuschristischoolct.com. Mrs. Ann Theresa Sarpu, Prin. Lay Teachers 23; Students 348.
Catechesis Religious Program—Students 126.

2—INCARNATION (1963)
544 Prospect St., Wethersfield, 06109-3609.
Tel: 860-529-2533; Fax: 860-721-6595; Email: incarnation@aohct.org. Rev. James M. Moran
Legal Title: The Church of the Incarnation Corporation
Catechesis Religious Program—Tel: 860-529-6765; Email: gotellit15@gmail.com. Noranne Wamester, D.R.E. Students 449.

3—SACRED HEART (1876) Merged with Corpus Christi, Wethersfield and St. Luke, Hartford to form Christ the King Parish.

4—SACRED HEART OF JESUS KOREAN CATHOLIC PARISH CORPORATION
56 Hartford Ave., Wethersfield, 06109.
Tel: 860-529-1456; Email: ctkoreancatholic@gmail.com. Rev. John Gye Lee.

WINDSOR, HARTFORD CO.

1—SAINT DAMIEN OF MOLOKAI PARISH CORPORATION
379 Broad St., Windsor, 06095. Tel: 860-688-4905; Fax: 860-688-2638; Email: office@windsorcatholic.org. Revs. John P. Melnick; Dairo E. Diaz, Parochial Vicar.
School—St. Gabriel School, (Grades K-8), 77 Bloomfield Ave., Windsor, 06095. Tel: 860-688-6401; Fax: 860-298-8668; Email: pmartin@stgabrielschool.org; Web: www.stgabrielschool.org. Patricia Martin, Prin. Lay Teachers 14; Students 191.

2—ST. GABRIEL (1894) Merged with St. Joseph, Windsor to form Saint Damien of Molokai Parish, Windsor.

3—ST. GERTRUDE (1947)
550 Matianuck Ave., Windsor, 06095-3599.
Tel: 860-522-6163; Fax: 860-525-2320; Email: stgertrude@aohct.org. Rev. Maurice J. Barry
Legal Title: The Saint Gertrude's Church Corporation of Windsor
Catechesis Religious Program—Teri Coughlin, D.R.E.

WINDSOR LOCKS, HARTFORD CO.

1—MARY, GATE OF HEAVEN PARISH CORPORATION
42 Spring St., Windsor Locks, 06096-2311.
Tel: 860-623-2524. Revs. Robert A. O'Grady; Timothy A. O'Brien, Parochial Vicar; Deacon Ronald Biamonte, M.A.
Parish Center—45 Church St., Windsor Locks, 06096. Tel: 860-627-9469.
Catechesis Religious Program—Marilyn Stratton, D.R.E. Students 50.

2—ST. MARY (1852) [CEM] Merged with St. Robert Bellarmine Parish, Windsor Locks to form Mary, Gate of Heaven,Windsor Locks.

3—ST. ROBERT BELLARMINE (1962) Merged with St. Mary, Windsor Locks to form Mary, Gate of Heaven, Windsor Locks.

WINSTED, LITCHFIELD CO., ST. JOSEPH aka St. Joseph Roman Catholic Church (1853) [CEM]
31 Oak St., Winsted, 06098. Tel: 860-379-3369; Email: stjosephwinsted@aohct.org. 186 Main St., Winsted, 06098. Revs. Bruce C. Czapla, O.F.M.; Roger L. Hall, O.F.M., Parochial Vicar
Legal Title: St. Josephs Roman Catholic Church Corporation, Winsted, Connecticut
Res.: 66 Oak St., Winsted, 06098.
Fax: info@stjoseph-winsted.org.
School—St. Anthony, (Grades PreK-8), 55 Oak St., Winsted, 06098. Tel: 860-379-7521;
Fax: 860-379-7523; Email: mrhowe@sas-winsted.org. Louis Howe, Prin.; Scott Norton. Lay Teachers 11; Students 180.
Catechesis Religious Program—Tel: 860-469-2292; Email: lrodgers@stjoseph-winsted.org. Lindsay Rogers, D.R.E. Students 175.

WOLCOTT, NEW HAVEN CO.
1—SAINT BASIL THE GREAT PARISH CORPORATION (2017)
525 Woodtick Rd., Wolcott, 06617-2898.
Tel: 203-879-2544; Email: stbasilthegreat@aohct.org. Rev. Kevin G. Donovan.
2—ST. MARIA GORETTI (1973) Merged with St. Pius X, Wolcott, to form Saint Basil the Great Parish, Wolcott.
3—ST. PIUS X (1956) Merged with St. Maria Goretti, Wolcott, to form Saint Basil the Great Parish, Wolcott.
WOODBRIDGE, NEW HAVEN CO., CHURCH OF THE ASSUMPTION (1924)
81 Center Rd., Woodbridge, 06525-1699.
Tel: 203-387-7119; Fax: 203-387-4281; Email: assumptionwoodbridge@aohct.org; Email: fr.ford@aohct.org; Web: www.assumptionchurch.com. Very Rev. Christopher M. Ford, J.C.L.; Rev. Joseph Sidera, C.S.C., Parochial Vicar; Deacon John Mordecai
Legal Title: The Church of the Assumption, Woodbridge
Church: 1700 Litchfield Tnpke., Woodbridge, 06525.
Catechesis Religious Program—Tel: 203-389-9863. Sr. Dorellen Sullivan, R.S.M., D.R.E. Students 413.
WOODBURY, LITCHFIELD CO.
1—PRINCE OF PEACE PARISH CORPORATION (2017)
494 Main St. S., Woodbury, 06798. Tel: 203-263-2008 ; Email: princeofpeace@aohct.org; Web: princeofpeaceparish-aohct.org. Rev. James T. Gregory
Legal Title: Prince of Peace Parish Corporation.
2—ST. TERESA OF AVILA (1902) Merged with Church of the Nativity, Bethlehem to form Prince of Peach Parish, Woodbury.
YALESVILLE, NEW HAVEN CO., OUR LADY OF FATIMA (1956)
382 Hope Hill Rd., Yalesville, 06492-7565.
Tel: 203-265-0961; Email: ourladyoffatimayalesville@aohct.org; Web: www.ladyoffatimaparish.org. P.O. Box 4518, Yalesville, 06492-7565. Rev. Robert N. Landback
Legal Title: The Our Lady of Fatima Church Corporation of Yalesville, Connecticut
Catechesis Religious Program—Tel: 203-265-6426; Fax: TracySB1123@aol.com. Tracy Blum, D.R.E., Tel: 203-265-6426, Ext. 4. Students 267.

Chaplains of Public Institutions

HARTFORD. *Hartford Correctional Institution*, 177 Weston St., 06120. Tel: 860-240-1857. Rev. Zacharias Pushpanathan, Chap., Sr. Jerilyn Hunihan, A.S.C.J., Chap.
Hartford Hospital, 80 Seymour St., 06102-5037.
Tel: 860-545-2251; Fax: 860-545-3594. Rev. Nicola N.H. Tran, Chap.
BRISTOL. *Bristol Hospital*, Brewster Rd., Bristol, 06011-0977. Tel: 860-585-3431. Rev. J. Richard Fowler, Interfaith Chap., (United Church of Christ).
CHESHIRE. *Cheshire Correctional Institution*, 900 Highland Ave., Cheshire, 06410-1698.
Tel: 203-250-2787. Rev. Robert Villa, Chap., Deacon Jose Robles.
Manson Youth Institution, 42 Jarvis St., Cheshire, 06410-1545. Tel: 203-806-2508. Deacon Leo B. Conard III, Chap.
ENFIELD. *Carl Robinson Correctional Institution*, P.O. Box 1400, Enfield, 06083-1400. Tel: 860-253-8389. Rev. Robert Vujs, M.M., Deacon Michael Torres.
Willard-Cybulski Correction Institute, 391 Shaker Rd., P.O. Box 2400, Enfield, 06082.
Tel: 860-763-6559. Rev. Robert Villa, Deacon Michael Torres.
MANCHESTER. *Manchester Memorial Hospital*, 71 Haynes St., Manchester, 06040-4188.
Tel: 860-646-1222, Ext. 2137. Rev. Louis D. Cremonie, Chap.
NEW BRITAIN. *The Hospital of Central Connecticut (New Britain General Hospital)*, 100 Grand St., New Britain, 06050-2016. Tel: 860-224-5011;
Fax: 860-224-5740. Rev. Ronald T. Smith, Chap.
Res.: 396 Church St., P.O. Box 515, New Britain, 06050-0515. Tel: 860-224-0341.
NEW HAVEN. *New Haven Correctional Center*, 245 Whalley Ave., New Haven, 06511. Rev. Zacharias Pushpanathan.
Yale-New Haven Hospital, 20 York St., New Haven, 06504-1001. Tel: 203-688-2151; Fax: 203-688-3478. Revs. William Maguire, C.P., Chap., Geoffrey C. Smith, Chap., Tel: 203-688-7031, Sr. Carole Hermann, O.P., Tel: 203-688-7032.
ROCKY HILL. *Veterans' Home and Hospital*, 287 West St., Rocky Hill, 06067-3902.
Tel: 860-529-2571, Ext. 2386.
SUFFIELD. *Macdougall - Walker Correctional Institute*, 1153 E. St. S., Suffield, 06080-0002.
Tel: 860-627-2148 Mac Dougall;
Tel: 860-292-3429 Walker;
Fax: 860-627-2152 Mac Dougall. Rev. Zacharias Pushpanathan, Deacon Henry J. Szumowski.
WATERBURY. *Waterbury Hospital*, 64 Robbins St., Waterbury, 06721-2600. Tel: 203-573-7213;
Fax: 203-573-7326; Fax: 203-573-6000. Deacon Neil Culhane, Chap., Email: nculhane@wtbyhosp.org.
WEST HAVEN. *V.A. CT Health Care System*, 950 Campbell Ave., West Haven, 06516-2700.
Tel: 203-932-5711, Ext. 2422. Rev. Msgr. Stephen Adu-Kwaning, (Ghana), Rev. Cosmas Archibong.
WETHERSFIELD. *Connecticut Department of Correction*, 24 Wolcott Hill Rd., Wethersfield, 06109-1152.
Tel: 860-692-7577; Fax: 860-692-6263. Deacon Michael Torres, Catholic Chaplain Liaison, Rev. Charles Williams, Dir. Religious Svcs.

Special and other Archdiocesan Assignments:
Rev. Msgr.—
Schmitz, Gerard G., Interim Chap., (Retired), St. Thomas More Chapel and Golden Center, 268 Park St., New Haven, 06511-4714. Tel: 203-777-5537
Very Revs.—
Mukuka, George S., J.C.L., Ph.D., Judicial Vicar, 467 Bloomfield Ave., Bloomfield, 06002. Tel: 860-242-5573
Shanley, James A., Secretariat for Communications and Public Rels., 134 Farmington Ave., 06105. Tel: 860-541-6491
Vargo, Robert B., J.C.L., Vicar for Clergy, 134 Farmington Ave., 06105
Revs.—
Casey, Michael T., Dir. Vocations, 467 Bloomfield Ave., Bloomfield, 06002. Tel: 860-242-5573
Daly, Shawn T., Office of Minister for Priests, 626 Willard Ave., Newington, 06111
Dolan, Michael J., Dir. of Interreligious Affairs, 2819 Whitney Ave., Hamden, 06518-2598. Tel: 203-248-0141
Donahue, Aidan N., Dir. of Formation for the Permanent Diaconate, 70 Gulf St., Milford, 06460. Tel: 203-878-3571
Gatzak, John P., Exec. Dir., Office of Radio/Television, 15 Peach Orchard Rd., Prospect, 06712-1052
Kinnane, James F., J.C.L., Adjutant Judicial Vicar, 467 Bloomfield Ave., Bloomfield, 06002. Tel: 860-242-5573
Lerner, Ryan M., Chancellor & Sec. to the Archbishop, 134 Farmington Ave., 06105-3784. Tel: 860-541-6491
Whyte, Michael G., Dir., Continuing Formation of Priests, 265 Stratton Brook Rd., P.O. Box 184, West Simsbury, 06092. Tel: 860-658-1642.

On Duty Outside the Archdiocese:
Rev. Msgr.—
Sokolowski, Robert S., Catholic University of America, School of Philosophy, Washington, DC 20064
Revs.—
Leavitt, Robert F., S.S., St. Mary Seminary, 5400 Roland Ave., Baltimore, MD 21210
McKearney, James L., S.S., St. Patrick Seminary, 320 Middlefield Rd., Menlo Park, CA 94025
Thayer, David D., S.S., Theological College of Catholic University of America, 401 Michigan Ave., N.E., Washington, DC 20064.

Medical Leave:
Revs.—
DeVito, Michael C.
Forsyth, Kevin J.
Mitchell, Thomas R.
Vincenzo, Dennis J.
Williams, John L.

Leave of Absence:
Revs.—
Echavarria, Carlos Andres
Garcia, Ramon Israel
Gingras, Dennis C.
Gotta, Paul A.

Unassigned:
Rev.—
Hanley, Dennis P.

Retired:
Rev. Msgrs.—
Bevins, John J., (Retired), 184 Monroe Ave., Waterbury, 06705
Coleman, James G., (Retired), 133 Piping Rock Rd., Waterbury, 06706
Conte, John P., (Retired), 16 First St., West Haven, 06516
Schmitz, Gerard G., (Retired), 31 C Harbour Village, Branford, 06405
Walker, David M., (Retired), 29 Acorn Rd., Branford, 06488
Revs.—
Altermatt, Gregory M., (Retired)
Archambault, James H., (Retired), 2003 49th St. W., Bradenton, FL 34209
Balchunas, Henry A., (Retired), 11 Sunrise Ave., Niantic, 06357
Baldyga, William L., (Retired), Sacred Heart Rectory, 158 Broad St., New Britain, 06053
Berberich, Thomas E., (Retired), Pilgrim Manor, Rm. 30, Covenant Village, 12 Missionary Rd., Cromwell, 06406-6669
Birmingham, Robert F., (Retired), 9220 Mojave Pl., New Port Richey, FL 34655
Blackall, Randall L., D.Min., (Retired), St. Mary Home, 2021 Albany Ave., West Hartford, 06107
Bock, Lawrence R., (Retired), Holy Spirit Rectory, 183 Church St., Newington, 06111
Bonadies, Kenneth P., (Retired), 5402 Glenn Ivy Place, Pinellas Park, FL 33782
Borino, David J., (Retired), 100 York St., Apt. 5R, New Haven, 06511-8612
Bruno, Anthony J., (Retired), P.O. Box C, Somersville, 06072
Burbank, Robert J., (Retired), 27 Kelsey Rd., Clinton, 06413
Callahan, Francis X., (Retired), St. Agnes Rectory, 400 Merwin Ave., Milford, 06460
Cavagnuolo, Salvatore F., (Retired), 301 Songbird Ave., Southington, 06489
Cesaro, Nicholas J., (Retired), 467 Bloomfield Ave., Bloomfield, 06002
Cockayne, John E., (Retired), P.O. Box 716, Southington, 06489
Cody, Henry P., (Retired), 31 Quinn St., Naugatuck, 06670
Colicchio, Ralph M., (Retired), 126 Southwick Ct., Cheshire, 06410
Connaghan, Daniel H., (Retired)
Cooney, John M., (Retired), 69 Old South Rd., P.O. Box 701, Litchfield, 06759
Cretella, Joseph J., (Retired), 217 Trailing Creek Rd., Madison, AL 35757
Daly, John J., (Retired), 41 Kenton St., Kensington, 06037
DeCarolis, Joseph R., (Retired), St. Mary Home, 2021 Albany Ave., West Hartford, 06117
DeCarolis, Vito C., (Retired), 124 Farrell Rd., Waterbury, 06706
DuPont, Arthur J., (Retired), 467 Bloomfield Ave., Bloomfield, 06002
Fador, Francis R., (Retired), 1352 Torringford West St., Torrington, 06790
Ferraro, Ronald A., (Retired), 180 Scott Rd., Waterbury, 06705
Frascadore, Henry C., (Retired), Bushnell Towers, 1 Gold St., Apt. 4C, 06103. Tel: 860-904-3301
Grant, Robert J., (Retired), 467 Bloomfield Ave., Bloomfield, 06002
Hagearty, Charles B., (Retired), 39 Carriage Dr., Naugatuck, 06770. Tel: 203-592-7749
Halovatch, Paul J., (Retired), 25 Hamden Hills Rd., Unit 52, Hamden, 06518
Heffernan, Robert G., (Retired), 25 Hamden Hill Dr., Unit 13, Hamden, 06518
Jaksina, Edward S., (Retired), 25 Nash St., New Britain, 06053
Johnson, Francis P., (Retired), 30 Echo Ln., West Hartford, 06107-3698
Kaminsky, Joseph T., (Retired), 4930 Coquina Crossing Dr., Elkton, FL 32033
Karwowski, Edmund K., (Retired), 12 N. Elm St., Wallingford, 06492
Keane, John J., (Retired), 205 Hazard Ave., Enfield, 06082
Kenefick, Paul F., (Retired), 21 Windy Hill Dr., South Windsor, 06074
Killeen, William J., (Retired), 185 Ridge Rd., Hamden, 06517-3511
Kinnane, James R., (Retired), Holy Spirit Rectory, 183 Church St., Newington, 06111
Krugel, Stephen A., (Retired), 456 Plains Rd., Milford, 06461
Krupnik, Marion I., (Retired), St. Lucian's Residence, 532 Burritt St., New Britain, 06053-3699
Kurnath, Joseph G.M., (Retired), P.O. Box 12, Lakeville, 06039
Kvedas, Leonard J., Holy Rosary Rectory, 10 Father Salemi Dr., Ansonia, 06401
Laliberte, George G., (Retired), 467 Bloomfield Ave., Bloomfield, 06002

Langlois, Frederick M., (Retired), 5631 Longford Ter. #205, Fitchburg, WI 53711
LaPlante, Roland M., (Retired), 467 Bloomfield Ave., Bloomfield, 06002-2999
Lauretti, George F., (Retired), 6 Father Crudele Dr., Bristol, 06010
Leary, James F., (Retired), Ardon Courts of Farmington, 45 South Rd., Farmington, 06032
Lewandowski, David J., (Retired), 24 Woodhaven Rd., Bristol, 06010
Looney, Joseph E., (Retired), Archbishop Daniel A. Cronin Res., Bloomfield, 06002
MacDonald, Hugh J., (Retired), Church of the Resurrection Rectory, 115 Pond Hill Rd., Wallingford, 06492
Malave, Will-Roger, (Retired), 43 Norton St., Torrington, 06790
Mangiafico, Paul J., (Retired), 8408 Annwood Rd., Largo, FL 33777-2026
Maroney, Maurice J., (Retired), 850 Viscount Dr., Apt. 24, Milford, 06460
Masters, Gerard G., (Retired), 506 New Rd., Northfield, 08225
McHugh, John P., (Retired), 555 Asylum Ave.
Meehan, Timothy A., (Retired), in res., St. Bernadette, New Haven
Montgomery, Joseph T., (Retired), 30 Royal Oak Rd., New Britain, 06053
Morrison, Douglas A., (Retired), 24 Courthouse Sq., Apt. 805, Rockville, MD 20850
Moskus, John T., (Retired), 42 Maplewood Ave., Storrs, 06268
Nadolny, Edmund S., (Retired), 467 Bloomfield Ave., Bloomfield, 06002
Neumann, Richard J., (Retired), 43 Tinsmith Crossing, Wethersfield, 06109
Nock, James J., (Retired), 1 Lexington St., Wethersfield, 06109
O'Brien, Edmund M., (Retired), 467 Bloomfield Ave., Bloomfield, 06002
O'Keefe, William F., (Retired), St. Joseph Residence, 1365 Enfield St., Enfield, 06082
O'Rourke, Thomas J., (Retired), 2464 Australia Way E, Apt. 78, Clearwater, FL 33763
Padelli, Emilio P., (Retired), 43 Old Farm Rd., Somers, 06071
Pahl, John E., (Retired), 54 Hardwick Rd., Bristol
Pettit, Joseph H., (Retired), 180 Scott Rd., Waterbury, 06705
Pilon, James F., (Retired), 331 Songbird Ln., Southington, 06489
Pogorzelski, Andrzej, Sts. Cyril and Methodius Rectory, 55 Charter Oak Ave., 06106
Rosa, Salvatore J., (Retired), 467 Bloomfield Ave., Bloomfield, 06002
Sharkey, Philip J., (Retired), 512 A Kettletown Rd., Southbury, 06488
Sheridan, Philip A., (Retired), 20 Carmel Ridge Estates, Trumbull, 06611-2072
Smolenski, Stanley, (Retired), 300C Ashton Ave., Kingstree, SC 29556
Sobiecki, Peter S., (Retired), 49 Hillhurst Ave., New Britain, 06053
Sokolowski, William R., (Retired), P.O. Box 283, Terryville, 06786
Spodnik, A. Leo, (Retired), St. Lucian Home, 532 Burritt St., New Britain, 06053
St. Martin, Robert J., (Retired), P.O. Box 193, Hebron, 06248
Sullivan, Daniel James, (Retired), 3 Whiting Ct., Northford, 06472
Sullivan, Daniel Jeremiah, (Retired), 194 Webster Hill Blvd., West Hartford, 06107
Sullivan, John P., (Retired), 194 Webster Hill Blvd., West Hartford, 06107
Taberski, Richard M., (Retired), 41 Torrington Heights Rd., Torrington, 06790
Traxl, William L., (Retired), 1177 Hebron Ave., Glastonbury, 06033
Valla, Dominic J., (Retired), 49B Heritage Village, Southbury, 06405
Vujs, Joseph E., (Retired), 14 Hawley St., Newington, 06111
Wrenn, Lawrence G., (Retired), 8941 Veranda Way, #522, Sarasota, FL 34238-3372.

Permanent Deacons:
Abdalla, John, (Senior Status)
Albert, Roger R., (Senior Status)
Arena, James V., St. Aloysius, Plantsville
Armstrong, Brian, St. Matthew, Forestville
Baldwin, Alan C., (Inactive)
Bandeira, Francis X., (Senior Status)
Bangs, Kenneth, St. Patrick, Collinsvile
Barry, Robert J., St. Patrick, Farmington
Bartlett, William H., St. Edmund Campion, East Hartford
Beecher, Stephen M. Sr., (Senior Status)
Bernd, Robert E., (Senior Status)
Berube, Robert A., (Senior Status)
Bevvino, Frank J., Our Lady of Victory & St. John Vianney, West Haven
Biamonte, Ronald, M.A., Mary Gate of Heaven, Windsor Locks
Bicknell, Ronnie, St. Elizabeth of the Trinity, North Haven
Bilbraut, Victor C., Our Lady of Sorrows, Hartford
Bilodeau, Steven, St. Elizabeth of the Trinity, North Haven
Blair, Robert N., (Senior Status)
Blanchette, James, Annunciation, Newington
Bossidy, John P., (Senior Status)
Boucher, Richard F., (Senior Status), St. Bernard, Enfield
Breen, Thomas F. III
Cabeen, Thomas, St. Raphael, Milford
Camerota, Daniel A., (Senior Status), St. John the Evangelist, Watertown
Cardona, Raul, St. Rose of Lima, Meriden
Carrero, Adolfo G., (Senior Status)
Carter, Robert, St. Michael the Archangel, Derby
Cassella, Michael E., Christ the King, Wethersfield
Clifford, Thomas J., St. Francis of Assisi, Naugatuck
Colella, Charles G., Mary Mother of the Church, Waterbury
Conard, Leo B. III, St. Maximilian Kolbe, Thomaston
Cooke, Joseph J., (Senior Status)
Coppola, Angelo J., St. Thomas, Southington
Corraro, Dominic, Holy Trinity, Wallingford
Coyne, Joseph F., (Senior Status)
Croce, Emil P., St. Basil the Great, Wolcott
Croll, Calvin S., (Senior Status)
Culhane, Neil, Waterbury Hospital, Waterbury
Cunniff, Charles E. Jr., (Senior Status)
Delehanty, Thomas F., (Senior Status)
Diorio, Nicholas J., (Senior Status)
DiRienzo, Mario, (Senior Status)
Dlugokinski, Jose L., (Senior Status)
DosSantos, Kenneth, St. Maximilian Kolbe, Thomaston
Doyle, Henry, (Senior Status), St. Gabriel, Milford
Driscoll, Frank M., (Senior Status)
Dungan, Roy C., (Senior Status)
Dziatko, William, St. Paul/St. Augustine, Glastonbury/South Glastonbury
Elder, William A., (Senior Status)
English, Seth M., (Senior Status)
Ewaskie, Kenneth E., (Medical Leave)
Farrell, William A., (Senior Status), St. Patrick, Farmington
Ferguson, Dennis R., St. Timothy, West Hartford; Permanent Deacon for Deaf Apostolate
Florio, Louis J., (Senior Status)
Fracasso, Robert G., (Senior Status)
Frederick, George W., Our Lady Queen of Angels, Meriden
Fugere, Raymond J. Jr., (Senior Status), St. Gianna (Beretta Molla), West Hartford
Fusco, Louis P., (Senior Status)
Fusco, Salvatore F., Mary our Queen, Plantsville
Genovese, Nicholas A., Precious Blood, Milford
Germain, Alan A., St. James, Manchester
Giard, Edward J., St. Junipero Serra, South Windsor
Gilles, William J., St. Teresa of Calcutta, Manchester
Gonzalez, Emilio, Christ the Bread of Life, Hamden
Gordon, Robert D., St. John the Evangelist, Watertown
Gosselin, Philip, St. Edmund Campion, East Hartford
Griffin, Wayne F., St. Francis of Assisi, New Britain
Gurr, Ronald B., Christ the Bread of Life, Hamden
Guzauckas, Joseph, (Senior Status)
Guzzardi, Carmelo A., (Senior Status), St. Paul, Kensington
Haines, Michael D., Junipero Serra, South Windsor
Hajjar, George D., (Senior Status)
Hamel, Richard H., St. John the Great, Torrington
Hart, John L., (Senior Status)
Healy, Timothy E., St. Ann, Avon
Hernandez, Carmelo, St. Augustine, Hartford
Hickey, James E. Jr., (Senior Status)
Hilliard, Robert J., (Senior Status)
Hoffman, Harold J. Jr., Precious Blood, Milford
Hyde, Peter R., St. John the Great, Torrington
Iadarola, Paul P., St. Bridget of Sweden, Cheshire
Iassogna, Nicholas J. Jr., (Senior Status)
Johnson, Robert C., Our Lady Queen of the Apostles, Derby
Kane, Joseph K., Divine Providence, New Britain
Kensah, Edward, North American Martyrs, East Hartford
Kieda, Rene J., (Senior Status)
Krasnicki, Frank J., (Senior Status)
Kulas, Michael J., (Senior Status)
Kulas, Paul J., St. Dominic, Southington
Lambert, Robert E., (Senior Status)
LaRocque, Leo R., St. James, Manchester
Lauer, Paul B., (Senior Status)
LeBlanc, Gaspard D., (Senior Status)
Lembo, Victor M., St. Michael, Beacon Falls
Lickwar, R. Carl, (Senior Status), St. Damien of Molokai, Windsor
Lopez, Alexander Jr., All Saints, Waterbury
Lopez, Edwin, All Saints, Waterbury
Lovelace, William J., (Senior Status)
Lovett, John J., (Senior Status), St. Francis de Sales, Bristol
Lynch, Michael, Holy Rosary, Ansonia
Macaluso, Robert J., St. John Bosco, Branford
Macchio, Dean A., Our Lady of Victory, West Haven
Maffeo, John R., (Senior Status), St. Louis de Montfort, Litchfield
Magnuson, Robert A., (Out of Archdiocese)
Makara, John W., (Leave of Absence)
Mancini, Edward J., (Senior Status), (Out of Archdiocese)
Marcarelli, Julius R., (Senior Status)
Marenna, Joseph P., St. Ambrose, North Branford
Maturana, Julio C., North American Martyrs, East Hartford
Mazurek, Joseph S., Holy Trinity, Wallingford
McCarroll, George E., (Leave of Absence)
McCluskey, James P., St. Matthew, Forestville
McCormack, James J., St. Gianna (Beretta Molla)
McGivney, Raymond J. Jr., (Inactive)
McGrath, William M., (Senior Status)
McKaig, John W., St. John Fisher, Marlborough
Michaele, Adam J., St. Margaret, Madison
Miller, Arthur L., St. Mary, Simsbury; Dir. Campus Min., Capital Community College
Miller, Roland G., (Senior Status)
Mitchell, Victor C. Jr., St. John the Evangelist, Watertown
Moran, P. Terrence, Campus Ministry, Southern CT University, New Haven
Mordecai, John, Assumption, Woodbridge
Moriello, Angelo, All Saints, Waterbury
Motto, Vincent J., St. Jeanne Jugan, Enfield
Muszynski, Jacek, Sacred Heart, New Britain
Mylott, John J., (Senior Status)
Nebiolo, Eugene P., (Senior Status)
Newbery, Robert D., (Senior Status)
Nolan, Terence M., (Leave of Absence)
Nwankwo, Anthony, Sacred Heart, Bloomfield
O'Connor, Martin J., St. Mary, New Haven
O'Donovan, John C., (Senior Status)
O'Toole, Michael J., (Senior Status)
Ortiz, Edwin, Maria Reina de la Paz, Hartford
Ossa, Tullio V., Our Lady of Guadalupe, New Haven
Pagliaro, Ernest H. Jr., Our Lady of Mt. Carmel, Waterbury
Pallotti, Robert M., St. Peter Claver, West Hartford
Pantalena, Edward J., (Senior Status), Christ the King, Wethersfield
Papillo, James F., Basilica of the Immaculate Conception, Waterbury
Parkinson, William H., St. Pio of Pietrelcina, East Haven
Perez, Valentin, Our Lady of Sorrows, Hartford
Pettinico, George M., (Senior Status)
Phaneuf, Eugene E., (Senior Status)
Piotrowski, Stanley J. Jr., St. Gregory the Great, Bristol
Prete, Paul V., (Senior Status)
Ramos, Edmund J., (Senior Status)
Regan, Joseph M. Jr., (Senior Status)
Renker, Richard W., (Senior Status), Holy Rosary, Ansonia; St. Anthony, Ansonia
Rescildo, Ralph J., St. Teresa, Woodbury
Reynolds, David, Our Lady of Hope, New Hartford
Richter, Neil B., (Senior Status), St. Joseph, Bristol
Riotte, Eugene C., (Senior Status), Most Holy Trinity, Wallingford
Rivera, Pedro L., (Senior Status)
Robert, Paul, St. Raymond of Penafort, Enfield
Robles, José Alberto, Our Lady Queen of Angels, Meriden; Chap., Cheshire Correctional Institute
Rosado, Ramon A., St. Justin-St. Michael, Hartford; Chap., Osborn Institution
Rosello, Modesto A., (Senior Status), Mary Mother of the Church, Waterbury
Roy, Reginald, (Senior Status)
Rubitz, Michael, Holy Cross, New Britain
Ryzewski, Joseph R., Divine Mercy, Hamden
Sabo, Paul E., (Senior Status)
Sandford, Wayne E., St. Pio of Pietrelcina, East Haven
Santos, Richard D., Sacred Heart, Bloomfield
Sartor, George G., St. Raphael, Milford
Savarese, Stephen L., St. John of the Cross, Middlebury
Sayles, William J., Christ the Redeemer, Milford
Scanlon, Thomas P., (Senior Status)
Scrivani, Ernest, T.O.C., St. Elizabeth of the Trinity, North Haven
Sennett, Richard M., (Senior Status)
Shelto, Michael A., (Senior Status)
Shiels, James H., Annunciation, Newington
Singer, Norman H., (Senior Status)

Smith, Donald H. Jr., Our Lady Queen of Angels, Meriden
Solli, Anthony P., Our Lady of Mount Carmel, Hamden
St. Jean, Stephen E., (Inactive)
Stanley, James H., (Senior Status)
Stevens, Mark J., St. Blaise, Waterbury
Stolfi, Domenic N., (Senior Status)
Streib, George H., (Senior Status)
Sullivan, Joseph D., Holy Infant, Orange
Sutak, Thomas S., St. Mary, Unionville
Sutherland, Jeffrey B., St. Ann, Avon
Sweeney, John M., (Leave of Absence)
Szumowski, Henry J., St. Dunstan, Glastonbury; Chap., MacDougall-Walker, Osborn, & Northern Correctional Institutions
Tanguay, James F., Annunciation, Newington
Tartaris, Robert P., (Senior Status)
Taylor, James P., (Senior Status)
Taylor, Norris, Cathedral of St. Joseph, Hartford
Thermer, C. Eric, St. Timothy, West Hartford
Thompson, Bruce R., (Senior Status)
Thorney, Vincent M., (Senior Status)
Torres, Michael, Chap. and Catholic Liasion, Enfield Correctional Institution; St. Martha, Enfield
Twerago, John P., (Senior Status)
Vazquez, Julio, (Senior Status)
Vecca, Carl M., Mary Mother of the Church, Waterbury
Vigliotta, Crescenzo, St. Jeanne Jugan, Enfield
Violette, Carroll, (Inactive)
Wallin, Robert F., All Saints, Waterbury
Walsh, Michael J., St. John of the Cross, Middlebury
Ward, Michael J., St. Josephine Bakhita, Rocky Hill
Weaver, Stephen L., Sts. Isidore and Maria, Glastonbury
Wilber, Richard, St. Bridget of Sweden, Cheshire
Wilcox, William H., (Senior Status)
Wisniewski, Richard J., St. Stanislaus, Bristol
Yatcko, Stephen, Our Lady of Mount Carmel, Hamden
Yergeau, Laurent, Assumption, Ansonia.

INSTITUTIONS LOCATED IN DIOCESE

[A] SEMINARIES, ARCHDIOCESAN

BLOOMFIELD. *St. Thomas Seminary*, 467 Bloomfield Ave., Bloomfield, 06002-2999. Tel: 860-242-5573; Fax: 860-242-4886; Email: info@stseminary.org; Web: stseminary.org. Sr. Mary Grace Walsh, A.S.C.J., Ph.D., Pres.; Steven Rugens, Admin.; Revs. Nicholas J. Cesaro, In Res., (Retired); Kevin J. Gray, In Res.; George G. Laliberte, In Res., (Retired); Roland M. LaPlante, In Res., (Retired); Joseph E. Looney, In Res., (Retired); Most Rev. Christie A. Macaluso, D.D., V.G., In Res.; Revs. Edmund S. Nadolny, In Res., (Retired); Salvatore J. Rosa, In Res., (Retired); Most Rev. Peter A. Rosazza, D.D., In Res.

[B] SEMINARIES, RELIGIOUS OR SCHOLASTICATES

CHESHIRE. *Novitiate of the Legion of Christ*, 475 Oak Ave., Cheshire, 06410. Tel: 203-271-0805; Fax: 203-271-3845; Email: cheshire@legionaries.org; Web: www.facebook.com/lccheshire. Revs. Kevin Meehan, L.C., Rector; John Budke, L.C., Vice Rector; Joseph Brickner, L.C., Novice Instructor; Christopher O'Connor, L.C., Prof.; Tarsicio Samaniego, L.C.; Simon Devereux, L.C.; Andrew La Budde, L.C. Lay Teachers 9; Priests 13; Religious 90; Students 21; Religious Teachers 5; Clergy / Religious Teachers 13.

Studies: Revs. Andreas Kramarz, L.C., Dean Studies; Walter Schu, L.C., Prof.; Raymond Cosgrave, L.C.; John Curran, L.C.; John Sweeney, L.C.; Kermit Syren, L.C.

[C] COLLEGES AND UNIVERSITIES

HAMDEN. *Mt. Sacred Heart College*, 295 Benham St., Hamden, 06514-2801. Tel: 203-248-4225; Fax: 203-230-8341; Email: secretary@ascjus.org. Sisters Ritamary Schulz, A.S.C.J., Contact Person; Sharon Kalert, A.S.C.J., Sec. Chartered by the State of Connecticut for Sisters of Community of Apostles of the Sacred Heart of Jesus.
Corporation Name: Apostles of the Sacred Heart of Jesus, Incorporated.

CHESHIRE. *Legion of Christ College, Inc.*, 475 Oak Ave., Cheshire, 06410. Tel: 203-271-0805; Fax: 203-271-3845; Email: eramirez@arcol.org; Web: www.lccollege.org. Rev. Frank Formolo, L.C., Contact Person. Brothers 73; Lay Teachers 9; Priests 13; Students 90; Clergy / Religious Teachers 13.

NEW HAVEN. *Albertus Magnus College* (1925) 700 Prospect St., New Haven, 06511-1189. Tel: 800-578-9160; Fax: 203-773-5248; Email: admissions@albertus.edu; Web: www.albertus.edu. Marc Camille, Pres.; Dr. Sean O'Connell, Vice Pres. Academic Affairs; William Guerrero, Vice Pres., Fin., & Treas.; Melissa DeLucia, Registrar; Andrew Foster, Vice Pres., Student Svcs.; Anne Leeny-Panagrossi, Librarian. Dominican Sisters (Dominican Sisters of Peace, Columbus, OH). Clergy 7; Lay Teachers 45; Sisters 1; Students 1,650.

WEST HARTFORD. *University of Saint Joseph* (1932) 1678 Asylum Ave., West Hartford, 06117. Tel: 860-232-4571; Fax: 860-233-5695; Email: admissions@usj.edu; Web: www.usj.edu. Rhona Free, Ph.D., Pres.; Michelle Kalis, Ph.D., Provost; Marjorie Pinney, Vice Pres. Inst. Advancement; Shawn Harrington, Senior Vice Pres., Finance & Strategy; Sharon Brewer, Registrar. Sisters of Mercy.Co-Ed Undergraduate & Graduate School.; Chartered by the State of Connecticut. Lay Teachers 129; Priests 2; Sisters 3; Students 2,463; Undergraduates Men 28; Undergraduates Women 907; Graduates Coed 2,117; School for Young Children 112; Gengras Center for Exceptional Children 112; Clergy / Religious Teachers 4.

[D] HIGH SCHOOLS, ARCHDIOCESAN

BRISTOL. *St. Paul Catholic High School*, 1001 Stafford Ave., Bristol, 06010-3894. Tel: 860-584-0911; Fax: 860-585-8815; Email: cdupont@spchs.com; Web: www.spchs.com. Mr. Cary Dupont, Pres. & Chief Admin.; James Cooper, Dean, Academic Life; Albert Wallace, Dean, Student Life; Revs. Gary F. Simeone, Chap.; Hector G. Rangel, Chap. Faculty 39; Lay Teachers 38; Sisters 1; Students 450.

MANCHESTER. *East Catholic High School*, 115 New State Rd., Manchester, 06042-1898. Tel: 860-649-5336; Fax: 860-649-7191; Email: hintonr@echs.com; Web: ECHS.com. Mr. Ryan Hinton, Prin.; Susan Perillo, Vice Prin.; Thomas Maynard, Headmaster; Constance Jurczak, Library/Media Dir. Lay Teachers 50; Sisters of Notre Dame de Namur 2; Students 650; Clergy / Religious Teachers 3.

WATERBURY. *Sacred Heart High School*, 142 S. Elm St., Waterbury, 06706. Tel: 203-753-1605; Fax: 203-597-1686; Email: aazzara@sacredhearthighschool.org; Email: eregan@sacredhearthighschool.org; Web: sacredhearthighschool.org. Anthony R. Azzara, Prin.; Mrs. Eileen Regan, Pres. & Chief Admin.; Debora Taylor, Dir. Student Activities; Jane Scully-Parshall, Librarian; Rev. Elkin Mauricio Galvis, Chap. Lay Teachers 28; Priests 1; Students 354.

WEST HARTFORD. *Northwest Catholic High School* (1961) 29 Wampanoag Dr., West Hartford, 06117-1299. Tel: 860-236-4221; Fax: 860-586-0911; Email: ccashman@nwcath.org; Web: www.northwestcatholic.org. Christian J. Cashman, Pres.; Mr. Christopher Stuck, Dean; Mrs. Jennifer Montoney, Dean. Lay Teachers 55; Students 516; Clergy / Religious Teachers 2.

[E] HIGH SCHOOLS, PRIVATE

HAMDEN. *Sacred Heart Academy*, 265 Benham St., Hamden, 06514-2833. Tel: 203-288-2309; Fax: 203-230-9680; Email: soneill@sacredhearthamden.org; Web: www.sacredhearthamden.org. Sisters Sheila O'Neill, A.S.C.J., Pres. & Contact; Kathleen Mary Coonan, A.S.C.J., Prin.; Maureen Hayes, Librarian. Apostles of the Sacred Heart of Jesus. Lay Teachers 40; Sisters 7; Students 490.

MILFORD. *Academy of Our Lady of Mercy*, Lauralton Hall, 200 High St., Milford, 06460-3262. Tel: 203-877-2786; Fax: 203-876-9760; Email: nbenson@lauraltonhall.org; Web: www.lauraltonhall.org. Elizabeth Miller, Pres.; Theresa Lawler, Librarian; Nicole Benson, Contact Person. Sisters of Mercy of the Americas, N.E. Community Lay Teachers 46; Students 456.

NEW MILFORD. *Canterbury School*, 101 Aspetuck Ave., New Milford, 06776-1739. Tel: 860-210-3800; Fax: 860-350-4425; Email: admissions@cbury.org; Web: www.cbury.org. Rachel E. Stone, Head of School; Ellen O'Meara, Librarian. Coed Boarding & Day Students Lay Teachers 85; Priests 1; Students 320; Clergy / Religious Teachers 1.

WATERBURY. *Holy Cross High School* (1968) 587 Oronoke Rd., Waterbury, 06708. Tel: 203-757-9248 ; Fax: 203-757-3423; Email: mleger@holycrosshs-ct.com; Web: HolyCrosshs-ct.com. Mrs. Margaret Leger, Prin.; Louis Howe, Dir. Campus Min.; Roseanne Billias, Library & Media. Brothers of the Congregation of Holy Cross, conducted in cooperation with Sisters of the Congregation of Notre Dame. Lay Teachers 47; Sisters 1; Students 489.

WEST HAVEN. *Notre Dame High School*, 1 Notre Dame Way, West Haven, 06516-2499. Tel: 203-933-1673; Fax: 203-933-2474; Email: info@notredamehs.com; Web: www.notredamehs.com. Mr. Robert Curis, Pres.; Mrs. Kathleen Wielk, Vice Pres. for Advancement; Mr. Joseph Ramirez, Vice Pres. for Student Success; Katie Saxon, Vice Pres. for Academics; Bro. George C. Schmitz, C.S.C., Dir. of Planned Giving
Legal Title: Congregation of Holy Cross Brothers 1; Lay Teachers 45; Students 550; Clergy / Religious Teachers 1.

Notre Dame Loyalty & Endowment Fund, Inc., One Notre Dame Way, West Haven, 06516. Tel: 203-933-1673; Fax: 203-933-2474; Email: colt@notredamehs.com. Mr. Robert Curis, Pres.

[F] DAY CARE CENTER

HAMDEN. *Apostles of the Sacred Heart Clelian Center, Inc.* (1988) 261 Benham St., Hamden, 06514-2898. Tel: 203-288-4151; Fax: 203-288-0551; Email: info@cleliancenter.org; Web: www.cleliancenter.org. Mrs. Patricia Scafariello, Dir. A day health care facility for the elderly (interdenominational).
Legal Title: Apostles of the Sacred Heart of Jesus Capacity 70; Tot Asst. Annually 90; Total Staff 15; Total Assisted 60.

Sacred Heart Manor Nursery and Kindergarten, 261 Benham St., Hamden, 06514. Tel: 203-230-4889; Email: masharron@ascjus.org. Sr. Mary Anne Sharron, A.S.C.J., Dir. & Contact. Lay Teachers 5; Religious 1; Students 55; Apostles of the Sacred Heart of Jesus 1; Total Assisted 55.

[G] GENERAL HOSPITALS

HARTFORD. *Saint Francis Hospital and Medical Center*, 114 Woodland St., 06105-1299. Tel: 860-714-4000; Fax: 860-714-8030; Email: jrodis@stfranciscare.org; Web: www.stfranciscare.com. John Rodis, M.D., Pres.; Suzanne Nolan, Dir. Pastoral Care & Chap.; Suzanne Carnes, Chap.; Rev. Mark Bonsignore, Chap.; Vincent Gierer, Chap.; Fiona Phelan, Media Rels. Mgr.; Elizabeth Price, Supvr. Clinical Pastoral Ed.; Rev. Kevin J. Gray, Chap. Bassinets 65; Bed Capacity 617; Tot Asst. Annually 330,149; Total Staff 4,132; Licensed Beds 617; Outpatient Visits 297,814; Inpatient Visits 32,335; Observation 6,414. In Res. Rev. Elias Menuba, Chap.

The Women's Auxiliary of Saint Francis Hospital and Medical Center, Tel: 860-714-4558; Fax: 860-714-7809. Judith Levi, Pres.

Asylum Hill Family Medicine Center, Inc., Tel: 860-714-4212; Fax: 860-714-8079; Web: stfranciscare.org.

Saint Francis Care, Inc., 114 Woodland St., 06105. Tel: 860-714-4000; Email: fphelan@stfranciscare.org. Fiona Phelan, Contact Person. Bed Capacity 617; Tot Asst. Annually 330,149; Total Staff 4,312.

Saint Francis Medical Group, Inc., 114 Woodland St., 06105. Tel: 860-714-4000; Email: fphelan@stfranciscare.org. Fiona Phelan, Contact Person.

Saint Francis Emergency Medical Group, Inc., 114 Woodland St., 06105. Tel: 860-714-4000; Email: fphelan@stfranciscare.org. Fiona Phelan, Contact Person.

Saint Francis Hospital and Medical Center Foundation, Inc., 95 Woodland St., 06105-1299. Tel: 860-714-4900; Fax: 860-714-8069; Email: fphelan@stfranciscare.org; Web: stfranciscare.org. Lynn Rossini, Vice PRes., Chief Devel. Officer.

Mount Sinai Rehabilitation Hospital, Inc., 490 Blue Hills Ave., 06112. Tel: 860-714-3500; Fax: 860-714-8550; Email: lrossini@stfranciscare.org; Web: stfranciscare.org. Lynn Rossini, Contact Person. Bed Capacity 200; Tot Asst. Annually 10,000; Total Staff 4,300.

NEW HAVEN. *Saint Regis Health Center, Inc.* dba Sister Anne Virginia Grimes Health Center, 1354 Chapel St., New Haven, 06511. Tel: 203-867-8300; Fax: 203-867-8345; Email: jtarutis@srhs.org; Web: www.srhs.org. John Tarutis, Exec. Dir.; Donna Wade, Dir., Nursing; Lisa Irish, Chap. 122-bed skilled nursing facility.; Religious Community: Srs. of Charity of St. Elizabeth Bed Capacity 122; Tot Asst. Annually 800; Total Staff 152.

WATERBURY. *Saint Mary's Hospital*, 56 Franklin St., Waterbury, 06706-1200. Tel: 203-709-6000; Fax: 203-709-3238; Email: community@stmh.org; Web: stmh.org. Dr. Steven Schneider, Pres.; Rev. Joseph Pullikattil, Chap.; Sr. Dolores Lahr, C.S.J., Dir., Mission Integration. Catholic Health MinistriesSaint Mary's Hospital Foundation, Inc., (Nonprofit corporations for the exclusive benefit of Saint Mary's Hospital). Bassinets 32; Bed Capacity 202; Patients Asst Anual. 230,000; Sisters 1; Tot

Asst. Annually 230,000; Total Staff 2,000; Licensed 347; Neonatal ICU 8.

Saint Mary's Hospital Foundation, Inc., 56 Franklin St., Waterbury, 06706. Tel: 203-709-6390 ; Fax: 203-709-3272; Email: community@stmh.org. Carrie McMahon, Exec. Dir.

[H] SPECIAL HOSPITALS

HARTFORD. **Malta House of Care, Inc.*, 19 Woodland St., Ste. 21, 06105. Tel: 860-725-0171; Fax: 860-725-0191; Email: tcaputomd@maltahouseofcare.org; Web: www.maltahouseofcare.org. Robert Voight, Chm.; Luis Diez-Morales, M.D., Board Pres.; Pauline Olsen, M.D., Clinical Supvr. To deliver charitable primary and/or preventative medical health care to the needy uninsured of the Greater Hartford region. Total Staff 6; Total Assisted 4,500.

[I] HOMES FOR AGED

ENFIELD. *The Home for the Aged of the Little Sisters of the Poor* (1839) Incorporated Operating as St. Joseph's Residence 1365 Enfield St., Enfield, 06082-4925. Tel: 860-741-0791; Fax: 860-265-1891; Email: enmothersuperior@littlesistersofthepoor.org. Sr. Genevieve Nugent, L.S.P., Supr. & Contact; Dolores D'Agostino, Contact Person; Rev. Richard Testa, In Res. Bed Capacity 83; Lay Staff 103; Residents 83; Little Sisters of the Poor 10; Tot Asst. Annually 100.

NEW BRITAIN. *St. Lucian's Residence, Inc.*, 532 Burritt St., New Britain, 06053-3699. Tel: 860-223-2123; Fax: 860-612-0321; Email: stlucians@comcast.net. Mother Mary Jennifer Carroll, D.M., Admin. & Contact; Rev. Joseph Tran, Chap., Immaculate Conception Friary. Daughters of Mary of the Immaculate Conception. Residents 42; Tot Asst. Annually 42; Total Staff 22.

Monsignor Bojnowski Manor, Inc. (1974) 50 Pulaski St., New Britain, 06053. Tel: 860-229-0336; Fax: 860-229-3252; Email: mjulmisse@mbmanor.org. Martin Julmisse, Dir. Owned and operated by the Daughters of Mary of the Immaculate Conception. Skilled Nursing Beds 60; Total Staff 85.

WEST HARTFORD. *Saint Mary Home*, 2021 Albany Ave., West Hartford, 06117-2796. Tel: 860-570-8300; Fax: 860-233-8849; Email: mreardon@mchc.org; Web: www.themercycommunity.org. Sr. Maureen Reardon, R.S.M., Ph.D., Senior Vice Pres.; Mrs. Patricia Russell, Dir. Nursing Svcs. Bed Capacity 256; Patients Asst Anual. 652; Total Staff 360; Sisters of Mercy 2; Sisters in Residence 38; Residents (Frances Warde Apts.) 97; Skilled Nursing 256.

Sedgwick Cedars Corporation, 27 Park Rd., West Hartford, 06119. Tel: 860-231-8678; Email: sbamcsj@gmail.com. Sr. Barbara Mullen, C.S.J., Prov. Bed Capacity 24; Tot Asst. Annually 30; Total Staff 18.

[J] HEALTH CARE CENTERS FOR AGED

WEST HARTFORD. *McAuley Center, Inc.* (1988) 275 Steele Rd., West Hartford, 06117. Tel: 860-570-8300; Fax: 860-233-8849; Email: mreardon@mchct.org. David Stevens, Exec.; Susan LeMay, Dir. Continuing care retirement community; Sisters of Mercy. 229 residential apartment units for individuals age 62 and over. Nursing care at St. Mary's Home included. Total in Residence 202.

[K] MONASTERIES AND RESIDENCES OF PRIESTS AND BROTHERS

HARTFORD. *Missionaries of La Salette Province of Mary, Mother of the Americas*, 915 Maple Ave., 06114-2330. Tel: 860-956-8870; Fax: 860-956-8849; Email: mlsadmin@aol.com; Web: www.lasalette.org. Very Rev. Rene J. Butler, M.S., Prov. Supr.; Revs. John R. Nuelle, M.S., In Res.; Raymond G. Cadran, M.S., In Res. Province of Mary, Mother of the Americas.

The Missionaries of La Salette Corporation.

MLS Religious Trust Priests 3. *Missionaries of LaSalette*, 85 New Park Ave., 06106-2184. Tel: 860-523-8275; Fax: 860-586-0754; Email: msladmin@aol.com. Revs. Salvatore D. Altavista, M.S.; Paul N. Belhumeur, M.S.; Richard R. Boucher, M.S.; Victor W. Chaupetta, M.S.; Frederick R. Flaherty, M.S.; John M. Garvey, M.S.; Clifford P. Hasler, M.S.; John F. Higgins, M.S.; Leo Holleran, M.S.; Maurice F. Linehan, M.S.; Alan B. McGuirk, M.S.; William W. Mulcair, M.S.; John A. Paninski, M.S.; Daniel J. Scott, M.S.; Thomas G. Sickler, M.S.; Donald D. Simonds, M.S.; Donald K. Thomas, M.S.; Bros. Gerald B. Buraczewski, M.S.; Jean Paul Champagne, M.S.; David J. Cook, M.S.; Mark L. Gallant, M.S.; Andre J. Hamel, M.S.; Paul Maceyka, Oblate; Leonard Melanson, M.S.; Edmund A. Normantowicz, M.S.; Robert Russell, M.S. Priests 20; Oblates 8.

Priests-Brothers of Province Serving Abroad: Revs. Joseph Bachand, M.S.; Bernard Baris, M.S.; Norman H. Butler, M.S.; Robert R. Butler, M.S.; Neil G. Jones, M.S. *Our Lady of Sorrows Rectory*, 16 Greenwood St., 06106-2109. Tel: 860-233-4424; Fax: 860-236-0149; Email: mlsadmin@aol.com; Web: www.lasalette.org. Rev. James J. Aherne, M.S. *North American La Salette Mission Center*, 915 Maple Ave., 06114-2330. Tel: 860-956-8870; Fax: 860-956-8849; Email: mlsadmin@aol.com; Web: www.lasalette.org. Rev. Thomas Vellappallil, M.S., Dir.; Mrs. Connie Evans, Sec.

St. Patrick-St. Anthony Friary (Holy Name Prov.) 285 Church St., 06103-1196. Tel: 860-756-4034; Fax: 860-249-6487; Email: info@spsact.org; Web: spsact.org. Revs. Thomas M. Gallagher, O.F.M., Pastor & Guardian; Cidouane C. Joseph, O.F.M., Parochial Vicar; John J. Leonard, O.F.M., Parochial Vicar; Bro. John Gill, O.F.M., Pastoral Assoc.; Rev. James P. Kelly, O.F.M., In Res. Franciscan Friars. Brothers 1; Priests 5.

CHESHIRE. *Legionaries of Christ*, 475 Oak Ave., Cheshire, 06410. Tel: 203-271-0805; Fax: 203-271-3845; Email: cheshire@legionaries.org; Web: www.legionofchrist.org. Revs. Andreas Kramarz, L.C., Dean; John Budke, L.C., Admin.; Joseph Brickner, L.C., Dir.; Kevin Meehan, L.C., Rector; John Bender, Asst. Supt.; John Sweeney, L.C., Registrar; Raymond Cosgrave, L.C., Spiritual Advisor/Care Svcs.; John Curran, L.C., Chap.; Eric Nielsen, Chap.; Kermit Syren, L.C., Chap.; Christopher O'Connor, L.C., Prof.; Tarsicio Samaniego, L.C., Prof.; Miguel de la Torre, Prof.

LITCHFIELD. *Montfort Missionaries*, 83 Montfort Rd., Litchfield, 06759. Tel: 860-567-8434; Fax: 860-567-9670; Email: lourdesshrinect@gmail.com; Web: www.shrinect.org. P.O. Box 667, Litchfield, 06759. Revs. Donald Lasalle, S.M.M., Supr.; William Considine, S.M.M., Asst. Priests 2.

Lourdes in Litchfield, Tel: 860-567-1041; Fax: 860-567-9670.

Lourdes Shrine Guild, Inc. Montfort House (Center for Spiritual Renewal), Tel: 860-567-8434; Fax: 860-567-9670.

KENSINGTON. *St. Paul Friary* (1985) 479 Alling St., Kensington, 06037-2100. Tel: 860-828-0331; Fax: 860-828-7620; Email: stpaul@aohct.org. Revs. Robert Schlageter, O.F.M. Conv.; Charles Jagodzinski, O.F.M.Conv., Parochial Vicar; Timothy Lyons, O.F.M.Conv., Parochial Vicar; Raymond Borkowski, O.F.M. Conv., In Res.

Legal Title: St. Paul Parish Corporation.

MANCHESTER. *DePaul Provincial Residence* (1995) 234 Keeney St., Manchester, 06040-7048. Tel: 860-643-2828; Fax: 860-533-9462; Email: nepcm1@cox.net. Revs. Marek Sadowski, C.M., Prov. & Contact; Edmund Gutowski, C.M.; Roman Kmiec, C.M.; Chester R. Mrowka, C.M.; Stanley Staniszewski, C.M.; Michael Wanat, C.M.; Bro. Joseph S. Zurowski, C.M. Congregation of the Mission, New England Province.(Vincentian Fathers and Brothers)

The New England Province of the Congregation of the Mission IncorporatedNew England Province of the Congregation of the Mission, Inc., 32 Jewett St., Ansonia, 06401. Fax: 203-734-4884; Email: nepcm1@ox.net. Rev. Marek Sadowski, C.M., Prov. The St. Joseph Church Corporation of Ansonia owns the rectory building. *Charitable Trust of the New England Province of the Congregation of the Mission. St. Joseph Rectory*, 32 Jewett St., Ansonia, 06401. Fax: 203-734-4884; Email: nepcm1@cox.net. *St. Michael the Archangel Rectory*, 75 Derby Ave., Derby, 06418-2098. Tel: 203-734-0005; Fax: 203-736-2044; Email: stmichaelsderby@sbcglobal.net. Rev. A. Rafal Kopystynski, C.M. Students 136; Adult Enrollment 1,500. *St. Stanislaus Rectory* (1904) 9 Eld St., New Haven, 06511-3899. Tel: 203-562-2828; Fax: 203-752-0217; Email: fr.maciejewski@aohct.org. Revs. Tadeusz Maciejewski, C.M.; Anthony F. Kuzia, C.M.; Stanley Miekina, C.M.

MERIDEN. *Franciscan Brothers of the Eucharist*, 173 Goodspeed Ave., Meriden, 06451. Tel: 203-237-3601; Fax: 203-237-4217; Email: brothers@fbecommunity.org; Web: www.fbecommunity.org. Bro. Leo Maneri, F.B.E., Pres.

NEW BRITAIN. *Conventual Franciscans* (1979) 532 Burritt St., New Britain, 06053-2869. Tel: 860-225-5786; Email: smjenifferc@yahoo.com; Web: stlucianresidence.com. Rev. Joseph Tran, Chap. Daughters of Mary Motherhouse.In Res. Rev. Joseph Tran.

NEW HAVEN. *St. Mary Priory*, 5 Hillhouse Ave., New Haven, 06511. Tel: 203-562-6193; Fax: 203-562-1273; Email: church@stmarys-priory.com; Email: stmarynewhaven@aohct.org; Web: www.stmarys-priory.com. Revs. John Paul Walker, O.P.; Elias Alan Henritzy, O.P.; Jonathan Kalisch, O.P.; James Lenaghan, O.P., Chap.; Henry A. Camacho, O.P., In Res.; Bro. Patrick Foley, O.P. Order of Preachers (Dominicans). Total in Residence 6.

Priests of the Congregation of Holy Cross, 203 Maple St., New Haven, 06511. Tel: 203-623-5623; Fax: 203-776-2405; Email: johnlmyoung@msn.com. Rev. John L. Young, C.S.C.

NORTH GUILFORD. *Our Lady of Grace Monastery* (1947) 11 Race Hill Rd., North Guilford, 06437-1099. Tel: 203-457-0599; Fax: 888-959-0643; Email: gracemonastery@comcast.net; Web: www.ourladyofgracemonastery.org. Sr. Claire Lavoie, Prioress. Order of Preachers (Dominicans). Total in Residence 24.

WATERBURY. *Basilica of the Immaculate Conception Rectory*, 74 W. Main St., Waterbury, 06702. Tel: 203-574-0017; Fax: 203-756-8748; Web: www.TheImmaculate.com. Very Rev. Christopher M. Ford, J.C.L.; Rev. Joseph Karikunnel, C.S.T., Parochial Vicar. Missionaries of the Holy Apostles.

WEST HARTFORD. *Holy Family Monastery/Retreat*, 303 Tunxis Rd., West Hartford, 06107. Tel: 860-521-0440; Fax: 860-521-1929; Email: info@holyfamilyretreat.org; Web: www.holyfamilyretreat.org. Rev. David Cinquegrani, C.P., Dir.; Bros. Michael Moran, C.P.; Terence Skorka, C.P.; Rev. Terence J. Kristofak, C.P., In Res. Congregation of the Passion of Jesus Christ.

Legal Title: Passionist Fathers of CT, Inc. (dba Holy Family Passionist Monastery & Retreat Center) Brothers 2; Total in Community 4.

WEST HAVEN. *Brothers of Holy Cross*, 10 Ricardo St., West Haven, 06516-2499. Tel: 570-417-0638; Fax: 203-933-2474; Email: gcscsc@gmail.com. Bros. George C. Schmitz, C.S.C.; Joseph J. Walsh, C.S.C.; Lawrence Lussier, C.S.C. Brothers of Holy Cross. Brothers 3.

[L] CONVENTS AND RESIDENCES FOR SISTERS

HARTFORD. *The Community of the Dominican Daughters of Our Lady of Nazareth Corporation*, 510 New Britain Ave., 06106. Tel: 860-249-2912; Email: 74srlucy@gmail.com. Sr. Lucia Silva, O.P., Pres. Sisters 2.

Medical Mission Sisters (1925) 100 Girard Ave., 06105. Tel: 860-233-0875; Fax: 860-509-9509; Email: mtwinter@hartsem.edu; Email: mms@hartsem.edu; Web: mtwinter.hartsem.edu. Sr. Miriam Therese Winter, M.M.S., Ph.D. Sisters 1.

Mercyhouse (2002) 102 Putnam St., 06106-1390. Tel: 860-560-9590; Email: smjenniferc@yahoo.com. Mother Mary Jennifer Carroll, D.M., Contact Person. Sisters of Mercy of the Americas. Sisters 2.

Sisters of Mercy of the Americas Northeast Community (1831) Mercyhouse, 102 Putnam St., 06106-1390. Tel: 860-560-9590; Email: jgough@mercyhousing.org. Mother Mary Jennifer Carroll, D.M., Contact Person. Sisters 128.

Sisters of St. Joseph of Chambery (1650) 27 Park Rd., West Hartford, 06119. Tel: 860-233-5126; Fax: 860-232-4649; Email: csjusa@yahoo.com; Web: sistersofsaintjoseph.org. Mrs. Mary D'Arcangelo, Contact Person. Sisters 2. 27 Park Rd., West Hartford, 06119. Tel: 860-233-5126; Fax: 860-232-4649; Email: sbamcsj@gmail.com. Sr. Barbara Mullen, C.S.J., Prov. Sisters 83. 145 Elizabeth St., 06105. Tel: 860-523-5704; Email: csjusa@yahoo.com. Sisters 1. 73 Cannon Rd., East Hartford, 06108. Tel: 860-291-8998; Email: businessmanager@namct.org. Rev. William Agyemang. Sisters 1. *Formation Community Convent*, 407 McClintock St., New Britain, 06053. Tel: 860-505-8100; Email: csjusa@yahoo.com; Web: sistersofsaintjoseph.org. Mrs. Mary D'Arcangelo, Contact Person. Sisters 1.

Shalom Community Convent, 33 Freeman St., 06114. Tel: 860-956-9247; Email: csjusa@yahoo.com. Mrs. Mary D'Arcangelo, Contact Person. Sisters 2.

BETHLEHEM. *Abbey of Regina Laudis* (1946) 273 Flanders Rd., Bethlehem, 06751. Tel: 203-266-7727; Fax: 203-266-5915; Email: sr.rachel@icloud.com; Web: www.abbeyofreginalaudis.com. Mother Lucia Kuppens, O.S.B., Abbess & Mailing Contact; Olivia Frances Arnold, O.S.B., Prioress; Telchide Hinckley, O.S.B.; Maria Immaculata Matarese, O.S.B.; Margaret Georgina Patton, O.S.B., Subprioress; Augusta Collins, O.S.B.; Rachel Morfesi, O.S.B. Benedictine Nuns of the Primitive Observance. Novices 5; Postulants 2; Sisters 7; Professed Nuns 28; In First Vows 1.

BLOOMFIELD. *Sisters of Mercy of the Americas Northeast Community*, 5 Garrison Ter., Bloomfield, 06002-3005. Tel: 860-243-8524; Email: lvh52@aol.com. Sr. Irene Holowesko, R.S.M., Contact. Sisters 2.

Sisters of Notre Dame de Namur (Connecticut Province) 5 Garrison Ter., Bloomfield, 06002. Tel: 860-243-8524; Fax: 860-683-1351; Email: sndbloom@aol.com. Sr. Ellen Agritelly, Contact Person. Sisters 3; Total in Residence 3.

BRANFORD. *Benedictines of Jesus Crucified*, Monastery of the Glorious Cross, 61 Burban Dr., Monastery of

the Glorious Cross, Branford, 06405-4003.
Tel: 203-315-9964; Fax: 203-488-0352; Email: monasterygc@juno.com. Sr. Marie Zita Wenker, O.S.B., Prioress & Dir.

BRISTOL. *Sisters of St. Joseph of the Third Order of St. Francis*, 500 Stafford Ave., Apt. A12, Bristol, 06010. Tel: 860-621-7011; Email: ctmlw@comcast.net. Sr. Mary Lou Wojtusik, C.S.J., Contact Person. Sisters 1.

EAST HARTFORD. *Sisters of Notre Dame de Namur*, 21 Highview St., East Hartford, 06108-2983.
Tel: 860-289-5295; Email: spesnd@sbcglobal.net. Sr. Peggy Evans, S.N.D., Contact. Sisters 1. 50 Larrabee St., #G, East Hartford, 06108.
Tel: 860-289-2421; Email: spesnd@sbcglobal.net. Sisters Peggy Evans, S.N.D., Contact Person; Mary Janson-LaPalme, S.N.D., Contact Person. Sisters 2. 908 Forbes St., East Hartford, 06118.
Tel: 860-568-6958; Email: mrcsnd@sbcglobal.net. Sr. Mary Rose Crowley, S.N.D., Contact Person. Sisters 2.

Sisters of Notre Dame de Namur, 908 Forbes St., East Hartford, 06118-1924. Tel: 860-568-6958; Email: mrcsnd@aol.com. Sr. Mary Rose Crowley, S.N.D., Contact. Sisters 2; Total in Residence 2.

EAST HAVEN. *Provincial House Sisters of Charity of Our Lady, Mother of Mercy*, 32 Tuttle Pl., East Haven, 06512. Tel: 203-469-7872;
Fax: 203-469-8819; Email: scmm@comcast.net; Web: www.sistersofcharity.net. Sr. Barbara Connell, S.C.M.M., Contact. Sisters 1.

ENFIELD. *Felician Sisters - Our Lady of the Angels Convent*, 1315 Enfield St., Enfield, 06082-4929.
Tel: 860-745-7791; Tel: 860-745-4946;
Fax: 860-741-0819; Email: sconniet@feliciansisters.org; Email: ladyofangels@feliciansisters.org; Web: www.feliciansistersna.org. Sr. Mary Christopher Moore, C.S.S.F., Prov. Min. Felician Sisters of the Order of St. Francis of Connecticut. Sisters 45.

Enfield Convent (1932) Tel: 860-745-7791;
Fax: 860-741-0819. Sr. Mary Christopher Moore, C.S.S.F., Prov. Min.; Rev. Noel Danielewicz, O.F.-M.Conv. Felician Sisters. Total Felician Sisters of North America, Our Lady of Hope Province 593; Professed Sisters 45.

Felician Senior Services, Inc. (1990) 1333A Enfield St., Enfield, 06082-4929. Tel: 860-745-2542;
Fax: 860-745-2542; Email: enfieldccnurse@feliciansisters.org. Karen Enderle, Dir. Felician Sisters.A day respite health care facility for caregivers of the frail, elderly and Alzheimer clients. Total Staff 9; Total Assisted 30.

Felician Sisters Care Center (1938) 1315 Enfield St., Enfield, 06082-4929. Tel: 860-745-0217;
Fax: 860-741-6474; Email: enfieldccnurse@feliciansisters.org. Sr. Mary Christopher Moore, C.S.S.F., Prov.

Mother Angela Residence (1964) 1333-B Enfield St., Enfield, 06082-4929. Tel: 860-745-5705; Email: smchristopher@feliciansisters.org; Web: feliciansistersna.org. Sr. Mary Christopher Moore, C.S.S.F., Prov.

Enfield Montessori School (1965) 1325 Enfield St., Enfield, 06082-4929. Tel: 860-745-5847;
Fax: 860-745-2010; Email: info@enfieldmontessorischool.org. Cliona Beaulieu, Dir. & Contact. Clergy 1; Students 128.

Little Sisters of the Poor (1839) 1365 Enfield St., Enfield, 06082-4925. Tel: 860-741-0791;
Fax: 860-741-3982; Email: enmothersuperior@littlesistersofthepoor.org; Web: www.littlesistersofthepoorconneticut.org. Sr. Genevieve Nugent, L.S.P., Supr. Sisters 10.

FARMINGTON. *Maryknoll Sisters of St. Dominic* (1920) 275 Main St. #A1, Farmington, 06032-2930.
Tel: 860-678-1971; Email: kmageemm@yahoo.com; Web: maryknollsisters.org. Kathleen A. Magee, Contact Person. Sisters 2.

Sisters of the Cross and Passion (1852) St. Gabriel's House, 31 Colton St., Farmington, 06032-2381.
Tel: 201-320-3323; Fax: 860-677-2873; Email: maureenobriencp@gmail.com; Web: passionistsisters.org. Sisters Mary O'Brien, C.P., Contact; Mary Ann Strain. Sisters 2.

GUILFORD. *Immaculate Heart of Mary Convent*, 581 Jennifers Dr., Guilford, 06437. Tel: 203-689-5845. Sr. Carol Sansone, A.S.C.J., Contact Person. Sisters 1.

HAMDEN. *Mary, Mother of the Church Convent*, 115 Denslow Hill Rd., Hamden, 06514.
Tel: 203-407-1042; Email: secretary@ascjus.org. Sr. Anne D'Alessio, A.S.C.J., Supr. Sisters 3.

Mount Sacred Heart Provincialate Convent, 295 Benham St., Hamden, 06514-2801.
Tel: 203-248-4225; Fax: 203-230-8341; Email: secretary@ascjus.org; Web: www.ascjus.org. Sisters Ritamary Schulz, A.S.C.J., Prov. Supr.; Virginia Herbers, A.S.C.J., Vicaress; Sharon Kalert, A.S.C.J., Sec.
Corporation Name: Apostles of the Sacred Heart of Jesus, Incorporated. Novices 3; Professed 115; Sisters in Province 115.

Sacred Heart Academy Convent, 265 Benham St., Hamden, 06514. Tel: 203-288-9408; Email: soneill@ascjus.org. Sr. Sheila O'Neill, A.S.C.J., Supr. Sisters 5.

Sacred Heart Manor, Inc., 261 Benham St., Hamden, 06514. Tel: 203-248-4031; Email: secretary@ascjus.org. Sr. Barbara Matazzaro, A.S.C.J., Pres. Sisters 26.

Sisters of Mercy of the Americas Northeast Community, 2809 Whitney Ave., Hamden, 06518-2544. Tel: 203-287-9017; Email: annoneillrsm@juno.com. Sr. Ann O'Neill, R.S.M., Contact Person. Sisters 2.

Sr. Antonine Signorelli Formation House, 295 Benham St., Hamden, 06514. Tel: 203-281-2572; Email: secretary@ascjus.org. Sr. Mary Lee, A.S.C.J., Dir., Novices. Novices 4; Sisters 1.

LITCHFIELD. *Daughters of Wisdom* (1949) 229 E. Litchfield Rd., Litchfield, 06759. Tel: 860-567-3163 ; Fax: 860-567-3166; Email: rg@wisdomhouse.org; Web: www.wisdomhouse.org. Deborah Kelly; Sr. Jo-Ann Iannotti, O.P. Sisters 3.

Daughters of Wisdom, 12 Clark Rd., Litchfield, 06759-2808. Tel: 860-529-8419; Fax: 860-529-8419; Email: rg@wisdomhouse.org; Web: daughtersofwisdom.org. Sisters Jo-Ann Iannotti, O.P., Contact Person; Ann Casagrande, Contact Person. Sisters 3.

MADISON. *Sisters of Mercy of the Americas Northeast Community*, 167 Neck Rd., Madison, 06443-2725.
Tel: 203-245-4261; Email: emmanuel115@juno.com. Sisters Mary C. Daly, R.S.M.; Ann McGovern, R.S.M. Sisters 4.

MERIDEN. *Generalate of the Franciscan Sisters of the Eucharist* (1973) Mailing Address: The Franciscan Sisters of the Eucharist, 405 Allen Ave., Meriden, 06451. Tel: 203-237-0841; Fax: 203-238-9801; Email: fseinfo@fsecommunity.org; Web: fsecommunity.org. Mother Miriam Seiferman, F.S.E., Supr.; Sisters Barbara Johnson, F.S.E., Vicar; Suzanne Gross, F.S.E.; Mother Clare Hunter; Raffaella Petrini; Mary Richards. The Institute of the Franciscan Sisters of the Eucharist.
Franciscan Sisters of the Eucharist, Inc. Novices 1; Sisters 82; Professed Sisters 81. 275 Finch Ave., Meriden, 06451. Tel: 203-238-2400;
Fax: 203-237-3739; Email: chiaracenter@fsecommunity.org. Sr. Mary Elizabeth Endee, F.S.E., Supr. Sisters 5. 269 Finch Ave., Meriden, 06451. Tel: 203-630-1771;
Fax: 203-630-1776; Email: fsepaulvi@fsecommunity.org. Sr. Suzanne Gross, F.S.E., Supr. Sisters 7.

NEW BRITAIN. *Motherhouse of Daughters of Mary of the Immaculate Conception* (1904) 314 Osgood Ave., New Britain, 06053. Tel: 860-225-9406;
Fax: 860-225-4321; Email: smjenniferc@yahoo.com; Web: www.crossfire.org/daughtersofmary. Mother Mary Jennifer Carroll, D.M., Supr. Gen. Daughters of Mary of the Immaculate Conception. Sisters in Community 22.

St. Lucian's Residence, 532 Burritt St., New Britain, 06053-3699. Tel: 860-223-2123; Email: stlucians@comcast.net. Mother Mary Jennifer Carroll, D.M., Contact Person. Sisters 2.

Marian Heights, 314 Osgood Ave., New Britain, 06053. Tel: 860-225-9406; Fax: 860-225-4321; Email: smjenniferc@yahoo.com. Mother Mary Jennifer Carroll, D.M., Supr. Sisters 22.

Sacred Heart Convent (1904) 23 Orange St., New Britain, 06053. Tel: 860-225-3989; Email: smjenniferc@yahoo.com. Mother Mary Jennifer Carroll, D.M., Contact Person.

Msgr. Bojnowski Manor (1974) 50 Pulaski St., New Britain, 06053. Tel: 860-229-0336;
Fax: 860-229-3252; Email: smjenniferc@yahoo.com; Web: www.crossfire.org. Mother Mary Jennifer Carroll, D.M., Contact Person. Sisters 1.

Sisters of Mercy of the Americas Northeast Community, 37 Carlton St., New Britain, 06053.
Tel: 860-229-7575; Email: info@mercyne.org. Sr. Barbara Kowalski, R.S.M., Contact. Sisters 128.

Sisters of St. Joseph of Chambery, Cana, 1190 Slater Rd., New Britain, 06053-1614. Tel: 860-826-1655; Email: csjusa@yahoo.com. Sr. Suzanne Brazauskas, C.S.J., Contact Person. Sisters of St. Joseph of Chambery. Sisters 2; Total in Residence 2.

Sisters of St. Joseph of Chambery, 407 McClintock St., New Britain, 06053. Tel: 860-827-0479; Email: csjusa@yahoo.com. Mrs. Mary D'Arcangelo, Contact Person. Sisters 2; Total in Residence 2.

Sisters of St. Joseph of Chambery, 126 Texas Dr., New Britain, 06052. Tel: 860-348-0449; Email: csjusa@yahoo.com. Sr. Suzanne Brazauskas, C.S.J., Contact Person. Sisters 2; Total in Residence 2.

Sisters of the Cross and Passion (1849) 16 Hunters Ridge, Apt. 16, Unionville, 06085.
Tel: 860-472-7260; Email: maureenobriencp@gmail.com. Sr. Ann Rodgers, C.P., Contact. Sisters 1.

NEW HARTFORD. *Missionary Servants of the Most Blessed Trinity*, 595 Town Hill Rd., New Hartford, 06057. Tel: 860-379-4329; Fax: 860-379-4329; Email: trinita@charter.net. Sr. Christine Cusati, M.S.B.T., Contact Person. Sisters 2; Total in Residence 2.

NEW HAVEN. *Dominican Sisters of Peace* (1901) St. Mary's Convent, 15 Lincoln St., New Haven, 06511. Tel: 203-865-7305; Email: barbdecrosta@att.net. Sisters Barbara DeCrosta, O.P., Contact; Ellen McNulty, O.P.; Maureen O'Brien, O.P.; Margaret Mary Kennedy, O.P.; Janie Kennoy, O.P. Sisters 5.

Dominican Sisters of Peace, 15 Eld St., New Haven, 06511-3815. Tel: 203-865-7305; Email: barbdecrosta@att.net. Sr. Barbara DeCrosta, O.P., Contact Person. St. Stanislaus Church of New Haven owns the convent building. Sisters 2.

Dominican Sisters of Peace, St. Mary's Convent, 15 Lincoln St., New Haven, 06511. Tel: 203-865-7305; Email: barbdecrosta@att.net. Sr. Barbara DeCrosta, O.P., Contact Person. Dominican Sisters of Peace (Columbus, OH). Sisters 1.

NORTH GUILFORD. *Monastery of Our Lady of Grace* (1947) 11 Race Hill Rd., North Guilford, 06437-1099. Tel: 203-457-0599; Fax: 888-959-0643; Email: gracemonastery@comcast.net; Web: www.ourladyofgracemonastery.org. Sr. Mary Ann Dunn, O.P., Prioress. Dominican Contemplative Nuns (Cloistered). Sisters 27; Professed Sisters 25.
A contemplative community with solemn vows and papal enclosure. Perpetual Adoration. Sr. Claire, O.P., Prioress & Contact.
Dominican Contemplative Nuns (Cloistered). Sr. Claire, O.P., Prioress & Contact.

NORTH HAVEN. **St. Frances Cabrini Convent*, 94 Chapel Hill Rd., North Haven, 06473.
Tel: 203-239-8012; Fax: 203-891-5748; Email: fr.santiago@aohct.org. Sr. Ambrogia Alderuccio, S.S.H.J., Contact Person. Sisters of the Sacred Heart of Jesus of Ragusa. Sisters 5; Total in Residence 5.

WALLINGFORD. *Holy Trinity Convent*, 247 S. Main St., Wallingford, 06492. Tel: 203-265-6999;
Fax: 203-294-4983; Email: sisterkatiekelly@snet.net. Sr. Kathleen Kelly, R.S.M., Contact Person. Sisters of Mercy of the Americas of Connecticut. Sisters 1.

WATERBURY. *Notre Dame Convent*, 119 Southmayd Rd., Waterbury, 06705. Tel: 203-753-1095; Email: pjamele@yahoo.com. Sr. Eleanor Verrastro, C.N.D., Local Leader. Sisters of the Congregation of Notre Dame. Sisters 3. 587 Oronoke Rd., Waterbury, 06708. Tel: 203-755-8828; Email: pjamele@yahoo.com. Patricia Jamele, Contact Person. Sisters 6.

Sisters of Notre Dame de Namur (1804) 131 Herschel Ave., Waterbury, 06708. Tel: 203-757-1444; Email: mary.farren@sndden.org. Sr. Mary Beth Johnson, S.N.D., Contact. Sisters 2.

Sisters of St. Joseph of Chambery, 284 Windy Dr., Waterbury, 06705-2543. Tel: 203-573-9848; Email: csjusa@yahoo.com. Sr. Sandra Shaw, C.S.J. Sisters 2.

Sisters of St. Joseph of Chambery, 116 New Haven Ave., Waterbury, 06708. Tel: 203-527-8321; Email: csjusa@yahoo.com. Sr. Lucy Scata, C.S.J., Contact Person. Sisters 2.

WATERTOWN. *St. John the Evangelist Convent*, 9 Academy Hill, Watertown, 06795-2101.
Tel: 860-274-1820; Fax: 860-945-6418; Email: bvaluckassnd@gmail. com. Rev. Anthony J. Smith, Contact Person. School Sisters of Notre Dame. Sisters 2.

WEST HARTFORD. *Convent of Mary Immaculate, Provincial House of the Sisters of St. Joseph of Chambery* (1650) (North American Province) 27 Park Rd., West Hartford, 06119. Tel: 860-233-5734 ; Fax: 860-232-4649; Email: csjusa@yahoo.com; Email: sbamcsj@gmail.com; Web: www.sistersofsaintjoseph.org. 650 Willard Ave., Newington, 06111. Sr. Barbara Mullen, C.S.J., Prov.; Mrs. Mary D'Arcangelo, Admin. Asst. & Contact. Sisters of St. Joseph of Chambery.In Community:
The Sisters of St. Joseph Corporation Sisters 78; Professed Sisters 78.

The Sisters of St. Joseph Corporation, 650 Willard Ave., Newington, 06111. Tel: 959-200-4086; Email: csjusa@yahoo.com. Sr. Barbara Mullen, C.S.J., Prov. St. Mary's Church Corporation of Newington owns the convent building. Sisters 6.

Religious Trust of the Sisters of St. Joseph of Chambery (the "Trust"), Tel: 860-231-8678.

Dominican Sisters, 78 Westpoint Ter., West Hartford, 06107. Tel: 860-521-8296;
Fax: 860-521-8296. Sr. Magdalene Nguyen, O.P., Supr. & Contact. Sisters 2; Total in Residence 2.

Saint Mary Home, 2021 Albany Ave., West Hartford, 06117. Tel: 860-570-8200; Fax: 860-570-8501; Email: mreardon@mchct.org; Web: www.mchct.org. Sr. Maureen Reardon, R.S.M. Sisters 22; Total Apartments 97.

Sisters of Mercy of the Americas - Northeast Community, Inc., 25 Prescott St., 1st Fl., West Hartford, 06110-2335. Tel: 860-594-8619; Fax: 860-310-2177; Email: tharris@mercyne.org. Sisters Elizabeth deManbey, R.S.M., Local Coord.; Dorellen Sullivan, R.S.M., Local Coord. Sisters 100.

Sisters of Mercy of the Americas of Connecticut, 132 Milton St., West Hartford, 06119-1218. Tel: 860-523-0707; Email: pcolla@yahoo.com. Sr. Patricia Colla, R.S.M., Contact Person. Sisters 128.

University of Saint Joseph, Lourdes Hall, 1678 Asylum Ave., West Hartford, 06117-2791. Tel: 860-232-6730; Email: edemanbey@comcast.net. Sr. Elizabeth deManbey, R.S.M., Contact Person. 54 Boulanger Ave. #1, West Hartford, 06110-1103. Tel: 860-231-8472; Email: pcolla@yahoo.com. Sr. Patricia Colla, R.S.M., Contact Person. Sisters 1. 54 Boulanger Ave. #2, West Hartford, 06110-1103. Tel: 860-233-6679; Email: pcolla@yahoo.com. Sr. Patricia Colla, R.S.M., Contact Person. Sisters 1.

Visitation Plaza, 54 Boulanger Ave., #1, West Hartford, 06110. Tel: 203-755-7236. Sr. Mary Etta Higgins, R.S.M., Life & Ministry Admin., (Srs. of Mercy). Sisters 1.

WEST HAVEN. *Our Lady of Victory Convent*, 634 Jones Hill Rd., West Haven, 06516-6398. Tel: 203-934-8601; Email: fr.dillon@aohct.org. Sr. Denise Farrands, O.S.U. Ursuline Sisters of the Congregation of Tildonk, Belgium. Sisters 2.

Sisters of Charity of St. Elizabeth, Convent Station, 101 W. Prospect St., West Haven, 06516. Tel: 203-397-5243; Email: srjean@sbcglobal.net. Sr. Jean Trainor, S.C., Contact Person. Sisters 2.

WINCHESTER CENTER. *Villa Ferretti, Religious Teachers Filippini*, 438 Winchester Rd., Box 55, Winchester Center, 06094. Tel: 860-379-3279; Fax: 860-379-6479. Sr. Angela Bulla, M.P.F., Contact Person. Sisters 1.

WINDSOR. *The Connecticut Province of the Sisters of Notre Dame de Namur, Inc.*, Admin. Offices, 468 Poquonock Ave., Windsor, 06095-2473. Tel: 860-688-1832; Fax: 860-683-1741; Email: anne.malone@sndden.org; Web: www.sndden.org. Sisters Anne Malone, S.N.D.deN., Leadership Team & Contact; Mary Farren, S.N.D.deN., Leadership Team; Barbara Barry, S.N.D.deN., Leadership Team, Tel: 860-285-8901; Edie Daly, S.N.D.deN., Leadership Team, Tel: 860-285-8441; Barbara English, S.N.D.deN., Leadership Team; Catherine Waldren, S.N.D.deN., Leadership Team. Sisters 61.

Julie House, Inc., 425 Poquonock Ave., Windsor, 06095-2465. Tel: 860-298-8320; Fax: 860-683-1351 ; Email: dina.karvelis@sndden.org. Dina Karvelis, Admin. Assisted living home for S.N.D.'s only. Residents 14; Total Staff 5.

Sisters of St. Joseph of Chambery, 67 Bloomfield Ave., Windsor, 06095. Tel: 860-285-0890; Email: windwomen@att.net. Sr. Anne Kane, C.S.J., Contact Person. Sisters 2.

WOLCOTT. *Contemplative Sisters of the Good Shepherd*, 5 Carriage Hill Dr., Wolcott, 06716. Tel: 203-879-6330; Fax: 203-879-5920; Email: gdshep620@sbcglobal.net; Web: www.sistersofthegoodshepherdcontemplatives.org. Sr. Carol Anne Seigel, C.G.S., Contact Person & Coord. Sisters 1.

Daughters of Wisdom, 18 Munson Rd., #2, Wolcott, 06716. Tel: 203-879-3432; Email: dguerettedw@comcast.net. Sr. Diane Guerrette, D.W., Contact Person. Sisters 1.

[M] COUNSELING CENTERS

MERIDEN. *Franciscan Life Center*, 271 Finch Ave., Meriden, 06451. Tel: 203-237-8084; Fax: 203-639-1333; Web: www.flcenter.org; Email: sbarbara@flcenter.org. Chris LaRiviere, Exec. Dir. *Franciscan Life Center Network, Inc.* Franciscan Sisters of the Eucharist 8; Total Staff 21; Total Assisted 3,000.

[N] ADOPTION SERVICES-HOME CARE

MERIDEN. *Franciscan Family Care Center* (1979) 267 Finch Ave., Meriden, 06451. Tel: 203-238-1441; Fax: 203-686-0807; Email: ssuzanne@franciscanhc.org. Sr. Suzanne Gross, F.S.E., Admin. Franciscan Home Hospice Care & Contact, Tel: 203-237-8084; Fax: 203-639-1333

Legal Title: Franciscan Family Care Center, Inc. (dba Franciscan Home Care and Hospice Care) Franciscan Sisters of the Eucharist 6; Tot Asst. Annually 800; Total Staff 6; Total Assisted 800.

[O] RETREAT HOUSES-RENEWAL CENTERS

FARMINGTON. *Our Lady of Calvary Retreat Center*, 31 Colton St., Farmington, 06032. Tel: 860-677-8519; Fax: 860-677-2873; Email: olcretreat@sbcglobal.net; Web: www.ourladyofcalvary.com. Sisters Ann Rodgers, C.P., Dir.; Kathleen FitzSimons, C.N.D., Admin. & Contact Person; Maria Descy, Contact Person; Kathy Irr. Conducted by the Sisters of the Cross and Passion for Religious and Lay Persons.

LITCHFIELD. *Wisdom House Retreat Center* (1949) 229 E. Litchfield Rd., Litchfield, 06759-3002. Tel: 860-567-3163; Fax: 860-567-3166; Email: dkelly@wisdomhouse.org; Web: www.wisdomhouse.org. Deborah Kelly, Exec. Dir. A retreat center which presents programs in spirituality, education & the arts. Use of space is available for nonprofit organizations when their purpose corresponds to the Mission of Wisdom House. The Center is a sponsored ministry of the Daughters of Wisdom.

MADISON. *Mercy Center, Incorporated*, 167 Neck Rd., Madison, 06443. Tel: 203-245-0401; Fax: 203-245-8718; Email: info@mercybythesea.org; Web: www.mercybythesea.org. Sr. Eileen Dooling, R.S.M. Sisters of Mercy-Northeast Community Sisters 4; Total Staff 14.

WEST HARTFORD. *Holy Family Passionist Retreat Center*, 303 Tunxis Rd., West Hartford, 06107. Tel: 860-521-0440; Fax: 860-521-1929; Email: info@holyfamilyretreat.org; Web: www.holyfamilyretreat.org. Revs. David Cinquegrani, C.P., Retreat Dir.; Terence J. Kristofak, C.P., In Res.; Sr. Elaine Betoncourt, C.S.J., Retreat Team; Brandon Nappi, D.Min., Retreat Team; Colin Petramale, Retreat Team; Bill Heiden, Retreat Team; Liza Peters, M.Div., Youth Min.; Kasia Owczarek, Special Events. For laymen and laywomen. Conducted by the Passionist Community

Legal title: Passionist Fathers of CT, Inc. (dba Holy Family Passionist Retreat Center) Lay Staff 25; Priests 2; Sisters 1.

[P] NEWMAN CENTERS

HARTFORD. *Capital Community College*, 950 Main St., 06103. Tel: 860-906-5000; Web: www.ccc.commnet.edu. Deacon Arthur L. Miller, Chap.

University of Hartford Newman Center, 200 Bloomfield Ave., 06117-1599. Tel: 860-768-4899; Email: uhacatholicmin@aol.com. Rev. Patrick M. Kane, Chap.

Trinity College Chapel, 300 Summit St., 06106-3186. Tel: 860-297-2015; Email: campusministry5@aol.com; Web: www.trincoll.edu/orgs/newman-club. Rev. Ryan M. Lerner, Chap.; Elliot Levesque, Contact Person.

HAMDEN. *Quinnipiac Catholic Chaplaincy*, 275 Mt. Carmel Ave., Hamden, 06518-1908. Tel: 203-582-8257. Rev. James Lenaghan, O.P., Chap. & Contract, St. Mary's Priory, 5 Hillhouse Ave., New Haven, 06505.

NEW BRITAIN. *Central Connecticut State University Newman House*, 145 Paul J. Manafort Dr., New Britain, 06053-2552. Tel: 860-832-3795; Tel: 860-225-6449; Fax: 860-225-2315; Email: fr.casey@aohct.org. Rev. Michael T. Casey, Chap.

St. Francis of Assisi Friary, 1755 Stanley St., New Britain, 06053-2099. Tel: 860-225-6449; Fax: 860-225-2315; Email: fr.casey@aohct.org. Rev. Michael T. Casey.

NEW HAVEN. *Southern Connecticut State University Catholic Center*, 129 Edwards St., New Haven, 06511. Tel: 203-392-5331; Tel: 203-624-5297; Email: furlongj1@southernct.org. Rev. Eric Zuniga, Chap.; Deacon P. Terrance Moran, Campus Min.; James Furlong, Inter Faith Office.

Yale University-St. Thomas More Catholic Center and Chapel (1957) 268 Park St., New Haven, 06511-4714. Tel: 203-777-5537; Fax: 203-777-0144; Email: danielle.wilson@yale.edu; Web: www.stm.yale.edu. Rev. Msgr. Gerard G. Schmitz, Chap., (Retired); Rev. Karl Davis, Campus Min.; Sr. Jennifer Schaaf, Campus Min.; Carlene Demiany, Campus Min.; Allan Esteron, Campus Min.

[Q] ORGANIZED CHARITIES

HARTFORD. *Catholic Charities, Inc. - Archdiocese of Hartford* Administrative Office 839-841 Asylum Ave., 06105. Tel: 860-493-1841; Email: akarpiej@ccaoh.org; Web: www.ccaoh.org. Marek Kukulka, CEO. Tot Asst. Annually 20,000; Total Staff 421.

13 Wolcott St., Waterbury, 06702. Tel: 203-596-9359; Fax: 203-757-9753.

WATERBURY. *St. Vincent de Paul Mission of Waterbury, Inc.*, P.O. Box 1612, Waterbury, 06721. Tel: 203-754-0000; Fax: 203-756-0865; Email: st.vincent.depaul@snet.net; Web: svdpmission.org. Deacon Paul P. Iadarola, Exec. Dir. & Contact Person.

[R] SOCIAL SERVICE CENTERS FOR LIFE, FAMILY, AND CULTURE

BLOOMFIELD. *Office for Faith and Culture*, 134 Farmington Ave., Bloomfield, 06002-2999. Tel: 860-541-6491; Email: sr.clare.millea@aohct.org. Sr. Clare Millea, A.S.C.J., Dir. Tot Asst. Annually 538,000; Total Staff 1.

WATERBURY. *Spanish-Speaking Center*, 13 Wolcott St., Waterbury, 06702-1790. Tel: 203-756-4439; Email: fr.jimenez@aohct.org. Rev. Diego A. Jimenez. Tot Asst. Annually 1,000; Total Staff 1; Total Assisted 350.

[S] MISCELLANEOUS

HARTFORD. *134 Farmington Avenue, Inc.*, The Chancery, 134 Farmington Ave., 06105. Tel: 860-541-6491; Fax: 860-541-6309; Email: laurie.deluca@aohct.org. Laurie R. DeLuca, Contact Person.

Archdiocese of Hartford Multi-Employer Health Benefits Trust (2017) 134 Farmington Ave., 06105. Tel: 860-541-6491; Email: linda.carroll@aohct.org; Email: laurie.deluca@aohct.org. Matthew A. Byrne, CPA, M.B.A., Exec.

Archdiocese of Hartford Retired Priests Health and Benefits Trust (2017) 134 Farmington Ave., 06105. Tel: 860-541-6491; Email: linda.carroll@aohct.org; Web: chancellor@aohct.org. Matthew A. Byrne, CPA, M.B.A., Exec.

Cathedral Indemnity Company, The Chancery, 134 Farmington Ave., 06105. Tel: 860-541-6491; Fax: 860-541-6309; Email: matt.byrne@aohct.org; Email: linda.carroll@aohct.org. Matthew A. Byrne, CPA, M.B.A., Contact Person.

Hartford Educational Broadband, Inc., 134 Farmington Ave., 06105-3784. Tel: 860-541-6491; Fax: 860-541-6309; Email: matt.byrne@aohct.org. Matthew A. Byrne, CPA, M.B.A., CFO. Purpose: to provide broadband capacity to archdiocesan educational institutions, license the excess broadband capacity and provide funds generated for the support of the Archdiocesan educational mission.

House of Bread, Inc., 1453 Main St., 06120-2726. Tel: 860-549-4188; Fax: 860-249-4656; Email: hobread@aol.com. Sisters Maureen Faenza, C.S.J., Co-Dir.; Theresa Fonti, C.S.J., Co-Dir.

Jubilee House, Inc., 40 Clifford St., 06114. Tel: 860-247-3030; Fax: 860-548-9635; Email: hobread@aol.com. Sr. Jeanne Paulella, C.S.J., Dir.

Malta House of Care Foundation, Inc., 19 Woodland St., Ste. 21, 06105. Tel: 860-461-0965; Email: mmurphy@maltahouseofcare.org; Web: www.maltahouseofcare.org. Robert O'Hara, Chm.; Filomena Soyster, Board Pres.; Sr. Michelle Anne Murphy, Exec. Dir.; Pauline Olsen, M.D., Exec.

Mercy Housing and Shelter Corporation, 211 Wethersfield Ave, 06114. Tel: 860-808-2040; Fax: 860-548-0692; Email: dmartineau@mercyhousingct.org; Web: www.mercyhousingct.org. David Martineau, Pres. & Exec. Dir.; Stephen Abshire, Treas. & Dir. Finance; Henrietta Rand, Sec. & Exec. Asst. Homeless Services Total Staff 68; Total Assisted 4,661.

MLS Religious Trust, 915 Maple Ave., 06114-2330. Tel: 860-956-8870; Fax: 860-956-8849; Email: mlsfo@aol.com. Sr. Carmel Caputo, C.N.D., Contact.

North American La Salette Mission Center, Inc. (1996) 915 Maple Ave., 06114-2330. Tel: 860-956-8870; Fax: 860-956-8849; Email: lsmc2@charter.net; Web: www.lsmc.org. Rev. Thomas Vellappallil, M.S., Dir.; Mrs. Connie Evans, Sec.

St. Augustine Foundation, Inc. (2017) 134 Farmington Ave., 06105. Tel: 860-541-6491; Email: linda.carroll@aohct.org. Matthew A. Byrne, CPA, M.B.A., Dir.

St. Joseph's Community Center, Inc., 29 John St., Waterbury, 06708. Tel: 860-728-2562; Email: akarpiej@ccaoh.org. Alyson Karpiej, Contact Person.

The Archdiocese of Hartford Investment Trust, 134 Farmington Ave., 06105-3784. Tel: 860-541-6491; Fax: 860-541-6309; Email: matt.byrne@aohct.org. Matthew A. Byrne, CPA, M.B.A., Trustee/Trust Investment Officer.

The Benevolent Association for Priests of The Archdiocese of Hartford, Incorporated, 134 Farmington Ave., 06105-3784. Tel: 860-541-6491; Fax: 860-541-6309; Email: matt.byrne@aohct.org. Matthew A. Byrne, CPA, M.B.A., Dir.

The Hartford Bishops' Foundation, Inc., 134 Farmington Ave., 06105. Tel: 860-541-6491. Lisa Owens, Contact Person.

The Hartford Roman Catholic Diocesan Corporation (1911) 134 Farmington Ave., 06105. Tel: 860-541-6491; Email: matt.byrne@aohct.org. Matthew A. Byrne, CPA, M.B.A., Contact Person.

BLOOMFIELD. *Foundation for the Advancement of Catholic Schools*, 467 Bloomfield Ave., Bloomfield, 06002-2999. Tel: 860-761-7499; Fax: 860-242-0361; Email: cbhoward@facshartford.org; Web: www.facshartford.org. Cynthia Basil Howard, Exec. Dir.; Marie M. Dussault, Assoc. Dir.

BRISTOL. *Magnificat-Mother of Divine Mercy Corporation, Bristol, CT*, 129 Strawberry Hill Rd., Bristol, 06010. Tel: 860-589-7405; Email: maryleblanc48@gmail.com. Mary LeBlanc, Pres. Purpose: to foster the work of intercession; to conduct prayer focused meetings and to serve the needy.

HAMDEN. *Sacred Heart Academy Endowment Fund, Inc.*, 265 Benham St., Hamden, 06514.
Tel: 203-288-9408; Email: soneill@sacredhearthamden.org. Sr. Sheila O'Neill, A.S.C.J., Pres.

LITCHFIELD. *Lourdes Shrine Guild, Inc.* (1946) 83 Montfort Rd., Litchfield, 06759. Tel: 860-567-1041; Fax: 860-567-9670; Email: lourdesshrinect@gmail.com. P.O. Box 667, Litchfield, 06759. Rev. Donald Lasalle, S.M.M., Supr. Priests 1.

MERIDEN. *Franciscan Life Center Network, Incorporated*, 405 Allen Ave., Meriden, 06451.
Tel: 203-237-8084; Fax: 203-639-1333; Email: sistersuzanne@prolifeministry.org; Web: www.flcenter.org. Sr. Suzanne Gross, F.S.E., Sec.

Franciscan Ever There Care, 273 Finch Ave., Meriden, 06451. Tel: 203-630-2881;
Fax: 203-639-0831; Email: Clientservices@franciscanetc.org; Web: www.franciscanetc.org. Christopher LaRiviere, Exec. Dir.

Franciscan Life Center, 271 Finch Ave., Meriden, 06451. Tel: 203-237-8084; Fax: 203-639-1333; Email: clariviere@franciscanetc.org.

Franciscan Life Process Center, 11650 Downes St., Lowell, MI 49331. Tel: 616-897-7842;
Fax: 616-897-7054; Email: flpc@lifeprocesscenter.org; Web: lifeprocesscenter.org. Sr. Colleen Ann Nagle, F.S.E., Dir.

Franciscan Montessori Earth School, 14750 S.E. Clinton St., Portland, OR 97236.
Tel: 503-760-8220; Fax: 503-760-8333; Email: prolife@flcenter.org. Sr. Therese Gutting, F.S.E., Admin. Clergy 1; Students 10.

NEW BRITAIN. *Charitable Trust of the Daughters of Mary of the Immaculate Conception*, 314 Osgood Ave., New Britain, 06053. Tel: 860-225-9406; Email: smjenniferc@yahoo.com; Web: www.crossfire.org/daughtersofmary. Mother Mary Jennifer Carroll, D.M., Contact Person.

Marian Heights, Incorporated, 314 Osgood Ave., New Britain, 06053. Tel: 860-225-9406; Email: conventheights@yahoo.com; Web: www.crossfire.org. Mother Mary Jennifer Carroll, D.M., Contact Person. Purpose: home is limited for low income elderly, adult day care, child day care, convent.

Retirement Trust of the Daughters of Mary of the Immaculate Conception (2016) 314 Osgood Ave., New Britain, 06053. Tel: 860-225-9406; Email: smjenniferc@yahoo.com. Mother Mary Jennifer Carroll, D.M., Prov. Total in Community 22.

Siena Learning Center, 29 Edson St., New Britain, 06051-3001. Tel: 860-348-0622. Sr. Virginia Bruen, Dir. Dominican Sisters of Peace, Inc.

NEW HAVEN. *Apostle Immigrant Services, Corporation*, 81 Saltonstall Ave., New Haven, 06513.
Tel: 203-752-9068; Fax: 203-752-9136; Email: smeburns@ascjus.org. Sr. Mary Ellen Burns, A.S.C.J., Dir. & Contact Person.

Springs Learning Center, 115 Blatchley Ave., New Haven, 06513-4206. Tel: 203-787-1025; Email: springslearning@oppeace.org. Sr. Margaret Mary Kennedy, O.P., Dir. Dominican Sisters of Peace, Inc.

WATERBURY. *Francis Xavier Plaza, Inc.*, 605 Baldwin St., Waterbury, 06706-1501. Tel: 860-728-2562; Email: akarpiej@ccaoh.org. Alyson Karpiej, Contact Person. Providing housing opportunities for low income and homeless persons, potentially homeless persons or elderly, disabled or otherwise disadvantaged persons.

WEST HARTFORD. **Intensive Education Academy, Inc.*, 840 N. Main St., West Hartford, 06117-2026.
Tel: 860-236-2049; Fax: 860-231-2843; Email: jodonnell@le-academy.org. Jill O'Donnell, Dir. of Education.

Mercy Community Health, Inc., 2021 Albany Ave., West Hartford, 06117-2796. Tel: 860-570-8301;
Fax: 860-233-8849; Email: mreardon@mchct.org; Web: www.themercycommunity.org. David Stevens, Pres.

RELIGIOUS INSTITUTES OF MEN REPRESENTED IN THE ARCHDIOCESE

For further details refer to the corresponding bracketed number in the Religious Institutes of Men or Women section.

[0200]—*Benedictine Monks*—O.S.B.
[0600]—*Brothers of Holy Cross* (Notre Dame, IN)—C.S.C.
[1100]—*Brothers of the Sacred Heart*—S.C.
[0275]—*Carmelites of Mary Immaculate*—C.M.I.
[0610]—*Congregation of the Holy Cross*—C.S.C.
[1330]—*Congregation of the Mission (Vincentian Fathers)*—C.M.
[1000]—*Congregation of the Passion* (Prov. of St. Paul of the Cross)—C.P.
[0480]—*Conventual Franciscans* (St. Anthony of Padua Prov.)—O.F.M.Conv.
[]—*Franciscan Brothers of the Eucharist*—F.B.E.
[0520]—*Franciscan Friars* (Immaculate Conception, Holy Name Provs.)—O.F.M.
[0730]—*Legionaries of Christ*—L.C.
[0780]—*Marist Fathers*—S.M.
[0800]—*Maryknoll*—M.M.
[0720]—*The Missionaries of Our Lady of La Salette* (Prov. O.L. of Seven Dolors)—M.S.
[0590]—*Missionaries of the Holy Apostles*—M.S.A.
[0870]—*Montfort Missionaries*—S.M.M.
[0910]—*Oblates of Mary Immaculate*—O.M.I.
[093]—*Oblates of St. Joseph*—O.S.J.
[0430]—*Order of Preachers-Dominicans* (Eastern Prov.)—O.P.
[1190]—*Salesians of St. John Bosco*—S.D.B.
[1240]—*Servites (Order of Friar Servants of Mary)*—O.S.M.
[0760]—*Society of Mary (Marianists)*—S.M.
[]—*Sons of Charity*—S.C.

RELIGIOUS INSTITUTES OF WOMEN REPRESENTED IN THE ARCHDIOCESE

[0130]—*Apostles of the Sacred Heart of Jesus*—A.S.C.J.
[0180]—*Benedictine Nuns of the Primitive Observance*—O.S.B.
[2250]—*Congregation of Benedictines of Jesus Crucified*—O.S.B.
[1830]—*Contemplative Sisters of the Good Shepherd*—C.G.S.
[0860]—*Daughters of Mary of the Immaculate Conception*—D.M.
[0820]—*Daughters of the Holy Spirit*—D.H.S.
[0960]—*Daughters of Wisdom*—D.W.
[1050]—*Dominican Contemplative Nuns*—O.P.
[]—*Daughters of Our Lady of Nazareth* (Madrid, Spain)—O.P.
[]—*Dominican Sisters (Congregation of St. Catherine of Siena)*—O.P.
[1070-15]—*Dominican Sisters of Hope*—O.P.
[]—*Dominican Sisters of Our Lady of the Springs of Bridgeport*—O.P.
[1115]—*Dominican Sisters of Peace*—O.P.
[1170]—*Felician Sisters* (Our Lady of the Angels Province)—C.S.S.F.
[1250]—*Institutes of the Franciscan Sisters of the Eucharist*—F.S.E.
[2340]—*Little Sisters of the Poor*—L.S.P.
[2470]—*Maryknoll Sisters of St. Dominic*—M.M.
[2490]—*Medical Mission Sisters*—M.M.S.
[2790]—*Missionary Servants of the Most Blessed Trinity*—M.S.B.T.
[3430]—*Religious Teachers Filippini*—M.P.F.
[]—*Sisters Minor of the Mary Immaculate*—S.M.M.I.
[0520]—*Sisters of Charity of Our Lady, Mother of Mercy*—S.C.M.M.
[0590]—*Sisters of Charity of Saint Elizabeth, Convent Station*—S.C.
[2575]—*Sisters of Mercy of the Americas* (Albany, Vermont, Detroit & Connecticut)—R.S.M.
[3000]—*Sisters of Notre Dame de Namur* (Connecticut, Boston, California & Base Community)—S.N.D.deN.
[1650]—*Sisters of St. Francis of Philadelphia*—O.S.F.
[3850]—*Sisters of St. Joseph of Chambery*—C.S.J.
[3930]—*Sisters of St. Joseph of the Third Order of St. Francis*—S.S.J.-T.O.S.F.
[2980]—*Sisters of the Congregation de Notre Dame*—C.N.D.
[3180]—*Sisters of the Cross and Passion*—C.P.
[]—*Sisters of the Sacred Heart of Jesus of Ragusa*—S.S.H.J.
[]—*Society of the Sisters of the Church*—S.S.C.
[4060]—*Society of the Holy Child Jesus*—S.H.C.J.
[4130]—*Ursuline Sisters of The Congregation of Tildonk, Belgium*—O.S.U.

ARCHDIOCESAN CEMETERIES

HARTFORD. *Catholic Cemeteries Association of the Archdiocese of Hartford, Inc.*, 700 Middletown Ave., P.O. Box 517, North Haven, 06473-0517.
Tel: 203-239-2557; Fax: 203-239-5035; Email: cca@ccaem.org; Web: www.ccacem.org. John Pinone, Dir.

Holy Trinity, 346 North Colony St., Wallingford, 06492. Tel: 203-237-3226; Fax: 203-327-3226; Email: sverespie@ccacem.org. 250 Gypsy Ln., Meriden, 06450-7938. Mr. Scott Verespie, Dir.

St. Patrick, Wall St., Meriden, 06450.
Tel: 203-237-3226; Email: sverespie@ccacem.org. 250 Gypsy Ln., Meriden, 06450. Mr. Scott Verespie, Dir.

ANSONIA. *St. Mary*, Division St., Ansonia, 06401.
Tel: 203-735-8026; Email: kgerckens@ccacem.org. 219 New Haven Ave., Derby, 06418. Mr. Kevin Gerckens, Dir.

Old St. Mary, 1309 Stanley St., New Britain, 06051.
Tel: 860-225-1938; Email: ppiscitelli@ccacem.org. 1141 Stanley St., New Britain, 06051. Mr. Paul Piscitelli, Dir. Total Plots 71

BLOOMFIELD. *Mount Saint Benedict*, One Cottage Grove Rd., Bloomfield, 06002-3398.
Tel: 860-242-0738; Fax: 860-242-0738; Email: rmaher@ccacem.org. Mr. Robert Maher, Dir.

DERBY. *Mount St. Peter*, 219 New Haven Ave., Derby, 06418. Tel: 203-735-8026; Fax: 203-734-2831; Email: kgerckens@ccacem.org. Mr. Kevin Gerckens, Dir.

Old St. Mary Cemetery, 930 Burnside Ave., East Hartford, 06108. Tel: 860-646-3772; Email: bmccann@ccacem.org. 368 Broad St., Manchester, 06040. Mr. Bruce McCann, Dir.

EAST HARTFORD. *St. Mary*, 1411 Stanley St., New Britain, 06051. Tel: 860-225-1938; Email: ppiscitelli@ccacem.org. Mr. Paul Piscitelli, Dir.

GLASTONBURY. *Holy Cross*, 1318 Hebron Ave., Glastonbury, 06033. Tel: 860-646-3772;
Fax: 860-646-3772; Email: bmcann@ccacem.org. 368 Broad St., Manchester, 06040-4033. Mr. Bruce McCann, Dir.

MANCHESTER. *St. Bridget*, 180 Oakland St., Manchester, 06040. Tel: 860-646-3772; Email: bmccann@ccacem.org. 368 Broad St., Manchester, 06040. Mr. Bruce McCann, Dir.

St. James, 360 Broad St., Manchester, 06040.
Tel: 860-646-3772; Email: bmccann@ccacem.org. 368 Broad St., Manchester, 06040. Mr. Bruce McCann, Dir.

MERIDEN. *St. Patrick*, 103-199 F D Oates Ave., 06112.
Tel: 860-242-0738; Email: rmaher@ccacem.org. 1 Cottage Grove Rd., Bloomfield, 06002. Mr. Robert Maher, Dir.

Sacred Heart, 250 Gypsy Ln., Meriden, 06450.
Tel: 203-237-3226; Email: sverespie@ccacem.org. Mr. Scott Verespie, Dir.

NAUGATUCK. *St. Francis*, Cemetery Rd., Naugatuck, 06770. Tel: 203-754-9105; Email: skomar@ccacem.org. 2324 E. Main St., Waterbury, 06705. Steven Komar, Dir. (New Haven Region)

St. James, 155-241 Cross St., Naugatuck, 06770.
Tel: 203-754-9105; Email: skomar@ccacem.org. 2324 E. Main St., Naugatuck, 06770. Steven Komar, Dir.

NEW BRITAIN. *St. Mary*, 1309 Stanley St., New Britain, 06051. Tel: 860-225-1938; Email: ppiscitelli@ccacem.org. 1141 Stanley St., New Britain, 06051. Mr. Paul Piscitelli, Dir. Plots Available 71

Old St. Mary, 177 Wakelee Ave., Ansonia, 06401.
Tel: 203-735-8026; Email: kgerckens@ccacem.org. 219 New Haven Ave., Derby, 06418. Mr. Kevin Gerckens, Dir.

NEW HAVEN. *St. Bernard*, 520 Columbus Ave., New Haven, 06519. Tel: 203-624-3980; Email: ajeanette@ccacem.org. 280 Derby Ave., West Haven, 06516. Anthony Jeanette, Dir.

NORTH HAVEN. *All Saints*, 700 Middletown Ave., P.O. Box 517, North Haven, 06473-0517.
Tel: 203-239-2557; Fax: 203-239-5035; Email: cgrzywacz@ccacem.org. Chuck Grzywacz, Contact Person. Plots Available 1; Total Plots 1

TORRINGTON. *St. Francis*, 863 S. Main St., Torrington, 06070. Tel: 860-482-4670; Email: lrichards@ccacem.org. Lisa Richards, Dir.

Old St. Francis, Willow St., Torrington, 06790.
Tel: 860-482-4670; Email: lrichards@ccacem.org. 863 S. Main St., Torrington, 06790. Lisa Richards, Dir.

St. Peter, 236 E. Pearl Rd., Torrington, 06790.
Tel: 860-482-4670; Email: lrichards@ccacem.org. 863 S. Main St., Torrington, 06790. Lisa Richards, Dir.

WALLINGFORD. *Holy Trinity*, 32 Mather St., 06120.
Tel: 860-242-0738; Fax: 860-242-0738; Email: rmaher@ccacem.org. One Cottage Grove Rd., Bloomfield, 06002-3398. Mr. Robert Maher, Dir.

St. John, Christian St., Wallingford, 06492.
Tel: 203-237-3226; Email: sverespie@ccacem.org. 250 Gypsy Ln., Meriden, 06450. Mr. Scott Verespie, Dir.

WATERBURY. *Calvary*, 945 Hamilton Ave., Waterbury, 06076. Tel: 203-754-9105; Email: skomar@ccacem.org. 2324 E. Main St., Waterbury, 06705-2691. Steven Komar, Dir.

St. Joseph, 945 Hamilton Ave., Waterbury, 06706.
Tel: 203-754-9105; Email: skomar@ccacem.org. 2324 E. Main St., Waterbury, 06705. Steven Komar, Dir.

Old St. Joseph, Hamilton Ave. and Silver St., Waterbury, 06706. Tel: 203-754-9105; Email: skomar@ccacem.org. 2324 E. Main St., Waterbury, 06705. Steven Komar, Dir.

WATERTOWN. *Mount Olivet*, 451-675 Platt Rd., Watertown, 06795. Tel: 860-274-4641; Email: rgambordella@ccacem.org. 669 Platt Rd., Watertown, 06795. Mr. Robert Gambordella, Dir.

WEST HAVEN. *St. Lawrence*, 280 Derby Ave., West Haven, 06516. Tel: 203-624-3980; Email: ajeanette@ccacem.org. Anthony Jeanette, Dir.

NECROLOGY

† Liptak, David Q., (Retired), Died Jan. 1, 2018
† Regan, John D., (Retired), Died Aug. 5, 2018
† Beloin, Robert L., Ph.D., New Haven, CT St. Thomas More Chapel, Died Sep. 23, 2018
† Burns, William L., (Retired), Died Jan. 1, 2018
† Karpiey, Daniel J., (Retired), Died Jan. 27, 2018
† Russo, Robert T., (Retired), Died Oct. 28, 2018

An asterisk (*) denotes an organization that has established tax-exempt status directly with the IRS and is not covered by the USCCB Group Ruling.

Diocese of Helena

(Diocesis Helenensis)

Erected March 7, 1884.

Square Miles 51,922.

Comprises the western part of the State of Montana, and is made up of the following Counties: Lewis and Clark, Glacier, Pondera, Flathead, Lake, Lincoln, Missoula, Mineral, Sanders, Powell, Granite, Ravalli, Deer Lodge, Silver Bow, Jefferson, Broadwater, Gallatin, Madison, Beaverhead, Meagher, Wheatland and parts of Teton and Toole.

Diocesan Legal Title–Roman Catholic Bishop of Helena, Montana, a Corporation Sole.

For legal titles of parishes and diocesan institutions, consult the Chancery Office.

(VACANT SEE)

Chancery: 515 N. Ewing, P.O. Box 1729, Helena, MT 59624-1729. Tel: 406-442-5820; Fax: 406-442-5191.

Web: www.diocesehelena.org

Email: chancery@diocesehelena.org

STATISTICAL OVERVIEW

Personnel	
Priests: Diocesan Active in Diocese	36
Priests: Diocesan Active Outside Diocese	2
Priests: Retired, Sick or Absent	30
Number of Diocesan Priests	68
Religious Priests in Diocese	3
Total Priests in Diocese	71
Extern Priests in Diocese	6
Ordinations:	
Transitional Deacons	1
Permanent Deacons in Diocese	40
Total Brothers	1
Total Sisters	21
Parishes	
Parishes	58
With Resident Pastor:	
Resident Diocesan Priests	29
Resident Religious Priests	1
Without Resident Pastor:	
Administered by Priests	25
Administered by Religious Women	1
Administered by Lay People	2
Missions	38
Professional Ministry Personnel:	
Brothers	1
Sisters	12
Lay Ministers	57
Welfare	
Catholic Hospitals	3
Total Assisted	250,765
Day Care Centers	3
Total Assisted	144
Special Centers for Social Services	2
Total Assisted	2,600
Educational	
Diocesan Students in Other Seminaries	5
Total Seminarians	5
Colleges and Universities	1
Total Students	1,268
High Schools, Diocesan and Parish	2
Total Students	280
High Schools, Private	1
Total Students	42
Elementary Schools, Diocesan and Parish	4
Total Students	937
Elementary Schools, Private	1
Total Students	158
Catechesis/Religious Education:	
High School Students	732
Elementary Students	2,620
Total Students under Catholic Instruction	6,042
Teachers in the Diocese:	
Brothers	1
Sisters	1
Lay Teachers	257
Vital Statistics	
Receptions into the Church:	
Infant Baptism Totals	584
Minor Baptism Totals	195
Adult Baptism Totals	89
Received into Full Communion	126
First Communions	496
Confirmations	421
Marriages:	
Catholic	136
Interfaith	59
Total Marriages	195
Deaths	771
Total Catholic Population	45,400
Total Population	619,667

Former Bishops—Rt. Revs. JOHN B. BRONDEL, cons. Bishop of Victoria, V.I., Dec. 14, 1879; appt. Vicar Apostolic of Montana, April 17, 1883; Bishop of Helena, March 7, 1884; died Nov. 3, 1903; JOHN P. CARROLL, D.D., cons. Bishop of Helena, Dec. 21, 1904; died Nov. 4, 1925; Most Revs. GEORGE J. FINNIGAN, C.S.C., D.D., cons. Bishop of Helena, Aug. 1, 1927; died Aug. 14, 1932; RALPH L. HAYES, D.D., cons. Bishop of Helena, Sept. 21, 1933; transferred to Rectorship North American College, Rome, Italy, Sept. 11, 1935; transferred to Titular See of Hierapolis, Oct. 26, 1935; transferred to Davenport, Nov. 16, 1944; appt. Assistant at the Pontifical Throne, April 30, 1958; transferred to Titular See of Naraggara and retired, Oct. 20, 1966; died July 4, 1970; JOSEPH M. GILMORE, S.T.D., cons. Bishop of Helena, Feb. 19, 1936; died April 2, 1962; RAYMOND G. HUNTHAUSEN, ord. June 1, 1946; appt. July 8, 1962; cons. Bishop of Helena, Aug. 30, 1962; transferred to Archdiocese of Seattle, Feb. 25, 1975; installed Archbishop of Seattle, May 22, 1975; retired Aug. 21, 1991; died July 22, 2018; ELDEN F. CURTISS, D.D., ord. May 24, 1958; appt. March 4, 1976; cons. Bishop of Helena, April 28, 1976; transferred to Archdiocese of Omaha, May 4, 1993; installed Archbishop of Omaha, June 25, 1993; retired June 3, 2009.; ALEXANDER J. BRUNETT, Ph.D., ord. July 13, 1958; appt. April 19, 1994; cons. Bishop of Helena, July 6, 1994; transferred to Archdiocese of Seattle Oct. 28, 1997; installed Archbishop of Seattle Dec. 18, 1997; retired Sept. 16, 2010.; ROBERT C. MORLINO, ord. June 1, 1974; cons. Bishop of Helena Sept. 21, 1999; transferred to Diocese of Madison May 23, 2003; installed Bishop of Madison Aug. 1, 2003; died Nov. 24, 2018; GEORGE LEO THOMAS, D.D., Ph. D., ord. May 22, 1976; appt. Auxiliary Bishop of Seattle Nov. 19, 1999; appt. Bishop of Helena March 23, 2004; installed June 4, 2004; appt. Bishop of Las Vegas Feb. 28, 2018; installed May 15, 2018.

Diocesan Administrator—Rev. Msgr. KEVIN S. O'NEILL, Tel: 406-442-5820; Email: koneill@sthelenas.org.

Administrator's Delegate—Rev. BART TOLLESON, Email: btolleson@diocesehelena.org.

Delegate for Clergy—Mailing Address: 730A Missy's Way, Missoula, 59801. Tel: 406-396-3811. Rev. GARY W. RELLER, (Retired), Email: greller@diocesehelena.org.

Director for Ministry to Priests—Rev. THOMAS P. HAFFEY, 2100 Farragut, Butte, 59701. Tel: 406-723-4303; Email: ftphaffey@bresnan.net.

Delegate for Senior Status Priests—Rev. Msgr. JOSEPH D. HARRINGTON, (Retired), 1726 Cannon St., Helena, 59601. Tel: 406-449-7025.

Delegate for Canonical Services—Rev. JOHN W. ROBERTSON, P.O. Box 1729, Helena, 59624. Tel: 406-442-5820; Fax: 406-442-1085; Email: jrobertson@diocesehelena.org.

Chancery Services—515 N. Ewing St., P.O. Box 1729, Helena, 59624. Tel: 406-442-5820; Fax: 406-442-5191; Email: chancery@diocesehelena.org; Web: www.diocesehelena.org.

Director—Rev. JOHN W. ROBERTSON.

Administrative Assistant—KRISTI IRWIN.

Chancellor—Rev. JOHN W. ROBERTSON.

Pastoral and Renewal Services—VACANT.

Pastoral Planning Services—VACANT, Dir.; KRISTI IRWIN, Administrative Asst.

Archivist—VACANT.

Financial Services—JIM CARNEY, Diocesan Financial Svcs. Officer, 515 N. Ewing St., P.O. Box 1729, Helena, 59624. Tel: 406-442-5820; Fax: 406-442-5191.

Development Services—Mailing Address: P.O. Box 1729, Helena, 59624. Tel: 406-442-5820; Fax: 406-442-5191. VACANT, Dir.

Stewardship Services—GLENDA SEIPP, Dir. Stewardship & Annual Giving, Mailing Address: P.O. Box 1729, Helena, 59624. Tel: 406-442-5820; Fax: 406-442-5191.

Diocesan Tribunal—Rev. JOHN W. ROBERTSON, P.O. Box 1729, Helena, 59624. Tel: 406-442-5820; Fax: 406-442-1085.

Notaries (Tribunal)—JOANNA HADDON; KRISTI IRWIN.

Judicial Vicar—Rev. JOHN W. ROBERTSON.

Associate Judges—Revs. THOMAS P. HAFFEY; MATTHEW P. HUBER.

Promoter of Justice—Rev. ROBERT GROSCH, J.C.L.

Defenders of the Bond—Revs. JEFFREY M. FLEMING; GARY W. RELLER, (Retired).

Diocesan Consultors—Revs. PATRICK BERETTA; BRIAN BERGERON; EDWARD HISLOP; RODERICK ERMATINGER; THOMAS P. HAFFEY; GARY W. RELLER, (Retired); BART TOLLESON; VALENTINE D. ZDILLA; JOHN W. ROBERTSON, Chancellor & Sec.

Diocesan Finance Council—JIM CARNEY; TERRY B. COSGROVE, Chm.; LORI MURPHY-MOULLET; Rev. Msgrs. KEVIN S. O'NEILL; JOSEPH D. HARRINGTON, (Retired); CATHY GIVLER; PETER JOHNSON; Rev.

JOHN W. ROBERTSON; RON SCHAFER; DAVE ROBERTS; RICK AHMANN.

Deaneries—Rev. EDWARD KOHLER, Conrad; Rev. Msgr. KEVIN S. O'NEILL, Helena; Revs. EDWARD HISLOP, Missoula; CRAIG HANLEY, Kalispell; THOMAS P. HAFFEY, Butte; VALENTINE D. ZDILLA, Bozeman.

Personnel Board—Rev. Msgr. KEVIN S. O'NEILL; Revs. GARY W. RELLER, (Retired); THOMAS P. HAFFEY; Rev. Msgr. JOSEPH D. HARRINGTON, (Retired); Revs. LEO J. PROXELL; JOHN DARRAGH, (Retired); DOUGALD MCCALLUM; MARC J. LENNEMAN; SEAN RAFTIS; JOHN W. ROBERTSON, Sec.

Interdiocesan Organizations

Montana Catholic Conference—Mailing Address: 1313 11th Ave., P.O. Box 1708, Helena, 59624. Tel: 406-442-5761; Fax: 406-442-9047; Email: director@montanacc.org; Web: www.montanacc.org. MATTHEW BROWER, Exec. Dir.

Catholic Social Services for Montana, Inc.—1301 11th Ave., P.O. Box 907, Helena, 59624. Tel: 406-442-4130; Fax: 406-442-4192; Email: twila@cssmt.org; Web: www.cssmt.org. TWILA COSTIGAN, Exec. Dir. Coordinates and supervises all Catholic Social welfare in the State of Montana.

Helena Office—Mailing Address: P.O. Box 907, Helena, 59624. Tel: 406-442-4130. TWILA COSTIGAN, Dir., Adoptions; JANN PETEK, Social Worker; SENJA LINJANEN, Exec. Asst.; SUSAN GLIKO, Rachel's Hope Prog. Coord.

Billings Office—1048 N. 30th St., Billings, 59101. Tel: 406-252-3399. Social Worker: MICHELLE PERLICK, (Billings).

Great Falls Office—410 Central Ave., Ste. 601, Great Falls, 59401. VACANT.

Missoula Office—420 W. Pine St., Missoula, 59802. JENNY GREENWOOD, Social Worker, Tel: 406-728-5429.

Diocesan Offices and Organizations

Borromeo Pre-Seminary Program—Rev. MARC J. LENNEMAN, 1601 N. Benton Ave., Helena, 59625. Tel: 406-447-4869.

Catholic Campaign for Human Development—Deacon JAMES BUTTS, P.O. Box 277, Bigfork, 59911.

Catholic Committee on Scouting—MIKE MORGAN, Mailing Address: 23 Laurin Loop, Sheridan, 59749. Tel: 406-842-5085.

Catholic Youth Coalition—Mailing Address: P.O. Box 1729, Helena, 59624. Tel: 406-442-5820. KEVIN MOLM, Contact.

Charismatic Renewal—VACANT, P.O. Box 1729, Helena, 59624. Tel: 406-442-5820.

Christian Family Movement—VACANT, Contact, P.O. Box 1729, Helena, 59624.

Continuing Formation of the Clergy—Rev. THOMAS P. HAFFEY, Dir., 2100 Farragut, Butte, 59701. Tel: 406-723-4303.

Delegate for Religious—Mailing Address: P.O. Box 1729, Helena, 59624. Tel: 406-442-5820. VACANT.

Cursillo Movement, Journey and Search—Mailing Address: P.O. Box 1729, Helena, 59624. Tel: 406-442-5820. Deacon DOUG CAMERON; MARILYN CAMERON.

Daughters of Isabella—CAROLYN SMITH, Regent, 51100 Mt. Hwy. 200, Ovando, 59854.

Diocesan Attorney—WILLIAM DRISCOLL, Mailing Address: Franz & Driscoll, P.L.L.P., P.O. Box 1155, Helena, 59624. Tel: 406-442-0005.

Diocesan Buildings—Mailing Address: P.O. Box 1729, Helena, 59624. JIM CARNEY, Mgr.

Diocesan Council of Catholic Women—148 Drew Lane, Bigfork, 59911. SUSAN PORROVECCHIO.

Diocesan Ecumenical Officer—Diocese of Helena: P.O. Box 1729, Helena, 59624-1729. Tel: 406-442-5820. DAN BARTLESON, Email: dbartleson@diocesehelena.org.

Friends of The Catholic University—Rev. Msgr. JOSEPH D. HARRINGTON, Chm., (Retired), 1601 N. Benton Ave., Helena, 59625. Tel: 406-447-4459.

Guatemala Missions—Mailing Address: P.O. Box 1729, Helena, 59624. Tel: 406-442-5820. Deacon MICHAEL SEIPP, Dir.

Holy Childhood Association—VACANT.

Legendary Lodge (Diocesan Summer Camp)—DAN BARTLESON, Mailing Address: P.O. Box 1729, Helena, 59624. Tel: 406-442-5820.

Marriage Encounter—CHRIS STOKES; ANGIE STOKES, 1718 Wicks Ln., Billings, 59105. Tel: 406-534-2391.

Office of Due Process—Rev. JOHN W. ROBERTSON, P.O. Box 1729, Helena, 59624. Tel: 406-442-5820.

Permanent Deacons—Mailing Address: P.O. Box 1729, Helena, 59624. Tel: 406-442-5820. Deacon MICHAEL SEIPP, Dir.

Program of Formation for Lay Ministry—DAN BARTLESON, Mailing Address: P.O. Box 1729, Helena, 59624. Tel: 406-442-5820.

Program of Formation for the Permanent Diaconate—Mailing Address: P.O. Box 1729, Helena, 59624. Tel: 406-442-5820. Deacon MICHAEL SEIPP, Dir.

Liturgical Commission—Rev. EDWARD HISLOP, Chm., 1475 Eaton St., Missoula, 59801. Tel: 406-721-2405. Members: JOSEPH BEAUSOLEIL; Deacon JAMES BUTTS; JASON PHILLIPS; Rev. JEFFREY M. FLEMING; Sr. MARY AGNES HOGAN, S.C.L.; TERRY ORR; Deacon BERNARD MCCARTHY; Sr. MARY JO QUINN, S.C.L.; VICKI BURGMEIER; Rev. BRIAN BERGERON; Sr. GRETCHEN WAGNER, C.S.J. Consultant: Rev. MICHAEL DRISCOLL.

Propagation of the FaithMailing Address: Diocese of Helena, P.O. Box 1729, Helena, 59624-1729. Tel: 406-442-5820; Email: chancery@diocesehelena.org. Rev. JOHN W. ROBERTSON, Chancellor.

Catholic Formation Department—515 N. Ewing St., P.O. Box 1729, Helena, 59624. Tel: 406-442-5820. KEVIN MOLM, Dir.

Superintendent of Schools—TIMOTHY UHL, Ed.D., 1313 11th Ave., P.O. Box 1708, Helena, 59601. Tel: 406-442-5761; Fax: 406-442-9047.

Third Order of St. Francis—TONY POELMAN, 1702 Peosta, Helena, 59601.

Victim Assistance Coordinator—HELEN BEAUSOLEIL, Mailing Address: P.O. Box 1729, Helena, 59624. Tel: 406-459-0513; Email: victimassistant@diocesehelena.org.

Vocations Office—Mailing Address: P.O. Box 1729, Helena, 59624. Tel: 406-442-5820. Rev. MARC J. LENNEMAN, 1601 N. Benton Ave., Helena, 59625. Tel: 406-447-4869.

Communications Director—DAN BARTLESON, Mailing Address: P.O. Box 1729, Helena, 59624. Tel: 406-442-5820; Email: dbartleson@diocesehelena.org.

CLERGY, PARISHES, MISSIONS AND PAROCHIAL SCHOOLS

CITY OF HELENA

(LEWIS AND CLARK COUNTY)

1—CATHEDRAL OF ST. HELENA (1866)
530 N. Ewing St., 59601. Tel: 406-442-5825; Email: tcorbett@sthelenas.org. Rev. Msgr. Kevin S. O'Neill; Rev. Christopher Lebsock, Parochial Vicar; Deacon Bob Fishman; Michael Vreeberg, Pastoral Assoc.; Jason Phillips, Pastoral Assoc.
Catechesis Religious Program—Email: bfishman@sthelenas.org. Students 166.
Good Samaritan Thrift Store—3067 N. Montana Ave., 59601. Tel: 406-442-0780; Email: theresa@goosamministries.org. Theresa Ortega, Dir. (Assistance to those in need.).

2—ST. MARY (1910)
1700 Missoula Ave., 59601. Tel: 406-442-5268; Fax: 406-449-0860; Email: smcc@stmaryhelena.org; Web: www.stmaryhelena.org. Rev. Richard Francesco; Deacon Michael Seipp.
Catechesis Religious Program—Deb Kralicek, D.R.E. Students 88.

3—OUR LADY OF THE VALLEY
1502 Shirley Rd., 59602. Tel: 406-458-6114; Fax: 406-458-8179; Email: olvoffice@olvmt.org; Web: www.olvmt.org. Rev. Daniel B. Shea; Deacons Randy Fraser; Stephen Barry; Margaret Brennan, Music Min.; Nelson Cathleen, Business Mgr.; Pamela Banning, Office Mgr.; Tim Harris, RCIA Coord.; Pete Oljar, Pastoral Council Chair; Chris Jensen, Finance Council Chair; Valerie Bright, Custodial; Marty Heaton, Custodial/Grounds.
Catechesis Religious Program—David Casey, Youth Min.; Cyndi Krings, Youth Min. Students 140.
Mission—Sacred Heart, 125 Walsh St., Wolf Creek, 59648.

OUTSIDE THE CITY OF HELENA

ANACONDA, DEER LODGE CO.

1—ANACONDA CATHOLIC COMMUNITY aka Holy Family Catholic Church, St. Peter's Catholic Church (1980) Serves the entire community of Anaconda.
217 W. Pennsylvania, Anaconda, 59711. Tel: 406-563-8406; Email: anacondacatholic@qwestoffice.net; Web: anacondacatholiccommunity.com. Rev. Dougald McCallum.
Holy Family—
St. Peter, 405 Alder St., Anaconda, 59711.
Catechesis Religious Program—Ashley See, D.R.E. Students 83.

2—ST. JOSEPH'S (1957) Closed. 1977. For inquiries for parish records contact Anaconda Catholic Community, Anaconda.

3—ST. PAUL'S (1888) Closed. 1980. For inquiries for parish records contact Anaconda Catholic Community, Anaconda.

4—ST. PETER'S (1898) Closed. 1980. For inquiries for parish records contact Anaconda Catholic Community, Anaconda.

BELGRADE, GALLATIN CO., ST. JOHN VIANNEY PARISH
609 N. Quaw Blvd., Belgrade, 59714. Tel: 406-388-1290; Fax: 406-388-2321; Email: sjvbelgrade@gmail.com; Web: www.sjvbelgrade.org. Rev. Eric C. Gilbaugh; Deacon Warner Holm.
Catechesis Religious Program—Email: sjvre.belgrade@gmail.com. Meredith Beery, D.R.E. Students 89.

BIGFORK, FLATHEAD CO., SAINT JOHN PAUL II (1958)
195 Coverdell Rd., Bigfork, 59911. Tel: 406-837-4846 ; Fax: 406-755-5591; Email: johnpaul2@centurytel.net; Web: www.saintjp2.org. P.O. Box 277, Bigfork, 59911. Rev. Craig Hanley; Deacon James Butts, Pastoral Assoc.; Mrs. Dawn Lembke, Business Mgr.
Catechesis Religious Program—Sierra Butts, D.R.E. Students 71.

BONNER, MISSOULA CO., ST. ANN (1940)
9015 Hwy. 200 E., Bonner, 59823. Tel: 406-258-6815; Email: stannparish5@gmail.com; Web: www.stannbonner.org. P.O. Box 1008, Bonner, 59823. Rev. Jozef Perehubka, (Poland); Mr. Doug Lawrence, Pres.; Anne Wright, Music Min.; Ms. Jill Frohlich, Youth Min.; Mrs. Rory Page, Sec.
Catechesis Religious Program—Donna Fuller, D.R.E. Students 29.
Mission—Living Water, 152 S.O.S. Rd., Seeley Lake, 59868. Tel: 406-677-2688; Email: livingwatermission@diocesehelena.org. P.O. Box 995, Seeley Lake, 59868. Mrs. Marilyn Niklas, Pres.; Mrs. Velma Burnett, D.R.E.; Chris Flinders, Music Min.; Mrs. Rita Rossi, Sec.

BOULDER, JEFFERSON CO., ST. CATHERINE (1894)
214 S. Elder St., Boulder, 59632. Tel: 406-225-3222; Email: saintcatherineschurch@gmail.com. P.O. Box 205, Boulder, 59632. Revs. Thomas P. Haffey; Elias Kabuk.
Mission—St. John the Evangelist, Hwy. 69, Boulder Valley, 59632.

BOZEMAN, GALLATIN CO.

1—HOLY ROSARY (1885)
220 W. Main St., P.O. Box 96, Bozeman, 59771-0096. Tel: 406-587-4581; Email: hrp@holyrosarybozeman.org; Web: holyrosarybozeman.org. Rev. Leo J. Proxell; Deacon Vern Korchinski.
Catechesis Religious Program—Students 222.

2—RESURRECTION UNIVERSITY CATHOLIC PARISH (1965) (Newman Parish)
1725 S. 11th Ave., Bozeman, 59715. Tel: 406-589-9243; Web: www.resurrectionbozeman.org. Rev. Valentine D. Zdilla; Deacon Steven Buckner.

BROWNING, GLACIER CO., LITTLE FLOWER PARISH (1904)
202 1st St. N.W., Browning, 59417. Tel: 406-338-5775; Fax: 406-338-5775; Email: lfpblackfeet@gmail.com. P.O. Box 529, Browning, 59417. Revs. Edward Kohler; Joseph Paddock, Parochial Vicar; Deacon John Gobert.
School—De La Salle Blackfeet Middle School, (Grades 4-8), 104 First St. N.W., Browning, 59417. Tel: 406-338-5290; Email: brodale@dlsbs.org; Web: www.dlsbs.org. P.O. Box 1489, Browning, 59417. Bro. Dale Mooney, F.S.C., Pres.; Michael O'Brien, Prin. Lay Teachers 13; Students 70; Clergy / Religious Teachers 2.
Catechesis Religious Program—Ronnalea Gallagher, D.R.E. Students 26.
Missions—Sacred Heart—Starr School Road, Starr School, 59417.
Chapel of the Ascension, South East Corner, East Glacier, 59434.

BUTTE, SILVER BOW CO.

1—ST. ANN (1917)
2100 Farragut Ave., Butte, 59701. Tel: 406-723-4303; Fax: 406-723-5172; Email: stannparish@bresnan.net; Web: www.stannsbutte.org. Revs. Thomas P. Haffey; Kirby Longo, Parochial Vicar; Deacons Bernard McCarthy, Parish Admin.; John Uggetti.
Catechesis Religious Program—2100 Farragut, Butte, 59701. Rosalie Stimatz-Richards, D.R.E. Students 75.

2—BUTTE CATHOLIC COMMUNITY CENTRAL, Includes St. Joseph and St. John the Evangelist Parishes. See individual listings.
1500 Cobban, Butte, 59701. Tel: 406-782-8349; Email: stjohnparish@bresnan.net; Email: bschwartzmiller22@gmail.com. Rev. Robert Hall, Admin.

3—BUTTE CATHOLIC COMMUNITY NORTH, Includes Immaculate Conception and St. Patrick Parishes. See individual listings.
102 S. Washington St., Butte, 59701.

Tel: 406-723-5407; Fax: 406-782-5408; Email: bccn@diocesehelena.org; Web: www.butteccn.org. Rev. Patrick Beretta; Deacon Bernard McCarthy; Ms. Seaneen Prendergast, Pastoral Assoc.; Mr. John Brown, Business Mgr.; Mrs. Julie Brinton, Sec.
Catechesis Religious Program—Ms. Seaneen Prendergast, D.R.E. Students 63.

4—St. Helena (1921) Closed. 1966. For inquiries for parish records contact Butte Catholic Community North, Butte.

5—Holy Savior (1904) Closed. Closed in 1974. For inquiries for parish records contact Butte Catholic Community North, Butte.

6—Holy Spirit (1978)
3930 E. Lake St., Butte, 59701. Tel: 406-494-5078; Fax: 406-494-5726; Email: holyspiritbutte@q.com; Web: www.holyspiritbutte.org. Revs. Thomas P. Haffey; Kirby Longo; William Dornbos, Pastoral Assoc.; Deacon Doug Cameron; Maureen Richardson, Sec.
Catechesis Religious Program—Email: rcrosby@q.com. Rene Crosby, D.R.E. & Youth Min. Students 12.

7—Immaculate Conception (1907) (Butte Catholic Community North)
102 S. Washington, Butte, 59701. Tel: 406-723-5407; Fax: 406-782-5408; Email: bccn@diocesehelena.org. Rev. Patrick Beretta.

8—St. John the Evangelist (1917)
1500 Majors Ave., Butte, 59701. Tel: 406-782-8349; Email: stjohnparish@bresnan.net; Email: bschwartzmiller22@gmail.com. 1500 Cobban St., Butte, 59701. Rev. Robert Hall, Admin. (A Part of Butte Catholic Community Central).

9—St. Joseph (1905) (A Part of Butte Catholic Community Central)
Utah & 2nd St., Butte, 59701. Tel: 406-782-8349; Email: stjohnparish@bresnan.net; Email: bschwartzmiller22@gail.com. 1500 Cobban St., Butte, 59701. Rev. Robert Hall, Admin.

10—St. Mary (1903) Closed. 1986. For inquiries for parish records contact Butte Catholic Community North, Butte.

11—St. Patrick (1881) (Butte Catholic Community North)
329 W. Mercury St., Butte, 59701. Tel: 406-723-5407; Email: bccn@diocesehelena.org. Mailing Address: 102 S. Washington St., Butte, 59701. Rev. Patrick Beretta.

12—Sacred Heart Parish (1903) Closed. 1970. For inquiries for parish records contact Butte Catholic Community North, Butte.

Choteau, Teton Co., St. Joseph (1898)
320 Main St. N., Choteau, 59422. Tel: 406-466-2961; Email: ltoeckes@3rivers.net; Web: www.jmjparishes.com. P.O. Box 640; Choteau, 59422. Rev. Brian Bergeron.
Catechesis Religious Program—Tel: 406-463-2586. Laura Toeckes, D.R.E. Students 25.

Columbia Falls, Flathead Co., St. Richard (1941)
Mailing Address: 1210 9th St. W., P.O. Box 2073, Columbia Falls, 59912. Tel: 406-892-5142; Fax: 406-892-2147; Email: strichards@bresnan.net; Web: www.strichardsparish.org. Rev. Sean Raftis; Deacon Doug Cordier, Pastoral Assoc.
Catechesis Religious Program—Raven Dryden-Woelkers, D.R.E.; Lynette Smith, Youth Min. Students 47.
Station—West Glacier Mission, Apgar Ampitheather, Apgar, 59936.

Conrad, Pondera Co., St. Michael the Archangel (1909)
106 S. Maryland St., Conrad, 59425.
Tel: 406-278-7517; Email: stmike.conrad@gmail.com. P.O. Box 577, Conrad, 59425. Revs. Timothy J. Moriarty; John Abutu; Yovin Shayo; Deacon Marcus Raba.
Catechesis Religious Program—Tanya Mycke, D.R.E. Students 27.

Cut Bank, Glacier Co., St. Margaret aka St. Margaret Catholic Community (1914)
129 Second Ave. S.E., Cut Bank, 59427.
Tel: 406-873-4413; Email: stmarg207@gmail.com; Web: www.stmargaretcatholiccommunity.org. P.O. Box 207, Cut Bank, 59427. Revs. Timothy J. Moriarty; Peter Mikwabe, Parochial Vicar; Sr. Gretchen Wagner, C.S.J., Parish Life Coord.; Mr. Clint Augare, Fin. Council Contact; Ms. Carolyn Holm, Bookkeeper; Mrs. Elaine Blomquist, Pastoral Council Contact; Ms. Pauline Nygaard, Music Min.; Ms. Dorothy Johnson, Liturgy Dir.
Catechesis Religious Program—Mrs. Juanita Meeks, D.R.E. Students 49.

Deer Lodge, Powell Co., Immaculate Conception (1911)
605 Clark St., P.O. Box 786, Deer Lodge, 59722.
Tel: 406-846-4114; Email: icdeerlodge@outlook.com; Web: www.icdeerlodge.org. Rev. Joseph Fleming; Chris Dubay, Pastoral Assoc.
Catechesis Religious Program—Joan Sewell, D.R.E.; Ann Marie Thomas, Youth MIn. Students 29.

Dillon, Beaverhead Co., St. Rose of Lima (1901)
226 S. Atlantic St., Dillon, 59725. Tel: 406-683-4391; Fax: 406-683-6244; Email: strosedillon2015@gmail.com. Rev. Pascal Kasanziki; Deacon Paul Rust; Mr. Mike Thornton, RCIA Coord.; Ms. Mary Hartman, Youth Min.
Catechesis Religious Program—Nancy Johnson, D.R.E. Students 50.
Missions—St. John The Apostle—Frontage Rd., Melrose, 59743. Email: strosedillon@gmail.com.
Lima Mission, Lima Fire Hall, Lima, 59739.
Tel: 406-276-3376; Email: strosedillon@gmail.com. Kathy Stosich, Contact Person.

Drummond, Granite Co., St. Michael (1919)
12 Main St., Drummond, 59832. Tel: 406-241-3604; Email: vburgmeier@blackfoot.net. P.O. Box 329, Drummond, 59832. Deacon Chris Burgmeier; Vicki Burgmeier, Parish Admin.
Catechesis Religious Program—Students 4.
Mission—St. Mary, Church Rd., Gold Creek, 59733.

Dutton, Teton Co., St. William (1962)
20 1st Ave. N.E., Dutton, 59433. Tel: 406-476-3429; Email: deaconmarcus@me.com. P.O. Box 18, Dutton, 59433. Revs. Timothy J. Moriarty; John Abutu, Parochial Vicar; Yovin Shayo, Parochial Vicar; Deacon Marcus Raba; Pam Raba, Pastoral Assoc.
Mission—Guardian Angel, 104 Central Ave., Power, 59468. Tel: 406-463-2450; Email: deaconmarcus@me.com. P.O. Box 105, Power, 59468.

East Helena, Lewis and Clark Co., SS. Cyril and Methodius (1907)
120 W. Riggs St., P.O. Box 1110, East Helena, 59635. Tel: 406-227-5334; Fax: 406-227-5891; Email: parishoffice@sscyril.org; Web: www.sscyril.org. Rev. Bart Tolleson; Deacon Iver Johnson.
Catechesis Religious Program—Email: chris@sscyril.org; Email: marie@sscyril.org. Marie Moran, D.R.E.; Christopher Hammen, Youth Min. Students 141.
Missions—St. John's—5 S. Main, Clancy, 59634.
Our Lady of the Lake, 8375 Canyon Ferry Rd., Lewis and Clark Co. 59602.

Eureka, Lincoln Co., Our Lady of Mercy (1916)
500 Dewey Ave., Eureka, 59917. Tel: 406-297-2118; Fax: 406-297-5247; Email: olm@interbel.net; Web: olmeurekamt.org. P.O. Box 626, Eureka, 59917-0626. Rev. Gregory Lively; Mrs. Lisa Stein, Office Mgr.
Catechesis Religious Program—Tel: 406-297-2118. Holly Oncken, D.R.E. Students 14.

Fairfield, Teton Co., St. John the Evangelist (1941)
519 First Ave. S., Fairfield, 59436. Tel: 406-466-2961; Email: ltoeckes@3rivers.net; Web: www.jmjparishes.com. P.O. Box 397, Fairfield, 59436. Rev. Brian Bergeron.
Catechesis Religious Program—Tel: 406-463-2586. Laura Toeckes, D.R.E. Students 21.
Mission—St. Matthias, 508 Broadway, Augusta, 59410.

Frenchtown, Missoula Co., St. John the Baptist (1884) [CEM]
Mailing Address: 16680 Main St., P.O. Box 329, Frenchtown, 59834. Tel: 406-626-4492; Fax: 406-620-1970; Email: stjohnthebaptist@hotmail.com; Web: www.clarkforkcatholic.com. Revs. Jeffrey M. Fleming; Cody Williams.
Catechesis Religious Program—Jodi Todd, D.R.E. Students 7.
Missions—St. Mary Queen of Heaven—204 2nd Ave. E., Superior, 59872.
St. Albert the Great, 117 Railroad St., Alberton, 59820.

Hamilton, Ravalli Co., St. Francis of Assisi (1896)
411 S. 5th St., Hamilton, 59840. Tel: 406-363-1385; Fax: 406-363-1451; Email: mail@stfrancishamilton.org; Web: www.stfrancishamilton.org. P.O. Box 593, Hamilton, 59840. Rev. James Connor; Deacon Jim Kaney; Sr. Margaret Hogan, S.C.L., Pastoral Assoc.; Diane Tredik, Youth Min.; Craig Tredik, Youth Min.
Catechesis Religious Program—Sara Morin, D.R.E. Students 28.
Mission—St. Philip Benizi, 312 Miles Ave., Darby, 59829.

Harlowton, Wheatland Co., St. Joseph (1909)
26 Third St. N.W., Box 286, Harlowton, 59036.
Tel: 406-632-5538; Email: stjosephparish-harlowton@diocesehelena.org. Revs. David Severson; Micah Bagayang.
Catechesis Religious Program—Ms. Kristi Lane, D.R.E.; Ms. Gwen Begger, Youth Min. Students 4.
Missions—Immaculate Conception—304 Louis Ave., Judith Gap, 59453. Email: holycrossmt@gmail.com.
Blessed Sacrament, 203 W. 1st St., Shawmut, 59078.

Heart Butte, Glacier Co., St. Anne (Blackfeet Reservation) (1911)
BIA Rd. #1, Heart Butte, 59448. Tel: 406-338-2312; Fax: 406-338-2362; Email: stannes@3rivers.net. P.O. Box 160, Heart Butte, 59448. Revs. Edward Kohler; Joseph Paddock.
Catechesis Religious Program—Students 30.
Mission—Holy Family Mission, [CEM] Joe Show E. Rd., Heart Butte, 59448. Email: lfpblackfeet@gmail.com. P.O. Box 529, Browning, 59417.

Helmville, Powell Co., St. Thomas the Apostle (1889) [CEM]
108 Main St., Helmville, 59843. Tel: 406-793-5697; Email: momannx22@gmail.com. P.O. Box 90, Helmville, 59843. Rev. John W. Robertson.
Catechesis Religious Program—Maureen Mannix, D.R.E.
Mission—St. Jude's, 100 Main St., Lincoln, 59639. Tel: 406-362-3210; Email: jrobertson@diocesehelena.org. P.O. Box 802, Lincoln, 59639. Families 15.

Kalispell, Flathead Co.

1—St. Matthew (1895)
602 S. Main St., Kalispell, 59901. Tel: 406-752-6788; Fax: 406-756-8248; Email: parish@stmattsaints.org; Web: www.stmatthewskalispell.org. Rev. Roderick Ermatinger; Deacon Charles Harball; Jeanne O'Connell, Pastoral Min./Coordinator; Michael HueKhang, Pastoral Min./Coordinator; Mrs. Megan Holt, Business Mgr.; Kim Maes, Music Min.; Ruby Reiner, Sec.
Catechesis Religious Program—Mrs. Megan Holt, D.R.E. Students 101.

2—Risen Christ (1978)
65 W. Evergreen Dr., Kalispell, 59901.
Tel: 406-752-4219; Fax: 406-752-4226; Email: rcparish@montanasky.us; Web: risenchristkalispell.org. Rev. Stanislaw Rog, Admin.
Catechesis Religious Program—Katherine Louden, D.R.E. Students 25.

Libby, Lincoln Co., St. Joseph (1911)
719 Utah Ave., Libby, 59923. Tel: 406-293-4322; Email: stjosephlibby@gmail.com. Revs. Richard Kluk, Admin.; Sean Raftis, S.J.; Mike Noble, Youth Min.; Leona LeRoy, Business Mgr.
Catechesis Religious Program—Theresa Purdy, D.R.E. Students 17.
Mission—Immaculate Conception, 756 Hwy. 2 W., Troy, 59935.

Missoula, Missoula Co.

1—St. Anthony (1921)
217 Tremont St., Missoula, 59801. Tel: 406-543-3129; Fax: 406-549-6009; Email: office@stacp.org; Web: www.stacp.org. Rev. Michael Drury; Terry Jimmerson, Pastoral Assoc.
Catechesis Religious Program—Debbie Dube, D.R.E. Students 19.

2—Blessed Trinity Parish (1971)
1475 Eaton St., Missoula, 59801. Tel: 406-721-2405; Email: office@blessedtrinitymissoula.org; Web: blessedtrinitymissoula.org. Rev. Edward Hislop; Deacon Ronald Butler; Sr. Mary Jo Quinn, S.C.L., Pastoral Assoc.; Daniel Hampson, Music Min.; Jim McDonald, Business Mgr.; Carol Lemieux, Sec.
Catechesis Religious Program—Email: judyc@blessedtrinitymissoula.org. Judy Cooney, D.R.E. Students 83.
Mission—Spirit of Christ, 5475 Farm Ln., Lolo, Missoula Co. 59847. Tel: 406-273-2748. Cheryl Russell, Pastoral Min./Coord.

3—Christ the King (1966) (Newman Parish)
1400 Gerald Ave., Missoula, 59801.
Tel: 406-728-3845; Email: office@ctkmsla.org. Revs. Jeffrey M. Fleming; Cody Williams; Bridgette Bannick, Campus Min.; Shai LaFleur, Youth Min.
Catechesis Religious Program—Email: pcassidy@ctkmsla.org. Patti Cassidy, D.R.E. Students 23.

4—St. Francis Xavier (1881)
420 W. Pine St., Missoula, 59802. Tel: 406-542-0321; Fax: 406-327-8537; Email: stfrancisxavier@sfxmissoula.org; Web: www.sfxmissoula.org. Revs. Joseph Carver, S.J.; Richard Perry, S.J.; Deacons Michael Bloomdahl; Carlton Quamme, Sr. Status; Colin McCormack, Parish Admin.
Catechesis Religious Program—Spiritual Exercises in Everyday Life (S.E.E.L.), Email: lukelarson@sfxmissoula.org. Brian Johnson, D.R.E. Students 21.

5—Holy Family (1972) Closed. For inquiries contact Blessed Trinity Parish.

Philipsburg, Granite Co., St. Philip (1892)
308 W. Kearney, Philipsburg, 59858. Cell: 406-241-3604. Mailing Address: P.O. Box 329, Drummond, 59832. Deacon Chris Burgmeier; Vicki Burgmeier, Parish Admin.

Plains, Sanders Co., St. James (1889)
109 W. Meany St., Plains, 59859. Tel: 406-826-3668; Email: jbenusa@diocesehelena.org; Web: www.sccthompsonfalls.parishesonline.com. P.O. Box 745, Plains, 59859. Rev. Jeffrey M. Benusa; Deacon Lynn F. McAtee.
Catechesis Religious Program—Linda Black, Youth Min. Students 8.
Mission—Sacred Heart, 22 First Ave., Hot Springs, 59845.

Polson, Lake Co., Immaculate Conception (1909) [CEM 3]
1002 4th Ave. E., Polson, 59860. Tel: 406-883-2506; Fax: 406-883-4649; Email:

lakecountyromancatholic@gmail.com; Web: www.lakecountyromancatholic.org. P.O. Box 1477, Polson, 59860. Rev. Kevin Christofferson; Deacon Wesley Vert, Sr. Status.
Catechesis Religious Program—Deanna McElwee, D.R.E. Students 74.

RONAN, LAKE CO., SACRED HEART (1911)
35933 Round Butte Rd., Ronan, 59864.
Tel: 406-883-2506; Fax: 406-883-4649; Email: lakecountyromancatholic@gmail.com. Mailing Address: P.O. Box 1477, Polson, 59860. Rev. Kevin Christofferson.
Mission—St. Joseph's, 53099 Main St. N., Charlo, 59824. Tel: 406-676-4511.

ST. IGNATIUS, LAKE CO., ST. IGNATIUS MISSION (1854)
300 Beartrack Ave., P.O. Box 667, St. Ignatius, 59865. Tel: 406-745-2768; Fax: 406-745-0010; Email: mission7@blackfoot.net; Web: www.stignatiusmission.org. Rev. Craig Hightower; Sr. Margaret Hillary, Admin. & D.R.E.
Catechesis Religious Program—Email: ashchurch@blackfoot.net. Students 58.
Missions—Sacred Heart—112 Taelman, Arlee, 59821. Tel: 406-726-3540; Email: ashchurch@blackfoot.net.
St. John Berchman's, Agency Road, Jocko, 59821. P.O. Box 270, Arlee, 59821.

SHELBY, TOOLE CO., ST. WILLIAM (1924)
531 Main St., Shelby, 59474. Tel: 406-434-2988; Fax: 406-434-9133; Email: saintwm@3rivers.net. Revs. Timothy J. Moriarty; Peter Mikwabe, Parochial Vicar.
Catechesis Religious Program—Emily McDermott, D.R.E. Students 36.
Mission—St. Thomas Aquinas (1917) 120 1st St. S., Sunburst, 59482. Tel: 406-434-9133.

SHERIDAN, MADISON CO., MADISON COUNTY CATHOLIC COMMUNITY, Comprised of St. Mary of the Assumption, Laurin; St. Joseph, Sheridan; and St. Patrick, Ennis.
105 Poppleton, P.O. Box 17, Sheridan, 59749.
Tel: 406-842-5588. Rev. John Crutchfield.
Catechesis Religious Program—Margaret Stecker, Parish Youth Ministry & Parish Junior High Coord. Students 19.
Mission—Notre Dame.

STEVENSVILLE, RAVALLI CO., ST. MARY (1842) [CEM]
333 Charlos St., Stevensville, 59870.
Tel: 406-777-5257; Fax: 406-777-1032; Email: stmarystevi@gmail.com; Web: www.stmarymissionchurch.org. Rev. Matthew P. Huber; James Gablick, Grounds & Maintenance; Theresa Endecott, Sec.
Catechesis Religious Program—Derek Wherley, D.R.E. Students 17.
Mission—St. Joseph, 224 Linder St., Florence, 59833.

SWAN VALLEY, LAKE CO., OUR LADY OF SWAN VALLEY MISSION, Mission of Saint John Paul II, Bigfork.
21592 Sycamore Tree Ln., Swan Lake, 59911.
Tel: 406-837-4846; Fax: 406-755-5591. P.O. Box 277, Bigfork, 59911. Rev. Craig Hanley; Deacon James Butts, Pastoral Admin.; Mrs. Dawn Lembke, Business Mgr.

THOMPSON FALLS, SANDERS CO., ST. WILLIAM (1955)
416 Preston Ave., Thompson Falls, 59873.
Tel: 406-827-4433; Email: stwilliam@blackfoot.net; Web: www.scccthompsonfalls.parishesonline.com. P.O. Box 186, Thompson Falls, 59873. Rev. Jeffrey M. Benusa; Deacon Ronald Kazmierczak; Mrs. Sandra Wulfekuhle, Sec.
Catechesis Religious Program—John Bennett, Youth Min.; Sherri Koskela, Youth Min.; Mandy Helvey, Youth Min.; Dennis Wulfekuhle, Youth Min. Students 18.
Mission—Noxon Mission, 200 Broadway, Noxon, 59853.

THREE FORKS, GALLATIN CO., HOLY FAMILY (1886)
104 E. Birch St., P.O. Box 99, Three Forks, 59752.
Tel: 406-285-3592; Email: holyfamily@q.com; Web: www.holyfamilymt.org. Rev. Eric C. Gilbaugh; Deacon Robert Lane.
Catechesis Religious Program—Carolyn Nealen, D.R.E. Students 10.

TOWNSEND, BROADWATER CO., HOLY CROSS (1903)
101 S. Walnut, P.O. Box 610, Townsend, 59644.
Tel: 406-266-4811; Email: holycrossmt@gmail.com; Web: holycrossmt.org. Revs. David Severson; Micah Bagayang.
Catechesis Religious Program—Shawna Wickens, D.R.E. Students 46.

VALIER, PONDERA CO., ST. FRANCIS (1909)
616 4th St., P.O. Box 338, Valier, 59486.
Tel: 406-279-3327; Email: stfrancis@3rivers.net. Rev. Timothy J. Moriarty; Sr. Gretchen Wagner, C.S.J., Pastoral Assoc. & D.R.E.; Mary Jean Brophy, Pastoral Assoc.
Catechesis Religious Program—Ms. Janet Stokes, D.R.E. Students 45.
Mission—Holy Cross.

WALKERVILLE, SILVER BOW CO., ST. LAWRENCE O'TOOLE (1896) Closed. 1986. For inquiries for parish records contact Butte Catholic Community North, Butte.

WEST YELLOWSTONE, GALLATIN CO., OUR LADY OF THE PINES
437 Madison Ave., P.O. Box 577, West Yellowstone, 59758. Tel: 406-646-7755; Email: ptoeckes@gmail.com. Sr. Patricia Toeckes, S.C.L., Pastoral Admin. & D.R.E.
Catechesis Religious Program—Students 27.
Mission—St. Joseph of Big Sky, 510 Little Coyote Rd., P.O. Box 161738, Big Sky, 59716.
Tel: 406-995-4697; Email: bscm@3rivers.net.

WHITE SULPHUR SPRINGS, MEAGHER CO., ST. BARTHOLOMEW (1916)
407 Second Ave. S.E., P.O. Box 422, White Sulphur Springs, 59645. Tel: 406-547-3737; Email: stbartholomewparish-whitesulphursprings@diocesehelena.org. Revs. David Severson; Micah Bagayang, Parochial Vicar.
Catechesis Religious Program—Email: holycrossmt@gmail.com. Ms. Helen Hanson, D.R.E. Students 8.

WHITEFISH, FLATHEAD CO., ST. CHARLES BORROMEO (1890)
230 Baker Ave., Whitefish, 59937. Tel: 406-862-2051; Fax: 866-948-8416; Email: stcharles@stcharleswhitefish.net; Web: www.stcharleswhitefish.org. P.O. Box 128, Whitefish, 59937. Rev. Kenneth E. Fortney.
Catechesis Religious Program—Email: office@stcharleswhitefish.net. Lynn Beck, D.R.E.; Mr. Greg Cantrell, Youth Min. Students 70.

WHITEHALL, JEFFERSON CO., ST. TERESA OF AVILA (1911)
107 Second Ave. E., P.O. Box 337, Whitehall, 59759.
Tel: 406-287-3893; Fax: 406-287-9213; Email: stteresa6@q.com. Revs. Thomas P. Haffey; Elias Kabuk; Mrs. Sherre Mead, Sec.
Catechesis Religious Program—Email: jaynelkd@aol.com. Students 15.

DIOCESAN MISSIONS

GUATEMALA, SANTO TOMAS
515 N. Ewing St., P.O. Box 1729, 59624-1729.
Tel: 406-442-5820; Email: chancery@diocesehelena.org. Deacon Michael Seipp, Dir.

HELENA, LEWIS AND CLARK CO., GUATEMALA MISSION MEDICAL FUND
515 N. Ewing St., 59624. Tel: 406-442-5820; Email: mseipp@diocesehelena.org; Web: www.diocesehelena.org. P.O. Box 1729, 59624-1729. Deacon Michael Seipp, Dir.

Chaplains of Public Institutions

HELENA. *U.S. Veteran's Hospital*, Fort Harrison, 59626. Served by Helena Area Parishes.

BOULDER. *Boulder River School and Hospital.* Attended from St. Catherine, Boulder.

DEER LODGE. *Montana State Prison.* Attended from Immaculate Conception Parish, Deer Lodge. Rev. Joseph Fleming.

WARM SPRINGS. *Warm Springs State Hospital.* Rev. Joseph Fleming.

Special Assignments:
Rev.—
Robertson, John W., Delegate for Canonical Svcs., Chancellor & Judicial Vicar, P.O. Box 1729, 59624.

On Duty Outside the Diocese:
Rev. Msgr.—
McCarthy, John F., P.A., Oblates of Wisdom, P.O. Box 13230, St. Louis, MO 63157
Revs.—
Driscoll, Michael, Notre Dame University, Department of Theology, South Bend, IN 46617
Flynn, Thomas, Emory University, 1278 Oakdale Rd., N.E., Atlanta, GA 30307.

Military Chaplains:
Revs.—
Diphe, Juan M., U.S. Air Force
Severson, David, Chap., Montana National Guard.

Retired:
Rev. Msgr.—
Harrington, Joseph D., (Retired), 1726 Cannon St., 59601
Revs.—
Bullman, Rudolph, (Retired), P.O. Box 1729, 59624-1729
Byrne, Joseph L., (Retired), 35 Carroll Dr., Townsend, 59644
Darragh, John, (Retired), 730 B Missy's Way, Missoula, 59801
Dornbos, William, 100 E. Broadway, Butte, 59701
Finnegan, Joseph, (Retired), P.O. Box 503, Whitehall, 59759
Hannigan, Raymond, (Retired), 848 S. 79th Pl., Mesa, AZ 85208
Hazelton, James, (Retired)
Hogan, James J., (Retired), 901 S. Higgins # 301, Missoula, 59801
Hunthausen, John F., (Retired), 15 Bumblebee Ct., Apt. A, 59601
Langhans, Victor E., (Retired), 640 SW Nottingham Ln., Dallas, OR 97338
McCormick, Frank, (Retired), 2409 Mary Jane Blvd., Missoula, 59808
Miller, John P., (Retired), 410 W. Artemas Dr., Missoula, 59803
Murray, John E., (Retired), 901 Pennsylvania Ave., Deer Lodge, 59722
O'Donnell, Thomas M., (Retired), 1701 Prospect Ave., #3H, 59601
Oblinger, Joseph B., (Retired), 2219 W. Oak St. #307, Bozeman, 59718
Patton, Patrick G., (Retired), 2405 Ridgeside Dr., Apopka, FL 32713
Pins, Herbert J., (Retired)
Poole, Michael, (Retired)
Smith, Michael M., (Retired)
Sullivan, Jeremiah, (Retired), 18 Bumblebee Ct., 59601
Tallman, Stephen, (Retired), 5630 Lower Woodchuck Rd., Florence, 59833
Wang, John, (Retired), 425 Ford St., Missoula, 59801.

Permanent Deacons:
Barry, Stephen, Our Lady of the Valley, Helena
Biedermann, John, (Senior Status)
Bloomdahl, Michael, St. Francis Xavier, Missoula
Buckner, Steven, Resurrection Parish, Bozeman
Burgmeier, Chris, Flint Creek Catholic Community, Hall
Butler, Ronald, Blessed Trinity Parish, Missoula
Butts, James, St. John Paul II Parish, Bigfork
Cameron, Doug, Holy Spirit, Butte
Casazza, Dan, (Senior Status)
Cordier, Doug, St. Richard, Columbia Falls
Dorrington, Andrew, (Senior Status)
Duvernay, J. Anthony, (Senior Status)
Fishman, Bob, Cathedral of St. Helena, Helena
Fournier, Ronald, (Senior Status)
Fraser, Randall, (Senior Status)
Gobert, John, Little Flower, Browning
Gullotta, Daniel, (Senior Status)
Harball, Charles, St. Matthew, Kalispell
Holm, Warner, St. John Vianney, Belgrade
Johnson, Iver, SS. Cyril & Methodius, Helena
Kaney, Jim, St. Francis of Assisi, Hamilton
Kazmierczak, Ronald, St. William, Thompson Falls
Korchinski, Vern, Holy Rosary Parish, Bozeman
Lane, Robert, (Senior Status)
McAtee, Lynn F., St. James, Plains
McCarthy, Bernard, Butte Catholic Community North
McCarthy, Thomas, (Senior Status)
McCubbins, Floyd, Risen Christ, Kalispell
McGrath, Daniel, (Senior Status)
Miller, Richard, (Senior Status)
Miller, Robert J., (Senior Status)
Pearce, Robert, (Senior Status)
Quamme, Carlton, (Senior Status)
Raba, Marcus, St. Michael the Archangel, Conrad; St. William, Dutton; Guardian Angel Mission, Power
Rust, Paul
Seipp, Michael, St. Mary Catholic Community, Deacon Director
Uggetti, John, St. Ann, Butte
Vert, Wesley, (Senior Status).

INSTITUTIONS LOCATED IN DIOCESE

[A] SEMINARIES, DIOCESAN

HELENA. *Carroll College*, 1601 N. Benton Ave., 59625.
Tel: 406-447-4300; Email: mlenneman@carroll.edu. Rev. Marc J. Lenneman, Pastor. Clergy 1; Students 5; Clergy / Religious Teachers 1.

[B] COLLEGES AND UNIVERSITIES

HELENA. *Carroll College* (1909) 1601 N. Benton Ave., 59625. Tel: 406-447-4300; Fax: 406-447-4533; Email: news@carroll.edu; Email: mjlarson@carroll.

edu; Web: www.carroll.edu. Dr. John Cech, Pres.; Lori Peterson, Vice Pres. Finance & Admin.; Dr. James Hardwick, Vice Pres. Student Life; Rev. Marc J. Lenneman, Dir. Campus Ministry Programs & Chap. Four-year Diocesan, liberal arts, and pre-professional college. Clergy 1; Priests 1; Students 1,268; Total Staff 155; Lay Professors 93; Clergy / Religious Teachers 1.

[C] HIGH SCHOOLS, DIOCESAN

BUTTE. *Central High School* aka Butte Central Catholic High School (1924) 9 S. Idaho St., Butte, 59701. Tel: 406-782-6761; Fax: 406-723-3873; Email: jpwilliams@buttecentralschools.org; Web: www.buttecentralschools.org. Mr. John (JP) Williams, Prin.

Legal Title: Butte Central Catholic High School Lay Teachers 25; Students 125; Clergy / Religious Teachers 1.

MISSOULA. *Loyola Sacred Heart High School* (Missoula Catholic Schools) 320 Edith St., Missoula, 59801. Tel: 406-549-6101; Fax: 406-542-1432; Web: www.mcsmt.org. Debra Jones, Exec. Dir. MCS Foundation; Timothy Uhl, Ed.D., Supt.; Kathy Schneider, Pres.; Carla Mendenhall, Business Mgr.; Patrice Schwenk, Librarian. Clergy 1; Lay Teachers 21; Students 155; Clergy / Religious Teachers 3.

[D] SCHOOLS, ELEMENTARY

BROWNING. *De La Salle Blackfeet School*, (Grades 4-8), 104 First St. N.W., Browning, 59417. Tel: 406-338-5290; Fax: 406-338-7900; Email: info@dlsbs.org; Web: www.dlsbs.org. P.O. Box 1489, Browning, 59417. Bro. Dale Mooney, F.S.C., Pres.; Michael O'Brien, Prin.; Shelly Hall, Librarian. Brothers 2; Lay Teachers 10; Students 77.

BUTTE. *Butte Central Elementary School*, (Grades PreK-5), 1100 Delaware Ave., Butte, 59701. Tel: 406-782-4500; Fax: 406-723-4845; Email: susie.hogart@buttechentralschools.org; Web: www.buttecentral.org. Don Peoples Jr., Pres.; Susie Hogart, Prin.; Sue Burt, Sec. Day Care 40; Lay Teachers 20; Sisters 1; Students 264.

After School Care (Daycare, Preschool & Grades K-8) Tel: 406-782-4500; Fax: 406-723-4845. Pam Olson, Dir. Students 20.

Central Junior High School, (Grades 6-8), 1100 Delaware Ave., Butte, 59701. Tel: 406-782-4500; Fax: 406-723-4845; Email: info@buttecentralschools.org; Web: www.buttecentralschools.org. Susie Hogart, Prin. Clergy 1; Lay Teachers 5; Students 88.

KALISPELL. *St. Matthew School* (1917) (Grades PreK-8), 602 S. Main St., Kalispell, 59901. Tel: 406-752-6303; Fax: 406-756-8248; Email: office@stmattsaints.org; Web: www.stmattsaints.org. Lauren Smith, Prin.; Margaret Stell, Librarian; Myrna Matulevich, Science & Tech. Clergy 2; Lay Teachers 22; Preschool 51; Sisters 1; Students 156; Clergy / Religious Teachers 2.

Day Care Center, 602 S. Main St., Kalispell, 59901. Tel: 406-756-6807; Fax: 406-756-8248; Email: office@stmattsaints.org. Rosanne Herne, Dir. (Ages 2-6) Students 51.

MISSOULA. *St. Joseph Elementary School* (1873) (Grades PreK-8), (Missoula Catholic Schools) 503 Edith St., Missoula, 59801. Tel: 406-549-1290; Fax: 406-543-4034; Email: tina.mcgill@mcsmt.org; Email: sjs.secretary@mcsmt.org; Web: www.mcsmt.org. Christina Vierra McGill, Prin. Lay Teachers 26; Preschool 36; Students 265; Personnel 6.

Child Care Center, 503 Edith St., Missoula, 59801. Tel: 406-549-1290; Fax: 406-543-4034; Email: amanda.wiseman@mcsmt.org. Launa Beamon, Dir.; Amanda Wiseman, Dir. (Ages 3-4) Students 38.

[E] GENERAL HOSPITALS

BUTTE. *St. James Health Care, Sisters of Charity of Leavenworth Health System*, 400 S. Clark St., Butte, 59701. Tel: 406-723-2500; Fax: 406-723-2443; Email: dana.penrose@sclhs.net; Web: www.stjameshealthcare.org. P.O. Box 3300, Butte, 59702. Jay Doyle, Pres.; Tracy Neary, Regl. Vice Pres., Mission Integration; Rev. Robert G. Porter, Chap.; Deacon John Uggetti, Chap. Bed Capacity 100; Sisters of Charity of Leavenworth 1; Tot Asst. Annually 11,000; Total Staff 560.

MISSOULA. *Providence Health & Services - Montana* dba St. Patrick Hospital, 500 W. Broadway, Missoula, 59802. Tel: 406-329-5630; Fax: 406-329-5693; Email: info@saintpatrick.org; Web: www.saintpatrick.org. P.O. Box 4587, Missoula, 59806. Joyce Dombrouski, CEO. Bed Capacity 253; Tot Asst. Annually 188,467; Total Staff 2,126.

POLSON. *St. Joseph Medical Center* (1916) #6 Thirteenth Ave. E., Polson, 59860. Tel: 406-883-5680; Fax: 406-883-8488; Web: montana.providence.org/hospitals/st-joseph/. P.O. Box 1010, Polson, 59860. Joyce Dombrouski, CEO. Bed Capacity 22; Tot Asst. Annually 51,298; Total Staff 273.

[F] HERMITAGES

EUREKA. *Regina Coeli Hermitage*, 194 Northgate Rd., Eureka, 59917. Tel: 406-889-8084; Email: pidacaritas@gmail.com. Rev. Bro. Timothy Marie Pida, Er.Dio., Diocesan Hermit.

[G] HOUSES OF PRAYER

SWAN LAKE. *The Sycamore Tree Catholic Retreat Center*, 21592 Sycamore Tree Ln., Swan Lake, 59911. Tel: 406-754-2429; Fax: 406-754-2429; Email: email@sycamoretreeretreat.org; Web: www.sycamoretreeretreat.org. Michelle Jenkins, Dir.; Mrs. Christina Farrier, Bookkeeper.

[H] NEWMAN CHAPLAINS

BOZEMAN. *Resurrection Catholic Campus Ministry* (Newman Program) 1725 S. 11th Ave., Bozeman, 59715-4218. Tel: 406-586-9243; Email: office@resurrectionbozeman.org; Email: vzdilla@resurrectionbozeman.org; Web: www.resurrectionbozeman.org. Rev. Valentine D. Zdilla; Deacon Steven Buckner; Mary Shaun Mize, Contact Person.

BUTTE. *Montana College of Mineral Science and Technology*, 102 S. Washington St., Butte, 59701. Tel: 406-723-5407; Fax: 406-723-5408; Email: bccn@diocesehelena.org; Web: www.butteccn.org. Rev. Patrick Beretta, Chap.; Ms. Seaneen Prendergast, Campus Min.

DILLON. *University of Montana - Western*, 226 S. Atlantic St., Dillon, 59725. Tel: 406-683-4391; Fax: 406-683-6244; Email: strosedillon2015@gmail.com. Rev. Pascal Kasanziki, Pastor.

MISSOULA. *University of Montana* (Christ the King Parish) 1400 Gerald Ave., Missoula, 59801-4230. Tel: 406-728-3845; Web: www.umccm.org. Revs. Jeffrey M. Fleming, Pastor; Cody Williams, Assoc. Pastor; Bridgette Bannick, Campus Min.

[I] FOUNDATIONS

HELENA. **Foundation for the Diocese of Helena, Inc.*, 515 N. Ewing, 59601. Tel: 406-442-5820; Fax: 406-442-5191; Email: jsaarinen@diocesehelena.org; Web: www.fdoh.org. P.O. Box 1729, 59624. Pete Ridgeway, Pres.; Jeanne Saarinen, Exec. Dir.

Legal Title: Western Montana Catholic Foundation.

BUTTE. *St. James Healthcare Foundation*, 425 W. Porphyry St., Butte, 59701. Tel: 406-782-5640; Fax: 406-782-5643; Email: stjamesfoundation@sclhs.net; Web: www.sclhealth.org/locations/st-james-healthcare-foundation. Lauri Yelenich, Chm.

MISSOULA. *Providence Montana Health Foundation*, 502 W. Spruce St., Missoula, 59802. Tel: 406-329-5640; Fax: 406-327-3058; Email: fran.albrecht@providence.org; Web: www.supportpmhf.org. P.O. Box 4587, Missoula, 59806. Fran Albrecht, Exec.

[J] MISCELLANEOUS

HELENA. **St. Andrew School*, (Grades K-12), 1900 Floweree St., 59601. Tel: 406-449-3201; Fax: 406-449-0129; Email: standrew@standrewschool.org; Web: www.standrewschool.org. P.O. Box 231, 59624. Donna Smillie, Prin. Lay Teachers 22; Students 200.

**The Julius Foundation*, 3312 Dunlap Dr., 59602-7754. Tel: 406-465-8312; Email: thejuliusfoundation@outlook.com; Web: thejuliusfoundation.org. Teresa Kaiserski, Sec.

BROWNING. *St. Vincent de Paul Thrift Store*, 112 1st Ave. N.W., Browning, 59417. Tel: 406-338-5403; Email: chall@dlsbs.org. P.O. Box 974, Browning, 59417. Clarice Hall, Mgr.

BUTTE. *Central Education Foundation*, P.O. Box 634, Butte, 59703-0634. Tel: 406-723-6706; Fax: 406-782-4026; Email: dpeoples@buttecentralfoundation.org; Web: www.buttecentral.org/foundation. Don Peoples Jr., Exec.

**Maternal Life International* (1996) 326A S. Jackson St., Butte, 59701-8804. Tel: 406-782-1719; Email: maternallifeinfo@gmail.com; Web: www.mlicares.org. Dr. George Mulcaire-Jones, Dir.

MISSOULA. *Loyola Sacred Heart High School Foundation* aka Missoula Catholic Schools Foundation (1960) Serving Missoula Catholic Schools. 300 Edith St., Missoula, 59801. Tel: 406-541-2858; Fax: 406-542-9900; Web: www.mcsmt.org. Debra Jones, Dir.; Mr. Martin Lecholat, Chm.

Legal Title: Missoula Catholic Schools Foundation.

STEVENSVILLE. *Historic St. Mary's Mission*, 315 Charlo St., Stevensville, 59870. Tel: 406-777-5734; Email: stmary@cybernet1.com; Web: saintmarysmission.org. P.O. Box 211, Stevensville, 59870-0211. Colleen Meyer, Dir.

RELIGIOUS INSTITUTES OF MEN REPRESENTED IN THE DIOCESE

For further details refer to the corresponding bracketed number in the Religious Institutes of Men or Women section.

[]—*Apostolic Life Community of Priests in the Opus Spiritus Sancti* (Moshi, Tanzania)—A.L.C.P./O.S.S.

[0330]—*Brothers of the Christian Schools* (Midwest Prov.)—F.S.C.

[0690]—*Jesuit Fathers and Brothers* (USA West Prov.)—S.J.

RELIGIOUS INSTITUTES OF WOMEN REPRESENTED IN THE DIOCESE

[1070-03]—*Dominican Sisters*—O.P.

[1070-14]—*Dominican Sisters*—O.P.

[2575]—*Institute of the Sisters of Mercy of the Americas* (Cedar Rapids, IA)—R.S.M.

[0440]—*Sisters of Charity of Cincinnati, Ohio*—S.C.

[0480]—*Sisters of Charity of Leavenworth, Kansas*—S.C.L.

[3840]—*Sisters of St. Joseph of Carondelet.*

DIOCESAN CEMETERIES

HELENA. *Resurrection Cemetery*, 3685 N. Montana Ave., 59604. Tel: 406-442-1782; Cell: 406-439-1821; Fax: 406-443-7036; Email: lkops@cfcsmission.org; Web: www.diocesehelena.org. P.O. Box 5029, 59604-5029. Laurie Kops, Dir.; Karen Putman, Contact Person; John Bibler, Contact Person. Plots Available 4,000; Total Plots 11,852

Resurrection Cemetery Association (Corporate Name for Diocesan Cemeteries) 3685 N. Montana Ave., 59604. Tel: 406-442-1782; Cell: 406-439-1821; Fax: 406-443-7036; Email: lkops@cfcsmission.org; Web: www.diocesehelena.org. P.O. Box 5029, 59604. Laurie Kops, Dir.

BUTTE. *Holy Cross Cemetery*, 4700 Harrison Ave., Butte, 59701. Tel: 406-494-3812; Fax: 406-494-2475; Email: ddriver@mtcatholiccemeteries.org. Laurie Kops, Dir.; Kenny Martz, Mgr.; Donna Driver, Family Svc. Advisor. Plots Available 10,000; Total Plots 29,200

St. Patrick Cemetery, 4700 Harrison Ave., Butte, 59701. Tel: 406-494-3812; Fax: 406-494-2475; Email: ddriver@mtcatholiccemeteries.org. Laurie Kops, Dir.; Kenny Martz, Mgr.; Donna Driver, Family Svc. Advisor. Plots Available 2,000; Total Plots 16,000

MISSOULA. *St. Mary Cemetery*, 641 Turner St., Missoula, 59802. Tel: 406-543-7951; Fax: 406-829-3817; Email: ddattilo@mtcatholiccemeteries.org. Laurie Kops, Dir.; Mike Hamlin, Cemetery Sexton; Diana Dattilo, Family Svc. Advisor. Plots Available 800; Total Plots 9,300

NECROLOGY

† Noonan, Robert, (Retired), Died Aug. 10, 2018

An asterisk (*) denotes an organization that has established tax-exempt status directly with the IRS and is not covered by the USCCB Group Ruling.

Diocese of Honolulu

(Dioecesis Honoluluensis)

Most Reverend

CLARENCE R. SILVA

Bishop of Honolulu; ordained May 2, 1975; appointed Bishop of Honolulu May 17, 2005; consecrated July 21, 2005. *Bishop's Office: 1184 Bishop St., Honolulu, HI 96813.*

Chancery Office: 1184 Bishop St., Honolulu, HI 96813. Tel: 808-585-3300; Fax: 808-521-8428.

Web: catholichawaii.org

Square Miles 6,435.

Corporate Title: The Roman Catholic Church In The State Of Hawaii.

Comprises all of the Hawaiian Islands.

The Hawaiian Islands were annexed as a Territory of the United States in 1898. Hawaii became the 50th State of the Union on August 21, 1959.

In 1826, a Prefecture-Apostolic was erected for the Hawaiian Islands and entrusted to the Fathers of the Sacred Hearts of Jesus and Mary (Picpus). The Very Rev. Alexis Bachelot, SS.CC., was the first Prefect-Apostolic. He arrived with his companions in Honolulu on the 7th of July, 1827. In 1844, the Islands were erected a Vicariate Apostolic. Diocese erected Sept. 10, 1941.

For legal titles of parishes and diocesan institutions, consult the Chancery Office.

STATISTICAL OVERVIEW

Personnel	
Bishop	1
Priests: Diocesan Active in Diocese	34
Priests: Diocesan Active Outside Diocese	3
Priests: Retired, Sick or Absent	23
Number of Diocesan Priests	60
Religious Priests in Diocese	45
Total Priests in Diocese	105
Extern Priests in Diocese	30
Ordinations:	
Diocesan Priests	1
Transitional Deacons	1
Permanent Deacons in Diocese	74
Total Brothers	23
Total Sisters	137
Parishes	
Parishes	66
With Resident Pastor:	
Resident Diocesan Priests	25
Resident Religious Priests	21
Without Resident Pastor:	
Administered by Priests	20
Missions	25
Professional Ministry Personnel:	
Brothers	6
Sisters	26
Lay Ministers	68
Welfare	
Health Care Centers	3
Total Assisted	700
Homes for the Aged	1
Total Assisted	182
Day Care Centers	1
Total Assisted	37
Special Centers for Social Services	2
Total Assisted	44,500
Residential Care of Disabled	1
Total Assisted	1,095
Educational	
Diocesan Students in Other Seminaries	11
Total Seminarians	11
Colleges and Universities	1
Total Students	1,800
High Schools, Diocesan and Parish	3
Total Students	572
High Schools, Private	4
Total Students	1,554
Elementary Schools, Diocesan and Parish	21
Total Students	3,433
Elementary Schools, Private	1
Total Students	1,398
Catechesis/Religious Education:	
High School Students	1,650
Elementary Students	4,053
Total Students under Catholic Instruction	14,471
Teachers in the Diocese:	
Brothers	14
Sisters	39
Lay Teachers	710
Vital Statistics	
Receptions into the Church:	
Infant Baptism Totals	1,635
Minor Baptism Totals	124
Adult Baptism Totals	90
Received into Full Communion	180
First Communions	1,385
Confirmations	3,716
Marriages:	
Catholic	295
Interfaith	97
Total Marriages	392
Deaths	1,495
Total Catholic Population	112,961
Total Population	1,428,000

Former Prelates—Very Rev. ALEXIS BACHELOT, SS.CC., ord. 1820; appt. Pref. Apost. 1826; died Dec. 5, 1837; Most Revs. LOUIS MAIGRET, SS.CC., ord. Sept. 23, 1828; appt. Pref. Apost. 1838; appt. Vicar Apost. 1844; consecrated at Santiago Oct. 31, 1847; Titular Bishop of Arathia; died June 11, 1882.; HERMAN KOECKEMANN, SS.CC., ord. May 31, 1862; appt. Coadjutor May 17, 1881; cons. at San Francisco Aug. 21, 1881; Titular Bishop of Olba; Succeeded June 11, 1882; died Feb. 22, 1892.; GULSTAN ROPERT, SS.CC., ord. May 26, 1866; cons. at San Francisco, Sept. 12, 1892; Titular Bishop of Panopolis; died Jan. 4, 1903.; LIBERT H. BOEYNAEMS, SS.CC., ord. Sept. 11, 1881; cons. at San Francisco, July 25, 1903; Titular Bishop of Zeugma; died May 13, 1926.; STEPHEN P. ALENCASTRE, SS.CC., ord. April 5, 1902; cons. at Los Angeles as Coadjutor, Aug. 24, 1924; Titular Bishop of Arabissus; Vicar Apost. May 13, 1926; died Nov. 9, 1940.; JAMES J. SWEENEY, ord. June 20, 1925; appt. May 20, 1941; cons. at San Francisco, July 25, 1941; died June 19, 1968; JOHN J. SCANLAN, ord. June 22, 1930; cons. Sept. 21, 1954 as Auxiliary Bishop; appt. Apostolic Admin. Nov. 10, 1967; succeeded to see March 6, 1968; retired June 30, 1981; died Jan. 31, 1997; JOSEPH A. FERRARIO, ord. May 19, 1951; cons. Jan. 13, 1978 as Auxiliary Bishop; succeeded to see June 25, 1982; retired Oct. 12, 1993; died Dec. 12, 2003; FRANCIS X. DILORENZO, ord. May 18, 1968; cons. March 8, 1988 as Auxiliary Bishop of Scranton; appt. Apostolic Admin. Oct. 12, 1993; succeeded to See November 29, 1994; appt. Bishop of Richmond March 31, 2004; installed May 24, 2004; died Aug. 17, 2017.

Offices at the Chancery

Chancery—1184 Bishop St., Honolulu, 96813-2858. Tel: 808-585-3300; Fax: 808-521-8428.

Office of the Bishop—Most Rev. CLARENCE (LARRY) R. SILVA, Email: bishop@rcchawaii.org; DENISE OLIVEIRA, Admin. Asst./Ecclesial Notary, Tel: 808-585-3356; Email: doliveira@rcchawaii.org.

Vicar General and Moderator of the Curia—Very Rev. Msgr. GARY L. SECOR, Email: gsecor@rcchawaii.org; ELINA SIMON, Administrative Asst./Notary Pub./Eccles. Notary, Tel: 808-585-3346; Email: esimon@rcchawaii.org.

Episcopal Vicar for Clergy—Rev. GREGORIO S. HONORIO, M.S., Email: ghonorio@rcchawaii.org; DARLENE CACHOLA, Administrative Asst./Eccles. Notary, Tel: 808-585-3343; Email: dcachola@rcchawaii.org.

Director of Vocations—Rev. RHEO OFALSA, Tel: 808-585-3355; Email: rofalsa@rcchawaii.org.

Worship—Deacon MODESTO R. CORDERO, Dir., Tel: 808-585-3342; Email: mcordero@rcchawaii.org.

Hawaii Catholic Herald—Tel: 808-533-1791; Fax: 808-585-3381. PATRICK DOWNES, Editor, Email: pdownes@rcchawaii.org.

Finance—Tel: 808-585-3300; Fax: 808-521-8428. LISA SAKAMOTO, Diocesan Finance Officer, Email: lsakamoto@rcchawaii.org; MARVIN CHOY, Controller, Email: marvin@rcchawaii.org.

Human Resources—DARA PERREIRA, PHR, Dir., Tel: 808-585-3306; Email: dperreira@rcchawaii.org.

Facilities Management—VINCENT A. VERNAY, Mgr., Tel: 808-585-3334; Email: vvernay@rcchawaii.org.

Land Asset Management—MARLENE DECOSTA, Dir., Tel: 808-585-3332; Email: mdecosta@rcchawaii.org.

Offices at St. Stephen Diocesan Center

St. Stephen Diocesan Center—6301 Pali Hwy., Kaneohe, 96744-5224. Tel: 808-203-6724; Fax: 808-261-7022. SABRINA IZAGUIRRE, Asst. Admin., Tel: 808-203-6724; Email: sizaguirre@rcchawaii.org. Office Hours: Mon.-Fri. 8-4.

Tribunal/Canonical Affairs—Send prenuptial files to this address: 6301 Pali Hwy., Kaneohe, HI 96744. Tel: 808-203-6766. Very Rev. MARK J. GANTLEY, J.C.L., Judicial Vicar & Dir. Canonical Affairs, Email: mgantley@rcchawaii.org; ANNE KIRBY, J.C.L., Defender of the Bond; MARY L. DUDDY, Moderator of the Tribunal Chancery/Notary Pub., Email: mary_duddy@rcchawaii.org; Rev. STEVE NGUYEN, J.C.L., Defender of the Bond & Promoter of Justice, Email: snguyen@rcchawaii.org.

Hawaii Catholic Schools—MICHAEL M. ROCKERS, Ed. D., Supt., Tel: 808-203-6764; Email: mrockers@rcchawaii.org.

Chancellor & Archivist—Deacon KEITH CABILES, Tel: 808-203-6715; Email: kcabiles@rcchawaii.org.

Hawaii Catholic Conference—EVA MARIE ANDRADE, Dir., Tel: 808-203-6704; Email: eandrade@rcchawaii.org.

Respect Life/Natural Family Planning—PAULETTE VERNAY, Dir., Tel: 808-203-6722; Email: pvernay@rcchawaii.org.

Religious Education—JAYNE MONDOY, M.A., Dir., Tel: 808-203-6745; Email: jmondoy@rcchawaii.org.

Youth & Young Adult Ministry—LISA GOMES, Dir., Tel: 808-203-6743; Email: lgomes@rcchawaii.org.

Deacon Formation—Deacon JOHN A. COUGHLIN, Dir., Tel: 808-203-6729; Email: jcoughlin@rcchawaii.org; KATHLEEN COUGHLIN, Dir., Tel: 808-203-6717.

Safe Environment—KRISTEN LEANDRO, Dir., Tel: 808-203-6719; Email: kleandro@rcchawaii.org.

Stewardship and Development—MARK J. CLARK, Dir., Tel: 808-203-6728; Email: mclark@rcchawaii.org.

Social Ministry—Rev. ROBERT STARK, S.S.S., Dir., Tel:

808-203-6734; Email: rstark@rcchawaii.org; IWIE TAMASHIRO, Parish Social Ministry & Persons with Disabilities Dir., Tel: 808-203-6702; Email: itamashiro@rcchawaii.org; DAVID COLEMAN, M.A., Ph.D., Dir. Catholic Relief Svcs., Email: dcoleman@chaminade.edu.

Pastoral Planning—JAMES P. WALSH, Dir., Tel: 808-203-6733; Email: jwalsh@rcchawaii.org.

Information Technology—FRANCIS KUNG, Mgr., Tel: 808-203-6730; Email: ithelpdesk@rcchawaii.org.

Other Diocesan Officials

Vicars Forane—Rev. DONG MIN (PAUL) LI, East Hawaii, Email: pli@rcchawaii.org; Rev. Msgr. TERRENCE A.M. WATANABE, Maui, Lanai, Email: twatanabe@rcchawaii.org; Revs. LANE K. AKIONA, SS.CC., East Honolulu, Email: lakiona@rcchawaii.org; EDMUNDO N. BARUT JR., Leeward Oahu, Email: ebarut@rcchawaii.org; KONELIO FALETOI, West Hawaii, Email: lfaletoi@rcchawaii.org; GREGORIO S. HONORIO, M.S., West Honolulu, Email: ghonorio@rcchawaii.org; WILLIAM J. KUNISCH II, Central Oahu, Molokai, Email: wkunisch@rcchawaii.org; PETER MITI, Windward Oahu, Email: pmiti@rcchawaii.org; ANTHONY W. RAPOZO, Kauai, Email: arapozo@rcchawaii.org.

Permanent Deacons—Deacon CLARENCE DECAIRES, Dir., Email: cdecaires@rcchawaii.org.

Censor Liborum—Rev. Msgr. JOHN MUTISO MBINDA, Email: jmbinda@rcchawaii.org.

Diocesan Ecumenical and Interfaith Director—Rev. JACK RYAN, (Retired), Email: jryan@rcchawaii.org.

Councils and Boards

College of Consultors—Very Rev. Msgr. GARY L. SECOR; Rev. Msgr. TERRENCE A.M. WATANABE; Very Rev. MARK J. GANTLEY, J.C.L.; Revs. LANE K. AKIONA, SS.CC.; EDMUNDO N. BARUT JR.; KONELIO FALETOI; MANUEL HEWE; GREGORIO S. HONORIO, M.S.; WILLIAM J. KUNISCH II; DONG MIN (PAUL) LI; PETER MITI; ANTHONY W. RAPOZO.

Presbyteral Council—Very Rev. Msgr. GARY L. SECOR; Rev. Msgr. TERRENCE A.M. WATANABE; Revs. PASCUAL ABAYA, Vice Chm.; LANE K. AKIONA, SS.CC.; EDMUNDO N. BARUT JR.; MICHEL DALTON, O.F.M.Cap., Vice Chair; KONELIO FALETOI, Chm.; ALFRED GUERRERO; MANUEL A. HEWE; GREGORIO S. HONORIO, M.S.; KHANH HOANG; ALAPAKI KIM, Sec.; WILLIAM J. KUNISCH II; STEPHEN A. MACEDO; DONG MIN (PAUL) LI; PETER MITI; ANTHONY W. RAPOZO; E.J. IKAIKA RESINTO.

Diocesan Pastoral Council—Very Rev. Msgr. GARY L. SECOR, Ex Officio; JAMES P. WALSH, Staff; RYAN AGCAOILI; RAINA BAUTISTA; Bro. DANIEL J. CASEY, C.F.C.; Sr. WILLIAM MARIE ELENIKI, O.S.F.; Rev. ALFRED GUERRERO; Deacon WILLIAM FRIESE; CRAIG HIGAKI; RUPERT S. HUNT SR.; CHRISTOPHER KALILI, Vice Chair; FAITH LEASIOLAGI; ZACHARY RAMONES; JOSEPHINE REYES; PABLO RODRIGUEZ; EUGENE SANTIAGO; LLEWELLYN YOUNG, Ph.D., Chair.

Diocesan Finance Council—Very Rev. Msgr. GARY L. SECOR, Ex Officio; LISA SAKAMOTO, Staff; MARLENE DE COSTA, Staff; ROBERT BRUCE GRAHAM JR., Esq., Counsel; PAUL DE VILLE; RALPH MESICK; ARNOLD MARTINES; ELLIOT MILLS; DIANE MURAKAMI, Vice Chair; CELESTE ODA; RICHARD STACK JR., Sec.; Rev. FRANCISCO DE LOS REYES, S.S.S.; MARY PAT WATERHOUSE; MICHAEL YEE.

Hawaii Catholic Conference Board—Most Rev. CLARENCE (LARRY) R. SILVA, Ex Officio Chair; Very Rev. Msgr. GARY L. SECOR; EVA MARIE ANDRADE, Dir.; DAVID COLEMAN, M.A., Ph.D.; PATRICK DOWNES; Very Rev. MARK J. GANTLEY, J.C.L.; ANNE HARPHAM; BETTY LOU LARSON; SHAWN LUIZ, Esq.; MICHAEL M. ROCKERS, Ed.D.; GARY SIMON; Rev. ROBERT STARK, S.S.S.; TERRY WALSH.

CLERGY, PARISHES, MISSIONS AND PAROCHIAL SCHOOLS

ISLAND OF OAHU

CITY OF HONOLULU

1—CATHEDRAL BASILICA OF OUR LADY OF PEACE (1843)
1184 Bishop St., 96813-2838. Tel: 808-536-7036; Fax: 808-585-3383; Email: coolop@rcchawaii.org; Web: www.cathedralofourladyofpeace.com. Very Rev. Msgr. Gary L. Secor; Revs. Marvin Samiano, J.C.L., Parochial Vicar; Norlito Conception, In Res.; Manuel A. Hewe, In Res.; Rheo Ofalsa, In Res.; Deacon Jose Almuena.
Catechesis Religious Program—Email: mbauer@rcchawaii.org. Mr. Michael Bauer, D.R.E. Students 44.

2—CO-CATHEDRAL OF ST. THERESA OF THE CHILD JESUS (1931)
712 N. School St., 96817. Tel: 808-521-1700; Fax: 808-599-3629; Email: rmendoza@rcchawaii.org; Web: cocathedral.org. Rev. Gregorio S. Honorio, M.S.; Deacons Rafael Mendoza, Business Mgr.; Francis Leasiolagi; Roy T. Matsuo.
School—St. Theresa of the Child Jesus School, (Grades K-8), Tel: 808-536-4703; Fax: 808-524-6861; Email: cgora@rcchawaii.org; Web: www.cocathedral.org/103. Conception Gora, Prin.
Catechesis Religious Program—Email: mestrella@rcchawaii.org. Sr. Mercedita B. Estrella, S.P.C., D.R.E. Students 224.
Convent—Tel: 808-533-3101; Email: stccsj38@twc.com. Sisters of St. Joseph of Carondelet 3; Sisters of St. Paul of Chartes 1.
Vietnamese Holy Martyrs Community—
Tel: 808-536-0046; Email: vietholymartyrs@gmail.com; Web: www.vietmartyrs-honolulu.net. Rev. Dominic Hoan Nguyen, Chap.; Deacon Anthony Nguyen.

3—ST. ANTHONY (1916)
640 Puuhale Rd., 96819. Tel: 808-845-3255; Fax: 808-845-3664; Email: stanthonyhonolulu@gmail.com; Web: saintanthonykalihi.org. Revs. Arnel Soriano, M.S.; Edwin Conselva, M.S., Parochial Vicar; Francisco Nicomedes S. Sanchez, In Res.
Catechesis Religious Program—Leeza Agpaoa, D.R.E. Students 79.
Convent—702 Puuhale Rd., 96819. St. Paul of Chartres 3.

4—ST. AUGUSTINE BY THE SEA (1854)
130 Ohua Ave., 96815. Tel: 808-923-7024; Fax: 808-922-4086; Email: staugustinebythesea@gmail.com; Web: staugustinebythesea.com. Rev. Lane K. Akiona, SS.-CC.; Deacon Keith Cabiles.
Catechesis Religious Program—Students 40.

5—BLESSED SACRAMENT (1938)
2124 Pauoa Rd., 96813. Tel: 808-531-6980; Email: bscpauoa@rcchawaii.org; Web: blessedsacramentpauoa.org. Rev. Steve Nguyen, J.C.L.; Deacon Joseph Soon.
Catechesis Religious Program—Students 15.

6—HOLY FAMILY (1950)
830 Main St., 96818. Tel: 808-422-1135; Email: info@holyfamilyhonolulu.org; Web: holyfamilyhonolulu.org. Revs. John R. LeVecke, Admin.; John B. Weling, In Res.; Deacon Michael Brown.
School—Holy Family Catholic Academy, (Grades K-8), Tel: 808-423-9611; Fax: 808-422-5030; Email: lpatiak@rcchawaii.org; Web: hfcahawaii.org. Leilani Patiak, Dir. Students 370.
Child Care—Early Learning Center,
Tel: 808-421-1265; Email: elc@hfcahawaii.org. Leilani Patiak, Dir. Lay Teachers 3; Students 67.
Catechesis Religious Program—Diane Fujinaga, C.R.E. Students 81.

7—HOLY TRINITY (1939)
5919 Kalanianaole Hwy., 96821. Tel: 808-396-0551; Fax: 808-396-1380; Email: holytrinity@rcchawaii.org; Email: jweaver@rcchawaii.org; Web: holytrinitychurchhi.org. Rev. Michel Dalton, O.F.M.-Cap.; Deacons Stephen Kula; Fernando V. Ona.
Catechesis Religious Program—

8—ST. JOHN THE BAPTIST (1844) [CEM]
2324 Omilo Ln., 96819. Tel: 808-845-0984; Fax: 808-841-6643; Email: sjbkalihi@gmail.com; Web: saintjohnthebaptisthawaii.org. Rev. Moses Akebule, Admin.; Deacons Peter Soumwei; Ricardo Burgos.
School—St. John the Baptist School, (Grades PreK-8), 2340 Omilo Ln., 96819. Tel: 808-841-5551; Fax: 808-842-6104; Email: cchong@sjbcs.org; Web: www.sjbcs.net. Carol Chong, Prin.; Ms. Gloria Ilae, Librarian. Lay Teachers 9; Dominican Sisters 3; Students 108.
Catechesis Religious Program—Danielle Burgos, D.R.E. Students 0.
Convent—2330 Omilo Ln., 96819. Tel: 808-845-2622; Web: www.ophawaiiregion.com. Dominican Sisters of the Most Holy Rosary 4.

9—MARY, STAR OF THE SEA (1946)
4470 Aliikoa St., 96821. Tel: 808-734-0396; Fax: 808-744-2008; Email: sarahbryant.starofthesea@hawaii.rr.com; Web: starofthesea honolulu.com. Revs. Francisco De Los Reyes, S.S.S.; Paterno B. Labasano, S.S.S., Parochial Vicar.
School—Mary, Star of the Sea School, (Grades 1-8), 4469 Malia St., 96821. Tel: 808-734-0208; Fax: 808-735-9790; Email: star@starofthesea.org; Web: www.starofthesea.org. Margaret Rufo, Prin. Lay Teachers 24; Students 159.
Child Care—Early Learning Center, (Grades PreK-K), 4470 Aliikoa St., Ste. 100, 96821.
Tel: 808-734-3840; Fax: 808-732-1738; Email: elc@starofthesea.org; Web: www.staroftheseaelc.org. Lisa Foster, Prin. Lay Teachers 11; Students 205.
Catechesis Religious Program—Tel: 808-349-2009; Email: darlenealoha@gmail.com. Darlene Ah Yo, D.R.E. Students 52.

10—NEWMAN CENTER-HOLY SPIRIT PARISH (1981)
1941 East West Rd., 96822-2321. Tel: 808-988-6222; Email: info@newmanhawaii.org. Rev. Alfred Guerrero.
Res.: Dever House, 2727 Pamoa Rd., 96822.
Catechesis Religious Program—Email: religiousedu@newmanhawaii.org. Dr. Anna Viggiano, D.R.E. Students 43.

11—OUR LADY OF THE MOUNT (1870) [CEM]
1614 Monte St., 96819. Tel: 808-845-0828; Fax: 808-845-0828; Email: olm@rcchawaii.org; Web: ourladyofthemountkalihi.org. Revs. Edgar B. Brillantes; Adrian R. Gervacio, Pastor Emeritus, (Retired).
Catechesis Religious Program—Email: srclemencespc@yahoo.com. Ms. Lucille Mohika, D.R.E. Students 55.

12—ST. PATRICK (1929)
1124 Seventh Ave., 96816. Tel: 808-732-5565; Fax: 808-737-2477; Email: church@saintpatrickhawaii.org; Email: school@saintpatrickhawaii.org; Web: saintpatrickhawaii.org. Revs. Clarence L. Guerreiro, SS.CC.; Bertram Lock, SS.CC., Parochial Vicar; Santtosh Thotankara, Parochial Vicar.
Catechesis Religious Program—Tel: 808-734-8979; Email: adecosta@saintpatrickhawaii.org. Sr. Anne Clare De Costa, SS.CC., D.R.E. Students 78.

13—SS PETER AND PAUL (1969)
800 Kaheka St., 96814. Tel: 808-941-0675; Fax: 808-945-0689; Email: sspeterpaul@hawaii.rr.com; Web: sspeterpaulhawaii.org. Revs. Khanh Pham Nguyen; Siegfred Dosdos, Parochial Vicar; Deacons Richard Abel; Angken Xymoon.
Res.: 1561 Kanunu St., #1006, 96814.
Catechesis Religious Program—Yvonne Toma, D.R.E. Students 92.

14—ST. PHILOMENA (1942)
3300 Ala Laulani St., 96818-2837. Tel: 808-839-1876; Fax: 808-834-6888; Email: sp.hawaii.receptionist@gmail.com; Email: lhiga@rcchawaii.org; Web: stphilomenahawaii.org. Revs. Rico Bernadez, Admin.; Mario Palanca, In Res.
Child Care—Early Learning Center,
Tel: 808-833-8080; Fax: 808-834-3438. Peter Tedtaotao, Dir. Lay Teachers 42; Students 124.
Catechesis Religious Program—Jenny Pavao, C.R.E.; Kurt Meyer, Youth Min. Students 75.

15—ST. PIUS X (1958)
2821 Lowrey Ave., 96822-1644. Tel: 808-988-3308; Fax: 808-973-2209; Email: general@mp-cc.net; Web: mp-cc.net. Rev. Thomas P. Joseph, Ph.D., Admin.; Deacon Vince Wozniak.
Catechesis Religious Program—
Korean Catholic Community—2949 Kahawai St., 96822. Tel: 808-988-9678. Rev. YoungKun Kim, Chap.

16—SACRED HEART (1914)
1701 Wilder Ave., 96822. Tel: 808-973-2211; Fax: 808-973-2209; Email: general@mp-cc.net; Web: mp-cc.net. Rev. EJ Racinto; Deacon Vince Wozniak.
School—Maryknoll School, (Grades K-12), 1526 Alexander St., 96822. Tel: 808-952-8400; Tel: 808-952-7100; Fax: 808-952-7331; Email: admission@maryknollschool; Web: www.maryknollschool.org. Perry K. Martin, Pres.; Shana Tong, Vice Pres.; Chris Loomis, Prin.; John Madriaga, Prin.; Thomas Furtado, H.S. Vice Prin.; Michelle Gabriel, Grade School Vice Prin. Lay Teachers 78; Students 1,079; High School Students 501; Grade School Students 722.
Catechesis Religious Program—Tel: 808-952-7120; Fax: 808-952-2009. Becky Kotake, D.R.E. Students 1,141.

17—ST. STEPHEN (1932)
2747 Pali Hwy., 96817. Tel: 808-595-3105; Email: ssccpali@rcchawaii.org; Web: ssccpali.net. Rev. Mario Raquepo; Deacon Ronald Choo.
Catechesis Religious Program—

OUTSIDE THE CITY OF HONOLULU
County of Honolulu

AIEA, ST. ELIZABETH (1926) 99-312 Moanalua Rd., Aiea, 96701. Tel: 808-487-2414; Email: stelizabe001@hawaii.rr.com; Web: stelizabethaiea.com. Revs. Arnold Ortiz; Samuel E. Loterte, S.S.S., Parochial Vicar; Deacon Frederico Carahasen Jr.
School—St. Elizabeth School, (Grades K-8), 99-310 Moanalua Rd., Aiea, 96701.
Tel: 808-488-5322; Fax: 808-486-0856; Email: info@steliz-hi.org; Web: www.steliz-hi.org. Sr. Bernarda Sindol, O.P., Prin. Lay Teachers 5; Sisters 6; Students 152.
Catechesis Religious Program—
Email: umeristella@gmail.com. Sr. Meristella Umdor, M.S.M.H.C., D.R.E. Students 169.
Convent—

Tel: 808-487-3131. Dominican Sisters of the Most Holy Rosary 5.

EWA, IMMACULATE CONCEPTION CHURCH (1929) 91-1298 Renton Rd., Ewa, 96706. Tel: 808-681-3701; Fax: 808-681-3117; Email: iccewa@rcchawaii.org; Web: immaculateconceptionewa.org. Rev. Nicholas Brown; Deacons Jonathan Ocampo; Avaletalia Huhkin.
Catechesis Religious Program—
Tel: 808-954-1730; Email: ewaccd@gmail.com. Shirley Sunio, D.R.E. Students 171.

EWA BEACH, OUR LADY OF PERPETUAL HELP (1969) 91-1004 North Rd., Ewa Beach, 96706-2796.
Tel: 808-689-8681; Fax: 808-689-1954; Email: olph@rcchawaii.org; Web: olphewabeach.org. Revs. Edmundo N. Barut Jr.; Constantino Atenaja Jr., Parochial Vicar; Deacons Ronald Paglinawan; Eric Kim.
Res.: 91-1037 Makekula Pl., Ewa Beach, 96706.
School—Our Lady of Perpetual Help School, (Grades K-8),
91-1010 North Rd., Ewa Beach, 96706.
Tel: 808-689-0474; Fax: 808-689-4847; Email: info@olphschoolewabeachhi.com; Web: olphschoolewabeachhi.com. Sr. Davilyn AhChick, O.S.F., Prin. Lay Teachers 10; Students 150.
Catechesis Religious Program—
Email: jtorres@rcchawaii.org. Julia Torres, D.R.E. Students 65.

KAHUKU, ST. ROCH (1917) [CEM] 56-350 Kamehameha Hwy., P.O. Box 295, Kahuku, 96731.
Tel: 808-293-5026; Fax: 808-293-1737; Email: saintrochkahuku@gmail.com; Web: strochkahuku.com. Rev. Anastacio Postrano.
Catechesis Religious Program—Ms. LaVerne Rivas, D.R.E. Students 23.
Mission—St. Joachim (1917)
53-536 Kamekameha Hwy., Punaluu, 96717. Punaluu.

KAILUA
1—ST. ANTHONY OF PADUA (1933) 148 Makawao St., Ste. A, Kailua, 96734-2334. Tel: 808-266-2222;
Tel: 808-791-6523; Fax: 808-266-2229; Email: frontdesk@stanthonyskailua.org; Email: accounting@atanthonyskailua.org; Web: stanthonyskailua.org. Revs. Exsequel Tuyor, Admin.; Joseph A. Diaz, Parochial Vicar; Marlon Belmonte, Parochial Vicar; Deacons Ernest F. Carlbom; Michael Weaver.
Res.: 116 Makua St., Kailua, 96734.
School—St. Anthony of Padua School, (Grades K-8),
148 Makawao St., Kailua, 96734-2334.
Tel: 808-261-3331; Fax: 808-263-3518; Email: info@saskailua.org; Web: www.saskailua.org. Bridget Olsen, Prin. Lay Teachers 25; Students 275.
Child Care—Early Learning Center, Lay Teachers 4; Students 65.
Catechesis Religious Program—
Tel: 808-791-6525. Donna Estomago, C.R.E. Students 123.
2—ST. JOHN VIANNEY (1962) 920 Keolu Dr., Kailua, 96734-3842. Tel: 808-262-8317; Fax: 808-261-4039; Email: cclarke@rcchawaii.org; Web: saintjohnvianneyhawaii.org. Rev. Peter Miti; Deacons Walter H. Yoshimitsu; Clarence DeCaires; Jerry L. Tokars.
School—St. John Vianney School, (Grades PreK-8),
940 Keolu Dr., Kailua, 96734-3842.
Tel: 808-261-4651; Email: sjvkailua@hawaii.rr.com; Web: sjvkailua.org. Caryn DeMello, Prin.; Annie Chee, Contact Person. Lay Teachers 19; Students 174.
Catechesis Religious Program—Ms. Steffanie Beissel, D.R.E. Students 110.

KANEOHE, ST. ANN (1841) [CEM] 46-129 Haiku Rd., Kaneohe, 96744. Tel: 808-247-3092;
Fax: 808-235-0717; Email: stanns@saintannhawaii.org; Web: www.saintannhawaii.org. Revs. Richard McNally, SS.CC.; Edward Popish, SS.CC., Parochial Vicar; Deacon Billy Whitfield.
School—St. Ann School, (Grades PreK-8),
46-125 Haiku Rd., Kaneohe, 96744. Email: schooloffice@saintannhawaii.org; Web: www.saintannhawaii.org. Mandy Thronas-Brown, Prin.; Cynthia Achong, Dir. Lay Teachers 18; Students 190.
Child Care—Early Learning Center
Tel: 808-247-3092, Ext. 103; Email: elcoffice@saintannhawaii.org. Cynthia Achong, Dir. Lay Teachers 6; Students 102.
Catechesis Religious Program—
Tel: 808-247-3092, Ext. 104. Mr. Robert Noguchi, D.R.E. Students 220.

KAPOLEI, ST. JUDE (1988) 92-455 Makakilo Dr., Kapolei, 96707. Tel: 808-672-9041;
Fax: 808-672-3779; Email: nwheeler@rcchawaii.org; Web: stjudehawaii.org. Revs. Khanh Hoang; Ramesh Martin Devadoss, Parochial Vicar; Deacons William Friese; John A. Coughlin; Raul Perez.
Res.: 92-104 Leipapa Way, Kapolei, 96707.
Catechesis Religious Program—
Tel: 808-672-8669; Email: bboquer@rcchawaii.org. Bonnie Boquer, D.R.E. Students 298.

MILILANI TOWN, ST. JOHN APOSTLE AND EVANGELIST (1969) 95-370 Kuahelani Ave., Mililani Town, 96789.
Tel: 808-623-3332; Fax: 808-623-3286; Email: sjaeinfo@rcchawaii.org; Web: stjohnmililani.org. Rev. Msgr. John Mutiso Mbinda; Rev. Joseph Ayinpuusa, Parochial Vicar; Deacons Modesto R. Cordero; Romeo Ganibe.
Child Care—St. John Catholic Preschool (1979)
Tel: 808-623-3332, Ext. 200; Fax: 808-623-6496; Email: mscat@sjcpmililani.org. Catherine Awong, Dir. Lay Teachers 3; Students 20.
Catechesis Religious Program—Julie Quiroz-Zamora, D.R.E. Students 275.

NANAKULI, ST. RITA (1963) 89-318 Farrington Hwy., Nanakuli, 96792. Tel: 808-668-7833;
Fax: 808-688-7716; Email: strita_nanakuli@rcchawaii.org; Web: stritananakuli.org. Rev. Alapaki Kim; Deacon Harold S. Levy Jr.
Res.: 87-1511 Nakii St., Waianae, 96792.
Catechesis Religious Program—
Tel: 808-668-7833; Email: strita_nanakuli@rcchawaii.org. Karen Victor, D.R.E.

PEARL CITY, OUR LADY OF GOOD COUNSEL (1958) [CEM] 1525 Waimano Home Rd., Pearl City, 96782.
Tel: 808-455-3012; Email: office@olgcchurchpc.org; Web: olgcchurch.org. Revs. Pascual Abaya; Ernesto A. Juarez Jr., Parochial Vicar; Deacons Thomas Miyashiro; Efrain Andrews; Raymond Lamb.
School—Our Lady of Good Counsel School, (Grades PreK-8),
1530 Hoolana St., Pearl City, 96782.
Tel: 808-455-4533; Fax: 808-455-5587; Email: inquire@olgchawaii.org; Web: olgchawaii.org. Chantelle Luarca, Prin. Lay Teachers 12; Students 162.
Catechesis Religious Program—

WAHIAWA, OUR LADY OF SORROWS (1939) 1403-A California Ave., Wahiawa, 96786-2595.
Tel: 808-621-5109; Fax: 808-622-5073; Email: ourladyofsorrows@rcchawaii.org; Web: olswahiawa.org. Rev. Ajith Kumar Antony Dass, SS.CC.; Deacons Celestino Emwalu; Wally Mitsui.
Catechesis Religious Program—
Email: info@olswahiawa.org. Shirley Caban, C.R.E. Students 75.

WAIALUA, ST. MICHAEL (1853) [CEM] 67-390 Goodale Ave., Waialua, 96791. Tel: 808-637-4040;
Fax: 808-637-4287; Email: stsmichaelpeter_paul@hawaii.rr.com; Web: stsmichaelpeterpaul.org. Rev. Joseph Pasala.
School—St. Michael School, (Grades PreSchool-8),
67-340 Haona St., Waialua, 96791. Tel: 808-637-7772 ; Fax: 808-637-7722; Email: stmichaelhi@hawaii.rr.com; Web: stmichaelschoolhi.com. Kainoa Fukumoto, Prin. Clergy 1; Lay Teachers 8; Students 91.
Catechesis Religious Program—Ms. Beverly Orillo, D.R.E. Students 90.
Mission—SS. Peter and Paul
59-810 Kamehameha Hwy., Haleiwa, 96712. Email: jpasala@rcchawaii.org.

WAIANAE, SACRED HEART (1838) [CEM] 85-786 Old Government Rd., Waianae, 96792. Tel: 808-696-3773 ; Fax: 808-696-2242; Email: office.shcwaianae@gmail.com. Rev. Santiago A. Agoo Jr., Admin.; Deacons Jerome Vito; Morton Zabala.
Catechesis Religious Program—
Tel: 808-861-3747; Email: lefua77@yahoo.com. Rosalina Lefu'a, D.R.E. Students 115.

WAIKANE, OUR LADY OF MT. CARMEL (1867) [CEM] 48-422 Kamehameha Hwy., Kaneohe, 96744.
Tel: 808-239-9269; Fax: 808-239-8561; Email: olmc001@hawaii.rr.com; Web: mtcarmelhawaii.com. P.O. Box 6581, Kaneohe, 96744. Rev. Paulo R. Kosaka, O.F.M.Cap.

WAIMANALO, ST. GEORGE (1954) 41-1323 Kalanianaole Hwy., Waimanalo, 96795. Tel: 808-259-7188;
Fax: 808-259-0169; Email: stgeorge@rcchawaii.org; Web: stgeorge96795.com. Rev. Raymund Ellorin; Deacon Edward Cho.
Catechesis Religious Program—
Email: kulani48@hawaii.rr.com. Victoria DeSilva, D.R.E. Students 100.

WAIPAHU, ST. JOSEPH (1940) [CEM] 94-675 Farrington Hwy., Waipahu, 96797. Tel: 808-677-4276;
Fax: 808-671-3215; Web: stjosephchurchwaipahu.org. Revs. Efren A. Tomas, M.S.; Geronimo Castro, M.S., Parochial Vicar; Anton Nyo, Parochial Vicar; Deacons Keith Galang; Sanele Paselio.
School—St. Joseph School, (Grades PreK-8),
94-651 Farrington Hwy., Waipahu, 96797.
Tel: 808-677-4475; Fax: 808-677-8937; Email: sjs@stjosephwaipahu.org; Web: www.stjosephwaipahu.org. Beverly Sandobal, Prin.; Agnes Simpliciano, Librarian (Part-time). Lay Teachers 19; Sisters 2; Students 280.
Catechesis Religious Program—
Tel: 808-676-3493; Fax: 808-676-3493. Geraldine Simbahon, D.R.E. Students 402.

WAIPIO, RESURRECTION OF THE LORD (1986) 94-1260 Lumikula St., Waipahu, 96797. Tel: 808-676-4700;
Fax: 808-676-4534; Email: zramones@rcchawaii.org; Web: resurrectionhawaii.org. Rev. William Kunisch II; Deacons Jose Ancheta; Gary Streff.
Res.: 94-1245 Lumikula St., Waipahu, 96797.
Catechesis Religious Program—
Email: reanalex@hotmail.com. Roeana Alexander, C.R.E. Students 162.

ISLAND OF HAWAII
County of Hawaii

HAWI, SACRED HEART (1905) [CEM] 55-3374 Akoni Pule Hwy., P.O. Box 220, Hawi, 96719-0220.
Tel: 808-889-6436; Email: shchawi@hawaii.twcbc.com; Web: sacredhearthawi.com. Rev. Elias F. Escanilla, Admin.; Deacon Thomas J. Adams.
Catechesis Religious Program—Mrs. Evie Adams, D.R.E. Students 29.

HILO, ST. JOSEPH (1860) [CEM] 43 Kapiolani St., Hilo, 96720. Tel: 808-935-1465; Fax: 808-969-1665; Email: dwatson@stjoehilo.com; Web: stjoehilo.com. Revs. Wilbert A. Laroga, S.S.S.; Apolinario Ty, S.S.S., Parochial Vicar.
School—St. Joseph School, (Grades PreK-12),
High School: 1000 Ululani St., Hilo, 96720.
Tel: 808-961-0424 (Pre-school);
Tel: 808-935-4935 (Elementary School);
Tel: 808-935-4936 (High School);
Fax: 808-443-0294 (Elementary);
Fax: 808-443-0294 (High School); Email: tfuata@rcchawaii.org; Web: www.sjshilo.com. Llewellyn Young, Ph.D., Prin.; Marie Roberts, Preschool Dir.; Theresa Burian, Elem. Vice-Prin.; Ann Wilson, Elem. School Librarian; Miri Sumida, High School Librarian. Lay Teachers 35; Students 295.
Catechesis Religious Program—
Email: cvillena@stjoehilo.com. Chrislyn Villena, C.R.E. & Youth & Young Adult Min. Students 136.

HONAUNAU, ST. BENEDICT (1899) [CEM] 84-5140 Painted Church Rd., Captain Cook, 96704.
Tel: 808-328-2227; Fax: 808-328-8482; Email: st.benedict@rcchawaii.org; Web: thepaintedchurchhawaii.org. Rev. Ornoldo Cherrez, Admin.; Deacon Craig Camello.
Catechesis Religious Program—Edwina Fujimoto, D.R.E. Students 69.
Mission—St. John the Baptist
81-6402 Mamalahoa Hwy., Kealakekua, 96750. Kealakekua.

HONOKAA, OUR LADY OF LOURDES (1870) [CEM 6] 54-5028 Plumeria St., P.O. Box 129, Honokaa, 96727.
Tel: 808-775-9591; Email: ourladyof001@hawaii.rr.com. Rev. Anselmo Bobier, Admin.
Catechesis Religious Program—
45-5028 Plumeria Rd., Honokaa, 96727. Dolores Whaley, D.R.E. Students 55.

KAILUA, ST. MICHAEL THE ARCHANGEL (1840) 75-5769 Alii Dr., Kailua-Kona, 96740. Tel: 808-326-7771; Email: stmichaelarchangel@rcchawaii.org; Web: konacatholicchurch.net. Revs. Konelio Faletoi; Diego Restrepo, Parochial Vicar; Deacon Michael Ross.
Catechesis Religious Program—Students 136.
Missions—Holy Rosary—
73-4179 Mamalahoa Hwy., Kalaoa, 96740. Kalaoa.
Immaculate Conception
76-5960 Mamalahoa Hwy., Holualoa, 96725. Holualoa.
St. Paul
79-7234 St. Paul's Rd., Honalo, 96740. Honalo.
St. Peter by the Sea
78-6684 Alii Dr., Kahaluu, 96740. Kahaluu.

KEAUKAHA, MALIA PUKA O KALANI (MARY GATE OF HEAVEN) (1929) 326 Desha Ave., P.O. Box 222, Hilo, 96721. Tel: 808-935-9338; Email: maliapastor@gmail.com; Web: maliapukaokalani.com. Rev. Michael G. Scully, S.J., Admin.
Catechesis Religious Program—
Email: kmg2011@yahoo.com. Karen Gerkey, D.R.E. Students 16.

LAUPAHOEHOE, ST. ANTHONY (1926) [CEM] 35-2095 Old Mamalohoa Hwy., P.O. Box 339, Laupahoehoe, 96764. Tel: 808-962-6538; Fax: 808-962-6971; Email: saintpadua@hotmail.com; Web: hamakuacatholic.org. Rev. Temistocles Tuyac, Admin.

MOUNTAIN VIEW, ST. THERESA (1930) 18-1355 Volcano Hwy., P.O. Box 37, Mountain View, 96771.
Tel: 808-968-6233; Email: stcmv1@gmail.com; Web: stcmv.org. Rev. Dong Min (Paul) Li; Deacons Jim Dougherty; David Watson.
Catechesis Religious Program—Ms. Ceraida Amar, D.R.E.; Ms. Roquita Kaisen, D.R.E. Students 55.
Mission—Holy Rosary
16-537 Laukaki Pl., Keaau, 96749. Tel: 808-968-8233 .

NAALEHU, SACRED HEART (1846) [CEM] 95-5558 Mamalahoa Hwy., P.O. Box 760, Naalehu, 96772.
Tel: 808-928-8208; Email: hrc.shc@gmail.com. Rev. Martin Mwanshibula, Admin.; Deacon Joseph Aglia.
Catechesis Religious Program—Nellie Davis, D.R.E. Students 6.

PAHALA, HOLY ROSARY (1885) [CEM] 96-3143 Pikake St., P.O. Box 760, Pahala, 96777. Tel: 808-928-8208;

Fax: 808-928-8208; Email: hrc.shc@gmail.com. Rev. Martin Mwanshibula, Admin.; Deacon Joseph Aglia.
Catechesis Religious Program—Jeanette Castillo, C.R.E. Students 16.

PAHOA, SACRED HEART (1882) [CEM] 15-3003 Pahoa Village Rd., Pahoa, 96778. Tel: 808-965-8202; Fax: 808-965-5144; Email: shpahoa@gmail.com; Web: pahoasacredheart.com. Rev. John Molina, Admin.
Catechesis Religious Program—
Tel: 808-896-1148; Email: mnaiga03@gmail.com. Malia Naiga, C.R.E. Students 45.

PAPAIKOU, IMMACULATE HEART OF MARY (1923) [CEM] 27-186 Kaapoko Homestead Rd., P.O. Box 79, Papaikou, 96781. Tel: 808-964-1240; Fax: 808-964-1240; Email: ihmparish@hotmail.com; Web: hamakuacatholic.org. Rev. Temistocles Tuyac, Admin.; Deacon LeRoy Andrews.
Catechesis Religious Program—
Tel: 808-938-3295; Email: dcnandrews@gmail.com. Deacon LeRoy Andrews, D.R.E. Students 57.
Mission—Good Shepherd, [CEM]
28-640 Government Main Rd., Honomu, 96728. Patricia Phillips, Contact Person. Honomu.

WAIMEA, ANNUNCIATION (1965) [CEM] 65-1235 Kawaihae Rd., P.O. Box 301, Kamuela, 96743. Tel: 808-887-1220; Email: annchhi@hawaiiantel.net; Web: bigislandcatholicchurch.org. Rev. Stephen A. Macedo.
Catechesis Religious Program—
Tel: 808-887-1203; Email: annunciationwaimeare@gmail.com. Jane Aganus, D.R.E. Students 99.
Mission—Ascension
69-1789 Puako Beach Dr., Puako, 96743. Puako.

ISLAND OF KAUAI
County of Kauai

KALAHEO, HOLY CROSS (1909) [CEM] 2-2370 Kaumualii Hwy., P.O. Box 487, Kalaheo, 96741-0487. Tel: 808-332-8011; Email: holycrosschurch@hawaii.rr.com. Rev. Danilo C. Galang, M.S.; Deacon Andres Emayo.
Catechesis Religious Program—Students 114.
Mission—Sacred Heart
2626 Melemele Rd., Eleele, 96705. Eleele.

KAPAA, ST. CATHERINE (1887) [CEM] 5021-A Kawaihau Rd., Kapaa, 96746. Tel: 808-882-7900; Tel: 808-822-4804; Fax: 808-822-3014; Email: arapozo@rcchawaii.org; Web: kauaistcatherine.church. Revs. Anthony W. Rapozo; William Tulua, Parochial Vicar.
School—St. Catherine School, (Grades PreK-12), 5021 Kawaihau Rd., Kapaa, 96746.
Tel: 808-822-4212; Fax: 808-823-0991; Email: scsoffice@st-catherineschool.org; Web: www.kawaistcatherine.org/school. Britt Cocumelli, Prin. Clergy 1; Lay Teachers 20; Preschool 57; Students 169.
Catechesis Religious Program—
Tel: 808-822-7900; Email: mcruz@rcchawaii.org. Michael Cruz, D.R.E. Students 53.
Missions—St. Sylvester, Kilauea—
2390 Kolo Rd., Kilauea, 96754. Kilauea.
St. William, Hanalei
5292-A Kuhio Hwy., Hanalei, 96714. Hanalei.

KEKAHA, ST. THERESA (1944) [CEM] 8343 Kaumualii Hwy., P.O. Box 159, Kekaha, 96752. Tel: 808-337-1548; Email: sttheresac@yahoo.com; Web: kekahacatholic.com. Rev. Emerson de los Reyes, Admin.; Deacon James Bostick.
School—St. Theresa School, (Grades PreK-8), 8320 Elepaio Rd., Kekaha, 96752. Tel: 808-337-1351; Fax: 808-337-1714; Email: office@sttheresakanai.com; Web: www.sttheresakanai.com. Wendy Castillo, Prin.; Adela Chavez, Librarian. This school belongs to St. Theresa Church Kekaha (Kauai) Lay Teachers 9; Students 131.
Catechesis Religious Program—
Tel: 808-639-7067; Email: mary47@hawaii.rr.com. Maryann McMillen, D.R.E. Students 117.
Convent—
P.O. Box 489, Kekaha, 96752. Tel: 808-337-9661. Sr. Janet Rose, O.S.F., Supr. Franciscan Sisters of Christian Charity 4.
Mission—Sacred Hearts
9496 Kaumualii Hwy., Waimea, 96796.
Tel: 808-337-1784; Email: edelosreyes@rcchawaii.org. Waimea.

KOLOA, ST. RAPHAEL (1841) [CEM] 3011 Hapa Rd., Koloa, 96756. Tel: 808-742-1955; Email: straphael@rcchawaii.org; Web: st-raphael-kauai.org. Rev. Arlan Intal, M.S.
Catechesis Religious Program—Mrs. Allison Carveiro, D.R.E. Students 60.

LIHUE, IMMACULATE CONCEPTION (1884) [CEM 2] 4453 Kapaia Rd., Lihue, 96766. Tel: 808-245-2432; Fax: 808-246-2571; Email: icchurchkauai@rcchawaii.org; Web: icchurchlihue.com. Rev. Edison Pamintuan, M.S.; Deacons William A. Farias; David E. Kane.
Catechesis Religious Program—
Tel: 808-635-6874; Email: sgina0814@yahoo.com. Sr. Gina Senapio, O.P., D.R.E. Students 143.
Convent—
3343 Kanakolu St., Lihue, 96766. Dominican Sisters of St. Catherine of Siena 2.

ISLAND OF LANAI
County of Maui

LANAI CITY, SACRED HEARTS (1930) [CEM] 815 Fraser Ave., P.O. Box 630784, Lanai City, 96763.
Tel: 808-565-7070; Email: sacredheartslanai@yahoo.com; Web: sacredheartslanai.org. Rev. Jose Macoy.
Catechesis Religious Program—Jessie Myers, D.R.E.; Wilma Koep, Asst. D.R.E. Students 70.

ISLAND OF MAUI
County of Maui

HAIKU, ST. RITA (1922) 655 Haiku Rd., Haiku, 96708. Tel: 808-575-2601; Fax: 808-575-2063; Email: stritahaiku@gmail.com; Web: stritahaiku.com. Rev. Chacko Muthoottil, M.F.
Catechesis Religious Program—Christine Matheis, D.R.E. Students 18.
Mission—St. Gabriel, [CEM] Keanae.
Wailuanui Rd., Keanae, 96708.

HANA, ST. MARY (1859) [CEM] 5000 Hana Hwy., P.O. Box 219, Hana, 96713. Tel: 808-248-8030; Fax: 808-248-8042; Email: hanastmary@gmail.com. Rev. Drexel Ramos, Admin.
Res.: 5065 Hana Hwy., Hana, 96713.
Catechesis Religious Program—
Tel: 808-248-8422. Helen Cosma, D.R.E. Students 22.
Missions—St. Peter—
47699 Hana Hwy., Puuiki, 96713. Puuiki.
St. Paul
41145 Hana Hwy., Kipahulu, 96713. Kipahulu.
St. Joseph
33622 Piilani Hwy., Kaupo, 96790. Kaupo.

KAHULUI, CHRIST THE KING (1932) [CEM] 20 W. Wakea Ave., Kahului, 96732. Tel: 808-877-6098; Fax: 808-463-3747; Email: info@ctkchurchmaui.org; Email: mildred@ctkchurchmaui.org; Web: ctkchurchmaui.org. Rev. Augustine Uthuppu, M.S.; Deacons Cornelio Pulido; Kenneth Bissen Jr.
School—Child Development Center (Pre-School)
211 S. Kaulawahine St., Kahului, 96732.
Tel: 808-877-3587; Fax: 808-871-8101; Email: ctkps@hawaii.rr.com. Carole Arakawa, Dir.
Christ the King Child Development Center Lay Teachers 8; Students 45.
Catechesis Religious Program—
Tel: 808-877-3674; Email: fabrizi42@yahoo.com. Sr. Angela Laurenzo, C.S.J, D.R.E. Students 240.
Convent—Sisters of St. Joseph of Carondelet
35 Hololea St., Apt. D206, Kahului, 96732.

KIHEI, MAUI CO., ST. THERESA (1928) 25 W. Lipoa St., Kihei, 96753. Tel: 808-879-2649; Fax: 808-879-0045; Email: mafalekaono@rcchawaii.org; Web: saint-theresa.com. Rev. Msgr. Terrence A.M. Watanabe; Rev. Noe Acosta Perez, Chap.
Catechesis Religious Program—
Tel: 808-879-4844; Email: kmartin@rcchawaii.org. Kalae Martin, D.R.E. Students 164.

KULA, HAWAII CO., OUR LADY QUEEN OF THE ANGELS (1940) [CEM] 9177 Kula Hwy., Kula, 96790-9464. Tel: 808-878-1261; Fax: 808-878-3105; Email: kccchurch@rcchawaii.org; Web: kulacatholiccommunity.org. Rev. Adondee Arrellano, M.S.
Catechesis Religious Program—
Tel: 808-283-7545; Email: dabegas@hotmail.com. Mary Jean Bega, D.R.E. Students 49.
Missions—Holy Ghost— (1899)
4300 Lower Kula Rd., Waiakoa, 96790. Waiakoa.
St. James the Less (1851)
Piilani Hwy., Ulupalakua, 96790. Ulupalakua.

LAHAINA, MAUI CO., MARIA LANAKILA (VICTORIOUS MARY) (1846) [CEM] 712 Wainee St., Lahaina, 96761-1511. Tel: 808-661-0552; Fax: 808-661-1670; Email: info@marialanakila.org; Web: marialanakila.org. Revs. Joseph Pathiyil, M.F.; Sebastian Kumar Soosai, M.F., Parochial Vicar.
School—Sacred Hearts School, (Grades PreK-8), 239 Dickenson St., Lahaina, 96761.
Tel: 808-661-4720; Fax: 808-667-5363; Email: bspitznagel@shsmaui.org; Web: www.shsmaui.org. Becky Spitznagel, Prin. Clergy 2; Lay Teachers 17; Students 214.
Catechesis Religious Program—
Email: tlolesio@shsmaui.org. Tonata Lolesio, D.R.E. Students 114.
Convent—Missionary Sisters of Faith 3.
Mission—Sacred Hearts
500 Office Rd., Kapalua, 69761. Honokahua (Kapalua).

MAKAWAO, HONOLULU, ST. JOSEPH (1851) [CEM] 1294 Makawao Ave., Makawao, 96768. Tel: 808-572-7652; Fax: 808-573-2278; Email: stjosephmakawao@rcchawaii.org; Web: sjcmaui.org. Revs. Jaime Jose; Michael Tolentino, Parochial Vicar; Deacon Patrick Constantino.
School—St. Joseph Early Learning Center
Tel: 808-572-6235; Email: stjoe@sjsmaui.org; Web: sjsmaui.org. Helen Souza, Dir. Students 42.
Catechesis Religious Program—
Tel: 808-572-2273; Email: sharris@rcchawaii.org. Sheri Harris, D.R.E. Students 102.

PAIA, MAUI CO., HOLY ROSARY (1866) [CEM] 954 Baldwin Ave., Paia, 96779-9605. Tel: 808-579-9551; Email: calnas@rcchawaii.org. Rev. Cipriano Alnas, Admin.; Deacon Christopher Rubican.
Catechesis Religious Program—Ms. Cyrila Pascual, D.R.E. Students 12.

WAIHEE, HONOLULU, ST. ANN (1935) [CEM] 40 Kuhinia St., Waihee, 96793-9216. Tel: 808-244-3284; Email: info@saint-ann-maui.org; Email: stannwaihee@gmail.com; Web: saint-ann-maui.org. Rev. Oliver J. Ortega, Admin.
Catechesis Religious Program—Students 33.
Mission—St. Francis Xavier, [CEM]
Kahekili Hwy., Kahakuloa, 96793. Kahakuloa.

WAILUKU, MAUI CO., ST. ANTHONY OF PADUA (1846) [CEM] 1627 B Mill St., Wailuku, 96793-1999. Tel: 808-244-4148; Fax: 808-242-9375; Email: info@stanthonymaui.org; Web: stanthonymaui.org. Revs. Roland Bunda, S.M.; Sylverius Kerketta, S.M., Parochial Vicar; Deacon Stephen Maglente.
School—St. Anthony of Padua School, (Grades PreK-12),
1627A Mill St., Wailuku, 96793.
Tel: 808-244-4976 (Elementary);
Tel: 808-244-4190 (High School);
Tel: 808-242-9024 (PreK);
Fax: 808-242-8081 (High School); Fax: 808-244-7950; Email: sas@sasmaui.org; Web: sasmaui.org. Timothy Cullen, Head of School. Lay Teachers 31; Students 307.
Catechesis Religious Program—
Tel: 808-242-6040. Sr. Eva Joseph Mesina, C.S.J., D.R.E. Students 183.

ISLAND OF MOLOKAI
County of Kalawao

KALAUPAPA, ST. FRANCIS (1873) Kamehameha St., P.O. Box 9, Kalaupapa, 96742. Tel: 808-567-6238; Email: pkilililea@rcchawaii.org; Web: damienchurchmolokai.org/wp/saint-francis-church. Rev. Patrick J. Killilea, SS.CC.
Mission—St. Philomena, Kalawao
Damien Rd., Kalawao, 96742.

County of Maui

KAUNAKAKAI, MAUI CO., ST. DAMIEN (1874) [CEM 2] 115 Ala Malama St., P.O. Box 1948, Kaunakakai, 96748-1948. Tel: 808-553-5220; Fax: 808-553-3534; Email: molocath1@hawaiiantel.net; Web: damienchurchmolokai.org. Rev. Sioneata Kaitapu, SS.CC.; Deacon Michael K. Shizuma.
Res.: 5900 Kamehameha V Hwy., P.O. Box 1948, Kaunakakai, 96748.
Catechesis Religious Program—Roseline Brito, D.R.E., High School; Grace Kashiwamura, D.R.E., PreK/K-Elementary. Students 83.
Missions—Our Lady of Seven Sorrows, Kaluaaha—
8033 Kamehameha V Hwy., Kaluaaha, 96748.
St. Joseph, Kamalo
Kamehameha V Hwy., Kamalo, 96748.
St. Vincent Ferrer, Maunaloa
274 Maunaloa Rd., Maunaloa, 96770.

Additional Clergy

Apostleship of the Sea. Deacons Joaquin Borja, Vince Wozniak.
Hospital Ministry. Revs. Antonio D. Bobis, Diocesan Hospital Chap., Ramon Danilo Laeda, St. Francis Healthcare Chap., Victor Lanuevo, St. Francis Healthcare Chap., (Retired), Francisco Nicomedes S. Sanchez, Diocesan Hospital Chap. Dir.
Prison Ministry, 6301 Pali Hwy., Kaneohe, 96744. Tel: 808-203-6722. Deacon Efrain Andrews, Diocesan Coord.

Priests On Duty Elsewhere:
Revs.—
Coughlin, Thomas, Archdiocese of San Antonio
Dumag, Peter, Military Archdiocese, U.S. Air Force
Mamo, Nathan, Diocese of Reno.

Retired Priests:
Revs.—
Berger, John W., (Retired), 1435 Midway Pkwy., St. Paul, MN 55108
Bush, Scott, (Retired), 1184 Bishop St., 96813
Butler, John J., (Retired), Dayton, OH
Carvalho, Gordian, (Retired)
Chacko, Sebastian V., (Retired), 98-209 Kanuku St., Aiea, 96701
Colton, Gary P., (Retired), 160 Keonekai Rd., #27-1019, Kihei, 96753

Evers, Paul H., P.O. Box 943, Masontown, WV 26542
Fernandez, Sydney, (Retired), 801 S. King St., #1003, 96813
Fisher, Clarence L., (Retired), 99-727 Malae Pl., Aiea, 96701
Freitas, Patrick, (Retired), 801 S. King St., 96813
Gervacio, Adrian R., (Retired), 1614 Monte St., 96819
Grimaldi, Joseph A., J.C.L., M.A., (Retired), P.O. Box 7199, Bloomfield Hills, MI 48302
Gross, Thomas L., (Retired), 5419 W. Tropicana Ave., #2503, Las Vegas, NV 89103
Hennen, Joseph, (Retired), 1766 Cobblestone Ct., Red Wing, MN 55066
Koshko, Dennis, (Retired), 801 South King St., #1010, 96813
Lanuevo, Victor, (Retired)
Orsini, James, (Retired), P.O. Box 1743, Wailuku, 96793
Owens, Michael J., (Retired), 6301 Pali Hwy., Kaneohe, 96744
Rebuldela, Alfred, (Retired), P.O. Box 253, Papaikou, 96781
Ryan, Jack, (Retired), 801 S. King St., 96813
Shannon, William, (Retired), 801 S. King St., #1006, 96813
Smith, Paul, (Retired), 1330 Ala Moana Blvd., #2602, 96814
Yim, Louis H., (Retired), 801 S. King St., #1002, 96813.

Deacons on Duty Elsewhere:
Deacon—
Archer, Wayne C., 4200 Timber Brook Dr., San Antonio, TX 78238.

Retired Deacons:
Awana, Benjamin A., 89-104 A Haleakala Ave., Nanakuli, 96792
Bostick, James E., P.O. Box 894, Kekaha, 96752
Calunod, Andres J., 1434 Gregory St., 96817
Cho, Edward, 41-1403 Kumuula St., Waimanalo, 96795
Cyr, Robert, 15-2811 Opakapaka St., Pahoa, 96778-8611
Franco, Lawrence Stanley, 452 Kaiola Pl., Kihei, 96753
Guinaugh, Daniel R., 571 Lexington Pkwy., Apopka, FL 93712
Hope, Jack M., 845 E. Silverado Ranch Rd., #1277, Las Vegas, NV 89183
Ignacio, Lawrence, P.O. Box 317, Paauilo, 96776
Kang, Dominic S.
Libarios, Ernest Sr., 98-1470 Kaonohi St., Aiea, 96701
Matsuo, Roy T., 1755 Mahani Loop, 96819
Mitsui, Wallace M., 95-690 Lewanuu St., Mililani, 96789
Pascua, Manuel, 380 Kaima Pl., Kapaa, 96746
Phillips, Albert C., 3297 Haleakala Hwy., Makawao, 96768
Port, Richard J., 1600 Ala Moana Blvd., #3100, 96815
Thorp, George Jr., 1459 Akamai St., Kailua, 96734
Victor, Leslie, 7255 Kuhono St., 96825
Yoshimitsu, Walter H., 681 Akoakoa St., Kailua, 96734.

INSTITUTIONS LOCATED IN DIOCESE

[A] COLLEGES AND UNIVERSITIES

HONOLULU. **Chaminade University of Honolulu* (1955) 3140 Waialae Ave., 96816. Tel: 808-735-4711; Fax: 808-735-7748; Email: admissions@chaminade.edu; Web: www.chaminade.edu. Lynn Babington, Pres.; Bro. Edward Brink, Vice Pres. Brothers 8; Priests 2; Students 1,927; Total Enrollment 1,800; Total Staff 344; Clergy / Religious Teachers 13.

[B] SCHOOLS

ISLAND OF OAHU. HONOLULU

Damien Memorial School (1962) (Grades 6-12), 1401 Houghtailing St., 96817. Tel: 808-841-0195; Fax: 808-847-1401; Web: www.damien.edu. Wes Reber Porter, Pres.; Dr. Kyle Atabay, Prin.; Cheryle O'Brien, Librarian. Brothers 2; Lay Teachers 55; Students 638; Students Grades 6-8 193; High School Students 445.

St. Francis School (1924) (Grades PreK-12), 2707 Pamoa Rd., 96822. Tel: 808-988-4111; Fax: 808-988-5497; Email: admin@stfrancis-oahu.org; Email: lgerboc@stfrancis-oahu.org; Web: www.stfrancis-oahu.org. Sr. Joan of Arc Souza, O.S.F., Prin.; Louise Gerboc, Contact Person. Lay Teachers 44; Preschool 49; Sisters 1; Students 451; Students Grades K-8 196; High School Students 255.

**St. Louis School*, (Grades K-12), 3142 Waialae Ave., 96816-1578. Tel: 808-739-7777; Fax: 808-739-4853; Email: info@saintlouishawaii.org; Web: www.saintlouishawaii.org. Glenn Medeiros, Pres. Lay Teachers 59; Priests 2; Students 853; Students Grades K-8 369; High School Students 484; Clergy / Religious Teachers 4.

St. Patrick School, (Grades PreK-8), 3320 Harding Ave., 96816. Tel: 808-734-8979; Fax: 808-732-2851; Email: adecosta@saintpatrickhawaii.org; Web: www.saintpatrickhawaii.org. Rev. Clarence L. Guerreiro, SS.CC., Pres.; Sr. Anne Clare DeCosta, SS.CC., Vice Pres. Clergy 1; Lay Teachers 39; Sisters 1; Students 316; Clergy / Religious Teachers 1.

Sacred Hearts Academy (1909) (Grades PreK-12), 3253 Waialae Ave., 96816. Tel: 808-734-5058; Fax: 808-737-7867; Email: bwhite@sacredhearts.org; Web: www.sacredhearts.org. Betty White, Head of School; Dr. Brandy Sato, Vice Prin.; Kellie Fase, Librarian; Laurel Oshiro, Librarian. Lay Teachers 80; Preschool 50; Sisters 2; Support Staff, Counselors, Administrators 30; Students Grades K-8 530; High School Students 400.

EWA BEACH.

St. Francis Preschool, 91-1758 Oohao St., Ewa Beach, 96706. 2226 Liliha St., Ste. 227, 96817. Tel: 808-681-0100; Email: info@stfrancishawaii.org. Rochelle Takata, Mgr. Lay Teachers 9; Sisters 1; Students 60.

WAIPIO.

Rosary Preschool, 94-1249 Lumikula St., Waipahu, 96797. Tel: 808-676-1452; Email: rosarypreschool@rcchawaii.org; Web: rosarypreschool.com. Sr. Cecilia Fabular, O.P., Dir. Clergy 5; Lay Teachers 4; Sisters 5; Students 50.

[C] HEALTHCARE INSTITUTES

HONOLULU. *St. Francis Healthcare System of Hawaii*, 2226 Liliha St., Ste. 227, 96817. Tel: 808-547-6500; Fax: 808-547-8018; Email: info@stfrancishawaii.org; Web: www.stfrancishawaii.org. Jerry J. Correa Jr., CEO. Total Staff 272.

The St. Francis International Center for Healthcare Ethics, 2226 Liliha St.,Ste. 227, 96817. Tel: 808-547-6500; Email: info@stfrancishawaii.org. Patty Martin, Vice Pres.

SFMC Joint Ventures, LLC, 2226 Liliha St., Ste. 227, 96817. Tel: 808-547-6500; Email: info@stfrancishawaii.org. Jerry Correa Jr., Mgr.

St. Francis Development Corporation, 2226 Liliha St., Ste. 227, 96817. Tel: 808-547-6500; Fax: 808-547-8018; Email: info@stfrancishawaii.org; Web: stfrancishawaii.org. Jerry Correa Jr., Pres.

St. Francis Community Health Services, 2226 Liliha St., Ste. 227, 96817. Tel: 808-595-7566; Fax: 808-547-8149; Email: mahhomauga@stfrancishawaii.org. Melissa Ah Ho-Mauga.

St. Francis Hospice Home Setting Program, 2226 Liliha St., Ste. 227, 96817.

Health Services for Senior Citizens, 2228 Liliha St., Ste. 408, 96817. 2226 Liliha St., Ste. 227, 96817. Tel: 808-547-6121; Fax: 808-676-1220; Email: info@stfrancishawaii.org. Melissa Ah Ho-Mauga, Vice Pres. Tot Asst. Annually 522; Total Staff 19.

Sister Maureen Keleher Center St. Francis Hospice Nuuanu, 24 Puiwa Rd., 96817. 2226 Liliha St., Ste. 227, 96817. Tel: 808-595-7566; Fax: 808-676-1220; Email: info@stfrancishawaii.org. Melissa Ah Ho-Mauga, Vice Pres. Bed Capacity 12; Tot Asst. Annually 170; Total Staff 38.

The Maurice J. Sullivan Family Hospice Center, 91-2127 Fort Weaver Rd., Ewa Beach, 96706. 2226 Liliha St., Ste. 227, 96817. Tel: 808-595-7566; Fax: 808-676-6885; Email: info@stfrancishawaii.org. Melissa Ah Ho-Mauga. Total Staff 76.

St. Francis Medical Center, 2226 Liliha St., Ste. 227, 96817. Tel: 808-547-6500; Email: info@stfrancishawaii.org. Jerry Correa Jr., Pres.

MOB Management, LLC, 2226 Liliha St., Ste. 227, 96817. Tel: 808-547-6500; Email: info@stfrancishawaii.org. Jerry Correa Jr., Member.

St. Francis Medical Center West, 2226 Liliha St., Ste. 227, 96817. Tel: 808-547-6500; Email: info@stfrancishawaii.org. Jerry Correa Jr., Pres.

St. Francis Residential Care Community dba Franciscan Vistas, 2226 Liliha St., Ste. 227, 96817. Tel: 808-547-6500; Fax: 808-547-8018; Email: info@stfrancishawaii.org. Jerry Correa Jr., Pres. Total Staff 1; Residents Assisted Annually 182.

St. Francis Healthcare Foundation of Hawaii, 2228 Liliha St., Ste. 205, 96817. Tel: 808-547-6500; Fax: 808-547-8034; Email: info@stfrancishawaii.org. 2226 Liliha St., Ste. 227, 96817. Leslie Lam. Total Staff 5.

Blessings House, 91-019 Popoi Pl., Ewa Beach, 96706. 2226 Liliha St., Ste. 227, 96817. Tel: 808-547-6500; Email: info@stfrancishawaii.org. Sr. Beatrice Tom, O.S.F., Pres. Staff 4.

Franciscan Care Services, 2226 Liliha St., Ste. 227, 96817. Tel: 808-547-6500; Fax: 808-676-1220; Email: info@stfrancishawaii.org. Jerry Correa Jr., Pres.

Sister Maureen Intergenerational Learning Environment aka Franciscan Adult Day Center, 2715 Pamoa Rd., 96822. 2226 Liliha St., Ste. 227, 96817. Tel: 808-988-5678; Fax: 808-988-1179; Email: info@stfrancishawaii.org. Melissa Ah Ho-Mauga. Capacity 33; Total Staff 8.

St. Francis Adult Day Center aka St. Francis Intergenerational Center, 91-1758 Oohao St., Ewa Beach, 96706. 2226 Liliha St., Ste. 227, 96817. Tel: 808-681-0100; Email: info@stfrancishawaii.org. Melissa Ah Ho-Mauga, Vice Pres. Please refer to section [B] Schools for St. Francis Preschool Capacity 42; Staff 9.

Hawaii Bone Marrow Donor Registry, 2228 Liliha St., Ste. 105, 96817. Tel: 808-547-6154; Fax: 808-547-6979; Email: rchung@stfrancis.org. 2226 Liliha St., Ste. 227, 96817. Renee Chung, Donor Prog. Mgr.

Our Lady of Keaau, Waianae, Keaau Homesteads Rd., Waianae, 96792. P.O. Box 1475, Waianae, 96792. Tel: 808-696-7255; Fax: 808-696-5672; Email: info@stfrancishawaii.org. Sisters Beatrice Tom, O.S.F., Pres.; Donna Marie Evans, O.S.F.

[D] MONASTERIES AND RESIDENCES OF PRIESTS AND BROTHERS

HONOLULU. *Christian Brothers of Ireland*, 1840 Owawa St., 96819. Email: samp@damien.edu. Bros. Bernard S. Samp, C.F.C, Contact Person; Daniel J. Casey, C.F.C.; Bruce John Cullerton, C.F.C.; Liam V. Nolan, C.F.C.; Kevin J. Reilly, C.F.C. Brothers 5.

Marianist Communities, 3140 Waialae Ave., 96816-1578. Tel: 808-738-5887; Fax: 808-732-3374; Email: brohoppe@aol.com. Bro. Dennis Schmitz, S.M., Spiritual Adviser / Care Svcs. Please refer to the following parish for additional residence: St. Anthony, Wailuku.3140 Waialae Ave., 96816-1578.

Center Marianist Community, 3140 Waialae Ave., 96816. Tel: 808-739-8500; Fax: 808-739-8501; Email: george.cerniglia@chaminade.edu. Revs. George J. Cerniglia, S.M., Dir.; Robert Bouffier, Prof.; Paul Fitzpatrick, S.M., Prof. Brothers 5; Priests 2. *Marianist Hall Community*, Marianist Hall, 3140 Waialae Ave., 96816. Tel: 808-739-8300; Fax: 808-739-8320; Email: frankdamm31@gmail.com. Revs. Patrick McDaid, S.M., Dir.; James Allen DeLong, S.M. Brothers 7; Priests 2.

KANEOHE. *Sacred Hearts Center, Congregation of the Sacred Hearts of Jesus and Mary and of Perpetual Adoration*, 45-713 Pookela St., Kaneohe, 96744. Tel: 808-235-5035; Fax: 808-235-8849; Web: www.sscc.org. P.O. Box 1365, Kaneohe, 96744. Revs. Herman Gomes, SS.CC., Prov.; Joseph Bukoski III, SS.CC., In Res., (Retired); Bro. Richard Kupo, SS.-CC., In Res. Please refer to the following parishes for additional residences: Our Lady of Sorrows, Wahiawa; St. Anne, Kaneohe; St. Augustine, Honolulu; St. Damien, Kaunakakai; St. Francis, Kalaupapa; St. Michael, Waialua

Legal Titles: Sacred Hearts Missions; Sacred Hearts Fathers Brothers 1; Priests 2. *St. Patrick's Monastery*, 1124-A 7th Ave., 96816. Tel: 808-732-0281; Fax: 808-737-2477; Email: clancy@hawaii.rr.com. Revs. Clarence Guerreiro, Supr.; Albert Garcia, SS.CC., Member; Christopher Keahi, SS.CC., Member; William F. Petrie, SS.CC., Member. Priests 4.

WAIALUA. *Benedictine Monastery of Hawaii / Mary, Spouse of the Holy Spirit* (1984) 67-290 Farrington Hwy., P.O. Box 490, Waialua, 96791. Tel: 808-637-7887; Fax: 808-637-8601; Email: monastery@hawaiibenedictines.org; Web: www.hawaiibenedictines.org. Rev. David Barfknecht, O.S.B., Prior; Sr. Mary Jo McEnany, O.S.B., Subprioress; Rev. Michael Sawyer, O.S.B.; Sisters Geralyn Spaulding, O.S.B.; Celeste Cabral, O.S.B. Public Association of the Faithful of Diocesan Right.

Public Association of the Faithful of Diocesan Right.

[E] CONVENTS AND RESIDENCES FOR SISTERS

HONOLULU. *Congregation of the Sacred Hearts of Jesus and Mary and of Perpetual Adoration* (1800) Tel: 808-737-5822; Email: reginasscc@cs.com; Web:

www.ssccpicpus.com. Sr. Regina Mary Jenkins, SS.CC., Prov. Sisters of the Congregation of the Sacred Hearts of Jesus and Mary and of Perpetual Adoration, SS.CC. Sisters 5.

Regina Pacis Community, 1120 Fifth Ave., 96816. Tel: 808-737-5822; Fax: 808-735-0878; Email: reginasscc@cs.com. Sr. Regina Mary Jenkins, SS.-CC., Prov. Sisters 5.

Puawakea Community, Puawakea Community, 3351 Kalihi St., 96819. Tel: 808-845-4353; Fax: 808-848-2696; Email: sisteranneclare@gmail.com. Sr. Anne Clare DeCosta, SS.CC., Contact Person. Sisters 3.

Paewalani Community, 45-901 Wailele Rd., Kaneohe, 96744. Tel: 808-247-3688; Email: sisteranneclare@gmail.com; Web: sistersofthesacredhearts.org. Sr. Anne Clare DeCosta, SS.CC., Contact Person. Sisters 2.

Malia o ka Malu Community, 1117 Fourth Ave., 96816. Tel: 808-734-2048; Fax: 808-735-0878; Email: helenew@hawaii.rr.com. Sr. Helene Wood, SS.CC., Supr. & Contact Person. Sisters 11.

Moloka'i Sisters Community, 405 Palapalai Pl., Kaunakakai, 96748. Tel: 808-553-4303; Email: jessiealai@hotmail.com. P.O. Box 1237, Kaunakakai, 96748. Sr. Jessie Kai, SS.CC., Supr. Sisters 3.

Daughters of St. Paul Convent, 1143 Bishop St., 96813. Tel: 808-521-2731; Fax: 808-523-3685; Email: honolulu@paulinemedia.com; Web: daughtersofstpaul.org. Sr. Patricia Maresca, Supr. Sisters 4.

Maryknoll Sisters of St. Dominic, 125 Ainoni St., Kailua, 96734-2138. Tel: 808-261-6356; Fax: 808-988-8089; Email: mkainoni@yahoo.com. Sr. Bitrina Kirway, M.M., Contact Person. Sisters 12. *Maryknoll Sisters Residence*, 2880 Oahu Ave., 96822-1732. Tel: 808-988-6540; Fax: 808-988-8089; Email: mkmanoa@hawaii.rr.com. Sr. Bitrina Kirway, M.M., Regl. Communicator. Sisters 4. *Maryknoll Sisters Residence*, 1570 Mokulua Dr., Kailua, 96734-3254. Tel: 808-261-1674; Email: mkslanikai@yahoo.com. Sr. Bitrina Kirway, M.M., Regl. Communicator. Sisters 3.

Sisters of St. Francis of the Neumann Communities (1883) St. Francis Convent, 2715 Pamoa Rd., 96822-1885. Tel: 808-988-4432; Fax: 808-687-8695; Email: pschofield@sosf.org. Sr. Patricia Schofield, O.S.F., Regl. Min. Sisters of St. Francis of the Neumann Communities (O.S.F.); St. Francis Healthcare System of Hawaii; St. Francis School. Sisters 25.

Sisters of St. Joseph of Carondelet, Carondelet Center, 5311 Apo Dr., 96821-1829. Tel: 808-373-8801; Fax: 808-373-8803; Email: hvpmae@gmail.com. Sr. Brenda Lau, C.S.J., Dir. Sisters 19.

St. Joseph by the Sea Community, 206 Kailua Rd., Kailua, 96734-2398. Tel: 808-262-0575; Email: hvpmae@gmail.com. Sr. Brenda Lau, C.S.J., Member. Please refer to the following parish convents for additional residences: Co-Cathedral, Honolulu; Christ the King, Kahului. Sisters 3.

KANEOHE. *Carmel of the Holy Trinity (Carmelite Monastery)*, 6301 Pali Hwy., Kaneohe, 96744-5224. Tel: 808-261-6542; Email: carmeltrinityhawaii@outlook.com. Sr. Agnella Iu, Delegate. Order of Discalced Carmelite Nuns of Our Lady of Mount Carmel (O.C.D.). Sisters 3.

WAIANAE. *House of Aloha*, 86-569 Paheehee Rd., Waianae, 96792. Tel: 808-696-3021; Email: srermiet@yahoo.com. Sr. Ermelinda Tagnipez, Dir.

WAIPIO. *Dominican Center Hawaii*, 94-1249 Lumikula St., Waipahu, 96797. Tel: 808-676-1452; Tel: 808-677-1202; Fax: 808-677-1202; Email: srbsindol@hotmail.com; Web: www.ophawiiregion.com. Sisters Bernarda Sindol, O.P., Supr.; Cecilia Fabular, O.P., Contact Person. Please refer to the following parish convents for additional residences: St. Elizabeth, Aiea; St. John, Honolulu. Sisters 20.

[F] CHARITIES

HONOLULU. **Catholic Charities Hawaii*, 1822 Keeaumoku St., 96822. Tel: 808-524-4673; Fax: 808-521-4357; Email: info@catholiccharitieshawaii.org; Web: catholiccharitieshawaii.org. Ms. Stella M. Wong, M.S.W., Acting Pres./CEO; Ms. Tina Andrade, Vice Pres./Mission Integration; Ms. Mary Saunders, Vice Pres./Philanthropy; Ms. Celine Allouchery, Exec. Asst. Persons Served 40,000.

HILO. *Hope Services Hawaii*, 296 Kilauea Ave., Hilo, 96720. Tel: 808-935-3050; Fax: 808-935-3794; Email: info@hopeserviceshawaii.org; Web: hopeserviceshawaii.org. Brandee Menino, CEO. Bed Capacity 163; Tot Asst. Annually 2,800; Total Staff 58; Volunteers 253.

[G] RETREAT AND SPIRITUAL CENTERS

HONOLULU. *St. Anthony Retreat Center* (1909) 3351 Kalihi St., 96819. Tel: 808-845-4353; Email: sarc3351@gmail.com; Web: www.saintanthonyretreat.org. Sr. Anne Clare DeCosta, SS.CC., Admin. Staff 14.

**Marianist Center of Hawaii* (1986) 3140 Waialae Ave., 96816. Tel: 808-738-5887; Fax: 808-732-3374; Email: baldschmitz@aol.com; Email: mchwjcampbell@chaminade.edu. Bros. Dennis Schmitz, S.M., Dir.; William Campbell, Dir. Total Staff 4.

Mystical Rose Oratory, 3140 Waialae Ave., 96816. Tel: 808-739-4738; Tel: 808-738-5887 (direct line); Fax: 808-732-3374; Email: george.cerniglia@chaminade.edu. Rev. George J. Cerniglia, S.M., Chap.

KANEOHE. *St. Stephen Diocesan Center*, 6301 Pali Hwy., Kaneohe, 96744-5298. Tel: 808-203-6724; Fax: 808-261-7022; Email: sizaguirre@rcchawaii.org. Sabrina Izaguirre, Asst. Admin., Tel: 808-203-6724.

[H] FOUNDATIONS

HONOLULU. *Foundation for Maryknoll School*, 1526 Alexander St., 96822. Tel: 808-952-7310; Email: development@maryknollschool.org. Stacey Wong, Chm.

**Hawaii Catholic Community Foundation*, 1184 Bishop St., 96813. Tel: 808-585-3307; Email: marvin@rcchawaii.org; Email: financeoffice@rcchawaii.org. Lisa Sakamoto, 1184 Bishop St., 96813.

KANEOHE. *Augustine Educational Foundation* (1984) St. Stephen Diocesan Center, 6301 Pali Hwy., Kaneohe, 96744. Tel: 808-203-6736; Tel: 808-203-6748; Email: sue@augustinefoundation.org; Email: tonya@augustinefoundation.org; Email: info@augustinefoundation.org; Web: www.augustinefoundation.org. Susan Ferandin, Exec. Dir.; Tonya Stevenson, Assoc. Dir.

WAILUKU. *St. Anthony School of Maui Foundation* (2018) 1618 Lower Main St., Wailuku, 96793. Rev. Roland Bunda, S.M.

RELIGIOUS INSTITUTES OF MEN REPRESENTED IN THE DIOCESE

For further details refer to the corresponding bracketed number in the Religious Institutes of Men or Women section.

[0310]—*Congregation of Christian Brothers*—C.F.C.
[1140]—*Congregation of the Sacred Hearts of Jesus and Mary and of Perpetual Adoration*—SS.CC.
[0220]—*Congregation of the Blessed Sacrament*—S.S.S.
[]—*Congregation of the Mother of the Redeemer*—C.R.M.
[]—*Missionaries of Faith*—M.F.
[0720]—*Missionaries of Our Lady of La Salette*—M.S.
[0470]—*Order of Friars Minor Capuchin*—O.F.M.Cap.
[]—*Order of St. Augustine*—O.S.A.
[0690]—*Society of Jesus (Jesuits)*—S.J.
[0760]—*Society of Mary (Marianists)*—S.M.

RELIGIOUS INSTITUTES OF WOMEN REPRESENTED IN THE DIOCESE

[3690]—*Congregation of the Sacred Hearts of Jesus and Mary and of Perpetual Adoration*—SS.CC.
[0950]—*Daughters of Saint Paul*—F.S.P.
[]—*Dominican Sisters of St. Catherine of Siena*—O.P.
[1070-03]—*Dominican Sisters of the Most Holy Rosary (Sinsinawa)*—O.P.
[]—*Little Sisters of Mary Immaculate of Galu*—L.S.M.I.G.
[2470]—*Maryknoll Sisters of St. Dominic*—M.M.
[]—*Missionary Sisters of Faith*—S.M.F.
[]—*Missionary Sisters of Mary Help of Christians*—M.S.M.H.C.
[0420]—*Order of Discalced Carmelite Nuns*—O.C.D.
[0430]—*Sisters of Charity of the Blessed Virgin Mary*—B.V.M.
[0990]—*Sisters of Divine Providence*—C.D.P.
[3980]—*Sisters of St. Paul of Chartres*—S.P.C.
[1805]—*Sisters of St. Francis of the Neumann Communities*—O.S.F.
[3840]—*Sisters of St. Joseph of Carondelet*—C.S.J.
[]—*Sisters of the Holy Family*—S.H.F.

NECROLOGY

† Turner, Edward, (Retired), Died Aug. 7, 2018

An asterisk (*) denotes an organization that has established tax-exempt status directly with the IRS and is not covered by the USCCB Group Ruling.

Diocese of Houma-Thibodaux

(Dioecesis Humensis-Thibodensis)

Most Reverend

SHELTON J. FABRE, D.D.

Bishop of Houma-Thibodaux; ordained August 5, 1989; appointed Auxiliary Bishop of New Orleans and Titular Bishop of Prudenziana December 13, 2006; ordained February 28, 2007; appointed Fourth Bishop of Houma-Thibodaux September 23, 2013; installed October 30, 2013. *Office: 2779 Hwy. 311, Schriever, LA 70395.*

Most Reverend

SAM G. JACOBS, D.D.

Retired Bishop of Houma-Thibodaux; ordained June 6, 1964; appointed Bishop of Alexandria July 1, 1989; ordained and installed August 24, 1989; appointed third Bishop of Houma-Thibodaux August 1, 2003; installed October 10, 2003; retired September 23, 2013. *Office: 2779 Hwy. 311, Schriever, LA 70395.*

Diocesan Pastoral Center: P.O. Box 505, Schriever, LA 70395. Tel: 985-868-7720; Fax: 985-868-7727.

Email: bishopsec@htdiocese.org

ERECTED JUNE 5, 1977.

Square Miles 3,500.

Comprises the parishes of Lafourche, Terrebonne, parts of St. Mary, Jefferson, St. Martin and Assumption.

For legal titles of parishes and diocesan institutions, consult the Pastoral Center.

STATISTICAL OVERVIEW

Personnel	
Bishop	1
Retired Bishops	1
Priests: Diocesan Active in Diocese	33
Priests: Diocesan Active Outside Diocese	4
Priests: Retired, Sick or Absent	18
Number of Diocesan Priests	55
Religious Priests in Diocese	7
Total Priests in Diocese	62
Extern Priests in Diocese	3
Ordinations:	
Diocesan Priests	2
Transitional Deacons	2
Permanent Deacons	4
Permanent Deacons in Diocese	36
Total Brothers	5
Total Sisters	18
Parishes	
Parishes	39
With Resident Pastor:	
Resident Diocesan Priests	32
Resident Religious Priests	6
Without Resident Pastor:	
Administered by Priests	1
Missions	3
Pastoral Centers	2
Professional Ministry Personnel:	
Sisters	5
Lay Ministers	150
Welfare	
Homes for the Aged	1
Total Assisted	60
Day Care Centers	1
Total Assisted	73
Specialized Homes	1
Total Assisted	40
Educational	
Diocesan Students in Other Seminaries	14
Total Seminarians	14
High Schools, Diocesan and Parish	3
Total Students	1,665
Elementary Schools, Diocesan and Parish	10
Total Students	3,405
Catechesis/Religious Education:	
High School Students	1,673
Elementary Students	3,113
Total Students under Catholic Instruction	9,870
Teachers in the Diocese:	
Brothers	3
Lay Teachers	351
Vital Statistics	
Receptions into the Church:	
Infant Baptism Totals	872
Minor Baptism Totals	76
Adult Baptism Totals	47
Received into Full Communion	45
First Communions	1,067
Confirmations	939
Marriages:	
Catholic	216
Interfaith	40
Total Marriages	256
Deaths	1,217
Total Catholic Population	92,350
Total Population	210,512

Former Bishops—Most Revs. WARREN L. BOUDREAUX, J.C.D., D.D., First Bishop of Houma-Thibodaux; ord. May 30, 1942; retired Dec. 29, 1992; died Oct. 6, 1997; MICHAEL JARRELL, D.D., Second Bishop of Houma-Thibodaux; ord. June 3, 1967; appt. Dec. 29, 1992; cons. and installed March 4, 1993; appt. 6th Bishop of Lafayette, Louisiana Nov. 8, 2002; SAM G. JACOBS, ord. June 6, 1964; appt. Bishop of Alexandria July 1, 1989; ord. and installed Aug. 24, 1989; appt. third Bishop of Houma-Thibodaux Aug. 1, 2003; installed Oct. 10, 2003; retired Oct. 30, 2013.

Pastoral Center

Diocesan Pastoral Center—Address all correspondence to: P.O. Box 505, Schriever, 70395. Office: 2779 Hwy. 311, Schriever, 70395. Tel: 985-868-7720; Fax: 985-868-7727. Office Hours: Mon.-Fri. 8:30-4:30.

Vicar General for Administration—Very Rev. SIMON PETER ENGURAIT, V.G.

Vicar General for Parish Life—Very Rev. MARK TOUPS, V.G.

Chancellor—Very Rev. ALEX GAUDET.

Judicial Vicar—Very Rev. ERIC LEYBLE, J.V.

Vicar for Clergy—Very Rev. JAY BAKER, V.C.

Finance Officer—VACANT.

Ecclesiastical Tribunal

Director of Tribunal—Very Rev. ERIC LEYBLE, J.V.

Tribunal Specialist and Notary—VERONICA SONGE.

Auditor—Rev. JACOB LIPARI III.

Diocesan Tribunal—Address all correspondence to Very Rev. ERIC LEYBLE, J.V., Mailing Address: P.O. Box 505, Schriever, 70395. Office: 2779 Hwy. 311, Schriever, 70395. Tel: 985-850-3126.

Judges—Very Revs. ERIC LEYBLE, J.V.; JAY BAKER, V.C.; VICENTE DELA CRUZ, J.V.

Defender of the Bond—VACANT.

Departments of the Diocesan Curia

Department of Administration Ministries

Counselor—VACANT.

Priests Council—Mailing Address: P.O. Box 505, Schriever, 70395. 2779 Hwy. 311, Schriever, 70395. Rev. P. J. MADDEN; THOMAS KURIAKOSE; JOSEKUTTY VARGHESE; ALEXIS LAZARRA; CODY CHATAGNIER; BRICE HIGGINBOTHAM; WILMER TODD, Ex Officio; Very Revs. MARK TOUPS, V.G.; SIMON PETER ENGURAIT, V.G.; ALEX GAUDET.

College of Consultors—Very Revs. JAY BAKER, V.C.; SIMON PETER ENGURAIT, V.G.; CLYDE MAHLER, V.F.; CHARLES J. PERKINS, V.F.; MARK TOUPS, V.G.; Revs. THOMAS KURIAKOSE; MITCHEL SEMAR.

Deans—

Upper Lafourche Deanery—Very Rev. CLYDE MAHLER, V.F., 2100 Cedar St., Unit 3, Morgan City, 70301.

South Lafourche Deanery—Very Rev. CHARLES J. PERKINS, V.F., 3500 Hwy. 1, Raceland, 70394.

Terrebonne Deanery—Very Rev. MIKE TRAN, V.F., 2011 Acadia Dr., Houma, 70363.

Diocesan Finance Council—Rev. MICHAEL BERGERON, (Retired); Very Rev. SIMON PETER ENGURAIT, V.G., Ex Officio; ANGELIQUE BARKER; RODNEY WHITNEY; ROBERT NAQUIN; QUINT OCKER; TIM ROBICHAUX; CRAIG STAGNA.

Accounting, Business Office, Finance—2779 Hwy. 311, Schriever, 70395. Tel: 985-868-7720. *Mailing Address: P.O. Box 505, Schriever, 70395.* APRIL LEBOUEF, Comptroller.

Archives and Historical Research Center—KEVIN ALLEMAND, Dir., 205 Audubon St., Thibodaux, 70301. Tel: 985-446-2383.

Building Commission—JAMES J. DANOS, Dir., 2779 Hwy. 311, Schriever, 70395. Mailing Address: P.O. Box 505, Schriever, 70395. Tel: 985-868-7720.

Cemeteries—949 Menard St., Thibodaux, 70301. Tel: 985-446-0280. KAYLA BRUNET.

Child and Youth Protection—2779 Hwy. 311, Schriever, 70395. Tel: 985-868-7720. *Mailing Address: P.O. Box 505, Schriever, 70395.* MELISSA R. ROBERTSON, PHR, SHRM-CP.

Legal Services—Watkins, Walker, Eroche & Hoychick, 1340 W. Tunnel Blvd., Ste. 306, Houma, 70360. Very Rev. SIMON PETER ENGURAIT, V.G., Dir., 2779

Hwy. 311, Schriever, 70395. Mailing Address: P.O. Box 505, Schriever, 70395. Tel: 985-868-7720.

Stewardship and Development—2779 Hwy. 311, Schriever, 70395. Tel: 985-868-7720. *Mailing Address: P.O. Box 505, Schriever, 70395.* AMY PONSON.

Human Resources & Employment Benefits—MELISSA R. ROBERTSON, PHR, SHRM-CP, 2779 Hwy. 311, Schriever, 70395. Mailing Address: P.O. Box 505, Schriever, 70395. Tel: 985-868-7720.

Insurance - Property, Casualty & Liability—2779 Hwy. 311, Schriever, 70395. Tel: 985-868-7720. *Mailing Address: P.O Box 505, Schriever, 70395.*

Operations - Computers & Technology—HOLLY BECNEL, Dir., 2779 Hwy. 311, Schriever, 70395. Mailing Address: P.O. Box 505, Schriever, 70395. Tel: 985-868-7720.

Department for Clergy and Religious

Coordinator—Very Rev. JAY BAKER, V.C., 2779 Hwy. 311, Schriever, 70395. Mailing Address: P.O. Box 505, Schriever, 70395. Tel: 985-868-7720.

Clergy Personnel—Very Rev. JAY BAKER, V.C., Mailing Address: P.O. Box 505, Schriever, 70395. Tel: 985-868-7720.

Continuing Education of the Clergy-Ministry to Priests Program—Very Rev. ALEX GAUDET, Mailing Address: P.O. Box 505, Schriever, 70395. Tel: 985-868-7720.

Vicar for Priests—Mailing Address: P.O. Box 505, Schriever, 70395. Very Rev. JAY L. BAKER, V.C.

Permanent Diaconate—2779 Hwy. 311, Schriever, 70395. Mailing Address: P.O. Box 505, Schriever, 70395. Tel: 985-868-7720. Deacon STEPHEN BRUNET, Dir., Tel: 985-876-0842.

Vocations—Mailing Address: P.O. Box 505, Schriever, 70395. Tel: 985-850-3157. Rev. JOHN DAVID MATHERNE, Dir.

Seminarians—Mailing Address: P.O. Box 505, Schriever, 70395. Tel: 985-850-3157. Revs. ANDRE MELANCON, Dir., Notre Dame Seminarians; MITCHEL SEMAR, Dir., St. Joseph Seminarians.

Women Religious—Mailing Address: P.O. Box 505, Schriever, 70395. Sr. CARMELITA CENTANNI, M.S.C.

Department of Formation Ministries

Coordinator—Very Rev. SIMON PETER ENGURAIT, V.G., 2779 Hwy. 311, Schriever, 70395. Tel: 985-868-7720. P.O. Box 505, Schriever, 70395.

Campus Ministry—Mailing Address: P.O. Box 2051, Thibodaux, 70310. Tel: 985-446-6201. Rev. MITCHEL SEMAR, N.S.U.

Catholic Schools—SUZANNE TROXCLAIR, 2779 Hwy. 311, Schriever, 70395. Tel: 985-868-7720. Mailing Address: P.O. Box 505, Schriever, 70395.

Communications, Public Relations, Publications, Radio & Television—Mailing Address: P.O. Box 505, Schriever, 70395. Tel: 985-868-7720. LONNIE THIBODEAUX.

Bayou Catholic—(Diocesan Magazine)– LAWRENCE CHATAGNIER, Editor, 2779 Hwy. 311, Schriever, 70395. Tel: 985-868-7720. P.O. Box 505, Schriever, 70395.

Religious Education—VACANT, 2779 Hwy. 311, Schriever, 70395. Tel: 985-868-7720. Mailing Address: P.O. Box 50, Schriever, 70395.

Youth Ministries—Mailing Address: P.O. Box 505, Schriever, 70395. Tel: 985-868-7720. Rev. JOHN DAVID MATHERNE.

Worship—Rev. GLENN LECOMPTE, Dir., 2779 Hwy. 311, Schriever, 70395. Tel: 985-868-7720. Mailing Address: P.O. Box 505, Schriever, 70395.

Rite of Christian Initiation of Adults—Deacon LEE CROCHET, 121 Kellie Dr., Houma, 70360. Tel: 985-855-1063.

Department of Social Ministries

Coordinator of Social Ministries—MR. ROBERT D. GORMAN, L.C.S.W., A.C.S.W., 1220 Aycock St., Houma, 70360. Tel: 985-876-0490.

Catholic Charities—1220 Aycock St., Houma, 70360. Tel: 985-876-0490. MR. ROBERT D. GORMAN, L.C.S.W., A.C.S.W., Exec. Dir.

Programs of Catholic Charities:—

Adoption—1220 Aycock St., Houma, 70360. Tel: 985-876-0490. MR. ROBERT GORMAN, L.C.S.W., A.C.S.W.

Assisi Bridge House—600 Bull Run Rd., Schriever, 70395. Tel: 985-872-5529. MS. MONIQUE ALBARADO, L.P.C., Dir.

Catholic Campaign for Human Development—1220 Aycock St., Houma, 70360. Tel: 985-876-0490. MS. AGNES BITATURE, Assoc. Dir.

Catholic Community Center—9018 Avenue A, Galliano, 70354. Tel: 985-632-6859. MS. SUSAN TERREBONNE, Mgr.

Catholic Housing Services—1220 Aycock St., Houma, 70360. Tel: 985-876-0490. MS. PAULA RINGO, Assoc. Dir.

Catholic Relief Services—1220 Aycock St., Houma, 70360. Tel: 985-876-0490. MS. AGNES BITATURE, Assoc. Dir.

C.E.N.T.S. Micro Enterprise Program—1220 Aycock St., Houma, 70360. Tel: 985-876-0490. MS. PAULA RINGO, Assoc. Dir.

Disaster Preparedness & Relief/Matthew 25—1220 Aycock St., Houma, 70360. Tel: 985-876-0490. MS. AGNES BITATURE, Assoc. Dir.

Foster Grandparent Program—1220 Aycock St., Houma, 70360. Tel: 985-876-0490. MR. VAN JOHNSON, Assoc. Dir.

Good Samaritan Raceland Food Bank—2084 Hwy. 182, Raceland, 70394. Tel: 985-537-7706. MS. LESLIE ROBICHAUX, Mgr.

Good Samaritan Thibodaux Food Bank—100 Birch St., Thibodaux, 70301. Tel: 985-447-9776. MS. KRISTIN LAFLEUR, Mgr.

Individual and Family Assistance—1220 Aycock St., Houma, 70360. Tel: 985-876-0490. MS. JENNIFER GAUDET, Assoc. Dir.

Parish Social Ministry/Justice & Peace—1220 Aycock St., Houma, 70360. Tel: 985-876-0490. MS. AGNES BITATURE, Assoc. Dir.

St. Lucy Child Development Center—MS. DANIELLE DAVIS, Dir., 1224 Aycock St., Houma, 70360. Tel: 985-876-1246.

Other Offices and Commissions

Charismatic Renewal—PENNY ANTILL, Charismatic Renewal Liaison, 4065 Bayou Black Dr., Houma, 70360. Tel: 985-856-4269.

Cursillo—Ponderosa Ln., Gray, 70364. Tel: 985-850-3132. Deacon LLOYD DUPLANTIS, Dir.

Ecumenism—VACANT, P.O. Box 505, Schriever, 70395. Tel: 985-868-7720.

Pontifical Missionary Union of Priests and ReligiousMissionary Childhood Association; Society of St. Peter the Apostle. Rev. ROBERT JOEL CRUZ, Dir., 1220 Aycock St., Houma, 70360. Tel: 985-850-0035; Fax: 985-850-0063.

Lumen Christi Retreat Center—100 Lumen Christi Ln., Hwy. 311, Schriever, 70395. Tel: 985-868-1523; Fax: 985-868-1525. CHRIS DOMINGUE, Admin.

Scouting—Mailing Address: P.O. Box 505, Schriever, 70395. Tel: 985-868-7720; Fax: 985-850-3215. Deacon GARY LAPEYROUSE, Dir.

Organizations

Catholic Daughters of the Americas—Very Rev. CHARLES PERKINS, Spiritual Advisor, 3500 Hwy. 1, Raceland, 70394.

Diocesan Council of St. Vincent de Paul Societies—Mailing Address: P.O. Box 3620, Houma, 70361. MR. PAUL MACLEAN.

Knights of Columbus—Rev. JACOB LIPARI III, Diocesan Chap., Mailing Address: 2100 Cedar St., Unit 3, Morgan City. Tel: 985-384-3551.

St. Vincent de Paul Store—MR. PETE CAVALIER, Pres.; MR. ROY BURNS, Vice Pres.; PHYLLES LAGARDE, Treas. Store Managers: JIM LAGARDE; PHYLLES LAGARDE, 107 Point St., Houma, 70360. Tel: 985-872-9373; Fax: 985-223-1931.

Victim Assistance Coordinator—Sr. CARMELITA CENTANNI, M.S.C., Tel: 985-850-3172; Email: ccentanni@htdiocese.org.

CLERGY, PARISHES, MISSIONS AND PAROCHIAL SCHOOLS

CITY OF HOUMA

(PARISH TERREBONNE)

1—CATHEDRAL OF ST. FRANCIS DE SALES (1847) [CEM 2]
400 Verret St., Houma, 70360. Tel: 985-876-6904; Email: admin@stfrancisdesaleshouma.org; Web: www.stfrancisdesaleshouma.org. P. O. Box 4014, Houma, 70361. Very Rev. Jay L. Baker, V.C., Rector; Rev. Jean-Marie Nsambu; Deacon Lee Crochet.
Res.: 500 Goode St., Houma, 70360.
School—Cathedral of St. Francis De Sales School, (Grades PreK-7), 300 Verret St., Houma, 70360. Tel: 985-868-6646; Fax: 985-851-5896; Email: stfrancis@htdiocese.org. Kelli Cazayoux, Prin. Lay Teachers 32; Students 627.
Catechesis Religious Program—Jane Lirette, D.R.E. Students 246.

2—ANNUNZIATA (1963)
2011 Acadian Dr., Houma, 70363. Tel: 985-876-2971; Fax: 985-868-6414; Email: annunziatach@comcast.net; Web: www.annunziatacatholic.org. Very Rev. Mike Tran, V.F.; Deacon Raymond Bourg Jr.; Ms. Whitney Fairchild, Youth Min.; Ms. Lisa Bourg, Office Mgr.; Mrs. Maria Escobedo, Hispanic Sec. & Receptionist.
Catechesis Religious Program—Mrs. Heather Anderton, D.R.E. Students 925.

3—ST. BERNADETTE aka St. Bernadette Soubirous Church (1958)
409 Funderburk Ave., Houma, 70364. Tel: 985-879-1506; Email: vbreaux@htdiocese.org. Revs. Andre Melancon; Paul Birdsall; Deacons James Brunet Jr.; James Lefevre; Gerald Rivette, (Retired), (Retired).
School—St. Bernadette School, (Grades PreSchool-7), 309 Funderburk Ave., Houma, 70364. Tel: 985-872-3854; Fax: 985-872-5780; Email: stbernelm@htdiocese.org; Web: saintbernadettepandas.org. Lydia Landry, Prin.; Dale Ford, Librarian; Mrs. Amanda Robertson, Admin. Lay Teachers 30; Students 445.
Catechesis Religious Program—Wanda Fos, C.R.E. Students 480.

4—ST. GREGORY BARBARIGO (1963)
1005 Williams Ave., Houma, 70364. Tel: 985-876-2047; Email: ddehart@htdiocese.org. Rev. Alexis Lazarra; Deacon Dennis Dupre, (Retired).
Res.: 439 Sixth St., Houma, 70364.
School—St. Gregory Barbarigo School, (Grades PreSchool-7), 441 Sixth St., Houma, 70364. Tel: 985-876-2038; Fax: 985-879-2789; Email: stgregoryschool@htdiocese.org; Web: www.htdioceseschools.org/st-gregory-barbarigo. Cindy Martin, Prin. Lay Teachers 10; Students 137.
Catechesis Religious Program—Students 76.

5—ST. LOUIS (1965) [CEM]
2226 Bayou Blue Rd., Houma, 70364. Tel: 985-876-3449; Email: stlouisch@comcast.net. Rev. Robert C. Rogers.
Catechesis Religious Program—Tel: 985-976-3438; Email: poincotamc@comcast.net. Andrea C. Poincot, C.R.E. Students 231.

6—ST. LUCY
Mailing Address: 1214 Aycock St., Houma, 70361. Tel: 985-879-2632; Fax: 985-879-2402; Email: stlucychurch@htdiocese.org. Rev. Msgr. Cletus Egbi, Admin.; Most Reverend Shelton J. Fabre, D.D.
Church: 1224 Aycock St., Houma, 70360.
Catechesis Religious Program—Wildred Miller, D.R.E. Students 29.

7—MARIA IMMACOLATA (1963)
246 Corporate Dr., Houma, 70364. Tel: 985-876-3313; Email: mmoss@htdiocese.org. Rev. Joseph Pilola; Deacons William Dunkelman; Chris A. Prestenback.
Res.: 326 Estate Dr., Houma, 70364.
Tel: 985-876-3313; Email: mmoss@htdiocese.org.
School—Maria Immacolata School, (Grades PreSchool-7), 324 Estate Dr., Houma, 70364. Tel: 985-876-1631; Fax: 985-876-1608; Email: dbergeron@htdiocese.org. Prissy Davis, Prin.; Karen DeBlieux, Librarian. Lay Teachers 15; Students 175.
Catechesis Religious Program—Fern Tabor, D.R.E. Students 224.

8—OUR LADY OF THE MOST HOLY ROSARY (1948) [CEM] (Holy Rosary Church)
8594 Main St., Houma, 70363. Tel: 985-876-7652; Email: angie.naquin@htdiocese.org. Rev. Rholando Grecia.
Catechesis Religious Program—Tel: 985-879-2815; Email: wmoore1048@aol.com. Wanda Moore, D.R.E. Students 105.

CITY OF THIBODAUX

(LAFOURCHE PARISH)

1—ST. CHARLES BORROMEO (1912) [CEM]
1985 Hwy. 308, Thibodaux, 70301. Tel: 985-446-6663; Fax: 985-447-3348; Email: stcharles@htdiocese.org. Very Rev. Carl Collins, V.F.
Catechesis Religious Program—Email: lwhitman@htdiocese.org. Lisa Whitman, D.R.E. Students 135.

2—CHRIST THE REDEEMER (1983) [CEM]
720 Talbot Ave., Thibodaux, 70301. Tel: 985-447-2013; Email: ctrchurch@htdiocese.org; Web: www.ctr-htdiocese.org. Very Rev. Mark Anthony Toups; Rev. Samuel Higginbotham.

3—ST. GENEVIEVE (1959)
815 Barbier Ave., Thibodaux, 70301. Tel: 985-446-5571; Email: stgenevievechurch@htdiocese.org; Web: www.stgenevievechurch.com. Rev. Romeo "Billy" Velasco; Very Rev. Eric Leyble, J.V.; Deacon Irving Daigle, (Retired).
School—St. Genevieve School, (Grades K-7), 807 Barbier Ave., Thibodaux, 70301. Tel: 985-447-9291; Fax: 985-447-9883; Email: stgenelm@htdiocese.org. Chris Knobloch, Prin.; Cheryl Thibodaux, Asst. Prin.;

Christie Montgomery, Librarian. Lay Teachers 30; Students 463.
Catechesis Religious Program—Tel: 985-446-5127. Sr. Lauren Lindee, O.P., D.R.E. Students 126.
4—ST. JOHN THE EVANGELIST (1919) [CEM]
2085 St. Mary St., Thibodaux, 70301.
Tel: 985-447-3995; Email: sjechurch@charter. Rev. Josekutty Varghese; Sheryl Chauvin, Pastoral Assoc.
Catechesis Religious Program—Susie Richard, D.R.E. Students 101.
5—THE CONGREGATION OF ST. JOSEPH'S ROMAN CATHOLIC CATHEDRAL (1817)
721 Canal Blvd., P.O. Box 966, Thibodaux, 70302.
Tel: 985-446-1387; Tel: 985-446-1388;
Fax: 985-446-6571; Email: stjosephcc@htdiocese.org; Web: www.stjoseph-cc.org. Revs. Vincente DeLa Cruz; Aurelio Luzon Jr.; Joseph Tregre, Chap.; Deacons Ambrose J. Ayzinne; Joseph Bourgeois.
School—St. Joseph Catholic Elementary School, (Grades PreK-7), 501 Cardinal Dr., Thibodaux, 70301. Tel: 985-446-1346; Fax: 985-449-0760; Email: stjoeelm@htdiocese.org; Web: www.stjosephcesthibodaux.org. Gerard Rodrigue Jr., Prin.; Mrs. Betty Danos, Admin. Lay Teachers 40; Students 676.
Catechesis Religious Program—Mrs. Susan Manning, D.R.E. Students 70.
6—ST. LUKE (1923) (African American)
300 E. 11th St., Thibodaux, 70301. Tel: 985-446-0487 ; Email: stlukecatholicchurch@htdiocese.org; Web: stlukethibodaux.com. 1100 Bourbon St., Thibodaux, 70301. Most Rev. Shelton J. Fabre; Rev. Msgr. Cletus Egbi, Admin.
Catechesis Religious Program—1100 Bourbon Street, Thibodaux, 70301. Email: cstreams@htdiocese.org. Christine Streams, D.R.E. Students 18.
7—ST. THOMAS AQUINAS (1970)
P.O. Box 2051, Thibodaux, 70310. Tel: 985-446-6201; Email: st.thomas@htdiocese.org; Web: www.stthomasthibodaux.org; Web: www.nsucatholics.org. 204 Madewood Drive, Thibodaux, 70301. Rev. Mitchel Semar.
Catechesis Religious Program—
Fax: eevans@htdiocese.org. Eve Evans, D.R.E. Students 114.

OUTSIDE THE CITIES OF HOUMA AND THIBODAUX

AMELIA, ST. MARY PARISH
1—ST. ANDREW (1965) [CEM]
833 Julia St., Amelia, 70340. Tel: 985-631-2333; Email: st.andrew@teche.net; Web: st.andrewcentral.org. P.O. Box 310, Amelia, 70340. Rev. Robert Joel Cruz.
Catechesis Religious Program—Pam Benoit, D.R.E. Students 50.
2—THANH GIA (1981) Personal Parish for Vietnamese Community.
1115 Lake Palourde Rd., Morgan City, 70340.
Tel: 985-631-3194; Fax: 985-631-2634. P.O. Box 338, Amelia, 70340. Revs. James Nguyen Van Thien, C.M.C.; John Bosco.
Res.: 711 Magnolia St., Morgan City, 70380.
Catechesis Religious Program—Students 11.
Missions—Vietnam's Martyrs—406 N. Main Project Rd., 70395.
St. Holy Rosary, 3593 Friendswood Dr., Houma, 70363. Tel: 985-580-4101.
St. Peter, 13040 Hwy. 308, Larose, 70373.
Tel: 985-693-5575.
BAYOU BLACK, TERREBONNE PARISH, ST. ANTHONY OF PADUA (1876)
3897 Bayou Black Dr., Houma, 70360.
Tel: 985-872-0922; Fax: 985-872-2001; Email: stanthonybayoublack@htdiocese.org; Web: stanthonybayoublack.org. Rev. Carlos Talavera; Deacon Brent Bergeron.
Catechesis Religious Program—Students 220.
BOURG, TERREBONNE PARISH, ST. ANN (1908) [CEM]
4355 Hwy. 24, Bourg, 70343. Rev. Cody Chatagnier, Admin.
Catechesis Religious Program—Tel: 985-594-5088. Mrs. Melba Stringer, D.R.E. Students 283.
CHACAHOULA, TERREBONNE PARISH, ST. LAWRENCE (1858) [CEM 2]
2128 Bull Run Rd., 70395. Tel: 985-448-2165;
Fax: 985-448-2166; Email: saintlawch@htdiocese.org. Rev. Blair Sabaricos.
Catechesis Religious Program—Students 42.
CHACKBAY, LAFOURCHE PARISH, OUR LADY OF PROMPT SUCCOR (1892) [CEM 2]
529 Hwy. 20, Thibodaux, 70301. Tel: 985-633-2903; Email: nancyabenoit@charter.net. Rev. Sabino B. Rebosura II.
Catechesis Religious Program—Students 351.
CHAUVIN, TERREBONNE PARISH, ST. JOSEPH (1948) [CEM]
5232 Hwy. 56, Chauvin, 70344. Tel: 985-594-5859; Email: saintjosephchurch@charter.net; Web: saintjosephchurch5.wixsite.com/saintjosephchurch. Rev. Baby V. Kuruvilla; Deacon Gary Lapeyrouse.
Catechesis Religious Program—Carla Babin, D.R.E. Students 288.
CUT-OFF, LAFOURCHE PARISH, SACRED HEART aka The Congregation of the Sacred Heart Roman Catholic Church, Cut Off, Louisiana (1923) [CEM]
15300 W. Main, Cut-Off, 70345. Tel: 985-632-3858;
Tel: 985-632-6322; Fax: 985-632-4452; Email: mforet@htdiocese.org; Email: cduet@htdiocese.org. Revs. Gregory Perkins Fratt; Joey Lirette.
Catechesis Religious Program—Tel: 985-632-6322; Email: kmayberry@htdiocese.org. Mrs. Kathy Mayberry, D.R.E. Students 320.
GALLIANO, LAFOURCHE PARISH, ST. JOSEPH (1958) [CEM]
17980 West Main St., P.O. Box 519, Galliano, 70354.
Tel: 985-242-4099; Email: stjosephgalliano@mobiletel.com. Rev. Peter Tai Thanh Le.
Catechesis Religious Program—Students 207.
GHEENS, LAFOURCHE PARISH, COMMUNITY OF ST. ANTHONY (1987) [CEM] (Quasi Parish)
333 Twin Oaks Dr., Raceland, 70394.
Tel: 985-537-6002; Fax: 985-537-4408; Email: galario@htdiocese.org; Web: sthilaryht.org. Revs. Patrick J. Madden; Noas Kerketta; Mrs. Gretchen Alario, Sec.
Catechesis Religious Program—Mrs. Diane Melancon, D.R.E.; Mrs. Sarah Salinas, D.R.E. Students 98.
GIBSON, TERREBONNE PARISH
1—THE CHAPEL OF THE BLESSED SACRAMENT
P.O. Box 587, Gibson, 70356. Tel: 985-575-3551. Rev. Van Constant, Chap. Personal Parish for the Extraordinary form of the Roman Rite.
2—ST. PATRICK (1920) Merged with St. Lawrence, Chacahoula.
GOLDEN MEADOW, LAFOURCHE PARISH, OUR LADY OF PROMPT SUCCOR (1916) [CEM]
723 N. Bayou Dr., Golden Meadow, 70357.
Tel: 958-475-5428; Email: tduet@htdiocese.org. Rev. Joseph Henry Sebastian.
Catechesis Religious Program—Tel: 985-696-8007; Email: gwen@viscom.net. Students 70.
GRAND CAILLOU, TERREBONNE PARISH, HOLY FAMILY (1952) [CEM 2]
6641 Grand Caillou Rd., Dulac, 70353.
Tel: 985-563-2325; Fax: 985-563-4980; Email: holyfamilychurch@htdiocese.org. P.O. Box 87, Dulac, 70353. Deacons Jesse LeCompte; Bernard A. Harold Fanguy.
Catechesis Religious Program—Rita Duplantis, D.R.E. Students 70.
GRAND ISLE, WEST JEFFERSON PARISH, OUR LADY OF THE ISLE (1933) [CEM]
195 Ludwig Lane, Grand Isle, 70358.
Tel: 985-787-2385; Email: oloti@htdiocese.org. P.O. Box 885, Grand Isle, 70358. Rev. Joseph P. Chacko, I.M.S.
Catechesis Religious Program—Tel: 985-787-4530. Students 45.
KRAEMER, LAFOURCHE PARISH, ST. LAWRENCE THE MARTYR (1962) [JC2]
3723 Hwy. 307, Thibodaux, 70301. Tel: 985-633-9431 ; Email: stlstjchurch@htdiocese.org. Rev. Thomas Kuriakose.
Mission—St. James, [CEM] Thibodaux, 74072.
Tel: 985-633-9431; Email: stlstjchurch@htdiocese.org.
Catechesis Religious Program—Tel: 985-633-5714. Students 118.
LAROSE, LAFOURCHE PARISH, OUR LADY OF THE ROSARY (1873) [CEM]
12911 E. Main, P.O. Box 10, Larose, 70373.
Tel: 984-693-3433; Tel: 985-693-8850;
Fax: 985-693-7551; Email: holyrosarylarose@htdiocese.org; Web: www.ourladyoftherosarychurch.org. Rev. Duc Bui.
Res.: 12937 E. Main, P.O. Box 10, Larose, 70373.
School—Holy Rosary, (Grades PreK-8), P.O. Box 40, Larose, 70373. Tel: 985-693-3342; Fax: 985-693-3348 ; Email: holyroselm@htdiocese.org; Web: www.htdioceseschools.org/holy-rosary. Scott Bouzigard, Prin.; Donna Darda, Business Mgr. Lay Teachers 18; Students 210.
Catechesis Religious Program—Email: olrccd@htdiocese.org. Jennifer Sanamo, D.R.E. Students 193.
LOCKPORT, LAFOURCHE PARISH, HOLY SAVIOR (1850) [CEM]
612 Main St., Lockport, 70374. Tel: 985-532-3533; Web: holysaviorchurch.com; Email: holysaviorchurch@htdiocese.org; Web: holysaviorchurch.com. Rev. Thankachan (John) Nambusseril, C.M.I.
Catechesis Religious Program—Tel: 985-532-6111; Fax: 985-532-2010. Students 337.
MONTEGUT, TERREBONNE PARISH, SACRED HEART (1864) [CEM 2]
1113 Hwy. 55, P.O. Box 2, Montegut, 70377.
Tel: 985-594-5856; Fax: 985-594-8087; Email: sacredheartch@htdiocese.org; Web: www.shmontegut.org. Rev. Rajasekar Karumelnathan, Admin.
Catechesis Religious Program—Students 56.
MORGAN CITY, ST. MARY PARISH
1—HOLY CROSS (1964)
2100 Cedar St. Unit #3, Morgan City, 70380.
Tel: 985-384-3551; Email: holycrosschurch@htdiocese.org. Very Rev. Clyde Mahler, V.F.; Deacon Vic Bonnaffee.
School—Holy Cross School, (Grades PreSchool-6), 2100 Cedar St., Unit 2, Morgan City, 70381.
Tel: 985-384-1933; Fax: 985-384-3270; Email: hceoffice@htdiocese.org; Web: holycrosselementary.org. Amanda Talbot, Prin. Lay Teachers 13; Students 238.
Catechesis Religious Program—Students 230.
Mission—St. Rosalie, 1315 Stephensville Rd., Morgan City, St. Mary Parish 70380.
2—SACRED HEART OF JESUS (1859)
415 Union St., P.O. Box 632, Morgan City, 70381.
Tel: 985-385-0770; Email: shcsecretary@htdiocese.org; Web: www.sacredheartmc.org. Revs. Wilfredo Decal; Evelio Buenaflor Jr.; Deacons Larry Callais; Randall Jennings.
Catechesis Religious Program—Email: shcdre@htdiocese.org. Amanda Jennings, D.R.E. Students 133.
POINTE-AUX-CHENES, LAFOURCHE PARISH, ST. CHARLES BORROMEO (1971) [CEM]
1237 Hwy. 665, Montegut, 70377. Tel: 985-594-6801; Email: st.charleschurch@att.net; Web: www.stcharlespac.com. Rev. Rajasekar Karumelnathan, Admin.
Catechesis Religious Program—Students 80.
RACELAND, LAFOURCHE PARISH
1—ST. HILARY OF POITIERS (1965)
333 Twin Oaks, Raceland, 70394. Tel: 985-537-6002; Email: galario@htdiocese.org; Web: sthilaryht.org. Revs. Patrick J. Madden; Noas Kerketta; Mrs. Gretchen Alario, Sec.
Catechesis Religious Program—Email: dmelancon@htdiocese.org. Mrs. Diane Melancon, D.R.E. Students 325.
2—ST. MARY'S NATIVITY (1850) [CEM]
3500 Hwy. 1, Raceland, 70394. Tel: 985-537-3204;
Fax: 985-537-3235; Email: stmarylmz@bellsouthl.net; Email: stmarysec@bellsouth.net; Web: www.stmnparish.org. Very Rev. Charles Perkins.
School—St. Mary's Nativity School, (Grades PreK-8), 3492 Nies St., Raceland, 70394. Tel: 985-537-7544; Fax: 985-537-4020; Email: mbagala@htdiocese.org. Marissa Bagala, Prin.; Jackie Jackson, Librarian. Lay Teachers 15; Students 254.
Catechesis Religious Program—Students 149.
SCHRIEVER, TERREBONNE PARISH, ST. BRIDGET (1911) [CEM]
100 Hwy. 311, 70395. Tel: 985-446-6801; Email: stbridgetchurch@htdiocese.org. Very Rev. Simon Peter Engurait, V.G.; Deacon Stephen Brunet.
Catechesis Religious Program—Tel: 985-446-1985. Bernadette Mabile, D.R.E. Students 127.
THERIOT, TERREBONNE PARISH, ST. ELOI (1875) [CEM]
1335 Bayou Dularge Rd., Theriot, 70397.
Tel: 985-872-2946; Email: steloichurch@htdiocese.org. Very Rev. Dean Danos, V.F.; Deacons Daniel Bascle; Glenn Porche.
Catechesis Religious Program—Tel: 985-851-6893. Students 99.

Chaplains of Public Institutions

HOUMA. *Terrebonne General Medical Center*. Rev. Sovi Devasia, Chap.
Terrebonne Parish Sheriff Police and Fire Departments. Deacon Linwood Liner, Chap.
THIBODAUX. *Lafourche Parish Sheriff, Police and Fire Departments*. Vacant.
Thibodaux Regional Medical Center. Rev. Joseph Tregre, Chap.
CUT OFF. *Our Lady of the Sea General Hospital*, 200 W. 134 Pl., Cut Off, 70345. Tel: 985-632-6401. Vacant.

On Duty Outside the Diocese:
Very Rev.—
Rodrigue, Joshua J., S.T.L.
Revs.—
Boquet, Shenan J.
Bouterie, Thomas
Dugas, Scott
King, Stuart.

Retired:
Rev. Msgrs.—
Bergeron, Albert G., (Retired), 546 Ave. B, Marrero, 70072
Brunet, Frederic, (Retired)
Ledet, Donald, (Retired), 1201 Cardinal Dr., Thibodaux, 70301
Revs.—
Bergeron, Michael, (Retired)

Cruz, Domingo, (Retired)
Naquin, Roch, (Retired), 539 Island Rd., Montegut, 70377
Nguyen, Ty Van, (Retired)
Santiago, Florentino F., (Retired)
Silva, Caesar, (Retired)
Timbre, Roland, (Retired)
Todd, Wilmer, (Retired)
Villarrubia, Roger Jr., (Retired), 8594 Main St., Houma, 70363.

Permanent Deacons:
Haddad, Gregory, Gray
Andry, Malcolm, Our Lady of the Most Holy Rosary, Houma
Authement, Douglas, (Retired), Cathedral of St. Francis de Sales, Houma
Ayzinne, Ambrose Joseph, St. Joseph, Thibodaux
Bascle, Daniel, (Retired), St. Eloi, Theriot
Belanger, Gerald, (Retired), Bourg
Bergeron, Brent, St. Anthony, Bayou Black
Bonnaffee, Vic, Principal, Holy Cross, Morgan City
Bourg, Raymond, Annunziata, Houma
Bourgeois, Brent P., St. Charles Borromeo, St. Charles
Bourgeois, Joseph, St. Joseph Co-Cathedral, Thibodaux
Brunet, James Jr., Co-Dir. Continuing Formation, St. Bernadette, Houma
Brunet, Stephen, Co-Dir., Permanent Diaconate Formation
Burregi, Sam J., (Retired), Sacred Heart, Cut-Off
Cantrelle, Michael, (Retired), Holy Rosary, Larose
Crochet, Lee, Cathedral of St. Francis de Sales, Houma
Daigle, Irving, (Retired), St. Genevieve, Thibodaux
Dickerson, Martin, St. Luke, Thibodaux
Doucet, Davis, Our Lady of the Rosary, Larose
Dragna, Andrew J., (Retired), Holy Cross, Morgan City
Dunkelman, William, Maria Immacolata, Houma
Duplantis, Lloyd, Crusillo Chap., St. Bridget, Schriever
Dupre, Dennis, St. Gregory, Houma
Fanguy, Bernard A. Harold, (Retired), Holy Family, Grand Caillou
Giroir, Charles, (Retired), Christ the Redeemer, Thibodaux
Jennings, Randall, Sacred Heart, Morgan City
Landry, Alduce, (Retired), Thibodaux
Lapeyrouse, Gary, Boy Scouts Chap., St. Joseph, Chauvin
LeCompte, Jesse, St. Anthony of Padua, Bayou Black
Liner, Linwood Paul Sr., Asst. Dir., Personnel, Permanent Diaconate
Marts, Melvin, Shalom Catholic Ministries
Mattingly, John, Our Lady of the Rosary, Houma
Pitre, Jeff, Sacred Heart, Cut Off
Porche, Glenn, St. Eloi, Theriot
Prestenback, Chris A., Maria Immacolata, Houma
Rivette, Gerald, (Retired), (Retired), St. Bernadette, Houma
Uzee, Dickey, (Retired), Raceland
Weigand, Joseph Jr., (Retired), Cathedral of St. Francis de Sales, Houma.

INSTITUTIONS LOCATED IN DIOCESE

[A] HIGH SCHOOLS, DIOCESAN

HOUMA. *Vandebilt Catholic High School*, (Grades 8-12), 209 S. Hollywood Rd., Houma, 70360.
Tel: 985-876-2551; Fax: 985-868-9774; Email: vandebilthi@htdiocese.org; Web: www.vandebiltcatholic.org. Mr. David Boudreaux, Pres.; Mr. Jeremy Gueldner, Prin.; Danae Jackson, Librarian. Brothers of the Sacred Heart. Lay Teachers 70; Students 905; Clergy / Religious Teachers 1.

THIBODAUX. *Edward Douglas White Catholic High*, (Grades 8-12), (Coed) 555 Cardinal Dr., Thibodaux, 70301. Tel: 985-446-8486; Fax: 985-448-1275; Email: edwhitehi@htdiocese.org; Web: www.edwhite.org. Michelle Chiasson, Prin.; Tim Robichaux, Pres. Brothers of the Sacred Heart. Brothers 3; Lay Teachers 53; Students 709; Clergy / Religious Teachers 6.

E.D. White Catholic High School Foundation, Inc., Thibodaux. Tel: 985-446-8486; Fax: 985-446-5444.

E.D. White Catholic High School Alumni Assn., Thibodaux. Tel: 985-446-8486; Fax: 985-448-1275; Email: edwalumni@htdiocese.org.

MORGAN CITY. *Central Catholic School*, (Grades 7-12), 2100 Cedar St., Unit 1, Morgan City, 70380.
Tel: 985-385-5372; Fax: 985-385-3444; Email: centcathi@htdiocese.org; Web: www.cchseagles.com. Deacon Vic Bonnaffee, Prin.; Karen Tycer, Senior High & Guidance Counselor; Anna Saleme, Librarian. Lay Teachers 22; Students 220.

[B] DAY CARE CENTERS

HOUMA. *St. Lucy Child Development Center*, 1224 Aycock St., Houma, 70360. Tel: 985-876-1246;
Fax: 985-876-7751; Web: htdiocese.org/st-lucy-child-development-center. 1220 Aycock St., Houma, 70360. Ms. Danielle Davis, Assoc. Dir. Children 42; Total Staff 7.

[C] RETREAT CENTERS

SCHRIEVER. *Lumen Christi Retreat Center*, 100 Lumen Christi Ln., Hwy. 311, 70395. Tel: 985-868-1523;
Fax: 985-868-1525; Email: lumenchristi@htdiocese.org. Chris Fomangue, Admin.

[D] PRIVATE ASSOCIATIONS OF THE FAITHFUL

THIBODAUX. MARIAN SERVANTS OF THE WORD, 506 Cardinal Dr., Thibodaux, 70301. Tel: 985-447-6564 ; Cell: 985-226-1890; Email: marianservants@att.net; Email: clairely1@comcast.net. Claire Joller, Dir.; Mrs. Sally Sobert, Treas.

[F] MISCELLANEOUS

THIBODAUX. *The Diocese of Houma-Thibodaux Historical Research Center*, 205 Audubon Ave., Thibodaux, 70301. Tel: 985-446-2383;
Fax: 985-449-0574; Email: kallemand@htdiocese.org. Very Rev. Alex Gaudet, Chancellor.

St. Joseph Manor (Retirement Community) 1201 Cardinal Dr., Thibodaux, 70301. Tel: 985-446-9050 ; Fax: 985-449-0047; Email: annt@stjosephmanor.org; Web: www.stjosephmanor.org. Ann Thibodaux, Admin.

Magnificat of the Houma-Thibodaux Diocese, 830 Laurel Valley Rd., Thibodaux, 70302.
Tel: 985-446-5001; Fax: 985-447-4261. P.O. Box 702, Thibodaux, 70302. Mrs. Mina McKee, Dir.

SCHRIEVER. *Cemeteries Trust*, P.O. Box 505, 70395.
Tel: 985-850-3112; Fax: 985-868-7727. Very Rev. Simon Peter Engurait, V.G., Dir.

RELIGIOUS INSTITUTES OF MEN REPRESENTED IN THE DIOCESE

For further details refer to the corresponding bracketed number in the Religious Institutes of Men or Women section.

[1100]—*Brothers of the Sacred Heart*—S.C.

RELIGIOUS INSTITUTES OF WOMEN REPRESENTED IN THE DIOCESE

[]—*Daughters of Our Lady of the Holy Rosary*.
[]—*Dominican Contemplative Sisters*.
[]—*Little Friars and Nuns of Jesus and Mary*.
[]—*Marianites of Holy Cross*—M.S.C.
[]—*Missionary Catechists of the Sacred Heart*—M.C.S.H.
[3830]—*Sisters of St. Joseph*—C.S.J.

NECROLOGY

† O'Brien, Patrick, (Retired), Died Apr. 12, 2018

An asterisk (*) denotes an organization that has established tax-exempt status directly with the IRS and is not covered by the USCCB Group Ruling.

Archdiocese of Indianapolis

(Archidioecesis Indianapolitana)

CHRIST THE CORNERSTONE

Most Reverend

CHARLES C. THOMPSON

Archbishop of Indianapolis; ordained May 30, 1987; appointed Bishop of Evansville April 26, 2011; ordained June 29, 2011; appointed Archbishop of Indianapolis June 13, 2017; installed July 28, 2017. *Office: 1400 N. Meridian St., Indianapolis, IN 46202-2367.*

The Archbishop Edward T. O'Meara Catholic Center: 1400 N. Meridian St., Indianapolis, IN 46202-2367. Tel: 317-236-1400; Fax: 317-236-1401.

Web: www.archindy.org

Email: chancery@archindy.org

Square Miles 13,758.

Established a Diocese in 1834; established an Archdiocese December 19, 1944 by decree of Pope Pius XII.

Comprises the Counties of Bartholomew, Brown, Clark, Clay, Crawford, Dearborn, Decatur, Fayette, Floyd, Franklin, Hancock, Harrison, Hendricks, Henry, Jackson, Jefferson, Jennings, Johnson, Lawrence, Marion, Monroe, Morgan, Ohio, Orange, Owen, Parke, Perry, Putnam, Ripley, Rush, Scott, Shelby, Switzerland, Union, Vermillion, Vigo, Washington and Wayne, and the township of Harrison in Spencer County, in the southern part of Indiana.

For legal titles of parishes and archdiocesan institutions, consult the Chancery Office.

STATISTICAL OVERVIEW

Personnel	
Archbishops	1
Abbots	1
Retired Abbots	3
Priests: Diocesan Active in Diocese	90
Priests: Diocesan Active Outside Diocese	3
Priests: Retired, Sick or Absent	54
Number of Diocesan Priests	147
Religious Priests in Diocese	86
Total Priests in Diocese	233
Extern Priests in Diocese	19
Ordinations:	
Diocesan Priests	1
Permanent Deacons in Diocese	64
Total Brothers	38
Total Sisters	452
Parishes	
Parishes	121
With Resident Pastor:	
Resident Diocesan Priests	90
Resident Religious Priests	9
Without Resident Pastor:	
Administered by Priests	12
Administered by Deacons	2
Administered by Religious Women	6
Administered by Lay People	2
Missions	5
Closed Parishes	1
Professional Ministry Personnel:	
Brothers	1
Sisters	27
Lay Ministers	228
Welfare	
Catholic Hospitals	2
Total Assisted	925,464
Homes for the Aged	2
Total Assisted	209
Day Care Centers	3
Total Assisted	234
Specialized Homes	2
Total Assisted	1,882
Special Centers for Social Services	37
Total Assisted	210,044
Educational	
Seminaries, Diocesan	1
Students from This Diocese	13
Students from Other Diocese	31
Diocesan Students in Other Seminaries	10
Seminaries, Religious	1
Students Religious	106
Total Seminarians	129
Colleges and Universities	2
Total Students	4,647
High Schools, Diocesan and Parish	7
Total Students	3,692
High Schools, Private	4
Total Students	2,349
Elementary Schools, Diocesan and Parish	57
Total Students	16,983
Elementary Schools, Private	1
Total Students	82
Catechesis/Religious Education:	
High School Students	3,200
Elementary Students	10,636
Total Students under Catholic Instruction	41,718
Teachers in the Diocese:	
Priests	15
Sisters	12
Lay Teachers	1,858
Vital Statistics	
Receptions into the Church:	
Infant Baptism Totals	3,238
Minor Baptism Totals	504
Adult Baptism Totals	321
Received into Full Communion	480
First Communions	4,134
Confirmations	2,897
Marriages:	
Catholic	633
Interfaith	281
Total Marriages	914
Deaths	1,892
Total Catholic Population	213,807
Total Population	2,621,455

The Diocese of Vincennes (now Indianapolis) was established by decree of Pope Gregory XVI, May 6, 1834, and the See was fixed at Vincennes. The territory then comprised the entire State of Indiana and the eastern third of Illinois. By decree of Pope Pius IX, January 8, 1857, the northern half of the State became the Diocese of Fort Wayne. The southern half of the State remained the Diocese of Vincennes.

The second Bishop of Vincennes, by Apostolic Brief, was permitted to establish his residence either at Vincennes, Madison, Lafayette or Indianapolis; the See City, however, was to remain at Vincennes. This permission was renewed to the fourth Bishop, with the exception of Lafayette. On the appointment of the fifth Bishop, he was directed to fix his residence at Indianapolis, but the Cathedral and title of the See were continued at Vincennes. By an Apostolic Brief dated March 28, 1898, the title of the Diocese was changed to that of "Diocese of Indianapolis" with the city of Indianapolis as the Episcopal See. By the same Brief the Patron Saint of the Diocese was to remain St. Francis Xavier, the title of the old Cathedral in Vincennes.

On December 19, 1944, Most Reverend Amleto Giovanni Cicognani, Apostolic Delegate to the United States, solemnly proclaimed the Papal Decree of Pope Pius XII in SS. Peter and Paul Cathedral, Indianapolis, elevating Indianapolis to the status of an Archdiocese, the State of Indiana being the Metropolitan Area. The Dioceses of Evansville and Lafayette-in-Indiana were created by the same decree and were made Suffragan Sees of Indianapolis. Upon the establishment of the Diocese of Gary on December 17, 1956, it too became a Suffragan See.

Former Bishops—Rt. Revs. SIMON GUILLAUME GABRIEL BRUTE DE REMUR, S.S., D.D., ord. 1808; cons. 1834; died 1839; CELESTIN DE LA HAILANDIERE, D.D., ord. 1825; cons. 1839; resigned 1847; died in France, 1882; JOHN S. BAZIN, D.D., ord. 1822; cons. 1847; died 1848; MAURICE DE SAINT PALAIS, D.D., ord. 1836; cons. Jan. 14, 1849; died June 28, 1877; FRANCIS SILAS CHATARD, D.D., ord. 1862; cons. May 12, 1878; died Sept. 7, 1918; Most Revs. JOSEPH CHARTRAND, D.D., ord. Sept. 24, 1892; cons. Titular Bishop of Flavias and Coadjutor Bishop, Sept. 15, 1910; succeeded to the See of Indianapolis, Sept. 7, 1918; died Dec. 8, 1933; JOSEPH ELMER RITTER, S.T.D., ord. May 30, 1917; cons. Titular Bishop of Hippo and Auxiliary Bishop, March 28, 1933; succeeded to the See March 24, 1934; installed as Archbishop Dec. 19, 1944; transferred to Metropolitan See of St. Louis, July 20, 1946; named Cardinal, Jan. 16, 1961; died June 10, 1967; PAUL C. SCHULTE, D.D., ord. June 11, 1915; cons. Bishop of Leavenworth, Sept. 21, 1937; appt. Archbishop of Indianapolis, July 20, 1946; installed Oct. 10, 1946; resigned Jan. 14, 1970; died Feb. 17, 1984; GEORGE J. BISKUP, ord. March 19, 1937; cons. Titular Bishop of Hemeria and Auxiliary of Dubuque, April 24, 1957; transferred to Des Moines Feb. 3, 1965; transferred to Indianapolis "cum jure successionis," July 26, 1967; succeeded to See Jan. 14, 1970; resigned March 26, 1979; died Oct. 17, 1979; EDWARD T. O'MEARA, S.T.D., ord. Dec. 21, 1946; appt. Titular Bishop of Thisiduo and Auxiliary of St. Louis Jan. 28, 1972; consecrated in the Basilica of St. Peter, Rome, Feb. 13, 1972; appt. Archbishop of Indianapolis Nov. 27, 1979; installed Jan. 10, 1980; died Jan. 10, 1992; DANIEL MARK BUECHLEIN, O.S.B., ord. May 3, 1964; appt. to Memphis Jan. 16, 1987; cons. Bishop March 2, 1987; installed March 2, 1987; appt. Archbishop of Indianapolis July 14, 1992; installed Sept. 9, 1992; retired Sept. 21, 2011; died Jan. 25, 2018.; His Eminence JOSEPH CARDINAL TOBIN, C.Ss.R., Professed Perpetual Vows as a member of the Congregation of the Most Holy Redeemer (Redemptorists), Aug. 21, 1976; ord. June 1, 1978; served as Provincial Consultor for the Redemptorists, 1984-1990; served as General Consultor for the Redemptorists, Rome 1991-1997; elected and served as Superior General, Congregation of the Most Holy Redeemer, Rome, 1997-2009; named Secrectary of the Congregation for Institutes of Consecrated Life and Societies of Apostolic Life and Titular Archbishop of Obba, by Pope Benedict XVI, Aug. 2, 2010; ord. Bishop in St. Peter's Basilica, Rome, Oct. 9, 2010; named sixth Archbishop of Indianapolis Oct. 18, 2012; installed as Archbishop of Indianapolis, Dec. 3, 2012; named to the College of Cardinals by Pope Francis, Oct. 9, 2016 and elevated to the college of cardinals Nov. 19, 2016; appt. to the Archdiocese of Newark Oct. 22, 2016; installed Jan. 6, 2017.

Archdiocesan Administration—Secretariats/ Vicariates/Agencies and Offices can be contacted through The Archbishop Edward T. O'Meara Catholic Center. *Mailing Address: 1400 N. Meridian St., Indianapolis, 46202.*
Tel: 317-236-1400; Fax: 317-236-1401.

Vicar General and Moderator of the Curia—Rev. Msgr. WILLIAM F. STUMPF, Ph.D.

Chancellor—ANNETTE (MICKEY) LENTZ.

Vice Chancellor—Very Rev. ERIC M. JOHNSON, M.A., M.Div., V.E.

Chief Financial Officer—BRIAN BURKERT.

Board of Consultors—Most Rev. CHARLES C. THOMPSON; Rev. Msgr. WILLIAM F. STUMPF, Ph.D.; Revs. JOSEPH M. FELTZ, M.A., M.Div.; STEPHEN W. GIANNINI, M.A., M.S., M.Div.; TODD M. RIEBE; JEFFREY H. GODECKER, (Retired); JOHN J. HOLLOWELL; JONATHAN P. MEYER.

Deaneries and Deans—Very Rev. GUY R. ROBERTS, V.F., Indianapolis North; Rev. Msgr. PAUL D. KOETTER, V.F., Indianapolis East; Very Rev. ROBERT J. ROBESON, Ph.D., V.F., Indianapolis South; Rev. MICHAEL E. O'MARA, V.F., Indianapolis West; Very Rev. DANIEL J. STAUBLIN, V.F., Seymour; Rev. RICHARD W. ELDRED, Bloomington; Very Rev. DUSTIN M. BOEHM, V.F., Connersville; VACANT, New Albany; Very Rev. MICHAEL T. KEUCHER, M.A., M.Div., V.F., Batesville; Rev. SENGOLE THOMAS GNANARAJ, (India) V.F., Tell City; Very Rev. MARTIN DAY, O.F.M.Conv., V.F., Terre Haute.

Finance Council—Most Rev. CHARLES C. THOMPSON; BRIAN BURKERT, CFO; GREG MONTE, Chair; J. PATRICK BYRNE; PATRICK CARNEY; KEVIN HALLORAN; ANDY RINZEL; JEFF WHITING; DANIEL RILEY; LANCE LYDAY; Rev. Msgr. WILLIAM F. STUMPF, Ph.D.

Council of Priests—Most Rev. CHARLES C. THOMPSON; Rev. Msgr. WILLIAM F. STUMPF, Ph.D., Vicar Gen./ Moderator of the Curia; Very Rev. ERIC M. JOHNSON, M.A., M.Div., V.E.; ANNETTE "MICKEY" LENTZ, Chancellor; Very Rev. DUSTIN M. BOEHM, V.F.; Rev. CHRISTOPHER A. CRAIG; Very Revs. SEAN R. DANDA, V.F.; DENNIS M. DUVELIUS, V.F.; Revs. D. MICHAEL WELCH, (Retired); JOHN J. HOLLOWELL; TODD MICHAEL GOODSON, V.F.; DANIEL J. MAHAN; JONATHAN P. MEYER; ERIC "RICK" NAGEL, M.A., M.Div.; Very Rev. JOSEPH L. NEWTON, J.C.L., M.Div., V.J.; Revs. MICHAEL HOYT; CHRISTOPHER WADELTON.

Priests' Personnel Board—Most Rev. CHARLES C. THOMPSON; Rev. THOMAS E. CLEGG; Very Rev. ERIC M. JOHNSON, M.A., M.Div., V.E.; Revs. H. MICHAEL HILDERBRAND, M.A., M.Div., M.S., Ed.S.; JOHN P. MCCASLIN, M.A., M.Div.; JONATHAN P. MEYER; Very Rev. JOSEPH B. MORIARTY; Rev. ROBERT W. SIMS; Rev. Msgr. ANTHONY R. VOLZ.

Deacons' Personnel Board—Very Rev. ERIC M. JOHNSON, M.A., M.Div., V.E., Chm.; Deacon MICHAEL EAST, Vice Chair; LYNN BOWER; MARY ELLEN HENN; Deacons THOMAS HORN; RONALD PIRAU; WAYNE DAVIS.

Archdiocesan Review Board—MARY ANN RANSDELL; IDA LAMBERTI; EILEEN AHRENS; MARY CATHERINE HORTY; EDMUND C. HASKINS, Ph.D.; Rev. Msgr. ANTHONY R. VOLZ.

Bishop Simon Brute College Seminary—Very Rev. JOSEPH B. MORIARTY, Rector, Tel: 317-924-4100.

Secretariat for Catholic Charities—DAVID BETHURAM, M.A., M.Min, Exec. Dir., Tel: 317-236-7325.
Catholic Charities Social Concerns—
Tel: 317-473-0413. THERESA CHAMBLEE.
Catholic Campaign for Human Development—
Catholic Relief Services—
Parish Social Ministry—
Justice for Immigrants—
Catholic Charities Indianapolis—DAVID BETHURAM, M.A., M.Min, Indianapolis Agency Dir., Tel: 317-236-1500.
Catholic Charities Terre Haute—JOHN C. ETLING, Terre Haute Agency Dir., Tel: 812-232-1447.
Catholic Charities New Albany—MARK CASPER, New Albany Agency Dir., Tel: 812-949-7305.
Catholic Charities Bloomington—O'CONNEL CASE, Clinical Dir., Tel: 812-332-1262.
Catholic Charities Tell City—JOAN HESS, Tell City Agency Dir., Tel: 812-547-0903.
St. Elizabeth Coleman Pregnancy and Adoption Services—DAVID BETHURAM, M.A., M.Min, Agency Dir., Tel: 317-787-3412.
St. Elizabeth's Regional Maternity Center—MARK CASPER, Agency Dir., Tel: 812-949-7305.

Secretariat for Catholic Schools—GINA FLEMMING, Supt., Catholic Schools, Tel: 317-592-4051.
Office of Catholic Schools—MARY MCCOY, Asst. Supt., Elementary Education; BEN POTTS, Asst. Supt., Secondary Education, Tel: 317-236-1440; ROB RASH, Asst. Supt., Personnel & Legal Support, Tel: 317-236-1544.
Catholic Education, School Improvement—GINA KUNTZ FLEMING, Supt. Catholic Schools, Tel: 317-592-4051.
Notre Dame Ace Academies—GINA KUNTZ FLEMING, Exec. Dir., Tel: 317-592-4051.
Catholic Youth Organization—580 E. Stevens St., Indianapolis, 46203. Tel: 317-632-9311. BRUCE SCIFRES, Dir.
St. Mary's Child Center, Inc.—CONSTANCE SHERMAN, Dir., 901 Dr. Martin Luther King, Jr. St., Indianapolis, 46202. Tel: 317-635-1491.

Secretariat for Communications—GREG A. OTOLSKI, Exec. Dir., Tel: 317-236-1585.
Archdiocesan Newspaper, "The Criterion"—GREG A. OTOLSKI, Assoc. Publisher; MICHAEL A. KROKOS, Editor, Tel: 317-236-1570.
Catholic Communications Center—GREG A. OTOLSKI, Exec. Dir., Tel: 317-236-1585.

Secretariat for Finance and Administrative Services—BRIAN BURKERT, CFO & Exec. Dir., Tel: 317-236-1410.
Accounting Services—BRIAN SCHMIDT, Controller, Tel: 317-236-1410.
Information Services—AME Group
Tel: 317-261-3379. Deacon RONALD PIRAU, Chief Information Officer.
Management Services—ERIC L. ATKINS, Dir., Tel: 317-236-1452.
Purchasing Office—STEPHEN M. JAMES, Dir., Tel: 317-236-1451.
Catholic Cemeteries Assoc.—TONY LLOYD, Buchanan Group, 9001 N. Haverstick Rd., Indianapolis, 46240. Tel: 317-574-8898.
Roman Catholic Archdiocese of Indianapolis Properties, Inc.—Most Rev. CHARLES C. THOMPSON, Pres.; ANNETTE "MICKEY" LENTZ, Sec.; BRIAN BURKERT, Treas., Tel: 317-236-1410.

Secretariat for Pastoral Ministries—Deacon MICHAEL BRAUN, Dir.
Office for Intercultural Ministry—Tel: 317-261-3380. OSCAR J. CASTELLANOS, Dir.
Office of Human Life and Dignity—
Tel: 317-236-1569. BRIE ANNE EICHHORN, R.N., C.F.C.P., Coord.
Office of Marriage and Family Life—
Tel: 317-236-1521. VACANT, Dir.
Office of Youth Ministry—Tel: 317-236-1442. SCOTT WILLIAMS, Dir.
Young Adult and College Campus Ministry—MATTHEW FALEY, Dir., Tel: 317-236-1436.
Archdiocesan Office of Inter-Religious Affairs and Ecumenism—Very Rev. RICHARD GINTHER, V.F., Dir.
Archives—Tel: 317-236-1429. JULIE MOTYKA, Archivist.
Archdiocesan Historian—Rev. JACK W. PORTER, (Retired).
Human Resources—ED ISAKSON, Dir., Tel: 317-236-1594.
Parish Planning and Organizational Development—ANNETTE "MICKEY" LENTZ, Dir.

Secretariat for Worship and Evangelization—Very Rev. PATRICK J. BEIDELMAN, S.T.L., Exec. Dir., Tel: 317-236-1483.
Archdiocesan Cathedral—Very Rev. PATRICK J. BEIDELMAN, S.T.L., Pastor & Rector.
Office of Catechesis—KEN OGOREK, Dir. Catechesis, Tel: 317-236-1446.
Ministry to Persons with Special Needs—ERIN JEFFRIES, Coord., Tel: 317-236-1448.
Evangelization Commission—Very Rev. PATRICK J. BEIDELMAN, S.T.L., Exec. Dir.
Office of Worship—Very Rev. PATRICK J. BEIDELMAN, S.T.L., Exec. Dir., Tel: 317-236-1483; MR. ANDREW MOTYKA, Dir. Archdiocesan & Cathedral Liturgical Music.
Retreat & Renewal Ministries and Fatima Retreat House—GEORGENE BEIRIGER, Dir., 5353 E. 56th St., Indianapolis, 46226. Tel: 317-545-7681; Fax: 317-545-0095.

Secretariat for Stewardship and Development—JOLINDA MOORE, Exec. Dir., Tel: 317-236-1462.
Office of Stewardship and Development—JOLINDA MOORE, Exec. Dir. Stewardship & Devel., Tel: 317-236-1462; RON GREULICH, Catholic Philanthropic Advisor, Tel: 317-236-1426; DANA TOWNSEND, Dir., Donor Svcs., Tel: 317-236-1498; MICHAEL KIRK, Catholic Philanthropic Advisor, Tel: 317-236-1546; JAMES MASLAR, Catholic Philanthropic Advisor, Tel: 317-236-1588; KIM PAHOVEY, Dir. Mission Advancement for Catholic Education, Tel: 317-236-1568; CHERI BUSH, Dir. Mission Advancement for Catholic Charities, Tel: 317-236-1411; DANA STONE, Dir. Appeals and Creative Svcs., Tel: 317-236-1591.
Catholic Community Foundation, Inc.—ELISA SMITH, Dir., Tel: 317-236-1427.
Mission Office—Rev. GERALD J. KIRKHOFF, Tel: 317-236-1489.

Vicariate for Clergy, Religious and Parish Life Coordinators—Very Rev. ERIC M. JOHNSON, M.A., M.Div., V.E., Vicar.
Deacons, Office of—Deacon MICHAEL EAST, Dir.
Deacon Formation, Office of—Deacon KERRY BLANDFORD, Dir., Tel: 317-236-1490.
Advocacy for Priests—Revs. GERALD J. KIRKHOFF, Tel: 317-236-1489; JOSEPH F. RAUTENBERG, Ethics & Bioethics Consultant, Tel: 317-236-1449.
Personnel: Priests, Religious and Parish Life Coordinators—Very Rev. ERIC M. JOHNSON, M.A., M.Div., V.E., Tel: 317-236-1495.
Priestly and Religious Vocations—Rev. ERIC M. AUGENSTEIN, M.A., M.Div., Dir., Tel: 317-236-1490; ANDY MILLER, Assoc. Dir.

Vicar Judicial Metropolitan Tribunal—Very Rev. JOSEPH L. NEWTON, J.C.L., M.Div., V.J., Vicar Judicial, Tel: 317-236-1460.
Adjunct Vicars Judicial—Revs. ROBERT J. GILDAY, S.T.B.; PAUL M. SHIKANY, J.C.L.; Rev. Msgr. FREDERICK EASTON, J.C.L., Adjunct Vicar Judicial, Judicial Vicar Emeritus.
Judge Instructors and Assessors—ANN TULLY, B.S., M.T.S.; NANCY THOMPSON.
Ecclesiastical Notary/Assessor—MS. KAY SUMMERS, B.A., M.A.
Defender of the Bond—Rev. JAMES R. BONKE, J.C.L., (Retired), (Part-time).
Promoter of Justice—VACANT.
Archdiocesan Judge—Rev. STEPHEN W. GIANNINI, M.A., M.S., M.Div.
Auditor—Sr. PAULA MODAFF, S.P., J.C.L.
Advocates—JOSEPH R. GEHRET, B.A.; DANIEL ROSS, B.A.
Ecclesiastical Notaries—TARA SHERINGER, B.S.; PERRY LANGLEY, B.A.

Victim Assistance Coordinator—CARLA HILL, Tel: 317-236-1548; Tel: 800-382-9836, Ext. 1548.

Victim Assistance Review Board—EILEEN AHRENS, Chm.; EDMUND C. HASKINS, Ph.D.; MARY CATHERINE HORTY; IDA LAMBERTI; MARY ANN RANSDELL; Rev. Msgr. ANTHONY R. VOLZ.

CLERGY, PARISHES, MISSIONS AND PAROCHIAL SCHOOLS

CITY OF INDIANAPOLIS

(MARION COUNTY)

1—SS. PETER AND PAUL CATHEDRAL, INDIANAPOLIS, INC. (1892) [JC] Very Rev. Patrick J. Beidelman, S.T.L., Rector; Rev. Eric M. Augenstein, M.A., M.Div., In Res.; Very Rev. Joseph L. Newton, J.C.L., M.Div., V.J., In Res.; Deacons Stephen Hodges, Pastoral Assoc.; Nathan C. Schallert.
Res.: 1347 N. Meridian St., 46202. Tel: 317-634-4519 ; Email: info@ssppc.org; Web: www.ssppc.org.

2—ST. ANDREW THE APOSTLE (1946) Deacon Kerry Blandford, Parish Life Coord.; Rev. James M. Farrell, S.T.B., Mod.
Legal Name: St. Andrew the Apostle Catholic Church, Indianapolis, Inc.
Parish Office: 4052 E. 38th St., 46218-1444.
Tel: 317-546-1571; Email: lisa.standrew@gmail.com.
Catechesis Religious Program—Email: rdecker@standrewstrita.org. Students 17.

3—ST. ANN CATHOLIC CHURCH, INDIANAPOLIS, INC. (1917) [JC] Rev. Robert T. Hausladen; Deacon Joseph J. Beauchamp.
Office & Mailing Address: 6350 S. Mooresville Rd., 46221-4519. Tel: 317-821-2909; Email: saintannchurc@aol.com; Web: www.st-ann-rcindy.org.
Catechesis Religious Program—Tel: 317-821-2909; Email: st-ann-ff@comcast.net. Kelly O'Brien, C.R.E. Students 50.

4—ST. ANTHONY CATHOLIC CHURCH, INDIANAPOLIS, INC. (1891) [JC]
337 N. Warman Ave., 46222-4094. Tel: 317-636-4828 ; Fax: 317-636-3140; Email: saintanthonybusiness@gmail.com; Web: www.saintanthonyindy.org. Rev. Juan Jose Valdes, Admin.; Deacon Oscar Morales.
Catechesis Religious Program—Email: escmcfadden@gmail.com. Emily McFadden, D.R.E. Students 310.

5—ST. BARNABAS CATHOLIC CHURCH, INDIANAPOLIS, INC. (1965) Rev. Msgr. Anthony R. Volz; Rev.

Matthew Tucci; Deacons Patrick Bower; Jerome R. Matthews.
Res.: 8300 Rahke Rd., 46217-4999. Tel: 317-882-0724 ; Email: twarner@stbindy.org.
School—St. Barnabas School, (Grades PreK-8), Tel: 317-881-7422; Email: twarner@stbindy.org. Carissa Maddox, Prin. Lay Teachers 31; Students 530.
Catechesis Religious Program—Students 165.

6—CHRIST THE KING (1939)
Tel: 317-255-3666. Rev. Todd M. Riebe
Legal Name: Christ The King Catholic Church, Indianapolis, Inc.
Parish Office: 5884 Crittenden Ave., 46220.
Tel: 317-255-3666; Email: ctk@ctk-indy.org; Web: www.ctk-indy.org.
School—Christ the King School, 5858 Crittenden Ave., 46220. Tel: 317-257-9366; Fax: 317-475-6581; Email: info@ctk-indy.org. Ed Seib, Prin. Lay Teachers 25; Students 314.
Catechesis Religious Program—Students 35.

7—ST. CHRISTOPHER (Speedway City) (1937) Revs. Paul M. Shikany, J.C.L.; Jude Meril Sahayam; Sisters Mary DeFazio, S.P., Pastoral Assoc.; Kathleen Morrissey, O.P., Pastoral Assoc.; Mr. Bill Szolek Van Valkenburgh, Pastoral Assoc.
Legal Name: St. Christopher Catholic Church, Indianapolis, Inc.
Res.: 5301 W. 16th St., 46224-6497.
Tel: 317-241-6314; Email: pshikan@aol.com.
School—St. Christopher School, 5335 W. 16th St., 46224. Fax: 317-244-6678; Email: kking@stchrisindy.org. Karen King, Prin. Lay Teachers 18; Students 225.
Catechesis Religious Program—Thomas Steiner, Youth Min.; Nancy Links, Music Min. Students 205.

8—ST. GABRIEL (1963) Rev. Michael E. O'Mara, V.F.
Legal Name: St. Gabriel the Archangel Catholic Church, Indianapolis, Inc.
Parish Center: 6000 W. 34th St., 46224-1297.
Tel: 317-291-7014; Email: parish@stgabrielindy.org; Web: www.stgabrielindy.org.
See School under St. Michael the Archangel, Indianapolis for details.
Catechesis Religious Program—Tel: 317-299-9924. Mrs. Teresa Keith, Dir. Faith Formation. Students 159.

9—GOOD SHEPHERD (1993) [JC] (St. Catherine, 1909, and St. James the Greater, 1951, were closed, merged, and renamed in 1993.)
2905 S. Carson Ave., 46203-5216. Tel: 317-783-3158; Email: goodshepherdcc@sbcglobal.net. Very Rev. Robert J. Robeson, Ph.D., V.F., Parochial Admin.; Rev. John Beitans, In Res., (Retired)
Legal Name: Good Shepherd Roman Catholic Church, Indianapolis, Inc.
School—Central Catholic School, (Grades K-8), 1155 E. Cameron St., 46203. Tel: 317-783-7759; Fax: 317-781-5964; Email: rhurrle@centralcatholicindy.org. Ruth Hurrle, Prin. Students 248.
Catechesis Religious Program—Students 10.

10—HOLY ANGELS CATHOLIC CHURCH, INDIANAPOLIS, INC. (1903) (African American)
Tel: 317-926-3324. Rev. Kenneth Taylor, V.F.; Deacon Wilfredo R. de la Rosa; Sr. Gail Trippett, C.S.J., Pastoral Assoc.
Res.: 740 W. 28th St., 46208-5099. Tel: 317-926-3324 ; Email: holyangelsbulletin@hotmail.com; Web: www.holyangelsindy.org.
School—Holy Angels Catholic Church, Indianapolis, Inc. School, (Grades K-6), 2822 Dr. Martin Luther King, Jr. St., 46208. Tel: 317-926-5211; Fax: 317-926-5219; Email: mgoddard@holyangelscatholicschool.org. Justin Armitage, Prin.; Mrs. Jude Mitchell, Librarian. Lay Teachers 8; Sisters of I.H.M. Reparatrix 1; Students 155.
Catechesis Religious Program—Stephanie Whitley, D.R.E. Students 33.

11—HOLY SPIRIT CATHOLIC CHURCH, INDIANAPOLIS, INC. (1946) Rev. Msgr. Paul D. Koetter, V.F.; Rev. Nicholas Ajpacaja Tzoc; Deacon Michael Slinger.
Res.: 7243 E. 10th St., 46219-4990.
Tel: 317-353-9404; Email: parishoffice@holyspirit.cc; Web: www.holyspirit-indy.org.
School—Holy Spirit Catholic Church, Indianapolis, Inc. School, (Grades PreK-8), 7241 E. 10th St., 46219. Tel: 317-352-1243; Fax: 317-351-1822; Email: parishoffice@holyspirit.cc. Rita Parsons, Prin. Lay Teachers 23; Students 413.
Catechesis Religious Program—Tel: 317-357-6915. Students 500.

12—IMMACULATE HEART OF MARY (1946) [JC] Rev. Robert W. Sims
Legal Name: Immaculate Heart of Mary Catholic Church, Indianapolis, Inc.
Parish Center: 5692 Central Ave., 46220-3012.
Tel: 317-257-2266; Email: churchinfo@ihmindy.org.
School—Immaculate Heart of Mary School, 317 E. 57th St., 46220. Tel: 317-255-5468; Fax: 317-475-7379; Email: schoolinfo@ihmindy.org. Ronda Swartz, Prin. Lay Teachers 30; Students 434.
Catechesis Religious Program—Students 103.

13—ST. JOAN OF ARC (1921) [JC] Very Rev. Guy R. Roberts, V.F.
Legal Name: St. Joan of Arc Catholic Church, Indianapolis, Inc.
Res.: 4217 Central Ave., 46205-1896.
Tel: 317-283-5508; Email: groberts@stjoa.org.
School—St. Joan of Arc School, (Grades PreK-8), 500 E. 42nd St., 46205. Tel: 317-283-1518; Fax: 317-931-3380; Email: jandriole@sjoa.org. Janet Andriole, Prin. Lay Teachers 9; Students 331.
Catechesis Religious Program—Students 65.

14—ST. JOHN THE EVANGELIST (1837) Rev. Rick Nagel; Deacon David J. Bartolowits
Legal Name: St. John the Evangelist Catholic Church, Indianapolis, Inc.
Res.: 126 W. Georgia St., 46225-1004.
Tel: 317-635-2021; Email: office@stjohnsindy.org.
Catechesis Religious Program—

15—ST. JOSEPH CATHOLIC CHURCH, INDIANAPOLIS, INC. (1949) [JC] Rev. Robert T. Hausladen.
Res.: 1375 S. Mickley Ave., 46241-3219.
Church, Office & Mailing Address: 1401 S. Mickley Ave., 46241. Tel: 317-244-9002; Email: stjosephschurch@hotmail.com.
Catechesis Religious Program—Judy Meyers, C.R.E. Students 41.

16—ST. JUDE CATHOLIC CHURCH, INDIANAPOLIS, INC. (1959) Very Rev. Stephen J. Banet, V.F.; Deacon David Henn.
Res.: 5353 McFarland Rd., 46227-7098.
Tel: 317-786-4371; Email: sbanet@stjudeindy.org.
School—St. Jude Catholic Church, Indianapolis, Inc. School, 5375 McFarland Rd, 46227.
Tel: 317-784-6828; Fax: 317-780-7594; Email: jshelburn@sjsindy.org. Mr. Joseph Shelburn, Prin. Lay Teachers 24; Students 500.
Catechesis Religious Program—Tel: 317-780-7591. Students 162.

17—ST. LAWRENCE CATHOLIC CHURCH, LAWRENCE, INC. (1949) Revs. Thomas L. Schliessmann, M.N.; Martin Rodriguez, B.A., S.T.B.; Jiho (Peter) Son, Korean Community, Korean Chapel, Tel: 317-542-0863; Deacon Thomas Ward.
Office: 6944 E. 46th St., 46226-3704.
Tel: 317-546-4065; Email: kczachura@saintlawrence.net; Web: www.saintlawrence.net.
School—St. Lawrence Catholic Church, Lawrence, Inc. School, 6950 E. 46th St., 46226.
Tel: 317-543-4923; Fax: 317-543-4929; Email: kczachura@saintlawrence.net. Sarah J. Watson, Prin. Lay Teachers 31; Students 265.
Catechesis Religious Program—Email: cdiaz@saintlawrence.net. Claudia Diaz, D.R.E. Students 235.

18—SAINT LUKE CATHOLIC CHURCH, INDIANAPOLIS, INC. (1961) [JC]
7575 Holliday Dr. E., 46260-3697. Tel: 317-259-4373; Email: patrickj@stluke.org; Web: www.stluke.org. Rev. Msgr. Joseph F. Schaedel, M.S., M.Div.; Rev. Joby Puthussery; Mrs. Diane Schafer, Pastoral Min./Coord.; Mr. Stephen Jendraszak, Business Mgr.; Mr. Thomas Nichols, Music Min.
Res.: 7550 Holliday Dr. E., 46260.
Schools—Saint Luke Catholic Church, Indianapolis, Inc. School—7650 N. Illinois St., 46260.
Tel: 317-255-3912; Email: patrickj@stluke.org; Web: www.stluke.org. Mrs. Elizabeth Kissel, Prin. Lay Teachers 40; Students 572.
St. Luke Preschool, 7711 Holliday Dr E, 46260.
Tel: 317-259-4373.
Catechesis Religious Program—Email: dcarollo@stluke.org. Sr. Diane Carollo, S.G.L., D.R.E. Students 100.

19—ST. MARK THE EVANGELIST (1946) Revs. William G. Marks; David Bu Nyar; Deacon Paul F. Fisherkeller
Legal Name: St. Mark the Evangelist Catholic Church, Indianapolis, Inc.
Res.: 535 E. Edgewood Ave., 46227-2099.
Tel: 317-787-8246; Email: frbill@stmarkindy.org; Email: aarcher@stmarkindy.org.
School—St. Mark the Evangelist School, 541 E. Edgewood Ave., 46227. Tel: 317-786-4013; Fax: 317-783-9574; Email: frbill@stmarkindy.org. Rusty Albertson, Prin. Lay Teachers 19; Students 263.
Catechesis Religious Program—Tel: 317-784-7155; Email: mlcav@stmarkindy.org. Students 167.

20—SAINT MARY OF THE IMMACULATE CONCEPTION (1858) [JC] (Hispanic) Rev. Carlton J. Beever
Legal Name: Saint Mary of the Immaculate Conception Catholic Church, Indianapolis, Inc.
Res.: 311 N. New Jersey St., 46204-2174.
Tel: 317-637-3983; Email: palejo@saintmarysindy.org; Web: www.saintmarysindy.org.
Catechesis Religious Program—*The Marian Center*, Students 125.

21—ST. MATTHEW CATHOLIC CHURCH, INDIANAPOLIS, INC. (1958) Rev. J. Nicholas Dant, M.Div., S.T.L.; Loral Tansy, Pastoral Assoc.
Res.: 4100 E. 56th St., 46220-5599.
Tel: 317-257-4297; Email: ltansy@saintmatt.org.
School—St. Matthew School, (Grades K-8), Tel: 317-251-3997; Email: ltansy@saintmatt.org. David Smock, Prin. Lay Teachers 31; Religious 1; Students 380.
Catechesis Religious Program—
Tel: 317-257-4297, Ext. 2215; Email: jlengerich@saintmatt.org. Students 97.

22—ST. MICHAEL THE ARCHANGEL (1948) Rev. John Kamwendo, B.Ed., M.Th., S.T.B., M.Div., D.Th., Th. D.
Legal Name: St. Michael the Archangel Catholic Church, Indianapolis, Inc.
Res.: 3354 W. 30th St., 46222-2183.
Tel: 317-926-7359; Email: bulletin@saintmichaelindy.org; Email: rectory@saintmichaelindy.org.
School—St. Michael-St. Gabriel Archangels School, 3352 W. 30th St., 46222. Tel: 317-926-0516; Fax: 317-921-3280; Email: bulletin@saintmichaelindy.org. Liz Ramos, Prin. Lay Teachers 24; Students 326.
Catechesis Religious Program—Tel: 317-921-3284; Email: mhawkins@saintmichaelindy.org. Students 58.

23—ST. MONICA CATHOLIC CHURCH, INDIANAPOLIS, INC. (1956) Revs. Todd Michael Goodson, V.F.; Jeffrey Dufresne; Deacons Robert J. Beyke; John R. McShea.
Res.: 6131 N. Michigan Rd., 46228-1298.
Tel: 317-253-2193; Email: parishoffice@stmonicaindy.org.
School—St. Monica School, Tel: 317-255-7153; Email: parishoffice@stmonicaindy.org. Eric Schommer, Prin. Lay Teachers 33; Students 395.
Catechesis Religious Program—Tel: 317-253-2193; Email: mjthomasday@stmonicaindy.org. Mary Jo Thomas-Day, D.R.E. Sisters 1; Students 700.

24—NATIVITY OF OUR LORD JESUS CHRIST (1947) [JC] 7225 Southeastern Ave., 46239-1209.
Tel: 317-357-1200; Email: tmarlin@nativityindy.org; Web: www.nativityindy.org. Rev. Eric M. Augenstein, M.A., M.Div.; Deacon John E. Hosier
Legal Name: Nativity of Our Lord Jesus Christ Catholic Church, Indianapolis, Inc.
School—Nativity of Our Lord Jesus Christ School, 3310 S. Meadow Dr., 46239. Tel: 317-357-1459; Fax: 317-357-9175; Email: tbianchini@nativity.org. Terri Bianchini, Prin. Lay Teachers 25; Students 385.
Catechesis Religious Program—Tel: 317-359-6075; Email: mross@nativityindy.org. Students 114.

25—OUR LADY OF LOURDES (1909)
5333 E. Washington St., 46219-6492.
Tel: 317-356-7291; Email: parishsecretary@ollindy.org; Web: www.ollindy.org. Rev. Richard M. Ginther, V.F.
Legal Name: Our Lady of Lourdes Catholic Church, Indianapolis, Inc.
School—Our Lady of Lourdes School, 30 S. Downey Ave., 46219. Tel: 317-357-3316; Fax: 317-357-0980; Email: ckolakovich@ollindy.org. Chris Kolakovich, Prin. Lay Teachers 20; Students 242.
Catechesis Religious Program—Email: parishsecretary@ollindy.org. Students 8.

26—OUR LADY OF THE MOST HOLY ROSARY (1909) [JC] (Italian) Rev. C. Ryan McCarthy, S.T.D., B.A., M.Div.; Very Rev. Joseph L. Newton, J.C.L., M.Div., V.J., Sacramental Min.
Legal Name: Our Lady of the Most Holy Rosary Catholic Church, Indianapolis, Inc.
Office: 520 Stevens St., 46203-1737.
Tel: 317-636-4478; Email: info@holyrosaryindy.org; Web: www.holyrosaryindy.org.
Catechesis Religious Program—Teresa Gorsage, C.R.E.

27—ST. PATRICK CATHOLIC CHURCH, INDIANAPOLIS, INC. (1865) (Irish—Hispanic) Revs. Lawrence R. Janezic, O.F.M.; Dennis Schafer, O.F.M.
Church: 950 Prospect St., 46203-1897.
Tel: 317-631-5824; Email: sheartparish@sbcglobal.net.
See Central Catholic Consolidated, Indianapolis under Good Shepherd, Indianapolis for details.
Catechesis Religious Program—Sisters 1; Students 299.

28—ST. PHILIP NERI (1909) [JC] (Irish—Hispanic) Rev. Christopher Wadelton
Legal Name: St. Philip Neri Catholic Church, Indianapolis, Inc.
Res.: 550 N. Rural St., 46201-2497.
Tel: 317-631-8746; Email: info@stphilipneri-indy.org.
School—St. Philip Neri School, 545 N. Eastern Ave., 46201. Tel: 317-636-0134; Fax: 317-636-3231; Email: info@stphilipneri-indy.org. Kari Buchinger, Prin. Lay Teachers 14; Students 290.
Catechesis Religious Program—Students 175.

29—ST. PIUS X CATHOLIC CHURCH, INDIANAPOLIS, INC. (1955) Revs. James M. Farrell, S.T.B.; David Bu Nyar; Deacon Richard J. Wagner.
Res.: 7200 Sarto Dr., 46240-3599. Tel: 317-255-4534; Email: jfarrell@spxparish.org; Web: www.spxparish.org.
School—St. Pius X Catholic Church School,

Tel: 317-466-3361; Email: jfarrell@spxparish.org. Alec Mayer, Prin. Lay Teachers 28; Students 413.
Catechesis Religious Program—Tel: 317-257-1085; Fax: 317-466-3377. Students 219.

30—ST. RITA CATHOLIC CHURCH, INDIANAPOLIS, INC. (1919) [JC] (African American)
1733 Dr. Andrew J. Brown Ave., 46202-1998.
Tel: 317-632-9349; Email: stritasecretary71@yahoo.com; Web: www.stritachurch-indy.org. Rev. Kenneth Taylor, V.F.; Deacon Oliver L. Jackson.
Catechesis Religious Program—Students 53.

31—ST. ROCH CATHOLIC CHURCH, INDIANAPOLIS, INC. (1922) [JC] Rev. Douglas Hunter, Admin.
Res.: 3600 S. Pennsylvania St., 46227-1299.
Tel: 317-784-1763; Email: church@strochindy.org.
School—St. Roch Catholic Church, Indianapolis, Inc. School, 3603 S. Meridian St., 46217.
Tel: 317-784-9144; Email: strochchurch@comcast.net. Amy Wilson, Prin. Lay Teachers 21; Students 305.
Catechesis Religious Program—Students 47.

32—SACRED HEART OF JESUS (1875) [CEM 2] [JC] (German) Revs. Lawrence R. Janezic, O.F.M.; Dennis Schafer, O.F.M., Parochial Vicar; Bro. Gary Jeriha, O.F.M., Pastoral Assoc.; Revs. Justin Belitz, O.F.M., In Res.; Tom Fox, O.F.M., In Res.; Bro. Guillermo Morales, O.F.M., In Res.
Legal Name: Sacred Heart of Jesus Catholic Church, Indianapolis, Inc.
Res.: 1530 S. Union St., 46225-1697.
Tel: 317-638-5551; Email: sheartparish@sbcglobal.net.
See Central Catholic School, Indianapolis under Good Shepherd, Indianapolis and Roncalli High School in the Institution Section for details.
Catechesis Religious Program—Students 6.

33—ST. SIMON THE APOSTLE (1961) Revs. John P. McCaslin, M.A., M.Div.; Santhosh Yohannan; Deacon Michael Braun
Legal Name: St. Simon the Apostle Catholic Church, Indianapolis, Inc.
Church & Office: 8155 Oaklandon Rd., 46236-8578.
Tel: 317-826-6000; Email: jmccaslin@saintsimon.org.
School—St. Simon the Apostle School, (Grades PreSchool-8), Tel: 317-826-6000; Email: cdarragh@saintsimon.org. Cathlene Darragh, Prin. Lay Teachers 37; Students 717.
Catechesis Religious Program—
Tel: 317-826-6000, Ext. 113. Students 420.

34—ST. THERESE OF THE INFANT JESUS (1925) [JC] Rev. Robert J. Gilday, S.T.B.
Legal Name: St. Therese of the Infant Jesus Catholic Church, Indianapolis, Inc.
Res.: 4720 E. 13th St., 46201-1798.
Tel: 317-357-8352; Email: tcostello@littleflower.org; Email: parishoffice@littleflowerparish.org.
School—St. Therese of the Infant Jesus School, (Grades PreSchool-8), 1401 N. Bosart Ave, 46202.
Tel: 317-353-2282; Fax: 317-322-7702; Email: tcostello@littleflower.org; Web: www.littleflowerparish.org/school. Kevin Gawrys, Prin. Lay Teachers 16; Students 336.
Catechesis Religious Program—Students 60.

35—SAINT THOMAS AQUINAS (1939) Rev. Michael Hoyt
Legal Name: Saint Thomas Aquinas Catholic Church, Indianapolis, Inc.
Office: 4625 N. Kenwood Ave., 46208-3599.
Tel: 317-253-1461; Email: mhoyt@staindy.org.
Res.: 4650 N. Illinois St., 46208.
School—Saint Thomas Aquinas School, 4600 N. Illinois St., 46208. Tel: 317-255-6244;
Fax: 317-255-6106; Email: rsochacki@staschool-indy.org; Web: www.staschool-indy.org. Cara Swinefurth, Prin. Lay Teachers 21; Students 207.
Catechesis Religious Program—Students 40.

OUTSIDE THE CITY OF INDIANAPOLIS

AURORA, DEARBORN CO., ST. MARY IMMACULATE CONCEPTION (1857) Rev. Stephen D. Donahue
Legal Name: St. Mary Immaculate Conception Catholic Church, Aurora, Inc.
Parish Office: 203 Fourth St., Aurora, 47001-1298.
Tel: 812-926-0060; Email: frstephen.donahue@mystmarys.com; Email: Kelly.rose@mystmarys.com.
School—St. Mary Immaculate Conception School, (Grades K-8), 211 Fourth St., Aurora, 47001.
Tel: 812-926-1558; Fax: 812-926-4439; Email: stmary@uswebmail.biz; Web: www.stmaryschoolaurora.com. Bob Brookbank, Prin. Lay Teachers 9; Students 131.
Catechesis Religious Program—Email: carolynmeyer@uswebmail.biz.

BATESVILLE, RIPLEY CO., ST. LOUIS CATHOLIC CHURCH, BATESVILLE, INC. (1868) [CEM] (German) Very Rev. Stanley Pondo, J.D., J.C.D., M.Div.; Deacon Ronald Freyer.
Res.: 13 St. Louis Pl., Batesville, 47006-1393.
Tel: 812-934-3204; Email: frstanleypondo@yahoo.com; Web: www.stlouis-batesville.org.
Schools—Preschool—200 S. Walnut St., Batesville, 47006. Tel: 812-932-1731; Email: bmoll@st.louisschool.org. Brenda Moll.
St. Louis Catholic Church, Batesville, Inc. School, 17 St. Louis Pl., Batesville, 47006. Tel: 812-934-3310; Fax: 812-934-6202; Email: cmoeller@st.louisschool.org. Chad M. Moeller, Prin. Lay Teachers 28; Students 356.
Catechesis Religious Program—
Tel: 812-934-3204, Ext. 249; Email: amytongesreligioused@st.louisschool.org. Amy Tonges, D.R.E. Students 188.

BEDFORD, LAWRENCE CO., ST. VINCENT DE PAUL CATHOLIC CHURCH, BEDFORD, INC. (1864) Rev. Richard W. Eldred; Deacons David Reising; Thomas Scarlett.
Parish/Mailing Office: 1723 I St., Bedford, 47421-4221. Tel: 812-275-6539; Email: parish@svsbedford.org; Web: www.yourcclc.org.
Rectory—St. Mary of the Assumption, 777 S. 11th St., Mitchell, 47446.
School—St. Vincent de Paul Catholic Church, Bedford, Inc. School, (Grades PreK-8), 923 18th St., Bedford, 47421. Tel: 812-279-2540;
Fax: 812-276-4880; Email: parish@svsbedford.org. Teresa Underwood, Prin.; Millie Castagnier, Librarian. Lay Teachers 14; Students 167.
Catechesis Religious Program—Email: warem@svsbedford.org. Michael Ware, D.R.E. Students 54.

BEECH GROVE, MARION CO., HOLY NAME OF JESUS (1908) [JC] Very Rev. Robert J. Robeson, Ph.D., V.F.
Legal Name: Holy Name of Jesus Catholic Church, Indianapolis, Inc.
Res.: 89 N. 17th Ave., Beech Grove, 46107-1531.
Tel: 317-784-5454 (Parish Office); Email: frrobeson@holyname.cc; Web: www.holyname.cc.
School—Holy Name of Jesus School, 21 N. 17th Ave., Beech Grove, 46107. Tel: 317-784-9078 (Office);
Tel: 317-788-3617 (School Cafeteria);
Tel: 317-788-3618; Fax: 317-788-3616; Email: rkitchens@holyname.cc; Web: www.holyname.cc/school.htm. Mr. Robert Kicthens, Prin. Lay Teachers 21; Students 252.
Catechesis Religious Program—
Tel: 317-784-5454, Ext. 5; Email: sabb@holyname.cc; Web: www.holyname.cc. Students 50.

BLOOMINGTON, MONROE CO.

1—ST. CHARLES BORROMEO (1864) [JC]
Mailing Address: 2222 E. 3rd St., Bloomington, 47401-5385. Tel: 812-336-6846; Email: frkovatch@stcharlesbloomington.org. Rev. Thomas G. Kovatch, B.S., M.Div.; Deacon Marc Kellams, JD
Legal Name: St. Charles Borromeo Catholic Church, Bloomington, Inc.
Res.: 2001 Southdowns Dr., Bloomington, 47401-5385.
School—St. Charles Borromeo School, (Grades PreK-8), 2224 E. 3rd St., Bloomington, 47401.
Tel: 812-336-5853; Fax: 812-349-0300; Email: frkovatch@stcharlesbloomington.org. Madonna Paskash, Prin.; Ruth Gleason, Librarian. Lay Teachers 32; Students 450.
Catechesis Religious Program—Tel: 812-334-1664. Rose Johnson, D.R.E.; Ashley Barnett, D.R.E. Students 230.

2—ST. JOHN THE APOSTLE (1970) Rev. Daniel J. Mahan; Deacon Richard Stanford
Legal Name: St. John the Apostle Catholic Church, Bloomington, Inc.
Res.: 4607 W. State Rd. 46, Bloomington, 47404-9255. Tel: 812-876-1974; Email: info@sjabloomington.org.
Catechesis Religious Program—
Tel: 812-876-0718, Ext. 203. Scott Benningfield, D.R.E. Students 63.

3—ST. PAUL CATHOLIC CENTER, BLOOMINGTON, INC. (1969) Rev. John J. Meany, O.P.; Friars Patrick Hyde, O.P.; Joseph Minuth, O.P.; Deacon Ronald Reimer.
Res.: 1413 E. 17th St., Bloomington, 47408-1602.
Tel: 812-339-5561; Email: pastor@hoosiercatholic.org; Web: www.hoosiercatholic.org.
Catechesis Religious Program—Email: bmcintyre@hoosiercatholic.org. Students 215.

BRADFORD, HARRISON CO., ST. MICHAEL CATHOLIC CHURCH, BRADFORD, INC. (1835) [CEM]
Mailing Address: 11400 Farmers Ln., N.E., Greenville, 47124. Tel: 812-364-6646;
Fax: 812-364-6614; Email: stmichaels@mw.twcbc.com; Web: saintmichaelschurch.net. Rev. Aaron J. Pfaff; Deacon John R. Jacobi.
Catechesis Religious Program—Tel: 812-364-6173; Email: johnjacobi@insightbb.com. Students 105.

BRAZIL, CLAY CO., ANNUNCIATION CATHOLIC CHURCH, BRAZIL, INC. (1866)
Tel: 812-448-1901; Email: annunciationchurch@msn.com. Rev. John J. Hollowell.
Office: 19 N. Alabama St., Brazil, 47834-2399.
Tel: 812-448-1901; Email: annunciationchurch@msn.com.
Child Care—Preschool, 415 E. Church St., Brazil, 47834. Fax: 812-443-2403. Jane Osborn, Admin.
Catechesis Religious Program—Students 26.

BRIGHT, DEARBORN CO., ST. TERESA BENEDICTA OF THE CROSS, BRIGHT, INDIANA (2000) Rev. Randall R. Summers, M.B.A., M.A., M.Div.; Deacon Steven C. Tsuleff.
Parish Office: 23455 Gavin Ln., Lawrenceburg, 47025-8372. Tel: 812-656-8700; Email: parishoffice@stteresab.com.
Catechesis Religious Program—Students 90.

BROOKVILLE, FRANKLIN CO.

1—ST. MICHAEL THE ARCHANGEL (1845) [CEM] (German) Rev. Vincent P. Lampert
Legal Name: St. Michael the Archangel Catholic Church, Brookville, Inc.
Church: 145 St. Michael Blvd., Brookville, 47012.
Tel: 765-647-5462; Email: stmichael@etczone.com.
School—St. Michael the Archangel School,
Tel: 765-647-4961; Email: stmichael@etczone.com. Cynthia Johnson, Prin. Lay Teachers 13; Sisters of the Third Order Regular of St. Francis 2; Students 223.
Catechesis Religious Program—Students 48.

2—ORATORY OF SS. PHILOMENA AND CECILIA (2010)
Mailing Address: 16194 St. Mary's Rd., Brookville, 47012. Tel: 765-647-0310; Email: fishingpadre1971@gmail.com. Revs. Brian Austin, F.S.S.P., Assoc. Admin.; Howard Remski, F.S.S.P., Asst. Admin.
Legal Name: Oratory of SS. Philomena and Cecilia Catholic Church, Brookville, Inc.

BROWNSBURG, HENDRICKS CO., ST. MALACHY CATHOLIC CHURCH, BROWNSBURG, INC. (1869) [CEM 2] (Irish) Very Rev. Sean R. Danda, V.F.; Rev. Xavier Raj; Deacons Daniel Collier; Rick Renzi.
Church & Mailing Address: 9833 E. Co. Rd. 750 N., Brownsburg, 46112-9633. Tel: 317-852-3195; Email: jkiefer@stmalachy.org.
School—St. Malachy Catholic Church, Brownsburg, Inc. School, (Grades K-8), 7410 N. Co. Rd. 1000 E., Brownsburg, 46112. Tel: 317-852-2242;
Fax: 317-852-3604; Email: abostrom@stmalachy.org. Angela Bostrom, Prin.; Saundra Kennison, Vice Prin.; Katie Buck, Librarian. Lay Teachers 30; Students 456.
Catechesis Religious Program—Students 450.

CAMBRIDGE CITY, WAYNE CO., ST. ELIZABETH OF HUNGARY (1852)
333 W. Maple St., Cambridge City, 47327-1130.
Tel: 765-478-3242; Fax: 765-478-3585; Email: frjhall@gmail.com; Web: www.st-eliz.org. Rev. John M. Hall, V.F.
Legal Name: St. Elizabeth of Hungary Catholic Church, Cambridge City, Inc.
Catechesis Religious Program—Email: syanos@nlte.net. Students 52.

CANNELTON, PERRY CO., ST. MICHAEL CATHOLIC CHURCH, CANNELTON, INC. (1859) [CEM] Rev. Sengole Thomas Gnanaraj, (India) V.F., Admin.
Parish Office: c/o Catholic Ministry Center, 824 Jefferson St., Tell City, 47586-2114.
Tel: 812-547-7994; Email: stmichaelch@yahoo.com.
Res.: 814 Jefferson St., Tell City, 47586.
Tel: 812-547-9901.
Church: Eighth St., Cannelton, 47520.
Catechesis Religious Program—Students 11.

CHARLESTOWN, CLARK CO., ST. MICHAEL CATHOLIC CHURCH, CHARLESTOWN, INC. (1860) [CEM] Rev. Henry F. Tully.
Res.: 101 St. Michael Dr., Charlestown, 47111-1635.
Tel: 812-256-3200; Email: michaelsecretary@mw.twcbc.com.
Child Care—Child Care Center, 102 St. Michael Dr., Charlestown, 47111. Tel: 812-256-3503. Rita Poff, Dir. (PreK-K) Students 75.
Catechesis Religious Program—Students 79.

CLARKSVILLE, CLARK CO., ST. ANTHONY OF PADUA (1851) [CEM] Revs. Joseph West, O.F.M.Conv.; Robert St. Martin, O.F.M.Conv., In Res.; Florian Tiell, O.F.M.Conv., In Res.; Friar Mark Weaver, O.F.M.Conv., In Res.; Mark Clements, Business Mgr.; Stacy Gillenwater, Youth Min.; Dr. Timothy Glasscock, Music Min.
Legal Name: St. Anthony of Padua Catholic Church, Clarksville, Inc.
Res.: 316 N. Sherwood Ave., Clarksville, 47129-2724.
Tel: 812-282-2290; Email: parish.office@stanthony-clarksville.org; Web: www.stanthony-clarksville.org.
School—St. Anthony of Padua School, (Grades K-8), 320 N. Sherwood Ave., Clarksville, 47129.
Tel: 812-282-2144; Fax: 812-282-2169; Email: s.tucker@stanthony-clarksville.org; Web: www.stap.us. Stephany Tucker, Prin. Lay Teachers 27; Students 240.
Catechesis Religious Program—Students 15.

CLINTON, VERMILLION CO., SACRED HEART CHURCH, CLINTON, INC. (1891)
610 S. 6th St., Clinton, 47842-2016.
Tel: 765-832-8468; Email: sacredheartclinton@sbcglobal.net. Rev. Varghese Maliakkal.
Rectory—558 Nebeker St., Clinton, 47842.
Catechesis Religious Program—Students 59.

COLUMBUS, BARTHOLOMEW CO., ST. BARTHOLOMEW CATHOLIC CHURCH, COLUMBUS, IN (1994) St. Bartholomew (1841) and St. Columba (1963) were closed, merged, and renamed St. Bartholomew.
Mailing Address: 1306 27th St., Columbus, 47201-6375. Tel: 812-379-9353; Fax: 812-375-0720; Email: mjanes@stbparish.net; Web: www.saintbartholomew.org. Revs. Clement T. Davis, M.Div.; Kyle Rodden; Deacons William Jones; Juan Carlos Ramirez.
School—St. Bartholomew School, (Grades K-8), 1306 27th St., Columbus, 47201. Fax: 812-376-0377; Email: mjanes@stbparish.net. Helen Heckman, Prin. Lay Teachers 26; Students 372.
Catechesis Religious Program—Students 418.

CONNERSVILLE, FAYETTE CO., ST. GABRIEL CATHOLIC CHURCH, CONNERSVILLE, INC. (1851) [JC] Very Rev. Dustin M. Boehm, V.F.; Pamela S. Rader, Business Mgr.
Res.: 232 W. Ninth St., Connersville, 47331-2099. Tel: 765-825-8578; Email: dboehm@stgabrielconnersville.org.
School—St. Gabriel Catholic Church, Connersville, Inc. School, (Grades PreK-6), 224 W. Ninth St., Connersville, 47331. Tel: 765-825-7951; Fax: 765-827-4347; Email: sbarth@stgabrielconnersville.org; Web: www.stgabriel.k12.in.us. Sue Barth, Prin. Lay Teachers 8; Students 158.
Catechesis Religious Program—Students 40.

CORYDON, HARRISON CO., ST. JOSEPH CATHOLIC CHURCH, CORYDON, INC. (1896) [CEM] Rev. Robert Jason Hankee.
Res.: 312 E. High St., Corydon, 47112-1299. Tel: 812-738-2742; Email: parish.office@catholic-community.org.
School—St. Joseph Catholic Church, Corydon, Inc. School, 512 N. Mulberry St., Corydon, 47112. Tel: 812-738-4549; Fax: 812-738-2722; Email: parish.office@catholic-community.org. Julie Crone, Prin. Lay Teachers 12; Students 117.
Catechesis Religious Program—Tel: 812-738-2759. Students 140.

DANVILLE, HENDRICKS CO., MARY. QUEEN OF PEACE (1939) Rev. Michael C. Fritsch, M.Div., V.F.
Legal Name: Mary. Queen of Peace Catholic Church, Danville, Inc.
Res.: 1005 W. Main St., Danville, 46122-1025. Tel: 317-745-4284; Email: frfritsch@gmail.com.
Catechesis Religious Program—Tel: 317-745-4284, Ext. 13; Email: polycarp11@iquest.net. Matthew Fallon, D.R.E.; Beth Dieckmann, Youth Min. Students 153.

DEARBORN, DEARBORN CO., ALL SAINTS CATHOLIC CHURCH, DEARBORN, INC. (2014)
25743 State Rte. 1, Guilford, 47022-8979. Tel: 812-576-4302; Fax: 812-576-2324; Email: emilyalig.asp@gmail.com. Rev. Jonathan P. Meyer; Deacon Robert W. Decker.
School—All Saints Catholic Academy, (Grades K-PreK), Tel: 812-576-0104; Email: emilyalig.asp@gmail.com. Emily Alig, Contact Person. Students 80.

DECATUR, DECATUR CO., ST. CATHERINE OF SIENA PARISH, DECATUR, INC. (2014) [CEM]
9995 E. Base Rd., Greensburg, 47240-8406. Tel: 812-934-2880; Email: stcatherine47240@gmail.com; Web: www.stcatherinesparish.org. Rev. William L. Ehalt.
Catechesis Religious Program—1963 N. St. John St., Greensburg, 47240. Tel: 812-663-4754; Email: stcatherinevs@gmail.com. Vicki Schwering, D.R.E. Students 176.

EDINBURGH, JOHNSON CO., HOLY TRINITY CATHOLIC CHURCH, EDINBURGH, INC. (1851)
100 Keeley St., P.O. Box 216, Edinburgh, 46124-0216. Tel: 812-526-9460; Email: parishoffice@holytrinityedinburgh.net. Rev. Clement T. Davis, M.Div., Mod.; Deacon Russell B. Woodard, Parish Life Coord.
Res.: 114 Lancelot Dr., Franklin, 46131. Tel: 317-738-3929; Fax: 812-526-2477; Email: hilltop1851@gmail.com.
Catechesis Religious Program—Tel: 812-526-9460. Students 60.

FORTVILLE, HANCOCK CO., ST. THOMAS THE APOSTLE, FORTVILLE, INC. (1919) Rev. George Joseph Nangachiveettil, (India); Deacon Anthony E. Lewis.
Res.: 523 S. Merrill St., Fortville, 46040-1428. Tel: 317-485-5102; Email: secretary@stthomasfortville.com.
Catechesis Religious Program—Tel: 317-485-5103. Students 74.

FRANKLIN, JOHNSON CO., ST. ROSE OF LIMA CATHOLIC CHURCH, FRANKLIN, INC. (1868) Rev. Steven Schaftlein.
Res.: 114 Lancelot Dr., Franklin, 46131-8806. Tel: 317-738-3929; Email: yburgener@stroselions.net.
School—St. Rose of Lima School, (Grades PreK-8), Tel: 317-738-3451; Email: yburgener@stroselions.net. Rebecca Floyd, Prin. Students 194.
Catechesis Religious Program—Tel: 317-736-6754. Students 88.

FRENCH LICK, ORANGE CO., OUR LADY OF THE SPRINGS (1887) Rev. John Peter Gallagher
Legal Name: Our Lady of the Springs Catholic Church, French Lick, Inc.
Res.: 8796 W. State Rd. 56, French Lick, 47432-9391. Tel: 812-936-4568; Email: ols936@bluemarble.net; Web: occ-indy.org.
Catechesis Religious Program—Students 12.
Mission—Our Lord Jesus Christ the King (1948) Hwy 150, E., Paoli, Orange Co. 47454.
Catechesis Religious Program—

FRENCHTOWN, HARRISON CO., ST. BERNARD CATHOLIC CHURCH, FRENCHTOWN, INC. (1849) [CEM] Rev. Aaron J. Pfaff; Deacon John R. Jacobi, D.R.E.
Church: 7600 Hwy. 337 N.W., Depauw, 47115-8558. Tel: 812-347-2326; Email: SaintBernardCatholicChurch@gmail.com.
Res.: 11400 Farmers Ln., Greenville, 47124. Tel: 812-364-6646; Fax: 812-364-6614.
Catechesis Religious Program—Students 35.

FULDA, SPENCER CO., ST. BONIFACE CATHOLIC CHURCH, FULDA, INC. (1847) [CEM]
Mailing Address: P.O. Box 8, St. Meinrad, 47577. Rev. Anthony Vinson, O.S.B., Admin.
Church: 1559 N. State Rd. 545, Fulda, 47536. Tel: 812-357-5533; Fax: 812-357-2862; Email: smeinrad@psci.net.
Catechesis Religious Program—Students 64.

GREENCASTLE, PUTNAM CO., ST. PAUL THE APOSTLE (1853) Rev. John J. Hollowell
Legal Name: St. Paul the Apostle Catholic Church, Putnam County, Inc.
Res.: 202 E. Washington St., Greencastle, 46135-1549. Tel: 765-653-5678; Email: stpauloffice202@gmail.com.
Catechesis Religious Program—Students 118.

GREENFIELD, HANCOCK CO., ST. MICHAEL CATHOLIC CHURCH, GREENFIELD, INC. (1860) Rev. Aaron M. Jenkins; Deacon Wayne Davis.
Res.: 519 Jefferson Blvd., Greenfield, 46140-1899. Tel: 317-462-4240; Email: parishsecretary@stmichaelsgrfld.org; Email: rgriffis@stmichaelsgrfld.org; Web: www.stmichaelsgrfld.org.
School—St. Michael Catholic School, (Grades PreK-8), 515 Jefferson Blvd., Greenfield, 46140. Tel: 317-462-6380; Fax: 317-467-2864; Email: rhittel@stmichaelsgrfld.org; Web: www.school-stmichaelsgrfld.org. Ruth Hittel, Prin. Lay Teachers 21; Students 161.
Catechesis Religious Program—Email: prichey@stmichaelsgrfld.org. Students 220.

GREENSBURG, DECATUR CO., ST. MARY CATHOLIC CHURCH, GREENSBURG, INC. (1858) [CEM] Revs. John A. Meyer, V.F., 1331 E. Hunter. Robbins Way, Greensburg, 47240; Adam L. Ahern, M.Div.; Deacon Bradley Anderson.
Church: 1331 E. Hunter Robbins Way, Greensburg, 47240-2197. Tel: 812-663-8427; Fax: 812-663-6088; Email: frmeyer@etczone.com.
School—St. Mary Catholic Church, Greensburg, Inc. School, (Grades PreK-7), Tel: 812-663-2804; Email: nbuening@stmarysgreensburg.com. Nancy Buening, Prin. Lay Teachers 17; Students 314.
Catechesis Religious Program—Students 167.

GREENWOOD, JOHNSON CO.
1—SS. FRANCIS AND CLARE OF ASSISI CATHOLIC CHURCH, GREENWOOD, INC. (1993) Revs. Stephen W. Giannini, V.E.; David J. Marcotte, B.A., M.Div., Sacramental Min.; Deacon Ronald Pirau.
Church & Parish Office: 5901 Olive Branch Rd., Greenwood, 46143-8181. Tel: 317-859-4673; Fax: 317-859-4678; Email: jbiasi@ss-fc.org; Web: www.ss-fc.org.
School—SS. Francis and Clare of Assisi Catholic Church, Greenwood, Inc. School, (Grades PreK-8), Tel: 317-215-2826; Email: ssfcschool@ss-fc.org. Betty Popp, Prin. Lay Teachers 60; Students 570.
Catechesis Religious Program—Email: pmcgill@ss-fc.org. Patricia McGill, D.R.E. Students 680.
2—OUR LADY OF THE GREENWOOD CATHOLIC CHURCH, INC. (1948) [JC] Rev. Msgr. Mark Svarczkopf; Revs. Anthony Hollowell; Mauro G. Rodas, Sacramental Min., (Retired); Deacon Reynaldo Nava.
Res.: 335 S. Meridian St., Greenwood, 46143-1698. Tel: 317-888-2861; Email: info@olgreenwood.org.
School—Our Lady of the Greenwood Catholic Church, Inc. School, (Grades PreK-8), 399 S. Meridian St., Greenwood, 46143. Tel: 317-888-2861; Email: info@olgreenwood.org. Kent Clady, Prin.; Paula Howard, Librarian. Clergy 5; Lay Teachers 30; Students 366.
Catechesis Religious Program—Sisters 1; Students 200.

HENRYVILLE, CLARK CO., ST. FRANCIS CATHOLIC CHURCH, HENRYVILLE, INC. (1869)
Mailing Address: 101 St. Michael Dr., Charlestown, 47111. Rev. Henry F. Tully.
Church: 101 N. Ferguson Dr., Henryville, 47126. Tel: 812-294-4682; Email: michaelsecretary@insightbb.com.
Catechesis Religious Program—Students 50.

JEFFERSONVILLE, CLARK CO.
1—ST. AUGUSTINE (1851) [CEM] Rev. Douglas W. Marcotte, B.S., M.A., S.T.B.; Deacon John Thompson, Pastoral Assoc.
Legal Name: St. Augustine Catholic Church, Jeffersonville, Inc.
Res.: 315 E. Chestnut St., P.O. Box 447, Jeffersonville, 47131-0447. Tel: 812-282-2677; Email: kueding@jeffersonvillecatholic.org.
Catechesis Religious Program—316 E. Maple St.. Tel: 812-282-1231; Fax: 812-282-1605. Students 34.
2—SACRED HEART CATHOLIC CHURCH, JEFFERSONVILLE, INC. (1953) Rev. Douglas W. Marcotte, B.S., M.A., S.T.B.; Deacon John Thompson.
Church & Parish Office: 1840 E. 8th St., Jeffersonville, 47130-4897. Tel: 812-282-2677; Email: kueding@jeffersonvillecatholic.org.
School—Sacred Heart Catholic Church, Jeffersonville, Inc. School, 1842 E. 8th St., Jeffersonville, 47130. Tel: 812-283-3123; Email: fbarlag@sacredheartschool.us. Frank Barlag, Prin. Lay Teachers 18; Students 254.
Catechesis Religious Program—Students 104.

LANESVILLE, HARRISON CO., ST. MARY CATHOLIC CHURCH, LANESVILLE, INC. (1843) [CEM] (German) Rev. Robert St. Martin, O.F.M.Conv.; Deacon Richard Cooper.
Res.: 2500 St. Mary's Dr., Lanesville, 47136. Tel: 812-952-2853 (Parish Office); Email: rphillips@frontier.com.
Catechesis Religious Program—Email: faithformation@frontier.com. Students 124.

LAWRENCEBURG, DEARBORN CO., ST. LAWRENCE CATHOLIC CHURCH, LAWRENCEBURG, INC. (1842) (German) Rev. Benjamin D. Syberg, B.A., M.Div.
Parish Office—Parish Office: 542 Walnut St., Lawrenceburg, 47025-1861. Tel: 812-537-3992; Email: stlawrenceparish@comcast.net.
Rectory—526 Walnut St., Lawrenceburg, 47025. Tel: 812-537-1297.
School—St. Lawrence Catholic Church, Lawrenceburg, Inc. School, 524 Walnut St., Lawrenceburg, 47025. Tel: 812-537-3690; Fax: 812-537-9685; Email: admin@sls-apps.org. Michael Odar, Prin. Lay Teachers 17; Students 211.
Catechesis Religious Program—Tel: 812-537-1112. Students 50.

LEOPOLD, PERRY CO., ST. AUGUSTINE CATHOLIC CHURCH, LEOPOLD, INC. (1837) [CEM] Rev. Brian G. Esarey.
Res.: 18020 Lafayette St., Leopold, 47551. Tel: 812-843-5143; Email: staughc@psci.net.
Catechesis Religious Program—Students 76.

LIBERTY, UNION CO., ST. BRIDGET CATHOLIC CHURCH, LIBERTY, INC. (1854) [CEM]
404 E. Vine St., P.O. Box 112, Liberty, 47353. Tel: 765-825-8578; Email: dboehm@stgabrielconnersville.org. 232 W. 9th St., Connersville, 47331. Very Rev. Dustin M. Boehm, V.F.
Catechesis Religious Program—Tel: 765-458-5412. Students 43.

MADISON, JEFFERSON CO., PRINCE OF PEACE CATHOLIC CHURCH, MADISON, INC. (1993) [CEM 3] St. Michael (1837), St. Mary (1851), St. Patrick (1853), Madison, and St. Anthony, China (1861) were closed, merged and renamed Prince of Peace.
305 W. State St., Madison, 47250. Tel: 812-265-4166; Fax: 812-273-3427; Email: parishoffice@popeace.org; Web: www.popeace.org. Rev. Christopher A. Craig; Deacon Michael Gardner.
School—Pope John XXIII, (Grades PreSchool-6), 221 State St., Madison, 47250. Tel: 812-273-3957; Fax: 812-265-4566. Curt Gardner, Prin.; Karen Terlinden, Librarian. Students 348.
High School—Shawe Memorial Junior-Senior High School, 201 W. State St., Madison, 47250. Tel: 812-273-2150; Fax: 812-273-2013; Email: shaweprincipal@popeace.org. Steve Hesse, Prin. Students 258.
Catechesis Religious Program—Students 50.

MARENGO, CRAWFORD CO., ST. JOSEPH CATHOLIC CHURCH, MARENGO, INC. (1855) [CEM] Attended by St. Bernard, Frenchtown.
State Rd. 66, Marengo, 47115. Tel: 812-347-2326; Email: stbernardcatholicchurch@gmail.com. Mailing Address: 7600 Hwy. 337, N.W., Depauw, 47115. Rev. Aaron J. Pfaff, Admin.
Church: 341 S. State Rd. 66, Marengo, 47140.
Catechesis Religious Program—Students 10.

MARTINSVILLE, MORGAN CO., ST. MARTIN OF TOURS (1848) [CEM]
1720 E. Harrison St., Martinsville, 46151-1844. Rev. Jegan Peter; Deacon Tim Harte

Legal Name: St. Martin of Tours Catholic Church, Martinsville, Inc.
Res.: 1709 E. Harrison St., Martinsville, 46151-1844. Tel: 765-342-6379; Email: secretarysm@att.net; Web: www.stmartins-martinsville.org.
Catechesis Religious Program—Tel: 765-352-0602; Fax: 765-342-1263. Students 66.

MILAN, RIPLEY CO., ST. CHARLES CATHOLIC CHURCH, MILAN, INC. (1908) [CEM 2]
Mailing Address: 213 Ripley St., P.O. Box 813, Milan, 47031-0813. Tel: 812-654-7051; Email: st.charleschurch@yahoo.com. Rev. John Meyer, Mod.; Gary Taylor, D.Min., Parish Life Coord.
Catechesis Religious Program—Tel: 812-654-7015. Gary Taylor, D.R.E. Students 45.

MILLHOUSEN, DECATUR CO., IMMACULATE CONCEPTION (1834) [CEM]
Mailing Address: 2081 E. County Rd., 820 S., Greensburg, 47240-9636. Tel: 812-591-2362; Fax: 812-591-2362; Email: sisterdonna@millhousenchurch.com; Web: millhousenchurch.com. Very Rev. Sean R. Danda, V.F., Mod.; Revs. John F. Geis, Sacramental Min., (Retired); William J. Turner, Sacramental Min., (Retired), Email: wjturner77@gmail.com; Sr. Donna M. Prickel, O.S.F., Parish Life Coord.
Legal Name: Immaculate Conception Catholic Church, Millhousen, Inc.
Catechesis Religious Program—Students 65.

MITCHELL, LAWRENCE CO., ST. MARY OF THE ASSUMPTION (1869) Rev. Richard W. Eldred; Deacons David Reising; Thomas Scarlett
Legal Name: St. Mary of the Assumption Catholic Church, Mitchell, Inc.
Res.: 777 S. 11th St., Mitchell, 47446-1643.
Tel: 812-849-3570; Email: stmarysmitchell@frontier.com.
Catechesis Religious Program—Students 18.

MOORESVILLE, MORGAN CO., ST. THOMAS MORE CATHOLIC CHURCH, MOORESVILLE, INC. (1967) Rev. Francis Joseph Kalapurackal, Admin.
Res.: 1200 N. Indiana St., Mooresville, 46158.
Tel: 317-831-4142; Email: kphillips@stm-church.org.
Catechesis Religious Program—Students 215.

MORRIS, RIPLEY CO., ST. ANTHONY OF PADUA CATHOLIC CHURCH, MORRIS, INC. (1856) [CEM] Rev. Shaun P. Whittington.
Parish Office: 4781 E. Morris Church St., Morris, 47033. Tel: 812-934-6218; Email: parishoffice@stanthonymorris.org.
Catechesis Religious Program—Students 112.

NAPOLEON, RIPLEY CO., ST. MAURICE CATHOLIC CHURCH, NAPOLEON, INC. (1848) [CEM]
Mailing Address: 8874 Harrison St., P.O. Box 17, Napoleon, 47034-0017. Tel: 812-852-4237; Email: srsgerth@hotmail.com. Revs. John A. Meyer, V.F., Mod.; John F. Geis, Sacramental Min., (Retired); William J. Turner, Sacramental Min., (Retired); Sr. Shirley Gerth, O.S.F., Parish Life Coord.
Catechesis Religious Program—Fax: 812-852-4235. Sisters 1; Students 106.

NASHVILLE, BROWN CO., ST. AGNES CATHOLIC CHURCH, NASHVILLE, INC. (1940) [JC]
Mailing Address: 1008 McLary Rd., P.O. Box 577, Nashville, 47448-0577. Tel: 812-988-2778; Email: stagnesnashville@gmail.com; Web: www.stagneschurchnashville.org. Revs. Daniel Mahan, Mod.; Eric Johnson, Sacramental Min.; Sr, Susan Hooks, O.S.B., Parish Life Coord.
Catechesis Religious Program—Tel: 812-988-1432. Sisters 1; Students 60.

NAVILLETON, FLOYD CO., ST. MARY OF THE ANNUNCIATION (1845) [CEM] (German) Rev. Pius Poff, O.F.M.Conv.
Legal Name: St. Mary of the Annunciation Catholic Church, Navilleton, Inc.
Res.: 7500 Navilleton Rd., Floyds Knobs, 47119-8603. Tel: 812-923-5419; Email: stmarynavilleton@mw.twcbc.com.
Catechesis Religious Program—Students 102.

NEW ALBANY, FLOYD CO.

1—HOLY FAMILY CATHOLIC CHURCH, NEW ALBANY, INC. (1954) [JC] Very Rev. Jeremy M. Gries, V.F.
Res.: 129 W. Daisy Lane, New Albany, 47150.
Tel: 812-944-8283; Email: info@holyfamilynewalbany.org.
School—Holy Family Catholic Church, New Albany, Inc. School, (Grades PreSchool-8), 217 W. Daisy Ln., New Albany, 47150. Tel: 812-944-6090; Fax: 812-944-7299; Email: info@holyfamilynewalbany.org; Web: www.holyfamilyeagles.com. Gerald Ernstberger, Prin.; Kerri Tomlin, Librarian. Lay Teachers 23; Students 401.
Catechesis Religious Program—Students 70.

2—ST. MARY OF THE ANNUNCIATION (1858) [CEM] [JC] (German) Friar Mark Weaver, O.F.M.Conv.; Deacon Martin Ignacio
Legal Name: St. Mary of the Annunciation Catholic Church, New Albany, Inc.
Res.: 415 E. Eighth St., New Albany, 47150-3299.
Tel: 812-944-0417; Email: info@stmarysna.org.
Catechesis Religious Program—Students 123.

3—OUR LADY OF PERPETUAL HELP (1950) Very Rev. Joseph M. Feltz, M.Div., M.A.; Deacon Jeffrey Powell
Legal Name: Our Lady Of Perpetual Help Catholic Church, New Albany, Inc.
Res.: 1752 Scheller Ln., New Albany, 47150-2423.
Tel: 812-944-1184; Email: mcampbell@olphna.org.
School—Our Lady of Perpetual Help School, Tel: 812-944-7676; Email: sbeyl@olphna.org. Steve Beyl, Prin. Lay Teachers 25; Students 351.
Catechesis Religious Program—Tel: 812-948-0185. Students 177.

NEW CASTLE, HENRY CO., ST. ANNE CATHOLIC CHURCH, NEW CASTLE, INC. (1873) [CEM] Rev. John M. Hall, V.F.
Parish Office: 102 N. 19th St., New Castle, 47362-3999. Tel: 765-529-0933; Email: stannechurch@hotmail.com.
Catechesis Religious Program—Tel: 765-529-8976; Email: kaitblandford@gmail.com. Students 50.

NEW MIDDLETOWN, HARRISON CO.

NORTH VERNON, JENNINGS CO., ST. MARY CATHOLIC CHURCH, NORTH VERNON, INC. (1861) [CEM]
212 Washington St., North Vernon, 47265-1199.
Tel: 812-346-3604; Fax: 812-346-3506; Email: sharlot01@gmail.com; Web: www.stmaryscc.org. Rev. Jerry L. Byrd, M.A., M.Div.; Deacon Lawrence French.
School—St. Mary Catholic Church, North Vernon, Inc. School, (Grades K-8), 209 Washington St., North Vernon, 47265. Tel: 812-346-3445; Fax: 812-346-5930; Email: stmarys@seidata.com; Web: www.stmarysnv.com. Lisa Vogel, Prin. Lay Teachers 8; Students 230.
Catechesis Religious Program—Students 130.

OLDENBURG, FRANKLIN CO., HOLY FAMILY CATHOLIC CHURCH, OLDENBURG, INC. (1837) [CEM] Revs. Carl Langenderfer, O.F.M., Parochial Admin.; Joe Nelson, O.F.M., In Res.; Robert Weakley, O.F.M., In Res.; Michael Chowning, O.F.M., In Res.; Neri Greskoviak, O.F.M., In Res.
Res.: Main St., P.O. Box 98, Oldenburg, 47036-0098.
Tel: 812-934-3013; Email: holyfamilyjo@etczone.com.
Catechesis Religious Program—Students 300.

OSGOOD, RIPLEY CO., ST. JOHN THE BAPTIST CATHOLIC CHURCH, OSGOOD, INC. (1867) [CEM] Revs. John A. Meyer, V.F., Mod.; John F. Geis, Sacramental Min., (Retired); William J. Turner, Sacramental Min., (Retired); Sr. Shirley Gerth, O.S.F., Parish Life Coord.
Res.: 331 S. Buckeye St., Osgood, 47037-1305.
Tel: 812-689-4244; Email: srsgerth@hotmail.com.
Catechesis Religious Program—Email: srsgerth@hotmail.com. Twinned with St. Maurice Parish, Napoleon. Sisters 1; Students 25.

PAOLI, ORANGE CO., OUR LORD JESUS CHRIST THE KING (1948) Attended from Our Lady of the Springs, French Lick.
Mailing Address: P.O. Box 544, Paoli, 47454. Rev. John Peter Gallagher
Legal Name: Our Lord Jesus Christ the King Catholic Church, Paoli, Inc.
Church: Hwy. 150 E., Paoli, 47454.
Tel: 812-723-3900; Email: christtheking1948@gmail.com.
Catechesis Religious Program—Tel: 812-723-5506. Jim O'Connell, D.R.E. Students 31.

PLAINFIELD, HENDRICKS CO., ST. SUSANNA CATHOLIC CHURCH, PLAINFIELD, INC. (1953) Rev. Glenn L. O'Connor; Deacon Charles J. Giesting.
Res.: 1210 E. Main St., Plainfield, 46168-1797.
Tel: 317-839-3333; Email: info@saintsusanna.com; Web: www.saintsusannachurch.com.
School—St. Susanna Catholic Church, Plainfield, Inc. School, (Grades PreSchool-8), 1212 E. Main St., Plainfield, 46168. Tel: 317-839-3713; Fax: 317-838-7718; Email: info@saintsusanna.com. Michele Tillery, Prin. Lay Teachers 25; Students 225.
Catechesis Religious Program—Tel: 317-838-7722; Email: keffron@saintsusanna.com. Kevin Effron, C.R.E. Students 450.

RICHMOND, WAYNE CO., ST. ELIZABETH ANN SETON CATHOLIC CHURCH, RICHMOND, INC. (1846) [JC]
Email: seas@setonparishes.org. Rev. Kevin Morris; Deacons James Miller; Frank Roberts.
Res.: 720 A North St., Richmond, 47374.
Church: 235 S. 5th St., Richmond, 47374-5418.
Parish Center & Mailing Address: 240 S. 6th St., Richmond, 47374. Tel: 765-962-3902; Fax: 765-966-0820; Email: rcco@richmondcatholiccommunity.com.
School—St. Elizabeth Ann Seton aka Seton Catholic Schools, (Grades PreK-6), 801 W. Main St., 700 North A St., Richmond, 47374. Tel: 765-962-4877; Tel: 765-962-5010; Email: kbecker@setonschools.org. Kimberley Becker, Prin. Lay Teachers 17; Students 253.
See Seton Catholic High School, Richmond under High Schools, Inter-Parochial in the Institution section.

Catechesis Religious Program—Marcy Valentini, C.R.E. Students 106.

ROCKVILLE, PARKE CO., ST. JOSEPH CATHOLIC CHURCH, ROCKVILLE, INC. (1867) [CEM] Rev. Varghese Maliakkal.
Res.: 201 E. Ohio St., Rockville, 47872-1898.
Tel: 765-569-5406; Email: stjoerockville@yahoo.com.
Catechesis Religious Program—Tel: 765-597-2474. Twinned with Sacred Heart, Clinton. Students 11.

RUSHVILLE, RUSH CO., ST. MARY CATHOLIC CHURCH, RUSHVILLE, INC. (1857) [CEM] Very Rev. Jeremy M. Gries, V.F.
Res.: 512 N. Perkins St., Rushville, 46173-1692.
Tel: 765-932-2588; Email: frgries@stmaryrush.org; Email: dspaeth@stmaryrush.org.
School—St. Mary Catholic Church, Rushville, Inc. School, (Grades PreK-6), 226 E. 5th St., Rushville, 46173. Tel: 765-932-3639; Fax: 765-938-1322; Email: dspaeth@stmaryrush.org; Web: www.stmaryrush.org. Janna Stonebraker, Prin. Lay Teachers 7; Students 118.
Catechesis Religious Program—Students 100.

ST. ANN, JENNINGS CO., ST. ANN CATHOLIC CHURCH, JENNINGS COUNTY, INC. (1841) [CEM] Attended from St. Joseph, North Vernon.
Mailing Address: 629 Clay St., North Vernon, 47265.
Tel: 812-346-4783. Rev. Jerry L. Byrd, M.A., M.Div.; Deacon Lawrence French.
Church: 4570 N. County Rd. 150 E., North Vernon, 47265-7564. Tel: 812-346-3604; Fax: 812-346-3506; Email: sharlot01@gmail.com; Web: www.stjoefourcorners.org.
Catechesis Religious Program—Students 19.

ST. CROIX, PERRY CO.

1—HOLY CROSS CATHOLIC CHURCH, ST. CROIX, INC. (1860) [CEM]
Mailing Address: 12239 State Rd. 62, St. Croix, 47576-9999. Tel: 812-843-5701; Email: staughc@psci.net. Rev. Brian G. Esarey.
Res.: 18020 Lafayette St., Leopold, 47551.
Tel: 317-625-6329; Web: www.catholic-church.org/holycrossparish.
Catechesis Religious Program—Students 25.

2—ST. ISIDORE THE FARMER (1968) [CEM] St. John, (1875), and St. Joseph, (1891), Perry Co., were closed, merged and renamed St. Isidore in 1968.
6501 St. Isidore Rd., P.O. Box 54, Bristow, 47515.
Tel: 812-843-5713; Email: saintisidore@psci.net. Rev. Luke Waugh, O.S.B., Admin.
Legal Name: St. Isidore the Farmer Catholic Church, Bristow, Inc.
Catechesis Religious Program—Students 71.

ST. JOSEPH, JENNINGS CO., ST. JOSEPH CATHOLIC CHURCH, JENNINGS COUNTY, INC. (1850) [CEM 2]
Mailing Address: 629 Clay St., North Vernon, 47265.
Tel: 812-346-4783; Fax: 812-352-9033; Email: sharlot01@gmail.com; Web: www.stjoefourcorners.org. Rev. Jerry L. Byrd, M.A., M.Div.; Deacon Lawrence French.
Church: 1875 S. County Rd. 700 W., North Vernon, 47265.
Catechesis Religious Program—Students 45.

ST. MARK, PERRY CO., ST. MARK'S CATHOLIC CHURCH, PERRY COUNTY, INC. (1863) [CEM] [JC] (German) Very Rev. Dennis M. Duvelius, V.F.
Res.: 5377 Acorn Rd., Tell City, 47586-9738.
Tel: 812-836-2481; Email: stmark@psci.net.
Catechesis Religious Program—Students 32.

ST. MARY-OF-THE-KNOBS, FLOYD CO., ST. MARY-OF-THE-KNOBS (1823) [CEM] Rev. H. Michael Hilderbrand, M.A., M.Div., M.S., Ed.S.
Legal Name: St. Mary-of-the-Knobs Catholic Church, Floyds Knobs, Inc.
Res.: 3033 Martin Rd., Floyds Knobs, 47119-9107.
Tel: 812-923-3011; Email: frmike@twc.com.
School—St. Mary-of-the-Knobs School, (Grades PreSchool-6), Tel: 812-923-3011; Email: frmike@twc.com. Tracy Jansen, Prin. Students 207.
Catechesis Religious Program—Students 192.

ST. MARY-OF-THE-WOODS, VIGO CO., ST. MARY-OF-THE-WOODS CATHOLIC CHURCH, INC. (1837) [CEM]
Mailing Address: 3827 N. Arms Pl., P.O. Box 155, St. Mary of the Woods, 47876-0155. Tel: 812-535-1261; Email: jslobigsp@aol.com; Web: stmarysvillagechurch.org. Revs. Daniel E. Bedel, B.A., M.Div., Mod.; Darvin E. Winters, Sacramental Min.; Sr. Joan Slobig, S.P., Parish Life Coord.
Catechesis Religious Program—Email: mamabird82@hotmail.com. Diana Bird, C.R.E. Students 55.

ST. MEINRAD, SPENCER CO., ST. MEINRAD CATHOLIC CHURCH, INC. (1854) [CEM]
Mailing Address: P.O. Box 8, St. Meinrad, 47577. Rev. Anthony Vinson, O.S.B., Admin.
Church: 19630 N. 4th St., St. Meinrad, 47577.
Tel: 812-357-5533; Fax: 812-357-2862; Email: smeinrad@psci.net.
Catechesis Religious Program—Students 47.

ST. NICHOLAS, RIPLEY CO., ST. NICHOLAS CATHOLIC CHURCH, SUNMAN, INC. (1836) [CEM]
6461 E. St. Nicholas Dr., Sunman, 47041.

Tel: 812-623-2964; Fax: 812-623-0066; Email: parishoffice@stanthonymorris.org. Rev. Shaun P. Whittington.
School—St. Nicholas Catholic Church, Sunman, Inc. School, (Grades K-8), 6459 E. St. Nicholas Dr., Sunman, 47041. Tel: 812-623-2348; Email: Principal@stnicholas-sunman.org. Sherri Kirschner, Prin.; Lisa Weisbrod, School Sec.; Annette Rees, Librarian. Lay Teachers 9; Students 139.
Catechesis Religious Program—Renee Jackson, D.R.E. Students 51.

ST. PETER, FRANKLIN CO., ST. PETER CATHOLIC CHURCH, FRANKLIN COUNTY, INC. (1838) [CEM] (German) Rev. Vincent P. Lampert.
Res.: 1207 East Rd., Brookville, 47012-9365.
Tel: 765-647-5462; Email: stpeter@etczone.com.
Catechesis Religious Program—Tel: 812-623-4051. Students 76.

ST. PETER, HARRISON CO.

ST. VINCENT DE PAUL, SHELBY CO., ST. VINCENT DE PAUL (1837) [CEM] Very Rev. Michael T. Keucher, M.A., M.Div., V.F., Sacramental Min.; Sr. Joan Miller, O.S.F., Parish Life Coord.
Legal Name: St. Vincent De Paul Catholic Church, Shelby County, Inc.
Res.: 4218 E. Michigan Rd., Shelbyville, 46176-9242.
Tel: 317-398-4028; Email: stvincent4218@gmail.com.
Catechesis Religious Program—Tel: 317-392-3879; Fax: 317-392-3879. Students 57.

SALEM, WASHINGTON CO., ST. PATRICK CATHOLIC CHURCH, SALEM, INC. (1942) [CEM]
208 S. Shelby St., P.O. Box 273, Salem, 47167-0273.
Tel: 812-752-3693; Email: amartyrs@Frontier.com. Rev. Joseph L. Villa.
Catechesis Religious Program—Tel: 812-883-3589. Students 21.

SCOTTSBURG, SCOTT CO., CHURCH OF THE AMERICAN MARTYRS, SCOTTSBURG, INC. (1938)
270 S. Bond St., Scottsburg, 47170-2009.
Tel: 812-752-3693; Fax: 812-752-0969; Email: amartyrs@frontier.com; Web: www.amartyrs.org. Rev. Joseph L. Villa.
Parish Office & Mailing Address: 262 W. Cherry St., Scottsburg, 47170-2013.
Catechesis Religious Program—Students 29.

SELLERSBURG, CLARK CO., ST. JOHN PAUL II CATHOLIC CHURCH, SELLERSBURG, INC. (2014) [CEM] Rev. Thomas E. Clegg.
Church - St. Paul Campus: 216 Schellers Ave., Sellersburg, 47172-1241. Tel: 812-246-3522; Email: bsmith@stjohnpaulparish.org; Web: www.stjohnpaulparish.org.
School—St. John Paul II Catholic School, (Grades K-6), 105 St. Paul St., Sellersburg, 47172.
Tel: 812-246-3266; Fax: 812-246-7632; Email: office@stjohnpaulschool.org; Web: www.stjohnpaulschool.org. Karen Haas, Prin. Lay Teachers 19; Students 364.
Catechesis Religious Program—Tel: 812-246-2512; Email: kseipel@stjohnpaulparish.org. Kristina Seipel, D.R.E. Students 110.

SEYMOUR, JACKSON CO., ST. AMBROSE CATHOLIC CHURCH, SEYMOUR, INC. (1860) [CEM] Very Rev. Daniel J. Staublin, V.F.; Deacons John D. Cord; Michael East.
Res.: 325 S. Chestnut St., Seymour, 47274-2329.
Tel: 812-522-5304; Email: saintambrosebulletin@gmail.com.
School—St. Ambrose Catholic Church, Seymour, Inc. School, (Grades PreK-8), 301 S. Chestnut St., Seymour, 47274. Tel: 812-522-3522; Email: saintambrosebulletin@gmail.com. Michelle Neibert-Levine, Prin. Lay Teachers 13; Students 155.
Catechesis Religious Program—Tel: 812-522-2686; Tel: 812-522-5304, Ext. 322. Students 145.
Mission—Our Lady of Providence (1934) Merged 325 S. Chestnut St., Brownstown, Jackson Co. 47274.

SHELBYVILLE, SHELBY CO., ST. JOSEPH CATHOLIC CHURCH, SHELBYVILLE, INC. (1868) [CEM] [JC]
125 E. Broadway, Shelbyville, 46176-1498.
Tel: 317-398-8227; Email: rebecca@sjsshelbyville.org; Web: www.stjoeshelby.org. 228 E. Hendricks St., Shelbyville, 46176-1498. Very Rev. Michael T. Keucher, M.A., M.Div., V.F.; Deacon Thomas Hill.
Res.: 220 E. Hendricks St., Shelbyville, 46176-1498.
School—St. Joseph Catholic Church, Shelbyville, Inc. School, (Grades PreK-5), 127 E. Broadway, Shelbyville, 46176. Tel: 317-398-4202; Fax: 317-398-0270; Email: office@sjsshelbyville.org. James Tush, Prin. Lay Teachers 10; Students 129.
Catechesis Religious Program—Tel: 317-398-8227; Fax: 866-988-7561; Email: rebecca@sjsshelbyville.org; Web: www.stjosephshelby.org. Students 230.

SPENCER, OWEN CO., ST. JUDE CATHOLIC CHURCH, SPENCER, INC. (1951)
300 W. Hillside Ave., P.O. Box 317, Spencer, 47460-0317. Tel: 812-829-3082; Fax: 812-829-0888; Email: stjudespencer@sbcglobal.net. Rev. Daniel J. Mahan.
Catechesis Religious Program—Students 30.

STARLIGHT, CLARK CO., ST. JOHN THE BAPTIST CATHOLIC CHURCH, STARLIGHT, INC. (1861) [CEM] [JC] (German) Very Rev. Wilfred E. Day, V.F., Admin.
Legal Name: St. John the Baptist Catholic Church, Starlight, Inc.
Res.: 8310 St. John Rd., Floyds Knobs, 47119-8545.
Tel: 812-923-5785; Fax: 812-923-2015; Email: stjohnstarligth@aol.com; Web: www.stjohnstarlight.org.
Catechesis Religious Program—Students 68.

TELL CITY, PERRY CO., ST. PAUL CATHOLIC CHURCH, TELL CITY, INC. (1859) [CEM] Very Rev. Dennis M. Duvelius, V.F.; Rev. Sengole Thomas Gnanaraj, (India) V.F., In Res.; Deacon Kenneth C. Smith.
Parish Office: Catholic Ministry Center, 824 Jefferson St., Tell City, 47586. Tel: 812-547-7994; Email: stpaulch@psci.net.
Church: 814 Jefferson St., Tell City, 47586.
Tel: 812-547-9901.
Catechesis Religious Program—Tel: 812-547-7102. Students 252.

TERRE HAUTE, VIGO CO.

1—ST. BENEDICT CATHOLIC CHURCH, TERRE HAUTE, INC. (1865) [JC] (German) Very Rev. Martin Day, O.F.M.Conv., V.F.
Church & Parish Office: 111 S. Ninth St., Terre Haute, 47807-3711. Tel: 812-232-8421; Email: pastor@stbenedictth.org.
Catechesis Religious Program—(pre-grade 8) 77.
Mission—St. Benedict Soup Kitchen, 128 S. 9th St., Terre Haute, Vigo Co. 47807. Tel: 812-238-9109; Email: terran@stbenedictth.org.

2—ST. JOSEPH UNIVERSITY CATHOLIC CHURCH (1837) [JC] Revs. Savio Manavalan; Cyprian Uline, O.F.M.Conv.
Legal Name: St. Joseph University Catholic Church, Terre Haute, Inc.
Res.: 118 S. 9th St., Terre Haute, 47807.
Tel: 812-232-5075; Web: www.stjoeup.org.
Church & Mailing Address: 113 S. 5th St., Terre Haute, 47807-3577. Tel: 812-232-7011; Email: parishoffice@stjoeup.org.
Catechesis Religious Program—Email: reled@stjoeup.org. Joint Program H.S. (5 parishes) 179; (Pre-school-8th) 113.

3—ST. MARGARET MARY (1920) [JC]
Mailing Address: 2405 S. Seventh St., Terre Haute, 47802-3599. Tel: 812-232-3512; Email: mcoad@smmth.org; Email: bdetamore@saintpat.org; Web: www.smmth.org. Rev. Daniel E. Bedel, B.A., M.Div.; Deacon Michael Stratman; Mr. Jerry Moorman, Pastoral Assoc.
Legal Name: St. Margaret Mary Catholic Church, Terre Haute, Inc.
Res.: 2421 S. Seventh St., Terre Haute, 47802.
Catechesis Religious Program—Email: dre@saintpat.org. Jillian Vandermarks, D.R.E. Students 58.

4—ST. PATRICK CATHOLIC CHURCH, TERRE HAUTE, INC. (1881) Rev. Daniel E. Bedel, B.A., M.Div.; Deacon Michael Stratman; Brittany Detamore, Business Mgr.
Church: 1807 Poplar St., Terre Haute, 47803-2196.
Tel: 812-232-8518; Email: dbedel@saintpat.org.
School—St. Patrick Catholic Church, Terre Haute, Inc. School, (Grades PreK-8), 449 S. 19th St., Terre Haute, 47803. Tel: 812-232-2157; Fax: 812-478-9384; Email: dbedel@saintpat.org. Patty Mauer, Prin.; Dallas Wright, Asst. Prin. Lay Teachers 23; Students 344.
Catechesis Religious Program—Students 74.

5—SACRED HEART OF JESUS (1924) Revs. Daniel E. Bedel, B.A., M.Div., Mod.; Darvin E. Winters, Sacramental Min.; Barbara Black, Parish Life Coord.
Legal Name: Sacred Heart of Jesus Catholic Church, Terre Haute, Inc.
Res.: 2322 N. 13 1/2 St., Terre Haute, 47804-2498.
Tel: 812-466-1231; Email: secretary@shjth.org.
Catechesis Religious Program—Students 70.

TROY, PERRY CO., ST. PIUS V CATHOLIC CHURCH, TROY, INC. (1849) [CEM 2] Rev. Sengole Thomas Gnanaraj, (India) V.F.
Parish Office & Mailing Address: Catholic Ministry Center, 824 Jefferson St., Tell City, 47586.
Tel: 812-547-7994; Email: st.piuschurch@yahoo.com.
Church: State Rd. 66, Troy, 47588.
Catechesis Religious Program—Students 51.

VEVAY, SWITZERLAND CO., MOST SORROWFUL MOTHER OF GOD (1876)
Ferry Street, P.O. Box 257, Vevay, 47043.
Tel: 812-265-4166; Fax: 812-273-3427; Email: parishoffice@popeace.org. Rev. Christopher A. Craig; Deacon Michael Gardner
Legal Name: Most Sorrowful Mother of God Catholic Church, Vevay, Inc.
Church: 513 Ferry St., Vevay, 47043.

Chaplains of Public Institutions

INDIANAPOLIS. *Indianapolis Fire Department*. Rev. John P. McCaslin, M.A., M.Div.
Indianapolis International Airport. Rev. Glenn L. O'Connor.
Indianapolis Metropolitan Police Department. Rev. Steven C. Schwab, (Retired).
Indiana University Health Methodist Hospital. Rev. Emmanuel C. Nyong.
Veterans' Administration Hospital. Rev. Charles Smith, S.V.D.

PUTNAMVILLE. *Putnamville Correctional Facility*. Rev. John J. Hollowell.

RICHMOND. *Richmond State Hospital*. Rev. Kevin Morris.

On Special or Other Archdiocesan Assignment:
Revs.—
Bramlage, Gregory D., Diocese of Colorado Springs, CO for Missionary Ministry
Kappes, Christiaan W., Byzantine Seminary, Pittsburg, PA
Porter, Jack W., Archdiocesan Historian, (Retired)
Wysciskalla, Timothy M., Pontifical North American College, Rome.

Retired:
Rev. Msgrs.—
Easton, Frederick C., (Retired), 3315 S. Commons Dr., Bloomington, 47401
Knueven, Harold L., (Retired), 1602 Conwell St., Connersville, 47331
Moran, Lawrence J., (Retired), P.O. Box 10099, Terre Haute, 47801
Richart, Paul F., (Retired), 7360 W. Pedora School Rd., Eckerty, 47116
Riedman, Joseph G., (Retired), 1413 Westwood Blvd., Connersville, 47331
Revs.—
Ashmore, Ronald M., (Retired), 5315 N. 14 1/2 St., Terre Haute, 47805
Atkins, J. Daniel, (Retired), 2800 Charlestown Rd., New Albany, 47150
Beitans, John, (Retired), 2905 S. Carson Ave., 46203
Bonke, James R., J.C.L., (Retired), 600 N. Alabama St., Ste. 1000, 46204
Bryan, Francis E., (Retired), 488 North 24th Ave., Beech Grove, 46107
Buchanan, Donald E., LCDR, CHC, USN, (Retired), P.O. Box 367, Austin, 47102-0367
Cox, Bernard, (Retired), 1375 Legendary Blvd., Clermont, FL 34711
Dede, Paul M., (Retired), 2442 Stonelake Cir., Bloomington, 47404
Denison, Frederick J., (Retired), 50 Lonnie Lawson Ct., Brandenburg, KY 40108
Donohoo, Daniel B., M.A., M.Div., (Retired), St. Patrick Seminary, Menlo Park, CA
Eckstein, Francis J., (Retired), 10325 N. St. Nicholas Rd., Sunman, 47041
Ernst, William W., (Retired), 1118 Creekview Cir., New Albany, 47150
Fink, John L., (Retired), 220 Sky Park Dr., Corydon, 47112
Geis, John F., (Retired), 853 N. County Rd., 950 E., Greensburg, 47240
Godecker, Jeffrey H., (Retired), 5353 E. 56th St., 46226
Hartzer, John, (Retired), 909 Ridge Ave., Lawrenceburg, 47025
Herber, Stanley J., M.A., V.F., (Retired), St. Paul Hermitage, 501 N. 17th St., Beech Grove, 46107
Hulsman, Paul E., (Retired), 7402 Lasane Dr., Louisville, KY 40214
Jarrell, Stephen T., (Retired), 5548 Greenhill Pl., Apt. G, 46237
Kirkhoff, Gerald J., V.F., (Retired), 6745 Valley Brooke Way, 46237
Landwerlen, Paul E., (Retired), 2479 McKay Rd., Shelbyville, 46176
Lawler, David J., (Retired), 7426 Lionshead Dr., 46260
Luerman, John H., (Retired), 823 S.W. 15th St., Richmond, 47374
Lutz, Herman, (Retired), St. Paul Hermitage, 501 N. 17th Ave., Beech Grove, 46107-1196
Mader, Joseph E., (Retired), 315 S. Flagler Dr., Rm. 317, Palm Beach, FL 33401
Manna, Louis M., (Retired), 217 Maplewood Dr., Clarksville, 47129
Maung, John S., (Retired), 4524 Wentworth Blvd., 46201
Munshower, William G., (Retired), 1123 Edmonson Ave., Bldg. 1, Apt. 29A, 46219
Peter, Martin A., (Retired), 12935 Sawmill Rd., Columbus, 47201
Porter, Jack W., (Retired), St. Paul Hermitage, 501 N. 17th Ave., Beech Grove, 46107-1196
Rautenberg, Joseph F., (Retired), 1052 Lincoln Park E. Dr., Greenwood, 46142
Richardt, J. Lawrence, M.A., S.T.L., (Retired), 1223 N. Edmonson Ave. C1, 46219
Rightor, Harold W. II, (Retired), 2850 S. Holt St., 46241

Ripperger, William, (Retired), Magnolia Springs, 8225 Whipps Mill Rd., Louisville, KY 40245
Rodas, Mauro G., (Retired), 4002 Oakfield Dr., 46237
Schafer, Raymond E., (Retired), 7195 New Cut Rd., Scottsburg, 47170
Schwab, Steven C., (Retired), 2833 Thornton Ln., 46268
Sheets, Joseph B., (Retired), 436 Mutton Creek Dr., Seymour, 47274
Stepanski, Thomas K., (Retired), 687 Aspen Ct., Danville, 46122
Turner, William J., (Retired), 7972 W. County Rd. 350 N., St. Paul, 47272
Vogelsang, Clifford R., (Retired), 9140 Cinnebar Dr., 46268
Welch, D. Michael, (Retired), 8905 Stepping Stone Way, Avon, 46123
Wilmoth, James R., V.F., (Retired), St. Paul Hermitage, 501 N. 17th St., Beech Grove, 46107.

Permanent Deacons:
Deacons—
Anderson, Bradley, St. Mary Parish, Greensburg
Bartolowits, David J., St. John the Evangelist Parish, Indianapolis
Beauchamp, Joseph J., St. Ann Parish, Indianapolis
Beyke, Robert J., St. Monica Parish, Indianapolis
Blackwell, Gary M., Holy Name of Jesus Parish, Beech Grove
Blandford, Kerry, Dir., Deacon Formation, St. Andrew the Apostle, Indianapolis
Bower, Patrick, St. Barnabas; Methodist, IU & Riley Hospitals, Indianapolis
Braun, Michael, St. Simon the Apostle Parish, Indianapolis; Community Hospital East, Indianapolis; Community Hospital North & East, Indianapolis; Re-Entry Education Facility, Indianapolis
Chlopecki, John J., (Retired)
Collier, Daniel, St. Malachy, Brownsburg; Indianapolis Women's Correction Facility
Cooper, Richard, St. Mary Parish, Lanesville; hospital, nursing home and bereavement ministry
Cord, John D., St. Ambrose Parish, Seymour
Davis, Wayne, St. Michael, Greenfield; New Castle Correctional Facility
de la Rosa, Wilfredo R., Church of the Holy Angels Parish, Indianapolis
Decker, Robert W., All Saints, Dearborn
East, Michael, Dir., Deacons, St. Ambrose, Seymour; Jackson County Jail
Ferrer-Soto, Emilio, St. Patrick; Wishard Hospital, Indianapolis
Fisherkeller, Paul F., St. Mark the Evangelist Parish, Indianapolis
French, Lawrence, St. Joseph & St. Ann, Jennings County; St. Mary, North Vernon; St. Vincent Hospital, North Vernon; Patriot Academy, Muscatatuck Urban Training Center, Butlerville
Freyer, Ronald, St. Louis Parish, Batesville; hospital and nursing homes
Gardner, Michael, Prince of Peace, Madison; Most Sorrowful Mother of God, Vevay; Madison State Hospital
Giesting, Charles J., St. Susanna Parish, Plainfield
Gretencord, Steven, Sacred Heart Parish, Terre Haute; Ryves Youth Center of Catholic Charities Terre Haute, Terre Haute; U.S. Penitentiary, Terre Haute
Harte, Tim, St. Martin of Tours Parish, Martinsville; Man of Mission Ministry; nursing homes and with the homebound; Habitat for Humanity
Henn, David, St. Jude, Indianapolis; Archdiocese Office of Worship
Hill, Thomas, St. Joseph Parish, Shelbyville; Pregnancy Care Centers of South-Central Indiana; Salvation Army, Bartholomew County
Hodges, Stephen, SS. Peter & Paul Cathedral, Indianapolis; Chaplain for Courage Ministry
Horn, Thomas, Our Lady of Lourdes Parish, Indianapolis
Hosier, John E., Nativity of Our Lord Jesus Christ Parish, Indianapolis
House, Steven, Annapolis, MD
Ignacio, Martin, St. Mary Parish, New Albany
Jackson, Oliver L., St. Rita Parish, Indianapolis
Jacobi, John R., St. Michael Parish, Greenville
Jones, Wesley, Ph.D., (Retired)
Jones, William, St. Bartholomew, Columbus; Substance Addiction Ministry
Kellams, Marc, JD, St. Charles Borromeo, Bloomington; hospitals & nursing homes, Monroe Co.
Klauder, Francis C., (Retired)
Lewis, Anthony E., St. Thomas the Apostle Parish, Fortville
Matthews, Jerome R., St. Barnabas Parish, Indianapolis
McShea, John R., St. Monica Parish, Indianapolis
Miller, James, St. Elizabeth Ann Seton Parish, Richmond; Richmond nursing homes
Morales, Oscar, Marion County Jail #2, Indianapolis; St. Anthony Parish, Indianapolis
Nava, Reynaldo, Our Lady of the Greenwood Parish, Greenwood
Pirau, Ronald, SS. Francis and Clare of Assisi Parish, Greenwood; Johnson County Jail; Dismas Ministry, Johnson County & the south side of Indianapolis
Powell, Jeffrey, Our Lady of Perpetual Help Parish, New Albany; Hospitals and Nursing Homes, Floyd County
Ramirez, Juan Carlos, St. Bartholomew Parish, Columbus
Reimer, Ronald, St. Paul Catholic Center, Bloomington and ministry of charity for the sick and homebound of the parish
Reising, David, St. Vincent de Paul, Bedford; St. Mary, Mitchell; Lawrence County Jail, Bedford
Renzi, Rick, St. Malachy Parish, Brownsburg; Beds and Britches, Etc. program
Roberts, Frank, St. Elizabeth Ann Seton Parish, Richmond; Richmond nursing homes
Scarlett, Matthew T., St. Vincent de Paul Parish, Bedford
Schallert, Nathan C., SS. Peter and Paul Catherdral, Indianapolis
Slinger, Michael, Holy Spirit Parish, Indianapolis; Holy Family Shelter, Indianapolis; Metropolitan Tribunal
Smith, Kenneth C., St. Paul Parish, Tell City
Stratman, Michael, St. Patrick, St. Margaret Mary, Union Hospital, Terre Haute
Thompson, John, St. Augustine Parish, Sacred Heart Parish Jeffersonville; Clark County Jail
Tsuleff, Steven C., St. Teresa Benedict of the Cross Parish, Bright
Wagner, Richard J., St. Pius X Parish, Indianapolis; St. Augustine Home for the Aged, Indianapolis; Helping Our Own People (HOOP)
Ward, Thomas, St. Vincent New Hope, Indianapolis; St. Lawrence Parish, Indianapolis
Woodward, Russell, Holy Trinity, Edinburgh; Edinburgh Correctional Facility.

INSTITUTIONS LOCATED IN DIOCESE

[A] SEMINARIES, RELIGIOUS OR SCHOLASTICATES

INDIANAPOLIS. *Bishop Simon Bruté College Seminary, Inc.*, 2500 Cold Spring Rd., 46222. Tel: 317-924-4100; Fax: 317-924-4140; Email: skuhn@archindy.org. Very Rev. Joseph B. Moriarty, Rector; Rev. Justin DuVall, O.S.B., Vice Rector; Dr. John Cadwallader, Dir. Counseling & Personal Devel.; Revs. Jonathan Fassero, O.S.B., Assoc. Dir. of Spiritual Formation; Andrew W. Syberg, M.A., M.Div., Formation Dean. Clergy 5; Seminarians 43; Clergy / Religious Teachers 5.

SAINT MEINRAD. *Saint Meinrad School of Theology*, 200 Hill Dr., St. Meinrad, 47577. Tel: 812-357-6611; Fax: 812-357-6964; Email: rector@saintmeinrad.edu; Web: www.saintmeinrad.edu. Rev. Denis Robinson, O.S.B., Pres. & Rector; Dr. Robert Alvis, Academic Dean & Assoc. Prof., Church History; Mrs. Lisa Castlebury, Treas. & Business Mgr.; Rev. Tobias Colgan, O.S.B., Vice Rector; Sr. Jeana Visel, O.S.B., Dir. Graduate Theology Programs. School of Theology. Administrators 30; Faculty 10; Students 173; Clergy / Religious Teachers 8; Staff 12.

[B] COLLEGES AND UNIVERSITIES

INDIANAPOLIS. *Marian University* (Coed) 3200 Cold Spring Rd., 46222. Tel: 317-955-6000; Fax: 317-955-6448; Web: www.marian.edu. Mr. Adam Setmeyer, Vice Pres.; Sr. Jean Marie Cleveland, O.S.F., Vice Pres. Mission Effectiveness; Dr. Thomas Enneking, Ph.D., Provost; Daniel J. Elsener, Pres.; Rev. Leopold Keffler, O.F.M.Conv.; Rhonda Huisman, Librarian; Rev. Dr. William Stang, Chap. Sisters of the Third Order Regular of St. Francis. Clergy 4; Lay Teachers 150; Priests 2; Sisters 4; Students 3,527; Clergy / Religious Teachers 4.

SAINT MARY-OF-THE-WOODS. *Saint Mary-of-the-Woods College* (1840) 1 St. Mary of the Woods, St. Mary of the Woods, 47876. Tel: 812-535-5273; Fax: 812-535-5005; Email: mking2@smwc.edu; Web: www.smwc.edu. Dr. Dottie King, Ph.D., Pres.; Judy Tribble, Librarian. Sponsored by the Sisters of Providence, St. Mary-of-the-Woods. Lay Staff 245; Lay Teachers 167; Students 1,120.

[C] HIGH SCHOOLS, INTER-PAROCHIAL

INDIANAPOLIS. *Bishop Chatard High School, Inc.* (1961) 5885 Crittenden Ave., 46220. Tel: 317-251-1451; Fax: 317-254-5427; Email: jhansen@bishopchatard.org; Web: www.bishopchatard.org. William Bill Sahm, Pres.; Deacon Richard J. Wagner, Vice Pres., Mission & Ministry, Prin.; Tyler Mayer, Vice Pres. of Institutional Advancement; Joe Hansen, Prin.; Ann Taylor, Asst. Prin. Deacons 1; Lay Teachers 52; Sisters of St. Benedict 1; Students 700.

Father Thomas Scecina Memorial High School, Inc., 5000 Nowland Ave., 46201-1836. Tel: 317-356-6377; Fax: 317-322-4287; Email: jbrettnacher@scecina.org; Web: www.scecina.org. Mr. Joseph Therber, Pres.; Joe Brettnacher, Prin.; Sr. Sheila Hackett, Librarian; Rev. Aaron M. Jenkins, Chap. Lay Teachers 28; Priests 1; Students 425; Clergy / Religious Teachers 1.

Roncalli High School, Inc., 3300 Prague Rd., 46227. Tel: 317-787-8277; Fax: 317-788-4095; Email: cweisenbach@roncalli.org; Web: www.roncalli.org. Dr. Joseph D. Hollowell, Pres.; Rev. David J. Marcotte, B.A., M.Div., Chap.; Charles Weisenbach, Prin.; Tim Printarelli, Dean of Students; Terese Carson, Vice Pres. for Institutional Advancement; Dave Gervasio, Vice Pres. Finance and Facilities; Bob Tully, Vice Pres.for Missions and Ministry. Lay Teachers 100; Priests 2; Students 1,194.

West Deanery Unified Catholic Schools, Inc. dba Cardinal Ritter High School & St. Michael-St. Gabriel Elementary School, 3360 W. 30th St., 46222. Tel: 317-924-4333; Fax: 317-927-7822; Email: momara@stgabrielindy.org. Matt Hollowell, Prin.; E. Jo Hoy, B.S., M.S., Pres.; Rev. Matthew Tucci, Chap.; Elizabeth Jessen, Librarian. Lay Teachers 50; Students 652.

CLARKSVILLE. *Our Lady of Providence Junior - Senior High School, Inc.*, 707 Providence Way, Clarksville, 47129. Tel: 812-945-2538; Fax: 812-945-3460; Email: mernstberger@providencehigh.net; Web: www.providencehigh.net. Dr. Melinda Ernstberger, Prin.; Mr. Stephen Williamson, Pres.; Rev. Eric Johnson, Chap. Lay Teachers 38; Priests 1; Students 386; Students (9-12) 459; Students (7-12) 518; Clergy / Religious Teachers 1.

MADISON. *Shawe Memorial Junior-Senior High School* (1954) 201 W. State St., Madison, 47250. Tel: 812-273-2150; Fax: 812-273-2013; Email: shaweprincipal@popeace.org. Phil Kahn, Pres.; Steve Hesse, Prin.; Rev. Christopher A. Craig, Chap. Lay Teachers 18; Priests 1; Students 166; Chaplains 1.

RICHMOND. *Seton Catholic High School*, 233 S. 5th St., Richmond, 47374. Tel: 765-965-6956; Fax: 765-966-0820; Email: jmarkward@setoncatholichighschool.org. Rick Ruhl, Pres.; Rev. Kevin Morris, Chap.; John Markward, Prin. Lay Teachers 10; Priests 1; Students 154.

[D] HIGH SCHOOLS, PRIVATE

INDIANAPOLIS. *Brebeuf Jesuit Preparatory School, Inc.* (1962) 2801 W. 86th St., 46268-1926. Tel: 317-524-7050; Fax: 317-524-7142; Email: rgalle@brebeuf.org; Web: www.brebeuf.org. Revs. William Verbryke, S.J., Pres.; Christopher Johnson, Vice Pres.; Greg VanSlambrook, Prin. Society of Jesus Community. Lay Teachers 67; Priests 2; Students 790; Clergy / Religious Teachers 5.

Cathedral High School (Cathedral Trustees, Inc.) (1918) 5225 E. 56th St., 46226. Tel: 317-542-1481; Fax: 317-542-1484; Email: dworland@gocathedral.com; Web: www.gocathedral.com. Robert Bridges, Pres.; David Worland, Prin.; Jennifer Herron, Librarian. Brothers 1; Lay Teachers 97; Sisters 1; Students 1,104.

Providence Cristo Rey High School, Inc., 75 N. Belleview Pl., 46222-4145. Tel: 317-860-1000; Fax: 317-860-1004; Email: info@pcrhs.org; Web: www.pcrhs.org. Dr. Margie Crooks, Pres.; Leslie Napora, Prin. Lay Teachers 10; Students 232.

OLDENBURG. *Oldenburg Academy of the Immaculate Conception*, One Twister Cir., P.O. Box 200, Oldenburg, 47036-0200. Tel: 812-934-4440; Fax: 812-934-4838; Email: dlaake@oldenburgacademy.org; Web: www.oldenburgacademy.org. Diane H. Laake, Pres.; Brian McFee, Prin. Lay Teachers 19; Students 216.

[E] RELIGIOUS EDUCATION CENTERS

SELLERSBURG. *Aquinas Center for Continuing Religious Education*, 2609 W. St. Joe Rd., Sellersburg, 47172. Tel: 812-246-5044; Email: aquinasctr@sbcglobal.net; Web: aquinascenter.org. Ms. Christina Flum, Dir. Catechetical Ministry.

TERRE HAUTE. *Terre Haute Deanery Pastoral Center*, 1801 Poplar St., Terre Haute, 47803. Tel: 812-232-8400; Email: louise@thdeanery.org;

Web: www.thdeanery.org. Louise Meneghini, Admin. Total Staff 1.

[F] GENERAL HOSPITALS

INDIANAPOLIS. *Central Indiana Health System Cardiac Services, Inc.* (1991) 10330 N. Meridian St., 46290. Tel: 317-583-3289; Fax: 317-583-3285. Jonathan Nalli, Chm.

Franciscan Health (1914) Franciscan Health Indianapolis, 8111 S. Emerson Ave., 46237. Tel: 317-528-5000; Tel: 317-834-1160; Fax: 317-528-6696; Fax: 317-831-9315; Email: James.Callaghan@franciscanalliance.org; Web: www.franciscanalliance.org. Dr. James Callaghan, B.S., M.B.A., M.D., Pres. & CEO; Sr. Marcene Franz, B.Ed., M.Ed., Vice Pres., Mission Integration Svcs.; Revs. Mike O. Onwuegbuzie, B.D., M.Ed., M.Admin., Chap.; George F. Plaster, M.Div., Chap.; Michael E. Burns, S.D.S., M.Div., M.A.R., Chap.; Thomas Perrin, Chap. Franciscan Alliance Bassinets 55; Bed Capacity 600; Priests 4; Sisters 4; Tot Asst. Annually 463,213; Total Staff 4,320.

Franciscan Health Mooresville, 1201 Hadley Rd., Mooresville, 46158. Tel: 574-254-6273; Fax: 574-257-8669; Web: www.franciscanalliance.org.

St. Vincent Hospital and Health Care Center, Inc. (1884) 2001 West 86th St., 46260. Tel: 317-583-3289; Fax: 317-583-3285; Web: www.stvincent.org. Cheryl Harmon, Pres.; Rev. Ben Okonkwo, Chap.; Deacon Rick Renzi, Chap.; Lucia Hamilton, Dir. Daughters of Charity of St. Vincent de Paul. Bed Capacity 833; Tot Asst. Annually 49,814; Total Staff 4,669.

St. Vincent Seton Specialty Hospital, Inc., 8050 Township Line Rd., 46260. Tel: 317-415-8500. Penny Harper, Dir.

BEDFORD. *St. Vincent Dunn Hospital Inc.*, 1600 23rd St., Bedford, 47421. Tel: 812-275-3331; Fax: 812-276-1265; Web: www.stvincent.org. Jerry R. Laue, Admin. Bed Capacity 25; Tot Asst. Annually 4,080; Total Staff 84.

BRAZIL. **St. Vincent Clay Hospital, Inc.* (A member of St. Vincent Health & Ascension Health.) 1206 E. National Ave., P.O. Box 489, Brazil, 47834. Tel: 812-442-2500; Fax: 812-442-2605. Jerry R. Laue, Admin. Bed Capacity 25; Tot Asst. Annually 3,419; Total Staff 65.

NORTH VERNON. *St. Vincent Jennings Hospital Foundation, Inc.*, 301 Henry St., North Vernon, 47265. Tel: 812-352-4200; Fax: 812-352-4201; Email: noemail@donotpublish.com. Joseph B. Ford, Admin.

**St. Vincent Jennings Hospital, Inc.* (A member of St. Vincent Health & Ascension Health.) 301 Henry St., North Vernon, 47265. Tel: 812-352-4200; Fax: 812-352-4201. Dana Muntz, Admin. Bed Capacity 17; Tot Asst. Annually 4,775; Total Staff 54.

SALEM. *St. Vincent Salem Hospital, Inc.*, 911 N. Shelby St., Salem, 47167. Tel: 812-883-5881; Fax: 812-883-8563. Dana Muntz, Admin. Bed Capacity 25; Tot Asst. Annually 3,084; Total Staff 72.

[G] PROTECTIVE INSTITUTIONS

TERRE HAUTE. *Gibault Children's Services*, 6401 S. U.S. Hwy. 41, Terre Haute, 47802. Tel: 812-299-1156; Fax: 812-298-3044; Email: gibault@gibault.org; Web: www.gibault.org. Michele Madley, M.S., L.M.H.C., C.C.B.T., C.C.T.P., Pres. & CEO. Residential treatment facility for males and females between the ages of 6 and 21, sponsored by the Knights of Columbus of Indiana. Bed Capacity 114; Tot Asst. Annually 164; Total Staff 244; Licensed Youth 114.

[H] HOMES FOR AGED

INDIANAPOLIS. *St. Augustine Home, Little Sisters of the Poor* (1873) 2345 W. 86th St., 46260. Tel: 317-415-5767; Fax: 317-415-6282; Email: 'bkindianapolis@littlesistersofthepoor.org. Sr. Francis Gabriel, L.S.P., Dir. Bed Capacity 96; Residents 96; Sisters 8; Tot Asst. Annually 121; Total Staff 122.

BEECH GROVE. *St. Paul Hermitage, LLC*, 501 N. 17th Ave., Beech Grove, 46107. Tel: 317-786-2261; Fax: 317-782-1411; Email: administrator@stpaulhermitage.org. Sr. Rebecca Marie Fitterer, O.S.B., Admin.; Revs. Herman Lutz, In Res., (Retired); Jack W. Porter, Ph.D., M.A., In Res.; James Wilmoth, V.F., In Res.; Stanley J. Herber, M.A., V.F., In Res., (Retired)

Sisters of St. Benedict of Beech Grove, Ind., Inc. Bed Capacity 109; Residents 98; Sisters 4; Tot Asst. Annually 105; Total Staff 100.

NEW ALBANY. *Providence Retirement Home Auxiliary, Inc.*, 4915 Charlestown Rd., New Albany, 47150. Tel: 812-535-4001. Sr. Suzanne Dailey, S.P., Admin.

[I] RETREAT HOUSES

INDIANAPOLIS. **Our Lady of Fatima Retreat House, Inc.* (1950) 5353 E. 56th St., 46226. Tel: 317-545-7681; Fax: 317-545-0095; Email: fatima@archindy.org; Web: www.archindy.org/fatima. Georgene Beiriger, Dir. Used by both clergy and laity. Priests 1; Total Staff 20; Served 10,000.

BEECH GROVE. *Benedict Inn Retreat & Conference Center* (1981) 1402 Southern Ave., Beech Grove, 46107-1197. Tel: 317-788-7581; Fax: 317-782-3142; Email: benedictinn@benedictinn.org; Web: www.benedictinn.org. Sr. Carol Falkner, O.S.B., Admin. Retreats and workshops for clergy, religious, and laity. Sisters 3.

MOUNT SAINT FRANCIS. *Mount Saint Francis Friary and Retreat Center* (1896) 101 St. Anthony Dr., Mount St. Francis, 47146-9999. Tel: 812-923-8817; Fax: 812-923-0177; Email: retreats@mountsaintfrancis; Web: mountsaintfrancis.org. Revs. Wayne Hellmann, O.F.M.Conv., Prof., St. Louis Univ.; Kenneth Davis, O.F.M.Conv. Total in Residence 15; Total Staff 9. In Res. Deacon Nicholas Wolfla, O.F.M.Conv., J.C.L., Province Sec. & Judge, Metropolitan Tribunal of Louisville; Revs. Regis Schlagheck, O.F.M.Conv., Prov. Treas.; John Bamman, O.F.M.Conv., Vocation Dir.; Bros. Robert Baxter, O.F.M.Conv., Guardian & Dir. Retreats; Paul Clark, O.F.M.Conv., Province Sec.; Revs. Maurus Hauer, O.F.M.Conv.; Ken Bartsch, O.F.M.Conv.; Bro. Dennes Moses, O.F.M.Conv.; Revs. John Elmer, O.F.M.Conv.; David Lenz, O.F.M.Conv.; Kenneth Gering, O.F.M.Conv.; Pius Poff, O.F.M.Conv.; Leopold Keffler, O.F.M.Conv.

Province of Our Lady of Consolation, Inc., 101 St. Anthony Dr., Mount Saint Francis, 47146. Tel: 812-923-8444; Fax: 812-923-8145; Email: secretaryolc@franciscansusa.org. Very Rev. James Kent, O.F.M.Conv., Prov.; Friar Mark Weaver, O.F.M.Conv., Vicar Prov.; Deacon Nicholas Wolfla, O.F.M.Conv., J.C.L., Province Sec. (Provincial Office).

SAINT MEINRAD. *Archabbey Guest House & Retreat Center*, 200 Hill Dr., St. Meinrad, 47577. Tel: 812-357-6585; Tel: 800-581-6905; Fax: 812-357-6841; Email: mzoeller@saintmeinrad.edu; Web: www.saintmeinrad.edu. Bro. Maurus Zoeller, O.S.B., Retreat Dir. & Guest Master. Retreat House for Men, Women, Couples Rooms 31.

[J] MONASTERIES AND RESIDENCES OF PRIESTS AND BROTHERS

BLOOMINGTON. *Marian Friary of Our Lady Coredemptrix, Franciscans of the Immaculate*, 8212 W. Hendricks Rd., Bloomington, 47403. Tel: 812-825-4742; Fax: 812-825-6742; Email: ffi.bloomington@gmail.com. Rev. Ignatius Manfredonia, F.I., Father Guardian; Friars Roderic Mary Burke, F.I.; Gabriel Francis Mary Cortes, F.I., Vicar Econom. Brothers 2; Priests 2.

MOUNT SAINT FRANCIS. *Provincial Headquarters, Our Lady of Consolation Province, Conventual Franciscans*, 101 Anthony Dr., Mount St. Francis, 47146. Tel: 812-923-8444; Fax: 812-923-8145; Email: secretaryolc@franciscansusa.org; Web: www.franciscansusa.org. Very Rev. James Kent, O.F.M.Conv., Prov.; Deacon Nicholas Wolfla, O.F.M.Conv., J.C.L., Province Sec.

Province of Our Lady of Consolation Brothers 29; Deacons 1; Novices 3; Postulants 1; Priests 67. *Development Office*, 101 St. Anthony Dr., Mount St. Francis, 47146. Tel: 812-923-5250; Fax: 812-923-3200; Email: noemail@donotpublish.com. Rev. John Elmer, O.F.M.Conv., Devel. Spiritual Dir. Priests 1; Total Staff 6. *Vocation Office - Our Lady of Consolation Province*, Tel: 502-933-4439; Fax: 502-933-7747. Revs. John Bamman, O.F.M.Conv., Dir., Vocation, St. Francis of Assisi Friary, 2225 Lower Hunters Trace, Louisville, KY 40216. Tel: 502-447-5566; Andrew Martinez, O.F.M.Conv., Assoc. Vocation Dir. Priests 2; Total Staff 3. *Curia Generalizia*.

SAINT MEINRAD. *St. Meinrad Archabbey* (1854) 100 Hill Dr., St. Meinrad, 47577. Tel: 812-357-6611; Fax: 812-357-6551; Email: abbot@saintmeinrad.edu; Web: www.saintmeinrad.org. Revs. Denis Robinson, O.S.B., Rector; Brendan Moss, O.S.B., M.Div., Rector; Very Rev. Godfrey Mullen, O.S.B., Rector; Rev. Kurt Stasiak, O.S.B., Abbot, (Retired); Very Rev. John McMullen, O.S.B., Prior; Revs. Guerric DeBona, O.S.B., Subprior; Raymond Studzinski, O.S.B., Admin.; Peduru Fonseka, Coord.; Ephrem Carr, O.S.B., Prof.; Patrick Cooney, O.S.B., J.C.L., Vicar; Matthias Neuman, O.S.B., Chap.; Mark O'Keefe, O.S.B., Chap.; Aurelius Boberek, O.S.B.; Meinrad Brune, O.S.B.; Adrian Burke, O.S.B., V.F., P.O. Box 8, Saint Meinrad, 47577. Tel: 812-357-5533; Fax: 812-357-2862; Bede Cisco, O.S.B., St. Michael Parish, 3354 W. 30th St., 46222; Tobias Colgan, O.S.B.; Joseph Cox, O.S.B.; Augustine Davis, O.S.B.; Justin Duvall, O.S.B.; Jonathan Fassero, O.S.B.; Colman Grabert, O.S.B.; Thomas Gricoski, O.S.B.; Louis Hacker, O.S.B.; Harry Hagan, O.S.B.; Warren Heitz, O.S.B.; Eugene Hensell, O.S.B.; Sean Hoppe, O.S.B., St. Augustine Church, General Delivery, Leopold, 47551; Jeremy King, O.S.B.; Pius Klein, O.S.B., St. Mary Rectory, 313 Washington St., Huntingburg, 47542; Rt. Rev. Bonaventure Knaebel, O.S.B.; Revs. Micheas Langston, O.S.B.; Sebastian Leonard, O.S.B., Canterbury School, Aspetuck Ave., New Milford, CT 06776; Edward Linton, O.S.B.; Guy Mansini, O.S.B.; Benedict Meyer, O.S.B.; Noel Mueller, O.S.B.; Louis Mulcahy, O.S.B.; Paul Nord, O.S.B.; Julian Peters, O.S.B.; Denis Quinkert, O.S.B.; Christian Raab, O.S.B.; David Rabenecker, O.S.B.; Rt. Rev. Lambert Reilly, O.S.B.; Revs. Germain Swisshelm, O.S.B.; Vincent Tobin, O.S.B.; Anthony Vinson, O.S.B.; Luke Waugh, O.S.B.; Samuel Weber, O.S.B. Archabbey of the Order of St. Benedict, including School of Theology (St. Meinrad Seminary). Brothers 28; Priests 50.

[K] CONVENTS AND RESIDENCES FOR SISTERS

INDIANAPOLIS. *Servants of the Gospel of Life, Inc.*, 7575 Holliday Dr. E., 46260. Tel: 317-509-3256; Email: dcarollo@stluke.org. Sr. Diane Carollo, S.G.L., Sister Servant. Sisters 1.

Missionaries of Charity, 2424 E. 10th St., 46201. Tel: 317-916-6753. Sisters M. Jonathan, Regl. Supr.; M. Salvinette, M.C., Supr. Sisters 4.

BEECH GROVE. *Our Lady of Grace Monastery*, 1402 Southern Ave., Beech Grove, 46107-1197. Tel: 317-787-3287; Fax: 317-780-2368; Email: olgprioress@benedictine.com; Web: www.benedictine.com. Sr. Jennifer Mechtild Horner, O.S.B., Prioress

Sisters of St. Benedict of Beech Grove, Ind., Inc. Sisters 53. 1414 Southern Ave., Beech Grove, 46107-1197. Tel: 317-786-0338; Fax: 317-780-2368; Email: mneuman204@att.net. Rev. Matthias Neuman, O.S.B., Chap. Sisters 58.

GREENWOOD. *F.I.H. Convent - Franciscan Sisters of the Immaculate Heart of Mary* (1998) 345 S. Meridian St., Greenwood, 46143. Tel: 317-865-6013; Fax: 317-885-5006; Email: srushatta@gmail.com. Sr. Ushatta Mary, F.I.H., Supr. Franciscan Sisters of the Immaculate Heart of Mary. Sisters 13.

OLDENBURG. *Motherhouse of the Congregation of the Sisters of the Third Order of St. Francis*, 22143 Main St., P.O. Box 100, Oldenburg, 47036. Tel: 812-934-2475; Fax: 812-933-6403; Email: osf@oldenburgosf.com; Web: www.oldenburgfranciscans.org. Sr. Christa Franzer, O.S.F., M.S.A., Congregational Min. Sisters 189; Total in Residence 119; Professed Sisters in Congregation 189; Professed Sisters in Archdiocese 141.

Sisters of St. Francis Community Support Trust, Oldenburg. Tel: 812-934-2475. Sr. Maureen Irvin, O.S.F., Subprior. Total in Residence 118; In Congregation 197.

Michaela Farm, Oldenburg, 47036. Tel: 812-933-0260; Email: noemail@donotpublish.com. Sr. Maureen Irvin, O.S.F., Congregational Min.

Oldenburg Franciscan Center, Oldenburg, 47036. Tel: 812-933-6437; Email: noemail@donotpublish.com. Sr. Maureen Irvin, O.S.F., Congregational Min.

Sisters of Our Lady of Mount Carmel Carmelite Monastery (1922) Carmelite Sisters, 22143 Main St., P.O. Box 260, Oldenburg, 47036. Tel: 812-212-5901; Email: jeanmcgoff@gmail.com. Sr. Jean Alice McGoff, O.C.D., Prioress. Sisters 5; Professed Religious 5.

SAINT MARY-OF-THE-WOODS. *Sisters of Providence General Administration*, one Sisters of Providence Rd, St. Mary of the Woods, 47876. Tel: 812-535-2864; Fax: 812-535-1011; Email: ma@spsm.org; Web: www.sistersofprovidence.org. Sr. Dawn Tomaszewski, S.P., Gen. Supr.; Rev. Daniel R. Hopcus, Chap. Novices 2; Sisters 183; Professed in Congregation 300; Professed Residing in Archdiocese 196.

TERRE HAUTE. *Sisters of Our Lady of Mount Carmel of Terre Haute, Carmelite Monastery* (1947) Carmelite Monastery, 59 Allendale, Terre Haute, 47802-4751. Tel: 812-299-1410; Fax: 812-299-5820; Email: carmelth@heartsawake.org; Web: www.heartsawake.org. Mother Anne Brackmann, O.C.D., Prioress. Sisters 18; Solemnly Professed 12.

[L] ARCHDIOCESAN CHARITIES

INDIANAPOLIS. *A Caring Place - Adult Day Services*, c/o Fairview Presbyterian Church, 4609 N. Capitol Ave., 46208. Tel: 317-466-0015; Fax: 317-475-3093; Email: asczesny@archindy.org. Amy J. Sczesny, L.C.S.W., Prog. Dir. Total Staff 13.

Catholic Charities Indianapolis, Inc., The Catholic

Center, 1400 N. Meridian St., 46202.
Tel: 317-236-1500; Fax: 317-261-3375; Email: dbethuram@archindy.org; Web: www.catholiccharitiesindpls.org. David Bethuram, M.A., M.Min, Agency Dir.

St. Elizabeth/Coleman Pregnancy & Adoption Services, 2500 Churchman Ave., 46203.
Tel: 317-787-3412; Fax: 317-787-0482; Email: stelizabeths@stelizabeths.org; Web: www.stelizabeths.org. David Bethuram, M.A., M.Min, Agency Dir.

Holy Family Services, 907 N. Holmes Ave., 46222.
Tel: 317-635-7830; Fax: 317-684-9702; Email: bbickel@archindy.org; Web: www.catholiccharitiesindpls.org. Bill Bickel, M.T.S., Dir. Total Staff 16; Total Assisted 1,000.

BLOOMINGTON. *Catholic Charities Bloomington, Inc.*, 803 N. Monroe St., Bloomington, 47404.
Tel: 812-332-1262; Fax: 812-334-8464; Email: occase@ccbin.org. O'Connell Case, Clinical Dir.

NEW ALBANY. *St. Elizabeth Catholic Charities, Inc.*, Mailing Address: 702 E. Market St., New Albany, 47150. Tel: 812-949-7305; Fax: 812-941-7008; Email: info@stelizabethcatholiccharities.org; Web: www.stelizabethcatholiccharities.org. Mark Casper, Dir. Total Staff 26; Total Assisted 607.

St. Elizabeth's Regional Maternity Center, Mailing Address: 702 E. Market St., New Albany, 47150.
Tel: 812-949-7305; Fax: 812-941-7008; Email: info@stelizabethcatholiccharities.org; Web: www.stelizabethcatholicharities.org. Mark Casper, Dir. Full-range maternity home and adoption agency offering residential and outreach services. Total Staff 26; Total Assisted 607.

TELL CITY. *Catholic Charities Tell City, Inc.*, 802 9th St., Tell City, 47586. Tel: 812-547-0903;
Fax: 812-547-0903; Email: info@catholiccharitiestellcity.org; Web: www.catholiccharitiestellcity.org. Joan Hess, Agency Dir.

TERRE HAUTE. *Catholic Charities Terre Haute, Inc.*, 1801 Poplar St., Terre Haute, 47803.
Tel: 812-232-1447; Fax: 812-478-1363; Email: jetling@ccthin.org; Web: www.ccthin.org. John C. Etling, Dir. Tot Asst. Annually 39,500; Total Staff 29.

Bethany House, 1402 Locust Ave., Terre Haute, 47807. Tel: 812-232-4978; Email: noemai@donotpoublish.com. Danielle Elkins, Prog. Dir. Tot Asst. Annually 2,000; Total Staff 6.

Christmas House, 1440 Locust St., Terre Haute, 47807. Tel: 812-234-7372; Email: noemail@donotpublish.org. Tot Asst. Annually 2,432; Total Staff 1.

Household Exchange, 1402 Locust St., Terre Haute, 47807. Tel: 812-232-4978; Email: noemail@donotpublish.com. Danielle Elkins, Prog. Dir. Tot Asst. Annually 100; Total Staff 1.

Ryves Youth Center at Etling Hall, 1356 Locust St., Terre Haute, 47807. Tel: 812-235-1265; Email: noemail@donotpublish.com. Jim Edwards, Prog. Dir. Students 1,012; Total Staff 6.

**Terre Haute Catholic Charities Foodbank, Inc.*, 1356 Locust St., Terre Haute, 47807.
Tel: 812-235-3424; Email: info@ccthin.org; Web: ccthin.org. John C. Etling, Dir. Tot Asst. Annually 35,000; Total Staff 12.

[M] CATHOLIC YOUTH ORGANIZATIONS

INDIANAPOLIS. *Catholic Youth Organization of the Archdiocese of Indianapolis, Inc.*, 580 E. Stevens St., 46203. Tel: 317-632-9311; Email: noemail@donotpublish.com; Web: www.cyoarchindy.org. Bruce Scifres, Dir.; Mr. Gerald R. Ross, Assoc. Dir.

NASHVILLE. *C.Y.O. Camp Rancho Framasa, Inc.* (1946) 2230 N. Clay Lick Rd., Nashville, 47448-8638.
Tel: 888-988-2839; Fax: 812-988-4842; Email: info@campranchoframasa.org; Web: www.campranchoframasa.org. Mr. Kevin Sullivan, Camp Dir.

OLDENBURG. *Camp River Ridge*, 6145 Harvey Branch Rd., Oldenburg, 47036. Email: campriverridge@gmail.com; Web: www.campriverridge.org. Lucio Boccacci, Dir. (Branch of Mission Networks Activities USA, Inc., Archdiocese of New York) Boys 500; Clergy 8; Girls 500; Students 1,000.

[N] CAMPUS MINISTRIES

INDIANAPOLIS. *Butler Catholic Community*, c/o Center for Faith and Vocation, 4600 Sunset Ave., 46208.
Tel: 317-509-6012; Email: noemail@donotpublish.com. Rev. Michael Hoyt, Chap.; Emily Hitchens.

University of Indianapolis Newman Center, c/o SS. Francis and Clare of Assisi, Greenwood: 5901 Olive Branch Rd.,, Greenwood, 46143. Tel: 317-859-4673 . Rev. David J. Marcotte, B.A., M.Div., Chap.

BLOOMINGTON. *Indiana University, Bloomington*, c/o St. Paul Catholic Center, 1413 E. 17th St., Bloomington, 47408. Tel: 812-339-5561; Email: noemail@donotpublish.com; Web: www.hoosiercatholic.org. Fr. Patrick Hyde, O.P.

FRANKLIN. *Franklin College* (1834) c/o St. Rose of Lima Parish, 114 Lancelot Dr., Franklin, 46131.
Tel: 317-738-3929; Fax: 317-738-3583; Email: noemail@donotpublish.com. Rev. Steven Schaftlein, Chap.

GREENCASTLE. *DePauw University*, c/o St. Paul the Apostle Parish, 202 E. Washington St., Greencastle, 46135. Tel: 765-653-5678; Email: noemail@donotpublish.com. Rev. John J. Hollowell, Chap.

MADISON. *Hanover College*, c/o Prince of Peace Parish, 305 W. State St., Madison, 47250.
Tel: 812-944-1184; Email: noemail@donotpublish.com. Rev. Adam Ahern, Chap.

RICHMOND. *Earlham College*, c/o St. Andrew Parish, 240 S. 6th St., Richmond, 47374. Tel: 765-962-3902 ; Email: noemail@donotpublish.com. Rev. Kevin Morris.

TERRE HAUTE. *St. Joseph University Parish*, St. Joseph University Parish, 113 S. Fifth St., Terre Haute, 47807. Tel: 812-232-7011; Email: parishoffice@stjoeup.org. Rev. Cyprian Uline, O.F.-M.Conv., Campus Min.

[O] MISCELLANEOUS

INDIANAPOLIS. **The Catholic Writers Guild Inc.*, P.O. Box 39326, 46239-0326. Tel: 877-829-5500. Paula Harrell, Contact Person.

Hearts and Hands Corporation of Indiana, 337 N. Warman, 46222. Tel: 317-636-4828; Email: noemail@donotpublish.com. Rev. John P. McCaslin, M.A., M.Div.

**Inter Mirifica, Inc.*, 7340 E. 82nd St., Ste. A, 46256.
Tel: 317-598-6700; Fax: 317-598-6701; Email: bob@teipencpa.com; Web: www.catholicradioindy.org. Robert C. Teipen, Chm.

**St. Marys Child Center, Inc.*, 901 Dr. Martin Luther King Jr. St., 46202. Tel: 317-635-1491;
Fax: 317-635-1493; Email: nneedham@smccindy.org; Web: www.smccindy.org. Constance Sherman, Dir. A not-for-profit education center that is focused on helping young children who are at great risk to experience success in school and in life.

Mother Theodore Catholic Academies, Inc. dba Notre Dame ACE Academies (2010) 1400 N. Meridian St., 46202-1410. Tel: 317-236-1400; Email: rspringman@archindy.org. Gina Kuntz Fleming, Exec. Dir., Tel: 317-236-7322.

Society of St. Vincent de Paul, Archdiocesan Council of Indianapolis, Inc., 3001 E. 30th St., 46218.
Tel: 317-924-5769; Fax: 317-924-5781; Web: www.svdpindy.org. Mr. Jake Asher, Pres. Total Assisted 67,000.

**St. Vincent Health, Inc.*, 10330 N. Meridian St., 46290. Tel: 317-583-3289; Fax: 317-583-3285; Email: michael.wessel@ascension.org; Web: www.stvincent.org. Jonathan Nalli, CEO; Mike Wessel, Mgr. Finance & Contact Person.

St. Vincent Medical Group, 8333 Naab Rd., Ste. 200, 46260. Tel: 317-583-3073; Fax: 317-583-3102; Email: ann.varner@ascension.org. Richard I. Fogel, M.D., CEO.

Criterion Press, Inc., 1400 N. Meridian St., 47206-1410. Tel: 317-236-1579. Michael A. Krokos, Editor.

BEECH GROVE. *Charitable Trust of the Monastery of Our Lady of Grace* (1989) 1402 Southern Ave., Beech Grove, 46107-1197. Tel: 317-787-3287;
Fax: 317-780-2368; Email: olgpriores@benedictine.com; Email: olgmbusoff@gmail.com; Web: www.benedictine.com. Sisters Maureen Cooney, Treas.; Jennifer Mechtild Horner, O.S.B., Prioress

Charitable Trust of the Monastery of Our Lady of Grace, Sisters of the Order of St. Benedict.

Franciscan Alliance Information Services, 1500 Albany St., Beech Grove, 46107. Tel: 317-532-7800; Fax: 317-532-7801; Web: www.franciscanalliance.org. Mr. Charles Wagner, Exec. Sponsored by Franciscan Alliance, Inc.

BLOOMINGTON. *Heart of Mercy Solitude, Inc.*, 1150 Charles Lee Ct., Greenwood, 46143.
Tel: 317-581-9446; Email: noemail@donotpublish.com. Sr. Judith Ayres, H.S., Dir.

**St. Paul Street Evangelization*, 8220 W. State Rd. 48, Bloomington, 47404. Tel: 657-777-2963. Steve Dawson, Dir.

GEORGETOWN. *Providence Self-Sufficiency Ministries, Inc.* (1994) 8037 Unruh Dr., Georgetown, 47122-8759. Tel: 812-951-1878; Fax: 812-951-1659; Email: sbarbara@pssmsi.org; Web: www.pssm.org. Sr. Barbara Ann Zeller, Pres. & CEO. Sponsored by The Sisters of Providence, Saint Mary-of-the-Woods. Total Assisted Historically 125,843; Personnel 133; Volunteers 48; Total Assisted 2014-15 2,233.

MOORESVILLE. *St. Thomas More Free Clinic, Inc.*, 1125 N. Indiana St., P.O. Box 935, Mooresville, 46158. Tel: 317-831-1697; Email: jbuckner@crowntech.com. Jeff Buckner, Bd. Member.

MOUNT SAINT FRANCIS. *Mount Saint Francis Sanctuary, Inc.*, Sec. Mailing Address: Marian University, 3200 Cold Spring Rd., 46222.
Tel: 812-923-8817; Fax: 812-923-0177; Email: noemail@donotpublish.com. Tony Perkins, Pres.; Chris Jones, Vice Pres.; Thomas A. Smith, O.F.M.-Conv., Treas.; Rev. Leopold Keffler, O.F.M.Conv., Sec.

New Albany Deanery-Catholic Youth Ministries, 101 St. Anthony Dr., Mount Saint Francis, 47146.
Tel: 812-923-8355; Email: sandy@nadyouth.org; Web: www.nadyouth.org.

OLDENBURG. *Association of Contemplative Sisters*, Carmelite Sisters, 22143 Main St., P.O. Box 260, Oldenburg, 47036-0260. Tel: 812-932-2075; Email: jeanmcgoff@gmail.com. Marilyn Webb, Pres. Membership 184.

SAINT MARY-OF-THE-WOODS. **Guerin Outreach Ministries, Inc.*, 1 Sisters of Providence, St. Mary of the Woods, 47876. Tel: 812-535-2864;
Fax: 812-535-1011. Sr. Dawn Tomaszewski, S.P., General Supr.

Providence Health Care, Inc., 1 Sisters of Providence, P.O. Box 97, St. Mary of the Woods, 47876.
Tel: 812-535-4001; Fax: 812-535-1005; Email: CGROVER@PHCWOODS.ORG; Email: MLYNCH@PHCWOODS.ORG; Web: phcwoods.com. Mrs. Mandy Lynch, Pres.; Mrs. Christina Grover, Exec.; Mrs. Kim Wright, Dir. Sponsored by the Sisters of Providence of Saint Mary-of-the-Woods. Bed Capacity 107; Employees 104; Skilled Nursing Beds 25.

Sisters of Providence Community Support Trust, St. Mary of the Woods, 47876-1007. Tel: 812-535-4193; Fax: 812-535-1011; Email: noemail@donotpublish.com; Web: www.sistersofprovidence.org. Sr. Suzanne Dailey, S.P., Gen. Sec.

Women of Providence in Collaboration, Inc., 1 Sisters of Providence, St. Mary of the Woods, 47876.
Tel: 812-535-2639; Fax: 812-535-1011. Sr. Dawn Tomaszewski, S.P., Supr.

SAINT MEINRAD. *Swiss-American Benedictine Congregation, Inc.*, 100 Hill Dr., St. Meinrad, 47577. Tel: 630-966-7750; Fax: 630-897-7086; Email: vbataille@marmion.org; Web: www.swissamericanmonks.org. 850 Butterfield Rd., Aurora, IL 60502-9743. Rt. Rev. Vincent Bataille, O.S.B., Abbot Pres.

WEST TERRE HAUTE. *Providence Food Pantry of West Terre Haute, Indiana, Inc.* (2017) 701 W. National Ave., West Terre Haute, 47885. Tel: 812-535-2855; Email: jhagelskamp@spsmw.org. Sr. Jeanette Hagelskamp, S.P., Gen. Councilor.

WHEATON. *Indianapolis Ministries 1, Inc.*, 26W171 Roosevelt Rd., P.O. Box 667, Wheaton, IL 60187. Steven Battenburg, Contact Person.

Indianapolis Ministries 2, Inc., 26W171 Roosevelt Rd., P.O. Box 667, Wheaton, IL 60187.
Tel: 414-271-6560; Email: noemail@donotpublish.com. Steven Battenburg, Contact Person.

[Q] CLOSED PARISHES, SCHOOLS AND OTHER INSTITUTIONS

INDIANAPOLIS. *Archives of the Archdiocese of Indianapolis*, 1400 N. Meridian St., 46202.
Tel: 317-236-1538; Email: archives@archindy.org; Web: www.archindy.org/archives/index.html. Julie Motyka, Archivist.

Closed Parishes and Missions (Sacramental and other records may be found where indicated):

Indianapolis:

Assumption (1894-1994) Merged with St. Anthony, where sacramental records are kept.

St. Bernadette (1952-2014) Merged with Our Lady of Lourdes where sacramental records are kept.

St. Bridget (1880-1994) Merged with SS. Peter & Paul, where sacramental records are kept.

St. Catherine of Siena (1909-1993) Merged with St. James and renamed Good Shepherd, where sacramental records are kept.

St. Francis de Sales (1881-1983) Merged with four neighboring parishes. Sacramental records are located in the archives.

Church of the Holy Cross (1895-2014) Merged with St. Philip Neri, where sacramental records are kept.

Holy Trinity (1909-2014) Merged with St. Anthony where sacramental records are kept.

St. James the Greater (1951-1993) Merged with St. Catherine and renamed Good Shepherd, where sacramental records are kept.

St. Joseph (1873-1949) Sacramental records kept at the new St. Joseph parish.

Acton:

St. John the Evangelist (1855-1936) Sacramental records are located in the archives.

Adyeville:

St. Jude Thaddeus (1889-1898).

Bainbridge:

St. Patrick (1865-1973) .
Batesville:
St. Mary of the Rock (1844-2013) Merged into Holy Family, Oldenburg where sacramental records are kept.
Blanford:
Queen of the Most Holy Rosary (1917-1942) .
Brownstown:
Our Lady of Providence (1934-2016) Sacramental records kept at St. Ambrose, Seymour.
Cannelton:
St. Patrick (1847-1902) Merged with St. Michael, Cannelton, where sacramental records are kept.
Carbon:
St. Joseph (1870-1970) Sacramental records are located in the archives.
Cedar Grove:
Holy Guardian Angels (1874-2013) Merged into St. Michael, Brookville where sacramental records are kept.
Centenary:
St. Anthony (1917-1942) .
China:
St. Anthony (1861-1993) Merged with Prince of Peace, Madison, where sacramental records are kept.
Columbus:
St. Columba (1963-1994) Merged with St. Bartholomew, Columbus, where sacramental records are kept.
Cypress Dale:
Sacred Heart (1868-1918) .
Derby:
St. Mary (1824-1973) Sacramental records kept at St. Augustine, Leopold.
Diamond:
St. John Baptist (Greek Uniate Catholic) (1897-1926) Sacramental records are located in the archives.
St. Mary (1897-1991) Sacramental records are located in the archives.
Dogwood:
St. Michael (1820-1928) .
Dover:
St. John the Baptist (1824-2013) .
Dugger:
Our Lady of Perpetual Help (1911-1982) Sacramental records kept at St. Mary, Sullivan Co., Diocese of Evansville.
Elizabeth:
St. Peter Catholic Church, Elizabeth (1849) Sacramental records are located in the archives.
Ellsworth:
St. John (1910-1912) .
Enochsburg:
St. John the Evangelist (1844-2014) .
Eureka:
Mattingly Chapel (1874-1886) .
Fontanet:
St. Augustine (1891-1980) Sacramental records are located in the archives.
Hamburg:
St. Anne (1869-2013) Merged into Holy Family, Odenburg where sacramental records are kept.
Hovey:
All Souls Chapel (1900-1915) .
Indian Creek:
St. Columban (1848-1868) .
Jennings Co.:
St. Denis (1894-2013) Merged into Immaculate Conception, Millhousen where sacramental records are kept.
Knightstown:
St. Rose of Lima (1872-2016) Sacramental records kept at St. Anne, New Castle.
Knightsville:
St. Patrick (1868-1890) .
Laconia:
Sacred Heart of Mary (1854-1922) .
Laurel:
St. Raphael (1869-1958) Sacramental records kept at St. Gabriel, Connersville.
Lexington:
Mother of God (1854-1941) .
Locust Point:
St. Joachim (1888-1930) .
Madison:
St. Mary (1851-1993) Merged with St. Patrick (1853-1993) and St. Michael (1837-1993) and renamed Prince of Peace, where sacramental records are kept.
Magnet:
Sacred Heart of Jesus Sacramental records kept at St. Augustine, Leopold.
McCutcheonville:
St. Patrick (1842-1881) .
Mecca:
St. Mary (1905-1936) .
Milltown:
St. Joseph (1855-1974) Sacramental records kept at St. Joseph, Crawford Co..
Montezuma:
Immaculate Conception (1867-2001) Sacramental records kept at St. Joseph, Rockville.
Mount Erin:
St. John the Baptist (1852-1885) .
Mount Pleasant:
St. Rose (1821-1883) .
Nebraska:
St. Bridget (1845-1936) .
New Albany:
Holy Trinity (1836-1975) Merged with St. Mary, New Albany, where sacramental records are kept.
New Alsace:
St. Paul (1833-2013) .
New Middletown
Most Precious Blood (1880) Sacramental records are located in the archives.
New Marion:
St. Mary Magdalene (1847-2013) Merged into Prince of Peace, Madison where sacramental records are kept.
Perry Co.:
St. Rose (1840-1903) Merged with St. Thomas, Knox Co., Diocese of Evansville, where sacramental records are kept.
St. Peter (See St. Peter, Rome, IN).
Ripley Co.:
St. Pius (1859-2014) Merged into St. Charles Borromeo, Milan where sacramental records are kept.
Rome:
St. Peter (1868-1885) Sacramental records are located in the archives.
St. Catherine (1841-1871) Sacramental records are located in the archives.
St. James (1844-1850) Merged with St. Joseph, Perry Co. (1891-1968) and renamed St. Isidore, Perry Co., where sacramental records are kept.
St. Magdalen (1847-1941) Sacramental records kept at St. John, Osgood.
St. Paul (1859-1996) Sacramental records kept at St. Vincent, Shelby Co.
St. Maurice:
St. Maurice (1859-2014) .
Salem:
St. Mary (1871-1902) .
Scipio:
St. Patrick (1841-1958) Sacramental records are located in the archives.
Seelyville:
Holy Rosary (1908-2012) Sacramental records are in the archives.
Shelburn:
St. Ann (1909-1978) Sacramental records kept at St. Mary, Sullivan, Diocese of Evansville.
Shirley:
Mother of God (1900-1920) Sacramental records are located in the archives.
Siberia:
St. Martin of Tours Catholic Church, Siberia (1869) Sacramental records are located in the archives.
Taylorsville (Selvin):
St. Thomas (1845-1875) .
Terre Haute:
St. Ann Catholic Church, Terre Haute, Inc. (1876-2012) Sacramental records are at St. Joseph University Parish, Terre Haute.
Universal:
St. Joseph Catholic Church, Universal, Inc. (1920-2012) Sacramental records kept at Sacred Heart Church, Clinton.
Valley Mills:
St. John the Baptist (1855-1903) Sacramental records are located in the archives.
West Baden Springs:
Our Lady of Lourdes (1900-1929) .
West Harrison (St. Leon):
St. Joseph (1841-2013) .
West Terre Haute:
St. Leonard of Port Maurice (1912-2011) Sacramental records kept at St. Mary of the Woods Parish.
Willow Valley:
St. Stephen (1906-1944) .
Yorkville:
St. Martin (1850-2013) .
Closed Parish Grade Schools:
Indianapolis:
Assumption, St. Anthony (Consolidated) School, 75 N. Belleview Pl., 46222. Tel: 317-636-3739; Email: cgreer@stanthonyindy.org. Cynthia L. Greer, Prin.
Holy Rosary, Holy Rosary Rectory, 520 Stevens St., 46203. Tel: 317-636-4478; Email: info@holyrosaryindy.org. Rev. C. Ryan McCarthy.
Holy Trinity, St. Anthony (Consolidated) School, 75 N. Belleview Pl., 46222. Tel: 317-636-3739.
Sacred Heart, Sacred Heart Rectory, 1530 Union St., 46225. Tel: 317-638-5551. Rev. Lawrence Janezik, O.F.M.
St. Ann, St. Ann Rectory, 2862 S. Holt Rd., 46241. Tel: 317-244-3750. Rev. Robert T. Hausladen.
St. Anthony, All Saints Catholic School, 75 N. Belleview Pl., 46222. Tel: 317-636-3739.
St. Bernadette.
St. Bridget Sacramental records are located in the archives.
St. Catherine, Central Catholic School, 1155 Cameron St., 46203. Tel: 317-783-7759.
St. Francis de Sales Sacramental records are located in the archives.
St. James the Greater, Central Catholic School, 1155 Cameron St., 46203. Tel: 317-783-7759.
St. Joseph, 349 N Warman Ave, 46222.
Tel: 317-636-3740. Cynthia L. Greer, Prin.
St. Mary, Holy Cross Central School, 125 N. Oriental St., 46201. Tel: 317-638-9068; Email: mgring@holycrossindy.org. Matthew Gring, Prin.
St. Patrick, Central Catholic School, 1155 Cameron St., 46203. Tel: 317-783-7759; Email: rhurrle@centralcatholicindy.org. Ruth Hurrle, Prin.
Madison:
St. Mary; St. Michael, Pope John XXIII Grade School, 221 State St., Madison, 47250.
Tel: 812-273-3957; Email: pjprincipal@popeace.org. Curt Gardner, Prin.
Morris:
St. Anthony, St. Anthony Rectory, P.O. Box 3, Morris, 47033. Tel: 812-934-6218.
New Castle:
St. Anne, St. Anne Rectory, 102 N. 19th St., New Castle, 47362. Tel: 765-529-0933. Rev. John M. Hall, V.F.
New Albany:
St. Mary Grade School (Closed July 2013).
Richmond:
Holy Family; St. Andrew; St. Mary, Elizabeth Ann Seton School, 801 W. Main St., Richmond, 47374. Tel: 765-962-4877.
Terre Haute:
St. Ann; St. Joseph, Student Services, Vigo County School Corp., P.O. Box 3703, Terre Haute, 47803. Tel: 812-462-4224.
St. Benedict, Terre Haute. Sacramental records are located in the archives.
St. Margaret Mary, St. Margaret Mary Rectory, 2405 S. Seventh St., Terre Haute, 47802.
Tel: 812-232-3512; Email: mcoad@smmth.org. Rev. Daniel E. Bedel, B.A., M.Div.
Closed High Schools and Academies.
Indianapolis:
Cathedral, Holy Cross Central School, 125 N. Oriental St., 46201. Tel: 317-638-9068; Email: mgring@holycrossindy.org. Matthew Gring, Prin.
St. John; St. Agnes; Ladywood; Ladywood/St. Agnes Academies, Sisters of Providence, Records Office - Owens Hall, St. Mary of the Woods, 47876. Tel: 812-535-3131.
St. Mary Academy, Registrar, Franciscan Motherhouse. Tel: 812-934-2475.
Beech Grove:
Our Lady of Grace Academy, Our Lady of Grace Monastery, 1402 Southern Ave., Beech Grove, 46107. Tel: 317-787-3287.
Terre Haute:
Central Catholic High School for Girls.
St. Patrick High School for Girls.
St. Vincent Academy Renamed St. Joseph Academy.
Schulte High School, Student Services, Vigo County School Corp., P.O. Box 3703, Terre Haute, 47803. Tel: 812-462-4224.
Other Closed Institutions:
Indianapolis:
Sisters of the Good Shepherd Convent Sacramental records are located in the archives.
Angel Guardian School for Orphans Entrance records, 1924-1937, are located in the archives.
Marydale School For Girls Sacramental records, 1875-1953, are located in the archives. School records are located in the archives of the Archdiocese of Indianapolis.
New Albany:
St. Edward Hospital, New Albany, Box 766, Mishawaka, 46546. Tel: 219-259-5427.
Terre Haute:
St. Anthony Hospital Baptismal records are located in the archives.

RELIGIOUS INSTITUTES OF MEN REPRESENTED IN THE ARCHDIOCESE

For further details refer to the corresponding bracketed number in the Religious Institutes of Men or Women section.
[0200]—*Benedictine Monks of St. Meinrad*—O.S.B.
[0480]—*Conventual Franciscans* (Our Lady of Consolation Prov.)—O.F.M.Conv.

[0520]—*Franciscan Friars (St. John the Baptist, Sacred Heart Province & Albuquerque Province)*—O.F.M.
[]—*Franciscans of the Immaculate*—F.I.
[]—*Glenmary Home Missioners* (Cincinnati, OH)—G.H.M.
[0690]—*Jesuit Fathers and Brothers* (Chicago Prov.)—S.J.
[0430]—*Order of Preachers Central Province*—O.P.
[1065]—*Priestly Fraternity of Saint Peter*—F.S.S.P.
[]—*Society of the Divine Savior*—S.D.S.
[0420]—*Society of the Divine Word* (Chicago Province)—S.V.D.

RELIGIOUS INSTITUTES OF WOMEN REPRESENTED IN THE ARCHDIOCESE

[0230]—*Benedictine Sisters of Pontifical Jurisdiction* (Ferdinand, IN)—O.S.B.
[]—*Congregation of St. Joseph* (Cleveland, OH)—C.S.J.
[1920]—*Congregation of the Sisters of the Holy Cross*—C.S.C.
[1730]—*Congregation of the Sisters of the Third Order of St. Francis, Oldenburg, IN*—O.S.F.
[]—*Daughters of Mary Mother of Mercy* (Umuahia, Abia State, Nigeria)—D.M.M.M.
[0420]—*Discalced Carmelite Nuns*—O.C.D.
[1070-03]—*Dominican Sisters*—O.P.
[]—*Franciscan Religious of Our Lady of Refuge* (Jalisco, Mexico)—R.F.R.
[]—*Franciscan Sisters of the Immaculate Heart of Mary* (Kerala, India)—F.I.H.
[2340]—*Little Sisters of the Poor* (Baltimore, MD)—L.S.P.
[2710]—*Missionaries of Charity*—M.C.
[2820]—*Missionary Sisters of Our Lady of Africa* (American Headquarters, Winooski, VT)—M.S.O.L.A.
[]—*New Evangelization Sisters of Mother of Perpetual Help*—N.E.S.
[]—*Servants of the Gospel of Life*—S.G.L.
[0500]—*Sisters of Charity of Nazareth* (Nazareth, KY)—S.C.N.
[]—*Sisters of Loretto at the Foot of the Cross* (Littleton, CO)—S.L.
[2990]—*Sisters of Notre Dame* (Toledo, Ohio)—S.N.D.
[3360]—*Sisters of Providence of Saint Mary-of-the-Woods*—S.P.
[]—*Sisters of St. Benedict of Our Lady of Grace Monastery* (Beech Grove, IN)—O.S.B.
[1640]—*Sisters of St. Francis of Perpetual Adoration*—O.S.F.
[3840]—*Sisters of St. Joseph Carondelet* (St. Louis, MO)—C.S.J.

ARCHDIOCESAN CEMETERIES

INDIANAPOLIS. **Archdiocese of Indianapolis Cemeteries, Inc.*, 1400 N. Meridian St., 46202. Tel: 317-236-1453; Email: eatkins@archindy.org. Eric L. Atkins, Dir.
Catholic Cemeteries, 9001 Haverstick Rd., 46240. Tel: 317-581-2643; Email: lsilver@catholiccemeteries.cc. Larry Silver, Contact Person.
Indianapolis South Deanery
Holy Cross Indianapolis
St. Joseph Indianapolis
Calvary Indianapolis
Indianapolis North Deanery
Our Lady of Peace Indianapolis
Indianapolis West Deanery
St. Malachy Brownsburg
St. Malachy Pittsboro

BATESVILLE. *Batesville Deanery*
St. Ann Hamburg
St. Anthony Morris
St. Cecilia Oak Forest
Cemetery (North end of Brookville) Brookville
St. Charles Milan
Holy Family Oldenburg
Holy Family Shrine Oldenburg
Holy Guardian Angels Cedar Grove
Immaculate Conception Millhousen
St. John Dover
St. John Enochsburg
St. John Osgood
St. Joseph St. Leon
St. Joseph Shelbyville
St. Louis Batesville
St. Martin Yorkville
St. Mary Greensburg
St. Mary of the Rock St. Mary of the Rock
St. Maurice Napoleon
St. Maurice St. Maurice
St. Michael Brookville
St. Paul New Alsace
St. Paul St. Paul
St. Peter St. Peter
St. Pius St. Pius
St. Raphael Laurel
St. Vincent de Paul St. Vincent de Paul

BLOOMINGTON. *Bloomington Deanery*
Catholic South of Martinsville
St. Martin Martinsville
Our Lady of Springs French Lick

CONNERSVILLE. *Connersville Deanery*
St. Anne New Castle
St. Andrew Richmond
St. Bridget Liberty
Calvary Rushville
St. Mary Richmond

NEW ALBANY. *New Albany Deanery*
St. Anthony Jeffersonville
St. Bernard Frenchtown
St. Bernard, Old Frenchtown
Cemetery Southwest of Bradford
St. Francis Henryville
Holy Trinity New Albany
St. Joachim Locust Point
St. John Starlight
St. Joseph Corydon
St. Joseph St. Joseph Hill
St. Mary Lanesville
St. Mary New Albany
St. Mary Navilleton
St. Mary of the Knobs Floyds Knobs
Mary, Queen of Heaven Jeffersonville
St. Michael Bradford
St. Michael Charlestown
St. Michael Dogwood
Most Precious Blood New Middleton
St. Peter Taylor Township

SEYMOUR. *Seymour Deanery*
St. Ambrose Seymour
St. Anne Jennings Co.
St. Anthony China
St. Bridget Nebraska
St. Catherine of Siena St. Catherine
St. Dennis Jennings Co.
St. Joseph Madison
St. Joseph St. Joseph
St. Magdalen Madison
St. Mary North Vernon
Old St. James St. James
St. Patrick Madison
St. Patrick Salem
St. Patrick Scipio

TELL CITY. *Tell City Deanery*
St. Augustine Leopold
St. Boniface Fulda
St. Croix Cemetery on original parish site. St. Croix
Holy Cross St. Croix
St. Isidore Bristow
St. John St. John
St. Joseph Milltown
St. Joseph St. Croix
St. Joseph St. Joseph
St. Martin Siberia
St. Mary Derby
St. Mary Tell City
St. Meinrad St. Meinrad
St. Michael Cannelton
Old St. Patrick Cannelton
St. Paul Cemetery Tell City
St. Peter Cannelton

TERRE HAUTE. *Terre Haute Deanery*
Annunciation Brazil
Catholic Armiesburg
Calvary Terre Haute
Greek Catholic Perth
Immaculate Conception Montezuma
St. John Greek Diamond
St. Joseph Terre Haute
St. Mary-of-the-Woods St. Mary-of-the-Woods

NECROLOGY

† Burkert, Gerald F., (Retired), Died May. 13, 2018
† Evard, Paul A., (Retired), Died Mar. 19, 2018
† Pesola, Joseph G., (Retired), Died Jul. 22, 2018

An asterisk (*) denotes an organization that has established tax-exempt status directly with the IRS and is not covered by the USCCB Group Ruling.

Diocese of Jackson

(Dioecesis Jacksoniensis)

Most Reverend

JOSEPH R. KOPACZ, PH.D.

Bishop of Jackson; ordained May 7, 1977; appointed Bishop of Jackson December 12, 2013; consecrated and installed February 6, 2014. *Mailing Address: P.O. Box 2248, Jackson, MS 39225-2248.*

Most Reverend

JOSEPH N. LATINO, D.D.

Retired Bishop of Jackson; ordained May 25, 1963; appointed Bishop of Jackson January 3, 2003; consecrated and installed March 7, 2003; retired December 12, 2013. *Mailing Address: P.O. Box 2248, Jackson, MS 39225-2248.*

Chancery Office: 237 E. Amite St., P.O. Box 2248, Jackson, MS 39225-2248. Tel: 601-969-1880; Fax: 601-960-8455.

Web: www.jacksondiocese.org

Email: chancery@jacksondiocese.org

Square Miles 37,643.

Established July 28, 1837 as Diocese of Natchez. Name changed to Diocese of Natchez-Jackson, March 7, 1957. Name changed to Diocese of Jackson, June 6, 1977.

Comprises 65 Counties in the State of Mississippi, namely: Adams, Alcorn, Amite, Attala, Benton, Bolivar, Calhoun, Carroll, Chickasaw, Choctaw, Claiborne, Clarke, Clay, Coahoma, Copiah, De Soto, Franklin, Grenada, Hinds, Holmes, Humphreys, Issaquena, Itawamba, Jasper, Jefferson, Kemper, Lafayette, Lauderdale, Leake, Lee, Leflore, Lincoln, Lowndes, Madison, Marshall, Monroe, Montgomery, Neshoba, Newton, Noxubee, Oktibbeha, Panola, Pike, Pontotoc, Prentiss, Quitman, Rankin, Scott, Sharkey, Simpson, Smith, Sunflower, Tallahatchie, Tate, Tippah, Tishomingo, Tunica, Union, Warren, Washington, Webster, Wilkinson, Winston, Yalobusha and Yazoo.

Legal Title: "Catholic Diocese of Jackson".

STATISTICAL OVERVIEW

Personnel	
Bishop	1
Retired Bishops	1
Retired Abbots	1
Priests: Diocesan Active in Diocese	30
Priests: Diocesan Active Outside Diocese	2
Priests: Retired, Sick or Absent	19
Number of Diocesan Priests	51
Religious Priests in Diocese	24
Total Priests in Diocese	75
Extern Priests in Diocese	13
Ordinations:	
Diocesan Priests	2
Transitional Deacons	2
Permanent Deacons in Diocese	10
Total Brothers	5
Total Sisters	100
Parishes	
Parishes	72
With Resident Pastor:	
Resident Diocesan Priests	34
Resident Religious Priests	11
Without Resident Pastor:	
Administered by Priests	11
Administered by Deacons	3
Administered by Religious Women	1
Administered by Lay People	5
Administered by Pastoral Teams, etc.	6
Completely Vacant	1
Missions	19
Pastoral Centers	2
Professional Ministry Personnel:	
Brothers	2
Sisters	9
Lay Ministers	9
Welfare	
Catholic Hospitals	1
Total Assisted	378,054
Homes for the Aged	1
Total Assisted	490
Residential Care of Children	3
Total Assisted	70
Day Care Centers	2
Total Assisted	108
Specialized Homes	6
Total Assisted	719
Special Centers for Social Services	12
Total Assisted	1,705
Residential Care of Disabled	1
Total Assisted	16
Educational	
Diocesan Students in Other Seminaries	6
Total Seminarians	6
High Schools, Diocesan and Parish	4
Total Students	930
Elementary Schools, Diocesan and Parish	10
Total Students	2,003
Elementary Schools, Private	2
Total Students	474
Catechesis/Religious Education:	
High School Students	1,117
Elementary Students	3,364
Total Students under Catholic Instruction	7,894
Teachers in the Diocese:	
Brothers	1
Sisters	6
Lay Teachers	361
Vital Statistics	
Receptions into the Church:	
Infant Baptism Totals	738
Minor Baptism Totals	65
Adult Baptism Totals	55
Received into Full Communion	198
First Communions	814
Confirmations	564
Marriages:	
Catholic	127
Interfaith	105
Total Marriages	232
Deaths	438
Total Catholic Population	43,563
Total Population	2,167,132

Former Bishops—Rt. Revs. JOHN J. CHANCHE, S.S., D.D., ord. June 5, 1819; cons. March 14, 1841; died July 22, 1852; J. O. VAN DE VELDE, S.J., D.D., ord. Sept. 25, 1827; appt. Bishop of Chicago Dec. 1, 1848; cons. Feb. 11, 1849; appt. Bishop of Natchez July 29, 1853; died Nov. 13, 1855.; Most Revs. WILLIAM HENRY ELDER, D.D., ord. March 29, 1846; cons. May 3, 1857; transferred to Cincinnati, 1880; died Oct. 31, 1904; FRANCIS JANSSENS, D.D., ord. Dec. 21, 1867; cons. May 1, 1881; transferred to New Orleans, Aug. 7, 1888; died June 9, 1897; Rt. Revs. THOMAS HESLIN, D.D., ord. Sept. 18, 1869; cons. June 18, 1889; died Feb. 22, 1911; JOHN EDWARD GUNN, S.M., D.D., ord. Feb. 2, 1890; cons. Aug. 29, 1911; died Feb. 19, 1924; Most Revs. RICHARD OLIVER GEROW, LL.D., S.T.D., ord. June 5, 1909; appt. June 25, 1924; cons. Oct. 15, 1924; retired Dec. 2, 1967; died Dec. 20, 1976; JOSEPH B. BRUNINI, D.D., LL.D., J.C.D., ord. Dec. 5, 1933; cons. Jan. 29, 1957; appt. Bishop, Dec. 2, 1967; installed Jan. 29, 1968; retired Jan. 24, 1984; died Jan. 7, 1996; WILLIAM R. HOUCK, D.D., ord. May 19, 1951; appt. Auxiliary Bishop of Jackson and Titular Bishop of Allessano on March 28, 1979; cons. May 27, 1979; appt. Bishop of Jackson April 24, 1984; installed June 5, 1984; retired Jan. 3, 2003; died March 9, 2016; JOSEPH N. LATINO, D.D., (Retired), 237 E. Amite St., P.O Box 2248, Jackson, 39225-2248. ord. May 25, 1963; appt. Bishop of Jackson Jan. 3, 2003; cons. March 7, 2003; retired Dec. 12, 2013.

Chancery Office—237 E. Amite St., P.O. Box 2248, Jackson, 39225-2248. Tel: 601-969-1880;
Fax: 601-960-8455. The telephone number for all Diocesan Offices is 601-969-1880, unless otherwise listed. Office Hours: 8:30 am-4:30 pm.

Office of the Bishop—Most Rev. JOSEPH R. KOPACZ, Ph. D., D.D., 237 E. Amite St., P.O. Box 2248, Jackson, 39225-2248.

Office of Vicar General—237 E. Amite St., P.O. Box 2248, Jackson, 39225-2248. Rev. KEVIN SLATTERY, J.C.L.

Moderator of the Curia—Rev. KEVIN SLATTERY, J.C.L.

Vicar for Clergy—Rev. MICHAEL O'BRIEN.

Chancellor—MS. MARY WOODWARD, 237 E. Amite St., P.O. Box 2248, Jackson, 39225-2248.

Archivist—MS. MARY WOODWARD.

Vice Chancellor—Very Rev. JEFFREY WALDREP, S.T.L., J.C.L.

Ecumenism—MS. MARY WOODWARD.

Parish Pastoral Councils—Rev. KEVIN SLATTERY, J.C.L., Dir.

Propagation of the FaithRev. KEVIN SLATTERY, J.C.L., Dir., Mailing Address: P.O. Box 2248, Jackson, 39225-2248.

Judicial Vicar—237 E. Amite St., P.O. Box 2248, Jackson, 39225-2248. Very Rev. JEFFREY WALDREP, S.T.L., J.C.L.

Adjutant Judicial Vicars—Rev. Msgr. MICHAEL FLANNERY, J.C.L., (Retired); Rev. KEVIN SLATTERY, J.C.L.

Judges—Rev. Msgr. MICHAEL FLANNERY, J.C.L., (Retired); Very Rev. JEFFREY WALDREP, S.T.L., J.C.L.

Defenders of the Bond—Revs. THOMAS MCGING, J.C.L.; KEVIN SLATTERY, J.C.L., at First Instance.; Sr. JOYCE HOBEN, S.N.D.N., J.C.L.; MRS. JACQUELINE RAPP, J.C.L.

Ecclesiastical Notaries—Very Rev. ANTHONY QUYET; MS. FABVIENEN TAYLOR; MS. MARY WOODWARD.

Promoter of Justice—Rev. THOMAS MCGING, J.C.L.
Approved Advocate and Auditors—Revs. BRIAN KASKIE; JOSEPH TONOS.
Office of Child Protection—MRS. VICKIE CAROLLO.
Office of Vocations—Revs. JOSE DE JESUS SANCHEZ, Dir.; AARON M. WILLIAMS, Liaison to Seminarians.
Director of Permanent Diaconate—Deacon JOHN T. MCGREGOR, St. Jude Church, P.O. Box 5526, Pearl, 39288-5526.
Department of Communications—MRS. MAUREEN SMITH, Dir., Mailing Address: P.O. Box 2130, Jackson, 39225-2130.
Mississippi Catholic—MRS. MAUREEN SMITH, Editor.
Department of Evangelization—237 E. Amite St., P.O. Box 2248, Jackson, 39225-2248. MS. CATHERINE D. COOK, Dir.
Superintendent of Schools—MS. CATHERINE D. COOK.
Early Child Development, Health and Education Projects—MS. CATHERINE D. COOK.
Department of Faith Formation—MS. FRAN LAVELLE, Dir., 237 E. Amite St., P.O. Box 2248, Jackson, 39225-2248.
Director of Spring Hill Theology Program—MS. FRAN LAVELLE.
Black Catholic Ministry—MR. WILL JEMISON, Coord.
Marriage & Family Ministry—MRS. CHARLENE BEARDEN, Coord.
Engaged Encounter—Very Rev. JEFFREY WALDREP, S.T.L., J.C.L., Dir.
Hispanic Ministry—Bro. THEODORE DAUSCH, C.F.C., Coord.
Campus Ministry—Rev. RUSTY VINCENT, Coord.
Charismatic Renewal—Rev. WILLIAM F. HENRY.
Youth Ministry—MRS. ABBEY SCHUHMANN, Coord.
Department of Stewardship - Development—MRS. REBECCA HARRIS, Dir.
Catholic Foundation—MRS. REBECCA HARRIS, Dir., 237 E. Amite St., P.O. Box 2248, Jackson, 39225-2248.
Department of Temporal Affairs—237 E. Amite St., P.O. Box 2248, Jackson, 39225-2248. Rev. LINCOLN DALL, Interim. Dir.
Catholic Charities, Inc.—850 E. River Pl., Jackson, 39202. Tel: 601-355-8634; Fax: 601-960-8493.
Executive Director—Most Rev. JOSEPH R. KOPACZ, Ph.D., D.D.
Chief Operating Officer—MR. JOHN LUNARDINI.
Division of Children's and Mental Health Services—MS. AMY TURNER, LMSW, Dir.
Division of Parish and Community Engagement Ministries (PACEM)—MS. DOROTHY BALSER, Dir.
Development—MR. MICHAEL THOMAS, Dir.
Finance—MRS. DIRA LAY, Dir.
Human Resources—MRS. SANDRA HENDERSON, Dir.
Victim Assistance Coordinator—MS. VALERIE MCCLELLAN, Tel: 601-326-3728.
Consultative Boards—
Association of Priests—Most Revs. JOSEPH R. KOPACZ, Ph.D., D.D., Co-Chm.; LOUIS F. KIHNEMAN III, Co Chm.; Revs. PATRICK MOCKLER, Pres.; JASON JOHNSTON, Sec., Treas. & Pres.-Elect. Trustees: Revs. THOMAS CONWAY; LINCOLN DALL; Rev. Msgr. MICHAEL THORNTON; Rev. RUSTY VINCENT.
Continuing Formation Committee—MR. LORENZO AJU; Revs. KENT BOWLDS; JASON JOHNSTON; Deacon JOHN T. MCGREGOR; MRS. PAMELA MINNINGER; Revs. PETER PHONG NGUYEN, S.V.D.; KEVIN SLATTERY, J.C.L.; SURESH REDDY THIRUMALAREDDY; RUSTY VINCENT.
Diocesan Consultors—Most Rev. JOSEPH R. KOPACZ, Ph.D., D.D., Pres.; Revs. MICHAEL O'BRIEN; KEVIN SLATTERY, J.C.L.; Rev. Msgr. ELVIN SUNDS; Rev. JOSEPH TONOS; Very Rev. JEFFREY WALDREP, S.T.L., J.C.L.
Finance Council—Most Rev. JOSEPH R. KOPACZ, Ph. D., D.D.; JOHN AGOSTINELLI; PATRICIA CASKEY; MONA COBB; JAMES COOPER; Rev. LINCOLN DALL; ED HANNAN; RUSTY HAYDEL; CHAD HIRN; RHOSHUNDA KELLY; HIBBETT NEEL; RILEY NELSON; BILL PHILIPP; Rev. KEVIN SLATTERY, J.C.L.; SR. DOROTHEA SONDGEROTH; LUIS TERRAZAS; Very Rev. JEFFREY WALDREP, S.T.L., J.C.L.; LEE WHITE.
Pastor Review Board—Revs. THOMAS LALOR; JOSEPH TONOS.
Personnel Board—Revs. MICHAEL O'BRIEN, Dir.; JASON JOHNSTON; THOMAS MCGING, J.C.L.; TIMOTHY MURPHY, M.A.; KEVIN SLATTERY, J.C.L., Ex Officio; SCOTT THOMAS; JOSEPH TONOS.
Priests' Council—Most Rev. JOSEPH R. KOPACZ, Ph. D., D.D., Pres.
Deanery Representatives—
Deanery I—Rev. Msgr. ELVIN SUNDS, Chm.
Deanery II—Rev. DAVID O'CONNOR.
Deanery III—Rev. THOMAS A. MULLALLY, S.V.D.
Deanery IV—Rev. GREGORY SCHILL, S.C.J.
Deanery V—Rev. TIMOTHY MURPHY, M.A., Sec.
Deanery VI—Rev. AUGUSTINE PALIMATTAM POULOSE.
Appointed Members—Revs. JASON JOHNSTON; SCOTT THOMAS; JOSEPH TONOS; ALBEENREDDY VATTI, (India).
Ex Officio—Revs. MICHAEL O'BRIEN; KEVIN SLATTERY, J.C.L.; Very Rev. JEFFREY WALDREP, S.T.L., J.C.L.

CLERGY, PARISHES, MISSIONS AND PAROCHIAL SCHOOLS

CITY OF JACKSON

(HINDS COUNTY)

1—ST. PETER CATHEDRAL (1846)
123 N. West St., P.O. Box 57, 39205-0057. Tel: 601-969-3125; Email: stpeters@comcast.net. Very Rev. Anthony Quyet, Rector.
Catechesis Religious Program—Hope Johnson, D.R.E. Students 169.

2—CHRIST THE KING (1945)
2303 John R. Lynch St., 39209. Tel: 601-948-8867; Email: ctkcatholicchurch@comcast.net. Rev. Jeremy Tobin, O.Praem., Sacramental Min.; Deacon Denzil Lobo, Ecclesial Min.
School—Sister Thea Bowman School, (Grades PreK-6), 1217 Hattiesburg St., 39209-7411. Tel: 601-352-5441; Fax: 601-352-5136. Mrs. Shae Goodman-Robinson, Prin.; Mrs. Ollie W. Johnson, Admin. Asst. Lay Teachers 6; Students 40.
Catechesis Religious Program—Dana Barnes, D.R.E. Students 28.

3—HOLY FAMILY (1957)
820 Forest Ave., 39206-3299. Tel: 601-362-1888; Email: holyfamilycc@comcast.net. Rev. Xavier Amirtham, O.Praem.
Catechesis Religious Program—Joyce Adams, C.R.E.; Gladys Russell, C.R.E. Students 4.

4—HOLY GHOST (1908)
1151 Cloister St., 39202. Tel: 601-353-1339; Email: 1151cloister@earthlink.net. Rev. Alfred Ayem, S.V.D.
Catechesis Religious Program—Melanie Norwood, D.R.E. Students 16.

5—ST. MARY (1948) Closed. Parish merged with St. Therese, Jackson.

6—ST. RICHARD OF CHICHESTER (1953)
1242 Lynnwood Dr., P.O. Box 16547, 39236-6547. Tel: 601-366-2335; Email: secretary@saintrichard.com. Revs. John Bohn; Nicholas Warren Adam.
School—St. Richard of Chichester School, (Grades PreK-6), 100 Holly Dr., 39206-6037. Tel: 601-366-1157; Fax: 601-366-4344; Email: jdavid@strichardschool.org; Web: www.strichardschool.org. Mrs. Jennifer David, Prin. Lay Teachers 22; Students 228.
St. Richard's School Special Kids Program—Email: sk@saintrichard.com. Turner Kim, Dir. Lay Teachers 4; Students 10.
Catechesis Religious Program—Tara Clifford, C.R.E. Students 236.

7—ST. THERESE (1955)
309 W. McDowell Rd., P.O. Box 8642, 39284-8642. Tel: 601-372-4481; Email: sttherese@jacksondiocese.org. Rev. Msgr. Elvin Sunds; Sr. Lourdes Gonzalez, M.G.Sp.S., Pastoral Hispanic Min.
Catechesis Religious Program—Sr. Magdalena Carillo, D.R.E. Students 159.

OUTSIDE THE CITY OF JACKSON

ABERDEEN, MONROE CO., ST. FRANCIS OF ASSISI (1977)
108 S. James St., P.O. Box 134, Aberdeen, 39730-0134. Tel: 662-813-2295; Email: saintfrancisaberdeen@gmail.com. Rev. Antony Chakkalakkal.
Catechesis Religious Program—102 S. James St., Aberdeen, 39730. Students 4.
Mission—Immaculate Heart of Mary (1942) 818 N. Jackson St., P.O. Box 309, Houston, Chickasaw Co. 38851-0309. Tel: 662-456-5450; Email: ihmcatholicchurch@att.net. Mr. Lorenzo Aju, Lay Ecclesial Min.
Catechesis Religious Program—Students 66.
Chapel—St. Theresa, 116 N. Fleming St., Okolona, Chickasaw Co. 38860.

AMORY, MONROE CO., ST. HELEN (1977)
401 Eighth Ave. S., P.O. Box 97, Amory, 38821-0097. Tel: 662-256-8392; Email: sisterlael@yahoo.com. Sr. Lael Niblick, C.S.A., Ecclesial Min.
Catechesis Religious Program—14 Annabelle Cove, Amory, 38821. Tel: 662-305-5551. Nancy Hoang, D.R.E. Students 43.

BATESVILLE, PANOLA CO., ST. MARY (1960)
120 Hwy. 35 N., Batesville, 38606-0569. Tel: 662-563-2273; Email: saintmarycc@bellsouth.net. P.O. Box 569, Batesville, 38606. Rev. Pradeep K. Thirumalareddy.
Catechesis Religious Program—Robin Ridge, D.R.E. Students 49.
Mission—St. John the Baptist, 110 N. Main St., Sardis, Panola Co. 38666.

BELZONI, HUMPHREYS CO., ALL SAINTS (1953)
200 Bowles St., Belzoni, 39038-3602. Tel: 662-247-1408; Email: allsaintsbelzoni@att.net. Rev. Panneer Selvam Arockiam.
Catechesis Religious Program—Joy Bellipanni, Sec. Students 6.

BOONEVILLE, PRENTISS CO., ST. FRANCIS OF ASSISI (1962)
721 N. College St., P.O. Box 654, Booneville, 38829. Tel: 662-728-7509; Email: stfrancisbv@att.net. Joel P. Schultz, Lay Ecclesial Min.
Catechesis Religious Program—Students 16.
Mission—St. Mary, 205 Eastport St. E., P.O. Box 651, Iuka, Tishomingo Co. 38852. Tel: 662-423-9358; Fax: 662-423-9358; Email: stmarycatho78710@bellsouth.net.

BROOKHAVEN, LINCOLN CO., ST. FRANCIS OF ASSISI (1887)
227 E. Cherokee St., P.O. Box 196, Brookhaven, 39602-0196. Tel: 601-833-1799; Email: office@stfrancisbrookhaven.org. Rev. Henry Shelton, (Retired).
Catechesis Religious Program—Tel: 601-754-0963. Erin Womack, D.R.E. Students 49.

BRUCE, CALHOUN CO., ST. LUKE THE EVANGELIST (1997) Closed. Mission of St. John, Oxford.

CAMDEN, MADISON CO., SACRED HEART (1850)
1493 Hwy. 17, Camden, 39045. Tel: 662-468-2354; Email: sacredheartcamden@gmail.com. Revs. Raul A. Ventura, S.T.; Odel Medina, S.T.
Catechesis Religious Program—Sr. Mary Anne Poeschl, R.S.M., D.R.E. Students 15.

CANTON, MADISON CO.

1—HOLY CHILD JESUS (1946)
315 Garrett St., P.O. Box 366, Canton, 39046-0366. Tel: 601-859-2957; Email: venturra@hotmail.com. Revs. Raul A. Ventura, S.T.; Odel Medina, S.T.
Catechesis Religious Program—Email: smapoeschl@hotmail.com. Sr. Mary Anne Poeschl, R.S.M., D.R.E. Students 9.

2—SACRED HEART (1859)
238 E. Center St., P.O. Box 361, Canton, 39046-0361. Tel: 601-859-3749; Email: office@sacredheart. Rev. Michael O'Brien.
Catechesis Religious Program—Email: peralta22b@gmail.com. Blanca Pealta, D.R.E. Students 66.

CARTHAGE, LEAKE CO., ST. ANNE (1954) [CEM]
207 Red Dog Rd., Carthage, 39051-3113. Tel: 601-297-7190; Email: stannecatholicchurch@gmail.com. Revs. Odel Medina, S.T.; Raul A. Ventura, S.T.
Catechesis Religious Program—Terrica Dawson, D.R.E. Students 12.

CHARLESTON, TALLAHATCHIE CO., ST. JOHN (1973)
304 W. Cypress St., P.O. Box 30, Charleston, 38921-0030. Tel: 662-647-3170; Email: bro.senan.gallagher@gmail.com. Bro. Senan Gallagher, S.T., Deacon Ecclesial Min.

CHATAWA, PIKE CO., ST. TERESA OF AVILA (1868)
3167 Old Hwy. 51 S., Osyka, 39657. Tel: 601-783-5931; Email: stalphonsusmccomb@gmail.com. Rev. Suresh Reddy Thirumalareddy.
Mission—St. James, 125 E. Bay St., Magnolia, Pike Co. 39652. Tel: 601-783-3494.

CLARKSDALE, COAHOMA CO.

1—ST. ELIZABETH (1891)
130 Florence Ave., Clarksdale, 38614-2720. Tel: 662-624-4301; Email: secretary@stelizabethclarksdale.org. Rev. Scott Thomas.
School—St. Elizabeth School, (Grades PreK-6), 150 Florence Ave., Clarksdale, 38614-2720. Tel: 662-624-4239; Fax: 662-624-2072; Email: solivi@seseagles.com. Sally Olivi, Prin. Lay Teachers 11; Students 124.
Catechesis Religious Program—Sarah Cauthen, D.R.E. Students 47.

2—IMMACULATE CONCEPTION (1945)
510 Ritchie Ave., Clarksdale, 38614. Tel: 662-624-4029; Email: secretary@stelizabethclarksdale.org. Rev. Scott Thomas.

CLEVELAND, BOLIVAR CO., OUR LADY OF VICTORIES (1924)
215 Bishop Rd., Cleveland, 38732-2446. Tel: 662-846-6273; Fax: 662-846-6270; Email: olvcc@att.net; Web: www.olvcleveland.com. Rev. Kent Bowlds.
Catechesis Religious Program—Jenifer Jenkins, D.R.E. Students 135.

CLINTON, HINDS CO., HOLY SAVIOR (1966)
714 Lindale St., P.O. Box 85, Clinton, 39060-0085. Tel: 601-924-6344; Email: holysavior@att.net; Web:

www.holy-savior-ms.org. Rev. Thomas McGing, J.C.L.
Catechesis Religious Program—Email: RE_holysavior@outlook.com. Rita Haselhorst, C.R.E.; Trish Ballard, C.R.E. Students 138.
Mission—Immaculate Conception, 232 Main St., Raymond, Hinds Co. 39154.

COLUMBUS, LOWNDES CO., ANNUNCIATION (1863)
823 College St., Columbus, 39701-5804.
Tel: 662-328-2927, Ext. 11; Email: annunchr@bellsouth.net. Very Rev. Jeffrey Waldrep, S.T.L., J.C.L.
School—Annunciation School, (Grades PreK-8), 223 N. Browder St., Columbus, 39702-5236.
Tel: 662-328-4479; Fax: 662-328-0430. Mrs. Joni House, Prin. Lay Teachers 23; Students 218.
Catechesis Religious Program—Gina Phillips, D.R.E. Students 80.

CORINTH, ALCORN CO., ST. JAMES THE LESS (1956)
3189 N. Harper Rd., P.O. Box 660, Corinth, 38835-0660. Tel: 662-331-5184; Email: stjamesc@comcast.net. Rev. Mario Solorzano.
Catechesis Religious Program—Tel: 601-331-5184; Email: stjamesccorinth@comcast.net. Luis Rosales, D.R.E. Students 135.

CRYSTAL SPRINGS, COPIAH CO., ST. JOHN THE EVANGELIST (1953)
221 E. Georgetown St., P.O. Box 167, Crystal Springs, 39059-0167. Tel: 601-892-1717; Email: stjohncatholic@msn.com. Rev. Thomas Delaney, Sacramental Min.; Janice Stansell, Lay Ecclesial Min.
Catechesis Religious Program—Students 6.
Mission—St. Martin of Tours, 113 E. Conway, Hazlehurst, Copiah Co. 39083.

EUPORA, WEBSTER CO., ST. JOHN NEUMANN (1990) Closed. For inquiries for parish records contact the chancery.

FAYETTE, JEFFERSON CO., ST. ANNE (1969)
89 Harriston Rd., P.O. Box 159, Fayette, 39069.
Tel: 601-455-5700; Email: stannefay@gmail.com. Rev. George B. Ajuruchi, S.S.J.

FLOWOOD, RANKIN CO., ST. PAUL (1978)
5971 Hwy. 25, Flowood, 39232-7101.
Tel: 601-992-9547; Email: office@saintpaulcatholicchurch.com. Rev. Gerard Hurley.
Child Care—Learning Center, 5969 Hwy. 25, Flowood, 39232-7101. Tel: 601-992-2876. Jennifer Henry, Dir. Lay Teachers 34; Students 107.
Catechesis Religious Program—5971 Hwy. 25, Flowood, 39232. Renee Borne, D.R.E. Students 246.

FOREST, SCOTT CO., ST. MICHAEL (1957)
Hwy. 80 E., Forest, 39074. Tel: 601-469-1916; Email: stmichael@stmichaelms.org. P.O. Box 388, Forest, 39074. Rev. Roberto Mena, Sacramental Min.; Deacon Edwin Santos, Admin.
Catechesis Religious Program—Liz Edmundson, D.R.E. Students 76.
Mission—St. Anne, 608 Decatur St., Newton, Newton Co. 39345. Liz Edmundson, Contact Person.
Station—Centro San Martin De Porres, Hwy. 80 W., Morton, 39117.

GLUCKSTADT, MADISON CO., ST. JOSEPH (1905)
127 Church Rd., Gluckstadt, 39110.
Tel: 601-856-2054; Fax: 601-856-2029; Email: pam@stjosephgluckstadt.com; Web: www.stjosephgluckstadt.com. Rev. Kevin Slattery, J.C.L., Sacramental Min.; Mrs. Pamela Minninger, Lay Ecclesial Min.
Catechesis Religious Program—Karen Worrell, C.R.E. Students 209.

GREENVILLE, WASHINGTON CO.

1—ST. JOSEPH (1868)
412 Main St., P.O. Box 1220, Greenville, 38702-1220. Tel: 662-335-5251; Email: parish@stjosephgreenville.org. Revs. William F. Henry; Aaron M. Williams.
High School—St. Joseph Catholic Unit School, (Grades K-12), 1501 VFW Rd., Greenville, 38701-5841. Tel: 662-378-9711; Fax: 662-378-3496; Email: swies@stjoeirish.org. Steve Wies, High School Prin.; Jo Anne Heisterkamp, Elementary School Prin. Lay Teachers 30; Students 257; Clergy / Religious Teachers 1.
Catechesis Religious Program—Mary Ann Barker, D.R.E. Students 20.

2—SACRED HEART (1913)
560 E. Gloster St., Greenville, 38701-3836.
Tel: 662-332-0891; Email: shcchurch@gmail.com. Revs. Thomas A. Mullally, S.V.D.; Cyriaque Sounou.
Catechesis Religious Program—Bynarozelle Mitchell, D.R.E. Students 25.

GREENWOOD, LEFLORE CO.

1—ST. FRANCIS OF ASSISI (1951)
2613 Hwy. 82 E., Greenwood, 38930-5966.
Tel: 662-453-0623; Email: sfgwparish@gmail.com. Revs. Joachim Studwell, O.F.M.; Camillus Janas, O.F.M.
School—St. Francis of Assisi School, (Grades PreK-6), 2607 Hwy. 82 E., Greenwood, 38930-5966.
Tel: 662-453-9511; Fax: 662-453-1366; Email: stfrancisgreenwood@gmail.com; Web: www.sfgwschool.org. Mrs. Jackie Lewis, Prin. Lay Teachers 5; Sisters 3; Students 79.
Catechesis Religious Program— (Combined with Immaculate Heart of Mary, Greenwood) Sr. Kathleen Murphy, O.S..F., D.R.E. Students 58.
Convent—Franciscan Sisters of Christian Charity, 2603 Hwy. 82 E., Greenwood, 38930-5966.
Tel: 662-453-1221. Sr. Annette Kurey, Dir. Sisters 4.

2—IMMACULATE HEART OF MARY (1909)
511 W. Washington St., P.O. Box 313, Greenwood, 38935-0313. Tel: 662-453-3980; Email: ihmeditor@gmail.com. Revs. Joachim Studwell, O.F.M.; Camillus Janas, O.F.M.
Catechesis Religious Program— (Combined with St. Francis of Assisi, Greenwood.) Sandra Correro, D.R.E. Students 51.

GRENADA, GRENADA CO., ST. PETER (1943)
320 College Blvd., Grenada, 38901-3808.
Tel: 662-226-2490; Email: stpeter@cableone.net. Rev. Arokia Savio.
Catechesis Religious Program—Annette Tipton, D.R.E. Students 23.

HERNANDO, DESOTO CO., HOLY SPIRIT (1961)
545 E. Commerce St., P.O. Box 424, Hernando, 38632-0424. Tel: 662-429-7851; Email: holyspiritchurch@shsm.org. Revs. Thi Pham, S.C.J.; Gregory Schill, S.C.J.; David Szatkowski, S.C.J., J.C.D.
Catechesis Religious Program—Amanda Ready, C.R.E. Students 127.

HOLLY SPRINGS, MARSHALL CO., ST. JOSEPH (1857)
305 E. Van Dorn Ave., P.O. Box 430, Holly Springs, 38635-0430. Tel: 662-252-3138; Email: fathermoderator6@gmail.com. Revs. Thi Pham, S.C.J.; Gregory Schill, S.C.J.; David Szatkowski, S.C.J., J.C.D.; Sr. Rose Hacker, S.S.S.F., Pastoral Assoc.
Catechesis Religious Program—Tel: 662-252-3138. Sr. Emily Morgan, R.S.M., D.R.E. Students 41.

INDIANOLA, SUNFLOWER CO.

1—ST. BENEDICT THE MOOR (1953)
403 Church St., P.O. Box 407, Indianola, 38751-0407. Tel: 662-887-4659; Email: icindianola2@att.net. Rev. Peter Nyugen.

2—IMMACULATE CONCEPTION (1955)
700 N. Sunflower Ext. Hwy. 448, P.O. Box 944, Indianola, 38751-0944. Tel: 662-887-4659; Email: icindianola2@att.net. Rev. Peter Nyugen.
Catechesis Religious Program—Rosemary Miller, D.R.E. Students 23.

KOSCIUSKO, ATTALA CO., ST. THERESE (1956)
108 Bell St., P.O. Box 628, Kosciusko, 39090-0628.
Tel: 662-289-1193; Email: sttheresecatholicchurch@gmail.com. Revs. Odel Medina, S.T.; Raul A. Ventura, S.T.
Catechesis Religious Program—Marline Tully, D.R.E. Students 39.

LELAND, WASHINGTON CO., ST. JAMES (1944)
312 E. Third St., P.O. Box 352, Leland, 38756-0352.
Tel: 662-686-7352; Email: stjamesleland@gmail.com. Rev. Alphonse Arulanandu.
Missions—Immaculate Conception—Hwy. 12 E., Hollandale, Washington Co. 38748.
Our Mother of Mercy, 119 Jefferson St., Anguilla, Sharkey Co. 38721.

LEXINGTON, HOLMES CO., ST. THOMAS (1966)
200 Boulevard St., Lexington, 39095-3531.
Tel: 662-453-0623; Email: sfgwparish@gmail.com. Rev. Joachim Studwell, O.F.M., Admin.
Mission—Sacred Heart, 304 Jones St., Winona, Montgomery Co. 38967-2238. Tel: 601-591-8254. Mr. Marvin Edwards, Lay Ecclesial Min.
Station—Mississippi State Penitentiary, Parchman, 38738.

LOUISVILLE, WINSTON CO., SACRED HEART (1966)
410 N. Spring Ave., Louisville, 39339-2222.
Tel: 662-773-6062; Email: sacredheart39339@yahoo.com. Rev. Darnis Selvanayakam, Sacramental Min.; Paula Fulton, Lay Ecclesial Min.

MADISON, MADISON CO., ST. FRANCIS OF ASSISI (1983)
4000 W. Tidewater Ln., Madison, 39110-8942.
Tel: 601-856-5556; Email: contact.us@stfrancismadison.org. Revs. Albeenreddy Vatti, (India); Jason Johnston.
School—St. Anthony Catholic School, (Grades PreK-6), 1585 Old Mannsdale Rd., Madison, 39110.
Tel: 601-607-7054; Fax: 601-853-9687; Email: jbell@stanthonyeagles.org; Web: www.stanthonyeagles.org. Jim Bell, Prin. Lay Teachers 23; Students 254.
Child Care—Assisi Early Learning Center,
Tel: 601-856-9494; Email: aelcmadison@jacksondiocese.org. Sr. Paula Blouin, S.S.N.D., Dir. Lay Teachers 32; Sisters 1; Students 144.
Catechesis Religious Program—Mary Catherine George, D.R.E. Students 234.

MAGEE, SIMPSON CO., ST. STEPHEN (1968)
594 Simpson Hwy. 149, P.O. Box 427, Magee, 39111-0427. Tel: 601-849-3237; Email: stephenstchurch@aol.com. Rt. Rev. Thomas DeWane, O.Praem., Sacramental Min.; Kelleigh Wilson, Lay Ecclesial Min.
Catechesis Religious Program—Kenny McDonald, D.R.E. Students 13.

MCCOMB, PIKE CO., ST. ALPHONSUS (1876)
501 Delaware Ave., P.O. Box 1105, McComb, 39649-1105. Tel: 601-684-5648; Email: stalphonsusmccomb@gmail.com. Rev. Brian Kaskie.
Catechesis Religious Program—Amy Tisdale, D.R.E. Students 130.

MERIDIAN, LAUDERDALE CO.

1—ST. JOSEPH (1910)
1914 18th Ave., P.O. Box 532, Meridian, 39302-0532. Tel: 601-484-8953; Email: donna@catholicmeridian.org. Revs. Matthew P. Simmons; Jose de Jesus Sanchez.

2—ST. PATRICK (1865)
P.O. Box 529, Meridian, 39302-0529.
Tel: 601-693-1321; Email: donna@catholicmeridian.org. Revs. Matthew P. Simmons; Jose de Jesus Sanchez.
Res.: 204-39th Ct., Meridian, 39301.
School—St. Patrick School, (Grades PreK-7), 2700 Davis St., Meridian, 39301-5707. Tel: 601-482-6044; Fax: 601-485-2762; Email: mfrias@stpatrickcatholicschool.org; Web: www.stpatrickcatholicschool.org. Montse Frias, Prin.; Helen Reynolds, Sec. Lay Teachers 9; Students 116.
Catechesis Religious Program—2601 Davis St., Meridian, 39301. Email: sister@catholicmeridian.org. Sr. Marilyn Winkel, D.R.E. Students 138.

MOUND BAYOU, BOLIVAR CO., ST. GABRIEL (1949) [CEM] Closed. For inquiries for parish records contact the chancery.

NATCHEZ, ADAMS CO.

1—ASSUMPTION OF THE B.V.M. (1957)
10 Morgantown Rd., Natchez, 39120-2788.
Tel: 601-442-7250; Email: assumptionchurch@cableone.net. Rev. David O'Connor.

2—HOLY FAMILY (1891)
16 Orange Ave., Natchez, 39120-3647.
Tel: 601-445-5700; Email: holyfamilynatchez@gmail.com. Rev. George B. Ajuruchi, S.S.J.
School—Holy Family Early Childhood Center, (Grades PreK-K), 8 Orange Ave., Natchez, 39120-3647. Tel: 601-442-3947; Fax: 601-442-3973; Email: holyfamily82608@bellsouth.net. Mrs. Ira Young, Co-Dir.; Sr. Dympna Clarke, Co-Dir. Lay Teachers 5; Sisters 2; Students 57.
Convent—Sisters of the Holy Spirit, 26 Orange Ave., Natchez, 39120. Tel: 601-445-6785;
Fax: 601-442-3973; Email: holyfamily82608@bellsouth.net. Sisters Dympna Clarke, Dir.; Louise McLoughlin, Asst. Sisters 2.
Mission—St. John the Baptist, 260 Cranfield Rd., Cranfield, Adams Co. 39661.

3—ST. MARY BASILICA (1842)
107 S. Union St., P.O. Box 1044, Natchez, 39121-1044. Tel: 601-445-5616; Email: stmarybasilica@cableone.net. Rev. David O'Connor.
High School—Cathedral School, (Grades PreK-12), (Coed) 701 Martin Luther King, Jr. St., Natchez, 39120-2962. Tel: 601-442-2531; Fax: 601-442-2179; Email: chs@cathedralgreenwave.com. Norman Yvon, High School Prin.; Mrs. Kimberly Burkley, Elementary School Prin. Lay Teachers 50; Students 693.
Catechesis Religious Program—(Grades K-12), 105 S. Union St., Natchez, 39120. Donna Martello, D.R.E. Students 18.

NEW ALBANY, UNION CO., ST. FRANCIS OF ASSISI (1949)
1507 S. Central Ave., P.O. Box 887, New Albany, 38652-0887. Tel: 662-534-4654; Email: stfrancisparish@bellsouth.net. Rev. Jesuraj Xavier.
Catechesis Religious Program—Ronnie Rossetti, D.R.E. Students 90.
Missions—St. Christopher—431 Pine Ridge Dr., P.O. Box 67, Pontotoc, Pontotoc Co. 38863-0067.
Tel: 662-489-7749; Email: stchristopher@juno.com. Rev. Timothy Murphy, M.A.
Catechesis Religious Program—Students 28.
St. Matthew Catholic Mission, 15710 Hwy. 15 N., P.O. Box 452, Ripley, 38663. Tel: 662-993-8862; Email: stmatthewcatholicchurch@ripleycable.net.

OLIVE BRANCH, DESOTO CO., QUEEN OF PEACE (1983)
8455 Germantown Rd., P.O. Box 65, Olive Branch, 38654-0065. Tel: 662-895-5007; Email: queenop@shsm.org. Revs. Thi Pham, S.C.J.; David Szatkowski, S.C.J., J.C.D.; Gregory Schill, S.C.J.; Sisters Rose Hacker, S.S.S.F., Pastoral Assoc.; Emily Morgan, R.S.M., Pastoral Assoc.
Catechesis Religious Program—Mrs. Victoria Stirek, D.R.E. Students 187.

OXFORD, LAFAYETTE CO., ST. JOHN THE EVANGELIST (1943)
416 S. 5th St., Oxford, 38655-3806.
Tel: 662-234-6073; Email: office@stjohnoxford.org. Rev. Joseph Tonos.
Catechesis Religious Program—Tara Luber, C.R.E. Students 218.
Mission—St. Luke the Evangelist, Public Sq., Bruce,

38915. Tel: 662-234-6073; Email: office@stjohnoxford.org. Rev. Michael McAndrew, C.Ss.R., Sacramental Min.

PAULDING, JASPER CO., ST. MICHAEL (1843)
Mailing Address: P.O. Box 388, Forest, 39074-0388. Tel: 601-469-1916. 1823 Hwy. 503, Paulding, 39348. Liz Edmundson, Business Mgr.

PEARL, RANKIN CO., ST. JUDE (1962)
399 Barrow St., P.O. Box 5526, Pearl, 39288-5526. Tel: 601-939-3181; Email: kmcgregor@stjudepearl.org. Rev. Lincoln Dall; Deacon John T. McGregor.
Catechesis Religious Program—Email: ccd@stjudepearl.org. Stacy Wolf, C.R.E. Students 138.

PHILADELPHIA, NESHOBA CO.
1—HOLY CROSS (1860)
406 Wilson St., Philadelphia, 39350-2906. Tel: 601-656-1841; Email: darnis72@gmail.com. Rev. Darnis Selvanayakam.
Catechesis Religious Program—10400 Road 612, Philadelphia, 39350. Emily Moran, D.R.E. Students 89.
2—HOLY ROSARY (Tucker Community) (1884)
10131 Holy Rosary Rd., Philadelphia, 39350-0037. Tel: 601-656-2880; Email: bgst1@aol.com. P.O. Box 37, Philadelphia, 39350. Rev. Robert Goodyear, S.T.
Catechesis Religious Program—Students 9.
Missions—St. Catherine—9857 Hwy. 489, Conehatta, Newton Co. 39057.
St. Therese, 0110 BIA Rd. 2213, Choctaw, Neshoba Co. 39350.

PORT GIBSON, CLAIBORNE CO., ST. JOSEPH (1849) [CEM]
411 Coffee St., P.O. Box 1012, Port Gibson, 39150-1012. Tel: 601-437-5790; Email: fstnmskb@yahoo.com. Rev. Faustin Misakabo, O.Praem.

RIPLEY, TIPPAH CO., ST. MATTHEW (1997) Closed. Mission of St. Francis, New Albany.

ROBINSONVILLE, TUNICA CO., GOOD SHEPHERD CATHOLIC CHURCH (2009)
1329 Casino Center Dr. Ext., P.O. Box 70, Robinsonville, 38664-0070. Tel: 662-342-7733; Email: ctkshaven@aol.com. Revs. Thi Pham, S.C.J.; David Szatkowski, S.C.J., J.C.D.; Gregory Schill, S.C.J.
Mission—Sacred Heart Chapel, 6473 Hwy. 161 N., P.O. Box 190, Walls, DeSoto Co. 38680-0190. Tel: 662-357-0250.

ROSEDALE, BOLIVAR CO., SACRED HEART (1968)
113 Railroad St., P.O. Box 307, Rosedale, 38769-0307. Tel: 662-846-7136; Email: tomek@bellsouth.net. Rev. Thomas A. Mullally, S.V.D., Sacramental Min.; Dr. James Tomek, Lay Ecclesial Min.

SENATOBIA, TATE CO., ST. GREGORY THE GREAT (1978)
705 Strayhorn St., Senatobia, 38668. Tel: 662-342-1073; Email: ctkshaven@aol.com. Mailing Address: Christ the King Church, 785 Church Rd. W., Southaven, 38671. Revs. Thi Pham, S.C.J.; David Szatkowski, S.C.J., J.C.D.; Gregory Schill, S.C.J.; Sr. Rose Hacker, S.S.S.F., Pastoral Assoc.
Catechesis Religious Program—707 Strayhorn, Senatobia, 38668. Sr. Emily Morgan, R.S.M., D.R.E. Students 47.

SHAW, BOLIVAR CO., ST. FRANCIS OF ASSISI (1949)
301 Dean Blvd., P.O. Box 239, Shaw, 38773-0239. Tel: 662-754-5561; Email: stfrancisassissi@gmail.com. Rev. Thomas A. Mullally, S.V.D.

SHELBY, BOLIVAR CO., ST. MARY (1905)
900 Martin Luther King St., P.O. Box 208, Shelby, 38774-0208. Tel: 662-398-7964; Email: saintmary700@att.net. Rev. Scott Thomas, Sacramental Min.

SOUTHAVEN, DESOTO CO., CHRIST THE KING (1974)
785 Church Rd. W., Southaven, 38671. Tel: 662-342-1073; Email: ctkshaven@aol.com. Revs. Thi Pham, S.C.J.; David Szatkowski, S.C.J., J.C.D.; Gregory Schill, S.C.J.; Deacon Ted Schreck; Sisters Rose Hacker, S.S.S.F., Pastoral Assoc.; Emily Morgan, R.S.M., Pastoral Assoc.
Catechesis Religious Program—Tel: 662-342-7733. Donna Williamson, D.R.E.; Sr. Emily Morgan, R.S.M., RCIA Coord. Students 279.

STARKVILLE, OKTIBBEHA CO., ST. JOSEPH (1930)
607 University Dr., Starkville, 39759. Tel: 662-323-2257; Email: demidunne@hotmail.com; Web: www.stjosephstarkville.org. Revs. Lenin Vargas; Roy Russel Vincent; Deacons Jeff Artiques; John A. McGinley.
Catechesis Religious Program—Email: officejeff@hotmail.com. Deacon Jeff Artigues, D.R.E. Students 117.
Mission—Corpus Christi, 206 N. Washington St., Macon, 39341. P.O. Box 533, Macon, Noxubee Co. 39341.
Chaplaincy—Mississippi State University, Starkville, 39760. Email: dawn.mcginley@gmail.com. Dawn McGinley, Advisor.

TUPELO, LEE CO., ST. JAMES (1908)
1911 N. Gloster St., P.O. Box 734, Tupelo, 38802-0434. Tel: 662-842-4881; Email: st_james_parish@comcast.net. Rev. Timothy Murphy, M.A.
Res.: 757 Lakeshire Dr., Tupelo, 38804. Tel: 662-840-7628.
Catechesis Religious Program—Dawn Steinman, D.R.E. Students 311.
Mission—Christ the King, 100 E. Main St., P.O. Box 614, Fulton, Itawamba Co. 38843-0614. Tel: 662-862-2239; Email: christking@nexband.com. Joan Shell, Pastoral Assoc.
Chapel—St. Thomas Aquinas, 612 County Rd. 683, Saltillo, Lee Co. 38866.

VICKSBURG, WARREN CO.
1—ST. MARY (1906)
1512 Main St., Vicksburg, 39183-2652. Tel: 601-636-0115; Email: stmarysvicksburg@gmail.com. Rev. Joseph Minh Nguyen.
Catechesis Religious Program—Fax: 601-661-0677. Dr. Josephine Calloway, D.R.E. Students 7.
2—ST. MICHAEL (1966)
100 St. Michael Pl., Vicksburg, 39180-8246. Tel: 601-636-3445; Email: office@stmichaelvicksburg.org. Rev. Robert Dore.
Catechesis Religious Program—Helen Benson, D.R.E. Students 68.
3—ST. PAUL (1839) [CEM]
713 Crawford St., Vicksburg, 39180-0646. Tel: 601-636-0140; Email: stpaulvick@att.net. Rev. Thomas Lalor.

WALLS, DESOTO CO., SACRED HEART (1944) Closed. Now a mission of Good Shepherd, Robinsonville.

WEST POINT, CLAY CO., IMMACULATE CONCEPTION (1965)
26707 E. Main St., West Point, 39773-7545. Tel: 662-494-3486; Email: westpoint@jacksondiocese.org. Rev. Binh Chau Nguyen.
Catechesis Religious Program—Penny Elliott, D.R.E. Students 24.

WOODVILLE, WILKINSON CO., ST. JOSEPH (1873)
338 Church St., P.O. Box 668, Woodville, 39669-0668. Tel: 601-888-3261; Email: stjoewms@bellsouth.net. Rev. Scott Dugas.
Catechesis Religious Program—338 Church St., Woodville, 39669. Ferguson Margo, D.R.E. Students 16.
Mission—Holy Family, 242 Main St., P.O. Box 548, Gloster, Amite Co. 39638-0548.

YAZOO CITY, YAZOO CO.
1—ST. FRANCIS (1940) Closed. For inquiries for parish records contact the chancery.
2—ST. MARY (1851)
129 N. Washington St., P.O. Box 27, Yazoo City, 39194-0027. Tel: 662-746-1680; Email: yazoocitystm@jacksondiocese.org. Rev. Panneer Selvam Arockiam.
Catechesis Religious Program—Diane Melton, D.R.E. Students 20.

Chaplains of Public Institutions

JACKSON. *Institute for the Blind, Institute for the Deaf and Speech Impaired*. Rev. John Bohn.
University of Mississippi Medical Center. Rev. Alfred L. Camp, (Retired).
Veterans Administration Hospital. Rt. Rev. E. Thomas De Wane, O.Praem.
MERIDIAN. *East Mississippi State Hospital*. Rev. Augustine Palimattam Poulose, Chap.
PEARL. *Rankin County Prison*. Rev. Lincoln Dall, Chap.
SANATORIUM. *Boswell Retardation Center*. Kelleigh Wilson.
WHITFIELD. *Mississippi State Hospital*. Rev. Lincoln Dall, Chap.

Serving Outside the Diocese:
Revs.—
Daniels, Jerrell Michael
Simmons, Matthew P.

On Leave:
Rev.—
Phipps, Ricardo M.

Retired:
Most Rev.—
Latino, Joseph N., D.D., (Retired)
Rev. Msgrs.—
Farrell, Patrick, (Retired)
Flannery, Michael, J.C.L., (Retired)
Revs.—
Balser, Edward, (Retired)
Bucciantini, Charles, (Retired)
Camp, Alfred L., (Retired)
Carroll, Brian, (Retired)
Corcoran, Frank, (Retired)
Cosgrove, Francis J., (Retired)
Cullen, William, (Retired)
Curley, P. J., (Retired)
Dyer, Joseph, (Retired)
Gallagher, Daniel, (Retired)
Johnson, Howard, (Retired)
Lopez, Jose, (Retired)
Messina, Samuel, (Retired)
Niemira, Thomas, (Retired)
Pentony, Liam, (Retired)
Prendergast, Noel, (Retired).

Permanent Deacons:
Artiques, Jeff, St. Joseph, Starkville
Babin, Henry, (Retired)
Gallagher, Senan, S.T., St. John, Charleston
Gruseck, David J., Annunciation, Columbus
Klingen, Dr. Theodore, (Retired)
Lobo, Denzil, St. Francis of Assisi, Madison
McGinley, John A., St. Joseph, Starkville
McGregor, John T., St. Jude, Pearl
Santos, Edwin, St. Michael, Forest
Schreck, Ted, Christ the King, Southaven.

INSTITUTIONS LOCATED IN DIOCESE

[A] HIGH SCHOOLS, INTER-PAROCHIAL

MADISON. *St. Joseph Catholic School* (1870) (Grades 7-12), (Coed) 308 New Mannsdale Rd., Madison, 39110. Tel: 601-898-4800; Fax: 601-898-4689; Web: www.stjoebruins.com. Dena Kinsey, Prin. Brothers 2; Lay Teachers 48; Students 386; Clergy / Religious Teachers 1.

VICKSBURG. *Vicksburg Catholic School*, (Grades PreK-12), (Coed) 1900 Grove St., Vicksburg, 39183-3181. Tel: 601-636-2256; Fax: 601-631-0430; Email: buddy.strickland@vicksburgcatholic.org; Web: www.vicksburgcatholic.org. Dr. Virgil "Buddy" Strickland, High School Prin.; Mrs. Mary Arledge, Elementary School Prin. Interparochial Lay Teachers 52; Students 538.

[B] ELEMENTARY SCHOOLS INTER-PAROCHIAL

HOLLY SPRINGS. *Holy Family School*, (Grades PreK-8), 395 N. West St., Holly Springs, 38635-1922. Tel: 662-252-1612; Fax: 662-252-3694; Email: cisom@shsm.org; Web: hfamilyschool.org. Clara Isom, Prin. Lay Teachers 17; Students 169; Clergy / Religious Teachers 1.

SOUTHAVEN. *Sacred Heart School* (1947) (Grades PreK-8), 5150 Tchulahoma Rd., Southaven, 38671-9726. Tel: 662-349-0900; Fax: 662-349-0690; Email: bmartin@shsm.org; Web: www.sheartschool.org. Ms. Bridget Martin, Prin.; Rae Davis, Librarian. Lay Teachers 25; Sisters 2; Students 312.

[C] GENERAL HOSPITALS

JACKSON. *St. Dominic-Jackson Memorial Hospital* (1946) 969 Lakeland Dr., Jackson, 39216-4699. Tel: 601-200-6848; Fax: 601-200-6800; Email: ldiamond@stdom.com; Web: www.stdom.com. Mr. Lester K. Diamond, Pres.; Sr. Mary Trinita Eddington, Prioress. Bed Capacity 571; Sisters 9; Tot Asst. Annually 378,054; Total Staff 3,602.

[D] ORPHANAGES AND INFANT HOMES

JACKSON. *St. Mary Orphan Home, Inc.*, P.O. Box 2248, 39225. Tel: 601-355-8634; Fax: 601-960-8493; Email: michaelthomas@ccjackson.org. Most Reverend Joseph R. Kopacz, Ph.D.

[E] MONASTERIES AND RESIDENCES OF PRIESTS AND BROTHERS

GREENWOOD. *St. Francis of Assisi Friary* (1951) 2613 Hwy. 82 E., Greenwood, 38930-5966. Tel: 662-453-0623; Fax: 662-453-9060; Email: sfgwparish@gmail.com. Bro. Craig Wilking, O.F.M., Local Supr.; Revs. Joachim Studwell, O.F.M., Pastor; Camillis Janus, Assoc. Pastor. Franciscan Friars - O.F.M.
Redemptorists of Greenwood, 1500 Levee Rd., P.O. Box 9462, Greenwood, 38930-9462. Tel: 662-451-7980; Email: frscottkatz@cox.net; Email: cssrdelta@gmail.com. Revs. Scott Katzenberger, C.Ss.R., Supr.; Michael McAndrew, C.Ss.R., Vicar; Kevin Zubel, Treas.; Theodore Dorcey, C.Ss.R., Sec.

MADISON. *Christian Brothers Residence*, 103 Brittany Way, Madison, 39110-7928. Tel: 601-949-6931; Email: ted.dausch@jacksondiocese.org. Bros. John Brennan, C.F.C.; Theodore Dausch, C.F.C. Congregation of Christian Brothers.

NESBIT. *St. Michael Community House*, 1360 Nesbit Rd., P.O. Box 38, Nesbit, 38651. Tel: 662-429-8424; Fax: 662-429-8423; Email: thiphamj@yahoo.com.

Revs. Thi Pham, S.C.J., Supr.; Jack Kurps, S.C.J., Exec. Dir.; Gregory Schill, S.C.J., Pastoral Team; David Szatkowski, S.C.J., J.C.D., Pastoral Team.

RAYMOND. *Priory of St. Moses the Black*, 7100 Midway Rd., Raymond, 39154. Tel: 601-857-0157; Fax: 601-857-5076; Email: et.dewane@norbertines.org. Rt. Rev. E. Thomas De Wane, O.Praem., Abbot/Prior; Revs. Norbert N'Zilamba Malonga Vindu, O.Praem.; Jeremy Tobin, O.Praem. Canons Regular of Premontre (The Premonstratensian Fathers). Priests 3.

[F] CONVENTS AND RESIDENCES FOR SISTERS

JACKSON. *St. Dominic Convent*, 969 Lakeland Dr., 39216. Tel: 601-200-6729; Email: sisterd@stdom.com; Web: www.stdom.com. Dorothea Sonderoth, OP, Prioress; Sr. Mary Dorothea Sondgeroth, O.P., Asst. Dir. Health Svcs. & Foundation. Sisters 9.

Our Lady of Mount Carmel and Little Flower Monastery (1951) 2155 Terry Rd., 39204. Tel: 601-373-1460; Fax: 601-372-1369; Email: carmelshop@aol.com. Sr. Mary Jane Agonoy, O.C.D., Prioress. Discalced Carmelites. Nuns with Solemn Vows 5.

CHATAWA. *St. Mary of the Pines*, 3167 Old Hwy. 51 S., Osyka, 39657. Tel: 601-783-5121; Fax: 601-783-0401; Email: dmheffner@ssndcp.org. Sr. Dana Marie Heffner, S.S.N.D., Admin. Home for the Retired Sisters of the Dallas Province of the School Sisters of Notre Dame. Retreat Center for Lay and Religious Groups. Sisters in Residence 44.

GREENWOOD. *St. Francis Convent*, 2603 Hwy. 82 E., Greenwood, 38930-5966. Tel: 662-453-1221; Fax: 662-453-1366. Sr. Annette Kurey, Dir. Franciscan Sisters of Christian Charity 4.

[G] RETREAT CENTERS

BROOKSVILLE. *The Dwelling Place*, 2851 Dwelling Place Rd., Brooksville, 39739-9174. Tel: 662-738-5348; Fax: 662-738-5345; Email: dwellpl@gmail.com; Web: www.dwellingplace.com. Clare Van Lent, Dir.

CHATAWA. *St. Mary of the Pines*, 3167 Old Hwy. 51 S., Osyka, 39657. Tel: 601-783-5121; Fax: 601-783-0401; Email: dmheffner@ssndcp.org. Sr. Dana Marie Heffner, S.S.N.D., Admin. Home for the Retired Sisters of the Dallas Province of the School Sisters of Notre Dame. Retreat Center for Lay and Religious Groups. Sisters in Residence 44.

[H] NEWMAN CENTERS

JACKSON. *Belhaven College Catholic Student Association*, P.O. Box 57, 39205-0057. Tel: 601-969-3125; Fax: 601-969-3130; Email: info@cathedralsaintpeter.org. Very Rev. Anthony Quyet.

Millsaps College Catholic Student Association, P.O. Box 57, 39205-0057. Tel: 601-969-3125; Fax: 601-969-3130; Email: info@cathedrdalsaintpeter.org. Very Rev. Anthony Quyet.

Tougaloo College Newman Center, Holy Ghost Church, 1151 Cloister St., 39202-2296. Tel: 601-353-1339; Fax: 601-353-9607; Email: 1151cloister@earthlink.net. Rev. Alfred Ayem, S.V.D., Contact Person.

University of Mississippi Medical Center - Catholic Student Association, P.O. Box 57, 39205-0057. Tel: 601-969-3125; Email: info@cathedralsaintpeter.org. Very Rev. Anthony Quyet.

BOONEVILLE. *Northeast Mississippi Community College Catholic Student Center*, St. Francis of Assisi, P.O. Box 654, Booneville, 38829. Tel: 662-728-7509; Email: stfrancisbv@att.net; Web: www.stfrancisbooneville.com. Joel P. Schultz, Contact Person.

BROOKHAVEN. *Lincoln Junior College Newman Center*, P.O. Box 196, Brookhaven, 39602-0196. Tel: 601-833-1799; Email: office@stfrancisbrookhaven.org. Rev. Henry Shelton, (Retired).

CLEVELAND. *Delta State University Newman Center*, Our Lady of Victories, 215 Bishop Rd., Cleveland, 38732-2446. Tel: 662-846-6273; Email: olvcc@att.net. Rev. Kent Bowlds, Pastor.

CLINTON. *Mississippi College Catholic Student Association*, Holy Savior Church, P.O. Box 85, Clinton, 39060. Tel: 601-924-6344; Email: holysavior@att.net. Rev. Thomas McGing, J.C.L.

COLUMBUS. *Mississippi University for Women Student Center*, Annunciation Church, 823 College St., Columbus, 39701. Tel: 662-328-2927; Email: annunchr@bellsouth.net; Web: www.annunciationcatholicchurch.com. Very Rev. Jeffrey Waldrep, S.T.L., J.C.L., Pastor.

FOREST. *East Central Community College Newman Center*, St. Michael's Church, P.O. Box 388, Forest, 39074. Tel: 601-469-1916; Fax: 601-469-1815; Email: foreststmichael@att.net. Rev. Roberto Mena.

GOODMAN. *Holmes Community College Newman Center*, St. Thomas, 200 Boulevard St., Lexington, 39095. Tel: 662-453-0623. Rev. Joachim Studwell, O.F.M.

HOLLY SPRINGS. *Rust College Newman Center*, St. Joseph's, P.O. Box 430, Holly Springs, 38635. Tel: 662-252-3138; Email: st930@bellsouth.net. Mr. James Rayford Sr.

OXFORD. *Ole Miss Campus Ministries*, St. John Church, 416 S. 5th St., Oxford, 38655. Tel: 662-234-6073; Fax: 662-234-6079; Email: office@stjohnoxford.org. Rev. Joseph Tonos.

STARKVILLE. *Mississippi State University Catholic Campus Ministry*, St. Joseph Church, 607 University Dr., Starkville, 39759. Tel: 662-323-2257; Fax: 662-323-2258; Web: msstateccm.org. Deacon John A. McGinley, Deacon; Dawn McGinley, Campus Min.

[I] MISCELLANEOUS

JACKSON. *Jackson Diocese Educational Services, Inc.*, 237 E. Amite Street, 39201-2168. Tel: 601-960-6930; Fax: 601-960-8469; Email: karla.luke@jacksondiocese.org; Email: cathy.cook@jacksondiocese.org; Web: schools.jacksondiocese.org/. P.O. Box 2248, 39225-2248. Ms. Catherine D. Cook, Supt.; Mrs. Karla Luke, Asst. Supt.

Parroquia De San Miguel Arcangel, P.O. Box 2248, 39225-2248. Tel: 601-969-1880; Email: mary.woodward@jacksondiocese.org. Rev. David Martinez Rubio, Admin. Saltillo Mission Sponsored by Dioceses of Jackson and Biloxi.
Av. Central 4649 y Calle 44, Col. Vista Hermosa, Saltillo, Coahuila, Mexico C.P. 25010. Tel: 011-52-84-44-82-2207.

Pax Christi Franciscans (1952) LaVerna House, 2108 Alta Woods Blvd., 39204. Tel: 601-373-4463. Kathleen Feyen, Pres. A Private Association of the Christian Faithful, living a consecrated life, engaged in social and educational works. Consecrated Members 3.

MADISON. **St. Catherine's Village, Inc.* (1988) 200 Dominican Dr., Madison, 39110. Tel: 601-856-0100; Fax: 601-200-0823; Email: village@stdom.com; Web: www.stcatherinesvillage.com. Rev. Albeenreddy Vatti, (India) Chap. Assisted Annually 450.

PONTOTOC. *Catholic Committee of the South, Inc.*, St. Christopher Mission, P.O. Box 67, Pontotoc, 38863. Tel: 662-489-7749; Email: stchristopher@juno.com. Sr. Mary Priniski, O.P., Coord.

WALLS. *Sacred Heart Southern Missions Housing Corporation*, 9260 McLemore Drive, P.O. Box 365, Walls, 38680-0365. Tel: 662-781-1516; Fax: 662-781-0886; Email: cloyd@shsm.org. Andrea Vincent, Pres.

Sacred Heart Southern Missions, Inc. (1942) 6050 Hwy. 161 N., P.O. Box 190, Walls, 38680-0190. Tel: 662-781-1360; Fax: 662-342-3390; Web: www.shsm.org. Rev. Jack Kurps, S.C.J., Exec. Dir.

RELIGIOUS INSTITUTES OF MEN REPRESENTED IN THE DIOCESE

For further details refer to the corresponding bracketed number in the Religious Institutes of Men or Women section.

[0900]—*Canons Regular of Premontre*—O.Praem.
[0310]—*Congregation of Christian Brothers*—C.F.C.
[1130]—*Congregation of the Priests of the Sacred Heart*—S.C.J.
[0520]—*Franciscan Friars* (Pulaski, WI)—O.F.M.
[0840]—*Missionary Servants of the Most Holy Trinity*—S.T.
[1070]—*Redemptorist Fathers* (Denver)—C.Ss.R.
[0420]—*Society of the Divine Word*—S.V.D.
[0700]—*St. Joseph's Society of the Sacred Heart*—S.S.J.

RELIGIOUS INSTITUTES OF WOMEN REPRESENTED IN THE DIOCESE

[3710]—*Congregation of the Sisters of Saint Agnes*—C.S.A.
[1780]—*Congregation of the Sisters of the Third Order of St. Francis of Perpetual Adoration*—F.S.P.A.
[0760]—*Daughters of Charity of St. Vincent de Paul*—D.C.
[0420]—*Discalced Carmelite Nuns*—O.C.D.
[1070-10]—*Dominican Sisters* (Springfield, IL)—O.P.
[1230]—*Franciscan Sisters of Christian Charity*—O.S.F.
[1310]—*Franciscan Sisters of Little Falls, Minnesota*—O.S.F.
[1845]—*Missionaries Guadalupanas of the Holy Spirit*—M.G.Sp.S.
[]—*Religious of St. Joseph* (Australia)—R.S.J.
[2970]—*School Sisters of Notre Dame* (Baltimore, St. Louis)—S.S.N.D.
[1680]—*School Sisters of St. Francis*—O.S.F.
[]—*Sisters of Charity* (Halifax)—S.C.
[0500]—*Sisters of Charity of Nazareth* (Kentucky)—S.C.N.
[2100]—*Sisters of Humility of Mary*—C.H.M.
[2575]—*Sisters of Mercy of the Americas* (Belmont, NC)—R.S.M.
[1650]—*Sisters of Saint Francis* (Philadephia, PA)—O.S.F.
[3830-13]—*Sisters of Saint Joseph* (Baden, PA)—C.S.J.
[1570]—*Sisters of St. Francis of the Holy Family* (Dubuque)—O.S.F.
[3840]—*Sisters of St. Joseph of Carondelet* (St. Louis)—C.S.J.
[1990]—*Sisters of the Holy Names of Jesus and Mary* (U.S. - Ontario)—S.N.J.M.
[2050]—*Sisters of the Holy Spirit and Mary Immaculate*—S.H.Sp.
[3320]—*Sisters of the Presentation of the BVM*—P.B.V.M.
[3330]—*Union of Sisters of the Presentation of the BVM*—P.B.V.M.

An asterisk (*) denotes an organization that has established tax-exempt status directly with the IRS and is not covered by the USCCB Group Ruling.

Diocese of Jefferson City

(Dioecesis Civitatis Jeffersoniensis)

Most Reverend

W. SHAWN MCKNIGHT

Bishop of Jefferson City; ordained May 28, 1994; appointed Bishop of Jefferson City November 21, 2017; consecrated February 6, 2018. *Res.: P.O. Box 104900, Jefferson City, MO 65110-4900.*

Catholic Center: Alphonse J. Schwartze Memorial, 2207 W. Main St., P.O. Box 104900, Jefferson City, MO 65110-4900. Tel: 573-635-9127; Fax: 573-635-0386.

Web: www.diojeffcity.org

ESTABLISHED JULY 2, 1956.

Square Miles 22,127.

Comprises the Counties of Adair, Audrain, Benton, Boone, Callaway, Camden, Chariton, Clark, Cole, Cooper, Crawford, Gasconade, Hickory, Howard, Knox, Lewis, Linn, Macon, Maries, Marion, Miller, Moniteau, Monroe, Montgomery, Morgan, Osage, Pettis, Phelps, Pike, Pulaski, Putnam, Ralls, Randolph, Saline, Schuyler, Scotland, Shelby and Sullivan in the State of Missouri.

For legal titles of parishes and diocesan institutions, consult the Chancery Office.

STATISTICAL OVERVIEW

Personnel	
Bishop	1
Retired Bishops	1
Priests: Diocesan Active in Diocese	51
Priests: Diocesan Active Outside Diocese	2
Priests: Retired, Sick or Absent	20
Number of Diocesan Priests	73
Religious Priests in Diocese	4
Total Priests in Diocese	77
Extern Priests in Diocese	18
Ordinations:	
Transitional Deacons	1
Permanent Deacons in Diocese	87
Total Brothers	1
Total Sisters	31
Parishes	
Parishes	95
With Resident Pastor:	
Resident Diocesan Priests	44
Resident Religious Priests	3
Without Resident Pastor:	
Administered by Priests	42
Administered by Deacons	3
Administered by Religious Women	3
Missions	14
Professional Ministry Personnel:	
Brothers	1
Sisters	14
Lay Ministers	94
Welfare	
Catholic Hospitals	2
Total Assisted	288,190
Health Care Centers	13
Total Assisted	122,358
Special Centers for Social Services	2
Total Assisted	48,073
Educational	
Diocesan Students in Other Seminaries	9
Total Seminarians	9
High Schools, Diocesan and Parish	3
Total Students	1,540
Elementary Schools, Diocesan and Parish	37
Total Students	5,809
Catechesis/Religious Education:	
High School Students	1,694
Elementary Students	3,129
Total Students under Catholic Instruction	12,181
Teachers in the Diocese:	
Brothers	1
Sisters	9
Lay Teachers	628
Vital Statistics	
Receptions into the Church:	
Infant Baptism Totals	929
Minor Baptism Totals	176
Adult Baptism Totals	121
Received into Full Communion	218
First Communions	1,172
Confirmations	1,205
Marriages:	
Catholic	247
Interfaith	145
Total Marriages	392
Deaths	768
Total Catholic Population	76,283
Total Population	922,351

Former Bishops—Most Revs. JOSEPH M. MARLING, C.PP.S., D.D., ord. Feb. 21, 1929; appt. Auxiliary of Kansas City, June 9, 1947; cons. Aug. 6, 1947; appt. Bishop of Jefferson City, Aug. 24, 1956; retired July 2, 1969; died Oct. 2, 1979; MICHAEL F. MCAULIFFE, S.T.D., ord. May 31, 1945; appt. July 2, 1969; cons. Aug. 18, 1969; retired Aug. 27, 1997; died Jan. 9, 2006; JOHN RAYMOND GAYDOS, ord. Dec. 20, 1968; appt. June 25, 1997; cons. Aug. 27, 1997; retired Nov. 21, 2017.

Vicar General—Mailing Address: P.O. Box 104900, Jefferson City, 65110-4900. Rev. Msgr. ROBERT A. KURWICKI, V.G.

Chancery Office—2207 W. Main St., P.O. Box 104900, Jefferson City, 65110-4900. Tel: 573-635-9127; Fax: 573-635-0386. All offices are at this address unless noted otherwise.

Chancellor—Sr. KATHLEEN WEGMAN, S.S.N.D.

Vice-Chancellor—Very Rev. MARK A. PORTERFIELD, J.C.L.

Moderator of the Curia—Rev. GREGORY C. MEYSTRIK.

Diocesan Tribunal—All marriage papers should be sent to the attention of Diocesan Tribunal Office.

Judicial Vicar—Very Rev. MARK A. PORTERFIELD, J.C.L.

Adjutant Judicial Vicar—Rev. Msgr. GREGORY L. HIGLEY.

Defenders of the Bond—MRS. CONSTANCE SCHEPERS.

Promoter of Justice—Very Rev. MARK A. PORTERFIELD, J.C.L.

Judge—Rev. MICHAEL F. QUINN.

Notary—MRS. TERESA VIGNOLA.

Diocesan Consultors—Rev. Msgr. ROBERT A. KURWICKI, V.G.; Very Rev. MARK A. PORTERFIELD, J.C.L.; Rev. Msgr. GREGORY L. HIGLEY; Revs. GREGORY C. MEYSTRIK; JASON T. DOKE; MATTHEW J. FLATLEY; DONALD J. ANTWEILER.

Deans—I. Columbia: Rev. PHILIP E. NIEKAMP, Dean: Boonville, Columbia, Fayette, Moberly, Pilot Grove, Brunswick, Glasgow, Indian Grove, Salisbury, Slater, Marshall. II. Hannibal: Rev. JASON T. DOKE, Dean: Canton (La Grange), Ewing, Hannibal, Indian Creek, Kahoka (Wayland), Louisiana (Clarksville), Monroe City, Palmyra, Perry (Paris), St. Clement, St. Patrick, Vandalia (Laddonia). III. Jefferson City: Rev. LOUIS M. NELEN, Dean: California, Holts Summit, Jefferson City, Russellville, St. Martins, Taos, Wardsville. IV. Kirksville: Deacon COLIN P. FRANKLIN, Dean: Baring, Edina, Kirksville (Novinger), Memphis, Milan (Unionville), Brookfield, Clarence, Macon (Bevier), Marceline, Shelbina. V. Mexico: Rev. Msgr. GREGORY L. HIGLEY, Dean: Centralia, Fulton, Hermann, Jonesburg, Martinsburg, Mexico, Mokane, Montgomery City, Rhineland, Wellsville. VI. Rolla: Rev. MATTHEW J. FLATLEY, Dean: Belle, Bourbon, Brinktown, Crocker, Cuba, Dixon, Owensville, Richland, Rolla, Rosati, St. James, Steelville, Vienna, St. Robert. VII. Sedalia/Lake Ozark: Rev. ANTHONY R. RINALDO, Dean: Camdenton, Eldon, Laurie (Versailles), Hermitage (Climax Springs), Lake Ozark, Mary's Home, St. Anthony, St. Elizabeth, Sedalia, Tipton, Warsaw. VIII. Westphalia: Rev. DANIEL J. MERZ, S.L.D., Dean: Argyle (Koeltztown), Bonnots Mill, Chamois, Folk, Frankenstein, Freeburg, Linn, Loose Creek, Meta, Rich Fountain, Westphalia, Morrison, Osage Bend, St. Thomas. IX. International Priests: Rev. ROBERTO M. IKE, Dean.

Masters of Ceremonies—

To The Bishop—Revs. MICHAEL W. PENN; JOSHUA J. DUNCAN.

Personnel Board—Most Rev. W. SHAWN MCKNIGHT; Rev. Msgr. MICHAEL T. FLANAGAN; Very Rev. MARK A. PORTERFIELD, J.C.L.; Rev. Msgr. ROBERT A. KURWICKI, V.G.; Revs. DONALD J. ANTWEILER; MICHAEL W. PENN; CHRISTOPHER L. CORDES; STEPHEN W. JONES.

Presbyteral Council—Most Rev. W. SHAWN MCKNIGHT, Pres. Deans: Revs. PHILIP E. NIEKAMP; JASON T. DOKE; LOUIS M. NELEN; Rev. Msgr. GREGORY L. HIGLEY; Revs. MATTHEW J. FLATLEY; COLIN P. FRANKLIN; ANTHONY R. RINALDO; DANIEL J. MERZ, S.L.D.; ROBERTO M. IKE. Representatives: Revs. DONALD J. ANTWEILER; FRANCIS W. DOYLE; JOHN J. SCHMITZ; DYLAN SCHRADER. Religious Representative: Rev. REGINALD WOLFORD, O.P. Ex Officio Members: Rev. Msgr. ROBERT A. KURWICKI, V.G.; Very Rev. MARK A. PORTERFIELD, J.C.L.

Diocesan Offices and Directors

Buildings and Properties—Rev. GREGORY C. MEYSTRIK; MR. BRAD COPELAND, Dir.

Campus Ministry—MRS. ANGELLE HALL, Dir.

Cemeteries—Deacon ALAN D. SIMS, Dir.

Charismatic Renewal Program—Deacon KENNETH BERRY, Diocesan Representative, 201 N. Cottey, Edina, 63537. Tel: 660-397-2636.

Communication—MRS. HELEN OSMAN, Dir. Diocesan Communications; MRS. JILL ALBERTI, Dir. Parish Communications.

Cursillo Movement—MS. BETH SCHROEDER, Lay Dir.; Rev. JOSEPH S. COREL, Spiritual Dir.

Chief Financial Officer—Deacon JOSEPH M. BRADDOCK, CPA.

Diaconate Office—Rev. DANIEL J. MERZ, S.L.D., Dir.; Deacon RAYMOND L. PURVIS, Coord.

Engaged Encounter—Coordinators: Deacon BURDETT WILSON; JOYCE WILSON, 4755 County Rd. 2130,

Huntsville, 65259; Rev. Michael F. Quinn, Spiritual Dir.

Finance—Deacon Joseph Braddock, CPA, CFO.

Finance Committee—Most Rev. W. Shawn McKnight; Deacon Joseph M. Braddock, CPA, CFO; Rev. Msgr. Michael T. Flanagan; Mr. Michael Kelly; Mr. Charles Cassmeyer; Ms. Barbara Reichart; Mrs. Arlene Vogel; Mr. Harold Westhues; Mr. Gary Wilbers; Mr. Matthias Tolksdorf; Rev. Gregory C. Meystrik; Rev. Msgr. Robert A. Kurwicki, V.G.; Mrs. Betty Zimmerman; Sr. Kathleen Wegman, S.S.N.D.

Hispanic Ministry—Mr. Enrique Castro, Dir.

Historical Archives—Sr. Kathleen Wegman, S.S.N.D., Contact.

Parish Services—Sr. Kathleen Wegman, S.S.N.D., Chancellor.

Legion of Mary—Deacon David Thompson, Spiritual Dir.

Liturgical Commission—Rev. Daniel J. Merz, S.L.D.

Mediation and Arbitration Board—Vacant.

Marriage Encounter—Chair Couple: Mr. Brit Smith; Mrs. Candi Smith, 215 Boonville Rd., Jefferson City, 65109. Tel: 573-636-3712; Rev. Gregory C. Meystrik, Spiritual Dir.

Marriage Tribunal—Mrs. Constance Schepers, Admin.

Ministry Formation—Revs. Christopher M. Aubuchon; Joshua J. Duncan; Louis M. Nelen.

Ministry to Priests—Most Rev. W. Shawn McKnight; Rev. Msgr. Robert A. Kurwicki, V.G., Chair; Very Rev. Mark A. Porterfield, J.C.L.; Rev. Gregory C. Meystrik; Rev. Msgr. Gregory L. Higley; Revs. Matthew J. Flatley; Daniel J. Merz, S.L.D.; Louis M. Nelen; Philip E. Niekamp; Jason T. Doke; Colin P. Franklin; Anthony R. Rinaldo; Roberto M. Ike.

Mission OfficeMr. Mark D. Saucier, Dir.

Newspaper-"The Catholic Missourian"—Mr. Jay Nies, Editor, Mailing Address: P.O. Box 104900, Jefferson City, 65110-4900.

Priestly and Religious Vocations Committee—Most Rev. W. Shawn McKnight; Revs. Christopher M. Aubuchon; Francis W. Doyle; Colin P. Franklin; Louis M. Nelen; Stephen W. Jones; Anthony R. Rinaldo; Anthony J. Viviano; Joshua J. Duncan; Paul J. Clark; Jason T. Doke.

Priests' Mutual Benefit Society—Board of Trustees: Most Rev. W. Shawn McKnight; Revs. Christopher L. Cordes, Sec.; Gregory C. Meystrik, Chair; Rev. Msgr. Robert A. Kurwicki, V.G.; Revs. Jeremy A. Secrist; Michael W. Penn.

Religious Education Office—Mr. John DeLaporte, Coord.

School Office—Sisters Elizabeth Youngs, S.C.L., Supt.; Julie Brandt, S.S.N.D., Assoc. Supt.

Diocesan Schools Technology Foundation—Vacant, 2207 W. Main St., P.O. Box 104900, Jefferson City, 65110-4900. Tel: 573-635-9127; Fax: 573-635-2286.

Scouting—600 Wildwood Ln., Waynesville, 65583. Tel: 573-774-4152. Deacon Rick L. Vise Sr., Chap.

Teens Encounter Christ (TEC)—Mr. Steve Maxwell, Lay Dir., 364 County Rd. 634, Freeburg, 65035; Rev. Michael A. Coleman, Spiritual Dir.

Risk Management—Mrs. Kathy Smith, Contact; Deacon Joseph M. Braddock, CPA, CFO & Contact.

Victim Assistance Coordinator—Mrs. Nancy Hoey, Tel: 573-694-3199; Email: reportabuse@diojeffcity.org.

Youth Ministry—Mr. John DeLaporte, Coord.

CLERGY, PARISHES, MISSIONS AND PAROCHIAL SCHOOLS

JEFFERSON CITY

(Cole County)

1—St. Joseph Cathedral (1959) [JC]
2305 W. Main St., 65109. Tel: 573-635-7991; Fax: 573-635-0842; Email: info@cathedraljc.org; Web: www.cathedraljc.org. Revs. Louis M. Nelen; Joshua J. Duncan; Deacons Robert J. Rackers, (Retired); Alvin J. Brand; Dana K. Joyce; James L. Kliethermes; R. Christopher Baker; John A. Schwartze; Tyler McClay.
School—St. Joseph Cathedral School, (Grades PreK-8), 2303 W. Main St., 65109. Tel: 573-635-5024; Fax: 573-635-5238; Email: sallen@sjcsmo.org; Web: www.sjcsmo.org. Spencer L. Allen, Prin.; Mrs. Gina Bailey, Asst. Prin. Lay Teachers 33; Students 455.
Catechesis Religious Program—Students 74.

2—Immaculate Conception (1913) [JC]
1206 E. McCarty St., 65101. Tel: 573-635-6143; Fax: 573-635-6036; Email: icchurch@icangels.com; Web: www.icangels.com. Revs. Donald J. Antweiler; Geoffrey Brooke Jr.; Deacons Mark Aulbur; Raymond L. Purvis; Kenneth V. Wildhaber Jr.
School—Immaculate Conception School, (Grades PreK-8), 1208 E. McCarty St., 65101. Tel: 573-636-7680; Fax: 573-635-1833; Email: hschrimpf@icangels.com; Web: www.icangels.com. Mrs. Heather Schrimpf, Prin.; Charlene Connor, Librarian. Lay Teachers 31; Students 296.
Catechesis Religious Program—Students 65.

3—St. Peter (1846) [JC]
216 Broadway, 65101. Tel: 573-636-8159; Fax: 573-634-6079; Email: parish@saintpeterjc.org; Web: www.stpeterjc.org. Rev. Charles D. Pardee; Deacons Thomas M. Whalen; Thomas M. Fischer; David Thompson; Philip Garcia; Ric Telthorst.
School—St. Peter School, (Grades K-8), 314 W. High St., 65101. Tel: 573-636-8922; Fax: 573-636-8410; Email: saints@saintpeterjc.org; Web: www.stpeterjc.org. Mrs. Gayle Trachsel, Prin.; Heather Luebbert, Librarian. Lay Teachers 40; Students 511.
Catechesis Religious Program—Students 89.

OUTSIDE JEFFERSON CITY

Argyle, Osage Co., St. Aloysius (1910) [CEM 2]
1 Church Lane, Argyle, 65001. Tel: 573-728-6975; Email: secretarysasb@gmail.com. P.O. Box 6, Argyle, 65001. Rev. Gregory C. Meystrik.
Catechesis Religious Program—Rachel Heimericks, D.R.E. Students 51.
Mission—St. Boniface (1866) 3982 Hwy. T, Koeltztown, 65001.

Baring, Knox Co., St. Aloysius (1894) [CEM]
Attended by Edina
509 N. Main St., Edina, 63537-1239.
Tel: 660-397-2183; Fax: 660-397-3680; Email: stjoeal@marktwain.net; Web: knoxcountycatholic.org. Rev. Colin P. Franklin; Deacon Kenneth Berry.
Catechesis Religious Program— Twinned with St. Joseph, Edina. Students 4.

Belle, Maries Co., St. Alexander (1910) [CEM]
Attended by Immaculate Conception, Owensville.
400 W. Third St., Belle, 65013. Tel: 573-859-6231; Email: icchurch@fidnet.com. P.O. Box 606, Belle, 65013. Rev. Wayne M. Boyer.
Catechesis Religious Program—Students 12.

Bonnots Mill, Osage Co., St. Louis of France (1905) [CEM]
211 Church Hill St., Bonnots Mill, 65054.
Tel: 573-897-2922; Fax: 573-897-4271; Email: icparish1845@gmail.com. Mailing Address: P.O. Box 8, Loose Creek, 65054. Rev. Callistus Okoroji; Deacon Larry Hildebrand.
Catechesis Religious Program—Students 8.

Boonville, Cooper Co., SS. Peter and Paul (1856) [CEM]
322 7th St., Boonville, 65233. Tel: 660-882-6468; Email: ssppchurch@socket.net; Web: www.stsppchurch.net. Rev. R. William Peckman; Deacon David Miller.
School—SS. Peter and Paul School, (Grades PreK-8) 502 7th St., Boonville, 65233. Tel: 660-882-2589; Fax: 660-882-2476; Email: alammers@sssppschool.net; Web: www.stsppschool.net. Mr. Alan Lammers Prin. Lay Teachers 12; Students 182.
Catechesis Religious Program—Email: ssppdre@socket.net. Theresa Krebs, D.R.E. Students 58.

Bourbon, Crawford Co., St. Francis Caracciolo (1915) [CEM 2]
1050 Old Hwy. 66, Bourbon, 65441.
Tel: 573-265-7250; Email: icchurch@centurylink.net; Web: www.icchurchstjames.org. Mailing Address: 316 E. Scioto, St. James, 65559. Rev. Henry Ussher, Admin.
Church: 1080 Old Hwy. 66 W., Bourbon, 65441.
Tel: 573-885-3520; Email: hcccuba@gmail.com; Web: www.holycrosscubamo.org.

Brinktown, Maries Co., Holy Guardian Angels (1891) [CEM] Attended by Visitation, Vienna.
37515 Hwy. N., Brinktown, 65443. Tel: 573-422-3950; Email: vgasecretary@att.net. 108 N. Coffey St., P.O. Box 226, Vienna, 65582. Rev. Matthew J. Flatley; Deacon Doug Hemke.
Catechesis Religious Program—Mendy James, D.R.E. Students 15.

Brookfield, Linn Co., Immaculate Conception (1859) [CEM]
313 N. Livingston St., Brookfield, 64628.
Tel: 660-258-2507; Email: rectory@icbrookfield.org; Web: www.icbrookfield.org. Rev. Gerald J. Kaimann; Sr. Mary Rost, S.S.N.D., Admin.
Catechesis Religious Program—Students 58.

Brunswick, Chariton Co., St. Boniface (1860) [CEM]
203 E. Harrison St., Brunswick, 65236.
Tel: 660-548-3267; Email: stboniface@centurylink.net. Rev. Boniface Kasiita Nzabonimpa.
Catechesis Religious Program—Students 20.
Mission—St. Joseph (1870)
Catechesis Religious Program—Students 6.

California, Moniteau Co., Annunciation (1872) [CEM]
310 S. Mill St., California, 65018. Tel: 573-796-4842; Email: annunciati@socket.net; Web: www.annunciationcatholicchurch.org. Rev. Anthony R. Rinaldo; Sr. Mary Ruth Wand, S.S.N.D., Pastoral Min.; Deacon Edwin Schepers.
Catechesis Religious Program—Students 100.

Camdenton, Camden Co., St. Anthony (1946)
1874 N. Business Rte. 5, Camdenton, 65020.
Tel: 573-346-2716; Fax: 573-346-0625; Email: stanthonys@sbcglobal.net; Web: www.stanthonyschurch.org. Rev. Daniel I.J. Lueckenotte; Deacon Stan Buczko.
Catechesis Religious Program—Mildred Webb, D.R.E. Students 150.

Canton, Lewis Co., St. Joseph (1865)
812 Lewis St., Canton, 63435. Tel: 573-288-3198; Email: stjosephcanton@centurytel.net. Rev. Robert H. Fields, Admin.
Catechesis Religious Program—Students 25.
Mission—Notre Dame (1868) 714 Rte. C, La Grange, Lewis Co. 63448. Tel: 573-655-4296. Donna Howe, Contact Person.

Centralia, Boone Co., Holy Spirit (1897)
404 S. Rollins St., Centralia, 65240.
Tel: 573-682-2815; Email: office@holyspiritcentralmo.org. Rev. Michael A. Coleman.
Catechesis Religious Program—Tel: 573-682-3507; Email: cagoosey@gmail.com. Ann Goosey, D.R.E. Students 104.

Chamois, Osage Co., Most Pure Heart of Mary (1865) [CEM 2]
106 W. 2nd St., P.O. Box 156, Chamois, 65024.
Tel: 573-763-5345; Email: mphsec@mostpureheart.org; Web: www.MostPureHeart.org. Rev. David A. Means, Canonical Admin.
Catechesis Religious Program—Students 15.

Clarence, Shelby Co., St. Patrick (1884) [CEM]
201 Grand St., Clarence, 63468. Tel: 573-588-4498; Fax: 573-588-4728; Email: stpatricksclarence@gmail.com. P.O. Box 306, Shelbina, 63468. Rev. Simeon A. Etonu, Admin.; Deacons John DeGraff; Larry W. Mitchell.
Catechesis Religious Program—Students 10.

Columbia, Boone Co.

1—Our Lady of Lourdes (1958)
903 Bernadette Dr., Columbia, 65203.
Tel: 573-445-7915; Fax: 573-446-7402; Email: office2@ourladyoflourdes.org; Web: www.ourladyoflourdes.org. Revs. Christopher L. Cordes; Leonard Mukiibi; Rev. Msgr. Michael T. Flanagan, In Res.; Deacons Joseph Puglis; James Leyden; Joseph M. Braddock, CPA.
School—Our Lady of Lourdes Interparish School, (Grades PreK-8), 817 Bernadette Dr., Columbia, 65203. Tel: 573-445-6516; Fax: 573-445-9887; Email: ehassemer@ollisk8.org; Web: ollisk8.org. Elaine Hassemer, Prin.; Sharon Schauwecker, Librarian. Lay Teachers 44; Students 635.
Catechesis Religious Program—Email: reddirector@ourladyoflourdes.org. Kathleen Armistead, D.R.E. Students 290.

2—Sacred Heart (1876)
105 Waugh St., Columbia, 65201. Tel: 573-443-3470; Fax: 573-442-1082; Web: www.sacredheart-church.org. Rev. Francis W. Doyle; Deacon Bill Caubet.
Catechesis Religious Program—Students 60.

3—St. Thomas More Newman Center (1963)
602 Turner Ave., Columbia, 65201.
Tel: 573-449-5424; Fax: 573-874-2777; Email: reception@comonewman.org. Revs. Richard F. Litzau, O.P.; Christopher M. Aubuchon; Joachim Culotta, O.P.; Reginald Wolford, O.P.; Sr. Karen Freund, O.P., Pastoral Assoc.; Deacons Francis Ruggiero; Gene Kazmierczak
Legal Name: St. Thomas More Newman Center, University of Missouri
Res.: 905 S. Greenwood, Columbia, 65203.
Catechesis Religious Program—Students 153.

Crocker, Pulaski Co., St. Cornelius (1966) [CEM]
Attended by St. Theresa, Dixon.
506 W. 2nd St., Dixon, 65459. Tel: 573-759-7521; Email: st.theresa@windstream.net. P.O. Box 310, Dixon, 65459-0310. Rev. Joseph Hoi.
Catechesis Religious Program—Tel: 573-621-5200. John Markusic, D.R.E. Students 3.

Cuba, Crawford Co., Holy Cross (1880) [CEM]
415 W. School Ave., Cuba, 65453. Tel: 573-885-3520; Fax: 573-885-3501; Email: hcccuba@gmail.com;

Web: www.holycrosscubamo.org. Revs. David J. Veit; Paul J. Clark; Sr. Karen Thein, Pastoral Min./Coord.
School—Holy Cross School, (Grades PreK-5), Tel: 573-885-4727; Fax: 573-885-3501; Email: holycrossschoolcuba@gmail.com; Web: www.holycrosscubamo.org. Deacon Michael S. Brooks, Prin.; Mrs. Rita May, Librarian. Lay Teachers 4; Students 51.
Catechesis Religious Program—Mrs. JoAnn Bayless, D.R.E.; Teresa Leicht, D.R.E. (Teen On Target). Students 27.

DIXON, PULASKI CO., ST. THERESA (1928) [CEM]
506 Oak St., Dixon, 65459. Tel: 573-759-7521; Email: st.theresa@windstream.net. P.O. Box 310, Dixon, 65459. Rev. Joseph Hoi.
Catechesis Religious Program—

EDINA, KNOX CO., ST. JOSEPH (1844) [CEM 2]
509 N. Main St., Edina, 63537-1239.
Tel: 660-397-2183; Fax: 660-397-3680; Email: stjoeal@marktwain.net; Web: www.knoxcountycatholic.org. Rev. Colin P. Franklin; Deacon Kenneth Berry.
Catechesis Religious Program—Students 58.

ELDON, MILLER CO., SACRED HEART (1910)
540 N. Mill St., Eldon, 65026. Tel: 573-392-5334; Fax: 573-395-3493; Email: sacred540@sbcglobal.net; Web: www.sacredhearteldon.org. Rev. Alexander Gabriel; Deacons Gary Christoff; Chet L. Zuck Jr.; Amy Frank, Sec.
Catechesis Religious Program—Students 55.

EWING, LEWIS CO., QUEEN OF PEACE (1887) [CEM 2]
307 N. Main St., Ewing, 63440. Tel: 573-209-3343; Email: qofpeace@marktwain.net. P.O. Box 347, Ewing, 63440-0347. Sr. Jane Weisgram, Parish Life Coord.
310 N. Main St., Ewing, 63440.
Catechesis Religious Program—Students 21.

FAYETTE, HOWARD CO., ST. JOSEPH (1956)
300 S. Cleveland Ave., Fayette, 65248.
Tel: 660-248-2439; Fax: 660-248-2439; Email: stjoseph-fayette@socket.net; Web: www.stjosephcath.org. Rev. R. William Peckman.
Catechesis Religious Program—Sandy Dorson, D.R.E. Students 31.

FOLK, OSAGE CO., ST. ANTHONY OF PADUA (1905) [CEM]
255 Hwy. EE, Folk, 65085. Tel: 573-455-2888; Email: folkchurch@yahoo.com. P.O. Box 157, Westphalia, 65085. Rev. Anthony J. Viviano. Mission parish of St. Joseph Catholic Church, Westphalia.
Catechesis Religious Program—Students 40.

FRANKENSTEIN, OSAGE CO., OUR LADY HELP OF CHRISTIANS (1863) [CEM 3]
1665 Hwy. C, Bonnots Mill, 65016. Tel: 573-897-2587 ; Email: olohc@hotmail.com. Rev. Daniel J. Merz, S.L.D.
School—St. Mary School, Tel: 573-897-2567. Janice Markway, Prin. Lay Teachers 5; Students 26.
Catechesis Religious Program—Students 25.

FREEBURG, OSAGE CO., HOLY FAMILY (1904) [CEM]
104 Oliver St., Freeburg, 65035. Tel: 573-744-5254; Email: cathedralofozarks@att.net. P.O. Box 9, Freeburg, 65035. Rev. William D. Debo.
School—Holy Family School, (Grades PreK-8), 110 West Oliver St., P.O. Box 156, Freeburg, 65035.
Tel: 573-744-5200; Email: hfsdreinkemeyer@gmail.com. Debbie Reinkemeyer, Prin. Clergy 1; Lay Teachers 8; Sisters 1; Students 88.
Catechesis Religious Program—Students 54.

FULTON, CALLAWAY CO., ST. PETER (1875)
700 State Rd. Z, Fulton, 65251. Tel: 573-642-5562; Tel: 573-642-2839; Email: stpeterparishoffice@stpeterfultonmo.org; Email: stpeterschooloffice@stpeterfultonmo.org; Web: stpeterfultonmo.org. Rev. Joseph A. Abah; Deacon John L. Neudecker, Parish Life Coord.
School—St. Peter School, (Grades PreK-8), Teresa Arms, Prin. Lay Teachers 12; Students 110.
Catechesis Religious Program—Students 43.

GLASGOW, HOWARD CO., ST. MARY (1866) [CEM]
421 Third St., Glasgow, 65254. Tel: 660-338-2053; Fax: 660-338-2598; Email: glasgowcatholicchurch@yahoo.com; Web: www.glasgowstmary.com. Rev. Paul M. Hartley.
School—St. Mary School, (Grades K-8), 501 3rd St., Glasgow, 65254. Kent Monnig, Prin. Lay Teachers 11; Students 105.
Catechesis Religious Program—Students 41.

HANNIBAL, MARION CO., HOLY FAMILY (1845) [JC]
218 S. Maple Ave., Hannibal, 63401.
Tel: 573-221-1078; Email: miller@myholyfamily.com. 1111 Broadway, Hannibal, 63401. Rev. Michael F. Quinn; Deacon Troy K. Egbert; Sr. Mary Essner, S.S.N.D., Pastoral Min.
School—Holy Family School, (Grades 1-8), 1113 Broadway, Hannibal, 63401. Tel: 573-221-0456; Fax: 573-221-6357; Email: sbuchytil@myholyfamily.com. Sr. Betty Uchytil, S.S.N.D., Prin. Lay Teachers 18; Sisters 1; Students 174.
Catechesis Religious Program—Email: maryssnd@hotmail.com. Students 65.

HERMANN, GASCONADE CO., ST. GEORGE CATHOLIC CHURCH (1845) [CEM]
128 W. 4th St., Hermann, 65041-1099.
Tel: 573-486-2723; Email: church@stgparish.com; Web: www.stgparish.com. Rev. Msgr. Gregory L. Higley.
School—St. George School, (Grades PreK-8), Tel: 573-486-5914; Email: office@stgparish.com; Web: www.stgeorgeschool-hermann.com. Julie Clingman, Prin. Lay Teachers 11; Students 161.
Catechesis Religious Program—Students 35.

HERMITAGE, HICKORY CO., ST. BERNADETTE (1973)
Hwy. 254, Hermitage, 65668. Tel: 417-745-6361; Email: stbernadettechurch@hotmail.com. P.O. Box 167, Hermitage, 65668. Deacon Kent Boettger, Parish Life Coord.
Catechesis Religious Program—Students 6.
Mission—Our Lady of the Snows, Coffman Bend Rd & 51 Grace Ln., Climax Springs, 65324.
Tel: 573-345-4223. P.O. Box 21, Climax Springs, 65324.

HOLTS SUMMIT, CALLAWAY CO., ST. ANDREW (1975) [CEM]
400 St. Andrew Dr., Holts Summit, 65043.
Tel: 573-896-5010; Email: standrew@embarqmail.com; Web: www.standrew.weconnect.com. Rev. Joseph S. Corel; Deacons Daniel J. Ramsay; Edward D. Stroesser.
Catechesis Religious Program—Students 30.

ILASCO, RALLS CO., HOLY CROSS, Closed. For inquiries for parish records please see Holy Family, Hannibal.

INDIAN CREEK, MONROE CO., ST. STEPHEN (1833) [CEM]
27519 Monroe Rd. 533, Monroe City, 63456.
Tel: 573-735-2541; Email: churchst.stephen@gmail.com; Web: www.ststephencatholicchurch.org. Rev. P. Gregory Oligschlaeger; Deacon L. Michael Long.
Catechesis Religious Program—

INDIAN GROVE, CHARITON CO., ST. RAPHAEL (1886) [CEM] Attended by St. Boniface, Brunswick.
203 E. Harrison St., Brunswick, 65236.
Tel: 660-548-3267; Email: stboniface@centurylink.net. Rev. Kasita Nzabonimpa, Admin.
Catechesis Religious Program—

JONESBURG, MONTGOMERY CO., ST. PATRICK (1862) [CEM]
505 First St., Jonesburg, 63351. Tel: 636-488-5623; Email: stpats@centurytel.net. Rev. Augustine Azubuike Okoli.
Catechesis Religious Program—Students 17.

KAHOKA, CLARK CO.
1—ST. MICHAEL THE ARCHANGEL (1891)
622 W. Exchange St., Kahoka, 63445.
Tel: 660-727-3472; Fax: 660-727-1183; Email: stmichel@centurytel.net. Rev. Robert H. Fields, Admin.
Catechesis Religious Program—Students 12.
2—THE SHRINE OF ST. PATRICK (1839) [CEM] Attended by Kahoka.
622 W. Exchange, Kahoka, 63445. Tel: 660-727-3472; Fax: 660-727-1183; Email: stmichel@centurytel.net. Rev. Robert H. Fields, Admin.
Catechesis Religious Program—Students 9.

KIRKSVILLE, ADAIR CO., MARY IMMACULATE (1888) [CEM]
716 E. Washington St., Kirksville, 63501.
Tel: 660-665-2466; Fax: 660-665-8955; Web: www.miparish.org. Rev. Msgr. David D. Cox; Deacon David D. Ream.
School—Mary Immaculate School, (Grades PreSchool-8), 712 E. Washington St., Kirksville, 63501. Tel: 660-665-1006; Fax: 660-665-3621; Email: ann.gray@miparish.org. Mrs. Ann Gray, Prin. Lay Teachers 10; Students 75.
Catechesis Religious Program—Tel: 660-665-2466. Students 96.
Mission—St. Rose of Lima (1903) 911 Rombauer, Novinger, Adair Co. 63559.

LAKE OZARK, MILLER CO., OUR LADY OF THE LAKE (1940)
2411 Bagnell Dam Blvd., Lake Ozark, 65049.
Tel: 573-365-2241; Email: ourladylake@sbcglobal.net. P.O. Box 2390, Lake Ozark, 65049. Rev. Msgr. Marion J. Makarewicz.
Catechesis Religious Program—Students 105.

LAURIE, MORGAN CO., ST. PATRICK (1870) [CEM]
176 Marian Dr., Laurie, 65038. Tel: 573-374-7855; Fax: 573-374-0627; Email: parishsecretary@shrineofstpatrick.com; Web: www.shrineofstpatrick.org. Rev. John J. Schmitz; Deacon David Lovell.
Catechesis Religious Program—Tel: 573-372-8594; Email: psr-dre@shrineofstpatrick.com. Michele Haggerty, D.R.E. Students 28.
Mission—St. Philip Benizi (1963) 17034 Hwy. D, Versailles, 65084. Tel: 573-374-6835; Fax: 573-378-4002.
Catechesis Religious Program— (Combined with Shrine of St. Patrick, Laurie)
Tel: 573-378-5958.
Shrine—The National Shrine of Mary, Mother of the Church, P.O. Box 1250, Laurie, 65038.

LINN, OSAGE CO., ST. GEORGE (1866) [CEM]
613 E. Main St., Linn, 65051. Tel: 573-897-2293; Email: stgeorgeparish@att.net; Web: church.saint-george-parish.org. P.O. Box 49, Linn, 65051. Rev. Daniel J. Merz, S.L.D.; Deacon Anthony J. Valdes.
School—St. George School, (Grades PreK-8), Tel: 573-897-3645; Tel: 573-897-2293; Email: lgrellner@saint-george-parish.org. Ms. Lisa Grellner, Prin. Lay Teachers 12; Students 167; Clergy / Religious Teachers 2.
Catechesis Religious Program—Tel: 573-897-2293. Students 24.

LOOSE CREEK, OSAGE CO., IMMACULATE CONCEPTION (1845) [CEM 2]
121 County Rd. 402, Loose Creek, 65054.
Tel: 573-897-2922; Fax: 573-897-4528; Email: icparish1845@gmail.com. P.O. Box 8, Loose Creek, 65054. Rev. Chinedu Callistus Okoroji; Deacon Larry Hildebrand.
School—Immaculate Conception School, (Grades PreK-8), 147 Co. Rd. 402, P.O. Box 68, Loose Creek, 65054. Tel: 573-897-3516; Email: stiefermann@radiowire.net. Rita Stiefermann, Prin. Lay Teachers 10; Students 134.
Catechesis Religious Program—Students 50.

LOUISIANA, PIKE CO., ST. JOSEPH (1865) [CEM]
508 N. 3rd St., Louisiana, 63353. Tel: 573-754-4757. Rev. William L. Korte, Admin.; Deacons Mark J. Dobelmann; James P. Davies.
Catechesis Religious Program—Terry Stark, D.R.E. Students 16.
Mission—Mary Queen of Peace (1951) .

MACON, MACON CO., IMMACULATE CONCEPTION (1857) [CEM]
402 N. Rollins St., Macon, 63552. Tel: 660-385-3792; Email: icchurchmacon@gmail.com. Rev. Benjamin E. Nwosu; Deacons Bernhard Toll; Lloyd Collins; William B. Tull III; Bruce Mobley.
School—Immaculate Conception School, (Grades PreK-8), 403 Rubey St., Macon, 63552.
Tel: 660-385-2711; Email: ics.macon.principal@gmail.com. Mrs. Teresa Marie Thrasher, Prin. Lay Teachers 8; Students 71.
Catechesis Religious Program—Students 27.
Mission—Sacred Heart (1880) .

MARCELINE, LINN CO., ST. BONAVENTURE (1888) [CEM 2]
409 S. Kansas Ave., Marceline, 64658-1301.
Tel: 660-376-3239; Email: stbon@mcmsys.com; Web: stbon.net. Rev. Gerald J. Kaimann.
School—Fr. McCartan Memorial School, (Grades PreK-8), 327 S. Kansas Ave., 409 S. Kansas Ave, Marceline, 64658. Tel: 660-376-3580;
Fax: 660-376-2836; Email: dillon@fathermccartan.com. Mr. Casey S. Dillon, Prin. Lay Teachers 7; Students 72.
Catechesis Religious Program—Students 40.

MARSHALL, SALINE CO., ST. PETER (1870) [CEM]
1801 S. Miami Ave., Marshall, 65340.
Tel: 660-886-7960; Fax: 660-886-7954; Email: stpeter.office@att.net; Web: www.stpeterchurch-marshallmo.org. P.O. Box 220, Marshall, 65340. Revs. Mark S. Smith, J.C.L., Admin.; Thomas L. Alber; Deacon Joseph R. Mitchell.
School—St. Peter School, (Grades PreK-8), 368 S. Ellsworth St., Marshall, 65340. Tel: 660-886-6390; Fax: 660-866-6606; Email: marmccoy@stpeterchurch-marshallmo.org. Mrs. Mary McCoy, Prin. Lay Teachers 20; Students 193.
Catechesis Religious Program—Students 94.
Mission—Holy Family (1945) 200 Ruby St., Sweet Springs, Saline Co. 65351.

MARTINSBURG, AUDRAIN CO., ST. JOSEPH (1876) [CEM]
408 E. Kellett, Martinsburg, 65264.
Tel: 573-492-6595; Email: parish@stjosephmb.org; Web: www.stjosephmb.org. Rev. Augustine Azubuike Okoli; Deacon Ronald E. Deimeke.
School—St. Joseph School, (Grades PreK-8), 401 E. Kellett, Martinsburg, 65264. Tel: 573-492-6283; Email: sjssecretary@stjosephmb.org; Email: mhombs@stjosephmb.org; Web: stjosephmb.org. Mrs. Michelle Hombs, Prin. Lay Teachers 7; Students 57.
Catechesis Religious Program—Students 30.

MARY'S HOME, MILLER CO., OUR LADY OF THE SNOWS (1883) [CEM]
Mailing Address: 274 Hwy. H, Eugene, 65032-4231.
Tel: 573-498-3820; Fax: 573-498-3779; Email: olosparish@gmail.com; Web: olosmaryshome.net. Rev. Alexander Gabriel; Deacon Stephen Schwartze; Mrs. Karen Harms, C.F.O.
Res.: 272 Hwy. H, Eugene, 65032.
School—Our Lady of the Snows School, (Grades PreK-8), 276 Hwy. H, Eugene, 65032.
Tel: 573-498-3574; Fax: 573-498-3776; Email: olosschool@gmail.com; Web: www.oloscougars.org. Mr. Joshua Vandike, Prin. Lay Teachers 6; Students 65.
Catechesis Religious Program—Tel: 573-498-3470;

Email: carolannplank@gmail.com. Carol Plank, D.R.E. Students 106.
MEMPHIS, SCOTLAND CO., ST. JOHN (1952) [CEM]
Mailing Address: 547 N. Clay St., Memphis, 63555. Tel: 660-465-7130; Email: stjohns@nemr.net. Rev. Colin P. Franklin.
Res.: 509 N. Main St., Edina, 63537.
Catechesis Religious Program—Laurie Jack, D.R.E. Students 11.
META, OSAGE CO., ST. CECILIA (1904) [CEM]
106 E. 6th St., Meta, 65058. Tel: 573-477-3315; Web: stceciliameta.net. P.O. Box 146, St. Thomas, 65076. Rev. Jeremy A. Secrist.
Catechesis Religious Program—Students 45.
MEXICO, AUDRAIN CO., ST. BRENDAN (1857) [CEM]
615 S. Washington St., Mexico, 65265-2658.
Tel: 573-581-4720; Email: parishoffice@saintbrendans.org. Rev. Dylan Schrader; Deacons Louis J. Leonatti; James Farnell.
School—St. Brendan School, (Grades PreK-8), 620 S. Clark St., Mexico, 65265. Tel: 573-581-2443;
Fax: 573-581-2571; Email: kcoulson@saintbrendans.org. Ms. Kathy Coulson, Prin. Clergy 1; Lay Teachers 15; Students 174; Clergy / Religious Teachers 1.
Catechesis Religious Program—Students 17.
MILAN, SULLIVAN CO., ST. MARY (1868) [CEM 2]
101 W. Baker St., Milan, 63556. Tel: 660-265-4110; Email: deacon@stmarymilan.com; Web: www.stmary.church. P.O. Box 147, Milan, 63556. Rev. Patrick G. Dolan, Sacramental Min.; Deacon John D. Weaver, Parish Life Coord.
Catechesis Religious Program—Students 67.
Mission—St. Mary (1868) 1118 Main St. Hwy. 136 E., Unionville, Putnam Co. 63565. Tel: 660-947-2599; Email: deacon@stmarymilan.com.
MOBERLY, RANDOLPH CO., ST. PIUS X (1870) [CEM]
201 S. Williams St., Moberly, 65270.
Tel: 660-263-5243; Fax: 660-263-0101; Email: stpiusxchurch@mcmsys.com; Web: www.stpiusxmoberly.com. P.O. Box 310, Moberly, 65270. Rev. Philip E. Niekamp; Deacons John F. Hill Jr.; Burdett E. Wilson; Samantha Rowland, D.R.E.; Mary Brink, Sec.; Paula Heath, Sec.
Res.: 217 S. Williams St., Moberly, 65270.
Tel: 660-263-7017; Email: niekamppe@gmail.com.
School—St. Pius X School, (Grades K-8), 210 S. Williams St., Moberly, 65270. Tel: 660-263-5500;
Fax: 660-263-5744; Email: maulbur@spxmoberly.eduk12.net. Mr. Michael Aulbur, Prin. Lay Teachers 15; Students 84.
Child Care—St. Pius X Early Childhood Center, Johnna Schumann, D.R.E. Lay Teachers 14; Students 60.
MOKANE, CALLAWAY CO., ST. JUDE THADDEUS (1900)
401 Adams St., Mokane, 65251. Tel: 573-642-5562; Email: stpeterparishoffice@stpeterfultonmo.org. 700 State Rd. Z, Fulton, 65251. Rev. Joseph A. Abah; Deacon John L. Neudecker.
Catechesis Religious Program—Students 6.
MONROE CITY, MONROE CO., HOLY ROSARY (1884) [CEM]
405 S. Main St., Monroe City, 63456.
Tel: 573-735-4718; Fax: 573-735-0713; Email: hrosarymc@gmail.com; Web: www.holyrosarymc.org. Rev. P. Gregory Oligschlaeger; Deacon L. Michael Long.
School—Holy Rosary School, (Grades 1-8), 415 S. Locust St., Monroe City, 63456. Tel: 573-735-2422; Email: hrssw@socket.net. Sr. Suzanne Walker, O.P., Prin.; Rev. Michael W. Penn. Clergy 1; Lay Teachers 11; Students 174; Clergy / Religious Teachers 1.
Catechesis Religious Program—Email: deaconmikelong@gmail.com. Students 54.
MONTGOMERY CITY, MONTGOMERY CO., IMMACULATE CONCEPTION (1861) [CEM 2]
307 N. Walker St., Montgomery City, 63361.
Tel: 573-564-2375; Email: imm-con@sbcglobal.net. Rev. Augustine Azubuike Okoli; Deacon Wayne W. Korte.
School—Immaculate Conception School, (Grades PreK-8), 407 W. Third St., Montgomery City, 63361.
Tel: 573-564-2679; Fax: 573-564-2305; Email: immaculateconception@icschool-mc.org; Web: immaculateconception@icschool-mc.org. Aggie Baldetti, Librarian; Dianne Talley, Librarian. Lay Teachers 9; Students 54.
Catechesis Religious Program—Bonnie Walker, D.R.E. Students 41.
MORRISON, GASCONADE CO., ASSUMPTION (1875) [CEM 2] Attended by Most Pure Heart of Mary, Chamois.
Mailing Address: P.O. Box 156, Chamois, 65024.
Tel: 573-763-5345; Email: mphsec@mostpureheart.org; Web: www.assumptionmorrison.org. 155 Morrison Avenue, Morrison, 65061. Rev. David A. Means, Canonical Admin.
Catechesis Religious Program—106 W. Second St., Chamois, 65024. Students 2.
OSAGE BEND, COLE CO., ST. MARGARET OF ANTIOCH (1907) [CEM]
12025 Rte. W., 65101. Tel: 573-496-3404; Email: stmargaretob@gmail.com. Rev. Ignazio C. Medina, Canonical Pastor & Sacramental Min.; Deacon Fred Schmitz, Pastoral Admin.
Catechesis Religious Program—Students 40.
OWENSVILLE, GASCONADE CO., IMMACULATE CONCEPTION (1893) [CEM 2]
Mailing Address: 103 E. Jefferson St., Owensville, 65066. Tel: 573-437-3086; Email: icchurchowensville@outlook.com. Rev. Wayne M. Boyer.
Res.: 404 S. First St., Owensville, 65066.
Catechesis Religious Program—Melinda Gibson, D.R.E. Students 71.
PALMYRA, MARION CO., ST. JOSEPH (1866)
400 S. Lane St., Palmyra, 63461. Tel: 573-769-3270; Email: office@stjoepalmyra.org; Web: www.stjoepalmyra.org. P.O. Box 606, Palmyra, 63461. Rev. Basil Eruo, Admin.; Deacon Robert A. Leake.
Catechesis Religious Program—Email: youth@stjoepalmyra.org. Cathy Fohey, D.R.E. Students 83.
PERRY, RALLS CO., ST. WILLIAM (1901) [CEM]
P.O. Box 339, Perry, 63462. Rev. John A. Henderson.
Catechesis Religious Program—
Missions—St. Frances Cabrini— (1953) 25560 Business Hwy. 24, Paris, Monroe Co. 65275.
St. Paul (Historic Church), 22520 St. Paul Dr., Center, Ralls Co. 63436.
PILOT GROVE, COOPER CO., ST. JOSEPH (1894) [CEM 3]
407 Harris St., Pilot Grove, 65276. Tel: 660-834-5600; Fax: 660-834-5601; Email: dgerkestjoe@gmail.com; Web: www.stjosephparishpg.catholicweb.com. Rev. Philip M. Kane.
School—St. Joseph School, (Grades PreK-8), 405 Harris St., Pilot Grove, 65276. Email: nwatring@stjosephcougars.com; Web: www.stjosephcougars.com. Nichole Watring, Prin. Clergy 1; Lay Teachers 6; Students 59; Clergy / Religious Teachers 1.
Catechesis Religious Program—Students 30.
Stations—St. John the Baptist— (1840) Clear Creek, 65276. (Mass).
St. Joseph, Otterville, 65348. (Mass).
RHINELAND, MONTGOMERY CO., CHURCH OF THE RISEN SAVIOR (1979) [CEM 2]
605 Bluff St., Rhineland, 65069. Tel: 573-236-4390; Email: risensav@ktis.net. Rev. Msgr. Gregory L. Higley; Deacons Joseph E. Horton; Gerald W. Korman; Sharon Buckner, Sec.
Catechesis Religious Program—Students 11.
Pilgrimage Site— (1888) Shrine of Our Lady of Sorrows, Starkenburg, 65069.
RICH FOUNTAIN, OSAGE CO., SACRED HEART (1838) [CEM]
Mailing Address: 4277 Hwy. U, Freeburg, 65035. Rev. William D. Debo.
School—Sacred Heart School, (Grades 1-8), 4309 Hwy. U, Freeburg, 65035. Tel: 573-744-5896;
Fax: 573-744-5761; Email: shsrf@sacredheartrf.com; Web: www.sacredheartrf.com. Linda Neuner, Prin. Lay Teachers 4; Sisters of Notre Dame 1; Students 24; Clergy / Religious Teachers 1.
Catechesis Religious Program—Students 50.
RICHLAND, PULASKI CO., ST. JUDE (1972)
Hwy. 7, Richland, 65556. Tel: 573-336-3662, Ext. 120; Email: strobert@fidmail.com. 367 Old Rte. 66, St. Robert, 65584. Rev. John W. Groner; Deacon Rick L. Vise Sr.
Catechesis Religious Program—Students 4.
ROLLA, PHELPS CO., ST. PATRICK (1862) [CEM]
17 St. Patrick Ln., Rolla, 65401. Tel: 573-364-1435; Fax: 573-364-2073; Email: bookkeeper@stpatrolla.org; Email: frdave98@gmail.com; Email: receptionist@stpatsrolla.org; Web: church.stpatsrolla.org. Revs. David J. Veit; Paul J. Clark; Deacons Michael S. Brooks; Thomas C. Manion; Matthew McLaughlin; Chad R. Lewis.
School—St. Patrick School, (Grades PreK-8), 19 St. Patrick Ln., Rolla, 65401. Tel: 573-364-1162;
Fax: 573-364-0679; Email: dbackesdelp@stpatrickrolla.org; Web: school.stpatsrolla.org. Deacon Michael Brooks, Prin. Lay Teachers 19; Students 162.
Catechesis Religious Program—Students 89.
ROSATI, PHELPS CO., ST. ANTHONY (1906) [CEM]
316 E. Scioto St., St. James, 65559.
Tel: 573-265-7250; Email: icchurch@centurylink.net. Rev. Henry Ussher, Admin.; Deacon Lawrence L. Clark.
Catechesis Religious Program—
RUSSELLVILLE, COLE CO., ST. MICHAEL (1906) [CEM 2]
5214 N. Hatler St., Russellville, 65074-1214.
Tel: 573-782-3171; Email: smcach@centurylink.net; Web: www.stmichaelschurchrlv.weebly.com. 13321 Railroad Ave., Russellville, 65074. Rev. Msgr. Robert A. Kurwicki, V.G.; Mrs. Kathy Wildhaber, Sec.
Catechesis Religious Program—Students 48.
ST. ANTHONY, MILLER CO., ST. ANTHONY (1906) [CEM]
132 Main St., Iberia, 65486. Tel: 573-793-6550; Email: stanthonyofpaduachurch@hotmail.com. P.O. Box 128, St. Elizabeth, 65075. Rev. Joby Parakkacharuvil Thomas, Canonical Admin.
Res.: 246 Main St., P.O. Box 128, Saint Elizabeth, 65075.
Catechesis Religious Program—Students 51.
ST. CLEMENT, PIKE CO., ST. CLEMENT (1871) [CEM 2]
21509 Hwy. 161, Bowling Green, 63334.
Tel: 573-324-5545; Web: 573-324-5155; Email: stclementparish@gmail.com; Web: www.stclementmo.org. Rev. Jason T. Doke.
School—St. Clement School, (Grades 1-8), Mailing Address: 21493 Hwy. 161, Bowling Green, 63334.
Tel: 573-324-2166; Fax: 573-324-6159; Email: stclementschool@gmail.com. Laurie Schuckenbrock, Prin. Clergy 1; Lay Teachers 6; Students 75; Clergy / Religious Teachers 1.
Catechesis Religious Program—Students 58.
ST. ELIZABETH, MILLER CO., ST. LAWRENCE (1871) [CEM]
246 Main, St. Elizabeth, 65075. Tel: 573-793-6550; Email: stlawrencegridiron@hotmail.com. P.O. Box 128, St. Elizabeth, 65075. Rev. Joby Parakkacharuvil Thomas, Canonical Admin.; Deacon Stephen Schwartze.
Catechesis Religious Program—Tel: 573-793-6550. Students 154.
ST. JAMES, PHELPS CO., IMMACULATE CONCEPTION (1870)
316 E. Scioto, St. James, 65559. Tel: 573-265-7250; Email: icchurch@centurylink.net; Web: www.icchurchstjames.org. Rev. Henry Ussher, Admin.; Deacon Lawrence L. Clark.
Catechesis Religious Program—Students 32.
ST. MARTINS, COLE CO., ST. MARTIN (1885) [CEM]
7148 Business 50 W., 65109. Tel: 573-893-2923; Email: stmartinparishoffice@gmail.com; Web: www.stmartinjc.org. 7148 St. Martins Blvd., 65109. Very Rev. Mark A. Porterfield, J.C.L.; Deacons Francis J. Butel; Stephan J. Kliethermes.
School—St. Martin School, (Grades PreK-8), 7206 St. Martins Ave., 65109. Tel: 573-893-3519;
Fax: 573-893-7404; Email: emulholland@stmartin.eduk12.net. Mr. Edmund Mullholland, Prin. Lay Teachers 17; Students 243.
Catechesis Religious Program—Tel: 573-893-2352;
Fax: 573-893-9587; Email: stmartinssnd@gmail.com. Mr. Mark McGuire, Pastoral Min./Coord. Students 26.
ST. ROBERT, PULASKI CO., ST. ROBERT BELLARMINE (1941) [CEM]
367 Old Rte. 66, St. Robert, 65584. Tel: 573-336-3662; Email: strobert@fidmail.com. Rev. John W. Groner; Deacon Rick L. Vise Sr.
Catechesis Religious Program—Students 78.
ST. THOMAS, COLE CO., ST. THOMAS THE APOSTLE (1869) [CEM]
14814 Rt. B, St. Thomas, 65076. Tel: 573-477-3315; Email: stthomasoffice@embarqmail.com; Web: stthomasapostle.net. P.O. Box 146, St. Thomas, 65076. Rev. Jeremy A. Secrist.
School—St. Thomas the Apostle School, (Grades PreSchool-8), 14830 Rte. B, P.O. Box 211, St. Thomas, 65076. Tel: 573-477-3322;
Fax: 573-477-3700; Email: lheckemeyer@embarqmail.com; Web: www.stthomasapostleschool.net. Mr. Leroy Heckemeyer, Prin. Lay Teachers 9; Students 88; Clergy / Religious Teachers 1.
Catechesis Religious Program—Students 78.
SALISBURY, CHARITON CO., ST. JOSEPH (1870) [CEM]
301 W. Williams, Salisbury, 65281.
Tel: 660-388-5590; Email: saintjosephcatholicchurch@hotmail.com. Rev. Michael P. Murphy.
School—St. Joseph School, (Grades K-8), 105 N. Willie Ave., Salisbury, 65281-1457. Mrs. Cathy Fuemmeler, Prin. Lay Teachers 12; Students 110; Clergy / Religious Teachers 1.
Catechesis Religious Program—Students 23.
SEDALIA, PETTIS CO.
1—ST. PATRICK (1866)
415 E. Fourth St., Sedalia, 65301. Tel: 660-826-2062;
Fax: 660-829-1085; Email: dee.stpatrickschurch@gmail.com; Web: www.catholicsedalia.org. Revs. Mark Miller, C.PP.S; Brendan Griffey; Deacons Arvol Bartok; Jerome Connery; Turf D. Martin; Christopher Wickern.
Catechesis Religious Program—Students 106.
2—SACRED HEART (1882) [CEM]
421 W. Third St., Sedalia, 65301. Tel: 660-827-2311;
Fax: 660-827-3941; Email: shparishsedalia@gmail.com; Web: www.catholicsedalia.org. Revs. Mark Miller, C.PP.S; Brendan Griffey; Deacons Arvol Bartok; Jerome Connery; Turf D. Martin; Christopher Wickern.
School—Sacred Heart School, (Grades PreK-8), 416 W. Third St., Sedalia, 65301. Tel: 660-827-3800;
Fax: 660-827-3806; Email: mregister@gogremlins.com. Dr. Mark Register, Prin. Lay Teachers 28; Students 256.
High School—Sacred Heart School,
Tel: 660-827-3800; Fax: 660-827-3806; Email: mregister@gogremlins.com; Email:

sjones@gogremlins.com; Web: www.gogremlins.com. Dr. Mark Register, Prin. Lay Teachers 33; Students 82.
Catechesis Religious Program—Students 22.
Mission—St. John (1845) Hwy. V & M, Bahner, Pettis Co. Hwy V & M.
Legal Title: St. John the Evangelist.

SHELBINA, SHELBY CO., ST. MARY (1879) [CEM]
307 E. Chestnut St., Shelbina, 63468.
Tel: 573-588-4498; Fax: 573-588-4498; Email: stmaryshelbina@gmail.com; Web: stmaryshelbina.org. P.O. Box 306, Shelbina, 63468. Rev. Simeon A. Etonu, Admin.; Deacons John DeGraff; Larry W. Mitchell.
Catechesis Religious Program—Students 96.

SLATER, SALINE CO., ST. JOSEPH (1882) Attended by Glasgow.
325 W. Emma St., Slater, 65349. Tel: 660-529-2588; Email: stjoseph1927@sbcglobal.net; Web: www.stjosephslater.net. Rev. Paul M. Hartley.
Catechesis Religious Program—Students 7.

STEELVILLE, CRAWFORD CO., ST. MICHAEL (1949)
Hwy. 8 E., Steelville, 65559. Email: icchurch@centurylink.net; Web: www.icchurchstjames.org. 316 E. Scioto, St. James, 65559. Tel: 573-265-7250. Rev. Henry Ussher, Admin.
Res.: 415 W. School St., Cuba, 65453.
Catechesis Religious Program—Students 5.

TAOS, COLE CO., ST. FRANCIS XAVIER (1838) [CEM]
7319 Rte. M, 65101. Tel: 573-395-4401;
Fax: 573-395-4302; Email: sfxchurch1@embarqmail.com; Web: www.sfxtaosmo.org. Rev. Michael W. Penn; Deacon James Haaf.
Res.: 7318 Rte. M, 65101. Email: clock@sfxtaos.com; Email: lherzing@sfxtaos.com.
School—St. Francis Xavier School, (Grades PreK-8), 7307 Rt. M., 65101. Tel: 573-395-4612;
Fax: 573-395-4017; Email: mbuskirk@sfxtaos.com; Web: www.sfxtaos.org. Mr. Michael Buskirk, Prin. Lay Teachers 16; Students 132.
Catechesis Religious Program—Students 60.

TIPTON, MONITEAU CO., ST. ANDREW (1857) [CEM]
106 W. Cooper St., Tipton, 65081-8210.
Tel: 660-433-2162; Email: sac_rectory@outlook.com; Web: www.standrewtipton.org. Rev. Anthony R. Rinaldo; Deacon Robert W. Reinkemeyer.
School—St. Andrew School, (Grades K-8), 118 E. Cooper St., Tipton, 65081-0617. Tel: 660-433-2232;
Fax: 660-433-5432; Email: sas118_school@outlook.com; Email: sas118_principal@outlook.com; Web: www.standrewtipton.org. Abby Martin, Prin. Lay Teachers 12; Students 111.
Catechesis Religious Program—Students 66.

VANDALIA, AUDRAIN CO., SACRED HEART (1891)
203 W. Home St., Vandalia, 63382.
Tel: 573-594-2717; Email: shccastj@windstream.net. P.O. Box 29, Vandalia, 63382. Rev. Jason T. Doke.
Catechesis Religious Program—Students 16.
Mission—St. John (1889) 601 W. Elm St., Laddonia, Audrain Co. 63352.
Catechesis Religious Program—

VIENNA, MARIES CO., VISITATION OF THE BLESSED VIRGIN MARY (1867) [CEM]
101 N. Main St., Vienna, 65582. Tel: 573-422-3950; Email: vgasecretary@att.net. 108 N. Coffey St., P.O. Box 171, Vienna, 65582. Rev. Matthew J. Flatley; Deacon Doug Hemke.
105 N. Main St., Vienna, 65582.
School—Visitation Inter-Parish School, (Grades K-8), Tel: 573-422-3375; Email: vips.principal@att.net. Marilyn Bassett, Prin. Lay Teachers 5; Students 51.
Catechesis Religious Program—Mendy James, D.R.E. Students 18.

WARDSVILLE, COLE CO., ST. STANISLAUS (1880) [CEM]
6418 Rte. W., Wardsville, 65101. Tel: 573-636-4925;
Fax: 573-636-2534; Email: ststansec@socket.net; Web: www.ststan.net. Rev. Ignazio C. Medina; Deacon Alan D. Sims.
School—St. Stanislaus School, (Grades PreK-8), 6410 Rte. W., Wardsville, 65101. Tel: 573-636-7802;
Fax: 573-635-4782; Email: nancyh@ststan.net; Web: www.ststan.net. Nancy Heberlie, Prin.; Ms. Laura Rudolph, Librarian. Lay Teachers 15; Students 191; Clergy / Religious Teachers 1.
Catechesis Religious Program—Email: ststanleann@socket.net. LeAnn Korsmeyer, D.R.E. Students 85.

WARSAW, BENTON CO., ST. ANN (1945) [CEM]
30455 W. Dam Access Rd., Warsaw, 65355.
Tel: 660-438-3844; Email: stannwarsaw1@gmail.com. Rev. Alexuis Ekka.
Catechesis Religious Program—Tel: 660-438-3843. Students 24.
Mission—SS. Peter & Paul (1878) 30455 W. Dam Access Rd., Warsaw, 65355. Tel: 660-668-3468; Email: spapcolecampmo@gmail.com. P.O. Box 248, Cole Camp, Benton Co. 65325.

WELLSVILLE, MONTGOMERY CO., CHURCH OF THE RESURRECTION (1873) [CEM]
409 E. Bates, Wellsville, 63384. Tel: 573-492-6595. 408 E. Kellett, Martinsburg, 65264-2012. Rev. Augustine Azubuike Okoli; Deacon Ronald E. Deimeke.
Catechesis Religious Program—

WESTPHALIA, OSAGE CO., ST. JOSEPH (1835) [CEM 2]
125 E. Main St., Westphalia, 65085.
Tel: 573-455-2320; Fax: 573-455-2974; Email: parishoffice@stjosephwestphalia.org; Web: www.stjosephwestphalia.org. P.O. Box 116, Westphalia, 65085. Rev. Anthony J. Viviano.
School—St. Joseph School, (Grades K-8), 123 E. Main, P.O. Box 205, Westphalia, 65085.
Tel: 573-455-2339; Fax: 573-455-2287; Email: schooloffice@stjosephwestphalia.org. Ms. Tammy Ogden, Prin. Lay Teachers 15; Students 193; Clergy / Religious Teachers 1.
Catechesis Religious Program—Students 97.

WIEN, CHARITON CO., ST. MARY OF THE ANGELS (1876) [CEM 2]
12520 St. Mary's Ave., New Cambria, 63558-3418.
Tel: 660-226-5243; Email: parishstmaryoftheangels@gmail.com. Rev. Michael P. Murphy.
Catechesis Religious Program—Tel: 660-651-7749; Email: jjbertsch@cvalley.net. Joe Bertsch, D.R.E. Students 40.

Chaplains of Public Institutions.

Hospitals and Schools

COLUMBIA AND JEFFERSON CITY. *Liaison to Healthcare.* Mr. Mike Berendzen, Interim Coord., Sr. Kathleen Wegman, S.S.N.D., Chancellor.

On Duty Outside the Diocese:
Revs.—
Anicama, Cesar
Reid, Nicholas J., CH(1st Lt.).

Absent on Leave:
Revs.—
Behan, Hugh F., (Removed from Ministry)
Clohessy, Kevin, (Removed from Ministry)
Daly, Manus P., (Removed from Ministry)
Doyle, Brendan P., (Retired), (Removed from Ministry)
Duesdieker, Robert W., (Removed from Ministry)
Fischer, John, (Removed from Ministry)
Hereford, Thomas D., (Leave of Absence)
Lahr, Mel, (Removed from Ministry)
Long, John, (Retired), (Removed from Ministry)
Schlachter, Eric A., (Removed from Ministry)
Schutty, John J., (Removed from Ministry)
Seifner, Thomas J., (Removed from Ministry)
Tatro, Timothy M., (Removed from Ministry)
Wallace, Donald L., (Removed from Ministry)
Whiteley, John, (Removed from Ministry).

Retired:
Rev. Msgrs.—
Lammers, Donald W., (Retired), 2305 W. Main St., 65109
McCorkle, Louis W., (Retired), P.O. Box 501, Conception, 64433. Tel: 660-944-2898
Wilbers, Michael T., (Retired), P.O. Box 2390, Lake Ozark, 65049. Tel: 573-693-9644
Revs.—
Behan, Hugh F.
Cronin, Richard, (Retired), 1899 Hwy. 63, Westphalia, 65085. Tel: 573-455-2280
Doyle, Edward A., (Retired), #9 Garden Place, Montgomery City, 63361. Tel: 573-564-2497
Elskamp, Frederick J., (Retired), 610 Belair, 65109
Frank, Richard W., (Retired), 803 Air View Dr., 65109
Gormley, Kevin W., (Retired), 15941 Little Buck Blvd., Boonville, 65233-2716
Jones, Paul W., (Retired), HC 77, P.O. Box 536, Pittsburg, 65724. Tel: 573-852-4601
Judge, Russell R., (Retired), 3782 Double Tree Ln., St. Charles, 63303
Kramer, George, (Retired), P.O. Box 68, Bonnots Mills, 65018. Tel: 573-897-2061
Maher, J. David, (Retired), 1899 Hwy. 63, Westphalia, 65085. Tel: 573-455-2280
McGrath, Thomas E., (Retired), 207 Norris Dr., 65109. Tel: 573-761-9180
Ryan, C. Duane, (Retired)
Steinhauser, Kenneth B., (Retired), 6201 Loran Ave., Apt. A, St. Louis, 63109
Wiederholt, Clarence E., (Retired), 1818 Almarie Ct., 65101. Tel: 573-636-4303.

Permanent Deacons:
Anderberg, Peter K., (Retired)
Aulbur, Mark
Baker, R. Christopher
Bartok, Arvol
Berry, Kenneth
Bilgrien, Kenneth D., (On Duty Outside the Diocese)
Boettger, Kent
Braddock, Joseph M., CPA
Brand, Alvin J.
Breazile, James E., (Retired)
Brooks, Michael
Buczko, Stan
Butel, Francis J., (Retired)
Caubet, William
Chaplin, Mark, (On Duty Outside the Diocese)
Christoff, Gary, (Retired)
Clark, Lawrence L.
Collins, Lloyd
Connery, Jerome
Daly, Michael M., (Retired)
Davies, James P.
DeGraff, John
Deimeke, Ronald E.
DePyper, Robert R., (Retired)
Dobelman, Mark J.
Dulle, Robert L., (Retired)
Egbert, Troy K.
Farnell, James
Fischer, Thomas M.
Fritsch, Frederick, (Retired)
Garcia, Philip
Haaf, James
Hemke, Doug
Hildebrand, Larry
Hill, John F. Jr.
Horsefield, Earl R., (Retired)
Horton, Joseph E.
Houston, John D., (Retired)
Joyce, Dana K.
Kazmierczak, Eugene S., (Retired)
Kliethermes, James L., (Retired)
Kliethermes, Stephan J.
Korman, Gerald W.
Korte, Wayne W.
Leake, Robert A.
Leonatti, Louis J.
Lewis, Chad R.
Leyden, James
Linhardt, Wayne, (Retired)
Long, Michael L.
Lovell, David
Manion, Thomas C.
Martin, Turf D.
McClay, Tyler
McLaughlin, Matthew
Miller, David
Mitchell, Joseph R., (Retired)
Mitchell, Larry W.
Mobley, Bruce
Neudecker, John L.
Poulter, Paul
Puglis, Joseph
Purvis, Raymond L.
Rackers, Robert J., (Retired)
Ramsay, Daniel J.
Ream, David D.
Reibenspies, Terence L., (Retired)
Reinkemeyer, Robert W.
Ruggiero, Frank
Schepers, Edwin
Schmitz, Fred
Schwartze, John A.
Schwartze, Stephen
Sims, Alan D.
Skahan, James E., (On Duty Outside the Diocese)
Stahl, Theodore E., (Retired)
Steffes, Gary D., (On Duty Outside the Diocese)
Stroesser, Edward D.
Telthorst, Ric
Thompson, David
Toll, Bernhard F., (Retired)
Tull, William B.
Vise, Rick L. Sr.
Visot, Luis R., (Retired)
Von Gunten, Richard A., (Retired)
Wand, Mark A.
Warden, Donald E., (Retired)
Watson, G. Robert, (Retired)
Weaver, John D.
Weisel, Fred M., (Retired)
Whalen, Tom, (Retired)
Wickern, Christopher
Wildhaber, Kenneth V. Jr.
Wilson, Burdett E.
Zuck, Chet L. Jr.

INSTITUTIONS LOCATED IN DIOCESE

[A] HIGH SCHOOLS, DIOCESAN

JEFFERSON CITY. *Helias Catholic High School*, 1305 Swift's Hwy., 65109. Tel: 573-635-6139; Fax: 573-635-5615; Email: info@heliascatholic.com; Web: www.heliascatholic.com. Rev. Stephen W. Jones, Pres.; Miss Kenya Fuemmeler, Prin.; Sr. Jean Dietrich, S.S.N.D., Asst. Prin.; Maureen Quinn, Dir. Campus Ministry; Revs. Christopher M. Aubuchon, Chap.; Joshua J. Duncan, Chap.; Brad Dempsey, Activities Dir.; Ms. Michelle Oliver, Librarian. Brothers of the Christian Schools 1; Lay Teachers 46; School Sisters of Notre Dame 1; Students 729.

COLUMBIA. *Fr. Augustine Tolton Regional Catholic High School*, 3351 E. Gans Rd., Columbia, 65201. Tel: 573-445-7700; Fax: 573-445-7703; Web: www.toltoncatholic.org. Deacon Dana K. Joyce, Pres.; Mrs. Gwenn Roche, Prin.; Rev. Michael A. Coleman, Chap.; Marigrace Powers, Librarian. Lay Teachers 26; Students 729.

[B] CATHOLIC HOSPITALS

JEFFERSON CITY. *SSM Health - St. Mary's Hospital*, 2505 Mission Dr., 65109. Tel: 573-681-3000; Fax: 573-681-3603; Email: SSMHealthCareOfficialCatholicDirectoryNotices@ssmhealth.com; Web: www.ssmhealthmidmo.com. Revs. Joshua Allee, Chap.; Paul Deutsch, Chap. Member of SSM Health Bed Capacity 154; Tot Asst. Annually 225,439; Total Staff 991; Clinics 13; Clinic Visits 122,358.

MEXICO. **SSM Audrain Health Care, Inc.*, 620 E. Monroe St., Mexico, 65265. Tel: 573-582-5000; Email: contact.midmo@ssmhealth.com; Web: www.ssmhealth.com. Donna Jacobs, Pres. Member of SSM Health Bed Capacity 88; Nurses 86; Tot Asst. Annually 62,751; Total Staff 382.

[C] CONVENTS AND RESIDENCES FOR SISTERS

JEFFERSON CITY. *Discalced Carmelite Monastery*, 1106 Swifts Highway, 65109. Tel: 573-636-3430; Email: carmelofjc.prayers@gmail.com. Mother Marie Therese Dubois, O.C.D., Prioress. Professed of Solemn Vows 4.

[D] NEWMAN CENTERS

COLUMBIA. *St. Thomas More Newman Center*, 602 Turner Ave., Columbia, 65201. Tel: 573-449-5424; Fax: 573-874-2777; Email: reception@comonewman.org; Web: www.comonewman.org. Revs. Richard F. Litzau, O.P.; Christopher M. Aubuchon; Reginald Wolford, O.P.; Sr. Karen Freund, O.P., Pastoral Assoc.; Mrs. Angelle Hall, Dir.

KIRKSVILLE. *Catholic Newman Center, Truman State University*, 709 S. Davis, Kirksville, 63501. Tel: 660-665-4357; Fax: 660-665-3592; Email: tsnewman@socket.net; Web: www.kirksvillenewman.truman.edu. Chris Korte, Dir.; Rev. Colin P. Franklin, Chap.

ROLLA. *Catholic Newman Center, Missouri University of Science and Technology*, 1607 N. Rolla St., Rolla, 65402. Tel: 573-364-2133; Fax: 573-368-3560; Email: newman@mst.edu; Web: www.rollanewman.org. P.O. Box 838, Rolla, 65402. Revs. David J. Veit, Pastor; Paul J. Clark, Campus Min.

[E] SOCIAL SERVICES

JEFFERSON CITY. *El Puente - Hispanic Ministry*, 1102 E. McCarty St., 65101. Tel: 573-635-2540; Fax: 573-365-4744; Web: www.el-puente-mo.org. Sr. Barbara Neist, S.S.N.D., Dir.

Samaritan Center, 1310 E. McCarty St., 65101. Tel: 573-634-7776; Fax: 573-761-5948; Email: samaritan@midmosamaritan.org; Web: www.midmosamaritan.org. P.O. Box 1687, 65102. Marylyn DeFeo, Exec. Dir. Tot Asst. Annually 35,000; Total Staff 8.

LINN. *Good Shepherd Center*, 1117 Adams St., P.O. Box 763, Linn, 65051. Tel: 573-897-0525; Email: info@diojeffcity.org. Bill Voss, Volunteer Dir. Tot Asst. Annually 13,073.

[F] MISCELLANEOUS

JEFFERSON CITY. *Catholic Charities of Central and Northern Missouri*, P.O. Box 104626, 65110-4626. Mr. Daniel C. Lester, Exec. Dir.; Ms. Lorna Tran, Dir., Refugee & Immigration Svcs.

Catholic Diocese of Jefferson City Fund, Inc., 2207 W. Main St., 65110-4900. Tel: 573-635-9127; Fax: 573-635-0386; Email: cfo@diojeffcity.org; Web: www.diojeffcity.org. P.O. Box 104900, 65110-4900. Deacon Joseph Braddock, CPA, Sec.

Diocesan Excellence in Education Fund, Inc., P.O. Box 104900, 65110-4900. Deacon Joseph Braddock, CPA, Contact Person.

Diocese of Jefferson City Parish Development Corporation, P.O. Box 104900, 65110-4900. Deacon Joseph Braddock, CPA, Contact Person.

Diocese of Jefferson City Real Estate Corporation, P.O. Box 104900, 65110-4900. Deacon Joseph Braddock, CPA, Contact Person.

Diocese of Jefferson City Real Estate Trust, P.O. Box 104900, 65110-4900. Deacon Joseph Braddock, CPA, Contact Person.

Fr. Augustine Tolton Regional Catholic High School Foundation, 3351 E. Gans Rd., Columbia, 65201. Tel: 573-445-7700; Fax: 573-445-7703; Email: bnaumann@toltoncatholic.org; Web: www.toltoncatholic.org. Bernie Naumann, Contact Person.

Jefferson City Diocese Chancery Building Fund, 2207 W. Main St., 65109. Tel: 573-635-9127; Fax: 573-635-0386; Email: cfo@diojeffcity.org. P.O. Box 104900, 65110-4900. Deacon Joseph M. Braddock, CPA, Contact Person.

Jubilee Retirement Trust Fund, 2207 W. Main St., 65109. Tel: 573-635-9127; Fax: 573-635-0386; Email: cfo@diojeffcity.org; Web: www.diojeffcity.org. P.O. Box 104900, 65110-4900. Deacon Joseph Braddock, CPA, Contact Person.

St. Mary's Health Center, Jefferson City, Missouri, Foundation, 2505 Mission Dr., 65109. Tel: 573-681-3743; Fax: 573-681-3654; Web: www.ssmhealth.com. Mr. Philip Gustafson, Pres. Member of SSM Health Bed Capacity 154; Employees 992; Tot Asst. Annually 225,439.

Missouri Catholic Conference, 600 Clark Ave., 65101. Tel: 573-635-7239; Fax: 573-635-7431; Email: mocatholic@mocatholic.org; Web: www.mocatholic.org. P.O. Box 1022, 65102. Deacon Tyler McClay, Exec.

St. Peter School Foundation, 368 S. Ellsworth St., Marshall, 65340. Tel: 660-886-6390; Fax: 660-886-6606; Email: marmccoy@stpeterchurch-marshallmo.org. Mrs. Mary McCoy, Prin.

Priests' Mutual Benefit Society, Inc., 2207 W. Main St., 65109. Tel: 573-635-9127; Fax: 573-635-0386; Email: cfo@diojeffcity.org. P.O. Box 104900, 65110-4900. Deacon Joseph Braddock, CPA, Contact Person.

RELIGIOUS INSTITUTES OF MEN REPRESENTED IN THE DIOCESE

For further details refer to the corresponding bracketed number in the Religious Institutes of Men or Women section.

[0330]—*Brothers of the Christian Schools* (Midwest Prov.)—F.S.C.

[]—*Order of Preachers* (Central Province)—O.P.

[1060]—*Society of the Precious Blood* (Kansas City Prov.)—C.PP.S.

RELIGIOUS INSTITUTES OF WOMEN REPRESENTED IN THE DIOCESE

[0460]—*Congregation of the Sisters of Charity of the Incarnate Word* (San Antonio, TX)—C.C.V.I.

[0420]—*Discalced Carmelite Nuns (Second Order of the Carmel)* Jefferson City, MO—O.C.D.

[1070-11]—*Dominican Sisters* (Sparkill, NY)—O.P.

[1115]—*Dominican Sisters of Peace* (Columbus, OH)—O.P.

[1070-10]—*Dominican Sisters of Springfield, IL* (Springfield, IL)—O.P.

[2970]—*School Sisters of Notre Dame* (Central Pacific Prov.)—S.S.N.D.

[]—*Sisters of Charity of Leavenworth, KS* (Leavenworth, KS)—S.C.L.

[]—*Sisters of St. Benedict* (Ferdinand, IN)—O.S.B.

[3270]—*Sisters of the Most Precious Blood* (O'Fallon, MO)—C.PP.S.

DIOCESAN CEMETERIES

JEFFERSON CITY. *St. Peter's Catholic Cemetery Association*, c/o Resurrection Cemetery, 3015 W. Truman Blvd., 65109. Tel: 573-893-2751; Fax: 573-893-5026; Email: info@rccjc.org. Mr. Alan Lepper, Gen. Mgr.

An asterisk (*) denotes an organization that has established tax-exempt status directly with the IRS and is not covered by the USCCB Group Ruling.

Diocese of Joliet in Illinois

(Dioecesis Joliettensis in Illinois)

Most Reverend

R. DANIEL CONLON

Bishop of Joliet; ordained January 15, 1977; appointed Bishop of Steubenville May 22, 2002; consecrated and installed August 6, 2002; appointed Bishop of Joliet May 17, 2011; installed July 14, 2011. *Blanchette Catholic Center: 16555 Weber Rd., Crest Hill, IL 60403.* Tel: 815-221-6100; Fax: 815-221-6101.

Blanchette Catholic Center, 16555 Weber Rd., Crest Hill, IL 60403. Tel: 815-221-6100; Fax: 815-221-6101.

Web: www.dioceseofjoliet.org

Email: dcastronovo@dioceseofjoliet.org

ESTABLISHED BY BULL DATED DECEMBER 11, 1948.

Square Miles 4,218.

Canonically Erected March 24, 1949.

Comprises the Counties of Du Page, Kankakee, Will, Grundy, Ford, Iroquois and Kendall in the State of Illinois.

Patron of Diocese: St. Francis Xavier.

For legal titles of parishes and diocesan institutions, consult the Chancery.

STATISTICAL OVERVIEW

Personnel	
Bishop	1
Retired Bishops	1
Abbots	1
Retired Abbots	2
Priests: Diocesan Active in Diocese	104
Priests: Diocesan Active Outside Diocese	7
Priests: Retired, Sick or Absent	63
Number of Diocesan Priests	174
Religious Priests in Diocese	93
Total Priests in Diocese	267
Extern Priests in Diocese	21
Ordinations:	
Diocesan Priests	7
Religious Priests	1
Transitional Deacons	3
Permanent Deacons	25
Permanent Deacons in Diocese	282
Total Brothers	46
Total Sisters	366
Parishes	
Parishes	117
With Resident Pastor:	
Resident Diocesan Priests	75
Resident Religious Priests	24
Without Resident Pastor:	
Administered by Priests	18
Missions	7

Professional Ministry Personnel:	
Brothers	2
Sisters	69
Lay Ministers	402
Welfare	
Catholic Hospitals	2
Total Assisted	298,962
Homes for the Aged	14
Total Assisted	2,927
Day Care Centers	3
Total Assisted	889
Special Centers for Social Services	4
Total Assisted	68,484
Residential Care of Disabled	1
Total Assisted	125
Educational	
Diocesan Students in Other Seminaries	37
Total Seminarians	37
Colleges and Universities	3
Total Students	14,440
High Schools, Diocesan and Parish	3
Total Students	1,544
High Schools, Private	5
Total Students	3,324
Elementary Schools, Diocesan and Parish	45
Total Students	12,232
Elementary Schools, Private	2

Total Students	385
Catechesis/Religious Education:	
High School Students	3,343
Elementary Students	33,066
Total Students under Catholic Instruction	68,371
Teachers in the Diocese:	
Priests	14
Brothers	32
Sisters	18
Lay Teachers	1,968
Vital Statistics	
Receptions into the Church:	
Infant Baptism Totals	5,799
Minor Baptism Totals	131
Adult Baptism Totals	238
Received into Full Communion	446
First Communions	6,808
Confirmations	6,610
Marriages:	
Catholic	992
Interfaith	194
Total Marriages	1,186
Deaths	3,290
Total Catholic Population	564,709
Total Population	1,950,354

Former Bishops—Most Revs. MARTIN D. MCNAMARA, D.D., appt. first Bishop of Joliet; ord. Dec. 3, 1922; appt. Dec. 17, 1948; cons. March 7, 1949; died May 23, 1966; ROMEO BLANCHETTE, D.D., appt. Auxiliary Bishop of Joliet and Titular Bishop of Maxita Feb. 8, 1965; cons. April 3, 1965; appt. Bishop of Joliet July 19, 1966; installed Aug. 31, 1966; resigned Jan. 30, 1979; died Jan. 10, 1982; JOSEPH L. IMESCH, ord. Dec. 16, 1956; ord. Auxiliary Bishop of Detroit April 3, 1973; appt. Bishop of Joliet June 30, 1979; installed Aug. 28, 1979; retired May 16, 2006; died Dec. 22, 2015.; JAMES PETER SARTAIN, D.D., S.T.L., ord. July 15, 1978; appt. Bishop of Little Rock Jan. 4, 2000; cons. and installed March 6, 2000; appt. Bishop of Joliet May 16, 2006; installed June 27, 2006; appt. Archbishop of Seattle Sept. 16, 2010.

Office of the Bishop—

Diocesan Bishop—Most Rev. R. DANIEL CONLON, D.D., J.C.D., Ph.D., Tel: 815-221-6185; Fax: 815-722-6632.

Vicar General—Very Rev. RICHARD L. SMITH, J.C.L., Tel: 815-221-6184; Fax: 815-722-6632.

Executive Assistant to Bishop and Media Relations—MR. ALEX RECHENMACHER, Tel: 815-221-6180; Fax: 815-722-6632.

Diocesan Pastoral Council—

Chair—MRS. MADELINE MCNICHOLAS, Tel: 815-221-6180.

Presbyteral Council—

Chair—Very Rev. JOHN KLEIN, Tel: 815-725-1527; Fax: 815-730-9907.

Curia Council—Most Rev. R. DANIEL CONLON, D.D., J.C.D., Ph.D.; MR. MICHAEL BAVA; Sr. JUDITH A. DAVIES, O.S.F.; Rev. BURKE MASTERS; MR. PETER NEWBURN; MR. ALEX RECHENMACHER; DR. DAVID CASTRONOVO, J.D., J.C.D.; MR. GLENN VAN CURA.

Board of Conciliation and Arbitration—

Chair—Sr. JUDITH A. DAVIES, O.S.F., Tel: 815-221-6118.

Deans—Very Revs. THOMAS PAUL, (East Dupage); JOHN BALLUFF, (West Dupage); PAUL HOTTINGER, (South DuPage); DENNIS PAUL, (North Will/ Kendall); RICHARD L. SMITH, J.C.L., (South Will-Grundy); CHRISTOPHER GROH, (Joliet); ALBERT J. HEIDECKE, (Kankakee); MICHAEL POWELL, (Ford-Iroquois).

Diocesan Offices

Unless otherwise indicated, diocesan offices are located at the Blanchette Catholic Center, 16555 Weber Rd., Crest Hill, IL 60403. Tel: 815-221-6100; Fax: 815-221-6101.

Secretariat for Administration

Secretary—MR. MICHAEL BAVA.

Buildings and Properties—MR. CHRIS NYE, Tel: 815-221-6195; Fax: 815-221-6087.

Catholic Cemeteries—MR. MICHAEL HACKIEWICZ, 200 W. Romeo Rd., Romeoville, 60446. Tel: 815-886-0750; Fax: 815-886-8711.

Development/Stewardship—MR. TONY BRANDOLINO, Tel: 815-221-6191; Fax: 815-838-8108.

Employee Benefits & Pension—MR. BRIAN SCHROEDER, Tel: 815-221-6203; Fax: 815-221-6083.

Finance - Diocesan—MR. BRIAN SCHROEDER, Tel: 815-221-6203; Fax: 815-221-6083.

Finance - Parish—MR. MARK JANUS, Tel: 815-221-6210; Fax: 815-221-6083.

Human Resources—MRS. NANCY SIEMERS, Tel: 815-221-6198; Fax: 815-221-6107.

Information Technology—MR. MICHAEL SEKULA, Tel: 815-221-6222; Fax: 815-221-6087.

Insurance—MR. BRIAN SCHROEDER, Tel: 815-221-6203; Fax: 815-221-6083.

Legal Services—MS. MAUREEN HARTON, Tel: 815-221-6211; Fax: 815-221-6083.

Secretariat for Chancery and Tribunal

Secretary—DR. DAVID CASTRONOVO, J.D., J.C.D.

Chancery & Archives—DR. DAVID CASTRONOVO, J.D., J.C.D., Tel: 815-221-6148; Fax: 815-221-6086. Office Hours: Mon.-Thurs. 8 a.m.-4:30 p.m., Fri. 8 a.m.-1 p.m.

Child and Youth Protection—MRS. MOLLY FARA, L.C.S.W., Tel: 815-221-6116; Fax: 815-221-6086.

Christ Our Hope Magazine—MR. CARLOS BRICENO, Tel: 815-221-6112; Fax: 815-221-6086.

Victim Assistance—MRS. LORRE CHASSEE, Tel: 815-263-6467; Fax: 815-221-6086.

Tribunal—

Judicial Vicar—Very Rev. JOSEPH J. TAPELLA, J.C.L., Tel: 815-221-6163; Fax: 815-221-6086.

Adjutant Judicial Vicar—Very Rev. GRZEGORZ PODWYSOCKI, J.C.L., Tel: 815-221-6163; Fax: 815-221-6086.

Advocates—SR. DOMINIC DYBEL, O.S.F., Tel: 815-221-

6168; Fax: 815-221-6086; MRS. NANCY HAUCH, Tel: 815-221-6163; Fax: 815-221-6086.
Defender of the Bond—Sr. ELAINE KERSCHER, O.S.F., J.C.L., Tel: 815-221-6163; Fax: 815-221-6086.
Judges—Very Revs. JOSEPH J. TAPELLA, J.C.L.; GRZEGORZ PODWYSOCKI, J.C.L.; MR. THOMAS E. KERBER, J.C.L.; The Honorable RICHARD J. SIEGL, J.D., Tel: 815-221-6163; Fax: 815-221-6086.
Notaries—MRS. HOPE DICK; MRS. NANCY HAUCH, Tel: 815-221-6163; Fax: 815-221-6086.

Secretariat for Clergy and Religious

Secretary—Sr. JUDITH A. DAVIES, O.S.F.
Clergy Life and Formation—Rev. DAVID MOWRY, Tel: 815-221-6184; Fax: 815-722-6632.
Delegate for Religious—Sr. JUDITH A. DAVIES, O.S.F., Tel: 815-221-6118; Fax: 815-722-6632.
Permanent Diaconate—Deacon JOHN FREUND, Tel: 815-221-6174; Fax: 815-838-8129.
Vicar for Priests—Very Rev. JOHN BALLUFF, Tel: 815-221-6171; Fax: 815-838-8129.
Vocations—Rev. STEVEN BORELLO, Tel: 815-221-6171; Fax: 815-838-8129.

Secretariat for Christian Formation

Secretary—Rev. BURKE MASTERS.
Catholic Education Foundation—MR. JOSEPH LANGENDERFER, Tel: 815-221-6127; Fax: 815-588-6007.
Catholic Schools Office—Rev. JOHN BELMONTE, S.J., Tel: 815-221-6126; Fax: 815-838-2182.
Adult Formation—Rev. BURKE MASTERS, Tel: 815-221-6147; Fax: 815-838-2182.
Youth Formation—MR. RYAN PURCELL, Tel: 815-221-6147; Fax: 815-838-2182.

Secretariat for Pastoral Concerns

Secretary—MR. PETER NEWBURN.
Council of Catholic Women—MRS. VANESSA LOPATKA, Tel: 815-221-6249; Fax: 815-221-6089.
Divine Worship—Sr. SHARON MARIE STOLA, O.S.B., Tel: 815-221-6231; Fax: 815-221-6089.
Ecumenism—MR. PETER NEWBURN, Tel: 815-221-6238; Fax: 815-221-6089.
Hispanic & Ethnic Ministry—VACANT.
Family Ministry—DR. JAMES HEALY, Tel: 815-838-5334; Fax: 815-221-6089.
Young Adult Ministry—MRS. SHEILA STEVENSON, Tel: 815-221-6234; Fax: 815-221-6089.

Secretariat for Social Concerns

Secretary—MR. GLENN VAN CURA.
Catholic Charities & Health Affairs—Legal Title: Catholic Charities of the Diocese of Joliet. MR. GLENN VAN CURA, Tel: 815-724-1159; Fax: 815-723-3452.
Human Dignity—MR. THOMAS GARLITZ, Tel: 815-221-6251; Fax: 815-221-6088.
Jail & Prison Ministry—MR. MICHAEL BEARY, Tel: 815-221-6251; Fax: 815-221-6088.
Justice and Peace; CCHD; CRS—MS. EDITH AVILA OLEA, Tel: 815-221-6251; Fax: 815-221-6088.
Missions—Deacon BRUCE CARLSON; Sr. NANCY ROBERTA SCHRAMM, O.S.F., Tel: 815-221-6251; Fax: 815-221-6088.
Respect Life—MS. ALEXANDRA FEDOSENKO, Tel: 815-221-6251; Fax: 815-221-6088.

CLERGY, PARISHES, MISSIONS AND PAROCHIAL SCHOOLS

CITY OF JOLIET

(WILL COUNTY)

1—THE CATHEDRAL OF ST. RAYMOND (1917)
604 N. Raynor Ave., Joliet, 60435. Tel: 815-722-6653; Email: info@straymond.net; Web: www.straymond.net. Very Rev. William G. Dewan, Rector; Revs. Ryan Adorjan; Burke Masters, In Res.
School—The Cathedral of St. Raymond School, (Grades PreSchool-8), 608 N. Raynor Ave., Joliet, 60435. Tel: 815-722-6626; Fax: 815-727-4668; Email: cprieboy@csrn.org. Marjorie Hill, Prin. Lay Teachers 28; Students 417.
Catechesis Religious Program—Fax: 815-722-3137; Email: re@straymond.net; Web: straymond.net/RE. Christine Pershey, D.R.E. Students 220.

2—ST. ANTHONY (1902) (Italian)
Mailing Address: 100 N. Scott St., Joliet, 60432-4210. Tel: 815-722-1057; Fax: 815-722-9805; Email: saintanthonyjoliet@hotmail.com. Very Rev. John Balluff.

3—ST. BERNARD (1921) Very Rev. Christopher Groh; Ms. Margaret Trepal, Pastoral Assoc.
Rectory & Mailing Address: 127 S. Briggs St., Joliet, 60433. Tel: 815-726-4474; Fax: 815-724-1720; Email: magdalenechurch@aol.com.
Church: Sterling Ave. & High St., Joliet, 60433.

4—SS. CYRIL AND METHODIUS (1900) (Slovak), Closed. For inquiries for parish records contact the chancery.

5—ST. FRANCIS XAVIER (2002) [CEM]
Mailing Address: 2500 Arbeiter Rd., Joliet, 60431. Tel: 815-609-8077; Fax: 815-609-8078; Email: office@st-francis-xavier.com; Web: www.st-francis-xavier.com. Rev. Karl Langsdorf.
Catechesis Religious Program—Email: nanagiunta@gmail.com. Mrs. Penny Giunta, C.R.E. Students 285.

6—HISTORIC ST. JOSEPH (1891) [CEM] (Slovenian)
416 N. Chicago St., Joliet, 60432. Tel: 815-727-9378; Email: jhalsne@stjosephjoliet.org; Web: www.stjosephjoliet.org. Rev. Timothy P. Andres, O.Carm.
Catechesis Religious Program—Email: cgimbel@stjosephjoliet.org. Cherie Gimbal, D.R.E. Students 88.

7—HOLY CROSS (1893) [JC] (Polish)
830 Elizabeth St., Joliet, 60435. Tel: 815-726-4031; Fax: 815-727-4393; Email: mnemanich@smncs.com; Email: amurphy@smncs.com. 830 Elizabeth Street, Joliet, 60435. Revs. Jerome Kish; Julian Kaczowka, S.Ch.
Catechesis Religious Program— Please see St. Mary Nativity, Joliet. Students 200.

8—ST. JOHN THE BAPTIST (1852) [CEM]
404 N. Hickory St., Joliet, 60435. Tel: 815-727-4788; Tel: 815-727-4786; Fax: 815-727-1729; Email: stjohnbap@church404.comcastbiz.net; Web: sjbcatholic.org. Revs. Herbert Jones, O.F.M.; More Torres Torres, Parochial Vicar; Bro. Edward Arambasich, O.F.M., In Res.; Rev. David Rodriguez, O.F.M., In Res.; Deacons Jose Lopez; James Janousek, Business Mgr.
Catechesis Religious Program—403 N. Hickory St., Joliet, 60435. Tel: 815-727-9077. Students 500.

9—ST. JUDE (1954)
2212 McDonough St., Joliet, 60436. Tel: 815-725-2209; Email: parishsecretary@stjudejoliet.net. Rev. Michael Lane; Mrs. Paula Bucciferro, Business Mgr.
School—St. Jude School, (Grades PreK-8), 2204 McDonough St., Joliet, 60436. Tel: 815-729-0288; Fax: 815-729-0344; Email: lstangler@stjudejoliet.net; Web: stjudejoliet.net. Lucas Stangler, Prin. Clergy 2; Lay Teachers 11; Dominican Sisters of St. Cecilia 2; Students 169.
Catechesis Religious Program—Email: rc@stjudejoliet.net. Sarah Reznicek, D.R.E. Students 180.

10—ST. MARY CARMELITE, Closed. For inquiries for parish records contact the chancery.

11—ST. MARY MAGDALENE (1953)
127 S. Briggs St., Joliet, 60433. Tel: 815-722-7653; Fax: 815-724-1720; Email: magdalenechurch@aol.com; Web: www.stmarymagdalenechurch.com. Very Rev. Christopher Groh; Deacon John Mele; Ms. Margaret Trepal, Pastoral Assoc.
Catechesis Religious Program—201 S. Briggs St., Joliet, 60433. Tel: 815-727-4600. Sr. Jude Marie Naiden, S.S.F.C.R., D.R.E. Students 57.

12—ST. MARY NATIVITY (1906) [JC] (Croatian)
706 N. Broadway, Joliet, 60435. Tel: 815-726-4031; Email: amurphy@smncs.com; Email: mnemanich@smncs.com. Revs. Jerome Kish; Julian Kaczowka, S.Ch.; Deacon Daniel Mahoney Sr. In Res., Rev. Julian Kaczowka, S.Ch.
School—St. Mary Nativity School, (Grades PreSchool-8), 702 N. Broadway, Joliet, 60435. Tel: 815-722-8518; Email: lwhite@stmarynativity.org. Mr. Larry White, Prin., Email: lwhite@stmarynativity.org. Lay Teachers 13; Students 167.
Catechesis Religious Program—Tel: 815-726-4073; Email: nsmith@stmarynativity.org. Nanci Lukasik-Smith, D.R.E. Students 56.
Convent—700 N. Hickory St., Joliet, 60435.

13—OUR LADY OF MOUNT CARMEL (1939) (Mexican-American)
407 Irving St., Joliet, 60432. Tel: 815-727-7187; Email: mountcarmel@ourladymtcarmel.net; Web: www.ourladymtcarmel.net. Revs. Jose Luis Torres, O.Carm.; Jose Cilia, O.Carm.; Edward Ward, O.Carm.
Weekend Svcs.: 205 E. Jackson St., Joliet, 60432.
Daily Mass: 405 E. Irving St., Joliet, 60432.
Res.: 409 Irving St., Joliet, 60432. Tel: 815-726-5208; Email: Jolutorres@hotmail.com.
Catechesis Religious Program—Tel: 815-727-6330; Email: anamtzsolano@hotmail.com. Anatolia Martinez, D.R.E. Students 740.

14—ST. PATRICK (1838)
710 W. Marion St., Joliet, 60436-1556. Tel: 815-727-4746; Email: stpatrectory0710@sbcglobal.net; Web: www.stpatsjoliet.com. Very Rev. Gregor Gorsic; Deacons Felix Dominguez, RCIA Coord.; Paul Kolodziej; Darrell Kelsey. In Res., Rev. Michael Pennock.
Catechesis Religious Program—Email: juliedillenburg@stpatsjoliet.com. Julie Dillenburg, D.R.E. Students 287.

15—ST. PAUL THE APOSTLE (1950)
18 Woodlawn Ave., Joliet, 60435. Tel: 815-725-1527; Email: parishsec@stpauljoliet.com; Web: stpauljoliet.com. Very Rev. John Klein; Deacon John Freund; Rev. John Belmonte, S.J., In Res.
School—St. Paul the Apostle School, (Grades PreSchool-8), 130 Woodlawn Ave., Joliet, 60435. Tel: 815-725-3390; Fax: 815-725-3180; Email: calimento@stpauljoliet.com; Web: www.stpauljoliet.com. Mrs. Corrine Alimento, Prin. Clergy 2; Lay Teachers 17; Students 255.
Catechesis Religious Program—120 Woodlawn Ave., Joliet, 60435. Email: jjones@stpauljoliet.com. Mrs. Jennifer Jones, D.R.E. Students 255.

16—SACRED HEART (1886) (African American)
337 S. Ottawa St., Joliet, 60436. Tel: 815-722-0295; Email: pastorsacredheart337@gmail.com. Very Rev. William G. Dewan; Rev. Ryan Adorjan, Parochial Vicar; Deacon Ralph Bias.
Catechesis Religious Program—Students 13.

17—ST. THADDEUS (1927) (Polish), Closed. For inquiries for parish records contact the chancery.

OUTSIDE THE CITY OF JOLIET

ADDISON, DU PAGE CO.

1—ST. JOSEPH (1956) (Hispanic)
330 E. Fullerton, Addison, 60101. Tel: 630-279-6553; Fax: 630-279-4925; Email: parish@stjosephaddison.org; Web: www.stjoeaddison.com. Rev. Luis Gutierrez; Deacon Philip Marrow.
See Holy Family Catholic School, Bensenville under St. Charles Borromeo, Bensenville for details.
Catechesis Religious Program—Tel: 630-832-5514; Email: carlo@stjosephaddison.org. Mr. Carlo Zeffiro, C.R.E. Students 350.

2—ST. PHILIP THE APOSTLE (1963)
1223 W. Holtz Ave., Addison, 60101. Tel: 630-543-4130; Email: jnoonan@st-phil.org. Rev. Steven Bondi; Deacons Philip Heitz; Sean McGreal.
School—St. Philip the Apostle School, (Grades PreSchool-8), 1233 W. Holtz Ave., Addison, 60101. Tel: 630-543-4130; Fax: 630-458-8750; Email: jnoonan@st-phil.org; Web: st-phil.org/school. Julie Noonan, Prin. Lay Teachers 14; Students 228.
Catechesis Religious Program—Tel: 630-543-1754; Email: nmcknight@st-phil.org. Mrs. Nancy McKnight, D.R.E. Students 256.

ASHKUM, IROQUOIS CO., ASSUMPTION OF THE BLESSED VIRGIN MARY (1903) [CEM] [JC2]
208 N. Second St., Box 218, Ashkum, 60911. Tel: 815-698-2262; Email: debbie_assumption@comcast.net. Rev. Douglas L. Hauber.
Catechesis Religious Program—Students 60.
Mission—St. John the Baptist (1856) 1500 E. 2700 N. Rd., Clifton, 60927. Tel: 815-698-2262.

AURORA, DU PAGE CO., OUR LADY OF MERCY (1988)
701 S. Eola Rd., Aurora, 60504. Revs. Don E. McLaughlin; Mark Bernhard, Parochial Vicar; Deacons Robert Vavra, (Retired); Philip Rehmer; Timothy Kueper; Tony Martini; Arturo Tiongson; Mike Plese.
Res.: 801 S. Eola Rd., Aurora, 60504.
Tel: 630-851-3444; Email: parishoffice@olmercy.com; Web: www.olmercy.com.
Catechesis Religious Program—
Tel: 630-851-3444, Ext. 222. Students 1,146.

BEAVERVILLE, IROQUOIS CO., ST. MARY (1857) [CEM]
308 St. Charles St., Beaverville, 60912. Tel: 815-435-2432; Email: stmaryschurchbeaverville@yahoo.com; Web: www.stmaryschurchbeaverville.com. P.O. Box 152, Beaverville, 60912. Rev. Daniel R. Belanger, C.S.V.; Ryan Loy, Pastoral Assoc.
Catechesis Religious Program—Tel: 815-486-7144; Email: teacherdad79@yahoo.com. Students 46.

BENSENVILLE, DU PAGE CO.

1—ST. ALEXIS (1926)
400 W. Wood St., Bensenville, 60106. Tel: 630-766-3530; Email: secretaryalexis@yahoo.com. Rev. Matthew Nathan.
Catechesis Religious Program—410 W. Wood St., Bensenville, 60106. Tel: 630-766-4417. Anthony Holmes, C.R.E.; Deacon Sergio Gonzalez, C.R.E. Students 36.

2—ST. CHARLES BORROMEO (1959)
1135 Daniel, Bensenville, 60106. Tel: 630-860-1120; Email: sheila@stcbparish.org; Web: www.stcbparish.org. Rev. Joshua Miller; Deacon Timothy Taylor.
School—Holy Family Catholic School, (Grades PreK-8), 145 E. Grand Ave., Bensenville, 60106. Tel: 630-766-0116; Fax: 630-766-0181; Email: officeeast@hfcatholic.org; Web: www.hfcatholic.org. Mrs. Linda Kelly, Prin. Lay Teachers 14; Students 137.
Catechesis Religious Program—Tel: 630-766-8822; Fax: 630-766-3481. Students 145.

BLOOMINGDALE, DUPAGE CO., ST. ISIDORE (1920)

[CEM]
427 W. Army Trail Rd., Bloomingdale, 60108-1390.
Tel: 630-529-3045; Email: jmcdaniel@stisidoreparish.org; Web: www.stisidoreparish.org. Revs. James Murphy; Juan Jose Hernandez, Parochial Vicar; Clive Otieno, Parochial Vicar; Deacons Terry Cummiskey; Oscar Monterroso; Joanna McDaniel, Admin.
School—St. Isidore School, (Grades PreSchool-8), 431 W. Army Trail Rd., Bloomingdale, 60108-1390.
Tel: 630-529-9323; Email: cyndicollins@saintisidoreschool.org. Mrs. Cyndi Collins, Prin. Lay Teachers 25; Students 256.
Catechesis Religious Program—Tel: 630-529-9191. Students 950.

BOLINGBROOK, WILL CO.
1—ST. DOMINIC (1964)
Mailing Address: 440 E. Briarcliff Rd., Bolingbrook, 60440. Revs. Franklin Duran; James Olofson; Deacons Lorenzo Chaidez; Arturo Chacon; Robert Wallace; Paul Walen.
Res.: 408 E. Briarcliff Rd., Bolingbrook, 60440.
Tel: 630-739-5703; Email: stdominic@comcast.net.
School—St. Dominic School, (Grades PreSchool-8), 420 E. Briarcliff Rd., Bolingbrook, 60440.
Tel: 630-739-1633; Fax: 630-739-5989; Email: stdominicschool@comcast.net. Sr. Marie Isaac Staub, O.P., Prin.; Susan Meifert, Librarian. Clergy 2; Lay Teachers 14; Students 224.
Catechesis Religious Program—
Tel: 630-739-5703, Ext. 23; Email: c.hannigan.wiehn@sdominic.com. Chris Hannigan-Wiehn, D.R.E. Students 602.

2—ST. FRANCIS OF ASSISI (1980)
1501 W. Boughton Rd., Bolingbrook, 60490.
Tel: 630-759-7588; Fax: 630-759-5257; Email: gmempin@stfrancisbb.og; Email: jchamberlain@stfrancisbb.org; Email: dblumenstein@stfrancisbb.org; Web: stfrancisbb.org. Revs. Herbert Essig; Patrick Murphy, Parochial Vicar; Deacons John Blumenstein; Raymond Hamilton; Marco Lovero; Michael McGuire; Genaro Mempin; Anthony Osei; Gregory Gresik, Pastoral Assoc.
Catechesis Religious Program—Email: tpalicka@stfrancisbb.org. Theresa Palicka, D.R.E. Students 649.

BOURBONNAIS, KANKAKEE CO., MATERNITY OF THE BLESSED VIRGIN MARY (1847) [CEM]
308 E. Marsile St., Bourbonnais, 60914.
Tel: 815-933-8285; Email: maternitybvm1847@yahoo.com; Web: www.mbvmchurch.org. Revs. Jason Nesbit, C.S.V.; Daniel Lydon, Parochial Vicar; Deacon Patrick Skelly.
Catechesis Religious Program—
Tel: 815-933-8285, Ext. 226; Email: mpallissard@mbvm.org. Maria Pallissard, D.R.E.

BRADLEY, KANKAKEE CO., ST. JOSEPH (1904)
211 N. Center Ave., Bradley, 60915.
Tel: 815-939-3573; Email: pstorer@stjosephbradley.org; Web: www.stjosephbradley.org. Rev. Anthony A. Nugent; Deacons Leon Fritz; Gregory Clodi, Pastoral Assoc.
Catechesis Religious Program—Students 182.

BRAIDWOOD, WILL CO., IMMACULATE CONCEPTION (1869) [CEM] (Irish—Italian)
110 S. School St., Braidwood, 60408.
Tel: 815-458-2125; Email: office@icbraidwood.org; Web: www.icparishbraidwood.org. Rev. Robert Noesen.

CABERY, FORD CO., ST. JOSEPH (1867) [CEM] (German), Closed. For inquiries for parish records contact St. Margaret Mary Parish, Herscher, IL.

CAROL STREAM, DU PAGE CO.
1—CORPUS CHRISTI (1989)
1415 W. Lies Rd., Carol Stream, 60188.
Tel: 630-483-4673; Email: corpuschristicc@sbcglobal.net. Rev. Marek Jurzyk; Deacons Thomas R. Thiltgen; William Thomas; Elizabeth Mazur, Pastoral Assoc.
Catechesis Religious Program—
Tel: 630-483-4222 (RE); Tel: 630-483-4226 (YM); Email: ccedu@sbcglobal.net; Email: ccym@sbcglobal.net. Students 406.

2—ST. LUKE (1963)
421 Cochise Ct., Carol Stream, 60188.
Tel: 630-668-1325; Email: stloff@aol.com; Web: www.stlukecarolstream.org. Rev. Danilo Soriano, C.P.
Catechesis Religious Program—Tel: 630-665-2322; Email: stlrfp@aol.com. Mark Donovan, D.R.E. Students 50.

CHANNAHON, WILL CO., ST. ANN PARISH (1990)
24500 S. Navajo Dr., Channahon, 60410.
Tel: 815-467-6962; Email: parishoffice@stannchannahon.org; Web: www.stannchannahon.org. Rev. Peter Jarosz.
Catechesis Religious Program—Email: tom@stannchannahon.org. Tom Uraski, D.R.E. Students 10.

CHEBANSE, IROQUOIS CO., SS. MARY AND JOSEPH (1869) [CEM]
P.O. Box 25, Clifton, 60927. Tel: 815-698-2262; Email: debbie_assumption@comcast.net. 525 S. Chestnut, Chebanse, 60922. Rev. Douglas Hauber.
Res.: 450 E. 3rd Ave., P.O. Box 25, Clifton, 60927.
Tel: 815-694-2027; Email: frdoug.hauber@yahoo.com.
Catechesis Religious Program—Students 30.

CLARENDON HILLS, DU PAGE CO., NOTRE DAME (1954)
64 Norfolk Ave., Clarendon Hills, 60514.
Tel: 630-654-6635; Email: parishoffice@notredameparish.org; Web: notredameparish.org. Rev. David Medow; Deacon Timothy Nickels.
School—Notre Dame School, (Grades PreK-8), 64 Norfolk Ave., Clarendon Hills, 60514.
Tel: 630-323-1642; Email: school@notredameparish.org. Ms. Mary Ann Feeney, Prin. Clergy 1; Lay Teachers 21; Students 203.
Catechesis Religious Program—
Tel: 630-654-3365, Ext. 237. Students 470.

CLIFTON, IROQUOIS CO., ST. PETER'S (1869) [CEM]
450 E. Third Ave., P.O. Box 25, Clifton, 60927-0025.
Tel: 815-694-2027; Email: frdoug.hauber@yahoo.com. Rev. Douglas L. Hauber.
Catechesis Religious Program—Tel: 815-694-2970; Email: stspmj@comcast.net. Students 35.

COAL CITY, GRUNDY CO., ASSUMPTION OF THE BLESSED VIRGIN MARY (1889)
Mailing Address: 195 S. Kankakee St., Coal City, 60416. Tel: 815-634-4171; Email: secretary@stmaryassumptionparish.org; Web: stmaryassumptionparish.org/conc/. Rev. Robert Noesen; Deacon William F. Bevan III.
Catechesis Religious Program—Tel: 815-518-5775; Email: deacon.bill.assumption@gmail.com. Deacon William Dunn, Dir. of Catechesis & Evangelization. Students 166.

CREST HILL, WILL CO.
1—ST. AMBROSE (1965)
1711 Burry Cir., 60403. Tel: 815-722-3222; Email: StAnneStAmbrose@rcdoj.org. Rev. Thomas Cargo.
Catechesis Religious Program—Tel: 815-722-9193; Email: SrAnneStAmbrose@rcdoj.org. Sr. Mary Frances Werner, D.R.E. Students 144.

2—ST. ANNE (1953)
1711 Burry Cir., 60403. Tel: 815-722-3222; Email: StAnneStAmbrose@rcdoj.org. 1800 Dearborn St., 60403. Rev. Thomas Cargo.

DARIEN, DU PAGE CO.
1—OUR LADY OF MOUNT CARMEL (1970)
8404 Cass Ave., Darien, 60561. Tel: 630-852-3303; Email: receptionist@ourladyofmtcarmel.org; Web: www.ourladyofmtcarmel.org. Revs. Michael O'Keefe, O.Carm.; Robert Carroll, O.Carm., Parochial Vicar; Deacons James Foody; Edward Ptacek.
Catechesis Religious Program—Tel: 630-963-3053; Email: dre@ourladyofmtcarmel.org. Sherry Rochford, D.R.E. Students 727.

2—OUR LADY OF PEACE (1970)
701 Plainfield Rd., Darien, 60561. Tel: 630-323-4333; Email: wdziordz@olopdarien.org. Revs. Walter Dziordz, M.I.C.; Mark Baron, M.I.C., Parochial Vicar; Deacons Frank Vonesh; Larry Fudacz; Patrick Kenny.
School—Our Lady of Peace School, (Grades PreK-8), 709 Plainfield Rd., Darien, 60561. Tel: 630-325-9220; Fax: 630-325-1995; Email: egray@olopdarien.org. Religious Teachers 1; Lay Teachers 15; Students 254.
Catechesis Religious Program—(Grades K-8), Tel: 630-986-8430; Email: religioused@olopdarien.org. Students 218.

DOWNERS GROVE, DU PAGE CO.
1—DIVINE SAVIOR (1968)
6700 Main St., Downers Grove, 60516. Email: marianne@divinesavior.net. Rev. Agustin Ortega-Ruiz; Deacons Paul S. Newey; Michael Januszewski; Marianne Treacy, Business Mgr.
Res.: 1200 67th St., Downers Grove, 60516.
Tel: 630-969-1532, Ext. 121; Email: parish@divinesavior.net; Web: www.divinesavior.net.
Catechesis Religious Program—Email: maureen@divinesavior.net. Mrs. Maureen Januszewski, D.R.E. Students 250.

2—ST. JOSEPH (1907)
4824 Highland Ave., Downers Grove, 60515.
Tel: 630-964-0216; Email: bharbauer@sjpdg.org; Web: www.stjosephdg.org. 4801 Main St., Downers Grove, 60515. Rev. John Phan.
School—St. Joseph School, (Grades PreSchool-8), 4832 Main St., Downers Grove, 60515.
Tel: 630-969-4306; Email: schooloffice@stjosephdg.org; Web: stjosephdg.com. Rita Stasi, Prin. Clergy 1; Lay Teachers 28; Students 432.
Catechesis Religious Program—Jacqueline M Lackaff, D.R.E.; Marta Spiezio, Youth Min. Students 382.

3—ST. MARY OF GOSTYN (1891)
445 Prairie St., Downers Grove, 60515.
Tel: 630-969-1063; Email: parish@stmarygostyn.org; Web: www.stmarygostyn.org. Revs. James Schwab; Shaun Cieslik, Parochial Vicar; Deacons Steven DeSitter; Albert Agurkis; Robert Miciunas; Steve Bisaillon, Music Dir.; LaVonne Czech, Marketing Dir.; Kelly Johnson, Adult Faith Formation Dir.; Terri O'Dekirk, Devel. Dir. & Plant Mgr.
Res.: 444 Wilson St., Downers Grove, 60515.
Tel: 630-960-3565.
School—St. Mary of Gostyn School, (Grades PreSchool-8), 440 Prairie Ave., Downers Grove, 60515. Tel: 630-968-6155; Fax: 630-968-6208; Email: school@stmarygostyn.org. Mr. Christopher Tiritilli, Prin.; Jamie Belcastro, Librarian. Lay Teachers 28; Students 465.
Catechesis Religious Program—Mary Jame Wahl, D.R.E.; Claire Simeo, Youth Min. Students 520.

ELMHURST, DU PAGE CO.
1—IMMACULATE CONCEPTION (1876)
134 Arthur St., Elmhurst, 60126. Tel: 630-530-8515; Email: info@icelmhurst.org. Very Rev. Thomas Paul; Rev. Christopher Lankford, Parochial Vicar; Deacon John Feely.
School—Immaculate Conception School, (Grades PreSchool-8), 132 Arthur St., Elmhurst, 60126.
Tel: 630-530-3490; Fax: 630-530-9787; Email: clinely@icgradeschoolelmhurst.org. Mrs. Cathy Linley, Prin. Lay Teachers 34; Students 487.
High School—IC Catholic Prep, 217 Cottage Hill Ave., Elmhurst, 60126. Tel: 630-530-3460;
Fax: 630-530-2290; Email: plevar@iccatholicprep.org. Ms. Pamela M. Levar, Prin. Lay Teachers 28; Students 313.
Catechesis Religious Program—Tel: 630-530-3483; Email: srmaryfrancis@icelmhurst.org; Email: jbastianoni@icelmhurst.org. Students 516.

2—MARY, QUEEN OF HEAVEN (1956)
442 N. West Ave., Elmhurst, 60126-2128. Rev. Jason Stone.
Res.: 426 N. West Ave., Elmhurst, 60126-2128.
Tel: 630-279-5700; Email: parishoffice@maryqueen.org; Web: maryqueen.org.
Catechesis Religious Program—Tel: 630-832-8962; Email: mglaudell@maryqueen.org. Mary Gluadell, D.R.E. Students 333.

3—VISITATION (1953)
779 S. York St., Elmhurst, 60126. Tel: 630-834-6700; Fax: 630-834-6711; Email: welcome@visitationcc.org; Web: Visitationparish.org. Revs. Greg Skowron; Michael Kearney; Deacons Jay Janousek; Anthony Spatafore; James Eaker; Michael Iozzo; Michael O'Ryan.
School—Visitation School, (Grades PreSchool-8), 851 S. York, Elmhurst, 60126. Tel: 630-834-4931;
Fax: 630-834-4936; Email: cdransoff@visitationelmhurst.org; Email: kmcvey@visitationelmhurst.org; Web: www.visitationelmhurst.org. Dr. Christopher Dransoff, Prin. Lay Teachers 26; Students 424.
Catechesis Religious Program—Students 679.

FRANKFORT, WILL CO., ST. ANTHONY (1929)
7659 W. Sauk Tr., Frankfort, 60423.
Tel: 815-469-3750; Email: jeanne@stanthonyfrankfort.com. Very Rev. Richard L. Smith, J.C.L.; Rev. John Sponder, Parochial Vicar; Deacons Donald Berkey; Daniel Danahey; Richard Rosko; William Boucek; Joseph Johnson, Pastoral Assoc.; Anthony Schlott, D.R.E. & A.F.F.
Catechesis Religious Program—Tel: 815-469-6198; Email: tony@stanthonyfrankfort.com. Students 590.

GIBSON CITY, FORD CO., OUR LADY OF LOURDES (1875) [JC]
534 N. Wood St., Gibson City, 60936.
Tel: 217-784-4671; Email: pastor@ololgc.org. Rev. Dong Bui.
Catechesis Religious Program—Alyce Hafer, D.R.E. Students 115.

GILMAN, IROQUOIS CO., IMMACULATE CONCEPTION (1872) [CEM] (Our Lady of Guadalupe)
224 N. Secor St., Gilman, 60938. Tel: 815-265-7236; Email: icccgilman@gmail.com. Revs. Marek Herbut; John Horan, Hispanic Min.
Catechesis Religious Program—Tel: 815-383-5819; Email: anitamelgoza5@gmail.com. Anita Melgoza, D.R.E. Students 82.
Mission—Immaculate Conception, 202 E. Green St., Roberts, 60962. 534 N. Wood St., Gibson City, 60936.

GLEN ELLYN, DU PAGE CO.
1—ST. JAMES THE APOSTLE (1965)
480 S. Park Blvd., Glen Ellyn, 60137.
Fax: 630-469-7590. Very Rev. David J. Hankus, D.Min.
Res.: 579 Prince Edward Rd., Glen Ellyn, 60137.
Tel: 630-469-7540, Ext. 201; Email: frdavid@stjamesge.org.
School—St. James the Apostle School, (Grades PreK-8), 490 S. Park Blvd., Glen Ellyn, 60137.
Tel: 630-469-8060; Fax: 630-469-1107; Email: pkirk@stjamesge-school.org. Paul Kirk, Prin. Clergy 1; Lay Teachers 12; Students 198.
Catechesis Religious Program—Tel: 630-858-5646; Email: lweesner@stjamesge.org. Lisa Weesner, D.R.E. Students 575.

2—ST. PETRONILLE (1925)
420 Glenwood Ave, Glen Ellyn, 60137-4506. Revs.

James Dougherty; Marcin Michalak, Parochial Vicar; Deacons Ronald Yurcus; John Spiezio; Bob Cassey. In Res., Revs. John D. Sullivan, (Retired); Arthur Maher, (Retired).
Res.: 412 Prospect Ave., Glen Ellyn, 60137.
Tel: 630-469-9494, Ext. 0; Email: office@stpetschurch.org.
School—St. Petronille School, (Grades K-8), 425 Prospect Ave., Glen Ellyn, 60137. Tel: 630-469-5041; Fax: 630-469-5071; Email: gronwickk@stpetschool.org; Web: www.stpetschool.org. Ms. Maureen Aspell, Prin. Lay Teachers 31; Students 492.
Catechesis Religious Program—
Tel: 630-858-3796, Ext. 4000; Email: tutajs@stpetschurch.org. Susan Tutaj, D.R.E. Students 517.
3—QUEENSHIP OF MARY (1993) [JC] (Vietnamese)
219 Armitage Ave., Glen Ellyn, 60137.
Tel: 630-752-0332; Cell: 847-833-0679; Email: dahhh1@wowway.com. Revs. Tri Van Tran; Nguyen Huy Quyen, In Res., (Retired).
Catechesis Religious Program—Tel: 630-752-0332. Students 129.
GLENDALE HEIGHTS, DU PAGE CO., ST. MATTHEW (1960)
1555 Glen Ellyn Rd., Glendale Heights, 60139.
Tel: 630-469-6300; Email: info@stmatthewchurch.org; Web: www.stmatthewchurch.org. Revs. Anthony Taschetta, Admin., (Retired); Michal Twaruzek, Parochial Vicar; Deacons Robert Malek; Lindsey Parsons; Gabriel Gamba; Michael Ruddle. In Res., Revs. Richard Cilano; Sundar Raj Kocherla, (India) (Retired).
School—St. Matthew School, (Grades PreK-8), 1555 Glen Ellyn Rd., Glendale Hts, 60139.
Tel: 630-858-3112; Email: info@stmatthewschool.org. Rev. Jerome Kish, Prin.; Mrs. Regina Pestrak, Prin. Lay Teachers 17; Students 236.
Catechesis Religious Program—Email: mruddle@stmatthewchurch.org. Students 309.
GOODRICH, KANKAKEE CO., SACRED HEART (1895) [CEM]
588 S. 10000 W. Road, Bonfield, 60913-7019.
Tel: 815-426-2550; Email: smm_sja-sh@yahoo.mail. Rev. Show Reddy Allum.
Catechesis Religious Program—Students 15.
HERSCHER, KANKAKEE CO., ST. MARGARET MARY, [CEM]
207 E. Fifth St., Herscher, 60941. Tel: 815-426-2550; Email: smm_sja_sh@yahoo.com. Rev. Show Reddy Allum.
Catechesis Religious Program—Tel: 815-426-2550. Stacie Powers, D.R.E. Students 74.
HINSDALE, DU PAGE CO., ST. ISAAC JOGUES (1930) (Irish—Italian)
306 W. Fourth St., Hinsdale, 60521.
Tel: 630-323-1248; Email: cathy@sijhinsdale.com; Web: www.sij.net. Revs. William DeSalvo; Rodolphe Arty, C.S.C., Parochial Vicar.
School—St. Isaac Jogues School, (Grades K-8), 421 S. Clay St., Hinsdale, 60521. Tel: 630-323-3244; Fax: 630-655-6676; Email: cburlinski@sijschool.org; Web: sijschool.org. Mrs. Carol Burlinski, Prin. Lay Teachers 33; Students 496.
Catechesis Religious Program—427 S. Clay St., Hinsdale, 60521. Tel: 630-323-0265;
Fax: 630-655-5539. Helen Johnson, Elementary D.R.E.; Mike Kuhn, Asst. Youth Ministry Coord. (6-8th grades). Students 530.
HOMER GLEN, WILL CO.
1—ST. BERNARD (1978)
14135 Parker Rd., Homer Glen, 60491.
Tel: 708-301-3020; Email: st.bernardsrectory@comcast.net. 13030 W. 143rd St., Homer Glen, 60491. Rev. Joseph McCormick, D.R.E.; Deacons Kevin Ryan; Christopher McCaffrey.
Catechesis Religious Program—Email: st.bernardsrep@comcast.net. Patricia Bass, D.R.E. Students 232.
2—OUR MOTHER OF GOOD COUNSEL (1996)
16043 S. Bell Rd., Homer Glen, 60491.
Tel: 708-301-6246; Tel: 708-301-0214; Email: omgccc@comcast.net; Email: frjoseph@omgccc.org; Web: www.omgccc.org. Rev. Joseph G. Broudou, O.S.A.; Deacon Fredrick Filippo; Revs. Terry A. Deffenbaugh, O.S.A., In Res.; Thomas L. Osborne, O.S.A., In Res.
Catechesis Religious Program—Tel: 708-301-0214; Email: janet.re@omgccc.org. Janet Litterio, D.R.E. Students 494.
IRWIN, KANKAKEE CO., ST. JAMES THE APOSTLE, [CEM]
4372 Main St., Irwin, 60901. Email: smm_sja_sh@yahoo.com. Res. & Mailing Address: St. Margaret Mary Parish, 207 E. Fifth St., Herscher, 60941. Tel: 815-426-2153. Rev. Show Reddy Allum.
Catechesis Religious Program—Tel: 815-933-5443. Allicia Miller, D.R.E. Students 60.
ITASCA, DU PAGE CO.
1—ST. ANDREW KIM (1981) [JC] (Korean)
1275 N. Arlington Hts. Rd., Itasca, 60143.
Tel: 630-250-0576; Email: standrewkimchicago@gmail.com; Web: www.standrewkimchicago.org. Rev. Ji Kim.
2—ST. PETER THE APOSTLE (1956)
524 N. Rush St., Itasca, 60143-1698.
Tel: 630-773-1272; Email: office@stpeteritasca.com; Web: stpeteritasca.com. Rev. Slawomir Ignasik.
Catechesis Religious Program—
Tel: 630-773-1272, Ext. 216. Students 243.
KANKAKEE, KANKAKEE CO.
1—ST. JOHN PAUL II PARISH
956 S. 10th Ave., Kankakee, 60901.
Tel: 815-933-7683; Email: dworth@jp2kankakee.org; Web: jp2kankakee.org. Revs. Santos Castillo; John Horan, Parochial Vicar.
Catechesis Religious Program—Students 225.
2—ST. MARTIN OF TOURS (1950) [JC] Merged with St. Rose of Lima and St. Teresa, Kankakee to form St. John Paul II Parish, Kankakee.
3—ST. PATRICK (1893) (Irish)
428 S. Indiana Ave., Kankakee, 60901.
Tel: 815-932-6716; Email: stpatskan@ameritech.net. Rev. John N. Peeters, C.S.V.; Sr. Theresa Galvan, C.N.D., Pastoral Min.; Marilyn Mulcahy, Pastoral Assoc.; Revs. Donald R. Wehnert, C.S.V., In Res., (Retired); Richard Pighini, C.S.V., In Res.
Catechesis Religious Program—Tel: 815-216-7267; Email: repfaith13@gmail.com. Mrs. Marcia Brown Medina, D.R.E. Students 24.
4—ST. ROSE OF LIMA (1857) Merged with St. Martin of Tours and St. Teresa, Kankakee to form St. John Paul II Parish, Kankakee.
5—ST. STANISLAUS, (Polish), Closed. For inquiries for parish records contact the chancery.
6—ST. TERESA (1949) [CEM] Merged with St. Martin of Tours and St. Rose of Lima, Kankakee to form St. John Paul II Parish, Kankakee.
KINSMAN, GRUNDY CO., SACRED HEART (1880)
219 W. Emmett Street, P.O. Box 824, Kinsman, 60437. Tel: 815-392-4245; Fax: 815-237-2201; Email: stlawrenceswilm@yahoo.com; Web: swkrcatholics.org. Rev. Stanley Drewniak, (Poland).
Res.: c/o 165 Rice St., P.O. Box 190, South Wilmington, 60474.
Catechesis Religious Program—Students 36.
LISLE, DU PAGE CO., ST. JOAN OF ARC (1924)
820 Division St., Lisle, 60532. Tel: 630-963-4500; Fax: 630-963-4568; Email: info@sjalisle.org; Web: www.sjalisle.org. Revs. Gabriel Baltes, O.S.B.; Kenneth Zigmond, O.S.B., Parochial Vicar; Deacons Denis Stucko; Gregory Razka.
School—St. Joan of Arc School, (Grades PreSchool-8), 4913 Columbia, Lisle, 60532. Tel: 630-969-1732; Fax: 630-353-4590; Email: stjoanofarcschool@sjalisle.org; Web: school.sjalisle.org. Mr. Michael Sweeney, Prin. Lay Teachers 30; Students 366.
Catechesis Religious Program—Email: caswrite@aol.com; Email: agervacio@sjalisle.org; Email: dpointner@sjalisle.org. Dolly Pointner, D.R.E. (Elementary Religious Formation); Mr. Alex Gervacio, Youth Min. & RCIA Coord.; Cheryl Basile, Coord., Sunday School. Students 629.
LOCKPORT, WILL CO.
1—ST. DENNIS (1846)
1214 Hamilton St., Lockport, 60441.
Tel: 815-838-2592; Email: secretary@saint-dennis.org. Rev. James Curtin; Matthew Furjanic, Pastoral Assoc.; Deacon Guadalupe Villarreal.
School—St. Dennis School, (Grades PreSchool-8), 1201 S. Washington St., Lockport, 60441.
Tel: 815-838-4494; Fax: 815-838-5435; Email: school@saint-dennis.org; Web: www.saint-dennis.org. Mrs. Lisa Smith, Prin. Lay Teachers 14; Students 218.
Catechesis Religious Program—
Tel: 815-838-2592, Ext. 113; Email: vwozniak@saint-dennis.org. Venus Wozniak, Dir. Faith Formation.
2—ST. JOHN VIANNEY (1958)
401 Brassel, Lockport, 60441. Tel: 815-723-3291; Email: saintjohnvianney50@att.net. Very Rev. Grzegorz Podwysocki, J.C.L.
Catechesis Religious Program—Bernadetta Kopinski, D.R.E. Students 32.
3—ST. JOSEPH (1868)
410 S. Jefferson St., Lockport, 60441.
Tel: 815-838-0187; Email: stjoelockport@comcast.net; Web: www.stjosephlockport.org. Rev. Gregory Rothfuchs.
School—St. Joseph School, (Grades PreSchool-8), 529 Madison St., Lockport, 60441. Tel: 815-838-8173; Fax: 815-838-0504; Email: Blueribbonprincipal@stjoeschool.com; Web: www.stjoeschool.com. Miss Lynne Scheffler, Prin. Religious Teachers 1; Lay Teachers 13; Students 228.
Catechesis Religious Program—Tel: 815-838-2112; Email: stjosephlockportdre@gmail.com. Deacon Dennis Stolarz, D.R.E. Students 200.
4—OUR LADY OF KOREAN MARTYRS MISSION (1999) (Korean)
224 Bruce Rd., Lockport, 60441. Tel: 708-990-3007; Email: ourladyc7121@gmail.com. Rev. Sangil Park.
Catechesis Religious Program—Phillip Yang, D.R.E. Students 12.
LOMBARD, DU PAGE CO.
1—CHRIST THE KING (1960)
1501 S. Main St., Lombard, 60148. Tel: 630-629-1717; Email: carol@ctklombard.org. Rev. Jeffery Stoneberg; Deacons Frank Lillig; Peter Robinson; Anthony Clishem; Matthew Novak.
Catechesis Religious Program—Tel: 630-396-6078; Email: loretta@ctklombard.org. Loretta Crotty, D.R.E. Students 175.
2—DIVINE MERCY PARISH (1997)
21W411 Sunset Ave., Lombard, 60148.
Tel: 630-268-8766; Fax: 630-268-8712; Email: parafia@milosierdzie.us; Web: www.milosierdzie.us. Revs. Miroslaw Stepien; Piotr Janas; Tomasz Pietrzak; Piotr Nowacki, S.Ch.
Catechesis Religious Program—Tel: 630-830-2669. Mrs. Fryderyka Kubica, D.R.E. Students 1,200.
3—ST. PIUS X (1954)
1025 E. Madison, Lombard, 60148.
Tel: 630-627-4526; Fax: 630-495-5926; Email: parishoffice@stpiuslombard.org; Web: www.stpiuslombard.org. Rev. Jerzy Zieba, C.R.; Deacons Armando Herrera; John Chan; Thomas Rachubinski; Ron Knecht; Larry Lissak.
School—St. Pius X School, (Grades PreSchool-8), 601 S. Westmore, Lombard, 60148. Tel: 630-627-2353; Fax: 630-627-1810; Email: schooloffice@stpiuslombard.org; Web: www.stpiuslombard.org/school/. Toni Miller, Prin. Lay Teachers 27; Students 429.
Catechesis Religious Program—Email: jconnolly@stpiuslombard.org; Email: spxhispano@aol.com; Email: ebecerra@stpiuslombard.org. Elizabeth Becerra, Dir. of Faith Formation; Abraham Rodriguez, D.R.E.; Jill Connolly, D.R.E. Students 336.
4—SACRED HEART (1912)
114 S. Elizabeth St., Lombard, 60148.
Tel: 630-627-0687; Email: rditta@shclombard.org; Web: www.sacredheartlombard.org. Rev. Thomas Botheroyd; Deacons William H. Crane; Robert Krol; David Mahoney; Christopher Mazzacano.
School—Sacred Heart School, (Grades PreSchool-8), 322 W. Maple St., Lombard, 60148.
Tel: 630-629-0536; Fax: 630-629-4752; Email: info@shslombard.org; Web: www.shslombard.org. Joy Packard-Higgins, Ph.D., Prin. Lay Teachers 16; Students 205.
Catechesis Religious Program—Tel: 630-495-0843. Dr. Linda Andrejek, D.R.E. Students 287.
MANHATTAN, WILL CO., ST. JOSEPH (1891) [CEM 2]
235 W. North, P.O. Box 25, Manhattan, 60442.
Tel: 815-478-3341; Email: sjpoffice@sjpmanhattan.org; Web: www.sjpmanhattan.org. Rev. John Lindsey; Deacon Patrick Forsythe.
School—St. Joseph School, (Grades PreSchool-8), 275 W. North St., P.O. Box 70, Manhattan, 60442.
Tel: 815-478-3951; Fax: 815-478-7412; Email: principal@sjsmanhattan.org; Web: sjsmanhattan.org. Mrs. Colleen Domke, Prin. Clergy 1; Lay Teachers 12; Students 103.
Catechesis Religious Program—Tel: 815-478-4452; Email: religiousedl@sjpmanhattan.org. Kelly Hoehn, D.R.E. Students 320.
MANTENO, KANKAKEE CO., ST. JOSEPH (1855) [CEM]
207 S. Main St., Manteno, 60950. Tel: 815-468-3403; Email: stjosephmanteno@gmail.com; Web: www.stjosephmanteno.com. 175 S. Main St., Manteno, 60950. Very Rev. Albert J. Heidecke.
Catechesis Religious Program—Tel: 815-468-8116; Email: stjoesre8116@yahoo.com. Jessica Dickson, D.R.E. Students 206.
MINOOKA, GRUNDY CO., ST. MARY (1862) [CEM] (Irish)
303 W. St. Mary St., P.O. Box 456, Minooka, 60447.
Tel: 815-467-2233; Email: stmarysbusiness@gmail.com; Web: stmarysminooka.com. Rev. Tuan Van Nguyen.
Catechesis Religious Program—Tel: 815-467-2769. Students 511.
MOKENA, WILL CO., ST. MARY CHURCH (1864) [CEM]
P.O. Box 2, Mokena, 60448-0002. Tel: 708-326-9300; Email: secretary@stmarymokena.org; Web: www.stmarymokena.org. 19626 115th Ave., Mokena, 60448. Revs. Dindo Billote; Raed Bader; Deacons Robert Kaminski; Gary Bednar; Nabil Halaby; John Rex.
School—St. Mary Church School, (Grades PreK-8), 11409 W. 195th St., Mokena, 60448.
Tel: 708-326-9330; Fax: 708-326-9331; Email: school@stmarymokena.org; Web: stmaryschoolmokena.org. Beth Cunningham, Prin.; Jeanne Wolski, Admin. Lay Teachers 24; Franciscan Sisters of the Sacred Heart 1; Students 467.
Catechesis Religious Program—11409 W. 195th St., Mokena, 60448. Tel: 708-326-9351; Email: nbrockmann@stmarymokena.org. Nicole Brochmann, D.R.E. Students 754.
MOMENCE, KANKAKEE CO., ST. PATRICK (1859) [CEM]
119 Market St., Momence, 60954. Tel: 815-472-2864;

Email: stpatsrectory@mchsi.com. Rev. Daniel Hessling.
Catechesis Religious Program—Students 50.
Mission—Sacred Heart, P.O. Box 557, Hopkins Park, Kankakee Co. 60944.

MONEE, WILL CO., ST. BONIFACE (1868) [JC] (German—Polish)
5304 W. Main St., Monee, 60449. Tel: 708-534-9682; Email: office@stboniface.comcastbiz.net; Web: stbonifacemonee.org. P.O. Box 217, Monee, 60449. Rev. Roger Kutzner; Deacon Mark Otten.
Catechesis Religious Program—Students 52.

MORRIS, GRUNDY CO., IMMACULATE CONCEPTION OF THE BLESSED VIRGIN MARY (1852) [CEM]
516 E. Jackson St., Morris, 60450. Tel: 815-942-0620; Email: gfolkers@ics1.org; Web: icmorris.org. 600 E. Jackson St., Morris, 60450. Rev. Edward Howe, C.R.; Deacons Santos H. Martinez; Paul Jung; Deaon Arnulfo Cisneros. In Res., Rev. Gerald Watt, C.R.
School—Immaculate Conception of the Blessed Virgin Mary School, (Grades PreSchool-8), 505 E. North St., Morris, 60450. Tel: 815-942-4111; Fax: 815-942-5094; Email: kdeslaur@ics1.org; Web: www.ics1.org. Mr. Kim DesLauriers, Prin. Clergy 1; Lay Teachers 13; Students 191.
Catechesis Religious Program—Tel: 815-942-4177; Email: jdillenburg@ics1.org. Julie Dillenburg, D.R.E. Students 231.

NAPERVILLE, DUPAGE CO.
1—ST. ELIZABETH SETON (1986)
2220 Lisson Rd., Naperville, 60565.
Tel: 630-416-3325; Email: stelizabethseton@gmail.com. Rev. Scott Huggins; Deacons Thomas Ross; Gerard Erickson; Scott Pace; Robert Larkin; John Ripoll.
Catechesis Religious Program—Tel: 630-416-1992; Fax: 630-416-4086. Peggy Idstein, D.R.E. Students 617.
2—HOLY SPIRIT CATHOLIC COMMUNITY (1998)
2003 Hassert Blvd., Naperville, 60564.
Tel: 630-922-0081; Email: welcome@hscc.us; Web: hscc.us. Rev. Dennis Lewandowski.
Rectory—2228 Snow Creek Rd., Naperville, 60564.
Catechesis Religious Program—Students 1,165.
3—ST. MARGARET MARY (1980)
1450 Green Trails Dr., Naperville, 60540.
Tel: 630-369-0777; Fax: 630-369-1493; Email: info@smmp.com; Web: smmp.com. Very Rev. Paul Hottinger; Sr. Madelyn Gould, S.S.S.F., Pastoral Assoc.; Deacons Kenneth J. Miles; Terry Taylor; Fred Straub; Joseph Ferrari; Donald Helgeson.
Catechesis Religious Program—Email: sdavey@smmp.com. Sue Davey, D.R.E. Students 709.
4—STS. PETER AND PAUL (1856) [CEM]
36 N. Ellsworth St., Naperville, 60540.
Tel: 630-355-1081; Fax: 630-355-1179; Email: ckennedy@sspeterandpaul.net; Web: www.sspeterandpaul.net. Very Rev. Brad Baker; Revs. Tomy Chellakandathil, C.M.I., (India) Parochial Vicar; Thomas Theneth, C.M.I., Parochial Vicar; John T. McGeean, (In Res.), (Retired); Deacons Ronald Brown; Roger Novak; Michael Crowell; Joseph Verdico; Kevin Neis; Wilfredo Marrero; Thomas Rehak.
School—Saints Peter and Paul School, (Grades K-8), 201 E. Franklin, Naperville, 60540.
Tel: 630-355-0113; Fax: 630-355-9803; Email: kmeskill@sspeterandpaulschool.com; Web: www.sspeterandpaulschoolcom. Mrs. Karen Meskill, Prin. Clergy 2; Lay Teachers 27; Students 417.
Catechesis Religious Program—36 N. Ellsworth St., Ste. 104, Naperville, 60540. Students 481.
5—ST. RAPHAEL (1963)
Mailing Address: 1215 Modaff Rd., Naperville, 60540-7818. Revs. Daniel Bachner; John Honiotes, Parochial Vicar; Deacons Kurt Lange; Daniel Doheny; Ciro Afeltra; Leonard Penkala; John Gustin.
Tel: 630-355-4545; Fax: 630-355-7470; Email: admin@st-raphael.com; Web: www.st-raphael.com.
School—St. Raphael School, (Grades K-8), 1215 Modaff Rd., Naperville, 60540-7818.
Tel: 630-355-1880; Email: dking@st-raphaelschool.org. Mavis DeMar, Prin. Lay Teachers 23; Students 300.
Catechesis Religious Program—Tel: 630-615-7642; Email: msadler@st-raphael.com. Michelle Sadler, D.R.E. Students 826.
6—ST. THOMAS THE APOSTLE (1984)
1500 Brookdale Rd., Naperville, 60563.
Tel: 630-355-8980; Email: jsimmons@stapostle.org; Web: www.stapostle.org. Revs. Philip M. Danaher; Joseph Kappilumakkal, C.M.I.; Deacons Charles Lane, (Retired); James Breen; Lawrence Kearney; Michael Barrett, Email: meabarrett@att.net; Patrick Lennon; Joseph Cuzzone.
Catechesis Religious Program—Tel: 630-305-6318; Email: pdougherty@stapostle.org. Students 853.

NEW LENOX, WILL CO., ST. JUDE (1934)
241 W. Second Ave., New Lenox, 60451.
Tel: 815-485-8049; Email: BulletinEditor@stjudes.org; Web: www.stjudes.org. Revs. Robert Basler, O.S.A.; R. William Sullivan, O.S.A., Parochial Vicar; John J. Sotak, O.S.A., Parochial Vicar; Deacons Robert Fitt; William Ciston; Dennis Theriault; George Goes; Mark Armamentos. In Res., Revs. James Friedel, O.S.A.; John M. Ohner, O.S.A.
School—St. Jude School, (Grades PreK-8),
Tel: 815-463-4254; Email: kwinters@stjudes.org; Web: stjudes.org/school. Mrs. Kathy Winters, Prin. Clergy 4; Lay Teachers 12; Students 191.
Catechesis Religious Program—Email: kneu@stjudes.org. Katie Neu, D.R.E. Students 238.

OAKBROOK TERRACE, DUPAGE CO., ASCENSION OF OUR LORD (1967)
1 S. 314 Summit Ave., Oakbrook Terrace, 60181.
Tel: 630-629-5810; Email: welcome@ascensionofourlord.net; Web: www.ascensionofourlord.net. Rev. Jose Kadukunnel, C.M.I.; Deacon Peter Rooney; Mr. Edward Rylko, Business Mgr.; Darlene Crilly, Music Min.
Catechesis Religious Program—Email: vzaprzal@ascensionofourlord.net. Mr. Vincent Zaprzal, D.R.E. Students 62.

OSWEGO, KENDALL CO., ST. ANNE (1963)
551 Boulder Hill Pass, Oswego, 60543. P.O. Box 670, Oswego, 60543-0670. Tel: 630-554-3331; Email: stanne@stanneparish.org; Web: www.stanneparish.org. Rev. John J. Ouper; Deacons David Brockman; Duane Wozek; James Perry; Gary Wooley.
Catechesis Religious Program—Tel: 630-554-1425; Fax: 630-554-9797; Email: reo@stanneparish.org. Students 1,090.

PARK FOREST, WILL CO., ST. MARY (1959)
227 Monee Rd., Park Forest, 60466.
Tel: 708-748-6686; Email: cbartels@stmaryparkforest.org; Web: www.stmaryparkforest.org. Rev. Stephen Eickhoff; Deacons John Drechny; Edward Szymanski.
Catechesis Religious Program—Students 15.

PAXTON, FORD CO., ST. MARY (1910)
407 W. Pells, Paxton, 60957-1290. Tel: 217-379-4033; Email: frbui@stmarypaxton.org; Web: www.stmarypaxton.org. Rev. Dong Bui.
Mission—St. Joseph.
Catechesis Religious Program—Tel: 217-892-4877; Email: dan.schneider@lgseeds.com. Dan Schneider, D.R.E. Students 92.

PEOTONE, WILL CO., ST. PAUL THE APOSTLE (1961)
511 N. Conrad St., Peotone, 60468. Rev. Roger Kutzner; Deacon James Kelly, D.R.E.; Paula Prium, Business Mgr.
Res.: 501 N. Conrad St., Peotone, 60468.
Tel: 708-258-6917; Tel: 708-258-9580; Email: stpauloffice@att.net.
Catechesis Religious Program—Tel: 708-258-9580; Email: StPaulRe@att.net. Students 132.

PIPER CITY, FORD CO., ST. PETER (1887) [CEM]
Mailing Address: 224 N. Secor St., Gilman, 60938. Rev. Marek Herbut.
Res.: 212 Pine St., Piper City, 60959.
Tel: 815-265-7236; Email: lhayslett@frontier.com; Email: rbtreyes948@yahoo.com.
Catechesis Religious Program—1245 E. 2800 N., Piper City, 60959. Students 10.

PLAINFIELD, WILL CO., ST. MARY IMMACULATE (1908) [CEM]
15629 S. Route 59, Plainfield, 60544.
Tel: 815-436-2651; Email: moleary@smip.org; Web: www.smip.org. Revs. Patrick M. Mulcahy; Michael McMahon; Deacons James Sossong; Victor Puscas; Patrick Lombardo; Thomas O'Connell; Michael Perkins; Thomas Schroeder; Denise Rowan, Business Mgr. In Res., Rev. John Regan.
School—St. Mary Immaculate School, (Grades PreSchool-8), Tel: 815-436-3953; Email: jgarvey@smip.org; Fax: 815-439-8045. Mr. John Garvey, Prin.; Jennifer Errthum, Vice Prin.; Lisa Kissel, Librarian. Lay Teachers 25; Students 412.
Catechesis Religious Program—Tel: 815-436-4501; Fax: 815-439-2304; Email: gmorse@smip.org. Students 974.

PLANO, KENDALL CO., ST. MARY (1885) [CEM]
901 N. Center St., Plano, 60545. Tel: 630-552-3448; Email: info@saintmaryplano.com; Web: www.saintmaryplano.com. Revs. Andy Davy, M.I.C.; Gabriel Cillo, M.I.C., Parochial Vicar; Deacon Eduardo Murillo. In Res., Rev. Matthew Lamoureux, M.I.C.
School—St. Mary School, (Grades K-8), 817 N. Center Ave., Plano, 60545. Tel: 630-552-3345; Fax: 630-552-4385; Email: royals@saintmaryplano.com; Web: smplano.com. Mr. Joseph Scarpino, Prin. Lay Teachers 17; Students 205.
Catechesis Religious Program—Email: eduardomurillo@saintmaryplano.com. Students 198.

ROCKDALE, WILL CO., ST. JOSEPH CHURCH (1914)
1329 Belleview Ave., Rockdale, 60436-2577.
Tel: 815-725-4469; Email: michael_magiera@hotmail.com; Web: fsspjoliet.wordpress.com. Rev. Michael Magiera.
Catechesis Religious Program—Tel: 815-729-9149; Email: StJosephRep@hotmail.com. Elizabeth Kelch, D.R.E. Students 21.

ROMEOVILLE, WILL CO., ST. ANDREW THE APOSTLE (1959)
530 Glen Ave., Romeoville, 60446. Tel: 815-886-4165; Email: office@andrewcc.org; Web: andrewcc.org. Revs. Maciej Stelmach; Jesus Oliveros; Deacons Herb Waldron; Rich Ford; Jerry Clark; Jesse Tagle; Felix Dominguez; Ricardo Marquez; Rigoberto Padilla.
School—St. Andrew the Apostle School, (Grades PreSchool-8), 505 Kingston Dr., Romeoville, 60446.
Tel: 815-886-5953; Fax: 815-293-2016; Email: schooloffice@andrewcc.org; Email: principal@andrewcc.org. Carol Albreski, Prin.; Mrs. Jill Briceno. Lay Teachers 12; Students 161.
Catechesis Religious Program—Tel: 815-886-5962; Email: faithformation@andrewcc.org; Email: adultff@andrewcc.org. Elena Ibarra, D.R.E. (Faith Formation); Barbara Sanders, RCIA Coord. Students 407.

ROSELLE, DU PAGE CO., ST. WALTER (1946)
130 W. Pine Ave., Roselle, 60172. Tel: 630-894-2461; Email: mpusateri@stwalterchurch.com; Web: www.stwalterchurch.com. Revs. Mario S. Quejadas; Clive Otieno; Deacons Ron Searls; Michael Kowalchik; Michael Butz; Joseph Pusateri; Maria Pusateri, Business Mgr.
School—St. Walter School, (Grades PreSchool-8), 201 W. Maple Ave., Roselle, 60172. Tel: 630-529-1721; Fax: 630-529-9290; Email: swsoffice@stwalterschool.com; Web: www.stwalterschool.com. Mary Kathryn Warco, Prin.; Julie Olzen, Librarian. Lay Teachers 30; Students 571.
Catechesis Religious Program—140 W. Pine, Roselle, 60172. Valerie Della Penna, D.R.E.; Kenneth Ortega, Dir. Faith Formation. Students 661.

ST. ANNE, KANKAKEE CO., ST. ANNE (1865) [CEM] (French-Canadian)
230 N. Sixth Ave., St. Anne, 60964.
Tel: 815-427-8265; Email: stanneca@sbcglobal.net. Rev. James Fanale, C.S.V.
Catechesis Religious Program—Students 60.

ST. GEORGE, KANKAKEE CO., ST. GEORGE (1853) [CEM] (French-Canadian)
5272 E. 5000 North Rd., Bourbonnais, 60914-9725.
Tel: 815-939-1851; Fax: 815-939-2777; Email: stgeorge@stgeorgeil.com; Web: www.stgeorgeil.com. Rev. Daniel R. Belanger, C.S.V.; Deacons Joseph Cotugno; Milton Leppert.
Catechesis Religious Program—Students 111.

SHOREWOOD, WILL CO., HOLY FAMILY (1959)
600 Brook Forest Ave., Shorewood, 60404.
Tel: 815-725-6880; Email: ppucel@holyfamilyshorewood.org; Web: holyfamilyshorewood.org. Very Rev. Dennis Paul; Rev. Thomas Dunn; Deacons Karl Huebner; Thomas Paluch; Paul Schneider; Manuel Guerrero; Steve Gerding. In Res., Rev. Vytas Memenas, Senior Priest, (Retired).
School—Holy Family School, (Grades PreK-8), 600 Brook Forest Ave., Shorewood, 60404.
Tel: 815-725-8149; Email: asimone@holyfamilyshorewood.org; Web: holyfamilyshorewood.org. Mr. Anthony Simone, Prin.; Erick Passarelli, Vice Prin. Lay Teachers 15; Students 316.
Catechesis Religious Program—Tel: 815-730-8691; Email: lkrauledis@holyfamilyshorewood.org. Leslie Krauledis, D.R.E. Students 825.

SOUTH WILMINGTON, GRUNDY CO., ST. LAWRENCE (1904)
165 Rice St., Box 190, South Wilmington, 60474.
Tel: 815-237-2230; Fax: 815-237-2201; Email: stlawrenceswilm@yahoo.com. Rev. Stanley Drewniak, (Poland).
Catechesis Religious Program—Students 81.
Mission—St. Mary (1899) 216 E. Lincoln St., P.O. Box 16, Reddick, Kankakee Co. 60961.

STEGER, WILL CO., ST. LIBORIUS (1902)
71 W. 35th St., Steger, 60475. Tel: 708-754-1363; Email: parish@stliborius.org; Web: www.stliborius.org. Rev. Stephen Eickhoff.
School—Mother Teresa Catholic Academy, (Grades PreSchool-8), 24201 S. Kings Rd., Crete, 60417.
Tel: 708-672-3093; Fax: 708-367-0640; Email: info@mtcacademy.org; Web: www.mtcacademy.org. Annie Murray, Prin. (Steger Campus) Lay Teachers 15; Students 260.
Catechesis Religious Program—Tel: 708-754-3460. Students 181.

VILLA PARK, DU PAGE CO.
1—ST. ALEXANDER (1924)
300 S. Cornell Ave., Villa Park, 60181.
Tel: 630-833-7730; Email: office@stalexanderparish.org; Web: www.stalexanderparish.org. Rev. Mark Rosenbaum; Deacons Julio Jimenez; Christopher Cochran; James Krueger; Matthew Tretina.
Catechesis Religious Program—130 S. Cornell Ave., Villa Park, 60181. Tel: 630-834-3787; Email: akreuger@stalexanderparish.org. Ann Krueger, D.R.E. Students 135.
2—ST. JOHN THE APOSTLE (1959) (Italian—Polish-

Hispanic)
330 N. Westmore, Villa Park, 60181.
Tel: 630-279-7404; Email: sttacc@comcast.net; Web: www.stjohnvillapark.org. Rev. Mark Rosenbaum; Deacon Ronald Madsen.
Catechesis Religious Program—Tel: 630-279-7433. Dolly Foley, D.R.E. Students 120.
WARRENVILLE, DU PAGE CO., ST. IRENE (1927)
28 W. 441 Warrenville Rd., Warrenville, 60555.
Tel: 630-393-2400; Email: parishoffice@st-irene.org. Rev. James Antiporek; Deacons William Murphy, Pastoral Assoc.; Joseph Urso, Pastoral Assoc.; Bradley Hentz, Pastoral Assoc.; Annette Kubalanza, Pastoral Assoc.
School—St. Irene School, (Grades PreSchool-8), 3S601 Warren Ave., Warrenville, 60555.
Tel: 630-393-9303, Ext. 116;
Tel: 630-393-9303, Ext. 136; Fax: 630-393-7009; Email: SaintIreneSchool@aol.com; Email: M.Detwiler@st-ireneschool.org; Web: www.st-ireneschool.org. Mrs. Maggie Detwiler, Prin. Lay Teachers 14; Students 153.
Catechesis Religious Program—
Tel: 630-393-2400, Ext. 22. Pamela Keating, Co-D.R.E.; Mary Kravchuk, Co-D.R.E. Students 175.
WATSEKA, IROQUOIS CO., ST. EDMUND (1872)
219 E. Locust St., Watseka, 60970. Tel: 815-432-3274 ; Email: churchlady97@sbcglobal.net. Very Rev. Michael Powell.
Catechesis Religious Program—Tel: 815-432-5569; Email: pattiduffy@ymail.com. Students 68.
Mission—St. Joseph, P.O. Box 173, Crescent City, Iroquois Co. 60928.
WAYNE, DU PAGE CO., RESURRECTION CATHOLIC CHURCH (1968)
30W350 Army Trail Rd., Wayne, 60184.
Tel: 630-289-5400; Fax: 630-289-5407; Email: resacc@sbcglobal.net; Web: www.resurrectioncc.com. Rev. Tri Van Tran.
Catechesis Religious Program—
Tel: 630-289-5400, Ext. 215; Email: resff@outlook.com. Students 314.
WEST CHICAGO, DU PAGE CO., ST. MARY (1894) [CEM]
140 N. Oakwood Ave., West Chicago, 60185.
Tel: 630-231-0013; Email: Parish.Office@stmarywc.org; Web: srmarywc.org. Revs. David Lawrence; Anthony Nyamai; Deacons Bruce Carlson; Luis Saltigerald; Daniel Culloton.
Catechesis Religious Program—
Tel: 630-231-0013, Ext. 233. Students 446.
WESTMONT, DU PAGE CO., HOLY TRINITY (1938)
25 E. Richmond St., Westmont, 60559. Web: www.holytrinitywestmont.org. Revs. Rafal Wasilewski, C.R.; Marion Wroblewski, C.R., Parochial Vicar; Most Rev. Robert Kurtz, In. Res.; Deacons William Casey; Thomas Jagielo; Patrick Blaney; Anthony Lenard.
Res.: 111 S. Cass Ave., Westmont, 60559.
Tel: 630-968-1366; Email: htparish@comcast.net.
School—Holy Trinity School, (Grades PreK-8), 108 S. Linden Ave., Westmont, 60559. Tel: 630-971-0184; Fax: 630-971-1175; Email: schooloffice@holytrinitywestmont.org; Web: www.holytrinitywestmont.org/school. Dr. Pamela Simon, Prin. Lay Teachers 18; Students 172.
Catechesis Religious Program—Tel: 630-968-5978; Email: jgregoire@holytrinitywestmont.org. Joanne Gregoire, D.R.E. Students 233.
WHEATON, DU PAGE CO.
1—ST. DANIEL THE PROPHET CHURCH (1989)
101 W. Loop Rd., Wheaton, 60189. Tel: 630-384-0123 ; Email: Info@StDaniel.org; Web: www.StDaniel.org. Rev. James Dvorscak; Karen Gulvas, Preschool Dir.; William Runge, Dir. of Music; Daniel Sledz, Business Mgr.; Gina Wiedeman, Youth Min.; Diane Ahlemeyer, D.R.E.
2—ST. MARK (1962)
303 E. Parkway Dr., Wheaton, 60187.
Tel: 630-665-0030; Email: office@stmarkwheaton.org. 300 E. Cole Ave., Wheaton, 60187. Rev. Andrew Lewandowski, C.R.
Catechesis Religious Program—Students 50.
3—ST. MICHAEL (1882) [CEM]
310 S. Wheaton Ave., Wheaton, 60187.
Tel: 630-462-5000; Email: churchoffice@stmichaelcommunity.org; Web: www.stmichaelcommunity.org/. Revs. Daniel Hoehn; Max Behna; Deacons Daniel Aderholdt; Kenneth Kubica; Daniel Simmet.
School—St. Michael School, (Grades PreSchool-8), 314 W. Willow Ave., Wheaton, 60187.
Tel: 630-665-1454; Fax: 630-665-1491; Email: schooloffice@stmichaelschoolwheaton.org; Web: www.stmichaelschoolwheaton.org. Adam Ferguson, Prin. Lay Teachers 29; Students 570.
Catechesis Religious Program—317 Willow Ave., Wheaton, 60187. Email: mglaz@stmichaelcommunity.org. Magdalena Glaz, D.R.E. Students 1,071.
WILMINGTON, WILL CO., ST. ROSE (1855) [CEM]
603 S. Main St., Wilmington, 60481.
Tel: 815-476-7491; Email: strose603@aol.com. Rev. Sebastian Gargol.
School—St. Rose School, (Grades PreK-8), 626 Kankakee St., Wilmington, 60481. Tel: 815-476-6220 ; Fax: 815-476-2154; Email: lblandstrose@gmail.com; Web: www.stroseschoolwilmington.org/. Linda Bland, Prin. Lay Teachers 8; Students 80.
Catechesis Religious Program—Tel: 815-476-7491. Sarah Enz, D.R.E. Students 115.
WILTON CENTER, WILL CO., ST. PATRICK (1905) [CEM] (Irish)
14936 Wilmington Peotone Rd., Manhattan, 60442.
Tel: 815-478-3440; Email: stpatrickwilton@aol.com. Rev. Sebastian Gargol.
Catechesis Religious Program—Students 43.
WINFIELD, DU PAGE CO., ST. JOHN THE BAPTIST (1867) [CEM] [JC2]
O.S. 233 Church St., Winfield, 60190.
Tel: 630-668-0918; Email: contactus@stjohnwinfield.org; Web: www.stjohnwinfield.org. Revs. Matthew Pratscher; Keith Wolfe, Parochial Vicar; Deacon David Ritter.
School—St. John the Baptist School, (Grades PreK-8), O.S. 259 Church St., Winfield, 60190.
Tel: 630-668-1074; Fax: 630-668-7176; Email: terih@stjohnwinfield.org. Joanne Policht, Prin. Lay Teachers 14; Students 129.
Catechesis Religious Program—Maureen Brennan, D.R.E. Students 396.
WOOD DALE, DU PAGE CO., HOLY GHOST (1946)
254 N. Wood Dale Rd., Wood Dale, 60191.
Tel: 630-860-2975; Email: tbero@holyghostparish.org; Web: www.holyghostparish.org. Rev. John Joseph Hornicak; Deacons Dino Franch, Pastoral Assoc.; Robert Lasica, Pastoral Assoc.
Catechesis Religious Program—Tel: 630-766-1045; Email: kgrant@holyghostparish.org. Mrs. Kathy Grant, D.R.E. Students 162.
WOODRIDGE, DU PAGE CO.
1—CHRIST THE SERVANT PARISH (1990)
Mailing Address: 8700 Havens Dr., Woodridge, 60517. Tel: 630-910-0770; Fax: 630-910-6060; Email: ctsoffice@ctswoodridge.org; Web: www.ctswoodridge.org. Rev. Robert Duda; Deacons Thomas Fricke; Rod Accardi.
Catechesis Religious Program—Students 210.
2—ST. SCHOLASTICA (1962)
7800 S. Janes Ave., Woodridge, 60517.
Tel: 630-985-2351; Email: Ritaramsey@stscholasticaparish.org. Rev. Norbert Raszeja, C.R.; Deacons Gerald G. Christensen; Thomas Marciani; George Soloy; Ms. Lianda Valentine, Business Mgr.; Mary Ellen Upchurch, Music Min.
School—St. Scholastica School, (Grades K-8), 7720 Janes Ave., Woodridge, 60517. Tel: 630-985-2515; Fax: 630-985-2395; Email: ldriscoll@stscholasticaschool.org; Email: agosewehr@stscholasticaschool.org. Elizabeth Driscoll, Prin.; Ms. Alison Gosewehr; Barbara Stance, Librarian. Lay Teachers 15; Students 213.
Catechesis Religious Program—Tel: 630-985-9255; Email: bcartner@stscholasticaparish.org. Beth Cartner, Dir. Faith Formation; Jennifer Michalik-Olson, Youth Min.; Shawn Denning, RCIA Coord. Students 455.
YORKVILLE, KENDALL CO., ST. PATRICK (1885) [CEM] [JC]
406 Walnut St., Yorkville, 60560. Rev. Matthew Lamoureux, M.I.C.; Deacons Dale Metcalfe; Doug Wells; Bill Johnson.
Res.: 901 N. Center St., Plano, 60545.
Tel: 630-553-6671, Ext. 16; Email: susansmerz@stpatrickyorkville.org; Web: www.StPatrickYorkville.org.
Catechesis Religious Program—Email: michelegonzales@stpatrickyorkville.org. Michele Gonzales, D.R.E. Students 525.

Chaplains of Public Institutions

JOLIET. *Illinois State Penitentiary*, P.O. Box 112, Joliet, 60434. Vacant.
DOWNERS GROVE. *Good Samaritan Hospital*, 3821 Highland Ave., Downers Grove, 60515. Vacant.
ELMHURST. *Elmhurst Memorial Hospital*, 200 Berteau Ave., Elmhurst, 60126. Vacant, Chap.
HINSDALE. *Hinsdale Hospital*, 120 N. Oak, Hinsdale, 60521. Vacant.
KANKAKEE. *Riverside Medical Center*, 350 N. Wells, Kankakee, 60901. Vacant.
Shapiro Development Center, 100 E. Jeffery, Kankakee, 60901. Rev. Richard Jacklin.
NAPERVILLE. *Edward Hospital*, S. Washington St., Naperville, 60540. Rev. Lee Bacchi, Chap.
WINFIELD. *Central DuPage Hospital*, 0N025 Winfield Rd., Winfield, 60190. Vacant.

On Duty Outside the Diocese:
Revs.—
Dieter, Thomas M.
Martis, Douglas, Ph.D., S.T.D., Pontifical College Josephinum, Columbus, OH 43235
Pennock, Michael
Schoenstene, Robert L., M.A., S.S.L., St. Mary of the Lake Seminary, Mundelein, 60060.

Leave of Absence:
Revs.—
Buczyna, Andrew L.
Burnett, James R.
Collogan, Robert
Dennerlein, Arno A.
Flores, Alejandro
Infanger, Frank
Legarreta, Felipe DeJesus
McCawley, Scott M.
Nowak, James
Simonelli, Gerald
Vagenas, William.

Retired:
Rt. Revs.—
Anderson, Hugh R., O.S.B., (Retired)
Kalcic, Dismas B., O.S.B., (Retired)
Revs.—
Arseneau, Vernon, (Retired)
Bowden, Lloyd, (Retired)
Coleman, Robert J., (Retired)
Conway, William, (Retired)
Corbino, Thomas, (Retired)
Dennerlein, John L., (Retired)
Dillon, David, O.Carm., (Retired)
Donnelly, William, (Retired)
Doyle, John J., (Retired)
Farrell, Kevin R., (Retired)
Fortier, Joel, (Retired)
Fullmer, Hugh, (Retired)
Gabel, Martin M., (Retired)
Graziano, J. Damien, (Retired)
Hemrick, Eugene F., (Retired)
Heramb, James, (Retired)
Hoffenkamp, Robert A., (Retired)
Holup, James, (Retired)
Hurley, George, (Retired)
Huy Quyen, Nguyen, (Retired)
Kelpsas, A., M.I.C., (Retired)
Kocher, Donald, (Retired)
Kocherla, Sundar Raj, (India) (Retired)
Kostelz, Richard F., (Retired)
Kucera, Edward J., O.S.B., (Retired)
LaPore, Arthur, (Retired)
Lennon, James M., (Retired)
Lescher, Raymond C., (Retired)
Maher, Arthur, (Retired)
McGeean, John T., (Retired)
McGivney, Thomas Jr., (Retired)
Memenas, Vytas, (Retired)
Menezes, Mark, (Retired)
Micka, Alphonse, M.I.C., (Retired)
Mumper, Edward, (Retired)
O'Shea, William J., (Retired)
Poff, Edward, (Retired)
Prodehl, Richard B., (Retired)
Randall, Jude D., O.S.B., (Retired)
Riva, Gerald, (Retired)
Ross, Richard, (Retired)
Sebahar, John, (Retired)
Stempora, Daniel F., (Retired)
Sullivan, John D., (Retired)
Taschetta, Anthony, (Retired)
Testa, Jess, (Retired)
Tivy, Gerald, (Retired)
Valente, Michael, (Retired)
Wehnert, Donald R., C.S.V., (Retired)
Weitzel, Theodore, (Retired)
Welch, John, O.Carm., (Retired)
Wheeler, Charles, (Retired)
Yarno, Kenneth, C.S.V., (Retired).

Permanent Deacons:
Doyle, Michael, St. Daniel the Prophet, Wheaton
Accardi, Rodger F., Central DuPage Hospital; Christ the Servant, Woodridge
Aderholdt, Daniel, St. Michael, Wheaton
Afeltra, Ciro, St. Raphael, Naperville
Agurkis, Albert, St. Mary of Gostyn, Downers Grove
Anchor, Robert, (On Duty Outside the Diocese)
Armamentos, Mark, St. Jude, New Lenox
Balgeman, Richard, (Retired)
Barrett, Michael, St. Thomas, Naperville
Beabout, Norman, (On Duty Outside the Diocese)
Bednar, Gary, St. Mary, Mokena
Berkey, Donald, St. Anthony, Frankfort
Bernardin, Donald, (Leave of Absence)
Bevan, William F. III, Assumption, Coal City
Bias, Ralph, Sacred Heart, Joliet
Blaney, Patrick, Holy Trinity, Westmont
Blumenstein, John, St. Francis of Assisi, Bolingbrook

Boucek, William, St. Anthony, Frankfort
Bowns, Loren, (On Duty Outside the Diocese)
Boyle, John R., St. Alexander, Villa Park
Breen, James, St. Thomas the Apostle, Naperville
Brockman, David, St. Anne, Oswego
Brown, Ronald, Sts. Peter & Paul, Naperville
Busato, Rocco, St. John Paul II, Kankakee
Butz, Michael, St. Walter, Roselle
Carlson, Bruce, St. Mary, West Chicago
Carson, Neill, (Retired)
Casey, William, (Retired)
Cassey, Robert, St. Petronille, Glen Ellyn
Cerrato, Dominic, St. Joseph, Lockport
Chacon, Arturo, St. Dominic, Bolingbrook
Chaidez, Lorenzo, St. Dominic, Bolingbrook
Chambers, Frank A., (On Duty Outside the Diocese)
Chan, John, St. Pius X, Lombard
Christensen, Gerald G., St. Scholastica, Woodridge
Cirmo, Andrew, (On Duty Outside the Diocese)
Cisneros, Arnulfo, Immaculate Conception, Morris
Ciston, William, St. Jude, New Lenox
Clark, Gordon, (Retired)
Clark, Raymond, Leave of Absence
Clishem, Anthony, Christ the King, Lombard
Clodi, Gregory, St. John Paul II, Kankakee
Cochran, Christopher, St. Alexander, Villa Park
Cole, John, (Unassigned); (On Duty Outside the Diocese)
Cooley, Stephen, (On Duty Outside the Diocese)
Cotugno, Joseph, St. George, St. George
Cozzens, John, St. Michael, Wheaton
Crane, William H., Sacred Heart, Lombard
Crowell, Michael, Sts. Peter & Paul, Naperville
Culloton, Daniel, St. Mary, West Chicago
Cummins, Gregory, Immaculate Conception, Braidwood
Cummiskey, Terry, St. Isidore, Bloomingdale
Cuzzone, Joseph, St. Thomas the Apostle, Naperville
Cyr, Donald, (Retired)
Dalpiaz, Joseph C., Mother of Good Counsel, Homer Glen
Danahey, Daniel, St. Anthony, Frankfort
Darschewski, Ronald, (On Duty Outside the Diocese)
Defino, Daniel, St. Isidore, Bloomingdale
DeSitter, Steven, St. Mary of Gostyn, Downers Grove
Dixon, James A., (On Duty Outside the Diocese)
Doheny, Daniel, St. Raphael, Naperville
Dominguez, Felix, St. Andrew, Romeoville
Drechny, John, (Retired)
Duncan, Robert, St. Ann, Channahon
Dunn, William, Assumption, Coal City
Eaker, James, Visitation, Elmhurst
Eastburn, Lloyd D., St. Edmund, Watseka
Ellman, Edward, (On Duty Outside the Diocese)
Erickson, Gerard, St. Elizabeth Seton, Napervile
Feely, John, Immaculate Conception, Elmhurst
Ferrari, Joseph, St. Margaret Mary, Naperville
Filippo, Fredrick, Mother of Good Council, Homer Glen
Fitt, Robert, St. Jude, New Lenox
Foody, James, Our Lady of Mt. Carmel, Darien
Ford, Richard, St. Andrew, Romeoville
Forsythe, Patrick, St. Joseph, Manhattan
Fox, Steven A., (On Duty Outside the Diocese)
Foy, Richard, (Leave of Absence)
Franch, Dino J., Holy Ghost, Wood Dale
Frazier, Steven, (On Duty Outside of Diocese)
Freund, John, St. Paul the Apostle, Joliet
Fricke, Thomas E., Christ the Servant, Woodridge
Fritz, Leon P., St. Joseph, Bradley
Fudacz, Larry, Our Lady of Peace, Darien
Gagnon, Ronnie, St. Margaret Mary, Herscher
Gamboa, Gabriel, St. Matthew, Glendale Heights
Gerding, Stephen, Holy Family, Shorewood
Goebel, Thomas, Immaculate Conception, Elmhurst
Goes, George, St. Jude, New Lenox
Gonzalez, Sergio, St. Alexis, Bensenville
Gregoire, Jerome, (Leave of Absence)
Grozik, Alexander, Mary Queen of Heaven, Elmhurst
Guerrero, Manuel, (Retired)
Gustin, John, St. Raphael, Naperville
Hahn, Duane, (Leave of Absence)
Halaby, Nabil, St. Mary, Mokena
Hamilton, Raymond, (Retired)
Heitschmidt, Jerome, (On Duty Outside the Diocese)
Heitz, Philip, St. Philip, Addison
Helgeson, Donald, St. Margaret Mary, Naperville
Henrissey, Francis R., (Leave of Absence)
Hentz, Bradley, St. Irene, Warrenville
Herrera, Armando, St. Pius X, Lombard
Hill, Steven, (On Duty Outside the Diocese)
Huebner, Karl, Holy Family, Shorewood
Iozzo, Michael, Visitation, Elmhurst
Jackson, Kenneth, (Retired)
Jagielo, Thomas, Holy Trinity, Westmont
Janousek, James, St. John the Baptist, Joliet
Janousek, Jay, (Retired)
Januszewski, Michael, Divine Savior, Downers Grove
Jimenez, Julio, St. Alexander, Villa Park
Johnson, Joseph, St. Anthony, Frankfort
Jung, Paul, Immaculate Conception, Morris
Kaminski, Robert, St. Mary, Mokena
Kearney, Lawrence, St. Thomas, Naperville
Kelly, James, St. Paul the Apostle, Peotone
Kelly, Paul, St. Isaac Jogues, Hinsdale
Kelly, William, (On Duty Outside the Diocese)
Kelsey, Darrell, St. Patrick, Joliet
Kenny, Patrick, Our Lady of Peace, Darien
Kim, Paul, (Retired)
Kinsella, James, (Leave of Absence)
Knecht, Ronald, St. Pius X, Lombard
Kobs, Dennis, (On Duty Outside the Diocese)
Kolodziej, Paul, St. Patrick, Joliet
Koster, Kevin, Resurrection, Wayne
Kowalchik, Michael, St. Walter, Roselle
Koza, Joseph, (On Duty Outside the Diocese)
Kozar, Francis, St. Joseph, Downers Grove
Krol, Robert, Sacred Heart, Lombard
Krueger, James, St. Alexander, Villa Park
Kubica, Kenneth, St. Michael, Wheaton
Kueper, Timothy, Our Lady of Mercy, Aurora
LaMotte, Robert, St. Joseph, Bradley
Lane, Charles, (Retired)
Lange, Kurt, St. Raphael, Naperville
Larkin, Robert, St. Elizabeth Seton, Naperville
Lasica, Robert, Holy Ghost, Wood Dale
Legner, Neil, (On Duty Outside the Diocese)
Lenard, Anthony, Holy Trinity, Wesmont
Lennon, Patrick, St. Thomas the Apostle, Naperville
Leonardelli, Mark, (On Duty Outside the Diocese)
Leppert, Milton, St. George, Bourbonnais
Lifka, David, (Leave of Absence)
Lillig, Francis, Christ the King, Lombard
Lissak, Lawrence, St. Pius X, Lombard
Lombardo, Patrick, St. Mary Immaculate, Plainfield
Lopez, Jose L., St. John the Baptist, Joliet
Lovero, Marco, St. Francis of Assisi, Bolingbrook
Madsen, Ronald, St. John the Apostle, Villa Park
Mahoney, Daniel Sr., St. Mary Nativity, Joliet
Mahoney, David, Sacred Heart, Lombard
Maier, Frederick, St. Peter the Apostle, Itasca
Malek, Robert, St. Matthew, Glendale Heights
Marciani, Thomas, St. Scholastica, Woodridge
Marlowe, David, St. John Pual II, Kankakee
Marquez, Ricardo, St. Andrew, Romeoville
Marrero, Wilfredo, Sts. Peter & Paul, Naperville
Marrow, Philip, St. Joseph, Addison
Martinez, Artemio, St. John the Baptist, Joliet
Martinez, Santos H., Immaculate Conception, Morris
Martini, Anthony, Our Lady of Mercy, Aurora
Mazzacano, Christopher, Sacred Heart, Lombard
McCaffrey, Christopher, Cathedral of St. Raymond, Joliet
McDonnell, Joseph, (On Duty Outside the Diocese)
McGreal, Sean, St. Philip, Addison
McGuire, Michael, St. Francis of Assisi, Bolingbrook
Meador, David, (Leave of Absence)
Means, James, Resurrection, Wayne
Mele, John, St. Mary Magdalene, Joliet
Mempin, Genaro, St. Francis of Assisi, Bolingbrook
Metcalfe, Dale R., St. Patrick, Yorkville
Miciunas, Robert, St. Mary of Gostyn, Downers Grove
Miles, Kenneth J., St. Margaret Mary, Naperville
Moeller, John, (On Duty Outside the Diocese)
Monahan, Kevin, (On Duty Outside the Diocese)
Monterroso, Oscar, St. Isidore, Bloomingdale
Murillo, Eduardo, St. Mary, Plano
Murphy, William E., St. Irene, Warrenville
Neary, Terrance, St. Isadore, Bloomingdale
Neher, Norman, (Retired)
Neis, Kevin, Sts. Peter & Paul, Naperville
Newey, Paul, Divine Savior, Downers Grove
Nguyen, Anthony, (On Duty Outside the Diocese)
Nickels, Timothy, Notre Dame, Clarendon Hills
Nolan, Thomas J., Mary, Queen of Heaven, Elmhurst
Novak, Matthew, Christ the King, Lombard
Novak, Roger, Sts. Peter and Paul, Naperville
O'Connell, Thomas, (Retired)
O'Ryan, Michael, Visitation, Elmhurst
Osei, Anthony, St. Francis of Assisi, Bolingbrook
Otten, Mark, St. Boniface, Monee
Ouska, Gregory, St. Joseph, Downers Grove
Pace, Scott, St. Elizabeth Seton, Naperville
Padilla, Rigoberto, St. Andrew the Apostle, Romeoville
Pallo, Daniel, (On Duty Outside the Diocese)
Paluch, Thomas, Holy Family, Shorewood
Parsons, Lindsey, St. Matthew, Glendale Heights
Penkala, Leonard, St. Raphael, Naperville
Perkins, Michael, St. Mary Immaculate, Plainfield
Perry, James, St. Anne, Oswego
Petak, Edwin, Cathedral of St. Raymond, Joliet
Peterson, Charles M., St. Patrick, Joliet
Pidgeon, Matthew, (On Duty Outside the Diocese)
Pistorio, Charles, (Unassigned Outside of Diocese)
Plese, Anthony, St. Rose, Wilmington
Plese, Michael, Our Lady of Mercy, Aurora
Prete, David, St. Liborius, Steger
Principe, Michael, (Retired)
Ptacek, Edward, Our Lady of Mt. Carmel, Darien
Pusateri, Joseph, St. Walter, Roselle
Puscas, Victor, St. Mary Immaculate, Plainfield
Putman, John, St. Mary, Minooka
Rachubinski, Thomas, St. Pius X, Lombard
Randolph, Donald, Resurrection, Wayne
Raskowski, David, (Retired)
Razka, Gregory, St. Joan of Arc, Lisle
Rehak, Thomas, Sts. Peter & Paul, Naperville
Rehmer, Philip, Our Lady of Mercy, Aurora
Rex, John, St. Mary, Mokena
Ripoll, John, St. Elizabeth Seton, Naperville
Rittenhouse, Daniel, (On Duty Outside of Diocese)
Ritter, David, St. John the Baptist, Winfield
Robinson, Peter, Christ the King, Lombard
Rooney, Peter, Ascension, Oakbrook Terrace
Rosko, Richard, St. Anthony, Frankfort
Ross, Thomas, St. Elizabeth Seton, Naperville
Ruddle, Michael, St. Matthew, Glendale Heights
Ryan, Kevin, St. Bernard, Homer Glen
Ryba, Michael, (On Duty Outside of Diocese)
Safko, Terry L., (Retired)
Sagenbrecht, Thomas, St. Francis Xavier, Joliet
Saltigerald, Luis, St. Mary, West Chicago
Sarantakos, Paul, Our Lady of Lourdes, Gibson City
Schlott, Anthony, St. Anthony, Frankfort
Schneider, Paul A., (Retired)
Schroeder, Thomas, St. Mary Immaculate, Plainfield
Schumacher, Carl, St. Joseph, Downers Grove
Searls, Ronald, St. Walter, Roselle
Sebastian, John, St. Isaac Jogues, Hinsdale
Shea, John, Cathedral of St. Raymond, Joliet
Sheridan, Thomas, (Retired)
Simmet, Daniel, St. Michael, Wheaton
Skelly, Patrick, Maternity BVM, Bourbonnais
Soloy, George, St. Scholastica, Woodridge
Sossong, James R., St. Mary Immaculate, Plainfield
Spatafore, Anthony, Visitation, Elmhurst
Spiezio, John, St. Petronille, Glen Ellyn
Starasinich, Douglas, St. Joseph, Joliet
Stevens, Richard R., (On Duty Outside the Diocese)
Stolarz, Dennis, St. Joseph, Lockport
Storrs, Wayne, Christ the King, Lombard
Straub, Fred, (Retired)
Stroner, William, St. Michael, Wheaton
Stucko, Denis, (Retired)
Sullivan, Robert, St. Joseph, Downers Grove
Szymanski, Edward, St. Mary, Park Forest
Tagle, Jesse, St. Andrew, Romeoville
Taylor, Terrance, St. Margaret Mary, Naperville
Taylor, Timothy, St. Charles Borromeo, Bensenville
Tetrault, Robert L., (On Duty Outside the Diocese)
Theriault, Dennis, St. Jude, New Lenox
Thiltgen, Thomas R., Corpus Christi, Carol Stream
Thomas, William, Corpus Christi, Carol Stream
Tiongson, Arturo, Our Lady of Mercy, Aurora
Tretina, Matthew, St. Alexander, Villa Park
Troy, Daniel, (Retired)
True, Robert, (Retired)
Uffmann, William, (Leave of Absence)
Urso, Joseph, St. Irene, Warrenville
Valdez, George, (Leave of Absence)
Vavra, Robert, Our Lady of Mercy, Aurora
Verdico, Joseph, Sts. Peter & Paul, Naperville
Villarreal, Guadalupe, St. Dennis, Lockport
Volker, Jeffrey, (On Duty Outside the Diocese)
Vonesh, Frank, Our Lady of Peace, Darien
Waldron, Herbert, St. Andrew, Romeoville
Walen, Paul J. Sr., (Retired)
Wallace, Robert, St. Dominic, Bolingbrook
Waring, Robert, St. Isaac Jogues, Hinsdale
Wells, Douglas, St. Patrick, Yorkville
Wharry, James, (On Duty Outside the Diocese)
Woods, Charles, (Retired)
Wooley, Gary, St. Anne, Oswego
Wozek, Duane, St. Anne, Oswego
Yarshen, Richard, Sts. Peter & Paul, Naperville
Yurcus, Ronald J., St. Petronille, Glen Ellyn
Zarembka, Terrance, St. Scholastica, Woodridge
Ziomek, Robert, St. Peter the Apostle, Itasca.

INSTITUTIONS LOCATED IN DIOCESE

[A] COLLEGES AND UNIVERSITIES

JOLIET. *University of St. Francis* (1920) 500 N. Wilcox, Joliet, 60435. Tel: 800-735-7500; Fax: 815-740-4285; Email: information@stfrancis.edu; Web: www.stfrancis.edu. Dr. Arvid C. Johnson, Ph.D., Pres.; Sisters Mary Elizabeth Imler, O.S.F., B.S., M.S., M.A., Vice Pres., Mission Integration and Ministry; Margaret Karwowski, O.S.F., Ph.D., Adjunct Instructor; Rev. Terry A. Deffenbaugh, O.S.A., Chap. & Theology Instructor; Ms. Shannon Wenzel, Dir. Lib. Serv.; Sr. Gayle Rusbasan Sr., Campus Min. A coed residence and commuter school. Clergy 1; Lay Teachers 106; Priests 1; Students 3,527; Total Staff 307; Franciscan Sisters of the Sacred Heart 2.

LISLE. *Benedictine University*, 5700 College Rd., Lisle, 60532-0900. Tel: 630-829-6600; Fax: 630-960-1126; Email: dturner@ben.edu; Web: www.ben.edu. Rt. Rev. Austin G. Murphy, O.S.B., Chancellor; Mr. Charles Gregory, Acting Pres.; Miroslava Krug, Vice Pres., Finance; Leonard Bertolini, Vice Pres., Univ. Devel.; Dr. James Payne, Provost & Vice Pres., Academic Affairs; Dr. David Sonnenerger, Ph.D., Assoc. Provost; Dr. Peter Huff, Chief Mission Officer; Rev. David Turner, O.S.B., Asst. to Pres. for History & Mission; Marco Macini, Vice Pres., Student Life; Michelle Koppitz, Vice Pres., Adult & Prof. Prog.; Cindy Lambert, Registrar; Carrie Roberts, Dir., Campus Min.; Dr. Christopher Duffrin, Dean, College of Education & Health Svcs.; William Law, Dean, College of Science; Joseph Incandala, Dean, College of Liberal Arts; Dr. Darrell Radson, Dean, College Business; Revs. Philip S. Timko, O.S.B., Sacramental Min.; John Palmer, C.S.V., Campus Min.; James Flint, O.S.B., Campus Min.; Rt. Revs. Hugh R. Anderson, O.S.B., Campus Min., (Retired); Dismas B. Kalcic, O.S.B., Campus Min., (Retired); Bro. Richard Poro, O.S.B., Student Life Assoc.; Rev. Julian von Duerbeck, O.S.B., Adjunct Prof., Rel. Studies; Bro. Augustine Mallak, O.S.B., Adjunct Prof., Music; Mark McHorney, Athletic Dir.; Jack Fritts, Librarian. Administrators 319; Brothers 2; Religious Teachers 2; Lay Teachers 414; Priests 7; Sisters 1; Students 4,413.

Founders Woods, Ltd., 5700 College Rd., Lisle, 60532. Tel: 630-829-6400; Fax: 630-829-6340; Email: dturner@ben.edu. Rev. David Turner, O.S.B., Contact Person.

ROMEOVILLE. *Lewis University* (Coed University) One University Pkwy., Romeoville, 60446-2200. Tel: 815-838-0500; Fax: 815-838-5561; Email: chead@lewisu.edu; Web: www.lewisu.edu/. Bro. Stephen Zlatic, Dir., Univ. Ministry. De La Salle Christian Brothers 22; Clergy 6; Lay Teachers 263; Priests 1; Students 6,500.

[B] HIGH SCHOOLS, DIOCESAN

KANKAKEE. *Bishop McNamara Catholic High School* (1922) 550 W. Brookmont Blvd., Kankakee, 60901. Tel: 815-932-7413; Fax: 815-932-0926; Email: tgranger@bmcss.org; Web: www.bishopmac.com. Terry Granger, Prin.; Tricia Surprenant, Dir., Finance; Sr. Maureen Fallon, Asst. Prin., Curriculum & Instruction. Lay Teachers 27; Priests 1; Sisters 1; Students 343; Total Staff 52.

[C] HIGH SCHOOLS, PRIVATE

JOLIET. *Joliet Catholic Academy* (Coed) 1200 N. Larkin Ave., Joliet, 60435. Tel: 815-741-0500; Fax: 815-741-9530; Email: jbudz@jca-online.org; Web: www.jca-online.org. Jeffrey Budz, Pres. & Prin.; William Pender, Vice Prin.; Laura Pahl, Vice Prin. Carmelites & Joliet Franciscans. Religious Teachers 1; Lay Teachers 44; Priests 3; Sisters 1; Students 615.

LISLE. *Benet Academy* (1887) 2200 Maple Ave., Lisle, 60532. Tel: 630-719-2782; Fax: 630-719-2849; Email: smarth@benet.org; Web: www.benet.org. Rt. Rev. Austin G. Murphy, O.S.B., Chancellor; Mr. Stephen A. Marth, Prin.; Mr. James Brown, Asst. Prin.; Mr. William Myers, Asst. Prin.; Mrs. Kathleen Swanson, Librarian; Michelle Renicker, Business Mgr. Brothers 3; Religious Teachers 1; Lay Teachers 81; Priests 3; Students 1,341.

LOMBARD. *Montini Catholic High School* (1996) 19 W. 070 16th St., Lombard, 60148-4797. Tel: 630-627-6930; Fax: 630-627-0537; Email: moneill@montini.org; Web: www.montini.org. James F. Segredo, Pres.; Kevin Beirne, Prin.; Sara Lhotka, Vice Prin. Lay Teachers 568; Students 575.

NEW LENOX. *Providence Catholic High School* (1918) (Coed) 1800 W. Lincoln Hwy., New Lenox, 60451. Tel: 815-485-2136; Fax: 815-485-2709; Email: jmerkelis@providencecatholic.org; Web: www.providencecatholic.org. John Harper, Prin.; Mrs. Janlyn Auld, Vice Prin.; Revs. John D. Merkelis, O.S.A., Pres. & Dir.; Richard Young, O.S.A., Prior. Religious Teachers 2; Lay Teachers 57; Priests 2; Students 885. In Res. Revs. John A. Kret, O.S.A.; Gerald Nicholas, O.S.A.; Joseph G. Broudou, O.S.A.

WHEATON. *St. Francis High School* (1956) 2130 W. Roosevelt Rd., Wheaton, 60187. Tel: 630-668-5800; Fax: 630-668-5893; Email: rhuhn@sfhscollegeprep.org; Web: www.sfhscollegeprep.org. Dr. Betsy Ackerson, Pres.; Raeann Huhn, Prin. Lay Teachers 61; Students 716.

[D] ELEMENTARY SCHOOLS, DIOCESAN

BOURBONNAIS. *Bishop McNamara Catholic School*, (Grades PreSchool-6), (f/k/a Maternity B.V.M. School) 324 E. Marsile St., Bourbonnais, 60914. Tel: 815-933-7758; Fax: 815-933-1884; Email: ngernon@bmcss.org. Mrs. Nicole Gernon, Prin. Lay Teachers 22; Students 311.

BRADLEY. *Bishop McNamara Catholic School*, (Grades PreSchool-6), (f/k/a St. Joseph School) 247 N. Center Ave., Bradley, 60915. Tel: 815-933-8013; Fax: 815-933-2775; Email: dberg@bmcss.org; Web: www.stjosephschoolbradley.org. Mrs. Dana Berg, Prin. Clergy 1; Lay Teachers 10; Sisters 1; Students 153.

KANKAKEE. *Bishop McNamara Catholic School*, (Grades 7-12), 550 E. Brookmont Blvd., Kankakee, 60901. Tel: (815) 932-7413; Email: tgranger@bmcss.org. Terry Granger, Pres. Clergy 1; Lay Teachers 27; Students 493.

NAPERVILLE. *All Saints Catholic Academy*, (Grades PreK-8), 1155 Aurora Ave., Naperville, 60540. Tel: 630-961-6125; Fax: 630-961-3771; Email: msantos@ascacademy.org; Web: ascacademy.org. Very Rev. Paul Hottinger, Pres.; Rev. Scott Huggins; Melissa K. Santos, Prin.; Revs. Mark Bernhard, Chap.; Philip M. Danaher. Religious Teachers 4; Lay Teachers 37; Students 443.

[E] AGENCIES AND INSTITUTIONS OF THE CHARITIES OF THE DIOCESE

CREST HILL. *Catholic Charities, Diocese of Joliet*, 16555 Weber Rd., 60403. Tel: 815-723-3405; Fax: 815-723-3452; Email: gvancura@cc-doj.org; Email: info@cc-doj.org; Web: www.catholiccharitiesjoliet.org. Mr. Glenn Van Cura, Exec. Dir. Administrative Office for Will, Grundy and Kendall Counties. Tot Asst. Annually 64,000; Total Staff 250.

DOWNERS GROVE. *Catholic Charities, Diocese of Joliet*, 3130 Finley Rd., Ste. 520, Downers Grove, 60515. Tel: 630-495-8008; Fax: 630-495-9854; Email: info@cc-doj.org; Web: www.catholiccharitiesjoliet.org. Mr. Glenn Van Cura, Exec. Regional Office for DuPage County. Tot Asst. Annually 64,000; Total Staff 250.

KANKAKEE. *Catholic Charities, Diocese of Joliet*, 249 S. Schuyler Ave., Ste. 300, Kankakee, 60901. Tel: 815-933-7791; Fax: 815-932-3030; Email: info@cc-doj.org; Web: www.catholiccharitiesjoliet.org. Mr. Glenn Van Cura, Exec. Regional Office for Kankakee, Ford, and Iroquois Counties. Tot Asst. Annually 64,000; Total Staff 250.

[F] PROTECTIVE INSTITUTIONS

MOMENCE. **Good Shepherd Manor* (1971) P.O. Box 260, Momence, 60954. Tel: 815-472-6492; Tel: 815-472-3700; Fax: 815-472-2160; Email: info@goodshepherdmanor.org; Web: www.goodshepherdmanor.org. Mr. Bruce Fitzpatrick, Pres.; Rev. Wolf V.K. Werling, Chap.; Bro. Alphonsus Brown, O.H., Asst. Admin. Adult Male DD-MR. Bed Capacity 125; Hospitaller Brothers of St. John of God 2; Priests 1; Tot Asst. Annually 125; Total Staff 145; Permanent Residents 125.

[G] DAY CARE

JOLIET. *Vilaseca Josephine Center* (1974) 351 N. Chicago St., Joliet, 60432. Tel: 815-727-1467; Fax: 815-727-1480; Email: josemvilaseca@hotmail.com. Sisters Araceli Perez, Dir.; Judith Perez, Sub-Dir. Josephine Sisters. Students 85.

[H] LEARNING CENTERS

KANKAKEE. *Presence Fortin Villa Learning Center*, 1025 N. Washington Ave., Kankakee, 60901. Tel: 815-932-8411; Fax: 815-936-3275; Email: Judy.MacPhersonSchumacher@presencehealth.org. Stacey Fox, Dir. Childcare with Preschool for children 6 weeks to 12 years.

Presence Life Connections dba Presence Fortin Villa Learning Center Students 106; Total Staff 21.

[I] GENERAL HOSPITALS

JOLIET. *Presence Saint Joseph Medical Center*, 333 N. Madison St., Joliet, 60435-6595. Tel: 815-725-7133; Fax: 815-741-7579; Email: melissa.kulik@amitahealth.org; Email: kathleen.carlson@amitahealth.org; Web: www.presencehealth.org/locations/hospitals/presence-saint-joseph-medical-center. Robert Erickson, Pres. & C.E.O.; Daniel Cunningham, Spiritual Care Mgr. Sponsored by Ascension Health Ministries (Ascension Sponsor), a public juridic person

Presence Central and Suburban Hospitals Network dba Presence Saint Joseph Medical Center Bed Capacity 498; Patients Asst Anual. 211,607; Priests 1; Sisters 2; Total Staff 2,016.

Presence Industrial Rehabilitation Center, Joliet, Tel: 815-741-7416; Fax: 815-741-0774.

Presence Physical Rehab & Sports Injury Center, Joliet, Tel: 815-741-7114; Fax: 815-725-6997.

KANKAKEE. *Presence St. Mary's Hospital*, 500 W. Court St., Kankakee, 60901. Tel: 815-937-2400; Fax: 815-937-3535; Email: melissa.kulik@amitahealth.org; Email: kathleen.carlson@amitahealth.org; Web: www.presencehealth.org/locations/hospitals/presence-st-marys-hospital. Christopher Shride, Regl. Pres. & CEO; Deacon Patrick Skelly, Chap. Sponsored by Ascension Health Ministries (Ascension Sponsor), a public juridic person.

Presence Central and Suburban Hospitals Network dba Presence St. Mary Hospital Bed Capacity 182; Tot Asst. Annually 87,355; Total Staff 685.

MOKENA. *Presence Central and Suburban Hospitals Network* (1997) 18927 Hickory Creek Dr., Ste. 300, Mokena, 60448. Tel: 312-308-3200; Fax: 312-308-3396; Email: melissa.kulik@amitahealth.org; Email: kathleen.carlson@amitahealth.org; Web: www.presencehealth.org. Dana Gilbert, Pres. Sponsored by Ascension Health Ministries (Ascension Sponsor), a public juridic person.

[J] HOMES FOR AGED

JOLIET. *Our Lady of Angels Retirement Home*, 1201 Wyoming Ave., Joliet, 60435. Tel: 815-725-6631; Fax: 815-725-1451; Email: phargis@olaretirement.org. George Block, Admin.; Marguerite Kronberger, Dir. Sisters of St. Francis of Mary Immaculate. Residents 121; Sisters 2; Total Staff 175; Retired Sisters 47. In Res. Sr. Rosemary Huzl.

Presence Villa Franciscan, 210 N. Springfield Ave., Joliet, 60435. Tel: 815-725-3400; Fax: 815-725-2160; Email: david.green@presencehealth.org; Web: www.presencehealth.org/lifeconnections/body.cfm?id=2045. Christopher Green, Admin.; David Green, Chap., Spiritual Health Dir. Extended, Intermediate, and Skilled Care, Respite Care.

Presence Life Connections dba Presence Villa Franciscan Bed Capacity 154; Tot Asst. Annually 833; Total Staff 167.

BOURBONNAIS. *Presence Our Lady of Victory Nursing Home*, 20 Briarcliff Ln., Bourbonnais, 60914. Tel: 815-937-2022; Fax: 815-936-3231; Email: Judy.MacPhersonSchumacher@presencehealth.org; Web: www.presencehealth.org. Marcita Carter, Admin.; Sr. Martha Harrington, Spiritual Care Dir.

Presence Life Connections dba Our Lady of Victory Nursing Home Bed Capacity 107; Sisters 1; Tot Asst. Annually 212; Total Staff 99.

CLIFTON. *Presence Merkle-Knipprath Countryside*, 1190 E. 2900 N Rd., Clifton, 60927-7103. Tel: 815-694-2306; Fax: 815-694-2818; Email: Antoinette.Potts@Presencehealth.org; Email: Karen.Grillion@Presencehealth.org. Bro. Damien DeBraekeleer, O.S.F., Spiritual Care Dir.; Karen Grillion, Admin. Apartment Community and Nursing Center. Bed Capacity 114; Tot Asst. Annually 118; Total Staff 76.

KANKAKEE. *Presence Heritage Lodge*, 995 N. Entrance Ave., Kankakee, 60901. Tel: 815-939-4506; Fax: 815-939-4761; Email: Judy.MacPhersonSchumacher@presencehealth.org. Robin Gifford, Admin.

Presence Life Connections dba Presence Heritage Lodge Bed Capacity 26; Tot Asst. Annually 37; Total Staff 17.

Presence Life Connections, Tel: 815-939-4506; Fax: 815-939-4761.

Ascension Health Senior Care, 901 N. Entrance Ave., Kankakee, 60901. Tel: 815-939-4506; Fax: 815-939-4761; Email: robin.gifford@presencehealth.org; Web: www.provena.org/lifeconnections/body.cfm?id=2008. Robin Gifford, Admin.; Carole DiZeo, Spiritual Care Dir.

Presence Life Connections dba Presence Heritage Village Bed Capacity 87; Tot Asst. Annually 369; Total Staff 83.

LEMONT. *Franciscan Communities, Inc.* dba Marian Village, 11500 Theresa Dr., Lemont, 60439. Tel: 708-226-3780; Fax: 708-226-3781; Email: dbannon@francicancommunities.com; Web: www.franciscancommunities.com. 15624 Marian Dr., Homer Glen, 60491. Daniel Bannon, Exec. Dir.; Elizabeth Pienta, Dir., Mission Integration & Pastoral Care; Rev. Jacob Kolawole.

LISLE. *Villa St. Benedict*, 1920 Maple Ave., Lisle, 60532. Tel: 630-725-7000; Fax: 630-852-3196; Email: kdicristina@villastben.org; Web: www.villastben.org. Ms. Kathy DiCristina, Admin. Continuing Care Retirement Bed Capacity 261; Total Assisted 135.

NAPERVILLE. *St. John Vianney Villa*, 1464 Green Trails Dr., Naperville, 60540-8372. Tel: 630-983-0533; Fax: 630-983-6375; Email: frscott@rcdoj.org. Revs. Lee Bacchi, Hospital Chap.; Scott M. McCawley; John Sebahar, (Retired); Daniel F. Stempora, (Retired); Jess Testa, (Retired); James Radek; Donald Kocher, (Retired); Martin M. Gabel, (Retired). Retirement home for priests. Residents 9; Tot Asst. Annually 12.

St. Patrick's Residence, 1400 Brookdale Rd., Naperville, 60563-2126. Tel: 630-416-6565; Fax: 630-416-8755; Email: info@stpatricksresidence.org; Web: www.stpatricksresidence.org. Mrs. Marilyn Daley, Admin. Bed Capacity 209; Residents 193; Carmelite Sisters 4; Total Staff 285.

OAKBROOK. *Franciscan Tertiary Province of the Sacred Heart, Inc.* dba Mayslake Village Inc., 1801 35th St., Oak Brook, 60523. Tel: 630-850-8232; Fax: 630-850-8233; Email: kmaxwell@mayslake.com; Web: www.mayslake.com. Mr. Michael A. Frigo, Pres. & CEO. Senior Citizen Retirement Community.

Mayslake Annex II, NFP, 1801 35th St., Oak Brook, 60523. Tel: 630-850-8232; Fax: 630-850-8233; Email: kmaxwell@mayslake.com; Web: www.mayslake.com. Mr. Michael A. Frigo, Pres. & CEO.

Mayslake East Wing, Inc., 1801 35th St., Oak Brook, 60523. Tel: 630-850-8232; Fax: 630-850-8233; Email: kmaxwell@mayslake.com; Web: www.mayslake.com. Mr. Michael A. Frigo, Pres. & CEO.

WHEATON. *Marian Park, Inc.* (1972) 2126 W. Roosevelt Rd., Wheaton, 60187. Tel: 630-665-9100; Tel: 630-909-6933; Fax: 630-665-9357; Email: mhingtgen@mercyhousing.org; Web: www.mercyhousing.org. Melissa Clayton, Vice Pres. Units 209.

[K] MONASTERIES AND RESIDENCES OF PRIESTS AND BROTHERS

JOLIET. *St. Elias Carmelites*, 3504 Lake Shore Dr., Joliet, 60431-8819. Tel: 815-439-8246; Email: steliascarmelites@comcast.net. Revs. Donald W. Buggert, O.Carm.; Jeffery Smialek, O.Carm.; Edward Ward, O.Carm.; John Welch, O.Carm., (Retired); Bros. Lawrence Fidelus, O.Carm.; Dominic Soganich, O.Carm.; Rev. Rolf Willemsen. Brothers 2; Priests 5.

St. John the Baptist Friary, 404 N. Hickory St., Joliet, 60435-7554. Tel: 815-727-9783; Tel: 217-316-4335; Fax: 815-727-1729; Email: eja1951@gmail.com. Bro. Edward Arambasich, O.F.M., Guardian; Revs. Herbert Jones, O.F.M.; Lawrence Jagdfeld, O.F.M., Business Mgr.; David Rodriguez, O.F.M.; More Torres Torres, Assoc. Pastor. Brothers 1; Priests 4.

BURR RIDGE. *Christian Brothers Provincial Office (Midwest Province)* (1995) 7650 S. County Line Rd., Burr Ridge, 60527-7959. Tel: 630-323-3725; Fax: 630-323-3779; Email: info@cbmidwest.org; Web: www.cbmidwest.org. Bros. Larry Schatz, F.S.C., Prov. & Brother Visitor; Joseph Saurbier, F.S.C., Treas.; Michael Kadow, F.S.C., Prov. Asst.; Bede Baldry, F.S.C., Prov. Asst.; Dr. Scott Kier, Supt., Lasallian Educ.

DARIEN. *Carmelite Provincial Office*, 1317 Frontage Rd., Darien, 60561. Tel: 630-971-0050; Fax: 630-971-0195; Email: provincial@carmelnet.org; Web: www.carmelnet.org. Very Revs. William Harry, O.Carm., Prior Provincial; Joseph Atcher, O.Carm., Vice Prior Provincial & Provincial Treas.; Revs. John Benedict-Weber, O.Carm.; Robert Boley, O.Carm.; Kevin McBrien, O.Carm.; Jorge Remuzgo, O.Carm.; Bro. Robert Murphy, O.Carm.; Revs. Gavin Quinn, O.Carm.; Thomas Alkire, O.Carm., (Retired); Very Rev. Carl J. Markelz, O.Carm., Vice Prior Prov.; Rev. Felix Prior, O.Carm.
The Society of Mt. Carmel

Carmelites Serving in Italy: Rev. Raul Maravi, O.Carm., Email: rmaravi@carmelnet.org; Very Rev. Carl J. Markelz, O.Carm.; Rev. Craig Morrison, O.Carm.

Carmelites Serving in Canada: Revs. Marc Bell, O.Carm.; John J. Comerford, O.Carm.; Thomas Hakala, O.Carm.; Leo Huard, O.Carm., (Retired); Christopher Kulig, O.Carm.; Stanley Makacinas, O.Carm., Acting Dir. Mt. Carmel Spiritual Center, (Retired); Anthony McNamara, O.Carm., (Retired); Gerard Power, O.Carm.; Michael Wastag, O.Carm.

Carmelites Serving in Peru: Revs. Edward Adelmann, O.Carm.; Miguel Bacigalupo; Salvador Bartolo, O.Carm., (Retired); Floristan Guerrero, O.Carm.; James Geaney, O.Carm., (Retired), Prelate Nullius, Sicuani, Peru. Tel: 011-51-8-435-11611; Fax: 011-51-8-435-1089; Enrique Laguna-Vargas, O.Carm.; Adolfo Medrano Bellido, O.Carm.; Gerald Payea, O.Carm.; Eduardo Rivero, O.Carm.; Jorge Villegas, O.Carm.; Bro. Rodolfo Aznaran, O.Carm.

Carmelites Serving in Australia: Bro. Sean Keefe, O.Carm.

Carmelites Serving in Mexico: Revs. Jesus Larios Avila, O.Carm.; Rogelio Garcia, O.Carm.; Peter Hinde, O.Carm.; Mario Loya, O.Carm.; Emilio Rodriguez, O.Carm.; Bro. Mario Cadena, O.Carm.

Carmelites Serving in El Salvador: Revs. David Blanchard, O.Carm.; Alfredo Guillen, O.Carm.; Bros. Jesus Paz, O.Carm.; Benjamin Salas, O.Carm.; Oscar Salazar, O.Carm.; Rev. Tracy O'Sullivan, O.Carm.

Carmelites Serving Elsewhere: Revs. Emil Agostino, O.Carm., (Retired); Timothy P. Andres, O.Carm.; Nelson Belizario, O.Carm.; Kyrin Caggiano, O.Carm., (Retired); Warren Carlin, O.Carm., (Retired); Marcel Dube, O.Carm., (Retired); Michael Flynn, O.Carm.; Niles Gillen, O.Carm., (Retired); Myron Judy, O.Carm.; Albert P. Koppes, O.Carm., (Retired); James Lewis, O.Carm.; Blaise McInerney, O.Carm., (Retired); Michael Mulhall, O.Carm., (Retired); Henry Ormond, O.Carm.; Clyde Ozminkowski, O.Carm., (Retired); Paul Robinson, O.Carm., (Retired); Thomas Walsh, O.Carm., (Retired); Frank Weil, O.Carm.; Valentine Boyle, O.Carm., (Retired); Augustine Carter, O.Carm., (Retired); Stephen Cooley, O.Carm., (Retired); Matthias Ewing, O.Carm., (Retired); Peter Liuzzi, O.Carm., (Retired); Joseph McGowan, O.Carm., (Retired); Most Rev. Michael LaFay, O.Carm., (Retired).

St. Simon Stock Priory (1959) 8501 Bailey Rd., Darien, 60561. Tel: 630-971-0050; Email: provincial@carmelnet.org. Revs. Bernhard Bauerle, O.Carm.; Robert E. Colaresi, O.Carm., Prior; William Harry, O.Carm., Prov.; Gavin Quinn, O.Carm.; Glenn Snow, O.Carm.; Raymond Clennon, O. Carm.; Terrence Cyr, O.Carm.; Robert Traudt, Priest. Priests 6.

Titus Brandsma Priory (1979) 8423 Bailey Rd., Darien, 60561-5361. Tel: 630-971-0050; Tel: 773-410-0211; Fax: 630-971-0195; Email: pmcgarry@carmelnet.org; Web: www.carmelites.org. Revs. David Dillon, O.Carm., (Retired); Peter McGarry, O.Carm., Prior; Bruce Taggart, O.Carm. Carmelite Priory of the Society of Mount Carmel
Society of Mount Carmel.

LISLE. *St. Procopius Abbey*, 5601 College Rd., Lisle, 60532. Tel: 630-969-6410; Fax: 630-969-6426; Email: assistant@procopius.org; Email: gjelinek@procopius.org; Web: www.procopius.org. Rt. Rev. Austin G. Murphy, O.S.B., Abbot; Very Ven. Guy Jelinek, O.S.B., Prior & Business Mgr.; Revs. Anthony J. Jacob, O.S.B.; Thomas Chisholm, O.S.B., Subprior, (Retired); Joseph Chang, O.S.B.; Julian von Duerbeck, O.S.B.; James Flint, O.S.B., Procurator & Treas.; T. Becket Franks, O.S.B., Chap.; Rt. Rev. Dismas B. Kalcic, O.S.B., Chap., (Retired); Rev. Edward J. Kucera, O.S.B., (Retired); Bro. Gregory Perron; Revs. Jude D. Randall, O.S.B., (Retired); Philip S. Timko, O.S.B.; David Turner, O.S.B.; Kenneth Zigmond, O.S.B., Parochial Vicar; Rt. Rev. Hugh R. Anderson, O.S.B., Chap., Benet Academy, (Retired); Rev. Gabriel Baltes, O.S.B.; Bros. Kevin Coffey, Teacher; Elias Dicosola, Junior; Richard Poro, O.S.B., Campus Min.; Augustine Mallak, O.S.B., Teacher; Raphael Kozel, (Retired); Charles Hlava, Teacher. Benedictine Monks. Brothers 7; Priests 15; Junior 1. *Benedictine Chinese Mission*, 5601 College Rd., Lisle, 60532. Tel: 630-969-6410; Fax: 630-969-6426 ; Email: secretary@procopius.org; Email: gjelinek@procopius.org. Rt. Rev. Austin G. Murphy, O.S.B. *Slav Missions*, 5601 College Rd., Lisle, 60532. Tel: 630-969-6410; Fax: 630-969-6426; Email: gjelinek@procopius.org; Email: secretary@procopius.org. Rt. Rev. Austin G. Murphy, O.S.B. *St. Procopius Abbey Endowment*, 5601 College Rd., Lisle, 60532. Tel: 630-969-6410; Fax: 630-969-6426; Email: gjelinek@procopius.org; Email: secretary@procopius.org. Rt. Rev. Austin G. Murphy, O.S.B.

MOMENCE. *Brother Mathias Barrett Inc. of Illinois*, 114 W. Washington St., P.O. Box 736, Momence, 60954. Tel: 815-472-3131; Fax: 815-472-6914; Email: judy@sjog-na.org. Bro. Alphonsus Brown, O.H., Pres. Brothers 2.

NEW LENOX. *Augustinian Friary*, 1800 W. Lincoln Hwy., New Lenox, 60451. Tel: 815-485-6880; Fax: 815-485-2709; Email: gnicholas@ameritech.net. Revs. Richard Young, O.S.A., Chm.; Joseph G. Broudou, O.S.A., In Res.; John A. Kret, O.S.A., Treas.; John D. Merkelis, O.S.A., Prov. Asst.; Gerald Nicholas, O.S.A., Prior. (See separate listing for Providence High School).

ROMEOVILLE. *La Salle Community* (1996) 100 Faculty Ln., Romeoville, 60446-1178. Tel: 815-836-5402; Fax: 815-836-5858; Email: brjgaff@lewisu.edu. Bros. Pierre St. Raymond, F.S.C., Dir.; Thomas Dupre, F.S.C.; Christopher Ford, F.S.C.; James Gaffney, F.S.C.; Peter Hannon, F.S.C.; Philip Johnson, F.S.C.; Leo Jones, F.S.C., Email: LJones9911@aol.com; Joseph Martin, F.S.C.; Raphael Mascari, F.S.C.; Raymond McManaman, F.S.C.; Lawrence Oelschlegel, F.S.C.; Bernard Rapp, F.S.C.; John Vietoris, F.S.C.; John Blease, F.S.C.; Getachew Nadew. Brothers 15.

WESTMONT. *Westmont North Community* (2002) 222 S. Cass Ave., Westmont, 60559. Tel: 630-724-1976; Email: scutuma@yahoo.com. Bros. Kenneth Arnold, F.S.C., Dir.; David Kuebler, F.S.C.; Richard Geimer, F.S.C.; Thomas Dominic Vance, F.S.C. Brothers 4.

[L] CONVENTS AND RESIDENCES FOR SISTERS

JOLIET. *St. Clare House of Prayer* (1968) 1320 Franciscan Way, Joliet, 60435-3956. Tel: 815-725-1455; Email: stclarehouse@aol.com. Sr. Lourdes Boyer, O.S.F., Contact Person. Sisters of St. Francis of Mary Immaculate 3.

Josephine Sisters (1872) 351 N. Chicago St., Joliet, 60432. Tel: 815-727-1467; Fax: 815-727-1480; Email: josephinesis@hotmail.com. Sr. Judith Perez, Supr. Josephine Sisters of Mexico (Hermanas Josefinas). Sisters 4.

Sisters of St. Francis of Mary Immaculate (1865) 1433 Essington Rd., Joliet, 60435-2873. Tel: 815-725-8735; Fax: 815-725-8648; Email: dzemont@jolietfranciscans.org; Web: www.jolietfranciscans.org. Sr. Dolores Zemont, O.S.F., M.S.A., M.P.S., Pres.
Congregation of the Third Order of St Francis of Mary Immaculate, Joliet, IL. Sisters 134.

FRANKFORT. *Franciscan Sisters of the Sacred Heart* (1866) 9201 W. St. Francis Rd., Frankfort, 60423-8330. Tel: 815-469-4895; Fax: 815-464-3809; Email: joyce.shanabarger@presencehealth.org; Web: www.fssh.net. Sr. Joyce Shanabarger, O.S.F., Gen. Supr.
An Association of Franciscan Sisters of the Sacred Heart and Franciscan Foundation. Sisters 61.

KANKAKEE. *Servants of the Holy Heart of Mary, Holy Family Prov., U.S.A.* (1889) Provincial Administration, 2041 W. State Rt. 113, Kankakee, 60901. Tel: 815-937-2380; Fax: 815-937-5520; Email: cmkarnitsky@gmail.com; Email: lrentas@sscm-usa.org; Web: www.sscm-usa.org. Sr. Carol Karnitsky, S.S.C.M., Prov.
Servants of the Holy Heart of Mary Charitable Trust Sisters 1; Professed Sisters 25.

LISLE. *Benedictine Sisters of the Sacred Heart, Sacred Heart Monastery* (1895) 1910 Maple Ave., Lisle, 60532-2164. Tel: 630-725-6000; Fax: 630-969-5814; Email: mbratrsovsky@shmlisle.org; Web: www.shmlisle.org. Sr. Mary Bratrsovsky, O.S.B., Prioress
Benedictine Sisters of the Sacred Heart Professed Sisters 27.

MINOOKA. *The Poor Clares of Joliet, Annunciation Monastery*, 6200 E. Minooka Rd., Minooka, 60447. Tel: 815-467-0032; Fax: 815-467-4080; Email: poorclaresofjoliet@att.net; Web: www.poorclaresjoliet.org. Sr. M. Dorothy Urschalitz, P.C.C., Contact Person. Sisters 10.

NEW LENOX. *Mother of Good Counsel Monastery*, 440 N. Marley Rd., New Lenox, 60451. Tel: 815-463-9662; Email: augustiniannuns@sbcglobal.net. Sr. Mary Grace Kuppe, O.S.A., Prioress. Augustinian Cloistered Nuns, Inc. Solemnly Professed Sisters 4.

PLAINFIELD. *Mantellate Sisters Servants of Mary of Plainfield*, 16949 S. Drauden Rd., Plainfield, 60586. Tel: 815-436-5796; Fax: 815-436-7486; Email: srloustu@yahoo.com. Sr. Louise Staszewski, O.S.M., Rel. Supr. Sisters 4.

Mantellate Sisters Servants of Mary, U.S.A., 16949 S. Drauden Rd., Plainfield, 60586-9168. Tel: 815-436-5796; Fax: 815-436-7486; Email: srloustu@yahoo.com. Sr. Louise Staszewski, O.S.M., Regl. Supr. Homes for the Aged and Foreign Missions. Sisters 5.

WHEATON. *St. Clara Province Charitable Trust*, 26 W. 171 Roosevelt Rd., P.O. Box 667, Wheaton, 60187-0667. Tel: 630-909-6600; Fax: 630-462-7148; Email: joliverio@wfsisters.org. John D. Oliverio, Dir.

Convent of Our Lady of the Angels Motherhouse and Novitiate (1860) Franciscan Sisters, Daughters of the Sacred Hearts of Jesus and Mary (Wheaton, IL) 26 W. 171 Roosevelt Rd., P.O. Box 667, Wheaton, 60187. Tel: 630-909-6600; Fax: 630-468-7148; Email: cmorgan@wfsisters.org; Web: www.wheatonfranciscan.org. Sr. Melanie Paradis, O.S.F., Prov. Dir.
Wheaton Franciscan Sisters Corp. Sisters 45.

Religious of the Institute of the Blessed Virgin Mary, P.O. Box 508, Wheaton, 60187-0508. Tel: 630-653-6113; Fax: 630-653-4886; Email:

ibvmbarb@aol.com; Web: www.ibvm.us. Sisters Judy Illig, I.B.V.M., Prov.; Constance Steffen, Vicar; Barbara Nelson, Treas.; Claire Vandborg. Sisters 51.

Office of Development, Tel: 630-682-9097; Fax: 630-653-0826; Email: development@ibvm.org.

United States Province Administration, 26W171 Roosevelt Rd., Wheaton, 60187. Tel: 630-665-3814 (Prov. Leader); Tel: 630-653-6113 (Prov. Treas.); Tel: 630-868-2904 (Sec.); Fax: 630-868-2852; Email: ibvmbarb@aol.com.

Mary Ward Center, Tel: 773-734-2420; Fax: 773-734-2990; Email: mwcmaryhoward@aol.com.

[M] HOUSES OF RETREAT/PRAYER

DARIEN. *Carmelite Spiritual Center*, 8419 Bailey Rd., Darien, 60561. Tel: 630-969-4141; Fax: 630-969-3376; Email: retreats@carmelitespiritualcenter.org. Revs. Robert E. Colaresi, O.Carm., Dir.; Glenn Snow, O.Carm. Total Staff 16.

DOWNERS GROVE. *Mayslake Ministries, Inc.* (1991) 718 Ogden Ave., Ste. 200, Downers Grove, 60515. Tel: 630-852-9000; Fax: 630-852-9009; Email: mamore@mayslakeministries.org; Web: mayslakeministries.org. Rev. Thomas Borkowski, (Retired); Mary Amore, D.Min., Exec. Dir. Lay Staff 1; Priests 2.

FRANKFORT. *Portiuncula Center for Prayer* (1990) 9263 W. St. Francis Rd., Frankfort, 60423-8330. Tel: 815-464-3880; Fax: 815-469-4880; Email: info@portforprayer.org; Web: www.portforprayer.org. Mary Lou Nugent, Dir.

KANKAKEE. *One Heart, One Soul Spirituality Center*, 2041 State Rte. 113, Kankakee, 60901. Tel: 815-937-2344; Email: ohos@sscm-usa.org; Web: www.sscm-usa.org. Sr. Carol Karnitsky, Prov.

PLANO. *La Salle Manor Christian Brothers Retreat House* (1957) 12480 Galena Rd., Plano, 60545. Tel: 630-552-3224, Ext. 101; Fax: 630-552-9160; Email: info@lasallemanor.org; Web: www.lasallemanor.org. Robert Dressel, Pres.

[N] MISCELLANEOUS

JOLIET. *Diocesan Educational Endowment Fund*, 16555 Weber Rd., 60403. Tel: 815-221-6100; Email: mjanus@dioceseofjoliet.org. Mr. Mark Janus, Contact Person.

Presence Home Care Joliet, 1060 Essington Rd., Joliet, 60435. Tel: 815-741-7371; Fax: 815-741-7372; Email: Judy.MacPhersonSchumacher@presencehealth.org; Web: www.presencehealth.org. Michael Gordon, Pres.; Jan Cotter, Dir.

Presence Home Care dba Presence Home Care Joliet.

**The Upper Room Crisis Hotline (TURCH)*, P.O. Box 3572, Joliet, 60434. Tel: 815-727-4367; Tel: 888-808-8724 (Hotline); Fax: 815-726-5004; Email: catholichotline@gmail.com; Web: www.theupperroomcrisishotline.org. Sr. Mary Frances Seeley, O.S.F., Ph.D., Pres.

AURORA. *Assisi Homes - Constitution House, Inc.* (1995) 401 N. Constitution Dr., Aurora, 60506. Tel: 303-830-3300; Tel: 630-896-2100; Email: mrankin@mercyhousing.org; Web: www.mercyhousing.org. Melissa Clayton, Contact Person. Units 232.

BURR RIDGE. *Christian Brothers Fund, Inc.*, 7650 S. County Line Rd., Burr Ridge, 60527-7959. Tel: 630-323-3725; Fax: 630-323-3779; Email: info@cbmidwest.org; Web: cbmidwest.org. Bros. Larry Schatz, F.S.C., Pres.; Joseph Saurbier, F.S.C., Treas.; Samantha VenHuizen.

CREST HILL. *The Catholic Education Foundation of the Diocese of Joliet*, 16555 Weber Rd., 60403. Tel: 815-221-6127; Fax: 815-588-6007; Email: jgeorgis@dioceseofjoliet.org; Web: CEFJoliet.org. Mr. Joseph Langenderfer, CEO.

Diocese of Joliet Catholic Cemetery Perpetual Care Trust, 16555 Weber Rd., 60403. Tel: 815-933-2342; Email: eholloway@dioceseofjoliet.org. Eric Holloway, Dir.

Diocese of Joliet Seminarian Education Endowment Trust, 16555 Weber Rd., 60403. Tel: 815-221-6100; Email: bschroeder@dioceseofjoliet.org. Mr. Brian Schroeder, Contact Person.

National Association of Catholic Nurses-U.S.A., c/o Diocese of Joliet, 16555 Weber Rd., 60403. Tel: 578-462-0899; Fax: 578-462-2892; Email: catholicnurses@nacn-usa.org; Web: www.nacn-usa.org. Diana Ruzicka, Pres.

DARIEN. *Association of Our Lady of Mount Carmel*, 1317 N. Frontage Rd., Darien, 60561. Tel: 800-341-5950; Email: info@associationofmtcarmel.org; Web: www.associationofmtcarmel.org. Rev. William Harry, O.Carm., Pres.

National Shrine Museum of St. Therese of Lisieux, 8501 Bailey Rd., Darien, 60561. Tel: 630-969-3311; Fax: 630-969-5536; Email: webmaster@sainttherese.org; Web: www.saint-therese.org. Rev. Bernhard Bauerle, O.Carm., Shrine Dir.

Provincial Office of Lay Carmelites and Scapular Center, 8501 Bailey Rd., Darien, 60561. Tel: 630-969-5050; Fax: 630-969-7519; Email: laycarmelites@carmelnet.org; Web: laycarmelitespcm.org. Rev. Peter McGarry, O.-Carm., Prov. Delegate; Sr. Libby Dahlstrom, O.-Carm., Assoc. Prov. Delegate; Cindy Perazzo, Prov. Coord.

Society of the Little Flower (1923) 1313 N. Frontage Rd., Darien, 60561-5341. Tel: 630-968-9400; Fax: 630-968-9542; Email: webmaster@littleflower.org; Web: www.littleflower.org. Rev. Robert E. Colaresi, O.Carm., Dir.

FRANKFORT. *Presence Care @ Home*, 18927 Hickory Creek Dr., Mokena, 60448-8507. Tel: 708-478-7900 ; Fax: 708-478-5143; Email: Judy.MacPhersonSchumacher@presencehealth.org; Web: www.presencehealth.com. Michael Gordon, Pres.

KANKAKEE. *Azzarelli Clinic*, 341 S. St. Joseph Ave., Kankakee, 60901. Tel: 815-928-6093; Email: dgeistwhite@jp2kankakee.org. Delynn Geistwhite, Dir. Tot Asst. Annually 2,000; Total Staff 1.

Lisieux Pastoral Center, 371 N. St. Joseph Ave., Kankakee, 60901-2741. Tel: 815-939-2913; Email: ksw1153@outlook.com. Kathy Wade, Dir. Tot Asst. Annually 275; Total Staff 3.

Presence Heritage Day Break, 1025 N. Washington, Kankakee, 60901. Tel: 815-937-2447; Fax: 815-936-3245; Email: Judy.MacPhersonSchumacher@presencehealth.org; Web: www.presencehealth.org. Rebecca Barney, Admin.

Presence Life Connections dba Presence Heritage Day Break Bed Capacity 40; Tot Asst. Annually 11; Total Staff 9.

MOKENA. *Presence Life Connections*, 18927 Hickory Creek Dr., Ste. 300, Mokena, 60448-8507. Tel: 708-478-7900; Fax: 708-478-5143; Email: tiffany.buecher@ascension.org; Web: www.presencehealth.org. Michael Gordon, Pres.

MOMENCE. *B.G.S. Charitable Trust*, 114 W. Washington St., P.O. Box 736, Momence, 60954-0736. Tel: 815-472-3131; Fax: 815-472-6914; Email: judy@sjog-na.org. Michael Brown, Contact Person.

Hospitaller Order of St. John of God Province of the Good Shepherd in NA, Inc., 114 W. Washington St., P.O. Box 736, Momence, 60954. Tel: 815-472-3131; Fax: 815-472-6914; Email: judy@sjog-na.org; Web: www.sjog-na.org. Bro. Justin Howson, O.H., Prov.

Little Brothers of the Good Shepherd, Inc., 114 W. Washington St., P.O. Box 736, Momence, 60954. Tel: 815-472-3131; Fax: 815-472-6914; Email: judy@sjog-na.org; Web: www.sjog-na.org. Bro. Richard MacPhee, Treas. Gen.

NAPERVILLE. *Catholic CEO Healthcare Connection (CCHC)* (1985) 50 S. Main St., Ste. 200, Naperville, 60540. Tel: 630-352-2220; Fax: 630-352-2301; Email: roger.butler@cchcforum.org. Mr. Roger N. Butler, Exec. Dir.

OAK BROOK. *Mayslake Center II, N.F.P.*, 1801 35th St., Oak Brook, 60523. Tel: 630-850-8232; Fax: 630-850-8233; Email: kmaxwell@mayslake.com. Mr. Michael A. Frigo, Pres. & CEO.

MV Benevolent Fund, Inc. (2003) 1801 35th St., Oak Brook, 60523. Tel: 630-850-8232; Fax: 630-850-8233; Email: kmaxwell@mayslake.com. Mr. Michael A. Frigo, Pres. & CEO.

ROMEOVILLE. *Charitable Trust of the Brothers of the Christian Schools*, 1205 Windham Pkwy., Romeoville, 60446-1679. Tel: 630-378-2900; Fax: 630-378-2501; Email: info@cbservices.org; Web: www.cbservices.org. Michael Quirk, CEO.

Christian Brothers Employee Benefit Trust, 1205 Windham Pkwy., Romeoville, 60446-1679. Tel: 630-378-2900; Fax: 630-378-2501; Email: info@cbservices.org; Web: www.cbservices.org. Michael Quirk, CEO.

Christian Brothers Employee Retirement Plan Trust, 1205 Windham Pkwy., Romeoville, 60446-1679. Tel: 630-378-2900; Fax: 630-378-2501; Email: info@cbservices.org; Web: www.cbservices.org. Michael Quirk, CEO.

Christian Brothers Religious Medical Trust, 1205 Windham Pkwy., Romeoville, 60446-1679. Tel: 630-378-2900; Fax: 630-378-2501; Email: info@cbservices.org; Web: www.cbservices.org. Michael Quirk, CEO.

Christian Brothers Retirement Savings Plan Trust, 1205 Windham Pkwy., Romeoville, 60446-1679. Tel: 630-378-2900; Fax: 630-378-2501; Email: info@cbservices.org; Web: www.cbservices.org. Michael Quirk, CEO.

**Christian Brothers Services*, 1205 Windham Pkwy., Romeoville, 60446-1679. Tel: 630-378-2900; Fax: 630-378-2501; Email: info@cbservices.org; Web: www.cbservices.org. Bro. Michael Quirk, F.S.C., Pres. & CEO.

Religious & Charitable Risk Pooling Trust of the Brothers of the Christian Schools, 1205 Windham Pkwy., Romeoville, 60446-1679. Tel: 630-378-2900; Fax: 630-378-2501; Email: info@cbservices.org; Web: www.cbservices.org. Michael Quirk, CEO.

WESTMONT. *The League of the Miraculous Infant Jesus of Prague*, P.O. Box 1045, Westmont, 60559-8245. Tel: 800-447-3436; Email: info@infantprague.org. Very Rev. William Harry, O.Carm., Dir.

WEST CHICAGO. **The Society of St. Vincent de Paul of the Joliet Diocesan Council, Inc.*, 213 Main St., West Chicago, 60185. Tel: 630-293-9755; Fax: 630-293-9881; Email: svdpjoliet@sbcglobal.net. Deacon William Thomas, Dir.

WHEATON. *Assisi Homes of Illinois, Inc.* (1974) 2126 W. Roosevelt Rd., Wheaton, 60187-0667. Melissa Clayton, Vice Pres. Units 65.

**Assisi Homes - LaSalle Manor Inc.*, 1135 10th St., LaSalle, 61301. Tel: 630-909-6900; Fax: 630-909-6933; Email: mhingtgen@mercyhousing.org; Web: www.mercyhousing.org. Melissa Clayton, Vice Pres.

Canticle Place, Inc. (1994) 26 W. 105 Roosevelt Rd., Wheaton, 60187. Tel: 630-665-9100; Fax: 630-665-9357; Email: mhingtgen@mercyhousing.org; Web: www.mercyhousing.org. Melissa Clayton, Vice Pres. Units 12.

Franciscan Health & Education Corp., Inc., 26 W. 171 Roosevelt Rd., P.O. Box 667, Wheaton, 60187. Tel: 630-909-6600; Fax: 630-462-7148; Email: joliverio@wfsisters.org. Sr. Melanie Paradis, O.S.F., Pres.

Franciscan Ministries, Inc. (1983) Property & Mailing Address: 26 W. 171 Roosevelt Rd., P.O. Box 667, Wheaton, 60187-0667. Tel: 630-909-6900; Fax: 630-462-7148; Email: joliverio@wfsisters.org; Web: www.wheatonfranciscan.org. John D. Oliverio, Pres.

Institute of the Blessed Virgin Mary Charitable Trust, P.O. Box 508, Wheaton, 60187. Tel: 630-653-6113; Fax: 630-653-4886; Email: ibvmbarb@aol.com; Web: www.ibvm.us. Sr. Barbara Nelson, Treas.

Wheaton Franciscan Services, Inc. (1983) 26 W. 171 Roosevelt Rd., P.O. Box 667, Wheaton, 60187. Tel: 630-909-6600; Fax: 630-462-7148; Email: joliverio@wfsisters.org; Web: www.wheatonfranciscan.org. John D. Oliverio, Pres. & CEO.

RELIGIOUS INSTITUTES OF MEN REPRESENTED IN THE DIOCESE

For further details refer to the corresponding bracketed number in the Religious Institutes of Men or Women section.

[0140]—*The Augustinians* (Mother of Good Counsel Prov.)—O.S.A.
[0200]—*Benedictine Monks*—O.S.B.
[0330]—*Brothers of the Christian Schools* (Midwest Prov.)—F.S.C.
[0270]—*Carmelite Fathers & Brothers* (Prov. of Pure Heart of Mary)—O.Carm.
[0275]—*Carmelites of Mary Immaculate*—C.M.I.
[1320]—*Clerics of St. Viator*—C.S.V.
[0310]—*Congregation of Christian Brothers*—C.F.C.
[1080]—*Congregation of the Resurrection*—C.R.
[0540]—*Franciscan Missionary Brothers of the Sacred Heart of Jesus*—O.S.F.
[0520]—*Franciscans* (Order of Friars Minor, Sacred Heart Prov.)—O.F.M.
[0670]—*Hospitaller Brothers of St. John of God*—O.H.
[]—*Legionaries of Christ*—L.C.
[0740]—*Marian Fathers* (Prov. of St. Casimir)—M.I.C.
[1065]—*Priestly Fraternity of St. Peter*—F.S.S.P.
[0610]—*Priests of the Congregation of Holy Cross*—C.S.C.
[1260]—*Society of Christ*—S.Ch.
[0690]—*Society of Jesus* (Chicago, St. Louis Prov. & Wisconsin)—S.J.
[2010]—*Society of the Precious Blood*—C.PP.S.

RELIGIOUS INSTITUTES OF WOMEN REPRESENTED IN THE DIOCESE

[160]—*Augustinian Nuns of Contemplative Life*—O.S.A.
[0230]—*Benedictine Sisters of Pontifical Jurisdiction* (Lisle, IL)—O.S.B.
[0330]—*Carmelite Sisters for the Aged and Infirm* (Germantown, NY)—O.Carm.
[0400]—*Congregation of Our Lady of Mount Carmel* (Lacombe, LA)—O.Carm.
[3110]—*Congregation of Our Lady of the Retreat in the Cenacle*—R.C.
[1070]—*Congregation of St. Cecilia*—O.P.
[3710]—*Congregation of the Sisters of Saint Agnes*—C.S.A.
[3832]—*Congregation of the Sisters of St. Joseph*—C.S.J.

[1710]—*Congregation of the Third Order of St. Francis of Mary Immaculate, Joliet, IL*—O.S.F.
[1070-03]—*Dominican Sisters* (Sinsinawa)—O.P.
[1070-13]—*Dominican Sisters* (Adrian)—O.P.
[1070-10]—*Dominican Sisters* (Springfield)—O.P.
[1450]—*Franciscan Sisters of the Sacred Heart* (Frankfort)—O.S.F.
[1240]—*Franciscan Sisters, Daughters of the Sacred Hearts of Jesus and Mary* (Wheaton)—O.S.F.
[1910]—*Hermanas Josefinas*—H.J.
[2370]—*Institute of the Blessed Virgin Mary (Loretto Sisters)*—I.B.V.M.
[2575]—*Institute of the Sisters of Mercy of the Americas* (Chicago, IL)—R.S.M.
[3570]—*Mantellate Sisters, Servants of Mary* (Plainfield, IL)—O.S.M.
[2865]—*Missionaries of the Sacred Heart of Jesus & Our Lady of Guadalupe*—M.S.C.Gpe.
[2084]—*Missionary Sisters of Christ the King*—M.Ch. R.
[]—*Missionary Sisters of the Holy Family* (Komorrow-Warsaw, Poland)—M.S.F.
[3050]—*Oblate Sisters of the Sacred Heart*—O.S.H.J.
[3760]—*Order of St. Clare*—P.C.C.
[3230]—*Poor Handmaids of Jesus Christ*—P.H.J.C.
[2970]—*School Sisters of Notre Dame* (Chicago Prov.)—S.S.N.D.
[1680]—*School Sisters of St. Francis* (U.S. Prov.)—O.S.F.
[3590]—*Servants of Mary* (Ladysmith, WI)—O.S.M.
[3520]—*Servants of the Holy Heart of Mary*—S.S.C.M.
[]—*Sisters for the Christian Community*—S.F.C.C.
[0460]—*Sisters of Charity of Incarnate Word*—C.C.V.I.
[0430]—*Sisters of Charity of the Blessed Virgin Mary*—B.V.M.
[2350]—*Sisters of Living Word*—S.L.W.
[3000]—*Sisters of Notre Dame de Namur* (Cincinnati Prov.)—S.N.D.deN.
[3360]—*Sisters of Providence of Saint Mary-of-the-Woods, IN*—S.P.
[1705]—*The Sisters of St. Francis of Assisi* (St. Francis)—O.S.F.
[1520]—*Sisters of St. Francis of Christ the King*—S.S.F.C.R.
[1570]—*Sisters of St. Francis of Dubuque* (Iowa)—O.S.F.
[]—*Sisters of St. Francis of the Neumann Communities* (Syracuse, NY)—O.S.F.
[3930]—*Sisters of St. Joseph of the Third Order of St. Francis* (Prov. of Immaculate Conception)—S.S.J.-T.O.S.F.
[]—*Sisters of the Blessed Korean Martyrs*—S.K.M.
[2980]—*Sisters of the Congregation de Notre Dame*—C.N.D.
[1720]—*Sisters of the Third Order Regular of St. Francis of the Congregation of Our Lady of Lourdes* (Rochester, MN)—O.S.F.
[2150]—*Sisters Servants of the Immaculate Heart of Mary*—I.H.M.
[1890]—*Society of Helpers*—H.H.S.
[]—*Trinitarian Daughters of the Mother of God* Columbia—H.M.D.

DIOCESAN CEMETERIES

JOLIET. *SS. Cyril and Methodius Cemetery*, Rte. 6 Maple Rd., Joliet, 60432. Tel: 815-886-0750; Fax: 815-886-8711; Email: eholloway@dioceseofjoliet.org; Web: www.dioceseofjoliet.org/cemeteries. Eric Holloway, Dir.

Holy Cross Cemetery, Theodore St., 60403. Tel: 815-886-0750; Fax: 815-886-8711; Email: eholloway@dioceseofjoliet.org. Eric Holloway, Dir.

St. John the Baptist Cemetery, Ruby St. & Clements St., Joliet, 60435. Tel: 815-886-0750; Fax: 815-886-8711; Email: eholloway@dioceseofjoliet.org; Web: www.dioceseofjoliet.org/cemeteries. Eric Holloway, Dir.

St. Mary Nativity Cemetery, Caton Farm Rd. & Oakland Ave., 60435. Tel: 815-886-0750; Fax: 815-886-8711; Email: eholloway@dioceseofjoliet.org; Web: www.dioceseofjoliet.org/cemeteries. Eric Holloway, Dir.

Mount Olivet Cemetery, 1320 E. Cass St., Joliet, 60432. Tel: 815-726-7444; Fax: 815-726-7468; Email: eholloway@dioceseofjoliet.org; Web: www.dioceseofjoliet.org/cemeteries. Eric Holloway, Dir.

St. Patrick Cemetery, Hunter St. & Jefferson St., Joliet, 60436. Tel: 815-886-0750; Fax: 815-886-8711; Email: eholloway@dioceseofjoliet.org; Web: www.dioceseofjoliet.org/cemeteries. Eric Holloway, Dir.

BOURBONNAIS. *All Saints Cemetery*, 1839 W. Rte. 102, Bourbonnais, 60914. Tel: 815-933-2342; Tel: 815-886-0750; Fax: 815-937-0166; Fax: 815-886-8711; Email: eholloway@dioceseofjoliet.org; Web: www.dioceseofjoliet.org/cemeteries. Eric Holloway, Dir.

Maternity/BVM Cemetery, Canterberry Ln., Bourbonnais, 60914. Tel: 815-933-2342; Fax: 815-937-0166; Email: eholloway@dioceseofjoliet.org; Web: www.dioceseofjoliet.org/cemeteries. Eric Holloway, Dir.

CAROL STREAM. *St. Stephen Cemetery*, St. Charles Rd., Carol Stream, 60188. Tel: 815-886-0750; Fax: 815-886-8711; Email: eholloway@dioceseofjoliet.org; Web: www.dioceseofjoliet.org/cemeteries. Eric Holloway, Dir. Merged as Holy Family Cemetery.

DOWNERS GROVE. *Holy Family Cemetery*, 1501 Hobson Rd., Downers Grove, 60517. Tel: 815-886-0750; Fax: 815-886-8711; Email: eholloway@dioceseofjoliet.org; Web: www.dioceseofjoliet.org/cemeteries. Eric Holloway, Dir.

ELMHURST. *St. Mary Cemetery*, 310 W. Alexander Blvd., Elmhurst, 60126. Tel: 630-668-3313; Fax: 630-668-0204; Email: eholloway@dioceseofjoliet.org; Web: www.dioceseofjoliet.org/cemeteries. Eric Holloway, Dir.

KANKAKEE. *Mt. Calvary Cemetery*, 2000 E. Court St., Kankakee, 60901. Tel: 815-933-2342; Fax: 815-937-0166; Email: eholloway@dioceseofjoliet.org; Web: www.dioceseofjoliet.org/cemeteries. Eric Holloway, Dir.

St. Rose Cemetery, Rte. 50, Kankakee, 60901. Tel: 815-933-2342; Tel: 815-886-0750; Fax: 815-937-0166; Email: eholloway@dioceseofjoliet.org. Eric Holloway, Dir.

LOCKPORT. *Calvary Cemetery*, Rte. 171 & High Rd., Lockport, 60441. Tel: 815-886-0750; Fax: 815-886-8711; Email: eholloway@dioceseofjoliet.org. Eric Holloway, Dir.

LOCKPORT SOUTH. *Lockport South Cemetery*, 16th St. & Washington St., Lockport, 60441. Tel: 815-886-0750; Fax: 815-886-8711; Email: eholloway@dioceseofjoliet.org. Eric Holloway, Dir.

LOMBARD. *St. Mary Cemetery*, Finley Rd., Lombard, 60148. Tel: 815-886-0750; Fax: 815-886-8711; Email: eholloway@dioceseofjoliet.org. Eric Holloway, Dir.

NAPERVILLE. *SS. Peter & Paul Cemetery*, Columbia St. & North Ave., Naperville, 60563. Tel: 630-668-3313; Fax: 630-668-0204; Email: eholloway@dioceseofjoliet.org; Web: www.dioceseofjoliet.org/cemeteries. Eric Holloway, Dir.

OSWEGO. *Risen Lord Cemetery*, 1501 Simons Rd., Oswego, 60543. Tel: 630-554-7590; Fax: 630-554-7592; Email: eholloway@dioceseofjoliet.org; Web: www.dioceseofjoliet.org/cemeteries. Eric Holloway, Dir.

ROMEOVILLE. *Catholic Cemeteries Monument Sales*, 200 W. Romeo Rd., Romeoville, 60446-2264. Tel: 815-886-0750; Fax: 815-886-8711; Email: eholloway@dioceseofjoliet.org; Web: www.dioceseofjoliet.org/cemeteries. Eric Holloway, Dir.

Resurrection Cemetery, 200 W. Romeo Rd., (135th) at Rt. 53, Romeoville, 60446. Tel: 815-886-0750; Fax: 815-886-8711; Email: eholloway@dioceseofjoliet.org; Web: www.dioceseofjoliet.org/cemeteries. Eric Holloway, Dir.

WHEATON. *Assumption Cemetery*, One S. 510 Winfield Rd., Wheaton, 60189. Tel: 630-668-3313; Tel: 815-886-0750; Fax: 630-668-0204; Fax: 815-886-8711; Email: eholloway@dioceseofjoliet.org; Web: www.dioceseofjoliet.org/cemeteries. Eric Holloway, Dir.

WINFIELD. *St. John the Baptist*, Garymills Rd. & Summit Dr., Winfield, 60190. Tel: 630-668-3313; Tel: 815-886-0750; Fax: 630-668-0204; Fax: 815-886-8711; Email: eholloway@dioceseofjoliet.org; Web: www.dioceseofjoliet.org/cemeteries. Eric Holloway, Dir.

NECROLOGY

† Norbeck, Ernest, (Retired), Died Mar. 7, 2018
† Settles, Dennis, (Retired), Died Sep. 16, 2018
† Sularz, Thomas, (Retired), Died Jul. 15, 2018
† White, Denis, (Retired), Died Dec. 4, 2018
† Wilkening, Henry, (Retired), Died Apr. 17, 2018

An asterisk (*) denotes an organization that has established tax-exempt status directly with the IRS and is not covered by the USCCB Group Ruling.

Diocese of Juneau

(Dioecesis Junellensis)

Most Reverend

ANDREW E. BELLISARIO, C.M.

Bishop of Juneau; ordained June 16, 1984; appointed Bishop of Juneau July 11, 2017; ordained and installed October 10, 2017. *Office: 415 Sixth St., #300, Juneau, AK 99801.*

Chancery: 415 Sixth St., #300, Juneau, AK 99801. Tel: 907-586-2227; Fax: 907-463-3237.

Web: www.dioceseofjuneau.org

Email: communication@dioceseofjuneau.org

ESTABLISHED JUNE 23, 1951.

Square Miles 37,566.

Corporate Title: "Corporation of the Catholic Bishop of Juneau."

Comprises the entire southeastern part of the State of Alaska known legally as The First Judicial District.

For legal titles of parishes and diocesan institutions, consult the Chancery Office.

STATISTICAL OVERVIEW

Personnel	
Bishop	1
Priests: Diocesan Active in Diocese	5
Priests: Diocesan Active Outside Diocese	2
Priests: Retired, Sick or Absent	2
Number of Diocesan Priests	9
Religious Priests in Diocese	3
Total Priests in Diocese	12
Permanent Deacons in Diocese	6
Parishes	
Parishes	9
With Resident Pastor:	
Resident Diocesan Priests	6
Resident Religious Priests	2
Without Resident Pastor:	
Administered by Priests	1
Missions	17

Welfare	
Catholic Hospitals	1
Total Assisted	10,462
Special Centers for Social Services	1
Total Assisted	10,000
Other Institutions	1
Total Assisted	15,000
Educational	
Diocesan Students in Other Seminaries	3
Total Seminarians	3
Elementary Schools, Diocesan and Parish	1
Total Students	80
Catechesis/Religious Education:	
High School Students	54
Elementary Students	287
Total Students under Catholic Instruction	424

Teachers in the Diocese:	
Lay Teachers	7
Vital Statistics	
Receptions into the Church:	
Infant Baptism Totals	53
Minor Baptism Totals	9
Adult Baptism Totals	8
Received into Full Communion	13
First Communions	69
Confirmations	55
Marriages:	
Catholic	11
Interfaith	5
Total Marriages	16
Deaths	23
Total Catholic Population	7,249
Total Population	75,000

Former Bishops—Most Revs. DERMOT O'FLANAGAN, D.D., ord. Aug. 27, 1929; appt. Bishop July 9, 1951; cons. Oct. 3, 1951; resigned June 19, 1968; appt. Titular Bishop of Trecalae; died Dec. 31, 1972; FRANCIS T. HURLEY, D.D., ord. June 16, 1951; appt. Titular Bishop of Daimlaig and Auxiliary of Juneau, Feb. 4, 1970; cons. March 19, 1970; Ordinary of See, July 20, 1971; appt. Archbishop of Anchorage, May 4, 1976; installed July 8, 1976; retired March 3, 2001; died Jan. 10, 2016; MICHAEL H. KENNY, D.D., ord. March 30, 1963; appt. March 20, 1979; cons. May 27, 1979; installed June 15, 1979; died Feb. 19, 1995; MICHAEL W. WARFEL, ord. April 26, 1980; appt. Nov. 19, 1996; installed Dec. 17, 1996; appt. Bishop of Great Falls-Billings Nov. 20, 2007.; EDWARD J. BURNS, ord. June 25, 1983; appt. Bishop of Juneau Jan. 19, 2009; ord. March 3, 2009; installed April 2, 2009; appt. Bishop of Dallas Dec. 13, 2016; installed Feb. 9, 2017.

Diocesan Offices

Chancery—415 Sixth St., #300, Juneau, 99801. Tel: 907-586-2227; Fax: 907-463-3237.

Vicar General/Chancellor—Rev. PATRICK J. TRAVERS, J.C.L., J.D., Tel: 907-723-7303; Email: pjtravers@att.net.

Administration—415 Sixth St., #300, Juneau, 99801. Tel: 907-586-2227; Fax: 907-463-3237.

Business Manager and Finance Officer—Deacon MIKE MONAGLE, Tel: 907-586-2227, Ext. 27.

Director of Administrative Services/Assistant to the Bishop—MS. ROBERTA IZZARD, Tel: 907-586-2227, Ext. 25.

Assistant to the Finance Officer—MS. RUTH VINCENT, Tel: 907-586-2227, Ext. 30.

Information Systems and Maintenance—MR. NEAL ARNOLD, Tel: 907-586-2227, Ext. 34.

Safe Environment and Victim Assistance Coordinator—MS. ROBERTA IZZARD, Tel: 907-586-2227, Ext. 25.

Director of Office of Communications—DOMINIQUE JOHNSON, Tel: 907-586-2227, Ext. 32.

Editor, Diocesan Publication "Southeast Alaska Catholic"—Tel: 907-586-2227, Ext. 32. DOMINIQUE JOHNSON.

Office of Ministries and Missions—415 Sixth St., #300, Juneau, 99801. Tel: 907-586-2227, Ext. 23; Fax: 907-463-3237. Deacon CHARLES H. ROHRBACHER, Dir., Tel: 907-586-2227, Ext. 29.

Shrine of St. Therese—JOSEPH SEHNERT, Exec. Dir., Tel: 907-586-2227, Ext. 24.

Office of Archives & Special Projects—MRS. PEGGY MATTSON, Tel: 907-586-2227, Ext. 31.

Diocesan Tribunal—9055 Atlin Dr., Juneau, 99801. Tel: 907-789-7330; Fax: 907-790-3430.

Judicial Vicar—Rev. PATRICK J. TRAVERS, J.C.L., J.D.

Tribunal Assistant and Notary—MR. CHARLES VANKIRK.

Defender of the Bond—DANIELA KNEPPER, J.C.L.

Advisory Bodies

College of Consultors—Revs. STEVEN P. GALLAGHER; PETER F. GORGES, (Retired); PERRY M. KENASTON; EDMUND J. PENISTEN; SCOTT R. SETTIMO; PATRICK J. TRAVERS, J.C.L., J.D.

Presbyteral Council—Revs. PATRICK T. CASEY, O.M.I.; STEVEN P. GALLAGHER; PETER F. GORGES, (Retired); PERRY M. KENASTON; EDMUND J. PENISTEN; SCOTT R. SETTIMO; PATRICK J. TRAVERS, J.C.L., J.D.; AUGUSTINE MINN, K.M.S.; DWIGHT HOEBERECHTS, O.M.I.

Finance Council—Deacon MIKE MONAGLE; MR. BRIAN GOETTLER; MR. HUGH GRANT; Revs. PATRICK J. TRAVERS, J.C.L., J.D.; PERRY M. KENASTON; JAMES DONAGHEY; LISA LINDEMAN; GREG SAMORAJSKI.

Shrine of Saint Therese Board—MRS. JANICE BURNS BUYARSKI; MR. BRIAN FLORY; Rev. PATRICK J. TRAVERS, J.C.L., J.D.; MS. NORA TONER; DOMINIQUE JOHNSON; LEORA HOUTARY; NICOLE MILLER; ANN KLAUSNER; JANET OLMSTEAD.

Review Board for the Protection of Children and Young People—MR. PAUL DESLOOVER; MRS. DEBORAH FAGNANT; MS. ANN TURNER OLSON; DR. DESTINY SARGEANT; DR. DOUGLAS SMITH, M.D.; Rev. PATRICK J. TRAVERS, J.C.L., J.D.; MRS. MARILYN MONAGLE; MR. NICK POLASKY; MRS. PAM MCANDREWS.

Other Catholic Agencies Operating Within the Diocese

Catholic Community Service, Inc.—419 Sixth St., Juneau, 99801. Tel: 907-463-6151.

Executive Director—ERIN WALKER-TOLLES.

Board of Directors—Most Rev. ANDREW E. BELLISARIO, C.M., Pres.; Rev. PATRICK J. TRAVERS, J.C.L., J.D., Ex Officio; MR. LARRY BUSSONE; MR. JON BOLLING; MS. JAN BURKE; MR. JAMES CARROLL; Deacon MICHAEL MONAGLE; MR. JOHN GREELY; MR. CHARLES HORAN; MS. PATRICIA DAVIDSON; MS. LORI ORTIZ; Deacon VINCENT G HANSEN; MARIA LISOWSKI; MR. CHRISTOPHER GIANOTTI.

Includes Southeast Senior Services; Child Care and Family Resources; and Hospice and Home Care of Juneau—

St. Vincent de Paul Society, Diocesan Council of Southeast Alaska, Inc.—8617 Teal St., Juneau, 99801. Tel: 907-789-5535.

General Manager—BRADLEY PERKINS.

**PeaceHealth Ketchikan Medical Center—3100 Tongass Ave., Ketchikan, 99901.* Tel: 907-225-5171 ; Fax: 907-228-8322.

Chief Administrative Officer—LIZ DUNNE, Pres. & CEO.

CLERGY, PARISHES, MISSIONS AND PAROCHIAL SCHOOLS

CITY AND BOROUGH OF JUNEAU

1—CATHEDRAL OF THE NATIVITY OF THE BLESSED VIRGIN MARY

416 Fifth St., 99801. Tel: 907-586-1513; Email: cathedral@dioceseofjuneau.org. Rev. Patrick T.

Casey, O.M.I.; Deacon Charles H. Rohrbacher; Sr. Marie Lucek, O.P., Pastoral Assoc.
Catechesis Religious Program—
Tel: 907-586-1317; Email: cathedraldre@acsalaska.net. Bridget Goertzen, D.R.E. Students 46.
2—ST. PAUL THE APOSTLE
9055 Atlin Dr., 99801. Tel: 907-789-7307, Ext. 2; Email: stpauls@ptialaska.net; Web: www.stpaulsjuneau.org. Rev. Michael D. Galbraith, Admin.; Deacons Gary Horton; Mike Monagle.
Catechesis Religious Program—
Tel: 907-789-7303. Kimberly Watt, D.R.E. Students 167.

OUTSIDE THE CITY AND BOROUGH OF JUNEAU

HAINES, SACRED HEART
Box 326, Haines, 99827. Tel: 907-766-2241; Fax: 907-766-2275; Email: sacredheart@aptalaska.net; Web: www.sacredhearthaines.org. Rev. Perry M. Kenaston; Deacon Vincent G Hansen.
Missions—St. Therese of the Child Jesus—P.O. Box 496, Skagway, 99840. Tel: 907-983-2271.
Kluckwan.
KETCHIKAN, HOLY NAME
433 Jackson St., Ketchikan, 99901.
Tel: 907-225-2570; Email: churchoffice@holynamektn.org. Revs. Patrick J. Travers, J.C.L., J.D.; Augustine Minn, K.M.S.
Corporation of the Catholic Bishop of Juneau
School—Holy Name School, (Grades 1-6),
Tel: 907-225-2400; Email: schooloffice@holynamektn.org; Web: www.holynameschoolketchikan.org. Nicole Miller, Prin. Lay Teachers 7; Students 82.
Catechesis Religious Program—Fax: 907-225-2120; Email: v.marcantonio@holynamektn.org. Vincent Marcantonio, D.R.E. Students 45.
Mission—Holy Family, Metlakatla.
KLAWOCK, ST. JOHN BY THE SEA
6840 Michigan Ave., Klawock, 99925.
Tel: 907-755-2345; Email: saintjohnbythesea@dioceseofjuneau.org; Web: www.dioceseofjuneau.org/saint-john-by-the-sea-parish. P.O. Box 245, Klawock, 99925. Rev. Edmund J. Penisten.
Catechesis Religious Program—Students 12.
PETERSBURG, ST. CATHERINE OF SIENA
306 N. Third St., P.O. Box 508, Petersburg, 99833. Web: www.stcatherineofsienapetersburg.com. Rev. Steven P. Gallagher.
SITKA, ST. GREGORY OF NAZIANZEN
P.O. Box 495, Sitka, 99835-0495. Tel: 907-747-8371; Email: saintgregory@dioceseofjuneau.org. Revs. Andrew Sensenig, O.M.I.; Peter F. Gorges, Pastor Emeritus, (Retired).
Mission—Kake.
WRANGELL, ST. ROSE OF LIMA
120 Church St., Box 469, Wrangell, 99929. Rev. Steven P. Gallagher.
Res.: Box 469, Wrangell, 99929. Tel: 907-874-3771; Email: Strosewrg@gmail.com.
Catechesis Religious Program—Tel: 907-470-4220; Email: trophymtn@aol.com. Peggy Mitchell, D.R.E.
YAKUTAT, ST. ANN
P.O. Box 323, Yakutat, 99689. Tel: 907-784-3287; Email: commissions@dioceseofjuneau.org. Deacon Charles H. Rohrbacher, Dir. Northern Missions.

DIOCESAN MISSIONS

JUNEAU, DIOCESAN MISSIONS
415 Sixth St., Ste. 300, 99801. Tel: 907-586-2227; Email: commissions@dioceseofjuneau.org. Deacon Charles H. Rohrbacher, Dir. Estimated Number of Catholics 50.
ELFIN COVE, Deacon Charles H. Rohrbacher, Dir.
EXCURSION INLET, Deacon Charles H. Rohrbacher, Dir.
GUSTAVUS, Deacon Charles H. Rohrbacher, Dir.
SACRED HEART, Hoonah. Deacon Charles H. Rohrbacher, Dir.
KAKE, Deacon Charles H. Rohrbacher, Dir.
PELICAN, Deacon Charles H. Rohrbacher, Dir.
ST. FRANCIS, Tenakee Springs. Deacon Charles H. Rohrbacher, Dir.

On Duty Outside the Diocese:
Rev.—
Saba, Joseph, 5660 W. Placita Del Risco, Tucson, AZ 85745.

Retired:
Revs.—
Gorges, Peter F., (Retired), St. Gregory, P.O. Box 495, Sitka, 99835-0495
Konda, Bernard, (Retired), Priests Retirement Center, 6900 E. 45th St. N. F-1, Bel Aire, KS 67226.

Permanent Deacons:
Hansen, Vincent G, Sacred Heart, Haines
Horton, Gary, St. Paul the Apostle, Juneau
Matthews, Ron, St. Gregory Nazianzen, Sitka
Monagle, Michael, St. Paul the Apostle, Juneau
Olmstead, Steven B., St. Paul the Apostle, Juneau
Rohrbacher, Charles H., Cathedral of the Nativity of the Blessed Virgin Mary, Juneau.

INSTITUTIONS LOCATED IN DIOCESE

[A] CONVENTS AND RESIDENCES FOR SISTERS

JUNEAU. *St. Joseph Convent*, Mailing Address: 416 5th St., 99801. 2971 Douglas Hwy., 99801.
Tel: 907-586-1340. Ms. Roberta Izzard, Contact Person. Intercommunity residence of various religious orders of women.

RELIGIOUS INSTITUTES OF MEN REPRESENTED IN THE DIOCESE
For further details refer to the corresponding bracketed number in the Religious Institutes of Men or Women section.
[0910]—*Oblates of Mary Immaculate*—O.M.I.
[]—*Korean Missionary Society*—K.M.S.

An asterisk (*) denotes an organization that has established tax-exempt status directly with the IRS and is not covered by the USCCB Group Ruling.

Diocese of Kalamazoo

(Dioecesis Kalamazuensis)

Most Reverend

PAUL J. BRADLEY

Bishop of Kalamazoo; ordained May 1, 1971; appointed Titular Bishop of Afufenia and Auxiliary Bishop of Pittsburgh December 16, 2004; ordained February 2, 2005; appointed Bishop of Kalamazoo April 6, 2009; installed June 5, 2009.

Most Reverend

JAMES A. MURRAY

Retired Bishop of Kalamazoo; ordained June 7, 1958; appointed Bishop of Kalamazoo November 18, 1997; ordained and installed January 27, 1998; retired April 6, 2009. Email: jmurray@dioceseofkalamazoo.org.

ESTABLISHED JULY 21, 1971.

Square Miles 5,337.

Comprises the following nine Counties in the State of Michigan: Allegan, Barry, Berrien, Branch, Calhoun, Cass, Kalamazoo, St. Joseph and Van Buren.

For legal titles of parishes and diocesan institutions, consult the Diocesan Pastoral Center.

Diocesan Pastoral Center: 215 N. Westnedge Ave., Kalamazoo, MI 49007-3760. Tel: 269-349-8714; Fax: 269-349-6440.

Web: dioceseofkalamazoo.org

STATISTICAL OVERVIEW

Personnel	
Bishop	1
Retired Bishops	1
Priests: Diocesan Active in Diocese	38
Priests: Diocesan Active Outside Diocese	3
Priests: Retired, Sick or Absent	18
Number of Diocesan Priests	59
Religious Priests in Diocese	14
Total Priests in Diocese	73
Extern Priests in Diocese	7
Permanent Deacons in Diocese	54
Total Brothers	1
Total Sisters	161
Parishes	
Parishes	46
With Resident Pastor:	
Resident Diocesan Priests	23
Resident Religious Priests	7
Without Resident Pastor:	
Administered by Priests	7
Administered by Religious Women	2
Completely Vacant	7
Missions	13
Pastoral Centers	1
Professional Ministry Personnel:	
Brothers	1
Sisters	10
Lay Ministers	169
Welfare	
Catholic Hospitals	2
Total Assisted	4,955,299
Homes for the Aged	3
Total Assisted	827
Specialized Homes	16
Total Assisted	400
Special Centers for Social Services	7
Total Assisted	29,557
Educational	
Diocesan Students in Other Seminaries	6
Total Seminarians	6
High Schools, Diocesan and Parish	3
Total Students	437
Elementary Schools, Diocesan and Parish	22
Total Students	1,761
Catechesis/Religious Education:	
High School Students	525
Elementary Students	2,302
Total Students under Catholic Instruction	5,031
Teachers in the Diocese:	
Priests	3
Lay Teachers	118
Vital Statistics	
Receptions into the Church:	
Infant Baptism Totals	808
Minor Baptism Totals	73
Adult Baptism Totals	92
Received into Full Communion	113
First Communions	1,048
Confirmations	849
Marriages:	
Catholic	168
Interfaith	85
Total Marriages	253
Deaths	753
Total Catholic Population	95,831
Total Population	959,496

Former Bishops—Most Revs. PAUL V. DONOVAN, D.D., ord. May 20, 1950; appt. Bishop of Kalamazoo June 15, 1971; ordained and installed July 21, 1971; resigned Nov. 22, 1994; died April 28, 2011.; ALFRED J. MARKIEWICZ, D.D., ord. June 6, 1953; appt. Titular Bishop of Afufenia and Auxiliary to the Bishop of Rockville Centre, July 7, 1986; ord. Bishop, Sept. 17, 1986; appt. Bishop of Kalamazoo, Nov. 22, 1994; installed Jan. 31, 1995; died Jan. 9, 1997; JAMES A. MURRAY, J.C.L., ord. June 7, 1958; appt. Bishop of Kalamazoo Nov. 18, 1997; ord. and installed Jan. 27, 1998; retired April 6, 2009.

Vicars General—Rev. Msgrs. MICHAEL D. HAZARD, V.G., St. Joseph Church, 936 Lake St., Kalamazoo, 49001. Tel: 269-343-6256; Fax: 269-343-1214; MICHAEL A. OSBORN, V.G., J.C.D., Moderator of the Curia, Diocese of Kalamazoo: 215 N. Westnedge Ave., Kalamazoo, 49007. Tel: 269-903-0185; Fax: 269-349-6440.

Diocesan Pastoral Center—215 N. Westnedge Ave., Kalamazoo, 49007-3760. Tel: 269-349-8714; Fax: 269-349-6440; Web: dioceseofkalamazoo.org. Office Hours: 8:30-4.

Chancellor—MR. MICHAEL R. EMMONS, 215 N. Westnedge Ave., Kalamazoo, 49007-3760. Tel: 269-903-0213; Fax: 269-349-6440.

Vicar for Canonical Concerns—Rev. Msgr. THOMAS A. MARTIN, J.C.D., 215 N. Westnedge Ave., Kalamazoo, 49007-3760. Tel: 269-903-0179; Fax: 269-349-6440.

Direct Communications regarding Marriage Dispensations to Vicar for Canonical Concerns. *Diocesan Pastoral Center, 215 N. Westnedge Ave., Kalamazoo, 49007-3760.* Tel: 269-903-0179; Fax: 269-349-6440.

Vicar for Clergy—St. Joseph Parish, 220 Church St., St. Joseph, 49085. Tel: 269-983-1575. Very Rev. ROBERT F. CREAGAN, E.V., V.F.

Vicars Forane—Very Revs. JAMES RICHARDSON, M.A., V.F., Central Deanery; MARK VYVERMAN, V.F., Eastern Deanery; ROBERT F. CREAGAN, E.V., V.F., Western Deanery; FABIO H. GARZON, V.F., Northern Deanery.

Diocesan Tribunal—Diocesan Pastoral Center, 215 N. Westnedge Ave., Kalamazoo, 49007-3760. Tel: 269-903-0189; Fax: 269-349-6440.

Judicial Vicar—Rev. Msgr. THOMAS A. MARTIN, J.C.D.

Defender of the Bond—Rev. MICHAEL A. HACK, J.C.D.

Assessor—Rev. KENNETH W. SCHMIDT, J.C.D., M.A., L.P.C., N.L.L.

Promoter of Justice—Rev. Msgr. MICHAEL A. OSBORN, V.G., J.C.D.

Judge—Deacon HALLIE BOHAN, J.C.L.

Court Experts—MRS. CARLA FALLON, M.A., L.L.P.; MRS. PHYLLIS FLORIAN, Psy.D., L.P.; MRS. JILLIAN PEYERK.

Chief Notary and Administrative Assistant—MRS. PATRICIA TULEJA.

Ecclesiastical Notary/Instructor—MRS. PATRICIA TULEJA.

Direct communications regarding Marriage Dispensations to: Vicar for Canonical Concerns *Diocesan Pastoral Center, 215 N. Westnedge, Kalamazoo, 49007-3760.* Tel: 269-903-0179; Fax: 269-349-6440.

Diocesan Consultors—Rev. Msgrs. MICHAEL D. HAZARD, V.G.; THOMAS A. MARTIN, J.C.D.; MICHAEL A. OSBORN, V.G., J.C.D.; Very Revs. ROBERT F. CREAGAN, E.V., V.F.; MARK J. VYVERMAN, V.F.; Revs. KENNETH W. SCHMIDT, J.C.D., M.A., L.P.C., N.L.L.; LAWRENCE M. FARRELL.

Presbyteral Council Members—Rev. Msgrs. MICHAEL D. HAZARD, V.G.; THOMAS A. MARTIN, J.C.D.; MICHAEL A. OSBORN, V.G., J.C.D.; Rev. LAWRENCE M. FARRELL; Very Rev. MARK J. VYVERMAN, V.F.; Rev. KENNETH W. SCHMIDT, J.C.D., M.A., L.P.C., N.L.L.; Very Rev. JAMES RICHARDSON, M.A., V.F.; Rev. FRANCIS A. MAROTTI; Very Revs. ROBERT F. CREAGAN, E.V., V.F.; FABIO H. GARZON, V.F.; Revs. JOHN PETER AMBROSE, M.S.F.S., (India); WILLIAM JACOBS JR., S.S.; THOMAS MCNALLY.

Staff to the Presbyteral Council—MR. MICHAEL R. EMMONS; MR. T. EDWARD CAREY JR.

Diocesan Finance Council—Rev. WILLIAM JACOBS JR., Sr. Parochial Vicar, St. Catherine of Siena, Portage; Rev. Msgr. MICHAEL A. OSBORN, V.G., J.C.D., Rector, St. Augustine Cathedral; Deacon ALFRED BELL, Retired Bookkeeper for St. Catherine of Siena, Portage; Sr. ELIZABETH VEENHUIS, C.S.J., Former Pres. Sisters of St.

Joseph, Kalamazoo; MR. ROBERT WHEELER, Vice Pres. A.M. Todd; MR. JERRY B. LOVE, CPA, Arcadia Investment Mgmt. Corp., Kalamazoo; MRS. BOBBIE OTTO, CPA, South Haven, MI. Staff to Finance Council: MR. MICHAEL R. EMMONS, Chancellor, Diocese of Kalamazoo; MR. T. EDWARD CAREY JR., CFO.

Diocesan Pastoral Council Membership—

Parish Members—MR. CHARLES YOUNG, Chm., St. Ann, Augusta.; CECILIA GARCIA, San Felipe de Jesus, Fennville; MARTY KLUBECK, St. Mary, Niles.; SARAH ROBINSON, St, Philip, Battle Creek.; BECKY CARR, St. Ambrose, Parchment.; JOHN ARMOCK, St. Mary Visitation, Byron Ctr.; MS. MICHELLE SMITH, St. Augustine Cathedral, Kalamazoo.; KATHI LOVELL, St. Martin of Tours, Vicksburg.; LIZBETH FUENTES, St. Joseph, Kalamazoo.; GABRIEL ALVEZ, Holy Angels, Sturgis.; MIKE ZENK, St. Anthony, Buchanan.; DAVID RHOA, St. Mary, Paw Paw.; MICHAEL LAH, Ss. John & Bernard, Benton Harbor.; SANDRA FRANCO, Immaculate Conception, Hartford.; RAYITO TAPIA, Holy Angels, Sturgis.; JAN KUHTIC, St. Therese, Wayland.; PHIL GREEN, St. Rose of Lima, Hastings.; BILL BOYD, Our Lady Queen of Peace, Bridgman.; BECKY BORGLIN, St. Mary of the Lake, New Buffalo.; NORB STROBEL, St. Charles Borromeo, Coldwater.; STEVE HAGEMAN, St. Mary, Marshall.; JOHN HARTMAN, Our Lady of the Lake, Edwardsburg.; SHARON HARTMAN, Our Lady of the Lake, Edwardsburg.; JIM GRACE, St. Thomas More, Kalamazoo.; MARY REDMOND, St. Monica, Kalamazoo.; COLLEEN SEMLER, St. Catherine of Siena, Portage.; MIKE SCHUMACHER, Immaculate Conception, Three Rivers.

Religious Member—SR. KATHLEEN KAISER, C.S.J.

Clergy Members—Rev. Msgrs. MICHAEL D. HAZARD, V.G., St. Joseph, Kalamazoo.; THOMAS MARTIN, St. Augustine, Kalamazoo.; MICHAEL A. OSBORN, V.G., J.C.D.; Deacon JASON AIELLO, St. Monica, Kalamazoo.

Diocesan Staff Members—MRS. VICKI CESSNA; MR. TIMOTHY LIESER; MR. MICHAEL R. EMMONS; MRS. MARGARET ERICH; MR. T. EDWARD CAREY JR.; MR. JAMIN HEROLD; MR. THOMAS DOWDALL.

Diocesan Secretariats and Offices

All Diocesan Offices are located at 215 N. Westnedge Ave., Kalamazoo, MI 49007 unless otherwise noted.

Office of the Bishop—

Bishop—Most Rev. PAUL J. BRADLEY, Tel: 269-903-0153.

Executive Assistant—MRS. LEXIE SHOEMAKER-FATH, Tel: 269-903-0153.

Chancellor—MR. MICHAEL R. EMMONS, Tel: 269-903-0213.

Chief Finance Officer—MR. T. EDWARD CAREY JR., Tel: 269-903-0191.

Director of Stewardship and Development— Tel: 269-903-0196. MR. THOMAS DOWDALL; MRS. KRISTIN CORRA, Support Specialist, Tel: 269-903-0150.

Vicars General—Rev. Msgrs. MICHAEL D. HAZARD, V.G., Tel: 269-343-6256; MICHAEL A. OSBORN, V.G., J.C.D., Tel: 269-903-0185.

Judicial Vicar—Rev. Msgr. THOMAS MARTIN, Tel: 269-903-0179.

Vicar for Clergy—Very Rev. ROBERT F. CREAGAN, E.V., V.F., Tel: 269-327-5165.

General Secretariat—

General Secretary/Executive Director of Administration/Moderator of the Curia—Rev. Msgr. MICHAEL A. OSBORN, V.G., J.C.D., Tel: 269-903-0185.

Office of Vocations—Rev. Msgr. MICHAEL A. OSBORN, V.G., J.C.D.; Rev. THOMAS MCNALLY, Tel: 269-903-0203; MRS. ANNETTE BRENNAN, Support Specialist, Tel: 269-903-0203.

Business Office—MR. T. EDWARD CAREY JR., CFO, Tel: 269-903-0191; MS. TAMMI WACHTERHAUSER, Accounting Clerk, Tel: 269-903-0211; MRS. JEANNETTE MATTHEIS, Bishop's Annual Appeal/ Assoc. Account Clerk, Tel: 269-903-0187; MR. JIM WARREN, Sr. Accountant, Tel: 269-903-0149.

Deacon Formation—Rev. GERMAN PEREZ-DIAZ, Ph. D., Dir., Tel: 269-903-0151. Assistant Directors: Rev. JOSE HARO; Deacon DAVID GUIDO.

Deacon Personnel—Deacon JOHN RYDER, Dir., Tel: 269-903-0169. Associate Director: Deacon JAMES MELLEN, Tel: 269-838-3078.

Immigration Assistance Program—MRS. SAMANTHA LINDBERG, J.D., Dir., Tel: 269-903-0135.

Support Specialist—MS. KARINA MAZEI-PUNG, Tel: 269-903-0137.

Priestly Life and Ministry—Rev. KENNETH W. SCHMIDT, J.C.D., M.A., L.P.C., N.L.L., Tel: 269-381-8917.

Victim Assistance Coordinator—Deacon PATRICK HALL, Tel: 269-903-0175.

Worship & Liturgy—MR. MICHAEL R. EMMONS, Tel: 269-903-0213.

Additional Key Responsibility Areas: Catholic Community Center, Clergy Personnel, Facilities Management, Human Resources, Information Technology, Catholic Cemeteries.

Society for the Propagation of Faith—Rev. LAWRENCE M. FARRELL.

Trauma Recovery Program—Rev. KENNETH W. SCHMIDT, J.C.D., M.A., L.P.C., N.L.L., Tel: 269-381-8917; SHARON FROOM, Tel: 269-381-8917, Ext. 222.

Secretariat for Catholic Education and New Evangelization—

Executive Director—MRS. MARGARET ERICH, Tel: 269-903-0165.

Catholic Schools—MRS. MARGARET ERICH, Supt., Tel: 269-903-0165; DR. JILLIAN KELLOUGH, Assoc. Dir., Tel: 269-903-0181.

Associate Director of Catechesis and Youth Ministry—MR. GEORGE DRAGAN, Tel: 269-903-0141.

Enrollment and Retention—MRS. NINA LANEY.

Safe Environment/Child & Youth Protection—MS. MARINA SHOUP, Tel: 269-903-0171.

Support Specialist—MS. LAURIE TICHVON, Tel: 269-903-0207.

Secretariat for Communications and Public Affairs—

Executive Director—MRS. VICKI CESSNA, Tel: 269-903-0163.

Associate Director—MRS. TERRY HAGEMAN, Tel: 269-903-0173.

Southwest Michigan Catholic - Editor—MRS. VICKI CESSNA, Tel: 269-903-0163.

Communications Assistant—MRS. SARAH DEMOTT, Tel: 269-903-0144.

Legislative Relations/Public Affairs—MRS. VICKI CESSNA, Tel: 269-903-0163.

Additional Key Responsibility Areas: Advertising, Creative Services, Marketing and Promotional Graphics, Media Relations, Website; Social Media.

Secretariat for Parish Life and Lay Leadership—

Executive Director—MR. JAMIN HEROLD.

Domestic Church (Marriage Preparation)—MRS. SOCORRO TRUCHAN, Assoc. Dir., Tel: 269-903-0199.

Lay Ecclesial Ministry Formation—MR. JAMIN HEROLD, Tel: 269-903-0183.

Multicultural and Hispanic Ministry—DR. ANGELICA VALDES, Support Specialist.

Director of Hispanic-Latino Ministry—MRS. VERONICA RODRIGUEZ, Dir., Tel: 269-903-0197; MARIA MARCELLA TRUMM, Support Specialist; Very Rev. FABIO H. GARZON, V.F., Clergy.

Sanctity of the Human Person (Respect Life)—MISS LISA IRWIN, Assoc. Dir., Tel: 269-903-0177; Tel: 269-903-0177.

Young Adult and Adult Ministry—MR. TIM MCNAMARA, Assoc. Dir., Tel: 269-903-0139; MRS. JOAN JACONETTE, Support Specialist, Tel: 269-903-0147.

Other Catholic Institutions

Catholic Charities Diocese of Kalamazoo—MR. TIMOTHY LIESER, Exec. Dir., Tel: 269-381-9800; Email: timlieser@ccdok.org.

The Ark Services for Youth—

Baraga Manor—

Bridges Mental Health Counseling—

Caring Network—

Inner City Ministry—Sr. MAUREEN MCGRATH, O.P., Catholic Community Center, 589 Pearl St., Benton Harbor, 49022. Tel: 269-926-6424; Fax: 269-926-2870.

CLERGY, PARISHES, MISSIONS AND PAROCHIAL SCHOOLS

CITY OF KALAMAZOO

(KALAMAZOO COUNTY)

1—ST. AUGUSTINE CATHEDRAL (1856)
542 W. Michigan Ave., 49007. Tel: 269-345-5147; Email: msaliwanchik@stakalamazoo.org; Web: stakalamazoo.org. Rev. Msgr. Michael A. Osborn, V.G., J.C.D., Rector; Revs. Thomas McNally, Associate Rector; James Vinh Le, Parochial Vicar; Deacon Don Bouchard.
School—St. Augustine Cathedral School, 600 W. Michigan Ave., 49007. Tel: 269-349-1945; Fax: 269-349-1085; Email: azommers@stakzoo.org; Web: www.stakzoo.org. Andra Zommers, Prin. Lay Teachers 16; Students 349.
Catechesis Religious Program—Email: bsunnerville@stakalamazoo.rog. Bret Sunnerville, D.R.E. Students 62.

2—ST. JOSEPH (1904)
936 Lake St., 49001. Tel: 269-343-6256; Fax: 269-343-1214; Email: mail.stjoekal@gmail.com. Rev. Msgr. Michael D. Hazard, V.G.; Rev. Andrew Raczkowski, Parochial Vicar; Deacons John Ryder; Timothy Kistka.
Catechesis Religious Program—Students 184.

3—ST. MARY (1935)
939 Charlotte, 49048. Tel: 269-342-0621; Email: office@stmarykazoo.org; Web: www.stmarykazoo.org. Very Rev. James Richardson, M.A., V.F.; Rev. Harold G. Potter, In Res.; Deacon Patrick Hall, Parish Coord.
Catechesis Religious Program—Email: dre@stmarykzoo.org. Nicki Herold, D.R.E. & D.Y.M.; George Bugaj, Music Dir. Students 27.

4—ST. MONICA (1955)
4408 S. Westnedge, 49008. Tel: 269-345-4389; Fax: 269-345-5211; Web: stmonicachurchkzoo.com. Very Rev. Lawrence Farrell, V.F.; Revs. James Adams, Parochial Vicar; Daniel E. Doctor, O.D., Parochial Vicar; Robert E. Consani, In Res., (Retired); Deacons Jason Aiello; Walter Brockmeyer; Kurt Lucas.
Res.: 534 W. Kilgore Rd., 49008.
School—St. Monica School, 530 W. Kilgore Rd., 49008. Tel: 269-345-2444; Fax: 269-345-8534; Email: breits@stmonicakzoo.org; Web: www.csgk.org\st-monica-welcome. Mrs. Rebecca Reits, Prin. Clergy 1; Lay Teachers 15; Students 292; Clergy / Religious Teachers 1.
Catechesis Religious Program—Students 363.

5—ST. THOMAS MORE STUDENT PARISH (1956)
421 Monroe St., 49006. Tel: 269-381-8917; Email: sttoms@sttomskazoo.org. Rev. Daniel W. Hyman; Deacons Frank Sila, B.A., Pastoral Assoc.; Joe Schmitt, M.A., Pastoral Assoc.
Catechesis Religious Program—542 W. Michigan Ave., 49007. Tel: 269-345-5147; Email: bsunnerville@stakalamazoo.org. Bret Sunnerville, D.R.E. Students 47.

OUTSIDE THE CITY OF KALAMAZOO

ALBION, CALHOUN CO., ST. JOHN THE EVANGELIST (1873) [CEM]
1020 Irwin Ave., Albion, 49224. Tel: 517-629-4532; Email: mary@stjohn-church.org; Web: www.stjohn-church.org. Very Rev. Craig Lusk, V.F.; Rev. Joseph B. Gray, Pastor Emeritus, (Retired); Deacon Kenneth Snyder.
Res.: 879 Finley Dr., Albion, 49224.
Catechesis Religious Program—Jaime Stevens, D.R.E. Students 51.

ALLEGAN, ALLEGAN CO., BLESSED SACRAMENT (1934) [CEM]
110 N. Cedar, Allegan, 49010-1246.
Tel: 269-673-4455; Email: blsacch@frontier.com; Web: www.blessedsacrament-allegan.org. Rev. Simon Joseph Chummar Manjooran, S.B.D., (India); Deacons James Bauer; Eugene Haas.
Res. & Church: 429 Trowbridge St., Allegan, 49010-1246. Fax: 616-673-5869.
Catechesis Religious Program—Students 70.

AUGUSTA, KALAMAZOO CO., ST. ANN (1958)
12648 E. D Ave., Augusta, 49012. Tel: 269-731-4721. Rev. Francis A. Marotti; Deacon Michael Carl.
School—St. Ann School aka Light of Christ Academy, (Grades PreK-K), Tel: 269-731-0281; Email: school@stannaugusta.org; Web: lightofchristacademy.org. Carrie Jewett, Admin. Aides 7; Lay Teachers 9; Students 70; Clergy / Religious Teachers 1.
Catechesis Religious Program—Email: pvanderpool@stannaugusta.org. Patricia Vanderpool, D.R.E. Students 168.

BANGOR, VAN BUREN CO., SACRED HEART OF JESUS (1932) [CEM]
201 S. Walnut St., Bangor, 49013. Tel: 269-427-7514; Email: sacredheartbangor@yahoo.com; Web: ichartford.com. Rev. German Perez Diaz; Deacon Arthur Morsaw.

BATTLE CREEK, CALHOUN CO.

1—ST. JEROME (1955) [JC]
229 Collier Ave., Battle Creek, 49017.
Tel: 269-968-2218; Email: stjeromechurch22@aol.com; Web: stjeromebc.org. Rev. Christopher J. Ankley; Deacon Gary Wright, (Retired).
Res.: 61 N. 23rd St ., Battle Creek, 49015.
Catechesis Religious Program—(In programs at St. Joseph, St. Philip or Catholic schools).

2—ST. JOSEPH (1942) [JC]
61 23rd St. N., Battle Creek, 49015.
Tel: 269-962-0165; Fax: 269-962-5937; Email: frchris@bcacs.org; Email: frjose@bcacs.org; Web: stjosephbc.org. Revs. Christopher J. Ankley; Jose de Jesus Haro Gomez, Parochial Vicar; Deacons James Nelson; David Krajewski.
School—St. Joseph School, (Grades PreK-8), 47 N. 23rd, Battle Creek, 49015. Tel: 269-965-7749;

Fax: 269-965-0790; Web: bcacs.org. Mrs. Sara Myers, Prin. Lay Teachers 12; Students 240; Clergy / Religious Teachers 1.
Catechesis Religious Program—Tel: 269-965-4079; Email: bkincaid@bcacs.org. Students 278.
3—ST. PHILIP (1869) [CEM]
112 Capital Ave., N.E., Battle Creek, 49017.
Tel: 269-968-6645; Email: admin@stphilipbc.org. Very Rev. John D. Fleckenstein; Revs. Robert J. Johansen; Pangiraj Nathan; Deacons Alfred Bell; Albert Patrick.
Res.: 126 Capital Ave., N.E., Battle Creek, 49017.
Catechesis Religious Program—Tel: 269-962-9506. Students 100.
BENTON HARBOR, BERRIEN CO.
1—ST. BERNARD, Merged with St. John, Benton Harbor.
2—SS. JOHN & BERNARD (1996) [CEM]
580 Columbus Ave., Benton Harbor, 49022.
Tel: 269-925-2425; Email: ssjbbusmgr@gmail.com; Web: www.ssjohnandbernard.org. Very Rev. Robert F. Creagan, E.V., V.F.; Rev. Benjamin Joseph Huynh, Parochial Vicar.
Res.: 600 Columbus Ave., Benton Harbor, 49022. Email: fatherben14@gmail.com.
Catechesis Religious Program—220 Church St., St. Joseph, 49085. Students 217.
3—ST. JOHN THE EVANGELIST, Merged with St. Bernard, Benton Harbor.
BRIDGMAN, BERRIEN CO., OUR LADY QUEEN OF PEACE (1939)
3903 Lake St., Bridgman, 49106-0747.
Tel: 269-465-6252; Fax: 269-465-4930; Email: pastor@olqop.org. Rev. Arthur Howard, O.D.
Catechesis Religious Program—Students 39.
BRONSON, BRANCH CO., ST. MARY ASSUMPTION (1867) [CEM] (Polish)
602 W. Chicago St., Bronson, 49028.
Tel: 517-369-2120; Email: stmarybronson@yahoo.com; Web: stmarysbronson.org. Very Rev. Mark J. Vyverman, V.F.; Revs. Paul Redmond, Parochial Vicar; Rajain Mathias, Parochial Vicar; Deacons James Lavelline; Alan Sosinski; John Wielgos.
School—St. Mary Assumption School, 204 Albers Rd., Bronson, 49028. Tel: 517-369-4625; Fax: 517-369-1652; Email: principal@stmarybronson.org. Mr. David Kubel, Prin. Lay Teachers 7; Students 77.
Catechesis Religious Program—Tel: 260-829-6243. John Stukey, D.R.E. Students 88.
BUCHANAN, BERRIEN CO., ST. ANTHONY (1941) [CEM]
509 W. 4th St., Buchanan, 49107. Tel: 269-695-3863; Email: office@stanthonybuchanan.com. Rev. Leo Cartagena; Deacon Alberto Rivera-Gutierrez.
Catechesis Religious Program—Patti Mitchell, D.R.E. Students 60.
Mission—St. Gabriel Mission Church, 429 Rose Hill, Berrien Springs, Berrien Co. 49103.
BYRON CENTER, ALLEGAN CO., ST. MARY'S VISITATION (1866) [CEM 2] [JC2] (German)
2459 146th Ave., Byron Center, 49315.
Tel: 616-681-9701, Ext. 100; Email: parishsec@smvchurch.org; Email: gandres@smvchurch.org; Web: www.smvchurch.org. Revs. Stephen Rodrigo, (India); Christopher Derda, Admin.; Deacon Edward LaRoche.
School—St. Mary's Visitation School, 2455 146th Ave., Byron Center, 49315. Tel: 616-681-9701; Email: secretary@smvschool.org; Web: smvschool.org. Christopher Hurley, Prin. Lay Teachers 7; Students 79.
Catechesis Religious Program—
Tel: 616-681-9701, Ext. 203; Email: jim.nachtegall@gmail.com. Jim Nachtegall, D.R.E. Students 76.
CASSOPOLIS, CASS CO., ST. ANN (1915)
421 N. Broadway, P.O. Box 247, Cassopolis, 49031.
Tel: 269-445-3000; Email: cantos2@comcast.net. Rev. Robert E. Flickinger.
Catechesis Religious Program—Email: dillonsolol@gmail.com. Students 5.
COLDWATER, BRANCH CO., ST. CHARLES BORROMEO (1849)
150 Taylor St., Coldwater, 49036. Tel: 517-278-2650; Email: scbparishoffice@gmail.com; Web: st-charlescoldwater.org. Very Rev. Mark J. Vyverman, V.F.; Revs. Paul Redmond, Parochial Vicar; Rajain Mathias, Parochial Vicar; Deacons James Lavelline; Alan Sosinski; John Wielgos.
School—St. Charles Borromeo School, 79 Harrison St., Coldwater, 49036. Tel: 517-279-0404; Fax: 517-278-0505; Email: mescherb@scbelementary.org; Web: www.st-charlescoldwater.org. Brenda Mescher, Prin. Lay Teachers 13; Students 165.
Catechesis Religious Program—Email: stcharlesdre@gmail.com. Angela Richards, D.R.E. Students 57.
Mission—Our Lady of Fatima, 8220 M-60, Union City, Branch Co. 49094. Email: alichristo422@gmail.com. Alice Christopher, Contact Person.

DECATUR, VAN BUREN CO., HOLY FAMILY (1938)
500 W. St. Mary St., Decatur, 49045.
Tel: 269-783-4223; Email: holyfamilydecatur@gmail.com. Rev. Michael Rejent, O.S.F.S., In Res.
Catechesis Religious Program—Students 25.
DELTON, BARRY CO., ST. AMBROSE (1950)
11137 Floria Rd., Delton, 49046. Tel: 269-623-2490; Fax: 269-623-2498; Email: stambrose@mei.net. Sr. Constance Fifelski, O.P., Parish Coord.
Res.: 11252 Floria Rd., Delton, 49046.
Catechesis Religious Program—Students 28.
Mission—Our Lady of Great Oak, Lacey, Barry Co.
DORR, ALLEGAN CO., ST. STANISLAUS (1892) [CEM] (Polish)
1871 136th Ave., Dorr, 49323. Tel: 269-793-7268; Email: gandres@st-stans.net; Email: Rectory@st-stans.net; Web: www.st-stans.net. Revs. Stephen Rodrigo, (India); Christopher Derda, Admin.; Deacon Russell Pogodzinski.
School—St. Stanislaus School, (Grades PreSchool-8), 1861 136th Ave., Dorr, 49323. Tel: 269-793-7204; Fax: 269-793-3264; Email: murphy@st-stans.net; Web: st-stans.net. Rev. Christopher Derda, Admin. Lay Teachers 5; Students 58.
Catechesis Religious Program—Tel: 616-681-9701; Email: jim.nachtegall@gmail.com. Jim Nachtegall, D.R.E. Students 85.
Mission—Sacred Heart, 2036 20th Ave., Allegan, 49010. Tel: 269-793-7268, Ext. 246.
DOUGLAS, ALLEGAN CO., ST. PETER (1894) [CEM]
100 St. Peter Dr., P.O. Box 248, Douglas, 49406-0248. Tel: 269-857-7951; Email: marianne.hoffman@stpeter-douglas.org; Web: stpeter-douglas.org. Very Rev. Fabio H. Garzon, V.F.; Deacon Anthony Nethercott.
Catechesis Religious Program—Students 75.
Mission—San Felipe de Jesus, 5586 117th Ave., Fennville, 49408.
DOWAGIAC, CASS CO., HOLY MATERNITY OF MARY (1892) [CEM]
210 N. Front St., Dowagiac, 49047.
Tel: 269-782-2808; Tel: 269-782-9034;
Fax: 269-782-3558; Email: holymaternity@yahoo.com; Web: holymotherparishes.com. Rev. John Tran, Admin.; Deacon Philip Sirk.
Catechesis Religious Program—Email: maludvik@aol.com. Melissa Stanger, D.R.E. Students 63.
EDWARDSBURG, CASS CO., OUR LADY OF THE LAKE (1923)
24832 US Hwy. 12, Edwardsburg, 49112.
Tel: 269-699-5870; Email: cantos2@comcast.net; Web: www.ourladyedwardsburg.org. Rev. Robert E. Flickinger.
Catechesis Religious Program—Students 112.
GOBLES, VAN BUREN CO., ST. JUDE (1985)
13809 M-40 N., Gobles, 49055. Tel: 269-628-2219; Email: st.judeparishgobles@gmail.com; Web: www.stjudeparishgobles.com. P.O. Box 102, Gobles, 49055. Rev. Joseph Xavier, M.S.F.S.; Deacon John R. Bodway, Pastoral Admin.
Catechesis Religious Program—Cindy Carroll, D.R.E. Students 20.
HARTFORD, VAN BUREN CO., IMMACULATE CONCEPTION (1946) (Hispanic)
63559 60th Ave., Hartford, 49057. Tel: 269-621-4106; Fax: 269-308-3046; Email: ic.hartfordchurch@gmail.com; Web: ichartford.com. Rev. German Perez; Deacons Arthur Morsaw; James Rauner.
HASTINGS, BARRY CO., ST. ROSE OF LIMA (1873) [CEM]
805 S. Jefferson Ave., Hastings, 49058.
Tel: 269-945-4246; Email: pastorstrose2015@gmail.com. Rev. Stephan Philip, M.S.F.S.; Deacons Gene Haas; James Mellen.
School—St. Rose of Lima School, (Grades PreK-6), 707 S. Jefferson St., Hastings, 49058.
Tel: 269-945-3164; Fax: 269-945-0509; Email: info@srlsh.org; Web: stroseschoolhastings.com. Lori Pearson, Prin. Clergy 4; Lay Teachers 4.5; Students 70.
Catechesis Religious Program—Students 71.
Mission—St. Cyril, 203 N. State St., Nashville, Barry Co. 49073.
MARSHALL, CALHOUN CO., ST. MARY (1852) [CEM]
212 W. Hanover St., Marshall, 49068.
Tel: 269-781-3949; Email: stmarymarshall@aol.com; Web: stmarymarshall.org. Very Rev. Craig Lusk, V.F.
Res.: 214 S. Eagle St., Marshall, 49068.
Catechesis Religious Program—Tel: 269-781-5656. Students 131.
MATTAWAN, VAN BUREN CO., ST. JOHN BOSCO (1953)
23830 Front Ave., Mattawan, 49071.
Tel: 269-668-3312; Email: ltoso2015@outlook.com; Web: stjohnbosco.com. Rev. Alan P. Jorgensen; Deacon Louis Zemlick.
Catechesis Religious Program—Email: sjboscore@gmail.com; Email: mawhitney@earthlink.net. Johnna Makuch, D.R.E. (SJB); Mary Whitney, D.R.E. (SMM). Students 135.

Mission—St. Margaret Mary, 296 E. Dibble St., Marcellus, Cass Co. 49067.
MENDON, ST. JOSEPH CO., ST. EDWARD (1872) [CEM]
332 W. State St., P.O. Box 368, Mendon, 49072.
Tel: 269-496-3525; Email: stedwardchurch@msn.com. Rev. Msgr. Thomas A. Martin, J.C.D.
Catechesis Religious Program—Lyn Wilson, D.R.E. Students 7.
NEW BUFFALO, BERRIEN CO., ST. MARY OF THE LAKE (1857)
718 W. Buffalo St., New Buffalo, 49117.
Tel: 269-469-2637; Email: stmarynewbuffalo@gmail.com; Web: www.stmarynewbuffalo.org. Revs. John Peter Ambrose, M.S.F.S., (India); Vanathaiyan Savarimuthu.
Catechesis Religious Program—Students 42.
NILES, BERRIEN CO.
1—ST. MARK (1955)
3 N. 19th St., Niles, 49120-2117. Tel: 269-683-8650; Email: stmark319@yahoo.com; Web: stmarkparishofniles.org. Rev. Thomas King, C.S.C.; Bro. Dennis Meyers, Assoc.
Catechesis Religious Program—Students 27.
2—ST. MARY OF THE IMMACULATE CONCEPTION CHURCH (1870) [CEM 2]
203 S. Lincoln Ave., Niles, 49120-2862.
Tel: 269-683-5087; Fax: 269-683-5089; Email: stmaryniles@sbcglobal.net; Web: stmarysniles.org. 219 S. State St., Niles, 49120-2862. Very Rev. Christian R. Johnston, V.F.; Deacon Roger Gregorski, D.R.E.
Res.: 211 S. Lincoln Ave., Niles, 49120.
School—St. Mary of the Immaculate Conception Church School, (Grades PreK-8), 217 S. Lincoln Ave., Niles, 49120. Tel: 269-683-9191; Fax: 269-683-8118; Email: l.johnson@stmarysschoolniles.org; Web: www.stmarysschoolniles.org. Ms. Leslie Johnson, Prin. Lay Teachers 5; Students 81.
Catechesis Religious Program—Students 87.
CHRISTIAN SERVICE CENTER, 322 Clay St., Niles, 49120. Tel: 269-684-0637. Tot Asst. Annually 2,100; Total Staff 30.
OTSEGO, ALLEGAN CO., ST. MARGARET (1887) [CEM]
766 S. Farmer St., Otsego, 49078. Tel: 269-694-6311; Email: stmbook@yahoo.com. Rev. Simon Joseph Chummar Manjooran, S.B.D., (India); Deacons James Bauer; Eugene Haas; Dean Herman.
Res.: 110 N. Cedar St., Allegan, 49010.
School—St. Margaret School, 736 S. Farmer, Otsego, 49078. Tel: 269-694-2951; Fax: 269-694-4520; Email: jhall@stmargaretschool.net; Web: www.stmargaretschool.net. Lay Teachers 5; Students 54.
Catechesis Religious Program—Tel: 269-694-6311; Email: jumpinjoy@sbcglobal.net; Email: joyvlivingston@gmail.com. Students 176.
PARCHMENT, KALAMAZOO CO., ST. AMBROSE (1955)
1628 E. G Ave., Parchment, 49004.
Tel: 269-385-4152; Tel: 269-343-0099; Email: ambroseparchment@sbcglobl.net; Web: stambroseparchment.com. Revs. James S. O'Leary; Kevin Covert, In Res.; Deacons Hallie Bohan, J.C.L.; Alfred Radford; David Bartholomew, (Retired).
Catechesis Religious Program—Email: ambrosedre@sbcglobal.net. Amy Miles, D.R.E. Students 47.
PAW PAW, VAN BUREN CO., ST. MARY (1887) [CEM]
209 S. Brown St., Paw Paw, 49079.
Tel: 269-657-4459; Fax: 269-657-4260; Email: stmarypawpaw@bloomingdalecom.net; Web: stmarypawpaw.com. Mailing Address: 500 Paw Paw St., Paw Paw, 49079. Rev. Joseph Xavier, M.S.F.S.; Deacon Duane Poage.
Res.: 214 S. Brown St., Paw Paw, 49079.
School—St. Mary School, 508 Paw Paw St., Paw Paw, 49079. Tel: 269-657-3750; Email: mradomsky@saintmarypawpaw.org. Lay Teachers 7; Students 86.
Catechesis Religious Program—Email: drestmarypawpaw@bloomingdalecom.net. Jackie Marshall, D.R.E. Students 135.
PEARL, ALLEGAN CO., SAN FELIPE DE JESUS (1986) (Hispanic)
Mailing Address: 5586 117th Ave., P.O. Box 588, Fennville, 49408. Tel: 269-561-5029;
Fax: 269-561-2192; Email: joe.marble@stpeter-douglas.org; Web: www.sanfelipe-fennville.org. Very Rev. Fabio H. Garzon, V.F.; Deacon Maximino Rodriguez.
PORTAGE, KALAMAZOO CO., ST. CATHERINE OF SIENA (1966)
1150 W. Centre St., Portage, 49024-5385.
Tel: 269-327-5165; Email: info@stcatherinesiena.org; Web: stcatherinesiena.org. Revs. Kenneth W. Schmidt, J.C.D., M.A., L.P.C., N.L.L.; William Jacobs Jr., Parochial Vicar; Sahaya Lopez, Parochial Vicar; Albert Kemboi, Parochial Vicar; Deacons Edward Feltes; Brian Kaluzny; Jack Prendergast.
Catechesis Religious Program—Karen Galloway, Pastoral Assoc. Students 381.
ST. JOSEPH, BERRIEN CO., ST. JOSEPH (1720) [CEM]
201 Church St., St. Joseph, 49085. Tel: 269-983-1575

; Email: sjcath1@att.net; Web: www.stjoestjoe.church. 220 Church St., St. Joseph, 49085. Very Rev. Robert F. Creagan, E.V., V.F.; Rev. Arul Lazar, Parochial Vicar; Deacons Michael Gallagher; Edward Nickel.
Res.: 211 Church St., St. Joseph, 49085.
Catechesis Religious Program—Email: timsmith752@gmail.com. Tim Smith, D.R.E. Students 221.

SILVER CREEK, CASS CO., SACRED HEART OF MARY (1838) [CEM] (Native American)
51841 Leach Rd., Dowagiac, 49047.
Tel: 269-782-8048; Email: sacredheart2002b@gmail.com; Web: www.holymothersparishes.com. Rev. Michael Rejent, O.S.F.S., Parochial Vicar.

SOUTH HAVEN, VAN BUREN CO., ST. BASIL (1900) [CEM]
513 Monroe Blvd., South Haven, 49090.
Tel: 269-637-2404; Email: info@saintbasilcatholicchurch.org. Rev. James A. Morris; Deacon John Lohrstorfer.
Res.: 634 Kentucky Ave., South Haven, 49090.
School—St. Basil School, (Grades PreK-6), 94 Superior St., South Haven, 49090. Tel: 269-637-3529; Email: camilledelano@saintbasilcatholic.org; Web: www.saintbasilcatholic.org. Camille DeLano, Admin. Lay Teachers 7; Students 91.
Catechesis Religious Program—Students 75.

STURGIS, ST. JOSEPH CO., HOLY ANGELS (1879)
402 S. Nottawa St., Sturgis, 49091.
Tel: 269-651-5200, Ext. 101; Email: gabe@holyangelssturgis.org. Rev. Evelio Rios Ramirez; Deacon Lawrence M. Kasuboski.
Catechesis Religious Program—Tel: 269-651-5520; Email: dre@holyangelssturgis.org. Rayito Tapia, D.R.E. Students 278.

THREE OAKS, BERRIEN CO., ST. MARY OF THE ASSUMPTION (1880)
28 W. Ash St., Three Oaks, 49128. Tel: 269-756-2041; Email: st.maryassumption@att.net. Revs. John Peter Ambrose, M.S.F.S., (India); Vanathaiyan Savarimuthu.
Catechesis Religious Program—Students 18.
Mission—St. Agnes, Sawyer, Berrien Co.

THREE RIVERS, ST. JOSEPH CO., IMMACULATE CONCEPTION (1885)
645 S. Douglas Ave., Three Rivers, 49093.
Tel: 269-273-8953; Email: iccatholicchurch@catholicweb.com; Web: iccollaborative.com. Rev. Antony Rajesh.
School—Immaculate Conception School, 601 S. Douglas Ave., Three Rivers, 49093-2044.
Tel: 269-273-2085; Email: principal@iccatholicschool.com. Sharon Voege, Prin. Lay Teachers 3; Students 31; Pre-School Aide 4.
Catechesis Religious Program—Tel: 269-816-5773; Email: josephgraber@gmail.com. Joe Graber, D.R.E. Students 47.
Missions—St. Barbara—479 S. Burr Oak Rd., Colon, St. Joseph Co. 49040.
St. Clare, 23126 M-86, Centreville, St. Joseph Co. 49032.

VICKSBURG, KALAMAZOO CO., ST. MARTIN OF TOURS (1951)
5855 E. W Ave., P.O. Box 264, Vicksburg, 49097-0264. Tel: 269-649-1629; Email: ctakacs@stmartinvicksburg.org. Rev. Msgr. Thomas Martin; Deacons David Guido; Thomas Thamann.
Catechesis Religious Program—Email: dre@stmartinvicksburg.org. Clare Zemlick, D.R.E. Preschool 5; Students 122.

WATERVLIET, BERRIEN CO., ST. JOSEPH (1896) [CEM]
157 Lucinda Ln., Watervliet, 49098.
Tel: 269-463-5470, Ext. 100; Email: sjcatholicwatervliet@gmail.com; Web: stjcatholic.net. Very Rev. Robert F. Creagan, E.V., V.F.; Rev. Patrick H. Craig, O.D., Admin.
Res.: 179 Lucinda Ln., Watervliet, 49098.
Catechesis Religious Program—Students 25.

WAYLAND, ALLEGAN CO.
1—SS. CYRIL AND METHODIUS (1917) [CEM]
159 131st Ave., Wayland, 49348. Tel: 269-792-3543; Email: info@sscmparish.org; Web: www.sscmparish.org. Rev. Alphonse Savarimuthu, M.S.F.S., (India); Deacon Jeffrey Ryan.
Catechesis Religious Program—Students 63.
2—ST. THERESE OF LISIEUX (1942)
128 Cedar St., Wayland, 49348. Tel: 269-792-2138; Email: sttparish1@gmail.com; Web: sttparishwayland.org. Rev. Alphonse Savarimuthu, M.S.F.S., (India); Deacons Mark Chrusciel; Jeffrey Ryan.
School—St. Therese of Lisieux School, 430 S. Main St., Wayland, 49348. Tel: 269-792-2016;
Fax: 269-792-6778; Email: sttoffice1@gmail.com; Email: sttprincipal1@gmail.com; Web: www.sttthereseschoolwaylandmi.org. Mr. Hank Leverette, Prin. Clergy 1; Lay Teachers 5; Students 42.
Catechesis Religious Program—
Tel: 269-792-2016, Ext. 27; Email: bg14alldre@yahoo.com; Web: www.stl.catholicweb.com. Students 79.

WHITE PIGEON, ST. JOSEPH CO., ST. JOSEPH (1832) [CEM]
16603 US Hwy. 12, White Pigeon, 49099.
Tel: 269-483-7621; Fax: 269-483-7891; Email: saintjoewp@comcast.net; Web: www.stjosephwhitepigeon.org. Rev. Evelio Rios Ramirez.
Catechesis Religious Program—Email: lauren@holyangelssturgis.org. Ms. Lauren Coates, D.R.E. Students 49.

Chaplains of Public Institutions

COLDWATER. *Florence Crane Correctional Facility for Women.*
Lakeland Correctional Facility for Men.

Continuing Studies:
Revs.—
Hanley, Jeffrey David, (Rome)
Nightingale, Maxmilian Jacob, (Rome).

Retired:
Rev. Msgrs.—
Bogdan, Leonard A., (Retired), 16611 N.W. Point Pkwy. - C115, Surprise, AZ 85374
Sears, Eugene A., (Retired), 302 Anchor's Way, Saint Joseph, 49085
Revs.—
Barth, Raymond J., (Retired), P.O. Box 186, Baroda, 49101
Consani, Robert E., (Retired), 4408 S. Westnedge Ave., 49008
Fischer, Charles H., (Retired), 7361 Cactus Cove S.W., Byron Center, 49315
Fritz, Richard A., (Retired), St. Augustine Cathedral, 542 W. Michigan Ave., 49007
Gray, Joseph B., (Retired), 1020 Irwin Ave., Albion, 49224
Howell, Michael J., (Retired), 818 S. Park St., 49001
Illikattil, Mathew K., (Retired), 11348 Holly Dr., Riverview, FL 33578
Klingler, Donald P., (Retired), 6309 Overdale Manor, 49009
Valls, Richard, (Retired), 10552 Rancho Carmel, San Diego, CA 92128
Wieber, Donald A., (Retired), Grace Haven, 1507 Glastonbury Dr., St. Johns, 48879
Young, John, (Retired), 15485 Blue Star Hwy., South Haven, 49090.

Permanent Deacons:
Aiello, Jason, St. Monica, Kalamazoo
Bartholomew, David, St. Ambrose, Parchment
Bauer, James, Blessed Sacrament, Allegan; St. Margaret, Otsego
Bell, Alfred, St. Philip, Battle Creek
Bodway, John, St. Jude Mission, Gobles
Bohan, Hallie, J.C.L., St. Ambrose, Parchment
Bouchard, Don, St. Augustine Cathedral, Kalamazoo
Brockmeyer, Walter, St. Monica, Kalamazoo
Carl, Michael, St. Ann, Augusta
Chrusciel, Mark, St. Theresa and Sts. Cyril & Methodius, Wayland
Connelly, Bart, Immaculate Conception, Three Rivers
DeMars, Richard, Diocese of Rochester, NY
Feltes, Edward, St. Catherine of Siena, Portage
Gallagher, Michael, St. Joseph, St. Joseph
Gregorski, Roger, St. Mary, Niles
Guido, David, St. Martin of Tours, Vicksburg; St. Edwards, Mendon
Haas, Eugene
Hall, Patrick, St. Mary, Kalamazoo
Hermann, Dean, St. Margaret, Otsego
Herrera, Manuel, Diocese of Grand Rapids, MI
Kaluzny, Brian, St. Catherine of Siena, Portage
Kasuboski, Lawrence M., Holy Angels, Sturgis
Kimmerly, James
Kistka, Timothy, St. Joseph, Kalamazoo
Krajewski, David, St. Joseph, Battle Creek
LaRoche, Edward, St. Mary Visitation, Byron Center
Lavelline, James, St. Charles Borromeo, Coldwater
Lohstorfer, John, St. Basil, South Haven
Lucas, Kurt, St. Monica, Kalamazoo
Mellen, James, St. Rose of Lima, Hastings
Middleton, Allan, Diocese of Grand Rapids, MI
Moreno, Michael, St. Mary, Marshall
Morsaw, Arthur, Immaculate Conception, Hartford
Nelson, James, St. Joseph, Battle Creek
Nethercott, Anthony, (Retired)
Nickel, Edward, S.S. John & Bernard, Benton Harbor
Patrick, Albert, St. Philip, Battle Creek
Poage, Duane, St. Mary, Paw Paw
Pogodzinski, Russell, St. Stanislaus, Dorr
Prendergast, Jack, (Retired)
Radford, Alfred, St. Ambrose, Parchment
Rauner, James, Immaculate Conception, Hartford
Rivera-Gutierrez, Alberto, St. Gabriel, Berrien Springs
Rodriguez, Maximino, (Retired)
Ryan, Jeffrey, St. Theresa and S.S. Cyril & Methodius, Wayland
Ryder, John, St. Joseph, Kalamazoo
Schmitt, Joe, M.A., St. Thomas More, Kalamazoo
Sila, Frank, B.A., St. Thomas More, Kalamazoo
Sirk, Philip, Holy Maternity of Mary, Dowagiac
Snyder, Kenneth, St. John, Albion
Sosinski, Alan, St. Mary of the Assumption, Bronson
Thamann, Thomas, St. Martin of Tours, Vicksburg
Van Dril, William, (Retired)
Vogel, Richard, Archdiocese of Galveston-Houston
Wesolowski, Frank, (Retired)
Wielgos, John, St. Mary's Assumption, Bronson
Wright, Gary, St. Jerome, Battle Creek
Zemlick, Louis, St. John Bosco, Mattawan.

INSTITUTIONS LOCATED IN DIOCESE

[A] HIGH SCHOOLS, DIOCESAN

KALAMAZOO. *Msgr. John R. Hackett High School* (1964) 1000 W. Kilgore Rd., 49008. Tel: 269-381-2646; Fax: 269-381-3919; Email: hackett@hackettcp.org; Web: www.hackettcatholicprep.org. Very Rev. John D. Fleckenstein, Admin.; Rev. Thomas McNally, Chap.; Mr. Brian Kosmerick, Prin. Deacons 1; Lay Teachers 22; Priests 1; Students 236; Clergy / Religious Teachers 1.

BATTLE CREEK. *St. Philip Catholic Central High School*, 20 Cherry St., Battle Creek, 49017. Tel: 269-963-4503; Fax: 269-965-5590; Email: vgroat@bcacs.org; Web: bcacs.org. Vicky Groat, Prin. Lay Teachers 12; Students 115; Clergy / Religious Teachers 2.

ST. JOSEPH. *Lake Michigan Catholic Middle and High School*, (Grades 6-12), 915 Pleasant St., St. Joseph, 49085. Tel: 269-983-2511; Fax: 269-983-0883; Email: jberlin@lmclakers.org; Web: www.lmclakers.org. Mr. Joseph Schmidt, Prin. Lay Teachers 18; Students 169.

[B] GRADE SCHOOLS, INTERPAROCHIAL

ST. JOSEPH. *Lake Michigan Catholic Schools*, (Grades PreK-5), 3165 Washington Ave., St. Joseph, 49085. Tel: 269-429-0227; Fax: 269-429-1461; Web: lmclakers.org. Larry Hoskins, Prin.; Janice Mathews, Librarian. Lay Teachers 21; Students 282.

[C] CATHOLIC SOCIAL AGENCIES

KALAMAZOO. *Catholic Charities Diocese of Kalamazoo*, 1819 Gull Rd., 49048. Tel: 269-381-9800; Fax: 269-381-2932; Email: info@ccdok.org; Web: www.ccdok.org. Mr. Timothy Lieser, Pres. & CEO. Tot Asst. Annually 8,500; Total Staff 45.

[D] GENERAL HOSPITALS

DOWAGIAC. *Ascension Borgess-Lee Hospital*, 420 W. High St., Dowagiac, 49047. Tel: 269-782-8681; Fax: 269-783-3044; Web: www.borgesslee.com. Kathy Young, Pres. Bed Capacity 25; Tot Asst. Annually 155,299; Total Staff 186.

[E] HOMES FOR SENIOR CITIZENS

KALAMAZOO. *Borgess Gardens* aka Borgess Place, 3057 Gull Rd., 49048. Tel: 269-552-6500; Fax: 269-552-6510; Email: carly.macdonald@ascension.org; Web: www.ascension.org. Carly MacDonald, Admin. Skilled Nursing Facility specializing in Short Term Rehab. Bed Capacity 101; Total Staff 130; Total Assisted 600.
Dillon Complex for Independent Living, Inc. Nonprofit housing corporation Dillon Hall, 3301 Gull Rd., #308, 49048. Tel: 269-342-0263; Fax: 269-342-1814; Email: lisaw@lmc-mi.com; Email: kdavis@csjinitiatives.org; Web: www.dillonhall.org. Ms. Denise Gannon, CEO. Sponsored by the Congregation of the Sisters of St. Joseph ministry CSJ Initiatives, Inc. Tot Asst. Annually 78; Total in Residence 90; Total Staff 5; Apartments 72.

OTSEGO. *Otsego Senior Apts., Inc.*, Baraga Manor Apts., 301 Washington St., Otsego, 49078. Tel: 269-694-9711; Fax: 269-694-5857; Email: baraga@medallionmgmt.com; Web: catholicfamilyservices.org. Ms. Carol Dennis, Dir. Managed by Medallion Management, Inc. Tot Asst. Annually 59; Total Staff 6; Rental Units 48.

1819 Gull Rd., 49048. Tel: 269-694-9711; Fax: 269-694-5857. Apartments 48.

[F] CONVENTS AND RESIDENCES FOR SISTERS

NAZARETH. *Congregation of the Sisters of St. Joseph* (1889) 3427 Gull Rd., Nazareth, 49074. Tel: 269-381-6290; Fax: 269-381-4909; Web: www.csjoseph.org. Sr. Marjorie Bassett, C.S.J., Contact Person. Sisters 151.

[G] NEWMAN CENTERS

KALAMAZOO. *Western Michigan University, Kalamazoo College, Kalamazoo Valley Community College*, 421 Monroe St., 49006. Tel: 269-381-8917; Fax: 269-381-0195; Email: sttoms@sttomskazoo.org; Web: www.sttomskazoo.org. Rev. Daniel W. Hyman, Chap.; Deacons Frank Sila, B.A., Pastoral Assoc.; Joe Schmitt, M.A., Pastoral Assoc.

[H] MISCELLANEOUS LISTINGS

KALAMAZOO. *Ascension Borgess Hospital* (1889) 1521 Gull Rd., 49048. Tel: 269-226-4800; Fax: 269-226-7396; Web: www.borgess.com. Jerry Love, Chm. Borgess Health is a Health Care System sponsored by Ascension Health which operates Borgess Ambulatory Care, Inc., Borgess Foundation, Borgess Medical Center, Borgess Gardens, Borgess-Pipp Hospital, Borgess-Lee Memorial Hospital, ProMed Healthcare, Borgess Health Park, Textile Systems, Inc. and other related companies. Incorporated in the State of Michigan. Tot Asst. Annually 4,800,000; Total Staff 2,998.

The Catholic Foundation of Southwestern Michigan, 215 N. Westnedge Ave., 49007. Tel: 269-349-8714; Fax: 269-349-6440; Email: LShoemaker@diokzoo.org. Mr. Thomas Dowdall, Dir.

Catholic Schools of Greater Kalamazoo, 1000 W. Kilgore Rd., 49008. Tel: 269-381-2646; Fax: 269-381-3919; Email: manderegg@csgk.org. Very Rev. Lawrence Farrell, V.F.

Diocesan Council of St. Vincent dePaul, 2400 Joni Ln., Stevensville, 49127. Tel: 269-449-8838; Fax: 269-388-4511; Email: svdpkal@att.net. Patricia Worick, Pres. Total Assisted 16,127.

Kalamazoo Regional Catholic Schools Foundation, 1000 W. Kilgore Rd., 49008. Tel: 269-381-2646; Fax: 269-381-3919; Email: kwillard@csgk.org; Email: sharding@csgk.org; Web: csgk.org. Steven Johnson, Pres.

BATTLE CREEK. *BCACS Foundation, Inc.* (Battle Creek Area Catholic Schools Foundation, Inc.) 63 N. 24th St., Battle Creek, 49015. Tel: 269-963-4771; Fax: 269-963-3917; Email: lmcintyre@bcacs.org; Web: bcacs.org/bcacs-foundation. Mrs. Louanne McIntyre, Dir.

HASTINGS. *St. Rose Lima Trust Fund*, 805 S. Jefferson St., Hastings, 49058. Tel: 269-945-4246; Fax: 269-945-0005; Email: pltwoods@yahoo.com. Patricia Woods, Chm.

ST. JOSEPH. *Lake Michigan Catholic School Fund* (1971) 515 Ship St., Ste. #202, St. Joseph, 49085. Tel: 269-470-8891; Email: tcacsf@comcast.net. Sarah Jollay, Pres.; Kelli Corning, Dir.

SOUTH HAVEN. *St. Basil Educational Endowment Fund*, 94 Superior St., South Haven, 49090. Tel: 269-637-3529; Tel: 269-637-4272; Fax: 269-639-1242; Email: principal@saintbasilcatholic.org; Web: www.saintbasilcatholic.org. Mr. Frank Overton, Pres.; Megan Akami, Sec.; Mrs. Chris Filbrandt, Treas.; Jim Marcoux, Contact Person.

RELIGIOUS INSTITUTES OF MEN REPRESENTED IN THE DIOCESE

For further details refer to the corresponding bracketed number in the Religious Institutes of Men or Women section.

[1330]—*Congregation of the Mission*—C.M.
[1080]—*Congregation of the Resurrection*—C.R.
[]—*Missionaries of St. Frances de Sales*—M.S.F.S.
[0920]—*Oblates of St. Francis de Sales* (Toledo-Detroit Prov.)—O.S.F.S.
[0610]—*Priests of the Congregation of the Holy Cross* (Indiana Prov.)—C.S.C.

RELIGIOUS INSTITUTES OF WOMEN REPRESENTED IN THE DIOCESE

[3832]—*Congregation of the Sisters of St. Joseph*—C.S.J.
[1070-05]—*Dominican Sisters*—O.P.
[1070-13]—*Dominican Sisters*—O.P.
[1070-14]—*Dominican Sisters*—O.P.
[2575]—*Sisters of Mercy of the Americas*—R.S.M.
[3930]—*Sisters of St. Joseph of the Third Order of St. Francis*—S.S.J.-T.O.S.F.
[3260]—*Sisters of the Precious Blood* (Dayton, OH)—C.PP.S.
[2150]—*Sisters, Servants of the Immaculate Heart of Mary* (Monroe, MI)—I.H.M.

An asterisk (*) denotes an organization that has established tax-exempt status directly with the IRS and is not covered by the USCCB Group Ruling.

Archdiocese of Kansas City in Kansas

(Archidioecesis Kansanopolitana in Kansas)

Most Reverend

JOSEPH F. NAUMANN

Archbishop of Kansas City in Kansas; ordained May 24, 1975; appointed Titular Bishop of Caput Cilla and Auxiliary Bishop of St. Louis July 9, 1997; consecrated September 3, 1997; appointed Coadjutor Archbishop of Kansas City in Kansas January 7, 2004; installed March 19, 2004; succeeded to See January 15, 2005.

Most Reverend

JAMES P. KELEHER, S.T.D.

Archbishop Emeritus of Kansas City in Kansas; ordained April 12, 1958; appointed Bishop of Belleville October 23, 1984; consecrated December 11, 1984; appointed Archbishop of Kansas City in Kansas June 28, 1993; installed September 8, 1993; retired January 15, 2005.

Catholic Chancery Offices: 12615 Parallel Pkwy., Kansas City, KS 66109. Tel: 913-721-1570; Fax: 913-721-1577.

Web: www.archkck.org

Email: archkck@archkck.org

Square Miles 12,524.

Established Vicariate Apostolic July 19, 1850. Diocese of Leavenworth established May 22, 1877. See changed to Kansas City in Kansas May 10, 1947; created Archdiocese August 9, 1952.

Comprises the following 21 Counties of Kansas: Anderson, Atchison, Brown, Coffey, Doniphan, Douglas, Franklin, Jackson, Jefferson, Johnson, Leavenworth, Linn, Lyon, Marshall, Miami, Nemaha, Osage, Pottawatomie, Shawnee, Wabaunsee and Wyandotte.

Patrons of the Diocese: I. Blessed Virgin Mary (Immaculate Conception); II. St. John Baptist Vianney.

For legal titles of institutions, please contact the Catholic Chancery Offices.

STATISTICAL OVERVIEW

Personnel	
Archbishops	1
Retired Archbishops	1
Abbots	1
Retired Abbots	2
Priests: Diocesan Active in Diocese	72
Priests: Diocesan Active Outside Diocese	6
Priests: Retired, Sick or Absent	27
Number of Diocesan Priests	105
Religious Priests in Diocese	57
Total Priests in Diocese	162
Extern Priests in Diocese	19
Ordinations:	
Diocesan Priests	2
Transitional Deacons	5
Permanent Deacons in Diocese	42
Total Brothers	15
Total Sisters	393
Parishes	
Parishes	106
With Resident Pastor:	
Resident Diocesan Priests	57
Resident Religious Priests	9
Without Resident Pastor:	
Administered by Priests	40
Professional Ministry Personnel:	
Brothers	1
Sisters	13
Lay Ministers	154
Welfare	
Catholic Hospitals	1
Health Care Centers	4
Total Assisted	11,719
Homes for the Aged	3
Total Assisted	973
Special Centers for Social Services	9
Total Assisted	527,065
Educational	
Diocesan Students in Other Seminaries	30
Students Religious	4
Total Seminarians	34
Colleges and Universities	3
Total Students	4,240
High Schools, Diocesan and Parish	5
Total Students	3,247
High Schools, Private	1
Total Students	205
Elementary Schools, Diocesan and Parish	36
Total Students	9,520
Elementary Schools, Private	2
Total Students	108
Catechesis/Religious Education:	
High School Students	1,557
Elementary Students	10,298
Total Students under Catholic Instruction	29,209
Teachers in the Diocese:	
Sisters	9
Lay Teachers	999
Vital Statistics	
Receptions into the Church:	
Infant Baptism Totals	2,821
Minor Baptism Totals	219
Adult Baptism Totals	199
Received into Full Communion	342
First Communions	2,946
Confirmations	3,070
Marriages:	
Catholic	573
Interfaith	217
Total Marriages	790
Deaths	1,402
Total Catholic Population	190,624
Total Population	1,387,343

Predecessors—Most Revs. J. B. MIEGE, S.J., cons. Bishop of Messenia, Vicar-Apostolic, March 25, 1851; resignation accepted by Pope Pius IX Nov. 8, 1874; died July 21, 1884; LOUIS M. FINK, O.S.B., D.D., cons. Bishop of Eucarpia June 11, 1871; appt. first Bishop of Leavenworth May 22, 1877; died March 17, 1904; THOMAS F. LILLIS, O.D., cons. Bishop of Leavenworth, Dec. 27, 1904; appt. Coadjutor Bishop of Kansas City, with right of succession March 14, 1910; succeeded to the See of Kansas City, Feb. 21, 1913; JOHN WARD, D.D., ord. July 17, 1884; appt. Bishop of Leavenworth Nov. 25, 1910; cons. Feb. 22, 1911; died April 20, 1929; Most Revs. FRANCIS JOHANNES, D.D., LL.D., cons. May 1, 1928; succeeded to the See, April 20, 1929; died March 13, 1937; PAUL C. SCHULTE, D.D., ord. June 11, 1915; appt. Bishop of Leavenworth May 29, 1937; cons. Sept. 21, 1937; appt. Archbishop of Indianapolis July 20, 1946; installed Oct. 10, 1946; GEORGE J. DONNELLY, S.T.D., ord. June 12, 1921; appt. Titular Bishop of Coela and Auxiliary of St. Louis March 19, 1940; cons. April 23, 1940; appt. Bishop of Leavenworth Nov. 9, 1946; died Dec. 13, 1950; EDWARD J. HUNKELER, D.D., ord. June 14, 1919; appt. Bishop of Grand Island March 10, 1945; cons. May 1, 1945; transferred to Kansas City March 28, 1951; elevated to Archiepiscopal dignity Aug. 9, 1952; retired Sept. 10, 1969; died Oct. 1, 1970; IGNATIUS J. STRECKER, D.D., S.T.D., ord. Dec. 19, 1942; appt. Bishop of Springfield-Cape Girardeau April 7, 1962; cons. June 20, 1962; transferred to Kansas City Sept. 10, 1969; retired Sept. 8, 1993; died Oct. 16, 2003; JAMES P. KELEHER, S.T.D., ord. April 12, 1958; appt. Bishop of Belleville Oct. 23, 1984; cons. Dec. 11, 1984; appt. Archbishop of Kansas City in Kansas June 28, 1993; installed Sept. 8, 1993; retired Jan. 15, 2005.

Catholic Chancery Offices—12615 Parallel Pkwy., Kansas City, 66109. Tel: 913-721-1570; Fax: 913-721-1577. Office Hours: 8:30-5.

Vicars General—Revs. GARY PENNINGS, V.G.; BRIAN SCHIEBER.

Chancellor—Rev. JOHN A. RILEY.

Metropolitan Tribunal—12615 Parallel Pkwy., Kansas City, 66109. Tel: 913-721-1570; Fax: 913-721-1577.

Judicial Vicar—Rev. JOSEPH ARSENAULT, S.S.A., J.C.L.

Adjutant Judicial Vicar—Rev. BRUCE ANSEMS, J.C.L.

Judges—Rev. Msgr. GARY APPLEGATE, J.C.L.; Revs. DENIS MEADE, O.S.B., J.C.D.; JOSEPH ARSENAULT, S.S.A., J.C.L.; BRUCE ANSEMS, J.C.L.

Defender of the Bond—Rev. Msgr. RAYMOND BURGER, (Retired).

Advocates—Selected Priests & Selected Lay Advocates.

Notary—JANIE SNEAD.

Archdiocesan Consultors—Rev. Msgr. THOMAS TANK; Rev. GARY PENNINGS, V.G.; Rt. Rev. JAMES R. ALBERS, O.S.B.; Revs. BRIAN SCHIEBER; PATRICK SULLIVAN; JOHN A. RILEY; ANDREW STROBL; MARK MERTES; OSWALDO SANDOVAL; JOSEPH ARSENAULT, S.S.A., J.C.L.

Archdiocesan Council on Finances—Rev. JOHN A. RILEY, Chancellor; MR. STEPHEN CLIFFORD; MR. GARY DAVIS; MR. KELLY DUBBERT; MR. MICHAEL EASTERDAY; MS. CARLA MILLS, CFO; MS. NANCY MELLARD; MR. KEVIN KELLY; MS. KATHLEEN LUSK; Rev. GARY PENNINGS, V.G.; MRS. LESLE KNOP; MS. JEANNE GORMAN; MR. JOHN SEITZER; MS. THERESA GORDZICA; MS. JULIE NEWMASTER; MR. MICHAEL SCHEOPNER; MR. MARK LESTER; MS. MARY STADLER; MR. JOHN CATON; MR. STEVE FRANKE; MRS. BETH COLEMAN; MR. JIM SCHMANK.

Archdiocesan Finance Officer—MS. CARLA MILLS.

Regional Pastoral Leaders—Revs. DANIEL GARDNER, Atchison; ANDREW STROBL, Johnson Co.; JEFFREY A. ERNST, O.F.M.Cap., Lawrence; RICHARD MCDONALD, Leavenworth; JOHN PILCHER, Topeka; BRANDON FARRAR, Southern; VACANT, Nemaha-Marshall; Rev. MARK MERTES, Wyandotte Co.

Archdiocesan Pastoral Council—Most Rev. JOSEPH NAUMANN; BART BASKA; BILL COCHRAN; JANE SHRIVER; STAN NILL; Sr. ANNE SHEPARD, O.S.B.; JANA BERSTED; ANABELLE WASSERMAN; BARBARA DEHAEMERS; SHANNON GOMEZ; KEN GUDENKAUF; BRIAN LILLIE; Sr. ELENA MORCELLI, A.V.I.; GAIL O'CONNOR; PHIL PUNSWICK; MATT RAMAGE; RHONDA SMITH; MIKE STADLER. Ex Officio: Revs. GARY PENNINGS, V.G., Vicar Gen.; JOHN RILEY, Chancellor; MR. STEVE EHART, Lead Consultant, Mission Strategy.

Catholic Foundation of Northeast Kansas—12615 Parallel Pkwy., Kansas City, 66109.

Catholic Education Foundation—12615 Parallel Pkwy., Kansas City, 66109.

Archdiocesan Archivist—(contact Chancellor's Office).

Archdiocesan Offices and Directors

Savior Pastoral Center—12601 Parallel, Kansas City, 66109. Tel: 913-721-1097; Fax: 913-721-2339; Email: savior@archkck.org; Web: www.saviorpastoralcenter.org. MR. TIMOTHY CHIK, Dir.

Black Catholics—BARBARA BAILEY, 2203 Parallel, Kansas City, 66104. Tel: 913-321-1958.

Evangelization—Deacon DANA NEARMYER, Dir.

Youth Evangelization—MR. RICK CHEEK, Consultant.

Adult Evangelization—MRS. EMILY LOPEZ, Lead Consultant; MS. KIMBERLY ZUBILLAGA, Consultant.

Prairie Star Ranch—12615 Parallel Pkwy., Kansas City, 66109. Tel: 913-721-1570; Fax: 913-721-2680. MR. GREGORY WELLNITZ, Dir.

Deaf Ministry—MS. KATIE LOCUS, Consultant.

Marriage and Family Life—Deacon TONY ZIMMERMAN, Lead Consultant. Consultants: BRAD DUPONT; LIBBY DUPONT; SAM MEIER, (Sacred Sexuality: Happier Marriages, Safer Families).

Liturgy and Sacramental Life—MR. MICHAEL PODREBARAC.

Pro-life / Respect Life—DEBRA NIESEN.

Social Justice—MR. BILL SCHOLL.

Special Needs—MR. TOM RACUNAS.

Hispanic Ministry—Rev. GIANANTONIO BAGGIO, Dir.

Administrative Services—MRS. RITA HERKEN.

Human Resources—MICHELE KOOIMAN.

Stewardship and Development—MRS. LESLE KNOP, Dir., 12615 Parallel Pkwy., Kansas City, 66109. Tel: 913-721-1570.

Catholic Youth Organization—5041 Reinhardt Dr., Mission, 66205. JOHN MCGOLDRICK, Exec. Dir., Email: john@cyojwa.org.

Catholic Charities of Northeast Kansas, Inc.—See Institution section H.

Council for Catholic Charismatic Renewal—Rev. ANTHONY OUELLETTE.

Archdiocesan Council of Catholic Women (ACCW)—VACANT, Spiritual Moderator.

Catholic Charities Foundation of Northeast Kansas—See Institution section H.

Catholic Neighborhood Outreach, Inc.—See Institution section H.

Communications—ANITA MCSORLEY, Media Liaison, 12615 Parallel Pkwy., Kansas City, 66109. Tel: 913-721-1570.

Catholic Committee on Scouting—Rev. SHAWN TUNINK, J.C.L., Chap.

Holy Childhood Association—Rev. RICHARD HALVORSON, 12615 Parallel Pkwy., Kansas City, 66109. Tel: 913-721-1570.

Kansas Catholic Conference—204 S.W. 8th Ave., Topeka, 66603. Tel: 785-227-9247; Web: www.kscathconf.org. GERALD "CHUCK" WEBER JR., Exec. Dir.

Legion of Mary—Rev. QUENTIN SCHMITZ, Spiritual Dir.

Newspaper "The Leaven"—Rev. MARK GOLDASICH, Editor, Mailing Address: 12615 Parallel Pkwy., Kansas City, 66109. Tel: 913-721-1570; Fax: 913-721-5276.

Presbyteral Council—Rev. PATRICK SULLIVAN, Chm.

Pontifical Mission Societies in the United States—Rev. RICHARD HALVORSON, 12615 Parallel Pkwy., Kansas City, 66109.

Office of Child & Youth Protection—Rev. JOHN RILEY.

Schools—DR. KATHLEEN O'HARA, Supt.; ALLISON CARNEY, Assoc. Supt.; DR. KAREN KROH, Assoc. Supt. for Student Svcs., 12615 Parallel Pkwy., Kansas City, 66109. Tel: 913-721-1570.

Victim Assistance Coordinator—LINDA SLATER-TRIMBLE, Tel: 913-298-9244.

Vocations Office—Rev. DANIEL MORRIS, Dir.

CLERGY, PARISHES, MISSIONS AND PAROCHIAL SCHOOLS

CITY OF KANSAS CITY

(WYANDOTTE COUNTY)

1—CATHEDRAL OF ST. PETER THE APOSTLE (1907)
409 N. 15th St., 66102. Tel: 913-371-0840. Revs. Harold F. Schneider; John C. Reynolds, Sacramental Asst.; Deacon Michael Hill.
See Resurrection Catholic School at the Cathedral under Elementary Schools, Interparochial in the Institution Section.
Catechesis Religious Program—Tel: 816- 200-4636; Email: mramirez@cthedralkck.org. Martha Ramirez, D.R.E. Students 139.

2—ALL SAINTS (2007)
811 Vermont Ave., 66101. Tel: 913-371-1837; Tel: 913-573-2067; Fax: 913-621-2709; Email: secretary@allsaintsparishkck.org. Revs. Oswaldo Sandoval; Salvador Diaz Llamas, Parochial Vicar; Nancy Luna-Loera, Pastoral Min./Coord.; Mrs. Lazara Beatriz Camareno, Catechism Coord.; Mrs. Diana Rocha, Sec.
See Resurrection Catholic School at the Cathedral under Elementary Schools, Interparochial in the Institution Section.

3—BLESSED SACRAMENT (1899)
2203 Parallel Ave., 66104. Tel: 913-321-1958. Revs. Mark Mertes; Thomas Kearns, In Res., (Retired); John C. Reynolds, In Res.
Catechesis Religious Program—Lucy Bernal, M.A., D.R.E. Students 118.

4—CHRIST THE KING (1939)
3024 N. 53rd St., 66104. Tel: 913-287-8823; Email: ctkkcks@gmail.com. Rev. Mark Mertes.
School—Christ the King School, (Grades PreK-8), 3027 N. 54th St., 66104. Tel: 913-287-8883; Fax: 913-287-7409; Web: www.ctkkck.eduk12.org. Cathy Fithian, Prin.; Elizabeth Rebeck, Librarian. Lay Teachers 13; Students 233.
Catechesis Religious Program—Sue Reaves, D.R.E., Email: suereaves60@gmail.com. Students 61.

5—SS. CYRIL AND METHODIUS (1904) (Slovak), Merged with St. Joseph and St. Benedict, Kansas City to form All Saints, Kansas City.

6—HOLY FAMILY (1907) (Slovenian)
274 Orchard Ave., 66101. Tel: 913-371-1561. Rev. Peter Jaramillo, S.S.A.
See Resurrection Catholic School at the Cathedral under Elementary Schools, Interparochial in the Institution Section.

7—HOLY NAME (1876)
1001 Southwest Blvd., 66103. Tel: 913-236-9219; Email: holynamechurchkck@gmail.com; Web: www.holynameparish.org. 16 S. Iowa St., 66103. Rev. Anthony Ouellette
Legal Title: Holy Name of Jesus Parish
School—Holy Name School, (Grades PreSchool-8), 1007 S.W. Blvd., 66103. Tel: 913-722-1032; Fax: 913-722-4175; Email: holyname@archkcks.org; Web: www.holynamecatholicschool.org. Amanda Vega-Mavec, Prin. Lay Teachers 10; Students 116.
Catechesis Religious Program—Jennifer Starcke, D.R.E. Students 11.

8—ST. JOHN THE BAPTIST (1898) (Croatian)
708 N. Fourth St., 66101. Tel: 913-371-0627. Rev. Peter Jaramillo, S.S.A.
See Resurrection Catholic School at the Cathedral under Elementary Schools, Interparochial in the Institution Section.

9—ST. JOHN THE EVANGELIST, Merged with Sacred Heart, Kansas City to form Our Lady of Unity, Kansas City.

10—ST. JOSEPH AND ST. BENEDICT, Merged with SS. Cyril and Methodius, Kansas City to form All Saints, Kansas City.

11—ST. MARY-ST. ANTHONY (1858)
632 Tauromee, 66101. Tel: 913-371-1408; Email: smsakcks@gmail.com. Revs. Peter Jaramillo, S.S.A.; John Melnick, S.S.A.; Joseph Arsenault, S.S.A., J.C.L.
Res.: 615 N. Seventh St., 66101. Tel: 913-621-2120.
Catechesis Religious Program—Ricardo Gomez, D.R.E. Students 48.

12—OUR LADY AND ST. ROSE, Attended by Blessed Sacrament, Kansas City.
8th & Quindero, 66104. Tel: 913-321-1958. c/o Blessed Sacrament, 2203 Parallel, 66104. Rev. Mark Mertes.
Church: 2300 N. Eighth St., 66101.
Catechesis Religious Program—Tel: 913-321-1958; Fax: 913-321-1997. Franchiel Nyakatura, D.R.E. Students 23.

13—OUR LADY OF UNITY (2007)
2910 Strong Ave., 66106. Tel: 913-677-4621. Revs. John Cordes; Oscar Garavito, Parochial Vicar; Deacon Keith Geary.
See Our Lady of Unity School, Kansas City under Elementary Schools, Interparochial located in the Institution section.
Catechesis Religious Program—Diana Ortega, D.R.E., Email: olureligiondirector@gmail.com; Lety Fernandez, D.R.E., Email: leticiasoliso4@gmail.com. Students 252.

14—ST. PATRICK'S (1873)
1086 N. 94th St., 66112. Tel: 913-299-3370; Email: tsmith@archkckcs.org; Email: stpatrickchurchkck@archkckcs.org. Rev. John Riley, Parochial Admin.; Rev. Msgr. Gary Applegate, J.C.L., Sacramental Min.; Revs. Agustin Martinez, Parochial Vicar; Michael Van Lian; Deacon David Cresswell.
School—St. Patrick's School, (Grades K-8), 1066 N. 94th, 66112. Tel: 913-299-8131; Fax: 913-299-2845; Email: ftorres@stpatrickkck.eduk12.net. Felicia Torres, Prin.; Emily Yantz, Librarian. Lay Teachers 22; Students 262.
Catechesis Religious Program—Tel: 913-299-3728. Betty Ann Battson, D.R.E., Email: bbattson@stpatrickkck.eduk12.net. Students 214.

15—SACRED HEART, Merged with St. John the Evangelist, Kansas City to form Our Lady of Unity, Kansas City.

16—ST. THOMAS THE APOSTLE, Closed. For inquiries for parish records contact the chancery.

OUTSIDE THE CITY OF KANSAS CITY

ALMA, WABAUNSEE CO., HOLY FAMILY (1874) [CEM]
Attended by Served from St. Bernard, Wamego.
1st & Kansas, Alma, 66401. Tel: 785-449-2537; Email: holyfamilyparishalma@gmail.com. P.O. Box 128, Alma, 66401. Rev. Michael Peterson.
Catechesis Religious Program—c/o St. Bernard, 17665 Old Post Rd., Wamego, 66547. Dan Deiter, D.R.E. Students 22.

ATCHISON, ATCHISON CO.

1—ST. BENEDICT (2013) [JC]
1001 N. 2nd St., Atchison, 66002. Tel: 913-367-0671; Email: lcross@benedictine.edu; Web: www.stbenedictatchison.org. Very Rev. Jeremy Heppler, O.S.B.
Church: 1000 N. 2nd St., Atchison, 66002.
Tel: 913-360-8543.
St. Joseph Church, 845 Spring Garden, Atchison, 66002.
St. Patrick Church, 19384 234th Rd., Atchison, 66002.
School—St. Benedict School, (Grades PreK-8), 201 Division, Atchison, 66002. Tel: 913-367-3503; Fax: 913-367-9324; Email: dliebsch@benedictine.edu; Web: www.stbenedictatchison.org/school. Diane Liebsch, Prin. Religion Teacher 1; Lay Teachers 13; Students 182.
Catechesis Religious Program—Paige Rioux, C.C.D. Dir. Students 54.
Mission—St. John's.

2—ST. JOSEPH (1949) [JC] Merged with St. Benedict's, Atchison, Sacred Heart, Atchison and St. Patrick, St. Patrick to form St. Benedict, Atchison.

3—SACRED HEART (1892) [JC] Merged with St. Benedict's, Atchison, St. Joseph, Atchison and St. Patrick, St. Patrick to form St. Benedict, Atchison.

AXTELL, MARSHALL CO., ST. MICHAEL
504 6th St., Axtell, 66403. Tel: 785-736-2220; Fax: 785-736-2230; Email: jshau47@gmail.com. P.O. Box K, Axtell, 66403. Rev. James Shaughnessy.
Catechesis Religious Program—Tel: 785-736-2260. Kathleen Heiman, D.R.E., Tel: 785-736-2373; Email: heiman@bluevalley.net. Students 81.

BAILEYVILLE, NEMAHA CO., SACRED HEART (1912) [CEM]
357 Third St., P.O. Box 36, Baileyville, 66404.
Tel: 785-336-6464; Email: pastor@shbaileyville.com. Rev. Reginald Saldanha.
Catechesis Religious Program—Alicia Keegan, D.R.E. Students 45.

BALDWIN, DOUGLAS CO., ANNUNCIATION (1859) [CEM]
Mission: St. Francis of Assisi, Lapeer.
740 N. 6th St., Baldwin City, 66006.
Tel: 785-594-3700; Web: annunciationchurchks.org. Rev. Jomon Palatty, M.S.F.S., Parochial Admin.
Catechesis Religious Program—Students 61.

BASEHOR, LEAVENWORTH CO., HOLY ANGELS (1866) [CEM]
15438 Leavenworth Rd., Basehor, 66007.
Tel: 913-724-1665; Email: holyangelsbasehor@gmail.com. Rev. Richard J. McDonald.
Res.: 15440 Leavenworth Rd., Basehor, 66007.

Tel: 913-724-3122; Fax: 913-724-4148; Web: www.HolyAngelsBasehor.org.
Catechesis Religious Program—Cathy Kern, D.R.E. Students 221.

BEATTIE, MARSHALL CO., ST. MALACHY (1880) [CEM] Attended by Served from St. Gregory, Marysville.
1012 Main St., Beattie, 66406. Tel: 785-562-3302. c/o St. Gregory Church, 207 N. 14th St., Ste. B, Marysville, 66508. Rev. Nathan Haverland.
Catechesis Religious Program—Students 10.

BENDENA, DONIPHAN CO., ST. BENEDICT (1855) [CEM] Attended by Served from St. Joseph Parish in Wathena.
676 St. Benedict Rd., Bendena, 66008.
Tel: 785-359-6725. P.O. Box 128, Bendena, 66008. Rev. Francis Bakyor, (Ghana).
Catechesis Religious Program—Tel: 785-359-6725. B.J. Spiker, D.R.E. Students 32.

BLAINE, POTTAWATOMIE CO., ST. COLUMBKILLE, Attended by Served from Annunciation in Frankfort.
13311 Hwy. 16, Blaine, 6666549. Tel: 785-292-4462; Email: annparfrankfort@bluevalley.net. Mailing Address: c/o Annunciation, 213 E. 5th St., Frankfort, 66427. Rev. Anthony Chendumalli, Parochial Admin.
Catechesis Religious Program—Sally Olson, D.R.E. Students 27.

BLUE RAPIDS, MARSHALL CO., ST. MONICA - ST. ELIZABETH, Attended by
1007 East Ave., Blue Rapids, 66411.
Tel: 785-292-4462; Email: annparfrankfort@bluevalley.net. Mailing Address: c/o Annunciation, 213 E. 5th St., Frankfort, 66427. Rev. Anthony Chendumalli, Parochial Admin. Served from Annunciation, Frankfort.
Catechesis Religious Program—Sarah Toerber, D.R.E. Students 24.

BURLINGTON, COFFEY CO., ST. FRANCIS XAVIER (1871) [CEM]
214 Juniatta, Burlington, 66839. Tel: 620-364-5671; Email: stfrancisoffice@embarqmail.com. Rev. Quentin Schmitz.
Catechesis Religious Program—Jessica Beyer, D.R.E.; Angela Myers, Youth Min. Students 59.

CORNING, NEMAHA CO., ST. PATRICK (1890) [CEM] Attended by
1387 56th Rd., Corning, 66417. Tel: 785-868-2790. Rev. Gova Narisetty, Parochial Admin. Served from St. Vincent de Paul, Onaga.
Church: 6606 Atlantic, Corning, 66417. Email: 3parishassistant@gmail.com; Web: www.3catholicparishkck.com.
Catechesis Religious Program—Ann Stallbaumer, D.R.E.; Candice Schmitz, D.R.E. Students 151.

DELIA, JACKSON CO., SACRED HEART OF JESUS, Closed. For inquiries for parish records contact Immaculate Conception, St. Marys.

DONIPHAN, DONIPHAN CO., ST. JOHN, Closed. For inquiries for parish records contact St. Benedict's, Atchison.

EASTON, LEAVENWORTH CO.
1—ST. JOSEPH-ST. LAWRENCE (2009) [CEM]
211 W. Riley St., P.O. Box 129, Easton, 66020.
Tel: 913-773-5712; Fax: 913-773-8401; Email: sjslparish@gmail.com. Rev. Mathew Francis.
St. Joseph of the Valley Church: 31151 207th St., Leavenworth, 66048.
Catechesis Religious Program—Jennifer Roggenkamp, D.R.E. Students 73.
2—ST. LAWRENCE (1878) [CEM] Merged with St. Joseph of the Valley, Leavenworth to form St. Joseph-St. Lawrence, Easton.

EDGERTON, JOHNSON CO., ASSUMPTION (1857) [CEM] Merged with Sacred Heart, Gardner to form Divine Mercy, Gardner.

EFFINGHAM, ATCHISON CO., ST. ANN, [CEM]
301 Williams St., Box 54, Effingham, 66023.
Tel: 913-833-5660. Rev. Daniel Gardner, Parochial Admin.
Catechesis Religious Program—Jill Thorne, D.R.E. Students 35.

EMERALD, ANDERSON CO., ST. PATRICK
33721 NW Crawford Rd., Williamsburg, 66095.
Tel: 620-364-5671; Email: stfrancisoffice@embarqmail.com. Mailing Address: c/o St. Francis Xavier, 214 Juniatta, Burlington, 66839. Rev. Quentin Schmitz. Served from St. Francis Xavier, Burlington.

EMMETT, POTTAWATOMIE CO., HOLY CROSS, Merged with Immaculate Conception, St. Marys.

EMPORIA, LYON CO.
1—ST. CATHERINE (1923) [CEM] Attended by
205 S. Lawrence St., Emporia, 66801.
Tel: 620-342-1368; Email: saintcatherineemporia@gmail.com. Rev. Nicholas Blaha.
Catechesis Religious Program—Sr. Aurora Villamar, D.R.E. Students 167.
2—SACRED HEART (1874) [CEM]
27 Cottonwood St., Emporia, 66801.
Tel: 620-342-1061; Fax: 620-342-0450; Email: loiss@shemporia.org; Email: marciel@shemporia.org. Rev. Brandon Farrar.
School—Sacred Heart School, (Grades K-6), 102 Cottonwood St., Emporia, 66801. Tel: 620-343-7394; Email: mbarnhart@shemporia.org; Web: www.shsemporia.eduk12.net. Darby O'Neill, Prin.; Becky DeJesus, Librarian. Lay Teachers 8; Students 67.
Catechesis Religious Program—Tel: 620-342-1061. Joan Dold, D.R.E. Students 124.

ESKRIDGE, WABAUNSEE CO., ST. JOHN VIANNEY, Closed. For inquiries on parish records, contact Immaculate Conception, St. Marys.

EUDORA, DOUGLAS CO., HOLY FAMILY (1859) [CEM]
820 Birch St., Eudora, 66025. Tel: 785-542-2788. Rev. Michael Scully, O.F.M.Cap.
Catechesis Religious Program—Molly Pratt, D.R.E., Email: mollypratt.holyfamilychurch@gmail.com. Students 171.

FIDELITY, BROWN CO., ST. AUGUSTINE (1860) [CEM] Attended by Served from Sacred Heart, Sabetha
1948 Acorn Rd., Sabetha, 66534. Tel: 785-284-0888; Email: jzarse@archkck.org. 1031 S. 12th St., Sabetha, 66534. Rev. Jaime Zarse.

FLUSH, POTTAWATOMIE CO., ST. JOSEPH, Attended by Served from St. Bernard in Wamego.
8965 Flush Rd., St. George, 66535. Tel: 785-494-8234; Fax: 785-456-7869; Email: stbernard66547@gmail.com; Web: www.saintbernardwamego.com. Mailing Address: c/o St. Bernard, 17665 Old Post Rd., Wamego, 66547. Revs. Michael Peterson, Tel: 785-456-7869; Carl Dekat, In Res., (Retired).
Catechesis Religious Program—Students 79.

FRANKFORT, MARSHALL CO., ANNUNCIATION (1880) [CEM]
213 E. Fifth St., Frankfort, 66427. Tel: 785-292-4462; Email: annparfrankfort@bluevalley.net. Rev. Anthony Chendumalli, Parochial Admin.
Catechesis Religious Program—Jan Stallbaumer, D.R.E. (Elementary). Students 97.

GARDNER, JOHNSON CO., DIVINE MERCY (2011) [CEM]
555 W. Main St., Gardner, 66030. Tel: 913-856-7781; Email: secretary@divinemercyks.org; Web: www.divinemercyks.org. Rev. Adam Wilczak.
Sacred Heart Church—Email: info@divinemercyks.org.
Assumption Church, 114 E. Nelsom, Edgerton, 66021.
Catechesis Religious Program—Email: maria@divinemercyks.org. Maria Lopeman, D.R.E. Students 439.

GARNETT, ANDERSON CO., HOLY ANGELS, [CEM]
5500 E. 4th Ave., Garnett, 66032. Tel: 785-448-1686; Email: office@hasjparishes.com; Web: hasjparishes.com. 520 E. 4th Ave., Garnett, 66032. Rev. Daniel Stover.
Res.: 514 E. Fourth, Garnett, 66032.
Tel: 785-448-3846.
See St. Rose Philippine Duchesne School under Elementary Schools, Interparochial located in the Institution Section.

GREELEY, ANDERSON CO., ST. JOHN THE BAPTIST (1881) [CEM] Attended by Served from Holy Angels, Garnett.
427 S. Prairie, P.O. Box 94, Greeley, 66033.
Tel: 785-448-1686; Email: office@hasjparishes.com; Web: www.hasjparishes.com. 520 E. 4th Ave., Garnett, 66032. Rev. Daniel Stover.
See St. Rose Philippine Duchesne School under Elementary Schools, Interparochial located in the Institution Section.
Catechesis Religious Program—Tel: 785-448-1686. Joyce Burris, D.R.E. Students 3.

HARTFORD, LYON CO., ST. MARY, [CEM] Attended by
501 Mechanic St., Hartford, 66854.
Tel: 620-475-3326. 308 Iowa St., Olpe, 66865. Revs. Brandon Farrar, Parochial Admin.; Ratna Nannam, Parochial Vicar. St. Joseph Church, Olpe KS
Catechesis Religious Program—P.O. Box 147, Hartford, 66854. Students 6.

HIAWATHA, BROWN CO., ST. ANN (1882)
800 Hiawatha Ave., Hiawatha, 66434.
Tel: 785-742-3010; Email: stanns@rainbowtel.net. Rev. Daniel Gardner.
Catechesis Religious Program—Brian Lillie, D.R.E.; Kim Lillie, D.R.E.; Kevin Hill, D.R.E.; Ellen Hill, D.R.E. Students 77.

HOLTON, JACKSON CO., ST. DOMINIC (1870) [CEM]
115 E. 5th St., Holton, 66436. Tel: 785-364-3262; Web: www.jacocatholics.org. Rev. Jonathan Dizon.
Res.: 416 Ohio Ave., Holton, 66436.
Tel: 785-362-7026.
Catechesis Religious Program—Barbara Berg, D.R.E. Students 89.
Mission—Our Lady of the Snows Oratory, Potawatomi Reservation, Mayetta, Jackson Co. 66509.

HORTON, BROWN CO., ST. LEO (1887) [CEM 3] Attended by Served from St. Ann, Hiawatha.
1340 First Ave. E., Horton, 66439. Tel: 785-486-3971; Email: smslchurch@rainbowtel.net. Rev. Daniel Gardner.
Catechesis Religious Program—Rhonda Smith, D.R.E. Students 58.

KELLY, NEMAHA CO., ST. BEDE (1901) [CEM] Attended by Served from St. Vincent de Paul in Onaga.
7344 Drought St., Kelly, 66538. Tel: 785-889-4896. c/o Vincent de Paul: 809 Clifton St., P.O. Box 396, Onaga, 66521. Rev. Gova Narisetty, Parochial Admin.
Catechesis Religious Program—Sonny Gore, D.R.E.; Colette Hermesch, D.R.E.; Janice Kramer, D.R.E. Students 55.

LACYGNE, LINN CO., OUR LADY OF LOURDES (1982) Attended by Served from St. Philip Neri, Osawatomie.
819 N. 5th St., La Cygne, 66040. Tel: 913-755-2652; Email: bclayton@archkck.org; Web: www.miamilinncatholics.org. Mailing Address: P.O. Box 4, Osawatomie, 66064. Rev. Barry R. Clayton.
Catechesis Religious Program—Allyson James, D.R.E. Students 8.

LANSING, LEAVENWORTH CO., ST. FRANCIS DE SALES (1886)
900 Ida St., Lansing, 66043. Tel: 913-727-3742; Email: parish@stfrancislansing.org; Web: stfrancislansing.org. Rev. William McEvoy; Sr. Josephine Macias, C.D.P., D.R.E.
Catechesis Religious Program—Students 137.

LAPEER, DOUGLAS CO., ST. FRANCIS OF ASSISI (1863) [CEM] Attended by Served from Annunciation in Baldwin City
452 E. 300 Rd., Overbrook, 66524. Tel: 785-594-3700; Email: baldwincitycatholics@gmail.com. Mailing Address: c/o Annunciation, 740 N. 6th St., Baldwin City, 66006. Rev. Jomon Palatty, M.S.F.S., Parochial Admin.

LAWRENCE, DOUGLAS CO.
1—CORPUS CHRISTI (1981) [JC]
6001 Bob Billings Pkwy., Lawrence, 66049-5200.
Tel: 785-843-6286; Email: church@cccparish.org. Rev. Michael Mulvany; Rev. Msgr. Vincent E. Krische, (Retired).
School—Corpus Christi School, (Grades PreK-8), Tel: 785-331-3374; Email: marym@cccparish.org; Web: www.cccparish.org. Mary Mattern, Prin. Lay Teachers 27; Students 256.
Catechesis Religious Program—Sr. Doris Engeman, F.S.H.F., D.R.E. Students 110.
2—ST. JOHN THE EVANGELIST (1858) [CEM]
1229 Vermont St., Lawrence, 66044.
Tel: 785-843-0109; Fax: 785-749-5064. Revs. Jeffrey A. Ernst, O.F.M.Cap.; Barnabas Eichor, O.F.M.Cap., Parochial Vicar; Michael Scully, O.F.M.Cap., In Res.
School—St. John the Evangelist School, (Grades PreK-8), 1208 Kentucky, Lawrence, 66044.
Tel: 785-843-9511; Fax: 785-843-7143; Email: newton@saint-johns.net; Web: www.saint-johns.net/school. Patricia Newton, Prin.; Karen Rinke, Librarian. Lay Teachers 22; Students 266.
Catechesis Religious Program—Lois Mersmann, D.R.E., Email: lmersmann@saint-johns.net. Students 200.

LEAVENWORTH, LEAVENWORTH CO.
1—ST. CASIMIR, (Polish), Merged with Sacred Heart, Leavenworth to form Sacred Heart-St. Casimir, Leavenworth.
2—IMMACULATE CONCEPTION (1855) Merged with St. Joseph's, Leavenworth to form Immaculate Conception-St. Joseph, Leavenworth.
3—IMMACULATE CONCEPTION-ST. JOSEPH (2007) (Old Cathedral)
747 Osage, Leavenworth, 66048. Tel: 913-682-3953; Email: icsj@sbcglobal.net. Rev. David McEvoy, O.-Carm.; Bro. David McGinnis, O.Carm., Pastoral Assoc.; Deacons Timothy McEvoy, Pastoral Assoc.; Dean Gilbert, Pastoral Assoc.
Immaculate Conception Church: 711 N. 5th St., Leavenworth, 66048.
St. Joseph Church: 306 N. Broadway, Leavenworth, 66048.
Rectory—300 N. Broadway, Leavenworth, 66048. Tel: 913-682-0809.
See Xavier Elementary School, Leavenworth under Elementary Schools, Interparochial located in the Institution section.
Catechesis Religious Program—Students 91.
Mission—Sacred Heart, Leavenworth, Kickapoo Twp. 66048.
4—ST. JOSEPH (1858) Merged with Immaculate Conception, Leavenworth to form Immaculate Conception-St. Joseph's, Leavenworth.
5—ST. JOSEPH OF THE VALLEY (1863) [CEM] Consolidated with St. Lawrence, Easton to form St. Joseph-St. Lawrence, Easton.
6—SACRED HEART OF JESUS, [CEM] Merged with St. Casimir, Leavenworth to form Sacred Heart-St. Casimir, Leavenworth.
7—SACRED HEART-ST. CASIMIR (2007)
521 Linn St., Leavenworth, 66048. Tel: 913-772-2424. Rev. John Riley, Parochial Admin.; Deacon Robert D. Zbylut; James Skahan.

Res.: 1401 Second Ave., Leavenworth, 66048.
Tel: 913-772-1787; Fax: 913-651-2150.
Sacred Heart Church: 1405 2nd Ave., Leavenworth, 66048.
St. Casimir Church: 715 Pennsylvania, Leavenworth, 66048.
See Xavier Elementary School, Leavenworth under Elementary Schools, Interparochial located in the Institution section.
Catechesis Religious Program—Tel: 913-772-1787. Students 28.

LEAWOOD, JOHNSON CO.

1—CHURCH OF THE NATIVITY (1986)
3800 W. 119th St., Leawood, 66209.
Tel: 913-491-5017; Email: info@kcnativity.org. Revs. Michael Hawken; Alfred Rockers, In Res., (Retired); Deacons Michael Schreck; Ralph Schramp.
School—Church of the Nativity School, (Grades PreK-8), 3700 W. 119th St., Leawood, 66209.
Tel: 913-338-4330; Fax: 913-338-2050; Email: nativityparishschool@kcnativity.org; Web: www.nativityparishschool.com. Mr. David Kearney, Prin.; Jean Stump, Librarian. Lay Teachers 26; Students 267.
Catechesis Religious Program—Sr. Helen Smith, D.R.E. Students 227.
Christian Formation Office—

2—CURE OF ARS (1959)
9401 Mission Rd., Leawood, 66206.
Tel: 913-649-1337; Email: cureparish@cureofars.com; Web: cureofars.com. Revs. Richard Storey; Justin Hamilton, Parochial Vicar; Deacons Phillip Nguyen; Stephen White.
School—Cure of Ars School, (Grades K-8), 9403 Mission Rd., Leawood, 66206. Tel: 913-648-2620; Fax: 913-648-3810; Email: school@cureofars.com. Andrew Legler, Prin.; Josephine Nigro, Librarian. Lay Teachers 43; Students 582.
Catechesis Religious Program—Bernadette Myers, D.R.E. Students 167.

3—ST. MICHAEL THE ARCHANGEL (1999)
14251 Nall Ave., Overland Park, 66223.
Tel: 913-402-3900. Revs. Brian Schieber; Matthew Nagle, Parochial Vicar; Shawn Tunink, J.C.L., Parochial Vicar; Deacons Mark Stukel; John Weist.
School—St. Michael the Archangel School, (Grades K-8), 14201 Nall Ave., Leawood, 66223.
Tel: 913-402-3950; Fax: 913-851-8221; Email: molly.mincher@stmichaelcp.org; Web: https://stmichael.eduk12.net. Michael Cullinan, Prin.; Janet O'Connell, Asst. Prin.; Elaine Glenski, Librarian. Lay Teachers 34; Students 533.
Catechesis Religious Program—Shawna Davidson, D.R.E., Tel: 913-402-3963; Email: shawna.davidson@stmichaelcp.org. Students 707.

LENEXA, JOHNSON CO., HOLY TRINITY (1880)
9150 Pflumm Rd., Lenexa, 66215. Tel: 913-888-2770. Revs. Michael Koller; Gerard Alba, Parochial Vicar; Deacons Dana Nearmyer; Stuart Holland, Dir. of Christian Formation & Lit.
School—Holy Trinity School, (Grades K-8), 13600 W. 92nd St., Lenexa, 66215. Tel: 913-888-3250; Fax: 913-438-2572; Email: smerfen@htslenexa.org; Web: www.htslenexa.org. Scott Merfen, Prin.; Kelly Kinnan, Librarian; Susan Gasper, Librarian; Lori Lorg, Librarian. Lay Teachers 40; Students 594.
Catechesis Religious Program—Students 297.

LILLIS, MARSHALL CO., ST. JOSEPH, [CEM] Closed. For inquiries for parish records contact Annunciation, Frankfort.

LOUISBURG, MIAMI CO., IMMACULATE CONCEPTION (1887) [CEM]
Office: 602 S. Elm, Louisburg, 66053.
Tel: 913-837-2295; Email: iccc@mokancomm.net. P.O. Box 118, Louisburg, 66053. Rev. Msgr. Robert Bergman; Deacon George Karnaze.
Catechesis Religious Program—Students 123.

MARYSVILLE, MARSHALL CO., ST. GREGORY (1862) [CEM]
1310 Carolina, Marysville, 66508. Tel: 785-562-3302; Email: parishoffice@stgregorychurch.org; Web: www.stgregorychurch.org. 207 N. 14th, Ste. B, Marysville, 66508. Rev. Nathan Haverland.
Res.: 206 N. 14th, Marysville, 66508.
Tel: 785-562-2989.
School—St. Gregory School, (Grades PreK-6), 207 N. 14th, Marysville, 66508. Tel: 785-562-2831; Email: kfarrell@stgregorychurch.org; Web: www.stgregorychurch.org/school. Karen Farrell, Prin. Lay Teachers 9; Students 93.
Catechesis Religious Program—Allyson Lauer, D.R.E. Students 21.

MAYETTA, JACKSON CO., ST. FRANCIS XAVIER, [CEM] Attended by Served from St. Dominic in Holton.
Mailing Address: c/o St. Dominic, 115 E. Fifth St., Holton, 66436. Tel: 785-364-3262; Email: parish@jacocatholics.org; Web: www.jacocatholics.org. Rev. Jonathan Dizon.
Catechesis Religious Program—Tel: 785-966-2690. Barbara Berg, D.R.E. Students 34.

MERIDEN, JEFFERSON CO., ST. ALOYSIUS (1882) [CEM] Attended by St. Theresa, Perry.
615 Wyandotte St., Meriden, 66512.
Tel: 785-484-3312; Email: stalsmer@yahoo.com. P.O. Box 364, Meriden, 66512. Rev. James Moster, O.F.M.Cap.
Catechesis Religious Program—Tel: 785-383-3035. Cassandra Bevitt, D.R.E. Students 56.

MISSION, JOHNSON CO., ST. PIUS X (1954)
5500 Woodson Rd., Mission, 66202.
Tel: 913-432-4808; Email: spxchurch@archkckcs.org; Web: spxmission.org. Rev. Kenneth W. Kelly.
Res.: 5601 Woodson Rd., Mission, 66202.
Fax: 913-432-2086.
See John Paul II School under Elementary Schools, Interparochial located in the Institution Section.
Catechesis Religious Program—Kathleen O'Bryan, D.R.E. Students 55.

MOONEY CREEK, JEFFERSON CO., CORPUS CHRISTI (1857) [CEM] Attended by Served from St. Joseph, Nortonville.
Mailing Address: 18760 Rogers Rd., Atchison, 66002. Tel: 913-886-2030; Email: sj.ic.cc.parishoffice@gmail.com. Rev. Lazar Carasala, (India) Parochial Admin.
Catechesis Religious Program—Lisa Kramer, D.R.E. Students 27.

MOUND CITY, LINN CO., SACRED HEART SHRINE TO ST. PHILIPPINE DUCHESNE (1942) [CEM] Attended by Attended by St. Philip Neri, Osawatomie.
729 W. Main St., Mound City, 66056.
Tel: 913-755-2652; Email: bclayton@archkck.org; Web: www.miamilinncatholics.org. P.O. Box H, Mound City, 66056. Rev. Barry R. Clayton; Deacon Don Poole.
Catechesis Religious Program—Tel: 913-795-2724. Jeff Dawson, D.R.E. Students 27.

NORTONVILLE, JEFFERSON CO., ST. JOSEPH, [CEM]
221 N. Sycamore, Nortonville, 66060.
Tel: 913-886-2030; Email: sj.ic.cc.parishoffice@gmail.com. Rev. Lazar Carasala, (India) Parochial Admin.
Catechesis Religious Program—Donna Noll, D.R.E. Students 36.

OLATHE, JOHNSON CO.

1—ST. JOHN PAUL II CATHOLIC CHURCH
16680 S. Lind Rd., Olathe, 66062. Tel: 913-747-9636; Email: office@jp2kc.org; Web: www.jp2kc.org. Rev. Andrew Strobl; Deacons Charles Cecil; Joseph Allen; Cindy Quirk, Business Mgr.
Catechesis Religious Program—Web: www.jp2kc.org/parish-faith-formation. Curtis Keddy, D.R.E., Email: curtiskeddy@jp2kc.org. Home-based religious education program; no enrollment.

2—ST. PAUL (1860) [JC]
21650 W. 115th Ter., Olathe, 66061.
Tel: 913-764-0323; Web: www.spcatholic.org. Rev. Michael Hermes; Deacon W.A. (Mike) Moffitt.
School—St. Paul School, (Grades PreK-8),
Tel: 913-764-0619; Fax: 913-768-6040; Web: www.spcatholic.org/school. Dr. Ann Connor, Prin. Lay Teachers 13; Students 174.
Catechesis Religious Program—Karla Melgar, C.R.E. Students 515.

3—PRINCE OF PEACE (1979)
16000 W. 143rd St., Olathe, 66062.
Tel: 913-782-8864; Email: parishoffice@popolathe.org. Revs. Gerald Volz; Agustin Martinez, Parochial Vicar; Deacons Gary (Mike) Denning; Chris Slater.
School—Prince of Peace School, (Grades K-8),
Tel: 913-764-0650; Fax: 913-393-0819; Email: jshriver@popolathe.org. Jane Shriver, Prin.; Melinda Yaklin, Asst. Prin.; Pam Schuetz, Librarian. Lay Teachers 35; Students 512.
Catechesis Religious Program—Tel: 913-829-1147; Fax: 913-747-7747. Shannon Cardaronella, Dir. Child Ministry; Kyle Kuckelman, High School Youth Min.; Martha Tonn, Pastoral Assoc. Faith Formation. Students 462.

OLPE, LYON CO., ST. JOSEPH (1885) [CEM]
306 Iowa, P.O. Box 165, Olpe, 66865.
Tel: 620-475-3326. Revs. Brandon Farrar, Parochial Admin.; Ratna Nannam, Parochial Vicar.
Catechesis Religious Program—Rose Redeker, D.R.E. Students 99.

ONAGA, POTTAWATOMIE CO., ST. VINCENT DE PAUL (1881) [CEM]
809 Clifton St., Onaga, 66521. Tel: 785-889-4896. Box 396, Onaga, 66521. Rev. Gova Narisetty, Parochial Admin.
Church Site: 308 E. 3rd St.
Catechesis Religious Program—Amber Magnet, D.R.E. Students 45.

OSAGE CITY, OSAGE CO., ST. PATRICK (1911) [CEM 3]
c/o St. Patrick, 309 S. 6th St., Osage City, 66523.
Tel: 785-528-3424; Fax: 785-528-3381; Email: bulletin@stpatrickchurches.org; Web: www.stpatrickchurches.org. Rev. Konda Nusi, Parochial Admin.
Catechesis Religious Program—Students 56.

OSAWATOMIE, MIAMI CO., ST. PHILIP NERI (1889)
514 Parker Ave., Osawatomie, 66064.
Tel: 913-755-2652; Email: bclayton@archkck.org; Web: www.miamilinncatholics.org. Mailing Address: P.O. Box 4, Osawatomie, 66064. Rev. Barry R. Clayton.
Church: 500 Parker Ave., Osawatomie, 66064. Email: cvitt@miamilinncatholics.org.
Catechesis Religious Program—Mary Alice Heppler, D.R.E. Students 23.
Chaplaincy—State Hospital for Mentally Ill, Osawatomie, 66064.

OTTAWA, FRANKLIN CO., SACRED HEART, [CEM]
408 S. Cedar St., Ottawa, 66067. Tel: 785-242-2174; Tel: 785-242-7258; Tel: 785-242-4297;
Fax: 785-242-2351; Email: shcottawa@gmail.com; Email: shcreled@sacredheartottawa.org. Rev. William Fisher.
School—Sacred Heart School, (Grades PreK-5), 426 S. Cedar, Ottawa, 66067. Tel: 785-242-4297; Fax: 785-242-0820; Email: lblaes@sacredheartottawa.eduk12.net; Web: sacredheartottawa.eduk12.net. Lisa Blaes, Prin.; Erin Zuelke, Librarian. Lay Teachers 6; Students 67.
Catechesis Religious Program—Tel: 785-242-7258. Carmelita Sieg, D.R.E. Students 56.

OVERLAND PARK, JOHNSON CO.

1—CHURCH OF THE ASCENSION (1991)
9510 W. 127th St., Overland Park, 66213.
Tel: 913-681-3348; Email: ascensionchurch@kcascension.org; Web: www.kcascension.org. Rev. Msgrs. Thomas Tank; Charles McGlinn, Sr. Parochial Vicar/In Res., (Retired); Rev. Michael Guastello, Parochial Vicar; Deacon John Stanley.
School—Church of the Ascension School aka Ascension Catholic School, (Grades PreK-8),
Tel: 913-851-2531; Fax: 913-851-2518; Email: bwright@acseagles.org; Web: www.acseagles.org. Becky Wright, Prin. Lay Teachers 37; Students 551.
Catechesis Religious Program—Tel: 913-681-7683; Email: woleary@kcascension.org. William O'Leary, D.R.E. Students 721.

2—HOLY CROSS aka Church of the Holy Cross (1968)
8311 W. 93rd St., Overland Park, 66212.
Tel: 913-381-2755; Email: churchoffice@holycrossopks.org; Web: holycrossopks.org. Revs. Michael C. Stubbs; Juan Carlos Franco, M.N.M., Parochial Vicar; Anthony C. Williams, In Res.
Res.: 8315 W. 93rd St., Overland Park, 66212.
Tel: 913-341-5618.
School—Holy Cross School, (Grades K-8), 8101 W. 95th, Overland Park, 66212. Tel: 913-381-7408; Fax: 913-381-1312; Email: gradeschool@hccsmail.com; Web: www.holycrosscatholicschool.com. Karen Hopson, Prin. Lay Teachers 24; Students 280.
Catechesis Religious Program—Tel: 913-381-2755. Robert Bacic, D.R.E., Email: rbacic@holycrossopks.org. Students 90.

3—HOLY SPIRIT (1981)
11300 W. 103rd St., Overland Park, 66214.
Tel: 913-492-7318; Fax: 913-492-7370. Revs. Richard Halvorson; Alessandro Borraccia.
School—Holy Spirit School, (Grades PreK-8),
Tel: 913-492-2582; Fax: 913-492-9613; Email: mwatson@hscatholic.org; Web: www.hscatholic.org. Michele Watson, Prin. Lay Teachers 26; Students 328.
Catechesis Religious Program—Tel: 913-492-7382. Sr. M. Teresa Pandl, F.S.G.M., D.R.E. Students 238.

4—QUEEN OF THE HOLY ROSARY (1944)
7023 W. 71st St., Overland Park, 66204.
Tel: 913-432-4616. Rev. William Bruning; Rev. Msgr. Gary Applegate, J.C.L., Sacramental Min.; Deacon Jim Lavin.
See John Paul II School under Elementary Schools, Interparochial located in the Institution Section.
Catechesis Religious Program—Tel: 913-722-2206. Denise Godinez, D.R.E. Students 132.

PAOLA, MIAMI CO., HOLY TRINITY (1859) [CEM]
400 S. East. St., Paola, 66071. Tel: 913-557-5067. Rev. Peter O'Sullivan.
School—Holy Trinity School, (Grades PreK-8), 601 E. Chippewa, Paola, 66071. Tel: 913-294-3286; Fax: 913-294-5286; Email: htsecretary@holytrinitypaola.org. Michelle Gavin, Prin. Lay Teachers 9; Students 97.
Catechesis Religious Program—Tel: 913-294-5492. Brian Bollinger, D.R.E.; Jenn Bollinger, D.R.E. Students 63.

PAXICO, WABAUNSEE CO., SACRED HEART (1884) [CEM] Served from St. Bernard, Wamego.
c/o St. Bernard, 22298 Newbury Rd., Paxico, 66526.
Tel: 785-636-5578; Email: sacredheartpaxico@gmail.com. Rev. Michael Peterson.
Catechesis Religious Program—Michelle Stuhlsatz, D.R.E. Students 31.

PERRY, JEFFERSON CO., ST. THERESA, [CEM 2]
209 Third, Perry, 66073. Tel: 785-597-5558; Email: rellis107@yahoo.com. P.O. Box 42, Perry, 66073. Rev. James Moster, O.F.M.Cap.
Catechesis Religious Program—Tel: 785-597-5558. Jill Guilfoyle, D.R.E. (K-12). Students 39.

PRAIRIE VILLAGE, JOHNSON CO., ST. ANN (1949) [CEM]

7231 Mission Rd., Prairie Village, 66208.
Tel: 913-660-1182; Email: stanncatholicchurch@stannpv.org; Web: www.stannpv.org. Rev. Craig Maxim; Deacons Todd Brower; Stephen Nguyen.
School—St. Ann School, (Grades K-8), 7241 Mission Rd., Prairie Village, 66208. Tel: 913-660-1101; Fax: 913-660-1132; Email: mriley@stannpv.org; Web: www.school.stannpv.org. Mike Riley, Prin.; Donna O'Connor, Librarian. Lay Teachers 30; Students 380.
Catechesis Religious Program—Tel: 913-660-1195. Maureen Leach, D.R.E. Students 160.

PURCELL, DONIPHAN CO., ST. MARY (1858) [CEM] Attended by Served from St. Ann, Effingham.
c/o St. Ann, Box 54, Effingham, 66023.
Tel: 913-833-5660. Rev. Daniel Gardner, Parochial Admin.
Church Site: 446 Hwy. 137, Purcell, 66041. Email: monkbt1958@gmail.com.

READING, LYON CO., ASSUMPTION, Closed. For inquiries for parish records contact the chancery.

RICHMOND, FRANKLIN CO., ST. THERESE (1929) Attended by Served from St. Boniface, Scipio.
544 E Central, Richmond, 66080. Tel: 785-835-6273; Fax: 785-835-6112. 32292 N.E. Norton Rd., Garnett, 66032. Revs. J. Gerald Williams, O.Carm.; David Simpson, O.Carm., In Res.

ROELAND PARK, JOHNSON CO., ST. AGNES (1923)
5250 Mission Rd., Roeland Park, 66205.
Tel: 913-262-2400; Fax: 913-262-1050; Email: church@stagneskc.org; Web: www.stagneskc.org. Revs. William Porter; Bruce Ansems, J.C.L., In Res.; Mike Gomez, Business Mgr./Dir. Parish Ministries; Kristen Beeves, Music Min.; Teresa Youngstrom, Parish Sec.
School—St. Agnes School, (Grades PreK-8), 5130 Mission Rd., Roeland Park, 66205. Tel: 913-262-1686 ; Fax: 913-384-1567; Email: sullivan.jane@stagneskc.org; Web: www.stagneskc.org. Jane Sullivan, Prin. Lay Teachers 27; Students 261.

ROSSVILLE, SHAWNEE CO., ST. STANISLAUS, Attended by Served from Immaculate Conception, St. Marys.
703 Main St., Rossville, 66533. Tel: 785-584-6612; Email: ssparish1899@gmail.com; Web: www.ststansrossville.org. P.O. Box 794, Rossville, 66533. Rev. Raymond May Jr.
Catechesis Religious Program—Tel: 785-584-6612. Connie Fischer, D.R.E. Students 98.

SABETHA, NEMAHA CO., SACRED HEART
1031 S. 12th, Sabetha, 66534. Tel: 785-284-0888; Web: www.NEKansasCatholics.org. Rev. Jaime Zarse.
Res.: 1042 S. 14th, Sabetha, 66534.
Catechesis Religious Program—Religious Education, Gina Sallman, Dir. of Faith Formation. Students 102.

ST. BENEDICT, NEMAHA CO., ST. MARY'S CATHOLIC CHURCH (1859) [CEM] Attended by Served from Sacred Heart, Baileyville.
9208 Main St., St. Benedict, 66538.
Tel: 785-336-6464; Email: stmstb.org@gmail.com. Rev. Reginald Saldanha.
Catechesis Religious Program—Diane Schmitz, D.R.E. Students 28.

ST. LOUIS, ATCHISON CO., ST. LOUIS, [CEM] Attended by St. Ann's, Effingham.
11321 Morton Rd., Good Intent, 66002.
Tel: 913-833-5660; Email: info@stanneffingham.org. Mailing Address: c/o St. Anne, 301 William, P.O. Box 54, Effingham, 66023. Rev. Daniel Gardner, Parochial Admin.
Catechesis Religious Program—Becky Finnegan, D.R.E., Tel: 913-370-2985; Email: rebecca.finnegan@lvpioneers.org. Students 43.

ST. MARYS, POTTAWATOMIE CO., IMMACULATE CONCEPTION (1849) [CEM]
208 W. Bertrand, St. Marys, 66536.
Tel: 785-437-2408; Email: icgeneral64@gmail.com. Rev. Raymond May Jr.
Catechesis Religious Program—Mrs. Alice Bordelon, D.R.E. Students 109.

ST. PATRICK, ATCHISON CO., ST. PATRICK (1857) [CEM] Consolidated with St. Benedict's, Atchison, Sacred Heart, Atchison and St. Joseph, Atchison to form St. Benedict, Atchison.

SCIPIO, ANDERSON CO., ST. BONIFACE (1858) [CEM]
32292 N.E. Norton Rd., Garnett, 66032.
Tel: 785-835-6273; Fax: 785-835-6112; Email: gwilliams@archkck.org. Revs. J. Gerald Williams, O.-Carm.; David Simpson, O.Carm., In Res.
Catechesis Religious Program— Combined program with St. Therese, Richmond. Margaret Mechnig, D.R.E. Students 67.

SCRANTON, OSAGE CO., ST. PATRICK (1868) [CEM] Attended by
302 S. Boyle, Scranton, 66537. Tel: 785-528-3424; Fax: 785-528-338; Email: office@stpatrickchurches.org; Web: www.stpatrickchurches.org. Mailing Address: c/o St. Patrick, 309 S. 6th St., Osage City, 66523. Rev. Konda Nusi, Parochial Admin. Served from St. Patrick's, Osage City.
Catechesis Religious Program—Students 24.

SENECA, NEMAHA CO., SS. PETER AND PAUL (1869) [CEM]
411 Pioneer, Seneca, 66538. Tel: 785-336-2128; Fax: 785-336-2307. Rev. Arul Carasala, (India).
School—SS. Peter and Paul School, (Grades PreK-8), 409 Elk St., Seneca, 66538. Tel: 785-336-2727; Fax: 785-336-3817; Email: tleonard@sppschool.com; Web: www.sppschool.com. Todd Leonard, Prin.; Rosalie Divelbiss, Librarian. Lay Teachers 16; Students 204.
Catechesis Religious Program—Shannon Holthaus, D.R.E. Students 120.

SHAWNEE, JOHNSON CO.
1—GOOD SHEPHERD (1973)
12800 W. 75th St., Shawnee, 66216.
Tel: 913-631-7116; Email: church@gsshawnee.org; Web: www.gsshawnee.org. Revs. Kent O'Connor; Daniel Coronado, Parochial Vicar; Deacons Steve Lemons; Marcos Navarro.
Res.: 7511 Canenen Lake Rd., Lenexa, 66216.
Tel: 913-631-5661.
School—Good Shepherd School, (Grades PreK-8), Tel: 913-631-0400; Fax: 913-631-3539; Email: amcguff@gsshawnee.org. Ann McGuff, Prin.; Jennifer Smith, Librarian. Lay Teachers 27; Students 322.
Catechesis Religious Program—Tel: 913-563-5303; Email: info@gsshawnee.org. Nicholas Moragues, D.R.E. Students 325.
2—ST. JOSEPH (1868)
5901 Flint St., Shawnee, 66203. Tel: 913-631-5983; Fax: 913-631-3562. Rev. Scott Wallisch; Rev. Msgr. Michael Mullen, Sr. Parochial Vicar/In Res.; Deacon Tom Mulvenon.
School—St. Joseph School, (Grades K-8), 11505 Johnson Dr., Shawnee, 66203. Tel: 913-631-7730; Fax: 913-631-3608; Email: shill@stjoeshawnee.org; Web: www.stjoeshawnee.org. Dr. Stephanie Hill, Prin.; Sue Carter, Asst. Prin. Lay Teachers 26; Students 421.
Child Care—Early Education Center, 11525 Johnson Dr., Shawnee, 66203. Tel: 913-631-0004; Fax: 913-631-4362. (Day Care & Preschool) Students 142; Auxiliary Teachers 30.
Catechesis Religious Program—Tel: 913-631-8923. Beth Bracken, D.R.E. Students 187.
3—SACRED HEART (1900)
5501 Monticello Rd., Shawnee, 66226.
Tel: 913-422-5700. Revs. Patrick Sullivan; Viet Nguyen, Parochial Vicar; Deacon Nicholas Moragues.
School—Sacred Heart School, (Grades PreK-8), 21801 Johnson Dr., Shawnee, 66218.
Tel: 913-422-5520; Fax: 913-745-0290; Email: maureen.engen@shoj.org; Web: www.shoj.org. Kathy Rhodes, Prin.; Kathy Clevinger, Librarian. Lay Teachers 27; Students 418.
Catechesis Religious Program—Tel: 913-422-5700. Emily Dumler, D.R.E. (K-6); Kelly Kmieck, D.R.E. (7-8). Students 642.

SUMMERFIELD, MARSHALL CO., HOLY FAMILY, Attended by Served from St. Michael, Axtell.
c/o St. Michael, 504 6th St., Axtell, 66403.
Tel: 785-736-2220; Fax: 785-736-2230; Email: jshau47@gmail.com. P.O. Box K, Axtell, 66403. Rev. James Shaughnessy.
Church: 600 Main St., Summerfield, 66541. Email: gnarisetty@archkck.org.

TONGANOXIE, LEAVENWORTH CO., SACRED HEART (1874) [CEM]
1100 West St., P.O. Box 539, Tonganoxie, 66086-0539. Tel: 913-369-2851; Email: mgoldy@sunflower.com; Web: www.shcct.com. Rev. Mark Goldasich; Deacon Ron Zishka.
Catechesis Religious Program—Tel: 913-369-3176; Email: cfoure6@msn.com. Jennifer Eastes, D.R.E.; Nancy Lanza, D.R.E. Students 151.

TOPEKA, SHAWNEE CO.
1—ASSUMPTION (1862) Consolidated with Holy Name, Topeka to form Mater Dei, Topeka.
2—CHRIST THE KING (1977)
5973 S.W. 25th St., Topeka, 66614.
Tel: 785-273-0710; Fax: 785-273-4766; Email: parishoffice@ctktopeka.org; Web: CTKTOPEKA.ORG. Rev. Matthew Schiffelbein; Rev. Carter Zielinski, Parochial Vicar. Church, School and Early Education Center
Res.: 5972 S.W. 25th St., Topeka, 66614.
School—Christ the King School, (Grades K-8), Tel: 785-272-2220; Email: reynosor@ctktopeka.eduk12.net. Relynn Reynoso, Prin. Lay Teachers 23; Students 268.
Catechesis Religious Program—Deb Frost, D.R.E., Email: dfrost@ctktopeka.org. Students 202.
3—HOLY NAME, Consolidated with Assumption, Topeka to form Mater Dei, Topeka.
4—ST. JOSEPH (1887) Consolidated with Sacred Heart, Topeka to form Sacred Heart-St. Joseph, Topeka.
5—MATER DEI (2006)
911 S.W. Clay, Topeka, 66606. Tel: 785-232-7744; Web: www.materdeiparish.org. Rev. John Pilcher; Deacon Chris Seago.
Worship Sites—
Mater Dei Assumption Church—8th & Jackson St., Topeka, 66603.
Mater Dei Holy Name Church, 10th & Clay St., Topeka, 66604.
School—Mater Dei School, (Grades PreK-8), 934 S.W. Clay St., Topeka, 66606. Tel: 785-233-1727; Fax: 785-233-1728; Email: hilleberta@materdeischool.org. Andrea Hillebert, Prin. (Elementary & Middle School). Lay Teachers 14; Students 166.
Catechesis Religious Program—Students 53.
6—ST. MATTHEW (1955)
2700 S.E. Virginia Ave., Topeka, 66605.
Tel: 785-232-5012; Fax: 785-232-0028; Email: parishoffice@saintmatthews.org; Email: jtorrez@archkck.org; Web: www.saintmatthews.org. Rev. John Torrez; Mr. Bob Broxterman, Business Mgr.
School—St. Matthew School, (Grades K-8), 1000 S.E. 28th, Topeka, 66605. Tel: 785-235-2188; Fax: 785-235-2207; Email: school@saintmatthews.org; Web: www.saintmatthews.org. Theresa Lein, Prin.; Debbie Otting, Librarian. Lay Teachers 13; Students 187.
Catechesis Religious Program—Email: llopez@saintmatthews.org. Linette Lopez, D.R.E.; Mrs. Maureen Leiker, Sec. Students 205.
7—MOST PURE HEART OF MARY (1946) [JC]
3601 SW 17th St., Topeka, 66604. Tel: 785-272-5590; Email: parish@mphm.com; Web: www.mphm.com. 1800 S.W. Stone Ave., Topeka, 66604. Revs. Gregory Hammes; Karl Good, Parochial Vicar; Deacon Dan Ondracek.
School—Most Pure Heart of Mary School, (Grades K-8), 1750 S.W. Stone, Topeka, 66604.
Tel: 785-272-4313; Fax: 785-272-1138; Email: ewhite@mphm.com; Web: www.mphm.com/school. Eric White, Prin.; Judy Desetti, Librarian. Lay Teachers 25; Students 361.
Catechesis Religious Program—Kristi Gosser, D.R.E. Students 119.
8—MOTHER TERESA OF CALCUTTA (2004)
Mailing Address: 2014 N.W. 46th St., Topeka, 66618.
Tel: 785-286-2188; Fax: 785-286-2803; Email: office@mtcctopeka.org; Web: www.mtcctopeka.org. Rev. Thomas Reddy Aduri; Deacons Timothy Ruoff; Bradley Sloan.
Res.: 4609 N.W. Kendall Dr., Topeka, 66618.
Catechesis Religious Program—Beth Mercer, D.R.E. Students 245.
9—OUR LADY OF GUADALUPE, [CEM]
134 N.E. Lake St., Topeka, 66616. Tel: 785-232-5088. Revs. Gerardo Arano-Ponce; Jesus Perez Casallas, Parochial Vicar; Deacon Porfido Ray Delgado.
Consolidated with Sacred Heart School and renamed Holy Family School. See Elementary Schools Interparochial located in the Institution section.
Catechesis Religious Program—Tel: 785-233-9171. Andrea Valdez, D.R.E., Email: olgparishsor@olgparish.com. Students 318.
10—SACRED HEART (1919) Consolidated with St. Joseph, Topeka to form Sacred Heart-St. Joseph, Topeka.
11—SACRED HEART-ST. JOSEPH (2006)
227 S.W. VanBuren, Topeka, 66603.
Tel: 785-232-2863; Tel: 785-234-3338. Rev. Timothy A. Haberkorn.
Worship Site: Sacred Heart Church, 312 N.E. Freeman Ave., Topeka, 66616.
See Holy Family School under Elementary Schools, Interparochial located in the Institution Section.
Catechesis Religious Program—Tel: 785-357-0293. Paul Allen, D.R.E. Students 90.

TROY, DONIPHAN CO., ST. CHARLES, [CEM] Attended by Served from St. Joseph Parish, Wathena.
520 W. Chestnut, Troy, 66087. Tel: 785-985-2271; Fax: 785-985-2666. Mailing Address: P.O. Box 456, Troy, 66087. Rev. Francis Bakyor, (Ghana).
Catechesis Religious Program—Barb Greaser, D.R.E.

VALLEY FALLS, JEFFERSON CO., ST. MARY'S IMMACULATE CONCEPTION, [CEM] Attended by Served from St. Joseph, Nortonville.
905 Broadway St., Valley Falls, 66088.
Tel: 913-886-2030; Email: sj.ic.cc.parishoffice@gmail.com. P.O. Box 176, Valley Falls, 66088. Rev. Lazar Carasala, (India) Parochial Admin.
Catechesis Religious Program—Tel: 785-945-3787; Fax: 785-945-4021. Dawna Edmonds, D.R.E. Students 38.

WAMEGO, POTTAWATOMIE CO., ST. BERNARD (1898) [CEM]
17665 Old Post Rd., Wamego, 66547.
Tel: 785-456-7869; Email: stbernard66547@gmail.com. Rev. Michael Peterson.
Catechesis Religious Program—Students 222.

WATERVILLE, MARSHALL CO., ST. MONICA, Closed. For inquiries see St. Monica - St. Elizabeth, Blue Rapids.

WATHENA, DONIPHAN CO., ST. JOSEPH (1869) [CEM]

102 S. 7th St., P.O. Box 159, Wathena, 66090. Tel: 785-989-4818; Email: stjosephwathena@outlook.com; Web: www.stjosephwathena.com. Rev. Francis Bakyor, (Ghana).

Catechesis Religious Program—Mary Kay Nold, D.R.E. Students 31.

WAVERLY, COFFEY CO., ST. JOSEPH, Attended by Served from St. Francis Xavier, Burlington.

508 Pearson Ave., Waverly, 66871. Tel: 620-364-5671 ; Email: stfrancisoffice@embarqmail.com. Mailing Address: c/o St. Francis Xavier, 214 Juniatta, Burlington, 66839. Rev. Quentin Schmitz.

Catechesis Religious Program—Jill Barnhart, D.R.E. Students 38.

WEA, MIAMI CO., QUEEN OF THE HOLY ROSARY (1869) [CEM]

22779 Metcalf Ave., Bucyrus, 66013.

Tel: 913-533-2494; Tel: 913-533-2464; Email: ndoyle@qhrwea.org. Rev. Gary Pennings, V.G.

School—Queen of the Holy Rosary School, (Grades PreK-8), Email: nick@qhrwea.org; Web: www.qhrwea.org. Nick Antista, Prin. Lay Teachers 15; Students 144.

Catechesis Religious Program—Tel: 913-533-2462. Mark Schuetz, Adult Faith Formation & D.R.E. Students 95.

WESTPHALIA, ANDERSON CO., ST. TERESA, Attended by Served from St. Francis Xavier, Burlington.

404 Garrison Ave., Westphalia, 66093.

Tel: 620-364-5671; Email: stfrancisoffice@embarqmail.com. Mailing Address: c/o St. Francis Xavier, 214 Juniatta St., Burlington, 66839. Rev. Quentin Schmitz.

Catechesis Religious Program—Marilyn Brooks, D.R.E., Tel: 785-489-2324. Students 39.

WETMORE, NEMAHA CO., ST. JAMES (1874) Attended by Served from Sacred Heart, Sabetha.

512 Kansas Ave., Wetmore, 66550. Tel: 785-284-0888 ; Web: www.nekansascatholics.org. c/o Sacred Heart, 1031 S. 12th, Sabetha, 66534. Rev. Jaime Zarse.

Catechesis Religious Program—Gina Sallman, Email: gina@nekansascatholics.org. Students 30.

WHEATON, POTTAWATOMIE CO., ST. MICHAEL, Closed. For inquiries for parish records contact the chancery. Rev. Michael Scully, O.F.M.Cap.

Chaplains of Public Institutions

KANSAS CITY. *K.U. Medical Center and Chapel*. Rev. Rafi Kuttukaran, Chap.

LAWRENCE. *Haskell Institute*. Rev. Michael Scully, O.F.M.Cap., Chap.(Government Indian School).

Special Assignment:

Revs.—

Chontos, Joseph, Part-Time Chap., Kansas Juvenile Correctional Complex, Topeka, KS; Kansas Air National Guard 190th Air Refueling Wing, Topeka, KS

Williams, Anthony C., Chap., St. Joseph Medical Center, MO 64114.

On Duty Outside the Archdiocese:

Revs.—

Ahn, Edward, A.V.I., Kenrick-Glennon Seminary

Beseau, Steven, S.T.D., Faculty member, Athenaeum of Ohio, Mount St. Mary's Seminary, Archdiocese of Cincinnati

Klingele, Brian, Chap., USAF

Saiki, Anthony, Pontifical Gregorian University, Rome (Further Studies)

Sosio, Mirco, A.V.I., Kenrick-Glennon Seminary.

Administrative Leave:

Rev.—

Cramer, Joseph.

Medical Leave:

Rev.—

Lunsford, Keith.

Inactive:

Revs.—

Kallal, Scott, A.V.I.

Rossman, Christopher

Seuferling, George, (Retired)

Ziegler, Michael Tod.

Retired:

Rev. Msgrs.—

Burger, Raymond, (Retired), Olathe, KS

Krische, Vincent E., (Retired), Lawrence, KS

McGlinn, Charles, (Retired), Overland Park, KS

Revs.—

Albertson, Lawrence, (Retired), Overland Park, KS

Burger, Francis, (Retired), Overland Park, KS

Cullen, Donald, (Retired), Kansas City, MO

Dekat, Carl, (Retired), St. George, KS

Dekat, Earl, (Retired), St. George, KS

Dolezal, Thomas H., (Retired), Lenexa, KS

Hasenkamp, Robert, (Retired), Lecompton, KS

Kearns, Thomas, (Retired), Kansas City, KS

Lickteig, Anthony, (Retired), Overland Park, KS

Livojevich, Ronald, (Retired), Overland Park, KS

Ludwikoski, James E., (Retired)

Melchior, Thomas, (Retired), Topeka, KS

Pflumm, Robert, (Retired), Olathe, KS

Rockers, Alfred, (Retired), Leawood, KS

Tillia, Marc, (Retired), Bahia, Brazil; Bahia, Brazil

Wait, Dennis, (Retired), Kansas City, KS

Winkelbauer, Phillip J., (Retired), Olathe, KS.

Permanent Deacons:

Deacons—

Allen, Joseph, St. John Paul II, Olathe

Berry, Guy

Brower, Todd, St. Ann Parish, Prairie Village

Cecil, Charles, St. John Paul II, Olathe

Cresswell, David, St. Patrick, Kansas City

Delgado, Porfido Ray, Our Lady of Guadalupe, Topeka

Denning, Gary (Mike), Prince of Peace, Olathe

Geary, Keith, Our Lady of Unity, Kansas City

Gilbert, Dean, Immaculate Conception-St. Joseph, Leavenworth

Hill, Michael, Cathedral of St. Peter, Kansas City; Cursillo Movement - Asst. to Spiritual Advisor

Holland, Stuart, Holy Trinity Parish, Lenexa

Karnaze, George, Immaculate Conception, Louisburg

Lavin, Jim, Queen of the Holy Rosary, Overland Park

Lemons, Steve, Good Shepherd, Shawnee

McEvoy, Timothy, Immaculate Conception-St. Joseph, Leavenworth

Moffitt, W.A. (Mike), St. Paul, Olathe

Moragues, Nicholas, Sacred Heart of Jesus, Shawnee

Mulvenon, Tom, St. Joseph Parish, Shawnee

Navarro, Marcos, Good Shepherd, Shawnee

Nearmyer, Dana, Dir. of Evangelization and Prairie Star Ranch; Holy Trinity Parish, Lenexa

Nguyen, Phillip, Cure of Ars, Leawood

Nguyen, Stephen, St. Ann, Prairie Village

O'Connor, Arthur, Divine Mercy, Gardner

Ondracek, Dan, Most Pure Heart of Mary, Topeka

Peterson, Daniel, (Retired)

Poole, Don, Sacred Heart Parish, Mound City

Rothermich, Tom, (Archdiocese of St. Louis); Queen of the Holy Rosary, Wea

Ruoff, Timothy, Mother of Teresa of Calcutta, Topeka

Schramp, Ralph, Church of the Nativity, Leawood

Schreck, Michael, Church of the Nativity, Leawood

Seago, Chris, Mater Dei Parish, Topeka

Skahan, James E., (Diocese of Jefferson City); Sacred Heart-St. Casimir, Leavenworth

Slater, Chris, Prince of Peace, Olathe

Sloan, Bradley, Mother of Teresa of Calcutta, Topeka

Stanley, John, Church of the Acension, Overland Park

Stukel, Mark, St. Michael the Archangel, Leawood

Weist, John, St. Michael the Archangel, Leawood

White, Stephen, Cure of Ars, Leawood

Zbylut, Robert, (Diocese of Galveston-Houston); Sacred Heart-St. Casimir, Leavenworth

Zimmerman, Tony, (Diocese of Kansas City-St. Joseph); Marriage and Family Life Lead Consultant, Kansas City

Zishka, Ron, Sacred Heart, Tonganoxie.

INSTITUTIONS LOCATED IN DIOCESE

[A] COLLEGES AND UNIVERSITIES

KANSAS CITY. *Donnelly College*, 608 N. 18th St., 66102. Tel: 913-621-6070; Fax: 913-621-8719; Email: admissions@donnelly.edu; Web: www.donnelly.edu. Rev. Msgr. Stuart Swetland, Pres.; Jennifer Bales, Registrar; Jane Ballagh de Tovar, Librarian. Clergy 2; Lay Teachers 82; Priests 2; Sisters 1; Students 1,030; Clergy / Religious Teachers 3.

ATCHISON. *Benedictine College*, 1020 N. 2nd St., Atchison, 66002. Tel: 913-367-5340;

Fax: 913-367-6566; Web: www.benedictine.edu. Stephen D. Minnis, J.D., Pres.; Ron Olinger, CFO; Pete Helgesen, Dean Enrollment Mgmt.; Kimberly C. Shankman, Ph.D., Dean of College; Joseph Wurtz, Ed.D., Dean of Students; Tom Hoopes, Vice Pres. College Relations; Linda Henry, Ed.D., Vice Pres. Student Life; Kelly J. Vowels, Vice Pres. Advancement; Charlie Gartenmayer, Dir. Athletics; Revs. Meinrad Miller, O.S.B., Theology; Blaine Schultz, O.S.B., Prof. Emeritus Music; Sr. Linda Herndon, O.S.B., Assoc. Dean of Academic Records & Registrar; David Trotter, Dir. Mission & Min.; Bro. Joseph Ryan, O.S.B., Mailroom Clerk; Steven Gromatzky, Librarian; Deacon Dana Nearmyer, Adjunct, Theology; Sr. Cecilia Olson, O.S.B., Adjunct, Theology; Revs. Marion Charboneau, O.S.B., Adjunct, History; Simon Baker, O.S.B., Chap.; Jay Kythe, O.S.B., Asst. Chap.; Sr. Kathleen Flanagan, O.S.B., Circulation Coord., Library. Coed College of St. Benedict's & Mount St. Scholastica. Brothers 1; Deacons 1; Priests 5; Benedictine Sisters 3; Students 1,956; Lay Persons 122; Clergy / Religious Teachers 10.

LEAVENWORTH. *University of Saint Mary*, 4100 S. 4th St. Trafficway, Leavenworth, 66048.

Tel: 913-682-5151; Fax: 913-758-6140; Email: admiss@stmary.edu; Web: www.stmary.edu. Sr. Diane Steele, S.C.L., Ph.D., Pres.; Michelle Metzinger, Provost & Acadmic Vice Pres., Provost & Academic Vice Pres.; Danielle Dion, Librarian & Vice Pres. of Student Life. Lay Teachers 159; Sisters of Charity of Leavenworth 3; Students 1,254.

[B] HIGH SCHOOLS, INTERPAROCHIAL

KANSAS CITY. *Bishop Ward High School*, 708 N. 18th St., 66102. Tel: 913-371-1201; Fax: 913-371-2145; Email: wardhigh@wardhigh.org; Web: www.wardhigh.org. Mr. James (Jay) Dunlap Jr., Pres.; Michelle Olson, Prin.; Rev. Agustin Martinez, Chap. Lay Teachers 26; Students 281; Carmelites 1; Clergy / Religious Teachers 1.

Bishop Ward High School Foundation,

Tel: 913-371-1201; Fax: 913-371-2145.

LENEXA. *St. James Academy* (2005) 24505 Prairie Star Pkwy., Lenexa, 66227. Tel: 913-254-4200;

Fax: 913-254-4221; Email: atylicki@sjakeepingfaith.org; Web: www.sjakeepingfaith.org. Andy Tylicki, Pres.; Shane Rapp, Prin.; Rev. Viet Nguyen, Chap. Lay Teachers 60; Sisters 1; Students 900; Clergy / Religious Teachers 2.

OVERLAND PARK. *Saint Thomas Aquinas High School, Inc.* (1988) 11411 Pflumm Rd., Overland Park, 66215. Tel: 913-345-1411; Fax: 913-345-2319; Email: wpford@stasaints.net; Web: www.stasaints.net. Dr. William P. Ford, Pres.; Rev. Matthew Nagle, Chap.; Dr. Michael Sullivan, Prin.; Mr. Brian Schenck, Prin.; Mr. Craig Moss, Prin.; Amanda Davis, Librarian. Lay Teachers 79; Priests 1; Students 951.

St. Thomas Aquinas High School Foundation,

Tel: 913-345-1411; Fax: 913-345-2319.

ROELAND PARK. *Bishop Miege High School* (1958) 5041 Reinhardt Dr., Shawnee Mission, 66205.

Tel: 913-262-2700; Fax: 913-262-2752; Web: www.bishopmiege.com. Randy Salisbury, Pres.; Maureen Engen, Prin.; Joe Schramp, Assoc. Prin; Mr. Andrew Groene, Asst. Prin./Athletic Dir.; Rev. Justin Hamilton, Chap. Lay Teachers 43; Students 679.

Bishop Miege High School Foundation,

Tel: 913-262-2700; Fax: 913-262-3754.

TOPEKA. *Hayden High School* (1911) 401 Gage Blvd., Topeka, 66606. Tel: 785-272-5210;

Fax: 785-272-2975; Email: sandstromj@haydencatholic.net; Web: www.haydencatholic.org. Mrs. Shelly Buhler, Pres.; Mr. James Sandstrom, Prin.; Rev. Carter Zielinski, Chap. Lay Teachers 35; Students 440; Clergy / Religious Teachers 1.

Hayden High School Foundation, Tel: 785-272-5210 ; Fax: 785-272-2975.

[C] HIGH SCHOOLS, PRIVATE

ATCHISON. *Maur Hill - Mount Academy*, 1000 Green St., Atchison, 66002. Tel: 913-367-5482;

Fax: 913-367-5096; Email: admissions@mh-ma.com; Web: www.mh-ma.com. Phil Baniewicz, Pres.; Monika King, Prin.; Richard Hunninghake, Asst. Prin. Brothers 1; Lay Teachers 20; Priests 1; Sisters 2; Students 205; Clergy / Religious Teachers 3.

[D] ELEMENTARY SCHOOLS, INTERPAROCHIAL

KANSAS CITY. *Our Lady of Unity School*, (Grades K-8), 2646 S. 34th, 66106. Tel: 913-262-7022;

Fax: 913-262-7836. Cally Dahlstrom, Prin.; Linda Hutzenbuhler, Librarian. Lay Teachers 8; Students 137; Religious Teachers 1; Clergy / Religious Teachers 1.

Resurrection Catholic School at the Cathedral, (Grades PreK-8), (Merger of Cathedral, St. John/Holy Family and All Saints Schools) 425 N. 15th St., 66102. Tel: 913-371-8101; Fax: 913-371-2151; Email: lhiggins@rcskck.org; Web: www.rcskck.org. Lynda Higgins, Prin.; Allie Dorsey, Librarian. Lay

Teachers 19; Sisters 1; Students 261; Clergy / Religious Teachers 1.

GARNETT. *St. Rose Philippine Duchesne School*, (Grades K-8), 530 E. Fourth, Garnett, 66032. Tel: 785-448-3423; Fax: 785-448-3164; Email: kwoelken@archkckcs.org; Web: strosegarnett.eduk12.net/. Kelli Woelken, Prin. Lay Teachers 6; Students 81.

LEAVENWORTH. *Xavier Elementary School*, (Grades PreK-6), Admin. Office: 1409 2nd Ave., Leavenworth, 66048. Tel: 913-682-7801; Fax: 913-682-5262; Tel: 913-682-3135; Email: lrcsadmin@leavenworthcatholicschools.org; Web: leavenworthcatholicschools.org. 541 Muncie Rd., Leavenworth, 66048. Evelyn Porter, Prin.; Cindi Thiele, Librarian. Consolidation of the following parishes: St. Casimir; Sacred Heart; St. Joseph; and Immaculate Conception, St. Ignatius, St. Francis de Sales, St. Lawrence, St. Joseph of the Valley, and Holy Angels (Basehor) Administrators 1; Lay Teachers 15; Students 136; Staff 3.

OVERLAND PARK. *John Paul II Catholic School*, (Grades PreK-8), 6915 W. 71st., Overland Park, 66204. Tel: 913-432-6350; Fax: 913-432-5081; Web: www.johnpaul2opks.com; Email: jyankovich@archkckcs.org. Jenny Yankovich, Prin.; Joanne Rineman, Librarian. Lay Teachers 18; Students 157.

TOPEKA. *Holy Family Catholic School*, (Grades PreSchool-8), K-8 Building: 1725 N.E. Seward Ave., Topeka, 66616. Tel: 785-234-8980; Fax: 785-234-6778; Email: mcbrides@holyfamilytopeka.net; Web: www.holyfamilytopeka.com. Pre-School Building: 210 N.E. Branner, Topeka, 66616. Tel: 785-233-9171. Nick Anderson, Prin.; Nancy Walker, Librarian. Lay Teachers 10; Students 168.

[E] ELEMENTARY AND SECONDARY SCHOOLS, PRIVATE

KANSAS CITY. *Our Lady's Montessori School*, (Grades Day Care-K), 3020 S. 7th St., 66103. Tel: 913-403-9550; Fax: 913-403-9540; Email: sralison@olmskc.org; Email: srmarymediatrix@gmail.com; Email: showard@olmskc.org; Email: lsharpe@olmskc.org; Web: olmskc.org. Sr. Alison Marie Conemac, S.O.L.T., Dir. Clergy 3; Lay Teachers 13; Sisters 4; Students 66.

MAPLE HILL. *St. John Vianney School* (2000) (Grades K-12), 14611A Waterman Crossing Rd., Maple Hill, 66507. Tel: 785-207-5927; Email: sjvs.cristeros@gmail.com. Revs. Eric Flood, F.S.S.P., Chap.; Martin Adams, Assoc. Chap. Lay Teachers 3; Priests 2; Students 42; Clergy / Religious Teachers 2.

[F] GENERAL HOSPITALS

TOPEKA. *St. Francis Health Center, Inc.*, 534 S. Kansas Ave., Ste. 1000, Topeka, 66603. Tel: 303-813-5190; Email: OCD-Contact@sclhs.net. Ms. Marla DeMicco, Contact Person. No longer operating as a hospital after divestiture of assets on 11/1/2017.

[G] NURSING HOMES

OLATHE. *Villa St. Francis Catholic Care Center, Inc.* (1945) 16600 W. 126th St., Olathe, 66062. Tel: 913-829-5201; Fax: 913-829-5399; Email: contactus@villasf.org; Web: www.villasf.org. Rodney Whittington. Owned and operated by Villa St. Francis, Inc.; Skilled nursing care; memory care unit, long term care, respite care, rapid recovery with PT/OT speech therapy. Bed Capacity 170; Total in Residence 163; Total Staff 250; Total Assisted 375.

OVERLAND PARK. *Carondelet Long Term Care Facilities, Inc.* dba St. Joseph Place, 11901 Rosewood, Overland Park, 66209. Tel: 913-345-1745; Fax: 913-345-1346; Email: traney@ascension.org. Daniel Stricker, Exec. Bed Capacity 132; Total Staff 80; Total Assisted 280.

[H] CATHOLIC CHARITIES

KANSAS CITY. *Catholic Charities of Northeast Kansas, Inc.*, 9720 W. 87th St., Overland Park, 66212. Tel: 913-433-2100; Fax: 913-433-2101; Email: info@catholiccharitiesks.org; Web: www.CatholicCharitiesKS.org. Mrs. Lauren Solidum, Pres./CEO. Tot Asst. Annually 527,065; Total Staff 234.

Catholic Charities Foundation of Northeast Kansas, 9720 W. 87th St., Overland Park, 66212. Tel: 913-433-2100; Fax: 913-433-2101.

Catholic Community Hospice, 9740 W. 87th St., Overland Park, 66212. Fax: 913-371-3080; Email: info@catholiccharitiesks.org. Tot Asst. Annually 382.

Catholic Neighborhood Outreach, Inc. (2004) 9750 W. 87th St., Overland Park, 66212. Tel: 913-648-6795; Email: mflorea@catholiccharitiesks.org. Total Staff 2.

Catholic Neighborhood Outreach, Inc., 11310 W. 135th St., Overland Park, 66221. Tel: 913-909-2485; Email: mflorea@catholiccharitiesks.org.

Emergency Assistance Center - Atchison, 502 Kansas Ave., Atchison, 66002. Tel: 913-367-5070; Email: info@catholiccharitiesks.org; Web: www.catholiccharitiesks.org. Tot Asst. Annually 2,160; Total Staff 1.

Emergency Assistance Center - Lawrence, 1525 W. 6th St., Lawrence, 66044. Tel: 785-856-2694; Email: info@catholiccharitiesks.org. Tot Asst. Annually 4,997; Total Staff 2.

Emergency Assistance Center - Leavenworth, 716 N. 5th St., Leavenworth, 66048. Tel: 913-651-8060; Email: info@catholiccharitiesks.org.

Emergency Assistance Center - North Johnson County, 9806 W. 87th St., Overland Park, 66212. Tel: 913-384-6608; Email: info@catholiccharitiesks.org. Tot Asst. Annually 10,233; Total Staff 5.

Emergency Assistance Center - South Johnson County, 333 E. Poplar, Olathe, 66061. Tel: 913-782-4077; Email: info@catholiccharitiesks.org. Tot Asst. Annually 9,528; Total Staff 4.

Emergency Assistance Center - Topeka, 234 S. Kansas Ave., Topeka, 66603. Tel: 785-233-6300; Email: info@catholiccharitiesks.org. Tot Asst. Annually 11,176; Total Staff 5.

Emergency Assistance Center - Wyandotte County, 2220 Central Ave., 66102. Tel: 913-621-3445; Email: info@catholiccharitiesks.org. Tot Asst. Annually 15,226; Total Staff 4.

Hope Distribution Center, 1708 Steele Rd., 66106. Tel: 913-432-3141; Email: info@catholiccharitiesks.org. Tot Asst. Annually 11,095; Total Staff 3.

Shalom House Men's Shelter (1971) 2100 N. 13th St., 66104. Tel: 913-321-2206; Email: mflorea@catholiccharitiesks.org. c/o Catholic Charities: 9720 W. 87th St., Overland Park, 66212. Tot Asst. Annually 89; Total Staff 1.

[I] MONASTERIES AND RESIDENCES FOR PRIESTS AND BROTHERS

ATCHISON. *St. Benedict's Abbey* (1857) 1020 N. 2nd St., Atchison, 66002. Tel: 913-367-7853; Fax: 913-367-6230; Email: jalbers@kansasmonks.org; Email: frgabriellandis@gmail.com; Web: www.kansasmonks.org. Rt. Revs. James R. Albers, O.S.B., Abbot; Ralph Koehler, O.S.B., (Retired Abbot), (Retired); Revs. Meinrad Miller, O.S.B., Novice Master; Maurice C. Haefling, O.S.B., Business Mgr.; Rt. Rev. Barnabas Senecal, O.S.B., Retired Abbot, (Retired); Very Rev. Jeremy Heppler, O.S.B.; Friar Jay Kythe, O.S.B., Novice Master, Priest of the Archdiocese of Minneapolis - St. Paul in temporary vows as a monk.; Rev. Simon Baker, O.S.B., Junior Master; Very Rev. Gabriel Landis, O.S.B., Prior; Revs. Josias Dias da Costa, O.S.B.; Carlos Nogueira Filho, O.S.B.; Joaquim Carvalho, O.S.B.; Marion Charboneau, O.S.B.; Roderic Giller, O.S.B.; Matthew Habiger, O.S.B.; Albert Hauser, O.S.B.; Daniel McCarthy, O.S.B.; Denis Meade, O.S.B., J.C.D.; Rodrigo Perissinotto, O.S.B.; Aaron Peters, O.S.B.; Donald Redmond, O.S.B, (Retired); Vinicius de Queiroz Rezende; Brendan Rolling, O.S.B.; Duane Roy, O.S.B.; Blaine Schultz, O.S.B.; Paul Steingreaber, O.S.B.; Benjamin Tremmel, O.S.B.; Michael Zoellner, O.S.B.; Bros. Leven Harton, O.S.B., Subprior; Placidus Lee, O.S.B.; Timothy McMillan, O.S.B.; John Peto, O.S.B.; Joseph Ryan, O.S.B.; Thiago Ferreira Silva, O.S.B.; Christopher Start, O.S.B.; Karel Soukup, O.S.B.; Luke Turner, O.S.B.; Anthony Vorwerk, O.S.B. Brothers 14; Priests 28.

LAWRENCE. *St. Conrad Friary* (1990) (Capuchins) 745 Tennessee, Lawrence, 66044. Tel: 785-843-0188; Fax: 785-843-2214; Email: dfreinert@gmail.com; Web: www.capuchins.org. Revs. Curtis Carlson, O.F.M.Cap., In Res.; Barnabas Eichor, O.F.M.Cap., In Res.; Jeffrey A. Ernst, O.F.M.Cap., In Res.; Duane F. Reinert, O.F.M.Cap., In Res.; Michael Scully, O.F.M.Cap., In Res. Priests 5.

[J] CONVENTS AND RESIDENCES FOR SISTERS

KANSAS CITY. *Little Sisters of the Lamb*, Provincial House: 36 S. Boeke St., 66101. Tel: 913-621-1727; Email: lumenchristi@communityofthelamb.org. Sr. Benedicte Bertrand, O.P., Prioress. Sisters 7; Aspirants 2.

Servants of Mary, Ministers to the Sick, 800 N. 18th St., 66102. Tel: 913-371-3423; Tel: 913-621-1147; Fax: 913-621-4962; Email: mprovincialsdemkc@yahoo.com. Sisters Alicia Hermosillo, S.deM., Prov.; Lucero Garcia, Local Supr.; Rev. Joseph Arsenault, S.S.A., J.C.L., Chap. Ministers to the Sick, Motherhouse of the Congregation for the United States.; Nurses, private duty, and visiting nursing in the homes. Professed Sisters 26.

ATCHISON. *Dooley Center, Inc.* (1993) 801 S. Eighth St., Atchison, 66002. Tel: 913-360-6200; Fax: 913-360-6275; Web: www.mountosb.org. Sr. Esther Fangman, O.S.B., Admin. Benedictine Sisters of Mount St. Scholastica, Inc., Atchison, KS. Nursing care facility for the aged/infirm members of this religious community. Sisters 36.

Mount St. Scholastica (1863) 801 S. 8th St., Atchison, 66002. Tel: 913-360-6200; Fax: 913-360-6190; Email: esther@mountosb.org; Web: www.mountosb.org. Sr. Esther Fangman, Prioress. Motherhouse of the Sisters of St. Benedict. Novices 1; Sisters 117; Professed Sisters 116.

LEAVENWORTH. *Motherhouse of the Sisters of Charity of Leavenworth*, 4200 S. 4th St., Leavenworth, 66048-5054. Tel: 913-758-6501; Fax: 913-364-5401; Email: cphelps@scls.org; Web: www.scls.org. Sisters Constance Phelps, S.C.L., Community Dir.; Lucy Walter, S.C.L., Local Coord.; Margaret Finch, S.C.L., Mother House Admin.; Rev. Dennis Schaab, C.PP.S., Chap. Sisters 207; Total in Residence 89.

OVERLAND PARK. *Association of the Apostles of the Interior Life*, 10300 Cody St., Overland Park, 66214. Tel: 913-261-9692; Email: susanmarie.avi@gmail.com; Web: www.apostlesofil.com. Sr. Susan Pieper, Supr. Sisters 6.

[K] PRIVATE ASSOCIATIONS OF THE FAITHFUL

KANSAS CITY. *SOCIETY OF ST. AUGUSTINE - PUBLIC ASSOCIATION OF THE FAITHFUL (2000) 2601 Ridge Ave., 66102. Tel: 913-321-4673; Email: pmjaramillo@msn.com; Web: www.augustinian.us. Revs. Peter Jaramillo, S.S.A., Prior; John Melnick, S.S.A., Sub Prior; Joseph Arsenault, S.S.A., J.C.L., Novice Master. Novices 1; Priests 3; Professed 1.

SHAWNEE MISSION. FRANCISCAN SERVANTS OF THE HOLY FAMILY - PUBLIC ASSOCIATION OF THE FAITHFUL (2001) P.O. Box 7251, Shawnee Mission, 66207. Tel: 785-218-2894; Email: srdoris@kcfranciscans.org; Web: www.kcfranciscans.org. Sr. Doris Engeman, F.S.H.F., Sister Servant. Mission: Helping families grow in holiness and unity.

[L] CLERICAL ASSOCIATIONS OF THE CHRISTIAN FAITHFUL

OVERLAND PARK. *Association of Priests of the Apostles of the Interior Life*, 10513 Ballentine St., Overland Park, 66214. Tel: 913-800-0355; Email: apostles.kansas@gmail.com. Rev. Vincent Huber, A.V.I. Priests 5.

[M] CAMPUS MINISTRY

EMPORIA. *Didde Catholic Campus Center, Emporia State University*, Office: 1415 Merchant St., Emporia, 66801. Tel: 620-343-6765; Fax: 620-343-6792; Email: contact@diddecenter.org; Web: www.diddecenter.org. Rev. Nicholas Blaha, Chap.

1102 Neosho St., Emporia, 66801. Rev. Nicholas Blaha, Chap. Total Staff 7.

LAWRENCE. *Haskell Catholic Campus Center* (1985) 2301 Barker Ave., Lawrence, 66046-4813. Tel: 785-842-2401; Email: finchjean@yahoo.com. Jean Finch, Dir.; Rev. Michael Scully, O.F.M.Cap., Chap. Total Staff 1.

St. Lawrence Catholic Campus Center at the University of Kansas and Residence, 1631 Crescent Rd., Lawrence, 66044. Tel: 785-843-0357; Email: kucatholic@kucatholic.org; Web: www.kucatholic.org. Rev. Mitchel Zimmerman, Chap. & Dir. Total Staff 11.

TOPEKA. *Catholic Campus Center at Washburn University*, 1633 S.W. Jewell, Topeka, 66604. Tel: 785-233-2204; Fax: 785-233-2205; Email: wucatholic@hotmail.com; Web: www.wucatholic.com. Patti Lyon, O.F.S., B.A., M.S., Dir.; Rev. Jonathan Dizon, Chap.

[N] MISCELLANEOUS LISTINGS

KANSAS CITY. *Catholic Care Campus, Inc.* dba Santa Marta (2004) 13800 W. 116th St., Olathe, 66062. Tel: 913-906-0990; Fax: 913-906-0911; Email: csurmaczewicz@santamartaretirement.com; Web: www.santamartaretirement.com. Chet Surmaczewicz, Exec. Dir.; Rev. Msgr. Raymond Burger, Chap., (Retired). Independent, assisted living, memory support, skilled nursing. Total Staff 196; Total Assisted 318.

The Catholic Foundation of Northeast Kansas, 12615 Parallel, 66109. Tel: 913-647-3062; Fax: 913-647-0333; Email: cfnek@archkck.org; Web: www.cfnek.org. Mrs. Lesle Knop, Dir. (Formerly known as Archdiocesan Foundation).

Catholic Housing of Wyandotte County, 2 S. 14th St., 66102. Tel: 913-342-7580; Fax: 913-342-7581; Email: bcrawford@chwckck.org; Web: www.chwckck.org. Rev. Gary Pennings, V.G.

The Cursillo Movement of the Archdiocese of Kansas City in Kansas (1974) 2601 Ridge Ave., 66102. Tel: 913-321-4673; Email: dwait@archkck.org; Web: www.cursillokcks.com. Rev. Dennis Wait, Spiritual Advisor, (Retired); Gail Shepard, Lay Dir.; Deacon Michael Hill, Asst. Spiritual Advisor.

Duchesne Clinic (1989) 636 Tauromee Ave., 66101. Tel: 913-321-2626; Fax: 913-321-2651; Email: jennifer.wewers@caritasclinics.org; Web: www.duchesneclinic.org. George M. Noonan, Exec. Dir. A division of Caritas Clinics, Inc., Leavenworth, KS. Patients Asst Anual. 1,425; Total Staff 20.

**El Centro, Inc.*, 650 Minnesota Ave., 66101. Tel: 913-677-0100; Fax: 913-362-8513; Email: icaudillo@elcentroinc.com; Web: www.elcentroinc.com. Irene Caudillo, Pres. & CEO.

St. Joseph Adoption Referral Service, Inc. (2001) 8160 Parallel Pkwy., Ste. 103, 66112. Tel: 913-299-5222; Tel: 800-752-1737; Fax: 913-299-5111; Email: apeacefulblessing@yahoo.com; Web: www.catholicadoptionministry.org. Sisters Janet Fleischhacker, C.S.J., Pres. & Contact Person; Dolora May, Dir. Tot Asst. Annually 20; Total Staff 3.

Lay and Deacon and Priest Retirement Plans of the Archdiocese of Kansas City in Kansas (1978) 12615 Parallel Pkwy., 66109. Tel: 913-721-1570; Fax: 913-721-2680; Email: cmills@archkck.org; Web: www.archkck.org. Ms. Carla Mills, CFO.

Little Brothers of the Lamb, Inc., 801 Vermont Ave., 66101. Tel: 913-998-6644; Email: littlebrotherskansas@communityofthelamb.org. Christophe Laurent, Contact Person. Brothers 3; Priests 1.

ATCHISON. *The Maur Hill Prep School Endowment Association, Inc.*, 1000 Green St., Atchison, 66002. Tel: 913-367-5482; Fax: 913-367-5096; Email: philb@mh-ma.com. Phil Baniewicz, Pres.

Maur Hill-Mount Academy School Endowment Association, Inc., 1000 Green St., Atchison, 66002. Tel: (913) 367-5482; Email: philb@mh-ma.com. Phil Baniewicz, Pres.

EASTON. *Christ's Peace House of Prayer* (1972) 22131 Meagher Rd., Easton, 66020. Tel: 913-773-8255; Email: info@christspeace.com; Web: www.christspeace.com. Vincent Eimer, Dir. Total in Residence 1; Total Staff 2.

LEAVENWORTH. *Caritas Clinics, Inc.*, 818 N. 7th St., Leavenworth, 66048. Tel: 913-651-8860; Fax: 913-682-4409; Email: george.noonan@caritasclinics.org; Email: jennifer.wewers@caritasclinics.org; Web: www.caritasclinics.org. George M. Noonan, Exec. Dir. Sisters of Charity of Leavenworth.Administrative structure for Saint Vincent Clinic, Leavenworth, Duchesne Clinic, Kansas City. Total Staff 5.

Saint Vincent Clinic (1986) 818 N. 7th St., Leavenworth, 66048. Tel: 913-651-8860; Fax: 913-682-4409; Email: george.noonan@caritasclinics.org; Email: jennifer.wewers@caritasclinics.org; Web: www.saintvincentclinic.org. George M. Noonan, Exec. Dir. (A division of Caritas Clinics, Inc., Leavenworth, KS) Patients Asst Anual. 375; Total Staff 5.

Xavier Corporation, 4200 S. 4th St., Ste. 309, Leavenworth, 66048. Tel: 913-758-6502; Email: katherinefranchett@yahoo.com. Sr. Katherine Franchett, Chmn.

MAYETTA. *Our Lady of the Snows Oratory*, Potawatomi Reservation, Mayetta, 66509. Mailing Address: c/o St. Dominic, 115 E. 5th St., Holton, 66436. Tel: 785-364-3262; Fax: 785-364-1499; Email: parish@jacocatholics.org. Rev. Jonathan Dizon, Chap. Attended by: St. Dominic, Holton, KS.

OVERLAND PARK. *Holy Family School of Faith*, 13240 Craig St., Overland Park, 66213. Tel: 913-310-0014; Email: support@schooloffaith.com; Web: www.schooloffaith.com. Michael Scherschligt, Exec. Dir.

PRAIRIE VILLAGE. *School of Love, Inc.*, 5105 Tomahawk Rd., Prairie Village, 66208. Tel: 913-221-3959; Email: mike@schooloflovekc.com; Web: www.schooloflovekc.com. Mike Dennihan, Exec. Dir.

TOPEKA. *El Centro de Servicios Para Hispanos* dba El Centro of Topeka (1971) 134 N.E. Lake, Topeka, 66616. Tel: 785-232-8207; Fax: 785-232-8834; Email: lmunoz@elcentrooftopeka.org. Mr. Lalo Munoz, Admin.

St. Francis Health Center Foundation, 534 S. Kansas Ave., Ste. 1000, Topeka, 66603. Tel: 303-813-5190; Email: OCD-Contact@sclhs.net. 500 Eldorado Blvd., Ste. 4300, Broomfield, CO 80021. Carl Baranowski, Sec.

Marian Clinic, Inc., 3164 E. 6th St., Topeka, 66607. Tel: 785-233-2800; Fax: 785-233-5116; Email: krista.hahn@mariandental.org; Web: www.mariandental.org. Krista Hahn, CEO; Patty Vasquez, Office Mgr. Affiliate of Sisters of Charity of Leavenworth Health System Total Patients 8,885; Total Patient Visits 8,571.

RELIGIOUS INSTITUTES OF MEN REPRESENTED IN THE ARCHDIOCESE

For further details refer to the corresponding bracketed number in the Religious Institutes of Men or Women section.

[]—*Apostles of the Interior Life*—A.V.I.
[0200]—*Benedictine Monks* (St. Benedict's Abbey)—O.S.B.
[0470]—*The Capuchin Friars* (Holy Family)—O.F.M.Cap.
[0270]—*Carmelite Fathers & Brothers* (American Prov.)—O.Carm.
[1330]—*Congregation of the Mission of St. Vincent de Paul*—C.M.
[1000]—*Congregation of the Passion*—C.P.
[]—*Little Brothers of the Lamb*—O.P.
[1210]—*Missionaries of St. Charles-Scalabrinians*—C.S.
[0485]—*Missionaries of St. Francis de Sales*—M.S.F.S.
[]—*Missionary Fathers of the Nativity of Mary*—M.N.M.
[]—*Order of Augustinian Recollects*—O.A.R.
[]—*Poor of Jesus Christ*—P.J.C.
[1065]—*Priestly Fraternity of St. Peter*—F.S.S.P.
[]—*Society of Jesus*—S.J.
[]—*Society of St. Augustine*—S.S.A.
[1060]—*Society of the Precious Blood*—C.PP.S.

RELIGIOUS INSTITUTES OF WOMEN REPRESENTED IN THE ARCHDIOCESE

[0100]—*Adorers of the Blood of Christ*—A.S.C.
[]—*Apostles of the Interior Life* (Public Association of the Faithful)—A.V.I.
[]—*Augustinian Recollect Missionary Sisters*—A.R.M.S.
[0230]—*Benedictine Sisters of Pontifical Jurisdiction*—O.S.B.
[3832]—*Congregation of the Sisters of St. Joseph of Wichita*—C.S.J.
[]—*Franciscan Servants of Holy Family (Public Association of the Faithful).*
[1430]—*Franciscan Sisters of Our Lady of Perpetual Help*—O.S.F.
[]—*Fraternity, The Poor of Jesus Christ*—P.J.C.
[]—*Little Sisters of the Lamb*—O.P.
[]—*Marian Sisters of the Diocese of Lincoln.*
[2500]—*Medical Sisters of St. Joseph*—M.S.J.
[]—*Missioneras Guadalupanos de Cristo Rey.*
[0480]—*Sisters of Charity of Leavenworth, Kansas*—S.C.L.
[]—*Sisters of Divine Providence*—C.D.P.
[]—*Sisters of St. Anne*—C.S.S.A.
[1600]—*Sisters of St. Francis of the Martyr St. George*—F.S.G.M.
[3840]—*Sisters of St. Joseph of Carondelet* (St. Louis, MO)—C.S.J.
[3105]—*Sisters of the Society of Our Lady of the Most Holy Trinity* Corpus Christi, TX—S.O.L.T.
[3600]—*Sisters, Servants of Mary*—S.M.
[4120-05]—*Ursuline Nuns of Mount Saint Joseph*—O.S.U.

ARCHDIOCESAN CEMETERIES

KANSAS CITY. *Gate of Heaven, St. John, Mount Calvary*, Catholic Cemeteries: 1150 N. 38th St., 66102. Tel: 913-371-4040; Fax: 913-621-2862; Email: rchenoweth@cathcemks.org; Web: www.cathcemks.org. P.O. Box 2327, 66110. Mr. Robert Chenoweth, Dir.

SHAWNEE, JOHNSON COUNTY. *Resurrection, Shawnee, St. Joseph's, Shawnee, St. John, Lenexa, Mount Calvery, Olathe*, Catholic Cemeteries: 1150 N. 38th St., 66102. Tel: 913-371-4040. P.O. Box 2327, 66110. Mr. Robert Chenoweth, Dir.

ATCHISON. *Mount Calvary*
LEAVENWORTH. *Mount Calvary*
TOPEKA. *Mount Calvary*

NECROLOGY

† Klasinski, George, (Retired), Died Apr. 14, 2018
† Schwalm, Donald, (Retired), Died Feb. 14, 2018

An asterisk (*) denotes an organization that has established tax-exempt status directly with the IRS and is not covered by the USCCB Group Ruling.

Diocese of Kansas City-St. Joseph

(Dioecesis Kansanopolitanae Sancti Josephi)

Most Reverend

JAMES V. JOHNSTON, JR., D.D., J.C.L.

Bishop of Kansas City-Saint Joseph; ordained June 9, 1990; appointed Bishop of Springfield-Cape Girardeau January 24, 2008; ordained March 31, 2008; appointed Bishop of Kansas City-Saint Joseph September 15, 2015; installed November 4, 2015. *Chancery: 20 W. 9th St., Ste. 200, Kansas City, MO 64105. Mailing Address: P.O. Box 419037, Kansas City, MO 64141-6037.* Tel: 816-756-1850; Fax: 816-756-2105; Email: bishopsoffice@diocesekcsj.org.

Most Reverend

ROBERT W. FINN, D.D.

Resigned Bishop of Kansas City-St. Joseph; born April 2, 1953; ordained July 7, 1979; appointed Coadjutor Bishop of Kansas City-St. Joseph March 9, 2004; installed May 3, 2004; succeeded to See May 24, 2005; resigned April 21, 2015. *Mailing Address: 4100 S.W. 56th St., Lincoln, NE 68522.*

CARITAS CHRISTI URGET NOS

Mailing Address: P.O. Box 419037, Kansas City, MO 64141-6037. Chancery: 20 W. 9th St., Ste. 200, Kansas City, MO 64105

Square Miles 15,429.

Diocese of Kansas City Established September 10, 1880; Diocese of St. Joseph Established March 3, 1868.

Redesignated Diocese of Kansas City-St. Joseph August 29, 1956.

Comprises the Counties of Andrew, Atchison, Bates, Buchanan, Caldwell, Carroll, Cass, Clay, Clinton, Daviess, DeKalb, Gentry, Grundy, Harrison, Henry, Holt, Jackson, Johnson, Lafayette, Livingston, Mercer, Nodaway, Platte, Ray, St. Clair, Vernon and Worth in the State of Missouri.

For legal titles of parishes and diocesan institutions, consult the Chancery Office.

STATISTICAL OVERVIEW

Personnel	
Bishop	1
Retired Bishops	1
Abbots	1
Priests: Diocesan Active in Diocese	69
Priests: Diocesan Active Outside Diocese	3
Priests: Retired, Sick or Absent	38
Number of Diocesan Priests	110
Religious Priests in Diocese	59
Total Priests in Diocese	169
Extern Priests in Diocese	7
Ordinations:	
Diocesan Priests	3
Transitional Deacons	4
Permanent Deacons	11
Permanent Deacons in Diocese	72
Total Brothers	19
Total Sisters	210
Parishes	
Parishes	88
With Resident Pastor:	
Resident Diocesan Priests	53
Resident Religious Priests	14
Without Resident Pastor:	
Administered by Priests	20
Administered by Deacons	1
Missions	10
Professional Ministry Personnel:	
Sisters	2
Lay Ministers	366
Welfare	
Catholic Hospitals	1
Total Assisted	51,292
Homes for the Aged	13
Total Assisted	3,362
Day Care Centers	9
Total Assisted	370
Special Centers for Social Services	8
Total Assisted	153,771
Residential Care of Disabled	1
Total Assisted	362
Other Institutions	1
Total Assisted	88
Educational	
Seminaries, Diocesan	1
Students from This Diocese	6
Students from Other Diocese	57
Diocesan Students in Other Seminaries	21
Total Seminarians	27
Colleges and Universities	2
Total Students	5,251
High Schools, Diocesan and Parish	3
Total Students	817
High Schools, Private	4
Total Students	2,344
Elementary Schools, Diocesan and Parish	24
Total Students	5,520
Elementary Schools, Private	1
Total Students	243
Catechesis/Religious Education:	
High School Students	583
Elementary Students	5,185
Total Students under Catholic Instruction	19,970
Teachers in the Diocese:	
Priests	5
Sisters	4
Lay Teachers	372
Vital Statistics	
Receptions into the Church:	
Infant Baptism Totals	1,717
Minor Baptism Totals	216
Adult Baptism Totals	141
Received into Full Communion	377
First Communions	1,808
Confirmations	1,772
Marriages:	
Catholic	468
Interfaith	230
Total Marriages	698
Deaths	1,155
Total Catholic Population	123,441
Total Population	1,568,149

Former Bishops—Most Revs. JOHN JOSEPH HOGAN, D.D., born May 5, 1829; ord. April 10, 1852; cons. Bishop of St. Joseph, MO, Sept. 13, 1868; transferred to Kansas City, Sept. 10, 1880; died Feb. 21, 1913; THOMAS F. LILLIS, D.D., born March 3, 1861; ord. Aug. 15, 1885; cons. Bishop of Leavenworth, Dec. 27, 1904; appt. Coadjutor to the Bishop of Kansas City, "cum jure successionis," March 14, 1910; Bishop of Kansas City, Feb. 21, 1913; appt. assistant at the Pontifical Throne, Aug. 19, 1935; died Dec. 29, 1938; EDWIN V. O'HARA, D.D., born Sept. 6, 1881; ord. June 10, 1905; appt. Bishop of Great Falls, MT, August 1, 1930; cons. Oct. 28, 1930; transferred to the See of Kansas City, April 15, 1939; made assistant at the Pontifical Throne, Jan. 5, 1949; appt. Archbishop "ad personam," June 29, 1954; died Sept. 11, 1956; His Eminence JOHN CARDINAL CODY, D.D., S.T.D., born Dec. 24, 1907; ord. Dec. 8, 1931; appt. Titular Bishop of Appollonia and Auxiliary Bishop of St. Louis, May 14, 1947; cons. July 2, 1947; promoted to coadjutor of St. Joseph "cum jure successionis," Jan. 27, 1954; appt. to Diocese of Kansas City-St. Joseph, Aug. 24, 1956; succeeded to See Sept. 11, 1956; transferred to Archdiocese of New Orleans as Coadjutor Archbishop "cum jure successionis," Aug. 10, 1961; acceded to the See of New Orleans, Nov. 8, 1964; transferred to the Archdiocese of Chicago, June 16, 1965; created Cardinal Priest, June 26, 1967; died April 25, 1982; Most Revs. CHARLES H. HELMSING, D.D., born March 23, 1908; ord. June 10, 1933; appt. Titular Bishop of Axomis and Auxiliary Bishop of St. Louis, March 17, 1949; cons. April 19, 1949; appt. Bishop of Springfield-Cape Girardeau, Aug. 24, 1956; transferred to Diocese of Kansas City-St. Joseph, Jan. 27, 1962; retired Aug. 17, 1977; died Dec. 20, 1993; JOHN J. SULLIVAN, D.D., born July 5, 1920; ord. Sept. 23, 1944; appt. Bishop of Grand Island, July 25, 1972; cons. Sept. 19, 1972; installed Grand Island, Sept. 21, 1972; appt. Bishop of Kansas City-St. Joseph, June 27, 1977; installed Aug. 17, 1977; retired Sept. 9, 1993; died Feb. 8, 2001; RAYMOND J. BOLAND, D.D., born Feb. 8, 1932; ord. June 16, 1957; appt. Bishop of Birmingham Feb. 2, 1988; cons. March 25, 1988; appt. Bishop of Kansas City-St. Joseph June 22, 1993; installed Sept. 9, 1993; retired May 24, 2005; died Feb. 27, 2014.; ROBERT W. FINN, born April 2, 1953; ord. July 7, 1979; appt. Coadjutor Bishop of Kansas City-St. Joseph March 9, 2004; installed May 3, 2004; succeeded to See May 24, 2005; resigned April 21, 2015.

Former Bishops of Diocese of St. Joseph, MO—Most Revs. JOHN J. HOGAN, D.D., born May 5, 1829; ord. April 10, 1852; appt. first Bishop of St. Joseph, March 3, 1868; consecrated Sept. 13, 1868; transferred to See of Kansas City, Sept. 10, 1880; administrator of St. Joseph until 1893; died Feb. 21, 1913; MAURICE F. BURKE, D.D., born May 5, 1844; ord. May 22, 1875; appt. first Bishop of Cheyenne, WY, Aug. 9, 1887; consecrated Oct. 28, 1887; transferred to St. Joseph, June 19, 1893; died March 17, 1923; FRANCIS GILFILLAN, D.D., born Feb. 16, 1872; ord. June 24, 1895; appt. Titular Bishop of Spigas and Coadjutor with the right of succession to the See of St. Joseph, July 8, 1922; consecrated Nov. 8, 1922; succeeded to the See of St. Joseph, March 17, 1923; died Jan. 13, 1933; CHARLES H. LEBLOND, D.D., born Nov. 18,

1883; ord. Oct. 27, 1909; appt. Bishop of St. Joseph, July 21, 1933; consecrated Sept. 21, 1933; resigned as Bishop of St. Joseph and appointed Titular Bishop of Orcistus, Aug. 24, 1956; died Dec. 30, 1958.

Chancery—Mailing Address: P.O. Box 419037, Kansas City, 64141-6037. Tel: 816-756-1850; Fax: 816-756-0878. All official matters should be sent to this address.

Vicar General - Chancellor & Moderator of the Curia— Rev. KENNETH A. RILEY, J.C.L., V.G.

*Vicar General - Vicar for Clergy—*Rev. CHARLES N. ROWE, S.T.D.

*Finance Officer—*DAVID A. MALANOWSKI.

*Judicial Vicar—*Rev. KENNETH A. RILEY, J.C.L., V.G., Chancellor.

*College of Consultors—*Revs. J. KENNETH CRIQUI; RONALD J. ELLIOTT; Rev. Msgr. ROBERT S. GREGORY, (Retired); Revs. THOMAS W. HERMES; JOSEPH POWERS; KENNETH A. RILEY, J.C.L., V.G., Chancellor; MATTHEW ROTERT; CHARLES N. ROWE, S.T.D., V.G.

*Presbyteral Council—*Revs. MATTHEW BRUMLEVE, Chm.; ANDRES MORENO, Vice Chm.; GABRIEL LICKTEIG, Ordained Ten Years & Under; ANDREW MATTINGLY, Sec. & Treas.; TERRY BRUCE, Retired Priests' Representative, (Retired); KENNETH A. RILEY, J.C.L., V.G., Chancellor & Ex Officio; CHARLES N. ROWE, S.T.D., V.G., Ex Officio; ALBERT BRUECKEN, O.S.B.; JOSEPH BATHKE, C.PP.S.; WILLIAM T. SHEAHAN, S.J.

*Deans—*Revs. MICHAEL ROACH, Deanery I; ANDREW MATTINGLY, Deanery II; ANDRES MORENO, Deanery III; GREGORY HASKAMP, Deanery IV; DAVID L. HOLLOWAY, Deanery V; MICHAEL CLARY, Deanery VI; JOSEPH BATHKE, C.PP.S., Deanery VII; DEVASAHAYAM GUDIME, Deanery VIII; JOSEPH TOTTON, Deanery IX; ALBERT BRUECKEN, O.S.B., Deanery X; JOSEPH POWERS, Deanery XI; CHRISTIAN J. MALEWSKI, Deanery XII; MATTHEW BRUMLEVE, Deanery XIII; MICHAEL ROACH, Deanery XIV.

Diocesan Offices and Directors

*Archivist—*ZACHARY DAUGHTREY, Ph.D.

Bright Futures FundJEREMY LILLIG, Dir.

*Building Commission—*Deacon MICHAEL LEWIS, Chm.; BOB DRAKE; BILL GAGNON; JOHN GIACOMO; JOSEPH W. HARRIS; BERNARD JACQUINOT; MARTHA C. KAUFFMAN; DAVE KOPEK; DAVID A. MALANOWSKI; THOMAS STRAHAN; Rev. PAUL TURNER, S.T.D.

Catholic Charities Foundation—4001 Blue Pkwy., Kansas City, 64130. Tel: 816-221-4377; Fax: 816-472-5423. CHRISTOPHER ICE, CEO.

Catholic Charities of Kansas City-St. Joseph, Inc.—4001 Blue Pkwy., Kansas City, 64130. Tel: 816-221-4377; Fax: 816-472-5423. SUNNY JONES, COO. Northwest Missouri Branch Office: JAN MOTL, Dir., 1123 S. 10th St., St. Joseph, 64503-2506. Tel: 816-232-2885.

*Catholic Healthcare Office—*JOHN F. MORRIS, Ph.D., Dir.

*The "Catholic Key" Diocesan Newspaper—*JACK SMITH, Editor.

*Cemeteries (Catholic Cemeteries Associated, Diocese of Kansas City-St. Joseph, Inc.)—*MR. STEPHEN REYES, Gen. Mgr., 7601 Blue Ridge, Kansas City, 64138. Cemeteries: Kansas City, Mt. Olivet; Mt. St. Mary; Resurrection; St. Joseph, Mt. Olivet.

*Censor Librorum—*Rev. Msgr. WILLIAM J. BLACET, P.A., J.C.L., (Retired).

*Communications—*JACK SMITH, Dir.; MEGAN MARLEY, Digital/Social Media Coord.

*Consecrated Life Office—*Sr. CONNIE BOULCH, O.S.F., Dir.

*Construction Management Office/Building Commission—*MARTHA C. KAUFFMAN, Construction Mgr.; LISA GRABLE, Coord., Fax: 816-756-5572.

*Divine Worship—*Rev. PAUL TURNER, S.T.D., Dir.; MARIO PEARSON, Ph.D., Music Coord.

Disability & Deaf Services—4001 Blue Pkwy., Kansas City, 64130. ASHLEY DOOLEY WOHLGEMUTH, Dir.

*Diocesan Special Events Office—*Deacon RALPH L. WEHNER, Coord.

*Domestic Church & Discipleship—*DINO DURANDO, Dir.

*Ecumenical/Interreligious Commission Officer & Chair—*Rev. PAUL TURNER, S.T.D.

*Facilities and Real Estate Management—*BILL GAGNON, Dir.; LISA GRABLE, Coord., Fax: 816-756-5572.

*Family Life Office—*DINO DURANDO, Dir.

*Finance Council—*Most Rev. JAMES V. JOHNSTON JR., D.D., J.C.L.; DAVID BRAIN; JOHN CROWE; CHRISTINE DEMAREA; JOHN DeSTEFANO; Rev. PATRICK J. RUSH, (Retired); JEREMY LILLIG, Non-Voting Member; THERESA HUPP; EILEEN HUTCHINSON; ALAN LANKFORD; THOMAS A. MCCULLOUGH; GEORGE MCLINEY; MARGO SHEPARD; JIM VANDYKE. Staff Representatives: MONICA ADAMS; DAVID A. MALANOWSKI.

*Finance Office—*DAVID A. MALANOWSKI, Finance Officer; MONICA ADAMS, Internal Auditor; DONNA LEWIS, Accounting Mgr.

*General Counsel—*PATRICK MILLER.

*Hispanic Ministry—*MIGUEL SALAZAR, Dir.

*Human Resources—*BOB ROPER, Dir.

*Human Rights Office—*BILL FRANCIS, Dir.

*Insurance Office—*MONICA ADAMS, Risk Mgr.

*Legion of Mary—*Rev. DONALD E. STURM, Dir., (Retired).

*Permanent Diaconate—*Deacons PAUL MULLER, Dir. Diaconate Prog.; KENNETH ALBERS, Formation Dir.; MICHAEL LEWIS, Asst. Dir.-Ordained; JAMES OLSHEFSKI, Asst. Dir.-Candidates; Revs. CHARLES N. ROWE, S.T.D., V.G., Vicar for Clergy; JOSEPH CISETTI, Dir. Spiritual Formation.

*Priestly Life and Ministry—*Rev. JUSTIN E. HOYE, Dir.

*Priests' Pension Plan—*Administrative Committee: Revs. CHARLES N. ROWE, S.T.D., V.G., Chm.; ERNEST P. DAVIS; GREGORY HASKAMP; M. JEFFREY STEPHAN; Deacon JOSEPH WHISTON; DAVID A. MALANOWSKI; BOB ROPER; NICK HADLEY.

*Priests' Purgatorial Society—*Rev. CHARLES N. ROWE, S.T.D., V.G., Sec.

Propagation of the Faith(Pontifical Society for the Propagation of the Faith, Missionary Union of the Clergy and Religious, The Pontifical Society of St. Peter the Apostle for Native Clergy, Missionary Childhood Association, and Daily World Missionaries) Rev. CHARLES N. ROWE, S.T.D., Dir.

*Office of Child and Youth Protection—*CARRIE COOPER, Dir.; SHERRY HUFFMAN, Safe Environment Prog. Coord.; JENIFER VALENTI, Independent Ombudsman; KATHLEEN CHASTAIN, Victim Svcs. Coord.

*Respect Life Office—*BILL FRANCIS, Dir.

*School Office—*DAN PETERS, Ed.D., Supt.; PAT BURBACH, Assoc. Supt.

*Stewardship and Development—*JEREMY LILLIG, Dir.; LAURA GRAY, Dir. Planned Giving; KEN KREMER, Dir. Devel.; THERESA SCHUMAN, Dir. Annual Catholic Appeal.

Tribunal—Mailing Address: P.O. Box 419037, Kansas City, 64141-6037. Tel: 816-756-1850.

*Judicial Vicar—*Rev. KENNETH A. RILEY, J.C.L., V.G., Chancellor.

*Defenders of the Bond—*Revs. ANTHONY J. PILEGGI, J.C.L.; ALEX KREIDLER, J.C.L.

*Director/Auditor—*DONETTA K. SHAW.

*Auditor—*BEATRIZ LIVINGSTON.

*Vocation Office—*Rev. ADAM JOHNSON, Dir.

*Young Adult & Campus Ministry Office—*Rev. ANDREW MATTINGLY, Dir.

*Youth Office—*MICHAEL NATIONS, Dir.

CLERGY, PARISHES, MISSIONS AND PAROCHIAL SCHOOLS

KANSAS CITY

(JACKSON COUNTY)

1—CATHEDRAL OF IMMACULATE CONCEPTION (1882)
416 W. 12th St., 64105. Tel: 816-842-0416; Email: info@kcgolddome.org. Revs. Paul Turner, S.T.D.; Anthony J. Pileggi, J.C.L., In Res.; Kenneth A. Riley, J.C.L., V.G., In Res.; Deacons Stephen W. Livingston; James Olshefski.

2—ST. ALOYSIUS (1886) (Hispanic), Closed. For inquiries for parish records contact Archives, Catholic Chancery.

3—ST. ANTHONY (1991)
318 Benton Blvd., 64124. Tel: 816-231-5445; Email: stanthony318@gmail.com; Web: www.stanthonykc.org. Rev. Andres Moreno; Deacon Thomas D. Powell.
*Catechesis Religious Program—*Students 48.

4—ST. BERNADETTE'S (1958)
9020 E. 51st Ter., 64133. Tel: 816-356-3700; Email: stbkcmo@gmail.com; Web: www.stbernadettekcmo.org. Revs. David L. Holloway; Philip Luebbert, Parochial Vicar.
Res.: 9021 E. 51st Ter., 64133.
*Catechesis Religious Program—*Email: linda@stbernadettekcmo.org. Linda Sapenaro, D.R.E. Students 14.

5—BLESSED SACRAMENT, Closed. For inquiries for parish records contact Archives, Catholic Chancery.

6—ST. CATHERINE OF SIENA (1926)
4101 E. 105th Ter., 64137-1649. Tel: 816-761-5483; Email: anitaosb@saintcatherine.com; Web: www.saintcatherine.com. Rev. Sunoj Thomas, O.S.B., Parochial Admin.; Deacon David Healy.
Catechesis Religious Program—

7—ST. CHARLES BORROMEO (1947)
900 N.E. Shady Lane Dr., 64118-4742.
Tel: 816-436-0880; Email: ngirton@stcharleskc.com; Web: www.stcharleskc.com. Rev. Donald P. Farnan; Deacons Joseph Whiston; Victor Quiason.
School—St. Charles Borromeo School, (Grades PreK-8), 804 N.E. Shady Lane Dr., Oakview, 64118.
Tel: 816-436-1009; Fax: 816-436-6293; Email: alachowitzer@stcharleskc.com; Web: stcharleskcschool.weconnect.com. Ann Lachowitzer, Prin. Lay Teachers 17; Students 190.
*Catechesis Religious Program—*Email: bdarnell@stcharleskc.com. Benjamin Darnell, D.R.E. Students 67.

8—CHRIST THE KING (1938)
Mailing Address: 8510 Wornall Rd., 64114.
Tel: 816-363-4888; Fax: 816-363-2315; Email: frlock@ctkkcmo.org; Email: wendy@ctkkcmo.org; Web: www.ctkkcmo.org. Revs. Gregory J. Lockwood; Louis Farley, In Res.
Res.: 504 W. 85th Terr., 64114.
Child Care—Preschool, Tel: 816-984-8768; Email: stacy@ctkkcmo.org. (Infant/Toddler & Preschool) Lay Teachers 20; Students 71; Clergy / Religious Teachers 1.
*Catechesis Religious Program—*Email: s.w.d@svcglobal.net; Email: justinbolson1987@gmail.com. Susan Dietchman, D.R.E.; Justin Olson, RCIA Coord. Students 115.

9—CHURCH OF THE HOLY MARTYRS (1991) (Vietnamese)
7801 Paseo Blvd., 64131. Tel: 816-333-3214; Email: giaoxukcmk@gmail.com; Web: giaoxukcmk.org. Rev. Duc Nguyen; Deacon Doan Tran.
*Catechesis Religious Program—*Tel: 816-333-5349. Students 181.

10—ST. ELIZABETH (1917)
2 E. 75th St., 64114. Tel: 816-523-2405; Email: info@stekc.org; Web: www.stekc.org. Rev. Gregory Haskamp; Deacon Michael McLean.
School—St. Elizabeth's School, (Grades PreK-8), 14 W. 75th St., 64114. Tel: 816-523-7100;
Fax: 816-523-2566; Email: pkollasch@stekc.org; Web: stekcschool.org. Pat Kollasch, Prin. Lay Teachers 32; Students 424.
*Catechesis Religious Program—*Students 19.

11—ST. FRANCIS SERAPH, Closed. For inquiries for parish records contact St. Anthony, Kansas City.

12—ST. FRANCIS XAVIER (1909)
1001 E 52 St, 64110. Tel: 816-523-5115; Email: parish@sfx-kc.org; Web: www.sfx-kc.org. Revs. Stephen T. Yavorsky, S.J.; Robert A. Hagan, S.J., Parochial Vicar.
*Catechesis Religious Program—*Tel: 816-381-9163; Email: mccormally@sfx-kc.org. Mariann Mccormally, D.R.E. Students 23.

13—ST. GABRIEL ARCHANGEL (1956)
4733 N. Cleveland Ave., 64117.
Tel: 816-453-1183, Ext. 200; Email: lori.langner@stgabrielskc.net; Web: www.stgabrielskc.net. Rev. Joseph M. Sharbel; Deacons Larry West; Daniel Brink.
School—St. Gabriel Archangel School, (Grades K-8), 4737 N. Cleveland Ave., 64117. Tel: 816-453-4443; Email: amy.hogan@outlook.com. Mrs. Amy Hogan, Prin. Lay Teachers 12; Students 96.
Child Care—Early Childhood Learning Center, Tel: 816-453-1153. Mrs. Amy Hogan, Prin. Lay Teachers 14; Students 35.
Catechesis Religious Program—
Tel: 816-453-1183, Ext. 217. Students 153.

14—GUARDIAN ANGELS (1909)
1310 Westport Rd., 64111. Tel: 816-931-4351; Email: tgutierrez@guardianangelskc.org. Revs. Garry Richmeier, C.PP.S., Sacramental Min.; Carlito Saballo, S.O.L.T., Parochial Vicar; Deacon Tyrone Gutierrez, Pastoral Admin.
School—Our Lady of Hope School, (Grades K-8), 4232 Mercier, 64111. Tel: 816-931-1693;
Fax: 816-931-6713; Email: mdelac@olhkcmo.org; Email: lklein@olhkcmo.org; Web: www.olhkcmo.org. Mary Delac, Prin.; Lillian Klein, Business Mgr. Clergy 3; Lay Teachers 12; Students 185; Clergy / Religious Teachers 1.
*Catechesis Religious Program—*Students 20.

15—HOLY CROSS (1902)
5106 St. John Ave., 64123. Tel: 816-231-4845;
Fax: 816-483-0900; Email: holycrosskc@juno.com. Rev. Thomas Holder, Parochial Admin.; Deacon Daniel Esteban.
*Catechesis Religious Program—*Students 176.

16—HOLY FAMILY (1980)

919 N.E. 96th St., 64155. Tel: ; Web: www.holyfamily.com. Rev. Philip Egan.
17—HOLY ROSARY (1890) (Italian)
911 Missouri Ave., 64106. Tel: 816-842-5440; Fax: 816-474-3806; Email: holyrosarykc@gmail.com; Web: www.hrkcmo.org. Revs. Abner Ables Jr.; Giannantonio Baggio, C.S., In Res.
Catechesis Religious Program—Students 5.
18—HOLY TRINITY, Closed. For inquiries for parish records contact Our Lady of Peace, Kansas City.
19—ST. JAMES (1906)
3909 Harrison St., 64110. Tel: 816-561-8512; Email: parish@stjkc.org; Web: www.stjkc.org. Revs. Michael Roach; Garry Richmeier, C.PP.S., Sacramental Min.
Catechesis Religious Program—Students 20.
20—ST. JOHN FRANCIS REGIS (1964)
8941 James A. Reed Rd., 64138. Tel: 816-761-1608; Email: cmelchior@regischurch.org; Web: www.stregischurch.com. Rev. Sean P. McCaffery; Deacons Samuel Adams; Kenneth Albers; Robert Falke.
School—St. John Francis Regis School, Tel: 816-763-5837; Web: www.regischurch.org. Ms. Robin Sowders, Prin. Lay Teachers 14; Students 140.
Catechesis Religious Program—Email: sduerr@regischurch.org. Susan Duerr, D.R.E. Students 27.
21—ST. JOHN THE BAPTIST, Closed. For inquiries for parish records contact St. Anthony, Kansas City, Tel: 816-231-5445.
22—ST. LOUIS (1919) (African American)
5930 Swope Pkwy., 64130. Tel: 816-444-6535; Fax: 816-444-6027; Email: SaintLouisKCMO@yahoo.com. Rev. Carlito Saballo, S.O.L.T.; Deacon John Purk
Legal Title: St. Louis Catholic Church
Catechesis Religious Program—
23—ST. MATTHEW APOSTLE (1964)
8001 Longview Rd., 64134. Tel: 816-763-0208; Fax: 816-765-2617. Rev. Richard D. Rocha; Deacon Ralph Joseph McNeal.
Catechesis Religious Program—Students 63.
24—ST. MICHAEL ARCHANGEL, Closed. For inquiries for parish records contact Our Lady of Peace, Kansas City, Tel: 816-231-0953.
25—ST. MONICA (1910) (African American)
1616 Paseo Blvd., 64108. Tel: 816-471-3696; Email: stmonica1616kc@hotmail.com. 1400 E. 17th St., 64108. Rev. Leonard Gicheru; Deacons Kenneth Greene; Darwin Dupree.
Catechesis Religious Program—Ramonda Doakes, D.R.E. Students 38.
26—ORATORY OF OLD ST. PATRICK (2005) Traditional Latin Mass Community.
Mailing Address: P.O. Box 414237, 64141-4237. 806 Cherry St., 64106. Tel: 816-931-5612; Email: oldstpatrick@institute-christ-king.org; Web: www.institute-christ-king.org/kansascity/. Rev. Canon Altiere, Rector
Institute of Christ the King
Catechesis Religious Program—Students 15.
27—OUR LADY OF GOOD COUNSEL (1866)
3934 Washington, 64111-2904. Tel: 816-561-0400; Email: kathy@olgckc.org. Revs. Adam Johnson; Alex Kreidler, J.C.L.; Andrew Mattingly; Deacon Ralph L. Wehner, Lit. Dir.
28—OUR LADY OF GUADALUPE, Closed. For inquiries for parish records contact Sacred Heart - Guadalupe, Kansas City, Tel: 816-842-6146.
29—OUR LADY OF PEACE (1991) (Hispanic)
1029 Bennington Ave., 64126. Tel: 816-231-0953; Email: admin@olopkc.org; Web: www.olopkc.org. Rev. Thomas Holder, Parochial Admin.; Sr. Greta Chavarria, Pastoral Assoc.; Deacon Alfred Santellan.
Catechesis Religious Program—1001 Bennington Ave., 64126-2299. Students 74.
30—OUR LADY OF PERPETUAL HELP (1878)
3333 Broadway Blvd., 64111. Tel: 816-561-3771; Email: alicea@olphkc.org. Revs. Gary Ziuraitis, C.Ss.R.; Andrew Thompson; Terry McCloskey, C.Ss.R.; John Tran; Eugene Harrison, C.Ss.R., In Res.; Frank Kriski, C.Ss.R., In Res.; Gregory Schmitt, In Res.
Catechesis Religious Program—Students 23.
31—OUR LADY OF SORROWS (1890)
2552 Gillham Rd., 64108. Tel: 816-421-2112; Email: oloskc@oloskc.org. Rev. Randolph Sly; Deacon Scott McKellar.
Catechesis Religious Program— Attend Our Lady of Perpetual Help Catholic Church, Kansas City.
32—ST. PATRICK (1924)
1357 N.E. 42nd Ter., 64116. Tel: 816-453-5510; Tel: 816-453-0971; Fax: 816-453-4458; Web: www.stpatrickkc.com. Rev. Matthew Brumleve; Deacons Jim Koger, Pastoral Assoc.; Michael Lewis, Pastoral Assoc.
School—St. Patrick School, (Grades PreK-8), 1401 N.E. 42nd Ter., 64116. Tel: 816-453-0971; Email: mragan@stpatrickkc.com; Web: stpatrickkc.com. Mary Ragan, Dir.; Kaci Monaghan, Prin. Lay Teachers 13; Students 112.
Catechesis Religious Program—Tel: 816-453-0971; Email: jfolken@stpatrickkc.com. Jean Folken, D.R.E. Students 69.
33—ST. PETER'S (1925)
701 E. Meyer Blvd., 64131. Tel: 816-363-2320; Email: communications@stpeterskc.org; Web: www.stpkc.org. 815 E. Meyer Blvd., 64131. Revs. Matthew Rotert; William Fox; Terry Bruce, In Res., (Retired). Res.: 6415 Holmes Rd., 64131. Email: mpfeifer@stpeterskc.org.
School—St. Peter's School, (Grades PreK-8), 6400 Charlotte St., 64131. Tel: 816-523-4899; Fax: 816-523-1248; Email: ameyer@Stpeterskc.org; Email: mstewart@stpeterskc.org; Web: www.stpkc.org. Mrs. Angie Meyer, Prin.; Mary Stewart, Vice Prin. Clergy 2; Lay Teachers 36; Students 513.
Catechesis Religious Program—Email: teresa@church.visitation.org. Ms. Teresa Albright, Pastoral Assoc. Students 16.
34—ST. RAPHAEL THE ARCHANGEL (1963) Closed. For inquiries for parish records contact Archives, Catholic Chancery.
35—SACRED HEART-GUADALUPE (1887) (Hispanic)
Tel: 816-842-6146, Ext. 22; Tel: 816-599-7242, Ext. 21; Email: aracelib@Sacredheartguadalupe.org; Email: ramonaarroyo@sacredheartguadalupe.org; Email: frfelipes@sacredheartguadalupe.org; Web: www.sacredheartguadalupe.org. Revs. Paul Turner, S.T.D., Parochial Admin.; Luis Felipe Suarez, Parochial Vicar; Mrs. Araceli Bernardino, Business Mgr. Res.: 907 Avenida Cesar Chavez, 64108.
Catechesis Religious Program—Ms. Ramona Arroyo, D.R.E. Students 25.
36—ST. STANISLAUS, Closed. For inquiries for parish records contact Our Lady of Peace, Kansas City, Tel: 816-231-0953.
37—ST. THERESE LITTLE FLOWER (1925)
5814 Euclid Ave., 64130. Tel: 816-444-5406; Fax: 816-444-9345; Email: mrotert@stlfkc.org; Web: www.stlfkc.org. Revs. Matthew Rotert; William Fox.
Catechesis Religious Program—Students 21.
38—ST. THERESE PARISH (Kansas City North) (1949)
7207 Hwy. 9, N.W., 64152.
Tel: 816-741-2800 Parish Office;
Tel: 816-746-1500 Early Ed Center;
Fax: 816-741-4959; Email: sttheresenorth@sttheresenorth.org; Web: www.sttheresenorth.org. Revs. Joseph Cisetti; Randolph Sly, Parochial Vicar; Ryan Koster, Parochial Vicar; Deacons Doug Warrens, RCIA Coord.; Scott McKellar, Pastoral Assoc.; Tony Zimmerman; Rick Boyle.
School—St. Therese Parish School, (Grades K-8), 7277 Hwy. 9, N.W., 64152. Tel: 816-741-5400; Fax: 816-741-0533; Email: sttheresenorth@sttheresenorth.org; Web: www.sttheresenorth.org. Theresa Roth, Prin. Lay Teachers 37; Students 660.
Catechesis Religious Program—
Tel: 816-741-5400, Ext. 107; Email: jdavis@sttheresenorth.org. Jennifer Davis, D.R.E. Students 400.
39—ST. THOMAS MORE (1964)
11822 Holmes Rd., 64131.
Tel: 816-942-2492, Ext. 202; Email: information@stmkc.com; Web: stmkc.com. Revs. Justin E. Hoye; Gabriel Lickteig, Parochial Vicar; Deacon Kevin Cummings.
School—St. Thomas More School, (Grades PreK-8), 11800 Holmes Rd., 64131. Tel: 816-942-5581; Email: smith_randy@stmcyclones.org; Web: stmkc.com. Mr. Randy Smith, Prin.; Mrs. Kathy O'Sullivan, Vice Prin. Lay Teachers 41; Students 491.
Catechesis Religious Program—Email: gbash@stmkc.com. Gabrielle Bash, D.R.E. Students 17.
40—VISITATION OF THE BLESSED VIRGIN MARY (1909) (Irish)
Mailing Address: 5141 Main St., 64112.
Tel: 816-753-7422; Fax: 816-753-5505; Email: paula@church.visitation.org; Web: www.visitation.org. Rev. Msgr. Bradley S. Offutt.
School—Visitation of the Blessed Virgin Mary School, 5134 Baltimore Ave., 64112.
Tel: 816-531-6200; Fax: 816-531-8045; Email: vcascone@school.visitation.org. Vincent Cascone, Prin. Clergy 1; Lay Teachers 39; Students 521.
Catechesis Religious Program—Email: tina@church.visitation.org. Students 58.

CITY OF ST. JOSEPH

(BUCHANAN COUNTY)
ST. JOSEPH
1—CO-CATHEDRAL OF ST. JOSEPH (1845) 519 N. 10th St., St. Joseph, 64501. Tel: 816-232-7763; Email: pbokay@cathedralsj.org; Web: www.cathedralsj.org. Revs. Stephen Hansen; Jayson Becker; Deacons Joshua Fultz; Steven Welsh.
School—Co-Cathedral of St. Joseph School, (Grades PreK-8),
Tel: 816-232-8486; Fax: 816-232-8793. Mrs. Rebecca Evans, Prin. Clergy 2; Lay Teachers 17; Students 234.
Catechesis Religious Program—
Tel: 816-232-7763, Ext. 103; Email: kspafford@cathedralsj.org. Kathryn Spafford, Contact Person. Students 28.
2—ST. FRANCIS XAVIER (1890) 2618 Seneca St., St. Joseph, 64507. Tel: 816-232-8449; Email: jlutz@sfxstjoe.com; Web: www.sfxstjoe.com. Revs. Joseph Miller, C.PP.S.; William Walter, C.PP.S., In Res.
School—St. Francis Xavier School, (Grades PreK-8), 2614 Seneca St., St. Joseph, 64507.
Tel: 816-232-4911; Fax: 816-364-0263; Email: admissions@sfxstjoe.com; Web: www.stfranstjo.com. Mr. Darin Pollard, Prin. Lay Teachers 24; Students 273.
Catechesis Religious Program—Students 34.
3—ST. JAMES (1900) 5814 King Hill Ave., St. Joseph, 64504. Tel: 816-238-0853; Email: fgirard@saintjamessaintjoseph.org. Revs. Evan Harkins; Jonathan Davis, Parochial Vicar.
School—St. James School
120 Michigan Ave., St. Joseph, 64504.
Tel: 816-238-0281. Mrs. Gerre Martin, Prin. Clergy 1; Lay Teachers 10; Students 141.
Catechesis Religious Program—Students 30.
4—ST. MARY CATHOLIC CHURCH (1891) 1606 N. 2nd St., St. Joseph, 64505. Tel: 816-279-1154; Email: email.stmary@gmail.com. Revs. Stephen Hansen, Admin.; Jayson Becker, Parochial Vicar.
Catechesis Religious Program—Students 16.
5—OUR LADY OF GUADALUPE (1982) 4503 Frederick Blvd., St. Joseph, 64506. Tel: 816-232-2847; Fax: 816-232-0269; Email: ahurst@olog.org; Email: cmalewski@olog.org; Email: kpowers@olog.org; Web: www.olog.org. Revs. Christian J. Malewski; Samuel Miloscia; Kathy Powers, Pastoral Assoc.; Angela Hurst, Business Mgr.
Catechesis Religious Program—Tina Dotson, Family Catechesis Coord.; Ally Goetz, Youth Min. Students 115.
6—ST. PATRICK (1869) 1723 S. 12th St., St. Joseph, 64503. Tel: 816-279-2594. Revs. Evan Harkins, Parochial Admin.; Jonathan Davis, Parochial Vicar; Deacons John Nash; Marcelino Canchola.
Catechesis Religious Program—Students 7.
7—QUEEN OF THE APOSTLES, Closed. For inquiries for parish records contact the Co-Cathedral of St. Joseph, Kansas City, Tel: 816-232-7763.

OUTSIDE THE CITIES OF KANSAS CITY AND ST. JOSEPH

BELTON, CASS CO., ST. SABINA'S (1944)
700 Trevis Ave., Belton, 64012. Tel: 816-331-4713; Fax: 816-322-6196; Email: frjeff@stsabinaparish.org; Web: www.stsabinaparish.org. Rev. M. Jeffrey Stephan; Deacon Michael Gates
Legal Title: St. Sabina Catholic Church, Belton.
BETHANY, HARRISON CO., BLESSED SACRAMENT (1945) [JC2]
Mailing Address: 1208 S. 25th St., P.O. Box 166, Bethany, 64424. Tel: 660-425-8160; Email: cathlc@grm.net. Rev. Sebastian Allgaier, O.S.B. Res.: P.O. Box 501, Conception, 64433. Web: www.blessedsacramentbethany.parishesonline.com.
Catechesis Religious Program—Students 12.
BLUE SPRINGS, JACKSON CO.
1—ST. JOHN LA LANDE (1938)
805 NW R.D. Mize Rd., Blue Springs, 64015.
Tel: 816-229-3378. Rev. Ronald J. Elliott; Deacons Douglas Myler; Shane Voyles.
School—St. John LaLande School, 801 N.W. R.D. Mize Rd., Blue Springs, 64015. Tel: 816-228-5895; Fax: 816-228-8979; Email: awright@sjlparish.org; Web: www.stjohnlalandeschool.com. Ann Wright, Prin. Lay Teachers 16; Students 218; Staff 4.
Catechesis Religious Program—Students 150.
2—ST. ROBERT BELLARMINE (1983)
4313 S.W. State Rte. 7, Blue Springs, 64014-5701.
Tel: 816-229-5168; Fax: 816-229-3981;
Tel: 816-229-3552; Email: john_bolderson@msn.com; Email: edwills@robertbellarmine.org; Email: office@robertbellarmine.org; Email: susan@robertbellarmine.org; Email: michael@robertbellarmine.org; Web: www.robertbellarmine.org. Revs. John D. Bolderson; Edward Wills, Business Mgr.; Deacon Michael Elsey, Chap.
Res.: 4112 S.W. 9th St., Blue Springs, 64015. Email: judy@robertbellarmine.org.
Catechesis Religious Program—Students 169.
BUCKNER, JACKSON CO., CHURCH OF THE SANTA FE (1965)
231 S. Sibley Street, P.O. Box 317, Buckner, 64016-0317. Tel: 816-650-9341; Email: barbarablando@gmail.com. Rev. Msgr. Ralph L. Kaiser.
Catechesis Religious Program—
BUTLER, BATES CO., ST. PATRICK'S (1882)
400 W. Nursery St., Butler, 64730. Tel: 660-679-4482

; Email: stpatrickbutler@embarqmail.com. Rev. Jason Koch.
Catechesis Religious Program—Students 38.

CAMERON, CLINTON CO., ST. MUNCHIN (1867) [CEM 2] (German—Irish)
301 N. Cedar St., Cameron, 64429. Tel: 816-632-2768 ; Fax: 816-632-7997; Email: stmunchin@centurytel.net; Web: www.munchin.net. Rev. Thomas K. Ludwig.
Res.: 316 W. 3rd St., Cameron, 64429.
Catechesis Religious Program—Email: maryfmorgan@centurytel.net. Mary Morgan, D.R.E. Students 47.
Mission—St. Aloysius, 301 S. Water, Maysville, DeKalb Co. 64469.

CARROLLTON, CARROLL CO., ST. MARY'S (1867) [CEM]
211 E. Shanklin St., Carrollton, 64633.
Tel: 660-542-1259; Email: stmary2007@sbcglobal.net. Rev. J. Kenneth Criqui; Deacon Gary Kappler.
Catechesis Religious Program—Students 59.
Mission—Sacred Heart, 403 S. Walnut, Norborne, Carroll Co. 64668.

CHILLICOTHE, LIVINGSTON CO., ST. COLUMBAN (1857) [CEM 2]
1111 Trenton St., Chillicothe, 64601-1499.
Tel: 660-646-0190; Email: kim@stcolumbanonline.org; Web: stcolumbanonline.org. Rev. Benjamin Kneib.
School—Bishop Hogan Memorial School, 1114 Trenton St., Chillicothe, 64601. Tel: 660-646-0705; Email: kidsareus@bishophogan.org; Web: www.bishophogan.org. Mrs. Pam Brobst, Prin. Lay Teachers 12; Students 118.
Catechesis Religious Program—Students 52.

CLINTON, HENRY CO., HOLY ROSARY (1875)
610 S. 4th St., Clinton, 64735. Tel: 660-885-4523; Email: holyrosary@hrclinton.com; Web: www.trumanlakecatholic.com. Rev. James Taranto; Deacon Steven Carter.
Res.: 401 E. Allen, Clinton, 64735.
School—Holy Rosary School, 400 E. Wilson, Clinton, 64735. Tel: 660-885-4412; Email: hrsecretary@hrclinton.net. Mrs. Andrea Harris, Prin. Clergy 2; Lay Teachers 12; Students 102; Clergy / Religious Teachers 2.
Catechesis Religious Program—Students 15.
Missions—St. Catherine's—605 Walnut St., Osceola, St. Clair Co. 64776. Tel: 660-885-4523; Email: holyrosary@hrclinton.com. 610 S. 4th, Clinton, 64735.
St. Bartholomew.

CONCEPTION JUNCTION, NODAWAY CO., ST. COLUMBA (1860) [CEM]
311 Roosevelt, P.O. Box 127, Conception Junction, 64434. Tel: 660-944-2301. Rev. Allan Stetz, O.S.B.
Catechesis Religious Program—Students 76.

EASTON, BUCHANAN CO., ST. JOSEPH'S (1830) [CEM] (Irish—German)
107 S Shortridge, Easton, 64443. Tel: 816-473-2011; Email: stjosephchurch@centurytel.net; Web: stjosepheaston.org. Mailing Address: P.O. Box 197, Easton, 64443. Rev. Joseph Totton; Christine Ottinger, Music Min.; Penny Harrison, Sec.
Catechesis Religious Program—Email: baskets105@gmail.com. Amy Adams, D.R.E. Students 5.

EXCELSIOR SPRINGS, CLAY CO., ST. ANN (1889)
1503 Tracy, Excelsior Springs, 64024.
Tel: 816-630-6659; Email: stannparishoffice@gmail.com. Rev. M. Christopher Smith.
Catechesis Religious Program—Chris Sanders, D.R.E. & Pastoral Care. Students 130.

GALLATIN, DAVIESS CO., MARY IMMACULATE (1950)
409 S. Main, Gallatin, 64640. Tel: 816-663-2146; Email: shmichurch@gmail.com; Web: maryimmaculategallatin.org. Mailing Address: P.O. Box 188, Hamilton, 64644-0188. Rev. Thomas W. Hermes.
Catechesis Religious Program—Tel: 660-663-5199; Email: jarboe@windstream.net. Mary Jarboe, D.R.E. Students 14.

GLADSTONE, CLAY CO., ST. ANDREW THE APOSTLE (1964)
6415 NE Antioch Rd., Gladstone, 64119.
Tel: 816-453-2089; Fax: 816-453-6393; Email: jrobertson@sataps.com; Web: www.sataps.com. Revs. Vincent M. Rogers; Eric Schneider, Parochial Vicar.
School—St. Andrew the Apostle School, (Grades PreK-8), 6415 N.E. Antioch Rd., Gladstone, 64119.
Tel: 816-454-7377; Email: spalmarine@sataps.com; Web: www.sataps.com. Mr. Tony Calcara, Prin. Administrators 3; Clergy 1; Lay Teachers 20; Students 280.
Catechesis Religious Program—
Tel: 816-454-7377, Ext. 107. Donna Geisinger, D.R.E. (K-5th Grade; Carolyn Anch, D.R.E. (Middle-High School). Students 177.

GRANDVIEW, JACKSON CO., CORONATION OF OUR LADY (1958)
13000 Bennington Ave., Grandview, 64030.
Tel: 816-761-8811; Email: coronation@coronationofourlady.org. Rev. Adam Haake; Deacon Michael Dennis.
Res.: 12937 Craig Dr., Grandview, 64030.
Fax: 816-761-8812; Email: coronation@kc.rr.com; Web: www.coronationofourlady.org.
Catechesis Religious Program—Students 41.

HAMILTON, CALDWELL CO., SACRED HEART (1921)
205 E Middle St., Hamilton, 64644-0188.
Tel: 816-583-1117; Email: shmichurch@gmail.com. P.O. Box 188, Hamilton, 64644. Revs. Thomas W. Hermes; John H. Zupez, S.J., In Res.
Res.: 209 E. Middle St., Hamilton, 64644-0188. Web: sacredheart-hamilton.org.
Catechesis Religious Program—Tel: 816-695-5736; Email: spschwery@yahoo.com. Sabrina Banks, D.R.E. Students 10.

HARRISONVILLE, CASS CO., OUR LADY OF LOURDES aka Our Lady of Lourdes Catholic Church, Harrisonville (1941)
2700 E. Mechanic, Harrisonville, 64701.
Tel: 816-380-5744; Email: ollinfo@embarqmail.com; Web: www.ourladyoflourdesharrisonville.org. Rev. Michael Clary, Admin.
Mission—Holy Trinity, 1372 NW Graham Rd., Urich, 64788.

HIGGINSVILLE, LAFAYETTE CO., ST. MARY'S (1879) [CEM]
401 W. Broadway, Higginsville, 64037.
Tel: 660-584-3038. Rev. Thomas J. D. Hawkins.
Catechesis Religious Program—Students 32.

HURLINGEN, BUCHANAN CO., SEVEN DOLORS (1872) [CEM] [JC] (German)
12750 NE Hurlingen Rd, Hurlingen, 64443.
Tel: 816-232-2847; Fax: 816-232-0269; Email: ahurst@olog.org; Email: cmalewski@olog.org. 4503 Frederick Blvd., St. Joseph, 64506. Revs. Christian J. Malewski, Parochial Admin.; Samuel Miloscia, Parochial Vicar.
Res.: 2618 Seneca St., St. Joseph, 64507.
Catechesis Religious Program—

HOLDEN, JOHNSON CO., ST. PATRICK'S (1869) [CEM 2]
703 S. Olive St., Holden, 64040-1443.
Tel: 816-540-4563; Web: www.stpatrickholden.org. St Bridget Catholic Church, Pleasant Hill: 2103 Lexington Rd., Pleasant Hill, 64080. Rev. Curt Vogel, Parochial Admin.
Catechesis Religious Program—Kathleen Bryant, D.R.E. Students 36.

INDEPENDENCE, JACKSON CO.

1—ST. ANN'S (1915)
10113 E. Lexington Ave., Independence, 64053.
Tel: 816-252-1160; Email: saintanns64053@yahoo.com. Rev. James F. Carlyle.

2—ST. JOSEPH THE WORKER (1976)
2200 N. Blue Mills Rd., Independence, 64058.
Tel: 816-796-6877; Email: Pastor@sjtw.us; Web: www.sjtw.us. Revs. Joseph Powers; Timothy Leete, Parochial Vicar.
Catechesis Religious Program—Janice McQuillan, Faith Formation Coord. Students 20.

3—ST. MARK (1965)
3736 S. Lees Summit Rd., Independence, 64055.
Tel: 816-373-2600; Email: cmasuch@stmarksparish.com. Revs. Joseph Powers; Timothy Leete, Parochial Vicar; Deacon Kenneth Fuenfhausen, Director of Youth Min.
Catechesis Religious Program—Email: jarthur@stmarksparish.com; Email: jpowers@stmarksparish.com; Email: kfuenfhausen@stmarksparish.com. Joyce Arthur, D.R.E. Students 406.

4—ST. MARY'S (1823) [CEM]
600 N. Liberty St., Independence, 64050.
Tel: 816-252-0121; Email: mbartulica@hotmail.com; Web: www.saintmarysparish.org. Rev. Matthew Bartulica.
Catechesis Religious Program—Debra Gilbert, D.R.E. Students 30.

5—NATIVITY OF MARY PARISH (1938)
Mailing Address: 10017 E. 36th Ter. S., Independence, 64052. Tel: 816-353-2184; Email: parish@nativityofmary.org; Web: Nativityofmary.org. Rev. Robert Stone.
Res.: 10015 E. 36th Ter. S., Independence, 64052. Email: mclancy@nativityofmary.org.
School—Nativity of Mary Parish School, (Grades PreK-8), 10021 E. 36th Ter. S., Independence, 64052. Tel: 816-353-0284; Fax: 816-356-0286; Email: school@nativityofmary.org. Mrs. Mary Parrish, Prin. Clergy 1; Lay Teachers 14; Students 186.
Catechesis Religious Program—Preschool 16; Students 212.

KEARNEY, CLAY CO., CHURCH OF THE ANNUNCIATION (1980)
Mailing Address: 701 N. Jefferson, P.O. Box 599, Kearney, 64060-0599. Tel: 816-628-5030; Email: annunciation@fairpoint.net; Web: annunciationkearney.com. Rev. Al Ebach, C.PP.S.
Catechesis Religious Program—Students 200.

LEES SUMMIT, JACKSON CO.

1—HOLY SPIRIT (1979)
1800 S.W. State Rte. 150, Lees Summit, 64082.
Tel: 816-537-6990; Fax: 816-272-6291; Email: parish@holyspiritmo.org; Web: www.holyspiritmo.org. Rev. Michael Clary; Deacons Richard Akins; Don Schmidt; Fred Lange.
Res.: 1137 S.W. Georgetown Dr., Lees Summit, 64082.
Catechesis Religious Program—Email: mstewart@holyspiritmo.org. Michelle Stewart, D.R.E. Students 308.

2—ST. MARGARET OF SCOTLAND CATHOLIC CHURCH (1999)
777 N.E. Blackwell Rd., Lees Summit, 64086.
Tel: 816-246-6800; Email: fr.ernie.davis@stmos.org; Web: www.stmos.org. Rev. Ernest P. Davis; Deacons Paul Muller; David Rennicke; Sue Nichols, Parish Mgr.
Catechesis Religious Program—Tel: 816-272-0125; Email: cliccar@stmos.org. Cathie Liccar, D.R.E. Students 253.

3—OUR LADY OF THE PRESENTATION (1896)
130 N.W. Murray Rd., Lees Summit, 64081.
Tel: 816-251-1100; Email: cchristianson@olpls.org. Revs. Thomas Holder; Olvin Giron, Parochial Vicar; Deacons Keith Hoffman; Mike Peterson.
School—Our Lady of the Presentation School, 150 N.W. Murray Rd., Lees Summit, 64081.
Tel: 816-251-1150; Email: jbriggs@olpls.org; Web: www.olpls.org. Jody Briggs, Prin. Lay Teachers 36; Students 471.
Catechesis Religious Program—Tel: 816-251-1135. Jo Engert, D.R.E. Students 226.

LEXINGTON, LAFAYETTE CO., IMMACULATE CONCEPTION (1842) [CEM]
107 N. 18th St., Lexington, 64067. Tel: 660-259-3043 ; Email: iccc@embarqmail.com. Rev. Devasahayam Gudime.
Catechesis Religious Program—Students 45.

LIBERTY, CLAY CO., ST. JAMES (1840)
309 S. Stewart Rd., Liberty, 64068.
Tel: 816-781-4343; Email: daryl.sweetland@stjames-liberty.org; Web: www.stjames-liberty.org. Revs. Michael Roach; Timothy Armbruster, C.PP.S.; Deacon Charles Koesterer.
School—St. James School, (Grades PreK-8), 309 S. Stewart Rd., Liberty, 64068. Tel: 816-781-4428; Email: jennifer.smith@stjames-school.org; Web: www.stjames-school.org. Mrs. Jennifer Scanlon-Smith, Prin. Lay Teachers 31; Students 358.
Catechesis Religious Program—Students 445.

MARYVILLE, NODAWAY CO., ST. GREGORY BARBARIGO (1858) [CEM 2] [JC]
333 S. Davis St., Maryville, 64468. Tel: 660-582-3833 ; Fax: 660-582-5914; Email: rankindevinsg@gmail.com; Email: vansicklepamsg@gmail.com; Web: www.stgregorysmaryville.org. Rev. Albert Bruecken, O.S.B.
Res.: 825 E. Edwards St., Maryville, 64468.
School—St. Gregory Barbarigo School, (Grades PreK-8), 315 S. Davis St., Maryville, 64468.
Tel: 660-582-2462; Fax: 660-582-2496; Email: sstiens@stgregorysschool.org; Email: smartin@stgregorysschool.org. Mrs. Shelly Stiens; Susan Martin, Prin. Lay Teachers 16; Students 155.
Catechesis Religious Program—Students 15.

MONTROSE, HENRY CO., IMMACULATE CONCEPTION (1876) [CEM] [JC2] (German)
606 Kansas Ave., Montrose, 64770-9601.
Tel: 660-693-4651; Email: theresam.iccmo@embarqmail.com. Rev. Jason Koch.
School—St. Mary School, (Grades PreK-8), 608 Kansas Ave., Montrose, 64770. Tel: 660-693-4502; Email: theresam.iccmo@embarqmail.com. Rev. Thomas W. Hermes, Prin.; Mr. Phillip Landers, Prin. Clergy 1; Lay Teachers 4; Students 39; Clergy / Religious Teachers 1.
Catechesis Religious Program—Email: frtomh@embarqmail.com. Students 39.

NEVADA, VERNON CO., ST. MARY (1887) [CEM]
330 N. Main St., Nevada, 64772. Tel: 417-667-7517; Email: stmarysnevada@sbcglobal.net. Rev. Peter M. Savidge.
School—St. Mary School, (Grades PreK-5), 330 N. Main St., Nevada, 64772. Tel: 417-667-7517; Email: stmarysnevada@sbcglobal.net. Ms. Amanda Prine, Prin. Lay Teachers 3; Students 13.
Catechesis Religious Program—Tel: 417-549-6166; Email: abcdhab@gmail.com. Colleen Haberkorn, D.R.E. Students 15.
Mission—St. Bridget's, 9th & E. Walnut St., Rich Hill, Bates Co. 64779.

OAK GROVE, ST. JUDE THE APOSTLE (1973)
2001 S. Broadway, P.O. Box 590, Oak Grove, 64075.
Tel: 816-690-3165; Email: contact@stjudeoakgrove.com; Web: www.stjudeoakgrove.org. Rev. Bryan C. Amthor, Parochial Admin.
Res.: 716 S. Third St., Odessa, 64076.
Catechesis Religious Program—Email: corriosn@stjudeoakgrove.com. Connie Orrison, D.R.E. Students 20.

ODESSA, LAFAYETTE CO., ST. GEORGE (1882)

716 S. Third, Odessa, 64076. Tel: 816-230-4127; Tel: 816-633-7475; Email: stgeorgeodessa@gmail.com; Web: stgeorgeodessamo.org. Rev. Bryan C. Amthor, Admin.

Catechesis Religious Program—Tel: 816-633-7475; Email: stgeorgeodessa@gmail.com. Students 63.

PARNELL, NODAWAY CO., ST. JOSEPH'S (1891) [CEM 2] [JC]

411 S. Main, P.O. Box 78, Parnell, 64475. Tel: 660-986-3305. Rev. Allan Stetz, O.S.B.

Catechesis Religious Program—Students 61.

PLATTE CITY, PLATTE CO., TWELVE APOSTLES PARISH (2008)

17900 Humphrey's Rd., Platte City, 64079. Mailing Address: 407 Cherry St., Weston, 64098. Tel: 816-640-2206; Fax: 816-640-2209; Email: secyhtxii@kc.rr.com; Web: www.twelveapostlescatholic.org. Rev. Steven C. Rogers.

Catechesis Religious Program—Mrs. Katherine Daughtrey, D.R.E. Students 137.

PLATTSBURG, CLINTON CO., ST. ANN'S (1866) [CEM] (Irish)

700 W. Maple St., Plattsburg, 64477. Tel: 816-539-2634; Email: stannplattsburg@gmail.com; Web: stannplattsburg.org. Rev. Joseph Totton, Parochial Admin.

Catechesis Religious Program—Roxanne Durando, D.R.E. Students 35.

PLEASANT HILL, CASS CO., ST. BRIDGET CATHOLIC CHURCH, PLEASANT HILL (1884)

2103 N. Lexington, Pleasant Hill, 64080. Tel: 816-540-4563; Fax: 816-540-2162; Email: stbridgetparish@embarqmail.com; Web: stbridgetph.weconnect.com. Rev. Curt Vogel.

Catechesis Religious Program—Melissa Thornsberry, D.R.E. Students 85.

RAYTOWN, JACKSON CO., OUR LADY OF LOURDES (1948)

7009 Blue Ridge Blvd., Raytown, 64133. Tel: 816-353-2380; Email: office@ollraytown.com; Web: www.ollraytown.com. 7049 Blue Ridge Blvd., Raytown, 64133. Rev. David L. Holloway; Deacons Richard Gross; Joseph Zager.

Catechesis Religious Program—Catechesis of the Good Shepherd, Mrs. Wanda Demoss, Contact Person. Students 5.

RICHMOND, RAY CO., IMMACULATE CONCEPTION (1869) [CEM]

602 S. Camden, Richmond, 64085. Tel: 816-776-6870 ; Email: richmondcatholic@sbcglobal.net. Rev. Devasahayam Gudime.

Res.: 107 N. 18th St., Lexington, 64067.

Catechesis Religious Program—Students 14.

SAVANNAH, ANDREW CO., ST. ROSE OF LIMA (1898)

707 S. Hall Ave., Savannah, 64485. Tel: 816-324-5700; Email: srlp@stjoelive.com. Rev. Joshua Barlett, Admin.

St Patrick Parish: 303 Grand Ave., Forest City, 64451.

Catechesis Religious Program—Students 75.

Mission—St. Patrick, 303 Grand Ave., Forest City, Holt Co. 64451.

SMITHVILLE, CLAY CO., CHURCH OF THE GOOD SHEPHERD (1974)

18601 N. 169 Hwy., Smithville, 64089. Tel: 816-532-4344; Email: gsccmo@gmail.com; Web: www.gsccmo.org. Rev. Terrell M. Finnell; Deacons Michael Koile; John Wichmann.

Catechesis Religious Program—Email: chelsea@voboril.org. Chelsea Voboril, D.R.E. Students 116.

STANBERRY, GENTRY CO., ST. PETER'S (1880) [CEM]

614 N. Alanthus Ave., Stanberry, 64489. Tel: 660-783-2159. Rev. Pachomius Meade, O.S.B.

Catechesis Religious Program—Students 65.

Mission—St. Patrick's, 4201 State Hwy. AA, King City, Gentry Co. 64463.

Catechesis Religious Program—Students 13.

SUGAR CREEK, JACKSON CO., ST. CYRIL (1912) (Croatian—Slovak)

11231 Chicago Ave., Sugar Creek, 64054. Tel: 816-252-9564; Email: jascarlyle@gmail.com. Rev. James F. Carlyle.

Catechesis Religious Program—Students 2.

TARKIO, ATCHISON CO., ST. PAUL THE APOSTLE (1890) [JC]

908 Elm St., Tarkio, 64491. Tel: 660-736-4342; Email: stpaulstben@gmail.com. St. Paul the Apostle Parish: P.O. Box 5, Tarkio, 64491. Rev. Peter Ullrich, O.S.B.

Catechesis Religious Program—St. Paul, Students 5.

Mission—St. Benedict Catholic Church.

TRENTON, GRUNDY CO., ST. JOSEPH'S CATHOLIC CHURCH (1872) [CEM]

1728 St. Joseph St., Trenton, 64683. Tel: 660-359-2841; Email: stjosephtrenton@gmail.com. Rev. Kevin Drew.

Mission—Immaculate Heart of Mary Catholic Church, Email: kevdrew11@yahoo.com.

Catechesis Religious Program—Students 28.

WARRENSBURG, JOHNSON CO., SACRED HEART (1865)

300 S. Ridgeview Dr., Warrensburg, 64093. Tel: 660-747-6154; Email: Parish@shcatholic.com; Web: www.shcatholic.com. Rev. Joseph Bathke, C.PP.S.

Catechesis Religious Program—Email: psr@shcatholic.com. Ramona Baldwin, D.R.E. Students 140.

WESTON, PLATTE CO., HOLY TRINITY (1842) [JC]

407 Cherry St., Weston, 64098. Tel: 816-640-2206; Web: www.holytrinitycatholic.org. Rev. Steven C. Rogers.

Catechesis Religious Program—Mrs. Katherine Daughtrey, D.R.E. Students 62.

Special Assignment:

Revs.—

Amthor, Bryan C., Chap., St. Pius High School
Davis, Jonathan, Chap., Bishop LeBlond High School
Farley, Louis, Chap., St. Joseph's Medical Ctr. and St. Mary's Medical Ctr.
Gicheru, Leonard, Chap., Veterans Administration Medical Ctr.
Haake, Adam, Chap., St. Michael the Archangel High School
Johnson, Adam, Vocation Dir.
Kreidler, Alex, J.C.L., Tribunal Judge
Luebbert, Philip, Chap., Little Sisters of the Poor
Mattingly, Andrew, Dir. Young Adult Office & Campus Ministries
Pileggi, Anthony J., J.C.L., Tribunal, Defender of the Bond
Riley, Kenneth A., J.C.L., V.G., V.G.-Chancellor & Mod. of the Curia, Judicial Vicar
Rowe, Charles N., S.T.D., Vicar for Clergy
Sly, Randolph, Pres., St. Michael the Archangel High School.

On Duty Outside the Diocese:

Revs.—

Benjamin, Matthew, Archdiocese for Military Svcs.
Reardon, Daniel, Archdiocese for Military Svcs.

Retired:

Rev. Msgrs.—

Blacet, William J., P.A., J.C.L., Emeritus, (Retired), 3934 Washington, 64111
Caldwell, William, S.T.B., (Retired), Excelsior Springs Residential Center, 1700 Rainbow Dr., Rm. 606, Excelsior Springs, 64024
Gregory, Robert S., (Retired), 23 Janssen Pl., 64109-2622
Leitner, John E., (Retired), 12100 Wornall Rd., #357, 64145

Revs.—

Borkowski, Thomas, (Retired), Wheaton Franciscan Sisters, 2S436 Emerald Green Dr. #A, Warrenville, IL 60555
Bruce, Terry, (Retired), 6415 Holmes Rd., 64131
Coleman, C. Michael, J.C.L., (Retired), 1546 Homestead Rd., LaGrange Park, IL 60526
Cronin, Thomas, (Retired), 143 Desert Lakes Dr., Fernley, NV 89408
Deming, Robert N., (Retired), 7927 Bristol Ct., Prairie Village, KS 66208
Gauthier, Ernest, L.C.S.W., (Retired), 2920 S.E. Bingham Ct., Lee's Summit, 64063
Gillgannon, Michael, (Retired), 8300 E. 88th Tr., Apt. #1006, 64138
Hanh, Joseph Phan Trong, (Retired), 11619 Minor Dr., 64114
Hart, James, B.A., M.A., (Retired), 8300 E. 88th Ter., #2006, 64138
Healy, James E., (Retired), 207 N.W. Birch St., Lees Summit, 64064
Kerr, Robert, (Retired), 8607 Jarboe, 64114-2748
Mahoney, Robert J., Ph.D., (Retired), 4550 Warwick, #905, 64111
Matt, Joseph H., J.C.L., (Retired), 3221 Gateway Dr., Independence, 64057-3322
McCormack, John, M.S., (Retired), 8300 E. 88th Ter., #2010, 64138-4490
Moscaritolo, Mario, (Retired), 30 Chelsea St., #708, Everett, MA 02149
Opoka, Lloyd E., (Retired), 9401 Madison Ave., 64114-3206
Rice, Michael D., (Retired), 1650 Shawnee Bend Rd., Sunrise Beach, 65079
Rost, Robert A., D.Min., (Retired), 553 Lake Viking Ter., Gallatin, 64640
Rush, Patrick J., (Retired), 2900 W. 53rd St., Fairway, KS 66205
Ryan, C. Duane, (Retired), 263 Bello Point Dr., Sunrise Beach, 65079
Schuele, John, (Retired), Villa Ventura,12100 Wornall Rd., #264, 64145
Sinclair, Alexander B., (Retired), 4545 Wornall Rd., #608, 64111
Sturm, Donald E., (Retired), 2830 Angelique St., Saint Joseph, 64501
Tobin, Charles P., (Retired), P.O. Box 502, Conception, 64433
Walker, Michael, (Retired), P.O. Box 665, Green Mountain Falls, CO 80819
Waris, Gerald R., (Retired), 7300 W. 107th St., #418, Overland Park, KS 66212
Wiederholt, Thomas W., (Retired), 514 W. 26th St., 4-N, 64108.

Permanent Deacons:

Adams, Samuel
Akins, Richard
Albers, Kenneth
Beaudoin, Philip Ross, (Retired)
Boyle, Rick
Brink, Daniel
Buckner, Brian
Canchola, Marcelino
Carter, Steven
Clough, Richard, (Retired)
Cummings, Kevin
Davis, F. Jerry, (Retired)
Dennis, Michael
Dupree, Darwin
Elsey, Michael
Esteban, Daniel
Falke, Robert
Fuenfhausen, Kenneth
Fultz, Joshua
Gates, Michael
Greene, Kenneth
Gross, Richard
Gutierrez, Tyrone
Healy, David
Hemke, Douglas
Hoffman, Keith
Kappler, Gary
Koesterer, Charles
Koger, Jim
Lange, Fred
Lauhoff, John D., (Retired)
LeMay, Joseph
Lewis, Michael
Livingston, Stephen W.
Madden, Donald
McCandless, Donald L., (Retired)
McKay, Clarence W., (Retired)
McKellar, Scott, (Ordinariate of the Chair of St. Peter)
McLean, Michael
McMenamy, Justin M., (Retired)
McNeal, Ralph Joseph
Muller, Paul
Myler, Douglas
Nash, John
Nguyen, Dien
Nguyen, Paul
Olshefski, James
Peak, Frank L., (Retired)
Peterson, Mike
Pham, Tuyen, (Retired)
Powell, D. Thomas, (Retired)
Quiason, Victor
Rennicke, James III
Reynolds, James III
Schieber, Martin L., (Retired)
Schmidt, Donald J.
Schneider, Lawrence, (Retired)
Tran, Doan
Warrens, Doug
Wehner, Ralph L.
Welsh, Steven
West, Larry
Whiston, Joseph
Wichmann, John
Williams, Jerry, (Retired)
Zagar, Joseph
Zimmerman, Tony.

INSTITUTIONS LOCATED IN DIOCESE

[A] SEMINARIES, RELIGIOUS OR SCHOLASTICATES

KANSAS CITY. *Gaspar Mission House*, 5221 Rockhill Rd., 64110. Tel: 816-333-7980. Revs. Richard Bayuk, C.PP.S.; Garry Richmeier, C.PP.S. Priests 2; Clergy / Religious Teachers 2.

CONCEPTION. *Conception Seminary College*, 37174 State Hwy. VV, P.O. Box 502, Conception, 64433-0502. Tel: 660-944-3105; Fax: 660-944-2829; Email: seminary@conception.edu; Web: conception.edu. Very Rev. Brendan Moss, O.S.B., Rector, (St. Meinrad Archabbey); Rev. Peter Ullrich, O.S.B.,

Vice Pres.; Most Rev. Jerome Hanus, O.S.B.; Revs. Albert Bruecken, O.S.B.; Timothy M. MyViet Tran, C.M.C., J.C.L.; Enrique Garcia, Chap., Diocese of Des Moines; Bro. Etienne Huard, O.S.B., Chap.; Revs. Victor Schinstock, O.S.B., Chap.; Scott Boeckman, Chap.; Xavier Nacke, O.S.B.; Benedict Neenan, O.S.B., Abbot - Chancellor; Daniel Petsche, O.S.B., Dir. of Spiritual Formation; Duane F. Reinert, O.F.M.Cap.; John Rini, (Retired); Adam Ryan, O.S.B.; Paul Sheller, O.S.B.; Stephen Keusenkothen; Martin DeMeulenaere, O.S.B., Pastoral Min./Coord.; Charles P. Tobin, Spiritual Advisor/ Care Svcs., (Retired). Brothers 11; Clergy 19; Lay Professors 11; Priests 21; Sisters 1; Students 70; Total Staff 46; Clergy / Religious Teachers 19.

LIBERTY. *Society of the Precious Blood Provincial Offices* (1965) P.O. Box 339, Liberty, 64069-0339. Tel: 816-781-4344; Fax: 816-781-3639; Email: communications@kcprovince.org. Revs. Joseph Nassal, C.PP.S., Prov. Dir.; Richard Bayuk, C.PP.S., Vice Prov.; Joseph Miller, C.PP.S., 3rd Councilor. Brothers 1; Priests 44; Candidates 1; Bishops 1.

[B] COLLEGES AND UNIVERSITIES

KANSAS CITY. *Avila University*, 11901 Wornall Rd., 64145-1698. Tel: 816-942-8400; Fax: 816-501-2451; Email: david.armstrong@avila.edu; Web: www.avila.edu. Ronald A. Slepitza, Ph.D., CSJA, Pres.; Cathryn Pridal, Ph.D., Provost & Vice Pres. for Academic Affairs; Paul Toler, Vice Pres. for Finance & Admin. Svcs.; Sue King, Ph.D., Vice Pres. Information Svcs. & Vice Provost; David Armstrong, Dir. Campus Ministry & Mission Effectiveness; Darby Gough, Dean of Students; Angie Heer, Vice Pres., Advancement & External Rels. Lay Teachers 71; Students 1,818.

Rockhurst University (1910) 1100 Rockhurst Rd., 64110-2561. Tel: 816-501-4000; Fax: 816-501-4241; Email: decla.tyler-simpson@rockhurst.edu; Web: www.rockhurst.edu. Kermit J. Fendler, Chm. Bd. of Trustees; Rev. Thomas B. Curran, S.J., Pres.; Douglas Dunham, Ph.D., Vice Pres., Academic Affairs; Gerald Moench, Chief Fin. Officer; Laurie Hathman, M.L.S., Dir. of the Library; Kris Pace, Controller; Ellen Spake, Ph.D., Asst., Pres. for Mission & Ministry; Matthew Quick, Ph.D., Vice Pres., Student Devel., Athletics, & Campus Ministry & Dean of Students; Matt Heinrich, Assoc. Vice Pres., Facilities & Tech.; Matt Ellis, Assoc. Vice Pres. Enrollment. Clergy 5; Priests 2; Students 3,433; Lay Professors 238; Clergy / Religious Teachers 5.

College of Arts and Sciences, Tel: 816-501-4075; Fax: 816-501-4169; Web: www.rockhurst.edu/academic/deansoffice/index.asp. Pedro Maligo, Ph. D., Dean.

College of Health and Human Services, Tel: 816-501-4686; Fax: 816-501-4615; Web: www.rockhurst.edu/academic/SGPS/index.asp.

Helzberg School of Management, Tel: 816-501-4087; Fax: 816-501-4650; Web: www.rockhurst.edu/HSOM/index.asp. Cheryl McConnell, Ph.D., Dean.

Research College of Nursing, 2525 E. Meyer Blvd., 64132. Tel: 816-995-2800; Fax: 816-995-2817; Email: info@rockhurst.edu; Web: www.researchcollege.edu. Nancy DeBasio, Ph.D., R.N., Pres.

[C] HIGH SCHOOLS, DIOCESAN

KANSAS CITY. *St. Pius X High School*, 1500 NE 42nd Ter., 64116. Tel: 816-453-3450; Fax: 816-452-7099; Email: jmonachino@stpiusxhs-kc.com; Web: www.stpiusxhs-kc.com. Joseph Monachino Jr., Prin. Lay Teachers 23; Students 330.

ST. JOSEPH. *Bishop LeBlond High School*, 3529 Frederick Ave., St. Joseph, 64506. Tel: 816-279-1629; Fax: 816-279-5488; Email: jsullivan@bishopleblondhs.com; Web: bishopleblond.com. Jeffrey Sullivan, Prin.; Rev. Jonathan Davis, Chap. Lay Teachers 18; Priests 1; Students 153.

LEES SUMMIT. *St. Michael the Archangel High School* (2014) 2901 N.W. Lees Summit Rd., Lees Summit, 64064. Tel: 816-763-4800; Tel: 816-499-8601; Email: jmaddox@smacatholic.org; Email: contact@smacatholic.org; Web: www.smacatholic.org. Rev. Randy Sly, Pres.; Jodie Maddox, Prin. Lay Teachers 32; Students 334; Clergy / Religious Teachers 5.

[D] HIGH SCHOOLS, PRIVATE

KANSAS CITY. *Cristo Rey Kansas City High School*, 211 W. Linwood Blvd., 64111-1327. Tel: 816-457-6044; Fax: 816-457-6046; Email: joconnor@cristoreykc.org; Web: www.cristoreykc.org. Mr. John O'Connor, Pres.; Mr. Michael Padow, Prin. Lay Staff 58; Lay Teachers 25; Sisters 3; Students 349.

Notre Dame de Sion High School (1912) 10631 Wornall Rd., 64114-5096. Tel: 816-942-3282; Fax: 816-942-4052; Email: sioncommunications@ndsion.edu; Web: www.ndsion.edu. Alicia Kotarba, Pres.; Natalie McDonough, Prin.; Elizabeth Middleton, Registrar; Annie Riggs, Mission Dir.

Legal Title: Affiliated with Sisters of Notre Dame de Sion Lay Teachers 45; Students 345.

Rockhurst High School (1910) 9301 State Line Rd., 64114-3229. Tel: 816-363-2036; Fax: 816-363-3764; Email: gharkness@rockhursths.edu; Web: www.rockhursths.edu. Revs. William T. Sheahan, S.J., Pres.; Vincent Giacabazi, S.J.; Gregory Harkness, Prin.; Amy Gansner, Librarian; Rev. Daniel J. Tesvich, S.J. Lay Teachers 136; Students 999; Jesuit Priests 3; Clergy / Religious Teachers 3.

St. Teresa's Academy, 5600 Main St., 64113-1298. Tel: 816-501-0011; Fax: 816-817-9395; Email: nbone@stteresasacademy.org; Email: krohr@stteresasacademy.org; Email: lbaker@stteresasacademy.org; Email: bmccormick@stteresasacademy.org; Web: www.stteresasacademy.org. Mrs. Nan Bone, Pres.; Dr. Elizabeth Baker, Prin., Student Affairs; Barbara McCormick, M.A., Prin., Academic Affairs. Affiliated with Sisters of St. Joseph of Carondelet. Lay Teachers 57; Students 620.

[E] CONSOLIDATED SCHOOLS

KANSAS CITY. *Holy Cross School*, (Grades PreK-8), 121 N. Quincy Ave., 64123-1399. Tel: 816-231-8874; Fax: 816-231-7258; Email: bdeane@hcskcmo.org; Web: www.hcskcmo.org. Barb Deane, Prin. Lay Teachers 14; Students 171.

Our Lady of Hope School, (Grades K-8), 4232 Mercier, 64111. Tel: 816-931-1693; Fax: 816-931-6713; Email: mdelac@olhkcmo.org; Email: lklein@olhkcmo.org; Web: www.olhkcmo.org. Mary Delac, Prin.; Lillian Klein, Business Mgr.

Legal Title: Our Lady of the Angels Clergy 1; Lay Teachers 13; Students 185; Clergy / Religious Teachers 9.

[F] ELEMENTARY SCHOOLS, PRIVATE

KANSAS CITY. *Notre Dame de Sion Elementary School* (1912) 3823 Locust St., 64109-2697. Tel: 816-753-3810; Fax: 816-753-0806; Web: www.ndsion.edu. Alicia Kotarba, Pres.; Dr. Paola Clark, Middle School Prin.; Annie Riggs, Mission Dir. Affiliated with Sisters of Notre Dame de Sion. Lay Teachers 33; Students 244.

[G] GENERAL HOSPITALS

KANSAS CITY. *St. Joseph Medical Center Foundation*, 1000 Carondelet Dr., 64114. Tel: 314-733-8000; Email: jenna.mihm@ascension.org; Web: www.ascension.org. 4600 Edmundson Rd., St. Louis, 63134. Jenna Mihm, Vice Pres. Legal Svcs. & Assoc. Gen. Counsel. Sponsored by Ascension Health Ministries.

MARYVILLE. *SSM Health St. Francis Hospital - Maryville* (1894) 2016 S. Main, Maryville, 64468. Tel: 660-562-2600; Tel: 660-562-7900; Fax: 660-562-7911; Email: SSMHealthCareOfficialCatholicDirectoryNotices@ssmhealth.com; Web: www.ssmhealthstfrancis.com. Michael A. Baumgartner, Pres. Member of SSM Health Care. Sponsored by Franciscan Sisters of Mary, St. Louis, MO. Acute care facility. Bed Capacity 81; Tot Asst. Annually 51,031; Total Staff 503.

[H] SPECIAL CARE UNITS

KANSAS CITY. *Carondelet Manor* dba Carondelet Place, 621 Carondelet Dr., 64114. Tel: 816-941-1300; Fax: 816-941-7007; Email: traney@ascension.org. Daniel Stricker, Exec. Member of Ascension Health Bed Capacity 162; Tot Asst. Annually 396; Total Staff 120.

BLUE SPRINGS. *St. Mary's Village* (1987) 111 Mock Ave., Blue Springs, 64014. Tel: 816-228-5655; Fax: 816-228-8480; Email: shannon.wakeman@ascension.org. Daniel Stricker, Exec. Long term care facility with skilled nursing care and residential care. Member of Ascension Health.

Carondelet Long Term Care Facilities, Inc. Bed Capacity 187; Tot Asst. Annually 751; Total Staff 130; Skilled Care 130; Assisted Living 57.

LIBERTY. *Life Unlimited* (1981) 2135 Manor Way, Liberty, 64068-9397. Tel: 816-781-4332; Fax: 816-781-8820; Email: info@imanor.org. Julie Edlund, Exec. Dir. Residential and day habilitation services for people with developmental disabilities; Operated by the Life Unlimited of Directors. Residents 134; Tot Asst. Annually 362; Total Staff 280.

[I] HOMES FOR THE ELDERLY

KANSAS CITY. *Cathedral Square Towers*, 444 W. 12th St., 64105. Tel: 816-471-6555; Fax: 816-421-1279; Email: cathedral01@kc.rr.com. Jan Carson, Mgr. Apartment residence for the elderly and handicapped. Total in Residence 154; Total Staff 12; Units 156.

Columbus Park Plaza, 801 Pacific, 64106. Tel: 816-472-0887; Fax: 816-472-6105; Email: columbuspark@dalmarkgroup.com. Janice Davis, Property Mgr. Apartment residence for elderly and handicapped. Total in Residence 56; Total Staff 2; Units 56.

Jeanne Jugan Center, 8745 James A. Reed Rd., 64138-4490. Tel: 816-761-4744; Fax: 816-761-8313; Email: adkansascity@littlesistersofthepoor.org; Web: www.littlesistersofthepoorkansascity.org. Sr. Marguerite McCarthy, Pres.; Rev. Philip Luebbert, Chap. Little Sisters of the Poor.

Little Sisters of the Poor Bed Capacity 74; Sisters 12; Total in Residence 107; Total Staff 112; Apartments 33; Total Assisted 107.

Marlborough Manor, 1818 E. 79th St., 64132. Tel: 816-333-7761; Fax: 816-523-2388; Email: marlborough@dalmarkgroup.com. Toinette Freeman, Property Mgr. Rental housing for low income (a 31-unit apartment residence for the elderly and disabled). Total in Residence 31; Total Staff 3.

Red Bridge Place, 11300 Colorado, 64137. Tel: 816-761-4667; Fax: 816-761-4769; Email: redbridge@dalmarkgroup.com. Toinette Freeman, Mgr. Total Staff 3; Total Assisted 46.

Tremont Place (1994) 6161 N. Chatham Ave., 64151. Tel: 816-587-7637; Fax: 816-587-7707; Email: tremontapts01@gmail.com. Shaun Forgey, Mgr. A 50-unit apartment residence for the elderly and disabled. Must be sixty-two or over. Bed Capacity 50; Tot Asst. Annually 50; Total Staff 3.

ST. JOSEPH. *The Living Community of St. Joseph* (2004) 1202 Heartland Rd., St. Joseph, 64506. Tel: 816-671-8500; Fax: 816-671-8571; Email: chris.kerns@bhshealth.org; Web: www.lcosj.com. Christine Kerns, Admin./CEO. Bed Capacity 131; Tot Asst. Annually 7,158; Total Staff 187.

CAMERON. *St. Patrick's Manor*, 514 Northland Dr., Cameron, 64429. Tel: 816-632-1684; Fax: 816-632-7624; Email: stpatricksmanor@dalmarkgroup.com. Mr. Christopher Freeman, Mgr. A 31-unit apartment residence for the elderly and disabled. Bed Capacity 31; Total Staff 3.

LIBERTY. *Our Lady of Mercy Country Home*, 2115 Maturana Dr., Liberty, 64068. Tel: 816-781-5711; Fax: 816-792-0179; Email: dtrimmer@ourladyofmercy.net; Web: ourladyofmercy.net. Sr. Sandra Thibodeaux, M.M.B., Regl. Mod. Mercedarian Missionaries of Berriz. Bed Capacity 106; Sisters 9; Tot Asst. Annually 525; Total Staff 68; Guest Capacity 106.

[J] MONASTERIES AND RESIDENCES OF PRIESTS

KANSAS CITY. *Redemptorists Fathers of Kansas City, Missouri*, 3333 Broadway Blvd., 64111. Tel: 816-561-3771; Fax: 816-561-3704; Email: info@olphkc.org. Revs. Frank Kriski, C.Ss.R.; J. Terrence McCloskey, C.Ss.R.; Richard Quinn, C.Ss.R; Gary Ziuraitis, C.Ss.R.; Eugene Harrison, C.Ss.R.; Andrew Thompson, Parochial Vicar. Priests 6. In Res. Revs. Nghia Cao, C.Ss.R.; Eugene Harrison, C.Ss.R.

Rockhurst Jesuit Community, 5133 Forest Ave., 64110-2513. Tel: 816-501-3232; Fax: 816-501-3250; Email: wsheahan@jesuits.org; Web: www.rockhurst.edu/jesuitcommunity. Revs. William T. Sheahan, S.J., Rector; Thomas B. Curran, S.J.; Vincent Giacabazi, S.J.; Robert A. Hagan, S.J.; Vernon R. Heinsz, S.J.; Daniel J. Tesvich, S.J.; James J. White, S.J.; Stephen T. Yavorsky, S.J.; John H. Zupez, S.J.; Carl Heumann, S.J.; Brian Frain, Prof. Total in Residence 11.

Society of Our Lady of the Most Holy Trinity, 3705 Tracy Ave., 64109. Tel: 816-392-8516; Email: frcarlito64@yahoo.com.ph; Web: www.solt.net. Rev. Carlito Saballo, S.O.L.T., KC Ecclesial Team Servant & Leader. Deacons 2; Priests 2; Sisters 4; Laity 21.

CONCEPTION. *Conception Abbey*, 37174 State Hwy. V V, Conception, 64433. Tel: 660-944-3100; Fax: 660-944-2800; Email: communications@conception.edu; Web: www.ConceptionAbbey.org. Revs. Benedict Neenan, O.S.B., Abbot; Daniel Petsche, O.S.B., Prior; Bro. Bernard Montgomery, O.S.B.; Most Rev. Jerome Hanus; Rt. Rev. Marcel Rooney, O.S.B., (Retired); Revs. Anthony Shidler, O.S.B.; Norbert Schappler, O.S.B.; Donald Grabner, O.S.B., (Retired); Richard Cleary, O.S.B.; Kenneth Reichert, O.S.B.; Rene Guesnier, O.S.B.; Roger Schmit, O.S.B.; Reginald Sander, O.S.B.; Xavier Nacke, O.S.B.; Karl Barmann, O.S.B.; Bro. Blaise Bonderer, O.S.B.; Revs. Quentin Kathol, O.S.B.; Allan Stetz, O.S.B.; Isaac True, O.S.B.; Bro. Thomas Sullivan, O.S.B.; Revs. Martin DeMeulenaere, O.S.B.; Albert Bruecken, O.S.B.; Peter Ullrich, O.S.B., Email: peter@conception.edu; Samuel Russell, O.S.B.; Bros. Justin Hernandez, O.S.B.; Michael Marcotte, O.S.B.; Jonathan Clark, O.S.B.; Rev. Adam Ryan,

O.S.B.; Bros. Cyprian Langlois, O.S.B.; Jude Person, O.S.B.; Jacob Kubajak, O.S.B.; Rev. Sebastian Allgaier, O.S.B.; Bro. Elias Zaczkiewicz, O.S.B.; Revs. Pachomius Meade, O.S.B.; Guerric Letter, O.S.B.; Macario Martinez, O.S.B.; Bros. Anselm Broom, O.S.B., Subprior; David Wilding, O.S.B.; Revs. Victor Schinstock, O.S.B.; Paul Sheller, O.S.B.; Bros. Maximilian Burkhart, O.S.B.; Placid Dale, O.S.B.; Etienne Huard, O.S.B. Benedictine Monks. Brothers 17; Priests 35. Junior Monks Bros. Placid Dale, O.S.B.; Maximilian Burkhart, O.S.B.; Etienne Huard, O.S.B.; Luke Kral, O.S.B.

LIBERTY. *Precious Blood Center* (1991) 2130 Saint Gaspar Way, Liberty, 64068-7941.
Tel: 816-781-4344; Fax: 816-781-3639; Email: communications@preciousbloodkc.org. Rev. Michael Goode, C.PP.S. Religious 14.

Society of the Precious Blood Provincial Office (1965) P.O. Box 339, Liberty, 64069-0339.
Tel: 816-781-4344; Fax: 816-781-3639; Email: communications@preciousbloodkc.org. Revs. Joseph Nassal, C.PP.S., Prov. Dir.; Richard Bayuk, C.PP.S., Prov. Treas.; Joseph Miller, C.PP.S. Clergy 1; Deacons 3.

[K] CONVENTS AND RESIDENCES FOR SISTERS

KANSAS CITY. *Benedictines of Mary, Queen of Apostles* Priory of Our Lady of Ephesus 8005 N.W. 316th St., Gower, 64454. Mother Cecilia Snell, O.S.B., Abbess. Novices 10; Postulants 10; Sisters 24.

Sisters of the Society of Our Lady of the Most Holy Trinity (1958) 3738 Tracy Ave., 64109.
Tel: 816-561-8849; Email: kcecclesialteam@gmail.com; Email: conventkansascity@gmail.com; Web: solt.net. Sr. Alison Marie of Abba Father Conemac, S.O.L.T., House Servant. Society of Apostolic Life. Families 15; Lay Staff 10; Priests 1; Sisters 4.

CLYDE. *Benedictine Convent of Perpetual Adoration* (1874) 31970 State Hwy. P, Clyde, 64432.
Tel: 660-944-2221; Fax: 660-944-2133; Email: sister@benedictinesisters.org; Web: www.benedictinesisters.org. Sr. Dawn Mills, Prioress Gen. Attended by Conception Abbey; One other interdependent monastery: Tucson, AZ. Sisters 52.

INDEPENDENCE. *St. Francis Convent Novitiate and Prayer Center* (Switzerland 1378, U.S. 1892) 2100 N. Noland Rd., Independence, 64050.
Tel: 816-252-1673; Fax: 816-252-5574; Email: STFRAN2100@aol.com; Web: www.osfholyeucharist.org. Sr. M. Connie Boulch, O.S.F., Supr. Motherhouse of the Sisters of St. Francis of the Holy Eucharist. Sisters 13.

LIBERTY. *Mercedarian Missionaries of Berriz*, 2115 Maturana Dr., 101B, Liberty, 64068-7985.
Tel: 816-781-8202; Email: mmbus@sbcglobal.net; Web: mmberriz.com. Sr. Sandra Thibodeaux, M.M.B., Regl. Coord. Mercedarian Mission. Mercedarian Missionaries of Berriz 3.

Mercedarian Missionaries of Berriz (M.M.B.), 2116 Maturana Dr. 101B, Liberty, 64068.
Tel: 816-781-8202; Email: mmbus@sbcglobal.net. Sisters Linda Teegarden, M.M.B., Local Coord.; Sandra Thibodeaux, M.M.B., Business Mgr. Mercedarian Mission. Sisters 3.

Mercedarian Missionaries of Berriz (M.M.B.), 2120 Maturana Dr., Liberty, 64068. Tel: 816-415-3133; Email: sf_thib@att.net. Sr. Sandra Thibodeaux, M.M.B., Local Coord. Mercedarian Mission. Sisters 3.

Queen of Angels Monastery - Benedictine Sisters, 23615 N.E. 100th St., Liberty, 64068-8716.
Tel: 816-750-4618; Fax: 816-750-4620; Email: sisters@libertyosb.org; Email: anitabenedictine@gmail.com; Web: libertyosb.org. Sr. Anita Helgenberger, Treas. Sisters 4; Total in Residence 5.

RAYTOWN. *Sisters in Jesus the Lord*, 7009 Blue Ridge Blvd., Raytown, 64133-5629. Tel: 816-353-2177; Web: www.cjd.cc. Sr. Julia Mary Kubista, Supr. Novices 1; Postulants 1; Sisters 6.

SAVANNAH. *Sisters of St. Francis Provincial House* (1922) 908 Franciscan Way, P.O. Box 488, Savannah, 64485-0488. Tel: 816-324-3179;
Fax: 816-324-7264; Web: sistersofstfrancis.org. Rev. Donald Grabner, O.S.B., Chaplain, (Retired); Sr. Christine Martin, O.S.F., Prov. Sisters of St. Francis of Savannah, MO. Motherhouse and Novitiate. Sisters 7.

[L] SERVICES

KANSAS CITY. *Bishop Sullivan Center* (1972) 6435 Truman Rd., 64126. Tel: 816-231-0984;
Tel: 816-561-8515; Email: donations@bishopsullivan.org; Tel: 913-906-8938;
Fax: 816-231-3096; Web: www.bishopsullivan.org. Thomas W. Turner, Dir. Tot Asst. Annually 18,000; Total Staff 19; Volunteers 300; Total Assisted 18,000.

Redemptorist Social Services Center, Inc., 207 W. Linwood Blvd., 64111-1327. Tel: 816-931-9942;
Fax: 816-531-0583; Email: info@kcsocialservices.org; Web: www.kcsocialservices.org. Diana Kennedy, Dir. Tot Asst. Annually 15,450; Total Staff 5; Total Assisted 5,684.

**Seton Center*, 2816 E. 23 St., 64127.
Tel: 816-231-3955; Fax: 816-231-1894; Email: lcolwell@setonkc.org; Web: www.setonkc.org. Sr. Loretto Marie Colwell, S.C.L., Exec. Dir. Total Staff 14; Total Assisted 21,756.

[M] NEWMAN CENTERS

KANSAS CITY. *Avila University Campus Ministry*, 11901 Wornall Rd., 64145. Tel: 816-501-2423;
Fax: 816-501-2454; Email: david.armstrong@avila.edu; Email: Julie.Cowley@avila.edu; Web: www.avila.edu. David Armstrong, Dir. Campus Ministry. Staff 4; Total Assisted 1,200.

ST. JOSEPH. *Newman Club, Missouri Western State University*, 4518 Mitchell, St. Joseph, 64507.
Tel: 816-298-0445. Mr. Leeds Haroldson, Campus Min. Clergy 1; Faculty 2.

MARYVILLE. *Newman Catholic Center, Northwest Missouri State University*, 606 College Ave., Maryville, 64468. Tel: 660-582-7373; Email: newman@nwmissouri.edu; Web: www.northwestnewman.com. Maximilian Kolbe Pawlowski, Campus Min. Total Staff 1; Total Assisted 500.

WARRENSBURG. *Newman Center Catholic Campus Ministry for University of Central Missouri*, 106 Broad St., Warrensburg, 64093. Tel: 660-747-6997; Fax: 660-362-0243; Email: catholicmules@gmail.com. Michael McCormick, Dir. Total Staff 1; Total Assisted 200.

[N] MISCELLANEOUS

KANSAS CITY. **Alexandra's House*, 638 W. 39th Ter., 64111-2914. Tel: 816-931-2539; Email: care@alexandrashouse.com; Web: www.alexandrashouse.com. Patti Lewis, Dir. Perinatal hospice and infant care system.

St. Anthony's Home, 20 W. 9th St., Ste. 200, P.O. Box 419037, 64141-6037. Tel: 816-756-1850; Email: malanowski@diocesekcsj.org. Dave Malanowski, Dir.

Carondelet Health, 621 Carondelet Dr., 64114.
Tel: 314-733-8000; Fax: 314-733-8013; Email: jenna.mihm@ascension.org; Web: www.ascension.org. Jenna Mihm, Vice Pres. Legal Svcs. & Assoc. Gen. Counsel. Parent Co. Sponsored by Ascension Health Ministries. Ascension Health is sole member. Bed Capacity 142; Tot Asst. Annually 300; Total Staff 110.

Catholic Charities Foundation, 4001 Blue Pkwy, 64130. Tel: 816-221-4377; Fax: 816-472-5423; Email: shilliard@ccharities.com; Web: www.catholiccharities-kcsj.org. Stephen Hilliard, Exec. Dir. Tot Asst. Annually 8,401; Total Staff 13.

Catholic Community Hospice, 8510 Wornall Rd., 64114. Tel: 816-523-5634; Email: emark@catholiccommunityhospice.com; Web: www.catholiccommunityhospice.com. Edra Mark, Dir.

Catholic Diocese of Kansas City-St. Joseph Deposit and Loan Fund, 20 W. 9th St., Ste. 200, 64105.
Tel: 816-756-1850; Fax: 816-756-0878; Email: malanowski@diocesekcsj.org. David A. Malanowski, Dir.

Cristo Rey Kansas City Corporate Internship Program, 211 W. Linwood Blvd., 64111.
Tel: 816-457-6044; Fax: 816-457-6046; Email: joconnor@cristoreykc.org; Web: www.cristoreykc.org. Mr. John O'Connor, Pres.

Cursillo, 7724 N. Broadway, 64118.
Tel: 816-803-3517; Email: gabelick@gmail.com; Web: www.diocese-kcsj.org/igm/familylife/index.htm. Rev. Gabriel Lickteig, Spiritual Advisor.

**De La Salle Alumni Association*, P.O. Box 380083, 64138. Tel: 816-767-9800; Email: johnlouis1945@gmail.com. Mr. John Delgado, Contact Person.

Diocesan Council of Catholic Women, 20 W. 9th St., Ste. 200, P.O. Box 419037, 64141-6037.
Tel: 816-756-1850; Email: blando@diocesekcsj.org. Kathy Philpott, Pres.

Diocese of Kansas City-St. Joseph Real Estate Corporation, 20 W. 9th St., Ste. 200, 64105.
Tel: 816-756-1850; Fax: 816-756-0878; Email: rowe@diocesekcsj.org. Rev. Charles N. Rowe, S.T.D., Vice Pres.

Diocese of Kansas City-St. Joseph Real Estate Trust, 20 W. 9th St., Ste. 200, 64105. Tel: 816-756-1850;
Fax: 816-756-0878; Email: rowe@diocesekcsj.org. Rev. Charles N. Rowe, S.T.D., Vice Pres.

Endowment Trust Fund for Catholic Education (1989) 20 W. 9th St., Ste. 200, 64105.
Tel: 816-756-1850; Fax: 816-756-5089; Email: lillig@diocesekcsj.org; Web: www.diocese-kcsj.org. P.O. Box 419037, 64141-6037. Jeremy Lillig, Dir. Stewardship & Devel.

**Jerusalem Farm, Inc.*, 520 Garfield Ave., 64124.
Tel: 816-421-1855; Email: community@jerusalemfarm.org; Web: www.jerusalemfarm.org. Jessie Schiele, Dir.; Jordan Schiele, Dir. Intentional Catholic community centered on prayer, community, service and simplicity, providing home repair and retreats in the Historic Northeast of Kansas City Missouri.

Knights of St. Peter Claver (K.P.C.), 1600 Paseo, St. Monica Parish, 64108. Tel: 816-471-3696;
Fax: 816-471-1100. Deacon Kenneth Greene, Contact Person. Ladies Auxiliary of St. Peter Claver.

Ladies of Charity of Metropolitan Kansas City (1952) P.O. Box 480753, 64148-0753. Tel: 913-268-8652; Email: rosemary.nelson17@gmail.com; Web: www.ladiesofcharitykc.org. Mrs. Rosemary Nelson, Pres. A group of volunteers who work and raise money to help the poor and those in need for the benefit of Seton Center, Duchesne Clinic, Villa St. Francis and other agencies in the greater Kansas City area.

Marillac Home for Children, P.O. Box 419037, 64141-6037. Tel: 816-756-1850; Email: malanowski@diocesekcsj.org. Dave Malanowski, Dir.

Our Lady of Perpetual Help Charitable Trust (1978) 3333 Broadway, 64111. Tel: 816-561-3771;
Fax: 816-561-3704; Email: gziuraitis@olphkc.org; Web: www.redemptoristkc.org. Rev. Gary Ziuraitis, C.Ss.R., Supr.

Siena Club, 20 W. 9th St., Ste. 200, P.O. Box 419037, 64141-6037. Tel: 816-756-1850.

CONCEPTION. **The St. Benedict Education Foundation*, Conception Abbey Office, 37174 State Hwy V V, P.O. Box 16, Conception, 64433. Tel: 660-944-2832; Fax: 660-944-2800; Email: jacob@conception.edu; Web: www.stbenedictfoundation.org. Rev. Benedict Neenan, O.S.B.

LIBERTY. **St. Gaspar Society* (1991) P.O. Box 339, Liberty, 64069. Tel: 816-781-4344;
Fax: 816-781-3639; Email: communications@kcprovince.org. Revs. Joseph Nassal, C.PP.S., Pres.; Michael Goode, C.PP.S., Treas.; Fr. Lau Pham, C.P.P.S., Sec.; Rev. Richard Bayuk, C.PP.S.

Our Lady of Mercy Home, 2115 Maturana Dr., Liberty, 64068-9469. Tel: 816-781-5711;
Fax: 816-792-0179; Email: dtrimmer@ourladyofmercy.net. Sr. Sandra Thibodeaux, M.M.B., Regional Coord.

**Queen of Angels Foundation, Inc.*, 23615 N.E. 100th St., Liberty, 64068. Tel: 816-750-4618;
Fax: 816-750-4620; Email: sisters@libertyosb.org; Email: anitabenedictine@gmail.com. Sr. Anita Helgenberger, Treas.

MARYVILLE. *St. Francis Hospital Foundation*, 2016 S. Main, Maryville, 64468. Tel: 660-562-7933; Email: Rita.Miller@ssmhealth.com. Michael A. Baumgartner, Exec.

RAYMORE. *St. Francis de Sales Association*, 1800 N. Jeter Rd., Raymore, 64083. Tel: 816-331-4831; Email: willabird1@juno.com. Barbara McClung, Group Dir.

RELIGIOUS INSTITUTES OF MEN REPRESENTED IN THE DIOCESE

For further details refer to the corresponding bracketed number in the Religious Institutes of Men or Women section.

[0200]—*Benedictine Monks* (Conception Abbey)—O.S.B.
[0330]—*Christian Brothers of the Midwest, Burr Ridge*—F.S.C.
[1210]—*Congregation of the Missionaries of St. Charles*—C.S.
[]—*Congregation of the Mother of the Redeemer*—C.R.M.
[0305]—*Institute of Christ the King-Sovereign Priest*—I.C.R.S.S.
[0690]—*Jesuit Fathers and Brothers* (USA Central and S. Prov.)—S.J.
[1070]—*Redemptorist Fathers of Kansas City, Missouri* (Denver Prov.)—C.SS.R.
[0975]—*Society of Our Lady of Most Holy Trinity*—S.O.L.T.
[1060]—*Society of the Precious Blood* (Kansas City Prov.)—C.PP.S.

RELIGIOUS INSTITUTES OF WOMEN REPRESENTED IN THE DIOCESE

[0230]—*Benedictine Sisters of Pontifical Jurisdiction* (Atchinson, KS; Liberty, MO)—O.S.B.
[]—*Benedictines of Mary, Queen of Apostles*—O.S.B.
[0397]—*Congregation of Mary Queen* (Springfield, MO)—C.M.R.
[0220]—*Congregation of the Benedictine Sisters of Perpetual Adoration of Pontifical Jurisdiction*—O.S.B.
[3832]—*Congregation of the Sisters of St. Joseph* (Wichita, KS)—C.S.J.
[1070-10]—*Dominican Sisters* (Springfield, IL)—O.P.
[]—*Franciscan Sisters of Mary Immaculate*—F.M.I.
[2575]—*Institute of the Sisters of Mercy of the Americas* (Omaha, NE)—R.S.M.

[]—*Labor Mariae* (Independence, MO)—L.M.
[2340]—*Little Sisters of the Poor*—L.S.P.
[2510]—*Mercedarian Missionaries of Berriz*—M.M.B.
[2960]—*Notre Dame Sisters* (Omaha, NE)—N.D.
[]—*School Sisters of Christ the King*—C.K.
[]—*Sisters in Jesus the Lord*—C.J.D.
[0480]—*Sisters of Charity of Leavenworth, Kansas*—S.C.L.
[0430]—*Sisters of Charity of the Blessed Virgin Mary*—B.V.M.
[2360]—*Sisters of Loretto at the Foot of the Cross*—S.L.
[1670]—*Sisters of St. Francis of Savannah, MO*—O.S.F.
[1560]—*Sisters of St. Francis of the Holy Eucharist* (Independence, MO)—O.S.F.
[3830-15]—*Sisters of St. Joseph* (Concordia, KS)—C.S.J.
[3840]—*Sisters of St. Joseph of Carondelet*—C.S.J.
[3105]—*Society of Our Lady of the Most Holy Trinity*—S.O.L.T.

DIOCESAN CEMETERIES

ST. JOSEPH. *Mount Olivet*, 26th and Lovers Ln., St. Joseph, 64506. Tel: 816-353-1900; Email: sreyes@cemeterieskcsj.org; Web: www.cemeterieskcsj.org. Mr. Stephen Reyes, General Mgr.

KANSAS CITY. *Mount Olivet & Mount St. Mary*, 7601 Blue Ridge Blvd, 64506. Mr. Stephen Reyes, Business Mgr.

KANSAS CITY NORTH. *Resurrection*, 5001 N.E. Cookingham Dr., 64156. Tel: 816-734-2356; Email: sreyes@cemeterieskcsj.org; Web: www.cemeterieskcsj.org. 7601 Blue Ridge Blvd., 64138. Mr. Stephen Reyes, Business Mgr.

NECROLOGY

† Karels, Ambrose G., (Retired), Died Apr. 7, 2018

An asterisk (*) denotes an organization that has established tax-exempt status directly with the IRS and is not covered by the USCCB Group Ruling.

Diocese of Knoxville

Most Reverend

RICHARD F. STIKA

Third Bishop of Knoxville; ordained December 14, 1985; appointed third Bishop of Knoxville January 12, 2009; ordained and installed March 19, 2009. *Office: 805 S. Northshore Dr., Knoxville, TN 37919.*

Chancery Office: 805 S. Northshore Dr., Knoxville, TN 37919. Tel: 865-584-3307

Web: www.dioknox.org

ESTABLISHED SEPTEMBER 8, 1988.

Square Miles 14,242.

Comprises the Counties of Anderson, Bledsoe, Blount, Bradley, Campbell, Carter, Claiborne, Cocke, Cumberland, Fentress, Grainger, Greene, Hamblen, Hamilton, Hancock, Hawkins, Jefferson, Johnson, Knox, Loudon, McMinn, Marion, Meigs, Monroe, Morgan, Pickett, Polk, Rhea, Roane, Scott, Sequatchie, Sevier, Sullivan, Unicoi, Union and Washington in the State of Tennessee.

For legal titles of parishes and diocesan institutions, consult the Chancery Office.

STATISTICAL OVERVIEW

Personnel	
Bishop	1
Priests: Diocesan Active in Diocese	50
Priests: Diocesan Active Outside Diocese	3
Priests: Retired, Sick or Absent	16
Number of Diocesan Priests	69
Religious Priests in Diocese	16
Total Priests in Diocese	85
Extern Priests in Diocese	6
Ordinations:	
Transitional Deacons	1
Permanent Deacons in Diocese	75
Total Brothers	9
Total Sisters	49
Parishes	
Parishes	50
With Resident Pastor:	
Resident Diocesan Priests	35
Resident Religious Priests	6
Without Resident Pastor:	
Administered by Priests	9
Missions	1
Pastoral Centers	2
Professional Ministry Personnel:	
Brothers	4
Sisters	44
Lay Ministers	78
Welfare	
Catholic Hospitals	1
Total Assisted	171,104
Health Care Centers	1
Total Assisted	518
Homes for the Aged	1
Total Assisted	338
Specialized Homes	2
Total Assisted	141
Special Centers for Social Services	7
Total Assisted	72,768
Educational	
Diocesan Students in Other Seminaries	13
Total Seminarians	13
High Schools, Diocesan and Parish	2
Total Students	1,020
Elementary Schools, Diocesan and Parish	8
Total Students	1,857
Catechesis/Religious Education:	
High School Students	1,075
Elementary Students	4,017
Total Students under Catholic Instruction	7,982
Teachers in the Diocese:	
Priests	3
Scholastics	28
Sisters	13
Lay Teachers	289
Vital Statistics	
Receptions into the Church:	
Infant Baptism Totals	1,012
Minor Baptism Totals	151
Adult Baptism Totals	103
Received into Full Communion	213
First Communions	1,292
Confirmations	1,986
Marriages:	
Catholic	203
Interfaith	73
Total Marriages	276
Deaths	408
Total Catholic Population	67,575
Total Population	2,458,717

Former Bishops—Most Revs. ANTHONY J. O'CONNELL, ord. March 30, 1963; appt. Bishop of Knoxville May 27, 1988; installed Sept. 8, 1988; appt. Bishop of Palm Beach Nov. 11, 1998; installed Jan. 14, 1999; resigned March 8, 2002; died May 4, 2012.; JOSEPH E. KURTZ, ord. 1972; appt. Bishop of Knoxville Oct. 26, 1999; ord. and installed Dec. 8, 1999; appt. Archbishop of Louisville June 12, 2007.

Vicars General—Very Revs. DAVID BOETTNER, V.G.; DOUGLAS OWENS, V.G.

Episcopal Vicar for Priests—Rev. Msgr. G. PATRICK GARRITY, V.E., (Retired).

Deans of the Diocese—Revs. MICHAEL E. CUMMINS, V.F., Five Rivers Deanery; CHARLES BURTON, V.F., Chattanooga Deanery; JAMES BRENT SHELTON, V.F., Cumberland Mtn. Deanery; RONALD A. FRANCO, C.S.P., V.F., Smoky Mtn. Deanery.

Chancery Office—805 S. Northshore Dr., Knoxville, 37919. Tel: 865-584-3307; Fax: 865-584-7538. Office Hours: Mon.-Fri. 9-5All official business should be directed to this office.

Moderator of the Curia—Very Rev. DOUGLAS OWENS, V.G.

Chancellor and Chief Operating Officer—Deacon SEAN K. SMITH.

Assistant to the Bishop—Deacon SEAN K. SMITH.

Vice Chancellor for Canonical Affairs—Very Rev. J. DAVID CARTER, J.C.L.

Vice Chancellor for Administration—PAUL SIMONEAU.

Auditors—All priests on assignment in the diocese.

Presbyteral Council—Rev. BEDE C. ABOH, (Nigeria); Very Rev. DAVID BOETTNER, V.G., Ex Officio; Rev. CHARLES BURTON, V.F.; Very Rev. J. DAVID CARTER, J.C.L.; Revs. THOMAS CHARTERS, G.H.M.; MICHAEL E. CUMMINS, V.F., Chm.; RONALD A. FRANCO, C.S.P., V.F.; Rev. Msgr. T. ALLEN HUMBRECHT; Revs. CHRISTOPHER MANNING; WILLIAM L. MCKENZIE; MICHAEL F. NOLAN; Very Rev. DOUGLAS OWENS, V.G., Ex Officio; Revs. JOSEPH REED; JAMES BRENT ALLEN SHELTON, V.F., Vice Chm.; ARTHUR TORRES BARONA, (Colombia); ALEX WARAKSA, Recording Sec.; MIGUEL VELEZ-CARDONA, (Colombia); JAMES L. VICK.

Diocesan Consultors—Very Rev. DAVID BOETTNER, V.G.; Rev. CHARLES BURTON, V.F.; Very Rev. J. DAVID CARTER, J.C.L.; Rev. MICHAEL E. CUMMINS, V.F.; Rev. Msgr. T. ALLEN HUMBRECHT; Very Rev. DOUGLAS OWENS, V.G.; Revs. JOSEPH REED; JAMES BRENT SHELTON, V.F.; ALEX WARAKSA.

Diocesan Finance Council—JERRY BODIE; Very Rev. DAVID BOETTNER, V.G., Ex-Officio, Vicar Gen.; J. MICHAEL CONNOR; MR. JOHN DEINHART, Ex Officio; SHARON FOLK, Chm.; PAUL GREEN; VINCE FUSCO; SHANNON HEPP, Ex Officio, Diocesan Finance Officer; CHRIS LIPOSKY; ANDY LORENZ; Very Rev. DOUGLAS OWENS, V.G., Ex Officio, Vicar Gen.; EDWARD PHILLIPS, Ex Officio, Diocesan Attorney; WILLIAM RISKO; ALAN SEFTON, Vice Chm.; Deacon SEAN K. SMITH, Ex Officio; FRAN THIE.

Diocesan Offices and Directors

Archives—Deacon SEAN K. SMITH, 805 S. Northshore Dr., Knoxville, 37919. Tel: 865-584-3307.

Campus Ministries—

East Tennessee State University—Rev. BEDE C. ABOH, (Nigeria) Chap., Catholic Center, 734 W. Locust St., Johnson City, 37604. Tel: 423-926-7061.

University of Tennessee-Chattanooga—

Chattanooga Deanery Priests (Sacramental Ministry)—514 Palmetto St., Chattanooga, 37403. Tel: 423-618-9062. Rev. COLIN BLATCHFORD, Chap.; Deacon BRIAN GABOR, Part Time Campus Min.; DONNA GABOR, Part Time Campus Min.

University of Tennessee-Knoxville—Rev. DONALD ANDRIE, C.S.P., Dir., 1710 Melrose Pl., Knoxville, 37916. Tel: 865-523-7931.

Catholic Schools Office—Sr. MARY MARTA ABBOTT, R.S.M., Ed.S., Supt., 805 S. Northshore Dr., Knoxville, 37919. Tel: 865-584-3307.

Catholic Charities of East Tennessee, Inc.—119 Dameron Ave., Knoxville, 37917. Tel: 865-524-9896 ; Fax: 865-971-3575; Web: ccetn.org. LISA HEALY, Interim Exec. Dir. The umbrella agency for all Catholic Charities of the diocese.

Catholic Campaign for Human Development—119 Dameron Ave., Knoxville, 37917. Tel: 865-524-9896 . LISA HEALY, Interim Dir.

Catholic Charities (Chattanooga Area)—5720 Uptain Rd., Bldg. 6100, Ste. 4200, Chattanooga, 37411. VACANT, Devel. Coord.

Catholic Charities (Knoxville Area)—LISA INGLE, Dir. Oper., 119 Dameron Ave., Knoxville, 37917. Tel: 865-524-9896; Fax: 865-971-3575.

Catholic Charities (Upper East Tennessee Area)—1409 W. Market St., #109, Johnson City, 37604. Tel: 865-524-9896.

Cemeteries—Deacon SEAN K. SMITH, Dir., 805 S. Northshore Dr., Knoxville, 37919. Tel: 865-584-3307; Very Rev. J. DAVID CARTER, J.C.L., Contact, Mt. Olivet Cemetery, 4159 Ringgold Rd., Chattanooga, 37412. Tel: 423-266-1618; DAVID E. HALE, Supt., Tel: 423-622-0728; Rev. RONALD A. FRANCO, C.S.P., V.F., Contact, Calvary Cemetery in Knoxville, 1916 Martin Luther King Jr. Ave., Knoxville, 37915. Mailing Address: c/o Immaculate Conception Church, 414 W. Vine Ave., Knoxville, 37902-1327. Tel: 865-522-1508.

Chancellor and Chief Operating Officer—Deacon SEAN K. SMITH, 805 S. Northshore Dr., Knoxville, 37919. Tel: 865-584-3307.

Censor Librorum—Sr. MARY TIMOTHEA ELLIOTT, R.S.M. Contact: Deacon SEAN K. SMITH, 805 S. Northshore Dr., Knoxville, 37919. Tel: 865-584-3307.

Christian Formation—805 S. Northshore Dr., Knoxville, 37919. Sr. ANNA MARIE MCGUAN, R.S.M., Dir.; Rev. RICHARD G. ARMSTRONG JR.,

Asst. Dir.; Sr. MARY TIMOTHEA ELLIOTT, R.S.M., Theological Consultant.

Communications Office—JIM WOGAN, Dir. Communications, 805 S. Northshore Dr., Knoxville, 37919-7551. Tel: 865-584-3307; Email: jwogan@dioknox.org.

Diaconate and Deacon Formation—Deacon TIM ELLIOTT, Dir., 805 S. Northshore Dr., Knoxville, 37919. Tel: 865-584-3307.

Diocesan Council of Catholic Women—Rev. DAN G. WHITMAN, Diocesan Spiritual Moderator, 212 Mount Bethel Rd., Greeneville, 37745. Tel: 423-639-9381.

Ecumenism—Rev. Msgr. T. ALLEN HUMBRECHT, Dir., 805 S. Northshore Dr., Knoxville, 37919. Tel: 865-584-3307.

Finance Office—SHANNON HEPP, Diocesan Finance Officer, 805 S. Northshore Dr., Knoxville, 37919. Tel: 865-584-3307.

Hispanic Ministry—Chancery Office: 805 S. Northshore Dr., Knoxville, 37919. BLANCA PRIMM, Dir.

Human Resources Office—JENNIFER MILLS, Dir., Chancery Office, 805 S. Northshore Dr., Knoxville, 37919. Tel: 865-584-3307.

Justice and Peace Office—PAUL SIMONEAU, Dir., Chancery Office: 805 S. Northshore Dr., Knoxville, 37919. Tel: 865-584-3307.

Marriage Tribunal—Very Revs. DEXTER BREWER, J.C.L., J.V., 2800 McGavock Pike, Nashville, 37214. Tel: 615-783-0273; J. DAVID CARTER, J.C.L., Adjutant Judicial Vicar, 214 E. 8th St., Chattanooga, 37402. Tel: 423-266-1618. Diocesan marriage tribunal is shared with the Diocese of Nashville.

Ministries of the Chattanooga Deanery—Rev. CHARLES BURTON, V.F., 930 Ashland Terr., Chattanooga, 37415. Tel: 423-870-2386; JANE HUBBARD, Deanery Coord., 5720 Uptain Rd., Bldg. 6100, Ste. 4200, Chattanooga, 37411. Tel: 423-267-9878.

Ministries of the Five Rivers Deanery—Rev. MICHAEL E. CUMMINS, V.F., 2517 John B. Dennis Hwy., Kingsport, 37660. Tel: 423-288-8101.

Ministries of the Cumberland Mtn. Deanery—327 Vermont Ave., Oak Ridge, 37830. Tel: 865-482-2875. Rev. JAMES BRENT SHELTON, V.F.

Ministries of the Smoky Mtn. Deanery—Rev. RONALD A. FRANCO, C.S.P., V.F., 414 W. Vine Ave., Knoxville, 37902-1327. Tel: 865-522-1508.

Moderator of the Curia—805 S. Northshore Dr., Knoxville, 37919. Very Rev. DOUGLAS OWENS, V.G.

Priestly Life and Ministry—Rev. Msgr. G. PATRICK GARRITY, V.E., Dir., (Retired), P.O. Box 3755, Knoxville, 37927. Tel: 865-310-6146.

Propagation of the FaithPAUL SIMONEAU, Dir., 805 S. Northshore Dr., Knoxville, 37919. Tel: 865-584-3307.

Scouting—Rev. DUSTIN ALAN COLLINS, Scout Chap., 858 Louisville Rd., Alcoa, 37701. Tel: 865-982-3672.

Diocesan Catholic Committee on Scouting—GEORGE C. LECRONE SR., Chm., 10700 Leeward Ln., Knoxville, 37934. Tel: 865-974-0050; CHRIS MANNING, Vice Chm., 7000 Westland Dr., Knoxville, 37919; Rev. DUSTIN ALAN COLLINS, Chap., 858 Louisville Rd., Alcoa, 37701. Tel: 865-982-3672.

Stewardship and Strategic Planning—MR. JOHN DEINHART, Dir., Email: jdeinhart@dioknox.org; ALLISON DIGENNARO, Asst. Dir., 805 S. Northshore Dr., Knoxville, 37919. Tel: 865-584-3307.

The East Tennessee Catholic—(Diocesan Magazine-Newspaper). BILL BREWER, Editor, 805 S. Northshore Dr., Knoxville, 37919. Tel: 865-584-3307; Email: bbrewer@dioknox.org.

Victim Assistance Coordinator—MARLA LENIHAN, 400 Laboratory Rd., Ste. 103, Oak Ridge, 37830. Tel: 865-482-1388.

Vocations—Rev. JOSEPH REED, Vocation Dir.; Very Rev. J. DAVID CARTER, J.C.L., Deanery Coord. for Vocations, Tel: 423-802-6889; Sr. MARY CHARLES MAYER, R.S.M., Delegate for Consecrated Life, Vocation Promotion for Rel., 805 S. Northshore Dr., Knoxville, 37919. Tel: 865-584-3307.

Worship and Liturgy—805 S. Northshore Dr., Knoxville, 37919. Revs. JOSEPH REED, Diocesan Dir.; RANDY STICE, Advisor.

Youth and Young Adult Ministry—Deacon AL FORSYTHE, Diocesan Coord., 805 S. Northshore Dr., Knoxville, 37919. Tel: 865-584-3307; DONNA L. JONES, Coord. Chattanooga Deanery, 859 McCallie Ave., Ste. 302, Chattanooga, 37403. Tel: 423-267-9878; Deacons G. JAMES FAGE II, Coord., Five Rivers Deanery, 780 Roddy Dr., Morristown, 37814. Tel: 423-587-4925; DAN HOSFORD, Coord. Cumberland Mtn. Deanery, 102 Pheasant Rd., Clinton, 37716. Tel: 865-603-9682; BETH PARSONS, Coord. Smoky Mtn. Deanery, 37803, 2822 Country Meadows Ln., Maryville; BRITTANY GARCIA, Hispanic Youth & Young Adult Min., 805 S. Northshore Dr., Knoxville, 37919. Tel: 865-584-3307.

CLERGY, PARISHES, MISSIONS AND PAROCHIAL SCHOOLS

CITY OF KNOXVILLE

(KNOX COUNTY)

1—CATHEDRAL OF THE MOST SACRED HEART OF JESUS (1956) [JC]
417 Erin Dr. Ste. 120, 37919. Tel: 865-588-0249; Email: shcathedral@shcknox.org; Web: shcathedral.org/. Very Rev. David Boettner, V.G., Rector; Rev. Arthur Torres Barona, (Colombia); Deacons Ben Johnston; Dan Alexander; Glenn Kahler, Dir. Liturgy & Music; Deacons Joel Livingston Jr.; Walt Otey.
School—Sacred Heart Cathedral School, (Grades PreK-8), 711 S. Northshore Dr., 37919.
Tel: 865-588-0415; Fax: 865-558-4139; Email: dpatterson@shcknox.org; Web: www.shcschool.org. Daniel J. Breen, Prin.; Rachel Best, Librarian; Nicloe Erwin, Librarian. Clergy 1; Lay Teachers 37; Students 617.
Catechesis Religious Program—Dave Wells, Dir. Adult & Young Adults. Students 230.

2—ST. ALBERT THE GREAT CHURCH (2007)
7200 Brickey Ln., 37918. Tel: 865-689-7011; Email: office@satgknox.org; Web: www.satgknox.org. Rev. Chris Michelson; Rev. Msgrs. William H. Gahagan, Sacramental Min., (Retired); G. Patrick Garrity, V.E., Sacramental Min., (Retired); Rev. William L. McKenzie, Sacramental Min.; Deacons Michael Eiffe; Patrick Murphy-Racey; Robert Smearing; Michael Duncan.
See Saint Joseph School of Knoxville under Elementary Schools Regional located in the Institution Section.
Catechesis Religious Program—Students 135.

3—ALL SAINTS CATHOLIC CHURCH (1994) [JC]
Mailing Address: 620 N. Cedar Bluff Rd., 37923.
Tel: 865-531-0770; Fax: 865-531-1009; Email: admin@allsaintsknoxville.org; Web: www.allsaintsknoxville.com. Very Rev. Douglas Owens, V.G.; Revs. Miguel Velez-Cardona, (Colombia); Adam Kane; Deacons Tim Elliott; David J. Lucheon; Fredy Vargas.
Catechesis Religious Program—Email: Carrie.Manabat@allsaintsknoxville.com. Carrie Manabat, D.R.E. Students 659.

4—CHURCH OF DIVINE MERCY (2012) [JC]
Mailing Address: 10919 Carmichael Rd., 37932. Rev. Hoan Dinh, O.F.M., (Vietnam).
Catechesis Religious Program—Tel: 865-437-7136. Students 55.

5—HOLY GHOST (1908) [JC]
Mailing Address: 111 Hinton Ave., 37917. Email: hgchurch@bellsouth.net; Web: holyghostknoxville.org. 1041 N. Central St., 37917. Tel: 865-522-2205. Revs. John R. Dowling; Michael Hendershott; Deacon Gordon Lowery.
Catechesis Religious Program—Elizabeth Bunker, D.R.E.; Anita Gouge, D.R.E. Students 80.

6—IMMACULATE CONCEPTION (1852) [CEM]
414 W. Vine Ave., 37902-1327. Tel: 865-522-1508; Email: icoffice@bellsouth.net; Web: www.icknoxville.org. Revs. Ronald A. Franco, C.S.P., V.F.; Timothy Sullivan, C.S.P., Parochial Vicar; Deacons Joseph Hieu Vinh; Joe Stackhouse, Ph.D.; Doug Bitzer; Revs. James A. Haley, C.S.P., In Res., (Retired); Donald Andrie, C.S.P., In Res.
Res.: 707 E. Scott Ave., 37917. Tel: 347-886-4270; Email: rfrancocsp@aol.com.
See Saint Joseph School of Knoxville under Elementary Schools Regional located in the Institution Section.
Catechesis Religious Program—Brigid Johnson, D.R.E. & Faith Formation. Students 24.

7—ST. JOHN NEUMANN (1977)
Mailing Address: 633 St. John Ct., 37934-1555.
Tel: 865-966-4540; Email: sjncoffice@sjnknox.org; Web: www.sjnknox.org. Revs. Joseph Reed; Christopher Manning; Michael R. Maples; Scott Russell; Deacons Donald Amelse, M.P.S.; Marquis Syler; Al Forsythe; Mike Humphreys; Mike Gouge. In Res., Rev. Joseph Hammond, C.H.S., (Ghana).
School—St. John Neumann School, (Grades PreK-8), 625 St. John Ct., 37934-1555. Tel: 865-777-0077; Fax: 865-777-0087; Email: sjns@sjncs-knox.org; Web: www.sjncs-knox.org. Bill Derbyshire, Prin.; Sabrina Talley, Dean; Diane Schukman, Librarian. Clergy 2; Lay Teachers 23; Students 276.
Catechesis Religious Program—Marilyn Derbyshire, D.R.E.; Sr. Elizabeth Wanyoike, RCIA. Students 229.

8—SAINT JOHN XXIII UNIVERSITY PARISH (1968) [CEM] (Non-territorial parish for the University of Tennessee at Knoxville).
1710 Melrose Pl., 37916. Tel: 865-523-7931; Email: john23@utk.edu. Revs. Donald Andrie, C.S.P.; Robert J. O'Donnell; Deacon Robert Ketteringham, Pastoral Assoc.
Legal Name: Saint John XXIII University Parish / Catholic Center
Catechesis Religious Program—Email: andrea@john23rd.org. Andrea Sirek, D.R.E. Students 33.

OUTSIDE THE CITY OF KNOXVILLE

ALCOA, BLOUNT CO., OUR LADY OF FATIMA (1950)
858 Louisville Rd., Alcoa, 37701. Tel: 865-982-3672; Fax: 865-977-4183; Email: khalligan@ourladyoffatima.org; Web: ourladyoffatima.org. Revs. William J. McNeeley, Admin.; Dustin Alan Collins, Parochial Vicar; Deacons William Jacobs; Scott Maentz.
Res. & Rectory: 860 Louisville Rd., Alcoa, 37701.
Catechesis Religious Program—Email: smygillen@ourladyoffatoma.org. Sr. Yvette Gillen, R.S.M., Faith Formation. Students 273.

ATHENS, MCMINN CO., ST. MARY (1968)
1291 E. Madison Ave., Athens, 37303.
Tel: 423-745-4277; Email: stmaryathenstn@att.net; Web: www.stmaryathenstn.org. Rev. John Arthur Orr, Ph.D.; Deacon Erasmo Hernandez.
Catechesis Religious Program—
Tel: 423-745-4277, Ext. 2. Oneta Fioravanti, D.R.E. Students 86.

CHATTANOOGA, HAMILTON CO.

1—BASILICA OF STS. PETER AND PAUL (1852) [JC]
214 E. 8th St., Chattanooga, 37402.
Tel: 423-266-1618; Email: office@stspeterandpaulbasilica.com; Web: www.stspeterandpaulbasilica.com. Very Rev. J. David Carter, J.C.L., Rector; Rev. Colin Blatchford; Deacons Gaspar DeGaetano; Hicks Armor; Thomas McConnell.
Catechesis Religious Program—Email: dre@stspeterandpaulbasilica.com. Danielle Stradley, D.R.E.; Michael Stradley, D.R.E. Students 309.

2—ST. JUDE (1958) [JC]
930 Ashland Ter., Chattanooga, 37415.
Tel: 423-870-2386; Email: info@stjudechattanooga.org; Web: www.stjudechattanooga.org. Revs. Charles Burton, V.F.; Moises Moreno-Urzua, (Mexico); Deacons Brian Gabor; Paul Nelson; Bernard (Butch) Feldhaus. In Res., Rev. Paul J. Valleroy, (Retired).
School—St. Jude School, (Grades PreSchool-8), 930 Ashland Ter., Chattanooga, 37415.
Tel: 423-877-6022; Email: goodhardj@mysjs.com; Web: www.mysjs.com. Jamie Goodhard, Prin. Lay Teachers 35; (Including Preschool) 345.
Catechesis Religious Program—Kyra Niemann Ross, D.R.E. Students 215.

3—OUR LADY OF PERPETUAL HELP (1937)
501 S. Moore Rd., Chattanooga, 37412.
Tel: 423-622-7232; Email: franklin_olph@hotmail.com; Web: www.myolph.com. Revs. James L. Vick; Adam Royal; Deacon Dennis Meinert.
Res.: 501 S. Moore Rd., Chattanooga, 37412.
Tel: 423-622-7232; Email: franklin_olph@hotmail.com; Web: www.myolph.com.
School—Our Lady of Perpetual Help School, (Grades PreK-8), 505 S. Moore Rd., Chattanooga, 37412.
Tel: 423-622-1418; Fax: 423-622-2016; Email: lfox@myolph.com. Ms. Leslie Fox, Prin. Lay Teachers 26; Students 275.
Catechesis Religious Program—Corinne Hennen, D.R.E. Students 125.

4—ST. STEPHEN (1961) [JC]
7111 Lee Hwy., Chattanooga, 37421.
Tel: 423-892-1261; Email: secretary@ststephenchatt.org; Email: bookkeeper@ststephenchatt.org; Web: www.ststephenchatt.org. Revs. Manuel Perez, (Mexico); Christopher Floersh; Deacon Gary Brinkworth.
Catechesis Religious Program—Email: cre@ststephenchatt.org. Karen Underwood, C.R.E. Students 175.

CLEVELAND, BRADLEY CO., ST. THERESE OF LISIEUX (1914)
900 Clingan Ridge Dr., N.W., Cleveland, 37312.
Tel: 423-476-8123; Email: secretary@stthereseclevelandtn.org; Web: www.StThereseCatholicChurch.org. Revs. Michael F. Nolan; Michael Creson, (Retired); Deacons Stephen Ratterman; Barry Maples.
Catechesis Religious Program—Email: dre@stthereseclevelandtn.org. Marietta Giraldo, D.R.E. Students 287.

CLINTON, ANDERSON CO., ST. THERESE (1971)

701 S. Charles G. Seivers Blvd., Clinton, 37716.
Tel: 865-457-4073; Email: bookkeeper@saintthereseclinton.org; Web: www.saintthereseclinton.org. Rev. Richard G. Armstrong Jr., Admin.
Catechesis Religious Program—Cathy Hundley, D.R.E. Students 26.

COPPERHILL, POLK CO., ST. CATHERINE LABOURE (1977)
Mailing Address: P.O. Box 1165, Copperhill, 37317.
Tel: 423-496-3498; Email: sclcchurch@etcmail.com; Web: www.sclccopperhill.org. 115 E. Main St., Copperhill, 37317. Rev. Thomas W. Moser; Deacon Loris Sinanian; Mr. Michael Regan, Spanish Contact.
Catechesis Religious Program—Email: cmcamberjones@yahoo.com. Amber Jones, D.R.E. Students 24.

CROSSVILLE, CUMBERLAND CO., ST. ALPHONSUS (1948)
151 St. Alphonsus Way, Crossville, 38555.
Tel: 931-484-2358; Web: www.stalonline.org. Rev. James P. Harvey II, Email: stalphonsus@stalonline.org; Deacon Peter Minneci.
Catechesis Religious Program—Tel: 931-456-5227; Fax: 931-484-7407; Email: sara@stalonline.org. Sara Carey, D.R.E. Students 85.

DAYTON, RHEA CO., ST. BRIDGET (1968)
320 Walnut Grove Church Rd., P.O. Box 106, Dayton, 37321. Tel: 423-775-2664; Email: dre@saintbridget.net; Web: www.saintbridget.net. Rev. Samuel L. Sturm.
Catechesis Religious Program—Rhonda Schalk, D.R.E. Students 59.

DUNLAP, SEQUATCHIE CO., SHEPHERD OF THE VALLEY (1997)
Mailing Address: 6191 Hwy. 28, P.O. Box 1747, Dunlap, 37327-1747. Tel: 423-949-6903; Email: shepherdofthevalleyindunlap@yahoo.com; Web: www.sotvcc.weebly.com. Rev. Mark A. Scholz.
Catechesis Religious Program—Lisa Tuggle, D.R.E. Students 25.

ELIZABETHTON, CARTER CO., ST. ELIZABETH (1923)
510 W. C St., P.O. Box 7, Elizabethton, 37644-0007.
Tel: 423-543-3412; Email: stelizabeth@chartertn.net. Rev. Dennis Kress; Deacon Richard Carner.
Catechesis Religious Program—Linda D. Muraski, D.R.E., Email: linda5rivers@hotmail.com. Students 24.

ERWIN, UNICOI CO., ST. MICHAEL THE ARCHANGEL CATHOLIC CHURCH (2011)
Mailing Address: P.O. Box 1009, Erwin, 37650.
Tel: 423-735-0484; Email: stmichaeltheangeluc@gmail.com. 657 N. Mohawk Dr., Erwin, 37650. Rev. Thomas Charters, G.H.M.
Catechesis Religious Program—Students 97.

FAIRFIELD GLADE, CUMBERLAND CO., ST. FRANCIS OF ASSISI (1983) [CEM]
7503 Peavine Rd., Fairfield Glade, 38558.
Tel: 931-484-3628; Email: stfrancis@frontiernet.net; Web: saintfrancisfairfield.org. Rev. Michael Woods.
Res.: 7505 Peavine Rd., Fairfield Glade, 38558.
Tel: 931-456-0415; Fax: 931-707-0186; Email: stfrancis@frontiernet.net; Web: www.saintfrancisfairfield.org.

GATLINBURG, SEVIER CO., ST. MARY (1935)
304 Historic Nature Tr., Gatlinburg, 37738.
Tel: 865-436-4907; Email: saintmaryg1@gmail.com. Rev. Antony Punnackal, C.M.I., (India).
Catechesis Religious Program—Stacy Champagne, D.R.E., Email: stacy@pixdipity.com. Students 88.

GREENEVILLE, GREENE CO., NOTRE DAME (1955)
212 Mt. Bethel Rd., Greeneville, 37745.
Tel: 423-639-9381; Email: notredametn@embarqmail.com; Web: notredamechurchtn.org. Rev. Dan G. Whitman; Deacon Wil Johnson.
Catechesis Religious Program—Susan Collins, D.R.E. Students 111.

HARRIMAN, ROANE CO., BLESSED SACRAMENT (1908)
535 Margrave Dr., Harriman, 37748-2118.
Tel: 865-882-9838; Email: blessedsacramentoffice@gmail.com; Web: www.blessedsacramentchurchandmissions.com. Rev. Michael Sweeney.
Catechesis Religious Program—Alicia Laffoon, D.R.E. Students 18.
Station—Morgan County State Prison, Wartburg. Tel: 423-346-1300.

HELENWOOD, SCOTT CO., ST. JUDE PARISH (1982)
Mailing Address: 13067 Scott Hwy., P.O. Box 555, Helenwood, 37755. Tel: 423-569-9584 (Church); Email: ssmith@dioknox.org. Rev. Albert C. Sescon, (Philippines); Sr. Patricia Soete, R.S.M., Pastoral Assoc.
Catechesis Religious Program—

JAMESTOWN, FENTRESS CO., ST. CHRISTOPHER CATHOLIC CHURCH (1975)
160 Holt Spur Dr., Jamestown, 38556.
Tel: 931-879-4146; Web: www.saintchristopherjamestown.com. c/o Jim Romer, 204 Anderson Tinch Ave., Jamestown, 38556-5221.
Tel: 931-879-4146. Rev. Michael Sweeney.

JEFFERSON CITY, JEFFERSON CO., HOLY TRINITY CATHOLIC CHURCH (1997)
475 N. Hwy. 92, Jefferson City, 37760. Web: htjctn.org. P.O. Box 304, Jefferson City, 37760.
Tel: 865-471-0347; Fax: 865-471-0349; Email: holytrinity.jeffcity@gmail.com. Rev. W. Patrick Resen; Deacons Jim Prosak; Jack Raymond; David Oatney; Matt Pidgeon. In Res., Rev. Alex J. Waraksa.
Catechesis Religious Program—Valerie Mulligan, Catechetical Leader; Scott Mulligan, Catechetical Leader. Students 46.
Mission—Saint John Paul II Catholic Mission, 7735 Rutledge Pike, Rutledge, Grainger Co. 37861.
Tel: 865-992-7222.

JOHNSON CITY, WASHINGTON CO., ST. MARY'S CATHOLIC CHURCH (1906)
2211 E. Lakeview Dr., Johnson City, 37601.
Tel: 423-282-6367; Fax: 423-282-6145; Email: mildret.godwin@stmarysjc.org; Web: stmarysjc.org. Revs. Peter J. Iorio; Jesus Guerrero Rodriguez; Deacons Michael Jacobs; Donald Griffith; John Hackett.
School—St. Mary's Catholic Church School, (Grades K-8), Tel: 423-282-3397; Email: David.Arwood@stmarysjc.org. David Arwood, Prin. Lay Teachers 26; Students 147.
Catechesis Religious Program—Tel: 423-282-6367. Judy Holt, D.R.E.; Stephanie Mann, Youth Min. Students 261.
Mission—ETSU Catholic Center, 734 W. Locust St., Johnson City, 37601.

KINGSPORT, SULLIVAN CO., ST. DOMINIC (1941)
2517 John B. Dennis Hwy., Kingsport, 37660.
Tel: 423-288-8101; Fax: 423-288-7183; Email: stdomchurch@aol.com; Web: www.saintdominickpt.org/. Revs. Michael E. Cummins, V.F.; Emmanuel Massawe; Deacons Frank Fischer; Robert Lange; Stephan Helmbrecht.
School—St. Dominic School, (Grades PreK-5), 1474 E. Center St., Kingsport, 37664. Tel: 423-245-8491; Fax: 423-245-2907; Email: stdomchurch@aol.com. Mr. Tucker Davis, Prin.; Dusty Newman, Librarian. Lay Teachers 15; Students 76.
Catechesis Religious Program—Karen Lewicki, D.R.E. Students 154.

LA FOLLETTE, CAMPBELL CO., OUR LADY OF PERPETUAL HELP (1904)
Mailing Address: 1142 E. Elm St., La Follette, 37766. Tel: 423-562-0312; Email: OLPHLaFollette@dioknox.org; Email: lodge1053@yahoo.vom; Web: OLPHtrio.org. Rev. Albert C. Sescon, (Philippines).
Catechesis Religious Program—

LANCING, MORGAN CO., ST. ANN (1982) Attended by Blessed Sacrament, Harriman.
Mailing Address: 535 Margrave Dr., Harriman, 37748. Tel: 865-882-9838; Email: saintannlancing@gmail.com. 198 Ridge Rd., Lancing, 37770. Rev. Michael Sweeney.
Catechesis Religious Program—P.O. Box 77, Lancing, 37770.

LENOIR CITY, LOUDON CO., ST. THOMAS THE APOSTLE (1973)
Mailing Address: 1580 St. Thomas Way, Lenoir City, 37772. Revs. Ray Powell; Julian Cardona, (Colombia); Deacons Sean K. Smith; Thomas Bomkamp; John Krepps.
Res.: 1570 St. Thomas Way, Lenoir City, 37772.
Tel: 865-986-9885; Email: info@sthomaslc.com; Web: www.sthomaslc.com.
Catechesis Religious Program—Email: jill@sthomaslc.com. Jill St. Ives, D.R.E. Students 232.

MADISONVILLE, MONROE CO., ST. JOSEPH THE WORKER (1992) [CEM]
Mailing Address: 649 Old Tellico Hwy. N., Madisonville, 37354. Tel: 423-442-7273; Email: sjtwrcc@bellsouth.net; Web: www.saintjosephtheworker.net. Rev. Julius Abuh, (Nigeria).
Catechesis Religious Program—Sue Mangiaracina, D.R.E. Students 51.

MAYNARDVILLE, UNION, CO., SAINT TERESA OF KOLKATA CHURCH (2011)
Mailing Address: 4365 Maynardville, P.O. Box 1076, Maynardville, 37807. Tel: 865-992-7222; Email: blessed_teresa@att.net; Web: www.btcmaynardvillecatholicchurch.com. 4365 Maynardville Hwy., Maynardville, 37807. Rev. Steven Pawelk, G.H.M.; Deacon Larry Rossini; Bro. Joe Steen, G.H.M.
Catechesis Religious Program—iRMA Morales, D.R.E. Students 52.

MORRISTOWN, HAMBLEN CO., ST. PATRICK (1959)
2518 W. Andrew Johnson Hwy., Morristown, 37814.
Tel: 423-586-9174, Ext. 7; Fax: 423-318-7044; Email: stpatricktn@gmail.com; Web: stpatrickmorristowntn.org. Rev. Patrick Brownell; Deacon Gerald James Fage.
Catechesis Religious Program—Tel: 423-586-4091. Veronica Galvan, D.R.E. Students 400.

MOUNTAIN CITY, JOHNSON CO., ST. ANTHONY OF PADUA CATHOLIC CHURCH (1995)
833 W. Main St., Mountain City, 37683.
Tel: 423-727-5156; Email: stelizabeth@chartertn.net. Rev. Dennis Kress.
Res.: 641 Hemlock St., Mountain City, 37683.
Catechesis Religious Program—Leni Smith, D.R.E. Students 15.

NEWPORT, COCKE CO., GOOD SHEPHERD (1967)
Mailing Address: 2361 Cosby Hwy., P.O. Box 1894, Newport, 37822. Tel: 423-623-5051; Email: rhoffstetter121@comcast.net. Rev. Msgr. Robert J. Hofstetter, V.F.; Deacon Otto Preske.
Catechesis Religious Program—Nancy Soesbee, D.R.E. Students 34.

NORRIS, ANDERSON CO., ST. JOSEPH (1949) [CEM]
3425 Andersonville Hwy. 61, Norris, 37828.
Tel: 865-494-7746; Email: stjosephnorris1@comcast.net; Web: www.sjnorris.ort. P.O. Box 387, Norris, 37828. Rev. Richard G. Armstrong Jr., Admin.
Catechesis Religious Program—Cheryl Ridenour, D.R.E. Students 34.

OAK RIDGE, ANDERSON CO., ST. MARY (1943)
327-B Vermont Ave., Oak Ridge, 37830.
Tel: 865-482-2875; Email: office@stmarysoakridge.org; Web: www.stmarysoakridge.org. Revs. James Brent Shelton, V.F.; Pontian Kiyimba, A.J., (Uganda); Deacons Gary Sega; John DeClue.
School—St. Mary School, (Grades PreK-8), 323 Vermont Ave., Oak Ridge, 37830. Tel: 865-483-9700; Fax: 865-483-8305; Email: srmarieblanchette@stmarysoakridge.org; Web: school.stmarysoakridge.org/. Sr. Marie Blanchette Cummings, O.P., Prin.; Kim Bellofatto, Librarian. Religious Teachers 4; Lay Teachers 19; Sisters 4; Students 190.
Catechesis Religious Program—
Tel: 865-482-2875, Ext. 8386; Email: DRE@stmarysoakridge.org. Cyndi Panter, D.R.E. Students 124.

PIGEON FORGE, SEVIER CO., HOLY CROSS (1992)
144 Wears Valley Rd., Pigeon Forge, 37863.
Tel: 865-429-5587; Fax: 865-453-8951; Email: hcpftn@gmail.com; Web: www.holycrosscatholicchurchtn.org. Rev. Ronald Stone; Deacon Steve May.
Catechesis Religious Program—Patty Whaley, D.R.E., Email: downtownpb@msn.com. Students 43.

ROGERSVILLE, HAWKINS CO., ST. HENRY (1981)
112-114 Hwy. 70 N., Rogersville, 37857-4000.
Tel: 423-272-6897; Email: admin@sainthenrychurch.org. Rev. Bartholomew Okere, (Nigeria).
Catechesis Religious Program—Patt Knopp, D.R.E. Students 13.

RUTLEDGE, GRAINGER, SAINT JOHN PAUL II CATHOLIC MISSION (2011)
Mailing Address: 7735 Rutledge, P.O. Box 1076, Maynardville, 37807. Tel: 865-992-7222; Email: spawelk@glenmary.org; Web: stjohnpaulcatholic.com. 7735 Rutledge Pk., Rutledge, 37861. Revs. Steven Pawelk, G.H.M.; Alex Waraska.
Catechesis Religious Program—Nancy Cervantes, D.R.E. Students 39.

SEYMOUR, SEVIER CO., HOLY FAMILY (1984)
Mailing Address: 307 Black Oak Ridge Rd., Seymour, 37865. Tel: 865-573-1203; Fax: 865-579-3645; Email: secretary@holyfamilyseymour.org; Web: www.holyfamilyseymour.org. Rev. Gilbert M. Diaz; Deacons Dean Burry; Gil Campos.
Catechesis Religious Program—Tel: 865-573-4597. Bill Voight, D.R.E. Students 43.

SIGNAL MOUNTAIN, HAMILTON CO., ST. AUGUSTINE (1938) [CEM]
1716 Anderson Pike, Signal Mountain, 37377.
Tel: 423-886-3424; Email: parishoffice@staugustinecatholic.org; Web: www.staugustinecatholic.org. Rev. Joseph Kuzhupil, M.S.F.S., (India); Deacon Tom Tidwell.
Catechesis Religious Program—Email: heather@staugustinecatholic.org. Heather Wilson, D.R.E. Students 125.

SNEEDVILLE, HANCOCK CO., ST. JAMES THE APOSTLE (1982) Attended by St. Henry, Rogersville.
3652 Main St., P.O. Box 93, Sneedville, 37869. Rev. Bartholomew Okere, (Nigeria).
Res.: 112-114 Hwy. 70 N., Rogersville, 37857.
Tel: 423-272-6897; Email: barthnneji07@gmail.com.

SODDY DAISY, HAMILTON CO., HOLY SPIRIT CATHOLIC CHURCH (1999)
Mailing Address: P.O. Box 1015, Soddy Daisy, 37384.
10768 Dayton Pike, Soddy Daisy, 37379.
Tel: 423-332-5300; Fax: 423-332-5391; Email: hscc_parish@holyspirittn.com; Web: www.holyspiritsoddydaisy.com. Rev. Msgr. T. Allen Humbrecht; Deacons Michael Kucharzak; Noel W. Spencer Jr., Ph.D.
Res.: 10812 Dayton Pike, Soddy Daisy, 37379.
Tel: 423-332-8283.
Catechesis Religious Program—Helen Barbeauld, D.R.E. Students 103.

SOUTH PITTSBURG, MARION CO., OUR LADY OF LOURDES

(1899)
704 Holly Ave., South Pittsburg, 37380.
Tel: 423-837-7068; Email: olol704@hotmail.com. Rev. Mark A. Scholz.
Mission—Virgin of the Poor Shrine.
Catechesis Religious Program—Students 7.

TAZEWELL, CLAIBORNE CO., CHRIST THE KING (1990) Attended by Our Lady of Perpetual Help Church, LaFollette
P.O. Box 404, Tazewell, 37879. 816 Blue Top Rd., Tazewell, 37879. Tel: 423-562-0312; Email: OLPHLaFollette@dioknox.org; Web: www.OLPHTrio.org. Rev. Albert C. Sescon, (Philippines).
Catechesis Religious Program—Heather McLean, D.R.E.

TOWNSEND, BLOUNT CO., ST. FRANCIS OF ASSISI (1961)
Mailing Address: 7719 River Rd., Townsend, 37882.
Tel: 865-448-6070; Email: stfrancistownsend@comcast.net; Web: stfrancistownsend.org. Rev. Antonio Giraldo.
Catechesis Religious Program—

Retired:
Rev. Msgrs.—
Gahagan, William H., (Retired), P.O. Box 902, Norris, 37828
Garrity, G. Patrick, V.E., (Retired), P.O. Box 3755, 37927
Revs.—
Brando, Joseph J., (Retired), 2146 Floyd Porter Rd., Maryville, 37803
Hostettler, Paul A., (Retired), 34 White Bridge Rd., Rm. 105, Nashville, 37205
Jennings, Michael T., (Retired), 329 Boyd St., Apt. 34, Rogersville, 37857
Neuzil, Gregory, (Retired), 6114 Lausche Ave., Apt. 103, Cleveland, OH 44103
O'Connell, Thomas P., (Retired), 8458 Gleason Dr., Apt. 335, 37919
Valleroy, Paul J., (Retired), 930 Ashland Ter., Chattanooga, 37415.

Permanent Deacons:
Alexander, Dan, Cathedral of the Most Sacred Heart of Jesus, Knoxville
Amelse, Donald, M.P.S., St. John Neumann, Knoxville
Armor, Hicks, Basilica of Sts. Peter & Paul, Chattanooga
Bitzer, Doug, Immaculate Conception, Knoxville
Bomkamp, Thomas, St. Thomas the Apostle, Lenoir City
Brinkworth, Gary, St. Stephen, Chattanooga
Burry, Dean, Holy Family, Seymour
Campos, Gil, Holy Family, Seymour
Carner, Richard, St. Elizabeth, Elizabethton
DeClue, John, St. Mary, Oak Ridge
DeGaetano, Gaspar, Basilica of Sts. Peter & Paul, Chattanooga
Diesing, William, (Retired)
Duncan, Michael, St. Albert the Great, Knoxville
Eiffe, Michael, St. Albert the Great, Knoxville
Elliott, Tim, All Saints, Knoxville
Fage, G. James II, St. Patrick, Morristown
Farber, Keith S., (Retired)
Feldhaus, Butch, St. Jude, Chattanooga
Fischer, Frank, St. Dominic, Kingsport
Fischer, Robert W., (Retired)
Forsythe, Al, St. John Neumann, Knoxville
Frazier, J. Michael
Fredericks, George III, St. Mary, Johnson City
Gabor, Brian, St. Jude & U.T.C. Catholic Center, Chattanooga
Gouge, Mike, St. John Neumann, Knoxville
Griffith, Donald, St. Mary, Johnson City
Grossmayer, Simon Jr., St. Augustine, Signal Mountain
Hackett, John, St. Mary, Johnson City
Helmbrecht, Stephan, St. Dominic, Kingsport
Hernandez, Erasmo, St. Mary, Athens
Hosford, Dan, St. Therese and St. Joseph
Humphreys, Mike, St. John Neumann, Knoxville
Jacobs, Michael, St. Mary, Johnson City
Jacobs, William, Our Lady of Fatima, Alcoa
Johnson, Wil, Notre Dame, Greeneville
Johnston, Ben
Ketteringham, Robert, St. John XXIII, Knoxville
Kiefer, Thomas, (Retired)
Kilburn, Gordon, St. Augustine, Signal Mountain
Krepps, John, St. Thomas the Apostle, Lenoir City
Kucharzak, Michael, (Retired)
Lange, Robert, St. Dominic, Kingsport
Lawson, James, (Retired)
Livingston, Joel Jr., Cathedral of the Most Sacred Heart of Jesus, Knoxville
Long, Kenneth, (Retired)
Lowery, Gordon, Holy Ghost, Knoxville
Lucheon, David J., All Saints, Knoxville
Maentz, Scott, Our Lady of Fatima, Alcoa
Maples, Barry, St. Therese of Lisieux, Cleveland
May, Steve, Holy Cross, Pigeon Forge
McConnell, Thomas, Basilica of Sts. Peter & Paul, Chattanooga
Meinert, Dennis, Our Lady of Perpetual Help, Chattanooga
Minneci, Peter, St. Alphonsus, Crossville
Murphy-Racey, Patrick, St. Albert the Great, Knoxville
Nelson, Paul, St. Jude, Chattanooga
Nestor, Michael, (Retired)
Oatney, David, Holy Trinity, Jefferson City
Otey, Walt, Cathedral of the Most Sacred Heart of Jesus, Knoxville
Pecot, David E., (Retired)
Preske, Otto F., Good Shepherd, Newport
Prosak, Jim, Holy Trinity, Jefferson City
Ratterman, Steve, St. Therese of Lisieux, Cleveland
Raymond, Jack, Holy Trinity, Jefferson City
Rivera, Jose, (Retired)
Rossini, Larry, St. Teresa of Kolkata, Maynardville
Rust, Robert, All Saints, Knoxville
Sega, Gary, St. Mary, Oak Ridge
Sinanian, Loris, St. Catherine, Copperhill
Smearing, Robert, St. Albert the Great, Knoxville
Smith, Sean K., St. Thomas the Apostle, Lenoir City
Spencer, Noel W. Jr., Ph.D., Holy Spirit, Soddy Daisy
Stackhouse, Joe, Ph.D., Immaculate Conception, Knoxville
Syler, Marquis E., St. John Neumann, Knoxville
Tidwell, Tom, St. Augustine, Signal Mountain
Vargas, Fredy, All Saints, Knoxville
Vinh, Joseph, Immaculate Conception, Knoxville
West, James Larry.

INSTITUTIONS LOCATED IN DIOCESE

[A] HIGH SCHOOLS, DIOCESAN

KNOXVILLE. *Knoxville Catholic High School* (1932) 9245 Fox Lonas Rd., 37923. Tel: 865-560-0313; Fax: 865-560-0314; Email: info@knoxvillecatholic.com; Web: knoxvillecatholic.com. Mr. Dickie Sompayrac, Pres., Tel: 865-560-0518; Fax: 865-560-0591; Rev. Christopher Manning, Chap., Tel: 865-560-0510; Fax: 865-560-0314; Dawn Harbin, Librarian, Tel: 865-560-0313, Ext. 2412; Fax: 865-560-0314. Religious Teachers 7; Lay Teachers 57; Priests 2; Sisters 2; Students 624; Total Staff 78.
Knoxville Catholic High School Development Board of Trust, 9245 Fox Lonas Rd., 37923.
Tel: 865-560-0509; Fax: 865-560-0314; Email: info@knoxvillecatholic.com. Mr. Dickie Sompayrac, Pres.

CHATTANOOGA. *Notre Dame High School* (1876) 2701 Vermont Ave., Chattanooga, 37404.
Tel: 423-624-4618; Fax: 423-624-4621; Email: valadie@myndhs.com; Web: www.myndhs.com. George Valadie, Pres.; Becky Light, Librarian; Rev. Christopher Floersh, Chap. Religious Teachers 4; Lay Teachers 34; Priests 2; Sisters 3; Students 396; Total Staff 12.
Notre Dame High School Financial Board of Trustees, 2701 Vermont Ave., Chattanooga, 37404. Tel: 423-624-4618; Email: valadie@myndhs.com. George Valadie, Pres.

[B] ELEMENTARY SCHOOL, REGIONAL

KNOXVILLE. *Saint Joseph School of Knoxville*, (Grades PreK-8), Parochial-Regional School for Holy Ghost Church, Immaculate Conception Church & St. Albert the Great Church. 1810 Howard Dr., 37918. Tel: 865-689-3424; Fax: 865-687-7885; Email: azengel@sjsknox.org; Web: www.sjsknox.org. Rev. Chris Michelson, Pres.; Mr. Andy Zengel, Prin.; Julie Duncan, Librarian. Lay Teachers 17; Students 240.

[C] GENERAL HOSPITALS

CHATTANOOGA. *Memorial Health Care System, Inc.* aka CHI Memorial (1952) 2525 De Sales Ave., Chattanooga, 37404. Tel: 423-495-2525; Fax: 423-495-8937; Email: tammy_singleton@memorial.org; Email: lisa_sheets@memorial.org; Web: www.memorial.org. Janelle Reilly, CEO; Robert V. Scheri, B.C.C., Vice Pres. Mission Integratoion/Spiritual Care. (Member of Catholic Health Initiatives) Bed Capacity 405; Sisters 2; Tot Asst. Annually 171,104; Total Staff 3,252.
Memorial Health Care System Foundation, Inc. aka CHI Memorial (2001) 2525 De Sales Ave., Chattanooga, 37404. Tel: 423-495-2525; Fax: 423-495-7726; Email: jennifer_nicely@memorial.org. Janelle Reilly, CEO.

[D] SPECIAL HOSPITALS

SIGNAL MOUNTAIN. *Alexian Village Health and Rehabilitation Center* (1938) 635 Alexian Way, Signal Mountain, 37377. Tel: 423-517-9500; Fax: 423-517-0318; Email: dawn.salyer@ascension.org; Web: www.alexianvillage.net. Doug Malin, Admin. Licensed Skilled & Intermediate Care Nursing Home. Bed Capacity 114; Brothers 8; Tot Asst. Annually 518; Total Staff 105; Assisted Living 32.

[E] MOBILE HEALTH CLINIC

KNOXVILLE. *St. Mary's Legacy Clinic, Inc.*, 805 S. Northshore Dr., 37919. Tel: 865-212-5570; Email: srmariana@dioknox.org; Web: www.stmaryclinic.org. Sr. Mariana Koonce, R.S.M., M.D., Exec. Dir.

[F] HOMES FOR THE AGED

SIGNAL MOUNTAIN. *Alexian Village of Tennessee* (1983) 437 Alexian Way, Signal Mountain, 37377.
Tel: 423-886-0100; Fax: 423-886-0561; Email: dawn.salyer@ascension.org; Web: ascensionliving.org. Rev. Mitred Archpriest Arokiaselvam Nithiyaselvam, Chap.; Rev. Valerie Carnes, Chap.; Terry Thompkins, Exec. Retirement Community & Healthcare Center. Total in Residence 338; Total Staff 300; Life Care Units 308.

[G] PROTECTIVE INSTITUTIONS

KNOXVILLE. *Columbus Home*, 3227 Division St., 37919. Tel: 865-971-3560; Fax: 865-544-0538; Email: bbeverly@ccetn.org. Ms. Brenda Beverly. Bed Capacity 14; Tot Asst. Annually 133; Total Staff 18.

[H] MONASTERIES AND RESIDENCES OF PRIESTS AND BROTHERS

KNOXVILLE. *Paulist Fathers* dba Missionary Society of St. Paul the Apostle, 707 E. Scott Ave., 37917.
Tel: 347-886-4270; Email: rfrancocsp@aol.com; Web: www.paulistfathers.org. Revs. Ronald A. Franco, C.S.P., V.F., Supr.; Donald Andrie, C.S.P.; Timothy Sullivan, C.S.P.; James A. Haley, C.S.P., (Retired); Robert J. O'Donnell, Vicar. Priests 5.

SIGNAL MOUNTAIN. *Alexian Brothers*, 198 James Blvd., Signal Mountain, 37377-1816. Tel: 423-551-3982; Email: blowe@alexianbrothers.net; Web: www.alexianbrothers.org/. Bros. Andrew Thome, C.F.A., Patient Visitor; Lawrence Krueger, C.F.A., Supr. Gen.; Thomas Klein, C.F.A., Mission Coord.; Richard Lowe, C.F.A., Dir.; Richard Kane. Brothers 5.

[I] CONVENTS AND RESIDENCES FOR SISTERS

KNOXVILLE. *Mary, Mother of Mercy Convent*, 6832 S. Northshore Dr., 37919. Tel: 865-690-9266; Email: srannamarie@dioknox.org. Sr. Anna Marie McGuan, Supr. Religious Sisters of Mercy of Alma, Michigan (R.S.M.) Sisters 8.
Sisters of Mercy of the Americas (1831) (South Central Region) St. Mary's Convent, 701 E. Oak Hill Ave., 37917. Tel: 865-621-8854; Email: mnaber@mercysc.org. Sr. Albertine Paulus, Supr. Sisters 2.

HELENWOOD. *Sisters of Mercy*, 13071 Scott Hwy., P.O. Box 555, Helenwood, 37755. Tel: 423-569-9584. Rev. Albert C. Sescon, (Philippines). Sisters 1.
St. Jude Church, 13067 Scott Hwy., Helenwood, 37755. Tel: 423-569-9584; Email: pasoete@highland.net. Sr. Patricia Soete, R.S.M., Pastoral Assoc., Tel: 423-569-3492.

NEW MARKET. *Handmaids of the Precious Blood Corp.*, 596 Callaway Ridge Rd., New Market, 37820-3446. Tel: 423-241-7065; Email: mothermarietta@gmail.com; Web: www.nunsforpriests.org. Rev. Mother Marietta, H.P.B., Mother Prioress. Motherhouse & Novitiate of the Handmaids of the Precious Blood. Perpetually Professed Sisters 15.

OAK RIDGE. *Dominican Sisters (St. Cecilia Congregation)* (1860) 323 Vermont Ave., Oak Ridge, 37830. Tel: 865-483-0720; Email: oakridge@op-tn.org. Sr. John Kennedy, Supr. Sisters 6.

[J] NEWMAN CENTERS

KNOXVILLE. *UT-Knoxville, Newman Foundation, Inc.* (1968) St. John XXIII University Parish / Catholic Center, 1710 Melrose Pl., 37916. Tel: 865-523-7931 ; Fax: 865-523-7979; Email: john23@utk.edu; Web: www.john23rd.org. Revs. Donald Andrie, C.S.P.; Robert J. O'Donnell, Assoc. Pastor; Deacon Robert Ketteringham, Pastoral Assoc.

CHATTANOOGA. *Newman Foundation of Chattanooga,*

Inc., 514 Palmetto St., Chattanooga, 37403. Tel: 423-618-9062; Email: bjgabor@comcast.net; Web: www.utccatholic.org. Rev. Colin Blatchford, Sacramental Min.; Deacon Brian Gabor, PT Campus Min.; Donna Gabor, PT Campus Min., Dir. Total Staff 3.

JOHNSON CITY. *ETSU-Catholic Center*, 734 W. Locust St., Johnson City, 37604. Tel: 423-926-7061; Email: etsucatholiccenter@yahoo.com; Web: www.catholiccenteratetsu.com. Rev. Bede C. Aboh, (Nigeria) Chap. Total Staff 1.

[K] FOUNDATIONS AND ENDOWMENTS

KNOXVILLE. *The Catholic Diocese of Knoxville Foundation, Inc.*, 805 S. Northshore Drive, 37919. Tel: 865-584-3307; Fax: 865-584-7538; Email: shepp@dioknox.org. Deacon Sean K. Smith, Chancellor.

Catholic Foundation of East Tennessee, 805 S. Northshore Drive, 37919. Tel: 865-584-3307; Fax: 865-584-7538; Email: jdeinhart@dioknox.org. Mr. John Deinhart, Dir.

St. Mary's Legacy Foundation of East Tennessee, Inc., 805 S. Northshore Drive, 37919. Tel: 865-584-3307; Email: jdeinhart@dioknox.org; Web: dioknox.org/offices-ministries/st-marys-legacy-foundation/. Mr. John Deinhart, Dir.; Most Reverend Richard F. Stika, Chm.; Sally Sefton, Pres. Members of the Corporation Most Reverend Richard F. Stika; Very Rev. David Boettner, V.G.; Deacons Sean K. Smith; David J. Lucheon; Clara Mathien.

[L] RETREAT HOUSES

BENTON. *Christ Prince of Peace Retreat Center*, 250 Locke Ln., Benton, 37307. Tel: 865-584-3307; Tel: psimoneau@dioknox.org; Web: www.dioknox.org. Paul Simoneau.

[M] MISCELLANEOUS

KNOXVILLE. *Diocesan Council of Catholic Women*, 805 S. Northshore Drive, 37919. Tel: 865-386-5784; Email: kvacaliuc@gmail.com. Rev. Dan G. Whitman, Deanery Spiritual Mod., Five Rivers; Rev. Msgr. T. Allen Humbrecht, Deanery Spiritual Mod., Chattanooga; Revs. Michael Woods, Deanery Spiritual Mod., Cumberland Mountain; Joseph J. Brando, Deanery Spiritual Mod., (Retired).

The Diocese of Knoxville Paraclete Bookstore, Inc., Mailing Address: 805 S. Northshore Drive, 37919. Tel: 865-588-0388; Tel: 800-333-2097; Email: theparaclete@dioknox.org. 417 Erin Drive, Ste. 110, 37919. Deacon Sean K. Smith, Chancellor.

**Ladies of Charity Knoxville* (1942) 120 W. Baxter Ave., 37917-6401. Tel: 865-247-5790 Thrift Shop; Tel: 865-474-9329 Emergency Assistance; Fax: 865-474-9367; Email: ladiesofcharityknox@gmail.com; Web: ladiesofcharityknox.org. Rev. John R. Dowling, Spiritual Mod. Tot Asst. Annually 66,135; Total Staff 11.

Ladies of Charity- Pantry, 120 W. Baxter Ave., 37917. Tel: 865-474-9348; Fax: 865-474-9367; Email: ladiesofcharityeap@comcast.net. Laura Deubler, Contact Person.

CHATTANOOGA. *Ladies of Charity*, 2821 Rossville Blvd., Chattanooga, 37407. Tel: 423-698-2846; Tel: 423-313-7348; Fax: 423-622-7035; Email: jan.clark11@yahoo.com. Rev. James L. Vick, Spiritual Mod. Assistance by appointment only with social worker, food, medicine, clothing, doctor co-pay, layettes for newborns, utility assistance, vision, dental, etc. Tot Asst. Annually 3,015.

St. Alexuis Outreach Ministries, Inc., 250 E. 10th St., Chattanooga, 37402-4241. Tel: 423-755-3430; Fax: 423-634-2049; Email: schill@alexianbrothers.net. Bro. Richard Lowe, C.F.A., Chm.; Susan Chill, Pres.

RELIGIOUS INSTITUTES OF MEN REPRESENTED IN THE DIOCESE

For further details refer to the corresponding bracketed number in the Religious Institutes of Men or Women section.

[0120]—*Alexian Brothers*—C.F.A.

[]—*Apostles of Jesus*—A.J.

[]—*Carmelites of Mary Immaculate*—C.M.I.

[]—*Crusaders of the Holy Spirit*—C.H.S.

[]—*Franciscan Friars Minor (Franciscan Friars)*—F.F.M.

[0570]—*The Glenmary Home Missioners*—Glmy.

[0840]—*Missionary Servants of the Most Holy Trinity*—S.T.

[]—*Order of Missionaries of St. Francis de Sales*—M.S.F.S.

[1030]—*Paulist Fathers*—C.S.P.

RELIGIOUS INSTITUTES OF WOMEN REPRESENTED IN THE DIOCESE

[1070-07]—*Dominican Sisters (St. Cecilia Congregation)*—O.P.

[1860]—*Handmaids of the Precious Blood of Jesus*—H.P.B.

[2575]—*Institute of the Sisters of Mercy of the Americas* (South Central)—R.S.M.

[]—*Missionary Congregation of the Evangelizing Sisters of Mary* (Uganda)—E.S.M.

[]—*Missionary Sisters of the Sacred Heart of Jesus "Ad Gentes"*—M.A.G.

[2519]—*Religious Sisters of Mercy of Alma, Michigan*—R.S.M.

[0500]—*Sisters of Charity of Nazareth*—S.C.N.

[]—*Sisters of St. Francis of the Martyr St. George*—F.S.G.M.

[3930]—*Sisters of St. Joseph, Third Order of St. Francis*—S.S.J.-T.O.S.F.

[0970]—*Sisters of the Divine Compassion*—R.D.C.

[]—*Sisters of the Good Shepherd* (Mid-North America Province)—R.G.S.

[]—*Sisters of the Presentation of the Blessed Virgin Mary*—P.B.V.M.

INTERPAROCHIAL CEMETERIES

KNOXVILLE. *Calvary Cemetery*, 1916 Martin Luther King Jr. Ave., 37915. Tel: 865-522-1508; Email: icoffice@bellsouth.net. c/o Immaculate Conception Church, 414 West Vine Ave., 37902-1327. Rev. Ronald A. Franco, C.S.P., V.F.

CHATTANOOGA. *Mount Olivet Cemetery*, One Mount Olivet Dr., Chattanooga, 37412. Tel: 423-622-0728; Fax: 509-693-8902; Tel: 423-266-1618; Email: encompass@prodigy.net; Email: business@stspeterandpaulbasilica.com; Web: www.mountolivet.com. 214 E. 8th St., Chattanooga, 37402. Very Rev. J. David Carter, J.C.L.; David E. Hale, Supt.

An asterisk (*) denotes an organization that has established tax-exempt status directly with the IRS and is not covered by the USCCB Group Ruling.

Diocese of La Crosse

(Dioecesis Crossensis)

Most Reverend

WILLIAM P. CALLAHAN, O.F.M.CONV.

Bishop of La Crosse; ordained April 30, 1977; appointed Auxiliary Bishop of Milwaukee and Titular Bishop of Lares October 30, 2007; ordained December 21, 2007; appointed Bishop of La Crosse June 11, 2010; installed August 11, 2010. *Chancery Office: 3710 East Ave. S., P.O. Box 4004, La Crosse, WI 54602-4004.*

Holy Cross Diocesan Center: 3710 East Ave. S., P.O. Box 4004, La Crosse, WI 54602-4004. Tel: 608-788-7700; Fax: 608-788-8413.

Web: diolc.org

Email: mailbox@diolc.org

Square Miles 15,078.

Erected March 3, 1868. Subdivided May 3, 1905. Subdivided January 15, 1946.

Comprises the following 19 Counties in the State of Wisconsin: Adams, Buffalo, Chippewa, Clark, Crawford, Dunn, Eau Claire, Jackson, Juneau, La Crosse, Marathon, Monroe, Pepin, Pierce, Portage, Richland, Trempealeau, Vernon and Wood.

For legal titles of parishes and diocesan institutions, consult the Chancery Office.

STATISTICAL OVERVIEW

Personnel	
Bishop	1
Priests: Diocesan Active in Diocese	84
Priests: Diocesan Active Outside Diocese	3
Priests: Diocesan in Foreign Missions	1
Priests: Retired, Sick or Absent	49
Number of Diocesan Priests	137
Religious Priests in Diocese	7
Total Priests in Diocese	144
Extern Priests in Diocese	29
Ordinations:	
Diocesan Priests	2
Transitional Deacons	2
Permanent Deacons	4
Permanent Deacons in Diocese	59
Total Brothers	2
Total Sisters	244
Parishes	
Parishes	159
With Resident Pastor:	
Resident Diocesan Priests	94
Resident Religious Priests	1
Without Resident Pastor:	
Administered by Priests	64
New Parishes Created	1
Professional Ministry Personnel:	
Brothers	1
Sisters	3
Lay Ministers	116
Welfare	
Catholic Hospitals	6
Total Assisted	214,131
Health Care Centers	1
Homes for the Aged	7
Day Care Centers	4
Specialized Homes	4
Special Centers for Social Services	4
Total Assisted	5,080
Residential Care of Disabled	1
Total Assisted	9
Other Institutions	1
Total Assisted	22
Educational	
Diocesan Students in Other Seminaries	28
Total Seminarians	28
Colleges and Universities	1
Total Students	2,101
High Schools, Diocesan and Parish	7
Total Students	1,219
High Schools, Private	1
Total Students	9
Elementary Schools, Diocesan and Parish	52
Total Students	5,440
Elementary Schools, Private	1
Total Students	76
Catechesis/Religious Education:	
High School Students	2,827
Elementary Students	7,473
Total Students under Catholic Instruction	19,173
Teachers in the Diocese:	
Sisters	3
Lay Teachers	506
Vital Statistics	
Receptions into the Church:	
Infant Baptism Totals	1,439
Minor Baptism Totals	59
Adult Baptism Totals	80
Received into Full Communion	128
First Communions	1,702
Confirmations	1,773
Marriages:	
Catholic	342
Interfaith	157
Total Marriages	499
Deaths	1,928
Total Catholic Population	149,025
Total Population	913,448

Former Bishops—Most Rev. MICHAEL HEISS, D.D., cons. Sept. 6, 1868; appt. Titular Archbishop of Hadrianople, and coadjutor to the Metropolitan of Milwaukee March 14, 1880; promoted to Milwaukee, Sept. 1881; died March 26, 1890; Rt. Revs. KILIAN CASPAR FLASCH, D.D., ord. Dec. 16, 1859; cons. Aug. 24, 1881; died Aug. 3, 1891; JAMES SCHWEBACH, D.D., ord. June 16, 1870; cons. Feb. 25, 1892; died June 6, 1921; Most Revs. ALEXANDER J. MCGAVICK, D.D., LL.D., cons. Titular Bishop of Marcopolis and Auxiliary Bishop of Chicago, May 1, 1899; transferred to See of La Crosse, Nov. 21, 1921; died Aug. 25, 1948; JOHN P. TREACY, S.T.D., cons. Titular Bishop of Metelis and Coadjutor of La Crosse "cum jure successionis," Oct. 2, 1945; succeeded to the See, July 23, 1946; died Oct. 11, 1964; FREDERICK W. FREKING, D.D., J.C.D., cons. Bishop of Salina, KS, Nov. 30, 1957; transferred to the See of La Crosse, Dec. 30, 1964; installed La Crosse, Feb. 24, 1965; retired May 10, 1983; died Nov. 28, 1998; JOHN J. PAUL, appt. Titular Bishop of Lambese and Auxiliary Bishop of La Crosse, May 17, 1977; cons. Aug. 4, 1977; appt. to the Residential See of La Crosse, Oct. 18, 1983; installed as Bishop of La Crosse, Dec. 5, 1983; retired Dec. 10, 1994; died March 5, 2006; His Eminence RAYMOND LEO CARDINAL BURKE, D.D., J.C.D., appt. to the Residential See of La Crosse Dec. 10, 1994; cons. Jan. 6, 1995; installed as Eighth Bishop of La Crosse Feb. 22, 1995; appt. Archbishop of the Archdiocese of St. Louis Dec. 2, 2003; installed Jan. 26, 2004; appt. Prefect of the Apostolic Signatura June 27, 2008; elevated to Cardinal Nov. 20, 2010; appt. Patron of the Sovereign Military Order of Malta Nov. 8, 2014; appt. to the Congregation for the Causes of Saints Sept. 26, 2015.; Most Rev. JEROME E. LISTECKI, D.D., J.C.D., ord. May 14, 1975; appt. Auxiliary Bishop of Chicago and Titular Bishop of Nara Nov. 7, 2000; cons. Jan. 8, 2001; appt. Bishop of La Crosse Dec. 29, 2004; installed March 1, 2005; appt. Archbishop of Milwaukee Nov. 14, 2009; installed Jan. 4, 2010.

Holy Cross Diocesan Center—3710 East Ave. S., P.O. Box 4004, La Crosse, 54602-4004. Tel: 608-788-7700; Fax: 608-788-8413. Office Hours: Mon.-Fri. 8-4:30.

Vicars General—Very Rev. WILLIAM A. DHEIN, V.G., J.C.L.; Rev. Msgrs. JOSEPH G. DIERMEIER, V.G., J.C.L.; MICHAEL J. GORMAN, V.G., J.C.L.

Finance—MR. KURT JERECZEK, Office for Temporalities, Tel: 608-791-0171; Web: diolc.org/temporalities.

Consultative Bodies—

Building Commission—Very Rev. WILLIAM A. DHEIN, V.G., J.C.L.; MR. CHRISTOPHER CARSTENS; MR. THOMAS REICHENBACHER.

College of Consultors—Most Rev. WILLIAM P. CALLAHAN, O.F.M.Conv.; Rev. Msgrs. JOSEPH G. DIERMEIER, V.G., J.C.L.; MICHAEL J. GORMAN, V.G., J.C.L.; Very Rev. WILLIAM A. DHEIN, V.G., J.C.L.; Revs. WILLIAM P. FELIX; ROBERT M. LETONA; WILLIAM G. MENZEL, (Retired); DANIEL L. THELEN.

Deans—Very Rev. SEBASTIAN J. KOLODZIEJCZYK, Arcadia Deanery; Revs. JUSTIN J. KIZEWSKI, Chippewa Falls Deanery; DEREK J. SAKOWSKI, Eau Claire Deanery; Rev. Msgr. CHARLES D. STOETZEL, La Crosse Deanery; Very Revs. SAMUEL A. MARTIN, Marshfield Deanery; JAMES C. WEIGHNER, Prairie du Chien Deanery; Rev. Msgr. ROGER J. SCHECKEL, Richland Center Deanery; Very Rev. DANIEL H. HACKEL, Stevens Point Deanery; Rev. VARKEY VELICKAKATHU, Thorp Deanery; Very Rev. JOHN A. POTACZEK, Tomah Deanery; Rev. Msgr. MARK R. PIERCE, J.C.L., Wausau Deanery; Very Rev. G. VALENTINE JOSEPH, Wisconsin Rapids Deanery; Rev. ERIC AWORTE-DADSON, (Ghana) Durand Deanery.

Diocesan Pastoral Council—Very Rev. WILLIAM A. DHEIN, V.G., J.C.L., Exec. Sec., Mailing Address: P.O. Box 4004, La Crosse, 54602-4004.

Personnel Council—Most Rev. WILLIAM P. CALLAHAN, O.F.M.Conv., Pres.; Very Rev. SAMUEL A. MARTIN, Chm.; Revs. BRIAN D. KONOPA; DEREK J. SAKOWSKI; EDWARD J. SHUTTLEWORTH. Ex Officio: Rev. Msgrs. JOSEPH G. DIERMEIER, V.G., J.C.L.; MICHAEL J. GORMAN, V.G., J.C.L., Sec.; DAVID C. KUNZ; Very Rev. WILLIAM A. DHEIN, V.G., J.C.L.; Rev. ALAN P. WIERZBA.

Presbyteral Council—Most Rev. WILLIAM P. CALLAHAN, O.F.M.Conv., Pres.; Very Rev. ALLAN L. SLOWIAK; Revs. WILLIAM P. FELIX; ALAN T. BURKHARDT; BRIAN D. KONOPA; ROBERT C. THORN; KEITH J. KITZHABER; ROBERT M. LETONA; DANIEL L. THELEN; WILLIAM G. MENZEL, (Senior Priests), (Retired); LOUIS D. BRITTO SUSAIRAJ, (International Priests).

Ex Officio—Very Rev. WILLIAM A. DHEIN, V.G.,

J.C.L.; Rev. Msgrs. JOSEPH G. DIERMEIER, V.G., J.C.L.; MICHAEL J. GORMAN, V.G., J.C.L.; DAVID C. KUNZ; Rev. BRIAN D. KONOPA.

Offices of the Diocesan Curia

Chancellor—Very Rev. WILLIAM A. DHEIN, V.G., J.C.L., Tel: 608-791-2655; Email: wdhein@diolc.org. Vice Chancellor: Rev. KURT J. APFELBECK, Tel: 608-791-0177; Email: kapfelbeck@diolc.org. Administrative Assistant: MARY JO WILSON, Email: mwilson@diolc.org; Web: diolc.org/chancery.

Archives—Rev. KURT J. APFELBECK, Archivist, Email: archives@diolc.org; Web: diolc.org/archives.

Bishop's Office—BRIAN T. LOGUE, Chief of Staff, Tel: 608-791-0172; Email: blogue@diolc.org; DEBORAH BRANNON, Administrative Asst., Tel: 608-788-7700; Fax: 608-788-4689; Email: dbrannon@diolc.org.

Catholic Charities of the Diocese of La Crosse, Inc.—ROBERTO PARTARRIEU, Exec. Dir., 3710 East Ave., P.O. Box 266, La Crosse, 54602-0266. Tel: 608-782-0710; Fax: 608-782-0702; Web: cclse.org.

Catholic Committee on Scouting—Web: diolc.org/scouting/scouting. Committee Chair: Deacon JASON C. HUTZLER, N 2148 Valley Rd., La Crosse, 54601. Tel: 608-787-0407. Committee Chaplain: Very Rev. JAMES F. ALTMAN, Mailing Address: 1032 Caledonia St., La Crosse, 54603. Tel: 608-782-7557.

Diocesan Council of Catholic Women—Web: www.ldccw.org/directory.

Diocesan Program for Permanent Deacons—Rev. WILLIAM P. FELIX, Dir., Tel: 715-644-5435; MR. CHRISTOPHER J. RUFF, Assoc. Dir., Tel: 608-791-0161; Fax: 608-791-2675; Email: ministries@diolc.org; Web: diolc.org/ministries/ministry-formation/diaconate.

Diocesan School of Biblical Studies—611 Stark St., Wausau, 54403. Tel: 715-842-4283. Rev. Msgr. MARK R. PIERCE, J.C.L., Dir.

Diocesan Tribunal—3710 East Ave. S., P.O. Box 4004, La Crosse, 54602-4004. Tel: 608-791-2684; Email: tribunal@diolc.org; Web: diolc.org/tribunal.

Judicial Vicar—Rev. Msgr. ROBERT P. HUNDT, J.C.L., (Retired).

Judges—Rev. Msgrs. ROBERT P. HUNDT, J.C.L., (Retired); MICHAEL J. GORMAN, V.G., J.C.L.

Defender of the Bond—Rev. WILLIAM J. KULAS.

Promoter of Justice—Rev. Msgr. JOSEPH G. DIERMEIER, V.G., J.C.L.

Auditor—Sr. DONNA KRZMARZICK, I.S.S.M.

Hispanic Ministry—Rev. TIMOTHY L. OUDENHOVEN, Abbotsford; Very Rev. SEBASTIAN J. KOLODZIEJCZYK, Arcadia; Rev. DEREK J. SAKOWSKI, Eau Claire; JUAN PEDRO ROBLEZ BALTAZAR, Sparta; Rev. ROBERT C. THORN, Wausau.

Hospitals and Health Affairs—Mailing Address: P.O. Box 436, Colby, 54421. Tel: 715-223-3048. Rev. D. JOSEPH REDFERN.

International Priests—Rev. Msgr. DAVID C. KUNZ, Tel: 608-791-2679; Email: dkunz@diolc.org. Responsible for the recruitment and retention of international priests who serve in the Diocese; Oversees all legal aspects of hosting international priests including visas, travel documents and residency;; Facilitates initial and ongoing orientation within parishes and the Diocese; Maintains relationships with foreign bishops and religious superiors to ensure fruitful, pastoral rapport.

Mission Office/Propagation of the FaithVery Rev. WOODROW H. PACE, Dir., Tel: 608-791-2676; Web: diolc.org/missions.

Holy Childhood Association—Very Rev. WOODROW H. PACE.

Moderator of the Curia—Very Rev. WILLIAM A. DHEIN, V.G., J.C.L.

Native Americans, Apostolate for—ELEANOR ST. JOHN, Coord., Tel: 608-788-7700.

Office for Catechesis and Evangelization—ANN C. LANKFORD, Dir., Tel: 608-791-2658; Email: alankford@diolc.org; Web: diolc.org/catechesis; Web: diolc.org/evangelization.

Hmong Faith Formation Coordinator—LOR THAO, Contact, Mary Mother of Good Help Parish, 2221 B Grand Ave., Wausau, 54403. Tel: 715-849-5664; Email: fral@marymotherofgoodhelp.org.

Hmong Pastoral Care Coordinator—PASHING LO, Mary Mother of Good Help Parish, 2221 B Grand Ave., Wausau, 54403. Email: fral@marymotherofgoodhelp.org.

Office for Catholic Schools—MR. THOMAS REICHENBACHER, Supt., Tel: 608-788-7707; Fax: 608-788-7709; Email: treichenbacher@diolc.org; JESSICA WILLIAMS, Asst. Supt., Email: jwilliams@diolc.org; Web: diolc.org/schools.

Office for Communications and Public Relations—JACK FELSHEIM, Tel: 608-791-2657; Email: jfelsheim@diolc.org.

Diocesan Magazine "Catholic Life"—Tel: 608-788-1524; Email: catholiclife@diolc.org; Web: catholiclife.diolc.org. Most Rev. WILLIAM PATRICK CALLAHAN, Publisher.

Office for Consecrated Life—Sr. DONNA KRZMARZICK, I.S.S.M., Dir., Tel: 608-791-2690; Email: dkrzmarzick@diolc.org; Web: diolc.org/consecratedlife.

Office for Diocesan Buildings and Grounds—KATHY HAVERLAND, Contact Person, Tel: 608-791-2692; Email: khaverland@diolc.org; Web: diolc.org/buildings.

Office for Ecumenism—Very Rev. SAMUEL A. MARTIN, Diocesan Officer, Ecumenical Questions, Tel: 715-384-3252.

Office for Marriage & Family Life—ALICE HEINZEN, Dir., Mailing Address: P.O. Box 4004, La Crosse, 54602-4004. Tel: 608-791-2673; Email: familylife@diolc.org; Web: diolc.org/marriage.

Natural Family Planning Program—ALICE HEINZEN, Dir., 711 24th St. N.E., Menomonie, 54751. Tel: 715-235-6226; Email: nfp@diolc.org; Web: diolc.org/marriage/natural-family-planning; DAN KITZHABER, Asst. Dir., Email: dkitzhaber@diolc.org; JEFF ARROWOOD, Educator, Email: arrowood@catholicexchange.com.

Office for Ministries and Social Concerns—MR. CHRISTOPHER J. RUFF, Dir., Tel: 608-791-0161; Email: ministries@diolc.org; Web: diolc.org/ministries; Web: diolc.org/social-concerns; Web: diolc.org/social-concerns/respect-life.

Office for Sacred Worship—MR. CHRISTOPHER J. CARSTENS, Dir., Tel: 608-791-2674; Email: ccarstens@diolc.org; Web: diolc.org/sacredworship.

Office for Safe Environment—Rev. Msgr. DAVID C. KUNZ, Tel: 608-791-2679; Fax: 608-791-0165; Email: safeenvironment@diolc.org; Web: diolc.org/safe-environment.

Office for Temporalities—MR. KURT JERECZEK, Contact Person, Tel: 608-791-2668; Fax: 608-787-9802; Web: diolc.org/temporalities.

Office for Vocations—Rev. ALAN P. WIERZBA, Dir., Tel: 608-791-2667; Fax: 608-791-0165; Email: vocations@diolc.org; Web: diolc.org/priesthood.

Mater Redemptoris House of Formation—Sr. M. CONSOLATA CREWS, F.S.G.M., Dir., Tel: 608-788-4530; Email: materredemptoris@gmail.com; Web: materredemptoris.blogspot.com. Provides a home to help form women in the process of discerning religious life.

Office for Youth & Young Adult Ministry—CHRISTOPHER J. ROGERS, Dir., Tel: 608-791-2652; Email: crogers@diolc.org.

St. Joseph's Priest Fund, Inc., (Benevolent Society)—Rev. BRIAN J. JAZDZEWSKI, Pres.; Rev. Msgr. MICHAEL J. GORMAN, V.G., J.C.L., Exec. Sec., Tel: 608-791-2655.

Vicar for Clergy—Rev. Msgr. DAVID C. KUNZ, Tel: 608-791-2679; Fax: 608-791-0165. Handles all matters regarding suitability letters for priests and deacons.

Vicar for Senior Priests—Rev. BRIAN D. KONOPA, Mary, Mother of the Church, 2006 Weston St., La Crosse, 54601. Tel: 608-788-5483.

Victim Assistance Coordinator—Deacon DAVID J. ALLEN, Blessed Sacrament Parish, 130 Losey Blvd. S., La Crosse, 54601. Tel: 608-792-9684.

CLERGY, PARISHES, MISSIONS AND PAROCHIAL SCHOOLS

CITY OF LA CROSSE

(LA CROSSE COUNTY)

1—ST. JOSEPH THE WORKMAN CATHEDRAL (1860) [CEM 2]
530 Main St., 54601. Tel: 608-782-0322; Email: office@cathedralsjworkman.org; Web: www.cathedralsjworkman.org. Rev. Msgr. Charles D. Stoetzel, Rector; Deacons Joseph A. Richards; Thomas H. Skemp.
See Aquinas Catholic Schools, LaCrosse under Unified Catholic School Systems located in the Institution section.
Catechesis Religious Program—Tel: 608-782-2953; Fax: 608-785-1064. Students 17.

2—BLESSED SACRAMENT (1937) [CEM 2]
130 Losey Blvd. S., 54601. Tel: 608-782-2953; Email: office@bsplacrosse.org; Web: bsplacrosse.org. Rev. Peter Mariasamy; Deacon David J. Allen.
See Aquinas Catholic Schools, LaCrosse under Unified Catholic School Systems located in the Institution section.

3—HOLY CROSS, Closed. For inquiries for parish records contact the Diocesan Archive, P.O. Box 4004, La Crosse, WI 54602-4004 Tel: 608-788-7700.

4—HOLY TRINITY (1887) [JC]
1333 13th St. S., 54601. Tel: 608-782-2028; Email: htparish@outlook.com; Web: www.parishesonline.com/find/holy-trinity-church-54601. Rev. G. Richard Roberts.
Catechesis Religious Program—Email: holytrinityreled@charter.net. Students 68.

5—ST. JAMES THE LESS (1886)
1032 Caledonia St., 54603. Tel: 608-782-7557; Email: saintjameslacrosse@gmail.com; Web: www.saintjameslax.com. Very Rev. James F. Altman; Deacon Jason C. Hutzler. Extraordinary and Forms of the Mass.
Catechesis Religious Program—Students 36.

6—ST. JOHN THE BAPTIST, Closed. For inquiries for parish records contact Diocesan Archives, P.O. Box 4004, La Crosse, WI 54602-4004 Tel: 608-788-7700.

7—ST. MARY, Closed. For inquiries for parish records contact The Diocesan Archives, P.O. Box 4004, La Crosse, WI 54602-4004 Tel: 608-788-7700.

8—MARY, MOTHER OF THE CHURCH (2000)
2006 Weston St., 54601. Tel: 608-788-5483; Fax: 608-519-1792; Email: secretary@mmoclacrosse.org; Web: www.mmoclacrosse.org. Rev. Brian D. Konopa; Deacon Richard R. Sage.
See Aquinas Catholic Schools, LaCrosse under Unified Catholic School Systems located in the Institution section.
Catechesis Religious Program—Therese Van Oss, D.R.E.

9—ST. PIUS X, Closed. For inquiries for parish records contact Mary, Mother of the Church, 2006 Weston St., La Crosse, WI 54601 Tel: 608-788-5483.

10—RONCALLI NEWMAN PARISH aka Roncalli Newman Center (1976)
1732 State St., 54601. Tel: 608-784-4994; Email: roncalli@roncallinewmancenter.org; Web: www.roncallinewmancenter.com. Rev. Billy J. Dodge; Deacon David J. Belland. Serving Univ. of Wisconsin-La Crosse and Western Technical College.

11—ST. THOMAS MORE, Closed. For inquiries for parish records contact Mary, Mother of the Church, 2006 Weston St., La Crosse, WI 54601. Tel: 608-788-5483.

12—ST. WENCESLAUS, Closed. For inquiries for parish records contact The Diocesan Archives, P.O. Box 4004, La Crosse, WI 54602-4004 Tel: 608-788-7700.

OUTSIDE THE CITY OF LA CROSSE

ABBOTSFORD, CLARK CO., ST. BERNARD (1904) [JC]
400 N. 2nd Ave., Abbotsford, 54401.
Tel: 715-223-4026; Email: ellie@abbydore.org. Rev. Timothy L. Oudenhoven. Also serves St. Louis, Dorchester.
Catechesis Religious Program—Students 177.

ADAMS, ADAMS CO., ST. JOSEPH (1884) [CEM]
807 W. Lake St., Friendship, 53934. 166 N. Main St., P.O. Box 310, Adams, 53910. Rev. Francis Xavier Dias; Deacon David L. Kennedy.
Catechesis Religious Program—Students 81.

ALMA, BUFFALO CO., ST. LAWRENCE (1867)
206 S 2nd St, P.O. Box 246, Alma, 54610.
Tel: 608-687-8418; Email: tresecclesiae@gmail.com; Web: tresecclesiae.org. Rev. Prince Amala Jesuraja; Deacon Edward D. Wendt. Serves Immaculate Conception, Fountain City and St. Boniface, Waumandee.

ALMA CENTER, JACKSON CO., IMMACULATE CONCEPTION (1882) [CEM]
Mailing Address: 341 W. Main St., P.O. Box 188, Alma Center, 54611. Tel: 715-964-5201; Email: icjosephjohn@hotmail.com. Rev. Daniel L. Thelen, Parochial Admin. Serves St. John Cantius, Fairchild; St. Joseph, Fairview.

ALMOND, PORTAGE CO., HOLY GUARDIAN ANGELS, Closed. For inquiries for parish records contact St. Maximilian Maria Kolbe, Southeastern Portage County.

ALTDORF, WOOD CO., ST. JOSEPH, Closed. For inquiries for parish records contact St. Joachim, Pittsville.

ALTOONA, EAU CLAIRE CO., ST. MARY (1902) [JC]
1812 Lynn Ave., Altoona, 54720. Tel: 715-855-1294; Email: stmarypar@gmail.com; Web: www.stmarys-altoona.com. Revs. Derek J. Sakowski; Daniel J. Sedlacek. Also serves St. Raymond of Penafort in Fall Creek.
See Regis Catholic Schools, Eau Claire under Unified Catholic School Systems located in the Institution section.
Catechesis Religious Program—Tel: 715-855-1294. Mary Kneer, D.R.E. Students 280.

AMHERST, PORTAGE CO., ST. JAMES (1905) [CEM]
453 S. Main, P.O. Box 280, Amherst, 54406-0280.
Tel: 715-824-3455; Email: catholiccentral54406@gmail.com; Web: sjsmmcc.

weconnect.com. Very Rev. Daniel H. Hackel. Also serves St. Mary of Mount Carmel, Fancher.
Catechesis Religious Program—Email: sjsmdre.plc@gmail.com. Students 23.
ARCADIA, TREMPEALEAU CO.
1—HOLY FAMILY (2000) [CEM]
223 E. Maple St., Arcadia, 54612. Tel: 608-323-7116; Fax: 608-323-8346; Email: secretary@holyfam.com; Web: www.holyfam.com. Very Rev. Sebastian J. Kolodziejczyk; Rev. Kyle N. Laylan. Also serves Sacred Heart, Pine Creek (Dodge)
School—Holy Family Catholic School, (Grades PreK-8), 532 Mc Kinley St., Arcadia, 54612.
Tel: 608-323-3676; Fax: 608-323-7386; Email: nimichalak@holyfam.com. Nikki Michalek, Prin. Clergy 1; Lay Teachers 11; Students 146.
Catechesis Religious Program—Students 112.
2—OUR LADY OF PERPETUAL HELP, Closed. For inquiries for parish records contact Holy Family, Arcadia.
3—ST. STANISLAUS, Closed. For inquiries for parish records contact Holy Family, Arcadia.
ARKANSAW, PEPIN CO., ST. JOSEPH (1913) [CEM 2]
W7805 County Rd. Z, Arkansaw, 54721.
Tel: 715-647-2901; Email: saintjoseph@nelson-tel.net. Rev. Joseph Okine-Quartey. Also serves St. John the Baptist, Plum City.
ARPIN, WOOD CO., ST. FRANCIS, Closed. For inquiries for parish records contact St. James, Vesper.
ATHENS, MARATHON CO., ST. ANTHONY DE PADUA (1881) [JC]
417 Caroline St., P.O. Box 206, Athens, 54411.
Tel: 715-257-7684; Email: tricia.rogaczewski@staathens.org. Rev. George Nelson Graham.
School—St. Anthony de Padua School, (Grades K-8), Tel: 715-257-7541. Luke Knoedler, Prin. Lay Teachers 7; Students 54.
AUBURNDALE, WOOD CO., NATIVITY OF THE BLESSED VIRGIN MARY (1886) [CEM 2]
5866 Main St., P.O. Box 177, Auburndale, 54412-0177. Tel: 715-652-2806; Email: saintsmmk@gmail.com; Web: www.saintsmmk.com. Rev. A. Antony Arokiyam. Also serves St. Kilian, Blenker; St. Michael, Hewitt
Catechesis Religious Program—Sherrie Weber, D.R.E. Students 101.
AUGUSTA, EAU CLAIRE CO., ST. ANTHONY DE PADUA, Closed. For inquiries for Parish Records contact St. Raymond of Penafort, Southern Eau Claire County.
BABCOCK, WOOD CO., ALL SAINTS, Closed. For inquiries for Parish Records contact Saint Joachim, Pittsville.
BAKERVILLE, WOOD CO., CORPUS CHRISTI 1873 Attended by
10075 County Hwy. BB, Marshfield, 54449.
Tel: 715-384-3213; Email: SacredHeartMarshfield@gmail.com; Web: sacredheartmarshfield.org. 112 E 11th St., Marshfield, 54449. Rev. Keith J. Kitzhaber; Deacon Raymond R. Draeger. Also serves Sacred Heart, Marshfield.
See Columbus Catholic Schools, Marshfield under Unified Catholic School Systems located in the Institution section.
BANGOR, LA CROSSE CO., ST. MARY (1899) [CEM] Attended by
Mailing Address: 210 Hamlin St W, West Salem, 54669-1139. Tel: 608-786-0610; Email: stleomaryoffice@gmail.com; Web: www.westsalembangorcatholic.org. 303 16th Ave S, Bangor, 54614. Rev. Raja Arul Samy; Deacon Robert J. Zietlow. Also serves St. Leo the Great, West Salem.
BEAR VALLEY, RICHLAND CO., ST. KILIAN, Closed. For inquiries for parish records contact Nativity, B.V.M., Keyesville.
BEVENT, MARATHON CO., ST. LADISLAUS (1886) [CEM] Attended by
173141 State Hwy. 153, Hatley, 54440.
Tel: 715-446-3060; Fax: 715-446-2668; Email: parishsecretary@stladislaus.org; Web: stladislaus.weebly.com. Rev. Augustine Kofi Bentil; Sr. Mary Ellen Diermeier, S.S.J.-T.O.S.F., Pastoral Assoc.; Deacon David L. Ashenbrenner. Also serves St. Joseph, Galloway.
BIG RIVER, PIERCE CO., NATIVITY OF THE BLESSED VIRGIN MARY (1872) [CEM 2]
W10137 570th Ave., River Falls, 54022.
Tel: 715-425-5806; Email: stmarys@dishup.us; Web: www.stmarysbigriver.com. Very Rev. Kevin C. Louis, S.T.L.; Deacon Daniel A. Gannon.
Catechesis Religious Program—Cynthia Beurskens, D.R.E. Students 78.
BLACK RIVER FALLS, JACKSON CO.
1—GUARDIAN ANGELS (1857) [CEM 2]
507 Main St., Black River Falls, 54615-1647.
Tel: 715-284-5613; Email: parishoffice@guardianangelscathparish.org; Web: www.guardianangelscathparish.org. Rev. Emmanuel Famiyeh. Founded in 2017, the merger of St. Joseph in Black River Falls (1857) and St. Kevin in Melrose (1963).
Legal Titles: St. Joseph; St. Kevin
Catechesis Religious Program—Students 79.
2—ST. JOSEPH, Merged with St. Kevin, Melrose to form Guardian Angels, Black River Falls.
BLAIR, TREMPEALEAU CO., ST. ANSGAR (1961) Attended by
Mailing Address: 22650 Washington St., Ettrick, 54627. Tel: 608-525-3811; Email: stbridgets@centurytel.net. 607 E Olson St, Blair, 54616. Rev. Amalraj Antony, Parochial Admin. Also serves St. Bridget, Ettrick
Catechesis Religious Program—Rev. Delrose Patzner-Hansen, C.R.E. Students 15.
BLENKER, WOOD CO., ST. KILIAN (1882) [CEM] Attended by
Mailing Address: 3872 County Rd. P, P.O. Box 125, Blenker, 54415. Tel: 715-652-2806; Email: saintsmmk@gmail.com; Web: www.saintsmmk.com. Rev. A. Antony Arokiyam. Also serves Nativity of the BVM, Auburndale and St. Michael, Hewitt.
Catechesis Religious Program—Joyce Martin, C.R.E. Students 85.
BLOOMER, CHIPPEWA CO., ST. PAUL (1902) [CEM 3]
1222 Main St., Bloomer, 54724. Tel: 715-568-3255; Email: stpaulreoffice@bloomer.net; Web: stpauls.bloomertel.net. Rev. Victor C. Feltes; Deacon Richard J. Kostner.
School—St. Paul School, (Grades PreK-8), 1210 Main St., Bloomer, 54724. Tel: 715-568-3233; Fax: 715-568-3244; Email: stpaulad@bloomer.net. Jacqueline Peterson, Prin. Lay Teachers 14; Students 112.
Catechesis Religious Program—Tel: 715-568-3256. Kelly Barrick, C.R.E. Students 133.
BOYCEVILLE, DUNN CO., ST. LUKE (1964) [JC] Attended by
919 Center St., P.O. Box 316, Boyceville, 54725.
Tel: 715-643-3081; Email: stlukebv@yahoo.com; Web: www.saintlukebv.org. Rev. Arockia Stanislaus. Also serves Sacred Heart, Elmwood; Sacred Heart of Jesus, Spring Valley.
Catechesis Religious Program—Lori Boesl, D.R.E. Students 11.
BOYD, CHIPPEWA CO., SACRED HEART OF JESUS-ST. JOSEPH (1996) [CEM 2] Merged with St. Rose of Lima, Cadott & Holy Family, Stanley in 2013 to form All Saints, Stanley. Parish suppressed. For parish sacramental records contact All Saints, Stanley.
BRACKETT, EAU CLAIRE CO., HOLY GUARDIAN ANGELS, Closed. For inquiries for Parish Records contact St. Raymond of Penafort, Southern Eau Claire County.
BROOKS, ADAMS CO., ST. ANN 1912 [CEM] Closed. St. Ann Parish suppressed July 1, 2016 and St. Ann Oratory established. Effective on that same date the civil corporation known as St. Ann Parish was dissolved and St. Ann Oratory Trust established. Sacramental records are kept at St. Joseph Parish, Adams.
BUENA VISTA, PORTAGE CO., ST. MARTIN, Closed. For inquiries for parish records contact St. Maximilian Maria Kolbe, Southeastern Portage County.
CADOTT, CHIPPEWA CO., ST. ROSE OF LIMA, [CEM] Merged with Holy Family, Stanley & Sacred Heart of Jesus-St. Joseph, Boyd in 2013 to form All Saints, Stanley. Parish suppressed. For sacramental records contact All Saints, Stanley.
CAMP DOUGLAS, JUNEAU CO., ST. JAMES (1857) [CEM]
100 Bartell St., P.O. Box 199, Camp Douglas, 54618.
Tel: 608-427-6762; Fax: 608-427-6438; Email: stjames@mwt.net; Web: www.mjpcatholic.com. Rev. Robert M. Letona. Also serves St. Michael, Indian Creek and St. Paul, New Lisbon.
CASHTON, MONROE CO., SACRED HEART OF JESUS (1918) [CEM 3]
1205 Front St., Cashton, 54619. Tel: 608-654-5654; Email: smash3psecretary@mwt.net; Email: smash3ppastor@mwt.net; Web: www.smash3p.org. Rev. Michael E. Klos; Deacon Samuel G. Schmirler. Also serves St. Augustine, Norwalk; Nativity of the Blessed Virgin Mary, St. Mary's Ridge.
School—Sacred Heart of Jesus School, (Grades PreK-8), 710 Kenyon St., Cashton, 54619.
Tel: 608-654-7733; Fax: 608-654-5760; Email: smash3pschool@mwt.net. Jayme Klinge, Head Teacher. Lay Teachers 5; Students 45; Clergy / Religious Teachers 1.
CASSEL, MARATHON CO., SACRED HEART 1886 [CEM] Also serves St. Patrick, Halder.
222761 County Rd. S., Marathon, 54448.
Tel: 715-443-3675; Email: sacredheartcassel@gmail.com. Rev. Felix Tigoy.
CASTLE ROCK LAKE, JUNEAU CO.
CAZENOVIA, RICHLAND CO., ST. ANTHONY DE PADUA (1857) [CEM] [JC] Also serves Sacred Heart, Lone Rock and St. Mary, Keyesville.
32505 County Hwy. V, Cazenovia, 53924.
Tel: 608-983-2367; Email: bulletintriparish@gmail.com. Rev. Irudayanathan Thainase, O.F.M.Cap.
CHILI, CLARK CO., ST. STEPHEN, Closed. For inquiries for Parish Records contact Archives, P.O. Box 4004, La Crosse, WI 54602-4004.
CHIPPEWA FALLS, CHIPPEWA CO.
1—ST. CHARLES BORROMEO (1884) [JC] Also serves St. Peter, Tilden.
810 Pearl St., Chippewa Falls, 54729.
Tel: 715-723-4088; Email: StChrls723@gmail.com; Web: www.stcharles-cf.com. Rev. Msgr. Michael J. Gorman, V.G., J.C.L.; Rev. Mark A. Miller; Deacon Daniel J. Rider.
See McDonell Area Catholic Schools, Chippewa Falls under Unified Catholic School Systems located in the Institution section.
Catechesis Religious Program—Greg Gilbertson, D.R.E. Students 72.
2—HOLY GHOST (1886) [JC] Also serves St. Bridget, Springfield.
412 S. Main St., Chippewa Falls, 54729.
Tel: 715-723-4890; Fax: 715-723-7358; Email: holyghostsecretary@gmail.com; Web: holyghostchurchcf.com. Rev. Justin J. Kizewski.
See McDonell Area Catholic Schools, Chippewa Falls under Unified Catholic School Systems located in the Institution section.
Catechesis Religious Program—Paula Hanson, C.R.E. Students 119.
3—NOTRE DAME (1856) [JC]
117 Allen St., Chippewa Falls, 54729-2899.
Tel: 715-723-7108; Fax: 715-723-7523; Email: parishoffice@thechurchofnotredame.org; Web: www.thechurchofnotredame.org. Rev. Jesse D. Burish.
See McDonell Area Catholic Schools, Chippewa Falls under Unified Catholic School Systems located in the Institution section.
Catechesis Religious Program—Email: religioused@thechurchofnotredame.org. Angela Katz, D.R.E. Students 61.
COLBY, CLARK CO., ST. MARY HELP OF CHRISTIANS (1877) [CEM]
205 S. 2nd St., P.O. Box 436, Colby, 54421.
Tel: 715-223-3048; Email: catholiccentral@gmail.com; Web: centraloffice.weconnect.com. Rev. D. Joseph Redfern; Deacon Michael J. Schaefer.
School—St. Mary Help of Christians School, (Grades PreK-8), Tel: 715-223-3033. Nancy Zygarlicke, Prin. Lay Teachers 10; Students 100.
Catechesis Religious Program—
Tel: 715-223-3048, Ext. 4. Jenessa Freidhof, Contact Person. Students 104.
COOKS VALLEY, CHIPPEWA CO., ST. JOHN THE BAPTIST (1884) [CEM]
Mailing Address: 4540 State Hwy. 40, Bloomer, 54724. Tel: 715-568-3778; Email: stjohns@bloomer.net; Web: stjohns.bloomertel.net. Rev. Victor C. Feltes. Also serves St. Paul, Bloomer.
COON VALLEY, VERNON CO., ST. MARY 1910 [CEM]
904 Central Ave., Coon Valley, 54623.
Tel: 608-452-3841; Email: stmaryscv@mwt.net; Web: www.stmarycv.org. Rev. Matthew N. Marshall.
Catechesis Religious Program—Jodie Holdorf, D.R.E. Students 27.
CORNELL, CHIPPEWA CO., HOLY CROSS (1915) [CEM 2]
107 8th St., P.O. Box 68, Cornell, 54732.
Tel: 715-239-6826; Email: holycross107@centurytel.net. Rev. Eric G. Linzmaier; Deacon Dennis Rivers. Also serves: St. Anthony, Drywood; Sacred Heart, Jim Falls
Catechesis Religious Program—Tel: 715-239-2123; Email: riversdennis3@gmail.com. Betty Rivers, D.R.E. Students 69.
CUSTER, PORTAGE CO., IMMACULATE CONCEPTION (1875) [CEM] Also serves Sacred Heart, Polonia
7176 Esker Rd., Custer, 54423. Tel: 715-592-4330; Email: stmary@wi-net.com; Web: www.stmaryscuster.com. Rev. Gregory A. Michaud.
CZESTOCHOWA, CLARK CO., ST. MARY OF CZESTOCHOWA, Closed. For inquiries for parish records contact Diocesan Archives, P.O. Box 4004, La Crosse, WI 54602-4004, Tel. (608) 788-7700.
DE SOTO, CRAWFORD CO., SACRED HEART, Closed. For inquiries for parish records contact St. Charles Borromeo, Genoa.
DILLY, VERNON CO., ST. JOHN NEPOMUCENE, Closed. For inquiries for parish records contact Diocesan Archives, P.O. Box 4004, La Crosse, WI 54602-4004 Tel: 608-788-7700.
DORCHESTER, CLARK CO., ST. LOUIS (1878) [JC]
133 N 3rd St., Dorchester, 54425. Tel: 715-223-4026; Email: ellie@abbydore.org. 400 N 2nd Ave., Abbotsford, 54405. Rev. Timothy L. Oudenhoven. Also serves St. Bernard of Abbotsford.
Catechesis Religious Program—Tel: 715-654-5467. Students 45.
DRYWOOD, CHIPPEWA CO., ST. ANTHONY (1886) [CEM] Attended by
13981 250th St, Cadott, 54729. Tel: 715-382-4422; Tel: 715-239-6826; Email: sacredheartparishjimfalls@yahoo.com. Mailing Address: 13989 195th St., P.O. Box 68, Jim Falls, 54748. Rev. Eric G. Linzmaier; Deacon Dennis Riv-

ers. Also serves Holy Cross, Cornell and Sacred Heart, Jim Falls.

DURAND, PEPIN CO., ST. MARY'S ASSUMPTION (1860) [CEM]
911 W. Prospect St., P.O. Box 188, Durand, 54736.
Tel: 715-672-5640; Fax: 715-672-4193; Email: sanns@nelson-tel.net; Web: catholictriparish.org. Rev. Paul Bosco Anthony; Deacons James A. Weingart; Robert J. Hansen, St. Mary's Assumption, Durand; Holy Rosary, Lima; Sacred Heart, Mondovi; Prefect for Perm. Deacon Life and Ministry.
School—St. Mary's Assumption School, (Grades 4-8), 901 W. Prospect St., Durand, 54736.
Tel: 715-672-5617; Fax: 715-672-3931; Email: assumption4-8@nelson-tel.net. Mary Lansing, Prin. Lay Teachers 10; Students 84.
Catechesis Religious Program—Tel: 715-672-4668; Email: triparishre@nelson-tel.net. Linda Schaub, D.R.E. Students 152.

EASTMAN, CRAWFORD CO., ST. WENCESLAUS (1883) [CEM] Also serves Sacred Heart of Jesus, Wauzeka.
28075 State Hwy. 27, P.O. Box 109, Eastman, 54626.
Tel: 608-874-4151; Email: stwenceslaus@centurytel.net. Rev. Anandan Rajendran.
Catechesis Religious Program—Tel: 608-874-4221. Barbara Martin, D.R.E. Students 64.

EAU CLAIRE, EAU CLAIRE CO.

1—IMMACULATE CONCEPTION (1945)
1712 Highland Ave., Eau Claire, 54701.
Tel: 715-835-9935; Email: immaculateconceptionec@gmail.com; Web: www.ic-ec.us. Rev. Francis Thadathil; Deacon Gregory J. Power.
See Regis Catholic Schools, Eau Claire under Unified Catholic School Systems located in the Institution section.
Catechesis Religious Program—Tel: 715-835-7721; Fax: 715-830-9846. Linda Corey, D.R.E.; Barb Brandner, D.R.E. Students 269.

2—ST. JAMES THE GREATER (1948) [JC]
2502 11th St. Ste. 1, Eau Claire, 54703.
Tel: 715-835-5887; Email: stjameseac@aol.com; Web: stjameseauclaire.org. Rev. Thomas J. Krieg.
See Regis Catholic Schools, Eau Claire under Unified Catholic School Systems located in the Institution section.
Catechesis Religious Program—
Tel: 715-835-5887, Ext. 120; Email: beaudrie.kelly@gmail.com. Kelly Beaudrie, C.R.E. Students 164.

3—NEWMAN COMMUNITY (1969) [JC]
110 Garfield Ave., Eau Claire, 54701-4042.
Tel: 715-834-3399; Email: parishoffice@newmanec.com; Web: newmanec.com. Rev. Daniel E. Oudenhoven.
Catechesis Religious Program—Savannah Siegler, D.R.E. Students 69.

4—ST. OLAF 1952 [JC]
3220 Monroe St., P.O. Box 1203, Eau Claire, 54702.
Tel: 715-832-2504; Fax: 715-832-0742; Email: solaf@saintolafparish.org; Web: www.saintolafparish.org. Rev. James J. Kurzynski.
See Regis Catholic Schools, Eau Claire under Unified Catholic School Systems located in the Institution section.
Catechesis Religious Program—Kathy Pichler. Students 153.

5—ST. PATRICK, Merged with Sacred Heart of Jesus, Eau Claire to form Sacred Heart of Jesus-St. Patrick, Eau Claire. For inquiries for parish records contact Sacred Heart of Jesus-St. Patrick, Eau Claire.

6—SACRED HEART OF JESUS, Merged with St. Patrick, Eau Claire to form Sacred Heart of Jesus-St. Patrick, Eau Claire. For inquiries for parish records contact Sacred Heart of Jesus-St. Patrick, Eau Claire.

7—SACRED HEART OF JESUS-ST. PATRICK (1999) [CEM 2]
322 Fulton St., Eau Claire, 54703. Tel: 715-835-0925; Email: office@shspec.org; Web: www.shspec.org. Rev. Brian J. Jazdzewski. Founded in 1999, the merger of St. Patrick, Eau Claire (1865) and Sacred Heart of Jesus, Eau Claire (1875).
Res.: 416 N. Dewey St., Eau Claire, 54703.
See Regis Catholic Schools, Eau Claire under Unified Catholic School Systems located in the Institution section.
Sacred Heart Church—418 N. Dewey St., Eau Claire, 54703.
St. Patrick Church, 316 Fulton St., Eau Claire, 54703.

EAU GALLE, DUNN CO., ST. HENRY (1856) [CEM]
N460 County Rd. D, Eau Galle, 54737.
Tel: 715-283-4448; Email: sthenry@wwt.net. Rev. Jerome G. Hoeser.
Catechesis Religious Program—Tel: 715-283-4451. Rosemary Asher, C.R.E. Students 89.

EDGAR, MARATHON CO., ST. JOHN THE BAPTIST (1900) [CEM] (German—Polish) Also serves Holy Family, Poniatowski.
103 N. 4th Ave., P.O. Box 35, Edgar, 54426.
Tel: 715-352-3011; Email: parishadmin@stjohnedgar.org; Web: www.church.stjohnedgar.org. Rev. Thomas M. Huff; Deacon Gregory W. Kaiser.
School—St. John the Baptist School, (Grades PreK-8), 125 N. 4th Ave., P.O. Box 66, Edgar, 54426.
Tel: 715-352-3000; Email: secretary@stjohnedgar.org. Jeff Gulan, Prin.; Marie Stubbe, Sec. Clergy 2; Lay Teachers 8; Students 53.
Catechesis Religious Program—Nancy Hackel, C.R.E. Students 156.

ELK MOUND, DUNN CO., ST. JOSEPH (1959) [CEM]
417 W. Menominee St., P.O. Box 275, Elk Mound, 54739. Tel: 715-875-4539; Email: stjosephemwi@gmail.com. Rev. Joseph C. Nakwah. Also serves St. Joseph, Rock Falls.
Catechesis Religious Program—Sharon Biegel, D.R.E. Students 77.

ELLSWORTH, PIERCE CO., ST. FRANCIS OF ASSISI (1897) [CEM] [JC4]
264 S. Grant St., P.O. Box 839, Ellsworth, 54011.
Tel: 715-273-4774; Email: stfrancisrectory@sbcglobal.net; Web: www.stfrancisellsworth.com. Rev. Eric Aworte-Dadson, (Ghana).
School—St. Francis of Assisi School, (Grades PreK-5), 244 W. Woodworth St., P.O. Box 250, Ellsworth, 54011. Tel: 715-273-4391; Fax: 715-273-6374; Email: cbuckel@stfrancisellsworth.org. Charles Buckel, Prin. Lay Teachers 8; Students 85.
Catechesis Religious Program—Cell: 715-338-1199; Email: cfoley@dishup.us. Joan Foley, D.R.E. Students 208.

ELMWOOD, PIERCE CO., SACRED HEART (1913) [CEM]
106 W. Wilson Ave., Elmwood, 54740.
Tel: 715-778-5519; Email: admin@svecatholic.org; Web: www.svecatholic.org. S105 Sabin Ave., P.O. Box 456, Spring Valley, 54767. Rev. Arockia Stanislaus. Also serves St. Luke, Boyceville and Sacred Heart of Jesus, Spring Valley.
Res.: 114 W. Wilson Ave., Elmwood, 54740-8603.
Catechesis Religious Program—Marilyn Bowell, D.R.E. Students 55.

ELROY, JUNEAU CO., ST. PATRICK (1877) [CEM] Attended by
110 Spring St., Elroy, 53929. Tel: 608-462-5875; Email: stjosephkendall@centurytel.net. 307 Spring St., Box 155, Kendall, 54638. Rev. John Peter Anthonisamy Chinnappan. Also serves St. Joseph, Kendall and St. John the Baptist, Wilton.
Catechesis Religious Program—Diane Hansen, C.R.E. Students 39.

ETTRICK, TREMPEALEAU CO., ST. BRIDGET (1869) [CEM]
22650 Washington St., Ettrick, 54627.
Tel: 608-525-3811; Email: stbridgets@centurytel.net. Rev. Amalraj Antony. Also serves St. Ansgar, Blair.

FAIRCHILD, EAU CLAIRE CO.

1—ST. JOSEPH (1870) [CEM]
N13740 Fairview Rd., Fairchild, 54741.
Tel: 715-964-5201; Email: icjosephjohn@hotmail.com. 341 W. Main St., P.O. Box 188, Alma Center, 54611. Rev. Daniel L. Thelen, Parochial Admin. Also serves Immaculate Conception, Alma Center and St. John Cantius, Fairchild.

2—ST. JOHN CANTIUS 1887 [CEM] Attended by
306 2nd St., Fairchild, 54741. Tel: 715-964-5201; Email: icjosephjohn@hotmail.com. 341 W. Main St., P.O. Box 188, Alma Center, 54611. Rev. Daniel L. Thelen, Parochial Admin. Also serves Immaculate Conception, Alma Center; St. Joseph, Fairview.

FAIRVIEW.

FALL CREEK, EAU CLAIRE CO.

1—ST. JOHN THE APOSTLE, Closed. For inquiries for Parish Records contact St. Raymond of Penafort, Southern Eau Claire County.

2—ST. RAYMOND OF PENAFORT (1998) [CEM]
E10455 Mallard Rd., Fall Creek, 54742.
Tel: 715-877-3400; Email: straymondparish@gmail.com; Web: www.straymond.us. Revs. Derek J. Sakowski; Daniel J. Sedlacek. Also serves St. Mary, Altoona. Founded in 1998, the merger of St. Anthony, Augusta (1857), Holy Guardian Angels, Brackett (1903), St. John the Apostle, Fall Creek (1967).

FANCHER, PORTAGE CO., ST. MARY OF MOUNT CARMEL (1884) [CEM] Attended by
3995 County Rd. K, Amherst, 54406.
Tel: 715-824-3455; Email: catholiccentral54406@gmail.com; Web: sjsmmcc.weconnect.com. 453 S. Main St., P.O. Box 280, Amherst, 54406. Very Rev. Daniel H. Hackel. Also serves St. James, Amherst.
Catechesis Religious Program—Tel: 715-316-7056; Email: sjsmdre.plc@gmail.com. Students 76.

FOUNTAIN CITY, BUFFALO CO., IMMACULATE CONCEPTION (1857) [CEM] Also serves St. Lawrence, Alma and St. Boniface, Waumandee.
2 N Hill St, P.O. Box 218, Fountain City, 54629.
Tel: 608-687-8418; Email: tresecclesiae@gmail.com; Web: tresecclesiae.org. Rev. Prince Amala Jesuraja; Deacon Edward D. Wendt.

GALESVILLE, TREMPEALEAU CO., ST. MARY (1904) Attended by
20354 W. Ridge Ave., Galesville, 54630.
Tel: 608-534-6652; Email: stmarygalesville@triwest.net; Web: www.saintbartholomew.net. 11646 South St., Trempealeau, 54661. Rev. Antony Joseph, (India). Also serves St. Bartholomew, Trempealeau.
Catechesis Religious Program—Kent Jacobsen, C.R.E. Students 26.

GALLOWAY, MARATHON CO., ST. JOSEPH (1921) [CEM] Also serves St. Ladislaus, Bevent.
182590 County Rd. C, Wittenberg, 54499.
Tel: 715-454-6431; Email: stjosephchurchgalloway@gmail.com; Web: www.stjosephgalloway.com. Rev. Augustine Kofi Bentil; Sr. Mary Ellen Diermeier, S.S.J.-T.O.S.F., Pastoral Assoc.; Deacon David L. Ashenbrenner.
Catechesis Religious Program—Tel: 715-454-6432. Mary Uttecht, C.R.E. Students 50.

GAYS MILLS, CRAWFORD CO., ST. MARY (1908) [JC] Also serves St. Philip, Rolling Ground and St. Patrick, Seneca.
115 School St., Gays Mills, 54631. Tel: 608-735-4420; Email: stmary@mwt.net. Rev. Zacharie Beya-Tshingimba.
Catechesis Religious Program—Tel: 608-624-5633; Email: marscars@mwt.net. Marguerite Carstens, D.R.E. Students 2.

GENOA, VERNON CO., ST. CHARLES BORROMEO 1862 [CEM]
Mailing Address: 701 Walnut St., P.O. Box 130, Genoa, 54632. Tel: 608-689-2646; Fax: 608-689-2811; Email: stcharle@mwt.net; Web: www.mwt.net/~st.charl/. Rev. Nathaniel Kuhn.
School—St. Charles School, (Grades PreK-6), 707 Eagle St., P.O. Box 130, Genoa, 54632.
Tel: 608-689-2642; Fax: 608-689-2811; Email: stcharle@mwt.net. Patricia Hytry, Head Teacher. Lay Teachers 5; Students 32.
Catechesis Religious Program—Jayne Bellwahn, D.R.E. Students 34.

GREENWOOD, CLARK CO., ST. MARY HELP OF CHRISTIANS (1903) [CEM]
123 N. Main St., P.O. Box 129, Greenwood, 54437.
Tel: 715-255-8017; Email: stap1931@gmail.com; Web: stanthonyloyal.org. Rev. Leo Stanislaus. Also serves St. Anthony, Loyal and Holy Family, Willard.
School—St. Mary Help of Christians School, (Grades 1-6), 119 N. Main, P.O. Box 129, Greenwood, 54437.
Tel: 715-267-6477; Fax: 715-267-6477; Email: stmarys.gr.office@tds.net. Jeannine Raycher, Prin. Lay Teachers 3; Students 26.

HALDER, MARATHON CO., ST. PATRICK 1871 [CEM] Also serves Sacred Heart, Cassel.
136058 Halder Dr., Mosinee, 54455.
Tel: 715-693-2765; Email: stpats@mtc.net. Rev. Felix Tigoy.
Catechesis Religious Program—Jackie Martin, D.R.E. Students 45.

HATLEY, MARATHON CO., ST. FLORIAN (1885) [CEM]
500 Church Ln., P.O. Box 100, Hatley, 54440.
Tel: 715-446-3085; Email: officemanager@stflos.org; Web: www.stflos.org. Rev. Gregory J. Bohren. Also serves St. Agnes, Weston.

HEFFRON, PORTAGE CO., ST. JOHN THE BAPTIST, Closed. For inquiries for parish records contact St. Archiver, P.O. Box 4009, La Crosse WI 54602.

HEWITT, WOOD CO., ST. MICHAEL (1888) [JC]
11100 Main St., Hewitt, 54441. Tel: 715-652-2806; Email: saintsmmk@gmail.com; Web: www.saintsmmk.com. Rev. A. Antony Arokiyam. Also serves Nativity of the BVM, Auburndale and St. Kilian, Blenker.
Catechesis Religious Program—Angela Bloczynski, C.R.E. Students 48.

HILLSBORO, VERNON CO., ST. ALOYSIUS (1905) [JC]
545 Prairie Ave., P.O. Box 466, Hillsboro, 54634.
Tel: 608-489-2580; Email: saintals@mwt.net. Rev. Donald J. Bauer. Also serves St. Jerome, Wonewoc & Oratory of St. Teresa of Avila Oratory, Union Center.
Catechesis Religious Program—Tel: 608-489-3544. Students 57.

HOLMEN, LA CROSSE CO., ST. ELIZABETH ANN SETON (1983)
515 N. Main St., Holmen, 54636-9387.
Tel: 608-526-4424; Email: office@seasholmen.org. Rev. John L. Parr; Sr. Bridget Donaldson, O.S.B., Pastoral Assoc.
Res.: 704 Hillcrest Dr., Holmen, 54636-9745.
Catechesis Religious Program—Students 428.

INDEPENDENCE, TREMPEALEAU CO., SS. PETER AND PAUL (1875) [CEM]
36028 Osseo Rd., P.O. Box 430, Independence, 54747. Tel: 715-985-2227; Email: ssppchurch@ssppwi.org; Web: ssppwi.org. Very Rev. Woodrow H. Pace.
School—SS. Peter and Paul School, (Grades PreK-8), 36100 Osseo Rd., P.O. Box 430, Independence, 54747. Tel: 715-985-3719. Tresa Van Roo, Prin. Lay Teachers 8; Students 80.

INDIAN CREEK, MONROE CO., ST. MICHAEL (1869) [CEM]
18316 County Hwy. N., Tomah, 54660.

Tel: 608-427-6762; Email: stjames@mwt.net; Web: www.mjpcatholic.com. 100 Bartell St., P.O. Box 199, Camp Douglas, 54618. Rev. Robert M. Letona. Also serves St. Michael, Indian Creek and St. Paul, New Lisbon.
Res.: 408 W. River St., New Lisbon, 53950.
Catechesis Religious Program—Deb Granger, D.R.E. Students 23.

JIM FALLS, CHIPPEWA CO., SACRED HEART OF JESUS 1886
13989 195th St., P.O. Box 68, Jim Falls, 54748.
Tel: 715-382-4422 (Office); Email: sacredheartparishjimfalls@yahoo.com. Rev. Eric G. Linzmaier; Deacon Dennis Rivers. Also serves Holy Cross, Cornell and St. Anthony, Drywood.
Res.: 107 S. 8th St., P.O. Box 68, Cornell, 54732.

JUNCTION CITY, PORTAGE CO., ST. MICHAEL (1884) [CEM]
324 Main St., P.O. Box 128, Junction City, 54443.
Tel: 715-457-2314; Email: kmwparishes@tds.net. Rev. John Ofori-Domah; Deacon Richard Rozumalski. Also serves St. Bartholomew, Mill Creek and St. Wenceslaus, Milladore.
Catechesis Religious Program—Students 56.

KENDALL, MONROE CO., ST. JOSEPH (1883) [CEM] Also serves St. Patrick, Elroy, and St. John the Baptist, Wilton.
307 Spring St., P.O. Box 155, Kendall, 54638.
Tel: 608-463-7120; Email: stjosephkendall@centurytel.net. Rev. John Peter Anthonisamy Chinnappan.
Catechesis Religious Program—Diane Hansen, C.R.E. Students 13.

KEYESVILLE, RICHLAND CO., NATIVITY OF THE BLESSED VIRGIN MARY 1856 [CEM]
32605 Durst Ln., Richland Center, 53581.
Tel: 608-585-4846. Rev. Irudayanathan Thainase, O.F.M.Cap. Also serves St. Anthony de Padua, Çazenovia and Sacred Heart, Lone Rock.

KNOWLTON, MARATHON CO., ST. FRANCIS XAVIER (1853) [CEM] Also serves St. John the Baptist, Peplin.
150051 Mead Ln., Mosinee, 54455. Tel: 715-693-3120 ; Fax: 715-693-6291; Email: sfxknowl@mtc.net. Rev. James F. Trempe.

LANARK, PORTAGE CO., ST. PATRICK, Closed. For inquiries for parish records contact Archiver P.O. Box 4004 La Crosse, WI 54602.

LIMA, PEPIN CO., HOLY ROSARY 1886 [CEM]
N6235 County Rd. V., Box 188, Durand, 54736.
Tel: 715-672-5640; Fax: 715-672-4193; Email: sanns@nelson-tel.net; Web: www.catholictriparish.org. 911 W. Prospect St., P.O. Box 188, Durand, 54736. Rev. Paul Bosco Anthony; Deacons James A. Weingart; Robert J. Hansen. Also serves St. Mary's Assumption, Durand; Sacred Heart, Mondovi
School—Holy Rosary School, (Grades K-3),
Tel: 715-672-4276; Email: assumptionk-3@nelson-tel.net. Mary Lansing, Prin. Clergy 1; Lay Teachers 4; Students 47.
Catechesis Religious Program—Tel: 715-672-4668; Email: triparishre@nelson-tel.net. Linda Schaub, D.R.E. Students 57.

LONE ROCK, RICHLAND CO., SACRED HEART 1901
417 S. Oak St., Lone Rock, 53556. Tel: 608-983-2367; Email: grrottwi@gmail.com. 32505 County Hwy. V, Cazenovia, 53924. Rev. Irudayanathan Thainase, O.-F.M.Cap. Also serves St. Anthony, Cazenovia and Nativity of the BVM, Keyesville.

LOYAL, CLARK CO., ST. ANTHONY OF PADUA (1893) [CEM] Also serves St. Mary Help of Christians Church, Greenwood & Holy Family, Willard.
407 N. Division St., P.O. Box 69, Loyal, 54446-0069.
Tel: 715-255-8017; Email: stap1931@gmail.com; Web: www.stanthonyloyal.org. Rev. Leo Stanislaus.
School—St. Anthony of Padua School, (Grades K-6), 208 W. Spring St., Loyal, 54446. Tel: 715-255-8636; Fax: 715-255-8636. Barbara Kingsbury, Prin. Lay Teachers 4; Students 29.
Catechesis Religious Program—
Tel: 715-255-8636, Ext. 109. Margie Ouimette, D.R.E. Students 112.

LYNDON STATION, JUNEAU CO., ST. MARY 1851 [CEM]
117 Juneau St. N., P.O. Box 303, Lyndon Station, 53944. Tel: 608-666-2421; Email: stmaryparishlyndon@gmail.com; Web: stmaryparishlyndon.com. Rev. Clayton R. Elmhorst.
Catechesis Religious Program—Sandra Madland, C.R.E. Students 33.

MARATHON CITY, MARATHON CO., NATIVITY OF THE BLESSED VIRGIN MARY (1856) [CEM]
712 Market St., P.O. Box 7, Marathon, 54448.
Tel: 715-443-2045; Email: bvmparish@stmarysmarathon.org; Web: stmarysmarathon.weconnect.com. Rev. Msgr. Joseph G. Diermeier, V.G., J.C.L.; Deacons Bryan K. Hilts; John P. Bourke.
School—St. Mary's School, (Grades K-8), 716 Market St., P.O. Box 102, Marathon, 54448-0102.
Tel: 715-443-3430; Fax: 715-443-2989; Email: jkoch@stmarysmarathon.org. Joseph Koch, Prin. Lay Teachers 14; Students 174.
Catechesis Religious Program—Tel: 715-443-2433; Fax: 715-443-2575. Students 130.

MARSHFIELD, WOOD CO.
1—ST. JOHN THE BAPTIST (1877) [JC] Also serves Christ the King, Spencer.
201 W. Blodgett St., Marshfield, 54449.
Tel: 715-384-3252; Email: mjgouin@frontier.com; Web: www.stjohnsmarshfield.org. Very Rev. Samuel A. Martin; Rev. Barry P. Saylor; Deacon Jeffrey L. Austin.
See Columbus Catholic Schools, Marshfield under Unified Catholic School Systems located in the Institution section.
Catechesis Religious Program—Tel: 715-384-3919. Debra Mlsna, D.R.E. Students 155.

2—OUR LADY OF PEACE (1947) [JC]
1414 W. 5th St., Marshfield, 54449.
Tel: 715-384-9414; Email: office@olpmarshfield.com; Web: olpmarshfield.com. 510 S. Columbus Ave., Marshfield, 54449. Rev. Douglas C. Robertson.
See Columbus Catholic Schools, Marshfield under Unified Catholic School Systems located in the Institution section.
Catechesis Religious Program—Tel: 715-676-2549. Corinne Johnson, D.R.E. Students 217.

3—SACRED HEART OF JESUS (1916) [JC] Also serves Corpus Christi, Bakerville.
112 E. 11th St., Marshfield, 54449.
Tel: 715-384-3213; Email: SacredHeartMarshfield@gmail.com; Web: sacredheartmarshfield.org. Rev. Keith J. Kitzhaber; Deacon Raymond R. Draeger.
See Columbus Catholic Schools, Marshfield under Unified Catholic School Systems located in the Institution section.

MAUSTON, JUNEAU CO.
1—OUR LADY OF THE LAKE 1962 [CEM]
6865 Evergreen St., Mauston, 53948.
Tel: 608-565-2488; Email: stfrancisnecedah@tds.net; Web: stfrancisnecedah.org. 2001 S. Main St., Necedah, 54646. Rev. Wesley Janowski, C.R.; Deacon Glen J. Heinzl. Also serves St. Francis, Necedah.

2—ST. PATRICK (1901) [CEM 2]
401 Mansion St., Mauston, 53948. Tel: 608-847-6054; Email: stpatrickparishmauston@gmail.com; Web: www.stpatricksmauston.com. Very Rev. John A. Potaczek; Deacon Juan A. Delgado.
School—St. Patrick School, (Grades PreK-8), 325 Mansion St., Mauston, 53948. Tel: 608-847-5844; Fax: 608-847-4103; Email: frjohnpotaczek@stpatricksmauston.com. Lay Teachers 12; Students 133.
Catechesis Religious Program—Students 53.

MELROSE, JACKSON CO., ST. KEVIN 1963 [JC] Merged with St. Joseph, Black River Falls to form Guardian Angels, Black River Falls.

MENOMONIE, DUNN CO., ST. JOSEPH (1861) [CEM]
910 Wilson Ave., Menomonie, 54751.
Tel: 715-232-4922; Email: mary.allison@menomoniecatholic.org; Web: www.menomoniecatholic.org. Rev. John Muthu Vijayan.
School—St. Joseph School, (Grades PreK-6),
Tel: 715-232-4920; Email: keila.drout@menomoniecatholic.org. Mrs. Keila Drout, Prin. Lay Teachers 14; Students 126.
Catechesis Religious Program—Emily Revak, D.R.E.; Pam Sirinek, Youth Min. Students 205.

MIDDLE RIDGE, LA CROSSE CO., ST. PETER (1869) [CEM]
W695 State Rd. 33, Rockland, 54653.
Tel: 608-486-2180; Email: stpetersrectory@centurytel.net; Web: www.saintpetersparish.net. Rev. Timothy J. Welles. Also serves St. Joseph Parish in St. Joseph's Ridge.

MILAN, MARATHON CO., ST. THOMAS (1913) [CEM] Also serves St. Anthony, Athens.
5363 Vilas St., Milan, 54411. Tel: 715-257-7684; Email: tricia.stanthonyathens@gmail.com; Web: www.stanthonyathens.com. Mailing Address: 417 Caroline St., P.O. Box 206, Athens, 54411. Rev. George Nelson Graham.

MILL CREEK, PORTAGE CO., ST. BARTHOLOMEW 1883 [CEM] Also serves St. Michael, Junction City and St. Wenceslaus, Milladore.
2493 County Rd. M, Stevens Point, 54481.
Tel: 715-457-2314; Email: kmwparishes@tds.net. 146 Main St., Milladore, 54454. Rev. John Ofori-Domah; Deacon Richard Rozumalski.

MILLADORE, WOOD CO., ST. WENCESLAUS (1883) [CEM] Also serves St. Bartholomew, Mill Creek, and St. Michael, Junction City.
146 Main St., Milladore, 54454. Tel: 715-457-2314; Email: kmwparishes@tds.net. Rev. John Ofori-Domah; Deacon Richard Rozumalski.
Catechesis Religious Program—Students 59.

MONDOVI, BUFFALO CO., SACRED HEART OF JESUS (1896) [JC]
453 W. Hudson St., Mondovi, 54755.
Tel: 715-672-5640; Fax: 715-672-4193; Email: sanns@nelson-tel.net; Web: www.catholictriparish.org. 911 W. Prospect St., P.O. Box 188, Durand, 54736. Rev. Paul Bosco Anthony; Deacons James A. Weingart; Robert J. Hansen. Also serves St. Mary's Assumption, Durand; Holy Rosary, Lima
Catechesis Religious Program—Tel: 715-672-4668; Email: triparishre@nelson-tel.net. Linda Schaub, D.R.E. Students 123.

MOSINEE, MARATHON CO., ST. PAUL (1878) [CEM]
603 4th St., Mosinee, 54455. Tel: 715-693-2650; Email: parish@stpaulmosinee.org; Web: www.stpaulmosinee.org. Very Rev. Donald L. Meuret; Deacon Kevin J. Breit.
School—St. Paul School, (Grades PreK-8), 404 High St., Mosinee, 54455. Tel: 715-693-2675;
Fax: 715-693-1332; Email: school@stpaulmosinee.org. Lay Teachers 4; Students 27.
Catechesis Religious Program—Tel: 715-693-4030. JoAnn Sondelski, D.R.E. Students 220.

NECEDAH, JUNEAU CO., ST. FRANCIS OF ASSISI (1876) [CEM]
2001 S. Main St., Necedah, 54646. Tel: 608-565-2488 ; Email: stfrancisnecedah@tds.net; Web: www.saintfrancisnecedah.org. Rev. Wesley Janowski; Deacon Glen J. Heinzl. Offering ordinary and extraordinary forms of the Mass. Also serves Our Lady of the Lake, Castle Rock Lake.
Catechesis Religious Program—Kristen Taubel, D.R.E. Students 120.

NEILLSVILLE, CLARK CO., ST. MARY (1878) [CEM]
1813 Black River Rd., Neillsville, 54456.
Tel: 715-743-3840; Email: stmaryneillsville@tds.net; Web: stmaryneillsville.weebly.com. Rev. Varkey Velickakathu.
Catechesis Religious Program—Stephanie Hannasch, D.R.E. Students 142.

NEKOOSA, WOOD CO., SACRED HEART OF JESUS (1900) [JC] Also serves St. Alexander, Port Edwards.
711 Prospect Ave., Nekoosa, 54457.
Tel: 715-886-3422; Email: sacredht@wctc.net; Web: sachtnek.com. Rev. R. John Swing; Deacons Mark C. Quayhackx; Richard Skifton.
See Assumption Catholic Schools, Wisconsin Rapids under Unified Catholic School Systems located in the Institution section.
Catechesis Religious Program—Peggy Wettstein, D.R.E. Students 119.

NEW AUBURN, CHIPPEWA CO., ST. JUDE, Closed. For inquiries for parish records contact the chancery.

NEW LISBON, JUNEAU CO., ST. PAUL (1862) [CEM]
408 W. River St., New Lisbon, 53950.
Tel: 608-562-3125; Email: st.paul@mwt.net; Web: www.mjpcatholic.com. Rev. Robert M. Letona. Also serves St. James, Camp Douglas and St. Michael, Indian Creek.
Catechesis Religious Program—Tel: 608-562-5482. Sue La Budda, C.R.E. Students 33.

NORTH CREEK, TREMPEALEAU CO., ST. MICHAEL (1875) Closed. For inquiries for parish records contact the chancery.

NORWALK, MONROE CO., ST. AUGUSTINE OF HIPPO (1903) [CEM] Attended by
W109 County Hwy. U, Norwalk, 54648.
Tel: 608-654-5654; Email: smash3psecretary@mwt.net; Email: smash3ppastor@mwt.net; Web: smash3p.org. 1205 Front St., Cashton, 54619. Rev. Michael E. Klos; Deacon Samuel G. Schmirler. Also serves Sacred Heart of Jesus, Cashton and Nativity of the BVM, St. Mary's Ridge.

ONALASKA, LA CROSSE CO., ST. PATRICK (1949) [JC]
1031 Main St., Onalaska, 54650. Tel: 608-783-5535; Email: sj6340@yahoo.com; Web: www.stpatsonalaska.com. Rev. Msgr. Steven J. Kachel; Deacon Frank J. Abnet.
See Aquinas Catholic Schools, LaCrosse under Unified Catholic School Systems located in the Institution section.
Catechesis Religious Program—Tel: 608-783-1099. Cathryn Olson, D.R.E. Students 533.

OWEN, CLARK CO., HOLY ROSARY (1920)
415 W. 3rd St., P.O. Box 309, Owen, 54460.
Tel: 715-229-0606; Email: holyrosaryowen@gmail.com; Web: stbernardsthedwig.org. Rev. Baskaran Sandhiyagu. Also serves St. Bernard-St. Hedwig, Thorp
Catechesis Religious Program—Jean Gokey, D.R.E. Students 54.

PEPLIN, MARATHON CO., ST. JOHN THE BAPTIST (1916) [CEM] Attended by
3308 State Hwy. 153, Mosinee, 54455.
Tel: 715-693-3120; Email: sfxknowl@mtc.net. 150051 Mead Ln., Mosinee, 54455. Rev. James F. Trempe. Also serves St. Francis Xavier, Knowlton.

PINE CREEK, TREMPEALEAU CO., MOST SACRED HEART (1864) [CEM]
N20555 County Rd. G, Dodge, 54625-9721.
Tel: 608-539-3704; Email: rmspittler@triwest.net. Very Rev. Sebastian J. Kolodziejczyk; Rev. Kyle N. Laylan. Also serves Holy Family, Arcadia.

PITTSVILLE, WOOD CO., ST. JOACHIM 1879 [CEM]
5312 3rd Ave., P.O. Box 69, Pittsville, 54466.
Tel: 715-884-6815; Email: friarjo@tds.net. Rev. Ama-

lanathan Malaiyappan. Also serves Holy Rosary, Sigel and St. James, Vesper.
Catechesis Religious Program—Tel: 715-884-2115. Judy Gachnang, D.R.E. Students 129.

PLOVER, PORTAGE CO., ST. BRONISLAVA (1896) [JC]
3200 Plover Rd., P.O. Box 158, Plover, 54467.
Tel: 715-344-4326; Email: parishoffice@stbrons.com; Web: stbrons.com. Revs. Edward J. Shuttleworth; Charles J. Richmond; Deacon Vernon R. Linzmeier.
See Pacelli Catholic Schools, Stevens Point, under Unified Catholic School Systems located in the Institution section.
Catechesis Religious Program—Tel: 715-341-6700. Jody Glodowski, D.R.E.; Julie Studinski, D.R.E. Students 296.

PLUM CITY, PIERCE CO., ST. JOHN THE BAPTIST (1872) [JC]
212 Church Rd., Plum City, 54761.
Tel: 715-647-2901; Email: 11stjohn@centurylink.net. Rev. Joseph Okine-Quartey. Also serves St. Joseph, Arkansaw.
Catechesis Religious Program—Sherry Schlosser, D.R.E. Students 31.

POLONIA, PORTAGE CO., SACRED HEART 1864 [CEM]
7375 Church St., Custer, 54423. Tel: 715-592-4221; Email: parishoffice@sacredheartpolonia.com; Web: www.sacredheartpolonia.com. Rev. Gregory A. Michaud.
School—Sacred Heart School, (Grades PreK-6), 7379 Church St., Custer, 54423. Tel: 715-592-4902; Email: tmccann@sacredheartpolonia.org. Mr. Thomas McCann, Prin. Lay Teachers 4; Students 34.

PONIATOWSKI, MARATHON CO., HOLY FAMILY (1877) [CEM 2]
R444 County Road U, Edgar, 54426.
Tel: 715-352-3011; Email: holyfamilychurchponiatowski@gmail.com. 103 N. 4th Ave., P.O. Box 35, Edgar, 54426. Rev. Thomas M. Huff. Also serves St. John the Baptist, Edgar.
Catechesis Religious Program—Students 52.

PORT EDWARDS, WOOD CO., ST. ALEXANDER (1941) [JC]
880 1st St., Port Edwards, 54469. Tel: 715-887-3012; Email: stalexander@wctc.net; Web: saintalexander.weebly.com. Rev. R. John Swing; Deacon Mark C. Quayhackx. Also serves Sacred Heart, Nekoosa.

PRAIRIE DU CHIEN, CRAWFORD CO.
1—ST. GABRIEL (1817) [CEM 2] Merged with St. John Nepomucene, Prairie du Chien in 2012 to form Holy Family Parish, Prairie du Chien.
2—HOLY FAMILY PARISH
710 S. Wacouta Ave., Prairie Du Chien, 53821.
Tel: 608-326-6511; Email: lgratace@prairiecatholic.org; Web: prairiecatholic.org. Very Rev. James C. Weighner; Deacon Mark Grunwald.
School—Prairie Catholic School, (Grades PreK-8), 515 N. Beaumont Rd., Prairie du Chien, 53821.
Tel: 608-326-8624; Web: prairiecatholic.org. Mary Henry, Prin. Clergy 1; Lay Teachers 13; Students 97.
3—ST. JOHN NEPOMUCENE (1891) Merged with St. Gabriel, Prairie du Chien in 2012 to form Holy Family Parish, Prairie du Chien.

PRESCOTT, PIERCE CO., ST. JOSEPH 1868 [CEM]
269 Dakota St. S., Prescott, 54021. Tel: 715-262-5310 ; Email: stjosephprescott@comcast.net; Web: stjosephprescott.com. Rev. George R. Szews; Deacon Gerald T. Rynda.
School—St. Joseph School, (Grades PreK-6), 281 Dakota St. S., Prescott, 54021. Tel: 715-262-5912; Fax: 715-262-5901; Email: school.office@stjosephprescott.com. Chris Magee, Prin. Lay Teachers 10; Students 79.
Convent—268 Dakota St. S., Prescott, 54021. Tel: 715-262-5105.

RICHLAND CENTER, RICHLAND CO., ST. MARY (ASSUMPTION OF B.V.M.) 1858 [CEM]
160 W. 4th St., Richland Center, 53581.
Tel: 608-647-2621; Email: cheryl.blankenship@stmarysrc.com; Web: stmarysrc.com. Rev. Msgr. Roger J. Scheckel; Deacon Donald Tully.
School—St. Mary (Assumption of B.V.M.) School, (Grades K-8), 155 W. 5th St., Richland Center, 53581. Tel: 608-647-2422; Fax: 608-647-5914; Email: vicki.faber@stmaryrc.com. Vicki Faber, Prin. Lay Teachers 12; Students 158.
Catechesis Religious Program—155 W. 5th St., Richland Center, 53581. Tel: 608-647-0400; Email: re@stmarysrc.com. Candace McGrath, C.R.E. Students 42.

RISING SUN, CRAWFORD CO., ST. JAMES, Closed. For inquiries for parish records contact The Diocesan Archive, P.O. Box 4004, La Crosse, WI, 54602-4004.

ROCK FALLS, DUNN CO., ST. JOSEPH (1905) [CEM]
E9265 State Rd. 85, Mondovi, 54755.
Tel: 715-875-4539; Email: stjosephrf@gmail.com. Rev. Joseph C. Nakwah. Also serves St. Joseph, Elk Mound.
Catechesis Religious Program—Amy Mayer, C.C.D. Coord., Tel: 715-875-4527. Students 23.

ROLLING GROUND, CRAWFORD CO., ST. PHILIP (1857) [CEM]
42678 Church Rd., Soldiers Grove, 54655.
Tel: 608-735-4420; Email: stmary@mwt.net. 115 School St., Gays Mills, 54631. Rev. Zacharie Beya-Tshingimba. Also serves St. Mary, Gays Mills and St. Patrick, Seneca.
Catechesis Religious Program—Tel: 608-624-5633; Email: marscars@mwt.net. Marguerite Carstens, D.R.E. Students 23.

ROSHOLT, PORTAGE CO., ST. ADALBERT (1898) [CEM]
3315 St Adalberts Rd, Rosholt, 54473.
Tel: 715-677-4519; Email: parish@rosholtcatholic.org; Web: www.rosholtcatholic.org. Rev. Jeffrey W. Hennes. Also serves St. Mary (Immaculate Conception) Torun.
School—St. Adalbert School, (Grades PreK-8), 3314 St. Adalbert Rd., Rosholt, 54473. Tel: 715-677-4517; Email: school@rosholtcatholic.org; Web: www.rosholtcatholic.org/school. Mr. Thomas McCann, Prin. Lay Teachers 6; Students 48; Clergy / Religious Teachers 1.

ROTHSCHILD, MARATHON CO., ST. MARK (1960)
602 Military Rd., Rothschild, 54474.
Tel: 715-359-5206; Email: stmarkroths@smproths.org; Web: www.smproths.org. Very Rev. Allan L. Slowiak; Deacon Patrick J. McKeough.
See Newman Catholic Schools, Wausau under Unified Catholic School Systems located in the Institution section.
Catechesis Religious Program—Mary Hart, D.R.E. Students 155.

ROZELLVILLE, MARATHON CO., ST. ANDREW 1881 [CEM]
Attended by St. Joseph, Stratford.
D1868 County Rd. C, P.O. Box 106, Stratford, 54484.
Tel: 715-687-2404; Email: stjosephoffice1@gmail.com; Web: www.stjosephstratford.org. Rev. Sengole Vethamanickam.

RUDOLPH, WOOD CO., ST. PHILIP 1884 [CEM]
6957 Grotto Ave., P.O. Box 165, Rudolph, 54475.
Tel: 715-435-3286; Email: stphilipchurch@gmail.com; Web: www.saint-philip.org. Rev. David P. Bruener; Deacon Kevin R. Ray. Also serves St. Lawrence, Wisconsin Rapids.
Res.: 530 Tenth Ave. N., Wisconsin Rapids, 54495.
See Assumption Catholic Schools, Wisconsin Rapids under Unified Catholic School Systems located in the Institution section.

SAINT JOSEPH RIDGE, LA CROSSE CO., ST. JOSEPH (1866) [CEM] Also serves St. Peter, Middle Ridge.
W2601 State Rd. 33, 54601. Tel: 608-788-1646; Email: sjrp2601@gmail.com; Web: www.saintjosephridgeparish.com. Rev. Timothy J. Welles.

SAINT MARY'S RIDGE, MONROE CO., NATIVITY OF THE BLESSED VIRGIN MARY (1856) [CEM]
26400 County Rd. U, Cashton, 54619-9157.
Tel: 608-654-5654; Email: smash3psecretary@mwt.net; Email: smash3ppastor@mwt.net; Web: www.smash3p.org. 1205 Front St., Cashton, 54619. Rev. Michael E. Klos; Deacon Samuel G. Schmirler. Also serves St. Augustine, Norwalk; Sacred Heart, Cashton.

SCHOFIELD, MARATHON CO., ST. THERESE OF THE CHILD JESUS (1937) [CEM]
113 Kort St. W., Rothschild, 54474.
Tel: 715-359-2421; Email: colleen@sttheresecc.org; Web: sttheresecc.org. 112 Kort St. W., Schofield, 54476. Rev. Louis D. Britto Susairaj; Deacon Michael Lambrecht.
See Newman Catholic Schools, Wausau under Unified Catholic School Systems located in the Institution section.
Catechesis Religious Program—Students 221.

SENECA, CRAWFORD CO., ST. PATRICK (1872) [CEM]
106 Main St., Seneca, 54654. Tel: 608-735-4420; Email: stmary@mwt.net. 115 School St., Gays Mills, 54631. Rev. Zacharie Beya-Tshingimba. Also serves St. Mary, Gays Mills and St. Philip, Rolling Ground.
Catechesis Religious Program—Tel: 608-734-3009; Email: sdgarfoot@yahoo.com. Sue Garfoot, D.R.E. Students 44.

SIGEL, WOOD CO.

SOUTHEASTERN PORTAGE COUNTY, PORTAGE CO., ST. MAXIMILIAN MARIA KOLBE (1996) [CEM 4]
8611 State Rd. 54, Almond, 54909. Tel: 715-824-3380 ; Email: angie@stmaxkolbe.org; Web: www.stmaxkolbe.org. Rev. Peter M. Manickam. Founded in 1996, the merger of Holy Guardian Angels, Almond (1914), St. Martin, Buena Vista (1862), St. John the Baptist, Heffron (1967), St. Patrick, Lanark (1888).

SPARTA, MONROE CO., ST. PATRICK (1876) [CEM] Also serves St. John the Baptist, Summit Ridge.
118 S K St., Sparta, 54656. Tel: 608-269-2655, Ext. 1; Email: strectory@stpats.net; Web: stpatricksparish.weconnect.com. 319 W. Main St., Sparta, 54656. Very Rev. Eric R. Berns; Juan Pedro Roblez Baltazar.
School—St. Patrick School, (Grades K-8), 100 S. L St., Sparta, 54656. Tel: 608-269-4748; Email: jeansuttie@stpatricksparta.net. Jean Suttie, Prin. Lay Teachers 11; Students 132.
Catechesis Religious Program—Tel: 608-269-7500. David Schmidt, D.R.E. Students 164.

SPAULDING-CITY POINT, JACKSON CO., NORTH AMERICAN MARTYRS, Closed. For inquiries for parish records contact St. Joachim, Pittsville.

SPENCER, MARATHON CO., CHRIST THE KING (1938) [JC]
Also serves St. John the Baptist, Marshfield.
107 E. Wendell St, P.O. Box 156, Spencer, 54479.
Tel: 715-659-4480; Email: office@ctkspencer.net; Web: www.ctkspencer.net. Very Rev. Samuel A. Martin; Rev. Barry P. Saylor; Deacon Jeffrey L. Austin.
Catechesis Religious Program—101 Wendell St., P.O. Box 156, Spencer, 54479-0156. Students 126.

SPRING VALLEY, PIERCE CO., SACRED HEART OF JESUS (1884) [CEM 2]
S105 Sabin Ave., P.O. Box 456, Spring Valley, 54767.
Tel: 715-778-5519; Email: admin@svecatholic.org; Web: www.svecatholic.org. Rev. Arockia Stanislaus. Also serves St. Luke, Boyceville and Sacred Heart, Elmwood.
Catechesis Religious Program—Laura Buchal, D.R.E.

SPRINGFIELD, EAU CLAIRE CO., ST. BRIDGET (1859) [CEM]
2801 N. 110th Ave., Chippewa Falls, 54729.
Tel: 715-723-4890; Email: yhiess@ssndcp.org; Web: www.parishesonline.com/find/st-bridget. 412 S. Main, Chippewa Falls, 54729. Rev. Justin J. Kizewski. Also serves Holy Ghost, Chippewa Falls.
Catechesis Religious Program—Jennifer Reetz, D.R.E. Students 32.

STANLEY, CHIPPEWA CO.
1—ALL SAINTS 2013 [CEM]
226 E. 3rd Ave., P.O. Box 125, Stanley, 54768.
Tel: 715-644-5435; Email: info@allsaintscathcom.com; Web: allsaintscathcom.com. Rev. William P. Felix; Deacon Ned L. Willkom.
Catechesis Religious Program—Sara Rykal, D.R.E. Students 180.
2—HOLY FAMILY (1896) Merged with Sacred Heart of Jesus-St. Joseph, Boyd & St. Rose of Lima, Cadott in 2013 to form All Saints, Stanley.

STEVENS POINT, PORTAGE CO.
1—ST. CASIMIR (TOWNSHIP OF HULL) (1871) [CEM]
203 Casimir Rd., Stevens Point, 54481.
Tel: 715-344-9582; Email: saintcasimirparish@gmail.com. Rev. Arul Joseph Visuvasam; Deacon Ray J. Heitzinger. Also serves St. Peter, Stevens Point.
2—HOLY SPIRIT PARISH 2015
838 Fremont St, Stevens Point, 54481.
Tel: 715-344-9117; Email: contact@holyspiritstevenspoint.org; Web: www.holyspiritstevenspoint.org. Very Rev. Steven J. Brice; Rev. Todd A. Mlsna, Tel: 715-252-8157; Deacon Richard Letto. Founded in 2015, the merger of St. Stanislaus Kostka, Stevens Point (1917) and Newman University Parish, Stevens Point (1970)
Campus Ministry Center, Newman Catholic Center & Res.: 2108 Fourth Ave., Stevens Point, 54481.
See Pacelli Catholic Schools, Stevens Point under Unified Catholic School Systems located in the Institution section.
3—ST. JOSEPH (1884) [JC]
1709 Wyatt Ave., Stevens Point, 54481-3615.
Tel: 715-341-1617, Ext. 101; Email: rschneeberg@stjoespoint.org; Web: www.stjoespoint.org. Revs. Jerzy Rebacz; Fernando Lara Hernandez; Todd A. Mlsna; Deacons Michael Horgan; Arthur J. Schaller.
See Pacelli Catholic Schools, Stevens Point under Unified Catholic School Systems located in the Institution section.
Catechesis Religious Program—
Tel: 715-341-1617, Ext. 101. Lynn Meyer, C.R.E. Students 84.
4—NEWMAN UNIVERSITY PARISH (1970) [JC] Merged with St. Stanislaus Kostka, Stevens Point in 2015 to form Holy Spirit Parish, Stevens Point.
5—ST. PETER (1876) [JC]
800 4th Ave., Stevens Point, 54481.
Tel: 715-344-6115; Email: stpeters@pacellicatholicschools.com; Web: stpeter.us. Revs. Arul Joseph Visuvasam; Todd A. Mlsna; Deacon Ray J. Heitzinger. Also serves St. Casimir, Stevens Point.
See Pacelli Catholic Schools, Stevens Point under Unified Catholic School Systems located in the Institution section.
Catechesis Religious Program—Shirley Wanserski, D.R.E.; Marie Von Rueden, Youth Min. Students 110.
6—ST. STANISLAUS (1917) [JC] Merged with Newman University Parish, Stevens Point in 2015 to form Holy Spirit Parish, Stevens Point.
7—ST. STEPHEN (1852) [CEM]
1401 Clark St., Stevens Point, 54481.
Tel: 715-344-3319, Ext. 101; Email: ststephensp@gmail.com; Web: saintstephenparish.webs.com. Revs. Jerzy Rebacz; Fernando Lara Hernandez; Todd A. Mlsna; Deacons Arthur J. Schaller; Michael Horgan. Also serves St. Joseph, Stevens Point.
See Pacelli Catholic Schools, Stevens Point under

Unified Catholic School Systems located in the Institution section.
Catechesis Religious Program—1709 Wyatt Ave., Stevens Point, 54481. Tel: 715-341-1617; Email: lmeyer@stjoespoint.org. Lynn Meyer, D.R.E. Students 110.

STRATFORD, MARATHON CO., ST. JOSEPH (1900) [CEM 3] Also serves St. Andrew, Rozellville.
119200 Larch St., P.O. Box 6, Stratford, 54484.
Tel: 715-687-2404; Email: stjosephoffice1@gmail.com; Web: www.stjosephstratford.org. Rev. Sengole Vethamanickam.
School—St. Joseph School, (Grades PreK-8), Tel: 715-687-4145; Fax: 715-257-7791; Email: principal@ststratford.org. Michele Novak, Prin. Lay Teachers 7; Students 40.
Catechesis Religious Program—Tel: 715-687-3392. Ruth Gawlikoski, D.R.E. Students 134.

SUMMIT RIDGE, MONROE CO., ST. JOHN THE BAPTIST (1877) [CEM] Served from St. Patrick, Sparta.
16585 Kellogg Ave., Norwalk, 54648.
Tel: 608-269-2655; Email: stprectory@stpats.net; Web: www.stpatricksparish.weconnect.com. 319 W. Main St., Sparta, 54656. Very Rev. Eric R. Berns; Juan Pedro Roblez Baltazar.

THORP, CLARK CO., ST. BERNARD-ST. HEDWIG PARISH (1884) [CEM] Also serves Holy Rosary, Owen.
109 N. Church St., Box 329, Thorp, 54771.
Tel: 715-669-5526; Email: thorp.parish@yahoo.com; Web: www.stbernardsthedwig.org. Rev. Baskaran Sandhiyagu.
School—St. Bernard-St. Hedwig Parish School aka Thorp Catholic School, (Grades K-8), 411 E. School St., Thorp, 54771. Tel: 715-669-5530; Email: tcsfriedel@gmail.com. Mario Friedel, Prin. Lay Teachers 7; Students 68; Clergy / Religious Teachers 1.
Catechesis Religious Program—Tel: 715-669-7302. Leeann Klapatauskas, D.R.E. Students 229.

TILDEN, CHIPPEWA CO., ST. PETER (1869) [CEM]
11358 County Hwy. Q, Chippewa Falls, 54729.
Tel: 715-723-4088; Email: StCharles723@gmail.com. 810 Pearl St., Chippewa Falls, 54729. Rev. Msgr. Michael J. Gorman, V.G., J.C.L.; Rev. Mark A. Miller; Deacon Daniel J. Rider. Also serves St. Charles Borromeo, Chippewa Falls.
School—St. Peter School, (Grades 1-8), 11370 County Hwy. Q, Chippewa Falls, 54729. Tel: 715-288-6250; Email: cprincipalc@gmail.com; Web: stpeterschooltilden.com. Tommy Christopher, Prin. Lay Teachers 5; Students 55.
Catechesis Religious Program—Greg Gilbertson, D.R.E. Students 18.

TOMAH, MONROE CO.
1—ST. MARY (IMMACULATE CONCEPTION) (1867) [CEM] Merged with St. Andrew, Warrens to form Queen of the Apostles Parish, Tomah.
2—QUEEN OF THE APOSTLES PARISH 2015
Mailing Address: 303 W. Monroe St., Tomah, 54660.
Tel: 608-372-4516; Fax: 608-372-4440; Email: psecretary@queenoftheapostlestomah.com; Web: www.queenoftheapostlestomah.com. Rev. Msgr. Richard W. Gilles, J.C.L.; Deacon Robert G. Riedl.
School—Queen of the Apostles Parish School, (Grades PreK-8), 315 W. Monroe St., Tomah, 54660. Tel: 608-372-5765; Email: school@queenoftheapostlestomah.com. Sandra Murray, Prin. Lay Teachers 12; Students 140.
Catechesis Religious Program—Tel: 608-372-0825; Email: wthorson@queenoftheapostlestomah.com. Wanda Thorson, D.R.E. Students 93.

TORUN, PORTAGE CO., ST. MARY (IMMACULATE CONCEPTION) 1897 [CEM]
5589 Dewey Dr., Stevens Point, 54482.
Tel: 715-344-2599; Email: parish@toruncatholic.org; Web: www.toruncatholic.org. Rev. Jeffrey W. Hennes. Also serves St. Adalbert, Rosholt.
Res.: 3315 St. Adalbert Rd., Rosholt, 54473-8948.

TREMPEALEAU, TREMPEALEAU CO., ST. BARTHOLOMEW (1869) [CEM 2] Also serves St. Mary, Galesville
11646 South St., Trempealeau, 54661.
Tel: 608-534-6652; Email: stmarygalesville@triwest.net; Web: saintbartholomew.net. Rev. Antony Joseph, (India); Deacons Russell E. Cabak; Kent L. Jacobson.
Catechesis Religious Program—Mike Maier, C.R.E. Students 93.

UNION CENTER, JUNEAU CO., ST. THERESA OF AVILA, Closed. For inquiries for parish records contact St. Aloysius, Hillsboro.

VESPER, WOOD CO., ST. JAMES 1909 [CEM]
6631 Church Ave., P.O. Box 68, Vesper, 54489.
Tel: 715-884-6815; Email: stjames@tds.net; Web: www.parishesonline.com/find/ss-joachim-james-holy-rosary. Rev. Amalanathan Malaiyappan. Also serves Holy Rosary, Sigel and St. Joachim, Pittsville.
Catechesis Religious Program—Annette Molepske, D.R.E. Students 58.

VIROQUA, VERNON CO., ANNUNCIATION OF THE BLESSED VIRGIN MARY (1906)
400 Congress Ave., Viroqua, 54665-1309.
Tel: 608-637-7711; Email: stmaryparish@mwt.net; Web: saintmaryviroqua.org. Rev. Janusz A. Kowalski.
Catechesis Religious Program—Tel: 608-634-3033. Dennis Olson, C.R.E. Students 211.

WARRENS, MONROE CO., ST. ANDREW (1896) Merged with St. Mary (Immaculate Conception), Tomah to form Queen of the Apostles Parish, Tomah.

WAUMANDEE, BUFFALO CO., ST. BONIFACE (1867) [CEM 2]
S2022 County Road U, Waumandee, 54622.
Tel: 608-626-2611; Email: tresecclesiae@gmail.com; Web: tresecclesiae.org. Rev. Prince Amala Jesuraja; Deacon Edward D. Wendt. Serves St. Lawrence, Alma and Immaculate Conception, Fountain City.
School—St. Boniface School, (Grades PreK-8), Tel: 608-626-2611; Email: stbonschool@mwt.net. Carrie Venner, Head Teacher. Lay Teachers 3; Students 19.

WAUSAU, MARATHON CO.
1—ST. ANNE (1949) [JC]
700 W. Bridge St., Wausau, 54401. Tel: 715-849-3930; Web: www.stanneswausau.org. Very Rev. Thomas F. Lindner; Deacon Ervin A. Burkhardt.
See Newman Catholic Schools, Wausau under Unified Catholic School Systems located in the Institution section.
Catechesis Religious Program—Email: johns@stanneswausau.org. John Schmitt, D.R.E. Students 266.
2—CHURCH OF THE RESURRECTION (1998) [JC]
Mailing Address: 621 N. 2nd St., Wausau, 54403.
Tel: 715-845-6715; Email: croffice@eastsideparishes.org; Web: eastsideparishes.org. Rev. Msgr. Mark R. Pierce, J.C.L.; Deacons Peter A. Burek; Michael Maher Jr. Also serves St. Michael, Wausau
Previous Names: St. James, St. Mary (Immaculate Conception)
See Newman Catholic Schools, Wausau under Unified Catholic School Systems located in the Institution section.
3—HOLY NAME OF JESUS (1946)
1104 S. 9th Ave., Wausau, 54401. Tel: 715-842-4543; Email: judy@holynamewausau.com; Web: holynamewausau.com. Revs. Robert C. Thorn; Peter Kieffer; Deacon Thomas J. Tierney. Also serves St. Matthew, Wausau.
See Newman Catholic Schools, Wausau under Unified Catholic School Systems located in the Institution section.
4—ST. JAMES THE GREATER, Closed. For inquiries for Parish Records contact Church of the Resurrection, Wausau.
5—ST. MARY (IMMACULATE CONCEPTION), Closed. For inquiries for Parish Records contact Church of the Resurrection, Wausau.
6—MARY, MOTHER OF GOOD HELP PARISH 2018
2221B Grand Ave., Wausau, 54401.
Tel: 715-298-9055; Fax: 715-298-9055. Rev. Alan T. Burkhardt.
Res.: 1104 S. 9th Ave., Wausau, 544001.
7—ST. MATTHEW (1958) Also serves Holy Name of Jesus, Wausau.
229 S. 28th Ave., Wausau, 54401. Tel: 715-842-3148; Email: anngn@stmatthewwausau.org; Web: www.stmatthewwausau.org. Revs. Robert C. Thorn; Peter Kieffer; Deacon Thomas J. Tierney.
Catechesis Religious Program—Patricia Cicha, D.R.E. Students 110.
8—ST. MICHAEL (1887) [CEM]
611 Stark St., Wausau, 54403. Tel: 715-842-4283; Email: smoffice@eastsideparishes.org; Web: www.eastsideparishes.org. Rev. Msgr. Mark R. Pierce, J.C.L.; Deacons Peter A. Burek; Michael Maher Jr.
See Newman Catholic Schools, Wausau under Unified Catholic School Systems located in the Institution section.
Catechesis Religious Program—Tel: 715-842-1810; Email: faithform@eastsideparishes.org. Students 160.

WAUZEKA, CRAWFORD CO., SACRED HEART (1881) [CEM]
711 E. Main St., P.O. Box 237, Wauzeka, 53826.
Tel: 608-874-4151; Email: shwauzeka@gmail.com. Rev. Anandan Rajendran. Also serves St. Wenceslaus, Eastman.

WEST SALEM, LA CROSSE CO., ST. LEO THE GREAT (1957) Also serves St. Mary, Bangor.
210 Hamlin St. W., West Salem, 54669.
Tel: 608-786-0610; Email: stleomaryoffice@gmail.com; Web: westsalembangorcatholic.org. Rev. Arulsamy Raja Kennedy; Deacon Robert J. Zietlow.
Catechesis Religious Program—Sarah Reischl, D.R.E. Students 153.

WESTON, MARATHON CO., ST. AGNES (1910) [CEM]
6101 Zinser St., Weston, 54476. Tel: 715-359-5675; Email: deb@stagnescatholicparish.com; Web: www.stagnescatholicparish.com. Rev. Gregory J. Bohren. Also serves St. Florian, Hatley.
Catechesis Religious Program—Students 215.

WHITEHALL, TREMPEALEAU CO., ST. JOHN THE APOSTLE (1948)
35900 Lee St., P.O. Box 566, Whitehall, 54773.
Tel: 715-538-4607; Email: sjawhitehall@gmail.com; Web: www.ssppwi.org. Very Rev. Woodrow H. Pace; Rev. Emmanuel Asamoah-Bekoe.

WILLARD, CLARK CO., HOLY FAMILY (1912) [CEM]
W8170 Main St., Willard, 54493. Tel: 715-255-8017; Email: stap1931@gmail.com; Web: stanthonyloyal.org. 407 N. Division St., P.O. Box 69, Loyal, 54446. Rev. Leo Stanislaus. Also serves St. Mary, Help of Christians, Greenwood and St. Anthony, Loyal.

WILSON, EAU CLAIRE CO., ST. PETER, Closed. For inquiries for parish records contact All Saints, Stanley.

WILTON, MONROE CO., ST. JOHN THE BAPTIST (1875) [CEM] Attended by
504 Enderby St., Wilton, 54670. Tel: 608-435-6456; Email: stjosephkendall@centurytel.net. 307 Spring St., P.O. Box 155, Kendall, 54638. Rev. John Peter Anthonisamy Chinnappan. Also serves St. Patrick, Elroy and St. Joseph, Kendall.
Catechesis Religious Program—Tel: 608-463-7120. Diane Hansen, D.R.E. Students 40.

WISCONSIN RAPIDS, WOOD CO.
1—HOLY ROSARY (1881) [CEM]
6190 Chapel Rd., Wisconsin Rapids, 54495.
Tel: 715-884-6815; Email: friarjo@tds.net; Web: www.parishesonline.com/find/ss-joachim-james-holy-rosary. Mailing Address: 5312 3rd Ave., P.O. Box 69, Pittsville, 54466-0069. Rev. Amalanathan Malaiyappan. Also serves St. Joachim, Pittsville and St. James, Vesper.
2—ST. LAWRENCE 1900 [JC] Also serves St. Philip, Rudolph.
Tel: 715-421-5777; Email: slparishwr@gmail.com; Web: www.saintlawrencewr.org. Rev. David P. Bruener; Deacon Kevin R. Ray.
See Assumption Catholic Schools, Wisconsin Rapids under Unified Catholic School Systems located in the Institution section.
3—OUR LADY, QUEEN OF HEAVEN (1947) [JC]
750 10th Ave. S., Wisconsin Rapids, 54495.
Tel: 715-423-1251; Email: olqh@solarus.net; Web: www.our-lady.org. Very Rev. G. Valentine Joseph; Rev. Aaron Becker.
See Assumption Catholic Schools, Wisconsin Rapids under Unified Catholic School Systems located in the Institution section.
Catechesis Religious Program—Email: reoffice@solarus.net. Rosemary Hokamp, D.R.E. Students 153.
4—SS. PETER AND PAUL (1837) [CEM]
1150 2nd St. N., Wisconsin Rapids, 54494.
Tel: 715-423-1351; Email: kaitlyn@ssppwisrapids.org; Web: www.ssppwisrapids.org. Rev. Robert A. Schaller; Deacon Jerome Ruesch.
Catechesis Religious Program—Students 25.
5—ST. VINCENT DE PAUL (1956)
820 13 St. S., Wisconsin Rapids, 54494.
Tel: 715-423-2111; Email: stvin@wctc.net; Web: stvincentdepaulparish.weebly.com. Rev. Jerome Patric.
See Assumption Catholic Schools, Wisconsin Rapids under Unified Catholic School Systems located in the Institution section.
Catechesis Religious Program—Tel: 715-213-8276. Mary Jo Sigourney, D.R.E. Students 108.

WONEWOC, JUNEAU CO., ST. JEROME 1883 [CEM]
528 Center St., Wonewoc, 53968. Tel: 608-489-2580; Email: saintals@mwt.net. 545 Prairie Ave., P.O. Box 466, Hillsboro, 54634-0466. Rev. Donald J. Bauer. Also serves St. Aloysius, Hillsboro.

WUERZBURG, MARATHON CO., ST. JOHN THE BAPTIST (1904) Closed. For inquiries for parish records contact the Diocesan Archives.

YUBA, RICHLAND CO., ST. WENCESLAUS, Closed. For inquiries for parish records contact The Diocesan Archives.

Chaplains of Public Institutions

OXFORD. *Federal Correctional Institute*, Oxford. Rev. James P. McNamee, (Retired), Tel: 608-297-2790.

TOMAH. *Veterans Administration Medical Center*, 500 E. Veterans St., Tomah, 54660. Tel: 608-372-3971. Rev. G. Richard Roberts, Part-time Chap., Tel: 608-782-2028.

Special Assignment:
Rev. Msgrs.—
Burrill, Jeffrey D., Assoc. Gen. Sec, U.S. Conference of Catholic Bishops, 3211 4th St. N.E., Washington, DC 20017
Hundt, Robert P., J.C.L., Judicial Vicar, (Retired), P.O. Box 4004, 54602-4004
Kunz, David C., Vicar for Clergy, P.O. Box 4004, 54602-4004. Tel: 608-791-2667
Very Rev.—
Dhein, William A., V.G., J.C.L., Vicar Gen., Chancellor & Mod. the Curia, P.O. Box 4004, 54602. Tel: 608-791-2655

Revs.—
Apfelbeck, Kurt J., Archivist & Vice Chancellor, P.O. Box 4004, 54602. Tel: 608-791-0177
Benzmiller, James T., P.O. BOX 41, Boyd, 54726
Czerwonka, Paul G., 713 West Ave. S., 54601. Disability Leave
Dickman, Richard C., (Retired), 211 W. Oak St., Sparta, 54656
Dodge, Billy J., Dir. Vocation Recruitment; Dir. Continuing Ed. & Formation, P.O. Box 4004, 54602
Genovesi, James, 3500 County Rd. 5 N., Custer, 54423-9514. 3500 County H., Custer, 54423
Gilbert, John Mary, Chap., Institute of St. Joseph, 31360 County Hwy. MM, Boyd, 54726
Guanella, Alan M., Catholic Univ., Curley Hall, 620 Michigan Ave. N.E., Washington, DC 20064. Grad. Studies in Canon Law, Catholic Univ.
Olson, David P., Instructor & Formation Advisor, Mundelein Seminary-Faculty, Mundelein Seminary, 1000 E. Maple Ave., Mundelein, IL 60060
Wierzba, Alan P., Dir. Vocations, P.O. Box 4004, 54602-4004. Tel: 608-791-2667.

Foreign Missions:
Most Rev.—
Flock, Robert H., Bishop, San Ignacio De Valasco, Email: rflock06@gmail.com. Bishop of San Ignacio de Valasco, Bolivia, South America
Rev. Msgr.—
Hirsch, Joseph W., Email: director@homeajpm.org; Web: www.homeajpm.org/our-mission. Casa Hogar Juan Pablo II; Lurin, Peru, South America.

Leave of Absence:
Revs.—
Apfelbeck, Keith J.
Konopacky, Joseph R.
Neis, William P.
O'Hara, Joseph M.
Olson, Randy G.
Stashek, Brian E.
Wolf, Anthony J.

Absent:
Rev.—
Moreno, Hector C.

Retired:
Rev. Msgrs.—
Hundt, Robert P., J.C.L., (Retired), P.O. BOX 4004, 54602-4004. Tel: 608-791-2684
Malin, Delbert J., (Retired), 909 Western Ave., Holmen, 54636. Tel: 608-526-4908
Malnar, Matthew G., (Retired), (Diocese of Amarillo), P.O. Box 4004, 54602
McGarty, Bernard O., (Retired), 109 S. 14th St., 54601. Tel: 608-784-4473
Revs.—
Beckfelt, John W., (Retired), 935 Kenwood Ave., #345, Duluth, MN 55811. Tel: 218-723-6408
Berger, Lawrence B., (Retired), 518 10th Pl., Onalaska, 54650
Blenker, Ambrose J., (Retired), 3750 Blue Violet Ln., #205, Wisconsin Rapids, 54494
Boneck, Norman D., (Retired), 603 4th St., Mosinee, 54455. Tel: 715-693-2650
Cook, Robert J., (Retired), 100 6th St. N., Apt. 406, 54601
Corradi, Frank, (Retired), 317 W. Grand Ave., P.O. Box 247, Chippewa Falls, 54729
Dickman, Richard C., (Retired), 211 W. Oak St., Sparta, 54656
Doerre, Edmund J, (Retired), 3141 East Ave. S., Unit #3, 54601
Follmar, A. Joseph, (Retired), 110 Shiela St., P.O. Box 113, Manhattan, IL 60442
Grevatch, William N., (Retired), 621 N. 2nd St., Wausau, 54403
Heagle, John L., (Retired), 3447 El Dorado Loop 5, P.O. Box 3094, Salem, OR 97302
Hegenbarth, Robert S., (Retired), 12756 State Hwy. 27, Sparta, 54656
Hiebl, Charles J., (Retired), 101 W. Cedar St., Abbotsford, 54405
Hoffman, Paul E., (Retired), 4115 Jeffers Rd., Apt. 209, Eau Claire, 54703. Tel: 715-514-5507
Jablonske, William, (Retired), 2815 County Hwy I, #224, Chippewa Falls, 54729
Kelly, Daniel J., (Retired), 1111 Burlington Ave., Unit 312, Lisle, IL 60532. Tel: 630-698-1927
Kulas, William, (Retired), (Diocese of Winona-Rochester), 20582 W. Gale Ave., Galesville, 54630
Lesczynski, James J., (Retired), 2883 County Rd. Z., Adams, 53910. Tel: 715-321-1002
Logan, James J., (Retired), 706 Palmetto Ave., Marshfield, 54449. Tel: 715-389-1396
Lynch, Dennis J., (Retired), 1408 Strongs Ave., Apt. 304, Stevens Point, 54481. Tel: 715-630-9120
McNamee, James P., (Retired), 246 Clay St., Montello, 53949. Tel: 608-297-2790
Menzel, William G., (Retired), 2511 8th St. S., PMB 136, Wisconsin Rapids, 54494
Monti, Robert M., (Retired), 3333 N.E. 34th St., Apt. 1616, Fort Lauderdale, FL 33308
Nelson, Robert W., (Retired), 7054 Lundberg Rd., Wisconsin Rapids, 54495
Pedretti, Robert F., (Retired), 491 Red Tail Dr., Amherst, 54406. Tel: 715-824-5808
Przybylski, Donald L., (Retired), 1020 1st St., Apt 212, Stevens Point, 54481-2654
Redmond, Arthur S., (Retired), 606 Ranger St., Mosinee, 54455
Rybicki, David G., (Retired), 2411 Monique Ln., Apt. 4, Marshfield, 54449
Schaefer, James F., (Retired), P.O. Box 1552, Wausaukee, 54402-1552
Schulte, Lyle L., (Retired), Whispering Pines, 340 Bridlewood Dr., #203, P.O. Box 287, Plover, 54467
Schultz, John A., (Retired), S10444 US Hwy. 53, Fall Creek, 54742. Tel: 715-271-0018
Sonnberger, Albert W., (Retired), 1900 Priddy St., Apt. 37, Bloomer, 54724. Tel: 715-568-2503
Steiner, John W., (Retired), Capitol Lake Terraces, 345 W. Main St., Madison, 53703-3114
Streveler, Robert A., (Retired), 300 E. 4th St., Marathon, 54448. Tel: 715-443-2236
Witucki, Roy R., (Retired), 7176 Esker Rd., Custer, 54423
Wolf, Eugene J., (Retired), P.O. Box 4004, 54602-4004
Zimmerman, Rex A., (Retired), 823 Indiana Ave., Stevens Point, 54481. Tel: 715-344-9718.

Permanent Deacons:
Abnet, Frank J., 509 12th Ave. N., Onalaska, 54650. Tel: 608-783-5535. St. Patrick, Onalaska
Agema, Larry J., Senior Deacon, 727 Farr Ct., Eau Claire, 54701. Tel: 715-901-0962
Allen, David J., Victim Assistance Coord., 224 S. 21st St., 54601. Tel: 608-792-9684
Anderson, Thomas C., 1130 25th Pl., Wisconsin Rapids, 54494. Our Lady Queen of Heaven, Wisconsin Rapids
Ashenbrenner, David L., 204955 State Hwy. 49, Wittenberg, 54499. Tel: 715-454-6353. St. Ladislaus, Bevent; St. Joseph, Galloway
Austin, Jeffrey L., 8689 Richfield Dr., Marshfield, 54449. Tel: 715-676-3186. St. John the Baptist, Marshfield; Christ the King, Spencer
Belland, David J., 1514 King St., 54601. Tel: 608-796-4423. Roncalli Newman Center, La Crosse
Bourke, John P., 15701 Evergreen Dr., Marathon, 54448. Tel: 715-443-6238. Nativity of the BVM, Marathon
Breit, Kevin J., 146115 Bison Dr., Mosinee, 54455. St. Paul, Mosinee
Brunner, Norbert J., 23 Fairview Trl., Waunakee, 53597. Tel: 608-850-4669. St. John the Baptist, Waunakee, WI
Burek, Peter A., 1602 Burek Ave., Wausau, 54401. Church of the Resurrection, Wausau, WI; St. Michael, Wausau
Burkhardt, Ervin A., 1509 Golden Meadow St., Wausau, 54401. Tel: 715-675-1979
Cabak, Russell E., (Diocese of Superior), N7068 Sunrise Ln., Holmen, 54636-9417. Tel: 608-797-2277. St. Mary, Galesville; St. Bartholomew, Trempealeau
Chittendon, Robert W., Senior Deacon, 204 E. Clairemont Ave., Eau Claire, 54701. Tel: 715-833-1369
Delgado, Juan A., 346 Grayside Dr., Mauston, 53948. Tel: 608-847-6178. St. Patrick, Mauston
Draeger, Raymond R., 401 S. Adams Ave., Marshfield, 54449. Tel: 715-207-6085. Corpus Christi, Bakerville; Sacred Heart, Marshfield
Gannon, Daniel A., N4470 1130th St., Prescott, 54021. Tel: 715-425-5806. Nativity of the BVM, Big River
Green, William, Senior Deacon, 1680 Short St., Schofield, 54476. Tel: 715-298-2541. (Diocese of Marquette)
Grunwald, Mark, 304 S. Jackson St., Prairie du Chien, 53821. Tel: 608-326-5459. Holy Family, Prairie du Chien
Hansen, Robert J., N5804 Albany N., Mondovi, 54755. St. Mary's Assumption, Durand; Holy Rosary, Lima; Sacred Heart, Mondovi; Prefect for Deacon Life & Ministry
Heinzl, Glen J., N11015 19th Ave., P.O. Box 499, Necedah, 54646. Tel: 715-565-7771. Our Lady of the Lake, Castle Rock Lake; St. Francis of Assisi, Necedah
Heitzinger, Ray J., 1908 Strongs Ave., Stevens Point, 54481. Tel: 715-343-6370. St. Peter, Stevens Point; St Casimir (Township of Hull), Stevens Point
Hilts, Bryan K., 223100 Greentree Rd., Marathon, 54448. Tel: 715-443-6633. Nativity of the Blessed Virgin Mary, Marathon
Horgan, Michael, 5419 Pinewood Dr., Stevens Point, 54482-8818. Tel: 715-344-5050. St. Joseph, Stevens Point; St. Stephen, Stevens Point; Chairman, Catholic Committee on Scouting.
Hutzler, Jason C., N2148 Valley Rd., 54601. Tel: 608-787-0407. St. James the Less, La Crosse
Jacobson, Kent L., N21229 County Rd. T, Ettrick, 54627. St. Mary, Galesville; St Bartholomew, Trempealeau
Jolliffe, Garry, Senior Deacon, 2550 S. Ellsworth Rd., Unit 434, Mesa, AZ 85209. Tel: 480-792-9221
Kaiser, Gregory W., 214710 Cardinal Ln., Edgar, 54426. Tel: 715-687-4669. St. John the Baptist, Edgar
Kennedy, David L., 2285 11th Ave., Adams, 53910. Tel: 608-339-7264. St. Joseph, Adams; (Archdiocese of Milwaukee)
Kinnick, Thomas M., 4380 Steinbeck Way, Ave Maria, FL 54142. Tel: 715-404-0480
Kostner, Richard J., 908 18th Ave., Bloomer, 54724. Tel: 715-568-5978. St. Paul, Bloomer
Koza, J. Michael, 2110 NW 91st Ln., Coral Springs, FL 33071. Tel: 507-895-3377
Lambrecht, Michael, 136 W. Charles St., Schofield, 54476. Tel: 715-254-4064. St. Therese, Scofield
Landry, James L., Senior Deacon, 4520 Whip-or-Will Ln., Wisconsin Rapids, 54494. Tel: 715-421-5067
Letto, Richard, 6921 Country Beautiful Ln., Stevens Point, 54482-9761. Tel: 715-345-1798. Holy Spirit, Stevens Point
Linzmeier, Vernon R., 1010 Ashwood Dr., Plover, 54467. Tel: 715-344-4326. St. Bronislava, Plover
Ludick, Matthew R., 401 4th Ave. S.E., Apt. 357, Saint Joseph, MN 56374
Maher, Michael Jr., 203 Kent St., Wausau, 54403-6925. Tel: 715-843-7933. Church of the Resurrection, Wausau; St. Michael, Wausau;
McKeough, Patrick J., 609 Becker St., Rothschild, 54474. Tel: 715-359-7430. St. Mark, Rothschild
Power, Gregory J., 1706 Sherwin Ave., Eau Claire, 54701-4378. Tel: 715-831-9119. Immaculate Conception, Eau Claire
Quayhackx, Mark C., 880 First St., Port Edwards, 54469. Tel: 715-887-3012. Sacred Heart, Nekoosa; St. Alexander, Port Edwards
Ray, Kevin R., Dir. Deacon Personnel, 1473 Rapids Trail, Nekoosa, 54457. Tel: 608-498-1060. St. Philip, Rudolph; St. Lawrence, Wisconsin Rapids
Richards, Joseph A., N1673 Breidel Coulee Rd., 54601. Tel: 608-780-1669. St. Joseph the Workman Cathedral, La Crosse; Building Dir. Holy Cross Diocesan Center
Rider, Daniel J., 15429 County Hwy. UN, Chippewa Falls, 54729. Tel: 715-215-0102. St. Charles Borromeo, Chippewa Falls; St. Peter, Tilden
Riedl, Robert G., 32001 County Hwy. P, Kendall, 54638. Tel: 608-463-7662. Queen of the Apostles, Tomah
Rivers, Dennis, 501 Main St., P.O. Box 195, Cornell, 54732. Tel: 715-239-2123. Holy Cross, Cornell; St. Anthony, Drywood; Sacred Heart of Jesus, Jim Falls
Rozumalski, Richard, 2229 Bear Creek Rd., Stevens Point, 54481. Tel: 715-344-0008. St. Michael, Junction City; St. Bartholomew, Mill Creek; St. Wenceslaus, Milladore
Ruesch, Jerome, 3811 Parkland Ln., Wisconsin Rapids, 54494. Tel: 715-323-5174. SS. Peter & Paul, Wisconsin Rapids
Rynda, Gerald T., 175 Tower Heights Ct., Prescott, 54021. Tel: 715-262-3065. St. Joseph, Prescott; Coord. Pastoral Field Educ. for Deacon Formation
Sage, Richard R., 3315 Solaris Ln., 54601. Tel: 608-796-1688. Mary, Mother of the Church, La Crosse
Schaefer, Michael J., 401 N. 2nd St., Colby, 54421. Tel: 715-223-5985. St. Mary Help of Christians, Colby
Schaller, Arthur J., 6822 Country Beautiful Ln., Stevens Point, 54483. Tel: 715-592-3692. St. Joseph, Stevens Point; St. Stephen, Stevens Point
Schmirler, Samuel G., E7490 Lars Hill Rd., Westby, 54667. Tel: 608-634-2001. Sacred Heart, Cashton; St. Augustine of Hippo, Norwalk; Nat. of the BVM, St. Mary's Ridge
Skemp, Thomas H., 2130 King St., 54601. Tel: 608-385-7466. St. Joseph the Workman Cathedral, La Crosse
Skifton, James D., 515 Highland Ave., Nekoosa, 54427. Tel: 715-886-4705. Sacred Heart, Nekoosa; St. Alexander, Port Edwards
Tierney, Thomas J., 2408 N. 76th Ave., Wausau, 54401. Tel: 715-297-5976. Holy Name of Jesus, Wausau; St. Matthew, Wausau
Trzinski, James, 145 Saint Claude St., P.O. Box 787, Denmark, 54408. Tel: 920-240-1968
Tully, Donald, S6634 County Rd. J, Viroqua, 54665.

Tel: 608-675-3111. Assumption of the Blessed Virgin Mary, Richland Center

Walker, Hugh D., Senior Deacon, 41 Odessa Ct., Stevens Point, 54481. Tel: 715-344-3970

Weingart, James A., 401 1st Ave., P.O. Box 211, Durand, 54736. Tel: 715-672-4412. St. Mary's Assumption, Durand; Holy Rosary, Lima; Sacred Heart, Mondovi

Wendt, Edward D., S2022 County Rd. U, Waumandee, 54622. Tel: 608-626-2611, Ext. 3. St. Lawrence, Alma; Immaculate Conception, Fountain City; St. Boniface, Waumandee (Diocese of Rockford)

Willkom, Ned L., P.O. Box 136, Cadott, 54727. Tel: 715-289-3339. All Saints, Stanley

Zietlow, Robert J., 1273 Bentgrass Ct., Onalaska, 54650. Tel: 608-780-4751. St. Mary, Bangor; St. Leo the Great, West Salem

Knauf, LeRoy, Senior Deacon, 625 S. 68th Ave., #2, Wausau, 54401. Tel: 715-298-3196.

INSTITUTIONS LOCATED IN DIOCESE

[A] SEMINARIES, DIOCESAN

LA CROSSE. *Holy Cross Seminary House of Formation*, 3710 East Ave. S., P.O. Box 4004, 54602-4004. Tel: 608-791-2667; Fax: 608-791-0165; Email: rorth@diolc.org. Rev. Alan P. Wierzba, Dir. Clergy 3; Students 3.

[B] COLLEGES AND UNIVERSITIES

LA CROSSE. *Viterbo University*, 900 Viterbo Dr., 54601-8804. Tel: 608-796-3000; Fax: 608-796-3050; Email: smseverson@viterbo.edu; Web: www.viterbo.edu. Dr. Glena Temple, Pres.; Emilio Alvarez, Dir. Campus Min.; Sheila Severson, Exec. Admin. Asst.; Rev. Conrad Targonski, Chap. Founded in 1890 by the Franciscan Sisters of Perpetual Adoration, Viterbo Univ. is a Catholic, Franciscan Univ. Comprised of Five Undergraduate Schools, A Graduate School, and a Center for Adult Learning. Lay Teachers 285; Priests 1; Sisters 3; Students 2,766.

[C] UNIFIED CATHOLIC SCHOOL SYSTEMS

LA CROSSE. *Aquinas Catholic Schools, Inc.*, (Grades PreK-12), 315 11th St. S., Ste. 2200, 54601. Tel: 608-784-8585; Fax: 608-784-9988; Email: ted.knutson@aquinasschools.org; Web: www.aquinasschools.org. Mr. Ted Knutson, Pres.

Aquinas High School, 315 S. 11th St., 54601. Tel: 608-784-0287; Fax: 608-782-8851; Email: denise.ring@aquinasschools.org; Web: www.aquinasschools.org. Mrs. Denise Ring, Prin.; Revs. Matthew N. Marshall, Chap.; Nathaniel Kuhn, Chap. Clergy 2; Lay Teachers 29; Students 288.

Aquinas Middle School (1999) (Grades 7-8), 315 S. 11th St., 54601. Tel: 608-784-0156; Fax: 608-784-0229; Email: denise.ring@aquinasschools.org; Web: www.aquinascatholicschools.org. Mrs. Denise Ring, Prin.; Rev. Matthew N. Marshall, Chap. Lay Teachers 15; Students 156.

Blessed Sacrament School, (Grades 3-6), 2404 King St., 54601. Tel: 608-782-5564; Fax: 608-782-7765; Email: kay.berra@aquinasschools.org; Web: www.aquinascatholicschools.org. Kay Berra, Prin. Lay Teachers 17; Students 201.

St. Joseph Cathedral School, (Grades PreK-2), 1319 Ferry St., 54601. Tel: 608-782-5998; Email: Patty.gk@aquinasschools.org; Web: www.aquinasschools.org. Mrs. Patricia A. Gallagher-Kosmatka, Prin. Lay Teachers 13; Students 150.

St. Patrick School, (Grades PreK-6), 127 11th Ave. N., Onalaska, 54650. Tel: 608-783-5483; Fax: 608-783-2128; Email: Sue.amble@aquinasschools.org; Web: www.aquinasschools.org. Susan Amble, Prin. Lay Teachers 17; Students 192.

CHIPPEWA FALLS. *McDonell Area Catholic Schools*, (Grades PreK-12), Central Office 1316 Bel Air Blvd., Chippewa Falls, 54729. Tel: 715-723-0538; Fax: 715-723-1501; Email: k.adams@macs.k12.wi.us; Web: www.macs.k12.wi.us. Jeffrey Heinzen, Pres.

Holy Ghost Elementary School, (Grades 3-5), 436 S. Main St., Chippewa Falls, 54729. Tel: 715-723-6478; Fax: 715-723-8990; Email: k.bahnub@macs.k12.wi.us. Kayla Bahnub, Prin. Clergy 1; Lay Teachers 7; Students 85.

McDonell Central Catholic High School, 1316 Bel Air Blvd., Chippewa Falls, 54729. Tel: 715-723-9126, Ext. 2200; Fax: 715-723-3024; Email: principal@macs.k12.wi.us. Brian Schulner, Prin.; Rev. Mark A. Miller, Chap. Lay Teachers 16; Students 147.

Notre Dame Middle School, (Grades 6-8), 1316 Bel Air Blvd., Chippewa Falls, 54729. Tel: 715-723-4777; Fax: 715-723-3024; Email: principal@macs.k12.wi.us. Brian Schulner, Prin.; Rev. Mark A. Miller, Chap. Clergy 1; Lay Teachers 9; Students 93.

St. Charles Primary School, (Grades K-2), 429 Spruce St., Chippewa Falls, 54729. Tel: 715-723-5827; Fax: 715-723-2109; Email: k.bahnub@macs.k12.wi.us. Kayla Bahnub, Prin. Clergy 1; Lay Teachers 10; Students 83.

EAU CLAIRE. *Regis Catholic Schools*, (Grades PreK-12), Central Office: 2728 Mall Dr., Ste. 200, Eau Claire, 54701. Tel: 715-830-2273; Fax: 715-835-4658; Email: mgobler@regiscatholicschools.com; Web: www.regiscatholicschools.org. Mark Gobler, Pres. Central Office

Genesis Child Development Center, 418 N. Dewey St., Eau Claire, 54703-3241. Tel: 715-830-2275; Email: gcdc@regiscatholicschools.com; Web: www.regiscatholicschools.com. Gayle Flaig, Admin. Clergy 1; Students 72.

Immaculate Conception School, (Grades K-5), 1703 Sherwin Ave., Eau Claire, 54701. Tel: 715-830-2276; Fax: 715-830-9846; Email: rcassidy@regiscatholicschools.com; Web: www.regiscatholicschools.com/schools/immaculate-conception. Renee Cassidy, Prin. Lay Teachers 20; Students 200.

Regis Child Development Center, 418 N. Dewey St., Eau Claire, 54703. Tel: 715-830-2275; Fax: 715-830-0541; Email: gflaig@regiscatholicschools.com; Web: www.regiscatholicschools.com/schools/child-dev-center. Gayle Flaig, Admin. Students 93.

Regis High School, 2100 Fenwick Ave., Eau Claire, 54701. Tel: 715-830-2271; Email: ppedersen@regiscatholicschools.com; Web: www.regiscatholicschools.com. Paul Pedersen, Prin. Lay Teachers 12; Students 220.

Regis Middle School, (Grades 6-8), 2100 Fenwick Ave., Eau Claire, 54701. Tel: 715-830-2272; Fax: 715-830-5461; Email: ppedersen@regiscatholicschools.com; Web: www.regiscatholicschools.com/schools/regis-middle-school. Paul Pedersen, Prin.; Rev. Daniel J. Sedlacek, Chap. Lay Teachers 8; Students 176.

St. James School, (Grades PreK-5), 2502 Eleventh St., Eau Claire, 54703. Tel: 715-830-2277; Fax: 715-858-3478; Email: kmechelke@regiscatholicschools.com; Web: www.regiscatholicschools.com/schools/stjames-elementary. Jacqueline Lutz, Prin.; Kelly Mechelke, Prin. Lay Teachers 9; Students 127.

St. Mary School, (Grades PreK-5), 1828 Lynn Ave., Altoona, 54720. Tel: 715-830-2278; Fax: 715-858-3478; Email: csmiskey@regiscatholicschools.com; Web: www.regiscatholicschools.com/schools/stmarys-elementary. Carisa Smiskey, Prin. Lay Teachers 9; Students 169.

MARSHFIELD. *Columbus Catholic Schools (CCS)*, (Grades PreK-12), 710 S. Columbus Ave., Marshfield, 54449. Tel: 715-387-1177; Fax: 715-384-4535; Email: eaton.david@columbusdons.org; Web: www.columbuscatholicschools.org. Mr. David Eaton, Pres.

Columbus Catholic High School, 710 S. Columbus Ave., Marshfield, 54449-3413. Tel: 715-387-1177; Fax: 715-384-4535; Email: vanwyhe.steven@columbusdons.org; Web: www.columbuscatholicschools.org. Steven Van Wyhe, Prin.; Revs. Daniel J. Sedlacek, Chap.; Barry P. Saylor, Chap. Clergy 1; Lay Teachers 27; Students 125.

Columbus Catholic Middle School, (Grades 6-8), 710 S. Columbus Ave., Marshfield, 54449. Tel: 715-384-7184; Fax: 715-384-4535; Email: vanwyhe.steven@columbusdons.org; Web: www.columbusdons.org. Steven Van Wyhe, Prin.; Revs. Daniel J. Sedlacek, Chap.; Barry P. Saylor, Chap. Clergy 1; Lay Teachers 8; Students 110.

Our Lady of Peace School, (Grades 3-5), 1300 W. 5th St., Marshfield, 54449. Tel: 715-384-5474; Fax: 715-387-8697; Email: heise.shirley@columbusdons.org; Web: www.columbuscatholicschools.org. Shirley Heise, Prin. Lay Teachers 8; Students 98.

St. John the Baptist Primary School, (Grades PreK-2), 307 N. Walnut Ave., Marshfield, 54449. Tel: 715-384-4989; Fax: 715-387-8697; Email: heise.shirley@columbusdons.org; Web: www.columbuscatholicschools.org. Shirley Heise, Prin. Lay Teachers 11; Students 175.

STEVENS POINT. *Pacelli Catholic Schools*, (Grades PreSchool-12), Central Office: 1301 Maria Dr., Stevens Point, 54481. Tel: 715-341-2445; Fax: 715-342-2001; Email: ghansel@pacellicatholicschools.com; Web: www.pacellicatholicschools.com. Mr. Gregg Hansel, Dir. of Education. Clergy 1; Lay Teachers 56; Students 619.

St. Bronislava School, (Grades PreK-4), 3301 Willow Dr., Plover, 54467. Tel: 715-342-2015; Fax: 715-342-2016; Email: ghansel@pacellicatholicschools.com; Web: pacellicatholicschools.com. Mr. Gregg Hansel, Prin. Lay Teachers 10; Students 85.

Pacelli Catholic High School, 1301 Maria Dr., Stevens Point, 54481. Tel: 715-341-2442; Fax: 715-341-6799; Email: ltheiss@pacellicatholicschools.com; Web: pacellicatholicschools.com. Lawrence Theiss, Prin.; Rev. Charles J. Richmond, Chap. Clergy 1; Lay Teachers 20; Students 212.

Pacelli Catholic Early Childhood Center- St. Stanislaus, (Grades PreK-PreK), 2150 High St., Stevens Point, 54481. Tel: 715-341-2878; Email: lsvihel@pacellicatholicschools.com; Web: pacellicatholicschools.com. Lesley Lingofelt-Svihel, Prin.; Mr. Gregg Hansel, Dir. Educ. Lay Teachers 10; Students 79.

Pacelli Catholic Elementary: St. Stephen, (Grades K-4), 1335 Clark St., Stevens Point, 54481. Tel: 715-344-3751; Fax: 715-344-3766; Email: ghansel@pacellicatholicschools.com; Web: pacellicatholicschools.com. Mr. Gregg Hansel, Prin. Lay Teachers 6; Students 143.

Pacelli Catholic Middle School: St. Peter, (Grades 6-8), 708 1st St., Stevens Point, 54481. Tel: 715-344-1890; Fax: 715-342-2005; Email: elopas@pacellicatholicschools.com; Web: pacellicatholicschools.com. Mrs. Ellen Lopas, Prin.; Rev. Charles J. Richmond, Chap. Clergy 1; Lay Teachers 10; Students 167.

WAUSAU. *Newman Catholic Schools*, (Grades PreK-12), 619 Stark St., Wausau, 54403. Tel: 715-845-5735; Fax: 715-848-3582; Email: mmartin@newmancatholicschools.com; Web: www.newmancatholicschools.com. Michael Martin, Pres.

Newman Catholic High School (NCS), 1130 W. Bridge St., Wausau, 54401. Tel: 715-845-8274; Fax: 715-842-1302; Email: dsullivan@newmancatholicschools.com; Web: www.newmancatholicschools.com. Daniel Sullivan, Prin.; Rev. Peter Kieffer, Chap. Lay Teachers 14; Students 122.

Newman Catholic Early Childhood Center: St. Michael, 615 Stark St., Wausau, 54403. Tel: 715-848-0206; Fax: 715-845-3582; Web: www.newmancatholicschools.com. Terry Vechinski, Prin.; Jacci Lepack, Site Dir. Lay Teachers 1; Students 21.

Newman Catholic Elementary School at St. Anne Parish, (Grades K-5), 604 N. 6th Ave., Wausau, 54401. Tel: 715-845-5754; Fax: 715-848-3582; Email: tvechinski@newmancatholicschools.com; Web: www.newmancatholicschools.com. Terry Vechinski, Prin. Lay Teachers 16; Students 190.

Newman Catholic Elementary School at St. Mark Parish, (Grades PreK-5), 602 Military Rd., Rothschild, 54474. Tel: 715-359-9662; Fax: 715-355-8904; Email: tmeyer@newmancatholicschools.com; Web: www.newmancatholicschools.com. Tina Meyer, Prin. Lay Teachers 15; Students 97.

Newman Catholic Middle School (NCMS), (Grades 6-8), 1130 W. Bridge St., Wausau, 54401. Tel: 715-345-8274; Email: amcmanus@newmancatholicschools.com; Web: www.newmancatholicschools.com. Ann McManus, Prin.; Rev. Peter Kieffer, Chap. Lay Teachers 8; Students 143.

WISCONSIN RAPIDS. *Assumption Catholic Schools, Inc. (ACS-WR)*, (Grades PreK-12), Central Office 445 Chestnut St., Wisconsin Rapids, 54494. Tel: 715-422-0900; Fax: 715-422-0935; Email: dminter@assumptioncatholicschools.org; Web: www.assumptioncatholicschools.org. Daniel Minter, Pres.

Legal Title: Wisconsin Rapids Area Catholic Schools.

Assumption High School, 445 Chestnut St., Wisconsin Rapids, 54494. Tel: 715-422-0910; Fax: 715-422-0936; Web: assumptioncatholicschools.org. Anne Zacher, Prin.

Assumption Middle School, (Grades 6-8), 440 Mead St., Wisconsin Rapids, 54494. Tel: 715-422-0950; Fax: 715-422-0936; Web: assumptioncatholicschools.org. Anne Zacher, Prin.; Joan Bond, Prin., Email: jbond@assumptioncatholicschools.org. Clergy 1; Lay Teachers 6; Students 101.

Our Lady Queen of Heaven School, (Grades K-3), 750 10th Ave. S., Wisconsin Rapids, 54495. Tel: 715-422-0982; Fax: 715-424-0936; Email: rgudelis@assumptioncatholicschools.org; Web: assumptioncatholicschool.org. Rebecca Gudelis, Prin. Lay Teachers 8; Students 76.

St. Lawrence Early Childhood Center, 551 10th Ave. N., Wisconsin Rapids, 54495. Tel: 715-422-0990; Fax: 715-422-0936; Web: assumptioncatholicschools.org. Laura Cronan, Dir. Ages 6 weeks to 5 years. Lay Teachers 5; Students 50.

St. Vincent de Paul School, (Grades 3-5), 831 12th St. S., Wisconsin Rapids, 54494. Tel: 715-422-0962 ; Fax: 715-422-0936; Email: pfochs@assumptioncatholicschools.org; Web: assumptioncatholicschools.org. Pam Fochs, Prin. Lay Teachers 11; Students 99.

[D] GENERAL HOSPITALS

LA CROSSE. *Mayo Clinic Health System - Franciscan Healthcare, La Crosse Campus Medical Center*, 700 West Ave. S., 54601-4783. Tel: 608-785-0940; Fax: 608-791-9429; Email: hansen.julie@mayo.edu; Web: www.mayohealthsystem.org. Timothy Johnson, M.D., Pres. & CEO. Franciscan Sisters of Perpetual Adoration and Mayo Foundation. Bed Capacity 331; Tot Asst. Annually 28,553; Total Staff 3,925.

CHIPPEWA FALLS. *St. Joseph's Hospital of the Hospital Sisters of the Third Order of St. Francis* (1888) 2661 County Hwy. I, Chippewa Falls, 54729. Tel: 715-717-7200; Fax: 715-717-1694; Web: www.stjoeschipfalls.com. Andrew Bagnall, CEO; Revs. Biju Chennala Kunjukutty, M.S.F.S., Chap.; John A. Schultz, Chap., (Retired). Hospital Sisters of the Third Order of St. Francis.Hospital Sisters Health System. Bed Capacity 102; Tot Asst. Annually 69,358; Total Staff 356.

EAU CLAIRE. *HSHS Sacred Heart Hospital*, 900 W. Clairemont Ave., Eau Claire, 54701-4121. Tel: 715-717-4131; Fax: 715-717-6076; Web: www.sacredhearteauclaire.org. Mary Ellen Bliss, Dir. of Pastoral Care; Revs. Biju Chennala Kunjukutty, M.S.F.S., Chap., Congregation of Missionaries of St. Francis de Saler, NE India Province; John A. Schultz, Chap., (Retired). Hospital Sisters of the Third Order of St. FrancisHospital Sisters Health System Bed Capacity 222; Tot Asst. Annually 118,104; Total Staff 1,154.

MARSHFIELD. *Saint Joseph's Hospital of Marshfield, Inc.*, c/o Ascension St. Clare's Hospital, 3400 Ministry Pkwy., Weston, 54476. Tel: 715-393-3000; Fax: 715-359-1087; Email: timothy.waldoch@ascension.org; Web: healthcare.ascension.org. Debra Standridge, Regl. Pres.; Mr. Timothy Waldoch, Chief Mission Integration Officer; Antonina Olszewski, Dir. Spiritual Care. Sponsored by Ascension Health Ministries (Ascension Sponsor), a public juridic personTraining School for Nurses (Affiliated with U.W.-Eau Claire).

SPARTA. *Mayo Clinic Health System - Franciscan Healthcare, Sparta Campus Hospital*, 310 W. Main St., Sparta, 54656-2142. 700 West Ave., S., 54601. Tel: 608-269-2132; Fax: 608-269-4562; Email: hansen.julie@mayo.edu; Web: www.mayohealthsystem.org. Kimberly A. Hawthorne, Admin. Franciscan Sisters of Perpetual Adoration and Mayo Foundation. Bed Capacity 25; Tot Asst. Annually 600; Total Staff 84; Patient Days 750.

STANLEY. **Ascension Our Lady of Victory Hospital, Inc.*, 1120 Pine St., Stanley, 54768-0220. Tel: 715-644-5571; Fax: 715-644-6221; Email: timothy.waldoch@ascension.org; Web: healthcare.ascension.org. Debra Standridge, Regl. Pres.; Mr. Timothy Waldoch, Chief Mission Integration Officer; Antonina Olszewski, Dir. Spiritual Care. Sponsored by Ascension Health Ministries (Ascension Sponsor), a public juridic person
Legal Title: Our Lady of Victory Hospital, Inc. Bed Capacity 24; Tot Asst. Annually 1,762; Total Staff 59.

STEVENS POINT. *Ascension St. Michael's Hospital, Inc.*, 900 Illinois Ave., Stevens Point, 54481. Tel: 715-346-5000; Fax: 715-346-5088; Email: timothy.waldoch@ascension.org; Web: healthcare.ascension.org. Debra Standridge, Regl. Pres.; Mr. Timothy Waldoch, Chief Mission Integration Officer; Antonina Olszewski, Dir. Spiritual Care. Sponsored by Ascension Health Ministries (Ascension Sponsor), a public juridic person
Legal Title: St. Michael's Hospital of Stevens Point, Inc. Bed Capacity 93; Tot Asst. Annually 15,301; Total Staff 425.

Ascension Medical Group - Northern Wisconsin, Inc., 824 Illinois Ave., Stevens Point, 54481. Tel: 715-342-7500; Fax: 715-346-5088; Email: timothy.waldoch@ascension.org; Web: healthcare.ascension.org. Mary Beth McDonald, Pres.; Mr. Timothy Waldoch, Chief Mission Integration Officer; Antonina Olszewski, Dir. Spiritual Care. Sponsored by Ascension Health Ministries (Ascension Sponsor), a public juridic person
Former Name: Ministry Medical Group, Inc. Tot Asst. Annually 217,760; Total Staff 637.

WESTON. *Ascension St. Clare's Hospital, Inc.* (2002) 3400 Ministry Pkwy., Weston, 54476. Tel: 715-393-3000; Fax: 715-359-1087; Email: timothy.waldoch@ascension.org; Web: healthcare.ascension.org. Debra Standridge, Regl. Pres.; Mr. Timothy Waldoch, Chief Mission Integration Officer; Antonina Olszewski, Dir. Spiritual Care. Sponsored by Ascension Health Ministries (Ascension Sponsor), a public juridic person
Legal Title: Saint Clare's Hospital of Weston, Inc. Bed Capacity 98; Tot Asst. Annually 9,006; Total Staff 317.

[E] REHABILITATION FACILITIES

CHIPPEWA FALLS. *L.E. Phillips Libertas Treatment Center* (1977) 2661 County Hwy. I, Chippewa Falls, 54729. Tel: 715-723-5585; Tel: 800-680-4578; Fax: 715-726-3504; Email: deon.dachel@hshs.org; Web: www.libertascenter.org. Andrew Bagnall, Pres. & CEO; Toni Simonson, Exec. Dir. Hospital Sisters Health System, Hospital Sisters of the Third Order of St. Francis. Bed Capacity 38; Tot Asst. Annually 1,500; Total Staff 45.

[F] HOMES FOR AGED

LA CROSSE. *Benedictine Manor*, 2902 East Ave. S., 54601. Tel: 608-788-9870; Fax: 608-787-8889; Email: john.padjen@bhshealth.org. John Padjen, CEO, Admin. Sponsored by the Benedictine Sisters of St. Scholastica Monastery. Tot Asst. Annually 186; Total Staff 177; Units 66.

Benedictine Villa, 2904 East Ave., S., 54601. Tel: 608-788-7489; Fax: 608-788-0857; Email: john.padjen@bhshealth.org. John Padjen, CEO, Admin. Sponsored by the Benedictine Sisters of St. Scholastica Monastery. Tot Asst. Annually 50; Total Staff 20; Units 43.

Bethany St. Joseph Care Center, 2501 Shelby Rd., 54601. Tel: 608-788-5700; Email: info@bsjcorp.com. Mr. Craig Ubbelohde, Admin. Bed Capacity 140; Tot Asst. Annually 350.

EAU CLAIRE. *St. Francis Apartments* (1986) 851 University Dr., Eau Claire, 54701. Tel: 715-834-1338; Email: therese.martens@hshs.org. Therese Martens, Mng. Agent
Hospital Sisters Health Care-West, Inc. Total in Residence 75; Units 60.

WAUSAU. *Benedictine Living Community of Wausau*, 1821 N. 4th Ave., Wausau, 54401. Tel: 715-675-9451; Fax: 715-675-4051; Email: gary.hixon@bhshealth.org. Gary Hixon, Admin. Sponsored by the Benedictine Sisters of St. Scholastica Monastery. Tot Asst. Annually 257; Total Staff 196; Units 82.

[G] RETREAT HOUSES

LA CROSSE. *Franciscan Spirituality Center*, 920 Market St., 54601-8809. Tel: 608-791-5295; Fax: 608-782-6301; Email: fscenter@fspa.org; Web: www.fscenter.org. Audrey Lucier, Dir.
Legal Title: Franciscan Sisters of Perpetual Adoration.

MARATHON. *St. Anthony's of Marathon, Inc.*, 300 E. 4th St., P.O. Box 86, Marathon, 54448-0086. Tel: 715-443-2236; Fax: 715-443-2235; Email: info@sarcenter.com; Email: lrandall@sarcenter.com; Web: www.sarcenter.com. Lori Randall, Dir.; Rev. Robert A. Streveler, In Res., (Retired).

[H] MONASTERIES AND RESIDENCES OF PRIESTS AND BROTHERS

LA CROSSE. *Holy Cross (Seminary) Diocesan Center*, 3710 East Ave. S., P.O. Box 4004, 54602-4004. Tel: 608-788-7700; Fax: 608-788-8413; Email: jrichards@diolc.org; Web: diolc.org. Deacon Joseph A. Richards, Building Dir.; Rev. Kurt J. Apfelbeck, In Res.; Very Rev. William A. Dhein, V.G., J.C.L., In Res.; Rev. Msgrs. Robert P. Hundt, J.C.L., In Res., (Retired); David C. Kunz, In Res.; Matthew G. Malnar, In Res., (Retired); Revs. Alan P. Wierzba, In Res.; Eugene J. Wolf, In Res., (Retired).

SPRING VALLEY. *Brothers of St. Pius X*, Woodland View Apts., W346 N. 2nd St., P.O. Box 284, Spring Valley, 54767. Tel: 715-778-4999; Email: mand30mb@frontiernet.net. Bro. Michael Mandernach, Contact Person.

WAUSAU. *St. Mary's Roman Catholic Oratory*, 408 Seymour St., Wausau, 54403-6266. Tel: 715-842-9995; Fax: 715-848-5615; Email: stmarysoratory@institute-christ-king.org; Web: www.institute-christ-king.org. Rev. Heitor Matheus, Vicar; Rev. Canon Aaron Huberfield, Rector
Legal Title: Institute of Christ the King Sovereign Priest. Offering the extraordinary form of the Mass.

[I] CONVENTS AND RESIDENCES FOR SISTERS

LA CROSSE. *St. Rose Convent*, 912 Market St., 54601-4782. 912 Market St., 54601-8800. Tel: 608-782-5610; Fax: 608-782-6301; Email: fspa@fspa.org; Web: www.fspa.org. Sr. Karen Lueck, F.S.P.A., Pres.; Rev. Richard Tulko, O.F.M., Chap. Motherhouse and Novitiate of the Congregation of the Franciscan Sisters of Perpetual Adoration. Sisters 206; In Motherhouse 54.

Villa St. Joseph, W2658 State Rd. 33, 54601-2625. Tel: 608-788-5100; Fax: 608-788-7360; Email: drydberg@villastj.org; Web: www.fspa.org. Sr. Delores Rydberg, F.S.P.A., Admin. Franciscan Sisters of Perpetual Adoration.A Retirement home for aged and convalescent Franciscan Sisters of Perpetual Adoration. Lay Staff 117; Sisters 3; Under Care 45.

CUSTER. *St. Clare Convent* (1874) (Felician Sisters) 7381 Church St., Custer, 54423. Tel: 715-592-4213. Sr. Mary Moore, Prov. Placement City: Polonia.

STEVENS POINT. *St. Joseph Motherhouse* (1901) Attn: Cindy Matteson, 1300 Maria Dr., Stevens Point, 54481-1141. Tel: 715-344-2830; Tel: 715-341-8457, Ext. 1; Fax: 715-344-2380; Email: cindy@ssj-tosf.org; Web: www.ssj-tosf.org. Ms. Cindy Matteson, CEO; Rev. Todd A. Mlsna, Chap., Tel: 715-344-8346. Residence of the Sisters of St. Joseph of the Third Order of St. Francis. Sisters 25.

[J] SOCIAL SERVICE AGENCIES

LA CROSSE. *Catholic Charities of the Diocese of La Crosse, Inc.* (1932) 3710 East Ave. S., P.O. Box 266, 54602-0266. Tel: 608-782-0710; Fax: 608-782-0702; Email: info@cclse.org; Web: www.cclse.org. Roberto Parterrieu, Exec. Dir. Adoption Services, Disability Services, Disaster Relief, Emergency Svcs., Fin. Counseling, Pregnancy & Parenting Svcs., Adoption Placement, Immigration Svcs., Disability Svcs., St. Lawrence Community Svcs., Homeless Shelters. Tot Asst. Annually 6,813; Total Staff 100.

WAUSAU. *Northland House*, 325 N. 1st Ave., Ste. 202B, P.O. Box 231, Wausau, 54401-0231. Tel: 715-845-4898; Fax: 715-848-0498; Email: nhgh@dwave.net; Web: www.northlandhouse.org. Kelli Anderson, Admin. Sponsored by the Benedictine Sisters of St. Scholastica Monastery.A subsidiary of Benedictine Health System. Tot Asst. Annually 97; Total Staff 8; Units 12.

[K] NEWMAN CAMPUS MINISTRY

EAU CLAIRE. *Newman Parish*, 110 Garfield Ave., Eau Claire, 54701-4042. Tel: 715-834-3399; Email: parishoffice@newmanec.com; Web: www.newmancc.com. Rev. Daniel E. Oudenhoven. Serving Univ. of Wisconsin-Eau Claire and Chippewa Valley Technical College.

MENOMONIE. *Newman Center at University of Wisconsin - Stout*, 710 2nd St. E., Menomonie, 54751-1808. Tel: 715-235-4258; Email: director@stoutcatholic.org; Web: stoutcatholic.org. Rev. John Muthu Vijayan, Chap.; Steven Drapalik, Campus Min.

[L] FOUNDATIONS, FUNDS & TRUSTS

LA CROSSE. *Aquinas Catholic Schools Foundation*, 315 S. 11th St., 54601. Tel: 608-784-8585 Business Office; Tel: 608-784-0707 Development Office; Email: brad.reinhart@aquinasschools.org. Rev. Msgr. Charles D. Stoetzel, Dean.

Bishop John J. Paul Scholarship Endowment Trust, 3710 East Ave. S., P.O. Box 4004, 54602-4004. Tel: 608-791-0171. Mr. Kurt Jereczek, Contact Person.

Bishop's Education Endowment Trust, 3710 East Ave. S., P.O. Box 4004, 54602-4004. Tel: 608-791-0171. Mr. Kurt Jereczek, Contact Person.

Blessed Sacrament Parish Endowment Trust, 130 Losey Blvd. S., 54601. Tel: 608-782-2953; Fax: 608-785-1064; Email: bspchurch@yahoo.com; Web: www.bsplacrosse.org. Mrs. Eileen Francksen, Contact Person.

Caritas Endowment Trust, 3710 East Ave. S., P.O. Box 266, 54602-0266. Tel: 608-782-0710; Fax: 608-782-0702; Email: lnigon@cclse.org. Lori Nigon, Fin. Dir.

Cathedral of St. Joseph the Workman Endowment Trust, 530 Main St., 54601-4033. Tel: 608-782-0322; Fax: 608-782-8228; Email: office@cathedralsjworkman.org. Rev. Msgr. Charles D. Stoetzel, Rector.

Diocese of La Crosse Youth Ministry Endowment Trust, Office of Youth Ministry, 3710 E. Ave. S., P.O. Box 4004, 54602-4004. Tel: 608-791-0171. Mr. Kurt Jereczek, Contact Person.

Father Joseph Walijewski Orphanage Endowment Trust, 3710 East Ave. S., P.O. Box 4004, 54602. Tel: 608-791-2685; Email: jreiter@diolc.org; Web: www.frjoesguiild.org. Jeffrey Reiter, Devel. Dir.

Holy Cross Seminary Education Fund Endowment Trust, 3710 East Ave S., P.O. Box 4004, 54602-4004. Tel: 608-791-0171; Email: kjereczek@diolc.org. Rev. Alan P. Wierzba, Vocation Dir.; Mr. Kurt Jereczek, Contact Person.

Holy Trinity Catholic Church Endowment Trust,

1333 13th St. S., 54601. Tel: 608-782-2028; Email: htparish@outlook.com. Rev. G. Richard Roberts.

St. James Parish Endowment Trust, 1032 Caledonia St., 54603-2510. Tel: 608-782-7557; Fax: 608-796-0086; Email: saintjameslacrosse@gmail.com. Very Rev. James F. Altman.

La Crosse Deanery Catholic Education Endowment Trust, 3710 East Ave S., P.O. Box 4004, 54602-4004. Tel: 608-788-7700; Email: treichenbacher@diolc.org; Web: diolc.org. Mr. Thomas Reichenbacher, Supt.

Mary, Mother of the Church Parish Endowment Trust, 2006 Weston St., 54601-6526. Tel: 608-788-5483; Fax: 608-788-4070; Email: secretary@mmoclacrosse.org; Web: www.mmoclacrosse.org. Rev. Brian D. Konopa.

Mayo Clinic Health System - Franciscan Healthcare Foundation, Inc., 700 West Ave. S., 54601. Tel: 608-784-6449; Fax: 608-791-9799; Email: grabow.peter@mayo.edu; Email: hansen.julie@mayo.edu; Web: www.mayohealthsystem.org. Julie Hansen, CFO; Peter Grabow, Dir.

Roncalli Newman Parish Student Endowment Trust, 1732 State St., 54601. Tel: 608-784-4994; Fax: 608-784-0230; Email: ckaufman@roncallinewmancenter.org; Web: www.roncallinewmancenter.com. Rev. Billy J. Dodge.

ALMOND. *St. Maximilian Kolbe Church Endowment Trust*, 8611 State Rd. 54, Almond, 54909-9704. Tel: 715-824-3380; Email: angie@stmaxkolbe.org; Web: www.stmaxkolbe.org. Rev. Peter M. Manickam.

ALTOONA. *St. Mary Parish Endowment Trust*, 1812 Lynn Ave., Altoona, 54720. Tel: 715-855-1294; Fax: 715-855-8664; Email: stmarypar@gmail.com. Rev. Derek J. Sakowski.

ARCADIA. *Holy Family School Endowment Trust Fund*, 532 E. McKinley St., Arcadia, 54612-1522. Tel: 608-323-3676; Email: barb@holyfam.com; Web: www.holyfam.com. Very Rev. Sebastian J. Kolodziejczyk, Dean; Mrs. Nicole Michalak, Prin.; Rev. Kyle N. Laylan.

Franciscan Skemp Foundation of Arcadia, Inc., 700 West Ave. S., 54601. Tel: 608-392-9710; Email: hansen.julie@mayo.edu; Web: www.mayoclinichealthsytems.org. Julie Hansen, CFO.

ATHENS. *Saint Anthony Parish Endowment Trust*, 417 Caroline St., P.O. Box 206, Athens, 54411. Tel: 715-257-7684; Fax: 715-257-7791; Email: tricia.rogaczewski@staathens.org. Rev. George Nelson Graham.

AUBURNDALE. *St. Mary Education Endowment Trust*, 5866 Main St., P.O. Box 177, Auburndale, 54412-0177. Tel: 715-652-2806; Fax: 715-652-8020; Email: saintsmmk@gmail.com; Web: www.saintsmmk.com. Rev. A. Antony Arokiyam.

BEVENT. *St. Ladislaus Parish Bevent Endowment Trust*, 173141 State State Hwy. 153, Hatley, 54440. Tel: 715-446-3060; Fax: 715-446-2668; Email: parishsecretary@stladislaus.org; Web: stladislaus.weebly.com. Rev. Augustine Kofi Bentil; Sr. Mary Ellen Diermeier, S.S.J.-T.O.S.F., Pastoral Assoc.

BIG RIVER. *The St. Mary's-Big River Endowment Trust*, Pastor, W10137 570th Ave., River Falls, 54022-4933. Tel: 715-425-5806; Email: stmarys@dishup.us; Web: www.stmarysbigriver.com. Very Rev. Kevin C. Louis, S.T.L. Placement City: Big River.

BLAIR. *The St. Ansgar Catholic Church Endowment Trust*, 607 E. Olson St., Blair, 54616. Tel: 608-525-3811; Email: stbridgets@centurytel.net. 22650 Washington St., Ettrick, 54627-9598. Rev. Amalraj Antony.

BLOOMER. *St. Paul Catholic Parish of Bloomer Wisconsin Endowment Trust*, 1222 Main St., Bloomer, 54724-1325. Tel: 715-568-3255; Email: stpaulreoffice@bloomer.net; Web: stpauls.bloomertel.net. Rev. Victor C. Feltes.

CASHTON. *Holy Family Endowment Trust Fund*, 1205 Front St., Cashton, 54619-8029. Tel: 608-654-5654; Email: smash3ppastor@mwt.net. Rev. Michael E. Klos.

Sacred Heart of Jesus Education Endowment Trust, 1205 Front St., Cashton, 54619. Tel: 608-654-5654; Fax: 608-654-5760; Email: smash3pfinance@mwt.net. Rev. Michael E. Klos.

CHIPPEWA FALLS. *St. Charles Future Fund Trust*, 810 Pearl St., Chippewa Falls, 54729-1729. Tel: 715-723-4088; Fax: 715-723-2195; Email: StChrls723@gmail.com. Rev. Msgr. Michael J. Gorman, V.G., J.C.L.

The Education/Sustaining Endowment Trust, 412 Main St., Chippewa Falls, 54729. Tel: 715-723-4890; Fax: 715-723-7358. Rev. Justin J. Kizewski.

St. Joseph's Foundation, 2661 County Hwy. I, Chippewa Falls, 54729. Tel: 715-717-7397; Fax: 715-717-7258; Email: cheryl.halida@hshs.org; Web: www.stjoeschipfalls.com. Cheryl Halida, Contact Person.

McDonell Catholic Schools Endowment Trust, 1316 Bel Air Blvd., Chippewa Falls, 54729. Tel: 715-723-0538, Ext. 2200; Fax: 715-723-1501; Email: president@macs.k12.wi.us. Jeffrey Heinzen, Pres.; Teresa Dachel, Business Mgr.

Notre Dame Children's Endowment Trust, 117 Allen St., Chippewa Falls, 54729-2899. Tel: 715-723-7108; Fax: 715-723-7523; Email: parishoffice@thechurchofnotredame.org. Rev. Jesse D. Burish.

Notre Dame Parish Endowment Trust, 117 Allen St., Chippewa Falls, 54729-2899. Tel: 715-723-7108; Fax: 715-723-7523; Email: parishoffice@thechurchofnotredame.org. Rev. Jesse D. Burish.

COLBY. *St. Mary's Catholic School, Colby Endowment Trust*, 205 S. 2nd St., Colby, 54421. 205 S. 2nd St., P.O. Box 436, Colby, 54421-0436. Tel: 715-223-3048; Email: catholiccentral@gmail.com. Rev. D. Joseph Redfern.

DURAND. *St. Mary Catholic School Endowment Trust*, 901 W. Prospect St., Durand, 54736. P.O. Box 188, Durand, 54736-0188. Tel: 715-672-5640; Email: sanns@nelson-tel.net. Rev. Paul Bosco Anthony.

EAU CLAIRE. *Friends of St. James the Greater Catholic School at Eau Claire Tuition Endowment Trust*, 2502 11th St., Ste. 1, Eau Claire, 54703-2700. Tel: 715-835-5887; Email: stjameseac@aol.com; Web: www.stjameseauclaire.org. Rev. Thomas J. Krieg.

Hospital Sisters of St. Francis Foundation, Inc., 900 W. Clairemont Ave., Eau Claire, 54701. Tel: 715-717-4925; Email: Amy.Bulpitt@hshs.org; Web: www.sacredhearteauclaire.org. Ann Carr, Treas. HSHS Sacred Heart Foundation (a division of Hospital Sisters of St. Francis Foundation, Inc.).

The St. James the Greater Catholic Church Endowment Trust, 2502 11th St., Ste. 1, Eau Claire, 54703-2700. Tel: 715-835-5887; Fax: 715-835-3110; Email: stjameseac@aol.com; Web: www.stjameseauclaire.org. Rev. Thomas J. Krieg.

St. Olaf Parish Endowment Trust, 3220 Monroe St., P.O. Box 1203, Eau Claire, 54703-1203. Tel: 715-832-2504; Fax: 715-832-0742; Email: stolaf@saintaolafparish.org; Web: www.saintolafparish.org. Rev. James J. Kurzynski.

St. Patrick of Eau Claire Endowment Trust, 322 Fulton St., Eau Claire, 54703-5323. Tel: 715-832-0925; Email: office@shspec.org; Web: www.shspec.org. Rev. Brian J. Jazdzewski.

Regis Catholic Schools Educational Endowment Trust (Case Endowment Fund) 2728 Mall Dr., Ste. 200, Eau Claire, 54701. Tel: 715-878-9495; Email: foundation@regiscatholicschools.com. Todd Hehli, Foundation Pres.

Regis Catholic Schools Foundation, 2728 Mall Dr., Ste. 200, Eau Claire, 54701. Tel: 715-878-9495; Email: foundation@regiscatholicschools.com; Web: www.regiscatholicschoolsfoundation.com. Todd Hehli, Foundation Pres.

The Sacred Heart Parish Endowment Trust, 322 Fulton St., Eau Claire, 54703. Tel: 715-832-0925; Fax: 715-832-0366; Email: office@shspec.org. Rev. Brian J. Jazdzewski.

ELLSWORTH. *The St. Francis Parish Endowment Trust*, 264 S. Grant, P.O. Box 839, Ellsworth, 54011. Tel: 715-273-4774; Fax: 715-273-4066; Email: stfrancisrectory@sbcglobal.net. Rev. Eric Aworte-Dadson, (Ghana).

HOLMEN. *St. Elizabeth Ann Seton Endowment Trust*, 515 N. Main St., Holmen, 54636. Tel: 608-526-4424 ; Fax: 608-526-3177; Email: office@seasholmen.org. Rev. John L. Parr.

INDEPENDENCE. *The SS. Peter & Paul Parish-Independence Education Endowment Trust*, 36028 Osseo Rd., P.O. Box 430, Independence, 54747-0430. Tel: 715-985-2227; Fax: 715-985-2649. Very Rev. Woodrow H. Pace.

MARATHON. *Nativity of the Blessed Virgin Mary, Marathon Endowment Trust*, 712 Market, P.O. Box 7, Marathon, 54448-0007. Tel: 715-443-2045; Email: bvmparish@stmarysmarathon.org; Web: stmarysmarathon.weconnect.com. Rev. Msgr. Joseph G. Diermeier, V.G., J.C.L.

MARSHFIELD. *Columbus High School Foundation*, 710 S. Columbus Ave., Marshfield, 54449. Tel: 715-387-2444; Fax: 715-384-4535; Email: vicky.tracy@columbusdons.org; Web: www.columbuscatholicschools.org. Victoria Tracy, Devel. Coord.

Foundation of Saint Joseph's Hospital of Marshfield, Inc., 3400 Ministry Pkwy., Weston, 54476. Tel: 715-393-2604; Fax: 715-359-1087; Email: timothy.waldoch@ascension.org; Web: healthcare.ascension.org/donate. Patti Shafto-Carlson, Dir.; Mr. Timothy Waldoch, Chief Mission Integration Officer; Mrs. Lisa Froemming, Vice Pres. for Philanthropy. Sponsored by Ascension Health Ministries (Ascension Sponsor), a public juridic person.

St. John the Baptist Educational Endowment Trust, 201 W. Blodgett St., Marshfield, 54449. Tel: 715-384-3252; Fax: 715-384-3252; Email: mjgouin@frontier.com. Very Rev. Samuel A. Martin.

St. John the Baptist Maintenance Endowment Trust, 201 W. Blodgett St., Marshfield, 54449. Tel: 715-384-3252; Fax: 715-384-3252; Email: mjgouin@frontier.com. Very Rev. Samuel A. Martin.

Marshfield Area Catholic Schools Endowment Trust, 710 S. Columbus Ave., Marshfield, 54449. Tel: 715-387-2444; Email: eaton.david@columbusdons.org. Victoria Tracy, Devel. Coord.

The Our Lady of Peace Endowment Trust, 510 S. Columbus Ave., Marshfield, 54449. Tel: 715-384-9414; Fax: 715-384-6606; Email: office@olpmarshfield.com; Web: www.olpmarshfield.com. Rev. Douglas C. Robertson.

MAUSTON. *St. Patrick's Congregation Trust*, 401 Mansion St., Mauston, 53948-1367. Tel: 608-847-6054; Fax: 608-847-3288; Email: stpatrickparishmauston@gmail.com; Web: www.stpatrickmauston.com. Very Rev. John A. Potaczek.

MENOMONIE. *The St. Joseph School at Menomonie Endowment Trust*, 910 Wilson Ave., Menomonie, 54751. Tel: 715-232-4922; Fax: 715-232-4923; Email: mary.allison@menomoniecatholic.org; Web: menomoniecatholic.org. Mrs. Keila Drout, Prin.; Rev. John Muthu Vijayan; Mrs. Carol Stratton, Business Mgr.

MOSINEE. *St. Paul Parish Endowment Trust*, 603 4th St., Mosinee, 54455. Tel: 715-693-2650; Email: parish@stpaulmosinee.org. Very Rev. Donald L. Meuret.

NEILLSVILLE. *The St. Mary's Catholic Church Endowment Trust*, 1813 Black River Rd., Neillsville, 54456-1033. Tel: 715-743-3840; Fax: 715-743-7963; Email: stmaryneillsville@tds.net; Web: stmaryneillsville.weebly.com. Rev. Varkey Velickakathu.

ONALASKA. *Charles Simpson of St. Patrick Parish, Onalaska Endowment Trust*, 1031 Main St., Onalaska, 54650-2742. Tel: 608-783-5535; Email: sj6340@yahoo.com; Web: www.stpatsonalaska.com. Deacon Frank J. Abnet, Contact Person.

Father John Rossiter and Friends Endowment Trust of St. Patrick Parish, 1031 Main St., Onalaska, 54650-2742. Tel: 608-783-5535; Email: sj6340@yahoo.com; Web: www.stpatsonalaska.com. Rev. Msgr. Steven J. Kachel; Deacon Frank J. Abnet, Fin. Officer.

PITTSVILLE. *St. Joachim's Parish Endowment Trust*, 5312 3rd Ave., P.O. Box 69, Pittsville, 54466. Tel: 715-884-6815; Email: friarjo@tds.net. Rev. Amalanathan Malaiyappan.

PLOVER. *St. Bronislava Parish, Plover Endowment Trust*, 3200 Plover Rd., P.O. Box 158, Plover, 54467-0158. Tel: 715-344-4326; Fax: 715-344-6121; Email: parishoffice@stbrons.com; Web: stbrons.com. Rev. Edward J. Shuttleworth.

POLONIA. *Sacred Heart School, Polonia Endowment Trust*, 7379 Church St., Custer, 54423. Tel: 715-592-4902; Email: tmccann@sacredheartpolonia.org. Mr. Thomas McCann, Prin. Placement City: Polonia.

PORT EDWARDS. *St. Alexander's Church, Port Edwards Endowment Trust*, 880 First St., Port Edwards, 54469. Tel: 715-887-3012; Fax: 715-887-3748; Email: stalexander@wctc.net; Web: saintalexander.weebley.com. Rev. R. John Swing.

PRAIRIE DU CHIEN. *The St. Gabriel's Endowment Trust*, 506 N. Beaumont Rd., Prairie du Chien, 53821. Tel: 608-326-2404; Email: sgp@prairiecatholic.org; Web: prairiecatholic.org. Very Rev. James C. Weighner.

The St. John's Endowment Trust, 710 S. Wacouta Ave., Prairie du Chien, 53821. Tel: 608-326-6511; Email: lgratace@prairiecatholic.org; Web: prairiecatholic.org. Very Rev. James C. Weighner.

RICHLAND CENTER. *The Assumption of the Blessed Virgin Mary Parish Endowment Trust*, 160 W. 4th St., Richland Center, 53581. Tel: 608-647-2621; Fax: 608-647-6029; Email: cheryl.blankenship@stmarysrc.com; Web: stmarysrc.com. Rev. Msgr. Roger J. Scheckel.

ROTHSCHILD. *The St. Mark Catholic Parish Endowment Trust*, 602 Military Rd., Rothschild, 54474-1523. Tel: 715-359-5206; Fax: 715-355-8904; Email: stmarkroths@smproths.org; Web: www.smproths.org. Very Rev. Allan L. Slowiak.

SCHOFIELD. *St. Therese Catholic Church Endowment Fund*, 112 Kort St. W, Schofield, 54476. Tel: 715-359-2421; Fax: 715-355-3088; Email: colleen@sttheresecc.org; Web: sttheresecc.org. Rev. Louis Britto D. Susairaj.

SPARTA. *Endowment Trust of the Friends and Parishioners of St. Patrick Parish*, 319 W. Main St., Sparta, 54656-2143. Tel: 608-269-2655; Email:

stprectory@stpats.net; Web: stpatricksparish.weconnect.com. Very Rev. Eric R. Berns.

Mayo Clinic Health System - Franciscan Healthcare Foundation of Sparta, Inc., 310 W. Main St., Sparta, 54656-2142. 700 West Ave., S., 54601. Tel: 608-269-2132; Fax: 608-269-4562; Email: hawthorne.kimberly@mayo.edu; Web: www.mayohealthsystem.org. Kimberly A. Hawthorne, Admin.; Robert O'Brien, Contact Person.

STANLEY. *St. Rose of Lima Catholic Church Endowment Trust*, 226 E. 3rd Ave., P.O. Box 125, Stanley, 54768-0125. Tel: 715-644-5435; Email: info@allsaintscathcom.com. Rev. William P. Felix.

STEVENS POINT. *Catholic Schools Endowment Trust in Portage County, Wisconsin*, 1301 Maria Dr., Stevens Point, 54481. Tel: 715-341-2445; Fax: 715-342-2001; Email: ghansel@pacellicatholicschools.com; Web: www.pacellicatholicschools.com. Hannah Henderson, Devel. Dir.

Saint Michael's Foundation of Stevens Point, Inc., 900 Illinois Ave., Stevens Point, 54481. Tel: 715-343-3259; Fax: 715-343-3330; Email: timothy.waldoch@ascension.org; Web: healthcare.ascension.org/Donate. Margo Willard, Dir.; Mr. Timothy Waldoch, Chief Mission Integration Officer; Mrs. Lisa Froemming, Vice Pres. for Philanthropy. Sponsored by Ascension Health Ministries (Ascension Sponsor), a public juridic person.

Newman Campus Ministry Endowment Trust, 838 Fremont St., Stevens Point, 54481. Tel; 715-344-9117; Email: contact@holyspiritstevenspoint.org; Web: www.holyspiritstevenspoint.org. Very Rev. Steven J. Brice.

Pacelli High School Foundation, 1301 Maria Dr., Stevens Point, 54481. Tel: 715-341-2445; Fax: 715-342-2001; Email: ghansel@pacellicatholicschools.com; Web: www.pacellicatholicschools.com. Hannah Henderson, Devel. Dir.; Mr. Gregg Hansel, Dir. Educ.; LouAnn Shulfer, Vice Chair.

St. Joseph Parish, Stevens Point Endowment Trust, 1709 Wyatt Ave., Stevens Point, 54481-3615. Tel: 715-341-1617; Email: rschneeberg@stjoespoint.org; Web: www.togetherinfaith.org. Revs. Todd A. Mlsna; Jerzy Rebacz.

St. Stanislaus Kostka Congregation, Stevens Point Endowment Trust, 838 Fremont St., Stevens Point, 54481. Tel: 715-344-9117; Email: contact@holyspiritstevenspoint.org. Very Rev. Steven J. Brice.

St. Stephen Parish Endowment Trust, 1401 Clark St., Stevens Point, 54481-2906. Tel: 715-344-3319; Fax: 715-344-6101; Email: ststephensp@gmail.com; Web: www.saintstephenparish.webs.com. Rev. Jerzy Rebacz.

STRATFORD. *St. Joseph Parish Endowment Trust*, 420 E. Larch St., P.O. Box 6, Stratford, 54484. Tel: 715-687-2404; Email: stjosephoffice1@gmail.com. Rev. Sengole Vethamanickam.

TILDEN. *St. Peter Parish Endowment Trust*, 11358 County Hwy. Q, Chippewa Falls, 54729. 810 Pearl St., Chippewa Falls, 54729-1729. Tel: 715-723-4088; Fax: 715-723-2195; Email: StChrls723@gmail.com. Rev. Msgr. Michael J. Gorman, V.G., J.C.L.

TOMAH. *The St. Mary's Catholic Church Educational Endowment Trust*, 303 W. Monroe St., Tomah, 54660. Tel: 608-372-4516; Fax: 608-372-4440; Email: cbailey@queenoftheapostlestomah.com. Rev. Msgr. Richard W. Gilles, J.C.L.

VIROQUA. *St. Mary's Parish Viroqua Endowment Trust*, 400 Congress Ave., Viroqua, 54665. Tel: 608-637-7711; Email: stmaryparish@mwt.net. Rev. Janusz A. Kowalski.

WAUMANDEE. *St. Boniface Parish Catholic School Endowment Trust Fund*, S2022 County Rd. U, Waumandee, 54622. Tel: 608-626-2621; Email: tresecclesiae@gmail.com. Rev. Prince Amala Jesuraja.

WAUSAU. *Church of the Resurrection Parish Church Building Endowment Trust*, 621 N. 2nd St., Wausau, 54403-4802. Tel: 715-845-6715; Email: finance@eastsideparishes.org. Rev. Msgr. Mark R. Pierce, J.C.L.

St. Michael Parish Endowment Trust, 611 Stark St., Wausau, 54403-3577. Tel: 715-842-4283; Email: vicki@eastsideparishes.org; Web: www.eastsideparishes.org. Rev. Msgr. Mark R. Pierce, J.C.L.

**Newman Catholic Schools Endowment Trust*, 619 Stark St., Wausau, 54403. Tel: 715-845-5735; Fax: 715-848-3582; Email: mmartin@newmancatholicschools.com; Web: www.newmancatholicschools.com. Michael Martin, Pres.

WESTON. *Foundation of Saint Clare's Hospital of Weston, Inc.*, 3400 Ministry Pkwy., Weston, 54476. Tel: 715-393-2604; Fax: 715-393-2645; Email: timothy.waldoch@ascension.org; Web: healthcare.ascension.org/Donate. Patti Shafto-Carlson, Dir.; Mr. Timothy Waldoch, Chief Mission Integration Officer; Mrs. Lisa Froemming, Vice Pres. for Philanthropy. Sponsored by Ascension Health Ministries (Ascension Sponsor), a public juridic person.

WHITEHALL. *St. John Parish Endowment Trust*, 35900 Lee St., P.O. Box 566, Whitehall, 54773. Tel: 715-538-4607; Fax: 715-538-9236; Email: sjawhitehall@gmail.com. Very Rev. Woodrow H. Pace.

WILLARD. *Holy Family Parish, Willard Endowment Trust*, W8170 Main St., Willard, 54493. Tel: 715-255-8017; Email: stap1931@gmail.com. 407 N. Division St., P.O. Box 69, Loyal, 54446. Rev. Leo Stanislaus.

WISCONSIN RAPIDS. *St. Lawrence Parish, Wisconsin Rapids Endowment Trust*, 530 10th Ave. N., Wisconsin Rapids, 54495-2566. Tel: 715-421-5777; Email: slparishwr@gmail.com. Rev. David P. Bruener.

Our Lady Queen of Heaven Parish Endowment Trust, 750 10th Ave. S., Wisconsin Rapids, 54495. Tel: 715-423-1251; Fax: 715-423-9407; Email: olqh@solarus.net; Web: www.our-lady.org. Rev. G. Valentine Joseph.

St. Vincent de Paul Parish, Wisconsin Rapids Endowment Trust, 820 13th St. S., Wisconsin Rapids, 54494. Tel: 715-423-2111; Email: stvin@wctc.net. Rev. Jerome Patric.

Assumption Catholic Schools Endowment, 445 Chestnut St., Wisconsin Rapids, 54494. Tel: 714-422-0910; Web: assumptioncatholicschools.org. Daniel Minter, Pres.

[M] ASSOCIATIONS OF THE FAITHFUL

LA CROSSE. SOCIETY OF THE OBLATES OF WISDOM, 119 Sheridon Rd., Eastman, 54626-8702. Tel: 608-874-5221; Tel: 314-621-2055; Email: jfmccarthy1@sbcglobal.net; Email: materdei82@hotmail.com; Web: www.rtforum.org. P.O. Box 13230, St. Louis, MO 63157. Rev. Msgr. John F. McCarthy, P.A., J.C.D., S.T.D., Dir.; Rev. Brian Harrison, First Asst. to the Dir. Gen.

Marian Academy of the Oblates of Holy Tradition, P.O. Box 13230, 54602-4004. Tel: 970-586-5689; Cell: 970-412-7420; Email: jfmccarthy1@sbcglobal.net; Email: materdei82@hotmail.com. 119 Sheridon Rd., Eastman, 54626-8702.

BOYD. INSTITUTE OF ST. JOSEPH, 31360 County Hwy. MM, Boyd, 54726-5988. Tel: 715-667-3372; Email: writeus@isjoseph.com. Revs. William P. Felix, Moderator; John Mary Gilbert, Chap.

[N] MISCELLANEOUS LISTINGS

LA CROSSE. *St. Ambrose Financial Services, Inc.*, 3710 East Ave., S., P.O. Box 4004, 54602-4004. Tel: 608-791-2669; Email: dherricks@stambrosefinancial.com; Web: stambrosefinancial.com. Dennis Herricks, Exec. Dir.

La Crosse Guild of the Catholic Medical Association, W5560 County Rd. MM, 54601-2209. Tel: 608-788-5052; Email: slpavela@gmail.com. Stephen Pavela, Pres.

The Marian Catechist Apostolate, 5250 Justin Rd., P.O. Box 637, 54602-0637. Tel: 608-782-0011; Fax: 608-796-0086; Email: InternationalOffice@MarianCatechist.com; Web: mariancatechist.com. His Eminence Raymond Leo Cardinal Burke, D.D., J.C.D., Intl. Dir. & Episcopal Mod.; Theresa Ann Knothe, Dir.

Marian Catechist Apostolate, Inc., 5250 Justin Rd., P.O. Box 637, 54601-0637. Tel: 608-782-0011; Email: InternationalOffice@MarianCatechist.com; Web: www.mariancatechist.com. Theresa Ann Knothe, Intl. Coord.

Mater Redemptoris House of Formation, 3730 East Ave. S., P.O. Box 4004, 54602-4004. Tel: 608-788-4530; Fax: 608-788-4571; Email: materredemptoris@gmail.com; Web: www.materredmptoris.org. Sr. M. Consolata Crews, F.S.G.M., Supr.

**Mayo Clinic Health System - Franciscan Healthcare, Inc., Corporate Office*, 700 West Ave. S., 54601-4783. Tel: 608-785-9710; Fax: 608-791-9429; Email: hansen.julie@mayo.edu; Web: www.mayohealthsystem.org. Timothy Johnson, M.D., Pres. & CEO, Integrated Healthcare Delivery System. Sponsored by the Congregation of the Sisters of the Third Order of St. Francis of Perpetual Adoration (Franciscan Sisters of Perpetual Adoration) and Mayo Foundation.

**Mayo Clinic Health System - Franciscan Medical Center, Inc.*, 700 West Ave. S., 54601-4796. Tel: 608-785-0940; Fax: 608-791-9429; Email: hansen.julie@mayo.edu; Web: www.mayohealthsystem.org. Timothy Johnson, M.D., Regl. Vice Pres. Bed Capacity 331; Total Staff 3,925.

Gerard Hall, 940 Division St., 54401. Tel: 608-791-3985; Email: renley.vanessa@mayo.edu. Vanessa Renley, Admin. 8 bed home for women with AODA, MH, or Pregnancy and Parenting Issues. Bed Capacity 8; Tot Asst. Annually 44; Total Staff 5.

Men's Recovery House, 1005 Jackson St., 54601. Tel: 608-392-4542. A 9-bed facility for treating men with substance abuse and serious mental illness. Bed Capacity 9; Total Staff 6; Patient Days 1,546.

St. Clare Health Mission, 916 Ferry St., 54601. Tel: 608-392-9544; Fax: 608-392-9570; Email: schmschedule@aol.com; Web: www.stclarehealthmission.org. Sandy Brekke, Clinic Dir. A non-profit organization run by volunteers to bring free health care to those most in need.

Women's Recovery House, 1005 Jackson St., 54601. Tel: 608-392-4578; Tel: 608-392-6872. An 8-bed treatment facility for women with substance abuse and also serious mental illness. Bed Capacity 8; Total Staff 5; Patient Days 1,743.

Shrine of Our Lady of Guadalupe, 5250 Justin Rd., P.O. Box 1237, 54602-1237. Tel: 608-782-5440; Fax: 608-782-3104; Email: larvidson@guadalupeshrine.org; Web: www.guadalupeshrine.org. Mr. Leif E. Arvidson, Exec. Dir.

We Belong To Christ Campaign, Inc., 3710 East Ave. S., P.O. Box 4004, 54602-4004. Tel: 608-7910-2685; Fax: 608-788-3854; Email: jreiter@diolc.org. Jeffrey Reiter, Dir.

EAU CLAIRE. *Hospital Sisters Health Care-West, Inc.*, St. Francis Apartments, 851 University Dr., Eau Claire, 54701. Tel: 217-523-4747; Email: Amy.Bulpitt@hshs.org. Ann Carr, Treas.

GENOA. *The Hermitage of St. Mary, Inc.* (1997) W1498 Spring Coulee Rd., Genoa, 54632. Tel: 608-386-5143; Email: hermitageofst.mary@hotmail.com. Sr. Mary Dawiczyk, H.S.M., Pres. & Treas.

STEVENS POINT. *Ascension at Prentice Street Department of Ascension Saint Michael's Hospital*, 209 Prentice St. N., Stevens Point, 54481. Tel: 715-344-4611; Fax: 715-344-8127; Email: todd.kuhn@ascensionhealth.org; Web: healthcare.ascension.org. Laurie Roberts, Exec. Dir. Corporate Sponsor: Ministry Health Care, Inc. (Milwaukee, WI); Sponsored by Sisters of the Sorrowful Mother.

WILLARD. *The Christine Center*, W8303 Mann Rd., Willard, 54493. Tel: 715-267-7507; Fax: 715-267-7512; Email: christinecenter@tds.net; Web: www.christinecenter.org. Russell King, Exec. Dir.

RELIGIOUS INSTITUTES OF MEN REPRESENTED IN THE DIOCESE

For further details refer to the corresponding bracketed number in the Religious Institutes of Men or Women section.

[1180]—*Brothers of Saint Pius X* (La Crosse)—C.S.P.X.

[0485]—*Congregation of Missionaries of St. Francis de Sales* (N.E. India Prov.)—M.S.F.S.

[0480]—*Conventual Franciscans*—O.F.M.Conv.

[0520]—*Franciscan Friars* (Assumption of the B.V.M. Prov.)—O.F.M.

[0533]—*Franciscan Friars of the Immaculate*—F.I.

[0305]—*Institute of Christ the King*—I.C.

RELIGIOUS INSTITUTES OF WOMEN REPRESENTED IN THE DIOCESE

[1780]—*Congregation of the Sisters of the Third Order of St. Francis of Perpetual Adoration* (La Crosse, WI)—F.S.P.A.

[1820]—*Hospital Sisters of the Third Order of St. Francis* (Springfield, IL)—O.S.F.

[]—*Presentation Sisters of the Blessed Virgin Mary* (Philippines).

[2970]—*School Sisters of Notre Dame* (Milwaukee Prov.)—S.S.N.D.

[]—*Secular Institute of Schoenstatt Sisters of Mary*—I.S.S.M.

[3590]—*Servants of Mary* (Ladysmith, WI)—O.S.M.

[1600]—*Sisters of St. Francis of the Martyr St. George* (Alton, IL)—F.S.G.M.

[3930]—*Sisters of St. Joseph - Third Order Regular* (Stevens Point, WI)—S.S.J.-T.O.S.F.

[0230]—*Sisters of the Order of St. Benedict* (St. Joseph, MN)—O.S.B.

[4100]—*Sisters of the Sorrowful Mother* (U.S./Caribbean Prov.)—S.S.M.

DIOCESAN CEMETERIES

LA CROSSE. *Catholic Cemetery*, 519 Losey Blvd. S., 54601. Tel: 608-782-0238; Email: jreinhart1@yahoo.com. Jeffrey Reinhart, Supt. Gate of Heaven Cemetery; French Island Cemetery; Catholic Cemetery.

Woodlawn, 3636 Mormon Coulee Rd., 54601. Tel: 608-788-0980; Email: jreinhart1@yahoo.com. John Reinhart, Supt., Tel: 608-792-2555

CHIPPEWA FALLS. *Chippewa Catholic Cemetery Assoc., Inc.*, 418 N. State St., Chippewa Falls, 54729.

Tel: 715-723-0792; Email: cfcatholiccemetery@gmail.com. Peter J. Danielson, Supt.

EAU CLAIRE. *Calvary Cemetery Association*, 4100 S. Hastings Way, P.O. Box 633, Eau Claire, 54702-0633. Tel: 715-831-2156; Email: managercccec@gmail.com. Jim Theisen, Pres.; Peter Wagener, Mgr.; Diane Dingman, Treas.

MARSHFIELD. *Gate of Heaven*, 1100 St. Joseph Ave., Marshfield, 54449. 7883 Hwy. 80, Marshfield, 54449. Tel: 715-486-2098; Tel: 715-676-2629; Email: zif00@hotmail.com; Email: hilltop@ci.marshfield.wi.us. Dennis Wolf, Pres.; Michael Baltus, Sexton

STEVENS POINT. *Stevens Point Area Catholic Cemetery Association, Inc.*, 1232 Wilshire Blvd., Stevens Point, 54481. Tel: 715-341-3236; Email: spacca@att.net; Web: www.stevenspointcatholiccemetery.com. John Okonek, Supt. Serves St. Bronislava, St. Joseph, St. Peter, St. Stephen & Holy Spirit parishes.

NECROLOGY

† DuChez, Daniel B., (Retired), Died Mar. 1, 2018
† Finucan, J. Thomas, (Retired), Died May. 14, 2018
† Grassl, Joseph Alfred, (Retired), Died Jan. 18, 2018
† Keating, Joseph R., (Retired), Died Sep. 29, 2018
† Pedretti, Raymond J., (Retired), Died May. 10, 2018
† Smith, Thomas J., (Retired), Died Oct. 11, 2018
† Thome, Edwin J., (Retired), Died May. 9, 2018

An asterisk (*) denotes an organization that has established tax-exempt status directly with the IRS and is not covered by the USCCB Group Ruling.

Diocese of Lafayette

(Dioecesis Lafayettensis)

Most Reverend

J. DOUGLAS DESHOTEL

Bishop of Lafayette; ordained priest May 13, 1978; appointed Auxiliary Bishop of Dallas and Titular Bishop of Cova, March 11, 2010; Episcopal ordination April 27, 2010; appointed Bishop of Lafayette February 17, 2016; installed April 15, 2016. *Office: 1408 Carmel Dr., Lafayette, LA 70501-5298.*

CARITAS CHRISTI URGET ME

Most Reverend

MICHAEL JARRELL, D.D.

Retired Bishop of Lafayette; ordained June 3, 1967; ordained to the episcopacy and installed as second Bishop of Houma-Thibodaux March 4, 1993; appointed sixth Bishop of Lafayette November 8, 2002; installed December 18, 2002; retired February 17, 2016. *Office: 1408 Carmel Dr., Lafayette, LA 70501-5298.*

ESTABLISHED JANUARY 11, 1918.

Square Miles 5,777.

Comprises the civil parishes (Counties) of Acadia, Evangeline, Iberia, Lafayette, St. Landry, St. Martin and St. Mary (west of Atchafalaya River) and Vermilion in the south central part of the State of Louisiana.

For legal titles of Diocese, parishes and diocesan institutions, consult the Chancery Office.

Administrative Offices: Diocesan Office Building, 1408 Carmel Dr., Lafayette, LA 70501-5298. Tel: 337-261-5500; Fax: 337-261-5603.

Web: www.diolaf.org

Email: rstevenson@diolaf.org

STATISTICAL OVERVIEW

Personnel	
Bishop	1
Retired Bishops	1
Abbots	1
Priests: Diocesan Active in Diocese	105
Priests: Diocesan Active Outside Diocese	5
Priests: Retired, Sick or Absent	44
Number of Diocesan Priests	154
Religious Priests in Diocese	58
Total Priests in Diocese	212
Extern Priests in Diocese	8
Ordinations:	
Diocesan Priests	7
Transitional Deacons	3
Permanent Deacons in Diocese	111
Total Brothers	6
Total Sisters	106
Parishes	
Parishes	121
With Resident Pastor:	
Resident Diocesan Priests	84
Resident Religious Priests	15
Without Resident Pastor:	
Administered by Priests	22
Missions	28
Professional Ministry Personnel:	
Sisters	4
Lay Ministers	256
Welfare	
Catholic Hospitals	1
Total Assisted	109,022
Homes for the Aged	31
Total Assisted	4,978
Special Centers for Social Services	15
Total Assisted	187,371
Educational	
Diocesan Students in Other Seminaries	40
Seminaries, Religious	1
Students Religious	20
Total Seminarians	60
High Schools, Diocesan and Parish	9
Total Students	3,306
High Schools, Private	1
Total Students	153
Elementary Schools, Diocesan and Parish	26
Total Students	9,086
Elementary Schools, Private	2
Total Students	530
Catechesis/Religious Education:	
High School Students	5,134
Elementary Students	11,435
Total Students under Catholic Instruction	29,704
Teachers in the Diocese:	
Sisters	1
Lay Teachers	878
Vital Statistics	
Receptions into the Church:	
Infant Baptism Totals	2,787
Minor Baptism Totals	140
Adult Baptism Totals	74
Received into Full Communion	217
First Communions	281
Confirmations	2,560
Marriages:	
Catholic	785
Interfaith	105
Total Marriages	890
Deaths	3,219
Total Catholic Population	253,035
Total Population	647,108

Former Bishops—Most Revs. JULES B. JEANMARD, D.D., LL.D., ord. June 11, 1903; appt. first Bishop of Lafayette, July 18, 1918; cons. Dec. 8, 1918; installed as first Bishop of Lafayette, Dec. 12, 1918; appt. Assistant at the Pontifical Throne, Dec. 8, 1943; resigned and named Titular Bishop of Bareta, March 13, 1956; died Feb. 23, 1957; ROBERT E. TRACY, D.D., LL.D., Auxiliary Bishop of Lafayette, March 18, 1959; appt. first Bishop of Baton Rouge, Aug. 10, 1961; died April 4, 1980; WARREN L. BOUDREAUX, D.D., J.C.D., Auxiliary Bishop of Lafayette, May 19, 1962; appt. second Bishop of Beaumont, Texas, June 4, 1971; died Oct. 6, 1997; MAURICE SCHEXNAYDER, D.D., ord. April 11, 1925; appt. Titular Bishop of Tuscamia and Auxiliary of Lafayette, Dec. 11, 1950; cons. Feb. 22, 1951; appt. second Bishop of Lafayette, March 13, 1956; installed May 24, 1956; resigned Nov. 7, 1972; died Jan. 23, 1981; GERARD L. FREY, D.D., appt. third Bishop of Lafayette, Nov. 7, 1972; installed Jan. 7, 1973; resigned May 13, 1989; died Aug. 16, 2007; HARRY J. FLYNN, D.D., ord. May 28, 1960; appt. Coadjutor Bishop of Lafayette, April 19, 1986, fourth Bishop of Lafayette, May 13, 1989; appt. Coadjutor Archbishop of St. Paul and Minneapolis, Feb. 22, 1994; EDWARD JOSEPH O'DONNELL, D.D., ord. April 6, 1957; appt. Titular Bishop of Britonia and Auxiliary Bishop of St. Louis Dec. 6, 1983; cons. Feb. 10, 1984; appt. fifth Bishop of Lafayette Nov. 8, 1994; installed Dec. 16, 1994; retired Nov. 8, 2002; died Feb. 1, 2009; CHARLES MICHAEL JARRELL, D.D., ord. June 3, 1967; ord. to the episcopacy and installed as second Bishop of Houma-Thibodaux March 4, 1993; appt. sixth Bishop of Lafayette Nov. 8, 2002; installed Dec. 18, 2002; retired Feb. 17, 2016.

Bishop's Office—Mailing Address: Diocesan Office Building, 1408 Carmel Dr., Lafayette, 70501-5298. Tel: 337-261-5614; Fax: 337-261-5603.

Administrative Offices—Diocesan Office Building, 1408 Carmel Dr., Lafayette, 70501-5298. Tel: 337-261-5500; Fax: 337-261-5603.

Vicar General—Very Rev. Msgr. WILLIAM CURTIS MALLET, J.C.L., V.G., Tel: 337-261-5611; Fax: 337-261-5603.

Vicar for Special Projects for the Bishop—Very Rev. Msgr. H. A. LARROQUE, J.C.D.

Chancellor—MRS. MAUREEN K. FONTENOT, Tel: 337-261-5613; Fax: 337-261-5693.

Presbyteral Council—Rev. JAMES BRADY, J.C.L.

Diocesan Pastoral Council—Mailing Address: 1408 Carmel Dr., Lafayette, 70501. Tel: 337-261-5613. MRS. MAUREEN K. FONTENOT, Chancellor.

Clergy Personnel Advisory Board—1408 Carmel Dr., Lafayette, 70501. Tel: 337-261-5690; Fax: 337-261-5603. Very Rev. JARED G. SUIRE, V.E.

Office of Dean—Very Revs. CHESTER C. ARCENEAUX, V.F., Central Deanery, Cathedral of St. John the Evangelist, Lafayette; WILLIAM C. BLANDA, V.F., South Deanery, St. Peter Church, New Iberia; LOUIS J. RICHARD, V.F., West Deanery, St. Mary Magdalen Church, Abbeville; THOMAS P. VOORHIES, V.F., North Deanery, Sacred Heart of Jesus Church, Ville Platte.

Finance Officer—Deacon JEFF TRUMPS, Diocesan Finance Officer & Dir., Mailing Address: 1408 Carmel Dr., Lafayette, 70501-5298. Tel: 337-261-5632; Fax: 337-735-9442.

Vicar for Clergy—Very Rev. JARED G. SUIRE, V.E.

Victims' Assistance Coordinator—MR. JOSEPH PISANO JR., Tel: 337-298-2987.

Abuse Review Board—Mailing Address: 1408 Carmel Dr., Lafayette, 70501-5298. Tel: 337-261-5611. Very Rev. Msgr. WILLIAM CURTIS MALLET, J.C.L., V.G.

Tribunal

Tribunal—Mailing Address: 1408 Carmel Dr., Lafayette, 70501-5298. Tel: 337-261-5623; Fax: 337-261-5646.

Judicial Vicar—VACANT.
Adjutant Judicial Vicar—Very Rev. VINH DINH LUU, J.C.L., Tel: 337-261-5623; Fax: 337-261-5646.
Assessors—MR. JOHN AMOS, J.C.D.
Auditor/Instructor—MRS. KRISTI G. MUNZING.
Promoter of the Justice—Very Rev. Msgr. WILLIAM CURTIS MALLET, J.C.L., V.G.
Judge—Very Rev. VINH DINH LUU, J.C.L., Tel: 337-261-5623; Fax: 337-261-5646.
Defenders of the Bond—Tel: 337-261-5613. Revs. KEN BROUSSARD, J.C.L.; O. JOSEPH BREAUX; Very Rev. Msgr. H. A. LARROQUE, J.C.D.
Advocates—Revs. JAMES BRADY, J.C.L.; BILL JOHN MELANCON.
Notary—MRS. CAROLYN A. TRAHAN.
Diocesan Consultors—Very Rev. Msgr. WILLIAM CURTIS MALLET, J.C.L., V.G.; Very Revs. CHESTER C. ARCENEAUX, V.F.; WILLIAM C. BLANDA, V.F.; LOUIS J. RICHARD, V.F.; Revs. JAMES BRADY, J.C.L.; STEVEN C. LEBLANC; MARK H. MILEY.

Diocesan Secretariats, Offices and Directors

Catholic Charities of Acadiana—MRS. KIM BOUDREAUX, Dir.
Catholic Relief Services—1408 Carmel Dr., Lafayette, 70501. MRS. KIM BOUDREAUX, Diocesan Coord.
Migration and Refugee Services—MS. TINA QUESADA, Dir., 1408 Carmel Dr., Lafayette, 70501-5298. Tel: 337-261-5535.
Persons with Disabilities—MS. JULIE CAILLOUET, Prog. Coord., 1408 Carmel Dr., Lafayette, 70501-5298. Tel: 337-232-3463; Tel: 337-261-5548.
Secretariat of Ministries—1408 Carmel Dr., Lafayette, 70501-5298. Tel: 337-261-5609. Deacon JAMES KINCEL, Dir.
Black Catholic Ministry—MRS. STEPHANIE BERNARD, Prog. Coord., 1408 Carmel Dr., Lafayette, 70501-5298. Tel: 337-261-5694.
Catechetics—1408 Carmel Dr., Lafayette, 70501-5298. Tel: 337-261-5550. CHAD JUDICE, Dir.
Hispanic Ministry—Deacon JUAN CARLOS PAGAN, Prog. Coord., 1408 Carmel Dr., Lafayette, 70501-5298. Tel: 337-261-5542.
Justice and Peace—MRS. STEPHANIE BERNARD, Prog. Coord., 1408 Carmel Dr., Lafayette, 70501-5298. Tel: 337-261-5694.
Marriage and Family Life Ministry & Pro-Life Activities—MRS. KELLEY CHAPMAN, Dir.; Rev. JUDE HALPHEN, Ph.D., Counselor, 1408 Carmel Dr., Lafayette, 70501-5298. Tel: 337-261-5653.
Office of Worship—1408 Carmel Dr., Lafayette, 70501-5298. Tel: 337-261-5554. Rev. DUSTIN DOUGHT, Dir.
Religious Brothers and Sisters—1408 Carmel Dr., Lafayette, 70501-5298. Tel: 337-261-5609. Sr. CELESTE D. LARROQUE, S.E.C., Dir.
Vietnamese Catholic Ministry—1408 Carmel Dr., Lafayette, 70501-5298. Tel: 337-893-0244. Deacon TAM MINH TRAN, Prog. Coord.
Secretariat of Catholic Schools—1408 Carmel Dr., Lafayette, 70501-5298. Tel: 337-261-5568. MS. ANNA LARRIVIERE, Supt.
Catholic Schools—MS. ANNA LARRIVIERE, Supt., 1408 Carmel Dr., Lafayette, 70501-5298. Tel: 337-261-5529.
Secretariat of Community Services—MRS. MAUREEN K. FONTENOT, Chancellor & Dir. Human Resources, 1408 Carmel Dr., Lafayette, 70501-5298. Tel: 337-261-5613.
Archives - Research and Information—MRS. BARBARA C. DEJEAN, Archivist & Dir., 1408 Carmel Dr., Lafayette, 70501-5298. Tel: 337-261-5639; Tel: 337-261-5667.
Auxiliary Services—MS. PATSY ARWOOD, Coord., 1408 Carmel Dr., Lafayette, 70501-5298. Tel: 337-261-5600.
Human Resources—MRS. MAUREEN K. FONTENOT, Chancellor & Dir., 1408 Carmel Dr., Lafayette, 70501-5298. Tel: 337-261-5526.
Pontifical Mission Societies—1408 Carmel Dr., Lafayette, 70501-5298. Tel: 337-261-5613. MRS. MAUREEN K. FONTENOT, Chancellor & Dir.
Safe Environment—1408 Carmel Dr., Lafayette, 70501-5298. MRS. MAUREEN K. FONTENOT, Chancellor & Dir., Tel: 337-261-5526; MRS. LISA FREDERICK, Prog. Coord., Tel: 337-735-9434; MR. JOSEPH PISANO JR., Victim Asst. Coord., Tel: 337-298-2987.
Secretariat of Communications—1408 Carmel Dr., Lafayette, 70501-5298. Tel: 337-261-5612. MRS. BLUE ROLFES, Dir.
Office of Communications—1408 Carmel Dr., Lafayette, 70501-5298. Tel: 337-261-5612. MRS. BLUE ROLFES, Dir.
Acadiana Catholic Magazine—MS. STEPHANIE MARTIN, Mng. Editor, 1408 Carmel Dr., Lafayette, 70501-5298. Tel: 337-261-5512.
Radio-TV—MR. DAVID MERGIST, Producer & Dir., 1408 Carmel Dr., Lafayette, 70501-5298. Tel: 337-261-5626.
Social Media Specialist—MRS. JULIE D. MIRE, 1408 Carmel Dr., Lafayette, 70501-5298. Tel: 337-261-5518.
Website Coordinator—1408 Carmel Dr., Lafayette, 70501-5298. Tel: 337-261-5512. MRS. BLUE ROLFES.
Secretariat of Financial Affairs—Deacon JEFF TRUMPS, Dir. & Diocesan Finance Officer, 1408 Carmel Dr., Lafayette, 70501-5298. Tel: 337-261-5632.
Building & Grounds Manager—MR. ANTHONY BOUDREAUX, Prog. Coord., 1408 Carmel Dr., Lafayette, 70501-5298. Tel: 337-261-5605.
Building & Renovations—MR. AL LANDRY, Architect, 1408 Carmel Dr., Lafayette, 70501-5298. Tel: 337-735-9429; Tel: 337-261-5565.
Financial Affairs—Deacon JEFF TRUMPS, Diocesan Finance Officer & Dir., 1408 Carmel Dr., Lafayette, 70501-5298. Tel: 337-261-5632.
Accounting—1408 Carmel Dr., Lafayette, 70501-5298. Tel: 337-261-5627. MR. ERIC GUIDRY, Controller.
Information Technology—MR. ROBIN STEVENSON, Dir., 1408 Carmel Dr., Lafayette, 70501-5298. Tel: 337-261-5516.
Parish & School Finance—MR. JOHN PEULER, 1408 Carmel Dr., Lafayette, 70501-5298. Tel: 337-735-9436.
Property/Liability Insurance Program—MR. RYAN FITZGERALD, Risk Mgr., 1408 Carmel Dr., Lafayette, 70501-5298. Tel: 337-735-9449.
Stewardship & Development—1408 Carmel Dr., Lafayette, 70501-5298. Tel: 337-261-5641. VACANT.
Vicar for Clergy—Very Rev. JARED G. SUIRE, V.E.
Ongoing Formation of Priests—1408 Carmel Dr., Lafayette, 70501. Tel: 337-261-5690; Fax: 337-261-5603. Very Rev. JARED G. SUIRE, V.E.
Permanent Diaconate—Deacon JAMES KINCEL, Dir., 1408 Carmel Dr., Lafayette, 70501-5298. Tel: 337-261-5609.
Vocations—1408 Carmel Dr., Lafayette, 70501. Tel: 337-261-5690; Fax: 331-261-5603. Rev. PATRICK BROUSSARD.
Seminarians—1408 Carmel Dr., Lafayette, 70501. Tel: 337-261-5690; Fax: 331-261-5603. Rev. KEVIN BORDELON.

Miscellaneous

Catholic Charismatic Renewal—Office: 1408 Carmel Dr., Lafayette, 70501. Tel: 337-288-9402. MR. JOHN LISTI, Office Admin., Email: johnlisti@gmail.com.
Catholic Daughters of America—Diocesan Co Chaplains: Revs. HERBERT BENNERFIELD; CEDRIC SONNIER.
Credit Union—Pelican State Credit Union, 1600 N. Bertrand Dr., Lafayette, 70506. Tel: 337-261-1151.
Cursillo—Rev. THEODORE BROUSSARD JR., Spiritual Dir., Tel: 337-543-7425; Tel: 337-543-7591.
Diocesan Disaster Coordinators—1408 Carmel Dr., Lafayette, 70501-5298. Tel: 337-735-9449; Tel: 337-261-5565. MR. RYAN FITZGERALD; MRS. KIM BOUDREAUX.
Hospitals—Rev. M. KEITH LABOVE, Coord. Health Affairs, Mailing Address: 406 E. Pinhook Rd., Lafayette, 70501. Tel: 337-237-0988.
Knights of Columbus—Rev. MARK DERISE, State Chap.
Retreats—Mailing Address: P.O. Box D, Grand Coteau, 70541-1003. Tel: 337-662-5410. MR. PETER BAUDOIN, Dir., Our Lady of the Oaks Retreat House, Grand Coteau, LA.
Scouting—552 Main St., Cankton, 70584. Rev. KENNETH J. DOMINGUE, Assoc. Scout Chap.
Catholic Committee on Scouting—MR. ROBERT T. CLEMENTS, Diocesan Lay Chm., 204 Crawford, Lafayette, 70506-6028.

CLERGY, PARISHES, MISSIONS AND PAROCHIAL SCHOOLS

CITY OF LAFAYETTE

(LAFAYETTE PARISH)

1—CATHEDRAL OF ST. JOHN THE EVANGELIST (1821) [CEM]
515 Cathedral St., 70501. Tel: 337-232-1322; Email: dhuval@saintjohncathedral.org. Very Rev. Chester C. Arceneaux, V.F.; Revs. Patrick Broussard, Parochial Vicar; Andrew Philip Schumacher; Cyprian Eze, In Res.; Deacon George Bernard Jourdan.
Church: 914 St. John St., 70501.
School—Cathedral-Carmel Elementary, (Grades PreK-8), 848 St. John St., 70501. Tel: 337-235-5577; Fax: 337-261-9493; Email: kaillet@cathedralcarmel.com; Web: www.cathedralcarmel.com. Mary Catherine "Kay" Aillet, Prin.; Menard Christine, Admin.; Jill Spikes, Admin.; Nicole White, Admin.; Jan Johnson, Librarian. Lay Teachers 49; Priests 2; Students 773.
Catechesis Religious Program—Tel: 337-232-1325; Email: bprimeaux@saintjohncathedral.org. Brittany Primeaux, D.R.E. Students 213.

2—ST. ANTHONY (1955) [JC] (African American)
615 Edison St. Lafayette, 70501. Tel: 337-234-5855; Fax: 327-264-1507; Email: stanthonychurch@bellsouth.net. Clifton Labbe, S.V.D.; Deacon Albert Marcel Jr.
Legal Title: St. Anthony Catholic Church.
Catechesis Religious Program—Email: taym822@gmail.com. Tammy Marcel, D.R.E. Students 91.

3—ST. EDMOND (1974)
4131 W. Congress St., 70506. Tel: 337-981-0874; Email: secretary@st-edmond.org. Rev. Gilbert J. Dutel; Deacon Frank Cormier.
Catechesis Religious Program—
Tel: 337-981-0874, Ext. 274; Email: religioused@st-edmond.org. Rosemary Benoit, D.R.E. Students 236.

4—ST. ELIZABETH SETON (1975)
610 Raintree Tr., 70507. Tel: 337-235-1483; Email: pastor@setonchurch.org. Rev. David B. Hebert; Deacons Nelson Joseph Schexnayder Jr.; Ronald Paul Chauvin.
Catechesis Religious Program—Email: nelsonschexnayder@yahoo.com. Gerry Baumboree, D.R.E. Students 153.

5—ST. GENEVIEVE (1929) [CEM]
417 E. Simcoe, 70501. Tel: 337-234-5147; Fax: 337-234-8654; Email: stgenevieve@cox.net; Web: www.stgens.net. Rev. Brian Taylor.
Schools—St. Genevieve Elementary School—(Grades PreK-4), 201 Elizabeth St., 70501. Tel: 337-234-5257; Email: sgscardinals@stgen.net; Web: www.stgen.net. Becky Trouille, Prin. Lay Teachers 17; Students 300.
St. Genevieve Middle School, (Grades 5-8), 91 Teurlings Dr., 70501. Tel: 337-266-5553; Fax: 337-266-5775; Email: sgscardinals@stgen.net; Web: www.stgen.net. Mrs. Julie Zaunbrecher, Prin. Lay Teachers 15; Students 248.
See Teurlings Catholic High under High Schools, Interparochial located in the Institution section.
Endowment—St. Genevieve School Foundation, Inc., 91 Teurlings Dr., 70501. Tel: 337-266-5553.
Catechesis Religious Program—
Tel: 337-234-5147, Ext. 121. Nicole Osmer, D.R.E. Students 30.

6—HOLY CROSS (1965)
415 Robley Dr., 70503. Tel: 337-984-9636; Email: kborah@holycrosslafayette.com. Rev. Howard Blessing; Deacons Robert Charles Klingman Jr., Business Mgr.; James Kincel; Scotty James Baudoin.
Catechesis Religious Program—
Tel: 337-988-3790, Ext. 1101. Students 474.

7—IMMACULATE HEART OF MARY (1934) [CEM] (African American)
818-12th St., 70501. Tel: 337-235-4518; Email: smyladiyil@diolaf.org. Revs. Sebastian Myladiyil, S.V.D.; Leon wa Tshianga Ngandu, S.V.D.; Ryszard Kalinowski, S.V.D., In Res.
Catechesis Religious Program—Tel: 337-235-6323; Fax: 337-235-6321. Students 129.

8—ST. JULES (1962)
116 St. Jules St., 70506. Tel: 337-234-2727; Email: gporche@diolaf.org. Revs. J. Daniel Edwards; Joseph Sai Tran, S.V.D., Priest in Service to the Vietnamese Community in Lafayette; Thomas Finley, In Res., (Retired); Deacons Jose Vicente Blanco; Jose Luna-Becerra; Reginald A. Bollich.
Catechesis Religious Program—Email: dedwards@diolaf.org. Students 175.

9—ST. LEO THE GREAT (1960)
300 W. Alexander St., 70501. Tel: 337-232-2404; Email: pastor@stleolafayette.com; Web: www.stleolafayette.com. Rev. Dustin Dought.
School—Sts. Leo-Seton, (Grades PreK-8), 502 St. Leo St., 70501. Tel: 337-234-5510; Fax: 337-234-3676; Email: kgothreaux@leoseton.org. Kimberly Gothreaux, Prin.; Kellie Plaisance, Librarian; Mrs. Kathy Schaub, Business Mgr. Lay Teachers 34; Students 515.
Catechesis Religious Program—Students 47.

10—ST. MARY MOTHER OF THE CHURCH (1975)
419 Doucet Rd., 70503. Tel: 337-981-3379; Email: deb58@cox.net. Rev. Harold Trahan; Deacon Michael Wayne Crain.
Child Care—St. Mary Early Learning Center, 419 Doucet Rd., 70503. Tel: 337-984-3750; Email: dnmsix@bellsouth.net. Michelle Guidry, Prin. Students 227.
Catechesis Religious Program—Cindy Guidry, D.R.E. Students 167.

11—OUR LADY OF FATIMA (1949)

2319 Johnston St., 70503. Tel: 337-232-8945; Email: administrator@fatimalafayette.org; Web: www.fatimalafayette.org. Revs. Michael Russo; Nathan A. Comeaux; Deacons Timothy Maragos; Edward J. Boustany.

School—Our Lady of Fatima School, (Grades PreK-8), 2315 Johnston St., 70503. Tel: 337-235-2464; Fax: 337-235-1320; Email: aisaacs@olf.org; Web: www.fatimawarrior.com. Angela Isaacs, Prin.; Shannon Biggs, Librarian; Melissa Olivier, Librarian. Special Ed. offered. Lay Teachers 80; Students 870.

Catechesis Religious Program—Tel: 337-235-2464; Email: lmelancon@olf.org. Lisa Melancon, D.R.E. Students 18.

12—OUR LADY OF WISDOM, UNIVERSITY OF LOUISIANA (1942)
501 East Saint Mary Blvd., 70504-3599.
Tel: 337-232-8742; Fax: 337-236-6737; Email: wisdom@ourladyofwisdom.org; Web: www.ourladyofwisdom.org. P.O. Box 43599, 70504-3599. Revs. Bryce Sibley; René Pellessier, Parochial Vicar; Deacons Juan Carlos Pagan; Coby Brandon Thomas.

Catechesis Religious Program—Tel: 337-501-7730; Email: mchtpa@aol.com. Michelle Hernandez, D.R.E. Students 110.

13—OUR LADY QUEEN OF PEACE (1969) [CEM] (African American)
145 Martin Luther King Jr. Dr., 70501.
Tel: 337-233-1591; Email: queenofpeace1969@gmail.com. P.O. Box 90740, 70509. Rev. F. Hampton Davis III; Deacon Louis J. Lloyd.

Rectory—415 Cooper St., 70501.

Catechesis Religious Program—Email: fhdavis3@bellsouth.net. Gail Lee, D.R.E. Students 142.

14—ST. PATRICK (1952)
406 E. Pinhook Rd., 70501. Tel: 337-237-0988; Email: stpat.org@gmail.com; Web: stpat.org. Rev. M. Keith LaBove.

15—ST. PAUL THE APOSTLE (1911) (African American)
326 S. Washington St., 70501. Tel: 337-235-0272; Email: tonanala@yahoo.com. Rev. Anthony A. Anala, S.V.D.

Catechesis Religious Program—Cassandra Griffin, D.R.E. Students 100.

Mission—Our Lady of Good Hope, Lafayette Parish.

16—ST. PIUS X (1968) [JC]
201 E. Bayou Pkwy., 70598-0489. Tel: 337-232-4656; Email: info@stpiusxchurch.org. P.O. Box 80489, 70598-0489. Revs. James Brady, J.C.L.; Joel Christopher Faulk, Parochial Vicar; Deacons Samuel Joseph Russo Jr.; Philip Lizotte; Jeffrey Paul Trumps.

School—St. Pius Elementary School, (Grades PreK-8), 205 E. Bayou Pkwy., 70508. Tel: 337-237-3139; Fax: 337-232-3455; Email: donna_lemaire@stpiuselementary.org; Web: www.stpiuselementary.org. Miss Donna Lemaire, Prin.; Judice Kay, Lib. Lay Teachers 56; Students 680.

Catechesis Religious Program—Email: blakeph@stpiusxchurch.org; Email: youthminister@stpiusxchurch.org. Blake P. Harson, D.R.E.; James Opdenhoff, Youth Min. Students 237.

OUTSIDE THE CITY OF LAFAYETTE

ABBEVILLE, VERMILION PARISH

1—ST. MARY MAGDALEN (1844) [CEM 2]
300 Pere Megret, P.O. Box 1507, Abbeville, 70510.
Tel: 337-893-0244; Fax: 337-893-0427; Email: parish@stmarymagdalenparish.org; Web: www.stmarymagdalenparish.org. Very Rev. Louis J. Richard, V.F.; Revs. James B. Nguyen, Priest in Service to the Vietnamese Community in Abbeville; Michael Richard, Parochial Vicar; Deacons Tam Tran; William Merrill Vincent; Khang Francis Xavier Van Cao.

School—Mt. Carmel School, (Grades PreK-8), 405 Park Ave., Abbeville, 70510. Tel: 337-898-0859; Fax: 337-893-5968; Email: carmel@mceschool.org; Web: www.mceschool.org. Sr. Janet LeBlanc, O.-Carm., Pres.; Jackie Trahan, Prin.; Tiffany Abshire, Librarian. Lay Teachers 26; Sisters 1; Students 360.

High School—Vermilion Catholic, 425 Park Ave., Abbeville, 70510. Tel: 337-893-6636; Fax: 337-898-0394; Email: mikeguilbeaux@vermilioncatholic.com; Web: www.vermilioncatholic.com. Mr. Mike Guilbeaux, Prin. Lay Teachers 22; Students 242.

St. Mary Magdalen Christian Service Center—701 Chevis St., Abbeville, 70510.

Catechesis Religious Program—Email: rlivers@diolaf.org. Renella Livers, D.R.E. Students 209.

2—ST. THERESA OF THE CHILD JESUS (1959)
Mailing Address: P.O. Box 609, Abbeville, 70511-0609. Tel: 337-893-5631; Fax: 337-893-9168; Email: lgayneaux@diolaf.org; Web: sttheresaabbeville.com. 101 N. Leonard St., Abbeville, 70510. Rev. Francois Sainte-Marie.

Catechesis Religious Program—Loretta Gayneaux, D.R.E. Students 142.

ARNAUDVILLE, ST. LANDRY PARISH

1—ST. CATHERINE (1949) (African American)
242 Pine St., Arnaudville, 70512. Tel: 337-754-5912; Fax: 337-754-7203; Email: bsanders@arnaudvillecatholic.org; Email: sgresko@arnaudvillecatholic.org; Web: arnaudvillecatholic.org. P.O. Box 351, Arnaudville, 70512. Rev. Travis Abadie.

Catechesis Religious Program—Tel: 337-754-5912; Email: sgresko@diolaf.org. Sheila Gresko, D.R.E. Students 26.

2—ST. JOHN FRANCIS REGIS (1853) [CEM]
232 Main St, Arnaudville, 70512. Tel: 337-754-5912; Fax: 337-754-7203; Email: bsanders@arnaudvillecatholic.org; Email: sgresko@arnaudvillecatholic.org; Email: hwyble@arnaudvillecatholic.org; Web: arnaudvillecatholic.org. P.O. Box 649, Arnaudville, 70512. Rev. Travis Abadie; Deacon John Kenneth Arnaud.

Catechesis Religious Program—Email: sgresko@diolaf.org. Sheila Gresko, D.R.E. Students 213.

BALDWIN, ST. MARY PARISH, SACRED HEART (1906) [CEM]
414 Martin Luther King, P.O. Box 308, Baldwin, 70514. Tel: 337-923-7781; Fax: 337-923-4966; Email: sacred_heart07@bellsouth.net. Rev. Cedric Sonnier; Deacon Richard Picard.

Catechesis Religious Program— Twinned with Immaculate Conception, Charenton, LA. Kathy Sanders, D.R.E. Students 53.

BASILE, EVANGELINE PARISH, ST. AUGUSTINE (1921) [CEM]
2717 Dr. Bobby Deshotel Ave., Basile, 70515.
Tel: 337-432-6817; Email: staugustinecc@ymail.com. Rev. Keenan Wynn Brown.

Catechesis Religious Program—Email: kbrown@diolaf.org. Students 245.

BAYOU VISTA, ST. MARY PARISH, ST. BERNADETTE (1963) [CEM]
1112 Saturn Rd., Morgan City, 70380.
Tel: 985-395-2470; Email: stbern@teche.net. Rev. William G. Rogalla.

Catechesis Religious Program—Becky Blanchard, D.R.E. Students 106.

BERWICK, ST. MARY PARISH, ST. STEPHEN (1950)
3217 Second St., Berwick, 70342. Tel: 985-385-1280; Email: ststephenchurch@atvci.net; Web: ststephenberwick.org. Rev. Msgr. J. Douglas Courville, J.C.L.

Catechesis Religious Program—Tel: 985-385-1283. Debbie Monceaux, D.R.E. Students 202.

BREAUX BRIDGE, ST. MARTIN PARISH

1—ST. BERNARD (1847) [CEM 2] [JC2]
Mailing Address: 219 E. Bridge St., Breaux Bridge, 70517. Tel: 337-332-2159; Email: michele@stbernardch.com; Web: stbernardch.com. Revs. Garrett K. McIntyre; Stephen Pellessier; Deacons Marcel P. Hebert Jr.; Jim Davis; Kenneth E. Soignier.

Res.: 204 N. Main St., Breaux Bridge, 70517.

School—St. Bernard School, (Grades PreK-8), 251 E. Bridge St., Breaux Bridge, 70517. Tel: 337-332-5350; Fax: 337-332-5894; Email: jpmasterson@sbscrusaders.com; Web: www.sbscrusaders.com. John Paul Masterson, Prin.; Marty Heintz, Vice Prin. Lay Teachers 35; Students 436.

Catechesis Religious Program—Students 367.

2—ST. FRANCIS OF ASSISI (1923) [CEM] (African American)
610 N. Main St., Breaux Bridge, 70517.
Tel: 337-332-2250; Email: bettyjohn@cox.net; Email: nwaigwejerome@yahoo.com. Rev. Ugochukwu Cletus.

Catechesis Religious Program—Cheryl Ozen, D.R.E. Students 67.

BROUSSARD, LAFAYETTE PARISH

1—ST. JOSEPH (1952) [CEM 2] (African American)
Mailing Address: P.O. Box 278, Broussard, 70518.
Tel: 337-837-6218; Fax: 337-837-2072; Email: stjosant@yahoo.com. Rev. Thomas James, S.V.D., V.E.

Res.: 232 St. DePorres St., Broussard, 70518. Email: tjames@diolaf.org.

Catechesis Religious Program—Charlotte Milson, D.R.E. Students 73.

Mission—St. Anthony, 1639 Old Spanish Hwy., Cade, St. Martin Parish 70519.

2—SACRED HEART OF JESUS (1883) [CEM]
200 W. Main St., Broussard, 70518.
Tel: 337-837-1864; Fax: 337-837-1703; Email: tracy@shbroussard.org; Email: bookkeeper@shbroussard.org; Web: shbroussard.org. P.O. Box 737, Broussard, 70518. Revs. Michael L. Delcambre; Joseph Kyle White.

School—St. Cecilia, (Grades PreK-8), 302 W. Main St., Broussard, 70518. Tel: 337-837-6363; Fax: 337-837-3688; Email: gfontenot@scsbluejays.org; Web: scsbluejays.org. Mr. George Fontenot, Prin. Lay Teachers 28; Students 483.

Catechesis Religious Program—Email: frmichael@shbroussard.org. Paige Billeaud, D.R.E. Students 298.

CANKTON, ST. LANDRY PARISH, ST. JOHN BERCHMANS (1925) [CEM]
552 Main St., Cankton, 70584-9722.
Tel: 337-668-4413; Fax: 337-668-4505; Email: stjb@centurytel.net; Web: stjberchmans.com. Rev. Kenneth J. Domingue.

Catechesis Religious Program—Tel: 337-837-1864; Fax: 337-837-1703. Students 279.

CARENCRO, LAFAYETTE PARISH

1—OUR LADY OF THE ASSUMPTION (1925) [CEM] (African American)
410 N. Michaud St., P.O. Box 130, Carencro, 70520-0130. Tel: 337-896-8304; Email: deaconsenegal@yahoo.com. Rev. Msgr. Ronald Broussard; Deacon Nolton J. Senegal.

Catechesis Religious Program—Sarah Robert, D.R.E. Students 25.

2—ST. PETER (1874) [CEM]
102 N. Church St., P.O. Box 40, Carencro, 70520.
Tel: 337-896-9408; Fax: 337-896-9414; Email: mledoux@diolaf.org; Web: www.sprcc.org. Rev. Mark Ledoux; Deacon Barney Dale Lejeune.

School—Carencro Catholic, (Grades PreK-8), 200 W. St. Peter St., Carencro, 70520. Tel: 337-896-8973; Fax: 337-896-1931; Email: pfrederick@carencrocatholic.org; Web: www.carencrocatholic.org. Andre Angelle, Prin.; Sandie Enlund, Librarian; Paula Frederick, Devel. Dir. Clergy 1; Lay Teachers 24; Students 300.

Catechesis Religious Program—Students 84.

CATAHOULA, ST. MARTIN PARISH, ST. RITA (1952) [CEM]
1006 St. Rita Hwy., St. Martinville, 70582.
Tel: 337-394-4679; Email: church@strita.brcoxmail.com. Rev. Bill John Melancon.

Catechesis Religious Program—Tel: 337-394-4030; Email: rlatiolais67@gmail.com. Raymond Latiolais Jr., D.R.E. Students 218.

CECILIA, ST. MARTIN PARISH

1—ST. JOSEPH (1893) [CEM] [JC]
2250 Cecilia High School Hwy, P.O. Box 279, Cecilia, 70521. Tel: 337-667-6344; Fax: 337-667-7073; Email: pastor@stjosephcecilia.com. Rev. Gregory P. Cormier.

Catechesis Religious Program—Students 206.

2—ST. ROSE OF LIMA (1944) [CEM] (African American)
2184 Bushville Hwy., P.O. Box 126, Cecilia, 70521.
Tel: 337-667-6555; Fax: 337-667-6686; Email: st.roseoflimacatholicchurch@yahoo.com; Email: pastor@stjosephcecilia.com. Rev. Gregory P. Cormier.

Catechesis Religious Program—Traci Sassau, D.R.E. Students 59.

CENTERVILLE, ST. MARY PARISH, ST. JOSEPH (1953) [CEM]
132 Hwy. 317, P.O. Box 280, Centerville, 70522.
Tel: 337-836-5659; Fax: 337-836-5659; Email: sjcc@cox-internet.com. Revs. Salvino Primor; Ruben Primor, D.R.E.

Catechesis Religious Program—Students 35.

CHARENTON, ST. MARY PARISH, IMMACULATE CONCEPTION (1844) [CEM]
Mailing Address: 3041 Chitamacha Tr., P.O. Box 278, Charenton, 70523. Tel: 337-923-4281; Email: csonnier@diolaf.org; Web: www.icsee.com. Rev. Cedric Sonnier.

Catechesis Religious Program— Twinned with Sacred Heart of Jesus, Baldwin.

CHATAIGNIER, EVANGELINE PARISH, OUR LADY OF MOUNT CARMEL (1869) [CEM] (French)
5706 Vine St., P.O. Box 100, Chataignier, 70524.
Tel: 337-885-3223; Fax: 337-885-3223; Email: deldridge@diolaf.org. Rev. Darren J. Eldridge.

Catechesis Religious Program—Email: seldridge@diolaf.org. Students 26.

CHURCH POINT, ACADIA PARISH

1—OUR LADY OF THE SACRED HEART (1873) [CEM 3] [JC]
118 N. Rogers St., Church Point, 70525.
Tel: 337-684-5494; Fax: 337-684-2133; Email: jdeblanc@diolaf.org. P.O. Box 403, Church Point, 70525. Rev. Msgr. Jefferson J. DeBlanc Jr.; Rev. David Rozas, Parochial VIcar; Deacon Francis Douglas Wimberly.

School—Our Mother of Peace, (Grades PreK-8), 218 N. Rogers St., Church Point, 70525.
Tel: 337-684-5780; Fax: 337-684-5780; Email: dfontenot@ompwildcats.com; Web: www.ompwildcats.com. Debbie Fontenot, Prin.; Jill Myers, Librarian. Clergy 3; Lay Teachers 18; Students 264.

Catechesis Religious Program—Email: jwyble@diolaf. Deacon Jerry Wayne Wyble. Students 307.

Chapel—Lewisburg, St. John Chapel, 374 Bourque Rd., Church Point, 70525. Email: jdeblanc@diolaf.org.

2—OUR MOTHER OF MERCY (1941) [JC] (African American)
693 N. Main St., P.O. Box 237, Church Point, 70525.

Tel: 337-684-2319; Email: ourmotherofmercychurchpoint41@gmail.com. Rev. Emmanuel Awe, S.S.J.
Catechesis Religious Program—Tel: 337-684-6832. Linda Brooks, D.R.E. Students 12.
COTEAU HOLMES, ST. MARTIN PARISH, ST. ELIZABETH (1956) [CEM]
1006 St. Elizabeth St., St. Martinville, 70582.
Tel: 337-394-6684; Email: jpadin@diolaf.org. Rev. Joseph L.F. Padinjarepeedika, C.M.I., (India).
Catechesis Religious Program—Students 13.
COTEAU, IBERIA PARISH, OUR LADY OF PROMPT SUCCOR (1934) [CEM]
2409 Coteau Rd., New Iberia, 70560.
Tel: 337-369-6993; Email: secretary@olps-coteau.org. Rev. Brian Harrington.
Catechesis Religious Program—Email: cmouton@diolaf.org. Cathy Mouton, D.R.E. Students 195.
COW ISLAND, VERMILION PARISH, ST. ANNE (1933) [CEM] [JC3]
17315 Lionel Rd., Abbeville, 70510.
Tel: 337-643-7714; Email: stanne@kaplantel.net. Rev. Matthew Barzare.
Catechesis Religious Program—Londa Touchet, D.R.E. Students 155.
Mission—Sacred Heart, 28220 W. Hwy 82, Pecan Island, Vermilion Parish 70510.
CROWLEY, ACADIA PARISH
1—IMMACULATE HEART OF MARY (1959)
901 E. Elm St., Crowley, 70526. Tel: 337-783-3498; Email: parish@ihmcrowley.org. Rev. Jason Vidrine.
Res.: 825 E. Elm St., Crowley, 70526.
School—Redemptorist Catholic Elementary School, (Grades PreK-8), 606 South Ave. N., Crowley, 70526. Tel: 337-783-4466; Fax: 337-788-0961; Email: chabetz@redemptorist-catholic.org; Web: www.redemptorist-catholic.org. Cindy D. Habetz, Prin.; Melissa Dooley, Admin. Acct. Lay Teachers 16; Students 116.
Catechesis Religious Program—Email: ihmcatholicchurch@cox-internet.com. James Franke, D.R.E. Students 65.
2—ST. MICHAEL ARCHANGEL (1895)
224 W. 5th Street, P.O. Box 406, Crowley, 70527. Tel: 337-783-7394; Fax: 337-788-0237; Email: stmichaelcrowley@gmail.com; Web: stmichaelcrowley.org. Revs. Mikel Anthony Polson; Brent Smith, Parochial Vicar; Deacon Daniel Peter Didier.
School—St. Michael's Catholic School, (Grades PreK-8), 805 E. Northern Ave., Crowley, 70526. Tel: 337-783-1410; Fax: 337-783-8547; Email: hbroussard@stmike.net. Jeanne Nickel, Librarian; Sandi Dore', Prin. Lay Teachers 26; Students 391.
Catechesis Religious Program—Eva Cormier, D.R.E. Students 89.
3—ST. THERESA (1920) (African American) Rev. Godwin Imoru.
Res.: 417 W. 3rd St., Crowley, 70526.
Tel: 337-783-1880; Email: st.theresachurch@hotmail.com.
Catechesis Religious Program—Verila Cormier, D.R.E. Students 80.
DELCAMBRE, VERMILION PARISH
1—SAINT MARTIN DE PORRES (1948) [JC] (African American)
Mailing Address: 206 W. Church St., Delcambre, 70528. Tel: 337-685-4426; Fax: 337-685-4424; Email: mike.reeser2@yahoo.com; Email: frbbreaux@gmail.com; Web: www.delcambrechurches.weconnect.com. 608 Martin Luther King Dr., Delcambre, 70528. Rev. John Breaux.
Catechesis Religious Program—Castel School of Religion, 208 S. Peter St., Delcambre, 70528. Email: delcambrechurches@yahoo.com. Students 20.
2—OUR LADY OF THE LAKE (1897) [CEM]
206 W. Church St., Delcambre, 70528.
Tel: 337-685-4426; Email: mike.reeser2@yahoo.com. Rev. John Breaux.
Catechesis Religious Program—Castel School of Religion, 208 South St. Peter St., Delcambre, 70528. Email: delcambrechurches@yahoo.com. Students 189.
DURALDE, EVANGELINE PARISH, ANNUNCIATION OF THE B.V.M. (1964) (Acadian)
4476 Duralde Hwy., Eunice, 70535.
Tel: 337-457-4849; Email: annunciation@hughesnet.com. Rev. Msgr. J. Robert Romero, V.E.; Revs. Matthew Hebert, Parochial Vicar; Darren J. Eldridge, D.R.E.; Deacon James Cormier, Pastoral Assoc.
Catechesis Religious Program—Students 96.
DUSON, LAFAYETTE PARISH
1—ST. BENEDICT THE MOOR aka St. Benedict Church, [CEM] (African American)
9135 Cameron St., Duson, 70529. Tel: 337-873-6772; Fax: 337-873-3023. P.O. Box 8, Duson, 70529-0008. Revs. Aaron Melancon; Louis Allen Breaux.
Catechesis Religious Program—Students 118.
2—ST. THERESA OF THE CHILD JESUS aka St. Theresa Church (1928) [CEM]
209 C St., Duson, 70529. Tel: 337-873-4962; Fax: 337-873-3023; Email: amelancon@diolaf.org. P.O. Box 8, Duson, 70529-0008. Revs. Aaron Melancon; Louis Allen Breaux; Deacon Steve Simon.
Catechesis Religious Program—Email: sbcdus@bellsouth.Net. Students 74.
ERATH, VERMILION PARISH, OUR LADY OF LOURDES (1928) [CEM 2]
700 S. Broadway, Erath, 70533. Tel: 337-937-6888; Email: ftoups@gmail.com. Rev. Andre R. Metrejean; Deacon Timothy Isidore Marcantel.
Catechesis Religious Program—Frances Toups, D.R.E. Students 481.
EUNICE, ACADIA PARISH, ST. THOMAS MORE (1967)
1011 Sittig St., P.O. Box 1022, Eunice, 70535.
Tel: 337-457-8107; Fax: 337-457-1735; Email: stthomasmore.eunice@gmail.com; Web: www.stthomasmorecatholicchurch-eunice.org. Rev. Clinton M. Sensat; Deacon David W. Guillory.
Catechesis Religious Program—Yolanda Thibodeaux, D.R.E. Students 259.
EUNICE, ST. LANDRY PARISH
1—ST. ANTHONY OF PADUA (1902) [CEM]
Mailing Address: 310 W. Vine Ave., P.O. Box 31, Eunice, 70535. Tel: 337-457-5285; Fax: 337-457-7904 ; Email: stanthony@stanthonyeunice.org. Rev. Msgr. J. Robert Romero, V.E.; Rev. Matthew Hebert, Parochial Vicar; Deacon Gary Gaudin.
School—St. Edmund Catholic School, (Grades PreK-12), 351 W. Magnolia St., Eunice, 70535.
Tel: 337-457-2592; Tel: 337-457-3777;
Fax: 337-457-5989; Email: charles.hazard@stedmund.com; Web: stedmund.com. Mrs. Katie Cormier, Librarian; Charles Hazard, Prin. Lay Teachers 30; Students 408.
High School—St. Edmund Catholic School, (Grades 7-12), 351 W. Magnolia St., Eunice, 70535.
Tel: 337-457-2592; Fax: 337-457-2510; Email: charles.hazard@stedmund.com. Lay Teachers 36; Students 427.
Catechesis Religious Program—Tel: 337-457-7505; Email: dreangieag@yahoo.com. Angie Aguillard, D.R.E. Students 139.
2—ST. MATHILDA (1939) [CEM] (African American)
800 E. Laurel Ave., Eunice, 70535. Tel: 337-457-3286 ; Fax: 337-457-3274; Email: stmathildaeunice@gmail.com. Mailing Address: P.O. Box 346, Eunice, 70535. Rev. D. Blaine Clement.
Res.: 130 N. Martin L. King Dr., Eunice, 70535.
Catechesis Religious Program—Eltra Jordan, D.R.E. Students 45.
EVANGELINE, ACADIA PARISH, ST. JOSEPH (1938) [CEM 2]
Mailing Address: 1400 Old Evangeline Hwy., P.O. Box 183, Evangeline, 70537. Tel: 337-824-4995; Fax: 337-824-4995; Email: plafleur@diolaf.org. Rev. Paul J. LaFleur.
Catechesis Religious Program—Students 82.
Mission—St. Jules, Riverside Rd., Petit Mamou, Acadia Parish.
FOUR CORNERS, ST. MARY PARISH, ST. PETER THE APOSTLE (1960)
Mailing Address: 1325 Big Four Corners Rd., Franklin, 70538. Tel: 337-276-5256;
Fax: 337-276-5256; Email: spta4c@yahoo.com. Rev. Francis Damoah, S.V.D.
Catechesis Religious Program—Email: akedati@diolaf.org. Students 14.
Mission—St. Joan of Arc, (Closed) Glencoe, St. Mary Parish.
FRANKLIN, ST. MARY PARISH
1—ASSUMPTION B.V.M. (1852)
Mailing Address: 211 Iberia St., Franklin, 70538.
Tel: 337-828-3869; Fax: 337-828-3872; Email: marysassumption@yahoo.com; Web: www.churchofassumption.com. Rev. Lloyd F. Benoit Jr.
School—St. John Elementary, (Grades PreK-5), 924 Main St., Franklin, 70538. Tel: 337-828-2648; Fax: 337-828-2112; Email: shigdon@stjohnelem.com; Web: www.stjohnelem.com. Mrs. Sheri Higdon, Prin. Lay Teachers 10; Students 119.
High School—Hanson High School, (Grades 6-12), 903 Anderson St., Franklin, 70538.
Tel: 337-828-3487; Fax: 337-828-0787; Email: kadams@hansonmemorial.com; Web: www.hansonmemorial.com. Mrs. Kim Adams, Prin. Lay Teachers 22; Students 182.
Catechesis Religious Program—Ricky Pellerin, D.R.E. Students 59.
2—ST. JULES (1950) [CEM]
631 Magnolia St., Franklin, 70538.
Tel: 337-828-1714; Email: stjuleschurch@hotmail.com. Rev. Peter Emusa; Deacon Joseph C. Thomas.
Catechesis Religious Program—Students 30.
Mission—Immaculate Conception, 601 Magnolia, Verdunville, St. Mary Parish.
GRAND COTEAU, ST. LANDRY PARISH, ST. CHARLES BORROMEO (1819) [CEM] [JC]
P.O. Box A, Grand Coteau, 70541. Tel: 337-662-5279; Fax: 337-662-5270; Email: stcharles1819@gmail.com; Web: www.st-charles-borromeo.org. Revs. Derrick Weingartner, S.J.; Clyde LeBlanc, S.J.; Michael Wegenka; Deacons Herd Guilbeau; Guy Anthony Kilchrist.
Res.: 174 Church St., Grand Coteau, 70541.
School—St. Ignatius School, (Grades PreK-8), 180 Church Street, Grand Coteau, 70541.
Tel: 337-662-3325; Fax: 337-662-3349; Email: cindyp@siscardinals.org; Web: siscardinals.org. P.O. Drawer J, Grand Coteau, 70541. Mrs. Cynthia Prather, Prin. Lay Teachers 24; Students 408.
Catechesis Religious Program—252 A Church St., Grand Coteau, 70541. Tel: 337-662-5271; Email: stcharlesrec@gmail.com. P.O. Drawer A, Grand Coteau, 70541. Students 293.
Mission—Christ the King, Opelousas.
GRAND PRAIRIE, ST. LANDRY PARISH, ST. PETER (1951) [CEM 2] [JC]
1074 Hwy. 748 (Grand Prairie), Washington, 70589-4541. Tel: 337-826-5635; Email: dpicard@diolaf.org. Rev. Daniel Picard; Deacon Malcolm Shawn Melancon.
Catechesis Religious Program—Students 90.
GUEYDAN, VERMILION PARISH, ST. PETER THE APOSTLE (1907) [JC]
603 Main St., Gueydan, 70542. Tel: 337-536-9258; Web: www.saintpeterchurch.org. P.O. Box 28, Gueydan, 70542. Rev. Corey Campeaux.
Catechesis Religious Program—Students 27.
Mission—St. David, 13022 Hwy. 3093, Kaplan, Vermilion Parish 70548.
HENDERSON, ST. MARTIN PARISH, OUR LADY OF MERCY (1962) [CEM] [JC]
Mailing Address: P.O. Box 587, Breaux Bridge, 70517. Tel: 337-228-2352; Fax: 337-228-2372; Email: sacredmercy@yahoo.com. Rev. Garrett Savoie.
Res.: 1454 Henderson Hwy., Henderson, 70517.
Catechesis Religious Program—Email: gsavoie@diolaf.org. Donna Lacombe, D.R.E. Students 89.
Mission—Sacred Heart, Butte La Rose, St. Martin Parish.
HENRY, VERMILION PARISH, ST. JOHN (1939) [CEM] (French-Acadian)
18534 La. Hwy. 689, Erath, 70533. Tel: 337-937-5108 ; Email: stjohns5108@yahoo.com. Rev. Emmanuel Fernandez.
Catechesis Religious Program—21125 LA Hwy. 333, Abbeville, 70510. Linda Choate, D.R.E. Students 43.
Mission—St. James, 21125 LA Hwy. 333, Abbeville, 70510.
IOTA, ACADIA PARISH, ST. JOSEPH (1892) [CEM]
Mailing Address: 604 St. Joseph Ave., Iota, 70543.
Tel: 337-779-2627; Fax: 337-779-2632; Email: stjosephiota@gmail.com; Web: www.stjosephiota.org. Rev. Jude W. Thierry.
School—St. Francis, (Grades PreK-8), 490 St. Joseph Ave., Iota, 70543. Tel: 337-779-2527; Email: st_francis@centurytel.net; Web: stfranciswolves.com. Mr. Michael Darbonne, Admin. Clergy 1; Lay Teachers 12; Students 153.
Catechesis Religious Program—Email: jthierry@diolaf.org. Students 406.
Mission—St. Michael, Egan, Acadia Parish.
JEANERETTE, IBERIA PARISH
1—ST. JOHN THE EVANGELIST (1879) [CEM]
1510 Church St., Jeanerette, 70544.
Tel: 337-276-4576; Email: stjohnev@yahoo.com; Web: www.stjohnjeanerette.org. Rev. Alexander Albert.
Catechesis Religious Program—Patti Bonin, D.R.E. Students 95.
2—OUR LADY OF THE ROSARY (1945) [CEM] [JC] (African American)
11200 Old Jeanerette Rd., Jeanerette, 70544.
Tel: 337-276-6900; Fax: 337-276-6931; Email: olrjean@yahoo.com. Rev. Francis Damoah, S.V.D.
Catechesis Religious Program—Students 10.
JUDICE, LAFAYETTE PARISH, ST. BASIL (1970) [CEM]
1803 Duhon Rd. (Judice), Duson, 70529.
Tel: 337-984-2179; Email: stbasil@cox.net. Rev. Steven C. LeBlanc.
Catechesis Religious Program—Cindy Richardson, D.R.E. Students 71.
KAPLAN, VERMILION PARISH, OUR LADY OF THE HOLY ROSARY (1896) [JC]
Mailing Address: 603 N. Herbert Ave., Kaplan, 70548. Tel: 337-643-6472; Fax: 337-643-2516; Email: hrcc@kaplantel.net; Web: www.holyrosarycabrini.org. Revs. Mark H. Miley; Arockia Palthasar; Deacon David L. Vaughn.
School—Maltrait Memorial, (Grades PreK-8), One Crusader Square, Kaplan, 70548. Tel: 337-643-7765; Fax: 337-643-7765; Email: mmcscrusader@kaplantel.net. 612 N. Hebert, Kaplan, 70548. Mrs. Renee C. Meaux, Prin. Clergy 3; Lay Teachers 14; Students 118.
Catechesis Religious Program—Jerry Abshire, D.R.E. Students 337.
Mission—St. Frances Xavier Cabrini, 901 N. Frederick Ave., Kaplan, Vermilion Parish 70548.
KROTZ SPRINGS, ST. LANDRY PARISH, ST. ANTHONY OF PADUA (1958)

Mailing Address: 219 Eighth Ave., P.O. Box 425, Krotz Springs, 70750. Tel: 337-566-3527; Fax: 337-566-2803; Email: mdeblanc@diolaf.org. Rev. Michael DeBlanc III.
Catechesis Religious Program—Sabrina Ardoin, D.R.E. Students 110.

LAWTELL, ST. LANDRY PARISH

1—ST. BRIDGET (1920) [CEM 2]
3933 Hwy. 35, P.O. Box 156, Lawtell, 70550. Tel: 337-543-7591; Email: tjbroussard@diolaf.org. Rev. Ted Broussard.
Catechesis Religious Program—Margaret Mounier, D.R.E. Students 104.
Mission—Sacred Heart, 3681 Hwy 104, Prairie Ronde, St. Landry Parish 70550.

2—HOLY FAMILY (1953) (African American)
Mailing Address: P.O. Box 310, Lawtell, 70550. Tel: 337-543-2366; Email: baubespin@diolaf.org; Web: www.holyfamilysaintann.org. 283 Thibodeaux St., Lawtell, 70550. Rev. Borgia Aubespin, S.V.D.
Catechesis Religious Program— Combined with St. Ann, Mallet. Antoinette Rene, D.R.E.

LEBEAU, ST. LANDRY PARISH, IMMACULATE CONCEPTION (1897) [CEM] (African American)
Mailing Address & Office: 103 Lebeau Church Rd., Lebeau, 71345. Tel: 337-623-0303; Fax: 337-623-0675; Email: jfallon@diolaf.org; Web: www.lebeauchurch.com. Rev. James P. Fallon, S.S.J., Admin.
Rectory—P.O. Box 6, Lebeau, 71345.
Catechesis Religious Program—Email: jpfallon@hotmail.com. Jane Edwards, D.R.E. Students 32.

LEONVILLE, ST. LANDRY PARISH

1—ST. CATHERINE (1952) [JC] (African American)
4399 Hwy 31, Leonville, 70551. Tel: 337-879-2365; Fax: 337-879-3050; Email: stleochurch126@gmail.com. P.O. Box 547, Leonville, 70551. Rev. Darren J. Eldridge.
Catechesis Religious Program— Twinned with St. Leo the Great, Leonville. Deacon Dwayne Boudreaux, D.R.E. Students 219.
Mission—St. Jules, 6098 Hwy 31, Prairie Laurent, St. Landry Parish 70551.

2—ST. LEO THE GREAT (1896) [CEM] [JC]
126 Church Rd., Leonville, 70551. Tel: 337-879-2365; Fax: 337-879-3050; Email: stleochurch126@gmail.com. Mailing Address: P.O. Box 544, Leonville, 70551. Rev. Darren J. Eldridge.
Catechesis Religious Program—Religious Education, Twinned with St. Catherine, Leonville. Deacon Dwayne Boudreaux, D.R.E.; Mrs. Peggy Lalonde, Contact Person. Students 241.

LEROY, VERMILION PARISH, OUR LADY OF PERPETUAL HELP (1922) [CEM] Rev. Johnathan J. Janise.
Res.: 12995 Louisiana Hwy. 699, Maurice, 70555. Tel: 337-893-0610; Email: jjanise@diolaf.org.
Catechesis Religious Program—Bonnie Bergeron, D.R.E. Students 71.

LOREAUVILLE, IBERIA PARISH

1—ST. JOSEPH (1873) [CEM] [JC2]
117 S. Main St., Loreauville, 70552. Tel: 337-229-4254; Fax: 337-229-4255; Email: bcrochet@diolaf.org; Web: stjosephparishonline.org. P.O. Box 365, Loreauville, 70552. Revs. Barry F. Crochet; Godwin O. Nzeh, C.M.F., Parochial Vicar.
Catechesis Religious Program—Students 383.

2—OUR LADY OF VICTORY (1953) [CEM 2] [JC] (African American)
120 Daigre St., Loreauville, 70552. Tel: 337-229-8284 ; Fax: 337-229-8254; Email: olv_loreauville@yahoo.com; Web: ourladyofvictory-loreauville.com. P.O. Box 387, Loreauville, 70552. Revs. Barry F. Crochet; Godwin O. Nzeh, C.M.F., Parochial Vicar.
Catechesis Religious Program—Email: bcrochet@diolaf.org. Mary Claire Collins, D.R.E. Students 64.

LOUISA, ST. MARY PARISH, ST. HELENA (1890) [CEM]
108 St. Helen's Church Ln., Franklin, 70538. Tel: 337-867-4378; Email: sacred_heart07@bellsouth.net. Rev. Richard Broussard; Deacon Gerald Joseph Bourg.
Chapel—St. Francis, Cypremort Point.

LYDIA, IBERIA PARISH, ST. NICHOLAS (1867) [CEM 2]
7809 Weeks Island Rd., Lydia, 70569. Tel: 337-369-7510; Fax: 337-369-7413; Email: blabiche@diolaf.org. P.O. Box 369, Lydia, 70569. Rev. Gregory Chauvin.
Catechesis Religious Program—7819 Weeks Island Rd., New Iberia, 70560. Tel: 337-369-3837. Students 60.

LYONS POINT, ACADIA PARISH, ST. JOHN THE BAPTIST (1952) [CEM]
Mailing Address: 8021 Lyons Point Hwy., Crowley, 70526. Tel: 337-783-2968; Fax: 337-783-2065. Rev. Neil Pettit.
Catechesis Religious Program—Deanna Spell, D.R.E. Students 72.

MALLET, ST. LANDRY PARISH, ST. ANN (1856) [CEM] (African American)
Mailing Address: P.O. Box 310, Lawtell, 70550. Tel: 337-543-2366; Fax: 337-841-0210; Email: baubespin@diolaf.org. 8348 Hwy. 190, Lawtell, 70550. Rev. Borgia Aubespin, S.V.D.
Catechesis Religious Program— Combined with Holy Family, Lawtell. Antoinette Rene, D.R.E. Students 88.

MAMOU, EVANGELINE PARISH, ST. ANN (1914) [CEM]
716 Sixth St., Mamou, 70554. Tel: 337-468-3159; Fax: 337-468-3427; Email: catholicmamou@gmail.com; Web: www.saintannmamou.org. Rev. William Massie.
Catechesis Religious Program—Tel: 337-543-2366; Email: baubespin@diolaf.org. Antoinette Rene, D.R.E. Students 195.
Mission—Holy Spirit, 5023 Vidrine Rd., Ville Platte, 70586.

MAURICE, VERMILION PARISH

1—ST. ALPHONSUS (1893) [CEM]
8700 Maurice Ave., P.O. Box 190, Maurice, 70555. Tel: 337-893-4099; Email: STALPHONSUS@COX-INTERNET.COM. Rev. Paul G. Bienvenu; Deacon Byron James Soley.
Catechesis Religious Program—Chris Guidry, D.R.E. Students 541.

2—ST. JOSEPH (1948) [JC] (African American)
8005 Maurice Ave., P.O. Box 250, Maurice, 70555-0250. Tel: 337-893-5428; Fax: 337-893-5441; Email: stjosephchurchmaurice@yahoo.com. Rev. Stanley Jawa, S.V.D.
Catechesis Religious Program—Email: sjawa@diolaf.org. Students 70.

MELVILLE, ST. LANDRY PARISH, ST. JOHN THE EVANGELIST (1931) [CEM]
Mailing Address: 318 First St., P.O. Box 256, Melville, 71353-0256. Tel: 337-623-4957; Fax: 337-623-4970; Email: stjohnmelville@gmail.com. Rev. Stephen Chibunda Ugwu, Admin.
Catechesis Religious Program—Students 27.
Mission—St. Thomas, the Apostle, Palmetto, St. Landry Parish.

MERMENTAU, ACADIA PARISH, ST. JOHN THE EVANGELIST (1882) [CEM]
707 Orange St., Mermentau, 70556. Tel: 337-824-2278; Tel: 337-824-2245; Fax: 337-824-9624; Email: kbenoit@diolaf.org. P.O. Box 340, Mermentau, 70556. Rev. Randy Moreau.
Catechesis Religious Program—Amy Mouton, D.R.E. Students 64.
Mission—St. Margaret, 322 Miller St., Estherwood, Acadia Parish 70534. Katrina Benoit, Contact Person.

MILTON, LAFAYETTE PARISH, ST. JOSEPH (1977) [CEM]
100 E. Milton Ave., P.O. Box 299, Milton, 70558. Tel: 337-856-5997; Fax: 337-856-5955; Email: secretary@stjo-milton.org; Web: www.stjo-milton.org. Rev. William Schambough.
Catechesis Religious Program—Kayla Robles, D.R.E. Students 488.

MIRE, ACADIA PARISH, ASSUMPTION OF THE BLESSED VIRGIN MARY (1954) [CEM]
6080 Mire Hwy., Church Point, 70525. Tel: 337-873-6574; Email: emeche@diolaf.org. Rev. Michael Arnaud.
Catechesis Religious Program—Email: emeche@diolaf.org. Edna Meche, D.R.E. Students 177.

MORROW, ST. LANDRY PARISH, ST. PETER (1947) [CEM] (French)
111 St. Peter Ln., P.O. Box 319, Morrow, 71356. Tel: 318-346-7010; Fax: 318-346-7080; Email: stpeters319@att.net. Rev. Donavan J. Labbe.
Catechesis Religious Program—Students 5.
Mission—Resurrection.

MORSE, ACADIA PARISH, IMMACULATE CONCEPTION (1956)
Mailing Address: 123 N. Jules Ave., P.O. Box 297, Morse, 70559-0297. Tel: 337-783-2968; Fax: 337-783-2965; Email: ctrahan@diolaf.org; Web: www.icc-sjtb.org. Rev. Neil Pettit.
Catechesis Religious Program—Deanna Spell, D.R.E. Students 103.
Mission—St. Aloysius, 218 2nd St., Midland, 70559.

MOWATA, ACADIA PARISH, ST. LAWRENCE (1905) [CEM 2] Rev. Joseph Sai Tran, S.V.D.
Res.: 29031 Crowley-Eunice Hwy., Eunice, 70535. Tel: 337-457-2739; Email: jtran@diolaf.org; Email: jostran76@yahoo.com.
Catechesis Religious Program—Tina Johnson, D.R.E. Students 65.

NEW IBERIA, IBERIA PARISH

1—ST. EDWARD (1917) [CEM] [JC]
201 Ambassador W. Lemelle Dr., New Iberia, 70560. Tel: 337-369-3101; Fax: 337-369-3118; Email: stedwardcc@cox.net. Rev. Thomas H. Vu.
School—St. Edward School, (Grades PreK-3), 175 Porter St., New Iberia, 70560. Tel: 337-369-6764; Fax: 337-369-9534; Email: questions@sespandas.com; Web: www.SESPandas.com. Mrs. Karen Bonin, Prin.; Mrs. Lorita Cruz, Librarian. Lay Teachers 20; Students 320.
Catechesis Religious Program—Tel: 337-412-7881. Elizabeth Harris, D.R.E. Students 75.
Mission—St. Jude, New Iberia, Iberia Parish 70560.

2—NATIVITY OF OUR LADY (1964) [CEM]
130 N. Richelieu Cir., New Iberia, 70560. Tel: 337-364-8360; Fax: 337-364-1509; Email: nativity@ni.brcoxmail.com; Web: www.nativityni.org. Revs. Mario P. Romero; Eugene R. Tremie, In Res., (Retired).
Catechesis Religious Program—Tel: 337-365-3759; Email: nativityccd@ni.brcoxmail.com. Brenda Romero, D.R.E. Students 315.

3—OUR LADY OF PERPETUAL HELP (1949) [JC]
1303 St. Jude Ave., New Iberia, 70560. Tel: 337-365-5481; Email: olphni@gmail.com. Revs. Bill John Melancon; Korey LaVergne, Pastoral Assoc.; Deacon Durwood Gerard Viator.
Catechesis Religious Program—Email: ptauzin@diolaf.org. Peggy Tauzin, D.R.E. Students 94.

4—ST. PETER (1838) [CEM] [JC] (Hispanic—Acadian)
108 E. St. Peter St., New Iberia, 70562. Tel: 337-369-3816; Fax: 337-369-3192; Email: stpeter@cox-internet.com; Web: www.stpetersofnewiberia.com. P.O. Box 12507, New Iberia, 70562. Very Rev. William C. Blanda, V.F.; Rev. Alexander Albert, Parochial Vicar; Deacons Wade Joseph Broussard; Patrick D. Burke, Email: deaconburke.stpeters@yahoo.com; Martin Ancil Cannon.
Catechesis Religious Program—Email: srmarypeter@stpeterofnewiberia.com. Sr. Mary Peter Sealey, D.R.E. Students 155.

5—SACRED HEART OF JESUS (1960)
2514 Old Jeanerette Rd., New Iberia, 70563. Tel: 337-364-4439; Email: sacredheartofjesusdre@gmail.com. Rev. Michael Keith Landry; Peter Derouen, Youth Min.; Darrell Francois, Bookkeeper; Ms. Mindy Domingue, Receptionist.
Res.: 4000 Walnut Dr., New Iberia, 70563.
Catechesis Religious Program—Robin Landry, D.R.E. Students 395.

OPELOUSAS, ST. LANDRY PARISH

1—HOLY GHOST (1920) [JC] (African American)
Mailing Address: P.O. Box 1785, Opelousas, 70571-1785. Tel: 337-942-2732; Email: pastor@hgcatholic.org. Revs. Lambert Lein, S.V.D.; Rofinus Jas, S.V.D.; Deacon Charles Richard.
Res.: 747 N. Union St., Opelousas, 70570. Web: www.hgcatholic.org.
Catechesis Religious Program—Tel: 337-945-3824; Email: dre@hgcatholic.org. Tamara Broussard, D.R.E.; Barbara Butler, D.R.E. Students 170.

2—ST. LANDRY (1776) [CEM] [JC]
1020 N. Main St., Opelousas, 70570. Tel: 337-942-6552; Email: djoubert@diolaf.org; Web: Stlandrycatholicchurch.com. Rev. Msgr. Russell J. Harrington; Deacons Dwayne Paul Joubert, Pastoral Assoc.; Samuel Diesi; John W. Miller.

3—OUR LADY OF MERCY (1942)
1432 W. Landry St., Opelousas, 70570. Tel: 337-942-4174; Email: olomcamille@yahoo.com. 207 N. Camille St., Opelousas, 70570. Rev. Gregory M. Simien; Deacons J. Ulysse Joubert; Thomas Lindsey.
Res.: 124 N. Camille St., Opelousas, 70570.
Catechesis Religious Program—1407 Alberta St., Opelousas, 70570. Email: gsimien@diolaf.org. Students 85.

4—OUR LADY QUEEN OF ANGELS (1967) [JC]
2125 S. Union St., Opelousas, 70570. Tel: 337-942-5628; Email: secretary@queenofangelschurch.org. Rev. Msgr. Keith J. DeRouen; Deacon Jerome Collins.
Catechesis Religious Program—Email: kjdmartin@aol.com. Students 142.

PARKS, ST. MARTIN PARISH, ST. JOSEPH (1938)
Mailing Address: 1034 Bridge St., Parks, 70582. Tel: 337-845-4168; Fax: 337-845-5079; Email: parkschurches@gmail.com. Rev. Nicholas Dupre, C.J.C.; Deacons Dennis Joseph Landry; Joseph Philip Liuzza III.
Catechesis Religious Program—Students 160.
Mission—St. Louis, Parks, St. Martin Parish.

PATTERSON, ST. MARY PARISH, ST. JOSEPH (1848) [CEM] Rev. Herbert Bennerfield.
Res.: 1011 Frist St., P.O. Box 219, Patterson, 70392-0219. Tel: 985-395-3616; Email: stjoepat@cox-internet.com; Web: www.stjosephpatla.org.
Catechesis Religious Program—Tel: 985-395-3881; Email: stjoedre@teche.net. Mamie Perry, D.R.E. Students 116.

PINE PRAIRIE, EVANGELINE PARISH, ST. PETER (1924) [CEM 2]
Mailing Address: 1325 1st St., P.O. Box 709, Pine Prairie, 70576. Tel: 337-599-2224; Fax: 337-599-3003 ; Email: kmayne@diolaf.org. Rev. Kenneth Mayne.
Mission—St. Theresa, 2117 St. Landry Hwy., Evangeline Parish, LA.
Catechesis Religious Program—Email:

stpeterinpineprairie@yahoo.com. Barry Bonnett, D.R.E. Students 175.

PLAISANCE, ST. LANDRY PARISH, ST. JOSEPH (1949) [CEM] (African American)
3283 Hwy. 167, Opelousas, 70570. Tel: 337-826-3395; Email: dthomas@diolaf.org. Rev. Taj Van Courtlan Glodd.
Catechesis Religious Program—Tel: 337-826-3395. Students 15.
Mission—St. Ann, Frilot Cove, Evangeline Parish.

PORT BARRE, ST. LANDRY PARISH
1—ST. MARY (1952) [CEM] [JC] (African American)
4827 Hwy. 103, P.O. Box 338, Port Barre, 70577. Tel: 337-585-2315; Email: smc_pb@yahoo.com. Rev. Clint James Trahan.
Catechesis Religious Program—Students 50.
2—SACRED HEART OF JESUS (1871) [CEM] [JC]
417 Salzan St., P.O. Box 129, Port Barre, 70577. Tel: 337-585-2279; Fax: 337-585-5377; Email: dpicard@diolaf.org. Rev. Clint James Trahan.
Catechesis Religious Program—Email: sacredrectory@bellsouth.net. Dee Jesclard, D.R.E. Students 100.

RAYNE, ACADIA PARISH
1—ST. JOSEPH (1872) [CEM 2] [JC2]
Mailing Address: 401 S. Adams, P.O. Box 199, Rayne, 70578. Tel: 337-334-2193; Fax: 337-334-2199; Email: stjoseph1872@diolaf.org. Revs. Kevin P. Bordelon; Christopher Cambre, Parochial Vicar; Deacons Barry Joseph LeBlanc; Denis Francis LaCroix.
School—Rayne Catholic Elementary, (Grades PreK-8), 407 S. Polk St., Rayne, 70578. Tel: 337-334-5657; Tel: 337-334-5658; Fax: 337-334-3301; Email: rdaigle@raynecatholic.org; Web: www.raynecatholic.org. Mr. Gregory Dubois, Prin. Clergy 2; Lay Teachers 22; Students 287.
Catechesis Religious Program—Email: dbordelon@diolaf.org. Georgette Richard, D.R.E. Students 433.
2—OUR MOTHER OF MERCY (1924) [CEM] (African American)
707 Lyman Ave., Rayne, 70578. Tel: 337-334-3516; Email: rwagner@diolaf.org. Rev. Richard F. Wagner, S.S.J.
Catechesis Religious Program—Tel: 337-207-4092. Students 83.

RICHARD, ACADIA PARISH, ST. EDWARD (1939) [CEM] [JC]
1463 Charlene Hwy., Church Point, 70525. Tel: 337-684-5991; Email: jgary2@diolaf.org. Rev. Wayne J. Duet.
Catechesis Religious Program—Monica Rougeau, D.R.E. Students 200.
Mission—St. Thomas, 802 Tasso Loop, Savoy, St. Landry Parish 70525.

ROBERTS COVE, ACADIA PARISH, ST. LEO IV (1883) [CEM] (German)
7166 Roberts Cove Rd., Rayne, 70578-8912. Tel: 337-334-5056; Email: josette@stsleoandedmund.org. Rev. Paul Broussard; Deacon Joshua Reed LeBlanc.
Catechesis Religious Program—Email: jbroussard@diolaf.org. Students 51.
Mission—St. Edmund Chapel, Branch, Acadia Parish.

RYNELLA, IBERIA PARISH, ST. MARCELLUS (1960) [CEM]
6100 Avery Island Rd., New Iberia, 70560. Tel: 337-364-0818; Email: stmarcellusc@aol.com. Rev. James B. Nguyen.
Catechesis Religious Program—Tel: 337-364-9419; Email: ylhebert@diolaf.org. Yvonne Hebert, D.R.E. Students 122.

ST. MARTINVILLE, ST. MARTIN PARISH
1—ST. MARTIN DE TOURS (1765) [CEM]
133 S. Main St., P.O. Drawer 10, St. Martinville, 70582. Tel: 337-394-6021; Email: tamlebsmdt@gmail.com; Web: www.saintmartindetours.org. Rev. Rusty P. Richard.
Catechesis Religious Program—Email: rrichard@diolaf.org. Tilly Duplechein, D.R.E. Students 91.
2—NOTRE DAME DE PERPETUEL SECOURS (1938) [CEM] [JC] (African American)
201 Gary St., St. Martinville, 70582. Tel: 337-394-3084. P.O. Box 677, St. Martinville, 70582. Revs. Michael M. Sucharski, S.V.D.; Darrell Kelley, S.V.D., In Res.; Deacons David Chambers; Carlton J. Lee Sr.
Catechesis Religious Program—Mrs. Glenda Sonnier, D.R.E. Students 144.

SCOTT, LAFAYETTE PARISH
1—SAINT MARTIN DE PORRES (1961) [CEM] (African American)
1100 Chaisson St., P.O. Box 1347, Scott, 70583-1347. Tel: 337-232-1968; Fax: 337-266-8922; Email: deporres@bellsouth.net. Rev. Msgr. Ronald Broussard.
Catechesis Religious Program—Tel: 337-258-1667; Email: deaconsenegal@yahoo.com. Brenda Dugas, D.R.E. Students 65.
2—STS. PETER AND PAUL (1904) [CEM]
Mailing Address: P.O. Box 610, Scott, 70583. Tel: 337-235-2433; Fax: 337-233-4868; Email: stspeterandpaulscott@hotmail.com; Web: www.stspeterandpaulscott.org. Revs. Mark Derise; Arockiadass Thanaraj; Most Rev. Charles Michael Jarrell, D.D., Former Bishop; Deacons Arthur Francis Bakeler Jr.; Clifford Jude Tanner.
School—Sts. Peter and Paul Catholic School, (Grades PreK-8), 1301 Old Spanish Tr., Scott, 70583. Tel: 337-504-3400; Fax: 337-504-4995; Email: info@sts-peter-paul.org; Web: www.sts-peter-paul.org. Mrs. Danielle Babineaux, Prin.; Mrs. Rachel Kimble, Admin. Lay Teachers 24; Students 371.
Catechesis Religious Program—1110 Old Spanish Tr., Scott, 70583. Email: mderise@diolaf.org. Students 255.

VILLE PLATTE, EVANGELINE PARISH
1—ST. JOSEPH (1947) [CEM] (African American)
708 E. Main St., Ville Platte, 70586. Tel: 337-506-2400; Fax: 337-506-2400; Email: frtom@sacredheartvp.com; Email: srdarens@yahoo.com. Very Rev. Thomas P. Voorhies, V.F.; Rev. Blake Dubroc; Sr. Rita Darensbourg, S.S.F., Pastoral Assoc.
Church: 1107 Dr. Martin Luther King Jr. Dr., Ville Platte, 70586.
Catechesis Religious Program—Email: srdarens@yahoo.com. Students 4.
2—OUR LADY QUEEN OF ALL SAINTS (1969)
1012 Dardeau St., Ville Platte, 70586. Tel: 337-363-5167; Fax: 337-363-5179; Email: olqasec@centurytel.net. Rev. Mitchell Guidry; Deacons Eugene LeBoeuf; John Bennett Soileau Jr.
Catechesis Religious Program—1220 Dardeau St., Ville Platte, 70586. Tiffany Alfred, D.R.E. Students 120.
3—SACRED HEART OF JESUS (1854) [CEM]
708 E. Main St., Ville Platte, 70586. Tel: 337-363-2989. Very Rev. Thomas P. Voorhies, V.F.; Rev. Blake Dubroc, Parochial Vicar.
School—Sacred Heart Elementary School, (Grades K-8), 161 Bourgeois St., Ville Platte, 70586. Tel: 337-363-3445; Fax: 337-363-3551; Email: virginia.morein@shsvp.com. Virginia Morein, Elementary Prin.; Rebecca Buller, Librarian. Lay Teachers 22; Students 385.
High School—Sacred Heart High School, 114 Trojan Ln., Ville Platte, 70586. Tel: 337-363-1475; Fax: 337-363-0348; Email: dawn.shipp@shsvp.com. Mrs. Dawn C. Shipp, Prin.; Laura Daire, Librarian. Lay Teachers 14; Students 199.
Catechesis Religious Program—Email: frtom@sacredheartvp.com. Tiffany Alfred, D.R.E. Students 53.
Chapel—Belaire Cove Chapel, 2003 Belaire Cove Rd., Ville Platte, 70586.

WASHINGTON, ST. LANDRY PARISH
1—HOLY TRINITY (1950) (African American)
Mailing Address: 414 E. St. Mitchell Street, P.O. Box 186, Washington, 70589. Tel: 337-826-3376; Fax: 337-826-3376; Email: Sherolyn.Boutte@diolaf.org. Rev. Matthew P. Higginbotham.
Catechesis Religious Program—Students 13.
2—IMMACULATE CONCEPTION (1854)
314 E. Moundville St, P.O. Box 116, Washington, 70589. Tel: 337-826-7396; Fax: 337-826-0099; Email: Immaculateconceptionchurch@yahoo.com. Rev. Matthew P. Higginbotham.
Catechesis Religious Program—Katie Fontenot, D.R.E.

YOUNGSVILLE, LAFAYETTE PARISH, ST. ANNE (1859) [CEM]
201 Church St., P.O. Box 410, Youngsville, 70592. Tel: 337-856-8212; Fax: 337-856-8277; Email: stanne@stannechurch.net; Web: www.stannechurch.net. Rev. Thomas Jason Mouton; Deacon Wynard Joseph Mitchell Boutte.
Catechesis Religious Program—Tel: 337-857-6382; Email: dre@stannechurch.net. Jessica Currier, D.R.E. Students 417.

On Special Assignment:
Very Rev. Msgrs.—
Larroque, H. Alexandre, J.C.D., Vicar for Special Projects
Mallet, William Curtis, J.C.L., V.G., Vicar General
Very Rev.—
Suire, Jared G., V.E., Vicar for Clergy
Revs.—
Akalawu, Ambrose, Chap., Our Lady of Lourdes.
Boyer, Millard G., Chap., Tel: 337-289-7483. Lafayette General Medical Center, Lafayette
Broussard, Ken, J.C.L., Tribunal Office
Eze, Cyprian, Hospital Ministry - Lafayette General Southwest, Lafayette
Finley, John Thomas, Diocesan Chap., Bethany Health Care, Lafayette
Guillory, Brad D., 4109 Lew Wallace Dr., Clovis, NM 88101. Special Assignment, Archdiocese of the Military Services
Guillory, Joshua P., Special Assignment, Rome
Halphen, Jude, Ph.D., Dir., Marriage, Family Life & Pro-Life Activities, Dir., Marriage & Family Life Office, Diocese of Lafayette
Kalinowski, Ryszard, S.V.D., Rel. Chap., Lafayette area hospitals
Luu, Vinh Dinh, J.C.L., Adjutant Judicial Vicar, extern
Meaux, Glenn, SOLT Haiti Mission
Ofodum, Anselm I., Chap., Our Lady of Lourdes Regional Medical Center, Lafayette
Pitre, Benjamin, Pontifical North American College, Rome.

On Leave / Administrative Leave:
Very Rev. Msgr.—
Robichaux, Robie E., J.C.L.
Rev. Msgr.—
Herpin, Michael
Revs.—
Alexander, Joseph
Arceneaux, Jules
Broussard, David
Gearheard, William, (Working Outside of Diocese)
Simoneaux, Jody.

Retired:
Rev. Msgrs.—
Greene, Richard, (Retired), New Iberia
Mallet, Charles J., (Retired)
Metrejean, Paul, (Retired), Opelousas
Revs.—
Abara, Lawrence N., (Retired), South Carolina
Bergeron, C. Paul, (Retired), Houma
Bertrand, Conley, (Retired), 1804 W. University Ave., 70506
Bienvenu, Kenneth A., (Retired), St. Martinville
Breaux, Overton Joseph, (Retired), Maurice
Broussard, A. Rex Jr., (Retired), Lafayette
Broussard, Henry J., (Retired), Eunice
Broussard, Richard Dale, Admin, (Retired), Louisa
Brown, Wilbur J., (Retired), Eunice
Calais, Floyd J., (Retired), Lafayette
Courville, Robert, (Retired), Alexandria
Cremaldi, Angelo, (Retired), Patterson
Degeyter, Edward, (Retired), St. Martinville, LA
Downs, Gregory Todd, (Retired), Ville Platte
Dugas, Willard, (Retired), Lafayette
Fabre, Richard, (Retired), New Iberia
Finley, Thomas, (Retired), in residence, St. Jules, Lafayette
Hebert, T. J., (Retired), Lafayette
Landry, Oneil Anthony, (Retired), P.O. Box 202, Centerville, 70522
Langlois, Charles, (Retired), New Iberia
LeDoux, Louis Vernon, (Retired), New York
Leger, Austin, (Retired), Opelousas
Montelaro, Thomas, (Retired), Nevada
Nguyen, Thomas Thanh, (Retired)
Pelous, Donald, (Retired), P.O. Box 852, Breaux Bridge, 70517
Ruskoski, William Paul, (Retired), Franklin
Stemmann, Joseph, (Retired), New Iberia
Trahan, Charles N., (Retired), New Iberia
Tremie, Eugene R., (Retired), New Iberia
Vidrine, Richard, (Retired), Ville Platte.

Permanent Deacons:
Adams, Thomas E. Sr., (Unassigned)
Arnaud, John Kenneth, St. Francis Regis, Arnaudville
Bakeler, Arthur Francis Jr., (Unassigned)
Baudoin, Scotty James, Holy Cross, Lafayette
Bergeron, Harris, (Retired)
Bertrand, Glen, Come Lord Jesus Program, Lafayette
Besse, Daniel Lee, (Retired)
Blanco, Jose Vicente, St. Jules, Lafayette
Bollich, Reginald A., St. Jules, Lafayette
Boudreaux, F. Dwayne, St. Leo the Great, Leonville
Bourg, Gerald Joseph, St. Helena, Louisa
Boustany, Edward Jules, Our Lady of Fatima, Lafayette
Boutte, Wynard Joseph Mitchell, St. Anne, Youngsville
Broussard, Wade, St. Peter's, New Iberia
Burke, Patrick Douglas, St. Peter, New Iberia
Cannon, Martin Ancil, St. Peter, New Iberia
Cao, Khang Francis Xavier Van, St. Mary Magdalen, Abbeville
Chambers, David Brodrick, Notre Dame, St. Martinville
Chauvin, Ronald Paul, St. Elizabeth Seton, Lafayette
Collins, Jerome, Our Lady Queen of Angels, Opelousas
Cormier, Frank Alex, St. Edmond, Lafayette
Cormier, James, Annunciation BVM, Duralde
Crain, Michael Wayne, St. Mary Mother of the Church, Lafayette

Darce, Harry, Our Lady of Perpetual Help, Maurice
David, Kenneth James, (Unassigned)
Davis, James, (Unassigned)
DeJean, Alvin Ray, (Unassigned)
Derouen, Raymond Charles, (Retired)
Didier, Daniel Peter, St. Michael the Archangel, Crowley
Diesi, Samuel Charles, St. Landry, Opelousas Church
Doumit, Christopher, St. Joseph, Loreauville
Duhon, Keith Anthony, St. Joseph, Milton
Eleazar, Paul, (Retired)
Faber, Kyle Joseph, St. Genevieve, Lafayette
Gaudin, Gary Michael, St. Anthony, Eunice
Guidry, Perry John, Our Lady of Mercy, Henderson
Guilbeau, Joseph Herd, St. Charles Borromeo, Coteau
Guillory, David W., St. Thomas More, Eunice
Hayes, Russell James, Chap., Our Lady of Lourdes & Our Lady of the Lake, Delcambre Regional Medical Center
Hebert, Clifford Mitchell Jr., Sacred Heart of Jesus, Port Barre
Hebert, Douglas, (Retired)
Hebert, Joseph, St. Peter's, Gueydan
Hebert, Marcel, St. Bernard, Breaux Bridge
Hyde, Randy Eugene, (Unassigned)
Jeanlouis, Roland James, Our Lady of Victory, Loreauville
Joubert, Dwayne Paul, St. Landry, Opelousas
Joubert, J. Ulysse, Our Lady of Mercy, Opelousas
Jourdan, George Bernard, Cathedral of St. John the Evangelist, Lafayette
Kilchrist, Guy Anthony, (Unassigned)
Kincel, James, Dir. & Permanent Diaconate
Kirk, Brian Thomas, moved to Lake Charles
Klingman, Robert Charles Jr., Holy Cross, Lafayette
LaCroix, Denis Francis, St. Joseph, Rayne
Landry, Dennis Joseph, St. Joseph, Parks
LeBlanc, Barry Joseph, St. Joseph, Rayne
LeBlanc, Joshua Reed, St. Leo IV, Roberts Cove
Lebouef, Eugene J., Queen of All Saints, Ville Platte
Ledet, Timothy Francis, St. Joseph, Rayne
Lee, Carlton J. Sr., Notre Dame, St. Martinville
Leger, Robert Lee, St. Joseph, Iota
Lejeune, Barney Dale, St. Peter, Carencro
LeJeune, J. Leon, (Retired)
Lindsey, Thomas, Our Lady of Mercy, Opelousas
Liuzza, Joseph Philip III, St. Joseph, Parks
Lizotte, Philippe Eugene Ronald, St. Pius X, Lafayette
Lloyd, Louis, Our Lady Queen of Peace, Lafayette
Luna-Becerra, Jose, St. Jules, Lafayette
Maragos, Timothy, Our Lady of Fatima, Lafayette
Marcantel, Timothy Isidore, Our Lady of Lourdes, Erath
Marcel, Albert Jr., St. Anthony, Lafayette
Matte, Paul, (Unassigned)
McDonner, Robert, (Unassigned)
Melancon, Douglas J., (Retired)
Miller, Cody, (Unassigned)
Miller, John W., St. Landry, Opelousas
Morrison, Michael Raymond, Immaculate Heart of Mary, Lafayette
Mouton, Chris, (Leave of Absence)
Nguyen, Tuan Anh, St. Jules, Lafayette, Vietnamese Ministry
Ortego, Charles (Chuck), Our Lady of Mt. Carmel, Chataignier
Pagan, Juan Carlos, Our Lady of Wisdom, Lafayette
Perron, Roderick P., (Retired)
Peyton, Scott Ellis, Sacred Heart, Ville Platte
Picard, Richard, Sacred Heart of Jesus, Baldwin
Pollingue, William Logan, Our Lady Queen of Angels, Opelousas
Rabailais, Bert, (Retired)
Richard, Charles Ray, Holy Ghost, Opelousas
Richard, Thomas, (Retired)
Rogers, Steve Anthony, St. Edward, New Iberia
Russo, Samuel Joseph Jr., St. Pius X, Lafayette
Sarkies, John, (Retired)
Schexnayder, Nelson Joseph Jr., St. Elizabeth Seton, Lafayette
Senegal, Nolton J., Our Lady of the Assumption, Carencro
ShawnMalcolm Melancon, St. Peter, Washington
Simon, Steve, St. Theresa, Duson
Smith, Charles J., (Retired)
Soignier, Kenneth E., St. Bernard, Breaux Bridge
Soileau, John Bennett Jr., Our Lady Queen of All Saints, Ville Platte
Soley, Byron James, St. Alphonsus, Maurice
Sommers, Thomas Richard, St. John the Baptist, Lyons Point
Tanner, Clifford Jude, Sts. Peter and Paul, Scott
Thomas, Coby Brandon, Our Lady of Wisdom, Lafayette
Thomas, Joseph C., St. Peter the Apostle, Four Corners
Trahan, Joseph, Sacred Heart, Broussard
Tran, Tam Minh, St. Mary Magdalen, Abbeville
Trumps, Jeffrey Paul, Diocesan Fin. Officer
Van Cleve, Stephen Glenn, Nativity of Our Lady, New Iberia
Vaughn, David Lee, Our Lady of the Holy Rosary, Kaplan
Viator, Durwood Gerard, Our Lady of Perpetual Help, New Iberia
Vincent, William Merrill, St. Mary Magdalen, Abbeville
Wimberly, Francis Douglas, Our Lady of the Sacred Heart, Church Point
Winn, Byrne James, St. John Berchmans, Cankton
Wyble, Jerry Wayne, Our Lady of the Sacred Heart, Church Point
Yenik, Michael Robert, Houston, TX.

INSTITUTIONS LOCATED IN DIOCESE

[A] SEMINARIES, RELIGIOUS OR SCHOLASTICATES

GRAND COTEAU. *St. Charles College*, 313 E. Martin Luther King Dr., P.O. Box C, Grand Coteau, 70541-1003. Tel: 337-662-5251; Fax: 337-662-3187; Email: derricksj@yahoo.com. Revs. Mark E. Thibodeaux, S.J., Dir., Novices; Andrew R. Kirschman, S.J., Dir.; Derrick Weingartner, S.J., Rector & Supr., Jesuit Spirituality Center. Novitiate of U.S. Central and Southern Province of the Society of Jesus. Novices 20; Priests 2; Students 20; Clergy / Religious Teachers 2.

Saint Alphonsus Rodriguez Pavilion Revs. A. Ferdinand Derrera, S.J.; Rodney T. Kissinger, S.J.; Roland J. Lesseps, S.J.; Bert Mead, S.J.; Paul V. Osterle, S.J.; John F. Paul, S.J.; Herve Rachivitch, S.J.; Edmundo Rodriguez, S.J.; Paul W. Schott, S.J.; Bros. Joseph Martin, F.S.C., (Retired); John Puza, S.J.

Jesuit Spirituality Center Revs. Thomas J. Madden, S.J.; Hernando J. Ramirez, S.J.

Novitiate Revs. James F. Goeke, S.J.; Mark E. Thibodeaux, S.J.

[B] HIGH SCHOOLS, INTERPAROCHIAL

LAFAYETTE. *Teurlings Catholic High School* (1955) 139 Teurlings Dr., 70501. Tel: 337-235-5711; Fax: 337-234-8057; Email: mboyer@tchs.net; Web: www.tchs.net. Mr. Michael H. Boyer, Prin. Lay Teachers 46; Students 744.

St. Thomas More, 450 E. Farrel Rd., 70508. Tel: 337-988-3700; Fax: 337-988-2911; Email: kelley.leger@stmcougars.net; Web: www.stmcougars.net. Rev. Michael Russo, Chancellor; Richard Lavergne, Pres.; Kelley Leger, Prin. Lay Teachers 88; Students 971; Total Staff 117.

CROWLEY. *Notre Dame High School of Acadia Parish*, 910 N. Eastern Ave., Crowley, 70526. Tel: 337-783-3519; Fax: 337-788-2115; Email: cistre@ndpios.com; Email: jmouton@ndpios.com; Web: www.ndpios.com. Ms. Cindy M. Istre, Prin.; Rev. Mikel Anthony Polson, Chancellor. Lay Teachers 32; Students 370.

NEW IBERIA. *Catholic High School*, (Grades 4-12), 1301 DeLaSalle Dr., New Iberia, 70560. Tel: 337-364-5116; Fax: 337-364-5041; Email: esegura@chspanthers.com; Web: chspanthers.com. Dr. Stella Arabie, Prin.; Penny Smith, Librarian. Lay Teachers 59; Priests 2; Sisters 1; Students 701; Total Staff 73; Clergy / Religious Teachers 2.

OPELOUSAS. *Opelousas Catholic School* (1971) (Grades PreK-12), Elementary: (PreK-5) High School: (6-12) 428 E. Prudhomme St., Opelousas, 70570. Tel: 337-942-5404; Fax: 337-942-5922; Email: ocsvikings@yahoo.com. Marty Heintz, Prin.; Rose Lalonde, Dir.; Leslie Carlos, Librarian. Administrators 5; Lay Teachers 46; Students 580.

[C] ELEMENTARY SCHOOLS, INTERPAROCHIAL

LAFAYETTE. *Holy Family School* (1903) (Grades PreK-8), 200 St. John St., 70501. Tel: 337-235-0267; Fax: 337-235-0558; Email: rgriffin@holyfamilycs.com; Web: www.hfcsonline.com. Roger Griffin, Prin.; Cynthia Cluse, Librarian. Sisters of the Holy Family. Clergy 4; Lay Teachers 14; Sisters 4; Students 285; Clergy / Religious Teachers 4.

[D] ELEMENTARY SCHOOLS, PRIVATE

ABBEVILLE. *Mt. Carmel School* aka Mount Carmel School of Abbeville, Inc. (1885) (Grades PreK-8), 405 Park Ave., Abbeville, 70510. Tel: 337-898-0859 ; Fax: 337-893-5968; Email: jtrahan@mceschool.com; Web: www.mceschool.org. Sr. Janet LeBlanc, O.Carm., Pres.; Jackie Trahan, Prin.; Tiffany Abshire, Librarian. Lay Teachers 24; Sisters of Mt. Carmel 1; Students 322.

[E] HIGH AND ELEMENTARY SCHOOLS, PRIVATE

GRAND COTEAU. *Academy of the Sacred Heart*, (Grades PreK-12), 1821 Academy Road, P.O. Box 310, Grand Coteau, 70541. Tel: 337-662-5275; Fax: 337-662-3011; Email: yadler@sshcoteau.org; Web: www.sshcoteau.org. Yvonne Adler, Ph.D., Headmaster; Bonnie Hale, Registrar; Angela Hymel, Contact Person; Jeanne-Marie Meaux, Librarian. Day School for both divisions (girls-boys) are single gender. Boarding facilities for girls 7th-12th grade. Clergy 4; Lay Teachers 42; Students 254; Religious of the Sacred Heart 2.

Berchmans Academy of the Sacred Heart, (Grades PreK-12), (Day school for boys) Tel: 337-662-5275; Email: aboagni@sshcoteau.org. Yvonne Adler, Ph. D., Headmaster; Angie Boagni, Contact Person. Clergy 2; Lay Teachers 22; Students 123.

[F] GENERAL HOSPITALS

LAFAYETTE. *Our Lady of Lourdes Regional Medical Center, Inc.* (1949) 4801 Ambassador Caffery Pkwy., 70508. Tel: 337-470-2100; Fax: 337-470-2574; Web: www.lourdes.net. Bryan Lee, CEO; Mr. Robert Mahtook, Chm. Bed Capacity 186; Tot Asst. Annually 111,775; Total Staff 1,543.

[G] HOMES FOR THE AGED INFIRM

LAFAYETTE. *Bethany M.H.S. Health Care Center* (1962) 406 St. Julien Street, P.O. Box 2308, 70502. Tel: 337-234-2459; Fax: 337-234-9483; Email: srddornan@gmail.com. Sr. Diane Dornan, M.H.S., Contact Person. Bed Capacity 42; Sisters 7; Total Staff 74; Total Assisted 42.

Village du Lac, Inc., 1404 Carmel Dr., 70501. Tel: 337-234-5106; Fax: 337-234-2630; Email: eboustany@diolaf.org. Deacon Edward J. Boustany, Dir. The DioceseCommunity housing for the handicapped and elderly with low income. Bed Capacity 200; Tot Asst. Annually 476; Total Staff 4.

NEW IBERIA. *Consolata Home* (1960) 2319 E. Main St., New Iberia, 70560. Tel: 337-365-8226; Fax: 337-365-8626; Email: chasdel@cox.net. Charles L. Delahoussaye, Admin.; Rev. Charles Langlois, Chap., (Retired). Bed Capacity 120; Residents 114; Total Staff 107; Clergy Apartments 6; Total Assisted 165.

OPELOUSAS. *C'est La Vie Center of the Sisters Marianites of Holy Cross* dba C'est la Vie Independent Living Apartments, 960 E. Prudhomme St., Opelousas, 70570. Tel: 337-942-8154; Fax: 337-942-8279; Email: mike@promptsuccor.com; Web: www.promptsuccor.com. Michael Purser, Admin.; Sisters Ann Arno, M.S.C., Coord.; Mary Kay Kinberger, M.S.C., Asst. Admin. Independent living for the elderly and handicapped. Bed Capacity 34; Patients Asst Anual. 50; Sisters 6; Total Staff 6.

Prompt Succor Nursing Home Corporation dba Our Lady of Prompt Succor Nursing Facility, 954 E. Prudhomme St., Opelousas, 70570. Tel: 337-948-3634; Fax: 337-942-8279; Email: mike@promptsuccor.com; Web: www.promptsuccor.com. Michael Purser, Admin.; Sr. Mary Kay Kinberger, M.S.C., Asst. Admin. Bed Capacity 120; Patients Asst Anual. 200; Sisters 40; Total Staff 165.

[H] MONASTERIES AND RESIDENCES OF PRIESTS AND BROTHERS

GRAND COTEAU. *St. Charles College*, 313 E. Martin Luther King, P.O. Box C, Grand Coteau, 70541-1003. Tel: 337-662-5251; Fax: 337-662-3187; Email: derricksj@yahoo.com. Revs. Mark E. Thibodeaux, S.J., Dir.; James P. Bradley, S.J., Dir.; Derrick Weingartner, S.J., Rector/Supr.; Bro. Anthony S. Coco, S.J.; Rev Andrew Kirschman, Dir. A Jesuit Community for Jesuits working in the Grand Coteau ministries.

OPELOUSAS. *Mother of the Redeemer Monastery* (1990) 168 Monastery Ln., Opelousas, 70570. Tel: 337-543-2237; Fax: 337-543-7752; Email: plaisance_monks@yahoo.com; Web: www.motheroftheredeemer.org. Rev. James Liprie, O.S.B., Supr.; Bros. Gregory Foret, O.S.B., Sec./Treas.; Laurent Abila, O.S.B., Member; Rev. Bernard V. Lebiedz, O.S.B., Member; Bro. Martin des Porres, Temp. Member. Brothers 3; Priests 2.

[I] CONVENTS AND RESIDENCES FOR SISTERS

LAFAYETTE. *Discalced Carmelites* Monastery of Mary, Mother of Grace. 1250 Carmel Dr., 70501-5299. Tel: 337-232-4651; Fax: 337-232-3540; Email: srmj@lafayettecarmel.com; Web: lafayettecarmelites.org. Very Rev. Msgr. H. A. Larroque, J.C.D., Chap.; Mother Regina Mullins, O.C.D., Prioress. Novices 3; Sisters 15; Solemnly Professed 11; Cloistered Nuns 13; Extern. Sisters 1.

Franciscan Missionaries of Our Lady, 101 Sandbar Ln., 70508. Tel: 337-504-5949. Sr. Uyen Vu, Contact Person. Sisters 2.

Marianites of Holy Cross, 1417 St. John St., 70506. Tel: 337-234-5454; Email: marlabmsc@juno.com. Sr. Margaret Cano, Contact Person. Sisters 3.

Missionaries of Charity, 904 Jack St., 70501. Tel: 337-233-3929. Sisters M. Jonathan, MC, Regl. Supr.; M. Annaleah, MC, Regl. Supr.; M. Romero, MC, Supr. Sisters 4.

Sisters of Divine Providence (1866) 317 Guilbeau Rd., Apt. 101-E, 70506. Tel: 337-984-8520; Email: mildredleonards@cox.net. Sr. Mildred Leonards, Contact Person. Sisters 1.

Sisters of Mt. Carmel (1846) 2326 Camilla St., Abbeville, 70510. Tel: 337-385-2834; Email: leahsellers@cox.net. Sr. Leah Sellers, Contact Person. Sisters 3.

Sisters of the Most Holy Sacrament (1872) Convent, Generalate & Administrative Offices, 313 Corona Dr., P.O. Box 90037, 70509-0037. Tel: 337-981-8475; Fax: 337-981-9128; Email: dmholysisters@bellsouth.net. Sisters Diane Dornan, M.H.S., Provincial; Ann Lacour. Sisters 11.

GRAND COTEAU. *Religious of the Sacred Heart*, 376 E. Martin Luther King Drive, P.O. Box 4292, Grand Coteau, 70541. Tel: 337-662-5526; Email: slasseigne@rscj.org; Web: www.rscj.org. Sr. Sheila Hammond, Prov. Sisters 4.

Sisters of the Holy Spirit, P.O. Box 115, Lebeau, 71345. Tel: 337-623-5540; Email: jprejean@diolaf.org. Sr. Martha Readore, Contact Person. Sisters 1.

NEW IBERIA. *School Sisters of Notre Dame*, 501 Darby Ln., Apt. 102, New Iberia, 70560. Tel: 337-504-4360; Email: krausbar2@gmail.com. Sr. Barbara Kraus, S.S.N.D., Contact Person. Sisters 1.

Sisters of Providence, 213 Oak Hill Rd., New Iberia, 70563. Tel: 337-364-3142; Email: jprejean@diolaf.org. Sisters 1.

OPELOUSAS. *Marianites of the Holy Cross*, 1417 St. John Street, 70501. Tel: 337-234-5454; Email: smrcno@yahoo.com. Sr. Margaret Cano, Contact Person. Sisters 3.

Sisters of the Holy Family, 708 E. Main St., Ville Platte, 70586. Tel: 337-506-2400; Tel: 504-241-3088; Email: emartinssfd@aol.com. Sr. E. Martin, Contact Person. Sisters 2.

[J] RETREAT HOUSES

GRAND COTEAU. *Jesuit Spirituality Center (St. Charles College)*, P.O. Box C, Grand Coteau, 70541-1003. Tel: 337-662-5251; Fax: 337-662-3187; Email: office@jesuitspiritualitycenter.org; Web: jesuitspiritualitycenter.org. Rev. Anthony H. Ostini, S.J., Dir.; Mr. Easton Hebert, Retreat Dir.; Revs. Hernando J. Ramirez, S.J., Dir.; John Callahan, Retreat Dir.; Mrs. Nelda Turner, Retreat Dir. Year-round directed retreats of 3, 5, 8, or 30 days plus a variety of weekend retreats and/or programs open to men and women. (Full-time) 2; Priests 3.

Our Lady of the Oaks Retreat House, P.O. Box D, Grand Coteau, 70541. Tel: 337-662-5410; Fax: 337-662-5331; Email: oloaks@centurytel.net; Web: www.ourladyoftheoaks.com. Revs. Lou McCabe, Retreat Dir.; Steven E. Kimmons, S.J., Retreat Dir.; Joseph A. Tetlow, S.J., Retreat Dir. Jesuit Fathers.Preached retreats for men, women and married couples.

ST. MARTINVILLE. *Our Lady of Sorrows Retreat Center*, 103 Railroad Ave., St. Martinville, 70582. Tel: 337-394-6550; Email: frchampagne@yahoo.com; Web: www.jesuscrucified.net. Rev. Michael Champagne, C.J.C., S.T.D., Spiritual Advisor/Care Svcs.

[K] CURSILLO CENTERS

OPELOUSAS. *Cursillo Center*, 3651 Hwy. 104 (Prairie Ronde), Opelousas, 70570. Tel: 337-543-7425; Fax: 337-543-2100; Email: rctomlinson@bellsouth.net; Web: www.whowillsit.com. Rev. Theodore Broussard Jr., Dir.

[L] NEWMAN CENTERS

LAFAYETTE. *Our Lady of Wisdom Catholic Student Center*, 501 East Saint Mary Blvd., 70503. Univ. of Louisiana, P.O. Box 43599, 70504. Tel: 337-232-8741; Tel: 337-232-8742; Fax: 337-236-6737; Email: wisdom@ourladyofwisdom.org; Web: ragincajuncatholics.org. Revs. Bryce Sibley, Pastor; René Pellessier, Assoc. Pastor.

EUNICE. *Catholic Student Center-Louisiana State Univ.-Eunice*, P.O. Box 1129, Eunice, 70535. Tel: 337-457-8107; Fax: 337-457-1735; Email: lsuecatholic.stm@gmail.com. Josh Brumfield, Admin. & Campus Min. Total in Residence 1; Total Staff 1.

[M] MISCELLANEOUS

LAFAYETTE. *St. Augustine Trust Fund*, P.O. Box 90037, 70509-0037. Tel: 337-981-8475; Fax: 337-981-9128; Email: srddornan@gmail.com. Sr. Diane Dornan, M.H.S., Pres. Sisters of the Most Holy Sacrament.

Come Lord Jesus! Inc. (1974) 1804 W. University Ave., 70506. Tel: 337-233-6277; Email: comelordjesusprogram@gmail.com; Web: www.comelordjesus.com. Rev. Conley Bertrand, Dir. Priests 1; Total Staff 4.

Community of Jesus Crucified, 103 Railroad Ave., St. Martinville, 70582. Tel: 337-394-6550; Email: frchampagne@yahoo.com; Web: www.jesuscrucified.net. Rev. Michael Champagne, C.J.C., S.T.D., Spiritual Advisor/ Care Svcs. Brothers 3; Priests 1; Seminarians 1; Sisters 4.

Lourdes Foundation, Inc., 4801 Ambassador Caffery Pkwy., 70508. Tel: 337-470-4610; Fax: 337-470-2574; Email: jeigh.stipe@fmolhs.org; Web: www.lourdes.net. Jeigh O. Stipe, Exec. Dir.; Mike Moncla, Chm.

Sisters of the Eucharistic Covenant, 105 Upperline Ave., 70501. Tel: 337-233-2226; Fax: 337-233-2226; Email: clarr0101@gmail.com; Web: secsisters.org. Sr. Celeste D. Larroque, S.E.C., Pres.

NEW IBERIA. *Progressive Education Program, Inc.* (1976) P.O. Box 10237, New Iberia, 70562-0237. Tel: 337-365-0933; Fax: 337-364-2555; Email: pepitc1990@gmail.com. Sr. Barbara Kraus, S.S.N.D., Dir.

SAINT MARTINVILLE. *Community of Jesus Crucified - Priest Brother and Sister Servants*, 103 Railroad Ave., Saint Martinville, 70582.

**Witness to Love Marriage Prep Renewal Ministry*, 1039 Rue Maline, Saint Martinville, 70582.

[N] CATHOLIC SOCIAL SERVICE CENTERS

LAFAYETTE. *Catholic Services of Acadiana, Inc.* (1973) 405 St. John St., 70502-3177. Tel: 337-235-4972; Fax: 337-234-0953; Web: www.catholicservice.org. P.O. Box 3177, 70502. Sarah Clement, Dir. Tot Asst. Annually 4,462; Total Staff 36; Full-time Employees 33; Part-time Employees 3.

Service Centers: Mrs. Kim Boudreaux, Exec. Dir.

Bishop O'Donnell Housing, Tel: 337-235-4972; Fax: 337-234-0953; Email: kboudreaux@catholicservice.org; Web: www.catholicservice.org. Mrs. Kim Boudreaux, Exec.

Msgr. A. O. Sigur Service Center, 401 St. John St., 70501. Tel: 337-235-4972; Fax: 337-234-0953; Email: kboudreaux@catholicservice.org; Web: www.catholicservice.org. Mrs. Kim Boudreaux, Exec. Tot Asst. Annually 1,576; Total Staff 9.

St. Joseph Shelter for Men, 425 St. John St., 70501. Tel: 337-233-6816; Email: mhinman@catholicservice.org; Web: www.catholicservice.org. Mrs. Kim Boudreaux, Exec. Bed Capacity 30; Tot Asst. Annually 118; Total Staff 4.

St. Joseph Diner, 613 W. Simcoe, 70501. Tel: 337-235-4972; Fax: 337-234-0953; Email: kboudreaux@catholicservice.org; Web: www.catholicservice.org. Mrs. Kim Boudreaux, Exec. Number of Meals 112,000.

New Life Center, 1000 E. Willow St., 70501. Fax: 337-948-0011; Email: mhinman@catholicservice.org; Web: www.catholicservice.org. Mrs. Kim Boudreaux, Exec. Tot Asst. Annually 159; Total Staff 6.

Stella Maris Center, 615 Simcoe St., 70501. Tel: 337-235-4972, Ext. 118; Fax: 337-234-0953; Email: mhinman@catholicservice.org; Web: www.catholicservice.org. Mrs. Kim Boudreaux, Exec. Shower Services 4,128; Laundry Services 1,886.

St. Michael Center for Veterans, 425 St. John St., 70501. Tel: 337-233-6816; Fax: 337-233-6829; Email: mhinman@catholicservice.org; Web: www.catholicservice.org. Mrs. Kim Boudreaux, Exec. Tot Asst. Annually 24; Total Staff 4.

CROWLEY. *Crowley Christian Care Center* (1987) 726 W. 7th St., P.O. Box 686, Crowley, 70527-0686. Tel: 337-783-5811; Fax: 337-783-5813; Email: edboustany@diolaf.org. Deacon Edward Jules Boustany, Contact Person. Total Staff 3; Total Assisted 4,800.

NEW IBERIA. *Social Service Center* (1975) 432 Bank Ave., New Iberia, 70560. Tel: 337-369-6384; Fax: 337-369-7522; Email: eboustany@diolaf.org. Shirley DeClouet, Dir. Total Staff 30; Total Families Assisted 5,000.

VILLE PLATTE. *Christian Care and Share Center* (1985) 129 W. Main St., P.O. Box 901, Ville Platte, 70586. Tel: 337-363-8041; Email: eboustany@diolaf.org. Mr. Eugene S. Fontenot, Chm. Tot Asst. Annually 1,500; Total Staff 8.

[O] CLOSED INSTITUTIONS

LAFAYETTE. *Diocese of Lafayette, Department of Archives*, Research & Information, 1408 Carmel Dr., P.O. Box 3387, 70501. Tel: 337-261-5639; Fax: 337-261-5508; Tel: 337-261-5667; Email: bdejean@diolaf.org; Web: www.diolaf.org. Mrs. Maureen K. Fontenot, Chancellor; Very Rev. Msgr. William Curtis Mallet, J.C.L., V.G., Vicar; Mrs. Barbara C. DeJean, Archivist. The following parish, school or institution records may be requested from the above address unless otherwise indicated.

Assumption School, Carencro.
Christ the King School, Bellevue.
Holy Rosary Institute, Lafayette.
Little Flower School, Arnaudville.
Mercy Convent School, St. Martinville.
Mercy Elementary School, St. Martinville.
Notre Dame School, St. Martinville.
St. Ann School, Carencro.
St. Elizabeth School, Prairie Basse.
St. Joseph School, Jeanerette.
St. Mathilda School, Eunice.
St. Peter Claver School, Grand Coteau.
St. Pierre School, Carencro.
Trinity Catholic School, St. Martinville.

The closed schools listed below do not have any records kept with the Diocesan Archives:.

Black School, Segura.
Colored School, Delcambre.
Holy Cross College, New Iberia.
Immaculate Conception School, Lebeau.
Marianite Holy Cross Convent, Arnaudville.
Mount Carmel Academy, Washington.
Our Lady of Lourdes School, Abbeville.
Our Lady of the Rosary School, Jeanerette.
St. Ann School, Mallet.
St. Benedict the Moor School, Duson.
St. Francis of Assisi School, Beaux Bridge.
St. Joseph Convent School, Opelousas.
St. Joseph Institute, Opelousas.
St. Joseph School, Arnaudville.
St. Joseph School, Charenton.
St. Joseph School, Broussard.
St. Joseph School, Mamou.
St. Joseph School, St. Martinville.
St. Katherine School, Cankton (Coulee Croche).
St. Katherine School, Leonville.
St. Leo School, Roberts Cove.
St. Mathilda School, Eunice.
St. Monica School, Tyrone.
St. Peter College, New Iberia.
St. Peter School, Four Corners.
St. Peter School, Glencoe.
St. Philomena School, Gueydan.
St. Stephen Kindergarten, Berwick.
St. Theresa School, Crowley.
Seton Elementary, Abbeville.
Immaculate Minor Seminary, Lafayette.

St. Mary's Home, Lafayette Contact Catholic Services of Acadiana, Inc.

Our Lady of Lourdes Church, Abbeville Contact St. Mary Magdalen Church, Abbeville.

Atchafalya Basin Missions Bayou Benoit, Bayou Chene, Diamond Slough, Bayou Little Pigeon, Chene au Tigre, Shaw's Island, Hogs Island Pass, Lake Round, Whiskey Bay, Lake Chicot, Lake Dautrieve, Bayou Smith, Lake Long, Grand Bayou, Bayou Catfish, Butte La Rose. Contact Immaculate Conception Church, Charenton and/or Our Lady of Mercy, Henderson.

Assumption Chapel, Basile Closed 2012. Contact Our Lady of Mount Carmel Church, Chataignier.

St. Julien Chapel, Basile Closed 1967. Contact Our Lady of Mount Carmel Church, Chataignier.

Immaculate Conception Chapel, Forked Island Closed 2008. Contact St. Anne Church, Cow Island.

St. Agnes Chapel, Garland Closed 2003. Conatct Immaculate Conception Church, Washington.

Mother of Mercy Chapel, Weeks Island Contact St. Helena Church, Louisa.

St. Joseph Chapel, Bayou Current Had been attached to three different church parishes: Immaculate Conception Church, Le Beau; Sacred Heart Church, Port Barre; St. John Evangelist Church, Melville.

St. Agnes Chapel, Eunice Became the church parish of St. Thomas More, Eunice.

St. Anthony Chapel, Gradney Island Had been attached to two separate parishes: St. Joseph Church, Plaisance; Holy Ghost Church, Opelousas.

St. Mary Chapel, Habetz Cove Contact St. Leo IV, Roberts Cove.

St. John Vianney, Lafayette Attached to two separate church parishes: Our Lady Queen of Peace, Lafayette & Immaculate Heart of Mary, Lafayette.

St. John of the Cross Chapel, Le Blanc Contact St. Anne Church, Youngsville.

Long Plantation Chapel, Lafayette Contact St. Paul Church, Lafayette.

Little Flower Chapel, Pins Claire Attached to three separate church parishes: St. Peter Church, Pine Prairie; St. Ann Church, Mamou & St. Joseph Church, Ville Platte.

St. Andre Chapel, Plaisance Contact St. Peter Church, Grand Prairie.

St. Theresa Chapel, Prairie Basse Contact Assumption Church, Carencro.

Prairie Jean Reed Chapel Contact St. Ann Church, Mamou.

St. Catherine Chapel, Rosa Contact Immaculate Conception Church, Washington.

St. John Levert Chapel, St. Martinville Contact St. Martin de Tours, St. Martinville.

St. Agatha Chapel, Swords Attached to two separate church parishes: Our Lady of Mount Carmel Church, Chataignier & St. Bridget Church, Lawtell.

St. Monica Chapel, Tyrone Contact St. Mathilda Church, Eunice.

Mother of Mercy Chapel, Nina Contact Mother of Mercy Church, Henderson.

RELIGIOUS INSTITUTES OF MEN REPRESENTED IN THE DIOCESE

For further details refer to the corresponding bracketed number in the Religious Institutes of Men or Women section.

[0200]—*Benedictines (Olivetan, Subiaco Congregation)*—O.S.B.
[]—*Carmelites of Mary Immaculate*—C.M.I.
[0740]—*Congregation of Marians of the Immaculate Conception*—M.I.C.
[]—*Congregation of the Holy Spirit (Holy Ghost Fathers)*—C.S.Sp.
[0585]—*Heralds of Good News*—H.G.N.
[0690]—*Jesuit Fathers and Brothers* (New Orleans Prov.)—S.J.
[0730]—*Legionaries of Christ*—L.C.
[0420]—*Society of the Divine Word*—S.V.D.
[0700]—*St. Joseph's Society of the Sacred Heart (Josephite Fathers)* (Baltimore Prov.)—S.S.J.

RELIGIOUS INSTITUTES OF WOMEN REPRESENTED IN THE DIOCESE

[0400]—*Congregation of Our Lady of Mount Carmel*—O.Carm.
[2410]—*Congregation of the Marianites of Holy Cross*—M.S.C.
[1950]—*Congregation of the Sisters of the Holy Family*—S.S.F.
[0420]—*Discalced Carmelite Nuns*—O.C.D.
[1380]—*Franciscan Missionaries of Our Lady*—O.S.F.
[2710]—*Missionaries of Charity* (Bronx, NY)—M.C.
[4070]—*Religious of the Sacred Heart*—R.S.C.J.
[2970]—*School Sisters of Notre Dame* (South Central)—S.S.N.D.
[]—*Sisters for Christian Community*—S.F.C.C.
[0990]—*Sisters of Divine Providence* (San Antonio, TX)—C.D.P.
[]—*Sisters of Eucharistic Covenant*—S.E.C.
[2050]—*Sisters of the Holy Spirit and Mary Immaculate*—S.H.Sp.
[2940]—*Sisters of the Most Holy Sacrament*—M.H.S.
[3658]—*Sisters of the Sacred Heart of Jesus*—S.S.H.J.

NECROLOGY

† Angelle, Robert G., (Retired), Died May. 11, 2018
† Warren, Arthur, (Retired), Died Aug. 28, 2018

An asterisk (*) denotes an organization that has established tax-exempt status directly with the IRS and is not covered by the USCCB Group Ruling.

Diocese of Lafayette in Indiana

(Dioecesis Lafayettenis in Indiana)

Most Reverend

TIMOTHY L. DOHERTY, S.T.L., PH.D.

Bishop of Lafayette in Indiana; ordained Priest June 26, 1976; appointed Sixth Bishop of Lafayette in Indiana May 12, 2010; ordained and installed as Bishop July 15, 2010. *Office: P.O. Box 260, Lafayette, IN 47902-0260.*

Most Reverend

WILLIAM L. HIGI, D.D.

Bishop Emeritus of Lafayette in Indiana; ordained May 30, 1959; appointed Bishop of Lafayette in Indiana April 7, 1984; consecrated and installed June 6, 1984; retired May 12, 2010. *Res.: 1743 Mill Pond Ln., Lafayette, IN 47905-5578.*

CANONICALLY ERECTED OCTOBER 21, 1944.

Square Miles 9,832.

Comprises the Counties of Benton, Blackford, Boone, Carroll, Cass, Clinton, Delaware, Fountain, Fulton, Grant, Hamilton, Howard, Jasper, Jay, Madison, Miami, Montgomery, Newton, Pulaski, Randolph, Tippecanoe, Tipton, Warren and White in the State of Indiana.

For legal titles of parishes and diocesan institutions, consult the Bishop's Office (Chancery).

Office of Bishop and Chancery: P.O. Box 260, Lafayette, IN 47902-0260. Tel: 765-742-0275; Fax: 765-742-7513.

Web: www.dol-in.org

STATISTICAL OVERVIEW

Personnel	
Bishop	1
Retired Bishops	1
Priests: Diocesan Active in Diocese	66
Priests: Diocesan Active Outside Diocese	5
Priests: Retired, Sick or Absent	24
Number of Diocesan Priests	95
Religious Priests in Diocese	8
Total Priests in Diocese	103
Extern Priests in Diocese	4
Ordinations:	
Diocesan Priests	2
Transitional Deacons	2
Permanent Deacons	7
Permanent Deacons in Diocese	28
Total Brothers	2
Total Sisters	29
Parishes	
Parishes	61
With Resident Pastor:	
Resident Diocesan Priests	48
Resident Religious Priests	3
Without Resident Pastor:	
Administered by Priests	8
Professional Ministry Personnel:	
Sisters	7
Welfare	
Catholic Hospitals	11
Total Assisted	759,734
Health Care Centers	2
Total Assisted	482
Educational	
Diocesan Students in Other Seminaries	14
Total Seminarians	14
Colleges and Universities	1
Total Students	14,300
High Schools, Diocesan and Parish	2
Total Students	1,223
Elementary Schools, Diocesan and Parish	15
Total Students	3,687
Catechesis/Religious Education:	
High School Students	2,468
Elementary Students	7,501
Total Students under Catholic Instruction	29,193
Teachers in the Diocese:	
Priests	2
Sisters	10
Lay Teachers	397
Vital Statistics	
Receptions into the Church:	
Infant Baptism Totals	1,343
Minor Baptism Totals	79
Adult Baptism Totals	114
Received into Full Communion	146
First Communions	1,880
Confirmations	1,692
Marriages:	
Catholic	204
Interfaith	154
Total Marriages	358
Deaths	828
Total Catholic Population	94,100
Total Population	1,290,812

Former Bishops—Most Rev. JOHN GEORGE BENNETT, D.D., LL.D., ord. June 27, 1914; appt. First Bishop of Lafayette Nov. 11, 1944; cons. Jan. 10, 1945; died Nov. 20, 1957; His Eminence JOHN CARDINAL CARBERRY, D.D., S.T.D., J.C.D., Ph.D., ord. July 28, 1929; appt. Coadjutor with Right of Succession Aug. 22, 1956; appt. Bishop of Lafayette in Indiana Nov. 20, 1957; transferred to Diocese of Columbus, Jan. 20, 1965; transferred to the Archdiocese of St. Louis March 24, 1968; created Cardinal April 28, 1969; retired July 31, 1979; died June 17, 1998; Most Revs. RAYMOND J. GALLAGHER, D.D., ord. March 25, 1939; appt. Bishop of Lafayette in Indiana June 23, 1965; cons. Aug. 11, 1965; installed Aug. 23, 1965; resigned Oct. 26, 1982; retired April 13, 1983; died March 7, 1991; GEORGE A. FULCHER, S.T.D., D.D., ord. Feb. 28, 1948; appt. Auxiliary Bishop of Columbus, OH and Titular Bishop of Morosbido May 24, 1976; cons. July 18, 1976; appt. Bishop of Lafayette in Indiana Feb. 8, 1983; installed April 14, 1983; died Jan. 25, 1984; WILLIAM L. HIGI, ord. May 30, 1959; appt. Bishop of Lafayette in Indiana April 7, 1984; cons. and installed June 6, 1984; retired May 12, 2010.

Vicar General—Very Rev. THEODORE C. DUDZINSKI, J.C.L., V.G.

Chancellor and Moderator of the Curia—Very Rev. THEODORE C. DUDZINSKI, J.C.L., V.G.

Vice Chancellor—Rev. ANDREW R. DEKEYSER, J.C.L.

Vicar for Clergy—Very Rev. DALE W. EHRMAN, V.E.

Judicial Vicar—Very Rev. TIMOTHY M. ALKIRE, J.C.L., V.J.

Office of Bishop and Chancery—Mailing Address: P.O. Box 260, Lafayette, 47902-0260. Tel: 765-742-0275; Fax: 765-742-7513.

Deans—Very Revs. ERIC C. UNDERWOOD, V.F., Lafayette Deanery; ROBERT J. BERNOTAS, V.F., Fowler Deanery; THEODORE D. ROTHROCK, V.F., Carmel Deanery; MICHAEL A. MCKINNEY, V.F., Logansport Deanery; ANDREW J. DUDZINSKI, V.F., Muncie Deanery.

Diocesan Consultors—Very Revs. THEODORE C. DUDZINSKI, J.C.L., V.G.; DANIEL B. GARTLAND, V.F.; THEODORE D. ROTHROCK, V.F.; MICHAEL A. MCKINNEY, V.F.; ROBERT J. BERNOTAS, V.F.; DENNIS J. GOTH, V.F.; Rev. Msgr. ROBERT L. SELL III, J.C.L., V.G.

Diocesan Administrative & Pastoral Offices

Department of Finance and Administration—MR. MATTHEW MCKILLIP, Dir. & CFO. Conducts the financial affairs of the diocese; oversees employee benefit program.

Office of Administration—Mailing Address: P.O. Box 260, Lafayette, 47902-0260. Tel: 765-742-4852. ANDREW A. GULJAS, Facilities Mgmt. Coord., Email: aguljas@dol-in.org; ROBIN CALDANARO, Controller; KENT MIKESELL, Maintenance; AMY LUCAS, Staff Accountant.

Office of Stewardship and Development—Mailing Address: Bishop's Office, P.O. Box 1687, Lafayette, 47902-1687. Tel: 765-742-7000; Fax: 765-742-7513. MIKE MACNULTY, Dir.; VACANT, Major and Planned Gifts Officer. Administrative Assistants: KARLA ICSMAN. Oversees the Biennial Fruitful Harvest Appeal; organizes and presents estate planning programs, the Annual Seminary Fund Appeal and Diocesan Capital Campaigns.

Office of Technology, Communications & Planning—Mailing Address: P.O. Box 1603, Lafayette, 47902-1603. Tel: 765-742-2050. *Shipping Address: 610 Lingle Ave., Lafayette, 47901-1740.* Deacon MIKE MESCALL, Dir.; GABBY HLAVEK, Communications Mgr.; MELINDA MCPHERSON, Social Media & Website Coord.; LAURIE CULLEN, Administrative Asst.; Very Vacant See VACANT, Asst. Editor; VACANT, Business Applications Specialist.

Publisher- "The Catholic Moment"—Most Rev. TIMOTHY L. DOHERTY, S.T.L., Ph.D.; GABBY HLAVEK, Communications Mgr.; VACANT, Asst. Editor. Advertising/Circulation; Coordinates pastoral planning; serves the communications needs of the diocese primarily through "The Catholic Moment".

Newspaper "The Catholic Moment"—P.O. Box 1603, Lafayette, 47902. GABBY HLAVEK, Editor; VACANT, Asst. Editor, Advertising.

Department of Pastoral Ministries—JONATHAN SULLIVAN, Dir.; VACANT, Administrative Asst.

Office of Catechesis—JONATHAN SULLIVAN, Dir.; EVELYN BURTON, Adult & Lay Formation Specialist; PAUL SIFUENTES, Youth & Young Adult Formation Specialist; VACANT, Administrative Asst. Provides formational opportunities for adults; prepares men and women for lay ministry in the diocese and the

Catholic church through human, spiritual, pastoral and intellectual formation.

Office of the Ecclesial Lay Ministry Program—Mailing Address: 2300 9th St., Lafayette, 47909-2400. Tel: 765-269-4650; Tel: 888-544-1684; Fax: 765-269-4651. JONATHAN SULLIVAN, Dir.; EVELYN BURTON, Adult & Lay Formation Specialist; VACANT, Administrative Asst.

Office of Catholic Schools—DR. PEG DISPENZIERI, Supt.; ANDREW KREMER, Assoc. Supt. Administrative Assistants: SHERRY YOUNG; TRICIA RAUSCH; NOREEN BEARDMORE, Schools Health Coord.

Office of Family Life & Hispanic Ministry—Catholic Pastoral Center, 2300 S. Ninth St., Lafayette, 47909-2400. Tel: 765-269-4675; Fax: 765-269-4676. DR. DORA TOBAR, Mgr. Family Life & Hispanic Ministry.

Hispanic Ministry—Deacon DOMINGO C. CASTILLO, Tel: 765-506-3968; Email: dcastillo@dol-in.org; CLAUDIA SADOWSKI, Hispanic Ministry Specialist; Deacon JOSE D. MUNOZ, Cell: 765-491-0363; Email: jmunoz@dol-in.org.

Administrative Assistant—CLAUDIA CASTILLO, Tel: 765-269-4662; SUSAN HOEFER, NFP Coord., Tel: 765-421-1998; VACANT, Project Giana Coord., Tel: 765-427-3410. Promotes the dignity of the family and all human life through promotion and coordination of programs dealing with family life, marriage preparation and pro-life activities.; ELSA SAMORA, Hispanic Project Rachel, Tel: 765-701-0620; KATHY LEHE, English Project Rachel, Tel: 765-414-3072.

Office of Divine Worship & The Catechumenate—Catholic Pastoral Center, 2300 S. Ninth St., Lafayette, 47909-2400. Tel: 765-269-4677; Fax: 765-269-4661. SANDRA SANTUCCI, Mgr. Divine Worship.

Tribunal—Catholic Pastoral Center, 2300 S. Ninth St., Lafayette, 47909-2400. Tel: 765-474-0506.

Judicial Vicar—Very Rev. TIMOTHY M. ALKIRE, J.C.L., V.J.

Ecclesiastical Tribunal—

Judges—Revs. SAMUEL J. KALU, J.C.L.; DAVID L. RASNER, J.C.L.

Judge Instructor—Rev. SAMUEL J. KALU, J.C.L.

Defender of the Bond—Rev. ANDREW R. DEKEYSER, J.C.L.

Auditor—Rev. STEPHEN J. DUQUAINE, M.A., M.Div.

Ecclesiastical Notary—NIALL HICKEY.

Full-Time Advocates—LINDA O'GARA; LOU COFFING; VERNA S. MEEK, Records & Archive Coord.

Office Manager—LINDA O'GARA.

Administrative Causes—Very Rev. THEODORE C. DUDZINSKI, J.C.L., V.G.

Other Offices and Directors

Aquinas Educational Foundation, Inc.—Rev. PATRICK H. BAIKAUSKAS, O.P., Res. Agent, 535 State St., West Lafayette, 47906. Tel: 765-743-4653.

Archivist—VACANT.

Building Commission—NORBERT STRANSKY, Chm.; Very Rev. THEODORE C. DUDZINSKI, J.C.L., V.G., Ex Officio; ANDREW A. GULJAS, Facilities Mgmt. Coord. & Ex Officio; DEBRA KUNCE; MICHAEL L. GIBSON; STEPHAN GOFFINET; DR. DOUGLAS SUTTON; WILL WRIGHT; ANDRE MAUE.

Catholic Charities Central Office—Refer to Diocesan Pastoral Office.

Censor Librorum—Rev. DAVID L. RASNER, J.C.L., Catholic Pastoral Center, 2300 S. Ninth St., Lafayette, 47909-2400. Tel: 765-474-0506.

Corporation—Roman Catholic Diocese of Lafayette in Indiana, Inc. (Incorporated, March 21, 1958). Most Rev. TIMOTHY L. DOHERTY, S.T.L., Ph.D., Pres. & Treas.; Very Rev. THEODORE C. DUDZINSKI, J.C.L., V.G., Sr. Vice Pres. & Sec.; MR. MATTHEW MCKILLIP, Vice Pres., Asst. Sec. & Treas.

D.C.C.W.—BETH KEELE, Pres., 1016 Coin Dr., Frankfort, 46041.

Eucharistic League—The Chancery, P.O. Box 260, Lafayette, 47902.

Fruitful Harvest Office—Mailing Address: P.O. Box 1687, Lafayette, 47902. Tel: 765-269-4608.

Finance Council—Most Rev. TIMOTHY L. DOHERTY, S.T.L., Ph.D., Ex Officio; Very Rev. THEODORE C. DUDZINSKI, J.C.L., V.G., Ex Officio; MR. MATTHEW MCKILLIP, Dir. Pastoral Office for Admin. & Ex Officio; LEO DIERCKMAN; LYNN LAYDEN; MARIANNE MCLEAN; MARY PIANTEK; TOM PARENT, Legal Advisor & Ex Officio; KARLA SCHLICHTE.

Greater Lafayette Catholic School Board—J. ERIC DAVIS, Exec. Dir. Lafayette Catholic School System, Tel: 765-474-7500.

Greater Lafayette Area Catholic School Foundation, Inc.—MICHAEL L. GIBSON, 428 N. 4th St., Lafayette, 47901.

Holy Childhood Association—VACANT.

Human Resources Department—Mailing Address: P.O. Box 260, Lafayette, 47902-0260. Tel: 765-742-0275. JEANNE K. LAUSTEN, Dir.; ERICA WETLI, Payroll & Benefits Coord.

Newman Apostolate, Purdue University—Rev. PATRICK H. BAIKAUSKAS, O.P., Dir., 535 State St., West Lafayette, 47906. Tel: 765-743-4652.

Newman Foundation, Ball State, Inc.—Rev. BRIAN M. DOERR, 1200 Riverside Ave., Muncie, 47303. Tel: 765-288-6180.

Pastoral Office for Catholic Outreach—VACANT, Dir.

Ecumenical & Interreligious Officer—Deacon JAMES B. RUSH, Tel: 765-742-2107, Ext. 974.

Office of the Permanent Diaconate—Mailing Address: P.O. Box 677, Cicero, IL 46034. Tel: 765-269-4603; Fax: 765-742-7513. Very Rev. DALE W. EHRMAN, V.E., Dir. Associate Directors: Deacons STEPHEN P. MILLER, Dir. Formation, Email: dcn.smiller@dol.in.org; D. MICHAEL GRAY, Assoc. Dir. Personnel, Email: dcn.mgray@dol-in.org; WILLIAM T. REID, Coord. Pastoral Field Educ. & Vocation Recruitment, Email: dcn.wreid@dol-in.org; Very Rev. DALE W. EHRMAN, V.E., Dir. Spiritual Formation.

Presbyteral Council—Most Rev. TIMOTHY L. DOHERTY, S.T.L., Ph.D., Pres.; Revs. ADAM G. MAUMAN, Chm.; ANTHONY T. ROWLAND, Vice Chair; CHRISTOPHER R. SHOCKLEE, Sec.

Members—Very Revs. THEODORE C. DUDZINSKI, J.C.L., V.G.; DALE W. EHRMAN, V.E.; ROBERT J. BERNOTAS, V.F.; ERIC C. UNDERWOOD, V.F.; MICHAEL A. MCKINNEY, V.F.; THEODORE D. ROTHROCK, V.F.; ANDREW J. DUDZINSKI, V.F.; Rev. Msgr. ROBERT L. SELL III, J.C.L., V.G.; Revs. RICHARD J. DOERR; MARTIN J. SANDHAGE; KYLE P. NETERER; PETER F. LOGSDON.

Propagation of the FaithVery Rev. THEODORE C. DUDZINSKI, J.C.L., V.G., Co-Dir.; KAREN MALKE, Co-Dir. Refer to the Bishop's office.

Religious Education Dept.—Refer to Pastoral Office for Catechesis.

Schools—The Catholic Pastoral Center, 2300 S. Ninth St., Lafayette, 47909-2400. Tel: 765-269-4670. DR. PEG DISPENZIERI, Supt.; ANDREW KREMER, Assoc. Supt.

St. Joseph Retreat & Conference Center—1440 W. Division Rd., Tipton, 46072. Tel: 765-551-9570; Web: www.stjosephretreat.org. SAMIR AZER, Dir. Opers. & Hospitality; Rev. DAVID G. HUEMMER, Spiritual Dir./Chap.; TWYLA ARNOLD, Mktg. Specialist.

Vicar for Clergy—Mailing Address: Sacred Heart of Jesus, P.O. Box 677, Cicero, 46034. Tel: 765-269-4603. Very Rev. DALE W. EHRMAN, V.E.; BECKY THESIER, Exec. Asst.

Victim Assistance Coordinator—DORIS MAY, Tel: 765-464-4988.

Vocation Director—2300 S. 9th St., Lafayette, 47902. Tel: 765-269-4652. Revs. CLAYTON D. THOMPSON, Dir. Vocations; DEREK AARON, Assoc. Dir. Vocations; VACANT, Admin. Asst.

CLERGY, PARISHES, MISSIONS AND PAROCHIAL SCHOOLS

CITY OF LAFAYETTE

(TIPPECANOE COUNTY)

1—ST. MARY CATHEDRAL (1843) [JC]
1212 South St., 47901. Tel: 765-742-4440; Email: stmparish@lcss.org. Revs. Dominic C. Petan; Kyle P. Neterer; Deacons John R. Jezierski; Joseph F. Poremski.
School—St. Mary Cathedral School, (Grades PreK-3), Tel: 765-742-6302; Fax: (765) 742-7060; Web: stmar.lcss.org. Kim Delaney, Prin. Lay Teachers 19; Students 221.
Catechesis Religious Program—
Tel: 765-742-4440, Ext. 228. Students 213.

2—ST. ANN (1884) [JC]
612 Wabash Ave., 47905-1096. Tel: 765-742-7031; Email: dominic@stannli.comcastbiz.net. Rev. Dominic G. Young.
Catechesis Religious Program—Students 47.

3—ST. BONIFACE (1853) [CEM] (German)
318 N. Ninth St., 47904-2597. Tel: 765-742-5063; Email: bonioffice@comcast.net. Very Rev. Timothy M. Alkire, J.C.L., V.J.; Revs. Mark D. Walter, Parochial Vicar; Stephen J. Duquaine, M.A., M.Div., (In Res.); Deacons Ronald D. Nevinger; Jose D. Munoz; Michael D. Gray; Stanislaw H. Zak.
School—St. Boniface Middle School, (Grades 4-6), Tel: 765-742-7913; Fax: 765-423-4988; Email: srlenore@lcss.org; Web: stbon.lcss.org. Sr. M. Lenore Schwartz, O.S.F., Prin. Lay Teachers 13; Sisters 1; Students 127.
Catechesis Religious Program—Tel: 765-742-1351; Email: haroreled@comcast.net. Students 324.
Convent—Sisters of St. Francis of Perpetual Adoration Convent, 1106 State St., 47905.
Tel: 765-742-8081.

4—ST. LAWRENCE (1895)
1916 Meharry St., 47904-1442. Tel: 765-742-2107; Email: info@saintlawrencechurch.net; Web: www.saintlawrencechurch.net. Very Rev. Eric C. Underwood, V.F.; Rev. Cole Daily, Parochial Vicar; Deacons Jim B. Rush; Edward R. Boes.
School—St. Lawrence School, 1902 Meharry St., 47904-1497. Tel: 765-742-4450; Email: williams@lcss.org. Jody Williams, Prin. Lay Teachers 18; Students 280.
Catechesis Religious Program—Email: hillman@saintlawrencechurch.net; Email: dward@saintlawrencechurch.net; Email: hsyouth@saintlawrencechurch.net. Ryan Hillman, D.R.E.; Ms. Dawn Ward, D.R.E.; Lyn Bordenet, Youth Min.; Bill Bayley, Youth Min.; Sue Bayley, Youth Min. Students 132.

OUTSIDE THE CITY OF LAFAYETTE

ALEXANDRIA, MADISON CO., ST. MARY (1896)
820 W. Madison St., Alexandria, 46001-1520.
Tel: 765-724-2483; Email: mking@maryandjosephchurches.com; Email: fr.dduff@dol-in.org; Web: maryandjosephchurches.com. Rev. Daniel J. Duff.
School—St. Mary School, (Grades PreK-8), Email: stmary820@comcast.net; Email: mbudzenski@maryandjosephchurches.com. Rev. Daniel J. Duff, Pastor. Lay Teachers 10; Students 90.
Catechesis Religious Program—Students 38.

ANDERSON, MADISON CO.

1—ST. AMBROSE (1947)
2801 Lincoln St., Anderson, 46016-5068.
Tel: 765-644-5956; Web: www.stambrosestmary.org. Rev. Msgr. Robert L. Sell III, J.C.L., V.G.; Rev. Daniel P. Shine, Parochial Vicar.
School—Holy Cross School, (Grades PreK-8), Combined St. Mary and St. Ambrose, Anderson. 2825 Lincoln St., Anderson, 46016.
Tel: 765-642-8428; Fax: 765-643-6470;
Tel: 765-642-1848; Fax: 765-642-1828; Email: tneal@holycrossschool-anderson.org; Web: www.holycrossschool-anderson.com. 321 E. 11th St., Anderson, 46016. 1115 Pearl St., Anderson, 46016. Tina Neal, Prin. Clergy 12; Lay Teachers 21; Students 200.
Catechesis Religious Program—Tel: 765-644-8467; Email: stmarysminister@catholicweb.com. Janice Storey, D.R.E. Students 33.

2—ST. MARY (1858) [CEM]
1115 Pearl St., Anderson, 46016-1789.
Tel: 765-644-8467; Web: stambrosestmary.org. Rev. Msgr. Robert L. Sell III, J.C.L., V.G.; Rev. Daniel P. Shine, Parochial Vicar; Janice Storey, Pastoral Assoc.
School—Holy Cross School, (Grades PreK-8), with St. Ambrose, Anderson. Tel: 765-642-1848; Email: tneal@holycrossschool-anderson.org; Email: agranger@holycrossschool-anderson.org; Web: www.holycrossschool-anderson.com/. Tina Neal, Prin. Lay Teachers 18; Students 200.
Catechesis Religious Program—Email: stmarys.minister@catholicweb.com. Students 107.

ATTICA, FOUNTAIN CO., ST. FRANCIS XAVIER (1862) [CEM]
407 S. Perry St., Attica, 47918-0001.
Tel: 765-762-3330; Email: samuelfutral3@gmail.com. P.O. Box 55, Attica, 47918. Rev. Samuel F. Futral.
Catechesis Religious Program—Eileen Hays, D.R.E. Students 34.

BRYANT, JAY CO., HOLY TRINITY (1861) [CEM] (German)
7321 E. SR 67, Bryant, 47326-9636.
Tel: 260-997-6450. Rev. Kenneth Alt.
Catechesis Religious Program—Linda Wellman, D.R.E. Students 85.

CARMEL, HAMILTON CO.

1—ST. ELIZABETH ANN SETON (1981)
10655 Haverstick Rd., Carmel, 46033-3800.
Tel: 317-846-3850; Tel: 317-816-0045;
Fax: 317-846-3710; Email: parish@setoncarmel.org; Web: setoncarmel.org. Very Rev. Theodore D. Rothrock, V.F.; Revs. John Nguyen, Parochial Vicar; Thomas J. Haan, In Res.; Deacons William T. Reid; Bob Angelich.
Catechesis Religious Program—Students 1,718.

2—OUR LADY OF MOUNT CARMEL (1955)
14598 Oak Ridge Rd., Carmel, 46032-1201.
Tel: 317-846-3475; Email: OLMCparish@olmc1.org; Web: www.olmc1.org. Revs. Richard J. Doerr; Alejandro M. Paternoster; Kevin H. Hurley; Christian M.

DeCarlo; Deacons William H. Rahill; Paul S. Lunsford.
School—Our Lady of Mount Carmel School, (Grades K-8), 14596 Oak Ridge Rd., Carmel, 46032-1198.
Tel: 317-846-1118; Fax: 317-582-2375; Web: www.school.olmc1.org. Lay Teachers 32; Dominican Sisters of St. Cecilia 4; Students 654.
Catechesis Religious Program—Email: ponchakt@olmc1.org. Tom Ponchak, D.R.E. Students 1,470.
Convent—Dominican Sisters of St. Cecilia Congregation, 40 Bennet Rd., Carmel, 46032.
CICERO, HAMILTON CO., SACRED HEART OF JESUS (1898) (German—Irish)
410 S. Pearl St., Cicero, 46034-0889.
Tel: 317-984-2115; Tel: 317-606-8153;
Fax: 317-984-7185; Email: shjc@dol-in.org; Web: www.sacredheartcicero.org. P.O. Box 889, Cicero, 46034-0889. Very Rev. Dale W. Ehrman, V.E.; Deacon John P. Etter.
Res.: 359 S. Pearl St., P.O. Box 889, Cicero, 46034-0889. Tel: 317-984-5117.
Catechesis Religious Program—Email: shjcpre@dol-in.org. Rachel Woods, D.R.E. Students 73.
COVINGTON, FOUNTAIN CO., ST. JOSEPH (1861) [CEM]
308 Pearl St., Covington, 47932-1062.
Tel: 765-793-3289; Email: samuelfutral3@gmail.com. Rev. Samuel F. Futral.
Catechesis Religious Program—Jennifer Goeppner, D.R.E. Students 23.
CRAWFORDSVILLE, MONTGOMERY CO., ST. BERNARD (1859) [CEM]
1306 E. Main St., Crawfordsville, 47933-2001.
Tel: 765-362-6121; Email: parish@stbernardcville.org; Web: stbernardcville.org. Rev. Christopher R. Shocklee.
Catechesis Religious Program—
Tel: 765-362-6121, Ext. 217; Email: dre@stbernardcville.org. Anne Wolfley, D.R.E. Students 185.
DE MOTTE, JASPER CO., ST. CECILIA (1952) [CEM]
334 Fifteenth St. SW, DeMotte, 46310.
Tel: 219-987-3511; Email: saint1@netnitco.net; Web: www.stceciliademotte.org. Mailing Address: P.O. Box 700, DeMotte, 46310. Very Rev. Dennis A. Faker, V.F.
Catechesis Religious Program—Email: saint2@netnitco.net. Margaret Tuohy, D.R.E. Students 127.
DELPHI, CARROLL CO., ST. JOSEPH (1859) [CEM]
207 N. Washington St., Delphi, 47923.
Tel: 765-564-2407; Email: office@stjosephdelphi.org. Rev. Clayton D. Thompson.
Catechesis Religious Program—Tel: 765-564-3601; Email: dre@stjosephdelphi.org. Paula Iunghuhn, D.R.E. Students 36.
DUNKIRK, JAY CO., ST. MARY (1896)
346 S. Broad St., Dunkirk, 47336-0286.
Tel: 765-768-6157; Email: stmaryjohn@att.net; Web: stmaryjohn.org. P.O. Box 286, Dunkirk, 47336. Rev. David J. Newton.
Catechesis Religious Program—Wendy Stout, D.R.E. Students 15.
DUNNINGTON, BENTON CO., ST. MARY (1876) [CEM]
Physical Address: 2961 South SR71, Ambia, 47917.
Tel: 765-884-1818; Email: sheart18@sacredheartsite.com. Mailing Address: 107 E. Main St., Fowler, 47944. Rev. Peter J. Vanderkolk, Admin.
Catechesis Religious Program—Students 5.
EARL PARK, BENTON CO., ST. JOHN THE BAPTIST (1888) [CEM]
Mailing Address: P.O. Box 131, Kentland, 47951-0131. Tel: 219-474-5514. Very Rev. Robert J. Bernotas, V.F.
Church: 205 S. Chestnut St., Earl Park, 47942-8692.
Catechesis Religious Program—Combined with Sacred Heart, Fowler & St. Joseph, Kentland.
ELWOOD, MADISON CO., ST. JOSEPH (1889) [CEM] [JC] (Irish—German)
1306 S. A St., Elwood, 46036-1941. Tel: 765-552-6753 ; Web: maryandjosephchurches.com. Rev. Daniel J. Duff.
Catechesis Religious Program—Students 26.
FISHERS, HAMILTON CO.
1—HOLY SPIRIT CHURCH (1991)
10350 Glaser Way, Fishers, 46037.
Tel: 317-849-9245. Very Rev. Daniel B. Gartland, V.F.; Rev. Coady Owens, Parochial Vicar.
Catechesis Religious Program—Tel: 317-849-8016. Students 1,689.
2—ST. JOHN VIANNEY PARISH (2005)
15176 Blessed Mother Blvd., Fishers, 46037.
Tel: 317-485-0150; Fax: 317-588-1486; Email: dduquaine@sjvfishers.com; Email: lkunkel@sjvfishers.com; Web: www.sjvfishers.com. Revs. Anthony T. Rowland; Sean V. Pogue, Parochial Vicar; Ms. Jennifer Duquaine, Music Min.; Mrs. Gloria Hughey, Youth MIn.; Mr. Larry Kunkel, Business Mgr.; Mrs. Debbie Duquaine, Sec.; Ms. Helen Storms, Sec.
Catechesis Religious Program—Email: idipsumsapere@att.net. Timothy O'Donnell, D.R.E.; Mrs. Christine Vincent-Rodas, D.R.E. Students 133.
3—ST. LOUIS DE MONTFORT (1978)
11441 Hague Rd., Fishers, 46038-1876.
Tel: 317-842-6778. Revs. Patrick R. Click; Travis R. Stephens.
School—St. Louis de Montfort School, (Grades K-8), 11421 Hague Rd., Fishers, 46038. Tel: 317-842-1125; Fax: 317-842-1126; Email: sstewart@sldmfishers.org. Scott Stewart, Prin. Lay Teachers 30; Students 494.
Catechesis Religious Program—Students 400.
FOWLER, BENTON CO., SACRED HEART OF JESUS (1872) [CEM]
107 E. Main St., Fowler, 47944-1148.
Tel: 765-884-1818; Email: sheart18@sacredheartsite.com. Rev. Peter J. Vanderkolk.
School—Sacred Heart of Jesus School, (Grades PreK-6), Tel: 765-884-0710; Email: kgross@sacredheartsite.com; Web: www.sacredheartschoolfowler.org. Kristina Gross, Prin. Lay Teachers 7; Students 106.
Catechesis Religious Program—Students 31.
Mission—St. Mary's Church, 2961 S. State Rd. 71, Ambia, 47917-8516.
FRANCESVILLE, PULASKI CO., ST. FRANCIS SOLANO (1867)
217 W. Montgomery St., Francesville, 47946.
Tel: 574-946-4906; Email: stpete4906@embarqmail.com; Web: preciousbloodcluster.org. 401 N. Monticello St., Winamac, 46996. Rev. Leroy G. Kinnaman, Admin.
FRANKFORT, CLINTON CO., ST. MARY (1875) [CEM]
600 St. Mary's Ave., Frankfort, 46041-2735.
Tel: 765-654-5796; Email: stmaryfrankfort@gmail.com. Rev. Christopher T. Miller.
Catechesis Religious Program—Email: stmarysjohnpaul@gmail.com. Lori Stover, D.R.E. Students 351.
GAS CITY, GRANT CO., HOLY FAMILY (1908)
325 E. North A St., Gas City, 46933-1431.
Tel: 765-674-2605; Email: hcatholicchurch@indy.rr.com. Rev. Christopher G. Roberts.
Catechesis Religious Program—Students 30.
GOODLAND, NEWTON, SS. PETER AND PAUL (1880) [CEM]
Mailing Address: P.O. Box 131, Kentland, 47951-1322. Tel: 219-474-5514; Email: fr.rbernotas@dol-in.org. Very Rev. Robert J. Bernotas, V.F.
Church: 421 S. Newton St., Goodland, 47948-8156.
Catechesis Religious Program—Combined with St. Joseph, Kentland.
HARTFORD CITY, BLACKFORD CO., ST. JOHN THE EVANGELIST (1865)
209 S. Spring St., Hartford City, 47348-2551.
Tel: 765-348-3889; Email: stmaryjohn@att.net. Rev. David J. Newton.
Catechesis Religious Program—Tel: 765-348-3889. Claire Aulbach, D.R.E. Students 51.
KENTLAND, NEWTON, ST. JOSEPH (1864) [CEM]
409 E. Allen St., P.O. Box 131, Kentland, 47951-1322. Tel: 219-474-5514; Email: fr.rbernotas@dol-in.org. Very Rev. Robert J. Bernotas, V.F.
Endowment—St. Joseph School Foundation, Inc.
Catechesis Religious Program—Mrs. Linda Robertson, D.R.E. Students 48.
KEWANNA, FULTON CO., ST. ANN (1857) [CEM]
415 Logan St., Kewanna, 46939. Tel: 574-223-2808; Email: stjoseph@rtcol.com. 1310 Main St., Rochester, 46975. Very Rev. Michael A. McKinney, V.F., Admin.
Catechesis Religious Program—Tel: 574-946-3453; Fax: 574-946-3563. Attend the program at St. Peter's, Winamac.
KOKOMO, HOWARD CO.
1—ST. JOAN OF ARC (1927)
3155 S. 200 W., Kokomo, 46902-9611.
Tel: 765-865-9964. Rev. Matthew J. Arbuckle.
Res.: 1307 Bagley Dr., Kokomo, 46902. Email: diana@saintjoan.org; Web: www.saintjoan.org.
School—Sts. Joan of Arc & Patrick, (Grades 3-8),
Tel: 765-865-9960 (St. Joan of Arc);
Fax: 765-865-9962; Web: www.stsjp.org. Nick Kanable, Prin. (Consolidated School) Lay Teachers 15; Students 156.
Catechesis Religious Program—Email: cgrube@saintjoan.org. Chad Grube, D.R.E. Students 67.
2—ST. PATRICK (1859) [JC]
1229 N. Washington St., Kokomo, 46901.
Tel: 765-452-6021. 1204 N. Armstrong St., Kokomo, 46901. Revs. Brian A. Dudzinski; David G. Huemmer, In Res.; Deacon Ronald L. Morrow.
School—Sts. Joan of Arc & Patrick, 1230 N. Armstrong St., Kokomo, 46901. Tel: 765-459-4769; Fax: 765-457-3096; Web: www.stsjp.org. Nick Kanable, Prin. (St. Patrick Campus) Lay Teachers 11; Students 116.
Catechesis Religious Program—Students 130.
LAKE VILLAGE, NEWTON, ST. AUGUSTA (1947) [JC]
3228 W. St. Rd. 10, Lake Village, 46349-9706. Rev. Martin J. Sandhage.
Res.: 3491 W. St. Rd. 10, Lake Village, 46349-9706.
Tel: 219-992-3220; Tel: 219-992-3333;
Fax: 219-992-9332; Email: staugust@parish.dol-in.org; Web: www.staugustalv.org.
Catechesis Religious Program—Tel: 219-992-9010; Email: catholiccrafter25@gmail.com. Mrs. Jeanette Marter, D.R.E. Students 36.
LEBANON, BOONE CO., ST. JOSEPH (1862) [CEM]
319 E. South St., Lebanon, 46052-0309.
Tel: 765-482-5558; Fax: 765-482-1436; Email: stjoe@stjoeleb.org; Web: www.stjoeleb.org. P.O. Box 309, Lebanon, 46052. Rev. Richard J. Weisenberger.
Res.: 310 E. Pearl St., Lebanon, 46052-2684.
Catechesis Religious Program—Email: religioused@stjoeleb.org. Students 153.
LOGANSPORT, CASS CO., ALL SAINTS (1985) [JC]
Consolidation of the following three parishes (Legal Titles): St. Bridget (1875); St. Joseph (1868); and St. Vincent de Paul (1838).
112 E. Market St., Logansport, 46947-3428.
Tel: 574-722-4080; Fax: 574-722-5426; Email: jklepinger@allsaintslogansport.com; Web: www.allsaintslogansport.com. Revs. Jeffrey D. Martin; Gustavo Lopez, Parochial Vicar.
Catechesis Religious Program—Email: jtumasian@allsaintslogansport.com. Joseph Tumasian, D.R.E. Students 330.
LUCERNE, CASS CO., ST. ELIZABETH (1953) Closed. For inquiries for parish records, please see All Saints Church, Logansport.
MARION, GRANT CO.
1—OUR LADY OF GUADALUPE, (Hispanic), Closed. For inquiries for parish records contact St. Paul, Marion.
2—ST. PAUL (1868)
1031 W. Kem Rd., Marion, 46952. Tel: 765-664-6345; Web: stpaulcatholicmarion.org. Rev. Christopher G. Roberts.
School—St. Paul School, (Grades PreK-6), 1009 Kem Rd., Marion, 46952. Tel: 765-662-2883;
Fax: 765-664-5953; Email: info@stpaulcatholicmarion.com; Web: stpaulcatholicmarion.org. Rebecca Spitznagel, Prin. Clergy 1; Lay Teachers 9; Students 129.
Catechesis Religious Program—
Tel: 765-662-2883, Ext. 117; Email: nreynolds@stpaulcatholicmarion.com. Nora Reynolds, D.R.E. Students 68.
MEDARYVILLE, PULASKI CO., ST. HENRY (1868) [CEM] Closed. For inquiries for parish records see St. Peter, Winamac.
MONTEREY, PULASKI CO., ST. ANNE (1851) [CEM 2] (German)
6894 N. Walnut St., Monterey, 46960-0096.
Tel: 574-223-2808; Email: stjoseph@rtcol.com; Web: www.stannechurchmonterey.org. 1310 Main St., Rochester, 46975. Very Rev. Michael A. McKinney, V.F., Admin.
Catechesis Religious Program—Tel: 219-542-4711. Students 9.
MONTICELLO, WHITE CO., OUR LADY OF THE LAKES (1948)
543 S. Main St., Monticello, 47960-2948.
Tel: 574-583-6790 Parish Office;
Tel: 574-583-5724 Rectory Phone (Priest);
Fax: 574-583-4112 Fax Machine (parish Office); Email: ladyofthelakes@lightstreamin.com; Web: www.ourladyofthelakesmonticello.com. Rev. David L. Rasner, J.C.L.; Kathy Diener, Business Mgr.
Res.: 543 S. Main St., Monticello, 47960-2948.
Tel: 574-583-5724; Tel: 574-583-6790;
Fax: 574-583-4112; Email: ladyofthelakes@lightstreamin.com; Email: kdiener@lightstreamin.com; Web: www.ourladyofthelakesmonticello.com.
Catechesis Religious Program—Tel: 574-583-6790. Teresa DeMien, D.R.E.; Ary Nelson, Liturgy & Worship Dir.; Kathy Diener, Admin. Students 166.
MONTPELIER, BLACKFORD CO., ST. MARGARET OF SCOTLAND (1864) [CEM] Closed. For sacramental records contact 209 S. Spring St., Hartford City, IN 47348.
MUNCIE, DELAWARE CO.
1—ST. FRANCIS OF ASSISI (1973) (Ball State University Parish)
1200 W. Riverside Ave., Muncie, 47303.
Tel: 765-288-6180; Email: stfrancisnewman@parish.dol-in.org; Web: www.stfrancisnewman.org. Rev. Brian M. Doerr.
Catechesis Religious Program—Email: afeola@parish.dol-in.org. Anthony Feola, D.R.E. Students 88.
2—ST. LAWRENCE (1869)
820 E. Charles St., Muncie, 47305-2699.
Tel: 765-288-9223; Email: jcarnes@parish.dol-in.org; Web: stlawrencemuncie.com. Revs. David E. Hellmann; Robert L. Williams, V.F., In Res., (Retired); Richard Shirey, Business Mgr.; Jason Hart, Liturgy Dir.
School—St. Lawrence Catholic School, (Grades K-5), 2801 E. 16th St., Muncie, 47302. Tel: 765-282-9353; Fax: 765-282-0475; Email: r.frey@stlawrencemuncie.

org; Web: www.stlawrencemuncie.org. Rob Frey, Prin. Lay Teachers 8; Students 57; Clergy / Religious Teachers 1.
Catechesis Religious Program—Susan Wilhelm, Faith Formation Dir.; Sheila Henry, D.R.E. (Grades K-5). Students 32.
3—ST. MARY (1930)
2300 W. Jackson St., Muncie, 47303-4797.
Tel: 765-288-5308; Fax: 765-288-6357; Email: parishoffice@stmarymuncie.org; Web: stmarymuncie.org. Very Rev. Andrew J. Dudzinski, V.F.
Schools—St. Mary School—(Grades PreK-8), 2301 W. Gilbert St., Muncie, 47303-4797.
Tel: 765-288-5878; Fax: 765-284-3685; Web: www.stmarymuncie.org/school. Elisha Schlabach, Prin. Lay Teachers 13; Students 128.
Pope John Paul II Middle School, (Grades 6-8), 2301 W. Gilbert St., Muncie, 47303-4797.
Tel: 765-288-5878; Fax: 765-284-3685; Web: stmarymuncie.org/school. Elisha Schlabach, Prin. Lay Teachers 6; Students 37.
Catechesis Religious Program—Email: religioused@stmarymuncie.org. Ms. Katie Hazen, D.R.E.; Tammy Laudicina, Family Life Dir./Youth Min. Students 71.
NOBLESVILLE, HAMILTON CO., OUR LADY OF GRACE (1944)
9900 E. 191st St., Noblesville, 46060-1520.
Tel: 317-773-4275; Email: churchoffice@ologn.org; Web: ologn.org. Revs. Thomas H. Metzger; Michael Bower; Michael J. Witka, Dir. Business & Admin.; Barb Leap, Dir. Music & Liturgy.
School—Our Lady of Grace School, (Grades PreK-8), Tel: 317-770-5660; Fax: 317-770-5663; Web: www.olmcschool.org. Michelle Boyd, Prin. Lay Teachers 28; Students 415.
Catechesis Religious Program—Tel: 317-773-0291; Email: bwhampton@ologn.org. Becky Hampton, C.R.E. (Elementary). Students 503.
OTTERBEIN, BENTON CO., ST. CHARLES (1902) [JC]
109 N. Meadow, Otterbein, 47970. Tel: 765-385-2587 ; Email: spchurch@localline.com; Web: www.stcharlesotterbein.com. 502 S. Michigan St., Oxford, 47971. Rev. Robert W. Klemme.
Church: 108 N. Meadow St., Otterbein, 47970-0661.
Catechesis Religious Program—Jennifer Senesac, D.R.E. Students 95.
OXFORD, BENTON CO., ST. PATRICK (1867) [CEM] [JC] (Irish)
502 S. Michigan St., Oxford, 47971-8562.
Tel: 765-385-2587; Fax: 765-385-0225; Email: spchurch@localline.com; Web: www.stpatrickoxford.com. Rev. Robert W. Klemme.
Catechesis Religious Program—Barbara Richardson, D.R.E. Students 56.
PERU, MIAMI CO., ST. CHARLES BORROMEO (1860) [CEM]
58 W. 5th St., Peru, 46970. Tel: 765-473-5543. 80 W. 5th St., Peru, 46970. Rev. Adam G. Mauman; Deacon Truman T. Stevens.
Catechesis Religious Program—Email: rcook@stcharlesperu.org. Rita Cook, D.R.E. Students 31.
PORTLAND, JAY CO., IMMACULATE CONCEPTION (1876) (German)
506 E. Walnut St., Portland, 47371-1599.
Tel: 260-726-7341; Email: fr.rmoran@dol-in.org; Web: icportland.org. Rev. Robert E. Moran, V.F.
Catechesis Religious Program—Tel: 260-726-4371. Francis Albert, D.R.E. Students 178.
REMINGTON, JASPER CO., SACRED HEART OF JESUS (1875) [CEM] (German—French)
124 New York St., Remington, 47977-0159.
Tel: 219-261-2302. P.O. Box 159, Remington, 47977. Rev. Paul C. Hudson.
Catechesis Religious Program—Tel: 219-208-0008. Students 43.
RENSSELAER, JASPER CO., ST. AUGUSTINE (1883) [CEM]
318 N. McKinley Ave., Rensselaer, 47978-2599.
Tel: 219-866-5351. Rev. Donald J. Davison, C.PP.S.
School—St. Augustine School, 328 N. Mckinley Ave., Rensselaer, 47978. Tel: 219-866-5480;
Fax: 219-866-5663; Email: schooler@s-augustine.org; Web: www.s-augustine.org. Mr. W. Schooler, Prin. Lay Teachers 7; Religious 1; Students 101.
Catechesis Religious Program—Email: rensselaerdre@gmail.com. Anthony Butler, D.R.E. Students 86.
REYNOLDS, WHITE CO., ST. JOSEPH (1866) [CEM]
601 S. Kenton St., Reynolds, 47980-8098.
Tel: 219-984-5401. Rev. John J. Cummings, Admin.
Catechesis Religious Program—Students 25.
ROCHESTER, FULTON CO., ST. JOSEPH (1900)
1310 Main St., Rochester, 46975-2108.
Tel: 574-223-2808; Email: stjoseph@rtcol.com; Web: www.parishesonline.com/find/st-joseph-catholic-church. Very Rev. Michael A. McKinney, V.F., Pastor & Admin.
Catechesis Religious Program—Students 97.
STAR CITY, PULASKI CO., ST. JOSEPH (1851) [CEM 2]
5895 S. State Rd. 119, Star City, 46985.
Tel: 574-946-4906; Email: stpete4906@embarqmail.com; Web: preciousbloodcluster.org. 401 N. Monticello St., Winamac, 46996. Rev. Leroy G. Kinnaman, Admin.
TIPTON, TIPTON CO., ST. JOHN THE BAPTIST (1866) [CEM]
Mailing Address: 335 Mill St., Tipton, 46072-1403.
Tel: 765-675-2422; Email: businessmanager@stjohnstipton.com. Very Rev. Dennis J. Goth, V.F.
Res.: 340 N. Mill St., Tipton, 46072-1403. Email: father@stjohnstipton.com; Web: www.stjohnstipton.com.
School—St. John the Baptist School, 323 Mill St., Tipton, 46072. Fax: 765-675-2163; Email: g.king@stjohnstipton.com. Very Rev. Dennis J. Goth, V.F., Pastor. Lay Teachers 2; Students 20.
Catechesis Religious Program—Email: slpowell_2000@yahoo.com. Shelly Powell, D.R.E. Students 41.
UNION CITY, RANDOLPH CO., ST. MARY (1865) [CEM] (Irish—German)
425 W. Hickory St., Union City, 47390-1301.
Tel: 765-964-4202; Email: stmaryuc@embarqmail.com; Web: StMUC-StJW.org. Rev. Peter F. Logsdon.
Catechesis Religious Program—Karen Johnston, D.R.E. & Parish Sec. Students 29.
WEST LAFAYETTE, TIPPECANOE CO.
1—BLESSED SACRAMENT (1957)
2224 Sacramento Dr., West Lafayette, 47906-1998.
Tel: 765-463-5733; Email: receptionist@parish.dol-in.org. Very Rev. Theodore C. Dudzinski, J.C.L., V.G.; Rev. Andrew R. DeKeyser, J.C.L., In Res.; Deacon Matthew (Mike) C. Mescall.
Catechesis Religious Program—Students 337.
Station—Indiana Veterans' Home, West Lafayette.
2—ST. THOMAS AQUINAS (1951) (Purdue University Parish)
535 W. State St., West Lafayette, 47906-3541.
Tel: 765-743-4652. Revs. Patrick H. Baikauskas, O.P., Pastor & Dir. Campus Ministry; Cassian K. Sama, O.P.; Timothy M. Combs, O.P.; Deacon Charles A. Jindrich.
Catechesis Religious Program—Email: john@boilercatholics.org. John Strong, D.R.E. Students 348.
WESTFIELD, HAMILTON CO., ST. MARIA GORETTI (1995)
17102 Spring Mill Rd., Westfield, 46074.
Tel: 317-867-3213; Web: www.smgonline.org. Revs. Kevin J. Haines; Derek Aaron; Michael J. McKinley; Deacon Stephen P. Miller, Pastoral Assoc.
School—St. Maria Goretti School, (Grades K-8), 17104 Spring Mill Rd., Westfield, 46074.
Tel: 317-896-5582; Fax: 317-867-0783; Email: v.barnes@smgonline.org. Vince Barnes, Prin. Lay Teachers 30; Students 422.
Catechesis Religious Program—Email: s.maue@smgonline.org. Sue Maue, D.R.E. Students 521.
WHEATFIELD, JASPER CO., SORROWFUL MOTHER (1887) [CEM]
165 Grace St., P.O. Box 248, Wheatfield, 46392-0248.
Tel: 219-956-3343. Rev. Paul W. Cochran.
Catechesis Religious Program—Tel: 219-956-3347. Students 116.
WINAMAC, PULASKI CO., ST. PETER (1859) [CEM]
401 N. Monticello St., Winamac, 46996-1327.
Tel: 574-946-4906; Email: stpete4906@embarqmail.com; Web: preciousbloodcluster.org. Rev. Leroy G. Kinnaman.
Catechesis Religious Program—424 N. Market St., Winamac, 46996. Students 59.
WINCHESTER, RANDOLPH CO., ST. JOSEPH (1952)
514 W. Washington St., Winchester, 47394.
Tel: 765-964-4202; Email: smbookkeeper@embarqmail.com. 425 W. Hickory St., Union City, 47390. Rev. Peter F. Logsdon.
Catechesis Religious Program—Karen Johnston, D.R.E.; Paula Dirksen, Asst. to D.R.E., Tel: 765-584-1084. Students 32.
ZIONSVILLE, BOONE CO., ST. ALPHONSUS LIGUORI (1945) [JC]
1870 W. Oak St., Zionsville, 46077-1894.
Tel: 317-873-2885; Fax: 317-873-8746; Email: parishsecretary@zionsvillecatholic.com; Web: www.zionsvillecatholic.com. Revs. Dennis J. O'Keeffe; James De Oreo; Deacon Timothy J. Perry.

Chaplains of Public Institutions

LAFAYETTE. *Indiana Veterans' Home, Queen of the Universe Chapel*. Attended from Blessed Sacrament Church, West Lafayette.
GRISSOM. *Grissom Air Force Base, St. Michael's Chapel*, 434 Air Refueling Wing, 7088 S. Tanker St., Grissom, 46971. Tel: 765-688-2191; Email: Alex.jack@us.af.mil. Rev. Adam G. Mauman, Auxiliary Civilian Chap.
LOGANSPORT. *Logansport State Hospital*. Attended from All Saints Church, Logansport.
MARION. *U.S. Veteran's Hospital*. Vacant, Auxiliary Chap.
PENDLETON. *Correctional Industrial Complex Ecumenical Chapel*, P.O. Box 601, Pendleton, 46064. Tel: 765-778-8011.
Indiana State Reformatory, St. Christopher Chapel, 4490 W Reformatory Rd, P.O. Box 28, Pendleton, 46064. Tel: 765-778-2107.

On Duty Outside the Diocese:
Revs.—
Comeau, Ronald R., 6 Johnson Rd., Aurora, ON Canada L4C 2A2. Tel: 416-772-1965
Westfall, Joseph B., 160 Barger St., Putnam Valley, NY 10579-3409.

Military Chaplains:
Revs.—
Janko, Joshua, Air Force Academy, Colorado
Kinney, John M., 2743 Trinity View, San Antonio, TX 78261-2557. Tel: 210-488-3989
Mahalic, Philip A., 2749 Artillery Post Rd., Apt. D, Fort Sam Houston, TX 78234-2682. Tel: 810-289-0573.

Retired:
Most Rev.—
Higi, William Leo, D.D., (Retired), 1743 Mill Pond Ln., 47905-5578. Tel: 765-427-4991
Very Rev. Msgr.—
Borawski, Gerald J., V.F., (Retired), 7821 Lake Ave., Apt. 422, Cleveland, OH 44102. Tel: 765-742-4440
Rev. Msgr.—
Duncan, John C., (Retired), 9257 Golden Leaf Way, Indianapolis, 46260-5071
Revs.—
Bates, James R., (Retired), 8810 Colby Blvd. Apt. 340, Indianapolis, 46268-1388. Tel: 317-876-2884
Bowers, Philip T., (Retired), 8121 Foxchase Dr., Indianapolis, 46256-4812. Tel: 317-441-0745
Clegg, Timothy W., (Retired), 13135 Charlton Dr., Brooksville, FL 34614-1931
Cover, Phillip B., (Retired), 3300 N.E. 36th St., #401, Ft. Lauderdale, FL 33308
Fox, Thomas E., V.F., (Retired), 401 E. Appaloosa Tr., 47905
Funk, C. Alan, (Retired), 8237 N. U.S. Hwy. 41, Earl Park, 47942-8619. Tel: 219-474-5227
Goodrum, James R., (Retired), 112B Williams St., Monticello, 47960-1675. Tel: 574-583-5755
Gross, Donald L., V.F., (Retired), 700 S. Sharon Ave., Fowler, 47944-1670
Holbrook, William M., (Retired), 5136 Nottingham Ave., Chicago, IL 60656-3639. Tel: 773-622-5900, Ext. 6. 5900 W. Barry Ave., Chicago, IL 60634-5728
Hosey, P. Keith, (Retired), 5353 E. 56th St., Indianapolis, 46226-1486. Tel: 317-545-7681
Kettron, W. Michael, (Retired), St. Paul Hermitage, 501 N. 17th Ave., Beech Grove, 46107. Tel: 317-376-5322
Kiefer, John D., (Retired), 2200 S. 625 E., Selma, 47383
Mannion, John H., B.S., M.Div., (Retired), 5361 Spring Creek Rd., Indianapolis, 46254
Puetz, Richard W., (Retired), 701 Armory Rd., Rm. 409, Delphi, 46923-1915. Tel: 765-564-2182
Williams, Robert L., V.F., (Retired), St. Lawrence Church, 820 E. Charles St., Muncie, 47305-2699.

Permanent Deacons:
Bock, Christopher D., St. Louis de Montfort, Fishers
Boes, Edward R., St Lawrence, Lafayette
Castillo, Domingo C., St. Paul, Marion
Etter, John P., Sacred Heart of Jesus, Cicero
Gray, D. Michael, St. Boniface, Lafayette
Jezierski, John R., Cathedral of St. Mary, Lafayette
Jindrich, Charles A., St. Thomas Aquinas, West Lafayette
Kuenz, Gary J., St. Mary, Muncie
Lunsford, Paul S., Our Lady of Mount Carmel, Noblesville
Mescall, Matthew (Mike) C., Church of the Blessed Sacrament, West Lafayette
Miller, Stephen P., St. Maria Goretti, Westfield
Morrow, Ronald L., St. Patrick, Kokomo
Munoz, Jose D., St. Boniface, Lafayette

Nevinger, Ronald D., St. Boniface, Lafayette
Perry, Timothy J., St. Alphonsus Ligouri, Zionsville
Poremski, Joseph F., Cathedral of St. Mary, Lafayette
Rahill, William H., Our Lady of Mount Carmel, Carmel
Reid, William T., St. Elizabeth Seton, Carmel
Rush, James B., St. Lawrence, Lafayette
Seitz, Steven D., St. Louis de Montfort, Fishers
Springer, Charles L., St. Patrick, Kokomo; Miami Correctional Facility
Stevens, Truman T., St. Charles Borromeo, Peru
Van Schepen, Joseph D., St. Cecilia, DeMotte
Zak, Stanislaw H., St. Boniface, Lafayette.

INSTITUTIONS LOCATED IN DIOCESE

[A] COLLEGES AND UNIVERSITIES

RENSSELAER. *Saint Joseph's College* (1889) 1027 S. College Ave., Rensselaer, 47978. Tel: 219-866-6000 ; Email: bfischer@saintjoe.edu; Web: www.saintjoe.edu. Bros. Timothy P. Hemm, C.PP.S.; Robert Reuter, C.PP.S., Ph.D. The Society of the Precious Blood. Brothers 2.

[B] HIGH SCHOOLS, INTER-PAROCHIAL

LAFAYETTE. *Central Catholic Junior-Senior High School*, 2410 S. Ninth St., 47909-2499.
Tel: 765-474-2496; Fax: 765-474-8752; Email: nwagner@lcss.org; Web: www.lcss.org. Mr. Neil R. Wagner, Prin.; Melissa Robertson, Asst. Prin.; Caitie Rose Beardmore, Campus Min. Administrators 3; Lay Staff 9; Lay Teachers 35; Sisters 2; Students 463; Asst. Campus Minister 1; Clergy / Religious Teachers 5.

NOBLESVILLE. *Hamilton County Catholic High School Corporation* dba St. Theodore Guerin High School, 15300 N. Gray Rd., Noblesville, 46062.
Tel: 317-582-0120; Fax: 317-219-0582; Web: www.guerincatholic.org. P.O. Box 557, Fishers, 46038. Dr. John Atha, Pres.; James M. McNeany Jr., Prin.; Rev. Thomas J. Haan, Chap.
Legal Titles: Guerin Catholic High School; Blessed Theodore Guerin High School. Administrators 3; Faculty 57; Lay Teachers 54; Priests 1; Sisters 2; Students 755; Non-Teaching Staff 44; Clergy / Religious Teachers 3.

[C] GENERAL HOSPITALS

LAFAYETTE. *Franciscan Health Lafayette Central* (1874) 1501 Hartford St., P.O. Box 7501, 47903.
Tel: 765-423-6011; Fax: 765-502-4455; Email: Terry.Wilson@franciscanalliance.org; Web: www.franciscanhealth.org. Terrance E. Wilson, Pres. & CEO. Franciscan Alliance, Inc. Bed Capacity 14; Students 126; Tot Asst. Annually 15,331; Total Staff 473.
St. Elizabeth School of Nursing, 1501 Hartford St., 47904. Tel: 765-423-6408; Fax: 765-423-6364; Web: www.franciscanste.org. Students 150.
Franciscan Health Lafayette East, 1701 S. Creasy Ln., 47905. Tel: 765-502-4000; Fax: 765-502-4455; Email: Terry.Wilson@franciscanalliance.org; Web: www.franciscanhealth.org. Terrance E. Wilson, Pres. & CEO; Sisters M. Ann Kathleen Magiera, O.S.F., Vice Pres. Mission Integration; Aline Shultz, Vice Pres.; Revs. David Buckles, J.C.L., Chap.; Paul M. Graf, Chap.; Michael Winstead, Admin. Owned by Franciscan Alliance, Inc. Bassinets 36; Bed Capacity 203; Sisters 2; Tot Asst. Annually 291,292; Total Staff 1,361.

ANDERSON. *St. Vincent Anderson Regional Hospital, Inc.*, 2015 Jackson St., Anderson, 46016.
Tel: 765-646-8373; Fax: 765-646-8504; Email: michael.schroyer@stvincent.org; Web: www.stvincent.org/andersonregional. Mr. Michael K. Schroyer, Pres.; Sr. Eileen Wrobleski, C.S.C., Vice Pres., Mission Integration. Bed Capacity 193; Sisters of the Holy Cross 4; Tot Asst. Annually 189,177; Total Staff 1,172.

CARMEL. *Franciscan Health Indianapolis at Carmel*, 12188B N. Meridian St., Carmel, 46032.
Tel: 317-705-4520; Fax: 317-705-4599; Email: stephen.wheatley@franciscanalliance.org; Web: www.franciscanhealth.org. Stephen Wheatley, Dir. Bed Capacity 6; Tot Asst. Annually 3,741; Total Staff 42.
St. Vincent Carmel Hospital, Inc. (1985) 13500 N. Meridian St., Carmel, 46032-1903.
Tel: 317-582-7137; Fax: 317-582-7744; Email: jclandry@stvincent.org; Web: www.stvincent.org. Gary Fammartino, Pres.; Carey Landry, Certified Chap. (A member of St. Vincent Health, Inc. and Ascension Health.) Bed Capacity 145; Tot Asst. Annually 11,129; Total Staff 466; Total Pastoral Care Staff 2.

CRAWFORDSVILLE. *Franciscan Health Crawfordsville*, 1710 Lafayette Rd., Crawfordsville, 47933.
Tel: 765-362-2800; Fax: 765-364-3189; Email: terrence.klein@franciscanalliance.org; Web: www.franciscanhealth.org. Sr. Cheryl Dazey, Dir.; Terrence L. Klein, Vice Pres. & COO. Franciscan Alliance, Inc. Bed Capacity 40; Tot Asst. Annually 128,333; Total Staff 223; Licensed Beds 103; Professed Sisters 1.

ELWOOD. *St. Vincent Mercy Hospital* (1926) St. Vincent Madison County Health System, Inc. 1331 South A St., Elwood, 46036-1942. Tel: 765-552-4600;
Fax: 765-552-4700; Email: ACYates@stvincent.org; Web: mercy.stvinent.org. Ann C. Yates, R.N., Dir., Patient Care, Email: ACYates@stvincent.org; Francis "Cheech" Albarano, Admin. Bed Capacity 25; Tot Asst. Annually 43,078; Total Staff 165.

FISHERS. *St. Vincent Fishers Hospital, Inc.*, 13861 Olio Rd., Fishers, 46037. Tel: 317-415-9000;
Fax: 317-415-9049; Email: gafammar@stvincent.org. Gary Fammmartino, Admin. A member of St. Vincent Health, Inc. and Ascension Health Bed Capacity 46; Tot Asst. Annually 5,552; Total Staff 166.

KOKOMO. *St. Vincent Kokomo* St. Joseph Hospital and Health Center, Inc. 1907 W. Sycamore St., Kokomo, 46901. Tel: 765-452-5611;
Tel: 765-456-5300 (Administration);
Fax: 765-456-5083; Email: margaret.johnson@stvincent.org; Web: www.stvincent.org/stjoseph. Margaret M. Johnson, Pres. St. Vincent NW. Region; Mark Deckinga, M.Div., B.C.C., Dir., Pastoral Care. Bed Capacity 138; Tot Asst. Annually 15,456; Total Staff 562.
Saint Joseph Foundation of Kokomo, Indiana, Inc., 1907 Sycamore St., Kokomo. Tel: 765-456-5406;
Fax: 765-456-5387; Email: todd.moser@stvincent.org; Web: stvincent.org/stjoseph. Todd Moser, Dir. St. Joseph Foundation.

RENSSALAER. *Franciscan Health Rensselaer* dba Franciscan Health Rensselaer, 1104 E. Grace St., Rensselaer, 47978-3296. Tel: 219-866-5154;
Fax: 219-866-3234; Email: carlos.vasquez@franciscanalliance.org; Web: FranciscanHealth.org/Rensselaer. Carlos Vasquez, Vice Pres. Critical access hospital. Bed Capacity 46; Tot Asst. Annually 51,719; Total Staff 253.

WILLIAMSPORT. *St. Vincent Williamsport Hospital, Inc.*, 412 N. Monroe St., Williamsport, 47993-1097.
Tel: 765-762-4000; Fax: 765-762-4126; Email: mjcraigi@stvincent.org; Web: www.stvincent.org. Jane Craigin, CEO; Rev. Don Williams, Chaplain. Bed Capacity 16; Priests 1; Tot Asst. Annually 4,926; Total Staff 116.

[D] NURSING HOMES

LAFAYETTE. *St. Anthony Health Care*, 1205 N. 14th St., 47904. Tel: 765-423-4861; Fax: 765-742-8790; Email: admin@sahc.net; Web: www.saintanthonycares.com. Rev. Samuel J. Kalu, J.C.L., Liturgy Dir., Liturgy Dir. Bed Capacity 120; Residents 90; Tot Asst. Annually 300; Total Staff 172.

[E] MONASTERIES AND RESIDENCES OF PRIESTS AND BROTHERS

LAFAYETTE. *Emmaus House*, 2500 S. Ninth St., 47909.
Tel: 765-477-6441; Email: skalu@dol-in.org. Rev. Samuel J. Kalu, J.C.L., Tribunal Assoc. Judge. Priests 1.

[F] CONVENTS AND RESIDENCES FOR SISTERS

ANDERSON. *Congregation of the Sisters of the Holy Cross*, 2115 Meridian St., Anderson, 46016.
Tel: 765-642-2427. Sr. Suzanne Brennan, Treas.
Sisters of the Holy Cross, Inc. Sisters 2.

KOKOMO. *Maria Regina Mater Monastery* (1959) 1175 N. 300 W., Kokomo, 46901-1799. Tel: 765-457-5743 ; Fax: 765-457-5743; Web: www.thepoorclares.org. Mother Miriam, P.C.C., Abbess. Monastery of Poor Clares of the Reform of St. Colette. Sisters 9; Solemnly Professed Nuns in Cloister 8; Other (Junior) 1.

[G] NEWMAN CENTERS

MUNCIE. *Newman Foundation-Ball State University* (1973) 1200 W. Riverside Ave., Muncie, 47303.
Tel: 765-288-6180; Fax: 765-288-7777; Email: stfrancisnewman@parish.dol-in.org; Web: www.stfrancisnewman.org. Rev. Brian M. Doerr, Chap. Students 1,300.

WEST LAFAYETTE. *St. Thomas Aquinas Parish and Foundation for Catholic Students Attending Purdue University* (1951) 535 W. State St., West Lafayette, 47906-3541. Tel: 765-743-4652;
Fax: 765-743-0426; Email: mailbox@boilercatholics.org; Web: www.boilercatholics.org. Rev. Patrick H. Baikauskas, O.P., Pastor & Dir. Campus Ministry; Dee Bernhardt, Asst. Dir., Campus Min. & D.R.E. Students 13,000.

[H] MISCELLANEOUS

LAFAYETTE. *Caregiver Companion, Inc.*, 612 Wabash Ave., 47905. Tel: 765-423-1879; Email: caregiver95@gmail.com; Web: www.caregivercompanion.org. Diana F. Salazar, Exec. Dir. & Contact Person; Lauren Frecker, Dir.
**Franciscan Health Foundation Western Indiana*, 1501 Hartford St., 47904. Tel: 765-423-6810;
Fax: 765-423-6898; Email: WIFoundation@franciscanalliance.org; Web: www.franciscanalliance.org/foundation. Susan Howarth, Exec. A regional office & division of Franciscan Alliance Foundation, Inc. Staff 3.
Lafayette Diocesan Foundation, Inc., P.O. Box 1687, 47902-1687. Tel: 765-742-7000; Fax: 765-742-7513; Web: www.dol-in.org/diocesan-staff. Mike MacNulty, Dir.; William Gettings, Chm. Bd. Total Staff 2.

ANDERSON. *St. Vincent Anderson Regional Hospital Foundation, Inc.*, 2015 Jackson St., Anderson, 46016. Tel: 765-646-8373; Fax: 765-646-8504; Email: michael.schroyer@stvincent.org; Web: www.stvincent.org/andersonregional. Mr. Michael K. Schroyer, Pres.

LEMONT. **University Place, Inc.*, 1700 Lindberg Rd., West Lafayette, 47906. Tel: 765-464-5600; Web: www.franciscancommunities.com. 11500 Theresa Dr., Lemont, IL 60439. David Kinder, Exec. Dir.; Melissa Smith, Dir. of Mission Integration & Pastoral Care. Sponsored by the Franciscan Sisters of Chicago. Independent Living 106; Assisted Living 46; Skilled Nursing 30.

NOBLESVILLE. *Hamilton County Catholic High School Corporation* dba St. Theodore Guerin High School; Guerin Catholic High School, 15300 N. Gray Rd., Noblesville, 46062. Tel: 317-582-0120;
Fax: 317-219-0582; Web: www.guerincatholic.org. P.O. Box 557, Fishers, 46038. Most Rev. Timothy L. Doherty, S.T.L., Ph.D.; Very Rev. Theodore C. Dudzinski, J.C.L., V.G.; Dr. Peg Dispenzieri, Vice Prin.; G. Gary Malone
Legal Titles: St. Theodore Guerin High School, Guerin Catholic High School, formerly Blessed Theodore Guerin High School High School Students 755.

PERU. *St. Charles Conference of the Society of St. Vincent DePaul, Inc.*, 30 W. 7th St., Peru, 46970.
Tel: 765-472-1855. Sara Welke, Contact Person.

WEST LAFAYETTE. *Dominicans, Community of St. Thomas Aquinas, Inc.*, 2535 Newman Rd., West Lafayette, 47906-4537. Tel: 765-743-3795; Email: fr.tcombs@dol-in.org. Revs. Patrick H. Baikauskas, O.P.; Timothy M. Combs, O.P.; Cassian K. Sama, O.P.

RELIGIOUS INSTITUTES OF MEN REPRESENTED IN THE DIOCESE

For further details refer to the corresponding bracketed number in the Religious Institutes of Men or Women section.

[0520]—*Order of St. Francis Minors*—O.F.M.
[1060]—*Society of the Precious Blood*—C.PP.S.

RELIGIOUS INSTITUTES OF WOMEN REPRESENTED IN THE DIOCESE

[3832]—*Congregation of the Sisters of St. Joseph*—C.S.J.
[1920]—*Congregation of the Sisters of the Holy Cross*—C.S.C.
[1070-09]—*Dominican Sisters of St. Cecilia*—O.P.
[]—*Our Lady of Victory Missionary Sisters*—O.L.V.M.
[3230]—*Poor Handmaids of Jesus Christ*—P.H.J.C.
[]—*Sisters of Providence* (Crawfordsville, IN).
[]—*Sisters of St. Francis of Clinton* (Iowa)—O.S.F.
[1640]—*Sisters of St. Francis of Perpetual Adoration*—O.S.F.
[]—*Sisters of the Third Order of St. Francis of Penance and Charity*—O.S.F.

NECROLOGY

† Askar, George F., (Retired), Died Feb. 27, 2018
† Grace, Joseph W., (Retired), Died Jul. 2, 2018
† Haslinger, Philip S., (Retired), Died Dec. 3, 2018
† Kroeger, Timothy D., (Retired), Died Dec. 9, 2018
† Ondo, Michael A., (Retired), Died Jun. 27, 2018
† Ziegler, Ambrose M., (Retired), Died Oct. 22, 2018

Diocese of Lake Charles

Most Reverend

GLEN JOHN PROVOST

Bishop of Lake Charles; ordained June 29, 1975; appointed Bishop of Lake Charles March 6, 2007; ordained April 23, 2007. *Chancery Office: 414 Iris St., P.O. Box 3223, Lake Charles, LA 70602.* Tel: 337-439-7400; Fax: 337-439-7413.

Chancery Office: 414 Iris St., P.O. Box 3223, Lake Charles, LA 70602. Tel: 337-439-7400; Fax: 337-439-7413.

Web: lcdiocese.org

Email: info@lcdiocese.org

ESTABLISHED APRIL 25, 1980.

Square Miles 5,313.

Comprises the civil parishes (or counties) of Allen, Beauregard, Calcasieu, Cameron and Jefferson Davis in the State of Louisiana.

For legal titles of parishes and diocesan institutions, consult the Chancery Office.

STATISTICAL OVERVIEW

Personnel	
Bishop	1
Priests: Diocesan Active in Diocese	29
Priests: Diocesan Active Outside Diocese	1
Priests: Retired, Sick or Absent	14
Number of Diocesan Priests	44
Religious Priests in Diocese	19
Total Priests in Diocese	63
Extern Priests in Diocese	5
Ordinations:	
Diocesan Priests	1
Transitional Deacons	1
Permanent Deacons in Diocese	36
Total Brothers	1
Total Sisters	18
Parishes	
Parishes	39
With Resident Pastor:	
Resident Diocesan Priests	28
Resident Religious Priests	11
Without Resident Pastor:	
Administered by Priests	3
Missions	7
Professional Ministry Personnel:	
Sisters	9
Lay Ministers	1,112
Welfare	
Catholic Hospitals	2
Total Assisted	136,272
Homes for the Aged	1
Total Assisted	55
Day Care Centers	1
Total Assisted	130
Special Centers for Social Services	3
Total Assisted	23,905
Educational	
Diocesan Students in Other Seminaries	13
Total Seminarians	13
Colleges and Universities	1
Total Students	14,505
High Schools, Diocesan and Parish	1
Total Students	591
Elementary Schools, Diocesan and Parish	6
Total Students	2,008
Catechesis/Religious Education:	
High School Students	1,710
Elementary Students	4,196
Total Students under Catholic Instruction	23,023
Teachers in the Diocese:	
Priests	1
Sisters	3
Lay Teachers	149
Vital Statistics	
Receptions into the Church:	
Infant Baptism Totals	823
Adult Baptism Totals	98
Received into Full Communion	236
First Communions	943
Confirmations	895
Marriages:	
Catholic	234
Interfaith	69
Total Marriages	303
Deaths	794
Total Catholic Population	67,405
Total Population	303,027

Former Bishops—Most Revs. JUDE SPEYRER, D.D., ord. July 25, 1953; appt. First Bishop of Lake Charles Jan. 29, 1980; ord. and installed April 25, 1980; resigned Dec. 12, 2000; died July 21, 2013.; EDWARD K. BRAXTON, ord. May 13, 1970; appt. Auxiliary Bishop of St. Louis March 28, 1995; ord. Auxiliary Bishop of St. Louis May 17, 1995; appt. Bishop of Lake Charles Dec. 12, 2000; installed Feb. 22, 2001; appt. Bishop of Belleville March 15, 2005.

Bishop's Office—414 Iris St., P.O. Box 3223, Lake Charles, 70602. Tel: 337-439-7400, Ext. 204.

Chancery Office—414 Iris St., P.O. Box 3223, Lake Charles, 70602. Tel: 337-439-7400; Fax: 337-439-7413. Office Hours: Mon.-Fri. 8:30-4:30.

Bishop Perry Building—411 Iris St., Lake Charles, 70601. Tel: 337-439-7426; Fax: 337-439-7428. Office Hours: Mon.-Fri. 8:30-4:30.

Vicar General—Rev. Msgr. DANIEL A. TORRES, V.G., Mailing Address: P.O. Box 3223, Lake Charles, 70602. Tel: 337-439-7400.

Moderator of the Curia and Vice Chancellor—Very Rev. RUBEN J. BULLER.

Chancellor—Deacon GEORGE STEARNS, P.O. Box 3223, Lake Charles, 70602. Tel: 337-439-7400, Ext. 220.

Tribunal—414 Iris St., P.O. Box 3223, Lake Charles, 70602. Tel: 337-439-7400, Ext. 210. Very Rev. WILLIAM ELDER, J.C.L., Judicial Vicar.

Judges—Rev. Msgr. JACE F. ESKIND, J.C.L.; MS. BONNIE LANDRY, J.C.L.; Revs. JOHN PAYNE, J.C.L.; RUBEN VILLARREAL, J.C.L.

Advocates—Sr. MARIA REGINA OSONDU, D.M.M.M.; Deacon GEORGE K. CARR.

Defenders of the Bond—Rev. ALBERT W. BOREL, J.C.L.; Rev. Msgr. HARRY D. GREIG II.

Notary—MRS. DEBRA FOREMAN.

Promoter of Justice—Rev. ALBERT W. BOREL, J.C.L.

Deans—Very Revs. EDWARD J. RICHARD, M.S., M.S., West Deanery; ANTHONY M. FONTENOT, South Deanery; MARCUS JOHNSON, Central Deanery; JACOB SCOTT CONNER, East Deanery.

Presbyteral Council—Very Revs. AUBREY V. GUILBEAU, Chm.; ANTHONY M. FONTENOT; MARCUS JOHNSON; Rev. ROJO ANTONY PALATTY KOONATHAN, H.G.N.; Very Rev. RUBEN J. BULLER, Sec.; Rev. JOSE VATTAKUNNEL, M.C.; Rev. Msgrs. RONALD GROTH, (Retired); JAMES GADDY, (Retired); Rev. BRIAN MADISON KING; Very Rev. EDWARD J. RICHARD, M.S., M.S.; Rev. Msgr. DANIEL A. TORRES, V.G.; Very Rev. JACOB SCOTT CONNER.

Diocesan Consultors—Rev. Msgr. DANIEL A. TORRES, V.G.; Very Revs. ANTHONY M. FONTENOT; MARCUS JOHNSON; JACOB SCOTT CONNER; AUBREY V. GUILBEAU; RUBEN J. BULLER; Rev. Msgr. JAMES GADDY, (Retired), (convener of the college); Rev. ROLAND G. VAUGHN, (Retired).

Offices, Boards, Commissions, Committees

Black Catholics—Deacon EDWARD LAVINE, P.O. Box 3223, Lake Charles, 70601. Tel: 337-439-7436, Ext. 11.

Clergy Formation—Rev. NATHAN LONG, 411 Iris St., Lake Charles, 70601. Tel: 337-439-7400.

Communications—MORRIS LEBLEU, Mailing Address: P.O. Box 3223, Lake Charles, 70601. Tel: 337-439-7400, Ext. 304.

Counseling—Rev. WHITNEY MILLER, St. Charles Retreat Center, 2151 Sam Houston Jones Pkwy., Moss Bluff, 70611.

Deaf Apostolate—Very Rev. AUBREY V. GUILBEAU, 418 Iris St., Lake Charles, 70601. Tel: 337-439-4373.

Development Office—STEPHANIE RODRIGUE, Dir. Devel., Tel: 337-439-7400 Ext. 307; MORRIS LEBLEU, Assoc. Dir., Mailing Address: P.O. Box 3223, Lake Charles, 70602. Tel: 337-439-7400, Ext. 304.

Diocesan Building Commission—Deacon GEORGE STEARNS, Chm., P.O. Box 3223, Lake Charles, 70602. Tel: 337-439-7400, Ext. 204.

Vocation Director & Director of Seminarians—Rev. JEFFERY PAUL STARKOVICH, 414 Iris St., Lake Charles, 70601. Tel: 337-439-7400.

Education—MRS. KIMBERLEE GAZZOLO, Supt., Mailing Address: P.O. Box 3223, Lake Charles, 70602. Tel: 337-439-7426, Ext. 18.

Evangelization—411 Iris St., Lake Charles, 70601. Sr. MARIROSE RUDEK, R.S.M.

Fiscal Administration—MS. PATRICIA MYERS, Mailing Address: P.O. Box 3223, Lake Charles, 70602. Tel: 337-439-7400, Ext. 203.

Hispanic Ministry—Deacon JOSUE CANELO, Dir., Saint Henry Catholic Church, 1021 8th Ave., Lake Charles, 70601. Tel: 337-436-7223.

Office of Liturgy—Very Rev. RUBEN J. BULLER, Dir., Diocese of Lake Charles: 414 Iris St., Lake Charles, 70601. Tel: 337-439-7400, Ext. 217.

Parish Boundaries Commission—Rev. Msgr. DANIEL A. TORRES, V.G., Chm., Mailing Address: P.O. Box 3223, Lake Charles, 70602. Tel: 337-439-7400, Ext. 204.

Permanent Diaconate—Deacon JAMES DALE DESHOTEL, Chm.

Personnel Board—Rev. Msgr. DANIEL A. TORRES, V.G.; Very Revs. AUBREY V. GUILBEAU; MARCUS JOHNSON; JACOB SCOTT CONNER; ANTHONY M. FONTENOT; Rev. MATTHEW CORMIER; Very Rev. EDWARD J. RICHARD, M.S., M.S.

Propagation of the FaithVery Rev. ANTHONY M. FONTENOT, Mailing Address: 7680 Gulf Hwy., Lake Charles, 70607. Tel: 337-478-0213; Fax: 337-478-0793.

Religious Education—411 Iris St., Lake Charles, 70601. Sr. MARIROSE RUDEK, R.S.M.

Relief Services Catholic—Very Rev. ANTHONY M.

FONTENOT, Mailing Address: 7680 Gulf Hwy., Lake Charles, 70607.

St. Charles Retreat Center—Rev. WHITNEY MILLER, Dir., 2151 Sam Houston Jones Pkwy., Lake Charles, 70611. Tel: 337-855-1232.

Sea, Apostleship of the—Very Rev. ROMMEL P. TOLENTINO, Chap.; Deacon PATRICK LAPOINT, Dir., 160 Marine St., Lake Charles, 70601. Tel: 337-436-1315.

Catholic Charities—1225 Second St., Lake Charles, 70601. Tel: 337-439-7436. Sr. MIRIAM MACLEAN, R.S.M., Dir.

Pastoral Services, Catholic—1225 Second St., Lake Charles, 70601. Sr. MIRIAM MACLEAN, R.S.M., Sec.

Scouting—617 W. Claude St., Lake Charles, 70605. Rev. SAM ANGE III, Chap.

Vocation Director—Rev. JEFFERY PAUL STARKOVICH. Vocation Recruiter: Rev. NATHAN LONG

CLERGY, PARISHES, MISSIONS AND PAROCHIAL SCHOOLS

LAKE CHARLES

(CALCASIEU PARISH)

1—IMMACULATE CONCEPTION CATHEDRAL (1869) [CEM] Mailing Address: P.O. Box 1029, 70602.
Tel: 337-436-7251; Fax: 337-436-7240; Email: iccathedral@structurex.net; Web: immaculateconceptioncathedral.com. Very Rev. Rommel P. Tolentino, Email: rommel.tolentino@lcdiocese.org; Deacon Christopher Fontenot; Very Rev. Ruben J. Buller, In Res.
Church: 935 Bilbo, 70601.
School—Immaculate Conception Cathedral School, (Grades PreK-8), 1536 Ryan St., 70601.
Tel: 337-433-3497; Fax: 337-433-5056; Email: rviau@iccschool.org; Web: www.iccschool.org. Mrs. Christi Jarreau, Prin.; Ms. Tenia Fuselier, Librarian. Lay Teachers 36; Students 405.

2—CHRIST THE KING (2002) Very Rev. Anthony M. Fontenot.
Res.: 7680 Gulf Hwy., 70607. Tel: 337-478-0213; Email: adminassit@suddenlink.net.
Catechesis Religious Program—JoAnna Bearb, D.R.E. (Elementary); Tammy Duhon, D.R.E. (Jr. High & Sr. High). Students 103.

3—ST. HENRY (1958) [JC]
1021 8th Ave., 70601. Tel: 337-436-7223; Email: pkittling@sthenry.church. Rev. Matthew Cormier; Deacons Josue Canelo, Pastoral Min.; Patrick Hebert.
Catechesis Religious Program—Email: pkittling@sthenry.church. Phyllis Kittling, D.R.E. Students 32.

4—IMMACULATE HEART OF MARY (1953) (African American) Revs. V. Wayne LeBleu; Joby Kaniyamparambil Mathew, H.G.N., Parochial Vicar.
Res.: 2031 Opelousas St., 70601. Tel: 337-436-8093; Email: ihmchurch@suddenlink.net.
Catechesis Religious Program—Jacqueline Mathews, D.R.E. Students 120.
Mission—Our Lady of Fatima Chapel, 1700 Graham St., Calcasieu Parish 70601.

5—ST. MARGARET (1940)
2500 Enterprise Blvd., 70601. Tel: 337-439-4585; Email: info@stmargaret.church; Web: www.stmargaret.church. Very Rev. Marcus Johnson; Revs. Vijaya Prakash Peddoju, H.G.N., Parochial Vicar; Samuel Orsot; Deacons Dan Landry, (Retired); Raymond Menard; Anthony Pousson.
School—St. Margaret School, (Grades PreK-8),
Tel: 337-436-7959; Fax: 337-436-9932. Lay Teachers 27; Students 288.
Catechesis Religious Program—Tel: 337-436-6358. Joanne Schwem, D.R.E. Students 59.

6—ST. MARTIN DEPORRES (2002)
5495 Elliott Rd., 70605. 5383 Elliott Rd., 70605. Rev. Msgr. Jace F. Eskind, J.C.L.; Deacon Richard E. Donahoe.
Res.: 2503 Vogue Dr., 70605. Tel: 337-478-3845; Email: info@smdpcatholic.com.
Catechesis Religious Program—Mrs. Denise Donahoe, D.R.E. Students 215.

7—OUR LADY OF GOOD COUNSEL (1957) Rev. Nathan Long.
Res.: 221 Aqua Dr., 70605. Tel: 337-477-1434; Email: nathan.long@lcdiocese.org.
Catechesis Religious Program—Students 77.

8—OUR LADY QUEEN OF HEAVEN (1957) [CEM]
617 W. Claude St., 70605. Tel: 337-477-1236; Email: OLQH@lcdiocese.org; Web: olqh.org. Rev. Msgr. Daniel A. Torres, V.G.; Rev. Trey Ange, Parochial Vicar; Deacons George K. Carr, (Retired); Harold Nixon; Brian Kirk; Revs. Charles Okorougo, In Res.; Ruben Villarreal, J.C.L., In Res.
School—Our Lady Queen of Heaven School, (Grades PreK-8), 3908 Creole St., 70605. Tel: 337-477-7349; Fax: 337-477-7384. Ms. JoAnn Wallwork, Prin.; Diane Oden, Librarian. Lay Teachers 65; Students 648.
Catechesis Religious Program—3909 Creole St., 70605. Tel: 337-477-3937. Pamela Alston, D.R.E. (Grades 7-12); Mrs. Robin Suire, D.R.E. (Grades 1-6). Students 406.

9—SACRED HEART OF JESUS (1919) [CEM] (African American)
1102 Mill St., 70601. Tel: 337-439-2646;
Fax: 337-439-2650; Email: Sacredheart-lc@suddenlinkmail.com. Rev. Richard U. Adiukwu; Deacons Ed Lavine; Erroll DeVille.
Catechesis Religious Program—Barbara Batiste, D.R.E. Students 58.

10—ST. THEODORE (1974)
Mailing Address: 785 Sam Houston Jones Pkwy., 70611. Tel: 337-855-6662; Email: sttheodorecommunuity@yahoo.com; Web: mossbluffcatholic.org. P.O. Box 12726, 70612. Very Rev. Aubrey V. Guilbeau; Rev. Albert Borel, J.C.L.; Deacon Leo Anthony Hebert.
Res.: 413 Longleaf Dr., 70611.
School—St. Theodore School, (Grades PreK-8),
Tel: 337-855-9465; Fax: 337-855-2809. Lay Teachers 17; Students 180.
Catechesis Religious Program—Email: theodoreccd@yahoo.com. Sherry Livingston, D.R.E. Students 482.

OUTSIDE THE CITY OF LAKE CHARLES

BELL CITY, CALCASIEU PARISH, ST. JOHN VIANNEY (1939) [CEM]
7120 Hwy. 14 E., Bell City, 70630. Tel: 337-358-2502; Tel: 337-358-2504; Email: stjohnvianney1939@yahoo.com; Email: sjv.julieracca@gmail.com; Web: www.sjv-bc.com. 7120 Hwy. 14 E., Bell City, 70630. Rev. John Payne, J.C.L.
Catechesis Religious Program—7120 Hwy 14 E., Bell City, 70630. Paige Myers, D.R.E. Students 211.

BIG LAKE, CAMERON PARISH, ST. MARY OF THE LAKE (1938) Rev. Msgr. James M. Gaddy.
Res.: 11054 Hwy. 384 (Big Lake), 70607.
Tel: 337-598-3101; Email: stmarysla@aol.com.
Catechesis Religious Program—Felisha Nunez, D.R.E. Students 200.
Mission—St. Patrick's, Sweet Lake, Cameron Parish.

CAMERON, CAMERON PARISH, OUR LADY STAR OF THE SEA (1961) Rev. Babasino Fernandes.
Church & Res.: 5250 W. Creole Hwy., Cameron, 70631. Tel: 337-542-4795; Email: sacredheartchurch@camtel.net.
Catechesis Religious Program— (Combined with Sacred Heart of Jesus, Creole).

CREOLE, CAMERON PARISH, SACRED HEART OF JESUS (1890) [CEM 3] Rev. Babasino Fernandes.
Church & Res.: 5250 W. Creole Hwy., Cameron, 70631. Tel: 337-542-4795; Email: sacredheart@camtel.net.
Catechesis Religious Program—Email: stephaniedrodrigue@gmail.com. Stephanie Rodrigue, D.R.E. Students 87.

DEQUINCY, CALCASIEU PARISH, OUR LADY OF LA SALETTE (1955)
203 S. Grand, DeQuincy, 70633. Tel: 337-786-3500; Fax: 337-786-4222; Email: lasalettedequincy@yahoo.com. Rev. Vincent Vadakkedath.
Catechesis Religious Program—Mark Peloquin. Students 64.

DE RIDDER, BEAUREGARD PARISH, ST. JOSEPH'S (1938) Rev. Jude Brunnert, M.S.; Deacon Al Weinnig.
Res.: 1125 Blankenship Dr., De Ridder, 70634.
Tel: 337-463-6878; Email: jpbrunnert@yahoo.com; Email: sandraskyle45@hotmail.com; Email: cjhoerner@gmail.com; Web: www.stjosephderidder.org.
Catechesis Religious Program—Mrs. Theresa Pendley, D.R.E. Students 175.

ELTON, JEFFERSON DAVIS PARISH
1—ST. JOSEPH'S (1950) [CEM] (African American) Rev. Jose Vattakunnel, M.C.
Res.: 209 N. Washington St., P.O. Box 789, Elton, 70532. Tel: 337-584-2818; Email: jose.vattakunnel@lcdiocese.org.
Catechesis Religious Program— (combined with St. Paul's religious program) Lezlie LaFosse, D.R.E.
2—ST. PAUL (1913) [CEM]
Mailing Address: P.O. Box 129, Elton, 70532. 1100 St. Mary St., Elton, 70532. Tel: 337-584-2818; Email: stpaul-elton@hotmail.com. Rev. Jose Vattakunnel, M.C.; Deacons John Eaves; Michael Paul Guillory.
Catechesis Religious Program—Lezlie LaFosse, D.R.E. Students 161.

FENTON, JEFFERSON DAVIS PARISH, ST. CHARLES BORROMEO (1980)
804 Third Ave., P.O. Box 309, Fenton, 70640.
Tel: 337-756-2529; Email: stcharles02@yahoo.com. Rev. Rojo Anthony Palatty Koonathan, H.G.N.
Catechesis Religious Program—Email: scbccd@gmail.com. Susan Augustine, D.R.E. Students 57.
Mission—St. John the Evangelist, 306 Ann St., P.O. Box 124, Lacassine, Jefferson Davis Parish 70650.
Tel: 337-588-4606; Email: stjohnlacassine@gmail.com.
Catechesis Religious Program—Cindy Scharff, D.R.E. Students 150.

GRAND CHENIER, CAMERON PARISH, ST. EUGENE (1962) [CEM 3]
5035 Grand Chenier Hwy., Grand Chenier, 70643.
Tel: 337-538-2245; Email: steugene@camtel.net. Rev. Clyde Thomas.
Catechesis Religious Program—Shari Richard, D.R.E. Students 6.

HACKBERRY, CAMERON PARISH, ST. PETER THE APOSTLE (1955) [CEM] Rev. Arvind Minz.
Res.: 1210 Main St., P.O. Box 372, Hackberry, 70645. Tel: 337-762-3365; Email: stpeterschurch@camtel.net.
Catechesis Religious Program—Tammy Welch, D.R.E.; Trisha Savoie, D.R.E. Students 82.
Mission—Our Lady of the Assumption, 6470 Gulf Beach Hwy., Johnsons Bayou, 70631.
Catechesis Religious Program—Cheyenne Sandifer, D.R.E.; Cindy McGee, D.R.E. Students 28.

IOWA, CALCASIEU PARISH, ST. RAPHAEL (1931)
Mailing Address: 213 S. Thomson Ave., P.O. Drawer 849, Iowa, 70647. Tel: 337-582-3503; Email: straphael-iowa@hotmail.com. Rev. Dismas L. Mauk, S.V.D. In Res., Rev. Benignus Lambertus Wego, S.V.D.
Res.: 918 Dorothy St., P.O. Drawer 849, Iowa, 70647.
Catechesis Religious Program—Brittany Foreman, D.R.E. Students 223.
Mission—St. Joseph.

JENNINGS, JEFFERSON DAVIS PARISH
1—IMMACULATE CONCEPTION (1956)
515 Bryan St., Jennings, 70546. Tel: 337-824-1164; Email: icchurchjennings@yahoo.com. Rev. Marion Susil Fernando; Deacon Bennett McNeal, D.R.E.
Catechesis Religious Program—Email: icchurchjennings@yahoo.com. Students 81.
2—OUR LADY HELP OF CHRISTIANS (1891) [CEM] Rev. Charles McMillin.
Res.: 710 State St., P.O. Drawer 1170, Jennings, 70546. Tel: 337-824-0168; Email: secretary@olhcjennings.com.
School—Our Lady Help of Christians School, 600 Roberts Ave., Jennings, 70546. Tel: 337-824-1743; Fax: 337-824-1752; Email: rchapman@olischool.org. Rebecca Chapman, Prin. Clergy 1; Lay Teachers 25; Students 237.
Catechesis Religious Program—Melody Trahan, D.R.E. (PreK-8th); Debbie Davis, D.R.E. (PreK-8th). Students 208.
3—OUR LADY OF PERPETUAL HELP (1941) [CEM]
920 S. Broadway, P.O. Box 1331, Jennings, 70546.
Tel: 337-824-3182; Fax: 337-824-3186; Email: olphjennings@att.net. Rev. Jude Fernando, T.O.R.
Catechesis Religious Program—Tel: 337-824-3703. Ella Dartest-Williams, D.R.E. Students 28.

KINDER, ALLEN PARISH, ST. PHILIP NERI (1937) [CEM] (Acadian—French)
607 4th Ave., P.O. Box 146, Kinder, 70648.
Tel: 337-738-5612; Email: Keith.Pellerin@lcdiocese.org; Web: www.spnerichurch.com. Rev. Keith Pellerin; Deacon Roy Nash.
Catechesis Religious Program—317 7th St., P. O. Box 146, Kinder, 70648. Tel: 337-738-5535; Email: stphilipneri@centurytel.net. Laurie Pickle, D.R.E. Students 231.

LAKE ARTHUR, JEFFERSON DAVIS PARISH, OUR LADY OF THE LAKE (1922) [CEM] [JC3] Rev. Jay Alexius.
Res.: 203 Commercial Ave., Lake Arthur, 70549.
Tel: 337-774-2614; Fax: 337-774-3793; Email: ollsecretary@bellsouth.net; Web: www.ourladyofthelake.church.
Catechesis Religious Program—309 Lake St., Lake Arthur, 70549. Tel: 337-774-2675. Students 207.

OAKDALE, ALLEN PARISH, SACRED HEART (1948) [CEM]
Mailing Address: P.O. Box 926, Oakdale, 71463-0926. Rev. Vijaya Peddoju, H.G.N.
Res.: 1208 E. Seventh Ave., Oakdale, 71463.
Tel: 318-335-3780; Email: oakdalesacredheart@yahoo.com.
Catechesis Religious Program—Diane Bacon, D.R.E. Students 60.
Mission—St. Frances, 204 Poplar St., P.O. Box 926, Elizabeth, Allen Parish 70638.

OBERLIN, ALLEN PARISH, ST. JOAN OF ARC (1920) [CEM]
110 W. Fifth Ave., P.O. Box 479, Oberlin, 70655.
Tel: 337-639-4399; Email: secretary@sjoaoberlin.com; Web: sjoaoberlin.com. Very Rev. Jacob Scott Conner; Deacons Norris Chapman, (Retired); James Dale Deshotel.
Catechesis Religious Program—Students 88.

RAGLEY, BEAUREGARD PARISH, ST. PIUS X CATHOLIC CHURCH (2014)
16816 Hwy. 171, Ragley, 70657. Tel: 337-725-3719;

Fax: 337-725-6248; Email: secretary@spx.church; Email: bookkeeper@spx.church; Web: spx.church. Rev. Jeffery Paul Starkovich.
Catechesis Religious Program—Email: stpiusred@centurytel.net. Students 181.

RAYMOND, JEFFERSON DAVIS PARISH, ST. LAWRENCE (1951) Rev. William Miller.
Res.: 5505 Pine Island Hwy., Jennings, 70546.
Tel: 337-584-2700; Fax: 337-584-3990; Email: stlawrencecc@yahoo.com.
Catechesis Religious Program—Tel: 337-584-2002; Fax: 337-584-3990. Students 174.

SULPHUR, CALCASIEU PARISH

1—IMMACULATE CONCEPTION OF THE B.V.M. (1959)
2700 Maplewood Dr., Sulphur, 70663.
Tel: 337-625-3364; Email: church@icsulphur.org. Rev. Timothy Goodly; Deacon Chris Gregory.
Catechesis Religious Program—Tel: 337-527-5261; Email: olps1@olpssulphur.com. Paula Hunter, D.R.E. Students 308.

2—OUR LADY OF LASALETTE (1961) [CEM]
602 N. Claiborne St., Sulphur, 70663.
Tel: 337-527-6722; Email: olls@suddenlinkmail.com. Rev. Andrews Kollannoor, M.S. In Res., Rev. Lawrence A. Kohler, M.S.
Catechesis Religious Program—Tel: 337-527-8307. Cay Gibson, D.R.E. Students 192.

3—OUR LADY OF PROMPT SUCCOR (1919)
1109 Cypress St., Sulphur, 70663. Tel: 337-527-5261; Email: olps1@olpssulphur.com; Web: www.olpssulphur.com. Very Rev. Edward J. Richard, M.S., M.S.; Revs. Paul Jussen, M.S., Parochial Vicar; Luis Tigga, H.GN.; Deacon Patrick LaPoint; Msgr. Arthur B. Calkins, In Res.
School—Our Lady of Prompt Succor School, (Grades K-8), 1111 Cypress St., Sulphur, 70663.
Tel: 337-527-7828; Fax: 337-528-3778. Mr. Trevor Donnelly, Prin.; Ms. Stephanie Viator, Librarian. Lay Teachers 25; Students 279.
Catechesis Religious Program—1029 Lasalette Dr., Sulphur, 70663. Tel: 337-527-9964. Patsy Hebert, D.R.E.; Terry Sittig, D.R.E. Students 198.

4—ST. THERESA (1971)
4822 Carlyss Dr., Sulphur, 70665. Tel: 337-583-4800; Email: sthresa1@camtel.net; Web: st-theresa-parish.org. Revs. Jom Joseph, H.G.N.; Luke Krzanowski; Deacon Keith Ellender.
Catechesis Religious Program—Tel: 337-583-4800. Angie Clark, D.R.E. Students 395.

VINTON, CALCASIEU PARISH, ST. JOSEPH (1920) Rev. Carlos Garcia Cardona; Deacon Jesse Menard.
Res.: 1502 Industrial St., Vinton, 70668.
Tel: 337-589-7358; Email: stjosephvinton@hotmail.com.
Catechesis Religious Program—Rhonda Guidry, D.R.E. Students 137.

WELSH, JEFFERSON DAVIS PARISH

1—ST. JOSEPH (1941) [JC] (African American)
310 N. Sarah St., Welsh, 70591. Tel: 337-434-3673; Email: stjosephwelsh@gmail.com. Rev. Jude Fernando, T.O.R.
Mission—St. Peter Claver, 400 W. 2nd St., Iowa, Calcasieu Parish 70547. Fax: 337-734-4435.
Catechesis Religious Program—Students 7.

2—OUR LADY OF SEVEN DOLORS (1904) [CEM] [JC]
Tel: 337-734-3446; Email: OLDS@centurytel.net. Rev. Alan P. Trouille; Deacons Richard Hinchee; Wayne Chapman.
Catechesis Religious Program—Rachelle Trahan, D.R.E. Students 242.

WESTLAKE, CALCASIEU PARISH, ST. JOHN BOSCO (1955) Rev. Jenesh Joseph, H.G.N.; Deacons Fred Reed Jr.; Garrett Caraway Jr.; Rev. Michael J. Barras, In Res.
Res.: 1301 Sampson St., Westlake, 70669.
Tel: 337-433-2467; Email: cgcampbell@yahoo.com.
Catechesis Religious Program—Email: bhogan@st.johnboscochurch.com. Barbara Hogan, D.R.E. Students 280.

Chaplains of Public Institutions

LAKE CHARLES. *Lake Charles Memorial Hospital*. Rev. Benignus Lambertus Wego, S.V.D.

SULPHUR. *West Calcasieu Cameron Hospital*. Rev. Michael J. Barras.

Graduate Studies:
Rev.—
Thompson, Dean Brian, Catholic University, Washington, DC, Holy Comforter-St. Cyprian Parish, 1357 E. Capitol St., S.E., Anacostia, Washington, DC 20003.

On Leave:
Rev.—
DesOrmeaux, Scott, P.O. Box 3223, 70602-3223.

Retired:
Rev. Msgrs.—
Dubois, Charles J., (Retired), P.O. Box 1924, 70602
Groth, Ronald, (Retired), 122 New Orleans Ave., Lake Arthur, 70549
Revs.—
Boulet, Marshall, (Retired), 230 Fairway Dr., Crowley, 70526
Harris, Whitney G., (Retired), 233 Dogwood Ct., Canton, MI 48187-3971. Tel: 651-201-1800. Wells Fargo Place, 30 7th St. E., St. Paul, 55101-7804
Mancuso, Henry, (Retired), 858 Kirby St., 70601
Marco, Alfredo, (Retired), #9 Std. Domingo St., Bombon, Camarines Sur Philippines. Tel: 011-63-54-471-65-24
McGrath, Joseph, (Retired), 805 Willow Springs Rd., Sulphur, 70663
Mulanjanany, Augustine, (Retired), 1019A Daoust Dr., Alexandria, 71303
Mullen, Thomas G., (Retired), 15115 Interlachen Dr., Unit 712, Silver Spring, MD 20906-5642. Tel: 301-598-1922; Email: waverlywoods@earthlink.net
Piraro, Don, (Retired), 3905 Kingston St., Box 36, 70605
Poerio, John, (Retired), 3905 Kingston St., 70605
Russi, Fred, (Retired), 3905 Kingston St., 70605
Sedita, Vincent, (Retired), 4411 Monticello St., 70605
Smit, Gerard C., (Retired), 147 W. State St., Apt. 109, Kennett Square, PA 19348. (Non-Active)
Vaughn, Roland G., (Retired), P.O. Box 231, Lacassine, 70650.

Permanent Deacons:
Bertrand, Glen
Bushnell, Joseph
Canelo, Josue, St. Henry Catholic Church, Lake Charles
Caraway, Julius G. Jr., St. John Bosco Church, Westlake
Carr, George K., (Retired), Our Lady Queen of Heaven, LC
Chapman, Norris, (Retired)
Chapman, Wayne, Our Lady of Seven Dolors, Welsh
Deshotel, Dale, St. Joan of Arc, Oberlin; (Chairperson)
DeVille, Erroll Joseph, Sacred Heart of Jesus Catholic Church, Lake Charles
Donahoe, Richard E., St. Martin de Porres Catholic Church, Lake Charles
Eaves, John, St. Paul, Elton
Ellender, Keith, St. Theresa of the Child Jesus, Carlyss
Fontenot, Christopher
Gregory, Chris, Immaculate Conception, Sulphur
Guillory, Michael Paul, St. Paul Catholic Church, Elton
Harmon, Glenn
Hebert, Leo Anthony, St. Theodore Catholic Church, Moss Bluff
Hebert, Patrick, St. Henry Catholic Church, Lake Charles
Hinchee, Richard, Our Lady of Seven Dolors, Welsh
Kirk, Brian, Our Lady Queen of Heaven, Lake Charles
Landry, Dan, (Retired), St. Margaret, Lake Charles
LaPoint, Patrick, Our Lady of Prompt Succor, Sulphur; (Vice-Chairperson)
Lavine, Edward, Sacred Heart, Lake Charles
McNally, Edward, (Retired), Immaculate Conception, Jennings
McNeal, Bennett, Immaculate Conception, Jennings
Menard, Jesse, St. Joseph, Vinton
Menard, Raymond, St. Margaret, LC
Nash, Roy, St. Philip Neri, Kinder
Nixon, Harold, Our Lady Queen of Heaven, Lake Charles
Pousson, Anthony, St. Margaret of Scotland, Lake Charles
Reed, Frederick, (Retired), St. John Bosco, Westlake
Serice, Maurice, (Retired), Our Lady of LaSalette, Sulphur
Soileau, Brian, Camp Karol Retreat Center
Starr, Stephen, St. Raphael Catholic Church, Iowa, LA
Stearns, George, Chancellor & Archivist
Tramel, Michael, St. Lawrence, Jennings
Wagner, Harry E. Jr., (Retired), Immaculate Conception, Sulphur
Weinnig, Albert, St. Joseph Catholic Church, DeRiddler.

INSTITUTIONS LOCATED IN DIOCESE

[A] HIGH SCHOOLS, INTERPAROCHIAL

LAKE CHARLES. *St. Louis Catholic High School*, 1620 Bank St., 70601. Tel: 337-436-7275;
Fax: 337-436-6792; Email: abradley@slchs.org; Web: www.slchs.org. Andrew Bradley, Prin.; Revs. Nathan Long, Rector; Ruben Villarreal, J.C.L., Chap.; Melanie Lejeune, Librarian. Religious Teachers 3; Lay Teachers 47; Students 577.

[B] GENERAL HOSPITALS

LAKE CHARLES. *CHRISTUS Health Southwestern Louisiana* dba CHRISTUS Ochsner St. Patrick Hospital & CHRISTUS Ochsner Lake Area Hospital, 524 Dr. Michael DeBakey Dr., 70601.
Tel: 337-436-2511; Fax: 337-491-7157; Email: joy.huff@christushealth.org; Web: www.christusstpatrick.org. Kevin Holland, CEO; Joy Huff, Vice Pres., Mission Integration; Revs. Brian Madison King, Chap.; Charles Okorougo, Chap.; Sisters Leonie Iweh, D.M.M.M., Chap.; Mary Kamara, Chap.; Ethel Puno, Chap. Sponsored by Christus Health System, Irving, TX. Bed Capacity 318; Sisters 3; Tot Asst. Annually 209,141; Total Staff 1,391.

[C] RETREAT HOUSES

LAKE CHARLES. *St. Charles Center*, 2151 Sam Houston Jones Pkwy., 70611. Tel: 337-855-1232;
Fax: 337-855-9062; Email: michelle.monceaux@lcdiocese.org; Web: www.stcharlescenter.com. Rev. Whitney Miller, Dir.; Deacon Brian Soileau.

[D] SPECIAL RESIDENCES

LAKE CHARLES. *Our Lady Queen of Heaven Manor*, Villa Maria, 3905 Kingston St., 70605.
Tel: 337-478-4780; Fax: 337-474-8822; Email: villamaria@suddenlinkmail.com. Becky See, Dir. Bed Capacity 118; Tot Asst. Annually 65; Total Staff 33; Units 61.

[E] NEWMAN CENTERS

LAKE CHARLES. *Catholic Student Center*, McNeese State University, 221 Aqua Dr., 70605.
Tel: 337-477-1434; Fax: 337-479-2129; Email: nathan.long@lcdiocese.org; Web: www.cowboycatholics.com. Rev. Nathan Long; Sr. Shirley Gobert, S.E.C., Pastoral Assoc.
Center for Catholic Studies, McNeese State University, 221 Aqua Dr., 70605.
Tel: 337-477-1434; Fax: 337-479-2129; Email: nathan.long@lcdiocese.org. Sr. Marirose Rudek, R.S.M., Dir.

[F] HOUSE OF DISCERNMENT

LAKE CHARLES. *Vianney House of Discernment*, 1624 Bank St., 70601. Tel: 337-493-5252; Email: nathan.long@lcdiocese.org. Rev. Nathan Long, Dir.

[G] SOCIAL SERVICE CENTERS

LAKE CHARLES. *Catholic Charities Southwest Louisiana*, 1225 2nd St., 70601. Tel: 337-439-7436; Fax: 337-439-7435; Email: jessica.watson@lcdiocese.org. Sr. Mary Vianney Walsh, R.S.M., Dir. Catholic Charities. Tot Asst. Annually 21,643; Total Staff 4.

[H] MISCELLANEOUS

LAKE CHARLES. *Catholic Daughters of America*, 7506 Cardiff Ave., Baton Rouge, 70808.
Tel: 225-769-0122; Email: conniecda@yahoo.com. Very Rev. Edward J. Richard, M.S., M.S., Chap.
CHRISTUS St. Patrick Foundation dba CHRISTUS Ochsner Southwestern Louisiana Foundation, 524 Doctor Michael DeBakey Dr., 70601.
Tel: 337-430-5353; Fax: 337-430-5352; Email: kay.barnett@christushealth.org; Web: www.christusochsnerswlafoundation.org. Kay Barnett, Exec.
CHRISTUS St. Patrick Home Care,
Tel: 337-395-5600; Email: laurie.jones2@lhcgroup.com. Deloris Parnell, Regl. Admin.
School Food Services of Lake Charles, Inc., 1112 Bilbo St., 70601. Tel: 337-433-9640, Ext. 202;
Fax: 337-433-9685; Email: edrie.durio@lcdiocese.org.
Society of Roman Catholic Church of the Dioceses of Lake Charles, 414 Iris St., 70601.
Tel: 337-439-7400; Email: daniel.torres@lcdiocese.org; Web: www.lcdiocese.org. P.O. Box 3223, 70602-3223. Rev. Msgr. Daniel A. Torres, V.G., Vicar Gen.

RELIGIOUS INSTITUTES OF MEN REPRESENTED IN THE DIOCESE

For further details refer to the corresponding bracketed number in the Religious Institutes of Men or Women section.

[]—*The Herald of Good News* (Odisha, India)—H.G.N.
[]—*Missionaries of Compassion* (Andhra Pradesh, India)—M.C.

[0720]—*The Missionaries of Our Lady of La Salette* (Hartford, CT)—M.S.

[]—*Society of the Divine Word* (Bay Saint Louis, MS)—S.V.D.

RELIGIOUS INSTITUTES OF WOMEN REPRESENTED IN THE DIOCESE

[0470]—*Congregation of the Sisters of Charity of the Incarnate Word, Houston, Texas*—CCVI.

[]—*Daughters of Mary, Mother of Mercy* (Prov. of U.S.A./Canada)—D.M.M.M.

[]—*Religious Sisters of Mercy of Alma* (Alma, MI)—R.S.M.

NECROLOGY

† Melancon, Louis, (Retired), Died Jun. 30, 2018

An asterisk (*) denotes an organization that has established tax-exempt status directly with the IRS and is not covered by the USCCB Group Ruling.

Diocese of Lansing

(Dioecesis Lansingensis)

Most Reverend

EARL A. BOYEA

Bishop of Lansing; ordained May 20, 1978; appointed Auxiliary Bishop of Detroit and Titular Bishop of Siccenna July 22, 2002; consecrated September 13, 2002; appointed Bishop of Lansing February 27, 2008; installed April 29, 2008. *Chancery: 228 N. Walnut St., Lansing, MI 48933.* Tel: 517-342-2452; Fax: 517-342-2505.

Most Reverend

CARL F. MENGELING, D.D., S.T.D.

Retired Bishop of Lansing; ordained May 25, 1957; appointed Bishop of Lansing November 7, 1995; consecrated and installed January 25, 1996; retired February 27, 2008. *Chancery: 228 N. Walnut St., Lansing, MI 48933.* Tel: 517-342-2452; Fax: 517-342-2505.

ESTABLISHED MAY 22, 1937.

Square Miles 6,218.

Canonically Erected August 4, 1937.

Comprises the Counties of Clinton, Eaton, Genesee, Hillsdale, Ingham, Jackson, Lenawee, Livingston, Shiawassee and Washtenaw, in the State of Michigan.

For legal titles of parishes and diocesan institutions, consult the Chancery Office.

Chancery: 228 N. Walnut St., Lansing, MI 48933. Tel: 517-342-2440; Fax: 517-342-2519.

Web: www.dioceseoflansing.org

Email: chancery@dioceseoflansing.org

STATISTICAL OVERVIEW

Personnel	
Bishop	1
Retired Bishops	1
Priests: Diocesan Active in Diocese	79
Priests: Diocesan Active Outside Diocese	7
Priests: Retired, Sick or Absent	65
Number of Diocesan Priests	151
Religious Priests in Diocese	33
Total Priests in Diocese	184
Extern Priests in Diocese	14
Ordinations:	
Diocesan Priests	1
Permanent Deacons in Diocese	128
Total Brothers	3
Total Sisters	419
Parishes	
Parishes	74
With Resident Pastor:	
Resident Diocesan Priests	55
Resident Religious Priests	2
Without Resident Pastor:	
Administered by Priests	9
Pastoral Centers	1
Closed Parishes	5
Professional Ministry Personnel:	
Sisters	7
Lay Ministers	348
Welfare	
Catholic Hospitals	4
Total Assisted	1,953,172
Health Care Centers	3
Total Assisted	30,739
Homes for the Aged	3
Total Assisted	204
Specialized Homes	1
Total Assisted	85
Special Centers for Social Services	9
Total Assisted	286,257
Residential Care of Disabled	1
Total Assisted	65
Educational	
Diocesan Students in Other Seminaries	22
Total Seminarians	22
Colleges and Universities	1
Total Students	2,433
High Schools, Diocesan and Parish	4
Total Students	2,203
High Schools, Private	1
Total Students	35
Elementary Schools, Diocesan and Parish	28
Total Students	5,675
Elementary Schools, Private	5
Total Students	663
Catechesis/Religious Education:	
High School Students	917
Elementary Students	8,241
Total Students under Catholic Instruction	20,189
Teachers in the Diocese:	
Priests	7
Sisters	26
Lay Teachers	714
Vital Statistics	
Receptions into the Church:	
Infant Baptism Totals	1,815
Minor Baptism Totals	157
Adult Baptism Totals	213
Received into Full Communion	339
First Communions	2,086
Confirmations	2,334
Marriages:	
Catholic	451
Interfaith	159
Total Marriages	610
Deaths	1,906
Total Catholic Population	185,580
Total Population	1,813,907

Former Bishops—Most Revs. JOSEPH H. ALBERS, D.D., J.C.D., appt. Titular Bishop of Lunda and Auxiliary to the Archbishop of Cincinnati, Dec. 16, 1929; cons. Dec. 27, 1929; appt. first Bishop of Lansing, Aug. 4, 1937; died Dec. 1, 1965; ALEXANDER M. ZALESKI, D.D., S.S.L., appt. Titular Bishop of Lyrbe and Auxiliary of Detroit, March 28, 1950; cons. May 23, 1950; transferred to Lansing Oct. 7, 1964; acceded to the See Dec. 1, 1965; died May 16, 1975; KENNETH J. POVISH, D.D., appt. Bishop of Crookston, July 28, 1970; cons. Sept. 29, 1970; appt. Bishop of Lansing, Oct. 8, 1975; installed Dec. 11, 1975; retired Nov. 7, 1995; died Sept. 5, 2003; CARL F. MENGELING, D.D., S.T.D., ord. May 25, 1957; appt. Bishop of Lansing Nov. 7, 1995; cons. and installed Jan. 25, 1996; retired Feb. 27, 2008.

Chancery—228 N. Walnut St., Lansing, 48933. Tel: 517-342-2440; Fax: 517-342-2519. (see Diocesan Departments for additional Fax numbers) Office Hours: Mon.-Fri. 8-12 & 1-4:30.Address all communications to this office.

Bishop's Office—228 N. Walnut St., Lansing, 48933. Tel: 517-342-2452; Fax: 517-342-2505. MR. MICHAEL ANDREWS, Chancellor, Tel: 517-342-2454; Rev. Msgr. GEORGE C. MICHALEK, J.C.L., Vice Chancellor, Tel: 517-485-9902; DEBORAH AMATO, Chief of Staff, Tel: 517-342-2512.

Vicar General—Rev. TIMOTHY E. MACDONALD, 606 S. Wisner, Jackson, 49203. Tel: 517-783-2748.

Regional Vicars—Revs. JAMES F. EISELE, Ingham/Eaton/Clinton; ANDREW A. CZAJKOWSKI, Genesee; TIMOTHY E. MACDONALD, Jackson; DANIEL F. WHEELER, Lenawee/Hillsdale; DAVID J. SPEICHER, Livingston; BRENDAN J. WALSH, Washtenaw.

College of Consultors—Most Rev. EARL A. BOYEA; Revs. LOUIS T. EKKA, (India); PAUL E. ERICKSON; JOSEPH J. KRUPP; SHAUN D. LOWERY; TIMOTHY A. NELSON; JONATHAN P. PERROTTA; DAVID M. REAMSNYDER; THOMAS W. THOMPSON, (Retired); TIMOTHY E. MACDONALD; KARL L. PUNG.

Vicar for Charismatic Communities—St. Mary: 10601 Dexter-Pinckney Rd., Pinckney, 48169. Tel: 734-878-3161; Fax: 734-878-2383. Rev. DANIEL J. KOGUT.

Delegate for Consecrated Life—Sr. RITA WENZLICK, O.P., Tel: 517-342-2502.

Ecumenical Officer—Holy Family, 11804 S. Saginaw St., Grand Blanc, 48439. Tel: 810-694-4891; Fax: 810-694-1583. Rev. WILLIAM WEGHER.

Commissions and Councils—

Presbyteral Council—Revs. MATHIAS D. THELEN, Chair; DAVID M. REAMSNYDER, Vice Pres.; DENIS R. SPITZLEY, Corresponding Sec., (Retired).

Board of Education and Catechesis—1514 E. Michigan Ave., Lansing, 48912. Rev. STEVEN M. MATTSON, Pres.

Building Commission—St. John the Evangelist Church: 404 N. Dayton St., Davison, 48423. Rev. ANDREW A. CZAJKOWSKI.

Cursillo—Rev. DAVID B. ROSENBERG, Spiritual Dir., St. Francis Retreat Ctr., 703 E. Main St., Dewitt, 48820. Tel: 517-669-8321.

Finance Council—MR. TOM SMITH, Chm., Tel: 517-377-0866.

Priest Pension Board—Rev. RYAN L. RILEY.

Priests' Assignment Commission—Revs. CHARLES CANOY; JAMES F. EISELE; EDWARD O. FRIDE; JONATHAN P. PERROTTA; ROBERT J. PIENTA; JAMES R. ROLPH; MATHIAS D. THELEN; ERIC C. WEBER; DANIEL J. WESTERMANN.

Diocesan Offices And Departments

Victim Assistance Coordinator—CHERYL WILLIAMS-HECKSEL, LMSW, Tel: 888-308-6252; Email: cwilliamshecksel@dioceseoflansing.org.

Diocesan Archivist—Rev. Msgr. GEORGE C. MICHALEK, J.C.L., 228 N. Walnut St., Lansing, 48933. Tel: 517-342-2540; Fax: 517-342-2544.

Diocesan Mission Office—(Includes Propagation of the Faith, Holy Childhood Assoc., Inter-Parish Sharing) *228 N. Walnut St., Lansing, 48933.* Tel: 517-342-2510; Tel: 517-342-2541; Fax: 517-342-2468; Fax: 517-342-2542. ANN RIVET.

General Counsel—WILLIAM R. BLOOMFIELD, Tel: 517-342-2522.

Human Resources—LISA KUTAS, Dir., Tel: 517-342-2511; Fax: 517-342-2527.

Office of Child & Youth Protection—REBA SOMMER, Coord., Tel: 517-342-2551; Fax: 517-342-2505.

Worship Office—JEREMY PRIEST, Dir., Tel: 517-342-2476.

Worship Commission—Rev. ANTHONY J. STROUSE.

Director of Properties—ALAN OLSEN, Tel: 517-342-2534; Fax: 517-342-2468.

Diocesan Tribunal—

Judicial Vicar—228 N. Walnut St., Lansing, 48933. Tel: 517-342-2560; Fax: 517-342-2561. Rev. DAVID W. HUDGINS, J.C.L. (Address all rogatory commissions to the Diocesan Tribunal).

Adjunct Judicial Vicar—Rev. Msgr. GEORGE C. MICHALEK, J.C.L.; Rev. NATHANIEL J. SOKOL, J.C.L.

Tribunal Judges—Rev. Msgrs. RAYMOND J. GOEHRING, J.C.L.; GEORGE C. MICHALEK, J.C.L.; Revs. DAVID W. HUDGINS, J.C.L.; NATHANIEL J. SOKOL, J.C.L.

Defenders of the Bond—Deacon JOHN M. CAMERON, J.C.L.; Rev. MARK J. RUTHERFORD, J.C.L.

Assessor—LESLIE FLOETER, J.D.

Promoter of Justice—Rev. JAMES P. CONLON.

Court Experts—Rev. GEORGE R. DAISY; ANGELA FOWLER, L.C.S.W.; PAUL JOHNSTON, M.A., M.S.W., LMSW, ACSW.

Notaries—DEBORAH AMBROSE; AVA JO PUNG.

Christian Initiation Advisory Committee—JEREMY PRIEST, Chm., Tel: 517-342-2479.

Faith Magazine—See Miscellaneous Listings: Faith Publishing Service.

Department of Catholic Charities—Deacon JAMES KASPRZAK, Tel: 517-342-2462; Fax: 517-342-2446.

Alcoholism and Other Drugs—Deacon JAMES KASPRZAK, Tel: 517-342-2462.

Catholic Campaign for Human Development—ANN RIVET, Tel: 517-342-2510.

Catholic Relief Services—ANN RIVET, Tel: 517-342-2510.

Courage and Encourage—Rev. STEVEN M. MATTSON, Tel: 517-482-4749.

Marriage and Family Life—RICHARD BUDD, Tel: 517-342-2471.

Natural Family Planning—JENNY INGLES, Tel: 517-342-2587.

Life Justice—JENNY INGLES, Tel: 517-342-2587.

Restorative Justice—Deacon KENNETH PREISS, Tel: 517-342-2451.

Separated & Divorced Ministry—RICHARD BUDD, Tel: 517-342-2471.

Project Rachel (Post-Abortion Counseling)—JENNY INGLES, Tel: 517-342-2587.

Ministry with Persons with Disabilities—Deacon JAMES KASPRZAK, Tel: 517-342-2462.

Catholic Deaf/Hard of Hearing Ministry—Deacon JAMES KASPRZAK, Tel: 517-342-2462.

Diocesan Cemeteries—TIMOTHY BAZANY, Tel: 517-484-2500.

Department of Communication—MICHAEL D. DIEBOLD, Chm., Tel: 517-853-7660; Fax: 517-853-7616.

Department of Education and Catechesis—THOMAS P. MALONEY, Tel: 517-342-2483; Fax: 517-342-2468.

Superintendent of Schools—THOMAS P. MALONEY, Tel: 517-342-2483; Fax: 517-342-2468; SEAN COSTELLO.

Associate Superintendent—RAYMOND RZEPECKI, Tel: 517-342-2481; Fax: 517-342-2468.

Director of Curriculum, Assessment, Instruction—THERESE EDWARDS, Tel: 517-342-2486.

Catechesis—TIMOTHY CARPENTER, Tel: 517-342-2479.

Youth Ministry—BRIAN FLYNN, Tel: 517-342-2584.

Young Adult Ministry—DAWN HAUSMANN, Tel: 517-342-2506.

Campus Ministry—BRIAN FLYNN, Tel: 517-342-2584; KATIE DILLER, Tel: 517-337-9778, Ext. 133.

Department of Finance—GEORGE LANDOLT, Chm. & Finance Officer, Tel: 517-342-2442; Fax: 517-342-2527.

Technology Administrator—ALAN OLSEN, Tel: 517-342-2534; Fax: 517-342-2468; PETER FRAHM, Tel: 517-342-2538.

Department of Formation—Rev. JOHN LINDEN, Chm., Tel: 517-342-2507; Fax: 517-342-2468.

Director of Vocations/Seminarians—Rev. JOHN LINDEN, Tel: 517-342-2507.

Lay Ecclesial Ministry—DEBORAH AMATO, Dir.; BERT SCHOMBERGER, Coord., Tel: 517-342-2521; Tel: 517-304-3521.

Permanent Diaconate—Deacons KENNETH PREISS, Tel: 517-342-2451; RANDAL DESROCHERS, Diaconal Formation, Tel: 517-342-2571.

Priestly Life and Ministry—Rev. KARL L. PUNG, Dir., Tel: 810-229-9863; Fax: 810-220-0730.

Consecrated Vocations—DAWN HAUSMANN, Dir., Tel: 517-342-2506.

New Evangelization—CRAIG POHL, Dir., Tel: 517-342-2509.

Discernment Houses—

Emmaus House—DAWN HAUSMANN, Dir., 228 N. Walnut St., Lansing, 48933. Tel: 517-342-2506.

Father McGiveny House—Rev. WILLIAM A. ASHBAUGH, Dir., St. Thomas the Apostle Church, 530 Elizabeth St., Ann Arbor, 48104. Tel: 734-761-8606.

St. Catherine House—Rev. WILLIAM A. ASHBAUGH, Dir., St. Thomas the Apostle Church, 530 Elizabeth St., Ann Arbor, 48104. Tel: 734-761-8606.

CLERGY, PARISHES, MISSIONS AND PAROCHIAL SCHOOLS

CITY OF LANSING

(INGHAM COUNTY)

1—ST. MARY CATHEDRAL (1866)
219 Seymour, 48933. Tel: 517-484-5331; Fax: 517-484-0475; Email: kpung@stmarylansing.org; Web: stmarylansing.org. Rev. Karl L. Pung; Deacon Joseph Jong; Sr. Joan Meerschaert, O.P., Pastoral Min.
Catechesis Religious Program—Students 37.

2—ST. ANDREW DUNG-LAC (1998) (Vietnamese)
1611 W. Oakland Ave., 48915. Tel: 517-580-7557; Email: kinhvu1611@gmail.com. Rev. Joseph S. Kim.
Catechesis Religious Program—Students 67.

3—ST. CASIMIR (1921)
Mailing Address: 815 Sparrow Ave., 48910-8003. Tel: 517-482-1346; Fax: 517-482-1313; Email: office@stcas.org; Web: www.stcas.org. Rev. William R. Lugger.
Catechesis Religious Program—Students 85.

4—CRISTO REY (1961) (Hispanic)
201 W. Miller Rd., 48911. Tel: 517-394-4639; Email: veronicam@cristoreychurch.org; Web: www.cristoreychurch.org. Rev. Frederick L. Thelen; Deacon Rogelio Alfaro.
Res.: 6121 Rosedale Rd., 48911.
Catechesis Religious Program—Students 194.

5—ST. GERARD (Delta Township, Eaton Co.) (1958) [JC]
4437 W. Willow Hwy., 48917. Tel: 517-323-2379; Email: bpdroste@stgerard.org; Web: stgerard.org. Rev. John P. Klein; Vincent Richardson; Deacon Jim Corder.
School—St. Gerard School, (Grades PreK-8), 4433 W. Willow Hwy., 48917. Tel: 517-321-6126; Fax: 517-323-8046; Email: spiecuch@stgerardlansing.org; Web: stgerardlansing.org. Michelle Piecuch, Prin. Lay Teachers 30; Students 484.
Catechesis Religious Program—Tel: 517-321-4179. Students 330.

6—IMMACULATE HEART OF MARY (1949)
3815 S. Cedar, 48910. Tel: 517-393-3030; Email: marshb@ihmlansing.org. Revs. John Byers; George R. Daisy, In Res.; Deacons William Fudge III; John M. Cameron, J.C.L.
School—Immaculate Heart of Mary School, (Grades PreK-8), 3830 Rosemont St., 48910-4525. Tel: 517-882-6631; Fax: 517-882-5536; Email: wilcoxc@ihmlansing.org; Web: www.ihmlansing.org. Karen Hicks, Prin. Lay Teachers 12; Students 180.
Catechesis Religious Program—Tel: 517-393-3033. Students 67.

7—RESURRECTION (1922)
1505 E. Michigan Ave., 48912. Tel: 517-482-4749; Email: info@corlansing.org; Web: www.corlansing.org. Mailing Address: 1514 E. Michigan Ave., 48912-2221. Rev. Steven M. Mattson.
Res.: 1715 E. Jerome St., 48912.
School—Resurrection School, (Grades PreK-8), 1527 E. Michigan Ave., 48912. Tel: 517-487-0439; Fax: 517-487-3198; Email: school@resurrectionlansing.org; Web: resurrectionlansing.org. Jacob Allstott, Prin. Clergy/Religious Teachers 1; Lay Teachers 16; Sisters 2; Students 157; Librarians 1.
Catechesis Religious Program—Email: aamburn@corlansing.org; Email: jjong@corlansing.org. Angie Amburn, Dir. Faith Formation; Jay Jong, Faith Formation. Students 34.

8—ST. THERESE (1949) [CEM]
102 W. Randolph St., 48906. Tel: 517-487-3749; Fax: 517-487-3755; Email: secretary@sttherese.org; Web: www.sttherese.org. Rev. John M. Fain; Deacon David Borzenski.
Catechesis Religious Program—Tel: 517-487-3730. Ms. Patricia Droste, D.R.E. Students 50.

OUTSIDE THE CITY OF LANSING

ADRIAN, LENAWEE CO.

1—ST. JOSEPH (1863) [CEM] Merged with St. Mary of Good Counsel to form Holy Family Parish Adrian.

2—HOLY FAMILY PARISH ADRIAN (1853) [CEM]
305 Division St., Adrian, 49221. Tel: 517-263-4681; Email: office@stmarysadrian.com; Web: www.holyfamilyadrian.com. Revs. John J. Loughran, O.S.F.S.; Timothy McIntire, O.S.F.S., Parochial Vicar; Deacon Richard Bayes Jr., (Sr. Status).
Catechesis Religious Program—
Tel: 517-263-4681, Ext. 207; Email: discipleship@stmarysadrian.com. Katie Love, D.R.E. Students 126.
St. Mary of Good Counsel, (Worship Site).
ST. JOSEPH ORATORY, 415 Ormsby St., Adrian, OH 49221.

ANN ARBOR, WASHTENAW CO.

1—CHRIST THE KING PARISH ANN ARBOR (1981)
4000 Ave Maria Dr., Ann Arbor, 48105.
Tel: 734-665-5040; Fax: 734-663-3735; Email: kbogan@ctkcc.net; Web: www.ctkcc.net. Rev. Edward O. Fride; Deacons Daniel R. Foley; Gerald P. Holowicki; Louis J. Russello, Pastoral Assoc.; Larry Randolph, Pastoral Assoc.; John Ozog; Wayne Slomiany.
Catechesis Religious Program—Tel: 734-929-0977; Email: jhoving@ctkcc.net. Students 401.

2—ST. FRANCIS OF ASSISI PARISH ANN ARBOR (1950) [CEM]
2250 E. Stadium Blvd., Ann Arbor, 48104.
Tel: 734-821-2100; Fax: 734-821-2102; Email: parishoffice@stfrancisa2.org; Web: www.stfrancisa2.com. Mailing Address: 2150 Frieze Ave., Ann Arbor, 48104. Revs. James P. Conlon; Shaun D. Lowery; Terrence J. Dumas, In Res.; Deacons Richard Badics; Gene Leger
St. Francis of Assisi Catholic Church; St. Francis of Assisi Catholic Parish; St. Francis of Assisi Catholic Church Educational Trust Fund; St. Francis of Assisi Catholic School; St. Francis of Assisi Catholic School Tuition Assistance Fund
School—St. Francis of Assisi School, (Grades PreK-8), 2270 E. Stadium Blvd., Ann Arbor, 48104.
Tel: 734-821-2200; Fax: 734-821-2202; Email: school@stfrancisaa.org; Web: www.stfrancisa2.com/school/. Julia Pritzel, Prin. Clergy/Religious Teachers 1; Lay Teachers 31; Students 412; Pre-K Enrollment 26.
Catechesis Religious Program—Tel: 734-821-2132; Tel: 734-821-2125; Email: ward@stfrancisa2.org; Email: mlucas@stfrancisa2.org. Ellen Ward, D.R.E.; Marty Lucas, RCIA Coord. Students 657.

3—ST. MARY STUDENT PARISH ANN ARBOR (1915)
Serving students, faculty, and staff at the University of Michigan.
331 Thompson St., Ann Arbor, 48104-2295.
Tel: 734-663-0557, Ext. 232; Email: stmarys@umich.edu; Web: www.stmarystudentparish.org. Revs. James Gartland, S.J., Admin.; Dennis T. Dillon, S.J.; Joseph F. Wagner, S.J., Campus Min.; Patrick Casey, S.J., Pastoral Assoc.; Deacon Romolo J. Leone, Pastoral Assoc.; Jennifer Line, Campus Min.; Allison Reis, Campus Min.; Brian Cerabona, Campus Min.; Julie Mussio, Marriage Prep Coord.; Lori Feiler, Family Min. Prog. Coord.; Amy Ketner, Hispanic/Latino Min. Coord.; Kristin Berger, Music Coord.; Danielle Kopin, Stewardship Dir.; Alicia Frenette, Controller; Lanette Mele, Office Mgr. & Liturgy Asst.
Catechesis Religious Program—Rita Zyber, RCIA Coord. Students 371.

4—ST. PATRICK PARISH ANN ARBOR (1831) [CEM]
5671 Whitmore Lake Rd., Ann Arbor, 48105.
Tel: 734-662-8141; Email: info@stpatricka2.org; Web: www.stpatricka2.org. Rev. Thomas Wasilewski; Deacon Frank Joseph Papp.
Catechesis Religious Program—Students 49.

5—ST. THOMAS THE APOSTLE PARISH ANN ARBOR (1835) [CEM]
530 Elizabeth St., Ann Arbor, 48104.
Tel: 734-761-8606; Fax: 734-997-8432; Email: info@stthomasannarbor.org; Web: www.sta2.org. Revs. William A. Ashbaugh; Anthony Smela; Deacons James Miles; Warren Hecht; Thomas Loewe; Kathy Grisdela, Business Mgr.
School—St. Thomas the Apostle School, (Grades PreK-8), 540 Elizabeth St., Ann Arbor, 48104.
Tel: 734-769-0911; Fax: 734-769-9078; Email:

kgrisdela@sta2.org. Tim DiLaura, Prin. Lay Teachers 19; Students 168.
Catechesis Religious Program—Email: mpope@sta2.org. Monica Pope, Dir. Faith Formation. Students 125.
BELLEVUE, EATON CO., ST. ANN (1923) Merged with and became an Oratory of St. Mary, Charlotte.
BLISSFIELD, LENAWEE CO., ST. PETER THE APOSTLE (1910) Merged with St. Alphonsus Parish, Deerfield to form Light of Christ Parish, Deerfield.
BRIGHTON, LIVINGSTON CO.
1—HOLY SPIRIT PARISH BRIGHTON (1979)
9565 Musch Rd., Brighton, 48116. Tel: 810-231-9199; Email: parishoffice@holyspiritrcs.org; Web: www.hsrcc.net. Rev. John George Rocus; Deacon Gerald Brennan.
School—Holy Spirit School, (Grades PreK-8), 9565 Musch Rd., Brighton, 48116. Tel: 810-900-9050; Email: office@holyspiritrcs.org; Web: wps.holyspiritrcs.org. Christine Blandino, Prin. Lay Teachers 6; Students 79.
Catechesis Religious Program—
Tel: 810-231-9199, Ext. 209; Email: mbastian@holyspiritrcs.org. Mary Anne Bastian, D.R.E. Students 37.
2—ST. MARY MAGDALEN PARISH BRIGHTON (1993)
2201 S. Old U.S. 23 Hwy., Brighton, 48114.
Tel: 810-229-8624; Fax: 810-229-6471; Email: pastor1@saintmarymagdalen.org; Web: www.saintmarymagdalen.org. Rev. David F. Howell; Deacons H. David Scharf; James M. Chevalier; Gary W. Prise; P. Devon Wolfe.
Catechesis Religious Program—Email: dre1@saintmarymagdalen.org. Roxanne Hundsrucker, D.R.E. Students 810.
3—ST. PATRICK PARISH BRIGHTON (1832) [CEM] (Irish)
711 Rickett Rd., Brighton, 48116. Tel: 810-229-9863; Fax: 810-229-4221; Email: lynn@stpatchurch.org; Web: www.stpatchurch.org. Revs. Mathias D. Thelen; Joseph Campbell, Parochial Vicar; Deacons Michael Gilbert; David Lawrence; Patrick A. McDonald; Tom Rea; Anne Guminik, Pastoral Min./Coord.; Stephen Royal, Pastoral Min.; H. William Smeal, Pastoral Min.
Res.: 129 Becker, Brighton, 48116-9863.
School—St. Patrick School, (Grades PreK-8), 1001 Orndorf Dr., Brighton, 48116. Tel: 810-229-7946; Fax: 810-229-6206; Email: principal@stpatschool.org; Web: www.stpatschool.org. Jeanine Kenny, Prin. Lay Teachers 24; Students 432; Unique Clergy / Religious Teachers.
Catechesis Religious Program—710 Rickett Rd., Brighton, 48116. Tel: 810-229-4221; Email: khoover@stpatchurch.org. Kurt Hoover, D.R.E. Students 465.
BROOKLYN, LENAWEE CO., ST. JOSEPH SHRINE (Irish Hills) (1854) [CEM]
8743 U.S. 12, Brooklyn, 49230. Tel: 517-467-2183; Email: sjshrine@frontiernet.net; Web: www.stjosephbrooklynmi.com. Rev. Robert J. Pienta; Deacon Gene Hausmann.
Catechesis Religious Program—Tel: 517-467-2106; Email: faithformationsjs@gmail.com. Jill Page, D.R.E. Students 12.
BURTON, GENESEE CO.
1—BLESSED SACRAMENT (1957) Merged with and became an Oratory of St. John the Evangelist, Davison.
2—HOLY REDEEMER (1940)
1227 E. Bristol Rd., Burton, 48529.
Tel: 810-743-3050; Email: kbeamer.hrc@gmail.com; Web: holyredeemerburton.org. Rev. Steven D. Anderson; Deacon Kenneth Preiss.
Catechesis Religious Program—Tel: 810-742-9460. Paul Schlegelmilch, D.R.E./Pastoral Assoc.; Emily Arthur, Adult Faith Formation/RCIA; David Schmit, Music & Youth Coord.; Rafael Urgino, Dir. Evangelization/Formation. Students 250.
CHARLOTTE, EATON CO., ST. MARY (1868)
807 St. Mary Blvd., Charlotte, 48813.
Tel: 517-543-4319; Email: parishoffice@stmarycharlotte.org; Web: www.stmarycharlotte.org. Rev. Dwight M. Ezop; Deacon Thomas Fogle.
School—St. Mary School, (Grades K-8), 905 St. Mary Blvd., Charlotte, 48813. Tel: 517-543-3460; Email: mwildern@stmarycharlotte.org; Web: stmarycharlotte.org. Amanda Wildern, Prin. Lay Teachers 8; Students 113.
ST. ANN ORATORY (1923) 312 S. Main St., Bellevue, 49021.
CHELSEA, WASHTENAW CO., ST. MARY PARISH CHELSEA (1845) [CEM] [JC]
14200 E. Old U.S. Hwy. 12, Chelsea, 48118.
Tel: 734-475-7561; Email: smcch@aol.com; Web: stmarychelsea.org. Very Rev. William J. Turner; Deacons Thomas Franklin; D. Michael Martin.
Catechesis Religious Program—Tel: 734-475-8164; Fax: 734-475-5835. Students 453.
CLARKLAKE, JACKSON CO., ST. RITA (1916) [JC]
10516 Hayes Rd., Clarklake, 49234.
Tel: 517-592-5470; Fax: 517-592-3779; Email: stritasclarklake@gmail.com; Web: www.stritacatholicparish.com. Rev. Thomas J. Helfrich, O.S.F.S.; Deacons Louis Weitzel; Christopher Vida.
Res.: 10720 Hayes Rd., Clarklake, 49234.
Catechesis Religious Program—Tel: 517-592-5718; Email: louannealber@gmail.com. Louanne Alber, D.R.E. Students 127.
CLIO, GENESEE CO., SS. CHARLES AND HELENA (1953)
230 E. Vienna St., Clio, 48420-1423.
Tel: 810-686-9861; Email: parishssch@catholicweb.com. Rev. Kenneth F. Coughlin; Deacon Raymond Ellingson.
CONCORD, JACKSON CO., ST. CATHERINE LABOURE (1953)
211 Harmon Ave., Concord, 49237. Tel: 517-524-7578 ; Fax: 517-524-7518; Email: stcatherine92@yahoo.com; Web: www.stcatherinelaboureconcord.org. Rev. Timothy D. Krzyzaniak; Deacon Thomas Arehart.
Res.: 312 Kryst St., Concord, 49237.
Catechesis Religious Program—Leslie Reagle, D.R.E. Students 23.
DAVISON, GENESEE CO., ST. JOHN THE EVANGELIST (1871) [CEM]
404 N. Dayton St., Davison, 48423-1397.
Tel: 810-653-2377; Fax: 810-658-1123; Email: lmiles@stjohndavison.org; Email: sschroeder@stjohndavison.org; Web: www.stjohndavison.org. Revs. Andrew A. Czajkowski; John Machiorlatti, Parochial Vicar; Deacon Dan Fairweather.
Rectory—316 N. Dayton St., Davison, 48423.
Catechesis Religious Program—505 N. Dayton, Davison, 48423. Laurie Miles, D.R.E.; Elaine Ouellette, D.R.E.; Denise Fabian, Coord. Middle School Ministry; Becky Beck, Coord. Youth Min. Students 397.
BLESSED SACRAMENT ORATORY (1957) 6340 Roberta St., Burton, 48509.
DEWITT, CLINTON CO., ST. JUDE (1971)
409 Wilson St., De Witt, 48820. Rev. Robert L. Irish.
Res.: 414 N. Bridge St., De Witt, 48820.
Tel: 517-669-8335; Email: robstrouse@stjudedewitt.com.
Catechesis Religious Program—Tel: 517-669-8341. Students 354.
DEERFIELD, LENAWEE CO.
1—LIGHT OF CHRIST PARISH (2010)
222 Carey St., Deerfield, 49238. Tel: 517-447-3500; Email: lightofchristparish@gmail.com. Rev. Jeffrey A. Poll.
St. Peter the Apostle, (Worship Site) 309 S. Lane, Blissfield, 49228-1244. Tel: 517-486-2156; Fax: 517-486-2157.
Catechesis Religious Program—Email: deannabdre@gmail.com. Deanna Burke, D.R.E. Students 97.
2—ST. ALPHONSUS, Merged with St. Peter the Apostle Parish, Blissfield, to form Light of Christ Parish, Deerfield.
DEXTER, WASHTENAW CO., ST. JOSEPH PARISH DEXTER (1840) [CEM]
6805 Mast Rd., Dexter, 48130. Tel: 734-426-8483; Fax: 734-426-6451; Email: info@stjos.com; Web: www.stjos.com. Mailing Address: 3430 Dover St., Dexter, 48130. Rev. Brendan J. Walsh; Deacons Romolo Leone; Randal Desrochers.
Catechesis Religious Program—Tel: 734-426-2674; Email: michelle_hochrein@stjos.com. Michelle Horchrein, D.R.E. Students 306.
DURAND, SHIAWASSEE CO., ST. MARY & ST. JOSEPH (1900)
700 Columbia Dr., Durand, 48429. Tel: 855-288-6701 ; Email: stmarydurand@gmail.com; Web: stmarystjoseph.org. Rev. Daniel J. Westermann, Admin.
Catechesis Religious Program—Email: smsjdre@gmail.com. Robin Doyle, D.R.E. Students 25.
ST. JOSEPH ORATORY, 9450 Duffield Rd., Gaines, 48436.
EAST LANSING, INGHAM CO.
1—ST. JOHN THE EVANGELIST CHURCH AND STUDENT CENTER (1958) Merged with and became an Oratory of St. Thomas Aquinas, East Lansing.
2—ST. THOMAS AQUINAS (1940)
955 Alton Rd., East Lansing, 48823.
Tel: 517-351-7215; Fax: 517-351-7271; Email: jderengoski@elcatholics.org; Web: www.elcatholics.org. Revs. Gordon P. Reigle; Gerald Ploof, Sacramental Asst., (Retired); Gary K. Koenigsknecht, Pastoral Assoc.; Deacons David Drayton; James Kasprzak; David Zygmontowicz; Ms. Alexandra Darley, Music Min.; Katie Diller, Dir. Campus Ministry; Denise Waytes, Dir. Liturgy; Denise Zakerski, Communications Mgr.; Keith Tharp, Dir. Admin.; Judy Crabtree, Accountant; Joy Derengoski, Admin. Asst.; Josh Hamilton, Youth Min.; Joe Reis, Campus Min.; Pete Ries, RCIA Coord.; Dian Silvey, Formation Asst.; Al Weilbaecher, Adult Faith Formation.
Rectory—987 Longfellow Dr., East Lansing, 48823.
School—St. Thomas Aquinas School, (Grades PreK-8), 915 Alton Rd., East Lansing, 48823.
Tel: 517-332-0813; Fax: 517-332-9490; Email: mclinton@elcatholics.org; Email: mkrusky@elcatholics.org. Meghan Loughlin-Krusky, Prin.; Kerri Wilcox, Admin.; MaryJo Lounds, Business Mgr.; Marilyn Clinton, Sec.; Kathleen Mayotte, Librarian. Lay Teachers 26; Students 350.
Catechesis Religious Program—Email: dlewis@elcatholics.org. Debra Lewis, D.R.E. Students 359.
ST. JOHN THE EVANGELIST CHURCH AND STUDENT CENTER (1958) 327 M.A.C., East Lansing, 48823. (East Lansing).
EATON RAPIDS, EATON CO., ST. PETER (1891)
515 E. Knight St., Eaton Rapids, 48827.
Tel: 517-663-4735; Email: spceatonrapidsoffice@gmail.com; Web: www.spceatonrapids.org. Rev. George Puthenpeedika.
Catechesis Religious Program—Email: spceatonrapidsfaithformation@gmail.com. Jessica Schaub, D.R.E. Students 78.
FENTON, GENESEE CO., ST. JOHN THE EVANGELIST (1843) [CEM 2]
600 N. Adelaide St., Fenton, 48430.
Tel: 810-629-2251; Email: mfrench@stjohnfenton.org; Web: www.stjohnfenton.org. Revs. Robert F. Copeland; Ryan L. Riley; Deacons Terry Carsten, Email: terrycars10@aol.com; Daniel Medich.
School—St. John the Evangelist School, (Grades PreK-8), 514 Lincoln St., Fenton, 48430.
Tel: 810-629-6551; Fax: 810-629-2213; Email: rjodway@stjohnfenton.com; Web: www.stjohnfenton.com. Rosanne Jodway, Prin. Lay Teachers 15; Students 300.
Catechesis Religious Program—Tel: 810-629-1850; Email: annie@stjohnfenton.org. Annie Kitching, D.R.E. Students 393.
FLINT, GENESEE CO.
1—CHRIST THE KING (1929) (African American)
1811 Seymour Ave., Flint, 48503. Tel: 810-233-0402; Fax: 810-233-0466; Email: ccatholic@att.net. Rev. Philip Schmitter.
Rectory—1832 Seymour Ave., Flint, 48503.
Catechesis Religious Program—Suzanne Kelly, D.R.E. Students 10.
2—HOLY ROSARY (1951)
5199 Richfield Rd., Flint, 48506. Tel: 810-736-4040; Fax: 810-736-1064; Email: holyrosaryflint@yahoo.com; Web: holyrosaryflint.com. Rev. Roy Horning.
Res.: 3166 Mac Ave., Flint, 48506.
School—Holy Rosary School, (Grades K-8), 5199 Richfield Rd., Flint, 48506. Tel: 810-736-4220; Email: kkallas@holyrosarycatholic.com; Web: holyrosaryflint.org. Mark Callahan, Prin. Lay Teachers 5; Students 57.
Catechesis Religious Program—Mrs. Pamela Sneller, D.R.E. Students 89.
3—ST. JOHN VIANNEY (1941)
2415 Bagley St., Flint, 48504-4613.
Tel: 810-235-1812; Fax: 810-235-4911; Email: stjohnvianney@comcast.net; Web: www.flintcatholic.org. Revs. Thomas Firestone; James V. Mangan, Parochial VIcar; Paul Joseph Donnelly; James R. Rolph, Chap.; Mrs. Melinda Holm, Business Mgr.
School—St. John Vianney School, (Grades PreK-8), 2319 Bagley St., Flint, 48504. Tel: 810-235-5687; Fax: 810-235-2811; Email: business@sjvkids.org; Web: www.sjvkids.org. Theresa Marshall, Prin. Lay Teachers 11; Students 150; Total Staff 7.
Catechesis Religious Program—Email: sjvyouthgroup@yahoo.com. Maureen Kelsey, D.R.E. Students 75.
ST. MARY ORATORY, 2500 N. Franklin, Flint, 48506. Tel: 810-232-4012.
ST. MICHAEL ORATORY, 609 E. Fifth Ave., Flint, 48503.
4—ST. MATTHEW (1911) Merged with and became an oratory of St. John Vianney, Flint.
706 Beach St., Flint, 48502. Tel: 810-232-0880; Email: stmatthew@flintcatholic.org. Mailing Address: 2415 Bagley St, Flint, 48504. Revs. Thomas M. Firestone; James V. Mangan, Parochial Vicar; Mrs. Melinda Holm, Business Mgr.
5—OUR LADY OF GUADALUPE (1957) (Latino)
G-2316 W. Coldwater Rd., Flint, 48505.
Tel: 810-787-5701; Email: ologflint@gmail.com. Rev. Paul Joseph Donnelly, Parochial Vicar.
Catechesis Religious Program—Students 111.
6—ST. PIUS X (1955)
G-3139 Hogarth Ave., Flint, 48532.
Tel: 810-235-8574; Fax: 810-235-2675; Email: spxparish@gmail.com; Web: www.spxparish.com. Rev. Anthony J. Strouse; Deacon David Jansen.
School—St. Pius X School, (Grades PreK-8),
Tel: 810-235-8572; Email: principal@stpiusxcatholic.org; Web: spxes.schoolwires.net. Lay Teachers 13; Students 160.
FLUSHING, GENESEE CO., ST. ROBERT (1875) [CEM]
310 N. Cherry St., Flushing, 48433.
Tel: 810-659-2501; Email: info.strobert@gmail.com;

Web: www.strobertparish.org. Revs. Jonathan P. Perrotta; Anthony Brooks, Parochial Vicar; Deacon Richard Rymar.
School—St. Robert School, (Grades PreK-8), 214 E. Henry, Flushing, 48433. Tel: 810-659-2503; Fax: 810-659-4002; Email: srsoffice@aol.com; Web: www.strobertschool.com. Matthew Ralbusky, Prin. Lay Teachers 15; Students 224.
Catechesis Religious Program—Tel: 810-659-8556; Email: hturchi@strobertschool.com. Hannah Turchi, D.R.E. Students 343.

FOWLER, CLINTON CO., MOST HOLY TRINITY (1881) [CEM] (German)
545 N. Maple St., Fowler, 48835. Tel: 989-593-2162; Email: office@mhtparish.com. Rev. Dennis J. Howard.
School—Most Holy Trinity School, (Grades 1-8), 11144 Kent St., Fowler, 48835. Tel: 517-593-2616; Fax: 989-593-2801; Email: principal@mhtparish.com. Anne K. Hufnagel, Prin. Lay Teachers 5; Students 96.
Catechesis Religious Program—Tel: 989-593-3174; Email: mhtdre@gmail.com. Paul Fahey, D.R.E. Students 225.

FOWLERVILLE, LIVINGSTON CO., ST. AGNES PARISH FOWLERVILLE (1891) [CEM 2]
855 E. Grand River Ave., Fowlerville, 48836. Tel: 517-223-8684; Fax: 517-223-0813; Email: stagnesfowlerville@sbcglobal.net; Web: stagnesmi.weconnect.com. Rev. Nathaniel J. Sokol, J.C.L.; Deacons Roger Cahaney; Peter Guditas.
Catechesis Religious Program—Email: msheridandre@gmail.com. Marie Sheridan, D.R.E. Students 263.

GAINES, GENESSEE CO., ST. JOSEPH (1871) [CEM] Merged with and became an Oratory of St. Mary, Durand, MI.

GRAND BLANC, GENESEE CO.
1—HOLY FAMILY (1946)
11804 S. Saginaw St., Grand Blanc, 48439. Tel: 810-694-4891; Email: holyfamily@hfgb.org; Web: hfgb.org. Revs. Joseph J. Krupp; Peter Lawrence, P.V., Parochial Vicar.
School—Holy Family School, (Grades PreK-8), 215 Orchard St., Grand Blanc, 48439. Tel: 810-694-9072; Fax: 810-694-9405; Email: info@hfsgb.org; Web: hfsgb.org. Theresa Purcell, Prin. Clergy/Religious Teachers 1; Lay Teachers 25; Students 456.
Catechesis Religious Program—Tel: 810-694-9072, Ext. 101; Email: jgravel@hfgb.org. Jan Gravel, D.R.E. Students 208.
2—ST. MARK THE EVANGELIST (1978)
7296 Gale Rd., Grand Blanc, 48439. Tel: 810-636-2216; Email: sgriffith@stmarkgoodrich.org; Web: www.stmarkgoodrich.org. Revs. Joseph J. Krupp; Peter Lawrence, P.V., Parochial Vicar; Deacon Ronald Kenney.
Catechesis Religious Program—Email: stmarkdff@hotmail.com. Deacon Ronald Kenney, D.R.E. Students 21.

GRAND LEDGE, EATON CO., ST. MICHAEL (1901)
345 Edwards St., Grand Ledge, 48837. Tel: 517-627-8493; Fax: 517-627-1289; Email: terimarshall@stmichaelgl.org; Web: www.stmichaelgl.org. Rev. James F. Eisele.
Res.: 405 Edwards St., Grand Ledge, 48837.
School—St. Michael School, (Grades PreK-8), 325 Edwards St., Grand Ledge, 48837. Tel: 517-627-2167; Email: lauriecathcart@stmichaelgl.org. Laurie Cathcart, Prin. Lay Teachers 9; Students 131; Librarians/Aides 3.
Catechesis Religious Program—Email: jennifernelson@stmichaelgl.org. Lay Teachers 11; Students 99.

HILLSDALE, HILLSDALE CO., ST. ANTHONY (1853) [CEM]
11 N. Broad St., Hillsdale, 49242. Tel: 517-437-3305; Email: st.anthonycatholicchurch@yahoo.com; Web: stanthonyhillsdale.com. Rev. David M. Reamsnyder, Parochial Admin.
Catechesis Religious Program—Tel: 517-437-2777. Students 152.

HOWELL, LIVINGSTON CO.
1—ST. AUGUSTINE PARISH HOWELL (1843) [CEM] (Quasi Parish)
6481 Faussett Rd., Howell, 48855. Tel: 517-546-9807; Email: st.augustinechurch@att.net; Web: www.staugustinehowell.com. Rev. Gregg Pleiness; Deacons William Sirl; Jeffrey Southerland.
Res.: 8011 Faussett Rd., Fenton, 48430.
Parish House—Howell. Tel: 810-750-0354.
Catechesis Religious Program—Donna Griffin, D.R.E. Students 66.
2—ST. JOHN THE BAPTIST PARISH HOWELL (1843) [CEM] (Irish—German)
2099 N. Hacker Rd., Howell, 48855. Tel: 517-546-7200; Email: fgeorge@stjohnhowell.com; Web: www.stjohnhowell.com. Rev. Francis M. George; Deacons David Piggot; William Russell.
Res.: 1951 N. Hacker Rd., Howell, 48855.
Catechesis Religious Program—Email: ksmall@stjohnhowell.com. KIm Kaye-Small, D.R.E. Students 383.
3—ST. JOSEPH PARISH HOWELL (1888) [CEM]
440 E. Washington St., Howell, 48843. Tel: 517-546-0090; Fax: 517-546-3126; Email: michelle@stjosephhowell.com; Web: www.stjosephhowell.com. Revs. David J. Speicher; Prabhu Lakra, Parochial Vicar; Deacons Endre Doran; Frank Wines Sr., D.R.E.; Ray Kunik.
School—St. Joseph Catholic School, (Grades PreK-8), 425 E. Washington St., Howell, 48843. Tel: 517-546-0090, Ext. 200; Fax: 517-546-8939; Email: rhornby@stjosephhowell.com; Email: amsmullen@stjosephhowell.com. Ms. Renee Hornby, Prin. Lay Teachers 10; Students 175.
Catechesis Religious Program—Tel: 517-546-0090, Ext. 400; Email: deaconfrank@stjosephhowell.com. Students 175.

HUDSON, LENAWEE CO., SACRED HEART (1846) [CEM]
207 S. Market St., Hudson, 49247. Tel: 517-448-3811; Email: info@sacredhearthudson.org. Rev. Todd W. Koenigsknecht, Admin.; Deacon John Amthor.
School—Sacred Heart School, (Grades K-6), Tel: 517-448-6405; Email: aatkin@sacredhearthudson.org; Web: www.sacredhearthudson.org. Anne Atkin, Prin. Lay Teachers 5; Preschool 30; Students 43.
Catechesis Religious Program—Web: www.sacredhearthudson.org/catechism. Students 55.

JACKSON, JACKSON CO.
1—ST. JOHN THE EVANGELIST (1856) [CEM] [JC]
711 N. Francis St., Jackson, 49201. Tel: 517-784-0553; Email: info@stjohnjackson.org; Web: www.stjohnjackson.org. Rev. Charles Canoy; Deacons Albert Krieger; Michael McCormick; David Etters.
School—St. John the Evangelist School, (Grades PreSchool-6), 405 E. North St., Jackson, 49202. Tel: 517-784-1714; Fax: 517-788-5382; Email: tklavon@myjacs.org; Web: www.jcsstjohn.org/. Kristi Blair, Prin. Lay Teachers 19; Students 208.
Catechesis Religious Program—Email: todd@saintjohnjackson.org. Todd Gale, D.R.E. St. Joseph & St. John joint CCD program. Students 757.
ST. JOSEPH THE WORKER (1902) 705 N. Waterloo Ave., Jackson, 49202.
2—ST. MARY STAR OF THE SEA (1881)
120 E. Wesley St., Jackson, 49201. Tel: 517-784-7184; Email: suzannestmarys@gmail.com; Web: www.stmaryjackson.com. Revs. Timothy A. Nelson; Richard Eberle, O.S.F.S., In Res.; Deacons Carol Franssen; Vincent C. Genco; Matthew Shannon.
Res.: 301 S. Mechanic St., Jackson, 49201.
School—St. Mary Star of the Sea School, (Grades PreK-6), 116 E. Wesley St., Jackson, 49201. Tel: 517-784-8811; Fax: 517-788-3425; Email: stmaryschool@myjacs.org. Matthew Berkemeier, Prin. Lay Teachers 8; Students 157.
Catechesis Religious Program—Tel: 517-788-6153; Email: stmaryjacksondre@tds.net. Students 120.
ST. STANISLAUS KOSTA ORATORY, 608 S. Elm Ave., Jackson, 49203.
3—QUEEN OF THE MIRACULOUS MEDAL (1934)
606 S. Wisner, Jackson, 49203. Tel: 517-783-2748; Email: jlienhart@queenschurch.com. Rev. Timothy E. MacDonald; Deacons Jack Kowalski; Patrick Gorczyca.
School—Queen of the Miraculous Medal School, (Grades K-6), 811 S. Wisner, Jackson, 49203. Tel: 517-782-2664; Fax: 517-782-3570; Email: lhartley@myjacs.org. Elizabeth Hartley, Prin. Lay Teachers 21; Students 270.
Catechesis Religious Program—Students 102.

LAINGSBURG, SHIAWASSEE CO., ST. ISIDORE (1902) [CEM]
310 Crum St., Laingsburg, 48848. Tel: 517-651-6722; Email: parishhq1@juno.com; Web: stisidorechurch.org. Rev. Robert Crowley Bacik.
Catechesis Religious Program—Email: marystevens@stisidorechurch.org. Mary Stevens, D.R.E. Students 60.

LESLIE, INGHAM CO., SS. CORNELIUS AND CYPRIAN (Bunker Hill) (1863) [CEM] Merged with St. James, Mason to form the Catholic Community of Saints James, Cornelius & Cyprian.

MANCHESTER, WASHTENAW CO., ST. MARY PARISH MANCHESTER (1871) [CEM]
210 W. Main St., P.O. Box 249, Manchester, 48158. Tel: 734-428-8811; Email: stmarymanchester@gmail.com; Web: stmarymanchester.org. Rev. Bosco Padamattummal, (India) Parochial Admin.; Deacon R. Dennis Walters.
Catechesis Religious Program—Students 61.

MANITOU BEACH, LENAWEE CO., ST. MARY ON THE LAKE (1956)
450 Manitou Rd., Manitou Beach, 49253. Tel: 517-547-7496; Email: office@stmarymanitoubeach.org; Web: www.saintmarymanitoubeach.org. Rev. Todd W. Koenigsknecht, Admin.; Deacon John Amthor, Pastoral Assoc.
Catechesis Religious Program—Tel: 734-904-0637; Email: deaconjohn@sacredhearthudson.org. Students 27.

MASON, INGHAM CO., THE CATHOLIC COMMUNITY OF SAINTS JAMES, CORNELIUS & CYPRIAN (1942)
1010 S. Lansing St., Mason, 48854. Tel: 517-676-9111; Email: stsccblms@gmail.com; Web: saintsjcc.org. Rev. Kusitino Cobona; Deacons Thomas Feiten; Albert Turkovich.
Catechesis Religious Program—Maureen Stockwell, D.R.E. Students 191.
SS. CORNELIUS AND CYPRIAN ORATORY, 1320 Catholic Church Rd., Leslie, 49251.

MICHIGAN CENTER, JACKSON CO., OUR LADY OF FATIMA (1954)
913 Napoleon Rd., Michigan Center, 49254. Tel: 517-764-2088; Email: linda@fatimaparish.net; Web: www.fatimaparish.net. Rev. Satheesh C. Alphonse, S.D.C.
Catechesis Religious Program—Tel: 517-764-1321; Email: val@fatimaparish.ent. Valerie Prettenhofer, D.R.E. Students 67.

MILAN, WASHTENAW CO., IMMACULATE CONCEPTION PARISH MILAN (1854)
420 North St., Milan, 48160. Tel: 734-439-2030; Fax: 734-439-5659; Email: cjnovara@gmail.com; Web: www.iccmilan.com. Rev. Vincent VanDoan; Deacon John Flanagan.
Catechesis Religious Program—Email: valeriew@live.com. Valerie Wilson, D.R.E. Students 110.

MONTROSE, GENESEE CO., GOOD SHEPHERD (1979)
400 N. Saginaw, P.O. Box 3274, Montrose, 48457-0974. Tel: 810-639-7600; Fax: 810-639-3245; Email: goodshepherdofmontrose@gmail.com; Web: www.goodshepherdmontrose.org. Revs. Jonathan P. Perrotta; Anthony Brooks, Parochial Vicar; Deacon Bryan Root.
Catechesis Religious Program—Students 70.

MORRICE, SHIAWASSEE CO., ST. MARY (1875) [CEM]
509 N. Main St., P.O. Box 310, Morrice, 48857. Tel: 517-625-4260; Email: lnebo@catholicweb.com; Email: cgarrison@catholicweb.com; Web: www.stmarymorrice.org. Rev. Msgr. George C. Michalek, J.C.L.
Catechesis Religious Program—Tel: 517-625-6140. Students 70.

MOUNT MORRIS, GENESEE CO., ST. MARY (1867) [CEM]
11110 Saginaw St., Mount Morris, 48458. Tel: 810-686-3920; Fax: 810-686-0759; Email: rslattery1955@gmail.com; Web: stmarymountmorris.org. Rev. Roy Theodore Horning.
School—St. Mary School, (Grades PreK-8), 11208 N. Saginaw, Mount Morris, 48458. Tel: 810-686-4790; Fax: 810-686-4749; Email: pmccracken@stmaryshome.org; Web: www.saintmaryscatholic.com. Rexford Hart, Prin. Lay Teachers 11; Students 104.
Catechesis Religious Program—Tel: 810-686-3920, Ext. 112. Melisa Lee, D.R.E. Students 27.

OKEMOS, INGHAM CO., ST. MARTHA (1988)
1100 W. Grand River, Okemos, 48864. Tel: 517-349-1763; Email: ilolson@st-martha.org; Web: www.st-martha.org. Revs. Michael A. Murray; David W. Hudgins, J.C.L., In Res.; Deacons Carl Boehlert; John Finn.
School—St. Martha School, (Grades PreK-8), Tel: 517-349-3322; Email: schoolprincipal@st-martha.org. Monica Dowell, Prin.; Lynn Collom, Sec. Lay Teachers 7; Students 119.
Catechesis Religious Program—Email: jrosalez@st-martha.org. Jackie Rosalez, D.R.E. Students 160.

OTISVILLE, GENESEE CO., ST. FRANCIS XAVIER (1947)
212 Center St., Otisville, 48463. Tel: 810-631-6305; Tel: 810-686-9861; Tel: 810-631-8306; Fax: 810-631-4412; Email: office212.sfx@gmail.com; Email: parishssh@catholicweb.com; Web: www.sfxotisville.org. Rev. Kenneth F. Coughlin.
Catechesis Religious Program—Email: dre.sfx@gmail.com. Students 54.

OVID, SHIAWASSEE CO., HOLY FAMILY (1966)
510 N. Mabbitt Rd., Ovid, 48866. Tel: 989-834-5855; Email: holyfamilyovid@gmail.com; Web: www.stisidorechurch.org/hf. Revs. Robert Crowley Bacik, Admin.; Raymond J. Urbanek, In Res., (Retired).
Catechesis Religious Program—Ginger Kusnier, D.R.E. Students 24.

OWOSSO, SHIAWASSEE CO.
1—ST. JOSEPH (1923) Merged with and became an oratory of St. Paul Church, Owosso.
2—ST. PAUL (1871) [CEM 2]
111 N. Howell St., Owosso, 48867. Tel: 989-723-4277; Fax: 989-723-9503; Email: secretary@stpaulowosso.org; Web: www.stpaulowosso.org. Revs. Michael O'Brien; Dieudonne Ntakarutimana, Parochial Vicar; Deacon Gary Edington.
School—St. Paul School, (Grades K-8), 718 W. Main St., Owosso, 48867. Tel: 989-725-7766; Fax: 989-725-9824; Email: stpaulschool@spsowosso.

org; Web: www.spsowosso.org. Laura Heatwole, Prin. Lay Teachers 8; Students 66.
Catechesis Religious Program—Tel: 989-723-4765; Email: religioused@stpaulowosso.org. Sharon Hardenbergh, D.R.E. Students 103.
ST. JOSEPH ORATORY, 915 E. Oliver St., Owosso, 48867. Tel: 989-725-5215.

PINCKNEY, LIVINGSTON CO., ST. MARY PARISH PINCKNEY (1867) [CEM]
10601 Dexter-Pinckney Rd., Pinckney, 48169.
Tel: 734-878-3161; Email: info@stmarypinckney.org; Web: www.stmarypinckney.org. Rev. Daniel J. Kogut.
School—St. Mary School, (Grades PreK-8), Tel: 734-878-5616; Email: mrskinsey@stmarypinckey.org; Web: www.stmarypinckney.org. Lay Teachers 11; Students 135.
Catechesis Religious Program—Tel: 734-878-2217; Tel: 734-878-5616; Email: ssalow@stmarypinckney.org; Email: mrskinsey@stmarypinckney.org. Sarah Salow, D.R.E. Students 155.

ST. JOHNS, CLINTON CO., ST. JOSEPH (1874)
109 Linden St., St. Johns, 48879. Tel: 989-224-8994; Email: stjosephchurchstjohns@gmail.com; Web: www.stjoecatholic.com. Rev. Michael J. Williams; Deacons Marvin Robertson; Gerald Fust.
School—St. Joseph School, (Grades K-6), 201 E. Cass St., Saint Johns, 48879. Tel: 989-224-2421; Fax: 989-224-1900; Email: principal@stjoecatholicschool.org; Web: www.stjoecatholic.com. Christopher O. Wells, Prin. Lay Teachers 12; Students 201.
Catechesis Religious Program—Tel: 989-224-8537; Email: dre.stjoseph@gmail.com. Michelle Parker, D.R.E. Students 215.

SALINE, WASHTENAW CO., ST. ANDREW PARISH SALINE (1968) [CEM]
910 Austin Dr., Saline, 48176. Tel: 734-429-5210; Email: office@standrewsaline.org; Web: www.standrewsaline.org. Rev. James G. McDougall, Admin., (Retired); Deacons Douglas Cummings; Paul Ellis.
Catechesis Religious Program—Email: k-8@standrewsaline.org. Janet Cook, Dir. of Faith Formation (K-8). Students 410.

SWARTZ CREEK, GENESEE CO., ST. MARY OF ANGELS (1912) [CEM] (Czech)
4413 Morrish Rd., Swartz Creek, 48473.
Tel: 810-635-3240; Email: info@smqa.net; Web: www.smqa.net. Rev. Louis T. Ekka, (India); Deacon Rodney Amon.
Res.: 7563 Mary St., Swartz Creek, 48473.
Catechesis Religious Program—Email: vstandley@smqa.net. Valerie Standley, D.R.E. Students 82.

TECUMSEH, LENAWEE CO., ST. ELIZABETH (1947)
506 N. Union St., Tecumseh, 49286.
Tel: 517-423-2447; Email: steliz50@aol.com; Web: www.stelizabethstdominic.org. Rev. Daniel F. Wheeler; Deacons James Nicholson; Ray Pizana.
Catechesis Religious Program—512 N. Union St., Tecumseh, 49286. Kimberly Bauer, D.R.E.; Heather Marsh, Youth Min. Students 223.
ST. DOMINIC ORATORY (1853) Clinton.

WESTPHALIA, CLINTON CO., ST. MARY (1836) [CEM] (German)
201 N. Westphalia St., Westphalia, 48894.
Tel: 989-587-4201; Email: mlenneking@stmarychurch.net; Web: www.stmarychurch.net. Mailing Address: P.O. Box 267, Westphalia, 48894. Rev. Eric C. Weber; Deacon Chuck Thelen.
School—St. Mary School, (Grades K-6), 209 N. Westphalia St., Westphalia, 48894.
Tel: 989-587-3702; Fax: 989-587-3706; Email: dlthelen@stmaryschool.us. Mailing Address: P.O. Box 270, Westphalia, 48894. Darren Thelen, Prin. Lay Teachers 14; Students 281; Total Staff 23; Librarian 1.
Catechesis Religious Program—Email: jlspitzley@stmarychurch.net. Jordan Spitzley, D.R.E. Students 224.

WILLIAMSTON, INGHAM CO., ST. MARY (1869) [CEM]
157 High St., Williamston, 48895. Tel: 517-655-2620; Email: maryannduffy.stmary@gmail.com; Web: www.saint-mary.church. Rev. Mark J. Rutherford, J.C.L.; Deacon Stephen Hilker, Business Mgr.
Res.: 505 Red Cedar Blvd., Williamston, 48895.
School—St. Mary School, (Grades PreK-5), 220 Cedar St., Williamston, 48895. Tel: 517-655-4038; Fax: 517-655-3855; Email: stmarywilliamston.rj@gmail.com; Email: stmarys@wowway.biz. R. J. Lomas, Prin. Lay Teachers 5; Students 74.
Catechesis Religious Program—Tel: 517-655-2520; Fax: 517-655-3433. Nancy Duey, D.R.E. Students 160.

YPSILANTI, WASHTENAW CO.
1—ST. JOHN THE BAPTIST PARISH YPSILANTI (1858) [CEM]
411 Florence St., Ypsilanti, 48197. Tel: 734-483-3360 ; Fax: 734-483-0712; Email: sjbreceptionist@gmail.com; Web: www.ypsilanticatholic.com. Rev. Robert Roggenbuck; Deacons Wayne Charlton; Mark Millage; Curtis Scholl; Steve Thomashefski.
Rectory—410 W. Cross St., Ypsilanti, 48197.
Catechesis Religious Program—Students 130.
2—ST. JOSEPH PARISH YPSILANTI (1889) [CEM]
9425 Whittaker Rd., Ypsilanti, 48197.
Tel: 734-461-6555; Email: stjosephypsi@comcast.net; Web: www.stjosephypsilanti.com. Rev. Pieter van-Rooyen; Deacons Stanley Kukla, Admin.; Richard Giesige.
Catechesis Religious Program—Tel: 734-480-9491; Tel: 734-480-9491; Email: belinzy532@gmail.com; Email: belinzy532@gmail.com. Betty Linzy, D.R.E. Students 50.

Chaplains of Public Institutions.

Hospitals

LANSING. *Sparrow Hospital*, Tel: 517-364-1000. Vacant.
ANN ARBOR. *St. Joseph Mercy Hospital*. Deacon Steve Thomashefski, Chap.
University of Michigan Hospitals/Pastoral Dept.. Rev. Lewis Eberhart, Deacon Wayne Charlton, Tel: 734-730-4582.
VA Hospital. Deacon John Ozog, Tel: 734-657-5386.
CHELSEA. *St. Joseph Mercy Hospital*. Deacon Tom Franklin, Tel: 734-657-5386.
FLINT. *Hurley Regional Medical Center*. Deacon Michael Dear, Tel: 810-429-2230.
McLaren Regional Medical Center. Deacon Anthony Verdun, Tel: 810-655-4059.
GRAND BLANC. *Genesys Regional Medical Center*. Vacant.
JACKSON. *Allegiance Health*, 205 N. East Ave., Jackson, 49201. Vacant.

Prisons

ADRIAN. *Gus Harrison Regional Facility*. Rev. James McHugh, O.S.F.S., Deacons Len Brown, Tel: 517-442-8971, Ray Pizana, Tel: 517-442-5558.
Parr Hwy. Correctional Facility. (Consolidated with Gus Harrison) (Vacant).
JACKSON. *Cotton Facility*. Rev. James McHugh, O.S.F.S.
Egeler Correctional Facility. Rev. Timothy E. MacDonald.
Parnall Facility. Rev. Timothy A. Nelson, Tel: 517-784-7184, Deacon Matthew Shannon, Tel: 517-789-6260.
MILAN. *Federal Correctional Institution*. Rev. James McHugh, O.S.F.S.

Special Alternative Incarceration

CHELSEA. *Camp Cassidy Lake*. Very Rev. William J. Turner, Tel: 734-475-1697.
JACKSON. *Duane Waters Hospital*. (Hospice for Inmates) Rev. Satheesh C. Alphonse, S.D.C.
WHITMORE LAKE. *Woodland Correctional Facility*. (Vacant).

On Duty Outside the Diocese:
Revs.—
Bui, Vincent, S.S., 3776 Raven Ct., San Jose, CA 95127
Fons, David Michael, Piazza della Pilotta 1, 00187 Rome, Italy
Gawronski, Gerald, Iraq
Kersten, Jay J., Navy Chap.
Kropf, Richard, Star Rte. 1, P.O. Box 629, Johannesburg, 49751
Mabee, Zachary M., University of Reading/Christ the King Parish, 408 Northumberland Ave., Whitley, South Reading, England RG2 8NR
Whitlock, John J., St. John Vianney Seminary, 2115 Summit Ave., St. Paul, MN 55105.

On Leave of Absence:
Revs.—
Carlos, Miguel
Dehetre, Mark
Njus, Jeffrey
Thomsen, Steven, (New Zealand).

Retired:
Rev. Msgrs.—
Goehring, Raymond, (Retired), 901 Brookside Dr., Apt. 205, 48917
Groshek, Richard, (Retired), 5201 Woodhaven Ct., Apt. 601, Flint, 48532
Lunsford, Robert D., (Retired), 401 E. Madison, #A, Dewitt, 48820
Murphy, Michael D., (Retired), 703 E. Main St., #100, Dewitt, 48820. Tel: 517-342-2450
Reilly, Bernard, (Retired), 402 E. Madison #A, DeWitt, 48820
Revs.—
Aubin, Joseph, (Retired), 402 E. Madison, #B, Dewitt, 48820
Beiter, Eugene J., (Retired), 402 E. Madison, #D, Dewitt, 48820
Brennan, Thomas, (Retired), 468 Lancaster Ct., Saline, 48176
Clark, Peter J., (Retired), 220 Brown St., Clinton, 49236
Cummings, Paul J., (Retired), 401-B E. Madison St., DeWitt, 48820
Czarnota, Stanislaus, (Retired), 401 Madison, Apt. C, Dewitt, 48820
Dombrowski, Timothy, (Retired), 5341 McAuley Dr., Ypsilanti, 48197
Dougherty, C. Peter, (Retired), P.O. Box 14062, 48901
Dumas, Terrence J., 2150 Frieze Ave., Ann Arbor, 48104
Faraci, Francis, (Retired), 1504 S. Vassar Rd., Unit 2, Burton, 48519
Fedewa, Matthew, (Retired), 395 E. Madison, Apt. B, Dewitt, 48820. 4437 W. Willow, 48917
Fisher, David E., (Retired)
Foglio, John, (Retired), P.O. Box 4098, East Lansing, 48826
Gerl, Robert, D.Min., Ph.D., (Retired), 1538 Evanston, Kalamazoo, 49008
Harvey, David W., (Retired), 6320 Bollard Rd., Fenton, 48430
Irvin, Charles, (Retired), Fairview, P.O. Box 40, Grand Ledge, 48837
Koenigsknecht, William J., (Retired), 10809 E. 3rd St., Fowler, 48835
Kolenski, Robert D., (Retired), 3375 N. Linden Rd., #205, Flint, 48504
Kuchar, Michael W., (Retired), 4838 Skyline Dr., Perrinton, 48871
Lorenzo, Eduardo, (Retired), 6073 Ballard, Flint, 48505
Madey, Louis, (Retired), 1504 S. Vassar Rd., Unit 5, Burton, 48519
Makranyi, Steven F., (Retired), 3096 Vineyard Ln., Flushing, 48433
McDonald, Kenneth, (Retired), 402 E. Madison, #D, DeWitt, 48820
McDougall, James G., (Retired), 600 W. Huron, #520, Ann Arbor, 48103
McGraw, Robert H., (Retired), 1504 S. Vassar Rd., Unit 6, Burton, 48519
Nenneau, Thomas D., (Retired), 1504 S. Vassar Rd., Unit 3, Burton, 48519
Osborn, Douglas, (Retired), 402-C E. Madison, Dewitt, 48820
Pamment, Duaine H., (Retired), 8527 Woodruff Dr., S.W., Byron Center, 49315
Petroski, Michael A., (Retired), 163 Oakwood, Saline, 48176
Ploof, Gerald, (Retired), 395 E. Madison, Apt. D, Dewitt, 48820
Robert, Darin T., (Retired), 1020 Wing Dr., Ann Arbor, 48103
Rusch, Donald, (Retired), P.O. Box 399, East Pointe, 48021
Schweda, Phillip, J.C.L., (Retired), 1000 Pinebrook Rd., Venice, FL 33980
Sessions, Phillip D., (Retired), P.O. Box 703, Palm Desert, CA 92261
Shaver, James, (Retired), 1320 Catholic Church Rd., Leslie, 49251
Simon, Carl, (Retired), 1504 S. Vassar Rd., Unit 4, Burton, 48519
Spitzley, Denis R., (Retired), 1504 S. Vassar Rd., Unit 1, Burton, 48519
Stevenson, William J., (Retired), P.O. Box 1882, Brighton, 48116
Swiat, James R., (Retired), 1209 S. Union St., Traverse City, 49684
Taylor, Jon, (Retired), 222 Broadway, Apt. 410, Eugene, OR 97402
Thompson, Thomas W., (Retired), 395 E. Madison, Apt. C, Dewitt, 48820
Tran, Joseph, (Retired), Fairview, P.O. Box 40, Grand Ledge, 48837
Tyler, Bernard L., (Retired), 112 McKee St., Houghton Lake, 48629
Urbanek, Raymond J., (Retired), P.O. Box 612, Ovid, 48866-0612
Wakefield, Alan, (Retired), 235 N. Whittaker, #36, New Buffalo, 49117
Wehrle, Jonathan, (Retired), 1400 Noble Rd., Williamston, 48895.

Permanent Deacons:
Alfaro, Rogelio, Senior Status
Amon, Rodney, St. Mary Queen of Angels, Swartz Creek
Amthor, John, Sacred Heart, Hudson

Arehart, Thomas, St. Catherine Laboure, Concord
Arquette, Lester, St. Thomas the Apostle, Ann Arbor
Badics, Richard, St. Francis of Assisi, Ann Arbor
Barrett, David, Senior Status
Bauer, Robert, St. Michael, Grand Ledge
Bayes, Richard, Senior Status
Blondin, Lawrence, Holy Family, Grand Blanc
Boehlert, Carl, St. Martha, Okemos
Borzenski, David, St. Therese, Lansing
Brennan, Gerald, Holy Spirit, Brighton
Brown, James, Senior Status
Brown, Leonard C., St. Joseph, Adrian
Butler, Gerald, Serving in Diocese of Cleveland
Cahaney, Roger, St. Agnes, Fowlerville
Cameron, John M., J.C.L., Diocese of Lansing Tribunal; Immaculate Heart of Mary, Lansing
Carsten, Terry, St. John the Evangelist, Fenton
Charlton, Wayne, St. John the Baptist, Ypsilanti
Chevalier, James M., Senior Status
Coffelt, Randy, St. Mary, Pinckney
Corder, James, St. Gerard, Lansing
Corrion, Wayne, St. Mary & St. Joseph, Durand
Crowley, John D., St. Joseph, Adrian
Cummings, Doug, St. Andrew, Saline
Dear, Michael, St. John Vianney, Flint
Desrochers, Randal, Dir. of Diaconal Formation; St. Joseph, Dexter
Doran, Endre, Senior Status
Drayton, David, St. Thomas Aquinas / St. John, East Lansing
Edington, Gary, St. Paul, Owosso
Ellingson, Raymond, SS. Charles & Helena, Clio
Ellis, Paul, St. Andrew, Saline
Epley, John, Senior Status
Etters, David, St. John the Evangelist, Jackson
Fairweather, Daniel, St. John the Evangelist, Davison
Feiten, Thomas, St. James, Mason
Finn, John, St. Martha, Okemos
Fitch, John II, Senior Status
Flanagan, John, Immaculate Conception, Milan
Fogle, Thomas, St. Mary, Charlotte
Foley, Daniel R., Christ the King, Ann Arbor
Franklin, Thomas, St. Mary, Chelsea
Franssen, Carol, St. Catherine Laboure, Concord
Fudge, William, Senior Status
Fust, Gerald, St. Joseph, St. Johns
Gallagher, Gary, Holy Redeemer, Burton
Genco, Vincent, St. Mary Star of the Sea, Jackson
Giesige, Richard, St. Joseph, Ypsilanti
Gilbert, Michael, St. Patrick, Brighton
Gorczyca, Patrick, Queen of the Miraculous Medal, Jackson
Gudaitis, Peter, St. Agnes, Fowlerville
Hall, Daniel, St. Mary, Pinckney
Hausmann, Gene, St. Joseph Shrine, Brooklyn
Hecht, Warren, St. Thomas the Apostle, Ann Arbor
Herzog, Robert, Senior Status
Heutsche, Ted, St. Jude, Dewitt
Hilker, Stephen, St. Mary, Williamston
Holowicki, Gerry, Christ the King, Ann Arbor
Jansen, David, St. Pius X, Flint
Jong, Joseph, St. Mary Cathedral & MSU Chinese Community
Kasprzak, James, St. Thomas Aquinas, East Lansing
Kenney, Ronald, St. Mark the Evangelist, Grand Blanc
Kilburn, Gordon, Serving in the Diocese of Knoxville
Kowalski, John, Queen of the Miraculous Medal, Jackson
Krieger, Albert, Senior Status
Kukla, Stanley, St. Joseph, Ypsilanti
Lawrence, Dave, St. Patrick, Brighton
Leger, Gene, St. Francis of Assisi, Ann Arbor
Leone, Romolo, St. Joseph, Dexter
Loewe, Thomas, St. Thomas the Apostle, Ann Arbor
Marsal, Gideon, Senior Status
Marsh, John, St. Isidore, Laingsburg
Martin, Michael, St. Mary, Chelsea
Martinez, James, Senior Status
McCarthy, John, St. Michael, Grand Ledge
McCormick, Michael, St. John the Evangelist, Jackson
McCrandall, Michael, Serving in the Archdiocese of Detroit
McDonald, Patrick, St. Patrick, Brighton
McPhilamy, Robert, Senior Status
Medich, Daniel, St. John the Evangelist, Fenton
Michael, Donald, St. Anthony, Hillsdale
Middleton, Greg, St. Mary and St. Joseph, Durand
Miles, James, St. Thomas the Apostle, Ann Arbor
Millage, Mark, St. John the Baptist, Ypsilanti
Nguyen, Dom Chuong, St. Casimir, Lansing
Nicholson, James, St. Elizabeth, Tecumseh
Odette, Omar, Holy Redeemer, Burton
Ozog, John, Christ the King, Ann Arbor
Papp, Frank Joseph, Senior Status
Pennell, Dennis, Holy Family, Grand Blanc
Petersen, Aaron, St. Anthony of Padua, Hillsdale
Piggot, David, St. John the Baptist, Hartland
Pizana, Eulalio, St. Elizabeth, Tecumseh
Poole, Gregory, Serving in the Diocese of Fort Wayne-South Bend
Preiss, Kenneth, Holy Redeemer, Burton
Preston, Richard, Senior Status
Prise, Gary W., St. Mary Magdalen, Brighton
Randolph, Larry, Christ the King, Ann Arbor
Rea, Tom, St. Patrick, Brighton
Robertson, Marvin, Senior Status
Root, Bryan, Good Shepherd, Montrose
Rowe, Ronald, Serving in the Diocese of Gaylord
Russell, William, St. John the Baptist, Howell
Russello, Lou, Christ the King, Ann Arbor
Rymar, Richard, St. Robert Bellarmine, Flushing
Savage, Richard, Senior Status
Scharf, David, Senior Status
Scholl, Curtis, St. John the Baptist, Ypsilanti
Shaneyfelt, Richard, Senior Status
Shannon, Matthew, St. Mary Star of the Sea, Jackson
Simmon, Mark, Senior Status
Simon, Edward, Serving in the Diocese of Grand Rapids
Sirl, William, St. Augustine, Deerfield Twp.
Slomiany, Wayne, Christ the King, Ann Arbor
Southerland, Jeffrey, St. Augustine, Howell
Spaulding, Kenneth, Queen of the Miraculous Medal, Jackson
Stanford, Richard, Serving in the Archdiocese of Indianapolis
Sullivan, Michael, Serving in the Diocese of Gaylord
Sundwick, John, Our Lady of Guadalupe, Flint
Tardif, Andre, St. Michael, Grand Ledge
Thelen, Chuck, St. Mary, Westphalia
Thomashefski, Stephen A., St. John the Baptist, Ypsilanti
Turkovich, Al, Senior Status
Verdun, Anthony, St. John Vianney, Flint
Vida, Christopher, St. Rita, Clarklake
Walters, Dennis, St. Mary, Manchester
Washington, Oliver, Senior Status
Weitzel, Louis, Senior Status
Wendell, Max, Senior Status
Wines, Frank Sr., St. Joseph, Howell
Wolfe, P. Devon, St. Mary Magdalen, Brighton
Zygmontowicz, David, St. Thomas Aquinas, East Lansing.

INSTITUTIONS LOCATED IN DIOCESE

[A] COLLEGES AND UNIVERSITIES

ADRIAN. *Siena Heights University*, 1247 E. Siena Heights Dr., Adrian, 49221-1796. Tel: 517-263-0731; Fax: 517-264-7702; Email: dkeller@sienaheights.edu; Web: www.sienaheights.edu. Sisters Peg Albert, O.P., Ph.D., Pres.; Sharon R. Weber, O.P., Ph.D., Vice Pres., Academics. Sponsored by the Adrian Dominican Sisters. Clergy / Religious Teachers 3; Faculty 88; Sisters 5; Students 2,433; Total Staff 177.

[B] HIGH SCHOOLS, DIOCESAN

LANSING. *Lansing Catholic High School*, 501 Marshall St., 48912. Tel: 517-267-2100; Fax: 517-267-2135; Email: cecilia.draminski@lansingcatholic.org; Web: www.lansingcatholic.org. Douglas Moore, Prin.; Rev. Paul Erikson, Chap. Lansing Catholic Central Board of Education Lay Teachers 33; Priests 1; Sisters 2; Students 519; Clergy / Religious Teachers 1.

ANN ARBOR. *Father Gabriel Richard High School* (1867) 4333 Whitehall Dr., Ann Arbor, 48105. Tel: 734-662-0496; Fax: 734-662-4133; Email: fgoffice@fgrhs.org; Web: www.fgrhs.org. Christopher Dotson, Prin.; Rev. Richard C. Lobert, Chap. Gabriel Richard Board of Education Clergy / Religious Teachers 6; Lay Teachers 38; Priests 1; Sisters 5; Students 559.

FLINT. *Powers Catholic High School*, 1505 W. Court St., Flint, 48503. Tel: 810-591-4741; Fax: 810-591-1794; Email: sbartos@powerscatholic.org; Web: www.powerscatholic.org. Rory Mattar, Pres.; Mrs. Sally Bartos, Prin.; Rev. James R. Rolph, Chap. Powers Catholic Board of Education Lay Teachers 38; Priests 1; Students 660; Total Staff 82.

JACKSON. *Lumen Christi Catholic School*, (Grades 7-12), 3483 Spring Arbor Rd., Jackson, 49203. Tel: 517-787-0630; Fax: 517-787-1066; Email: lcadv@myjacs.org; Web: www.jcslumenchristi.org. Rev. Daniel Lannen, O.S.F.S.; Ms. Elaine Crosby, Pres.; Mrs. Stephanie Kristovic, Prin.; Rev. Brian Lenz, P.V., Chap. Lay Teachers 46; Priests 1; Students 465; Clergy / Religious Teachers 1.

[C] SCHOOLS, PRIVATE

ANN ARBOR. **Spiritus Sanctus Academy*, (Grades PreSchool-8), 4101 E. Joy Rd., Ann Arbor, 48105. Tel: 734-996-3855; Fax: 734-996-4270; Email: mpauze@spiritussanctus.org; Web: www.spiritussanctus.org. Sr. John Dominic Rasmussen, O.P., Prin. Clergy 1; Lay Teachers 13; Sisters 5; Students 180; Clergy / Religious Teachers 1; Staff 4.

BURTON. *St. Thomas More Academy* (1989) (Grades K-12), 6456 E. Bristol Rd., Burton, 48519. Tel: 810-742-2411; Email: k12.stma@gmail.com; Web: stma-mi.org. Dan Le Blanc, Prin. Administrators 4; Lay Teachers 13; Priests 9; Students 106; Total Staff 15.

PLYMOUTH. **Spiritus Sanctus Academy*, 10450 Joy Rd., Plymouth, 48170. Tel: 734-414-8430; Fax: 734-414-8495; Email: srmariafaustina@spiritussanctus.org; Email: szawacki@spiritussanctus.org; Web: www.spiritussanctus.org. Sr. Maria Faustina, O.P., Prin.; Rev. Nicholas S. Seggobe, Chap. Lay Teachers 16; Priests 1; Sisters 4; Students 175; Clergy / Religious Teachers 5.

YPSILANTI. **HVS Corp. (Huron Valley Catholic School)* (2000) (Grades PreK-8), 1300 N. Prospect, Ypsilanti, 48198-3093. Tel: 734-483-0366; Fax: 734-483-0372; Email: khall@hvcatholicschool.org; Web: www.huronvalleycatholicschool.org. Timothy F. Kotyuk, Prin.; Becky Tepen, Business Mgr. Admin. Personnel 1; Lay Teachers 11; Sisters 1; Students 171; Clergy / Religious Teachers 1; Total Staff 16.

[D] SPECIALIZED CHILD CARE FACILITIES & SCHOOLS

CHELSEA. *St. Louis Center for Exceptional Children & Adults*, 16195 Old U.S. 12, Chelsea, 48118. Tel: 734-475-8430; Fax: 734-475-0310; Email: frjoe@stlouiscenter.org; Email: frenzo@stlouiscenter.org; Web: www.stlouiscenter.org. Revs. Joseph Rinaldo, S.D.C., Prov. Treas.; Enzo Addari, S.D.C., M.Div., M.Ed, Admin.; David Stawasz, S.D.C., R.N., Medical Prog.; Rayapillai Amalorpavanathan, S.D.C., B.A., Catholic Chap., Children's Section; Michael Irudayanathan Franklin Arolaiadoss, S.D.C., B.B.M., Catholic Chap., Adults Units Prog. Operated by the Servants of Charity. Clergy / Religious Teachers 5; Residents 65; Students 18; Total Staff 90.

JACKSON. *St. Joseph Home for Children, Inc.* dba Felician Children's Center, 205 Seymour Ave., Jackson, 49202. Tel: 517-841-3876; Tel: 734-793-3852; Email: k.richter@feliciansisters.org; Web: felicianchildrenscenter.org; Email: tjackson@feliciansisters.org. P.O. Box 532437, Livonia, 48153. Tracy Smith-Jackson, Pres. Felician Sisters (C.S.S.F.)Child Care Center for Children, Preschool & Montessori Preschool and Kindergarten. Lay Teachers 29; Sisters 2; Students 85.

[E] CATHOLIC CHARITIES & SERVICE AGENCIES

LANSING. **Cristo Rey Community Center*, 1717 N. High St., 48906. Tel: 517-372-4700; Fax: 517-372-8499; Email: jgarcia@cristoreycommunity.org; Web: www.cristoreycommunity.org. Joseph Garcia, Exec. Dir. Tot Asst. Annually 39,500; Total Staff 23.

St. Vincent Catholic Charities (1948) 2800 W. Willow, 48917. Tel: 517-323-4734; Fax: 517-886-1150; Web: www.stvcc.org. Andrea E. Seyka, CEO. Tot Asst. Annually 3,045; Total Staff 175.

Adoption, 2800 W. Willow, 48917. Tel: 517-323-4734 ; Fax: 517-886-1168; Email: snoeyig@stvcc.org. Andrea E. Seyka, CEO. Tot Asst. Annually 78; Total Staff 6.

Children's Home, 2828 W. Willow St., 48917. Tel: 517-323-4734; Fax: 517-323-0257; Email: snoeyig@stvcc.org. Andrea E. Seyka, CEO. Residents 40; Tot Asst. Annually 85; Total Staff 79.

Counseling Services, 2800 W. Willow, 48917. Tel: 517-323-4734; Fax: 517-886-1158; Email: Carrerj@stvcc.org. Andrea E. Seyka, CEO. Tot Asst. Annually 548; Total Staff 11.

Foster Care Includes case management and licensing 2800 W. Willow, 48917. Tel: 517-323-4734; Fax: 517-886-1168; Email: snoeyig@stvcc.org. Andrea E. Seyka, CEO. Total Staff 11; Total Assisted 341.

Immigration Law Clinic, 2800 W. Willow, 48917. Tel: 517-323-4734; Fax: 517-886-1191; Email: glennol@stvcc.org. Andrea E. Seyka, CEO. Tot Asst. Annually 1,391; Total Staff 9.

Refugee Resettlement Includes Reception, Placement, Health & Employment 2800 W.

Willow, 48917. Tel: 517-323-4734; Fax: 517-853-0031; Email: harrisj@stvcc.org. Andrea E. Seyka, CEO. Tot Asst. Annually 602; Total Staff 29.

ADRIAN. *Catholic Charities of Jackson, Lenawee & Hillsdale Counties* (1958) 199 N. Broad St., Adrian, 49221. Tel: 517-263-2191; Email: slewis@catholiccharitiesjlhc.org; Web: www.catholiccharitiesjlhc.org. Sue Lewis, B.A., Exec. Dir. Tot Asst. Annually 12,139; Total Staff 67.

3425 Francis St., Jackson, 49203. Tel: 517-782-2551; Fax: 517-783-1986; Email: slewis@catholiccharitiesjlhc.org; Web: www.catholiccharitiesjlhc.org. Sue Lewis, B.A., Exec. Tot Asst. Annually 5,691; Total Staff (Jackson Site) 27.

ANN ARBOR. *Catholic Charities of Michigan* (2000) 4925 Packard St., Ann Arbor, 48108. Tel: 734-223-1844; Fax: 734-973-2138; Email: ceo@catholiccharities-mi.org; Web: www.catholiccharities-mi.org. Roberto M. Javier, M.H.A., CEO. Total Staff 3.

Catholic Social Services of Washtenaw County, 4925 Packard Rd., Ann Arbor, 48108. Tel: 734-971-9781; Fax: 734-971-2730; Email: development@csswashtenaw.org; Web: www.csswashtenaw.org. David Garvin, M.S.W., L.M.S.W., Admin. Tot Asst. Annually 9,379; Total Staff 144.

DAVISON. *Outreach East*, 425 N. Genesee St., P.O. Box 61, Davison, 48423. Tel: 810-653-7711; Fax: 810-309-1083; Email: outreacheast@gmail.com. Jan Lebert, Dir. Tot Asst. Annually 6,108; Total Staff 1.

FLINT. *Catholic Charities of Shiawassee & Genesee Counties - North End Soup Kitchen Programs*, 735 Stewart Ave., Flint, 48504. Tel: 810-232-9950; Fax: 810-232-9110; Web: www.ccsgc.org. Mailing Address: 901 Chippewa St., Flint, 48503. Vicky L. Schultz, Pres. & CEO. Tot Asst. Annually 185,018; Total Staff 13; Community Closet 31,944; Warming Center 8,147.

Catholic Charities of Shiawassee and Genesee Counties (1941) 901 Chippewa St., Flint, 48503. Tel: 810-232-9950; Fax: 810-232-9110; Web: www.ccsgc.org. Vicky L. Schultz, Pres. & CEO. Tot Asst. Annually 22,429; Total Staff 67.

HOWELL. *Livingston County Catholic Charities* (1985) 2020 E. Grand River Ave., Ste. 104, Howell, 48843. Tel: 517-545-5944; Fax: 517-545-7390; Email: mark@livingstoncatholiccharities.org; Web: www.livingstoncatholiccharities.org. Mark T. Robinson, A.C.S.W., Exec. Dir. Tot Asst. Annually 3,876; Total Staff 45.

OWOSSO. *Catholic Charities of Shiawassee & Genesee Counties*, 1480 N. M-52, Ste. 1, Owosso, 48867. Tel: 989-723-8239; Fax: 989-723-8230; Email: dsummers@ccsgc.org; Web: www.ccsgc.org. Vicky L. Schultz, Pres. & CEO. Tot Asst. Annually 4,763; Total Staff 15.

[F] GENERAL HOSPITALS

LANSING. **Migrant Clinic-Cristo Rey Community Center*, 1717 N. High St., 48906. Tel: 517-371-1700; Fax: 517-371-4245; Email: jgarcia@cristoreycommunity.org; Web: www.cristoreycommunity.org. Joseph Garcia, Exec. Dir. Tot Asst. Annually 6,900; Total Staff 11.

ANN ARBOR. *Catherine McAuley Health Services Corporation* (Subsidiary of Trinity Health) 5305 E. Huron River Dr., P.O. Box 992, Ann Arbor, 48106. Tel: 734-712-3791; Fax: 734-712-5459; Web: www.stjoeshealth.org. Robert Casalou, CEO. Health Care Center, Ancillary Care Systems: (Primary Care Physician Practices).

Saint Joseph Mercy Chelsea, Inc. (A Member of Trinity Health) 1600 S. Canton Center Rd., Ste. 310, Canton, 48188. Tel: 734-398-0628; Fax: 734-398-0640. Robert Casalou, Pres. & CEO. Bed Capacity 1,110; Tot Asst. Annually 2,120,691; Total Staff 16,000; General Hospitals 4.

St. Joseph Mercy Hospital, 5301 E. Huron River Dr., P.O. Box 995, Ann Arbor, 48106. Tel: 734-712-3791; Fax: 734-712-5459; Email: ann.yarbrough@stjoeshealth.org. David Brooks, Pres. Bed Capacity 537; Tot Asst. Annually 1,114,251; Total Staff 4,853; General Hospitals 1.

CHELSEA. *Chelsea Community Hospital* (A member of Trinity Health) 775 S. Main, Chelsea, 48118. Tel: 734-475-3912; Fax: 734-475-4066; Email: sheena.coburn@stjoeshealth.org; Web: www.stjoeshealth.org. Nancy Graebner, Pres. & CEO; Kathy Schell, Chap. Bed Capacity 133; Tot Asst. Annually 336,960; Total Staff 1,028.

GRAND BLANC. *Ascension Genesys Hospital*, 1 Genesys Pkwy., Grand Blanc, 48439. Tel: 810-606-5000; Fax: 810-603-8906; Email: paula.caruso@ascension.org; Web: www.genesys.org. Christopher J. Palazzolo, CEO & Pres. An affiliate of Genesys Health System; Acute care hospital. Bed Capacity 400; Tot Asst. Annually 226,697; Total Staff 2,976.

Genesys Ambulatory Health Services, Inc. (1981) An affiliate of Genesys Health System 5445 Ali Dr., Grand Blanc, 48439-5193. Tel: 810-603-8686; Fax: 810-603-8906; Web: genesys.org. JoAnne Herman, Vice Pres. Provides private duty home care services and manages shared services. Tot Asst. Annually 13,797; Total Staff 158.

PACE - Program of All Inclusive for the Elderly, 412 E. First St., Flint, 48503. Tel: 810-236-7500; Email: Annette.Sivertson@Ascension.org. Annete Siverston, Dir. Adult Enrollment 62.

Genesys Health System, 5445 Ali Dr., Grand Blanc, 48439. Tel: 810-603-8686; Fax: 810-603-8906; Email: paula.caruso@ascension.org; Web: genesys.org. Mailing Address: 1 Genesys Pkwy., Grand Blanc, 48439. Christopher J. Palazzolo, Pres. & CEO. Bed Capacity 412; Tot Asst. Annually 240,556; Total Staff 3,160.

HOWELL. *Saint Joseph Mercy Livingston Hospital* (A member of Trinity Health) 620 Byron Rd., Howell, 48843-1093. Tel: 517-545-6000; Fax: 517-545-6192; Email: jessica.gobbo@stjoeshealth.org; Web: trinity-health.org/stjoeshealth.org. Deacon Tom Rea, Chap.; Rev. Dale Hedblad, Chap.; Carolyn White, Chap. Bed Capacity 136; Tot Asst. Annually 275,264; Total Staff 614; General Hospitals 1.

[G] HOMES FOR THE AGED & CONVALESCENT

ANN ARBOR. *Servants of God's Love Ministries: Emmanuel House* (1999) 475 Evergreen, Ann Arbor, 48103. Tel: 734-528-9031; Email: ehypsi@gmail.com; Web: emmanuel-house.org. Sr. Fran DePuydt, S.G.L., Admin. Bed Capacity 4; Tot Asst. Annually 4; Volunteers 60.

GRAND BLANC. *Genesys Short Term Rehabilitation Center* (1980) An affiliate of Genesys Health System One Genesys Pkwy., Grand Blanc, 48439. Tel: 810-603-8686; Tel: 810-606-6190; Email: paula.caruso@ascension.org; Web: genesys.org. Raquel Largent, Admin. Skilled nursing facility. Bed Capacity 12; Tot Asst. Annually 196; Total Staff 20.

YPSILANTI. *Emmanuel House II* (2002) 3341 Hillside Dr., Ypsilanti, 48197. Tel: 734-528-9031; Email: ehypsi@juno.com; Web: emmanuel-house.org. Sr. Mary Zielinski, Admin. Bed Capacity 4; Total Staff 45; Total Assisted 4.

[H] HOSPICES

LANSING. **Mother Teresa House for the Care of the Terminally Ill*, 308 N. Walnut St., P.O. Box 13004, 48901. Tel: 517-484-5494; Web: motherteresahouse.org. Karen Bussey, Dir. Total Staff 8; Total Assisted 42.

[I] MONASTERIES AND RESIDENCES OF PRIESTS AND BROTHERS

ANN ARBOR. *USA Midwest Province of the Society of Jesus - Jesuit Residence*, 1919 Wayne St., Ann Arbor, 48104. Tel: 734-663-0557; Fax: 734-663-2756; Email: a2jesuits@gmail.com. Revs. Joseph F. Wagner, S.J., Supr.; Richard Baumann, S.J., In Res.; Patrick Casey, S.J., In Res.; Richard D'Souza, S.J., In Res.; Dennis T. Dillon, S.J., In Res.; James Gartland, S.J., In Res.

BROOKLYN. *Oblate Fathers of St. Francis De Sales, Inc.*, 3403 Loren Dr., Jackson, 49203. Tel: 517-592-8218; Cell: 517-414-0784; Email: jmslc@earthlink.net; Email: mckenna@oblates.us; Web: www.desales.org. Very Rev. Kenneth N. McKenna, O.S.F.S., Prov. Total in Residence 4.

Thorrez Vocational Trust, Ltd., 1124 Ventura Dr., Brooklyn, 49230. Tel: 517-592-8218; Cell: 517-414-07847; Email: jmslc@earthlink.net; Email: mckenna@oblates.us; Web: www.desales.org. Rev. James McHugh, O.S.F.S., Contact Person.

[J] CONVENTS AND RESIDENCES FOR SISTERS

LANSING. *Congregation of the Passion* (1984) St. Therese Convent, 109 E. Randolph, 48906-4042. Tel: 517-372-5849. Sr. Clareth Chavarrio Porras, C.F.P., Prioress. Sisters 4.

ADRIAN. *Adrian Dominican Office of Development* (1987) 1257 E. Siena Heights. Dr., Adrian, 49221-1793. Tel: 517-266-3480; Fax: 517-266-3524; Email: development@adriandominicans.org; Web: www.adriandominicans.org. Amy Palmer, Dir. Adrian Dominican Sisters. Sisters 624.

Dominican Sisters of Adrian, MI, Inc. (1998) 1257 E. Siena Heights Dr., Adrian, 49221. Tel: 517-266-3570; Email: CMBollin@adriandominicans.org. Siemen Patricia, O.P., Prioress. Sisters 624.

Motherhouse of the Sisters of St. Dominic, Congregation of the Most Holy Rosary (1923) 1257 E. Siena Heights Dr., Adrian, 49221-1793. Tel: 517-266-3400; Fax: 517-266-3545; Email: info@adriandominicans.org; Web: www.adriandominicans.org. Patricia Siemen, O.P., Prioress; Rev. James Hug, S.J., Chap. Sisters 624.

Dominican Life Center (1926) 1277 E. Siena Heights Dr., Adrian, 49221-1755. Tel: 517-266-3650; Fax: 517-266-3656; Email: cpickney@adriandominicans.org. Cheryl Pickney, Admin.

ANN ARBOR. *Dominican Sisters of Mary, Mother of the Eucharist* (1997) 4597 Warren Rd., Ann Arbor, 48105. Tel: 734-994-7437; Fax: 734-994-7438; Email: sjab@sistersofmary.org; Web: www.sistersofmary.org. Mother Mary Assumpta Long, O.P., Prioress Gen. Novices 11; Postulants 14; Sisters 136; Final Professed 72; Temporary Professed 39.

Dominican SMME Corporation (2002) c/o Dominican Sisters of Mary, Mother of the Eucharist, 4597 Warren Rd., Ann Arbor, 48105. Tel: 734-994-7437; Fax: 734-994-7438; Email: sjab@sistersofmary.org. Mother Mary Assumpta Long, O.P., Pres. Sisters 135.

**Servants of God's Love* (1975) 4399 Ford Rd., Ann Arbor, 48105. Tel: 734-663-6128; Fax: 734-663-6128; Email: srdorcee@att.net; Web: www.servantsofgodslove.net. Sr. Dorcee Clarey, Supr. Sisters 18.

DE WITT. *St. Albert the Great Convent*, 217 Schavey Rd., De Witt, 48820. Tel: 517-669-2277; Fax: 517-669-8123; Email: saintalberts@rsmofalma.org; Web: rsmofalma.org. Sr. Miriam MacLean, Supr. Sisters 5.

[K] PASTORAL CENTERS

FLUSHING. *Mt. Zion Catholic Community* (1988) 8228 N. McKinley Rd., Flushing, 48433. Tel: 810-639-7175; Fax: 810-639-5262; Email: mtzion@centurytel.net; Web: www.mtzioncatholiccommunity.com. Salvador Barba, Contact Person.

Res.: 8236 N. McKinley Rd., Flushing, 48433. Fax: 810-639-5262; Email: mtzion@centurytel.net. Salvitor Barba, Dir.

JACKSON. *Sacred Heart Chapel*, c/o St. Stanislaus Oratory, 608 Elm Ave., Jackson, 49203. Tel: 517-783-2772; Email: sacred.heart32@gmail.com. Sr. Clareth Chavarrio Porras, C.F.P., Pastoral Assoc.; Angeline V. Medina, Treas.

[L] RETREAT CENTERS

ADRIAN. *Weber Retreat Center* (1970) 1257 E. Siena Heights Dr., Adrian, 49221-1793. Tel: 517-266-4000; Fax: 517-266-4004; Email: webercenter@adriandominicans.org; Web: www.adriandominicans.org/weber. Sr. Janet Doyle, O.P., Dir.

BROOKLYN. *Lake Vineyard Camps, Inc., (De Sales Center)*, 1124 Ventura, Brooklyn, 49230-9078. Tel: 517-592-8218; Cell: 517-414-0784; Email: jmslc@earthlink.net; Email: mckenna@oblates.us; Web: www.desales.org. Rev. James McHugh, O.S.F.S., Dir. De Sales Center is a Catholic Retreat Center operated by Lake Vineyard Camps, Inc. for the Oblates of St. Francis de Sales, Inc. Also on the property is the Novitiate House for the Toledo-Detroit Province of the Oblates of St. Francis de Sales. Priests 1; Total Staff 25; Total Assisted 2,000.

DE WITT. *St. Francis Retreat Center DeWitt*, 703 E. Main St., DeWitt, 48820. Tel: 517-669-8321; Tel: 866-669-8321 (Toll Free); Fax: 517-669-2708; Email: information@stfrancis.ws; Web: www.stfrancis.ws. Rev. David B. Rosenberg, Dir., DeWitt, MI St. Francis Retreat Center; Michael Kutas, Opers. Mgr. Total in Residence 1; Total Staff 51.

Bethany House (Spiritual Life Center for Youth) (2001) St. Francis Retreat Center, 703 E. Main St., DeWitt, 48820. Tel: 517-669-8321; Fax: 517-669-2708; Email: information@stfrancis.ws. Rev. David B. Rosenberg, Dir.

[M] CAMPUS MINISTRY

ADRIAN. *Siena Heights University*, 1247 E. Siena Heights Dr., Adrian, 49221. Tel: 517-264-7192; Fax: 517-264-7745; Email: tpuszcze@sienaheights.edu; Web: www.sienaheights.edu. Tom Puszczewicz, Campus Min. Campus Ministry.

ANN ARBOR. *St. Mary Student Parish*, 331 Thompson St., Ann Arbor, 48104-2295. Tel: 734-663-0557; Fax: 734-663-2756; Email: stmarys@umich.edu; Web: www.stmarystudentparish.org. Revs. Benjamin B. Hawley, S.J., Pastor; Dennis T. Dillon, S.J., Pastoral Assoc.; Joseph F. Wagner, S.J., Campus Min. Serving the University of Michigan. Total Staff 27.

Refer to the parish section for complete campus ministry staff.

[N] ENDOWMENTS AND TRUSTS

LANSING. *Chancery Office*, 300 W. Ottawa, 48933. Tel: 517-342-2440.

Blessed Sacrament Educational Trust Fund,

Tel: 810-742-3151; Fax: 810-742-1409. (Blessed Sacrament Parish, Burton).

Church of the Resurrection Educational Trust Fund (Church of the Resurrection, Lansing), Tel: 517-482-4749; Fax: 517-484-4740.

Father Al Miller Educational Trust Fund (St. Mary Parish, Westphalia), Tel: 517-587-4201; Fax: 517-587-3838.

Father Gabriel Richard High School Trust Fund (Fr. Gabriel Richard H.S., Ann Arbor), Tel: 734-662-0496; Fax: 734-662-4133.

Holy Redeemer Educational Trust Fund (Holy Redeemer Parish, Burton), Tel: 810-743-3050; Fax: 810-743-4381.

Immaculate Heart of Mary St. Casimir School Mary Goeddeke Educational Trust Fund (IHM-St. Casimir School, Lansing) Tel: 517-882-6631.

Luke M. Powers Educational Trust Fund (Flint), Tel: 810-591-4741; Fax: 810-591-0383.

Lumen Christi High School Endowment Fund (Lumen Christi H.S., Jackson), Tel: 517-787-0630; Fax: 517-787-1066.

Most Holy Trinity Educational Trust Fund (Most Holy Trinity Church, Fowler), Tel: 517-593-2616; Fax: 517-593-2801.

Msgr. Lawrence H. Soest Educational Trust Fund (St. Mary Parish, Flint), Tel: 810-232-4012; Fax: 810-232-4013.

Rev. Joseph R. Robb Educational Trust Fund (Holy Rosary Parish, Flint), Tel: 810-736-4040; Fax: 810-736-9129.

Sacred Heart Educational Fund (Sacred Heart Parish, Hudson), Tel: 517-448-3811.

St. Francis of Assisi Educational Trust Fund (St. Francis of Assisi Parish, Ann Arbor), Tel: 734-821-2200; Fax: 734-821-2202.

St. Gerard Educational Trust Fund (St. Gerard Parish, Lansing), Tel: 517-323-2379; Fax: 517-886-1394.

St. John the Evangelist Parish Educational Trust Fund (St. John the Evangelist Parish, Jackson), Tel: 517-784-0553; Fax: 517-788-5381.

St John School Educational Foundation, Inc. (St. John Parish, Fenton), Tel: 810-629-2251; Fax: 810-629-2302.

St. John Vianney Educational Trust Fund (St. John Vianney Parish, Flint), Tel: 810-235-1812; Fax: 810-235-4911.

St. Joseph Church of Howell Trust Fund (St. Joseph Church, Howell), Tel: 517-546-0090.

St. Joseph Educational Trust Fund (St. Joseph Church, Owosso), Tel: 517-725-5215; Fax: 517-725-1519.

St. Joseph Educational Trust Fund (St. Joseph Church, St. Johns), Tel: 517-224-8994; Fax: 517-224-3475.

St. Louis Center for Exceptional Children & Adults Endowment Trust Agreement (St. Louis Center, Chelsea) Tel: 734-475-8430; Fax: 734-475-0310.

St. Mary Educational Trust Fund (St. Mary Parish, Mt. Morris), Tel: 810-686-3920; Fax: 810-686-0759.

St. Mary Parish Educational Trust Fund (St. Mary Parish, Charlotte), Tel: 517-543-4319; Fax: 517-543-9078.

St. Mary Star of the Sea Educational Trust Fund (St. Mary Star of the Sea Parish, Jackson), Tel: 517-784-7184; Fax: 517-783-2571.

St. Michael's School Endowment Fund Policy (St. Michael School, Grand Ledge), Tel: 517-627-2167.

St. Patrick Parish Educational Trust Fund (St. Patrick Parish, Brighton), Tel: 810-229-9863; Fax: 810-220-0730.

St. Paul's School Education Trust Fund (St. Paul Parish, Owosso), Tel: 517-723-4277; Fax: 517-723-9503.

St. Pius X Church Educational Trust Fund (St. Pius X Church, Flint), Tel: 810-235-8574; Fax: 810-235-8580.

St. Robert Bellarmine/Fr. Charles Jacobs Educational Trust Fund (St. Robert Bellarmine Parish, Flushing), Tel: 810-659-2501; Fax: 810-659-2564.

St. Therese Educational Trust Fund (St. Therese Parish, Lansing), Tel: 517-487-3749; Fax: 517-487-3755.

St. Thomas Aquinas Educational Foundation Trust (St. Thomas Aquinas Parish, East Lansing), Tel: 517-351-7215; Fax: 517-351-7271.

St. Thomas Grade School Trust Agreement (St. Thomas the Apostle Parish, Ann Arbor), Tel: 734-761-8606; Fax: 734-997-8432.

St. Thomas Scholarship Trust for Father Gabriel Richard H.S. (St. Thomas the Apostle Parish, Ann Arbor) 517 Elizabeth St., Ann Arbor, 48104. Tel: 734-769-0911; Fax: 734-997-8432.

Parish Savings & Loan Trust (2018) 228 N.Walnut St., 48933.

[O] PRIVATE ASSOCIATION OF THE FAITHFUL

ANN ARBOR. *Catholic Men's Movement* (1997) 1 Ave Maria Dr., P.O. Box 466, Ann Arbor, 48106. Tel: 734-930-4524; Email: cmmdesk@gmail.com; Web: www.catholic-men.org. Peter Ziolkowski, Dir.; Bob Roleke, Admin.

[P] PUBLIC ASSOCIATIONS OF THE FAITHFUL

LANSING. *Catholic Lay Association of the Holy Spirit Oratory* (1999) Immaculate Heart of Mary, 3815 S. Cedar St., 48910. Tel: 517-393-3030; Fax: 517-393-0855; Email: frjbyers@ihmlansing.org. Rev. John Byers, Chap.

Saint John XXIII Community (2010) 219 Seymour St., 48933. Tel: 517-589-8211; Email: fr@getholy.com; Web: www.getholy.com. Rev. Jeffrey Robideau, Chap., Tel: 517-817-0636.

FENTON. *Alma Redemptoris Mater*, 7381 Turner Rd., Fenton, 48430. Tel: 810-397-4657; Email: tmf734@netzero.com. Rev. Thomas Firestone, Contact Person; Bro. Gary Pearce.

[Q] MISCELLANEOUS LISTINGS

LANSING. *The Catholic Foundation of the Diocese of Lansing*, 228 N. Walnut St., 48933. Tel: 517-342-2503; Email: mhufnagel@dioceseoflansing.org. John Madigan, Pres.; Matt Hufnagel, Vice Pres.

Catholic Lawyers Guild (1985) 1812 N. Genesee Dr., 48915. Tel: 517-402-2880; Email: lclguild@gmail.com; Web: www.lansingcatholiclawyersguild.com. Diane Arzberger, Exec. Dir.

Charismatic Renewal Diocesan Service Committee (Catholic Charismatic Renewal) 835 Maycroft Rd., 48917. Tel: 517-256-7223; Email: rstamford@hotmail.com. Rev. Benjamin B. Hawley, S.J., Bishop's Liaison, St. Mary Student Parish, Ann Arbor; Ralph Stamford, Treas., Email: rstamford@hotmail.com; Connie McClanahan, Sec. Communications & Assoc. Liaison; Debbie McPherson, Vice Chairperson; Debbie Hawley, Chairperson & Co. Representative to MI Committee.

FAITH Catholic, 1500 E. Saginaw St., 48906. Tel: 517-853-7600; Fax: 517-853-7616; Email: pobrien@faithcatholic.com; Web: www.faithcatholic.com. Patrick O'Brien, Pres. & CEO; Elizabeth Solsburg, Vice Pres. & Editorial Dir.; Peter Wagner, Treas.

Diocesan Communications, Tel: 517-853-7660. Michael D. Diebold, Dir., Communications, Diocese of Lansing.

FAITH Magazine Rev. Dwight M. Ezop, Editor-in-Chief.

Liturgical Products Cynthia Vandecar, Dir., Production & Customer Svc.

Web Solutions Peter Wagner, CFO & Dir., Technology.

Mass Times Trust, Web: masstimes.org.

Catholic Event Finder, Web: www.catholiceventfinder.com.

Michigan Catholic Conference (1963) 510 S. Capitol Ave., 48933. Tel: 517-372-9310; Fax: 517-372-3940; Email: plong@micatholic.org; Web: www.micatholic.org. Paul A. Long, Pres. & CEO.

ADRIAN. *Adrian Dominican Montessori Teacher Education Institute*, 1257 E. Siena Heights Dr., Adrian, 49221. Tel: 517-266-3415; Fax: 517-266-3545; Email: info@admtei.org; Web: www.admtei.org. Sr. Leonor J. Esnard, O.P., Ph. D., Dir.

Adrian Rea Literacy Center, 1257 E. Siena Heights Dr., Adrian, 49221-1793. Tel: 517-264-7320; Fax: 517-264-7321; Email: cmaly@adriandominicans.org. Sr. Carleen Maly, O.P., Dir.

ANN ARBOR. *Education in Virtue*, 4597 Warren Rd., Ann Arbor, 48105. Tel: 734-996-4245; Email: sjdr@educationinvirtue.com; Web: educationinvirtue.com. 4101 E. Joy Rd., Ann Arbor, 48105. Sr. John Dominic Rasmussen, O.P., Pres.

Lumen Ecclesiae Press (2017) 4597 Warren Rd., Ann Arbor, 48105.

The Marnee and John DeVine Foundation, 4925 Packard, Ann Arbor, 48108. Tel: 734-971-9781; Fax: 734-926-0160; Email: development@csswashtenaw.org; Email: janw@csswashtenaw.org; Web: www.csswashtenaw.org. Jan Wisniewski, Contact Person. Philanthropic arm of Catholic Social Services of Washtenaw County.

Renewal Ministries Inc. (1980) 230 Collingwood Blvd., Ste. 250, Ann Arbor, 48103. Tel: 734-662-1730; Fax: 734-662-4697; Email: gseromik@renewalministries.net; Web: www.renewalministries.net. Ralph Martin, Pres. Total Staff 15.

FLINT. *St. Luke N.E.W. Life Center*, 3115 Lawndale Ave., Flint, 48504. Tel: 810-239-8710; Fax: 810-239-8726; Email: mmotley@stlukenewlifecenter.com. Sr. Judith A. Blake, C.S.J., Dir.; Carol Weber, Dir.

GRASS LAKE. *The Pious Union of St. Joseph*, 953 E. Michigan Ave., Grass Lake, 49240-9210. Tel: 517-522-8017 (Voice/TDD); Fax: 517-522-8387; Email: piousunion@pusj.org; Web: www.piousunionofstjoseph.org. Revs. Leo Joseph Xavier, S.D.C., Admin.; Satheesh C. Alphonse, S.D.C., Vocations Ministry; Sr. Margaret Ann Hubler, Pastoral Asst.

Now and at the Hour Magazine, Grass Lake. Tel: 517-522-8017; Fax: 517-522-8387; Email: piousunion@pusj.org; Web: pusj.org.

HILLSDALE. *St. Anthony Family Center*, 11 N. Broad St., Hillsdale, 49242. Tel: 517-437-3305; Fax: 517-437-0034; Email: st.anthonycatholicchurch@yahoo.com. Michelle Taylor, Dir. Food pantry serving all of Hillsdale Co. Total Staff 1; Total Assisted 1,500.

RELIGIOUS INSTITUTES OF MEN REPRESENTED IN THE DIOCESE

For further details refer to the corresponding bracketed number in the Religious Institutes of Men or Women section.

[]—*Alma Redemptoris Mater*—A.R.M.
[]—*Detroit Province of the Society of Jesus*—S.J.
[]—*Legionaries of Christ*—L.C.
[0485]—*Missionaries of St. Francis de Sales*—M.S.F.S.
[0920]—*Oblates of St. Francis de Sales*—O.S.F.S.
[0940]—*Oblates of the Virgin Mary*—O.M.V.
[]—*Polish Order of the Society of Christ*—S.CHR.
[]—*Priests of the Congregation of Holy Cross*—C.S.C.
[1220]—*Servants of Charity*—S.D.C.
[]—*Society of the Priests of Saint Sulpice*—S.S.
[]—*Work of Mary Mediatrix*—O.M.M.

RELIGIOUS INSTITUTES OF WOMEN REPRESENTED IN THE DIOCESE

[]—*Congregation of the Passion*—C.F.P.
[3832]—*Congregation of the Sisters of St. Joseph*—C.S.J.
[1070-13]—*Dominican Sisters* (Adrian)—O.P.
[1070-14]—*Dominican Sisters* (Grand Rapids)—O.P.
[]—*Dominican Sisters of Mary, Mother of the Eucharist* (Ann Arbor)—S.M.M.E.
[]—*Dominican Sisters of Peace* (Columbus, OH)—O.P.
[]—*Felician Sisters of North America* Livonia, MI—C.S.S.F.
[]—*Franciscan Sisters of the Atonement*—S.A.
[2575]—*Institute of the Sisters of Mercy of the Americas*—R.S.M.
[]—*Religious Sisters of Mercy* (Alma, MI)—R.S.M.
[]—*Servants of God's Love*—S.G.L.
[0440]—*Sisters of Charity of Cincinnati, Ohio*—S.C.
[1560]—*Sisters of St. Francis of the Holy Eucharist*—O.S.F.
[]—*Sisters of St. Joseph*—T.O.S.F.
[]—*Sisters of St. Paul de Chartres* (Vietnam)—S.P.C.
[2260]—*Sisters of the Lamb of God*—A.D.
[3260]—*Sisters of the Precious Blood (Dayton, OH)*—C.PP.S.
[3320]—*Sisters of the Presentation of the Blessed Virgin Mary*—P.B.V.M.
[2150]—*Sisters Servants of the Immaculate Heart of Mary*—I.H.M.

CLOSED PARISHES & INSTITUTIONS

The Sacramental Records of the following Parishes and Institutions are kept at the Archives of the Diocese of Lansing with the exceptions as listed. The Archives address is: 228 N. Walnut St., Lansing, MI 48933. Tel: 517-342-2450; Fax: 517-342-2544. Available on Tuesdays only from 9:30 a.m. to 4:30 p.m.

LANSING. *Holy Cross Church* Sept. 1924-July 2009 (Baptisms after Dec. 31, 1967 at St. Mary Cathedral).

Lansing & Olivet Newman Centers Jan. 1974-Oct. 1976.

St. Lawrence Hospital Aug. 1936-Feb. 1998.

GENESEE. *St. Agnes Church, Flint* July 1928-Aug. 2008.

St. Francis of Assisi Church, Flint
July 1949-June 1985; August 1921-March 1973.

St. Joseph Church, Flint (Hungarian).

St. Leo the Great Church, Flint June 1957-Dec. 2008 (Baptisms after Aug. 1973 at Holy Rosary, Flint).

St. Luke Church, Flint July 1950-Aug. 2008.

Sacred Heart Church, Flint July 1928-Aug. 2008.

INGHAM. *St. Joseph Church, Leslie* 1869-1904 (Always a Mission, request assistance from Archives).

JACKSON. *St. Agnes, Brooklyn* 1913-1931 (Records at St. Joseph Shrine, Brooklyn).

LIVINGSTON. *St. Joseph Church, Cohoctah* 1880-1904 (Records at St. Joseph, Howell).

St. Joseph/St. Patrick Church, Green Oak Township 1838-1856 (Records at St. John, Fenton).

SHIAWASSEE. *Annunciation to the Blessed Virgin Mary Church, Corunna* 1857-1907 (Records at St. Paul, Owosso.

St. Patrick Church, Woodhull Township 1847-1932 (Always a Mission, request assistance from Archives).

WASHTENAW. *St. Alexis Church Ypsilanti* June 1966-Jan.1994.

St. Francis Borgia Church, Freedom Township 1874-1938 (Records at St. Mary, Manchester).

Transfiguration Church, Ypsilanti Jan. 1994-Sept. 2009.

St. Ursula Church, Ypsilanti June 1960-Jan. 1994 (Baptisms after Aug. 1978 at St. John the Baptist, Ypsilanti).

CLOSED HIGH SCHOOLS

All surviving high school student records of the following were transferred to the regional high schools.

LANSING. *St. Mary Cathedral High School, Lansing* 1904-1963 (Records at Lansing Catholic Central High School, Lansing).

Msgr. John A. Gabriels High School, Lansing 1964-1970 (Records at Lansing Catholic Central High School, Lansing).

Msgr. John A. Rafferty High School, Lansing 1964-1970 (Records at Lansing Catholic Central High School, Lansing).

Resurrection High School, Lansing 1939-1963 (Records at Lansing Catholic Central High School, Lansing).

GENESEE. *St. Agnes High School, Flint* 1954-1970 (Records at Fr. Luke M. Powers High School, Flint).

All Saints High School, Flint 1939-1954 (Records at Fr. Luke M. Powers High School, Flint).

Holy Redeemer High School, Burton 1956-1970 (Records at Fr. Luke M. Powers High School, Flint).

Holy Rosary High School, Flint 1964-1992 (Records at Fr. Luke M. Powers High School, Flint).

St. John Vianney High School, Flint 1955-1970 (Records at Fr. Luke M. Powers High School, Flint).

St. Mary High School, Flint 1929-1971 (Records at Fr. Luke M. Powers High School, Flint).

St. Mary High School, Mt. Morris 1930-1970 (Records at Fr. Luke M. Powers High School, Flint).

St. Matthew High School, Flint 1919-1970 (Records at Fr. Luke M. Powers High School, Flint).

St. Michael High School, Flint 1919-1970 (Records at Fr. Luke M. Powers High School, Flint).

Sacred Heart High School, Flint 1946-1967 (Records at Fr. Luke M. Powers High School, Flint).

JACKSON. *St. John the Evangelist High School, Jackson* 1892-1968 (Records at Lumen Christi High School, Jackson).

St. Mary Star of the Sea High School, Jackson 1892-1968 (Records at Lumen Christi High School, Jackson).

WASHTENAW. *St. John the Baptist High School, Ypsilanti* 1961-1970 (Records at Fr. Gabriel Richard High School, Ann Arbor).

St. Thomas the Apostle High School, Ann Arbor 1887-1977 (Records at Fr. Gabriel Richard High School, Ann Arbor).

The following high schools have no succeeding institutions. Contact the local parish for records.

Adrian Catholic Central High School, Adrian 1955-1969 (Records at St. Mary, Adrian).
Sacred Heart High School, Hudson 1933-1946.
St. Joseph High School, Adrian 1927-1954.
St. Mary High School, Adrian 1933-1954.
St. Mary, Chelsea 1916-1934.
St. Alphonsus High School, Deerfield 1918-1937.
St. Joseph High School, Dexter 1926-1927.
St. Paul High School, Owosso 1905-1971.
St. Mary High School, Westphalia 1936-1961.

DIOCESAN CEMETERIES

LANSING. *St. Joseph*
LAINGSBURG. *St. Patrick*
FLINT. *St. Michael Byzantine*
New Calvary
Old Calvary

NECROLOGY

† Howard, Vincent, (Retired), Died Dec. 6, 2018
† Butler, Thomas W., (Retired), Died May. 3, 2018
† Constantine, Bennett P., (Retired), Died Feb. 19, 2018
† Mossholder, Francis D., Saline, MI St. Andrew, Died Sep. 11, 2018
† Werner, Benjamin, (Retired), Died Dec. 25, 2018

An asterisk (*) denotes an organization that has established tax-exempt status directly with the IRS and is not covered by the USCCB Group Ruling.

Diocese of Laredo

Most Reverend

JAMES A. TAMAYO, D.D.

Bishop of Laredo; ordained Priest June 11, 1976; appointed Titular Bishop of Ita and Auxiliary Bishop of Galveston-Houston January 26, 1993; consecrated March 10, 1993; appointed first Bishop of Diocese of Laredo July 3, 2000; installed August 9, 2000. *Office: 1901 Corpus Christi St., Laredo, TX 78043.* Tel: 956-727-2140; Fax: 956-727-2777.

Chancery Office: 1901 Corpus Christi St., Laredo, TX 78043. Tel: 956-727-2140; Fax: 956-727-2777. . *Mailing Address: P.O. Box 2247, Laredo, TX 78044-2247*

ESTABLISHED AUGUST 9, 2000.

Square Miles 10,905.

Comprises the Counties of Webb, Zapata, Jim Hogg, La Salle, Maverick, Zavala and Dimmitt.

STATISTICAL OVERVIEW

Personnel	
Bishop	1
Priests: Diocesan Active in Diocese	26
Priests: Retired, Sick or Absent	5
Number of Diocesan Priests	31
Religious Priests in Diocese	14
Total Priests in Diocese	45
Extern Priests in Diocese	9
Ordinations:	
Diocesan Priests	2
Permanent Deacons in Diocese	33
Total Brothers	7
Total Sisters	43
Parishes	
Parishes	32
With Resident Pastor:	
Resident Diocesan Priests	23
Resident Religious Priests	8
Without Resident Pastor:	
Administered by Priests	1
Missions	17
Professional Ministry Personnel:	
Brothers	1
Sisters	5
Lay Ministers	11
Welfare	
Health Care Centers	1
Total Assisted	29,872
Residential Care of Children	1
Total Assisted	42
Specialized Homes	1
Total Assisted	1,629
Special Centers for Social Services	2
Total Assisted	28,287
Educational	
Diocesan Students in Other Seminaries	7
Total Seminarians	7
High Schools, Diocesan and Parish	1
Total Students	330
Elementary Schools, Diocesan and Parish	5
Total Students	935
Elementary Schools, Private	1
Total Students	438
Catechesis/Religious Education:	
High School Students	2,620
Elementary Students	5,227
Total Students under Catholic Instruction	9,557
Teachers in the Diocese:	
Priests	5
Sisters	18
Lay Teachers	126
Vital Statistics	
Receptions into the Church:	
Infant Baptism Totals	2,046
Minor Baptism Totals	263
Adult Baptism Totals	63
Received into Full Communion	77
First Communions	2,384
Confirmations	1,768
Marriages:	
Catholic	351
Interfaith	14
Total Marriages	365
Deaths	1,086
Total Catholic Population	348,060
Total Population	382,484

Chancery—1901 Corpus Christi St., Laredo, 78043. Tel: 956-727-2140; Fax: 956-727-2777. *Mailing Address: P.O. Box 2247, Laredo, 78044-2247.*

Vicar General—Very Rev. R. ANTHONY MENDOZA, V.G., 1901 Corpus Christi St., Laredo, 78043. Tel: 956-727-2140; Fax: 956-727-2777. P.O. Box 2247, Laredo, 78044-2247.

Chancellor—ROMEO RODRIGUEZ JR., M.S., 1201 Corpus Christi St., Laredo, 78040. Tel: 956-727-2140; Fax: 956-764-7842.

Vice Chancellor—Rev. IDEN BELLO MIQUILENA, J.C.L., 1201 Corpus Christi St., Laredo, 78040. Tel: 956-727-2140; Fax: 956-764-7842.

Tribunal—Very Rev. OLIVER ANGEL, J.C.L., Judicial Vicar, 1901 Corpus Christi St., Laredo, 78043. Tel: 956-727-2140; Fax: 956-712-1343.

Fiscal Officer—CECILIA MORENO, M.B.A., M.P.H., 1901 Corpus Christi St., Laredo, 78043. Tel: 956-727-2140; Fax: 956-523-0828.

Presbyteral Council—Most Rev. JAMES A. TAMAYO, D.D., Pres.; Revs. IDEN BELLO MIQUILENA, J.C.L., Chm.; TORIBIO C. GUERRERO, Vice Chm.; FRANCISCO QUIROZ, Sec. Ex Officio Members: Revs. JERZY KRZYWDA, Dean, Northern Deanery; WOJCIECH PRZYSTASZ, Dean, Central Deanery; EVENCIO HERRERA, O.F.M., Dean, Southern Deanery; Very Rev. R. ANTHONY MENDOZA, V.G., Vicar Gen. Elected Members: Revs. AGUSTIN ESCALANTE; JANUSZ GLABINSKI; TORIBIO C. GUERRERO; JOSE M. GUEVARA; FRANCISCO QUIROZ; JOSE G. CADENA; JAMES FEE, O.M.I.; ANGEL VALENCIANO. Appointed Member: Rev. Msgr. JAMES E. HARRIS.

College of Consultors—Revs. IDEN BELLO MIQUILENA, J.C.L.; JOSE MARIA GUEVARA; Very Rev. R. ANTHONY MENDOZA, V.G.; Revs. AGUSTIN ESCALANTE; JAMES FEE, O.M.I.; Rev. Msgr. JAMES E. HARRIS; Rev. WOJCIECH PRZYSTASZ.

Diocesan Offices and Directors

Laredo Catholic Communications, Inc.—BENNETT MCBRIDE, Exec. Vice Pres. & Gen. Mgr., 1901 Corpus Christi St., Laredo, 78043. Tel: 956-722-4167; Fax: 956-722-4464; Email: khoy@khoy.org; Web: www.khoy.org.

Communications Department—1901 Corpus Christi St., Laredo, 78043. Tel: 956-722-4167; Fax: 956-722-4464. BENNETT MCBRIDE, Dir., Email: bmcbride@dioceseoflaredo.org; MARGARET MEDELLIN, Editor, La Fe Magazine, Email: mmedellin@dioceseoflaredo.org; ERICA JOHNSTON, Radio Broadcast & Sales Assoc., Email: ejohnston@dioceseoflaredo.org.

Stewardship and Development—1901 Corpus Christi St., Laredo, 78043. Tel: 956-727-2140; Fax: 956-523-0828. RENE GONZALEZ, Dir.

Catholic Charities—1919 Cedar St., Laredo, 78043. MR. BENJAMIN G. DE LA GARZA, Exec. Dir., Email: bdelagarza@ccdol.org.

Social and Human Services—LUIS RICARDO VALDEZ, Representative, Tel: 956-722-2443.

Immigration Services-Servicios Para Immigrantes—Servicios Para Inmigrantes: 1919 Cedar St., Laredo, 78040. Tel: 956-722-2443; Fax: 956-725-2238. EDITH CEDILLO, Dept. of Justice Accredited Representative Mgr., Email: ecedillo@ccdol.org.

Catholic Charities Senior Center—1717 Callaghan Ave., Laredo, 78040. Tel: 956-722-3629. JOE BARRON, Supvr.

Catholic Charities Humanitarian Relief Center—LUIS RICARDO VALDEZ.

Calvary Catholic Cemetery—ROSA ALDAPE, Mgr., 3600 McPherson, P.O. Box 2366, Laredo, 78040. Tel: 956-723-6811; Fax: 956-723-8726.

Our Lady of Refuge Cemetery—1679 Flowers, Eagle Pass, 78852. Tel: 830-773-4247. CELINA M. CARDENAS, Admin.

Sacred Heart Church Cemetery—51 N. IH 35, Cotulla, 78014. Tel: 830-879-2658. Rev. PAWEL ANTOSZEWSKI, Admin.

Charismatic Renewal—DAVID DANIEL; MICAELA DANIEL, 616 Santa Martha Blvd., Laredo, 78046. Tel: 956-568-4894; Tel: 956-999-0041.

Cursillo Movement—Rev. TORIBIO C. GUERRERO, Spiritual Dir., P.O. Box 1175, Laredo, 78042-1175. 2502 Zaragoza St., Laredo, 78040. Tel: 956-285-4839; Fax: 956-724-5581.

Diocesan Finance Council—HECTOR J. CERNA, Chm.; SAUL FERNANDEZ; PEDRO SAENZ JR., J.D.; Rev. P. NOLASCO HINOJOSA JR.; OSCAR O. LOPEZ, C.F.P.

Human Resources—1901 Corpus Christi St., Laredo, 78043. Tel: 956-727-2140; Fax: 956-727-9904. MELINDA SEPULVEDA, Dir.

Family Life Ministry—MARTHA E. MILLER, Dir., 1201 Corpus Christi St., Laredo, 78040. Tel: 956-727-2140; Fax: 956-764-7842.

Natural Family Planning and Understanding Sexuality—Family Life Office, 1201 Corpus Christi St., Laredo, 78040. Tel: 956-727-2140; Fax: 956-764-7842.

Office of Respect Life—Very Rev. R. ANTHONY MENDOZA, V.G., Spiritual Dir., 1201 Corpus Christi St., Laredo, 78040. Tel: 956-727-2140; Fax: 956-764-7842.

Sacramental Preparation Office—1201 Corpus Christi St., Laredo, 78040. Tel: 956-727-2140; Fax: 956-764-7842. JUAN CARLOS VERA JR., Dir., Email: jvera@dioceseoflaredo.org.

Persons with Special Needs—1201 Corpus Christi St., Laredo, 78040. Tel: 956-727-2140; Fax: 956-764-7842. JUAN CARLOS VERA JR., Email: jvera@dioceseoflaredo.org.

Religious Education for Adults—1201 Corpus Christi St., Laredo, 78040. Tel: 956-727-2140; Fax: 956-764-7842. Rev. FRANCISCO QUIROZ, Dir., Email: frfquiroz@dioceseoflaredo.org.

Priests Personnel Board—Revs. IDEN BELLO MIQUILENA, J.C.L.; JERZY KRZYWDA; Very Rev. R. ANTHONY MENDOZA, V.G.; Revs. WOJCIECH PRZYSTASZ; EVENCIO HERRERA, O.F.M.

Youth Ministry—GUSTAVO MARTINEZ, Dir., 1201 Corpus Christi St., Laredo, 78040. Tel: 956-727-2140; Fax: 956-764-7842.

C.Y.O.—1201 Corpus Christi St., Laredo, 78040. Tel: 956-727-2140; Fax: 956-764-7842; Email: cyo@dioceseoflaredo.org. COURTNEY WALKER, Coord.

Archives—ROMEO RODRIGUEZ JR., M.S., Chancellor; CELIA H. REYNA, Asst. Archivist, 1915 Laredo St., Laredo, 78043. Tel: 956-727-2140; Rev. JOSE ANGEL DE LEON JR.

Catholic Schools—

Superintendent's Office—1201 Corpus Christi St., Laredo, 78040. Tel: 956-753-5208; Fax: 956-753-5203. GUADALUPE M. PEREZ, Ed.D., Supt.

Safe Environment Coordinator—MELINDA SEPULVEDA, 1901 Corpus Christi St., Laredo, 78043. Tel: 956-727-2140.

Victim Assistance Coordinator—ROMEO RODRIGUEZ JR., M.S., 1201 Corpus Christi St., Laredo, 78040. Tel: 956-764-7825; Fax: 956-764-7842; Email: rrodriguez@dioceseoflaredo.org.

Vocations Office—1201 Corpus Christi St., Laredo, 78040. Tel: 956-727-2140; Fax: 956-764-7842. Rev. FRANCISCO QUIROZ, Dir., Email: frfquiroz@dioceseoflaredo.org.

Casa Guadalupe House of Discernment—2302 Corpus Christi St., Laredo, 78043. Tel: 956-727-2140; Fax: 956-764-7842. Rev. FRANCISCO QUIROZ, Dir., Email: frfquiroz@dioceseoflaredo.org.

Other Offices and Organizations

Equestrian Order of the Holy Sepulcher of Jerusalem—Southwestern Lieutenancy—SAUL FERNANDEZ, KC HS, Tel: 830-513-0984; Email: extact98@hotmail.com; Dame ROSANTINA FERNANDEZ, LC HS, 1980 Roberto Manuel Cr., Eagle Pass, 78852. Tel: 830-968-0568; Email: quichy_4@yahoo.com.

Knights of Columbus—ANGEL LUNA, Diocesan Deputy, 1650 Robins Row, Eagle Pass, 78852. Tel: 830-325-1788.

Catholic Daughters of the Americas—ELVA MEDINA, District Deputy #15, Court St. Isabella the Catholic #683, 305 Baffin Bay, Laredo, 78041. Tel: 956-436-4222.

CLERGY, PARISHES, MISSIONS AND PAROCHIAL SCHOOLS

CITY OF LAREDO

(WEBB COUNTY)

1—SAN AGUSTIN CATHEDRAL (1762) (Hispanic) 201 San Agustin Ave., 78040. Tel: 956-722-1382; Fax: 956-722-0441; Email: sec@sanagustincathedrallaredo.org. 214 San Bernardo Ave., 78040. Rev. Iden Jose Bello, Rector; Deacon Leonardo Aguillon.
Catechesis Religious Program—Miroslava Vargas, D.R.E. Students 130.

2—BLESSED SACRAMENT (1950) [CEM 2] (Hispanic) 2219 Galveston St., 78043. Tel: 956-722-1231; Fax: 956-722-2823. Rev. Wojciech Przystasz, Admin.; Deacon Rogelio Martinez Jr.
Catechesis Religious Program—Maria Teresa P. Hinojosa, D.R.E. Students 180.

3—CHRIST THE KING (1954) 1105 Tilden Ave., 78040. Tel: 956-723-4267; Fax: 956-791-8034; Email: sec@christthekinglaredo.org. Rev. Jose G. Cadena, Admin.; Deacon Alberto Brizuela.
Catechesis Religious Program—Tel: 956-286-6298. Laura Villalobos, D.R.E. Students 383.
Mission—San Carlos Mission (1993) Hwy 359, 78046. Tel: 956-286-6298. Laura Villalobos, Contact Person.
Catechesis Religious Program—Laura Villalobos, D.R.E. Students 69.

4—DIVINE MERCY (1998) 9350 Amber Ave., 78045. Tel: 956-726-0210; Email: FrMichael@dioceseoflaredo.org. Revs. Michael De Leon; Miguel Orzua, Parochial Vicar.
Catechesis Religious Program—Email: dre@divinemercylaredo.org. Sandra Vidal, D.R.E. Students 285.

5—ST. FRANCES CABRINI (1958) [CEM] (Hispanic) 3018 Davis Ave., 78040. Tel: 956-722-2919; Tel: 956-722-3481; Fax: 956-724-5232; Email: sec@stfrancescabrinilaredo.org; Web: www.stfrancescabrinilaredo.org. Rev. Msgr. James E. Harris, Admin.; Deacon Raymundo Guevara Jr.
Catechesis Religious Program—Tel: 956-722-8315. Johanna Puente, D.R.E. Students 142.

6—HOLY FAMILY (1984) (Hispanic) 2702 Stone Ave., 78040. Tel: 956-724-6881; Fax: 956-724-5581. 2705 McPherson Ave., 78040-5432. Rev. P. Nolasco Hinojosa Jr.; Deacon Hector D. Hernandez.
Catechesis Religious Program—Antonieta Palacios, D.R.E. Students 37.

7—HOLY REDEEMER (1940) [JC] (Hispanic) 1602 Garcia St., 78040. Mailing Address: P.O. Box 1087, 78042. Tel: 956-723-7171; Email: bk@holyredeemerlaredo.org; Web: www.holyredeemerlaredo.org. Rev. Francisco Leon, O.S.A.; Deacon Edmundo Lopez Jr.
Mission—Santa Cruz, 2002 Lee Ave., Webb Co. 78040.
Catechesis Religious Program—Cristina Lozano, D.R.E. Students 139.

8—ST. JOHN NEUMANN (1979) 102 W. Hillside Rd., 78041. Tel: 956-726-9488; Fax: 956-726-0540; Email: sec@sjnlaredo.org; Email: bk@sjnlaredo.org; Web: www.sjnlaredo.org. Rev. Salvador Pedroza; Deacon Gerardo Morales.
Catechesis Religious Program—
Fax: cre@sjnlaredo.org. Julie Rodriguez, D.R.E. Students 168.

9—ST. JOSEPH (1953) 109 N. Meadow Ave., 78040. Tel: 956-723-4172; Fax: 956-728-8824; Email: sec@stjosephlaredo.org. Rev. Janusz Glabinski; Deacon Crispin O. Soto.
Catechesis Religious Program—Tel: 956-740-2803. Julissa Liendo, D.R.E. Students 171.

10—ST. JUDE (1984) Mailing Address: 2031 Lowry Rd., 78045. Tel: 956-722-2280; Fax: 956-722-0209. Rev. Jose Maria Guevara.
Catechesis Religious Program—Aracely Juarez, D.R.E. Students 362.
Mission—Sagrado Corazon de Jesus (1994)
Catechesis Religious Program—Students 59.

11—NUESTRA SENORA DEL ROSARIO (2000) 420 Sierra Vista Blvd., 78046-7765. Tel: 956-753-8764; Fax: 956-753-9972; Email: sec@nuestrasenoradelrosariolaredo.org. Revs. Francisco Stodola; Wojciech Kosowicz, Ph.D., In Res.
Catechesis Religious Program—Mrs. Hassmany Meza, D.R.E.; Mr. Luis Meza, D.R.E.; San Juana Rodriguez, D.R.E. Students 453.

12—OUR LADY OF GUADALUPE (1926) [JC] 1718 San Jorge Ave., 78040. Tel: 956-723-6954. Rev. Leszek J. Waclawik; Deacon Ignacio Valdez.
Catechesis Religious Program—Amanda Cantu, D.R.E. Students 94.

13—ST. PATRICK (1970) 555 E. Del Mar Blvd., 78041. Tel: 956-722-6215 Main Office; Tel: 956-726-4644 Confirmation Office; Fax: 956-722-6266; Email: ministries@stpatricklaredo.org; Web: www.stpatricklaredo.org. Very Rev. R. Anthony Mendoza, V.G.; Revs. Pedro Mercado Jr., Parochial Vicar; Jacinto Olguin, Parochial Vicar; Deacons Joe Longoria; Miguel Robles.
Catechesis Religious Program—Email: franthonym@dioceseoflaredo.org; Email: creconfirmation@stpatricklaredo.org; Email: cre@stpatricklaredo.org. Students 555.

14—ST. PETER THE APOSTLE (1897) Mailing Address: 1510 Matamoros St., 78040. Tel: 956-723-6301; Fax: 956-723-6321. Rev. Agustin Escalante.
Catechesis Religious Program—Patricia Reyes Morales, D.R.E.; Rocio Ezeta, Adult Formation. Students 85.

15—SAN FRANCISCO JAVIER (1966) (Hispanic) Mailing Address: P.O. Box 1175, 78042-1175. 2502 Zaragoza St., 78042-1175. Tel: 956-723-3850; Fax: 956-725-6544; Email: sec@sanfranciscojavierloredo.org. Rev. Toribio C. Guerrero.
Catechesis Religious Program—Students 82.

16—SAN LUIS REY (1958) (Hispanic) 3502 Sanders Ave., 78040-1346. Tel: 956-723-6587; Web: www.dioceseoflaredo.org/parishes/san-luis-rey-church-laredo. Revs. Michael J. Gergen, S.D.B.; Thomas L. Juarez, S.D.B., Parochial Vicar; Jesús Villalobos, S.D.B., Parochial Vicar; Deacons Jose Rodriguez; Enrique Penunuri.
Catechesis Religious Program—Tel: 956-722-3323; Email: cre@sanluisreylaredo.org. Carlos Ochoa, D.R.E. Students 496.

17—SAN MARTIN DE PORRES (1979) (Hispanic) 1704 Sandman St., 78041. Mailing Address: P.O. Box 2666, 78044-2666. Tel: 956-723-5215; Fax: 956-723-9443; Web: www.san-martin.org. Rev. Msgr. Alejandro Salazar; Rev. Elias Sanchez Yanes, Parochial Vicar; Deacons Luis E. Raines, Deacon; Frank Idrogo; Enrique Mejia; Leonel San Miguel.
Catechesis Religious Program—Tel: 956-725-2440; Email: smartinccd@hotmail.com. Christopher Martinez, D.R.E. Students 555.
Mission—Santa Teresita (1996) Hwy. 59, 78044. Email: smpyvonne@gmail.com.
Catechesis Religious Program—Students 39.

18—SANTA MARGARITA DE ESCOCIA (1991) (Hispanic) 320 Segovia Dr., 78046. Tel: 956-724-9669; Fax: 956-791-2167; Email: sec@santamargaritadeescocia.org. Rev. Alirio Corrales, Admin.
Catechesis Religious Program—Martha Vasquez, D.R.E. Students 210.

19—SANTO NINO DE ATOCHA CATHOLIC CHURCH (1985) (Hispanic) Santo Nino Church, 2801 Cross St., 78046. Tel: 956-724-6638; Fax: 956-712-8096; Email: sec@santoninolaredo.org. Rev. Santiago Domingo, Admin.
Catechesis Religious Program—Tel: 956-763-8431; Email: cre@santoninolaredo.org. Lourdes Ramirez, D.R.E. Students 280.

20—ST. VINCENT DE PAUL (1969) (Hispanic) 2710 Boulanger St., 78043. Tel: 956-722-3034; Fax: 956-722-4829. Rev. Leonel Martinez, O.S.A.; Deacon Miguel Vallarta.
Catechesis Religious Program—Tel: 956-726-4134. Patricia Lopez, D.R.E. Students 388.

OUTSIDE THE CITY OF LAREDO

ASHERTON, DIMMIT CO., IMMACULATE CONCEPTION (1918) (Hispanic) 579 Crockett Street, Asherton, 78827-0008. Tel: 830-468-3343; Fax: 830-468-3342; Email: sec@immaculateconceptionasherton.org. P.O. Box 8, Asherton, 78827. Rev. Jan Ziemniak.
Catechesis Religious Program—Tel: 830-457-4720; Email: cre@immaculateconceptionasherton.org. Deolanda Saldivar, D.R.E. Students 66.
Missions—St. Michael—Sulema Herrera, Contact Person.
Catechesis Religious Program—Students 7.
St. Henry, Sulema Herrera, Contact Person.
Catechesis Religious Program—

CARRIZO SPRINGS, DIMMIT CO., OUR LADY OF GUADALUPE (1881) 1003 N. 6th St., Carrizo Springs, 78834. Tel: 830-876-2239; Fax: 830-876-5023; Email: sec@ourladyofguadalupecarrizo.org. Revs. Jerzy Krzywda, Admin.; Juan Mercado, Parochial Vicar; Deacon Jose F. Perez.
Catechesis Religious Program—Tel: 830-876-0153; Email: olog.ccd@sbcglobal.net. Diamantina Vargas, D.R.E. Students 217.

COTULLA, LA SALLE CO., SACRED HEART (1882) [JC] 307 S. Main St., Cotulla, 78014. Tel: 830-879-2658; Fax: 830-879-4916; Email: sec@sacredheartcotulla.org. Rev. Pawel Antoszewski.
Catechesis Religious Program—Tel: 830-879-3196; Email: sagradocorazon@sbcglobal.net. Sr. Marta P. Fernandez, M.P.S., D.R.E. Students 156.

CRYSTAL CITY, ZAVALA CO., SACRED HEART (1917) (Hispanic) 115 E. Kinney St., Crystal City, 78839. Tel: 830-374-3148; Email: sec@sacredheartcrystalcity.org. Rev. Gerardo Silos, Admin.; Deacons Frank Huerta; Antonio Rivera; Frank Solansky.
Catechesis Religious Program—Gilbert Martinez, D.R.E. Students 166.

EAGLE PASS, MAVERICK CO.

1—ST. JOSEPH (1967) (Hispanic) Mailing Address: 800 Comal St., Eagle Pass, 78852-4029. Tel: 830-773-6114; Fax: 830-773-6068. Rev. Richard Kulwiec, O.M.I.; Deacon Benito Ibarra.
Catechesis Religious Program—Tel: 830-773-6515; Fax: cre@stjosepheaglepass.org. Maria R. Hernandez, D.R.E. Students 189.

2—OUR LADY OF REFUGE (1859) [CEM] Mailing Address: 815 Webster, Eagle Pass, 78852. Tel: 830-773-8451 (Office); Tel: 830-773-8421 (Res.); Email: bk@ourladyofrefgueeaglepass.org. Revs. James Fee, O.M.I.; Stanislaw Zowada, Parochial Vicar; Deacons Michael Castillo; Carlos G. de la Pena; Juan Martinez; Keith Ayers.
Catechesis Religious Program—Email: bk@ourladyofrefugeeaglepass.org. Rev. James Fee, O.M.I., D.R.E. Students 447.
Missions—Our Lady of Lourdes—Seco Mines, Maverick Co..
Catechesis Religious Program—Students 211.
Our Lady of Guadalupe, Quemado, Maverick Co..
Catechesis Religious Program—Students 44.

3—SACRED HEART aka Parroquia Sagrado Corazon (1966) (Hispanic) 2055 Williams St., Eagle Pass, 78852-5099. Tel: 830-773-2451; Tel: 830-773-3628; Fax: 830-773-0643; Web: sacredheartchurch-eaglepass.org. Rev. Lawrence Mariasoosai, O.M.I.; Deacons Manuel Rene Cardona; Leandro Contreras Jr.; Hector Ricardo Martinez.
Catechesis Religious Program—Tel: 830-758-1681. Carmen Suarez, D.R.E. Students 608.
Mission—Our Lady of San Juan aka Mision de Nuestra Señora de San Juan, 18779 El Indio Highway, El Indio, Maverick Co. 78860. Sonia Belmonte, Contact Person.

ENCINAL, LA SALLE CO., IMMACULATE HEART OF MARY (1898) (Hispanic) Mailing Address: P.O. Box 5, Encinal, 78019-0005.

400 Santa Fe St., Encinal, 78019-0005.
Tel: 956-948-5328; Email: sec@immaculateheartofmaryencinal.org. Rev. P. Nolasco Hinojosa Jr., Admin.
Catechesis Religious Program—Tel: 956-489-3288; Email: cre@immaculateheartofmaryencinal.org. Maria Teresa Cassiano, D.R.E. Students 20.

HEBBRONVILLE, JIM HOGG CO., OUR LADY OF GUADALUPE (1926) [CEM]
504 E. Santa Clara St., Hebbronville, 78361.
Tel: 361-527-3865; Fax: 361-527-5548; Email: sec@ourladyofguadalupehebbronville.org. Revs. Evencio Herrera, O.F.M.; Jose Gloria, O.F.M., Parochial Vicar; Miguel Velasco, Parochial Vicar; Bro. Alberto Alvarado Vasquez, In Res.
Missions—St. Agnes—324 Liner St., Mirando City, Jim Hogg Co. 78369.
Catechesis Religious Program—Students 14.
St. Bridget, 115 Laurel Ave., Oilton, Jim Hogg Co. 78371.
Catechesis Religious Program—Students 12.
Sacred Heart, 211 N. Ave. G, Bruni, Jim Hogg Co. 78344.
Catechesis Religious Program—Students 21.
Catechesis Religious Program—Lazara Garcia, D.R.E. Students 147.

LA PRYOR, ZAVALA CO., ST. JOSEPH (1917) (Hispanic)
620 W. Benson St., La Pryor, 78872-0436.
Tel: 830-365-4107; Fax: 830-365-9367; Email: frgusortega@dioceseoflaredo.org; Email: sec@stjosephlapryor.org. P.O. Box 436, La Pryor, 78872. Rev. Gustavo Ortega Rodriguez, O.F.M., Admin.; Deacons Eugene F. Corrigan; Juan Gallegos.
Mission—St. Patrick, P.O. Box 83, Batesville, Zavala Co. 78829.
Catechesis Religious Program—Students 25.
Catechesis Religious Program—620 W. Benson St., La Pryor, 78872. Tel: 830-468-7097; Email: sec@stjosephlapryor.org. Terri Dube, D.R.E. Students 91.

RIO BRAVO, WEBB CO., SANTA RITA DE CASIA (1986)
1001 Espejo Molina, Rio Bravo, 78046.
Tel: 956-725-7215; Fax: 956-728-8539. Rev. Joel Perez, Admin.
Catechesis Religious Program—Students 181.
Mission—Santa Monica Mission, 507 Morales (El Cenizo), Rio Bravo, Webb Co. 78046.
Catechesis Religious Program—Students 60.

ZAPATA, ZAPATA CO., OUR LADY OF LOURDES (1940) (Spanish)
1610 Hidalgo Blvd., Zapata, 78076.
Tel: 956-765-4216; Fax: 956-765-6188; Email: sec@ourladyoflourdeszapata.org. Revs. Daniel Ramirez-Portugal; Noel Davis, Parochial Vicar; Angel Valenciano, Parochial Vicar.
Catechesis Religious Program—Sr. Maria de Jesus Callejas, HMRF, D.R.E. Students 364.
Missions—Our Lady of Refuge—Zapata, Zapata Co. 78076.
Catechesis Religious Program—Students 20.
San Pedro, Zapata, Zapata Co. 78076.
Catechesis Religious Program—Students 3.
Santa Ana, Zapata, Zapata Co. 78076.
Catechesis Religious Program—Students 8.

Chaplains of Public Institutions

LAREDO. *Webb County Jail*, 4402 Tilden Ave., 78041.
Tel: 956-723-5029. Deacons Enrique Penunuri, Jose Rodriguez, Prison Chap.Chaplaincy Apostolate to Refugees & Jail Ministry.

INSTITUTIONS LOCATED IN DIOCESE

[A] HIGH SCHOOLS

LAREDO. *St. Augustine High School* (Diocesan) 1300 Galveston St., 78040. Tel: 956-724-8131; Fax: 956-724-8770; Email: ogentry@st-augustine.org; Web: st-augustine.org. Mrs. Olga P. Gentry, Prin. Lay Teachers 26; Sisters 2; Students 330.

[B] JUNIOR HIGH AND ELEMENTARY SCHOOLS

LAREDO. *St. Augustine (Elementary School)* aka St. Augustine Elementary/Middle School (1927) (Grades PreK-8), (Diocesan) 1300 Galveston St., 78040. Tel: 956-724-1176; Fax: 956-724-9891; Email: bzurita@st-augustine.org; Web: www.st-augelem.org. Barbra Zurita, Prin.; Oralia Gallardo, Library Mgr. Religious Teachers 11; Lay Teachers 20; Students 300.
Blessed Sacrament School, (Grades PreK-8), 1501 N. Bartlett Ave., 78043. Tel: 956-722-1222; Fax: 956-712-2002; Email: ssantos@bsacramentschool.com. Selma J. Santos, Prin.; Ana L. Castro, Librarian. Lay Teachers 15; Students 300.
Mary Help of Christians School, (Grades PreK-8), (Private) 10 E. Del Mar Blvd., 78041.
Tel: 956-722-3966; Fax: 956-722-1413; Email: vdo@mhcslaredo.org; Email: anita.averill@mhcslaredo.org; Email: flor.ponce@mhcslaredo.org; Email: alheyda.guerra@mhcslaredo.org; Web: www.mhcslaredo.org. Sr. Vuong Do, F.M.A., Prin.; Flor Ponce, Vice Prin.; Anita Averill, Vice Prin.; Alheyda Guerra, Business Mgr. Religious Teachers 5; Lay Teachers 34; Sisters 5; Students 438.
Our Lady of Guadalupe School (1904) (Grades PreK-7), 400 Callaghan St., 78040-3834.
Tel: 956-722-3915; Fax: 956-727-2840; Email: hmartinez@ourladyofguadalupeschool.net; Web: www.ourladyofguadalupeschool.net/. Herlinda Martinez, Prin. Lay Teachers 9; Students 110.
St. Peter's Memorial, (Grades PreK-8), (Diocesan) 1519 Houston St., P.O. Box 520, 78040.
Tel: 956-723-6302; Fax: 956-725-2671; Email: jackie_marin@hotmail.com. Sr. Beth Yoest, Prin. Lay Teachers 9; Students 60.

EAGLE PASS. *Our Lady of Refuge* (1950) (Grades PreK-8), 577 Washington St., Eagle Pass, 78852. Tel: 830-773-3531; Fax: 830-773-7310; Email: ana.bermea@olorschoolep.org; Web: oloroschoolep.org. Ana Bermea, Prin.; Romana Rodriguez, Bookkeeper. Lay Teachers 13; Students 165.

[C] ORPHANAGES AND INFANT HOMES

LAREDO. *Sacred Heart Children's Home* (1907) 3310 S. Zapata Hwy., 78046. Tel: 956-723-3343; Email: magdasofiasscjp@gmail.com. Sr. Magdalena Juarez, Supr. Religious Teahers 9; Sisters 17; Students 42.

[D] MONASTERIES AND RESIDENCES OF PRIESTS AND BROTHERS

LAREDO. *Congregation of St. John* aka Brothers of Saint John, 505 Century Dr., S., 78046.
Tel: 956-635-6587; Email: accounting@communityofstjohn.com; Web: www.csjohn.org. Revs. John Michael Paul Bartz, C.S.J., Prior; Victor Shoemaker, C.S.J.; Bros. Esteban Gonzalez, C.S.J.; Gabriel Maria, C.S.J.; Michael Mary, C.S.J.; Bruno Thomas, C.S.J. Brothers 4; Priests 2; Total in Residence 6.
Marist Brothers, 1511 Cherry Hill Dr., 78041-3807.
Tel: 956-724-2651; Fax: 956-724-1963; Email: brojoeh@prodigy.net. Bros. Joseph E. Herrera, F.M.S., Dir.; Philip R. Degagne, F.M.S. Marist Brothers 2.

[E] CONVENTS AND RESIDENCES FOR SISTERS

LAREDO. *Daughters of Mary Help of Christians Convent* (1935) 10 E. Del Mar Blvd., 78045-2368.
Tel: 956-791-8617; Fax: 956-722-1413; Email: vdo@mhcslaredo.org; Email: loutrevino19@gmail.com; Web: www.mhcslaredo.org. Sr. Vuong Do, F.M.A., Supr. Daughters of Mary Help of Christians (Salesian Sisters). Sisters 5.
Daughters of Saint Joseph, 8986 Foggy Loop, 78045.
Tel: 956-717-5944; Email: laredotexasfsj@yahoo.com. Sr. Angeles Reyes, Supr. Sisters 4.
Eucharistic Missionary Society (EMS), 1101 Cortez St., 78040. Tel: 956-726-4085; Fax: 956-726-4085; Email: emisoc@laredo.globalpc.net. Sr. Maria Manuela Susana Pedroza, E.M.S. Sisters 1.
Mother of the Eucharist Convent Felician Sisters (1855) 705 Dellwood Dr., 78045-2114.
Tel: 956-568-1502; Email: feliciansisters@stx.rr.com; Web: feliciansistersna.org. Sr. Mary Christopher Moore, Prov. Sisters 2.
Order of St. Ursula, 136 Palencia, 78046.
Tel: 956-722-1101. Sisters 1.
Religious Sisters of Mercy Convent, 2905 Monterrey St., 78046. Tel: 956-721-7401; Fax: 956-721-7405; Email: maria.vera@mercy.net. Sr. Maria Luisa Vera, R.S.M., Dir. Sisters 4.
Servants of the Sacred Heart of Jesus and the Poor (1907) 3310 S. Zapata Hwy., 78046.
Tel: 956-723-3343; Email: regionyermousa@gmail.com. Mother Maria Marinelarena, S.S.H.J.P., Supr. Servants of the Sacred Heart of Jesus and of the Poor. Sisters 18.
Sisters of St. John (1992) 504 Century Dr., S., 78046.
Tel: 956-727-1028; Fax: 956-727-1028. Sr. Jean Marthe LaMore. Sisters 1; Total in Residence 1.

EAGLE PASS. *Missionary Sisters of Our Lady of Perpetual Help* (1934) 895 Webster, Eagle Pass, 78852. Tel: 830-773-8915; Email: garzamps@yahoo.com. Sr. Ana Popo, D.R.E. Sisters 5.
Order of St. Benedict (Mission work in Piedras Negras) 1080 Vista Hermosa, Eagle Pass, 78852.
Tel: 830-758-0812; Email: sisursie@hotmail.com. Sr. Ursula Herrera, Contact Person. Sisters 1.

ZAPATA. *Hermanas Misioneras del Rosario de Fatima*, 1609 Glenn St., Zapata, 78076. Tel: 956-765-4216; Email: mjcsmrf@hotmail.com. 1610 Hildalgo Blvd., Zapata, 78076. Sr. Maria de Jesus Callejas, HMRF, D.R.E. Sisters 3.

[F] RETREAT HOUSES

LAREDO. *Holy Spirit Retreat and Conference Center*, 501 Century Dr., S., 78046. Tel: 956-635-6587; Email: hsrc@communityofstjohn.com; Web: www.csjohn.org. Bro. Esteban Gonzalez, C.S.J., Dir. Brothers 4; Priests 2.

[G] MISCELLANEOUS

LAREDO. *St. Augustine School Endowment Fund, Inc.*, 1300 Galveston, 78040. Tel: 956-724-8131; Fax: 956-724-8770; Email: ogentry@st-augustine.org; Web: www.st-augustine.org. Mrs. Olga P. Gentry, Prin.
Campus Ministry, 1901 Corpus Christi, 78043.
Tel: 956-727-2140; Email: rrodriguez@dioceseoflaredo.org; Web: www.newmanclub.us. Laredo Community College; Texas A&M International University.
Casa de Misericordia (1998) P.O. Box 430175, 78043-0175. Tel: 956-712-9590; Tel: 877-782-2722; Fax: 956-791-1364; Email: marambula@casademisericordia.org; Email: marynell.ploch@mercy.net; Web: www.casademisericordia.org. Sr. Rosemary Welsh, R.S.M., Dir.; Maria Elena Arambula, Shelter Admin. Domestic Violence Shelter.
Diocese of Laredo Deposit and Loan Fund, Inc., 1901 Corpus Christi St., 78043. Tel: 956-727-2140; Fax: 956-523-0828; Email: cmoreno@dioceseoflaredo.org. Mrs. Maria Moreno, Admin.
Diocese of Laredo Perpetual Benefit Endowment Fund, Inc., 1901 Corpus Christi St., 78043.
Tel: 956-727-2140; Fax: 956-523-0828; Email: cmoreno@dioceseoflaredo.org. Mrs. Maria Moreno, Admin.
Mercy Ministries of Laredo (2003) 2500 Zacatecas, 78046. Tel: 956-718-6810; Fax: 956-721-7405; Email: mercy.laredo@mercy.net; Email: marynell.ploch@mercy.net; Web: mercy.net. Sr. Maria Luisa Vera, R.S.M., Pres. Total Unique Patients Served Annually 2,321.
Nocturnal Adoration Society of the United States (1900) 2219 San Dario, 78041. Tel: 956-701-3477; Email: info@nashqusa.org; Email: antonio.hernandez@nashqusa.org; Email: rosendo.hernandez@nashqusa.org; Web: Nationalnocturnaladorationsociety.org. Rev. Alirio Corrales, Dir.; Mr. Raul Mendoza, Pres.; Mr. Antonio Hernandez, Vice Pres.; Alfredo Equigua, Sec.; Francisco Gomez, Treas. Congregation of the Blessed Sacrament.

EAGLE PASS. *Our Lady of Refuge Cemetery*, 1679 Flowers, Eagle Pass, 78852. Tel: 830-773-4247; Email: cemetery@ourladyofrefugeeaglepass.org. Celina M. Cardenas, Admin.

RELIGIOUS INSTITUTES OF WOMEN REPRESENTED IN THE DIOCESE
For further details refer to the corresponding bracketed number in the Religious Institutes of Men or Women section.
[]—*Benedictine Sisters*—O.S.B.
[]—*Congregation of the Sisters of St. Felix (Felician Sisters)*—C.S.S.F.
[]—*Daughters of Mary Help of Christians*—F.M.A.
[]—*Daughters of Saint Joseph*—F.S.J.
[]—*Eucharistic Missionary Society*—E.M.S.
[]—*Hermanas Misioneras del Rosario de Fatima*—H.M.R.F.
[]—*Missionary Sisters of Our Lady of Perpetual Help*—M.P.S.
[]—*Order of St. Ursula*—O.S.U.
[]—*Servants of the Sacred Heart of Jesus and the Poor*—S.S.H.J.P.
[]—*Sisters of Mercy Convent*—R.S.M.
[]—*Sisters of St. John*—C.S.J.

An asterisk (*) denotes an organization that has established tax-exempt status directly with the IRS and is not covered by the USCCB Group Ruling.

Diocese of Las Cruces

(Dioecesis Las Cruces)

Most Reverend

PETER BALDACCHINO

Bishop of Las Cruces; ordained May 25, 1996; appointed Titular Bishop of Vatarba and Auxiliary Bishop of Miami February 20, 2014; ordained March 19, 2014; appointed Bishop of Las Cruces May 15, 2019; installed July 23, 2019. *The Pastoral Center, 1280 Med Park Dr., Las Cruces, NM 88005.*

Most Reverend

RICARDO RAMIREZ, C.S.B., D.D.

Retired Bishop of Las Cruces; ordained December 10, 1966; appointed Titular Bishop of Vatarba and Auxiliary of San Antonio October 27, 1981; consecrated December 6, 1981; appointed First Bishop of Las Cruces August 31, 1982; installed October 18, 1982; retired Jan. 10, 2013. *Res.: 2744 Morning Light Pl., Las Cruces, NM 88011.*

The Pastoral Center: 1280 Med Park Dr., Las Cruces, NM 88005. Tel: 575-523-7577; Fax: 575-524-3874.

Web: www.rcdlc.org

Email: pastoralcenter@rcdlc.org

ESTABLISHED OCTOBER 18, 1982.

Square Miles 44,483.

Comprises the Counties of Dona Ana, Hidalgo, Grant, Luna, Sierra, Otero, Lincoln, Chaves, Eddy and Lea in the State of New Mexico.

For legal titles of parishes and diocesan institutions, consult The Pastoral Center.

STATISTICAL OVERVIEW

Personnel	
Retired Bishops	1
Priests: Diocesan Active in Diocese	17
Priests: Diocesan Active Outside Diocese	4
Priests: Retired, Sick or Absent	16
Number of Diocesan Priests	37
Religious Priests in Diocese	23
Total Priests in Diocese	60
Extern Priests in Diocese	20
Ordinations:	
Transitional Deacons	1
Permanent Deacons in Diocese	43
Total Brothers	1
Total Sisters	38
Parishes	
Parishes	47
With Resident Pastor:	
Resident Diocesan Priests	15
Resident Religious Priests	6
Without Resident Pastor:	
Administered by Priests	23
Administered by Deacons	3
Missions	44
Professional Ministry Personnel:	
Brothers	1
Sisters	7
Lay Ministers	28
Welfare	
Day Care Centers	1
Total Assisted	95
Educational	
Diocesan Students in Other Seminaries	7
Total Seminarians	7
High Schools, Private	1
Total Students	16
Elementary Schools, Private	5
Total Students	553
Catechesis/Religious Education:	
High School Students	2,432
Elementary Students	4,438
Total Students under Catholic Instruction	7,446
Teachers in the Diocese:	
Lay Teachers	72
Vital Statistics	
Receptions into the Church:	
Infant Baptism Totals	1,252
Minor Baptism Totals	154
Adult Baptism Totals	70
Received into Full Communion	161
First Communions	1,411
Confirmations	1,623
Marriages:	
Catholic	226
Interfaith	21
Total Marriages	247
Deaths	1,014
Total Catholic Population	156,704
Total Population	555,454

Former Bishop—Most Revs. RICARDO RAMIREZ, C.S.B., D.D., ord. Dec. 10, 1966; appt. Titular Bishop of Vatarba and Auxiliary of San Antonio Oct. 27, 1981; cons. Dec. 6, 1981; appt. First Bishop of Las Cruces Aug. 31, 1982; installed Oct. 18, 1982; retired Jan. 10, 2013.; OSCAR CANTU, ordained May 21, 1994; appointed Auxiliary Bishop of San Antonio and Titular Bishop of Dardanus April 10, 2008; ordained June 2, 2008; appointed Apostolic Administrator of San Antonio May 26, 2010; resigned Apostolic Administrator October 14, 2010; appointed Bishop of Las Cruces January 10, 2013; installed Feb. 28, 2013; appt. Coadjutor Bishop of San Jose July 11, 2018.

The Pastoral Center—1280 Med Park Dr., Las Cruces, 88005. Tel: 575-523-7577; Fax: 575-524-3874. Office Hours: Mon.-Fri. 8:00am to 5:00pm.

Vicar General—VACANT.

Episcopal Vicar for Clergy and Personnel—Very Rev. Msgr. ROBERT L. GETZ, P.A., (Retired).

Episcopal Vicar for Consecrated Life—Very Rev. VALENTINE M. JANKOWSKI, O.F.M.Conv.

Chancellor—Very Rev. ENRIQUE LOPEZ-ESCALERA, J.C.L.

Director of Clergy Personnel—Rev. RICHARD CATANACH.

Diocesan Tribunal—1280 Med Park Dr., Las Cruces, 88005. Rev. CHRISTOPHER E. WILLIAMS, J.C.L., Judicial Vicar.

Promoter of Justice—Very Rev. ENRIQUE LOPEZ-ESCALERA.

Judge—Rev. JOSEPH L. PACQUING.

Defenders of the Bond—Very Rev. Msgr. JOHN E. ANDERSON, P.A., (Retired); Revs. RICHARD CATANACH; EMMANUEL EZENNEH; MICHAEL LINDSAY.

Administrative Director for Tribunal—VACANT.

Assesor—VACANT.

Advocate—VACANT.

Notary—DOROTHY MEDINA.

Vicars—Very Rev. WILLIAM MCCANN; Rev. MARTIN G. CORDERO; Very Revs. JUAN CARLOS RAMIREZ; MANUEL IBARRA; CARLOS A. ESPINOZA; Rev. CARLOS MARTINEZ, O.F.M.

Diocesan Consultors—Most Rev. GERALD F. KICANAS; Revs. RICHARD CATANACH; MARTIN G. CORDERO; Very Revs. ENRIQUE LOPEZ-ESCALERA; WILLIAM MCCANN; VALENTINE M. JANKOWSKI, O.F.M.Conv.

Presbyteral Council—Most Rev. GERALD F. KICANAS; Very Rev. JUAN CARLOS RAMIREZ; Rev. CHRISTOPHER E. WILLIAMS, J.C.L.; Very Rev. CARLOS A. ESPINOZA; Revs. GUILLERMO RIVERA, O.P.; MARTIN G. CORDERO; Very Rev. MANUEL IBARRA; Revs. CARLOS MARTINEZ, O.F.M.; HRUDAY PASALA; RICHARD CATANACH; MARTIN CORNEJO; Very Rev. VALENTINE M. JANKOWSKI, O.F.M.Conv.; Revs. EDUARDO ESPINOSA, O.F.M.; FRANCIS LAZER; ALEJANDRO URENA; Very Revs. ENRIQUE LOPEZ-ESCALERA; WILLIAM MCCANN.

Clergy Personnel Board—Rev. RICHARD CATANACH; Most Rev. GERALD F. KICANAS; Very Rev. ENRIQUE LOPEZ-ESCALERA; Revs. ALEJANDRO URENA; MARTIN CORNEJO; Very Revs. VALENTINE M. JANKOWSKI, O.F.M.Conv.; CARLOS A. ESPINOZA; MANUEL IBARRA.

Priestly Life and Ministry Committee—Rev. RICHARD CATANACH.

Priests Retirement Board—Most Rev. GERALD F. KICANAS; Rev. ALEJANDRO URENA; Very Rev. WILLIAM MCCANN; Rev. RICHARD CATANACH; Rev. Msgr. ROBERT L. GETZ, P.A., (Retired); Very Rev. VALENTINE M. JANKOWSKI, O.F.M.Conv.; MS. JENNIFER CANTRELL.

Permanent Deacon Council—Deacons ARTHUR GUTIERREZ; ROGELIO MONTES; KENNETH QUADE; JERRY PIERCE; LOUIS A. ROMAN; CHRISTOPHER GUTIERREZ.

Director of Deacon Formation—Very Rev. CARLOS A. ESPINOZA; Deacon LEONEL BRISENO.

Director of Deacons—Very Rev. CARLOS A. ESPINOZA.

Comptroller—MRS. BRENDA CLARK.

Human Resources—MS. MARGARITA MARTINEZ.

Finance Council—Most Rev. GERALD F. KICANAS; MR. JONATHAN BLAZAK, Finance Dir.; Very Rev. ENRIQUE LOPEZ-ESCALERA, Chancellor; MR. GREG CARRASCO; Rev. RICHARD CATANACH; Deacon

JAMES HOY; Very Rev. WILLIAM MCCANN; MRS. SUSAN ROBERTS; RICK KOLL.

Office of Development, Stewardship and Foundation—MRS. SUSAN ROBERTS, Exec. Dir.

Office of Insurance—MR. BRENT HATLEY, Risk Mgr./Insurance Admin.

Office of Buildings and Properties—MR. JUAN MORENO, Real Estate & Properties Technician/Construction Liaison.

Diocesan Ministries Offices and Directors

Office of Evangelization and Formation—MS. GRACE CASSETTA, Dir.

Office of Vocations—Rev. ALEJANDRO URENA; Very Rev. JUAN CARLOS RAMIREZ.

Art and Environment Committee—MRS. JOANNA HASTON.

Attorneys—Deacon DAVID MCNEILL JR.; MS. KATY MORROW; MR. ALAN GREEN.

Campus Ministry—Rev. ALEJANDRO URENA.

Judicial Vicar—Rev. CHRISTOPHER E. WILLIAMS, J.C.L.

Cursillo Secretariat—Deacon JESUS HERRERA, Spiritual Dir.; MR. PASCUAL MENDEZ, Sec.

Office of Children and Youth Catechesis—MS. GRACE CASSETTA.

Lay Ministry Formation—MS. GRACE CASSETTA, Dir.

Ecumenical Liaison—Deacon LEONEL BRISENO, Deputy.

Hispanic Ministry—VACANT.

Holy Childhood Association—Very Rev. Msgr. JOHN E. ANDERSON, P.A., (Retired).

Office of Liturgical Formation—MRS. JOANNA HASTON.

Propagation of the FaithRev. RICHARD CATANACH.

Rite of Christian Initiation of Adults (RCIA)—MRS. JOANNA HASTON.

Office of Youth, Young Adults and Pastoral Juvenile Ministry—VACANT.

Diocesan Pastoral Council—(On Hold) Most Rev. OSCAR CANTU, S.T.D. Member: Very Rev. ENRIQUE LOPEZ-ESCALERA, Chancellor.

Diocesan Archives—Very Rev. ENRIQUE LOPEZ-ESCALERA, Archivist; DONNA VARGAS.

Charismatic Renewal Liaisons—Rev. MARTIN G. CORDERO; MR. SAM TOME, (West); MRS. ENEDINA TOME, (West).

Agua Viva—Rev. MARTIN CORNEJO, Editor; CHRISTINA ANCHONDO, Mng. Editor/Graphic Designer.

Agua Viva Editorial Advisory Board—Most Rev. GERALD F. KICANAS; Sr. DOROTHY YOUNG, C.S.S.F.; MR. JONATHAN BLAZAK; CHRISTINA ANCHONDO; MRS. JOANNA HASTON; MS. JULIA FRACKER, M.B.A., M.A.; LOURDES RAMOS; MS. GRACE CASSETTA; MRS. FAVIOLA GODFREY, Translator.

Office of Prison and Jail Ministry—Deacon LEONEL BRISENO, Chap.

Office of Marriage and Family Life—Deacon LEONEL BRISENO.

Office of Catholic Schools—MS. JULIA FRACKER, M.B.A., M.A., Supt.

Pro-Life Coordinator—MS. GRACE CASSETTA.

Victim Assistance Coordinator—MS. MARGARITA MARTINEZ, Tel: 575-523-7577; Email: mmartinez@rcdlc.org.

CLERGY, PARISHES, MISSIONS AND PAROCHIAL SCHOOLS

CITY OF LAS CRUCES

(DONA ANA COUNTY)

1—CATHEDRAL OF THE IMMACULATE HEART OF MARY (1953)
1240 S. Espina St., 88001. Tel: 575-524-8563; Email: ihmcathedral@qwestoffice.net; Web: www.ihmcathedral.com. Very Rev. William McCann, Rector; Rev. Marcel Okonkwo, Parochial Vicar; Deacons Edward Misquez; Ruben Gutierrez.
Catechesis Religious Program—Email: patti.ihm@gmail.com. Ms. Patti Carrasco, D.R.E.

2—ST. ALBERT THE GREAT NEWMAN PARISH (1986) Serving New Mexico State University.
2615 S. Solano, 88001. Tel: 575-522-6202; Email: isabel@stalbertnewmancenter.org; Web: www.stalbertnewmancenter.org. Rev. Alejandro Urena; Deacon David McNeill Jr.
Catechesis Religious Program—Mr. Salvador Melendrez, D.R.E. Students 332.

3—ST. GENEVIEVE (1859) [CEM]
100 S. Espina, 88001. Tel: 575-524-9649; Email: sgcchurch@qwestoffice.net; Web: www.stgen.info. Most Rev. Joseph Mukala, Admin.; Revs. Rogelio Martinez, J.C.L.; Juan Moreno, In Res.; Deacons Louis A. Roman; Steve Apodaca; Magdalena Zubia-Candia, Business Mgr.

4—HOLY CROSS (1970)
1327 N. Miranda St., 88005. Tel: 575-523-0167; Email: info@hcclc.org; Web: www.holycrosslascruces.org. Rev. Richard Catanach; Deacon Francisco Gurrola.
Catechesis Religious Program—Virginia Smith, D.R.E. Students 107.

5—OUR LADY OF HEALTH (1956) [CEM]
1178 N. Mesquite, 88001. Tel: 575-526-9545; Email: oloh1178@yahoo.com. Rev. Ruben Romero, Parochial Admin.; Deacon Jim Brueggen.
Catechesis Religious Program—Anthony Rodriguez, D.R.E. Students 195.

6—SANTA ROSA DE LIMA (1982)
5035 Holsome Rd., 88011. Tel: 575-382-8123; Fax: 575-382-5481; Email: santarosadelimachurch@yahoo.com; Web: www.santarosadelimachurch.com. Rev. Mendoza Andres, Admin.; Deacon Leonel Briseno.

OUTSIDE THE CITY OF LAS CRUCES

ALAMOGORDO, OTERO CO.

1—IMMACULATE CONCEPTION (1900) [CEM]
705 Delaware Ave., Alamogordo, 88310.
Tel: 575-437-3291; Email: iccalamogordo@gmail.com. Rev. Martin Cornejo; Mrs. Irma Gallegos, D.R.E.; Mr. Lucas Gallegos, Business Mgr.; Deacon Peter Schumacher.
Mission—Our Lady of the Desert, (Closed) Boles Acres, Otero Co.

2—ST. JUDE (1965)
1404 College Ave., Alamogordo, 88310-4860.
Tel: 575-437-0238; Fax: 575-437-0267; Email: sjalamo@zianet.com. Rev. Thomas W. Hoffman, S.J.

ANTHONY, DONA ANA CO., ST. ANTHONY'S (1899) [CEM]
224 Lincoln St., P.O. Box 2624, Anthony, 88021.
Tel: 575-882-2239; Email: stanthonysnm@gmail.com. Revs. Jose Felix Troncoso; Juan Almarza, O.A.R., Parochial Vicar; Ricardo Hinojal, O.A.R., Parochial Vicar; Deacon Luis Padilla.
Convent—Hermanas Dominicas de la Doctrina Cristiana, 124 Tornillo, Chaparral, 88081. Tel: 575-824-0508.
Missions—Our Lady of Refuge—1320 Mercantil, La Union, Dona Ana Co. 88021. Tel: 505-589-0542. Deacon Jesse Sanchez, Admin.
Immaculate Conception, San Benito Rd., P.O. Box 2624, Anthony, Dona Ana Co. 88021. Cell: 575-496-0858.

ARTESIA, EDDY CO.

1—ST. ANTHONY (1905)
502 S. Ninth St., Artesia, 88210. Tel: 575-746-4471; Email: stanthonyartesia@yahoo.com. Rev. Francis Lazer; Deacon Antonio Torrez.

2—OUR LADY OF GRACE (1942)
1111 N. Roselawn Ave., Artesia, 88210.
Tel: 575-748-1356; Email: ourlady@pvtnetworks.net. Rev. Lurdhu Vijaya Amarlapudi, Admin.; Deacons Richard Rodriguez; Pablo Merjil.
Res.: 1110 N. Roselawn, Artesia, 88210.

BAYARD, GRANT CO., OUR LADY OF FATIMA (1950)
340 Mayo St., P.O. Box 1425, Bayard, 88023.
Tel: 575-537-2421; Email: ourladyoffatimabayard@gmail.com. Rev. Michael J. Williams, Admin.
Missions—St. Anthony—c/o Our Lady of Fatima, P.O. Box 1425, Bayard, 88023. Fierro, NM, Grant Co.
Holy Family.
San Lorenzo, Box 385, San Lorenzo, 88049. Tel: 575-313-4126.

CARLSBAD, EDDY CO.

1—ST. EDWARD (1893)
205 N. Guadalupe St., Carlsbad, 88220.
Tel: 575-885-6600; Email: workingforjesus@saintedward.net. Rev. Pasala Hruday Kumar, Admin.; Deacon Jerry Pierce; Kim Thompson, Contact Person.
Res.: 610 W. Stevens, Carlsbad, 88220.
Tel: 575-887-6486.

2—SAN JOSE (1902)
1002 DeBaca, Carlsbad, 88220. Tel: 575-885-5792; Email: sjcatholicchurch@windstream.net. Rev. Martin G. Cordero; Deacons Melvin Balderrama; Antonio Dominguez.
Religious Education Center—Tel: 575-887-1346. Patsy Grantner, D.R.E.

CARRIZOZO, LINCOLN CO., ST. RITA (1850) [CEM]
213 Birch St., Box 727, Carrizozo, 88301.
Tel: 575-648-2853; Email: santaritaparish@yahoo.com. Deacon Gilbert Chavez; Rev. Emmanuel Ezenneh, Admin.
Missions—Sacred Heart—Capitan, Lincoln Co.
St. Therese of the Little Flower, Corona, Lincoln Co.

CHAMBERINO, DONA ANA CO., SAN LUIS REY (1959)
206 S. San Luis Ave., P.O. Box 230, Chamberino, 88027. Tel: 575-233-3191. 353 E. Josephine St., La Mesa, 88044. Very Rev. Carlos A. Espinoza.
Church: 204 S. San Luis Ave., Chamberino, 88027. , Yolanda Gonzalez, D.R.E. Students 68.

CHAPARRAL, DONA ANA CO., ST. THOMAS MORE CHURCH (1977)
568 E. Lisa, Chaparral, 88081. Tel: 575-824-4433; Fax: 575-824-4433; Email: paristst.thomasmore@yahoo.com. Revs. Jose Yela; Jesus Martinez de Espronceda, O.A.R., Parochial Vicar; Deacon Roberto Mata.
Catechesis Religious Program—860 Desert Ln, Chaparral, 88081. Juana Chavez, D.R.E. Students 81.

DEMING, LUNA CO.

1—ST. ANN'S (1918)
400 S. Ruby St., Deming, 88030. Tel: 575-546-3343; Email: saintanndeming@me.com. Very Rev. Manuel Ibarra.
Catechesis Religious Program—Tel: 575-546-3905. Velia Legarda, D.R.E. Students 281.

2—HOLY FAMILY (1905)
612 S. Copper St., Deming, 88030-4115.
Tel: 575-546-9783; Email: hfcdeming@gmail.com. 615 S. Copper St., Deming, WA 88030-4115. Prakasham Naripogula, Admin.
Catechesis Religious Program—Samantha DeLao, D.R.E. Students 143.
Mission—

DEXTER, CHAVEZ CO., IMMACULATE CONCEPTION (1953)
400 W. Sixth St., P.O. Box 189, Dexter, 88230.
Tel: 575-734-5478; Tel: 575-910-2564; Email: munozmrosario@yahoo.com. Deacon Jesus Herrera, Admin.
Catechesis Religious Program—Maria Ramirez, D.R.E. Students 400.
Missions—Our Lady of Guadalupe—204 Broadway, Lake Arthur, Chavez Co. 88253. Tel: 575-308-3818; Email: acsalcido2002@yahoo.com. Adelina Salcido, Contact Person.
St. Catherine, 200 S. Texas, Hagerman, Chavez Co. 88232. Tel: 575-840-6720; Email: munozmrosario@yahoo.com. Mary Varela, Contact Person.

DONA ANA, DONA ANA CO., OUR LADY OF THE PURIFICATION (1860) [JC]
5525 Cristo Rey, Dona Ana, 88032.
Tel: 575-526-2114; Email: oloplcnm@gmail.com. P.O. Box 706, Dona Ana, 88032. Rev. Juan Camilo Montoya, Admin.; Deacon Leonel Briseno.
Mission—San Isidro, 3875 San Isidro Road, Dona Ana Co. 88007. Rev. Juan Camilo Montoya, O.F.M., Contact Person.

GARFIELD, DONA ANA CO., SAN ISIDRO (1945) [CEM]
2003 Loma Parda, HC 31, Box 43, Garfield, 87936-9701. Tel: 575-267-5111; Email: sanisidro.church@gmail.com. Deacon Manuel Madrid, Parish Life Coord.
Catechesis Religious Program—Dulce Carter, D.R.E. Students 20.
Missions—San Jose—HC31 BOX 43, Arrey, Sierra Co. 87930.
Our Lady of Guadalupe.

HATCH, DONA ANA CO., OUR LORD OF MERCY (1889)
117 Hartman St., Hatch, 87937. Tel: 575-267-4983; Email: olmsecretary@gmail.com; Web: olmhatch.org. P.O. Box 321, Hatch, 87937. Rev. Alejandro Reyes, Admin.; Deacon Timothy Flynn.
Catechesis Religious Program—Melissa Carson, D.R.E. Students 232.
Mission—Our Lady of All Nations, 1992 Rincon Rd., Rincon, Dona Ana Co.

HOBBS, LEA CO.

1—ST. HELENA (1951)
100 E. Bender Blvd., Hobbs, 88240.
Tel: 575-392-7551; Email: parishoffice@sthelenaparish.org. Rev. Joseph L. Pacquing, Parish Admin.

2—OUR LADY OF GUADALUPE (1981)
914 S. Selman, Hobbs, 88240. Tel: 575-393-4991; Fax: 575-397-1480; Email: ourladyparish@yahoo.com; Web: guadalupehobbs.com. Rev. Jose Agustin Segura, Parochial Admin.

HURLEY, GRANT CO., INFANT JESUS SHRINE (1916)
204 Cortez St., Box 97, Hurley, 88043.
Tel: 575-537-3691; Email: infantejesushurley@gmail.com. Rev. Michael J. Williams, Admin.; Deacon Arthur Gutierrez.
Missions—San Juan—2281 Hwy. 61, San Juan, Grant Co. 88041.
San Jose, 1071 Hwy. 61, Faywood, Luna Co. 88041. Tel: 505-259-9523.

JAL, LEA CO., ST. CECILIA (1941)
500 S. 6th St., P.O. Box 430, Jal, 88252.
Tel: 575-395-2431; Email: saintceciliacatholic@windstream.net. Rev. Jorge Vargas, Admin.
Mission—St. Clare, 3000 N. Main St., P.O. Box 1464, Eunice, 88252. Tel: 575-394-2198.

LA LUZ, OTERO CO., OUR LADY OF THE LIGHT (1874) [CEM]
La Luz Rd., P.O. Box 236, La Luz, 88337.
Tel: 575-434-9460; Email: olofthelt@hotmail.com.

Rev. Theophine Okafor, Admin.; Alicia McAninch, D.R.E.

Mission—Sacred Heart, Cloudcroft, Otero Co.

LA MESA, DONA ANA CO., SAN JOSE, [JC]
353 E. Josephine St., La Mesa, 88044.
Tel: 575-233-3191; Fax: 575-233-2834; Email: parishrectory@sanjosecatholicchurch.com. Very Rev. Carlos A. Espinoza, Admin.; Deacon Roger Montes.

Catechesis Religious Program—Elizabeth Serrano, D.R.E. Students 44.

Mission—San Pedro (Del Cerro), 137 Lomas Ave., Vado, Dona Ana Co. 88072.

LORDSBURG, HIDALGO CO., ST. JOSEPH (1900)
416 E. Second St., Lordsburg, 88045.
Tel: 575-542-3268; Email: stjosephcatholicparish416@gmail.com. Rev. Jude M. Okonkwo, Admin.

Missions—St. Jude—Cotton City, Hidalgo Co.

San Felipe de Neri, Rodeo, Hidalgo Co.

LOVING, EDDY CO., OUR LADY OF GRACE (1937)
301 4th St., P.O. Box 428, Loving, 88256.
Tel: 575-745-3341; Email: workingforjesus@saint-edward.net. Rev. Pasala Hruday Kumar, Admin.
Res.: 610 W. Stevens, Carlsbad, 88220.
Tel: 575-887-6486.

Mission—Cristo Rey, P.O. Box 69, Malaga, Eddy Co. 88263.

LOVINGTON, LEA CO., ST. THOMAS AQUINAS (1919)
1301 N. Ninth St., Lovington, 88260.
Tel: 575-396-4206; Email: stthomasholyrosary@gmail.com; Web: www.saintthomascatholicchurch.net. Petra Black, D.R.E.; Rev. Alonso Quinonez, Admin.; Llubia Rodriguez, Sec.; Maria Torres, Sec.

Mission—Our Lady of the Holy Rosary, Tatum, Lea Co.

MESCALERO, OTERO CO., ST. JOSEPH (1895) (Native American)
626 Mission Trail, Mescalero, 88340.
Tel: 575-464-4473; Email: st.josephapachemission@gmail.com. P.O. Box 187, Mescalero, 88340. Rev. Bryant Hausfeld, O.F.M., Sac. Min.; Sisters Robert Ann Hecker, O.S.F., Parish Life Coord.; Juanita Little, Min. Asst.; Harry Vasile, Min. Coord.; Una Lucero, Sec.

Missions—St. Patrick—Mailing Address: P.O. Box 187, Mescalero, Otero Co. 88304.

Our Lady of Guadalupe, Hwy. 70, Bent, Otero Co. 88340.

MESILLA PARK, DONA ANA CO., SHRINE AND PARISH OF OUR LADY OF GUADALUPE (1914)
3600 Parroquia St., P.O. Box 298, Mesilla Park, 88047. Tel: 575-526-8171; Email: pazkathy60@yahoo.com. Very Rev. Valentine M. Jankowski, O.F.M.Conv.; Deacons Leopoldo Moreno; Emilio Ramos. , Margie Graham, D.R.E. Students 126.

MESILLA, DONA ANA CO., BASILICA OF SAN ALBINO (1852) [CEM]
2280 Calle Principal, P.O. Box 26, Mesilla, 88046.
Tel: 575-526-9349; Email: basilica@sanalbino.org. Rev. Christopher E. Williams, J.C.L.

Mission—San Jose Mission, P.O. Box 502, Fairacres, Dona Ana Co. 88033. Tel: 575-312-4215. Sr. Marie-Paule Willem, F.M.M., Parish Life Coord.

ROSWELL, CHAVES CO.

1—ASSUMPTION OF THE BLESSED VIRGIN MARY (1963)
2808 N. Kentucky, Roswell, 88201.
Tel: 575-622-9895, Ext. 300, 302; Email: abvmmanager@gmail.com; Email: assumptionbvm@hotmail.com. Jaroslaw Nowacki, Admin.

2—ST. JOHN THE BAPTIST (1903) (Hispanic)
510 S. Lincoln, Roswell, 88203. Tel: 575-622-3531; Fax: 575-623-8933; Web: www.sanjuannm.org. 506 S. Lincoln Ave., Roswell, 88203. Deacon Ernesto Martinez, Admin.; Revs. Eduardo Espinosa, O.F.M.; Jorge Hernandez, O.F.M., Parochial Vicar; Deacon Louis Romero.

3—ST. PETER (1903)
111 E. Deming, Roswell, 88203. Tel: 575-622-5092; Email: stpeterchurchroswellnm@gmail.com. Rev. Carlos Martinez, O.F.M.; Deacons Howard Herring, Pastoral Assoc.; Frank Pitman; Christopher Gutierrez.

RUIDOSO, LINCOLN CO., ST. ELEANOR (1939)
207 Junction Rd., P.O. Box 8300, Ruidoso, 88355.
Tel: 575-257-2330; Email: steleanor@valornet.com. 120 Junction Rd., P.O. Box 8300, Ruidoso, 88355. Very Rev. Juan Carlos Ramirez.

Missions—St. Jude Thaddeus—[CEM] San Patricio, Lincoln Co.

San Juan, (Closed) Lincoln, Lincoln Co.

St. Joseph, Picacho, Lincoln Co.

San Ysidro, Glencoe, Lincoln Co.

SAN MIGUEL, DONA ANA CO.

1—SAN MIGUEL (1927)
19217 S. Hwy. 28, San Miguel, 88058. 353 E. Josephine St., La Mesa, 88044. Very Rev. Carlos A. Espinoza; Rev. Ringo Perea, Parochial Vicar.

Catechesis Religious Program—Elizabeth Serrano, D.R.E. Students 101.

Mission—Our Lady of Perpetual Help, 125 W. Mesquite St., Mesquite, 88048. Very Rev. Carlos A. Espinoza, Contact Person.

*Catechesis Religious Program*Elizabeth Serrano, D.R.E. Students 101.

SANTA CLARA, GRANT CO., SANTA CLARA (1888)
207 S. Bayard, P.O. Box 215, Santa Clara, 88026.
Tel: 575-537-3713; Email: santaclara_church13@yahoo.com. Rev. Robert L. Becerra, Church of St. Luke, 2892 S. Congress Ave., Palm Springs, FL 33461; Deacon Richard Rodriguez, D.R.E.

Catechesis Religious Program—Students 25.

SANTA TERESA, ST. JOHN PAUL II PARISH, INC. aka St. John Paul II
5290 McNutt Rd., P.O. Box 1530, Santa Teresa, 88008. Tel: 575-332-4496; Email: johnpauliifamily@gmail.com. Rev. Enrique López-Escalera, Diocesan Chancellor.

Catechesis Religious Program—Tel: 915-525-5384; Email: hcbalsiger1@aol.com. Christy Balsiger, D.R.E. Students 45.

SILVER CITY, GRANT CO.

1—ST. FRANCIS NEWMAN CENTER PARISH (1964) Serving Western New Mexico University.
914 W. 13th St., Silver City, 88061.
Tel: 575-538-3662; Email: stfrancisnewman@msn.com. Rev. Jarek Nowacki, Admin.; Deacon James Hoy.

2—ST. VINCENT DE PAUL (1874)
420 Market St., P.O. Box 1189, Silver City, 88062.
Tel: 575-538-9373; Fax: 575-388-0870; Email: svdp_nm@comcast.net. Rev. Oliver Obele, M.S.P., Admin.; Deacons William Holguin; Jeremiah Bustillos.

Missions—St. Isidore—Hwy. 211 N. #9 Turkey Creek, Gila, 88038. Tel: 575-538-9373; Fax: 575-388-0870.

Holy Cross, Pinos Altos, Grant Co..
Tel: 575-538-9373; Fax: 575-388-0870.

SUNLAND PARK, DONA ANA CO., ST. MARTIN DE PORRES (1964)
1885 McNutt Rd., Sunland Park, 88063.
Tel: 575-589-2106; Fax: 575-332-4922; Email: sanmartin@saintly.com. Rev. Guillermo Rivera, O.P., Admin.; Deacon Jesus Favela.

TRUTH OR CONSEQUENCES, SIERRA CO., OUR LADY OF PERPETUAL HELP (1916)
103 E. 6th Ave., Truth or Consequences, 87901.
Tel: 575-894-7804; Tel: 575-894-7805;
Tel: 575-894-0451; Email: olphviola@gmail.com. Revs. Marcos Reyna; Donald F. Hyatt, C.S.B.; Deacons James R. Winder, Parish Life Coord.; Adam L. Sanchez.

Missions—St. Jose—Cuchillo, Sierra Co.

San Ysidro, Las Palomas, Sierra Co.

St. Ignatius, Montecello, Sierra Co.

San Lorenzo, Placitas, Sierra Co.

Chapels—St. Gregory, Chapels Chiz—

San Miguel, Rancho de San Miguel.

Station—St. Jude, Winston.

TULAROSA, OTERO CO., ST. FRANCIS DE PAULA (1868) [CEM] [JC]
303 Encino, Tularosa, 88352. Tel: 575-585-2793; Email: francis@tularosa.net. Rev. Theophine Okafor, Admin.; Deacon Mariano Melendrez.

Mission—Santo Nino, Three Rivers, Otero Co. 88352.

On Duty Outside the Diocese:
Revs.—
Basso, Anthony, Orange Park, FL
Flores, Raymond J.

Absent On Leave:
Revs.—
Beggane, Thomas
Valdez, Jose Pedro
Weber, John, J.C.L., (Medical Leave).

Military:
Revs.—
Garcia, Alfredo, Sierra Chapel, WSMR, NM
Udechekwa, Bedemoore, St. Joseph Holloman AFB.

Retired:
Very Rev. Msgrs.—
Anderson, John E., P.A., (Retired)
Getz, Robert L., P.A., (Retired)
Revs.—
Bergs, David, (Retired)
Clark, Anthony, (Retired)
Galvan, Alfred, (Retired)
Kao, Paulus, (Retired)
Macaya, Miguel, (Retired)
Nichols, Roderick, (Retired).

Permanent Deacons:
Albin, Richard, Santa Teresa
Apodaca, Steve, St. Genevieve, Las Cruces
Balderrama, Mel L., San Jose, Carlsbad
Briseno, Leonel, Our Lady of Purification, Dona Ana
Brueggen, Jim, Our Lady of Health, Las Cruces
Bustillos, Jeramiah Gomes, St. Vincent de Paul, Silver City
Castanon, David M., (Retired), Santa Clara, Santa Clara
Chavez, Gilbert, St. Rita, Carrizozo
Chavez, Rigoberto, (Retired)
Dominguez, Antonio, San Jose, Carlsbad
Favela, Jesus, San Martin de Porres, Sunland Park
Flynn, Timothy, Our Lord of Mercy, Hatch
Gurrola, Francisco, Holy Cross, Las Cruces
Gutierrez, Arthur, Shrine Infant Jesus, Hurley
Gutierrez, Christopher, St. Peter, Roswell
Gutierrez, Ruben, Cathedral of IHM, Las Cruces
Herrera, Jesus, Immaculate Conception, Dexter; Admin.
Herring, Howard, St. Peter, Roswell
Holguin, William, St. Vincent de Paul, Silver City
Hoy, James, St. Francis Newman, Silver City
Madrid, Manuel, San Isidro, Garfield
Martinez, Ernesto, St. John the Baptist, Roswell
Mata, Roberto, St. Thomas More, Chaparral
McNeill, David Jr., Albert the Great Newman Center, Las Cruces
Melendrez, Mariano C., St. Francis de Paula, Tularosa
Merjil, Pablo, Our Lady of Grace, Artesia
Miller, Jerry, St. Francis Newman, Silver City
Misquez, Edward, IHM, Las Cruces
Montes, Rogelio, San Jose, La Mesa; San Miguel, San Miguel
Moreno, Leopoldo, San Jose, La Mesa; Shrine and Parish of Our Lady of Guadalupe, Mesilla Park
Navarrette, Sam, (Retired)
Padilla, Luis, St. Anthony, Anthony
Pierce, Jerry, St. Edward, Carlsbad
Pitman, Frank, St. Peter, Roswell
Quade, Kenneth, St. Joseph Holloman AFB
Ramos, Emilio, Our Lady of Guadalupe, Mesilla Park
Rodriguez, Richard, Our Lady of Grace, Artesia
Rodriguez, Richard Alires, (Retired)
Roman, Louis A., St. Genevieve, Las Cruces; Co-Dir., Deacon Formation
Romero, Louis, St. John the Baptist, Roswell
Sanchez, Adam L., (Retired)
Sanchez, Jesse, St. Anthony, Anthony
Schumacher, Peter, Immaculate Conception, Alamogordo
Shuster, John, (Retired)
Torrez, Antonio, St. Anthony, Artesia
Weiss, Andy, Our Lady of the Light, La Luz
Winder, Jim, Vice Chancellor, Our Lady of Perpetual Help, Truth or Consequences.

INSTITUTIONS LOCATED IN DIOCESE

[A] ELEMENTARY SCHOOLS, PRIVATE

LAS CRUCES. *Las Cruces Catholic School, Inc.*, (Grades PreK-12), 1331 N. Miranda, 88005.
Tel: 575-526-2517; Fax: 575-524-0544; Web: www.lascrucescatholicschool.com. Connie Limon, Prin.; Sr. Kathleen Corbett, Librarian. Religious Teachers 4; Lay Teachers 37; Students 277.

ALAMOGORDO. *Fr. James B. Hay, Inc.* (1956) (Grades PreK-6), 1000 E. Eighth St., Alamogordo, 88310.
Tel: 575-437-7821; Fax: 575-443-6129; Email: office@fjbhcatholic.org; Web: www.fjbhcatholic.org. Victor Gonzales, Prin. Religious Teachers 1; Lay Teachers 8; Students 66.

CARLSBAD. *St. Edward School, Inc.*, (Grades PreK-5), 805 Walter, Carlsbad, 88220. Tel: 575-885-4620;
Fax: 575-885-7706; Email: ofcstedward@bajabb.com; Email: st.edwardnmprincipal@gmail.com. Karen Faber, Admin. Religious Teachers 4; Lay Teachers 6; Students 56.

HOBBS. *St. Helena School of Hobbs, Inc.*, (Grades PreK-5), 105 E. St. Anne St., Hobbs, 88240.
Tel: 575-392-5405; Fax: 575-392-0128; Email: office@sthelenaschool.net; Web: www.sthelenaschool.net. Mr. Stephen Bridgforth, Prin.; Ms. Mayra Negrete, Sec. Lay Teachers 9; Students 67.

ROSWELL. *All Saints Catholic School*, (Grades PreK-8), 2700 N. Kentucky, Roswell, 88201.
Tel: 575-627-5744; Fax: 575-623-3906; Email: principal@allsaintsroswell.com; Web: www.

allsaintsschool.com. Kendra Mathison, Prin.; Anna Pabst, Librarian. Lay Teachers 12; Students 103.

[B] MONASTERIES & RESIDENCES OF PRIESTS AND BROTHERS

LAS CRUCES. *Basilian Fathers*, 1682 Alta Vista Pl., 88011. Tel: 575-521-4269; Email: ed.heidt@gmail.com; Web: www.basilian.org. Revs. Ed Heidt, C.S.B., Pres. of the Corporation; Donald F. Hyatt, C.S.B.; David O. Klein, C.S.B.; David L. Sharp, C.S.B.

MESILLA. *Augustinian Recollect Fathers* Province of St. Nicholas of Tolentine, Provincial Delegation in the South of U.S.A. San Alypius House, 2190 W. Side Rd., P.O. Box 310, Mesilla, 88046.
Tel: (575) 635-9778; Cell: (575) 571-9607; Email: jofetroncoso@gmail.com; Web: www.agustinosrecoletos.org. Rev. Jose Felix Troncoso, Admin.

[C] CONVENTS AND RESIDENCES FOR SISTERS

CHAPARRAL. *Dominicas De La Doctrina Cristiana*, 124 Tornillo, Chaparral, 88081. Tel: 575-824-0508; Email: araddcop@yahoo.com.mx. Sr. Araceli López. Novices 8; Professed 5; Sisters 13.

Religious of the Assumption (2001) 300-2 McCombs Rd., PMB #43, Chaparral, 88081.
Tel: 575-824-2850; Email: rachaparral@juno.com; Web: assumptionsisters.org. 629 Mesilla View Dr., Chaparral, 88081. Sr. Diana Wauters, R.A., Supr. Sisters 3.

ROSWELL. *The Community of Poor Clares of New Mexico, Inc.* aka Poor Clare Monastery of Our Lady of Guadalupe (1948) 809 E. 19th St., Roswell, 88201. Tel: 575-622-0868; Fax: 575-627-2184; Email: pccros@dfn.com; Web: www.poorclares-roswell.org. Sisters Angela Kelly, P.C.C., Abbess; Therese Passo, Vicar. Professed Nuns 22.

SILVER CITY. *Sisters of St. Joseph*, Tel: 575-538-3350; Email: stfrancisnewman@msn.com. Sisters Rosemary Farrell, C.S.J., 1410 W. 6th St., Apt. 2, Silver City, 88061. Tel: 575-538-3350; Rita Plante, C.S.J., 602 N. Arizona, Silver City, 88061. Tel: 575-313-2206. Sisters 2.

[D] RETREAT CENTERS

MESILLA PARK. *Holy Cross Retreat and Friary*, 600 Holy Cross Rd., Mesilla Park, 88047.
Tel: 575-524-3688; Fax: 575-524-3811; Email: director@holycrossretreat.org; Web: www.holycrossretreat.org. Rev. Thomas A. Smith, O.F.M.Conv., Dir.; Very Rev. Valentine M. Jankowski, O.F.M.Conv., Pastor; Friars Charles Henkle, Chap.; Peter Massengill, Sacramental Min.

SAN PATRICIO. *San Patricio Retreat Center*, 119 La Mancha, P.O. Box 102, San Patricio, 88348.
Tel: 575-653-4415; Email: sanpatricioretreat@gmail.com; Web: www.sanpatricioretreat.org. Guillermo Maldonado, Dir.

[E] MISCELLANEOUS

LAS CRUCES. *Catholic Charities of Southern New Mexico, Inc.*, 2215 S. Main St., Ste. B, 88005.
Tel: 575-527-0500; Fax: 575-526-9626; Email: kf@catholiccharitiesdlc.org; Web: www.catholiccharitiesdlc.org. Most Rev. Gerald F. Kicanas, Apostolic Admin.

Catholic Diocese of Las Cruces Foundation, Inc., 1280 Med Park Dr., 88005. Tel: 575-523-7577; Fax: 575-524-3874; Email: sroberts@rcdlc.org; Web: dioceseoflascruces.org. Mrs. Susan Roberts, Exec. Dir.

**Order of Secular Discalced Carmelites* (1989) 776 Montwood Ct., Alamogordo, 88810. Email: 1littlepoet@gmail.com. P.O. Box 1509, Mesilla, 88046. Therese Wiley, Pres.

The Priests' Retirement Plan of the Catholic Diocese of Las Cruces, Inc., 1280 Med Park Dr., 88005.
Tel: 505-503-8637; Fax: 575-524-3874; Email: jen@jcantrellcpa.com. 5024 4th St. NW, Albuquerque, 87101. Rev. Richard Catanach, Pres.

Secular Institute of Missionaries of the Kingship of Christ, 1012 Ivydale Dr., Apt. A, 88005-1260. Cell: 575-635-8488; Email: skclark3@gmail.com. Sandra Clark, Contact Person. Professed 3.

ALAMOGORDO. *Shroud Exhibit and Museum, Inc.*, 923 N. New York Ave., P.O. Box 1711, Alamogordo, 88310. Tel: 575-921-3505; Email: Webmaster@ShroudNM.com; Web: ShroudNM.com. Deacon Andy Weiss, Pres.

CARLSBAD. *San Jose Child Care Inc.*, 421 W. Fox St., Carlsbad, 88220. Tel: 575-628-1346; Fax: 575-628-1346; Email: sanjosedaycare1@windstream.net. Patsy Grantner, Prin. Religious Teachers 1; Students 95.

MESILLA. *Magnificat-Our Lady of the Cross Chapter, Inc.*, P.O. Box 1387, Mesilla, 88046. Cell: 575-640-5080; Tel: 575-647-2367; Email: loridahlstrom@live.com. Very Rev. William McCann, Spiritual Advisor; Elizabeth Behnke, Treas.; Amy Apodaca, Sec.; Lori Dahlstrom, Contact Person.

RELIGIOUS INSTITUTES OF MEN REPRESENTED IN THE DIOCESE

For further details refer to the corresponding bracketed number in the Religious Institutes of Men or Women section.

[0170]—*Basilian Fathers*—C.S.B.
[0480]—*Conventual Franciscans* (Our Lady of Guadalupe Custody)—O.F.M.Conv.
[0520]—*Franciscan Friars* (St. John the Baptist, Our Lady of Guadalupe, St. Barbara Provs.)—O.F.M.
[]—*Heralds of the Good News Missionary Society*—H.G.N.
[0690]—*Jesuit Fathers and Brothers* (New Orleans, Wisconsin Provs.)—S.J.
[]—*Order of Holy Cross*—O.S.C.
[]—*Order of Preachers*—O.P.
[0150]—*Order of the Augustinian Recollects*—O.A.R.
[0610]—*Priests of the Congregation of Holy Cross* (Southwest Prov.)—C.S.C.
[]—*Theatine Fathers*—C.R.

RELIGIOUS INSTITUTES OF WOMEN REPRESENTED IN THE DIOCESE

[]—*Discalced Carmelites.*
[]—*Discipulas Misioneras de la Virgen de Guadalupe*—D.M.V.G.
[1070]—*Dominicas de la Doctrina Cristiana*—O.P.
[]—*ECCE Franciscan Sisters.*
[1170]—*Felician Sisters, Immaculate Conception Convent*—C.S.S.F.
[1370]—*The Franciscan Missionaries of Mary*—F.M.M.
[1430]—*Franciscan Sisters of Our Lady of Perpetual Help*—O.S.F.
[]—*Our Lady of Sorrows*—O.L.S.
[3760]—*Poor Clares Monastery of Our Lady of Guadalupe*—P.C.C.
[]—*Religious of the Assumption*—R.A.
[3830-15]—*Sisters of St. Joseph*—C.S.J.

NECROLOGY

† Burke, Ronald, (Retired), Died Oct. 30, 2018

An asterisk (*) denotes an organization that has established tax-exempt status directly with the IRS and is not covered by the USCCB Group Ruling.

Diocese of Las Vegas

(Dioecesis Campensis)

Most Reverend

GEORGE LEO THOMAS

Bishop of Las Vegas; ordained May 22, 1976; appointed Auxiliary Bishop of Seattle November 19, 1999; appointed Bishop of Helena March 23, 2004; installed June 4, 2004; appointed Bishop of Las Vegas February 28, 2018; installed May 15, 2018. *Catholic Center, 336 Cathedral Way, Las Vegas, NV 89114-8316.*

Catholic Center: 336 Cathedral Way, Las Vegas, NV 89109. Tel: 702-735-3500; Fax: 702-735-8941.

Most Reverend

JOSEPH A. PEPE

Retired Bishop of Las Vegas; ordained May 16, 1970; appointed Bishop of Las Vegas April 6, 2001; ordained and installed May 31, 2001; retired Feb. 28, 2018. *Mailing Address: 336 Cathedral Way, Las Vegas, NV 89109.* Tel: 702-735-3500; Fax: 702-735-8941.

Square Miles 39,688.

Erected by His Holiness Pope Pius XI March 27, 1931.

Redesignated Diocese of Reno-Las Vegas by Pope Paul VI, October 13, 1976.

Redesignated Diocese of Las Vegas by His Holiness Pope John Paul II March 21, 1995.

For legal titles of parishes and diocesan institutions, consult the Chancery Office.

STATISTICAL OVERVIEW

Personnel	
Bishop	1
Retired Bishops	1
Priests: Diocesan Active in Diocese	20
Priests: Diocesan Active Outside Diocese	2
Priests: Retired, Sick or Absent	17
Number of Diocesan Priests	39
Religious Priests in Diocese	26
Total Priests in Diocese	65
Extern Priests in Diocese	24
Ordinations:	
Diocesan Priests	1
Permanent Deacons in Diocese	26
Total Brothers	5
Total Sisters	14
Parishes	
Parishes	30
With Resident Pastor:	
Resident Diocesan Priests	15
Resident Religious Priests	3
Without Resident Pastor:	
Administered by Priests	10
Administered by Deacons	2
Missions	5
Pastoral Centers	4
Professional Ministry Personnel:	
Brothers	3
Sisters	5
Lay Ministers	163
Welfare	
Catholic Hospitals	3
Total Assisted	198,350
Specialized Homes	1
Total Assisted	30,000
Special Centers for Social Services	15
Total Assisted	55,000
Educational	
Diocesan Students in Other Seminaries	6
Total Seminarians	6
High Schools, Diocesan and Parish	1
Total Students	1,477
Elementary Schools, Diocesan and Parish	6
Total Students	2,160
Catechesis/Religious Education:	
High School Students	3,691
Elementary Students	8,560
Total Students under Catholic Instruction	15,894
Teachers in the Diocese:	
Brothers	2
Lay Teachers	230
Vital Statistics	
Receptions into the Church:	
Infant Baptism Totals	4,378
Minor Baptism Totals	409
Adult Baptism Totals	161
Received into Full Communion	109
First Communions	4,226
Confirmations	2,094
Marriages:	
Catholic	432
Interfaith	84
Total Marriages	516
Deaths	831
Total Catholic Population	620,000
Total Population	2,263,946

Former Bishop—Most Revs. DANIEL F. WALSH, D.D., ord. March 30, 1963; appt. Titular Bishop of Tigia and Auxiliary of San Francisco Sept. 24, 1981; appt. Bishop of Reno-Las Vegas June 9, 1987; installed Aug. 6, 1987; appt. Bishop of Las Vegas March 21, 1995; installed July 28, 1995; appt. Bishop of Santa Rosa in California, April 11, 2000; installed May 22, 2000; JOSEPH A. PEPE, (Retired), ord. May 16, 1970; appt. Bishop of Las Vegas April 6, 2001; ord. and installed May 31, 2001; retired Feb. 28, 2018.

Catholic Center—Mailing Address: 336 Cathedral Way, Las Vegas, 89109. Tel: 702-735-3500; Fax: 702-735-8941; Web: www.dioceseoflasvegas.org. Office Hours: Mon.-Fri. 8-12 & 1-4.

Chancellor and Moderator of the Curia—Very Rev. ROBERT E. STOECKIG, V.G., Tel: 702-697-3903; Fax: 702-735-8941.

Vicar General—Very Rev. ROBERT E. STOECKIG, V.G., Tel: 702-697-3903; Fax: 702-735-8941.

Diocesan Tribunal Office-Judicial Vicar—Tel: 702-735-1210; Fax: 702-735-5146. Very Rev. ROBERT M. HERBST, O.F.M.Conv., J.C.D.

Promoter of Justice—Rev. THOMAS J. FRANSISCUS, C.SS.R., J.C.L.

Defenders of the Bond—MRS. DEBORAH BARTON, J.C.L.; Rev. Msgr. MICHAEL MORAN; Very Rev. MICHAEL J. IBACH, J.C.L.; Rev. JAMES SCHIFFER, S.S.C.; Bro. MANUEL RUIZ.

Diocesan Judges—Rev. Msgr. THOMAS F. DONOVAN, J.C.D.; Very Rev. LANGES J. SILVA, J.C.D.; Revs. CHARLES J. CHAFFMAN, J.C.D.; DAVID I. FULTON, S.T.D., J.C.L., J.C.D.

Diocesan Advocates—Deacon FELIPE RIVAS; MRS. PAM MORLEY, A.A.; MRS. LEONARDA SERNA; MRS. MARGARITA HERNANDEZ; Deacons JIM L. WIGGINS; RICK MINCH; JACOB FAVELA; Rev. SAMUEL MARTINEZ.

Presbyteral Council for the Diocese of Las Vegas—Very Rev. ROBERT E. STOECKIG, V.G.; Revs. JOHN T. ASSALONE, M.Div.; WILLIAM J.M. KENNY; Rev. Msgr. GREGORY W. GORDON, S.T.L.; Revs. JAMES MICHAEL JANKOWSKI; SAMUEL MARTINEZ; TADEUSZ WINNICKI, S.Chr.; STEVEN R. HOFFER; MIGUEL CORRAL; BRUNO MAURICCI, (Peru); GERRY GRUPCZNSKI, S.Chr.

Diocesan Offices and Directors

Catholic Charities of Southern Nevada—

President & CEO—Deacon THOMAS A. ROBERTS, 1501 Las Vegas Blvd. N., Las Vegas, 89101. Tel: 702-385-2662.

Chief Financial Officer—Deacon ARUNA I. SILVA, Tel: 702-735-7865.

Director of Clergy Education—Very Rev. ROBERT E. STOECKIG, V.G.

St. Thomas Aquinas Catholic Newman Community at UNLV—Rev. DANIEL ROLLAND, O.P., Dir. & Campus Minister, 4765 Brussels St., Las Vegas, 89119. Tel: 702-736-0887; Fax: 702-891-0615; Email: info@unlvnewman.com; Web: newman.unlv.edu.

Human Resources Department—Tel: 702-735-4570. JUDITH KOHL, Esq.

Legal Department—Tel: 702-735-2512. JUDITH KOHL, Esq., Gen. Counsel.

Department of Faith & Ministry Formation

Director for Faith and Ministry Formation—CONNIE CLOUGH, Tel: 702-735-6044.

Coordinator for Catholic Campaign for Human Development, Catholic Relief Services, Respect Life—Deacon TIM O'CALLAGHAN, Dir. Social Justice, 336 Cathedral Way, Las Vegas, 89109. Tel: 702-293-7500; Email: lvsocialaction@gmail.com.

Home and Foreign Missions—Very Rev. ROBERT E. STOECKIG, V.G., Tel: 702-697-3903.

Hospital Apostolate—VACANT.

Information, Communications and Media—Very Rev. ROBERT E. STOECKIG, V.G., Tel: 702-697-3903; Deacon TIM O'CALLAGHAN, Tel: 702-293-7500.

Italian Catholic Federation—Rev. SAMUEL J. FALBO.

Native American and Colored People Commission—Very Rev. ROBERT E. STOECKIG, V.G.

Missionary Childhood Association—Very Rev. ROBERT E. STOECKIG, V.E., V.G.

Propagation of the FaithVery Rev. ROBERT E. STOECKIG, V.E., V.G.

Priests' Pension Board—Deacon ARUNA I. SILVA, CFO;

Very Rev. ROBERT E. STOECKIG, V.G.; Rev. Msgr. GREGORY W. GORDON, S.T.L.; Revs. JOHN T. ASSALONE, M.Div.; WILLIAM KENNY.

Property Management—Deacon ARUNA I. SILVA, CFO.

Vocations—Very Rev. RON ZANONI, V.F., Dir.

Respect Life Liaison—MRS. KATHLEEN MILLER, 3510 Leor Ct., Las Vegas, 89121. Tel: 702-212-6472; Tel: 702-737-1672.

Natural Family Planning/Fertility Care—RUBY PALILEO, R.N.

Diocesan Finance Committee Members—Deacon ARUNA I. SILVA, CFO; PATRICIA MULROY; LEO FALKENSAMMER; Very Rev. ROBERT E. STOECKIG, V.E., V.G.; J. TITO TIBERTI; CHUCK KERZETSKI.

Catholic Charities of Southern Nevada—Board of Trustees: Most Rev. GEORGE LEO THOMAS, Ph.D., Chm.; Deacon THOMAS A. ROBERTS, Pres. & CEO, 1501 Las Vegas Blvd. N., Las Vegas, 89101. Tel: 702-385-2662; Very Rev. ROBERT E. STOECKIG, V.G.; JOHN P. HESTER, Pres.; Rev. SAMUEL MARTINEZ; TOM MCCORMICK; JOHN PAGE, Treas.; SCOTT WHITE; JULIE MURRAY; JIM KING; FRANCISCO AGUILAR; PATRICIA MULROY; WALTER SPANSEL; ROSSI RALENKOTTER; WILLIAM J. BULLARD; ROBERT M. BROWN; MARILYN SPIEGEL, Sec.; MARK J. RICCIARDI.

Victim Advocate & Safe Environment Coordinator—MR. RONALD VALLANCE, Tel: 702-235-7723.

Archivist—ARGIA KOPA, Tel: 702-735-2744.

CLERGY, PARISHES, MISSIONS AND PAROCHIAL SCHOOLS

CITY OF LAS VEGAS

(CLARK COUNTY)

1—GUARDIAN ANGEL CATHEDRAL (1963)
302 Cathedral Way, 89109. Tel: 702-735-5241; Web: www.gaclv.org. 336 Cathedral Way, 89109. Very Rev. Robert E. Stoeckig, V.E., V.G., Rector; Rev. Joseph Lai, Parochial Vicar.
Rectory—4433 Zev Ct., 89121.

2—ST. ANNE (1947)
1901 S. Maryland Pkwy., 89104. Tel: 702-735-0510; Fax: 702-735-5582; Email: parish@stannelvnv.org; Web: www.stannelvnv.org. Rev. Msgr. Gregory W. Gordon, S.T.L.; Revs. Gregorio Leon; Mugagga Lule; Deacon Santiago Guerrero.
School—St. Anne School, (Grades PreK-8), 1813 S. Maryland Pkwy., 89104. Tel: 702-735-2586; Fax: 702-735-8357; Email: school@stannelvnv.org. Mary Beth Zentner, Prin.; Susan McDonald, Office Mgr.; Sheila Solomon, Librarian. Lay Teachers 13; Students 256.
Catechesis Religious Program—Tel: 702-866-0008; Email: dre@stannelvnv.org. Silvia Corral, D.R.E. Students 1,510.

3—ST. ANTHONY OF PADUA (2006)
6350 N. Fort Apache Rd., 89149. Tel: 702-399-6897; Email: pat@saplv.com; Web: www.saplv.com. Rev. Robert W. Puhlman.
Rectory—5605 Rainbow Springs, 89149.
Catechesis Religious Program—Students 513.

4—ST. BRIDGET ROMAN CATHOLIC CHURCH (1945)
220 N. 14th St., 89101-4312. Tel: 702-384-3382; Email: abeers@stbridgetc.org. Revs. Rolando Rivera, M.Div., Admin.; Frank Yncierto, Parochial Vicar; Deacon Jim L. Wiggins.
Res.: 215 N. 14th St., 89101.
Catechesis Religious Program—Xavier Ceballos, Dir. of Faith Formation. Students 502.

5—CHRIST THE KING (1978)
4925 S. Torrey Pines Dr., 89118. Tel: 702-871-1904; Fax: 702-251-4935; Email: jacobf@ctkccnv.org; Web: www.ctklv.org. Rev. Ray Rioux, Admin.; Deacon Jacob Favela.
Catechesis Religious Program—
Tel: 702-871-1904, Ext. 230. Beth Thompson, D.R.E. Students 428.
Mission—St. Catherine of Siena, P.O. Box 19789, Sandy Valley, Clark Co. 89019. Tel: 702-858-3792; Email: rminch2@sbcglobal.net.

6—ST. ELIZABETH ANN SETON (1992)
1811 Pueblo Vista Dr., 89128. Tel: 702-228-8311; Fax: 702-228-8310; Email: seaschurch@seaslv.org; Web: www.seaslv.org. Revs. Bede Wevita; Lourdes Jayamanne, Parochial Vicar; David Kuttner, Parochial Vicar; Deacons Steve Doucet; Aruna I. Silva.
School—St. Elizabeth Ann Seton School, (Grades 1-8), 1807 Pueblo Vista Dr., 89128. Tel: 702-804-8328; Fax: 702-228-8906; Email: seasschool@seaslv.org. Nilakshi Helen Silva, Prin. Lay Teachers 26; Students 420.
Catechesis Religious Program—Helen Silva, Pastoral Associate, Faith Formation Dir., Tel: 702-804-8306; Fax: 702-228-8067; Meghan Hernandez, Dir. Youth & Young Adult Min., Tel: 702-804-8313; Fax: 702-363-4849; Marcie Wilske, Pastoral Assoc., Adult Faith Formation. Students 527.

7—ST. FRANCIS DE SALES (1964)
1111 Michael Way, 89108. Tel: 702-647-3440; Fax: 702-646-3587; Email: frbruno@sfdslv.org; Web: www.stfrancisdesaleslv.org. Revs. Bruno Mauricci, (Peru); Miguel Corral.
Res.: 1628 Desert Fort, 89128.
School—St. Francis de Sales School, (Grades K-8), Tel: 702-647-2828; Email: frbruno@sfdslv.org. Lay Teachers 16; Students 280.
Catechesis Religious Program—Tel: 702-646-2266; Fax: 702-647-6701. Mona Harris, D.R.E. Students 700.

8—HOLY FAMILY (1975)
4490 Mountain Vista, 89121. Tel: 702-458-2211; Fax: 702-458-0966; Email: fr.steve.hoffer@gmail.com; Web: www.holyfamilylv.org. Revs. Steven R. Hoffer; Tony Udoh; Deacons Eugene Krzeminski, RCIA Coord.; Daniel Maier, RCIA Coord.
Res.: 3879 Catamaran Cir., 89121.
Catechesis Religious Program—Email: esmesaldiaz@yahoo.com. Esmeralda Saldivar, D.R.E. Students 629.

9—HOLY SPIRIT CATHOLIC CHURCH (2007)
5830 Mesa Park Dr., 89135. Tel: 702-459-7778; Fax: 702-437-9548; Email: holyspiritlv@holyspiritlv.org; Web: www.holyspiritlv.org. Rev. William J.M. Kenny; Deacons Richard Green, RCIA Coord.; Daniel Powers; Doug Winston; Sr. Karen Crouse, Spiritual Advisor/Care Svcs.
Rectory—5585 Alden Bend Dr., 89135.
Catechesis Religious Program—Anna Forsberg, D.R.E. (K-5); Louie Latina, D.R.E. (6-12). Sisters 1; Students 775; Lay Ministers 3.

10—ST. JAMES THE APOSTLE (1942) (African American)
1920 N. Martin Luther King Blvd., 89106.
Tel: 702-648-6606; Email: stjames@sjtac.org. Revs. James Michael Jankowski; Lijo Abraham; Deacon James Marek.
Catechesis Religious Program—Email: aeagan@sjtac.org. Arsenia Eagan, D.R.E. Students 69.

11—ST. JOAN OF ARC (1908) [CEM]
315 S. Casino Center Blvd., 89101. Tel: 702-382-9909; Fax: 702-382-6655; Email: st.joanlv@gmail.com. Rev. Tadeusz Winnicki, S.Chr.

12—ST. JOSEPH, HUSBAND OF MARY (1989)
7260 W. Sahara Ave., 89117. Tel: 702-363-1902; Fax: 702-363-7976; Email: mhowes@stjosephhom.org; Web: www.stjosephhom.org. Rev. Marc C. Howes; Bro. Jose Unlayao, C.J.D.; Revs. Roy Kurian; Innocent Anyanwu, C.S.Sp., (Nigeria) Ph.D., Chap.; Deacons Thomas A. Roberts; Al Paduano; Vince Murone, Finance; Barbara Finn, Music Min.; Greg Sinclair, Pastoral Assoc.
Res.: 7761 Via Olivero Ave., 89117.
Catechesis Religious Program—Tel: 702-304-3005; Email: jwattenbarger@stjosephhom.org. Joshua Wattenbarger. Students 641.

13—ST. MARY THE VIRGIN (1983) Closed. For inquiries for parish records contact the chancery.

14—OUR LADY OF LA VANG (2003) (Vietnamese)
Vietnamese Community, 4835 S. Pearl St., 89121. Tel: 702-821-1459; Email: melavanglasvegas@gmail.com; Web: www.lavanglasvegas.com. Rev. Thomas Ha, Admin.
Catechesis Religious Program—Ron Tran, Parish Pastoral Council. Students 130.

15—OUR LADY OF LAS VEGAS (1957)
3050 Alta Dr., 89107. Tel: 702-802-2300; Email: ollvparish@ollv.org. Revs. Gerald Grupczynski, S.Chr.; Tomasz Ludwicki, S.Chr., Parochial Vicar.
School—Our Lady of Las Vegas School, (Grades PreK-8), 3046 Alta Dr., 89107. Tel: 702-802-2323; Fax: 702-802-2324; Email: ollvschool@ollv.org; Web: www.ollvschool.org. Phyllis Joyce, Prin. Lay Teachers 28; Students 469.
Catechesis Religious Program—Tel: 702-802-2362; Email: lizwilliams1234@hotmail.com. Students 147.

16—ST. PAUL JUNG-HA-SANG KOREAN CATHOLIC CHURCH (1987) (Korean)
Korean Community, 6080 S. Jones Blvd., 89118. Tel: 702-222-4349; Fax: 702-227-8817; Email: kimsjaug@gmail.com. Rev. Yung Yob Yun, Chap.
Catechesis Religious Program—Shin W. Lee, D.R.E. Students 11.

17—PRINCE OF PEACE (1981)
5485 E. Charleston Blvd., 89142. Tel: 702-431-2233; Email: cathy@poplv.org. Revs. Jose Rolando Rivera; Mark Ameh, Parochial Vicar; Deacons G. Miguel Torres; David Walker.
Catechesis Religious Program—Students 1,083.

18—SHRINE OF THE MOST HOLY REDEEMER (1991)
55 E. Reno Ave., 89119. Tel: 702-891-8600, Ext. 230; Tel: 702-891-8600, Ext. 229; Email: frmanuel@shrinelv.org; Email: mthompson@shrinelv.org. Rev. Manuel Quintero, Rector; Ms. Merlyn Thompson, Business Mgr.; Robert Grant, Music Min.

19—ST. VIATOR CATHOLIC COMMUNITY (1954)
2461 E. Flamingo Rd., 89121. Tel: 702-733-8323; Email: info@stviator.org; Web: www.stviator.org. Revs. Richard A. Rinn, C.S.V.; Lawrence Lentz, C.S.V.; Bro. Michael Rice, C.S.V.; Susan Lockett, Business Mgr.
School—St. Viator Catholic Community School, (Grades PreK-8), 4246 S. Eastern Ave., 89119-5426. Tel: 702-732-4477; Fax: 702-732-4418; Email: tbrunelle@stviator.org; Email: svsschool@stviator.org; Web: stviatorschool.org. Mrs. Tracy L. Brunelle, Prin.; Carolyn Wells, Librarian. Lay Teachers 29; Students 510.
Catechesis Religious Program—Tel: 702-733-0392. Rosy Hartz, D.R.E. Students 162.

OUTSIDE THE CITY OF LAS VEGAS

AMARGOSA VALLEY, NYE CO., CHRIST OF THE DESERT CATHOLIC CHURCH (1984) (Hispanic)
1730 E. White Sands, Amargosa Valley, 89020.
Tel: 775-372-5337; Tel: 775-727-4044; Email: frhpsalditos@yahoo.com. 1208 Joshua Rd., Amargosa Valley, 89020. Rev. Henry P. Salditos. Mission Church- Priest if from Our Lady of the Valley, Pahrump NV- Diocese of Las Vegas, NV.
Catechesis Religious Program—Students 10.

BOULDER CITY, CLARK CO., ST. ANDREW CATHOLIC COMMUNITY (1931) [JC]
1399 San Felipe Dr., Boulder City, 89005.
Tel: 702-293-7500; Email: standrewbc@gmail.com; Web: standrewbc.org. Deacon Tim O'Callaghan, Parish Life Coord.
Catechesis Religious Program—Email: standrew.dre@gmail.com. Jenifer Jefferies, D.R.E. Students 57.

CALIENTE, LINCOLN CO., HOLY CHILD (1870) [CEM]
Mailing Address: P.O. Box 748, Caliente, 89008-0748. Tel: 775-726-3669; Fax: 775-726-3669; Email: fitz_42@hotmail.com. Deacon Patrick R. Fitzsimons. Church: 80 Tennille St., Caliente, 89008-0748. Pager: 775-962-2443.
Catechesis Religious Program—Students 19.

ELY, WHITE PINE CO., SACRED HEART (1906)
900 E. 11th St., P.O. Box 151026, Ely, 89315.
Tel: 775-289-2207; Email: sacredheartchurchely@yahoo.com. Rev. John B. McShane.
Res.: 900 13th St., E., Ely, 89301.
Catechesis Religious Program—Jennifer Tallerico, Admin. Asst. Students 47.
Mission—St. Michael's.

HENDERSON, CLARK CO.

1—ST. FRANCIS OF ASSISI (2003)
2300 Sunridge Heights, Henderson, 89052.
Tel: 702-914-2175; Email: sfa@sfahdnv.org; Web: www.sfahdnv.org. Revs. John T. Assalone, M.Div.; Vicente Panaligan, Parochial Vicar.
Catechesis Religious Program—Tel: 702-914-3563; Email: king@sfahdnv.org. Craig King, D.R.E. Students 1,009.

2—ST. PETER THE APOSTLE (1943)
204 S. Boulder Hwy., Henderson, 89015.
Tel: 702-970-2500; Email: info@stpahend.org; Web: www.stpeterhenderson.org. Revs. Samuel Martinez; Shawn Dresden, Parochial Vicar.
Rectory—179 Mount St. Helen Dr., Henderson, 89012.
Catechesis Religious Program—Tel: 702-970-2525; Fax: 702-970-2565. Brothers 1; Sisters 2; Students 264.

3—ST. THOMAS MORE (1986)
130 N. Pecos Rd., Henderson, 89074.
Tel: 702-361-3022; Fax: 702-361-7784; Email: stmlv02@aol.com; Web: www.stmlv.org. Revs. Alan Syslo, C.S.V.; Michael P. Keliher, C.S.V.; Deacons Robert Rudloff Jr.; William McManus; Michael Underwood.
Catechesis Religious Program—Tel: 702-361-8840; Fax: 702-361-5992. Juliann Dwyer, D.R.E.; Dorothy Distel, D.R.E. Students 1,139.

LAUGHLIN, CLARK CO., ST. JOHN THE BAPTIST CATHOLIC CHURCH (1992)
3055 El Mirage Way, Laughlin, 89029.
Tel: 702-298-0440; Fax: 702-298-0279; Email: SJBLaughlin@gmail.com; Web: LaughlinCatholic.com. P.O. Box 31230, Laughlin, 89028. Rev. Charles B. Urnick, Admin.; Deacons Daniel McHugh; Richard Lambert.
Res.: 3115 Terrace View, Laughlin, 89029.
Catechesis Religious Program—Hope Castillo, D.R.E. Students 14.

MESQUITE, CLARK CO., LA VIRGEN DE GUADALUPE (1992)
401 Canyon Crest Blvd., Mesquite, 89027.
Tel: 702-346-7065; Email: lvdgoffice@mesquiteweb.com; Web: catholicchurch89027.org. Mailing Address: P.O. Box 300, Mesquite, 89024. Rev. Blaise

R. Baran, Admin.; Deacons John Lawrence Smith; Gary Jacobs; Jaime Marquez.
Res.: 121 Falcon St., Mesquite, 89027.
Education Center—Tel: 702-346-4460; Fax: 702-346-2156; Email: floresnev@yahoo.com.
Catechesis Religious Program—Students 234.

NORTH LAS VEGAS, CLARK CO.

1—ST. CHRISTOPHER (1953) [JC]
1840 N. Bruce St., North Las Vegas, 89030.
Tel: 702-642-1154; Fax: 702-642-0719; Email: eragland@stchrisnlv.org. Revs. M. Eugene Kinney; William H. Ortiz.
Res.: 1401 Flower Ave., North Las Vegas, 89030.
School—St. Christopher School, (Grades K-8), Tel: 702-657-8008; Email: principal@stchrisnlv.org. Mr. Christopher Zunno, Prin.; Ms. Dolce Martinez, Sec. Lay Teachers 12; Students 225.
Catechesis Religious Program—Tel: 702-657-6779; Fax: 702-657-8406. Cynthia Carrillo, D.R.E. Students 1,577.

2—ST. JOHN NEUMANN (1999)
2575 W. El Campo Grande Ave., North Las Vegas, 89031. Tel: 702-657-0200; Fax: 702-648-2327; Web: www.sjnc.org. Revs. James Michael Jankowski; Lijo Abraham, Parochial Vicar.
Catechesis Religious Program—Faith Formation Program, Tel: 702-657-0200, Ext. 210; Email: cathy.trawinski@sjnc.org. Students 694.

OVERTON, CLARK CO., ST. JOHN THE EVANGELIST (1959)
2955 St. Joseph St., Logandale, 89021.
Tel: 702-398-3998; Email: stjohn@mvdsl.com. Mailing Address: P.O. Box 457, Overton, 89040. Rev. Blaise R. Baran, Admin.
Res.: 3228 Taylor St., Logandale, 89021.
Catechesis Religious Program—Students 81.

PAHRUMP, NYE CO., OUR LADY OF THE VALLEY (1985)
781 E. Gamebird, Pahrump, 89048.
Tel: 775-727-4044; Email: our_lady781@yahoo.com; Web: ourladyof thevalley.org. Rev. Henry P. Salditos, Admin.; Deacon Rick Minch.
Catechesis Religious Program—Maria Gonzalez, D.R.E. Students 124.

TONOPAH, NYE CO., ST. PATRICK (1902)
144 South St., Tonopah, 89049. Tel: 775-482-6746; Fax: 775-482-8446; Email: stpatrickstonopah@frontier.com. Mailing Address: P.O. Box 325, Tonopah, 89049. Rev. Rey Salditos, Admin.
Catechesis Religious Program—Students 12.
Missions—St. Barbara—91 Hadley Cir., Round Mountain, 89045.
Our Lady of Guadalupe, SR 264, Fish Lake Community Center, Dyer, Esmeralda Co. 89010.

On Duty Outside the Diocese:
Rev. Msgr.—
McAuliffe, Kevin W., J.C.L., V.G.
Rev.—
Audet, Phil.

Unassigned:
Revs.—
Bedoya, Reuben
Chaanine, George
Petekiewicz, Robert P.
Roberts, Mark
Waters, Bernard F., (New Zealand).

Retired:
Revs.—
Alzate, Alberto, (Colombia) (Retired)
Annese, Joseph P., (Retired)
Anthony, Joseph, (Retired)
Bevan, James J. Jr., (Retired)
Casaleggio, Dave, (Retired)
Cortes, Jesse, (Retired)
Cruz, Gustavo, (Retired)
Hughes, Anthony, (Retired)
Nguyen, Joseph Trong, (Retired)
O'Donnell, Philip, (Retired)
Timoney, Francis, (Retired)
Wehn, Timothy, (Retired).

Permanent Deacons:
Avila, Antonio
Breeden, John
Cater, Patrick
Doucet, Steve
Fitzsimons, Patrick R.
Guerrero, Santiago
Maier, Daniel
Marek, James
McManus, William
Minch, Rick
Moreno, Jaime
Murone, Vincent
O'Callaghan, Tim
Paduano, Al
Powers, Daniel
Richard, Andre
Rivas, Felipe
Roberts, Thomas A.
Rodriguez Tarango, Jose
Rudloff, Robert Jr.
Silva, Aruna I.
Torres, G. Miguel
Underwood, Michael
Walker, David
Wiggins, Jim L.
Wilson, Tracy.

INSTITUTIONS LOCATED IN DIOCESE

[A] HIGH SCHOOLS, DIOCESAN

LAS VEGAS. *Bishop Gorman High School* (1954) 5959 S. Hualapai, 89148. Tel: 702-732-1945; Fax: 702-732-8830; Email: kkiefer@bishopgorman.org; Email: jkilduff@bishopgorman.org; Web: www.bishopgorman.org. Mr. John Kilduff, Pres.; Kevin Kiefer, Prin. Religious Brothers 2; Lay Teachers 106; Students 1,477.

NORTH LAS VEGAS. *Cristo Rey St. Viator Las Vegas Preparatory, Inc.*, 2880 N. Van Der Meer St., North Las Vegas, 89030. Tel: 702-844-2019; Email: tvonbehren@crsvlv.org; Web: www.cristoreylasvegas.org. Rev. Thomas von Behren, C.S.V., Pres. Lay Teachers 12; Students 125.

[B] GENERAL HOSPITALS

HENDERSON. *St. Rose Dominican Hospital, Rose de Lima Campus* (1947) 102 E. Lake Mead Pkwy., Henderson, 89015. Tel: 702-616-5000; Fax: 702-616-4699; Email: Robert.Sahagian@DignityHealth.org; Web: www.strosehospitals.org. Teressa Conley, Pres., NV Svc. Area. Sponsored by Sisters of St. Dominic, Congregation of the Most Holy Rosary Adrian, MI. Bed Capacity 110; Priests 1; Sisters 5; Tot Asst. Annually 35,263; Total Staff 475.

St. Rose Dominican Hospital, San Martin Campus, 8280 W. Warm Springs Rd., 89113. Tel: 702-492-8000; Fax: 702-492-8511; Email: Robert.Sahagian@DignityHealth.org; Web: www.strosehospitals.org. Lawrence Barnard, Pres. Sisters of St. Dominic, Congregation of the Most Holy Rosary, Adrian, MI. Bed Capacity 147; Priests 1; Tot Asst. Annually 44,824; Total Staff 803.

St. Rose Dominican Hospital, Siena Campus (2000) 3001 St. Rose Pkwy., Henderson, 89052-6178. Tel: 702-616-5000; Fax: 702-616-5511; Email: Robert.Sahagian@DignityHealth.org; Web: www.strosehospitals.org. Eugene Bassett, Pres. Sponsored by Sisters of St. Dominic, Congregation of the Most Holy Rosary Adrian, MI. Bed Capacity 326; Sisters 4; Tot Asst. Annually 118,263; Total Staff 2,232.

[C] MONASTERIES AND RESIDENCES OF PRIESTS AND BROTHERS

LAS VEGAS. *Clerics of St. Viator Retirement Home*, 4219 Pinecrest Cir. E., 89121. Tel: 702-699-5474; Email: silva@dolv.org. Rev. William F. Haesaert, C.S.V., (Retired). Brothers 2; Priests 2.

Dominican Rectory, Fra Angelico House (1998) 1701 Chapman Dr., 89104-3516. Tel: 702-369-1215; Fax: 702-369-3742; Email: aidsproject@dolv.org. Revs. Joseph O'Brien, O.P., Office, Supr., Email: aidsproject@dioceseoflasvegas.org; Daniel Rolland, O.P., Dir., Newman Center UNLV; Bro. Frederick W. Narbares, O.P., Prof.; Revs. Albert Felice-Pace, O.P.; Michael (Miguel) Rolland, O.P. (Western Dominican Province) Religious Brothers 1; Priests 4.

[D] CONVENTS AND RESIDENCES FOR SISTERS

LAS VEGAS. *The Franciscan Sisters of Perpetual Adoration* (1979) 1304 E. St. Louis Ave., 89104-3466. Tel: 702-735-5285; Email: lorforster1@aol.com. Sr. Lorraine Forster, Contact Person. Sisters 2.

[E] NEWMAN CENTERS

LAS VEGAS. *St. Thomas Aquinas Catholic Newman Community at UNLV*, 4765 Brussels St., 89119. Tel: 702-736-0887; Fax: 702-891-0615; Email: info@unlvnewman.com; Web: unlvnewman.com. Rev. Daniel Rolland, O.P., Dir. & Campus Min.

[F] MISCELLANEOUS

LAS VEGAS. *Bishop Gorman Assistance Corporation*, 336 Cathedral Way, 89109. Tel: 702-735-3500; Email: silva@dolv.org. Deacon Aruna Silva, Exec.

Bishop Gorman Development Corp., 336 Cathedral Way, 89109. Tel: 702-735-7865; Fax: 702-735-2996; Email: silva@dolv.org. Deacon Aruna I. Silva, Exec. Dir.

Catholic Charities of Southern Nevada (1941) 1501 Las Vegas Blvd., N., 89101. Tel: 702-385-2662; Fax: 702-384-0677; Email: abeltran@catholiccharities.com; Web: www.catholiccharities.com. Deacon Thomas A. Roberts, Pres. Tot Asst. Annually 55,000; Total Staff 223.

Adoption Services (1941) Tel: 702-385-3351; Fax: 702-388-8723; Email: troberts@catholiccharities.com; Web: www.catholiccharities.com. Deacon Thomas A. Roberts, CEO.

Immigration Services (1984) Tel: 702-383-8387; Fax: 702-436-1579; Email: troberts@catholiccharities.com; Web: www.catholiccharities.com.

Migration and Refugee Services (1975) Tel: 702-383-8387; Fax: 702-436-1579; Email: troberts@catholiccharities.com; Web: www.catholiccharities.com. Deacon Thomas A. Roberts, CEO.

English Language Program, Tel: 702-215-4732; Fax: 702-307-2265; Email: troberts@catholiccharities.com. Deacon Thomas A. Roberts, CEO.

Senior Nutrition & Meals-on-Wheels (1975) Tel: 702-385-5284; Fax: 702-385-3206; Email: troberts@catholiccharities.com; Web: www.catholiccharities.com. Deacon Thomas A. Roberts, CEO. Tot Asst. Annually 3,633; Total Staff 35; Unique 718,023.

Social Services (1941) Tel: 702-387-2291; Fax: 702-383-9031; Web: www.catholiccharities.com.

St. Vincent Lied Dining Facility (1965) Tel: 702-215-4727; Fax: 702-385-1173; Email: troberts@catholiccharities.com; Web: www.catholiccharities.com. Deacon Thomas A. Roberts, CEO. Tot Asst. Annually 187,877.

St. Vincent CCSN SRO Inc., Tel: 702-366-2090; Fax: 702-851-0820; Email: troberts@catholiccharities.com. Deacon Thomas A. Roberts, CEO.

Emergency Shelter, Tel: 702-387-2282; Email: troberts@catholiccharities.com; Fax: 702-384-0677. Deacon Thomas A. Roberts, CEO.

Resident Empowerment Program (1985) Tel: 702-387-2282; Fax: 702-558-1703; Email: troberts@catholiccharities.com; Web: www.catholiccharities.com. Deacon Thomas A. Roberts, CEO. Tot Asst. Annually 225; Total Staff 4.

Employment Services Center.

NCWB Housing, Inc. (1978) Stella Fleming Towers, 400 Brush St., 89107. Tel: 702-878-5398; Fax: 702-878-4579; Email: ncoleaia2@cox.net. Deacon Thomas A. Roberts, CEO.

CCSN Mojave Project, Inc. (1985) Monsignor Shallows Apartments, 561 N. Mojave Rd., 89101. Tel: 702-384-2643; Fax: 702-384-8759; Email: ncoleaia2@cox.net. Deacon Thomas A. Roberts, CEO.

CCSN McFarland Housing Development Corporation, Inc. (1997) 4988 Jeffreys St., 89119. Tel: 702-736-7596; Fax: 702-878-4579; Email: ncoleaia2@cox.net. Deacon Thomas A. Roberts, Pres.

CCSN McFarland Housing, Inc., 4988 Jeffreys St., 89119. Tel: 702-736-9596; Fax: 702-736-9579; Email: ncoleaia2@cox.net. Deacon Thomas A. Roberts, Pres.

Women, Infants, and Children (WIC), Tel: 702-366-2069; Fax: 702-366-9551; Email: troberts@catholiccharities.com; Web: www.catholiccharities.com. Deacon Thomas A. Roberts, CEO. Tot Asst. Annually 64,608; Total Staff 14.

Catholic Diocese of Las Vegas Capital Funding Corporation, 336 Cathedral Way, 89109. Tel: 702-735-3500; Email: silva@dolv.org. Deacon Aruna I. Silva, Exec.

Catholic Diocese of Las Vegas Capital Management Corporation, 336 Cathedral Way, 89109. Tel: 702-735-7865; Email: silva@dolv.org. Deacon Aruna I. Silva, Exec.

Diocesan Residence (1999) Diocese of Las Vegas, 336 Cathedral Way, 89109. Tel: 702-735-7865; Fax: 702-735-2996; Email: kroberts@dolv.org. Deacon Aruna I. Silva, Exec.

Serra House (Formation Residence) 9308 Harrow Rock St., 89143-1385. 336 Cathedral Way, 89109. Tel: 702-629-4438; Tel: 702-735-3500; Email: frron@dolv.org. Very Rev. Ron Zanoni, V.F., Vocations Dir.

Service Campaign Corporation, 336 Cathedral Way, 89109. Tel: 702-735-3500; Email: silva@dolv.org. Deacon Aruna I. Silva, Exec. Merged into the Roman Catholic Bishop of Las Vegas and His Successors, a Corporation Sole.

St. Thomas More Society of Nevada, P.O. Box 97404, 89193. Tel: 702-361-7480; Fax: 702-798-8653; Email: katrina@stmnevada.org; Web: www.stmnevada.org. Richard Gordon, Pres.

HENDERSON. *St. Rose Dominican Health Foundation*, 2865 Siena Hts. Dr., Ste. 300, Henderson, 89052. 3001 St. Rose Pkwy., Henderson, 89052. Tel: 702-616-5750; Fax: 702-616-5751; Email: Robert.Sahagian@DignityHealth.org; Web: www.supportstrose.org. Charles Guida, LAV, Pres.

Saint Therese Center (1998) HIV/AIDS Outreach Program 215 Palo Verde, Henderson, 89015. P.O. Box 90625, Henderson, 89015. Tel: 702-564-4224; Fax: 702-564-0604; Email: aidsproject@dolv.org; Web: sainttheresecenter.org. Rev. Joseph O'Brien, O.P., Exec. Dir. Patients Asst Anual. 30,000.

St. Therese HIV/AIDS Little Flower House, 241 Palo Verde Dr., Henderson, 89015. P.O. Box 90625, Henderson, 89009-0625. Tel: 702-564-4224; Fax: 702-564-0604; Email: aidsproject@dolv.org. Rev. Joseph O'Brien, O.P., Exec.

St. Therese HIV/AIDS Executive Office, 215 Palo Verde Dr., Henderson, 89015. P.O. Box 90625, Henderson, 89009. Tel: 702-564-4224; Fax: 702-564-0604; Email: aidsproject@dolv.org. Rev. Joseph O'Brien, O.P., Exec.

RELIGIOUS INSTITUTES OF MEN REPRESENTED IN THE DIOCESE

For further details refer to the corresponding bracketed number in the Religious Institutes of Men or Women section.

[]—*Canons Regular of Jesus the Lord*—C.J.D.
[1320]—*Clerics of St. Viator*—C.S.V.
[]—*Congregation of the Holy Spirit*—C.S.Sp.
[]—*Congregation of the Most Holy Redeemer (Extra Patriam)*—C.C.s.R.
[0480]—*Conventual Franciscans*—O.F.M. Conv.
[0854]—*Missionary Society of St. Paul*—M.S.P.
[]—*Order of the Most Holy Trinity and of the Captives*—O.S.S.T.
[]—*Society of Christ*—S.Chr.
[]—*Western Dominican Province*—O.P.

RELIGIOUS INSTITUTES OF WOMEN REPRESENTED IN THE DIOCESE

[1780]—*Congregation of the Sisters of the Third Order of St. Francis of Perpetual Adoration*—F.S.P.A.
[1070-04]—*Dominican Sisters*—O.P.
[]—*Franciscan Sisters of Charity and Penance*—O.S.F.
[]—*Lovers of the Holy Cross of Go Vap*—L.H.C.

An asterisk (*) denotes an organization that has established tax-exempt status directly with the IRS and is not covered by the USCCB Group Ruling.

Diocese of Lexington

ANNUNTIAMUS VERBUM VITAE

Most Reverend

JOHN STOWE, O.F.M. CONV.

Bishop of Lexington; ordained September 16, 1995; appointed Bishop of Lexington March 12, 2015; installed May 5, 2015. *The Catholic Center: 1310 W. Main St., Lexington, KY 40508-2048.*

The Catholic Center: 1310 W. Main St., Lexington, KY 40508-2048. Tel: 859-253-1993; Fax: 859-254-6284.

Web: www.cdlex.org

Email: webmaster@cdlex.org

ESTABLISHED MARCH 2, 1988.

Square Miles 16,423.

Comprises the counties of Anderson, Bath, Bell, Bourbon, Boyd, Boyle, Breathitt, Carter, Clark, Clay, Elliott, Estill, Fayette, Floyd, Franklin, Garrard, Greenup, Harlan, Jackson, Jessamine, Johnson, Knott, Knox, Laurel, Lawrence, Lee, Leslie, Letcher, Lincoln, McCreary, Madison, Magoffin, Martin, Menifee, Mercer, Montgomery, Morgan, Nicholas, Owsley, Perry, Pike, Powell, Pulaski, Rockcastle, Rowan, Scott, Wayne, Whitley, Wolfe and Woodford.

For legal titles of parishes and diocesan institutions, consult the Chancellor.

STATISTICAL OVERVIEW

Personnel	
Bishop	1
Priests: Diocesan Active in Diocese	37
Priests: Diocesan Active Outside Diocese	4
Priests: Retired, Sick or Absent	12
Number of Diocesan Priests	53
Religious Priests in Diocese	15
Total Priests in Diocese	68
Extern Priests in Diocese	2
Ordinations:	
Transitional Deacons	3
Permanent Deacons in Diocese	85
Total Sisters	41
Parishes	
Parishes	48
With Resident Pastor:	
Resident Diocesan Priests	31
Resident Religious Priests	10
Without Resident Pastor:	
Administered by Deacons	1
Administered by Religious Women	2
Administered by Lay People	4
Missions	11
Professional Ministry Personnel:	
Sisters	8
Lay Ministers	52
Welfare	
Catholic Hospitals	10
Total Assisted	1,404,381
Health Care Centers	4
Total Assisted	46,000
Homes for the Aged	1
Total Assisted	110
Special Centers for Social Services	1
Total Assisted	1,300
Educational	
Diocesan Students in Other Seminaries	8
Total Seminarians	8
High Schools, Diocesan and Parish	1
Total Students	834
High Schools, Private	1
Total Students	54
Elementary Schools, Diocesan and Parish	13
Total Students	2,493
Catechesis/Religious Education:	
High School Students	451
Elementary Students	2,007
Total Students under Catholic Instruction	5,847
Teachers in the Diocese:	
Priests	1
Sisters	2
Lay Teachers	370
Vital Statistics	
Receptions into the Church:	
Infant Baptism Totals	603
Minor Baptism Totals	58
Adult Baptism Totals	66
Received into Full Communion	125
First Communions	661
Confirmations	630
Marriages:	
Catholic	117
Interfaith	91
Total Marriages	208
Deaths	287
Total Catholic Population	46,205
Total Population	1,588,319

Former Bishop—Most Revs. JAMES K. WILLIAMS, D.D., ord. May 25, 1963; appt. Titular Bishop of Catula and Auxiliary Bishop of Covington on April 15, 1984; cons. June 19, 1984; appt. Bishop of Lexington Jan. 14, 1988; installed March 2, 1988; resigned June 11, 2002; RONALD WILLIAM GAINER, ord. May 19, 1973; appt. Bishop of Lexington Dec. 13, 2002; cons. Feb. 22, 2003; appt. Bishop of Harrisburg Jan. 24, 2014.

The Catholic Center—1310 W. Main St., Lexington, 40508-2048. Tel: 859-253-1993; Fax: 859-254-6284. Office Hours: Mon.-Fri. 8:30-4:30.

Bishop of Lexington—Most Rev. JOHN STOWE, O.F.M.Conv.

Vicar General—Rev. ROBERT H. NIEBERDING, V.G., (Retired).

Chancellor—KAREN ABBEY.

Bishop's Delegate for Administration—MR. DOUG CULP.

Executive Administrative Assistant To The Bishop—KAREN ABBEY.

Secretariat for Stewardship—MRS. DEBBIE SWISHER, Diocesan Finance Officer, 1310 W. Main St., Lexington, 40508-2048.

College of Consultors—Revs. PAUL PRABELL; LINH NGUYEN; ROBERT H. NIEBERDING, V.G., (Retired); MICHAEL J. RAMLER; DANIEL J. NOLL; FRANK C. OSBURG, (Retired), 1310 W. Main St., Lexington, 40508-2048.

Regional Councillors—Fayette: Rev. PAUL PRABELL. Bluegrass West: Rev. CHARLES W. HOWELL. Bluegrass East: Rev. TOM FARRELL. Mountain West: Rev. JAY VONHANDORF. Mountain East: Rev. JOHN RAUSCH, G.H.M. Big Sandy/Licking: Rev. RICHARD WATSON.

Diocesan Tribunal—1310 W. Main St., Lexington, 40508-2048. Tel: 859-253-1993; Fax: 859-259-0951.

Judicial Vicar—Rev. JOHN E. LIST, J.C.L., Email: jlist@cdlex.org.

Tribunal Director—RENATA BABICZ-BARATTO, J.U.D., J.C.L., Email: ribabicz@cdlex.org.

Associate Judges—Revs. VICTOR FINELLI, J.C.L.; BARRY WINDHOLTZ, J.C.L.; Very Rev. MICHAEL HACK, J.C.L.

Defenders of the Bond—Revs. MICHAEL WEGLICKI; AROKODIAS DAS, J.C.L.; Deacon MARCO RAJKOVICH, J.D.

Promoter of Justice—Rev. PAUL PRABELL.

Notaries—LORRAINE LEE; DONNA GOODMAN.

Priests' Retirement Committee—Revs. JOHN E. LIST; FRANK C. OSBURG, (Retired); MICHAEL J. RAMLER; STEVE L. ROBERTS; DANIEL P. SCHWENDEMAN; RICHARD WATSON; MR. GARY M. REICH; MR. NICK MEGGOS; MR. MALCOLM MERRILL; MS. KATHLEEN CHAPIN; MR. LOUIS FISTER; JEFF BRUALEY; JOB D. TURNER; MRS. DEBBIE SWISHER.

Diocesan Offices And Directors

Secretariat of the Vicar General—Rev. ROBERT H. NIEBERDING, V.G., (Retired).

Archives—KAREN ABBEY, 1310 W. Main St., Lexington, 40508-2048. Tel: 859-253-1993.

Campus Ministry—Newman Center Dir., Contact The Catholic Center, *1310 W. Main St., Lexington, 40508-2048.* Tel: 859-253-1993. Deacon JOHN ROBERT BRANNEN, Dir.

Catholic Scouting—Rev. MICHAEL WEGLICKI, Diocesan Dir., Tel: 606-464-3357.

Catholic Charities of Lexington—1310 W. Main St., Lexington, 40508-2048. Tel: 859-253-1993, Ext. 215; Email: gvicini@cdlex.org. GINNY VICINI, Dir.

Father Beiting Appalachian Mission Center—DOMINIC CAPRIA, Dir. Oper., Mailing Address: 332 River Bend Rd., Louisa, 41230. Tel: 606-638-0219.

Deaf Ministry—Masses: Sun. 11 am at Mary, Queen of the Holy Rosary, Lexington; Sun. 11:15 am at Sts. Peter and Paul, Danville.

Secretariat for Stewardship—MRS. DEBBIE SWISHER, DFO, 1310 W. Main St., Lexington, 40508-2048. Tel: 859-253-1993, Ext. 267.

Mission Office, Propagation of the Faith and The Holy Childhood1310 W. Main St., Lexington, 40508-2048. Tel: 859-253-1993. KAREN ABBEY.

Ecumenical Liaison—Rev. NICK A. PAGANO, 4001 Victoria Way, Lexington, 40515. Tel: 859-273-9999.

R.C.I.A.—KAREN ROOD, Coord., 1310 W. Main St., Lexington, 40508-2048. Tel: 859-253-1993, Ext. 251.

Secretariat for Pastoral Life—MR. DOUG CULP, 1310 W. Main St., Lexington, 40508-2048. Tel: 859-253-1993, Ext. 220.

Secretariat for Catholic Schools—Tel: 859-253-1993, Ext. 219. MR. TOM BROWN.

Director of Religious Formation & Adult Faith Formation—ROD STEARN, 1310 W. Main St., Lexington, 40508-2048. Tel: 859-253-1993, Ext. 221.

Cliffview Retreat Center—789 Bryant's Camp Rd., Lancaster, 40444. Tel: 859-792-3333. TISHA BRISTOW, Facilities Mgr., Tel: 859-792-1223.

Communications—1310 W. Main St., Lexington, 40508-2048. Tel: 859-253-1993, Ext. 220. MR. DOUG CULP.

Hispanic Ministry—MR. DOUG CULP, Dir.; Deacon EDUARDO FORTINI, Coord. Hispanic Ministry; Rev. CARLOS MARTINEZ.

Human Resources—JORDAN VICE, Interim Dir., 1310 W. Main St., Lexington, 40508. Tel: 859-253-193, Ext. 238; Email: jvice@cdlex.org.

Director of Family Life—MICHAEL ALLEN, Tel: 859-253-1993, Ext. 212.

Director of Youth & Young Adult Ministry—Deacon JOHN ROBERT BRANNEN, 1310 W. Main St., Lexington, 40508. Tel: 859-253-1993, Ext. 218; Email: jbrannen@cdlex.org.

HIV/AIDS Ministry—Rev. JOHN C. CURTIS, Diocesan Coord., (Retired).

Commission for African American Catholic Concerns—Contacts: MRS. BARBARA DEHAAN; MRS. CHRISTINA WEATHERS, Mailing Address: 410 Jefferson St., Lexington, 40508. Tel: 859-223-3703; Tel: 859-254-0030.

Regina Pacis Community—(Traditional Latin Mass Community) *4088 Frankfort Rd., Georgetown, 40324*. Tel: 859-268-5159. Rev. MARK FISCHER, Chap., Email: mfischer@cdlex.org.

Liturgy—KAREN ROOD, Dir., 1310 W. Main St., Lexington, 40508-2048. Tel: 859-253-1993, Ext. 251.

Newspaper "Cross Roads"—1310 W. Main St., Lexington, 40508-2048. Tel: 859-253-1993, Ext. 220; Fax: 859-259-0951. MR. DOUG CULP, Editor.

Permanent Diaconate—Co-Directors: Deacon PAUL S. ROOT; MS. JOAN ROOT, 4704 Windstar Way, Lexington, 40515. Email: proot@cdlex.org.

Magnificat-Lexington—NKECKI AMADIFE, Coord., 3023 Tim Tam Tr., Versailles, 40383. Tel: 859-533-8097; Email: nkeci.amadife@kysu.edu.

Ministry for Persons with Disabilities—JOE PETRY; MRS. MARY PETRY, 124 Rolling Hills, Danville, 40422. Tel: 859-936-8656.

Priests' Personnel—Rev. DANIEL J. NOLL, 601 Hill N Dale Rd., Lexington, 40503-2116. Tel: 859-983-2643.

Religious—SR. CLARA FEHRINGER, O.S.U., Delegate, 213 Taylor Dr., Lexington, 40507. Tel: 859-509-2662; Email: cfehringer@cdlex.org.

Respect Life—PEGGY SHEIKO, Diocesan Coord., Email: psheiko@cdlex.org.

Victim Assistance Coordinator—LAURA NAPORA, Tel: 859-338-5695; Email: victimsassistance@cdlex.org.

Vocations—Rev. ALAN CARTER, Dir., Tel: 859-253-1993, Ext. 247; Email: acarter@cdlex.org.

Coordinator of Vocation Programs—LOGAN HAIRE, 1310 W. Main St., Lexington, 40508. Tel: 859-253-1993, Ext. 248; Email: lhaire@cdlex.org.

CLERGY, PARISHES, MISSIONS AND PAROCHIAL SCHOOLS

CITY OF LEXINGTON

(FAYETTE COUNTY)

1—CATHEDRAL OF CHRIST THE KING (1945)
299 Colony Blvd., 40502. Tel: 859-268-2851; Fax: 859-268-8061; Email: CTKoffice@cdlex.org; Web: cathedralctk.org. Rev. Paul Prabell, Rector; Deacons Lee Ferguson; John Hinkel; Joe Spaulding; Al Wiemann; Arden Wolterman; Mark Stauffer; Timothy Weinmann, D.R.E.; John Robert Brannen; Paul Root; Sr. Georgette Andrade; Karen Sheppard, Dir. of Advancement; Karen Kirkland, Dir.; Robert Whitaker, Music Min.; Meg Campos, Dir.; Joseph Sandfort, Admin.; Mr. Joseph Buckman, Admin.; Ms. Jennifer McKenna, Business Mgr.
School—Cathedral of Christ the King School, (Grades PreK-8), 412 Cochran Rd., 40502.
Tel: 859-266-5641; Fax: 859-266-4547; Email: office@ckslex.org; Email: kthompson@ckslex.org; Email: psmith@ckslex.org; Web: ctkschool.net. Paula Smith, Prin. Lay Teachers 36; Students 485.
Catechesis Religious Program—Tel: 859-266-0302. Rebecca Whitney, Youth Min. Students 240.

2—ST. ELIZABETH ANN SETON (1980)
1730 Summerhill Dr., 40515. Tel: 859-273-1318; Email: seasparish@cdlex.org; Web: www.setonchurch.com. Rev. Daniel P. Schwendeman; Deacons Robert S. Joice; Matthew C. Coriale; Mark T. Woelfel; Spencer Parrott.
Res.: 1750 Summerhill Dr., 40515.
School—Seton Catholic School, (Grades PreSchool-8), 1740 Summerhill Dr., 40515. Tel: 859-273-7827; Fax: 859-272-0115; Email: amartin@cdlex.org; Web: www.setonstars.com. Anna Martin, Prin.; Susan Whalen, Librarian. Lay Teachers 55; Students 319.

3—HOLY SPIRIT CHURCH - THE NEWMAN CENTER (1963) Parish for Students, Faculty and Staff of the University of Kentucky.
320 Rose Ln., 40508. Tel: 859-255-8566; Email: psutherland@cdlex.org; Web: www.uknewman.com. Revs. Stephen Roberts; Terrence deSilva, Parochial Vicar; Deacon Bo Fugazzi.
Catechesis Religious Program—Sr. Ellen Kehoe, S.P., D.R.E. Students 140.

4—MARY, QUEEN OF THE HOLY ROSARY (1960)
601 Hill 'N Dale Rd., 40503. Tel: 859-278-7432; Email: mqhr@cdlex.org. Revs. Daniel J. Noll; Vitner Martinez; Deacons Jim Paris; Bob Kotzbauer; Bill Rood; Nick Nickl.
School—Mary, Queen of the Holy Rosary School, (Grades PreK-8), 605 Hill 'N Dale Rd., 40503.
Tel: 859-277-3030; Fax: 859-277-1784; Email: kpedroche@mq.cdlex.org; Web: www.maryqueenschool.org. Rebecca Brown, Prin.; Christine Hayes, Librarian. Lay Teachers 36; Students 400.
Catechesis Religious Program—Students 598.

5—ST. PAUL (1865) [JC]
425 W. Short St., 40507-1254. Tel: 859-252-0738; Email: saintpaul@cdlex.org. 501 W. Short St., 40507-1254. Revs. Catesby Clay Jr.; Carlos Martinez, Pastoral Assoc.; Deacons Ramon Alfaro; John F. Zeigler.
School—Sts. Peter & Paul Regional Elementary School - Main Campus, (Grades K-8),
Tel: 859-254-9257; Email: jburch@sppslex.org. Jamie Burch, Prin. Lay Teachers 32; Students 305.
Catechesis Religious Program—Carey Parker, Dir. Sacramental Prep. Students 185.

6—PAX CHRISTI CATHOLIC CHURCH (1994) [CEM]
4001 Victoria Way, 40515. Tel: 859-273-9999; Fax: 859-245-8123; Email: mholland@cdlex.org; Email: pstewart@cdlex.org; Web: paxchristilex.org. Rev. Patrick F. Stewart; Melissa Holland, Pastoral Assoc.
Catechesis Religious Program—Students 139.

7—ST. PETER (1812) [JC]
141 Barr St., 40507. Tel: 859-252-7551; Email: st.peter@cdlex.org; Web: cdlex.org/stpeter. 125 Barr St., 40507-1321. Rev. John E. List, J.C.L.; Deacons Philip Latiff; Bill Wakefield; Scott Allen Hunt; Ted Fraebel; Pam Berger, Pastoral Assoc.
Rectory: 153 Barr St., 40507-1321.
Fax: 859-252-1853.
School—Sts. Peter & Paul Regional School - Early Childhood Campus, Tel: 859-233-2235; Email: price@sppslex.org. Pam Rice, Dir. Lay Teachers 4; Students 171.
Catechesis Religious Program—Students 37.

8—ST. PETER CLAVER (1887) (Korean)
485 W. 4th St., 40508-1319. Tel: 859-254-0030; Email: jweathers@cdlex.org; Web: cdlex.org/stpeterclaver. Rev. Norman Fischer; Deacons James Weathers, Parish Life Dir.; Eddie H. Grider; Mrs. Christina Weathers, Business Mgr.
Catechesis Religious Program—Nita Clarke, D.R.E. Students 57.

OUTSIDE THE CITY OF LEXINGTON

ASHLAND, BOYD CO., HOLY FAMILY (1860) [CEM]
900 Winchester Ave., Ashland, 41101-7497.
Tel: 606-329-1607; Email: holyfamily@cdlex.org. Rev. Andy Garner; Deacon Robert Maher.
School—Holy Family School, (Grades PreK-12), 932 Winchester Ave., Ashland, 41101. Tel: 606-324-7040; Fax: 606-324-6288; Email: akempf@cdlex.org; Web: holyfamilyashland.weebly.com. Ann Kempf, Prin. Lay Teachers 15; Students 140.
Catechesis Religious Program—Students 35.
Mission—St. Lawrence, Greenup.

BARBOURVILLE, KNOX CO., ST. GREGORY (1910)
329 N. Sycamore Dr., Barbourville, 40906-1540.
Tel: 606-546-4461; Email: amuthu@cdlex.org. Rev. Anthony Muthu, H.G.N.
Catechesis Religious Program—Dee Crescitelli, D.R.E. Students 6.

BEATTYVILLE, LEE CO., QUEEN OF ALL SAINTS (1965)
90 Railroad St., P.O. Box 617, Beattyville, 41311-0563. Tel: 606-464-8695; Email: qas@cdlex.org. Rev. John Lijana.
Mission—Booneville Catholic Church of the Holy Family (1984) 1439 KY 11 S., Booneville, Owsley Co. 41314. Tel: 606-593-6948; Fax: 606-593-6948; Email: meilermanosf@yahoo.com. Sisters Angie Keil, O.S.F., Pastoral Assoc.; Marge Eilerman, O.S.F, Pastoral Assoc. Families 16.
ST. THERESE (1948) P.O. Box 563, Beattyville, Lee Co. 41311.

BEREA, MADISON CO., ST. CLARE (1950)
622 Chestnut St., Berea, 40403. Tel: 859-986-4633; Email: stclare@cdlex.org; Web: www.stclareberea.org. Rev. Gary Simpson; Deacon John Roche, Pastoral Assoc.
Catechesis Religious Program—Students 38.
Missions—Our Lady of Mt. Vernon— (1954) P.O. Box 1006, Mt. Vernon, Rockcastle Co. 40456.
Tel: 606-256-4170.
St. Paul (1973) P.O. Box 189, McKee, Jackson Co. 40456. Tel: 606-287-7601; Email: stpaulmk@prtnet.org. Rebecca Koury, Pastoral Assoc.

CARLISLE, NICHOLAS CO., SHRINE OF OUR LADY OF GUADALUPE (1962)
617 E. Main St., Carlisle, 40311. Rev. Daniel Fister.
Res.: 1007 Main St., Paris, 40361-1709.
Tel: 859-987-1571; Email: dfister@cdlex.org 8.
Catechesis Religious Program—Tel: 859-289-5586. Amy Switzer, C.R.E. Students 12.

CORBIN, KNOX CO., SACRED HEART (1902)
703 Master St., P.O. Box 455, Corbin, 40702.
Tel: 606-528-5222; Fax: 606-523-9901. Rev. Michael Weglicki; Deacon Kevin Gerald Meece.

CUMBERLAND, HARLAN CO., ST. STEPHEN (1940)
304 Central St., Cumberland, 40823. Rev. Mani George Thellikalayil, M.C., Email: tmgeorge@cdlex.org.

DANVILLE, BOYLE CO., SS. PETER & PAUL aka Ss. Peter & Paul Catholic Church (1807)
117 W. Main St., Danville, 40422. Tel: 859-236-2111; Email: ssppchurch@cdlex.org; Email: cunderwood@cdlex.org; Web: ssppdanville.org. Rev. Alan Carter; Deacons Jeremiah Noe; Dennis Chatham; Richard L. Abbey.
Catechesis Religious Program—Students 128.

FRANKFORT, FRANKLIN CO., GOOD SHEPHERD (1845)
70 Shepherd Way, Frankfort, 40601.
Tel: 502-227-4511; Fax: 502-875-9854; Email: gsc@gssfrankfort.org; Web: frankfortgoodshepherd.org. Rev. Charles W. Howell; Deacons Thomas Snyder; Michael Joseph Lynch; Thomas Wilhelm Kaldy.
Church & Office: 72 Shepherd Way, Frankfort, 40601.
School—Good Shepherd School, (Grades K-8), 75 Shepherd Way, Frankfort, 40601. Tel: 502-223-5041; Fax: 502-223-2755; Email: mulrich@gssfrankfort.org; Web: www.gssfrankfort.org. Dr. Michele Ulrich, Prin.; Carlee Cutchin, Librarian. Lay Teachers 22; Students 161; Clergy / Religious Teachers 1.

GEORGETOWN, SCOTT CO., SS. FRANCIS & JOHN CATHOLIC CHURCH (1869) [CEM]
604 E. Main St., Georgetown, 40324.
Tel: 502-863-3404; Fax: 502-863-2259; Email: parishoffice@ssfrancisjohn.org; Web: www.ssfrancisjohn.org. Revs. Linh Nguyen; Arokiades Arokisamy, Parochial Vicar; Deacons John Calandrella; Skip Olson; Tim Stout; Dallas Kelley.
School—St. John Catholic School, (Grades PreK-8), 106 Military St., Georgetown, 40324.
Tel: 502-863-2607; Email: office@stjohnschoolonline.org; Web: www.stjohnschoolonline.org. Dan Mardell, Prin. Lay Teachers 15; Students 163.
Catechesis Religious Program—Tel: 502-863-1213. Barbara Mandell, C.R.E.; Katharine Coleman, Youth Dir. Students 20.

GRAYSON, CARTER CO., SS. JOHN & ELIZABETH (1964)
799 State Hwy. 1947, Grayson, 41143.
Tel: 606-474-9979; Email: mflanagan@cdlex.org; Email: sje1947@cdlex.org. Rev. Michael D. Flanagan.
Res.: 303 Horton St., Grayson, 41143.
Catechesis Religious Program—Tel: 606-474-6440. Nancy Kozee, D.R.E., Email: nancykozee@gmail.com. Students 18.

HARLAN, HARLAN CO., HOLY TRINITY (1948)
2536 S. U.S. Hwy. 421, Harlan, 40831-1798.
Tel: 606-573-6311; Email: mgrieshop@cdlex.org; Web: holytrinity.catholicweb.com. Marjorie D. Grieshop, Parish Life Dir.; Rev. Mani George Thellikalayil, M.C.
The Learning Center—Tel: 606-573-3570; Email: holytrinitylearningcenter@harlanonline.net.
Catechesis Religious Program—Students 24.

HARRODSBURG, MERCER CO., ST. ANDREW (1858) [CEM]
1125 Danville Rd., Harrodsburg, 40330-9671.
Tel: 859-734-4270; Email: harrodsburg@cdlex.org; Email: mjtrimble@cdlex.org; Web: www.harrodsburgcatholic.com. Rev. Albert J. DeGiacomo; Deacons Brian Wayne Wentz; Bruce Browning.
Catechesis Religious Program—Mary Jane Trimble, D.R.E. Students 105.
Mission—St. Mary (1949) 307 S. Buell St., Perryville, Boyle Co. 40468.

HAZARD, PERRY CO., MOTHER OF GOOD COUNSEL (1913)
329 Poplar St., Hazard, 41701. Tel: 606-436-2533; Email: lhelfrich@cdlex.org; Web: mgccc.org. Lori Helfrich, Parish Life Dir.
Catechesis Religious Program—Students 22.

JACKSON, BREATHITT CO., HOLY CROSS (1923)
51 Brewers Dr., Jackson, 41339-9616.
Tel: 606-666-7871; Email: jvancleef@cdlex.org; Email: esalmivancleef@cdlex.org; Web: www.holycrossjackson.org. Rev. Neil Pezzulo, G.M.H., Sacramental Min.; Josh van Cleef, Parish Life Dir.; Ellen Salmi van Cleef, Parish Life Dir.
Mission—Catholic Church of the Good Shepherd (1987) 532 Main St., P.O. Box 742, Campton, Wolfe Co. 41301. Tel: 606-668-3731; Email: spleiss@cdlex.org. Sr. Susan Marie Pleiss, O.S.F., Parish Life Dir. (A Mission of Holy Cross, Jackson, KY).

JELLICO, WHITLEY CO., KY & CAMPBELL CO., TN, ST. BONIFACE (1886) [CEM]
76 W. Sycamore St., Williamsburg, 40769.
Tel: 606-549-2156; Email: olph.boniface@gmail.com. Rev. Jesuraj Mariasalethu, H.G.N.
Catechesis Religious Program—

JENKINS, LETCHER CO., ST. GEORGE (1912)
22 Dotty Ln., Jenkins, 41537. Tel: 859-285-0201; Email: radams@cdlex.org. P.O. Box 787, Jenkins, 41537. Revs. Richard Watson; Rob Adams, Parochial Vicar.
Mission—Holy Angels (1960) McRoberts, Letcher Co.

LANCASTER, GARRARD CO., ST. WILLIAM (1951)

224 Lexington St., Lancaster, 40444.
Tel: 859-792-4009; Email: pjoseph@cdlex.org; Web: www.cdlex.com/stwilliam. Rev. Peter Joseph KIzhakkeparambil, H.G.N.; Deacons Mark Averett, Music Min.; Dennis Arthur Dever; Ms. Rachel Waters, Sec.
Catechesis Religious Program—Tel: 859-792-4578. Joni Jordan, D.R.E. Students 14.

LAWRENCEBURG, ANDERSON CO., ST. LAWRENCE (1873)
120 N. Gatewood St., Lawrenceburg, 40342.
Tel: 502-839-6381; Email: stlawrencenews@cdlex.org; Web: www.saintlawrencecatholicchurch.org. Rev. Jeffrey Estacio; Deacon Chris Cecil.
Catechesis Religious Program—Students 42.

LONDON, LAUREL CO., ST. WILLIAM (1905) [CEM]
521 W. 5th St., London, 40741. Tel: 606-864-7500; Fax: 606-864-8263; Email: stwilliamlondon@cdlex.org; Web: cdlex.org/london. Rev. Conrad Sutter; Sr. Marjorie Manning, C.S.C., Pastoral Assoc.; Deacon Charles Kevin Black.
Res.: 605 W. 5th St., London, 40741. Email: stwilliam@windstream.net; Web: london.cdlex.org.
Catechesis Religious Program—Sr. Marjorie Manning, C.S.C. Students 51.
Mission—St. Ann (1952) 222 Town Branch Rd., Manchester, Clay Co. 40962-1322. Tel: 606-598-2718 ; Email: stannmanchester@cdlex.org. Sr. Alice Schmersal, Pastoral Assoc.
ST. SYLVESTER, EAST BERNSTADT.

LOUISA, LAWRENCE CO., ST. JUDE (1982)
1121 Meadowbrook Ln., Louisa, 41230.
Tel: 606-638-3409; Tel: 606-638-0418; Email: churchstjude@yahoo.com; Email: stjude@cdlex.org; Email: mramler@cdlex.org; Email: jdalton@cdlex.org; Email: pcataldi@cdlex.org; Web: www.cdlex.org/stjude. Rev. Michael J. Ramler; Deacon James Leonard Dalton; Sr. Patricia Cataldi, C.P.S., D.R.E.
Catechesis Religious Program—Faith Formation, Students 6.

LYNCH, HARLAN CO., CHURCH OF THE RESURRECTION (1917)
304 Central St., Cumberland, 40823.
Tel: 606-589-5616; Email: tmgeorge@cdlex.org. Rev. Mani George Thellikalayil, M.C.

MIDDLESBORO, BELL CO., ST. JULIAN (1890)
118 E. Chester Ave., Middlesboro, 40965.
Tel: 606-248-2068; Fax: 606-248-2207; Email: saintjuliancatho@bellsouth.net; Web: www.saintjuliancatholicchurch.com. Rev. John Moriarty.
Catechesis Religious Program—Tel: 423-869-9255. Theresa Tanner, C.R.E., Tel: 423-869-9555. Students 29.
Mission—St. Anthony (1889) .

MONTICELLO, WAYNE CO., ST. PETER (1967)
1139 Hwy. #3106, Monticello, 42633.
Tel: 606-348-9416; Cell: 773-595-5481. P.O. Box 669, Monticello, 42633. Rev. John L. Kieffer, S.J., Sacramental Min.; Clarita Lilia Encomio, Parish Life Dir.
Catechesis Religious Program—Students 30.

MOREHEAD, ROWAN CO., CHURCH OF JESUS OUR SAVIOR (1961)
315 Battson-Oates, Morehead, 40351.
Tel: 606-784-4392; Fax: 606-783-0190; Email: morehead@cdlex.org; Web: www.cdlex.org/morehead. P.O. Box 307, Morehead, 40351. Rev. Arturo Molina; Deacons William R. Grimes; Daniel Joseph Connell; William T. Buelterman, (Retired).
Res.: 404 N. Wilson Ave., Morehead, 40351.
Tel: 606-784-4392; Email: morehead@cdlex.org; Web: www.cdlex.org/morehead.
Catechesis Religious Program—Susette Redwine, D.R.E. Students 45.
Mission—St. Julie Catholic Church (1969) 77 E. Main St., Owingsville, 40360. Tel: 606-674-3261; Email: stjulie@gmail.com. P.O. Box 382, Owingsville, 40360.
Chapel—Morehead, St. Claire Medical Center, 222 Medical Cir., Morehead, 40351. Tel: 606-783-6500; Email: smjudilambert@yahoo.com; Web: www.st-claire.org. Sr. Judi Lambert, Pastoral Care Dir.

MOUNT STERLING, MONTGOMERY CO., ST. PATRICK (1868) [CEM]
139 W. Main St., Mount Sterling, 40353.
Tel: 859-499-1075; Tel: 859-498-0300;
Fax: 859-499-1742; Email: stpatmtsterling@gmail.com; Web: stpatrickmtsterling.com. Rev. Frank Brawner.
Catechesis Religious Program—Melissa Buttry-Facilita, Facilitator. Students 50.

NICHOLASVILLE, JESSAMINE CO., ST. LUKE (1867)
304 S. Main St., Nicholasville, 40356.
Tel: 859-885-4892; Fax: 859-885-6762; Email: stlukenicholasville@cdlex.org; Web: nicholasville.cdlex.org. Revs. William C. Bush; Nicholas A. Pagano Jr., Parochial Vicar; Deacons David Hanson; Frank Keller; Marco Michael Rajkovich Jr.; Gary Rudemiller.
Catechesis Religious Program—Marquita Stafford, D.R.E. Students 68.

OTTENHEIM, LINCOLN CO., ST. SYLVESTER (1885) [CEM]
224 Lexington St., Lancaster, 40444.
Tel: 859-792-4009; Email: stwlcath@cdlex.org. Rev. Peter Kizhakkeparambil; Deacons Mark Averett; Dennis Arthur Dever; Leia Lewis; Ms. Rachel Waters, Sec.
Catechesis Religious Program—Tel: 606-365-2902. Emily Abee, D.R.E. Students 11.

PAINTSVILLE, JOHNSON CO., ST. MICHAEL CATHOLIC CHURCH (1941)
720 Washington Ave., Paintsville, 41240.
Tel: 606-789-4455; Email: stmike@bellsouth.net. Rev. Terence E. Hoppenjans; Sr. Nancy Edwards, C.S.J., Pastoral Assoc.; Deacon Paul David Brown.
School—Our Lady of the Mountains, (Grades PreK-1), 405 3rd St., Paintsville, 41240. Tel: 606-789-3661; Fax: 606-789-3661; Email: jrunyon@cdlex.org. Jayme Runyon, Prin. Clergy 2; Lay Teachers 6; Students 34.
Catechesis Religious Program—Students 12.

PARIS, BOURBON CO., ANNUNCIATION OF THE BLESSED VIRGIN MARY (1856) [CEM]
1007 Main St., Paris, 40361. Tel: 859-987-1571; Email: annunciation@cdlex.org; Web: annunciationparis.org. Rev. Daniel Fister; Deacons Kenneth Rayfield; Ronald Sparks; Phil Hanrahan.
School—St. Mary, (Grades PreK-5), 1121 Main St., Paris, 40361. Tel: 859-987-3815; Fax: 859-987-3815; Email: stmary@cdlex.org; Email: kleer@cdlex.org; Web: sms-ky.org. Lucy Marsh, Admin. Clergy 1; Lay Teachers 8; Students 66.
Catechesis Religious Program—Jennifer Frye, D.R.E. Students 47.

PIKEVILLE, PIKE CO., ST. FRANCIS OF ASSISI (1949)
137 Bryan St., Pikeville, 41501-1656.
Tel: 606-437-6117; Fax: 606-437-6822; Email: rwatson@cdlex.org; Email: radams@cdlex.org; Web: rgriffith@cdlex.org. Revs. Richard Watson; Rob Adams, Parochial Vicar; Deacon Joseph Byron Jacobs.
School—St. Francis of Assisi School, (Grades K-6), 147 Bryan St., Pikeville, 41501. Tel: 606-437-6117; Fax: 606-437-6822; Email: awestgate@cdlex.org; Web: cdlex.org/stfrancisschool. Rev. Richard Watson, Prin.; Mr. Anne Westgate, Prin. Lay Teachers 3; Sisters 1; Students 30.

PRESTONSBURG, FLOYD CO., ST. MARTHA (1984)
60 Martha Vineyard, Prestonsburg, 41653.
Tel: 606-874-9526; Email: stmarthaprestonsburg@cdlex.org. Rev. Brandon Bigam.
Catechesis Religious Program—Patty McBride, D.R.E. Students 40.
Mission—St. Luke (1982) 1221 Parkway Dr., Salyersville, Floyd Co. 41465. Tel: 606-349-5320.
Chapel—Martin, St. Joseph Hospital,
Tel: 606-285-6400.

RAVENNA, ESTILL CO., ST. ELIZABETH OF HUNGARY (1932)
316 5th St., Ravenna, 40472-1312. Tel: 606-723-8216 ; Email: st.elizabeth@windstream.net. Rev. Albert Fritsch, S.J.
Catechesis Religious Program—Students 4.

RICHMOND, MADISON CO., ST. MARK (1867)
608 W. Main St., Richmond, 40475.
Tel: 859-623-2989, Ext. 2001; Email: tfarrell@cdlex.org; Web: www.saintmarkcatholicchurch.net. Rev. Thomas P. Farrell; Deacons James D. Bennett; John Robert Brannen.
School—St. Mark School, (Grades PreK-5), Tel: 859-623-2989, Ext. 4; Email: cathycornett@saintmarkcatholicschool.com; Web: www.saintmarkcatholicschool.com. Rev. Thomas P. Farrell. Clergy 1; Lay Teachers 6; Students 72.
Catechesis Religious Program—Students 125.

SOMERSET, PULASKI CO., ST. MILDRED (1887)
203 S. Central Ave., Somerset, 42501.
Tel: 606-678-5051; Email: mshull@cdlex.org; Web: www.saintmildred.com. Rev. Jay Von Handorf; Deacons Vincent E. Cheshire; Larry Cranfill.
Catechesis Religious Program—Students 58.
Mission—Good Shepherd Chapel, 130 N. Main St., Whitley City, 42653. Tel: 606-376-8728.

STANTON, POWELL CO., OUR LADY OF THE MOUNTAINS (1984)
1093 E. College Ave., P.O. Box 727, Stanton, 40380-2354. Tel: 606-663-5919. Rev. Albert Fritsch, S.J.; Sr. Mary Jane Kreidler, Parish Life Coord.
Catechesis Religious Program—Students 5.

VERSAILLES, WOODFORD CO., ST. LEO (1891)
295 Huntertown Rd., Versailles, 40383.
Tel: 859-873-4573; Email: stleo@cdlex.org; Web: saintleoparishky.org. Rev. Miguel Alvizures; Deacons Patrick David DeLuca; Jim Lafser; Lawrence Todd.
School—St. Leo School, (Grades K-8), 255 Huntertown Rd., Versailles, 40383.
Tel: 859-873-4591; Email: hdibiasie@saintleoky.org; Web: saintleoky.org. Dr. Helena DiBiasie, Interim Prin. Lay Teachers 16; Students 180.
Catechesis Religious Program—Pat Newell, D.R.E. Students 144.

WEST LIBERTY, MORGAN CO., PRINCE OF PEACE (1963)
163 Pine Acres Dr., P.O. Box 393, West Liberty, 41472. Tel: 606-743-3266; Email: mflanagan@cdlex.org. Rev. Michael D. Flanagan; Mrs. Brenda Morgan, Business Mgr.
Rectory—Tel: 606-743-4817.
Catechesis Religious Program— (1963) Students 4.

WILLIAMSBURG, WHITLEY CO., OUR LADY OF PERPETUAL HELP (1963)
76 W. Sycamore St., Williamsburg, 40769.
Tel: 606-549-2156; Email: olph.boniface@gmail.com. Rev. Jesuraj Mariasalethu, H.G.N.
Catechesis Religious Program—Students 7.

WINCHESTER, CLARK CO., ST. JOSEPH aka St. Joseph Catholic Church (1872)
248 S. Main St., Winchester, 40391.
Tel: 859-744-4917; Email: stjospeh@cdlex.org; Web: stjosephwinchester.com. Rev. Frank Brawner; Deacons Anthony R. Fritz; Ron Allen.
Res.: 254 S. Main St., Winchester, 40391.
School—St. Agatha Academy, (Grades K-8), 244 S. Main St., Winchester, 40391. Tel: 859-744-6484; Fax: 859-744-0268; Email: stagatha@bellsouth.net; Web: saintagathaacademy.org. John Pica, Prin.; Christy Hisle, Librarian. Montessori Preschool - 8th Grade Lay Teachers 16; Students 148.
Catechesis Religious Program—Kathie Schweikart, D.R.E., Email: kschweikart@cdlex.org. Students 22.

PARISH PILGRIMAGE SHRINES

CARLISLE, OUR LADY OF GUADALUPE SHRINE
617 E. Main St., Carlisle, 40311. Tel: 859-987-1571; Email: kleer@cdlex.org. Rev. Daniel Fister.

Chaplains of Public Institutions

LEXINGTON. *Federal Medical Center*, 3301 Leestown Rd., 40507. Vacant.
Veterans' Administration Hospital, Leestown Pk., 40511. Tel: 859-233-4511. Vacant.
ASHLAND. *Federal Correctional Institution*. Vacant.
MANCHESTER. *Federal Correction Institution*. Vacant.

Special Assignment:
Revs.—
Aduaka, Anthony, (On Duty Outside of Diocese)
Dreves, Mark, (Sabbatical)
Fitzsimons, Patrick, (On Duty Outside of Diocese)
Godinez, Eulices, (On Duty Outside of Diocese)
Sichko, James W., (Evangelization).

Retired:
Rev. Msgr.—
Rolf, John J., (Retired), 15 Lemans Dr., Naples, FL 34112
Revs.—
Curtis, John C., (Retired), 2720 Green Valley Ct., 40511
Dane, John, (Retired), 193 Barnsley Rd., Wombwell, Barnsley, South Yorkshire S73 8DR, England
Hehman, Lawrence W., (Retired), 1332 Viley Rd., 40504
Johnson, Carl, (Retired), 1520 Derby Dr., Henderson, NV 89002
Knight, Dennis, (Retired), 541 Hill'n Dale, 40503
Koury, Joseph, (Retired), P.O. Box 3385, Glen Allen, VA 23058
Nieberding, Robert H., V.G., (Retired), 2716 Green Vally Ct., 40511
Osburg, Frank C., (Retired), 2717 Bay Cedar Cove, 40511
Stratman, Raymond, (Retired), 1139 Providence Ln., 40502
Thai, Thomas V., Ph.D., (Retired), 4698 Long Dr., Hamilton, OH 45011.

Permanent Deacons:
Abbey, Richard L.
Agnoli, Francis L., Davenport
Alfaro, Ramon
Allen, Ron
Averett, Mark
Bennett, James D.
Black, Charles Kevin
Boduch, Robert
Brannen, John Robert
Brown, Paul David
Browning, Bruce
Buelterman, William
Calandrella, John
Cecil, Chris
Chatham, Dennis
Cheshire, Vincent
Coe, John C.
Connell, Daniel Joseph
Coriale, Matthew C.
Cranfill, Larry
Dalton, James Leonard
Daugherty, Gordon Joseph
Daukas, Michael R.
DeLuca, Patrick David
Dever, Dennis Arthur

Downey, Richard C.
Durbin, Larry Pierce
Ferguson, Lee
Flowers, Don K.
Fortini, Eduardo
Fraebel, William Theodore Jr.
Fritz, Anthony R.
Fugazzi, Frederick E. Jr.
Greenwell, William
Grider, Eddie H.
Grimes, William R.
Hanrahan, Phil
Hanson, David
Hester, Steven
Hinkel, John
Hunt, Scott Allen
Jacobs, Joseph Byron
Jahnige, Ralph B.
Joice, Robert S.
Kaldy, Thomas Wilhelm
Keller, William F.
Kelley, Dallas
Kimmerly, James Joseph
Kotzbauer, Robert N.
Lackney, Robert R., (Retired)
Lafser, Jim
Latiff, Philip
Lewis, John M.
Lynch, Michael Joseph
Maher, Robert J.
Martorano, Raymond D., (Retired)
Meece, Kevin Gerald
Mellenger, Karl, (Retired)
Myers, Reid Lawrence
Nickl, Nick
Noe, Jeremiah
O'Neil, Dennis J., (Retired)
Olson, Paul E.
Paris, Jim
Parrott, Spencer
Rajkovich, Marco Michael Jr.
Rayfield, Kenneth
Roche, John
Rohan, Thomas, (Retired)
Rood, William A.
Root, Paul S.
Rudemiller, Gary
Schueneman, Joseph T., (Retired)
Snyder, Thomas, (Retired)
Sparks, Ronald
Spaulding, Joe
Stout, Tim
Strauffer, Mark B.
Todd, Lawrence
Wagner, Thomas
Wakefield, Bill
Weathers, James
Weinmann, Timothy E.
Wentz, Brian Wayne
Wiemann, Al
Woelfel, Mark T.
Wolterman, Arden J.
Zeigler, John F.

INSTITUTIONS LOCATED IN DIOCESE

[A] HIGH SCHOOLS, DIOCESAN

LEXINGTON. *Lexington Catholic High School*, Lexington Catholic High School, 2250 Clays Mill Rd., 40503. Tel: 859-277-7183; Fax: 859-276-5086; Email: krookard@lexingtoncatholic.com; Web: www.lexingtoncatholic.com. Dr. Steven Angelucci, Pres.; Mathew George, Prin. Lay Teachers 81; Priests 1; Students 834.

[B] HIGH SCHOOLS, PRIVATE

HAGER HILL. *The Piarist School* (1990) (Grades 7-12), P.O. Box 369, Hagerhill, 41222. Tel: 606-789-1967; Fax: 606-789-1968; Email: piarist_adm@bellsouth.net; Web: www.piaristschool.org. Rev. Thomas R. Carroll, Sch.P., Prin. College Prep High School. Religious Teachers 2; Lay Teachers 16; Priests 1; Students 60.

[C] GENERAL HOSPITALS

LEXINGTON. *Continuing Care Hospital, Inc.* (2001) 1 St. Joseph Dr., 3rd & 4th Fls., 40504.
Tel: 859-967-5744; Fax: 859-313-3835; Email: bobdesotelle@sjhlex.org. Robert Desotelle, Pres. Bed Capacity 57; Tot Asst. Annually 8,974; Total Staff 76.

Saint Joseph Health System dba Saint Joseph East, 150 N. Eagle Creek Dr., 40509. Tel: 859-967-5000; Fax: 859-967-5766; Email: karacarr@sjhlex.org; Web: www.sjhlex.org/east. Eric Gilliam, Pres. Bed Capacity 217; Tot Asst. Annually 144,659; Total Staff 864.

St. Joseph Health System, Inc. dba Saint Joseph Hospital, 1 St. Joseph Dr., 40504.
Tel: 859-313-1000; Fax: 859-313-3000; Email: squinn@sjhlex.org; Email: clspitser@catholichealth.net. Bruce Tassin, Pres. (Member of Catholic Health Initiatives). Bed Capacity 433; Tot Asst. Annually 111,903; Total Staff 1,160.

ASHLAND. *Our Lady of Bellefonte Hospital, Inc.*, 1000 St. Christopher Dr., Ashland, 41101.
Tel: 606-833-3333; Fax: 606-833-3593; Email: careline@bshsi.org; Web: bonsecours.com/kentucky. Kevin Halter, CEO; Mr. Joseph Mazzawi, Vice Pres. Mission. (Member of Bon Secours Mercy Health System, Inc.) Bed Capacity 214; Tot Asst. Annually 469,504; Total Staff 1,300.

BEREA. *Saint Joseph-Berea*, 305 Estill St., Berea, 40403. Tel: 859-986-3151; Fax: 859-986-6768; Email: terrencedeis@sj-london.org. Terence Deis, Pres. A member of Catholic Health Initiatives. Bed Capacity 25; Tot Asst. Annually 53,570; Total Staff 240.

IRVINE. *Mercy Health - Marcum and Wallace Hospital, LLC*, 60 Mercy Ct., Irvine, 40336.
Tel: 606-723-2115; Fax: 606-723-2951; Email: sstarling@mercy.com; Web: www.mercy.com. Susan Starling, Pres. & CEO. (Member of Mercy Health System, Cincinnati, OH). Bed Capacity 25; Tot Asst. Annually 74,136; Total Staff 202.

LONDON. *Saint Joseph London*, 1001 Saint Joseph Ln., London, 40741. Tel: 606-330-6000;
Fax: 606-330-6020; Email: DebbieM@sj-london.org; Web: saintjoseph-london.org. Terence Deis, Pres. (Member of Catholic Health Initiatives). Bed Capacity 150; Tot Asst. Annually 108,920; Total Staff 722.

MARTIN. *Saint Joseph Martin*, 11203 Main St., Martin, 41649. P.O. Box 910, Martin, 41649.
Tel: 606-285-6400; Fax: 606-285-6409; Email: bobbyisaac@catholichealth.net; Email: kathystumbo@catholichealth.net; Web: www.kentuckyonehealth.org/martin. Ms. Kathy Stumbo, Pres. Member of KentuckyOne Health. Bed Capacity 25; Tot Asst. Annually 30,999; Total Staff 199.

MOREHEAD. *Saint Claire Regional Medical Center*, 222 Medical Cir., Morehead, 40351. Tel: 606-783-6500; Fax: 606-783-6503; Email: Mark.Neff@st-claire.org; Web: st-claire.org. Mr. Mark Neff, Pres. & CEO. Sisters of Notre Dame. Bassinets 10; Bed Capacity 159; Sisters 2; Tot Asst. Annually 352,606; Total Staff 1,222; Patients with Primary Care Centers 112,983.

MOUNT STERLING. *St. Joseph Hospital Mt. Sterling*, 225 Falcon Dr., Mount Sterling, 40353.
Tel: 859-497-5000; Fax: 859-497-5020; Email: janetcarr@catholichealth.net. Sr. Janet Carr, C.D.P., Chap. Bed Capacity 42; Patients Asst Anual. 63,334; Total Staff 350.

[D] PRIMARY HEALTH CARE SERVICES

FRENCHBURG. *St. Claire Family Medicine-Frenchburg*, 732 Hwy. 36, Frenchburg, 40322.
Tel: 606-768-2191; Fax: 606-768-6130; Email: wcwhitt@st-claire.org; Web: st-claire.org. Wendy Whitt, R.N., Clinic Coord. (Div. of St. Claire Regional Medical Center). Tot Asst. Annually 10,000; Total Staff 16.

OLIVE HILL. *St. Claire Family Medicine-Olive Hill*, 155 Bricklayer St., P.O. Box 1268, Olive Hill, 41164.
Tel: 606-286-4152; Fax: 606-286-2385; Email: Gloria.Riggs@st-claire.org. Janie Riggs, Clinic Coord. (Div. of St. Claire Medical Center). Tot Asst. Annually 13,000; Total Staff 16.

OWINGSVILLE. *St. Claire Family Medicine - Owingsville*, 632 Slate Ave., P.O. Box 1120, Owingsville, 40360. Tel: 606-674-6386;
Fax: 606-674-3096; Email: Angela.Fryman@st-claire.org. Lori Crouch, Clinic Coord. (Div. of St. Claire Medical Center). Tot Asst. Annually 13,000; Total Staff 14.

SANDY HOOK. *St. Claire Family Medicine-Sandy Hook*, 390 KY Hwy. 7 S., Sandy Hook, 41171. P.O. Box 748, Sandy Hook, 41171. Tel: 606-738-5155;
Fax: 606-738-5420; Email: Donna.Conkright@st-claire.org. Donna Conkright, R.N., Clinic Coord. (Div. of St. Claire Medical Center). Tot Asst. Annually 10,000; Total Staff 14.

[E] NURSING HOMES

VERSAILLES. *Taylor Manor*, 300 Berry Ave., Versailles, 40383. Tel: 859-873-4201; Fax: 859-873-4856; Email: srmaryfaustina@taylormanor.org; Web: www.taylormanor.org. Rev. Frank Sherry, C.P.M., Chap.; Sr. Mary Faustina Zugelder, S.J.W., Admin. Bed Capacity 82; Sisters of St. Joseph the Worker 5; Tot Asst. Annually 110.

[F] RESIDENCES OF PRIESTS

LEXINGTON. *Jesuit Fathers & Brothers* (1981) Lexington Jesuit Residence: 2900 Candlelight Way, 40502. Tel: 513-312-8695; Email: rjbueter@aol.com. Rev. Walter Bado, S.J., Supr. Priests in Residence 4.

PRESTONSBURG. *Piarist Fathers* (1989) P.O. Box 369, Hager Hill, 41222. Tel: 606-789-1967;
Fax: 606-789-1968; Email: tcarroll@cdlex.org. Rev. Thomas R. Carroll, Sch.P. Priests 1.

[G] MONASTERIES FOR SISTERS

MARTIN. *Mt. Tabor Benedictines-The Dwelling Place Monastery* (1982) 150 Mt. Tabor Rd., Martin, 41649. Tel: 606-886-9624; Fax: 606-886-6598; Email: mtabor150@hotmail.com; Web: www.geocities.com/athens/9871. Sr. Eileen Schepers, O.S.B., Prioress. Total number in Community (Perpetually Professed) 7.

[H] SECULAR INSTITUTES

LEXINGTON. *Society of St. Vincent de Paul*, 1730 Summerhill Dr., 40515. Tel: 859-266-8003; Email: svdplex@yahoo.com. Tim Lewis, Pres. District Council of Lexington.

[I] SOCIAL SERVICES

MOUNT VERNON. **Appalachia Science in the Public Interest*, 50 Lair St., Mount Vernon, 40456.
Tel: 606-256-0077; Fax: 606-256-2779; Email: aspi@a-spi.org; Web: www.appalachia-spi.org. Suzanne Van Etten, Exec. Dir.; Rev. John L. Kieffer, S.J. Tot Asst. Annually 3,000; Total Staff 3.

[J] RENEWAL CENTERS

HAZARD. *Father Farrell Spiritual Life Center*, 329 Poplar at Cedar, Hazard, 41701. Tel: 606-436-2533 ; Fax: 606-435-0171; Email: lhelfrich@cdlex.org. Lori Helfrich, Parish Life Coord.

LANCASTER. *Cliffview Retreat Center*, 789 Bryants Camp Rd., Lancaster, 40444-7028.
Tel: 859-792-3333; Tel: 877-792-3330;
Fax: 859-792-1223; Email: cliffctr@cdlex.org; Email: tbristow@cdlex.org; Web: www.cliffview.org. Tisha Bristow, Facilities Mgr., Tel: 859-792-1223.

MARTIN. *Mt. Tabor Retreat Center*, 150 Mt. Tabor Rd., Martin, 41649. Tel: 606-886-9624;
Fax: 606-886-6598; Email: mtabor150@hotmail.com. Sr. Jan Barthel, Contact Person. Staff Sisters 8.

[K] NEWMAN CENTERS

LEXINGTON. *Holy Spirit Parish Newman Center, University of Kentucky*, 320 Rose Ln., 40508.
Tel: 859-255-8566; Fax: 859-254-7519; Email: psutherland@cdlex.org. Revs. Stephen Roberts; Terrence deSilva, Assoc. Pastor.

BARBOURVILLE. *St. Gregory Church-Union College*, 329 N. Sycamore St., Barbourville, 40906-1540.
Tel: 606-546-4461; Fax: 606-546-4461; Email: stgreg@barbourville.com; Web: barbourville.catholicweb.com. Rev. Anthony Muthu, H.G.N.

BEREA. *St. Clare Church-Berea College*, 622 Chestnut St., Berea, 40403. Tel: 859-986-4633; Email: stclare@cdlex.org. Rev. Gary Simpson; Deacon John Roche, Campus Min.

MOREHEAD. *Catholic Student Center-Morehead State University*, 315 Battson-Oates Dr., Morehead, 40351. Tel: 606-784-4392; Fax: 606-783-0190; Email: morehead@cdlex.org; Web: www.cdlex.org/morehead. P.O. Box 307, Morehead, 40351. Rev. Arturo Molina.

RICHMOND. *Catholic Campus Ministry of St. Mark*, Eastern Kentucky University, 405 University Dr., Richmond, 40475-2154. Tel: 859-623-2989 (Center) ; Email: asiniger@cdlex.org; Web: www.saintmarkcatholicchurch.net. Rev. Thomas P. Farrell; Alanna Sininger, Campus Min.
St. Stephen the Martyr Newman Center.

[L] MISCELLANEOUS

LEXINGTON. *Catholic Way Bible Study*, P.O. Box 22324, 40522-2324. Tel: 859-552-6484; Email: teachingleader@cwbs.org; Web: www.cwbs.org. Lavinia Spirito, Teaching Leader.

CDLEX Management Services, Inc., 1310 W. Main St., 40508. Tel: 859-253-1993; Email: dswisher@cdlex.org. Mrs. Debbie Swisher, Admin.

**Newman Foundation, Inc.*, 528 N. Broadway, Ste. 303, 40508. Tel: 859-255-0880; Email: newmandirector@gmail.com; Web: www.newmanfnd.org. Maria Bane, Exec. Dir.

ASHLAND. *Bon Secours Kentucky Health System Foundation, Inc.* dba Our Lady of Bellefonte Hospital Foundation, 1000 Ashland Dr., Ashland, 41101. Tel: 606-833-3653; Email: Luann_Serey@bshsi.org; Web: www.olbhfoundation.org/OLBH. Mrs. Luann Serey, Dir. Foundation.

Bon Secours Kentucky Health System, Inc., 1000 St. Christopher Dr., Ashland, 41101.

Tel: 606-833-3333; Email: careline@bshsi.org. Kevin Halter, CEO; Mr. Joseph Mazzawi, Vice Pres. of Mission.

DAVID. **St. Vincent Mission Inc.*, 6359 Hwy. 404, P.O. Box 232, David, 41616. Tel: 606-886-2513; Fax: 606-889-0759; Email: stvm@stvincentmission.org; Email: kathleen@stvincentmission.org; Email: erin@stvincentmission.org; Web: stvincentmission.org. Ms. Erin Bottomlee, CEO; Sr. Kathleen Weigand, Contact Person.

STANTON. *The Catholic Committee of Appalachia* (1970) 150 Mt. Tabor Rd., Martin, 41649. Tel: 304-927-5798; Email: cca@ccappal.org. Jeannie Kirkhope, Catholic Worker, Coord.

RELIGIOUS INSTITUTES OF MEN REPRESENTED IN THE DIOCESE

For further details refer to the corresponding bracketed number in the Religious Institutes of Men or Women section.

[]—*Fathers of Mercy*—C.P.M.
[0570]—*Glenmary Home Missioners*—G.H.M.
[0585]—*Heralds of Good News* (India)—H.G.N.
[0690]—*Jesuit Fathers and Brothers* (Chicago & Detroit Provs.)—S.J.
[]—*Missionaries of Compassion* (India)—M.C.
[1040]—*Piarist Fathers* (U.S. Prov.)—Sch.P.
[1065]—*Priestly Fraternity of St. Peter*—F.S.S.P.

RELIGIOUS INSTITUTES OF WOMEN REPRESENTED IN THE DIOCESE

[0230]—*Benedictine Sisters of Pontifical Jurisdiction* (Covington, KY; Martin, KY)—O.S.B.
[1920]—*Congregation of the Sisters of the Holy Cross*—C.S.C.
[1730]—*Congregation of the Sisters of the Third Order of St. Francis* (Oldenburg, IN)—O.S.F.
[1070-13]—*Dominican Sisters* (Adrian, MI)—O.P.
[2080]—*Home Mission Sisters of America (Glenmary)*—G.H.M.S.
[2710]—*Missionaries of Charity*—M.C.
[2850]—*Missionary Sisters of the Precious Blood*—C.P.S.
[2070]—*Religious of the Holy Union of the Sacred Hearts*—S.U.S.C.
[0500]—*Sisters of Charity of Nazareth*—S.C.N.
[0580]—*Sisters of Charity of St. Augustine* (Rienfield, OH)—C.S.A.
[1680]—*School Sisters of St. Francis*—S.S.S.F.
[1000]—*The Sisters of Divine Providence of Kentucky*—C.D.P.
[2990]—*Sisters of Notre Dame* (Covington Prov.)—S.N.D.
[3360]—*Sisters of Providence of St. Mary-of-the-Woods, Indiana*—S.P.
[3830-05]—*Sisters of St. Joseph* (Brentwood, NY)—C.S.J.
[3920]—*Sisters of St. Joseph the Worker*—S.J.W.
[1760]—*Sisters of the Third Order of St. Francis of Penance and Charity* (Tiffin, OH)—O.S.F.
[]—*Ursuline Sisters of Louisville* (Louisville, KY)—O.S.U.

DIOCESAN CEMETERIES

LEXINGTON. *Calvary*, 874 W. Main St., 40508. Tel: 859-252-5415; Email: ccemetery@cdlex.org; Web: www.cdlex.org/calvary-cemetery. Mr. Doug Culp, Dir.; Mrs. Fran Borders, Sexton

ASHLAND. *Calvary*

MT. STERLING. *St. Thomas*, 538 N. Maysville Rd., US 460, Mount Sterling, 40353. 139 W. Main St., Mount Sterling, 40353. Tel: 859-498-0300; Email: stpatmtsterling@gmail.com. Rev. Frank Brawner

NECROLOGY

† Noe, John P., Ashland, KY Holy Family, Died Feb. 12, 2018
† Poole, William G., (Retired), Died Dec. 21, 2018

An asterisk (*) denotes an organization that has established tax-exempt status directly with the IRS and is not covered by the USCCB Group Ruling.

Diocese of Lincoln

(Dioecesis Lincolnensis)

Most Reverend

FABIAN W. BRUSKEWITZ, D.D., S.T.D.

Bishop Emeritus of Lincoln; ordained July 17, 1960; appointed Bishop of Lincoln March 24, 1992; consecrated May 13, 1992; retired September 14, 2012. *Mailing Address: 3400 Sheridan Blvd., Lincoln, NE 68506-6125.*

Most Reverend

JAMES D. CONLEY, D.D., S.T.L.

Bishop of Lincoln; ordained May 18, 1985; appointed Titular Bishop of Cissa and Auxiliary Bishop of Denver April 10, 2008; ordained May 30, 2008; appointed Bishop of Lincoln September 14, 2012; installed November 20, 2012. *Mailing Address: 3400 Sheridan Blvd., Lincoln, NE 68506-6125.*

Chancery: 3400 Sheridan Blvd., Lincoln, NE 68506-6125. Tel: 402-488-0921; Fax: 402-488-3569.

ERECTED AUGUST 2, 1887.

Square Miles 23,844.

Comprises that part of the State of Nebraska south of the Platte River.

Legal Title: "The Catholic Bishop of Lincoln." For legal titles of parishes and diocesan institutions, consult the Chancery.

STATISTICAL OVERVIEW

Personnel	
Bishop	1
Retired Bishops	1
Priests: Diocesan Active in Diocese	128
Priests: Diocesan Active Outside Diocese	10
Priests: Diocesan in Foreign Missions	0
Priests: Retired, Sick or Absent	25
Number of Diocesan Priests	163
Religious Priests in Diocese	10
Total Priests in Diocese	173
Extern Priests in Diocese	7
Ordinations:	
Diocesan Priests	2
Transitional Deacons	4
Permanent Deacons in Diocese	1
Total Brothers	11
Total Sisters	139
Parishes	
Parishes	134
With Resident Pastor:	
Resident Diocesan Priests	84
Resident Religious Priests	1
Without Resident Pastor:	
Administered by Priests	49
Missions	1
Pastoral Centers	7
Professional Ministry Personnel:	
Sisters	81
Lay Ministers	14
Welfare	
Catholic Hospitals	4
Total Assisted	178,938
Homes for the Aged	4
Total Assisted	295
Day Care Centers	1
Total Assisted	46
Specialized Homes	1
Total Assisted	110
Special Centers for Social Services	22
Total Assisted	35,000
Residential Care of Disabled	1
Total Assisted	18
Other Institutions	1
Total Assisted	2,798
Educational	
Seminaries, Diocesan	1
Students from This Diocese	18
Students from Other Diocese	39
Diocesan Students in Other Seminaries	24
Seminaries, Religious	1
Students Religious	79
Total Seminarians	121
High Schools, Diocesan and Parish	6
Total Students	1,868
Elementary Schools, Diocesan and Parish	25
Total Students	5,005
Non-residential Schools for the Disabled	1
Total Students	18
Catechesis/Religious Education:	
High School Students	1,430
Elementary Students	4,145
Total Students under Catholic Instruction	12,587
Teachers in the Diocese:	
Priests	55
Sisters	36
Lay Teachers	536
Vital Statistics	
Receptions into the Church:	
Infant Baptism Totals	1,211
Minor Baptism Totals	66
Adult Baptism Totals	82
Received into Full Communion	106
First Communions	1,308
Confirmations	1,548
Marriages:	
Catholic	260
Interfaith	123
Total Marriages	383
Deaths	673
Total Catholic Population	97,090
Total Population	617,658

Former Bishops—Most Revs. THOMAS BONACUM, D.D., Bishop of Lincoln; cons. Nov. 20, 1887; died Feb. 4, 1911; J. HENRY TIHEN, D.D., cons. Bishop of Lincoln, July 6, 1911; transferred to the See of Denver, Sept. 21, 1917; died Jan. 14, 1940; CHARLES J. O'REILLY, D.D., cons. Bishop of Baker City, Aug. 24, 1903; transferred to the See of Lincoln, March 20, 1918; died Feb. 4, 1923; FRANCIS J. L. BECKMAN, S.T.D., D.D., cons. Bishop of Lincoln, May 1, 1924; elevated to the Metropolitan See of Dubuque, Jan. 17, 1930; died Oct. 17, 1948; LOUIS B. KUCERA, D.D., cons. Bishop of Lincoln, Oct. 28, 1930; died May 9, 1957; JAMES V. CASEY, appt. Auxiliary of Lincoln April 5, 1957; cons. April 24, 1957; appt. Bishop of Lincoln June 14, 1957; promoted to Archbishop of Denver, Feb. 22, 1967; died March 14, 1986; GLENNON P. FLAVIN, D.D., appt. Titular Bishop of Joannina and Auxiliary Bishop of St. Louis April 24, 1957; cons. May 30, 1957; promoted to See of Lincoln, May 29, 1967; retired March 24, 1992; died Aug. 27, 1995; FABIAN W. BRUSKEWITZ, D.D., S.T.D., ord. July 17, 1960; appt. Bishop of Lincoln March 24, 1992; cons. May 13, 1992; retired Sept. 14, 2012.

Chancery—3400 Sheridan Blvd., Lincoln, 68506. Tel: 402-488-0921; Fax: 402-488-3569. Office Hours: 8:30-5.

Moderator of the Curia—Rev. NICHOLAS A. KIPPER.

Vicar General—Rev. Msgr. MARK D. HUBER, J.C.L.

Chancellor—Rev. DANIEL J. RAYER, J.C.L.

Finance Officer—TRACY LOCKWOOD.

Diocesan Tribunal—3400 Sheridan Blvd., Lincoln, 68506.

Officialis—Rev. STEVEN P. SNITILY, J.C.L.

Adjutant Judicial Vicar—Rev. MAURICE H. CURRENT, J.C.L.

Promoters Justitiae—Rev. Msgr. MARK D. HUBER, J.C.L.; Rev. GARY L. COULTER, J.C.L.

Defensores Vinculi—Rev. Msgr. TIMOTHY J. THORBURN, J.C.L.; Rev. GARY L. COULTER, J.C.L.

Judges—Rev. DANIEL J. RAYER, J.C.L.; Rev. Msgr. TIMOTHY J. THORBURN, J.C.L.; Rev. CRAIG A. DOTY, J.C.L.

Advocates—Revs. STEVEN A. MILLS; ADAM M. SPARLING; ERIC A. CLARK; CALEB J. LARUE; BENJAMIN J. RYNEARSON; MICHAEL A. VENTRE; DAVID K. GAYHART; JUSTIN R. FULTON; ADAM M. SUGHROUE; MATTHEW J. ZIMMER; Very Rev. RAFAEL RODRIGUEZ-FUENTES; Revs. STEPHEN L. GRAEVE; COREY R. HARRISON; RYAN A. KAUP; DENTON R. MORRIS; CYRUS R. ROWAN; RYAN L. SALISBURY; CHRISTOPHER E. STOLEY; MICHAEL J. ZIMMER; ANDREW J. HEASLIP; DOMINIC T.H. PHAN; PATRICK F. BARVICK; KENNETH J. WEHRS; SAMUEL BEARDSLEE; TIMOTHY DANEK; JASON DOHER; CHRISTOPHER ECKRICH; TIMOTHY COLE KENNETT; ANDREW LITT; EVAN WINTER.

Notaries—Rev. SEAN P. KILCAWLEY; Sisters COLLETTE BRUSKEWITZ, O.S.F.; KATHRYN MANEY, M.S.; MRS. MARILYN L. FRIESEN.

Diocesan Consultors—Rev. Msgr. TIMOTHY J. THORBURN, J.C.L.; Rev. DANIEL J. RAYER, J.C.L.; Rev. Msgr. JOSEPH J. NEMEC, V.F.; Very Rev. RANDALL L. LANGHORST; Rev. Msgr. JOHN J. PERKINTON; Rev. LEO D. KOSCH; Rev. Msgr. MARK D. HUBER, J.C.L.; Rev. ROBERT A. MATYA.

Presbyteral Council—Rev. Msgrs. TIMOTHY J. THORBURN, J.C.L.; ROBERT G. TUCKER; Revs. NICHOLAS A. KIPPER; DANIEL J. RAYER, J.C.L.; Rev. Msgr. MARK D. HUBER, J.C.L.; Revs. ROBERT A. MATYA; NICHOLAS J. BAKER, V.F., (Retired); MICHAEL R. CHRISTENSEN; ROBERT FERGUSON, F.S.S.P.; Very Rev. CHRISTOPHER P. GOODWIN; Revs. RONALD G. HOMES; CHRISTOPHER J. MILLER; STEVEN P. SNITILY, J.C.L.; ADAM M. SUGHROUE; MATTHEW J. VANDEWALLE; MICHAEL A. VENTRE; MATTHEW J. ZIMMER; BRADLEY J. ZITEK.

Vicar for Clergy—Very Rev. CHRISTOPHER P. GOODWIN.

Vicars For Religious—Rev. GARY L. COULTER; Rev. Msgr. TIMOTHY J. THORBURN, J.C.L.

Vicar for Hispanic Ministry—Very Rev. RAFAEL RODRIGUEZ-FUENTES.

Deaneries and Deans—Very Revs. STEVEN P. MAJOR, V.F., Crete; LEO V. SEIKER, V.F., David City; RUDOLF F. OBORNY, V.F., Fairbury; Rev. KENNETH F. HOESING, V.F., Falls City; Very Revs. MARK E. SEIKER, M.Div., Indianola; MATTHEW F. EICKHOFF, V.F., Grant; JOSEPH M. WALSH, V.F., Hastings; JAMES C. SCHRADER JR., V.F., Lawrence; Rev. Msgrs. JOSEPH J. NEMEC, V.F., Lincoln; PAUL K. WITT, V.F., Orleans; Very Revs. MICHAEL G. MCCABE, V.F., Plattsmouth; MICHAEL J. MORIN, V.F., Wahoo; M. JAMES DIVIS, S.T.L., V.F., York.

Diocesan Offices and Directors

Apostleship of Prayer—Very Rev. MICHAEL J. MORIN, V.F., Dir.

Apostolates to the Elderly—Revs. DAVID F. BOUREK; THOMAS S. MACLEAN; WILLIAM DAVID GRANT.

Apostolate to the Spanish Speaking—Rev. RAMON E. DECAEN; MR. RICARDO IZQUIERDO, Dir.; Revs. THOMAS B. DUNAVAN, M.A., M.Ed.; JULIUS P. TVRDY; MARK L. CYZA; Very Rev. RAFAEL RODRIGUEZ-FUENTES; Rev. CRAIG J. CLINCH; Very Rev. STEVEN P. MAJOR, V.F.

Apostolate of Suffering—Rev. CHRISTOPHER K. KUBAT, 3700 Sheridan Blvd., Lincoln, 68506. Tel: 402-489-1834; Fax: 402-489-2046.

Archivist—Sr. PATRICIA RADEK, M.S.

Bishop's Appeal for Vocations—Rev. ERIC A. CLARK, Dir.

Bishop's Pastoral Plan for Pro-Life Activities—TOM VENZOR, State Dir., 215 Centennial Mall S., Ste. 310, Lincoln, 68508.

Building Commission—Rev. Msgr. JOHN J. PERKINTON, Chm.; Rev. TROY J. SCHWEIGER; Rev. Msgrs. TIMOTHY J. THORBURN, J.C.L.; MARK D. HUBER, J.C.L.; MR. RON REHTUS; MR. BILL MINES; MR. JOHN SINCLAIRE; MR. JASON SUELTER.

Catholic Relief Services—Rev. DANIEL J. RAYER, J.C.L., Dir.

Cemeteries—Rev. Msgr. TIMOTHY J. THORBURN, J.C.L.

Censores Librorum—Very Rev. M. JAMES DIVIS, S.T.L., V.F.; Rev. SEAN P. KILCAWLEY; Rev. Msgrs. TIMOTHY J. THORBURN, J.C.L.; DANIEL J. SEIKER, J.C.L.

Catholic Social Services—*Pregnancy & Counseling Services, 3700 Sheridan Blvd., Ste. 1, Lincoln, 68506*. Tel: 402-489-1834; Tel: 800-961-6277; Fax: 402-489-2046. *Administrative Food Pantry, Housing Refugee & Emergency Services, 2241 O St., Lincoln, 68510*. Tel: 402-474-1600; Fax: 402-474-1612; Email: frckubat@cssisus.org. *Catholic Social Services, 333 W. 2nd St., Hastings, 68901*. Tel: 402-463-2112; Tel: 888-826-9629; Fax: 402-463-2322. *Thrift Store, 325 W. 2nd St., Hastings, 68901*. Tel: 402-463-2151; Email: frckubat@cssisus.org. *Catholic Social Services, 1014 Central Ave., Auburn, 68305*. Tel: 402-274-4818. *Catholic Social Services Thrift Store, 527 Broadway St., Imperial, 69033*. Tel: 308-882-3065. Revs. CHRISTOPHER K. KUBAT, Dir.; JUSTIN R. FULTON, Asst. Dir.

Clergy Relief Society-The Saint John Vianney Association—*Mailng Address: 3400 Sheridan Blvd., Lincoln, 68506-6125*. Rev. Msgr. MARK D. HUBER, J.C.L., Sec. & Treas.

Child and Youth Protection Office—*3700 Sheridan Blvd., Ste. 8, Lincoln, 68506*. Tel: 402-613-2488. JESSICA COMPTON-CROKER, Safe Environment Coord. & Victim Assistance Coord.

Commission on Alcohol and Drug Abuse—Very Revs. M. JAMES DIVIS, S.T.L., V.F., Dir.; JOHN C. ROONEY, V.F., 3400 Sheridan Blvd., Lincoln, 68506. Tel: 402-483-1941.

Commission for Sacred Liturgy and Sacred Music—Rev. DANIEL J. RAYER, J.C.L., Chm.; Rev. Msgrs. JOSEPH J. NEMEC, V.F.; TIMOTHY J. THORBURN, J.C.L.; Revs. BRENDAN R.J. KELLY; ERIC A. CLARK; Sr. MARY FIDELIS, C.K.; AMY FLAMMINIO; JESSICA LIGON; ELIZABETH LEMME; NICHOLAS LEMME; Bro. JOHN MARY CABALUNA, K.H.E.

Catholic Lawyers Guild—Rev. GARY L. COULTER, J.C.L.

Catholic Physicians Guild—Rev. CHRISTOPHER K. KUBAT, Spiritual Dir., 2241 O St., Lincoln, 68510. Tel: 402-474-1600.

Office of Religious Education (CCD)—Rev. ANDREW J. HEASLIP, Diocesan Dir., Tel: 402-488-2040.

Cursillo—Very Rev. MARK E. SEIKER, M.Div., Dir.; GREG VANDENBERG, Asst.

Deaf Ministry—Revs. ROBERT K. BARNHILL, Dir., Tel: 402-488-2040 (TTY); MICHAEL S. STEC, Asst. Dir.

Diocesan Council of Catholic Women—MRS. KAY WESSEL, Pres.; Very Rev. THOMAS J. LUX, V.F., Moderator; Rev. THOMAS D. MCGUIRE, Asst. Moderator.

Diocesan Director of Liturgy—Rev. DANIEL J. RAYER, J.C.L., 3400 Sheridan Blvd., Lincoln, 68506-6125.

Charity and Stewardship Appeal (DDP)—*Mailing Address: 3400 Sheridan Blvd., Lincoln, 68506-6125*. Rev. ERIC A. CLARK, Dir.

Diocesan Finance Council—Most Rev. JAMES D. CONLEY, D.D., S.T.L.; Rev. Msgr. MARK D. HUBER, J.C.L. Members: Very Rev. MICHAEL G. MCCABE, V.F.; TRACY LOCKWOOD; MONICA BALTERS; DAN MULHEISEN; DORIS ROBERTSON; ALAN SLATTERY; TONY FULTON, Chm.

Diocesan Health Ministries, Inc.—*Mailing Address: 3400 Sheridan Blvd., Lincoln, 68506-6125*. Tel: 402-488-0921. Most Rev. JAMES D. CONLEY, D.D., S.T.L., Pres.; Rev. Msgr. MARK D. HUBER, J.C.L., Vice Pres.

Diocesan Housing Ministries, Inc.—Most Rev. JAMES D. CONLEY, D.D., S.T.L., Pres.; Rev. Msgrs. TIMOTHY J. THORBURN, J.C.L.; MARK D. HUBER, J.C.L.; JOHN J. PERKINTON; Revs. DANIEL J. RAYER, J.C.L.; CHRISTOPHER K. KUBAT, Mailing Address: 3400 Sheridan Blvd., Lincoln, 68506-6125. Tel: 402-488-0921.

Ecumenical Affairs, Commission for—Rev. DOUGLAS D. DIETRICH, Chm.; Very Revs. MATTHEW F. EICKHOFF, V.F.; M. JAMES DIVIS, S.T.L., V.F., Chm.; Rev. Msgr. PAUL K. WITT, V.F.; Rev. MAURICE H. CURRENT, J.C.L.

Engaged Encounter—Rev. SEAN P. KILCAWLEY.

Evangelization Office—Rev. ANDREW J. HEASLIP, Dir.

Evangelization Committee—Rev. ANDREW J. HEASLIP, Chm., Tel: 402-488-2040; Rev. Msgrs. TIMOTHY J. THORBURN, J.C.L.; PAUL K. WITT, V.F.; Rev. CHRISTOPHER L. BARAK; Rev. Msgr. JOSEPH J. NEMEC, V.F.

Family Life Office—Rev. SEAN P. KILCAWLEY, Dir., 3700 Sheridan Blvd., Ste. 7, Lincoln, 68506-6100. Tel: 402-488-2040.

Health Care Facilities—Revs. STEPHEN A. COONEY, 1420 K St., Lincoln, 68508; JOSEPH S. STEELE, 5401 South St., Lincoln, 68506; JOSEPH P. FINN; THOMAS S. MACLEAN.

Office of Communications—*Mailing Address: 3400 Sheridan Blvd., Lincoln, 68506-6125*. Tel: 402-488-0921. Rev. NICHOLAS A. KIPPER, Dir.

Insurance—Rev. Msgr. MARK D. HUBER, J.C.L., Dir.; MRS. MARSHA BARTEK, Mailing Address: 3400 Sheridan Blvd., Lincoln, 68506-6125.

Legion of Mary—Revs. JEREMY L. HAZUKA, Spiritual Dir.; MARK L. CYZA, Asst. Spiritual Dir.; DEE GAETA, Pres.

Liturgical Ministries—Rev. ERIC A. CLARK.

Marriage Encounter—Rev. SEAN P. KILCAWLEY, Dir.

Mission Office—Rev. K. WILLIAM HOLOUBEK, Dir. Pontifical Mission Societies, Propagation of the Faith, Holy Childhood Assoc., Missionary Union of the Clergy, 3700 Sheridan Blvd., Ste. 6, Lincoln, 68506-6100. Tel: 402-473-0635; Email: fr.william-holoubek@cdolinc.net.

Natural Family Planning—Tel: 402-488-2040. Rev. SEAN P. KILCAWLEY, Diocesan Dir.; JENNIFER SVAGERA, Diocesan Coord.

Nebraska Catholic Conference—TOM VENZOR, Exec. Dir., 215 Centennial Mall S., Ste. 310, Lincoln, 68508. Tel: 402-477-7517; Fax: 402-477-1503.

Newman Center University of Nebraska—Rev. ROBERT A. MATYA, Chap., 320 N. 16th St., Lincoln, 68508. Tel: 402-474-7914.

Newspaper—The Southern Nebraska Register *Mailing Address: 3700 Sheridan Blvd., Ste. 10, Lincoln, 68506-6100*. CATHY BENDER, Editor.

Office of Stewardship & Development—*Mailing Address: 3400 Sheridan Blvd., Lincoln, 68506*. Tel: 402-488-0921; Fax: 402-488-3569. Very Rev. JOSEPH M. WALSH, V.F., Delegate.

Permanent Deacon Continuing Education Committee—Revs. DANIEL J. RAYER, J.C.L.; LAWRENCE J. STOLEY; ROBERT A. MATYA.

PREP—Rev. SEAN P. KILCAWLEY.

Priests' Continuing Education Committee—Revs. LAWRENCE J. STOLEY; GARY L. COULTER, J.C.L.; Rev. Msgr. TIMOTHY J. THORBURN, J.C.L.; Very Rev. JEFFREY R. EICKHOFF, Ph.L.; Revs. DANIEL J. RAYER, J.C.L.; SEAN P. KILCAWLEY; MAURICE H. CURRENT, J.C.L.; Rev. Msgrs. JOHN J. PERKINTON; MARK D. HUBER, J.C.L.; Revs. ROBERT A. MAYTA; JOHN R. SULLIVAN.

Pro Life—Very Rev. LEO V. SEIKER, V.F., Dir.; Rev. JONATHAN J. HASCHKE, Asst. Dir.

Project Rachel—*Catholic Social Services*. Tel: 800-964-3787.

Retreat Program—Rev. GARY L. COULTER, Dir., Our Lady of Good Counsel Retreat House. Tel: 402-786-2705.

Rural Life Conference—Rev. DAVID F. BOUREK, Mailing Address: 3400 Sheridan Blvd., Lincoln, 68506-6125. Tel: 402-488-0921.

Serra Club—Rev. ROBERT A. MATYA, Chap. & Spiritual Dir., Tel: 402-474-7914.

Schools—*Mailing Address: 3700 Sheridan Blvd., Ste. 4, Lincoln, 68506-6100*. Rev. Msgr. JOHN J. PERKINTON, Supt.; Rev. LAWRENCE J. STOLEY; Sr. COLLETTE, O.S.F., Asst. Supt.; MATTHEW HECKER, Chief Administrative Officer.

Scouting—Rev. MATTHEW J. ZIMMER.

Teens Encounter Christ (TEC)—MR. JEFF SCHINSTOCK, Dir.

1962 Mass Apostolate—*St. Francis of Assisi Church, 1145 South St., Lincoln, 68502*. Tel: 402-477-5145. Rev. MATTHEW MCCARTHY, F.S.S.P.

Vocations—Revs. ROBERT A. MATYA, Dir.; STEVEN A. MILLS, Asst., St. Thomas Aquinas Church, 320 N. 16th St., Lincoln, 68508. Tel: 402-474-7914.

CLERGY, PARISHES, MISSIONS AND PAROCHIAL SCHOOLS

CITY OF LINCOLN

(LANCASTER COUNTY)

1—CATHEDRAL OF THE RISEN CHRIST (1932) [JC]
3500 Sheridan Blvd., 68506. Tel: 402-488-0948; Email: church@crchrist-parish.org. Rev. Msgr. Joseph J. Nemec, V.F., Rector; Revs. Justin Wylie, Parochial Vicar; Joseph J. Bernardo, In Res.; Eric A. Clark, In Res.
School—Cathedral of the Risen Christ School, (Grades PreK-8), 3245 S. 37th, 68506. Tel: 402-489-9621; Fax: 402-489-9622; Email: jeremy-ekeler@cdolinc.net; Web: www.cathedraleagles.com. Mr. Jeremy Ekeler, Prin. Clergy 2; Lay Teachers 25; Preschool 44; Students 328.

2—ST. ANDREW DUNG LAC AND COMPANIONS
9230 1st St., 68526. Tel: 402-423-2005; Email: josthanh24@yahoo.com; Web: www.andrewdunglac.org. Rev. Joseph Nguyen
Legal Name: St. Andrew Dung Lac and Companions Catholic Church of Lincoln.

3—BLESSED SACRAMENT (1922) [JC]
1720 Lake St., 68502. Tel: 402-474-4249; Email: frjohnsullivan@blessedsacramentlincoln.org. Revs. John R. Sullivan; Samuel Beardslee.
School—Blessed Sacrament School, (Grades PreK-8), Tel: 402-476-6202; Email: frjohnsullivan@blessedsacramentlincoln.org; Web: blessed-sacrament-school.com/. Mrs. Danielle Miller, Prin. Lay Teachers 13; Students 172; Clergy / Religious Teachers 2.
Catechesis Religious Program—Students 155.

4—CRISTO REY (2002) (Hispanic)
4245 J St., 68510. Tel: 402-327-2170 (Rectory); Tel: 402-488-5087 (Parish Office); Fax: 402-488-8370; Email: sacerdos4life@hotmail.com; Email: cristorey@windstream.nett; Web: Cristoreylincoln.com. 4221 J St., 68510. Revs. Ramon E. Decaen; James E. Winter.
Catechesis Religious Program—Melania Palacios de Izquierdo, D.R.E. Students 320.

5—IMMACULATE HEART OF MARY (1979) (Vietnamese)
6345 Madison Ave., 68507. Tel: 402-465-8541; Email: giaoxukhiettamme@gmail.com; Web: giaoxukhiettamme.org. Rev. Thomas Tuan Van Nguyen, C.M.C.
Catechesis Religious Program—Students 263.

6—ST. JOHN THE APOSTLE (1959) [JC]
7601 Vine St., 68505. Tel: 402-489-1946; Email: jnelbulletin@cdolinc.net. Revs. Lyle Johnson; Christopher M. Eckrich, Parochial Vicar.
Res.: 611 Broadview Dr., 68505.
School—St. John the Apostle School, (Grades PreK-8), Tel: 402-486-1860; Email: dennis-martin@cdolinc.net. Mr. Dennis Martin, Prin. Lay Teachers 24; Sisters 3; Students 348; Clergy / Religious Teachers 1.
Catechesis Religious Program—Students 160.

7—ST. JOSEPH (1976) [JC]
7900 Trendwood Dr., 68506. Tel: 402-483-2288; Web: www.stjosephlnk.org. Very Rev. Michael G. McCabe, V.F.; Revs. Stephen L. Graeve; James J. Meysenburg, B.A., M.A., M.Div., M.Ed., In Res.
School—St. Joseph School, (Grades PreK-8), 1940 S. 77th St., 68506. Tel: 402-489-0341; Fax: 402-489-3260; Email: ann-wackel@cdolinc.net. Sr. Mary Cecilia Mills, Prin.; Rev. Msgr. Liam M.

Barr, V.F., Chief Admin. Officer. Lay Teachers 33; Sisters 5; Students 495.
Catechesis Religious Program—Students 316.
8—ST. MARY (1867) [JC]
1420 K St., 68508. Tel: 402-435-2125. Rev. Douglas D. Dietrich.
School—St. Mary School, (Grades K-8), 1434 K St., 68508. Tel: 402-476-3987; Fax: 402-476-0838; Email: nina-beck@cdolinc.net. Dr. Nina Beck, Prin. Clergy 1; Lay Teachers 10; Students 139.
Catechesis Religious Program—Students 17.
9—ST. MICHAEL (1909) [CEM]
9101 S. 78th St., 68516. Tel: 402-488-1313; Email: stmichaelchurch@cdolinc.net; Web: stmichaellincoln.org. Revs. Kenneth A. Borowiak; Jason Doher; Nicholas A. Kipper, In Res.
School—St. Michael School, (Grades K-8), Tel: 402-488-1313; Email: denise-ray@cdolinc.net.
Catechesis Religious Program—Students 100.
10—NORTH AMERICAN MARTYRS (1993) [JC]
1101 Isaac Dr., 68521. Tel: 402-476-8088; Email: fr.brian.connor@cdolinc.net. Revs. Brian P. Connor; Luke Fleck; Christopher K. Kubat, In Res.
School—North American Martyrs School, (Grades PreK-8), 1101 Issac Dr., 68521. Tel: 402-476-7373; Email: sr.janelle-buettner@cdolinc.net; Web: www.namartyrs.org. Sr. Janelle Buettner, M.S., Prin. Lay Teachers 20; Priests 2; Sisters 4; Students 570.
Catechesis Religious Program—Students 239.
11—ST. PATRICK'S (1893) [JC]
6111 Morrill Ave., 68507. Tel: 402-466-2752. Revs. Troy J. Schweiger; Ryan L. Salisbury; David F. Bourek, In Res.
School—St. Patrick's School, 4142 N. 61st St., 68507. Tel: 402-466-3710; Email: fr.troy-schweiger@cdolinc.net; Web: www.stpatricklincolnschool.com. Rev. Troy J. Schweiger, Supt. Clergy 2; Lay Teachers 12; Marian Sisters (Waverly, NE) 2; Students 153; Clergy / Religious Teachers 2.
Catechesis Religious Program—Students 85.
12—ST. PETER (1990) [JC]
4500 Duxhall Dr., 68516. Tel: 402-423-1239; Email: clieb@stpeterslincoln.com. Revs. Craig A. Doty, J.C.L.; Caleb J. LaRue.
School—St. Peter School, (Grades PreK-8), Tel: 402-421-6299; Email: maldridge@stpeterslincoln.com; Web: www.saintpeterslincoln.com/school.html. Rev. Charles L. Townsend, Supt. Clergy 6; Lay Teachers 31; Students 415.
Catechesis Religious Program—Students 245.
13—SACRED HEART (1919) [JC]
3128 S St., 68503. Tel: 402-476-2610; Email: sacredheartlincoln@outlook.com; Web: sacredheartlincoln.org. Revs. Leo D. Kosch; Lee T. Jirovsky, B.A., M.Div., M.Ed., In Res.
School—Sacred Heart School, Tel: 402-476-1783; Fax: 402-476-2610; Email: laura-knaus@cdolinc.net; Web: mysacredheartschool.com. Laura Knaus, Prin.; Rev. Leo D. Kosch, Admin. Clergy 1; Lay Teachers 14; Students 160.
Catechesis Religious Program—Students 35.
14—ST. TERESA'S (1926) [JC]
735 S. 36th St., 68510. Tel: 402-477-3979; Email: Fr. Jamie-Hottovy@cdolinc.net; Email: aubrey-potter@cdolinc.net; Email: patty-lang@cdolinc.net. Revs. Jamie Hottovy; Justin R. Fulton; Shravankumar Raminedi.
School—St. Teresa's School, (Grades PreK-8), 616 S. 36th St., 68510. Tel: 402-477-3358; Fax: 402-477-3361; Email: sr.anne-joelle@cdolinc.net. Sr. Anne Joelle, Prin. Clergy 2; Lay Teachers 18; Sisters 2; Students 260; Clergy / Religious Teachers 2.
Catechesis Religious Program—Students 373.
15—ST. THOMAS AQUINAS (1958) [JC]
320 N. 16th St., 68508. Tel: 402-474-7914; Fax: 402-476-2620; Email: newmancenter@unl.edu; Web: newmancenter.unl.edu. Revs. Robert A. Matya; Steven A. Mills.
Catechesis Religious Program—Emily Gratopp, D.R.E.

OUTSIDE THE CITY OF LINCOLN

ASHLAND, SAUNDERS CO., ST. MARY'S (1900)
1625 Adams St., Ashland, 68003. Tel: 402-944-3554; Email: stmaryashland@windstream.net. Rev. William Holoubek.
Catechesis Religious Program—Students 80.
Mission—St. Joseph's, Greenwood, Cass Co.
AUBURN, NEMAHA CO., ST. JOSEPH'S (1881) [CEM]
1306 23rd St., Auburn, 68305. Tel: 402-274-3733; Email: stjoseph@kc.twcbc.com; Web: auburnstjoseph.org. P.O. Box 406, Auburn, 68305. Rev. Karl T. Millis, Admin.
Catechesis Religious Program—Barb Billesbach, D.R.E. Students 90.
Mission—St. Clara, 604 6th St., Peru, Nemaha Co. 68421.
AURORA, HAMILTON CO., ST. MARY'S (1888)
1420 9th St., Aurora, 68818. Tel: 402-694-3427. P.O. Box 291, Aurora, 68818. Rev. Loras K. Grell.
Catechesis Religious Program—Students 125.
Mission—St. Joseph's, [CEM] Giltner, Hamilton Co.
BEATRICE, GAGE CO., ST. JOSEPH'S (1869) [CEM]
612 High St., Beatrice, 68310. Tel: 402-223-2923. Rev. Robert K. Barnhill.
School—St. Joseph's School, Tel: 402-223-5033; Email: andrew-haake@cdolinc.net. Lay Teachers 7; Students 102; Clergy / Religious Teachers 1.
Catechesis Religious Program—Students 147.
BEAVER CROSSING, SEWARD CO., SACRED HEART (1890) [CEM]
401 Dimery, Beaver Crossing, 68313.
Tel: 402-532-2545; Web: www.sacredheartcatholicbc.org. P.O. Box 208, Beaver Crossing, 68313. Rev. Maurice H. Current, J.C.L.
Catechesis Religious Program—Students 42.
Mission—St. Patrick's, [CEM 2] Utica, Seward Co.
BEE, SEWARD CO., ST. WENCESLAUS
350 Elm St., Bee, 68314. Tel: 402-643-9107; Email: stwenceslaus@lmnetworks.net. P.O. Box 146, Bee, 68314. Rev. Brendan R.J. Kelly.
BELLWOOD, BUTLER CO.
1—ST. PETER'S (1889) [JC]
211 Esplanade St., Bellwood, 68624-2402.
Tel: 402-538-3135; Email: saintpetersaintjoseph@gmail.com. Rev. Benjamin P. Holdren.
Catechesis Religious Program—Students 30.
Mission—St. Joseph's, Bellwood, Butler Co.
2—PRESENTATION (1874) [JC]
1291 41 Rd., Bellwood, 68624. Tel: 402-367-3666; Email: presentationparish-bellwood@lincolndiocese.org. Rev. Janusz Marzynski.
Catechesis Religious Program—Students 34.
BENKELMAN, DUNDY CO., ST. JOSEPH'S (1911) [CEM]
813 Cheyenne St., P.O. Box 447, Benkelman, 69021.
Tel: 308-423-2329; Email: mfeickhoff@hotmail.com; Web: www.stjosephsbenkelman.com. Rev. Matthew F. Eickhoff.
Catechesis Religious Program—Students 46.
Mission—St. Joseph's, Stratton, Hitchcock Co.
BRAINARD, BUTLER CO., HOLY TRINITY (1888) [CEM]
108 E. Brainard St., Brainard, 68626.
Tel: 402-545-2691. P.O. Box 39, Brainard, 68626. Rev. Steven P. Snitily, J.C.L.
Catechesis Religious Program—Students 56.
BRUNO, BUTLER CO., ST. ANTHONY (1899) [CEM]
405 Pine St., Bruno, 68014. Tel: 402-543-2233; Email: frhomes@juno.com. Rev. Ronald G. Homes.
Catechesis Religious Program—Tel: 402-543-2465. Students 49.
Mission—SS. Peter and Paul, [CEM 2] 222 Maple, Abie, Butler Co. 68036.
CAMBRIDGE, FURNAS CO., ST. JOHN'S (1883) [CEM]
815 Nelson, P.O. Box F, Cambridge, 69022.
Tel: 308-697-3722; Email: cchurch@swnebr.net. Rev. Kenneth J. Wehrs.
Catechesis Religious Program—Students 60.
Mission—St. Germanus, Arapahoe, Furnas Co.. Fax: 308-340-3920.
Catechesis Religious Program—Students 11.
CAMPBELL, FRANKLIN CO., ST. ANNE (1880) [CEM]
518 S. Stewart, P.O. Box 156, Campbell, 68932-0156.
Tel: 402-756-8006. Very Rev. James C. Schrader Jr., V.F.
Catechesis Religious Program—Students 53.
Mission—Holy Trinity, 513 S. Liberty, Blue Hill, Webster Co. 68930.
COLON, SAUNDERS CO., ST. JOSEPH'S (1919) [CEM]
111 Cherry St., P.O. Box 58, Colon, 68018.
Tel: 402-647-4901; Email: fr.david-gayhart@cdolinc.net. Rev. David K. Gayhart.
Catechesis Religious Program—Students 54.
Mission—St. Mary, [CEM] Cedar Bluffs, Saunders Co.
CORTLAND, GAGE CO., ST. JAMES (1882) [CEM]
155 N. Lincoln Ave., Cortland, 68331.
Tel: 402-798-7335; Email: frkipper@windstream.net. Rev. Nicholas A. Kipper.
Catechesis Religious Program—Students 86.
CRETE, SALINE CO., SACRED HEART (1873) [CEM]
515 E. 14th St., Crete, 68333. Tel: 402-826-2044; Email: jsec@cdolinc.net; Web: www.sacred-heart-crete.org. Very Rev. Steven P. Major, V.F.; Rev. Douglas Daro.
School—Sacred Heart School, (Grades K-6), Tel: 402-826-2318; Email: sr.mary-alma@cdolinc.net.
Catechesis Religious Program—Students 152.
CURTIS, FRONTIER CO., ST. JAMES (1914)
313 E. 6th St., P.O. Box 144, Curtis, 69025.
Tel: 308-367-4280; Email: stjames@curtis-ne.com. Rev. Bernard Kimminau.
Catechesis Religious Program—Students 16.
Missions—St. Joseph's—Farnam, Dawson Co.
St. William's, Wellfleet, Lincoln Co.
DAVEY, LANCASTER CO., ST. MARY'S (1876) [CEM]
17630 N. 3rd St., P.O. Box 37, Davey, 68336.
Tel: 402-785-3445; Email: stmarydavey@parishmail.com. Rev. Cyrus R. Rowan, Admin.
Catechesis Religious Program—Students 96.
DAVID CITY, BUTLER CO.
1—ST. FRANCIS (Center) (1878) [CEM]
3071 P Rd., David City, 68632. Tel: 402-367-4202. Rev. Sean M. Timmerman.
2—ST. MARY'S (1877) [CEM]
580 I St., David City, 68632. Tel: 402-367-3579; Email: stmarys.davidcity@gmail.com; Web: www.stmarysdavidcity.org. Revs. Jay M. Buhman; Corey R. Harrison, Parochial Vicar.
Catechesis Religious Program—Students 480.
Mission—Assumption (1878) David City, Butler Co. 68632.
DAWSON, RICHARDSON CO., ST. MARY'S (1873) [CEM]
312 4th St., Dawson, 68337. Tel: 402-855-3595; Email: fr.kenneth-hoesing@cdolinc.net; Web: www.lincolndiocese.org/directory/parishes/695-st-mary-dawson. P.O. Box 96, Dawson, 68337. Rev. Kenneth F. Hoesing, V.F.
Catechesis Religious Program—Students 50.
Mission—St. Anne's, [CEM 2] 507 Main St., Shubert, Richardson Co. 68437.
DENTON, LANCASTER CO., ST. MARY'S (1906)
7105 Cass, P.O. Box 406, Denton, 68339.
Tel: 402-797-2105; Email: stmarys@windstream.net; Web: www.dentonstmarys.com. Rev. Msgr. Mark D. Huber, J.C.L.
Catechesis Religious Program—Students 82.
DONIPHAN, HALL CO., ST. ANN'S (1888) [CEM]
202 N. 5th St., P.O. Box 407, Doniphan, 68832.
Tel: 402-845-4477; Email: stanns@cdolinc.net; Web: stannsdoniphan.org. Rev. Adam M. Sughroue.
Res.: 404 Cedar, Doniphan, 68832. Tel: 402-845-2707 .
Catechesis Religious Program—Students 90.
Mission—Sacred Heart, [CEM] 103 W. Pine St., Kenesaw, Seward Co. 68956. Web: sacredheartkenesaw.org.
DWIGHT, BUTLER CO., ASSUMPTION (1899) [CEM]
336 W. Pine, P.O. Box 70, Dwight, 68635.
Tel: 402-566-2765; Email: snatrectory@hotmail.com. Rev. Raymond L. Jansen.
Catechesis Religious Program—Students 79.
EXETER, FILLMORE CO., ST. STEPHEN'S (1871) [JC]
207 N. Union Ave., Exeter, 68351. Tel: 402-266-5581; Email: st.stephen_bulletin@yahoo.com. Rev. Msgr. Daniel J. Seiker, J.C.L., Admin.
Catechesis Religious Program—Students 32.
Mission—St. Wenceslaus, 703 Main St., Milligan, 68406.
FAIRBURY, JEFFERSON CO., ST. MICHAEL'S (1885) [CEM]
807 F St., P.O. Box 406, Fairbury, 68352.
Tel: 402-729-2058; Email: st.michael.fairbury@gmail.com; Web: www.stmichaelsfairbury.org. Rev. John B. Birkel.
Catechesis Religious Program—Students 36.
Mission—St. Mary's, 511 Amanda, Alexandria, Thayer Co. 68303.
FALLS CITY, RICHARDSON CO., SS. PETER AND PAUL (1871) [CEM 2]
1820 Fulton St., Falls City, 68355. Tel: 402-245-3002 ; Email: Deb-Lem@cdolinc.net. Revs. Thomas B. Dunavan, M.A., M.Ed.; Timothy Cole Kennett, Parochial Vicar.
School—SS. Peter and Paul School, (Grades PreK-12), Tel: 402-245-4151; Email: fr.thomas-dunavan@cdolinc.net. Mr. Douglas Goltz, M.A., Prin.
Catechesis Religious Program—Students 41.
FRIEND, SALINE CO., ST. JOSEPH'S (1874) [CEM]
405 S. Main St., Friend, 68359. Tel: 402-947-3651. Rev. Lawrence J. Stoley.
Catechesis Religious Program—Tel: 402-947-3657. Students 21.
GENEVA, FILLMORE CO., ST. JOSEPH'S (1898) [CEM 2]
831 E St., P.O. Box 383, Geneva, 68361.
Tel: 402-759-3225; Email: saint_joseph@windstream.net. Rev. Harlan D. P. Waskowiak.
Catechesis Religious Program—Students 85.
Mission—St. Mary, 703 Swartzendruber Dr., Shickley, Fillmore Co. 68436.
GRANT, PERKINS CO., MOTHER OF SORROWS (1928)
745 Garfield Ave., Grant, 69140. Tel: 308-352-4803. P.O. Box 536, Grant, 69140. Rev. Thomas B. Bush.
Catechesis Religious Program—Diana Tate, Catechetical Leader. Students 27.
Mission—Resurrection of Our Lord, 203 Grant St., Elsie, Perkins Co. 69134.
HARVARD, CLAY CO., ST. JOSEPH'S (1878)
605 N. Kearney, P.O. Box 70, Harvard, 68944.
Tel: 402-772-3511; Email: chris.stoley@gmail.com. Rev. Christopher E. Stoley.
Catechesis Religious Program—Students 65.
HASTINGS, ADAMS CO.
1—ST. CECILIA'S (1878) [JC]
301 W. 7th St., Hastings, 68901. Tel: 402-463-1336; Email: stcbulletin@windstream.net; Web: stceciliahastings.org. Very Rev. Joseph M. Walsh, V.F.; Revs. Ryan A. Kaup; Thomas S. Brouillette, In Res.
Catechesis Religious Program—Hastings Catholic

Schools, Tel: 402-462-2105; Fax: 402-462-2106. Students 285.

2—ST. MICHAEL'S (1945) [JC]
715 Creighton Ave., Hastings, 68901.
Tel: 402-463-1023; Email: stmichaelsparish1@stmhastings.net. Revs. Jeremy L. Hazuka; Nathan Hall, Parochial Vicar.
Catechesis Religious Program—Hastings Catholic Schools, 721 Creighton Ave., Hastings, 68901. Tel: 402-462-6310; Fax: 402-462-6035.

HEBRON, THAYER CO., SACRED HEART (1878) [CEM]
436 N. 3rd St., Hebron, 68370. Tel: 402-768-6293; Email: robornyhebron@yahoo.com. Very Rev. Rudolf F. Oborny, V.F.
Catechesis Religious Program—Students 62.

HOLDREGE, PHELPS CO., ALL SAINTS (1902)
1204 Logan St., Holdrege, 68949. Tel: 308-995-4590; Email: church@asholdrege.org; Web: www.ascholdrege.com. Very Rev. Thomas J. Lux, V.F., Pastor.
Res.: 1308 Logan St., Holdrege, 68949.
School—All Saints Catholic, (Grades PreK-4), 1206 Logan St., Holdrege, 68949. Tel: 308-995-4590; Email: school@asholdrege.org; Web: www.ascholdrege.com/ASCS. Lay Teachers 7; Students 58; Clergy / Religious Teachers 1.
Catechesis Religious Program—Tel: 308-995-4590. Kelsey Stevenson, Catechetical Leader; Mindy Pelster, Catechetical Leader. Students 84.
Mission—St. John's, 105 E. Niobrara St., Smithfield, Gosper Co. 68976.

IMPERIAL, CHASE CO., ST. PATRICK (1903)
126 E. 7th St., Imperial, 69033. Tel: 308-882-4995. P.O. Box 96, Imperial, 69033. Rev. Lothar M. Gilde.
Catechesis Religious Program—Students 127.

INDIANOLA, RED WILLOW CO., ST. CATHERINE'S (1888) [CEM]
815 D St., P.O. Box O, Indianola, 69034.
Tel: 308-364-2428; Email: st.catherine.church@hotmail.com. Rev. Gregory P. Pawloski.
Catechesis Religious Program—Students 49.

KENESAW, ADAMS CO., SACRED HEART (1908)
P.O. Box 407, Doniphan, 68832. Tel: 402-845-2707; Email: stanns@cdolinc.net; Web: stannsdoniphan.org. Rev. Adam M. Sughroue.
Res.: 404 Cedar, Doniphan, 68832.
Church: 103 W. Pine St., Kenesaw, 68956.
Catechesis Religious Program—Tel: 402-752-8149. Students 40.

LAWRENCE, NUCKOLLS CO., SACRED HEART (1893) [CEM 3]
250 N. Phillips St., P.O. Box 247, Lawrence, 68957. Tel: 402-756-7393; Email: bjrectory@gtmc.net. Rev. Thomas J. Schultes.
Res.: 141 E. 2nd St., Lawrence, 68957.
Catechesis Religious Program—Barb Janda, Catechetical Leader. Students 84.
Missions—Assumption—c/o P.O. Box 247, Lawrence, NE 68957: 506 Liberty St., Deweese, Clay Co. 68934.
St. Stephen's, 1838 Road 2600, P.O. Box 247, Lawrence, Nuckolls Co. 68957.

LOMA, BUTLER CO., ST. LUKE'S CZECH CATHOLIC SHRINE (1912) [CEM] (Czech)
Mailing Address: c/o Rev. Steven Smitily, P.O. Box 39, Brainard, 68626. Tel: 402-545-2691; Email: fr.steven-snitily@lincolndiocese.org. Rev. Steven P. Snitily, J.C.L., Dir.

MANLEY, CASS CO., ST. PATRICK'S (1881) [CEM]
101 N. Broadway, Manley, 68403. Tel: 402-234-3595. P.O. Box 27, Manley, 68403. Rev. Thomas L. Wiedel.
Catechesis Religious Program—Students 87.
Mission—St. Mary's, [CEM] 505 W. G St., Elmwood, Cass Co. 68349. Tel: 402-994-2485.

MCCOOK, RED WILLOW CO., ST. PATRICK (1886) [CEM]
612 E. 4th St., McCook, 69001. Tel: 308-345-6734; Tel: 308-345-4546. P.O. Box 1040, McCook, 69001. Revs. Gary G. Brethour; Andrew Litt, Parochial Vicar; Very Rev. Bernard A. Lorenz, V.F., In Res.
School—St. Patrick School, (Grades PreK-8), 401 E. F St., McCook, 69001. Tel: 308-345-4546; Fax: 308-345-4546; Email: Becky-Redl@cdolinc.net. Rev. Gary G. Brethour, CEO. Clergy 2; Lay Teachers 15; Priests 2; Students 150.
Catechesis Religious Program—Students 139.
Missions—Sacred Heart—McCook, Red Willow Co.
St. Ann's, [CEM] McCook, Red Willow Co.

MEAD, SAUNDERS CO., ST. JAMES (1882) [CEM 2]
213 E. 8th St., Mead, 68041. Tel: 402-624-3555; Email: casi-schmidt@cdolinc.net. Very Rev. Michael J. Morin, V.F.
Catechesis Religious Program—Students 58.

MINDEN, KEARNEY CO., ST. JOHN THE BAPTIST (1882)
624 N. Garber Ave., P.O. Box 245, Minden, 68959. Tel: 308-832-1245; Email: fr.tvrdy@gmail.com. Rev. Msgr. Paul K. Witt, V.F., Admin.
Catechesis Religious Program—Tel: 308-832-1626. Students 86.
Mission—Holy Family, Heartwell, Kearney Co.

MORSE BLUFF, SAUNDERS CO., ST. GEORGE (1945) [CEM]
260 Short St., Morse Bluff, 68648. Tel: 402-666-5280; Email: st.gmb@nntc.net. P.O. Box 98, Morse Bluff, 68648. Rev. Dennis Hunt.
Catechesis Religious Program—Students 3.
Mission—Sacred Heart, [CEM] .

NEBRASKA CITY, OTOE CO.
1—ST. BENEDICT'S (1856) [CEM]
411 5th Rue, Nebraska City, 68410.
Tel: 402-873-3047; Email: stbenedicts1856@gmail.com; Web: stbens.org. Revs. Michael A. Ventre, Admin.; Dominic T.H. Phan, Parochial Vicar.
See Lourdes Elementary and Lourdes Primary, Nebraska City under Elementary Schools, Interparochial located in the Institution section.
Catechesis Religious Program—Students 86.

2—ST. MARY'S (1869) [CEM]
218 N. 6th St., Nebraska City, 68410.
Tel: 402-873-3024; Email: sm22100@windstream.net; Web: stmarysnebraskacity.com. Revs. Jonathan J. Haschke; James Morin.
Catechesis Religious Program—Students 34.

NORTH PLATTE, LINCOLN CO., ST. ELIZABETH ANN SETON (1994)
3301 Echo Dr., North Platte, 69101.
Tel: 308-534-5461; Web: seas-np.org. Very Rev. Mark E. Seiker, M.Div.
Catechesis Religious Program—Students 41.

ORLEANS, HARLAN CO., ST. MARY'S (1878) [CEM]
109 W. Linn, P.O. Box 446, Orleans, 68966.
Tel: 308-473-3475; Email: blasenwitt@yahoo.com. Rev. Msgr. Paul K. Witt, V.F.
Catechesis Religious Program—Students 20.
Missions—St. Michael's—510 Central Ave., Oxford, Furnas Co. 68967.
St. Joseph's (1909) 810 4th St., P.O. Box 764, Alma, Harlan Co. 68920. Tel: 308-928-2575. In Res., Rev. Nicholas J. Baker, V.F., (Retired).
Catechesis Religious Program—Students 16.

OSCEOLA, POLK CO., ST. VINCENT FERRER (1946) [CEM]
751 S. Nance, P.O. Box 212, Osceola, 68651.
Tel: 402-747-3491; Email: cr62313@windstream.net. Very Rev. Valerian Bartek.
Catechesis Religious Program—Students 76.
Mission—St. Mary's (1893) Osceola, Polk Co.

PALMYRA, OTOE CO., ST. LEO'S (1874) [CEM 2]
330 W. 8th St., Palmyra, 68418-2537.
Tel: 402-780-5535; Email: stleopalmyra@gmail.com; Web: www.stleoandstmartin.com. Rev. Adam M. Sparling.
Catechesis Religious Program—Students 57.
Mission—St. Martin's, Douglas, Otoe Co.

PAUL, OTOE CO., ST. JOSEPH'S (1871) [CEM]
5592 O Rd., Nebraska City, 68410. Tel: 402-873-4569 ; Email: fr.michael-ventre@cdolinc.net. Rev. Michael A. Ventre.
Catechesis Religious Program—Students 6.
Mission—St. Bernard's, [CEM] .

PLATTSMOUTH, CASS CO., CHURCH OF THE HOLY SPIRIT (1862) [CEM]
520 S. 18th St., Plattsmouth, 68048.
Tel: 402-296-3139; Email: plattsmouthHSC@cdolinc.net. Very Rev. Michael K. Houlihan, V.F.; Rev. Timothy Danek.
School—St. John the Baptist School, (Grades K-8), Tel: 402-296-6230; Email: linda-monahan@cdolinc.net. Very Rev. Michael K. Houlihan, V.F., Supt. Lay Teachers 14; Students 185.
Catechesis Religious Program—Students 53.

PRAGUE, SAUNDERS CO., ST. JOHN'S (1901) [CEM]
122 W. Center Ave., P.O. Box 96, Prague, 68050.
Tel: 402-663-4615; Email: fr.ben-rynearson@cdolinc.net. Rev. Benjamin J. Rynearson.
Catechesis Religious Program—Students 12.
Mission—SS. Cyril and Methodius, [CEM] 2880 County Rd. O, Plasi, Saunders Co. 68050.

RED CLOUD, WEBSTER CO., SACRED HEART (1883) [CEM]
413 N. Seward St., Red Cloud, 68970.
Tel: 402-746-3750; Email: rcsacredheart@gmail.com. Rev. Paul G. Frank.
Catechesis Religious Program—Students 12.
Mission—St. Katharine Drexel, Franklin, Franklin Co. 68939.

ROSELAND, ADAMS CO., SACRED HEART (1921)
P.O. Box 67, Roseland, 68973. Tel: 402-756-6251; Email: shcc@gtmc.net. Rev. Thomas S. Brouillette, Admin.
Res.: 11814 W. Alexander, Roseland, 68973.
Tel: 402-756-6251; Email: shcc@gtmc.net.
Catechesis Religious Program—Students 66.
Mission—Assumption, [CEM] 12620 W. Assumption Rd., Roseland, Adams Co. 68973.

RULO, RICHARDSON CO., IMMACULATE CONCEPTION (1863) [CEM]
601 W. Rouleau St., Rulo, 68431. Tel: 402-245-4731; Email: fr.david-oldham@cdolinc.net. Rev. David A. Oldham.
Catechesis Religious Program—Tel: 402-245-3002. Students 31.
Mission—St. Mary's, Arago, Richardson Co.

SEWARD, SEWARD CO., ST. VINCENT DE PAUL (1878)
152 Pinewood Ave., Seward, 68434.
Tel: 402-643-3421; Email: gloria-schneider@cdolinc.net. Rev. Msgr. Robert G. Tucker.
School—St. Vincent de Paul School, (Grades K-5), Tel: 402-643-9525; Cell: msgrtucker@gmail.com.
Catechesis Religious Program—Tel: 402-643-3521. Students 245.

SHELBY, POLK CO., SACRED HEART (1898) [CEM]
210 S. Walnut St., Shelby, 68662-0340.
Tel: 402-527-5425; Email: sacredheartshelby@windstream.net; Web: www.shelbysacredheart.com. P.O. Box 340, Shelby, 68662-0340. Very Rev. Leo V. Seiker, V.F.

STEINAUER, PAWNEE CO., ST. ANTHONY (1882) [CEM]
310 Hickory St., Steinauer, 68441. Tel: 402-869-2256 ; Web: pcocatholics.com. Rev. Michael R. Christensen.
Catechesis Religious Program—Students 78.
Mission—Sacred Heart, [CEM] Burchard, Pawnee Co.

SUPERIOR, NUCKOLLS CO., ST. JOSEPH'S (1934)
1415 California, Superior, 68978-1019.
Tel: 402-879-3735; Email: bz2244@netzero.net. Rev. Ferdinand J. Boehme.
Catechesis Religious Program—Students 66.
Mission—Sacred Heart, Nelson, Nuckolls Co.

SUTTON, CLAY CO., ST. MARY'S (1876) [CEM]
312 S. Saunders Ave., P.O. Box 406, Sutton, 68979.
Tel: 402-773-5346; Email: stmaryssutton@gmail.com. Rev. Michael J. Zimmer.
Catechesis Religious Program—Students 90.
Mission—St. Helena's, 172 Jackson St., Grafton, Fillmore Co. 68365.

SYRACUSE, OTOE CO., ST. PAULINUS (1906)
Mailing Address: 863 5th St., Syracuse, 68446-9504.
Tel: 402-269-3382; Email: stpaulinuschurch@gmail.com; Web: paulinustrinity.weebly.com. Rev. Jerel A. Scholl.
Catechesis Religious Program—Students 104.
Mission—Holy Trinity, [CEM] 4456 Arbor Rd., Avoca, Cass Co. 68307.

TECUMSEH, JOHNSON CO., ST. ANDREW'S (1866) [CEM]
186 N. 5th St., P.O. Box 656, Tecumseh, 68450.
Tel: 402-335-3742; Email: fr.craig-clinch@cdolinc.net. Revs. Craig J. Clinch; Thomas D. McGuire, In Res.
School—St. Andrew's School, (Grades PreK-6), Tel: 402-335-2234; Email: fr.craig-clinch@cdolinc.net. Rev. Craig J. Clinch, Admin. Clergy 1; Lay Teachers 3; Students 23.
Catechesis Religious Program—Students 99.
Mission—St. Mary's, [CEM] St. Mary, Johnson Co.

TRENTON, HITCHCOCK CO., ST. JAMES (1894) [CEM]
117 W. B St., P.O. Box 488, Trenton, 69044.
Tel: 308-334-5328; Email: stjames@gpcom.net. Rev. Christopher J. Miller.
Catechesis Religious Program—Students 35.
Missions—Holy Family—Palisade, Hitchcock Co.
St. John's, [CEM] Wauneta, Chase Co.

ULYSSES, BUTLER CO., IMMACULATE CONCEPTION (1915) [CEM]
215 S. 6th St., Ulysses, 68669. Tel: 402-549-2437. Mailing Address: P.O. Box 128, Ulysses, 68669. Rev. Michael S. Stec.
Catechesis Religious Program—Students 24.

VALPARAISO, SAUNDERS CO., STS. MARY AND JOSEPH'S (1975) [CEM]
637 Iver St., Valparaiso, 68065. Tel: 402-784-2511; Web: www.stsmaryandjosephval.com. Rev. Matthew J. Zimmer.
Catechesis Religious Program—Students 159.

WAHOO, SAUNDERS CO., ST. WENCESLAUS (1877) [CEM 2]
211 E. 2nd St., Wahoo, 68066. Tel: 402-443-4235; Email: stwencoffice@wahoocatholic.org; Web: www.wahoocatholic.org. 214 E. 2nd St., Wahoo, 68066. Revs. Joseph J. Faulkner; Cyrus R. Rowan; Mark S. Pfeiffer, In Res.
School—St. Wenceslaus School, (Grades PreK-6), 108 N. Linden, Wahoo, 68066-1953. Very Rev. Michael J. Morin, V.F., Supt.; Mr. Mike Weiss, Admin. Lay Teachers 17; Students 283.
Catechesis Religious Program—Students 522.

WALLACE, LINCOLN CO., ST. MARY'S (1909)
209 N. Commercial Ave., Wallace, 69169.
Tel: 308-387-4441. P.O. Box 191, Wallace, 69169. Rev. Thomas B. Bush.
Catechesis Religious Program—Mrs. Terri Sullivan, Catechetical Leader. Students 16.

WESTON, SAUNDERS CO., ST. JOHN NEPOMUCENE (1885) [CEM 2]
450 School St., Weston, 68070. Tel: 402-642-5245; Email: StJohn-Weston@cdolinc.net. P.O. Box 10, Weston, 68070. Rev. Matthew J. Vandewalle.
School—St. John Nepomucene School, (Grades PreK-6), 130 N. Front St., Weston, 68070.
Tel: 402-642-5234; Email: fr.matthew-vandewalle@cdolinc.net. Rev. Matthew J. Vandewalle, Pres.; Linda Maly, Headmaster. Clergy 1; Lay Teachers 8; Students 84; Clergy / Religious Teachers 2.

Mission—St. Vitus, [CEM] N. Main St., Touhy, 68065.
Catechesis Religious Program—Students 13.

WILBER, SALINE CO., ST. WENCESLAUS (1878)
501 N. Wilson, Wilber, 68465. Tel: 402-821-2689; Email: office@stwenceslauswilber.org. P.O. Box 706, Wilber, 68465. Very Rev. Randall L. Langhorst, Admin.
Catechesis Religious Program—Students 86.
Mission—St. Joseph's, 511 N. Elm St., Tobias, Saline Co. 68465.

WYMORE, GAGE CO., ST. MARY'S (1881) [CEM 3]
107 N. 11th St., P.O. Box 295, Wymore, 68466. Tel: 402-645-3051; Email: stmarys1@windstream.net. Rev. Bala Raju Marneni, In Res.
Catechesis Religious Program—Students 41.
Missions—St. Joseph's—406 Wyatt St., Barneston, Gage Co. 68466.
St. Mary's, [CEM] 521 Perry St., Odell, Gage Co. 68415.

YORK, YORK CO., ST. JOSEPH'S aka St. Joseph Church & School (1878) [CEM]
505 N. East Ave., York, 68467. Tel: 402-362-4595; Email: stjoeyork@gmail.com. Rev. Msgr. James M. Reinert; Rev. Denton R. Morris, Parochial Vicar.
School—St. Joseph's School, (Grades K-8), Tel: 402-362-3021; Email: office@stjosephyork.org. Mrs. Rochelle Geiger, Prin.
Catechesis Religious Program—Students 89.
Mission—St. Patrick's, [CEM] 305 E. M St., Mc Cool Junction, York Co. 68401.
Catechesis Religious Program—Students 14.

Shrines

CRETE, SALINE CO., SCHOENSTATT SHRINE (2001) Sr. M. Marcia Vinje I, Contact Person.
Shrine—340 State Hwy. 103, Crete, 68333-5020. Tel: 402-826-3346; Email: srmarcia@schsrsmary.org; Web: www.cormariae.com.

Chaplains of Public Institutions

LINCOLN. *Nebraska Penal Complex*, 2241 O St., 68508. Tel: 402-474-1600; Email: frckubat@cssisus.org. Rev. Msgr. James M. Reinert, Revs. Craig J. Clinch, Chap., Scott M. Courtney, Christopher K. Kubat, Dir., Thomas S. MacLean.

On Duty Outside the Diocese:
Rev. Msgr.—
Fucinaro, Thomas J., Via della Nocetta, 63, 00164 Rome, Italy
Revs.—
Gross, Gary, Military Duty, 1700 George Dieter St., El Paso, TX 79936
Gyhra, Richard A., Secretariat of State, Holly See, Villa Stritch, Via della Nocetta 63, 00164 Rome, Italy CH1292
Menke, Andrew V., 4001 14th St., N.E., Washington, DC 20017
Panzer, Joel, Military Duty.

Graduate Studies:
Rev.—
Rolling, Matthew M., (Casa Santa Maria, Rome).

Retired:
Rev. Msgrs.—
Dawson, James D., (Retired), 5401 South St., 68506
Roh, Robert A., V.F., M.A., S.T.L., (Retired), 1820 Fulton St., Falls City, 68355
Vap, Ivan F., (Retired), 3301 Sheridan Blvd., 68506
Very Rev.—
O'Byrne, Patrick J., (Retired), West End Millstreet, Co. Cork Ireland
Revs.—
Baker, Nicholas J., V.F., (Retired), P.O. Box 764, Alma, 68920
Benton, James F., (Retired), 3301 Sheridan Blvd., 68506
Cooper, John A., (Retired), 3301 Sheridan Blvd., 68506
Copenhaver, John L., (Retired), 2938 Marianna Cir., Cedar Bluffs, 68015
Hotovy, Dennis W., (Retired), 2211 Sunset Dr., Beatrice, 68310
Kalin, William A., (Retired), 3301 Sheridan Blvd., 68506
Keefe, John J., (Retired), 3301 Sheridan Blvd., 68506
Murphy, Patrick F., (Retired), Bronacum House, 3301 Sheridan Blvd., 68506
O'Connor, James M., (Retired), 75 Carrowmore Meadows, Knock, County Mayo, Ireland
Rauth, Philip J., (Retired), 13305 William Cir., Omaha, 68144
Rutten, Paul J., (Retired), 3301 Sheridan Blvd., 68506
Stander, Edwin L., (Retired), 3301 Sheridan Blvd., 68506
Zastrow, John A., (Retired), 3301 Sheridan Blvd., 68506.

INSTITUTIONS LOCATED IN DIOCESE

[A] SEMINARIES, RELIGIOUS OR SCHOLASTICATES

DENTON. *Our Lady of Guadalupe Seminary, Inc.*, 7880 W. Denton Rd., P.O. Box 147, Denton, 68339. Tel: 402-797-7700; Fax: 402-797-7705; Email: vocations@fsspolgs.org; Email: seminary@fsspolgs.org; Web: www.fsspolgs.org. Very Rev. Josef Bisig, F.S.S.P., Rector; Revs. Robert Ferguson, F.S.S.P., Vice Rector/Prof.; Benoit Guichard, F.S.S.P., Prof.; William Lawrence, F.S.S.P., Prof.; Joseph Lee, F.S.S.P., Prof.; Rhone Lillard, F.S.S.P., Prof.; Charles Ryan, F.S.S.P., Prof.; Anthony Uy, F.S.S.P., Prof.
(Previous: Priestly Fraternity of St. Peter (Inc.) dba Our Lady of Guadalupe Seminary) Religious Teachers 8; Lay Faculty 4; Students 78; Adjunct Professors 3.

SEWARD. *St. Gregory the Great Seminary*, 800 Fletcher Rd., Seward, 68434. Tel: 402-643-4052; Fax: 402-643-6964; Email: sggs@sggs.edu; Web: sggs.edu. Very Rev. Rafael Rodriguez-Fuentes, Asst. Dean of Men; Rev. Lawrence J. Stoley, Academic Dean; Very Rev. M. James Divis, S.T.L., V.F., Spiritual Dir.; Rev. Msgr. Daniel J. Seiker, J.C.L., Asst. Spiritual Dir.; Very Rev. Jeffrey R. Eickhoff, Ph.L., Rector; Dr. Terrence Nollen, Ph.D., Librarian; Very Rev. John C. Rooney, V.F., Admin. Religious Teachers 10; Lay Staff 10; Priests 10; Seminarians 55; Sisters 3; Students 85; Total in Residence 65; Male Religious 3.
Newman Institute for Catholic Thought and Culture, c/o St. Gregory the Great Seminary, 800 Fletcher Rd., Seward, 68434-8146. Tel: 402-643-4052; Fax: 402-643-6964; Email: jfreeh@unl.edu. Mr. John Freeh, Dir.

[B] ELEMENTARY SCHOOLS, INTERPAROCHIAL

HASTINGS. *St. Michael's Elementary, Hastings Catholic Schools*, 721 Creighton Ave., Hastings, 68901. Tel: 402-462-6310; Fax: 402-462-6035; Email: carrie-rasmussen@cdolinc.net. Mrs. Carrie Rasmussen, Prin.; Sr. M. Francesca Santacroce, F.S.G.M., Librarian. Lay Teachers 21; Priests 6; Sisters 1; Students 232.

NEBRASKA CITY. *Lourdes Elementary* aka Lourdes Central Catholic School, (Grades PreK-5), 412 2nd Ave., Nebraska City, 68410. Tel: 402-873-3739; Fax: 402-873-3154; Email: Lourdes-office@cdolinc.net; Web: lourdescentralcatholic.org. Rev. Jonathan J. Haschke, Pres.; Curt Feilmeier, Prin.; Mrs. Kim Esser, Librarian. Religious Teachers 1; Lay Teachers 8; Students 133.

[C] HIGH SCHOOLS, INTERPAROCHIAL

LINCOLN. *Pius X Catholic High School*, 6000 A St., 68510. Tel: 402-488-0931; Fax: 402-488-1061; Tel: 402-473-5970, Ext. 56120; Email: webmaster@piusx.net; Web: www.piusx.net. Tom Korta, Prin.; Greg Lesiak, Asst. Prin.; Terry Kathol, Asst. Prin.; Revs. James J. Meysenburg, B.A., M.A., M.Div., M.Ed., Chief Admin. Officer; Lee T. Jirovsky, B.A., M.Div., M.Ed., Admin.; Jan Frayser, Admin.; Rev. Joseph J. Bernardo, Chap.; Clarie Howington, Campus Min.; Erin Willis, Librarian. Religious Teachers 16; Lay Teachers 76; Priests 16; Sisters 3; Students 1,209.

DAVID CITY. *Aquinas/St. Mary's Schools* (1899) (Grades PreK-12), 3420 MN Rd., P.O. Box 149, David City, 68632. Tel: 402-367-3175; Fax: 402-367-3176; Email: fr.sean-timmerman@cdonlinc.net; Web: www.aquinas-catholic.com. Mr. David G. McMahon, Prin. (Aquinas High School); Sarah Zook, Prin. (St. Mary); Revs. Ronald G. Homes, Chap.; Sean M. Timmerman, Admin.; Mrs. LouAnne Eller, Librarian. Religious Teachers 5; Lay Teachers 21; Priests 6; Students 268.

FALLS CITY. *Sacred Heart School*, 1820 Fulton St., Falls City, 68355. Tel: 402-245-4151; Fax: 402-245-5217; Email: doug-goltz@cdolinc.net; Web: www.fcsacredheart.org. Mr. Douglas Goltz, M.A., Prin.; Revs. David A. Oldham, Dir., Guidance; Thomas B. Dunavan, M.A., M.Ed., Chief Admin. Officer. Religious Teachers 4; Lay Teachers 20; Students 198.
High School, Web: fcsacredheart.org; Tel: 402-245-4151; Fax: 402-245-5217. Lay Teachers 9; Priests 3; Students 71.
Elementary School K-8 Mr. Douglas Goltz, M.A., Prin.; Angela Simon, Librarian. Lay Teachers 18; Priests 3; Students 168.

HASTINGS. *St. Cecilia's Middle School/High School*, (Grades 6-12), 521 N. Kansas, Hastings, 68901. Tel: 402-462-2105; Fax: 402-462-2106; Email: fr.tom-brouillette@cdolinc.net; Web: www.hastingscatholicschools.org. Sandy VanCura, Prin.; Rev. Thomas S. Brouillette, Chief Admin. Officer; Mrs. Marilyn Zysset, Librarian. Religious Teachers 5; Lay Teachers 18; Priests 5; Sisters 2; Students 240.

NEBRASKA CITY. *Lourdes Central Catholic Schools*, (Grades 6-12), 412 2nd Ave., Nebraska City, 68410. Tel: 402-873-6154; Fax: 402-873-3154; Email: lourdes-office@cdolinc.net; Web: lourdescentralcatholic.org. Rev. Jonathan J. Haschke, Pres.; Curt Feilmeier, Prin.; Mrs. Kim Esser, Librarian. Lay Teachers 20; Priests 4; Sisters 3; Students 185.

WAHOO. *Bishop Neumann Jr.-Sr. High School*, 202 S. Linden, Wahoo, 68066. Tel: 402-443-4151; Fax: 402-443-5551; Email: jennifer-benes@cdolinc.net; Web: bishopneumann.com. Very Rev. Michael J. Morin, V.F., Admin. Religious Teachers 4; Lay Teachers 25; Priests 6; Sisters 1; Students 266.

[D] GENERAL HOSPITALS

LINCOLN. *CHI Health Nebraska Heart*, 7500 S. 91st St., 68526. Tel: 800-644-3627; Fax: 402-483-8708; Email: btrausch@stez.org; Web: www.neheart.com. Derek Vance, Pres. Affiliate of Catholic Health Initiatives. Bed Capacity 63; Tot Asst. Annually 14,477; Total Staff 293.
CHI Health St. Elizabeth (1889) 555 S. 70th St., 68510. Tel: 402-219-8000; Fax: 402-219-8973; Email: dvance@stez.org; Email: btrausch@stez.org; Email: marlin@neheart.com; Web: www.saintelizabethonline.com. Derek Vance, Pres.; Rev. Stephen A. Cooney, Chap. Affiliate of Catholic Health Initiatives. Bed Capacity 258; Deacons 1; Priests 1; Tot Asst. Annually 93,020; Total Staff 949.

NEBRASKA CITY. *CHI Health St. Mary's*, 1301 Grundman Blvd., Nebraska City, 68410. Tel: 402-873-3321; Fax: 402-873-9033; Email: ddefreece@stez.org; Web: www.chihealthstmarys.com. P.O. Box 70, Nebraska City, 68410. Daniel DeFreece, Pres. Affiliate of Catholic Health Initiatives. Bed Capacity 18; Tot Asst. Annually 64,921; Total Staff 175.

[E] HOMES FOR AGED

LINCOLN. *Bonacum House* (1987) 3301 Sheridan Blvd., 68506. Tel: 402-483-0391; Fax: 402-483-0391; Email: priestshome@gmail.com. Sr. Andrea Goeckner, Contact Person; Rev. Msgr. Mark D. Huber, J.C.L., Admin. Residence for retired priests. Residents 10.
Madonna Rehabilitation Hospitals, 5401 South St., 68506. Tel: 402-413-3000; Tel: 800-676-5448; Fax: 402-413-4296; Email: info@madonna.org; Web: www.madonna.org. Revs. John R. Sullivan, Vice Pres.; Joseph S. Steele, Chap. Physical Medicine and Rehabilitation, Inpatient and Outpatient Services, Long-Term Care, and Assisted Living Transitional Care. Bed Capacity 328; Tot Asst. Annually 6,520.

DAVID CITY. *St. Joseph's Court, Inc.* (2000) 646 I St., David City, 68632. Tel: 402-367-4337; Fax: 402-367-4345; Email: assistedliving@saintjosephsvilla.org; Web: saintjosephsvilla.org. Christina Kadavy, Contact Person. Assisted Living Residents 26; Total Assisted 26.
St. Joseph's Villa, Inc., 927 7th St., David City, 68632. Tel: 402-367-3045; Fax: 402-367-3730; Email: administration@saintjosephvilla.org. Sandra Palmer, Admin.; Vicki Stout, Admin. Sisters Adorers of the Blood of Christ (St. Louis, MO). Residents 58; Total Staff 103; Total Assisted 72.

[F] RETREAT HOUSES

WAVERLY. *Our Lady of Good Counsel Retreat House*, 7303 N. 112th St., Waverly, 68462. Tel: 402-786-2705; Fax: 402-786-7211; Email: goodcounsel@cdolinc.net; Web: www.goodcounselretreat.com. Rev. Gary L. Coulter, J.C.L., Dir. Private Rooms 50. In Res. Rev. Msgr. John J. Perkinton.

[G] CONVENTS AND RESIDENCES FOR SISTERS

LINCOLN. *Adoration Convent and Church of Christ the King*, 1040 S. Cotner Blvd., 68510. Tel: 402-489-0765; Fax: 402-489-0864; Email: comedivineguest@gmail.com; Email:

adorechristk@gmail.com. Sr. Louise Mary, Supr.; Rev. Jamie Hottovy, Chap. Sister Servants of the Holy Spirit of Perpetual Adoration. Sisters 9; Professed Sisters 9.

St. Agnes Convent, 3405 Sheridan Blvd., 68506. Tel: 402-484-7348; Email: sr.collette@cdolinc.net. Sr. Collette Bruskewitz, O.S.F., Contact Person. Sisters 2; Professed Sisters 2.

Congregation of Missionary Sisters of the Blessed Virgin Mary, Queen of Mercy, 9141 S. 78th St., 68516. Tel: 402-421-1704; Fax: 402-473-5789; Email: srsqueenmercy@hotmail.com. Sr. Rosaria Hoang, Supr. Sisters 11; Professed Sisters 11.

School Sisters of Christ the King, Villa Regina Motherhouse & Novitiate (1976) 4100 S.W. 56th St., 68522-9261. Tel: 402-477-5232; Email: M. Joan-Paul@cdolinc.net; Web: www.cksisters.org. Mother Joan Paul, C.K., Supr. Sisters 29. In Res. Most Rev. Robert W. Finn, Tel: 402-477-1768.

CRETE. *Secular Institute of the Schoenstatt Sisters of Mary, ISSM*, 340 State Hwy. 103, Crete, 68333-5020. Tel: 402-826-3346; Email: marcia. schoenstatt@yahoo.com. Sr. M. Marcia Vinje I, Contact Person. Sisters 2.

NEBRASKA CITY. *The Franciscan Sisters of the Sorrowful Mother*, 1503 4th Corso, Nebraska City, 68410-2628. Tel: 402-873-3052; Email: fs93813@gmail.com. Sr. Kathleen Kilp, O.S.F., Supr. Sisters 3.

VALPARAISO. *Carmel of Jesus, Mary, and Joseph*, 9300 W. Agnew Rd., Valparaiso, 68065. Tel: 402-784-0375; Fax: 402-784-0375; Email: msgr.thorburn@lincolndiocese.org. Mother Teresa of Jesus, O.C.D., Prioress. Sisters 26.

WAVERLY. *Marian Sisters of the Diocese of Lincoln Motherhouse and Novitiate*, 6765 N. 112th St., Waverly, 68462-9762. Tel: 402-786-2750; Fax: 402-786-7256; Email: ceciliarezac1@gmail. com; Web: www.mariansisters.org. Sr. Cecilia Ann Rezac, M.S., Supr. Novices 3; Postulants 1; Professed 35; Sisters 39.

[H] SPECIAL EDUCATION

LINCOLN. *Villa Marie School and Home for the Educable Mentally Handicapped* (1964) 7205 N. 112th, Waverly, 68462. Tel: 402-786-3625; Fax: 402-488-6525; Email: sr.jeanette-rerucha@cdolinc.net. Sr. Jeanette Rerucha, M.S., Head Teacher; Rev. Msgr. John J. Perkinton, Dir. Marian Sisters (Waverly, NE). Sisters 3; Students 23.

[I] NEWMAN CENTERS

LINCOLN. *University of Nebraska, Newman Club*, 320 N. 16th St., 68508. Tel: 402-474-7914; Email: newmancenter@unl.edu; Web: newmancenter.unl. edu. Revs. Robert A. Matya, Vocation Dir.; Steven A. Mills. See also: St. Thomas Aquinas, Lincoln, NE.

[J] FUNDS, FOUNDATIONS AND TRUSTS

LINCOLN. *Chancery*, 3400 Sheridan Blvd., 68506. Tel: 402-488-0921; Fax: 402-488-3569; Email: fr. dan-rayer@lincolndiocese.org; Web: www. lincolndiocese.org. Rev. Msgr. Mark D. Huber, J.C.L., Vicar; Rev. Daniel J. Rayer, J.C.L., Chancellor.

Mass Stipends, 3400 Sheridan Blvd., 68506. Tel: 402-488-0921; Email: fr.dan-rayer@lincolndiocese.org. Rev. Daniel J. Rayer, J.C.L.

Mission Office Fund, 3700 Sheridan Blvd., Ste. 6, 68506. Tel: 402-473-0635; Email: fr.william-holoubek@cdolinc.net. Rev. William Holoubek, Dir.

The Catholic Foundation of Southern Nebraska, 3700 Sheridan Blvd., Ste. 9, 68506. Tel: 402-488-2142; Fax: 402-325-1351; Email: chris-raun@catholicgift.org; Web: catholicgift.org. Mr. Chris Raun, Dir.

Joy of the Gospel Campaign, Joy of the Gospel Campaign, 3400 Sheridan Blvd., 68506. Tel: 402-488-0921; Fax: 402-488-3569. Rev. Msgr. Timothy J. Thorburn, J.C.L.

Charity and Stewardship Appeal (DDP), Charity and Stewardship Appeal (DDP), 3400 Sheridan Blvd., 68506. Tel: 402-488-0921; Fax: 402-488-3569. Rev. Msgr. Timothy J. Thorburn, J.C.L.

[K] CATHOLIC SOCIAL SERVICES

LINCOLN. *Catholic Social Services*, Admin. Offices 2241 O St., 68510. Tel: 402-474-1600; Fax: 402-474-1612 ; Email: frckubat@cssisus.org; Web: www.cssisus. org. Rev. Christopher K. Kubat, Dir. (Social Services) Tot Asst. Annually 28,575; Total Staff 113.

Other Addresses:

Apostolate of Suffering, 2241 O St., 68510. Tel: 402-474-1600; Fax: 402-474-1612; Email: frckubat@cssisus.org. Rev. Christopher K. Kubat, Dir.

Counseling Svcs. 3700 Sheridan Blvd., 68506. Tel: 402-489-1834; Tel: 800-961-6277; Fax: 402-489-2046.

Catholic Social Svcs. 333 W. 2nd St., Hastings, 68901. Tel: 402-463-2112; Tel: 888-826-9629; Fax: 402-463-2322.

St. Francis Thrift Store and Services, 1014 Central Ave., Auburn, 68305. Tel: 402-274-4818; Email: ckrueger@cssisus.org. Rev. Christopher K. Kubat, Dir.

St. Isidore Thrift Store and Services, 527 Broadway St., Imperial, 69033. P.O. Box 1085, Imperial, 69033. Tel: 308-882-3065; Email: ckrueger@cssisus.org. Rev. Christopher K. Kubat, Dir.

[L] MISCELLANEOUS LISTINGS

LINCOLN. *Calvary Cemetery and Mausoleum*, 3880 L St., 68510. Tel: 402-476-8787; Email: msgr. thorburn@lincolndiocese.org. Rev. Msgr. Timothy J. Thorburn, J.C.L., Dir. Joint cemetery for Lincoln parishes.

Camp Kateri Tekakwitha, 1305 Rd. 3, P.O. Box 127, Mc Cool Junction, 68401. Tel: 402-366-9337; Email: CampKateriT@gmail.com; Web: www. campkateri.org. Russell Koos, Dir. Clergy 1; Religious Teachers 1; Students 800.

Ecclesial Carmelite Movement, 3745 S. 44th St., 68506. Email: carmelitemovement@gmail.com; Web: www.carmelitemovement.us. Rev. Msgr. Timothy J. Thorburn, J.C.L., Chap.

ST. FRANCIS OF ASSISI CHURCH, 1145 S. St., 68502. Tel: 402-477-5145; Email: rector@stfrancislincoln. org; Email: admin@stfrancislincoln.org; Web: www.stfrancislincoln.org. Rev. Matthew McCarthy, F.S.S.P., Chap.

John XXIII Diocesan Center (2001) 3700 Sheridan Blvd., 68506. Tel: 402-488-2040; Fax: 402-488-6525; Email: joan-penn@cdolinc.net. Rev. Nicholas A. Kipper, Mod.

Magnificat-Lincoln, 1101 N. 79th St., 68505-2008. Tel: 402-489-3819; Fax: 402-467-3293; Email: rhonda33.praising.him.4ever@gmail.com. Rhonda Litt, Coord.

Pius X Foundation and Pius X Endowment Fund, 6000 A St., 68510. Tel: 402-488-1046; Fax: 402-488-1061; Email: courtney. johnson@piusx.net; Email: emily.moore@piusx.net; Web: www.piusx.net. Mrs. Courtney Johnson, Dir. Advancement; Rev. James J. Meysenburg, B.A., M.A., M.Div., M.Ed., Sec.

**Society of St. Vincent de Paul - Lincoln Council*, P.O. Box 30145, 68503-0145. Tel: 402-435-7986 (Helpline); Email: svdplincolncouncil@gmail.com; Web: lincoln. svdcouncil.org. Denise Dean, Pres.; Rev. Ramon E. Decaen, Chap.; Angela Reiling, Sec.

CRETE. *Schoenstatt Shrine*, 340 State Hwy. 103, Crete, 68333-5020. Tel: 402-826-3346; Email: srmarcia@schsrsmary.org; Web: www.cormariae. org. Sr. M. Marcia Vinje I, Contact Person.

DAVID CITY. *Aquinas High School Endowment Fund*, 3420 MN Rd., David City, 68632. Tel: 402-367-3175; Fax: 402-367-3176; Email: fr. sean-timmerman@cdolinc.net; Web: www.aquinas-catholic.net. Rev. Sean M. Timmerman, Supt.

FALLS CITY. *Sacred Heart High School Endowment Fund*, 1820 Fulton St., Falls City, 68355. Tel: 402-245-4151; Fax: 402-245-5217; Email: fr. thomas-dunavan@cdolinc.net. Rev. Thomas B. Dunavan, M.A., M.Ed., Sec.

HASTINGS. *Hastings Catholic Schools Foundation* (1981) 521 N. Kansas, Hastings, 68901. Tel: 402-462-2105; Fax: 402-462-2106; Email: fr. tom-brouillette@cdolinc.net; Web: www. hastingscatholicschools.org. Rev. Thomas S. Brouillette, Sec.

NEBRASKA CITY. *Lourdes Central High School Endowment Fund*, 412 Second Ave., Nebraska City, 68410. Tel: 402-873-6154; Fax: 402-873-3154; Email: sm22100@windstream.net. Rev. Jonathan J. Haschke, Sec.

WAHOO. *Bishop Neumann High School Endowment Fund*, 202 S. Linden, Wahoo, 68066. Tel: 402-443-4151; Fax: 402-443-5551; Email: jennifer-benes@cdolinc.net; Web: bishopneumann. com. Very Rev. Michael J. Morin, V.F., Sec.

WAVERLY. **Knights of the Holy Eucharist, Inc.*, 7303 N. 112th St., Waverly, 68462. Tel: 402-786-2705; Email: knightsinfo@gmail.com. Bro. David Mary Fazzini, Supr.

RELIGIOUS INSTITUTES OF MEN REPRESENTED IN THE DIOCESE

For further details refer to the corresponding bracketed number in the Religious Institutes of Men or Women section.

[]—*Congregation of the Mother of the Redeemer* (Vietnamese)—C.M.C.

[1065]—*Priestly Fraternity of St. Peter*—F.S.S.P.

RELIGIOUS INSTITUTES OF WOMEN REPRESENTED IN THE DIOCESE

[0100]—*Adorers of the Blood of Christ*—A.S.C.

[]—*Benedictine Sisters of the Sacred Hearts* (Tulsa, OK)—O.S.B.

[0420]—*Carmelite Monastery of Jesus, Mary, and Joseph*—O.C.D.

[]—*Congregation of Missionary Sisters of the Blessed Virgin Mary, Queen of Mercy*.

[]—*Franciscan Apostolic Sisters*—F.A.S.

[]—*Franciscan Sisters of the Sorrowful Mother*—O.S.F.

[2575]—*Institute of the Sisters of Mercy of the Americas*—R.S.M.

[2400]—*Marian Sisters of the Diocese of Lincoln*—M.S.

[0460]—*Passionist Sisters*—C.F.P.

[]—*Schoenstatt Sisters of Mary*.

[]—*School Sisters of Christ the King*—C.K.

[1680]—*School Sisters of St. Francis*—O.S.F.

[1600]—*Sisters of St. Francis of Martyr St. George*—O.S.F.

[3540]—*Sister Servants of the Holy Spirit of Perpetual Adoration*—S.Sp.S.deA.

NECROLOGY

† Cooper, James W., (Retired), Died May. 21, 2018

† Porada, Casey, Lincoln, NE Blessed Sacrament, Died May. 25, 2018

† Rempe, Melvin, (Retired), Died Mar. 27, 2018

An asterisk (*) denotes an organization that has established tax-exempt status directly with the IRS and is not covered by the USCCB Group Ruling.

Diocese of Little Rock

(Dioecesis Petriculana)

Most Reverend

ANTHONY BASIL TAYLOR

Bishop of Little Rock; ordained August 2, 1980; appointed seventh Bishop of Little Rock March 18, 2008; consecrated & installed June 5, 2008. *Office: 2500 N. Tyler St., Little Rock, AR 72207. Res.: 1201 S. Van Buren, Little Rock, AR 72204.* Tel: 501-664-0340. *Mailing Address: P.O. Box 7565, Little Rock, AR 72217.*

THE HUMBLE SHALL INHERIT THE EARTH

Chancery: 2500 N. Tyler St., P.O. Box 7565, Little Rock, AR 72217. Tel: 501-664-0340

Web: www.dolr.org

ESTABLISHED NOVEMBER 28, 1843.

Square Miles 52,068.

Comprises the State of Arkansas.

For legal titles of parishes and diocesan institutions, consult the Chancery Office.

STATISTICAL OVERVIEW

Personnel	
Bishop	1
Abbots	1
Priests: Diocesan Active in Diocese	71
Priests: Retired, Sick or Absent	16
Number of Diocesan Priests	87
Religious Priests in Diocese	34
Total Priests in Diocese	121
Extern Priests in Diocese	18
Ordinations:	
Diocesan Priests	8
Religious Priests	2
Transitional Deacons	2
Permanent Deacons in Diocese	95
Total Brothers	25
Total Sisters	121
Parishes	
Parishes	90
With Resident Pastor:	
Resident Diocesan Priests	52
Resident Religious Priests	16
Without Resident Pastor:	
Administered by Priests	20
Administered by Deacons	2
Missions	39
Pastoral Centers	1
Professional Ministry Personnel:	
Sisters	21
Lay Ministers	141
Welfare	
Catholic Hospitals	14
Total Assisted	1,216,088
Health Care Centers	6
Total Assisted	8,957
Homes for the Aged	30
Total Assisted	1,141
Specialized Homes	1
Total Assisted	272
Special Centers for Social Services	6
Total Assisted	6,603
Educational	
Diocesan Students in Other Seminaries	21
Total Seminarians	21
High Schools, Diocesan and Parish	3
Total Students	969
High Schools, Private	3
Total Students	666
Elementary Schools, Diocesan and Parish	24
Total Students	5,008
Catechesis/Religious Education:	
High School Students	2,548
Elementary Students	8,236
Total Students under Catholic Instruction	17,448
Teachers in the Diocese:	
Priests	4
Brothers	1
Sisters	5
Lay Teachers	557
Vital Statistics	
Receptions into the Church:	
Infant Baptism Totals	1,967
Minor Baptism Totals	293
Adult Baptism Totals	152
Received into Full Communion	364
First Communions	2,597
Confirmations	2,198
Marriages:	
Catholic	372
Interfaith	157
Total Marriages	529
Deaths	836
Total Catholic Population	156,240
Total Population	3,013,825

Former Bishops—Rt. Revs. ANDREW BYRNE, D.D., cons. March 10, 1844; died in Helena, June 10, 1862; EDWARD FITZGERALD, D.D., preconized June 22, 1866; cons. Feb. 3, 1867; died in Hot Springs, Feb. 21, 1907; Most Revs. JOHN B. MORRIS, D.D., ord. June 11, 1892; cons. June 11, 1906; died in Little Rock, Oct. 22, 1946; ALBERT L. FLETCHER, D.D., ord. June 4, 1920; cons. April 25, 1940; appt. Bishop of Little Rock Dec. 7, 1946; retired July 3, 1972; died Dec. 6, 1979; ANDREW J. MCDONALD, D.D., J.C.D., ord. May 8, 1948; appt. Bishop of Little Rock July 4, 1972; cons. Sept. 5, 1972; installed Sept. 7, 1972; retired Jan. 4. 2000; died April 1, 2014; JAMES PETER SARTAIN, D.D., S.T.L., ord. July 15, 1978; appt. Bishop of Little Rock Jan. 4, 2000; cons. and installed March 6, 2000; transfer to Joliet in Illinois June 27, 2006; transfer to Seattle Dec. 1, 2010.

Pastoral Center—2500 N. Tyler St., P.O. Box 7565, Little Rock, 72217. Tel: 501-664-0340; Fax: 501-664-9075. Office Hours: Mon.-Fri. 8:30-5.

Vicar General—Rev. Msgr. R. SCOTT FRIEND, V.G.

Chancery Offices—Fax: 501-265-0108.

Chancellor for Ecclesial Affairs—Very Rev. Msgr. FRANCIS I. MALONE, J.C.L., P.A., V.F.

Chancellor for Canonical Affairs—Deacon MATTHEW A. GLOVER, J.D., J.C.L., Fax: 501-265-0108. This office also handles Archives.

Chancellor for Administrative Affairs—MR. DENNIS P. LEE, J.D.

Safe Environment Coordinator—SUSAN DAVID.

Finance Officer—MR. GREGORY C. WOLFE, CFO.

Diocesan Tribunal—

Judicial Vicar—Rev. GREGORY T. LUYET, J.C.L., J.V. Adjutant Judicial Vicars: Very Rev. Msgr. FRANCIS I. MALONE, J.C.L., P.A., V.F.; Rev. ANDREW P. HART, J.C.L.

Judge—Deacon JOHN M. MCALLISTER, J.D., J.C.L. Assessor: Rev. JUAN MANJARREZ, V.F.

Defenders of the Bond—Rev. JOHN K. ANTONY, J.C.L., V.F.; Deacon MATTHEW A. GLOVER, J.D., J.C.L.; ZABRINA DECKER, J.C.D.

Promoter of Justice—Very Rev. Msgr. FRANCIS I. MALONE, J.C.L., P.A., V.F.

Notaries—SUSI BLANCO; MARIA VELAZQUEZ; AMANDA CRAWFORD; VERONICA MENDEZ LEON.

Minister for Religious—Sr. MARY CLARE BEZNER, O.S.B.

Diocesan Consultors—Rev. Msgr. R. SCOTT FRIEND, V.G.; Very Rev. Msgr. FRANCIS I. MALONE, J.C.L., P.A., V.F.; Revs. JOHN K. ANTONY, J.C.L., V.F.; ERIK POHLMEIER; Very Rev. NORBERT F. RAPPOLD, V.F.; Revs. GREGORY T. LUYET, J.C.L., J.V.; JOHN M. CONNELL; D. MARK WOOD; Very Rev. Msgr. DAVID LESIEUR, V.F.; Rev. JEROME KODELL, O.S.B.

Deans—Very Rev. Msgr. FRANCIS I. MALONE, J.C.L., P.A., V.F., Central Deanery; Revs. WILLIAM WYATT BURMESTER, V.F., Ouachita Deanery; ALPHONSE GOLLAPALLI, (India) V.F., North Delta Deanery; Very Rev. NORBERT F. RAPPOLD, V.F., North Ozark Deanery; Very Rev. Msgr. JACK D. HARRIS, V.F., River Valley Deanery; Rev. JOSEPH P. MARCONI, V.F., South Delta Deanery; Very Rev. Msgr. DAVID LESIEUR, V.F., West Ozark Deanery; Rev. JOHN K. ANTONY, J.C.L., V.F., West River Valley Deanery.

Diocesan Offices and Directors

Unless otherwise indicated all Diocesan Offices and Directors are located at: *St. John Catholic Center, 2500 N. Tyler St., Little Rock, 72207.* Tel: 501-664-0340; Fax: 501-664-9075. *Mailing Address: P.O. Box 7565, Little Rock, 72217-7565.*

Adoption Services, Inc.—ANTJE HARRIS, Dir., Fax: 501-664-9186.

Diocesan Council for Black Catholics—Rev. WARREN HARVEY, Bishop's Liaison.

Building Commission—JIM DRIEDRIC, Exec. Sec., Fax: 501-664-1310.

Catholic Charities of Arkansas—PATRICK GALLAHER, J.D., Exec. Dir., This office also handles: Alcohol and Chemical Addiction Ministry; Adoption Services; Catholic Campaign for Human Development; Catholic Immigration Services - N.W. Arkansas; Catholic Immigration Services - Little Rock; Catholic Relief Services; Parish Social Ministry; Prison Ministry; Refugee Resettlement; Social Action; Westside Free Medical Clinic; Family Assistance., Fax: 501-664-9186.

Catholic Campus Ministry—LIZ TINGQUIST, Dir.

Catholic Immigration Services - Little Rock Office—Fax: 501-664-9186. JENNIFER VERKAMP, Dir.

Catholic Immigration Services - NW Arkansas Office—FRANK HEAD JR., Dir., Refugee Resettlement Program, 2022 W. Sunset Ave., Springdale, 72762. Tel: 479-927-1996; Fax: 479-927-2979.

Catholic Youth Ministry—LIZ TINGQUIST, Dir.

Calvary Cemetery, Greater Little Rock—MICHAEL CAGLE, Supt., W. Charles Bussey Ave. & S. Woodrow St., Little Rock, 72205. Mailing Address: Calvary Cemetery, Diocese of Little Rock, 2500 N. Tyler St., Little Rock, 72207. Tel: 501-664-0340; Fax: 501-664-1310; Email: lakel@dolr.org.

Charismatic Movement—Very Rev. NORBERT F. RAPPOLD, V.F., (English); Revs. SALVADOR VEGA-ALVARENGA, (El Salvador) (Spanish); ANTHONY M. ROBBINS, Gen. Coord., Email: tonyrobbins2010@yahoo.com; Web: www.arkcc.org.

Clergy Welfare Advisory Board—Rev. JOSHUA STENGEL, Chm.

Continuing Education for the Clergy—Very Rev. Msgr. DAVID LESIEUR, V.F., Dir.

Cursillo Movement—Rev. MARTIN SIEBOLD, Spiritual Advisor, Cursillo; Deacon TIMOTHY JAMES COSTELLO, Asst. Spiritual Advisor; MRS. NANCY CHRISTIAN, Lay Dir. English Cursillo Office, Tel: 501-664-0340; Fax: 501-664-5835; Email: lrcursillo@dolr.org; VACANT, Spanish Cursillo Office, Tel: 501-664-0340; Fax: 501-664-5835; Email: lrcursillo@dolr.org.

Stewardship and Development Office—DIANNE BRADY, Dir.

Diaconate Office—Deacon TIMOTHY JAMES COSTELLO, Min. to Permanent Deacons.

Director of Permanent Diaconate Formation Program—Rev. ERIK POHLMEIER.

Family Life Office: (Pre-Cana, Marriage Encounter, Retrouvaille, Natural Family Planning)—ELIZABETH REHA, Dir.

Hispanic Ministry—Sr. NORMA EDITH MUNOZ, M.C.P., Dir. Associate Directors: Sisters SILVIA GARZA, M.C.P.; ANA LUISA DIAZ VAZQUEZ, M.C.P.

Hospitals—Very Rev. Msgr. FRANCIS I. MALONE, J.C.L., P.A., V.F.

Office of Divine Worship—Rev. JUAN J. GUIDO.

Minister to Priests—Very Rev. Msgr. DAVID LESIEUR, V.F.; Rev. WARREN HARVEY, Asst. Min. to Priests.

Newspaper "Arkansas Catholic"—MALEA HARGETT, Editor, P.O. Box 7417, Little Rock, 72217.

Presbyteral Council—Rev. Msgr. R. SCOTT FRIEND, V.G.; Very Rev. Msgr. FRANCIS I. MALONE, J.C.L., P.A., V.F.; Rt. Rev. LEONARD WANGLER, O.S.B., V.F.; Very Rev. Msgr. JACK D. HARRIS, V.F.; Revs. ALPHONSE GOLLAPALLI, (India) V.F.; JOHN K. ANTONY, J.C.L., V.F.; Very Rev. NORBERT F. RAPPOLD, V.F.; Revs. JACK VU, (Vietnam) V.F.; ANDREW P. HART, J.C.L., Chm.; ERIK POHLMEIER; JOSEPH P. MARCONI, V.F.; Very Rev. Msgr. DAVID LESIEUR, V.F.; Revs. WILLIAM WYATT BURMESTER, V.F.; STEPHEN GADBERRY; JOSEPH T. CHAN.

Clergy Personnel Advisory Board (Diocesan)—Rev. Msgr. R. SCOTT FRIEND, V.G.; Very Rev. Msgrs. FRANCIS I. MALONE, J.C.L., P.A., V.F.; DAVID LESIEUR, V.F.; Revs. MAURICIO CARRASCO; JOSHUA STENGEL; RUBEN QUINTEROS; GREGORY T. LUYET, J.C.L., J.V.; Very Rev. Msgr. JACK D. HARRIS, V.F.; Rev. JOHN E. MARCONI; DR. SHERRY SIMON; Deacon MATTHEW A. GLOVER, J.D., J.C.L.

Propagation of the FaithVery Rev. Msgr. FRANCIS I. MALONE, J.C.L., P.A., V.F., Fax: 501-664-5835.

Refugee Resettlement Program—FRANK HEAD JR., Dir.

Faith Formation—Rev. ERIK POHLMEIER, Dir.

Respect Life Office and Project Rachel—CATHERINE PHILLIPS, Dir.

St. John Catholic Center/Office Services—Deacon TIMOTHY JAMES COSTELLO, Dir.

Schools—THERESA HALL, Supt., Fax: 501-603-0518.

Little Rock Scripture Study—CATHERINE UPCHURCH, Dir.; LILLY HESS, Assoc. Dir.; AMY EKEH, Asst. Editor & Prog. Devel.

Monsignor James E. O'Connell Diocesan Seminarian Fund, Inc.—Rev. Msgr. R. SCOTT FRIEND, V.G., Dir.

Parish Social Ministry—REBECCA CARGILE, Dir., 2415 N. Tyler St., Little Rock, 72207. Tel: 501-664-0340; Fax: 501-664-9186.

Victim Assistance Coordinators—DR. GEORGE SIMON; DR. SHERRY SIMON, Tel: 501-664-0340, Ext. 425; Email: vacoord@dolr.org.

Vocations—Rev. Msgr. R. SCOTT FRIEND, V.G., Dir.; Rev. ANDREW P. HART, J.C.L., Asst. Dir.

Assistant Director for Development and Academic Advising—Deacon CHARLES VICTOR ASHBURN.

Westside Free Medical Clinic—KAREN DIPIPPA, Dir., Fax: 501-664-9186.

CLERGY, PARISHES, MISSIONS AND PAROCHIAL SCHOOLS

GREATER LITTLE ROCK

(PULASKI COUNTY)

1—CATHEDRAL OF ST. ANDREW (1845) [JC]
617 Louisiana St., 72201. Tel: 501-374-2794; Email: info@csalr.org; Web: www.csalr.org. Revs. Jack Vu, (Vietnam) V.F., Rector; Joseph T. Chan; Deacons William J. Bowen; Charles Victor Ashburn.
Catechesis Religious Program—
Tel: 501-371-2794, Ext. 221. Students 38.

2—ST. ANNE (North Little Rock) (1935) [JC]
6150 Remount Rd., North Little Rock, 72118.
Tel: 501-753-3977; Email: secretary@saintannenlr.org; Web: www.saintannenlr.org. Revs. Toshio Sato, C.M.; Luis A. Ramirez, C.M.
Catechesis Religious Program—Belinda Kaye Ortner, D.R.E. Students 202.

3—ST. AUGUSTINE (1929) [JC] (African American)
1421 E. Second, North Little Rock, 72114.
Tel: 501-375-9617; Fax: 501-375-9617; Email: staugustine1929@att.net. Rev. Leon Ngandu, (Congo).
Catechesis Religious Program—Rosalyn G. Pruitt, D.R.E. Students 15.

4—ST. BARTHOLOMEW (1907) (African American)
1622 Marshall St., 72202. Tel: 501-372-4682. Rev. Leon Ngandu, (Congo).
Catechesis Religious Program—

5—CHRIST THE KING (1966) [JC]
4000 N. Rodney Parham Rd., 72212.
Tel: 501-225-6774; Fax: 501-225-7169; Email: parishsecretary@ctklr.org; Web: www.ctklr.org. Very Rev. Msgr. Francis I. Malone, J.C.L., P.A., V.F.; Rev. L. Tuyen Ngoc Do; Deacons John M. McAllister, J.D., J.C.L.; Richard Lewis Patterson; Curtis Don Greenway; William Johnson; Michael Lynn Rector; Matthew A. Glover, J.D., J.C.L.
School—Christ the King School, (Grades PreK-8), 4002 N. Rodney Parham Rd., 72212.
Tel: 501-225-7883; Fax: 501-225-1315; Email: khouse@ctklr.org. Mrs. Kathy House, Prin.; Jenny Wood, Librarian. Lay Teachers 42; Students 657.
Catechesis Religious Program—Students 220.
Endowment—Msgr. Hebert Endowment Fund,
Tel: 501-225-7883; Fax: 501-225-1315.

6—ST. EDWARD (1884) [JC]
815 Sherman St., 72202. Mailing Address: 801 Sherman St., 72202. Tel: 501-374-5767; Email: office@saintedwards.net; Web: www.saintedwards.net. Revs. Juan Manjarrez, V.F.; Keith Higginbotham; Deacons Daniel Thomas Hartnedy; Daniel James Hennessey III; Efrain Antonio Vargas Rodriguez.
School—St. Edward School, (Grades PreK-8), 805 Sherman St., 72202. Tel: 501-374-9166;
Fax: 501-907-9078; Email: school@saintedwards.net. Lay Teachers 10; Students 143.
Catechesis Religious Program—Lilia Hernandez, D.R.E. Students 293.

7—IMMACULATE CONCEPTION (1948) [JC]
7000 John F. Kennedy Blvd., North Little Rock, 72116. Tel: 501-835-4323; Email: administrativeassistant@iccnlr.org; Web: www.iccnlr.org. Rev. John Wakube, A.J., (Uganda); Deacons Chuck Arthur Farrar; Lowell Gene King.
School—Immaculate Conception School, (Grades PreK-8), c/o Immaculate Conception Parish, 7000 John F. Kennedy Blvd., North Little Rock, 72116.
Tel: 501-835-0771, Ext. 300; Email: mbrucks@icsnlr.org; Email: info@icsnlr.org; Web: icsnlr.org. Marcia Brucks, Prin. Lay Teachers 35; Students 394.
Catechesis Religious Program—
Tel: 501-835-4323, Ext. 30. Phyllis Eubanks, Dir. Faith Formation. Students 83.
Endowment—Immaculate Conception School Endowment Fund, Fax: 501-834-0165.

8—IMMACULATE HEART OF MARY (Marche) (1878) [CEM] (Polish)
7006 Jasna Gora Dr., North Little Rock, 72118.
Tel: 501-851-2763; Email: parish@ihmnlr.org; Web: www.ihmnlr.org. Revs. Ruben Quinteros; Nelson Rubio; Deacons Brunon John Strozyk; Timothy James Costello; John Augustine Hartnedy.
School—Immaculate Heart of Mary School, (Grades PreK-8), Tel: 501-851-2760; Email: principal@ihmnlr.org; Web: ihmnlr.org. Mr. Daniel Smith, Prin. Clergy 2; Lay Teachers 15; Students 135.
Catechesis Religious Program—Students 53.
Endowment—Immaculate Heart of Mary Educational Trust Fund for Immaculate Heart of Mary School, Tel: 501-851-2763.

9—ST. MARY (North Little Rock) (1897) (Polish)
1516 Parker St., North Little Rock, 72114.
Tel: 501-374-7123; Fax: 501-374-2792; Email: stmaryschurchnlr@comcast.net. Revs. Ruben Quinteros; Nelson Rubio; Deacon Ronald F. Stager.
School—North Little Rock Catholic Academy, (Grades PreK-8), 1518 Parker St., North Little Rock, 72114. Tel: 501-374-5237; Fax: 501-374-5237; Email: sharpmelody6@gmail.com. Denise Troutman, Prin.; Ashley Montgomery, Librarian. Lay Teachers 22; Students 182.
Catechesis Religious Program—Denise Troutman, D.R.E. Students 196.
Endowment—St. Mary's School Endowment Fund,
Tel: 501-758-2220; Fax: 501-753-6623.

10—OUR LADY OF GOOD COUNSEL (1894)
1321 S. Van Buren St., 72204. Tel: 501-666-5073;
Fax: 501-664-1964; Email: parishoffice@goodcounsellr.com; Web: www.goodcounsellr.com. Rev. Joshua Stengel.
Catechesis Religious Program—Kristin Ables, D.R.E. Students 247.

11—OUR LADY OF THE HOLY SOULS (1947)
1003 N. Tyler St., 72205. Tel: 501-663-8632; Email: office@holysouls.org; Web: www.holysouls.org. Rev. John Marconi; Deacon John Wesley Hall.
School—Our Lady of the Holy Souls School, (Grades PreK-8), 1001 N. Tyler St., 72205. Tel: 501-663-4513; Fax: 501-663-1014; Email: hss@holysouls.org; Web: arcathsch.org/hs/. Nancy Handloser, Prin.; Amber Bagby, Vice Prin. Lay Teachers 42; Students 465.
Catechesis Religious Program—Kay Kay Derossette, D.R.E.; Samantha Denefe, Dir. Faith Formation & Evangelization. Students 150.
Endowment—Monsignor Allen Trust Fund for Holy Souls School, Becky Neighbors, Contact Person.

12—ST. PATRICK (1880) [JC] Attended from St. Andrew Cathedral, Little Rock.
211 W. 19th St., North Little Rock, 72114.
Tel: 501-758-1155; Email: stpatrickschurch@comcast.net. Revs. Jack Vu, (Vietnam) V.F.; Joseph T. Chan.
Catechesis Religious Program—1921 Maple St., North Little Rock, 72114. Sr. Sandy Nguyen, F.M., D.R.E. & Vietnamese Prog. Students 40.
Endowment—St. Patrick's Educational Endowment Fund, Tel: 501-605-0008; Fax: 501-753-8251.

13—ST. THERESA (1954) [JC]
6219 Baseline Rd., 72209. Tel: 501-565-9198; Fax: 501-565-9198; Email: office@stclr.org; Web: www.stclr.org. Mailing Address: P.O. Box 194470, 72209. Revs. D. Mark Wood; Robert K. Cigainero; Joseph de Orbegozo; Deacon William Robert Wrape.
School—St. Theresa School, (Grades PreK-8), 6311 Baseline Rd., 72209. Kristy Dunn, Prin. Lay Teachers 23; Students 190.
Catechesis Religious Program—Students 387.

OUTSIDE THE CITY OF LITTLE ROCK

ALTUS, FRANKLIN CO., ST. MARY (1879) [CEM]
5118 St. Mary's Ln., Altus, 72821. Tel: 479-468-2585; Email: stmarysparish@centurytel.net; Web: www.stmarysaltus.org. Rev. Hugh Assenmacher, O.S.B., Sacramental Min.; Deacon Brian Albert Lachowsky, Parish Admin.
Catechesis Religious Program—Students 68.

ARKADELPHIA, CLARK CO., ST. MARY (1971)
249 N. 14th St., Arkadelphia, 71923. Mailing Address: P.O. Box 26, Arkadelphia, 71923.
Tel: 870-246-7575; Email: frreavesstsjbm@gmail.com. Rev. Phillip A. Reaves, V.F.; Deacon David Henry Evans.

ASHDOWN, LITTLE RIVER CO., ST. ELIZABETH ANN SETON CHURCH (1991) Mission of St. Edward, Texarkana.
1910 Rankin St., Ashdown, 71822. Mailing Address: P.O. Box 966, Ashdown, 71822. Tel: 870-898-8529; Email: office@saintedwardstexarkana.com. Rev. James P. West.
Catechesis Religious Program—Stephanie Eberwein, Catechetical Leader. Students 9.

ATKINS, POPE CO., ASSUMPTION B.V.M. (1878) [CEM] (German)
118 Ave. 3 N.E., Atkins, 72823. Mailing Address: P.O. Box 337, Atkins, 72823. Tel: 479-641-7179. Rev. Ernest L. Hardesty.
Catechesis Religious Program—Students 27.

BALD KNOB, WHITE CO., ST. RICHARD CHURCH, Attended from St. James, Searcy.
101 W. Cleveland St., Bald Knob, 72010. Mailing Address: P.O. Box 172, Searcy, 72145.
Tel: 501-268-5252 (Searcy); Email: stjames172@sbcglobal.net. Rev. Polycarp Ssebbowa, (Uganda).

BARLING, SEBASTIAN CO., SACRED HEART OF MARY (1902) [CEM]
1301 Frank St., Barling, 72923. Tel: 479-452-1795; Fax: 479-434-2513; Email: shmbarling@gmail.com; Web: shmbarling.org. Revs. G. Matthew Garrison; Peter Quang Le, (Vietnamese Catholic Community). Vietnamese Masses.
Catechesis Religious Program—Edwina Schwarz, D.R.E.; Dottie Hunter, D.R.E. Students 26.
Mission—SS. Sabina & Mary Church, 14304 Old Jenny Lind Loop, Fort Smith, 72916. Sheryl Hampton, D.R.E. (See listing under Fort Smith).

BATESVILLE, INDEPENDENCE CO., ST. MARY (1909)
3800 Harrison St., Batesville, 72501.
Tel: 870-793-7717 (Office); Fax: 870-793-7717; Email: stmarys@suddenlinkmail.com; Web: www.stmarysbatesville.com. Rev. Stephen Gadberry; Deacon Mike Comnock.
Catechesis Religious Program—Lourdes Woodruff, D.R.E. Students 35.
Mission—St. Cecilia, 2475 Galleria Dr., Newport, Jackson Co. 72112. Tel: 870-523-6542.

BELLA VISTA, BENTON CO., ST. BERNARD OF CLAIRVAUX (1980) [CEM]
1 St. Bernard Ln., Bella Vista, 72715.
Tel: 479-855-9069; Fax: 479-855-9067; Email:

office@bvstbernard.org; Web: www.bvstbernard.org. Rev. Barnabas Maria Susai, I.M.S.; Deacon Al Genna; Mr. Russell Anzalone, Business Mgr.; Ms. Roxanne Birchfield, Treas.; Mrs. Christina Laughlin, Sec.
Catechesis Religious Program— (Religious Education/Youth & RCIA) Students 54.

BENTON, SALINE CO., OUR LADY OF FATIMA (1942)
900 W. Cross St., Benton, 72015. Tel: 501-315-5186; Email: olfchurchsec@gmail.com; Web: www.ourladyoffatimabenton.com. Very Rev. Paul F. Worm; Deacon Marcelino Luna.
School—Our Lady of Fatima School, (Grades K-8), 818 W. Cross St., Benton, 72015. Tel: 501-315-3398; Email: holydays@swbell.net; Web: www.ourladyoffatimaschool.com. Jan Cash, Prin. Clergy 1; Lay Teachers 6; Students 40.
Catechesis Religious Program—Kath Dunlap, D.R.E. Students 142.
Endowment—Our Lady of Fatima School Endowment Trust Fund.

BENTONVILLE, BENTON CO., ST. STEPHEN (1989) [CEM]
1300 N.E. J St., Bentonville, 72712.
Tel: 479-273-1240; Fax: 479-464-0969; Email: ststephen@ststephenbentonville.com; Web: www.ststephenbentonville.com. Rev. Msgr. Scott L. Marczuk, J.C.L.
Rectory—906 N.E. Carnahan Ct., Bentonville, 72712.
Catechesis Religious Program—Students 631.

BERRYVILLE, CARROLL CO., ST. ANNE (1958) Attended by St. Elizabeth of Hungary, Eureka Springs.
614 S. Main, Berryville, 72616. Tel: 870-423-3927; Email: secretary@stannesberryville.com; Web: www.stanneschurchberryville.org. Rev. Joseph Archibong; Deacon Elias Rangel Flores.
Res.: 209 Champion Hills Dr., Berryville, 72616. Tel: 479-253-9853.
Catechesis Religious Program—Pam Richter, D.R.E. Students 171.

BIGELOW, PERRY CO., ST. BONIFACE (1879) [CEM] (German) Attends St. Elizabeth, Oppelo.
20 St. Boniface Dr., Bigelow, 72016.
Tel: 501-759-2371; Email: threeparishbulletin@gmail.com. Rev. Richard P. Davis.
Catechesis Religious Program—Students 55.
Mission—St. Francis of Assisi, Little Italy, Pulaski Co.

BLYTHEVILLE, MISSISSIPPI CO., IMMACULATE CONCEPTION (1894)
1301 W. Main St., Blytheville, 72315. Mailing Address: P.O. Box 747, Blytheville, 72316.
Tel: 870-762-2506; Email: icccbly@gmail.com; Web: www.icbly.com. Rev. Thomas Joseph Hart; Deacons William G. Brandon Jr.; Robert Edward Ward.
Catechesis Religious Program—Tel: 870-561-4120. Students 33.
Mission—St. Matthew, Osceola, 72370.

BOONEVILLE, LOGAN CO., CHURCH OF OUR LADY OF THE ASSUMPTION (1953) Also attends St. Jude Thaddeus, Waldron.
616 Cherry St., Booneville, 72927. Mailing Address: P.O. Box 298, Booneville, 72927. Tel: 479-675-3371; Email: assumptionboone@yahoo.com. Rev. Alejandro Puello; Deacon Kenneth Edward Stengel.
Catechesis Religious Program—Catherine Phillips, D.R.E. Students 44.

BRINKLEY, MONROE CO., ST. JOHN THE BAPTIST (1875) [CEM] Attended by St. Mary, Helena.
203 W. Ash, Brinkley, 72021-3201. Tel: 870-734-1202 ; Email: stjohnbrinkley@sbcglobal.net. Revs. Benoit Mukamba, C.S.Sp.; Gilbert Tairo, C.S.Sp., (Tanzania); James Uzoma Ibeh, C.S.Sp.
Catechesis Religious Program—Tel: 870-734-3392. Carl Frein, D.R.E. Students 8.

CABOT, LONOKE CO., ST. JOHN THE BAPTIST CATHOLIC CHURCH
106 Pin Oak Dr., Cabot, 72023. Tel: 501-941-1566; Email: info@arkansaslatinmass.com; Web: www.arkansaslatinmass.com. Revs. Paul McCambridge; Stephen Braun, F.S.S.P.

CAMDEN, OUACHITA CO., ST. LOUIS (1871)
202 Adams, N.W., Camden, 71701. Tel: 870-836-2426 ; Email: stlouiscc6674@sbcglobal.net. Rev. William Wyatt Burmester, V.F.
Res.: 962 Ridgeview, Camden, 71701.
Catechesis Religious Program—Tel: 870-444-4596; Email: srdesire@msn.com. Desiree Stipp-Bethune, D.R.E. Students 22.
Mission—Immaculate Heart of Mary, Magnolia, Columbia Co. 71753.

CARLISLE, LONOKE CO., ST. ROSE OF LIMA CHURCH (1895)
603 E. Park, Carlisle, 72024. Mailing Address: P.O. Box M, Carlisle, 72024. Tel: 870-552-3601; Email: strose011@centurytel.net. Rev. Shaun C. Wesley.
Catechesis Religious Program—Students 59.
Mission—Holy Trinity, England, Lonoke Co.

CENTER RIDGE, CONWAY CO., ST. JOSEPH (1881) [CEM] (Italian)
343 Catholic Point Rd., Center Ridge, 72027.
Tel: 501-893-2889; Email: stjosephoffice@2889@gmail.com. Rev. Aby Abraham. Attended from Sacred Heart, Morrilton
Catechesis Religious Program—Students 42.

CHARLESTON, FRANKLIN CO., SACRED HEART (1879) [CEM]
18 Prairie St., Charleston, 72933-9334. Mailing Address: P.O. Box 1087, Charleston, 72933.
Tel: 479-965-2532; Email: sacredheartcharleston@gmail.com. Rev. Patrick Watikha, A.J., (Uganda); Deacon Mark Joseph Verkamp.
Catechesis Religious Program—Anita Collier, D.R.E. Students 98.

CHEROKEE VILLAGE, SHARP CO., ST. MICHAEL (1939)
49 Tekakwitha Dr., Cherokee Village, 72529. Mailing Address: P.O. Box 970, Cherokee Village, 72525. Tel: 870-257-2850; Email: stmichaelcv@yahoo.com; Web: www.stmichaelscv.org. Rev. Amal Raju Punganoor. Also attends St. Mary of the Mount, Horseshoe Bend.
Res.: 12 Micanopy Cir., Cherokee Village, 72529.
Catechesis Religious Program—Students 29.
Mission—St. Mary of the Mount Church, Horseshoe Bend, Izard Co.
St. Michael Memorial Garden (Columbarium)—Tel: 870-257-2850.

CLARKSVILLE, JOHNSON CO., HOLY REDEEMER (1879) [CEM]
103 E. Main St., Clarksville, 72830.
Tel: 479-754-3610; Email: wgwosb@suddenlinkmail.com; Web: www.hrclarksville.org. Rev. William Wewers, O.S.B.
Catechesis Religious Program—Pamela Valencia, Catechetical Leader. Students 321.

CLINTON, VAN BUREN CO., ST. JUDE CHURCH (1988) Attended from St. Francis of Assisi, Fairfield Bay.
3178 Hwy. 65 S., Clinton, 72031. Mailing Address: P.O. Box 526, Clinton, 72031. Tel: 501-745-5716; Email: stjudechurch@artelco.com. Rev. Luke Womack, Admin.; Deacon Frank Zanoff.
Catechesis Religious Program—Toni (Marie A.) Loudon, D.R.E. Students 17.

CONWAY, FAULKNER CO., ST. JOSEPH (1878) [CEM]
1115 College Ave., Conway, 72032. Tel: 501-327-6568 ; Fax: 501-329-6305; Email: sjoffice@sjparish.org; Web: www.sjparish.org. Revs. Anthony M. Robbins; Chandra Kodavatikanti; Jeffrey Hebert; Deacons David Kirby Westmoreland; Richard John Papini; Gerald Joseph Harrison.
School—St. Joseph School, (Grades PreK-12), 502 Front St., Conway, 72032. Tel: 501-329-5741; Fax: 501-513-6804; Email: dwolfe@sjbulldogs.org; Web: www.stjosephconway.org. Diane Wolfe, Prin.; Matt Tucker, Asst. Prin. (Grades 4-6); Courtney Pope, Asst. Prin. (PreK-3); Karen Wilson, Librarian; Christy Pasierb, Librarian. Lay Teachers 42; Students 432.
Catechesis Religious Program—Tel: 501-513-6812. Students 257.

CORNING, CLAY CO., ST. JOSEPH THE WORKER CHURCH (1968) Mission of St. Paul the Apostle, Pocahontas.
1415 Harb S., Corning, 72422. Mailing Address: c/o 2CR 186, Corning, 72422. Tel: 870-892-3319; Email: saintpaul@suddenlink.net. Rev. Mariadass N. Vallapaneni, (India).
Catechesis Religious Program—Students 3.

CRAWFORDSVILLE, CRITTENDEN CO., SACRED HEART CHURCH, Mission of St. Michael, West Memphis.
216 S. Main St., Crawfordsville, 72327. Mailing Address: c/o St. Michael, P.O. Box 899, West Memphis, 72303. Tel: 870-733-1212 (West Memphis); Email: westmemphiscatholic@gmail.com. Very Rev. Charles Thessing, V.F.

CROSSETT, ASHLEY CO., HOLY CROSS, Attended by Our Lady of the Lake, Lake Village.
2400 S. Main St., Crossett, 71635. Mailing Address: P.O. Box 1184, Crossett, 71635. Tel: 870-364-4847; Email: pieronisue@yahoo.com. Rev. Stephen Hart, Admin.; Deacons David Bruce French; Timothy Gelio Sampolesi.
Catechesis Religious Program—204 Marias Saline Rd., Crossett, 71635. Tel: 870-304-9337. Students 28.

DANVILLE, YELL CO., SAINT ANDREW CHURCH (1996) Attended from St. John, Russellville. Mission of St. Augustine, Dardanelle.
1810 E. 8th St., Danville, 72833. Mailing Address: P.O. Box 1262, Danville, 72833. Tel: 479-967-3699; Tel: 479-495-3404 (Main); Fax: 479-967-6215; Email: catholicstandrew@gmail.com. Rev. Maurico Carrasco.
Catechesis Religious Program—Cynthia Solis, Catechetical Leader. Students 171.

DARDANELLE, YELL CO., ST. AUGUSTINE (1925)
1001 N. 2nd St., Dardanelle, 72834.
Tel: 479-229-3972; Email: staugustcatholic@gmail.com. Mailing Address: P.O. Box 460, Dardanelle, 72834. Rev. Mauricio Carrasco.
Catechesis Religious Program—Students 131.

DE QUEEN, SEVIER CO., ST. BARBARA (1911) [CEM] [JC]
Address: 503 W. DeQueen Ave., De Queen, 71832.
Tel: 870-642-2256; Email: st.barbaraparish@yahoo.com. Rev. Ramses Abian Mendieta Lacyo; Deacon Israel Sanchez.
Catechesis Religious Program—Students 458.
Mission—St. Juan Diego, 113 Main St., Wickes, 71973. Tel: 870-385-7402.

DUMAS, DESHA CO., HOLY CHILD CHURCH, (Hispanic) Mission of St. Mark, Monticello.
807 E. Waterman, Dumas, 71639. Mailing Address: c/o St. Mark, 1016 N. Hyatt St., Monticello, 71655. Tel: 870-367-5974; Tel: 870-367-2848 (Monticello); Tel: stmkoff@ccc-cable.net. Rev. Mark Abban, (Ghana).
Catechesis Religious Program—Students 17.

EL DORADO, UNION CO., HOLY REDEEMER (1923)
440 W. Main St., El Dorado, 71730.
Tel: 870-863-3620; Email: holyredeemer@suddenlinkmail.com; Web: www.holyredeemereldorado.org. Rev. Edward P. D'Almeida; Deacon Jose Guadalupe Luebanos.
Catechesis Religious Program—Students 191.
Mission—St. Luke, 508 W. Pine St., Warren, 71671.

ENGELBERG, RANDOLPH CO., ST. JOHN THE BAPTIST (1885) [CEM] (German), Attended by St. Paul the Apostle, Pocahontas.
4650 Engelberg Rd., Pocahontas, 72455.
Tel: 870-892-3319; Email: saintpaul@suddenlink.net. Rev. Mariadass N. Vallapaneni, (India).
Catechesis Religious Program—Tel: 870-810-2105. David Helms, D.R.E. Students 8.

ENGLAND, LONOKE CO., HOLY TRINITY CHURCH (1976) Mission of St. Rose of Lima, Carlisle.
1240 AR Hwy. 161 W., England, 72046. Mailing Address: P.O. Box 243, England, 72046.
Tel: 870-552-3601; Email: strose011@centurytel.net. Rev. Shaun C. Wesley.

EUREKA SPRINGS, CARROLL CO., ST. ELIZABETH OF HUNGARY (1909) Attended from St. Anne, Berryville.
30 Crescent Dr., Eureka Springs, 72632. Mailing Address: 232 Passion Play Rd., Eureka Springs, 72632. Tel: 479-253-2222; Email: st.elizabeth@cox.net; Web: stelizabethar.org. Rev. Joseph Archibong.
Catechesis Religious Program—Tel: 479-253-6742.

FAIRFIELD BAY, VAN BUREN CO., ST. FRANCIS OF ASSISI (1976)
250 Woodlawn Dr., Fairfield Bay, 72088.
Tel: 501-884-3349; Email: stfrancis@artelco.com. Rev. Luke Womack; Deacon Frank Zanoff.
Catechesis Religious Program—Tel: 501-884-7272. Deacon Frank Zanoff, D.R.E.
Mission—St. Jude, Clinton, Van Buren Co.

FAYETTEVILLE, WASHINGTON CO.
1—ST. JOSEPH (1844) [CEM]
1722 N. Starr Dr., Fayetteville, 72701.
Tel: 479-442-0890; Fax: 479-442-7887; Email: lworden@sjfay.com; Web: www.sjfay.com. Revs. Jason Tyler, S.T.L.; Jules Norbert Njopmo, (Cameroon); Alfones Perikala, (India); Deacons Bud Baldwin III; Marcelino Vazquez.
School—St. Joseph School, (Grades PreK-8), Tel: 479-442-4554; Email: school@sjfay.com; Web: www.sjfayschool.com. Jason Pohlmeier, Prin. Lay Teachers 29; Students 309.
Catechesis Religious Program—Email: mvazquez@sjfay.com. Maria Vazquez, Faith Formation. Students 460.
Endowment—St. Joseph Endowment and Educational Trust Fund, Tel: 479-442-4554.

2—ST. THOMAS AQUINAS UNIVERSITY PARISH (1960)
603 N. Leverett Ave., Fayetteville, 72701-3220.
Tel: 479-444-0223; Fax: 479-442-2633; Email: ccm@uark.edu; Web: www.catholichogs.com. Revs. Andrew P. Hart, J.C.L.; Jason Sharbaugh; Deacons Norman Francis DeBriyn; Bud Baldwin III; Adamn Koehler, Campus Min.; Juliane Pierini, Campus Min.

FORDYCE, DALLAS CO., GOOD SHEPHERD (1977) Mission of St. Mary, Arkadelphia.
410 N. Oak St., Fordyce, 71742. Tel: 870-352-2328; Email: goodshepherdcatholicchurch@windstream.net. Mailing Address: P.O. Box 565, Fordyce, 71742. Rev. Phillip A. Reaves, V.F.

FOREMAN, LITTLE RIVER CO., SACRED HEART CHURCH, A mission of St. Edward, Texarkana.
415 S. Bell St., Foreman, 71836. Mailing Address: P.O. Box 43, Foreman, 71836. Tel: 870-542-6846; Fax: 870-542-6715. Rev. James P. West.
Catechesis Religious Program—Students 5.

FORREST CITY, ST. FRANCIS CO., ST. FRANCIS OF ASSISI (1876) [JC] Attended by St. Mary, Helena.
621 S. Washington St., Forrest City, 72335. Mailing Address: P.O. Box 786, Forrest City, 72336-0786.
Tel: 870-633-1665; Email: stfrancis621@gmail.com. Revs. Benoit Mukamba, C.S.Sp.; Gilbert Tairo, C.S.Sp., (Tanzania); James Uzoma Ibeh, C.S.Sp.
Catechesis Religious Program—

FORT SMITH, SEBASTIAN CO.
1—ST. BONIFACE (1886) [JC]
1820 North B St., Fort Smith, 72901.
Tel: 479-783-6711; Email: stbonifaceoffice@gmail.

com; Web: www.stbonifacefortsmith.com. Rev. Mario Jacobo.
School—St. Boniface School, (Grades PreK-6), 201 N. 19th St., Fort Smith, 72901. Tel: 479-783-6601; Fax: 479-783-6605; Email: rkaelin@stbonifaceschool.org; Web: www.stbonifaceschool.org. Rebecca Kaelin, Prin.; Cindy Foss, Librarian. Lay Teachers 17; Students 128.
Catechesis Religious Program—Email: stbfacedre@gmail.com. Diane Willis, D.R.E. Students 144.
Endowment—St. Boniface Catholic School Endowment Fund.

2—CHRIST THE KING (1928) [CEM] [JC]
2112 S. Greenwood Ave., Fort Smith, 72901.
Tel: 479-783-7745; Email: ctk@ctkparishfs.com; Web: ctkparishfs.com. Revs. Juan J. Guido; Norman McFall; Deacon Thomas Jakobs.
School—Christ the King School, (Grades PreK-6), 1918 S. Greenwood, Fort Smith, 72901.
Tel: 479-782-0614; Fax: 479-782-1098; Email: jplake@ctk-school.com; Web: www.ctk-school.com. Jeffery Plake, Prin. Lay Teachers 24; Students 283.
Catechesis Religious Program—Laura McFall, D.R.E. Students 295.
Endowment—Christ the King Catholic School Trust and Endowment Fund, Tel: 479-783-1937.

3—IMMACULATE CONCEPTION (1849) [JC]
22 N. 13th St., Fort Smith, 72902. Mailing Address: P.O. Box 1866, Fort Smith, 72902-1866.
Tel: 479-783-7963; Fax: 479-783-7865; Email: ic@icchurch.com; Web: www.icchurch.com. Revs. John K. Antony, J.C.L., V.F.; Stephen Elser; Deacons Greg Pair; Charles Edward Kuehl; Cesar Augusto Villafranca.
School—Immaculate Conception School, (Grades PreK-6), 223 South 14th St., Fort Smith, 72901.
Tel: 479-783-6798; Fax: 479-783-0510; Email: sblentlinger@icschoolfs.org; Web: www.icschoolfs.org. Sharon Blentlinger, Prin.; Laura Kendall, Librarian. Lay Teachers 30; Students 340.
Catechesis Religious Program—Tel: 479-783-7497. Surennah Werley, D.R.E. Students 478.
Shrine—Our Lady of the Ozarks Shrine, 22741 N. Hwy. 71, Winslow, Crawford Co. 72959.
Endowment—Immaculate Conception School Educational Trust.

4—SS. SABINA AND MARY CHURCH, Mission of Sacred Heart of Mary, Barling.
14304 Old Jenny Lind Loop, Fort Smith, 72916. Mailing Address: 1301 Frank St., Barling, 72923.
Tel: 479-452-1795 (Barling); Fax: 479-434-2513; Email: shmbarling@gmail.com; Web: shmbarling.org. Rev. G. Matthew Garrison.

GLENWOOD, PIKE CO., OUR LADY OF GUADALUPE CHURCH
35 Kennedy Rd., Glenwood, 71943. Mailing Address: P.O. Box 426, Glenwood, 71943. Tel: 870-356-5185; Tel: 479-644-8748; Email: ologglenwood@outlook.com. Rev. Salvador Vega-Alvarenga, (El Salvador).
Catechesis Religious Program—Students 80.

GRADY, LINCOLN CO., BLESSED SACRAMENT CHURCH, Closed. For inquiries for parish records contact St. Peter, Pine Bluff.

HAMBURG, ASHLEY CO., HOLY SPIRIT CHURCH (1987) (Hispanic), Attended by Mission of Our Lady of the Lake, Lake Village.
1138 S. Main St., Hamburg, 71646. Mailing Address: P.O. Box 272, Lake Village, 71653. Tel: 870-265-5439 ; Fax: 870-265-5439; Email: pieronisue@yahoo.com; Web: ourladyofthelake.us. Rev. Stephen Hart, Admin.; Deacons David Bruce French; Timothy Gelio Sampolesi.
Catechesis Religious Program—Students 70.

HARRISON, BOONE CO., MARY, MOTHER OF GOD (1919)
1614 Maplewood Rd., Harrison, 72601. Mailing Address: P.O. Box 2150, Harrison, 72602.
Tel: 870-741-5234; Fax: 870-741-4234; Email: mmgchurch@yahoo.com; Web: www.harrisoncatholic.org. Rev. James M. Fanrak, V.F.; Deacon Mark Allen Scouten.
Mission—St Andrew, 1486 Hwy. 62 W., P.O. Box 197, Yellville, Marion Co. 72687.

HARTFORD, SEBASTIAN CO., ST. LEO (1901) A mission of Immaculate Conception, Fort Smith.
101 Locust St., Hartford, 72938. Tel: 479-966-5376. Mailing Address: St. Scholastica Monastery, 1301 S. Albert Pike Ave., Fort Smith, 72903. Rev. Leslie A. Farley.
Catechesis Religious Program—Students 5.

HEBER SPRINGS, CLEBURNE CO., ST. ALBERT CHURCH
21 Park Rd., Heber Springs, 72543. Mailing Address: P.O. Box 1198, Heber Springs, 72543.
Tel: 501-362-2914; Email: stalbert21@suddenlinkmail.com. Rev. Chanda Pillai PJ, I.M.S.; Deacon Robert L. Morris.
Catechesis Religious Program—Students 71.

HELENA, PHILLIPS CO., ST. MARY (1858) [CEM] Also attends St. John the Baptist, Brinkley; St. Francis of Assisi, Forrest City; St. Mary of the Lake, Horseshoe Lake; and St. Andrew, Marianna.
123 Columbia St., Helena, 72342. Tel: 870-338-6990; Email: wmstmaryschurch@yahoo.com; Web: www.stmaryshelena.org. Revs. Benoit Mukamba, C.S.Sp.; Gilbert Tairo, C.S.Sp., (Tanzania); James Uzoma Ibeh, C.S.Sp.
Catechesis Religious Program—Tel: 870-572-1188. Tina Grubbs, Catechetical Leader. Students 27.

HOPE, HEMPSTEAD CO., OUR LADY OF GOOD HOPE (1875) [CEM]
315 W. Walker St., Hope, 71802. Mailing Address: P.O. Box 517, Hope, 71802-0517. Tel: 870-777-3202; Email: ourladyofgoodhope@sbcglobal.net. Rev. Nirmalraj Mariadass Kambala, C.P.P.S., (India).
Catechesis Religious Program—Shirley McRoy, D.R.E. Students 162.

HORSESHOE BEND, IZARD CO., ST. MARY OF THE MOUNT (1974) [CEM] Attended by St. Michael, Cherokee Village.
1002 First St., Horseshoe Bend, 72512.
Tel: 870-670-5896; Email: mounts@centurytel.net. Rev. Amal Raju Punganoor.
Catechesis Religious Program—Tel: 870-994-2143. Billie Gibson, D.R.E., Email: bjg63@hotmail.com.

HORSESHOE LAKE, CRITTENDEN CO., ST. MARY OF THE LAKE CHURCH (1964) Attended by St. Mary, Helena.
626 Horseshoe Cir, Horseshoe Lake, 72348. Mailing Address: 123 Columbia St., Helena, 72342.
Tel: 901-734-5300; Fax: 870-338-6990; Email: wmstmaryschurch@yahoo.com; Email: pzanone@hotmail.com. Revs. Benoit Mukamba, C.S.Sp.; Gilbert Tairo, C.S.Sp., (Tanzania); James Uzoma Ibeh, C.S.Sp.

HOT SPRINGS, GARLAND CO.

1—ST. JOHN THE BAPTIST (1907)
589 W. Grand Ave., Hot Springs, 71901.
Tel: 501-623-6201; Fax: 501-318-0328; Email: saintjohn.secretary@gmail.com; Web: www.stjohnshotsprings.net. Revs. Chinnaiah Yeddanapalli, (India); Michael Johns; Deacons Robert James Standridge; Robert E. Wanless.
School—St. John the Baptist School, (Grades PreK-8), 583 W. Grand Ave., Hot Springs, 71901.
Tel: 501-624-3147; Fax: 501-624-3171; Email: pguildsjs@gmail.com. Paul Guild, Prin. Lay Teachers 16; Sisters of Mercy 3; Students 124.
Catechesis Religious Program—Teresa Miller, D.R.E. Students 56.
Endowment—St. John's School Endowment, Tel: 501-624-3171.

2—ST. MARY OF THE SPRINGS (1869) [JC]
100 Central Ave., Hot Springs National Park, 71901.
Tel: 501-623-3233; Email: stmcc@hotsprings.net; Email: stmccadmin@hotsprings.net; Web: www.stmaryofthesprings.org. Rev. George W. Sanders; Deacons Joe Dale Harrison; Lee Leckner.

HOT SPRINGS VILLAGE, GARLAND CO., SACRED HEART OF JESUS (1979)
295 Balearic Rd., Hot Springs Village, 71909.
Tel: 501-922-2062; Email: sacredheart@hsvsacredheart.com; Web: www.hsvsacredheart.com. Rev. William Elser; Deacons William Friedman; John Froning; Larry Lipsmeyer.
Rectory—293 Balearic Rd., Hot Springs Village, 71909.
Catechesis Religious Program—Rose Harrigan, D.R.E. Students 25.

HUNTSVILLE, MADISON CO., ST. JOHN THE EVANGELIST (1963) [JC] Attended from St. Joseph Church, Fayetteville.
411 Crossbow Rd., Huntsville, 72740. Mailing Address: P.O. Box 755, Huntsville, 72740.
Tel: 479-442-0890; Fax: 479-232-5790; Email: jtyler@sjfay.com. Revs. Jason Tyler, S.T.L.; Jules Norbert Njopmo, (Cameroon); Alfones Perikala, (India).
Catechesis Religious Program—Sara Sandoval, D.R.E. Students 24.

JACKSONVILLE, PULASKI CO., ST. JUDE THE APOSTLE (1966)
2403 McArthur Dr., Jacksonville, 72076.
Tel: 501-982-4891; Fax: 501-982-0821; Email: stjudeapostle@gmail.com. Rev. W. Andrew Smith; Deacons John M. Alberson; Max R. Elliott; Ernesto Corona Gallegos.
Catechesis Religious Program—Tel: 501-843-9467. Paula Price, D.R.E. Students 345.

JONESBORO, CRAIGHEAD CO.

1—BLESSED JOHN NEWMAN UNIVERSITY PARISH, Attended by Blessed Sacrament, Jonesboro.
2800 E. Johnson Ave., Jonesboro, 72401.
Tel: 870-972-1888; Fax: 870-972-6294; Email: director@astatecnc.com; Web: www.astatecnc.com. Rev. Alphonse Gollapalli, (India) V.F.; Brandon Weisenfels, Dir.

2—BLESSED SACRAMENT (1885) [CEM]
1101 E. Highland Dr., Jonesboro, 72403. Mailing Address: P.O. Box 1735, Jonesboro, 72401.
Tel: 870-932-2529; Email: office@catholicjonesboro.com; Web: www.catholicjonesboro.com. Revs. Alphonse Gollapalli, (India) V.F.; Francis Madanu, (India); Deacon Ramon Ramirez Fernandez.
School—Blessed Sacrament School, (Grades PreK-6), 1105 E. Highland Dr., Jonesboro, 72401.
Tel: 870-932-3684; Email: school@catholicjonesboro.com. Mary Kay Jones, Prin. Clergy 1; Lay Teachers 11; Students 124.
Catechesis Religious Program—Tel: 870-243-6661; Fax: 870-935-4444. Cindy Cole, Children & Youth Min. Students 265.
Endowment—Blessed Sacrament Educational Endowment Fund, Tel: 870-935-2871.

LAKE VILLAGE, CHICOT CO., OUR LADY OF THE LAKE (1866) [CEM 2] (Italian)
314 S. Lake Shore Dr., Lake Village, 71653. Mailing Address: P.O. Box 272, Lake Village, 71653.
Tel: 870-265-5439; Fax: 870-265-5663; Email: pieronisue@yahoo.com. Rev. Stephen Hart; Deacons David Bruce French; Timothy Gelio Sampolesi.
Catechesis Religious Program—Deborah Vaughn, D.R.E. Students 79.
Mission—Holy Spirit, 1138 S. Main St., Hamburg, 71646.

LEOLA, GRANT CO., BLESSED JUAN DIEGO CHURCH, Closed. For inquiries for parish records contact the chancery.

LINCOLN, WASHINGTON CO., SS. PETER AND PAUL CATHOLIC CHURCH
119 W. Bean St., Lincoln, 72744. c/o St. Joseph Church, 1722 N. Starr Dr., Fayetteville, 72701.
Tel: 479-442-0890; Email: jtyler@sjfay.com. Revs. Jason Tyler, S.T.L.; Jules Norbert Njopmo, (Cameroon); Alfones Perikala, (India).
Catechesis Religious Program—Students 39.

LITTLE ITALY (ROLAND), PULASKI CO., ST. FRANCIS OF ASSISI CHURCH (1922) Attended from St. Boniface, Bigelow.
33223 Hwy. 300, Roland, 72135. Tel: 501-759-2371. Mailing Address: c/o St. Boniface, 20 St. Boniface, Bigelow, 72016. Rev. Richard P. Davis.
Catechesis Religious Program—

MAGNOLIA, COLUMBIA CO., IMMACULATE HEART OF MARY (1946) Mission of St. Louis Church, Camden.
2114 N. Jackson St., Magnolia, 71753.
Tel: 870-901-3173; Email: ihom1949@yahoo.com. Rev. William Wyatt Burmester, V.F.
Catechesis Religious Program—Dee Guzman, D.R.E. Students 36.

MALVERN, HOT SPRING CO., ST. JOHN THE BAPTIST (1949)
1114 Pine Bluff St., Malvern, 72104. Mailing Address: P.O. Box 6, Malvern, 72104.
Tel: 501-332-6244; Email: frreavesstsjbm@gmail.com. Rev. Phillip A. Reaves, V.F.

MARIANNA, LEE CO., ST. ANDREW, Mission of St. Mary, Helena.
54 W. Tennessee St., Marianna, 72360. Mailing Address: P.O. Box 724, Marianna, 72360.
Tel: 870-338-6990 (Helena); Email: wmstmaryschurch@yahoo.com. Revs. Benoit Mukamba, C.S.Sp.; Gilbert Tairo, C.S.Sp., (Tanzania); James Uzoma Ibeh, C.S.Sp.
Catechesis Religious Program—

MARKED TREE, POINSETT CO., ST. NORBERT (1947) Mission
501 Normandy St., Marked Tree, 72365. Mailing Address: 507 Normandy St., Marked Tree, 72365.
Tel: 870-358-2135; Fax: 870-358-4055; Email: randyshinabery@yahoo.com. Rev. Michael Sinkler; Deacon Robert Edward Ward.

MCCRORY, WOODRUFF CO., ST. MARY CHURCH, Mission of St. Peter, Wynne.
Hwy. 64 E., McCrory, 72101. Mailing Address: P.O. Box 517, Wynne, 72396. Fax: 870-238-2613 (Wynne); Email: mglover@dolr.org. Rev. Balaraju Desam, (India).
Catechesis Religious Program—Students 3.

MCGEHEE, DESHA CO., ST. MARY (1906) Attended by St. Mark, Monticello.
401 N. 3rd St., McGehee, 71654.
Tel: 870-367-2848 (Monticello); Fax: 870-814-1419; Email: sharon.spurlock@yahoo.com. Rev. Mark Abban, (Ghana).

MENA, POLK CO., ST. AGNES (1896) [CEM]
203 8th St., Mena, 71953. Tel: 479-394-1017;
Fax: 479-394-2088; Email: saintagnesmena@sbcglobal.net; Web: www.stagneschurchmena.org. Rev. Joseph Shantiraj, (India); Deacon James Tony Salamone.
Catechesis Religious Program—Students 66.
Mission—All Saints, 708 Hwy. 270 E., Mount Ida, Montgomery Co. 71957.

MONTICELLO, DREW CO., ST. MARK (1975)
1016 N. Hyatt St., Monticello, 71655.
Tel: 870-367-2848; Fax: 870-367-5868; Email: stmkoff@ccc-cable.net; Web: www.stmkcatholic.com. Rev. Mark Abban, (Ghana).
Rectory—452 W. Jefferson, Monticello, 71655.
Tel: 870-367-5974.
Catechesis Religious Program—Melissa Prince, D.R.E. Students 62.
Missions—Holy Child—(See listing under Dumas) Dumas, Desha Co.

St. Mary, (See listing under McGehee) 401 3rd St., McGehee, 71654.

MORRILTON, CONWAY CO., SACRED HEART (1879) [CEM]
506 E. Broadway, Morrilton, 72110.
Tel: 501-354-4181; Email: sacred_heart@hotmail.com. Very Rev. Msgr. Jack D. Harris, V.F.; Rev. Aby Abraham; Deacon Stephen Bradley Mallett.
School—Sacred Heart School, (Grades K-6), Tel: 501-354-8113; Email: bgreeson@sacredheartmorrilton.org; Web: sacredheartmorrilton.org. Buddy Greesom, Prin. Clergy 2; Lay Teachers 21; Students 260.
Catechesis Religious Program—Students 134.
Endowment—Sacred Heart School Endowment.

MORRISON BLUFF, LOGAN CO., SS. PETER AND PAUL (1878) Attended by St. Ignatius, Scranton.
2216 N. State Hwy. 109, Morrison Bluff, 72863. Email: 3parishes@gmail.com. Mailing Address: P.O. Box 87, Scranton, 72863.
Tel: 479-938-2821 (Scranton); Web: www.stspeterpaulchurch.org. Rev. John Miranda, (India).
Res.: 108 E. Main St., Scranton, 72863.
Catechesis Religious Program—Ruth Beshoner, D.R.E. Students 18.

MOUNT IDA, MONTGOMERY CO., ALL SAINTS CHURCH, Mission of St. Agnes, Mena.
708 Hwy. 270 E., Mount Ida, 71957. Mailing Address: P.O. Box 724, Mount Ida, 71957.
Tel: 870-867-4644; Email: saintagnesmena@sbcglobal.net; Web: allsaintsmountida.org. Rev. Joseph Shantiraj, (India); Deacon Tony Salamone.
Catechesis Religious Program—

MOUNTAIN HOME, BAXTER CO., ST. PETER THE FISHERMAN (1959)
249 Dyer St., Mountain Home, 72653. Mailing Address: P.O. Box 298, Mountain Home, 72654.
Tel: 870-425-2832; Fax: 870-424-5172; Email: stpeters.spcc@centurytel.net; Web: www.spccmtnhome.org. Very Rev. Norbert F. Rappold, V.F.; Rev. Nazarus Maduba, (Nigeria); Deacons Richard Linstad; Robert Crawford.
Catechesis Religious Program—Christine Langley, D.R.E. Students 40.
Mission—St. Mary Church (1983) 17068 Hwy. 66 W., Mountain View, Stone Co. 72560.

MOUNTAIN VIEW, STONE CO., ST. MARY CHURCH (1982) Mission of St. Peter the Fisherman, Mountain Home.
17068 Hwy. 66 W., Mountain View, 72560. Mailing Address: P.O. Box 926, Mountain View, Stone Co. 72560. Tel: 870-269-5194; Email: saintmarybulletin@gmail.com. Very Rev. Norbert F. Rappold, V.F.; Revs. Nazarus Maduba, (Nigeria); Henry B. Mischkowiuski, In Res., (Retired).
Catechesis Religious Program—Maryanne Smith, D.R.E. Students 2.

NASHVILLE, HOWARD CO., ST. MARTIN CHURCH
1011 Leslie St., Nashville, 71852. Mailing Address: P.O. Box 1039, Nashville, 71852.
Tel: 870-845-3095 (Main); Tel: 870-451-1291; Email: clubcobb@sbcglobal.net. Rev. Salvador Vega-Alvarenga, (El Salvador).
Catechesis Religious Program—Nona Broussard, D.R.E. Students 61.

NEWPORT, JACKSON CO., ST. CECILIA, Mission of St. Mary's, Batesville.
2475 Galeria Dr., Newport, 72112. Tel: 870-523-6542 ; Email: stmarys@suddenlinkmail.com. Rev. Stephen Gadberry.
Catechesis Religious Program—Students 12.

OPPELO, PERRY CO., ST. ELIZABETH (1884) [CEM] (German), Attended by St. Boniface Church, Bigelow.
St. Elizabeth Rd., Oppelo, 72110. Mailing Address: 20 St. Boniface Dr., Bigelow, 72016.
Tel: 501-759-2371; Email: stbnewdixie@gmail.com. Rev. Richard P. Davis.
Catechesis Religious Program—Students 36.

OSCEOLA, MISSISSIPPI CO., ST. MATTHEW (1879) Mission of Immaculate Conception, Blytheville.
501 S. Ermen Ln., Osceola, 72370. Tel: 870-762-2506 ; Email: iccbly@gmail.com. Mailing Address: P.O. Box 583, Osceola, 72370. Rev. Thomas Joseph Hart; Deacon Robert Edward Ward.
Res.: 1301 W. Main St., Blytheville, 72315.
Tel: 870-762-2506; Fax: 870-762-2506.
Catechesis Religious Program—800 Betty Lynn, Osceola, 72370. Tel: 870-563-4889. Students 13.

PARAGOULD, GREENE CO., ST. MARY (1883) [CEM]
220 N. 2nd St., Paragould, 72450. Tel: 870-236-2568; Email: stmryoff@grnco.net; Web: www.stmarysparagould.org. Rev. Stephen Mallanga, A.J., (Uganda); Deacons John Charles Drake; Ricardo Jose Puello Brenes.
Church: 300 N. 2nd St., Paragould, 72450.
School—St. Mary School, (Grades PreK-6), Tel: 870-236-3681; Email: principal@stmarysparagould.org; Web: www.stmarysparagould.org. Clergy 1; Lay Teachers 6; Students 65.
Catechesis Religious Program—Tel: 870-239-3976. Sharon Goodson, D.R.E. Students 100.
Mission—Immaculate Heart of Mary, Walnut Ridge, Lawrence Co.
Endowment—St. Mary Educational Trust Fund.

PARIS, LOGAN CO., ST. JOSEPH (1879) [CEM] (German)
15 S. Spruce St., Paris, 72855. Tel: 479-963-2131; Email: stjosephchurch2131@centurytel.net; Web: www.stjosephparis.org. Rev. Eugene Luke, O.S.B.; Deacon Thomas J. Pohlmeier.
School—St. Joseph School, (Grades PreK-8), 25 S. Spruce St., Paris, 72855. Tel: 479-963-2119; Fax: 479-963-8039; Email: principal@SaintJosephSchoolAR.org; Web: www.SaintJosephSchoolAR.org. Mrs. Christy Koprovic, Prin. Lay Teachers 9; Students 95.
Catechesis Religious Program—Sharon Pohlmeier, D.R.E. Students 42.
Mission—St. Anthony, P.O. Box 60, Ratcliff, 72951.
Endowment—St. Joseph Endowment Fund.

PINE BLUFF, JEFFERSON CO.
1—ST. JOSEPH (1858) [CEM 5] [JC]
412 W. 6th Ave., Pine Bluff, 71601. Mailing Address: P.O. Box 7434, Pine Bluff, 71611. Tel: 870-534-4701; Fax: 870-534-4703; Email: sjccpb1838@gmail.com; Web: www.stjosephpinebluff.org. Rev. Joseph P. Marconi, V.F.; Deacon Noel F. "Bud" Bryant, Email: nfblaw@cablelynx.com.
Catechesis Religious Program—Tel: 870-536-6699. Students 41.
Missions—Holy Cross—Sheridan, Grant Co.
St. Mary Plum Bayou, P.O. Box 7434, Pine Bluff, Jefferson Co. 71611-7434.
2—ST. PETER (1894) (African American)
207 E. 16th Ave., Pine Bluff, 71601.
Tel: 870-534-6418; Email: st.peterpinebluff@gmail.com; Web: www.saintpeterpinebluff.com. Rev. Siprianus Ola Rotok, S.V.D., (Indonesia).
Catechesis Religious Program—Nola Harrison, D.R.E. Students 39.
Mission—St. Raphael, Pine Bluff, Jefferson Co.

POCAHONTAS, RANDOLPH CO., ST. PAUL THE APOSTLE (1868) [CEM] Attends St. John the Baptist, Engelberg.
1002 Convent St., Pocahontas, 72455.
Tel: 870-892-3319; Email: saintpaul@suddenlink.net; Web: saintpaulscatholicchurchpocahontas.com. Rev. Mariadass N. Vallapaneni, (India).
School—St. Paul the Apostle School, (Grades PreK-6), 311 Cedar St., Pocahontas, 72455.
Tel: 870-892-5639; Email: stpaulsch@suddenlink.net. Maria Dickson, Prin.; Kelly Throesch, Librarian. Clergy 2; Lay Teachers 12; Students 122.
Catechesis Religious Program—Tel: 870-892-3319. Monica Lloyd, D.R.E. Students 127.
Mission—St. Joseph the Worker, Corning, Clay Co.

PRAIRIE VIEW, LOGAN CO., ST. MEINRAD CHURCH (1913) Attended from St. Ignatius, Scranton and SS. Peter & Paul, Morrison Bluff.
35 St. Meinrad Loop, Prairie View, 72863. Mailing Address: P.O. Box 87, Scranton, 72863.
Tel: 479-938-2821; Email: 3parishes@gmail.com. Rev. John Miranda, (India).
Catechesis Religious Program—Heath Spellers, D.R.E. Students 14.

RATCLIFF, LOGAN CO., ST. ANTHONY (1879) [CEM] (German) Mission of St. Joseph, Paris.
470 W. Wilson St., Ratcliff, 72951. Mailing Address: P.O. Box 60, Ratcliff, 72951. Tel: 479-970-3063; Email: kstengel75@gmail.com. Rev. Eugene Luke, O.S.B., Sacramental Min.; Deacon Kenneth Edward Stengel, Pastoral Admin.
Catechesis Religious Program—Pat Stengel, D.R.E. Students 17.

ROGERS, BENTON CO., ST. VINCENT DE PAUL (1941) [CEM]
1416 W. Poplar St., Rogers, 72758. Tel: 479-636-4020 ; Fax: 479-631-2548; Email: information@svdprogers.com; Web: www.svdprogers.com. Very Rev. Msgr. David LeSieur, V.F.; Revs. Balaraju Akkala; Martin Siebold; Deacons Clarence Arthur Leis, (Retired); John Ray Pate; Arturo Castrejon; Silvestre Duran; Ronald William Hoyt.
School—St. Vincent de Paul School, (Grades PreK-8), 1315 W. Cypress St., Rogers, 72758.
Tel: 479-636-4421; Fax: 479-636-5812; Email: svdpinfo@svdpschool.net; Web: www.svdpschool.net. Alice Stautzenberger, Prin. Lay Teachers 24; Students 365.
Catechesis Religious Program—
Tel: 479-636-4020, Ext. 40; Email: kalisan@svdprogers.com. Students 1,239.
Endowment—St. Vincent de Paul Endowment Fund.

RUSSELLVILLE, POPE CO.
1—ST. JOHN (1950)
1900 W. Main St., Russellville, 72801.
Tel: 479-967-3699; Fax: 479-967-6215; Email: churchoffice@sjccr.org; Web: www.saintjohnrussellville.org. Revs. Jack Sidler; Mauricio Carrasco.
School—St. John School, (Grades PreK-5), 1912 W. Main St., Russellville, 72801. Tel: 479-967-4644; Fax: 479-967-4645; Email: schooloffice@sjccr.org. Mark Tyler, Prin. Lay Teachers 12; Students 93.
Catechesis Religious Program—Christi Lynn Priore, Catechetical Leader & Youth Min. Students 206.
Endowment—St. John's Educational Trust, 1900 W. Main St., Russellville, 72801.
2—ST. LEO THE GREAT UNIVERSITY PARISH, Attended by Assumption of the Blessed Virgin Mary, Atkins.
509 W. L St., Russellville, 72801. Mailing Address: P.O. Box 9033, Russellville, 72811. Tel: 479-968-8249 ; Email: stleosatu@gmail.com; Web: www.stleosatu.org. Rev. Ernest L. Hardesty.

ST. VINCENT (HATTIEVILLE), CONWAY CO., ST. MARY (1880) [CEM]
11 Kaufman Ln., Hattieville, 72063.
Tel: 501-354-3206; Fax: 501-354-4132; Email: saintmary@aristotle.net. Rev. James Burnie, C.S.Sp.
Catechesis Religious Program—Donna Burgerer, D.R.E. Students 58.

SCRANTON, LOGAN CO., ST. IGNATIUS (1913) [CEM] (German)
108 S. Main St., Scranton, 72863. Mailing Address: P.O. Box 87, Scranton, 72863. Tel: 479-938-2821; Email: mjspillers94@gmail.com. Rev. John Miranda, (India).
Catechesis Religious Program—Students 50.
Missions—St. Meinrad—Prairie View, Logan Co.
SS. Peter & Paul Church, Morrison Bluff, Logan Co.

SEARCY, WHITE CO., ST. JAMES (1915)
1102 Pioneer Rd., Searcy, 72143. Mailing Address: P.O. Box 172, Searcy, 72143.
Tel: 501-268-5252 (Office); Email: stjames172@sbcglobal.net; Web: www.stjamessearcy.org. Rev. Polycarp Ssebbowa, (Uganda); Deacon Robert L. Morris.
Catechesis Religious Program—Theresa Gilliam, D.R.E. Students 184.
Mission—St. Richard, Hickory & Cleveland Sts., Bald Knob, White Co. 72010.

SHERIDAN, GRANT CO., HOLY CROSS (1949) Mission of St. Joseph, Pine Bluff.
921 W. Vine St., Sheridan, 72150. Tel: 870-534-4701; Email: joesaia@att.net. Mailing Address: P.O. Box 624, Sheridan, 72150. Rev. Joseph P. Marconi, V.F.
Catechesis Religious Program—Tel: 870-942-2259. Mary Hale, Catechetical Leader. (Attended from St. Joseph, Pine Bluff). Students 20.

SHOAL CREEK (NEW BLAINE), LOGAN CO., ST. SCHOLASTICA (New Blaine) (1878) (German)
288 St. Scholastica Rd., New Blaine, 72851.
Tel: 479-938-7566; Email: stscholcreek@yahoo.com. Rev. Gregory Pilcher, O.S.B.
Catechesis Religious Program—

SILOAM SPRINGS, BENTON CO., ST. MARY (1963)
1998 Hwy. 412 E., Siloam Springs, 72761. Mailing Address: P.O. Box 118, Siloam Springs, 72761.
Tel: 479-524-8526; Fax: 479-524-5677; Email: secretary@stmarysiloam.com; Web: www.stmarysiloamsprings.com. Rev. Salvador Marquez-Munoz.
Catechesis Religious Program—Leticia Zavala, D.R.E. Students 227.
Mission—Blessed Stanley Rother Catholic Church, 758 Hill Ave., Decatur, 72722.

SLOVAK, PRAIRIE CO., SS. CYRIL AND METHODIUS, [CEM] Attended by St. Rose of Lima, Carlisle.
1852 Hwy. 86 W., Stuttgart, 72160.
Tel: 870-241-3359; Fax: 870-673-6701. Rev. Shaun C. Wesley.
Catechesis Religious Program—Students 24.

SPRINGDALE, WASHINGTON CO., ST. RAPHAEL (1949) [JC]
1386 S. West End St., Springdale, 72764.
Tel: 479-756-6711, Ext. 227; Email: rhodges@straphaelcc.org; Web: www.straphaelcc.org. Revs. John M. Connell; Rajasekhar Chittem; Daniel Ramos; Deacons Chuck Marino; Dan Cashman; Jesus Ramos.
Catechesis Religious Program—Tel: 479-756-6711. Darla Lucas, Catechetical Leader; Monica Lopez, Catechetical Leader. Students 1,513.

STAMPS, LAFAYETTE CO., ST. VINCENT DE PAUL, Closed. For inquiries for parish records contact the chancery.

STAR CITY, LINCOLN CO., ST. JUSTIN (1986) [CEM] [JC] Attended by St. Peter, Pine Bluff.
400 N. Drew St., Star City, 71667. Mailing Address: 207 E. 16th Ave., Pine Bluff, 71601.
Tel: 870-534-6418; Email: st.peterpinebluff@gmail.com. Rev. Siprianus Ola Rotok, S.V.D., (Indonesia).
Catechesis Religious Program— Through St. Peter, Pine Bluff.

STUTTGART, ARKANSAS CO., HOLY ROSARY (1887) [CEM]
1815 S. Prairie St., Stuttgart, 72160.
Tel: 870-673-8351; Email: holyrose@centurylink.net. Rev. Clayton Gould.
School—Holy Rosary School, (Grades PreK-6), 920 W. 19th St., Stuttgart, 72160. Tel: 870-673-3211; Email: holyrosary@centurytel.net; Web: wwww.holyrosarystuttgart.come. Kathy Lorince, Prin. Lay Teachers 4; Students 42.

Catechesis Religious Program—Students 35.

SUBIACO, LOGAN CO., ST. BENEDICT (1878) [CEM]
81 W. Parish Dr., Subiaco, 72865. Tel: 479-934-1169; Cell: 479-438-5072; Email: stengelmark@gmail.com. Rev. Mark Stengel, O.S.B.
Catechesis Religious Program—Donna Forst, D.R.E. Students 60.

TEXARKANA, MILLER CO., ST. EDWARD (1903) [CEM]
407 Beech St., Texarkana, 71854. Tel: 870-772-1115; Email: office@saintedwardstexarkana.com; Web: www.saintedwardstexarkana.com. Mailing Address: P.O. Box 1186, Texarkana, 71854. Revs. James P. West; Lawrence Chellaian, In Res.; Deacons David Fowler; Angel Guzman.
Catechesis Religious Program—Kelli Nugent, Dir. Faith Formation. Students 310.
Missions—St. Elizabeth Ann Seton—1910 Rankin, Ashdown, 71822. Mailing Address: P.O. Box 966, Ashdown, Little River Co. 71822. Tel: 870-898-8529.
Sacred Heart, 415 S. Bell St., Foreman, 71836. Mailing Address: P.O. Box 43, Foreman, Little River Co. 71836. Tel: 870-542-6846.

TONTITOWN, WASHINGTON CO., ST. JOSEPH (1898) [CEM] (Italian)
154 E. Henri de Tonti Blvd., Tontitown, 72770. Mailing Address: P.O. Box 39, Tontitown, 72762. Tel: 479-361-2612; Email: stjoetontitown1@att.net; Web: www.stjoetontitown.org. Revs. John M. Connell; Rajasekhar Chittem; Daniel Ramos; Deacon Dan Joseph Daily.
Catechesis Religious Program—David Burkemper, D.R.E. Students 187.

VAN BUREN, CRAWFORD CO., ST. MICHAEL (1872)
1019 E. Pointer Tr., Van Buren, 72956. Tel: 479-471-1211; Fax: 479-471-1219; Email: officemgr@stmichaelvanburen.com; Web: www.stmichaelvanburen.com. Rev. Charles R. Hobbs; Deacon Domingo Antonio Lopez.
Catechesis Religious Program—Email: religioused@stmichaelvanburen.com. Mayra Marciano, Catechetical Leader. Students 217.

WALDRON, SCOTT CO., ST. JUDE THADDEUS CHURCH (1947) Mission of Church of the Assumption, Booneville.
680 St. Jude Dr., Waldron, 72958. Mailing Address: P.O. Box 1688, Waldron, 72958. Tel: 479-207-2494; Email: waldronstjudecatholicchurch@yahoo.com; Web: www.waldronar.catholicweb.com. Rev. Alejandro Puello.
Catechesis Religious Program—Students 53.

WALNUT RIDGE, LAWRENCE CO., IMMACULATE HEART OF MARY (1925) Attended by St. Mary, Paragould.
320 Free St., Walnut Ridge, 72476. Mailing Address: P.O. Box 70, Walnut Ridge, 72476. Tel: 870-886-2119 ; Email: stmryoff@grnco.net. Rev. Stephen Mallanga, A.J., (Uganda); Deacon Marlyn Glenn Tate.
Catechesis Religious Program—Students 2.

WARREN, BRADLEY CO., ST. LUKE CHURCH, Attended by Holy Redeemer, El Dorado.
508 W. Pine St., Warren, 71671. Mailing Address: 440 W. Main St., El Dorado, 71730. Tel: 870-836-3620; Email: holyredeemer@suddenlinkmail.com. Rev. Edward P. D'Almeida.
Catechesis Religious Program—Students 50.

WEINER, POINSETT CO., ST. ANTHONY (1902) [CEM]
407 Kings Hwy., Weiner, 72479. Mailing Address: P.O. Box 76, Weiner, 72479. Tel: 870-684-2656; Email: sac@rittermail.com. Rev. Michael Sinkler.
Catechesis Religious Program—Tel: 870-578-4255. Students 37.

WEST MEMPHIS, CRITTENDEN CO., ST. MICHAEL (1914)
411 N. Missouri St., West Memphis, 72301. Mailing Address: P.O. Box 899, West Memphis, 72303. Tel: 870-733-1212; Email: westmemphiscatholic@gmail.com. Very Rev. Charles Thessing, V.F.
Res.: 208 W. Cooper Ave., West Memphis, 72301.
School—St. Michael School, (Grades PreK-6), 405 Missouri, West Memphis, 72303. 405 N. Missouri, West Memphis, 72301. Tel: 870-735-1730; Fax: 870-735-3017; Email: smcswm@sbcglobal.net; Web: stmichaelwm.org. Elizabeth Haney, Prin. Lay Teachers 13; Students 139.
Catechesis Religious Program—Libby Burroughs, D.R.E. Students 110.
Endowment—St. Michael's School Endowment and Charitable Trust.
Mission—Sacred Heart, Crawfordsville, Crittenden Co.

WINSLOW, CRAWFORD CO., OUR LADY OF THE OZARKS SHRINE (1946) [CEM] Attended by Immaculate Conception, Fort Smith.
22741 N. Hwy. 71, Winslow, 72959. Mailing Address: 3436 Breckenridge Dr., Fayetteville, 72701. Tel: 479-634-2181. Rev. John K. Antony, J.C.L., V.F.; Deacon Grant Michael Henry, Pastoral Admin.
Catechesis Religious Program—Tel: 479-530-3792; Fax: 479-439-4739. Students 11.

WYNNE, CROSS CO., ST. PETER (1921)
1695 N. Falls Blvd., Wynne, 72396. Mailing Address: P.O. Box 517, Wynne, 72396. Tel: 870-238-2613; Fax: 870-238-2613; Email: louisehess@sbcglobal.net. Rev. Balaraju Desam, (India); Deacon Carlos Guzman Beltran.
Catechesis Religious Program—Tel: 870-919-4066. Judy Locke, D.R.E. Students 66.
Mission—St. Mary, Hwy. 64 E., McCrory, Woodruff Co. 72101.

YELLVILLE, MARION CO., ST. ANDREW CHURCH (1980) Mission of Mary Mother of God, Harrison.
1486 Hwy. 62 W., Yellville, 72687. Mailing Address: P.O. Box 197, Yellville, 72687. Tel: 870-449-4850; Fax: 870-741-4234 (Harrison); Email: mmgchurch@yahoo.com; Web: harrisoncatholic.org. Rev. James M. Fanrak, V.F.

Retired:
Rev. Msgrs.—
Hebert, J. Gaston, (Retired), 11621 Woodmar Ln., N.E., Albuquerque, NM 87111
Mancini, James E., (Retired), 703 Mill St., Springdale, 72764
O'Donnell, John F., (Retired), P.O. Box 7565, 72217
Oswald, Richard S., (Retired), P.O. Box 7565, 72217
Very Rev.—
Atunzu, Kevin O., (Retired), St. John Manor, 2414 N. Tyler St., 72207
Revs.—
Dienert, Robert T., (Retired), St. John Manor, 2414 N. Tyler St., 72207
Do, Nho Duy, (Retired), St. John Manor, 2414 N. Tyler St., 72207
Esposito, Ralph J., (Retired), 220 Hillcrest Ave., New Castle, PA 16105
Graves, Edwin, (Retired), St. John Manor, 2414 N. Tyler St., 72207
Keller, Thomas W., (Retired), St. John Manor, 2414 N. Tyler St., 72207
McDougal, Jon, (Retired), 1386 15th Terr., Barling, 72923
Mischkowiuski, Henry B., (Retired), P.O. Box 926, Mountain View, 72560
Oswald, John, (Retired), St. John Manor, 2414 N. Tyler St., 72207
Pallo, Joseph L., (Retired), 17911 Bushard St., Fountain Valley, CA 92708
Rosenau, Alan, (Retired), 107 Siesta St., Hot Springs, 71913
Swiderski, Stan, (Retired), 1500 Inverness Dr., Mountain Home, 72653-4256.

Permanent Deacons:
Deacons—
Alberson, John M., St. Jude the Apostle, Jacksonville
Andrus, Charles, (Retired)
Ashburn, Charles Victor, Cathedral of St. Andrew, Little Rock; Catholic High School for Boys, Little Rock; Vocations, Little Rock
Baldwin, Warren Thomas, St. Joseph & St. Thomas Aquinas, Fayetteville
Bowen, William Joseph, Cathedral of St. Andrew, Little Rock
Brandon, William G. Jr., Immaculate Conception, Blytheville
Brust, Raymond Edward, (Retired)
Bryant, Noel F. "Bud", St. Joseph, Pine Bluff
Burns, John Joseph, (Retired)
Cashman, Dan Charles, St. Raphael, Springdale
Castrejon, Arturo, St. Vincent de Paul, Rogers
Costello, Timothy James, Immaculate Heart of Mary, North Little Rock
Cowie, Robert, (Retired)
Cranford, William, (Retired)
Crawford, Robert, St. Peter the Fisherman, Mountain Home
Cronan, Paul, (Retired)
Cumnock, Thomas Michael, St. Mary, Batesville; St. Cecelia, Newport
Daily, Dan Joseph, St. Joseph, Tontitown
DeBriyn, Norman Francis, St. Thomas Aquinas, Fayetteville
Drake, John Charles, St. Mary, Paragould
Duran, Silvestre, St. Vincent de Paul, Rogers
Elliott, Max Robert, St. Jude the Apostle, Jacksonville; Little Rock Air Force Base
Evans, David Henry, St. Mary, Arkadelphia
Farrar, Chuck Arthur, Immaculate Conception, North Little Rock
Fowler, David, St. Edward, Texarkana
French, David Bruce, Holy Cross, Crossett; Holy Spirit, Hamburg; Our Lady of the Lake, Lake Village
Friedman, William, Sacred Heart of Jesus, Hot Springs Village
Froning, John, Sacred Heart of Jesus, Hot Springs Village
Gallegos, Ernesto Corona, St. Jude the Apostle, Jacksonville
Genna, Al, St. Bernard of Clairveaux, Bella Vista
Gieringer, Wallace Arnold, (Retired)
Glover, Matthew A., J.D., J.C.L., Christ the King, Little Rock
Goetz, Roy E., Subiaco Abbey, Subiaco
Greenway, Curtis Don, Christ the King, Little Rock
Guzman, Angel, St. Edward, Texarkana
Guzman Beltran, Carlos, St. Peter, Wynne
Hall, John Wesley, Our Lady of the Holy Souls, Little Rock
Harrison, Elton Clement, (Retired)
Harrison, Gerald Joseph, St. Joseph, Conway
Harrison, Joe Dale, St. Mary of the Springs, Hot Springs
Hartnedy, Daniel Thomas, St. Edward, Little Rock
Hartnedy, John Augustine, Immaculate Heart of Mary, North Little Rock
Hatch, Larry, St. Agnes, Mena
Hennessey, Daniel James III, St. Edward, Little Rock
Henry, Grant Michael, St. Joseph, Fayetteville; Our Lady of the Ozarks Shrine, Winslow
Hoyt, Ronald William, St. Vincent de Paul, Rogers
Jakobs, Thomas, Christ the King, Fort Smith
Jegley, Lawrence H., (Retired)
Johnson, William Albert, Christ the King, Little Rock
King, Lowell Gene, Immaculate Conception, North Little Rock
Krug, John Thomas, (Retired)
Kuehl, Charles Edward, Immaculate Conception, Fort Smith
Lachowsky, Brian Albert, St. Mary, Altus
Leckner, Leland Paul, St. Mary of the Springs, Hot Springs
Leis, Clarence Arthur, (Retired)
Linstad, Richard, St. Peter the Fisherman, Mountain Home
Lipsmeyer, Lawrence Joseph, Sacred Heart of Jesus, Hot Springs Village
Lopez, Domingo Antonio, St. Michael, Van Buren
Luebanos, Jose Guadalupe, Holy Redeemer, El Dorado
Luna, Marcelino, St. Edward, Little Rock
Mallett, Stephen Bradley, Sacred Heart, Morrilton
Marino, Charles Jr., St. Raphael, Springdale
Massanelli, Garland Edward, (Retired)
McAllister, John M., J.D., J.C.L., Christ the King, Little Rock
Morris, Robert L., St. Albert, Heber Springs; St. James, Searcy; St. Richard, Bald Knob
Pair, Greg, Immaculate Conception, Fort Smith
Papini, Richard John, St. Joseph, Conway
Pate, John Ray, St. Vincent de Paul, Rogers
Patterson, Richard Lewis, Christ the King, Little Rock
Pohlmeier, Thomas J., St. Joseph, Paris
Post, Matthew Joseph, (Retired)
Puello Brenes, Ricardo Jose, St. Mary, Paragould
Ramirez Fernandez, Ramon, Blessed Sacrament, Jonesboro
Ramos, Jesus, St. Raphael, Springdale
Rangel Flores, Elias, St. Anne, Berryville
Rector, Michael Lynn, Christ the King, Little Rock
Salamone, James "Tony", St. Agnes, Mena
Sampolesi, Timothy Gelio, Holy Cross, Crossett; Holy Spirit, Hamburg; Our Lady of the Lake, Lake Village
Sanchez, Israel, St. Barbara, De Queen
Scouten, Mark Allen, Mary, Mother of God, Harrison
Stager, Ronald F., Immaculate Conception, North Little Rock
Standridge, Robert James, St. John the Baptist, Hot Springs
Stengel, Kenneth Edward, Our Lady of the Assumption, Booneville; St. Anthony, Ratcliff
Strozyk, Brunon John, Immaculate Heart of Mary, North Little Rock
Tate, Marlyn Glenn, Immaculate Heart of Mary, Walnut Ridge
Vargas Rodriguez, Efrain Antonio, St. Rose of Lima, Carlisle; St. Edward, Little Rock
Vazquez, Marcelino, St. Joseph, Fayetteville
Verkamp, Mark Joseph, Sacred Heart, Charleston
Villafranca, Cesar Augusto, Immaculate Conception, Fort Smith
Wanless, Robert E., (Retired)
Ward, Robert Edward, Immaculate Conception, Blytheville; St. Norbert, Marked Tree; St. Matthew, Osceola
Westmoreland, David Kirby, St. Joseph, Conway
Wrape, William Robert, (Retired)
Zanoff, Frank, St. Francis of Assisi, Fairfield Bay; St. Jude, Clinton.

INSTITUTIONS LOCATED IN DIOCESE

[A] SEMINARIES, RELIGIOUS OR SCHOLASTICATES

LITTLE ROCK. *Diocese of Little Rock House of Formation*, 1201 S. Van Buren, 72204. Tel: 501-418-8525. Rev. Gregory T. Luyet, J.C.L., J.V., Prefect; Rev. Msgr. Scott Friend, V.G., Vocations Dir.

Marylake - Carmelite Novitiate (1952) 5151 Marylake Dr., 72206. Tel: 501-888-3052; Fax: 501-888-3080; Email: carmelitesok@yahoo.com; Web: www.carmelitefriarsocd.com. Revs. Gregory Ross, O.C.D., Contact Person; Jerome Earley, O.C.D.; Sam Anthony Morello, O.C.D. Discalced Carmelite Friars of the Province of St. Therese, Little Rock. Priests 3.

[B] HIGH SCHOOLS, DIOCESAN

LITTLE ROCK. *Catholic High School*, 6300 Father Tribou St., 72205. Tel: 501-664-3939; Fax: 501-664-6549; Email: chs@lrchs.org; Web: www.lrchs.org. Mr. Steve Straessle, Prin.; Rev. Msgr. Lawrence A. Frederick, Rector; Rev. Patrick Friend

Catholic High School of Little Rock, AR Brothers 1; Lay Teachers 43; Priests 2; Students 757; Total Staff 56; Clergy / Religious Teachers 3.

CONWAY. *St. Joseph School*, (Grades K-12), 502 Front St., Conway, 72032-5408. Tel: 501-329-5741; Fax: 501-513-6804; Email: dwolfe@sjbulldogs.org; Web: www.stjosephconway.org. Courtney Pope, Prin.; Matthew Tucker, Asst. Prin. (Grades K-3); Mrs. Diane Wolfe, Prin.; Christy Pasierb, Librarian; Karen Wilson, Librarian (Grades 7-12). Lay Teachers 46; Students 523.

FORT SMITH. *Trinity Junior High*, (Grades 7-9), 1205 S. Albert Pike, Fort Smith, 72903. Tel: 479-782-2451; Fax: 479-782-7263; Email: frjohn@icchurch.com; Web: www.trinitycatholicjh.org. Karen Hollenbeck, Prin.; Rev. John K. Antony, J.C.L., V.F., Admin. Lay Teachers 24; Students 218; Total Staff 25.

Trinity Educational Trust Fund, Tel: 479-782-2451; Fax: 479-782-7263.

MORRILTON. *Sacred Heart Catholic School*, (Grades K-12), 106 N. St. Joseph St., Morrilton, 72110. Tel: 501-354-8113; Fax: 501-354-2001; Email: bgreeson@sacredheartmorrilton.org. Brian Bailey, Prin.; Patty Bottoms, Librarian. Lay Teachers 23; Students 255; Total Staff 23.

[C] HIGH SCHOOLS, PRIVATE

LITTLE ROCK. *Mount St. Mary Academy* (Girls) 3224 Kavanaugh Blvd., 72205. Tel: 501-664-8006; Fax: 501-666-4382; Email: kdavis@mtstmary.edu; Web: www.mtstmary.edu. Karen Flake, CEO; Angela Collins, Prin.; Alice W. Jones, Librarian. Lay Staff 54; Priests 1; Sisters of Mercy 1; Students 493.

Mount St. Mary Foundation Corporation, Tel: 501-664-8006; Fax: 501-664-4382.

SUBIACO. **Subiaco Academy*, (Grades 7-12), 405 N. Subiaco Ave., Subiaco, 72865. Tel: 479-934-1005; Tel: 800-364-7824 (Toll Free); Fax: 479-934-1033; Email: dwright@subi.org; Web: www.subiacoacademy.us. Mr. David Wright, Headmaster. Brothers 3; Lay Teachers 32; Students 158; Clergy / Religious Teachers 3.

[D] GENERAL HOSPITALS

LITTLE ROCK. *St. Vincent Infirmary Medical Center* (1888) No. 2 St. Vincent Cir., 72205. Tel: 501-552-3676; Fax: 501-552-8614; Email: kcullinan@stvincenthealth.com. Bed Capacity 615; Sisters 2; Tot Asst. Annually 183,616; Total Staff 2,159.

BOONEVILLE. *Mercy Hospital Booneville*, 880 W. Main St., Booneville, 72927. Tel: 314-628-3608; Email: Marynell.Ploch@Mercy.Net. Susan Hannasch, Reg. Gen. Counsel. Bed Capacity 25; Tot Asst. Annually 14,749; Total Staff 87.

FORT SMITH. *CHRISTUS Dubuis Hospital of Fort Smith* (Owned & operated by CHRISTUS Continuing Care, a Texas nonprofit corporation) 7301 Rogers Ave., 4th Fl., Fort Smith, 72903. Tel: 479-314-4900; Fax: 479-314-4999; Web: christusdubuis.org/fortsmith. John F. Brothers.

Mercy Hospital Fort Smith (1905) 7301 Rogers Ave., Fort Smith, 72903. Tel: 479-314-6000; Fax: 479-314-1770; Email: Marynell.Ploch@Mercy.Net; Web: www.mercy.net. Martin Schreiber. Bed Capacity 349; Tot Asst. Annually 200,000; Total Staff 1,800.

Mercy Health Foundation, Fort Smith, 7301 Rogers Ave., Fort Smith, 72903. Tel: 479-314-1133; Email: patrick.pendleton@mercy.net; Email: taylor.martinez2@mercy.net; Web: www.mercy.net/practice/mercy-health-foundation-fort-smith/. Martin Schreiber, Admin.

HOT SPRINGS. *CHI St. Vincent Hot Springs*, Mailing Address: P.O. Box 29001, Hot Springs National Park, 71903-9001. Tel: 501-622-1000; Fax: 501-622-1199; Email: anthonyhouston@stvincenthealth.com; Web: www.chistvincent.com. Anthony Houston, Pres.; Rev. George W. Sanders, Chap. Bed Capacity 279; Patients Asst Anual. 170,000; Total Staff 2,200.

CHRISTUS Dubuis Hospital of Hot Springs (Owned & operated by CHRISTUS Continuing Care, a Texas nonprofit corporation) 300 Werner St., 3rd Fl., Hot Springs, 71913. Tel: 501-609-4300; Fax: 501-623-2317; Web: christusdubuis.org/hotsprings. John F. Brothers.

JONESBORO. *St. Bernard Medical Center* (1900) 225 E. Jackson #84, Jonesboro, 72401. Tel: 870-972-4100; Tel: 870-207-4230; Fax: 870-974-7040; Email: sbriley@sbrmc.org; Web: stbernards.info. Chris Barber, Pres. Bed Capacity 438; Sisters 5; Tot Asst. Annually 331,566; Total Staff 2,443.

MORRILTON. *CHI St. Vincent Morrilton* (1925) 4 Hospital Dr., Morrilton, 72110-4510. Tel: 501-977-2300; Fax: 501-977-2400; Email: llyarbrough@stvincenthealth.com. Leslie Bubba Arnold, Pres. Sponsored by St. Vincent Health System, a division of Catholic Health Initiatives.

St. Anthony's Hospital Association Bed Capacity 25; Tot Asst. Annually 36,768; Total Staff 137.

OZARK. *Mercy Hospital Ozark*, 801 W. River St., Ozark, 72949. Tel: 479-667-4138; Fax: 479-667-4751; Fax: 479-667-9778; Email: Marynell.Ploch@Mercy.Net. Juli Stec, COO; Martin Schreiber. Bed Capacity 25; Tot Asst. Annually 14,722; Total Staff 56.

PARIS. *Mercy Hospital Paris*, 500 E. Academy, Paris, 72855. Tel: 479-963-6101; Fax: 479-963-6155; Email: Marynell.Ploch@Mercy.Net. Juli Stec, COO; Martin Schreiber. Bed Capacity 16; Tot Asst. Annually 9,800; Total Staff 47.

ROGERS. *Mercy Hospital Rogers*, 2710 Rife Medical Ln., Rogers, 72756. Tel: 479-338-2903; Fax: 479-338-2906; Email: Marynell.Ploch@Mercy.Net. Eric Pianalto, CEO; Sr. Anita DeSalvo, R.S.M., Sister of Mercy. Bed Capacity 175; Tot Asst. Annually 171,469; Total Staff 1,000.

Mercy Health Foundation Northwest Arkansas, 2710 Rife Medical Ln., Rogers, 72756. Tel: 479-338-8000; Fax: 479-338-2906; Email: Marynell.Ploch@Mercy.Net. Susan Hannasch, Reg. Gen. Counsel.

SHERWOOD. *St. Vincent Medical Center / Sherwood* (1999) 2215 Wildwood Ave., Sherwood, 72120. Tel: 501-552-7107; Fax: 501-552-8614. Bed Capacity 69; Tot Asst. Annually 36,053; Total Staff 189.

WALDRON. *Mercy Hospital Waldron*, 1341 W. 6th St., Waldron, 72958. Tel: 479-637-4135; Fax: 479-637-3523; Email: Marynell.Ploch@Mercy.Net. Teresa Williams, Admin.; Martin Schreiber. Bed Capacity 24; Tot Asst. Annually 30,000; Total Staff 56.

WYNNE. *St. Bernard Community Hospital Corporation* aka CrossRidge Community Hospital, 310 S. Falls Blvd., Wynne, 72396. Tel: 870-238-3300; Fax: 870-238-7432; Email: sbriley@sbrmc.org. Sr. Mary John Seyler, Chm. Bed Capacity 25; Tot Asst. Annually 24,000; Total Staff 158.

[E] HOMES FOR AGED

LITTLE ROCK. *Christopher Homes of Arkansas, Inc.*, 2417 N. Tyler St., 72207. Tel: 501-664-1881; Fax: 501-664-1631; Email: llopez@dolr.org. Elizabeth Lopez, Dir. Total in Residence 588.

Christopher Homes, Inc.

Christopher Homes of Augusta, Inc. (1989) 900 Carver N. St., Augusta, 72006. Tel: 870-347-2388; Fax: 870-347-2388; Email: aug@christopherhomesofarkansas.org. Elizabeth Lopez, Dir. Christopher Homes of Augusta, Inc. Units 20.

Christopher Homes of Brinkley, Inc. (1987) 900 W. 6th St., Brinkley, 72021. Tel: 870-734-2201; Fax: 870-734-2201; Email: bri@christopherhomesofarkansas.org; Web: www.christopherhomesofarkansas.org. Elizabeth Lopez, Dir. Christopher Homes of Brinkley, Inc. Units 20.

Camden (1988) 900 Sharp Ave., Camden, 71701. Tel: 870-837-1911; Fax: 870-837-1905; Email: cam@christopherhomesofarkansas.org. Elizabeth Lopez, Dir. Units 20.

Clarendon (1989) 400 Meadow Ln., Clarendon, 72029. Tel: 870-747-5441; Fax: 870-747-1345; Email: cla@christopherhomesofarkansas.org. Units 20.

De Queen (1986) 119 S. Lakeside Dr., De Queen, 71832. Tel: 870-642-6211; Fax: 870-642-2029; Email: deq@christopherhomesofarkansas.org. Units 20.

De Valls Bluff (1990) 119 W. Sycamore, De Valls Bluff, 72041. Tel: 870-998-7280; Fax: 870-998-7285; Email: dev@christopherhomesofarkansas.org. Units 15.

Christopher Homes of Elaine, Inc. (1988) 500 N. Pecan, P.O. Box 43, Elaine, 72333. Tel: 870-827-3705; Fax: 870-827-3083; Email: ela@christopherhomesofarkansas.org. Christopher Homes of Elaine, Inc. Units 20.

El Dorado (1985) 1323 W. 5th St., El Dorado, 71730. Tel: 870-862-9711; Fax: 870-862-9714; Email: eld@christopherhomesofarkansas.org. Units 40.

Christopher Homes of Forrest City, Inc. (1986) 805 Dawson Rd., Forrest City, 72335. Tel: 870-633-4804; Fax: 870-633-4804; Email: for@christopherhomesofarkansas.org. Christopher Homes of Forrest City, Inc. Units 20.

Christopher Homes of Horatio, Inc. (1988) 408 Bruce St., Horatio, 71842. Tel: 870-832-4014; Fax: 870-832-2526; Email: hor@christopherhomesofarkansas.org. Christopher Homes of Horatio, Inc. Units 19.

Christopher Homes of Jonesboro, Inc. (1988) 2204 Crescendo Dr., Jonesboro, 72401. Tel: 870-931-9575; Fax: 870-931-9575; Email: jon@christopherhomesofarkansas.org. Units 20.

Christopher Homes of Marianna, Inc. (1986) 238 Christopher Cove #1, Marianna, 72360. Tel: 870-295-6345; Fax: 870-295-6345; Email: mar@christopherhomesofarkansas.org. Christopher Homes of Marianna, Inc. Units 20.

Christopher Homes of Paragould, Inc. (1990) 1612 S. 9th St., Paragould, 72450. Tel: 870-239-8609; Fax: 870-239-8609; Email: par@christopherhomesofarkansas.org. Christopher Homes of Paragould, Inc. Units 18.

Christopher Homes of Parkin, Inc. (1990) 100 College St., P.O. Box 586, Parkin, 72373. Tel: 870-755-2939; Fax: 870-755-2939; Email: pkn@christopherhomesofarkansas.org. Christopher Homes of Parkin, Inc. Units 20.

Christopher Homes of Searcy, Inc. (1985) 17 Christopher Cr., Searcy, 72143. Tel: 501-268-7804; Fax: 501-278-5195; Email: ser@christopherhomesofarkansas.org. Christopher Homes of Searcy, Inc. Units 40.

Christopher Homes of West Helena, Inc. (1984) 13 Christopher Pl., West Helena, 72390. Tel: 870-572-9433; Fax: 870-572-9433; Email: whl@christopherhomesofarkansas.org. Christopher Homes of West Helena, Inc. Units 62.

Christopher Homes of Wynne, Inc. (1991) 21 Christopher Pl., Wynne, 72396. Tel: 870-238-3388; Fax: 870-238-3915; Email: wyn@christopherhomesofarkansas.org. Christopher Homes of Wynne, Inc. Units 20.

Christopher Homes of Hot Springs, Inc. (1997) 1010 Cones Rd., Hot Springs, 71901. Tel: 501-318-1317; Fax: 501-318-1317; Email: hot@christopherhomesofarkansas.org. Elizabeth Lopez, Dir. Units 20.

Christopher Homes of Little Rock, 9216 Lanehart Rd., 72204. Tel: 501-812-3442; Fax: 501-313-2303; Email: lil@christopherhomesofarkansas.org.

Christopher Homes of Monette, Inc. (1993) 21 Christopher Pl., Monette, 72447. Tel: 870-486-2748; Fax: 870-486-2748; Email: mon@christopherhomesofarkansas.org. Units 20.

Christopher Homes of North Little Rock, Inc. (1996) 656 Donovan Briley Blvd., North Little Rock, 72118. Tel: 501-758-8582; Fax: 501-753-4466; Email: nlr@christopherhomesofarkansas.org. Units 55.

Christopher Homes of Palestine, Inc. (1993) 21 Christopher Pl., Palestine, 72372. Tel: 870-581-2023; Fax: 870-581-2057; Email: pal@christopherhomesofarkansas.org. Units 20.

Christopher Homes of Strong, Inc. (1994) 21 Christopher Pl, Strong, 71765. Tel: 870-797-7525; Fax: 870-797-2162; Email: str@christopherhomesofarkansas.org. Units 20.

The Cottages at Delta Acres Inc., 721 N. 7th St., Clarendon, 72029. Tel: 870-747-5150; Fax: 870-747-5151. Units 19.

BARLING. *Mercy Crest Housing, Inc.* aka Mercy Crest Assisted Living, 1300 Strozier Ln., Barling, 72923. Tel: 479-478-3000; Fax: 479-452-8382; Email: administrator@mercycrest.com; Web: www.mercycrest.com. Cindy Taylor, Admin. Sponsored by the Religious Sisters of Mercy. Bed Capacity 102; Tot Asst. Annually 135; Total Staff 57; Assisted & Independent Living 98.

BERRYVILLE. *Mercy Home Health Berryville*, 804 W. Freeman, Ste. 4, Berryville, 72616. Tel: 866-433-6078 (toll free); Fax: 870-423-4367; Email: Marynell.Ploch@Mercy.Net. Susan Hannasch, Reg. Gen. Counsel. Tot Asst. Annually 420; Total Staff 14.

JONESBORO. *Benedictine Manor I*, 312 S. Bridge St., Jonesboro, 72401. Tel: 870-932-8141; Web: stbseniorhousing.com. Mr. Brian Rega, Admin.

(Affiliated with Olivetan Benedictine Sisters, Inc., Jonesboro, AR) Bed Capacity 20; Tot Asst. Annually 25; Total Staff 1.

Benedictine Manor II, 312 S. Bridge St., Jonesboro, 72401. Tel: 870-932-8141; Web: stbseniorhousing.com. Mr. Brian Rega, Admin. (Affiliated with Olivetan Benedictine Sisters, Inc., Jonesboro, AR) Bed Capacity 20; Tot Asst. Annually 25; Total Staff 1.

St. Bernard Village, Inc., 1606 Heern Dr., Jonesboro, 72401. Tel: 870-932-8141; Fax: 870-933-5563; Web: www.stbseniorhousing.com. Mr. Brian Rega, Dir.; Kevin Hodges. (Affiliated with Olivetan Benedictine Sisters, Inc., Jonesboro, AR) Bed Capacity 258; Total Staff 68; Total Assisted 350.

[F] MONASTERIES AND RESIDENCES FOR PRIESTS AND BROTHERS

LITTLE ROCK. *St. John Manor*, 2414 N. Tyler St., 72207. Tel: 501-664-0340; Fax: 501-664-9075; Email: tcostello@dolr.org. Rev. Msgrs. John F. O'Donnell, (Retired); Richard S. Oswald, (Retired); Revs. Kevin Atunzu, (Nigeria) V.F.; Robert T. Dienert, (Retired); Nho Duy Do, (Retired); Edwin Graves, (Retired); Warren Harvey; Thomas W. Keller, (Retired); John Oswald, (Retired); Mr. Jinho Zyung, Res. Mgr. Priests 9.

SUBIACO. *Subiaco Abbey*, 405 N. Subiaco Ave., Subiaco, 72865. Tel: 479-934-1000; Fax: 479-934-4328; Email: frleonard@subi.org; Web: www.subi.org. Rt. Rev. Leonard Wangler, O.S.B., V.F., Abbot; Revs. Reginald Udouj, O.S.B., Business Mgr.; Patrick Boland, O.S.B., In Res.; Jerome Kodell, O.S.B., In Res.; Eugene Luke, O.S.B., Member; David McKillin, O.S.B., In Res.; Brendan Miller, O.S.B., In Res.; Elijah Owens, O.S.B., Member; Gregory Pilcher, O.S.B., Member; Mark Stengel, O.S.B., In Res.; Richard Walz, O.S.B., In Res.; William Wewers, O.S.B., Member; Bros. Edward Fischesser, O.S.B, In Res.; Ephrem O'Bryan, O.S.B., In Res. Brothers 25; Non-Professed 5; Priests 11; Students 3; Abbots 1; Clergy / Religious Teachers 4.

[G] CONVENTS AND RESIDENCES FOR SISTERS

LITTLE ROCK. *Discalced Carmelite Nuns*, 7201 W. 32nd St., 72204-4716. Tel: 501-565-5121;
Fax: 501-565-3877; Email: Lrcarmel@comcast.net; Web: www.littlerockcarmel.org. Sisters Lucia Ellender, O.C.D., Prioress; Stephanie Turner, O.C.D., Councilor; Cecilia Chun, O.C.D., Councilor; Andrea Fulmer, O.C.D., Councilor. Attended from Catholic High School, Little Rock & Our Lady of the Holy Souls, Little Rock.

Discalced Carmelite Nuns of Little Rock Sisters 14; Nuns with Solemn Vows 13.

Missionaries of Charity, 1014 S. Oak St., 72204.
Tel: 501-666-9718 (Abba House);
Tel: 501-663-3596 (Convent); Email: scadiz7@hotmail.com. Sisters M. Jonathan, M.C., Regional Supr.; M. Annunciella, M.C., Supr. Convent and home for expectant mothers, homeless women & children. Bed Capacity 17; Sisters 4; Tot Asst. Annually 250; Total Staff 4.

Mt. St. Mary's Convent (1851) 3508 Kavanaugh Blvd., 72205. Tel: 501-747-2432;
Fax: 501-666-4382; Email: jkonecny@mercysc.org. Sr. Judith Marie Keith, Contact Person. Sisters 2.

BARLING. *McAuley Convent and Retirement Residence*, 1300 Strozier Ln., Barling, 72923.
Tel: 479-478-3002; Fax: 479-478-3006; Email: dallen@mercysc.org. Cindy Taylor, Admin. Bed Capacity 30; Sisters of Mercy 9; Number Served 9.

FORT SMITH. *St. Scholastica Monastery-Motherhouse* (1879) 1301 S. Albert Pike, P.O. Box 3489, Fort Smith, 72903. Tel: 479-783-4147;
Fax: 479-782-4352; Email: monastery@stscho.org; Web: www.stscho.org. Rev. Leslie A. Farley, Chap.; Sisters Maria Goretti DeAngeli, O.S.B., Prioress; Cecelia Marie Brickell, Archivist. Benedictine Professed Sisters 38.

Sisters of Mercy of St. Edward Convent (1905) 7315 Riviera Dr., Fort Smith, 72903. Tel: 479-314-6097; Fax: 479-452-1699; Email: srsjm@yahoo.com. Sr. Judith Marie Keith, Contact Person. Sisters of Mercy 2.

JONESBORO. *Holy Angels Convent-Motherhouse*, 1699 C.R. 766, Jonesboro, 72401-6981.
Tel: 870-935-5810; Fax: 870-935-4210; Email: olivben@olivben.org; Web: www.olivben.org. P.O. Box 1209, Jonesboro, 72403-1209. Mother Johanna Marie Melnyk, O.S.B., Prioress; Rev. Michael Sinkler, Chap. Olivetan Benedictine Sisters. Sisters 35.

[H] NEWMAN CENTERS

LITTLE ROCK. *Catholic Campus Ministry*, 2500 N. Tyler St., 72207. Tel: 501-664-0340, Ext. 333;
Fax: 501-664-0119; Email: ltingquist@dolr.org. Tricia Gentry, Prog. Coord.; Liz Tingquist, Dir.

Univ. of Arkansas at Little Rock Catholic Campus Ministry, Tel: 501-772-2512; Email: ualrcatholics@gmail.com; Email: susej_thompson@yahoo.com; Web: ualr.edu/catholic/. Susej Thompson, Campus Min.; Rev. Joshua Stengel, Chap.

BATESVILLE. *Lyons College Catholic Campus Ministry*, 2500 N. Tyler St., P.O. Box 7565, 72217. Email: brandi.allen@lyon.edu. Rev. Stephen Gadberry; Brandi Allen, Campus Min.

CLARKSVILLE. *University of Ozarks Catholic Campus Ministry (Clarksville)*, 3659 CR 5500, Ozone, 72854. Tel: 479-979-1434; Email: mlstickl@ozarks.edu. Melodye Stickley, Campus Min.

CONWAY. *University of Central Arkansas & Hendrix College Catholic Campus Ministry*, 2204 Bruce St., Conway, 72034. Tel: 501-336-9091;
Fax: 501-336-9091; Email: catholic@cyberback.com; Web: www.conwaycatholic.com. Kasey Miller, Campus Min., Tel: 804-366-9467; Rev. Anthony M. Robbins, Chap.; Deacon Richard John Papini, Dir.; Jennifer Brewer, Admin. Asst. (Conway).

FAYETTEVILLE. *University of Arkansas, St. Thomas Aquinas University Parish*, 603 N. Leverett Ave., Fayetteville, 72701. Tel: 479-444-0223;
Fax: 479-442-2633; Email: ccm@uark.edu; Web: www.catholichogs.com. Revs. Andrew P. Hart, J.C.L.; Jason Sharbaugh; Adamn Koehler, Campus Min.; Juliane Pierini, Campus Min.

FORT SMITH. *University of Arkansas at Fort Smith, Catholic Campus Ministry*, 22 N. 13th St., Fort Smith, 72901. Tel: 501-249-4881; Email: Me.naomilee@gmail.com; Web: www.uafscatholic.org. Jennifer Briselden, Campus Min.

JONESBORO. *Arkansas State University, Blessed John Newman University Parish*, 2800 E. Johnson Ave., Jonesboro, 72401. Tel: 870-972-1888;
Fax: 870-972-6294; Email: director@astatecnc.com; Email: finance@astatecnc.com; Web: www.astatecnc.com. Rev. Alphonse Gollapalli, (India) V.F.; Brandon Weisenfels, Dir. & Campus Min.; Patricia McCaughan, Bookkeeper & Sec.

RUSSELLVILLE. *St. Leo the Great University Parish*, 509 W. L St., Russellville, 72801. Tel: 479-968-8249; Email: stleoatu@gmail.com; Web: www.stleoatu.homestead.com/homepage. P.O. Box 9033, Russellville, 72811. Rev. Ernest L. Hardesty; Mrs. Pat Buford, Dir. Campus Ministry; Mary Buford Corkins, Devel.

SEARCY. *Harding University In Searcy/Arkansas State University at Beebe, Campus Ministry*, 109 Campbell Dr., Beebe, 72012. Tel: 501-230-2890; Fax: 501-882-5465. Flo Fitch, Campus Min.

[I] PUBLIC ASSOCIATIONS OF THE FAITHFUL

BERRYVILLE. *Brothers and Sisters of Charity at Little Portion*, 350 County Rd. 248, Berryville, 72616.
Tel: 479-253-0253; Fax: 888-420-5678; Email: info@littleportion.org; Web: www.littleportion.org. John Michael Talbot, B.S.C., Gen. Min.; Viola Talbot, B.S.C., Vicar Gen. Min.

[J] RETREAT CENTERS

BERRYVILLE. *Little Portion Hermitage* (Public Association of the Faithful) 350 CR 248, Berryville, 72616-8505. Tel: 479-253-7710; Fax: 888-420-5678; Email: info@littleportion.org; Web: www.LittlePortion.org. John Michael Talbot, B.S.C., Gen. Min.; Viola Talbot, B.S.C., Vicar

Brothers and Sisters of Charity at Little Portion, Inc.

FORT SMITH. *St. Scholastica Retreat Center*, 1205 S. Albert Pike, Fort Smith, 72903. Tel: 479-783-1135;
Fax: 479-783-8138; Email: retreats@stscho.org; Web: stscho.org. Kathy Schmelzer, Center Dir.; Sisters Madeline Bariola, O.S.B., Dir. Hospitality; Macrina Wiederkehr, O.S.B., Dir, Retreats.; Rachel Dietz, O.S.B., Dir., Spir. Direct Prog. Conducted by Benedictine Sisters.

SHOAL CREEK. *Hesychia House of Prayer* (1981) 204 St. Scholastica Rd., New Blaine, 72851.
Tel: 479-938-7375; Email: hesychia@stscho.org; Web: www.stscho.org. Sr. Louise Sharum, O.S.B., Dir.; Rev. Gregory Pilcher, O.S.B. Attended from Subiaco Abbey, Subiaco, AR. Benedictine Sisters 1.

[K] MISCELLANEOUS LISTINGS

LITTLE ROCK. *Arkansas Catholic* (1911) Published by Arkansas Catholic, Inc. of the Diocese of Little Rock. 2500 N. Tyler St., P.O. Box 7417, 72217.
Tel: 501-664-0340; Tel: 501-664-0125;
Fax: 501-664-6572; Email: mhargett@dolr.org; Web: www.arkansas-catholic.org. Malea Hargett, Editor.

Clergy Welfare Fund, Inc., P.O. Box 7565, 72217-7565. Tel: 501-664-0340; Fax: 501-664-1310; Email: gwolfe@dolr.org. Mr. Gregory C. Wolfe, Dir. Finance.

Diocese of Little Rock Catholic Schools Education Trust, 2500 N. Tyler St., 72207. Tel: 501-664-0340; Email: thall@dolr.org. Theresa Hall, Supt.; Marguerite Olberts, Asst. Supt.; Ileana Dobbins, Asst. Supt.

Ladies of Charity of Arkansas, 2500 N. Tyler St., 72207. Tel: 501-664-0340; Fax: 501-664-9075; Email: lcark@dolr.org. Mrs. Kristy Eanes, Pres.

Little Rock Scripture Study (1974) 2500 N. Tyler St., P.O. Box 7565, 72217. Tel: 501-664-0340;
Tel: 501-664-6102; Fax: 501-664-9075; Email: lrss@dolr.org; Web: www.littlerockscripture.org. Catherine Upchurch, Dir.

The Mary Raymond Trust, P.O. Box 7565, 72217-7565. Tel: 501-664-0340; Fax: 501-664-1310; Email: gwolfe@dolr.org. Mr. Gregory C. Wolfe, Dir. Finance.

Monsignor James E. O'Connell Diocesan Seminarian Fund, Inc., P.O. Box 7565, 72217.
Tel: 501-664-0340, Ext. 331; Fax: 501-664-9075; Email: sfriend@dolr.org. Rev. Msgr. Scott Friend, V.G., Vicar General.

St. Thomas More Society of Arkansas, Inc., P.O. Box 1426, North Little Rock, 72115.
Tel: 501-833-0168, Ext. 302; Fax: 501-833-0253; Email: vhankins@hankinslawfirm.net.

CHEROKEE VILLAGE. *Magnificat - Mary Ark of the Covenant Corp.*, 49 Tekakwitha Dr., Cherokee Village, 72529. Tel: 870-257-2850; Email: stmichaelcv@yahoo.com. P.O. Box 970, Cherokee Village, 72525. Cindy Harris, Coord.

CONWAY. *Magnificat - Central Arkansas Chapter*, 4 Terra Cove, Conway, 72034-7502.
Tel: 501-339-7632; Email: DEBBIEECKERT@CONWAYCORP.NET. Rev. John E. Marconi, Spiritual Adviser / Care Svcs.

DUMAS. *Daughters of Charity Services of Arkansas*, 161 S. Main St., Dumas, 71639. Tel: 870-382-3080;
Fax: 870-382-3085. Administrative Offices, P.O. Box 158, Dumas, 71639. Brenda Jacobs, CEO. Tot Asst. Annually 4,190; Total Staff 29.
Clinics:.

St. Elizabeth Health Center, 407 S. Gould Ave., Gould, 71643. P.O. Drawer 370, Gould, 71643.
Tel: 870-263-4317; Fax: 870-263-4782. Sr. Judy Warmbold, D.C., Mission Leader.

DePaul Health Center, 145 S. Waterman St., Dumas, 71639. Tel: 870-382-4878;
Fax: 870-382-4895. P.O. Box 158, Dumas, 71639. Sr. Judy Warmbold, D.C., Mission Leader.

Wellness Center, 405 S. Gould Ave., Gould, 71643.
Tel: 870-263-4748; Fax: 870-263-4233. P.O. Box 370, Gould, 71643.

JONESBORO. *St. Bernard Healthcare*, 225 E. Jackson Ave. #84, Jonesboro, 72401. Tel: 870-207-4230;
Fax: 870-974-7040; Email: sbriley@sbrmc.org; Web: www.stbernards.info. Mr. Robert S. Jones, Attorney.

Jonesboro Real Estate Holding Company, Inc., 225 E. Jackson St., Jonesboro, 72401. Tel: 870-207-4230;
Fax: 870-974-7040; Email: sbriley@sbrmc.org. Ralph Waddell, Legal Counsel.

Total Life Healthcare, Inc., 505 E. Matthews Ave., Jonesboro, 72401. Tel: 870-207-7500;
Tel: 870-207-4230; Fax: 870-207-0527; Email: sbriley@sbrmc.org. Chris Barber, CEO. Staff 60; Total Assisted 261.

NORTH LITTLE ROCK. *MVL-VLM, Inc.* (2014) 6150 Remount Rd., North Little Rock, 72118.
Tel: 501-753-3977; Email: catecismo@saintannenlr.org. Guillermo Bruzatori, Exec. Dir.

Priestly Fraternity of St. Peter, 106 Pin Oak Dr., Cabot, 72023. Tel: 501-941-1566; Email: fssp-arkansas@comcast.net. Rev. Paul McCambridge, Contact Person.

POCAHONTAS. *St. Paul the Apostle Catholic Church - Capital Improvement Trust Fund*, 1002 Convent St., Pocahontas, 72455. Tel: 870-892-3319;
Fax: 870-892-5199; Email: saintpaul@suddenlink.net; Web: saintpaulcatholicchurchpocahontas.com. Rev. Mariadass N. Vallapaneni, (India).

RELIGIOUS INSTITUTES OF MEN REPRESENTED IN THE DIOCESE

For further details refer to the corresponding bracketed number in the Religious Institutes of Men or Women section.

[]—*Apostles of Jesus*—A.J.
[0200]—*Benedictine Monks* (Subiaco Abbey)—O.S.B.
[]—*Brothers of the Poor of St. Francis*—C.F.P.
[1330]—*Congregation of the Mission*—C.M.
[0260]—*Discalced Carmelite Friars* (St. Therese Prov.)—O.C.D.
[0650]—*Holy Ghost Fathers* (Western Vice Prov.)—C.S.Sp.
[]—*Indian Missionary Society*—I.M.S.
[1065]—*Priestly Fraternity of St. Peter*—F.S.S.P.
[0420]—*Society of the Divine Word* (Techny, IL)—S.V.D.
[]—*Society of the Precious Blood*—C.P.P.S.

RELIGIOUS INSTITUTES OF WOMEN REPRESENTED IN THE DIOCESE

[0230]—*Benedictine Sisters of Pontifical Jurisdiction* (Fort Smith, AR)—O.S.B.

[]—*Catholic Teachers of the Sacred Heart of Jesus*—M.C.S.C.
[0760]—*Daughters of Charity of St. Vincent de Paul* (West Central Prov.)—D.C.
[0793]—*Daughters of Divine Love*—D.D.L.
[]—*Daughters of Mary Mother of Mercy*—D.M.M.M.
[0895]—*Daughters of Our Lady of the Holy Rosary*—F.M.S.R.
[0420]—*Discalced Carmelite Nuns* (Little Rock, AR)—O.C.D.
[1070-27]—*Dominican Sisters, Immaculate Conception Province*—O.P.
[]—*Dominican Sisters of Tam Hiep* (Vietnam)—O.P.
[2575]—*Institute of the Sisters of Mercy of the Americas* (St. Louis, MO)—R.S.M.
[]—*Misioneras Catequistas de los Pobres*—M.C.P.
[2710]—*Missionaries of Charity*—M.C.
[0390]—*Missionary Carmelites of St. Teresa*—C.M.S.T.
[0240]—*Olivetan Benedictine Sisters* (Jonesboro, AR)—O.S.B.
[0500]—*Sisters of Charity of Nazareth*—S.C.N.

CEMETERIES

LITTLE ROCK. *Calvary*, Wright Ave. & S. Woodrow St., 72205. 2500 N. Tyler St., 72207. Tel: 501-664-0340; Email: mbibb@dolr.org. Mr. Dennis P. Lee, J.D., Admin. Entrance: Charles Bussey Ave.

FORT SMITH. *Calvary*, c/o Immaculate Conception Church, P.O. Box 1866, Fort Smith, 72902. Tel: 479-783-7963; Email: ic@icchurch.com. Rev. John K. Antony, J.C.L., V.F.

An asterisk (*) denotes an organization that has established tax-exempt status directly with the IRS and is not covered by the USCCB Group Ruling.

Archdiocese of Los Angeles

(Archidioecesis Angelorum in California)

His Eminence

ROGER CARDINAL MAHONY, D.D., V.G.

Archbishop Emeritus of Los Angeles; ordained May 1, 1962; appointed Titular Bishop of Tamascani and Auxiliary Bishop of Fresno January 7, 1975; consecrated March 19, 1975; appointed Bishop of Stockton February 26, 1980; installed as the third Bishop of Stockton April 17, 1980; appointed Archbishop of Los Angeles July 16, 1985; installed as the fourth Archbishop of Los Angeles September 5, 1985; Created Cardinal June 28, 1991; retired March 1, 2011. *Res.: 10834 Moorpark St., North Hollywood, CA 91602-2206.* Tel: 818-290-2286.

Most Reverend

THOMAS J. CURRY, D.D., PH.D., V.G.

Retired Auxiliary Bishop of Los Angeles; ordained June 18, 1967; appointed Titular Bishop of Ceanannus Mor and Auxiliary Bishop of Los Angeles February 8, 1994; ordained Bishop March 19, 1994; retired April 3, 2018. *St. Augustine Parish, 3850 Jasmine Ave., Culver City, CA 90232-3106.* Tel: 310-838-2477; Fax: 310-838-3070.

Most Reverend

JOSEPH M. SARTORIS, D.D., V.G.

Retired Auxiliary Bishop of Los Angeles; ordained May 30, 1953; appointed Titular Bishop of Oliva and Auxiliary Bishop of Los Angeles February 8, 1994; ordained Bishop March 19, 1994; retired December 31, 2002. *Res.: 1988 Rolling Vista Dr., #21, Lomita, CA 90717.*

Most Reverend

GERALD E. WILKERSON, D.D., V.G.

Retired Auxiliary Bishop of Los Angeles; ordained May 1, 1965; appointed Titular Bishop of Vincennes and Auxiliary Bishop of Los Angeles November 5, 1997; ordained Bishop January 21, 1998; retired December 31, 2015. *Res.: 9329 Crebs Ave., Northridge, CA 91324-2909.* Tel: 818-967-3867.

Most Reverend

GABINO ZAVALA, D.D., J.C.L., V.G.

Retired Auxiliary Bishop of Los Angeles; ordained May 28, 1977; appointed Titular Bishop of Tamascani and Auxiliary Bishop of Los Angeles February 8, 1994; ordained Bishop March 19, 1994; resigned January 4, 2012.

Most Reverend

EDWARD W. CLARK, D.D., S.T.D., V.G.

Auxiliary Bishop of Los Angeles; ordained May 27, 1972; appointed Titular Bishop of Gardar and Auxiliary Bishop of Los Angeles January 16, 2001; ordained March 26, 2001. *Office: Regional Bishop, Our Lady of the Angels Pastoral Region, 5835 W. Slauson, Culver City, CA 90230-6505.* Tel: 310-215-0703; Fax: 310-215-0749.

Most Reverend

ALEXANDER SALAZAR, D.D., V.G.

Auxiliary Bishop Emeritus of Los Angeles; ordained June 16, 1984; appointed Titular Bishop of Nesqually and Auxiliary Bishop of Los Angeles September 7, 2004; ordained November 4, 2004; resigned December 19, 2018.

Most Reverend

JOSE H. GOMEZ

Archbishop of Los Angeles; ordained August 15, 1978; appointed Auxiliary Bishop of Denver and Titular See of Belali January 23, 2001; ordained March 26, 2001; appointed Archbishop of San Antonio December 29, 2004; installed February 15, 2005; Pallium conferred June 29, 2005; appointed Coadjutor Archbishop of Los Angeles April 6, 2010; Succeeded to the See March 1, 2011. *Office: 3424 Wilshire Blvd., Los Angeles, CA 90010-2241.* Tel: 213-637-7534; Fax: 213-637-6510.

Archdiocesan Catholic Center Office: 3424 Wilshire Blvd., Los Angeles, CA 90010-2241. Tel: 213-637-7000; Fax: 213-637-6000.

Web: www.LA-Archdiocese.org

Email: info@LA-Archdiocese.org

Most Reverend

ROBERT E. BARRON, D.D., S.T.D., V.G.

Auxiliary Bishop of Los Angeles; ordained May 24, 1986; appointed Titular Bishop of Macriana in Mauretania and Auxiliary Bishop of Los Angeles July 21, 2015; ordained September 8, 2015. *Office: Regional Bishop, Santa Barbara Pastoral Region, 3240 Calle Pinon, Santa Barbara, CA 93105-2760.* Tel: 805-682-0442; Fax: 805-682-7509.

Most Reverend

DAVID G. O'CONNELL, D.D., V.G.

Auxiliary Bishop of Los Angeles; ordained June 10, 1979; appointed Titular Bishop of Cell Ausaille and Auxiliary Bishop of Los Angeles July 21, 2015; ordained September 8, 2015. *Office: Regional Bishop, San Gabriel Pastoral Region, 16009 E. Cypress Ave., Irwindale, CA 91706-2122.* Tel: 626-960-9344; Fax: 626-962-0455.

Most Reverend

MARC V. TRUDEAU

Auxiliary Bishop of Los Angeles; ordained June 8, 1991; appointed Titular Bishop of Tinis in Proconsular and Auxiliary Bishop of Los Angeles April 5, 2018; ordained June 7, 2018. *Office: Regional Bishop, San Pedro Pastoral Region: 3555 St. Pancratius Pl., Lakewood, CA 90712-1416.* Tel: 562-634-0456; Fax: 562-531-4783.

Most Reverend

ALEJANDRO D. ACLAN

Auxiliary Bishop of Los Angeles; ordained June 5, 1993; appointed Titular Bishop of Rusicade and Auxiliary Bishop of Los Angeles March 5, 2019; installed May 16, 2019.

Square Miles 8,636.

Diocese Established 1840; an Archbishopric July 11, 1936.

Comprises the Counties of Los Angeles, Santa Barbara and Ventura in the State of California.

Patroness of the Archdiocese: Our Lady of the Angels.

Secondary Patroness and Patrons: St. Vibiana; St. Emydius; and St. Patrick.

Legal Titles:
The Roman Catholic Archbishop of Los Angeles, a Corporation Sole.
Archdiocese of Los Angeles Education and Welfare Corporation.
Archdiocese of Los Angeles Insurance Company.
Archdiocese of Los Angeles Risk Management Corporation.
Archdiocese of Los Angeles Funeral and Mortuary Services Corporation.
Our Lady Queen of Angels.
St. John's Seminary in California.
The Cardinal McIntyre Fund for Charity.
Catholic Charities of Los Angeles, Inc.
Catholic Charities Community Development Corporation.
The Tidings.
Vida Nueva.
Catholic Education Foundation.
Opus Caritatis.
Cathedral of Our Lady of the Angels.
For legal titles of parishes and archdiocesan institutions, consult the Chancery Office.

STATISTICAL OVERVIEW

Personnel	
Retired Cardinals	1
Archbishops	1
Auxiliary Bishops	5
Retired Bishops	5
Abbots	1
Retired Abbots	1
Priests: Diocesan Active in Diocese	318
Priests: Diocesan Active Outside Diocese	11
Priests: Retired, Sick or Absent	162
Number of Diocesan Priests	491
Religious Priests in Diocese	532
Total Priests in Diocese	1,023
Extern Priests in Diocese	120
Ordinations:	
Diocesan Priests	9
Transitional Deacons	3
Permanent Deacons	16
Permanent Deacons in Diocese	415
Total Brothers	81
Total Sisters	1,387
Parishes	
Parishes	288
With Resident Pastor:	
Resident Diocesan Priests	185
Resident Religious Priests	55
Without Resident Pastor:	
Administered by Priests	32
Administered by Deacons	3
Administered by Lay People	3
Administered by Pastoral Teams, etc.	10
Missions	10
Pastoral Centers	15
New Parishes Created	1
Professional Ministry Personnel:	
Brothers	14
Sisters	141
Lay Ministers	1,007
Welfare	
Catholic Hospitals	13
Total Assisted	1,647,661
Health Care Centers	2
Total Assisted	98,827
Homes for the Aged	6
Total Assisted	5,184
Residential Care of Children	1
Total Assisted	72
Day Care Centers	85

Total Assisted	4,972
Specialized Homes	1
Total Assisted	82
Special Centers for Social Services	31
Total Assisted	52,287
Educational	
Seminaries, Diocesan	1
Students from This Diocese	60
Students from Other Diocese	43
Diocesan Students in Other Seminaries	27
Seminaries, Religious	5
Students Religious	53
Total Seminarians	140
Colleges and Universities	4
Total Students	15,320
High Schools, Diocesan and Parish	26
Total Students	12,844
High Schools, Private	25
Total Students	12,546
Elementary Schools, Diocesan and Parish	207
Total Students	46,361
Elementary Schools, Private	8
Total Students	2,253
Catechesis/Religious Education:	
High School Students	34,048
Elementary Students	67,958
Total Students under Catholic Instruction	191,470
Teachers in the Diocese:	
Priests	26
Brothers	24
Sisters	98
Lay Teachers	4,692
Vital Statistics	
Receptions into the Church:	
Infant Baptism Totals	52,398
Minor Baptism Totals	3,053
Adult Baptism Totals	1,408
Received into Full Communion	3,103
First Communions	39,516
Confirmations	23,680
Marriages:	
Catholic	6,099
Interfaith	583
Total Marriages	6,682
Deaths	11,410
Total Catholic Population	4,044,742
Total Population	11,465,880

Former Bishops—Rt. Revs. FRANCIS GARCIA DIEGO Y MORENO, O.F.M., D.D., cons. Oct. 4, 1840; Bishop of both Californias; died at Santa Barbara, April 30, 1846; JOSEPH SADOC ALEMANY, O.P., D.D., cons. June 30, 1850; Bishop of Monterey; transferred to San Francisco, July 29, 1853; died in Valencia, Spain, April 14, 1888; THADDEUS AMAT, C.M., D.D., cons. March 12, 1854; died May 12, 1878; FRANCIS MORA, D.D., cons. Titular Bishop of Mosynopolis and Coadjutor to Bishop Amat, Aug. 3, 1873; resigned May 6, 1896; died Aug. 3, 1905 in Sarria, Barcelona, Spain; GEORGE MONTGOMERY, D.D., cons. April 8, 1894, Bishop of Tmul and Coadjutor-Bishop of Monterey and Los Angeles cum jure successionis; succeeded to May 6, 1896; appt. Coadjutor-Archbishop of San Francisco, Jan. 1, 1903; died in San Francisco, Jan. 10, 1907; THOMAS JAMES CONATY, D.D., ord. 1872; cons. Nov. 24, 1901, Titular-Bishop of Samos; appt. Bishop of Monterey and Los Angeles, March 27, 1903; died at Coronado, CA, Sept. 18, 1915; Most Rev. JOHN J. CANTWELL, D.D., LL.D., appt. Bishop of Monterey-Los Angeles, Sept. 21, 1917; cons. Dec. 5, 1917; appt. Assistant to the Pontifical Throne, Sept. 30, 1929; transferred to Los Angeles, June 1, 1922; elevated to Archepiscopal dignity, July 11, 1936; installed Dec. 3, 1936; died Oct. 30, 1947, at Los Angeles, CA; His Eminence JAMES FRANCIS MCINTYRE, D.D., appt. Auxiliary Bishop of New York, Nov. 16, 1940; cons. Jan. 8, 1941; promoted to Coadjutor Archbishop, July 20, 1946; appt. Archbishop of Los Angeles, Feb. 7, 1948; installed March 19, 1948; created Cardinal Priest, Jan. 12, 1953; resigned Jan. 21, 1970; died July 16, 1979; TIMOTHY CARDINAL MANNING, D.D., J.C.D., appt. Titular Bishop of Lesvi and Auxiliary Bishop of Los Angeles, Aug. 3, 1946; cons. Oct. 15, 1946; installed as first Bishop of Fresno, Dec. 15, 1967; appt. Titular Bishop of Capri and Coadjutor Archbishop of Los Angeles, May 26, 1969; appt. Archbishop of Los Angeles, Jan. 21, 1970; created a Cardinal Priest, March 5, 1973; retired Sept. 4, 1985; died June 23, 1989 at Los Angeles, CA; ROGER CARDINAL MAHONY, D.D., V.G., ord. May 1, 1962; appt. Titular Bishop of Tamascani and Auxiliary Bishop of Fresno Jan. 7, 1975; cons. March 19, 1975; appt. Bishop of Stockton Feb. 26, 1980; installed as the third Bishop of Stockton April 17, 1980; appt. Archbishop of Los Angeles July 16, 1985; installed as the fourth Archbishop of Los Angeles Sept. 5, 1985; Created Cardinal June 28, 1991; retired March 1, 2011.

Archdiocesan Catholic Center Office—3424 Wilshire Blvd., Los Angeles, 90010-2241. Tel: 213-637-7000; Fax: 213-637-6000.

Office of the Archbishop—3424 Wilshire Blvd., Los Angeles, 90010-2241. Tel: 213-637-7534. Most Rev. JOSE H. GOMEZ; Rev. BRIAN NUNES, Priest Sec. & Master of Ceremonies; BEATRIZ VELAZQUEZ, Exec. Coord.

Archdiocesan Pastoral Regions

Santa Barbara Region—Most Rev. ROBERT E. BARRON, D.D., S.T.D., V.G., 3240 Calle Pinon, Santa Barbara, 93105-2760. Tel: 805-682-0442; Fax: 805-682-7509.

Deanery 1—Rev. JOY LAWRENCE SANTOS, V.F., Queen of Angels, 3495 Rucker Rd., Lompoc, 93436-2199.

Deanery 2—Rev. JOHN W. LOVE, V.F., St. Mark University Parish, 6550 Picasso Rd., Goleta, 93117-4698.

Deanery 3—Rev. THOMAS J. ELEWAUT, V.F., San Buenaventura Mission, 211 E. Main St., Ventura, 93001-2691.

Deanery 4—Rev. Msgr. PAUL M. ALBEE, V.F., St. Maximilian Kolbe, 5801 Kanan Rd., Westlake Village, 91362-5499.

San Fernando Region—VACANT, Mailing Address: P.O. Box 7608, Mission Hills, 91346-7608. 15101 San Fernando Mission Blvd., Mission Hills, 91345-1109. Tel: 818-361-6009; Fax: 818-361-6270.

Deanery 5—Rev. DAVID C. LOFTUS, V.F., Our Lady of Lourdes, 18405 Superior St., Northridge, 91325-1798.

Deanery 6—VACANT.

Deanery 7—Rev. Msgr. VITO DE MARZIO, R.C.J., V.F., St. Elizabeth Parish, 6635 Tobias Ave., Van Nuys, 91405-4688.

Deanery 8—Rev. Msgr. CRAIG A. COX, J.C.D., D.Min., V.F., Our Lady of Perpetual Help Parish, 23045 Lyons Ave., Santa Clarita, 91321-2632.

San Gabriel Region—Most Rev. DAVID G. O'CONNELL, D.D., V.G., 16009 E. Cypress Ave., Irwindale, 91706. Tel: 626-960-9344.

Deanery 9—Rev. Msgr. JOHN T. MORETTA, V.F., Resurrection, 3324 E. Opal St., Los Angeles, 90023-2917.

Deanery 10—Rev. Msgr. AUSTIN C. DORAN, V.F., St. Anthony, 1901 S. San Gabriel Blvd., San Gabriel, 91776-3992.

Deanery 11—Rev. WILLIAM T. EASTERLING, V.F., Sacred Heart, 344 W. Workman St., Covina, 91723-3345.

Deanery 12—Rev. JOHN H. KEESE, V.F., St. Elizabeth Ann Seton, 1835 Larkvane Rd., Rowland Heights, 91748-2501.

Our Lady of the Angels Pastoral Region—Most Rev. EDWARD W. CLARK, D.D., S.T.D., V.G., 5835 Slauson Ave., Culver City, 90230-6505. Tel: 310-215-0703; Fax: 310-215-0749.

Deanery 13—Rev. Msgr. LIAM J. KIDNEY, V.F., Corpus Christi, 887 Toyopa Dr., Pacific Palisades, 90272-0887.

Deanery 14—Rev. Msgr. TERRANCE L. FLEMING, S.T.D., V.F., St. Brendan, 310 S. Van Ness Ave., Los Angeles, 90020-4613.

Deanery 15—Rev. DAVID GALLARDO, V.F., Cathedral of Our Lady of the Angels, 555 W. Temple St., Los Angeles, 90012-2707.

Deanery 16—Rev. MARCOS J. GONZALEZ, St. John Chrysostom, 546 E. Florence Ave., Inglewood, 90301-1497.

San Pedro Pastoral Region—Most Rev. MARC V. TRUDEAU, D.D., V.G., 3555 St. Pancratius Pl., Lakewood, 90712-1416. Tel: 562-634-0456; Fax: 562-531-4783.

Deanery 17—Rev. NABOR RIOS, V.F., St. Gertrude, 7025 Garfield Ave., Bell Gardens, 90201-3291.

Deanery 18—Rev. BRIAN CASTANEDA, V.F., St. Gregory the Great, 13935 Telegraph Rd., Whittier, 90604-2597.

Deanery 19—Rev. Msgr. MICHAEL W. MEYERS, V.F., St. James, 124 N. Pacific Coast Hwy., Redondo Beach, 90277-3194.

Deanery 20—VACANT.

Archdiocesan Catholic Center

Unless otherwise listed, all ACC offices are located at: *3424 Wilshire Blvd., Los Angeles, 90010-2241.* Tel: 213-637-7000; Fax: 213-637-6000.

African-American Catholic Center for Evangelization—ANDERSON SHAW, 9505 Haas Ave., Los Angeles, 90047-3439. Tel: 323-777-2106; Fax: 323-777-2151; Email: aaccfe@shcglobal.net.

AIDS/HIV Ministry—Rev. CHRISTOPHER D. PONNET, Liaison, 1911 Zonal Ave., Los Angeles, 90033. Tel: 323-223-9047; Email: cponnet@stcamillus.ftml.net; Web: www.stcamilluscenter.org.

Angelus (Archdiocesan Magazine)—Tel: 213-637-7360; Fax: 213-637-6360.

Annual Catholic Appeals—DEIRDRE SMITH, Dir., Tel: 213-637-7461; Fax: 213-637-6111.

Apostleship of the Sea—870 W. Eighth St., San Pedro, 90731-3091. Tel: 310-833-3541. Rev. FREDDIE T. CHUA, Maritime Chap.

Applied Technology—DAVID SCHMITT, Dir., Tel: 213-637-7526.

Archdiocesan Council of Catholic Women—Tel: 213-637-7394.

Archives—15151 San Fernando Mission Blvd., Mission Hills, 91345-2617. Tel: 818-365-1501; Fax: 818-361-3276. KEVIN FEENEY, Archivist.

Brothers Council, Religious—Bro. LARRY J. MOEN, C.M.F., Tel: 323-337-6776.

Liaison to Brothers' Council—Rev. BRIAN NUNES, Tel: 213-637-7479.

Canonical Services, Vicar for—Rev. JOSEPH FOX, O.P., J.C.D., Tel: 213-637-7210; Fax: 213-637-6178.

Canonical Services Coordinator—Rev. PATRICK J. HILL, J.C.L., D.Min., (Retired), Tel: 213-637-7888.

Cardinal Manning House of Prayer for Priests—Rev. Msgr. JOHN D. STOEGER, Dir.; Rev. CHRISTOPHER M. CARTWRIGHT, S.J., Assoc. Dir., 3441 Waverly Dr., Los Angeles, 90027-2526. Tel: 323-662-7966; Fax: 323-953-4802.

Cardinal McIntyre Fund for Charity—Rev. Msgr. FRANCIS J. HICKS, Dir., Tel: 213-637-7438.

Catholic Campaign for Human Development—KATHLEEN DOMINGO, Dir., Tel: 213-637-7236.

Catholic Charities of Los Angeles, Inc.—1531 James M. Wood Blvd., P.O. Box 15095, Los Angeles, 90015-0095. Tel: 213-251-3400; Fax: 213-380-4603.

Executive Director—Rev. Msgr. GREGORY A. COX, M.S.W., M.B.A., M.Div., Tel: 213-251-3464.

Chief Financial Officer—Tel: 213-251-3410. DANIEL P. O'BRIEN.

Chief Development and Communications Officer—ALEXANDRIA (SANDI) ARNOLD, M.S., Dir., Tel: 213-251-3495.

Department of Human Resources—LELAND R. RATLEFF, M.A., Dir., Tel: 213-251-3414.

Director of Intra-Agency Programs—MOISES CARRILLO, M.A., Tel: 213-251-3412.

Catholic Charities Regional Offices—

Our Lady of the Angels Region—Tel: 310-392-8701. LORRI PERREAULT, Regl. Dir.

San Fernando Region—SANDRA YANEZ, Regl. Dir., Tel: 213-251-3549.

San Gabriel Region—VACANT, Tel: 213-251-3582.

San Pedro Region—BRUCE HACKMAN, M.Div., M.S., M.S.W., Regl. Dir., Tel: 213-251-3429.

Santa Barbara Region—DANIEL J. GRIMM, J.D., M.A., M.F.T., Regl. Dir., Tel: 805-965-7045.

Catholic Education Foundation—THERESA FRAGOSO, Dir. Oper. & Programs, Tel: 213-637-7694.

Catholic Relief Services—KATHLEEN DOMINGO, Dir., Tel: 213-637-7236.

Cemeteries, Catholic—Tel: 213-637-7800; Fax: 213-637-6800.

Director of Community Outreach—BRIAN MCMAHON, Tel: 213-637-7815.

Chancellor—Sr. MARY ELIZABETH GALT, B.V.M., Tel: 213-637-7460.

Clergy, Vicar for—Rev. Msgr. JAMES L. HALLEY, V.F., Vicar; Rev. JAMES M. ANGUIANO, Assoc. Vicar, Tel: 213-637-7284.

Communication Office—CAROLINA GUEVARA, Chief Communication Officer, Tel: 213-637-7253.

Construction—JOHN CHEE, Dir., Tel: 213-637-7858.

Deacons in Ministry—Deacon SHANE CUDA, Dir., Tel: 213-637-7734.

Development Department—CINDY GALINDO, Chief Devel. Officer, Tel: 213-637-7517.

Diaconate Formation Office—Deacon BRIAN CONROY, Dir., Tel: 213-637-7282.

Digital Office—MATTHEW MEEKS, Chief Digital Officer, Tel: 213-637-7258.

Ecumenical and Interreligious Affairs—Rt. Rev. ALEXEI R. SMITH, Dir., c/o St. Andrew's Church, 538 Concord St., El Segundo, 90245. Tel: 310-322-1892; Fax: 310-322-1919.

Ethnic Ministry—Tel: 213-637-7356.

Family Life Office—JOAN T. VIENNA, Dir., Tel: 213-637-7227; Fax: 213-637-6681; Email: familylife@la-archdiocese.org.

Financial Services—Information Desk. Tel: 213-637-7500; Web: www.la-archdiocese.org/org/fs. MR. RANDOLPH STEINER, CFO, Tel: 213-637-7218.

Fingerprinting Department—Deacon JOHN WILLIAM BARRY, Dir., Tel: 213-637-7680.

General Counsel—MARGARET G. GRAF, Tel: 213-637-7511.

Government Funded Programs—LILIA CHAVEZ, Dir. School Food Svc., Tel: 213-637-7915; Fax: 213-637-6900.

Health Affairs—Sr. ANGELA HALLAHAN, C.H.F., Dir., Tel: 213-637-7538.

Holy Childhood Association—(See Mission Office).

Human Resources—ANNABELLE BALTIERRA, Dir., Tel: 213-637-7596; Fax: 213-637-6116.

Information—REBECCA GARCIA, Archdiocesan Catholic Center Switchboard, Tel: 213-637-7000.

Instructional Television—DAVID G. MOORE, Dir., Tel: 213-637-7312.

Insurance—LEVONTINE TOMACAN, Dir., Tel: 213-637-7279.

Ladies of Charity of St. Vincent de Paul—2131 W. Third St., Seton Hall, Los Angeles, 90057-0992. Tel: 213-413-3688.

Legal Counsel—(See General Counsel).

Life, Justice, and Peace—KATHLEEN BUCKLEY DOMINGO, Dir., Tel: 213-637-7236.

Marriage Encounter—Contacts: BOON HAZBOUN; GINNY HAZBOUN, Tel: 562-861-7562; Web: www.geocities.com/melawest. Marriage Encounter Weekends are offered in English, Spanish and Korean.

Marriage Tribunal—(See Tribunal).

Mission Office—Rev. Msgr. TERRANCE L. FLEMING, S.T.D., V.F., Exec. Dir.; LYDIA GAMBOA, Dir., Tel: 213-637-7223; Fax: 213-637-6223; Email: missionoffice@la-archdiocese.org.

Moderator of the Curia and Vicar General—Tel: 213-637-7506. Rev. Msgr. ALBERT M. BAHHUTH, V.F.

New Evangelization, Office of—Tel: 213-637-7474. Rev. JAMES CLARKE, Ph.D., Dir.

Newman Centers (Campus Ministry Sites)—

Claremont Colleges—McAllister Religious Activities, 919 N. Columbia, Claremont, 91711. Rev. JOSEPH FENTON, S.M., Dir.

Loyola Law School—919 S. Albany St., P.O. Box 15019, Los Angeles, 90019. Tel: 213-736-1000; Fax: 213-380-3769. Rev. BRYAN PHAM, S.J., J.C.D., J.D., Dir.

Loyola Marymount University—One L.M.U. Dr., Los Angeles, 90045-2659. Tel: 310-338-2700. Rev. JAMES ERPS, S.J., Dir.

Marymount California University—30800 Palos Verdes Dr. E., Rancho Palos Verdes, 90275-6299. Tel: 310-303-7342; Fax: 310-377-6223; Web: www.marymountpv.edu. Rev. MARK VILLANO, C.S.P., Chap.

Mount St. Mary's University—Chalon Campus: 12001 Chalon Rd., Los Angeles, 90049-1599. Tel: 310-954-4125; Fax: 310-954-4346. *Doheny Campus: 10 Chester Pl., Los Angeles, 90007-2598.* Tel: 213-477-2672; Fax: 213-477-2699. GAIL GRESSER, Dir.

Occidental College—Catholic Campus Ministry: 1600 Campus Rd., Los Angeles, 90041. Tel: 323-259-2621; Fax: 323-341-4959.

University of California at Los Angeles—University Catholic Center: 633 Gayley Ave., Los Angeles, 90024. Tel: 310-208-5015; Fax: 310-208-6077. Rev. JAMIE BACA, C.S.P., Dir.

University of California at Santa Barbara—St. Mark University Parish, 6550 Picasso Rd., Goleta, 93117. Tel: 805-968-1078; Fax: 805-968-3965. Rev. JOHN W. LOVE, V.F., Pastor.

University of La Verne—Campus Ministry: 1950 Third St., La Verne, 91750. Tel: 909-593-3511, Ext. 4320; Fax: 909-392-2753.

University of Southern California—Our Saviour University Parish, 844 W. 32nd St., Los Angeles, 90007. Tel: 213-749-5341. Rev. RICHARD SUNWOO, Pastor.

Operations—Director of Archdiocesan Catholic Center Facilities and Operations: EILEEN O'BRIEN, Tel: 213-637-7618.

Parish Life Office—KATHERINE RUSSELL ENRIGHT, Dir., Tel: 213-637-7533.

Purchasing/Mail Center—JOHN MARMOLEJO, Purchasing Mgr., Tel: 213-637-7281.

Queen of Angels Center for Priestly Formation—1103 W. 164th St., Gardena, 90247. Tel: 310-516-6671. Revs. RANDY RAUL CAMPOS, Dir.; RAYMOND MARQUEZ, Assoc. Dir.; JONATHON MEYER, Assoc. Dir.

Real Estate—MICHAEL T. DAVITT, Dir., Tel: 213-637-7273; Fax: 213-637-6273.

Religious Education—Rev. CHRISTOPHER BAZYOUROS, Dir., Tel: 213-637-7309; Fax: 213-637-6574; Web: ore.la-archdiocese.org.

Associate Directors—GIOVANNI PEREZ, Tel: 213-637-7344; PAULETTE SMITH, Tel: 213-637-7332.

Regional Offices for Religious Education—Our Lady of the Angels Region: DAVID LARA, 5835 W. Slauson Ave., Culver City, 90230. Tel: 310-216-9587. San Fernando Region: DANA COUSO, Mailing Address: P.O. Box 7608, Mission Hills, 91346. Tel: 818-365-5123; Fax: 818-361-4133. San Gabriel Region: KATHRYN TASSINARI, 16009 E. Cypress Ave., Irwindale, 91706. Tel: 626-960-9344; Fax: 626-962-0455. San Pedro Region: KARINA PLASCENCIA, 3555 St. Pancratius Pl., Lakewood, 90712. Tel: 562-630-6272; Fax: 562-531-4783. Santa Barbara Region: TERESA DURAN, 4032 La Colina Rd., Santa Barbara, 93110. Tel: 805-569-1135; Fax: 805-569-2746.

Restorative Justice—5011 White Oak Ave., Encino, 91316. GONZALO DE VIVERO, Dir., Tel: 818-201-3100, Ext. 2.

Safeguard the Children—JOAN T. VIENNA, Dir., Tel: 213-637-7227.

Schools, Department of Catholic—Tel: 213-637-7300; Fax: 213-637-6140.

Superintendent of Catholic Schools—DR. KEVIN BAXTER.

Deputy Superintendent of Elementary Schools—DR. ANTHONY GALLA.

Deputy Superintendent of High Schools—DR. DANIEL J. O'CONNELL.

Associate Superintendent of Leadership, Innovation, and Growth—DR. SUSAN ABELEIN.

Scouting, Camp Fire Ministry—Web: www.ccsala.org.

Catholic Committee for Girl Scouts and Camp Fire (Girls)—4811 N. Rimhurst Ave., Covina, 91724-1625. Tel: 626-825-6436. SHARON SHELLMAN, Chair.

Los Angeles Catholic Committee on Scouting (Boys)—1511 Gene Ave., Simi Valley, 93065-3701. Tel: 805-527-8356. THELMA REEVES, Chair.

Chaplain—5801 Kanan Rd., Westlake Village, 91362-5499. Tel: 805-991-3915, Ext. 151. Deacon CHRISTOPHER LALIBERTE.

Society of St. Vincent de Paul—210 N. Ave. 21, Los Angeles, 90031-1713. Tel: 323-224-6287; Tel: 800-974-3571. RAY SWEET, Pres.; DAVID R. FIELDS, Exec. Dir.

Special Services—Tel: 213-637-7520. JUDY DEROSA BROOKS, Dir.

Tribunal—

Judicial Vicar—Rev. REYNALDO B. MATUNOG, J.C.L.

Adjutant Judicial Vicar—Rev. GERARDO GALAVIZ, J.C.L.

Vice Chancellor for Communications—DAVID SCOTT, Tel: 213-637-7259.

Victims Assistance Ministry—Tel: 800-355-2545 (Hotline); Tel: 213-637-7650 (Office). DR. HEATHER BANIS, Email: hbanis@la-archdiocese.org.

Vida Nueva (Archdiocesan Spanish Newspaper)—Tel: 213-637-7360; Fax: 213-637-6360.

Vocations—Tel: 213-637-7248; Web: www.vocations.la-archdiocese.org. Revs. SAMUEL W. WARD, Dir.; MICHAEL PERUCHO, Assoc. Dir.

Women Religious, Vicar for—Tel: 213-637-7592; Fax: 213-637-6592. Sr. MARIA CARLOS, E.I.N.

Worship—Sr. ROSANNE BELPEDIO, C.S.J., Dir., Tel: 213-637-7262; Email: worship@la-archdiocese.org.

Archdiocesan Advisory Boards

Archdiocesan Pastoral Council—Most Rev. JOSE H. GOMEZ.

Moderator—VIRGINIA TANAWONG.

Vice Moderator—CLAUDIA AVILA TORRES.

Secretary—DAVID KENNEDY.

Cardinal McIntyre Fund for Charity - Board of Directors—Most Rev. JOSE H. GOMEZ, Chair; Rev. Msgr. ALBERT M. BAHHUTH, V.F., Pres.; Sr. MARY ELIZABETH GALT, B.V.M., Sec.; Rev. JOSEPH P. SHEA, V.F., Treas.; Rev. Msgr. FRANCIS J. HICKS, Prog. Dir.

Clergy Misconduct Oversight Board—RHODA CONDE, Admin.; DR. KATHLEEN MCKENNA, Chair; MARK WOOD, Esq., Vice Chair.

College of Consultors—Most Rev. JOSE H. GOMEZ, Archbishop/Pres.

Council of Priests—Most Rev. JOSE H. GOMEZ, D.D., S.T.D., V.G., Pres.; Rev. Msgrs. LIAM J. KIDNEY, V.F., Chair; AUSTIN C. DORAN, V.F., Vice Chair; Rev. WILLIAM T. EASTERLING, V.F., Sec./Treas.

Deacon Council—Deacons SHANE CUDA, Dir. Deacons in Ministry; MELECIO ZAMORA, Chair; RICARDO MORA, Sec.

Finance Council—

Chair—MICHAEL ENRIGHT, Exec. Vice Pres. Chartwell Partners, LLC.

H.I.V./AIDS Ministry Advisory Board—

Director/Archbishop's Liaison—Rev. CHRISTOPHER D. PONNET.

Executive Committee—FRANK GALVAN, Co Chair; MANUEL TORRES, Co Chair.

Medical Advisor—DR. ELIZABETH BREEN.

Liturgical Commission—Rev. RICHARD VEGA, Chair; JOSEPH BAZYOUROS, Vice Chair; MONICA HUGHES, Sec.; Sr. ROSANNE BELPEDIO, C.S.J., Admin.

Personnel Board—Chair: Rev. Msgr. TERRANCE L. FLEMING, S.T.D., V.F.

Priests' Pension Board—Rev. PAUL K. FITZPATRICK, Chair.

Sisters' Coordinating Council—Sr. MARYANNE O'NEILL, C.S.C., Chair.

Theological Commission—Sr. MARY LEANNE HUBBARD, S.N.D., D.Min., Co Chair; Rev. THOMAS P. RAUSCH, S.J., Ph.D., Co Chair; DR. DANIEL SMITH-CHRISTOPHER, Ph.D., Consultant.

CLERGY, PARISHES, MISSIONS AND PAROCHIAL SCHOOLS

CITY OF LOS ANGELES

(LOS ANGELES COUNTY)

1—CATHEDRAL OF OUR LADY OF THE ANGELS (2002)
555 W. Temple St., 90012. Tel: 213-680-5200; Email: parish-5460@la-archdiocese.org. Most Rev. Jose H. Gomez, D.D., S.T.D., V.G., Archbishop of Los Angeles; Revs. David Gallardo, V.F.; Brian Nunes, Priest Sec. to Archbishop; Juan Jose Ochoa.
Catechesis Religious Program—Michelle-Marie Youssef, Dir. Faith Formation; Claudia Avila Torres, Dir. Evangelization. Students 25.

2—ST. AGATHA (1923)
2610 S. Mansfield Ave., 90016. Revs. Anthony S. Lee, Ph.D., Admin.; Joseph M. Palacios, Ph.D., In Res.; Deacon Hosea Alexander Sr.
Parish Office: 2646 S. Mansfield Ave., 90016.
Tel: 323-935-8127; Fax: 323-939-3547; Email: parish-5320@la-archdiocese.org; Web: www.stagathas.org.
Catechesis Religious Program—Tel: 323-933-0963; Email: tamezcua@stagathas.org. Teresa Amezcua, D.R.E.; Gricelda de la Cerda, Asst. D.R.E. Students 257.

3—ST. AGNES (1903) (Hispanic—Korean)
2625 S. Vermont Ave., 90007. Tel: 323-731-2464; Email: stagneschurchla@yahoo.com; Email: parish-5330@la-archdiocese.org. Revs. David Matz, C.PP.S., Pastoral Admin.; Timothy Guthridge, C.PP.S., Parochial Vicar; DaeJe Choi, S.J., In Res.; Chang Hyon Lee, S.J., In Res.; Dien Truong, C.PP.S., In Res.
School—St. Agnes School, (Grades PreK-8), 1428 W. Adams Blvd., 90007. Tel: 323-731-2464;
Fax: 323-735-7719; Email: school-8460@la-archdiocese.org. Kevin Dempsey, Prin. Lay Teachers 10; Students 238.
Catechesis Religious Program—Email: lizbetholiva2004@yahoo.com. Mrs. Miriam Oliva, D.R.E. Students 317.

4—ALL SAINTS (1926) (Hispanic)
3431 Portola Ave., 90032-2215. Tel: 323-223-1101; Email: allsaintschurch@earthlink.net. Revs. Thomas C. Francis, O.M.; Jose L. Vega, O.M.; Mario Pisano, O.M.; Gino Vanzillotta, O.M., In Res.; Deacon Pedro Rojas.
School—All Saints School, (Grades PreK-8), 3420 Portola Ave., 90032. Tel: 323-225-7264;
Fax: 323-225-1240; Email: school-7520@la-archdiocese.org. Maria Palermo, Prin. Lay Teachers 7; Students 115.
Catechesis Religious Program—Tel: 323-225-5193; Email: parish-4310@la-archdiocese.org. Ana Sanchez, D.R.E. Students 251.

5—ST. ALOYSIUS GONZAGA (1908) [CEM] (Hispanic)
2023 E Nadeau St., 90001. Tel: 323-585-4485;
Fax: 323-589-8485; Email: parish-5770@la-archdiocese.org; Web: www.staloysiusla.org. 7814 Crocket Blvd., 90001. Revs. Pedro Antonio Esteban; Avelino S. Crisanto, O.deM.
School—St. Aloysius Gonzaga School, (Grades PreK-8), 2023 E. Nadeau St., 90001. Tel: 323-582-4965;
Fax: 323-589-8485; Email: school-8810@la-archdiocese.org. Mrs. Nicole Johnson, Prin. Lay Teachers 10; Students 249.
Catechesis Religious Program—2027 E. Nadeau St., 90001. Tel: 323-277-7824; Email: m.celis@staloysiusla.org. Manuela Celis, D.R.E. Students 305.

6—ST. ALPHONSUS (1935) (Hispanic)
5223 Hastings St., 90022-2625. Tel: 323-264-3353; Email: parish-4230@la-archdiocese.org. Revs. Alfonso Borgen, O.F.M.Conv.; Omoldo Cherrez; Gerardo Galaviz, J.C.L., In Res.
School—St. Alphonsus School, (Grades PreK-8), 552 S. Amalia Ave., 90022-2625. Tel: 323-268-5165;
Fax: 323-268-7784; Email: school-7470@la-

archdiocese.org. Minerva Munguia-Sanchez, Prin. Lay Teachers 9; Students 315.
Catechesis Religious Program—Tel: 323-266-0855; Email: restalphonsus@gmail.com. Maria Elena Jauregui, D.R.E. Students 459.
7—ST. ANASTASIA (1953)
7390 W. Manchester Ave., 90045. Tel: 310-670-2243; Email: parish@st-anastasia.org; Email: parish-4820@la-archdiocese.org; Web: www.st-anastasia.org. Revs. Leszek Semik; Thomas F. King, Pastor Emeritus, (Retired); Rev. Msgr. Gregory A. Cox, M.S.W., M.B.A., M.Div., In Res.
School—St. Anastasia School, (Grades PreK-8), 8631 S. Stanmoor Dr., 90045. Tel: 310-645-8816; Fax: 310-645-6923; Email: school@st-anastasia.org; Email: school-7960@la-archdiocese.org; Web: school.st-anastasia.org. Dr. Gavin Colvert, Prin. Lay Teachers 19; Students 305.
Catechesis Religious Program—
Tel: 310-670-2243, Ext. 36; Email: jonettemauch@gmail.com. Jonette Mauch, D.R.E. Students 230.
8—ST. ANN (1937)
1365 Blake Ave., 90031. Tel: 323-221-6368; Email: office@dssala.org; Email: parish-3600@la-archdiocese.org; Web: www.dssala.org. Revs. Albert Susai Pragasam, O.S.M.; SamyDurai Arockiam, O.S.M.
Catechesis Religious Program—2302 Riverdale Ave., 90031. Tel: 323-225-9181; Email: ccuevas@dssala.org. Claudia Cuevas, D.R.E. Students 57.
9—ST. ANSELM (1924)
2222 W. 70th St., 90043. Tel: 323-758-6729; Email: parish-5540@la-archdiocese.org; Web: StAnselmChurchLA.org.
Catechesis Religious Program—Email: soniamay59@yahoo.com. Sonia Hernandez, D.R.E. Students 110.
10—ST. ANTHONY (1910) (Croatian)
712 N. Grand Ave., 90012. Tel: 213-628-2938; Email: parish-5340@la-archdiocese.org. Rev. Zvonimir Coric.
Catechesis Religious Program—Students 14.
11—ASCENSION (1923) (Hispanic—African American)
517 W. 112th St., 90044. Tel: 323-754-2978; Fax: 323-754-3905; Email: ascens@pacbell.net. Rev. Joseph Lal, Admin.
School—Ascension School, (Grades PreK-8), 500 W. 111th Pl., 90044. Tel: 323-756-4064; Fax: 323-756-1060; Email: ascjcastellanos@gmail.com. Jesse Castellanos, Prin. Lay Teachers 12; Students 213.
Catechesis Religious Program—Email: sweetlupita@yahoo.com. Maria Lupe Sanchez, D.R.E. Students 450.
12—ASSUMPTION (1926) (Hispanic)
2832 Blanchard St., 90033. Tel: 323-269-8171; Fax: 323-269-0106; Email: assumptionchurch@sbcglobal.net. Revs. Javier Alvarez, O.F.M., Admin.; Luis Alberto Guzman, O.F.M.
School—Assumption School, (Grades PreK-8), 3016 Winter St., 90063. Tel: 323-269-4319; Fax: 323-269-2434; Email: school-7320@la-archdiocese.org. Carolina Gomez, Prin. Lay Teachers 6; Students 260.
Catechesis Religious Program—Tel: 323-269-5920. Sr. Maria Calvillo, E.I.N., D.R.E. Students 140.
13—ST. BASIL (1920)
637 S. Kingsley Dr., 90005. Tel: 213-381-6191; Email: parish-5090@la-archdiocese.org. Revs. Francis J. Hicks; Dae Duk Stephanus Park; Rev. Msgr. Terrence Richey, In Res., (Retired); Rev. Victor J. Ruvalcaba, In Res.
Catechesis Religious Program—Email: eccristobal@la-archdiocese.org. Edna Cristobal, CPA, M.B.A., D.R.E. Students 197.
14—ST. BERNADETTE (1947) (African American)
3825 Don Felipe Dr., 90008. Tel: 323-293-4877; Email: stbernadettecc@gmail.com; Email: parish-5350@la-archdiocese.org. Rev. Michael W. Meyer, Sacramental Min.; Deacons James Carper, Parish Life Coord.; Emile Adams, Sacramental Min.
Catechesis Religious Program—Tel: 323-293-4877; Email: normajean@pacbell.net. Norma Jean Jackson, D.R.E. Students 22.
15—ST. BERNARD (1924)
2500 W. Ave. 33, 90065. Tel: 323-255-6142; Fax: 323-255-2351; Email: parish-3620@la-archdiocese.org; Web: www.stbernard-parish.com. Rev. Perry D. Leiker.
School—St. Bernard School, (Grades PreK-8), 3254 Verdugo Rd., 90065. Tel: 323-256-4989; Fax: 323-256-4963; Email: school-6950@la-archdiocese.org. Mr. Philip McCreary, Prin. Lay Teachers 10; Students 185.
Catechesis Religious Program—2515 W. Ave. 33, 90065. Tel: 323-256-6242; Email: acepeida@stbernard-church.com. Amelia Cepeida, D.R.E. Students 229.
16—BLESSED SACRAMENT (1904)
6657 Sunset Blvd., 90028. Tel: 323-462-6311; Email: communications@blessedsacramenthollywood.org; Web: www.blessedsacramenthollywood.org. Yolanda S. Brown, D.Min., Parish Life Dir.; Revs. Leo P. Prengaman, S.J.; Augusto Berrio, S.J.; Martin O. Silva, S.J.; Ike Udoh, S.J.; Jan Sooter, Pastoral Assoc.; Nathan Sheets, Mng. Dir., Center at Blessed Sacrament, 6636 Selma Ave., 90028. Tel: 323-740-0464; Fax: 323-464-7796.
School—Blessed Sacrament School, (Grades PreK-8), 6641 Sunset Blvd., 90028. Tel: 323-467-4177; Fax: 323-467-6099; Email: school-8140@la-archdiocese.org; Web: www.schoolblessedsacrament.org. Danina Flores-Uy, Prin. Lay Teachers 13; Students 155.
Catechesis Religious Program—Tel: 323-463-9820; Email: religioused@blessedsacramenthollywood.org. Virginia Cipres, D.R.E. Students 113.
17—ST. BRENDAN (1915)
310 S. Van Ness Ave., 90020. Tel: 323-936-4656; Email: info@stbrendanmail.org; Email: parish-5100@la-archdiocese.org; Web: www.stbrendanchurch.org. Rev. Msgr. Terrance L. Fleming, S.T.D., V.F.; Revs. Joseph Fox, O.P., J.C.D., In Res.; Patrick J. Hill, J.C.L., D.Min., In Res., (Retired).
School—St. Brendan School, (Grades PreK-8), 238 S. Manhattan Pl., 90004. Tel: 213-382-7401; Fax: 213-382-8918; Email: school-8220@la-archdiocese.org. Sr. Maureen O'Connor, C.S.J., Prin. Lay Teachers 18; Students 310; Clergy / Religious Teachers 2.
Catechesis Religious Program—Students 106.
18—ST. BRIDGET (1940) [JC] (Chinese)
510 Cottage Home St., 90012. Tel: 323-222-5518; Fax: 323- 227-1310; Email: parish-5110@la-archdiocese.org; Web: www.stbridgetccc.com. Mailing Address: 445 Cottage Home St., 90012. Rev. John Lam, S.D.B.
Catechesis Religious Program—Email: stbridgetccc@gmail.com. Sr. Maria Lai, C.S.J., D.R.E.
19—ST. BRIGID (1920) (African American—Hispanic)
5214 S. Western Ave., 90062. Tel: 323-292-0781; Email: parish-5550@la-archdiocese.org. Revs. Michael Okechukwu, S.S.J.; Emmanuel Awe, S.S.J.
Catechesis Religious Program—Email: floy@floyhawkins.com. Floy Hawkins, D.R.E. Students 56.
20—ST. CAMILLUS CENTER FOR SPIRITUAL CARE (1954)
1911 Zonal Ave., 90033-1032. Tel: 323-225-4461; Fax: 323-225-9096; Email: parish-4250@la-archdiocese.org; Web: www.stcamilluscenter.org. Rev. Christopher D. Ponnet, Pastor, Dir. & Chap.; His Eminence Roger Cardinal Mahony, Chap., (Retired); Revs. Robert J. Jones, C.M., Chap.; Joshua Ronnie Alvero, Chap.; Sr. Janet Husung, C.S.J., Chap.; Mr. Symeon Rendall Yee, Chap.; Mr. Luis Manuel Torres, Chap.; Mr. John Carlos Greeley, Chap.; Mr. Nick Jordan, Chap.; Arely Deras, Chap.; Mr. Christopher Stephan, Office Mgr.
Catholics Against the Death Penalty Center—
Tel: 323-225-4461, Ext. 221.
Catholic HIV/AIDS Office—
Tel: 323-225-4461, Ext. 221.
Pax Christi Los Angeles—
Tel: 323-225-4461, Ext. 221.
Catholic Ministry with Lesbian & Gay Persons—
Tel: 323-225-4461, Ext. 221.
Consistent Life Ethics Institute—
Tel: 323-225-4461, Ext. 221.
Catechesis Religious Program—Rambhoru Brinkmann, C.P.E. (Clinical Pastoral Educ.). Students 18.
21—ST. CASIMIR (1946) (Lithuanian)
2718 St. George St., 90027. Tel: 323-664-4660; Email: st.casimir@gmail.com; Email: parish-5120@la-archdiocese.org. Rev. Tomas Karanauskas.
Catechesis Religious Program—Email: tkaranauskas@gmail.com. Students 50.
22—CATHEDRAL CHAPEL OF ST. VIBIANA (1927)
926 S. La Brea Ave., 90036. Tel: 323-930-5976; Email: parish-5020@la-archdiocese.org. Rev. Truc Q. Nguyen, J.C.L.; Most Rev. Edward W. Clark, D.D., S.T.D., V.G., In Res.
School—Cathedral Chapel of St. Vibiana School, (Grades PreK-8), 755 S. Cochran Ave., 90036. Tel: 323-938-9976; Fax: 323-938-9930; Email: school-8150@la-archdiocese.org; Web: cathedralchapelschool.org. Tina Kipp, Prin. Lay Teachers 14; Students 280.
Catechesis Religious Program—Email: religioused@cathedralchapel.org. Sr. Anna Tom, S.D.S.H., D.R.E. Students 60.
23—ST. CECILIA (1909) (African American—Hispanic)
4230 S. Normandie Ave., 90037. Tel: 323-294-6628; Email: parish-5370@la-archdiocese.org. Rev. Roman Arzate.
School—St. Cecilia School, (Grades PreK-8), 4224 S. Normandie Ave., 90037. Tel: 323-293-4266; Email: stceciliasprincipal@gmail.com; Email: school-8480@la-archdiocese.org. Norma Guzman, Prin. Lay Teachers 10; Students 175.
Catechesis Religious Program—Tel: 323-298-7721. Sr. Olivia Ramirez, H.A., D.R.E. Students 434.
24—CHRIST THE KING (1926)
624 N. Rossmore Ave., 90004. Tel: 323-465-7605; Email: christtheking@sbcglobal.net. Rev. Don Woznicki; Deacon Marco Garcia Bejarano.
School—Christ the King School, (Grades PreK-8), 617 N. Arden Blvd., 90004. Tel: 323-462-4753; Fax: 323-462-8475; Email: principal@cksla.com; Web: cksla.org. Mrs. Patty Hager, Prin. Lay Teachers 13; Students 200.
Catechesis Religious Program—Tel: 323-465-7084. Sr. Maria Alice Hernandez, C.V.D., D.R.E. Students 151.
25—ST. COLUMBAN (1945) (Filipino)
125 S. Loma Dr., 90026. Tel: 213-250-8818; Email: parish-5130@la-archdiocese.org. Rev. John Brannigan, S.S.C.; Deacon Felix Dumlao.
Catechesis Religious Program—Students 37.
26—ST. COLUMBKILLE (1921) (Hispanic—African American)
6315 S. Main St., 90003. Tel: 323-758-5540; Email: parish-5560@la-archdiocese.org. Revs. Ever Quintero; Jorge Onofre Salazar.
School—St. Columbkille School, (Grades PreK-8), 145 W. 64th St., 90003. Tel: 323-758-2284; Fax: 323-750-7141; Email: office@columbkille.org; Email: school-8630@la-archdiocese.org. Dr. Karen Holyk-Casey, Prin. Lay Teachers 10; Students 265; Clergy / Religious Teachers 1.
Catechesis Religious Program—Tel: 323-789-3344. Students 455.
27—CRISTO REY (1939) (Hispanic)
4343 Perlita Ave., 90039. Tel: 323-245-4585; Email: parish-3530@la-archdiocese.org. Rev. Michael Stechmann, O.A.R.; Bro. Jorge Valdivia, O.A.R.; Deacon Ascencion Esqueda, O.A.R.
Catechesis Religious Program—Email: parish-3530@la-archdiocese.org. Jose Torres, D.R.E. Students 197.
28—DIVINE SAVIOUR (1907) (Hispanic)
610 Cypress Ave., Los Angelas, 90065.
Tel: 323-225-9181; Email: office@dssala.org; Web: www.dssala.org. 2911 Idell St., 90065. Revs. Albert Susai Pragasam, O.S.M.; SamyDurai Arockiam.
School—Divine Saviour School, (Grades PreK-8), 624 Cypress Ave., 90065. Tel: 323-222-6077; Email: school@dssala.org; Web: www.divinesaviourschool.org. Mr. Armando Carvalho, Prin. Lay Teachers 6; Students 82.
Catechesis Religious Program—
Tel: 323-225-9181 Ext. 127, 128; Email: ccuevas@dssala.org; Web: www.dssala.org. Claudia Cuevas, D.R.E. Students 260.
29—DOLORES MISSION (1945) (Hispanic)
1901 E. 4th St., 90033. Tel: 323-881-0039; Email: parish-4070@la-archdiocese.org. Revs. Ted Gabrielli, S.J.; Michael Lee, S.J.; Brendan P. Busse, S.J.; Gregory Boyle, S.J., In Res.; Tri M. Dinh, S.J., In Res.; Mark Torres, In Res.; Ellie Hidalgo, Pastoral Assoc.; Jody Lozano, Business Mgr.
School—Dolores Mission School, (Grades PreK-8), 170 S. Gless St., 90033. Tel: 323-881-0001; Email: school-7330@la-archdiocese.org. Karina Moreno, Prin. Lay Teachers 9; Students 245.
Catechesis Religious Program—171 S. Gless St., Los Angelas, 90033. Email: aislas@dolores-mission.org. Alma Islas, D.R.E. Students 205.
30—ST. DOMINIC (1921)
2002 Merton Ave., 90041. Tel: 323-254-2519; Email: parish-3630@la-archdiocese.org. Very Rev. Michael Fones, O.P.; Revs. Francis Goode, O.P.; Thomas Saucier; Michael Chaberek, O.P.; Dominic DeLay, O.P., In Res.; Cassian Lewinski, O.P., In Res.; Denis Reilly, In Res.
School—St. Dominic School, (Grades PreK-8), 2005 Merton Ave., 90041. Tel: 323-255-5803; Email: school-6960@la-archdiocese.org. Mrs. Emily Diaz, Prin. Lay Teachers 10; Students 232.
Child Care—Pre-School, Tel: 323-255-5803. Lay Teachers 1; Students 21.
Catechesis Religious Program—Christina Garcia, D.R.E.; Michelle Perez, D.R.E. Students 175.
31—ST. EUGENE (1942)
9505 Haas Ave., 90047. Tel: 323-757-3121; Fax: 323-757-8872; Email: steugenechurch@sbcglobal.net; Email: parish-5570@la-archdiocese.org; Web: www.steugeneparish.org. Rev. Jude Umeobi.
School—St. Eugene School, 9521 Haas Ave., Los Angelas, 90047. Email: school-8640@la-archdiocese.org. Leona Sorrell, Prin. Lay Teachers 16; Students 238.
Catechesis Religious Program—Anthony Ikebudu, D.R.E. Students 45.
32—FORMER CATHEDRAL OF ST. VIBIANA (1876) Closed. For inquiries for Sacramental Records contact 555 W. Temple St., Los Angeles, CA 90012.
33—ST. FRANCES XAVIER CABRINI (1946) (African

American—Latino)
1440 W. Imperial Hwy., 90047. Tel: 323-757-0271; Email: fxcab@sbcglobal.net; Email: parish-5580@la-archdiocese.org. Rev. Juan Bosco Jimenez, S.D.B.
School—St. Frances Xavier Cabrini School, (Grades PreK-8), 1428 W. Imperial Hwy., 90047.
Tel: 323-756-1354; Fax: 323-756-1157; Email: school-8650@la-archdiocese.org; Web: sfxcabrini.org. Mrs. Carmen A. Orinoco-Hart, Prin. Lay Teachers 10; Students 220.
Catechesis Religious Program—1430 W. Imperial Hwy., 90047. Email: linacarbajal@yahoo.com. Carmen Carbajal, D.R.E. Students 460.

34—ST. FRANCIS OF ASSISI (1920)
1523 Golden Gate Ave., 90026. Tel: 323-664-1305; Email: sfaparish@gmail.com; Email: parish-5140@la-archdiocese.org. Rev. Enrique Huerta.
School—St. Francis of Assisi School, (Grades PreK-8), 1550 Maltman Ave., 90026. Tel: 323-665-3601; Email: cnunez@stfrancisla.com; Email: school-8240@la-archdiocese.org; Web: www.stfrancisla.com. Mr. Claro Patrick Nunez, Prin. Lay Teachers 6; Students 84.
Catechesis Religious Program—Tel: 323-662-3345; Email: vilmasierra77@yahoo.com. Vilma Sierra, D.R.E. Students 76.

35—ST. FRANCIS XAVIER CHAPEL (1912) (Japanese)
222 S. Hewitt St., 90012. Tel: 213-626-2279; Email: parish-5380@la-archdiocese.org. Revs. Doan T. Hoang, S.J.; Chu Ngo, S.J.
Catechesis Religious Program—Students 28.

36—ST. GERARD MAJELLA (1952)
4439 Inglewood Blvd., 90066-6209.
Tel: 310-390-5034; Email: stgerardmajella@ca.rr.com; Email: parish-4860@la-archdiocese.org; Web: stgerardla.com. Revs. Martin Slaughter; Gerardo Padilla; Deacon Carlos (Charlie) Echeverry.
Catechesis Religious Program—Tel: 310-391-9637. Gabriela Gudino, D.R.E. Students 275.

37—ST. GREGORY NAZIANZEN (1923)
900 S. Bronson Ave., 90019. Tel: 323-935-4224; Email: parish-5150@la-archdiocese.org. Revs. Augustine Chang; Luke HyunSoo Byun.
Catechesis Religious Program—Jenny Menendez, D.R.E. Students 275.

38—HOLY CROSS (1906) (African American—Hispanic)
4705 S. Main St., 90037. Tel: 323-234-5984; Email: parish-5490@la-archdiocese.org. Revs. Jose Alberto Pimentel, M.C.C.J., Admin.; Shane Degblor; Xavier Colleoni, M.C.C.J., (Italy) In Res.; Robert Kleiner, M.C.C.J., In Res.; Deacon Leonel Yoque.
Catechesis Religious Program—104 W. 47th Pl., 90037. Tel: 323-234-1005; Email: holycrosscatholicchurch@yahoo.com. Sr. Ligia Zambrano, D.R.E. Students 603.

39—HOLY NAME OF JESUS (1921) (African American)
2190 W. 31st St., 90018. Tel: 323-734-8888; Email: parish-5240@la-archdiocese.org. Rev. Stanley Ihuoma, S.S.J.; Deacons Hosea Alexander Sr.; Alejandro Marin; Douglass R. Johnson Sr.; Jose Ines Penate Mojica.
School—Holy Name of Jesus School, (Grades PreK-8), 1955 W. Jefferson Blvd., 90018. Tel: 323-731-2255 ; Email: school-8420@la-archdiocese.org; Web: hnojla.org. Mrs. Marva Belisle, Prin. Lay Teachers 10; Students 185.
Catechesis Religious Program—Email: holynamedre@gmail.com. Catherine Brown, D.R.E. Students 80.

40—HOLY SPIRIT (1926)
1425 S. Dunsmuir Ave., 90019-4031.
Tel: 323-935-1333; Email: parish-5250@la-archdiocese.org. Revs. Joseph Okech Adhunga, A.J., (Kenya); Macdonald Akuti, A.J.; Gabriel Emuria, A.J.
School—Holy Spirit School, (Grades PreK-4), 1418 S. Burnside Ave., 90019. Tel: 323-933-7775;
Fax: 323-933-7453; Email: holyspiritschoolla@yahoo.com; Web: holyspiritstmarymagdalen.org. Ms. Nuria Gordillo, Prin. Lay Teachers 6; Students 127.
Catechesis Religious Program—Email: srluzdelcarmen@holyspiritla.org. Sr. Luz Del Carmen Perez, D.R.E. Students 160.

41—HOLY TRINITY (1925) (Filipino—Hispanic)
3722 Boyce Ave., 90039. Tel: 323-664-4723; Email: parish-3570@la-archdiocese.org. Revs. Ricardo Henry Viveros; Jaehun Song; Deacon Rolando Bautista.
School—Holy Trinity School, (Grades PreK-8), 3716 Boyce Ave., 90039. Tel: 323-663-2064; Web: www.holytrinityla.com. Karen Lloyd, Prin. Lay Teachers 11; Students 155.
Catechesis Religious Program—Students 250.
Mission—Sung Sam Korean Catholic Center, 1230 N. San Fernando Rd., 90065. Tel: 323-221-8874; Email: office@sungsamkcc.com. Rev. Taehyun Gregory Yang, Chap.

42—ST. IGNATIUS OF LOYOLA (1911)
6024 Terrace Dr., 90042. Tel: 323-256-3041; Email: parish-3640@la-archdiocese.org. Rev. Edwin C. Duyshart.
School—St. Ignatius of Loyola School, (Grades PreK-8), 6025 Monte Vista St., 90042. Tel: 323-255-6456; Fax: 323-255-0959; Email: admin@stignatiusla.org; Email: school-6970@la-archdiocese.org; Web: www.stignatiusla.org. Mrs. Ileana Wade, Prin. Lay Teachers 10; Students 187; Clergy / Religious Teachers 1.
Catechesis Religious Program—Tel: 323-254-9073; Email: stignatiusre@yahoo.com. Sr. Gemma de la Trinidad, E.F.M.S., D.R.E. Students 350.

43—IMMACULATE CONCEPTION (1908) (Hispanic)
1433 James M. Wood Blvd., 90015.
Tel: 213-384-1019; Email: immaconc@sbcglobal.net. Revs. Jesus Francisco Garcia Aguilar, C.O.R.C., (Mexico); Abdias Gonzalez Gonzalez, C.O.R.C., (Mexico).
School—Immaculate Conception School, (Grades PreK-8), 830 Green St., 90017. Tel: 213-382-5931; Email: principal@ics-la.org; Web: www.ics-la.org. Ms. Mary Ann Murphy, Prin. Lay Teachers 12; Students 250.
Catechesis Religious Program—832 Green Ave., 90017. Tel: 213-389-7277; Email: parish-5260@la-archdiocese.org. Edith Cruz, D.R.E. Students 481.

44—IMMACULATE HEART OF MARY (1910)
4954 Santa Monica Blvd., 90029. Tel: 323-660-0034;
Fax: 323-660-0047; Email: ihmcbusinessmanager@ihmc-la.org; Web: ihmc-la.org. Revs. Rolando Clarin; Florentino Victorino, M.S.C.
School—Immaculate Heart of Mary School, (Grades PreK-8), 1055 N. Alexandria Ave., 90029.
Tel: 323-663-4611; Fax: 323-663-6216; Email: ihm1@pacbell.net; Web: www.ihmla.org. Allyson Alberto, Prin. Lay Teachers 10; Students 175.
Catechesis Religious Program—Email: ihmcla@gmail.com. Mariela Morales, D.R.E. Students 131.

45—ST. JEROME (1949)
5550 Thornburn St., 90045. Tel: 310-348-8212; Email: parish-4870@la-archdiocese.org. Rev. Bill Bolton, S.D.B.
School—St. Jerome School, (Grades PreK-8), 5580 Thornburn St., 90045. Tel: 310-670-1678;
Fax: 310-670-2170; Email: principal@stjeromewestchester.org; Web: www.stjeromeschool.org. Priscilla Doorbar, Prin. Lay Teachers 12; Students 120.
Catechesis Religious Program—Students 60.

46—ST. JOAN OF ARC (1943) (Spanish)
11534 Gateway Blvd., 90064. Tel: 310-479-5111; Email: parish-4880@la-archdiocese.org. Rev. Joseph Q. Nguyen.
Catechesis Religious Program—Email: torres@stjoanchurch.com. Paola Torres, D.R.E. Students 210.

47—ST. JOHN THE EVANGELIST (1909) (Hispanic—African American)
6028 S. Victoria Ave., 90043. Tel: 323-758-9161;
Fax: 323-758-0112; Email: parish-5600@la-archdiocese.org; Web: www.johnevangelist.org. Revs. Lester Alan Jenkins; Jerome Bai, In Res.
Catechesis Religious Program—Email: cherylfabien@gmail.com. Cheryl Fabien, D.R.E. Students 74.

48—ST. JOSEPH (1888) (Hispanic)
218 E. 12th St., 90015. Tel: 213-748-5394; Email: stjosephschurch@sbcglobal.net; Email: parish-5390@la-archdiocese.org. Rev. Rafael Casillas; Deacon Miguel Cruz.
School—St. Turibius School, (Grades PreK-8), 1524 Essex St., 90021. Tel: 213-749-8894;
Fax: 213-275-1016; Email: info@stturibius.org; Email: school-8500@la-archdiocese.org; Web: www.stturibius.org. Karina Mendez, Prin. Lay Teachers 9; Students 165.
Catechesis Religious Program—Tel: 213-663-6995; Email: ambrocioalonso3030@gmail.com. Ambrocio Alonso, D.R.E. Students 310.
Mission—St. Turibius Mission, 1530 Essex St., Los Angeles Co. 90021. Tel: 213-748-5394; Email: parish-5390@la-archdiocese.org.

49—ST. KEVIN (1923) (Hispanic—Filipino)
4072 Beverly Blvd., 90004. Tel: 213-909-1801; Email: parish-5160@la-archdiocese.org; Web: www.stkevinchurchla.org. Revs. Percy Juan Bacani, M.J.; Melanio Viuya Jr., M.J.; Crespo Lape, M.J.; Deacon Carlos Magos.
Catechesis Religious Program—Email: rendall75@gmail.com. Symeon Yee, D.R.E. Students 206.

50—ST. LAWRENCE OF BRINDISI (1908) (African American—Hispanic)
10122 Compton Ave., 90002. Tel: 323-567-1439; Email: parish-5610@la-archdiocese.org. Revs. Matthew Elshoff, O.F.M.Cap.; Joseph S. Dederick, O.F.-M.Cap.; Bro. Mark Mance, O.F.M.Cap., Pastoral Assoc.
School—St. Lawrence of Brindisi School, (Grades PreK-8), 10044 Compton Ave., 90002.
Tel: 323-564-3051; Email: school-8680@la-archdiocese.org. Alicia Camacho, Prin. Lay Teachers 10; Students 300.
Catechesis Religious Program—Tel: 323-567-4698. Leonor Casas, D.R.E. Students 984.

51—ST. LUCY (1981) [CEM] (Hispanic)
3945 City Terrace Dr., 90063. Tel: 323-266-0451; Email: parish-4260@la-archdiocese.org. 1419 N. Hazard Ave., 90063. Revs. Miguel Mascorro, Sch.P.; Josep M. Margalef, Sch.P.
Catechesis Religious Program—Leticia Robles, D.R.E. Students 180.

52—ST. MALACHY (1926) (Hispanic)
1221 E. 82nd St., 90001. Tel: 323-585-1437;
Fax: 323-277-4776; Email: st.malachychurch@gmail.com; Email: parish-5620@la-archdiocese.org. 1228 E. 81st St., 90001. Rev. Luis R. Lucchetti, (Peru).
Child Care—St. Malachy Preschool,
Tel: 323-582-3112.
School—St. Malachy School, (Grades PreK-8), 1200 E. 81st St., 90001. Tel: 323-582-3112;
Fax: 323-582-9340; Email: stmalachyschl@sbcglobal.net; Email: school-8690@la-archdiocese.org. Rocio Orozco, Prin. Lay Teachers 11; Students 215.
Catechesis Religious Program—Tel: 323-582-3024; Email: ordazmartha14@yahoo.com. Martha Ordaz, D.R.E. Students 350.

53—ST. MARTIN OF TOURS (1946)
11967 Sunset Blvd., 90049. Tel: 310-476-7403; Email: info@saintmartinoftours.com; Email: parish-4900@la-archdiocese.org; Web: www.saintmartinoftours.com. Revs. Ben Le; Donal Keohane, (Ireland).
School—St. Martin of Tours School, (Grades PreK-8), 11955 Sunset Blvd., 90049. Tel: 310-472-7419;
Fax: 310-440-2298; Email: school-8040@la-archdiocese.org; Web: smtschool.net. Dr. Gavin Colvert, Prin. Lay Teachers 22; Students 205; Clergy / Religious Teachers 1.
Catechesis Religious Program—
Tel: 310-476-7403, Ext. 225; Email: rhiannon@saintmartinoftours.com. Rhiannon Jensen, D.R.E. Students 143.

54—ST. MARY (1896)
407 S. Chicago St., 90033. Tel: 323-268-7432; Email: parish-4280@la-archdiocese.org. Revs. Jesse Montes, S.D.B.; Joseph Farias, S.D.B.; Alberto Chavez, S.D.B.
School—St. Mary School, (Grades PreK-8), 416 S. St. Louis St., 90033. Tel: 323-262-3395; Email: school-7490@la-archdiocese.org; Web: stmaryla.org. Jonathan Medina, Prin. Lay Teachers 8; Students 166; Clergy / Religious Teachers 4.
Catechesis Religious Program—Ramon Rodriguez, D.R.E.; Carlos Flores, D.R.E. Students 243.

55—ST. MARY MAGDALEN (1930)
1241 Corning St., 90035. Tel: 310-652-2444; Email: parish-4910@la-archdiocese.org. Revs. Joseph Okech Adhunga, A.J., (Kenya); Macdonald Akuti, A.J.; John Montag, S.J.
School—St. Mary Magdalen School, (Grades 5-8), 1223 Corning St., 90035. Ms. Nuria Gordillo, Prin. Lay Teachers 4; Students 65; Clergy / Religious Teachers 1.
Catechesis Religious Program—Email: srluzdelcarmen@holyspiritla.org. Sr. Luz Del Carmen Perez, D.R.E. Students 22.

56—ST. MICHAEL (1907) (Hispanic—African American)
1016 W. Manchester Ave., 90044. Tel: 323-753-2696;
Fax: 323-753-3475; Email: parish-5630@la-archdiocese.org. Rev. Peter Thang C. Ngo, J.C.L.
School—St. Michael School, (Grades K-8), 1027 W. 87th St., 90044. Tel: 323-752-6101;
Fax: 323-752-6785; Email: principal@stmichaelguardians.org; Email: school-8700@la-archdiocese.org; Web: www.stmichaelguardians.org. Anabel Rodriguez, Prin. Lay Teachers 10; Students 284.
Catechesis Religious Program—Tel: 323-753-2976; Email: ludavigu@yahoo.com. Sr. Luz Dari Villera-Guzman, D.R.E. Students 450.

57—MOTHER OF SORROWS (1923) (Hispanic—African American)
114 W. 87th St., 90003. Tel: 323-758-7697;
Fax: 323-758-7853; Email: moscatholicch@yahoo.com. Rev. Brian Chung.
School—Mother of Sorrows School, (Grades PreK-8), 100 W. 87th Pl., 90003. Tel: 323-758-6204;
Fax: 323-758-6203; Email: school-8590@la-archdiocese.org. Miss Griselda Villarreal, Prin. Lay Teachers 14; Students 235.
Catechesis Religious Program—Tel: 323-789-6316; Email: hnarosalidia@yahoo.com. Sr. Rosa Lidia Orellana, C.S.J., D.R.E. Students 390.

58—NATIVITY (1920) (Hispanic—African American)
953 W. 57th St., 90037. Tel: 323-759-1562; Email: parish-5510@la-archdiocese.org. Revs. Ever Quintero, Admin.; Jorge Onofre Salazar.
School—Nativity School, (Grades PreK-8), 944 W. 56th St., 90037. Tel: 323-752-0720;
Fax: 323-752-1945; Email: school-8600@la-

archdiocese.org; Web: http://www.nativityla.org. Yanira Gomez, Prin. Lay Teachers 11; Students 327.
Catechesis Religious Program—Tel: 323-753-9802; Email: columbkille-nativityconfirmation@yahoo.com. Juan Carlos Alvarado, D.R.E. Students 330.

59—ST. ODILIA (1926) (Hispanic)
5222 Hooper Ave., 90011-4807. Tel: 323-231-5930; Email: parish-5640@la-archdiocese.org. Rev. Juan Silva.
School—St. Odilia School, (Grades PreK-8), 5300 S. Hooper Ave., 90011. Tel: 323-232-5449;
Fax: 323-233-6154; Email: school-8710@la-archdiocese.org. Sima Saravia-Perez, Prin. Lay Teachers 10; Students 280.
Catechesis Religious Program—Email: odiliaccd2011@yahoo.com. Rosa Enriquez, D.R.E. Students 181.
Mission—St. John Bosco, 5516 Duarte St., Los Angeles Co. 90058.

60—OUR LADY HELP OF CHRISTIANS (MARIA AUXILIADORA) (1923) (Hispanic)
512 S. Ave. 20, 90031. Tel: 323-223-4153; Email: parish-4080@la-archdiocese.org. Revs. Manuel Sanahuja, Sch.P.; Federico Castillo, Sch.P., In Res.
Catechesis Religious Program—Tel: 323-225-2846; Email: chuy200@yahoo.com. Jesse Arellano, D.R.E. Students 150.

61—OUR LADY OF GUADALUPE (1923) (Hispanic)
4018 Hammel St., 90063. Tel: 323-261-8051;
Fax: 323-261-1259; Web: www.olghammel.org. Rev. Marco Solis.
School—Our Lady of Guadalupe School, (Grades PreK-8), 436 N. Hazard Ave., 90063.
Tel: 323-269-4998; Fax: 323-780-7001; Web: www.olglions.org. Nancy Figueroa, Prin. Lay Teachers 10; Students 135.
Catechesis Religious Program—Tel: 323-262-7957. Sr. Sandra Martinez, M.J.C., D.R.E. Students 340.
Mission—San Felipe, 738 N. Geraghty Ave., Los Angeles Co. 90063.

62—OUR LADY OF GUADALUPE (Rosehill) (1928) (Hispanic)
4509 Mercury Ave., 90032. Tel: 323-225-4201; Email: parish-4100@la-archdiocese.org. Rev. Nelson Trinidad.
School—Our Lady of Guadalupe School, (Grades PreK-8), 4522 Browne Ave., 90032.
Tel: 323-221-8187; Fax: 323-221-8197; Email: school-7360@la-archdiocese.org. Evie Lopez, Prin. Lay Teachers 6; Students 160.
Catechesis Religious Program—4504 Browne Ave., 90032. Tel: 323-225-4203; Email: srtherese@olgrosehill.com. Sr. Theresa Marie Cedillo, D.R.E. Students 194.

63—OUR LADY OF GUADALUPE SANCTUARY (1929) (Hispanic)
4100 E. Second St., 90063. Tel: 323-261-4365; Email: parish-4110@la-archdiocese.org. Rev. Leslie N. Delgado, (Panama).
Catechesis Religious Program—Alfredo Diaz, D.R.E.; Manuel S. Chavez, D.R.E. Students 176.

64—OUR LADY OF LORETTO (1905)
250 N. Union Ave., 90026. Tel: 213-483-3013; Email: loretto.losangeles@gmail.com; Web: www.loretto.la. Revs. Anh-Tuan Dominic Nguyen; Oscar Daniel Martinez Gutierrez.
School—Our Lady of Loretto School, (Grades PreK-8), 258 N. Union Ave., 90026. Tel: 213-483-5251;
Fax: 213-483-6709; Email: school-8190@la-archdiocese.org; Web: www.ourladyofloretto.org. Nivita Brito, Prin. Lay Teachers 10; Students 167.
Catechesis Religious Program—Tel: 213-483-5251; Email: mevelynmo@gmail.com. Evelyn Mendoza, D.R.E. Students 209.

65—OUR LADY OF LOURDES (1910)
3772 E. Third St., 90063-2408. Tel: 323-526-3800;
Fax: 323-526-3807; Email: parish-4120@la-archdiocese.org; Web: www.ollourdes.com. Revs. Jesus Zamarripa, S.V.D.; Benediktus Obon.
School—Our Lady of Lourdes School, (Grades PreK-8), 315 S. Eastman Ave., 90063. Tel: 323-526-3813;
Fax: 323-526-3814; Email: school-7370@la-archdiocese.org; Web: www.la-ourladyoflourdes.org. Veronica Carrillo, Prin. Lay Teachers 15; Students 180.
Catechesis Religious Program—
Tel: 323-526-3800, Ext. 122. Francisco Mendez, D.R.E. Students 360.

66—OUR LADY OF SOLITUDE (1925) (Hispanic)
4561 Cesar Chavez Ave., 90022. Tel: 323-269-7248; Email: parish-4140@la-archdiocese.org. Revs. Guillermo Martinez, M.S.P.; Armando Bernabe, M.S.P.; Deacon Sergio A. Perez.
Catechesis Religious Program—Tel: 323-407-3623. Martha Quijano, D.R.E. Students 390.

67—OUR LADY OF THE BRIGHT MOUNT (1925) (Polish)
Rev. Rafal Dygula.
Res.: 3424 W. Adams Blvd., 90018. Tel: 323-734-5249; Fax: 323-734-0046; Email: parish-5280@la-archdiocese.org; Web: www.polskaparafiala.org.
Catechesis Religious Program—Teresa Lezak, D.R.E. Students 130.

68—OUR LADY OF THE ROSARY OF TALPA (1928) (Spanish)
2914 E. Fourth St., 90033. Tel: 323-268-9176; Email: talpachurch@sbcglobal.net. Rev. Pedro A. Cobenas.
School—Our Lady of the Rosary of Talpa School, (Grades PreK-8), 411 S. Evergreen Ave., 90033.
Tel: 323-261-0583; Email: school-7400@la-archdiocese.org. Sr. Adella Armentrout, Prin. Lay Teachers 10; Students 297; Clergy / Religious Teachers 2.
Catechesis Religious Program—
Tel: 323-268-9176, Ext. 103. Students 275.
Mission—La Purisima Chapel, 3236 Inez St., Los Angeles Co. 90023. Tel: 323-268-9177.

69—OUR LADY OF VICTORY (1966) (Spanish)
1316 S. Herbert Ave., 90023. Tel: 323-268-9502; Email: elavictory@adelphia.net; Email: parish-4160@la-archdiocese.org. Rev. Armando Lopez, O.F.M.
Catechesis Religious Program—1317 S. Herbert Ave., 90023. Tel: 323-262-2101. Mary Valentino, D.R.E. Students 305.

70—OUR LADY QUEEN OF ANGELS (1781) (Spanish)
535 N. Main St., 90012. Tel: 213-629-3101; Email: parish-5290@la-archdiocese.org; Email: info@laplacita.org; Web: www.laplacita.org. Revs. Arturo N. Corral, V.F.; Heriberto Serrano; Roberto Raygoza.
Catechesis Religious Program—Nilza Valencia, D.R.E. Students 164.

71—OUR MOTHER OF GOOD COUNSEL (1925)
2060 N. Vermont Ave., 90027-1919.
Tel: 323-664-2111; Email: omgcparish@gmail.com; Email: parish-5050@la-archdiocese.org; Web: www.omogc.org. Revs. James A. Mott, O.S.A.; William Thomas Davis, O.S.A.; Alvin Paligutan; Mark Menegatti, In Res.; James P. Retzner, O.S.A., In Res.
School—Our Mother of Good Counsel School, (Grades PreK-8), 4622 Ambrose Ave., 90027.
Tel: 323-664-2131; Fax: 323-664-1906; Email: school@omgcschool.org; Email: school-8180@la-archdiocese.org; Web: www.omgcschool.org. Allison Essman, Prin. Lay Teachers 10; Students 120.
Catechesis Religious Program—Email: dre.omgcparish@gmail.com. Ava Haylock, D.R.E. Students 150.

72—OUR SAVIOR PARISH & U.S.C. CARUSO CATHOLIC CENTER (1957)
844 32nd St., 90007. Tel: 213-516-3959, Ext. 205; Email: info@catholictrojan.org; Email: parish-5300@la-archdiocese.org; Web: www.catholictrojan.org. James Cappetta, Pres.; Revs. Richard Sunwoo; Gregory Vance, Campus Min.; Deacon Paul Pesqueira, Dir. Sacramental Preparation; Sr. Jennifer Zimmerman, Campus Minister, Spiritual Life; Roseairol Shawver, Dir. Campus Ministry; Anthony Heim, Campus Min., Email: anthony@catholictrojan.org; Tricia Tembreull, Campus Min.; Yvette Cardona, Business Mgr.; Andrew Mountin, Dir. of Worship.

73—ST. PATRICK (1904) (Hispanic)
1046 E. 34th St., 90011. Tel: 323-234-5963; Email: parish-5400@la-archdiocese.org. Rev. Msgr. Timothy J. Dyer, V.F.; Rev. Moises R. Apolinar Jr.
Catechesis Religious Program—Tel: 323-232-5460. Enedina Perez, D.R.E. Students 540.

74—ST. PAUL (1917)
1920 S. Bronson Ave., 90018. Tel: 323-730-9490; Email: parish-5410@la-archdiocese.org. Revs. Erasmus B. Soriano; John S.H. Lee; Florentino Victorino, M.S.C.
School—St. Paul School, (Grades PreK-8), 1908 S. Bronson Ave., 90018. Tel: 323-734-4022;
Fax: 323-734-5057; Email: school-8510@la-archdiocese.org; Web: stpaulschoolla.org. Linda Guzman, Prin. Lay Teachers 12; Students 185.
Catechesis Religious Program—Tel: 323-737-1784. Sr. Antonieta M. Zapata, M.G.Sp.S., D.R.E. Students 249.

75—ST. PAUL THE APOSTLE (1928) Revs. Gilbert Martinez, C.S.P.; Ryan Casey; Gerard Tully, C.S.P.; Thomas C. Gibbons, C.S.P., In Res.; Peter Abdella, C.S.P., In Res.; Jamie Baca, C.S.P., In Res.; Thomas J. Clerkin, C.S.P., In Res.; Patrick E. Hensy, C.S.P., In Res., (Retired); Paul A. Lannan, In Res., (Retired); Theodore A. Vierra, In Res., (Retired); Mark Villano, C.S.P., In Res.; Edward D. Wrobleski, C.S.P., In Res., (Retired).
Res.: 10750 Ohio Ave., 90024. Tel: 310-474-1527;
Fax: 310-474-2897; Email: parishoffice@sp-apostle.org; Web: sp-apostle.org.
School—St. Paul the Apostle School, (Grades PreK-8), 1536 Selby Ave., 90024. Tel: 310-474-1588;
Fax: 310-474-4272; Email: info@sp-apostle.org; Web: www.sp-apostle.org. Mrs. Crystal Pinkofsky, Prin. Lay Teachers 37; Students 550; Clergy / Religious Teachers 3.
Catechesis Religious Program—Mrs. Irene Holly, D.R.E. Students 114.

76—ST. PETER aka St. Peter's Italian Church (1904) (Italian)
1039 N. Broadway, 90012-1429. Tel: 323-225-8119; Email: stpeterit@yahoo.com; Web: stpeteritalianchurchla.org. Rev. Louis Piran, C.S.
Catechesis Religious Program—Michelle Fanara, D.R.E. Students 32.
Mission—San Conrado, 1820 Bouett St., Los Angeles Co. 90012. Tel: 323-223-6581; Email: parish-5170@la-archdiocese.org.

77—PRECIOUS BLOOD (1923)
435 S. Occidental Blvd., 90057. Tel: 213-389-8439; Email: parish-5070@la-archdiocese.org; Web: www.preciousbloodchurchla.org. Revs. Percy Juan Bacani, M.J.; Crespo Lape, M.J.; Melanio Viuya Jr., M.J.; Deacon Carlos Magos.
School—Precious Blood School, (Grades K-8), 307 S. Occidental Blvd., 90057. Tel: 213-382-3345;
Fax: 213-382-2078; Email: school-8200@la-archdiocese.org; Web: www.preciousbloodschool.net. Maria Cunanan, Prin. Lay Teachers 9; Students 90.
Catechesis Religious Program—Email: preciousblood.la@gmail.com. Symeon Yee, D.R.E. Students 163.

78—PRESENTATION OF MARY (1925) (Hispanic)
6406 Parmelee Ave., 90001. Tel: 323-585-0570; Email: parish-5520@la-archdiocese.org; Email: presentationofmary@att.net. Rev. Fredy B. Rosales.
Catechesis Religious Program—Jazmin Munoz, D.R.E. Students 470.

79—ST. RAPHAEL (1924) (Hispanic—African American)
Revs. Michael Joseph Wu, O.Carm.; Miguel Mascorro, Sch.P, In Res.; Deacons Miguel Angel Martinez; Anthony Armstrong, In Res.; Mr. Harry Wiley, Dir. African American Ministry.
Res.: 942 W. 70th St., 90044. Tel: 323-758-7100;
Fax: 323-758-7134; Email: office@straphaelchurchla.org; Email: parish-5650@la-archdiocese.org; Web: www.straphaelchurchla.org.
School—St. Raphael School, Tel: 323-751-2774;
Fax: 323-751-1244; Email: school-8720@la-archdiocese.org; Web: www.straphaella.org. Allison Hurtt, Prin. Lay Teachers 25; Students 285.
Catechesis Religious Program—Tel: 323-752-5965; Email: reled@straphaelchurchla.org. Ms. Maria Rosalba Soto, D.R.E. Students 236.

80—RESURRECTION (1923) (Mexican)
3324 E. Opal St., 90023. Tel: 323-268-1141; Email: resurrectionla@yahoo.com; Email: parish-4170@la-archdiocese.org; Web: Resurrectionla.com. Rev. Msgr. John T. Moretta, V.F.; Rev. Gustavo Mejia.
School—Resurrection School, (Grades PreK-8), 3360 E. Opal St., 90023. Tel: 323-261-5750; Email: school-7410@la-archdiocese.org; Email: principal@resurrection-school.org; Web: www.resurrection-school.org. Catalina Saenz, Prin. Lay Teachers 13; Students 249; Clergy / Religious Teachers 3.
Catechesis Religious Program—Tel: 323-264-1963; Email: Lpinon56@aol.com. Letty Pinon, D.R.E. Students 600.

81—SACRED HEART (1887) (Hispanic)
2210 Sichel St., 90031-3030. Tel: 323-221-3179; Email: parish-4180@la-archdiocese.org. Revs. Tesfaldet Asghedom; Tesfaldet Tekie Tsada, (Eritrea); George E. Horan, In Res.; Reynaldo B. Matunog, J.C.L., In Res.
School—Sacred Heart School, 2109 Sichel St., 90031. Tel: 323-225-4177; Fax: 323-225-2615; Email: school-7420@la-archdiocese.org. Sr. Maria Elena Gutierrez, Prin. Lay Teachers 10; Students 222; Clergy / Religious Teachers 1.
Catechesis Religious Program—Tel: 323-223-7571; Email: sacredheartreled@att.net. Celia Gonzalez, D.R.E. Students 124.

82—SAN ANTONIO DE PADUA (1926) (Hispanic)
555 N. Fairview Ave., 90033. Tel: 323-225-1301; Email: parish-4190@la-archdiocese.org. Rev. Gustavo J. Ramon.
Child Care—San Antonio de Padua Preschool Academy, Tel: 323-226-0227. Sr. Mary Magdalene Acuna, O.S.F., Dir. Students 65; Clergy / Religious Teachers 1.
Catechesis Religious Program—1500 E. Bridge St., 90033. Students 108.

83—SAN CONRADO MISSION (1966) Closed. (See St. Peter, Los Angeles for details.).

84—SAN FRANCISCO (1982) [CEM] [JC] (Hispanic)
4800 E. Olympic Blvd., 90022. Tel: 323-262-4253; Email: parish-4200@la-archdiocese.org. Rev. Mario Arellano.
Catechesis Religious Program—Tel: 323-261-2447; Email: rel.ed.sfchurch@gmail.com. Eduviges Cerda, D.R.E. Students 370.

85—SAN MIGUEL (1927) (Hispanic)
10746 Juniper St, 90059. Tel: 323-569-5951;
Fax: 323-567-1850; Email: parish-5530@la-archdiocese.org; Email: sanmiguel-church@hotmail.com. 2214 E. 108th St., 90059. Revs. Jose Valdez Romo, M.S.C.; Emiliano Pozas Perez, Parochial Vicar.

School—San Miguel School, (Grades PreK-8), 2270 E. 108th St., 90059. Tel: 323-567-6892; Fax: 323-923-9763; Email: info@sanmiguelcatholicschool.com; Email: school-8610@la-archdiocese.org; Web: www.sanmiguelcatholicschool.com. Maryann Reynoso-Davis, Prin. Lay Teachers 10; Students 202.
Catechesis Religious Program—Tel: 323-569-5951; Email: parish-5530@la-archdiocese.org. Mrs. Teresa Reynoso, D.R.E.; Sisters Catherine Burke, RCIA Coord.; Jane Bonar, RCIA Coord. Students 305.

86—SANTA ISABEL (1915) (Mexican)
918 S. Soto St., 90023. Tel: 323-268-4065; Fax: 323-268-4180; Email: parish-4210@la-archdiocese.org; Web: www.santaisabelchurch.org. Revs. Jesus Herrera Garcia, M.S.P.; Armando Bernabe, M.S.P.
School—Santa Isabel School, (Grades PreK-8), 2424 Whittier Blvd., 90023. Tel: 323-263-3716; Email: school-7450@la-archdiocese.org. Hilda Orozco, Prin. Lay Teachers 10; Students 190.
Catechesis Religious Program—Tel: 323-268-3019. Rachel Silva, D.R.E. Students 280.

87—SANTA TERESITA (1923) (Hispanic)
2645 Zonal Ave., 90033. Tel: 323-221-2446; Email: parish-4220@la-archdiocese.org. Revs. Pedro Lucia, Sch.P.; Carlos E. Rojas, Sch.P.; Manoj John, Sch.P.
School—Santa Teresita School, (Grades PreK-8), 2646 Zonal Ave., 90033. Tel: 323-221-1129; Fax: 323-221-6339; Email: school-7460@la-archdiocese.org. Sr. Mary Catherine Antczak, Prin. Lay Teachers 9; Students 265; Clergy / Religious Teachers 2.
Catechesis Religious Program—Tel: 323-221-2511. Sr. Sandra Martinez, M.J.C., D.R.E. Students 110.

88—ST. SEBASTIAN (1924)
11607 Ohio Ave., 90025. Rev. German Sanchez, Admin.; Ms. Irma Lomelli, Sec.
Res.: 1453 Federal Ave., 90025-2301.
Tel: 310-478-0136; Email: stsebastianoffice@gmail.com; Web: www.stsebastianla.org.
School—St. Sebastian School, 1430 Federal Ave. W., 90025. Tel: 310-473-3337; Fax: 310-473-3178; Email: principal@saintsebastianschool.com; Email: school-8110@la-archdiocese.org; Web: saintsebastianschool.com. Mrs. Patricia Harty, Prin. Lay Teachers 14; Students 145.
Catechesis Religious Program—Tel: 310-479-7380; Email: stsebastianoffice@gmail.com. Sisters Posada Leidy, D.R.E.; Ivon Bruno, Rel. Ed. Asst. Students 85.

89—ST. STEPHEN OF HUNGARY (1928) (Hungarian—German)
1046 E. 34th St., 90011. Tel: 323-234-5963; Fax: 323-234-2455; Email: parish-4450@la-archdiocese.org. Rev. Msgr. Timothy J. Dyer, V.F.
Res.: 3705 Woodlawn Ave., 90011. Tel: 323-234-5963; Email: parish-4450@la-archdiocese.org.

90—ST. TERESA OF AVILA (1921) Revs. Roberto Pirrone; Jose Rueda, In Res.
Res.: 2216 Fargo St., 90039. Tel: 323-664-8426; Email: parish-5180@la-archdiocese.org.
School—St. Teresa of Avila School, (Grades K-8), 2215 Fargo St., 90039. Tel: 323-662-3777; Fax: 323-662-3420; Email: stapanthers@gmail.com; Email: school-8260@la-archdiocese.org; Web: www.stapanthers.org. Mrs. Christina Fernandez-Caso, Prin. Lay Teachers 9; Students 131.
Catechesis Religious Program—Francis Calderon, D.R.E. Students 44.
Convent—2223 Fargo St., 90039. Tel: 323-913-1510.

91—ST. THOMAS THE APOSTLE (1903) (Hispanic) Revs. Mario Torres; Rafael Garces; Javier Jara-Ramos; Deacon Daniel Bernal.
Res.: 2727 W. Pico Blvd., 90006. Tel: 323-737-3325.
School—St. Thomas the Apostle School, (Grades PreK-8), 2632 W. 15th St., 90006. Tel: 323-737-4730; Fax: 323-737-6348; Email: office@saintthomasla.org; Web: http://www.saintthomasla.org. Mr. Adrian Cuevas, Prin. Lay Teachers 10; Students 304.
Catechesis Religious Program—2632 W. 15th St., 90006. Claudia Marin-Austin, D.R.E. Students 688.

92—ST. TIMOTHY (1943) Rev. Paul E. Vigil.
Rectory—10425 W. Pico Blvd., 90064.
Tel: 310-474-1216; Fax: 310-475-6047; Email: sttimothychurchla@gmail.com; Email: parish-4950@la-archdiocese.org; Web: www.sttimothyla.org.
School—St. Timothy School, (Grades PreK-8), 10479 W. Pico Blvd., 90064. Tel: 310-474-1811; Email: school-8080@la-archdiocese.org; Web: sttimothy.org. Lena Randle, Prin. Lay Teachers 16; Students 228.
Catechesis Religious Program—Michelle Morrison, D.R.E. Students 117.

93—TRANSFIGURATION (1923) (African American)
2515 W. Martin Luther King Blvd., 90008-2728.
Tel: 323-291-1136; Email: parish-5530@la-archdiocese.org. Deacon Mark Race, Admin.; Revs. Joel Henson, In Res.; Michael P. McCullough, In Res.; Bernard Viagappan, In Res.
School—Transfiguration School, (Grades PreK-8), 4020 Roxton Ave., 90008. Tel: 323-292-3011; Fax: 323-292-1527; Email: school-8540@la-archdiocese.org; Web: www.transfigurationla.org. Mrs. Evelyn Rickenbacker, Prin. Lay Teachers 10; Students 225.
Catechesis Religious Program—Email: missmrg2@yahoo.com. Refugio Godinez, D.R.E. Students 25.

94—ST. VINCENT DE PAUL aka St. Vincent's Church (1887) (Hispanic) Revs. David G. Nations, C.M.; Jerome Herff, C.M., Parochial Vicar; Derek Swanson, Parochial Vicar; Bro. Anthony B. Wiedemer, C.M., In Res.
Res.: 621 W. Adams Blvd., 90007. Tel: 213-749-8950; Fax: 213-749-9137; Email: stvincentparishla@gmail.com.
School—St. Vincent De Paul School, 2333 S. Figueroa St., 90007. Tel: 213-748-5367; Fax: 213-748-5347; Email: principal@stvincentla.net; Web: stvincentla.net. Erika Avila, Prin. Lay Teachers 13; Students 291; Clergy / Religious Teachers 1.
Catechesis Religious Program—
Tel: 213-749-8950, Ext. 115; Email: parish-5440@la-archdiocese.org. Miriam Cruz, D.R.E. Students 250.
Mission—Santo Nino, 601 E. 23rd St., Los Angeles Co. 90011. Tel: 213-748-5246.

95—VISITATION (1943) [JC]
6561 W. 88th St., 90045. Tel: 310-216-1145; Email: Visitationchurch497@gmail.com; Email: parish-4970@la-archdiocese.org; Web: www.visitationchurch-la.com. Rev. Msgr. James Forsen; Revs. James M. Anguiano, In Res.; Timothy McGowan, In Res.
School—Visitation School, (Grades PreK-8), 8740 Emerson Ave., 90045. Tel: 310-645-6620; Email: school-8100@la-archdiocese.org; Web: www.visitationschool.org. Christopher Watson, Prin. Lay Teachers 25; Students 263.
Catechesis Religious Program—
Tel: 310-216-1145, Ext. 20; Email: religiouseducationvc@gmail.com. Debra Evans, D.R.E. Students 107.

OUTSIDE THE CITY OF LOS ANGELES

ALHAMBRA, LOS ANGELES CO.

1—ALL SOULS (1912)
1500 W. Main St., Alhambra, 91801. Rev. Patrick Mbazuigwe.
Res.: 29 S. Electric Ave., Alhambra, 91801.
Tel: 626-281-0466; Fax: 626-281-2163; Email: allsoulscc@allsouls-la.org; Web: www.allsouls-la.org.
School—All Souls Catholic School, (Grades PreK-8), Tel: 626-282-5695; Fax: 626-282-2260; Email: school-7530@la-archdiocese.org. Carrie Fuller, Prin. Lay Teachers 12; Students 180.
Catechesis Religious Program—
Tel: 626-281-0466, Ext. 214; Email: jsramirez@allsouls-la.org. J. Sergio Ramirez, D.R.E. Students 208.

2—ST. THERESE (1924)
510 N. El Molino St., Alhambra, 91801. Revs. Philip Sullivan, O.C.D.; Bernard Perkins, O.C.D.; David Guzman, O.C.D.
Res.: 520 N. Vega, Alhambra, 91801.
Tel: 626-282-2744; Fax: 626-282-7560; Email: parish-4460@la-archdiocese.org.
School—St. Therese School, (Grades PreK-8), 1106 E. Alhambra Rd., Alhambra, 91801.
Tel: 626-289-3364; Fax: 626-284-6700; Email: admin@sainttheresecarmeliteschool.com; Web: sainttheresecarmeliteschool.com. Alma Cornejo, Prin. Lay Teachers 18; Students 100; Clergy / Religious Teachers 3.
Catechesis Religious Program—
Tel: 626-284-0020, Ext. 225. Rhonda Storey, D.R.E. Students 127.

3—ST. THOMAS MORE (1948) Revs. Thai Le; Jeremiah O'Neill, Pastor Emeritus, (Retired); Deacon Rogelio Garcia; Sr. Andrea Johnson, C.S.H., Liturgy Dir.
Res.: 2510 S. Fremont Ave., Alhambra, 91803.
Tel: 626-284-8333; Fax: 626-282-4459; Email: parish-4470@la-archdiocese.org; Web: www.stmcatholicalhambra.org.
School—St. Thomas More School, (Grades PreK-8), Tel: 626-284-5778; Email: school-7660@la-archdiocese.org. Mrs. Judith Jones, Prin. Lay Teachers 9; Students 220.
Catechesis Religious Program—
Tel: 626-284-8333, Ext. 139; Email: stmdrealhambra@gmail.com. Mae Ho, D.R.E. Students 135.

ALTADENA, LOS ANGELES CO.

1—ST. ELIZABETH OF HUNGARY (1918) Rev. Modesto Lewis Perez, J.C.D.; Deacons Jose Gallegos; Charles A. Mitchell; Douglas Cremer.
Office: 1879 N. Lake Ave., Altadena, 91001.
Tel: 626-797-1167; Fax: 626-797-9245; Email: parish-4400@la-archdiocese.org; Web: saintelizabethchurch.org.
School—St. Elizabeth of Hungary School, (Grades PreK-8), 1840 N. Lake Ave., Altadena, 91001.
Tel: 626-797-7727; Fax: 626-797-6541; Email: school-7600@la-archdiocese.org; Web: saint-elizabeth.org. Richard Gruttadaurio, Prin. Lay Teachers 14; Students 221.
Catechesis Religious Program—
Tel: 626-797-1167, Ext. 15; Email: mgalindo@saintelizabethchurch.org. Ms. Cary Novellas, Admin. Students 225.

2—SACRED HEART (1935) (African American—Hispanic)
2889 N. Lincoln Ave., Altadena, 91001.
Tel: 626-794-2046; Fax: 626-794-8315; Email: sacredheartchurch@att.net; Web: sacredheartaltadena.com. Rev. Jose Vaughn Banal, Ph.D.; Rev. Msgr. Loreto Gonzales.
Catechesis Religious Program—Tel: 626-798-6961; Email: lindagutierrez95@yahoo.com. Florinda Gutierrez, D.R.E. Students 184.

ARCADIA, LOS ANGELES CO., HOLY ANGELS (1935)
Email: parish-4530@la-archdiocese.org. Revs. Kevin E. Rettig; Blaise N. Brockman; Deacons Arnaldo Lopez; Bruce Sago; Sergio Perez.
Res.: 370 Campus Dr., Arcadia, 91007.
Tel: 626-447-1671; Email: ha@holyangelsarcadia.org; Web: www.holyangelsarcadia.org.
School—Holy Angels School, (Grades PreK-8), 360 Campus Dr., Arcadia, 91007. Tel: 626-447-6312; Fax: 626-447-2843; Email: admin@holyangelsarcadia.org. Mrs. Aimee Dyrek, Prin. Lay Teachers 20; Students 305.
Catechesis Religious Program—Email: pp@holyangelsarcadia.org. Pat Perez. Students 395.

ARTESIA, LOS ANGELES CO., HOLY FAMILY (1931) Revs. John Cordero, M.M.H.C.; Joachim E. Ablanida, M.M.H.C.
Res.: 18708 S. Clarkdale Ave., Artesia, 90701.
Tel: 562-865-2185; Fax: 562-860-0718; Email: businessoffice@holyfamilyartesia.org; Email: parish-5910@la-archdiocese.org; Web: www.holyfamilyartesia.org.
School—Our Lady of Fatima, (Grades PreK-8), 18626 S. Clarkdale Ave., Artesia, 90701.
Tel: 562-865-1621; Email: olfbusinessoffice@olfartesia.org; Email: school-8970@la-archdiocese.org. Luis Hayes, Prin. Lay Teachers 10; Students 246.
Catechesis Religious Program—Tel: 562-860-5973; Email: teresap@holyfamilyartesia.org. Teresa Paulino, D.R.E. Students 732.

AVALON, LOS ANGELES CO., ST. CATHERINE OF ALEXANDRIA (1902)
Mailing Address: P.O. Box 735, Avalon, 90704. Rev. William E. Ruther.
Res.: 800 Beacon St., Avalon, 90704.
Tel: 310-510-0192; Fax: 310-510-8360; Email: stcatherineofavalon@gmail.com; Web: www.stcatherineoncatalinaisland.org.
Catechesis Religious Program—Lynda Poindexter, D.R.E.; Hermida Hernandez, D.R.E. Students 115.

AZUSA, LOS ANGELES CO., ST. FRANCES OF ROME (1908) [CEM] (Hispanic) Revs. Richard Vega; Michael S. Grieco; Roque A.D. Fernandes, (Retired); Deacons Ernesto Vital; Juan Rogelio Garcia.
Res.: 501 E. Foothill Blvd., P.O. Box 637, Azusa, 91702. Tel: 626-969-1829; Fax: 626-815-2755; Email: parish-4610@la-archdiocese.org.
School—St. Frances of Rome School, (Grades PreK-8), 734 N. Pasadena Ave., Azusa, 91702.
Tel: 626-334-2018; Fax: 626-815-2760; Email: school-7760@la-archdiocese.org. Dr. Brian Wagner, Prin. Lay Teachers 9; Students 210.
Catechesis Religious Program—508 N. Soldano, Azusa, 91702. Lupe Roberts, D.R.E. Students 720.

BALDWIN PARK, LOS ANGELES CO., ST. JOHN THE BAPTIST (1946) (Hispanic—Filipino) Revs. Michael D. Gutierrez; Jonathon Meyer; Cesar Fonseca; Jude Uche.
Res.: 3848 Stewart Ave., Baldwin Park, 91706.
Tel: 626-960-2795; Fax: 626-472-0029; Email: info@stjohnsbp.org.
School—St. John the Baptist School, 3870 Stewart Ave., Baldwin Park, 91706. Tel: 626-337-1421; Fax: 626-337-3733; Email: school-7770@la-archdiocese.org. Sr. Rosario Mediavilla, Prin. Lay Teachers 16; Students 550; Clergy / Religious Teachers 3.
Catechesis Religious Program—Tel: 626-962-1004. Briceida Bugarin, D.R.E. Students 466.
Convent—3963 Baldwin Park Blvd., Baldwin Park, 91706. Tel: 626-337-0527. Sisters 9.

BELL GARDENS, LOS ANGELES CO., ST. GERTRUDE (1938) Revs. Nabor Rios, V.F.; Robert McGowan.
Res.: 7025 Garfield Ave., Bell Gardens, 90201.
Tel: 562-927-4495; Fax: 562-927-5826; Email: parish-5820@la-archdiocese.org.
School—St. Gertrude School, (Grades K-8), 6824 Toler Ave., Bell Gardens, 90201. Tel: 562-927-1216; Email: principal@stgertrudethegreat.com; Web: www.stgertrudethegreat.org. Mary Flock, Prin. Lay Teachers 10; Students 200.
Catechesis Religious Program—Tel: 562-927-3185; Email: stgertrude@verizon.net. Students 226.

BELLFLOWER, LOS ANGELES CO.
1—ST. BERNARD (1923) Rev. Toribio Gutierrez, C.M., Admin.; Deacon Ralph Riera.
Res.: 9647 E. Beach St., Bellflower, 90706.
Tel: 562-867-2337; Fax: 562-867-4863; Email: parish-5790@la-archdiocese.org; Web: www.stbernard-bellflower.com.
School—St. Bernard School, (Grades PreK-8), 9626 Park St., Bellflower, 90706. Tel: 562-867-9410; Email: sbprincipal1946@gmail.com; Email: sboffice16@gmail.com. Mr. James Cordero, Prin. Lay Teachers 12; Students 161.
Catechesis Religious Program—Tel: 562-925-9886; Email: ron_armendariz@yahoo.com. Roy Armendariz, D.R.E. Students 495.
2—ST. DOMINIC SAVIO (1954)
13400 Bellflower Blvd., Bellflower, 90706. Revs. Chinh D. Nguyen, S.D.B.; Andrew Ng, S.D.B.; Luis Flores Farias; Roberto Ledezma.
Res.: 9720 Foster Rd., Bellflower, 90706.
Tel: 562-920-7796; Fax: 562-920-0149; Email: parish-5800@la-archdiocese.org; Web: saintdominicsavio.org.
School—St. Dominic Savio School, (Grades PreK-8), 9750 Foster Rd., Bellflower, 90706.
Tel: 562-866-3617; Fax: 562-867-0887; Email: savioschool@sdss-bellflower.org; Web: sdss-bellflower.org. Mrs. Maria Watson, Prin. Lay Teachers 12; Students 321; Clergy / Religious Teachers 1.
Catechesis Religious Program—
Tel: 562-920-7796, Ext. 317; Email: vitapalacios@gmail.com. Sr. Carmen Palacions, F.M.A., D.R.E. Students 691.
BEVERLY HILLS, LOS ANGELES CO., GOOD SHEPHERD (1923)
504 N. Roxbury Dr., Beverly Hills, 90210.
Tel: 310-285-5425; Fax: 310-285-5433; Email: info@gsbh.org; Web: www.gsbh.org. Revs. Edward C. Benioff; George Patrick O'Brien, In Res., (Retired); Colm O'Ryan, In Res., (Retired).
Res.: 505 N. Bedford Dr., Beverly Hills, 90210.
Email: parish-4800@la-archdiocese.org.
School—Good Shepherd School, (Grades PreK-8), 148 S. Linden Dr., Beverly Hills, 90212.
Tel: 310-275-8601; Fax: 310-275-0366; Email: school-7940@la-archdiocese.org; Web: www.gsbh.net. Danielle Colvert, Prin. Lay Teachers 16; Students 195.
Catechesis Religious Program—Wendy Rappe. Students 52.
BURBANK, LOS ANGELES CO.
1—ST. FINBAR (1938)
Tel: 818-940-3921. Revs. Francis Mendoza; Christopher Bazyouros, In Res.
Res.: 2010 W. Olive Ave., Burbank, 91506.
Tel: 818-846-6251; Fax: 818-846-1703; Email: parish-3740@la-archdiocese.org.
School—St. Finbar School, 2120 W. Olive Ave., Burbank, 91506. Tel: 818-848-0191;
Fax: 818-848-4315; Email: finbar4545@yahoo.com; Email: school-7070@la-archdiocese.org; Web: www.saintfinbar.org. Mr. Michael Marasco, Prin. Lay Teachers 30; Students 300; Clergy / Religious Teachers 1.
Catechesis Religious Program—Email: sally@stfinbarburbank.org. Sally Meyers, D.R.E. Students 330.
2—ST. FRANCIS XAVIER (1954) Revs. Sebastian Vettickal, C.M.I., Admin., Admin.; Benny George, C.M.I., (India); Deacons Jaime Abrera; James Roope; Rita Recker, Pastoral Assoc. & Business Mgr.
Res.: 3801 Scott Rd., Burbank, 91504.
Tel: 818-504-4400; Fax: 818-767-5096; Email: rectory@sfxburbank.com; Email: parish-3760@la-archdiocese.org; Web: www.sfxburbank.com.
School—St. Francis Xavier School, (Grades PreK-8), 3601 Scott Rd., Burbank, 91504. Tel: 818-504-4422; Email: school-7090@la-archdiocese.org. Dr. Paul Sullivan, Prin. Lay Teachers 10; Students 307.
Catechesis Religious Program—Tel: 818-504-4411; Email: religioused@sfxburbank.com. Rosie Roope, C.R.E. Students 142.
3—ST. ROBERT BELLARMINE (1907)
143 N. Fifth St., Burbank, 91501. Rev. John Collins; Rev. Msgr. Francis T. Wallace, J.C.L., (Retired).
Ministry Center (Offices):—520 E. Orange Grove Ave., Burbank, 91501. Tel: 818-846-3443;
Fax: 818-954-9441; Email: parish-3800@la-archdiocese.org.
Res.: 133 N. Fifth St., Burbank, 91501.
School—St. Robert Bellarmine School, (Grades PreK-8), 154 N. Fifth St., Burbank, 91501.
Tel: 818-842-5033; Fax: 818-842-9789; Email: info@strobertbellarmineburbank.com; Web: strobertbellarmineburbank.com. Angite Riggio, Prin. Lay Teachers 12; Students 200.
Catechesis Religious Program—Email: cgallagher@srbburbank.org. Carol Gallagher, D.R.E. Students 243.
CAMARILLO, VENTURA CO.
1—ST. JUNIPERO SERRA (1988)
5205 Upland Rd., Camarillo, 93012.
Tel: 805-482-6417; Email: parish-3320@la-archdiocese.org. Rev. Patrick Mullen; Deacons Isaac (Ike) Edie; Bob Fargo; Genaro Roy Gacasan; Neil Joseph Kingsley; Luc Papillon; John Picard; Jack William Redmond II; Arnold Peter Reyes; William Spies; Joseph Felix Torti.
Catechesis Religious Program—Tere Delgado, D.R.E. Students 510.
2—ST. MARY MAGDALEN (1940) Revs. Preston P. Passos; Fidelis C. Omeaku; Deacons George Bednar; George J. Esseff Jr.; Johnnie Hammonds; Larry Modugno; Anh Quoc Vu; Ronald Dale Moon; Andrew Cottam; Manuel J. Martinez.
Res.: 2532 Ventura Blvd., Camarillo, 93010.
Tel: 805-484-0532; Fax: 805-987-2941; Email: office@smmcam.org; Web: www.smmcam.org.
School—St. Mary Magdalen School, (Grades PreK-8), 2534 Ventura Blvd., Camarillo, 93010.
Tel: 805-482-2611; Fax: 805-987-8211; Email: school-6670@la-archdiocese.org; Email: office@smmschool.net; Web: www.smmschool.net. Michael Ronan, Prin. Lay Teachers 15; Students 280.
Catechesis Religious Program—Tel: 805-482-1219; Email: redirector@smmcam.org. Mrs. Colleen Schulze, D.R.E.; Mr. Jeremiah Shoop, Youth Min. Students 305.
CANOGA PARK, LOS ANGELES CO., OUR LADY OF THE VALLEY (1921)
22021 Gault St., Canoga Park, 91303-1804.
Tel: 818-592-2880; Fax: 818-592-0299; Email: receptionist@olvcp.org. Revs. Arturo Velasco; Raul Gatbonton, M.M.H.C.; Miguel Angel Cortes; Danilo Guinto.
School—Our Lady of the Valley School, 22041 Gault St., Canoga Park, 91303-1804. Tel: 818-592-2894; Email: principal@olvcrusaders.org; Web: www.olvcrusaders.org. Mr. Miguel Beltran, Prin. Lay Teachers 10; Students 192.
Catechesis Religious Program—Sr. Estrela del Bando, C.H.S., D.R.E. Students 638.
CARPINTERIA, SANTA BARBARA CO., ST. JOSEPH (1933)
1500 Linden Ave., Carpinteria, 93013.
Tel: 805-684-2181; Fax: 805-684-0534; Email: stjoseph@stjosephchurch.org; Email: martha@stjosephchurch.org; Email: parish-3060@la-archdiocese.org; Web: www.stjosephchurch.org. 1532 Linden Ave., Carpinteria, 93013. Rev. Msgr. Richard Martini; Revs. Jose Castaneda; David M. Velazquez, Pastor Emeritus; Deacons Genaro Aispuro; Michael Joseph Betliskey.
Catechesis Religious Program—
Tel: 805-684-2181, Ext. 115; Cell: 805-696-3773; Email: nancy@stjosephchurch.org. Nancy Perez, D.R.E. Students 210.
Chapel—4691 7th St., Carpinteria, 93013.
CARSON, LOS ANGELES CO., ST. PHILOMENA (1956) [CEM] Revs. Francis Ilano; Demetrio L. Bugayong, Pastor Emeritus, (Retired); Alidor Mikobi, C.J., (Democratic Republic of Congo); Mikaele Mataafa.
Res.: 21900 S. Main St., Carson, 90745.
Tel: 310-835-7161; Fax: 310-830-5494; Email: parish-6210@la-archdiocese.org; Web: www.StPhilomenaParish.org.
School—St. Philomena School, (Grades PreK-8), 21832 S. Main St., Carson, 90745. Tel: 310-835-4827; Fax: 310-835-1655; Email: school-9240@la-archdiocese.org; Web: www.stphilomenaschool.org. Sr. Mary John Schik, Prin. Lay Teachers 12; Students 325.
Catechesis Religious Program—Tel: 310-830-6180; Email: rmgrosa@yahoo.com. Rosa Garcia, D.R.E. Students 832.
Convent—21832 1/2 S. Main St., Carson, 90745.
Tel: 310-834-9180. Sisters 4.
CHATSWORTH, LOS ANGELES CO., ST. JOHN EUDES (1963)
9901 Mason Ave., Chatsworth, 91311. Revs. Lawrence Goodwin, C.J.M.; Carlos Valencia, C.J.M.; Ben Drapeau, C.J.M., In Res.; Rev. Msgr. Emigdio Herrera, Admin., (Retired).
Res.: 9943 Mason Ave., Chatsworth, 91311.
School—St. John Eudes School, 9925 Mason Ave., Chatsworth, 91311. Tel: 818-341-1454;
Fax: 818-341-3093; Email: Principal@school.stjohneudes.org; Web: http://sjeschool.net/. Barbara Danowitz, Prin. Lay Teachers 17; Students 310.
Catechesis Religious Program—Students 454.
CLAREMONT, LOS ANGELES CO., OUR LADY OF THE ASSUMPTION (1947) Revs. Charles J. Ramirez; Thuan Nguyen; Christopher Troxell; Ronald Lee Clark; Rev. Msgr. Peter A. O'Reilly, In Res., (Retired); Deacons Arthur Escovedo, (Retired); Robert Steighner; John Tullius; Joe Domond; James Allgaier.
Res.: 435 Berkeley Ave., Claremont, 91711.
Tel: 909-626-3596; Fax: 909-624-3680; Email: parish-4670@la-archdiocese.org; Web: www.olaclaremont.org.
School—Our Lady of the Assumption School, (Grades PreK-8), 611 W. Bonita Ave., Claremont, 91711.
Tel: 909-626-7135; Fax: 909-398-1395; Email: school-7840@la-archdiocese.org; Web: www.ola-ca.org. Bernadette Boyle, Prin. Lay Teachers 20; Students 415.
Catechesis Religious Program—Tel: 909-624-1360; Email: ffoffice@olaclaremont.org. Maria Elena Cardena, D.R.E. Students 440.
COMMERCE, LOS ANGELES CO., ST. MARCELLINUS (1957) Rev. Gilbert Cruz, Sacramental Min.; Dr. Humberto Ramos, Ph.D., Parish Life Dir.
Res.: 2349 Strong Ave., Commerce, 90040.
Tel: 323-269-2733; Fax: 323-269-2106; Email: Parish-4270@la-archdiocese.org; Web: marcellinus.org.
Catechesis Religious Program—Tel: 323-266-4938; Email: adq311@yahoo.com. Alejandra Duarte, D.R.E. Students 150.
COMPTON, LOS ANGELES CO.
1—ST. ALBERT THE GREAT (1949) [CEM] (Hispanic—African American)
804 E. Compton Blvd., Rancho Dominguez, 90220.
Tel: 310-329-7548; Email: parish-5760@la-archdiocese.org. Rev. Humberto Bernabe; Deacon Victor Cruz.
Schools—St. Albert the Great Elementary School—(Grades PreK-5), Tel: 310-323-4559; Email: school-8800@la-archdiocese.org; Web: www.stalbertthegreatschool.org. Tina Johnson, Prin. Lay Teachers 12; Students 120.
St. Albert the Great Middle School, (Grades 6-8), 823 E. Compton Blvd., Rancho Dominguez, 90220.
Tel: 310-515-3891; Email: school-9410@la-archdiocese.org; Web: www.stalbertthegreatms.com.
Catechesis Religious Program—Tel: 310-323-1599. Arturo Gallardo, D.R.E. Students 450.
2—OUR LADY OF VICTORY (1920) (Hispanic—African American) Revs. Francisco Valdovinos, S.T., (Mexico); Carlos Zacarias, S.T.; Charles Gordon, S.T.; Bro. Andres Rivera, S.T., Pastoral Assoc.
Res.: 519 E. Palmer St., Compton, 90221.
Tel: 310-631-3233; Fax: 310-886-5681; Email: ourladyofvictory@aol.com; Email: parish-5740@la-archdiocese.org.
School—Our Lady of Victory School, (Grades PreK-8), 601 E. Palmer St., Compton, 90221.
Tel: 310-631-1320; Fax: 310-631-4280; Email: principal@ourladyofvictorycatholicschool.org; Web: ourladyofvictorycatholicschool.org. Deacon Arturo Gonzalez, Prin. Lay Teachers 10; Students 218.
Catechesis Religious Program—Tel: 310-631-1831. Ana Aguilar, D.R.E. Students 232.
3—SAGRADO CORAZON, SACRED HEART (1956) (Hispanic) Rev. Victor Raul Ramos; Deacon Jose Oscar Barrera.
Res.: 1720 N. Culver Ave., Compton, 90222.
Tel: 310-635-5436; Fax: 310-635-2121; Email: Parish-5750@la-archdiocese.org.
Catechesis Religious Program—1705 N. Culver Ave., Compton, 90222. Students 290.
COVINA, LOS ANGELES CO.
1—ST. LOUISE DE MARILLAC (1963)
1720 E. Covina Blvd., Covina, 91724.
Tel: 626-915-7873; Fax: 626-332-4431; Email: info@stlouisedm.org; Web: www.stlouisedm.org. Revs. Robert P. Fulton; Joseph Richard McShane; Deacons Peter Brause; Alan Holderness; Al Valles; Omar Uriarte.
School—St. Louise de Marillac School, (Grades PreK-8), 1728 E. Covina Blvd., Covina, 91724. Ms. Joanne Testacross, Prin. Lay Teachers 10; Students 253; Clergy / Religious Teachers 6.
Catechesis Religious Program—Tel: 626-332-5822; Email: TeresaC@stlouisedm.org. Teresa Culjak, D.R.E. Students 358.
2—SACRED HEART (1927) Rev. William T. Easterling, V.F.; Rev. Msgr. Brian M. Cavanagh, (Retired); Revs. Gabriel Lui, (Retired); James J. Kelly; Spencer Mayer Lewerenz; Deacons John G. Horn; Ronald Butler; Rodolfo R. Leyva.
Res.: 344 W. Workman St., Covina, 91723.
Tel: 626-332-3570; Fax: 626-967-4884; Email: parish-4580@la-archdiocese.org.
School—Sacred Heart School, (Grades PreK-8), 360 W. Workman St., Covina, 91723. Tel: 626-332-7222; Fax: 626-967-8836; Email: shscovina@hotmail.com; Email: school-7730@la-archdiocese.org; Web: www.shs.cc. Mrs. Claudia Tice, Prin. Lay Teachers 19; Students 204.
Catechesis Religious Program—Tel: 626-331-7914; Fax: 626-966-7165. Students 517.
CUDAHY, LOS ANGELES CO., SAGRADO CORAZON Y SANTA MARIA DE GUADALUPE (1991) [JC] (Hispanic)
4235 Clara St., Cudahy, 90201. Tel: 323-562-3356; Email: parish-6040@la-archdiocese.org. Revs. Miguel Angel Gutierrez, M.S.C.; Adrian Lopez.
Catechesis Religious Program—Students 380.
CULVER CITY, LOS ANGELES CO., ST. AUGUSTINE (1919) Revs. Christopher B. Fagan; Timothy R. Grumbach; Most Rev. Thomas J. Curry, D.D., Ph.D., V.G., In Res., (Retired); Deacons Rafael A. Victorin; Sonal Seneviratne, Business Mgr.
Res.: 3850 Jasmine Ave., Culver City, 90232.
Tel: 310-838-2477; Fax: 310-838-3070; Email:

augustineadmin1A@sbcglobal.net; Web: st-augustine-church.org.
Child Care—St. Augustine Licenced Preschool, Email: mrubio@sasmail.org. Minerva Rubio, Dir.
School—St. Augustine School, (Grades PreK-8), 3819 Clarington Ave., Culver City, 90232.
Tel: 310-838-3144; Fax: 310-838-7479; Email: bnguyen@la-archdiocese.org; Email: mbriseno@sasmail.org; Web: www.staugustineschool.com. Mrs. Beate Nguyen, Prin. Lay Teachers 18; Students 206.
Catechesis Religious Program—
Tel: 310-838-2477, Ext. 404; Email: tannepalmer@staugustineadla.org. Mrs. Terri Palmer, D.R.E. Students 520.

DIAMOND BAR, LOS ANGELES CO., ST. DENIS (1971)
2151 S. Diamond Bar Blvd., Diamond Bar, 91765-2981. Tel: 909-861-7106; Email: parish-4690@la-archdiocese.org. Revs. John Palmer, Admin.; Vincent Arogyaswamy, Parochial Vicar; Deacons Alfred Guerrero; Tom Le Donne; Dennis Shin; Philip Luevanos.
Catechesis Religious Program—Celia Flores, D.R.E. Students 322.

DOWNEY, LOS ANGELES CO.
1—OUR LADY OF PERPETUAL HELP (1909)
Mailing Address: 10445 S. Downey Ave., Downey, 90241. Rev. Msgr. Lorenzo Miranda; Rev. Ambrose Udoji; Deacons Richard J. Medina; Carlos Origel, Email: origel@aol.com.
Res.: 10727 S. Downey Ave., Downey, 90241.
Tel: 562-923-3246; Fax: 562-862-7020; Email: olphoffice@ca.rr.com.
School—Our Lady of Perpetual Help School, 10441 S. Downey Ave., Downey, 90241. Tel: 562-869-9969; Fax: 562-923-0659; Email: school-8770@la-archdiocese.org; Web: ourladyschool.com. Theresa Voeltz, Prin. Lay Teachers 19; Students 328.
Catechesis Religious Program—Theresa Nicholas, D.R.E. Students 580.
2—ST. RAYMOND (1956) Revs. John Higgins; Paul Thomas Padinja-Nedumparambil, O.C.D.
Res.: 12348 Paramount Blvd., Downey, 90242.
Tel: 562-923-4509; Fax: 562-869-3359; Email: straydny@aol.com; Email: parish5870@la-archdiocese.org.
School—St. Raymond School, 12320 Paramount Blvd., Downey, 90242. Tel: 562-862-3210;
Fax: 562-862-6328; Web: www.straymondschool-downey.org/. Mrs. Claudia Rodarte, Prin. Lay Teachers 16; Students 350.
Catechesis Religious Program—Tel: 562-862-6959. Sr. Paula Strohfus, C.H.F., D.R.E. Students 441.

EL MONTE, LOS ANGELES CO.
1—NATIVITY (1923) Revs. Alberto Villalobos; Joseph Dang Kim Nguyen; Joseph Q. Nguyen, Pastoral Assoc.
Res.: 3743 N. Tyler Ave., El Monte, 91731.
Tel: 626-444-2511; Fax: 626-443-1417; Email: parish@mynativity.org.
School—Nativity School, 10907 St. Louis Dr., El Monte, 91731. Tel: 626-448-2414; Fax: 626-448-2763; Email: principal@nativityschoolelmonte.org; Web: www.nativityschoolelmonte.org. Sr. Stacy Reiniman, Prin. Lay Teachers 11; Students 265; Clergy / Religious Teachers 1.
Catechesis Religious Program—Tel: 626-448-8895. Sandra Jinesta, D.R.E. Students 253.
2—OUR LADY OF GUADALUPE (1973) (Hispanic) Revs. Nicolas Sanchez Toledano; Jesus Castrillo, C.M.F., (Spain); Deacon Jose Guadamuz, Business Mgr.
Res.: 11359 Coffield Ave., El Monte, 91731.
Tel: 626-448-1795; Fax: 626-448-9507; Email: parish-4560@la-archdiocese.org.
Catechesis Religious Program—Tel: 626-448-7131. Sr. Ines Arguello, D.R.E. Students 2,100.

EL SEGUNDO, LOS ANGELES CO.
1—ST. ANDREW (1936) (Russian—Greek) Rt. Rev. Alexei R. Smith.
Res.: 538 Concord St., El Segundo, 90245.
Tel: 310-322-1892; Fax: 310-322-1919; Email: frarsmith@la-archdiocese.org.
Catechesis Religious Program—
2—ST. ANTHONY (1925)
Mailing Address: 215 Lomita St., El Segundo, 90245. Revs. Robert Victoria; Henry L. Hernando, In Res., (Retired).
Res.: 710 E. Grand Ave., El Segundo, 90245.
Tel: 310-322-4392; Fax: 310-322-0797; Email: parish-6120@la-archdiocese.org; Web: www.stanthonyes.com.
School—St. Anthony School, 233 Lomita St., El Segundo, 90245. Tel: 310-322-4218; Email: school-9170@la-archdiocese.org; Web: saselsegundo.org. Sylvia Kawjaree, Prin. Lay Teachers 9; Students 92.
Catechesis Religious Program—
Tel: 310-322-4392, Ext. 444; Email: dre@stathonyes.com. Timothy Rodrick, D.R.E. Students 204.

ENCINO, LOS ANGELES CO.
1—ST. CYRIL (1949)
15520 Ventura Blvd., Encino, 91436. Revs. Eben MacDonald; Cyprian Carlo, In Res., (Retired).
Res.: 4601 Firmament Ave., Encino, 91436.
Tel: 818-986-8234; Fax: 818-986-3310; Email: parish@st-cyril.org; Web: www.st-cyril.org.
School—St. Cyril School, 4548 Haskell Ave., Encino, 91436. Tel: 818-501-4155; Fax: 818-501-8480; Email: school-6800@la-archdiocese.org; Web: www.stcyril.net. Ryan Halverson, Prin.; Angelica Pugliese, Vice Prin. Lay Teachers 16; Students 280.
Catechesis Religious Program—Ray Perry, D.R.E.; Rebekka Viera, D.R.E. Students 110.
2—OUR LADY OF GRACE (1945)
5001 White Oak Ave., Encino, 91316.
Tel: 818-342-4686; Fax: 818-342-6579; Web: www.ourladyofgrace.org. Rev. Msgr. Jarlath Cunnane, V.F.; Revs. Raul Gatbonton, M.M.H.C.; Thomas Feltz, Retired Priest, (Retired); Deacon Glen Heffernan; Jeanne Rogers, Liturgy Dir.; Jill Moore, Dir. of New Evangelization.
Res.: 5011 White Oak Ave., Encino, 91316.
School—Our Lady of Grace School, (Grades PreK-8), 17720 Ventura Blvd., Encino, 91316.
Tel: 818-344-4126; Fax: 818-344-1736; Web: www.ourladyofgrace.com. Joyce Cluess, Prin. Lay Teachers 18; Students 306.
Catechesis Religious Program—Email: dre@ourladyofgrace.org. Dr. Jesse Rodriguez, D.R.E. Students 380.

FILLMORE, VENTURA CO., ST. FRANCIS OF ASSISI (1926) [JC]
1048 W. Ventura St., Fillmore, 93015.
Tel: 805-524-1306; Fax: 805-524-0784; Email: stfrancisoffice@spcglobal.net. Revs. Bernard J. Gatlin, (Retired); Alejandro A. Amayun, (Philippines).
Catechesis Religious Program—Email: parish-3210@la-archdiocese.org. Michael Lara, D.R.E. Students 312.

GARDENA, LOS ANGELES CO.
1—ST. ANTHONY OF PADUA (1910) Rev. Msgr. Sabato "Sal" A. Pilato; Revs. Julio Domenech; Randy Raul Campos, In Res.; Jonathon Meyer, In Res.; Deacon Antonio Huerta.
Res.: 1050 W. 163rd St., Gardena, 90247.
Tel: 310-327-5830; Fax: 310-327-6440; Email: parish-5780@la-archdiocese.org; Web: www.saintanthonygardena.org.
School—St. Anthony of Padua School, 1003 W. 163rd St., Gardena, 90247. Tel: 310-329-7170;
Fax: 310-329-9843; Email: school-8820@la-archdiocese.org; Web: www.stanthonygardena.org. Mrs. Angela Grey, Prin. Lay Teachers 9; Students 231.
Catechesis Religious Program—Tel: 310-323-0860; Email: parish-5780@la-archdiocese.org. Madonna Castro, D.R.E. Students 702.
2—MARIA REGINA (1956) [CEM] Rev. Sang V. Tran, (Vietnam); Rev. Msgr. Thomas M. Acton, In Res., (Retired); Deacons Phuoc Van Nguyen; Ramon Nunez.
Res.: 2150 W. 135th St., Gardena, 90249.
Tel: 310-323-0030; Fax: 310-323-8081; Email: office@mariareginagardena.net; Web: www.mariareginagardena.net.
School—Maria Regina School, 13510 S. Van Ness Ave., Gardena, 90249. Tel: 310-327-9133;
Fax: 310-327-2636; Email: school-8760@la-archdiocese.org; Web: mregina.org. Lynette Lino, Prin. Lay Teachers 10; Students 217.
Catechesis Religious Program—Yolanda Marquez, D.R.E. Students 300.

GLENDALE, LOS ANGELES CO.
1—INCARNATION (1927)
121 W. Glenoaks Blvd., Glendale, 91202.
Tel: 818-242-2579; Fax: 818-507-4976; Email: receptionist@incaglendale.org. Rev. John Terrence O'Brien; Rev. Msgr. Helmut A. Hefner, J.C.L., In Res., (Retired); Deacons Serj Harutunian; Dominic Pontrelli.
Res.: 1001 N. Brand Blvd., Glendale, 91202-2979.
School—Church of the Incarnation School, (Grades PreK-8), 123 W. Glenoaks Blvd., Glendale, 91202-2908. Tel: 818-241-2269; Fax: 818-241-4734; Email: school-6920@la-archdiocese.org; Web: www.incaschool.org. Dr. Colby Boysen, Prin. Lay Teachers 17; Students 252.
Child Care—Pre-School, 214 W. Fairview, Glendale, 91202. Tel: 818-241-2264; Fax: 818-241-0876; Email: preschool@incaschool.org. Dr. Colby Boysen, Prin. Students 28; Clergy / Religious Teachers 4.
Catechesis Religious Program—Email: religioused@incaglendale.org. Gloria Figueroa, D.R.E. Students 212.
2—HOLY FAMILY (1907)
209 E. Lomita Ave., Glendale, 91205.
Tel: 818-247-2222; Email: parish@hfglendale.org; Web: www.hfglendale.org. Revs. James M. Bevacqua; Luis Espinoza; Marlon Mateo; Deacons John Steele; Ron Baker; Neon Recuenco.
Res.: 321 E. Elk Ave., Glendale, 91205. Email: parish-3550@la-archdiocese.org.
School—Holy Family Grade School, (Grades PreK-8), 400 S. Louise St., Glendale, 91205.
Tel: 818-243-9239; Email: fsuelto@la-archdiocese.org; Email: school-6890@la-archdiocese.org; Web: www.hfgsglendale.org. Dr. Fidela Suelto, Prin. Lay Teachers 18; Students 270.
High School—Holy Family High School, (Girls) College Prep 400 E. Lomita Ave., Glendale, 91205.
Tel: 818-241-3178; Fax: 818-241-7753; Email: jreiken@hfhsglendale.org; Web: hfhsglendale.org. Dr. Joe Reiken, Prin. Lay Teachers 18; Students 120.
Catechesis Religious Program—
Tel: 818-247-2222, Ext. 382 and ext. 381; Email: reled@hfglendale.org. Sandra Rodas, D.R.E. Students 405.

GLENDORA, LOS ANGELES CO., ST. DOROTHY (1958)
Tel: 626-914-3941, Ext. 117; Email: lneag@stdorothy.org. Rev. Raymont Medina; Rev. Msgr. Norman F. Priebe, V.F., Admin. Pro Tem, (Retired); Deacon Steve Marsh.
Res.: 241 S. Valley Center, Glendora, 91741-3854.
Tel: 626-914-3941; Fax: 626-335-0059; Email: parish-4600@la-archdiocese.org; Email: lneag@stdorothy.org; Web: www.stdorothy.org.
School—St. Dorothy School, (Grades PreK-8), 215 S. Valley Center Ave., Glendora, 91741.
Tel: 626-335-0772; Email: info@stdorothyschool.com; Web: www.stdorothyschool.com. Adrienne Ferguson, Prin. Lay Teachers 12; Students 175.
Catechesis Religious Program—Tel: 626-335-2811. Mrs. Bernadette M. Martin, D.R.E. Students 327.

GOLETA, SANTA BARBARA CO.
1—ST. MARK UNIVERSITY PARISH (1966) [CEM] Rev. John W. Love, V.F.
Res.: 6550 Picasso Rd., Goleta, 93117.
Tel: 805-968-1078; Fax: 805-968-3965; Email: parish-3070@la-archdiocese.org; Web: www.saint-marks.net.
Catechesis Religious Program— Twinned with St. Raphael, Goleta Maria Moreno, D.R.E. Students 45.
2—ST. RAPHAEL (1896) Rev. Msgr. Jon F. Majarucon, V.F.; Deacons Sergio López Macías; Wayne Rascati; Stephen Montross.
Res.: 5444 Hollister Ave., Santa Barbara, 93111-2308. Tel: 805-967-5641; Fax: 805-964-2988; Email: parish-3080@la-archdiocese.org; Email: Raphstgo@yahoo.com; Web: Straphaelsb.org.
School—St. Raphael School, (Grades PreK-8), 160 St. Joseph St., Santa Barbara, 93111.
Tel: 805-967-2115; Fax: 805-683-9765; Email: office@srs805.org; Web: straphaelschoolsb.org. Michelle Limb, Prin. Lay Teachers 15; Students 244.
Catechesis Religious Program—Ana Solis-Cervantes, C.R.E. (Bilingual); Karen Froelicher, C.R.E. (English). Students 800.

GRANADA HILLS, LOS ANGELES CO.
1—ST. EUPHRASIA (1963) Rev. Msgr. James C. Gehl.
Res.: 11766 Shoshone Ave., Granada Hills, 91344.
Tel: 818-360-4611; Fax: 818-360-2755; Email: parish-3890@la-archdiocese.org; Email: jcgste@hotmail.com.
School—St. Euphrasia School, 17637 Mayerling St., Granada Hills, 91344. Tel: 818-363-5515; Email: school-7200@la-archdiocese.org; Web: www.steuphrasiaschool.org. Mary Blair, Prin. Lay Teachers 12; Students 215; Clergy / Religious Teachers 1.
Catechesis Religious Program—Email: domingueze57@yahoo.com. Sr. Elizabeth Dominguez, D.R.E. Students 220.
2—ST. JOHN BAPTIST DE LA SALLE (1953) Rev. Ramon G. Valera; Rev. Msgr. Robert L. Milbauer, V.F., Pastor Emeritus, (Retired); Rev. Yesupadam Teneti; Deacons Samuel Frias; Dan Revetto.
Res.: 10738 Hayvenhurst Ave., Granada Hills, 91344. Tel: 818-363-2535; Fax: 818-360-7407; Web: parish-3910@la-archdiocese.org; Web: sjbdls.com.
School—St. John Baptist de la Salle School, 16535 Chatsworth St., Granada Hills, 91344.
Tel: 818-363-2270; Fax: 818-832-8950; Email: office@sjbdls.org; Web: www.sjbdls.org. Monica Castaneda, Prin. Lay Teachers 14; Students 380.
Catechesis Religious Program—Tel: 818-368-1514; Email: dre@sjbdls.org. Sandy Cole, D.R.E. Students 550.

GUADALUPE, SANTA BARBARA CO., OUR LADY OF GUADALUPE (1867) [JC] (Hispanic) Rev. Rolando A. Sierra.
Res.: 1164 Obispo St., P.O. Box 897, Guadalupe, 93434. Tel: 805-343-2181; Fax: 805-343-6642; Email: olgguadalupe@gmail.com.
Catechesis Religious Program—Tel: 805-343-4404; Email: dfunkhouser@la-archdiocese.org. Dawn Funkhouser, D.R.E. Students 229.

HACIENDA HEIGHTS, LOS ANGELES CO., ST. JOHN VIANNEY (1965) Rev. Msgr. Timothy E. Nichols; Revs. Chan Woo Lee; Patrick Nwokeogu; Egren Gomez; Deacons Jesse Martinez; Richard Noon.
Res.: 1345 Turnbull Canyon Rd., Hacienda Heights, 91745. Tel: 626-330-2269; Fax: 626-330-0220; Email: parish-4710@la-archdiocese.org; Web: sjvhh.org.
Catechesis Religious Program—Students 656.

HAWAIIAN GARDENS, LOS ANGELES CO., ST. PETER

CHANEL (1986) (Mexican—Filipino) Revs. Lawrence T. Darnell, O.M.V.; Edward Broom, O.M.V.; David Yankaukas, O.M.V.; Vincenzo Antolini, O.M.V.; Craig MacMahon, O.M.V.
Res. & Church: 12001 E. 214th St., Hawaiian Gardens, 90716-1117. Tel: 562-924-7591;
Fax: 562-402-9411; Email: parish-6020@la-archdiocese.org.
Catechesis Religious Program—Students 1,320.

HAWTHORNE, LOS ANGELES CO., ST. JOSEPH (1915)
11901 Acacia Ave., Hawthorne, 90250.
Tel: 310-679-1139; Fax: 310-679-3034; Email: parish-6170@la-archdiocese.org. Revs. Gregory C. King; Jorge Onofre Salazar; Jorge Luis Chalaco Vega.
Res.: 11854 Acacia Ave., Hawthorne, 90250.
School—St. Joseph School, (Grades PreK-8), 11886 Acacia Ave., Hawthorne, 90250. Tel: 310-679-1014; Fax: 310-679-1310; Email: office@saintjosephsschool.org; Web: www.saintjoe.online. Mr. Kevin Donohue, Prin. Lay Teachers 20; Students 325.
Catechesis Religious Program—
Tel: 310-679-1139, Ext. 103. Luz Maria Salgado, D.R.E. Students 1,256.

HERMOSA BEACH, LOS ANGELES CO., OUR LADY OF GUADALUPE (1927) [CEM]
244 Prospect Ave., Hermosa Beach, 90254.
Tel: 424-247-8121; Tel: 310-372-7077;
Fax: 310-798-4051; Email: abeuder@ourladyofguadalupeschool.org; Email: jodiscully@gmail.com; Email: office@olgmail.org; Web: ourladyofguadalupechurch.org. Revs. Paul Gawlowski; Joseph Kim, O.F.M.Conv.; Carlos Morales, O.F.M.Conv.; Bro. John Fleming, O.F.M.-Conv., In Res.; Revs. Stephen Gross, O.F.M.Conv., In Res.; Peter Mallin, O.F.M.Conv., In Res.
Child Care—Our Lady of Guadalupe Preschool, 340 Massy St., Hermosa Beach, 90254. Students 30.
School—Our Lady of Guadalupe School, 320 Massey Ave., Hermosa Beach, 90254. Tel: 310-372-7486;
Fax: 424-327-6793; Email: school-9150@la-archdiocese.org; Web: ourladyofguadalupeschool.org. Mrs. April Beuder, Prin. Lay Teachers 20; Students 230.
Catechesis Religious Program—Email: religioused@olgmail.org. Theresa Avila, D.R.E. Students 350.

HUNTINGTON PARK, LOS ANGELES CO.
1—ST. MARTHA (1913) (Hispanic)
6000 Seville St., Huntington Park, 90255. Mailing Address: 6019 Stafford Ave., Huntington Park, 90255. Revs. Julio Cesar Ramos Ortega, M.G.; Juan Jose Marquez Echeverria, M.G.; Jorge Cruz Avila, M.G.; Deacon Ciro Augusto Garza.
Res.: 6019 Stafford Ave., Huntington Park, 90255.
Tel: 323-585-0386; Fax: 323-585-4560; Email: stamartha@aol.com; Email: parish-5840@la-archdiocese.org.
Catechesis Religious Program—Students 493.
2—ST. MATTHIAS (1913) [JC] (Latino)
3095 E. Florence Ave., Huntington Park, 90255. Revs. Ruben D. Restrepo, C.M.; Keleohi Alozie.
Res.: 7125 Mission Pl., Huntington Park, 90255.
Tel: 323-588-2134; Fax: 323-588-4519; Email: sanmatias.hp@gmail.com.
School—St. Matthias School, 7130 Cedar St., Huntington Park, 90255. Tel: 323-588-7253;
Fax: 323-588-1136; Email: school-8880@la-archdiocese.org. Joe Gallardo, Prin. Lay Teachers 8; Students 171.
Catechesis Religious Program—Students 1,111.

INGLEWOOD, LOS ANGELES CO., ST. JOHN CHRYSOSTOM (1923) (Hispanic)
546 E. Florence Ave., Inglewood, 90301.
Tel: 310-677-2736; Email: parish-5590@la-archdiocese.org; Web: www.stjohnchrysostomparish.org. Revs. Marcos J. Gonzalez, V.F.; Javier Altuna, S.J., (Retired); Anthony Garcias; Jude Okonkwo, In Res.; Deacon Roberto Vasquez.
School—St. John Chrysostom School, (Grades PreK-8), 530 E. Florence Ave., Inglewood, 90301.
Tel: 310-677-5868; Fax: 310-677-0584; Email: info@stjohninglewood.org; Web: www.stjohninglewood.org. Jae Kim, Prin. Lay Teachers 11; Students 290.
Catechesis Religious Program—
Tel: 310-677-2736, Ext. 500; Email: dresjc@gmail.com. Amy Kim, D.R.E. Students 668.

IRWINDALE, LOS ANGELES CO., OUR LADY OF GUADALUPE (1964)
16025 E. Cypress St., Irwindale, 91706-2199.
Tel: 626-962-3649, Ext. 221; Email: olgirwindale@earthlink.net. Rev. Joseph Canna.
Catechesis Religious Program—Ana Juarez, D.R.E. Students 1,269.

LA CANADA FLINTRIDGE, LOS ANGELES CO., ST. BEDE THE VENERABLE (1951)
215 Foothill Blvd., La Canada Flintridge, 91011. Rev. Msgrs. Antonio Cacciapuoti; Albert M. Bahhuth, V.F., In Res.; Deacon Augie Won.
Res.: 4511 Daleridge Rd., La Canada, 91011.
Tel: 818-949-4300; Fax: 818-790-9520; Email: parish-3610@la-archdiocese.org; Email: lisa@bede.org.
School—St. Bede the Venerable School, (Grades K-8), 4524 Crown Ave., La Canada Flintridge, 91011.
Tel: 818-790-7884; Fax: 818-790-0699; Email: stbedeedcenter@yahoo.com; Email: school-6940@la-archdiocese.org; Web: stbedeschool.net. Ralph Valente, Prin. Lay Teachers 20; Students 250.
Catechesis Religious Program—Tel: 818-949-4322. Moira Arjani, D.R.E.; Jessica Gerhardt, Youth Min.; Diane Cwik, Confirmation Coord. Students 325.

LA CRESCENTA, LOS ANGELES CO., ST. JAMES THE LESS (1955)
4625 Dunsmore Ave., La Crescenta, 91214.
Tel: 818-248-3442; Email: fred@hr-sj.org; Web: www.hrsjcatholic.com. 4651 Dunsmore Ave, La Crescenta, 91214. Rev. Edward R. Dover, V.F.; Deacon Joe Hegenbart.
School—St. James Elementary School, (TK-8) 4635 Dunsmore Ave., La Crescenta, 91214.
Tel: 818-248-7778; Fax: 818-248-5242; Email: principal@sjhrschool.org; Web: www.sjhrschool.org. Susan Romero, Prin. Lay Teachers 10; Students 119.
Catechesis Religious Program— Religious Education & Confirmation program combined with Holy Redeemer, Montrose. Tel: 818-249-2008; Email: hrsjlifeteen@gmail.com. Leon Michael Paul. Students 100.

LA MIRADA, LOS ANGELES CO.
1—BEATITUDES OF OUR LORD (1964) Rev. Anthony J. Page; Deacons Hector M. Hidalgo; Gene Gleason.
Res.: 13013 S. Santa Gertrudes Ave., La Mirada, 90638. Tel: 562-943-1521; Fax: 562-902-7627; Email: bol@ca.rr.com; Web: bolchurch.net.
School—Beatitudes of Our Lord School, 13021 S. Santa Gertrudes Ave., La Mirada, 90638.
Tel: 562-943-3218; Email: office@bolschool.org; Web: bolschool.org. Mrs. Maria Watson, Prin. Lay Teachers 12; Students 257.
Catechesis Religious Program—Tel: 562-943-5678; Email: beatitudesreo@ca.rr.com. Sandra Rehder, D.R.E. Students 270.
2—ST. PAUL OF THE CROSS (1956) Rev. Joseph Visperas; Deacons Mark Orcutt; Timothy J. Roberto.
Res.: 14020 Foster Rd., La Mirada, 90638.
Tel: 562-921-2914; Fax: 562-926-1514; Email: church@stpaulofthecross.org; Email: parish-6010@la-archdiocese.org; Web: www.stpaulofthecross.org.
School—St. Paul of the Cross School, 14030 Foster Rd., La Mirada, 90638. Tel: 562-445-4542; Email: school-9050@la-archdiocese.org. Ms. Sandra Hernandez, Prin. Lay Teachers 11; Students 175.
Catechesis Religious Program—
Tel: 562-445-4542, Ext. 2. Theresa Bartolone, D.R.E. Students 180.

LA PUENTE, LOS ANGELES CO.
1—ST. JOSEPH (1919) Revs. Matthew T. Cumberland; Jose Jesus Martinez, Pastoral Assoc.; Rev. Msgr. Patrick Joseph Staunton, In Res., (Retired).
Res.: 550 N. Glendora Ave., La Puente, 91744.
Tel: 626-336-2001; Fax: 626-336-6010; Email: st.joseph.secretary@gmail.com.
School—St. Joseph School, 15650 E. Temple Ave., La Puente, 91744. Tel: 626-336-2821; Email: stjoseph1@gmail.com; Email: school-7870@la-archdiocese.org. Mrs. Diana Rosas, Prin. Lay Teachers 12; Students 156.
Catechesis Religious Program—Tel: 626-336-1191; Email: BVargas@la-archdiocese.org. Beatriz Vargas, D.R.E. Students 411.
2—ST. LOUIS OF FRANCE (1955)
Mailing Address: 630 Ardilla Ave., La Puente, 91746. Rev. Msgr. John S. Woolway; Revs. Lawrence J. Dowdel Jr.; Eric Anthony Lewis, In Res., (Retired); Michael Joseph Wu, O.Carm., In Res.; Deacons Jaime S. Guerrero; Bernardo Zavala; Jose Rodriguez; Agustin Jimenez.
Res.: 13935 E. Temple, La Puente, 91746-2098.
Tel: 626-918-8314; Fax: 626-917-8413; Email: saintlouisoffrance@gmail.com; Email: parish-4630@la-archdiocese.org; Web: www.stlouisoffrance.org.
School—St. Louis of France School, 13901 E. Temple Ave., La Puente, 91746-2021. Tel: 626-918-6210;
Fax: 626-918-9549; Email: school-7780@la-archdiocese.org; Web: www.slfschool.org. Richard Soto, Prin. Lay Teachers 10; Students 163.
Catechesis Religious Program—Tel: 626-918-7002. Dolores Lazcano, D.R.E. Students 965.

LAKE BALBOA, LOS ANGELES CO., ST. BRIDGET OF SWEDEN (1955)
7100 Whitaker Ave., Lake Balboa, 91406. Revs. Rufino Carlos Nava, O.M.I.; Rajan Sengol.
Res.: 16711 Gault St., Lake Balboa, 91406.
Tel: 818-782-7181; Fax: 818-782-7184; Email: stbridgrectory@yahoo.com; Email: parish-3420@la-archdiocese.org.
School—St. Bridget of Sweden School, 7120 Whitaker Ave., Lake Balboa, 91406.
Tel: 818-785-4422; Fax: 818-785-0490; Email: school-6780@la-archdiocese.org. Robert Pawlak, Prin. Lay Teachers 13; Students 215.
Catechesis Religious Program—Tel: 818-312-3142; Email: dresbos91406@gmail.com. Elizabeth Escamilla-Cruz, D.R.E. Students 227.

LAKEWOOD, LOS ANGELES CO., ST. PANCRATIUS (1953) Rev. Msgr. Joseph F. Greeley, V.F.; Rev. Christopher Iloha, In Res.; Deacons Samuel Montoya; Romeo (Romy) Ligot.
Res.: 3519 St. Pancratius Pl., Lakewood, 90712.
Tel: 562-634-3111; Fax: 562-634-7817; Email: stpanrectory@sbcglobal.net.
School—St. Pancratius School, (Grades PreK-8), 3601 St. Pancratius Pl., Lakewood, 90712.
Tel: 562-634-6310; Fax: 562-633-0731; Email: school-9400@la-archdiocese.org; Web: www.stpanschool.org. Kimberly French-Bruch, Prin. Lay Teachers 13; Students 180.
Catechesis Religious Program—Tel: 562-634-1611; Email: stpanre@sbcglobal.net. Andrew Coffey, D.R.E. Students 279.

LANCASTER, LOS ANGELES CO.
1—ST. JUNIPERO SERRA aka Congregation of St. Joseph (Quartz Hill) (1987)
42121 60th St. W., Lancaster, 93536.
Tel: 661-943-9314; Fax: 661-943-6863; Email: info@fatherserra.org; Web: www.saintserra.org. Revs. Leo Dechant, C.S.J.; Sylvan Schiavo, C.S.J.; Giampietro Gasparin, C.S.J., In Res.; Deacons Paul Schwerdt, Pastoral Min.; Rito R. Lopez, Pastoral Min.; Marvin Castillo, Pastoral Min.; Gary D. Poole, (Retired).
Res.: 6122 Azalea Dr., Lancaster, 93536-3700.
Tel: 661-943-6475 (Res.).
Catechesis Religious Program—Tel: 661-943-5912; Email: cortiz@fatherserra.org. Cassandra Ortiz, D.R.E. Students 710.
Mission—St. Elizabeth, 13845 Johnson Rd., Lake Hughes, Los Angeles Co. 93532.
2—SACRED HEART (1886) Revs. Hieu Chi Tran; Gerald Osuagwu; Deacons Ron Routolo, RCIA Coord.; Dale Reynolds, Bereavement Ministry Coord.; Fermin Herrera, Spanish RCIA; Gregory Halamicek, Serves Edwards AFB.
Res.: 565 W. Kettering St., Lancaster, 93534.
Tel: 661-942-7122; Fax: 661-945-4255; Email: sacredheartchurchav@gmail.com; Email: parish-3840@la-archdiocese.org; Web: sacredheartlancaster.org.
School—Sacred Heart School, 625 W. Kettering St., Lancaster, 93534. Tel: 661-948-3613;
Fax: 661-948-4486; Email: school-7170@la-archdiocese.org; Web: www.shsav.org. David Schatz, Prin. Lay Teachers 12; Students 275.
Catechesis Religious Program—Tel: 661-948-3011; Email: sacredheartdre@yahoo.com. Rosa Anna Cruz, D.R.E. Students 926.

LOMITA, LOS ANGELES CO., ST. MARGARET MARY ALACOQUE (1937) Revs. Paul O'Donnell, M.C.C.J.; Marinello Saguin; John Palmer; Deacons Craig Siegman; Rick Soria; Dan Wallace; Cheto Mendoza.
Res.: 25429 Eshelman Ave., Lomita, 90717.
Tel: 310-326-3364; Fax: 310-539-1570; Email: smmchur@yahoo.com; Email: parish-6190@la-archdiocese.org.
School—St. Margaret Mary Alacoque School, (TK-8) 25515 Eshelman Ave., Lomita, 90717.
Tel: 310-326-9494; Fax: 310-326-2711; Email: school-9230@la-archdiocese.org. Elisa Zimmerman, Prin. Lay Teachers 15; Students 305.
Catechesis Religious Program—25511 Eshelman Ave., Lomita, 90717. Tel: 310-326-3364, Ext. 17; Email: smmcym@yahoo.com. Joe Voight, D.R.E. Students 760.

LOMPOC, SANTA BARBARA CO.
1—LA PURISIMA CONCEPCION (1787) Rev. Michael J. Sezzi, Admin.
Pastoral Center & Rectory: 213 W. Olive Ave., Lompoc, 93436. Tel: 805-735-3068;
Fax: 805-735-7649; Email: parish-2910@la-archdiocese.org; Web: www.lapurisima.org.
Child Care—Little Saints Preschool, Terese Hill, Dir.
School—La Purisima Concepcion School, 219 W. Olive Ave., Lompoc, 93436. Tel: 805-736-6210; Email: school-6430@la-archdiocese.org. Orlando Leon, Prin. Lay Teachers 4; Students 53; Preschool 85.
Catechesis Religious Program—
Tel: 805-735-3068, Ext. 23; Email: leticia.diaz@lapurisima.org. Leticia Diaz, D.R.E. Students 208.
2—OUR LADY QUEEN OF ANGELS (1972) Rev. Joy Lawrence Santos, V.F.; Rev. Msgr. John Gerard Fitzgerald, V.F., Pastor Emeritus, (Retired); Deacons Michael Lujan; Fernando Calderon.
Res.: 3495 Rucker Rd., Lompoc, 93436.
Tel: 805-733-2735; Fax: 805-733-1235; Email: parish-2930@la-archdiocese.org; Email: qeenofangels@netzero.net.
Catechesis Religious Program—Tel: 805-733-3155;

Email: parish-2930@la-archdiocese.org. Mary Lujan, D.R.E. Students 195.

LONG BEACH, LOS ANGELES CO.

1—ST. ANTHONY (1902) Revs. George Aguilera; Henry L. Hernando, In Res., (Retired); Deacon Jorge Ramos.
Res.: 540 Olive Ave., Long Beach, 90802.
Tel: 562-590-9229; Fax: 562-590-9048; Email: secretary@saintanthonylongbeach.org; Web: www.stanthonylb.org.
School—St. Anthony School, (Grades PreK-8), 855 E. 5th St., Long Beach, 90802. Tel: 562-432-5946; Fax: 562-435-8606; Email: school@saintanthonylongbeach.org. Alison Kargas, Prin. Lay Teachers 12; Students 213.
Catechesis Religious Program—Tel: 562-590-9229, Ext. 105; Email: verbumdei@saintanthonylongbeach.org. Sr. Zulma Esquivel, D.R.E. Students 440.
Mission—Our Lady of Mt. Carmel Cambodian Catholic Center, 1851 Cerritos Ave., Long Beach, Los Angeles Co. 90806.

2—ST. ATHANASIUS (1933)
Web: www.stathanasius.us. Revs. Alfredo A. Vargas, C.M.F., Admin.; Francis Ilano, In Res.; Deacon Faustino Ciau.
Res.: 5390 Linden Ave., Long Beach, 90805.
Tel: 562-423-7986; Fax: 562-422-0306; Email: athanasius@charter.net; Email: church@stathanasius-lb.org; Web: www.stathanasius.us.
School—St. Athanasius School, 5377 Linden Ave., Long Beach, 90805. Tel: 562-428-7422; Email: school-9330@la-archdiocese.org; Web: www.sharkslongbeach.com. Ms. Stacey Stewart, Prin. Lay Teachers 9; Students 143.
Catechesis Religious Program—Email: parish-6270@la-archdiocese.org. Students 450.

3—ST. BARNABAS (1939) Rev. Antony J. Gaspar; Deacon Carlito De Los Reyes.
Res.: 3955 Orange Ave., Long Beach, 90807.
Tel: 562-424-8595; Fax: 562-595-7875; Email: church@stbarnabaslb.org; Email: parish-6280@la-archdiocese.org; Web: www.stbarnabaslb.org.
School—St. Barnabas School, (Grades PreK-8), 3980 Marron Ave., Long Beach, 90807. Tel: 562-424-7476; Fax: 562-981-3351; Email: school-9340@la-archdiocese.org; Web: www.school.stbarnabaslb.org. Jennifer Kellam, Prin. Lay Teachers 16; Students 301.
Catechesis Religious Program—Tel: 562-988-6855. Rita Coffey, D.R.E. Students 319.

4—ST. BARTHOLOMEW (1937)
5100 E. Broadway, Long Beach, 90803.
Tel: 562-438-3826; Fax: 562-438-2227; Email: KFlood@la-archdiocese.org; Web: www.stbartholomewcclb.org. 252 Granada Ave., Long Beach, 90803. Rev. Michael Reardon; Kathleen Flood, Business Mgr.
Catechesis Religious Program—Email: KDeLeo@la-archdiocese.org; Email: STetreault@la-archdiocese.org; Web: www.stbartholomewcclb.org. Kelli De Leo, D.R.E. Students 183.

5—ST. CORNELIUS (1951) Revs. Michael Gleeson, (Ireland); George Reynolds; Deacons Richard Boucher; Joseph Hamamoto.
Res.: 5500 Wardlow Rd., Long Beach, 90808.
Tel: 562-421-8966; Fax: 562-421-5096; Email: secretary.stcornelius@gmail.com; Web: stcorneliuslb.org.
School—St. Cornelius School, 3330 Bellflower Blvd., Long Beach, 90808. Tel: 562-425-7813; Fax: 562-425-2743; Email: school-9350@la-archdiocese.org. Nancy Hayes, Prin. Lay Teachers 14; Students 334.
Catechesis Religious Program—Tel: 562-420-7613. Evelyn Padian, D.R.E. Students 375.

6—ST. CYPRIAN (1944) Rev. Jason Souza.
Res.: 4714 Clark Ave., Long Beach, 90808.
Tel: 562-421-9487; Fax: 562-496-1024; Email: info@stcyprianchurch.org; Email: parish-6310@la-archdiocese.org; Web: www.StCyprianChurch.org.
School—St. Cyprian School, 5133 Arbor Rd., Long Beach, 90808. Tel: 562-425-7341; Email: principal@stcyprianschool.org; Web: www.stcyprianschool.org. Rachelle Riemersma, Prin. Lay Teachers 13; Students 236.
Catechesis Religious Program—Tel: 562-420-6885. Andy Hillsey, D.R.E. Students 252.

7—HOLY INNOCENTS (1923) Rev. G. Peter Irving III.
Res.: 425 E. 20th St., Long Beach, 90806.
Tel: 562-591-6924; Fax: 562-685-0556; Email: office@lbcatholic.com; Web: www.lbcatholic.com.
School—Holy Innocents School, 2500 Pacific Ave., Long Beach, 90806. Tel: 562-424-1018; Fax: 562-424-9250; Email: secretary@holyinnocentsschlb.org. Sr. Caridad Sandoval, Prin. Lay Teachers 8; Carmelite Sisters of the Most Sacred Heart 3; Students 198; Clergy / Religious Teachers 3.
Catechesis Religious Program—Maria Gonzalez, D.R.E. Students 219.

8—ST. JOSEPH (1955)
6180 E. Willow St., Long Beach, 90815.
Tel: 562-594-4657; Fax: 562-431-7424; Email: stjoseph@stjosephlb.org; Email: parish-6320@la-archdiocese.org; Web: www.stjosephlb.org. Rev. Msgr. Kevin J. Kostelnik; Deacons Shane Cuda; Don Gath; Thomas L. Halliwell.
School—St. Joseph School, (Grades PreK-8), 6200 E. Willow St., Long Beach, 90815. Tel: 562-596-6115; Fax: 562-596-6725; Email: school-9370@la-archdiocese.org; Web: www.sjknights.net. Margaret Alvarez, Prin. Lay Teachers 16; Students 303.
Catechesis Religious Program—Tel: 562-598-0519; Email: religioused@stjosephlb.org. Joe Voight, D.R.E. Students 212.

9—ST. LUCY (1944) Revs. John Quy V. Tran; Francis Espiga; Joseph Van Vu; Joseph Yang, In Res.; Deacons Thien Joseph Pham; Francisco J. Gonzalez.
Res.: 2344 Cota Ave., Long Beach, 90810.
Tel: 562-424-9051; Fax: 562-988-0376; Email: lucy2344@gmail.com; Email: parish-6330@la-archdiocese.org.
School—St. Lucy School, (Grades PreK-8), 2320 Cota Ave., Long Beach, 90810. Tel: 562-424-9062; Fax: 562-424-8572; Email: principal@stlucyschoollb.org; Web: www.st.lucyschoollb.org. Ms. Angelica Izquierdo, Prin. Lay Teachers 11; Students 178; Clergy / Religious Teachers 2.
Catechesis Religious Program—Tel: 562-997-0511; Email: santarb@hotmail.com. Santa Rivera, D.R.E. Students 386.

10—ST. MARIA GORETTI (1955)
3954 Palo Verde Ave., Long Beach, 90808-2298.
Tel: 562-425-7459; Email: parish-6340@la-archdiocese.org. Rev. John Schiavone, V.F.
School—St. Maria Goretti School, (Grades PreK-8), 3950 Palo Verde Ave., Long Beach, 90808-2298. Tel: 562-425-5112; Email: principal@smgschool.com; Web: www.smgschool.com. Kathleen Hernandez, Prin. Lay Teachers 10; Students 165.
Catechesis Religious Program—Humberto Arredondo, D.R.E. Students 101.

11—ST. MATTHEW (1920) Rev. Guillermo Rodriguez, (El Salvador).
Res.: 672 Temple Ave., Long Beach, 90814.
Tel: 562-439-0931; Fax: 562-434-7621; Email: stmatt@stmatthewlb.org; Web: stmatthewlb.org.
Catechesis Religious Program—Tel: 562-434-6402. Leticia Gonzalez, D.R.E. Students 366.

12—OUR LADY OF REFUGE (1948) Revs. Gerard O'Brien, Admin.; Raymond D. Morales; Rev. Msgr. William J. O'Keeffe, Pastor Emeritus; Deacon Roger Faubert.
Res.: 5195 E. Stearns St., Long Beach, 90815.
Tel: 562-498-6641; Fax: 562-498-3344; Email: parish-6250@la-archdiocese.org; Email: parish@start.olrs.org; Email: betty@start.olrs.org; Web: www.ourladyofrefuge.org.
School—Our Lady of Refuge School, (Grades PreK-8), 5210 Los Coyotes Diagonal, Long Beach, 90815. Tel: 562-597-0819; Fax: 562-597-1419; Email: admin@start.olrs.org; Web: www.olrs.org. Mrs. Patricia Holmquist, Prin. Lay Teachers 13; Students 248.
Catechesis Religious Program—Tel: 562-597-3102; Fax: 562-494-4381; Email: sre@start.olrs.org. Anna Marie Sharkany. Students 248.

LOS NIETOS, LOS ANGELES CO., OUR LADY OF PERPETUAL HELP (1958) (Hispanic) Revs. Jose A. Bautista; Josef Draugialis; Thomas Ernest Roide II.
Res.: 8545 S. Norwalk Blvd., Los Nietos, 90606.
Tel: 562-692-3758; Fax: 562-695-4068; Email: parish-5920@la-archdiocese.org.
Catechesis Religious Program—Tel: 562-463-3389. Virginia Farias, D.R.E. Students 800.

LYNWOOD, LOS ANGELES CO.

1—ST. EMYDIUS (1924) Revs. Rigoberto Rodriguez; Freddy D. Gonzalez; David Ochoa, (Mexico) In Res., (Retired).
Res.: 10900 California Ave., P.O. Box 100, Lynwood, 90262-2094. Tel: 310-637-7095; Fax: 310-637-3319; Email: stemydius@hotmail.com.
School—St. Emydius School, (Grades K-8), 10990 California Ave., Lynwood, 90262. Tel: 310-635-7184; Fax: 310-605-3041; Email: saintemydius84@yahoo.com; Email: school-8850@la-archdiocese.org; Web: www.saintemydiuscatholicschool.org. Socorro Mendoza, Prin. Lay Teachers 14; Students 242.
Catechesis Religious Program—Tel: 310-639-1249. Adela Saucedo, D.R.E. Students 1,637.
Convent—10950 California Ave., Lynwood, 90262. Tel: 310-635-3264. Missionaries of Charity 6.

2—ST. PHILIP NERI (1948) (Hispanic) Revs. Ernesto Jaramillo; Jose Maria Cuahutemoc Ramirez.
Res.: 4311 Olanda St., Lynwood, 90262.
Tel: 310-632-7179; Fax: 310-632-5119; Email: parish-5860@la-archdiocese.org.
School—St. Philip Neri School, 12522 Stoneacre Ave., Lynwood, 90262. Tel: 310-638-0341; Fax: 310-638-9805; Email: school-8890@la-archdiocese.org; Web: stphilipnerilynwood.com. Elvia Villasenor, Prin. Lay Teachers 10; Students 217.
Catechesis Religious Program—Maria Refugio Rosas, D.R.E. Students 821.

MALIBU, LOS ANGELES CO., OUR LADY OF MALIBU (1946) Rev. Msgr. Liam J. Kidney, V.F., Admin.; Rev. William F. Kerze, (Retired).
Res.: 3625 Winter Canyon Rd., Malibu, 90265.
Tel: 310-456-2361; Fax: 310-456-3942; Email: parish@olmalibu.org; Email: parish-4810@la-archdiocese.org; Web: www.olmalibu.org.
School—Our Lady of Malibu School, Tel: 310-456-8071; Fax: 310-456-7767; Email: school-7950@la-archdiocese.org; Web: www.olmalibuschool.org. Michael A. Smith, Prin. Lay Teachers 15; Students 111.
Catechesis Religious Program—Email: mslaton@olmalibu.org. Marie Slaton, D.R.E. Students 90.

MANHATTAN BEACH, LOS ANGELES CO., AMERICAN MARTYRS (1930)
624 15th St., Manhattan Beach, 90266.
Tel: 310-545-5651; Email: rectory@americanmartyrs.org. 700 15th Street, Manhattan Beach, 90266. Rev. Msgr. John F. Barry, V.F., P.A.; Revs. Richard Prindle; Joseph Kammerer; Deacons Derek A. Brown; Fred Rose; Richard (Dick) Williams.
School—American Martyrs School, 1701 Laurel Ave., Manhattan Beach, 90266-4805. Dr. Camryn Friel, Prin. Lay Teachers 46; Students 714.
Catechesis Religious Program—Tel: 310-546-4734; Email: pwilliams@americanmartyrs.org. Patti Williams, D.R.E. Students 1,111.
Spirituality Center—770 17th St., Manhattan Beach, 90266-4805.

MAYWOOD, LOS ANGELES CO., ST. ROSE OF LIMA (1922) (Hispanic)
4430 E. 60th St., Maywood, 90270. Tel: 323-560-2381; Email: parish-5880@la-archdiocese.org. Revs. R. Dario Miranda, V.F.; Edward P. Soto, (Retired); Primitivo Gonzalez; Martin Rodriguez, C.O.R.C.; Deacon Alberto Reyes.
School—St. Rose of Lima School, 4422 E. 60th St., Maywood, 90270. Tel: 323-560-3376; Email: school-8910@la-archdiocese.org. Laura Guzman, Prin. Lay Teachers 10; Students 155.
Catechesis Religious Program—Tel: 323-560-0187; Email: aguardado@sroflima.org. Alvaro Guardado, D.R.E. Students 620.

MISSION HILLS, LOS ANGELES CO., SAN FERNANDO REY MISSION (1797) Rev. Msgr. Francis J. Weber, Admin., (Retired); Kevin Feeney, Dir.
Res.: 15151 San Fernando Mission Blvd., Mission Hills, 91345. Tel: 818-361-0186; Fax: 818-361-3276; Email: info@archivalcenter.org; Email: kevin@archivalcenter.org.

MONROVIA, LOS ANGELES CO.

1—ANNUNCIATION (1949)
1307 E. Longden Ave., Arcadia, 91006-5501.
Tel: 626-447-6202; Fax: 626-447-9834; Email: parish-4510@la-archdiocese.org; Web: www.annunciationchurch.net. 2701 S. Peck Rd., Monrovia, 91016-5004. Revs. Eugene Herbert; Michael G. Callanan, M.M., In Res., (Retired); Ramon Marti, Sch.P., In Res.
Catechesis Religious Program—Tel: 626-446-1625; Email: togetherinfaith@gmail.com. Arcie Reza, D.R.E. Students 233.

2—IMMACULATE CONCEPTION aka Roman Catholic Archbishop of Los Angeles Corp Sole (1904) Revs. Joachim Lepcha, Admin.; Martin Gonzalez; Deacons Michael Salcido; Ronald Sanchez; Maria Natera, Business Mgr.
Res.: 740 S. Shamrock Ave., Monrovia, 91016.
Tel: 626-358-1166; Fax: 626-358-6466; Email: office@icmonrovia.org; Email: information@icmonrovia.org; Web: www.icmonrovia.org.
School—Immaculate Conception School, (Grades PreK-8), 726 S. Shamrock Ave., Monrovia, 91016. Tel: 626-358-5129; Fax: 626-358-3933; Email: clovano@icschoolmonrovia.org; Web: www.icschoolmonrovia.org. Carmela Lovano, Prin. Lay Teachers 10; Students 110.
Catechesis Religious Program—Tel: 626-357-3010; Email: mmota@icmonrovia.org. Margarita Mota, D.R.E. Students 110.

MONTEBELLO, LOS ANGELES CO.

1—ST. BENEDICT (1906) Revs. Michael Stechmann, O.A.R.; Dionisio Cacherco; Galo Espinoza, O.A.R., (Ecuador); Francisco Sandoval, O.A.R., In Res.; Deacons David J. Estrada; Alfonso Castillo; Joe Flores.
Res.: 1022 W. Cleveland Ave., Montebello, 90640.
Tel: 323-721-1184; Fax: 323-721-5075; Email: parish-4240@la-archdiocese.org; Email: stbenedict1022@hotmail.com; Web: st-benedict-church.com.
School—St. Benedict School, (Grades PreK-8), 217 N. 10th St., Montebello, 90640. Tel: 323-721-3348;

Fax: 323-721-8698; Email: school-7480@la-archdiocese.org. Frank Loya, Prin. Lay Teachers 27; Students 470.
Catechesis Religious Program—1009 W. Madison Ave., Montebello, 90640. Tel: 323-720-5760. Raymundo Garcia, D.R.E. Students 416.

2—OUR LADY OF THE MIRACULOUS MEDAL (1950) Revs. John M. Vianney, Admin.; Michael W. Meyer, Pastoral Assoc.; Deacons Fred Rios; Frederick Peter Lara.
Res.: 820 N. Garfield Ave., Montebello, 90640.
Tel: 323-725-7578; Fax: 323-722-2654; Email: parish-4130@la-archdiocese.org; Web: olmmparish.com.
School—Our Lady of the Miraculous Medal School, 840 N. Garfield Ave., Montebello, 90640.
Tel: 323-728-5435; Fax: 323-728-8038; Email: school-7380@la-archdiocese.org; Web: olmmschool.com. Analisa Moreno, Prin. Lay Teachers 22; Students 450; Clergy / Religious Teachers 1.
Catechesis Religious Program—
Tel: 323-725-7578, Ext. 312; Fax: 323-722-2654; Email: irmamontreal@yahoo.com. Irma Montreal, D.R.E. Students 274.

MONTEREY PARK, LOS ANGELES CO.

1—ST. STEPHEN MARTYR (1921)
320 W. Garvey Ave., Monterey Park, 91754.
Tel: 626-573-0427; Email: parish-4240@la-archdiocese.org. 122 S. Ramona Ave., Monterey Park, 91754. Rev. Joseph Magdaong, Admin.
School—St. Stephen Martyr School, (Grades PreK-8), 119 S. Ramona Ave., Monterey Park, 91754.
Tel: 626-573-1716; Email: frontoffice@stsmc.org; Web: www.stsmc.org. Debora Cilio, Prin. Lay Teachers 9; Students 138.
Catechesis Religious Program—Students 99.

2—ST. THOMAS AQUINAS (1960) Revs. John Kyebasuuta; Justin Liu Tian.
Res.: 1501 S. Atlantic Blvd., Monterey Park, 91754.
Tel: 323-264-4447; Fax: 323-264-2524; Email: sta91754@gmail.com; Web: STAMPK.ORG.
School—St. Thomas Aquinas School,
Tel: 323-261-6583; Email: school-7500@la-archdiocese.org. Gloria Castillo, Prin. Lay Teachers 9; Students 180.
Catechesis Religious Program—Tel: 323-264-1338; Email: stareligioused@gmail.com. Sr. Rocio Nieto, D.R.E. Students 137.

MONTROSE, LOS ANGELES CO., HOLY REDEEMER (1925) Twinned parish with St James the Less, La Crescenta. Rev. Edward R. Dover, V.F.
Res.: 2411 Montrose Ave., Montrose, 91020.
Tel: 818-249-2008; Fax: 818-249-5642; Email: parish-3560@la-archdiocese.org; Email: fred@hr-sj.org; Web: www.hrsjcatholic.com.
Catechesis Religious Program—Tel: 818-249-2008; Email: drehrsj@gmail.com. Trish Swords. Students 127.

MOORPARK, VENTURA CO., HOLY CROSS (1982) Rev. Msgr. Joseph F. Hernandez; Deacons J. Trinidad Andrade; Eduardo Castillo; Patrick Coulter; Derrel Craig; Michael Kromm; Kevin Barry Mauch.
Res., Parish Church & Administration Bldg.: 13955 Peach Hill Rd., Moorpark, 93021. Tel: 805-529-1397; Fax: 805-529-3939; Email: church@holycross-moorpark.org.
Catechesis Religious Program—Sue Jones, D.R.E. Students 516.

NEW CUYAMA, SANTA BARBARA CO., IMMACULATE CONCEPTION (1969)
4595 Hwy. 166, P.O. Box 265, New Cuyama, 93254.
Tel: 661- 766-2741; Fax: 661-766-2919; Email: parish-2900@la-archdiocese.org. Deacon Ricardo N. Barragan, Parish Life Coord.
Res.: 4793 Cebrian St., P.O. Box 265, New Cuyama, 93254.

NEWBURY PARK, VENTURA CO., ST. JULIE BILLIART (1969) Rev. Paul Hruby; Deacons Barry Harper; David Nicholas Smith; Kim Bond, Email: aka007@roadrunner.com; Claudio Selame.
Res. & Church: 2475 Borchard Rd., Newbury Park, 91320. Tel: 805-498-3602; Fax: 805-376-2332; Email: parish@stjulieschurch.org; Email: parish-3270@la-archdiocese.org; Web: www.stjulieschurch.org.
Catechesis Religious Program—
Tel: 805-498-3602, Ext. 105. Students 310.

NORTH HILLS, LOS ANGELES CO., OUR LADY OF PEACE (1944) Revs. Michael Perucho, Admin.; William Alberto Gil Londono, (Colombia); Kenneth Chukwu, In Res.; Deacons Doug Jones; Rey Guiao; Celso Roxas; Gilberto Hernandez.
Res.: 15444 Nordhoff St., North Hills, 91343.
Tel: 818-894-1176; Fax: 818-894-3838; Email: olpeace@olpeace.org; Email: parish-3700@la-archdiocese.org; Web: www.olpeace.org.
School—Our Lady of Peace School, 9022 Langdon Ave., North Hills, 91343. Tel: 818-894-4059;
Fax: 818-894-6759; Email: school@olpeace.org. Lourdes Jasso, Prin. Lay Teachers 11; Students 184.
Catechesis Religious Program—Sr. Clarinda Idea, D.R.E. Students 641.

NORTH HOLLYWOOD, LOS ANGELES CO.

1—ST. CHARLES BORROMEO (1921) Revs. Jose Magana, V.F.; Jeff Baker; His Eminence Roger Cardinal Mahony, In Res., (Retired); Rev. Msgr. Peter D. Nugent, In Res., (Retired); Deacons Ryan Adams; Louis N. Roche Jr.
Res.: 10828 Moorpark St., North Hollywood, 91602.
Parish Center: 10834 Moorpark St., North Hollywood, 91602. Tel: 818-766-3838;
Fax: 818-766-5711; Email: generalinfo@scbnh.com; Web: www.scbnh.org.
School—St. Charles Borromeo School, 10850 Moorpark St., North Hollywood, 91602.
Tel: 818-508-5359; Fax: 818-508-4511; Email: school-7050@la-archdiocese.org; Web: www.scb.school. John Genova, Prin. Lay Teachers 17; Students 276.
Catechesis Religious Program—Jean Essa, D.R.E. Students 355.

2—ST. JANE FRANCES DE CHANTAL (1948)
13001 Victory Blvd., North Hollywood, 91606.
Tel: 818-985-8600; Email: sjfdechantal@yahoo.com. Parish Center, 12930 Hamlin St., North Hollywood, 91606. Revs. Antonio Carlucci, R.C.J.; Jupeter Quinto, R.C.J.
School—St. Jane Frances de Chantal School, (Grades K-8), 12950 Hamlin St., North Hollywood, 91606. Tel: 818-766-1714; Email: school-7110@la-archdiocese.org; Web: www.stjanefrancesschool.org/. Bev Reyes, Prin. Lay Teachers 11; Students 246.
Catechesis Religious Program—Students 290.

3—ST. PATRICK (1948)
6153 Cahuenga Blvd., North Hollywood, 91606-5117.
Tel: 818-752-3440; Fax: 818-769-6174; Email: nicolas.sanchez@la-archdiocese.org; Web: stpatrickcatholicchurch.net. Rev. Nicolas Sanchez.
School—St. Patrick School, 10626 Erwin St., North Hollywood, 91606. Tel: 818-761-7363;
Fax: 818-761-6349; Email: parish-7120@la-archdiocese.org; Web: stpatrickcatholicschool.com. Raquel Shin, Prin. Lay Teachers 11; Students 190.
Catechesis Religious Program—
Tel: 818-752-3240, Ext. 1006; Email: parish-3790@la-archdiocese.org. Sr. Luz Maria Hernandez, O.S.F., Pastoral Assoc.; Ricardo Sifontes, Pastoral Min./Coord. Students 382.

NORTHRIDGE, LOS ANGELES CO., OUR LADY OF LOURDES (1958)
18400 Kinzie St., Northridge, 91325. Mailing Address: 18405 Superior St., Northridge, 91325.
Tel: 818-349-1500; Fax: 818-435-4284; Email: parishcenter@ollnr.org; Web: www.ollnr.org. Rev. David C. Loftus, V.F.; Rev. Msgr. Peter C. Moran, Pastor Emeritus, (Retired); Revs. Jeremiah E. O'Keeffe, In Res., (Retired); Daniel Curtis White; Deacon Juan Galido.
School—Our Lady of Lourdes School, 18437 Superior St., Northridge, 91325. Tel: 818-349-0245; Email: school-6750@la-archdiocese.org; Web: ollnr.org/school. Lay Teachers 15; Students 276.
Catechesis Religious Program—Tel: 818-349-2836; Email: re@ollnr.org. Sr. Frances Kennedy, S.D.S.H., Elementary Religious Educ.; Sage Hubacek, Youth Min.; Sr. Sharon Richards, S.D.S.H., RCIA. Students 227.

NORWALK, LOS ANGELES CO.

1—ST. JOHN OF GOD (1950)
13819 S. Pioneer Blvd., Norwalk, 90650.
Tel: 562-863-5721; Email: frontoffice@sjogparish.org. Revs. Raymond Vicente Decipeda, M.M.H.C.; Pius Noel Pareja, M.M.H.C.; Matthew Fernandez.
School—St. John of God School, 13817 S. Pioneer Blvd., Norwalk, 90650. Tel: 562-863-5722;
Fax: 562-406-3928; Email: school@sjogschool.com; Web: www.sjogschool.com. Elizabeth Mendez, Prin. Lay Teachers 9; Students 127; Clergy / Religious Teachers 3.
Catechesis Religious Program—
Tel: 562-863-5721, Ext. 231; Email: parish-5970@la-archdiocese.org. Alejandro Velasquez, D.R.E. Students 374.

2—ST. LINUS (1961)
Mailing Address: 13915 Shoemaker Ave., Norwalk, 90650. Tel: 562-921-6649; Fax: 562-921-5150; Email: a.engquist@stlinus.org; Email: stlinus@stlinus.org; Web: www.StLinus-Church.org. Revs. Christopher M. Felix, Admin.; Markos Villanueva; Brian Delaney, In Res.; Marco D. Reyes, In Res.; Deacons Chuck Baker; Mario Guerra; Mario Mejia. 24 hour Adoration Chapel, Tuesday 7:00 pm Mother of Perpetual Help Novena,First and Third Friday (en Espanol) Mass 7:00 p.m. with all night adoration, Sacrament of Penance on Tuesdays 6:30 pm to 8:00 pm and by appointment
School—St. Linus School, 13913 Shoemaker Ave., Norwalk, 90650. Tel: 562-921-0336;
Fax: 562-926-9077; Email: schooloffice@stlinuslions.com; Web: stlinuslions.com. Greg Climaco, Prin. Lay Teachers 15; Students 260.
Catechesis Religious Program—Tel: 562-921-5179; Email: cmay@stlinus.org. Christina May, D.R.E. Students 350.

OJAI, VENTURA CO., ST. THOMAS AQUINAS (1919)
185 St. Thomas Dr., Ojai, 93023. Tel: 805-646-4338; Email: parish-3230@la-archdiocese.org. Revs. Thomas G. Verber, O.S.A.; Fernando Lopez, O.S.A.
Catechesis Religious Program—Email: stacojai@gmail.com. Aina Yates, D.R.E. Students 165.

OXNARD, VENTURA CO.

1—ST. ANTHONY (1959)
2511 S. C St., Oxnard, 93033. Email: info@stanthonyoxnard.org. 2635 Maywood Way, Oxnard, 93033. Revs. Doan The Pham; Franklin Cubas; Porfirio Alvarez, In Res., (Retired); Deacons George Angel Garcia; James Henry; Joe Kennedy; Aurelio Robles Macias; Jon McPheeters; Donald Pinedo; Roy Edward Sadowski.
School—St. Anthony School, 2421 S. C. St., Oxnard, 93033. Deacon Henry Barajas Jr., Prin. Lay Teachers 12; Students 260.
Catechesis Religious Program—Tel: 805-486-0784; Email: jacklyn@stanthonyoxnard.org. Jacklyn Gonzalez, D.R.E. Students 700.

2—MARY STAR OF THE SEA (1963) (Filipino—Mexican)
463 W. Pleasant Valley Rd., Oxnard, 93033.
Tel: 805-486-6133; Email: marystar@marystaroxnard.com. Revs. Felizardo Daganta; Anthony Z. Palos, O.A.R.; Eric Antonio Crelencia, O.A.R.; Deacons Alfonso Flores; Jose Noe Morales; Richardo Copon Jr.
Catechesis Religious Program—Tel: 805-483-9313; Email: marystar@marystaroxnard.com. Sr. Rosa Hernandez, C.V.D., D.R.E. Students 1,120.

3—OUR LADY OF GUADALUPE PARISH (1958) (Hispanic)
500 N. Juanita Ave., P.O. Box 272, Oxnard, 93030.
Tel: 805-483-0987; Email: parish-3150@la-archdiocese.org. Revs. Manuel Rosiles, M.Sp.S., Admin.; Joel Quezada, M.Sp.S.; Vincente Gutierrez-Franco, M.Sp.S.; Deacons Arturo Godinez; Francisco Lopez; Henry Barajas; Alejandro Zendejas Marron.
School—Our Lady of Guadalupe Parish School, 530 N. Juanita Ave., Oxnard, 93030. Tel: 805-483-5116; Email: school-6560@la-archdiocese.org; Web: guadalupeschool.com. Dr. Julio Tellez, Prin. Lay Teachers 11; Students 207; Clergy / Religious Teachers 2.
Catechesis Religious Program—Email: olggladislemus@gmail.com. Sr. Gladis Lemus, D.R.E. Students 671.
Mission—Christ the King, 535 Cooper Rd., Oxnard, Ventura Co. 93030.

4—SANTA CLARA (1885)
323 S. E St., Oxnard, 93030. Tel: 805-487-3891; Email: parish-3190@la-archdiocese.org. Rev. Marco Antonio Ortiz, S.T.L.; Deacons Vincent Crawford; Michael Holguin; Vincent Charles Kelch; Leonardo Lacbain; Lawrence James Lopez; Fidel Ramirez; Dano L. Ramos; Milton Rosenberg, Ph.D.; Raymond Vasquez Jr.
School—Santa Clara School, 324 S. E St., Oxnard, 93030. Tel: 805-483-6935; Fax: 805-487-6686; Email: scesprin@santaclaraparish.org; Web: https://scesoxnard.weebly.com/. Dotty Massa, Prin. Lay Teachers 14; Students 241; Clergy / Religious Teachers 2.
Catechesis Religious Program—Tel: 805-330-8217; Email: letty@santaclaraparish.org. Leticia Cazares, D.R.E. Students 1,112.

PACIFIC PALISADES, LOS ANGELES CO., CORPUS CHRISTI (1950)
15100 Sunset Blvd., Pacific Palisades, 90272.
Tel: 310-454-1328; Fax: 310-573-5021; Email: parishmail@corpuschristichurch.com. 880 Toyopa Dr., Pacific Palisades, 90272. Rev. Msgr. Liam J. Kidney, V.F.; Rev. Dennis Mongrain.
School—Corpus Christi School, 890 Toyopo Dr., Pacific Palisades, 90272. Ryan Bushore, Prin. Lay Teachers 26; Sisters of St. Louis (Monaghan) 1; Students 246; Clergy / Religious Teachers 1.
Catechesis Religious Program—Tel: 310-454-1328; Email: jane@corpuschristichurch.com. Jane Young, D.R.E. Students 134.

PACOIMA, LOS ANGELES CO.

1—GUARDIAN ANGEL (1956) (Hispanic)
10886 Lehigh Ave., Pacoima, 91331.
Tel: 818-485-5207; Fax: 818-485-5087; Email: parish-3680@la-archdiocese.org. 10919 Norris Ave., Pacoima, 91331. Rev. Rafael Lara; Deacons Ruben Ochoa; Raul Chavez; Jesus Villegas; Ruben A. Cordero.
School—Guardian Angel School, (Grades PreK-8),
Tel: 818-485-5000; Email: principal@guardianangelcs.com; Email: office@guardianangelcs.com. Mario Landeros, Prin. Lay Teachers 10; Students 232.
Catechesis Religious Program—Tel: 818-899-8907. Students 230.

2—MARY IMMACULATE (1954) (Spanish)
10390 Remick Ave., Pacoima, 91331-3685.
Tel: 818-899-0278; Email: parish-3690@la-archdiocese.org; Web: maryimmaculateparish.org. Revs. Abel Loera; Walter Paredes; Jeyaraj Joseph Williams.

School—Mary Immaculate School, Tel: 818-834-8551 ; Email: school-7020@la-archdiocese.org. Federina Gullano, Prin. Lay Teachers 10; Students 200.
Catechesis Religious Program—Tel: 818-899-2111; Email: hermanaraquel@hotmail.com. Raquel Arroyo, First Communion; Javier Hinojoza, Confirmation; Carlos Ruiz, RCIA. Students 804; Adult Enrollment 1.

PALMDALE, LOS ANGELES CO., ST. MARY (1890)
1600 E. Ave., R-4, Palmdale, 93550.
Tel: 661-947-3306; Fax: 661-947-8687; Email: info@saintmarys-ave.org; Web: www.saintmarys-ave.org. Revs. Vaughn P. Winters, V.F.; Eder Tamara; Joshua Diener; Thomas White, In Res.; Deacons Elvys C. Perez; Ed Caputo; Efrain Calderon.
School—St. Mary School, Tel: 661-273-5555; Email: school-7230@la-archdiocese.org. Anna Maria Rios, Prin. Lay Teachers 9; Students 287.
Catechesis Religious Program—Tel: 661-273-5554; Fax: 661-273-5525; Email: agasca@saintmarys-ave.org. Astrid Gasca, D.R.E. Students 1,619.
Missions—Our Lady of the Desert—35647 87th St. E, Littlerock, Los Angeles Co. 93543. Tel: 661-269-8837; Email: mcamacho@saintmarys-ave.org. Maria Iboa, Sec.
St. John Paul II Mission, (at Lake Los Angeles School) 16310 E. Ave. Q, Palmdale, 93591.
Tel: 661-264-9166. Maria Iboa, Sec.
Acton Mission at High Desert Jr. High School, 3620 Antelope Valley Rd., Acton, 93510. Tel: 661-965-5699 ; Email: quiltingnani@gmail.com. Maria Iboa, Sec.

PANORAMA CITY, LOS ANGELES CO., ST. GENEVIEVE (1950)
14061 Roscoe Blvd., Panorama City, 91402.
Tel: 818-894-2261; Email: bgarcia@stgenparish.org. Revs. Alden J. Sison; Andrew Chung; Jonas Redulla; Deacon Paulino Juarez-Ramirez.
School—St. Genevieve Elementary School, 14024 Community St., Panorama City, 91402.
Tel: 818-892-3802; Fax: 818-893-8143; Email: school-7100@la-archdiocese.org; Web: spartansonline.org. Daniel Horn, Prin. Lay Teachers 26; Students 488.
High School—St. Genevieve High School, 13967 Roscoe Blvd., Panorama City, 91402.
Tel: 818-894-6417; Fax: 818-892-9853; Email: odonoghue@sgps.org; Web: www.sgps.org. Daniel Horn, Pres.; Amanda Allen, Exec. Dir. Lay Teachers 28; Students 560; Clergy / Religious Teachers 1.
Catechesis Religious Program—Email: jmorales@stgenparish.org. Judith Morales, D.R.E. Students 429.

PARAMOUNT, LOS ANGELES CO., OUR LADY OF THE ROSARY (1913) (Hispanic—Tongan)
14815 S. Paramount Blvd., Paramount, 90723.
Tel: 562-633-1126; Email: parish-5730@la-archdiocese.org. Revs. Jesse C. Galaz, V.F.; William Alberto Gil Londono, (Colombia) In Res.; Alojzy Luis Gryszko, S.D.B., (Poland) In Res.; Deacons Oscar A. Corcios; Jorge Perez.
School—Our Lady of the Rosary School, 14813 S. Paramount Blvd., Paramount, 90723.
Tel: 562-633-6360; Fax: 562-633-2641; Email: school-8780@la-archdiocese.org; Web: www.olrcatholicschool.com/home. Vanessa Rivas, Prin. Lay Teachers 11; Students 285.
Catechesis Religious Program—Students 884.

PASADENA, LOS ANGELES CO.
1—ST. ANDREW (1886)
311 North Raymond, Pasadena, 91103.
Tel: 626-792-4183; Fax: 626-792-4456; Email: info@standrewpasadena.org; Web: www.saintandrewpasadena.org. 140 Chestnut St., Pasadena, 91103. Revs. Paul A. Sustayta; Jose Corral.
School—St. Andrew School aka St. Andrew Catholic School, (Grades PreK-8), 42 Chestnut St., Pasadena, 91103. Tel: 626-796-7697; Fax: 626-796-1931; Email: school-7580@la-archdiocese.org; Web: www.saspasadena.com. Raphael Domingo, Prin. Lay Teachers 15; Students 225.
Catechesis Religious Program—Tel: 626-768-9376; Email: ispillane@standrewpasadena.org. Isabel Spillane, D.R.E. Students 500.

2—ASSUMPTION OF THE BLESSED VIRGIN MARY (1950)
2640 E. Orange Grove Blvd., Pasadena, 91107.
Tel: 626-792-1343; Email: church@abvmpasadena.org. Rev. Michael Ume; Sr. Susan M. Slater, S.H.C.J., Pastoral Assoc.
School—Assumption of the Blessed Virgin Mary School, 2660 E. Orange Grove Blvd., Pasadena, 91107. Tel: 626-793-2089; Fax: 626-793-4070; Email: school-7540@la-archdiocese.org; Web: www.abvm-school.org. Sr. Carol Ward, O.P., Prin. Lay Teachers 16; Students 265.
Catechesis Religious Program—Tel: 626-792-6844; Email: cvaldez@abvmpasadena.org. Cheli Valdez, D.R.E. Students 230.

3—ST. PHILIP THE APOSTLE (1921)
151 S. Hill Ave., Pasadena, 91106. Tel: 626-793-0693 ; Fax: 626-793-0733; Email: parish-4420@la-archdiocese.org. Revs. Anthony J. Gomez, V.F.; William Alberto Gil Londono, (Colombia); Deacon William Landa.
School—St. Philip the Apostle School, (Grades PreK-8), 1363 Cordova St., Pasadena, 91106.
Tel: 626-795-9691; Fax: 626-795-9946; Email: school-7620@la-archdiocese.org; Web: www.stphiliptheapostle.org/school. Jennifer Ramirez, Prin. Lay Teachers 31; Students 558.
Catechesis Religious Program—
Tel: 626-793-0693, Ext. 108; Email: RE@stphiliptheapostle.org. Susie Arevalos, D.R.E. Students 360.

PICO RIVERA, LOS ANGELES CO.
1—ST. FRANCIS XAVIER (1939)
4245 S. Acacia Ave., Pico Rivera, 90660.
Tel: 562-699-8527; Fax: 562-699-5331; Email: parish-5940@la-archdiocese.org. Revs. Martin Madero, Sch. P., Admin.; Carlos Villasano; Deacons Sergio Islas; Carlos R. Rivas; Joseph Bernal.
Catechesis Religious Program—Tel: 562-699-7517. Sr. Petra Lopez, D.R.E. Students 245.

2—ST. HILARY (1950)
5465 Citronell Ave., Pico Rivera, 90660.
Tel: 562-942-7300; Tel: 562-942-7310;
Fax: 562-948-3760; Email: parish-5960@la-archdiocese.org; Web: www.st-hilary.com. Revs. Diego Cabrera Rojas, S.S.C.; Gerard O'Shaughnessy, S.S.C.; Thomas Reynolds, S.S.C., In Res.; Deacon Salvador Aviles; Theresa Salas, Business Mgr.
School—St. Hilary School, (Grades PreK-8), 5401 Citronell Ave., Pico Rivera, 90660. Tel: 562-942-7361 ; Fax: 562-801-9131; Email: office@sthilarycougars.org; Email: school-9000@la-archdiocese.org; Web: www.sthilaryschool.com. Patricia Contreras-McJunkin, Prin. Lay Teachers 10; Students 172.
Catechesis Religious Program—Tel: 562-942-7018; Email: st.hilarydre@gmail.com. Mia Gonzalez, D.R.E.; Carlos Loaiza Sr., Youth Min. Students 316.

3—ST. MARIANA DE PAREDES (1951) (Hispanic)
7922 S. Passons Blvd., Pico Rivera, 90660.
Tel: 562-949-8240; Fax: 562-942-7402; Email: parish-5990@la-archdiocese.org; Email: parish@stmariana.org. Revs. Lazaro Revilla; Miguel Angel Menjivar, (El Salvador).
School—7911 Buhman Ave., Pico Rivera, 90660.
Tel: 562-949-1234; Fax: 562-948-3855; Email: school-9030@la-archdiocese.org. Dr. Frank Montejano, Ph. D., Prin. Lay Teachers 14; Students 260.
Catechesis Religious Program—7930 Passons Blvd., Pico Rivera, 90660. Teresa Duran, Dir., Faith Formation; Moises R. Vargas, RCIA Coord. Students 430.

POMONA, LOS ANGELES CO.
1—ST. JOSEPH (1886)
1150 W. Holt Ave., Pomona, 91768.
Tel: 909-629-4101; Email: parish-4720@la-archdiocese.org; Email: info@stjoseph-pomona.org; Web: stjoseph-pomona.org. Revs. Steven Guitron; Louis Gonsalves; Ala Alamat, In Res.; John G. Montejano, In Res.
School—St. Joseph School, 1200 W. Holt Ave., Pomona, 91768. Tel: 909-622-3365;
Fax: 909-524-4384; Email: school-7860@la-archdiocese.org; Web: stjosephschoolpomona.org. Mrs. Diane Gehner, Prin. Lay Teachers 7; Students 73.
Catechesis Religious Program—Tel: 909-629-1404; Email: cervantesstjosephchurch@gmail.com. Sylvia Garcia, D.R.E.; Lilian Cervantes, D.R.E. Students 456.

2—ST. MADELEINE (1963)
931 E. Kingsley Ave., Pomona, 91767.
Tel: 909-629-9495; Fax: 909-623-7148; Email: parish-4740@la-archdiocese.org. Rev. Adrian M. San Juan, Admin.; Rev. Msgr. Andrew Stanislaus Tseu, Pastor Emeritus, (Retired).
School—St. Madeleine School, 935 E. Kingsley Ave., Pomona, 91767. Tel: 909-623-9602; Email: school-7880@la-archdiocese.org. Maria Irma Jimenez, Prin. Lay Teachers 10; Students 78.
Catechesis Religious Program—Email: vrincon91@gmail.com. Veronica Rincon, Youth Min. Students 21.

3—SACRED HEART (1935)
1215 S. Hamilton Blvd., Pomona, 91766.
Tel: 909-622-4553; Email: parish-4680@la-archdiocese.org. Rev. Alberto Arreola; Deacons Carlos Madrigal; Miguel Galvez.
Catechesis Religious Program—Silvia Contreras, D.R.E. Students 928.

RANCHO PALOS VERDES, LOS ANGELES CO., ST. JOHN FISHER (1961)
5448 Crest Rd., Rancho Palos Verdes, 90275.
Tel: 310-377-5571; Email: parish-6160@la-archdiocese.org; Web: www.sjf.org. Rev. Msgr. David A. Sork; Rev. Bernard Kalu; Rev. Msgr. Eugene A. Gilb, Pastor Emeritus, (Retired); Rev. Francis V. Aguilar.
School—St. John Fisher School, 5446 Crest Rd., Rancho Palos Verdes, 90275. Tel: 310-377-2800;
Fax: 310-377-3863; Email: school-9200@la-archdiocese.org; Web: www.sjfpv.org. Anne-Marie Hudani, Prin. Lay Teachers 20; Students 195.
Catechesis Religious Program—5400 Crest Rd., Rancho Palos Verdes, 90275. Tel: 310-377-4573; Email: mjohnson@sjf.org. Margaret Johnson, D.R.E. Students 480.

REDONDO BEACH, LOS ANGELES CO.
1—ST. JAMES (1892)
415 Vincent St., Redondo Beach, 90277.
Tel: 310-372-5228; Fax: 310-379-5552; Email: office@saintjames.church; Email: parish-6150@la-archdiocese.org; Web: www.saintjames.church. 124 N. Pacific Coast Hwy., Redondo Beach, 90277. Rev. Msgr. Michael W. Meyers, V.F.; Revs. Emmanuel Konyeaso; James F. Kavanagh, Pastor Emeritus, (Retired); Ikechukwu Ikeocha, In Res.; Deacon Robert J. Miller.
Child Care—St. James Preschool, 126 N. Pacific Coast Hwy., Redondo Beach, 90277.
Tel: 310-376-5550; Email: barbara@saintjames.church. Wendy Bell. Students 110.
School—St. James School, 4625 Garnet St., Torrance, 90503. Tel: 310-371-0416;
Fax: 310-371-8377; Email: office@stjamesweb.com. Noreen Maricich, Prin. Lay Teachers 14; Students 256.
Catechesis Religious Program—Tel: 310-379-3221; Email: diana@saintjames.church. Diana Holly, D.R.E.; Vincent Dao, Youth Min. Students 362.

2—ST. LAWRENCE MARTYR (1955)
1940 S. Prospect Ave., Redondo Beach, 90277-6003.
Tel: 310-540-0329; Fax: 310-540-8999; Email: info@stlm.org; Email: parish-6180@la-archdiocese.org. Rev. Msgr. Paul T. Dotson; Rev. Patrick Torres, M.C.; Rev. Msgr. Peter A. O'Reilly, In Res., (Retired); Deacons James A. Egnatuk; Dale Sheckler; Donald Burt.
School—St. Lawrence Martyr School, 1950 Prospect Ave., Redondo Beach, 90277-6003. Tel: 310-540-3049 ; Fax: 310-316-0888; Email: school-9220@la-archdiocese.org. Diane Kaiser, Prin. Lay Teachers 25; Students 290.
Catechesis Religious Program—Tel: 310-316-0961; Email: caterina.clarke@stlm.org. Caterina Clarke, D.R.E. Students 317.

RESEDA, LOS ANGELES CO., ST. CATHERINE OF SIENA (1949)
18115 Sherman Way, Reseda, 91335.
Tel: 818-343-2110; Email: parish-3430@la-archdiocese.org. Revs. Mauricio O. Goloran III, (Philippines); Bernard Shaw Santiago; Deacons Son Hoang; Pedro Lira.
School—St. Catherine of Siena School, 18125 Sherman Way, Reseda, 91335. Tel: 818-343-9880;
Fax: 818-343-6851; Email: school-6790@la-archdiocese.org. Desiree Tedesco, Prin. Lay Teachers 14; Students 130.
Catechesis Religious Program—Tel: 818-996-4588; Email: tdelrio@catherineofsiena.org. Tony Del Rio, D.R.E. Students 745.

ROWLAND HEIGHTS, LOS ANGELES CO., ST. ELIZABETH ANN SETON (1981)
1835 Larkvane Rd., Rowland Heights, 91748.
Tel: 626-964-3629; Fax: 626-913-2209; Email: parish-4700@la-archdiocese.org. Revs. John H. Keese, V.F.; Dominic Su; Paolo Garcia; Rev. Msgr. Michael F. Killeen, Pastor Emeritus, (Retired); Deacons Steven V. Hillmann; Peter K. Chu; Ms. Fe Musgrave, Pastoral Assoc.
Catechesis Religious Program—Suzann Oseguera, D.R.E. Students 483.

SAN DIMAS, LOS ANGELES CO., HOLY NAME OF MARY (1957)
724 E. Bonita Ave., San Dimas, 91773.
Tel: 909-599-1243; Fax: 909-599-4230; Web: www.hnmparish.org. Revs. Richard J. Danyluk, SS.CC., Admin.; Jeremy Sabugo; Mario Lopez; Deacons Alfred H. Austin; Marv Estey; Jose Guadamuz; Amante Pulido.
Res.: 764 Dickens Ln., La Verne, 91750.
School—Holy Name of Mary School, 124 San Dimas Cyn. Rd., San Dimas, 91773. Tel: 909-542-0449;
Fax: 909-592-3884; Email: hnmschool@hnmschool.org; Web: www.hnmschool.org. Mrs. Deborah Marquez, Prin. Lay Teachers 16; Students 355.
Catechesis Religious Program—Email: parish-4660@la-archdiocese.org. Melanie Bailey, C.R.E. Students 625.

SAN FERNANDO, LOS ANGELES CO.
1—ST. FERDINAND (1902)
1109 Coronel St., San Fernando, 91340.
Tel: 818-365-3967; Fax: 818-365-0067; Email: parish-3900@la-archdiocese.org; Web: www.stferdinandchurch.org. Revs. Juan Ayala, O.M.I.; James Taggart, O.M.I.; John M. Curran, O.M.I.; Deacon Ricardo Mora.
School—St. Ferdinand School, 1012 Coronel St., San Fernando, 91340. Tel: 818-361-3264;
Fax: 818-361-5894; Email: principal@stferdinand.com; Web: www.stferdinand.com. Mr. Luis Gamarra,

Prin. Lay Teachers 11; Students 220; Clergy / Religious Teachers 1.
Catechesis Religious Program—Silvia Sanchez, D.R.E. Students 359.
2—SANTA ROSA (1927) (Hispanic) Revs. Porfirio Garcia, O.M.I.; John M. Curran, O.M.I., Admin.; Feliciano Lopez Ortiz, O.M.I.; Victor Patricio-Silva; Maricela Lopez, Business Mgr.
Res.: 668 S. Workman St., San Fernando, 91340.
Tel: 818-361-4617; Email: parish-3860@la-archdiocese.org.
School—Santa Rosa de Lima Catholic School, (Grades PreK-8), 1316 Griffith St., San Fernando, 91340. Tel: 818-361-5096; Email: tbecker@srdlcs.com. Mrs. Tammy Becker, Prin.
Legal Title: Santa Rosa Bishop Alemany Catholic School Lay Teachers 14; Students 174.
Catechesis Religious Program—Mr. Juan Meraz, Youth Min.; Mrs. Magdalena Reynoso, RCIA Coord. Students 825.
3—ST. VITUS
607 4th St., San Fernando, 91340. Tel: 323-454-1002; Email: parish-3810@la-archdiocese.org. Revs. James Fryar, F.S.S.P.; Frederico Masutti, F.S.S.P.
SAN GABRIEL, LOS ANGELES CO.
1—ST. ANTHONY (1945)
1901 S. San Gabriel Blvd., San Gabriel, 91776.
Tel: 626-288-8912; Email: parish-4390@la-archdiocese.org; Web: www.saintanthonyparishsg.org. Rev. Msgr. Austin C. Doran, V.F.; Revs. William Matthew Wheeler; James Clarke, Ph.D., In Res.
School—St. Anthony School, (Grades PreK-8), 1905 S. San Gabriel Blvd., San Gabriel, 91776.
Tel: 626-280-7255; Fax: 626-280-3870; Email: agutierrez@saintanthonysg.com; Email: school-7590@la-archdiocese.org; Web: http://www.stanthonyschoolsg.org/. Ms. Angela Mastantuono, Prin. Lay Teachers 9; Students 109; Clergy / Religious Teachers 1.
Catechesis Religious Program—Tel: 626-288-5511; Email: dre@saintanthonyparishsg.org. Stephanie Ramos, D.R.E.; Mrs. Leticia Saucedo, Youth Min. Students 400.
Convent—626 E. Marshall St., San Gabriel, 91776. Tel: 626-288-2200. Sisters Kathleen Callaway, S.N.J.M., Contact Person; Eddy Mark. Sisters 4.
2—SAN GABRIEL MISSION (1771) [CEM] (Old Mission)
428 S. Mission Dr., San Gabriel, 91776.
Tel: 626-457-3035; Fax: 626-282-5308; Email: parish-4360@la-archdiocese.org. Revs. Paulus Marandi, C.M.F.; Theo Fuentes, C.M.F.; Tony Diaz, C.M.F.; Valentin Ramon, C.M.F., In Res.
School—San Gabriel Mission Elementary School, 416 S. Mission Dr., San Gabriel, 91776.
Tel: 626-281-2454; Fax: 626-281-4817; Email: egarcia@sgmission.org; Email: school-7560@la-archdiocese.org. Sr. Sharon Dempsey, Prin. Lay Teachers 15; Students 205.
High School—San Gabriel Mission High School, 254 S. Santa Anita St., San Gabriel, 91776.
Tel: 626-282-3181; Fax: 626-282-4209; Email: msallo@sgmhs.org; Web: www.sgmhs.org. Dr. Marielle Sallo, Prin. Girls College Prep. Parish School Lay Teachers 17; Students 206; Clergy / Religious Teachers 1.
Catechesis Religious Program—Gigi Galardi, D.R.E. Students 393.
Convent—412 S. Mission Dr., San Gabriel, 91776. Tel: 626-284-9585.
SAN MARINO, LOS ANGELES CO., SS. FELICITAS AND PERPETUA (1938) Rev. Paul K. Fitzpatrick.
Res.: 1190 Palomar Rd., San Marino, 91108.
Tel: 626-796-0432; Fax: 626-796-0363; Email: parish-4370@la-archdiocese.org; Email: rectory@ssfp.org; Web: www.ssfp.org.
School—Saints Felicitas and Perpetua School, (Grades PreK-8), 2955 Huntington Dr., San Marino, 91108. Tel: 626-796-8223; Email: school-7570@la-archdiocese.org; Web: www.ssfp.org. Mary-Frances O'Neill, Prin. Lay Teachers 15; Students 204.
Catechesis Religious Program—Email: jackiew@ssfp.org; Tel: 626-796-0432, Ext. 114. Jackie Whitenack, D.R.E. Students 103.
SAN PEDRO, LOS ANGELES CO.
1—HOLY TRINITY (1924)
1292 W. Santa Cruz St., San Pedro, 90732.
Tel: 310-548-6535; Fax: 310-833-1134; Email: parishoffice@holytrinitysp.org;
Tel: www.holytrinitysp.org. Mailing Address: 209 N. Hanford Ave., San Pedro, 90732. Revs. Kevin L. Nolan, V.F., Admin.; Xavier D'Souza; Larry Neumeier; Deacons Walter John Lauderdale; Gaspar Munoz; Dr. Joy Jones, Pastoral Assoc.
School—Holy Trinity School, 1226 W. Santa Cruz St., San Pedro, 90732. Tel: 310-833-0703;
Fax: 310-833-5219; Email: HolyTrinitySchoolSecretary@yahoo.com; Email: school-9120@la-archdiocese.org. Dr. Linda Wiley, Prin. Lay Teachers 28; Students (incl. preschool) 527; Clergy / Religious Teachers 1.
Catechesis Religious Program—Email: parish-6070@la-archdiocese.org; Tel: 310-833-3500. Mrs. Molly Slaught, D.R.E. Students 395.
2—MARY, STAR OF THE SEA (1889)
877 W. 7th St., San Pedro, 90731. Tel: 310-833-3541; Fax: 310-833-9254; Email: office@marystar.org. Revs. Maurice D. Harrigan; Martin Benzoni, O. Praem; Raja Selvam; Freddie T. Chua, Chap.; Rev. Msgr. Timothy P. O'Connell, In Res., (Retired); Rev. Ivan Gerovac, S.J., In Res.; Deacon Jorge Enrique Malca.
Res.: 870 W. 8th St., San Pedro, 90731.
School—Mary, Star of the Sea School, (Grades PreK-8), 717 S. Cabrillo Ave., San Pedro, 90731.
Tel: 310-831-0875; Email: marystarelementary@sbcglobal.net; Email: school-9130@la-archdiocese.org; Web: marystarelementary.com. Mr. James Cordero, Prin. Lay Teachers 14; Students (incl. preschool) 227; Clergy / Religious Teachers 1.
High School—Mary, Star of the Sea High School, 2500 N. Taper Ave., San Pedro, 90731.
Tel: 310-547-1138; Fax: 310-547-1827; Email: rector@marystarhigh.com; Email: principal@marystarhigh.com; Email: info@marystarhigh.com; Web: www.marystarhigh.com. Ms. Rita Dever, Prin.; Rev. Nicholas Tacito, Rector. Lay Teachers 29; Priests 5; Sisters 1; Students 549; Clergy / Religious Teachers 3.
Catechesis Religious Program—Sr. Mary J. Glynn, S.J.C., D.R.E. Students 255.
3—ST. PETER (1966) (Hispanic) Rev. Joseph Scalco, C.S.J.
Res.: 338 N. Grand Ave., San Pedro, 90731-2006.
Tel: 310-831-5360; Fax: 310-831-0415; Email: parish-6200@la-archdiocese.org.
Catechesis Religious Program—Students 380.
SANTA BARBARA, SANTA BARBARA CO.
1—HOLY CROSS (1973) Rev. Rafael Marin-Leon, V.F.; Deacons Nicholas Curran; Randy Saake.
Res.: 1740 Cliff Dr., Santa Barbara, 93109.
Tel: 805-962-0411; Fax: 805-564-6921; Email: secretary@holycross.sbcoxmail.com; Email: parish-3000@la-archdiocese.org.
Catechesis Religious Program—Tel: 805-962-7311; Email: cre@holycross.sbcoxmail.com. Anne Luna, D.R.E. Students 138.
2—OLD MISSION SANTA BARBARA (1786) [CEM] Revs. Daniel Lackie; Larry Gosselin, O.F.M.
Res.: 2201 Laguna St., Santa Barbara, 93105.
Tel: 805-682-4151; Tel: 805-682-4713;
Fax: 805-687-7841; Email: parishoffice@saintbarbaraparish.org; Email: parish-3050@la-archdiocese.org; Web: www.saintbarbaraparish.org.
Catechesis Religious Program—Students 75.
3—OUR LADY OF GUADALUPE (1928) (Hispanic)
221 N. Nopal Street, Santa Barbara, 93103. Email: olg.parish.sb@gmail.com. Mailing Address: 227 N. Nopal St., Santa Barbara, 93103. Revs. Pedro J. Lopez, V.F.; Cesar Fonseca.
Res.: 801 Jennings Ave., Santa Barbara, 93103.
Tel: 805-965-4060; Fax: 805-965-3386; Email: parish-3010@la-archdiocese.org.
Catechesis Religious Program—Tel: 805-962-4441; Email: rcanseco@parishmail.com. Rafaela Canseco, D.R.E. Students 391.
4—OUR LADY OF MOUNT CARMEL (1856) Revs. Lawrence Seyer; Maurice K. O'Mahony, Pastor Emeritus, (Retired); Rev. Msgr. Stephen N. Downes, V.F., Pastor Emeritus, (Retired).
Res.: 1300 E. Valley Rd., Santa Barbara, 93108.
Tel: 805-969-6868; Email: parish-3020@la-archdiocese.org; Email: info@mtcarmelsb.com.
School—Our Lady of Mount Carmel School, 530 Hot Springs Rd., Santa Barbara, 93108.
Tel: 805-969-5965; Fax: 805-565-9841; Email: info@mountcarmelschool.net; Email: school-6480@la-archdiocese.org; Web: www.mountcarmelschool.net. Tracie Simolon, Prin. Lay Teachers 14; Students 203.
Catechesis Religious Program—Tel: 805-969-4868. Sr. Rosalie Callen, C.S.J., D.R.E. Students 124.
5—OUR LADY OF SORROWS (1856)
21 E. Sola St., Santa Barbara, 93101.
Tel: 805-963-1734; Email: office@olssb.org; Web: www.our-lady-of-sorrows-santa-barbara.com. Revs. Cesar Magallon; Mario Torrez; Ms. Cara Crosetti, Business Mgr.
School—Notre Dame, (Grades PreK-8), 33 E. Micheltorena St., Santa Barbara, 93101.
Tel: 805-965-1033; Email: cstefanec@notredamesb.org; Web: www.notredamesb.org. Ms. Christina Stefanec, Prin. Lay Teachers 10; Students 182.
Catechesis Religious Program—Tel: 805-966-4941; Email: religioused@olssb.org. Anabella Lehne, D.R.E. Students 287.
6—SAN ROQUE (1953) [JC] Rev. Bruce Correio; Rev. Msgr. Michael J. Jennett, S.T.D., Pastor Emeritus, (Retired).
Res.: 325 Argonne Cir., Santa Barbara, 93105.
Tel: 805-687-5215; Fax: 805-682-9778; Email: office@sanroqueparish.org; Web: sanroque.weconnect.com.
Catechesis Religious Program—Tel: 805-682-1097; Email: education@sanroqueparish.org. Noel Fuentes, D.R.E. Students 80.
SANTA CLARITA, LOS ANGELES CO.
1—ST. CLARE (1977) Revs. Olin Mayfield; Malcolm Ambrose.
Res.: 27341 Camp Plenty Rd., Santa Clarita, 91351.
Tel: 661-252-3353; Fax: 661-252-1539; Email: office@st-clare.org; Web: www.st-clare.org.
Catechesis Religious Program—Students 694.
2—ST. KATERI TEKAKWITHA (1998)
Mailing Address: 22508 Copper Hill Dr., Santa Clarita, 91350-4299. Tel: 661-296-3180;
Fax: 661-296-7854; Email: parish-3960@la-archdiocese.org; Web: saintkateriparish.org. Revs. Albert H. Avenido, Admin.; Joo Won (Gabriel) Kang; Rev. Msgr. Michael J. Slattery, Pastor Emeritus, (Retired); Deacons Terrence Raymond Irwin; Robert Seidler; Gabriel Aguilera Jr., (Retired).
Catechesis Religious Program—Tel: 661-296-6945. Laura Diaz, D.R.E. Students 614.
3—OUR LADY OF PERPETUAL HELP (1944)
23233 Lyons Ave., Santa Clarita, 91321.
Tel: 661-259-2276, Ext. 667. Rev. Msgr. Craig A. Cox, J.C.D., D.Min., V.F.; Revs. Gilbert Arthur Guzman; Ethan Southard; Deacons Richard Karl; Kevin McCarthy; Jay Reiser.
Res.: 23045 Lyons Ave., Santa Clarita, 91321-2632.
Tel: 661-259-2276; Fax: 661-259-1873; Email: olph@olphscv.org; Web: www.olphscv.org.
School—Our Lady of Perpetual Help School, 23225 Lyons Ave., Santa Clarita, 91321. Tel: 661-259-1141;
Fax: 661-259-8254; Email: principal@olphsc.org; Web: www.olphsc.org. Sharon Krahl, Prin. Lay Teachers 13; Students 238.
Catechesis Religious Program—Tel: 661-259-4266; Email: wendy.olphrcia@yahoo.com. Wendy Lucas, D.R.E. Students 259.
Missions—Val Verde Mission at Boys & Girls Club—30300 Arlington St., Val Verde, 91384-2481.
Castaic Mission at North Lake Hills Elementary, 32545 Ridge Route Rd., Castaic, 91384-4133.
Tel: 661-259-1141; Email: school-7160@la-archdiocese.org. Sharon Krahl, Prin.
SANTA FE SPRINGS, LOS ANGELES CO., ST. PIUS X aka STP (1954) (Hispanic) Revs. Artur Gruszka; Pedro G. Valdez; Francis Ty Bui; Deacon Ron Elchert; Ms. Rita Freeborg, Business Mgr.; Ms. Priscilla Galdamez, Sec.
Res.: 10827 Pioneer Blvd., Santa Fe Springs, 90670.
Tel: 562-863-8734; Fax: 562-868-0051; Email: parish-6030@la-archdiocese.org.
Child Care—St. Pius X Preschool, Email: preschool@spxraiders.com; Web: www.spxraiders.com/preschool/. Kristin Muniz, Dir. Lay Teachers 2; Students 16.
School—St. Pius X School aka St. Pius X Parish School, (Grades PreK-8), 10855 S. Pioneer Blvd., Santa Fe Springs, 90670. Tel: 562-864-4818;
Fax: 562-864-7120; Email: office@spxraiders.com; Web: www.spxraiders.com. Christine Huerta Soler, Prin. Lay Teachers 12; Students 200.
Catechesis Religious Program—Tel: 562-868-2389; Tel: 562-567-7242; Email: espinosa_susanna@yahoo.com. Rita Amador, D.R.E.; Mrs. Susanna Espinosa, D.R.E. Students 383.
SANTA MARIA, SANTA BARBARA CO.
1—ST. JOHN NEUMANN (Santa Barbara) (1986) Revs. Rolando A. Sierra, C.Ss.R., (Venezuela); Joseph Dadiri; Rafael Garces; Deacons Ricardo Berumen; Jose Ojeda; Roberto Lupian Valdez; Jose Ortiz.
Res.: 966 W. Orchard, Santa Maria, 93458-2063.
Tel: 805-922-7099; Fax: 805-346-1747; Email: parish-2950@la-archdiocese.org; Web: www.stneumann.com.
Catechesis Religious Program—Email: angelicag@stneumann.com. Angelica Gonzalez, D.R.E. Students 626.
2—ST. LOUIS DE MONTFORT (Santa Barbara) (1963) [JC] Revs. Aidan Peter Rossiter, C.J.; Mark L. Newman, C.J.; John A. Mayhew, C.J.; Alfred Verstreaken, C.J.; Deacons Raul Blanco; Christopher Boerger; Richard Carmody; Alfredo Espinoza; Douglas Halvorsen; Robert Maciel; Antonio Mejia; Robert Schaefer, Email: rmshaefer@live.com.
Res.: 5075 Harp Rd., Santa Maria, 93455.
Tel: 805-937-4555; Fax: 805-934-2805; Email: sldmchurch@sldm.org; Email: parish-2960@la-archdiocese.org; Web: www.sldm.org.
School—St. Louis de Montfort School, 5095 Harp Rd., Santa Maria, 93455. Tel: 805-937-5571;
Fax: 805-937-3181; Email: school_office@sldmschool.org; Email: school-6410@la-archdiocese.org; Web: www.sldmschool.org. Kathy Crow, Prin. Lay Teachers 9; Students 253.
Catechesis Religious Program—Tel: 805-937-8363; Email: david@sldm.org. David Stevens, D.R.E. Students 805.

Mission—St. Anthony's Church, 270 Helena St., Los Alamos, 93440. Tel: 805-344-1604.

3—ST. MARY OF THE ASSUMPTION (1905) [JC]
431 E. Church St., Santa Maria, 93454.
Tel: 805-922-5826; Email: parish@stmary-sm.org; Web: www.stmary-sm.org. Rev. Thomas S. Cook; Rev. Msgr. James Philip Colberg, Pastor Emeritus, (Retired); Rev. Joachim Lepcha; Deacons Zenon Nawrocik; Dennis Pearson; Francisco Lopez.
Rectory, 414 E. Church St., Santa Maria, 93454.
Tel: 805-922-5826; Email: parish@stmary-sm.org.
School—St. Mary of the Assumption School, (Grades K-8), 424 E. Cypress St., Santa Maria, 93454.
Tel: 805-925-6713; Fax: 805-925-3815; Email: office@stmarysschoolsm.com; Email: principal@stmarysschoolsm.com; Email: preschool@stmarysschoolsm.com; Web: www.stmarysschoolsm.com. Michelle Cox, Prin. Lay Teachers 10; Students 215.
Child Care—Preschool, 309 S. School St., Santa Maria, 93454. Tel: 805-346-6541; Fax: 805-347-7658; Email: preschool@stmarysschoolsm.com; Email: principal@stmarysschoolsm.com; Web: www.stmarysschoolsm.com/preschool. Mrs. Mary Rowell, Dir.
Legal Title: St. Mary's Preschool Students 45; Staff 8.
Catechesis Religious Program—Office of Religious Education, Email: juan.pablo@stmary-sm.org. MR. Juan Pablo Garcia, D.R.E. Students 557.

SANTA MONICA, LOS ANGELES CO.

1—ST. ANNE (1951) Revs. Jorge Guillen, S.D.B., In Res.; Christopher Onyenobi, In Res.; Deacon Raul Molina, Parish Life Coord.
Res.: 2011 Colorado Ave., Santa Monica, 90404.
Tel: 310-829-4411; Fax: 310-829-9006; Email: stanne-church1@gmail.com; Email: parish-4830@la-archdiocese.org; Web: www.stanneshrine.org.
School—St. Anne School, 2015 Colorado Ave., Santa Monica, 90404. Tel: 310-829-2775;
Fax: 310-829-3945; Email: school-7970@la-archdiocese.org; Web: www.saintanneschool.com. Mr. Michael Browning, Prin. Lay Teachers 10; Students 250.
Catechesis Religious Program—Tel: 310-829-4040; Email: stannere@gmail.com. Carolina Badillo, D.R.E. Students 200.

2—ST. CLEMENT (1904) Rev. Anthony Gonzalez.
Res.: 3102 Third St., Santa Monica, 90405.
Tel: 310-396-2679; Fax: 310-396-4239; Email: stclements.santamonica@gmail.com; Email: parish-4850@la-archdiocese.org.
Catechesis Religious Program—Ivonne Buenrosta, D.R.E. Students 90.

3—ST. MONICA (1886)
725 California Ave., Santa Monica, 90403.
Tel: 310-566-1500; Fax: 310-566-1510; Email: info@stmonica.net; Web: www.stmonica.net. Rev. Msgr. Lloyd A. Torgerson; Revs. Mark Martinez; Ian Hagen; William Eric Ian Hagan; David Guffey, C.S.C., In Res.; Vincent A. Kuna, C.S.C., In Res.
School—Elementary School, 1039 Seventh St., Santa Monica, 90403. Tel: 310-451-9801;
Fax: 310-394-6001; Email: school@stmonicaelem.com; Email: school-8060@la-archdiocese.org; Web: www.stmonicaelem.com. Neil Quinly, Prin. Lay Teachers 15; Students 322.
High School—St. Monica High School, 1030 Lincoln Blvd., Santa Monica, 90403. Tel: 310-394-3701;
Fax: 310-458-1353; Email: jspellman@stmonicahs.net; Web: www.stmonicahs.org. Mr. James Spellman, Prin. Lay Teachers 37; Students 412.
Catechesis Religious Program—Email: suzette@stmonica.net. Suzette Sornborger, D.R.E. Students 326.

SANTA PAULA, VENTURA CO.

1—OUR LADY OF GUADALUPE (1929) [CEM] (Hispanic) Rev. Charles R. Lueras, C.R.I.C.
Res.: 427 N. Oak St., Santa Paula, 93060.
Tel: 805-525-3716; Fax: 805-525-3788; Email: parish-3160@la-archdiocese.org.
Catechesis Religious Program—423 N. Oak St., Santa Paula, 93060. Sr. Encarnacion de los Santos, O.P., D.R.E.
Convent—432 N. Oak St., Santa Paula, 93060.
Tel: 805-525-9207; Fax: 805-933-2729; Email: opolgs@aol.com; Web: crmsdusadelegation.org. Sisters 1.

2—ST. SEBASTIAN (1896)
235 N. Ninth St., Santa Paula, 93060.
Fax: 805-933-6799; Email: ramonaguilin@gmail.com; Email: parish-3220@la-archdiocese.org. Revs. Pasquale Vuoso, C.R.I.C.; Thomas J. Dome, C.R.I.C.; Thaddeus Haynes, C.R.I.C.; Deacons Alfonso A. Guilin; Christopher A. Reeve, C.R.I.C.
Child Care—St. Sebastian Preschool,
Tel: 805-933-5518. Annette Romero, Dir. Students 44.
School—St. Sebastian School, 325 E. Santa Barbara St., Santa Paula, 93060. Tel: 805-525-1575;
Fax: 805-933-0190; Email: principal@spsaints.org; Web: http://spsaints.weebly.com/. Grace Kelly, Prin. Lay Teachers 10; Students 127.
Catechesis Religious Program—Tel: 805-525-3201; Email: stsebastianccd@verizon.net. Marisela Favila, D.R.E. Students 145.

SHERMAN OAKS, LOS ANGELES CO., ST. FRANCIS DE SALES (1938) Rev. Michael Wakefield; Rev. Msgr. Kevin John Larkin, Pastor Emeritus, (Retired); Rev. Michael J. Sezzi, In Res.
Res.: 13360 Valleyheart Dr., S., Sherman Oaks, 91423. Tel: 818-784-0105; Fax: 818-784-4807; Email: parish-3750@la-archdiocese.org; Web: www.sfdsparish.com.
Church: Moorpark St. at Dixie Canyon Ave., Sherman Oaks, 91423. Email: sfdschurch@sbcglobal.net.
School—St. Francis de Sales School, (Grades PreK-8), 13368 Valleyheart Dr., Sherman Oaks, 91423.
Tel: 818-784-9573; Fax: 818-784-9649; Email: school-7080@la-archdiocese.org; Web: www.saintfrancisdesalesschool.com. Ms. Elizabeth Gregg, Prin. Lay Teachers 18; Students 345; Clergy / Religious Teachers 1.
Catechesis Religious Program—Email: lathuras@msn.com. Jack Lathuras, D.R.E. Students 307.

SIERRA MADRE, LOS ANGELES CO., ST. RITA (1908)
318 N. Baldwin Ave., Sierra Madre, 91024.
Tel: 626-355-1292; Fax: 626-355-2290; Email: parish-4330@la-archdiocese.org; Web: st-rita.org. Mailing Address: 50 E. Alegria Ave., Sierra Madre, 91024. Rev. Thomas E. Baker, V.F.; Deacons Manuel Valencia; John Hull, (Retired).
School—St. Rita School, 322 N. Baldwin Ave., Sierra Madre, 91024. Tel: 626-355-6114; Fax: 626-355-0713; Email: stritaschsmd@la-archdiocese.org. Joanne Harabedian, Prin. Lay Teachers 18; Students 284.
Catechesis Religious Program—
Tel: 626-355-1292, Ext. 228; Email: eff@st-rita.org. Mandi Welman, D.R.E. Students 145.

SIMI VALLEY, VENTURA CO.

1—ST. PETER CLAVER (1972)
2680 Stow St., Simi Valley, 93063. Revs. Riz J. Carranza; Adrian M. San Juan; Deacons Brian Clements; Melecio Zamora.
Res.: 5649 E. Pittman St., Simi Valley, 93063.
Tel: 805-526-6499; Fax: 805-526-7233; Email: saintpeterclaver@aol.com; Email: parish-3300@la-archdiocese.org; Web: www.saintpeterclaver.org.
School—St. Peter Claver School, (Grades PreSchool-8), 5670 Cochran St, Simi Valley, 93063.
Tel: 805-526-2244; Email: lbalcaceres@stpeterclaverschool.org. Lauren Balcaceres, Prin. Lay Teachers 11; Students 77.
Catechesis Religious Program—Tel: 805-526-0680; Email: faithformation@saintpeterclaver.org. Bianca Langlois, D.R.E. Students 380.

2—ST. ROSE OF LIMA (1921) Revs. Joseph P. Shea, V.F.; Gregorio Hidalgo; Jim Maher, In Res.; John Moloney, In Res.; Deacons Peter Wilson Jr.; Terence Reibenspies; Louis Homero Fernandez; Dave Lawrence; Christopher Emmett Ryan.
Res.: 1305 Royal Ave., Simi Valley, 93065.
Tel: 805-526-1732; Fax: 805-526-0067; Email: parish-3310@la-archdiocese.org; Email: parish@strosesv.com; Web: www.strosesv.com.
School—St. Rose of Lima School, 1325 Royal Ave., Simi Valley, 93065. Tel: 805-526-5304;
Fax: 805-526-0939; Email: office@srls.org; Web: srls.org. Dr. Jayne Quinn, Prin. Lay Teachers 15; Students 240.
Catechesis Religious Program—Tel: 805-526-5513. Sandy Lemos, D.R.E. Students 372.

SOLVANG, SANTA BARBARA CO., OLD MISSION SANTA INES (1804) (Spanish) Revs. Robert A. Barbato, O.F.M.Cap.; James Johnson, O.F.M. Cap.; Gerald Barron, O.F.M.Cap., In Res.; Deacon Ancelmo Aguirre.
Res.: 1760 Mission Dr., P.O. Box 408, Solvang, 93464. Tel: 805-688-4815; Fax: 805-686-4468; Email: office@missionsantaines.org; Email: parish-2940@la-archdiocese.org; Web: www.missionsantaines.org.
Catechesis Religious Program—Tel: 805-688-4138. Sr. Carmen Acosta, S.D.S.H., D.R.E. Students 181.

SOUTH EL MONTE, LOS ANGELES CO., EPIPHANY (1956) (Hispanic) Revs. Juan Francisco Gonzalez; Jorge Onofre Salazar; Pius Noel Pareja, M.M.H.C.; Deacon Doroteo Gonzalez.
Res.: 10911 Michael Hunt Dr., South El Monte, 91733. Tel: 626-442-6262; Fax: 626-575-1738; Email: epiphanysem@att.net; Email: parish-4520@la-archdiocese.org.
School—Epiphany School, 10915 Michael Hunt Dr., South El Monte, 91733. Tel: 626-442-6264;
Fax: 626-442-6074; Email: school-7690@la-archdiocese.org. Gabriela Negrete, Prin. Lay Teachers 13; Students 153.
Catechesis Religious Program—Sr. Clara Luz Bolanos, E.F.M.S., D.R.E. Students 542.

SOUTH GATE, LOS ANGELES CO., ST. HELEN (1931)
8912 S. Gate Ave., South Gate, 90280. Revs. Angel Castro; Jesus Garcia; Pedro Saucedo; Deacons Cecilio G. Pena; Rogelio Ramirez.
Res.: 3170 Firestone Blvd., South Gate, 90280.
Tel: 323-563-3522; Fax: 323-563-0161; Email: info@sthelencc.org; Email: parish-5830@la-archdiocese.org; Web: www.sthelencc.org.
School—St. Helen School, 9329 Madison Ave., South Gate, 90280. Tel: 323-566-5491; Fax: 323-566-2810; Email: sthelen9329@Yahoo.com; Email: school-8870@la-archdiocese.org; Web: sthelensg.org. Kurt Spanel, Prin. Lay Teachers 12; Students 305.
Catechesis Religious Program—9314 Madison Ave., South Gate, 90280. Tel: 323-569-9550; Email: llopez@sthelencc.org. Laura Lopez, D.R.E. Students 708.

SOUTH PASADENA, LOS ANGELES CO., HOLY FAMILY (1910)
1501 Fremont Ave., South Pasadena, 91030. Email: patricia@holyfamily.org. Rev. Denis Maher, Sacramental Min.; Rev. Msgr. Clement J. Connolly, Pastor Emeritus, (Retired); Cambria Tortorelli, Parish Life Coord.
Pastoral Center—1527 Fremont Ave., South Pasadena, 91030. Tel: 626-799-8908;
Fax: 626-799-0423; Email: parish-4340@la-archdiocese.org; Email: reception@holyfamily.org; Web: www.holyfamily.org.
School—Holy Family School, 1301 Rollin St., South Pasadena, 91030. Tel: 626-799-4354;
Fax: 626-403-6180; Email: fmontejano@holyfamily.org; Email: school-7550@la-archdiocese.org; Web: www.school.holyfamily.org. Dr. Frank Montejano, Ph.D., Prin. Lay Teachers 15; Students 316.
Catechesis Religious Program—1301 Rollin St., South Pasadena, 91030. Tel: 626-403-6118; Email: cvillegas@holyfamily.org. Colette Villegas, D.R.E. Students 303.

SUN VALLEY, LOS ANGELES CO., OUR LADY OF THE HOLY ROSARY (1937) (Hispanic—Filipino) Revs. Marvin Ajic, C.S.; Abner Ables, C.S.
Res.: 7800 Vineland Ave., Sun Valley, 91352-4596.
Tel: 818-765-3350; Fax: 818-765-3170; Email: parishoffice@olhr.org; Email: parish-3710@la-archdiocese.org; Web: www.olhr.org.
School—Our Lady of the Holy Rosary School, 7802 Vineland Ave., Sun Valley, 91352. Tel: 818-765-4897;
Fax: 818-765-5791; Email: school-7040@la-archdiocese.org. Maria Aguilar, Prin. Lay Teachers 9; Servant Sisters of the Blessed Sacrament 4; Students 233; Clergy / Religious Teachers 3.
Catechesis Religious Program—Tel: 818-982-4248. Diana Cruz, D.R.E. Students 570.
Mission—Our Lady of Zapopan, 7824 Lankershim Blvd., North Hollywood, Los Angeles Co. 91605.
Tel: 818-503-8920.

SYLMAR, LOS ANGELES CO., ST. DIDACUS (1957) (Hispanic)
14339 Astoria St., Sylmar, 91342. Tel: 818-367-6181; Email: parish-3880@la-archdiocese.org. 14337 Astoria St., Sylmar, 91342. Revs. Robert E. J. Garon; Arturo Valadez; Rev. Msgr. Peter L. Amy, In Res., (Retired); Rev. Norman A. Supancheck, In Res., (Retired); Deacons Raymond Camacho; Fermin Gomez.
Child Care—St. Didacus Preschool,
Tel: 818-367-5296. Dolores Hernandez, Dir. Students 35.
School—St. Didacus School, 14325 Astoria St., Sylmar, 91342. Tel: 818-367-5886;
Fax: 818-364-5486; Email: school-7190@la-archdiocese.org; Web: www.stdidacusschool.org. Krishana Gonzales, Prin. Lay Teachers 10; Students 143.
Catechesis Religious Program—Tel: 818-367-4155; Email: theresagross01@gmail.com. Mrs. Theresa Gross, D.R.E. Students 822.

TEMPLE CITY, LOS ANGELES CO., ST. LUKE THE EVANGELIST (1946)
5605 Cloverly Ave., Temple City, 91780.
Tel: 626-291-5900; Fax: 626-287-2332; Email: parish-4410@la-archdiocese.org. Revs. Mark A. Strader; Nicholas Assi, Pastoral Assoc., (Retired).
School—St. Luke the Evangelist School, (Grades PreK-8), 5521 Cloverly Ave., Temple City, 91780.
Tel: 626-291-5959; Fax: 626-285-5367; Email: school-7610@la-archdiocese.org; Web: stlukelions.org. Yvette Jefferys, Prin. Lay Teachers 9; Students 134.
Catechesis Religious Program—
Tel: 626-291-5900, Ext. 227; Email: barbara@stluketemplecity.org. Barbara Hansen, D.R.E. Students 105.

THOUSAND OAKS, VENTURA CO., ST. PASCHAL BAYLON (1960)
155 E. Janss Rd., Thousand Oaks, 91360.
Tel: 805-496-0222, Ext. 101; Fax: 805-379-2506; Email: parish@stpaschal.org; Email: parish-3290@la-archdiocese.org. Revs. Michael Rocha; Luis Estrada; Alejandro Enriquez; Deacons Mitchell Ito; James Robinson; Guillermo Rodriguez.
School—St. Paschal Baylon School, (Grades K-8), 154 E. Janss Rd., Thousand Oaks, 91360.

Tel: 805-495-9340; Fax: 805-778-1509; Email: principal@stpaschal.org; Email: school-6680@la-archdiocese.org. Suzanne Duffy, Prin. Lay Teachers 32; Students 273.
Catechesis Religious Program—
Tel: 805-496-0222, Ext. 115. Jennifer McCarthy, D.R.E. Students 425.

TORRANCE, LOS ANGELES CO.

1—ST. CATHERINE LABOURE (1947)
3846 Redondo Beach Blvd., Torrance, 90504.
Tel: 310-323-8900; Email: parish-6140@la-archdiocese.org. Revs. Alfred Hernandez; Hoang Dang.
School—St. Catherine Laboure School,
Tel: 310-324-8732; Email: school-9180@la-archdiocese.org; Web: www.stcat.org. Mrs. Jennifer Meyer Bagheri, Prin. Lay Teachers 25; Students 470.
Catechesis Religious Program—16831 Ainsworth, Torrance, 90504. Angela Morvice, D.R.E. Students 408.

2—NATIVITY (1924)
1447 Engracia Ave., Torrance, 90501-3234.
Tel: 310-328-2776; Email: parish-6090@la-archdiocese.org. Revs. Hung Ba Tran; Gerhart Habison, (Retired).
School—Nativity School, 2371 Carson St., Torrance, 90501. Tel: 310-328-5387; Fax: 310-328-5365; Email: school-9140@la-archdiocese.org. Mrs. Michelle Wechsler, Prin. Lay Teachers 12; Students 269.
Catechesis Religious Program—Tel: 310-320-6673. Bertha Melendres, D.R.E. Students 419.

TUJUNGA, LOS ANGELES CO., OUR LADY OF LOURDES (1920)
7315 Apperson St., Tujunga, 91042. Mailing Address: 7344 Apperson St., Tujunga, 91042.
Tel: 818-352-3218; Fax: 818-352-2738; Email: parish-3590@la-archdiocese.org. Rev. Roland Astudillo; Deacon Marciano Enriquez.
School—Our Lady of Lourdes School, (Grades PreK-8), 7324 Apperson St., Tujunga, 91042.
Tel: 818-353-1106; Fax: 818-951-4276; Email: school-6930@la-archdiocese.org. Evelyn Cortez, Prin. Lay Teachers 23; Students 155.
Catechesis Religious Program—7355 Apperson St., Bldg. 3, Tujunga, 91042. Tel: 818-353-3053; Email: fzano89@yahoo.com. Flor Zano, D.R.E. Students 129.

VALINDA, LOS ANGELES CO., ST. MARTHA (1958) (Hispanic—Filipino)
444 N. Azusa Ave., Valinda, 91744-4299.
Tel: 626-964-4313; Email: parish-4750@la-archdiocese.org. Revs. Thomas Frederick Asia; Alfonso Abarca, S.D.B.; Deacon Victor Tiambeng.
School—St. Martha School, 440 N. Azusa Ave., Valinda, 91744-4299. Tel: 626-964-1093; Email: school-7890@la-archdiocese.org. Sr. Carmen Fernandez, Prin. Lay Teachers 20; Students 296.
Catechesis Religious Program—Tel: 626-912-2581; Email: smonte@stmarthaval.org. Sara Monte, D.R.E. Students 351.

VAN NUYS, LOS ANGELES CO., ST. ELISABETH (1919) (Hispanic)
14655 Kittridge St., Van Nuys, 91405.
Tel: 818-779-1756, Ext. 200; Email: irma.stelisabethchurch@gmail.com; Email: parish-3730@la-archdiocese.org. 6635 Tobias Ave., Van Nuys, 91405. Revs. Vito Di Marzio, R.C.J.; Antonio Fiorenza, R.C.J.
School—St. Elisabeth School, Tel: 818-779-1766; Email: school-7060@la-archdiocese.org. Sr. Marita A. Olango, F.D.Z., Prin. Lay Teachers 10; Students 184.
Catechesis Religious Program—Sr. Angelie Inoferio, F.D.Z. Students 617.

VENICE, LOS ANGELES CO., ST. MARK (1923)
940 Coeur d'Alene Ave., Venice, 90291.
Tel: 310-821-5058; Email: info@stmarkvenice.com; Email: parish-4890@la-archdiocese.org. Rev. Paul J. Spellman, V.F.
School—St. Mark School, 912 Coeur d'Alene Ave., Venice, 90291. Tel: 310-821-6612; Fax: 310-822-6101 ; Email: school-8030@la-archdiocese.org. Mary Ann McQueen, Prin. Lay Teachers 25; Students 268; Clergy / Religious Teachers 3.
Catechesis Religious Program—Tel: 310-822-1201. Judy Girard, D.R.E. Students 280.

VENTURA, VENTURA CO.

1—OUR LADY OF THE ASSUMPTION (1954)
3175 Telegraph Rd., Ventura, 93003-3283.
Tel: 805-642-7966; Email: parish-3140@la-archdiocese.org. Revs. Leon Hutton; Joseph Choi; Deacons Daniel Bojorquez; Michael Burns; Raul Gonzalez; Donald Huntley; Philip Joerger; Ed Mills; Charles Philip Wessler.
School—Our Lady of the Assumption School, 3169 Telegraph Rd., Ventura, 93003-3282.
Tel: 805-642-7198; Fax: 805-642-0966; Email: school-6550@la-archdiocese.org. Patricia Groff, Prin. Lay Teachers 11; Students 252.
Catechesis Religious Program—
Tel: 805-642-7966, Ext. 125; Email: parish@ola-vta.org. Mary Joerger, D.R.E. Students 490.

2—SACRED HEART (1966)
10800 Henderson Rd., Ventura, 93004.
Tel: 805-647-3235; Email: rectory@sacredheartventura.org; Email: parish-3170@la-archdiocese.org. Revs. Aloysius Ezeonyeka; Daniel A. O'Sullivan, Pastor Emeritus, (Retired); Deacons John William Barry; Philip Conforti; Fernando M. Flores; Humberto Guzman.
School—Sacred Heart School, (Grades K-8), 10770 Henderson Rd., Ventura, 93004. Tel: 805-647-6174; Fax: 805-647-2291; Email: office@sacredheartschoolventura.org; Email: principal@sacredheartschoolventura.org; Email: school-6570@la-archdiocese.org. Christine Benner, Prin. Lay Teachers 11; Students 210.
Catechesis Religious Program—
Tel: 805-647-3235, Ext. 306; Email: re@sacredheartventura.org. Sr. Margaret Mary Scott, S.N.D., D.R.E. Students 430.

3—MISSION SAN BUENAVENTURA aka Old Mission Church / San Buenaventura Mission (1782) (Hispanic)
211 E. Main St., San Buenaventura, 93001.
Tel: 805-643-4318; Email: parish-3180@la-archdiocese.org. Revs. Thomas J. Elewaut, V.F.; Albert van der Woerd; Peter Damian Fernando, In Res., (Retired); Deacons Mark Lawrence Banda; Teodoro Landeros; Alfonso Cruz Mendez; Gustavo Catipon.
School—Holy Cross School, Tel: 805-643-1500; Email: principal@holycrossventura.org; Email: school-6580@la-archdiocese.org. Ms. Edie Lanphar, Prin. Lay Teachers 7; Students 110.
Catechesis Religious Program—Email: sistermaryrose@sanbuenaventuramissiin.org. Sr. Mary Rose Chinn, J.M.J., D.R.E. Students 282.

VERNON, LOS ANGELES CO., HOLY ANGELS PARISH OF THE DEAF (1987)
4433 Santa Fe Ave., Vernon, 90058.
Tel: 323-587-2096; Fax: 855-580-5765; Email: info@hacofthedeaf.org; Email: parish-5890@la-archdiocese.org. P.O. Box 58423, Vernon, 90058. Rev. Thomas Schweitzer; Deacons David Rose; Lawrence McGloin; Roger Gomez; Tomas Garcia Jr.
Catechesis Religious Program—Email: mescobar@hacofthedeaf.org. Maricela Escobar, D.R.E. Students 65.

WALNUT, LOS ANGELES CO., ST. LORENZO RUIZ (1991)
747 Meadowpass Rd., Walnut, 91789.
Tel: 909-595-9545; Email: parish-4760@la-archdiocese.org. Revs. Tony P. Astudillo; Martin Madero, Sch.P.
Catechesis Religious Program—Tel: 909-468-1812; Email: gabycoria@saintlorenzo.org. Gaby Coria, D.R.E. Students 428.

WEST COVINA, LOS ANGELES CO., ST. CHRISTOPHER (1954)
629 S. Glendora Ave., West Covina, 91790.
Tel: 626-960-1805; Fax: 626-851-0595; Email: parish-4590@la-archdiocese.org. Revs. Joseph Dass; Huy Nhat Nguyen; Deacons Jesse Batacan; Andrew Cho; Douglas Moloney, (Retired); Loc Nguyen.
School—St. Christopher School, (Grades PreK-8), 900 W. Christopher St., West Covina, 91790.
Tel: 626-960-3079; Fax: 626-338-7910; Email: school-7740@la-archdiocese.org. Lucia Saborio, Prin. Lay Teachers 15; Students 207.
Catechesis Religious Program—Tel: 626-338-2937. Judi Pena, D.R.E. Students 254.

WEST HOLLYWOOD, LOS ANGELES CO.

1—ST. AMBROSE (1922)
Saint Ambrose Church: 1281 N. Fairfax Ave., West Hollywood, 90046-5205. Tel: 323-656-4433; Email: stambrosech@aol.com; Email: parish-5080@la-archdiocese.org. Rev. Dennis P. Marrell; Deacon Michael Morgan, Business Mgr. & Pastoral Assoc.
Catechesis Religious Program—Students 6.

2—ST. VICTOR (1906)
8634 Holloway Dr., West Hollywood, 90069.
Tel: 310-652-6477; Email: saintvictorparish@saintvictor.org; Email: parish-4960@la-archdiocese.org. Rev. John-Paul Gonzalez, Admin.
Catechesis Religious Program—Sr. Marta Ann Corta, C.S.J., D.R.E.

WESTLAKE VILLAGE, LOS ANGELES CO., ST. JUDE (1970)
32032 W. Lindero Canyon Rd., Westlake Village, 91361-4270. Tel: 818-889-1279; Email: parish@saintjudetheapostle.org; Email: parish-3470@la-archdiocese.org. Revs. James Stehly; Peter V. Foran, In Res., (Retired); Deacons Dick Dornan; Bill Smith; Jesse Pasos; Jerome Bettencourt.
School—St. Jude School, (Grades K-8), 32036 W. Lindero Canyon Rd., Westlake Village, 91361-4270.
Tel: 818-889-9483; Email: school-6830@la-archdiocese.org. Michele Schulte, Prin. Lay Teachers 15; Students 216.
Catechesis Religious Program—Tel: 818-889-0612; Email: cindy@saintjudetheapostle.org. Cindy Kozal, D.R.E. Students 372.

WESTLAKE VILLAGE, VENTURA CO., ST. MAXIMILIAN KOLBE (1992)
5801 Kanan Rd., Westlake Village, 91362.
Tel: 818-991-3915; Fax: (818) 991-7152; Email: Kolbe@stmaxchurch.org; Email: parish-3330@la-archdiocese.org. Rev. Msgr. Paul M. Albee, V.F.; Deacons John Kruer; Christopher Laliberte; Gary Malley.
Catechesis Religious Program—
Tel: 818-991-3915, Ext. 112. Amy Laliberte, D.R.E. Students 340.

WHITTIER, LOS ANGELES CO.

1—ST. BRUNO (1955)
15740 Citrustree Rd., Whittier, 90603.
Tel: 562-947-5637, Ext. 110; Email: stbruno@stbrunochurch.org; Email: parish-5930@la-archdiocese.org. Revs. David Heney; David L. Whorton, Sacramental Min.; Abebe Teklemariam Woldemariam; Deacon P. Michael Freeman, Pastoral Assoc.
School—St. Bruno School, 15700 Citrustree Rd., Whittier, 90603. Tel: 562-943-8812;
Fax: 562-943-2172; Email: school-8980@la-archdiocese.org. Catherine Carvalho, Prin. Lay Teachers 9; Students 278.
Catechesis Religious Program—Tel: 562-943-2510. Jason Manley, D.R.E. Students 580.

2—ST. GREGORY THE GREAT (1951)
13935 Telegraph Rd., Whittier, 90604.
Tel: 562-941-0115; Fax: 562-941-3785; Email: parish-5950@la-archdiocese.org. Revs. Brian Castaneda, V.F.; Huy Nhat Nguyen; Deacon William Pilkington.
School—St. Gregory the Great School, (Grades PreK-8), 13925 Telegraph Rd., Whittier, 90604.
Tel: 562-941-0750; Fax: 562-903-7325; Email: school-8990@la-archdiocese.org. Lay Teachers 14; Students 306.
Catechesis Religious Program—Tel: 562-944-8311; Email: children@sggcatholic.org. Candace Pedroza, D.R.E. Students 180.

3—ST. MARY OF THE ASSUMPTION (1893)
7215 Newlin Ave., Whittier, 90602-1266.
Tel: 562-698-0107; Email: parish-6000@la-archdiocese.org. Revs. Steven J. Nyl, C.Ss.R.; Marcel Okwara, C.Ss.R.; Gary Lauenstein, C.Ss.R.; Mark Scheffler, C.Ss.R., Chap.; Bro. Thomas Wright, C.Ss.R., Business Mgr.; Revs. William Adams, C.Ss.R., In Res., (Retired); Joseph Butz, C.Ss.R., In Res.; John Gouger, In Res.; Anthony Phuc Nguyen, C.Ss.R., In Res.; Luong Uong, In Res.; Bro. Paul Jorns, C.Ss.R., In Res.; Deacon Bruce Sago.
School—St. Mary of the Assumption School, (Grades K-8), 7218 S. Pickering Ave., Whittier, 90602.
Tel: 562-698-0253; Fax: 562-698-0206; Email: school-9040@la-archdiocese.org. Maria Isabel Ortiz-Lopez, Prin. Lay Teachers 12; Students 232.
Catechesis Religious Program—Tel: 562-693-3764; Email: drecruces@yahoo.com; Email: parish-6000@la-archdiocese.org. Lillian Cruces, D.R.E. Students 589.

WILMINGTON, LOS ANGELES CO.

1—HOLY FAMILY (1929) (Hispanic)
1011 E. L St., Wilmington, 90744. Revs. Ruben Rocha, (Mexico); Francisco Pineda Vitela; Jesus Garcia.
Catechesis Religious Program—Tel: 310-549-0011; Email: parish-6060@la-archdiocese.org. Sr. Ines Arguello, D.R.E. Students 450.

2—SS. PETER AND PAUL (1865)
515 W. Opp St., Wilmington, 90744.
Tel: 310-834-5215; Email: sppc@sbcglobal.net; Email: parish-6110@la-archdiocese.org. Revs. Michael U. Perea, O.Praem.; Hildebrand Garceau, O.Praem.; Adrian Sanchez, O.Praem; Brendan Hankins; Claude Williams, School Rector.
School—SS. Peter and Paul School, (Grades K-8), 706 Bayview Ave., Wilmington, 90744.
Tel: 310-834-5574; Fax: 310-834-1601; Email: school-9160@la-archdiocese.org. Nancy Kuria, Prin. Lay Teachers 13; Students 210; Clergy / Religious Teachers 3.
Catechesis Religious Program—1015 Lagoon Ave., Wilmington, 90744. Tel: 310-834-5215, Ext. 53; Email: parish-6110@la-archdiocese.org. Mrs. Elsa Acevedo, D.R.E. Students 246.

WINNETKA, LOS ANGELES CO., ST. JOSEPH THE WORKER (1956) (Hispanic—Vietnamese)
19855 Sherman Way, Winnetka, 91306.
Tel: 818-341-6634; Email: parish-3460@la-archdiocese.org. 19808 Cantlay St., Winnetka, 91306. Revs. Alberto Villalobos; Thuan Nguyen; Roberto Rueda Catetano; Deacon Gus Mora.
School—St. Joseph the Worker School, (Grades PreK-8), 19812 Cantlay St., Winnetka, 91306.
Tel: 818-341-6616; Fax: 818-341-1102; Email: school-6820@la-archdiocese.org. C.J. Kruska, M.A.Ed., Prin. Lay Teachers 12; Students 258; Clergy / Religious Teachers 2.
Catechesis Religious Program—
Tel: 818-341-6634, Ext. 1016. Bill Sparks, D.R.E. Students 363.

WOODLAND HILLS, LOS ANGELES CO.

1—ST. BERNARDINE OF SIENA (1962)

24410 Calvert St., Woodland Hills, 91367.
Tel: 818-888-8200; Email: parish-3410@la-archdiocese.org. Revs. Michael J. Evans; William R. Crowe; Rev. Msgr. Richard Hayes Murray, In Res., (Retired); Deacons Dale Taufer; Steven Ellms.
Child Care—St. Bernardine of Siena Preschool, 24425 Calvert St., Woodland Hills, 91367.
Tel: 818-716-4730; Fax: 818-716-4753; Email: cbarkes@stbernardine.org. Charlene Barkes, Dir. Lay Teachers 29; Students 210.
School—St. Bernardine of Siena School, (Grades K-8), 6061 Valley Circle Blvd., Woodland Hills, 91367.
Tel: 818-340-2130; Fax: 818-340-3417; Email: school-6770@la-archdiocese.org. Mrs. Katy Kruska, Prin. Lay Teachers 29; Students 224.
Catechesis Religious Program—Tel: 818-340-1440; Email: efewless@sbcglobal.net. Eileen Fewless, D.R.E., Tel: 818-340-1440. Students 283.

2—St. Mel (1955)
20870 Ventura Blvd., Woodland Hills, 91364.
Tel: 818-340-6020; Fax: 818-340-0261; Email: parish-3480@la-archdiocese.org. Revs. Stephen V. Davoren; Vivian B. Lima; Deacon Brian Conroy; Mrs. Rosemary McLarty, Business Mgr.
Child Care—St. Mel Preschool, 5130 Serrania Ave., Woodland Hills, 91364. Tel: 818-340-3180. Claudia Powell, Dir. Lay Teachers 18; Students 119.
School—St. Mel School, (Grades K-8), 20874 Ventura Blvd., Woodland Hills, 91364. Tel: 818-340-1924; Fax: 818-347-4426; Email: school-6840@la-archdiocese.org. Mary Beth Lutz, Prin. Lay Teachers 38; Students 550.
Catechesis Religious Program—Tel: 818-340-6020; Email: mmatthews@stmel.org; Email: parish-3480@la-archdiocese.org. Monica Matthews, Rel. Educ., Children. Students 214.

On Duty Outside the Archdiocese:
Rev. Msgrs.—
Chaffman, Charles
Spiteri, Laurence J.

Graduate Studies:
Revs.—
Nguyen, Bao Huy, Advanced Studies in Rome
Ortega, Leo, Advanced Studies in Rome
Velazquez, Paul Jesus, Advanced Studies in Rome.

Hospital Chaplains:
Revs.—
Alvero, Joshua Ronnie, Chap., Los Angeles County-University of Southern California Medical Center, Los Angeles
Avestruz, Lester S., Chap., Cedars-Sinai Medical Center, Los Angeles
Ciccone, Mark, S.J., Chap., Providence St. Joseph Medical Center, Burbank
Comerford, Patrick, Chap., St. John's Health Center, Santa Monica
Delaney, Brian, Chap., Metropolitan State Hospital, Norwalk
Florido, Robert, Chap., Veterans Administration Long Beach Healthcare System, Long Beach
Ikeocha, Ikechukwu, Chap., St. Mary Medical Center, Long Beach
Jones, Robert J., C.M., Chap., Los Angeles County-University of Southern California Medical Center, Los Angeles
Kuriakose, Siju, Chap., University of California at Los Angeles Medical Center, Los Angeles
Lowe, William C.B., Chap., St. John's Regional Medical Center, Oxnard; St. John's Pleasant Valley Hospital, Camarillo
Mallin, Peter, O.F.M.Conv., Chap., Providence Little Company of Mary Medical Center Torrance, Torrance
Nwakuna, Anselm, Chap., Providence Tarzana Medical Center, Tarzana
Onyenobi, Christopher, Chap., Providence Little Company of Mary Medical Center San Pedro, San Pedro
Ozoufuanya, Victor, Chap., St. Mary Medical Center, Long Beach
Ponnet, Christopher, Chap., Los Angeles County-University of Southern California Medical Center, Los Angeles
Saldua, Max E., Chap., Veterans Administration Greater Los Angeles Health System, Los Angeles
Sigler, John, F.S.P., Chap., Cedars Sinai Medical Center, Los Angeles.

Jail and Prison Chaplains:
Revs.—
Griesgraber, Paul Gerard, Chap., Los Angeles Men's Central Jail, Los Angeles
Horan, George E., Los Angeles Men's Central Jail, Los Angeles
Kennedy, Michael E., S.J., Barry J. Nidorf Juvenile Hall, Sylmar.

Military Chaplains:
Revs.—
Kelly, Thomas, Chap., Vandenberg Air Force
Nguyen, Long, Chap., Navy Chaplain.

Public Safety Chaplains:
Revs.—
Folbrecht, Robert, Chap., Los Angeles County Fire Department, Los Angeles
McCullough, Michael P., Los Angeles Police Department, Los Angeles.

On Active Leave:
Revs.—
Byrne, Keith
Carcerano, Michael J.
Collins, John Michael
Lui, Tovia
Marquez, Esteban.

On Sick Leave:
Rev. Msgr.—
Woolway, John S.
Revs.—
Cavanagh, James
Folbrecht, Robert A.
Nuanez, Anthony
Rendon, Samuel
Souza, Jason
Troxell, Christopher
Velazquez, David M.

On Administrative Leave:
Rev. Msgr.—
Zak, Steven B., J.C.L., V.F.
Revs.—
Cano, Juan
Garcia, Sergio E.
Juarez, Lucio
Monico Soltero, Gilberto
Sears, Michael J.
Song, Simeon.

Retired:
His Eminence—
Mahony, Roger Cardinal, (Retired), St. Charles Borromeo Catholic Church, 10834 Moorpark St., North Hollywood, 91602-2206
Most Revs.—
Curry, Thomas J., D.D., Ph.D., V.G., (Retired), St. Augustine Catholic Church, 3850 Jasmine Ave., Culver City, 90232-3190
Salazar, Alexander, D.D., V.G., (Retired)
Sartoris, Joseph M., D.D., V.G., (Retired), 1988 Rolling Vista Dr., #21, Lomita, 90717
Wilkerson, Gerald E., D.D., V.G., (Retired), 9329 Crebs Ave., Northridge, 91324-2909
Zavala, Gabino, (Retired)
Rev. Msgrs.—
Acton, Sean A., (Retired), Nazareth House, 3333 Manning Ave., 90064
Acton, Thomas M., (Retired), Maria Regina Catholic Church, 2150 W. 135th St., Gardena, 90249-2498
Amy, Peter L., (Retired), St. Didacus Catholic Church, 14339 Astoria St., Sylmar, 91342-4124
Bauler, Gary Patrick, (Retired), 16030 Marine Dr., Huntington Beach, 92649
Bell, Carl F., (Retired), 13821 Fresh Meadow Ln., Apt. #7D, Seal Beach, 90740
Bunny, J. Michael, V.F., (Retired), 21621 Sandia Rd., #167, Apple Valley, 92308
Cavanagh, Brian M., (Retired), Sacred Heart Catholic Church, 344 W. Workman St., Covina, 91723-3345
Cokus, Joseph J., (Retired), 3 La Serena, Irvine, 92612
Colberg, James Philip, (Retired), 414 E. Church St., Santa Maria, 93454
Connolly, Clement J., (Retired), Holy Family Catholic Church, 1527 Fremont Ave., South Pasadena, 91030-3736
Donnelly, Lawrence Edward, (Retired), 1065 W. Lomita Blvd., Space 411, Harbor City, 90710
Downes, Stephen N., V.F., (Retired), Our Lady of Mount Carmel Catholic Church, 1300 E. Valley Rd., Santa Barbara, 93108
Duc Minh, Joseph N., (Retired), 432 S. Harbor Blvd., Apt. #37, Santa Ana, 92704-1368
Fitzgerald, John Gerard, V.F., (Retired), Queen of Angels Catholic Church, 3495 Rucker Rd., Lompoc, 93436
Flanagan, Sean B., (Retired), Nazareth House, 3333 Manning Ave., 90064-4804
Gilb, Eugene A., (Retired), Nazareth House, 3333 Manning Ave., 90064
Gipson, Robert W., (Retired), 489 E. Laurel Cir., Palm Springs, 92262
Gomez, Henry, Proto Notary Apostolic, (Retired), 1401 Pebbledon St., Monterey Park, 91754
Hefner, Helmut A., J.C.L., (Retired), P.O. Box 6570, Pine Mountain Club, 93222-6570
Herrera, Emigdio, (Retired), 519 W. Taylor, Space 318, Santa Maria, 93458
Hill, Charles E., (Retired), 517 E. 220th St., Carson, 90745
Howard, Robert E., (Retired), 489 E. Laurel Cir., Palm Springs, 92263
Jennett, Michael J., S.T.D., (Retired), San Roque Catholic Church, 325 Argonne Cir., Santa Barbara, 93105
Killeen, Michael F., (Retired), Nazareth House, 3333 Manning Ave., 90064
Krekelberg, Richard G., V.F., (Retired)
Larkin, Kevin John, (Retired), St. Francis de Sales Catholic Church, 13360 Valleyheart Dr., Sherman Oaks, 91423-3287
Leheny, Bernard, E.V., (Retired), San Pedro Pastoral Region, 3555 Saint Pancratius Pl., Lakewood, 90712
Leser, William J., C.B., S.T.B., (Retired), 18550 W. Vincennes St., Apt. 108, Northridge, 91324
Loftus, Padraic, (Retired), 22046 Providencia St., Woodland Hills, 91364
Matas, Juan, (Retired), 1947 Palm Ave., Monterey Park, 91755
McNamara, Robert J., (Retired), St. Bernardine of Siena Catholic Church, 24410 Calvert St., Woodland Hills, 91367
McNulty, Patrick, (Retired), Nazareth House, 3333 Manning Ave., 90064-4804
Milbauer, Robert L., V.F., (Retired), St. John the Baptist de la Salle Catholic Church, 10738 Hayvenhurst St., Granada Hills, 91344
Montoya, Paul M., (Retired), P.O. Box 2008, Lucerne Valley, 92356
Moran, Peter C., (Retired), 9801 Canby Ave., Northridge, 91325
Mulcahy, Donal, (Retired), 1201 S. Olive St., 90015
Murray, Richard Hayes, (Retired), St. Bernardine of Siena Catholic Church, 24410 Calvert St., Woodland Hills, 91367-1099
Nugent, Peter D., (Retired), St. Charles Borromeo Catholic Church, 10834 Moorpark St., North Hollywood, 91602
O'Connell, Timothy P., (Retired), Mary Star of the Sea Catholic Church, 870 W. 8th St., San Pedro, 90731. Tel: 310-547-1930
O'Keefe, William Joseph, (Retired), Our Lady of Refuge Catholic Church, 5195 Stearns St., Long Beach, 90815-2901
O'Reilly, Peter A., (Retired), St. Lawrence Martyr Catholic Church, 1940 S. Prospect St., Redondo Beach, 90277
O'Toole, William P., (Retired), Marycrest Manor, 10664 Saint James Dr., Culver City, 90230
Priebe, Norman F., V.F., (Retired), St. Dorothy Catholic Church, 241 S. Valley Center Ave., Glendora, 91741
Richey, Terrence, (Retired), St. Basil Catholic Church, 637 S. Kingsley Dr., 90005-2392
Rodriguez, Benigno Antonio, (Retired), 12109 Bayla St., Norwalk, 90650
Royer, Ronald Edmund, (Retired), 40708-B Balch Park Rd., Springville, 93265
Schmit, Jerome L., (Retired), Sacred Heart Catholic Church, 1215 S. Hamilton Blvd., Pomona, 91766
Segaric, John, (Retired), Trg Sv Stosije 1, Zadar, Croatia 23000
Slattery, Michael J., (Retired), St. Kateri Tekakwitha Catholic Church, 22508 Copper Hill Dr., Santa Clarita, 91350-4299
Staunton, Patrick Joseph, (Retired), St. Joseph Catholic Church, 550 N. Glendora Ave., La Puente, 91744-5112
Steinbock, Leo E., (Retired), P.O. Box 1950, Covina, 91722
Tseu, Andrew Stanislaus, (Retired), St. Madeleine Catholic Church, 931 E. Kingsley Ave., Pomona, 91767-5098
Wallace, Francis T., J.C.L., (Retired), St. Robert Bellarmine Catholic Church, 133 N. 5th St., Burbank, 91501-2178
Weber, Francis J., (Retired), San Fernando Mission Catholic Church, 15151 San Fernando Mission Blvd., Mission Hills, 91345-2617
Welbers, Thomas, (Retired), Nazareth House, 3333 Manning Ave., 90064
Revs.—
Albarano, Richard, (Retired), Palm Canyon Villas #139, 5301 E. Waverly Dr., Palm Springs, 92264
Alvarez, Porfirio, (Retired), St. Anthony Catholic Church, 2511 S. C St., Oxnard, 93034-2215
Assi, Nicholas, (Retired), St. Luke the Evangelist Catholic Church, 5605 Cloverly Ave., Temple City, 91780-0798
Barnes, James H., (Retired), 5000 S. Centinela Ave., #332, 90066
Belletty, Emile Ignatius, (Retired), 22039 Mariposa Ave., Torrance, 90502

Blanco, Adalberto, (Retired), 3885 Samuel Dr. #179, Oxnard, 93033
Brincat, George, (Retired), Holy Redeemer Catholic Church, 2411 Montrose Ave., Montrose, 91020
Bugayong, Demetrio L., (Retired), St. Philomena Catholic Church, 21900 S. Main St., Carson, 90745-2998
Buhr, Eugene S., (Retired), Nazareth House, 3333 Manning Ave., 90064-4804
Carlo, Cyprian, (Retired), St. Cyril of Jerusalem Catholic Church, 4601 Firmament Ave., Encino, 91436
Castaneda, Severiano, (Retired), 1308 S. Ferris Ave., 90022
Ciordia, Pedro M., (Retired), Residencia Sacerdotal, Avenida Baja Navarra 64, Pamplona, Navarra, Spain
Colborn, Francis R., S.T.D., (Retired), 333 Old Mill Rd., #236, Santa Barbara, 93110
Connor, William Joseph, (Retired), 2500 E. 2nd St., #205, Long Beach, 90803
Coronado, Genaro, (Retired), St. John of God Retirement Center, 2468 South St. Andrews Pl., 90018
De Souza, Owen, (Retired), 22039 Mariposa Ave., Torrance, 90502
Deasy, Kenneth H., (Retired), 3909 Mahinahina St., Lahaina, HI 96761
Devine, Finbarr Columba, (Retired), Avila Gardens, 1171 Encanto Pkwy., Duarte, 91010
Dober, Edward J., (Retired), 10000 Imperial Way., Apt. E105, Downey, 90242
Dolan, Jarlath, (Retired), 32 Irena Ave., Camarillo, 93012
Doran, Brian D., (Retired), 3206 Vermont Ave., Costa Mesa, 92626
Elis, Tomas Alfonso, (Retired), 20520 Seaboard Rd., Malibu, 90265
Fahey, John Peter, (Retired), Santa Clara Catholic Church, 323 S. 'E' St., Oxnard, 93030
Feltz, Thomas, (Retired), Our Lady of Grace Catholic Church, 5011 White Oak Ave., Encino, 91316-3799
Fernandes, Roque A.D., (Retired), St. Frances of Rome Church Catholic Church, 501 E. Foothill Blvd., Azusa, 91702
Fernando, Damian, (Retired), San Buenaventura Mission Catholic Church, 211 E. Main St., Ventura, 93001
Foran, Peter V., (Retired), St. Jude Catholic Church, 32032 W. Lindero Canyon, Westlake Village, 91361-4270
Fox, Daniel A., (Retired), 10378 Lakeshore Dr., Apple Valley, 92308
Galaz, Jesse Cayetano, (Retired), 13637 Dunrobin Ave., Bellflower, 90706
Gannon, Patrick J., (Retired), Nazareth House, 3333 Manning Ave., 90064-4804
Garcia, Guillermo C., Ph.D., (Retired), 3824 Elm Ave., Long Beach, 90049
Gatlin, Bernard J., (Retired), 4045 E. Center St., Piru, 93040
Glynn, Thomas Joseph, (Retired), Nazareth House, 3333 Manning Ave., 90064
Habison, Gerhart, (Retired), Nativity Catholic Church, 1447 Engracia Ave., Torrance, 90501
Haefeli, Joaquin C., (Retired), Nazareth House, 3333 Manning Ave., 90064
Hernando, Henry L., (Retired), 4102 Michigan Dr., Unit C, Silverdale, WA 98315
Hill, Patrick J., J.C.L., D.Min., (Retired), 519 E. 220th St., Carson, 90745
Janowski, Rock J., (Retired), 1241 S. Petit Ave., #5, Ventura, 93004
Java, Miguel B., (Philippines) (Retired), St. Basil Catholic Church, 637 S. Kingsley Dr., 90005
Johnson, Henry Joseph, (Retired), 4676 Admiralty Way, Ste. 101, Marina Del Rey, 90292
Joy, Laurence, (Retired), P.O. Box 435090, San Ysidro, 92143
Kavanagh, James F., (Retired), St. James Catholic Church, 124 N. Pacific Coast Hwy., Redondo Beach, 90277-3194
Kelly, Paul Maurice, (Retired), 1211 N. Ogden Dr., West Hollywood, 90046
Kerze, William F., (Retired), Our Lady of Malibu Catholic Church, 3625 Winter Canyon Rd., Malibu, 90265-4834
King, Thomas F., (Retired), 32 Avenue 27, Venice, 90291
Lee, Joshua Peter, (Retired), 12850 E Ave. W11, Pearblossom, 93553
Lewis, Eric Anthony, (Retired), 837 W. 4th St., Azusa, 91702
Llanos, Phillip S., (Retired), P.O. Box 608, Edwards, 93523
Lui, Gabriel, (Retired), 5216 Future Dr., Las Vegas, NV 89130-0150
Madrigal, Ildefonso M., (Retired), Mary Health of the Sick Hospital, 2929 Theresa Dr., Newbury Park, 91320
Maher, James Joseph, (Retired), 2334 Wild Rose Ct., Mohave Valley, AZ 86440
McDonnell, Anthony, (Retired), 8745 S. Liberator Ave., Westchester, 90045
McLean, William, (Retired), 1460 Homewood Rd. #95K, Seal Beach, 90740
McNulty, Gerard J., (Retired), 2722 E. 20th St., Unit 204, Signal Hill, 90755
Menke, Paul F., (Retired), P.O. Box 39518, 90039
Merino, Santiago James, (Retired), 3156 Marybeth Ave., El Monte, 91733
Miskella, Richard, (Retired), Rathimney Gusserane, New Ross, County Wexford Ireland
Moniz, Joseph Vincent, (Retired), St. Philip the Apostle Catholic Church, 151 S. Hill Ave., Pasadena, 91106-3498
Neiman, John Warren, (Retired), 75-065 Muirfield Ct., Indiana Wells, 92210
O'Brien, George Patrick, (Retired), Good Shepherd Catholic Church, 504 N. Roxbury Rd., Beverly Hills, 90210-3227
O'Grady, James F., (Retired), Visitation Catholic Church, 6561 W. 88th St., 90045-3716
O'Keeffe, Jeremiah E., (Retired), Our Lady of Lourdes Catholic Church, 18405 Superior St., Northridge, 91325
O'Leary, Niall Finbarr, (Retired), 1000 El Centro, Apt. 101, South Pasadena, 91030
O'Mahony, Maurice K., (Retired), Our Lady of Mount Carmel Catholic Church, 1300 E. Valley Rd., Santa Barbara, 93108-1294
O'Neill, Jeremiah, (Retired), 2100 W. Carlos Ave., Alhambra, 91803-4321
O'Ryan, Colm, (Retired), Good Shepherd Catholic Church, 504 N. Roxbury Rd., Beverly Hills, 90210-3298
O'Shea, Michael, (Retired), 11 Taobh Linn, Kenmare, County Kerry Ireland
O'Sullivan, Daniel A., (Retired), Sacred Heart Catholic Church, 10800 Henderson Rd., Ventura, 93004-1895
Ochoa, David, (Mexico) (Retired), St. Emydius Catholic Church, 10900 California Ave., Lynwood, 90262
Phelan, Cornelius Noel, (Retired), Nazareth House, 3333 Manning Ave., 90064
Poljicak, Vlatko, (Retired), St. Anthony (Croatian) Church, 712 N. Grand Ave., 90012
Ramirez, Francisco X., (Retired), 1046 E. 34th St., 90011
Roebert, Michael, (Retired), St. John's Seminary, 5012 Seminary Rd., Camarillo, 93012
Roman, Julio, (Retired), P.O. Box 226934, 90022
Romero, Gilbert Claude, (Retired), 13220 Southport Ln., #170-E., Seal Beach, 90740-3361
Romero, Juan R., (Retired), 2347 Los Patos Dr., Palm Springs, 92264
Scott, Alfonso A., (Retired), 6246 Crystal Cove Lot #236, Long Beach, 90803
Shelton, Lawrence, (Retired), St. Anselm Catholic Church, 2222 W. 70th St., 90043
Siebenand, Paul Alcuin, (Retired), 81897Avenida Estuco, Indio, 92203-4338
Soto, Edward P., (Retired), St. Rose of Lima Catholic Church, 4450 E. 60th St., Maywood, 90270-3198
Supancheck, Norman A., (Retired), St. Didacus Catholic Church, 14339 Astoria St., Sylmar, 91342
Suquilvide, Abel, (Retired), Nazareth House, 3333 Manning Ave., 90064-4804
Thompson, Jerald Wayne, (Retired), P.O. Box 455, Concho, AZ 85924
Thompson, Jerome H., (Retired), 25501 Crown Valley Pkwy., #221, Ladera Ranch, 92694
Tran, John Nghi C., (Retired), P.O. Box 2068, Garden Grove, 92842
Tsang, Peter, (Retired), 1739 Bolanos Ave., Rowland Heights, 91748
Wah, Joseph C., (Retired), 1328 Teal Ave., Paso Robles, 93446
Walker, Gerald Bernard, (Retired), 2020 Via Mariposa E., Unit C, Laguna Woods, 92637-0890
Wolfe, William P., J.C.L., (Retired), 647 Willcox Ave., #3E, 90004
Wolkovits, Paul Dennis, (Retired), 406 Ravenshill Way, DeLand, FL 32724
Wu, Jay, (Retired), 19621 Searls Dr., Rowland Heights, 91748
Young, Gerald A., (Retired), 121 Vista View Dr., Montrose, CO 81401.

Permanent Deacons:
Abalos, Roland, St. Finbar Catholic Church, Burbank
Abrera, Jaime, St. Francis Xavier Catholic Church, Burbank
Adams, Ryan, St. Charles Borromeo Catholic Church, North Hollywood
Aguilera, Gabriel Jr., (Retired), St. Kateri Tekakwitha Catholic Church, Santa Clarita
Aguirre, Ancelmo, Old Mission Santa Ines, Solvang
Aispuro, Genaro, St. Joseph Catholic Church, Carpinteria
Alefosio, Maselino, St. Catherine Laboure Catholic Church, Torrance
Alexander, Hosea Sr., Holy Name of Jesus Catholic Church, Los Angeles
Allgaier, James, Our Lady of the Assumption Catholic Church, Claremont
Amantea, Chris, American Martyrs Catholic Church, Manhattan Beach
Amos, Daniel, St. Paul the Apostle Catholic Church, Los Angeles
Andrade, J. Trinidad, Holy Cross Catholic Church, Moorpark
Arana, Antonio, St. Clare Catholic Church, Santa Clarita
Aranda, Fernando Jr., San Gabriel Mission Catholic Church, San Gabriel
Arban, Wilfredo, St. Dominic Savio Catholic Church, Bellflower
Arias, Isaac, Our Lady of Guadalupe Catholic Church, El Monte
Ascencio, Juan Francisco, St. Cecilia Catholic Church, Los Angeles
Austin, Alfred H., Holy Name of Mary Catholic Church, San Dimas
Aviles, Salvador, St. Hilary Catholic Church, Pico Rivera
Baker, Ronald, Holy Family Catholic Church, Glendale
Banda, Mark Lawrence, San Buenaventura Mission Catholic Church, Ventura
Barajas, Henry Jr., Our Lady of Guadalupe Catholic Church, Oxnard
Barragan, Arturo, St. John the Baptist Catholic Church, Baldwin Park
Barragan, Ricardo N., St. Mary Magdalen Catholic Church, Camarillo
Barrera, Jose Oscar, Sagrado Corazon Catholic Church, Compton
Barrios, Margarito, St. Joseph Catholic Church, Pomona
Barry, John William, Sacred Heart Catholic Church, Ventura
Batacan, Jesse, St. Christopher Catholic Church, West Covina
Bautista, Rolando, Holy Trinity Catholic Church, Los Angeles
Benalcazar, Eudoro G., All Souls Catholic Church, Alhambra
Benavides, Jose de Jesus, St. Marcellinus, Los Angeles
Bernal, Daniel, St. Thomas the Apostle Catholic Church, Los Angeles
Bernal, Joseph, St. Francis Xavier Catholic Church, Pico Rivera
Bernal, Sergio, Our Lady of Guadalupe Catholic Church, Guadalupe
Berumen, Ricardo, St. John Neumann Catholic Church, Santa Maria
Betancourt, Guillermo, Our Lady of the Valley Catholic Church
Betliskey, Michael Joseph, St. Joseph Catholic Church, Carpinteria
Bettencourt, Jerome, Santa Clara Catholic Church, Oxnard
Bettencourt, Jerome, St. Jude Catholic Church, Westlake Village
Blanco, Raul, St. Louis de Montfort Catholic Church, Santa Maria
Boerger, Christopher, St. Louis de Montfort Catholic Church, Santa Maria
Bojorquez, Daniel, Our Lady of the Assumption Catholic Church, Ventura
Bond, Joseph, St. Julie Billiart Catholic Church, Newbury Park
Boucher, Richard, St. Cornelius Catholic Church, Long Beach
Brandlin, Thomas E., M.N.A., St. Teresa of Avila Catholic Church, Los Angeles
Brause, Peter, St. Louise de Marillac Catholic Church, Covina
Brenes, Francisco, St. Finbar Catholic Church, Burbank
Brown, Derek A., American Martyrs Catholic Church, Manhattan Beach
Burns, Michael, Our Lady of the Assumption Catholic Church, Ventura
Burt, Donald, St. Lawrence Martyr, Redondo Beach
Butler, Ronald, Sacred Heart Catholic Church, Covina
Cabello, Luis, Our Lady of Sorrows Catholic Church, Santa Barbara
Calderon, Efrain, St. Mary Catholic Church, Palmdale
Calderon, Fernando, Queen of Angels Catholic Church, Lompoc

Camacho, Raymond, St. Didacus Catholic Church, Sylmar
Caputo, Edward E., St. Mary Catholic Church, Palmdale
Carmody, Richard, St. Louis de Montfort Catholic Church, Santa Maria
Carper, James, St. Peter Claver Catholic Church, Simi Valley
Castillo, Alfonso, St. Benedict Catholic Church, Montebello
Castillo, Eduardo, Holy Cross Catholic Church, Moorpark
Castillo, Marvin, St. Junipero Serra Catholic Church, Lancaster
Castro, Carlos, St. Elizabeth, Van Nuys
Catipon, Gus, San Buenaventura Mission Catholic Church, Ventura
Ceja, Victor Alejandro, Out Lady of Perpetual Help, Downey
Chacon, Pedro, St. Alphonsus Catholic Church, Los Angeles
Chavez, Manuel, St. Anthony Catholic Church, San Gabriel
Chavez, Raul, Guardian Angel Catholic Church, Pacoima
Chevez, Roberto I., Our Lady of Guadalupe Catholic Church, Irwindale
Cho, Taejun, St. Christopher Catholic Church, West Covina
Chu, Peter, St. Elizabeth Ann Seton Catholic Church, Rowland Heights
Ciau, Faustino, St. Athanasius Catholic Church, Long Beach
Clements, Brian, St. Peter Claver Catholic Church, Simi Valley
Conforti, Philip, Sacred Heart Catholic Church, Ventura
Conroy, Brian, St. Mel Catholic Church, Woodland Hills
Copon, Ricardo Pareja Jr., Mary Star of the Sea Catholic Church, Oxnard
Corcios, Oscar A., Our Lady of the Rosary Catholic Church, Paramount
Cordero, Ruben A., Guardian Angel Catholic Church, Pacoima
Corletto, Juan, St. Ann Catholic Church, Santa Monica
Cottam, Andrew, St. Mary Magdalen Catholic Church, Camarillo
Coulter, Patrick, Holy Cross Catholic Church, Moorpark
Crawford, Vincent, Santa Clara Catholic Church, Oxnard
Cremer, Douglas, St. Elizabeth Catholic Church, Altadena
Cruz, Miguel, St. Joseph Catholic Church, Los Angeles
Cruz, Victor, St. Albert the Great Catholic Church, Rancho Domingue
Cuda, Shane, St. Joseph Catholic Church, Long Beach
De Leon, Pedro, St. Joseph Catholic Church, Hawthorne
De Los Reyes, Carlito, St. Barnabas Catholic Church, Long Beach
Diaz, Jose, Sacred Heart Catholic Church, Altadena
Dierking, John, St. Frances of Rome Catholic Church, Azusa
Domond, Joseph, Our Lady of the Assumption Catholic Church, Claremont
Dornan, Richard, St. Jude Catholic Church, Westlake Village
Dumlao, Felix, St. Columban Catholic Church, Los Angeles
Echeverry, Carlos (Charlie), St. Gerard Majella Catholic Church, Los Angeles
Edie, Isaac (Ike), St. Junipero Serra, Camarillo
Egnatuk, James A., St. Lawrence Martyr Catholic Church, Redondo Beach
Elchert, Ron, St. Pius X Catholic Church, Santa Fe Springs
Ellms, Steven, St. Bernardine of Siena Catholic Church, Woodland Hills
Enriquez, Marciano, Our Lady of Lourdes Catholic Church, Tujunga
Espinosa, Alfredo, St. Louis de Montfort Catholic Church, Santa Maria
Esseff, George J. Jr., St. Mary Magdalen Catholic Church, Camarillo
Estey, Marvin, Holy Name of Mary Catholic Church, San Dimas
Estrada, Armando, St. Stephen Catholic Church, Monterey Park
Estrada, David J., St. Benedict Catholic Church, Montebello
Fargo, Robert, St. Junipero Serra, Camarillo
Fermin, Gilberto, Our Lady of Guadalupe Catholic Church, Santa Barbara
Fernandez, Jesus, Santa Rosa Catholic Church, San Fernando
Fernandez, Louis Homero, St. Rose of Lima Catholic Church, Simi Valley
Finocchiaro, Michael, St. Dominic Catholic Church, Los Angeles
Flores, Alfonso, Mary Star of the Sea Catholic Church, Oxnard
Flores, Fernando, Sacred Heart Catholic Church, Ventura
Flores, Joseph, St. Benedict Catholic Church, Montebello
Flores, Michael, St. Frances of Rome Catholic Church, Azusa
Freeman, P. Michael, St. Bruno Catholic Church, Whittier
Frias, Sam, St. John the Baptist de la Salle Catholic Church, Granada Hills
Gacasan, Genaro Roy, St. Junipero Serra, Camarillo
Galido, Juan Jr., Our Lady of Lourdes Catholic Church, Northridge
Gallegos, Jose, St. Elizabeth Catholic Church, Altadena
Galvez, Miguel, Sacred Heart Catholic Church, Pomona
Garcia, Adan, Our Lady of Guadalupe Catholic Church, El Monte
Garcia, Armando, St. Marcellinus Catholic Church, Los Angeles
Garcia Bejarano, Marco Antonio, Christ the King Catholic Church, Los Angeles
Garcia Cruz, Juan Rogelio, St. Frances of Rome Catholic Church, Azusa
Garcia, George Angel, St. Anthony Catholic Church, Oxnard
Garcia, Jose, St. John the Baptist Catholic Church, Baldwin Park
Garcia, Rene, St. John of God Catholic Church, Norwalk
Garcia, Rogelio, St. Thomas More Catholic Church, Alhambra
Garcia, Tomas Jr., Holy Angels Church of the Deaf, Vernon
Gath, Don, St. Joseph Catholic Church, Long Beach
Girard, Joseph, St. Mark Catholic Church, Venice
Gleason, Eugene, Beatitudes of Our Lord Catholic Church, La Mirada
Godinez, Jose Arturo, Our Lady of Guadalupe Catholic Church, Oxnard
Gomez, Fermin, St. Didacus Catholic Church, Sylmar
Gomez, Roger, Holy Angels Church of the Deaf, Vernon
Gonzalez, Arturo, Our Lady of Sorrows Catholic Church, Santa Barbara
Gonzalez, Doroteo, Epiphany Catholic Church, South El Monte
Gonzalez, Francisco J., St. Lucy Catholic Church, Long Beach
Gonzalez, Frank, St. John of God Catholic Church
Gonzalez, Jose, Our Lady of the Assumption Catholic Church, Ventura
Gonzalez, Luis, St. Joseph Catholic Church, La Puente
Gonzalez, Roberto, Our Lady of Sorrows Catholic Church, Santa Barbara
Gorospe, Santiago, St. Madeleine Catholic Church, Pomona
Gosdschan, Falk, Our Lady of Guadalupe Catholic Church, Santa Barbara
Guadamuz, Jose, Holy Name of Mary Catholic Church, San Dimas
Guerra, Mario, St. Linus Catholic Church, Norwalk
Guerra-Ramos, Alfred William, St. Denis Catholic Church, Diamond Bar
Guerra-Ramos, Mauricio, St. Emydius Catholic Church, Lynwood
Guerrero, Jaime S., St. Louis of France Catholic Church, La Puente
Guiao, Rey, Our Lady of Peace Catholic Church, North Hills
Guilin, Alfonso, St. Sebastian Catholic Church, Santa Paula
Guzman, Felipe, Resurrection Catholic Church, Los Angeles
Guzman, Humberto, Sacred Heart Catholic Church, Ventura
Halliwell, Thomas L., St. Joseph Catholic Church, Long Beach
Halvorsen, Douglas A., St. Louis de Montfort Catholic Church, Santa Maria
Hamamoto, Joseph, St. Cornelius Catholic Church, Long Beach
Harper, John Barry, St. Julie Billiart Catholic Church, Newbury Park
Harutunian, Serj, Incarnation Catholic Church, Glendale
Heffernan, Glen, Our Lady of Grace Catholic Church, Encino
Hernandez, Roberto, Holy Spirit Catholic Church, Los Angeles
Herrera, Fermin, Sacred Heart Catholic Church, Lancaster
Herrera-Hernandez, Gilberto, Our Lady of Peace Catholic Church, North Hills
Hidalgo, Hector M., Beatitudes of Our Lord Catholic Church, La Mirada
Hillmann, Steven V., St. Elizabeth Ann Seton Catholic Church, Rowland Heights
Hoang, Son, St. Catherine of Siena Catholic Church, Reseda
Holderness, Alan, St. Louise de Marillac Catholic Church, Covina
Holguin, Michael, Santa Clara Catholic Church, Oxnard
Horn, John G., Sacred Heart Catholic Church, Covina
Huerta, Antonio, St. Anthony of Padua Catholic Church, Gardena
Huntley, Donald, Our Lady of the Assumption, Ventura
Irwin, Terrence Raymond, St. Kateri Tekakwitha Catholic Church, Santa Clarita
Islas, Sergio, St. Francis Xavier Catholic Church, Pico Rivera
Ito, Mitchell, St. Paschal Baylon Catholic Church, Thousand Oaks
Ixta, Ignacio, Mary Star of the Sea Catholic Church, Oxnard
Jaurequi, Raymond, Holy Angels Catholic Church, Arcadia
Jimenez, Agustin, St. Louis of France Catholic Church, La Puente
Joerger, Philip, Our Lady of the Assumption, Ventura
Johnson, Douglass R. Sr., Holy Name of Jesus Catholic Church, Los Angeles
Juarez-Ramirez, Paulino, St. Genevieve Catholic Church, Panorama City
Karl, Richard J., Our Lady of Perpetual Help Catholic Church, Santa Clarita
Kennedy, Joseph Charles, St. Anthony Catholic Church, Oxnard
Kingsley, Neil Joseph, St. Junipero Serra, Camarillo
Kromm, Michael, Holy Cross Catholic Church, Moorpark
Krueger, William, Holy Family Catholic Church, South Pasadena
Kruer, John, St. Maximilian Kolbe Catholic Church, Westlake Village
Lacbain, Leonardo, Santa Clara Catholic Church, Oxnard
Laliberte, Christopher, St. Maximilian Kolbe Catholic Church, Westlake Village
Landa, William, St. Philip the Apostle Catholic Church, Pasadena
Landeros, Teodoro, San Buenaventura Mission Catholic Church, Ventura
Lara, Frederick Peter, Our Lady of the Miraculous Medal Catholic Church, Montebello
Lauderdale, Walter John, Holy Trinity Catholic Church, San Pedro
Lawrence, David, St. Julie Billiart Catholic Church, Newbury Park
Lawrence, David Paul, St. Rose of Lima Catholic Church, Simi Valley
Ledonne, Tom, St. Denis Catholic Church, Diamond Bar
Lee, Paul D., St. Agnes Catholic Church, Los Angeles
Leyva, Rodolfo R., Sacred Heart Catholic Church, Covina
Ligot, Romeo (Romy), St. Pancratius Catholic Church, Lakewood
Lim, James, St. Joseph Korean Catholic Center, Canoga Park
Lira, Pedro, St. Catherine of Siena Catholic Church, Reseda
Lopez, Arnaldo, Holy Angels Catholic Church, Arcadia
Lopez, Francisco Javier, Our Lady of Guadalupe Catholic Church, Oxnard
Lopez, Jose de Jesus, Mary Immaculate Catholic Church, Pacoima
Lopez, Lawrence James, Santa Clara Catholic Church, Oxnard
Lopez, Rito R., St. Junipero Serra Catholic Church, Lancaster
Lopez, Sergio, St. Raphael Catholic Church, Santa Barbara
Luevanos, Philip, St. Denis Catholic Church, Diamond Bar
Lujan, Michael, Queen of Angels Catholic Church, Lompoc
Lumsdaine, Joseph, St. Dominic Savio Catholic Church, Bellflower
Mabansag, Romeo, St. Mary of the Assumption Catholic Church, Santa Maria
Macias, Aurelio Robles, St. Anthony Catholic Church, Oxnard
Madrigal, Carlos, Sacred Heart Catholic Church, Pomona

Magos, Carlos, Precious Blood Catholic Church, Los Angeles
Malca, Jorge Enrique, Mary Star of the Sea Catholic Church, San Pedro
Mallaley, Gary, St. Maximilian Kolbe Catholic Church, Westlake Village
Marin, Alejandro, Holy Name of Jesus Catholic Church, Los Angeles
Marquez, Miguel, La Purisima Concepcion Catholic Church, Lompoc
Marron, Alejandro Zendejas, Our Lady of Guadalupe Catholic Church, Oxnard
Marsh, Steven R., St. Dorothy Catholic Church, Glendora
Martinez, Jesse, St. John Vianney Catholic Church, Hacienda Heights
Martinez, Manuel J., St. Mary Magdalen Catholic Church, Camarillo
Martinez, Miguel Angel, St. Raphael Catholic Church, Los Angeles
Mauch, Kevin Barry, Holy Cross Catholic Church, Moorpark
McCarthy, Kevin, Our Lady of Perpetual Help Catholic Church, Santa Clarita
McGloin, Lawrence, Holy Angels of the Deaf, Vernon
Medina, Richard J., Our Lady of Perpetual Help Catholic Church, Downey
Mejia, Antonio, St. Louis de Montfort Catholic Church, Santa Maria
Mejia, Mario, St. Linus Catholic Church, Norwalk
Mendez, Alfonso Cruz, San Buenaventura Mission Catholic Church, Ventura
Mendoza, Anacleto, St. Margaret Mary Alacoque Catholic Church, Lomita
Miller, Robert J., St. James Catholic Church, Redondo Beach
Mills, Edgar, Our Lady of the Assumption Catholic Church, Ventura
Mitchell, Charles A., St. Elizabeth of Hungary Catholic Church, Altadena
Mizerski, Joseph R., St. Therese Catholic Church, Alhambra
Modugno, Larry, St. Mary Magdalen Catholic Church, Camarillo
Molina, Raul, St. Anne Catholic Church, Santa Monica
Montoya, Samuel, St. Pancratius Catholic Church, Lakewood
Montross, Stephen, St. Raphael Catholic Church, Santa Barbara
Moon, Ronald, St. Mary Magdalen Catholic Church, Camarillo
Mora, Augusto, St. Joseph the Worker Catholic Church, Winnetka
Mora, Ricardo, St. Ferdinand Catholic Church, San Fernando
Morales-Cabello, Jose Noe, Mary Star of the Sea Catholic Church, Oxnard
Morgan, Michael, St. Ambrose Catholic Church, West Hollywood
Munoz, David Joel, Our Lady of Sorrows Catholic Church, Santa Barbara
Munoz, Gaspar, Holy Trinity Catholic Church, San Pedro
Navarro, Juan Alfonso, St. Joseph Catholic Church, Hawthorne
Nelson, Phillip, St. Thomas Aquinas Catholic Church, Ojai
Nguyen, Loc, St. Christopher Catholic Church, West Covina
Nguyen, Long, St. Catherine Laboure Catholic Church, Torrance
Nguyen, Matthew Van, Maria Regina Catholic Church, Gardena
Nicastro, Paul, La Purisima Concepcion Catholic Church, Lompoc
Noon, Richard, St. John Vianney Catholic Church, Hacienda Heights
Nunez, Ramon, Maria Regina Catholic Church, Gardena
O'Malley, Thom, St. Finbar Catholic Church, Burbank
Ochoa, Ruben, Guardian Angel Catholic Church, Pacoima
Ojeda, Jose, St. John Neumann Catholic Church, Santa Maria
Orcutt, Mark A., St. Paul of the Cross Catholic Church, La Mirada
Origel, Carlos, Our Lady of Perpetual Help Catholic Church, Downey
Oropeza, Daniel Alexander, St. John the Baptist Catholic Church, Baldwin Park
Ortega, Carlos, St. Basil Catholic Church, Los Angeles
Ortiz Dominguez, David, St. Lawrence of Brindisi Catholic Church, Los Angeles
Ortiz, Jose, Mary Immaculate Catholic Church, Pacoima
Padilla, Francisco, Mother of Sorrows Catholic Church, Los Angeles
Palmer, William Scott, Our Lady of Guadalupe Catholic Church, Hermosa Beach
Papillon, Luc, St. Junipero Serra, Camarillo
Pardo, Rogelio, Our Lady of Perpetual Help Catholic Church, Los Nietos
Pasos, Jesus S., St. Jude Catholic Church, Westlake Village
Patterson, Gregory, Transfiguration Catholic Church, Los Angeles
Pearson, Dennis, St. Mary of the Assumption Catholic Church, Santa Maria
Pena, Cecilio G., St. Helen Catholic Church, South Gate
Penate-Mojica, Jose Inez, Holy Name of Jesus Catholic Church, Los Angeles
Perez, Elvys C., St. Mary Catholic Church, Palmdale
Perez, Jorge, Our Lady of the Rosary Catholic Church, Paramount
Perez, Sergio, Our Lady of Solitude Catholic Church, Los Angeles
Pesqueira, Paul, Our Savior Catholic Church, Los Angeles
Pham, Thien Joseph, St. Lucy Catholic Church, Long Beach
Pilkington, William, St. Gregory the Great Catholic Church, Whittier
Pinal, Leovigildo, St. Philip Neri Catholic Church, Lynwood
Pinedo, Donald, St. Anthony Catholic Church, Oxnard
Pontrelli, Dominic, Incarnation Catholic Church, Glendale
Porras, Carlos Guido, St. Dominic Savio Catholic Church, Bellflower
Posvar, Edward, St. Rose of Lima Catholic Church, Simi Valley
Pulido, Amante, Holy Name of Mary Catholic Church, San Dimas
Quiju, Juan Luis, St. Ignatius of Loyola Catholic Church, Los Angeles
Rac, Felix, Christ the King Catholic Church, Los Angeles
Race, Mark, Transfiguration Catholic Church, Los Angeles
Ramirez, Fidel M., Santa Clara Catholic Church, Oxnard
Ramirez, Jose Ascencion, Our Lady of Sorrows Catholic Church, Santa Barbara
Ramirez, Rogelio, St. Helen Catholic Church, Southgate
Ramirez, Salvador, St. John of God Catholic Church, Norwalk
Ramos, Benjamin, St. Anthony Catholic Church, Gardena
Ramos, Dano L., Santa Clara Catholic Church, Oxnard
Ramos, Jorge, St. Anthony Catholic Church, Long Beach
Ramos Samayoa, Omar, St. Finbar Catholic Church, Burbank
Rascati, Wayne, St. Raphael Catholic Church, Santa Barbara
Rayas, Paul, Our Lady of Sorrows Catholic Church, Santa Barbara
Recinos, Richard, St. Agatha Catholic Church, Los Angeles
Recuenco, Neon, Holy Family Catholic Church, Glendale
Redmond, Jack William II, St. Junipero Serra, Camarillo
Reiser, Jay, Our Lady of Perpetual Help Catholic Church, Santa Clarita
Revetto, Dan, St. John the Baptist de la Salle Catholic Church
Reyes, Alberto, Our Lady of Victory Catholic Church, Compton
Reyes, Arnold Peter, St. Junipero Serra, Camarillo
Reynolds, Harrell Dale Jr., Sacred Heart Catholic Church, Lancaster
Rico, Jesus, La Purisima Concepcion Catholic Church, Lompoc
Riera, Ralph, St. Bernard Catholic Church, Bellflower
Rios, Fred, Our Lady of the Miraculous Medal Catholic Church, Montebello
Rivas, Carlos R., St. Francis Xavier Catholic Church, Pico Rivera
Roberto, Timothy J., St. Paul of the Cross Catholic Church, La Mirada
Roche, Louis N. Jr., St. Charles Borromeo Catholic Church
Rodriguez, Angel, Divine Saviour Catholic Church, Los Angeles
Rodriguez, Jose, St. Louis of France Catholic Church, La Puente
Rodriguez, Raymond, St. Francis of Assisi Catholic Church, Fillmore
Rodriguez-Hernandez, Federico, St. Paschal Baylon Catholic Church, Thousand Oaks
Rojas, Pedro, All Souls Catholic Church, Alhambra
Romero, Miguel, St. Alphonsus Catholic Church, Los Angeles
Roope, James, St. Francis Xavier Catholic Church, Burbank
Rose, David, Holy Angels Church of the Deaf, Vernon
Rose, Frederick, American Martyrs Catholic Church, Manhattan Beach
Routolo, Ronald, Sacred Heart Catholic Church, Lancaster
Roxas, Celso, Our Lady of Peace Catholic Church, North Hills
Rubio, Orlando, St. Ferdinand Catholic Church, San Fernando
Ruelas, Hector, St. Lawrence of Brindisi Catholic Church, Los Angeles
Ryan, Christopher Emmett, St. Rose of Lima Catholic Church, Simi Valley
Saake, Randal, Holy Cross Catholic Church, Santa Barbara
Saavedra, Gabriel, St. Bruno Catholic Church, Whittier
Sabol, Thomas A., St. Timothy Catholic Church, Los Angeles
Sadowski, Roy Edward, St. Anthony Catholic Church, Oxnard
Sago, Bruce, St. Mary of the Assumption Catholic Church, Whittier
Sahagun, Luis, St. Ignatius of Loyola Catholic Church, Los Angeles
Salas, Santiago, St. Cyprian Catholic Church
Salazar, John Burgos, St. Francis of Assisi Catholic Church, Los Angeles
Salcido, Michael P., Immaculate Conception Catholic Church, Monrovia
Sanchez, Fausto, St. Andrew Catholic Church, Pasadena
Sanchez, Ronald, Immaculate Conception Catholic Church, Monrovia
Sandner, Christopher Alan, Our Lady of Sorrows Catholic Church, Santa Barbara
Schaefer, Robert, St. Louis de Montfort Catholic Church, Santa Maria
Schalow, Jason, Sacred Heart Catholic Church, Lancaster
Schwerdt, Paul, Blessed Junipero Serra Catholic Church, Lancaster
Sedano, Jose Mario, Our Lady of Perpetual Help Catholic Church, Los Angeles
Seidler, Robert, San Fernando Pastoral Region, Mission Hills
Selame, Claudio, St. Julie Billiart Catholic Church, Newbury Park
Seneviratne, Sonal, St. Augustine Catholic Church, Culver City
Sheckler, Dale, St. Lawrence Martyr Catholic Church, Redondo Beach
Shin, Dennis, St. Denis Catholic Church, Diamond Bar
Shinn, John, St. Joseph Korean Catholic Center, Canoga Park
Siegman, Craig A., St. Margaret Mary Alacoque Catholic Church, Lomita
Skupnik, Raymond P., St. Cyprian Catholic Church, Long Beach
Smith, David Nicholas, St. Julie Billiart Catholic Church, Newbury Park
Smith, William Richard, St. Jude Catholic Church, Westlake Village
Spies, William, St. Junipero Serra, Camarillo
Steighner, Robert, Our Lady of the Assumption Catholic Church, Claremont
Tchoi, Francis, The 103 Saints Korean Catholic Center, Torrance
Tiambeng, Victor, St. Martha Catholic Church, Valinda
Torrado, Miguel Angel, St. Bartholomew Catholic Church, Long Beach
Torti, Joseph Felix, St. Junipero Serra, Camarillo
Trujillo, Jose Antonio, Our Lady of Sorrows Catholic Church, Santa Barbara
Tullius, John, Our Lady of the Assumption Catholic Church, Claremont
Uriarte, Omar, St. Louise de Marillac Catholic Church, Covina
Valencia, Manuel, St. Rita Catholic Church, Sierra Madre
Valles, Al, St. Louise de Marillac Catholic Church, Covina
Vargas, Miguel, Our Lady of Guadalupe Catholic Church, El Monte
Vasquez, Raymond Jr., Santa Clara Catholic Church, Oxnard
Vazquez, Roberto L., St. John Chrysostom Catholic Church, Inglewood
Vedro, Shawn Stanley, Queen of Angels Catholic Church, Lompoc
Victorin, Rafael A., St. Augustine Catholic Church, Culver City
Villacorta, Ricardo, Christ the King Catholic Church, Los Angeles

Villegas, Jesus, Guardian Angel Catholic Church, Pacoima
Vital, Ernesto, St. Francis of Rome Catholic Church, Azusa
Vu, Anh Quoc, St. Mary Magdalen Catholic Church, Camarillo
Wallace, Daniel, St. Margaret Mary Alacoque Catholic Church, Lomita
Wessler, Charles Philip, Our Lady of the Assumption Catholic Church, Ventura
Williams, Richard (Dick), American Martyrs Catholic Church, Manhattan Beach
Wilson, Peter Jr., St. Rose of Lima Catholic Church, Simi Valley
Wolford, Charles, Santa Teresita Hospital, Duarte
Won, Augustine Y., St. Bede the Venerable Catholic Church, La Canada
Ye, Young, Holy Trinity Catholic Church, Los Angeles
Yoque, Leonel, Holy Cross Catholic Church, Los Angeles
Younan, Sargon, St. John Eudes Catholic Church, Chatsworth
Zamalloa, Guido, San Gabriel Mission Catholic Church, San Gabriel
Zamora, Melecio, St. Peter Claver Catholic Church, Simi Valley
Zavala-Dominguez, Bernardo, St. Louis of France Catholic Church, La Puente.

INSTITUTIONS LOCATED IN DIOCESE

[A] SEMINARIES, ARCHDIOCESAN

CAMARILLO. *St. John's Seminary*, 5012 Seminary Rd., Camarillo, 93012-2500. Tel: 805-482-2755; Fax: 805-484-4074; Email: rector@stjohnsem.edu; Web: www.stjohnsem.edu. Revs. Gustavo Castillo, Dir. Spirituality Formation; Timothy Clement Klosterman, Dir. of Students/Dir. of Human Formation; Marco Antonio Durazo, Rector; John P. Brennan, S.M.A., S.T.D.; Eugenio Cardenas, M.Sp. S.; Luke Dysinger, O.S.B., M.D., D.Phil.; Aelred Niespolo, O.S.B., M.A., B.Th., M.Th.; Timothy Peters; Thinh Duc Pham; Slawomir Szkredka; Steven Thoma, C.R.; Sr. Leanne Hubbard. Major Seminary of the Archdiocese of Los Angeles. Lay Teachers 12; Students 112; Clergy / Religious Teachers 18.

[B] SEMINARIES, RELIGIOUS OR SCHOLASTICATES

LOS ANGELES. *St. Joseph's Novitiate*, 2468 S. St. Andrews Pl., 90018. Tel: 323-734-0233; Fax: 323-731-5987; Email: usaprov-office@sbcglobal.net; Web: www.stjog.org. Bro. Stephen de la Rosa, O.H., Prov. & Formation Dir. Hospitaller Brothers of St. John of God. Brothers 12.

CULVER CITY. *Ignatius House, The Novitiate of the U.S. West Province, Society of Jesus*, 10775 Deshire Pl., Culver City, 90230. Tel: 310-815-0166, Ext. 235; Fax: 310-815-0170; Email: scorder@jesuits.org; Email: scoble@jesuits.org; Web: www.jesuitswest.org. P.O. Box 5166, Culver City, 90231-5166. Revs. Scott W. Coble, S.J., Min.; Stephen J. Corder, S.J., Dir. of Novices; Anton F. Harris, S.J., Asst. Dir. of Novices; Michael E. Kennedy, S.J., Dir. of Jesuit Restorative Justice Initiative; Tri M. Dinh, S.J., Co-Dir. CHRISTUS Ministries; Michael Pastizzo, Senior Priest in Res. Novices 13; Clergy / Religious Teachers 6.

SANTA MARIA. *St. Joseph Seminary (Josephite Fathers' Novitiate)*, 180 Patterson Rd., Santa Maria, 93455. Tel: 805-937-5378; Fax: 805-937-5759; Email: cjvocationseu@josephite.community; Web: josephite.community. Revs. Timothy R. Lane, C.J.; Charles L. Hofschulte, C.J., M.A.; Edward Jalbert, C.J.; Mark L. Newman, C.J.; Bros. Gerardo Toscano, C.J.; Romualdo Orozco, C.J.; Rev. Ludo DeClippel, C.J., (Belgium). Priests 5; Scholastics 2; Students 2; Total Staff 1; Clergy / Religious Teachers 5.

SANTA PAULA. *Canons Regular of the Immaculate Conception, (C.R.I.C.) Dom Grea House (House of Formation)* (1871) 601 Glade Dr., Santa Paula, 93060-1640. Tel: 805-933-5063; Email: cricusa@icloud.com; Web: cricusa.org. Rev. Thomas J. Dome, C.R.I.C., Dir. & Novice Master; Bro. Roger M. Proulx, C.R.I.C. Brothers 2; Priests 5; Seminarians 1; Students 1; Clergy / Religious Teachers 5.

SANTA YNEZ. *San Lorenzo Seminary - Novitiate*, Religious Formation House: 1802 Sky Dr., P.O. Box 247, Santa Ynez, 93460-0247. Tel: 805-688-5630; Fax: 805-686-0775; Email: stjw@slseminary.org; Email: finance@olacapuchins.org; Web: www.sanlorenzoseminary.org. Rev. Robert Stewart, Dir.; Bro. Lance Love, O.F.M.Cap, Vicar; Rev. Philip J. Bernier, O.F.M.Cap.; Bro. Alexander Rodriguez, In Res. Capuchin Franciscan Friars. Brothers 2; Novices 14; Priests 4; Students 14; Total Staff 4; Clergy / Religious Teachers 2; Total in Community 20.

SUN VALLEY. *Scalabrini House of Discernment (Seminary)*, 10651 Vinedale St., Sun Valley, 91352-2825. Tel: 818-504-9561; Fax: 818-504-9562; Email: parish-3710@la-archdiocese.org. Revs. Giovanni Bizzotto, C.S., Vocation Dir.; Ramiro V. Sanchez Chan, C.S., Dir. Discernment Prog. Seminarians 9; Students 9; Clergy / Religious Teachers 2.

Scalabrini Vocation Office, Tel: 323-216-6278; Fax: 818-504-9562.

[C] COLLEGES AND UNIVERSITIES

LOS ANGELES. **Loyola Marymount University*, One LMU Dr., Ste. 4844, 90045-2659. Tel: 310-338-2700; Email: president@lmu.edu; Web: www.lmu.edu (Including Law School). Timothy Law Snyder, Ph.D., Pres.; Rev. Patrick J. Cahalan, S.J., Chancellor; Dr. Joseph Hellige, Exec. Vice Pres. & Provost; Mr. Thomas O. Fleming Jr., Senior Vice Pres. & CFO; Dennis Slon, Senior Vice Pres., Univ. Rels.; Dr. Lane Bove, Senior Vice Pres., Student Affairs; Dr. Joseph LaBrie, Chief of Staff to the Pres.; Dr. Michael O'Sullivan, Vice Provost, Academic Affairs; Rev. Robert V. Caro, S.J., Vice Pres., Mission & Min.; Dr. Abbie Robinson-Armstrong, Vice Pres., Intercultural Affairs; Ms. Lynne Scarboro, Senior Vice Pres., Admin.; Kathy Reed, Registrar; Kristine Brancolini, Dean, Univ. Libraries; John Carfora, Assoc. Provost, Research Advancement & Compliance and Acting Dir., Office of Research & Sponsored Projects; Dr. Maureen Weatherall, Vice Provost, Enrollment Mgmt.; Rebecca Chandler, Vice Pres., Human Resources; Rev. Albert P. Koppes, O.-Carm., Assoc. Chancellor, (Retired); Dr. Dennis W. Draper, Dean, Business Admin.; Dr. Tina Choe, Dean, Science & Engineering; Dr. Robbin Crabtree, Dean, Bellarmine College of Liberal Arts; Dr. Bryant Alexander, Dean, Communication & Fine Arts; Mr. Stephen G. Ujlaki, Dean, School of Film & TV; Dr. Shane P. Martin, Dean, School of Educ.; Ricardo Machon, Spl. Asst. Undergraduate Educ.; David Sapp, Spl. Asst. Undergraduate Educ. Students 8,358; Part-time Faculty 470; Loyola Marymount & Loyola Law School Staff 1,270; Full-time Faculty 485.

Jesuit Community, One L.M.U. Dr., P.O. Box 45041, 90045-0041. Tel: 310-338-7445; Fax: 310-338-3002; Email: allan.deck@lmu.edu. Revs. Allan Figueroa Deck, S.J., Ph.D., S.T.D., Rector; James Erps, S.J., Dir. Campus Min.; John Galvan, S.J., Campus Min.; Marc Reeves, S.J., Assoc. Dir. Campus Ministry; Jose Ignacio Badenes, S.J., Assoc. Prof. Spanish; James McDermott, S.J., Asst. to the Rector; John T. Mitchell, S.J., Min. to the Jesuit Community; Edward J. Siebert, S.J., Pres. Loyola Productions and Lectr. Film & TV; Ramesh Vandan, S.J., Grad. Student; Paul H. Vu, S.J., Asst. Dean Student Affairs & Prof. Psychology; Sean T. Dempsey, S.J., Prof. History & Vocation Coord.; Chanh C. Nguyen, S.J., Vocation Promoter, CA & OR Provinces of the Society of Jesus & Ecclesiastical Asst., CLC West Coast; Christopher T. Nguyen, S.J., Vocation Dir., Provinces of CA & OR of the Society of Jesus; Thomas P. Rausch, S.J., Ph.D., Prof. In Res. Most Rev. Gordon D. Bennett, S.J., Bishop Emeritus, Mandeville, Jamaica; Revs. Mark Bandsuch, S.J., Assoc. Prof. Business Law; Patrick J. Cahalan, S.J., Chancellor, Loyola Marymount Univ.; Robert V. Caro, S.J., Vice Pres. Mission & Ministry; Philip J. Chmielewski, S.J., Sir. Thomas More Chair Engineering Ethics; Patrick Connolly, S.J., Prof. Emeritus Film & TV; William J. Fulco, S.J., NEH Prof. Ancient Mediterranean Studies; James H. Keene, S.J., Chap., Nazareth House of Los Angeles; Thomas P. Rausch, S.J., Ph. D., Marie Chilton Prof. Catholic Theology; Richard A. Robin, S.J., Alumni Chap.; Randall Roche, S.J., Dir. Center for Ignatian Spirituality; Richard W. Rolfs, S.J., Prof. Emeritus History; Kenneth Rudnick, S.J., Prof. Philosophy; Amaechi M. Ugwu, S.J., Grad. Student in Learning Technology, Pepperdine Univ.; Robert T. Walsh, S.J., Exec. Dir. Center for Catholic Educ., Loyola Marymount Univ.; Robert J. Welch, S.J., Prof. Emeritus Political Science; Lan Ngo, S.J., Post-Doctoral Teaching Fellow, Asian & Asian-American Studies; Bryan Pham, S.J., J.C.D., J.D., Prof. Canon Law, Staff Attorney at Loyola Law School Immigration Clinic & Marriage Tribunal, Archdiocese of LA.

The Sacred Heart of Mary and Sisters of St. Joseph of Orange, 440 S Batavia St., Orange, 92868. Tel: 714-633-8121. Sr. Eileen McNerney, Supr. *Communities of the Religious of the Sacred Heart of Mary and Sisters of St. Joseph of Orange.*

Loyola School of Law (1920) 919 S. Albany St., P.O. Box 15019, 90015. Tel: 213-736-1000; Email: admissions@lls.edu; Web: www.lls.edu. Michael Waterstone, Dean. Faculty 143; Priests 1; Students 1,034.

Mount Saint Mary's University (1925) 12001 Chalon Rd., 90049. Tel: 310-954-4010; Fax: 310-954-4019; Email: amcelaney@msmu.edu; Web: www.msmu.edu. Dr. Ann McElaney, Pres. Conducted by the Sisters of St. Joseph of Carondelet Students 3,554; Clergy / Religious Teachers 5.

Doheny Campus, 10 Chester Pl., 90007. Tel: 213-477-2500; Fax: 213-477-2519; Email: onlineadmissions@msmu.edu; Web: www.msmu.edu. Dr. Ann McElaney-Johnson, Pres.; Dr. Jane Lingua, Vice Pres. Student Affairs; Larry Smith, Vice Pres. Info. Support Svcs. & Enrollment; Brian O'Rourke, Vice Pres. Enrollment Mgmnt.; Dr. Robert J. Perrins, Provost & Academic Vice Pres.; Dr. Stephanie Cubba, Vice. Pres. Inst. Advancement; Mr. Dean Kilgour, Asst. Vice Pres. Enrollment Mgmt.; Dr. Michele Starkey, Assoc. Provost; Chris McAlary, Vice Pres. Admin. & Fin.; Ruth Jackson, Interim Dir. Libraries & Consultant. Lay Teachers 378; Priests 2; Sisters 4; Students 3,504.

RANCHO PALOS VERDES. *Marymount California University*, 30800 Palos Verdes Dr., E., Rancho Palos Verdes, 90275-6299. Tel: 310-377-5501; Fax: 310-265-0642; Email: kramsay@marymountcalifornia.edu; Web: www.marymountcalifornia.edu. Lucas Lamadrid, Pres.; Dr. Ariane Schauer, Provost; Jose Rincon, Librarian. Lay Teachers 122; Priests 3; Sisters 1; Students 1,000; Clergy / Religious Teachers 1.

SANTA PAULA. **Thomas Aquinas College* (1969) 10000 N. Ojai Rd., Santa Paula, 93060. Tel: 805-525-4417; Tel: 800-634-9797; Fax: 805-525-0620; Email: pr@thomasaquinas.edu; Web: www.thomasaquinas.edu. Dr. Michael F. McLean, Pres.; Mr. Peter L. DeLuca III, Vice Pres. Finance & Admin.; Dr. Paul O'Reilly, Vice Pres. Devel.; Revs. Cornelius M. Buckley, S.J., Chap.; David Gonzalez, O.Praem., Chap.; Paul Raftery, O.P., Chap.; Robert Marczewski, Chap.; Richena Curphey, Librarian; John Goyette, Dean. Lay Teachers 38; Students 354.

[D] HIGH SCHOOLS, ARCHDIOCESAN

LOS ANGELES. *Bishop Conaty-Our Lady of Loretto High School* (1923) 2900 W. Pico Blvd., 90006-3802. Tel: 323-737-0012; Fax: 323-737-1749; Email: ajenoff@bishopconatyloretto.org; Web: www.bishopconatyloretto.org. Andrea Jenoff, Prin.; Jacqueline Lucero, Admin. Lay Teachers 18; Students 310; Total Staff 29.

Bishop Mora Salesian High School aka Salesian High School (LA), 960 S. Soto St., 90023. Tel: 323-261-7124; Fax: 323-261-7600; Email: info@mustangsla.org; Web: www.mustangsla.org. Mr. Alex Chacon, Pres.; Rev. James Nieblas, S.D.B., Dir.; Mr. Mark Johnson, Prin.; Mr. Mike Castillo, Vice Prin. Salesians of Don Bosco. Lay Teachers 29; Priests 1; Students 420.

Sacred Heart High School, 2111 Griffin Ave., 90031. Tel: 323-225-2209; Fax: 323-225-5046; Email: mr.saborio@shhsla.org; Web: www.shhsla.org. Raymond Saborio, Prin.; Ms. Luz Vivas, Vice Prin. Lay Teachers 25; Students 260; Total Staff 5.

Verbum Dei High School (Boys) 11100 S. Central Ave., 90059-1199. Tel: 323-564-6651; Fax: 323-564-9009; Email: principal@verbumdei.us; Web: www.verbumdei.us. Rev. Michael Mandala, S.J., Dir. Community Rels.; Ms. Cristina Cuellar-Villanueva, Vice Pres. Corp. Work Study Prog.; Dr. Brandi Lucas, Chief Academic Officer; Rev. George Teodoro, Campus Min. Conducted by the Archdiocese of Los Angeles. Lay Teachers 22; Priests 2; Scholastics 1; Students 330; Total Staff 50.

Verbum Dei High School Work Study, Inc., 11100 S. Central Ave., 90059-1199. Tel: 323-564-6651; Fax: 323-564-9009; Email: school-9780@la-archdiocese.org. Ms. Cristina Cuellar-Villanueva, Dir.

BURBANK. *St. John Paul II STEM Academy at Bellarmine-Jefferson*, 465 E. Olive Ave., Burbank, 91501.

DOWNEY. *St. Pius X-St. Matthias Academy* aka PMA, 7851 E. Gardendale St., Downey, 90242. Tel: 562-861-2271; Fax: 562-869-8652; Email: principal@piusmatthias.org; Email: pmamarketing@piusmatthias.org; Email: erubalcava@piusmatthias.org; Email: vzozaya@piusmatthias.org; Web: www.piusmatthias.org. Erick A. Rubalcava, Pres.; Veronica Zozaya, Vice Prin. Lay Teachers 28; Students 390.

GARDENA. *Junipero Serra High School* (1950) 14830 S. Van Ness Ave., Gardena, 90249. Tel: 310-324-6675

; Fax: 310-352-4953; Email: principal@la-serrahs.org; Web: www.la-serrahs.org. Mr. Michael J. Guzman, Prin.; Nadi Wissa, Asst. Prin. Lay Teachers 32; Students 450; Total Staff 14.

LA PUENTE. *Bishop Amat Memorial High School*, 14301 Fairgrove Ave., La Puente, 91746.
Tel: 626-962-2495; Fax: 626-960-0994; Email: president@bishopamat.org; Web: www.bishopamat.org. Rev. Msgr. Aidan M. Carroll, Pres.; Mr. Richard Beck, Prin.; Ms. Deborah Oswald, Dir. of Finance & Devel.; Mr. Gabriel Escovar, Asst. Prin., Academics; Mrs. Ivette Salcedo, Asst. Prin. & Student Services; Dana Vasquez, Asst. Prin., Faculty Devel.; Mrs. Alma Lopez, Librarian. Lay Teachers 84; Priests 2; Students 1,350; Total Staff 28; Clergy / Religious Teachers 1.

LA VERNE. *Damien High School*, 2280 Damien Ave., La Verne, 91750. Tel: 909-596-1946;
Fax: 909-596-6112; Email: info@damien-hs.edu; Web: www.damien-hs.edu. Revs. Peadar Cronin, SS.CC., Pres.; John Roche, SS.CC., Chap.; Dr. Merritt V. Hemenway, Prin.; Mr. Jeff Coray, Vice Prin.; Mr. Jeff Grant, Athletic Dir.; Mr. Chris Douglas, Dean of Faculty; Ms. Jocelle Reyes, Fin. Officer; Alejandro Jimenez, Dean; Angela Curry, Dean; Melissa Pasillas, Dean; Junior Pro, Dean; Rich Vasquez, Dean. Conducted by the Archdiocese of Los Angeles.
Congregation of the Sacred Hearts, Inc. Lay Teachers 52; Priests 2; Students 846; Total Staff 74.

LAKEWOOD. *St. Joseph High School* (Girls) 5825 N. Woodruff Ave., Lakewood, 90713.
Tel: 562-925-5073; Fax: 562-925-3315; Email: glogsdon@sj-jester.org; Web: www.sj-jester.org. Dr. Terri Mendoza, Ph.D., Prin. Conducted by Archdiocese of Los Angeles. Lay Teachers 37; Sisters 1; Students 548; Total Staff 25.

LANCASTER. *Paraclete High School*, 42145 30th St. West, Lancaster, 93536. Tel: 661-943-3255;
Fax: 661-722-9455; Email: janson@paracletehs.org; Web: www.paracletehs.org. John W. Anson, M.Ed., Prin.; Rev. Giampietro Gasparin, C.S.J., Campus Min.; Venus Gutierrez, Librarian; Ms. Kathleen Troisi, Vice Prin. Lay Teachers 43; Priests 2; Students 675.

LONG BEACH. *St. Anthony High School*, 620 Olive Ave., Long Beach, 90802. Tel: 562-435-4496;
Fax: 562-437-3055; Email: president@longbeachsaints.org; Web: www.longbeachsaints.org. Gina Maguire, Pres.; Chris McGuiness, Prin. Lay Teachers 52; Students 565.

MISSION HILLS. *Bishop Alemany High School*, 11111 N. Alemany Dr., Mission Hills, 91345.
Tel: 818-365-3925; Fax: 818-365-2064; Email: dchambers@alemany.org; Web: www.alemany.org. Mr. David Chambers, Prin.; Mrs. Jan Galla, Vice Prin.; Mr. Randy Thompson, Asst. Prin. Opers.; Mr. Richard Guante, Asst. Prin. Academics. Lay Staff 46; Lay Teachers 73; Priests 1; Sisters 2; Students 1,250.

MONTEBELLO. *Cantwell Sacred Heart of Mary High School* (1946) 329 N. Garfield Ave., Montebello, 90640. Tel: 323-887-2066; Fax: 323-724-4332; Email: school-9570@la-archdiocese.org; Web: www.cshm.org. Robert Fraley, Prin. Lay Teachers 23; Students 446; Total Staff 44.

OXNARD. *Santa Clara High School*, 2121 Saviers Rd., Oxnard, 93033. Tel: 805-483-9502;
Fax: 805-486-7006; Email: guzman@santaclarahighschool.com; Email: mmullen@santaclarahighschool.com; Email: luna@santaclarahighschool.com; Email: palmisano@santaclarahighschool.com; Web: www.santaclarahighschool.com. Rev. Juan Jose Guzman, O.A.R., Prin. Lay Teachers 10; Students 285; Total Faculty & Staff 20; Clergy / Religious Teachers 3.

PLAYA DEL REY. *St. Bernard High School*, 9100 Falmouth Ave., Playa del Rey, 90293.
Tel: 310-823-4651; Fax: 310-827-3365; Email: rbillups@stbernardhs.org; Web: www.stbernardhs.org. Carter Paysinger, Pres.; Mr. Richard Billups, Prin.; Rosalie Roberts, Vice Prin. Lay Teachers 19; Priests 1; Students 211; Total Staff 29; Clergy / Religious Teachers 1.

POMONA. *Pomona Catholic High School* (Girls) 533 W. Holt Ave., Pomona, 91768. Tel: 909-623-5297;
Fax: 909-620-6057; Email: rarteaga@pomonacatholic.org; Email: admissions@pomonacatholic.org; Web: www.pomonacatholic.org. Mrs. Rebecca Arteaga, Prin. Lay Teachers 25; Sisters 1; Students 230; Total Staff 6.
*Pomona Catholic Middle School*Religious Teachers 1; Lay Teachers 20; Students 105.

SANTA FE SPRINGS. *St. Paul High School* (1956) 9635 S. Greenleaf Ave., Santa Fe Springs, 90670.
Tel: 562-698-6246; Fax: 562-696-8396; Email: kate.aceves@la-archdiocese.org; Web: www.stpaulhs.org. Mrs. Kate Aceves, Prin.; Mr. Robert Miller, Asst. Prin. Advancement; Mr. Matthew Elliot, Admin. Brothers 1; Lay Teachers 42; Priests 1; Sisters 1; Students 650; Total Staff 65.

SANTA MARIA. *St. Joseph High School* (1964) 4120 S. Bradley Rd., Santa Maria, 93455.
Tel: 805-937-2038; Fax: 805-937-4248; Email: sjhs@sjhsknights.com; Web: www.sjhsknights.com. Rev. Edward Jalbert, C.J., Chap.; Joanne Poloni, Prin.; Jennifer Perez, Vice Prin. Lay Teachers 28; Priests 1; Students 397.

TORRANCE. *Bishop Montgomery High School*, 5430 Torrance Blvd., Torrance, 90503.
Tel: 310-540-2021; Fax: 310-792-1273; Web: www.bmhs-la.org. James Garza, Prin. Lay Teachers 68; Students 827.

VENTURA. *St. Bonaventure High School* (1963) 3167 Telegraph Rd., Ventura, 93003-3281.
Tel: 805-648-6836; Fax: 805-648-4903; Email: office@saintbonaventure.com; Web: www.saintbonaventure.com. Marc Groff, Prin.; Christina Castro, Vice Prin. Lay Teachers 35; Students 450; Total Staff 7.

[E] HIGH SCHOOLS, PAROCHIAL

High Schools are maintained in the following parishes (for particulars refer to the individual parishes):.
Glendale: Holy Family; San Gabriel: San Gabriel Mission; San Pedro: Mary Star of the Sea; Santa Monica, St. Monica; Van Nuys: St. Genevieve.

[F] HIGH SCHOOLS, PRIVATE

LOS ANGELES. *Cathedral High School of Los Angeles, Incorporated* (1925) 1253 Bishops Rd., 90012.
Tel: 323-225-2438; Fax: 323-222-7223; Email: brjohnm@cathedralhighschool.org; Web: www.cathedralhighschool.org. Mr. Martin Farfan, Pres.; Bro. John Montgomery, F.S.C., Prin.
Conducted by the Brothers of the Christian Schools (F.S.C.) Brothers 6; Lay Teachers 40; Students 657; Total Staff 60.
**Immaculate Heart High School* (1906) 5515 Franklin Ave., 90028-5999. Tel: 323-461-3651;
Fax: 323-462-0610; Web: www.immaculateheart.org. Maureen Diekmann, Pres.; Naemah Morris, Prin. Lay Teachers 40; Students 465.
Loyola High School of Los Angeles, 1901 Venice Blvd., 90006. Tel: 213-381-5121;
Fax: 213-368-1758; Email: ggoethals@loyolahs.edu; Web: loyolahs.edu. Revs. Gregory M. Goethals, S.J., Pres.; Wayne R. Negrete, S.J., Supr. Jesuit Community; Mr. Frank Kozakowski, Prin.; Revs. Gerald Hudson, S.J., Faculty Mathematics Dept.; John Quinn, S.J., Photography Teacher; Mr. William Slocum, Exec. Dir. Advancement; Rev. Stephen A. Barber, S.J., Dir. Cura Personalis Prog., Loyola High School. Sponsored by the California Province of the Society of Jesus. Administrators 7; Lay Teachers 87; Priests 2; Scholastics 1; Students 1,246; Total Staff 177. In Res Rev. Michael Mandala, S.J., Pres. Verbum Dei High School.
Marymount High School, 10643 Sunset Blvd., 90077.
Tel: 310-472-1205; Fax: 310-476-0910; Email: reception@mhs-la.org; Web: www.mhs-la.org. Ms. Jacqueline L. Landry, Head; Sharon Dandort, Assoc. Head; Tika Martin, Academic Dean; Lori Paillet, Dir. Finance; Rebecca Bostic, Campus Min. Religious of the Sacred Heart of Mary. Lay Teachers 50; Sisters 1; Students 411; Total Staff 41.
Notre Dame Academy Schools of Los Angeles (1949) (Grades 9-12), 2851 Overland Ave., 90064.
Tel: 310-839-5289; Fax: 310-839-7957; Web: www.ndasla.org. Ms. Lilliam Paetzold, Pres.; Kristin Callaghan, Vice Pres.; Brad Fuller, Prin. Faculty 30; Lay Teachers 29; Sisters of Notre Dame of Los Angeles 2; Students 361.

ALHAMBRA. *Ramona Convent Secondary School, Ramona Convent of the Holy Names*, 1701 W. Ramona Rd., Alhambra, 91803-3099.
Tel: 626-282-4151; Fax: 626-281-0797; Email: ramona@ramonaconvent.org; Web: www.ramonaconvent.org. Sr. Kathleen Callaway, S.N.J.M., Pres.; Ms. Mary Mansell, Prin.; Halina Szymanski, Vice Prin. Lay Teachers 30; Sisters of the Holy Names of Jesus and Mary 3; Students 294; Total Staff 50; Clergy / Religious Teachers 2.

BELLFLOWER. *St. John Bosco High School*, 13640 S. Bellflower Blvd., Bellflower, 90706.
Tel: 562-920-1734; Fax: 562-867-5322; Email: cyeazel@bosco.org; Web: www.bosco.org. Rev. Nicholas Reina, S.D.B.; Mr. Casey Yeazel, Prin.; Mr. Dennis Mulhaupt, Pres.; Dr. Christian DeLarkin, Vice Prin. Academic Affairs; Mr. Memo Guiterrez, Vice Prin. Student Affairs. (Boys) Brothers 2; Lay Teachers 54; Priests 1; Students 850.

BURBANK. *Providence High School* (Coed) 511 S. Buena Vista St., Burbank, 91505. Tel: 818-846-8141;
Fax: 818-843-8421; Email: allison.castro@providencehigh.org; Web: www.providencehigh.org. Mr. Joe Sciuto, Head of School; Allison Castro, Prin.; Claire Hickey, Dir. Campus Ministry; Kerry Martin, Dean Studies; Ernest Sly, Dean Students. Lay Teachers 47; Sisters 2; Students 458; Total Staff 17.

CHATSWORTH. *Chaminade College Preparatory* (1952) Office of the President, 10210 Oakdale Ave., Chatsworth, 91311-3533. Tel: 818-360-4211;
Fax: 818-363-0127; Email: rwebb@chaminade.org; Email: egluvna@chaminade.org; Web: www.chaminade.org. Mr. Robert S. Webb, Pres.
Chaminade College Preparatory Brothers 5; Lay Teachers 146; Priests 2; Students 1,992; Total Staff 216.
Chatsworth Campus (Middle School), (Grades 6-8), 19800 Devonshire St., Chatsworth, 91311.
Tel: 818-363-8127; Fax: 818-363-1219; Email: school-2830@la-archdiocese.org. Mr. Michael Valentine, Prin. Clergy 1; Lay Teachers 3; Students 708.
West Hills Campus (High School, Grades 9-12), 7500 Chaminade Ave., West Hills, 91304.
Tel: 818-347-8300; Fax: 818-348-8374; Email: tfahy@chaminade.org. Bro. Thomas Fahy, O.S.F., Prin.

ENCINO. *Crespi Carmelite High School*, 5031 Alonzo Ave., Encino, 91316. Tel: 818-345-1672;
Fax: 818-705-0209; Email: info@crespi.org; Web: www.crespi.org. Mrs. Janet Nungester; Dr. Kenneth Foersch, Pres.; Dr. Liam Joyce, Prin. For further details about Our Lady of Mount Carmel Priory, Encino please see Monasteries and Residences of Priests and Brothers. Lay Teachers 55; Priests 2; Students 600.

GLENDORA. *St. Lucy's Priory High School* (Girls) 655 W. Sierra Madre Ave., Glendora, 91741.
Tel: 626-335-3322; Fax: 626-335-4373; Email: info@stlucys.com; Web: www.stlucys.com. Ms. Gina Giuliucci, Prin.; Sr. Helen Dziuk, O.S.B., Vice Prin. Benedictine Sisters of St. Lucy's Priory. Lay Teachers 35; Sisters 2; Students 633; Total Staff 54.

INGLEWOOD. *St. Mary's Academy* (Girls) 701 Grace Ave., Inglewood, 90301. Tel: 310-674-8470;
Fax: 310-674-6255; Email: mbatungbacal@smabelles.org; Web: www.smabelles.org. Mary Rose Batungbacal, Prin. Lay Teachers 20; Sisters 2; Students 266; 16 16; Clergy / Religious Teachers 4.

LA CANADA FLINTRIDGE. *Flintridge Sacred Heart Academy* (1931) 440 St. Katherine Dr., La Canada Flintridge, 91011. Tel: 626-685-8500;
Fax: 626-685-8555; Email: cmccormack@fsha.org; Web: www.fsha.org. Sr. Celeste Marie Botello, O.P., Prin.
Flintridge Sacred Heart Academy, A Corporation Lay Teachers 44; Dominican Sisters of Mission San Jose 4; Students 385.
St. Francis High School of La Canada-Flintridge, 200 Foothill Blvd., La Canada Flintridge, 91011.
Tel: 818-790-0325; Fax: 818-790-5542; Email: martit@sfhs.net; Web: sfhs.net. Rev. Antonio (Tony) Marti, O.F.M.Cap., Pres. St. Francis High School; Mr. Thomas G. Moran, Prin.; Revs. Chris Thiel, O.F.M.Cap.; Anthony Scannel, O.F.M.Cap.; Jesus Vela, O.F.M.Cap., Chap.
St. Francis High School of La Canada-Flintridge Brothers 2; Lay Teachers 56; Priests 4; Students 670; Total Staff 72; Clergy / Religious Teachers 4.

MONTROSE. **St. Monica Academy, Inc.*, 2361 Del Mar Rd., Montrose, 91020. Tel: 626-229-0351;
Fax: 626-229-0343; Email: headmaster@stmonicaacademy.com. Marguerite Grimm, Headmaster. Lay Teachers 12; Students 80; Staff 15.

OJAI. *Villanova Preparatory School in California*, 12096 N. Ventura Ave., Ojai, 93023-3999.
Tel: 805-646-1464; Fax: 805-646-4430; Email: info@villanovaprep.org; Web: www.villanovaprep.org. Ms. Nancy O'Sullivan, Pres. Conducted by Augustinians (Order of St. Augustine).
Villanova Preparatory School in California Brothers 1; Lay Teachers 28; Priests 1; Sisters 1; Students 260; Total Staff 59.

PASADENA. *La Salle High School* (1956) 3880 E. Sierra Madre Blvd., Pasadena, 91107. Tel: 626-351-8951;
Fax: 626-351-0275; Email: principal@lasallehs.org; Web: lasallehs.org. Mrs. Courtney Kassakhian, Prin.; Dr. Richard Gray, Pres. Lay Teachers 58; Students 649; Total Staff 58.
Mayfield Senior School of the Holy Child Jesus, 500 Bellefontaine St., Pasadena, 91105-2439.
Tel: 626-799-9121; Fax: 626-799-8576; Email: rita.mcbride@mayfieldsenior.org; Web: www.mayfieldsenior.org. Kate Morin, Prin.; Cynthia Riegsecker, Dir.; Toi Treister, Asst. Head for Academy. Lay Teachers 36; Sisters 1; Students 300.

ROSEMEAD. *Don Bosco Technical Institute*, 1151 San Gabriel Blvd., Rosemead, 91770-4251.
Tel: 626-940-2000; Fax: 626-940-2001; Email: xjimenez@boscotech.edu; Web: www.boscotech.edu. Mr. Xavier E. Jimenez, Prin.; William Marticorena, Chm.; Richard Ronan, Registrar. Sponsored by Salesians of St. John Bosco.

Administrators 4; Brothers 5; Lay Teachers 38; Priests 3; Students 400; Total Staff 27.

SANTA BARBARA. *Bishop Garcia Diego High School Inc.* (1959) 4000 La Colina Rd., Santa Barbara, 93110. Tel: 805-967-1266; Fax: 805-964-3178; Email: bishop@bishopdiego.org; Web: www.bishopdiego.org. Ms. Karen Regan, Headmaster; Mrs. Jennifer Winnewisser, Campus Min. Lay Teachers 31; Sisters 1; Students 265; Total Staff 41.

SHERMAN OAKS. *Notre Dame High School* (1947) 13645 Riverside Dr., Sherman Oaks, 91423. Tel: 818-933-3600; Fax: 818-501-0507; Email: sedano@ndhs.org; Web: www.ndhs.org. Mr. Brett A. Lowart, Pres.; Mrs. Alice Cotti, Prin. Lay Teachers 82; Students 1,225; Total Staff 124.

SIERRA MADRE. *Mt. Alverno High School* (Girls) 200 N. Michillinda Ave., Sierra Madre, 91024. Tel: 626-355-3463; Fax: 626-355-3153; Email: info@alvernoheights.org; Web: alvernoheightsacademy.org. Mrs. Julia Fanara, Headmaster; Ms. Megan Hoover, Admin.; Ms. Kari Irvin, Admin.; Ms. Sara McCarthy, Admin.; Mrs. Cameron Werley-Gonzales, Admin. Lay Teachers 18; Students 175; Total Staff 40.

THOUSAND OAKS. *La Reina High School & Middle School*, (Grades 6-12), (Girls, Grades 6-12) 106 W. Janss Rd., Thousand Oaks, 91360. Tel: 805-495-6494; Fax: 805-494-4966; Email: lpino@lareina.com; Web: www.lareina.com. Mrs. Emily Beutner, Dean Student Life; Mr. Anthony Guevara, Headmaster. Lay Teachers 45; Students 418; Total Staff 67; Clergy / Religious Teachers 1.

VENTURA. **Saint Augustine Academy, Inc.*, (Grades 4-12), 130 S. Wells Rd., Ventura, 93004. Tel: 805-672-0411; Fax: 805-672-0177; Email: Office@SaintAugustineAcademy.com; Web: www.saintaugustineacademy.com. Michael Van Hecke, Prin. Lay Teachers 10; Students 134; Clergy / Religious Teachers 2.

WOODLAND HILLS. *Louisville High School* (1960) 22300 Mulholland Dr., Woodland Hills, 91364. Tel: 818-346-8812; Fax: 818-346-9483; Email: kvercillo@louisvillehs.org; Web: louisvillehs.org. Kathleen Vercillo, Prin.; Sr. Donna Hansen, S.S.L., Pres.; Mrs. Therese Blair, Librarian. Lay Teachers 31; Sisters 1; Students 336; Total Staff 28.

[G] ELEMENTARY SCHOOLS, PRIVATE

LOS ANGELES. *Notre Dame Academy Schools of Los Angeles* (1949) (Grades PreK-8), 2911 Overland Ave., 90064. Tel: 310-287-3895; Fax: 310-838-8983; Web: www.ndasla.org. Ms. Lilliam Paetzold, Pres.; Kristin Callaghan, Vice Pres.; Ashley Hobbs, Prin.; Ms. Amy Hickl, Vice Prin. Lay Teachers 18; Sisters of Notre Dame of Los Angeles 1; Students 287; Clergy / Religious Teachers 1.

MONTROSE. **St. Monica Academy, Inc.*, (Grades 1-12), 2361 Del Mar Rd., Montrose, 91020. Tel: 818-369-7310; Fax: 818-369-7305; Email: headmaster@stmonicaacademy.com; Email: mondonedom@stmonicaacademy.com; Web: stmonicaacademy.com. Marguerite Grimm, Headmaster. Lay Teachers 31; Students 277.

PASADENA. *Mayfield Junior School of the Holy Child Jesus*, 405 S. Euclid Ave., Pasadena, 91101. Tel: 626-796-2774; Fax: 626-796-5753; Email: school-2803@la-archdiocese.org; Web: www.mayfieldjs.org. Joseph J. Gill, Headmaster. Lay Teachers 73; Students 518; Total Staff 27.

VENTURA. **Saint Augustine Academy, Inc.*, (Grades PreK-3), 130 S. Wells Rd., Ventura, 93004. Tel: 805-672-0411; Fax: 805-672-0177; Email: office@saintaugustineacademy.com; Web: www.saintaugustineacademy.com. Michael Van Hecke, Prin. Lay Teachers 2; Students 24; Clergy / Religious Teachers 1.

[H] ORPHANAGES AND INFANT HOMES

ROSEMEAD, LOS ANGELES. *Maryvale* (1953) 7600 E. Graves Ave., P.O. Box 1039, Rosemead, 91770-1003. Tel: 626-280-6510; Fax: 626-288-8903; Email: maryvale@maryvale.org; Web: www.maryvale.org. Steve Gunther, M.S.W., Pres. & Exec. Dir. Total Staff 286; Family Resource Center 571; Daughters of Charity 6; Transitional Housing Program 2; Children: Residential Treatment 137; Early Education 387; Total Assisted 1,242.

The Los Angeles Orphan Asylum (1856) 7600 E. Graves Ave., Rosemead, 91770. Tel: 626-280-6510; Fax: 626-288-8903; Email: trosales@maryvale.org. Steve Gunther, M.S.W., Dir. Clergy 2; Students 75.

Los Angeles Orphanage Guild (1951) 7600 E. Graves Ave., Rosemead, 91770. Tel: 626-280-6510; Fax: 626-288-8903; Email: sgunther@maryvale.org; Web: www.laorphanageguild.com. Steven Gunther, Pres. Students 72.

[I] DAY NURSERIES

LOS ANGELES. *Divine Providence Pre-school and Kindergarten* (1954) 2620 Monmouth Ave., 90007. Tel: 213-747-3074; Fax: 213-747-6468; Email: kschneider@odn-la.org; Web: www.companyofmary.us. K.J. Mayer, Dir. Children 80; Lay Teachers 6; Sisters of the Company of Mary 1; Students 80; Total Staff 4.

GARDENA. *St. Anthony's Day Nursery*, 1044 W. 163rd St., Gardena, 90247. Tel: 310-329-8654; Email: info@la-archdiocese.org. Sr. Yadira Villalobos, M.C., Prin. Children 90; Sisters 10; Total Staff 12.

SYLMAR. *Poverello of Assisi Preschool* (1964) 13367 Borden Ave., Sylmar, 91342. Tel: 818-364-7446; Fax: 818-364-8596; Email: principal@poverelloschool.com. Sr. Patricia Cerrillo, Prin. Franciscan Missionary Sisters of the Immaculate Conception. Children 120; Sisters 12; Students 120; Total Staff 15.

[J] GENERAL HOSPITALS

BURBANK. *Providence Saint Joseph Medical Center*, 501 S. Buena Vista St., Burbank, 91505. Tel: 818-843-5111; Fax: 818-847-3310; Email: psjmc@providence.org; Web: www.providence.org. Sr. Sheila Browne, R.S.M., Dir., Mission Leadership, Tel: 818-847-3356; Rev. Mark Ciccone, S.J., Mgr., Spiritual Care, Tel: 818-847-4735; Mr. R. Phillip Kiehl, Chap.; D'vorah McDonald, Chap.; Sevan Sankrim, Chap.; Sr. Blanca Sagles, S.P., Assoc. Chap.; Ms. Claire Richardson, Chap. Bed Capacity 446; Tot Asst. Annually 230,000; Total Staff 2,600.

CAMARILLO. *St. John's Pleasant Valley Hospital*, 2309 Antonio Ave., Camarillo, 93010. Tel: 805-389-5800; Fax: 805-383-7450; Email: Robert.Sahagian@DignityHealth.org; Web: https://www.dignityhealth.org/pleasantvalley. Darren Lee, Pres./CEO. Sponsored by Sisters of Mercy of the Americas West Midwest Community. Bed Capacity 155; Sisters 2; Tot Asst. Annually 42,779; Total Staff 590.

LONG BEACH. *St. Mary Medical Center* (1924) 1050 Linden Ave., Long Beach, 90813. Tel: 562-491-9000; Fax: 562-436-6378; Email: Robert.Sahagian@DignityHealth.org; Web: www.stmarymedicalcenter.org. Sr. Celeste Trahan, Vice Pres., Mission Integration & Dir. Spiritual Care. Bed Capacity 389; Sisters 3; Tot Asst. Annually 138,496; Total Staff 1,492.

St. Mary Professional Building, Inc., 1050 Linden Ave., Long Beach, 90813. Tel: 562-491-9000; Email: Robert.Sahagian@DignityHealth.org. Sr. Celeste Trahan, Vice Pres.

MISSION HILLS. *Providence Holy Cross Medical Center*, 15031 Rinaldi St., Mission Hills, 91345-1207. Tel: 818-365-8051; Fax: 818-496-4569; Email: phcfoundation@providence.org; Web: www.providence.org/holycross. Bernie Klein, M.D., Chief Exec.; Ronald Galt, Dir., Mission Leadership and Spiritual Care, Tel: 818-496-5000; Andrea Cammarota, Chap.; Rev. Christina Chambers, Senior Chap.; Helde Ford, Sr. Chap.; Michael Rightmyer, Chap.; Kristin Michaelson, Chap.; Sr. Teresa Welch, S.P., Chap.; Nathan Pelz, Chap.; Rebecca Hewitt-Newson, Chap.; Elizabeth Seder, Chap.; Richard Maciejewski, Chap. Bed Capacity 377; Tot Asst. Annually 86,571; Total Staff 2,083.

NORTH HOLLYWOOD. *Providence St. Elizabeth Care Center*, 10425 Magnolia Blvd., North Hollywood, 91601. Tel: 818-980-3872; Fax: 818-980-6349; Email: psjfoundation@providence.org. Mr. Samuel Scrivens, Chap.; Sr. Blanca Sagles, S.P., Assoc. Chap. Bed Capacity 52; Tot Asst. Annually 60; Total Staff 50.

OXNARD. *St. John's Regional Medical Center*, 1600 N. Rose Ave., Oxnard, 93030. Tel: 805-988-2500; Fax: 805-981-4440; Email: Robert.Sahagian@DignityHealth.org; Web: www.dignityhealth.org/stjohnsregional. Darren Lee, Pres./CEO; Rev. Calin Tamiian, Chap. (Byzantine Priest); Sr. Janet Furman, Chap. Sponsored by Sisters of Mercy of the Americas West Midwest Community. Bed Capacity 265; Sisters of Mercy 2; Tot Asst. Annually 119,398; Total Staff 1,383.

St. John's Healthcare Foundation (Oxnard and Pleasant Valley), 1600 N. Rose Ave., Oxnard, 93030. Tel: 805-988-2868; Fax: 818-409-5353; Email: Robert.Sahagian@DignityHealth.org; Web: supportstjohns.org. Deborah Klein, Vice Pres. Philanthropy. Bed Capacity 265; Staff 9.

SAN PEDRO. *Providence Little Company of Mary Medical Center San Pedro*, 1300 W. 7th St., San Pedro, 90732. Tel: 310-832-3311; Fax: 310-514-5314; Email: plcmfoundation@providence.org; Web: www.providence.org/sanpedro. Nancy Carlson, COO; Sr. Nancy Jurecki, O.P., Dir., Mission Leadership & Spiritual Care, Tel: 310-514-4364; Darrah Glynn, Chap. (Protestant); Judith Sommerstein, Chap. (Jewish); Rev. Christopher Onyenobi, Chap. Bed Capacity 210; Tot Asst. Annually 101,010; Total Staff 1,150.

Providence Little Company of Mary Peninsula Diagnostic Center, 1360 W. 6th St., Ste. 100, San Pedro, 90732. Tel: 310-831-0371; Fax: 310-514-8920; Email: plcmfoundation@providence.org. Nancy Carlson, Chief Operating Officer.

Providence Little Company of Mary Peninsula Recovery Center, 1386 W. 7th St., San Pedro, 90732. Tel: 310-832-3311; Fax: 310-514-5376; Email: plcmfoundation@providence.org. Nancy Carlson, Chief Operating Officer.

Providence Little Company of Mary San Pedro Peninsula Hospital Pavilion, 1322 W. Sixth St., San Pedro, 90732. Tel: 310-832-3311; Fax: 310-514-5332; Email: plcmfoundation@providence.org. Julie Theiring, Admin. Dir.; Revs. Joel R. Buchman, M.A., S.T.B., Dir. Spiritual Care; Frank Gordillo, Chap. (Protestant); Francis L. Shigo, S.V.D., Chap. Skilled Nursing Facility. Bed Capacity 128.

Providence Little Company of Mary Sub-Acute Center-South Bay, 1322 W. 6th St., San Pedro, 90732. Tel: 310-732-6700; Fax: 310-732-6719; Email: plcmfoundation@providence.org. La Verna McMiller, Admin. Dir.; Rev. Joel R. Buchman, M.A., S.T.B., Dir. Spiritual Care; Margaret O'Leary, Chap. Bed Capacity 120.

SANTA MARIA. *Marian Regional Medical Center*, 1400 E. Church St., Santa Maria, 93454. Tel: 805-739-3000; Fax: 805-739-3060; Email: Robert.Sahagian@DignityHealth.org; Web: www.marianmedicalcenter.org. Ms. Sue Anderson, Pres.; Rev. Matthew Kronberg, Central Coast Spiritual Dir., (Evangelical Covenant Church); Elizabeth Hillis, Staff Chap. Sponsored by Sisters of St. Francis of Penance and Christian Charity. Bed Capacity 388; Sisters 5; Tot Asst. Annually 358,254; Total Staff 2,329.

Marian Regional Medical Center Extended Care Facility, Tel: 805-739-3650; Fax: 805-922-9067. Skilled Nursing Facility. Beds 95.

Marian Residence Retirement Home, 124 S. College Dr., Santa Maria, 93454. Tel: 805-922-7731; Email: Robert.Sahagian@DignityHealth.org. Kerin Mase, Dir.

Marian Regional Medical Center Foundation, 1400 E. Church St., Santa Maria, 93454. Tel: 805-739-3595; Fax: 805-739-3599; Email: Robert.Sahagian@DignityHealth.org; Web: www.supportmarianmedical.org. Jessa Brooks, Vice Pres. Employees 5.

SANTA MONICA. *Providence Saint John's Health Center*, 2121 Santa Monica Blvd., Santa Monica, 90404. Tel: 310-829-5511; Email: saintjohnshealthcenter@providence.org; Web: https://california.providence.org/saint-johns/. Marcel Loh, CEO & Pres.; Rev. Patrick Comerford, Chap. Providence Health System, Southern California. Bed Capacity 266; Sisters 2; Tot Asst. Annually 191,036; Total Staff 1,800.

TARZANA. *Providence Tarzana Medical Center*, 18321 Clark St., Tarzana, 91356. Tel: 818-881-0800; Email: ptzfoundation@providence.org. Shawn Kiley, Chap., Tel: 818-881-0800; Rev. Kenneth Chukwu, Chap.; Sr. Loraine Polacci, C.S.J., Chap.; Rabbi Sara Berman, Chap.; Rev. Anselm Nwakuna, Chap. Bed Capacity 245; Tot Asst. Annually 117,845; Total Staff 3,700.

TORRANCE. *Providence Little Company of Mary Foundation*, 4101 Torrance Blvd., Torrance, 90503. Tel: 310-303-5340; Fax: 310-540-8664; Email: plcmfoundation@providence.org. Joseph M. Zanetta, Pres.

Providence Little Company of Mary Medical Center, 4101 W. Torrance Blvd., Torrance, 90503. Tel: 310-540-7676; Fax: 310-540-7659; Email: plcmfoundation@providence.org; Web: providence.org. Liz Dunne, CEO; Revs. Dan Hudson, Mgr., Spiritual Care, Tel: 310-303-6122; Peter Mallin, O.F.M.Conv., Chap. Bassinets 35; Bed Capacity 250; Tot Asst. Annually 137,085; Total Staff 3,700.

WEST COVINA. *Citrus Valley Medical Center, Queen of the Valley Campus*, 1115 S. Sunset Ave., P.O. Box 1980, West Covina, 91790. Tel: 626-962-4011; Fax: 626-814-2428; Email: catherine@cvhp.com; Web: cvhp.org. Rev. Eric Anthony Lewis, Chap., (Retired); Mr. James T. Yoshioka, CEO. Bed Capacity 325; Tot Asst. Annually 125,000; Total Staff 1,500.

[K] SPECIAL HOSPITALS AND SANATORIA FOR INVALIDS

LOS ANGELES. **Order of Malta Los Angeles Clinic, Inc.*, 2222 W. Ocean View, #112, 90057. Tel: 213-384-4323; Fax: 213-384-4097; Email: freemed112@sbcglobal.net. David Frelinger, M.D., K.M., Medical Dir.; David Johnson, Admin. Conducted by Order of Malta Los Angeles Clinic, Inc. Tot Asst. Annually 2,217; Total Staff 12.

CULVER CITY. **Marycrest Manor* (1956) 10664 St. James Dr., Culver City, 90230-5498. Tel: 310-838-2778;

Tel: 310-838-0016 (Carmelite Sisters);
Fax: 310-838-9647;
Fax: 310-838-0024 (Carmelite Sisters); Email: admin@marycrestculvercity.com. Sr. Veronica Del Carmen, O.C.D., Admin. Bed Capacity 57; Tot Asst. Annually 600; Total Staff 70.

NEWBURY PARK. *Mary Health of the Sick Convalescent and Nursing Hospital* (1964) 2929 Theresa Dr., Newbury Park, 91320. Tel: 805-498-3644;
Fax: 805-498-5112; Email: office@maryhealth.com; Web: maryhealth.com. Sr. Lourdes Lara, S.deM., Exec. Dir. Sisters Servants of Mary. Bed Capacity 61; Sisters 13; Tot Asst. Annually 127; Total Staff 94.

OJAI. *St. Joseph's Health and Retirement Center*, 2464 E. Ojai Ave., Ojai, 93023. Tel: 805-646-1466;
Fax: 805-646-1013; Email: brmichaeloh@yahoo.com. Bro. Michael Bassemier, O.H., Admin.; Rev. Thaddeus Bui, O.H., Prior & Chap. Hospitaller Brothers of St. John of God. Capacity 28; Total Staff 42; Independent Living 25.

TORRANCE. **Providence Trinity Care Hospice*, 5315 Torrance Blvd., Ste. B1, Torrance, 90503.
Tel: 800-829-8660; Tel: 310-543-3400; Email: plcmfoundation@providence.org; Web: www.trinitycarehospice.org. Liz Dunne, Dir. Tot Asst. Annually 1,677; Total Staff 160.

[L] HANDICAPPED

SANTA MONICA. *Saint John's Child Study Center, Saint John's Hospital & Health Center*, 1339 20th St., Santa Monica, 90404-2033. Tel: 310-829-8921;
Fax: 310-829-8455; Email: saintjohnshealthcenter@providence.org. Rev. Patrick Comerford, Chap.; Rebecca Refuerza, L.C.S.W., Dir. Conducted by Sisters of Charity of Leavenworth. Tot Asst. Annually 1,800; Total Staff 2; Children Treated Annually 1,800.

SUNLAND. **Tierra del Sol Foundation*, 9919 Sunland Blvd., Sunland, 91040. Tel: 818-352-1419;
Fax: 818-353-0777; Email: jestrada@tierradelsol.org; Web: tierradelsol.org. Stephen J. Miller, Exec. Dir.; Nancy Bissonette-Andrew, Clinical Dir. Licensed Capacity 304.

[M] VISITING NURSE SERVICES

LOS ANGELES. *Servants of Mary, Ministers to the Sick*, 2131 W. 27th St., 90018-3018. Tel: 323-731-5747;
Fax: 323-731-4251; Email: servantsofmaryla@aol.com. Sr. Lourdes Garcia, S.deM., Supr. Sisters 12; Total Staff 7; Total Assisted 50.

[N] PROTECTIVE INSTITUTIONS

LOS ANGELES. *St. Anne's*, 155 N. Occidental Blvd., 90026. Tel: 213-381-2931; Fax: 213-381-7804; Email: stannes@stannes.org; Web: www.stannes.org. Tony Walker, M.A., Pres. & CEO. Sponsored by the Franciscan Sisters of the Sacred Heart. Bed Capacity 50; Tot Asst. Annually 1,150; Total Staff 300; Beds Licensed for Children Under 18 years of age 50; Children Served Annually in Residential Care 125.
Support groups include:.
St. Anne's Foundation.
St. Anne's Guild.
Mabel Mosler Auxiliary.
Loretta Young Auxiliary.
*Sister Winifred Auxiliary*Total Staff 220; Residential 250; Prevention Education 2,000.

Convent of the Good Shepherd-Good Shepherd Shelter (1904) Mailing Address: P.O. Box 19487, 90019. Tel: 323-737-6111; Fax: 323-737-6113; Email: akelley@goodshepherdshelter.org; Web: www.goodshepherdshelter.org. Mark Rothman, Dir. Conducted by Sisters of the Good Shepherd. Bed Capacity 73; Children 58; Sisters 10; Tot Asst. Annually 73; Total Staff 3; Women Assisted Annually 15.

CHATSWORTH. **Rancho San Antonio Boys Home, Inc.*, 21000 Plummer St., Chatsworth, 91311.
Tel: 818-882-6400; Fax: 818-882-6404; Email: info@ranchosanantonio.org. Bro. John Crowe, C.S.C., Exec. Dir. Directed by the Brothers of Holy Cross. Bed Capacity 106; Brothers 1; Tot Asst. Annually 405; Total Staff 168; Boys (13-17 yrs.) 106; Families Assisted 405.

SANTA BARBARA. *St. Vincent's Institution*, 4200 Calle Real, Santa Barbara, 93110-1454.
Tel: 805-683-6381; Email: info@sv-sb.org; Web: www.stvincents-sb.org. Lee Hilton, Contact Person.

Family Strengthening Program (1996) 4200 Calle Real, Santa Barbara, 93110-1454.
Tel: 805-683-6381; Fax: 805-967-7508; Web: www.stvincents-sb.org. Joanne Sizemore, Dir. For single or pregnant moms and their children 5 years and under on welfare and/or very low income. Children 25; Conducted by Daughters of Charity of St. Vincent de Paul 4; Tot Asst. Annually 23; Total Staff 5; Mothers 19.

Early Childhood Education Center (1918) 4200 Calle Real, Santa Barbara, 93110-1454.
Tel: 805-683-6381, Ext. 211; Fax: 805-967-7508; Web: www.stvincents-sb.org. Susy Del Toro, Dir. For infants, toddlers, and preschoolers. Day Care 98; Daughters of Charity of St. Vincent de Paul 4; Total Staff 24.

Villa Caridad, 4202 Calle Real, Santa Barbara, 93110-1454. Tel: 805-683-4375; Fax: 805-683-4725 ; Email: info@sv-sb.org. Alicia Rivera, Dir. Affordable apartments for low-income seniors 95.

St. Vincent's Gardens, 4234 Pozzo Cir., Santa Barbara, 93110-1454. Tel: 805-967-4340;
Fax: 805-967-4311; Email: SVG@pshhc.org. Teresa Barron, Dir. Affordable apartments for Families 75. Affordable Apartments for Families 75.

Fr. Virgil Cordano Center, 4020 Calle Real, Santa Barbara, 93110-1454. Tel: 805-563-1051;
Fax: 805-563-1046; Web: frvirgilcordanocenter.org. Sr. Margaret Keaveney, D.C., Exec.

San Vicente Mobile Home Park, 340 Old Mill Rd. #135A, Santa Barbara, 93110-1454.
Tel: 805-964-9662; Fax: 805-964-0816. Mary Manzo, Vice Pres.

St. Vincent's Heart, Tel: 805-683-6381;
Fax: 805-967-7508; Email: info@sv-sb.org; Web: www.stvincents-sb.org.

Vincent's Ministries, LLC, 4200 Calle Real, Santa Barbara, 93110.

[O] HOMES FOR AGED

LOS ANGELES. *St. John of God Retirement and Care Center*, 2468 S. St. Andrews Pl., 90018.
Tel: 323-731-0641; Fax: 323-731-1452; Email: contactus@stjog.org. Bros. Michael Bassemier, O.H., CEO; Stephen de la Rosa, O.H., Prov.; Pablo Lopez, O.H., Provincial. Bed Capacity 298; Brothers 5; Patients Asst Anual. 297; Total Staff 321; SNF 156; Residential Care 142.
Supporting Organizations:
Women's League of St. John of God, Inc., Helpers Club of St. John of God, Inc., 2425 S. Western Ave., 90018. Tel: 323-731-7141; Fax: 323-731-5717; Email: USAProv-office@sbcglobal.net. Bro. Stephen de la Rosa, O.H., Dir.

Nazareth House (1946) 3333 Manning Ave., 90064.
Tel: 310-839-2361; Fax: 310-839-4204; Email: mwashington@nazarethhousela.org; Web: www.nazarethouse.org. Melanie Washington, Dir. Congregation of the Sisters of Nazareth. Retired Priests 1; Residents 125; Sisters 1; Total Staff 93.

SAN FERNANDO. *Mother Gertrude Home for Senior Citizens*, 11320 Laurel Canyon Blvd., San Fernando, 91340. Tel: 818-898-1546;
Fax: 818-365-6646; Email: email@mothergertrudehome.org. Sr. Elia Caro, Dir. Capacity 45; Total in Residence 45; Total Staff 19.

SAN PEDRO. *Little Sisters of the Poor of Los Angeles* (1979) Jeanne Jugan Residence, 2100 S. Western Ave., San Pedro, 90732. Tel: 310-548-0625;
Fax: 310-548-4504; Email: mssanpedro@littlesistersofthepoor.org; Web: www.littlesistersofthepoor.org. Sr. Margaret Lennon, L.S.P., Supr.
Little Sisters of the Poor of Los Angeles. A Corporation Priests 3; Residents 102; Sisters 9; Tot Asst. Annually 1,260; Total Staff 110; Lay Associates 30.

SUN VALLEY. *Villa Scalabrini*, 10631 Vinedale St., Sun Valley, 91352. Tel: 818-768-6500;
Fax: 818-768-0684; Email: laura@villascalabrini.com; Web: www.villascalabrini.com. Rev. Adilso Balen, C.S., Exec. Missionary Fathers of St. Charles. Bed Capacity 188; Total Staff 130; Retirement Center 130; Skilled Nursing Unit 58.

[P] MONASTERIES AND RESIDENCES OF PRIESTS AND BROTHERS

LOS ANGELES. *Brothers of St. John of God, Inc., The*, 2425 S. Western Ave., 90018-2608.
Tel: 323-734-0233; Fax: 323-978-5881; Email: usaprov-office@sbcglobal.net; Web: www.stjog.org. Bro. Stephen de la Rosa, O.H., Prov. *Grande Apartments-Los Angeles*, Tel: 323-730-4100;
Fax: 323-737-1452; Email: slopez@sjghcs.org; Web: stjog.org. *Helper's Club, Inc.*, 2468 S. St. Andrew's Pl., 90018. Tel: 323-731-7141; Fax: 323-731-5717. *Hospitaller Brothers Healthcare, Inc.*,
Tel: 323-734-0233; Fax: 323-731-5987; Email: usaprov-office@sbcglobal.net; Web: stjog.org. *Hospitaller Foundation of California, Inc.*,
Tel: 323-731-7141; Fax: 323-731-5717; Email: arlene@hospitallerfoundation.org; Web: hospitallers.org. *St. John of God Health Care Services*, Tel: 760-241-4917; Fax: 760-241-8911; Email: gbarnes@sjghcs.org; Web: stjog.org. *St. John of God Retirement & Care Center*, 2468 S. St. Andrew's Pl., 90018. Tel: 323-731-0641;
Fax: 323-737-1452; Email: usaprov-office@sbcglobal.net; Web: hospitallers.org. Bro. Michael Bassemier, O.H., CEO. *St. Joseph's Health & Retirement Center*, 2464 E. Ojai Ave., Ojai, 93023. Tel: 805-646-1466; Fax: 805-646-1013; Web: www.stjog.org. Rev. Ignatius Sudol, O.H., Prior. *Women's League of St. John of God, Inc.*, 2468 S. St. Andrew's Pl., 90018. Tel: 323-731-7141;
Fax: 323-731-5717; Web: www.stjog.org/foundation. Bro. Stephen de la Rosa, O.H., Prov. *Women's League of St. Joseph's Health & Retirement Center*, Tel: 805-646-1466; Fax: 805-646-1013 ; Web: stjog.org.

Colombiere House, 5322 Franklin Ave., 90027.
Tel: 323-466-3723; Fax: 323-466-3826. Revs. Augusto Berrio, S.J.; Frank C. Buckley, S.J.; Mark Ciccone, S.J., Supr.; William K. Delaney, S.J.; Robert G. Dolan, S.J.; Leo P. Prengaman, S.J.; Ike Udoh, S.J.; Timothy Meier, On Sabbatical. Jesuit Fathers. Priests 8.

Dominic Savio Salesian Residence (1958) P.O. Box 331059, 90033. Tel: 510-224-8122;
Fax: 323-266-3487; Email: nreina@mustangsla.org; Web: www.donboscowest.org. Rev. John Lam, S.D.B., Supr. In Res. Revs. John Lam, S.D.B., Pastor St. Bridgit; Andrew Ng, S.D.B.; Jesse Montes, S.D.B., Pastor St. Mary's Parish; Nicholas Reina, S.D.B., Supr. of Community, Salesian High School; Leo Baysinger, S.D.B., Assoc. St. Mary's Parish; Joseph Farias, S.D.B., Assoc. St. Mary's Parish; Bros. Steven Standard, S.D.B., Community Treas., Salesian Boys & Girls Club, Salesian Family Youth Center; Tom Mass, S.D.B., Salesian Boy's & Girl's Club, Salesian Family Youth Center & St. Mary's.

Franciscan Brothers of the Third Order Regular, 4522 Gainsborough Ave., 90027-1227.
Tel: 323-644-2740; Email: hoconnor@olacathedral.org. Bro. Hilarion O'Connor, O.S.F., Regl. Supr. Brothers 6.

Guadalupe Missioners Procure, 4714 W. 8th St., 90005. Tel: 323-937-2780; Fax: 323-937-2782; Email: munozymg@yahoo.com. Revs. Salvador Arufe Gil, M.G., Dir.; Abraham R. Garcia, M.G., Asst. Priests 2.

Hospitaller Brothers of St. John of God, 2468 S. St. Andrew's Pl., 90018. Tel: 323-731-0641;
Fax: 323-731-5987; Email: usaprov-office@sbcglobal.net; Web: www.stjog.org. Bro. Stephen de la Rosa, O.H., Prov. Brothers 12.

St. John of God Retirement and Care Center, 2468 S. St. Andrews Pl., 90018. Tel: 323-731-0641;
Fax: 323-737-1452; Web: www.stjog.org. Bros. Pablo Lopez, O.H., Supr.; Stephen de la Rosa, O.H., Prov. Brothers 5.

Maryknoll Fathers and Brothers (Catholic Foreign Mission Society of America) 222 S. Hewitt St. #6, 90012-4309. Tel: 213-747-9676; Fax: 213-908-2317; Email: losangeles@maryknoll.org; Web: www.maryknoll.org. Rev. Michael G. Callanan, M.M., Supr., (Retired). 2701 S. Peck Rd., Monrovia, 91016-5004.
Tel: 626-447-6202, Ext. 32 (Annunciation Parish, Arcadia). Rev. Michael G. Callanan, M.M., (Retired). 340 Norumbega Dr., Monrovia, 91016-2445. Tel: 626-358-1825. Rev. Gerald J. Persha, M.M., (Retired), 340 Norumbega Dr., Monrovia, 91016. Tel: 626-358-1825.

Minim Fathers, 3431 Portola Ave., 90032.
Tel: 323-223-1101; Fax: 323-223-9592; Email: allsaintschurch@earthlink.net; Web: www.allsaintsla.com. Revs. Mario Pisano, O.M., Supr.; Gino Vanzillotta, O.M.; Jose L. Vega, O.M.; Thomas C. Francis, O.M. Priests 4.

Missionaries of Charity Brothers (1975) 1316 S. Westlake Ave., 90006. Tel: 213-380-5225; Email: brosla@aol.com; Web: www.mcbrothers.org. Bro. Kevin Cannon, Supr. Brothers 4.

**Missionaries of Jesus, Inc.*, 435 S. Occidental Blvd., 90057. Tel: 213-389-8439; Fax: 213-389-1951; Email: info@missionariesofjesus.com; Web: www.missionariesofjesus.com. Revs. Joseph Ricardo Guerrero, M.J., Gen. Supr.; Manuel Gacad, M.J., Pastor & Gen. Counselor; Michael Montoya, M.J., Vice Supr.; Enrique Ymson, M.J., Assoc. Pastor; Melanio Viuya Jr., M.J., Dir. Mission Promotion Office & Treas. Priests 5.

Piarist Fathers, 512 S. Avenue 20, 90031.
Tel: 213-223-4153; Email: parish-4080@la-archdiocese.org. Revs. Raul Palma, Sch.P.; Juan Trenchs, Sch.P.; Miguel Campos, Sch.P. Priests 4.

The Society of St. Paul (1914) (Mexican Province) 112 Herbert St., 90063. Tel: 323-269-9814;
Fax: 323-269-0242; Email: marvences@hotmail.com. Revs. Marco Antonio Vences, S.S.P., Pres.; Francisco M. Rosas Zevada, S.S.P., Treas.

BALDWIN PARK. *Vietnamese Redemptorist Mission*, 3452 N. Big Dalton Ave., Baldwin Park, 91706.
Tel: 626-851-9020; Tel: 626-377-6540; Email: chaqhung@yahoo.com. Revs. Ngo Dinh Thoa, C.Ss.R.; Pham Quoc Hung, C.Ss.R.; John Cuong Ba Vu, C.Ss.R.; Doan Trong Son, C.Ss.R.; Bros. John M. Viet Hien, C.Ss.R.; Martin Nguyen Van Moi, C.Ss.R.
In Residence Elsewhere: Revs. Dang Phuoc Hoa, C.Ss.R., 8800 E. 22nd St., Tucson, AZ 85710. Tel:

602-751-2060; Tran Dinh Phuc, C.Ss.R., 22 Stone St., Salinas, 93901. Tel: 408-772-8227; Quang Minh Nguyen; Nguyen Duc Mau, C.Ss.R., 2458 Atlantic Ave., Long Beach, 90806. Tel: 562-424-2041; Fax: 562-424-2152; Phan Phat Huon, C.Ss. R., 2458 Atlantic Ave., Long Beach, 90806. Tel: 562-424-2041; Fax: 562-424-2152; Ngo Van Dao, C.Ss.R., 2458 Atlantic Ave., Long Beach, 90806. Tel: 562-424-2041; Fax: 562-424-2152; Nguyen Tat Hai, C.Ss.R., 2458 Atlantic Ave., Long Beach, 90806. Tel: 562-424-2041; Fax: 562-424-2152; Nguyen Truong Luan, 2458 Atlantic Ave., Long Beach, 90806. Tel: 562-424-2041; Fax: 562-424-2152; Dinh Minh Hai, C.Ss.R., 3910 S. Ledbetter Dr., Dallas, TX 75236. Tel: 972-438-4082; Bui Quang Tuan, C.Ss.R., 3910 S. Ledbetter Dr., Dallas, TX 75236. Tel: 972-438-4082; Nguyen Phi Long, C.Ss.R., 3910 S. Ledbetter Dr., Dallas, TX 75236. Tel: 972-438-4082; Chau Xuan Bau, C.Ss. R., 3417 W. Little York Rd., Houston, TX 77091. Tel: 214-321-9493; Fax: 713-686-4589; Nguyen Quoc Dung, C.Ss.R.; Nguyen Dinh Trung, C.Ss.R., 3417 W. Little York Rd., Houston, TX 77091. Tel: 214-321-9493; Fax: 713-686-4589; Bro. Nguyen Tran Duc, C.Ss.R.; Revs. Tung Duc Vu, C.Ss.R.; Dominic Pham, C.Ss.R.; Dinh Ngoc Que, C.Ss.R.; Le Trong Hung, C.Ss.R.; Dat Tan Nguyen, C.Ss.R.; Bros. Hanh Phuoc Nguyen, C.Ss.R.; Nguyen Ngoc Khanh, C.Ss.R.; Sang Thanh Vu, C.Ss.R.

CUDAHY. *Misioneros del Sagrado Corazon y Santa Maria de Guadalupe* (1938) 4235 Clara St., Cudahy, 90201. Tel: 323-562-3356; Email: miguelgmsc@hotmail.com. Rev. Antero Sanchez, M.S.C., Regl. Supr.

ENCINO. *Our Lady of Mount Carmel Priory*, 4966 Alonzo Ave., Encino, 91316. Tel: 818-345-6055; Email: jsprissler@crespi.org. Revs. Adrian Wilde, Treas.; Benjamin Aguilar; John Coleman, O.Carm.; Mario Lopez; Augustine W. Carter, O.Carm., (Retired); Matt J. Ewing, O.Carm., (Retired); Albert P. Koppes, O.Carm., (Retired); Peter J. Liuzzi, O.Carm., (Retired); Thomas Batsis, O.-Carm., (Retired); Deacon John Sprissler, Prior

Fathers of the Order of Mount Carmel, Corporation Priests 7.

LA VERNE. *Congregation of the Sacred Hearts of Jesus and Mary*, 2150 Damien Ave., La Verne, 91750-5114. Tel: 909-593-5441 (Regional Office); Fax: 909-593-3971; Email: ssccwest@gmail.com; Web: www.ssccusawest.org. P.O. Box 668, San Dimas, 91773. Revs. Peadar Cronin, SS.CC., Pres., Holy Name of Mary, San Dimas, CA; Richard J. Danyluk, SS.CC., Supr., Holy Name of Mary Parish, San Dimas, CA; Michael W. Barry, SS.CC., Dir., Mary's Mercy Center, Inc: Mary's Table & Veronica's Home of Mercy, San Bernardino, CA; William C. Moore, SS.CC., Ministry of the Arts, Ministry of the Arts, San Dimas, CA; Martin P. O'Loghlen, SS.CC., Treas., Sacred Hearts Community, Hemet, CA; Patrick Fanning, Novice Master; Jeremiah Holland, SS.CC., Asst. Novice Master, Sacred Hearts Community, Hemet, CA; Patrick Travers, SS.CC., Holy Innocents Church, Victorville, CA; Brian Guerrini, SS.CC., Our Lady of Grace, Artesia, NM; Jeremy Sabugo; John Roche, SS.CC., Campus Min., La Verne, CA; Patrick P. Coyle, SS.CC., (Retired), Twenty-Nine Palms, CA; Patrick J. Crowley, SS.CC., Sacred Hearts Community, Hemet, CA; Peter K. Dennis, SS.CC., La Verne, CA; Michael N. Maher, SS.CC, St. Louis, Cathedral City; Sacred Hearts Community, Hemet, CA; Very Rev. Donal McCarthy, SS.CC., (Retired), La Verne, CA; Revs. Henry Paul Murtagh, SS.CC.; Patrick J. O'Hagan, SS.CC., (Retired), St. Paul the Apostle, Chino Hills; Santa Clarita. Priests in Residence 4.

MONTEBELLO. *Congregation of the Mission Western Province* aka DePaul Center Residence, 1105 Bluff Rd., Montebello, 90640-6198. Cell: 303-589-9073; Email: prodrig357@aol.com; Web: www.vincentian.org. Rev. Prudencio Rodriguez de Yurre, C.M., Supr.

DePaul Center, a California Corporation; Congregation of the Mission, Western Province, California; Vincentian Province of the West Support Trust Fund; Vincentian Foreign Mission Society

Vincentian Foreign Mission SocietyDePaul Evangelization Center, 1105 Bluff Rd., Montebello, 90640-6198. Tel: 323-721-6060; Fax: 323-887-1765; Email: cmstlouis@vincentian.org. Revs. Prudencio Rodriguez de Yurre, C.M., Supr. & Dir.; Binh Van Nguyen, C.M.; Robert J. Jones, C.M.; Juan Antonio Ruiz, C.M.; Bro. David Berning, C.M. Brothers 1; Priests 4. *Amat Residence II*, 641 W. Adams Blvd., 90007-2546. Tel: 323-236-5128; Email: JROCM@Hotmail.com; Web: www.vincentian.org. Revs. Pedro Villarroya, C.M.; James Osendorf, C.M., Supr.; Roy A. Persich, C.M., (Retired). Priests 3.

OXNARD. *Order of Augustinian Recollects (O.A.R.), St. Augustine Priory* (1990) 400 Sherwood Way, Oxnard, 93033-7510. Tel: 805-486-7433; Fax: 805-487-2805; Email: saprovince@yahoo.com; Web: www.agustinosrecolectos.com. Revs. Marlon Beof, O.A.R., Prior; John Michael Rafferty, O.A.R., Subprior & Vocations Dir. Brothers 1; Deacons 1; Priests 8; Total in Residence 10. In Res. Revs. James V. Brown, O.A.R.; Joaquin Goni, O.A.R.; Fidel Hernandez, O.A.R.; Robert Huse, O.A.R.; Frank T. Wilder, O.A.R.; Bro. Mario Alvarez, O.A.R.; Deacon Ascencion Esqueda, O.A.R.

PASADENA. *Legionaries of Christ*, 1455 Sierra Madre Villa Ave., Pasadena, 91107. Tel: 678-232-0225; Web: www.legionofchrist.org. Revs. Donal O'Keeffe, L.C., Supr.; Mariano de Blas Saez, L.C., In Res.; Agustin De la Vega, L.C., In Res.; Peter Devereux, L.C., In Res.; Lorenzo Gomez Sotres, L.C., In Res.; John Hopkins, L.C., In Res.; Randall Meissen, L.C., In Res.; Bernardo Torres, L.C., In Res. Priests 8.

SANTA BARBARA. *Franciscan Friary, Order of Friars Minor (Old Mission)* (1786) 2201 Laguna St., Santa Barbara, 93105. Tel: 805-682-4713; Fax: 805-682-6067; Email: parish-3050@la-archdiocese.org. Revs. Larry Gosselin, O.F.M.; Kenan Osborne, O.F.M.; Bros. Angelo Cardinalli, O.F.M., Chap., Old Mission; Regan Chapman, O.F.M., Guardian; Freddy Rodriguez, O.F.M., Asst. Postulant Dir. Brothers 6; Priests 3. In Res. Rev. Adrian Peelo, O.F.M., Pastor; Bros. John Gutierrez, O.F.M., Postulant Dir.; Arturo Noyes, O.F.M.; Nicholas Ronalter, O.F.M.

SANTA PAULA. *Canons Regular of the Immaculate Conception* (1871) Dom Grea House of Formation & Novitiate, 601 Glade Dr., Santa Paula, 93060-1640. Tel: 805-933-5063; Fax: 805-525-5115; Email: cricusa@yahoo.com; Web: cricusa.org. Revs. Pasquale Vuoso, C.R.I.C., Supr., Tel: 805-525-2149; Fax: 805-933-5520; Thomas J. Dome, C.R.I.C., Dir. & Novice Master; Charles R. Lueras, C.R.I.C., Tel: 805-525-2149; Fax: 805-933-5520; William B. Ustaski, C.R.I.C., Tel: 661-252-3353; Fax: 661-252-1539; Thaddeus Haynes, C.R.I.C.; Bro. Roger M. Proulx, C.R.I.C.; Deacon Christopher A. Reeve, C.R.I.C. Brothers 2; Priests 4; Seminarians 2.

SIERRA MADRE. *Passionist Residence*, 700 N. Sunnyside Ave., Sierra Madre, 91024. Tel: 626-355-1740; Fax: 626-355-1744; Email: materdolorosa@materdolorosa.org. Very Rev. Alan Phillip, C.P., Supr.; Revs. Michael Higgins, C.P., Dir.; Bruno D'Souza, C.P.; Clemente Barron; Bro. John Rockenbach, C.P. Brothers 1; Priests 4.

TEMPLE CITY. *Claretian Missionaries - Western Province, Inc.* Affiliated with Claretian Missionaries - U.S.A. Province, Inc. (Chicago, IL) 10203 Lower Azusa Rd., Temple City, 91780. Tel: 626-443-2009; Fax: 626-443-2005; Email: usawestprov@earthlink.net; Web: www.claretian.com. Very Rev. Rosendo Urrabazo, C.M.F., Pres., San Gabriel Mission, 428 S. Mission Dr., San Gabriel, 91776. Tel: 626-457-3035. *Tepeyac House*, 6104 York Blvd., 90042. Tel: 323-254-0510; Email: usawestprov@earthlink.net. Bro. Larry J. Moen, C.M.F. *Educational and Renewal Center, Inc.*, 10203 Lower Azusa Rd., Temple City, 91780. Tel: 626-443-2009; Fax: 626-443-2005; Email: usawestprov@earthlink.net; Web: www.claretian.com. Very Rev. Rosendo Urrabazo, C.M.F., Dir. *Dominguez Seminary Inc.*, 18127 S. Alameda St., Rancho Dominguez, 90220. Tel: 310-631-5981; Tel: 310-631-8484; Fax: 310-638-1818; Email: usawestprov@earthlink.net. Rev. Frank Ferrante, C.M.F., Supr.; Bro. Rene LePage, C.M.F., Econome; Revs. Robert Billett, C.M.F., Vicar Supr.; Robert Bishop, C.M.F.; Carlos C. Castillo, C.M.F.; Salvatore Bonano, C.M.F., (Retired); Milton Alvarez, C.M.F.; Alberto Domingo, C.M.F., (Retired); Donald Lavelle, C.M.F.; John Hampsch, C.M.F.; Richard Wozniak, C.M.F.; Bros. Paul Roy, C.M.F.; Thomas Haerle, C.M.F. Brothers 3; Priests 11.

VALYERMO. *St. Andrew's Abbey*, 31001 N. Valyermo Rd., P.O. Box 40, Valyermo, 93563-0040. Tel: 661-944-2178; Fax: 661-944-1076; Email: information@saintandrewsabbey.com; Web: www.saintandrewsabbey.com. Revs. Damien Toilolo, O.S.B., Abbot; Francis Benedict, O.S.B., Abbot Emeritus; Patrick Sheridan, O.S.B., Subprior; Bros. John Mark Matthews, O.S.B.; Peter Zhou Bang-jiu, O.S.B.; Rev. Philip Edwards, O.S.B.; Bros. Dominic Guillen, O.S.B.; Benedict Dull, O.S.B.; Joseph Iarrobino, O.S.B.; Revs. Luke Dysinger, O.S.B., M.D., D.Phil.; Martin Yslas, O.S.B.; Isaac Kalina, O.S.B.; Carlos Lopez, O.S.B.; Joseph (Dennis) Brennan, O.S.B., Prior; Aelred Niespolo, O.S.B., M.A., B.Th., M.Th.; Matthew Rios, O.S.B.; Cassian DiRocco, O.S.B.; Angelus Echeverry, O.S.B.; Bros. Paul Ortega, O.S.B.; Columba Corrie. Benedictine Monks. Brothers 7; Priests 13.

VAN NUYS. *Rogationist Fathers* (2001) 6635 Tobias Ave., Van Nuys, 91405. Tel: 818-782-0184; Fax: 818-782-1794; Email: info@vocationsandprayer.org; Web: www.rogationists.org. Revs. Jupeter Quinto, R.C.J., Supr., St. Jane de Chantal, N. Hollywood; Vito Di Marzio, R.C.J., Pastor, St. Elizabeth, Van Nuys; Antonio Fiorenza, R.C.J., Supr.; Denny Joseph, R.C.J., Assoc. Pastor, St. Elizabeth, Van Nuys; Shinto Sebastian, R.C.J., Assoc. Pastor, St. Jane de Chantal, N. Hollywood; Antonio Carlucci, R.C.J., Pastor, St. Jane de Chantal, N. Hollywood; Renato Panlasigui, R.C.J., Vocation Dir. & Res. Priest, St. Elizabeth, Van Nuys

Congregation of Rogationists, Inc. Priests 7.

WHITTIER. *Redemptorists of Whittier*, 7215 S. Newlin Ave., Whittier, 90602-1266. Tel: 562-698-0107; Fax: 562-696-1617; Email: frgstmary@archdiocese-la.org; Web: www.stmaryschurch-whittier.org. Revs. Steven J. Nyl, C.Ss.R., Pastor; Joseph Butz, C.Ss.R., Assoc. Pastor; Marcel Okwara, C.Ss.R.; Bro. Thomas Wright, C.Ss.R., Business Mgr.; Revs. William Adams, C.Ss.R., (Retired); John Gouger; Bro. Paul Jorns, C.Ss.R.; Revs. Gary Lauenstein, C.Ss.R., Supr.; Anthony Phuc Nguyen, C.Ss.R.; Mark Scheffler, C.Ss.R., Hospital Chap.; Luong Uong. Brothers 2; Priests 9. In Res. Revs. Gary Lauenstein, C.Ss.R., Redemptorist Supr.; William Adams, C.Ss.R., (Retired); Mark Scheffler, C.Ss.R.; Anthony Phuc Nguyen, C.Ss.R.; Bro. Paul Jorns, C.Ss.R.

[Q] CONVENTS AND RESIDENCES FOR SISTERS

LOS ANGELES. **The Blessed Sacrament Sisters of Charity, Inc.*, 248 S. Mariposa Ave., 90004. Tel: 213-389-7760; Email: inbousa@yahoo.com. Sr. Theresa Kong, Local Supr. Sisters 4.

California Institute of the Sisters of the Immaculate Heart Mary (1848) Office of the Archbishop, 3424 Wilshire Blvd., 5th Fl., 90010-2241. Tel: 213-637-7000; Fax: 213-637-6000; Email: info@la-archdiocese.org. Most Rev. Jose Gomez, Ordinary. Pontifical Commissary of the Archbishop.

California Institute of the Sisters of the Most Holy and Immaculate Heart of the Blessed Virgin Mary Sisters 3.

Congregation of the Sisters of Nazareth Motherhouse, U.S.A., 3333 Manning Ave., 90064. Tel: 310-839-2361; Fax: 310-839-0648; Email: regional@nazarethhousela.org; Web: www.nazarethhouse.org. Sr. Marie McCormack, C.S.N., Regl. Supr. Sisters 8.

Eucharistic Franciscan Missionary Sisters, Motherhouse, 943 S. Soto St., 90023. Tel: 213-264-6556; Tel: 310-328-6725; Fax: 213-526-1655; Email: efms@earthlink.net. Rev. Mother Rose Seraphim, E.F.M.S., Supr. Gen. Sisters 23.

Hermanas Carmelitas de San Jose (1916) 141 W. 87th Pl., 90003. Tel: 323-758-6840; Email: sisterscsjla@yahoo.com; Email: hnarosalidia@yahoo.com. Sr. Rosa Lidia Orellana, C.S.J., Supr. Sisters 4.

Missionary Benedictine Sisters of Tutzing in Los Angeles, Inc. (2002) 912 S. Bronson Ave., 90019-1935. Tel: 323-939-3977; Tel: 323-937-7971; Fax: 323-939-3977; Email: osbgregory@hanmail.net. Sr. Pachomia Kim, O.S.B., Supr. & Contact Person.

Missionary Guadalupanas of the Holy Spirit, Inc., 5467 W. 8th St., 90036. Tel: 323-424-7208; Fax: 323-424-7498; Email: province@guadalupeusa.org; Web: www.mgsps.org. Sisters Ana Gabriela Castro, M.G.Sp.S., Provincial; Frances Aldama, Vicar; Yesenia Fernandez, M.G.Sp.S., Treas. Sisters 4.

Novitiate, 5465 W. 8th St., 90036. Tel: 323-363-1133 ; Email: novitiate@guadalupeusa.org. Sr. Lorena Sandoval, Contact Person. Sisters 2.

Missionary Sisters of Christ the King (Poland) (1959) 3424 W. Adams Blvd., 90018. Tel: 323-734-5249; Fax: 323-734-0046; Email: plchurchla@earthlink.net. Sisters Anna Kalinowski, M.S.C.K., Local Supr.; Jadwiga Kokolus, M.C.H.R., Parish Sec. Sisters working in Archdiocese of Los Angeles 3.

Monastery of the Angels (Contemplative), 1977 Carmen Ave., 90068. Tel: 323-466-2186; Fax: 323-466-6645; Email: monasteryprioress@gmail.com. Sr. Mary St. Pius, O.P., Prioress; Rev. Michael Carey, O.P., Chap. Nuns of the Order of Preachers. Sisters 17.

Pious Disciples of the Divine Master, 501 N. Beaudry Ave., 90012-1509. Tel: 213-250-7962 (Center); Tel: 213-977-0893 (Community); Fax: 213-977-0987; Email: lalitcenter@aol.com; Web: www.pddm.us. Sr. M. Lucille Van Hoogmoed, P.D.D.M., Local Supr. Sisters 7.

Servants of the Immaculate Child Mary, E.I.N. (Esclavas de la Inmaculada Nina) (1901) 5135 Dartmouth Ave., 90032-3323. Tel: 323-225-3279; Fax: 323-225-3279; Email: ein-la@hotmail.com. Sr. Raquel Diaz Sandoval, Supr. Sisters 337. 350 S.

Boyle Ave., 90033-3813. Tel: 323-269-7786; Fax: 323-269-7786; Email: ein-la@hotmail.com.

Sisters of Social Service of Los Angeles (1926) General Motherhouse, 4316 Lanai Rd., Encino, 91436. Tel: 818-285-3355; Fax: 818-285-3366; Email: SistersSocialService@gmail.com; Web: www.sssla.org. Sr. Michele Walsh, S.S.S., Gen. Dir.

Sisters of Social Service of Los Angeles, Inc. Sisters 63.

Sisters of Social Service, Formation, 4316 Lanai Rd., Encino, 91436. Tel: 818-285-3355; Fax: 818-285-3366; Email: SistersSocialService@gmail.com; Web: sssla.org. Sr. Michele Walsh, S.S.S., Dir. Tot Asst. Annually 18,000; Total Staff 23; In Formation 6.

Sisters of St. Joseph of Carondelet in California (1850) 11999 Chalon Rd., 90049-1524. Tel: 310-889-2100; Fax: 310-476-8735; Email: tkvale@csjla.org; Web: www.csjla.org. Sisters Angela Faustina, C.S.J., Team Member; Theresa Kvale, C.S.J., Team Member; Suzanne Jabro, C.S.J., Team Member; Sandra Williams, C.S.J., Team Member; Mary Ann Martin, C.S.J., Team Member. Sisters 295.

Sisters of St. Joseph in California, Tel: 310-889-2158; Fax: 310-472-5982.

Sisters of St. Joseph Ministerial Services, Tel: 310-889-2157; Fax: 310-476-8735.

Sisters of St. Joseph of Orange, 8000 Regis Way, 90045. Tel: 310-645-2514; Email: jdugan@csjorange.org. Judith Dugan, Dir. Sisters 4.

Sisters of the Company of Mary, 2634 Monmouth Ave., 90007. Tel: 213-747-3542; Email: kschneider@odn-la.org; Web: http://www.cdm.edu.co. Sisters Beatriz Guzman, O.D.N.; Kathy Schneider, O.D.N., Supr.; Sharon Lamprecht, O.D.N., School Support Staff. Sisters 8.

Sisters of the Good Shepherd (1904) 2561 W. Venice Blvd., 90019. Tel: 323-737-6111; Fax: 323-731-5014; Email: rgsla1@aol.com; Web: www.goodshepherdsisters.org. Sr. Regina Do, Supr. Sisters 7.

Sisters of the Guardian Angel (1838) 4529 New York St., 90022. Tel: 323-266-4431; Email: regipenin@yahoo.com. Jenny Areas, Dir. Sisters 5.

Sisters of the Immaculate Heart of Mary of Mirinae, I.H.M.M., 423 S. Commonwealth Ave., 90020. Tel: 213-738-1020; Fax: 213-381-6302; Email: laihmm@hanmail.net. Sr. Cyrilla Kim, I.H.M.M., Supr. Sisters 7.

Sisters of the Society Devoted to the Sacred Heart (1940) 869 S. Rimpau Blvd., 90005. Tel: 323-935-2372; Fax: 323-935-5943; Email: info@la-archdiocese.org; Web: www.sacredheartsisters.com. Sr. Yolanda Magallanes, Supr. Sisters 3.

ALHAMBRA. *Carmel of St. Teresa of Los Angeles* (1913) 215 E. Alhambra Rd., Alhambra, 91801. Tel: 626-282-2387; Fax: 626-282-0144; Email: teresacarm1913@gmail.com; Web: www.carmelteresa.org. Mother Brenda Marie Schroeder, O.C.D., Prioress. Discalced Carmelite Nuns of the Order of the Blessed Virgin Mary of Mt. Carmel. Sisters 14.

Carmelite Sisters of the Most Sacred Heart of Los Angeles (1941) 920 E. Alhambra Rd., Alhambra, 91801-2799. Tel: 626-289-1353; Fax: 626-308-1913; Email: gensecretary@carmelitesisters.com; Web: www.carmelitesistersocd.com. Sr. Marisa, O.C.D. Novices 7; Postulants 5; Sisters 125; Professed Sisters 125.

ALTADENA. *Franciscan Sisters of the Sacred Heart* (1866) Sacred Heart Convent, 579 W. Mariposa St., Altadena, 91001. Tel: 805-451-0365; Email: californiasister72@yahoo.com; Web: www.fssh.com. Sr. Joyce Shanabarger, O.S.F., Gen. Supr. Sisters 3.

BELLFLOWER. **Sisters of the Blessed Korean Martyrs, S.B.K.M.* (1946) 16276 California Ave., Bellflower, 90706. Tel: 562-461-8100; Email: sbkm.americas@gmail.com; Web: www.sbkm.kr. Sr. Hang Soon Agnes Park, Supr. Sisters 7.

CULVER CITY. *Daughters of St. Paul*, 3908 Sepulveda Blvd., Culver City, 90230. Tel: 310-390-4699; Fax: 310-397-8366; Email: culvercity@paulinemedia.com; Web: pauline.org. Sr. Marie James Hunt, F.S.P., Supr. Sisters 6.

Religious Sisters of Charity (1815) 10668 St. James Dr., Culver City, 90230-5461. Tel: 310-559-0176; Fax: 310-559-3530; Email: bermorganrsc@gmail.com; Web: www.rsccaritas.org. Sr. Bernadette Morgan, R.S.C., Pres. Sisters 26.

DOWNEY. *Sisters of the Holy Faith in California*, 12322 S. Paramount Blvd., Downey, 90242-3538. Tel: 562-869-6092; Fax: 562-869-4609; Email: shfaith@yahoo.com; Web: www.holyfaithsisters.com. Sr. Dolores Madden, C.H.F., Supr. Sisters 22.

Visitation Congregation of North America, 7845 Quill Dr., Downey, 90242. Tel: 562-862-7472; Fax: 562-862-7472; Email: lasvm2000@yahoo.com. Sr. Meera Parayil, Contact Person. Sisters 3.

GARDENA. *Lovers of the Holy Cross Sisters*, 14700 S. Van Ness Ave., Gardena, 90249. Tel: 310-516-0271 ; Email: graceducle@gmail.com; Web: www.lhcla.org. Sr. Grace Le Sr., Supr. Sisters 62.

St. Anselm Convent, 7023 Arlington Ave., 90043. Tel: 323-455-2103; Email: vannenguyen@gmail.com; Web: www.lhcla.org. Sr. Anne Tran, L.H.C., M.S.W., Supr. Sisters 5. *St. Bruno Convent*, 10734 S. Widener Ave., Whittier, 90603. Tel: 562-947-1177; Fax: 562-947-1177; Email: srthumai@lhcla.org; Web: www.lhcla.org. Sr. Theresa Nguyen, F.M.S.R., Supr. Novices 3; Postulants 1; Sisters 64; Aspirants 16.

Poor Clare Missionary Sisters, Inc., 1050 W. 161st St., Gardena, 90247. Tel: 310-323-9942; Email: blanca_lopez90@yahoo.com. Sr. Yanory Zuniga, M.C., Supr. Sisters 14.

GLENDORA. *St. Lucy's Priory* (1955) 19045 E. Sierra Madre Ave., Glendora, 91741. Tel: 626-335-1682; Fax: 626-914-9398; Email: stlucysebrown@aol.com; Web: www.stlucys.com. Sr. Elizabeth Brown, Prioress

St. Lucy's Priory of Glendora California, Inc. Sisters 8.

LONG BEACH. **Little Handmaids of the Most Holy Trinity, M.A.S.T.* (1988) 3716 Arabella St., Long Beach, 90805. Tel: 562-633-0640; Fax: 562-531-8773; Email: holytrinitylb@yahoo.com. Sr. Jean Regin, Supr. Sisters 5.

The Medical Sisters of St. Joseph, 3627 Lemon Ave., Long Beach, 90807. Tel: 562-426-8825; Email: msjnirmala.@aol.com; Web: www.msjnirmala.org. Sr. Dennis Punchakunnel, M.S.J. Sisters 3.

MONROVIA. *Maryknoll Sisters of St. Dominic, Inc.* (1912) 340 Norumbega Dr., Monrovia, 91016-2445. Tel: 626-358-1825; Fax: 626-358-1227; Email: mkmonrovia340@gmail.com. Sr. Judith Esmenda, Contact Person. Sisters 24.

MONTEBELLO. *Religious of the Sacred Heart of Mary*, Provincial Center, 441 N. Garfield Ave., Montebello, 90640-2901. Tel: 323-887-8821; Fax: 323-887-8952; Email: etuohy@earthlink.net; Web: www.rshm.org. Sr. Joan Treacy, R.S.H.M., Prov. Sisters 49.

NORTHRIDGE. *Mother of Mercy Convent*, 9329 Crebs Ave., Northridge, 91324. Tel: 818-882-4095; Email: info@dmmmg.com. Sr. Patricia Beirne, R.S.M., Supr. Sister of Mercy Burlingame.

Sisters of the Society Devoted to the Sacred Heart (1940) Motherhouse: 9814 Sylvia Ave., Northridge, 91324. Tel: 818-772-9961; Fax: 818-772-2742; Email: mhsdsh2@sbcglobal.net; Web: www.sacredheartsisters.com. Sr. Mary Tomasella, S.D.S.H., Supr. Gen. Sisters 46.

NORWALK. *Lovers of the Holy Cross Nha Trang* (1950) 11409 Gwynne Ave., Norwalk, 90650. Tel: 562-809-1570; Email: theresphuoc@gmail.com. Sr. Mary Men T. Pham, L.H.C.N.T., Reg. Supr. U.S. Community 6.

OJAI. *Sisters of Mary Mother of the Church*, 431 Montana Cir., Ojai, 93023. Tel: 805-640-1798; Email: contact@sistersofmarymc.org. Mother Kathryn Duddy, Supr. Sisters 11.

OXNARD. *Servants of Mary, Ministers to the Sick*, 140 North G St., Oxnard, 93030-5214. Tel: 805-486-5502; Fax: 805-486-0663; Email: superioraox@gmail.com. Sr. Elvia Navarro, S.deM., Mistress of Novices. Novices 4; Postulants 1; Sisters 15.

RANCHO PALOS VERDES. *Daughters of Mary & Joseph, D.M.J.* (1817) 5300 Crest Rd., Rancho Palos Verdes, 90275-5004. Tel: 310-377-9968; Fax: 310-541-5967; Email: leadershipteam@dmjca.org; Web: www.daughtersofmaryandjoseph.org. Sr. Linda Webb, D.M.J., Supr. Sisters 39.

Sisters of Charity of Rolling Hills, 28600 Palos Verdes Dr. E., Rancho Palos Verdes, 90275. Tel: 310-831-4104; Email: scrh1964@gmail.com. Sr. Virginia Buchholz, S.C.R.H., Supr. Gen. Sisters 6.

SAN PEDRO. *Little Sisters of the Poor* (1979) 2100 S. Western Ave., San Pedro, 90732. Tel: 310-548-0625 ; Fax: 310-548-4504; Email: adsanpedro@littlesistersofthepoor.org. Sr. Margaret Lennon, L.S.P., Supr. & Admin. Residents 102; Sisters 10; Total Staff 110; Lay Associates 20; Total Assisted 1,260.

Religious Sisters of Charity, 830 1/2 W. 14th St., San Pedro, 90731. Tel: 310-519-0721; Email: evabryrsc@gmail.com. Sr. Bernadette Morgan, R.S.C., Rel. Order Leader. Sisters 4.

SANTA BARBARA. *Monastery of Poor Clares* (1928) Cloistered Contemplative Monastery, 215 E. Los Olivos St., Santa Barbara, 93105. Tel: 805-682-7670; Fax: 805-682-8041; Email: john@thynelaw.com; Web: www.poorclaressantabarbara.org. Mother Aimee Marie of the Eucharist, Abbess. Attended by Franciscan Fathers of the Old Mission. Professed 13; Sisters 13.

SOLVANG. *Sisters of the Society Devoted to the Sacred Heart* (1940) 1762 Mission Dr., Solvang, 93463. Tel: 805-688-6158; Fax: 805-688-6158; Email: info@la-archdiocese.org. Sr. Catherine Marie Stewart, S.D.S.H., Supr. Sisters 3.

SYLMAR. *Franciscan Sisters of the Immaculate Conception* (1874) 13367 Borden Ave., Unit A, Sylmar, 91342. Tel: 818-364-5557; Fax: 818-362-7536; Email: provstclare@outlook.com. Sr. Yolanda Yanez, O.S.F., Supr.

Franciscan Missionary Sisters of the Immaculate Conception Novices 2; Postulants 2; Sisters 78; Candidates 2.

Poor Clare Missionary Sisters, P.O. Box 922046, Sylmar, 91392. Tel: 818-365-8307; Fax: 818-365-8307; Email: blanca_lopez90@yahoo.com; Web: www.cmswr.org. Sr. Elvira Duron, M.C., Supr. Sisters 7.

THOUSAND OAKS. *Sisters of Notre Dame* (1924) 1776 Hendrix Ave., Thousand Oaks, 91360. Tel: 805-496-3243; Fax: 805-379-3616; Email: acostello@sndca.org; Web: www.sndca.org. Sr. Mary Anncarla Costello, S.N.D., Prov. Supr. Sisters 52.

TORRANCE. *Little Company of Mary Convent*, 20552 Mansel Ave., Torrance, 90503. Tel: 310-214-3190; Fax: 310-921-3253; Email: srmildred@sbcglobal.net; Web: www.lcmglobal.org. Sr. Terrence Landini, Supr. Sisters 2. *Convent*, 20562 Mansel Ave., Torrance, 90503. Tel: 310-370-3992; Fax: 310-370-8452; Email: terrence.landini@providence.org. Sr. Sharon Walsh, Dir. Sisters 2.

VENTURA. *Congregation of the Sisters of the Holy Cross*, 1931 Poli St., Ventura, 93001-2360. Tel: 805-652-1700; Fax: 805-653-1354; Email: mclayton@cscsisters.org. Sr. Madeleine Marie Clayton, C.S.C., Supr.

Sisters of the Holy Cross, Inc. St. Catherine-by-the-Sea Convent 21.

WILMINGTON. *The Congregation of the Norbertine Sisters*, 943 Lagoon Ave., Wilmington, 90744. Tel: 310-952-0144; Email: norbertinesrswilm@gmail.com. Sr. Adriana Gacikova, Supr. Sisters 3.

WINNETKA. *Sisters of St. Louis*, 20253 Ingomar St., Winnetka, 91306-2521. Tel: 818-772-8959; Email: info@la-archdiocese.org. Sr. Margaret Fitzer, Dir. Ursuline Sisters.Presentation Sisters.Sisters of St. Louis. Sisters 4.

WOODLAND HILLS. *Sisters of St. Louis, Louisville Convent*, 22300 Mulholland Dr., Woodland Hills, 91364-4933. Tel: 818-883-1678; Fax: 818-346-6109; Email: sslca4@sistersofsaintlouis.com; Web: www.stlouissisters.org. Sr. Judith Dieterle, S.S.L., Regl. Leader. Sisters 42.

[R] SECULAR INSTITUTES

SIMI VALLEY. *Society of Our Lady of the Way*, 2725 Tumbleweed Ave., Simi Valley, 93065. Tel: 805-520-6942; Email: pearlinea@hotmail.com; Email: solw@cwjamaica.com. Pearline Archer, Dir.; Marlene Holman, Dir.

Society of Our Lady of the Way of Southern California, Inc.

WEST COVINA. *Fr. Kolbe Missionaries of the Immaculata* (1954) 531 E. Merced Ave., West Covina, 91790. Tel: 626-917-0040; Email: fkmissionaries@gmail.com; Web: www.kolbemission.org/en. Rumela Camanga, Dir.

[S] ASSOCIATIONS OF THE FAITHFUL

LOS ANGELES. **Servants of the Father of Mercy, Inc.*, P.O. Box 42001, 90042. Tel: 310-595-4175; Email: contact@servantsofthefather.org. Bro. Gary Joseph, Dir.

LONG BEACH. **Friars of the Sick Poor of Los Angeles, Inc.* (2002) 576 Hunter Dr., Fillmore, 93015. Tel: 562-822-6499; Email: rhirbefsp@gmail.com; Web: friarsofthesickpoor.org. Bro. Richard A. Hirbe, f.s.p., Min./General-Founder. Novices 1; Friars 9.

VENTURA. **Handmaids of the Triune God*, P.O. Box 2957, Ventura, 93002-2957. Sr. Mary Joseph Mei, Rel. Order Leader. Sisters 2.

TRINITAS, 10332 Darling Rd., Ventura, 93004-2425. Tel: 805-659-4158; Fax: 805-659-4158; Email: trinitascom@juno.com. Mary Ann Wixted, Dir.

WINNETKA. MISSIONARY COMMUNITY OF THE HOLY SPIRIT, 7239 Hatillo Ave., Winnetka, 91306. Tel: 915-598-8600; Tel: 562-296-8254; Email: sollano_aurora@yahoo.com. Sr. Aurora Sollano, Supr.

[T] RESIDENCES FOR WOMEN

LOS ANGELES. *St. Anne's*, 155 N. Occidental Blvd., 90026. Tel: 213-381-2931; Fax: 213-381-7804; Email: stannes@stannes.org; Web: www.stannes.org. Tony Walker, M.A., Dir. Group Home transitional housing, child care, mental health and family based services for pregnant, parenting teens, their children & families.

Bethany House, 850 N. Hobart Blvd., 90029. Tel: 323-665-6937; Fax: 323-664-0754; Email: hmas.bethania@hotmail.com. Sr. Leticia Gomez, C.V.D., Dir. Bed Capacity 32; Tot Asst. Annually 32; Total Staff 6.

Good Shepherd Center for Homeless Women and Children (1984) Languille Emergency Shelter, 267 N. Belmont Ave., 90026. Tel: 213-250-5241; Tel: 213-482-1834; Fax: 213-250-5073; Fax: 213-482-0522; Email: srannetran@gsohomeless.org; Web: www.gschomeless.org. Sr. Anne Tran, L.H.C., M.S.W., Dir. (A Program of Catholic Charities of Los Angeles, Inc.) Bed Capacity 93; Tot Asst. Annually 1,283; Total Staff 28.

Good Shepherd Center Hawkes Transitional Residence/Women's Village (1998) 1640 Rockwood St., 90026. Tel: 213-482-0281; Fax: 213-482-0299; Email: srannetran@gschomeless.org. Sr. Anne Tran, L.H.C., M.S.W., Dir. (A Program of Catholic Charities of Los Angeles, Inc.) Bed Capacity 30; Tot Asst. Annually 30; Total Staff 10; Women Sheltered Annually 45; Women in Residence 30.

Angel Guardian Home/Women's Village (2000) 1660 Rockwood St., 90026. Tel: 213-483-6654; Fax: 213-482-0522; Email: srannetran@gschomeless.org. Sr. Anne Tran, L.H.C., M.S.W., Dir. Bed Capacity 12; Tot Asst. Annually 42; Total Staff 1; Women & Children Sheltered Annually 40.

Good Shepherd Center Farley House/Women's Village, 1671 Beverly Blvd., 90026. Tel: 213-235-1460; Fax: 213-235-1480; Email: srannetran@gschomeless.org. Sr. Anne Tran, L.H.C., M.S.W., Dir. (A Program of Catholic Charities of Los Angeles, Inc.) Bed Capacity 22; Tot Asst. Annually 65; Total Staff 12; Women & Children Sheltered Annually 65; Women & Children in Residence 58.

St. Joseph's Residence (1957) 1124 W. Adams Blvd., 90007. Tel: 213-749-9577; Fax: 213-747-7713; Email: stjoseph1960@yahoo.com. Sr. Beatriz Guzman, O.D.N., Dir. Sisters of the Company of Mary. Bed Capacity 32; Tot Asst. Annually 25; Total Staff 1.

See Sr. Julia Mary Farley House and the Village Kitchen under Catholic Charities in the Institution Section.

[U] RESIDENCES FOR MEN

LOS ANGELES. *Catholic Kolping House*, 1225 S. Union Ave., 90015. Tel: 213-388-9438; Fax: 213-388-9438; Email: losangeleskolpinghouse@yahoo.com; Web: www.kolping.org. Mary Freidonni, Dir. Capacity 60.

[V] RETREAT HOUSES

ALHAMBRA. **Sacred Heart Retreat House, Inc.*, 920 E. Alhambra Rd., Alhambra, 91801. Tel: 626-289-1353; Fax: 626-281-3546; Email: contact@sacredheartretreathouse.com; Web: www.sacredheartretreathouse.com. Sr. Julianna Gonzalez, Dir. Carmelite Sisters of the Most Sacred Heart of Los Angeles. Overnight 85; Day Retreat 150; St. Joseph Campus Day Retreat 150.

ENCINO. **Holy Spirit Retreat Center*, 4316 Lanai Rd., Encino, 91436. Tel: 818-784-4515; Fax: 818-784-0409; Email: officemanager@hsrcenter.org; Web: www.hsrcenter.com. Sr. Chris Machado, S.S.S., Dir. Sisters of Social Service.

MALIBU. *Serra Retreat* (1942) 3401 Serra Rd., P.O. Box 127, Malibu, 90265. Tel: 310-456-6631; Fax: 310-456-9417; Email: frmel@serraretreat.com; Web: www.serraretreat.com. Revs. Melvin A. Jurisich, O.F.M., Dir.; Warren Rouse, O.F.M., Asst. Dir.; Michael Doherty, O.F.M., Retreat Master; Raymond Tintle, O.F.M., (Retired); Bros. Samuel Cabot, O.F.M., (Retired); Regan Chapman, O.F.M., Sabbatical. Franciscan Friars of California. Brothers 2; Priests 4.

MONTEBELLO. *DePaul Evangelization Center* (1987) 420 Date St., Montebello, 90640-6143. Tel: 323-721-6060; Fax: 323-887-0765; Email: depaulcenter@att.net; Web: depaulcenter.org. Revs. Prudencio Rodriguez de Yurre, C.M., Supr., Vincentian House; Robert J. Jones, C.M.; Hoan N. Nguyen, C.M.; Juan Antonio Ruiz Barbacil, C.M.; Perry F. Henry, C.M., Dir. DePaul Evangelization Center; Bro. Kenneth J. Lund, C.M.

RANCHO PALOS VERDES. *Mary & Joseph Retreat Center*, 5300 Crest Rd., Rancho Palos Verdes, 90275-5004. Tel: 310-377-4867; Fax: 310-541-1176; Email: pcraig@maryjoseph.org; Email: csanchirico@maryjoseph.org; Web: www.maryjoseph.org. Paul Craig, Dir.; Christine Sanchirico, Dir. Daughters of Mary and Joseph. Retreat Center Capacity 69.

ROSEMEAD. *St. Joseph's Salesian Youth Renewal Center*, 8301 Arroyo Dr., P.O. Box 1639, Rosemead, 91770. Tel: 626-280-8622; Fax: 626-280-0545; Email: info@sjscenter.org; Web: sjscenter.org. Revs. Paul M. Caporali, S.D.B.; Bill Bolton, S.D.B., Dir. Retreat Center; Ted Montemayor, S.D.B., Dir. & Supr.; Mel Trinidad, S.D.B., Youth Min.; Marc Rougeau, S.D.B., Treas. & Vice Dir.; Christian H. Woerz, S.D.B., Vocation Dir.; Bros. Phil Mandile, S.D.B.; Larry King, S.D.B. Conducted by Salesians of St. John Bosco. Brothers 2; Priests 6; Tot Asst. Annually 6,000; Total Staff 4.

SAN FERNANDO. *Poverello of Assisi Retreat House* (1962) 1519 Woodworth St., San Fernando, 91340. Tel: 818-365-1071; Fax: 818-361-2751; Email: poverelloretreathouse@hotmail.com. Sr. Mary Jesus, O.S.F., Dir. Franciscan Missionary Sisters of the Immaculate Conception. Capacity 112.

SANTA BARBARA. *St. Mary's Seminary Center*, 1964 Las Canoas Rd., Santa Barbara, 93105. Tel: 805-966-4829; Fax: 805-564-1662; Email: stmarysseminary@cox.net. Revs. Patrick J. Mullin, C.M., Dir.; Roy A. Persich, C.M., (Retired); Walter L. Housey, C.M., (Retired); John V. Shine, C.M., (Retired). Priests 4.

SIERRA MADRE. **Mater Dolorosa Passionist Retreat Center, Inc.*, 700 N. Sunnyside Ave., Sierra Madre, 91025. Tel: 626-355-7188; Fax: 626-355-0485; Email: materdolorosa@materdolorosa.org; Web: www.materdolorosa.org. Rev. Michael Higgins, C.P., Dir. Conducted by the Passionist Community. Brothers 1; Priests 4.

Retreat Team: Revs. Michael Higgins, C.P., Retreat Dir.; Michael Hoolahan, C.P.; Deacon Manuel Valencia, Assoc. Retreat Dir.; Bro. John Rockenbach, C.P.; Elizabeth Welch Velarde, Admin.; Rev. Bruno D'Souza, C.P., Retreat Preaching Team; Jean Bowler, Retreat Team; Dr. Michael Downey, Dir. Spiritual & Theological Formation.

VALYERMO. *St. Andrew's Abbey Retreat Center (All Groups)*, 31001 N. Valyermo Rd., P.O. Box 40, Valyermo, 93563. Tel: 661-944-2178; Fax: 661-944-2183; Email: retreats@valyermo.com; Web: www.saintandrewsabbey.com. Rev. Philip Edwards, O.S.B., Retreat House Chap., Tel: 661-944-2178, Ext. 0; Rita Jones, Youth Center Dir., Tel: 661-944-2734; Rev. Patrick Sheridan, O.S.B., Guestmaster. Conducted by the Benedictine Monks.

[W] PERSONAL PRELATURES

LOS ANGELES. *Prelature of the Holy Cross and Opus Dei*, 770 S. Windsor Blvd., 90005. Tel: 323-930-2844; Email: la.priest.scheduler@gmail.com. Very Rev. Luke Mata; Rev. John R. Meyer.

Tilden Study Center, 655 Levering Ave., 90024-2308. Tel: 310-208-0941; Fax: 310-208-6783; Email: office@tildensc.org; Web: www.tildensc.org. Revs. Mark Mannion, Spiritual Dir.; Paul A. Donlan.

[X] CATHOLIC CHARITIES

LOS ANGELES. *Catholic Charities of Los Angeles, Inc.*, 1531 James M. Wood Blvd., P.O. Box 15095, 90015-0095. Tel: 213-251-3400; Fax: 213-380-4603; Email: mruvalcaba@ccharities.org; Web: catholiccharitiesla.org. Most Rev. Jose H. Gomez, D.D., S.T.D., V.G.; Rev. Msgr. Gregory A. Cox, M.S.W., M.B.A., M.Div., Exec. Dir., Tel: 213-251-3464; Alexandria (Sandi) Arnold, M.S., Chief Development and Communications Officer; Moises Carrillo, M.A., Dir. of the Intra-Agency Dept.; Daniel P. O'Brien, Chief Financial Officer; Leland R. Ratleff, M.A., Dir. of Human Resources. Tot Asst. Annually 690,115; Total Staff 350.

Archdiocesan Youth Employment Services, 3250 Wilshire Blvd., Ste. 1010, 90010. Tel: 213-736-5456; Fax: 213-736-5654; Email: rgutierrez@ccharities.org. Robert L. Gutierrez, M.P.A., Prog. Dir. Total Staff 30.

Catholic Youth Organization, 1530 James M. Wood Blvd., 90015. Tel: 213-251-3454; Fax: 213-251-3552. Maria Ruvalcaba, Sec.

Central Administrative Offices, 1531 James M. Wood Blvd., P.O. Box 15095, 90015-0095. Tel: 213-251-3400; Email: mruvalcaba@ccharities.org; Web: CatholicCharitiesLA.org. Rev. Msgr. Gregory A. Cox, M.S.W., M.B.A., M.Div., Exec. Dir., Tel: 213-251-3464; Alexandria (Sandi) Arnold, M.S., Chief Devel. & Communications Officer, Tel: 213-251-3495; Leland R. Ratleff, M.A., Dir. of Human Resources, Tel: 213-251-3414; Moises Carillo, Dir. of the Intra-Agency Dept.; Daniel P. O'Brien, Chief Financial Officer. Total Staff 27.

Continuous Quality Improvement, 1530 James M. Wood Blvd., 90015. Tel: 213-251-3459; Email: enelson@ccharities.org. Edward Nelson, Ph.D., Performance Quality Improvement Dir., Tel: 213-251-3459. Total Staff 1.

Employment Support Partnership, 4322 San Fernando Rd., Glendale, 91204. Tel: 213-318-5716; Fax: 818-502-2004; Email: bthoma@ccharities.org. Brenda Thomas, Program Dir. Tot Asst. Annually 17,341; Total Staff 8.

Esperanza Immigrant Rights Project, 1530 James M. Wood Blvd., 90015. Tel: 213-251-3505; Email: portiz@ccharities.org. Patricia Ortiz, J.D., Prog. Dir. Tot Asst. Annually 1,463; Total Staff 30.

Immigration & Refugee Services, 1530 James M. Wood Blvd., 90015. Tel: 213-251-3411; Email: slee@ccharities.org. Evenson (Steve) Lee, Program Dir. Tot Asst. Annually 2,256; Total Staff 21.

Catholic Immigration Services, Tel: 213-251-3411; Fax: 213-251-3444. Maria Ruvalcaba, Sec.

Refugee Resettlement Program, Tel: 213-251-3411. Maria Ruvalcaba, Sec.

OUR LADY OF THE ANGELS REGION, 211 Third Ave., Venice, 90291. Tel: 310-392-8701; Fax: 310-399-4097; Email: lperreault@ccharities.org. Lorri Perreault, Regional Dir. (Los Angeles Inner City. Inglewood, Crenshaw District, Koreatown, West Los Angeles, Malibu & Los Angeles Airport region) Tot Asst. Annually 81,866; Total Staff 70.

ADESTE Child Care Program, 211 Third Ave., Venice, 90291. Tel: 310-392-8701; Fax: 310-399-4097; Email: LPearreault@CCharities.org. Lorri Perreault, Dir.

ADESTE Child Care Program at El Santo Nino Community Services Center, 601 E. 23rd St., 90011. Tel: 213-318-5705; Email: lperreault@ccharities.org. Lorri Perreault, Regional Dir.; Elizabeth Soriano, Program Dir. Tot Asst. Annually 5,965; Total Staff 1.

Angel's Flight - At Risk Youth Services, 357 S. Westlake Ave., 90057. Tel: 213-413-2311; Tel: 800-833-2499 (Hotline); Fax: 213-413-5690; Email: lperreault@ccharities.org. Patricia Chaidez, L.M.F.T., Program Dir. Tot Asst. Annually 132; Total Staff 16.

Angel's Flight at My Club at El Santo Nino Community Services Center, 357 South Westlake Ave., 90057. Tel: 213-413-2311; Tel: 800-833-2499; Fax: 213-413-5690; Email: pchaidez@ccharities.org. Patricia Chaidez, L.M.F.T., Program Dir. Tot Asst. Annually 7,797; Total Staff 15.

Archdiocesan Youth Employment Services (AYES), South Office: 3965 S. Vermont Ave., 90037. Tel: 323-731-8596; Fax: 323-731-2905; Email: Alma@aye-la.org; Email: Roberta@aye-la.org. Alma Diaz; Roberta Guillen. Tot Asst. Annually 1,673; Total Staff 2.

Catholic Counseling Services, 211 Third Ave., Venice, 90291. Tel: 310-392-8701; Fax: 310-399-4097; Email: lperreault@ccharities.org. Lorri Perreault, Regional Dir. Tot Asst. Annually 1,549; Total Staff 1.

Good Shepherd Center for Homeless Women and Children, 1671 Beverly Blvd., 90026. Tel: 213-235-1460; Tel: 213-250-5241; Email: evaldes@gschomeless.org. Sr. Anne Tran, L.H.C., M.S.W., Prog. Dir.; Elvia Valdez, Program Assoc. Dir. Tot Asst. Annually 1,283; Total Staff 28.

My Club Program, 8705 S. Vermont Ave., 90044. Tel: 323-751-2582; Email: pchaidez@ccharities.org. Patricia Chaidez, L.M.F.T., Program Dir.; Latoya Williams, Program Coord. Tot Asst. Annually 104; Total Staff 2.

St. Margaret's Community Services Center, St. Margaret's Center, 10217 S. Inglewood Ave., Lennox, 90304. Tel: 310-672-2208; Email: lperreault@ccharities.org. Mary Agnes, Program Dir.; Lorri Perreault, Regional Dir. Tot Asst. Annually 47,968; Total Staff 11.

St. Robert's Community Services Center, 211 3rd Ave., Venice, 90291. Tel: 310-392-8701; Email: lperreault@ccharities.org. Lorri Perreault, Regional Dir. Tot Asst. Annually 1,549; Total Staff 1.

See Angel Guardian Home for Homeless Disabled Mothers with Minor Children under Residences for Women in the Institution Section.

SAN FERNANDO REGION, 21600 Hart St., Canoga Park, 91303. Tel: 213-251-3578; Tel: 213-251-3549; Fax: 818-883-4122; Email: syanez@ccharities.org. Sandra Yanez, Regl. Dir. (Burbank, Glendale, Eagle Rock, Verdugo Hills, Antelope Valley, San Fernando Valley) Tot Asst. Annually 59,465; Total Staff 9.

Angel's Flight My Club at Guadalupe Center, 21600 Hart St., Canoga Park, 91303. Tel: 213-251-3566; Email: syanez@ccharities.org. Patricia Chaidez, L.M.F.T., Program Dir.; Charles Wrightson, Program Coord.; Sandra Yanez, Regional Dir. Tot Asst. Annually 2,453; Total Staff 6.

Employment Support Partnership, 21600 Hart St., Canoga Park, 91303. Tel: 213-251-3586; Fax: 818-883-4122; Email: syanez@ccharities.org. 4322 San Fernando Rd., Glendale, 91204. Sandra Yanez, Regional Dir. Tot Asst. Annually 11,206; Total Staff 5.

Glendale Community Services Center, 4322 San

Fernando Rd., Glendale, 91204. Tel: 213-318-5707; Fax: 818-956-1857; Email: syanez@ccharities.org. Sandra Yanez, Regional Dir. Tot Asst. Annually 17,341; Total Staff 8.

Guadalupe Community Services Center, 21600 Hart St., Canoga Park, 91303. Tel: 213-251-3549; Email: syanez@ccharities.org. Sandra Yanez, Regional Dir. Tot Asst. Annually 22,413; Total Staff 5.

Loaves and Fishes Community Services, 7309 Van Nuys Blvd, Van Nuys, 91405. Tel: 818-997-0943; Email: syanez@ccharities.org. Sandra Yanez, Regional Dir. Tot Asst. Annually 2,021; Volunteers 20.

Refugee Resettlement Program, 4322 San Fernando Rd., Glendale, 91204. Tel: 818-409-0057; Email: syanez@ccharities.org. Sandra Yanez, Regional Dir. Tot Asst. Annually 6,622; Total Staff 2.

Temporary Skilled Worker Center (Day Laborer Program) 1190 Flower St., Burbank, 91502. Tel: 818-566-7148; Email: syanez@ccharities.org. Sandra Yanez, Regional Dir. Tot Asst. Annually 8,154; Total Staff 2.

SAN GABRIEL REGION, 1307 Warren St., 90033. Tel: 213-251-3582; Fax: 323-266-3269; Email: mruvalcaba@ccharities.org. Maria Ruvalcaba, Sec. (San Gabriel Valley, Mt. Baldy, Pomona Valley, East Los Angeles). Tot Asst. Annually 62,562; Total Staff 9.

Brownson House Community Center, 1307 Warren Ave., 90033. Tel: 213-251-3512. Mary Romero, Regional Dir. Tot Asst. Annually 16,619; Total Staff 2.

Catholic Charities Parish Liaison Program (CCPal), 1307 Warren St., 90033. Tel: 213-251-3520; Cell: mruvalcaba@ccharities.org. Maria Ruvalcaba, Contact Person.

McGill Street House, Administrative Office: 1460 E. Holt Ave., Ste. 98, Pomona, 91767. Tel: 909-629-1335. Tot Asst. Annually 1,317; Total Staff 2.

Pomona Community Services, 1460 E. Holt Ave., Ste. 98, Pomona, 91767. Tel: 909-629-1331. Tot Asst. Annually 1,317; Total Staff 2.

San Juan Diego Center, 4171 N. Tyler Ave., El Monte, 91731. Tel: 626-575-7652; Email: mruvalcaba@ccharities.org. Tot Asst. Annually 37,387; Total Staff 2.

SAN PEDRO REGION, 123 E. 14th St., Long Beach, 90813. Tel: 213-251-3429; Fax: 562-591-2481; Email: bhackman@ccharities.org. Bruce Hackman, M.Div., M.S., M.S.W., Regl. Dir. (Long Beach, South Bay, Compton, Rio Hondo, Vernon, Huntington Park, Whittier, Pico Rivera). Total Staff 29.

Elizabeth Ann Seton Residence, 2198 San Gabriel Avenue, Long Beach, 90810. Tel: 562-388-7670; Email: bhackman@ccharities.org. Bruce Hackman, M.Div., M.S., M.S.W., Regional Dir. Tot Asst. Annually 98,350; Total Staff 9.

Gatekeeper Project, 123 E. 14th St., Long Beach, 90813. Tel: 213-251-3432; Email: bhackman@ccharities.org. Bruce Hackman, M.Div., M.S., M.S.W., Regional Dir. Tot Asst. Annually 720; Total Staff 2.

Long Beach Community Services Center, 123 E. 14th St., Long Beach, 90813. Tel: 213-251-3432. Bruce Hackman, M.Div., M.S., M.S.W., Regional Dir. Tot Asst. Annually 60,957; Total Staff 10.

Mahar House-MY CLUB, 1115 Mahar Ave., Wilmington, 90744. Tel: 213-251-3458. Bruce Hackman, M.Div., M.S., M.S.W., Regl. Dir. Tot Asst. Annually 2,744; Staff 1.

Pico Rivera Food Pantry and Resource Center, 5014 Passons Blvd., Pico Rivera, 90660. Tel: 562-949-0937. Tot Asst. Annually 5,000; Total Staff 2.

Project Achieve Emergency Shelter, Administrative Office: 1368 Oregon Ave., Long Beach, 90813. Tel: 562-218-9864; Email: bhackman@ccharities.org. Bruce Hackman, M.Div., M.S., M.S.W., Regional Dir. Total Staff 6.

SANTA BARBARA REGION: SANTA BARBARA COUNTY, 609 E. Haley St., Santa Barbara, 93103. Tel: 805-965-7045; Email: dgrimm@ccharities.org. Daniel J. Grimm, J.D., M.A., M.F.T., Regl. Dir. (Lompoc, Santa Maria, Santa Barbara, Carpinteria). Total Staff 3.

Carpinteria Community Services, 941 Walnut St., Carpinteria, 93013. Tel: 805-684-8621. Tot Asst. Annually 8,119; Total Staff 1.

Catholic Charities Thrift Stores (Santa Barbara) (Thrift Store) 609 E. Haley St., Santa Barbara, 93103. Tel: 805-966-9659. Tot Asst. Annually 859; Total Staff 4.

Catholic Charities Thrift Stores (Santa Maria) (Thrift Store) 607 W. Main St., Santa Maria, 93454. Tel: 805-922-4174. Daniel J. Grimm, J.D., M.A., M.F.T., Contact Person.

Cuyama Valley Mobile Food Distribution Site, 4711 Hwy. 166, New Cuyama, 93254. Tel: 805-922-2059.

Guadalupe Mobile Food Distribution Site, 4681 11th St., Guadalupe, 93434. Tel: 805-922-2059.

Isla Vista Mobile Food Distribution Site, 6647 El Colegio Rd., Isla Vista, 93117. Tel: 805-965-7045; Email: dgrimm@ccharities.org. Daniel J. Grimm, J.D., M.A., M.F.T., Regl. Dir.

Lompoc Community Services Center, 325 N. 2nd St., Lompoc, 93436. Tel: 805-736-6226. Tot Asst. Annually 4,943; Total Staff 3.

Santa Barbara Community Services Center, 609 E. Haley St., Santa Barbara, 93103. Tel: 805-965-7045; Fax: 805-963-2978; Email: dgrimm@ccharities.org. Daniel J. Grimm, J.D., M.A., M.F.T., Regional Dir. Tot Asst. Annually 24,071; Total Staff 3.

Santa Maria Community Services Center, 607 W. Main St., Santa Maria, 93454. Tel: 805-922-2059. Tot Asst. Annually 17,703; Total Staff 4.

SANTA BARBARA REGION: VENTURA COUNTY, 303 N. Ventura Ave., Ste. A, Ventura, 93001-1961. Tel: 805-965-7045; Fax: 805-641-1898 ; Email: dgrimm@ccharities.org. Daniel J. Grimm, J.D., M.A., M.F.T., Regl. Dir. (Camarillo, Moorpark, Oxnard, Thousand Oaks, Simi Valley, Ventura, Conejo Valley) Tot Asst. Annually 17,538; Total Staff 13.

Moorpark Community Services, 612 Spring Rd., Ste. 101, Moorpark, 93021. Tel: 805-529-0720; Tel: 805-520-3017; Email: dgrimm@ccharities.org. Daniel J. Grimm, J.D., M.A., M.F.T., Regional Dir. Tot Asst. Annually 36,113; Total Staff 2.

Older Adult Services and Intervention System (OASIS) - Camarillo, 2532 Ventura Blvd., Camarillo, 93010. Tel: 805-987-2083 (Main Office); Tel: 805-914-4277 (Santa Paula, Fillmore, Moor Park); Tel: 805-524-5443 (Ventura, Oxnard, Port Hueneme); Tel: 805-420-9608; Fax: 805-383-1318; Email: dgrimm@ccharities.org. Daniel J. Grimm, J.D., M.A., M.F.T., Regional Dir. Tot Asst. Annually 5,490; Total Staff 6.

Ventura Community Services Center, 303 N. Ventura Ave., Ventura, 93001. Tel: 805-643-4694; Email: dgrimm@ccharities.org. Daniel J. Grimm, J.D., M.A., M.F.T., Dir. Tot Asst. Annually 17,538; Total Staff 1.

[Y] SUMMER CAMPS

LOS ANGELES. *Scouting and Camp Fire Ministry/ Catholic Youth Camps*, 4811 Rimhurst Ave., Covina, 91724. Tel: 626-825-6436 (Girls); Tel: 323-255-3824 (Boys); Email: info@nfcym.org. Sharon Shellman, Chm. CLGScf, Tel: 626-967-1815; Fax: 626-966-9610; Maureen Brown, Vice Chm. Boys.

St. Vincent dePaul Ranch Camp, 210 N. Ave. 21st, 90031. Tel: 323-224-6213; Fax: 323-226-4997; Email: rlopez@svdpla.org. Raymond P. Lopez, Dir. Camp. (Boys, Ages 7-13); Sponsored by St. Vincent de Paul Society. Capacity 100.

Sacred Heart Retreat Camp, Camp Office, 896 Cienega Rd., P.O. Box 1795, Big Bear Lake, 92315-1795. Tel: 323-935-2372; Tel: 909-866-5696; Fax: 909-866-5650; Email: office@sacredheartretreatcamp.com; Web: www.sacredheartretreatcamp.com. Sr. Mary Tomasella, S.D.S.H., Supr. Girls Sessions, Ages 8-17 years.; Owned and operated by the Sisters of the Society Devoted to the Sacred Heart.; Located at Big Bear Lake.

ENCINO. *Camp Mariastella*, 4316 Lanai Rd., Encino, 91436. Tel: 818-285-1555; Fax: 818-285-1556; Email: campmariastella@aol.com. Sr. Jennifer Gaeta, S.S.S., Exec. Dir. Capacity 140; Students 100; Clergy / Religious Teachers 2.

[Z] ST. VINCENT DE PAUL SOCIETY

LOS ANGELES. **Society of Saint Vincent de Paul Council of Los Angeles*, 210 N. Avenue 21, 90031. Tel: 323-224-6287; Fax: 323-225-4997; Email: csariego@svdpla.org; Web: www.svdpla.org. David R. Fields, Exec. Dir., Tel: 323-224-6289; Email: dfields@svdpla.org; David Garcia, Deputy Exec. Dir.; Susana Santana, Deputy Exec. Dir.

**St. Vincent de Paul Ranch Camp & Retreat Center*, 2550 Hwy. 154, Santa Barbara, 93105. Tel: 323-224-6213; Fax: 323-225-4997; Email: circlev@svdpla.org. Raymond P. Lopez, Dir.

**St. Vincent's Cardinal Manning Center*, 231 Winston St., 90013. Tel: 213-229-9963; Fax: 213-620-9141; Email: dfields@svdpla.org. Lawrence Hurst, Dir. Social Svcs.

**St. Vincent de Paul Stores*, 210 N. Ave. 21, 90031. Tel: 323-224-6280; Fax: 323-225-4997; Email: dfields@svdpla.org. David R. Fields, Dir. For Pick Up: 323-224-6280; 800-974-3571.

[AA] MISCELLANEOUS LISTINGS

LOS ANGELES. **Archdiocese of Los Angeles Insurance Company*, 3424 Wilshire Blvd., 90010. Tel: 213-637-7000; Email: info@la-archdiocese.org. Randy Steiner, CFO.

**Archdiocese of Los Angeles Risk Management Corporation*, 3424 Wilshire Blvd., 90010. Tel: 213-637-7000; Email: info@la-archdiocese.org. Randy Steiner, CFO.

Catholic Big Brothers Big Sisters, Inc., 1530 James M. Wood Blvd., 90015. Tel: 213-251-9800; Tel: 213-251-7760 (TTY); Fax: 213-251-9855; Email: info@catholicbigbrothers.org; Web: www.catholicbigbrothers.org. Ken Martinet, Pres. & CEO.

Catholic Charities Community Development Corporation, Inc., 1531 James M. Wood Blvd., P.O. Box 15095, 90015-0095. Tel: 213-251-2400; Email: mruvalcaba@ccharities.org. Maria Ruvalcaba, Exec. Asst. Total Staff 1.

Charisma in Missions, La Porciuncula, 1059 S. Gage Ave., 90023. Tel: 323-260-7031; Fax: 323-260-7221; Email: charismisn@aol.com. Esther Garzon, Dir.

**Western U.S.A. Lieutenancy of the Equestrian Order of the Holy Sepulchre of Jerusalem*, 555 W. Temple St., 90012. Tel: 213-680-5200; Email: admin@khswesternusa.org; Web: www.eohsjwesternusa.org. H.E. Sir Michael Scottfeeley KGCHS, Lieutenant.

555 W. Temple St., 90012. Tel: 213-626-0776. Most Rev. Jose H. Gomez, Grand Prior.

**Estrella del Mar de Los Angeles, Inc.* dba Regis House Community Center (1949) 2212 W. Beverly Blvd., 90057. Tel: 213-380-8168; Fax: 213-380-8160; Email: regishousecc@att.net. Sisters Albertina Morales, S.S.S., Dir.; Teresita Saavedra, S.S.S., Prog. Dir. Sisters of Social Service 2.

**Federation of Oases of Koinonia John the Baptist*, 1016 W. Manchester Ave., 90044. Tel: 310-990-6362; Email: leg@koinoniagb.org. Sr. Maire S. Close, Contact Person.

The Focolare Movement, Men's Branch (California) (Work of Mary), 8016 Cowan Ave., 90045-1405. Tel: 310-670-6736; Email: focolare.mla@gmail.com; Web: www.focolare.org/usa. Mr. John Castanon, Co-Dir. Pacific Region.

The Focolare Movement, Women's Branch, 4560 Mount Vernon Dr., 90043. Tel: 323-815-9081; Email: wla.focolare@gmail.com. Maria C. Ferreira, Dir. West Coast.

St. Francis Center, 1835 S. Hope St., 90015. Tel: 213-747-5347; Fax: 213-765-8915; Email: info@sfcla.org; Web: www.sfcla.org. Jose Ramirez, Exec. Dir.; Faye A. Alpaugh, Asst. Exec. Dir.

**Friends of John Paul II Foundation of California*, 3424 W. Adams Blvd., 90018. Tel: 805-796-0960; Email: bogusia.doerr@gmail.com. Boguslawa Doerr, Pres.

**Hospitaller Foundation of California, Inc., The*, 2468 S. St. Andrew's Pl., 90018. Tel: 323-731-7141; Fax: 323-731-5717; Email: arlene@hospitallerfoundation.org; Web: www.stjog.org/foundation. Bro. Stephen de la Rosa, O.H., Pres. (Fundraising for St. John of God Retirement and Care Center)

Helpers Club of St. John of God, Tel: 323-731-7141; Fax: 323-731-5717.

Women's League of St. John of God, Tel: 323-731-7141; Fax: 323-731-5717.

Hotel Dieu, 265 S. Lake St., Ste. 202, 90057. Mary McKenna, CFO; Gwen Wilkerson, Exec. Dir.

**The Institute for Advanced Catholic Studies*, University Religious Center, 835 W. 34th St., Ste. 102, 90089-0751. Tel: 213-740-3055; Tel: 213-740-1864; Fax: 213-740-2179; Email: iacss@comcast.net; Web: www.instituteforadvancedcatholicstudies.com. Rev. James L. Heft, S.M., Contact Person.

Korean Catholic Renewal Movement of Southern California, 1230 San Fernando Rd., 90065. Tel: 323-221-8874; Fax: 323-221-6325; Email: parish-3570@la-archdiocese.org. Rev. Raphael Jaehun Song, (Korea, South) Chap.

**Lay Mission-Helpers Association*, 3435 Wilshire Blvd., Ste. 1940, 90010-1901. Tel: 213-368-1870; Fax: 213-368-1871; Email: info@laymissionhelpers.org; Web: www.laymissionhelpers.org. Chad Ribordy, Exec. Dir.; Janice England, Prog. Dir.

**Little Flower Center* dba Little Flower Educational Child Care & Little Flower Missionary House, 920 E. Alhambra Rd., Alhambra, 91801-2704. Tel: 323-221-9248; Fax: 323-221-9250; Email: administrator@littleflowerla.com; Web: www.littleflowerla.com. 2434 Gates St., 90031. Sr. Gabriela Sandoval, O.C.D., Admin. Sponsored by the Carmelite Sisters of the Most Sacred Heart of Los Angeles. Capacity 133; Lay Teachers 12; Sisters 6.

**Mission Doctors Association*, 3435 Wilshire Blvd., Ste. 1940, 90010. Tel: 213-368-1875; Fax: 213-368-1871; Email: info@missiondoctors.org; Web: www.missiondoctors.org. Elise Frederick, Exec. Dir.

Notre Dame Academy Facilities Corporation, 2851 Overland Ave., 90064. Tel: 310-839-5289. Cecilia Uribe, Pres.

Notre Dame Academy Schools Foundation, 2851 Overland Ave., 90064. Tel: 310-839-5289. Daniel Koskovich, Pres.

Opus Caritatis, Inc., 1531 James W. Wood Blvd., 90015-0095. Tel: 213-251-3464; Email: mruvalcaba@ccharities.org. Rev. Msgr. Gregory A. Cox, M.S.W., M.B.A., M.Div., Contact Person.

**Parish Catalyst*, 11100 Santa Monica Blvd., Ste. 1910, 90025. Tel: 310-500-4286; Email: info@parishcatalyst.org. William Simon, Dir.

Paulist Pictures (1985) 6430 Sunset Blvd., Ste. 1220, 90028. Tel: 310-454-0688; Fax: 310-459-6549; Email: paulistmail@paulistproduction.org; Web: www.paulistproductions.org. Mike Sullivan, Pres.

Paulist Productions (1968) 1328 Westwood Blvd., 90024. Tel: 310-454-0688; Email: assistant@paulistproductions.com; Web: www.paulistproductions.org. Dr. Michael O'Sullivan, Pres.; Rev. Thomas C. Gibbons, C.S.P., Dir.; David G. Moore, Admin.

**Salesian Boys & Girls Club of Los Angeles*, 3218 Wabash Ave., 90063. Tel: 323-263-7519; Fax: 323-263-8558; Email: tmass@salesianclubs-la.org; Web: www.salesianclubs-la.org. Juan Montenegro, Exec.

Salesian Family Youth Center, 2228 E. 4th St., 90033. Tel: 323-980-8551; Fax: 323-980-8594; Email: tmass@salesianclubs-la.org. Juan Montenegro, Exec. The Salesian Family Youth Center is an outreach site of the Salesian Boys and Girls Club of Los Angeles and forms a single corporate entity with the Salesian Boys and Girls Club of Los Angeles.

Serra Institute, 2060 N. Vermont Ave., 90027. Tel: 323-664-9292; Email: gcrye@aol.com; Web: quantumtheology.org. Rev. Gary Rye, Dir.

Servants of the Immaculate Child Mary, 5135 Dartmouth Ave., 90032. Tel: 323-225-3279; Fax: 323-225-3279; Email: ein-la@hotmail.com; Email: sr.mcarlos@la-archdiocese.org. Sr. Raquel Diaz Sandoval, Contact Person.

Sisters of Nazareth Foundation, Inc., 3333 Manning Ave., 90064. Tel: 310-839-2361; Email: mwashington@nazarethhousela.org. Melanie Washington, Dir.

**South Central Los Angeles Ministry Project* aka South Central LAMP (1993) 892 E. 48th St., 90011. Tel: 323-234-1471; Fax: 323-234-1472; Email: social@southcentrallamp.org; Web: www.southcentrallamp.org. Diana Z. Pinto, Exec. Dir.

St. Vincent Senior Citizen Nutrition Program, Inc. aka St. Vincent Meals on Wheels (1977) 2303 Miramar St., 90057. Tel: 213-484-7778; Fax: 213-484-7276; Email: svmcinfo@verity.org. Mary Eileen Drees, Dir. Tot Asst. Annually 1,095,000; Total Staff 90; Meals Served Daily 3,000; Volunteers 300.

Works in New Directions, Inc. (WIND), 4316 Lanai Rd., Encino, 91436. Tel: 818-285-3355; Fax: 818-285-3366; Email: officemanager@hsrcenter.com. Sr. Celeste Arbuckle, S.S.S., Contact Person.

AGOURA. **Conrad N. Hilton Fund for Sisters*, 30440 Agoura Rd., Agoura, 91301. Tel: 818-483-0485; Fax: 818-851-3895; Email: info@hiltonfundforsisters.org; Web: www.hiltonfundforsisters.org. Sr. Gina Blunck, Dir.

ALHAMBRA. **Carmelite Educational Centers, Inc.*, 920 E. Alhambra Rd., Alhambra, 91801. Tel: 626-289-1353; Fax: 626-308-1913; Email: gensecretary@carmelitesistersocd.com; Web: www.carmelitesistersocd.com. Sr. Marisa Ducote, Dir.

Carmelite Sisters Foundation, Inc., 920 E. Alhambra Rd., Alhambra, 91801. Tel: 626-289-1353; Fax: 626-308-1913; Email: advancement@carmelitesistersocd.com. Sr. Marisa Ducote, Dir.

Flos Carmeli Formation Centers, Inc., 920 E. Alhambra Rd., Alhambra, 91801. Tel: 626-289-1353; Fax: 626-308-1913; Email: gensecretary@carmelitesistersocd.com. Sr. Marisa Ducote, Dir.

Mount Carmel Health Ministries, Inc., 920 E. Alhambra Rd., Alhambra, 91801. Tel: 626-289-1353; Fax: 626-308-1913; Email: gensecretary@carmelitesistersocd.com. Sr. Marisa Ducote, Dir.

BALDWIN PARK. *The Redemptorist Vietnamese Mission Corporation*, 3452 N. Big Dalton Ave., Baldwin Park, 91706. Tel: 626-851-9020; Email: chaqhung@yahoo.com. Rev. Pham Quoc Hung, C.Ss.R., Pres.

BURBANK. *SCRC (Southern California Renewal Communities)*, 9795 Cabrini Dr., Ste. 208, Burbank, 91504-1740. Tel: 818-771-1361; Fax: 818-771-1379; Email: spirit@scrc.org; Web: www.scrc.org. Dominic Berardino, Pres.; Rev. William K. Delaney, S.J., Pastoral Coord.

CARPINTERIA. **International Theological Institute for Studies on Marriage and the Family*, 3299 Padaro Ln., Carpinteria, 93013. Tel: 805-649-2346; Fax: 706-867-6216; Email: betty-itius@msn.com. Betty Hartmann, Contact Person.

CHATSWORTH. **El Sembrador Ministries*, 20720 Marilla St., Chatsworth, 91311. Tel: 818-700-4938; Fax: 818-841-1486; Email: rosiegomez@elsembrador.org; Web: www.elsembrador.org. Noel Diaz, Pres. & Founder; Rosie Sayes, CEO.

Sacred Heart Retreat Apostolate (2004) 10480 1/2 Winnetka Ave., Chatsworth, 91311. Tel: 818-488-1357; Fax: 818-488-1189; Email: sdshtreasurer@gmail.com; Web: www.sacredheartretreatcamp.com. Sisters Susan Blaschke, S.D.S.H., Treas. Gen; Mary Tomasella, S.D.S.H., Supr. Gen., Email: mhsdsh2@sbcglobal.net.

COVINA. *Comboni Mission Center*, 645 S. Aldenville Ave., Covina, 91723. Tel: 626-339-1914; Fax: 626-974-4238; Email: comboni@verizon.net. Revs. Jorge Ochoa, M.C.C.J., Supr.; Modi Abel Nyorko, Community Member; Gerardo De Tomasi, M.C.C.J.; Paul Ewers; Aldo Pozza, M.C.C.J., Bursar.

CULVER CITY. **Catholics in Media Associates* (1992) 3908 Sepulveda Blvd., Culver City, 90230. Tel: 818-907-2734; Email: info@catholicsinmedia.org; Web: www.catholicsinmedia.org. Sr. Rose Pacatte, F.S.P., Pres.; Andrea Setterstrom, Treas., Tel: 323-997-0055.

Christus Ministries, 10755 Deshire Pl., Culver City, 90230. Tel: 310-919-8485; Email: contact@christusministries.org; Web: www.ChristusMinistries.org. Rev. Tri M. Dinh, S.J., Dir.

**Loyola Productions, Inc.*, 1 LMU Dr. MS 8427, 90045. Tel: 310-962-8089; Fax: 310-338-7884; Email: esiebert@loyolaproductions.com; Email: enid@loyolaproductions.com; Web: www.loyolaproductions.com. Rev. Edward J. Siebert, S.J., Pres.

EL MONTE. **Hombre Nuevo*, 12036 Ramona Blvd., El Monte, 91732. Tel: 626-444-4442; Fax: 626-444-1435; Web: www.hombrenuevo.net. Dr. Rene Heredia, Dir.

GARDENA. **LHC Ministries, Inc.*, 14700 S. Van Ness Ave., Gardena, 90249. Tel: 310-516-0271; Email: graceducle@gmail.com. Sr. Marypeace Ho.

GLENDALE. **Together in Christ* (1998) 311 E. Stocker St., Ste. 102, Glendale, 91207. Tel: 818-246-5582; Fax: 818-246-5582; Email: TogetherChrist1@gmail.com. Nancy Barona, Pres.

LA VERNE. *Picpus Charitable Trust* (1991) 2150 Damien Ave., La Verne, 91750. Tel: 909-227-9346; Fax: 760-955-2100; Email: ptravers37@gmail.com. Rev. Patrick Travers, SS.CC., Dir.

LAKE BALBOA. *Maria Auxiliadora Magnificat Chapter*, 6738 Aldea Ave., Lake Balboa, 91406. Tel: 818-708-9702. Rosemarie Leon, Contact Person.

LANCASTER. *Antelope Valley Magnificat*, 6116 Quail Ridge Ln., Lancaster, 93536-3714. Tel: 661-943-6402; Email: trabjack@yahoo.com; Web: magnificat-ministry.net. Rita Trabold, Contact Person.

**Our Lady of Charity, Conference of St. Vincent de Paul Society*, 45058 Trevor, Ste. B, Lancaster, 93534. Tel: 661-942-3222; Tel: 661-946-0125; Email: dfields@svdpla.org. P.O. Box 412, Lancaster, 93584. Donald Willey, Pres., Tel: 661-946-0125; David R. Fields, Dir.

LONG BEACH. *St. Mary Catholic Housing Corp.* dba St. Mary Tower, 1050 Linden Ave., Long Beach, 90813. Tel: 562-491-9189; Fax: 562-436-6378; Email: Robert.Sahagian@dignityhealth.org. Robert Sahagian, Contact Person.

St. Mary Medical Center Foundation, 1050 Linden Ave., Long Beach, 90813. Tel: 562-491-9225; Fax: 562-491-9888; Email: LaRae.Bechmann@DignityHealth.org; Web: www.supportstmary.org. Ms. LaRae Bechmann, Pres. Employees 8.

LYNWOOD. *St. Louise Resource Services*, 3663 Martin Luther King Jr. Blvd., Lynwood, 90262. Tel: 424-220-6647; Tel: 424-220-6645; Email: lramirez@stlrs.org. Sr. Marjory Ann Baez, CEO.

MONTEREY PARK. *Filipino Pastoral Ministry*, 320 W. Garvey Ave., Monterey Park, 91754. Tel: 213-587-2226; Email: fr.albert@yahoo.com. Rev. Albert H. Avenido, Spiritual Mod., Chap.

Theresian Sisters, 901 W. El Repetto Dr., Monterey Park, 91754. Tel: 213-637-7559; Email: info@la-archdiocese.org. Sr. Anna Thaolu, C.S.T., Contact Person.

NORTHRIDGE. **John Paul II Foundation for the New Evangelization*, 9227 Reseda Blvd., Apt. 260, Northridge, 91324. Email: ParishEvangelizationLeaders@gmail.com.

OJAI. **St. Joseph's H. & RC Foundation* (1996) 2464 Ojai Ave., Ojai, 93023. Tel: 805-646-1466; Fax: 805-646-1013; Email: igi@ojai.net. Rev. Ignatius Sudol, O.H., CEO & Pres. Priests 2; Total Assisted 50.

PALMDALE. **Koinonia John the Baptist California*, 30451 Aliso Canyon Rd., Palmdale, 93550.

PASADENA. **The Association of Catholic Student Councils*, 530 S. Lake Ave., Ste. 889, Pasadena, 91101-3515. Tel: 925-954-7048; Email: tacsc@tacsc.org; Web: http://www.tacsc.org. Heidi Johnson, Dir.

GRACE, 85 S. Grand Ave., Pasadena, 91105. Tel: 626-356-4200; Fax: 626-356-4219; Email: info@grace-inc.org. Conway Collis, Dir.

Ramona Blvd., Inc., 1455 Sierra Madre Villa Ave., Pasadena, 91107. Tel: 678-938-4500; Email: fformolo@legionaries.org. Rev. Frank Formolo.

PICO RIVERA. *Margaret Aylward Center*, 4270 Acacia Ave., Pico Rivera, 90660. Tel: 562-695-6621; Email: maylwardonline@gmail.com. Leticia Solis, Dir.

RANCHO PALOS VERDES. *Congregazione delle Figlie di Maria e di Giuseppe, Inc.*, 5300 Crest Rd., Rancho Palos Verdes, 90275-5004. Tel: 310-377-2154; Email: pcraig@maryjoseph.org. Paul Craig, Dir.

Filles de Marie et de Joseph en Afrique, Inc., 5300 Crest Rd., Rancho Palos Verdes, 90275-5004. Tel: 310-377-4867; Email: pcraig@maryjoseph.org. Paul Craig, Dir.

SAN FERNANDO. **Valley Family Center* (1987) 302 S. Brand Blvd., San Fernando, 91340. Tel: 818-365-8588; Fax: 818-898-3382; Email: info@valleyfamilycenter.org; Web: www.valleyfamilycenter.com. Sr. Carmel Somers, R.S.C., Exec. Dir. Religious Sisters of Charity.

SAN PEDRO. *Apostleship of the Sea, Catholic Maritime Ministry*, Mary, Star of the Sea Parish, 870 W. 8th St., San Pedro, 90731. Tel: 310-833-3541; Fax: 310-833-9254; Email: aoslalb@gmail.com. Rev. Freddie T. Chua, Dir. of Maritime Ministry/A.O.S. Chap.

Center, Berth 93A, World Cruise Center, Port of Los Angeles, San Pedro, 90731. Tel: 310-833-3541; Fax: 310-833-9254; Email: aoslalb@gmail.com. Rev. Freddie T. Chua, Dir.

SANTA BARBARA. **The Cause of Blessed Junipero Serra*, Old Mission Santa Barbara, 2201 Laguna St., Santa Barbara, 93105-3611. Tel: 805-682-4713; Email: kjlofm@aol.com. Revs. Ken Laverone, O.F.M., Vice Postulator; Melvin A. Jurisich, O.F.M., Dir.

SANTA MARIA. *American Region of the Josephite Fathers Charitable Trust*, 180 Patterson Rd., Santa Maria, 93455. Tel: 805-937-5378; Email: frcharles71@gmail.com; Web: www.josephite.community. Revs. Ludovic DeClippel, Supr.; Charles L. Hofschulte, C.J., M.A., Contact Person.

**Servants and Handmaids of the Sacred Heart of Jesus, Mary and Joseph*, 1157 E. Clark Ave., Ste. H, Santa Maria, 93455. Tel: 805-524-5890; Email: admin@theservantsandhandmaids.net; Web: www.theservantsandhandmaids.net. P.O. Box 2309, Santa Maria, 93457-2309. Ms. Jerrie Castro, Pres.; Ms. Mary Ann Maagdenberg, Vice Pres.; Ms. Mary Ann Armstrong, Sec.

SANTA SUSANA KNOLLS. *Magnificat, A Ministry to Catholic Women West San Fernando Valley Chapter* (1984) 6202 Wisteria Dr., Santa Susana Knolls, 93063. Tel: 805-527-3745; Email: terithompson@sbcglobal.net; Email: teri@magnificatsfv.org; Web: www.magnificatsfv.org. Rev. Robert E. J. Garon, Spiritual Advisor/Care Services; Debbie Haywood; Espe Martin, Admin.; Leslie Ozark, Treas.; Teri Thompson, Dir.

THOUSAND OAKS. *Notre Dame Learning Center*, 1776 Hendrix Ave., Thousand Oaks, 91360. Tel: 805-494-0304; Fax: 805-379-3616; Email: cpapet@yahoo.com. Sr. Carol Papet, Dir. Preschool 30.

University Series Foundation, Inc., 155 E. Janss Rd., Thousand Oaks, 91360. Tel: 805-496-0222; Email: parish-3290@la-archdiocese.org. Rev. Michael Rocha, Dir.

TORRANCE. *Claretian Teaching Ministry*, 20610 Manhattan Pl., #120, Torrance, 90501-1863. Tel: 310-782-6408; Fax: 310-782-8892; Email: ctmonline@catholicbooks.net; Web: www.catholicbooks.net. Rev. John Hampsch, C.M.F., Dir.

World Wide Marriage Encounter, 16706 Cerise Ave., Torrance, 90504. Tel: 310-515-3522; Email: media@wwme.org; Web: www.wwme.org. Anthony Mena, Contact; Vel Mena, Contact.

VENICE. *St. Joseph Center* (1976) 204 Hampton Dr., Venice, 90291-8633. Tel: 310-396-6468; Fax: 310-392-8402; Email: vadams@stjosephctr.com; Email: community@stjosephctr.org; Web: www.stjosephctr.org. Sr. Catherine Mary Bundon, C.S.J., Contact Person.

VENTURA. **CAREGIVERS: Volunteers Assisting the Elderly* (1984) 1765 Goodyear Ave., #205, Ventura, 93003. Tel: 805-658-8530; Fax: 805-658-8537;

Email: info@vccaregivers.org; Web: www.vccaregivers.org. Tammy Glenn, Dir.
*Institute for Catholic Liberal Education, Inc. dba Catholic Textbook Project, 130 S. Wells Rd., Ventura, 93004. Tel: 805-672-0411; Fax: 805-672-0177; Email: mvh@catholictextbookproject.com. Michael Van Hecke, Dir.
WEST COVINA. *Luz De Cristo USA*, 1151 E. Grovecenter St., West Covina, 91790. Tel: 626-966-7594; Email: aidaimiranda@gmail.com; Web: www.luzdecristousa.org. Aida Miranda, Dir.

[BB] LEGAL TITLES

LOS ANGELES. *Archdiocesan Catholic Center*, 3424 Wilshire Blvd., 90010-2241. Tel: 213-637-7000; Fax: 213-637-6000; Email: info@la-archdiocese.org; Web: www.la-archdiocese.org. Rev. Msgr. Albert M. Bahhuth, V.F., Mod. of the Curia / Vicar Gen.; Sr. Mary Elizabeth Galt, B.V.M., Chancellor; Most Rev. Jose H. Gomez, D.D., S.T.D., V.G., Ordinary. For further information contact the Chancery. Also see Miscellaneous for additional listings.
Congregation of the Sacred Heart of Jesus & Mary and of Perpetual Adoration, Inc., SS.CC., LaVerne, Tel: 909-593-5441; Fax: 909-593-3971.
Recollect Augustinian Fathers & Brothers, Province of St. Augustine, Inc., O.A.R., Oxnard (1990) Tel: 805-486-7433; Fax: 805-487-2805.
School Sisters of Notre Dame, Tel: 314-544-0455; Fax: 314-544-6754. Various Locations in the Archdiocese.
Sisters of St. Louis Monaghan, Inc., S.S.L., Woodland Hills, Tel: 818-883-1678; Fax: 818-346-6109.
Ursulines of the Western Province, Inc., O.S.U., Encino, Tel: 650-346-9897.

RELIGIOUS INSTITUTES OF MEN REPRESENTED IN THE ARCHDIOCESE

For further details refer to the corresponding bracketed number in the Religious Institutes of Men or Women section.

[]—*Apostles of Jesus.*
[0200]—*Benedictine Monks*—O.S.B.
[1160]—*Brothers of St. Patrick*—F.S.P.
[0330]—*Brothers of the Christian Schools* (De La Salle)—F.S.C.
[0600]—*Brothers of the Holy Cross*—C.S.C.
[]—*Canons Regular of the Immaculate Conception*—C.R.I.C.
[0470]—*Capuchin Franciscan Friars*—O.F.M.Cap.
[0260]—*Carmelite (Discalced) Frairs*—O.C.D.
[0270]—*Carmelite Fathers*—O.Carm.
[0275]—*Carmelites of Mary Immaculate*—C.M.I.
[0360]—*Claretian Missionaries*—C.M.F.
[0370]—*Columban Fathers (Society of St. Columban)*—S.S.C.
[0380]—*Comboni Missionaries* (Verona)—M.C.C.J.
[0450]—*Congregation of Jesus and Mary (Eudist Fathers)*—C.J.M.
[1150]—*Congregation of St. Joseph*—C.S.J.
[1080]—*Congregation of the Resurrection*—C.R.
[1140]—*Congregation of the Sacred Hearts of Jesus and Mary*—SS.CC.
[0480]—*Conventual Franciscan Friars* (St. Joseph Cupertino Prov.)—O.F.M.Conv.
[0420]—*Divine Word Missionaries*—S.V.D.
[0430]—*Dominican Friars*—O.P.
[0515]—*Franciscan Brothers*—O.S.F.
[0520]—*Franciscan Friars* (St. Barbara Prov.)—O.F.M.
[]—*Franciscans Poor of Jesus Christ*—P.J.C.
[]—*Guadalupe Missioners* (Mexico)—M.G.
[0610]—*Holy Cross Fathers*—C.S.C.
[0670]—*Hospitaller Brothers of St. John of God*—O.H.
[0690]—*Jesuits (Society of Jesus)*—S.J.
[0710]—*Josephite Fathers*—C.J.
[0700]—*Josephites (St. Joseph's Society of the Sacred Heart)*—S.S.J.
[0730]—*Legionaries of Christ*—L.C.
[]—*Marian Missionaries of the Holy Cross* (Philippines)—M.M.H.C.
[0760]—*Marianists (Society of Mary)*—S.M.
[0780]—*Marist Fathers*—S.M.
[0800]—*Maryknoll Missioners*—M.M.
[0835]—*Minim Fathers*—O.M.
[]—*Misioneros del Sagrado Corazon y Santa Maria de Guadalupe* (Mexico)—M.S.C.
[]—*Misioneros Servidores de la Palabra* (Mexico)—M.S.P.
[]—*Missionaries of Charity Brothers*—M.C.
[0852]—*Missionaries of Jesus*—M.J.
[0660]—*Missionaries of the Holy Spirit*—M.Sp.S.
[0840]—*Missionary Servants of Most Holy Trinity*—S.T.
[0900]—*Norbertine Fathers (Canons Regulars of Premontre)*—O.Praem.
[0910]—*Oblates of Mary Immaculate*—O.M.I.
[0940]—*Oblates of the Virgin Mary*—O.M.V.
[]—*Operarios del Reino de Cristo* (Mexico)—O.R.C.
[0150]—*Order of Augustinian Recollects*—O.A.R.
[0140]—*Order of St. Augustine*—O.S.A.
[1000]—*Passionist (Congregation of the Passion)*—C.P.
[1030]—*Paulist Fathers (Congregation of St. Paul)*—C.S.P.
[1040]—*Piarist Fathers*—Sch.P.
[1065]—*Priestly Fraternity of St. Peter*—F.S.S.P.
[1070]—*Redemptorist Fathers*—C.Ss.R.
[]—*Redemptorist Fathers* (Vietnamese Province)—C.Ss.R.
[1090]—*Rogationist Fathers*—R.C.J.
[1190]—*Salesians of Don Bosco*—S.D.B.
[1210]—*Scalabrinians (Missionaries of St. Charles)*—C.S.
[]—*Servites (Order of Servants of Mary, India Province)*—O.S.M.
[1260]—*Society of Christ*—S.Ch.
[1020]—*Society of St. Paul (Pauline Fathers)*—S.S.P.
[1060]—*Society of the Precious Blood*—C.PP.S.
[0840]—*Trinitarians (Missionary Servants of the Most Holy Trinity)*—S.T.
[]—*Vietnamese Redemptorists*—C.Ss.R.
[1330]—*Vincentian Brothers (Congregation of the Mission)*—C.M.

RELIGIOUS INSTITUTES OF WOMEN REPRESENTED IN THE ARCHDIOCESE

[2120]—*Armenian Sisters of the Immaculate Conception*—C.I.C.
[]—*Augustinian Recollect Sisters*—O.A.R.
[]—*Benedictine Sisters of Monastery of St. Gertrude*—O.S.B.
[0230]—*Benedictine Sisters of St. Lucy's Priory*—O.S.B.
[1810]—*Bernardine Franciscan Sisters*—O.S.F.
[]—*Blessed Sacrament Sisters of Charity*—B.B.S.
[2930]—*California Institute of the Sisters of the Most Holy and Immaculate Heart of the Blessed Virgin Mary*—I.H.M.
[1895]—*Carmelitas de San Jose*—C.S.J.
[0370]—*Carmelite Sisters of the Most Sacred Heart*—O.C.D.
[1940]—*Congregation of the Holy Faith*—C.H.F.
[0760]—*Daughters of Charity of St. Vincent de Paul*—D.C.
[]—*Daughters of Divine Zeal*—F.D.Z.
[0860]—*Daughters of Mary*—D.M.
[0880]—*Daughters of Mary and Joseph*—D.M.J.
[0850]—*Daughters of Mary Help of Christians (Salesian Sisters of St. John Bosco)*—F.M.A.
[]—*Daughters of St. Mary*—D.S.M.
[0950]—*Daughters of St. Paul*—F.S.P.
[0420]—*Discalced Carmelites*—O.C.D.
[1050]—*Dominican Nuns of the Order of Preachers*—O.P.
[]—*Dominican Sisters of Christian Doctrine*—O.P.
[1070-19]—*Dominican Sisters of Houston*—O.P.
[1070-12]—*Dominican Sisters of Mission San Jose*—O.P.
[1070-03]—*Dominican Sisters of Sinsinawa*—O.P.
[3615]—*Esclavas de la Inmaculada Nina (Servants of the Immaculate Child Mary)*—E.I.N.
[1150]—*Eucharistic Franciscan Missionary Sisters*—E.F.M.S.
[]—*Evangelizadoras Eucaristicas de los Pobres*—E.E.P.
[1170]—*Felician Sisters (Sisters of St. Felix)*—C.S.S.F.
[]—*Focolare.*
[]—*Fr. Kolbe Missionaries of the Immaculata*—F.K.M.
[1350]—*Franciscan Missionary Sisters of the Immaculate Conception*—O.S.F.
[1500]—*Franciscan Sisters of Mary Immaculate*—F.M.I.
[1630]—*Franciscan Sisters of St. Francis of Penance and Christian Charity*—O.S.F.
[1450]—*Franciscan Sisters of the Sacred Heart*—O.S.F.
[]—*Fraternity of the Poor of Jesus*—P.J.C.
[]—*Handmaids of the Triune God*—J.M.J.
[]—*Hermanas Misioneras Servidoras de la Palabra*—H.M.S.P.
[0157]—*Hermanitas de la Annuciacion*—H.A.
[]—*Institute of Our Lady of the Annunciation*—I.O.L.A.
[]—*Kkottongnae Sisters of Jesus*—C.K.S.J.
[]—*Koinonia John the Baptist.*
[0690]—*Little Handmaids of the Most Holy Trinity*—M.A.S.T.
[2340]—*Little Sisters of the Poor*—L.S.P.
[2390]—*Lovers of the Holy Cross*—L.H.C.
[2385]—*Lovers of the Holy Cross, Nha Trang Province*—L.H.C. (NT).
[]—*Mary Queen of Heaven Missionaries*—M.Q.H.M.
[2470]—*Maryknoll Sisters of St. Dominic*—M.M.
[2500]—*Medical Sisters of St. Joseph*—M.S.J.
[1845]—*Missionaries Guadalupanas of the Holy Spirit*—M.G.Sp.S.
[2710]—*Missionaries of Charity*—M.C.
[]—*Missionaries of Jesus Crucified*—M.J.C.
[0210]—*Missionary Benedictine Sisters*—O.S.B.
[]—*Missionary Community of the Holy Spirit*—M.C.H.S.
[]—*Norbertine Sisters*—S.Praem.
[0240]—*Olivetan Benedictine Sisters of Pusan*—O.S.B.
[3760]—*Poor Clare Colettines*—P.C.C.
[2840]—*Poor Clare Missionary Sisters*—M.C.
[]—*Puso Ng Carmelo Community*—P.C.C.
[1145]—*Religious Missionaries of St. Dominic*—O.P.
[3465]—*Religious of the Sacred Heart of Mary*—R.S.H.M.
[3400]—*Religious Sisters of Charity*—R.S.C.
[2970]—*School Sisters of Notre Dame*—S.S.N.D.
[3580]—*Servants of Mary, Ministers to the Sick*—S.de.M.
[0980]—*Sister Disciples of the Divine Master*—P.D.D.M.
[3499]—*Sister Servants of the Blessed Sacrament*—S.J.S.
[]—*Sisters for Christian Community*—S.F.C.C.
[0250]—*Sisters of Bethany*—C.V.D.
[]—*Sisters of Charity of Jesus*—S.C.G.
[0480]—*Sisters of Charity of Leavenworth, Kansas*—S.C.L.
[]—*Sisters of Charity of Rolling Hills*—S.C.R.H.
[0430]—*Sisters of Charity of the Blessed Virgin Mary*—B.V.M.
[0470]—*Sisters of Charity of the Incarnate Word*—C.C.V.I.
[]—*Sisters of Little Jesus*—S.L.J.
[2575]—*Sisters of Mercy of the Americas*—R.S.M.
[3242]—*Sisters of Nazareth*—C.S.N.
[2990]—*Sisters of Notre Dame*—S.N.D.
[3000]—*Sisters of Notre Dame de Namur*—S.N.D.deN.
[]—*Sisters of Our Lady of Perpetual Help*—S.O.L.P.H.
[3350]—*Sisters of Providence*—S.P.
[3360]—*Sisters of Providence of Saint Mary of the Woods, Indiana*—S.P.
[4080]—*Sisters of Social Service*—S.S.S.
[1620]—*Sisters of St. Francis of the Neumann Communities*—O.S.F.
[1760]—*Sisters of St. Francis, Oldenburg*—O.S.F.
[3860]—*Sisters of St. Joseph Congregation*—S.J.C.
[3840]—*Sisters of St. Joseph of Carondelet*—C.S.J.
[3860]—*Sisters of St. Joseph of Cluny*—S.J.C.
[3830-03]—*Sisters of St. Joseph of Orange*—C.S.J.
[3930]—*Sisters of St. Joseph of the Third Order of St. Francis*—S.S.J.-T.O.S.F.
[3935]—*Sisters of St. Louis*—S.S.L.
[]—*Sisters of the Blessed Korean Martyrs*—S.B.K.M.
[0700]—*Sisters of the Company of Mary*—O.D.N.
[1830]—*Sisters of the Good Shepherd*—R.G.S.
[1850]—*Sisters of the Guardian Angel*—S.A.C.
[1920]—*Sisters of the Holy Cross*—C.S.C.
[1990]—*Sisters of the Holy Names of Jesus and Mary*—S.N.J.M.
[]—*Sisters of the Immaculate Heart of Mary of Mirinae*—I.H.M.M.
[]—*Sisters of the Immaculate Heart of Mary, Mother of the Church*—M.M.C.
[2270]—*Sisters of the Little Company of Mary*—L.C.M.
[]—*Sisters of the Love of God*—R.A.D.
[3200]—*Sisters of the Pious Schools*—Sch.P.
[3320]—*Sisters of the Presentation of the Blessed Virgin Mary*—P.B.V.M.
[]—*Sisters of the Sacred Heart of Mary*—C.S.C.M.
[]—*Sisters of the Sick Poor of Los Angeles*—S.S.P.
[4050]—*Society Devoted to the Sacred Heart*—S.D.S.H.
[]—*Society of Our Lady of the Way*—S.O.L.W.
[4060]—*Society of the Holy Child Jesus*—S.H.C.J.
[0380]—*Theresian Sisters*—C.S.T.
[]—*Trinitarians of Mary*—T.M.
[]—*Trinitas.*
[3330]—*Union of Sisters of Presentation of the Blessed Virgin Mary*—P.B.V.M.
[4110]—*Ursuline Sisters of the Roman Union*—O.S.U.
[]—*Verbum Dei Missionary Fraternity*—V.D.M.F.
[4200]—*Visitation Congregation*—S.V.M.

ARCHDIOCESAN CEMETERIES AND MORTUARIES

LOS ANGELES. *Calvary Cemetery and Mortuary*, 4201 Whittier Blvd., 90023. Tel: 323-261-3106; Email: calvaryla@catholiccm.org. Olga Medina, Cemetery Mgr.; Sonyaann Sandoval-Carreon, Mortuary Mgr.
CULVER CITY. *Holy Cross Cemetery & Mortuary*, 5835 W. Slauson Ave., Culver City, 90230. Tel: 310-836-5500; Fax: 310-836-3560; Email: holycrosscc@catholiccemeteriesla.org. Kathy Silva, Cemetery Mgr.; Mark Neander, Mortuary Mgr.
LANCASTER. *Good Shepherd Cemetery & Mausoleum*, 43121 70th St. W., Lancaster, 93536. Tel: 661-722-0887; Fax: 661-722-5344; Email: goodshepherd@catholiccm.org. Daniel Rejniak, Cemetery Mgr.
LONG BEACH. *All Souls Cemetery and Mortuary*, 4400 Cherry Ave., Long Beach, 90807. Tel: 562-424-8601; Fax: 562-426-8065; Email: allsouls@catholiccemeteriesla.org. Maryann McAdams, Cemetery Mgr.; Deacon Dana Gutman-Wedge, Mortuary Mgr.
MISSION HILLS. *San Fernando Cemetery and Mission Hills Catholic Mortuary*, 11160 Stanwood Ave., Mission Hills, 91345. Tel: 818-361-7387; Fax: 818-365-6187; Email: sanfernando@CatholicCM.org; Web: www.

missionhillsmortuary.com. Iris Soriano-Ross, Cemetery Mgr.; Mark Neander, Mortuary Mgr.

OXNARD. *Santa Clara Cemetery and Mortuary*, 2370 North "H" St., Oxnard, 93036. Tel: 805-485-5757; Email: sclara@catholiccemeteriesla.org. Blanca Martinez, Cemetery Mgr.; Ruby Barrios, Mortuary Mgr.

POMONA. *Holy Cross Cemetery*, 444 E Lexington Ave, Pomona, 91766. Tel: 909-627-3602; Fax: 909-465-0690; Email: holycrosspom@catholiccemeteriesla.org. Olga Medina, Cemetery Mgr.

ROSEMEAD. *Resurrection Cemetery & Mausoleum*, 966 N. Potrero Grande Dr., Rosemead, 91770. Tel: 323-887-2024; Fax: 323-722-0874; Email: resurrection@catholiccemeteriesla.org; Web: www.lacatholiccemeteries.org. Eva Gamboa, Cemetery Mgr.

ROWLAND HEIGHTS. *Queen of Heaven Cemetery and Mortuary*, 2161 S. Fullerton Rd., Rowland Heights, 91748. Tel: 626-964-1291; Fax: 626-964-4325; Email: queenofheaven@CatholicCM.org. Norberta Orta, Cemetery Mgr.; Bart Torres, Mortuary Mgr.

SANTA BARBARA. *Calvary Cemetery & Mausoleum*, 199 N. Hope Ave., Santa Barbara, 93110. Tel: 805-687-8811; Fax: 805-569-5814; Email: calvarysb@catholiccm.org. Gwen Hueston, Cemetery Mgr.

SIMI VALLEY. *Assumption Cemetery*, 1380 Fitzgerald Rd., Simi Valley, 93065. Tel: 805-583-5825; Email: assumption@catholiccm.org. Blanca Martinez, Cemetery Mgr.

NECROLOGY

† Gallagher, Robert J., (Retired), Died Jul. 26, 2018
† Loughnane, James J., Diamond Bar, CA St. Denis, Died Sep. 17, 2018
† Reilly, Patrick, (Retired), Died Apr. 4, 2018
† Stetson, William, Los Angeles, CA Prelature of the Holy Cross and Opus Dei., Died Jan. 3, 2019
† Vadakin, Royale M., (Retired), Died Sep. 17, 2018
† Won, John P. H., (Retired), Died Jun. 7, 2018
† De Los Rios, Enrique, Altadena, CA St. Elizabeth Parish, Died Jul. 7, 2018
† Fremgen, Edward George, (Retired), Died Nov. 5, 2017
† Gorman, Rody Ignatius, (Retired), Died Mar. 14, 2018
† Guerrini, Roderic M., (Retired), Died Mar. 14, 2018
† Gutting, John C., (Retired), Died Jan. 28, 2018
† Iglesias, Fernando Gonzalez, (Retired), Died Apr. 23, 2018
† Kelly, Francis, (Retired), Died Feb. 1, 2018
† Landreau, Edward Joseph, (Retired), Died Mar. 31, 2018
† Peacha, Thomas James, (Retired), Died Mar. 4, 2018

An asterisk (*) denotes an organization that has established tax-exempt status directly with the IRS and is not covered by the USCCB Group Ruling.

Archdiocese of Louisville

(Archidioecesis Ludovicopolitana)

Most Reverend

JOSEPH E. KURTZ

Archbishop of Louisville; ordained 1972; appointed Bishop of Knoxville October 26, 1999; ordained and installed December 8, 1999; appointed Archbishop of Louisville June 12, 2007; installed August 15, 2007. *Pastoral Center, 3940 Poplar Level Rd., Louisville, KY 40213*. Tel: 502-585-3291.

Pastoral Center, 3940 Poplar Level Rd., KY 40213. Tel: 502-585-3291; Fax: 502-585-2466.

Web: www.archlou.org

Email: pastoralcenter@archlou.org

Square Miles 8,124.

Established at Bardstown April 8, 1808; Transferred to Louisville Feb. 13, 1841; created an Archdiocese Dec. 10, 1937.

Comprises the following twenty-four Counties in central Kentucky: Adair, Barren, Bullitt, Casey, Clinton, Cumberland, Green, Hardin, Hart, Henry, Jefferson, Larue, Marion, Meade, Metcalfe, Monroe, Nelson, Oldham, Russell, Shelby, Spencer, Taylor, Trimble and Washington.

For legal titles of parishes and archdiocesan institutions, consult the Chancery.

STATISTICAL OVERVIEW

Personnel	
Archbishops	1
Priests: Diocesan Active in Diocese	67
Priests: Diocesan Active Outside Diocese	6
Priests: Diocesan in Foreign Missions	1
Priests: Retired, Sick or Absent	61
Number of Diocesan Priests	135
Religious Priests in Diocese	49
Total Priests in Diocese	184
Extern Priests in Diocese	8
Ordinations:	
Diocesan Priests	5
Transitional Deacons	3
Permanent Deacons in Diocese	140
Total Brothers	40
Total Sisters	501
Parishes	
Parishes	101
With Resident Pastor:	
Resident Diocesan Priests	88
Resident Religious Priests	7
Without Resident Pastor:	
Administered by Priests	4
Administered by Deacons	1
Administered by Lay People	1
Missions	9
Pastoral Centers	1
Professional Ministry Personnel:	
Brothers	6
Sisters	17
Lay Ministers	165
Welfare	
Catholic Hospitals	2
Total Assisted	191,103
Health Care Centers	1
Total Assisted	12,875
Homes for the Aged	4
Total Assisted	866
Residential Care of Children	2
Total Assisted	1,291
Specialized Homes	1
Total Assisted	303
Special Centers for Social Services	5
Total Assisted	52,123
Residential Care of Disabled	1
Total Assisted	12
Educational	
Diocesan Students in Other Seminaries	14
Total Seminarians	14
Colleges and Universities	2
Total Students	5,440
High Schools, Diocesan and Parish	4
Total Students	2,023
High Schools, Private	5
Total Students	3,777
Elementary Schools, Diocesan and Parish	34
Total Students	12,230
Elementary Schools, Private	5
Total Students	1,002
Non-residential Schools for the Disabled	1
Total Students	73
Catechesis/Religious Education:	
High School Students	522
Elementary Students	4,783
Total Students under Catholic Instruction	29,864
Teachers in the Diocese:	
Priests	13
Brothers	9
Sisters	21
Lay Teachers	697
Vital Statistics	
Receptions into the Church:	
Infant Baptism Totals	1,852
Minor Baptism Totals	337
Adult Baptism Totals	194
Received into Full Communion	322
First Communions	2,238
Confirmations	2,166
Marriages:	
Catholic	371
Interfaith	122
Total Marriages	493
Deaths	1,516
Total Catholic Population	156,214
Total Population	1,411,376

Former Bishops—Rt. Revs. BENEDICT JOSEPH FLAGET, S.S., D.D., cons. Bishop of Bardstown, Nov. 4, 1810; died Feb. 11, 1850; JOHN B. DAVID, S.S., D.D., Coadjutor; cons. Aug. 15, 1819; died July 12, 1841; GUY IGNATIUS CHABRAT, S.S., D.D., Coadjutor; cons. July 20, 1834; died Nov. 21, 1868; MARTIN JOHN SPALDING, D.D., Coadjutor with right of succession; cons. Sept. 10, 1848; transferred to Baltimore, May 6, 1864; died Feb. 7, 1872; PETER JOSEPH LAVIALLE, D.D., cons. Sept. 24, 1865; died May 11, 1867; WILLIAM GEORGE McCLOSKEY, D.D., cons. May 24, 1868; died Sept. 17, 1909; DENIS O'DONAGHUE, D.D., ord. Sept. 6, 1874; cons. Titular Bishop of Pomario and Auxiliary of Indianapolis on April 25, 1900; transferred to Louisville, Feb. 7, 1910; transferred to the Titular See of Lebedus, July 26, 1924; died Nov. 7, 1925; Most Revs. JOHN A. FLOERSH, D.D., ord. June 10, 1911; appt. Titular Bishop of Lycopolis and Coadjutor Bishop of Louisville with right of succession, Feb. 6, 1923; cons. April 8, 1923; succeeded to See July 26, 1924; elevated to Archiepiscopal dignity Dec. 10, 1937; resigned and named to Titular See of Sistroniana, March 1, 1967; died June 11, 1968; THOMAS J. McDONOUGH, D.D., transferred to Louisville, May 2, 1967; resigned Sept. 29, 1981; died Aug. 4, 1998; THOMAS C. KELLY, O.P., ord. June 5, 1958; appt. Titular Bishop of Tusuro July 12, 1977; promoted Archbishop of Louisville Dec. 29, 1981; retired June 12, 2007; died Dec. 14, 2011.

Vicar General—Rev. MARTIN A. LINEBACH.

Pastoral Center—*3940 Poplar Level Rd., Louisville, 40213*. Tel: 502-585-3291; Fax: 502-585-2466. Office Hours: 8:30-4:30All applications for dispensations are to be sent to this office.

Chancellor—DR. BRIAN B. REYNOLDS.

Vice Chancellor—RICHARD "TINK" GUTHRIE.

Secretary to Archbishop—Sr. PAULA WOLFF, O.S.B.

Vicar for Priests—Rev. JEFFREY P. SHOONER.

Archivist—Rev. R. DALE CIESLIK.

Chief Financial Officer—ROBERT L. ASH.

Metropolitan Tribunal—*Pastoral Center: 3940 Poplar Level Rd., Louisville, 40213*. Tel: 502-585-3291.

Judicial Vicar and Director—Very Rev. R. PAUL BEACH, J.C.L.

Adjutant Judicial Vicar—VACANT.

Defenders of the Bond—Revs. FREDERICK W. KLOTTER, S.T.L., J.C.L.; J. WAYNE MURPHY, (Retired); ROBERT E. OSBORNE, (Retired); PATRICK J. DOLAN, Ph.D., S.T.D.; JOHN A. SCHWARTZLOSE; DR. ROBERT L. STENGER, S.T.D., J.D.

Associate Judges—Very Rev. R. PAUL BEACH, J.C.L.; Rev. KENNETH R. FORTENER; Deacon P. STEPHAN PHELPS, M.T.S./C.L.; Bro. NICK WOLFLA, O.F.M. Conv., J.C.L.; VICTORIA KACZMAREK.

Assessor and Associate Director—VICTORIA KACZMAREK.

Ecclesiastical Notary—LINDA D. THOMAN.

College of Consultors—Revs. TERRY L. BRADSHAW; WILLIAM D. HAMMER; MARTIN A. LINEBACH; KEVIN ANTHONY MCGRATH, O.P.; JEFFREY SCOTT NICOLAS; JEFFREY P. SHOONER; Very Rev. R. PAUL BEACH, J.C.L.; Revs. WILLIAM M. BOWLING; ANTHONY L. CHANDLER, M.A.

Deans—Revs. TERRY L. BRADSHAW, Bardstown Deanery; WILLIAM M. BOWLING, Lebanon Deanery; MARK M. HAMILTON, Lebanon Deanery; MARTIN A. LINEBACH, Elizabethtown Deanery.

Priest Personnel Commission—Revs. JEFFREY P. SHOONER, Dir.; R. DALE CIESLIK; STEVEN D. HENRIKSEN; J. RANDALL HUBBARD; BRIAN A. KENNEY; SAJU M. VADAKUMPADAN, C.M.I.; GERALD L. BELL, (Retired).

Priests' Council—Most Rev. JOSEPH E. KURTZ, D.D., Presider; Rev. ANTHONY L. CHANDLER, M.A., Pres. Ex Officio: Very Rev. R. PAUL BEACH, J.C.L.; Rev. JEFFREY P. SHOONER. Members: Revs. TERRY L. BRADSHAW; MATTHEW T. HARDESTY; DEVASSYA P. KANATTU, C.M.I.; PATRICK J. DOLAN, Ph.D., S.T.D.; MICHAEL T. WIMSATT; J. WAYNE JENKINS, (Retired); JEFFREY SCOTT NICOLAS; JEFFREY G. HOPPER; MARTIN A. LINEBACH; GARY T. PADGETT; SCOTT J. WIMSETT; KEVIN ANTHONY MCGRATH, O.P.; JOHN J. STOLTZ; WILLIAM D. HAMMER; WILLIAM M. BOWLING; GEORGE ILLIKKAL, C.M.I., (India).

Archdiocesan Examiners—Revs. WILLIAM L. FICHTEMAN, (Retired); THOMAS L. BOLAND, (Retired); GARY T. PADGETT.

Archdiocesan Offices and Directors

Archdiocesan Communications Center—CECELIA PRICE, Chief Communications Officer, Maloney

Center, 1200 S. Shelby St., Louisville, 40203. Tel: 502-636-0296; Fax: 502-636-2379.

Byzantine Rite Faithful—Rev. JOHN W. BIRK, Chap., (Retired), 2082 Douglass Blvd., #1, Louisville, 40205. Tel: 502-451-1555.

Catholic Cemeteries Office—JAVIER FAJARDO, Exec. Dir., 1600 Newburg Rd., P.O. Box 4096, Louisville, 40204. Tel: 502-451-7710; Fax: 502-456-9270.

Catholic Charities—2911 S. 4th St., Louisville, 40208. Tel: 502-637-9786; Fax: 502-637-9780. LISA DEJACO CRUTCHER, CEO & Exec. Dir.

Priest Personnel Office—Rev. JEFFREY P. SHOONER, Dir., Mailing Address: Pastoral Center, 3940 Poplar Level Rd., Louisville, 40213. Tel: 502-585-3291; Fax: 502-585-2466.

Clerical Aid—Pastoral Center, 3940 Poplar Level Rd., Louisville, 40213. Tel: 502-585-3291.

Continuing Education for Clergy-Ministry to Priests—Rev. JEFFREY P. SHOONER, Mailing Address: Pastoral Center, 3940 Poplar Level Rd., Louisville, 40213. Tel: 502-585-3291.

Cursillo Movement—Flaget Center, 1935 Lewiston Pl., Louisville, 40216. Tel: 502-448-8581. KENNETH JACKEY, Lay Dir.

Ecumenical and Interreligious Relations Officer—Rev. MARK M. HAMILTON.

Family Ministries Office—Deacon T. STEPHEN BOWLING, Exec. Dir., 1200 S. Shelby St., Louisville, 40203. Tel: 502-636-0296; Fax: 502-636-2379.

Holy Childhood Association—Pastoral Center, 3940 Poplar Level Rd., Louisville, 40213. DR. BRIAN B. REYNOLDS, Dir.

L.A.M.P.—(Louisville Archdiocesan Mission Promoters), *Pastoral Center, 3940 Poplar Level Rd., Louisville, 40213.* Tel: 502-585-3291. Most Rev. JOSEPH E. KURTZ, D.D.

Office of the Diaconate—Deacon DENNIS M. NASH, Dir., Maloney Center, 1200 S. Shelby St., Louisville, 40203. Tel: 502-636-0296; Fax: 502-636-2379.

Parish Leadership Development—Pastoral Center, 3940 Poplar Level Rd., Louisville, 40213. Tel: 502-585-3291; Fax: 502-585-2466. SAL DELLA BELLA, Dir.

Office of Catholic Schools—Mailing Address: Pastoral Center, 3940 Poplar Level Rd., Louisville, 40213. LEISA SCHULZ, Supt. Schools.

Office of Youth and Young Adult—1200 S. Shelby St., Louisville, 40203. KARL DOLSON, Dir.

Office of Faith Formation—1200 S. Shelby St., Louisville, 40203. ARTHUR TURNER, Dir.

Office of Multicultural Ministry—M. ANNETTE TURNER, Dir., Maloney Center, 1200 S. Shelby St., Louisville, 40203. Tel: 502-636-0296.

Office of Worship—DR. KAREN SHADLE, Dir., Maloney Center, 1200 S. Shelby St., Louisville, 40203. Tel: 502-636-0296; Fax: 502-636-2379.

Opportunities for Life—BRENDA THOMPSON, Coord., Louisville/Owensboro Diocese, 600 Locust St., Owensboro, 42301. Tel: 502-810-8764; Tel: 800-860-7165.

Personnel Office—Pastoral Center, 3940 Poplar Level Rd., Louisville, 40213.

Pro-Life Ministries—EDWARD HARPRING, Coord., Maloney Center, 1200 S. Shelby St., Louisville, 40203. Tel: 502-636-0296; Fax: 502-636-2379.

Propagation of the Faith(Missions Office), Mailing Address: Pastoral Center, 3940 Poplar Level Rd., Louisville, 40213. DR. BRIAN B. REYNOLDS, Dir.

Sacred Heart Enthronement Center—Rev. JEFFERY G. HOOPER, Dir., 1225 S. Wilson Rd., Radcliff, 40160.

Office of Mission and Advancement—Pastoral Center: 3940 Poplar Level Rd., Louisville, 40213. Tel: 502-585-3291; Fax: 502-585-2466. MELODY DENSON, Dir.

Vicar for Retired Clergy—Rev. J. ROY STILES, (Retired), 2042 Buechel Bank Rd., Louisville, 40218. Tel: 502-499-0868.

Victim Assistance Coordinator—MARTINE SIEGEL, Tel: 502-636-1044; Email: msiegel@archlou.org; Email: family@archlou.org.

Vocations—Very Rev. MICHAEL T. WIMSATT, Dir., Maloney Center, 1200 S. Shelby St., Louisville, 40203. Tel: 502-636-0296.

CLERGY, PARISHES, MISSIONS AND PAROCHIAL SCHOOLS

CITY OF LOUISVILLE

(JEFFERSON COUNTY)

1—CATHEDRAL OF THE ASSUMPTION (1852)
433 S. 5th St., Louisville, 40202. Tel: 502-657-5213; Tel: 502-582-2971; Email: administrator@cathedraloftheassumption.org; Web: www.cathedraloftheassumption.org. Very Rev. Michael T. Wimsatt; Deacons P. Stephan Phelps, M.T.S./C.L.; Christopher F. McDonell. In Res., Most Rev. Joseph E. Kurtz, D.D.
Catechesis Religious Program—Students 44.

2—ST. AGNES (1885)
1920 Newburg Rd., Louisville, 40205.
Tel: 502-451-2220; Email: jcecil@stagneslouisville.org; Web: stagneslouisville.org. Rev. David Colhour, C.P.
School—St. Agnes School, (Grades K-8), 1800 Newburg Rd., Louisville, 40205. Tel: 502-458-2850; Fax: 502-459-5215; Email: jackicecil@yahoo.com. Julianna Daly, Prin.; Elizabeth Hinkebein, Librarian. Lay Teachers 27; Students 453.
Catechesis Religious Program—Theresa Secord, D.R.E. Students 50.

3—ST. ALBERT THE GREAT (1959)
1395 Girard Dr., Louisville, 40222.
Tel: 502-425-3940; Email: ebowling@stalbert.org; Web: www.stalbert.org. Rev. David W. Harris; Deacon Stephen Marks, Admin.
School—St. Albert the Great School, (Grades PreK-8), Tel: 502-425-1804; Email: emartin@stalbert.org. Ellen Martin, Prin. Lay Teachers 32; Students 611.
Catechesis Religious Program—
Tel: 502-423-1590, Ext. 110. Students 120.

4—ASCENSION OF OUR LORD (1965)
4600 Lynnbrook Dr., Louisville, 40220.
Tel: 502-451-3860; Email: dschabel@ascension-parish.com; Web: www.ascension-parish.com. Rev. Steven D. Henriksen.
School—Ascension of Our Lord School, (Grades PreK-8), Tel: 502-451-2535; Email: terry@ascension-parish.com; Web: www.ascension-parish.com. Mr. Terry Mullaney, Prin. Lay Teachers 19; Students 228.
Catechesis Religious Program—
Tel: 502-451-3860, Ext. 12. Students 32.

5—ST. ATHANASIUS (1960)
5915 Outer Loop Dr., Louisville, 40219.
Tel: 502-969-3332; Email: secretary@staparish.com; Web: www.stathanasiuslouisville.com. Rev. Gary G. Davis; Deacons Jesse E. Schook; Sam King; James McCarty.
School—St. Athanasius School, (Grades PreK-8), 5915 Outer Loop Dr., Louisville, 40219.
Tel: 502-969-2345; Email: reecem@athanasiusschool.org; Web: saintathanasiuslouisville.com. Margie Reece, Prin.; Anne Bainbridge, Librarian. Clergy 2; Lay Teachers 21; Students 341.
Catechesis Religious Program—Email: dminton@staparish.com. Debbie Minton, D.R.E. Students 340.

6—ST. AUGUSTINE (1870)
1310 W. Broadway, Louisville, 40203.
Tel: 502-584-4602; Fax: 502-581-0893; Email: staugustine@mw.twcbc.com; Web: staugustinecatholiclou-ky.org. Revs. Charles D. Walker, Admin.; Thomas E. Gentile, (Retired); Deogratias Ssamba, A.J.; Deacons James Turner; Keith L. McKenzie.
Hines Center—Tel: 502-584-5463.

7—ST. BARTHOLOMEW (1941)
2042 Buechel Bank Rd., Louisville, 40218.
Tel: 502-499-0883; Email: chayslette@saintbarths.org; Web: www.saintbarths.org. Revs. Nicholas J. Brown; Robert Barnell; Deacon Francisco J. Villalobos. In Res., Rev. J. Roy Stiles, (Retired).
Catechesis Religious Program—2825 Klondike Ln., Louisville, 40218. Mrs. Becky Box, D.R.E. Students 12.

8—ST. BERNADETTE PARISH (2008)
6500 St. Bernadette Ave., Prospect, 40059.
Tel: 502-245-2210; Fax: 502-442-0065; Email: tinal@stb2008.org; Web: www.stb2008.org. Revs. Jeffrey Scott Nicolas; Brandon DeToma; Deacons Todd C. Auffrey; Jerome L. Buehner.
Catechesis Religious Program—Mrs. Elizabeth Auffrey, D.R.E. Students 277.

9—ST. BERNARD (1963)
7500 Tangelo Dr., Louisville, 40228.
Tel: 502-239-5178; Email: stbparish@stbernardlou.com; Web: stbernardlou.com. Rev. Robert L. Stuempel; Deacons Philip Hettich; Michael Edwards.
School—St. Bernard School, (Grades PreK-8), Email: fklausing@stbernardlou.com. Fred J. Klausing III, Prin. Lay Teachers 26; Students 414.
Catechesis Religious Program—
Tel: 502-239-5178, Ext. 125. Cyndi Marlow, D.R.E. Students 50.

10—SAINT TERESA OF CALCUTTA PARISH (2008)
903 Fairdale Rd., Fairdale, 40118. Tel: 502-363-9929; Fax: 502-363-9960; Email: teresaofcalcutta@att.net; Web: www.teresaofcalcuttafairdale.weebly.com. Rev. Patrick J. Dolan, Ph.D., S.T.D.
Catechesis Religious Program—Email: btoc.dre@att.net. Theresa Watson, D.R.E. Students 68.

11—ST. BONIFACE (1836)
531 E. Liberty St., Louisville, 40202-1107.
Tel: 502-584-4279; Email: patty@stbonifaceparish.com; Web: stbonifaceparish.com. Very Rev. J. Mark Spalding, J.C.L., Presbyteral Mod.; Revs. Jeffrey P. Shooner; Adam Carrico; Deacon David R. Tomes.

12—ST. BRIGID (1873)
1520 Hepburn Ave., Louisville, 40204.
Tel: 502-584-5565; Email: Stbrigidlou@stbrigidlou.org; Web: www.heartofthehighlands.org. Revs. Gary T. Padgett; Joseph H. Voor, (Retired); Deacon Will Tribbey.

13—CHRIST THE KING (1928)
718 S. 44th St., Louisville, 40211. Tel: 270-432-5024; Email: christtheheale@scrtc.com. Rev. John T. Judie; Deacon K. Michael Burchett.
Catechesis Religious Program—Tel: 502-772-7851. Loueva Moss, D.R.E.

14—ST. EDWARD (1884) [CEM]
9608 Sue Helen Dr., Louisville, 40299.
Tel: 502-267-7494; Fax: 502-267-7495; Email: churchoffice@stedward.church; Web: www.stedwardchurch.com. Rev. Troy D. Overton.
School—St. Edward School, (Grades PreK-8), 9610 Sue Helen Dr., Louisville, 40299. Tel: 502-267-6633; Fax: 502-267-4474; Web: www.stedwardchurch.com/school/. David Bennett, Prin.; Diane Walsh, Librarian. Clergy 6; Lay Teachers 26; Students 378.
Catechesis Religious Program—
Tel: 502-267-7494, Ext. 16; Email: ahopper@stedward.church. Amy Hopper, Interim Dir. Parish Catechesis, Email: ahopper@stedwardchurch.com. Students 153.

15—ST. ELIZABETH ANN SETON (1975)
11501 Maple Way, Louisville, 40229. Rev. Maurice Hayes, O.F.M.Conv.; Deacon James C. Olrich.
Res.: 11507 Maple Way, Louisville, 40229.
Tel: 502-969-0004; Email: parishoffice@easeton.com; Web: easeton.com.
Catechesis Religious Program—Sr. Karla Kaelin, O.S.U.M.S.J., D.R.E. Students 42.

16—ST. ELIZABETH OF HUNGARY (1906)
Mailing Address: 747 Harrison Ave., Louisville, 40217. Tel: 502-637-7600; Fax: 502-637-3794; Email: parishoffice@paxchristilou.org; Web: www.paxchristilou.org. 1020 E. Burnett Ave., Louisville, 40217. Revs. Christopher S. Rhodes; Robert B. Gray, (Retired); Deacons Timothy D. Golden; Timothy E. Stewart.

17—EPIPHANY CATHOLIC CHURCH (1971)
914 Old Harrods Creek Rd., Louisville, 40223.
Tel: 502-245-9733; Email: office@epiphanycatholicchurch.org; Web: www.epiphanycatholicchurch.org. Rev. J. Randall Hubbard; Deacon Trey Mobley.
Catechesis Religious Program—Students 160.

18—ST. FRANCES OF ROME (1887)
2119 Payne St., Louisville, 40206. Tel: 502-896-8401; Email: stfranrome@sfrlou.org; Web: www.stfrancesofrome.org. Rev. Louis J. Meiman; Sr. Carmelita Dunn, S.C.N., Pastoral Assoc.; Deacon Ralph E. Bartley.
Catechesis Religious Program—Email: srmjgramig@sfrlou.org. Sr. Mary Jo Gramig, O.S.U., D.R.E. Students 74.

19—ST. FRANCIS OF ASSISI (1886)
1960 Bardstown Rd., Louisville, 40205-1572.
Tel: 502-456-6394; Email: smcgarvey@ccsfa.org; Web: www.ccsfachurch.org. Rev. Jeffrey D. Gatlin; Deacons Lawrence Biven; Darryl J. Diemer; Michael Sowers. In Res., Rev. Joseph T. Merkt, (Retired).
School—St. Francis of Assisi School, (Grades PreK-8), 1938 Alfresco Pl., Louisville, 40205-1876.
Tel: 502-459-3088; Email: sfrommeyer@ccsfa.org. Steve Frommeyer, Prin.; Sara Elmore, Librarian. Lay Teachers 28; Students 250.
Catechesis Religious Program—Email: jjones@ccsfa.org. JoAnn Jones, D.R.E. Students 32.

20—ST. GABRIEL THE ARCHANGEL (1953)
5505 Bardstown Rd., Louisville, 40291.
Tel: 502-239-5481; Email: parish@stgabriel.net; Web: stgabriel.net. Revs. John A. Schwartzlose; Shibu P. Devassykutty, C.M.I.; Deacons T. Stephen Bowling, St. Gabriel, Louisville, Director of Family Ministries Office; Michael Fitzmayer.
School—St. Gabriel the Archangel School, (Grades PreK-8), 5503 Bardstown Rd., Louisville, 40291.
Tel: 502-239-5535; Tel: 502-239-1298;
Fax: 502-231-1464; Email: school@stgabriel.net; Web: www.stgabriel.net. Lara Krill, Prin.; Meredith Kilner, Librarian. Clergy 1; Lay Teachers 41; Students 726.
Catechesis Religious Program—Email: mchoi@stgabriel.net. Mary Jane Choi, D.R.E. Students 86.

21—GOOD SHEPHERD (2009)

3525 Rudd Ave., Louisville, 40212. Tel: 502-749-9780; Fax: 502-749-8935; Email: secretary@goodshepherdchurch.us; Web: www.goodshepherdchurch.us. Revs. Charles D. Walker; Deogratias Ssamba, A.J.
Church: 3511 Rudd Ave., Louisville, 40212-2150.
Catechesis Religious Program—Students 16.

22—GUARDIAN ANGELS (1957)
6000 Preston Hwy., Louisville, 40219.
Tel: 502-968-5421; Email: guardangels@att.net. Rev. Jeffrey P. Leger.
Catechesis Religious Program—

23—HOLY FAMILY (1929)
3938 Poplar Level Rd., Louisville, 40213-1463. Deacon J. Patrick Wright, Parish Admin.; Revs. John Pozhathuparambil, O.F.M.Conv., Sacramental Moderator; George Munjanattu, Sacramental Mod.
Res.: 3926 Poplar Level Rd., Louisville, 40213.
Tel: 502-459-6066; Email: peggyb@hofaky.org; Web: holyfamilyky.org.
Catechesis Religious Program—

24—HOLY NAME (1891)
c/o Holy Trinity, 501 Cherrywood Rd., Louisville, 40207. Tel: 502-637-5560; Email: info@holynamelouisville.org; Web: www.holynamelouisville.org/. 2914 S. 3rd St., Louisville, 40207. Rev. William M. Bowling, Admin.
Catechesis Religious Program—Students 73.

25—HOLY SPIRIT (1937)
3345 Lexington Rd., Louisville, 40206.
Tel: 502-893-3982; Email: jhertzman@hspirit.org; Web: www.hspirit.org. Rev. Frederick W. Klotter, S.T.L., J.C.L.; Deacons Robert Hall, Email: bobcheri@twc.com; Bryan Bush; Anthon Brown.
School—Holy Spirit School, (Grades PreK-8), 322 Cannons Ln., Louisville, 40206. Tel: 502-893-7700; Fax: 502-893-8078; Email: dswenson@hspiritschool.org. Doris Swenson, Prin.; Stacy Lohman, Librarian. Lay Teachers 30; Students 437.
Catechesis Religious Program—Email: cmagee@hspirit.org. Carole Magee, D.R.E. Students 27.

26—HOLY TRINITY (1882)
501 Cherrywood Rd., Louisville, 40207.
Tel: 502-897-5207; Fax: 502-897-0962; Email: bcobb@htparish.org; Web: www.htparish.org. Revs. William M. Bowling; Kien Nguyen; J. Wayne Jenkins, (Retired); Deacons Walton G. Jones; Jeremiah S. Babin; J. Andrew Heinsohn.
School—Holy Trinity School, (Grades PreK-8), 423 Cherrywood Rd., Louisville, 40207.
Tel: 502-897-2785; Fax: 502-896-0990; Email: jrichards@ht-school.org. Mr. Jack Richards, Prin.; D. Dee Hill, Librarian, Email: dhill@ht-school.org. Clergy 3; Lay Teachers 40; Students 672.
Catechesis Religious Program—
Tel: 502-897-5207, Ext. 125. Students 81.

27—ST. IGNATIUS (1963)
1818 Rangeland Rd., Louisville, 40219.
Tel: 502-964-5904; Email: marysecsti@yahoo.com; Web: stignatiusmartyr.com. Rev. David A. Cockson.
Catechesis Religious Program—
Tel: 502-964-5904, Ext. 10. Students 23.

28—IMMACULATE HEART OF MARY (1953)
1545 Louis Coleman Jr. Dr., Louisville, 40211.
Tel: 502-774-5772; Email: irectory@bellsouth. Revs. Charles D. Walker; Deogratias Ssamba, A.J.; Deacons K. Michael Burchett; James Turner.
Catechesis Religious Program—Students 1.

29—INCARNATION (1966)
2229 Lower Hunters Trace Rd., Louisville, 40216.
Tel: 502-447-2013; Email: incarnationcatho@bellsouth.net; Web: www.incarnationcatholicchurch.org/. Rev. Christian Moore, O.F.M.Conv.; Deacons Robert Markert; Mark Patterson.

30—ST. JAMES (1906)
1826 Edenside Ave., Louisville, 40204.
Tel: 502-451-1420; Email: ahess@stjameslou.org; Web: stjameslou.org. Revs. Gary T. Padgett; Joseph H. Voor, (Retired); Deacon Will Tribbey.
School—St. James School, (Grades PreSchool-8), 1818 Edenside Ave., Louisville, 40204.
Tel: 502-454-0330; Fax: 502-454-0330; Email: stjames@stjamesbluejays.com; Web: www.stjamesbluejays.com. Jennifer Zimmerman, Admin. Lay Teachers 15; Students 180.
Catechesis Religious Program—Students 3.

31—ST. JOHN PAUL II (1953)
3042 Hikes Ln., Louisville, 40220-2017.
Tel: 502-459-4251; Fax: 502-459-9815; Email: dhoard@stjpiiparish.com; Email: parishoffice@stjpiiparish.com; Web: www.stjpiiparish.com. Rev. William P. Burks; Deacons Bruce Warren; James I. McGoff.
Catechesis Religious Program—Email: cmeyers@stjpiiparish.com. Curt Meyers, D.R.E. Students 31.

32—ST. JOHN VIANNEY (1951) Rev. Anthony Chinh N'go.
Res.: 4839 Southside Dr., Louisville, 40214.
Tel: 502-366-5517; Email: franthonyngo@yahoo.com.
Catechesis Religious Program—Sr. Clare Nguyen, D.R.E.; Mr. Thang Ly, D.R.E. Students 115.

33—ST. JOSEPH (1866)
1406 E. Washington St., Louisville, 40206.
Tel: 502-583-7401; Tel: 502-583-0892; Email: parish@sjosephcatholic.org; Web: sjosephcatholic.org. Rev. David Sanchez; Deacon Michael Shumway; Jennifer Tanselle, Business Mgr.; Wilson Wilder, Music Min.
Catechesis Religious Program—1420 E. Washington St., Louisville, 40206. Students 64.

34—ST. LAWRENCE (1953)
1925 Lewiston Dr., Louisville, 40216.
Tel: 502-448-2122; Email: secretary.lawrence@gmail.com; Web: stl-lawrence.org. Rev. Thomas A. Smith; Deacons David Dalton; Wayne Thieneman.
Catechesis Religious Program—Email: stlbillunruh@gmail.com. William (Bill) Unruh, D.R.E. Students 35.

35—ST. LEONARD (1953)
440 Zorn Ave., Louisville, 40206. Tel: 502-897-2595; Email: stlparish@stleonardlouisville.org; Web: www.stleonardlouisville.org. Rev. Louis J. Meiman; Monika Vowels, Business Mgr.; Ms. Jacqueline Rapp, J.D., J.C.L., Pastoral Assoc.; Deacon Ralph E. Bartley; Laura Meyer, Music Min.
School—St. Leonard School, (Grades PreK-8),
Tel: 502-897-5265; Email: mparola@stleonardlouisville.org. Mary Parola, Prin. Lay Teachers 20; Students 142.
Catechesis Religious Program—

36—ST. LOUIS BERTRAND (1866)
1104 S. 6th St., Louisville, 40203. Tel: 502-583-4448; Fax: 502-589-0056; Email: stlouisbertrand@stlb.org. Very Rev. Edward M. Gorman, O.P.; Revs. Louis Bertrand Lemoine, O.P.; Leon Martin Martiny, O.P.; Joseph Anthony Breen, O.P., In Res.; Francis Ralph, O.P., In Res.; Dominic Bump, O.P., In Res.; Emmanuel Bertrand, O.P., In Res.; Deacon William Klump.
Shrines—Lourdes Rosary Shrine, Inc.—
Blessed Margaret Castello Shrine.

37—ST. LUKE (1965)
4211 Jim Hawkins Dr., Louisville, 40229.
Tel: 502-969-3291; Email: stluke40229@gmail.com. Rev. Joseph M. Rankin. In Res., Rev. Gerald L. Bell, (Retired).
Catechesis Religious Program—Debbie Minton, D.R.E. Students 12.

38—ST. MARGARET MARY (1950)
7813 Shelbyville Rd., Louisville, 40222.
Tel: 502-426-1588; Email: parish@stmm.org; Web: www.stmm.org. Revs. William D. Hammer; John Erdman; Deacons Charles T. Bent; Derrick A. Barnes; John C. Koenig.
School—St. Margaret Mary School, (Grades K-8), Tel: 502-426-2635; Email: wsims@stmm.org. Wendy Sims, Prin. Lay Teachers 46; Students 724.
Catechesis Religious Program—Students 72.

39—ST. MARTHA (1960)
2825 Klondike Ln., Louisville, 40218.
Tel: 502-491-8535; Email: mschardein@stmarthachurch.org; Web: www.stmarthalouisville.org. Rev. Seejo Thandiackal, C.M.I.; Deacons John P. Maher; Daniel G. Bisig Sr.
School—St. Martha School, (Grades PreK-8),
Tel: 502-491-3171; Fax: 502-495-6107; Email: mbickett@stmarthaschool.org; Web: www.stmartharocks.com. Michael Bickett, Prin. Clergy 1; Lay Teachers 27; Students 341; Parish Population 1.
Catechesis Religious Program—Students 50.

40—ST. MARTIN DE PORRES (1990)
3112 W. Broadway, Louisville, 40211.
Tel: 502-778-1118; Fax: 502-778-1048; Email: Parrishoffice@stmartindeporrescatholic.org; Web: www.stmartindeporrescatholic.org. Revs. Charles D. Walker; Thomas E. Gentile, (Retired); Deogratias Ssamba, A.J.; Deacons James Turner; Keith L. McKenzie.
Catechesis Religious Program—Tel: 502-418-3447. Shantia Gully, Parish Office Coord.

41—ST. MARTIN OF TOURS (1853) Very Rev. R. Paul Beach, J.C.L.; Rev. David J. Carr; Deacons Robert C. Bryant; Richard P. Zoldak.
Res.: 639 S. Shelby St., Louisville, 40202.
Tel: 502-582-2827; Fax: 502-582-1780; Email: secretary@stmartinoftourschurch.org.
Catechesis Religious Program—Email: cindyheckmann@stmartinoftourschurch.org. Cindy Heckmann, D.R.E. Students 76.

42—MARY QUEEN OF PEACE PARISH (2009)
4005 Dixie Hwy., Louisville, 40216.
Tel: 502-448-4008; Email: mqop@twc.com; Web: www.MQOPShivelyky.org. Rev. Peter Bucalo; Deacon William Niemeier.
Catechesis Religious Program—Students 8.

43—ST. MICHAEL (1975)
3705 Stone Lakes Dr., Louisville, 40299.
Tel: 502-266-5611; Email: frdick@stmichaellouisville.org; Web: www.stmichaelchurch.org/. Rev. J. Richard Sullivan; Deacons Martin J. Brown; Kenneth J. Carter; Mark Kelley.
School—St. Michael School, (Grades K-8), 3703 Stone Lakes Dr., Louisville, 40299.
Tel: 502-267-6155; Fax: 502-267-1652; Email: stackett@stmichaellouisville.org. Stacy Tackett, Prin., Email: stackett@stmichaellouisville.org. Lay Teachers 58; Students 725.
Catechesis Religious Program—Email: brickert@stmichaellouisville.org; Email: mrogg@stmichaellouisville.org. Brenda Rickert, D.R.E. & Pastoral Assoc.; Maureen Rogg, RCIA Coord. Students 175.

44—MOST BLESSED SACRAMENT (1937)
Mailing Address: 4335 Hazelwood Ave., Louisville, 40215. 3509 Taylor Blvd., Louisville, 40215.
Tel: 502-361-0149; Email: mbs3509@aol.com. Rev. Steephen Koola, C.M.I., (India).
Catechesis Religious Program—Tel: 502-361-0960; Email: blanford@louisville.edu. Sandra Blanford, D.R.E. Students 15.

45—OUR LADY OF LOURDES (1950)
508 Breckenridge Ln., Louisville, 40207.
Tel: 502-896-0241; Email: cindys@ourlourdes.org; Email: olol@ourlourdes.org; Web: ourlourdes.org. Rev. Scott J. Wimsett; Deacon Timothy B. Ayers.
School—Our Lady of Lourdes School, (Grades K-8), 510 Breckenridge Ln., Louisville, 40207.
Tel: 502-895-5122; Fax: 502-893-5051; Email: jenniferb@ourlourdes.org. Jeffrey Beavin, Prin.; Ashley Hogue, Librarian. Lay Teachers 28; Students 428.
Catechesis Religious Program—
Tel: 502-896-0241, Ext. 13. Doug Wolz, D.R.E.; Beth Freeman, D.R.E. Students 48.

46—OUR LADY OF MOUNT CARMEL (1957)
5505 New Cut Rd., Louisville, 40214.
Tel: 502-366-1463; Email: jstieren@southendcatholic.com. Rev. Philip Lee Erickson, J.C.L.; Deacons Michael A. Tolbert; Terry Maguire; W. Timothy Johnson; Johnny Fellonneav.
Catechesis Religious Program—6105 S. Third St., Louisville, 40214. Tel: 502-366-1463;
Fax: 502-366-1464. Students 50.

47—OUR MOTHER OF SORROWS (1937)
747 Harrison Ave., Louisville, 40217.
Tel: 502-637-7600; Fax: 502-637-3794; Email: parishoffice@paxchristilou.org; Web: www.paxchristilou.org. 760 Eastern Pkwy., Louisville, 40217. Revs. Christopher S. Rhodes; Robert B. Gray, (Retired); Deacons Timothy E. Stewart; Timothy D. Golden.

48—ST. PATRICK (1988)
1000 N. Beckley Station Rd., Louisville, 40245.
Tel: 502-244-6083; Email: ourparish@stpatlou.org; Web: www.stpatlou.org. Revs. Jeffrey P. Shooner; Robert E. Osborne, (Retired); Adam Carrico; Deacons Gregory M. Gitschier; Scott R. Haner; Mark J. Rougeux.
School—St. Patrick School, (Grades PreK-8),
Tel: 502-244-7083; Email: nsturtzel@stpatlou.org. Nathan Sturtzel, Prin. Lay Teachers 43; Students 619.
Catechesis Religious Program—R. Tim Grove, Dir.; Jonna O'Bryan, Dir. Students 250.

49—ST. PAUL (1851) [CEM]
6901 Dixie Hwy., Louisville, 40258.
Tel: 502-935-1223; Email: stpaulacct@mw.twcbc.com. Rev. Dismas J. Veeneman, O.F.M.Conv.; Deacons Charles Beckmann; Gary W. Fowler; Rev. Adam Bunnell, O.F.M.Conv., In Res.
School—St. Paul School, (Grades PreK-8),
Tel: 502-935-5511; Email: jen.burba@saintpaulschool.net. Jennifer Burba, Prin. Lay Teachers 21; Students 285.
Catechesis Religious Program—Tel: 502-935-1325. Amy Gaekle, Dir. Faith Formation. Students 41.

50—ST. PETER THE APOSTLE PARISH (2008)
Mailing Address: 5431 Johnsontown Rd., Louisville, 40272. Rev. Christopher B. Lubecke; Deacons Stephen Smith, Email: ssmith@saintpeterapostle.org; Gregory L. Klinglesmith.
Parish Office: 7718 Columbine Dr., Louisville, 40258.
Tel: 502-937-5920; Email: bcolyer@saintpeterapostle.org; Web: www.saintpeterapostle.org.
School—St. Andrew Academy, (Grades PreK-8), 7724 Columbine Dr., Louisville, 40258. Tel: 502-935-4578; Email: barbaraschrader@saintandrewacademy.com. Stuart Cripe, Prin.; Stephanie Blandford, Resource Teacher/Counselor; Doris Baines, Librarian. Sponsored by St. Peter the Apostle Parish. Lay Teachers 16; Students 279.
Catechesis Religious Program—Email: browland@saintpeterapostle.org. Betty Rowland, D.R.E. Students 60.

51—ST. RAPHAEL THE ARCHANGEL (1947)
Mailing Address: 2141 Lancashire Ave., Louisville, 40205. Fax: 502-458-8049; Fax: 502-458-2500; Email: sleon@sraparish.org. Rev. Shayne R. Duvall.
School—St. Raphael the Archangel School, (Grades

K-8), 2131 Lancashire Ave., Louisville, 40205.
Tel: 502-456-1541; Fax: 502-451-3632; Email: jtabor@straphaelschool.org. Ms. Michelle Brandle, Prin. Lay Teachers 29; Students 360.
Catechesis Religious Program—Students 6.

52—ST. RITA (1921)
8709 Preston Hwy., Louisville, 40219.
Tel: 502-969-4579; Email: wpuga@saintrita.net; Web: saintrita.net. Rev. Joseph M. Rankin; Deacons Aurelio A. Puga; Kenneth J. Mitchell. In Res., Rev. Gerald L. Bell, (Retired).
School—St. Rita School, (Grades PreK-8), Tel: 502-969-7067; Email: nhulsewede@stritacatholicschool.com. Neil Hulsewede, Prin. Lay Teachers 20; Students 309.
Catechesis Religious Program—Students 150.

53—SS. SIMON AND JUDE (1950)
4335 Hazelwood Ave., Louisville, 40215.
Tel: 502-368-4887; Email: simonandjude4335@aol.com. Rev. Stephen Koola, C.M.I., (India).
Catechesis Religious Program—Email: blanford@louisville.edu. Sandra Blanford, D.R.E. Students 13.

54—ST. STEPHEN, MARTYR (1948)
2931 Pindell Ave., Louisville, 40217.
Tel: 502-635-5813; Email: cbutler@ssmartyr.org. Rev. Harry J. Gelthaus, hgelthaus@ssmartyr.org; Deacons Sylvester Nitzken; Stephen J. DaPonte.
School—St. Stephen, Martyr School, (Grades PreK-8), Tel: 502-635-7141; Fax: 502-635-1576; Email: Bbritt@ssmartyr.org; Web: www.ssmartyr.org. Bridget Britt, Prin. Clergy 1; Lay Teachers 18; Students 291.
Catechesis Religious Program—Email: ssmith@ssmartyr.org. Stacey Smith, D.R.E. Students 2,797.

55—ST. THERESE (1908)
Mailing Address: 747 Harrison Ave., Louisville, 40217. Tel: 502-637-7600; Fax: 502-637-3794; Email: parishoffice@paxchristilou.org; Web: www.paxchristilou.org. 1010 Schiller Ave., Louisville, 40204. Revs. Christopher S. Rhodes; Robert B. Gray, (Retired); Deacons Timothy E. Stewart; Timothy D. Golden.

56—ST. THOMAS MORE (1944)
6105 S. Third St., Louisville, 40214.
Tel: 502-366-1463; Email: bcrask@southendcatholic.com. Rev. Philip Lee Erickson, J.C.L.; Deacons Michael A. Tolbert; Terry Maguire; W. Timothy Johnson.
Catechesis Religious Program—Email: jstieren@southendcatholic.com. Julie Stieren, D.R.E. Students 29.

57—ST. WILLIAM (1901)
1226 W. Oak St., Louisville, 40210.
Tel: 502-635-6307; Email: stwilliamchurchlouisville@gmail.com; Web: www.stwilliamchurch.org. Rev. John R. Burke, Sacramental Mod., (Retired); Sharan A. Benton, Pastoral Admin.; Dawn Dones, Pastoral Assoc.
Catechesis Religious Program—Joseph Grant, D.R.E. Students 30.

OUTSIDE THE CITY OF LOUISVILLE

ALBANY, CLINTON CO., EMMANUEL CATHOLIC (1975)
Mailing Address: P.O. Box 160, Albany, 42602. Hwy. 127 N., Albany, 42607. Tel: 606-387-7251; Email: emmanuelskm@windstream.net. Rev. Devassya P. Kanattu, C.M.I.
Catechesis Religious Program—
Mission—Holy Cross Catholic Church, 264 Glasgow Rd., Burkesville, 42717. Tel: 270-864-4107.

BARDSTOWN, NELSON CO.

1—BASILICA OF ST. JOSEPH PROTO-CATHEDRAL (1816) [CEM]
310 W. Stephen Foster Ave., P.O. Box 548, Bardstown, 40004. Tel: 502-348-3126; Email: stjoe@bardstown.com; Web: www.stjosephbasilica.org. Revs. Terry L. Bradshaw; Anthony Minh Vu; Deacons Richard J. Walsh; John Hamilton; Rev. C. Joseph Batcheldor, (Retired).
School—Basilica of St. Joseph Proto-Cathedral School, (Grades PreK-8), 320 W. Stephen Foster Ave., Bardstown, 40004. Tel: 502-348-5994; Fax: 502-348-4694; Email: mbowen@stjoeelem.ort. Margaret Bowen, Prin.; Tricia Payne, Librarian. Lay Teachers 22; Preschool 40; Students 386.
Child Care—St. Joseph Montessori Children's Center, 161 West Dr., Nazareth, 40048. Tel: 502-348-1548; Fax: 502-331-4050.
Catechesis Religious Program—Email: robin.mcleake@gmail.com. Robin Leake, D.R.E. Students 95.

2—ST. MONICA (1956)
407 S. Third St., Bardstown, 40004.
Tel: 502-348-5250; Email: saintmonicabardstown@gmail.com; Web: stmonicabardstown.org. Rev. James Jason Harris; Deacon Scott R. Turner.

BRANDENBURG, MEADE CO., ST. JOHN THE APOSTLE (1892) [CEM]
515 Broadway, Brandenburg, 40108.
Tel: 270-422-2196; Email: sjsecretary@bbtel.com. Rev. Kevin J. Bryan; Deacon J. Michael Jones.
Catechesis Religious Program—Monica Lucas, D.R.E. Students 208.

CALVARY, MARION CO., HOLY NAME OF MARY (1798) [CEM]
Mailing Address: 235 S. Spalding Ave., Lebanon, 40033. Tel: 270-692-3019; Tel: 270-692-6491; Email: andreaw@staugustinechurch.net; Email: staugustinechurch@staugustinechurch.net. 3295 Hwy. 208, Lebanon, 40033. Revs. Mark M. Hamilton; David Farrell, Parochial Vicar; Deacons Dennis May; Joseph R. Dant; Kathy Shannon, Pastoral Assoc.
Catechesis Religious Program—Email: mikel@staugustinechurch.net. Mike Luescher, D.R.E. Students 67.

CAMPBELLSVILLE, TAYLOR CO., OUR LADY OF PERPETUAL HELP (1879) [CEM]
213 University Dr., Campbellsville, 42719. 425 North Central Ave., Campbellsville, 42718.
Tel: 270-465-4282; Email: ourladycatholic@windstream.net; Web: www.onfirecatholic.com. Rev. Saju M. Vadakumpadan, C.M.I.
Catechesis Religious Program—429 N. Central Ave., Campbellsville, 42718. Students 31.
Mission—Our Lady of Fatima, 70566 Calvary Rd., Campbellsville, 42718.

CECILIA, HARDIN CO., ST. AMBROSE (1879)
Mailing Address: St. James Church, 611 E. Main St., Cecilia, 42727. Tel: 270-862-5343; Email: stambrose@windstream.net. 609 East Main St., Cecilia, 42724. Rev. Benedict J. Brown, Admin.
Catechesis Religious Program—

CLEMENTSVILLE, CASEY CO., ST. BERNARD (1802)
5075 KY 551, Liberty, 42539. Tel: 606-787-7570; Email: sbchurch1@windstream.net. Rev. George Otuma, A.J., Admin.
Catechesis Religious Program—Tel: 606-787-6600.
Mission—Sacred Heart, c/o 5075 KY 551, Liberty, Casey Co. 42539.

CULVERTOWN, NELSON CO., IMMACULATE CONCEPTION
Mailing Address: 413 First St., New Haven, 40051-6030. Tel: 502-549-3680; Email: parishoffice@saintcatherineschool.com; Web: stcatherinenewhaven.org. 8191 New Haven Rd., New Haven, 40051. Rev. Matthew T. Hardesty; Deacon William A. Downs.

EDMONTON, METCALFE CO., CHRIST THE HEALER (1975)
Mailing Address: P.O. Box 599, Edmonton, 42129. 1610 W. Stockton St., Edmonton, 42129.
Tel: 270-432-5024; Tel: 270-432-0686; Email: christtheheale@scrtc.com. Deacon John Froehlich, Admin.; Rev. Wilfredo Luder Fernandez, Admin.
Catechesis Religious Program—Tel: 270-452-5024. Emmert Dee, D.R.E. Students 20.
Mission—Christ the King, P.O. Box 518, Tompkinsville, Monroe Co. 42167. 1000 Celina Rd., Tompkinsville, 42167.

ELIZABETHTOWN, HARDIN CO., ST. JAMES (1851) [CEM]
307 W. Dixie Ave., Elizabethtown, 42701.
Tel: 270-765-6268; Email: parishoffice@stjames-etown.org; Web: www.stjames-etown.org. Revs. Martin A. Linebach; Michael Sanders; Deacons William Clark; Karl A. Drerup.
School—St. James School, (Grades PreK-8), 401 Robinbrooke Blvd., Elizabethtown, 42701.
Tel: 270-765-7011; Fax: 270-769-5745; Email: jzimmermansis@gmail.com. Martha West, Librarian. Lay Teachers 29; Students 503.
Catechesis Religious Program—Email: sranickel@stjames-etown.org. Sr. Augusta Nickel, O.P., D.R.E. Students 174.

FAIRFIELD, NELSON CO., ST. MICHAEL (1792) [CEM]
Mailing Address: P.O. Box 27, Fairfield, 40020. Rev. John R. Johnson.
Res.: 111 Church St., P.O. Box 27, Fairfield, 40020.
Tel: 502-252-0106; Email: office@stmichaelfairfield.org.
Catechesis Religious Program—Gilly Simpson, D.R.E. Students 48.

FINLEY, TAYLOR CO., OUR LADY OF THE HILLS (1908) [CEM]
213 University Dr., Campbellsville, 42718. 9259 Old Lebanon Rd., Finley, 42718. Tel: 270-465-4282; Email: ourladycatholic@windstream.net; Web: www.onfirecatholic.com. Rev. Saju M. Vadakumpadan, C.M.I.
Catechesis Religious Program—9259 Old Lebanon Rd., Campbellsville, 42718. Students 24.

FLAHERTY, MEADE CO., ST. MARTIN OF TOURS (1848) [CEM]
440 Saint Martin Rd., Vine Grove, 40175.
Tel: 270-828-2552; Email: stmartinfl@bbtel.com; Web: stmartinfl.org. Rev. Jeffrey G. Hopper; Deacons John R. Whelan; Joseph D. Calvert.
Catechesis Religious Program—Tel: 270-828-8484; Email: stmformation@bbtel.com. Regina Bennett, D.R.E. Students 106.

GLASGOW, BARREN CO., ST. HELEN (1893)
103 W. Brown St., Glasgow, 42141.
Tel: 270-651-5263; Email: sthelen@glasgow-ky.com. Revs. Ben Cameron, C.P.M.; Victor Moratin, C.P.M.; Deacons Lee Bidwell; David U. Smith.
Catechesis Religious Program—Students 55.
Mission—Our Lady of the Caves Church, 1010 S. Dixie St., Horse Cave, 42749.

GREENSBURG, GREEN CO., HOLY REDEEMER (1969)
Mailing Address: P.O. Box 190, Columbia, 42728.
Tel: 270-384-4528; Email: churchoffice@southernkycatholics.org. 110 Industrial Dr., Greensburg, 42743. Rev. Joseph Thomas, C.M.I.
Catechesis Religious Program—Students 4.

HODGENVILLE, LARUE CO., OUR LADY OF MERCY (1853) [CEM]
208 Walters Ave., Hodgenville, 42748.
Tel: 270-358-4697; Email: olmparish@windstream.net. Rev. Pablo A. Hernandez; Deacon James A. Cecil.
Catechesis Religious Program—Tel: 270-325-3801. Students 27.

HOLY CROSS, MARION CO., HOLY CROSS (1785) [CEM]
Mailing Address: 200 School Dr., P.O. Box 74, Loretto, 40037. Tel: 270-865-2521; Email: sfahc@richm.twcbc.com; Web: sfahc.com. 59 New Haven Rd., Loretto, 40037. Rev. Bryan Lamberson, Admin.
Catechesis Religious Program—Carol Blanford, D.R.E. Students 23.

HOWARDSTOWN, NELSON CO., ST. ANN (1862) [CEM]
7490 Howardstown Rd., Howardstown, 40051.
Tel: 502-286-3181; Email: staschool@hughes.net. Rev. Pablo A. Hernandez.
School—St. Ann School, Tel: 502-549-7210; Email: staschool@hughes.net. Lois Cecil, Prin. Lay Teachers 1; Students 15.

JAMESTOWN, RUSSELL CO., HOLY SPIRIT (1953)
Mailing Address: P.O. Box 190, Columbia, 42728. 406 N. Main St., Jamestown, 42629.
Tel: 270-343-3346; Email: churchoffice@southernkycatholics.org. Rev. Joseph Thomas, C.M.I.
Catechesis Religious Program—Students 48.
Mission—Good Shepherd (1964) 1221 Greensburg St., P.O. Box 190, Columbia, Adair Co. 42728.
Tel: 270-384-4528.

LAGRANGE, OLDHAM CO., IMMACULATE CONCEPTION (1962)
502 N. Fifth Ave., LaGrange, 40031.
Tel: 502-222-0255; Email: monica.breitholle@iclagrange.org; Web: iclagrange.org. Rev. Anthony L. Chandler, M.A.; Deacons Thomas M. McNally; Robert R. Caruso.
Catechesis Religious Program—Email: susan.ashby@iclagrange.org. Susan Ashby, Children's Family Min. Students 283.
Stations—Kentucky State Reformatory—LaGrange. Tel: 502-222-9441.
Cedar Lake Lodge, La Grange, 40032.
Tel: 502-222-7157.
Baptist Hospital Northeast, LaGrange.
Tel: 502-222-5388.
Richwood Nursing Home, La Grange, 40032.
Tel: 502-222-3186.

LEBANON JUNCTION, BULLITT CO., ST. BENEDICT (1907)
Mailing Address: 187 S. Plum St., Shepherdsville, 40165. Rev. Brian A. Kenney; Deacon Theodore C. Luckett.
Res.: 211 W. Oak St., Lebanon Junction, 40150.
Tel: 502-543-5918; Email: parish@stafalcons.com.
Catechesis Religious Program—Students 2.

LEBANON, MARION CO., ST. AUGUSTINE (1815) [CEM]
235 S. Spalding Ave., Lebanon, 40033.
Tel: 270-692-3019; Email: staugustinechurch@staugustinechurch.net; Web: staugustinechurch.net. Revs. Mark M. Hamilton; David Farrell; Deacons Joseph R. Dant; Dennis May; Kathy Shannon, Pastoral Assoc.
School—St. Augustine School, (Grades PreK-8), 236 S. Spalding Ave., Lebanon, 40033. Tel: 270-692-2063; Fax: 270-692-6597; Email: pterrell@saintaschool.net. Paul Terrell, Prin.; Paula Mattingly, Librarian. Lay Teachers 12; Students 177.
Catechesis Religious Program—Mike Luescher, D.R.E. Students 77.

MOUNT WASHINGTON, BULLITT CO., ST. FRANCIS XAVIER (1846) [CEM]
155 Stringer Ln., Mount Washington, 40047.
Tel: 502-538-4933; Email: frontoffice@sfxmw.com. Rev. R. Dale Cieslik; Deacons Gerald J. Mattingly; Stephen A. Age.
Catechesis Religious Program—Email: darlene.fowler@sfxmw.com. Darlene Fowler, D.R.E.

NEW HAVEN, NELSON CO., ST. CATHERINE (1844) [CEM]
Mailing Address: 413 First St., New Haven, 40051.
Tel: 502-549-3680; Email: parishoffice@saintcatherineschool.com; Web: stcatherinenewhaven.org. 174 N. Main St., New Haven, 40051. Rev. Matthew T. Hardesty.
School—St. Catherine School, (Grades PreK-8),

Email: jobryan@stcatherineacademy.net. Jo Renee O'Bryan, Prin. Lay Teachers 6; Students 90.

NEW HOPE, NELSON CO., ST. VINCENT DE PAUL (1820) [CEM]
Mailing Address: P.O. Box 58, New Hope, 40052.
Tel: 502-549-3680; Fax: 502-549-5410; Email: parishoffice@saintcatherineschool.com. 104 Church St., New Hope, 40052. Rev. Matthew T. Hardesty.
Catechesis Religious Program—Norine Masterson, D.R.E. Students 44.

PAYNEVILLE, MEADE CO., ST. MARY MAGDALEN OF PAZZI (1883) [CEM]
110 Hwy. 376, P.O. Box 110, Payneville, 40157.
Tel: 270-496-4333; Fax: 270-496-4790; Email: stmarymag@bbtel.com; Web: www.stmarypayneville.org. Rev. George Illikkal, C.M.I., (India); Deacon Gregory A. Beavin.
Catechesis Religious Program—200 Hwy 376, P.O. Box 110, Payneville, 40157. Tel: 270-496-4587. Susan McCoy, D.R.E. Students 122.

PEWEE VALLEY, OLDHAM CO., ST. ALOYSIUS (1871) [CEM]
212 Mount Mercy Dr., Pewee Valley, 40056.
Tel: 502-241-8452; Tel: 502-241-8516; Email: parishoffice@staloysiuspwv.org. Rev. John J. Stoltz; Deacons Charles Brown; Thomas L. Roth; Dan E. Parker; Phillip L. Noltemeyer.
School—St. Aloysius School, (Grades PreK-8), 122 Mt. Mercy Dr., Pewee Valley, 40056.
Tel: 502-241-8516; Fax: 502-243-2241; Email: schooloffice@staloysiuspwv.org. Maryann Hayslip, Prin.; Becky Johnson, Librarian. Lay Teachers 27; Students 417.
Catechesis Religious Program—
Tel: 502-241-8452, Ext. 1036. Students 205.
Mission—Korean Catholic Community.
Station—Kentucky Correctional Institute for Women, Pewee Valley. Tel: 502-241-8454.

RADCLIFF, HARDIN CO., ST. CHRISTOPHER (1958) [CEM]
1225 S. Wilson Rd., Radcliff, 40160.
Tel: 270-351-3706; Fax: 270-351-1225; Email: church@stchristopherparish.org; Web: www.stchristopherparish.org/. Rev. Jeffrey G. Hopper.
Catechesis Religious Program—Students 65.

RAYWICK, MARION CO., ST. FRANCIS XAVIER CHURCH (1837) [CEM] Rev. David W. Naylor.
Res.: 108 Main St., Raywick, 40060.
Tel: 270-692-2245; Email: raywickchurch@windstream.net.
Catechesis Religious Program—Students 65.

RHODELIA, MEADE CO., ST. THERESA (1818) [CEM]
9245 Rhodelia Rd., Payneville, 40157.
Tel: 270-496-4362; Fax: 270-496-4416; Email: sttheresa@bbtel.com; Web: www.sttheresarhodelia.org. Rev. George Illikkal, C.M.I., (India); Deacon Gregory A. Beavin.
Catechesis Religious Program— Twinned with St. Mary Magdalen of Pazzi 200 Hwy. 376, Payneville, 40157. Tel: 270-496-4333. Students 122.

ST. FRANCIS, MARION CO., ST. FRANCIS OF ASSISI CHURCH (1870) [CEM]
200 School Dr., P.O. Box 74, Loretto, 40037.
Tel: 270-865-2521; Email: sfahc@richm.twcbc.com. 6785 Hwy. 52, Loretto, 40037. Rev. Bryan Lamberson, Admin.
Res.: 6785 Hwy. 52, Loretto, 40037.
Tel: 270-865-2075; Email: sfahc@richm.twcbc.com; Web: sfahc.org.
Catechesis Religious Program—Carol Blanford, D.R.E. Students 85.

ST. JOHN, HARDIN CO., ST. JOHN THE BAPTIST (1829) [CEM]
c/o St. Brigid Church, 314 E, Main St., Vine Grove, 40175. Rev. Daniel L. Lincoln; Deacon Mike Ryan.
Res.: 657 St. John Church Rd., Elizabethtown, 42701. Tel: 270-862-9816; Email: brigidvg@bbtel.com.
Catechesis Religious Program—Tel: 270-735-6930; Email: mcnutt@bbtel.com. Lisa Thomas, D.R.E. Students 61.

ST. MARY, MARION CO., ST. CHARLES (1786) [CEM]
675 Hwy. 327, Lebanon, 40033. Tel: 270-692-4513; Fax: 270-638-6204; Email: saintcharles@windstream.net. Rev. David W. Naylor.
Catechesis Religious Program—Students 52.

ST. THOMAS, NELSON CO., ST. THOMAS (1812)
870 Saint Thomas Ln., Bardstown, 40004.
Tel: 502-348-3717; Email: stthomas@bardstown.com; Email: jjharrisjj@gmail.com. Rev. James Jason Harris, Admin.; Deacons Samuel R. Filiatreau; Scott R. Turner.
Catechesis Religious Program—Students 65.

SAMUELS, NELSON CO., ST. GREGORY (1845) [CEM]
330 Samuels Loop, Cox's Creek, 40013.
Tel: 502-348-6337; Email: stgregory@stgregoryparish.org; Web: www.stgregoryparish.org. Rev. Peter Quan Do.
School—St. Gregory School, (Grades PreK-8), 350 Samuel's Loop, Cox's Creek, 40013.
Tel: 502-348-9583; Fax: 502-348-9597; Email: camille.Boone@stgregoryparish.org. Camille Boone, Prin.; Sr. Rosemary Rule, Librarian. Lay Teachers 13; Students 200.
Catechesis Religious Program—Email: clara.fulkerson@stgregoryparish.org. Clara Fulkerson, D.R.E.; Renelle Stallings, Adult Faith Formation. Students 104.

SHELBYVILLE, SHELBY CO., ANNUNCIATION OF THE BLESSED VIRGIN MARY (1860)
120 Main St., Shelbyville, 40065. Tel: 502-633-1547; Email: parishoffice@ourcoa.org; Web: www.ourcoa.org. 105 Main St., Shelbyville, 40065. Rev. T. Michael Tobin, S.T.L., J.C.B.; Deacons Brendan Kinsella; Robert J. Hart; Joseph E. Bland.
Catechesis Religious Program—Students 245.
Mission—St. John Chrysostom (1873) 122 Penn St., P.O. Box 74, Eminence, Henry Co. 40019.
Tel: 502-845-7005.

SHEPHERDSVILLE, BULLITT CO., ST. ALOYSIUS (1911)
187 S. Plum St., Shepherdsville, 40165.
Tel: 502-543-5918; Email: parish@stafalcons.com. Rev. Brian A. Kenney; Deacon Theodore C. Luckett.
Catechesis Religious Program—Students 11.

SPRINGFIELD, WASHINGTON CO.
1—ST. DOMINIC (1843) [CEM]
303 W. Main St., Springfield, 40069.
Tel: 859-336-3569; Email: stdom@bellsouth.net. Rev. Trumie C. Elliott.
School—St. Dominic School, (Grades PreK-8), 312 W. High St., Springfield, 40069. Tel: 859-336-7165; Email: pbreunig@stdominicelementary.org. Pamela Breunig, Prin. Lay Teachers 15; Students 225.
Catechesis Religious Program—Email: stdomdre@bellsouth.net. Students 74.
2—HOLY ROSARY (1929)
Mailing Address: Box 146, Springfield, 40069.
Tel: 859-336-3898; Fax: 859-336-3893; Email: kyholyrosary3860@att.net. 378 Rosary Heights, Springfield, 40069. Rev. Kevin Anthony McGrath, O.P.
Catechesis Religious Program—378 Rosary Hts., Springfield, 40069. Email: plgrundy@bellsouth.net. Pamela Grundy, D.R.E. Students 38.
3—HOLY TRINITY (1883) [CEM]
306 Fredericktown Rd., Springfield, 40069.
Tel: 859-284-5242; Email: htr@bardstown.com. Rev. Michael Martin, C.M.I., Admin.; Deacon Richard Fagan.
Catechesis Religious Program—Chris Riley, D.R.E. Students 31.
Mission—Holy Rosary-Manton, [CEM] 6964 Cissellvile Rd., Springfield, Washington Co. 40069.
4—ST. ROSE (1806) [CEM]
868 Loretto Rd., P.O. Box 71, Springfield, 40069.
Tel: 859-336-3121; Email: strose3121@att.net. Revs. Kevin Anthony McGrath, O.P.; Edmund Ditton, O.P.; Deacon William D. Coulter; Rev. William Luke Tancrell, O.P., In Res.; Bro. Gerard Thayer, In Res.
Catechesis Religious Program—Students 62.

VINE GROVE, HARDIN CO., ST. BRIGID (1908) [CEM]
314 E. Main St., Vine Grove, 40175.
Tel: 270-877-2461; Email: brigidvg@bbtel.com; Web: stbrigidvg.org. Rev. Daniel L. Lincoln; Deacon Michael A. Ryan.
Catechesis Religious Program—Students 108.

WHITE MILLS, HARDIN CO., ST. IGNATIUS (1842) [CEM]
Mailing Address: P.O. Box 67, White Mills, 42788.
Cell: 270-234-4191; Email: kitamike@outlook.com. 7786 Sonora Hardin Springs Rd., White Mills, 42788. Rev. Benedict J. Brown.
Catechesis Religious Program—Students 6.

Chaplains of Public Institutions

LOUISVILLE. *Central State Hospital*. Rev. John R. Johnson.
Jewish Hospital and Sts. Mary & Elizabeth Hospital. Rev. David A. Cockson, Chap.
Norton Hospitals. Rev. Expedito Muwonge.

On Duty Outside the Archdiocese:
Revs.—
Bromwich, James S., P.O. Box 9036, Fort Wayne, IN 46899
Dittmeier, Charles R., 8905 Yellow Wood Pl., Louisville, 40242
Do, Tung Minh, 631 High St., Prahran East, Victoria Australia 3181
Langford, Terry L., 712 Anderman Ln., Apt. 102, Darien, IL 60561. 4121 E. Busch Blvd., Apt. 701, Tampa, FL 33617
Reinhart, James M., (Retired), 6024 Marshall Ave., Chicago Ridge, IL 60415
Stevens, Gladstone H., S.S., 320 Middlefield Rd., Menlo Park, CA 94025
Whelan, Daniel, P.O. Box 9036, Fort Wayne, IN 46899.

Retired:
Revs.—
Abel, Robert M., (Retired), 375 School Side Dr., Brandenburg, 40108
Batcheldor, C. Joseph, (Retired), P.O. Box 548, Bardstown, 40004
Bell, Gerald L., (Retired), 4211 Jim Hawkins Dr., Louisville, 40229
Birk, John W., (Retired), 2082 Douglass Blvd., #1, Louisville, 40205
Boland, Thomas L., (Retired), 11802 Big Horn Pl., Louisville, 40299
Breen, Bernard J., (Retired), 4875 Sherbur 3-B, Louisville, 40207
Burke, John R., (Retired), 1826 Edenside Ave., Louisville, 40204
Caldwell, John A., (Retired), 13618 Surefire Ln., #101, Louisville, 40245
Clark, Thomas R., (Retired), 407 D S. Third St., Bardstown, 40004
Cousens, Dennis L., (Retired), 7604 Cantrell Dr., Crestwood, 40014
Craycroft, Bernard L., (Retired), 388 University Dr., Radcliff, 40160
Crews, Clyde F., (Retired), 2001 Newburg Rd., Louisville, 40205
Deatrick, John D., (Retired), 3806 Village Green Dr., Louisville, 40299
Delahanty, Patrick D., (Retired), 613 Zane St., Louisville, 40203
Domhoff, Ronald J., (Retired), 903 Fairdale Rd., Fairdale, 40118
Eifler, John G., (Retired), 572 Upland Rd., Louisville, 40206
Fichteman, William L., (Retired), 3309 Heather Lane, Louisville, 40218
Flynn, James E., (Retired), Masonic Home Dr., #106, Bldg. 290, Masonic Home, 40041
Fowler, Joseph M., (Retired), 1718 Bonnycastle Ave., Louisville, 40213
Gentile, Thomas E., (Retired), 2603 Hardwood Ct., Louisville, 40214
Graf, James W., (Retired), 384 N. Hurricane Hills, Boston, 40107
Graffis, Joseph T., (Retired), 4112 Massie Ave., #2, Louisville, 40207
Gray, Robert B., (Retired), 1278 Parkway Gardens Ct., Louisville, 40217
Griner, William S., (Retired), 11110 Old Harrods Creek Ct., Louisville, 40223
Hackett, James F., (Retired), 740 Zorn Ave., #2B/C, Louisville, 40206
Hall, Joseph S., (Retired), 310 Boxwood Run Rd., Mt. Washington, 40047
Hayden, Joseph F., (Retired), 9208 Newbury Ct., Prospect, 40059
Hill, Donald M., (Retired), 5105 Gemma Way Apt. 108, Louisville, 40219
Jenkins, Wayne, (Retired), 501 Cherrywood Rd., Louisville, 40207
Kamber, Kenneth L., (Retired), 4029 Busath Ave., Louisville, 40218
Knott, J. Ronald, D.Min., (Retired), 1271 Parkway Gardens Ct., #106, Louisville, 40217
Lyon, Joseph A., (Retired), 2120 Payne St., Louisville, 40206
Merkt, Joseph T., (Retired), 1960 Bardstown Rd., Louisville, 40205
Miller, William, (Retired), 3517 Nanz Ave., Louisville, 40207
Mouser, Joseph Irvin, (Retired), 3940 Poplar Level Rd., Louisville, 40213
Mudd, James T., (Retired), 3817 Greenhurst, Louisville, 40299
Murphy, James Wayne, (Retired), 7908 Woodfern Way, Louisville, 40291
Osborne, Robert E., (Retired), 3910 Village Green Dr., Louisville, 40299
Ray, Robert E., (Retired), 4720 Southern Pkwy., Louisville, 40214
Reilly, Robert E., (Retired), 2120 Payne St., Louisville, 40206
Reinhart, James M., (Retired), 6024 Marshall Ave., Chicago Ridge, IL 60415
Reteneller, Charles E., (Retired), 2120 Payne St., Louisville, 40206
Rice, G. Nicholas, (Retired), 214 Eline Ave., Louisville, 40207
Ryan, Donald P., (Retired), 3525 Ephraim McDowell Dr., #128, Louisville, 40216
Scaglione, Paul A., (Retired), 4720 Southern Pkwy., Louisville, 40214
Scheich, Eugene, (Retired), P.O. Box 91348, Louisville, 40228
Spalding, Leon C., (Retired), 1305 Donard Park Way, Louisville, 40218
Springman, Donald W., (Retired), 8028 St. Andrews Village Dr., Louisville, 40241
Stiles, J. Roy, (Retired), 2042 Buechel Bank Rd., Louisville, 40218
Timmel, Gerald L., (Retired), 2120 Payne St., #329, Louisville, 40206

Volpert, Robert C., (Retired), 3004 Aspenwood Way, Louisville, 40241
Voor, Joseph H., (Retired), 1826 Edenside Ave., Louisville, 40204
Wagner, William F., (Retired), Casa Granada Bldg. 3, Breckenridge Ln. #136, Louisville, 40220
Wilson, Albert L., (Retired), 2120 Payne St., #312, Louisville, 40206
Zettel, David H., (Retired), 4011 Shelbyville Rd., Louisville, 40207.

Permanent Deacons:
Abell, James H., (Retired)
Age, Stephen A., All Saints, Taylorsville; St. Francis Xavier, Mt. Washington
Auffrey, Todd C., Louisville
Ayers, Timothy B., Our Lady of Lourdes, Louisville
Babin, Jeremiah S., Holy Trinity, Louisville
Barnes, Derrick A., St. Margaret Mary, Louisville
Bartley, Ralph E., St. Leonard; St. Frances of Rome, Louisville
Beavin, Gregory A., St. Mary Magdalen of Pazzi, Payneville; St. Theresa, Rhodelia
Becker, Gary Earle, (Retired), Santa Barbara, CA
Beckham, Stephen W., (Retired)
Beckmann, Charles, (Retired)
Bent, Charles T., St. Margaret Mary, Louisville
Bidwell, Lee G., St. Helen, Glasgow; Our Lady of the Caves, Horse Cave
Bissig, Paul F., Good Shepherd, Louisville
Biven, Lawrence, Nazareth Home, Louisville
Bland, Joseph E., Annunciation, Shelbyville; St. John Chrysostom, Eminence
Bowling, T. Stephen, Director of Family Ministries Office, St. Gabriel
Brown, Anthony T., Holy Spirit, Louisville
Brown, Charles, St. Aloysius, Pewee Valley
Brown, Martin J., St. Michael, Louisville
Bryant, Robert C., St. Martin of Tours, Louisville
Buehner, Jerome L., St. Bernadette, Prospect
Burchett, K. Michael, Christ the King; Immaculate Heart, Louisville
Bush, Bryan R., Holy Spirit, Louisville
Calvert, Joseph D., St. Martin of Tours, Flaherty
Carney, Edward P., (Retired)
Carter, Kenneth J., St. Michael, Louisville
Caruso, Lucio A., Epiphany, Louisville
Caruso, Robert R., Immaculate Conception, LaGrange
Caspar, Robert, St. James, Elizabethtown; St. Ambrose, Cecilia; St. Ignatius, White Mills
Cecil, James A., Our Lady of Mercy, Hodgenville
Churchill, John, (Retired)
Clark, George B., (On Leave)
Clark, William, St. James, Elizabethtown
Cooper, Ernest A., Holy Rosary, Springfield
Cottrell, Francis E., (Retired)
Coulter, William D., St. Rose, Springfield
Dalton, David, Dismas Charities, St. Lawrence
Dant, Joseph R., St. Augustine, Lebanon
DaPonte, Stephen J., St. Stephen Martyr & Holy Family, Louisville
Dever, Robert, (Retired)
Diemer, Darryl J., St. Francis of Assisi, Louisville
Downs, William A., Immaculate Conception, Culvertown
Drerup, Karl A., St. James, Elizabethtown
Dugan, Louis B., St. James & St. Brigid, Louisville
Edwards, Michael, St. Bernard, Louisville
Fagan, Richard, Holy Trinity, Fredricktown; Holy Rosary, Manton
Fahringer, Carl A., St. Francis Xavier, Mt. Washington; All Saints, Taylorsville
Fellonneau, John, St. Thomas More and Our Lady of Mt. Carmel, Louisville
Filiatreau, Samuel R., St. Thomas, Bardstown
Fitzmayer, Michael, St. Gabriel, Louisville
Flowers, Donald K., (Retired)
Fowler, Gary W., St. Paul, Louisville
Froehich, John, Christ the Healer, Edmonton
Gitschier, Gregory M., St. Patrick, Louisville; Metro Police Dept. Chaplain
Golden, Timothy D., Our Mother of Sorrows; St. Therese; St. Elizabeth
Hall, Robert, Vicar for Senior Deacons, Holy Spirit, Louisville
Hamilton, John, St. Joseph, Bardstown
Haner, Scott R., St. Patrick, Louisville
Harris, Patrick, St. Bernadette, Louisville
Hart, Robert J., Annunciation, Shelbyville; St. John Chrysostom, Eminence
Hasson, Anthony P., (Retired)
Heinsohn, J. Andrew, Holy Trinity, Louisville
Hettich, Philip, St. Bernard, Louisville; Louisville Metro Corrections
Hotz, R. David, Immaculate Conception, LaGrange
Houck, Peter L., (Retired)
Johnson, W. Timothy, Our Lady of Mt. Carmel; St. Thomas More, Louisville
Jones, J. Michael, St. John the Apostle, Brandenburg
Jones, Walton G., Holy Trinity, Louisville
Kampschaefer, Robert M., (Retired)
Karley, Brian, C.R.
Kelley, Mark, St. Michael, Fairfield
King, Sam, St. Athanasius, Louisville
Kinsella, Brendan, Annunciation, Shelbyville; St. John Chrysostom, Eminence
Klinglesmith, Gregory L., St. Peter the Apostle, Louisville
Klump, William, St. Louis Bertrand, Louisville
Koenig, John C., St. Margaret Mary, Louisville
Layman, Michael A., St. Albert, Louisville
Lewis, John M., Ascension, Louisville
Luckett, Theodore C., St. Aloysius, Shepherdsville; St. Benedict, Lebanon Junction
Maguire, Terry, Our Lady of Mt. Carmel; St. Thomas More, Louisville
Maher, John P., St. Martha, Louisville
Markert, Robert, Incarnation, Louisville; Catholic Cemeteries Chaplain
Marks, Stephen, St. Albert the Great & Metro Corrections
Masterson, Donald E., (On Leave)
Mattingly, Gerald J., St. Francis Xavier, Mt. Washington; All Saints, Taylorsville
Mattingly, Tom, (Retired)
May, Dennis, St. Augustine, Lebanon; Holy Name of Mary, Calvary
McCarty, James, St. Athanasius, Louisville
McDonell, Christopher F., Cathedral of the Assumption, Louisville
McGinty, David L., (retired)
McGoff, James I., St. John Paul II, Louisville
McKenzie, Keith L., St. Augustine; St. Martin de Porres, Louisville
McNally, Thomas M., Immaculate Conception, La Grange
Mitchell, Kenneth J., St. Rita & St. Luke, Louisville
Mobley, Joseph, St. Agnes, Louisville
Moore, Joseph F., St. Agnes, Louisville
Murphy, Michael, (On Duty Outside the Diocese)
Nash, Dennis M., Dir. Diaconate Office, St. Raphael, Louisville
Niemeier, William, Mary Queen of Peace, Louisville
Nitzken, Sylvester, St. Stephen Martyr, Louisville
Noltemeyer, Phillip L., St. Aloysius, Shepherdsville
Olrich, James C., St. Elizabeth Ann Seton Church, Louisville
Parker, Dan E., St. Aloysius, Pewee Valley
Patterson, Daniel, (Retired)
Patterson, Mark, Incarnation, Louisville
Phelps, P. Stephan, M.T.S./C.L., Cathedral of the Assumption, Louisville
Prestwood, Harry, (Retired)
Puga, Aurelio A., St. Rita, Louisville
Raibert, Joseph A., (Retired)
Ratterman, Cletus A., (Retired)
Roth, Thomas L., St. Aloysius, Pewee Valley
Rougeux, Mark J., St. Patrick, Louisville
Ryan, Michael A., St. Brigid, Vine Grove; St. John the Baptist, Rineyville
Schlueter, Timothy, Ascension, Louisville
Schook, Jesse E., St. Athanasius, Louisville
Shumway, Michael, St. Joseph, Louisville
Simpson, John L., (Retired)
Smith, David U., St. Helen, Glasgow; Our Lady of the Caves, Horse Cave
Smith, Stephen, St. Peter the Apostle, Louisville
Sowers, Michael, St. Francis of Assisi, Louisville
Stanford, James E., (Retired), Louisville
Stewart, Timothy E., Our Mother of Sorrows; St. Therese; St. Elizabeth, Louisville
Thieneman, Wayne, St. Lawrence, Louisville
Tolbert, Michael A., St. Thomas More; Our Lady of Mt. Carmel, Louisville
Tomes, David R., St. Boniface, Louisville
Tribbey, William, St. Brigid and St. James, Louisville
Turner, James R., St. Martin de Porres; St. Augustine, Louisville
Turner, Scott R., St. Thomas; St. Monica, Bardstown
Vessels, Michael J., St. John the Baptist, Rineyville; St. Brigid, Vine Grove
Villalobos, Francisco J., St. Bartholomew, Louisville
Waldon, F. Eugene, Our Lady of Lourdes, Louisville
Walsh, Richard J., St. Joseph, Bardstown
Warren, Bruce J., St. John Paul II, Louisville
Whelan, John R., (Retired)
Wolfa, Nicholas, O.F.M. Conv, J.C.L., Mt. St. Francis
Wright, J. Patrick, Holy Family
Zoldak, Richard P., St. Martin of Tours, Louisville.

INSTITUTIONS LOCATED IN DIOCESE

[A] COLLEGES AND UNIVERSITIES

LOUISVILLE. *Bellarmine University*, (Grades Associate-Doctorate), 2001 Newburg Rd., Louisville, 40205-0671. Tel: 502-272-8291; Fax: 502-272-8162; Email: president@bellarmine.edu; Web: www.bellarmine.edu. Priests 3; Students 3,369.

Administration Officers: Susan Donovan, Pres.; Revs. Clyde F. Crews, (Retired), 2001 Newburg Rd., Louisville, 40205; Isaac McDaniel; Dr. Carole Pfeffer, Provost & Vice Pres. Academic Affairs; Dr. Mark Wiegand, Dean of the Lansing School of Nursing; Mr. Glenn Kosse, Vice Pres. Devel. & Alumni Rels.; Mr. Tim Sturgeon, Dean of Admissions; Dr. Sean Ryan, Dean Continuing & Professional Studies; Mr. Robert L. Zimlich, Vice Pres., Admin. & Finance; Mr. Hunt Helm, Vice Pres. Communications & Public Affairs; Helen-Grace Ryan, Vice Pres.; Laura Kline, Dir.

**Spalding University*, (Grades Associate-Doctorate), 845 S. 3rd St, Louisville, 40203. Tel: 502-585-9911; Fax: 502-992-2404; Email: jhoward@spalding.edu; Web: www.spalding.edu. Tori Murden McClure, Pres.; Dr. Richard Hudson, Dean of Students; Joanne Berryman, Admin.; Chris Hart, Dean Enrollment Mgmt.; Bert Griffin, Dir.; Rick Barney, Dir.; Ezra Krumhansl, Dir.; Jennifer Brockhoff, Dir. of Human Resources; Roger Burkman, Dir.; Chandra Irvin, Dir.; Kurt Jefferson, Dean; Kay Vetter, Dir.; Dr. Tomarra Adams, Dean. Lay Teachers 111; Sisters 1; Students 2,071.

[B] HIGH SCHOOLS, ARCHDIOCESAN

LOUISVILLE. *St. Francis DeSales High School* aka DeSales High School, 425 W. Kenwood Dr., Louisville, 40214. Tel: 502-368-6519; Fax: 502-366-5400; Email: advancement@desaleshs.com; Web: www.desaleshighschool.com. Dr. Rick Blackwell, Pres.; Mrs. Anastasia Quirk, Prin. Religious Teachers 1; Lay Teachers 30; Students 337.

Holy Cross High School, 5144 Dixie Hwy., Louisville, 40216. Tel: 502-447-4363; Fax: 502-448-1062; Email: scrook@holycrosshs.com; Web: www.holycrosshs.com. Jennifer Barz, Prin.; Ms. Danielle Wiegandt, Pres. Lay Teachers 20; Sisters 1; Students 260.

Trinity High School, 4011 Shelbyville Rd., Louisville, 40207. Tel: 502-895-9427; Fax: 502-895-6837; Email: snyder@trinityrocks.com; Web: www.trinityrocks.com. Dr. Robert J. Mullen, Pres.; Mr. Daniel J. Zoeller, Prin.; Rev. David H. Zettel, Chap., (Retired); Tim Jones, Librarian. Lay Teachers 94; Priests 1; Sisters 1; Students 1,140.

BARDSTOWN. *Bethlehem High School*, 309 W. Stephen Foster Ave., Bardstown, 40004. Tel: 502-348-8594; Fax: 502-349-1247; Email: BHS@bethlehemhigh.org; Web: www.bethlehemhigh.org. Tom Hamilton, Prin.; Beth Trusley, Librarian; Rev. James Jason Harris, Chap. Religious Teachers 3; Lay Teachers 21; Students 280.

[C] HIGH SCHOOLS, PRIVATE

LOUISVILLE. *Academy of Our Lady of Mercy*, 5801 Fegenbush Ln., Louisville, 40228. Tel: 502-671-2010; Fax: 502-491-0661; Email: mlotz@mercyjaguars.com; Web: www.mercyacademy.com. Mr. Michael C. Johnson, Pres.; Amy B. Elstone, Prin.; Karen Alpiger, Asst. Prin. Lay Teachers 43; Sisters of Mercy 1; Students 521.

Assumption High School, 2170 Tyler Ln., Louisville, 40205. Tel: 502-458-9551; Fax: 502-454-8411; Email: mtedesco@ahsrockets.org; Web: www.ahsrockets.org. Mary Lang, Pres.; Martha Tedesco, Prin. Sisters of Mercy. Lay Teachers 81; Students 903.

**Presentation Academy*, 861 S. 4th St., Louisville, 40203. Tel: 502-583-5935; Fax: 502-583-1342; Email: mbruder@presentationacademy.org; Email: bnoonan@presentationacademy.org; Web: www.presentationacademy.org. Laura Dills, Pres.; Becca Noonan, Prin. Lay Teachers 27; Sisters 4; Students 230.

Sacred Heart Academy, 3175 Lexington Rd., Louisville, 40206. Tel: 502-897-6097; Fax: 502-893-0120; Email: katemple@shslou.org; Web: www.shslou.org/academy. Mrs. Mary Lee McCoy, Prin. Ursuline Sisters. Lay Teachers 77; Sisters 1; Students 815.

St. Xavier High School, Xaverian Brothers, 1609 Poplar Level Rd., Louisville, 40217. Tel: 502-637-4712; Fax: 502-634-2171; Email: psangalli@saintx.com; Web: www.saintx.com. Dr. Perry E. Sangalli, Pres.; Frank Espinosa, Prin.; Michele Metcalfe, Librarian. Lay Teachers 120; Students 1,288.

[D] ELEMENTARY SCHOOLS, PRIVATE

LOUISVILLE. **Holy Angels Academy, Inc.*, (Grades K-

12), 12201 Old Henry Rd., Louisville, 40223. Tel: 502-254-9440; Fax: 502-254-9907; Web: holyangelslouisville.com. Joseph M. Norton, Headmaster and Prin., Grade School; Brian J. Dubil, Prin., High School; Rev. Robert M. Gregor, C.P.M., Chap. Religious Teachers 1; Lay Teachers 13; Priests 1; Students 60.

Sacred Heart Model School, (Grades K-8), 3107 Lexington Rd., Louisville, 40206. Tel: 502-896-3931; Fax: 502-896-3932; Email: mbratcher@shslou.org; Web: www.shslou.org. Michael L. Bratcher, Prin. Religious Teachers 1; Lay Teachers 45; Sisters 1; Students 360.

Sacred Heart Preschool, 3105 Lexington Rd., Louisville, 40206. Tel: 502-896-3941; Email: lhoughlin@shslou.org; Web: www.shslou.org. Lisa Houghline, Dir. Lay Teachers 40; Students 255.

[E] REGIONAL SCHOOLS

LOUISVILLE. *John Paul II Academy*, (Grades PreK-8), 3525 Goldsmith Ln., Louisville, 40220. Tel: 502-452-1712; Fax: 502-451-2462; Email: lwilt@jp2a.org. Lynn Wilt, Prin. Lay Teachers 21; Students 182.

St. Nicholas Academy, (Grades PreK-8), 5501 New Cut Rd., Louisville, 40214. Tel: 502-368-8506; Fax: 502-380-5453; Email: kdelozier@snapanthers.org; Web: www.sna-panthers.org. Kathy DeLozier, Prin. Regional school sponsored by the four parishes. Lay Teachers 21; Students 306.

Notre Dame Academy, (Grades PreK-8), 1927 Lewiston Dr., Louisville, 40216. Tel: 502-447-3155; Fax: 502-447-5515; Email: b.scherr@ndasaints.org; Web: ndasaints.org. Bernice Scherr, Prin.; Mrs. Daivie Kay, Librarian. Lay Teachers 25; Students 496.

PROSPECT. *Saint Mary Academy*, (Grades PreSchool-8), 11311 Saint Mary Ln., Prospect, 40059. Tel: 502-315-2555; Fax: 502-326-3655; Email: lisa.kelly@saintmaryacademy.com. Mrs. Lisa Kelly, Prin. Lay Teachers 33; Students 543.

[F] SPECIAL SCHOOLS

LOUISVILLE. *St. Joseph Child Development Center*, 2823 Frankfort Ave., Louisville, 40206. Tel: 502-893-0241; Fax: 502-896-2394; Email: aprilm@sjkids.org; Web: www.sjkids.org. April Manning, C.D.C. Dir. Students 150; Teachers 45.

**Nativity Academy* dba Nativity Academy at St. Boniface, (Grades 5-8), 529 E. Liberty St., Louisville, 40202. Tel: 502-855-3300; Fax: 502-562-2192; Email: cnord@nativityacademy.org; Web: nativitylouisville.org. Carol Nord, Exec. Dir.; Jessica Farrell, Prin. Students 82.

Pitt Academy, 7515 Westport Rd., Louisville, 40222. Tel: 502-966-6979; Fax: 502-962-8878; Email: rdoty@pitt.com; Web: www.pitt.com. Renée Doty, Prin. Special needs school. Lay Teachers 7; Students 70; Total Staff 7.

Sacred Heart School for the Arts, 3105 Lexington Rd., Angela Hall Building #17, Louisville, 40206. Tel: 502-897-1816; Fax: 502-896-3927; Email: apaul@shslou.org; Web: www.shslou.org. Dr. Anna Jo Paul, Exec. Dir. Lay Teachers 24; Students 350; Total Staff 28.

[G] ORPHANAGES AND INFANT HOMES

LOUISVILLE. *St. Joseph Catholic Orphan Society*, 2823 Frankfort Ave., Louisville, 40206. Tel: 502-893-0241; Fax: 502-896-2394; Email: gracea@sjkids.org; Email: kathyo@sjkids.org; Web: www.sjkids.org. Chris Whelan, Pres. Tot Asst. Annually 50.

St. Thomas Orphan Society, Inc., 3940 Poplar Level Rd., Louisville, 40213. Tel: 502-585-3291; Email: pastoralcenter@archlou.org. Dr. Brian B. Reynolds, Chancellor.

St. Vincent's Orphan Society, Inc., 3940 Poplar Level Rd., Louisville, 40213. Tel: 502-585-3294; Email: lmclemore@archlou.org; Web: archlou.org. Dr. Brian B. Reynolds, Chancellor.

[H] GENERAL HOSPITALS

LOUISVILLE. *SS. Mary and Elizabeth Hospital*, 1850 Bluegrass Ave., Louisville, 40215. Tel: 502-361-6000; Fax: 502-361-6799; Email: kentuckyonehealth@gmail.com; Web: kentuckyonehealth.org. Jennifer Nolan, Pres. & CEO. Catholic Health Initiatives. Bed Capacity 298; Patients Asst Anual. 114,721; Sisters 4; Total Staff 75.

BARDSTOWN. *Flaget Healthcare, Inc.* dba Flaget Memorial Hospital, 4305 New Shepherdsville Rd., Bardstown, 40004. Tel: 502-350-5000; Fax: 502-350-5036; Email: famn.lem@flaget.com; Web: www.flaget.com. Rick Vancise, Exec. Catholic Health Initiatives.Attended from St. Joseph Church. Bassinets 8; Bed Capacity 52; Patients Asst Anual. 73,485; Sisters 2; Total Staff 330.

[I] SPECIAL HOSPITALS

LOUISVILLE. *Our Lady of Peace*, 2020 Newburg Rd., Louisville, 40205. Tel: 502-451-3330; Fax: 502-479-4140; Email: rebecca.kistler@kentuckyonehealth.org; Web: www.jhsmh.org. Jennifer Nolan, Pres. & CEO. Catholic Health Initiatives.Hospital for Psychiatric Illness. Bed Capacity 396; Sisters 1; Tot Asst. Annually 11,535; Total Staff 600.

[J] PROTECTIVE INSTITUTIONS

LOUISVILLE. *Boys & Girls Haven*, 2301 Goldsmith Ln., Louisville, 40218. Tel: 502-458-1171; Fax: 502-451-2161; Email: jhadley@boyshaven.org; Web: www.boyshaven.org. Jeff Hadley, CEO. For dependent, neglected, or abused boys and girls, 12 to 23 years of age. Total Assisted 1,242.

St. Joseph Children's Home, 2823 Frankfort Ave., Louisville, 40206. Tel: 502-893-0241; Fax: 502-896-2394; Email: gracea@sjkids.org; Web: www.sjkids.org. Grace Akers, M.Div., Exec. Dir. Children 48.

[K] NURSING HOMES

LOUISVILLE. *St. Joseph Home for the Aged* aka Little Sisters of the Poor, 15 Audubon Plaza Dr., Louisville, 40217. Tel: 502-636-2300; Fax: 502-636-2239; Email: bslouisville@littlesistersofthepoor.org; Web: www.littlesistersofthepoorlouisville.org. Sr. Paul Maggyar, Pres.

Home for the Aged of the Little Sisters of the Poor Bed Capacity 77; Sisters 11; Total Staff 87.

Nazareth Home, Inc., 2000 Newburg Rd., Louisville, 40205. Tel: 502-459-9681; Fax: 502-456-9077; Email: mhaynes@nazhome.org; Web: nazhome.org. Mary Haynes, Pres. & CEO; Bridget Bunning, Dir. Pastoral Care; Deacon Lawrence Biven, Chap. Sisters of Charity of Nazareth. Residents 168; Total Staff 260; Total Served Annually 971.

[L] MONASTERIES AND RESIDENCES OF PRIESTS AND BROTHERS

LOUISVILLE. *St. Francis of Assisi Friary*, 2225 Lower Hunters Trace, Louisville, 40216. Tel: 502-447-5566; Email: fran.voc@aol.com. Revs. Christian Moore, O.F.M.Conv.; John Bamman, O.F.M.Conv.; Dismas J. Veeneman, O.F.M.Conv.; Leo Payyappily, O.F.M.Conv.; John Pozhathuparambil, O.F.M.Conv.; Tony Vattaparambil, O.F.M.Conv.; Bros. Larry Eberhardt, O.F.M.Conv.; John Mauer, O.F.M.Conv.

St. Louis Bertrand Priory, 1104 S. Sixth St., Louisville, 40203. Tel: 502-583-4448; Fax: 502-589-0056; Email: stlouisbertrand@stlb.org. Very Rev. Edward M. Gorman, O.P., Prior; Revs. Louis Bertrand Lemoine, O.P., Assoc. Pastor; Joseph Anthony Breen, O.P., Chap.; Leon Martin Martiny, O.P.; Dominic Bump, O.P. Priests: see St. Louis Bertrand Parish Priests 5.

Sacred Heart Retreat, 1924 Newburg Rd., Louisville, 40205. Tel: 502-451-2330; Fax: 502-451-0192; Email: billbaalman@gmail.com; Web: www.passionist.org. Revs. Sebastian MacDonald, C.P.; Simon Herbers, C.P.; Alfonso San Juan, C.P.; Denis McGowan, C.P.; Bro. William Baalman, C.P. (Corporate Title: Congregation of the Passion, Sacred Heart Community) Brothers 4; Priests 13. In Res. Revs. David Colhour, C.P.; Ronald Corl, C.P.; Leonard Kosatka, C.P.; Emmet Linden, C.P.; Eric Meyer, C.P.; Joseph Mitchell, C.P.; Richard L. Parks, C.P.; Saji Thengumkudiyil, C.P.; Robert Weiss, C.P., Asst. Supr.; Bros. Jerome Milazzo, C.P.; John Monzyk, C.P., Local Supr.; Kurt Wernert, C.P.

TRAPPIST. *Abbey of Our Lady of Gethsemani, of the Order of Cistercians of the Strict Observance*, 3642 Monks Rd., Trappist, 40051. Tel: 502-549-3117; Fax: 502-549-4125; Email: trappists@monks.org. Rt. Revs. Elias Dietz, O.C.S.O., Abbot; Timothy Kelly, O.C.S.O., Abbot, (Retired); Revs. James Conner, O.C.S.O.; Alan Gilmore, O.C.S.O.; Michael Casagram, O.C.S.O.; Peter Tong, O.C.S.O.; Joachim Johnson, O.C.S.O.; Seamus Malvey, O.C.S.O.; Andrew McAughan, O.C.S.O.; Anton Rusnak, O.C.S.O.; Carlos Rodriguez, O.C.S.O.; Lawrence Morey, O.C.S.O. Brothers 31; Priests 12.

[M] CONVENTS AND RESIDENCES FOR SISTERS

LOUISVILLE. *Discalced Carmelite Nuns*, 1907 Lauderdale Rd., Louisville, 40205. Tel: 812-841-6731; Email: nreynolds@spsmw.org. Ms. Nancy Reynolds, S.P., Prioress. Sisters 6.

Sisters of Mercy, 2181 Tyler Ln., Louisville, 40205. Tel: 502-774-0839; Email: pdiebold@mercysc.org. Sr. Paulanne Diebold, R.S.M., Contact Person. Sisters in Residence 5.

Ursuline Sisters of the Immaculate Conception, 3115 Lexington Rd., Louisville, 40206. Tel: 502-897-1811; Fax: 502-896-3913; Email: webmaster@ursulineslou.org; Web: www.ursulinesisterslouisville.org. 3105 Lexington Rd., Louisville, 40206. Sr. Janet Marie Peterworth, O.S.U., Pres. Sisters 61.

NAZARETH. *Generalate, Motherhouse and Novitiate of the Sisters of Charity of Nazareth*, 200 Nazareth Dr., P.O. Box 172, Nazareth, 40048. Tel: 502-348-1555 (SCN Center & Generalate); Tel: 502-348-1500 (Motherhouse); Fax: 502-348-1502; Email: sangeeta@scnky.org; Web: www.scnfamily.org. Sr. Sangeeta Ayithamattam, Pres.; Rev. Gary Young, C.R., Chap., Motherhouse. Sisters 549; Nazareth Sadan 3; Sisters at Motherhouse 79; Sisters at David Hall 16; Guest Houses 2; Nazareth Villages 2.

NERINX. *Motherhouse and Novitiate of the Sisters of Loretto at the Foot of the Cross*, 515 Nerinx Rd., Nerinx, 40049. Tel: 270-865-5811; Fax: 270-865-2200; Email: shannondrury@lorettocommunity.org; Web: www.lorettocommunity.org. Sisters Anthony Mary Satorivs, S.L., Svcs. Coord.; Barbara Nicholas, S.L., Pres.; Shannon Drury, Treas. Sisters 77; Tot in Congregation 136.

ST. CATHARINE. *Dominican Sisters of Peace*, 2645 Bardstown Rd., St. Catharine, 40061. Tel: 859-336-9303; Fax: 859-481-6285; Email: bsullivan@oppeace.org; Web: www.oppeace.org. Sr. Barbara Sullivan, O.P., Mission Group Coord. St. Catharine Motherhouse Sisters 90.

Sansbury Care Center, Inc., 2625 Bardstown Rd., St. Catharine, 40061. Tel: 859-336-3974; Fax: 859-336-0401; Email: pbrooks@sansburycare.org. Sr. Joyce Montgomery, O.P., Mission Group Coord.; Mrs. Pamela Brooks, Admin. Sisters 40; Skilled Nursing Beds 48; Other (Lay Residents) 19; Personal Care Beds 11.

[N] HOMES FOR MEN AND WOMEN

LOUISVILLE. *Mercy Sacred Heart, Inc.*, 2120 Payne St., Louisville, 40206. Tel: 502-895-9425; Fax: 502-357-5551; Email: kthieneman@mercy.com. Kim Thieneman, Exec. Dir.; Lisa Biddle-Puffer. Sisters of Mercy.

Mercy Sacred Heart, Inc. Bed Capacity 168; Capacity 168; Priests 4; Residents 118; Sisters 21; Tot Asst. Annually 118; Total Staff 150.

Sacred Heart Village I, Inc. (Senior Housing Apartments) 2110 Payne St., Louisville, 40206. Tel: 502-895-6409; Fax: 502-895-8166; Email: tsteiden@mercyhousing.org. Bed Capacity 125; Tot Asst. Annually 103; Total Staff 15.

**Sacred Heart Village II, Inc.* (Senior Housing Apartments) 2108 Payne St., Louisville, 40206. Tel: 502-895-8085; Fax: 502-895-8039; Email: tsteiden@mercyhousing.org. Dora Caudill, Mgr. Bed Capacity 125; Apt. Capacity 49; Tot Asst. Annually 49; Total Staff 15; Staff 55.

**Sacred Heart Village III, Inc.* (Senior Housing Apartments) 3101 Wayside Dr., Louisville, 40216. Tel: 502-776-5004; Fax: 502-772-7695; Email: tsteiden@mercyhousing.org. Bed Capacity 125; Tot Asst. Annually 118; Total Staff 15.

[O] RETREAT HOUSES

LOUISVILLE. *Catholic Charismatic Renewal*, Maloney Center, 1200 S. Shelby St., Louisville, 40203. Tel: 502-636-0296; Email: mlarison@archlou.org. Maureen Larison, Contact Person, Tel: 502-448-8581.

Flaget Center, 1935 Lewiston Dr., Louisville, 40216. Tel: 502-448-8581; Email: krobbins@archlou.org. Kim Robbins, Contact Person.

CRESTWOOD. *Lake St. Joseph Center*, 5800 Old LaGrange Rd., Crestwood, 40014. Tel: 502-241-4469. Sr. Martha Leis, Admin.

NERINX. *Knobs Haven*, 515 Nerinx Rd., Nerinx, 40049. Tel: 270-865-2621; Email: knobshaven@yahoo.com. Jo Ann Gates, Dir.

[P] MISCELLANEOUS LISTINGS

LOUISVILLE. *Archdiocesan Marian Committee*, 306 Fredericktown Rd., Springfield, 40069. Tel: 502-968-2933; Email: htr@bardstown.com. Rev. Matthew T. Hardesty, Dir.

**Catholic Education Foundation*, 401 W. Main St., Ste. 806, Louisville, 40202. Tel: 502-585-2747; Fax: 502-583-4929; Email: riechleiter@ceflou.org. Richard A. Lechleiter, Pres.

Catholic Foundation of Louisville, Inc., 3940 Poplar Level Rd., Louisville, 40213. Tel: 502-585-3291; Email: bash@archlou.org. Rev. Martin A. Linebach, Vicar; Dr. Brian B. Reynolds, Dir.; Robert L. Ash, Dir.

**Center for Interfaith Relations*, 415 W. Muhammad Ali Blvd., Ste. 101, Louisville, 40202-2334. Tel: 502-583-3100; Fax: 502-583-8524; Email: interfaithrelations@interfaithrelation.org; Web: interfaithrelations.org. Mustafa Gouverneur; Sarah Reed Harris, Mng. Dir.

CHI Kentucky, Inc., 1850 Bluegrass Ave., Louisville,

40215. Tel: 303-383-2746; Fax: 303-383-2695; Email: peggymartin@catholichealth.net. Sr. Peggy Martin, O.P., Senior Vice Pres.

Community Catholic Center, Inc., P.O. Box 11065, Louisville, 40251. Tel: 502-424-9398; Email: raegiuffre@gmail.com. Heidi Imberi-Hamilton, Exec. Dir.

The St. Francis de Sales High School Foundation, Inc., 425 Kenwood Dr., Louisville, 40214. Tel: 502-368-6519; Fax: 502-366-6172; Email: Joshua.Blandford@DeSalesHS.com. Stephen James, Chm.

The Franciscan Foundation, Inc., 6901 Dixie Hwy., Louisville, 40258. Tel: 502-935-1223; Fax: 502-933-7747; Email: dismasv@aol.com; Email: secretary@francisfound.org; Web: www.francisfound.org. Rev. Dismas J. Veeneman, O.F.-M.Conv.

Franciscan Shelter House dba Franciscan Kitchen, 748 S. Preston St., Louisville, 40203. Tel: 502-589-0140; Fax: 502-589-1134; Email: francisankitchen@gmail.com; Web: franciscankitchen.org. Heather Benjamin, Business Mgr.; Chuck Mattingly, Opers. Mgr.

Saint Luke Center, 9400 Williamsburg Plaza, Ste. 300, Louisville, 40222-6016. Tel: 301-422-5410; Email: tarynm@sli.org. Taryn Millar, Contact Person.

Mass of the Air, 1200 S. Shelby St., Louisville, 40203. Tel: 502-893-5120; Email: massoftheair@gmail.com. Deacon Mark J. Rougeux, Exec. Dir.

Our Lady's Rosary Makers, P.O. Box 37080, Louisville, 40233. Tel: 502-968-1434; Fax: 502-969-8883; Email: mikeford@olrm.org; Email: info@olrm.com; Web: www.olrm.org. Michael Ford, Pres.

St. Patrick School Foundation, Inc., 1000 N. Beckley Station Rd., Louisville, 40245. Tel: 502-244-7083; Fax: 502-719-0359; Email: rmarkpage@aol.com; Web: www.stpatlou.org. R. Mark Page, Pres.

Perpetual Eucharistic Adoration, 3940 Poplar Level Rd, Louisville, 40213. Tel: 025-853-2915; Tel: 502-968-2933; Email: lmclemore@archlou.org. Rev. Gary T. Padgett, Admin.

Publication: "The Record", Maloney Center, 1200 S. Shelby St., Louisville, 40203-2600. Tel: 502-636-0296; Fax: 502-636-2379; Email: record@archlou.org; Web: therecordnewspaper.org. Marnie McAllister, Editor, Editor; Jennifer Jenkins, Dir. of Advertising. Official newspaper of the Archdiocese of Louisville (Weekly).

Sacred Heart Schools, Inc., 3177 Lexington Rd., Louisville, 40206. Tel: 502-896-3910; Fax: 502-895-0989; Email: shs@shslou.org; Web: www.shslou.org. Dr. Cynthia Crabtree, Pres. Sponsored by Ursuline Sisters.

Trinity High School Foundation, Inc., 4011 Shelbyville Rd., Louisville, 40207. Tel: 502-736-2100; Fax: 502-736-2190; Email: ths.foundation@thsrock.net. Joe Landenwich, Chm.

Ursuline Sisters of Louisville Charitable Trust, 3115 Lexington Rd., Louisville, 40206. Tel: 502-212-1751; Email: ballison@ursulineslou.org. Sr. Rita Wigginton, Trustee.

Ursuline Society and Academy of Education, 3115 Lexington Rd., Louisville, 40206. Tel: 502-897-1811; Fax: 502-896-3913; Email: webmaster@ursulineslou.org; Web: www.ursulinesisterslouisville.org. 3105 Lexington Rd., Louisville, 40206. Sr. Janet Marie Peterworth, O.S.U., Admin.

World Apostolate of Fatima (Blue Army), 306 Fredericktown Rd., Springfield, 40069. Tel: 502-968-2933; Email: mhardesty@archlou.org. Rev. Matthew T. Hardesty, Spiritual Dir.

Sacred Heart Apostolate, 1225 S. Wilson Rd., Radcliff, 40160. Tel: 270-351-3706; Email: church@stchristopherparish.org. Rev. Jeffrey G. Hopper, Dir.

BARDSTOWN. *Flaget Hospital Foundation, Inc.*, 4305 New Shepherdsville Rd., Bardstown, 40004. Tel: 502-350-5058; Fax: 502-350-5022; Email: foundation@flaget.com; Web: www.kentuckyonehealth.org/flaget-memorial-hospital-foundation. Sue Downs, Pres. & CEO.

LEBANON. *The Laura*, 220 Laura Ln., Lebanon, 40033. Tel: 270-692-1790; Email: mheleneking@windstream.net. Sisters Marilyn King, R.S.M., Dir.; Genevieve Durcan, O.C.S.O., Co-Dir.; Mary Louise Yurik, R.S.M.

LORETTO. *Holy Cross Cemetery Trust, Inc.*, 7945 Loretto Rd., Loretto, 40037. Tel: 502-348-5404; Email: FBallard@holycrosscemeterytrust.org. Fabian Ballard, Dir.

NAZARETH. *Sisters of Charity of Nazareth, Inc.*, Crimmins Hall, 135 West Dr., P.O. Box 187, Nazareth, 40048. Tel: 502-331-4072; Fax: 502-331-4073; Email: mmiller@scnky.org. Sr. Mary Miller, Prov.

NERINX. *Sisters of Loretto Charitable Trust*, 515 Nerinx Rd., Nerinx, 40049-9999. Tel: 270-865-5811; Fax: 270-865-2200; Email: shannondrury@lorettocommunity.org; Web: www.lorettocommunity.org. Shannon Drury, Treas.

NEW HOPE. *St. Martin De Porres Lay Dominican Community*, 3050 Gap Knob Rd., P.O. Box 10, New Hope, 40052. Tel: 270-325-3061; Fax: 270-325-3091 ; Email: djmusk@earthlink.net; Email: newhopepublications@gmail.com; Web: www.newhope-ky.org. Dennis J. Musk, Prior.

[Q] CLOSED PARISHES

LOUISVILLE. *St. Aloysius* For parish records please contact the Chancery office.

St. Andrew For parish records please contact the Chancery office.

St. Ann For parish records please contact the Chancery office.

St. Anthony (1867) For inquiries for parish records contact Good Shepherd, Louisville.

St. Barnabas For parish records contact St. John Paul II parish.

St. Basil For records please contact Mary Queen of Peace parish.

St. Benedict For records please contact Martin de Porres parish.

St. Cecilia (1873) For inquiries for parish records contact Good Shepherd, Louisville.

St. Charles Borromeo For records please contact St. Martin De Porres parish.

St. Clement (1956) For inquiries for parish records please see St. Peter the Apostle, Louisville.

St. Columba For parish records please contact the Chancery office.

St. Denis (1916) For inquiries for parish records please see Mary Queen of Peace, Louisville.

St. George For parish records please contact the Chancery office.

St. Helen (1897) For inquiries for parish records please see Mary Queen of Peace, Louisville.

Holy Cross For records contact St. Martin de Porres parish.

St. Jerome (1953) For inquiries for parish records please see St. Teresa of Calcutta, Louisville.

St. John For records contact St. Martin of Tours parish.

St. Leo the Great For parish records please contact the Chancery office.

St. Mary (1968) For inquiries for parish records please see St, Teresa of Calcutta, Louisville.

St. Mary Magdalen For parish records please contact the Chancery office.

St. Matthias (1950) For inquiries for parish records please see Mary Queen of Peace, Louisville.

Mother of Good Counsel (1959) For inquiries for parish records please see St. Bernadette, Louisville.

Our Lady (1839) For inquiries for parish records contact Good Shepherd, Louisville.

Our Lady Help of Christians (1957) For inquiries for parish records please see St. Peter the Apostle, Louisville.

Our Lady of Consolation (1959) For inquiries for parish records please see St. Peter the Apostle, Louisville.

St. Peter Claver (2008) For parish records please contact the Chancery office.

St. Philip Neri For records please contact the chancery office.

St. Pius X For parish records contact St. John Paul II parish.

St. Polycarp (1960) For inquiries for parish records please see St. Peter the Apostle, Louisville.

Resurrection D.N.J.C. For records please contact Guardian Angels parish.

St. Timothy (1963) For inquiries for parish records please see St. Peter the Apostle, Louisville.

St. Vincent De Paul For inquiries for parish records please contact the chancery office.

COLESBURG. *St. Clare* For inquiries for parish records contact St. Benedict, Lebanon Junction.

GOSHEN. *Transfiguration of Our Lord* (1983) For inquiries for parish records please see St. Bernadette, Louisville.

ST. JOSEPH. *St. Joseph* For records contact St. Francis Xavier, Raywick.

RELIGIOUS INSTITUTES OF MEN REPRESENTED IN THE ARCHDIOCESE

For further details refer to the corresponding bracketed number in the Religious Institutes of Men or Women section.

[]—*Apostles of Jesus*—A.J.

[1350]—*Brothers of St. Francis Xavier* (American Central Prov.)—C.F.X.

[0275]—*Carmelites of Mary Immaculate*—C.M.I.

[]—*Carmelites of Mary Immaculate* (Prov. Devamatha, India)—C.M.I.

[0350]—*Cistercians Order of the Strict Observance-Trappists*—O.C.S.O.

[0820]—*Congregation of the Fathers of Mercy*—C.P.M.

[1000]—*Congregation of the Passion* (Holy Cross Prov.)—C.P.

[1080]—*Congregation of the Resurrection* (Rome, Italy)—C.R.

[0480]—*Conventual Franciscans* (Prov. of Our Lady of Consolation)—O.F.M.Conv.

[]—*Conventual Franciscans* (Prov. St. Maximillian Kolb-India)—O.F.M.Conv.

[0430]—*Order of Preachers-Dominicans* (St. Joseph Prov.)—O.P.

RELIGIOUS INSTITUTES OF WOMEN REPRESENTED IN THE ARCHDIOCESE

[0230]—*Benedictine Sisters of Pontifical Jurisdiction*—O.S.B.

[2145]—*Congregation of Augustinian Sisters Servants of Jesus and Mary*—O.S.A.

[0420]—*Discalced Carmelite Nuns*—O.C.D.

[1070-13]—*Dominican Sisters of St. Cecilia*—O.P.

[1115]—*Dominican Sisters of Peace*—O.P.

[2575]—*Institute of the Sisters of Mercy of the Americas*—R.S.M.

[2340]—*Little Sisters of the Poor*—L.S.P.

[0670]—*Order of Trappistines*—O.C.S.O.

[]—*Servants of Jesus, the High-Priest* (Vietnam)—S.J.P.

[0500]—*Sisters of Charity of Nazareth*—S.C.N.

[2360]—*Sisters of Loretto At the Foot of the Cross*—S.L.

[3000]—*Sisters of Notre Dame de Namur*—S.N.D.deN.

[3360]—*Sisters of Providence of Saint Mary-of-the-Woods, IN* (St. Gabriel Prov.)—S.P.

[]—*Sisters of St. Dominic* (Adrian, MI)—O.P.

[4120-03]—*Ursuline Nuns, of the Congregation of Paris*—O.S.U.

[4120-05]—*Ursuline Sisters of Mt. St. Joseph*—O.S.U.M.S.J.

ARCHDIOCESAN CEMETERIES

Offices for all cemeteries: 1600 Newburg Rd., Louisville, KY 40205; Mailing Address: P.O. Box 4096, Louisville, KY 40204. Tel: 502-451-7710; Fax: 502-456-9270.

LOUISVILLE.

Calvary dba Archdiocesan Catholic Cemeteries, 1600 Newburg Rd., Louisville, 40205. Tel: 502-451-7710; Email: cemeteries@archlou.org; Web: www.catholiccemeterieslouisville.org. Francisco Fajardo-Ocana, Dir.

St. John, 2601 Duncan St., Louisville, 40212. Tel: 502-451-7710; Email: cemeteries@archlou.org; Web: www.catholiccemeterieslouisville.org. P.O Box 4096, Louisville, 40204. Francisco Fajardo-Ocana, Dir.

St. Louis, 1167 Barret Ave., Louisville, 40204. Tel: 502-451-7710; Email: cemeteries@archlou.org; Web: www.catholiccemeterieslouisville.org. Francisco Fajardo-Ocana, Dir.

St. Michael, 1153 Charles St., Louisville, 40204. Tel: 502-451-7710; Email: cemeteries@archlou.org; Web: www.catholiccemeterieslouisville.org. Francisco Fajardo-Ocana, Dir.

NECROLOGY

† Osborne, Stanley J., (Retired), Died Jul. 17, 2018

An asterisk (*) denotes an organization that has established tax-exempt status directly with the IRS and is not covered by the USCCB Group Ruling.

Diocese of Lubbock

Most Reverend

ROBERT M. COERVER

Bishop of Lubbock; ordained June 27, 1980; appointed Third Bishop of Lubbock September 27, 2016; installed Nov. 21, 2016. *Res.: 3505 37th St., Lubbock, TX 79413. Office: The Catholic Pastoral Center, P.O. Box 98700, Lubbock, TX 79499-8700.*

Most Reverend

PLACIDO RODRIGUEZ, C.M.F.

Bishop Emeritus of Lubbock; ordained May 23, 1968; consecrated December 13, 1983; installed Auxiliary Bishop of Chicago; appointed Second Bishop of Lubbock April 5, 1994; installed June 1, 1994; retired September 27, 2016. *Res.: Provincial House - CMF, 400 N. Euclid Ave., Oak Park, IL 60302.*

ESTABLISHED AND CREATED A DIOCESE, JUNE 17, 1983.

Square Miles 23,382.

Comprises the Counties of Bailey, Lamb, Hale, Floyd, Motley, Cottle, Cochran, Hockley, Lubbock, Crosby, Dickens, King, Yoakum, Terry, Lynn, Garza, Kent, Stonewall, Haskell, Gaines, Dawson, Borden, Scurry, Fisher and Jones.

Legal Title: Roman Catholic Diocese of Lubbock.

The Catholic Pastoral Center: P.O. Box 98700, Lubbock, TX 79499-8700. Tel: 806-792-3943; Fax: 806-792-8109.

Web: www.catholiclubbock.org

Email: lflores@catholiclubbock.org

STATISTICAL OVERVIEW

Personnel	
Bishop	1
Retired Bishops	1
Priests: Diocesan Active in Diocese	26
Priests: Diocesan Active Outside Diocese	3
Priests: Retired, Sick or Absent	16
Number of Diocesan Priests	45
Religious Priests in Diocese	18
Total Priests in Diocese	63
Permanent Deacons in Diocese	65
Total Sisters	26
Parishes	
Parishes	62
With Resident Pastor:	
Resident Diocesan Priests	36
Resident Religious Priests	26
Professional Ministry Personnel:	
Lay Ministers	55
Welfare	
Catholic Hospitals	2
Total Assisted	617,211
Health Care Centers	8
Total Assisted	62,378
Special Centers for Social Services	2
Total Assisted	52,000
Educational	
Diocesan Students in Other Seminaries	5
Total Seminarians	5
High Schools, Diocesan and Parish	1
Total Students	156
Elementary Schools, Diocesan and Parish	7
Total Students	169
Catechesis/Religious Education:	
High School Students	1,872
Elementary Students	3,103
Total Students under Catholic Instruction	5,305
Teachers in the Diocese:	
Sisters	3
Lay Teachers	47
Vital Statistics	
Receptions into the Church:	
Infant Baptism Totals	416
Minor Baptism Totals	107
Adult Baptism Totals	75
Received into Full Communion	164
First Communions	615
Confirmations	506
Marriages:	
Catholic	137
Interfaith	38
Total Marriages	175
Deaths	335
Total Catholic Population	136,894
Total Population	494,450

Former Bishops—Most Revs. MICHAEL J. SHEEHAN, S.T.L., J.C.D., ord. July 12, 1964; cons. and installed as the first Bishop of Lubbock, June 17, 1983; appt. Apostolic Administrator of Santa Fe, April 6, 1993; installed as the 11th Archbishop of Santa Fe, Sept. 21, 1993; PLACIDO RODRIGUEZ, C.M.F., (Retired), ord. May 23, 1968; cons. Dec. 13, 1983; installed Auxiliary Bishop of Chicago; appt. Second Bishop of Lubbock April 5, 1994; installed June 1, 1994; retired Sept. 27, 2016.

The Catholic Pastoral Center—4620 Fourth St., Lubbock, 79416. Mailing Address: P.O. Box 98700, Lubbock, 79499-8700. Tel: 806-792-3943; Fax: 806-792-8109; Fax: 806-792-2953 (Bishop's Office). Office Hours: Mon.-Fri. 8:30-4:30.

Chancellor—MR. B. MARTY MARTIN, Catholic Pastoral Center, P.O. Box 98700, Lubbock, 79499-8700. Tel: 806-792-3943, Ext. 212; Fax: 806-792-2953.

Moderator of the Curia—Rev. JOSE MATTHEW KOCHUPARAMBIL, J.V.

Chancellor's Administrative Assistant—BELINDA L. AGUIRRE.

Bishop's Executive Assistant—JUDY LEOS RODRIGUEZ.

Diocesan Tribunal—Mailing Address: P.O. Box 98700, Lubbock, 79499-8700. Tel: 806-792-3943.

Officialis—Rev. JOSE MATTHEW KOCHUPARAMBIL, J.V.

Tribunal Director—RITA ORTIZ.

Promoter of Justice—Rev. Msgr. DAVID CRUZ, V.G.

Defender of the Bond—Very Rev. WILLIAM J. ANTON.

Defender of the Bond-Appeal—Very Rev. WILLIAM J. ANTON.

Notaries—RITA ORTIZ; JUDY LEOS RODRIGUEZ; BELINDA L. AGUIRRE.

Presbyteral Council—Most Rev. ROBERT M. COERVER; MR. B. MARTY MARTIN, Chancellor; Rev. Msgrs. DAVID CRUZ, V.G.; GERALD LEATHAM, (Retired); Revs. JOHN RATHINAM, I.M.S.; GEORGE RONEY; GEORGE POONELY; EMILIANO ZAPATA, O.P.; SELVA NAYAGAM, H.G.N.; RENATO CRUZ; Very Revs. JAMES MCCARTNEY, Dean; ERNESTO LOPEZ, Dean; WILLIAM ANTON, Dean; Rev. JOSE MATTHEW KOCHUPARAMBIL, J.V.

Priests Personnel Board—Most Rev. ROBERT M. COERVER; MR. B. MARTY MARTIN, Chancellor; Rev. Msgrs. DAVID CRUZ, V.G.; GERALD LEATHAM, (Retired); Rev. JOSE MATTHEW KOCHUPARAMBIL, J.V.; Very Rev. WILLIAM J. ANTON, Dean; Revs. RAYMUNDO MANRIQUEZ; RENE PEREZ; MARTIN PINA; Deacon JUAN CAVAZOS; Sr. OLIVIA RICO.

Vicar General—Rev. Msgr. DAVID CRUZ, V.G.

Vicar of Priests—Rev. Msgr. GERALD LEATHAM, (Retired).

Vicar of Retired Priests—Rev. Msgr. GERALD LEATHAM, (Retired).

Vicars Forane—Very Revs. WILLIAM J. ANTON, Plainview Deanery; ERNESTO LOPEZ, Brownfield Deanery; JAMES MCCARTNEY, Lubbock Deanery; Rev. SELVA NAYAGAM, H.G.N., Snyder Deanery.

Superintendent of Schools—MRS. CHRISTINE WANJURA, Prin., 4011 54th St., Lubbock, 79413. P.O. Box 98700, Lubbock, 79499. P.O. Box 98700, Lubbock, 79499.

Director of Youth—Sr. PEGGY SZELJACK, C.V.

Campus Ministry—2305 Main St., Lubbock, 79401. Tel: 806-762-5225. VINCE PETTIJEAN.

Director of Scouting—MRS. CHRISTINE WANJURA.

Priests' Pension Board—Most Rev. ROBERT M. COERVER; MR. B. MARTY MARTIN, Chancellor; Very Revs. JAMES MCCARTNEY, Dean; ERNESTO LOPEZ, Dean; Revs. JOHN SMITH; RUDOLF CRASTA; BRIAN WOOD; RENE PEREZ; MRS. JUANITA PINEDA; MRS. ANNABELLE G. OCANAS, CFO; MR. SONNY GARZA; MR. ANTON BUXKEMPER; MR. DAVID POWELL; MR. PAUL AWTRY.

Diocesan Building Commission—Deacon SEVERO ALVARADO; MR. MARC CHAPMAN; MR. RAY ARIAS; MR. BERNARD GRADEL; MR. LYLE FETTERLY; MR. JOSEPH RAPIER; MR. ROLLO GURSS; CARLOS OLIVAREZ.

Diocesan Pastoral Liturgy Commission—Most Rev. ROBERT M. COERVER; MR. B. MARTY MARTIN, Chm.; ALICIA ALVAREZ; Deacon JUAN CAVAZOS; MRS. JANIE HERNANDEZ.

Evangelization & Family Faith Formation—Mailing Address: P.O. Box 98700, Lubbock, 79499. Tel: 806-792-3943. Sr. PEGGY SZELJACK, C.V.

Catholic Charities, Diocese of Lubbock, Inc.—CYNTHIA QUINTANILLA, Dir., 102 Ave. J, Lubbock, 79401. Tel: 806-765-8475.

Ecumenical Affairs—VACANT.

Diocesan Council of Catholic Women—Rev. JOSE DE DIOS GONZALEZ; SUSAN LUNA, Pres.

Director of Vocations—Rev. RENE PEREZ, Seminarian Formation & Dir. Vocations.

Diocesan Attorney—913 Texas Ave., Lubbock, 79401. VICTOR WANJURA.

Diocesan Health Coordinator—VACANT.

Propagation of the FaithMR. B. MARTY MARTIN, Chancellor.

Office of Peace & Justice—MR. B. MARTY MARTIN, Chancellor.

Catholic Campaign for Human Development—Mailing Address: P.O. Box 98700, Lubbock, 79499. MR. ROBERT HOGAN.

Director of the Permanent Diaconate—Deacon JUAN CAVAZOS, P.O. Box 98700, Lubbock, 79499. Tel: 806-792-3943.

Cursillo Movement—Very Rev. ERNESTO LOPEZ.

Newspaper—South Plains Catholic MR. LUCAS FLORES, Editor, Mailing Address: P.O. Box 98700, Lubbock, 79499. Tel: 806-792-3943.

Director of Communications—MR. LUCAS FLORES.

Office of Stewardship & Development—Mailing Address: P.O. Box 98700, Lubbock, 79499. Tel: 806-792-3943. MRS. RACHEL MARTINEZ.

Finance Office—MRS. ANNABELLE G. OCANAS, CFO, Mailing Address: P.O. Box 98700, Lubbock, 79499. Tel: 806-797-3943.

Facilities Director—Mailing Address: P.O. Box 98700, Lubbock, 79499. Tel: 806-792-3943. Deacon SEVERO ALVARADO.

Respect Life Office—VACANT.

Diocesan Rural Life Office—DOUG HLAVATY, 20407 Hwy. 87, Lubbock, 79423.

Victim Assistance Coordinator—4620 4th St., Lubbock, 79416. Tel: 806-543-9178. OSCAR REYES.

CLERGY, PARISHES, MISSIONS AND PAROCHIAL SCHOOLS

CITY OF LUBBOCK

(LUBBOCK COUNTY)

1—CATHEDRAL CHRIST THE KING (1958)
4011 54th St., 79413-4699. Tel: 806-792-6168; Fax: 806-792-1417; Web: www.ctkcathedral.org. Very Rev. John M. Ohlig; Rev. Rene Perez.
School—Christ the King Cathedral School, (Grades PreK-12), Tel: 806-795-8283; Email: cwanjura@ctkcathedralschool.org; Web: www.ctkcathedralschool.org. Mrs. Gail Ambrose, Prin. (PreK-8); Mrs. Christine Wanjura, Prin. (High School). Clergy 2; Lay Teachers 47; Students 372; Clergy / Religious Teachers 3.
Child Care—Early Childhood Development Center, 5502 Nashville, 79413. Tel: 806-771-2077; Email: ecdcchristtheking@gmail.com. Katie Huey, Dir.
Catechesis Religious Program—Mrs. Margo Gonzalez, P.C.L. Students 270.

2—ST. ELIZABETH UNIVERSITY PARISH (1935)
2305 Main St., 79401. Tel: 806-762-5225, Ext. 7294; Email: stelubbock@gmail.com; Web: www.stelizabethlubbock.com. Revs. Emiliano Zapata, O.P.; Carl Paustian; Robert U. Perry, O.P., In Res.; R.B. Williams, O.P., In Res.; Deacons Richard McCann; Jose Fernando Olascoaga; Jeffrey J. Church; Waldo Martinez; Mr. Kevin Mantooth, Dir.; Mr. Nelson Rodriguez, Youth Min.; Nathan Robinett, Dir. Devel.; Mr. Gregory Shehan, Business Mgr.
Catechesis Religious Program—
Tel: 806-762-5225, Ext. 7304; Fax: 806-741-1962; Email: Sylvia_mslt@outlook.com. Sr. Sylvia Salvan, M.S.L.T., D.R.E. Students 115.

3—HOLY SPIRIT (1998)
9821 Frankford Ave., 79424. Tel: 806-698-6400; Fax: 806-798-0646; Email: parish@holyspiritlubbock.org; Web: www.holyspiritcathparish.org. Rev. Rudolf Crasta; Deacons Rick Vasquez; Michael Kenny; Leo Cottenoir; Ralph Rosiles; Jerry Duenes; Sr. Madonna Canja, M.S.L.T., Parish Outreach Basic Ecclesial Comm.; Karen Macha, Sec.
Res.: 9819 Frankford Ave., 79424.
Catechesis Religious Program—Mary Ellen Doskocill, C.R.E. & C.C.E. Coord. Students 425.

4—ST. JOHN NEUMANN (1979)
5802 22nd, 79407-1721. Tel: 806-799-2649; Email: stjneumann79@gmail.com; Web: www.sjnlubbock.org. Rev. George Roney; Deacons Max Joseph Perea; Ed Sears; Kyle Broderson.
Catechesis Religious Program—Dawn Hyatt, D.R.E. Students 36.

5—ST. JOHN THE BAPTIST CATHOLIC CHURCH (2015)
9810 Indiana Ave., Ste. 150, Box #4, 79423.
Tel: 806-771-2673; Fax: 806-771-2674; Email: stjohnbaptistlbk@gmail.com. Rev. Msgr. David Cruz, V.G.; RoseMary Cardenas, Business Mgr.; Mrs. Terri Contreras, Registrar; Myrna Porras, Sec.
Res.: 3323 86th St., 79423. Tel: 806-747-5996.
Catechesis Religious Program—Nancy Sanchez, D.R.E. Students 135.

6—ST. JOSEPH'S (1924) (Hispanic)
102 N. Ave. P, 79401-1199. Tel: 806-765-9935; Fax: 806-740-0032. Rev. Raymundo Manriquez; Deacons Santos Chavez Jr.; Jesse Cantu.
Catechesis Religious Program—Tel: 806-763-9695; Fax: 806-740-0032. Students 542.

7—OUR LADY OF GRACE (1960) (Hispanic)
3111 Erskine St., 79415-1623. Tel: 806-763-4156; Fax: 806-763-2521; Email: ourladyofgrace@yahoo.com. Very Rev. James McCartney; Rev. Jose de Dios Gonzalez; Deacons Manuel R. Lopez Jr.; Daniel Romo; Ernest Hernandez, (Retired); Erasmo Rodriguez, (Retired); Joe Morin; Sylvia Rubio, Business Mgr.
Catechesis Religious Program—Tel: 806-763-8727. Veronica Lopez, C.C.E. (Elementary); Diane Ramos, C.C.E. (Middle/ High); Melinda Garcia, RCIA (Adult Formation). Students 363.

8—OUR LADY OF GUADALUPE (1980) [CEM] (Hispanic)
1120 52nd St., 79412. Tel: 806-763-0710; Email: info@lubbockolg.org; Web: www.lubbockolg.org. Rev. Martin Pina; Deacons Jose Mora; Joe Martinez; Isaac McDonald; Robert Lopez
Catechesis Religious Program—Email: jmora@lubbockolg.org. Students 400.

9—ST. PATRICK (1960)
1603 Cherry Ave., 79403-6001. Tel: 806-765-5123; Fax: 806-765-5123; Email: saintpatrickchurch@yahoo.com. Rev. Joseph Thanavelil.
Catechesis Religious Program—Tel: 806-765-6979. Sr. Patricia Esparza, D.R.E. Students 116.

10—ST. THERESA'S (1961) (Hispanic)
2202 Upland Ave., 79407. Tel: 806-795-2249; Fax: 806-793-4456; Email: sttheresalubbock@gmail.com. Rev. John Ohlig.
Catechesis Religious Program—Xochitl Martinez, P.C.L. Students 85.

OUTSIDE THE CITY OF LUBBOCK

ABERNATHY, LUBBOCK CO., ST. ISIDORE (1966)
17813 N. I-27, Abernathy, 79311. Tel: 806-298-4278; Fax: 806-853-9484; Email: emmanuel.jp50@yahoo.com. Rev. Jacob P. Puthuparambil, O.S.B., (India).
Catechesis Religious Program—Gloria Garibay, D.R.E. Students 108.
Mission—Sacred Heart, Petersburg.
Tel: 806-677-0063.
Catechesis Religious Program—Hermidie Zapata, D.R.E. Students 50.

ANSON, JONES CO., ST. MICHAEL (1960) [JC] (Hispanic)
2010 County Rd. 477, Anson, 79501.
Tel: 325-823-2777. Rev. Selva Pappu.
Catechesis Religious Program—Lisa Ramos, D.R.E.; Eloise Quintanilla, D.R.E. Students 55.
Mission—Holy Trinity (1926) 1400 N. Hwy. 83, Hamlin, Jones Co. 79520. Students 24.

BROWNFIELD, TERRY CO., ST. ANTHONY'S (1952)
1902 Levelland Hwy, P.O. Box 671, Brownfield, 79316. Tel: 806-637-2344; Tel: 806-637-6626; Email: saintanthonycatholicchurch@yahoo.com. Rev. Eduardo C. Teo; Deacons Martin Miranda; Israel Limon Jr.; George Holguin.
Catechesis Religious Program—Fax: 806-637-2356. Chris Martinez, P.C.L.; Elsa Martinez, P.C.L. Students 156.
Mission—San Francisco de Asis, P.O. Box 92, Ropesville, Hockley Co. 79358.
Catechesis Religious Program—Evelyn Gonzales, D.R.E. Students 12.

DENVER CITY, YOAKUM CO., ST. WILLIAM (1955)
401 Mustang Ave., Denver City, 79323-2749.
Tel: 806-592-2063; Fax: 806-592-2239; Email: stwilliamcc@gmail.com. Rev. Heriberto Mercado; Deacon Angel Hernandez, P.C.L.
Catechesis Religious Program—Students 420.
Mission—Sacred Heart, 1305 11th St., Plains, Yoakum Co. 79355. Tel: 806-456-7002.

FLOYDADA, FLOYD CO., ST. MARY MAGDALEN (1928) [JC]
309 S. Wall, Floydada, 79235. Tel: 806-983-5878; Tel: 806-983-3496; Email: stmarymagdalen@att.net. Rev. Jaya Chandra Ruban Selvaraj.
Res.: 809 W. Ross, Floydada, 79235.
Catechesis Religious Program—Laticia Tevino, D.R.E. Students 42.
Missions—Our Lady of Guadalupe—701 Bundy St., Matador, Motley Co. 79244. Annette Hollinsworth, Contact Person.
St. Elizabeth, Second St. & Clare St., Paducah, Cottle Co. 79348. Janie Canales, Contact Person.
San Jose de Calasanz, 303 S.E. Fourth, Lockney, Floyd Co. 79241. Tel: 806-652-2321 (Parish Hall).

IDALOU, LUBBOCK CO., ST. PHILIP BENIZI (1979) (Spanish)
722 Sixth Pl., P.O. Box 1337, Idalou, 79329-1337.
Tel: 806-892-2743; Tel: 806-892-2928;
Fax: 806-892-9001. Rev. Jose Matthew Kochuparambil, J.V.; Deacons Rudy Calsoncin; Steve Padilla.
Catechesis Religious Program—Terri Espinoza, D.R.E. Students 121.
Mission—San Lorenzo, Jackson & Monroe, P.O. Box 129, Lorenzo, Crosby Co. 79343.
Catechesis Religious Program—Students 55.

LAMESA, DAWSON CO., ST. MARGARET MARY (1929) [CEM]
911 S. 1st St., P.O. Box 599, Lamesa, 79331.
Tel: 806-872-7100; Tel: 806-853-8309;
Fax: 806-872-3630; Email: stmmolg@gmail.com. Rev. Joseph Kurumbel, O.S.B.; Deacons Daniel Valenzuela; Saul Hernandez; Elva Gutierrez, Parish Sec.
Catechesis Religious Program—Francis Garcia, D.R.E.; Maria Casillas, D.R.E. Students 264.
Mission—Our Lady of Guadalupe, 407 N. Hartford, P.O. Box 599, Lamesa, Dawson Co. 79331.
Fax: 806-872-7100.

LEVELLAND, HOCKLEY CO., ST. MICHAEL'S (1956)
319 E. Washington St., Levelland, 79336-2611.
Tel: 806-894-2268; Email: stmichaellevelland@gmail.com; Web: stmichaellevelland.org. Very Rev. Ernesto Lopez; Rev. Jonathan Phillips; Deacons Juan Cavazos; Sergio Vidales.
Catechesis Religious Program—Tel: 806-894-9880. Gracie Ruiz, D.R.E.; Jesse Moreno, Dir. Youth Min.; Monica Moreno, Dir. Youth Min. Students 252.
Mission—San Isidro, 1306 S. Slaughter, P.O. Box 764, Sundown, Hockley Co. 79372-0764.

LITTLEFIELD, LAMB CO., SACRED HEART (1921) [CEM]
1309 W. 8th St., P.O. Box 1347, Littlefield, 79339-4234. Tel: 806-385-6043; Email: sacheart@windstream.net; Web: sacredheartlittlefield.org. Rev. Brian Wood.
Catechesis Religious Program—Susan Craig, D.R.E.; Joann Cuerto, D.R.E. Students 101.

MORTON, COCHRAN CO., ST. ANN (1955)
105 N.E. 8th St., Morton, 79346. Tel: 806-266-8693; Fax: 806-266-8692; Email: stannchurchmorton@gmail.com. Very Rev. Ernesto Lopez.
Catechesis Religious Program—Alma Ornelas, D.R.E. Students 83.
Mission—St. Philip Neri, [CEM] Farm Rd. 303, P.O. Box 395, Pep, Hockley Co. 79353. Tel: 806-933-4355. Marcy Demel, Contact Person.

MULESHOE, BAILEY CO., IMMACULATE CONCEPTION (1956) [CEM 2] [JC] (Hispanic)
805 E Hickory Ave, Muleshoe, 79347.
Tel: 806-272-4384; Email: iccmuleshoe@gmail.com. Rev. Leonardo Pahamtang, (Philippines).
Catechesis Religious Program—Tel: 806-272-4167. Alma Orozco, D.R.E. Students 260.
Mission—St. Mary Magdalen.
Catechesis Religious Program—Patsy Garcia, D.R.E. Students 55.

O'DONNELL, LYNN CO., ST. PIUS X (1959) [CEM] (Hispanic)
3025 CR.P, O'Donnell, 79351. Tel: 806-428-3224; Email: stephengnan@gmail.com. Rev. John Rathinam, I.M.S.
Catechesis Religious Program—Maria Zorola, D.R.E. Students 19.
Mission—St. Jude Thaddeus Catholic Church (1951) P.O. Box 785, Tahoka, Lynn Co. 79373.
Tel: 806-561-4420.
Catechesis Religious Program—Students 86.

OLTON, LAMB CO., ST. PETER THE APOSTLE (1944)
Mailing Address: 206 E. 11th St., P.O. Box 655, Olton, 79064-0655. Fax: 806-285-2140;
Fax: 806-285-3140; Email: saintpeterolton@gmail.com. Rev. Sylvester Dsouza.
Mission—St. Theresa, 504 E. 13th St., P.O. Box 528, Hale Center, 79041. Tel: 806-839-2892; Email: siludesouza@yahoo.com. Mrs. Juanita Pineda, Contact Person.
Catechesis Religious Program—
504 E. 13th St., Half Center, 79041.
Tel: 806-292-5592; Email: mmartinez1001@yahoo.com. Minerva Martinez, D.R.E. Students 119.

PLAINVIEW, HALE CO.

1—ST. ALICE (1911)
Mailing Address: 1114 Houston St., Plainview, 79072-7124. Rev. Msgr. Nicolas Rendon, (Philippines).
Res.: 810 W. 11th St., Plainview, 79072-7124.
Tel: 806-293-1903.
Catechesis Religious Program—Tel: 806-293-2891. Joann Gamez, D.R.E. Students 75.

2—OUR LADY OF GUADALUPE aka Nuestra Señora de Guadalupe (1946) [CEM]
211 W. 7th St., Plainview, 79072. Tel: 806-293-0085; Fax: 806-293-4507; Email: wjanton@gmail.com. P.O.

Box 1269, Plainview, 79073. Very Rev. William J. Anton; Deacon Arturo Hinojosa, Youth Min.; Sr. Patricia Esparza, D.R.E.; Mrs. Marisol Benzor, Sec.
Catechesis Religious Program—Students 221.
3—SACRED HEART (1964) (Hispanic)
2801 N. Columbia, Plainview, 79072.
Tel: 806-296-2753; Email: shplainview@gmail.com. 400 W. 29th St., Plainview, 79072. Rev. George Poonely
Legal Title: Sacred Heart Church
Catechesis Religious Program—Students 221.
POST, GARZA CO., HOLY CROSS (1955) [JC]
P.O. Box 190, Post, 79356-0190. Tel: 806-495-2791. Rev. Joseph Thanavelil.
Catechesis Religious Program—Debbie K. Hernandez, D.R.E. Students 89.
Mission—Blessed Sacrament, P.O. Box 119, Wilson, Lynn Co. 79381-0119. Debbie Hernadez, D.R.E.
RALLS, CROSBY CO., ST. MICHAEL (1959) [JC] (Hispanic)
Mailing Address: 1210 4th Street, P.O. Box 906, Ralls, 79357-0906. Tel: 806-253-2008; Email: stmichaelralls@live.com. Rev. Samuel B. Oracion.
Catechesis Religious Program—Virginia Torres, D.R.E. Students 15.
Mission—St. Joseph, Crosby Co.
ROTAN, FISHER CO., ST. JOSEPH (1929)
303 E. Lee, Rotan, 79546-3011. Tel: 325-267-6413; Tel: 325-267-6412; Email: stjosephrotan@yahoo.com. Rev. Renato Cruz; Deacon Valentin Morin, Youth Min.
Catechesis Religious Program—Rosemary Carrillo, D.R.E. Students 51.
Missions—Sacred Heart—[CEM] Ranchito, Fisher Co.
St. Mary, Aspermont, Stonewall Co.
SEMINOLE, GAINES CO., ST. JAMES (1958)
1010 Hobbs Hwy., P.O. Box 898, Seminole, 79360-0898. Tel: 432-758-2371; Email: stjamescatholic@sbcglobal.net. Rev. Paul Karieakatt, (India).
Catechesis Religious Program—P.O. Box 898, Seagraves, 79359. Tel: 432-847-9493; Email: gomez_lucinda@att.net. Lucinda Gomez, D.R.E. Students 235.
Mission—St. Paul's, 805 12th St., Seagraves, Gaines Co. 79359. Cindy M Davila, Contact Person.
Catechesis Religious Program—Tel: 432-238-3478. Lydia Aguilar, D.R.E.; Valerie Bueno, Youth Dir.; Jose Bueno, Youth Dir. Students 72.
SHALLOWATER, LUBBOCK CO., ST. PHILIP BENIZI (1967) [JC] (Hispanic)
1314 6th St., Shallowater, 79363. Tel: 806-832-5915; Tel: 806-832-4088. Rev. George Poonely; Deacons Frank Lopez, (Retired); Tommy Alvarado.
Catechesis Religious Program—Carmen Behrens, C.R.E.; Yolanda Sanchez, C.R.E. Students 131.
Mission—St. Anthony of Padua (1966) 4th S. Lawrence, Box 545, Anton, Hockley, Co. 79313.
SLATON, LUBBOCK CO.
1—ST. JOSEPH'S (1912) [JC] (German)
205 S. 19th, Slaton, 79364-3755. Tel: 806-828-3944; Fax: 806-828-3944. Rev. Joseph Palacios; Deacons Leroy Behnke; Adam V. Behnke.
School—St. Joseph's School, (Grades PreK-8), 1305 W. Division St., Slaton, 79364. Tel: 806-828-6761; Fax: 806-828-5396. Sr. Brenda Haynes, S.N.D., Prin. Lay Teachers 5; Sisters 3; Students 43.
Catechesis Religious Program—Students 50.
2—OUR LADY OF GUADALUPE (1952) [JC]
705 S. Fourth, Slaton, 79364-5406. Tel: 806-828-5108 ; Email: olgslaton@yahoo.com. Rev. Angelo R. Consemino; Deacon Phillip Maldonado; Eva Diaz, Parish Sec.
Catechesis Religious Program—Tel: 806-828-4573; Fax: 806-828-5108. Students 98.
SNYDER, SCURRY CO.
1—ST. ELIZABETH'S (1952) [CEM]
3005 Ave. A, Snyder, 79549-3909. Tel: 325-573-8824; Email: snyderstelizabeth@gmail.com. Rev. Arsenio C. Redulla.
Catechesis Religious Program—Tel: 325-573-8824. Students 48.
Mission—St. John, 4125 County Rd., Hermleigh, 79526.
2—OUR LADY OF GUADALUPE (1955) [CEM] [JC2] (Hispanic)
1311 Ave. K, Snyder, 79549-9533.
Tel: 325-573-3866 (Office); Tel: 325-573-1569 (Res.); Fax: 325-573-7142; Email: ologsny@sbcglobal.net. Rev. Raj Arokiasamy.
Catechesis Religious Program—Tel: 325-574-1022. Irma Guerero, P.C.L. Students 289.
SPUR, DICKENS CO., ST. MARY (1948)
402 E. 6th St., Spur, 79370. Tel: 806-271-4830; Fax: 806-271-4385. P.O. Box 189, Spur, 79370-0189. Rev. Jaya Chandra Ruban Selvaraj; Deacons Pete Garcia, (Retired); Eddie Morales.
Catechesis Religious Program—Students 43.
Mission—Epiphany, [JC] Jayton, Kent Co.
STAMFORD, JONES CO., ST. ANN (1955) [CEM]
104 New Braunfels, Stamford, 79553-6415.
Tel: 325-773-2659; Email: stannschurch1@gmail.com. Rev. Chacko Thadathil.
Catechesis Religious Program—Students 40.
Mission—St. George, 901 N. 16th St., Haskell, Haskell Co. 79521-3340. Tel: 940-864-3171.
Catechesis Religious Program—Students 39.
WOLFFORTH, LUBBOCK CO., ST. FRANCIS OF ASSISI MISSION, See separate listing. See San Ramon, Woodrow for details. Rev. Joy Anthony Thachil, S.A.C., (India).
WOODROW, LUBBOCK CO., SAN RAMON (1974)
15706 Loop 493, 79423. Tel: 806-863-2201; Fax: 806-863-3435. Rev. Joy Anthony Thachil, S.A.C., (India); Deacons Ron Vowels; Isidoro Saldana.
Catechesis Religious Program—Students 138.
Mission—St. Francis of Assisi, P.O. Box 785, Wolfforth, Lubbock Co. 79382. Tel: 806-866-9007.

Retired:
Very Rev. Msgr.—
Kasteel, Ben, V.G., (Retired)
Rev. Msgrs.—
Buxkemper, Roland, (Retired), Mexico
Driscoll, Eugene J., (Retired)
James, Joseph W., (Retired), Our Lady of Mercy Retreat Center, P.O. Box 744, Slaton, 79364
Leatham, Gerald, (Retired)
O'Connor, James, (Retired), Ireland
Schwertner, Timothy, (Retired)
Revs.—
Cherolikal, John, (Retired)
Judd, Timothy, (Retired)
Maher, Patrick, (Retired), Ireland
Neyland, Malcolm, (Retired)
Ramirez, Cornelio C., S.A.C., (Retired), 8415 Fremont Ave., 79423.

Permanent Deacons:
Almager, Ramon, (Retired)
Alvarado, Tommy, St. Anthony, Anton
Bane, John
Behnke, Adam V.
Behnke, Leroy, St. Joseph, Slaton
Brito, Benny, St. Joseph, Lubbock
Broderson, Kyle, St. John Neumann, Lubbock
Bustamante, Juan, (Retired), St. Ann, Stamford
Calsoncin, Rudy
Canale, Randy, Christ the King, Lubbock
Cantu, Jesse
Cavazos, Juan, St. Michael, Levelland
Chavez, Santos Jr.
Church, Jeffrey J.
Close, David
Cochran, Clarke E., St. John Neumann, Lubbock
Cottenoir, Leo, St. Michael, Levelland
Diaz, Ramon
Dougherty, Christopher
Duenes, Jerry, On duty outside the Diocese
Esquivel, Jessie, On duty outside the Diocese
Estrada, Julian, St. George, Haskell
Flores, Richard, (Retired), St. Anthony, Anton
Garcia, Aureliano, St. Michael, Ralls
Garcia, Doroteo, Sacred Heart, Littlefield
Garibay, Roy
Gracia, Pedro, (Retired), St. Mary, Spur
Hernandez, Angel
Hernandez, Ernesto, (Retired), Our Lady of Grace, Lubbock
Hinojosa, Arturo
Holguin, George, St. Anthony, Brownfield
Juarez, Pedro, Sacred Heart, Littlefield; On Duty Outside the Diocese
Key, Billy, On Duty Outside the Diocese
Limon, Israel Jr.
Lopez, Frank, (Retired), St. Phillip, Shallowater
Lopez, Manuel R. Jr.
Lopez, Robert
Maldonado, Phillip, Our Lady of Guadalupe, Slaton
Marin, Manuel
Martinez, Joe, Our Lady of Guadalupe, Lubbock
Martinez, Waldo, St. Elizabeth, Lubbock
McCann, Richard, St. Elizabeth, Lubbock
McDonald, Isaac, Our Lady of Guadalupe, Lubbock
Miranda, Martin
Mora, Jose
Morales, Eddie, Church of the Epiphany, Jayton
Morin, Joe, Our Lady of Grace, Lubbock
Morin, Valentin
Murillo, Paul
Olascoaga, Jose Fernando
Ortegon, Frank, (Retired), Our Lady of Guadalupe, Snyder
Padilla, Steve
Paniagua, Pete M.
Perea, Max Joseph
Phillips, Benny P.
Ramirez, Robert, Our Lady of Guadalupe, Snyder
Ramon, Rene
Resendez, Simon, St. Pius X, O'Donnell
Rodriguez, Erasmo, (Retired)
Rodriguez, Jose Luis, St. Theresa, Lubbock
Rodriguez, Ramiro, St. Patrick's, Lubbock
Romo, Daniel
Rosiles, Ralph, Holy Spirit, Lubbock
Rubalcado, Nasario, St. Joseph, Ralls
Rubio, Jose, St. Phillip Benizi, Idalou
Saldana, Isidoro, St. Francis, Lubbock
Sears, Edward L.
Simmons, Gary
Tjia, Steve, (Retired)
Valenzuela, Daniel, St. Margaret Mary, Lamesa
Vasquez, Enrique, St. Mary Magdalen, Floydada
Vidales, Sergio
Vowels, Ron.

INSTITUTIONS LOCATED IN DIOCESE

[A] MONASTERIES & RESIDENCES OF PRIESTS AND BROTHERS

LUBBOCK. *Southern Dominican Fathers of Lubbock* (2010) 2305 Main St., 79401.
Tel: 806-762-5225, Ext. 7343; Fax: 806-741-1962; Email: stelubbock@gmail.com. Revs. Carl Paustian, Member; Robert U. Perry, O.P., Member; R.B. Williams, O.P., Member; Emiliano Zapata, O.P., Member. Total in Community 4.

[B] CONVENTS AND RESIDENCES FOR SISTERS

LUBBOCK. *Our Lady of Grace Convent*, 3101 Erskine, 79415. Tel: 806-747-7472. Missionary Catechists of the Sacred Hearts of Jesus and Mary 3.
PLAINVIEW. *St. Alice Convent*, 1114 Houston, Plainview, 79072. Tel: 806-296-5426. St. Francis Mission Community 3.
WOLFFORTH. *St. Francis Mission Community* (1981) Our Lady of the Angels Motherhouse, 8202 CR 7700, Wolfforth, 79382. Tel: 806-863-4904; Fax: 806-863-4906; Email: franciscan@erfwireless.net. Caroline Rejino, Treas. St. Francis Mission Community 17.

[C] CATHOLIC RENEWAL CENTERS

LUBBOCK. *Catholic Renewal Center*, P.O. Box 98700, 79499-8700. Tel: 806-792-3943, Ext. 203; Web: www.dioceseoflubbock.org. Total Staff 4.
Office for Cursillo Movement, P.O. Box 98303, 79499-8296. Tel: 806-792-4308. Deacon Joe Morin.

[D] RETREAT HOUSES

SLATON. *Our Lady of Mercy Retreat Center*, 605 S. 19th St., Slaton, 79364-0744. Tel: 806-828-6428; Fax: 806-828-4861; Email: mercyslaton@gmail.com; Web: mercyrc.com. P.O. Box 744, Slaton, 79364. Rev. Msgr. Joseph W. James, Founder, (Retired); Mark Meurer, Dir. Total in Residence 3; Total Staff 8.

[E] MISCELLANEOUS LISTINGS

LUBBOCK. *Catholic Foundation of the Diocese of Lubbock, Inc.*, P.O. Box 98700, 79499-8700. Tel: 806-792-3943; Fax: 806-771-7660; Email: foundation@catholiclubbock.org; Email: rmartinez@catholiclubbock.org; Web: www.catholicfoundationlubbock.org. 4620 4th St., 79416. Mrs. Rachel Martinez, Dir.
Christ the King Cathedral School Foundation, 4011 54th St., 79413. Tel: 806-795-8283; Fax: 806-795-9715; Email: cduran@ctkcathedralschool.org; Email: cwanjura@ctkcathedralschool.org; Web: www.CTKCathedralschool.org. Very Rev. John M. Ohlig, Pastor.
RELIGIOUS INSTITUTES OF WOMEN REPRESENTED IN THE DIOCESE
For further details refer to the corresponding bracketed number in the Religious Institutes of Men or Women section.

[2700]—*Missionary Catechists of the Sacred Hearts of Jesus and Mary*—M.C.S.S.C.C.J.M.
[]—*Missionary Sisters of the Lord's Table*—M.S.L.T.
[]—*Sisters of Charity of the Incarnate Word*—C.C.V.I.
[2575]—*Sisters of Mercy of the Americas*—R.S.M.
[1620]—*Sisters of Saint Francis the Neumann Communities*—O.S.F.
[]—*St. Francis Mission Community* (Wolfforth, TX)—O.S.F.

An asterisk (*) denotes an organization that has established tax-exempt status directly with the IRS and is not covered by the USCCB Group Ruling.

Diocese of Madison

(Dioecesis Madisonensis)

Most Reverend

DONALD J. HYING

Bishop of Madison; ordained May 20, 1989; appointed Auxiliary Bishop of Milwaukee and Titular Bishop of Regiae May 26, 2011; installed July 20, 2011; appointed Bishop of Gary November 24, 2014; installed January 6, 2015; appointed Bishop of Madison April 25, 2019; installed June 25, 2019. *Chancery: Bishop O'Connor Catholic Center, 702 S. High Point Rd., Ste. 225, Madison, WI 53719.*

Chancery: Bishop O'Connor Catholic Center, 702 S. High Point Rd., Ste. 225, Madison, WI 53719. Tel: 608-821-3000; Fax: 608-440-2809.

Web: www.madisondiocese.org

Email: diocese@madisondiocese.org

Established 1946.

Square Miles 8,046.

Corporate Title: "Roman Catholic Diocese of Madison, Inc."

Comprises the Counties of Columbia, Dane, Grant, Green, Green Lake, Iowa, Jefferson, Lafayette, Marquette, Rock and Sauk in the State of Wisconsin.

For legal titles of parishes and diocesan institutions, consult the Chancery.

STATISTICAL OVERVIEW

Personnel	
Bishop	1
Retired Abbots	1
Priests: Diocesan Active in Diocese	76
Priests: Diocesan Active Outside Diocese	9
Priests: Retired, Sick or Absent	42
Number of Diocesan Priests	127
Religious Priests in Diocese	10
Total Priests in Diocese	137
Extern Priests in Diocese	28
Ordinations:	
Diocesan Priests	3
Transitional Deacons	4
Permanent Deacons	1
Permanent Deacons in Diocese	22
Total Brothers	5
Total Sisters	364
Parishes	
Parishes	102
With Resident Pastor:	
Resident Diocesan Priests	101
Resident Religious Priests	1
Missions	1
Pastoral Centers	2
New Parishes Created	1
Closed Parishes	2
Professional Ministry Personnel:	
Brothers	4
Sisters	5
Lay Ministers	1,026
Welfare	
Catholic Hospitals	4
Total Assisted	538,559
Health Care Centers	3
Total Assisted	163,434
Homes for the Aged	7
Total Assisted	1,512
Residential Care of Children	5
Total Assisted	5
Day Care Centers	20
Total Assisted	1,124
Specialized Homes	2
Total Assisted	291
Special Centers for Social Services	20
Total Assisted	52,105
Residential Care of Disabled	90
Total Assisted	313
Other Institutions	6
Total Assisted	8,923
Educational	
Diocesan Students in Other Seminaries	24
Total Seminarians	24
Colleges and Universities	1
Total Students	2,190
High Schools, Private	3
Total Students	584
Elementary Schools, Diocesan and Parish	42
Total Students	4,589
Elementary Schools, Private	4
Total Students	377
Catechesis/Religious Education:	
High School Students	2,891
Elementary Students	7,975
Total Students under Catholic Instruction	18,630
Teachers in the Diocese:	
Sisters	5
Lay Teachers	716
Vital Statistics	
Receptions into the Church:	
Infant Baptism Totals	1,887
Minor Baptism Totals	163
Adult Baptism Totals	59
Received into Full Communion	77
First Communions	2,049
Confirmations	2,262
Marriages:	
Catholic	328
Interfaith	134
Total Marriages	462
Deaths	1,585
Total Catholic Population	182,129
Total Population	1,060,208

Former Bishops—Most Revs. WILLIAM P. O'CONNOR, D.D., Ph.D., ord. March 10, 1912; appt. Bishop of Superior, Dec. 31, 1941; cons. March 7, 1942; transferred to first Bishop of Madison, Feb. 22, 1946; resigned Feb. 22, 1967; died July 13, 1973; CLETUS F. O'DONNELL, D.D., J.C.D., ord. May 3, 1941; appt. Titular Bishop of Abrittum and Auxiliary of Chicago, Oct. 26, 1960; cons. Dec. 21, 1960; promoted to Bishop of Madison, Feb. 22, 1967; resigned April 18, 1992; died Aug. 31, 1992; WILLIAM H. BULLOCK, D.D., E.D.S., ord. June 7, 1952; appt. Auxiliary Bishop of St. Paul and Minneapolis and Titular Bishop of Natchez June 3, 1980; cons. Aug. 12, 1980; appt. Bishop of Des Moines Feb. 10, 1987; installed April 2, 1987; appt. Bishop of Madison April 13, 1993; installed June 14, 1993; retired May 23, 2003; died April 3, 2011.; ROBERT C. MORLINO, D.D., S.T.D., ord. June 1, 1974; appt. Bishop of Helena July 6, 1999; cons. and installed Sept. 21, 1999; appt. Bishop of Madison May 23, 2003; installed Aug. 1, 2003; died Nov. 24, 2018.

Diocesan Administrator—Rev. Msgr. JAMES R. BARTYLLA.

Chancery—Bishop O'Connor Catholic Center, 702 S. High Point Rd., Ste. 225, Madison, 53719. Office Hours: Mon.-Fri. 8-4:30.

Chancellor—MR. WILLIAM D. YALLALY, Tel: 608-821-3003.

Director of Finance—MR. JOHN C. PHILIPP, Tel: 608-821-3021.

Diocesan Tribunal—Bishop O'Connor Catholic Center, 702 S. High Point Rd., Ste. 225, Madison, 53719. Tel: 608-821-3060; Fax: 608-440-2813; Email: tribunal@madisondiocese.org.

Judicial Vicar—Very Rev. GABRIEL A. LOPEZ-BETANZOS, J.C.L.

Judges—Very Rev. GABRIEL A. LOPEZ-BETANZOS, J.C.L.; Rev. MATTHEW M. BERGSCHNEIDER, J.C.L.; MR. TIMOTHY J. CAVANAUGH, J.C.L.; MR. PAUL M. MATENAER, J.C.L.

Promoter of Justice—Rev. SCOTT J. EMERSON, J.C.L.

Defenders of the Bond—PROF. WILLIAM L. DANIEL, J.C.D.; Rev. SCOTT J. EMERSON, J.C.L.

Advocate/Procurator (cc.1481-1490)—LAURA L. MORRISON, J.D., J.C.D.; ANDREW BARTELL, J.D., J.C.L.; DANIEL P. QUINAN, J.C.L.; JENNA M. COOPER, J.C.L.; MATTHEW R. KUETTEL, J.C.L.; RICHARD J. VERVER, J.C.L.; ED F. CONDON, J.C.D.; TIMOTHY M. OLSON; TODD BURUD; Revs. ALEXANDER M. LASCHUK, Ph.D., J.C.D.; DAVID A. CARRANO; BRYNA K. FASSINO; MR. ALDEAN B. HENDRICKSON, J.C.L.; ANNETTE M. HRYWNA, J.C.L.; JOSH D. TAGGATZ, J.D.; AMANDA M. ZURFACE, J.C.L.; CHRISTINA HIP-FLORES, J.C.D.; VINCENT M. GARDINER.

Notaries—MR. GRANT R. EMMEL, P.E.; MS. BECCA FISCHER; MR. WILLIAM D. YALLALY; MR. NATE SIMMONS.

Diocesan Consultors—Rev. Msgrs. JAMES R. BARTYLLA; MICHAEL L. BURKE, (Retired); DANIEL T. GANSHERT; KEVIN D. HOLMES; Very Revs. JOHN M. MEINHOLZ, V.F.; PAUL U. ARINZE, V.F.; RICHARD M. HEILMAN, V.F.; Rev. BART D. TIMMERMAN; Very Rev. GREGORY S. IHM.

Personnel Board—Rev. BART D. TIMMERMAN; Very Rev. RANDY J. TIMMERMAN, V.F.; Rev. MICHAEL A. RESOP; Rev. Msgrs. LAWRENCE M. BAKKE; DANIEL T. GANSHERT; JAMES R. BARTYLLA, Diocesan Admin., Ex Officio, & Chm.; Very Rev. JAMES M. POSTER, V.F.; Revs. SCOTT M. JABLONSKI; MICHAEL R. RADOWICZ.

Director for Permanent Deacons—Rev. MICHAEL R. RADOWICZ, Mailing Address: Diocese of Madison, 702 S. High Point Rd., Ste. 225, Madison, 53719.

Vicar for Priests—Rev. Msgr. JAMES L. GUNN, Mailing Address: Diocese of Madison, 702 S. High Point Rd., Ste. 225, Madison, 53719.

Vicar for Religious—VACANT.

Vicariates Forane—Very Rev. DAVID J. GREENFIELD, V.F., Columbia North Vicariate Forane; Rev. Msgr. DUANE R. MOELLENBERNDT, V.F., East Dane Vicariate Forane; Very Revs. JOHN M. MEINHOLZ, V.F., Grant Vicariate Forane; PATRICK J. WENDLER, Jefferson Vicariate Forane; Rev. STEPHEN C. PETRICA, V.F., Lafayette Vicariate; Very Revs. RANDY J. TIMMERMAN, V.F., Madison Vicariate Forane; PAUL UGO ARINZE, V.F., Rock-Green Vicariate Forane; JAMES M. POSTER, V.F., Sauk Vicariate Forane; RICHARD M. HEILMAN, V.F., West Dane Vicariate Forane.

Diocesan Offices and Directors

Apostolate for Persons with Disabilities—Bishop O'Connor Catholic Center, 702 S. High Point Rd.,

Ste. 225, Madison, 53719. Tel: 608-821-3050; Email: apd@madisondiocese.org. Rev. Msgr. LAWRENCE M. BAKKE.

Apostolate to the Deaf—VACANT.

Archives—MS. PAT BORN, Archivist, Bishop O'Connor Catholic Center, 702 S. High Point Rd., Ste. 225, Madison, 53719. Tel: 608-821-3140; Fax: 608-440-2811.

Catholic Committee on Scouting—MR. MICHAEL KLECKNER, Chm., 5595 Longford Terr., Madison, 53711. Tel: 608-275-3344; Email: mkleckner@amfam.com.

Building Commission—Rev. THOMAS L. KELLEY; Rev. Msgrs. DUANE R. MOELLENBERNDT, V.F.; JAMES R. BARTYLLA; MR. JOHN C. PHILIPP, Chm.; MRS. JILL MCNALLY; DR. PATRICK GORMAN; MR. PETER SZOTKOWSKI; MR. GRANT R. EMMEL, P.E.; MR. ERIC SCHIEDERMAYER.

Camp Gray—*E10213 Shady Lane Rd., Reedsburg, 53959*. Tel: 608-356-8200; Fax: 608-356-5855; Email: bigfun@campgray.com. JEFF HOEBEN, Dir.

Catholic Relief Services—VACANT.

Department of Cemeteries—MR. JOHN MILLER, Diocesan Dir., Central Office, 2705 Regent St., Madison, 53705. Tel: 608-238-5561; Fax: 608-440-2810.

Catholic Charities—*Bishop O'Connor Catholic Center, 702 S. High Point Rd., Madison, 53719.* Tel: 608-826-8000. JACKSON FONDER, Pres. & CEO, Madison Offices, 702 S. High Point Rd., Ste. 201, Madison, 53719. Tel: 608-826-8111; Fax: 608-826-8026.

Office for the Continuing Formation of Priests—*Bishop O'Connor Catholic Center, 702 S. High Point Rd., Ste. 225, Madison, 53719.* Tel: 608-821-3006. Rev. SCOTT M. JABLONSKI, Dir.

Education—MICHAEL LANCASTER, Ed.S., Supt., Schools, Tel: 608-821-3180.

Saint Raphael Society Clergy Retirement Plan—*Bishop O'Connor Catholic Center, 702 S. High Point Rd., Ste. 225, Madison, 53719.* Tel: 608-821-3011. Rev. Msgr. JAMES R. BARTYLLA; Rev. DAVID A. CARRANO; Rev. Msgr. JAMES J. UPPENA, (Retired); Very Rev. PAUL UGO ARINZE, V.F.; Rev. BRIAN J. WILK, V.F.; MR. WILLIAM D. YALLALY, Chancellor; MR. JOHN C. PHILIPP, Dir. Finance; MR. TODD ARGALL.

Council of Catholic Women—Rev. Msgr. DUANE R. MOELLENBERNDT, V.F., Moderator, Sacred Hearts of Jesus & Mary, 221 Columbus St., Sun Prairie, 53590-2297. Tel: 608-837-7381, Ext. 232.

Director of Communications & Information—BRENT KING, Tel: 608-821-3033. Bishop O'Connor Catholic Center, 702 S. High Point Rd., Ste. 225, Madison, 53719.

Office of Worship—DR. PATRICK GORMAN, Bishop O'Connor Catholic Center, 702 S. High Point Rd., Ste. 225, Madison, 53719. Tel: 608-821-3080.

Madison Diocesan Choir—*Bishop O'Connor Catholic Center, 702 S. High Point Rd., Ste. 225, Madison, 53719.* Tel: 608-821-3080; Email: diocesanchoir@straphael.org; Web: www.madisondiocese.org. DR. PATRICK GORMAN, Dir.

Office of Justice—MR. NATE SIMMONS, Bishop O'Connor Catholic Center, 702 S. High Point Rd., Ste. 225, Madison, 53719. Tel: 608-821-3086.

Outreach—

Catholic Multicultural Center—ANDREW RUSSELL, Admin., Tel: 608-661-3512.

Centro Pastoral Guadalupano—*Catholic Multicultural Center, 1862 Beld St., Madison, 53713.* Tel: 608-661-3512, Ext. 102. STEVE MAURICE, Coord.

St. Martin House—*Catholic Multicultural Center, 1862 Beld St., Madison, 53713.* Tel: 608-661-3512, Ext. 200. STEVE MAURICE, Coord.

Hispanic Ministry—*Bishop O'Connor Catholic Center, 702 S. High Point Rd., Ste. 225, Madison, 53719.* Tel: 608-821-3015.

Evangelization and Catechesis Department—(Youth & Young Adult Ministry; Respect Life - Tel: 608-821-4544; Curriculum and Catechist Development; Newman Apostolate - Madison: Rev. Eric H. Nielsen, Dir.; St. Paul Univ. Catholic Center, 723 State St., Madison, WI, 53703. Tel: 608-258-3140. Platteville: Rev. John Del Priore, S.J.S.; St. Augustine Newman Center, 135 S. Hickory St., Platteville, WI 53818. Tel: 608-348-7530).

Newspaper—"Catholic Herald, Madison Edition" MARY UHLER, Editor, Bishop O'Connor Catholic Center, 702 S. High Point Rd., Ste. 121, Madison, 53719. Tel: 608-821-3070.

Victim Assistance Coordinator—MRS. CHERYL BARTOSZEK, Bishop O'Connor Catholic Center, 702 S. High Point Rd., Ste. 225, Madison, 53719. Tel: 608-821-3162.

Propagation of the FaithRev. CHAD M. DROESSLER, Dir., Bishop O'Connor Catholic Center, 702 S. High Point Rd., Ste. 225, Madison, 53719. Tel: 608-821-3052; Fax: 608-440-2811.

St. Vincent de Paul Society—EDWARD A. EMMENEGGER.

Serra Clubs—Madison: Very Rev. GREGORY S. IHM. Janesville: Very Rev. GREGORY S. IHM.

Vocations—Very Rev. GREGORY S. IHM, Dir., Bishop O'Connor Catholic Center, 702 S. High Point Rd., Ste. 225, Madison, 53719. Tel: 800-833-8452 (Toll Free); Fax: 608-440-2814; Email: vocations@madisondiocese.org; Web: www.madisondiocese.org.

Wisconsin Catholic Conference—KIM WADAS VERCAUTEREN, Exec. Sec., 131 W. Wilson St., Ste. 1105, Madison, 53703. Tel: 608-257-0004.

Office of Human Resources—JOHN B. MILLER, Dir., Bishop O'Connor Catholic Center, 702 S. High Point Rd., Ste. 225, Madison, 53719. Tel: 608-821-3047.

Office of Stewardship and Development—JILL MCNALLY, Dir., Mailing Address: Bishop O'Connor Catholic Center, 702 S. High Point Rd., Ste. 225, Madison, 53719. Tel: 608-821-3043.

CLERGY, PARISHES, MISSIONS AND PAROCHIAL SCHOOLS

CITY OF MADISON

(DANE COUNTY)

1—CATHEDRAL PARISH OF ST. RAPHAEL (1854) (Merger of St. Raphael, Madison, Holy Redeemer, 128 W. Johnson St., Madison & St. Patrick, 410 E. Main St., Madison)
404 E. Main St., 53703. Tel: 608-257-5000;
Fax: 844-272-6677; Email: cathedral@straphael.org; Web: www.isthmuscatholic.org. Rev. Msgr. Kevin D. Holmes, Rector; Rev. Jose Luis Vazquez, (Mexico); Deacon Christopher Schmelzer.
Res.: 120 W. Johnson St., 53703.
Catechesis Religious Program—Email: amber@isthmuscatholic.org. Amber Cerrato, D.R.E. Students 140.
Lumen House, LLC—142 W. Johnson St., 53703.

2—ST. BERNARD (1907) [JC]
2462 Atwood Ave., 53704. Tel: 608-249-9256;
Fax: 608-244-3773; Email: pastor@sbmsn.org; Email: office@sbmsn.org; Web: www.sbmsn.org. 2438 Atwood Ave., 53704. Rev. Michael R. Radowicz.
Catechesis Religious Program—Email: re@sbmsn.org. Gerianne Nehls, D.R.E. Students 70.

3—BLESSED SACRAMENT (1922) [JC]
Mailing Address: 2116 Hollister Ave., 53726-3958.
Tel: 608-238-3471; Fax: 608-238-4220; Email: info@blsacrament.org; Email: fr.andy@blsacrament.org; Web: www.blsacrament.org. 2121 Rowley Ave., 53726-3958. Revs. Andrew McAlpin, O.P.; Samuel Hakeem, Parochial Vicar; Patrick Norris, O.P., Prior.
School—*Blessed Sacrament School*, 2112 Hollister Ave., 53726. Tel: 608-233-6155; Email: efirst@school.blsacrament.org; Web: www.blsacrament.org. Mr. Steve Castrogiovanni, Prin.; Elizabeth First, Business Mgr. Lay Teachers 25; Students 200.
Catechesis Religious Program—Email: Peggie@blsacrament.org. Peggie Hansen, D.R.E. Students 98.

4—ST. DENNIS (1956) [JC]
505 Dempsey Rd., 53714. Tel: 608-246-5124;
Fax: 608-246-5138; Email: office@stdennisparish.org; Web: www.stdennisparish.org. 413 Dempsey Rd., 53714. Very Rev. Randy J. Timmerman, V.F.; Rev. Joji R. Allam, (India) Parochial Vicar; Deacon David J. Hendrickson
Legal Title: Saint Dennis Congregation.
Rectory I: 313 Dempsey Rd., 53714. Email: rjtimmerman@stdennisparish.org.
Rectory II: 3937 Tulane Ave., 53714.
Tel: 608-237-1996; Email: jrallam@stdennisparish.org.
School—*St. Dennis School*, (Grades K-8), 409 Dempsey Rd., 53714. Tel: 608-246-5121;
Fax: 608-246-5137; Email: principal@stdennisschool.org; Web: www.st-dennis school.org. Matt Beisser, Prin. Lay Teachers 25; Dominican Sisters (Sinsinawa, WI) 2; Students 272.
Catechesis Religious Program—Tel: 608-246-5123; Email: lisa_harms@yahoo.com. Lisa Harms, C.R.E. (K-8); David Hendrickson, Pastoral Min. & H.S. Faith Formation. Students 194.

5—GOOD SHEPHERD PARISH (1905)
1128 St. James Ct., 53715-1363. Tel: 608-268-9930; Email: goodshepherdmadison@straphael.org; Web: www.thegoodshepherdmadison.org. Rev. Msgr. Thomas F. Baxter; Rev. Manuel Mendez-Cobos, Parochial Vicar, Latino Ministry.
School—*Good Shepherd Parish School* aka St. James School, (Grades PreK-8), 1204 St. James Ct., 53715. Tel: 608-268-9935; Web: www.stjamesschool.org. Michael McCabe, Prin. Lay Teachers 18; Students 133.
Catechesis Religious Program—Tel: 608-268-9931; Email: Shawn.Willox@straphael.org. Shawn Willox, D.R.E. & Youth Min. Students 171.

6—HOLY REDEEMER (1857) Merged into Cathedral Parish of St. Raphael, Madison.

7—IMMACULATE HEART OF MARY (1950) [JC]
5101 Schofield St., Monona, 53716.
Tel: 608-221-1521; Email: ihmoffice@ihmparish.org. Rev. Chad M. Droessler.
School—*Immaculate Heart of Mary School*, (Grades PreK-8), 4913 Schofield St., 53716. Tel: 608-222-8831 ; Fax: 608-221-4492; Email: cmeiller@ihm-school.org; Web: www.ihmcatholicschool.org. Ms. Callie Meiller, Prin. Clergy 1; Lay Teachers 20; Students 175.
Catechesis Religious Program—Email: lsoldner@ihmparish.org; Email: sreinbold@ihmparish.org; Email: kmarshall@ihmparish.org. Laura Soldner, D.R.E. (Faith Formation); Shane Reinbold, D.R.E. (Middle/ High School); Kathy Marshall, RCIA Coord. Students 124.

8—ST. MARIA GORETTI (1959) [JC]
5313 Flad Ave., 53711. Tel: 608-271-7421; Email: parish@stmariagoretti.org; Web: www.stmariagoretti.org. Revs. Robert Evenson; Anthony Thirumalareddy, Parochial Vicar; Rev. Msgr. Michael L. Burke, Pastor Emeritus, (Retired); Deacons Jerome Buhman, Dir. of Pastoral Care; Richard Martin, Dir. of Outreach; Mark Shapleigh, Admin.; Denise Herrmann Sr., Liturgy Dir.; Denise Gorman, Dir. Liturgical Music; Terri Kysely, Parish Life Coord.; Josh Bruecken, Dir. of Maintenance and Facilities; Emilia Rothgery, Bookkeeper; Monica Silverwood, Payroll; Jon Silverwood, IT; Trish Schaefer, Sec.
School—*St. Maria Goretti School*, (Grades PreK-8), 5405 Flad Ave., 53711. Tel: 608-271-7551; Email: school@stmariagoretti.org; Web: www.stmariagoretti.org/school. Elizabeth Adams-Young, Admin.; Dianne Metz, Vice Prin.; Beth Wilson, Sec.; Maria Dulli, Sec. Lay Teachers 29; Preschool 28; Students 429.
Catechesis Religious Program—5405 Flad Ave., 53711. Tel: 608-271-8081; Email: faith@stmariagoretti.org; Web: stmariagoretti.org/rel-edym. Margaret Bruenig Clark, D.R.E.; Amelia Misiak, Youth Min. Students 426.

9—OUR LADY, QUEEN OF PEACE (1945) [JC]
401 S. Owen Dr., 53711. Tel: 608-231-4600;
Fax: 608-231-4606; Email: lisa.haas@qopc.org; Web: www.qopc.org. Revs. Msgrs. Kenneth J. Fiedler; James J. Uppena, In Res., (Retired).
School—*Our Lady, Queen of Peace School*, (Grades PreK-8), 418 Holly Ave., 53711. Tel: 608-231-4580; Fax: 608-231-4589; Email: maryjovitale@qopc.org; Web: www.qopc.org/K4-8_School. Mrs. Mary Jo Vitale, Prin. Lay Teachers 36; Students 475.
Catechesis Religious Program—Tel: 608-231-4610; Tel: 608-231-4616; Tel: 608-231-4609; Email: debra.schroeder@qopc.org; Email: kay.schachte@qopc.org; Email: cheryl.horne@qopc.org. Kay Schachte, D.R.E.; Cheryl Horne, Dir. Youth Ministry. Students 380.

10—ST. PATRICK (1888) [JC] Merged into Cathedral Parish of St. Raphael, Madison.

11—ST. PAUL UNIVERSITY PARISH, [JC]
723 State St., 53703. Tel: 608-258-3140; Email: om@uwcatholic.org; Web: www.uwcatholic.org. Revs. Eric H. Nielsen; Andrew J. Showers, Parochial Vicar; Luke Syse, Parochial Vicar.
Catechesis Religious Program—

12—ST. PETER (1967) [CEM]
5001 N. Sherman Ave., 53704-1440.
Tel: 608-249-6651; Fax: 608-249-6870; Web: www.stpetersofmadison.org. Rev. Msgr. O. Charles Schluter; Deacon Todd Martin.
Catechesis Religious Program—Email: pdickey23@yahoo.com. Peg Miller, D.R.E. Students 141.

13—ST. THOMAS AQUINAS, [JC]
602 Everglade Dr., 53717. Tel: 608-833-2600;
Fax: 608-833-1129; Email: parish@stamadison.org; Web: www.stamadison.org. Revs. Bart D. Timmerman; Steven J. Kortendick, In Res.
Res.: 6817 Old Sauk Ct., 53717.
Catechesis Religious Program—Tel: 608-833-2606; Email: lorianne@stamadison.org; Email: dominick@stamadison.org. Lorianne Aubut, D.R.E.; Dominick Meyer, D.R.E. Students 143.

OUTSIDE THE CITY OF MADISON

ARGYLE, LAFAYETTE CO., ST. JOSEPH (1898) [CEM 2] Merged with St. Michael, Yellowstone; St. Patrick, Hollandale & Immaculate Conception, Blanchardville to form Congregation of St. Isidore, Hollandale.

ASHTON, DANE CO., ST. PETER CATHOLIC CHURCH

(1861) [CEM] (Linked with St. Martin of Tours, Martinsville)
7121 County Rd. K, Middleton, 53562.
Tel: 608-831-4843; Tel: 608-831-4846; Email: info@ashtoncatholic.org; Web: ashtoncatholic.org. Rev. Christopher Gernetzke.
School—St. Peter Catholic Church School, (Grades PreSchool-5), Tel: 608-831-4846; Fax: 608-831-6095; Email: dkalscheur@stpetermiddleton.org; Web: www.saintpetersaintmartin.org. Ms. Kathi Klaas, Prin.; Rev. Christopher Gernetzke, Admin. Lay Teachers 7; Students 78; Clergy / Religious Teachers 1.
Catechesis Religious Program—Email: michellereligiousedu@gmail.com. Michelle Leveque, C.R.E. Students 76.

AVOCA, IOWA CO., ST. JOSEPH PARISH, AVOCA, Closed. For inquiries for parish records contact Corpus Christi Parish, Boscobel, WI.

BARABOO, SAUK CO., ST. JOSEPH (1859) [CEM]
Mailing Address: 300 2nd St., Baraboo, 53913.
Tel: 608-356-4773; Email: jayp@stjosephbaraboo.com; Web: baraboocatholic.org. Very Rev. James M. Poster, V.F.; Rev. Jared Holzhuter, Parochial Vicar.
Res.: 314 East St., Baraboo, 53913.
School—St. Joseph School, (Grades PreK-8), 310 2nd St., Baraboo, 53913. Email: info@stjosephbaraboo.org. Denise Brinker, Prin. Lay Teachers 14; Students 209; Clergy / Religious Teachers 2.
Catechesis Religious Program—Tel: 608-356-5353; Email: beckyt@stjosephbaraboo.com. Becky Thompson, Dir. Faith Formation. Students 113.

BARNEVELD, IOWA CO., IMMACULATE CONCEPTION (1886) [CEM] [JC] Merged with St. Bridget, Ridgeway to form St. Bernadette, Ridgeway.

BELLEVILLE, DANE CO., ST. FRANCIS OF ASSISI (2008) [CEM 3]
338 S. Harrison St., P.O. Box 349, Belleville, 53508.
Tel: 608-424-3831; Email: stfrancisbell@gmail.com; Web: www.stfrancisbelleville.com. Rev. Michael E. Moon.
Res.: 221 Frederick St., Belleville, 53508.
Catechesis Religious Program—Tel: 608-558-4998. Pamela Burke, D.R.E. (Pre-K to 11th). Students 121.

BELMONT, LAFAYETTE CO., ST. PHILOMENA (1957) [CEM] (Linked with St. Mary/St. Paul, Mineral Point)
338 Chestnut St., P.O. Box 345, Belmont, 53510.
Tel: 608-762-5446; Tel: 608-987-2026; Email: spbelmont5446@yahoo.com. Rev. Joseph Michael Tarigopula.
Catechesis Religious Program—Cecilia Fink, D.R.E. Also serves the mission: Immaculate Conception at Truman, WI. Students 74.

BELOIT, ROCK CO.

1—ST. JUDE (1908) (Linked With St. Thomas the Apostle, Beloit)
737 Hackett St., Beloit, 53511. Tel: 608-364-2820; Fax: 608-364-2822; Email: pquinn@stjudebeloit.org; Web: www.stjudebeloit.org. Rev. John H. Hedrick; Deacon James Davis.
Res.: 747 Hackett St., Beloit, 53511.
Catechesis Religious Program— Combined with St. Thomas the Apostle, Beloit. Email: religiouseducation@stjudebeloit.org. Erin Olver, D.R.E. Students 270.

2—OUR LADY OF THE ASSUMPTION (1953) [JC]
2222 Shopiere Rd., Beloit, 53511. Tel: 608-362-9066; Email: miker@olabeloit.com; Web: www.olabeloit.com. Rev. Michael A. Resop.
Res.: 2487 N. Bootmaker Dr., Beloit, 53511.
School—Our Lady of the Assumption School, (Grades PreK-8), Tel: 608-365-4014; Email: tseivert@olaschool.ws; Web: www.olaschool.ws. Mr. Trevor Seivert, Prin. Clergy 1; Lay Teachers 14; Students 126; Clergy / Religious Teachers 1.
Catechesis Religious Program—Email: robo@olabeloit.com. Rob Olsen, Dir. Faith Formation. Students 222.

3—ST. PAUL, Closed. 1988. For inquiries for parish records contact St. Thomas the Apostle, Beloit.

4—ST. THOMAS THE APOSTLE (1851) (Linked with St. Jude, Beloit)
822 E. Grand Ave., Beloit, 53511. Tel: 608-362-1034; Fax: 608-363-9931; Email: parishoffice@stthomasbeloit.org; Web: www.stthomasbeloit.org. Rev. John H. Hedrick.
Res.: 737 Hackett St., Beloit, 53511.
Catechesis Religious Program— Combined with St. Jude Parish. Email: religiouseducation@stjudebeloit.org. Erin Olver, D.R.E. Students 168.

BENTON, LAFAYETTE CO., ST. PATRICK (1845) [CEM] (Linked with St. Rose of Lima, Cuba City)
237 E. Main St., P.O. Box 3, Benton, 53803.
Tel: 608-759-2131; Email: stpatrickbenton@gmail.com. Rev. David J. Flanagan.
Catechesis Religious Program—218 N. Jackson St., Cuba City, 53807. Tel: 608-778-3577. Karrie Steinhart, D.R.E. Students 34.

BERLIN, GREEN LAKE CO.

1—ALL SAINTS (2001) [CEM 2]
N8566 State Rd. 49, Berlin, 54923-0269.
Tel: 920-361-5252; Email: parishoffice@allsaintsberlin.org. P.O. Box 269, Berlin, 54923. Very Rev. David J. Greenfield, V.F.; Deacon James Hoegemeier.
Res.: 167 N. Wisconsin, Berlin, 54923.
School—All Saints School, 151 S. Grove St., Berlin, 54923. Tel: 920-361-1781; Fax: 920-361-7379; Email: szangl@allsaintsberlin.org; Web: school.allsaintsberlin.org. Mr. Steve Zangl, Prin. Lay Teachers 14; Students 131.
Catechesis Religious Program—Email: jdahms@allsaintsberlin.org. Jana Dahms, D.R.E. Students 270.

2—ST. JOSEPH, Merged with St. Michael, Berlin and St. Stanislaus, Berlin to form All Saints, Berlin.

3—ST. MICHAEL, Merged with St. Joseph, Berlin and St. Stanislaus, Berlin to form All Saints, Berlin.

4—ST. STANISLAUS, Merged with St. Joseph, Berlin and St. Michael, Berlin to form All Saints, Berlin.

BLANCHARDVILLE, LAFAYETTE CO., IMMACULATE CONCEPTION (1898) [CEM] Merged with St. Patrick, Hollandale, St. Joseph, Argyle & St. Michael, Yellowstone to form Congregation of St. Isidore, Hollandale.

BLOOMINGTON, GRANT CO., ST. MARY (1898) [CEM 2] (Linked with St. John, Patch Grove; St. Charles, Cassville; St. Mary, Glen Haven)
535 Congress St., P.O. Box 35, Bloomington, 53804.
Tel: 608-994-2526; Fax: 608-994-2551; Email: sunday7@tds.net; Web: swwicatholicparishes.com. Very Rev. John M. Meinholz, V.F.
School—St. Mary School, 531 Congress St., P.O. Box 35, Bloomington, 53804. Tel: 608-994-2435; Email: stmarybl@tds.net. Ms. Julie Zenz, Prin. Lay Teachers 6; Students 30; Clergy / Religious Teachers 1.
Catechesis Religious Program—Laura Tolle, D.R.E. Students 105.

BOSCOBEL, GRANT CO.

1—CORPUS CHRISTI PARISH, BOSCOBEL, WI (2011) [CEM 3]
405 E. LeGrand St., Boscobel, 53805-1150.
Tel: 608-375-4257; Fax: 608-375-4255; Email: icchurch@centurytel.net. Revs. Christopher Padilla; James Kotch, Parochial Vicar; Deacon Lawrence Schmitt.
Catechesis Religious Program—Tel: 608-375-4256. Students 127.

2—IMMACULATE CONCEPTION PARISH, BOSCOBEL, WI, Closed. For inquiries for parish records contact Corpus Christi Parish, Boscobel, WI.

BRIGGSVILLE, MARQUETTE CO., ST. MARY HELP OF CHRISTIANS (1851) [CEM] (Linked with St. Mary of the Immaculate Conception, Portage)
N565 Hwy. A, P.O. Box 127, Briggsville, 53920-0127.
Tel: 608-981-2282; Email: stmaryhofc@maqs.net. Rev. Gary L. Krahenbuhl; Sr. Anita Henning, Pastoral Min.
Catechesis Religious Program—Email: teresa.smhoc@maqs.net. Teresa Romain, Dir. Faith Formation. Students 12.

BUFFALO TOWNSHIP, MARQUETTE CO., ST. ANDREW (1860) [CEM] Merged with St. Mary of the Most Holy Rosary, Pardeeville to form St. Faustina Congregation, Columbia/Marquette County, WI, Inc., Pardeeville. For inquiries for sacramental records contact St. Faustina Congregation, Columbia/Marquette County, WI, Inc., Pardeeville.

CALAMINE, LAFAYETTE CO., ST. MICHAEL (1916) [CEM] Merged with Holy Rosary, Darlington; St. Peter, Elk Grove; Our Lady of Hope, Seymour; Immaculate Conception, Truman to form Our Lady of Fatima Congregation, Lafayette County, WI, Inc., Darlington. For inquiries for sacramental records contact Our Lady of Fatima Congregation, Lafayette County, WI, Inc., Darlington.

CAMBRIDGE, DANE CO., ST. PIUS X (1955) [CEM]
701 W. Water St., Cambridge, 53523.
Tel: 608-423-3015; Email: parishstpiusx@gmail.com. Rev. Alex Carmel Mimimula Selvaraj, Admin.
Catechesis Religious Program—Email: hthompson@stpiusxcp.org. Hannah Thompson, D.R.E. Students 62.

CASSVILLE, GRANT CO., ST. CHARLES BORROMEO, [CEM 2] (Linked with St. Mary Help of Christians, Glen Haven, St. John, Patch Grove & St. Mary, Bloomington.)
Mailing Address: 605 E. Dewey St., P. O. Box 166, Cassville, 53806. Tel: 608-725-5595; Email: stchas@tds.net. Very Rev. John M. Meinholz, V.F.; Cheryl Junk, Parish Admin. Asst.
Res.: 535 Congress St., P.O. Box 35, Bloomington, 53804.
School—St. Charles Borromeo School, (Grades 1-8), 521 E. Dewey St., Cassville, 53806.
Tel: 608-725-5173; Fax: 608-725-5179; Email: julie.zenz@stcharlescassville.org. Ms. Julie Zenz, Prin. Clergy 1; Lay Teachers 4; Students 15.
Catechesis Religious Program—Students 31.
Mission—St. Mary Help of Christians.

CASTLE ROCK, GRANT CO., ST. JOHN NEPOMUCENE (1879) [CEM] Merged with St. Lawrence O'Toole, Mount Hope and St. Mary's Parish, Fennimore to form Queen of All Saints, Fennimore.

CLINTON, ROCK CO., ST. STEPHEN (1973)
716 Shu-Lar Ln., P.O. Box 399, Clinton, 53525.
Tel: 608-676-2241; Fax: 608-676-4981; Email: parish@ststephensclinton.com; Web: ststephen.weconnect.com. Rev. Msgr. Daniel T. Ganshert, Admin.
Res.: 714 Shu-Lar Ln., Clinton, 53525.
Catechesis Religious Program—Tel: 608-385-9359; Email: zonbon2220@gmail.com. Steve Zahn, D.R.E. Students 39.

CLYDE, DODGE CO., ST. MALACHY PARISH, CLYDE, WI, Closed. For inquiries for parish records contact Corpus Christi Parish, Boscobel, WI.

COLUMBUS, COLUMBIA CO., ST. JEROME (1856) [CEM] (Linked with St. Patrick, Doylestown)
1550 Farnham St., Columbus, 53925.
Tel: 920-623-3753; Email: parish@stjeromecolumbus.org; Web: www.sjcolumbus.org/parish. Rev. Garrett B. Kau; Mrs. Kristine Radtke, Business Mgr.; Mrs. Teresa Miller, Sec.
Res.: 329 Folsom St., Columbus, 53925.
School—St. Jerome School, (Grades PreK-8), Tel: 920-623-5780; Email: sjsoffice@stjeromecolumbus.org; Email: jcotter@stjeromecolumbus.org; Web: www.sjcolumbus.org/school. Mrs. Jamie Cotter, Prin.; Mrs. Kim Zittel, Sec. Lay Teachers 14; Students 118.
Catechesis Religious Program—Email: sking@stjeromecolumbus.org. Sarah King, D.R.E. Students 113.

COTTAGE GROVE, DANE CO., ST. PATRICK (1882) [CEM]
434 N. Main St., P.O. Box 400, Cottage Grove, 53527-0400. Tel: 608-839-3969; Fax: 608-839-3593; Email: father@st-patrick-parish.com; Web: www.st-patrick-parish.com. Rev. Brian D. Dulli, S.T.L.
Catechesis Religious Program—Email: dre@st-patrick-parish.com. Kristia Loeder, D.R.E.; Stephanie Beaver, D.R.E. Students 110.

CROSS PLAINS, DANE CO., ST. FRANCIS XAVIER (1853) [CEM]
2947 Thinnes St., Cross Plains, 53528.
Tel: 608-798-0100; Fax: 608-798-2976; Email: info@sfxcrossplains.org. Rev. Thomas L. Kelley.
School—St. Francis Xavier School, 2939 Thinnes St., Cross Plains, 53528. Tel: 608-798-2422; Fax: 608-798-0898; Email: robert.abshire@sfxcrossplains.org; Web: www.sfxcatholicshool.org. Robert Abshire, Prin. Lay Teachers 17; Students 136.
Catechesis Religious Program—Tel: 608-798-4824; Email: natasha.virnig@sfxcrossplains.org. Natasha Virnig, D.R.E. Students 130.

CUBA CITY, GRANT CO., ST. ROSE OF LIMA, [CEM] (Linked with St. Patrick, Benton)
519 W. Roosevelt, Cuba City, 53807.
Tel: 608-744-2010; Fax: 608-744-8449; Email: strosech@lagrant.net; Web: www.strosecubacity.4lpi.com. Rev. David J. Flanagan.
School—St. Rose of Lima School, (Grades PreK-8), 218 N. Jackson St., Cuba City, 53807.
Tel: 608-744-2120; Email: schneiderm@strose.us; Web: www.strose.us. Mary Schneider, Prin. Lay Teachers 10; Students 131.
Catechesis Religious Program—Email: steinhartk@strose.us. Karrie Steinhart, D.R.E. Students 199.

DANE, DANE CO., ST. MICHAEL, [CEM] Merged with St. Patrick, Lodi to form Blessed Trinity, Lodi.

DARLINGTON, LAFAYETTE CO.

1—HOLY ROSARY (1864) [CEM 2] Merged with St. Peter, Elk Grove; St. Michael, Calamine; Our Lady of Hope, Seymour; Immaculate Conception, Truman to form Our Lady of Fatima Congregation, Lafayette County, WI, Inc., Darlington. For inquiries for sacramental records contact Our Lady of Fatima Congregation, Lafayette County, WI, Inc., Darlington.

2—OUR LADY OF FATIMA CONGREGATION, LAFAYETTE COUNTY, WI, INC.
730 Wells St., Darlington, 53530. Tel: 608-776-4059; Email: hrosary@centurylink.net; Web: www.congregationolf.org. Rev. Joji Reddy Thirumalareddy, Admin.
Res.: 104 E. Harriet St., Darlington, 53530.
St. Peter, Elk Grove—
St. Michael, Calamine.
Our Lady of Hope, Seymour.
Immaculate Conception, Truman.
Holy Rosary, Darlington.
School—Holy Rosary School, (Grades K-4), 744 Wells St., Darlington, 53530. Tel: 608-776-3710; Email: hrschool@mediacombb.net; Web: olfhrschool.org. Tanya Horne, Prin. Lay Teachers 5; Students 66.
Catechesis Religious Program—Tel: 608-776-2258; Email: d.smith-hole@mediacombb.net. Diane Smith-Hole, D.R.E. Students 138.

DAYTON, GREEN CO., ST. JAMES PARISH, DAYTON,

Closed. For inquiries for parish records contact St. Francis of Assisi, Belleville.

DE FOREST, DANE CO., ST. OLAF (1948) [CEM] (Linked with St. Joseph, East Bristol)
623 Jefferson St., De Forest, 53532.
Tel: 608-846-5726; Email: pastor@saintolafchurch.org; Web: www.saintolafchurch.org. Rev. Vincent Brewer.
Catechesis Religious Program—Tel: 608-839-7149; Tel: 608-825-4934; Email: dre@saintolafchurch.org; Email: bill@ringelstetter.net. Bill Ringelstetter, D.R.E. Students 291.

DICKEYVILLE, GRANT CO., HOLY GHOST, [CEM] (Linked with Immaculate Conception, Kieler)
305 W. Main St., P.O. Box 429, Dickeyville, 53808.
Tel: 608-568-7519; Fax: 608-568-3872; Email: dietzell@hgicschool.com; Web: www.HolyGhostandImmaculateConceptionChurches.org. Rev. Bernard E. Rott; Deacon Lawrence Tranel.
School—Holy Ghost-Immaculate Conception School, (Grades PreSchool-3), 325 W. Main St., P.O. Box 40, Dickeyville, 53808. Tel: 608-568-7790;
Tel: 608-568-7220; Fax: 608-568-3872; Email: hesselingr@hgicschool.com; Web: hgicschool.com. Rita Hesseling, Prin. Lay Teachers 13; Students 132.
Catechesis Religious Program—Angela Snyder, D.R.E., (Grade School), Tel: 608-568-7925; Tina Tranel, D.R.E., (High School), Tel: 608-568-7530. Students 119.

DODGEVILLE, IOWA CO., ST. JOSEPH, [CEM 3]
305 E. Walnut St., Dodgeville, 53533-1799.
Tel: 608-930-3392; Fax: 608-930-1722; Email: sjoffice@mhtc.net; Web: www.stjosephsdodgeville.org. Rev. Tafadzwa Kushamba.
Res.: 418 E Ellwood St., Dodgeville, 53533.
School—St. Joseph School, (Grades PreSchool-8), Tel: 608-930-3392, Ext. 5; Email: stjoseph@mhtc.net. Mrs. Dana Graber, Admin. Clergy 1; Lay Teachers 12; Students 154.
Catechesis Religious Program—Jackie Boley, D.R.E. Students 44.

DOYLESTOWN, COLUMBIA CO., ST. PATRICK (1865) [CEM] (Linked with St. Jerome, Columbus)
N4085 Bruce St., P.O. Box 40, Doylestown, 53928.
Tel: 920-992-3343; Fax: 844-484-2211. Rev. Garrett B. Kau.
Catechesis Religious Program—Tel: 920-992-3549; Email: vangen.mar@gmail.com. Marcia Vange, D.R.E. Students 35.

DURWARD'S GLEN, COLUMBIA CO., ST. CAMILLUS, [CEM] Closed. For inquiries for parish records contact the chancery.

EAST BRISTOL, DANE CO., ST. JOSEPH (1847) [CEM] (Linked with St. Olaf, De Forest)
1935 Hwy. V, Sun Prairie, 53590. Tel: 608-846-5726; Email: pcsec@saintolafchurch.org. 630 Jefferson St., De Forest, 53532. Rev. Vincent Brewer.
Catechesis Religious Program—Tel: 608-825-4934; Email: bill@ringelstetter.net. Bill Ringelstetter, D.R.E. Students 71.

EDGERTON, ROCK CO., ST. JOSEPH, [CEM 2]
590 S. Saint Joseph Cir., Edgerton, 53534-1243.
Tel: 608-884-3038; Fax: 608-884-3298; Email: theresa@stjoeedgerton.org; Email: cre@stjoeedgerton.org; Email: frdave.timmerman1@gmail.com; Web: www.stjoeedgerton.org. Rev. David W. Timmerman.
Res.: 836 Neumann Ct., Milton, 53563. Email: maryann@stjoeedgerton.org.
Catechesis Religious Program—Tel: 608-884-6231; Email: cre@stjoeedgerton.org. Paul Jozwiak, D.R.E. Students 117.

ELK GROVE, LAFAYETTE CO., ST. PETER, [CEM] Merged with Holy Rosary, Darlington; St. Michael, Calamine; Our Lady of Hope, Seymour; Immaculate Conception, Truman to form Our Lady of Fatima Congregation, Lafayette County, WI, Inc., Darlington. For inquiries for sacramental records contact Our Lady of Fatima Congregation, Lafayette County, WI, Inc., Darlington.

EVANSVILLE, ROCK CO., ST. PAUL (1906) [CEM] (Linked with St. Augustine, Footville)
39 Garfield Ave., Evansville, 53536.
Tel: 608-882-4138; Email: stpaulevans@gmail.com. Rev. Kevin F. Dooley.
Res.: 35 Garfield Ave., Evansville, 53536.
Catechesis Religious Program—Email: carolreilly39@gmail.com. Students 89.

FENNIMORE, GRANT CO.
1—ST. MARY (1885) [CEM] Merged with St. Lawrence, Mount Hope and St. John Nepomucene, Castle Rock to form Queen of All Saints, Fennimore.
2—QUEEN OF ALL SAINTS (2013) [CEM 3]
960 Jefferson St., Fennimore, 53809.
Tel: 608-822-3520; Email: anavarro@slsonline.org; Web: queenofallsaints.net. Revs. Alex Navarro, S.J.S.; James Kotch, Parochial Vicar; Jeff Jackson, Chm.; Ms. Mary Ann Carmody, Business Mgr.; Mrs. Jeri Novinska, Trustee; Mrs. Carol Rogers, Trustee.
St. John Nepomuc—15055 Shemak Rd., Muscoda, 53573.
St. Lawrence O'Toole, 13814 Irish Ridge Rd., Mount Hope, 53816.
St. Mary, Fennimore, 53809. Tel: 608-822-3520.
Catechesis Religious Program—Cell: 608-732-5686; Cell: 608-778-6027; Email: barb@stmaryfennimore.org. Jeff Jackson, D.R.E.; Mrs. Barbara Kohout, D.R.E. Students 69.

FOOTVILLE, ROCK CO., ST. AUGUSTINE (1869) (Linked with St. Paul, Evansville)
280 Haberdale Dr., Footville, 53537.
Tel: 608-876-6252. P.O. Box 325, Footville, 53537-0325. Rev. Kevin F. Dooley.
Res.: 35 Garfield Ave., Evansville, 53536.
Catechesis Religious Program— Linked with St. Paul, Evansville. Tel: 608-876-6311; Email: amazgr8z@ticon.net. Janet Kassel, D.R.E. Students 30.

FORT ATKINSON, JEFFERSON CO., ST. JOSEPH (1884) [CEM]
Mailing Address: 1660 Endl Blvd., Fort Atkinson, 53538. Tel: 920-563-3029; Email: frpete@gmail.com; Email: frpete@stjosephfort.org; Web: stjosephfort.org. Rev. Peter Auer.
School—St. Joseph School, 1650 Endl Blvd., Fort Atkinson, 53538. Mrs. Kari Homb, Prin. Lay Teachers 14; Students 132.
Catechesis Religious Program—Tel: 608-371-5046; Email: youthministry@stjosephfort.org; Email: nmayans@stjosephfort.org. Gina McDonald, D.R.E.; Norma Mayans, D.R.E. Students 149.

GLEN HAVEN, GRANT CO., ST. MARY HELP OF CHRISTIANS (1864) [CEM 2] (Linked with St. Charles Borromeo, Cassville, St. John, Patch Grove & St. Mary, Bloomington.)
P.O. Box 166, Cassville, 53806. Tel: 608-725-5595; Email: stchas@tds.net. 8808 4th St., Glen Haven, 53810. Very Rev. John M. Meinholz, V.F.
Res.: 535 Congress St., Bloomington, 53804.

GRATIOT, LAFAYETTE CO., ST. JOSEPH (1869) [CEM] (Linked with St. John, South Wayne & St. Matthew's, Shullsburg)
344 N. Judgement St., Shullsburg, 53586.
Tel: 608-965-4518; Email: stmathewschurch@centurytel.net. Rev. Sudhakar Devarapu.
Catechesis Religious Program—5695 Main St., Gratiot, 53541. Students 25.

GREEN LAKE, GREEN LAKE CO., OUR LADY OF THE LAKE (1908)
530 Ruth St., P.O. Box 215, Green Lake, 54941.
Tel: 920-294-6440; Email: info@greenlakecatholic.org; Web: www.greenlakecatholic.org. Rev. Michelu Ragola.
Catechesis Religious Program—Alice Bartow, D.R.E. Students 20.

HAZEL GREEN, GRANT CO.
1—ST. FRANCIS DE SALES (1845) [CEM] (Linked with St. Joseph, Hazel Green)
2720 N. Percival St., Hazel Green, 53811-9681.
Tel: 608-854-2392; Email: kfrisch78@gmail.com. Rev. Kenneth J. Frisch.
Catechesis Religious Program—Tel: 608-854-2391. Students 118.
2—ST. JOSEPH, [CEM 2] (Linked with St. Francis de Sales, Hazel Green)
780 County Hwy. Z, Hazel Green, 53811-9709.
Tel: 608-748-4528; Web: www.stjosephscs.info. Rev. Kenneth J. Frisch.
Res.: 1720 26th St., Hazel Green, 53811.
School—St. Joseph School, (Grades PreK-6), Tel: 608-748-4442; Email: principalwills@stjosephscs.info. Ms. Barbara Wills, Prin. Lay Teachers 6; Students 52.
Catechesis Religious Program—St. Francis de Sales, 2720 N. Percival St., Hazel Green, 53811. Students 118.

HIGHLAND, IOWA CO., SS. ANTHONY AND PHILIP, [CEM 2] (Linked with St. Thomas, Montfort)
726 Main St., P.O. Box 306, Highland, 53543.
Tel: 608-929-7490; Fax: 608-929-7701; Email: jimmurphy@centurylink.net; Web: ssanthonyphilip.com. Rev. James H. Murphy.
Res.: 1023 Dodgeville St., Highland, 53543.
Catechesis Religious Program—Email: deggers@centurylink.net. Delores Eggers, D.R.E. Students 135.

HOLLANDALE, IOWA CO.
1—CONGREGATION OF ST. ISIDORE
601 Grover St., P.O. Box 37, Hollandale, 53544.
Tel: 608-967-2344; Email: abhy@straphael.org. Rev. Paul Eruva, (India).
Catechesis Religious Program—Students 58.
2—ST. PATRICK (1844) [CEM] Merged with Immaculate Conception, Blanchardville; St. Joseph, Argyle & St. Michael, Yellowstone to form Congregation of St. Isidore, Hollandale.

JANESVILLE, ROCK CO.
1—ST. JOHN VIANNEY (1955)
1250 E. Racine St., Janesville, 53545.
Tel: 608-752-8708; Fax: 608-752-1970; Email: parish@sjv.org; Web: www.sjv.org. Mailing Address: 1245 Clark St., Janesville, 53545. Very Rev. Paul Ugo Arinze, V.F.; Revs. Joseph Baker, Parochial Vicar; Thomas P. Marr, In Res., (Retired).
School—St. John Vianney School, (Grades PreK-8), Tel: 608-752-6802; Email: school@sjv.org; Web: www.sjv.org. Christine Silha, Prin. Lay Teachers 15; Students 197.
Catechesis Religious Program—1238 E. Racine St., Janesville, 53545. Tel: 608-755-1476. George Wollinger, D.R.E. Students 119.
2—NATIVITY OF MARY (1876) [JC]
313 E. Wall St., Janesville, 53545. Tel: 608-752-7861; Email: psec@nativitymary.org; Web: www.nativitymary.org. Rev. Robert J. Butz.
School—Nativity of St. Mary School, (Grades PreK-8), Tel: 608-754-5221; Email: principal@nativitymary.org; Web: www.stmaryschoolwi.com. Mr. Matthew Parrish, Prin. Lay Teachers 21; Students 133.
Catechesis Religious Program—
Tel: 608-752-7861, Ext. 29; Email: re@nativitymary.org. (Family Faith Formation) Students 70.
3—ST. PATRICK (1850) [JC]
315 Cherry St., Janesville, 53548. Tel: 608-754-8193; Email: stpatrickcj@gmail.com; Web: www.stpats.org. Rev. Timothy J. Renz; Deacon John Houseman, Pastoral Assoc.; Lori Reddy, Sec.
Catechesis Religious Program—Tel: 608-754-8093; Email: saintpatricksre.director@gmail.com. Mrs. Marie Wallace, D.R.E. Students 28.
4—ST. WILLIAM (1952) [JC]
1815 Ravine St., Janesville, 53548.
Tel: 608-755-5180, Ext. Option 3; Fax: 608-755-5190; Email: parish@stwilliam.net; Web: www.stwilliam.net. Rev. James R. Leeser.
School—St. William School, (Grades PreK-8), 1822 Ravine St., Janesville, 53548. Tel: 608-755-5184; Fax: 608-755-5181; Email: principal@stwilliam.net; Web: www.stwilliam.net. Diane Rebout, Prin. Lay Teachers 14; Students 198.
Catechesis Religious Program—Tel: 608-755-5183; Email: heidijegerllehner@stwilliam.net. Mary MacPherson; Heidi Jegerlener, D.R.E. Students 88.

JEFFERSON, JEFFERSON CO.
1—ST. FRANCIS OF ASSISI (1859) [CEM 2]
214 N. Sanborn Ave., Jefferson, 53549.
Tel: 920-674-2025; Email: bschweiger@stjohnbaptist.net; Email: stjohns@jefnet.com; Web: www.stjohnbaptist.net. 324 E. North St., Jefferson, 53549. Rev. Thomas J. Coyle.
School—St. John the Baptist School, (Grades PreK-8), 333 E. Church St., Jefferson, 53549.
Tel: 920-674-5821; Web: www.stjohnbaptist.net. Mr. William Bare, Prin. Clergy 1; Lay Teachers 17; Students 122.
Catechesis Religious Program—324 E. North St., Jefferson, 53549. Tel: 920-674-5433; Email: ttopel@stjohnbaptist.net; Email: jelberi@stjohnbaptist.net. Jodi El-Beri, C.R.E.; Tiffany Topel, D.R.E. Students 225.
2—ST. JOHN THE BAPTIST (1859) [CEM] Merged with St. Lawrence, Jefferson to form St. Francis of Assisi Parish, Jefferson. For inquiries for sacramental records contact St. Francis of Assisi, Jefferson.
3—ST. LAWRENCE (1850) [CEM] Merged with St. John the Baptist, Jefferson to form St. Francis of Assisi, Jefferson. For inquiries for sacramental records contact St. Francis of Assisi, Jefferson.

JOHNSON CREEK, JEFFERSON CO., ST. MARY MAGDALENE (1906) [CEM] Merged with St. Francis Xavier, Lake Mills to form St. Gabriel Congregation, Jefferson County, WI, Inc., Lake Mills. For inquiries for sacramental records contact St. Gabriel Congregation, Jefferson County, WI, Inc., Lake Mills.

KIELER, GRANT CO., IMMACULATE CONCEPTION, [CEM] (Linked with Holy Ghost, Dickeyville)
3685 Cty. HHH, P.O. Box 57, Kieler, 53812.
Tel: 608-568-7530; Fax: 608-568-3811; Email: icparish@tds.net. Rev. Bernard E. Rott, Admin.; Deacon Lawrence Tranel.
School—Immaculate Conception School, (Grades 4-8), P.O. Box 129, Kieler, 53812. Tel: 608-568-7220; Email: hesselingr@hgicschool.com. 3685 County Hwy. HHH, Kieler, 53812. Rita Hesseling, Prin. Consolidated with Holy Ghost, Dickeyville. Clergy 1; Lay Teachers 9; Students 67.
Catechesis Religious Program—3685 County HHH. Twinned with Holy Ghost, Dickeyville. Students 119.

KINGSTON, GREENLAKE CO., ST. MARY (1876) [CEM] Merged with St. Joseph, Markesan to form Holy Family Parish, Pardeeville.

LA VALLE, SAUK CO.
1—HOLY FAMILY (1917) Merged with St. Boniface, Lime Ridge and St. Patrick, Loreto to form Holy Angels Congregation, La Valle. For inquiries for sacramental records contact Holy Angels Congregation, La Valle.
2—HOLY ANGELS CONGREGATION, SAUK COUNTY WI, INC.
P.O. Box 166, La Valle, 53941. Tel: 608-985-7558;

Email: holyangels7558@gmail.com. Rev. Sanctus K. Ibe; Deacon Tom Fogarty.
Worship Sites—
St. Boniface, 105 Church St., Lime Ridge, 53942.
Holy Family, 310 Bluff St., La Valle, 53941.
St. Patrick, S8284 County Rd. G, Plain, 53577.

LAKE MILLS, JEFFERSON CO.
1—ST. FRANCIS XAVIER (1912) Merged with St. Mary Magdalene, Johnson Creek to form St. Gabriel Congregation, Jefferson County, WI, Inc., Lake Mills. For inquiries for sacramental records contact St. Gabriel Congregation, Jefferson County, WI, Inc., Lake Mills.
2—ST. GABRIEL PARISH (2015)
602 College St., Lake Mills, 53551. Tel: 920-648-2468 ; Email: saintgabriel.lmjc@yahoo.com; Web: www.catholiclmjc.org. Rev. David A. Wanish.
Catechesis Religious Program—Mrs. Natalie Raupp, D.R.E.; Mary Paulowske, Youth Min. Students 217.

LANCASTER, GRANT CO., ST. CLEMENT (1859) [CEM 2]
135 S. Washington St., Lancaster, 53813.
Tel: 608-723-4990; Fax: 608-723-4012; Email: st_clement@tds.net; Web: saintclementparish.com. Rev. William F. Vernon.
School—St. Clement School, (Grades K-6), 330 W. Maple St., Lancaster, 53813. Tel: 608-723-7474; Fax: 608-723-4424; Email: school@saintclementschool.com; Web: www.saintclementschool.com. Joshua Jensen, Prin. Lay Teachers 11; Students 123.
Catechesis Religious Program—Mrs. Rebecca Dean, Co-C.R.E (Grades K-6); Ms. Melissa Martin, Co-C.R.E (Grades K-6); Mr. Nick Crosby, C.R.E. (Grades 7-9). Students 83.

LIME RIDGE, SAUK CO., ST. BONIFACE (1912) Merged with Holy Family, La Valle and St. Patrick, Loreto to form form Holy Angels Congregation, La Valle. For inquiries for sacramental records contact Holy Angels Congregation, La Valle.

LODI, COLUMBIA CO.
1—BLESSED TRINITY PARISH (2012) [CEM 2]
521 Fair St., Lodi, 53555. Tel: 608-592-5711; Web: www.btcatholic.us. Rev. Scott M. Jablonski.
Res.: 515 Fair St., Lodi, 53555.
School—Blessed Trinity School, (Grades PreK-8), 109 S. Military Rd., Dane, 53529.
Tel: 608-849-5619, Ext. 7; Email: btschool@btcatholic.us; Email: jkarls@btcatholic.us; Web: www.btcatholic.us. Jeffrey Karls, Prin. Lay Teachers 6; Students 56; Clergy / Religious Teachers 1.
Catechesis Religious Program—
Tel: 608-592-5711, Ext. 4; Email: gfinn@btcatholic.us. Geno Finn, D.R.E. Students 182.
2—ST. PATRICK (1857) [CEM] Merged with St. Michael, Dane to form Blessed Trinity, Lodi.

LORETO, MANITOWOC CO., ST. PATRICK (1866) [CEM 2] (Irish—German), Merged with Holy Family, La Valle and St. Boniface, Lime Ridge to form Holy Angels Congregation, La Valle. For inquiries for sacramental records contact Holy Angels Congregation, La Valle.

MARKESAN, GREEN LAKE CO., ST. JOSEPH (1886) Merged with St. Mary, Kingston, to form Holy Family Parish, Pardeeville.

MARSHALL, DANE CO., ST. MARY OF THE NATIVITY, [CEM] Merged with St. Joseph, Waterloo to form Holy Family Parish, Waterloo.

MARTINSVILLE, DANE CO., ST. MARTIN OF TOURS (1850) [CEM] (Linked with St. Peter, Ashton)
5959 St. Martin Cir., Cross Plains, 53528-9312.
Tel: 608-798-2815; Email: martinsvillesmtp@straphael.org. Rev. Christopher Gernetzke.
Catechesis Religious Program—Michelle Leveque, D.R.E. Students 18.

MAZOMANIE, DANE CO.
1—ST. BARNABAS (1856) [CEM] Merged with St. John the Baptist, Mill Creek to form Holy Cross Parish, Mazomanie.
2—HOLY CROSS PARISH (1856) [CEM]
410 Cramer St., P.O Box 68, Mazomanie, 53560.
Tel: 608-795-4321; Email: holycrossparish113@gmail.com. Revs. Miguel Gálvez, Admin.; Osvaldo Briones, S.J.S., Parochial Vicar.
Res.: 115 Madison St., Sauk City, 53583. Web: www.holycrossparishmazo.com.
Catechesis Religious Program—
Mission—St. John the Baptist, County Hwy. H, Arena, Iowa Co. 53503.

MCFARLAND, DANE CO., CHRIST THE KING (1970)
5306 Main St., P.O. Box 524, McFarland, 53558.
Tel: 608-838-9797; Email: ctk@myparish.com; Web: www.myparish.com. Rev. D. Stephen Smith.
Catechesis Religious Program—Email: nicole@myparish.com. Maureen Nelson, D.R.E. (K-5); Nicole Davis, Youth Min. Students 111.

MERRIMAC, SAUK CO., ST. MARY, HEALTH OF THE SICK (1948) Merged with St. Aloysius, Sauk City to form Divine Mercy Parish, Sauk City. Rev. Pedro Escribano, (Spain) Parochial Vicar.

MIDDLETON, DANE CO., ST. BERNARD (1889) [CEM]
2015 Parmenter St., Middleton, 53562-0187.
Tel: 608-831-6531; Fax: 608-831-8101; Email: parish@stbmidd.org; Web: www.stbmidd.org. Rev. Brian J. Wilk, V.F.
Catechesis Religious Program—Students 364.

MILL CREEK, ST. JOHN THE BAPTIST, Merged with St. Barnabas, Mazomanie to form Holy Cross Parish, Mazomanie.

MILTON, ROCK CO., ST. MARY (1891) [CEM]
837 Parkview Dr., Milton, 53563. Tel: 608-868-3338; Fax: 608-868-3345; Email: stmarymilton@gmail.com; Web: saintmarymilton.org. Rev. David W. Timmerman.
Res.: 836 Neumann Ct., Milton, 53563.
Tel: 608-868-2338.
Catechesis Religious Program—Tel: 608-868-3334; Email: sabrina.elsen1@gmail.com. Sabrina Elsen, Faith Formation Coord., Tel: 608-868-3334. Students 269.

MINERAL POINT, IOWA CO., CONGREGATION OF ST. MARY-ST. PAUL (1870) [JC2]
224 Davis St., Mineral Point, 53565.
Tel: 608-987-2026; Tel: 608-987-3361; Email: stmarypaul@msn.com; Web: stmarysstpauls.org. Rev. Joseph Michael Tarigopula.
Catechesis Religious Program—216 Davis St., Mineral Point, 53565. Email: stmarypaulccd@gmail.com. Paula Schuette, D.R.E. Students 113.

MONROE, GREEN CO., ST. CLARE OF ASSISI PARISH (St. Victor, 1860; St. Clare of Assisi, 2011)
1760 14th St., Monroe, 53566-2149.
Tel: 608-325-9506; Web: www.stclaregreencounty.org. Rev. Msgr. Lawrence M. Bakke.
School—St. Clare of Assisi Parish School aka St. Victor School, (Grades K-5), Tel: 608-325-3395; Email: joepeters@stvictormonroe.org; Web: www.stclaregreencounty.org. Joseph Peters, Prin. Lay Teachers 16; Students 116.
Catechesis Religious Program—Email: betsyb@stclaregreencounty.org. Betsy Brennan, D.R.E. Students 174.

MONTELLO, MARQUETTE CO., ST. JOHN THE BAPTIST, [CEM] (Linked with Good Shepherd, Westfield)
277 E. Montello St., Montello, 53949.
Tel: 608-297-7423; Email: sjbgsparishoffice@gmail.com; Email: ydominicsavio@gmail.com; Web: www.marquettecountycatholic.org. Rev. Savio Yerasani.
Catechesis Religious Program—Email: sjbreled01@gmail.com. Tina Schoebel, D.R.E. Students 62.
Mission—Good Shepherd, 241 E. 6th St., Westfield, Marquette Co. 53964. Tel: 608-296-3631; Email: jenniebradburn@gmail.com.

MONTFORT, GRANT CO., ST. THOMAS aka St. Thomas the Apostle (1925) [CEM] (Linked with SS. Anthony and Philip, Highland)
104 Park St., P.O. Box 68, Montfort, 53569.
Tel: 608-943-6944; Email: officestthomastheapostle@gmail.com; Web: stthomasmontfort.org. Rev. James H. Murphy.
Catechesis Religious Program—Julie Hawes, C.R.E. Students 63.

MOUNT HOPE, GRANT CO., ST. LAWRENCE O'TOOLE (1884) [CEM] Merged with St. Mary, Fennimore and St. John Nepomucene, Castle Rock to form Queen of All Saints, Fennimore.

MOUNT HOREB, DANE CO.
1—ST. IGNATIUS, [CEM] Merged with Holy Redeemer, Perry to form St. Michael the Archangel Parish, Mount Horeb.
2—ST. MICHAEL THE ARCHANGEL, [CEM]
107 S. Seventh St., Mount Horeb, 53572-2050.
Tel: 608-437-5348; Fax: 608-437-7691; Email: stihr@mhtc.net; Web: stmichaelwi.com. Rev. Chahm Gahng.
Catechesis Religious Program—Thaddeus Griebel, D.R.E.; Sonja Preimesberger, C.R.E. Students 165.

NESHKORO, MARQUETTE CO., ST. JAMES, [CEM] (Linked with St. John the Baptist, Princeton)
315 N Main St., Neshkoro, 54968. Tel: 920-293-4211; Email: stjamesneshkoro@gmail.com. 1211 W. Main St., Princeton, 54968. Rev. Dale W. Grubba.
Catechesis Religious Program—Students 15.

OREGON, DANE CO., HOLY MOTHER OF CONSOLATION (1856) [CEM]
651 N. Main St., Oregon, 53575. Tel: 608-635-5763; Fax: 608-635-5764; Email: gary.wankerl@hmocchurch.org; Web: holymotherchurch.weconnect.com. Rev. Gary A. Wankerl.
Catechesis Religious Program—Tel: 608-835-5764. Students 416.

PALMYRA, JEFFERSON CO., ST. MARY (1911) [CEM] (Linked with St. Mary Help of Christians)
919 W. Main St., P.O. Box P, Palmyra, 53156.
Tel: 262-495-2395; Fax: 262-495-2533; Email: smarypal@gmail.com. Rev. Mariadas Bekala.

PAOLI, DANE CO., ST. WILLIAM, [CEM] Merged with St. Andrew, Verona to form St. Christopher, Verona.

PARDEEVILLE, COLUMBIA CO.
1—ST. FAUSTINA CONGREGATION, COLUMBIA/MARQUETTE COUNTY, WI, INC. (1903)
318 S. Main St., Pardeeville, 53954.
Tel: 608-429-3030; Fax: 608-429-3129; Email: stfaustina.holyfamily@frontier.com; Web: www.sfhfparish.com. Rev. Mark W. Miller.
Catechesis Religious Program—Email: sfhffaithkeeper@frontier.com. Alfred Nickel, C.R.E. Students 49.
2—HOLY FAMILY PARISH
318 S. Main St., Pardeeville, 53954.
Tel: 608-429-3030; Fax: 608-429-3129; Email: stfaustina.holyfamily@frontier.com; Web: www.sfhfparish.com. Rev. Mark W. Miller.
Catechesis Religious Program—45 St. Joseph St., Markesan, 53946. Email: sfhffaithkeeper@frontier.com. Alfred Nickel, D.R.E. Students 48.
Missions—St. Joseph Church—41 St. Joseph St., Markesan, 53946.
St. Mary Church, 177 W. Pearl St., Kingston, 53939.
3—ST. MARY OF THE MOST HOLY ROSARY (1903) Merged with St. Andrew, Buffalo to form St. Faustina Congregation, Columbia/Marquette County, WI, Inc., Pardeeville. For inquiries for sacramental records contact St. Faustina Congregation, Columbia/Marquette County, WI, Inc., Pardeeville.

PATCH GROVE, GRANT CO., ST. JOHN (1845) [CEM] (Linked with St. Mary, Bloomington; St. Charles, Cassville; St. Mary's, Glen Haven)
535 Congress St., P.O. Box 35, Bloomington, 53804-0035. Tel: 608-994-2526; Fax: 608-994-2551. Very Rev. John M. Meinholz, V.F.
Catechesis Religious Program—Twinned with St. Mary, Bloomington.

PERRY, HOLY REDEEMER (1859) [CEM] Merged with St. Ignatius, Mt. Horeb to form St. Michael the Archangel Parish, Mount Horeb.

PINE BLUFF, DANE CO., ST. MARY OF PINE BLUFF (1854) [CEM] (Linked with St. Michael the Archangel, Mount Horeb) Latin Tridentate Mass once a week.
3673 County Road P, Cross Plains, 53528-9179.
Tel: 608-798-2111; Fax: 608-798-2112; Email: catholic@tds.net; Web: www.stmarypb.org. Very Rev. Richard M. Heilman, V.F.
Catechesis Religious Program—Tel: 608-523-1796; Email: bethptak@yahoo.com. Beth Ptak, D.R.E. Students 45.

PLAIN, SAUK CO., ST. LUKE (1857) [CEM 2] [JC2] (German) (Linked with St. John the Evangelist, Spring Green)
1240 Nachreiner Ave., Plain, 53577.
Tel: 608-546-2482; Fax: 608-546-2616; Email: stlukesplain@charter.net; Web: www.stlukecatholicchurchplain.com. Rev. John A. Silva.
Res.: 1270 Nachreiner Ave., Plain, 53577.
School—St. Luke School, 1290 Nachreiner Ave., P. O. Box 205, Plain, 53577. Tel: 608-546-2963; Web: stlukes-plain.org. Diane Mueller, Prin. Clergy 1; Lay Teachers 10; Students 96.
Catechesis Religious Program—Tel: 608-574-1440; Email: angie.pulvy@gmail.com. Angie Pulvermacher, C.R.E. Students 83.

PLATTEVILLE, GRANT CO.
1—ST. AUGUSTINE UNIVERSITY PARISH (1974) (Linked with St. Mary, Platteville)
135 S. Hickory St., Platteville, 53818-3316.
Tel: 608-383-5574; Fax: 608-383-5574; Email: office@pioneercatholic.org; Web: pioneercatholic.org. 185 S. Hickory, Platteville, 53818. Rev. John Del Priore, S.J.P., Admin.; Deacon William Bussan, Pastoral Min.
Catechesis Religious Program—Students 2.
2—ST. MARY (1842) (Linked with St. Augustine University Parish, Platteville)
130 W. Cedar St., Platteville, 53818-2457.
Tel: 608-348-9735; Email: info@saintmaryplatteville.com. Rev. John Patrick Blewett, S.J.S.; Deacon William Bussan.
Catechesis Religious Program—Diane Drefcinski, D.R.E. Students 38.

PORTAGE, COLUMBIA CO., ST. MARY OF THE IMMACULATE CONCEPTION (1833) [CEM] (Linked with St. Mary Help of Christians, Briggsville)
309 W. Cook St., Portage, 53901-0216.
Tel: 608-742-6998; Email: portage.stmary@gmail.com; Web: www.stmaryportage.com. Rev. Gary L. Krahenbuhl; Deacons Dennis Sutter; Stephen Letourneaux.
Res.: 307 W. Cook St., Portage, 53901-0216.
School—St. Mary of the Immaculate Conception School, (Grades K-8), 315 W. Cook St., Portage, 53901. Tel: 608-742-4998; Email: jamhahn@stmarysportage.com; Web: www.stmarysportage.org. Jamie Hahn, Prin.; Josh Schuenemann, Vice Prin. Lay Teachers 11; Priests 1; Students 135.
Catechesis Religious Program—Email: Brenda.stmary@gmail.com. Brenda Collins, D.R.E. & Youth Min. Students 111.

POYNETTE, COLUMBIA CO., ST. THOMAS (1907) [JC] (Linked with St. Joseph, Rio)
655 S. Main, P.O. Box 310, Poynette, 53955-0310. Tel: 608-635-4326; Email: poynette.stp@charter.net. Rev. Balaraju Eturi, (India).
Catechesis Religious Program—651 S. Main St., Poynette, 53955. Email: rereligionclass7@gmail.com. Melinda Murray, C.R.E. Students 116.

PRINCETON, GREEN LAKE CO., ST. JOHN THE BAPTIST (1875) [CEM] (Linked with St. James, Neshkoro)
1211 W. Main, Princeton, 54968. Tel: 920-295-6209; Fax: 920-295-0231; Email: grubba@centurytel.net. Rev. Dale W. Grubba.
School—St. John the Baptist School, 125 Church St., Princeton, 54968. Tel: 920-295-3541; Fax: 920-295-0178; Web: stjohnprince.org. Lay Teachers 4; Students 37.
Catechesis Religious Program—Students 43.

REEDSBURG, SAUK CO., SACRED HEART (1878) [CEM 3]
624 N. Willow St., Reedsburg, 53959. Tel: 608-524-2412; Fax: 608-524-3831; Email: sheart@rucls.net; Web: www.shcreedsburg.org. Rev. David A. Carrano; Deacons Thomas Hale, Pastoral Assoc.; Ronald Pickar.
Res.: 852 8th St., Reedsburg, 53959.
School—Sacred Heart School, (Grades PreK-8), 545 N. Oak St., Reedsburg, 53959. Tel: 608-524-3611; Email: shs@rucls.net; Web: shsreedsburg.org. Karen Marklein, Prin. Lay Teachers 12; Students 144.
Catechesis Religious Program—Tel: 608-524-2412, Ext. 14; Email: faithformation@rucls.net. Patrick Andera, Dir. Faith Formation. Students 166.

RIDGEWAY, IOWA CO.
1—ST. BERNADETTE (2010) [CEM 2]
106 North St., Ridgeway, 53582. Tel: 608-924-2441; Cell: 608-574-1936; Email: stbernadette2010@aol.com; Email: steve.petrica@gmail.com; Email: gutzmere@gmail.com; Web: www.facebook.com/groups/StBernadetteParish/. Rev. Stephen C. Petrica, V.F.
Res.: 803 W. Main St., Ridgeway, 53582-9659.
Catechesis Religious Program—Email: elfering@mhtc.net. Lisa Elfering, D.R.E.; Jayne Fassbender, D.R.E. Students 61.
2—ST. BRIDGET (1850) [CEM] [JC] Merged with Immaculate Conception, Barneveld to form St. Bernadette, Ridgeway.

RIO, COLUMBIA CO., ST. JOSEPH (1902) [CEM 2] (Linked with St. Thomas the Apostle, Poynette)
514 Lincoln Ave., Rio, 53960. Tel: 608-635-4326; Email: parishstjoseph@gmail.com; Email: poynette.stp@charter.net. 655 S. Main St., P.O. Box 310, Poynette, 53955-0310. Rev. Balaraju Eturi, (India).
Catechesis Religious Program—Cell: 608-698-4339. Peggy Lapacek, D.R.E. Students 15.

ROXBURY, DANE CO., ST. NORBERT (1846) [CEM]
8944 County Rd. Y, Sauk City, 53583-9510. Tel: 608-643-6611; Email: jzhanay@slsonline.org; Web: www.saint-norbert.org. Revs. Miguel Gálvez, Admin.; Jerry O. Zhanay, S.J.S., Parochial Vicar; Pedro Escribano, (Spain) Parochial Vicar; Osvaldo Briones, S.J.S., Parochial Vicar; Faustino Ruiz, S.J.P., (Spain) Parochial Vicar.
Res.: 115 Madison St., Sauk City, 53583.
Catechesis Religious Program—Email: silvanna.navarro@gmail.com. Silvanna Navarro, C.R.E. Students 136.

SAUK CITY, SAUK CO.
1—ST. ALOYSIUS (1845) [CEM 2] Merged with St. Mary Health of the Sick, Merrimac to form Divine Mercy Parish, Sauk.
2—DIVINE MERCY PARISH, [CEM 2]
115 Madison Ave., Sauk City, 53583. Tel: 608-643-2449; Email: secretary@divinemercy-parish.org; Web: www.divinemercy-parish.org. Revs. Miguel Gálvez, Admin.; Jerry O. Zhanay, S.J.S., Parochial Vicar; Pedro Escribano, (Spain) Parochial Vicar; Osvaldo Briones, S.J.S., Parochial Vicar.
School—Divine Mercy Parish School, (Grades PreK-5), 608 Oak St., Sauk City, 53583. Tel: 608-643-6868; Email: info@saintaloysiusschool.org; Web: www.saintaloysiusschool.org. Ms. Daniela Saldana, Prin. Clergy 4; Lay Teachers 7; Students 70.
Catechesis Religious Program—Tel: 608-643-4062; Email: lisa.enerson@saintaloysiusschool.org. Lisa Enerson, D.R.E. Students 79.

SEYMOUR, LAFAYETTE CO., OUR LADY OF HOPE, [CEM] Merged with Holy Rosary, Darlington; St. Peter, Elk Grove; St. Michael, Calamine; Immaculate Conception, Truman to form Our Lady of Fatima Congregation, Lafayette County, WI, Inc., Darlington. For inquiries for sacramental records contact Our Lady of Fatima Congregation, Lafayette County, WI, Inc., Darlington.

SHULLSBURG, LAFAYETTE CO., ST. MATTHEW (1835) [CEM 2] [JC2] (Linked with St. John's, South Wayne & St. Joseph's, Gratiot)
344 Judgment St., Shullsburg, 53586. Tel: 608-965-4518; Email: stmathewschurch@centurytel.net. Rev. Sudhakar Devarapu, Parochial Admin.
Catechesis Religious Program—Tel: 608-482-1397; Email: dianeweiskircher@yahoo.com. Diane Weiskircher, D.R.E. Students 109.

SOUTH WAYNE, LAFAYETTE CO., ST. JOHN (1898) [CEM] (Linked with St. Joseph, Gratiot & St. Matthew's, Shullsburg)
304 E Pleasant St., South Wayne, 53587. Tel: 608-965-4518; Email: stmathewschurch@centurytel.net. 344 N. Judgement St., Shullsburg, 53586. Rev. Sudhakar Devarapu, Parochial Admin.
Catechesis Religious Program—Students 14.

SPRING GREEN, SAUK CO., ST. JOHN THE EVANGELIST (1866) [CEM] (Linked with St. Luke, Plain)
129 W. Daley St., Spring Green, 53588. Tel: 608-588-2028; Fax: 608-588-2648; Email: stjohnspringgreen@gmail.com. Mailing Address: P.O. Box 628, Spring Green, 53588. Rev. John A. Silva.
School—St. John the Evangelist School, (Grades PreSchool-5), P.O. Box 129, Spring Green, 53588. Tel: 608-588-2021; Fax: 608-588-9372; Email: tfeigl@stjohnspringgreen.com; Web: www.stjohnsspringgreen.org. 209 N. Washington St., Spring Green, 53588. Mrs. Theresa Feigl, Prin. Lay Teachers 10; Students 60.
Catechesis Religious Program—Tel: 608-574-1880; Email: angie.pulvy@gmail.com. Angie Pulvermacher, D.R.E. Students 58.

STOUGHTON, DANE CO., ST. ANN, [CEM]
323 N. Van Buren, Stoughton, 53589. Tel: 608-873-7633; Web: stannparish.weconnect.com. Rev. Randy J. Budnar.
Res.: 320 N. Harrison St., Stoughton, 53589.
School—St. Ann School, (Grades PreK-8), 324 N. Harrison St., Stoughton, 53589. Tel: 608-873-3343; Email: stanns@stanns-school.org. Mrs. Kara Roisum, Prin. Lay Teachers 20; Students 154.
Catechesis Religious Program—Email: shaun.kleitsch@stanns-school.org. Shaun Kleitsch, D.R.E.; Cathie Truehl, D.R.E. Students 208.

SULLIVAN, JEFFERSON CO., ST. MARY HELP OF CHRISTIANS (1854) [CEM]
W856 Hwy. 18, Sullivan, 53187. Tel: 262-593-2250; Fax: 262-593-2721. Mailing Address: P.O. Box 418, Sullivan, 53187. Rev. Mariadas Bekala.
Catechesis Religious Program—Tel: 920-285-4425; Email: Anne.auger@outlook.com. Anne Auger, D.R.E. Students 37.

SUN PRAIRIE, DANE CO.
1—ST. ALBERT THE GREAT (1967)
2420 St. Albert Dr., Sun Prairie, 53590. Tel: 608-837-3798; Web: www.saintalberts.org. Rev. Msgrs. Donald J. Heiar Jr.; Douglas L. Dushack, Pastor Emeritus, (Retired); Deacon Joseph Stafford.
Catechesis Religious Program—Email: bonnie@saintalberts.org. Zoe Bernard, D.R.E.; Peter Cooney, D.R.E. Students 417.
2—SACRED HEARTS OF JESUS AND MARY, [CEM]
221 Columbus St., Sun Prairie, 53590. Tel: 608-837-7381; Fax: 608-825-9585; Email: sacredhearts@sacred-hearts.org; Email: sharon.ouimette@sacred-hearts.org; Web: www.sacred-hearts.org. Rev. Msgr. Duane R. Moellenberndt, V.F.; Rev. Grant Thies, Vicar.
Rectory—227 Columbus St., Sun Prairie, 53590.
School—Sacred Hearts of Jesus and Mary School, (Grades PreK-8), 219 Columbus St., Sun Prairie, 53590. Tel: 608-837-8508; Email: kim.frederick@shjms.org; Web: sacredhearts.k12.wi.us. Mrs. Kimberlee Frederick, Prin. Lay Teachers 30; Students 305; Clergy / Religious Teachers 2.
Catechesis Religious Program—Tel: 608-837-8509; Email: brad.grobbel@sacred-hearts.org. Bred Grobbel, D.R.E.; Mrs. Hanna Lesniewski, D.R.E. Students 163.

TENNYSON-POTOSI, GRANT CO., SS. ANDREW AND THOMAS (1970) [CEM 2]
101 Church St., Potosi, 53820-9654. Tel: 608-763-2671; Email: frleffler@tds.net; Web: www.ssandrew-thomas.org. Rev. Richard J. Leffler.
School—SS. Andrew and Thomas School, 100 Hwy. 61 N., P.O. Box 160, Potosi, 53820. Tel: 608-763-2120 ; Fax: 608-763-4064; Email: ssandrew@ss-andrew-thomas.org; Web: www.ssandrew-thomas.org. Ms. Debra Pfab, Prin. Clergy 1; Lay Teachers 8; Students 51.
Catechesis Religious Program—Students 68.

TRUMAN, LAFAYETTE CO., IMMACULATE CONCEPTION (1856) [CEM] Merged with Holy Rosary, Darlington; St. Peter, Elk Grove; St. Michael, Calamine; Our Lady of Hope, Seymour to form Our Lady of Fatima Congregation, Lafayette County, WI, Inc., Darlington. For inquiries for sacramental records contact Our Lady of Fatima Congregation, Lafayette County, WI, Inc., Darlington.

VERONA, DANE CO.
1—ST. ANDREW (1917) [CEM] Merged with St. William, Paoli to form St. Christopher Parish, Verona.
2—ST. CHRISTOPHER PARISH (2010) [CEM 2]
301 N. Main St., Verona, 53593. Tel: 608-845-6613; Fax: 608-848-4293; Email: fr.johns@icloud.com; Email: office@saintichristopherparish.com; Web: www.saintchristopherparish.com. Rev. John J. Sasse.
Catechesis Religious Program—Tel: 608-845-6613; Email: lsabbar@saintchristopherparish.com; Email: dulaszek@saintchristopherparish.com. Laurie Sabbarese, Faith Formation Office Asst.; Doug Ulaszek, Youth Ministry, Confirmation & Adult Faith Coord. Students 142.
3—ST. WILLIAM, Merged with St. Andrew, Verona to form St. Christopher Parish, Verona.

WATERLOO, JEFFERSON CO.
1—HOLY FAMILY PARISH (2012) [CEM]
205 Milwaukee Ave., Waterloo, 53594-1329. Tel: 920-478-2032; Email: parish.office@holyfamily.info; Email: pastor@holyfamily.info; Web: www.holyfamily.info. Rev. Jorge A. Miramontes.
School—Holy Family Parish School, (Grades PreK-6), 387 S. Monroe St., Waterloo, 53594. Tel: 920-478-3221; Email: school.office@holyfamily.info; Web: www.holyfamily.info. Ms. Penny Hilgendorf, Acting Prin. Lay Teachers 5; Students 26; Clergy / Religious Teachers 1.
Catechesis Religious Program—Email: melinda.riley@holyfamily.info. Melinda Riley, C.R.E. (K-9). Students 73.
2—ST. JOSEPH (1868) [CEM] Merged with St. Mary of the Nativity, Marshall to form Holy Family Parish, Waterloo.

WATERTOWN, JEFFERSON CO.
1—ST. BERNARD (1843)
114 S. Church St., Watertown, 53094-4399. Tel: 920-261-5133; Email: stbernard@watertowncatholic.org; Web: www.watertowncatholic.org. Very Rev. Patrick J. Wendler; Rev. Miroslaw Szynal, Parochial Vicar.
School—St. Bernard School, (Grades PreK-3), Tel: 920-261-7204; Email: secretarystb@watertowncatholic.org; Web: www.watertowncatholic.org. Adrienne Van Norman, Prin. Lay Teachers 10; Students 104; Religious Education Teacher 1.
Catechesis Religious Program—Email: mmcfarland@watertowncatholic.org. Michele McFarland, D.R.E. Students 172.
2—ST. HENRY (1853) [CEM]
412 N. 4th St., Watertown, 53094. Tel: 920-261-7273; Fax: 920-261-3681; Email: sthenry@watertowncatholic.org; Web: www.watertowncatholic.org. Very Rev. Patrick J. Wendler; Rev. Miroslaw Szynal, Parochial Vicar.
School—St. Henry School, (Grades 4-8), 300 Cady St., Watertown, 53094. Tel: 920-261-2586; Web: www.watertowncatholic.org. Adrienne Van Norman, Prin.; Sherry Harms, Vice Prin. Lay Teachers 8; Students 93.
Catechesis Religious Program—Tel: 920-261-2586; Email: tweissenborn@watertowncatholic.org; Email: avannorman@watertowncatholic.org. Todd Weissenborn, C.R.E.; Adrienne Van Norman, D.R.E. Students 122.

WAUNAKEE, DANE CO., ST. JOHN THE BAPTIST (1874) [CEM]
209 South St., Waunakee, 53597. Tel: 608-849-5121; Fax: 608-849-5866; Email: stjohnparish@stjb.org; Web: www.stjb.org. Rev. Msgr. James L. Gunn; Very Rev. Gabriel A. Lopez-Betanzos, J.C.L., Parochial Vicar; Rev. Paulraj Sellam, (India) Parochial Vicar; Deacon Norbert Brunner; Jackie Nerat, Business Mgr.
School—St. John the Baptist School, 114 E. 3rd St., Waunakee, 53597. Tel: 608-849-5325; Web: www.stjb.org. Elizabeth Goldman, Prin. Lay Teachers 17; Students 210.
Catechesis Religious Program—114 E. 3rd St., Waunakee, 53597. Email: edaley@stjb.org. Eileen Daley, Coord. Evangelization & Catechesis (Grades 5K-12). Students 555.

WESTFIELD, MARQUETTE CO., GOOD SHEPHERD (1961) (Linked with St. John the Baptist, Montello)
277 E. Montello St., Montello, 53949. Tel: 608-296-3631; Tel: 608-297-7423; Email: gsreligiousedl@gmail.com; Email: sjbgsparishoffice@gmail.com; Web: www.marquettecountycatholic.org. Rev. Savio Yerasani.
Catechesis Religious Program—241 E. 6th St., Westfield, 53964. Email: jenniebradburn@gmail.com. Jennifer Bradburn, D.R.E. Students 58.

WESTPORT, DANE CO., ST. MARY OF THE LAKE (1866) [CEM]
5460 Mary Lake Rd., Waunakee, 53597. Tel: 608-849-4116; Fax: 608-849-4122; Email: stmaryparish@stjb.org. 209 South St., Waunakee, 53597. Rev. Msgr. James L. Gunn; Very Rev. Gabriel A. Lopez-Betanzos, J.C.L.; Rev. Paulraj Sellam, (India).

WISCONSIN DELLS, COLUMBIA CO., ST. CECILIA (1866) [CEM]
603 Oak St., Wisconsin Dells, 53965.
Tel: 608-254-8381; Email: freric@dellscatholic.com; Email: tdonnelly@dellscatholic.com; Web: www.dellscatholic.com. Rev. Eric G. Sternberg.
Res. & Office: 1612 Pleasant View Dr., Wisconsin Dells, 53965.
Catechesis Religious Program—Tel: 608-253-5621. David Kordell, D.R.E. Students 195.

YELLOWSTONE, LAFAYETTE CO., ST. MICHAEL (1870) [CEM] Merged with St. Joseph, Argyle; St. Patrick, Hollandale & Immaculate Conception, Blanchardville to form Congregation of St. Isidore, Hollandale.

Chaplains of Public Institutions

MADISON. *Columbia County Institution*. Attended from St. Mary's Church, Portage.
Dane County Institution. Attended from St. Christopher, Verona.
Grant County Institution. Attended from St. Clement Church, Lancaster.
Green County Institution. Attended from St. Victor Church, Monroe.
Iowa County Institution. Attended from St. Joseph Church, Dodgeville.
Madison-Meriter General Hospital. Attended from Cathedral Parish of St. Raphael.
Mendota State Hospital. Vacant.
University of Wisconsin Hospitals and Clinics. Rev. Steven J. Kortendick, Chap.
602 Everglade Dr., 53717.

JANESVILLE. *Jefferson County Institution*. Attended from St. John the Baptist Church, Jefferson.
LaFayette County Institution. Attended from Holy Rosary Church, Darlington.
Mercy Hospital. Attended from Janesville Parishes, Janesville.
Rock County Institution. Attended from Janesville Parishes, Janesville.
Sauk County Institution. Attended from St. Boniface Church, Lime Ridge.
Wisconsin State School for the Blind. Attended from St. Patrick's Church, Janesville.

Graduate Studies:
Revs.—
Baker, Joseph, Pontifical Athenaeum Regina Apostolorum, Rome
Lee, Peter, Pontifical University of St. Thomas Aquinas, Rome
Olson, Drew, Patristic Institute Augustinianum, Rome.

Leave of Absence:
Revs.—
Johannes, David G.
Schneider, Lance J.

Military Chaplains:
Rev. Msgr.—
Heiar, Donald J. Jr.
Revs.—
Brewer, Vincent
Hesseling, Jason E.

Retired:
Rev. Msgrs.—
Burke, Michael L., (Retired), Holy Name Heights, 702 S. High Point Rd., #301, 53719
Connors, Terrence L., (Retired), 188 Cannery Pl., #301, Sun Prairie, 53590
Dushack, Douglas L., (Retired), 2420 St. Albert Dr., Sun Prairie, 53590
Healy, Gerard M., (Retired), 8202 Highview Dr., #233, 53719
Hebl, John H., (Retired), W8595 Fern Rd., Oxford, 53952
Hippee, Michael E., J.C.L., (Retired), 340 Sunset Dr., Unit #1511, Fort Lauderdale, FL 33301
Kertz, Raymond N., (Retired), 2334 16th Ave., Rockford, IL 61104
Uppena, James J., (Retired), 401 S. Owen Dr., 53711
Revs.—
Borre, Robert J., (Retired), 2000 Glenview Rd., Glenview, IL 60025-2850
Connell, William, (Retired), St. Mary's Care Center, 3401 Maple Grove Dr., 53719
Dischler, Raymond J., (Retired), 3830 Anchor Dr., 53714
Doheny, Thomas R., (Retired), 3133 Stratton Way #112, 53719
Doherty, Patrick J., (Retired)
Gillespie, Thomas E., (Retired), 8202 Highview Dr., #52, 53719
Hennington, Bruce M., (Retired), 120 Rainbow Dr., #2022, Livingston, TX 77399
Hinnen, James W., J.C.L., (Retired), 8202 Highview Dr., #259, 53719
Hollfelder, Eugene F., (Retired), S. 2518 Vanhy St., Baraboo, 53913
Hower, William J., (Retired), 2430 Springmill Dr., Oshkosh, 54904
Hughes, Robert W., (Retired), 229 Tamarack Dr. #3, Lake Mills, 53551
Klink, Kenneth J., (Retired), 7610 Mid-Town Rd., 53719
Kuhn, James G., (Retired), 7824 Courtyard Dr., 53715
Lange, Donald F., (Retired), 1365 Cody Pkwy., Apt. #105, Platteville, 53818
Lesniak, Richard D., (Retired), 221 Vista Ct., Waupaca, 54981-1993
Maksvytis, Jerome J., (Retired), 2515 Deerfield St., Portage, 53901
Marr, Thomas P., (Retired)
McEnery, James G., (Retired), 57 Cherokee Cir., #204, 53704-1499
Meier, Laverne G., (Retired), 8202 Highview Dr., Apt. #205, 53719
Monaghan, Thomas J., (Retired), 3018 Saddle Ridge, Portage, 53901
Nilles, Roger G., (Retired), 57 Cherokee Cir., #204, 53704
Nolan, William A., (Retired)
Schmidt, Francis J., (Retired), 1934 Dolores Dr., 53716
Schmitt, Kent A., (Retired), 2004 14th St., Monroe, 53566
Schumacher, Anthony J., (Retired), 2976 Chapel Valley, #103, 53711
Steffen, Francis J., (Retired), Academy Apts. #110, 511 Co. Rd. Z, Hazel Green, 53811
Turner, Jerome R., (Retired), 5658 NE Michael's Way, Poulsbo, WA 98370-8934
Umhoefer, Stephen J., (Retired), 727 Lorillard Ct., #330, 53703
Weisensel, Cyril O., (Retired), 702 S. High Point Dr., 53719.

Permanent Deacons:
Deacons—
Brunner, Norbert, St. John the Baptist, Waunakee; (Diocese of La Crosse)
Buhman, Jerome, St. Maria Goretti, Madison
Bussan, William, St. Augustine Univ., Platteville
Davis, James, St. Jude, Beloit
Fernan, John K., (Retired)
Hale, Thomas, Sacred Heart, Reedsburg
Hendrickson, David J., St. Dennis, Madison
Hoegemeier, James, All Saints, Berlin
Houseman, John, St. Patrick, Janesville
Jozefowicz, Patrick, SS. Anthony & Philip, Highland; St. Thomas, Montfort
Letourneaux, Stephen, St. Mary of the Immaculate Conception, Portage (Diocese of Green Bay)
Lukesic, Raymond, Cathedral Parish of St. Raphael, Madison
Martin, Richard, St. Maria Goretti, Madison
Martin, Todd, St. Peter, Madison
Pickar, Ronald, Sacred Heart, Reedsburg
Reilly, Timothy, St. Bernard, Madison; (Diocese of Green Bay)
Schmelzer, Christopher, 5307 Autumn Ln., McFarland, 53558. Cathedral Parish of St. Raphael
Schmitt, Lawrence, Corpus Christi, Boscobel
Stafford, Joseph, St. Albert the Great, Sun Prairie
Sutter, Dennis, St. Mary of the Immaculate Conception, Portage
Tranel, Lawrence, Holy Ghost, Dickeyville.

INSTITUTIONS LOCATED IN DIOCESE

[A] COLLEGES

MADISON. *Edgewood College, Inc.*, 1000 Edgewood College Dr., 53711-1997. Tel: 608-663-2262; Fax: 608-663-6717; Email: sflanagan@edgewood.edu; Web: www.edgewood.edu. Scott Flanagan, Pres.; Sr. Maggie Hopkins, O.P., Asst. to Pres., Dominican Catholic Identity; Mary Klink, Assoc. Vice Pres., Dominican Life & Mission; Laurin Dodge, Asst. Dir., Dominican Life. Sponsored by the Dominican Sisters of Sinsinawa, Edgewood College, rooted in the Dominican tradition, engages students within a community of learners committed to building a just and compassionate world. Religious Teachers 1; Lay Teachers 152; Sisters 3; Students 2,190.

[B] HIGH SCHOOLS, PRIVATE

MADISON. **St. Ambrose Academy*, 602 Everglade Dr., 53717. Tel: 608-827-5863; Fax: 608-833-1129; Email: info@ambroseacademy.org; Web: www.ambroseacademy.org. David Stiennon, Pres.; Scott Schmiesing, Prin. Lay Teachers 18; Students 99.
Edgewood High School of the Sacred Heart, Inc., 2219 Monroe St., 53711. Tel: 608-257-1023; Fax: 608-257-9133; Email: jen.trost@edgewoodhs.org; Web: www.edgewoodhs.org. Michael G. Elliott, Pres.; Beth Steffen, Prin. Dominican Sisters, Sinsinawa. Lay Teachers 57; Students 514.

[C] ELEMENTARY SCHOOLS, PRIVATE

MADISON. *Edgewood Campus School, Inc.* (1881) 829 Edgewood College Dr., 53711. Tel: 608-663-4100; Fax: 608-663-4101; Email: apalzkill@edgewoodk8.com; Web: www.campusschool.org. Anne Palzkill, Pres. & Prin. Dominican Sisters, Sinsinawa. Lay Teachers 21; Students 287.

[D] GENERAL HOSPITALS

MADISON. *SSM Health St. Mary's Hospital-Madison*, 700 S. Park St., 53715. Tel: 608-251-6100; Fax: 608-258-6188; Email: augustine.duru@ssmhealth.com. Franciscan Sisters of Mary (St. Louis, MO).Member of SSM Health. Bed Capacity 440; Tot Asst. Annually 117,785; Total Staff 2,575.
Pastoral Care Department: Augustine Duru, Regl. Dir., Mission, Ethics & Pastoral Care; Rev. Patrick F. Norris, O.P., Ethicist & Priest Chap.; Sr. Pamela Moehring, S.S.N.D., Catholic Chap.; Rev. Melva Bishop, American Baptist; John Berg, E.L.C.A. Min.; Robert Vetter, E.L.C.A. Min.; Liz Allen, Catholic Chap.; Dennis Harrison-Noonan, Catholic Chap.; Aaron Alfred, (United Methodist); Andrew Karlson, (Unitarian Universalist).

BARABOO. *St. Clare Hospital*, 707 14th St., Baraboo, 53913. Tel: 608-356-1400; Fax: 608-356-1367; Email: Angela.Ebright@ssmhealth.com; Web: www.stclare.com. Laura Walczak, Pres.; Doug Shepherd, M.Div. Member of SSM Health Care. Bed Capacity 43; Tot Asst. Annually 105,599; Total Staff 406.

JANESVILLE. *SSM Health, St. Mary's Hospital - Janesville*, 3400 E. Racine St., Janesville, 53546. Tel: 608-373-8010; Fax: 608-373-8006; Email: ssmhealthcareofficialcatholicdirectorynotices@ssmhealth.com; Web: www.stmarysjanesville.com. Ben Layman, Pres. Sponsored by: Franciscan Sisters of Mary (St. Louis, MO). Member of SSM Health Care.(a division of SSM Health Care of Wisconsin, Inc.); Purpose: to provide health care, health education and related facilities and services as a Catholic hospital. Bed Capacity 50; Tot Asst. Annually 36,175; Total Staff 283.

MONROE. *The Monroe Clinic, Inc.*, 515 22nd Ave., Monroe, 53566. Tel: 608-324-1000; Fax: 608-324-1114; Email: mike.sanders@monroeclinic.org; Email: damond.boatwright@ssmhealth.com; Web: www.monroeclinic.org. 10101 Woodfield Ln., St. Louis, MO 63132. Michael B. Sanders, Pres. & CEO; Wade Weis, Dir. SSM Health Care of Wisconsin, Inc. Bed Capacity 95; Tot Asst. Annually 279,000; Total Staff 1,250.

PORTAGE. *Divine Savior Healthcare, Inc.*, 2817 New Pinery Rd., Portage, 53901. Tel: 608-742-4131; Fax: 608-742-6098; Email: mdnelson@dshealthcare.com. Mr. Michael Decker, Pres. & CEO. Sisters of the Divine Savior. Bed Capacity 52; Patients Asst Anual. 162,337; Sisters 2; Total Staff 940.

[E] HOMES FOR THE AGED

MADISON. *St. Mary's Care Center*, 3401 Maple Grove Dr., 53719. Tel: 608-845-1000; Fax: 608-845-1001; Email: karen.hayden@ssmhealth.com; Email: douglas.trost@ssmhealth.com. Karen Hayden, Dir.; Douglas Trost, Vice Pres. Member of SSM Health. Bed Capacity 184; Tot Asst. Annually 647; Total Staff 273.

BARABOO. *SSM Health St. Clare Meadows Care Center*, 1414 Jefferson St., Baraboo, 53913.
Tel: 608-356-4838; Fax: 608-356-8732; Email: SSMHealthCareOfficialCatholicDirectoryNotices@ssmhealth.com; Email: ron.schaetzl@ssmhealth.com; Email: douglas.trost@ssmhealth.com; Web: www.stclare.com/meadows. Douglas Trost, Vice Pres.; Ronnie E. Schaetzl, Dir. Member of SSM Health Care. Bed Capacity 117; Skilled Nursing Beds 102; Total Staff 195; Total Assisted 450.

JANESVILLE. *St. Elizabeth Home*, 109 S. Atwood Ave., Janesville, 53545. Tel: 608-752-6709; Fax: 608-752-1724; Email: MichelleGodfrey@stelizabethmanor.com; Web: www.saintelizabethhome.com. Michelle Godfrey, Admin. Aged Residents 43; Bed Capacity 43; Tot Asst. Annually 84; Total Staff 50.

PORTAGE. *Tivoli at Divine Savior Healthcare*, Mailing

Address: 2805 Hunters Tr., P.O. Box 387, Portage, 53901-0387. Tel: 608-745-5900; Fax: 608-745-5997; Web: dshealthcare.com. Mr. Michael Decker, CEO; Sr. Virginia Hornish, Prov. (See Divine Savior Healthcare, Portage.) Aged Residents 83; Bed Capacity 123; Tot Asst. Annually 325; Total Staff 145.

[F] MONASTERIES AND RESIDENCES OF PRIESTS

MADISON. *Holy Name Heights*, 702 S. High Point Rd., Ste. 225, 53719. Tel: 608-821-3000; Fax: 608-440-2808; Email: Vicargeneral@madisondiocese.org; Web: www.madisondiocese.org. In Res. Rev. Msgr. James R. Bartylla, Vicar General; Revs. John T. Zuhlsdorf, Pres., Tridentine Mass Society of Madison; Scott J. Emerson, J.C.L.

EDGERTON. *Koshkonong Pastoral Center*, 432 Liguori Rd., Edgerton, 53534. Tel: 608-884-3425; Fax: 608-884-9231; Email: jcaouette@legionaries.org. Revs. Janick Caouette, L.C.; Javier Gonzalez, L.C., Prin.; Aaron Loch, Chap.

[G] CONVENTS AND RESIDENCES FOR SISTERS

MADISON. *Secular Institute of Schoenstatt Sisters of Mary*, 5901 Cottage Grove Rd., 53718-1397. Tel: 608-222-7208; Email: schoenstattheights@schsrsmary.org. Sr. M. Gabriella Maschita, I.S.S.M., Supr. Sisters 5.

BELOIT. *Auxiliaries of the Blessed Sacrament*, 916 Bluff St., Beloit, 53511. Tel: 608-466-9751; Email: Pamala31@juno.com. Sr. Pauline Labrecque, R.N., Admin. Regional House of the Auxiliaries of the Blessed Sacrament. Sisters 3.

PRAIRIE DU SAC. *Valley of Our Lady Monastery*, E11096 Yanke Dr., Prairie du Sac, 53578-9737. Tel: 608-643-3520 (Altar Breads); Email: cisterciannuns@valleyofourlady.org; Web: www.valleyofourlady.org. Mother Anne Marie Joerger, O.Cist., Supr. Cistercian Nuns. Postulants 1; Solemnly Professed 18; Claustral Oblate 1; Regular Oblates (non-resident) 50.

SINSINAWA. *Dominican Motherhouse*, 585 County Rd. Z, Sinsinawa, 53824-9701. Tel: 608-748-4411; Fax: 608-748-4491; Email: toniharrisop@gmail.com; Web: www.sinsinawa.org. Sisters Antoinette Harris, O.P., Prioress of the Congregation; Maryann Tranel, O.P., Sec. of the Congregation; Revs. John C. Risley, O.P., Chap.; Daniel Davis, O.P., Chap.; Sisters Maryann Lucy, O.P., Prioress - Siena, St. Clara Community; Georgia Acker, Prioress - Mound; Patricia Rinn, O.P., Prioress. Sinsinawa Dominican Congregation of the Most Holy Rosary. Sisters 400.

[H] CHARITABLE INSTITUTIONS

MADISON. *Catholic Charities, Inc., Diocese of Madison Administrative Center*, 702 S. High Point Rd., Ste. 201, 53719. Tel: 608-826-8000; Fax: 608-826-8026; Email: ccharities@ccmadison.org; Web: www.ccmadison.org. Jackson Fonder, Pres. & CEO. Tot Asst. Annually 25,875; Total Staff 443.

Janesville District Office, 2200 W Court St #130, Janesville, 53545. Tel: 608-758-8180; Fax: 608-758-8654; Email: ccharities@ccmadison.org. Jackson Fonder, Pres.

Catholic Multicultural Center Our Lady Queen of Peace Parish/ Catholic Multicultural Center Our Lady Queen of Peace Parish/ Catholic Multicultural Center, 1862 Beld St., 53713. Tel: 608-661-3512; Fax: 608-661-0363; Email: andy@cmcmadison.org; Web: www.cmcmadison.org. Rev. Msgr. Kenneth J. Fiedler, Spiritual Dir.; Andrew Russell, Dir. Tot Asst. Annually 2,000,000; Total Staff 16.

Society of St. Vincent de Paul aka Society of St. Vincent de Paul - Madison (District Council of Madison, Inc.) 2033 Fish Hatchery Rd., P.O. Box 259686, 53725-9686. Tel: 608-442-7200; Email: manager@svdpmadison.org; Web: www.svdpmadison.org. James Oeth, Pres.; Ernest Stetenfeld, CEO. Tot Asst. Annually 28,000; Total Staff 250.

BARABOO. *Saint Vincent de Paul Society-Baraboo*, 100 S. Blvd., P.O. Box 233, Baraboo, 53913. Tel: 608-356-4649; Fax: 608-356-4430; Email: svdpbaraboo@centurytel.net. Mike Grogan, Contact Person. Sponsored by: Saint Vincent de Paul SocietyPurpose: To help the poor and needy in a Vincentian spirit and manner.

Legal Name: St. Vincent de Paul Society St. Joseph Conference, Inc.

JEFFERSON. *St. Coletta of Wisconsin, Inc.*, N4637 County Rd. Y, Jefferson, 53549. Tel: 920-674-4330; Email: rbaker@stcolettawi.org; Web: www.stcolettawi.org. Ted Behncke, Pres.; Robin Baker, Dir. of Marketing & Devel. Sponsored by the Sisters of St. Francis of Assisi. Milwaukee. Residents 280; Sisters 1; Tot Asst. Annually 300; Total Staff 435.

MIDDLETON. *Society of St. Vincent de Paul (Diocesan Council of Madison)*, 3805 Lexington Dr., Middleton, 53562. Tel: 608-712-1748; Email: edemmenegr@aol.com. Rev. Msgr. Kevin D. Holmes, Spiritual Advisor/Care Svcs.; Edward A. Emmenegger, Council Pres.

PRAIRIE DU SAC. **St. Vincent de Paul Society of Sauk-Prairie Roxbury Inc.*, 815 19th St., Prairie du Sac, 53578. Tel: 608-643-8905; Fax: 608-643-8905; Email: stvdpmanager@verizon.net. Victor Lochner, Pres. Sponsored by: Saint Vincent de Paul Society-Purpose: To help the poor and needy in a Vincentian spirit and manner.

[I] MISCELLANEOUS

MADISON. *All Saints Assisted Living Center, Inc.*, 519 Commerce Dr., 53719. Tel: 608-827-2990; Email: hstringham@elderspan.com; Web: ww.allsaintsneighborhood.org. Jackson Fonder, Pres. Bed Capacity 151; Tot Asst. Annually 151; Total Staff 100.

All Saints Retirement Center, Inc., 8202 Highview Dr., 53719. Tel: 608-827-2222; Email: mnaegle@elderspan.com; Web: www.allsaintsneighborhood.org. Jackson Fonder, Pres. Purpose: To own, operate and maintain apartment homes for the aged in the tradition of the Roman Catholic Church, having a Catholic identity, and serving the physical, mental, emotional and spiritual needs of residents of the Diocese of Madison, Wisconsin. Bed Capacity 144; Tot Asst. Annually 144; Total Staff 3.

Apostolate to the Handicapped, Inc. dba Apostolate for persons with Disabilities, 702 South High Point Rd., Ste. 225, 53719. Tel: 608-821-3050; Fax: 608-325-2061; Email: APD@madisondiocese.org; Web: www.apdmadisondiocese.com. Rev. Msgr. Lawrence M. Bakke, Dir. & Contact Person; Deacon James Hoegemeier, Assoc. Dir.; Kellie O'Brien, Project Mgr.

dba Apostolate for Persons with Disabilities - Diocese of Madison.

The Catholic Diocese of Madison Foundation, Inc., 702 S. High Point Rd., Ste. 223, 53719. Tel: 608-821-3046; Tel: 608-821-3049; Email: daun.maier@diocesemadisonfoundation.org; Email: nikki.pfleger@diocesemadisonfoundation.org; Web: www.diocesemadisonfoundation.org. Daun Maier, Exec. Dir.; Niki Pfleger, Devel. Impact Mgr. Purpose: to operate at all times hereafter, exclusively for religious charitable and educational purposes within the meaning of 501(c)(3) of the Internal Revenue Code of 1986 and to exclusively serve the Roman Catholic Diocese of Madison & its Bishop.

**The Evangelical Catholic, Inc.*, 6602 Normandy Ln., Fl. 2, 53719. Tel: 608-820-1288; Email: ec@evangelicalcatholic.org; Web: www.evangelicalcatholic.org. Jason J. Simon, M.Div., Exec. Dir., Email: jsimon@evangelicalcatholic.org; Andrew Ochalek, Dir. Opers.; Dave Chodorowski, Dir.; James Carrano, M.A., Assoc. Dir.; Tom Wierschem, Business Specialist.

Holy Name Catholic Center, Inc., 702 S. High Point Rd., Ste. 225, 53719. Tel: 608-821-3000; Fax: 608-709-7611; Email: John.Philipp@madisondiocese.org; Web: www.madisondiocese.org. Rev. Msgr. James R. Bartylla, Vicar; Mr. John C. Philipp, Treas.

Holy Name Seminary, Inc., 702 S. High Point Rd., Ste. 225, 53719. Fax: 608-440-2808; Email: vicargeneral@madisondiocese.org; Web: www.madisondiocese.org. Rev. Msgr. James R. Bartylla, Vicar Gen.; Mr. John C. Philipp, Treas.

dba St. Joseph Fund.

St. Mary's Janesville Foundation, Inc., 3400 E. Racine St., Janesville, 53546. Tel: 608-373-8015; Email: deborah.thielen@ssmhealth.com; Web: www.stmarysjanesville.com. Deborah Thielen, Exec. Franciscan Sisters of MaryPurpose: Organized to provide gifts, grants or other payments to SSM Health Care of Wisconsin, Inc. and other charitable, educational, scientific or religious organizations exclusively.

St. Mary's Foundation, Inc., 700 S. Park St., 53715. Tel: 608-258-5600; Fax: 608-229-8495; Email: ssmhealthcareofficialcatholicdirectorynotices@ssmhealth.com; Web: www.stmarysmadison.com. Sandra Lampman, Exec. Dir. Sponsored by the Franciscan Sisters of Mary.Purpose: To solicit, manage, invest and expend endowment funds and other gifts, grants and bequests primarily for the maintenance and benefit of St. Mary's Hospital and St. Mary's Care Center of Madison, WI; to support other medical research, educational or charitable programs or activities of St. Mary's in the Madison, WI area. Member of SSM Health.

**Orate Institute of Sacred Liturgy, Music, and Art, Inc.*, 722 S. High Point Rd., 53719. Tel: 608-203-6735; Email: mrark@hotmail.com. Rt. Rev. Marcel Rooney, Pres.; Jeffrey Karls, Vice Pres.

St. Paul University Catholic Foundation, Inc., 723 State St., 53703-1087. Tel: 608-258-3140; Email: om@uwcatholic.org; Email: enielsen@uwcatholic.org; Web: www.uwcatholic.org. Michael Gratz, Pres.; Alexandria Viegut, Sec.; John Drake, Treas.; Rev. Eric H. Nielsen, Dir. Purpose: to own and maintain the property on which resides the St. Paul University Parish and St. Paul Catholic Student Center, and assume fiduciary responsibility for the student ministry. Total Staff 20.

Roman Catholic Diocese of Madison Cemeteries, Inc., Central Office, 702 S. High Point Rd., Ste. 225, 53705. Tel: 608-821-3000; Fax: 608-709-7611; Email: John.Miller@madisondiocese.org; Web: www.madisondiocese.org. Mr. John C. Philipp, Treas.

SSM Health Care of Wisconsin, Inc., 1808 W. Beltline Hwy., 53713. Tel: 608-260-3500; Fax: 608-260-3575; Email: damond.boatwright@ssmhealth.com. Damond William Boatwright, Pres. & CEO. Sponsored by: Franciscan Sisters of Mary.Purpose: To provide either directly or in conjunction with other persons or organizations health care, health education and related facilities and services. Member of SSM Health Care.

BARABOO. *St. Clare Health Care Foundation, Inc.*, 707 14th St., Baraboo, 53913. Tel: 608-356-1449; Fax: 608-356-1367; Email: SSMHealthCareOfficialCatholicDirectoryNotices@ssmhealth.com; Web: www.stclare.com/foundation. Julia Randles, Foundation Dir. Sponsored by The Franciscan Sisters of Mary.Purpose: to solicit, manage, invest and expend endowment funds and other gifts, grants and bequests primarily for the maintenance and benefit of St. Clare Hospital and St. Clare Meadows Care Center of Baraboo, WI; to support other medical research, educational or charitable programs or activities in the Baraboo, Wisconsin Dells and Lake Delton, Wisconsin Area. Member SSM Health Care.

BLACK EARTH. *Dead Theologians Society*, P.O. Box 368, Black Earth, 53515-0368. Tel: (608) 843-2907; Email: Eddie@DeadTheologiansSociety.com; Web: www.deadtheologianssociety.com. Eddie Cotter Jr., Founder & Exec. Dir.

BROOKLYN. *Tridentine Mass Society of the Diocese of Madison*, 733 Struck St., PO Box 44603, 53711-6145. Tel: 608-228-5063; Email: james@litewire.net; Web: www.latinmassmadison.org. Rev. John T. Zuhlsdorf, Pres.; James Howard, Vice Pres. & Treas.

EDGERTON. *Oaklawn Academy*, 432 Liguori Rd., Edgerton, 53534. Tel: 608-884-3425; Fax: 608-884-8175; Email: info@oaklawnacademy.org; Web: www.oaklawnacademy.org. Rev. Javier Gonzalez, L.C., Prin. Lay Teachers 6; Elementary School Students 42; High School Students 19; Total Students 61.

Oaklawn Incorporated, 432 Liguori Rd., Edgerton, 53534. Tel: 608-884-3425; Fax: 608-884-8175; Email: oaklawnusa@aol.com; Web: www.oaklawnusa.com. Revs. Janick Caouette, L.C.; Javier Gonzalez, L.C., Prin.; Frank Formolo, L.C., Sec.

MONROE. **Monroe Clinic and Hospital Foundation, Inc.*, 515 22nd Ave., Monroe, 53566. Tel: 608-324-2868; Fax: 608-324-1447; Email: Damond.Boatwright@ssmhealth.com. 10101 Woodfield Ln., St. Louis, MO 63132. Jane Sybers, Exec. SSM Health Care of Wisconsin, Inc.

PLATTEVILLE. *St. Augustine Newman Center*, 135 S. Hickory, Platteville, 53818-3316. Tel: 608-348-7530; Fax: 608-348-7530; Email: jdp@slsonline.org; Web: pioneercatholic.org. Revs. John Del Priore, S.J.P., Admin.; James Kotch, Parochial Vicar. Please refer to St. Augustine University Parish, Platteville. Priests 1; Total Staff 4; Total Assisted 622.

130 W. Cedar St., Platteville, 53818-2457. Tel: 608-348-9735; Fax: 608-348-9920.

SINSINAWA. *The Dominican Outreach Foundation*, 585 County Rd. Z, Sinsinawa, 53824. Tel: 608-748-4411 ; Email: matranel@sinsinawa.org; Web: www.sinsinawa.org. Sr. Maryann Tranel, O.P., Sec. Sponsored by Sinsinawa DominicansPurpose: The Dominican Outreach Foundation is organized to support the sisters educational, religious and charitable ministries.

Mother Samuel Coughlin Charitable Trust, 585 County Rd. Z, Sinsinawa, 53824-9701. Tel: 608-748-4411; Fax: 608-748-5501; Email: matranel@sinsinawa.org; Web: www.sinsinawa.org. Sr. Anne Sur, O.P., Contact Person. Sponsored by: Sinsinawa Dominicans.Purpose: To provide financial support to the aged, infirm or disabled vowed members of the Sinsinawa Dominicans.

Sinsinawa Housing, Inc., 585 County Rd. Z, Sinsinawa, 53824-9701. Tel: 608-748-4411; Fax: 608-748-4491; Email: matranel@sinsinawa.

org; Web: www.sinsinawa.org. Sr. Maryann Tranel, O.P., Sec. of the Congregation. Sponsored by the Sinsinawa Dominicans.Purpose: To provide low- to moderate-income housing for senior residents of southwestern Wisconsin.

Sinsinawa Nursing, Inc., 585 County Rd. Z, Sinsinawa, 53824-9701. Tel: 608-748-4411; Fax: 608-748-4491; Email: toniharrisop@gmail.com; Web: www.sinsinawa.org. Sr. Maryann Tranel, O.P., Sec. of the Congregation. Sponsored by the Sinsinawa Dominicans.To organize, construct, operate and maintain a care center in southwestern Wisconsin for the elderly and infirm.

[J] CLOSED/MERGED PARISHES

Madison Diocesan Archives, 702 S. High Point Rd., Ste. 225, 53719. Tel: 608-821-3140; Fax: 608-440-2811; Email: Pat.Born@madisondiocese.org. Ms. Pat Born, Archivist. As the location of sacramental records can change periodically, inquiries for records of parishes on this list should be directed to the Madison Diocesan Archives.

Holy Family, La Valle Merged. Parish records located at Holy Angels Congregation, La Valle.

Holy Redeemer, Madison Merged. Parish records located at St. Raphael Cathedral Parish, Madison.

Holy Redeemer, Perry Merged. Parish records located at St. Michael the Archangel Parish, Mt. Horeb.

Holy Rosary, Darlington Merged. Parish records located at Our Lady of Fatima Congregation, Lafayette County, WI, Inc., Darlington.

Immaculate Conception, Barneveld Merged. Parish records located at St. Bernadette Parish, Ridgeway.

Immaculate Conception, Blanchardville Merged. Parish records located at St. Isidore, Hollandale.

Immaculate Conception, Boscobel Merged. Parish records located at Corpus Christi Parish, Boscobel.

Immaculate Conception, Truman Merged. Parish records located at Our Lady of Fatima Congregation, Lafayette County, WI, Inc., Darlington.

New Diggings, Benton Closed. Parish records are commingled at St. Patrick, Benton.

Our Lady of Guadalupe, Endeavor Closed. Parish records located at Archives, Diocese of Madison.

Our Lady of Hope, Seymour Merged. Parish records located at Our Lady of Fatima Congregation, Lafayette County, WI, Inc., Darlington.

Queen of Americas, Cambria Closed. Parish records located at St. Mary, Pardeeville; St. Patrick, Doylestown; St. Joseph, Rio & Archives, Diocese of Madison.

St. Aloysius, Sauk City Merged. Parish records located at Divine Mercy Parish, Sauk City.

St. Andrew, Buffalo Merged. Parish records located at St. Faustina Congregation, Columbia/Marquette County, WI, Inc., Pardeeville.

St. Andrew, Tennyson Merged. Parish records located at SS. Andrew and Thomas, Potosi.

St. Andrew, Verona Merged. Parish records located at St. Christopher Parish, Verona.

St. Anthony, Highland Merged. Parish records located at SS. Anthony and Philip, Highland.

St. Augustine, Wyocena (Rocky Run) Closed. Parish records located at St. Patrick, Doylestown & St. Joseph, Rio.

St. Barnabas, Mazomanie Merged. Parish records located at Holy Cross Parish, Mazomanie.

St. Boniface, Lime Ridge Merged. Parish records located at Holy Angels Congregation, La Valle.

St. Bridget, Ridgeway Merged. Parish records located at St. Bernadette Parish, Ridgeway.

St. Camillus, Durward's Glen Merged. Parish records located at Divine Mercy Parish, Sauk City.

St. Francis Xavier, Adams Closed. Parish records located at St. Joseph, Argyle & St. Clare of Assisi, Monroe.

St. Francis Xavier, Lake Mills Merged. Parish records located at St. Gabriel Congregation, Jefferson County, WI, Inc., Lake Mills.

St. Ignatius, Mt. Horeb Merged. Parish records located at St. Michael the Archangel Parish, Mt. Horeb.

St. James, Dayton Closed. Parish records located at St. Francis of Assisi, Belleville.

St. James, Madison (1905) Merged. Parish records located at Good Shepherd Parish, Madison.

St. James, Vermont Closed. Parish records located at St. Mary, Pine Bluff.

St. John Nepomucene, Castle Rock Merged. Parish records located at SS. Anthony & Philip, Highland; St. Thomas, Montfort & Queen of All Saints, Fennimore.

St. John the Baptist, Jefferson Merged. Parish records located at St. Francis of Assisi, Jefferson.

St. John the Baptist, Mill Creek Merged. Parish records located at Holy Cross Parish, Mazomanie.

St. John the Baptist, Muscoda (1854) Merged. Parish records located at Corpus Christi Parish, Boscobel.

St. John the Baptist, Union Mills Closed. Parish records located at St. Joseph, Dodgeville.

St. Joseph, Argyle Merged. Parish records located at St. Isidore, Hollandale.

St. Joseph, Avoca Merged. Parish records located at Corpus Christi, Boscobel.

St. Joseph, Berlin Closed. Parish records located at All Saints, Berlin.

St. Joseph, Madison Merged. Parish records located at Good Shepherd Parish, Madison.

St. Joseph, Markesan Merged. Parish records located at Holy Family Parish, Markesan.

St. Joseph, Waterloo Merged. Parish records located at Holy Family Parish, Waterloo.

St. Lawrence, Jefferson Merged. Parish records located at Holy Family, Waterloo.

St. Lawrence, O'Toole, Mt. Hope Merged. Parish records located at Queen of All Saints Parish, Fennimore.

St. Malachy, Clyde Merged. Parish records located at Corpus Christi Parish, Boscobel.

St. Mary, Fennimore Merged. Parish records located at Queen of All Saints Parish, Fennimore.

St. Mary, Kingston Merged. Parish records located at Holy Family Parish, Markesan.

St. Mary, Mineral Point Merged. Parish records located at Cong. of St. Mary's/St. Paul's, Mineral Point.

St. Mary, Monroe Closed. Parish records located at St. Clare of Assisi, Monroe.

St. Mary Health of the Sick, Merrimac Merged. Parish records located at Divine Mercy Parish, Sauk City.

St. Mary of Lourdes, Belleville Merged. Parish records located at St. Francis of Assisi, Belleville.

St. Mary Magdalene, Johnson Creek Merged. Parish records located at St. Gabriel Congregation, Jefferson County, WI, Inc., Lake Mills.

St. Mary of the Most Holy Rosary, Pardeeville Merged. Parish records located at St. Faustina Congregation, Columbia/Marquette County, WI, Inc., Pardeeville.

St. Mary of the Nativity, Marshall Merged. Parish records located at Holy Family Parish, Waterloo.

St. Methodius, Pilot Knob Closed. Parish records located at St. Mary Help of Christians, Briggsville.

St. Michael, Berlin Merged. Parish records located at All Saints, Berlin.

St. Michael, Calamine Merged. Parish records located at Our Lady of Fatima Congregation, Lafayette County, WI, Inc., Darlington.

St. Michael, Dane Merged. Parish records located at Blessed Trinity Parish, Lodi.

St. Michael, Yellowstone Merged. Parish records located at St. Isidore, Hollandale.

St. Patrick, Albany (1868) Merged. Parish records commingled with St. Rose of Lima Parish, Brodhead; Parish records located at St. Clare of Assisi, Belleville.

St. Patrick, Hollandale Merged. Parish records located at St. Isidore, Hollandale.

St. Patrick, Lodi Merged. Parish records located at Blessed Trinity Parish, Lodi.

St. Patrick, Loreto Merged. Parish records located at Holy Angels Congregation, La Valle.

St. Patrick, Madison Merged. Parish records located at St. Raphael Cathedral Parish, Madison.

St. Patrick, Princeton Closed. Parish records located at St. James, Neshkoro.

St. Paul, Beloit Closed. Parish records located at St. Thomas the Apostle, Beloit.

St. Paul, Mineral Point Merged. Parish records located at Cong. of St. Mary's/St. Paul's, Mineral Point.

St. Peter, Elk Grove Merged. Parish records located at Our Lady of Fatima Congregation, Lafayette County, WI, Inc., Darlington.

SS. Peter & Paul, Pleasant Ridge Closed. Parish records located at St. Joseph, Dodgeville.

St. Philip, Highland Merged. Parish records located at SS. Anthony & Philip, Highland.

St. Raphael Cathedral, Madison Merged. Parish records located at St. Raphael Cathedral Parish, Madison.

St. Rose of Lima, Brodhead Merged. Parish records located at St. Clare of Assisi, Monroe.

St. Stanislaus Kostka, Berlin Merged. Parish records located at All Saints, Berlin.

St. Thomas, Potosi Merged. Parish records located at SS. Andrew and Thomas, Potosi.

St. Victor, Monroe (1860) Merged. Parish records located at St. Clare of Assisi Parish, Monroe.

St. William, Paoli Merged. Parish records located at St. Christopher Parish, Verona.

RELIGIOUS INSTITUTES OF MEN REPRESENTED IN THE DIOCESE

For further details refer to the corresponding bracketed number in the Religious Institutes of Men section.

[0730]—*Legionaries of Christ*—L.C.
[0200]—*Order of Saint Benedict*—O.S.B.
[0430]—*Order of Preachers-Dominicans* (Prov. of St. Albert the Great)—O.P.

RELIGIOUS INSTITUTES OF WOMEN REPRESENTED IN THE DIOCESE

For further details refer to the corresponding bracketed number in the Religious Institutes of Women section.

[]—*Auxiliaries of the Blessed Sacrament*—A.B.S.
[0680]—*Cistercian Nuns*—O.Cist.
[3710]—*Congregation of the Sisters of Saint Agnes*—C.S.A.
[1070-03]—*Dominican Sisters*—O.P.
[1070-09]—*Dominican Sisters*—O.P.
[1230]—*Franciscan Sisters of Christian Charity*—O.S.F.
[]—*Franciscan Sisters of Our Lady*—F.S.O.L.
[1415]—*Franciscan Sisters of Mary*—F.S.M.
[2575]—*Institute of the Sisters of Mercy of the Americas*—R.S.M.
[2970]—*School Sisters of Notre Dame*—S.S.N.D.
[1680]—*School Sisters of St. Francis*—O.S.F.
[]—*Secular Institute of Schoenstatt Sisters of Mary*.
[3020]—*Sisters Oblates to the Blessed Trinity*—O.B.T.
[0530]—*Sisters of Charity of Our Lady, Mother of the Church*—S.C.M.C.
[]—*Sisters of Mary Morning Star*.
[3930]—*Sisters of St. Joseph of the Third Order of St. Francis* (Prov. of St. Joseph)—S.S.J.-T.O.S.F.
[1030]—*Sisters of the Divine Savior*—S.D.S.
[1705]—*Sisters of the Third Order of St. Francis of Assisi*—O.S.F.

DIOCESE OF MADISON CEMETERIES

MADISON. *Resurrection Cemetery*, 2705 Regent St., 53705. Tel: 608-238-5561; Fax: 608-238-5768; Email: irma.slawson@madisondiocese.org. Mr. John Miller, Dir.

BELOIT. *Calvary Cemetery*, 1801 Colley Rd., Beloit, 53511. Email: kathy.crane@madisondiocese.org. Mailing Address: 1827 N. Washington St., Janesville, 53547. Tel: 608-754-3472; Fax: 608-744-8715. Mr. John Miller, Dir.

Mount Thabor Cemetery, 2138 Shopiere Rd., Beloit, 53511. Email: kathy.crane@madisondiocese.org. Mt. Olvet Cemetery, 1827 N. Washington St., Janesville, 53548. Tel: 608-754-3472; Fax: 608-741-8715. Mr. John Miller, Dir.

JANESVILLE. *Mount Olivet Cemetery*, 1827 N. Washington St., Janesville, 53548. Tel: 608-754-3472; Fax: 608-744-8715. Mr. John Miller, Dir.

NECROLOGY

† Morlino, Robert C., Bishop of Madison, Died Nov. 24, 2018

An asterisk (*) denotes an organization that has established tax-exempt status directly with the IRS and is not covered by the USCCB Group Ruling.

Diocese of Manchester

(Dioecesis Manchesteriensis)

Most Reverend

PETER A. LIBASCI

Bishop of Manchester; ordained April 1, 1978; appointed Titular Bishop of Satafis and Auxiliary Bishop of Rockville Centre April 3, 2007; installed June 1, 2007; appointed Bishop of Manchester September 19, 2011; installed December 8, 2011. *Chancery Office: 153 Ash St., P.O. Box 310, Manchester, NH 03105.*

Most Reverend

JOHN B. MCCORMACK, D.D.

Bishop Emeritus of Manchester; ordained February 2, 1960; consecrated December 27, 1995; installed September 22, 1998; Bishop emeritus September 19, 2011.

Most Reverend

ODORE J. GENDRON, D.D.

Retired Bishop of Manchester; ordained May 31, 1947; appointed December 12, 1974; consecrated February 3, 1975; Bishop emeritus June 12, 1990. *Mailing Address: P.O. Box 310, Manchester, NH 03105-0310.*

Chancery Office: 153 Ash St., Manchester, NH 03104. Tel: 603-669-3100; Fax: 603-669-0377.

Web: www.catholicnh.org

Email: stjoseph_church@yahoo.com

Most Reverend

FRANCIS J. CHRISTIAN, PH.D.

Retired Auxiliary Bishop of Manchester; ordained June 29, 1968; appointed April 2, 1996; consecrated May 14, 1996; retired February 1, 2018.

ESTABLISHED 1884.

Square Miles 9,305.

Comprises the State of New Hampshire.

For legal titles of parishes and diocesan institutions, consult the Chancery Office.

STATISTICAL OVERVIEW

Personnel	
Bishop	1
Retired Bishops	3
Abbots	1
Priests: Diocesan Active in Diocese	73
Priests: Diocesan Active Outside Diocese	1
Priests: Retired, Sick or Absent	43
Number of Diocesan Priests	117
Religious Priests in Diocese	38
Total Priests in Diocese	155
Extern Priests in Diocese	26
Ordinations:	
Transitional Deacons	2
Permanent Deacons	1
Permanent Deacons in Diocese	73
Total Brothers	15
Total Sisters	299
Parishes	
Parishes	89
With Resident Pastor:	
Resident Diocesan Priests	73
Resident Religious Priests	8
Without Resident Pastor:	
Administered by Priests	8
Missions	12
Welfare	
Catholic Hospitals	2
Total Assisted	579,424
Health Care Centers	8
Total Assisted	1,316
Homes for the Aged	4
Total Assisted	108
Day Care Centers	1
Total Assisted	309
Special Centers for Social Services	18
Total Assisted	138,970
Educational	
Diocesan Students in Other Seminaries	14
Total Seminarians	14
Colleges and Universities	4
Total Students	4,870
High Schools, Diocesan and Parish	3
Total Students	967
High Schools, Private	3
Total Students	1,288
Elementary Schools, Diocesan and Parish	17
Total Students	2,221
Elementary Schools, Private	5
Total Students	858
Catechesis/Religious Education:	
High School Students	2,738
Elementary Students	9,528
Total Students under Catholic Instruction	22,484
Teachers in the Diocese:	
Priests	5
Sisters	4
Lay Teachers	576
Vital Statistics	
Receptions into the Church:	
Infant Baptism Totals	1,606
Minor Baptism Totals	61
Adult Baptism Totals	20
Received into Full Communion	118
First Communions	1,783
Confirmations	2,611
Marriages:	
Catholic	301
Interfaith	106
Total Marriages	407
Deaths	2,531
Total Catholic Population	248,681
Total Population	1,356,458

Former Bishops—Rt. Revs. DENIS M. BRADLEY, D.D., ord. June 3, 1871; first Bishop of Manchester; cons. June 11, 1884; died Dec. 13, 1903; JOHN B. DELANY, D.D., ord. May 23, 1891; cons. Sept. 8, 1904; died June 11, 1906; Most Revs. GEORGE ALBERT GUERTIN, D.D., cons. March 19, 1907; died Aug. 6, 1931; JOHN B. PETERSON, D.D., cons. Auxiliary Bishop of Boston, Nov. 10, 1927; transferred to See, May 13, 1932; died March 15, 1944; MATTHEW F. BRADY, D.D., cons. Oct. 26, 1938; transferred to See, Nov. 11, 1944; died Sept. 20, 1959; ERNEST J. PRIMEAU, S.T.D., appt. Nov. 27, 1959; resigned Jan. 30, 1974; died June 15, 1989; ODORE J. GENDRON, D.D., ord. May 31, 1947; appt. Dec. 12, 1974; cons. Feb. 3, 1975; retired June 12, 1990; LEO E. O'NEIL, D.D., ord. June 4, 1955; appt. Coadjutor Oct. 17, 1989; succeeded to See June 12, 1990; died Nov. 30, 1997; JOHN B. MCCORMACK, D.D., (Retired), ord. Feb. 2, 1960; cons. Dec. 27, 1995; installed Sept. 22, 1998; Bishop emeritus Sept. 19, 2011.

Priest Secretary—Very Rev. JASON Y. JALBERT, Email: jjalbert@rcbm.org.

Episcopal Master of Ceremonies—Very Rev. JASON Y. JALBERT, Email: jjalbert@rcbm.org.

Master of Ceremonies—MR. ANTHONY J. HALEY, Email: thaley@rcbm.org.

Auxiliary Bishop Emeritus—Most Rev. FRANCIS J. CHRISTIAN, Ph.D., D.D., 153 Ash St., Manchester, 03104. Tel: 603-669-3100.

Judicial Vicar—Very Rev. GEORGES F. DE LAIRE, M.Ed., M.Div., J.C.L.

Vicar for Canonical Affairs—Very Rev. GEORGES F. DE LAIRE, M.Ed., M.Div., J.C.L.

Adjutant Judicial Vicar—Rev. MICHAEL S. TAYLOR, M.Div., J.C.L.

Office of Canonical Services—MRS. WINIFRED MCGRATH, M.Th., Dir. Canonical Svcs.

Promoter of Justice—Rev. Msgr. PAUL L. BOUCHARD, S.T.L., J.C.L.

Advocates—Very Rev. SHAWN M. THERRIEN, M.A.; Revs. ERIC T. DELISLE, M.Div.; JOHN W. FLEMING, M.Div.; MICHAEL E. GENDRON; MICHAEL KERPER; Deacons RAMON ANDRADE; GEORGE J. BORKUSH; CHRISTOPHER M. EVERHART; RICHARD A. FALARDEAU; STEPHEN M. LABRIE; THOMAS LAVALLEE; WILLIAM R. LAVALLEE; JAMES E. PATTERSON; ROBERT R. POTVIN; MR. MICHAEL BRUNETTE; MS. PAMELA CASEY; MS. JOY DAVIS; MS. PHYLLIS DEMERS; MS. MARGARET DONAHUE-TURNER, M.Div.; MS. ANNE HOEING; MS. JAN RAJCHEL; MS. KATHRYN RYAN; MS. WINNIE SMITH; MS. MARY E. VIENS; MR. PAUL E. VIENS.

Defender of the Bond—Rev. Msgr. PAUL L. BOUCHARD, S.T.L., J.C.L.

Diocesan Judges—Very Rev. GEORGES F. DE LAIRE, M.Ed., M.Div., J.C.L.; Rev. Msgr. DONALD J. GILBERT, J.C.L., (Retired); Rev. MICHAEL S. TAYLOR, M.Div., J.C.L.; MRS. WINIFRED MCGRATH, M.Th.

Auditors—Revs. VOLNEY J. DEROSIA; JOHN W. FLEMING, M.Div.; Very Rev. MARC B. DROUIN, M.Div.; JANE COSMO; CHRISTINE PATTERSON, M.Div., M.A.

Notaries—KATHERINE HEBERT; MONIQUE KAMINSKI; CHRISTINE MARRA.

Experts—DAVID J. CORRISS, Ph.D.; KATHRYN MCGRATH, M.A., M.S.W.; THOMAS H. KELLEY, Ph.D.

Liaison for Women Religious—Very Rev. GEORGES F. DE LAIRE, M.Ed., M.Div., J.C.L.

Vicars General—Very Revs. SHAWN M. THERRIEN, M.A.; JASON Y. JALBERT.

Priest Personnel Assignment Board—Most Rev. PETER A. LIBASCI, D.D.; Rev. Msgr. C. PETER DUMONT; Very Rev. SHAWN M. THERRIEN, M.A.; Revs.

CHRISTOPHER M. MARTEL; MICHAEL S. TAYLOR, M.Div., J.C.L.; RICHARD E. ST. LOUIS JR.; MICHAEL E. GENDRON.

Priest Personnel Assignment Board Non-Priest Advisors—Deacon JAMES P. WILTON; MR. ROLLA "MAC" MCFALL BRYANT, CPA; MS. MARY ELLEN D'INTINO, M.Ed., L.S.W.; MR. DEREK MCDONALD; MS. MARY JANE SILVIA; MR. DAVID A. THIBAULT.

Office of Ordained Ministry & Formation—Very Revs. SHAWN M. THERRIEN, M.A.; JASON Y. JALBERT.

Coordinator for Institutional Ministries—Deacon RUSSELL MOREY.

Coordinator for International Priests—Rev. CHRISTOPHER M. MARTEL.

Coordinator for Retired Priests—Rev. Msgr. CHARLES E. DESRUISSEAUX, (Retired).

Office of Deacon Personnel—Very Revs. SHAWN M. THERRIEN, M.A.; JASON Y. JALBERT.

Office of Formation For Deacon Candidates—Very Revs. SHAWN M. THERRIEN, M.A.; JASON Y. JALBERT.

Permanent Deacon Advisory Board—Rev. Msgr. C. PETER DUMONT; Deacons ERIC M. LAMBERT; DENNIS W. MARQUIS; CHRISTOPHER PAUL; JAMES P. WILTON; MRS. LAURA LAMBERT; DEBRA THIBAULT.

Office of Seminary Formation—Very Rev. JASON Y. JALBERT, Dir., Email: jjalbert@rcbm.org.

Office of Vocations—Rev. MATTHEW J. MASON, Dir., Email: mmason@rcbm.org. Assistant Vocation Directors: Revs. MARCOS A. GONZALEZ-TORRES; VOLNEY J. DEROSIA.

Office for Worship—Very Rev. JASON Y. JALBERT, Dir., Email: jjalbert@rcbm.org.

Vicars Forane—Very Revs. RAYMOND A. BALL; ANDREW W. CRYANS; RICHARD H. DION; MARK E. DOLLARD; MARC B. DROUIN, M.Div.; MARC R. GAGNE; JOHN M. GRACE; SHAWN M. THERRIEN, M.A.; ALAN C. TREMBLAY.

Consultative Bodies

College of Consultors—Rev. JOHN BUCCHINO, O.F.M.; Very Revs. JASON Y. JALBERT; SHAWN M. THERRIEN, M.A.; MARC R. GAGNE; Rev. Msgr. C. PETER DUMONT, (Retired).

Presbyteral Council—Most Rev. PETER A. LIBASCI, D.D.; Very Revs. GEORGES F. DE LAIRE, M.Ed., M.Div., J.C.L., Ex-officio; SHAWN M. THERRIEN, M.A., Ex Officio; JASON Y. JALBERT, Ex Officio; RICHARD H. DION; MARC B. DROUIN, M.Div.; Rev. Msgr. C. PETER DUMONT, (Retired); Revs. DAVID L. KNEELAND; STEVEN M. KUCHARSKI; RAY J. LABRIE; JOHN BUCCHINO, O.F.M.; ANDREW NELSON; Revs. ADRIEN R. LONGCHAMPS; VOLNEY J. DEROSIA; MICHAEL S. TAYLOR, M.Div., J.C.L., Appointed Member.

Finance Council—Most Rev. PETER A. LIBASCI, D.D., Chm.; Deacon PAUL R. BOUCHER; Rev. MICHAEL E. GENDRON; MS. EVA MARTEL; MR. STEVEN R. MCMANIS; MR. THOMAS F. PARKS; MR. MICHAEL A. RICHARDS; MR. RONALD J. RIOUX; ANTHONY ANNINO; FREDERICK BRIGGS JR.; MS. STACY J. CLARK. Staff: MR. ROLLA "MAC" MCFALL BRYANT, CPA; MR. DAVID A. GABERT; MS. PATRICIA GONEAU; MR. DAVID D. SPONENBERG; MS. TERESA L. ALDRIDGE.

Diocesan Review Board—MR. MARK COLLOPY; Rev. MICHAEL E. GENDRON; MS. LISA D. JOBIN; MS. SUSAN N. STONE; MS. CHRISTINE O. TREMBLAY, Chm.; ROBERT CAREY ESQ.; Rev. JASON WELLS, S.C.P., (The Episcopal Church); MR. GARY RAINEY, L.I.C.S.W. Staff: MS. MARY ELLEN D'INTINO, M.Ed., L.S.W.; Rev. Msgr. PAUL L. BOUCHARD, S.T.L., J.C.L.; MR. JOSEPH P. NAFF, M.S.W.; MS. ANNETTE DESMOND; MR. DALE ROBINSON; MR. RICK NANAN; MR. CRAIG ROUSSEAU.

Operations and Administration—DENNIS HONAN, Dir.

Information Technologies—DENNIS HONAN.

Project Manager—PEG DUGGAN.

Bishops Secretaries—

Secretary to Bishop—MS. LOUISE LEDUC, Email: lleduc@rcbm.org.

Secretary to the Auxiliary Bishop—MS. FRANCEEN M. MORASSE, Email: fmorasse@rcbm.org.

Superintendent of Catholic Schools—MR. DAVID THIBAULT.

Director of Marketing, Enrollment and Development—MRS. ALISON MUELLER. Diocesan School Board: MRS. NATALIE BRANKIN, Chair; Very Rev. RICHARD H. DION; DR. MARY KATE DONAIS; MR. PETER DUFOUR; MS. KELLY MOORE DUNN; MS. LAURA EL-AZEM; MR. EDWARD J. LAPALME III; MR. DANIEL J. LAPLANTE, CFA; Rev. CHRISTOPHER M. MARTEL; MR. DOUG MCGINLEY; Revs. ANDREW NELSON; CHARLES H. PAWLOWSKI; MRS. SHANNON SULLIVAN; BRIAND T. WADE, Esq.; MS. CAROLANN WAIS; MR. DAVID A. THIBAULT; MRS. ALISON MUELLER.

Diocesan Camps—MR. DAVID THIBAULT, Chm. Bd.; MR. MICHAEL DRUMM, Exec. Dir., P.O. Box 206, Gilmanton Iron Works, 03837-0206. Tel: 603-364-5851; Fax: 603-364-5038.

Secretariat for Catholic Formation—MS. MARY ELLEN MAHON, Cabinet Sec., Email: memahon@rcbm.org.

Catholic Home School Liaison—MS. MARY ELLEN MAHON, Email: memahon@rcbm.org.

Catholic Youth Organization—MR. CHARLES COOK, Dir.

Catholic Scouting—Very Rev. RAYMOND A. BALL, Dir.

Ecumenical/Interreligious Affairs—Rev. Msgr. CHARLES E. DESRUISSEAUX, (Retired), 153 Ash St., Manchester, 03104. Tel: 603-669-3100.

Pastoral Ministry—MS. MARY ELLEN MAHON, Email: memahon@rcbm.org.

New Hampshire Diocesan Council of Catholic Women—HEATHER JOHNSON, Pres.

Office of Adult Faith Formation—MS. MARY JANE SILVIA, Dir., Email: mjsilvia@rcbm.org.

Office of Family Life Ministries—MR. DEREK MCDONALD, Dir., Email: dmcdonald@rcbm.org.

Respect Life—MR. DEREK MCDONALD, Diocesan Coord.

Project Rachel—MR. DEREK MCDONALD, Coord.

Parish Faith Formation—MS. KELLY GOUDREAU, Dir., Email: kgoudreau@rcbm.org.

Secretariat For Catholic Action—MR. THOMAS E. BLONSKI, Cabinet Sec., Email: tblonski@nh-cc.org.

New Hampshire Catholic Charities, Inc.—215 Myrtle St., Manchester, 03104. Tel: 603-669-3030; Fax: 603-626-1252. MR. THOMAS E. BLONSKI, Pres. & CEO; MS. DOMINIQUE A. RUST, Vice Pres. & COO, Email: drust@nh-cc.org; MR. DAVID TWITCHELL, Vice Pres., Human Resources, Email: dtwitchell@nh-cc.org; MR. DAVID HILDENBRAND, CFO, Email: dhildenbrand@nh-cc.org; MR. ALAIN BERNARD, Asst. Vice Pres. Healthcare Svcs., Email: abernard@nh-cc.org.

Development—MS. KAREN MOYNIHAN, Interim Senior Dir., Email: kmoynihan@nh-cc.org.

Marketing and Communication—MR. MICHAEL MCDONOUGH, Exec. Dir.

Immigration and Refugee Services—MS. CATHY CHESLEY, J.D., Ed.D., Dir.

Programs and Mission Integrity—STEVEN KNIGHT, M.B.A., M.A., Asst. Vice Pres.

Clinical Services—Rev. JOHN J. MAHONEY JR., J.C.L., M.A., L.C.M.H.C., Dir.

Adoption and Maternity Services—ELAINE C. LANGTON, B.S., Coord.

Our Place—KAREN MUNSELL, M.S.W., Supvr.

Parish and Community Outreach Services—MR. MARC COUSINEAU, Dir.

NH Food Bank—EILEEN GROLL LIPONIS, Exec. Dir.

Secretariat for Development and Communications—MS. BEVIN KENNEDY, Cabinet Sec., Email: bkennedy@rcbm.org.

Development—MS. BEVIN KENNEDY, Dir., Email: bkennedy@rcbm.org.

Communications—MR. THOMAS P. BEBBINGTON, Dir., Email: tbebbington@rcbm.org.

Catholic Relief Services—MS. BEVIN KENNEDY, Diocesan Coord.

Catholic Campaign for Human Development—MS. BEVIN KENNEDY, Diocesan Coord.

Propagation of the Faith—MS. BEVIN KENNEDY, Email: bkennedy@rcbm.org.

Secretariat for Temporalities—MR. ROLLA "MAC" MCFALL BRYANT, CPA, Cabinet Sec.

Finance—MR. ROLLA "MAC" MCFALL BRYANT, CPA, Finance Officer; MR. DAVID D. SPONENBERG, Dir. Parish & School Financial Svcs., Email: sponenberg@rcbm.org; MS. PATRICIA GONEAU, Controller, Email: pgoneau@rcbm.org; MARY AVERILL, Asst. Dir., Parish & School Financial Svcs., Email: maverill@rcbm.org; MR. PETER M. STAUBLE, Parish & School Business Analyst, Email: pstauble@rcbm.org.

Real Estate and Construction—MR. ROBERT EIB, Dir. Sec., Email: reib@rcbm.org.

Catholic Cemeteries—MR. DAVID A. GABERT, Dir., Email: dgabert@rcbm.org.

Human Resources—MS. CHRISTINE L. HAGEN, Dir., Email: chagen@rcbm.org.

Secretariat for Multicultural Ministries—Deacon RAMON ANDRADE, Cabinet Sec.

Assistant Director for Multicultural Ministry—WENDY GUERRERO.

Brazilian Apostolate—Saint John XXIII Parish @ Infant Jesus Church, 121 Allds St., Nashua, 03060-6395. Rev. Msgr. EDDY N. BISSON; Rev. CRISTIANO GUILHERNE BORRO-BARBOSA, Chap.

Hispanic Parish Ministry—Revs. SAMUEL FULLER, O.F.M.Cap., Admin., St. Anne-St. Augustin Church, 382 Beech St., Manchester, 03103; MARCOS A. GONZALEZ-TORRES, Pastor, St. Aloysius of Gonzaga Church, 50 W. Hollis St., Nashua, 03060; GARY J. BELLIVEAU, Pastor, Corpus Christi Parish @ Immaculate Conception Church, 98 Summer St., Portsmouth, 03801; JOHN SULLIVAN, M.S., Pastor, LaSalette Shrine, 410 NH Rte. 4A, Enfield, 03748.

Vietnamese Apostolate—Revs. SAMUEL FULLER, O.F.M.Cap., Admin.; THIEN NGUYEN, Chap., St. Anne-St. Augustine Church, 382 Beech St., Manchester, 03103; RICHARD J. KELLEY, Pastor, (Retired); THIEN NGUYEN, Chap., St. Christopher Church, 60 Manchester St., Nashua, 03064.

African Apostolate—St. Anne-St. Augustine Church, 382 Beech St., Manchester, 03103. Rev. SAMUEL FULLER, O.F.M.Cap., Admin.

Chancellor—MS. DIANE MURPHY QUINLAN, Esq., 153 Ash St., Manchester, 03104. Tel: 603-669-3100; Email: dquinlan@rcbm.org.

Vice Chancellor—MS. MEREDITH P. COOK, Esq., Email: mcook@rcbm.org.

Legal Services—MS. DIANE MURPHY QUINLAN, Esq.; MS. MEREDITH P. COOK, Esq.

Paralegal—MS. ANNETTE DESMOND.

Historical Archivist—MR. DENNIS W. PEDLEY.

Office for Ministerial Conduct—MS. MARY ELLEN D'INTINO, M.Ed., L.S.W., Bishop's Delegate for Safe Environment & Ministerial Conduct, Email: medintino@rcbm.org.

Office for Healing and Pastoral Care—MR. JOSEPH P. NAFF, M.S.W., Dir., Tel: 603-663-0125; Email: jnaff@rcbm.org.

Safe Environment—MS. MARY ELLEN D'INTINO, M.Ed., L.S.W., Bishop's Delegate for Safe Environment & Ministerial Conduct; MS. EVE MONGEAU, Safe Environment Asst.

Safe Environment Council—Sr. ROSEMARY CROWLEY, S.N.D.deN.; MS. JUANITA SWEET; MR. MARC COUSINEAU; MS. NANCY DEFILIPPIO; MS. SARA SMITH; MR. MICHAEL DRUMM; MS. NOREEN SWYMER; MS. MAUREEN SLAVIN. Staff: MS. MARY ELLEN D'INTINO, M.Ed., L.S.W.; MS. EVE MONGEAU.

Office of Public Policy—MS. MEREDITH P. COOK, Esq., Dir.

Public Policy Commission—Deacon RAMON ANDRADE; Revs. THOMAS L. DUSTON; FREDERICK J. PENNETT JR.; MR. MARC F. GUILLEMETTE; MR. THOMAS E. BLONSKI; MR. EDWARD KENNEDY; MS. SUSAN GABERT; MS. JENNIFER MARTIN; Sr. MARY ROSE REDDY, D.M.M.L.; MS. LAURA EL-AZEM. Staff: MS. MEREDITH P. COOK, Esq.; MS. DIANE MURPHY QUINLAN, Esq.; MR. ROBERT E. DUNN, Esq.; MICHAEL COUGHLIN.

CLERGY, PARISHES, MISSIONS AND PAROCHIAL SCHOOLS

CITY OF MANCHESTER

(HILLSBOROUGH COUNTY)

1—ST. JOSEPH CATHEDRAL (1869) [CEM]

145 Lowell St., 03104-6135. Tel: 603-622-6404; Fax: 603-622-4415; Email: lwelsch@stjosephcathedralnh.org. Very Rev. Jason Y. Jalbert; Revs. Eric T. Delisle, M.Div.; Jeffrey A. Paveglio, Parochial Vicar; Deacons Robert R. Potvin; Karl Cooper. In Res., Most Rev. John B. McCormack, D.D., (Retired); Rev. Msgr. Anthony R. Frontiero; Rev. Jeffrey P. Statz.

Chapel—Most Blessed Sacrament Chapel, Lowell St., 03104.

Catechesis Religious Program—Ms. Colleen B. Lang, Catechetical Leader.

2—ST. ANNE (1848) Unified in 2004 into St. Anne-St. Augustin, Manchester.

3—ST. ANNE-ST. AUGUSTIN (1871) [CEM]

383 Beech St., 03103-5350. Tel: 603-623-8809; Tel: 603-625-5655; Tel: 603-625-4603; Email: parishoffice@stasta.org. Rev. Samuel Fuller, O.F.M.-Cap., Admin.; Deacons Ramon Andrade; Lam Tran; Revs. Bernard J. Campbell, O.F.M.Cap, In Res.; Joseph Gurdak, O.F.M.Cap., In Res.

Catechesis Religious Program—

4—ST. ANTHONY OF PADUA (1899) (French)

172 Belmont St., 03103-4452. Tel: 603-625-6409; Fax: 603-625-0099; Email: saintanthony@comcast.net. Very Rev. Richard H. Dion; Rev. Theodore Mbaegbu, In Res.

Catechesis Religious Program—Ms. Colette Lemarier, Catechetical Leader (K-6); Colin Upham, Catechetical Leader (7-10).

5—BLESSED SACRAMENT (1907)

14 Elm St., 03103-7242. Tel: 603-622-5445; Fax: 603-622-5983; Email: lisa@blessedsacramentnh.org; Web: www.blessedsacramentnh.org. Rev. John Bucchino, O.F.M.

Catechesis Religious Program—Mr. Stephen Donohue, Catechetical Leader; Ms. Martha Donohue, Catechetical Leader.

Chapel: St. Theresa of Lisieux Adoration Chapel—

6—ST. CATHERINE OF SIENA (1954)
207 Hemlock St., 03104-3248. Tel: 603-622-4966; Email: parishoffice@scsnh.com; Web: www.saintcatherineparishnh.com. Rev. Christopher M. Martel; Deacon Edward P. Munz.

Catechesis Religious Program—Email: yff@scsnh.com. Lisa Daugherty, Catechetical Leader. Students 154.

7—ST. EDMUND (1914) Merged in 2002 with St. John the Baptist parish, Manchester and became Parish of the Transfiguration, Manchester.

8—ST. GEORGE (1890) Closed. Unified in 2002 with St. Joseph Cathedral, Manchester.

9—ST. HEDWIG (1902) [CEM] (Polish)
147 Walnut St., 03104-4225. Tel: 603-623-4835; Email: parishoffice@sthedwigparish.comcastbiz.net; Web: sainthedwignh.org. Rev. Eric T. Delisle, M.Div.

10—ST. JOHN THE BAPTIST (1914) Merged in 2002 with St. Edward parish, Manchester to form Parish of the Transfiguration, Manchester.

11—STE. MARIE (1880) [CEM 2] (French)
378 Notre Dame Ave., 03102-3793. Tel: 603-622-4615; Fax: 603-622-4732; Email: mandy@stemariechurch.com. Rev. Maurice R. Larochelle, V.F.; Deacons Frank Gallinaro, Pastoral Assoc.; Kevin Cody. In Res., Revs. Jean M. Lemay; Bartholomew Ogumelo; Richard E. St. Louis Jr.

Office: 133 Wayne St., 03102-3740.

Catechesis Religious Program—Ms. Terry Bolduc, Catechetical Leader.

Chapels—Chapel of North American Martyrs—

St. Joan of Arc.

Mother Rivier Eucharist Adoration Chapel, 133 Wayne St., 03102.

12—OUR LADY OF PERPETUAL HELP (1911) Unified in 2006 with St. Anthony of Padua, Manchester.

13—PARISH OF THE TRANSFIGURATION (2002)
107 Alsace St., 03102-3006. Tel: 603-623-4715; Fax: 603-623-4715; Email: office.transfiguration@comcast.net. Rev. John W. Fleming, M.Div.; Deacon Richard J. Shannon. In Res., Rev. John J. Mahoney Jr., J.C.L., M.A., L.C.M.H.C.

Catechesis Religious Program—Tel: 603-622-0504. Sr. Bernadette Turgeon, S.N.D.deN., Catechetical Leader.

14—ST. PATRICK (1898) [CEM] Merged Unified in 2007 with Parish of the Transfiguration, Manchester.

15—ST. PIUS X (1955)
575 Candia Rd., 03109-4735. Tel: 603-622-6510; Fax: 603-622-1323; Email: parishoffice@saintpiusxnh.org; Web: saintpiusxnh.org. Very Rev. Georges F. de Laire, M.Ed., M.Div., J.C.L.; Deacon James E. Patterson. In Res.

Catechesis Religious Program—Email: llambert@saintpiusxnh.org. Linda M. Lambert, D.R.E.

16—ST. RAPHAEL (1888) [CEM]
103 Walker St., 03102-4566. Tel: 603-623-2604; Email: admin@st-raphael-parish.org; Web: www.st-raphael-parish.org. Rev. Jerome J. Day, O.S.B.

Catechesis Religious Program—Tel: 603-647-2283; Email: therese.dame@st-raphael-parish.org. Therese Dame, Catechetical Leader. Students 74.

17—SACRED HEART PARISH (1911) (French)
247 S. Main St., 03102-4890. Rev. Stephen Marcoux III; Deacon Thomas Cloutier.

Church: 265 S. Main St., 03102. Tel: 603-625-9525; Email: sacredheartmanchester@comcast.net.

Catechesis Religious Program—Tel: 603-622-3312. Ms. Terry Bolduc, Catechetical Leader.

18—ST. THERESA, Closed. Unified in 2004 with Blessed Sacrament Manchester.

OUTSIDE THE CITY OF MANCHESTER

ALTON, BELKNAP CO.

1—ST. JOAN OF ARC (1961) Merged in 2003 with St. Cecilia Parish, Wolfelboro to form St. Katharine Drexel, Alton.

2—ST. KATHARINE DREXEL (2003)
Mailing Address: P.O. Box 180, Wolfeboro, 03894-0180. Tel: 603-875-2548; Fax: 603-875-4801; Email: office@stkdrexel.org; Web: stkdrexel.org. Rev. Robert F. Cole; Deacons Rick Hilton, Pastoral Assoc.; Charles Ferraro.

Res.: 50 Friar Tuck Way, Wolfeboro, 03894.

Church: 40 Hidden Springs Rd., Alton, 03809.

Catechesis Religious Program—Ms. Gertrude Hammond, Catechetical Leader.

ASHLAND, GRAFTON CO., ST. AGNES (1904) Merged in 2006 with St. Matthew, Plymouth and St. Timothy, Bristol to form Holy Trinity Parish, Plymouth.

AUBURN, ROCKINGHAM CO., ST. PETER (1948)
567 Manchester Rd., Auburn, 03032-3123. Tel: 603-623-5429; Email: stpeteraub@comcast.net; Web: stpeteraub.org. Rev. Michael E. Gendron; Deacon Christopher Paul.

Catechesis Religious Program—Sophia Kelly, D.R.E.

BEDFORD, HILLSBOROUGH CO., ST. ELIZABETH SETON (1964)
190 Meetinghouse Rd., Bedford, 03110-6027. Tel: 603-669-7444; Fax: 603-644-5371; Email: sesparish@comcast.net; Web: www.stelizabethsetonchurch.org. Rev. Msgr. John P. Quinn; Sr. Rosemary Crowley, S.N.D.deN., Pastoral Assoc.

Catechesis Religious Program—Email: sesgertrude@comcast.net. Ms. Gertrude Hammond, Catechetical Leader; Ms. Carrie Soucy, Catechetical Leader. Students 1,046.

BELMONT, BELKNAP CO., ST. JOSEPH (1949)
6 High St., P.O. Box 285, Belmont, 03220-0285. Tel: 603-267-8174; Fax: 603-267-1170; Email: stjoebel@metrocast.net; Web: www.stjosephbelmont.org. Very Rev. Marc B. Drouin, M.Div.

Catechesis Religious Program—Tel: 603-286-9995. Karen Ober, Catechetical Leader. Students 64.

BENNINGTON, HILLSBOROUGH CO., ST. PATRICK (1936) [CEM] Merged in 2006 with St. Denis, Harrisville and St. Peter, Peterborough in 2006 to form Divine Mercy Parish, Peterborough.

BERLIN, COOS CO.

1—ST. ANNE (1885) Merged in 2000 with Guardian Angel, St. Joseph and St. Kieran to form Good Shepherd Parish, Berlin.

2—GOOD SHEPHERD (2000)
Mailing Address: 151 Emery St., Berlin, 03570. Tel: 603-752-2880; Fax: 603-752-1855; Email: bgoudreau@berlingorhamcatholics.org; Web: berlingorhamcatholics.org. Revs. Kyle F. Stanton; Michael L. Sartori, Parochial Vicar; Deacon Michael C. Couture.

Res.: 162 Madison Ave., Berlin, 03570-2065.

Catechesis Religious Program—Email: ben@berlingorhamcatholics.org; Email: Clara@berlingorhamcatholics.org. Ben Robertson, D.R.E.; Clara Robertson, D.R.E. Students 260.

3—GUARDIAN ANGEL (1917) Merged in 2000 with St. Anne, St. Joseph and St. Kieran to form Good Shepherd parish, Berlin.

4—ST. JOSEPH (1943) Merged in 2000 with Guardian Angel, St. Anne and St. Kieran to form Good Shepherd parish, Berlin.

5—ST. KIERAN (1894) Merged in 2000 with Guardian Angel, St. Anne and St. Joseph to form Good Shepherd parish, Berlin.

BRISTOL, GRAFTON CO., ST. TIMOTHY (1953) Merged in 2006 with St. Agnes, Ashland and St. Matthew, Plymouth to form Holy Trinity Parish, Plymouth.

CANDIA, ROCKINGHAM CO., ST. PAUL (1971) Merged with St. Peter, Auburn. For sacramental records see St. Peter, Auburn.

CASCADE, COOS CO., ST. BENEDICT, Closed. For Sacramental records contact Good Shepherd, Berlin.

CENTER OSSIPEE, CARROLL CO., ST. JOSEPH (1965)
23 Moultonville Rd., P.O. Box 248, Center Ossipee, 03814-0248. Tel: 603-531-5036; Fax: 603-531-6295; Email: stjosephrco@gmail.com; Web: www.stanthonystjoseph.org. Rev. Patrick N. Gilbert.

Catechesis Religious Program—Ms. Beth Kilroy, Catechetical Leader.

CHARLESTOWN, SULLIVAN CO.

1—ALL SAINTS PARISH (2007)
P.O. Box 332, Charlestown, 03603-0332. Tel: 603-826-3359; Email: allsaints3@comcast.net; Web: www.allsaintsnh.net. Rev. John B. Loughnane; Deacon Kenneth Czechowicz.

St. Catherine of Siena Church—285 Main St., Charlestown, 03603.

St. Peter Church, 38 Church St., North Walpole, 03609-1715.

Catechesis Religious Program—Ms. Debra Piletz, Catechetical Leader.

2—ST. CATHERINE (1904) Merged in 2007 with St. Peter Parish, North Walpole to form All Saints Parish, Charlestown.

CLAREMONT, SULLIVAN CO.

1—ST. JOSEPH (1920) (Polish)
58 Elm St., P.O. Box 824, Claremont, 03743-0824. Tel: 603-542-5732; Fax: 603-543-3673; Email: stmarysclaremont@comcast.net. Very Rev. Shawn M. Therrien, M.A.; Rev. Arockia Antony, H.G.N.; Deacons Paul R. Boucher; James P. Wilton.

2—ST. MARY (1823) [CEM]
32 Pearl St., Claremont, 03743-2552. Tel: 603-542-9518; Fax: 603-542-9614; Email: stmarysclaremont@comcast.net; Web: www.stmaryparishnh.org. Very Rev. Shawn M. Therrien, M.A.; Rev. Arockia Antony, H.G.N.; Deacons Paul R. Boucher; James P. Wilton.

School—John Paul II Academy, 18 Central St., Claremont, 03743. Tel: 603-542-2157; Email: admin@jp2academynh.org. Religious Teachers 4; Lay Teachers 5; Priests 2; Students 30.

Catechesis Religious Program—Ms. Lisa Sweet, Catechetical Leader. Students 48.

Chapel—Old St. Mary, Old Church Rd., Claremont, Sullivan Co. 03743.

COLEBROOK, COOS CO.

1—ST. BRENDAN (1953) [CEM] Merged in 2007 with St. Albert Parish, West Stewartstown to form North American Martyrs Parish, Colebrook.

2—NORTH AMERICAN MARTYRS PARISH (2007)
55 Pleasant St., Colebrook, 03576-0065. Tel: 603-237-4342; Email: frchenenamp@myfairpoint.net; Web: www.namp.weconnect.com. Very Rev. Craig I. Cheney.

St. Albert Church—15 Church St., West Stewartstown, 03597.

St. Brendan Church.

Catechesis Religious Program—

Mission—St. Pius the Tenth, 108 Colebrook Rd., Errol, 03579.

CONCORD, MERRIMACK CO.

1—CHRIST THE KING PARISH (2011)
72 S. Main St., Concord, 03301-4830. Tel: 603-224-2328; Email: parish@christthekingnh.org; Web: www.christthekingnh.org. Rev. Richard A. Roberge; Deacons Winton P. DeRosia; Kenneth Mayfield. In Res., Rev. Maurice Abasilim, (Nigeria).

2—IMMACULATE HEART OF MARY (1956)
180 Loudon Rd., Concord, 03301-6028. Tel: 603-224-4393; Fax: 603-224-6229; Email: recoffice@ihmnh.org; Web: ihmnh.org. Very Rev. Raymond A. Ball; Deacon John Morrow.

Catechesis Religious Program—Tel: 603-225-2026. Ms. Sara Smith, Catechetical Leader (K-8); Kim Ostrowski, Catechetical Leader (9-12).

3—ST. JOHN THE EVANGELIST (1865) Merged with Sacred Heart, Concord and St. Peter, Concord to form Christ the King Parish, Concord. For sacramental records see Christ the King, Concord.

4—ST. PETER (1946) Merged with Sacred Heart, Concord and St. John the Evangelist, Concord to form Christ the King Parish, Concord. For sacramental records see Christ the King, Concord.

5—SACRED HEART (1892) (French), Merged with St. John the Evangelist, Concord and St. Peter, Concord to form Christ the King Parish, Concord. For sacramental records see Christ the King, Concord.

DERRY, ROCKINGHAM CO.

1—HOLY CROSS (1989)
187 Hampstead Rd., Derry, 03038-4835. Tel: 603-437-9544; Fax: 603-537-1208; Email: hcadmin@holycrossderry.org. Rev. Roger H. Croteau.

Res.: 4 Belle Brook Ln., Derry, 03038-4835.

Catechesis Religious Program—Ms. George Strout, Catechetical Leader.

2—ST. THOMAS AQUINAS (1888)
26 Crystal Ave., Derry, 03038-1799. Tel: 603-432-5000; Fax: 603-434-0518; Email: Staderry@stthomasderry.org; Web: stthomasderry.org. Rev. Philip Pacheco, O.F.M.; Rev/ Joaquin Mejia, O.F.M.; Deacon Joseph Dion.

School—St. Thomas Aquinas School, (Grades K-8), 3 Moody St., Derry, 03038. Tel: 603-432-2712; Fax: 603-432-2179; Email: mainoffice@staderry.com; Web: www.staderry.com. Sr. Lucy Veilleux, P.M., Prin. Lay Teachers 11; Sisters 1; Students 203.

Catechesis Religious Program—Email: ssherman@stthomasderry.org. Sandy Sherman, D.R.E. Students 340.

DOVER, STRAFFORD CO.

1—ST. CHARLES (1893) [CEM] (French), Merged with St. Joseph & St. Mary, Dover to form Parish of the Assumption, Dover.

2—ST. JOSEPH (1945) Merged with St. Charles & St. Mary, Dover to form Parish of the Assumption, Dover.

3—ST. MARY (1833) Merged with St. Charles & St. Joseph, Dover to form Parish of the Assumption, Dover.

4—PARISH OF THE ASSUMPTION (2009)
150 Central Ave., Dover, 03820-3464. Tel: 603-742-4837; Email: office@assumptiondovernh.org; Web: www.assumptiondovernh.org. Revs. Agapit H. Jean Jr., V.F.; Ethelbert C. Orabuche; Deacon Arnold J. A. Gustafson.

St. Joseph Church: 150 Central Ave., Dover, 03820.

St. Mary Church: Chestnut St. at Third St., Dover, 03820.

Chapel—Chapel of the Nativity, Rte. 9, Barrington, 03820.

Catechesis Religious Program—Megan Licata, Catechetical Leader; Ms. Sheila Cronin, M.S.W., Catechetical Leader.

DURHAM, STRAFFORD CO., ST. THOMAS MORE
6 Madbury Rd., Box 620, Durham, 03824-0620. Tel: 603-868-2666; Fax: 603-868-3725; Email: stmdurham@comcast.net. Very Rev. Andrew W. Cryans.

Catechesis Religious Program—Ms. Ann McGurty, Catechetical Leader.

ENFIELD, GRAFTON CO., ST. HELENA (1899)

36 Shaker Hill Rd., P.O. Box 1363, Enfield, 03766. Tel: 603-632-4263; Fax: 603-632-7874; Email: sthstm@gmail.com; Web: sthstm.org. Rev. Charles H. Pawlowski.
Catechesis Religious Program—Email: dffsheartlebanon@gmail.com. Amy Cheevers, D.R.E. Students 7.
Mission—St. Mary, 1157 Rte. 4, Canaan, Grafton Co. 03741.

EPPING, ROCKINGHAM CO., ST. JOSEPH (1898) [CEM]
198 Pleasant St., P.O. Box 337, Epping, 03042-0337. Tel: 603-679-8805; Email: nh337@comcast.net. Rev. Donald E. Clinton; Deacon Terry Sullivan.
Church: 200 Pleasant St., Rte. 27, P.O. Box 337, Epping, 03042-0337.
Catechesis Religious Program—Ms. Ann Ryan, Catechetical Leader.

EXETER, ROCKINGHAM CO., ST. MICHAEL PARISH (1859)
93 Front St., Exeter, 03833-3297. Tel: 603-772-2494; Fax: 603-772-1629; Email: stm@stmichaelparish.org. 9 Lincoln St., Exeter, 03833. Web: stmichaelparish.org. Revs. Marc R. Montminy; Bartholomew I. Okonkwo, (Nigeria); Deacon Eric M. Lambert.
Catechesis Religious Program—Ms. Susan Breton, Catechetical Leader.

FARMINGTON, STRAFFORD CO., ST. PETER (1920)
88 Central St., Farmington, 03835-0565. 71 Lowell St., Rochester, 03867. Tel: 603-755-2280; Email: stmary@metrocast.net; Web: stpeterchurch.m.webs.com. Rev. Thomas L. Duston; Deacon Richard A. Falardeau.
Catechesis Religious Program—Ms. Claire Moffett, Catechetical Leader.

FRANKLIN, MERRIMACK CO.
1—ST. GABRIEL (2013) Rev. Raymond E. Gagnon; Deacon Thomas F. Matzke.
Worship Sites—
St. Mary of the Assumption—16 Chestnut St., Tilton, 03276.
St. Paul, 106 School St., Franklin, 03235.
Res.: 110 School St., P.O. Box 490, Franklin, 03235-0490. Tel: 603-934-5013, Ext. 0; Email: office@stgabrielnh.org; Web: stgabrielnh.org.
Catechesis Religious Program—Tel: 603-934-4372. Ms. Mary Ellen Shaw, Catechetical Leader.
2—ST. PAUL (1884) [CEM] Merged with St. Mary of the Assumption, Tilton to form St. Gabriel, Franklin.

GOFFSTOWN, HILLSBOROUGH CO., ST. LAWRENCE (1955)
1 E. Union St., Goffstown, 03045-1644. Tel: 603-497-2651; Email: stlawrenceoffice@myfairpoint.net; Web: www.stlawrencegoffstown.org. Rev. Gerard L. Bertin; Gerald Bergeron, Pastoral Assoc.; Deacon Geoffrey L. Ashman.
Catechesis Religious Program—Ms. Margaret Tipping, Catechetical Leader.

GONIC, STRAFFORD CO., ST. LEO (1892) [CEM]
59 Main St., Gonic, 03839-5220. Tel: 603-332-1863; Fax: 603-330-0865; Email: pgousse@hrsl.org. Rev. Paul M. Gousse; Deacon Stephen M. Labrie.
Child Care—St. Leo Catholic Children's Center.
Catechesis Religious Program—Sr. Mary Rose Reddy, D.M.M.L., Catechetical Leader (K-5).

GORHAM, COOS CO., HOLY FAMILY (1876) [CEM]
151 Emery St., Berlin, 03570. Revs. Kyle F. Stanton; Michael L. Sartori, Parochial Vicar; Deacon Michael C. Couture.
Res.: 162 Madison Ave., Berlin, 03570-0265.
Church: 7 Church St., Gorham, 03581-1695.
Tel: 603-752-2880; Fax: 603-752-1855; Email: bgoudreau@berlingorhamcatholics.org; Web: berlingorhamcatholics.org.
Catechesis Religious Program—Email: ben@berlingorhamcatholics.org; Email: clara@berlingorhamcatholics.org. Ben Robertson, D.R.E.; Clara Robertson, D.R.E.

GREENVILLE, HILLSBOROUGH CO., SACRED HEART OF JESUS (1888) [CEM]
15 High St., Greenville, 03048-3121. Tel: 603-878-1121; Email: sacredheartgreenvillenh@comcast.net. Rev. Wilfred H. Deschamps.
Catechesis Religious Program—Tel: 603-878-2274. Ms. Lisa Kouropoulos, Catechetical Leader.

GROVETON, COOS CO.
1—ST. FRANCIS XAVIER (1899) [CEM] Merged in 2007 with Sacred Heart, North Stratford to form St. Marguerite d'Youville Parish, Groveton.
2—ST. MARGUERITE D'YOUVILLE PARISH (2007)
11 State St., P.O. Box 247, Groveton, 03582-0247. Tel: 603-636-1047; Email: stfxsh11@gmail.com. Rev. Daniel R. Deveau.
Sacred Heart Church—59 Main St., North Stratford, 03590.
St. Francis Xavier Church.
Catechesis Religious Program—

HAMPSTEAD, ROCKINGHAM CO., ST. ANNE (1979)
26 Emerson Ave., P.O. Box 339, Hampstead, 03841-0339. Tel: 603-329-5886; Fax: 603-329-4468; Email: psmith@saintannechurchnh.org. Very Rev. Marc R. Gagne; Deacon William E. Mullen.
Res.: 99 Emerson Ave., P.O. Box 339, Hampstead, 03841-0339.
Catechesis Religious Program—Ms. Cheryl Gottwald, Catechetical Leader; Ms. Pam Walsh, Catechetical Leader.

HAMPTON BEACH, ROCKINGHAM CO., ST. PATRICK (1914) Open in summer months. For all records contact O.L.M.M. Parish, Hampton
5 Williams St., Hampton, 03842-2722.
Tel: 603-860-6257; Email: m.dunker@yahoo.com. Very Rev. Jason Y. Jalbert, Admin.

HAMPTON, ROCKINGHAM CO., OUR LADY OF THE MIRACULOUS MEDAL (1949)
289 Lafayette Rd., Hampton, 03842-2109.
Tel: 603-926-2206; Fax: 603-926-8602; Email: office@olmmparish.org. Revs. Gary J. Kosmowski; Boniface Agbata; Deacons Dennis M. Jacobs; Stephen J. Kaneb. In Res., Rev. Stephen F. Concannon.
Catechesis Religious Program—Tel: 603-926-5573. Ms. Sherry Impostato, Catechetical Leader.
Mission—St. Elizabeth of Hungary (1956) 1 Lowell St., Seabrook, 03874.

HANOVER, GRAFTON CO., ST. DENIS (1907)
8 Sanborn Rd., Hanover, 03755-2182.
Tel: 603-643-2166; Fax: 603-643-9881; Email: admin.stdenis@gmail.com; Web: www.saintdenisparish.org. Rev. Brian Mulcahy, O.P.
Catechesis Religious Program—Email: faithformation.stdenis@gmail.com. Jessica DePrizio Cole, D.R.E. Students 160.

HARRISVILLE, CHESHIRE CO., ST. DENIS, Merged with St. Patrick, Bennington and St. Peter, Peterborough in 2006 to form Divine Mercy Parish, Peterborough.

HENNIKER, MERRIMACK CO., ST. THERESA (1945)
Mailing Address: 158 Old West Hopkinton Rd., P.O. Box 729, Henniker, 03242-0729. Tel: 603-428-3325; Email: parish.office@tds.net; Web: www.showerofroses.org. Rev. Marcel I. Martel; Deacon Wayne R. Bolduc.
Catechesis Religious Program—Ms. Mary Corsetti, Catechetical Leader.

HILLSBOROGH, HILLSBOROUGH CO., ST. MARY (1892) [CEM] [JC]
P.O. Box 729, Hillsborough, 03244-0907. Email: parish.office@tds.net; Web: www.showerofroses.org. 38 Church St., Hillsborough, 03244-0907.
Tel: 603-464-5565. Rev. Marcel I. Martel; Deacon Wayne R. Bolduc.
Catechesis Religious Program—Janna Andrus, Catechetical Leader.
Parish Hall—Tel: 603-464-6021.

HINSDALE, CHESHIRE CO.
1—ST. JOSEPH (1884) [CEM] Merged in 2006 with St. Stanislaus, Winchester to form Mary, Queen of Peace Parish, Hinsdale.
2—MARY, QUEEN OF PEACE PARISH (2006)
161 Main St., Ste. 201, Keene, 03431-3790.
Tel: 603-352-1311; Fax: 603-358-5250; Email: holyspirit.peace@gmail.com; Web: www.swnhcatholics.com. Revs. Britto Adaikalam, Admin.; Steven M. Kucharski; Deacons Fintan Moore Jr.; David L. Romano; Kenneth J. Swymer.
Res.: 173 Main St., Keene, 03431-3790.
St. Joseph Church—35 Brattleboro Rd., Hinsdale, 03451.
St. Stanislaus Church, 80 Richmond St., Winchester, 03470.
Catechesis Religious Program—

HOOKSETT, MERRIMACK CO., HOLY ROSARY (1886) [CEM]
21 Main St., Hooksett, 03106-1630.
Tel: 603-485-3523; Fax: 603-485-8435; Email: hrparishhook@comcast.net. Rev. Edmund G. Crowley; Deacon William R. Lavallee.
Catechesis Religious Program—Ms. Cathy Mazzaglia, Catechetical Leader.

HUDSON, HILLSBOROUGH CO.
1—ST. JOHN THE EVANGELIST (1949) Merged in 2007 with Infant Jesus, Nashua to form Blessed John XXIII Parish, Nashua.
2—ST. KATHRYN (1968)
4 Dracut Rd., Hudson, 03051-5006.
Tel: 603-882-7793; Fax: 603-595-1465; Email: charlene.maniotis@stkathryns.org; Web: www.stkathryns.org. Rev. Joseph M. Cooper; Deacon Raymond V. Marcotte.
Catechesis Religious Program—Email: sr.janice@stkathryns.org. Sr. Janice Rooney, S.N.D.-deN., D.R.E.; Deacon Raymond V. Marcotte, Catechetical Leader. Students 391.

JAFFREY, CHESHIRE CO., ST. PATRICK (1885) [CEM]
87 Main St., Jaffrey, 03452-6139. Tel: 603-532-6634; Fax: 603-532-6633; Email: stpatric@myfairpoint.net; Web: stpatricksjaffrey.com. Rev. Wilfred H. Deschamps.
Church: 89 Main St., Jaffrey, 03452.
Catechesis Religious Program—Email: laurie@myfairpoint.net. Ms. Laurie Mathieu, Catechetical Leader. Students 18.

KEENE, CHESHIRE CO.
1—ST. BERNARD (1862) [CEM] Merged with St. Margaret Mary, Keene to form Parish of the Holy Spirit, Keene.
2—ST. MARGARET MARY (1955) Merged with St. Bernard, Keene to form Parish of the Holy Spirit, Keene.
3—PARISH OF THE HOLY SPIRIT (2010)
161 Main St., Keene, 03431. Very Rev. Alan C. Tremblay; Rev. Steven M. Kucharski; Deacons Fintan Moore Jr.; David L. Romano; Kenneth J. Swymer.
Res.: 173 Main St., Keene, 03431-3790.
Tel: 603-352-3525; Email: holyspirit.peace@gmail.com.
Worship Sites—
St. Bernard Church—185 Main St., Keene, 03431.
St. Margaret Mary Church, 33-35 Arch St., Keene, 03431.
Immaculate Conception Church, 37 School St., Troy, 03465.
Catechesis Religious Program—Email: swymerken@gmail.com. Deacon Kenneth J. Swymer, Catechetical Leader. Students 83.

LACONIA, BELKNAP CO., ST. ANDRE BESSETTE (2010)
291 Union Ave., Laconia, 03246-3122.
Tel: 603-524-9609; Email: sacredheartlaconia@metrocast.net; Web: standrebessette.org. Very Rev. Marc B. Drouin, M.Div.; Deacon Russell Morey; Very Rev. Msgr. Richard B. Thompson, (Retired).
Rectory—30 Church St., Laconia, 03246.
Catechesis Religious Program—
Worship Sites:—
St. Joseph— (1871) with Sacred Heart, Laconia and Our Lady of the Lakes, Lakeport to form St. Andre Bessette, Laconia. For sacramental records see St. Andre Bessette, Laconia.
Sacred Heart (1891) with St. Joseph, Laconia and Our Lady of the Lakes, Lakeport to form St. Andre Bessette, Laconia. For sacramental records see St. Andre Bessette, Laconia.

LAKEPORT, BELKNAP CO., OUR LADY OF THE LAKES (1905) Merged with St. Joseph, Laconia and Sacred Heart, Laconia to form St. Andre Bessette, Laconia. For sacramental records see St. Andre Bessette, Laconia.

LANCASTER, COOS CO.
1—ALL SAINTS (1856) [CEM] Merged with St. Matthew, Whitefield to form Gate of Heaven, Lancaster.
2—GATE OF HEAVEN (2009)
163 Main St., Lancaster, 03584-3032.
Tel: 603-788-2083; Email: gateofheavennh@aol.com; Tel: www.gateofheavennh.org. Rev. Matthew Schultz; Deacon Michael H. Johnson.
All Saints Church: 161 Main St., Lancaster, 03584.
St. Matthew Church, St. Matthew Church: 9 Jefferson Rd., Whitefield, 03598-3101.
Missions—St. Agnes—297 Presidential Hwy. (Rte. 2), Jefferson, Coos Co. 03583.
St. Patrick, 65 St. Patrick Church Rd, Twin Mountain, Coos Co. 03595.
Shrine—Bretton Woods, Our Lady of the Mountains, 2470 Route 302 East, Bretton Woods, 03575.
Catechesis Religious Program—Ms. Diane Caruso, Catechetical Leader; Ms. Susan Tibbetts, Catechetical Leader.

LEBANON, GRAFTON CO., SACRED HEART (1876)
2 Hough St., P.O. Box 482, Lebanon, 03766-0482.
Tel: 603-448-1262; Fax: 603-448-3754; Email: sheartlebanon@gmail.com. Rev. Charles H. Pawlowski.
Catechesis Religious Program—7 Fairview Ave., Lebanon, 03766. Jesse Dow, Catechetical Leader.

LINCOLN, GRAFTON CO., ST. JOSEPH (1902) Rev. David L. Kneeland.
Res.: 25 Church St., P.O. Box 128, Lincoln, 03251-0128. Tel: 603-745-2266; Fax: 603-745-2888; Email: stjlincoln@hotmail.com.
Catechesis Religious Program—Paula King, Catechetical Leader.

LISBON, GRAFTON CO., ST. CATHERINE OF SIENA (1958)
c/o 21 Pine St., Woodsville, 03785-1215.
Tel: 603-747-2038; Fax: 603-747-8071; Email: stjoseph_church@yahoo.com. Rev. Maria Susairaj.
Church: 28 Highland Ave., Lisbon, 03585.
Catechesis Religious Program—Ms. Mary Cataldo, Catechetical Leader.

LITCHFIELD, HILLSBOROUGH CO., ST. FRANCIS OF ASSISI (1953)
Parish Office, 9 St. Francis Way, Litchfield, 03052-8050. Tel: 603-424-3456; Email: parish@stfrancisofassisi.net; Web: www.stfrancisofassisi.net. Rev. Jeffrey P. Statz; Deacon Frank Ottaviano.
Catechesis Religious Program—Tel: 603-424-9061. Ms. Vicki Isabelle, Catechetical Leader.

LITTLETON, GRAFTON CO., ST. ROSE OF LIMA (1882) [CEM]
77 Clay St., Littleton, 03561-1205. Tel: 603-444-2593 ; Fax: 603-444-3126; Email: srlandols@gmail.com; Web: strosechurchnh.org. Very Rev. Mark E. Dollard; Deacon Stephen M. Noyes.

Catechesis Religious Program—Mr. Nicholas DeMayo, Catechetical Leader.
Mission—Our Lady of the Snows, 403 Main St., Franconia, Grafton Co. 03580.

LONDONDERRY, ROCKINGHAM CO.

1—ST. JUDE (1962)
435 Mammoth Rd., Londonderry, 03053-2304.
Tel: 603-432-3333; Email: sgreen@stjudenh.com. Rev. Robert E. Gorski; Deacon Marc G. Payeur.
Catechesis Religious Program—Tel: 603-437-7026; Email: twoodward@stjudenh.com. Ms. Trish Woodward, Catechetical Leader.

2—ST. MARK THE EVANGELIST (1981)
1 South Rd., Londonderry, 03053-3814.
Tel: 603-432-8711; Fax: 603-434-6748; Email: info@stmarksnh.org. Rev. Michael S. Zgonc; Deacon Thomas P. Lavallee.
Res.: One Griffin Rd., Londonderry, 03053.
Catechesis Religious Program—Tel: 603-432-5711. Ms. Catherine Kinnon, Catechetical Leader.

MARLBOROUGH, CHESHIRE CO., SACRED HEART (1886) [CEM] Unified in 2006 with St. Bernard, Keene.

MEREDITH, BELKNAP CO., ST. CHARLES BORROMEO (1946)
300 NH Rte. 25, P.O. Box 237, Meredith, 03253-0237. Tel: 603-279-4403; Fax: 603-279-9924; Email: office@stcharlesnh.org; Web: www.stcharlesnh.org. Rev. Msgr. Gerald R. Belanger.
Res.: 8 Ridge Rd., P.O. Box 237, Meredith, 03253-0237.
Catechesis Religious Program—Ms. De-Anne Porter, Catechetical Leader.

MERRIMACK, HILLSBOROUGH CO.

1—ST. JOHN NEUMANN (1982)
708 Milford Rd., Merrimack, 03054.
Tel: 603-880-4689; Email: welcome@sjnnh.org; Web: www.sjnnh.org. Rev. Robert K. Glasgow; Deacon Mark A. De Rosch.
Res.: 208 Naticook Rd., Merrimack, 03054.
Catechesis Religious Program—Tel: 603-880-0825. Ms. Lucy Jones.

2—OUR LADY OF MERCY (1954)
16 Baboosic Lake Rd., Merrimack, 03054-3603.
Tel: 603-424-3757; Email: frpaul@olmnh.org; Web: www.olmnh.org. Rev. Msgr. Paul L. Bouchard, S.T.L., J.C.L.; Deacon John B. Castelot; Rev. Daniel A. St. Laurent, In Res., (Retired).
Catechesis Religious Program—Email: lpaison@olmnh.org. Laurie Paison, D.R.E.

MILFORD, HILLSBOROUGH CO., ST. PATRICK (1895) [CEM]
34 Amherst St., Milford, 03055. Tel: 603-673-1311; Fax: 603-673-3687; Email: diane.st.patoffice@gmail.com; Web: saintpatrickmilfordnh.org. Rev. Dennis J. Audet; Patti Hendrickson, P.A., Pastoral Assoc.
Catechesis Religious Program—Tel: 603-673-4797. Ms. Sue Pasquale, Catechetical Leader; Ms. Kathy Frye, Catechetical Leader.

NASHUA, HILLSBOROUGH CO.

1—ST. ALOYSIUS OF GONZAGA (1871) [CEM 3] (French)
48 W. Hollis St., Nashua, 03060-3286.
Tel: 603-882-4362; Fax: 603-886-8923; Email: businessmanager@stlouisnashua.org. Rev. Marcos A. Gonzalez-Torres; Deacon Richard E. Desmarais.
Catechesis Religious Program—Tel: 603-821-5192.
Convent—St. Stanislaus, 5 Green St., Nashua, 03064.
Chapel—Corpus Christi Chapel, 43 Franklin St., Nashua, 03064.

2—ST. CASIMIR, Unified in 2002 with St. Patrick, Nashua.

3—ST. CHRISTOPHER (1950)
Mailing Address: 60 Manchester St., Nashua, 03064.
Tel: 603-882-0632; Fax: 603-881-8728; Email: office@stchrisparishnh.org. Rev. David Harris, Admin.; Deacon James P. Daly. In Res., Rev. Bruce W. Collard.
Res.: 62 Manchester St., Nashua, 03064-6296.
Tel: 603-882-0632; Email: parish.office@stchrisparishnh.org.
Catechesis Religious Program—Email: cmercurio@stchrisparishnh.org. Deacon James P. Daly; Christine Mercurio, D.R.E. Students 80.

4—ST. FRANCIS XAVIER (1885) [CEM] Closed. Unified in 2003 with St. Aloysius, Nashua.

5—IMMACULATE CONCEPTION (1968)
216 E. Dunstable Rd., Nashua, 03062-2344.
Tel: 603-888-0321; Fax: 603-888-8407; Email: diane.st.patoffice@gmail.com. Revs. Ray J. Labrie; Dixon Choolakkal, C.R.S., Weekend Ministry; Deacons William McDermott; Christopher M. Everhart.
Catechesis Religious Program—214 E. Dunstable Rd., Nashua, 03062-2344. Ms. Jane Brihan, Catechetical Leader K-5; Ms. Carmen Rodriguez-Brick, Catechetical Leader 6-12.

6—INFANT JESUS (1909) Merged with St. John the Evangelist, Hudson to form Blessed John XXIII Parish, Nashua.

7—SAINT JOHN XXIII PARISH (2007)
121 Allds St., Nashua, 03060-6395.
Fax: 603-882-7104; Email: office@stjohnxxiiinh.org. Rev. Msgr. Eddy N. Bisson, Admin.; Revs. George Mattathilanikal; Christiana Barbosa; Deacons Randy O'Neil; Edmund C. Hilston, (Retired).
Infant Jesus Church—
St. John the Evangelist Church, 25 Library St., Hudson, 03051-4239.
School—Infant Jesus School, (Grades PreK-6), 3 Crown St., Nashua, 03060-6366. Tel: 603-889-2649; Fax: 603-594-9117; Email: ricci@ijschool.org; Web: www.ijschool.org. Kelly Veilleux, Prin. Clergy 2; Lay Teachers 15; Students 75.
Catechesis Religious Program—23 Library St., Hudson, 03051-4239.
Brazilian Outreach Office—
Tel: 603-882-2462, Ext. 105.

8—ST. JOSEPH THE WORKER (1955)
777 W. Hollis St., Nashua, 03062-3553.
Tel: 603-883-0757; Fax: 603-883-8057; Email: parishoffice@stjoenash.org. Most Rev. Francis J. Christian, Ph.D., D.D.; Deacons Raymond A. Wheeler; Roland Leduc. In Res.
Catechesis Religious Program—Email: janicemercure@stjoenash.org. Janice Mercure, D.R.E. Students 186.

9—PARISH OF THE RESURRECTION (1970)
Pastoral Center, 449 Broad St., Nashua, 03063-3412.
Tel: 603-882-0925; Email: rezparish@comcast.net; Web: parishoftheresurrection.org. Very Rev. John M. Grace; Deacon Steve Veneman.
Res.: 23 Parrish Hill Rd., Nashua, 03063-3412.
Catechesis Religious Program—Tel: 603-889-0012; Email: rezreligioused@comcast.net. Ms. Terry Root, Catechetical Leader. Students 353.

10—ST. PATRICK (1855) [CEM 2]
29 Spring St., Nashua, 03060-3490.
Tel: 603-882-2262; Fax: 603-577-9817; Email: office@stpatricksnashua.org. Rev. Michael Kerper. In Res., Rev. John E. Healey, (Retired).
Catechesis Religious Program—Tel: 603-882-5417; Email: faithformation.st.patrick@gmial.com. Marie Miller, D.R.E.

11—ST. STANISLAUS PARISH
5 Green St., Nashua, 03064. Rev. James Smith, Parochial Vicar.

NEW LONDON, MERRIMACK CO., OUR LADY OF FATIMA (1952)
724 Main St., New London, 03257-7821.
Tel: 603-526-4484; Fax: 603-526-8055; Email: olfic@comcast.net; Web: www.olfic.org. Rev. Robert G. Biron; Deacon Gregory R. McGinn.
Catechesis Religious Program—Ms. Teresa Jackson, Catechetical Leader.
Mission—Immaculate Conception, 12 Church Ln., Andover, 03216.

NEWMARKET, ROCKINGHAM CO., ST. MARY CHURCH (1878) [CEM]
P.O. Box 337, Newmarket, 03857-0337.
Tel: 603-659-3643; Email: stmarynh@gmail.com; Web: stmarynh.org. 182 Main St., Newmarket, 03857. Revs. Marc R. Montminy; Bartholomew I. Okonkwo, (Nigeria); Deacon Eric M. Lambert.
Catechesis Religious Program—Tel: 603-659-6474. Stacey Cooper-Jennings, Catechetical Leader; Ms. Nicole Benson, Catechetical Leader.

NEWPORT, SULLIVAN CO., ST. PATRICK (1902) [CEM]
32 Beech St., Newport, 03773-1416.
Tel: 603-863-1422; Fax: 603-863-7898; Email: office@saintpatrickparish.net; Web: www.saintpatrickparish.net. 40 School St., Newport, 03773-1416. Rev. Michael R. Monette.
Catechesis Religious Program—Charlotte Antal, Catechetical Leader.
Mission—St. Joachim, 5 Old Georges Mills Rd., Sunapee, Sullivan Co. 03782.

NEWTON, ROCKINGHAM CO., MARY, MOTHER OF THE CHURCH (1967) Merged with Holy Angels to form St. Luke the Evangelist Parish, Plaistow.

NORTH CONWAY, CARROLL CO., OUR LADY OF THE MOUNTAINS (1902) [CEM 2]
2905 White Mountains Hwy., North Conway, 03860.
Tel: 603-356-2535; Fax: 603-356-2877; Email: ourladynh@myfairpoint.net. Rev. Steven M. Lepine; Deacon John Carey.
Catechesis Religious Program—Joseph Grdinich, Catechetical Leader.

NORTH STRATFORD, COOS CO., SACRED HEART (1888) [CEM 2] (French), Merged with St. Francis Xavier, Groveton to form St. Marguerite d'Youville Parish, Groveton.

NORTH WALPOLE, CHESHIRE CO., ST. PETER (1878) [CEM] Merged with St. Catherine of Siena Parish, Charlestown to form All Saints Parish, Charlestown.

PELHAM, HILLSBOROUGH CO., ST. PATRICK (1946)
12 Main St., Pelham, 03076-3724. Tel: 603-635-3525; Fax: 603-635-3919; Email: therese42852@comcast.net; Web: www.stpatricks-pelham.com. Rev. Volney J. DeRosia; Deacon John F. Ross; Rev. Richard J. Kelley, In Res., (Retired).
Catechesis Religious Program—Tel: 603-635-1447; Email: faithlifeformation@comcast.net. Adam Castor, Catechetical Leader.

PENACOOK, MERRIMACK CO., IMMACULATE CONCEPTION (1880) [CEM]
9 Bonney St., Penacook, 03303-1654.
Tel: 603-753-4413; Fax: 603-753-4071; Email: pastor@icpenacook.org; Web: www.icpenacook.org. Rev. Raymond J. Potvin.
Catechesis Religious Program—

PETERBOROUGH, HILLSBOROUGH CO.

1—DIVINE MERCY PARISH (2006)
12 Church St., Peterborough, 03458.
Tel: 603-924-7647; Email: divinemercynh@comcast.net; Web: divinemercynh.org. Rev. Michael S. Taylor, M.Div., J.C.L.; Deacon Dennis W. Marquis.
Catechesis Religious Program—Email: maplemanse@aol.com. Ms. Jackie Capes, Catechetical Leader. Students 89.

2—ST. PETER (1900) [CEM] Merged in 2006 with St. Denis, Harrisville and St. Patrick, Bennington in 2006 to form Divine Mercy Parish, Peterborough.

PITTSFIELD, MERRIMACK CO., OUR LADY OF LOURDES (1889)
20 River Rd., Pittsfield, 03263-3314.
Tel: 603-435-6242; Fax: 603-435-5531; Email: ololstjoseph@metrocast.net; Web: ourladyoflourdes-stjosephs.org/oll. Rev. John B. MacKenzie.
Catechesis Religious Program—Tel: 603-942-8716. Ms. Regina Garcia, Catechetical Leader.
Mission—St. Joseph, [CEM] 844 1st NH Tpke. (Rte. 4), Northwood, Rockingham Co. 03261.

PLAISTOW, ROCKINGHAM CO.

1—HOLY ANGELS (1892) [CEM] Merged in 2007 with Mary, Mother of the Church, Newton to form St. Luke the Evangelist Parish, Plaistow.

2—ST. LUKE THE EVANGELIST PARISH (2007)
8 Atkinson Depot Rd. (Rte. 121), Plaistow, 03865-3103. Tel: 603-382-8324; Email: purchase@stluketheevangelist.net; Web: www.stlukenh.org. Rev. Albert J. Tremblay.
Res.: Mary, Mother of the Church, 12 Amesbury Rd., Newton, 03858.
Holy Angels Church—8 Atkinson Depot Rd., Plaistow, 03865.
Mary, Mother of the Church, 12 Amesbury Rd., Newton, 03858.
School—Holy Angels Pre-School, Tel: 603-382-9783; Email: jtremblay@stluketheevangelist.net. Ms. Jean Lanctot, Dir.
Catechesis Religious Program—Ms. Joyce Szczapa, Catechetical Leader.
Convent—6 Atkinson Depot Rd., Plaistow, 03865.

PLYMOUTH, GRAFTON CO.

1—HOLY TRINITY PARISH (2006)
46 Langdon St., Plymouth, 03264-1438.
Tel: 603-536-4700; Fax: 603-536-4709; Email: holytrinitynh@gmail.com; Web: holytrinityparishnh.org. Rev. Leo A. LeBlanc; Deacon Michael Guy.
St. Agnes Church—19 Hill Ave., Ashland, 03217.
St. Matthew Church, 11 School St., Plymouth, 03264.
Catechesis Religious Program—Ms. Maureen Ebner, Catechetical Leader; Ms. Amy Ulricson, Catechetical Leader.
Chapel—Our Lady of Grace, 2 W. Shore Rd., Bristol, 03222.

2—ST. MATTHEW (1916) Merged in 2006 with St. Timothy, Bristol and St. Agnes, Ashland to form Holy Trinity Parish, Plymouth.

PORTSMOUTH, ROCKINGHAM CO.

1—ST. CATHERINE OF SIENA (1951) Merged in 2006 with St. James and Immaculate Conception, Portsmouth to form Corpus Christi Parish, Portsmouth.

2—CORPUS CHRISTI PARISH (2006)
845 Woodbury Ave., Portsmouth, 03801-3213.
Tel: 603-436-4555; Fax: 603-433-4401; Email: parishmail.ccnh@gmail.com; Web: www.corpuschristinh.org. Rev. Gary J. Belliveau.
Res.: 98 Summer St., Portsmouth, 03801.
Immaculate Conception Church, 98 Summer St., Portsmouth, 03801-4398.
Catechesis Religious Program—Ms. Brenda Stinson, Catechetical Leader.

3—IMMACULATE CONCEPTION (1851) [CEM 2] Merged in 2006 with St. Catherine of Siena and St. James, Portsmouth to form Corpus Christi Parish, Portsmouth.

4—ST. JAMES (1958) [JC] Merged in 2006 with St. Catherine of Siena and Immaculate Conception, Portsmouth to form Corpus Christi Parish, Portsmouth.

ROCHESTER, STRAFFORD CO.

1—ST. MARY (1872) [CEM]
71 Lowell St., Rochester, 03867-5002.
Tel: 603-332-1869; Fax: 603-332-2040; Email: stmary@metrocast.net; Web: stmarychurchnh.org. Rev. Thomas L. Duston; Deacon Richard A. Falardeau.
Catechesis Religious Program—Sr. Lucie Ducas, C.S.C., P.A., Catechetical Leader; Anna Ingram, Catechetical Leader.

2—OUR LADY OF THE HOLY ROSARY (1883) [CEM] (French)

189 N. Main St., Rochester, 03867-1299.
Tel: 603-332-1863; Fax: 603-330-0865; Email: pgousse@hrsl.org; Web: www.hrsl.org. Rev. Paul M. Gousse; Deacon Stephen M. Labrie.
Child Care—St. Leo Catholic Children's Center, 59 Main St., Gonic, 03839-5220.
Catechesis Religious Program—Email: srmaryrose@hrsl.org. Sr. Mary Rose Reddy, D.M.M.L., Catechetical Leader (1-5). Students 157.

ROLLINSFORD, STRAFFORD CO., ST. MARY (1856) [CEM] c/o St. Ignatius of Loyola, 404 High St., Somersworth, 03878. Tel: 603-692-4367;
Tel: 603-692-2172; Email: r.stmartin@comcast.net; Web: www.stignatius-stmary.org. Church St., Rollinsford, 03869. Rev. Andrew Nelson; Deacon David Divins.
Res.: 120 Maple St., P.O. Box 70, Somersworth, 03878.
Church: 440 Church St., Rollinsford, 03869.
Catechesis Religious Program—Tel: 603-749-1666. Ms. Laurie Lambert, Catechetical Leader.

RYE BEACH, ROCKINGHAM CO., ST. THERESA (1979) 815 Central Rd., P.O. Box 482, Rye Beach, 03871-0482. Tel: 603-964-6440; Fax: 603-964-4139; Email: ljoyce@santtheresachurchrye.org. Rev. Gary J. Kosmowski.
Catechesis Religious Program—Tel: 603-964-9878. Mr. Gary Hodsdon, Catechetical Leader; Ms. Anne Hoeing.

SALEM, ROCKINGHAM CO.
1—SAINTS MARY AND JOSEPH (2010)
200 Lawrence Rd., Salem, 03079-3978.
Tel: 603-893-8661; Email: officeadmin@saintsmaryandjoseph.org; Web: saintsmaryandjoseph.org. Rev. Vincent Onunkwo, Admin.; Deacon Jay L. Cormier, Ph.D.
Rectory—33 Main St., Salem, 03079-1922.
Mary, Queen of Peace Church—
St. Joseph Church, 40 Main St., Salem, 03079.
Catechesis Religious Program—Ms. Marie Mullen, Catechetical Leader; Ms. Susan Levesque, Catechetical Leader.
Chapel—Holy Family, 40 Main St., Salem, 03079.
2—MARY, QUEEN OF PEACE (1966) Merged with St. Joseph, Salem to form Saints Mary and Joseph, Salem. For sacramental records see Saints Mary and Joseph, Salem.

SANBORNVILLE, CARROLL CO., ST. ANTHONY (1908) [CEM]
239 Meadow St., P.O. Box 490, Sanbornville, 03872-0490. Tel: 603-552-3304; Email: stanthony239@gmail.com; Web: www.stanthonystjoseph.org. Rev. Patrick N. Gilbert.
Catechesis Religious Program—Ms. Beth Kilroy, Catechetical Leader.

SOMERSWORTH, STRAFFORD CO.
1—HOLY TRINITY (1857) [CEM] Merged with St. Martin, Somersworth to form Saint Ignatius of Loyola, Somersworth.
2—SAINT IGNATIUS OF LOYOLA (2009)
404 High St., Somersworth, 03878.
Tel: 603-692-2172; Email: r.stmartin@comcast.net; Email: holytrinity.stmary@comcast.net; Web: www.stignatius-stmary.org. Rev. Andrew Nelson; Deacon David Divins.
Res.: St. Martin Church, 130 Maple St., Somersworth, 03878-1999.
Holy Trinity Church—
St. Martin Church, 120 Maple St., Somersworth, 03878.
Catechesis Religious Program—Tel: 603-692-4367. Ms. Janet Jacobson, Catechetical Leader.
3—ST. MARTIN (1882) [CEM] (French), Merged with Holy Trinity, Somersworth to form Saint Ignatius Loyola, Somersworth.

SUNCOOK, MERRIMACK CO., ST. JOHN THE BAPTIST (1873) [CEM 2]
10 School St., Suncook, 03275-1817.
Tel: 603-485-3113; Fax: 603-485-2113; Email: stjohnthebaptist@comcast.net. Rev. Adrien R. Longchamps, Admin.; Deacon William R. Lavallee. In Res., Rev. John B. Finnigan, (Retired).
Catechesis Religious Program—Tel: 603-485-3972. Ms. Cathy Mazzaglia, Catechetical Leader.

TILTON, BELKNAP CO., ST. MARY OF THE ASSUMPTION (1894) [CEM] Merged with St. Paul, Franklin to form St. Gabriel, Franklin.

TROY, CHESHIRE CO., IMMACULATE CONCEPTION (1903) [CEM] Merged with St. Bernard, Keene. For sacramental records see St. Bernard, Keene.

WEST LEBANON, GRAFTON CO., HOLY REDEEMER (1953) Closed. Unified in 2003 with Sacred Heart, Lebanon.

WEST STEWARTSTOWN, COOS CO., ST. ALBERT (1926) [CEM] Merged in 2007 with St. Brendan Parish, Colebrook to form North American Martyrs Parish, Colebrook.

WEST SWANZEY, CHESHIRE CO., ST. ANTHONY (1958) Unified in 2004 with St. Bernard Parish, Keene.

WHITEFIELD, COOS CO., ST. MATTHEW (1886) [CEM 2] Merged with All Saints, Lancaster to form Gate of Heaven, Lancaster.

WILTON, HILLSBOROUGH CO., SACRED HEART (1882) [CEM] Closed. Unified into Sacred Heart of Jesus, Greenville.

WINCHESTER, CHESHIRE CO., ST. STANISLAUS (1962) Merged in 2006 with St. Joseph, Hinsdale to form Mary, Queen of Peace Parish, Hinsdale.

WINDHAM, ROCKINGHAM CO., ST. MATTHEW (1962) [JC] 2 Searles Rd., Windham, 03087-1206.
Tel: 603-893-3336; Fax: 603-898-4008; Email: windstmatt@comcast.net; Web: www.stmatthew-nh.org. Rev. Brian Kennedy, C.Ss.R.; Deacon Leland Fastnach.
Res.: 5 Searles Rd., Windham, 03087-1206.
Catechesis Religious Program—Ms. Margaret Donahue-Turner, M.Div., Catechetical Leader; Ms. Mary Jude Donabedian, Catechetical Leader; Ms. Sandy Gibbons, Catechetical Leader.

WOLFEBORO, CARROLL CO., ST. CECILIA, Merged in 2003 with St. Joan of Arc Parish, Alton to form St. Katharine Drexel, Alton.

WOODSVILLE, GRAFTON CO., ST. JOSEPH (1896) [CEM] Rev. Maria Susairaj.
Res.: 21 Pine St., Woodsville, 03785-1215.
Tel: 603-747-2038; Fax: 603-747-8071; Email: stjoseph_church@yahoo.com.
Catechesis Religious Program—Ms. Mary Cataldo, Catechetical Leader.

Chaplains of Public Institutions

MANCHESTER. *Bishop Peterson Residence*. Deacon Richard J. Shannon.
Catholic Medical Center. Revs. Jean M. Lemay, Bartholomew Ogumelu, Sr. Eileen Auger, Mr. Marc F. Guillemette, Sr. Martha Mulligan, R.S.M.
Elliott Hospital. Revs. Eric T. Delisle, M.Div., Rev., Theodore Mbaegbu.
St. George Manor - Holy Cross Health Center. Rev. Bruce W. Collard.
Hanover Hill Health Care Center. Rev. Theodore Mbaegbu.
Hillsborough County Jail. Vacant.
Hillsborough County Nursing Home. Rev. Eric T. Delisle, M.Div.
St. Joseph Residence. Rev. Msgr. Charles E. DesRuisseaux, (Retired), Rev. Roland P. Cote, (Retired).
Maple Leaf Nursing Home. Rev. Eric T. Delisle, M.Div.
Monastery of the Precious Blood. Rev. Msgr. Charles E. DesRuisseaux, (Retired), Rev. Adrien R. Longchamps.
Mt. Carmel Rehabilitation and Nursing Center. Rev. Roland P. Cote, (Retired).
Saint Teresa Rehabilitation and Nursing Center. Rev. Msgr. Charles E. DesRuisseaux, (Retired), Rev. Norman J. Simoneau, (Retired).
Veterans Administration Medical Center. Rev. Thomas P. Steinmetz, Sr. Marguerite Gravel, C.S.C.
Youth Development Center. Vacant.

BERLIN. *Androscoggin Valley Hospital*. Deacon Michael CouturePriests of Good Shepherd Parish.
Northern New Hampshire Correctional Facility. Rev. Kyle F. Stanton.
Saint Vincent de Paul Rehabilitation and Nursing Center. Priests of Good Shepherd Parish.

BOSCAWEN. *Merrimack County House of Correction*. Capital Deanery Priests.

BRENTWOOD. *Rockingham County House of Corrections*. Rev. Donald E. Clinton.

CLAREMONT. *Sullivan County House of Corrections*. Very Rev. Shawn M. Therrien, M.A.

CONCORD. *Carmelite Monastery*. Rev. Maurice Abasilim, (Nigeria).
Concord Hospital. Rev. Maurice Abasilim, (Nigeria).
N.H. Prison for Men. Revs. Bernard J. Campbell, O.F.M.Cap, Richard A. Roberge, Deacon James P. Daly, Chap.
New Hampshire State Hospital. Rev. Maurice Abasilim, (Nigeria).

DOVER. *Riverside Rest Home*. Seacoast Deanery Priests.
Saint Ann Rehabilitation and Nursing Center. Seacoast Deanery Priests.
Strafford County House of Correction. Seacoast Deanery Priests.
Wentworth-Douglass Hospital. Seacoast Deanery Priests.

GOFFSTOWN. *New Hampshire State Prison for Women*. Vacant.

JAFFREY. *Good Shepherd Rehabilitation and Nursing Center*. Rev. Richard A. Smith, (Retired).

KEENE. *Cheshire County House of Corrections*. Very Rev. Alan C. TremblayMonadnock Deanery Priests.
Cheshire Medical Center/Dartmouth Hitchcock. Priests of Parish of the Holy Spirit.

LACONIA. *Belknap County House of Corrections*. Very Rev. Marc B. Drouin, M.Div.
Saint Francis Rehabilitation and Nursing Center. Priests of St. Andre Bessette Parish.

LEBANON. *Dartmouth-Hitchcock Medical Center*. Rev. Samuel Seyd, (Pakistan).

NASHUA. *St. Joseph Hospital and Southern N.H. Regional Medical Center*. Souhegan Deanery Priests.

NORTH HAVERHILL. *Grafton County House of Correction*. Rev. Sebastian Susairaj, H.G.N.

OSSIPEE. *Carroll County House of Correction*. Rev. Patrick N. Gilbert.

PORTSMOUTH. *Portsmouth Regional Hospital*. Seacoast Deanery Priests.

ROCHESTER. *St. Charles Children's Home*. Rev. Paul M. Gousse.

WEST STEWARTSTOWN. *Coos County House of Corrections*. Very Rev. Craig I. Cheney.

WINDHAM. *Warde Health Center*. Rev. Bruce W. Collard.

On Duty Outside the Diocese:
Rev. Msgr.—
Frontiero, Anthony R.
Revs.—
Cody, Kevin W.
Montesanti, Steven G.

Personal or Administrative Leave:
Revs.—
Baker, W. Pierre
Desmarais, Gerard R.
Lamy, Raymond J.
Pennett, Frederick J. Jr.
St. Louis, Richard E. Jr.

Senior Priests:
Rev. Msgr.—
Bisson, Eddy N.

Retired:
Very Rev. Msgr.—
Thompson, Richard B., (Retired)
Rev. Msgrs.—
DesRuisseaux, Charles E., (Retired), 51 River Front Dr., Apt. 3, 03102
Dumont, C. Peter, (Retired), P.O. Box 490, Winnisquam, 03289
Gilbert, Donald J., J.C.L., (Retired)
Kelley, Edward J., (Retired), P.O. Box 416, Dover, 03821-0416
Lamothe, Daniel O., (Retired), 89 Goodell Ave., Swanzey, 03446
Revs.—
Allard, Marcel M., (Retired), 378 Notre Dame Ave., 03102
Auger, Gerald E., (Retired)
Babicz, Edmund A., (Retired)
Bilodeau, Roger P., (Retired), 1 Gilson Rd., Hollis, 03049
Boisvert, Robert G., (Retired), 6 Faith Ln., Center Barnstead, 03225
Cote, Roland P., (Retired)
Coyne, Emmett A., (Retired), 153 Ash St., 03104
Desjardins, George A., (Retired), 6 Pleasant St., E-3, Hooksett, 03106-1421
Di Russo, Anthony, (Retired), 410 Chase Rd., Lunenburg, MA 01462
Dion, Gerard, (Retired), 153 Ash St., 03104
Dunn, Gerald R., (Retired), P.O. Box 7356, Gonic, 03839. Tel: 603-569-5058
Finnigan, John B., (Retired), 10 School St., Suncook, 03275-1917
Frechette, Leo L., (Retired), 5 Tampa Dr., Unit 6, Rochester, 03867
Gauthier, Donald F. Jr., (Retired)
Gregoire, Paul L., (Retired), 377 Wilson St., 03103
Healey, John E., (Retired)
Kelley, Richard J., (Retired)
Kelso, Francis E., (Retired), 774 Dana Hill Rd., New Hampton, 03256
Lampron, Maurice W., (Retired), P.O. Box 717, Wolfeboro Falls, 03896-0717
Marchand, Robert A., (Retired), P.O. Box 185, Moody, ME 04054
Oliviera, Humbert, (Retired), 9 Hollis St., Cambridge, MA 02140
Rundzio, Mark A., (Retired), 745 2nd Ave., Berlin, 03570
Silva, Eusebio F., (Retired)
Simoneau, Norman J., (Retired), 185 Eastern Ave., Unit 202, 03104
Smith, Richard A., (Retired), 47 Howard Hill Rd., Apt. 202, Jaffrey, 03452
Soberick, George J., (Retired), 153 Ash St., 03104
St. Laurent, Daniel A., (Retired), 153 Ash St., 03104
Tetu, Richard P., (Retired), 378 Notre Dame Ave., 03102.

Permanent Deacons:
Abbott, Leon E. Jr., (Retired)
Andrade, Ramon, St. Anne-St. Augustine, Manchester
Ashman, Geoffrey L., St. Lawrence, Goffstown
Bolduc, Wayne R., St. Theresa Parish, Henniker; St. Mary Parish, Hillsborough
Borkush, George J., (Retired), (Unassigned)
Borland, Joseph P., (Retired)
Boucher, Paul R., St. Mary, Claremont
Brown, William, (Retired)
Carey, John J., Our Lady of the Mountains, N. Conway
Castelot, John B., Our Lady of Mercy, Merrimack
Cloutier, Thomas, Sacred Heart, Manchester
Cody, Kevin, Sainte Marie, Manchester
Cooper, Karl, St. Joseph Cathedral, Manchester
Cormier, Jay L., Ph.D., Sts. Mary and Joseph Parish, Salem
Costello, David T., (Retired)
Couture, Michael J., Good Shepherd Parish, Berlin; Holy Family Parish, Gorham
Czchowicz, Kenneth, All Saints Parish, Charlestown
Daly, James P., St. Christopher Parish, Nashua
De Rosch, Mark A., St. John Neumann Parish, Merrimack
DeRosia, Winton P., Christ the King, Concord
Desmarais, Richard E., St. Aloysius of Gonzaga Parish, Nashua
Divins, David, St. Ignatius of Loyola, Somersworth
Everhart, Christopher M., Immaculate Conception Parish, Nashua
Falardeau, Richard A., St. Mary, Rochester and St. Peter, Farmington
Fastnacht, Leland, St. Matthew, Windham
Ferraro, Charles, St. Kathryn Drexel, Alton
Gagnon, Robert J., (Retired)
Gallinaro, Frank, Ste. Marie, Manchester
Gustafson, Arnold J. A., Assumption, Dover
Guy, Michael, Holy Trinity, Plymouth
Hilston, Edmund C., (Retired)
Hilton, Richard, St. Katharine Drexel, Alton
Hobson, Mark F., Ph.D.
Jacobs, Dennis M., Our Lady of the Miraculous Medal, Hampton
Johnson, H. Michael, Gate of Heaven Parish, Lancaster
Kaneb, Stephen J., Our Lady of the Miraculous Medal, Hampton
Kram, Harry A., (Retired)
LaBonte, Alfred A. Jr., (Retired)
Labrie, Stephen M., Our Lady of Holy Rosary Parish, Rochester
Lambert, Eric M., St. Michael Parish, Exeter
Lavallee, Thomas P., St. Mark the Evangelist, Londonderry
Lavallee, William R., Holy Rosary, Hooksett; St. John the Baptist, Suncook
Leduc, Ronald, St. Joseph the Worker, Nashua
MacDonald, Bernard, (Retired)
Marcotte, Raymond V., St. Kathryn, Hudson
Marquis, Dennis W., Divine Mercy Parish, Peterborough
Matzke, Thomas F., St. Gabriel Parish, Franklin
Mayfield, Kenneth, Christ the King, Concord
McCarty, William, St. Andre Bessette, Laconia
McDermott, William, Immaculate Conception, Nashua
McGinn, Gregory R., Our Lady of Fatima, New London
Moore, Fintan Jr., Holy Spirit, Keene
Morey, Russell, St. Andre Bessette, Laconia
Morrow, John, Immaculate Heart of Mary, Concord
Mullen, William E., St. Anne, Hampstead
Munz, Edward P., St. Catherine, Manchester
Noyes, Stephen M., St. Rose of Lima Parish, Littleton
Ottaviano, Frank, St. Anne - St. Augustine, Manchester
Patterson, James E., St. Pius X, Manchester
Paul, Christopher, St. Peter Parish, Auburn
Payeur, Marc G., St. Jude, Londonderry
Potvin, Robert R., (Retired)
Rich, William, (Retired)
Rock, James E., (Retired)
Romano, David L., Parish of the Holy Spirit, Keene; Mary, Queen of Peace Parish, Hinsdale
Ross, John F., St. Patrick, Pelham
Shannon, Richard J., Parish of the Transfiguration, Manchester
Swymer, Kenneth J., Parish of the Holy Spirit, Keene; Mary, Queen of Peace Parish, Hinsdale
Testa, Paul E., (Retired)
Tran, Lam, St. Anne-St. Augustin, Manchester
Turner, John R., (Retired)
Veneman, Steve, Resurrection, Nashua
Wheeler, Raymond A., St. Joseph the Worker, Nashua
Wilton, James P., Corpus Christi Parish, Portsmouth.

INSTITUTIONS LOCATED IN DIOCESE

[A] SEMINARIES, RELIGIOUS OR SCHOLASTICATES

MANCHESTER. *St. Anselm Abbey Seminary*, 100 St. Anselm Dr., 03102. Tel: 603-641-7652; Fax: 603-641-7267; Email: webmaster@anselm.edu; Web: www.anselm.edu. Rt. Rev. Mark A. Cooper, O.S.B. Order of St. Benedict.

[B] COLLEGES AND UNIVERSITIES

MANCHESTER. *Saint Anselm College*, 100 St. Anselm Dr., 03102. Tel: 603-641-7000; Fax: 603-641-7284; Email: sdisalvo@anselm.edu; Web: www.anselm.edu. Steven DiSalvo, Ph.D., Pres. Admin. & Faculty; Rt. Rev. Mark A. Cooper, O.S.B., Chancellor. Order of St. Benedict. Brothers 2; Religious Teachers 1; Lay Teachers 233; Priests 5; Students 1,964.

MERRIMACK. *The Thomas More College of Liberal Arts* (1978) 6 Manchester St., Merrimack, 03054. Tel: 603-880-8308; Fax: 603-880-9280; Email: mschneider@thomasmorecollege.edu; Web: www.thomasmorecollege.edu. William E. Fahey, Ph.D., Pres. Religious Teachers 1; Priests 6; Students 95; Total Staff 25.

NASHUA. *Rivier University* (1933) 420 S. Main St., Nashua, 03060-5086. Tel: 603-888-1311; Tel: 603-897-8202; Fax: 603-897-8812; Email: jhparker@rivier.edu; Email: dtilders@rivier.edu; Web: www.rivier.edu. Sr. Paula Marie Buley, I.H.M., Pres.; Bro. Paul R. Demers, S.C., Chap.; Daniel Speidel, Dir. of Library. Sisters of the Presentation of Mary. Religious Teachers 2; Lay Teachers 64; Sisters 10; Students 2,400.

WARNER. *Northeast Catholic College* (1973) 511 Kearsarge Mountain Rd., Warner, 03278-9206. Tel: 603-456-2656; Fax: 603-456-2660; Email: administration@northeastcatholic.edu; Web: www.northeastcatholic.edu. George A. Harne, Pres.; R. Daniel Peterson, COO; Brian FitzGerald, Dean; Marie Lasher, Librarian. Religious Teachers 2; Lay Teachers 15; Students 72; Total Staff 26.

[C] HIGH SCHOOLS, DIOCESAN

MANCHESTER. *Trinity High School*, 581 Bridge St., 03104-5395. Tel: 603-668-2910; Fax: 603-668-2913; Email: webmaster@trinity-hs.org; Web: www.trinity-hs.org. Steven Gadecki, Prin. Lay Teachers 34; Students 368.

CONCORD. *Bishop Brady High School*, 25 Columbus Ave., Concord, 03301. Tel: 603-224-7418; Fax: 603-228-6664; Email: info@bishopbrady.edu; Web: www.bishopbrady.edu. Andrea Elliot, Prin.; Michael Ling, Vice Prin.; Keith Bergeron, Dean of Students; Linda Fairbanks, Campus Min. Lay Teachers 33; Students 310.

DOVER. *St. Thomas Aquinas High School* (1960) 197 Dover Point Rd., Dover, 03820. Tel: 603-742-3206; Fax: 603-749-7822; Email: sta@stalux.org; Web: www.stalux.org. Kevin Collins, Prin. Lay Teachers 36; Students 432.

[D] HIGH SCHOOLS, PRIVATE

NASHUA. *Bishop Guertin High School* (1963) 194 Lund Rd., Nashua, 03060. Tel: 603-889-4107; Fax: 603-889-0701; Email: brodeurl@bghs.org; Email: strnistej@bghs.org; Web: www.bghs.org. Linda Brodeur, Pres.; Jason Strniste, Prin.; Bro. Paul Demers, S.C., Chap. Brothers of the Sacred Heart.(Coed) Brothers 5; Lay Teachers 70; Students 805.

SUNAPEE. *Mount Royal Academy*, (Grades PreK-12), 26 Seven Hearths Ln., P.O. Box 362, Sunapee, 03782. Tel: 603-763-9010; Fax: 603-763-5390; Email: dtremblay@mountroyalacademy.com; Web: www.mountroyalacademy.com. Derek Tremblay, Headmaster. Lay Teachers 22.

[E] REGIONAL AND PAROCHIAL ELEMENTARY SCHOOLS

MANCHESTER. *St. Benedict Academy* (1989) (Grades PreK-6), 85 Third St., 03102. Tel: 603-669-3932; Fax: 603-669-3932; Email: officeadmin@st.benedictacademy.org; Web: stbenedictacademy.org. Heather Silveira. Lay Teachers 12; Students 119.

St. Casimir School, (Grades K-8), 456 Union St., 03103. Tel: 603-623-6411; Fax: 603-623-3236; Email: stcasimirnh@comcast.net; Web: www.stcasimirnh.org. Wanda Caraballo, Prin. Clergy 1; Lay Teachers 9; Sisters 1; Students 70.

St. Catherine School, (Grades PreK-6), 206 North St., 03104. Tel: 603-622-1711; Fax: 603-624-4935; Email: kmeehan@scsnh.com; Email: office@scsnh.com; Web: www.scsnh.com. Catherine Meehan, Prin. Lay Teachers 20; Sisters 1; Students 236.

St. Joseph Regional Junior High, (Grades 7-8), 148 Belmont St., 2nd Fl., 03103. Tel: 603-624-4811; Fax: 603-624-6670; Email: dmailloux@stjoesjrhs.org; Web: www.stjoesjrhs.org. Mr. Denis Mailloux, Prin. Lay Teachers 9; Students 96.

CONCORD. *St. John Regional School* (1888) (Grades PreK-8), 61 S. State St., Concord, 03301. Tel: 603-225-3222, Ext. 100; Fax: 603-225-0195; Email: mrdonohue@stjohnregional.org; Web: stjohnregional.org. Mr. Stephen Donohue, Prin. Lay Teachers 16; Students 189.

DERRY. *St. Thomas Aquinas School*, (Grades PreK-8), 3 Moody St., Derry, 03038. Tel: 603-432-2712; Fax: 603-432-2179; Email: schooloffice@staderry.com; Web: www.staderry.com. Patricia Berthiaume, Prin. Lay Teachers 11; Students 183.

DOVER. *St. Mary Academy*, (Grades PreK-8), 222 Central Ave., Dover, 03820. Tel: 603-742-3299; Fax: 603-743-3483; Email: mmckernan@stmaryacademy.org; Web: www.saintmaryacademy.org. Blake McGurty, Prin. Lay Teachers 21; Students 287.

HAMPTON. *Sacred Heart School* (1962) (Grades PreK-8), 289 Lafayette Rd., Hampton, 03842. Tel: 603-926-3254; Fax: 603-929-1109; Email: tmorinbailey@shshampton.org; Web: www.shshampton.org. Ms. Teresa Morin Bailey, Prin. Clergy 4; Lay Teachers 20; Students 195.

KEENE. *Saint Joseph Regional School* (1886) (Grades PreK-8), 92 Wilson St., Keene, 03431. Tel: 603-352-2720; Fax: 603-358-5465; Email: csmith@stjosephkeene.org; Web: stjosephkeene.org. Christopher D. Smith, Prin. & Contact. Religious Teachers 5; Deacons 1; Lay Teachers 21; Students 178.

LACONIA. *Holy Trinity School* dba Holy Trinity School of Laconia NH (1971) (Grades PreK-8), 50 Church St., Laconia, 03246. Tel: 603-524-3156; Fax: 603-524-4454; Email: fyoung@htsnh.org; Web: www.holytrinitynh.com. Francine Young, Prin. Lay Teachers 14; Students 70; Total Staff 12.

LITCHFIELD. *St. Francis of Assisi School*, (Grades PreSchool-6), 9 St. Francis Way, Litchfield, 03052-8050. Tel: 603-424-3312; Fax: 603-424-9128; Email: schwerdtm@stfrancisschoolnh.org. Mr. Mark Schwerdt, Prin. Lay Teachers 9; Students 129.

NASHUA. *St. Christopher School* (1963) (Grades PreK-6), 20 Cushing Ave., Nashua, 03064. Tel: 603-882-7442; Fax: 603-594-9253; Email: principal@stchrisschoolnh.org; Email: cclarke@stchrisschoolnh.org; Web: www.stchrisschoolnh.org. Ms. Cynthia Vita Clarke, Prin. Lay Teachers 22; Students 350.

Infant Jesus School (1909) (Grades PreK-6), 3 Crown St., Nashua, 03060. Tel: 603-889-2649; Fax: 603-594-9117; Email: veilleux@ijschool.org; Web: www.ijschool.org. Kelly Veilleux, Prin. Lay Teachers 12; Students 77.

Nashua Catholic Regional Junior High School (1972) (Grades 7-8), 6 Bartlett Ave., Nashua, 03064-1602. Tel: 603-883-6707; Tel: 603-882-7011; Fax: 603-594-8955; Email: gmcfadden@ncrjhs.net; Web: www.ncrjhs.org. Ms. Glenda L. McFadden, O.F.S., Prin. Lay Teachers 15; Students 136.

ROCHESTER. *St. Elizabeth Seton School* (1886) (Grades K-8), 16 Bridge St., Rochester, 03867. Tel: 603-332-4803; Fax: 603-332-2915; Email: suzanne.boutin@sesschool.org; Web: www.sesschool.org. Suzanne T. Boutin, Prin. Religious Teachers 1; Lay Teachers 10; Students 87.

SALEM. *St. Joseph Regional Catholic School* (1959) (Grades PreK-8), 40 Main St., Salem, 03079. Tel: 603-893-6811; Fax: 603-893-6811; Email: mainoffice@sjrcs.com; Web: stjosepheagles.org. Mrs. Mary Croteau, Prin. Lay Teachers 14; Students 125; Total Staff 25.

[F] ELEMENTARY SCHOOLS, PRIVATE

MANCHESTER. *St. Augustin Pre-School*, 251 Merrimack St., 03103. Tel: 603-623-8800; Fax: 603-626-1517; Email: sapreschool@comcast.net. Crystal Elie, Dir. Boys 15; Girls 30; Lay Teachers 8.

Holy Cross Early Childhood Center, 420 Island Pond Rd., 03109-4812. Tel: 603-668-0510; Email: holycrossecc@yahoo.com. Cindy Wallace, Dir. Lay Teachers 5; Sisters 2; Students 30.

Mount Saint Mary Academy, (Grades PreK-6), 2291 Elm St., 03104. Tel: 603-623-3155; Fax: 603-621-9254; Email: principal@mtstmary.org; Web: www.mtstmary.org. Kate Segal, Prin. Lay Teachers 16; Sisters 1; Students 132.

HUDSON. *Presentation of Mary Academy* (1926) (Grades PreK-8), 182 Lowell Rd., Hudson, 03051. Tel: 603-889-6054; Fax: 603-595-8504; Email: pmaprincipal@comcast.net; Web: www.pmaschool.org. Sr. Maria Rosa, P.M., Prin.; Mrs. Susan Glasheen, Librarian. Sisters of the Presentation of Mary. Religious Teachers 2; Lay Teachers 31; Students 472.

SUNAPEE. *Mount Royal Academy*, (Grades PreK-12), 26 Seven Hearths Ln., P.O. Box 362, Sunapee, 03782. Tel: 603-763-9010; Fax: 603-763-5390; Email: dtremblay@mountroyalacademy.com; Web: www.mountroyalacademy.com. Derek Tremblay, Headmaster. Lay Teachers 20; Students 190.

[G] CATHOLIC CHARITIES

MANCHESTER. *Catholic Charities Administration* aka New Hampshire Catholic Charities, 215 Myrtle St., 03104. Tel: 603-669-3030; Fax: 603-626-1252; Email: info@nh-cc.org; Web: www.nh-cc.org. Mr. Thomas E. Blonski, Pres. & CEO; Mr. David Hildenbrand, Vice Pres.; Ms. Dominique A. Rust, Vice Pres. & COO; Mr. David Twitchell, Vice Pres., Human Res.;SHRM-SCP;CCP;CBP; Mr. Alain Bernard, Asst. Vice Pres., Healthcare Services; Mr. Marc Cousineau, Dir. Parish and Community Svcs.; Bob Germain, Dir. Information Technology; Rosemary Hendrickx, Dir., Devel.; Steven Knight, M.B.A., M.A., Dir. Programs Quality and Initiatives; Eileen Groll Liponis, Dir.; Rev. John J. Mahoney Jr., J.C.L., M.A., L.C.M.H.C., Dir. Clinical & Family Svcs.; Mr. Michael McDonough, Dir.; Ms. Michal Waterman, Dir., Human Res.; Ms. Cathy Chesley, J.D., Ed.D., Dir. Immigration & Refugee Svcs.; Ms. Karen Moynihan, Dir. Tot Asst. Annually 139,582; Total Staff 921.

District Offices:.

151 Emery St., Berlin, 03570-0182. Tel: 603-752-1325; Fax: 603-752-6174; Email: berlin@nh-cc.org. Nicole Plourde, Admin. Mgr. & Parish Outreach Coord.

176 Loudon Rd., Concord, 03301-6025. Tel: 603-228-1108; Fax: 603-228-6025. Su McKinnon, M.Ed., Admin. Mgr. & Parish Outreach Coord.

161 Main St., Ste. 200, Keene, 03431-3722. Tel: 603-357-3093; Fax: 603-357-7810; Email: keene@nh-cc.org. Sr. Kathleen Haight, R.C.D., P.A., Admin. Mgr. & Parish Outreach Coord.

17 Gilford Ave, Laconia, 03246-2827. Tel: 603-528-3035; Fax: 603-524-7153; Email: laconia@nh-cc.org. Leonard B. Campbell, Admin. Mgr. & Parish Outreach Coord.

24 Hanover St., #8, Lebanon, 03766-1334. Tel: 603-448-5151; Fax: 603-448-5155. Mr. Marc Cousineau, Admin. Mgr. & Dir. of Parish and Community Svcs.

41 Cottage St., P.O. Box 323, Littleton, 03561-0323. Tel: 603-444-7727; Fax: 603-444-7728; Email: littleton@nh-cc.org. Ms. Janice MacKenzie, Admn. Mgr., Licensed Clinical Social Worker.

325 Franklin St., 03101-1999. Tel: 603-624-4717; Fax: 603-624-4736; Email: manchester@nh-cc.org.

261 Lake St., Nashua, 03060-4127. Tel: 603-889-9431; Fax: 603-880-4643; Email: nashua@nh-cc.org.

23 Grant St., Rochester, 03867-3001. Tel: 603-332-7701; Fax: 603-332-9629; Email: rochester@nh-cc.org.

95 Stiles Rd., Ste. 108, Salem, 03079-4808. Tel: 603-893-1971; Fax: 603-898-8661; Email: salem@nh-cc.org.

Other Programs:.

Healthcare Services, 215 Myrtle St., 03104. Tel: 603-641-0577; Fax: 603-641-6210; Email: kblain@nh-cc.org. Mr. Alain Bernard, Asst. Vice Pres. Tot Asst. Annually 920; Total Staff 727.

Immigration and Refugee Services, 3 Crown St., Nashua, 03060-4127. Tel: 603-889-9431; Fax: 603-880-4643; Email: kgeorge@nh-cc.org. Ms. Cathy Chesley, J.D., Ed.D., Dir. Immigration & Refugee Svcs. Legal and case management services for immigrants and refugees. Tot Asst. Annually 1,200; Total Staff 7.

New Hampshire Food Bank, 700 E. Industrial Park Dr., 03109. Tel: 603-669-9725; Fax: 603-669-0270; Email: info@nh-cc.org; Web: www.nhfoodbank.org. Eileen Groll Liponis, Dir. Statewide food distribution to soup kitchens, food pantries and direct service programs. Tot Asst. Annually 120,000; Total Staff 25.

Our Place, 16 Oak St., 03104-4319. Tel: 603-647-2244; Fax: 603-647-9933; Email: info@nh-cc.org. Karen A. Munsell, Admin. Mgr. & Social Worker. Services for pregnant and parenting teens. Tot Asst. Annually 130; Total Staff 4.

Our Place, 3 Crown St., Nashua, 03060. Tel: 603-994-2699; Fax: 603-994-0287; Email: info@nh-cc.org. Karen Munsell, M.S.W., Contact Person. Tot Asst. Annually 15; Total Staff 2.

St. Charles Children's Home aka St. Charles School, 19 Grant St., Rochester, 03867-3001. Tel: 603-332-4768; Fax: 603-332-3948; Email: sma@stcharleshome.net. Sr. Mary Agnes Dombroski, Prog. Admin. School behavioral services Students 9; Total Staff 12.

Bishop Peterson Residence, 221 Orange St., 03104-4324. Tel: 603-641-6277; Fax: 603-641-0385; Email: bpr.marlene@nh-cc.org. Marlene Makowski, Admin. Tot Asst. Annually 15; Total Staff 21.

[H] CHILD CARE INSTITUTIONS

MANCHESTER. *St. Peter's Home* (1902) 300 Kelley St., 03102-3093. Tel: 603-625-9313; Fax: 603-625-1910; Email: sft@stpeterhome.com; Web: www.stpeterhome.com. Sr. Florence Therrien, S.C.S.H., Dir.; Mrs. Donna M. Vachon, Asst. Dir. Lay Teachers 50; Sisters of Charity (Grey Nuns) 1.

ALLENSTOWN. *Pine Haven Boys Center* (1963) 133 River Rd., P.O. Box 162, Allenstown, 03275. Tel: 603-485-7141; Email: paulriva68@hotmail.com; Web: www.pinehavenboyscenter.org. Rev. Paul Riva, C.R.S., Exec. Somascan Fathers.

ROCHESTER. *St. Charles Children's Home*, 19 Grant St., Rochester, 03867-3099. Tel: 603-332-4768; Fax: 603-332-3948; Email: sma@stcharleshome.net; Web: www.stcharleshome.org. Sr. Mary Agnes Dombroski, D.M.M.L., M.B.A., Admin. New Hampshire Catholic Charities. Sisters 2; Students 6.

[I] GENERAL HOSPITALS

MANCHESTER. *Catholic Medical Center*, 100 McGregor St., 03102. Tel: 603-668-3545; Fax: 603-663-6850; Email: carrie.perry@cmc-nh.org; Web: www.catholicmedicalcenter.org. Joseph Pepe, M.D., Pres. & CEO. Bed Capacity 330; Total Staff 2,535; Inpatient Admissions 12,332; Outpatient Admissions 174,788.

NASHUA. *St. Joseph Hospital*, 172 Kinsley St., Nashua, 03061. Tel: 603-882-3000; Fax: 603-889-1651; Email: dmoen@stjosephhospital.com; Web: www.stjosephhospital.com. John Jurczyk, Pres.; Kathleen Rice-Orshak. Sponsored by Covenant Health Inc., Tewksbury, MA. Bed Capacity 208; Tot Asst. Annually 186,130; Total Staff 1,247.

[J] HEALTH CARE FACILITIES

MANCHESTER. *Holy Cross Health Center, Inc.* (1984) 357 Island Pond Rd., 03109-4811. Tel: 603-628-3550; Fax: 603-626-6270; Email: swojtriewicz@holycrosshc.org. Scott Wojtkiewicz, N.H.A., Admin. Nursing home for women religious, managed by Sisters of Holy Cross.

St. Joseph Residence (1980) 495 Mammoth Rd., 03104-5463. Tel: 603-668-6011; Fax: 603-647-6648; Email: MJMakowski@presmarynh.org. Marlene Makowski, Admin. Sponsored by the Presentation of Mary Sisters.A Managed Home of New Hampshire Catholic Charities. Bed Capacity 22; Tot Asst. Annually 38; Total Staff 65; Resident Care 18.

Mt. Carmel Rehabilitation and Nursing Center, 235 Myrtle St., 03104-4314. Tel: 603-627-3811; Fax: 603-626-4696; Email: jbohunicky@nh-cc.org. Joe Bohunicky, Admin. New Hampshire Catholic Charities. Bed Capacity 120; Tot Asst. Annually 362; Total Staff 175.

St. Teresa Rehabilitation and Nursing Center (1948) 519 Bridge St., 03104-5337. Tel: 603-668-2373; Fax: 603-668-0059; Email: stt.administrator@nh-cc.org. Luanne Rogers, Admin. New Hampshire Catholic Charities Bed Capacity 51; Tot Asst. Annually 199; Total Staff 86.

Bishop Primeau Senior Living Community (1986) Tel: 603-668-2373; Fax: 603-668-0059. Linda Illg, Apartment Mgr. Bed Capacity 25; Tot Asst. Annually 34; Total Staff 3.

BERLIN. *St. Vincent de Paul Rehabilitation and Nursing Center*, 29 Providence Ave., Berlin, 03570-3130. Tel: 603-752-1820; Fax: 603-752-7149; Email: stv.administrator@nh-cc.org. Jeff Lacroix, Admin. New Hampshire Catholic Charities. Bed Capacity 80; Residents 80; Tot Asst. Annually 137.

DOVER. *St. Ann Rehabilitation and Nursing Center* (1958) 195 Dover Point Rd., Dover, 03820-4693. Tel: 603-742-2612; Fax: 603-743-3055; Email: sta.administrator@nh-cc.org. Rev. Donald McAllister, Chap., (Retired). New Hampshire Catholic Charities. Bed Capacity 54; Tot Asst. Annually 249; Total Staff 80.

Bishop Gendron Senior Living Community (1999) Tel: 603-742-2612; Fax: 603-743-3055. Kathleen Stillwell, Apartment Mgr. Bed Capacity 31; Tot Asst. Annually 43; Total Staff 2.

JAFFREY. *Good Shepherd Rehabilitation and Nursing Center*, 20 Plantation Dr., Jaffrey, 03452-6631. Tel: 603-532-8762; Fax: 603-593-0006; Email: gsh.administrator@nh-cc.org. Barbara Wilkins, Admin. New Hampshire Catholic Charities. Bed Capacity 83; Tot Asst. Annually 102; Total Staff 95.

LACONIA. *Bishop Bradley Senior Living Community*, 406 Court St., Laconia, 03246. Tel: 603-524-0466; Fax: 603-527-0884; Email: stf.administrator@nh-cc.org. Deb Sturgeon, Apartment Mgr. Bed Capacity 25; Tot Asst. Annually 29; Apartments 25.

St. Francis Rehabilitation and Nursing Center (1948) 406 Court St., Laconia, 03246-3600. Tel: 603-524-0466; Fax: 603-527-0884; Email: stf.administrator@nh-cc.org. Brenda Buttrick, RNC, NHA, Admin. New Hampshire Catholic Charities. Bed Capacity 51; Tot Asst. Annually 141; Total Staff 87.

*Bishop Bradley Senior Living Community*Total Staff 4; Apartments 25.

WINDHAM. *Warde Rehabilitation & Nursing Center*, 21 Searles Rd., P.O. Box 420, Windham, 03087-1203. Tel: 603-890-1290; Fax: 603-890-1293; Email: whc.administrator@nh-cc.org. Bret Pomeroy, Admin. Owned by New Hampshire Catholic Charities. Bed Capacity 32; Tot Asst. Annually 130; Total Staff 86; Assisted Living 36.

[K] MONASTERIES AND RESIDENCES OF PRIESTS AND BROTHERS

MANCHESTER. *St. Anselm Abbey* Of the Order of St. Benedict including Seminary and Formation Program 100 St. Anselm Dr., 03102. Tel: 603-641-7652; Email: abbey@anselm.edu; Web: www.saintanselmabbey.org. Rt. Rev. Mark A. Cooper, O.S.B., Abbot & Chancellor.

CENTER HARBOR. *L.C. Center Harbor, Inc.*, 109 Dane Rd., P.O. Box 936, Center Harbor, 03226. Tel: 603-253-7728; Fax: 603-253-8740; Email: jbudke@legionaries.org. Rev. Lino Otero, Sec. & Treas.

COLEBROOK. *Shrine of Our Lady of Grace*, P.O. Box 35, Colebrook, 03576. 60 Wyman St., Lowell, MA 01852. Rev. James Chambers, Treas. Oblates of Mary Immaculate (United States Province).

ENFIELD. *Shrine of Our Lady of La Salette*, 410 N.H. Rte. 4A, P.O. Box 420, Enfield, 03748-0420. Tel: 603-632-4301 (Gift Shop); Tel: 603-632-7087 (Business); Fax: 603-632-7648; Email: lasalette-enfield@comcast.net; Web: www.lasaletteofenfield.org. Revs. Joseph Gosselin, Supr.; John Sullivan, M.S., Shrine Dir.; Bros. David Carignan, M.S., Chap.; Raymond M. Tetreault, M.S.

La Salette of Enfield, Inc. Brothers 2; Priests 2; Total Staff 13.

HANOVER. *Order of Preachers*, St. Thomas Aquinas House, 2 Occom Ridge, P.O. Box 147, Hanover, 03755. Tel: 603-643-2154; Fax: 603-543-9411; Email: AQ@Dartmouth.edu. Revs. D. Brendan Murphy, O.P.; Brian Mulcahy, O.P.

NASHUA. *Brothers of the Sacred Heart*, 196 Lund Rd., Nashua, 03060. Tel: 603-883-3683; Email: unitedstatesprovince@gmail.com. Bros. Laurent Beaunoyer, S.C., Dir.; Paul R. Demers, S.C.; Ralph Lebel, S.C.; Bertrand Ouellette, S.C.; Gerald Provencher, S.C.; Normand Roux, S.C.; Donald Tardif, S.C. Brothers 7.

[L] CONVENTS AND RESIDENCES OF SISTERS

MANCHESTER. *Monastery of the Precious Blood* (1898) 700 Bridge St., 03104-5495. Tel: 603-623-4264; Fax: 603-647-8385; Email: superior@srspreciousbloodnh.org. Sr. Mary Clare, A.P.B., Supr.; Rev. Adrien R. Longchamps, Chap. Sisters Adorers of the Precious Blood. Sisters 25.

Missionary Rosebushes of St. Theresa (1922) 700 Bridge St., 03104-5495. Tel: 603-623-4264; Fax: 603-647-8385; Email: superior@srspreciousbloodnh.org. Sr. Mary Clare Bergeron, Supr.

Sisters of Holy Cross, No. American Region / U.S. Sector Office, 365 Island Pond Rd., 03109. Tel: 603-622-9504; Fax: 603-622-9782; Email: dydupere@srsofholycross.com; Web: sistersofholycross.org. Sr. Diane Dupere, C.S.C., Sector Leader. Total Staff 10.

136 Lynwood Ln., 03109.

113 Wedgewood Ln., 03109.

Fairview Rd., R.R. 1, Pittsfield, 03263.

5 Crosswoods Path Blvd., #13, Merrimack, 03054.

9 Crosswoods Path Blvd., #B3, Merrimack, 03054.

11 Crosswoods Path Blvd., #11 & #12, Merrimack, 03054.

St. George Manor / Holy Cross Health Center, 357 Island Pond Rd., 03109. Tel: 603-624-4557; Fax: 603-645-1516; Email: dydupere@srsofholycross.com. Sisters Marguerite Marie Fortier, C.S.C., Co-Animator; Lorraine G. Choiniere, C.S.C., Co-Animator. Sisters 37.

Sisters of the Presentation of Mary, 495 Mammoth Rd., 03104-5494. Tel: 603-669-1080; Fax: 603-222-2333; Email: pmtreasurer209@gmail.com; Web: www.presentationofmary-usa.org. Sr. Annette Laliberte, P.M., Treas. Sisters 53. *St. Joseph Residence* (1980) 495 Mammoth Rd., 03104-5494. Tel: 603-627-5831; Tel: 603-668-6011; Email: pmtreasurer209@gmail.com. Sisters Lorraine Letourneau, Supr.; Cecile Plasse, Supr. Sisters 37.

St. Marie Residence (1959) 495 Mammoth Rd., 03104-5494. Tel: 603-623-0671; Email: stemarieres@yahoo.com. Sr. Estelle Leveillee, Supr. Sisters 11. *Presentation of Mary Academy*

(1926) 182 Lowell Rd., Hudson, 03051-4987.
Tel: 603-883-8192; Fax: 603-595-5646; Email: pmtreasurer209@gmail.com. Sr. Jacqueline Levreault, Supr. Sisters 7. *Presentation of Mary House of Formation*, 186 Lowell Rd., Hudson, 03051-4908. Tel: 603-882-1347; Email: camiremargaret@hotmail.com. Sr. Margaret Camire, Supr. Sisters 5. *Our Lady of Hope House of Prayer* (1990) 400 Temple Rd., New Ipswich, 03071. Tel: 603-878-2346; Fax: 603-878-4552; Email: olhope1@yahoo.com; Web: ourladyhope.org. Sr. Rita Pay, P.M., Supr. Sisters 4. *Holy Angels Convent* (1996) 6 Atkinson Depot Rd., Plaistow, 03865. Tel: 603-382-2744; Email: shollypm@gmail.com. Sr. Holly Gauthier, Supr. Sisters 2.

CONCORD. *Monastery of Discalced Carmelites* (1946) 275 Pleasant St., Concord, 03301-2590.
Tel: 603-225-5791; Email: sisters@concordcarmel.org. Sr. Claudette M. Blais, O.C.D., Prioress. Novices 1; Professed Sisters 9.

LITTLETON. *Daughters of the Charity of the Sacred Heart of Jesus*, Provincial House, 226 Grove St., Littleton, 03561. Tel: 603-444-5346;
Fax: 603-444-5348; Web: www.fcscj.org. Sr. Bonita Cote, F.C.S.C.J., Supr. Sisters 24.

NEW IPSWICH. *Our Lady of Hope House of Prayer*, 400 Temple Rd., New Ipswich, 03071.
Tel: 603-878-2346; Fax: 603-878-4552; Email: olhope1@yahoo.com; Web: ourladyhope.org. Sr. Rita Pay, P.M., Local Supr. Sisters 4.

NASHUA. *Holy Infant Jesus Convent*, 3 Crown St., Nashua, 03060-6366. Tel: 603-882-0553; Email: lorrainecsc41@gmail.com. Rev. Msgr. Eddy N. Bisson, Admin. Sisters 5.

Sisters of Mercy of the Americas-Northeast Community, Inc., Life & Ministry Office, 11 Trafalgar Sq., Ste. 203, Nashua, 03063.
Tel: 603-402-2883; Fax: 603-589-9305; Email: tharris@mercyne.org. Sisters Rosemary Burnham, Local Coord.; Cecelia Ferland, Local Coord. Sisters 72.

Mount St. Mary Academy, Inc., 2291 Elm St., 03104. Tel: 603-623-3155; Fax: 603-621-9254; Email: ksegalk@mtstmary.org. Kate Segal, Prin.

Frances Warde House, 21 Searles Rd., P.O. Box 420, Windham, 03087. Tel: 603-893-6550;
Tel: 603-641-2163; Fax: 603-893-2413;
Fax: 603-641-1063; Email: mfastnacht@nh-cc.org. Bret Pomeroy, Admin.

McAuley Commons, 37 Searles Rd., #207, Windham, 03087. Tel: 603-641-2163;
Fax: 603-641-1063; Email: fmckone@mercyne.org. Sr. Mary Flatley, Res.

[M] ASSOCIATIONS OF THE CHRISTIAN FAITHFUL

ROCHESTER. **Daughters of Mary, Mother of Healing Love*, 19 Grant St., Rochester, 03867.
Tel: 603-332-4768; Fax: 603-332-3948; Email: srmaryrose@hrsl.org; Web: www.motherofhealinglove.org. Mother Paul Marie Santa Lucia, Supr. (Private Association of the Christian Faithful).

[N] RETREAT HOUSES

ENFIELD. *Shrine of Our Lady of La Salette*, 417 N.H. Rte. 4A, P.O. Box 420, Enfield, 03748.
Tel: 603-632-7087 (Business);
Tel: 603-632-4301 (Gift Shop); Fax: 603-632-7648; Email: lasalette-enfield@comcast.net; Web: www.lasaletteofenfield.org. Revs. Joseph Gosselin, Supr.; John Sullivan, M.S., Shrine Dir.; Bros. David J. Carignan, M.S.; Raymond M. Tetreault, M.S.
La Salette of Enfield, Inc Brothers 3; Priests 1; Total Staff 13.

PITTSFIELD. .

[O] CAMPUS MINISTRY AND NEWMAN CENTERS

DURHAM. *St. Thomas More Catholic Student Center at the University of New Hampshire*, 6 Madbury Rd., P.O. Box 620, Durham, 03824-0620.
Tel: 603-868-2666; Fax: 603-868-3765; Email: stmdurham@comcast.net. Very Rev. Andrew W. Cryans, Chap.; Colleen O'Leary, Campus Min.; Roberta MacBride, Pastoral Asst.

HANOVER. **The Catholic Student Center at Dartmouth, Aquinas House, Aquinas at Dartmouth, Inc.* (1953) 2 Occom Ridge, P.O. Box 147, Hanover, 03755.
Tel: 603-643-2154; Fax: 603-643-9411; Email: brendan.joseph.murphy@dartmouth.edu; Web: www.dartmouthcatholic.com. Rev. D. Brendan Murphy, O.P., Chap. Total Staff 2; Total Priests in Residence 2.

KEENE. *Catholic Newman Center for Keene State College*, 161 Main St., Ste. 11, Keene, 03431.
Tel: 603-357-1444; Fax: 603-352-7472; Email: director@newmancenterkeene.com. Cynthia Cheshire, Campus Min.

PLYMOUTH. *Plymouth State University Catholic Campus Ministry*, Plymouth State University, 19 Highland Ave., Ste. A6, Plymouth, 03264.
Tel: 603-535-2673; Email: kmtardif@plymouth.edu. Katherine Tardif, Dir., Campus Ministry, Tel: 603-535-2673.

[P] SPECIAL APOSTOLATE CENTERS

KEENE. *Catholic Faith Formation Center*, 161 Main St., Ste. 118, Keene, 03431. Tel: 603-352-7662;
Fax: 603-352-7662; Email: cffc.keene@gmail.com. Ann Ball, Contact Person.

[Q] CAMPS AND COMMUNITY CENTERS

EFFINGHAM. *Camp Marist* (1949) 22 Abel Blvd., Effingham, 03882. Tel: 603-539-4552;
Fax: 603-539-8318; Email: office@campmarist.org; Web: www.campmarist.org. Vincent Gschlecht, Summer Camp Dir. Total Staff 100; Total Assisted 250.

GILMANTON IRON WORKS. *Camp Bernadette (Girls)* (1953) 83 Richards Rd., Wolfeboro, 03894. 32 Fatima Rd., Gilmanton Iron Works, 03837.
Tel: 603-364-5851; Fax: 603-364-5038; Email: mdrumm@bfcamp.com; Web: www.bfcamp.com. Most Rev. Peter A. Libasci, D.D., Bd. Chm.; Mr. Michael Drumm, Dir. Religious Teachers 2; Students 1,000; Total Staff 80.

Summer Business Office for Camp Bernadette, 83 Richards Rd., Wolfeboro, 03894. Tel: 603-569-1692 ; Fax: 603-569-2560; Email: info@bfcamp.com; Web: www.bfcamp.com. 32 Fatima Rd., Gilmanton Iron Works, 03837. Mr. Michael Drumm, Dir. Clergy 2; Students 1,080; Total Staff 80; Total Assisted 1,080.

Camp Fatima (1949) (Boys) Business Office, 32 Fatima Rd., Gilmanton Iron Works, 03837.
Tel: 603-364-5851; Fax: 603-364-5038; Email: mdrumm@bfcamp.com; Web: www.bfcamp.com. Most Rev. Peter A. Libasci, D.D., Bd. Chm.; Mr. Michael Drumm, Dir. Religious Teachers 2; Students 1,100; Total Staff 80.

[R] MISCELLANEOUS

MANCHESTER. *Bishop's Charitable Assistance Fund* (2002) 153 Ash St., 03104. Tel: 603-669-3100;
Fax: 603-669-0377; Email: menglish@rcbm.org. Melanie P. English, Contact Person.

Catholic Lawyers Guild of New Hampshire, Inc., 153 Ash St., 03105. Tel: 603-410-1704; Email: rdunn@devinemillimet.com. Robert Dunn Jr., Pres.

CMC Healthcare System, 100 McGregor St., 03102.
Tel: 603-668-3545; Fax: 603-663-8850; Email: dorothy.welsh@cmc-nh.org. Joseph Pepe, M.D., Pres.

Catholic Medical Center, Tel: 603-668-3545;
Fax: 603-663-6850.

Alliance Ambulatory Services, Inc., 100 McGregor St., 03102. Tel: 603-668-3545; Fax: 603-663-6850; Email: dorothy.welsh@cmc-nh.org. Joseph Pepe, M.D., Pres. & CEO.

Alliance Resources Inc., 100 McGregor St., 03102.
Tel: 603-668-3545; Tel: 608-663-6850; Email: dorothy.welsh@cmc-nh.org. Joseph Pepe, M.D., Pres. & CEO.

St. Peter's Home, 300 Kelly St., 03102.
Tel: 603-669-1219; Email: lisa_stpeters@hotmail.com; Web: www.stpetershome.com. Sr. Florence Therrien, S.C.S.H., Contact Person.

Diocesan Cemetery Office, 153 Ash St., P.O. Box 310, 03105. Tel: 603-669-3100; Fax: 603-669-0377; Email: dgabert@rcbm.org. Mr. David A. Gabert, Dir.

St. Patrick Cemetery, Merrimack Rd., Amherst, 03031. Tel: 603-673-1311; Tel: 603-672-1254;
Fax: 603-673-3687; Email: diane.st.patoffice@gmail.com. Jerry Guthrie, Contact Person.

St. Joseph Cemetery, Rte. 302, Bartlett, 03812.
Tel: 603-356-2535; Fax: 603-356-2877; Email: ourladynh@myfairpoint.net. Louise Michaud, Business Mgr.

St. Joseph Cemetery, Monroe Rd., Bath, 03740.
Tel: 603-747-2038; Fax: 603-747-8071; Email: stjoseph_church@yahoo.com. Rev. Maria Susairaj.

St. Joseph Cemetery, 448 Donald St., Bedford, 03110. Tel: 603-622-9522; Fax: 603-644-0770; Email: director@stjcem.org. Rick Welsh, Dir.

St. Hedwig Cemetery, Old Bedford Rd., Bedford, 03110. Tel: 603-623-4835;
Fax: 603-623-4835 (Call first); Email: stcasimirnh@comcast.net. Eleanor Felch, Contact Person.

Mount Calvary Cemetery, Old Stagecoach Rd., Bennington, 03442. Tel: 603-924-7647;
Fax: 603-924-8365; Email: divinemercynh@comcast.net. Brenda Wesoly, Business Mgr.

Calvary Cemetery, E. Milan Rd., Berlin, 03570.
Tel: 603-752-2880; Fax: 603-752-1855; Email: bgoudreau@berlingorhamcatholics.org. Bridget Goudreau, Sec.

St. Anne Cemetery, E. Milan Rd., Berlin, 03570.
Tel: 603-752-2880; Fax: 603-752-1855; Email: bgoudreau@berlingorhamcatholics.org. Bridget Goudreau, Sec.

St. Kieran Cemetery, E. Milan Rd., Berlin, 03570.
Tel: 603-752-2880; Fax: 603-752-1855; Email: bgoudreau@berlingorhamcatholics.org. Bridget Goudreau, Sec.

Mount Calvary Cemetery, Cates Hill Rd., Berlin, 03570. Tel: 603-752-2880; Fax: 603-752-1855; Email: bgoudreau@berlingorhamcatholics.org. Bridget Goudreau, Sec.

Old St. Rose of Lima Cemetery, Brook Rd., Bethlehem, 03574. Tel: 603-444-2593;
Fax: 603-444-3126; Email: srlandols@gmail.com. Very Rev. Mark E. Dollard.

St. Margaret Cemetery, St. Margaret's Rd. (off Rte. 3), Carroll, 03598. Tel: 603-788-2083;
Fax: 603-788-5553 (Call first); Email: bgoudreau@berlingorhamcatholics.org. Bridget Goudreau, Sec.

St. Catherine Cemetery, S. West St., Charlestown, 03603. Tel: 603-826-3359; Fax: 603-826-5875; Email: allsaints3@comcast.net. Rev. John B. Loughnane.

St. Mary Cemetery, Plains Rd., Claremont, 03743.
Tel: 603-542-9518; Fax: 603-542-9614; Email: stmarysclaremont@comcast.net. Very Rev. Shawn M. Therrien, M.A.

St. Brendan Cemetery, S. Main St., Colebrook, 03576. Fax: 603-237-8580; Tel: 603-237-4342; Email: frcheneynamp@myfairpoint.net. Edward Poulin, Contact Person.

St. Charles Cemetery, Old Rochester Rd., Dover, 03822. Tel: 603-742-4837; Fax: 603-749-6779; Email: cemeteries@assumptiondovernh.org. Angela Fahy, Contact Person.

St. Mary Cemetery, Dover Point Rd., Dover, 03822.
Tel: 603-742-4837; Fax: 603-749-6779; Email: cemeteries@assumptiondovernh.org. Angela Fahy, Contact Person.

St. Peter Cemetery (Walpole) Rte. 123, Walpole, 03604. Tel: 603-826-3359; Fax: 603-826-5875; Email: allsaints3@comcast.net. Rev. John B. Loughnane.

St. Joseph Cemetery, Rte. 27, Epping, 03042.
Tel: 603-679-8805; Fax: 603-679-5192; Email: nh337@comcast.net. Mike Kappler, Contact Person.

St. Pius Forest Lawn Cemetery, Main St., Errol, 03579. Tel: 603-237-4342; Fax: 603-237-8580; Email: frcheneynamp@myfairpoint.net. Louise Cote, Contact Person.

Holy Cross Cemetery, 1 Carr St., Franklin, 03235.
Tel: 603-934-5013; Fax: 603-934-3469; Email: office@stgabrielnh.org. Claire Connify, Sec.

Mount Calvary Cemetery, Cemetery Rd. (Gonic), Rochester, 03839. Tel: 603-332-1863;
Fax: 603-330-0865; Email: nhamann@hrsl.org. Norbert Hamann, Contact Person.

Holy Family Cemetery, 9 Church St., Gorham, 03581. Tel: 603-752-2880; Fax: 603-752-1855; Email: bgoudreau@berlingorhamcatholics.org. Bridget Goudreau, Sec.

St. Francis Xavier Cemetery, Brown Rd., Groveton, 03582. Tel: 603-636-1047; Fax: 603-636-2549; Email: deveau.d.r@gmail.com. Rev. Daniel R. Deveau.

St. Denis, Nelson Rd., Harrisville, 03450.
Tel: 603-924-7647; Fax: 603-924-8365; Email: divinemercynh@comcast.net. Brenda Wesoly, Sec.

St. Mary Cemetery, Center Rd., Hillsborough, 03244-0729. Tel: 603-848-7829; Tel: 603-464-5565;
Fax: 603-428-4479; Email: office@StTheresaChurch.comcastbiz.net. Keith Wing Sr., Contact Person.

St. Joseph Cemetery, Plain Rd., Hinsdale, 03451.
Tel: 603-336-7090; Tel: 603-352-3525;
Fax: 603-352-7472; Email: holyspirit.peace@gmail.com. Mike Abbott, Contact Person.

Holy Rosary Cemetery, 21 Main St., Hooksett, 03106. Tel: 603-485-3523; Fax: 603-485-8435; Email: hrparishhook@comcast.net. Rev. Edmund G. Crowley.

Holy Cross Cemetery, Ledge Rd., Hudson, 03051.
Tel: 603-881-8131; Fax: 603-557-9817; Email: mmgray@stpatricksnashua.org. Margaret Gray, Sec.

St. Patrick Cemetery, Derry Rd., Hudson, 03051.
Tel: 603-881-8131; Fax: 603-577-9817; Email: mmgray@stpatricksnashua.org. Margaret Gray, Contact Person.

St. Patrick Cemetery, Hillcrest Rd., Jaffrey, 03452.
Tel: 603-532-6634; Tel: 603-532-6484;
Fax: 603-532-6633; Email: stpatric@myfairpoint.net. Marc Cournoyer, Contact Person.

St. Joseph Cemetery, 600 Main St., Keene, 03435.
Tel: 603-352-3525; Fax: 603-352-7472; Email: holyspirit.peace@gmail.com. Ms. Noreen Swymer, Sec.

Sacred Heart Cemetery, Garfield St., Laconia,

03247. Tel: 603-524-9609; Fax: 603-524-9620; Email: corylj88@yahoo.com. Cory Johnson, Contact Person.

St. Lambert Cemetery, Province St., Laconia, 03247. Tel: 603-524-9609; Fax: 603-524-9620; Email: corylj88@yahoo.com. Cory Johnson, Contact Person.

All Saints Cemetery, Water St., Lancaster, 03584. Tel: 603-788-2083; Fax: 603-788-5553; Email: gateofheavennh@aol.com. Kathi Marshall, Sec.

Calvary Cemetery, 378 N. Main St., Lancaster, 03584. Tel: 603-788-2083; Fax: 603-788-5553; Email: gateofheavennh@aol.com. Kathi Marshall, Sec.

New St. Rose of Lima Cemetery, W. Main St., Littleton, 03561. Tel: 603-444-2593; Fax: 603-444-3126; Email: srlandols@gmail.com. Very Rev. Mark E. Dollard.

Holy Cross Cemetery, Gilcrest Rd., Londonderry, 03053. Tel: 603-622-3215; Fax: 603-624-8638; Email: kccody@mtcalvarycem.org. Rev. Kevin W. Cody, Dir.

St. Augustine Cemetery, S. Beech St., 03103. Tel: 603-860-0386; Fax: 603-626-1517; Email: cornerstone.kr@comcast.net; Email: sta.sta@stannestaug.org. Keith Racine, Contact Person.

Mount Calvary Cemetery, 474 Goffstown Rd., 03102. Tel: 603-622-3215; Fax: 603-624-8638; Email: kccody@mtcalvarycem.org. Rev. Kevin W. Cody, Admin.

Mount Calvary Cemetery, (End of) Ling St., Marlborough, 03455. Tel: 603-352-3525; Fax: 603-352-7472; Email: holyspirit.peace@gmail.com. Ms. Noreen Swymer, Sec.

St. Louis de Gonzaga Cemetery, 752 W. Hollis St., Nashua, 03064. Tel: 603-886-1302; Fax: 603-886-5361; Email: cemetery@stlouisnashua.org. Donna Pratt, Contact Person.

St. Francis Xavier Cemetery, 32 Pine Hill Rd., Nashua, 03064. Tel: 603-886-1302; Fax: 603-886-5361; Email: cemetery@stlouisnashua.org. Donna Pratt, Contact Person.

St. Stanislaus Cemetery, 61 Pine Hill Rd., Nashua, 03064. Tel: 603-886-1302; Fax: 603-886-5361; Email: cemetery@stlouisnashua.org. Donna Pratt, Contact Person.

Sacred Heart of Jesus Cemetery, High St., New Ipswich, 03071. Tel: 603-878-1121; Fax: 603-878-1121; Email: sacredheartgreenvillenh@comcast.net. Kathy Caron, Sec.

Calvary Cemetery, Rte. 108, Newmarket, 03857. Tel: 603-659-3344; Fax: 603-659-3181; Email: info@kentandpelczarfh.com. Michael Pelczar, Admin.

St. Patrick Cemetery, Summer St., Newport, 03773. Tel: 603-863-1422; Fax: 603-863-7898; Email: office@saintpatrickparish.net. Rev. Michael R. Monette.

Our Lady of the Mountains Cemetery, Rte. 16, North Conway, 03860. Tel: 603-356-2535; Fax: 603-356-2877; Email: ourladynh@myfairpoint.net. Louise Michaud, Business Mgr.

Sacred Heart Cemetery, Rte. 3, North Stratford, 03590. Tel: 603-636-1047; Fax: 603-636-2549; Email: deveau.d.r@gmail.com. Rev. Daniel R. Deveau.

Calvary Cemetery, Village St. Rte. 3, Penacook, 03303. Tel: 603-753-4413 (Pastor); Tel: 603-230-3911 Burial Info; Concord; Email: pastor@icpenacook.org. Rev. Raymond J. Potvin.

St. Peter Churchyard Cemetery (old), 18 Vine St., Peterborough, 03458. Tel: 603-924-7647; Fax: 603-924-8365; Email: divinemercynh@comcast.net. Brenda Wesoly, Sec.

St. Peter Cemetery (new), High St., Peterborough, 03458. Tel: 603-924-7647; Fax: 603-924-8365; Email: divinemercynh@comcast.net. Brenda Wesoly, Sec.

Mount Calvary Cemetery, Norris Rd., Pittsfield, 03263. Tel: 603-435-6242; Fax: 603-435-9398; Email: ololstjoseph@metrocast.net. Rev. John B. MacKenzie.

Holy Angels Cemetery, 22 East Rd., Plaistow, 03865. Tel: 603-382-8324; Fax: 603-382-1113; Email: jtremblay@stluketheevangelist.net. Jackie Tremblay, Contact Person.

Calvary Cemetery, Intersection of Greenland Rd., Islington St. & Middle Rd., Portsmouth, 03804. Tel: 603-436-9239; Tel: 603-436-4555; Fax: 603-433-4401; Email: businessmgr.ccnh@gmail.com. Kate Gordon, Business Mgr.

St. Mary Cemetery, Intersection of Greenland Rd., Islington St. & Middle Rd., Portsmouth, 03804. Tel: 603-436-9239; Tel: 603-436-4555; Fax: 603-433-4401; Email: businessmgr.ccnh@gmail.com. Kate Gordon, Business Mgr.

Holy Rosary Cemetery, 133 Brook St., Rochester, 03839. Tel: 603-332-1863; Fax: 603-330-0865; Email: nhamann@hrsl.org. Norbert Hamann, Contact Person.

St. Mary's Cemetery, Lowell St., Rochester, 03839. Tel: 603-332-1863; Fax: 603-332-2040; Email: nhamann@hrsl.org. Norbert Hamann, Contact Person.

St. Patrick Cemetery, Silver St., Rollinsford, 03805. Tel: 603-692-0524; Tel: 603-692-2172; Fax: 603-692-2499; Email: r.stmartin@comcast.net. Sandy Libby, Sec.

Mount Calvary Cemetery, St. Anthony's Rd., Sanbornville, 03872. Tel: 603-522-3304; Fax: 603-522-8273; Email: stanthony239@gmail.com. Rev. Patrick N. Gilbert.

Holy Trinity Cemetery, 333 High St., Somersworth, 03878. Tel: 603-692-0524; Tel: 603-692-2172; Fax: 603-692-2499; Email: r.stmartin@comcast.net. Sandy Libby, Sec.

Mount Calvary Cemetery, Maple St., Somersworth, 03878. Tel: 603-692-2172; Tel: 603-692-0524; Fax: 603-692-2499; Email: r.stmartin@comcast.net. Sandy Libby, Sec.

St. John the Baptist Cemetery, River Rd., Suncook, 03275. Tel: 603-485-3113; Fax: 603-485-2113; Email: stjohnthebaptist@comcast.net. Michelle Petit, Contact Person.

St. John the Baptist Old Cemetery, Granite St. Ext., Suncook, 03275. Tel: 603-485-3113; Fax: 603-485-2113; Email: stjohnthebaptist@comcast.net. Michelle Petit, Contact Person.

St. John's Cemetery, Sanbornton Rd., Rte. 132, Tilton, 03299. Tel: 603-934-5013; Fax: 603-934-3469; Email: office@stgabrielnh.org. Claire Connifey, Sec.

Mount Carmel Cemetery, Marlborough Rd., Troy, 03465. Tel: 603-352-3525; Fax: 603-352-7472; Email: holyspirit.peace@gmail.com. Ms. Noreen Swymer, Sec.

St. Margaret Cemetery, St. Margaret Rd. (off Rte. 3), Carroll, 03595. Tel: 603-788-2083; Fax: 603-788-5533; Email: gateofheavennh@aol.com. Kathi Marshall, Sec.

St. Peter Cemetery (Drewsville) Rte. 123 Whitcomb Rd., Walpole, 03608. Tel: 603-826-3359; Fax: 603-826-5875; Email: allsaints3@comcast.net. Rev. John B. Loughnane.

St. Albert Cemetery, Rte. 3, West Stewartstown, 03597. Tel: 603-237-4342; Fax: 603-237-8580; Email: frcheneynamp@myfairpoint.net. Suzanne Madore, Contact Person.

St. Matthew Cemetery, Whitefield Rd., Whitefield, 03598. Tel: 603-788-2083; Fax: 603-788-5553; Email: gateofheavennh@aol.com. Kathi Marshall, Sec.

Mount Calvary Cemetery, Abbott Hill Rd., Wilton, 03086. Tel: 603-878-1121; Email: sacredheartgreenvillenh@comcast.net. Kathy Caron, Sec.

Diocesan Priest Retirement Plan and Trust, 153 Ash St., 03105. Tel: 603-669-3100; Email: webmaster@rcbm.org. Rolla Bryant, Contact Person.

Friends of Saint Patrick School Trust Fund, 153 Ash St., 03105-0310. Tel: 603-669-3100; Email: mbryant@rcbm.org. Rolla Bryant, Contact Person.

Friends of the St. Thomas Aquinas School Trust Fund c/o Roman Catholic Bishop of Manchester, a corporation sole 153 Ash St., 03104. Tel: 603-669-3100; Email: mbryant@rcbm.org; Web: www.catholicnh.org. Rolla Bryant, Contact Person.

Infant Jesus School Trust Fund c/o Roman Catholic Bishop of Manchester, a corporation sole 153 Ash St., 03104. Tel: 603-669-3100; Email: mbryant@rcbm.org; Web: www.catholicnh.org. Rolla Bryant, Contact Person.

The NH Guild for Catholic Healthcare Professionals, 153 Ash St., P.O. Box 4538, 03108-4538. Tel: 603-663-8706; Email: nancy.malo@cmc-nh.org. Nancy Malo, Pres.

Saint Jude Parish Capital Campaign Trust c/o Roman Catholic Bishop of Manchester, a corporation sole 153 Ash St., 03104. Tel: 603-669-3100; Email: mbryant@rcbm.org; Web: catholicnh.org. Rolla Bryant, Contact Person.

St. Thomas Aquinas High School Capital Campaign Trust Fund, 153 Ash St., 03105-0310. Tel: 603-669-3100; Email: mbryant@rcbm.org. Rolla Bryant, Contact Person.

St. Thomas Aquinas High School Tuition Endowment Trust Fund, 153 Ash St., 03105-0310. Tel: 603-669-3100; Email: mbryant@rcbm.org. Rolla Bryant, Contact Person.

Trinity High School Endowment Trust c/o Roman Catholic Bishop of Manchester, a corporation sole 153 Ash St., 03104. Tel: 603-669-3100; Email: mbryant@rcbm.org; Web: catholicnh.org. Rolla Bryant, Contact Person.

NASHUA. *Corpus Christi Food Pantry and Assistance, Inc.*, 3 Crown St., Nashua, 03060. Tel: 603-882-6372 (Pantry); Tel: 603-598-1641 (Assistance); Fax: 603-598-1640; Email: corpuschristifp@outlook.com; Web: www.corpuschristifoodpantry.org. Susan Dignan, Dir.

Marguerite's Place, 87 Palm St., Nashua, 03060. Tel: 603-598-1582; Fax: 603-598-7574; Email: balves@margueritesplace.org; Web: www.margueritesplace.org. Barbara A. Alves, CEO. Bed Capacity 30; Total Staff 17; Total Assisted 26.

RELIGIOUS INSTITUTES OF MEN REPRESENTED IN THE DIOCESE

For further details refer to the corresponding bracketed number in the Religious Institutes of Men or Women section.

[]—*Heralds of Good News-Mary Queen of Apostles Province*—H.G.N.

[0720]—*The Missionaries of Our Lady of La Salette* (Province for USA)—M.S.

[0470]—*Order of Friars Minor Capuchin Franciscans - Province of St. Mary of the Capuchin Order* (New York - New England)—O.F.M.Cap.

[0520]—*Order of Friars Minor Franciscan Friars* (Province of the Immaculate Conception)—O.F.M.

[]—*Order of Preachers* (Prov. of St. Joseph-Eastern Dominican Prov.)—O.P.

[0200]—*The Order of St. Benedict* (Saint Anselm Abbey)—O.S.B.

[]—*Legionaries of Christ-North American Territory*—L.C.

[]—*Province of the United States of the Brothers of the Sacred Heart*—S.C.

[]—*The Priestly Fraternity of St. Peter*—F.S.S.P.

[1070]—*Redemptorist Fathers* (Province of San Juan)—C.Ss.R.

[1250]—*Somascan Fathers U.S.A. Foundation*—C.R.S.

RELIGIOUS INSTITUTES OF WOMEN REPRESENTED IN THE DIOCESE

[]—*Congregation of the Sisters of St. Joseph of Boston*—C.S.J.

[0750]—*Daughters of the Charity of the Sacred Heart of Jesus*—F.C.S.C.J.

[0420]—*Discalced Carmelites Nuns*—O.C.D.

[1070-16]—*Dominican Sisters of Hope*—O.P.

[1170]—*Felician Sisters - Our Lady of Hope Province*—C.S.S.F.

[]—*Little Sisters of St. Francis*—O.S.F.

[3450]—*Religious of Jesus and Mary* (U.S. Province)—R.J.M.

[0110]—*Sisters Adorers of the Precious Blood*—A.P.B.

[0640]—*Sisters of Charity of St. Vincent De Paul, Halifax*—S.C.

[1930]—*Sisters of Holy Cross US Sector-North American Region*—C.S.C.

[2575]—*Sisters of Mercy of the Americas Northeast Community* (NH Area)—R.S.M.

[3000]—*Sisters of Notre Dame de Namur - US E.-W. Province*—S.N.D.deN.

[3310]—*Sisters of the Presentation of Mary*—P.M.

[]—*Sisters, Servants of the Immaculate Heart of Mary*—I.H.M.

NECROLOGY

† Boucher, Gerard A., (Retired), Died Dec. 28, 2018
† McHugh, Paul F., (Retired), Died Apr. 7, 2018
† Memolo, Rocco C., (Retired), Died Jun. 8, 2018
† Piwowar, Stanley J., (Retired), Died Mar. 20, 2018
† Polito, Victor V.J., (Retired), Died Jul. 5, 2018

Diocese of Marquette

(Dioecesis Marquettensis)

Most Reverend

JOHN F. DOERFLER

Bishop of Marquette; ordained July 13, 1991; appointed Bishop of Marquette; installed February 11, 2014. *Chancery: 1004 Harbor Hills Dr., Marquette, MI 49855.*

Most Reverend

JAMES H. GARLAND, M.A., M.S.W., D.D.

Retired Bishop of Marquette; ordained 1959; appointed Titular Bishop of Garriana and Auxiliary Bishop of Cincinnati June 2, 1984; consecrated July 25, 1984; appointed Bishop of Marquette October 6, 1992; installed November 11, 1992; retired December 13, 2005. *Res.: 300 Rock St., Marquette, MI 49855.* Tel: 906-225-1141.

Chancery: 1004 Harbor Hills Dr., Marquette, MI 49855. Tel: 906-225-1141; Fax: 906-225-0437.

Web: www.dioceseofmarquette.org

VICARIATE-APOSTOLIC JULY 29, 1853; DIOCESE 1857.

Square Miles 16,281.

Comprises the Upper Peninsula of the State of Michigan.

For legal titles of parishes and diocesan institutions, consult the Chancery.

STATISTICAL OVERVIEW

Personnel	
Bishop	1
Retired Bishops	1
Priests: Diocesan Active in Diocese	41
Priests: Diocesan Active Outside Diocese	3
Priests: Retired, Sick or Absent	28
Number of Diocesan Priests	72
Religious Priests in Diocese	5
Total Priests in Diocese	77
Extern Priests in Diocese	11
Ordinations:	
Diocesan Priests	1
Permanent Deacons in Diocese	38
Total Sisters	32
Parishes	
Parishes	72
With Resident Pastor:	
Resident Diocesan Priests	43
Resident Religious Priests	5
Without Resident Pastor:	
Administered by Priests	42
Administered by Deacons	1
Administered by Religious Women	2
Missions	21
Pastoral Centers	4
Professional Ministry Personnel:	
Sisters	5
Lay Ministers	33
Welfare	
Catholic Hospitals	1
Total Assisted	165,637
Homes for the Aged	1
Total Assisted	140
Specialized Homes	2
Total Assisted	49
Special Centers for Social Services	2
Total Assisted	1,436
Other Institutions	2
Total Assisted	27,012
Educational	
Diocesan Students in Other Seminaries	10
Total Seminarians	10
Elementary Schools, Diocesan and Parish	9
Total Students	1,099
Catechesis/Religious Education:	
High School Students	901
Elementary Students	2,077
Total Students under Catholic Instruction	4,087
Teachers in the Diocese:	
Sisters	1
Lay Teachers	89
Vital Statistics	
Receptions into the Church:	
Infant Baptism Totals	370
Minor Baptism Totals	49
Adult Baptism Totals	51
Received into Full Communion	59
First Communions	416
Confirmations	292
Marriages:	
Catholic	144
Interfaith	57
Total Marriages	201
Deaths	1,036
Total Catholic Population	66,001
Total Population	302,077

Former Bishops—Most Revs. FREDERIC BARAGA, D.D., first Bishop; cons. Nov. 1, 1853; died Jan. 19, 1868; IGNATIUS MRAK, D.D., cons. Feb. 7, 1869; resigned 1878; transferred to Antinoe 1879; died Jan. 2, 1901; JOHN VERTIN, D.D., cons. Sept. 14, 1879; died Feb. 26, 1899; FREDERICK EIS, D.D., cons. Aug. 24, 1899; made Asst. at the Pontifical Throne July 13, 1922; resigned July 8, 1922; appt. Titular Bishop of Bita; died May 5, 1926; PAUL JOSEPH NUSSBAUM, D.D., cons. Bishop of Corpus Christi May 20, 1913; resigned March 26, 1920; appt. Bishop of Marquette Nov. 14, 1922; died June 24, 1935; JOSEPH CASIMIR PLAGENS, D.D., LL.D., cons. Sept. 30, 1924, Auxiliary Bishop of Detroit; Titular Bishop of Rhodiopolis; appt. to See of Marquette Nov. 16, 1935; transferred to the See of Grand Rapids Dec. 16, 1940; died March 31, 1943; FRANCIS J. MAGNER, D.D., appt. Dec. 21, 1940; cons. Feb. 24, 1941; died June 13, 1947; THOMAS L. NOA, D.D., cons. March 19, 1946; Titular Bishop of Salona and Coadjutor Bishop of Sioux City; appt. Bishop of Marquette Aug. 20, 1947; retired March 25, 1968; died March 13, 1977; CHARLES A. SALATKA, D.D., appt. Titular Bishop of Cariana and Auxiliary of Grand Rapids Dec. 9, 1961; cons. March 6, 1962; appt. Bishop of Marquette Jan. 10, 1968; installed March 25, 1968; appt. Archbishop of Oklahoma City Oct. 11, 1977; installed Dec. 15, 1977; retired Nov. 24, 1992; died March 17, 2003.; MARK F. SCHMITT, D.D., appt. Titular Bishop of Kells and Auxiliary of Green Bay May 5, 1970; cons. June 24, 1970; appt. Bishop of Marquette March 21, 1978; installed May 8, 1978; retired Nov. 11, 1992; died Dec. 14, 2011.; JAMES H. GARLAND, M.A., M.S.W., D.D., ord. 1959; appt. Titular Bishop of Garriana and Auxiliary Bishop of Cincinnati June 2, 1984; cons. July 25, 1984; appt. Bishop of Marquette Oct. 6, 1992; installed Nov. 11, 1992; retired Dec. 13, 2005.; ALEXANDER K. SAMPLE, ord. June 1, 1990; appt. Bishop of Marquette Dec. 13, 2005; installed Jan. 25, 2006; appt. Archbishop of Portland in Oregon Jan. 29, 2013; installed April 2, 2013.

Chancery—1004 Harbor Hills Dr., Marquette, 49855. Tel: 906-225-1141; Fax: 906-225-0437. Office Hours: Mon.-Thurs. 8-4:30, Fri. 8-12.

Vicar General—Rev. Msgr. MICHAEL J. STEBER.

Chancellor & Vicar for Religious—Very Rev. DANIEL J. MOLL, J.C.L.

Vice Chancellor—MARYANN BERNIER, Tel: 906-227-9115; Email: mbernier@dioceseofmarquette.org.

Diocesan Tribunal—1004 Harbor Hills Dr., Marquette, 49855. Tel: 906-227-9131.

Judicial Vicar—Very Rev. DANIEL J. MOLL, J.C.L.

Diocesan Judge—Very Rev. DANIEL J. MOLL, J.C.L.

Defensore Vinculi—Revs. JOHN J. SHIVERSKI, (Retired); BENEDETTO J. PARIS, J.C.L.

Advocate—Rev. FRANCIS J. DEGROOT.

Administrator and Notary—SHEILA WICKENHEISER.

Promoter of Justice—Rev. BENEDETTO J. PARIS, J.C.L.

Priests' Council—Tel: 906-227-9115.

Executive Board—Revs. MARK A. MCQUESTEN, Chm.; COREY J. LITZNER, Vice Chm.

Vicars Forane—Revs. TIMOTHY W. HRUSKA, Holy Name of Mary Vicariate; MICHAEL OCRAN, St. John Neumann Vicariate; MICHAEL J. JACOBUS, St. Mary Rockland Vicariate; JOHN E. MARTIGNON, The Most Holy Name of Jesus Vicariate; FRANCIS J. DEGROOT, St. Joseph-St. Patrick Vicariate; Very Rev. ALLEN P. MOTT, St. Peter Cathedral Vicariate; Rev. MICHAEL A. WOEMPNER, St. Mary Norway Vicariate.

Consultors—Revs. MARK A. MCQUESTEN; TIMOTHY M. EKAITIS; GLENN J. THEORET; Very Rev. LARRY P. VAN DAMME; Rev. COREY J. LITZNER; Rev. Msgr. MICHAEL J. STEBER.

Diocesan Offices and Directors

Administration & Finance, Dept. of—TIMOTHY D. THOMAS, Exec. Dir.; CAROL J. PARKER, Dir. Accountant & Human Resource Coord., Tel: 906-227-9105; Fax: 906-225-0437.

Archives—347 Rock St., Marquette, 49855. Tel: 906-225-9115. MARYANN BERNIER, Vice Chancellor.

Catholic Social Services, Dept. of—KYLE RAMBO, Exec. Dir., 347 Rock St., Marquette, 49855. Tel: 906-227-9119; Fax: 906-228-2469. Branch Offices: Escanaba, Iron Mountain.

Communication Office—JOHN FEE, Exec. Dir., Tel: 906-227-9129.

Evangelization and Education—MARK SALISBURY, Exec. Dir., Mailing Address: 1004 Harbor Hills Dr., Marquette, 49855. Tel: 906-227-9127; Fax: 906-225-0437.

Youth, Young Adult, Family Ministry—GREG GOSTOMSKI, Dir., Tel: 906-227-9125; Email: ggostomski@dioceseofmarquette.org.

Catechesis and Adult Faith Formation—DENISE M. FOYE, Dir., Tel: 906-227-9130; Email: dfoye@dioceseofmarquette.org.

Newspaper "The U.P. Catholic"—JOHN FEE, Editor, 1004 Harbor Hills, Marquette, 49855. Tel: 906-227-9129; Fax: 906-225-0437; JAMIE GUALDONI, Asst. Editor, Tel: 906-227-9134.

Ministry Personnel Services, Dept. of—1004 Harbor Hills Dr., Marquette, 49855. Tel: 906-227-9155; Fax: 906-225-0437; Email: mtomasi@dioceseofmarquette.org.

Bishop Baraga Association—An organization to promote the cause for the canonization of the Most Rev. Frederic Baraga *615 S. Fourth St., Marquette, 49855.* Tel: 906-227-9117; Fax: 906-228-2469. MRS. LENORA MCKEEN, Exec. Dir.; DR. ANDREA AMBROSI, Postulator, Email: lmckeen@bishopbaraga.org.

Building Commission, Diocese of Marquette—TIMOTHY D. THOMAS, 1004 Harbor Hills Dr., Marquette, 49855. Tel: 906-227-9135.

Cemeteries—NEIL NEWCOMB, Dir. Diocesan Cemeteries, 1004 Harbor Hills Dr., Marquette, 49855. Tel: 906-225-0191.

Charismatic Prayer Groups—Rev. Msgr. MICHAEL J. STEBER, Liaison, St. Peter Cathedral, 311 W. Baraga Ave., Marquette, 49855. Tel: 906-226-6548.

Cursillo—Very Rev. TIMOTHY FERGUSON, Interim Dir., Marygrove, P.O. Box 38, Garden, 49835. Tel: 906-644-2771.

Knights of Columbus—Rev. COREY J. LITZNER, Diocesan Chap., 16 6th St., L'Anse, 49946. Tel: 906-524-6424.

Panama Mission Fund—Rev. PAUL G. MANDERFIELD, (Retired), 1004 Harbor Hills Dr., Marquette, 49855. Tel: 906-225-9104.

Permanent Diaconate Formation Program—1004 Harbor Hills Dr., Marquette, 49855. Tel: 906-227-9103; Fax: 906-225-0437. Deacon THOMAS W. MOSELEY JR., Dir., Email: tmoseley@dioceseofmarquette.org.

Propagation of the Faith1004 Harbor Hills Dr., Marquette, 49855. Tel: 906-227-9155; Fax: 906-225-0437; Email: mtomasi@dioceseofmarquette.org. VACANT; MARTHA TOMASI, Administrative Asst.

Retreats—Very Rev. TIMOTHY FERGUSON, Dir., Marygrove Retreat Center, Garden, 49835. Tel: 906-644-2771.

Victim Assistance Coordinators—MR. STEPHEN J. LYNOTT, M.S.W., M.P.S., 1004 Harbor Hills Dr., Marquette, 49855. Tel: 844-495-4330 (Toll Free); MS. DIANE TRYAN, L.M.S.W., 1100 Ludington St., Ste. 401, Escanaba, 49829. Tel: 844-694-4362 (Toll Free).

St. Joseph Association—An Association of the Priests of the Diocese to provide Retirement Benefits. Rev. DARRYL J. PEPIN, Pres., Mailing Address: St. Elizabeth Ann Seton Parish, P.O. Box 187, Bark River, 49807. Tel: 906-227-9135.

U.P. Catholic Services Appeal—WENDY J. NEGRI, Coord., 1004 Harbor Hills Dr., Marquette, 49855. Tel: 906-227-9104.

Vocation Office—Rev. BENJAMIN J. HASSE, Dir., 1004 Harbor Hills Dr., Marquette, 49855. Tel: 906-290-2434; Tel: 866-375-2643; Fax: 906-225-0437.

Women Religious—Bishop Noa Home, 2920 3rd Ave. S., Escanaba, 49829. Tel: 906-786-0292. Sr. GLORIA J. SCHULTZ, S.P.C.

CLERGY, PARISHES, MISSIONS AND PAROCHIAL SCHOOLS

CITY OF MARQUETTE

(MARQUETTE COUNTY)

1—ST. PETER CATHEDRAL (1853)
311 Baraga Ave., 49855. Tel: 906-226-6548; Fax: 906-226-8683; Email: secretary@stpetercathedral.org; Web: www.stpetercathedral.org. Rev. Msgr. Michael J. Steber; Aaron J. Nowicki; Deacons John S. Leadbetter; Lawrence H. Londo; Donald Thoren; Thomas E. Foye; Dean J. Jackson.
See Fr. Marquette Catholic Central Schools System, Marquette under Elementary Interparochial Schools located in the Institution section.
Catechesis Religious Program—Jenny Lochner, Faith Formation. Students 73.
Mission—St. Mary, 305 Bensinger, Big Bay, Marquette Co. 49808.

2—ST. CHRISTOPHER (1954)
2372 Badger St., 49855. Tel: 906-226-2265; Fax: 906-226-8678; Email: Stchristopher49855@gmail.com. Revs. Gregory R. Heikkala; Brandon Oman; Deacons Steven M. Gualdoni; Thomas W. Moseley Jr., Pastoral Assoc.; Ms. Katherine Barber, Sec.
Catechesis Religious Program—Sr. Colleen Sweeting, O.S.F., D.R.E., Email: colleensweeting@hotmail.com. Students 15.

3—ST. JOHN THE BAPTIST (1986) Closed. For inquiries for parish records, contact St. Peter's Cathedral, Marquette.

4—ST. LOUIS THE KING (HARVEY) (1954)
264 Silver Creek Rd., 49855. Tel: 906-249-1438; Email: secretary@sltkchurch.org; Web: sltkchurch.org. Rev. Glenn J. Theoret; Deacons Scott Jamieson; Warren K. Vonck; Gregg R. St. John.
See Fr. Marquette Catholic Central Schools System, Marquette under Elementary Interparochial Schools located in the Institution section.
Catechesis Religious Program—Edward Hueckel, D.R.E. Students 80.

5—ST. MICHAEL (1942)
401 W. Kaye Ave., 49855. Tel: 906-228-8180; Email: secretary@stmichaelmqt.org; Web: www.stmichaelmqt.com. Revs. Gregory R. Heikkala; Brandon Oman; Deacon Dennis R. Maki.
See Fr. Marquette Catholic Central Schools System, Marquette under Elementary Interparochial Schools located in the Institution section.

OUTSIDE THE CITY OF MARQUETTE

AHMEEK, KEWEENAW CO., OUR LADY OF PEACE, (Keweenaw Catholic Missions)
Mailing Address: P.O. Box 546, Calumet, 49913.
Tel: 906-337-0810; Fax: 906-337-6424; Email: secretary@keweenawcc.org; Web: www.keweenawcc.org. 2854 US Hwy. 41, Ahmeek, 49901. Rev. Abraham J. Mupparathara, M.C.B.S., (India); Deacon Arthur Stancher.
Missions—Holy Redeemer—507 South St., Eagle Harbor, Keweenaw Co. 49950.
Our Lady of the Pines, 443 1st St., Copper Harbor, Keweenaw Co. 49918.

ALPHA, IRON CO., ST. EDWARD, Closed. For inquiries for parish records contact the chancery.

BARAGA, BARAGA CO., ST. ANN
Mailing Address: 16 6th St., L'Anse, 49946.
Tel: 906-353-6565; Email: bccc@up.net; Web: www.baragacountycatholiccommunity.org. 322 Lyons St., Baraga, 49908. Rev. Corey J. Litzner.
Res.: 318 Lyons St., Baraga, 49908.
Tel: 906-524-6424; Fax: 906-524-7585.
Catechesis Religious Program—Mrs. Christy Miron, D.R.E. Students 114.

BARBEAU, CHIPPEWA CO., HOLY FAMILY MISSION
P.O. Box 39, Barbeau, 49710. Tel: 906-632-3213; Fax: 906-632-8490; Email: jshascall@sbcglobal.net. Rev. John S. Hascall, O.F.M.Cap.
Res.: 1529 Marquette Ave., Sault Sainte Marie, 49783.
Catechesis Religious Program—Tel: 906-647-9145. Linda Little, D.R.E. Students 15.

BARK RIVER, DELTA CO., ST. ELIZABETH ANN SETON (1995) Formerly St. George, Bark River, Sacred Heart of Jesus, Schaffer & St. Michael, Perronville.
1216 12th Rd., P.O. Box 187, Bark River, 49807.
Tel: 906-466-9938; Fax: 906-466-0194. Rev. Darryl J. Pepin.
Catechesis Religious Program—Kelley VanLanen, D.R.E. Students 120.
Mission—St. Joseph, W2332 Cemetery Rd., Foster City, Dickinson Co. 49834.

BESSEMER, GOGEBIC CO., ST. SEBASTIAN
210 E. Iron St., Bessemer, 49911. Tel: 906-667-0952; Email: office@stsebastianparish.com. Rev. Dominic Agyapong.
Catechesis Religious Program—Email: dre@stsebastianparish.com. Angie Mazurek, D.R.E. Students 52.

BRIMLEY, CHIPPEWA CO., ST. FRANCIS XAVIER
Mailing Address: c/o St. Joseph, 11509 W H-40, Rudyard, 49780. Tel: 906-248-3443; Email: stjosephsofrudyardmi@gmail.com. Rev. Edward Baah Baafi; Deacon Joseph A. LaPlante.

CALUMET, HOUGHTON CO.

1—ST. PAUL THE APOSTLE (1908)
301 Eight St., Calumet, 49913. Tel: 906-337-2044; Tel: 906-337-0810; Fax: 906-337-6424; Email: secretary@keweenawcc.org; Web: www.keweenawcc.org. Mailing Address: P.O. Box 546, Calumet, 49913. Rev. Abraham J. Mupparathara, M.C.B.S., (India); Deacon Arthur Stancher.

2—SACRED HEART (1868)
56512 Rockland St., Calumet, 49913.
Tel: 906-337-0810; Fax: 906-337-6424; Email: secretary@keweenawcc.org; Web: www.keweenawcc.org. P.O. Box 546, Calumet, 49913. Rev. Abraham J. Mupparathara, M.C.B.S., (India); Deacon Arthur Stancher.

CASPIAN, IRON CO., ST. CECILIA (1913)
Mailing Address: P.O. Box 517, Caspian, 49915.
Tel: 906-265-3777; Email: stagnesstcecilia@gmail.com. 510 Brady St., Caspian, 49915. Rev. Gregory L. Veneklase; Deacon Robert J. Kostka, (Retired).
Catechesis Religious Program—Students 27.

CHAMPION, MARQUETTE CO., SACRED HEART (1873) [CEM]
Mailing Address: P.O. Box 99, Champion, 49814.
Tel: 906-376-8475; Email: smargey@att.net. 1723 Main St., Champion, 49814. Very Rev. Daniel J. Moll, J.C.L., Sacramental Min.; Sr. Margey Schmelzle, O.S.F., Pastoral Coord.
Catechesis Religious Program—

CHANNING, DICKINSON CO., ST. ROSE
Mailing Address: P.O. Box 235, Channing, 49815.
Tel: 906-542-3215. 703 Bell Ave., Channing, 49815. Email: st.rosechurch@sbcglobal.net. Rev. Daniel L. Malone.
Catechesis Religious Program—Nancy Reese, D.R.E. Students 14.

CHASSELL, HOUGHTON CO., ST. ANNE (1887)
Mailing Address: 411 MacInnes Dr., Houghton, 49931. Tel: 906-523-4912; Fax: 908-482-5530; Email: stalbert@stal-mtu.com; Web: www.facebook.com/st.anne.chassell. 41903 Willson Memorial Dr., Chassell, 49916. Revs. Ben Hasse; Dustin Larson; Deacon Thomas F. Corrigan; Sisters Marcelyn Gervais, O.S.F., Pastoral Assoc.; Jacqueline Spaniola, D.R.E.
Missions—Sacred Heart—Painesdale, Houghton Co.. Closed. For inquiries for parish records contact St. Ignatius Loyola, Houghton.
Immaculate Heart of Mary, Donken, Houghton Co.. Closed. For inquiries for parish records contact St. Ignatius Loyola, Houghton.

COOKS, SCHOOLCRAFT CO., ST. MARY MAGDALENE, [CEM]
Mailing Address: P.O. Box 68, Garden, 49835.
Tel: 906-644-2626; Fax: 906-644-2626; Email: stjohns@centurytel.net. 1130S County Rd. 442, Cooks, 49817. Rev. John Essel.

CRYSTAL FALLS, IRON CO., GUARDIAN ANGELS (1887)
412 Crystal Ave., Crystal Falls, 49920.
Tel: 906-875-3019; Fax: 906-875-1034; Email: guardang@att.net. Rev. Daniel L. Malone.
Catechesis Religious Program—11 N. 5th St., Crystal Falls, 49920. Patrick Sommers, D.R.E.; Christine Sommers, D.R.E. Students 35.

DAGGETT, MENOMINEE CO., ST. FREDERICK, Closed. For inquiries for parish records contact Precious Blood Parish, Stephenson.

DETOUR, CHIPPEWA CO., SACRED HEART (1884)
Mailing Address: 12841 E. Traynor Rd., Goetzville, 49736. Tel: 906-297-5211; Fax: 906-297-5108; Email: 4parishoffice@centurylink.net. Rev. Jose Cherian.
Mission—St. Florence, 34138 S. Townline Rd., Drummond Island, Chippewa Co. 49726.

ENGADINE, MACKINAC CO., OUR LADY OF LOURDES, Closed. For parish records, contact St. Gregory Parish, Newberry.

ESCANABA, DELTA CO.

1—ST. ANNE (1888) [CEM]
817 S. Lincoln Rd., Escanaba, 49829.
Tel: 906-786-1421; Email: stannes@chartermi.net. Rev. Francis J. DeGroot; Deacons Lewis Vaillencourt; Terrance J. Saunders.
See Holy Name Central Grade School, Escanaba under Elementary Interparochial Schools located in the Institution section.
Catechesis Religious Program—Nick Moreno, C.R.E.; Matt Buchmiller, C.R.E. Students 130.

2—ST. JOSEPH & ST. PATRICK (1997) (Formerly St. Joseph, Escanaba; Formerly St. Patrick, Escanaba).
709 First Ave. S., Escanaba, 49829.
Tel: 906-789-6244; Fax: 906-789-1213; Email: sjsp@att.net. Rev. Eric E. Olson.
See Holy Name Grade School, Escanaba under Elementary Interparochial Schools located in the Institution section.
Catechesis Religious Program—Students 38.

3—ST. THOMAS THE APOSTLE (1948)
1820 Ninth Ave. N., Escanaba, 49829.
Tel: 906-786-4627; Fax: 906-789-5558; Email: beth.sviland@stanthonystthomas.org; Web: dioceseofmarquette.org/stthomasescanaba. Rev. Rick L. Courier.
See Holy Name Catholic School, Escanaba under Elementary Interparochial Schools located in the Institution section.
Catechesis Religious Program—409 S. 22nd St., Escanaba, 49829. Tel: 906-786-7550. Students 56.

EWEN, ONTONAGON CO., SACRED HEART (1892)
Mailing Address: P.O. Box 50, Ewen, 49925.
Tel: 906-988-2310; Email: shcewen@charter.net. 201 S. Birch St., Ewen, 49925. Rev. Binu Joseph.
Catechesis Religious Program—Students 8.

Mission—St. Ann, 480 Forest Ave., Bergland, Ontonagon Co. 49910.

GARDEN, DELTA CO., ST. JOHN THE BAPTIST
Mailing Address: P.O. Box 68, Garden, 49835.
Tel: 906-644-2626; Email: stjohns@centurytel.net. 6410 State St., Garden, 49835. Rev. John Essel.

GLADSTONE, DELTA CO.
1—ALL SAINTS (1889)
715 Wisconsin Ave., Gladstone, 49837.
Tel: 906-428-3199; Web: www.allsaintsgladstone.org. P.O. Box 392, Gladstone, 49837. Revs. James C. Ziminski, Tel: 906-227-9101; Peter H. Fosu, (Ghana); Deacon Michael LeBeau.
Catechesis Religious Program—Kathy Kohtala, D.R.E. Students 265.
2—HOLY FAMILY
4011 CO 416-20th Rd., Gladstone, 49837.
Tel: 906-786-1209; Email: secretary@holyfamilyparish.net. Rev. Francis G. Dobrzenski.
Catechesis Religious Program—Cathy Flagstadt, D.R.E. Students 64.

GOETZVILLE, CHIPPEWA CO., ST. STANISLAUS KOSTKA (1897) [CEM]
12841 E. Traynor Rd., Goetzville, 49736.
Tel: 906-297-5211; Fax: 906-297-5108; Email: 4parishoffice@centurylink.net. Rev. Jose Cherian.
Catechesis Religious Program—Barbara Storey, D.R.E. Students 10.
Mission—Our Lady of the Snows, P.O. Box 325, Hessel, Mackinac Co. 49745.

GRAND MARAIS, ALGER CO., HOLY ROSARY CHURCH (1895) [CEM]
Mailing Address: P.O. Box 424, Grand Marais, 49839. Tel: 906-494-2589; Fax: 906-494-2589; Email: hrosary@gmail.com. E21907 Grand Marais Ave., Grand Marais, 49839. Rev. Timothy W. Hruska.
Catechesis Religious Program—Students 11.
Mission—St. Timothy, N9153 County Rd. H-33, Curtis, Mackinac Co. 49839.

GWINN, MARQUETTE CO., ST. ANTHONY (1912)
280 N. Boulder, Gwinn, 49841. Tel: 906-346-5312; Email: stanthonygwinn@gmail.com. Very Rev. Allen P. Mott.
Catechesis Religious Program—Email: st.anthony.faithformation@gmail.com. Danyl Winkler, Catechetical Leader. Students 18.
Mission—St. Joseph, County Rd. 426, Northland, Marquette Co. 49801.

HANCOCK, HOUGHTON CO., RESURRECTION aka Church of the Resurrection, [CEM]
900 Quincy St., Hancock, 49930. Tel: 906-482-0215; Fax: 906-523-5485; Email: secretary@resurrectionhancock.org; Web: www.churchoftheresurrection.weebly.com. Rev. William Ssozi.
Catechesis Religious Program—Lois Gemignani, D.R.E. Students 71.
Mission—St. Francis of Assisi, 23176 Fir Ave., Dollar Bay, Houghton Co. 49922.
Catechesis Religious Program—Students 22.

HERMANSVILLE, MENOMINEE CO., ST. JOHN NEUMANN (1995) [CEM] [JC] (Formerly St. Mary, Hermansville; St. Francis Xavier, Spalding).
N16150 Maple St., Spalding, 49886.
Tel: 906-497-4578 (Rectory);
Tel: 906-497-5800 (Office); Fax: 906-497-4278; Email: spiritu@att.net. P.O. Box 135, Spalding, 49886. Rev. Jacek S. Wtyklo.
Catechesis Religious Program—Sandy Hancheck, D.R.E.; Danielle Chartier, D.R.E. Students 63.

HOUGHTON, HOUGHTON CO.
1—ST. ALBERT THE GREAT UNIVERSITY PARISH (1963) (Michigan Technological University)
411 MacInnes Dr., Houghton, 49931.
Tel: 906-482-5530; Fax: 906-482-5530; Email: stalbert@stal-mtu.com; Web: www.mtucatholic.org. Revs. Ben Hasse; Dustin Larson, Parochial Vicar; Sisters Marcelyn Gervais, O.S.F., Pastoral Assoc.; Jacqueline Spaniola, Pastoral Assoc.
2—ST. IGNATIUS LOYOLA
305 Portage St., Houghton, 49931. Tel: 906-482-0212 ; Fax: 906-482-8110; Email: annette_bookkeeper@stignatius-houghton.org. Rev. John E. Martignon.
Catechesis Religious Program—Annette Butina, Faith Formation. Students 147.
Mission—St. Mary, Atlantic Mine, Houghton Co.. Closed. For inquiries for parish records contact St. Ignatius Loyola, Houghton.

HUBBELL, HOUGHTON CO., ST. CECILIA, Closed. For parish records, contact St. Joseph, Lake Linden.

IRON MOUNTAIN, DICKINSON CO.
1—IMMACULATE CONCEPTION OF THE BLESSED VIRGIN MARY (1890)
Mailing Address: 500 E. Blaine St., Iron Mountain, 49801-1840. Tel: 906-774-0511; Fax: 906-779-9953; Email: ironmtic@ironmtn.net. Rev. Msgr. James A. Kaczmarek.
See Bishop Baraga Catholic School System, Iron Mountain under Elementary Interparochial Schools located in the Institution section.
Catechesis Religious Program—Students 53.
2—ST. MARY AND ST. JOSEPH (1939)
411 W. B St., Iron Mountain, 49801.
Tel: 906-774-2046; Fax: 906-774-6015. Rev. Janusz Romanek.
See Bishop Baraga Catholic School, Iron Mountain under Elementary Interparochial Schools located in the Institution section.
Catechesis Religious Program—Karen Druschke, D.R.E. (7-12); Maria Erickson, D.R.E. (K-6). Students 100.

IRON RIVER, IRON CO., ST. AGNES (1883)
702 N. Fourth Ave., Iron River, 49935-1304.
Tel: 906-265-4557; Fax: 906-265-7155. Rev. Gregory L. Veneklase; Deacon Robert J. Kostka.
Catechesis Religious Program—Students 24.

IRONWOOD, GOGEBIC CO.
1—ST. AMBROSE, Consolidated with Holy Trinity & St. Michael to form Our Lady of Peace Parish, 1986.
2—ST. MICHAEL, Consolidated with St. Ambrose & Holy Trinity to form Our Lady of Peace Parish, 1986.
3—OUR LADY OF PEACE (1986) Formerly Holy Trinity, St. Ambrose & St. Michael.
108 S. Marquette St., Ironwood, 49938.
Tel: 906-932-0174; Fax: 906-932-1019; Email: ktlolop@gmail.com. Rev. Robb M. Jurkovich; Deacons Robert A. Hamen; Charles H. Gervasio.
Catechesis Religious Program—Alison Schlag, Faith Formation Coord. Students 92.

ISHPEMING, MARQUETTE CO.
1—ST. JOHN THE EVANGELIST (1871)
325 S. Pine St., Ishpeming, 49849-2339.
Tel: 906-486-6212; Fax: 906-486-4244; Email: stjohnschurch325@yahoo.com. Rev. Ryan T. Ford.
Religious Education Center—Tel: 906-486-9361. Angela Johnson, D.R.E.; Jennifer Rapavi, Dir. of Leadership Devel. Students 104.
2—ST. JOSEPH (1890)
1889 Prairie Ave., Ishpeming, 49849-1045.
Tel: 906-485-4200; Email: stjoeparish@outlook.com; Web: www.ishpemingcatholic.com. Rev. Ryan T. Ford; Deacon Steven M. Schaffer.
Res.: 1890 Prairie Ave., Ishpeming, 49849-1044. Tel: 906-204-2460.
Catechesis Religious Program—Tel: 906-486-9361; Email: ishpemingfaithformation@gmail.com. Angela Johnson, D.R.E.; Jennifer Rapavi, Dir. of Leadership Devel. Students 33.
3—ST. PIUS X, Closed. For inquiries for parish records contact St. Joseph Church, 1889 Prairie Ave., Ishpeming, MI 49849.

KINGSFORD, DICKINSON CO.
1—AMERICAN MARTYRS
908 W. Sagola Ave., Kingsford, 49802.
Tel: 906-774-0630; Fax: 906-774-4417; Email: frjoe@att.net; Web: Americanmartyrskg.org. Rev. Joseph O. Gouin.
Catechesis Religious Program—Kim Harris, Catechetical Leader. Students 143.
2—ST. MARY QUEEN OF PEACE (1945)
600 Marquette Blvd., Kingsford, 49802.
Tel: 906-774-6122; Fax: 906-774-2349; Email: st.maryqueenofpeacechurch@chartermi.net. Rev. Michael A. Woempner.
Catechesis Religious Program—Mary Beth Casanova, D.R.E. Students 81.

L'ANSE, BARAGA CO., SACRED HEART (1894)
16 6th St., L'Anse, 49946. Tel: 906-524-6424;
Fax: 906-524-7585; Email: bccc@up.net; Web: baragacountycatholiccommunity.org. Rev. Corey J. Litzner.
Catechesis Religious Program—Mrs. Christy Miron, Faith Formation Dir. Students 56.

LAKE LINDEN, HOUGHTON CO., ST. JOSEPH (1871)
701 Calumet St., Lake Linden, 49945.
Tel: 906-296-6851; Email: churchlady@saintjosephll.com. Rev. Joseph Boakye Yiadom, (Ghana).
Catechesis Religious Program—Students 71.

MACKINAC ISLAND, MACKINAC CO., STE. ANNE DE MICHILIMACKINAC (1695)
Mailing Address: P.O. Box 537, Mackinac Island, 49757. Tel: 906-847-3507; Email: steannes@gmail.com; Web: steanneschurch.org. 6836 Huron St., Mackinac Island, 49757. Revs. Francis Ricca; John Essel.
Catechesis Religious Program—

MANISTIQUE, SCHOOLCRAFT CO., ST. FRANCIS DE SALES
330 Oak St., Manistique, 49854. Tel: 906-341-5355;
Fax: 906-341-3984; Email: sfparish1@gmail.com; Web: stfrancisofmanistique.weconnect.com. Rev. Benedetto J. Paris, J.C.L.
Catechesis Religious Program—Mrs. Patricia Peck-Faketty, Catechetical Leader, Email: ffc11.st.francis@gmail.com. Students 40.
Mission—Divine Infant of Prague, Gulliver, Schoolcraft Co.

MENOMINEE, MENOMINEE CO.
1—HOLY REDEEMER (Birch Creek)
W-5541 Birch Creek Rd., Menominee, 49858.
Tel: 906-863-6920; Email: holyredeemer1@gmail.com. Rev. Michael Ocran; Deacons Roland Chaltry; Stephen S. Gretzinger.
See Menominee Catholic Central, Menominee under Elementary Interparochial Schools located in the Institution section.
Catechesis Religious Program—Students 27.
2—HOLY SPIRIT (1972)
1016 10th Ave., Menominee, 49858.
Tel: 906-863-5239; Fax: 906-863-2249; Email: office@holyspiritonline.org; Web: www.holyspiritonline.org. Rev. Mark A. McQuesten; Deacons Stephen S. Gretzinger; Charles H. Gervasio.
Catechesis Religious Program—Tel: 906-863-2249. Students 24.
3—RESURRECTION
2607 18th St., Menominee, 49858. Tel: 906-863-3405; Fax: 906-863-9090; Email: resparish1@att.net. Rev. Brian C. Gerber; Deacons Vincent W. Beckley, (Retired); Stephen S. Gretzinger; Charles H. Gervasio.
See St. John Paul II Catholic Academy, Menominee under Elementary Interparochial Schools located in the Institution section.
Catechesis Religious Program—
Tel: 906-863-3405, Ext. 13. Students 26.

MORAN, MACKINAC CO., IMMACULATE CONCEPTION, [CEM]
120 Church St., St. Ignace, 49781. Tel: 906-643-7671; Fax: 906-643-7755; Email: stigchurch@lighthouse.net; Web: www.stigchurch.org. W1934 Church, Moran, 49760. Revs. Francis Ricca; Peter H. Fosu, (Ghana); Deacon Thomas McClelland.
Catechesis Religious Program—Tel: 906-643-8887; Email: stigfaithform8800@att.net. Tim LaJoice, Catechetical Leader. Students 6.

MUNISING, ALGER CO., SACRED HEART OF JESUS (1896)
110 W. Jewell St., Munising, 49862.
Tel: 906-387-4900. P.O. Box 99, Munising, 49862. Rev. Christopher B. Gardiner.
Catechesis Religious Program—Tel: 906-387-4901. Barbara Herman, D.R.E. Students 46.
Mission—St. Therese, E5420 Woodland Ave., Autrain, Alger Co. 49806.

NADEAU, MENOMINEE CO., ST. BRUNO (1887)
N13770 Old US Hwy. 41, P.O. Box 95, Nadeau, 49863. Tel: 906-639-2388; Fax: 906-639-2301; Email: stbruno@alphacomm.net. Rev. Jacek S. Wtyklo.
Catechesis Religious Program—Cindy Swille, D.R.E. Students 350.

NAHMA, DELTA CO., ST. ANDREW
8236 River St., Nahma, 49864. Tel: 906-644-2626; Email: stjohns@centurytel.net. P.O. Box 68, Garden, 49835. Rev. John Essel.

NEGAUNEE, MARQUETTE CO., ST. PAUL
202 W. Case St., Negaunee, 49866. Tel: 906-475-9969 ; Fax: 906-475-9987. Rev. Msgr. Peter Oberto, J.C.L., (Retired).
Catechesis Religious Program—Bill Barrette, D.R.E. Students 96.
Mission—Our Lady Perpetual Help, 201 Nicholas Ave., Palmer, Marquette Co. 49871.

NEWBERRY, LUCE CO., ST. GREGORY (1886)
212 W. Harrie St., Newberry, 49868.
Tel: 906-293-5511; Fax: 906-293-5560; Email: stgreg@sbcglobal.net. Rev. Martin Flynn.
Res.: 111 W. Harrie St., Newberry, 49868.
Catechesis Religious Program—Dawn Stephenson, D.R.E. Students 60.
Missions—Our Lady of Victory—7208 N M123, Paradise, Chippewa Co.
St. Stephen, Hwy. U.S. 2, Naubinway, Mackinac Co. 49762. Tel: 906-477-6117; Email: sawicker@lighthouse.net.

NORWAY, DICKINSON CO., ST. MARY (1878)
401 Main St., Norway, 49870. Tel: 906-563-9845;
Fax: 906-563-7623; Email: saintmary@norwaymi.com; Web: www.stmarybarbara.org. Rev. Timothy M. Ekaitis.
See Holy Spirit Central School, Norway under Elementary Interparochial Schools located in the Institution section.
Catechesis Religious Program—Nancy Degnan, D.R.E. Students 14.

ONTONAGON, ONTONAGON CO., HOLY FAMILY, [CEM]
515 Pine St., Ontonagon, 49953. Tel: 906-884-2569;
Fax: 906-884-6030; Email: hfcc@up.net. Rev. Michael J. Jacobus; Deacon Matthew P. Weaver, (Retired).
Catechesis Religious Program—Students 33.

PERKINS, DELTA CO., ST. JOSEPH (1901)
Mailing Address: 5803 Hwy. M-35, P.O. Box 22, Perkins, 49872. Tel: 906-359-4701;
Fax: 906-359-4701; Email: perkins_stjoes@hotmail.com. Rev. Joseph Augustine Vandannoor, M.S.T., (India).
Catechesis Religious Program—Students 46.

PERRONVILLE, MENOMINEE CO., ST. ELIZABETH ANN SETON, Closed. (See Bark River.).

QUINNESEC, DICKINSON CO., ST. MARY, Closed. For inquiries for parish records contact St. Mary Church, 401 Main St., Norway, MI 49870.

RAMSAY, GOGEBIC CO., CHRIST THE KING, Closed. For inquiries for parish records contact St. Sebastian, Bessemer.

RAPID RIVER, DELTA CO., ST. CHARLES BORROMEO
7860 River St., P.O. Box 247, Rapid River, 49878. Tel: 906-474-6606; Email: stcharles@stcharleschurch-rr.org. Rev. Joseph Augustine Vandannoor, M.S.T., (India).
Catechesis Religious Program—Email: stcharles@stcharleschurch-rr.org. Michelle Loper, D.R.E. Students 35.

REPUBLIC, MARQUETTE CO., ST. AUGUSTINE (1877) [CEM]
Mailing Address: 574 Kloman Ave., Republic, 49879. Tel: 906-376-8475; Email: smargey@att.net. 626 Kloman Ave., Republic, 49879. Very Rev. Daniel J. Moll, J.C.L., Sacramental Min.; Sr. Margey Schmelzle, O.S.F., Pastoral Coord.

ROCKLAND, ONTONAGON CO., ST. MARY
Mailing Address: Holy Family Parish, 515 Pine St., Ontonagon, 49953. Tel: 906-884-2569;
Fax: 906-884-6030; Email: smcc@up.net. 11 Elm St., Rockland, 49953. Rev. Michael J. Jacobus.

RUDYARD, CHIPPEWA CO., ST. JOSEPH
Mailing Address: 11509 W. H-40, Rudyard, 49780. Tel: 906-478-4331; Email: stjosephsofrudyardmi@gmail.com. Rev. Edward Baah Baafi.
Mission—St. Mary.
Stations—Kinross Correctional Facility—Kincheloe.
Chippewa East Correctional Facility, Kincheloe.
Chippewa West Correctional Facility, Kincheloe.

ST. IGNACE, MACKINAC CO., ST. IGNATIUS LOYOLA, [CEM]
120 Church St., St. Ignace, 49781. Tel: 906-643-7671; Fax: 906-643-7755; Email: stigchurch@lighthouse.net; Web: www.stigchurch.org. Revs. Francis Ricca; Peter H. Fosu, (Ghana); Deacon Thomas McClelland.
Catechesis Religious Program—Tel: 906-643-8887; Email: stigfaithform88@att.net. Tim LaJoice, D.R.E. Students 65.

SAULT SAINTE MARIE, CHIPPEWA CO.
1—HOLY NAME OF MARY
377 Maple St., Sault Sainte Marie, 49783. Tel: 906-632-3381; Fax: 906-632-0741; Email: Stmary377@gmail.com. Rev. Sebastian Kavumkal, M.S.T., (India).
Catechesis Religious Program—Students 34.
2—ST. JOSEPH (1941)
606 E. Fourth Ave., Sault Sainte Marie, 49783. Tel: 906-632-9625; Fax: 906-632-5122; Email: stjoseph.lewinski0@gmail.com; Web: stjosephssm.org. Rev. Michael D. Chenier; Deacon William J. Piche, (Retired).
Catechesis Religious Program—
Tel: 906-632-9625, Ext. 4; Fax: 906-632-5122. Danna Schmitter, D.R.E. Students 84.
3—NATIVITY OF OUR LORD, Closed. For inquiries for parish records contact St. Joseph, Sault Sainte Marie.

SCHAFFER, DELTA CO., ST. ELIZABETH ANN SETON, Closed. Formerly Sacred Heart of Jesus. See Bark River.

SOUTH RANGE, HOUGHTON CO., HOLY FAMILY
305 Portage St., Houghton, 49931. Tel: 906-482-0212 ; Email: annette_bookkeeper@stignatius-houghton.org. Rev. John E. Martignon.
Church: 107 Atlantic Ave., South Range, 49963.
Catechesis Religious Program—Students 49.

SPALDING, MENOMINEE CO., ST. FRANCIS XAVIER, Closed. St. John Neumann, P.O. Box 135, Spalding, MI 49886.

STEPHENSON, MENOMINEE CO., PRECIOUS BLOOD CHURCH (1880) [CEM]
S. 304 Bluff St., Stephenson, 49887. Tel: 906-753-2562; Fax: 906-753-2811; Email: pbchurch@304att.net. Rev. Ronald K. Timock; Deacon Thomas J. Rivard. Extraordinary Form Latin Mass
Catechesis Religious Program—Tel: 906-753-4771. Sharon Tebo, D.R.E. Students 80.

TRENARY, ALGER CO., ST. RITA (1947)
N1048 First Ave. E., P.O. Box 207, Trenary, 49891. Tel: 906-446-3350; Fax: 906-446-3523; Email: strita@tds.net. Rev. Joseph Augustine Vandannoor, M.S.T., (India).
Catechesis Religious Program—Heidi Swajaneu, D.R.E. Students 23.

VULCAN, DICKINSON CO., ST. BARBARA
W5058 Main St., Vulcan, 49892. Tel: 906-563-9845; Fax: 906-563-7623; Email: saintmary@norwaymi.com; Web: www.stmarybarbara.org. Mailing Address: 401 Main St., Norway, 49870. Rev. Timothy M. Ekaitis.
See Holy Spirit Central School, Norway under Elementary Interparochial Schools located in the Institution section.
Catechesis Religious Program—401 Main St., Norway, 49870. Email: religioused@norwaymi.com. Nancy Degnan, Catechetical Leader. Students 29.

WAKEFIELD, GOGEBIC CO., IMMACULATE CONCEPTION OF THE BLESSED VIRGIN MARY
407 Ascherman St., Wakefield, 49968. Tel: 906-224-7851; Fax: 906-224-9118; Email: office@stsebastianparish.com. Rev. Dominic Agyapong.
Rectory—210 E. Iron St., Bessemer, 49911. Tel: 906-667-0952; Fax: 906-667-0952.
Mission—St. Catherine, Marenisco, Gogebic Co.. Tel: 906-787-2258. Rev. Raymond F. Moncher, (Retired).
Catechesis Religious Program—Laura Yuchasz, C.R.E. Students 21.

WATERSMEET, GOGEBIC CO., IMMACULATE CONCEPTION
E23933 D Ave., P.O. Box 398, Watersmeet, 49969. Tel: 906-358-4360; Tel: 906-988-2310; Email: shcewen@charter.net. Mailing Address: P.O. Box 50, Ewen, 49925. Rev. Binu Joseph.
Catechesis Religious Program—201 South Birch St., Ewen, 49925. Tel: 906-988-2310; Email: shcewen@charter.net. Students 4.

WELLS, DELTA CO., ST. ANTHONY OF PADUA (1949)
Mailing Address: 1820 9th Ave. N., Escanaba, 49829. Tel: 906-786-4627; Fax: 906-789-5558; Email: beth.sviland@stanthonystthomas.org; Web: www.dioceseofmarquette.org/stanthony.org. 6596 N. 3rd St., Wells, 49894. Rev. Rick L. Courier.
Catechesis Religious Program—409 S. 22nd St., Escanaba, 49829. Tel: 906-233-9566. Students 33.

WHITE PINE, ONTONAGON CO., ST. JUDE (1956)
8 Cedar St., P.O. Box 427, White Pine, 49971. Tel: 906-885-5763. Rev. Michael J. Jacobus.
Catechesis Religious Program— Held at Holy Family, 515 Pine St., Ontonagon. Students 6.

Indian Missions

ASSININS, BARAGA CO., THE MOST HOLY NAME OF JESUS-SAINT KATERI TEKAKWITHA
Mailing Address: 16 S. Sixth, L'Anse, 49946. Tel: 906-524-6424; Email: bccc@up.net; Web: baragacountycatholiccommunity.org. 14808 Assinins Rd., Baraga, 49908. Rev. Corey J. Litzner.
Res.: 14813 Assinins Rd., Baraga, 49908.
Catechesis Religious Program—Tel: 906-524-5157. Mrs. Christy Miron, D.R.E. Students 56.

BAY MILLS, CHIPPEWA CO., SAINT KATERI TEKAKWITHA
Mailing Address: P.O. Box 429, Brimley, 49715. Tel: 906-633-3213; Email: jshascall@sbcglobal.net. 12014 W. Lakeshore Dr., Brimley, 49715. Rev. John S. Hascall, O.F.M.Cap.
Catechesis Religious Program—Mrs. Amy Perron, D.R.E. Students 37.

SAULT SAINTE MARIE, CHIPPEWA CO., ST. ISAAC JOGUES MISSION (1950)
1529 Marquette Ave., Sault Sainte Marie, 49783. Tel: 906-632-3213; Email: jshascall@sbcglobal.net. Rev. John S. Hascall, O.F.M.Cap.
Catechesis Religious Program—Tel: 906-632-2856. Leslie Ruditis, D.R.E. Students 4.

SUGAR ISLAND, CHIPPEWA CO., SACRED HEART, Indian Missionaries, East.
Mailing Address: 377 Maple St., Sault Sainte Marie, 49783. Tel: 906-632-3381; Email: stmary377@gmail.com. 3001 S. Westshore Dr., Sugar Island, 49783. Rev. Sebastian Kavumkal, M.S.T., (India).
Catechesis Religious Program—Students 3.

Chaplains of Public Institutions

IRON MOUNTAIN. *Veterans Administration Center*. Rev. Msgr. James A. Kaczmarek, Chap.

On Duty Outside the Diocese:
Revs.—
Murphy, Patrick E., 5500 Armstrong Rd., (118c), Battle Creek, 49016. Dept. of Veterans Affairs Medical Center.
Sjoquist, Bradley, Casa Santa Maria, Via Dell'Umilta, 30 00187, Rome, Italy
Thomas, Nicholas, St. Rose of Lima Parish, 355 S. Navajo St., Denver, CO 80223.

Special Assignment:
Revs.—
Ferguson, Timothy, Dir., Marygrove Retreat Center
Hasse, Benjamin J., Dir., Vocations.

Retired:
Rev. Msgrs.—
Desrochers, Timothy H., (Retired), P.O. Box 693, Gwinn, 49841
Oberto, Peter, J.C.L., (Retired), 33B Grand Canyon Dr., Apt. 104, Baraboo, WI 53913-3141
Patrick, John E., V.G., (Retired), P.O. Box 609, Gwinn, 49841
Revs.—
Bracket, Louis P., (Retired), 303 Brotherton St., Wakefield, 49968
Eddy, Corbin, (Retired), 624 Lake Ave., Hancock, 49930
Grambow, Arnold J., (Retired), 3300 Thorntree Dr., #48, Gladstone, 49837
Kurtz, Jeffrey A., (Retired), 1824 State Hwy. M69, P.O. Box 203, Crystal Falls, 49920
Landreville, Norbert B., (Retired), P.O. Box 345, St. Ignace, 49781
Lenz, Frank, (Retired), 456 Co. Rd. KB, 49855
Longbucco, John L., (Retired), St. Rose of Lima Parish, 355 S. Navajo St., Denver, CO 80223
Maki, George S., (Retired), 284 W. Sunset Lake Rd., Iron River, 49935
Manderfield, Paul G., (Retired), 406 Emerald St., Houghton, 49931
Mayotte, Allan J., (Retired), 300 Rock St., Apt. 2, 49855
Menapace, James L., (Retired)
Moncher, Raymond F., (Retired), 303 Brotherton St., Wakefield, 49968
Nomellini, Paul J., (Retired), 1826 Mary's Way, Kingsford, 49802
Norden, Emmett M., (Retired), P.O. Box 562, Escanaba, 49829
Poisson, Thomas L., (Retired), 300 Rock St., Apt. 2, 49855
Rupp, Daniel N., (Retired)
Schaeffer, Richard C., (Retired), P.O. Box 9, Roscommon, 48653-0009
Sedlock, David W., (Retired), 477 Adams, Gwinn, 49841
Shiverski, John J., (Retired), 2916 3rd Ave. S., Apt. 12, Escanaba, 49829
Valerio, Raymond A., (Retired), 831 E. Grant, Iron Mountain, 49801
Vichich, Michael T., (Retired), P.O. Box 15, Crystal Falls, 49920
Wantland, Thomas A., (Retired), 137 Drifting Sands Dr., Venice, FL 34293
Williams, James J., (Retired), 1203 Wenniway, Mackinaw City, 49701
Zaloga, Daniel S., (Retired), 12161 N. Whitefish Point Rd., P.O. Box 325, Paradise, 49768
Zeugner, Raymond L., (Retired), 7055 Fairview Village Cir., Winter Haven, FL 33881.

Permanent Deacons:
Adler, David, Bay City, MI
Beckley, Vincent W., Resurrection, Menominee
Bygrave, Roger A., St. Joseph, Rudyard
Cadeau, John M., Holy Name of Jesus/Blessed Kateri Tekakwitha, Assinins
Chaltry, Roland, Holy Redeemer, Menominee
Christy, Donald R., St. Mary-St. Joseph, Iron Mountain
Corrigan, Thomas F., St. Anne, Chassell
Foye, Thomas E., St. Peter Cathedral, Marquette
Gervasio, Charles H., Holy Spirit, Menominee
Green, William, St. Anne, Wausau, WI
Gretzinger, Stephen S., Holy Spirit, Menominee
Gualdoni, Steven J., St. Christopher, Marquette
Hamen, Robert, Our Lady of Peace, Ironwood
Jackson, Dean J., St. Peter Cathedral, Marquette
Jamieson, Scott A., St. Louis the King, Marquette
Kostka, Robert J., St. Cecilia, Caspian; St. Agnes, Iron River
La Cosse, Robert, St. Michael, Marquette
LaPlante, Joseph A., St. Francis Xavier, Brimley; Mission of Blessed Kateri Tekakwitha, Bay Mills
Leadbetter, John S., St. Peter Cathedral, Marquette
LeBeau, Michael, St. Anne, Escanaba
Londo, Lawrence H., St. Peter Cathedral, Marquette
Maki, Dennis R., St. Michael, Marquette
McClelland, Thomas, St. Ignatius Loyola, St. Ignace
Moseley, Thomas W. Jr., St. Christopher, Marquette
Piche, William J., St. Joseph, Sault Ste. Marie
Rivard, Thomas J., Precious Blood, Menominee
Roetzer, Gerald G., Resurrection, Menominee
Sanders, Claire W., St. Joseph Mission, Foster City
Saunders, Terrance J., St. Anne, Escanaba
Schaffer, Steven M., St. Joseph, Ishpeming
St. John, Gregg R., St. Louis the King, Marquette
Stancher, Arthur, St. Paul the Apostle, Calumet; Sacred Heart, Calumet
Talford, David A., St. Anthony of Padua, Wells
Thoren, Donald W., St. Peter Cathedral, Marquette
Vailliencourt, Lewis, St. Anne, Escanaba
Vonck, Warren K., St. Louis the King, Marquette
Weaver, Matthew P., Holy Family, Ontonagon
Wittak, Jay W., Union Grove, WI.

INSTITUTIONS LOCATED IN DIOCESE

[A] ELEMENTARY INTERPAROCHIAL SCHOOLS

MARQUETTE. *Father Marquette Catholic Academy*, (Grades PreK-8), 500 S. Fourth St., 49855. Tel: 906-225-1129; Fax: 906-225-1987; Email: jbetz@fathermarquette.org; Web: fathermarquette.org. Mary Jo Scamperle, Prin. Serving the following parishes: St. Peter's Cathedral; St. Louis; St. Michael; St. Christopher. Lay Teachers 12; Students 129.

ESCANABA. *Holy Name Catholic School*, (Grades PreK-8), 409 S. 22nd St., Escanaba, 49829. Tel: 906-786-7550; Fax: 906-786-7582; Email: office@holynamecrusaders.com; Web: holynamecrusaders.com. Joseph L. Carlson, Prin. Lay Teachers 20; Students 320.

IRON MOUNTAIN. *Bishop Baraga Catholic School*, (Grades PreK-8), 406 W. B St., Iron Mountain, 49801. Tel: 906-774-2277; Fax: 906-774-8704; Email: office@baragaup.com; Email: aoller@baragaup.com; Web: www.baragaup.com. Angela Oller, Prin.; Annette Meiner, Business Mgr. Lay Teachers 10; Students 103.

IRONWOOD. *All Saints Catholic Academy*, (Grades PreK-5), 106 S. Marquette St., Ironwood, 49938. Tel: 906-932-3200; Fax: 906-932-1019; Email: emily.gardner@snu.edu; Email: tammieruby906@gmail.com; Web: allsaintscatholic.homestead.com. Ms. Emily Lightfoot, Acting Prin. Serving Our Lady of Peace, Ironwood. Religious Teachers 1; Lay Teachers 5; Students 32.

L'ANSE. *Sacred Heart School*, (Grades K-8), 433 Baraga Ave., Lanse, 49946. Tel: 906-524-5157; Fax: 906-524-5154; Email: principal@sacredheartlanse.org; Email: secretary@sacredheartlanse.org; Web: www.sacredheartlanse.org. Christy Miron, Prin. Religious Teachers 1; Lay Teachers 4; Students 57.

MANISTIQUE. *St. Francis de Sales School*, (Grades PreSchool-8), 210 Lake St., Manistique, 49854. Tel: 906-341-5512; Fax: 906-341-3984; Email: don.erickson@sfdsraiders.com; Web: www.sfdsraiders.com. Don Erickson, Prin.; Karen Mooi, Librarian. Religious Teachers 1; Lay Teachers 12; Students 121.

MENOMINEE. *St. John Paul II Catholic Academy*, (Grades PreK-8), 2701 17th St., Menominee, 49858. Tel: 906-863-3190; Fax: 906-863-3990; Email: secretary@jpiicatholicacademy.org; Email: principal@jpiicatholicacademy.org; Email: bookkeeper@jpiicatholicacademy.org; Web: www.jpiicatholicacademy.org. Michael Muhs, Prin.; Diane Mielke, Librarian
Menominee Catholic Central School Lay Teachers 10; Students 128.

NORWAY. *Holy Spirit Central School*, (Grades PreK-8), 201 Saginaw St., Norway, 49870. Tel: 906-563-8817; Fax: 906-563-8854; Email: office@hscsnorway.org; Web: hscsnorway.org. Melissa Menghini, Prin. Religious Teachers 1; Lay Teachers 6; Students 64.

SAULT SAINTE MARIE. *St. Mary School*, (Grades PreK-8), 360 Maple St., Sault Sainte Marie, 49783. Tel: 906-635-6141; Fax: 906-635-6934; Email: hyanni@eupschools.org. Hedy Yanni, Prin.; Karen Shackleton, Librarian. Serves all area Catholic parishes students as well as non-Catholic students. Religious Teachers 1; Lay Teachers 10; Students 138.

[B] ENDOWMENT FUNDS

MARQUETTE. *Marquette Area Catholic Education Fund*, 401 W. Kaye Ave., 49855. Tel: 906-226-3900; Email: mhdavenport54@hotmail.com. Mrs. Maura Davenport, Pres.

Upper Peninsula Catholic Foundation, Inc. aka U.P. Catholic Foundation, 1004 Harbor Hills Dr., 49855. Tel: 906-227-9108; Fax: 906-225-0437; Email: tgadzinski@dioceseofmarquette.org; Web: upcatholicfoundation.org. Terri Gadzinski, Dir.

ESCANABA. *Holy Name Endowment Fund*, 409 S. 22nd St., Escanaba, 49829. Tel: 906-786-7550; Fax: 906-786-7582; Email: office@holynamecrusaders.com. Joseph L. Carlson, Prin.

Holy Name Scholarship Foundation, 409 S. 22nd St., Escanaba, 49829. Tel: 906-786-7550; Fax: 906-786-7582; Email: office@holynamecrusaders.com. Joseph L. Carlson, Prin.

IRON MOUNTAIN. *Bishop Baraga Catholic School Foundation*, 406 W. B St., Iron Mountain, 49801. Tel: 906-774-2277; Fax: 906-774-8704; Email: aoller@baragaup.com; Email: office@baragaup.com; Web: www.baragaup.com. Angela Oller, Prin.; Jerry Brien, Chm.

IRONWOOD. *Our Lady of Peace School Educational Fund*, 108 S. Marquette St., Ironwood, 49938-2060. Tel: 906-932-0174; Fax: 906-932-1019; Email: ktlolop@gmail.com. Rev. Robb M. Jurkovich.

MANISTIQUE. *St. Francis de Sales Education Foundation*, 330 Oak St., Manistique, 49854. Tel: 906-341-5355; Email: jimjweber52@gmail.com; Web: stfrancisofmanistique.weconnect.com. James Weber, Pres.

MENOMINEE. *Menominee Catholic Education Fund*, 2701 17th St., Menominee, 49858-2604. Tel: 906-863-3190; Fax: 906-863-3990; Email: bookkeeper@jpiicatholicacademy.org. Mary Fox, Business Mgr.

NEGAUNEE. *Negaunee St. Paul Endowment Fund*, 202 W. Case St., Negaunee, 49866. Tel: 906-475-9969; Email: stpaul@chartermi.net. Rev. Msgr. Peter Oberto, J.C.L., (Retired).

NORWAY. *Holy Spirit Central School Educational Fund*, 201 Saginaw, Norway, 49870. Tel: 906-563-8817; Fax: 908-563-8854; Email: info@hscsnorway.org. Melissa Menghini, Prin.

SAULT SAINTE MARIE. *St. Mary School Endowment Fund*, 360 Maple St., Sault Sainte Marie, 49783. Tel: 906-635-6141; Fax: 906-635-6934; Email: hyanni@eupschools.org. Hedy Yanni, Prin.

[C] GENERAL HOSPITALS

ESCANABA. *OSF HealthCare St. Francis Hospital & Medical Group* O.S.F. Healthcare System. 3401 Ludington, Escanaba, 49829. Tel: 906-786-3311; Fax: 906-786-4004; Email: robert.brandfass@osfhealthcare.org; Web: www.osfhealthcare.org. David S. Lord, Pres.; Rev. Emmett M. Norden, Chap., (Retired). Bed Capacity 25; Tot Asst. Annually 131,824; Total Staff 489.

[D] HOMES FOR THE AGED

ESCANABA. *Bishop Noa Home for Senior Citizens*, 2900 3rd Ave. S., Escanaba, 49829. Tel: 906-786-5810; Fax: 906-786-5372; Email: administration@bishopnoahome.com; Web: www.bishopnoahome.com. Elsie Stafford, Admin. Sisters of St. Paul de Chartres. Bed Capacity 109; Residents 129; Sisters 3; Tot Asst. Annually 33,813; Staff 139.

[E] CONVENTS AND RESIDENCES OF SISTERS

MARQUETTE. *Provincialate of the Sisters of St. Paul de Chartres*, 1300 County Rd. 492, 49855. Tel: 906-226-3932; Fax: 906-226-2139; Email: sregarcia@yahoo.com; Web: sistersofstpaulus.org. Sr. Estela Garcia, Supr. Sisters 12.

IRON MOUNTAIN. *Monastery of the Holy Cross*, N4028 Hwy. U.S. 2, Iron Mountain, 49801. P.O. Box 397, Iron Mountain, 49801-0397. Tel: 906-774-0561; Fax: 906-774-0561; Email: vocation@holycrosscarmel.com; Web: www.holycrosscarmel.com. Mother Maria of Jesus, O.C.D., Prioress. Discalced Carmelite Nuns. Sisters 3; Solemnly Professed 16.

[F] RETREAT HOUSES

GARDEN. *Marygrove Retreat Center*, 6411 State St., P.O. Box 38, Garden, 49835. Tel: 906-644-2771; Email: mgcbox38@centurylink.net; Web: www.marygrove.org. Very Rev. Timothy Ferguson, Rector. Retreats and workshops for priests, religious and laity.

[G] NEWMAN CLUBS

MARQUETTE. *Catholic Campus Ministry-Northern Michigan University*, 1200 Hebard Ct., 49855. 401 W. Kaye Ave., 49855. Tel: 906-228-3302; Fax: 906-228-5502; Email: ccm@nmu.edu; Web: www.nmuccm.com. Revs. Gregory R. Heikkala, Dir.; Brandon Oman, Campus Min.

HOUGHTON. *St. Albert the Great University Parish* aka Catholic Campus Ministry at Michigan Tech (1963) 411 MacInnes Dr., Houghton, 49931. Tel: 906-482-5530; Fax: 906-482-5530; Email: stalbert@stal-mtu.com; Web: www.mtucatholic.org. Rev. Ben Hasse, Email: benjhasse@yahoo.com.

SAULT SAINTE MARIE. *Lake Superior State University, Newman Center*, 517 W. Easterday Ave., Sault Sainte Marie, 49783. Tel: 906-253-1285; Email: catholicnewmancenterlssu@gmail.com. Rev. Michael D. Chenier; Danna Schmitter, Contact Person.

[H] ASSOCIATIONS OF THE FAITHFUL

PARADISE. *Companions of Christ the Lamb*, P.O. Box 12, Paradise, 49768. Tel: 906-492-3647; Fax: 906-492-3648; Email: communityofccl@gmail.com. Revs. John Fabian, Mod.; Jernej Sustar; Daniel S. Zaloga, (Retired).

RELIGIOUS INSTITUTES OF MEN REPRESENTED IN THE DIOCESE

For further details refer to the corresponding bracketed number in the Religious Institutes of Men or Women section.

[0470]—*The Capuchin Friars* (Detroit, MI)—O.F.M.Cap.

[]—*Missionary Congregation of the Blessed Sacrament* (Kerala, India)—M.C.B.S.

[]—*Missionary Society of St. Thomas the Apostle* (Kerala, India)—M.S.T.

RELIGIOUS INSTITUTES OF WOMEN REPRESENTED IN THE DIOCESE

[0420]—*Discalced Carmelite Nuns*—O.C.D.

[1630]—*Franciscan Sisters of Christian Charity*—O.S.F.

[3980]—*Sisters of St. Paul of Chartres*—S.P.C.

[2180]—*Sisters of the Immaculate Heart of Mary*—I.H.M.

DIOCESAN CEMETERIES

MARQUETTE. *Holy Cross Catholic Cemetery*, 1400 Wright St., 49855. Tel: 906-225-0191; Email: nnewcomb@dioceseofmarquette.org. Neil Newcomb, Dir.

ESCANABA. *Holy Cross Catholic Cemetery*, 3026 Lake Shore Dr., Escanaba, 49829. Tel: 906-786-4685; Email: tstannard@dioceseofmarquette.org. Tom Stannard, Business Mgr.

NECROLOGY

† Schiska, Paul A., (Retired), Died Sep. 4, 2018

An asterisk (*) denotes an organization that has established tax-exempt status directly with the IRS and is not covered by the USCCB Group Ruling.

Diocese of Memphis

(Memphitana in Tennesia)

Most Reverend

DAVID P. TALLEY

Bishop of Memphis; ordained June 3, 1989; appointed Titular Bishop of Lambaesis and Auxiliary Bishop of Atlanta January 3, 2013; ordained April 2, 2013; appointed Coadjutor Bishop of Alexandria September 21, 2016; installed November 7, 2016; Succeeded February 2, 2017; appointed Bishop of Memphis March 5, 2019; installed April 2, 2019.

Most Reverend

MARTIN D. HOLLEY, D.D.

Former Bishop of Memphis in Tennessee; ordained May 8, 1987; appointed Titular Bishop of Rusibisir and Auxiliary Bishop of Washington, DC July 2, 2004; appointed Bishop of Memphis in Tennessee August 23, 2016; installed October 19, 2016; removed October 24, 2018.

ESTABLISHED JANUARY 6, 1971.

Square Miles 10,682.

Comprises the Counties of Benton, Carroll, Chester, Crockett, Decatur, Dyer, Fayette, Gibson, Hardeman, Hardin, Haywood, Henderson, Henry, Lake, Lauderdale, McNairy, Madison, Obion, Shelby, Tipton and Weakley in the State of Tennessee.

For legal titles of parishes and diocesan institutions, consult the Chancery Office.

Catholic Center: P.O. Box 341669, Memphis, TN 38184-1669. Tel: 901-373-1200; Fax: 901-373-1269.

Web: www.cdom.org

STATISTICAL OVERVIEW

Personnel	
Bishop	1
Retired Bishops	2
Priests: Diocesan Active in Diocese	61
Priests: Diocesan Active Outside Diocese	3
Priests: Retired, Sick or Absent	17
Number of Diocesan Priests	81
Religious Priests in Diocese	10
Total Priests in Diocese	91
Extern Priests in Diocese	9
Ordinations:	
Diocesan Priests	1
Permanent Deacons in Diocese	74
Total Brothers	38
Total Sisters	37
Parishes	
Parishes	42
With Resident Pastor:	
Resident Diocesan Priests	36
Resident Religious Priests	5
Without Resident Pastor:	
Administered by Deacons	1
Missions	6
Pastoral Centers	1
Professional Ministry Personnel:	
Brothers	38
Sisters	37
Lay Ministers	71
Welfare	
Homes for the Aged	2
Day Care Centers	2
Total Assisted	650
Special Centers for Social Services	1
Total Assisted	27,292
Educational	
Diocesan Students in Other Seminaries	17
Total Seminarians	17
Colleges and Universities	1
Total Students	1,892
High Schools, Diocesan and Parish	3
Total Students	833
High Schools, Private	3
Total Students	1,303
Elementary Schools, Diocesan and Parish	17
Total Students	4,126
Elementary Schools, Private	1
Total Students	450
Catechesis/Religious Education:	
High School Students	221
Elementary Students	2,424
Total Students under Catholic Instruction	11,266
Teachers in the Diocese:	
Brothers	7
Sisters	7
Lay Teachers	566
Vital Statistics	
Receptions into the Church:	
Infant Baptism Totals	1,077
Minor Baptism Totals	164
Adult Baptism Totals	77
Received into Full Communion	184
First Communions	1,382
Confirmations	1,235
Marriages:	
Catholic	193
Interfaith	69
Total Marriages	262
Deaths	376
Total Catholic Population	61,793
Total Population	1,561,304

Former Bishops—Most Revs. CARROLL T. DOZIER, D.D., ord. March 19, 1937; appt. Nov. 17, 1970; cons. Jan. 6, 1971; retired July 27, 1982; died Dec. 7, 1985; J. FRANCIS STAFFORD, D.D., ord. Dec. 15, 1957; cons. Bishop Feb. 29, 1976; appt. Nov. 16, 1982; appt. to Archdiocese of Denver, June 3, 1986; DANIEL M. BUECHLEIN, O.S.B., D.D., ord. May 3, 1964; appt. to Memphis Jan. 16, 1987; cons. Bishop Marsh 2, 1987; installed March 2, 1987; appt. Archdiocese of Indianapolis, July 14, 1992; installed Sept. 9, 1992; retired Sept. 21, 2011; died Jan. 25, 2018.; J. TERRY STEIB, S.V.D., D.D., (Retired), ord. Jan. 6, 1967; appt. Titular Bishop of Fallaba and Auxiliary Bishop of St. Louis Dec. 6, 1983; cons. Feb. 10, 1984; appt. Bishop of Memphis March 23, 1993; installed May 5, 1993; retired Aug. 23, 2016.; MARTIN D. HOLLEY, (Retired), ord. May 8, 1987; appt. Titular Bishop of Rusibisir and Auxiliary Bishop of Washington, DC July 2, 2004; appt. Bishop of Memphis in Tennessee August 23, 2016; installed Oct. 19, 2016; retired Oct. 24, 2018.

Vicar General—Catholic Center, 5825 Shelby Oaks Dr., Memphis, 38134. Tel: 901-373-1200.

Moderator of the Curia—VACANT.

Chancellor—Very Rev. JAMES M. CLARK, J.C.L., J.V.

Diocesan Offices & Directors

All diocesan office addresses & phone numbers are the same as mentioned above under Catholic Center Offices unless otherwise noted.

Historical Archives—Rev. KRZYSZTOF PELCZAR, Historical Archivist.

Catholic Public Policy Commission of Tennessee—VACANT.

College of Consultors—Rev. Msgr. VICTOR P. CIARAMITARO, E.V.; Very Rev. CARL JUDE HOOD, E.V.; Revs. JOHN J. HOURICAN; JOHNNIE B. SMITH; FRANCIS CHIAWA, (Nigeria) S.T.D.; JOLLY SEBASTIAN, M.C.B.S., (India); JACEK L. KOWAL; ROBERT W. MARSHALL JR.; BENJAMIN P. BRADSHAW; PAUL D. WATKINS, O.P.; Very Rev. JAMES M. CLARK, J.C.L., J.V.

Episcopal Vicars for Clergy—VACANT.

Media Consultant—VACANT.

Director for Development—MR. JIM MARCONI, Tel: 901-373-1200; Fax: 901-373-1269.

Director of Communications—VACANT.

Magazine—Faith West Tennessee; Electronic Media: "West Tennessee Catholic" MRS. SUZANNE AVILES, Editor & Dir. Communications, Tel: 901-373-1213.

Continuing Education for Clergy—Rev. RICHARD L. MICKEY, M.Ed.

Formation of Permanent Deacons—Tel: 901-682-6606. Deacon JEFFREY DRZYCIMSKI.

Director of Permanent Deacons—Tel: 901-487-7238. Deacon WILLIAM (BILL) DAVIS.

Director of Seminarians—Very Rev. JAMES M. CLARK, J.C.L., J.V., Dir.

Director of Vocations—Revs. YOELVIS GONZALEZ, Dir.; DEXTER NOBLEFRANCA, Asst. Dir.

Episcopal Delegate for Religious—Rev. AUGUSTINE JOSEPH DEARMOND, O.P.

Villa Vianney Senior Priests Residence—Rev. RICHARD L. MICKEY, M.Ed., Dir., 10605 Bishop Dozier Dr., Cordova, 38016. Tel: 901-752-0766.

Multicultural Ministries—

African American Catholics Ministry—Deacon NORMAN ALEXANDER, Chm., Council of African American Catholic Ministry, 5854 Sun Cove, Memphis, 38134. Tel: 901-497-1132.

Filipino Catholic Ministry—DR. OLIVIA KABIGAO, Pres., Tel: 901-921-3719.

Korean Catholic Ministry—VACANT.

Native American Catholic Ministry—MR. JASON TERRELL, Chairperson, Tel: 901-730-6706.

Polish Catholic Ministry—MRS. BARBARA WALKOWC, Pres., Tel: 901-754-1649; Rev. ROBERT SZCZECHURA, M.Div., M.A., Spiritual Advisor, Tel: 901-382-2504.

Vietnamese Catholic Ministry—Rev. SIMON THOI HOANG, S.V.D., Tel: 901-726-1891.

African Catholic Ministry—Rev. FRANCIS CHIAWA, (Nigeria) S.T.D., Dir., Tel: 731-925-4852.

Hispanic Catholic Ministry—Mailing Address: Catholic Center, 5825 Shelby Oaks Dr., Memphis, 38134. Tel: 901-373-1224; Fax: 901-373-1269. MS. ALMA Q. ABUELOUF, B.S.N., R.N.

FOCCUS Training—(Hispanic) WENDY VAZQUEZ, Coord. Catholic Center Marriage Preparation Ministry, Tel: 901-373-1200.

Hispanic Marriage Enrichment—5825 Shelby Oaks Dr., Memphis, 38134. Tel: 901-373-1222; Fax: 901-373-1269. WENDY VAZQUEZ, Coord. Catholic Center Marriage Preparation Ministry.

Hispanic Marriage Preparation—WENDY VAZQUEZ, Coord. Catholic Center Marriage Preparation Ministry, Tel: 901-373-1200.

Tribunal

Judicial Vicar—Very Rev. JAMES M. CLARK, J.C.L., J.V.; MRS. ANNA M. LYNN, J.C.L.

Ecclesiastical Notaries—Very Rev. JAMES M. CLARK, J.C.L., J.V.; Rev. CARLOS DONATO; MRS. NANCY HENNESSEY.

Facilities

Facilities and Risk Management—5825 Shelby Oaks Dr., Memphis, 38134-1669. Tel: 901-373-1200; Fax: 901-373-1269. MR. JAMES E. HEIRIGS, Dir.

Catholic Cemeteries—Calvary, Memphis; All Saints, Memphis; Mount Calvary, Jackson, TN MR. PATRICK POSEY SR., Dir., 1663 Elvis Presley Blvd., Memphis, 38106. Tel: 901-948-1529.

Engineering & Maintenance—5825 Shelby Oaks Dr., Memphis, 38134-1669. Tel: 901-373-1200; Fax: 901-373-1269. MR. JAMES E. HEIRIGS, Dir.

Department of Human Resources

Director of Human Resources—MRS. SANDRA GOLDSTEIN, Dir.

Employee Benefits—MRS. SHARON ICHNIOWSKI.

Office for Professional Responsibilities/Child and Youth Protection—MRS. SANDRA GOLDSTEIN.

Technical Services—MS. KATHY SABA, M.C.S.E., Dir.

Department for Social Ministries

Catholic Charities of West Tennessee—1325 Jefferson Ave., Memphis, 38104. Tel: 901-722-4700; Fax: 901-722-4791; Web: www.ccwtn.org. RICHARD HACKETT, Exec. Dir.

Finance—MRS. BRENDA O'LOONEY, Dir. Finance & Admin., Tel: 901-722-4700; Fax: 901-722-4766.

Marketing & Public Relations—Tel: 901-722-4700; Fax: 901-722-4791. LEIGH ANN ROMAN, Dir. Communications & Devel.

Camp Love & Learn—MRS. VIRGINIA DAVENPORT, Camp Dir., Tel: 901-722-4700; Fax: 901-722-4791.

Immigration Services—MRS. CHRISTINE BUTSON, Prog. Dir., Tel: 901-722-4700; Fax: 901-722-4791.

Volunteer In-Kind—Tel: 901-722-4700; Fax: 901-722-4791. MRS. MANDY LAMEY, Coord. Supportive Svcs.

Community & Parish Social Services—MRS. THERESE GUSTAITIS, Dir. Parish Social Ministry, Tel: 901-722-4700; Fax: 901-722-4791.

Housing Ministries Director—Tel: 901-722-4700. MRS. DANA BROOKS.

Department of Education/Catholic Schools Office

Department of Education/Catholic Schools Office—5825 Shelby Oaks Dr., Memphis, 38134. Tel: 901-373-1200; Fax: 901-373-1223.

Superintendent of Catholic Schools—MRS. JANET M. DONATO, Supt., Tel: 901-373-1200; Email: janet.donato@cc.cdom.org; MRS. SONDRA MORRIS, Dir. Diocesan Athletics, Tel: 901-260-2840; DR. COLLEEN BUTTERICK, Dir. School Counseling Svcs., Tel: 901-373-1219; MRS. TALLIE HODGES, Administrative Asst., Tel: 901-373-1219.

Department for Finance

Chief Financial Officer—MR. RICK HETHERINGTON.

Controller—MS. PATTI MORRIS.

Senior Finance Accountant—REBECCA HOLDER.

Department of Pastoral Life Ministries

Director of Pastoral Life Ministries—MS. ALMA Q. ABUELOUF, B.S.N., R.N., Mailing Address: Catholic Center, 5825 Shelby Oaks Dr., Memphis, 38134. Tel: 901-373-1224; Fax: 901-373-1269.

Director of Campus & Young Adult Ministry—SAM MAUCK.

Campus & Young Adult Ministry—3625 Mynders Ave., Memphis, 38111. Tel: 901-323-3051. See Section (J) Newman Centers for additional information.

Community Health Ministry—(Ministry to Sick, Ministry for People with Disability and Special Needs, Mid-South Area Assoc. of Catholic Nurses, Health Ministries Network of the Mid-South, Mental Illness Ministry). MS. ALMA Q. ABUELOUF, B.S.N., R.N., Dir.

Evangelization—MS. ALMA Q. ABUELOUF, B.S.N., R.N., Dir.

Family Ministries—MS. ALMA Q. ABUELOUF, B.S.N., R.N., Dir., Mailing Address: 5825 Shelby Oaks Dr., Memphis, 38134. Tel: 901-373-1200; Email: alma.abuelouf@cc.cdom.org.

Bereavement Ministry—(for those grieving a loss through death) *Mailing Address: Catholic Center, 5825 Shelby Oaks Dr., Memphis, 38134*. Tel: 901-373-1224; Fax: 901-373-1269. MS. ALMA Q. ABUELOUF, B.S.N., R.N.

Catholic Divorce Care Ministry—(Ministry for Separated and Divorced) *Mailing Address: Catholic Center, 5825 Shelby Oaks Dr., Memphis, 38134*. Tel: 901-373-1224; Fax: 901-373-1269. MS. ALMA Q. ABUELOUF, B.S.N., R.N.

Beginning Experience—(a ministry for the Separated, Divorced, Widowed) *Mailing Address: Catholic Center, 5825 Shelby Oaks Dr., Memphis, 38134*. Tel: 901-373-1224; Fax: 901-373-1269. MS. ALMA Q. ABUELOUF, B.S.N., R.N.

Marriage Preparation Ministry (English)—WENDY VAZQUEZ, Coord. Catholic Center Marriage Preparation Ministry, Tel: 901-373-1200.

Marriage Encounter—Mailing Address: Catholic Center, 5825 Shelby Oaks Dr., Memphis, 38134. Tel: 901-373-1224; Fax: 901-373-1269. MS. ALMA Q. ABUELOUF, B.S.N., R.N.

Marriage Enrichment—Mailing Address: Catholic Center, 5825 Shelby Oaks Dr., Memphis, 38134. Tel: 901-373-1224; Fax: 901-373-1269. MS. ALMA Q. ABUELOUF, B.S.N., R.N.

Programs for the Engaged—WENDY VAZQUEZ, Coord. Catholic Marriage Preparation Ministry, Tel: 901-373-1200.

Sponsor Couple Training—(Couples working with those preparing for marriage). WENDY VAZQUEZ, Coord. Catholic Center Marriage Preparation Ministry, Tel: 901-373-1200.

Natural Family Planning Center/Pro Life Office & Chastity Education—WENDY VAZQUEZ, Coord. Catholic Center Marriage Preparation Ministry, Tel: 901-373-1200.

Rachel's Vineyard—Tel: 901-463-3595; 877 HOPE 4 ME; Email: RVMPHS@gmail.com.

Mother/Daughter and Father/Son Fertility Appreciation & Chastity Programs—(Chastity promotion materials). WENDY VAZQUEZ, Coord. Catholic Center Marriage Preparation Ministry, Tel: 901-373-1200.

Parish Pastoral Councils—MS. ALMA Q. ABUELOUF, B.S.N., R.N., Dir.

Prison Ministries—Deacon WILLIAM (BILL) DAVIS, Dir.

Youth Ministries—SAM MAUCK.

Search—Rev. MICHAEL E. WERKHOVEN, Spiritual Dir.

Scouting—MR. CHUCK SCHADRACK, Chm.; Rev. WAYNE H. ARNOLD, Chap.

Director for Development—MR. JIM MARCONI, Tel: 901-373-1200; Fax: 901-373-1269.

Our Lady Queen of Peace Retreat Center—3630 Dancyville Rd., Stanton, 38069-4711. Tel: 731-548-2500. Rev. COSMAS MABU, Spiritual Dir.

Charismatic Renewal—Deacon WERNER ROSE, Diocesan Liaison, Tel: 901-754-7146; SHARON REITER, Assoc. Liaison, Tel: 734-584-6459.

Cursillo—DAVID CARNEY, Lay Dir., Email: laydirector@memphiscursillo.com; Web: memphiscursillo.com; Revs. DENNIS L. SCHENKEL; ENRIQUE GRANADOS GARCIA.

CLERGY, PARISHES, MISSIONS AND PAROCHIAL SCHOOLS

CITY OF MEMPHIS

(SHELBY COUNTY)

1—CATHEDRAL OF THE IMMACULATE CONCEPTION (1921)
1695 Central Ave., 38104. Tel: 901-725-2700; Fax: 901-725-2709; Email: ronnie.vinson@ic.cdom.org; Web: www.iccathedral.org. Revs. Robert W. Marshall Jr.; Yoelvis Aloysius Gonzalez, Parochial Vicar; Deacons Alan Crone; Rick Martin; William Pettit.
School—Cathedral of the Immaculate Conception School, (Grades PreK-12), 1669 Central Ave., 38104. Tel: 901-725-2710; Fax: 901-725-2715; Email: info.iccs@ic.cdom.org; Web: myiccs.org. Karen Gephart, Prin. (Elementary); Tracey Ford, Interim High School Prin.; Nancy Miller, Librarian. Lay Teachers 36; Students 330.
High School—Cathedral of the Immaculate Conception High School, 1725 Central Ave., 38104. Tel: 901-725-2705; Email: tracey.ford@ic.cdom.org; Web: www.myiccs.org. High School Students 90.
Catechesis Religious Program—Tel: 901-435-5281; Email: aileen.palmer@ic.cdom.org. Aileen G. Palmer, D.R.E. Students 79.

2—ST. ANN (Bartlett) (1950)
St. Ann Catholic Church: 6529 Stage Rd., Bartlett, 38134. Tel: 901-373-6011; Fax: 901-373-9030; Email: info@stannbartlett.org; Web: www.stannbartlett.org. Revs. Ernie DeBlasio; William J. Parham; Deacons Chip Jones; Bob Skinner.
School—St. Ann School, (Grades PreK-8), Tel: 901-386-3328; Email: joey.harris@sascolts.org; Web: www.sascolts.org. Lay Teachers 21; Students 215.
Catechesis Religious Program—Email: kathy.schober@stannbartlett.org. Kathy Schober, D.R.E. Students 212.

3—ST. ANNE'S (1933)
706 S. Highland St., 38111. Tel: 901-323-3817; Email: sandra.swain@stannechurch.cdom.org; Web: stannehighland.net. Rev. R. Bruce Cinquegrani; Deacon David Woolley.
Catechesis Religious Program—Email: tobryan328@yahoo.com. Mr. Thomas O'Bryan, D.R.E. Students 80.

4—ST. AUGUSTINE (1937) (African American)
1169 Kerr Ave., 38106. Tel: 901-774-2297; Fax: 901-774-1067; Email: staug.info@staugustine.cdom.org; Web: www.staugustinememphis.net. Rev. Francis Chiawa, (Nigeria) S.T.D.; Deacons Norman Alexander; Curtiss J. Talley.
Catechesis Religious Program—Tel: 901-774-2298. Students 9.

5—BLESSED SACRAMENT (1912)
2564 Hale Ave., 38112. Tel: 901-452-1543; Fax: 901-452-1592; Email: catholicmidtown@comcast.net; Web: memphismidtowncatholic.com. Rev. Edward K. Fisher.
Catechesis Religious Program—Sr. Monica P. Darrichon, S.Sp.S., D.R.E. Students 160.

6—ST. BRIGID (1992)
7801 Lowrance Rd., 38125-2825. Tel: 901-758-0128; Email: rvictor@stbrigidmemphis.org; Email: frstewart@stbrigidmemphis.org; Web: www.stbrigidmemphis.org. Rev. Keith Stewart.
Res.: 4200 Thunderstone Cir. W., 38125-3108.
Catechesis Religious Program—Email: ktrouy@stbrigidmemphis.org. Kim Trouy, D.R.E. Students 110.

7—CHURCH OF THE ASCENSION (1974)
3680 Ramill Rd., 38128-3245. Tel: 901-372-1364; Fax: 901-372-9411; Email: office@ascensionmemphis.org; Web: ascensionmemphis.org. Rev. Dennis L. Schenkel; Deacons Harvey Stewart; Michael Richardson.
Catechesis Religious Program—Email: DRE@ascensionmemphis.org. Irma Hernandez, D.R.E. Students 100.

8—CHURCH OF THE HOLY SPIRIT (1975)
2300 Hickory Crest Dr., 38119-6805. Tel: 901-754-7146; Email: christine.nourse@hspirit.cdom.org; Web: www.hspirit.com. Revs. John J. Hourican; Ajesh Joseph, Parochial Vicar; Deacons Richard Griffith; Werner Rose.
Catechesis Religious Program—
Tel: 901-754-7146, Ext. 30. Cisa Linxwiler, D.R.E. Students 199.

9—CHURCH OF THE INCARNATION (1978)
360 Bray Station Rd., Collierville, 38017-3263. Tel: 901-853-7468; Fax: 901-854-0536; Email: front.desk@incarnationcollierville.org; Web: www.incarnationchurch.com. Revs. Jacek L. Kowal; Thang Du "Peter" Nguyen; Deacons Greg Thomas; Miles Merwin; Robert Walker.
School—Church of the Incarnation School, (Grades 1-8), Tel: 901-853-7804; Email: michael.zientek@incarnationcollierville.org; Web: www.goics.org. Lay Teachers 17; Students 102.
Catechesis Religious Program—Tel: 901-853-0135; Email: lea.weaver@incarnationcollierville.org. Lea Weaver, Dir. Children's Faith Formation. Students 527.

10—CHURCH OF THE NATIVITY (1979)
5955 St. Elmo Rd., Bartlett, 38135-1516. Tel: 901-382-2504; Email: Angie.oneill@nativity.cdom.org. Rev. Robert Szczechura, M.Div., M.A.; Deacons Franklin O. Larker; Christopher Frame; David Rosenthal.
Res.: 3830 Billy Maher Rd., Barlett, 38135-1516.
Catechesis Religious Program—Theresa Krier, D.R.E. Students 150.

11—CHURCH OF THE RESURRECTION (1973)
5475 Newberry Ave., 38115-3629. Tel: 901-794-8970; Fax: 901-794-8806; Email: resurrectionmemphis@comcast.net; Web: www.resurrectionmemphis.org. Revs. James J. Martell; Rito De Santiago-Carreon; Deacon Justin Mitchell.

Catechesis Religious Program—Email: predirector@comcast.net. Sara S. Westrich, D.R.E. Students 239.

12—ST. FRANCIS OF ASSISI (1985)
8151 Chimneyrock Blvd., Cordova, 38016.
Tel: 901-756-1213; Fax: 901-755-2168; Email: office@stfrancismemphis.org; Web: www.stfrancismemphis.org. Very Rev. Carl Jude Hood, E.V.; Revs. Carl Gregorich; Johnnie B. Smith, Senior Priest; Deacons William (Bill) Davis; Chuck Lightcap; Mick Hovanec; Anthony (Tony) Rudolph.
School—St. Francis of Assisi School, (Grades PreK-8), 2100 N. Germantown Pkwy., Cordova, 38016.
Tel: 901-388-7321; Fax: 901-388-8201; Email: alicia.brown@sfawolves.org; Web: www.sfawolves.org. Mrs. Alicia Brown, Prin.; Mrs. Antonia Corzine, Asst. Prin.; Mrs. Stephanie Jones, Asst. Prin.; Cynthia Lopez, Librarian. Lay Teachers 55; Students 532.
Catechesis Religious Program—Mrs. Betty Siano, D.R.E. Students 404.

13—HOLY NAMES OF JESUS AND MARY (1939)
697 Keel Ave., 709 Keel Ave., 38107-2599.
Tel: 901-525-9870; Fax: 901-527-7436; Email: angela.delaney@holynames.cdom.org. Rev. Francis Chiawa, (Nigeria) S.T.D.; Ms. Angela Delaney, Volunteer.
Catechesis Religious Program—

14—HOLY ROSARY (1955)
4851 Park Ave., 38117. Tel: 901-767-6949; Email: rayna.cobb@holyrosarymemphis.org; Web: www.holyrosarychurchmphs.org. Revs. Russell D. Harbaugh; Richard A. Cortese, Parochial Vicar; Jeo Poulose, Parochial Vicar; Deacons David Dierkes; Kenneth McCarver; Daniel Brown; G. Richmond Quinton; James McBride.
School—Holy Rosary School, (Grades PreK-8), 4841 Park Ave., 38117. Tel: 901-685-1231;
Fax: 901-818-0335; Email: darren.mullis@holyrosarychurchmemphis.org. Darren Mullis, Prin.; Kathy Elmer, Librarian. Lay Teachers 60; Students 426.
Catechesis Religious Program—Email: laina.haff@holyrosarymemphis.org. Laina Haff, D.R.E. Students 441.

15—ST. JAMES (1956)
4180 LeRoy, 38108. Tel: 901-767-8672;
Fax: 901-767-8576; Email: stjamescatholic@bellsouth.net. Rev. Gerald Azike, S.T.D.

16—ST. JOHN'S (1947)
2742 Lamar Ave., 38114. Tel: 901-480-7055;
Fax: 901-672-7622; Email: stjohnmemphis@gmail.com. Deacon Walt Bolton, Admin.

17—ST. JOSEPH CATHOLIC CHURCH (1878)
3825 Neely Rd., 38109. Tel: 901-396-9996;
Fax: 901-332-8691; Email: stjosephsecretary@hotmail.com; Web: www.stjosephccmemphis.org. Rev. Juan Antonio Romo-Romo, S.V.D.; Deacon James Calicott.
Catechesis Religious Program—Email: m_darrichon@yahoo.com.ar. Sr. Mónica Darrichón, D.R.E. Students 161.

18—ST. LOUIS (1957)
203 S. White Station Rd., 38117. Tel: 901-255-1950;
Email: jan.odonnell@stlouis.cdom.org; Web: stlouischurchmphs.org. Revs. Jolly Sebastian, M.C.B.S., (India); William F. Burke; Carlos Donato; Deacons Ralph Donati, (Retired); Michael d'Addabbo; Jeffrey Drzycimski; Rev. Ruben Villalon-Rivera.
School—St. Louis School, (Grades PreK-8), 5192 Shady Grove Rd., 38117. Tel: 901-255-1900;
Fax: 901-328-9798; Email: kpesce@stlouismemphis.org; Web: www.stlouismemphis.org. Teddi Niedzwiedz, Prin. Aides 8; Lay Teachers 38; Students 528; Clergy / Religious Teachers 1.
Catechesis Religious Program—Email: csusindr@hotmail.com. Sr. Ancilia Indrati, D.R.E. Students 130.

19—ST. MARY CHURCH (1860)
155 Market St., 38105. Tel: 901-522-9420; Email: nancythielemier@gmail.com. Rev. Gary Lamb.
Catechesis Religious Program—Students 26.

20—ST. MICHAEL CHURCH (1951)
3863 Summer Ave., 38122. Tel: 901-323-0896;
Tel: 901-399-8800; Fax: 901-323-3557; Web: stmichaelmemphis.org. 3848 Forrest Ave., 38122. Revs. Benjamin P. Bradshaw; Jose Cruz Zapata-Torres, Parochial Vicar.
Res.: 3867 Summer Ave., 38122.
School—St. Michael Church School, (Grades PreK-8), 3880 Forrest Ave., 38122. Tel: 901-323-2162;
Fax: 901-323-0481; Email: school@stmichaelmemphis.org. Mary Anne Chiozza, Prin. Lay Teachers 13; Students 146.
Catechesis Religious Program—Mrs. Connie Razura, D.R.E. Students 558.

21—OUR LADY OF PERPETUAL HELP (1950)
8151 Poplar Ave., Germantown, 38138.
Tel: 901-754-1204, Ext. 325;
Tel: 901-753-1181, Ext. 340; Fax: 901-754-0969; Email: csneed@olphgermantown.org; Email: jlucchesi@olphgermantown.org; Web: www.olphgermantown.org. Rev. Mathew Panackachira, M.C.B.S.; Very Rev. James M. Clark, J.C.L., J.V.; Revs. Cain Galicia-Ramirez; Eric Peterson; Rev. Msgr. Victor P. Ciaramitaro, E.V., Senior Priest; Deacons David Lucchesi; John Moskal; Stephen Mangin; Ben Legett, Music Dir.
School—Our Lady of Perpetual Help School, (Grades PreK-8), 8151 Poplar, Germantown, 38138.
Tel: 901-753-1181, Ext. 340; Fax: 901-754-1475; Email: csneed@olphgermantown.org; Web: www.olphowls.org. Cristy Sneed, Prin.; Mrs. Elise Rodriguez, Vice Prin.; Mrs. Angela Saba, Sec.; Mrs. Laurie Cotros, Librarian; Barbara Moranville, Librarian. Faculty 21; Lay Teachers 21; Students 230.
Catechesis Religious Program—Email: cdemille@olphgermantown.org. Mr. Craig DeMille, D.R.E. Students 154.

22—OUR LADY OF SORROWS (1926)
3700 Thomas St., 38127. Tel: 901-353-1530;
Fax: 901-353-1052; Email: carolyn.roberts@ols.cdim.org. Rev. Bryan P. Timby; Deacon Henry P. Littleton.
Catechesis Religious Program—Maria Roque, D.R.E. Students 41.

23—ST. PATRICK'S (1866)
277 S 4th St., 38126. Tel: 901-527-2542; Web: www.stpatsmemphis.org; Email: julie.boland@stpat.cdom.org. Rev. Msgr. Valentine N. Handwerker; Deacons Eugene Champion; Frank Williams.
Res.: 670 S. Highland St., 38111.
Catechesis Religious Program—Students 14.

24—ST. PAUL THE APOSTLE (1944)
1425 E. Shelby Dr., 38116. Tel: 901-346-2380;
Fax: 901-346-2385; Email: jackie@stpaulmemphis.org; Web: www.stpaulmemphis.org. Revs. Stephen K. Kenny; Heriberto Granados, Parochial Vicar; Deacons Patrick Lyons; Andrew J. Terry.
School—St. Paul the Apostle School aka St. Paul Catholic School, (Grades PreK-7), Tel: 901-346-0862; Email: secretary.stpaul@stpaul.cdom.org. Sr. Mary Wright, O.P., Prin. Clergy 2; Lay Teachers 17; Students 262; Clergy / Religious Teachers 2.
Catechesis Religious Program—Mrs. Maria Jimenez, D.R.E. Students 129.

25—ST. PETER CHURCH (1840)
190 Adams Ave., 38103. Tel: 901-527-8282;
Fax: 901-526-6882; Email: secretary@stpeterchurch.org; Web: www.stpeterchurch.org. Revs. Augustine Joseph DeArmond, O.P.; Paul D. Watkins, O.P., Supr.; Ramon Gonzalez, O.P., Vicar; Deacon Eddie Ramsey.
Catechesis Religious Program—Christina Klyce, D.R.E. Students 159.

26—SACRED HEART CHURCH (1899)
1336 Jefferson Ave., 38104. Tel: 901-726-1891;
Fax: 901-339-1347; Email: contactus@sacredheartmemphis.org; Web: sacredheartmemphis.org. 1324 Jefferson Ave., 38104-2012. Revs. Simon Thoi Hoang, S.V.D.; Raymond Akumbilim.
Catechesis Religious Program—Students 188.

27—ST. THERESE THE LITTLE FLOWER (1930)
1644 Jackson Ave., 38107. Tel: 901-276-1412;
Fax: 901-274-4476; Email: sttherese@stlfchurch.cdom.org; Web: littleflowermemphis.org. Rev. Patrick Gallagher; Deacon Bill Lifsey.

28—ST. WILLIAM (1951)
4932 Easley Ave., Millington, 38053.
Tel: 901-872-4099; Email: lisa.rhodes@stwilliam.cdom.org; Web: stwilliamcc.org. Rev. Michael E. Werkhoven.
Catechesis Religious Program—Email: debbiebreckenridge@earthlink.net. Debbie Breckenridge, D.R.E. Students 97.

OUTSIDE SHELBY COUNTY

BOLIVAR, HARDEMAN CO., ST. MARY CHURCH (1950)
223 Mecklenburg Dr., Bolivar, 38008-1736.
Tel: 901-658-4627; Email: stmary9@bellsouth.net. Rev. Wayne H. Arnold.
Catechesis Religious Program—Students 16.

BROWNSVILLE, HAYWOOD CO., ST. JOHN CHURCH (1949)
910 N. Washington, Brownsville, 38012-0872.
Tel: 731-668-2596; Email: mona.strazzella@stmarys.tn.org. P.O. Box 872, Brownsville, 38012-0872. Revs. David Graham; Tojan Abaraham; Francisco Arroyo.
Catechesis Religious Program—Email: tsellari@bellsouth.net. Tommy Sellari, D.R.E. Students 47.

CAMDEN, BENTON CO., ST. MARY CHURCH (1981)
220 W. Main St., Camden, 38320. Tel: 731-584-6459; Email: smchfhcatholic@gmail.com. Rev. Herbert Ene, (Nigeria); Deacon Wayne Tedford.
Catechesis Religious Program—Sandra Simpson, D.R.E. Students 28.
Mission—Holy Family Church, 265 Cotham Dr., Huntingdon, Carroll Co. 38344.

COVINGTON, TIPTON CO., ST. ALPHONSUS CHURCH (1952)
1225 Hwy 51 S., Covington, 38019.
Tel: 901-476-8140; Fax: 901-476-9650; Email: office@stalphonsuscovington.org; Web: www.stalphonsuscovington.org. P.O. Box 430, Covington, 38019. Rev. Robert Ballman.
Res.: 1512 Evergreen, Covington, 38019.
Catechesis Religious Program—Karen Clark, D.R.E. Students 29.
Mission—Ave Maria, 664 S. Washington, Ripley, Lauderdale Co. 38063.

DYERSBURG, DYER CO., HOLY ANGELS CHURCH (1938) [CEM]
535 Tucker St., Dyersburg, 38024. Tel: 731-287-8000 ; Email: hachurch@cableone.net; Web: www.holyangelscc.com. Rev. Patrick Hirtz.
Res.: 527 Tucker St., Dyersburg, 38024.
Catechesis Religious Program—Email: nanacbeld@yahoo.com. Carrie Beld, D.R.E. Students 91.

HUMBOLDT, GIBSON CO., SACRED HEART (1872)
2887 E. Main St., Humboldt, 38343.
Tel: 731-784-3904; Fax: 731-784-5048; Email: sacredheart@aeneas.net. Rev. Mauricio Abeldaño; Deacons Ed Kutz; JR Hobbs.
Res.: 2881 E. Main St., Humboldt, 38343.
Catechesis Religious Program—Students 25.
Mission—St. Matthew, 9060 Telecom Dr., Milan, Northern Gibson Co. 38358.

JACKSON, MADISON CO., ST. MARY CHURCH (1867) [CEM]
1665 Hwy. 45 Byp., Jackson, 38305.
Tel: 731-668-2596; Fax: 731-668-9809; Email: mona.strazzella@stmarys.tn.org. Revs. David Graham; Tojan Abaraham; Francisco Franquiz; Deacons Robert Russell; Eddy Koonce; Jim Moss; Dale Brown.
School—St. Mary Church School, (Grades PreK-8), Tel: 731-668-2525; Email: becky.dearmitt@stmarys.tn.org; Web: www.stmarysschool.tn.org. Mrs. Jo-Ann Wormer, Prin.; Mrs. Becky DeArmitt, Sec. Lay Teachers 16; Students 254.
Catechesis Religious Program—Email: derek.rotty@stmarys.tn.org. Derek Rotty, D.R.E. Students 14.
Missions—St. John Church—Mailing Address: P.O. Box 872, Brownsville, Haywood Co. 38012.
Tel: 731-780-4734; Email: tsellari@bellsouth.net. 910 N. Washington Ave., Brownsville, Haywood Co. 38012. Tommy Sellari, Contact Person.
Catechesis Religious Program—
Our Lady of Guadalupe Mission - Bells, Email: fr.david@stmarys.tn.org.
Catechesis Religious Program—Students 79.

LEXINGTON, HENDERSON CO., ST. ANDREW THE APOSTLE (1981)
895 N. Broad St., Lexington, 38351.
Tel: 731-968-6393; Email: saintandrewlex@outlook.com; Web: saintandrewcatholicchurch.org. Rev. Anthony Onyekwe, (Nigeria).
Res.: 901 N. Broad St., Lexington, 38351.
Tel: 731-968-7944.
Catechesis Religious Program—Students 28.
Mission—St. Regina, 108 Skyline Ln., Parsons, Decatur Co. 38363. Tel: 901-355-3791; Email: saintregina@outlook.com.
Catechesis Religious Program—Lois Freeland, D.R.E. Students 27.

MARTIN, WEAKLEY CO., ST. JUDE CATHOLIC CHURCH (1962)
435 Moody Ave., Martin, 38237. Tel: 731-587-9777;
Fax: 855-995-5595; Email: office@stjudemartin.org; Web: www.stjudemartin.org. Rev. David Michael Orsak; Deacon Rodney Freed.
Catechesis Religious Program—Stacy Freed, D.R.E. Students 75.

MILAN, GIBSON CO., ST. MATTHEW MISSION (1977)
9060 Telecom Dr., Milan, 38358. Tel: 731-784-3904;
Fax: 731-784-5048. Mailing Address: c/o Sacred Heart Church, 2887 E. Main St., Humboldt, 38343. Rev. Mauricio Abeldaño; Deacons Ed Kutz; JR Hobbs.
Catechesis Religious Program—Students 22.

PARIS, HENRY CO., HOLY CROSS (1921)
1210 E. Wood St., Paris, 38242. Tel: 731-642-4681; Email: officemanager@holycrossparis.org; Web: www.holycrossparis.org. Rev. Martin M. Orjianioke, (Nigeria); Deacon Rodney Seyller.
School—Holy Cross School, Tel: 731-642-4681; Email: agtaylor0120@yahoo.com. Angie Taylor, Dir.; Connie Bell, Assistant. Lay Teachers 2; Students 26.
Catechesis Religious Program—Email: kim.rutherford@holycross.cdom.org. Kim Rutherford, D.R.E. Students 84.

SAVANNAH, HARDIN CO., ST. MARY CHURCH (1948)
2315 Pickwick St., Savannah, 38372.
Tel: 731-925-4852; Fax: 731-925-9612; Email: smccsavannah1@gmail.com; Web: www.saintmarysavannah.com. Rev. Dexter Noblefranca.
Catechesis Religious Program—Jon Stang, D.R.E. Students 56.
Mission—Our Lady of the Lake, 10645, Counce, Hardin Co. 38326.

SELMER, MCNAIRY CO., ST. JUDE THE APOSTLE CATHOLIC CHURCH (1982)

1318 E. Poplar Ave., Selmer, 38375-1913.
Tel: 731-645-4188; Email: stjude9@bellsouth.net. Rev. Wayne H. Arnold; Deacon Jim Gray.
Catechesis Religious Program—Students 13.

SOMERVILLE, FAYETTE CO., ST. PHILIP THE APOSTLE (1981)
11710 Hwy. 64, Somerville, 38068. Tel: 901-465-8685 ; Fax: 901-466-1645; Email: spacc@saintphilipcc.org. Rev. Robert D. Favazza.
Catechesis Religious Program—Email: mlopez@saintphilipcc.org. Maribel Lopez, D.R.E. Students 63.

UNION CITY, OBION CO., IMMACULATE CONCEPTION (1891)
1303 E. Reelfoot Ave., Union City, 38261.
Tel: 731-885-0963; Fax: 731-885-9960; Email: nina.pierce@icuc.cdom.org; Web: www.icuctn.org. Rev. Joey Kaump.
School—Immaculate Conception School, (Closed).
Catechesis Religious Program—Email: teresa.vallee@icuc.cdom.org. Teresa Vallee, D.R.E. Students 111.

Chaplains of Public Institutions

MEMPHIS. *Federal Correctional Institute at Memphis*. Rev. Faustino Maramot, Chap.
Memphis VA Medical Center. Rev. Richard D. Coy, Chap., (Retired).

Retired:
Rev. Msgrs.—
Buchignani, Peter P., P.A., J.C.L., (Retired)
Creary, J. Edwin, (Retired)
Kirk, Albert E., (Retired)
Kirk, Thomas D., (Retired)
McArthur, John B., (Retired)
Revs.—
Byrnes, Edward, (Retired)
Callis, Elbert, (Retired)
Coy, Richard D., (Retired)
Danner, James L., (Retired)
Foley, David M., (Retired)
Knight, David B., (Retired)
Pugh, James L., (Retired)
Stellini, Robert J., (Retired)
Stewart, Michael L., (Retired)
Thomas, Thomas P., (Retired).

Liaison for Retired Priests:
Rev.—
Coy, Richard D., (Retired).

Permanent Deacons:
Abonetti, Earnest
Alexander, Norman
Bennis, Donald
Blome, Michael, (Retired)
Bolton, Walt
Bonaiuto, Nick, (Retired)
Brown, Dale
Brown, Daniel, (Retired)
Calicott, James
Champion, Eugene
Chitwood, Jack, (Retired)
Conrad, Jack
Cooley, Jim, (Retired)
Crone, Alan
d'Addabbo, Michael
Davis, William (Bill)
Dierkes, David
Donati, Ralph, (Retired)
Drzycimski, Jeffrey
Finnegan, William, (Retired)
Frame, Christopher
Freed, Rodney
Gore, Michael
Gray, Jim
Griffith, Richard
Herbers, Bill, (Retired)
Hicks, Joseph, (Retired)
Hivner, John, (Retired)
Hobbs, James
Horne, Jerry
Hovanec, Mick
Howell, Larry, (Retired)
Jones, Chip
Kang, John, (Retired)
Koonce, Edward
Kutz, Edward
Kuzio, Joseph (Joe)
Larker, Frank
Lifsey, William
Lightcap, Charles
Littleton, Henry P.
Lucchesi, David
Lyons, Patrick
Mangin, Stephen
Martin, Rick
McBride, James
McCarver, Kenneth, (Retired)
Mensi, Joseph, (Retired)
Merwin, Miles, (Retired)
Miller, James, (Inactive)
Mitchell, Justin
Moore, Philip
Morton, Wayne, (Retired)
Moskal, John
Moss, James
Nourse, Bill
Pettit, William
Piatchek, James
Quinton, G. Richmond
Ramsey, Eddie
Richardson, Michael
Rose, Werner
Rosenthal, David
Rudolph, Anthony (Tony)
Russell, Robert
Schmall, James, (Retired)
Schmnall, James
Seyller, Rod
Skinner, Robert
Stewart, Harvey
Talley, Curtiss J.
Tedford, Wayne
Terry, Andrew Jr.
Thomas, Gregory
Tucker, Jim
Walker, Robert
Wells, Charles, (Retired)
Williams, Frank
Winston, William
Woolley, David
Yarbrough, Harold, (Inactive).

INSTITUTIONS LOCATED IN DIOCESE

[A] COLLEGES AND UNIVERSITIES

MEMPHIS. **Christian Brothers University* (1871) 650 E. Parkway S., 38104. Tel: 901-321-3000; Fax: 901-321-3117; Email: admissions@cbu.edu; Web: www.cbu.edu. Dr. John Smarrelli Jr., Ph.D., Pres.; Bro. Ryan Anderson, Dir.; Ms. Melissa Andrews, Dir.; Mr. Robert Arnold, Dir.; Bros. Dominic Ehrmantraut, F.S.C., Dir.; Tom Sullivan, F.S.C., Dir.; Ms. Amy Ware, Dir.; Rev. William J. Parham, Chap.; Mr. Thomas Cochran, Controller; Ms. Kay Cunningham, Librarian; Mr. Stephen Crisman; Dr. Paul Haught; Carolyn Head; Dr. Anne Kenworthy. (Coed); Four-Year University with Schools of Business, Engineering, Arts, and Sciences. Graduate programs in Business, Engineering, Education, and Physician's Assistant Studies.
Christian Brothers Univ. (of Memphis, Tenn.) Brothers 12; Lay Teachers 200; Priests 2; Students 1,892.

[B] DIOCESAN SCHOOLS

MEMPHIS. *St. Augustine Catholic School*, (Grades PreK-6), 1169 Kerr Ave., 38106. Tel: 901-942-8002; Fax: 901-942-4564; Email: kelsey.bourquin@staug.cdom.org; Web: www.staugmemphis.org/. Mrs. Kelsey Bourquin, Prin.; Dawn Stevens, Librarian; Marilyn Taylor, Sec. Clergy 4; Lay Teachers 18; Students 120.
De La Salle Elementary at Blessed Sacrament (2000) (Grades K-8), 2540 Hale Ave., 38112.
Tel: 901-866-9084; Fax: 901-866-9086; Email: principal@delasallememphis.org. Christopher Reid, Prin.; Yolanda Scott, Sec. Clergy 4; Lay Staff 5; Lay Teachers 14.
St. John Catholic School, (Grades PreK-6), 2718 Lamar Ave., 38114. Tel: 901-743-6700;
Fax: 901-743-6720; Email: elizabeth.gonzalez@stjohn.cdom.org. Mrs. Elizabeth Gonzalez, Prin.; Akira Dickson, Librarian. (Reopened 2000) Lay Teachers 13; Students 194.
St. Joseph School, (Grades PreK-6), 3851 Neely Rd., 38109. Tel: 901-344-0021; Fax: 901-348-0787; Email: leslie.harden@stjoseph.cdom.org; Web: StJoememphis.org. Leslie Harden, Prin. Clergy 2; Lay Teachers 15; Priests 1; Students 196.
Little Flower School, (Grades PreK-2), 1666 Jackson Ave., 38107. Tel: 901-725-9900; Fax: 901-725-5779; Email: tunia.sangster@stlfschool.cdom.org. Tunia Sangster, Prin. Clergy 3; Lay Staff 5; Lay Teachers 7; Students 78.
Memphis Catholic Middle and High School, (Grades 7-12), 61 N. McLean Blvd., 38104.
Tel: 901-276-1221; Fax: 901-725-1447; Email: tschreck@memphiscatholic.org; Email: drobinson@memphiscatholic.org; Web: www.memphiscatholic.org. Deacon Ted Schreck, Dir.; Rev. Fausta Odinwankpa, Chap.; Rosie Jupson, Counselor; Debra Robinson, Admin. Lay Teachers 21; Students 240.
See Education That Works, LLC in the Institution Section under Miscellaneous.
Our Lady of Sorrows School, (Grades PreK-8), 3690 Thomas St., 38127. Tel: 901-358-7431;
Fax: 901-353-1153; Email: deacon.henry@ols.cdom.org; Web: jubileeschools.org. Deacon Henry P. Littleton, Admin. Religious Teachers 1; Lay Teachers 17; Students 200.
St. Patrick School (1867) (Grades PreK-6), 287 S. Fourth St., 38126. Tel: 901-521-3252;
Fax: 901-521-8265; Email: Susan.pittman@stpat.cdom.org. Susan Pittman, Prin. (Closed 1950; reopened 2003). Clergy 1; Lay Staff 4; Lay Teachers 13; Students 143.
Resurrection Catholic School, (Grades PreK-6), 3572 Emerald St., 38115. Tel: 901-546-9926;
Fax: 901-546-9928; Email: james.shelton@rcs.cdom.org; Web: www.resurrectionlions.org. Mr. James Shelton, Prin.; Mrs. Phyllis Hubbard, Librarian. Lay Teachers 16; Students 235.

CORDOVA. *St. Benedict at Auburndale High School*, 8250 Varnavas Dr., Cordova, 38016.
Tel: 901-260-2840; Fax: 901-260-2850; Email: morriss@sbaeagles.org; Web: www.sbaeagles.org. Mrs. Sondra Morris, Prin.; Rev. Msgr. Thomas D. Kirk, Chap., (Retired); Deacon Jeffrey Drzycimski, Campus Min. Special programs for gifted and learning disabled. Lay Teachers 80; Sisters 2; Students 850.

[C] HIGH SCHOOLS, PRIVATE AND PAROCHIAL

MEMPHIS. *St. Agnes Academy - St. Dominic School* (1851) (Grades PreK-12), 4830 Walnut Grove Rd., 38117. Tel: 901-767-1356; Fax: 901-435-5866; Email: thood@saa-sds.org; Email: jsmoore@saa-sds.org; Web: www.saa-sds.org. Mr. Tom Hood, Pres.; Mr. Chris Burke, Dean; Mrs. Joy Maness, Dean; Mrs. Kathy Toes-Boccia, Dean, Tel: 901-767-1377; Fax: 901-684-5316; Mrs. Gretchen K. Kirk, D.R.E. Dominican Sisters of Peace.Title of Incorporation: St. Agnes Academy - St. Dominic School Religious Teachers 2; Lay Teachers 95; Students 780.
**Christian Brothers High School* (1871) 5900 Walnut Grove Rd., 38120-2174. Tel: 901-261-4900;
Fax: 901-261-4909; Email: info@cbhs.org; Web: www.cbhs.org. Bro. Christopher Englert, F.S.C., Pres.; Mr. Chris Fay, Prin.; Bro. Philip Jones, F.S.C., Dir.; Patrice Gallagher, Librarian. Title of Incorporation: Christian Brothers (LaSalle) High School. Brothers 7; Lay Teachers 79; Students 868.
Immaculate Conception Cathedral School (1950) (Grades PreK-12), 1725 Central Ave., 38104.
Tel: 901-725-2705 High School;
Tel: 901-725-2710 Lower School;
Fax: 901-725-2701 High School;
Fax: 901-725-2715 Lower School; Email: tracey.ford@ic.cdom.org; Email: karen.gephart@cdom.org; Web: www.myiccs.org. Karen Gephart, Prin.; Tracey Ford, Prin.; Nancy Miller, Librarian. Lay Teachers 35; Students 327.

JACKSON. *Sacred Heart of Jesus High School*, 146 McClellan Rd., Jackson, 38305. Tel: 731-660-4774; Fax: 731-984-7200; Email: ann.keyl@shjhs.org; Web: www.shjhs.org. Mrs. Ann Keyl, Prin. Lay Teachers 12; Students 106.

[D] RESIDENCES OF PRIESTS AND BROTHERS

MEMPHIS. *Brothers of the Christian Schools (Mid-West Prov.), F.S.C., #343*, Christian Brothers University, 650 E. Parkway S., 38104.
Tel: 901-321-3520; Fax: 901-321-3290. Bro. Dominic Ehrmantraut, F.S.C., Dir. Brothers 18. Christian Brothers High School, 5900 Walnut Grove Rd., 38119. Tel: 901-261-4900;
Fax: 901-261-4909; Web: www.cbhs.org. Bro. Philip Jones, F.S.C., Dir. Brothers 6.
The Dominican Friars of Memphis, Inc., 190 Adams Ave., 38103. Tel: 901-527-8282; Fax: 901-526-6882; Email: dominicanmemphis@gmail.com. Revs. Paul D. Watkins, O.P., Supr.; Ramon Gonzalez, O.P., Sec.; Augustine Joseph DeArmond, O.P., Treas.
Society of the Divine Word (Chicago Province), Sacred Heart Church, 1324 Jefferson Ave., 38104.
Tel: 901-726-1891; Fax: 901-726-9272. Revs. Kazimierz Abrahamczyk, S.V.D., (Poland) St. John Church, 2742 Lamar Ave., 38114; Fidelis Armin, S.V.D., (Indonesia) St. John Church, 2742 Lamar Ave., 38114; Pio Estepa, S.V.D., Sacred Heart Church, 1324 Jefferson Ave., 38104; Simon Thoi Hoang, S.V.D., Sacred Heart Church, 1324 Jefferson Ave., 38104. Sacred Heart Church; Antonio

Romo-Romo, S.V.D., 3825 Neely Rd., 38109. St. Joseph Church. Priests 5.

Villa Vianney Senior Priests Residence, 10605 Bishop Dozier Dr., Cordova, 38016-5559.
Tel: 901-752-0766; Fax: 901-752-0633; Email: rick.mickey@cc.cdom.org. Rev. Richard L. Mickey, M.Ed., Dir. In Residence 4; Total Staff 1; Retired 2.

[E] CONVENTS AND RESIDENCES FOR SISTERS

MEMPHIS. *Missionaries of Charity*, 700 N. 7th St., 38107. Tel: 901-527-4947; Tel: 901-526-5456; Email: scadiz7@hotmail.com. Sisters M. Jonathan, M.C., Regional Supr.; M. Celine Rose, M.C., Supr. Bed Capacity 18; Sisters 4; Tot Asst. Annually 650; Total Staff 4.

Missionary Sisters Servants of the Holy Spirit, S.Sp.S., 5280 Brenton Ave., 38120. Tel: 901-685-3649; Fax: 901-685-3649; Email: monicad@ssps-usa.org. Sr. Monica P. Darrichon, S.Sp.S., Supr. Sisters 3.

Monastery Of St. Clare O.S.C. (1932) 1310 Dellwood Ave., 38127. Tel: 901-357-6662; Email: memphisclares@gmail.com; Web: www.poorclare.org/memphis. Sr. Mary Marguerite, O.S.C., Abbess. Sisters 5.

Sisters of St. Charles Borromeo, C.B., 4778 Normandy Ave., 38117. Tel: 901-818-9180; Email: csusindr@hotmail.com; Web: www.cbsisters.org. Sisters 2.

[F] CATHOLIC CAMPUS & YOUNG-ADULT MINISTRY

MEMPHIS. *Catholic Campus Ministry*, 3625 Mynders Ave., 38111. Tel: 901-323-3051; Email: info@ccm.cdom.org; Web: memphisccm.org. Sam Mauck, Dir.; Heather Beekman, Campus Min.; Sally Harlan, Asst. Campus Min. / Admin. Asst.

[G] MISCELLANEOUS

MEMPHIS. *St. Anne Lay Carmelite Community*, 2929 Baskin St., 38127. Tel: 901-830-7824; Email: carmemphis@gmail.com.

The Catholic Cafe, Inc., c/o Glankler Brown, PLLC, 6000 Poplar Ave., Ste. 400, 38119.
Tel: 901-576-1714; Fax: 901-525-2389; Email: rhutton@glankler.com; Web: www.thecatholiccafe.com. Robert Hutton, Pres.

Catholic Charities of West Tennessee, 1325 Jefferson Ave., 38104-2013. Tel: 901-722-4700;
Fax: 901-722-4791; Email: rachel.daddabbo@acc.cdom.org; Web: www.ccwtn.org. Richard Hackett, Dir. Tot Asst. Annually 27,292; Total Staff 34.

Diocesan Council of Catholic Women, 6161 Acorn Dr., Bartlett, 38134-4601. Tel: 901-213-4778; Email: presbred@aol.com.

Education That Works, LLC, 61 N. McLean Blvd., 38104. Tel: 901-276-1221; Fax: 901-725-1447; Email: tschreck@memphiscatholic.org; Web: www.memphiscatholic.org. Deacon Ted Schreck, Dir.; Mr. Didier Aur, Dir.

Knights of St. Peter Claver (3rd Degree St. Benedict the Black Council No. 188 & Assembly 26 Bishop James P. Lyke 4th Degree), 1169 Kerr Ave., 38106. Cell: 901-270-8164; Email: geowens1@comcast.net. George Owens, Exec.

Ladies of Charity of Memphis (1937) P.O. Box 17699, 38187-0699. Tel: 901-767-0207; Email: rosemariep@comcast.net; Web: www.famvin.org/lcusa. Mary Jo Hendricks, Pres.

**Lumen Civitatis Inc.*, 2542 Ridgeway Rd., Ste. 7, 38119. Tel: 901-219-4591; Email: andrew@lumencivitatis.org; Web: www.lumencivitatis.com. P.O. Box 771692, 38177-1692. Andrew Bowie, Contact Person.

**Madonna Circle, Inc.* (Catholic Women's Service Organization) 2300 Hickory Crest Dr., 38119.
Tel: 901-479-7870; Email: pblanch1@comcast.net; Web: www.madonnacircle.org. Gia Blanchard, Pres.; Nancy Williams.

St. Martin de Porres National Shrine & Institute, 190 Adams Ave., 38103. Tel: 901-578-2643;
Fax: 901-526-6882; Email: stmartinshrine@bellsouth.net; Web: www.stmartinshrine.org. Rev. Michael O'Rourke, O.P.

St. Patrick's Center, 277 S. Fourth St., 38126.
Tel: 901-543-9924; Email: euchampion@aol.com; Web: www.stpatsmemphis.org. Deacon Eugene Champion, Exec. Dir.

Serra Club of Memphis, c/o The Catholic Center, 5825 Shelby Oaks Dr., 38134. Tel: 901-481-1274; Email: thomas.joan6@gmail.com. 4366 W. Cherry Place Dr., 38117. Joan Thomas, Pres.; Rev. Yoelvis Gonzalez, Chap.

**Society of St. Vincent DePaul*, 1306 Monroe Ave., 38104. Tel: 901-722-4703; Tel: 901-274-2137; Email: ozanamcentercoord@gmail.com; Web: www.svdpmemphis.org. Richard Peyton, Pres.; Rev. Richard D. Coy, (Retired).

STANTON. *Our Lady Queen of Peace Retreat Center*, 3630 Dancyville Rd., Stanton, 38069-4711.
Tel: 731-548-2500; Fax: 731-548-2520; Email: debbie.voyles@olqp.cdom.org; Web: www.olqpretreats.com (Our Lady Queen of Peace Retreat Center). Rev. Cosmas Mabu, Dir.

RELIGIOUS INSTITUTES OF MEN REPRESENTED IN THE DIOCESE

For further details refer to the corresponding bracketed number in the Religious Institutes of Men or Women section.

[0330]—*Brothers of the Christian Schools* (Midwest Prov.)—F.S.C.
[]—*Missionary Congregation of the Blessed Sacrament*—M.C.B.S.
[0430]—*Order of Preachers (Dominicans)*—O.P.
[0420]—*Society of Divine Word*—S.V.D.

RELIGIOUS INSTITUTES OF WOMEN REPRESENTED IN THE DIOCESE

[1070-07]—*Dominican Sisters*—O.P.
[1115]—*Dominican Sisters of Peace* (Columbus, OH)—O.P.
[2710]—*Missionaries of Charity*—M.C.
[3530]—*Missionary Sisters Servants of the Holy Spirit*—S.Sp.S.
[3760]—*Order of St. Clare* (Memphis, TN)—O.S.C.
[0500]—*Sisters of Charity of Nazareth*—S.C.N.
[]—*Sisters of Charity of St. Charles Borromeo*—C.B.
[0430]—*Sisters of Charity of the Blessed Virgin Mary*—B.V.M.
[]—*Sisters of Mercy* (Ireland)—R.S.M.
[2575]—*Sisters of Mercy of the Americas*—R.S.M.
[]—*Sisters of the Blessed Sacrament*—S.B.S.
[3180]—*Sisters of the Cross and Passion*—C.P.

DIOCESAN CEMETERIES

MEMPHIS. *All Saints*, c/o Calvary Cemetery, 1663 Elvis Presley Blvd., 38106. Tel: 901-948-1529;
Fax: 901-948-1511; Email: pat.posey@cemeteries.cdom.org; Web: www.cdom.org. Mr. Patrick Posey Sr., Dir.

Calvary, 1663 Elvis Presley Blvd., 38106.
Tel: 901-948-1529; Fax: 901-948-1511; Email: pat.posey@cemeteries.cdom.org; Web: www.cdom.org/cemeteries. Mr. Patrick Posey Sr., Dir.

JACKSON. *Mount Calvary*, c/o Calvary Cemetery, 1663 Elvis Presley Blvd., 38106. 1665 Hwy. 45 Byp., Jackson, 38305-4414. Tel: 731-668-2596;
Fax: 731-668-9809; Email: pat.posey@cemeteries.cdom.org; Web: www.cdom.org/cemeteries. Mr. Patrick Posey Sr., Dir.

An asterisk (*) denotes an organization that has established tax-exempt status directly with the IRS and is not covered by the USCCB Group Ruling.

Diocese of Metuchen

Most Reverend

JAMES F. CHECCHIO, J.C.D., M.B.A.

Bishop of Metuchen; ordained June 20, 1992; appointed Rector of the Pontifical North American College 2006-2016; appointed Bishop of Metuchen March 8, 2016; installed May 3, 2016. *146 Metlars Lane, Piscataway, NJ 08854. Res.: 10 Library Pl., Metuchen, NJ 08840.*

Most Reverend

PAUL G. BOOTKOSKI, D.D.

Bishop Emeritus of Metuchen; ordained May 28, 1966; appointed Titular Bishop of Zarna and Auxiliary Bishop of Newark July 8, 1997; ordained September 5, 1997; appointed Fourth Bishop of Metuchen January 4, 2002; installed March 19, 2002; retired March 8, 2016.

ESTABLISHED NOVEMBER 19, 1981.

Square Miles 1,425.

Legal Corporate Title: The Diocese of Metuchen.

Comprises the Counties of Warren, Hunterdon, Somerset and Middlesex in the State of New Jersey.

146 Metlars Lane, Piscataway, NJ 08854. Tel: 732-562-1990; Fax: 732-562-1399. . *Mailing Address: St. John Neumann Pastoral Center, P.O. Box 191, Metuchen, NJ 08840.*

Web: www.diometuchen.org

STATISTICAL OVERVIEW

Personnel	
Bishop	1
Retired Bishops	1
Priests: Diocesan Active in Diocese	124
Priests: Diocesan Active Outside Diocese	9
Priests: Retired, Sick or Absent	30
Number of Diocesan Priests	163
Religious Priests in Diocese	33
Total Priests in Diocese	196
Extern Priests in Diocese	16
Ordinations:	
Diocesan Priests	2
Transitional Deacons	3
Permanent Deacons in Diocese	183
Total Brothers	8
Total Sisters	258
Parishes	
Parishes	90
With Resident Pastor:	
Resident Diocesan Priests	84
Resident Religious Priests	6
Pastoral Centers	4
Professional Ministry Personnel:	
Brothers	6
Sisters	116
Lay Ministers	349
Welfare	
Catholic Hospitals	1
Total Assisted	253,437
Health Care Centers	4
Total Assisted	24,199
Homes for the Aged	4
Total Assisted	130
Day Care Centers	1
Total Assisted	170
Specialized Homes	1
Total Assisted	9
Special Centers for Social Services	8
Total Assisted	31,017
Residential Care of Disabled	1
Total Assisted	8
Other Institutions	105
Total Assisted	23,277
Educational	
Diocesan Students in Other Seminaries	20
Total Seminarians	20
High Schools, Diocesan and Parish	2
Total Students	1,102
High Schools, Private	2
Total Students	886
Elementary Schools, Diocesan and Parish	23
Total Students	5,695
Catechesis/Religious Education:	
High School Students	783
Elementary Students	23,317
Total Students under Catholic Instruction	31,803
Teachers in the Diocese:	
Priests	3
Brothers	4
Sisters	19
Lay Teachers	605
Vital Statistics	
Receptions into the Church:	
Infant Baptism Totals	3,365
Minor Baptism Totals	278
Adult Baptism Totals	119
Received into Full Communion	210
First Communions	4,138
Confirmations	4,677
Marriages:	
Catholic	667
Interfaith	121
Total Marriages	788
Deaths	3,404
Total Catholic Population	564,035
Total Population	1,410,087

Former Bishops—THEODORE E. MCCARRICK, ord. May 31, 1958; appt. Titular Bishop of Rusibisir and Auxiliary to the Archbishop of New York, May 24, 1977; cons. June 29, 1977; appt. first Bishop of Metuchen, Nov. 19, 1981; installed Jan. 31, 1982; promoted to the Archdiocese of Newark, June 3, 1986; installed July 25, 1986; dismissed from the clerical state Feb. 15, 2019; Most Revs. EDWARD T. HUGHES, ord. May 31, 1947; appt. Auxiliary to Archbishop of Philadelphia and Titular Bishop of Segia June 14, 1976; cons. July 21, 1976; appt. Second Bishop of Metuchen Dec. 16, 1986; installed Feb. 5, 1987; retired Sept. 8, 1997; died Dec. 25, 2012.; VINCENT DEPAUL BREEN, D.D., ord. July 15, 1962; appt. Third Bishop of Metuchen July 8, 1997; cons. and installed Sept. 8, 1997; retired Jan. 4, 2002; died March 30, 2003; PAUL G. BOOTKOSKI, ord. May 28, 1966; appt. Titular Bishop of Zarna and Auxiliary Bishop of Newark July 8, 1997; ord. Sept. 5, 1997; appt. Fourth Bishop of Metuchen Jan. 4, 2002; installed March 19, 2002; retired March 8, 2016.

St. John Neumann Pastoral Center—Mailing Address: P.O. Box 191, Metuchen, 08840. Tel: 732-562-1990; Fax: 732-562-1399.

Vicar General—Rev. TIMOTHY A. CHRISTY, V.G.

Episcopal Vicars—Rev. Msgrs. SEAMUS F. BRENNAN, Somerset County; JOHN N. FELL, S.T.D., Health Care Apostolate; Revs. EDMUND J. SHALLOW, Middlesex County North; JOHN C. GRIMES, Middlesex County South; ANTONY AROCKIADOSS, Hunterdon and Warren Counties; Rev. Msgr. WILLIAM BENWELL, J.C.L., Episcopal Vicar for Canonical Services.

Diocesan Departments and Offices

Office of the Bishop—Most Rev. JAMES F. CHECCHIO, J.C.D., MBA; THOMAS G. PHILLIPS III, Vice Chancellor & Asst. for Administrative Matters.

Office of Bishop Emeritus—Most Rev. PAUL G. BOOTKOSKI, D.D.

Office of the Vicar General—Rev. TIMOTHY A. CHRISTY, V.G.

Office of Child and Youth Protection—CHRISTOPHER J. FUSCO, J.C.L., Esq., Dir.

Victim Assistance Coordinator—GINA CRISCUOLO, L.C.S.W., Tel: 908-722-1881; Email: gcriscuolo@ccdom.org.

Office of Internal Audit—RENATA BOVE, Internal Auditor; OSCAR MONTALVO, Internal Auditor.

Moderator of the Curia—Rev. TIMOTHY A. CHRISTY, V.G., Tel: 732-562-2439; Fax: 732-562-1427.

Office of the Chancellor—VACANT, Chancellor; CAROL M. MACDERMOTT, Vice Chancellor, Tel: 732-562-2439; Fax: 732-562-1427; Email: chancellor@diometuchen.org.

Office of the Diocesan General Counsel—MICHAEL K. LIGORANO, K.M., Esq., Gen. Counsel; CHRISTOPHER J. FUSCO, J.C.L., Esq., Assoc. Gen. Counsel St. Thomas More Society.

The Tribunal

The Diocesan Center—Mailing Address: P.O. Box 191, Metuchen, 08840. Tel: 732-562-1990; Fax: 732-562-1193. Very Rev. ROBERT B. KOLAKOWSKI, J.C.D., Judicial Vicar; Rev. Msgr. RICHARD J. LYONS, J.C.L., Judicial Vicar Emeritus; CHRISTOPHER J. FUSCO, J.C.L., Esq., Moderator of the Tribunal; MARGARET MANZA, Admin. Coord.

Canonical Staff—Rev. Msgr. WILLIAM BENWELL, J.C.L.; CHRISTOPHER J. FUSCO, J.C.L., Esq.; Rev. Msgr. RICHARD J. LYONS, J.C.L.; Rev. MATTHEW R. PARATORE, J.C.L.

Auditor—SARA T. ACEVEDO.

Psychological Consultants—MARY BERTANI, Ed.S., L.M.F.T.; Sisters ELIZABETH MONICA ACRI, I.H.M.; SUSAN HADZIMA, I.H.M.

Notaries—SARA T. ACEVEDO; MARGARET MANZA.

Vicariate for Clergy and Consecrated Life

Vicariate for Clergy and Consecrated Life—Rev. Msgr. EDWARD C. PULEO, Episcopal Vicar.

Office of Ministry to Priests—Rev. Msgr. JOSEPH M. CURRY, Dir.

Office for Priest Personnel—Rev. Msgr. JOHN N. FELL, S.T.D., Dir.

Office of the Diaconate—Deacon STEPHEN F. KERN, Dir.

Office for Religious—Sr. MARY AQUINAS SZOTT, C.S.S.F., Delegate for Rel.

Office of Vocations—Rev. MAURICIO TABERA-VASQUEZ, Dir.

Board for Seminary Education—Rev. MAURICIO TABERA-VASQUEZ, Chm.

Office of Hospital Chaplaincy—Rev. SEAN G. WINTERS, Coord.

Office of Prison Ministry—Rev. SEAN G. WINTERS, Dir.

Vicariate for Administration

Episcopal Vicar—Rev. Msgr. JOSEPH G. CELANO.

Executive Director—CAROL PURCELL.

Office of Cemeteries—Tel: 732-463-1424; Tel: 800-943-8400 (Sales); Fax: 732-463-8807. MARY ELLEN GERRITY, Dir.

Office of Finance—PATRICIA MURTHA, Controller.

Office of Human Resources—MELISSA PUJOLS, SHRM-CP, Dir.

Office of Information Systems—LEONARDO G. CORTELEZZI, Dir.

Office of Insurance—JACQUELINE GLACKIN, Dir.

Office of Property & Facility Ownership & Management—MONICA P. DEMKOVITZ, Dir.

Office of Stewardship & Development—Rev. EDMUND A. LUCIANO III, Dir. Donor Rels.; SUE MANTARRO, Dir. Stewardship; TAMARA HEMINGWAY, Coord. Institutional Advancement.

Department of Education

Department of Education—VACANT.

Office of the Schools—ELLEN AYOUB, Supt.

Catholic Scouting Apostolate—Rev. Msgr. MICHAEL J. CORONA, P.A., Moderator.

Vicariate for Evangelization and Communication

Episcopal Vicar—Rev. TIMOTHY A. CHRISTY, V.G.

Office of Communication & Public Relations—ERIN FRIEDLANDER, Dir.

Office of Evangelization—JODIE D'ANGIOLILLO, Dir.

Catholic Charismatic Renewal—Bro. JUDE LASOTA, B.H., Spiritual Moderator.

Office of Worship—TONY VARAS, Dir.; THOMAS A. DELESSIO, Coord. Liturgical Music.

Diocesan Eucharistic League—Rev. ROBERT G. GORMAN, Dir.

Diocesan Holy Name Societies—Rev. CHESTER H. CARINA, J.C.L., Moderator.

Divine Mercy Apostolate—Rev. JOHN C. GRIMES, Moderator.

Legion of Mary, Metuchen Comitium—Rev. JOHN J. BARBELLA, Spiritual Dir.

Office of RCIA—SARA SHARLOW, Dir.

Office of Pontifical Mission Societies—Rev. JOHN G. HILLIER, Ph.D., Dir.

The Catholic Spirit—Revs. TIMOTHY A. CHRISTY, V.G., Editor; GLENN J. COMANDINI, S.T.D., Mng. Editor.

Secretariat for Family and Pastoral Life

Family and Pastoral Life—Very Rev. BRIAN J. NOLAN, Theological & Pastoral Advisor; JENNIFER A. RUGGIERO, Sec.

Office for Cultural Diversity Ministries—Sr. RUTH BOLARTE, I.H.M., Dir.; Rev. JUAN CARLOS GAVIRIA, Coord., Hispanic Lay Formation.

African-American, African & Caribbean Apostolate—Rev. ALPHONSUS KARIUKI, Coord.; Deacon ENOCK BERLUCHE SR., Coord.

Chinese Apostolate—PHILIP WU, Coord.

Filipino Apostolate—Rev. GERARDO B. PADERON, Coord.

Hungarian Apostolate—Rev. IMRE JUHASZ, Coord.

Indian and Sri-Lankan Apostolate—VACANT.

Korean Apostolate—Rev. NAMWOONG LEE, Coord.

Polish Apostolate—Rev. WALDEMAR LATKOWSKI, C.Ss.R., Coord.

Portuguese & Brazilian Apostolate—VACANT, Coord.

Vietnamese Apostolate—Rev. PETER TRAN, Coord.

Indonesian Apostolate—IAN SUPARDI, Coord.

Office for Persons with Disabilities—Rev. JOHN G. HILLIER, Ph.D., Dir.

Catholic Rural Ministry—Rev. MICHAEL C. SAHARIC, Coord.

Office of Discipleship Formation for Children—CAROL MASCOLA, Dir.

Ecumenical & Interfaith Affairs—Rev. GUY W. SELVESTER, Diocesan Ecumenical Officer.

Office of Family Life Ministry—VACANT, Dir.

EnCourage—Rev. DAVID V. SKOBLOW, Chap.

Courage—Rev. THOMAS A. ODORIZZI, C.O., Chap., Apostolate for Military Veterans & Families.

Office of Human Life & Dignity—JENNIFER A. RUGGIERO, Dir.

Office of Ongoing Faith Formation—Rev. A. GREGORY UHRIG, Coord.

Office of Youth & Young Adult Ministry—JOHN GLYNN.

Campus Ministry Apostolate—Very Rev. BRIAN J. NOLAN, Liaison.

The Catholic Center at Rutgers University—84 Somerset St., New Brunswick, 08901. Tel: 732-545-6663; Fax: 732-545-3495; Web: www.catholic-center.rutgers.edu. Bro. PATRICK REILLY, B.H., Dir.

Department of Social Services

Department of Catholic Social Services—JULIO COTO, L.C.S.W., Acting Exec. Dir. (See category for Catholic Charities under Institutions located in the Diocese for the full listing).

Catholic Campaign for Human Development—Deacons MICHAEL R. MARTINI, Dir.; PETER BARCELLONA, Assoc. Dir., Tel: 732-545-1681.

Catholic Charities Solidarity Team—Tel: 732-545-1681 . Deacons MICHAEL R. MARTINI, Dir.; PETER BARCELLONA, Assoc. Dir.

Consultative Bodies

College of Consultors—Most Rev. JAMES F. CHECCHIO, J.C.D., MBA; Rev. Msgrs. JOSEPH G. CELANO, Sec.; WILLIAM BENWELL, J.C.L.; Rev. TIMOTHY A. CHRISTY, V.G.; Rev. Msgr. EUGENE PRUS, (Retired); Very Revs. JONATHAN S. TOBOROWSKY; ROBERT B. KOLAKOWSKI, J.C.D.; Rev. Msgrs. SEAMUS F. BRENNAN; JOHN N. FELL, S.T.D.; EDWARD C. PULEO; Rev. ANTHONY M. SIRIANNI. Liturgical Advisor: TONY VARAS.

Deans—Revs. ANTHONY SIRANNI, Cathedral Deanery; CHARLES T. O'CONNOR, Forsgate Deanery; JOHN J. BARBELLA, Morris Canal Deanery; THOMAS F. RYAN, Raritan Bay Deanery; FRANCIS G. HILTON, S.J., County Seat Deanery; Rev. Msgr. RANDALL J. VASHON, Somerset Hills Deanery; Rev. ABRAHAM ORAPANKAL, Round Valley Deanery; Rev. Msgr. JOHN B. GORDON, Deanery of the Cities of New Brunswick and Perth Amboy; Rev. JAMES F. CONSIDINE, Middlebrook Deanery.

Presbyteral Council—Most Rev. JAMES F. CHECCHIO, J.C.D., MBA, Pres.

Diocesan Pastoral Council—Most Rev. JAMES F. CHECCHIO, J.C.D., MBA.

CLERGY, PARISHES, MISSIONS AND PAROCHIAL SCHOOLS

BOROUGH OF METUCHEN

(MIDDLESEX COUNTY), CATHEDRAL OF ST. FRANCIS OF ASSISI (1871)

32 Elm Ave., 08840. Tel: 732-548-0100; Fax: 732-549-1033; Email: info@stfranciscathedral.org; Web: www.stfranciscathedral.org. Rev. Msgr. Robert J. Zamorski, Rector; Revs. Dawid Wejnerowski, Parochial Vicar; John J. Werner, Parochial Vicar; Timothy A. Christy, V.G., In Res.; Deacons Guido J. Brossoni; Frank J. Cammarano; Kenrick Fortune; Eduardo Olegario; Joseph P. Saggese; Paul G. Licameli.

Catechesis Religious Program—45 Elm Ave., 08840. Tel: 732-548-0100, Ext. 226; Email: religioused@stfranciscathedral.org. Debra Schurko, Catechetical Leader. Students 1,187.

School—St. Francis Cathedral School, (Grades PreK-8), 528 Main St., 08840. Tel: 732-548-3107; Fax: 732-548-5760; Web: www.stfranciscathedralschool.org. Ms. Ann Major, Prin.; Mrs. Judi Monteleone, Vice Prin.; Mrs. Laura Graziano, Dir. Tech..; Mrs. Patricia Guidi, Librarian. Lay Teachers 26; Preschool 50; Students 407; Clergy / Religious Teachers 3.

OUTSIDE THE BOROUGH OF METUCHEN

ALPHA, WARREN CO., ST. MARY (1902) [CEM]

830 Fifth Ave., Alpha, 08865. Tel: 908-454-0444; Fax: 908-454-7745; Email: office@stmaryrc.org; Web: www.stmaryrc.org. Rev. Msgr. Terrance M. Lawler; Rev. James Tucker; Deacons George L. Bolash; John B. Van Haute.

Catechesis Religious Program—Tel: 908-454-9595; Email: alphareled@verizon.net. Ms. MaryBeth Luzzetti, D.R.E. Students 659.

ANNANDALE, HUNTERDON CO., IMMACULATE CONCEPTION (1864) [CEM 2]

316 Old Allerton Rd., Annandale, 08801. Tel: 908-735-7319; Fax: 908-735-4552; Email: parishoffice@iccannadale.org. Very Rev. Jonathan S. Toborowsky; Rev. Edgar Madarang; Deacons Joseph P. Campbell; Michael R. Martini; Michael A. Meyer; Edward F. Ciszewski; Mark van Duynhoven.

School—Immaculate Conception School, (Grades PreK-8), 314 Old Allerton Rd., Annandale, 08801. Tel: 908-735-6334; Fax: 908-238-0724; Email: info@icsclinton.org; Web: www.icsannandale.org. Connie Fortunato, Prin. Lay Teachers 28; Students 330; Clergy / Religious Teachers 1.

Catechesis Religious Program—Coleen D'Amato, D.R.E. Students 663.

Station—Edna Mahan Correctional Facility for Women, Clinton. Tel: 908-735-7111; Fax: 908-735-5246.

AVENEL, MIDDLESEX CO., ST. ANDREW (1920)

244 Avenel St., Avenel, 07001. Tel: 732-634-4355; Fax: 732-750-5905; Email: our.church@standrewparish.com. Rev. David B. Kosmoski; Deacon Walter S. Maksimik.

Station—Woodbridge State School, Avenel.

Catechesis Religious Program—Tel: 732-636-4261. Elizabeth Vitale, Catechetical Leader. Students 135.

Station—Woodbridge Emergency Reception Center, Avenel, 07001. Tel: 732-636-4261.

BAPTISTOWN, HUNTERDON CO., OUR LADY OF VICTORIES (1973)

1005 Rte. 159, P.O. Box 127, Baptistown, 08803. Tel: 908-996-2068; Email: olvkris@yahoo.com; Web: www.olvbaptistown.com. Rev. Krzysztof Kaczynski; Deacons John T. Monahan; Michael Semko.

Catechesis Religious Program—Gloria Nardone, D.R.E. Students 147.

BASKING RIDGE, SOMERSET CO., ST. JAMES (1864)

184 S. Finley Ave., P.O. Box 310, Basking Ridge, 07920. Tel: 908-766-0888; Fax: 908-766-1815; Email: stjamesbr@optonline.net; Web: www.saintjamesbr.org. Rev. Msgr. Sylvester J. Cronin III; Rev. Krystian S. Burdzy, Parochial Vicar; Sr. Esther Falzone, S.C.C., Pastoral Assoc.; Deacons Peter J. DePrima Jr.; Thomas H. Klaas; Frank A. Sinatra.

School—St. James School, (Grades PreSchool-8), 200 S. Finley Ave., P.O. Box 310, Basking Ridge, 07920. Tel: 908-766-4774; Fax: 908-766-4432; Email: soffice@sjsbr.org; Web: www.sjsbr.org. Mrs. Suzanne Florendo, Prin.; Sr. Joann Marie Aumand, Dir. Clergy 1; Lay Teachers 21; Students 210.

Catechesis Religious Program—200 S. Finley Ave., P. O. Box 310, Basking Ridge, 07920. Tel: 908-766-4774, Ext. 29; Email: stjamesccd@yahoo.com. Sr. Donna Brady, D.R.E. Students 854.

BELVIDERE, WARREN CO., ST. PATRICK (1892)

327 Greenwich St., Belvidere, 07823. Tel: 908-475-2559; Fax: 908-750-4262; Email: kkelly1@comcast.net; Web: www.stpatrickrose.org. Rev. David J. Pekola; Deacons John F. Dumschat; William Kintis.

Catechesis Religious Program—Tracy Menza, D.R.E. Students 92.

BERNARDSVILLE, SOMERSET CO., OUR LADY OF PERPETUAL HELP (1898) [CEM]

111 Claremont Rd., Bernardsville, 07924. Tel: 908-766-0079; Fax: 908-766-1185; Email: olphemail@aol.com; Web: www.olphbernardsville.org. Revs. John C. Siceloff; Juan Carlos Gaviria, Parochial Vicar; Deacon Benigno Ruiz-Diaz.

School—School of St. Elizabeth, (Grades PreK-8), 30 Seney Dr., Bernardsville, 07924. Tel: 908-766-0244; Fax: 908-766-5372; Email: principal.stelizabeth@diometuchen.org; Web: www.steschool.org. Dawn Paskalides, Prin. Lay Teachers 16; Students 179; Clergy / Religious Teachers 2.

Convent—St. Elizabeth Convent, 30 Seney Dr., Bernardsville, 07924. Tel: 908-766-0266. Sr. Donna Brady, Local Supr. Sisters of Christian Charity 4.

Catechesis Religious Program—Michele Lobo, D.R.E. Students 325.

Chapel—Bernardsville, Sacred Heart (Chapel of Convenience).

BLAIRSTOWN, WARREN CO., ST. JUDE (1945)

7 Eisenhower Rd., P.O. Box N, Blairstown, 07825. Tel: 908-362-6444; Fax: 908-362-6862; Email: stjudech@ptd.net; Web: stjudech.org. Very Rev. Ronald L. Jandernoa.

Catechesis Religious Program—Tel: 908-362-1431. Marie Draghi, D.R.E. Students 280.

BLOOMSBURY, HUNTERDON CO., CHURCH OF THE ANNUNCIATION (1948)

80 Main St., P.O. Box 136, Bloomsbury, 08804-0136. Tel: 908-479-4905; Email: annunicationrcc@earthlink.net. Rev. Roberto Coruna.

Catechesis Religious Program—Tel: 908-479-6708; Email: annunciationccd64@yahoo.com. Donna Perrone, Catechetical Leader. Students 92.

BOUND BROOK, SOMERSET CO.

1—ST. JOSEPH (1876) [CEM]

124 E. Second St., P.O. Box 72, Bound Brook, 08805. Tel: 732-356-0027; Email: St.Joseph.Parish@sjcbb.net; Web: www.sjcbb.net. Revs. John R. Pringle, Admin.; Alfonso R. Condorson; Deacons Gary Newton; Gustavo Sandoval.

Res.: 909 W. Meadow Dr., Bound Brook, 08805.

Catechesis Religious Program—124 East Second St., P.O. Box 72, Bound Brook, 08805. Tel: 732-356-0027; Email: reled@sjcbb.net; Email: Ana.Valencia@sjcbb.net. Ana Valencia, D.R.E. Students 284.

2—St. Mary of Czestochowa (1914) (Polish)
201 Vosseller Ave., Bound Brook, 08805.
Tel: 732-356-0358; Fax: 732-356-5348; Email: stmarybb1@verizon.net; Web: www.stmarys-boundbrook.org. Rev. John Stec, Admin.
Res.: 193 W. High St., Bound Brook, 08805.

Bridgewater, Somerset Co.

1—St. Bernard of Clairvaux (1843) [CEM]
500 Rte. 22, Bridgewater, 08807. Tel: 908-725-0552; Fax: 908-725-4524; Email: office@stbernardbridgewater.org; Web: www.stbernardbridgewater.org. Rev. Msgr. Randall J. Vashon; Rev. Edmund A. Luciano III, Parochial Vicar; Deacons Patrick J. Cline; Gerard C. Sims.
Catechesis Religious Program—Karen Dill, Catechetical Leader. Students 650.

2—Holy Trinity (1948)
60 Maple St., Bridgewater, 08807. Tel: 908-526-2394; Fax: 908-526-5837; Email: htchurch08807@yahoo.com. Revs. John R. Pringle; Thomas Myladil, O.C.D., Weekend Clergy; Deacons Michael A. Forrestall; John Phalen.
Catechesis Religious Program—Tel: 908-725-6339; Email: htreoffice@yahoo.com. Nancy Cichocki, Catechetical Leader. Students 108.

Califon, Hunterdon Co., St. John Neumann (1982)
398 Country Rd. 513, Califon, 07830.
Tel: 908-832-2513; Fax: 908-832-7618; Email: sjn@ccsjn.org. P.O. Box 455, Califon, 07830. Rev. Abraham Orapankal; Deacon Earl J. Roberts III.
Res.: 390 County Rd. 513, P.O. Box 455, Califon, 07830. Web: www.ccsjn.org.
Catechesis Religious Program—Tel: 908-832-2162. Renee Ciszewski, D.R.E., Email: renee@ccsjn.org. Students 76.

Carteret, Middlesex Co.

1—Divine Mercy Parish (2010)
213 Pershing Ave., Carteret, 07008.
Tel: 732-541-5768; Fax: 732-541-5871; Email: dmpcarteret@gmail.com. Rev. Edmund J. Shallow.

2—St. Joseph (1893)
55 High St., Carteret, 07008. Tel: 732-541-8946; Fax: 732-541-0500. Rev. James W. McGuffey; Rev. Msgr. Pafnouti Wassef, Parochial Vicar; Rev. Sean G. Winters, In Res.; Deacons George F. Kimball; Ramon L. Torres.
Res.: 7 Locust St., Carteret, 07008.
School—St. Joseph School, (Grades PreK-8), 865 Roosevelt Ave., Carteret, 07008. Tel: 732-541-7111; Fax: 732-541-0676; Email: rjohnson@sjps.net; Web: www.sjps.net. Mrs. Roseann Johnson, Prin.; Lonie Yuschik, Librarian. Lay Teachers 15; Students 145.
Catechesis Religious Program—Tel: 732-969-8767; Email: stjosephreled@aol.com. Marcelle Doherty, D.R.E. Students 177.

Colonia, Middlesex Co., St. John Vianney (1959)
420 Inman Ave., Colonia, 07067. Tel: 732-574-0150; Fax: 732-574-0050; Email: ldunbar@sjvs.net; Web: parish.sjvianney.com. Rev. John C. Gloss; Rev. Msgr. Edward M. O'Neill, Pastor Emeritus, (Retired); Revs. Bede Kim, Parochial Vicar; Joseph Kubiak, O.F.M.-Cap., Parochial Vicar; Deacons Thomas N. Bresnan; Joseph D. Ragucci; Thomas S. Michnewicz.
School—St. John Vianney School, (Grades PreK-8), Tel: 732-388-1662; Fax: 732-388-1003; Email: ejude@sjvs.net; Web: www.sjvs.net. Sr. Eileen Jude Wust, S.S.J., Prin.; Gina Damanti, Librarian. Lay Teachers 26; Bernardine Sisters 2; Students 358.
Catechesis Religious Program—Tel: 732-388-1424; Email: mcowan@sjvs.net. Mary Cowan, D.R.E. Students 263.
Convent—St. John Vianney Convent, 440 Inman Ave., Colonia, 07067. Tel: 732-388-8740. Bernardine Franciscan Sisters 2; Sisters of St. Joseph of Chestnut Hill 2.

Dunellen, Middlesex Co., St. John the Evangelist (1879)
317 First St., Dunellen, 08812. Tel: 732-968-2621; Email: Stjev@verizon.net. Rev. Msgr. William Benwell, J.C.L., Admin.; Deacon Glenn Robitaille.
Catechesis Religious Program—Tel: 908-968-0233; Email: stjohnpcl@gmail.com. Sharon Sweeney, D.R.E. Students 200.

East Brunswick, Middlesex Co., St. Bartholomew (1959)
470 Ryders Ln., East Brunswick, 08816.
Tel: 732-257-7722; Email: bbunag@stbartseb.com. Very Rev. Thomas J. Walsh; Rev. Dario Endiape, Parochial Vicar; Deacons John H. Broehl; Anthony J. Gostkowski; John F. Kenny; Filippo Tartara.
Catechesis Religious Program—Tel: 732-390-0354; Email: bfitzgerald@stbartseb.com. Barbara Fitzgerald, Catechetical Leader. Students 700.
School—St. Bartholomew School, (Grades PreK-8), Tel: 732-254-7105; Fax: 732-254-6352; Web: www.stbartseb.com. Ann Wierzbicki, Prin. Lay Teachers 24; Students 363.

Edison, Middlesex Co.

1—Guardian Angels (1959) Merged with St. Paul the Apostle, Highland Park and Our Lady of Korea, Quasi-Parish, Woodbridge to form Transfiguration of the Lord Parish, Highland Park. Sacramental records retained at Transfiguration of the Lord Parish, Highland Park.

2—St. Helena (1965)
950 Grove Ave., Edison, 08820. Tel: 732-494-3399; Fax: 732-494-2076; Email: parishoffice@sthelenaedison.org; Web: www.sthelenaedison.org. Revs. Anthony M. Sirianni; Anthony Dukru, Parochial Vicar; Keith Cervine, In Res.; Deacon Robert G. Yunker.
School—St. Helena School, (Grades PreK-8), 930 Grove Ave., Edison, 08820. Tel: 732-549-6234; Fax: 732-549-6205; Web: www.sthelenaedison.org. Sr. Mary Charles Wienckoski, C.S.S.F., Prin.; Lynne Soltys, Librarian. Clergy 1; Lay Teachers 22; Felician Sisters 1; Students 226.
Catechesis Religious Program—Tel: 732-549-4660; Email: CFF@sthelenaedison.org; Web: www.sthelenaedison.org. Lynne Soltys, D.R.E. Students 156.

3—St. Matthew the Apostle (1952)
81 Seymour Ave., Edison, 08817. Tel: 732-985-5063; Fax: 732-985-9104; Email: frgeorge@stmatthewtheapostle.com. Revs. George Targonski; Alphonsus Kariuki, Parochial Vicar.
School—St. Matthew School, (Grades PreK-8), 100 Seymour Ave., Edison, 08817. Tel: 732-985-6633; Fax: 732-985-7748; Web: www.stmatthewtheapostle.com/school. Mrs. Joyce Schaefer, Prin. Lay Teachers 15; Students 148.
Catechesis Religious Program—Email: pcl@stmatthewtheapostle.com. Mrs. Alice Fogarty, D.R.E. Students 228.

Far Hills-Peapack, Somerset Co., St. Elizabeth - St. Brigid
129 Main St., Peapack, 07977. Tel: 908-234-1265; Tel: 908-234-0079; Fax: 908-234-2923; Email: ParishLife@saintEB.org; Web: www.saintelizabeth-saintbrigid.org. P.O. Box 33, Peapack, 07977. Rev. Msgr. Edward C. Puleo; Rev. John G. Hillier, Ph.D., In Res.
St. Elizabeth—34 Peapack Rd., Far Hills, 07931.
St. Brigid, 129 Main St., Peapack, 07977.
Catechesis Religious Program—Email: reled@sainteb.org. Denise O'Callaghan, D.R.E. Students 299.

Flemington, Hunterdon Co., St. Magdalen de Pazzi (1864) [CEM]
105 Mine St., Flemington, 08822. Tel: 908-782-2922; Fax: 908-782-0952; Email: ckinney@stmagdalen.org. Revs. Kenneth D. Brighenti; Wladyslaw Wiktorek, Parochial Vicar; Deacons Michael J. Bachynsky; Stephen F. Kern; Thaddeus Wislinski; David L. Urcinas.
Catechesis Religious Program—Bridget Rincon, D.R.E. Students 606.
St. Magdalen Convent, 83 Bonnell St., Flemington, 08822. Sr. Gloria Pighini, S.J.H., Servant Sister. Sisters of Christian Charity 3.

Fords, Middlesex Co., Our Lady of Peace (1919)
P.O. Box 69, Fords, 08863. Tel: 732-738-7940; Fax: 732-738-3848; Email: mail@olpfords.org; Web: www.olpfords.org. Revs. Matthew R. Paratore, J.C.L.; Robert V. Meyers, J.C.L., Parochial Vicar; Deacons James A. Kelly Jr.; John A. Raychel.
Res.: 26 Maple Ave., Edison, 08837.
Catechesis Religious Program—Tel: 732-738-7464; Email: prep@olpfords.org. Ms. Candida Gonzalez, D.R.E. Students 168.

Great Meadows, Warren Co., Ss. Peter and Paul (1921)
360 U.S. Hwy. 46, Great Meadows, 07838.
Tel: 908-637-4269; Fax: 908-637-6896; Email: stpeterandpaul@comcast.net. Rev. Grzegorz Podsiadlo, S.D.S., Admin.; Deacon Stephen Gunther.
Catechesis Religious Program—Diane Francis, D.R.E. Students 145.

Hackettstown, Warren Co., Assumption of the Blessed Virgin Mary (1864)
302 High St., Hackettstown, 07840-0547.
Tel: 908-852-3320; Fax: 908-852-2361; Email: secretary@assumptionbvmnj.org; Web: www.assumptionbvmnj.org. Rev. Antony Arockiadoss; Deacons Daniel Gallagher; Walter H. Pidgeon; David M. Waguespack.
Catechesis Religious Program—159 Liberty St., Hackettstown, 07840. Email: faithformation@assumptionbvmnj.org. Ann-Kathryn Daly, Catechetical Leader. Students 171.

Hampton, Hunterdon Co., St. Ann (1859) [CEM]
Office: 32 Main St., Hampton, 08827.
Tel: 908-537-2221. P.O. Box 405, Hampton, 08827. Rev. Michael C. Saharic.
Church: 6 Church St., Hampton, 08827.
Catechesis Religious Program—Tel: 908-537-1070. Maureen Hammond, Catechetical Leader. Students 210.

Helmetta, Middlesex Co., Holy Trinity (1911) [CEM] (Polish)
100 Main St., Helmetta, 08828. Tel: 732-521-0172; Fax: 732-521-0824; Email: htc100@verizon.net. Rev. Andrzej Wieliczko, Admin.
Catechesis Religious Program—Tel: 732-521-0100. Melkis Oelkers, Catechetical Leader. Students 100.

High Bridge, Hunterdon Co., St. Joseph (1880)
59 Main St., High Bridge, 08829. Tel: 908-638-6211; Fax: 908-638-5802; Email: parishoffice@sjchb.org. Rev. James A. Kyrpczak; Deacon Thomas McGovern.
Catechesis Religious Program—Shari Shultz, D.R.E. Students 125.

Highland Park, Middlesex Co.

1—St. Paul the Apostle (1912) Merged with Guardian Angels, Edison and Our Lady of Korea, Quasi-Parish, Woodbridge to form Transfiguration of the Lord Parish, Highland Park. Sacramental records retained at Transfiguration of the Lord Parish, Highland Park.

2—Transfiguration of the Lord Parish
23 S. Fifth Ave., Highland Park, 08904-2604.
Tel: 732-572-0977; Email: transfiguration.parish@verizon.net. Revs. Abraham Lotha; Pauly Thekkan, C.M.I., In Res.; Deacon Edward Krupa.
Res.: 37 Plainfield Ave., Edison, 08818.
Guardian Angels—
St. Paul the Apostle, 502 Raritan Ave., Highland Park, 08904.
Catechesis Religious Program—Tel: 732-572-0955. Carol Mascola, D.R.E. Students 125.

Hillsborough, Somerset Co.

1—St. Joseph (Millstone Borough) (1883)
34 Yorktown Rd., Hillsborough, 08844.
Tel: 908-874-3141. Revs. Francis G. Hilton, S.J.; Tholitho Tholitho, In Res.
Res.: 41 Yorktown Rd., Hillsborough, 08844.
Catechesis Religious Program—
Tel: 908-874-3141, Ext. 224. James Jungels, D.R.E., Email: jjungels@stjosephsparish.com. Students 471.

2—Mary, Mother of God (1948)
157 S. Triangle Rd., Hillsborough, 08844.
Tel: 908-874-8220; Fax: 908-874-4183; Email: mmghillsborough@aol.com; Web: marymotherofgod.org. Revs. John M. Rozembajgier; Alexander J. Carles, Parochial Vicar; Sean A. Broderick, C.S.Sp., In Res.; Deacons Salvatore J. Bonfiglio; Christopher Conroy, D.R.E.; James N. McCormick.
School—Mary, Mother of God School,
Tel: 908-874-8489; Email: office@marymotherofgod.org. Karen Duffy, Pre-K Coord.; Christine Powell, Kindergarten Enrichment. Lay Teachers 5; Students 80.
Catechesis Religious Program—Tel: 908-874-8604; Email: deaconchris@marymotherofgod.org. Students 750.

Hopelawn, Middlesex Co.

1—Good Shepherd Parish
625 Florida Grove Rd., Hopelawn, 08861.
Tel: 732-826-4859; Email: goodshepherd20@verizon.net; Web: goodshepherdpanj.org. Rev. Michael G. Krull; Deacons Samuel J. Costantino; Edward G. Rodes; Albert Coppola.
Catechesis Religious Program—Maria C. Arcelay, D.R.E. Students 133.
Our Lady of the Most Holy Rosary.

2—Our Lady of the Most Holy Rosary (1904) [CEM] Merged with Holy Spirit, Perth Amboy to form Good Shepherd Parish, Perth Amboy. Sacramental records retained at Good Shepherd Parish, Hopelawn.

Iselin, Middlesex Co., St. Cecelia (1923)
45 Wilus Way, Iselin, 08830. Tel: 732-283-2300; Fax: 732-283-3326; Email: ceceliaparish@gmail.com. Revs. Thomas Naduviledathu, S.D.V.; Vernon Kohlmann, S.D.V., Parochial Vicar; Deacons Richard Lutomski; Anthony J. Pepe.
Catechesis Religious Program—Tel: 732-283-2816; Email: stcre@yahoo.com. Sr. Mary Linda Szal, D.R.E. Students 133.
Stations—NJ State Home for Disabled Veterans—132 Evergreen Rd., Edison, 08818.
Roosevelt Care Center, 1 Roosevelt Dr., Edison, 08837.

Jamesburg, Middlesex Co., St. James the Less (1878) [CEM]
36 Lincoln Ave., Jamesburg, 08831.
Tel: 732-521-0100; Fax: 732-521-8287; Email: jamestheless1880@gmail.com; Web: stjamesthelesschurch.org. Revs. Michael Fragoso; Joseph Kabali, (In Res.); Deacon Patrick J. Smith.
Catechesis Religious Program—Tel: 732-521-1188; Email: jamesthelessccd@gmail.com. Kim Bohinski-Smith, D.R.E. Students 328.

Kendall Park, Middlesex Co., St. Augustine of Canterbury (1952)
45 Henderson Rd., Kendall Park, 08824.
Tel: 732-297-3000; Fax: 732-940-1746; Web: www.staugustinenj.org. Rev. Robert G. Lynam; Deacons James Rivera; Denis Mayer; Sisters Joanne Manns, M.P.F., Pastoral Min./Coord.; Ruthann McGoldrick, Pastoral Assoc.
School—St. Augustine of Canterbury School, (Grades

PreK-8), Tel: 732-297-6042; Email: ldeluca@staugustinenj.org. Sr. Mary Louise Shulas, M.P.F., Prin. Lay Teachers 27; Students 403; Clergy / Religious Teachers 2.
Catechesis Religious Program—Tel: 732-297-3011. Sisters Joanne Manns, M.P.F., Catechetical Leader; Diana Yodris, Dir. Students 205.
Convent—St. Augustine of Canterbury Convent, Tel: 732-798-6950. Religious Sisters Filippini 4.

LAMBERTVILLE, HUNTERDON CO., ST. JOHN THE EVANGELIST (1843) [CEM]
44 Bridge St., Lambertville, 08530.
Tel: 609-397-3350; Fax: 609-397-8713; Email: office@parishofsaintjohn.org; Web: parishofsaintjohn.org. 13 N. Main St., Lambertville, 08530. Very Rev. Robert B. Kolakowski, J.C.D.
Catechesis Religious Program—Email: dre@parishofsaintjohn.org. Veronica McCabe, D.R.E. Students 141.

LAURENCE HARBOR, MIDDLESEX CO., ST. LAWRENCE (1943)
109 Laurence Pkwy., Laurence Harbor, 08879.
Tel: 732-566-1093; Fax: 732-765-9311; Email: saintlawrenceharbor@gmail.com. Rev. Mark Kehoe, Admin.; Deacons Stephen J. Gajewski; Gregory Ris; Michael Abriola.
Catechesis Religious Program—Tel: 732-566-0226. Judy Logan, D.R.E. Students 98.

MANVILLE, SOMERSET CO.
1—CHRIST THE KING (1948) Merged with Sacred Heart of Jesus, Manville to form Christ the Redeemer, Manville. Sacramental records retained at Christ the Redeemer Parish, Manville.
2—CHRIST THE REDEEMER PARISH, [CEM]
98 S. Second Ave., Manville, 08835. Email: parish@ctrmanville.com; Web: www.ctrmanville.com. P.O. Box 924, Manville, 08835.
Tel: 908-725-0072; Fax: 908-685-3029. Revs. Stanislaw Slaby, C.Ss.R.; Wojciech Kusek, C.Ss.R., Parochial Vicar; Deacons Thomas J. Giacobbe; William G. Stefany.
Christ the King Church—211 Louis St., Manville, 08835. Tel: 908-231-1330.
Sacred Heart Church, 98 S. Second Ave., Manville, 08835.
Catechesis Religious Program—99 N. 13th Ave., Manville, 08835. Charlotte Snow, D.R.E. Students 149.
3—SACRED HEART OF JESUS (1919) [CEM] (Polish), Merged with Christ the King, Manville to form Christ the Redeemer, Manville. Sacramental records retained at Christ the Redeemer Parish, Manville.

MARTINSVILLE, SOMERSET CO., BLESSED SACRAMENT (1968)
1890 Washington Valley Rd., Martinsville, 08836.
Tel: 732-356-4442; Email: pmarshall@blessedsacramentnj.org. 852 Newmans Ln., P.O. Box 563, Martinsville, 08836. Revs. Richard M. Rusk; Lukasz Blicharski, Parochial Vicar; Deacon Louis Pizzigoni III.
Catechesis Religious Program—Mrs. Patricia Marshall, D.R.E. Students 426.

MIDDLESEX, MIDDLESEX CO., OUR LADY OF MOUNT VIRGIN (1943)
600 Harris Ave., Middlesex, 08846.
Tel: 732-356-2149; Fax: 732-356-1302; Email: efleming@olmv.net. Rev. David V. Skoblow, Admin.; Deacons Edgar R. Chaves; John R. Czekaj; Thomas G. Sommero; John R. Tietjen.
Catechesis Religious Program—
Tel: 732-356-2149, Ext. 2010. Dorothy Zmigrodski, Catechetical Leader. Students 267.
Convent—Petra House, 610 Harris Ave., Middlesex, 08846. Tel: 732-377-9933. Sr. Kathleen Rooney, S.S.J., Contact Sister. Sisters of St. Joseph Chestnut Hills 5.

MILFORD, HUNTERDON CO., ST. EDWARD THE CONFESSOR (1944)
61 Mill St., Milford, 08848. Tel: 908-995-4723; Email: stedwardmilford@gmail.com; Web: www.stedwardmilford.com. Rev. Krzysztof Kaczynski; Deacon William J. Barr.
Catechesis Religious Program—Email: stedgrowingfaith@gmail.com. Kristine Menard, D.R.E. Students 100.

MILLTOWN, MIDDLESEX CO., OUR LADY OF LOURDES (1921)
233 N. Main St., Milltown, 08850. Tel: 732-828-0011; Fax: 732-828-3133; Email: olol678@aol.com. Revs. Edward A. Czarcinski; Michael E. Crummy, In Res.; Deacon Robert Gerling.
Catechesis Religious Program—Tel: 732-421-6818. Renee Young, D.R.E. Students 144.

MONMOUTH JUNCTION, MIDDLESEX CO., ST. CECILIA (1914)
10 Kingston Ln., Monmouth Junction, 08852.
Tel: 732-329-2893; Email: parishsect@stceciliaparish.net. Rev. Charles T. O'Connor; Deacon Michael P. Murtha.
Res.: 46 Kingston Ln., Monmouth Junction, 08852.
Catechesis Religious Program—Tel: 732-329-1141; Email: dre@stceciliaparish.net. Willliam Cherepon, D.R.E. Students 218.

MONROE TOWNSHIP, MIDDLESEX CO., NATIVITY OF OUR LORD (1992)
185 Applegarth Rd., Monroe Township, 08831.
Tel: 609-371-0499, Ext. 10; Email: admin@nativitymonroe.org; Web: www.nativitymonroe.org. Rev. Edward R. Flanagan; Deacons John Bertrand; Robert E. Gatto; John H. Shelton; Sr. Mary L. Cooke, Sec.
Catechesis Religious Program—
Tel: 609-371-2518, Ext. 14,18; Email: pcl@nativitymonroe.org. Mary Kay Cullinan, D.R.E. Students 215.
Convent—Blessed Pauline Convent, 59A Essex Rd., Monroe Twp., 08831. Tel: 609-409-1254. Sisters of Christian Charity 2.

NEW BRUNSWICK, MIDDLESEX CO.
1—HOLY FAMILY PARISH
56 Throop Ave., New Brunswick, 08901. Email: hfpcenter@holyfamilyforall.org; Web: www.holyfamilyforall.org; Web: pl.holyfamilyforall.org. Rev. Msgr. Joseph J. Kerrigan; Rev. Imre Juhasz, Parochial Vicar; Deacon Nelson Torres.
Catechesis Religious Program—Catherine Kovarcik, Faith Formation. Students 270.
St. Joseph Church—15 Maple St., New Brunswick, 08901.
St. Ladislaus Church, 215 Somerset St., New Brunswick, 08901.
Sacred Heart Church, 56 Throop Ave., New Brunswick, 08901.
2—ST. JOHN THE BAPTIST (1867) [CEM] (German), Merged with St. Mary of Mount Virgin, New Brunswick to form Parish of the Visitation, New Brunswick. Sacramental records retained at Parish of the Visitation, New Brunswick.
3—ST. JOSEPH (1924) (Polish), Merged with St. Ladislaus, New Brunswick & Sacred Heart, New Brunswick to form Holy Family Parish, New Brunswick. Sacramental records retained at Holy Family Parish, New Brunswick.
4—ST. LADISLAUS (1904) (Hungarian), Merged with St. Joseph, New Brunswick & Sacred Heart, New Brunswick to form Holy Family Parish, New Brunswick. Sacramental records retained at Holy Family Parish, New Brunswick.
5—ST. MARY OF MOUNT VIRGIN (1904) (Italian), Merged with St. John the Baptist, New Brunswick to form Parish of the Visitation, New Brunswick. Sacramental records retained at Parish of the Visitation, New Brunswick.
6—OUR LADY OF MT. CARMEL (1977) (Hispanic)
75 Morris St., New Brunswick, 08901.
Tel: 732-846-5873; Fax: 732-846-5397; Web: www.olmtcarmelonline.com. Revs. Raymond L. Nacarino; Jose Lorente, Parochial Vicar; Manuel Lorente, Parochial Vicar.
Res.: 528 Ryders Ln., East Brunswick, 08816.
Catechesis Religious Program—Taty Alvarado, Catechetical Leader. Students 625.
7—PARISH OF THE VISITATION, [CEM]
192 Sandford St., New Brunswick, 08901.
Tel: 732-545-5090; Fax: 732-937-9290; Email: parishofthevisitation@gmail.com. Revs. Firmino Htwe, Parochial Vicar; Javier Flores, Parochial Vicar; Benny Chittilappilly, Admin.
St. John the Baptist Church—29 Abeel St., New Brunswick, 08901.
St. Mary of Mt. Virgin Church, 190 Sandford St., New Brunswick, 08901.
St. Theresa of the Infant Jesus, 15 Fox Rd., Edison, 08817.
Catechesis Religious Program—Amelia Johnson, MET, Catechetical Leader. Students 443.
Convent—St. Mary of Mount Virgin Convent, 198 Sandford St., New Brunswick, 08901.
Tel: 732-545-0514. Sisters 4.
8—ST. PETER THE APOSTLE aka St. Peter the Apostle University and Community Parish (1829) [CEM]
94 Somerset St., New Brunswick, 08901.
Tel: 732-545-6820; Tel: 732-545-6185;
Fax: 732-545-4069; Email: parishoffice@stpeternewbrunswick.org; Web: www.stpeternewbrunswick.org. Rev. Msgr. Joseph G. Celano; Revs. James De Fillipps, Parochial Vicar; Jason Pavich, Parochial Vicar; Deacons Patrick J. Gutsick; Helmut Wittreich.
Catechesis Religious Program—Anne Marie Calderone, D.R.E. Students 58.
9—SACRED HEART (1883) Merged with St. Joseph, New Brunswick & St. Ladislaus, New Brunswick to form Holy Family Parish, New Brunswick. Sacramental records retained at Holy Family Parish, New Brunswick.

NORTH BRUNSWICK, MIDDLESEX CO., OUR LADY OF PEACE (1969)
277 Washington Pl., North Brunswick, 08902.
Tel: 732-297-9680; Fax: 732-297-1024; Email: olop_church@yahoo.com; Web: olopnb.org. Rev. John V. Polyak; Deacons Francis D'Mello; David A. DeFrange.
Catechesis Religious Program—Steve Reitano, Catechetical Leader. Students 306.

NORTH PLAINFIELD, SOMERSET CO.
1—ST. JOSEPH (1882)
41 Manning Ave., North Plainfield, 07060.
Tel: 908-756-3383; Email: fathergeorgef@aol.com. 99 Westervelt Ave., North Plainfield, 07060. Rev. Msgr. Richard J. Lyons, J.C.L., In Res.; Revs. George A. Farrell; Ronald Machado, Pastoral Assoc.; Deacon Cesar Augusto Ortega; Sr. Susana Islas, D.R.E.
Catechesis Religious Program—Students 183.
2—ST. LUKE (1965)
300 Clinton Ave., North Plainfield, 07063.
Tel: 908-754-8811; Fax: 908-754-0120. Rev. Msgr. Michael J. Corona, P.A., Admin.
Catechesis Religious Program—Jeanne Enteman, D.R.E. Students 110.

OLD BRIDGE, MIDDLESEX CO.
1—ST. AMBROSE (1961)
83 Throckmorton Ln., Old Bridge, 08857.
Tel: 732-679-5666; Fax: 732-679-0853; Email: joan.abitabile@saintambroseparish.com. Revs. John C. Grimes; John J. O'Kane, Parochial Vicar; Deacon Thomas C. Yondolino.
Res.: 2 Awn St., Old Bridge, 08857.
School—St. Ambrose School, (Grades K-8), 81 Throckmorton Ln., Old Bridge, 08857.
Tel: 732-679-4700; Fax: 732-679-6062; Email: principal@stambroseschool.net; Web: www.stambroseschool.net. Dr. Theodore Kadela, Prin. Lay Teachers 18; Students 190.
Catechesis Religious Program—Fax: 732-679-3416;
Tel: 732-679-5580; Email: kathy.abair@saintambroseparish.com. Kathy Abair, Catechetical Leader. Students 702.
2—MOST HOLY REDEEMER (1983)
133 Amboy Rd., Matawan, 07747. Tel: 732-566-9334; Fax: 732-566-2245; Email: MHR1987@aol.com; Web: www.mhr-parish.org. Revs. Chester H. Carina, J.C.L.; Joseph L. Desmond, In Res.; Deacons Robert T. McGovern; A. Keith Berg; Frank C. D'Auguste.
Catechesis Religious Program—Tel: 732-566-5630; Email: mhrccd1993@aol.com. Deborah Dyson, D.R.E. Students 299.
3—ST. THOMAS THE APOSTLE (1921)
1 St. Thomas Plaza, Old Bridge, 08857.
Tel: 732-251-4000; Fax: 732-251-4946; Email: krisyuhas@optonline.net. Revs. Jerome A. Johnson; Frank W. Fellrath, Parochial Vicar; Gerardo B. Paderon, Parochial Vicar; Deacons Robert Bonfante Sr.; Scott D. Titmas; Patrick W. Hearty; Joseph C. Tobin.
School—St. Thomas the Apostle School, (Grades PreK-8), 333 Hwy. 18, Old Bridge, 08857.
Tel: 732-251-4812; Fax: 732-251-5315; Email: jkowit@diometuchen.org. Mrs. Joanne Kowit, Prin.; Donna Delfino, Librarian. Lay Teachers 25; Students 417.
Catechesis Religious Program—Tel: 732-251-1660; Email: dyesis@sttaob.com. Debbie Yesis, D.R.E. Students 686.

OXFORD, WARREN CO., ST. ROSE OF LIMA (1864) [CEM]
85 Academy St., Oxford, 07863. Tel: 908-475-2559;
Fax: 908-475-4919; Email: kkelly1@comcast.net; Web: www.stpatrickrose.org. 327 Greenwich St., Belvidere, 07823. Rev. David J. Pekola; Deacon Lawrence V. D'Andrea.

PARLIN, MIDDLESEX CO., ST. BERNADETTE (1956)
20 Villanova Rd., Parlin, 08859. Tel: 732-721-2772; Fax: 732-721-5188; Email: secy@optonline.net. Rev. James W. Hagerman; Rev. Msgr. Andrew L. Szaroleta.
Catechesis Religious Program—Tel: 732-727-4343. Lorna Francis, Catechetical Leader. Students 295.

PERTH AMBOY, MIDDLESEX CO.
1—HOLY SPIRIT (1944) Closed. Sacramental records retained at Good Shepherd Parish, Hopelawn.
2—HOLY TRINITY (1899) [CEM] (Slovak), Merged with Our Lady of Hungary and La Asuncion to form Most Holy Name of Jesus Parish, Perth Amboy. Sacramental records retained at Most Holy Name of Jesus Parish, Perth Amboy.
3—SAINT JOHN PAUL II PARISH
Mailing Address: 490 State St., Perth Amboy, 08861-3541. Tel: 732-826-1395; Fax: 732-826-4217; Email: pastor@johnpaulsecond.com; Web: www.johnpaulsecond.com. Revs. Waldemar Latkowski, C.Ss.R.; Lukasz Drozak, C.Ss.R., Parochial Vicar; Deacon Basilio A. Perez.
Res.: 97 Buckingham Ave., Perth Amboy, 08861.
Our Lady of the Rosary of Fatima—188 Wayne St., Perth Amboy, 08861.
St. Stephen.
Catechesis Religious Program—Millie Vazquez, Catechetical Leader. Students 97.
4—LA ASUNCION (1981) (Hispanic), Closed. Sacramental records retained at Most Holy Name of Jesus Parish, Perth Amboy.

5—St. Mary (1845) Closed. Sacramental records retained at St. John Paul II Parish, Perth Amboy.
6—Most Holy Name of Jesus Parish
697 Cortlandt St., Perth Amboy, 08861-2843.
Tel: 732-442-0512; Email: mostholynameofjesus@gmail.com. Rev. Msgr. John B. Gordon; Rev. Nicholas Norena, Parochial Vicar; Deacons Noe Cortez; Enrique Garcia; Sharon Salinas, Bookkeeper; Sonia Molina, Sec.
Our Lady of Hungary Church—
Holy Trinity Church, 315 Lawrie St., Perth Amboy, 08861.
La Asuncion Church, 777 Cortlandt St., Perth Amboy, 08861.
Catechesis Religious Program—474 Penn St., Perth Amboy, 08861. Tel: 732-442-3457; Email: dre.mhnoj@gmail.com. Estefany Abreu, Catechetical Leader. Students 433.
7—Our Lady of Fatima (1960) (Hispanic)
380 Smith St., Perth Amboy, 08861.
Tel: 732-442-6634; Email: olfperthamboy@gmail.com; Web: olfperthamboy.org. Revs. Alberto Ruiz, C.M.F.; José Chung, Parochial Vicar; Gilles D. Njobam, C.M.F., Parochial Vicar; Rohan Dominic, C.M.F., In Res.; Deacons Pablo Bencosme; Gregorio A. Rios; Herminio Rivera.
Catechesis Religious Program—Fe Morales, Catechetical Leader. Students 294.
8—Our Lady of Hungary (1902) [CEM] (Hungarian), Merged with La Asuncion and Holy Trinity to form Most Holy Name of Jesus Parish, Perth Amboy. Sacramental records retained at Most Holy Name of Jesus Parish, Perth Amboy.
9—Our Lady of the Rosary of Fatima (1981) (Portuguese), Merged with St. Stephen and St. Mary to form St. John Paul II Parish, Perth Amboy. Sacramental records retained at St. John Paul II Parish, Perth Amboy.
10—St. Stephen (1892) [CEM] (Polish), Merged with St. Mary and Our Lady of the Rosary of Fatima to form St. John Paul II Parish, Perth Amboy. Sacramental records retained at St. John Paul II Parish, Perth Amboy.

Phillipsburg, Warren Co.
1—SS. Peter and Paul (1913) (Slovak), Closed. Records at St. Philip & St. James, Phillipsburg.
2—St. Philip & St. James (1860) [CEM]
430 S. Main St., Phillipsburg, 08865-3094.
Tel: 908-454-0112; Fax: 908-454-0125; Email: pastor@spsj.org; Email: secretary@spsj.org; Web: www.spsj.org. Revs. John J. Barbella; Thomas P. Ganley, Parochial Vicar; Leopoldo S. Salvania, Parochial Vicar; Deacons Enock Berluche Sr.; Larry M. Bevilacqua; John T. Flynn, (Retired); Robert Fisher.
School—St. Philip and St. James School, (Grades PreK-8), 137 Roseberry St., Phillipsburg, 08865.
Tel: 908-859-1244; Fax: 908-859-1202; Email: sspjschool@spsj.org; Web: sspjnj.org. Mrs. Donna Kucinski, Prin.
Saints Philip & James School Lay Teachers 18; Students 184; Clergy / Religious Teachers 4.
Catechesis Religious Program—137 Roseberry St., Phillipsburg, 08865. Tel: 908-859-1244, Ext. 9; Email: religiouseducation@spsj.org. Jo-Ann Scott, D.R.E. Students 357.

Piscataway, Middlesex Co.
1—St. Frances Cabrini (1961)
208 Bound Brook Ave., 08854-4097.
Tel: 732-885-5313; Fax: 732-885-9031; Email: sfc208@yahoo.com. Rev. James F. Considine; Deacon Roger Ladao.
Catechesis Religious Program—Tel: 732-885-8996. Terri Abano, D.R.E. Students 121.
2—Our Lady of Fatima (1948)
50 Van Winkle Pl., 08854.
Tel: 732-968-5556, Ext. 1104; Email: Ghughes@olfparish.org; Web: www.olfparish.org. Revs. Arlindo Paul DaSilva; Virgilio T. Tolentino, Pastoral Assoc.; Charles A. Sabella, Pastoral Assoc.; A. David Chalackal, In Res.; Deacons Lawrence P. Reilly; William P. Rider; Mrs. Gloria Hughes, Sec.
Res.: 501 New Market Rd., 08854.
Catechesis Religious Program—Tel: 732-968-5555; Email: jhorai@olfparish.org. Jeanette Horai. Students 274.

Pittstown, Hunterdon Co., St. Catherine of Siena (1992)
2 White Bridge Rd., Pittstown, 08867-0245.
Tel: 908-735-4024; Tel: 908-735-5086;
Fax: 908-735-0355; Email: stcofs@embarqmail.com; Email: bulletinmary@yahoo.com; Web: www.scoschurch.org. P.O. Box 245, Pittstown, 08867. Rev. Czeslaw Zalubski; Deacon Stephen G. Kassebaum; Pat Prakopcyk, Music Min.; Mary Mitariten, Sec.
Res.: 4 Whitebridge Rd., Pittstown, 08867-0245.
Catechesis Religious Program—Email: stcsre@embarqmail.com. Judith La Tournous, Catechetical Leader. Students 188.
St. Catherine of Siena Pastoral Center—142 Perryville Rd., Hampton, 08827.
Station—Country Arch Nursing Home, 114 Pittstown Rd., Pittstown, 08867. Tel: 908-735-6600.

Plainsboro, Middlesex Co., Queenship of Mary (1982)
16 Dey Rd., Plainsboro, 08536. Tel: 609-779-5511; Fax: 609-779-8904; Email: parishoffice@qomchurch.org; Web: www.qomchurch.org. Rev. Msgr. Robert W. Medley; Deacons Hugo Simao; Thomas P. Boccellari.
Catechesis Religious Program—Tel: 609-799-1428; Email: reginafinn@qomchurch.org. Regina Finn, Faith Formation; Mr. Jay Vince-Cruz, Music Min. Students 223.

Port Murray, Warren Co., St. Theodore (1983)
855 Rte. 57, P.O. Box 146, Port Murray, 07865.
Tel: 908-689-8318; Fax: 908-689-9242; Email: sttheodorenj@gmail.com; Web: www.sttheodorenj.com. Rev. Damian Tomiczek, S.D.S., Admin.
Catechesis Religious Program—Ginny Moran, D.R.E. Students 125.

Port Reading, Middlesex Co., St. Anthony of Padua (1906)
436 Port Reading Ave., Port Reading, 07064.
Tel: 732-634-1403; Fax: 732-602-0119; Email: info.stanthony1@gmail.com; Web: www.saintanthonypadua.org. Rev. William J. Smith; Rev. Msgr. Pafnouti Wassef; Deacons Peter Barcellona; Michael Brucato; Kenneth J. Perlas.
Catechesis Religious Program—Students 170.
Worship Site: Our Lady of Mount Carmel, 267 E. Smith St., Woodbridge, 07095.

Raritan, Somerset Co.
1—The Catholic Church of St. Ann aka St. Ann, Raritan (1903) (Italian)
45 Anderson St., Raritan, 08869. Tel: 908-725-1008; Fax: 908-707-1915; Email: info@stannparish.com; Web: www.stannparish.com. Rev. Thomas A. Odorizzi, C.O.; Very Rev. Peter R. Cebulka, C.O., Parochial Vicar; Deacons Joseph Richard Stevens, Business Mgr.; John R. Pacifico; Roy Rabinowitz; Robert Sause.
School—St. Ann School, (Grades PreK-8), 29 2nd Ave., Raritan, 08869. Tel: 908-725-7787;
Fax: 908-541-9335; Email: principal.stannschool@diometuchen.org. Sr. Margaret Mary Hanlon, M.P.F., Prin. Lay Teachers 14; Students 115; Religious Teachers Filippini 1; Clergy / Religious Teachers 1.
Convent—St. Ann Convent, 29 Second Ave., Raritan, 08869. Tel: 908-725-2256. Sr. Margaret Mary Hanlon, M.P.F., Supr. Religious Sisters Filippini 3.
Catechesis Religious Program—Email: pvella@stannparish.com. Sr. Phyllis Vella, D.R.E. Students 195.
2—St. Joseph (1912) (Slovak)
16 E. Somerset St., Raritan, 08869.
Tel: 908-725-0163; Email: parishoffice@sjraritan.org; Web: stjosephraritan.weconnect.com. Rev. Kenneth R. Kolibas.
Catechesis Religious Program—Students 23.

Sayreville, Middlesex Co.
1—Our Lady of Victories (1885) [CEM]
42 Main St., Sayreville, 08872. Tel: 732-257-0077; Fax: 732-651-1898; Email: tryan@olvsayrenj.com; Web: www.olvsayrenj.com. Rev. Thomas F. Ryan; Deacon Edward J. Majkowski.
Res.: 24 Main St., Sayreville, 08872.
School—Our Lady of Victories School, (Grades PreK-8), 36 Main St., Sayreville, 08872. Tel: 732-254-1676; Fax: 732-254-5066; Web: www.olvnj.com. Cynthia Casciola-Kitts, Prin.; Mrs. Beth Lucas, Librarian. Lay Teachers 14; Students 150.
Catechesis Religious Program—Jamie Wojcik, D.R.E., Email: jwojcik@olvsayrenj.com. Students 269.
2—St. Stanislaus Kostka (1914) [CEM] (Polish)
225 MacArthur Ave., Sayreville, 08872.
Tel: 732-254-0212; Fax: 732-390-2989; Email: Saintstanislaus@optonline.net. Rev. Kenneth R. Murphy; Deacons David Mikolai; Andrew Ozga.
School—St. Stanislaus Kostka School, (Grades K-8), 221 MacArthur Ave., Sayreville, 08872.
Tel: 732-254-5819; Fax: 732-254-7220; Email: emalinconico@diometuchen.org; Web: www.sskschool.org. Mrs. Elena Malinconico, Prin. Clergy 1; Lay Teachers 16; Students 155.
Catechesis Religious Program—Email: iforet@sskschool.org. Irene Foret, D.R.E. Students 93.

Skillman, Somerset Co., St. Charles Borromeo (1982)
47 Skillman Rd., Skillman, 08558. Tel: 609-466-0300 ; Email: jdimeglio@borromeo.org; Web: www.borromeo.org. 376 Burnt Hill Rd., Skillman, 08558. Rev. Msgr. Gregory E. S. Malovetz.
Catechesis Religious Program—
Tel: 609-466-0399, Ext. 19. Cathy Souto, Faith Formation. Students 282.

Somerset, Somerset Co., St. Matthias (1962)
168 J.F. Kennedy Blvd., Somerset, 08873.
Tel: 732-828-1400; Fax: 732-828-0866; Web: www.stmatthias.net. Rev. Abraham Orapankal, Admin.; Deacons John M. Radvanski; Russell B. Demkovitz.
Res.: 166 J.F. Kennedy Blvd., Somerset, 08873.
School—St. Matthias School, (Grades PreK-8), 170 J.F. Kennedy Blvd., Somerset, 08873.
Tel: 732-828-1402; Fax: 732-846-3099; Email: ebrett@stmatthias.info; Web: www.stmatthias.info. Ms. Eileen Brett, Prin.; Mr. Joseph Gidaro, Vice Prin.; Stephanie Lanzalotto, Librarian. Lay Teachers 28; Preschool 37; K-8 Students 385; Clergy / Religious Teachers 1.
Catechesis Religious Program—Dolores Nann, D.R.E. Students 331.
Convent—St. Matthias Convent, 1 Leupp Ln., Somerset, 08873. Tel: 732-828-9545; Email: msherwood@smpo.us. Sr. Marie Therese Sherwood, Pastoral Min./Coord. School Sisters of S. Francis 2.

Somerville, Somerset Co., Immaculate Conception (1882) [CEM]
35 Mountain Ave., Somerville, 08876.
Tel: 908-725-1112; Email: cjanuse@icsomerville.org; Web: www.icsomerville.org. Rev. Msgr. Seamus F. Brennan; Revs. Robert Pinnisi, Parochial Vicar; Martin Espinoza, Parochial Vicar; Deacons Anthony Hancock; Frank J. Quinn; John R. Czekaj; Reynaldo Lopez.
Res.: 225 Altamont Pl., Somerville, 08876.
Fax: 908-725-6269; Web: www.immaculateconception.org.
School—Immaculate Conception School, (Grades PreK-8), 41 Mountain Ave., Somerville, 08876.
Tel: 908-725-6516; Fax: 908-725-3172; Email: dhollod@ics41mtn.org; Web: www.icsschool.org. Sr. Mary Chapman, I.H.M., Prin.; Danielle Sakitis, Librarian. Clergy 1; Lay Teachers 29; Sisters 3; Students 328; Clergy / Religious Teachers 1.
High School—Immaculata High School, 240 Mountain Ave., Somerville, 08876. Tel: 908-722-0200 ; Fax: 908-218-7765; Email: jsilo@immaculatahighschool.org; Web: www.immaculatahighschool.org. Joan Silo, Prin. Lay Teachers 59; Sisters 3; Students 434; Clergy / Religious Teachers 56.
Convent—Immaculata Faculty Residence, 230 Mountain Ave., Somerville, 08876. Tel: 908-722-6894 . Sr. Mary Virginia Quinn, Supr. Sisters, Servants of the Immaculate Heart of Mary 11.
Catechesis Religious Program—
Tel: 908-725-1112, Ext. 1119; Email: kbohler@icsomerville.org. Mrs. Karen Bohler, Children's Faith Formation. Students 490.

South Amboy, Middlesex Co.
1—St. Mary (1864) [CEM 2]
256 Augusta St., South Amboy, 08879.
Tel: 732-721-0179; Fax: 732-721-0360; Email: saintmarysa@aol.com; Web: saintmarysa.org. Revs. Dennis R. Weezorak; Glenn J. Comandini, S.T.D., In Res.; Deacons Stephen N. Laikowski; Richard O'Brien.
Catechesis Religious Program—Tel: 732-721-1514. Mr. Kevin Schnell, Catechetical leader. Students 165.
2—Sacred Heart (1895) [CEM] (Polish)
531 Washington Ave., South Amboy, 08879.
Tel: 732-721-0040; Email: sheart224@aol.com; Web: www.sacredheartsa.org. Revs. Stanley G. Gromadzki; Marian Drozd, Parochial Vicar; Deacon Serge Bernatchez.
Catechesis Religious Program—Shannon Liana, Catechetical Leader. Students 311.

South Bound Brook, Somerset Co., Our Lady of Mercy (1949)
122 High St., South Bound Brook, 08880.
Tel: 732-356-1037; Email: olmsecretary@optonline.net; Web: www.olmsbb.org. Rev. Namwoong Lee, Admin.; Rev. Msgr. John N. Fell, S.T.D., In Res.

South Plainfield, Middlesex Co.
1—Our Lady of Czestochowa (1943) (Polish)
857 Hamilton Blvd., South Plainfield, 07080.
Tel: 908-756-1333; Fax: 908-756-8557; Email: olcchurch@verizon.net; Web: www.olcsouthplainfield.weconnect.com. 120 Kosciusko Ave., South Plainfield, 07080. Revs. Peter Tran; J. Maciej Melaniuk, Sr. Priest; Deacon Richard A. Kenton.
Catechesis Religious Program—Students 65.
2—Sacred Heart (1906) [CEM 2]
149 S. Plainfield Ave., South Plainfield, 07080.
Tel: 908-756-0633, Ext. 110; Email: admin@churchofthesacredheart.net; Web: www.churchofthesacredheart.net. 200 Randolph Ave., South Plainfield, 07080. Revs. John Paul Alvarado; Pervais Indrias, Parochial Vicar; Deacon Gregory Caruso.
Catechesis Religious Program—
Tel: 908-756-0633, Ext. 143; Email: religiouseducation@churchofthesacredheart.net; Web: www.churchofthesacredheart.net. Mrs. Louise Timko, D.R.E. Students 422.

South River, Middlesex Co.
1—Corpus Christi (1944)

100 James St., South River, 08882.
Tel: 732-254-1800; Fax: 732-254-8063; Email: corpuschristichurch5@gmail.com. Rev. Damian B. Breen.
Catechesis Religious Program—Rosa Fernandes, D.R.E. (Portuguese); Susan Tatto, D.R.E. (English). Students 240.
2—ST. MARY OF OSTRABRAMA (1903) [CEM] (Polish)
30 Jackson St., South River, 08882.
Tel: 732-254-2220; Fax: 732-651-8182; Email: ostrabrama@stmarysr.org; Web: stmarysr.org. Rev. Michael J. Gromadzki; Deacons Thomas F. Dominiecki; Mark J. Hennicke.
Catechesis Religious Program—Mrs. Rosemary Eckert, D.R.E. Students 130.
3—ST. STEPHEN PROTOMARTYR (1907) (Hungarian)
20 William St., South River, 08882.
Tel: 732-257-0100; Tel: 732-766-3452; Email: SaintStephen1@aol.com. Rev. John Szczepanik.
Catechesis Religious Program—Students 128.
SPOTSWOOD, MIDDLESEX CO., IMMACULATE CONCEPTION (1946)
18 South St., Spotswood, 08884. Tel: 732-251-3110; Fax: 732-251-2407; Email: office@icspotswood.com; Web: www.chicspotswood.com. Rev. Msgr. Joseph M. Curry; Revs. Mhonchan Ezung, Parochial Vicar; Peter Akkanath Chakkunny, C.M.I., In Res.; Deacons Thomas Griffoul; Danilo C. San Jose.
School—Immaculate Conception School, (Grades PreK-8), 23 Manalapan Rd., Spotswood, 08884.
Tel: 732-251-3090; Fax: 732-251-8270; Email: merath@icsspotswood.com; Web: www.icsspotswood.org. Mary Erath, Prin.; Kathleen Gately, Librarian. Lay Teachers 16; Felician Sisters 1; Students 222; Clergy / Religious Teachers 1.
Catechesis Religious Program—Mark Sahli, Faith Formation. Students 625.
Convent—21 Manalapan Rd., Spotswood, 08884.
Tel: 732-251-3446. Sr. Marie Teresa Soltys, Local Min. Sisters 3.
THREE BRIDGES, HUNTERDON CO., ST. ELIZABETH ANN SETON (1984)
105 Summer Rd., Three Bridges, 08887-2307.
Tel: 908-782-1475; Email: parishoffice@easeton.net; Web: easeton.net. Rev. Thomas J. Serafin; Deacons Kevin M. Kilcommons; Paul Santella; Michael S. Tomcho.
Catechesis Religious Program—Tel: 908-284-2929; Email: seasrf@easeton.net. Mariam Nawab, D.R.E. Students 543.
WARREN, SOMERSET CO., OUR LADY OF THE MOUNT (1911)
167 Mount Bethel Rd., Warren, 07059.
Tel: 908-647-1075; Fax: 908-647-7885; Email: parishoffice@olmwarren.org; Web: ourladyofthemount.org. Rev. Sean W. Kenney; Deacon John M. Scansaroli.
Catechesis Religious Program—
Tel: 908-647-1075, Ext. 112. Emma DeBorja, Catechetical Leader. Students 402.
WASHINGTON, WARREN CO., ST. JOSEPH (1872) [CEM]
200 Carlton Ave., Washington, 07882.
Tel: 908-689-0058; Fax: 908-689-3436. Rev. Guy W. Selvester; Deacons Edmund Hartmann Jr.; Sylvan Webb.
Catechesis Religious Program—Tel: 908-689-0093. Joyce Rock, D.R.E. Students 180.
WATCHUNG, SOMERSET CO., ST. MARY-STONY HILL (1847) [CEM]
225 Mountain Blvd., Watchung, 07069.
Tel: 908-756-6524; Fax: 908-756-2111; Web: www.stmaryswatchung.org. Very Rev. Brian J. Nolan; Deacons Peter D'Angelo; Lawrence J. Duffy.
Catechesis Religious Program—Catherine Cooney, D.R.E. Students 286.
WHITEHOUSE STATION, HUNTERDON CO., OUR LADY OF LOURDES (1923)
390 County Rd. 523, White House Station, 08889.
Tel: 908-534-2319; Email: pastor@ollwhs.org; Web: www.ollwhs.org. P.O. Box 248, Whitehouse Station, 08889. Very Rev. Leonard F.A. Rusay; Deacon Charles Paolino.
Catechesis Religious Program—
Tel: 908-534-2319, Ext. 17; Email: faithformation@ollwhs.org. Nina Forestiere, Youth Faith Formation. Students 305.
WOODBRIDGE, MIDDLESEX CO.
1—ST. JAMES (1860) [CEM 2]
369 Amboy Ave., Woodbridge, 07095.
Tel: 732-634-0500, Ext. 100; Email: fathercharlie@stjamesonline.org; Web: www.stjamesonline.org. 148 Grenville St., Woodbridge, 07095. Rev. Msgr. Charles W. Cicerale; Revs. Nalaka Silva, O.M.I., Parochial Vicar; Sebastian D. Kaithackal, C.M.I., In Res.; Deacons Michael Choi; John DiJoseph; William F. Lange; Roel S. Mercado; Carl E. Psota.
Rectory—145 Grove St., Woodbridge, 07095.
School—St. James School, (Grades PreK-8), 341 Amboy Ave., Woodbridge, 07095. Tel: 732-634-2090; Email: fcomiskey@diometuchen.org. Mrs. Frances Comiskey, Prin.; Mrs. Lori Jensen, Librarian. Lay Teachers 20; Students 211.
Catechesis Religious Program—Tel: 732-634-3026; Email: ccd@stjamesonline.org. Mr. David Gerity, D.R.E. Students 350.
Convent—149 Grove St., Woodbridge, 07095.
Tel: 732-634-0176. Sisters 1; Sisters of Mercy 1.
2—OUR LADY OF KOREA, Merged with St. Paul the Apostle, Highland Park and Guardian Angels, Edison to form Transfiguration of the Lord Parish, Highland Park. Sacramental records retained at Transfiguration of the Lord Parish, Highland Park.
3—OUR LADY OF MOUNT CARMEL (1921) Merged with St. Anthony of Padua, Port Reading. Sacramental records retained at St. Anthony of Padua Parish, Port Reading.

Chaplains of Public Institutions

ANNANDALE. *Mountainview Youth Correctional Facility*, Annandale, 08801. Tel: 908-638-6191. Rev. Robert G. Gorman, Chap.Attended by Rev. Robert Gorman Immaculate Conception, Annandale.
AVENEL. *Adult Diagnostic & Treatment Center*. Revs. Robert G. Gorman, Chap., Sean G. Winters, Chap. Attended by Revs. Sean Winters and Robert Gorman.
SOMERSET. *Parker at McCarrick*, 15 Dellwood Ln., Somerset, 08873. Tel: 732-545-4200. Rev. Michael E. Crummy, Chap.Total Assisted 1,125.
BELLE MEAD. *Carrier Clinic*. Deacon Salvatore J. Bonfiglio, Chap.
BELVIDERE. *Warren Correctional Center*. Attended by St. Patrick, Belvidere.
CLINTON. *Edna Mahan Correctional Facility for Women*, Clinton. Tel: 908-735-7111. Attended by Immaculate Conception, Annandale.
Hunterdon Developmental Center. Attended by Immaculate Conception, Annandale. (908) 735-4031.
EDISON. *John F. Kennedy Medical Center*. Rev. Msgr. Pafnouti Wassef, Rev. Sebastian D. Kaithackal, C.M.I., Chap., Deacon Paul J. Sheptuck.
FLEMINGTON. *Hunterdon Medical Center*. Rev. John Primich, Chap.Attended by St. Magdalen de Pazzi.
HACKETTSTOWN. *Hackettstown Community Hospital*. Attended by Assumption of the Blessed Virgin Mary.
LYONS. *U.S. Veterans Medical Center*. Rev. Andrzej Kielkowski, S.D.S., Chap.
MENLO PARK. *Roosevelt State Hospital*. Attended by St. Cecelia, Iselin.
NEW BRUNSWICK. *Robert Wood Johnson University Hospital*. Rev. Pauly Thekkan, C.M.I., Chap.
Saint Peter's University Hospital. Revs. A. David Chalackal, C.M.I., Chap., Peter Suhaka, Chap.
NORTH BRUNSWICK. *Middlesex County Adult Detention Center*. Attended by Our Lady of Peace, North Brunswick.
OLD BRIDGE. *Raritan Bay Medical Center-Old Bridge*. Attended by St. Thomas the Apostle Parish, Old Bridge.
PERTH AMBOY. *Raritan Bay Medical Center*, Perth Amboy. Tel: 732-826-2771. Rev. Sean G. Winters.
PHILLIPSBURG. *Warren Hospital*, Phillipsburg, 08865.
Tel: 908-454-0112. Rev. Thomas P. Ganley, Chap.
PLAINSBORO. *University Medical Center of Princeton at Plainsboro*, 1 Plainsboro Rd., Plainsboro, 08536.
Tel: 609-853-6500. Rev. Peter Akkanath Chakkunny, C.M.I., Chap.
RAHWAY. *East Jersey State Prison*, Rahway.
Tel: 732-634-4355. Deacon Walter H. Pidgeon, Chap.Attended by Deacon Walter Pidgeon and St. Andrew Church, Avenel.
SKILLMAN. *NJ State Neuropsychiatric Institute*. Attended by St. Charles Borromeo.
SOMERVILLE. *Robert Wood Johnson at Somerset Medical Center*, Somerville. Tel: 908-526-2394. Rev. Lazaro Perez, Chap.Attended by Christ the Redeemer, Manville.
SOUTH AMBOY. *South Amboy Memorial Hospital*. Attended by St. Mary and Sacred Heart.

Absent on Sick Leave:
Revs.—
Bihuniak, Michael J.
Desmond, Joseph L.
Morley, John J.

On Leave:
Rev.—
Alvarez, Antonio M.

On Duty Outside the Diocese:
Revs.—
Abano, Edgardo D.
Baran, Blaise R., Diocese of Las Vegas, NV
Bochnak, Zenon A., Archdiocese for the Military Services, USA
Lambert, Timothy J., Diocese of Brooklyn
Leonard, Raymond J., Diocese of Charleston, SC
Salonga, Juan S., Archdiocese for the Military Services, USA
Venditti, J. Michael, Archdiocese of Washington.

Retired:
Rev. Msgrs.—
Capik, William J., (Retired)
Cole, Raymond L., (Retired)
Fulton, David I., J.C.D., J.C.L., S.T.D., (Retired)
Haughney, William J., (Retired)
Herlihy, Daniel J., (Retired)
Prus, Eugene, (Retired)
Revs.—
Aniszczyk, Leon S., (Retired)
Brundage, John L., (Retired)
Caceres, Marco A., (Retired)
Cornejo, Vincent C., (Retired)
Crowley, R. Kevin, (Retired)
Driscoll, Michael A., (Retired)
Giordano, John C., (Retired)
Hemmerling, Henry L., (Retired)
Jarosz, Stanley, (Retired)
Kearns, Edward A., (Retired)
Kelly, Charles F., (Retired)
Krajewski, Joseph A., (Retired)
McCord, Kent G., (Retired)
McLaughlin, James W., (Retired)
Mickiewicz, J. William, (Retired)
Roca, Albert L., (Retired)
Scillieri, Charles P., (Retired)
Sloan, Daniel, (Retired)
Stingel, Louis F., (Retired)
Struzik, Edward J., (Retired)
Vadakkekara, J. Philip, (Retired)
Walega, Stanley J., (Retired)
Warman, William C., (Retired).

Permanent Deacons:
Abatemarco, Michael, (In Ministry Outside Diocese)
Abriola, Michael, St. Lawrence, Laurence Harbor
Adolfo, Alfredo, (In Ministry Outside Diocese)
Bachynsky, Michael J., St. Magdalen de Pazzi, Flemington
Barcellona, Peter, St. Anthony of Padua, Port Reading
Barr, William J., St. Edward the Confessor, Milford
Bauer, William R., (Retired)
Bencosme, Pablo, Our Lady of Fatima, Perth Amboy
Berg, A. Keith, Most Holy Redeemer, Matawan
Berluche, Enock Sr., St. Philip & St. James, Phillipsburg
Bernatchez, Serge, Sacred Heart, South Amboy
Bertrand, John, Nativity of Our Lord, Monroe Township
Bevilacqua, Larry M., St. Philip & St. James, Phillipsburg
Blessing, Paul E., (In Ministry Outside Diocese)
Boccellari, Thomas P., Queenship of Mary, Plainsboro
Bolash, George L., St. Mary, Alpha
Bonfante, Robert Sr., St. Thomas the Apostle, Old Bridge
Bonfiglio, Salvatore J., Mary, Mother of God, Hillsborough
Bresnan, Thomas N., St. John Vianney, Colonia
Brigande, Vincent C., St. Helena, Edison
Broehl, John H., St. Bartholomew, East Brunswick
Brossoni, Guido J., (Retired)
Brucato, Michael, St. Anthony of Padua, Port Reading
Caimi, Ronald J., (Retired)
Cammarano, Frank J., (Retired)
Campbell, Joseph P., Immaculate Conception, Annandale
Caruso, Gregory, Sacred Heart, South Plainfield
Chaves, Edgar R., Our Lady of Mt. Virgin, Middlesex
Choi, Michael, St. James, Woodbridge
Ciszewski, Edward F., Immaculate Conception, Annandale
Cline, Patrick J., St. Bernard of Clairvaux, Bridgewater
Coleman, George D., (Retired)
Conroy, Christopher, Mary Mother of God, Hillsborough
Coppola, Albert, Good Shepherd, Hopelawn
Cortez, Noe, Most Holy Name of Jesus, Perth Amboy
Costantino, Samuel J., Good Shepherd, Perth Amboy
Craig, John, St. Joseph, Hillsborough
Czekaj, John R., Our Lady of Mount Virgin, Middlesex; Immaculate Conception, Somerville
D'Andrea, Lawrence V., St. Rose of Lima, Oxford
D'Angelo, Peter, St. Mary-Stony Hill, Watchung
D'Auguste, Frank C., Most Holy Redeemer, Matawan

D'Mello, Francis, Our Lady of Peace, North Brunswick
Daley, James M., (Retired)
Damiano, Samuel J., (Retired)
DeFrange, David A., Our Lady of Peace, North Brunswick
Deitchman, John, (In Ministry Outside Diocese)
DeLorenzo, Donald J., (In Ministry Outside Diocese)
Demkovitz, Russell B., St. Matthias, Somerset
DePrima, Peter J. Jr., St. James, Basking Ridge
Di Joseph, John, St. James, Woodbridge
Dominiecki, Thomas F., (Retired)
Duffy, Lawrence J., St. Mary-Stony Hill, Watchung
Dumschat, John F., (Retired)
Fisher, Robert, St. Philip and St. James, Phillipsburg
Flynn, John T., (Retired)
Forrestall, Michael J., (Retired)
Fortune, Kenrick, Cathedral of St. Francis of Assisi, Metuchen
Gajewski, Stephen J., St. Lawrence, Laurence Harbor
Gallagher, Daniel, Assumption of the Blessed Virgin Mary, Hackettstown
Garcia, Enrique, Most Holy Name of Jesus, Perth Amboy
Gatto, Robert E., Nativity of Our Lord, Monroe Township
Gerling, Robert, Our Lady of Lourdes, Milltown
Giacobbe, Thomas J., Christ the Redeemer, Manville
Gleason, Michael P., (Retired)
Gonzalez, Phillip, (In Ministry Outside Diocese)
Gostkowski, Anthony J., St. Bartholomew, East Brunswick
Griffoul, Thomas, Immaculate Conception, Spotswood
Gunther, Stephen, Ss. Peter & Paul, Great Meadows
Gutsick, Patrick J., St. Peter the Apostle, New Brunswick
Hally, Luke J., (Retired)
Hamilton, Kenneth, (On Leave)
Hancock, Anthony, Immaculate Conception, Somerville
Hartmann, Edmund Jr., St. Joseph, Washington
Hearty, Patrick W., St. Thomas the Apostle, Old Bridge
Heissenbuttel, Thomas A., (Retired)
Hendrix, James W., (Retired)
Hennicke, Mark J., St. Mary Ostrabrama, South River
Holzinger, Stephen J. II, Our Lady of Lourdes, Milltown
Kaseta, Richard R., (In Ministry Outside Diocese)
Kassebaum, Stephen G., St. Catherine of Siena, Pittstown
Kelly, James A. Jr., Our Lady of Peace, Fords
Kenny, John F., St. Bartholomew, East Brunswick
Kenton, Richard A., Our Lady of Czestochowa, South Plainfield
Kern, Stephen F., St. Magdalen de Pazzi, Flemington
Kilcommons, Kevin M., St. Elizabeth Ann Seton, Three Bridges
Kimball, George F., St. Joseph, Carteret
Kintis, William, St. Patrick, Belvidere
Klaas, Thomas H., St. James, Basking Ridge
Koy, Martin L., (Retired)
Krupa, Edward, Transfiguration of the Lord, Highland Park
La Police, George D., (Retired)
Ladao, Rogelio, St. Frances Cabrini, Piscataway
Laikowski, Stephen N., St. Mary, South Amboy
Lange, William F., St. James, Woodbridge
Lawless, Timothy A., St. Joseph, Hillsborough
Licameli, Paul G., (Retired)
Livingston, Joel R., (Retired)
Lopez, Reynaldo, Immaculate Conception, Somerville
Lutomski, Richard, St. Cecelia, Iselin
Majkowski, Edward J., Our Lady of Victories, Sayreville
Maksimik, Walter S., St. Andrew, Avenel
Marano, Francis J., (Retired)
Martini, Michael R., Immaculate Conception, Annandale
Maurer, Joseph S., (Retired)
Mayer, Denis, St. Augustine of Canterbury, Kendall Park
McCarron, Richard, (In Ministry Outside Diocese)
McCormick, James N., Mary, Mother of God, Hillsborough
McGovern, Robert T., Most Holy Redeemer, Matawan
McGovern, Thomas, St. Joseph, High Bridge
McGuire, John H., (Retired)
McShane, John P., (Retired)
Mercado, Roel S., St. James, Woodbridge
Meyer, Michael A., Immaculate Conception, Annandale
Michnewicz, Thomas S., St. John Vianney, Colonia
Mikolai, David, St. Stanislaus Kostka, Sayreville
Monahan, John T., Our Lady of Victories, Baptistown
Moral, Luis S., (Retired)
Moscinski, Joseph C., (Retired)
Murtha, Michael P., St. Cecilia, Monmouth Junction
Nardi, Samuel, (Retired)
Newton, Gary, St. Joseph, Bound Brook
O'Brien, Richard, St. Mary, South Amboy
Olegario, Eduardo, (Retired)
Ortega, Cesar Augusto, St. Joseph, North Plainfield
Otlowski, Wayne, Church of the Sacred Heart, South Plainfield
Ozga, Andrew, St. Stanislaus Kostka, Sayreville
Pacifico, John R., St. Ann, Raritan
Paolino, Charles, Our Lady of Lourdes, Whitehouse Station
Paulus, Conrad, (In Ministry Outside Diocese)
Payne, Alfred C. Jr., (In Ministry Outside Diocese)
Pepe, Anthony J., St. Cecelia, Iselin
Perez, Basilio A., St. John Paul II, Perth Amboy
Perlas, Kenneth J., St. Anthony of Padua, Port Reading
Phalen, John, Holy Trinity, Bridgewater
Pidgeon, Walter H., Assumption of the Blessed Virgin Mary, Hackettstown
Pizzigoni, Louis III, Blessed Sacrament, Martinsville
Psota, Carl E., St. James, Woodbridge
Quinn, Frank J., Immaculate Conception, Somerville
Rabinowitz, Roy, St. Ann, Raritan
Radvanski, John M., St. Matthias, Somerset
Ragucci, Joseph D., St. John Vianney, Colonia
Raychel, John A., Our Lady of Peace, Fords
Reilly, Lawrence P., Our Lady of Fatima, Piscataway
Rider, William P., Our Lady of Fatima, Piscataway
Rios, Gregorio A., Our Lady of Fatima, Perth Amboy
Ris, Gregory, St. Lawrence, Laurence Harbor
Rivera, Herminio, Our Lady of Fatima, Perth Amboy
Rivera, James, St. Augustine of Canterbury, Kendall Park
Roberts, Earl J. III, St. John Neumann, Califon
Robitaille, Glenn, St. John the Evangelist, Dunellen
Rodes, Edward G., Good Shepherd, Perth Amboy
Ruiz-Diaz, Benigno I., Our Lady of Perpetual Help, Bernardsville
Russo, Anthony, (In Ministry Outside Diocese)
Saggese, Joseph P., Cathedral of St. Francis of Assisi, Metuchen
San Jose, Danilo C., Immaculate Conception, Spotswood
Sandoval, Gustavo, St. Joseph, Bound Brook
Santella, Paul, St. Elizabeth Ann Seton, Three Bridges
Sause, Robert Jr., St. Ann Raritan
Scansaroli, John M., Our Lady of the Mount, Warren
Semko, Michael, Our Lady of Victories, Baptistown
Shelton, John H., Nativity of Our Lord, Monroe Township
Sheptuck, Paul J., JFK Medical Center, Edison
Sicola, Thomas, (Retired)
Simao, Hugo, Queenship of Mary, Plainsboro
Sims, Gerard C., St. Bernard of Clairvaux, Bridgewater
Sinatra, Frank A., St. James, Basking Ridge
Smith, Patrick J., St. James the Less, Jamesburg
Sommero, Thomas G., Our Lady of Mount Virgin, Middlesex
Stefany, William G., Sacred Heart, Manville
Stevens, Joseph Richard (Rick), St. Ann, Raritan
Strus, Andrew J., (Retired)
Tartara, Filippo, St. Bartholomew, East Brunswick
Tesoriero, James A., (In Ministry Outside Diocese)
Tietjen, John R., Our Lady of Mount Virgin, Middlesex
Titmas, Scott D., St. Thomas the Apostle, Old Bridge
Tobin, Joseph C., St. Thomas the Apostle, Old Bridge
Tomcho, Michael S., St. Elizabeth Ann Seton, Three Bridges
Torres, Nelson, Holy Family, New Brunswick
Torres, Ramon L., St. Joseph, Carteret
Urcinas, David L., St. Magdalen de Pazzi, Flemington
van Duynhoven, Mark, Immaculate Conception, Annandale
Van Haute, John B., St. Mary, Alpha
Waguespack, David M., Assumption of the Blessed Virgin Mary, Hackettstown
Webb, Sylvan, St. Joseph, Washington
Webster, Dennis K., (Retired)
Wislinski, Thaddeus, St. Magdalen de Pazzi, Flemington
Wittreich, Helmut, St. Peter the Apostle, New Brunswick
Wojcik, Michael, St. Elizabeth-St. Brigid, Far Hills-Peapack
Yondolino, Thomas C., St. Ambrose, Old Bridge
Youn, Seock Ro, Transfiguration of the Lord, Highland Park
Yuhas, Frank, Sacred Heart, South Plainfield
Yunker, Robert G., St. Helena, Edison
Zampella, Donald, St. Bernadette, Parlin.

INSTITUTIONS LOCATED IN DIOCESE

[A] HIGH SCHOOLS, DIOCESAN

EDISON. *Bishop Ahr High School* (1969) One Tingley Ln., Edison, 08820. Tel: 732-549-1108; Fax: 732-494-2229; Email: dtrukowski@diometuchen.org; Web: www.bgahs.org. Sr. Donna Marie Trukowski, C.S.S.F., Prin.; Harry Ziegler, Assoc. Prin.; Rev. Keith Cervine, Dir. Catholic Identity; Ms. Sharon Taub, Librarian. Religious Teachers 1; Lay Teachers 61; Felician Sisters 2; Students 668.

[B] HIGH SCHOOLS, PRIVATE

METUCHEN. *Saint Joseph High School*, 145 Plainfield Ave., 08840-1099. Tel: 732-549-7600; Fax: 732-549-0664; Email: mhutnick@stjoes.org; Web: www.stjoes.org. Mr. Justin Fleetwood, Pres. Brothers 5; Lay Teachers 38; Students 543; Staff 22.

WATCHUNG. *Mount St. Mary Academy* (1908) 1645 U.S. Hwy. 22, W., Watchung, 07069. Tel: 908-757-0108; Fax: 908-756-5751; Email: lgambacorto@mountsaintmary.org; Web: www.mountsaintmary.org. Sr. Lisa D. Gambacorto, R.S.M., E.D.S., Pres.; Rev. William T. Morris, Chap. College preparatory day school for girls. A sponsored work of the Sisters of Mercy of the Americas. Lay Teachers 43; Sisters of Mercy 3; Students 344.

[C] DIOCESAN ELEMENTARY SCHOOLS

PERTH AMBOY. *Perth Amboy Catholic Primary School*, (Grades PreK-3), 613 Carlock Ave., Perth Amboy, 08861. Tel: 732-826-5747; Fax: 732-826-6096; Email: bpolicastro@diometuchen.org; Web: www.pacatholic.org. Sr. Beverly Policastro, S.C., Prin. Lay Teachers 6; Students 92.

Perth Amboy Catholic School, (Grades 4-8), 500 State St., Perth Amboy, 08861. Tel: 732-826-1598; Fax: 732-826-7063; Email: bpolicastro@diometuchen.org; Web: www.pacatholicschool.org. Sisters Dorothy M. Sajczuk, C.S.S.F., Librarian; Beverly Policastro, S.C., Prin. Religious Teachers 1; Lay Teachers 11; Students 108.

SOUTH PLAINFIELD. *Holy Savior Academy*, (Grades PreK-8), 149 S. Plainfield Ave., South Plainfield, 07080-1179. Tel: 908-822-5890; Fax: 908-822-5891; Email: cwoodburn@holysavioracademy.com; Web: www.holysavioracademy.com. Mrs. Carol Woodburn, Prin.; Colleen Head, Librarian. Lay Teachers 14; Students 166.

[D] PRE-SCHOOLS

MARTINSVILLE. *Little Friends of Jesus Nursery School*, 1881 Washington Valley Rd., Martinsville, 08836. Tel: 732-667-5272; Fax: 732-667-5277; Email: vocationistsisters@gmail.com. Sr. Ermelita Gella, S.D.V., Prin. Religious Teachers 6; Lay Teachers 4; Students 57.

[E] CATHOLIC CHARITIES

PERTH AMBOY. *Catholic Charities Central Office*, 319 Maple St., Perth Amboy, 08861. Tel: 732-324-8200; Fax: 732-826-3549; Email: aplace@ccdom.org; Web: www.ccdom.org. Julio Coto, L.C.S.W., Exec. Dir.; Marci Booth, L.C.S.W., Dir., Progs.; Marie Zissler, CFO. Tot Asst. Annually 3,841; Total Staff 98.

Bridgewater Family Service Center, 540 U.S. Rte. 22 E., Bridgewater, 08807. Tel: 908-722-1881; Fax: 908-704-0215; Email: aplace@ccdom.org; Web: ccdom.org. Martha Rezeli, M.A., C.S.W., Svc. Area Dir. Tot Asst. Annually 2,123; Total Staff 60.

Catholic Charities, Edison Family Service Center, 26 Safran Ave., Edison, 08837. Tel: 732-738-1323; Fax: 732-738-3896; Email: aplace@ccdom.org; Web: www.ccdom.org. Jessica Polizzotto, Dir. Tot Asst. Annually 641; Total Staff 40.

East Brunswick Family Service Center, 288 Rues Ln., East Brunswick, 08816. Tel: 732-257-6100;

Fax: 732-651-9834; Email: aplace@ccdom.org. Angela Orth, Svc. Area Dir. Tot Asst. Annually 12,090; Total Staff 40.

Flemington Family Service Center, 6 Park Ave., Flemington, 08822. Tel: 908-782-7905; Fax: 908-782-5934; Email: aplace@ccdom.org. Martha Rezeli, M.A., C.S.W., Svc. Area Dir. Tot Asst. Annually 3,252; Total Staff 31.

Phillipsburg Family Service Center, 700 Sayre Ave., Phillipsburg, 08865. Tel: 908-454-2074; Fax: 908-454-9871; Email: aplace@ccdom.org. Martha Rezeli, M.A., C.S.W., Svc. Area Dir. Tot Asst. Annually 2,520; Total Staff 36.

Social Service Center (1982) 387 South St., Phillipsburg, 08865. Tel: 908-859-5447; Fax: 908-859-6375; Email: mpopovice@ccdom.org. Martha Rezeli, M.A., C.S.W., Srvc. Area Dir. Tot Asst. Annually 11,519; Total Staff 30.

The Ozanam Shelter for Families and Single Women, 89 Truman Dr., Edison, 08817. Tel: 732-985-0327; Fax: 732-985-2449; Email: aplace@ccdom.org. Rebecca Rhoads, Svc. Area Dir. Tot Asst. Annually 1,173; Total Staff 30.

Catholic Charities Ozanam Inn, 20-22 Abeel St., New Brunswick, 08901. Tel: 732-729-0850; Fax: 732-729-0794; Email: aplace@ccdom.org; Web: www.ccdom.org. Rebecca Rhoads, Svc. Area Dir. Tot Asst. Annually 194; Total Staff 20.

Community House at St. Thomas, 124 Bentley Ave., Old Bridge, 08857. Tel: 732-251-0022; Fax: 732-251-3482; Email: aplace@ccdom.org; Web: www.ccdom.org. Susan Kuzma, Case Mgr. Total Assisted 7.

Metuchen Community Services Corporation, 103 Center St., Perth Amboy, 08861. Tel: 732-324-4357 ; Email: aplace@ccdom.org. Joan Lorah, L.C.S.W., Exec. Dir.

Community Child Care Solutions, 103 Center St., Perth Amboy, 08861. Tel: 732-324-4357; Fax: 732-826-4136; Email: aplace@ccdom.org. Joan Lorah, L.C.S.W., Exec. Dir. Tot Asst. Annually 5,997; Total Staff 52.

[F] GENERAL HOSPITALS

NEW BRUNSWICK. *Saint Peter's Healthcare System, Inc.*, 254 Easton Ave., New Brunswick, 08901. Tel: 732-745-8600, Ext. 6080; Fax: 732-448-0332; Email: kkillion@saintpetersuh.com; Web: www.saintpetershcs.com. Leslie D. Hirsch, Pres. & Interim CEO.

Saint Peter's Foundation, 254 Easton Ave., New Brunswick, 08901. Tel: 732-745-8542; Fax: 732-745-7573; Email: jchoma@saintpetersuh.com; Web: www.saintpetershcs.com\donate. James Choma, Exec.

Saint Peter's Health & Management Services Corporation, 254 Easton Ave., New Brunswick, 08901. Tel: 732-745-8600, Ext. 6080; Fax: 732-448-0332; Email: kkillion@saintpetersuh.com. Alyssa Verderami, Exec.

Saint Peter's Properties Corporation, Inc., 254 Easton Ave., New Brunswick, 08901. Tel: 732-745-8600, Ext. 6080; Fax: 732-448-0332; Email: averderami@saintpetersuh.com. Alyssa Verderami, Exec.

Saint Peter's University Hospital (1907) 254 Easton Ave., New Brunswick, 08901. Tel: 732-745-8600; Fax: 732-448-0332; Email: kkillion@saintpetersuh.com; Web: www.saintpetersuh.com. Deacon James Rivera, Dir.; Revs. A. David Chalackal, C.M.I., Chap.; Peter Suhaka, Chap.; Virginia Grey, Pastoral Care; James Jones, Pastoral Care. Bassinets 77; Bed Capacity 478; Tot Asst. Annually 248,424; Total Staff 3,476; Neonatal Intensive Care Bassinets 35; Intermediate Care Bassinets 19.

[G] HOMES FOR AGED

WOODBRIDGE. *St. Joseph Assisted Living*, 1 St. Joseph Ter., Woodbridge, 07095. Tel: 732-634-0004; Fax: 732-634-4586; Email: info@stjosephseniorhome.org. Sr. Zdzislawa Krukowska, L.S.I.C., Admin.

St. Joseph Home, Assisted Living and Nursing Center Residents 56; Little Servant Sisters 14; Staff 102.

St. Joseph Nursing Home, 3 St. Joseph Ter., Woodbridge, 07095. Tel: 732-750-0077; Email: info@stjosephseniorhome.com. Sr. Elzbieta Lopatka, L.S.I.C., Admin.

[H] MONASTERIES AND RESIDENCES FOR PRIESTS AND BROTHERS

METUCHEN. *Brothers of the Sacred Heart* (1901) 103 Buchanan Rd., Edison, 08820. Tel: 732-548-2292; Fax: 732-548-3101; Email: lcouvillon@stjoes.org. Rev. Louis Couvillon, S.C., Dir.; Bros. Gary Humes, S.C., Sub-Dir.; Ronald Cairns, S.C., Res.; Richard Leven, S.C., Res.; Michael Migasz, S.C., Res. Brothers 5.

NEW BRUNSWICK. *The New Brunswick Congregation of the Oratory of St. Philip Neri*, 45 Anderson St., Raritan, 08869. Tel: 908-725-1008; Fax: 908-707-1915; Email: oratorians@nboratory.org; Web: www.nboratory.org. Very Rev. Peter Cebulka, C.O., Supr.; Revs. Jeffrey Calia, C.O., Vicar; Kevin Kelly, C.O.; Bro. Steven Bolton, C.O., Novice; Rev. Thomas A. Odorizzi, C.O., Sec.; Bro. John Triana Beltran, C.O. Novices 1; Priests 4; Seminarians 1.

RARITAN. *Clairvaux House*, 52 W. Somerset St., Raritan, 08869. Tel: 908-300-8167; Fax: 908-722-4189; Email: shrinechapel@yahoo.com; Web: shrinechapel.com. Rev. Robert G. Gorman.

NORTH BRUNSWICK. *Consolata Society for Foreign Missions* (1901) Provincial Headquarter, 2624 Rte. 27, North Brunswick, 08902. Email: superiorenordamerica@consolata.org; Email: cimcrao@aol.com. Mailing Address: P.O. Box 5550, Somerset, 08875-5550. Tel: 732-297-9191; Email: supreus@consolata.net; Web: www.consolata.us. Revs. Paolo Fedrigoni, I.M.C., Coord. U.S. Group; Timothy Kinyua Gatitu, I.M.C.; James Kingori, I.M.C., (Kenya); Jorge Arias Rojas.

SOMERSET. *Maria Regina Residence*, 5 Dellwood Ln., Somerset, 08873. Tel: 732-828-6800; Fax: 732-828-7206; Email: guhrig@diometuchen.org. Rev. Msgr. Edward M. O'Neill, (Retired); Rev. A. Gregory Uhrig, Liaison to Retired Priests; Rev. Msgr. William J. Haughney, (Retired); Revs. Marco A. Caceres, (Retired); Vincent P. Chen, (Retired); Henry L. Hemmerling, (Retired); Charles F. Kelly, (Retired); J. William Mickiewicz, (Retired); Daniel Sloan, (Retired); Louis F. Stingel, (Retired); Edward J. Struzik, (Retired). Retirement home for Diocesan priests.

[I] CONVENTS AND RESIDENCES FOR SISTERS

METUCHEN. *St. Clare Convent*, 52 Elm Ave., 08840. Tel: 732-549-7598; Email: kkwiatkowski@stfranciscathedral.org. Sr. Lynn Marie Zawacka, Local Min. Felician Sisters 2.

St. Francis Convent, 44 Elm Ave., 08840. Tel: 732-662-5729; Email: kkwiatkowski@stfranciscathedral.org. Sr. Mary Elizabeth McCauley, S.C.C., Supr. Sisters of Christian Charity 4.

BELVIDERE. *Immaculate Conception Convent - Augustinian Recollect Sisters*, 743 Water St., Belvidere, 07823. Tel: 908-475-9947; Email: sb_dejesus11@yahoo.com.mx. Mother Maria Del Raio Garcia, Prioress. Sisters 9.

EDISON. *St. Thomas Aquinas Convent* (1969) 15 Wren Ct., Edison, 08820. Tel: 732-321-0137; Email: srcynthia@bgahs.org. Sisters Cynthia Marie Babyak, C.S.S.F., Local Min.; Donna Marie Trukowski, C.S.S.F.; Mary Charles Wienckoski, C.S.S.F. Sisters 4.

FLEMINGTON. *The Carmel of Mary Immaculate and St. Mary Magdalen*, 26 Harmony School Rd., Flemington, 08822. Tel: 908-782-4802; Fax: 888-503-3091; Email: friendsofcarmel@gmail.com; Web: www.flemingtoncarmel.org. Mother Anne of Christ, Prioress; Rev. John Primich, Chap. Sisters 11; Nuns Professed with Solemn Vows 11.

MARTINSVILLE. *Vocationist Sisters Convent*, 1881 Washington Valley Rd., Martinsville, 08836. Tel: 732-667-5275; Fax: 732-667-5277; Email: vocationistsisters@gmail.com; Email: srperpetua@hotmail.com. Sr. Maria P. DaConceicao, Supr. Vocationist Sisters 7.

NORTH PLAINFIELD. *Congregation of the Servants of the Holy Child Jesus of the Third Order Regular of Saint Francis*, 99 Harrison Ave., North Plainfield, 07060. Tel: 908-370-3616; Email: antoniavm@aol.com. Sr. M. Antonia Cooper, Contact Person. Total Sisters in the American Region 7.

WATCHUNG. *McAuley Hall Inc.*, 1633 U.S. Hwy 22, Watchung, 07069-6505. Tel: 908-754-3663; Fax: 908-754-3502; Email: gkidney@mcauleyhall.org. Sr. Brenda Rowe, R.S.M., Life Coord. Bed Capacity 74; Sisters 43.

Sisters of Mercy of the Americas, Mid-Atlantic Community, Sisters of Mercy, 1645 U.S. Hwy. 22 W., Watchung, 07069-6587. Tel: 908-756-0994; Fax: 908-754-0164; Email: lcavallo@mercymidatlantic.org; Web: www.mercymidatlantic.org. Sr. Patricia Vetrano, R.S.M., Pres. Professed Sisters in Residence 42.

WOODBRIDGE. *St. Joseph Convent*, 184 Amboy Ave., Woodbridge, 07095. Tel: 732-634-0415; Fax: 732-634-7888; Email: lsiclucyna@aol.com. Sr. Lucyna Zugaj, Supr. Sisters 10.

St. Joseph Home Convent, 3 St. Joseph Ter., Woodbridge, 07095. Tel: 732-750-0077; Fax: 732-634-4586; Email: info@stjosephseniorhome.com. Sr. Elzbieta Lopatka, L.S.I.C., Supr. Little Servant Sisters 14.

[J] RETREAT HOUSES

BELVIDERE. *Augustinian Recollect Sisters*, 20 Manunka Chunk Rd., Belvidere, 07823. Tel: 908-475-9947; Email: sb_dejesus11@yahoo.com.mx. Mother Maria Del Raio Garcia, Contact Person. Sisters 9.

FLEMINGTON. *Our Lady of Providence*, 31 Britton Dr., Flemington, 08822. Tel: 908-581-4297; Email: fllsp@littlesistersofthepoor.org. Sr. Bernice Marie, L.S.P., Dir. Little Sisters of the Poor. Sisters 2.

WATCHUNG. *Mt. St. Mary House of Prayer* (1976) Retreat House. 1651 U.S. Hwy. 22, Watchung, 07069-6587. Tel: 908-753-2091; Fax: 908-279-7146; Email: msmhope@msmhope.org; Web: www.msmhope.org. Sisters Laura Arvin, O.P., Dir.; Mary Jo Kearns, R.S.M., Dir.; Eileen P. Smith, R.S.M., Dir. Sisters 3.

[K] SHRINES AND PUBLIC ORATORIES

BERNARDSVILLE. *Sacred Heart Chapel* (Chapel of Convenience) Bernards Ave., Bernardsville, 07924. Our Lady of Perpetual Help, 111 Claremont Ave., Bernardsville, 07924. Tel: 908-766-0079; Fax: 908-766-1185; Email: olphemail@aol.com. Rev. John C. Siceloff.

RARITAN. *Shrine Chapel of the Blessed Sacrament*, 50 W. Somerset St., Raritan, 08869. Tel: 908-300-8167; Fax: 908-722-4189; Email: shrinechapel@yahoo.com; Web: shrinechapel.com. Rev. Robert G. Gorman, Rector.

WASHINGTON. *National World Apostolate of Fatima, USA, Inc. Blue Army Shrine of the Immaculate Heart of Mary*, 674 Mountain View Rd. E., Asbury, 08802. P.O. Box 976, Washington, 07882. Tel: 908-689-1700; Fax: 908-689-0721; Email: service@bluearmy.com; Web: www.bluearmy.com. Rev. James Walling, Chap.

[L] PUBLIC ASSOCIATIONS OF THE FAITHFUL

BLOOMSBURY. SISTERS OF JESUS OUR HOPE (1992) 376 Bellis Rd., Bloomsbury, 08804. Tel: 908-995-7261; Fax: 908-995-7262; Email: sisterchristine@sistersofjesusourhope.org; Web: www.sistersofjesusourhope.org. Sr. Christine Quense, S.J.H., Supr. Sisters 9.

FLEMINGTON. DOMINICAN SISTERS OF DIVINE PROVIDENCE (1982) 25 Harmony School Rd., Flemington, 08822. Tel: 908-782-1504; Email: srmcath25@gmail.com. Sr. Mary Catherine Baidy, O.P., Prioress. Sisters 2.

NEW BRUNSWICK. SISTERS OF JESUS OUR HOPE, 51 Jefferson Ave., New Brunswick, 08901. Tel: 732-246-3065; Email: sisterclairemarie@sistersofjesusourhope.org; Web: www.sistersofjesusourhope.org. Sr. Claire Marie Lessard, S.J.H., Sister Servant. Sisters 5.

OXFORD. THE ANAWIM COMMUNITY (1975) 354 Jonestown Rd., Oxford, 07863-3137. P.O. Box 207, Oxford, 07863-0207. Tel: 908-453-3886; Fax: 908-453-3786; Email: oxford@anawim.com; Web: www.anawim.com. Revs. Daniel H. Healy, Dir.; Richard M. Rusk, Dir. Missions. Priests 2; Staff 15.

STEWARTSVILLE. *Society of Jesus Christ the Priest*, 70 Edison Rd., P.O. Box 157, Stewartsville, 08886. Tel: 908-213-1447; Fax: 908-329-6111; Email: meadwater@slsonline.org; Email: rnacarino@slsonline.org. Revs. Lope Pascual de La Parte, Dir.; Raymond L. Nacarino, Treas.; Jose Lorente; Manuel Lorente.

[M] CAMPUS MINISTRY

NEW BRUNSWICK. *Catholic Center at Rutgers University*, 84 Somerset St., New Brunswick, 08901. Tel: 732-545-6663; Fax: 732-545-3495; Email: colleen.a.donahue@gmail.com; Web: www.rutgerscatholic.org. Rev. Msgr. Joseph G. Celano, Pastor; Bro. Patrick Reilly, B.H., Dir.; Sr. Lorraine Doiron, S.J.H., Campus Min.; Rev. James De Fillipps, Chap.; Very Rev. Peter Cebulka, C.O., Chap.; Rev. Jason Pavich, Chap.; Bro. Joseph Donovan, B.H., Campus Min.; Laura Greey, Campus Min.

[N] MISCELLANEOUS LISTINGS

METUCHEN. *The Foundation for Catholic Education*, 146 Metlars Ln., 08854. P.O. Box 191, 08840. Tel: 732-562-1990; Email: administration@diometuchen.org. Carol Purcell, Contact Person.

The Fund for the Future, Inc., 146 Metlars Ln., 08854. P.O. Box 191, 08840. Tel: 732-562-1990; Email: administration@diometuchen.org. Michael K. Ligorano, K.M., Esq., Gen. Counsel; Carol Purcell.

The Priestly Education Fund, Inc., 146 Metlars Ln., 08854. P.O. Box 191, 08840. Tel: 732-562-1990; Email: administration@diometuchen.org. Carol Purcell.

The Retirement Plan for the Priests of the Diocese of Metuchen, P.O. Box 191, 08840. Tel: 732-562-1990; Email: administration@diometuchen.org. Carol Purcell, Contact Person.

SOMERSET. *The Center for Great Expectations, Inc.*, 19 B Dellwood Ln., Somerset, 08873.

Tel: 732-247-7003, Ext. 27; Fax: 732-247-7043; Email: pegw@cge-nj.org; Email: pdeluca@cge-nj.org; Web: www.cge-nj.org. Mrs. Peg Wright, Pres.

WOODBRIDGE. *Mt. Carmel Home Nursing Service*, 184 Amboy Ave., Woodbridge, 07095. Tel: 732-277-8569; Email: info@stjosephseniorhome.com. Sr. Maria Dziuban, L.S.I.C., Dir.

RELIGIOUS INSTITUTES OF MEN REPRESENTED IN THE DIOCESE

For further details refer to the corresponding bracketed number in the Religious Institutes of Men or Women section.

[0200]—*Benedictine Monks*—O.S.B.
[]—*Brotherhood of Hope*—B.H.
[1100]—*Brothers of the Sacred Heart*—S.C.
[0470]—*The Capuchin Friars*—O.F.M.Cap.
[0275]—*Carmelites of Mary Immaculate*—C.M.I.
[0360]—*Claretian Missionaries* (USA Prov.)—C.M.F.
[0650]—*Congregation of the Holy Spirit*—C.S.Sp.
[0390]—*Consolata Missionaries*—I.M.C.
[0950]—*Oratorians*—C.O.
[]—*Order of Discalced Carmelites*—O.C.D.
[]—*Order of Friars Minor Capachin*—O.F.M.Cap.
[1070]—*Redemptorist Fathers*—C.Ss.R.
[1190]—*Salesians of Don Bosco*—S.D.B.
[1340]—*Society of Divine Vocations*—S.D.V.
[]—*Society of Jesus Christ the Priest*.
[1200]—*Society of the Divine Savior*—S.D.S.
[1335]—*Vincentian Retreat Master*—V.C.

RELIGIOUS INSTITUTES OF WOMEN REPRESENTED IN THE DIOCESE

[]—*Augustinian Recollects*—O.A.R.
[1980]—*Congregation of the Servants of the Holy Child Jesus*—O.S.F.
[0420]—*Discalced Carmelite Nuns*—O.C.D.
[1070-18]—*Dominican Sisters* (Caldwell)—O.P.
[1070-05]—*Dominican Sisters of Amityville*—O.P.
[]—*Dominican Sisters of Divine Providence*—O.P.
[1070-06]—*Dominican Sisters of Hope* (Ossining, N.Y.)—O.P.
[1170]—*Felician Sisters* (Our Lady of Hope Prov.)—C.S.S.F.
[1180]—*Franciscan Sisters of Allegany* (St. Bonaventure, NY)—O.S.F.
[1425]—*Franciscan Sisters of Peace*—F.S.P.
[2575]—*Institute of the Sisters of Mercy of the Americas*—R.S.M.
[2300]—*Little Servant Sisters of the Immaculate Conception*—L.S.I.C.
[2340]—*Little Sisters of the Poor* (Brooklyn Prov.)—L.S.P.
[2700]—*Missionary Catechists of the Sacred Hearts of Jesus and Mary*—M.C.S.H.
[2810]—*Missionary Sisters of Mother of God* (Byzantine-Ukrainian)—M.S.M.G.
[2760]—*Missionary Sisters of the Immaculate Conception*—S.M.I.C.
[3430]—*Religious Teachers Filippini* (St. Lucy Prov.)—M.P.F.
[1690]—*School Sisters of the Third Order of St. Francis*—O.S.F.
[0590]—*Sisters of Charity of Saint Elizabeth, Convent Station*—S.C.
[0660]—*Sisters of Christian Charity* (North American Eastern Prov.)—S.C.C.
[]—*Sisters of Jesus Our Hope*—S.J.H.
[3893]—*Sisters of Saint Joseph of Chestnut Hill, Philadelphia*—S.S.J.
[]—*Sisters of St. Martha*—C.S.M.
[2170]—*Sisters Servants of the Immaculate Heart of Mary*—I.H.M.
[4060]—*Society of the Holy Child Jesus*—S.H.C.J.
[]—*Trinitarium Sisters of Redemptor Homini*—T.R.H.
[4210]—*Vocationist Sisters*—S.D.V.

DIOCESAN CEMETERIES

EAST BRUNSWICK. *The Crematory at Holy Cross Burial Park*, 840 Cranbury-S. River Rd., Jamesburg, 08831. Tel: 732-640-1533; Fax: 732-463-8807; Email: cemeteries@diometuchen.org. P.O. Box 191, 08840. Mary Ellen Gerrity, Dir.

JAMESBURG. *Holy Cross Burial Park*, 840 Cranbury-S. River Rd., Jamesburg, 08831. Tel: 732-463-1424; Fax: 732-463-8807; Email: cemeteries@diometuchen.org. P.O. Box 191, 08840. Mary Ellen Gerrity, Dir.

PISCATAWAY. *Resurrection Burial Park*, Resurrection Cemetery & Mausoleum, 899 Lincoln Ave., 08854. Tel: 732-463-1424; Fax: 732-463-8807; Email: cemeteries@diometuchen.org. Mary Ellen Gerrity, Dir.

NECROLOGY

† Szymanski, John B., (Retired), Died Jun. 28, 2018
† Perunilam, Thomas V., (Retired), Died Jul. 26, 2018

An asterisk (*) denotes an organization that has established tax-exempt status directly with the IRS and is not covered by the USCCB Group Ruling.

Archdiocese of Miami

(Archidioecesis Miamiensis)

Most Reverend

THOMAS G. WENSKI

Archbishop of Miami; ordained May 15, 1976; appointed Titular Bishop of Kearney and Auxiliary Bishop of Miami June 24, 1997; consecrated September 3, 1997; appointed Coadjutor Bishop of Orlando July 1, 2003; installed August 22, 2003; appointed Fourth Bishop of Orlando November 13, 2004; appointed Archbishop of Miami April 20, 2010; installed June 1, 2010.

Most Reverend

JOHN C. FAVALORA

Retired Archbishop of Miami; ordained December 20, 1961; appointed Bishop of Alexandria June 16, 1986; ordained and installed July 29, 1986; appointed Third Bishop of St. Petersburg March 7, 1989; installed May 16, 1989; appointed Third Archbishop of Miami November 3, 1994; installed December 20, 1994; retired April 20, 2010. *Office: 9401 Biscayne Blvd., Miami Shores, FL 33138.*

Pastoral Center: 9401 Biscayne Blvd., Miami Shores, FL 33138. Tel: 305-757-6241; Fax: 305-754-1897.

Web: www.archdioceseofmiami.org

Email: information@theadom.org

Most Reverend

ENRIQUE DELGADO

Second Auxiliary Bishop of Miami; ordained June 29, 1996; appointed Titular Bishop of Aquae Novae in Proconsulari and Auxiliary Bishop of Miami October 12, 2017; installed December 7, 2017.

ESTABLISHED AUGUST 13, 1958.

Square Miles 4,958.

Created an Archbishopric, June 13, 1968.

Comprises the Counties in the southern part of the State of Florida, namely, Broward, Miami-Dade and Monroe.

For legal titles of Parishes and Archdiocesan institutions, consult the Pastoral Center.

STATISTICAL OVERVIEW

Personnel	
Archbishops	1
Retired Archbishops	1
Auxiliary Bishops	2
Priests: Diocesan Active in Diocese	139
Priests: Diocesan Active Outside Diocese	10
Priests: Retired, Sick or Absent	75
Number of Diocesan Priests	224
Religious Priests in Diocese	30
Total Priests in Diocese	254
Extern Priests in Diocese	43
Ordinations:	
Diocesan Priests	4
Transitional Deacons	4
Permanent Deacons in Diocese	145
Total Brothers	43
Total Sisters	237
Parishes	
Parishes	102
With Resident Pastor:	
Resident Diocesan Priests	93
Resident Religious Priests	9
Missions	6
Pastoral Centers	1
Professional Ministry Personnel:	
Sisters	38
Lay Ministers	362
Welfare	
Catholic Hospitals	5
Total Assisted	587,798
Health Care Centers	5
Total Assisted	676,624
Homes for the Aged	6
Total Assisted	4,533
Day Care Centers	11
Total Assisted	3,051
Specialized Homes	1
Total Assisted	145
Special Centers for Social Services	26
Total Assisted	121,688
Residential Care of Disabled	3
Total Assisted	35
Other Institutions	7
Total Assisted	12,306
Educational	
Seminaries, Diocesan	2
Students from This Diocese	39
Students from Other Diocese	37
Diocesan Students in Other Seminaries	19
Total Seminarians	58
Colleges and Universities	2
Total Students	12,909
High Schools, Diocesan and Parish	8
Total Students	9,052
High Schools, Private	4
Total Students	3,383
Elementary Schools, Diocesan and Parish	48
Total Students	20,165
Elementary Schools, Private	2
Total Students	1,130
Non-residential Schools for the Disabled	1
Total Students	165
Catechesis/Religious Education:	
High School Students	3,380
Elementary Students	21,279
Total Students under Catholic Instruction	71,521
Teachers in the Diocese:	
Priests	22
Brothers	12
Sisters	41
Lay Teachers	2,729
Vital Statistics	
Receptions into the Church:	
Infant Baptism Totals	9,775
Minor Baptism Totals	775
Adult Baptism Totals	470
Received into Full Communion	623
First Communions	9,709
Confirmations	7,726
Marriages:	
Catholic	1,581
Interfaith	156
Total Marriages	1,737
Deaths	3,804
Total Catholic Population	489,148
Total Population	4,855,720

Former Archbishops—Most Revs. COLEMAN F. CARROLL, D.D., ord. June 15, 1930; appt. Titular Bishop of Pitanae and Auxiliary Bishop of Pittsburgh, Aug. 25, 1953; cons. Nov. 10, 1953; appt. first Bishop of Miami, Aug. 13, 1958; installed Oct. 7, 1958; appt. Archbishop of Miami, March 13, 1968; died July 26, 1977; EDWARD A. MCCARTHY, D.D., S.T.D., J.C.D., ord. May 29, 1943; appt. Coadjutor Archbishop of Miami "cum jure successionis," Sept. 17, 1976; appt. Archbishop of Miami, July 26, 1977; retired Nov. 3, 1994; died June 7, 2005; JOHN C. FAVALORA, D.D., S.T.L., M.Ed., (Retired), ord. Dec. 20, 1961; appt. Bishop of Alexandria June 16, 1986; ord. and installed July 29, 1986; appt. Third Bishop of St. Petersburg March 7, 1989; installed May 16, 1989; appt. Third Bishop of Miami Nov. 3, 1994; installed Dec. 20, 1994; retired April 20, 2010.

Pastoral Center—9401 Biscayne Blvd., Miami Shores, 33138. Tel: 305-757-6241; Fax: 305-754-1897.

Vicars General—Most Rev. ENRIQUE DELGADO, Ph.D., D.D., V.G.; Rev. Msgr. CHANEL JEANTY, J.C.L., V.G.

Chancellors—Sr. ELIZABETH ANNE WORLEY, S.S.J., Chancellor for Admin. & COO, Tel: 305-762-1284; Email: eworley@theadom.org; Rev. Msgr. CHANEL JEANTY, J.C.L., V.G., Chancellor for Canonical Affairs, Tel: 305-762-1262; Email: cjeanty@theadom.org.

Metropolitan Tribunal—Address all Rogatory commissions and matrimonial matters to the Tribunal, *9401 Biscayne Blvd., Miami Shores, 33138.* Tel: 305-762-1161; Fax: 305-762-1178; Email: tribunal@theadom.org.

Judicial Vicar—Rev. Msgr. GREGORY C. WIELUNSKI, J.C.D.

Adjutant Judicial Vicar—Rev. Msgr. MICHAEL A. SOUCKAR, J.C.D.

Judges—Rev. Msgrs. ANDREW L. ANDERSON, J.C.D., (Retired); CHANEL JEANTY, J.C.L., V.G.; Revs. LUIS RIVERO, J.C.L.; JUDE O. EZEANOKWASA, (Nigeria) J.C.D.; MATHEW THUNDATHIL, (India) J.C.D.; DR. STEFANO BENIGNI, J.C.D.; Rev. FRANCIS CANCRO, J.C.L.

Promoter of Justice—Rev. Msgr. KENNETH K. SCHWANGER, J.C.D., (non-matrimonial cases).

Defenders of the Bond—Very Rev. KENNETH D. WHITTAKER, J.C.L., V.F.; Chorbishop MICHAEL G. THOMAS, J.C.D.; Rev. MANUAL PUGA, J.C.L.

Notaries—MS. GORETTI ANTHONY; MS. MAITE LENOZ; MS. MONICA CABRERA.

Assessor—MR. ROBERTO AGUIRRE.

Advocates—Deacon ANTONIO MACEO; MRS. PAULETTE VITALE; MRS. LOURDES CHAVEZ; MRS. PAULINE CERVANTES; MR. CHARLES D'COMO; MR. JUAN DEL SOL; MR. OLIVER PARKER.

Counsel-Assistant to the Tribunal—MR. J. PATRICK FITZGERALD, Esq.

Consultors—Most Rev. ENRIQUE DELGADO, Ph.D., D.D., V.G.; Rev. Msgrs. CHANEL JEANTY, J.C.L., V.G.; PABLO A. NAVARRO, V.F.; ROBERTO GARZA; Very Rev. MICHAEL W. DAVIS, M.Ed.; Revs. ALEJANDRO J. RODRIGUEZ ARTOLA; PAUL V. VUTURO.

Priest Secretary to the Archbishop—Rev. RICHARD J. VIGOA, Tel: 305-762-1232; Email: rvigoa@theadom.org.

Deans and Deaneries—Very Revs. MICHAEL J. GREER, V.F., (Northeast Broward); KENNETH D.

WHITTAKER, J.C.L., V.F., (Northwest Broward); DAVID A. ZIRILLI, V.F., (Southeast Broward); ERNEST BIRIRUKA, (Burundi) V.F., (Southwest Broward); CHRISTOPHER B. MARINO, V.F., (Northeast Dade); VACANT, (East Dade); Very Revs. MARCOS A. SOMARRIBA, V.F., (West Dade); JOHN C. BAKER, V.F., (Monroe); Rev. Msgr. PABLO A. NAVARRO, V.F., (South Dade); Very Rev. JOSE ALVAREZ, V.F., (Northwest Dade).

Presbyteral Council—

*President—*Most Rev. THOMAS G. WENSKI, D.D.

*Chairman—*Rev. PAUL VUTURO.

*Secretary—*Rev. MICHAEL HOYER.

*Ex Officio—*Most Rev. ENRIQUE DELGADO, Ph.D., D.D., V.G.; Very Revs. CHRISTOPHER B. MARINO, V.F.; EMANUELE DENIGRIS; FERDINAND SANTOS, (Philippines); Rev. Msgrs. CHANEL JEANTY, J.C.L., V.G.; ROBERTO GARZA; Rev. RICHARD J. VIGOA.

*Northwest Broward Deanery—*Rev. Msgr. MICHAEL SOUCKAR, J.C.L., J.C.D.

*Northeast Broward Deanery—*Very Rev. MICHAEL J. GREER, V.F.

*Southeast Broward Deanery—*Rev. ROBERT M. AYALA.

*Southwest Broward Deanery—*Rev. STEVEN O'HALA, S.T.D.

*Northwest Dade Deanery—*Rev. JOSE N. ALFARO.

*Northeast Dade Deanery—*Rev. REGINALD JEAN-MARY.

*West Dade Deanery—*Very Rev. MARCOS A. SOMARRIBA, V.F.

*East Dade Deanery—*Rev. JOSE LUIS MENENDEZ.

*South Dade Deanery—*Rev. Msgr. PABLO A. NAVARRO, V.F.

*Monroe Deanery—*Very Rev. JOHN C. BAKER, V.F.

*Age Group I—*Rev. JOSE N. ALFARO.

*Age Group II—*Rev. MICHAEL HOYER.

*Age Group III—*Rev. Msgr. JAMES FETSCHER.

*Incardinated Priests—*Rev. Msgr. PABLO A. NAVARRO, V.F.

*Religious Priests—*Rev. STANISLAW RAKIEJ, S.Chr.

*Non-Incardinated Priests—*Rev. SAHAYANATHAN NATHAN.

*Incardinated Retired Priests—*Rev. PATRICK O'NEILL, (Retired).

*Appointed by the Archbishop—*Very Revs. CHRISTOPHER B. MARINO, V.F.; JOSE ALVAREZ, V.F.; DAVID A. ZIRILLI, V.F.; ERNEST BIRIRUKA, (Burundi) V.F.; KENNETH D. WHITTAKER, J.C.L., V.F.; Rev. PAUL VUTURO.

*Archdiocesan Attorney—*MR. PATRICK FITZGERALD, 110 Merrick Way, Ste. 3-B, Coral Gables, 33134. Tel: 305-443-9162; Fax: 305-443-6613.

*Catholic Legal Services, Archdiocese of Miami, Inc.—*RANDOLPH P. MCGRORTY, CEO; MS. MYRIAM MEZADIEU, COO, Main Office: Courthouse Plaza Bldg., 28 W. Flagler St., 10th Fl., Miami, 33130. Tel: 305-373-1073; Fax: 305-373-1173; Web: www.cclsmiami.org. Broward Office: 6565 Taft St., Ste. 401, Hollywood, 33024. Tel: 954-306-9537; Fax: 800-691-5203. Doral Office: USCCB Bldg., 7855 N.W. 12th St., Ste. 114, Miami, 33126. Tel: 305-887-8333; Fax: 305-541-2724.

Pax Catholic Communications, Inc.—1779 N.W. 28th St., Miami, 33142. Tel: 305-638-9729; Web: www.paxcc.org. Rev. Msgr. ROBERTO GARZA, Gen. Mgr., Email: garza@paxcc.org.

*Radio Paz - WACC 830 AM—*24-hour Spanish radio.

Secretariat for Administration

*Chancellor for Administration and Chief Operating Officer—*Sr. ELIZABETH ANNE WORLEY, S.S.J., Tel: 305-762-1284; Email: eworley@theadom.org.

*Finance Office—*MR. MICHAEL A. CASCIATO, CPA, CFO, Tel: 305-762-1242; Email: mcasciato@theadom.org; MR. JOSEPH M. CATANIA, CPA, M.H.A., Treas.

*Finance Council—*Members: Most Revs. THOMAS G. WENSKI, D.D.; ENRIQUE DELGADO, Ph.D., D.D., V.G.; MR. THOMAS BEIER, Chm.; Sr. ELIZABETH ANNE WORLEY, S.S.J.; Very Rev. DAVID A. ZIRILLI, V.F.; Revs. PAUL V. VUTURO; ALEJANDRO J. RODRIGUEZ ARTOLA; MR. ALBERT DEL CASTILLO; MR. SEAN CLANCY; MR. WILLIAM G. BENSON, CPA; MRS. CHRISTINA BROCHIN.

*Building and Property Office—*MR. DAVID PRADA, Senior Dir., Tel: 305-762-1033; Email: dprada@theadom.org; MR. CARLOS SANABRIA, Project Mgr., Tel: 305-762-1034; Tel: 305-206-1544; Email: csanabria@theadom.org.

*Human Resources Office—*MRS. LISA PINTO, Senior Dir., Tel: 305-762-1201; Email: lpinto@theadom.org.

*Archdiocesan Safe Environment Program—*MS. MARY ROSS AGOSTA, Dir., Tel: 305-762-1043; Email: mragosta@theadom.org; MR. PETER ROUTSIS-ARROYO, Victim Asst. Coord., Tel: 866-802-2873; Email: proutsis-arroyo@ccadm.org.

*Archdiocese of Miami Health Plan Trust—*VACANT, Chm.; MS. SUSAN WADDELL, Dir., Email: swaddell@adomhealthplan.org.

*Pension—*Most Rev. THOMAS G. WENSKI, D.D.; Rev. Msgr. KENNETH K. SCHWANGER, J.C.D., Chm.

*Communications - Media Relations—*MS. MARY ROSS AGOSTA, Dir., Tel: 305-762-1043; Email: ragosta@theadom.org; MARIA ALEJANDRA RIVAS, Media Coord. & Digital Media Specialist, Tel: 305-762-1046; Email: mrivas@theadom.org.

*Office of Ecumenical and Inter-Faith Relations—*Rev. PATRICK O'NEILL, Dir., (Retired), Tel: 305-762-1254; Email: rfernandez@theadom.org.

*The Florida Catholic—*Archdiocesan English Monthly Publication ANA RODRIGUEZ-SOTO, Editor, Tel: 305-762-1131; Fax: 305-762-1132; Email: arsoto@theadom.org.

*La Voz Catolica—*Archdiocesan Spanish Monthly Publication ANA RODRIGUEZ-SOTO, Exec. Editor, Tel: 305-762-1131; Email: arsoto@theadom.org; ROCIO GRANADOS, Editor, Tel: 305-762-1130; Email: rgranados@theadom.org.

Secretariat for Parish Life

*Cabinet Secretary—*MR. STEPHEN COLELLA, Tel: 305-762-1126; Email: scolella@theadom.org.

*Evangelization and Parish Life Office—*MS. MARY ANN WIESINGER, Dir., Tel: 305-762-1129; Email: mwiesinger@theadom.org.

*Mission Office—*Tel: 305-762-1236. VACANT, Dir.

Pontifical Mission SocietiesVery Rev. DAVID A. ZIRILLI, V.F.

Society for the Propagation of the FaithVery Rev. DAVID A. ZIRILLI, V.F., Dir.

*Holy Childhood Association—*Very Rev. DAVID A. ZIRILLI, V.F.

*The Society of St. Peter Apostle—*Very Rev. DAVID A. ZIRILLI, V.F.

*Missionary Union of Priests and Religious—*Very Rev. DAVID A. ZIRILLI, V.F.

*Priests Purgatorial Society—*Very Rev. DAVID A. ZIRILLI, V.F.

*Office of Marriage and Family Life—*MR. STEPHEN COLELLA, Dir., Tel: 305-762-1157; Email: scolella@theadom.org; Rev. LAZARUS J. GOVIN, Assoc. Dir., Tel: 305-751-0005; Email: frgovin@stmarthamiami.com; MRS. SUSANNA DIAZ, Coord., Tel: 305-762-1127; Email: sdiaz@theadom.org; Web: www.miamiarch.org/familylife.

*Office of Youth and Young Adult Ministry—*MRS. ROSEMARIE BANICH, Dir., Tel: 305-762-1189; Email: rbanich@theadom.org; MRS. MICHELLE DUCKER-LOPEZ, Coord., Tel: 305-762-1190; Email: mducker@theadom.org.

*Scouting—*Deacon EMILIO BLANCO, Chap., Tel: 305-762-1245; Email: emblancomd@comcast.net.

*Office of Campus Ministry—*VACANT, Archdiocesan Dir.

Campus Ministry - Colleges Directory—

St. Thomas University, Inc.—

*Director of Campus Ministry—*DR. CLAUDIA H. HERRERA, Tel: 305-628-6515; Fax: 305-628-6721; Email: cherrera7@stu.edu.

*University Chaplain—*Tel: 786-395-5145. VACANT.

Barry University—

*Director of Campus Ministry—*MS. KAREN J. STALNAKER, M.A., P.T., Tel: 305-899-3650; Email: kstalnaker@barry.edu.

*Chaplain—*Rev. CRISTOBAL TORRES, O.P., M.S.W., M.Div., M.A., Tel: 305-899-3836; Email: ctorres@barry.edu.

*Coordinator of Worship & Music Ministry—*MR. HAMILTON GUTIERREZ, Coord., Tel: 305-899-3650; Email: hgutierrez@barry.edu.

FIU-University Park Campus—

*Campus Minister—*Rev. SAHAYANATHAN NATHAN, Chap. & Campus Min., Tel: 305-222-1500; Email: frnathan1976@gmail.com.

*Director—*Very Rev. MARCOS A. SOMARRIBA, V.F., Email: rectory@stagathaonline.org. FIU; University Park Campus ministry is sponsored by St. Agatha Parish.

University of Miami—

*Chaplain—*Rev. PHILLIP H. TRAN, Tel: 305-284-3030; Email: ptran@theadom.org.

*St. Augustine Catholic Church Pastor—*VACANT. University of Miami Campus ministry is sponsored by the Archdiocese of Miami in collaboration with St. Augustine Church and Catholic Student Center.

Respect Life Ministry—4747 Hollywood Blvd., Ste. 103, Hollywood, 33021. Tel: 954-981-2922; Fax: 954-981-2901; Email: info@respectlifemiami.org; Web: www.respectlifemiami.org. MR. JUAN GUERRA, Tel: 305-202-4894; Email: jguerra@theadom.org.

*Project Rachel—*Post Abortion Healing and Reconciliation Program. Toll Free, Confidential Line: Tel: 888-456-4673; 954-981-2984.

Respect Life Pregnancy Help Centers—

North Dade Pregnancy Help Center, 1515 N.W. 167 St., Bldg. 4, Ste. 190, Miami Gardens, 33169. Tel: 305-653-2921; Email: respectlifeministry@comcast.net.

North Broward Pregnancy Help Center, 5115 Coconut Creek Pkwy., Margate, 33063. Tel: 954-977-7769; Email: nbrespectlife@att.net.

South Broward Pregnancy Help Center, 4747 Hollywood Blvd., Ste. 101, Hollywood, 33021. Tel: 954-963-2229; Email: sbrespect.life@att.net.

Central Broward Pregnancy Help Center, 525 N.E. 13th St., #527, Fort Lauderdale, 33304. Tel: 954-565-0229; Email: respectlifefll@att.net.

South Dade Pregnancy Help Center, 3410 S.W. 107 Ave., Miami, 33165-3633. Tel: 305-273-8507; Tel: 305-273-8508; Email: southdadepregnancyhelp@gmail.com.

Secretariat for Education

*Cabinet Secretary, Secretary for Education and Superintendent of Schools—*KIM PRYZBYLSKI, Ph. D., Tel: 305-762-1078; Email: kpryzbylski@theadom.org.

Office of Catholic Schools—

*Associate Superintendent of Schools—*DONALD EDWARDS, Ed.D., Tel: 305-762-1018; Email: dedwards@theadom.org.

*Office of Catechesis—*Sr. KAREN MUNIZ, S.C.T.J.M., Dir., Tel: 305-762-1090; Email: kmuniz@theadom.org.

*Office of Lay Ministry—*MR. ROGELIO ZELADA, Assoc. Dir., Tel: 305-762-1187; Email: rzelada@theadom.org.

Secretariat for Stewardship

*Archdiocese of Miami Development and Stewardship Office—*MRS. KATIE BLANCO BOURDEAU, J.D., C.F.R.E., Cabinet Sec., Chief Devel. Officer, & Pres. Devel. Corp., Tel: 305-762-1053; Email: kblanco@theadom.org.

*Archdiocese of Miami Endowment Fund, Inc.—*MR. WILLIAM G. BENSON, CPA; MRS. KAREY L. BOSACK GREENSTEIN, J.D., Exec. Dir., Tel: 305-762-1110; Email: kbosack@theadom.org.

*Archdiocese of Miami Development Corporation—*MRS. KATIE BLANCO BOURDEAU, J.D., C.F.R.E., Pres., 9401 Biscayne Blvd., Miami Shores, 33138. Tel: 305-762-1053; Email: kblanco@theadom.org; Web: www.adomdevelopment.org.

Catholic Community Foundation in the Archdiocese of Miami, Inc.— (1999) Email: info@the-ccf.org; Web: www.the-ccf.org. MR. WILLIAM G. BENSON, CPA, Chm.; MRS. MARIA ARAZOZA, C.F.P., C.I.M.A., Vice Chair; MRS. KAREY L. BOSACK GREENSTEIN, J.D., Exec. Dir., Tel: 305-762-1110; Email: kbosack@theadom.org.

Ministry of Persons—

*Vicar for Priests—*Rev. Msgr. ROBERTO GARZA, Tel: 305-318-9938.

*Office for Religious—*Sr. ANA MARGARITA LANZAS, S.C.T.J.M., Dir., Tel: 305-762-1082; Email: religious@theadom.org.

*Vocations—*Rev. ELVIS A. GONZALEZ, Dir., 9401 Biscayne Blvd., Miami, 33138. Tel: 305-762-1137; Email: egonzalez@theadom.org.

*Archdiocesan Vocations Review Board—*Sr. YAMILE SAIEH, F.M.A.; Rev. Msgr. CHANEL JEANTY, J.C.L., V.G.; Revs. JOSE N. ALFARO; MANUEL ALVAREZ; LUCIEN EUGENE PIERRE; STEVEN O'HALA, S.T.D.; ISRAEL E. MAGO; LUIS ROGER LARGAESPADA; JEFFREY MCCORMICK; Sr. CARMEN ORS, S.C.T.J.M.

Serra Club—

*Miami—*MARCIA PEREZ, Pres., 4857 S.W. 147th Ct., Miami, 33185. Email: mpmarcita@gmail.com.

*Broward—*MR. MALCOLM MEIKLE, Pres., 111 N. Pompano Beach Blvd., #914, Pompano Beach, 33062. Tel: 954-946-2551; Email: malcolm@meikle.com.

*Chaplain-Dade County - Serra Club—*Rev. ELVIS A. GONZALEZ.

*Chaplain-Broward County - Serra Club—*Rev. ANTHONY MULDERRY.

Office for Permanent Diaconate—9401 Biscayne Blvd., Miami, 33138. Tel: 305-762-1024; Email: vpimentel@theadom.org. Deacon VICTOR M. PIMENTEL, S.T.L., Dir.

*Permanent Diaconate Advisory Board—*Most Rev. THOMAS G. WENSKI, D.D.; Rev. Msgr. KENNETH K. SCHWANGER, J.C.D., Chm. Advisory Bd.; Deacon VICTOR M. PIMENTEL, S.T.L., Dir.

Ministry of Worship and Spiritual Life—

*Director—*Rev. RICHARD J. VIGOA, Tel: 305-762-1104; Email: rvigoa@theadom.org.

*Liturgical Music—*MR. GUSTAVO ZAYAS, Dir., Tel: 305-759-4531, Ext. 111; Email: gzayas@theadom.org.

*Spiritual Life Committee—*MS. MARY ANN WIESINGER.

Sacred Art & Architecture—Rev. JOSE LUIS MENENDEZ.
Committee on Popular Piety—Rev. JUAN J. SOSA, Chm., Tel: 305-866-6567.
Office of Black Catholic Ministry—MRS. KATRENIA C. REEVES-JACKMAN, Dir., 9401 Biscayne Blvd., Miami Shores, 33138. Tel: 305-762-1120; Fax: 305-758-2027; Email: blackcatholicministry@theadom.org.
Prison Ministry—9401 Biscayne Blvd., Miami, 33138. Tel: 305-762-1093. Deacons EDGARDO FARIAS, Dir., Email: efarias@theadom.org; RAFAEL CRUZ, Assoc.
Ministry to Professional Groups—
Catholic Educators' Guild—VACANT.
Catholic Funeral Directors' Guild—VACANT.
Catholic Lawyers' Guild—VACANT.
Miami Guild of the Catholic Medical Association—Rev. ALFRED CIOFFI, Chap.
Catholic Law Enforcement Ministry—VACANT, Voluntary Chap., Hollywood Police Dept. Chaplains: Rev. REGINALD JEAN-MARY, (City of Miami Police); VACANT, (Florida Hwy. Patrol, Troop K); Deacon JOSE ANTONIO SANTOS, (City of Miami Beach).
Catholic Fire Service Ministry—VACANT, Chap., Miami-Dade Fire Rescue; Very Rev. CHRISTOPHER B. MARINO, V.F., Chap., City of Miami; Rev. ROBERTO M. CID, Chap., Miami Beach; VACANT, Chap., City of Coral Gables; Rev. JAMES A. QUINN, Chap. Miami Office of the Federal Bureau of Investigations & Hallandale Beach Police Dept., (Retired).
Ministry to Pastoral Services—
Seaport/Airport Ministry—Rev. ROBERTO M. CID, Dir.
Stella Maris Seamen Center, Inc.—Rev. ROBERTO M. CID, Chap. & Archdiocesan Dir., 1172 S. America Way, Miami, 33132-2025. Tel: 305-372-0250; Fax: 305-538-3203.
Port Everglades—Seafarer's House/Casa del Marino, Port Everglades, 33316. Rev. YUNPING PETER LIN, Chap.; Deacons RANDY MILLIKIN; GERALD MCGUINN. Port of Miami: Rev. ROBERTO M. CID.
Rural Life Ministry—Rev. RAFAEL COS, Dir., Tel: 305-258-6998.
Chapels—Everglades Community Association: 19320 S.W. 380 Terr., Florida City, 33034. South Dade Camp: 31248 S.W. 134th Ave., Homestead, 33033. Redland Camp: 29200 S.W. 158th Ave., Leisure City, 33033. Tel: 305-258-6998.
St. Ann Mission—13875 S.W. 264th St., Naranja, 33032. Mailing Address: P.O. Box 924884, Princeton, 33092. Tel: 305-258-6998; Fax: 305-258-0834; Email: misionsantaananaranja@gmail.com. Rev. RAFAEL COS.
Lay Apostolic Movements and Associations—
Catholic Daughters of the Americas—Court 634, Regent: LANA JABOUR, The Basilica of St. Mary Star of the Sea, 1010 Windsor Ln., Key West, 33040. Tel: 305-942-6905. Vice-Regent: URSULA ELLIOTT. Local Chaplain: Very Rev. JOHN C. BAKER, V.F.
Cofradia de Nuestro Senora del Rosario, de Chiquinquira—Web: www.virgendechiquinquira.org. Rev. JULIO R. SOLANO, Dir., 2700 N. 29 Ave., Ste. 205, Hollywood, 33020. Tel: 954-821-0406; Email: j.solano@stanthonyftl.org.
Camino del Matrimonio (Spanish/English)—Mailing Address: 7700 S.W. 56 St., Miami, 33155. Tel: 305-226-4664; Email: caminodelmatrimonio@gmail.com; Web: www.caminodelmatrimonio.org. Rev. RAFAEL CAPO, Sch.P., Spiritual Dir.
Agrupacion Catolica Universitaria, Inc. (ACU)—12805 S.W. 6th St., Miami, 33184. Tel: 786-360-8004; Web: www.estovir.org. Rev. GUILLERMO GARCIA-TUNON, S.J.
Jesus Maestro, Inc.—12805 S.W. 6th St., Miami, 33184. Tel: 786-360-8004; Web: www.estovir.org. Rev. GUILLERMO GARCIA-TUNON, S.J., Dir.; ERIK VIEIRA, Contact Person, Email: evieira@estovir.org.
ACU Holdings, Inc.—12805 S.W. 6th St., Miami, 33184. Tel: 786-360-8004; Web: www.estovir.org. Rev. GUILLERMO GARCIA-TUNON, S.J., Dir.
ACU Properties, LLC—12805 S.W. 6th St., Miami, 33184. Tel: 786-360-8004; Web: www.estovir.org. Rev. GUILLERMO GARCIA-TUNON, S.J., Dir.
St. Martin de Porres Assoc.—LEONA H. COOPER, Pres., Mailing Address: P.O. Box 330102, Miami, 33133. Tel: 305-443-9466; Fax: 305-461-8669; Email: cooperleona@yahoo.com.
Miami Archdiocesan Council of Catholic Women (MACCW)—LISA SHELLY, Pres., 9011 N.W. 23rd St., Coral Springs, 33065. Tel: 954-775-5002; Email: smerdlap@mindspring.com; Web: www.maccw.org; Very Rev. MICHAEL J. GREER, V.F., Spiritual Advisor, 2001 S. Ocean Blvd., Lauderdale-By-The-Sea, 33062. Tel: 954-941-7647. Spiritual Advisors: Rev. Msgrs. MICHAEL SOUCKAR, J.C.L., J.C.D., North District of MACCW; KENNETH K. SCHWANGER, J.C.D., Co Advisor South District of MACCW; Rev. WILLIAM ELBERT, Central District of MACCW, (Retired).
Catholic Charismatic Services–Archdiocese of Miami—Rev. JOHN FINK, Spiritual Dir. & Treas., (Retired), P.O. Box 816128, Hollywood, 33081-0128. Tel: 954-961-1856; Fax: 954-961-1856; Email: jfink201170@yahoo.com; Web: www.miamiccr.com; Web: www.stbartholomew.com; MR. EMERY HORVATH, Dir., Email: crob1@att.net. Spanish: Rev. ARMANDO TOLOSA, Spiritual Dir.; LOURDES BRITO, Coord., Centro Carismatico Catolico: 500 N.W. 22 Ave., Miami, 33125. Tel: 305-631-1007; Fax: 305-642-0006; Email: rcch@renovacioncarismaticamiami.com; Web: www.renovacioncarismaticamiami.com.
Office of Ministry to (Non-Hispanic) Cultural Groups—31300 Overseas Hwy., Big Pine Key, 33043. Tel: 305-872-2537. Rev. JESUS S. (JETS) MEDINA, Dir., Email: frjets@stpeterbpk.org.
Nigerian Apostolate—Rev. FIDELIS NWANKWO, C.S.Sp., 15700 N.W. 20th Ave. Rd., Miami Gardens, 33054. Tel: 305-705-2010; Email: finenwankwo@yahoo.com.
Brazilian and Portuguese Apostolate—St. Vincent, 6350 N.W. 18th St., Margate, 33063-2320. Tel: 954-972-0434; Fax: 954-971-9411; Email: stvincent7@aol.com.
Chinese Apostolate—Rev. YUNPING PETER LIN, Tel: 954-734-1985; Cell: 305-283-7207; Email: plin@theadom.org; Deacon ALEX LAM, 7270 S.W. 120 St., Miami, 33156. Tel: 350-238-7562, Ext. 105; Email: alam777@aol.com; BERNADETTE CHIK, St. Jerome Parish. Tel: 954-801-1977; Email: bernc539@yahoo.com.
Filipino Apostolate—MS. JANET MACASERO, Asst., 6320 Plunkett St., Hollywood, 33023. Tel: 954-981-7843; Email: jgmacasero@gmail.com.
Haitian Apostolate—Rev. REGINALD JEAN-MARY, Notre Dame D'Haiti Mission, 110 N.E. 62 St., Miami, 33138. Tel: 305-751-6289; ANNETTE DECIUS, Tel: 786-541-7380; Email: annettedecius@ymail.com.
Indian Apostolate—Rev. KURIAKOSE KUMBAKEEL, Our Lady of Health (Syro-Malabar Church), 201 N. University Dr., Coral Springs, 33071. Tel: 954-227-6985; Email: frkuku@gmail.com.
Caribbean Apostolate—DR. PRINCE SMITH, 755 N.W. 184th Dr., Miami Gardens, 33169. Tel: 305-653-8492; Email: smith23ps@att.net; JOHN WEST, Tel: 786-597-3042; Email: johnwestcdg@yahoo.com.
St. Paul Chung Ha Sang Korean Mission—3600 S.W. 32 Blvd., West Park, 33023. Rev. JEONG-HOO CHO, Mailing Address: 14344 S. Royal Cove Cir., Davie, 33325. Tel: 954-894-2018; RAYMOND LEE, Tel: 305-343-6807; Email: raymond@rheegs.com.
Polish—Rev. STANISLAW RAKIEJ, S.Chr., Our Lady of Czestochowa Polish Mission, 2400 N.E. 12th St., Pompano Beach, 33062. Tel: 954-946-6347; Fax: 954-946-0512; Email: polishchurch@bellsouth.net.
Vietnamese—Rev. JOSEPH LONG NGUYEN, Our Lady of La Vang Vietnamese Catholic Mission, 123 N.W. 6th Ave., Hallandale Beach, 33009. Tel: 954-374-9100; Fax: 954-987-1638; Email: josephln@yahoo.com; TAM TRUONG, Tel: 954-636-9963; Email: baokimanh@gmail.com.
Christian Family Movement—Spanish: Movimiento Familiar Cristiano, *Casa Cana, 480 E. 8th St., Hialeah, 33010.* Tel: 305-888-4819. MR. ADAN ZUNIGA, Pres., Tel: 786-663-6021; OLGA BERMUDEZ, Tel: 786-399-9783; Web: www.casacana.org; Email: mfccasacana62@gmail.com.
Archicofradia Nuestra Senora de la Caridad (Spanish)—Email: santuario@ermita.org; Web: ermitadelacaridad.org.
Ministry to the Deaf or Disabled—Schott Memorial Center, Inc., 6591 S. Flamingo Rd., Cooper City, 33330-3915. Tel: 954-434-3306; Fax: 954-434-3307. MRS. ILEANA RAMIREZ-CUELI, Exec. Dir.; MR. PABLO A. CUADRA, Dir. Rel. Formation; MARY ROUKAS, Dir. Progs. & Residences; JERRY COHEN, Dir. Annual Fund & Stewardship; AUDREY BROWN, Dir. Finance & Administration, Tel: 954-434-3306; Fax: 954-434-3307; Web: www.schottcommunities.org.
Comunidad de Vida Cristiana, Regina Mundi, South Florida Region—Rev. MARCELINO GARCIA, S.J., Spiritual Dir., Casa Manresa, 12190 S.W. 56 St., Miami, 33175. Tel: 305-596-0001; Web: www.clcsfr.org.
Cursillo Movement—
Cursillos de Cristiandad (Spanish)—Casa Mons. Agustin Roman, 16250 S.W. 112th Ave., Miami, 33157. Tel: 305-235-7160; Web: www.cursillos.org. Rev. ELVIS A. GONZALEZ, Spiritual Dir., Email: gonzalez@theadom.org; ALFREDO JACOMINO, Lay Coord., Email: directorlaico@cursillos.org.
Cursillo (English)—DAZEL KNOX, Lay Coord., Email: dazknox@bellsouth.net; Web: www.cursillomiami.org; Deacon ROBERT BINDER, Spiritual Dir., Tel: 305-255-6642; Email: margedun@bellsouth.net.
Emmaus Experience Parish Retreats—MYRNA GALLAGHER, Contact, Tel: 786-258-3654; JUDITH PASOS, English & Spanish Contact, Tel: 786-258-3654; Email: pasos.bravo@gmail.com.
**Ignatian Spirituality Center, Inc.—Casa Manresa, P.O. Box 651512, Miami, 33265.* Tel: 305-596-0001; Fax: 305-596-9655; Web: www.ceimiami.org. Rev. MARCELINO GARCIA, S.J., Dir.
Encuentros Juveniles (Spanish and English)—9401 Biscayne Blvd., Miami Shores, 33138. Email: encuentros.juveniles@theadom.org. MARK GOMEZ, Group Leader, Tel: 305-338-2661; Email: markagomez95@gmail.com; Rev. JEAN STERLING LAURENT, Spiritual Dir., Tel: 305-607-7083; Email: frsterlingmc@yahoo.com.
Impactos de Cristiandad (English and Spanish)—VACANT, P.O. Box 440967, Miami, 33144. Tel: 305-571-7111; Email: impactos@impactos.org; Web: www.impactos.org.
Knights of Columbus (English and Spanish)—9401 Biscayne Blvd., Miami Shores, 33138. Tel: 305-762-1158; Web: www.floridakofc.org. Rev. Msgr. GREGORY C. WIELUNSKI, J.C.D., Archdiocesan Chap., Email: gwielunski@theadom.org.
La Nueva Jerusalen Community - Comunidad de Alianza—VACANT, Spiritual Dir., Tel: 305-274-8224; WILLIAM F. BROWN JR., Liaison with the Archdiocese of Miami, Tel: 305-206-0623; Email: wfbrownjr@gmail.com; YADER PORTOCARRERO, Sr. Coord., Tel: 786-543-9920; Email: pyader@gmail.com.
Legion of Mary—(English Speaking) Rev. RICHARD SOULLIERE, Spiritual Dir., (Retired). Lay Contacts: JUDITH PADRON, (Spanish), Tel: 305-283-3280; Email: jtp1227@aol.com; MARK STEELE, (English), Tel: 303-233-0082; Email: mandmsteele@yahoo.com.
Neocatechumenal Way—Archdiocesan Team: DR. STEFANO BENIGNI, J.C.D.; LUCIA BENIGNI, Tel: 305-898-0643; Email: stefanobenigni@gmail.com; Web: www.camminoneocatecumenale.it.
Franciscanos de Maria/Franciscans of Mary—a private international association of the faithful. ELENA SROUJI, Tel: 305-297-7804; Email: ecsrouji@gmail.com; CRIS GARCIA-CASSALS, Tel: 305-607-6726; Email: crisgc@bellsouth.net; JULIA HERDOCIA, Tel: 305-773-7431; Email: juliaherdocia@gmail.com.
Catholic Charities of the Archdiocese of Miami, Inc.—1505 N.E. 26th St., Wilton Manors, 33305. Tel: 305-754-2444; Fax: 305-754-6649; Web: www.ccadm.org. Rev. Msgr. ROBERTO GARZA, Chair, Bd. of Dirs. & Dir. Mission Effectiveness, Email: rgarza@paxcc.org; MR. PETER ROUTSIS-ARROYO, CEO, Email: parroyo@ccadm.org; JULES JONES, CFO, Email: jjones@ccadm.org; DEVIKA AUSTIN, C.A.O., Email: daustin@ccadm.org.
Social Advocacy—MR. PETER ROUTSIS-ARROYO.
Catholic Campaign for Human Development—1505 N.E. 26th St., Wilton Manors, 33305. Tel: 305-754-2444; Fax: 305-754-6649.
Miami-Dade Region—
Elderly Services Congregate Meals—2800 N.W. 18th Ave., Miami, 33142. Tel: 305-751-5203; Email: congregatemeals@ccadm.org.
Refugee Resettlement and Employment Services—7707 N.W. 2nd Ave., 2nd Fl., Miami, 33150. Tel: 305-883-4555; Fax: 305-883-4498; Email: refugee@ccadm.org.
Pierre Toussaint Haitian Center—7707 N.W. 2nd Ave., 2nd Fl., Miami, 33150. Tel: 305-759-3050; Fax: 305-754-7423; Email: pierretoussaint@ccadm.org.
Unaccompanied Refugee Minors Program—7300 N. Kendall Dr., Ste. 620, Miami, 33156. Tel: 305-883-3383; Email: urmp@ccadm.org.
Unaccompanied Minors—Mailing Address: P.O. Box 971580, Miami, 33157. Tel: 305-380-0141; Email: ump@ccadm.org.
Boystown of Florida, Inc.—1505 N.E. 26 St., Wilton Manors, 33305. Tel: 305-762-1332; Fax: 305-754-6649.
New Life Family Center—Tel: 305-573-3333; Fax: 305-576-5111; Email: newlife@ccadm.org.
Homeless Prevention/Rapid Re-Housing—3620 N.W. 1st Ave., Miami, 33127. Tel: 305-573-3333.
Counseling—9999 N.E. 2nd Ave., Ste. 215B, Miami Shores, 33138. Tel: 954-649-7785. *7300 N. Kendall Dr., Ste. 620, Miami, 33156.* Tel: 305-883-3383, Ext. 302; Email: counseling@ccadm.org.

Substance Abuse—
St. Luke's Center, Inc.—Addiction Recovery Center.
St. Luke's Prevention—7707 N.W. 2nd Ave., Miami, 33150. Tel: 305-795-0077; Fax: 305-795-0030; Email: stlukes@ccadm.org.

Child Development Services/Miami-Dade—
Centro Hispano Catolico—Child Development Center, 125 N.W. 25th St., Miami, 33127. Tel: 305-573-9093; Fax: 305-576-6446; Email: centrohispano@ccadm.org; Email: feccentrohispano@ccadm.org.
Good Shepherd Child Development Center—18601 S.W. 97th Ave., Perrine, 33157. Tel: 305-235-1756 ; Fax: 786-231-0049; Email: goodshepherd@ccadm.org; Email: fecgoodshepherd@ccadm.org.
Notre Dame Child Development Center—130 N.E. 62nd St., Miami, 33138. Tel: 305-751-6778; Fax: 305-751-6959; Email: notredame@ccadm.org; Email: fecnotredame@ccadm.org.
Holy Redeemer Child Development Center—1325 N.W. 71 St., Miami, 33147. Tel: 305-836-4971; Fax: 305-836-3323; Email: holyredeemer@ccadm.org; Email: fecholyredeemer@ccadm.org.
Sagrada Familia Child Development Center—970 S.W. 1st St., Miami, 33130. Tel: 305-324-5424; Fax: 305-325-0642; Email: sagradafam@ccadm.org; Email: fecsagradafamilia@ccadm.org.
South Dade Child Development Center—28520 S.W. 148th Ave., Leisure City, 33033. Tel: 305-245-0979; Fax: 305-242-8796; Email: southdade@ccadm.org; Email: fecsouthdade@ccadm.org.

Broward Region—
Counseling—1503 N.E. 26th St., Wilton Manors, 33305. Tel: 954-332-7070. *9900 W. Sample Rd., Coral Springs, 33065.* Tel: 786-774-1025; Email: counseling@ccadm.org.
Homeless Prevention/Rapid Re-Housing—1505 N.E. 26th St., Wilton Manors, 33305. Tel: 954-315-2624; Email: browardhousingservices@ccadm.org.

Adult Day Care Programs—
Central West—6915 Stirling Rd., Davie, 33314. Tel: 954-583-6446; Email: centralwest@ccadm.org.
Centro Oeste—6915 Stirling Rd., Davie, 33314. Tel: 954-581-9719; Email: centrooeste@ccadm.org.
Wilton Manors—1503 N.E. 26th St., Wilton Manors, 33305. Tel: 954-630-9501; Fax: 954-566-6026; Email: browardelderly@ccadm.org.
Monroe Region—Tel: 305-292-9790; Fax: 305-292-5257.
Homeless Prevention/Rapid Re-Housing—2706 Flagler Ave., Key West, 33040. Tel: 305-272-9790.
Theresa House—1621 Spaulding Ct., Key West, 33040. Tel: 305-292-9790.
Workforce Housing—2706 Flagler Ave., Key West, 33040. Tel: 305-292-9790.
St. Bede's Village—2706 Flagler Ave., Key West, 33040. Tel: 305-292-9790; Email: stbedes@ccadm.org.

Ministry of Catholic Health Services—
Catholic Health Services, Inc.—4790 N. State Rd. 7, Lauderdale Lakes, 33319. Tel: 954-484-1515. MR. RALPH LAWSON, Chm. Bd.; Sr. ELIZABETH ANNE WORLEY, S.S.J., Vice Chair & Sec.; VACANT, Archdiocesan Dir. Catholic Identity; MR. JOSEPH M. CATANIA, CPA, M.H.A., Pres. & CEO; MR. ARISTIDES PALLIN, COO. Priest Chaplains: Revs. JOHN MARY PEREZ, Catholic Hospice, Tel: 305-877-5920; RAUL PEREZ VASALLO, Catholic Hospice, Tel: 786-537-0693; M. PARKER OGBOE, Dir. Pastoral Care - Central/West Campus, Tel: 305-798-3776. Villa Maria Nursing Center, St. Catherine's Rehabilitation Hospital, St. Catherine's West Rehabilitation Hospital; MAREK WIORKIEWICZ, S.D.S., (Poland) Villa Maria Nursing Center; PATRICK J. NAUGHTON, St. Joseph Assisted Living Facility, St. Anthony's Rehabilitation Hospital, Tel: 954-648-2870; EDMUND AKU, Dir. Pastoral Care - South Campus, Tel: 323-515-5200. St. Anne Nursing Center and Residence; ANTONY VAYALIKAROTTU, Dir. Pastoral Care - North Campus, St. John's Nursing Center, Tel: 954-673-3198.
Catholic Health Services, Inc. d/b/a Catholic Health Services Medical Group—3487 N.W. 30 St., Lauderdale Lakes, 33311. MARITZA LUNA-HAIR, Practice Mgr., Tel: 954-641-4200.
Catholic Health Care Transitions Services, Inc.—3075 N.W. 35 Ave., Lauderdale Lakes, 33311. Tel: 954-486-6951. CAROL HYLTON, Exec. Dir. Home & Community Based Svcs.

Catholic Housing for the Elderly and Handicapped, Inc.—
Catholic Housing Management—JUANA MEJIA, Vice Pres. Housing Devel. & Oper., 11410 N. Kendall Dr., Ste. 306, Miami, 33176. Tel: 305-757-2824.
Archbishop Carroll Manor, Inc.—3667 S. Miami Ave., Miami, 33133. Tel: 305-854-8953. ROBERT PIEDRA, Mgr.
Archbishop Hurley Hall, Inc.—MRS. ALEXANDRA PEREZ, Mgr., 632 N.W. 1st St., Hallandale, 33009. Tel: 954-454-0855.
Miami Beach Marian Towers, Inc.—ADA G. HERNANDEZ, Mgr., 17505 N. Bay Rd., Sunny Isles Beach, 33160. Tel: 305-932-1300.
Archbishop McCarthy Residence, Inc.—13201 N.W. 28th Ave., Opa Locka, 33054. Tel: 305-688-2700. DOMINGA ACEVEDO, Mgr.
Palmer House, Inc.—1225 S.W. 107th Ave., Miami, 33174. Tel: 305-221-9566. MICHELLE TORREALBA, Mgr.
St. Andrew Towers, Inc.—2700 N.W. 99th Ave., Coral Springs, 33065. Tel: 954-752-3960. SAPRINA JOYNER, Mgr.
St. Dominic Gardens, Inc.—5849 N.W. 7th St., Miami, 33126. Tel: 305-262-0962. RUBEN PEREZ, Mgr.
St. Elizabeth Gardens, Inc.—801 N.E. 33rd St., Pompano Beach, 33064. Tel: 954-941-4597. VILMA LUGO, Mgr.
St. Joseph Towers, Inc.—DEBRA HAMELRATH, Mgr., 3475 N.W. 30th St., Lauderdale Lakes, 33311. Tel: 954-485-5150.
St. Mary Towers, Inc.—7615 N.W. 2nd Ave., Miami, 33150. Tel: 305-757-3190. ARIESKY (TONY) VAZQUEZ, Mgr.
Stella Maris House, Inc.—JOHANKA ALONSO, Mgr., 8638 Harding Ave., Miami Beach, 33141. Tel: 305-865-6841.
St. Anne's Gardens, Inc.—11800 Quail Roost Dr., Miami, 33177. Tel: 305-234-1994. LUISA UREA, Mgr.
St. Boniface Gardens, Inc.—8200 Johnson St., Pembroke Pines, 33024. Tel: 305-433-3899. VICTOR CORDERO, Mgr.
St. Vincent de Paul Gardens, Inc.—BLANCA ALBELO, 10160 N.W. 19th Ave., Miami, 33147. Tel: 305-639-1590.
St. Monica Gardens, Inc.—3425 N.W. 189th St., Miami Gardens, 33056. Tel: 305-628-2500; Fax: 305-628-2600. ISABEL SOTO NORIEGA, Mgr.
St. Joseph Haitian Mission Manor, Inc.— dba St. Joseph Manor*1220 N.W. 6th Ave., Pompano Beach, 33060.* Tel: 754-222-6893. PAULA MEJIA, Mgr.
CHS St. Andrew Towers I Development LLC—4790 N. State Rd. 7, Lauderdale Lakes, 33319. Tel: 954-484-1515.
CHS St. Andrew Towers II Development LLC—4790 N. State Rd. 7, Lauderdale Lakes, 33319. Tel: 954-484-1515.
CHS St. Elizabeth Gardens Development LLC—4790 N. State Rd. 7, Lauderdale Lakes, 33319. Tel: 954-484-1515.
CHS Miami Beach Marian Towers Development LLC—4790 N. State Rd. 7, Lauderdale Lakes, 33319. Tel: 954-484-1515.
CHS Casa Sant'Angelo Apartments Development, LLC—4790 N. State Rd. 7, Lauderdale Lakes, 33319. Tel: 954-484-1515.
Miramar Senior Housing Project, Inc.— dba Casa Sant' Angelo*4790 N. State Rd. 7, Lauderdale Lakes, 33319.* Tel: 954-484-1515; Fax: 954-484-5416.

Nursing and Retirement Centers—
BROWARD:
St. Joseph Residence, Inc.JAMIE BONAVITA-RHODES, Admin., 3485 N.W. 30th St., Lauderdale Lakes, 33311. Tel: 954-739-1483.
St. John's Rehabilitation Hospital and Nursing Center, Inc. dba St. John's Nursing Center*3075 N.W. 35th Ave., Lauderdale Lakes, 33311.* Tel: 954-739-6233. PAMELA GAMBARDELLA, Exec. Dir. & Nursing Home Admin.
St. John's Rehabilitation Hospital and Nursing Center, Inc. d/b/a St. Anthony's Rehabilitation HospitalPAMELA GAMBARDELLA, Admin., 3487 N.W. 30th St., Fort Lauderdale, 33311. Tel: 954-739-6233.
Catholic Hospice of Broward, Inc.*4790 N. State Rd. 7, Lauderdale Lakes, 33319.* Tel: 954-484-1515.
Catholic Home Health Medicare Services, Inc.*4790 N. State Rd. 7, Lauderdale Lakes, 33319.* Tel: 954-484-1515.
Catholic Home Health Services, Inc.*4790 N. State Rd. 7, Lauderdale Lakes, 33319.* Tel: 954-484-1515.
Catholic Home Health Services of Broward, Inc. CAROL HYLTON, Admin., 3075 N.W. 35th Ave., Lauderdale Lakes, 33311. Tel: 954-486-3660.
MIAMI-DADE:
*St. Anne's Nursing Center, St. Anne's Residence, Inc.ROSEMARIE BAILEY, Exec. Dir., 11855 Quail Roost Dr., Miami, 33177. Tel: 305-252-4000.
Miami-Dade Nursing Center, Inc.*c/o 4790 N. State Rd. 7, Lauderdale Lakes, 33319.* Tel: 954-484-1515.
Villa Maria Nursing and Rehabilitation Center, Inc. dba Villa Maria Nursing Center*1050 N.E. 125 St., North Miami, 33161.* Tel: 305-891-8850. MR. NATHANIEL JOHNSON, Admin.
Villa Maria Nursing and Rehabilitation Center, Inc. d/b/a Villa Maria West Skilled Nursing FacilitySANDRA CABEZAS, Admin., 8850 N.W. 122nd St., Hialeah Gardens, 33018. Tel: 305-351-7181.
Villa Maria Nursing and Rehabilitation Center, Inc. d/b/a St. Catherine's Rehabilitation HospitalMR. JAIME GONZALEZ, Admin., 1050 N.E. 125th St., North Miami, 33161. Tel: 305-357-1735.
Villa Maria Nursing and Rehabilitation Center, Inc. d/b/a St. Catherine's West Rehabilitation HospitalMR. JAIME GONZALEZ, Admin., 8850 N.W. 122nd St., Hialeah Gardens, 33018. Tel: 305-351-7181.
Villa Maria Health Care Services, Inc. dba Catholic Home Health Services of Miami-Dade County*1050 N.E. 125th St., North Miami, 33161.* Tel: 305-899-0400. BEATRICE VOLTAIRE, Admin.
Miami Lakes - Catholic Hospice, Inc.*14875 N.W. 77 Ave., Ste. 100, Miami Lakes, 33014.* Tel: 305-822-2380; Fax: 305-824-0665; Web: www.catholichospice.org. DIAN BACKOFF, Exec. Dir.
Catholic Palliative Care Services, Inc.*14875 N.W. 77 Ave., Ste. 100, Miami Lakes, 33014.* Tel: 305-822-2380; Fax: 305-824-0665.
Villa Maria Foundation, Inc.*1050 N.E. 125th St., North Miami, 33161.* Tel: 305-891-8850.

Catholic Cemeteries of the Archdiocese of Miami, Inc.—MARY JO FRICK, Exec. Dir., 11411 N.W. 25th St., Miami, 33172. Tel: 305-592-0521.
Archdiocesan Cemeteries—Administrative Managers: MARIA TRUJILLO, Our Lady of Mercy Cemetery, 11411 N.W. 25th St., Miami, 33172. Tel: 305-592-0521; OFELIA SPARDY, Our Lady Queen of Heaven Cemetery, 1500 S. State Rd. 7, North Lauderdale, 33068. Tel: 954-972-1234.

Catholic Elderly Services, Inc. d/b/a Catholic Health Services Foundation—4790 N. State Rd. 7, Lauderdale Lakes, 33319. Tel: 954-484-1515.

Centro Mater Child Care Services, Inc.—MR. JOSEPH M. CATANIA, CPA, M.H.A., Pres. & CEO; J. ABILIO RODRIGUEZ, Exec. Dir., 8298 N.W. 103 St., Hialeah Gardens, 33016. Tel: 305-357-4395.
Centro Mater Child Care Center—MADELYN RODRIGUEZ-LLANES, Prog. Dir., 418 S.W. 4th Ave., Miami, 33130. Tel: 305-545-6049; Fax: 305-324-6162.
Centro Mater Child Care Center II—421 S.W. 4th St., Miami, 33130. Tel: 305-545-6049; Fax: 305-324-6162.
Centro Mater West Child Care Center—8298 N.W. 103rd St., Hialeah Gardens, 33016. Tel: 305-357-4395; Fax: 305-357-4674. JULIETTA RIVERON-BELLO, Prog. Dir.
Centro Mater West II Child Care Center—7700 N.W. 98th St., Hialeah Gardens, 33016. Tel: 305-362-9701; Fax: 305-362-9731.
Centro Mater Walker Park—800 W. 29th St., Hialeah, 33010. Tel: 305-887-1140.

Special Apostolates—
Amor en Accion (Love in Action)—Mailing Address: 9401 Biscayne Blvd., Miami Shores, 33138. Tel: 305-762-1226; Email: amor.en.accion@theadom.org. JANELLE JAY, Coord. & Contact.
Downtown Senior Citizens' Community Center at Gesu Church—Sisters MARIA ISABEL RINCON, O.P.; CECILIA ALONSO, O.P.; JULIA BARRETO, O.P., 118 N.E. 2nd St., Miami, 33132. Tel: 305-374-6099.

CLERGY, PARISHES, MISSIONS AND PAROCHIAL SCHOOLS

CITY OF MIAMI

(DADE COUNTY)

1—ST. MARY'S CATHEDRAL (1930)
7525 N.W. 2nd Ave., Miami, 33150. Tel: 305-759-4531; Tel: 305-759-4532; Fax: 305-757-7456; Email:

frontoffice@thecathedralofstmary.org; Web: www.thecathedralofstmary.org. Very Rev. Christopher B. Marino, V.F., Rector; Rev. Lesly Jean, (Haiti) Parochial Vicar; Deacons Raul Flores; Sergio Rodicio, Business Mgr.
School—St. Mary's Cathedral School, 7485 N.W. Second Ave., Miami, 33150. Tel: 305-795-2000; Fax: 305-795-2013; Email: info@stmarycathedralschool.org; Web: www.stmarymiami.org. Eduardo Flor, Prin. Lay Teachers 22; Sisters 1; Students 390.
Catechesis Religious Program—Tel: 305-795-2016; Email: mnieves@stmarycathedralschool.org. Maria Nieves, D.R.E. Students 33.
Endowment—St. Mary's Cathedral Foundation Trust, 9401 Biscayne Blvd., 33138. Mike Casciato, Contact Person.

2—ST. AGATHA (1971)
1111 S.W. 107th Ave., Miami, 33174.
Tel: 305-222-1500; Fax: 305-225-2481; Email: rectory@stagathaonline.org. Very Rev. Marcos A. Somarriba, V.F.; Revs. Raul S. Soutuyo, Parochial Vicar; Sahayanathan Nathan, Parochial Vicar; Juan Carlos Salazar Gomez, Parochial Vicar; Deacons Angel Pintado, (Retired); Ernesto Del Riego; Manuel Perez; Hector Norat; Santos Feliciano; Sr. Teresa Urioste, S.C.T.J.M., D.R.E.
School—St. Agatha School, (Grades PreK-8), 1125 S.W. 107th Ave., Miami, 33174. Tel: 305-222-8751; Fax: 305-222-1517; Email: office@stagathaonline.com; Web: school.stagathaonline.org. Patricia Hernandez, Prin. Lay Teachers 29; Students 446.
Catechesis Religious Program—Tel: 305-222-8067. Students 278.

3—ST. BRENDAN (1954)
8725 S.W. 32nd St., Miami, 33165. Tel: 305-221-0881; Fax: 305-226-6249; Email: pastor@sbrendan.org. Revs. Miguel A. Sepulveda; Oscar A. Perez, Parochial Vicar; Warren Escalona, Parochial Vicar; Sergio Cabrera, In Res., (Retired); Deacons Billy Lannon Jr.; Edgar Kelly.
School—St. Brendan School, 8755 S.W. 32 St., Miami, 33165. Tel: 305-221-2722; Fax: 305-554-6726; Email: mcapote@stbrendanmiami.org; Web: www.stbrendanmiami.org. Maria Cristina Capote-Alonso, Prin. Lay Teachers 51; Students 778; Staff 8.
Catechesis Religious Program—Tel: 305-221-2861; Email: ggonzalez@sbrendan.org. Mr. Gerardo Gonzalez, D.R.E. Students 203.

4—ST. CATHERINE OF SIENA (1968)
9200 S.W. 107th Ave., Miami, 33176.
Tel: 305-274-6333; Fax: 305-274-6337; Email: Pastor@scsmiami.org; Email: hfujita@scsmiami.org. Revs. Rolando Cabrera Garcia; Raphael Sarkodie, In Res.; Deacons Vicente Moreno; Raimundo Santos.
Catechesis Religious Program—Tel: 305-274-6331; Email: lmayorga@scsmiami.org. Lydia Mayorga, C.R.E. Students 41.

5—CHRIST THE KING aka Christ the King Catholic Church (1961)
16000 S.W. 112th Ave., Miami, 33157.
Tel: 305-238-2485; Fax: 305-254-0330; Email: ctkcatholic@bellsouth.net. Rev. Ferry Brutus, (Haiti); Deacon George Gibson.
Catechesis Religious Program—Tel: 305-235-0293; Email: alphaglardia@yahoo.com. Deacon Alpha Fleurimond, D.R.E. Students 35.

6—CORPUS CHRISTI (1941)
3220 N.W. 7th Ave., Miami, 33127.
Tel: 305-635-1331; Fax: 305-635-2031; Email: corpuschristi@corpuschristimiami.org; Web: www.corpuschristimiami.org. Revs. Jose Luis Menendez; Joseph Jean-Louis, O.M.I., Parochial Vicar; Deacon Antonio Perez.
Catechesis Religious Program—Email: carmen@claretiansisters.org. Sr. Carmen Alvarez, R.M.I., Tel: 305-633-5824. Students 431.
Missions—San Francisco y Santa Clara—402 N.E. 29th St., Miami, 33137.
San Juan Bautista, 3116 N.W. 2nd Ave., Miami, 33127.
Nuestra Senora de Altagracia, 1779 N.W. 28th St., Miami, 33142.
La Milagrosa, 1860 N.W. 18th Ter., Miami, 33125.
St. Robert Bellarmine, 3405 N.W. 27 Ave., Miami, 33142.

7—ST. DOMINIC (1962)
5909 N.W. 7th St., Miami, 33126. Tel: 305-264-0181; Fax: 305-262-4685; Email: elogiste@gmail.com. Revs. Eduardo Logiste, O.P., M.Div., M.A.; Orlando Cardozo, O.P., Parochial Vicar.
Catechesis Religious Program—Email: rob18316@aol.com. Robert Cruz, D.R.E. Students 119.

8—EPIPHANY (1951)
8080 S.W. 54 Ct., Miami, 33143. Tel: 305-667-4911; Fax: 305-667-8067; Email: info@epiphanycatholicchurch.com; Web: epiphanycatholicchurch.com. Rev. Msgr. Jude O'Doherty; Rev. Alexander Rivera, Parochial Vicar; Deacons Eduardo Smith; Donald Livingstone; Norman Ruiz-Castaneda; Thomas V. Eagan; Marcos Perez.
School—Epiphany School, 5557 S.W. 84th St., Miami, 33143. Tel: 305-667-5251; Fax: 305-667-6828; Web: www.epiphanycatholicschool.com. Ms. Ana Oliva, Prin. Lay Teachers 81; Sisters Servants of the Immaculate Heart of Mary 1; Students 901.
Catechesis Religious Program—Tel: 305-665-0037; Email: mimip@epiphanycatholicschool.com. Isabel Prellezo, D.R.E. Students 245.
Endowment—Church of the Epiphany Parish Endowment Trust, 9401 Biscayne Blvd., 33138. Tel: 305-762-1294; Email: mcasciato@theadom.org. Mike Casciato, Contact Person.

9—ST. FRANCIS XAVIER (1927) Merged with and sacramental records at Gesu Parish, Miami.

10—GESU (1896)
118 N.E. 2nd St., Miami, 33132. Tel: 305-379-1424; Fax: 305-372-9544; Email: gesuchurch@yahoo.com. Revs. Eduardo Alvarez, S.J.; Sergio Figueredo, S.J., Parochial Vicar; James L. Lambert, S.J., Parochial Vicar; James A. Marshall, S.J., Parochial Vicar; Sr. Julia Barreto, O.P., D.R.E.
Catechesis Religious Program—Tel: 305-374-6099. Students 38.

11—GOOD SHEPHERD (1977)
14187 S.W. 72nd St., Miami, 33183.
Tel: 305-385-4320; Fax: 305-456-1341; Email: sue@gscatholic.org; Web: www.gscatholic.org. Very Rev. Jesus J. Arias, V.F.; Rev. Edivaldo Da Silva Oliviera, Parochial Vicar; Deacons Julio Zayas; Arthur Merkel; Guillermo Dutra.
School—Good Shepherd School, (Grades PreK-8), Tel: 305-385-7002; Email: office@good-shepherd-school.org; Web: www.good-shepherd-school.org. Mrs. Clara Cabrera, Prin. Lay Teachers 18; Students 255.
Catechesis Religious Program—
Tel: 305-385-4320, Ext. 212; Email: lydia@gscatholic.org. Lydia Navarro, C.R.E. Students 565.

12—HOLY REDEEMER (1950) (African American)
1301 N.W. 71st St., Miami, 33147. Tel: 305-691-1701; Email: hredeemr@bellsouth.net; Web: www.holyredeemercatholicchurch.com. Rev. Alexander Ekechukwu, C.S.Sp.
Catechesis Religious Program—Monique Delancy, D.R.E. Students 28.

13—ST. JAMES (1952)
540 N.W. 132nd St., Miami, 33168.
Tel: 305-681-7428; Fax: 305-685-0631; Web: www.stjamesnorthmiami.org. Rev. Msgr. Chanel Jeanty, J.C.L., V.G.; Rev. Juan Gomez Franyutty, Parochial Vicar.
School—St. James School, 601 N.W. 131st St., North Miami, 33168. Tel: 305-681-3822; Email: principal@stjamesmiami.net; Fax: 305-681-6435; Web: stjamesmiami.net. Sr. Stephanie Flynn, S.S.J., Prin. Lay Teachers 30; Sisters 1; Students 485.
Catechesis Religious Program—Tel: 305-364-5581. Mahalia Marcelin, D.R.E. Students 65.

14—ST. JOACHIM (1972)
11740 S.W. 192nd St., Miami, 33177.
Tel: 305-233-1278; Fax: 305-233-2573; Email: st.joachimcc@yahoo.com. Rev. Msgr. Roberto Garza.
Catechesis Religious Program—11720 S.W. 192nd St., Miami, 33029. Gloria Torres, D.R.E. Students 331.

15—ST. JOHN BOSCO (1962)
1358 N.W. First St., Miami, 33125.
Tel: 305-649-5464. Revs. Yader F. Centeno, Sch.P., (Nicaragua); Andy Lorenzo-Puga, Parochial Vicar; Deacon Alfredo Valle.
Catechesis Religious Program—Email: jalonso@sjbmiami.org. Joel Alonso, D.R.E. Students 183.

16—ST. JOHN NEUMANN (1980)
12125 S.W. 107th Ave., Miami, 33176.
Tel: 305-255-6642; Fax: 305-233-3742; Email: parishoffice@sjn-miami.org; Web: www.sjn-miami.org. Rev. Msgr. Pablo A. Navarro, V.F.; Rev. Matthew Gomez, Parochial Vicar; Deacons Robert Binder; Ralph Gazitua; Henri Gonzalez; Louis Phang Sang; Marco Fernandez; Jose Felipe Gomez.
School—St. John Neumann School, 12115 S.W. 107th Ave., Miami, 33176. Tel: 305-255-7315; Fax: 305-255-7316; Email: info@sjncs.org; Web: www.sjncs.org. Mrs. Maria Elena Vilas, Prin. Aides 8; Lay Teachers 29; Students 339.
Catechesis Religious Program—Tel: 305-253-3081; Email: dre@sjn-miami.org. John Fernandez, D.R.E. Students 578.

17—ST. KEVIN (1963)
12525 S.W. 42nd St., Miami, 33175.
Tel: 305-223-0633; Fax: 305-554-9950; Email: stkev@bellsouth.net. Revs. Jesus Saldana; Julio Fernandez, S.D.B., Parochial Vicar; Isidro Marcelino Perez, (Cuba) Parochial Vicar; Deacons Robert B. Dinsmore; Michael Fresneda.
School—St. Kevin School, 4001 S.W. 127 Ave., Miami, 33175. Tel: 305-227-7571; Fax: 305-227-7574; Email: stkevin@stks.org; Web: www.stks.org. Dr. Mayra R. Constantino, Prin.; Dr. Sharyn D. Henderson, Vice Prin. Lay Teachers 44; Students 701.
Catechesis Religious Program—Tel: 305-223-2469; Email: reled@stkevinrep.org; Web: www.stkevinrep.org. Mr. Daniel Mercado, C.R.E.; Mrs. Alidi Rivera, C.R.E. Students 415.

18—ST. KIERAN (1967)
3605 S. Miami Ave., Miami, 33133.
Tel: 786-254-2543; Fax: 786-254-2545; Email: secretary@stkierancatholicchurch.org. Revs. Adelson Moreira, O.S.S.T., Parochial Vicar; Carlos J. Cabrera, In Res.; Laurent Sterling, In Res.
Catechesis Religious Program—Tel: 786-333-3167; Email: lguerrero@stkierancatholicchurch.org. Lileida Guerrero, C.R.E. Students 35.

19—ST. LOUIS (1963)
7270 S.W. 120th St., Pinecrest, 33156.
Tel: 305-238-7562; Fax: 305-238-6844; Email: information@stlcatholic.org; Web: stlcatholic.org. Revs. Paul V. Vuturo; Gustavo Barros, Parochial Vicar; Henrick Jose, (India) Parochial Vicar; Pedro Toledo, In Res.; Deacons Thomas Hanlon; George Labelle; Alex Lam; John Peremenis; Jeffrey J. Reyes; Jose Villena; Robert Yglesias; James Dugard.
School—St. Louis School, (Grades PreK-8), Tel: 305-238-7562, Ext. 200; Fax: 305-238-4296; Email: egarcia@stlcatholic.org. Edward Garcia, Prin.; Julie Perdomo, Admin.
Legal Title: St. Louis Covenant School Lay Teachers 34; Students 525.
Catechesis Religious Program—
Tel: 305-238-7562, Ext. 1500; Email: mildred@stlcatholic.org. Mrs. Mildred Ratcliff, D.R.E. Students 487.

20—ST. MICHAEL THE ARCHANGEL (1947)
2987 W. Flagler St., Miami, 33135.
Tel: 305-649-1811; Fax: 305-642-6815; Email: agonzalez0761@yahoo.com; Web: www.stmichaelmiami.org. Rev. Francisco Gerardo Diaz; Deacon Ernesto Rodriguez.
School—St. Michael the Archangel School, (Grades PreK-8), 300 N.W. 28th Ave., Miami, 33125.
Tel: 305-642-6732; Fax: 305-649-5867; Email: Fermo@stmacs.org; Web: stmacs.org. Carmen Alfonso, Prin. Lay Teachers 30; Students 350.
Catechesis Religious Program—
Tel: 305-649-1811, Ext. 7011. Ramon Rivero, D.R.E. Students 167.

21—MOTHER OF CHRIST (1983)
14141 S.W. 26th St., Miami, 33175.
Tel: 305-559-6111; Email: info@motherofchrist.net; Web: motherofchrist.info. Revs. Jorge A. Carvajal, Parochial Admin.; Armando Tolosa, Parochial Vicar; Deacons Jose Leroy Martinez; Jose F. Rosado.
School—Mother of Christ School, (Grades PreK-8), Tel: 786-497-6111; Email: moc.principal@motherofchrist.net. Mrs. Rita Marti, Prin.; Mrs. Yesenia De La Torre, Vice Prin. Lay Teachers 15; Students 338.
Catechesis Religious Program—Tel: 305-559-0163. Laura Lantigua, D.R.E. Students 325.

22—NOTRE DAME D'HAITI (1981)
110 NE 62nd St., Miami, 33138. Tel: 305-751-6289; Email: info@notredamedhaiti.org; Web: www.notredamedhaiti.org. Rev. Reginald Jean-Mary.
Catechesis Religious Program—Tel: 786-597-3932; Email: rsllebreton@yahoo.com. Rosel Lebreton, D.R.E. Students 133.

23—OUR LADY OF DIVINE PROVIDENCE (1973)
10205 W. Flagler St., Miami, 33174.
Tel: 305-551-8113; Email: office@oldpmiami.org; Web: www.oldpmiami.org. Revs. Enrique J. Estrada; Pedro M. Corces, Parochial Vicar; Deacon Eduardo Panellas.
Catechesis Religious Program—
Tel: 305-551-8113, Ext. 2013; Email: zmurgado@oldpmiami.org. Zoila M. Murgado, D.R.E. Students 271.

24—OUR LADY OF GUADALUPE (2001)
11691 N.W. 25 St., Doral, 33172. Tel: 305-593-6123; Fax: 305-463-0542; Email: info@guadalupedoral.org; Web: www.guadalupedoral.org. Revs. Israel E. Mago; Luis Pavon, Parochial Vicar; Deacons William Bertot, Admin.; Manuel Jimenez; Juan Carlos Urquijo.
Catechesis Religious Program—
Tel: 305-593-6123, Ext. 204; Email: miguel.ruiz@guadalupedoral.org. Miguel Ruiz, D.R.E. Students 1,261.

25—OUR LADY OF LOURDES (1985)
11291 S.W. 142nd Ave., Miami, 33186.
Tel: 305-386-4121; Email: fanny@ololourdes.org. Rev. Msgr. Kenneth K. Schwanger, J.C.D.; Rev. Omar Ayubi Giraldo, Parochial Vicar; Deacons Michael Plummer, D.R.E.; Jose M. Naranjo; Isidoro Villa; Carlos Garcia; Ricardo Rauseo.
School—Our Lady of Lourdes School, 14000 S.W. 112th St., Miami, 33186. Tel: 305-386-8446; Fax: 305-386-6694; Email: thalfaker@ololjaguars.org; Web: www.ololjaguars.org. Thomas Halfaker, Prin.; Laura G. Sanchez, Asst. Prin. Lay Teachers 29; Students 487.

Catechesis Religious Program—Tel: 305-386-4121; Email: dcnplummer@ololourdes.org. Students 638.

26—OUR LADY OF THE HOLY ROSARY (1959) Merged with St. Richard, Miami to form Our Lady of the Holy Rosary-St. Richard Church, Miami.

27—OUR LADY OF THE HOLY ROSARY - ST. RICHARD CHURCH (2010)
7500 S.W. 152nd St., Palmetto Bay, 33157.
Tel: 305-233-8711; Email: info@hrsrcs.org; Web: www.hrsrcs.org. Revs. William J. Sullivan, O.SS.T.; Daniel Houde, O.S.S.T., Parochial Vicar; Deacon Robert F. O'Malley Jr.; Mrs. Rosa Scott, Music Min.
School—Our Lady of the Holy Rosary - St. Richard Catholic School, 18455 Franjo Rd., Cutler Bay, 33157. Tel: 305-235-5442; Fax: 305-235-5670; Web: www.hrsrcs.org. Ninnette Lozano, Prin.; Floredenis Brown, Vice Prin.; Mrs. Nancy Kennedy, Registrar. Lay Teachers 22; Students 286.
Catechesis Religious Program—
Tel: 305-233-8711, Ext. 115; Email: potero@hrsrcs.org. Mrs. Alicia Mendes, Registrar; Paul Otero, D.R.E. Students 364.

28—SS. PETER AND PAUL (1938)
900 S.W. 26th Rd., Miami, 33129. Tel: 305-858-2621; Fax: 305-858-8073; Email: elvyl2910@hotmail.com. Revs. Juan M. Lopez; Juan Luis Sanchez, Parochial Vicar.
School—SS. Peter and Paul School, 1435 S.W. 12th Ave., Miami, 33129. Tel: 305-858-3722; Fax: 305-856-4322; Email: cmorales@stspeter-paul.org; Web: www.stspeter-paul.org. Dr. Carlota Morales, Prin. Lay Teachers 30; Students 420.
Catechesis Religious Program—Email: ltm310@yahoo.com. Leyla Mazpule, D.R.E. Students 131.

29—PRINCE OF PEACE (1987)
12800 N.W. 6th St., Miami, 33182. Tel: 305-559-3171 ; Email: info@popmiami.net. Revs. Giovanni de Jesus Pena; Joaquin Perez-Pupo, (Cuba) In Res., (Retired); Deacons Manuel Castellanos; Jorge Prieto; Lazaro Ulloa.
Catechesis Religious Program—Email: vlprinceofpeace@yahoo.com. Vivian Lorenzo, D.R.E. Students 188.

30—ST. RAYMOND (1969)
3475 S.W. 17th St., Miami, 33145. Tel: 305-446-2427; Fax: 305-445-7448; Email: pastor@straymondchurch.com; Email: secretary@straymondchurch.com; Web: www.straymondchurch.com. Rev. Francisco J. Hernandez.
Catechesis Religious Program—Tel: 305-646-1130; Email: srelena@piercedhearts.org. Sr. Elena A. Castillo, S.C.T.J.M., D.R.E. Students 134.

31—ST. RICHARD (1969) Merged with Our Lady of the Holy Rosary, Miami to form Our Lady of the Holy Rosary-St. Richard, Miami.

32—ST. ROBERT BELLARMINE (1968) Merged with and sacramental records at Corpus Christi Parish, Miami.

33—ST. THOMAS THE APOSTLE CHURCH (1959)
7377 S.W. 64th St., Miami, 33143. Tel: 305-665-5600; Fax: 305-662-9034; Email: pastor@stamiami.org; Email: JCSalazar@stamiami.org; Web: www.stamiami.org. Revs. Alejandro J. Rodriguez Artola; Juan Carlos Salazar Gomez, Parochial Vicar; Deacons Carlos Pulido; Carlos Charur Jr.
School—St. Thomas the Apostle School,
Tel: 305-661-8591, Ext. 301; Fax: 305-661-2181; Email: lfigueredo@stamiami.com. Mrs. Lisa Figueredo, Prin. Lay Teachers 36; Students 472.
Catechesis Religious Program—Email: tgonzalez@stamiami.org. Tania Gonzalez, D.R.E. Students 235.

34—ST. TIMOTHY (1960)
5400 S.W. 102nd Ave., Miami, 33165.
Tel: 305-274-8224; Email: frontdesk@sainttimothycatholic.org; Email: pastor@sainttimothycatholic.org; Web: www.sainttimothycatholic.org. Revs. Jorge L. Rodriguez de la Viuda; John Wladyslaw Juszczak, C.Ss.R., (Poland) Parochial Vicar; Miguel Angel Blanco, Parochial Vicar; Deacons Nelson Diaz; Fernando Bestard; Manuel Buigas; Manuel Canovaca.
School—St. Timothy School, Tel: 305-274-8229; Email: information@sttimothymiami.org; Web: www.sttimothymiami.org. Mrs. Annie Seiglie, Prin. Lay Teachers 34; Students 637; Clergy / Religious Teachers 1.
Child Care—Sister Carolyn Learning Center,
Tel: 305-274-8229; Email: bperdomo@sttimothytmiami.orhg. Ms. Barbara Perdomo, Dir. (PreK-2) Lay Teachers 12; Students 70.
Catechesis Religious Program—Tel: 305-274-8225. Mrs. Dennys Cabrera, D.R.E. Students 340.

35—ST. VINCENT DE PAUL (1962) Merged with and sacramental records at Saint Rose of Lima Parish, Miami Shores.

36—VISITATION (1956)
100 N.E. 191st St., Miami, 33179. Tel: 305-652-3624; Fax: 305-652-5207; Email: office@visitationmiami.org. Rev. Msgr. George Puthusseril, J.C.D.
Catechesis Religious Program—Email: ccddre@visitationmiami.org. Mrs. Marcia Waite, D.R.E. Students 130.

METROPOLITAN DADE COUNTY

COCONUT GROVE, ST. HUGH (1959) (Hispanic)
3460 Royal Rd., Coconut Grove, 33133.
Tel: 305-444-8363; Email: sthughchrurch@st-hugh.org; Web: sthughmiami.com. Revs. Luis Roger Largaespada; Damian Flanagan, Parochial Vicar.
School—St. Hugh School, Tel: 305-448-5602; Email: sthugh@sthugh.org; Web: www.sthughmiami.org. Mrs. Mary E. Fernandez, Ed.S., Prin. Lay Teachers 35; Students 312.
Catechesis Religious Program—Tel: 305-301-1884; Email: dre@st-hugh.org. Patricia Zapatero, D.R.E. Students 314.

CORAL GABLES

1—ST. AUGUSTINE (1969) [CEM]
1400 Miller Rd., Coral Gables, 33146.
Tel: 305-661-1648; Web: www.saintaugustinechurch.org.
Catechesis Religious Program—Email: education@saintaugustinechurch.org. Ms. Sofia Acosta, D.R.E. Students 210.

2—LITTLE FLOWER (1926)
2711 Indian Mound Tr., Coral Gables, 33134.
Tel: 305-446-9950; Email: cvgmia@gmail.com. Very Rev. Michael W. Davis, M.Ed.; Rev. Luis Flores, Parochial Vicar; Deacons Miguel Parlade; Roberto Fleitas.
School—Little Flower School, 2701 Indian Mound Tr., Coral Gables, 33134. Tel: 305-446-1738; Fax: 305-446-2877; Email: principal@stscg.org. Sr. Rosalie Nagy, O.C.D., Prin. Lay Teachers 46; Sisters 4; Students 932; Religious Teachers 3.
Catechesis Religious Program—
Tel: 305-446-9950, Ext. 307; Email: jsantibanez@cotlf.org. Jorge Santibanez, D.R.E. Students 362.

HIALEAH

1—ST. BENEDICT (1973)
650 W. 80th St., Hialeah, 33014-4125.
Tel: 305-558-2150. 701 W. 77th St., Hialeah, 33014. Rev. Julio E. De Jesus; Deacon Emilio Blanco.
Catechesis Religious Program—Tel: 305-557-2511; Email: sori.stbenedictreled@gmail.com. Sori Govin, D.R.E. Students 160.

2—ST. CECILIA (1971)
1040 W. 29th St., Hialeah, 33012. Tel: 305-883-0003; Email: saintceciliacatholicchurch@gmail.com; Web: www.miamiarch.org/CatholicDiocese.php?op=Church_1112202597886_main. Very Rev. Emanuele DeNigris; Revs. Antonio Vicente, (Brazil) Parochial Vicar; Ivan M. Rodriguez, Parochial Vicar. Redemptoris Mater Missionary Seminary resides adjacent to St Cecilia; priests minister in both entities.
Catechesis Religious Program—Tel: 786-355-5423; Email: clisellot@hotmail.com. Lisellot Casasnovas, D.R.E. Students 90.

3—IMMACULATE CONCEPTION (1954)
4497 W. First Ave., Hialeah, 33012.
Tel: 305-822-2011; Fax: 305-821-3481; Email: icrectory@icsmiami.org. Revs. Manuel Alvarez; Ivan Toledo, (Cuba) Parochial Vicar; Deacons Manuel Alfonso; Felix Gonzalez.
School—Immaculate Conception School, 125 W. 45th St., Hialeah, 33012. Tel: 305-822-6461; Fax: 305-822-0289; Email: icschool@miamiarch.org. Mrs. Victoria Leon, Prin. Lay Teachers 27; Students 410.
Catechesis Religious Program—Tel: 305-823-9563; Email: nstanley@icsmiami.org. Nubia Stanley, D.R.E. Students 297.

4—ST. JOHN THE APOSTLE (1945)
475 E. 4th St., Hialeah, 33010. Tel: 305-888-9769; Fax: 305-888-9341; Email: sjamiami@gmail.com. Revs. Hector A. Perez; Salvador Diaz Guerra, Parochial Vicar; Deacon Julke Llorens.
School—St. John the Apostle School, Email: frhectorperez@yahoo.com. Mr. Robert F. Hernandez, Prin. Lay Teachers 14; Students 215.
Catechesis Religious Program—Email: mssarmiento@aol.com. Rita M. Sarmiento, RCIA Coord. Students 48.

5—MOTHER OF OUR REDEEMER (1988)
8445 N.W. 186th St., Hialeah, 33015.
Tel: 305-829-6141; Web: www.motherofourredeemer.org. Rev. Juan P. Hernandez-Alonso, (Spain).
School—Mother of Our Redeemer School, (Grades PreK-8), Tel: 306-829-3988; Fax: 305-829-3019; Email: acasariego@moorsch.org; Web: www.moorsch.org. Ms. Ana Casariego, Prin. Lay Teachers 16; Students 228.
Catechesis Religious Program—Tel: 305-356-8346; Email: LMARTORELLA@MOTHEROFOURREDEEMER.ORG. Liliana Martorella, D.R.E. Students 303.

6—SAN LAZARO (1982)
4400 W. 18 Ave., Hialeah, 33012. Tel: 305-556-1717; Fax: 305-556-8918; Email: parishsecretary@sanlazaro17.org; Web: sanlazaro17.org. Revs. Jose Espino; David Smith, In Res., (Retired).
Catechesis Religious Program—Tel: 305-558-4078; Email: cdcdirector@sanlazaro17.org. Mrs. Maritza Bonachea, C.R.E. Students 238.

7—SANTA BARBARA (1987)
6801 W. 30th Ave., Hialeah, 33018.
Tel: 305-556-4442; Tel: 305-698-5574;
Fax: 305-558-7256; Email: pilicamacho@hotmail.com. Rev. Alvaro Huertas, (Colombia).
Catechesis Religious Program—
Tel: 305-556-4442, Ext. 104; Email: pilicamacho@hotmail.com. Mrs. Carmen Camacho, D.R.E.; Libia Rodriguez, D.R.E. Students 194.

HOMESTEAD, SACRED HEART (1929)
106 S.E. First Dr., Homestead, 33030-7322.
Tel: 305-247-4405, Ext. 230. Revs. Luis R. Rivera; Jean Claude Jean-Philippe, Parochial Vicar.
Catechesis Religious Program—Tel: 786-272-2531; Email: yolanda@sacredhearthomestead.org. Yolanda Del Rivero, D.R.E.; Mr. John Mark Kaldahl, Youth Min. Students 613.

KEY BISCAYNE, ST. AGNES (1954)
100 Harbor Dr., Key Biscayne, 33149.
Tel: 305-361-2351; Email: info@stagneskb.org; Web: www.stakb.org. Revs. Juan Carlos Paguaga; Andrzej Foltyn, Parochial Vicar; Deacons Edgardo Farias; Adrian Zapatero.
School—St. Agnes School, (Grades PreK-8), 122 Harbor Dr., Key Biscayne, 33149. Tel: 305-361-3245; Fax: 305-361-6329; Email: ctorres@stagneskb.org; Email: srivera@stagneskb.org; Email: mheras@stagneskb.org; Web: www.stakb.org. Mrs. Susana T. Rivera, Prin.; Ms. Monica Garcia, Vice Prin.; Mrs. Cristina Torres, Reg. Lay Teachers 40; Students 497; Clergy / Religious Teachers 2.
Catechesis Religious Program—Tel: 305-361-1378; Email: akurzan@stagneskb.org; Web: www.stakb.org. Sr. Maria Andrea Oliver, S.C.T.J.M., D.R.E.; Mrs. Alida Kurzan, Admin. Students 580.

LEISURE CITY, ST. MARTIN DE PORRES CATHOLIC CHURCH (1990) (Hispanic)
14881 S.W. 288th St., Leisure City, 33033.
Tel: 305-248-5355; Fax: 305-245-3047; Email: stmartindeporrescc@gmail.com. Rev. Joaquin Rodriguez.
Catechesis Religious Program—Carmen Colon, D.R.E.; Omar Carrero, RCIA Coord. Students 320.

MIAMI BEACH

1—ST. FRANCIS DE SALES (1964)
621 Alton Rd., Miami Beach, 33139.
Tel: 305-672-0093; Fax: 305-673-8559; Email: secretary@saintfrancisonthebeach.com. Rev. Gabriel Vigues; Deacon Jose Irrizarry.
Catechesis Religious Program—Tel: 305-767-6582; Email: ccdstfrancis@gmail.com. Alicia Martinez, D.R.E. Students 89.

2—ST. JOSEPH (1942)
8670 Byron Ave., Miami Beach, 33141.
Tel: 305-866-6567; Fax: 305-864-1069; Email: cwilliamson@stjosephmiamibeach.com; Web: www.stjosephmiamibeach.com. Revs. Juan J. Sosa; Adonis Gonzalez, Parochial Vicar.
Catechesis Religious Program—Email: airizarry@stjosephmiamibeach.com. Adam Irizarry, D.R.E. Students 209.

3—ST. PATRICK (1926)
3716 Garden Ave., Miami Beach, 33140.
Tel: 305-531-1124; Email: parish@stpatrickmiamibeach.com; Web: stpatrickmiamibeach.com. Revs. Roberto M. Cid; Freddy A. Yara, Parochial Vicar.
School—St. Patrick School, (Grades K-8), 3700 Garden Ave., Miami Beach, 33140. Tel: 305-534-4616 ; Fax: 305-538-5463; Email: school@stpatrickmiamibeach.com; Email: bmoro@stpatrickmiamibeach.com; Web: www.stpatrickmiamibeach.com. Bertha Moro, Prin. Lay Teachers 19; Students 320.
Catechesis Religious Program—
Tel: 305-531-1124, Ext. 1077; Tel: 305-563-8546; Email: jmarcazzo@stpatrickmiamibeach.com. Mr. Jon Pierre Marcazzo, D.R.E. Students 129.

MIAMI GARDENS

1—ST. MONICA (1959)
3490 N.W. 191st St., Miami Gardens, 33056.
Tel: 305-621-9846; Fax: 305-621-5608; Email: pastor@saintmonica.org; Web: www.saintmonica.org. Rev. Samuel Muodiaju, C.S.Sp., (Nigeria); Deacon Marco Rosales.
Catechesis Religious Program—Email: isjrbblm@aol.com. Mrs. Doris Hernandez, D.R.E. Students 51.

2—ST. PHILIP NERI CATHOLIC CHURCH (1953)
15700 N.W. 20th Avenue Rd., Miami Gardens, 33054. Tel: 305-705-2010; Fax: 786-320-6055; Email: stphilipneri15700@comcast.net. Rev. Fidelis Nwankwo, C.S.Sp.
Catechesis Religious Program—Ms. Tricia Hendricks, D.R.E. Students 10.

MIAMI LAKES, OUR LADY OF THE LAKES (1967)

15801 N.W. 67 Ave., Miami Lakes, 33014.
Tel: 305-558-2202; Fax: 305-558-2631; Email: jalvarez@ollnet.com. Very Rev. Jose Alvarez, V.F.; Rev. Oswaldo Agudelo, Parochial Vicar; Deacons Roger Currier; Albert Mindel; Carlos Ramirez; Juan Gonzalez.
School—Our Lady of the Lakes School, 6600 Miami Lakeway N., Miami Lakes, 33014. Tel: 305-362-5315; Fax: 305-362-4573; Email: bpicazo@ollnet.com; Web: www.ollnet.com. Ricardo Briz, Prin. Clergy 1; Lay Teachers 34; Students 479.
Catechesis Religious Program—Email: jvazquez@ollnet.com. Josefina Vazquez, D.R.E. Students 234.

MIAMI SHORES

1—ST. MARTHA (1970)
9221 Biscayne Blvd., 33138. Tel: 305-751-0005; Fax: 305-756-1161; Email: frontoffice@stmarthamiami.com; Web: www.stmarthamiami.com. Rev. Lazarus J. Govin.
Catechesis Religious Program—Danilo Recinos, D.R.E. Students 70.

2—ST. ROSE OF LIMA (1946)
415 N.E. 105th St., 33138. Tel: 305-758-0539; Email: mpinder@srlchurch.com; Email: frgeorge@srlchurch.com; Web: www.stroseoflimamiamishores.org. Revs. George Packuvettithara; Manual Puga, J.C.L., Parochial Vicar.
School—St. Rose of Lima School, (Grades PreK-8), 425 N.E. 105th St., Miami, 33138. Tel: 305-751-4257; Email: sbrown@srlschool.com; Web: www.srlschool.com. Dr. Stephen Brown, Prin. Lay Teachers 30; Students 479.
Catechesis Religious Program—
Tel: 305-758-0539, Ext. 408; Email: amolleda@srlschool.com. Annie Molleda, D.R.E. Students 160.

NORTH MIAMI, HOLY FAMILY (1950)
14500 N.E. 11 Ave., North Miami, 33161.
Tel: 305-947-5043; Tel: 305-947-1471;
Fax: 305-949-5591; Email: hfccmia@gmail.com; Email: secretary.holyfamilynorthmiami@gmail.com. Rev. Fritzner Bellonce.
School—Holy Family School, 14650 N.E. 12th Ave., North Miami, 33161. Tel: 305-947-6535;
Fax: 305-947-1826; Email: droberts@holyfamilynorthmiami.org. Mrs. Doreen Roberts, Prin. Lay Teachers 15; Students 246.
Catechesis Religious Program—Tel: 305-947-7739; Fax: 305-947-1417. Mrs. Victor Manuela, D.R.E. Students 86.

NORTH MIAMI BEACH, ST. LAWRENCE (1956)
2200 N.E. 191st St., North Miami Beach, 33180.
Tel: 305-932-3560; Email: stlawrenceparish@stlaw.org; Email: pastor@stlaw.org. Rev. Cletus Oluwafemi Omode, Parochial Admin.; Deacon Clyde McFarland.
School—St. Lawrence School, (Grades K-8),
Tel: 305-932-4912; Email: schooloffice@stlaw.org. Mrs. Dian Hyatt, M.S., Prin. Lay Teachers 14; Students 146.
Child Care—Child Care Center, Tel: 305-932-5366; Fax: 305-932-2346; Email: stlawrenceccc@aol.com; Web: www.stlawrencechildcarecenter.com. Ms. Iliana Medolla, Dir. Lay Teachers 10; Students 63.
Catechesis Religious Program—Tel: 305-931-6650; Email: rel_ed@stlaw.org. Joanne Lambert, M.A., D.R.E. Students 152.

OPA LOCKA, OUR LADY OF PERPETUAL HELP CHURCH (1954) Merged with and sacramental records at Saint James Parish, North Miami.

PRINCETON, ST. ANN MISSION (1961)
Mailing Address: P.O. Box 924884, Princeton, 33092-4884. Tel: 305-258-6998; Fax: 305-258-0834; Email: misionsantaananaranja@gmail.com. 13875 S.W. 264 St., Naranja, 33032. Rev. Rafael Cos.
Catechesis Religious Program—Tel: 786-410-5168. Sr. Martha Maria Gomez-Chow, S.C.T.J.M., D.R.E. Students 333.

SUNNY ISLES BEACH, ST. MARY MAGDALEN (1955)
17775 N. Bay Rd., Sunny Isles Beach, 33160.
Tel: 305-931-0600; Fax: 305-931-0601; Email: parishoffice@stmmsib.org; Web: stmmsib.org. Revs. Bernard G. Kirlin, V.F.; Francis Nwakile, In Res.
Catechesis Religious Program—Mrs. Maria Cortese, D.R.E. Students 132.

VIRGINIA GARDENS, BLESSED TRINITY (1952)
4020 Curtiss Pkwy., Virginia Gardens, 33166.
Tel: 305-871-5780; Email: reception@blessed-trinity.org. Revs. Jose N. Alfaro; Pawel Duda, Parochial Vicar; Deacons Dennis E. Jordan; Jose Aleman; Javier Inda.
School—Blessed Trinity School, (Grades PreK-8),
Tel: 305-871-5766; Fax: 305-876-1755; Email: btschool@blessed-trinity.org; Web: www.blessed-trinity.org. Mrs. Maria Teresa Perez, Prin. Lay Teachers 30; Religious 1; Students 237.
Catechesis Religious Program—Olga Venegas, D.R.E. Students 164.

OUTSIDE METROPOLITAN DADE COUNTY

BIG PINE KEY, MONROE CO., ST. PETER (1962)
31300 Overseas Hwy., P.O. Box 430657, Big Pine Key, 33043. Tel: 305-872-2537; Email: nancy@stpeterbpk.org; Email: frjets@stpeterbpk.org; Web: www.stpeterbpk.org. Rev. Jesus S. (Jets) Medina.
Catechesis Religious Program—Email: nancy@stpeterbpk.org. Nancy McCrosson, D.R.E. Students 60.
Mission—Sugarloaf Firehouse.

COCONUT CREEK, BROWARD CO., ST. LUKE (1985) Merged with and sacramental records at Saint Vincent Parish, Margate.

CORAL SPRINGS, BROWARD CO.

1—ST. ANDREW (1969)
9950 N.W. 29th St., Coral Springs, 33065-6103.
Tel: 954-752-3950; Fax: 954-752-3986; Email: parish@saccs.org; Web: www.standrewparish.org. Rev. Msgr. Michael A. Souckar, J.C.D.; Revs. Isaac Arickappalil, Parochial Vicar; Pedro Freitez, Parochial Vicar; Deacons Frank Gonzalez; Denis Mieyal; Stephen Rynkiewicz.
School—St. Andrew School, 9990 N.W. 29th St., Coral Springs, 33065. Tel: 954-753-1280;
Fax: 954-753-1933; Email: khughes@saccs.org. Kristen Hughes, Prin. Lay Teachers 24; Students 363.
Catechesis Religious Program—Tel: 954-905-6324; Tel: 954-905-6332; Email: bcastro@saccs.org. Beatriz Castro, D.R.E.; Cecilia Sousa, D.R.E. Students 530.

2—ST. ELIZABETH ANN SETON (1985)
1401 Coral Ridge Dr., Coral Springs, 33071.
Tel: 954-753-3330; Fax: 954-753-8442; Email: setonparishoffice@gmail.com; Web: www.stelizabethannseton.org. Revs. Edward M. Kelly; Attila Frohlich, Parochial Vicar; Deacons John Friel; Mario Lopez.
Catechesis Religious Program—Tel: 954-345-7071; Email: setonre@gmail.com. Gladys Jacobs, D.R.E. Students 541.

DANIA BEACH, BROWARD CO.

1—CHURCH OF THE RESURRECTION (1958) Merged with and sacramental records at Saint Maurice Parish, Dania Beach.

2—ST. MAURICE AT RESURRECTION (1970) (French)
441 N. E. 2nd St., Dania, 33004. Tel: 954-961-7777; Fax: 954-961-4358; Email: vicki.smarcc@gmail.com; Email: jpierre.smarcc@gmail.com; Web: www.stmauriceatresurrection.org. Rev. Msgr. Jean Pierre.
Catechesis Religious Program—Tel: 954-990-9573; Email: msashley.stmccd@gmail.com. Ashley Ronnan, D.R.E. Students 50.

DAVIE, BROWARD CO., SAINT DAVID (1974)
3900 S. University Dr., Davie, 33328.
Tel: 954-475-8046; Fax: 954-370-0819; Email: stdavidchurch@saintdavid.org. Rev. Steven O'Hala, S.T.D.
School—Saint David School, Tel: 954-472-7086; Email: schoolinformation@saintdavid.org; Web: www.saintdavid.org. Mrs. Jane Broder, Prin. Lay Teachers 30; Students 435.
Catechesis Religious Program—Tel: 954-475-1521; Tel: 954-559-6379; Email: ppotenza@saintdavid.org; Email: mcarter-waren@stu.edu. Pat Potenza, D.R.E.; Mrs. Mary Carter Waren, D.R.E. Students 304.

DEERFIELD BEACH, BROWARD CO.

1—ST. AMBROSE (1962)
380 S. Federal Hwy., Deerfield Beach, 33441.
Tel: 954-427-2225; Fax: 954-421-1638; Email: stambrosedeerfield@yahoo.com; Web: stambrosedeerfieldbeach.com. Revs. Dariousz Zarebski, S.D.S., Vicar Econome; Long Do, Parochial Vicar.
School—St. Ambrose School, (Grades PreK-8), 363 S.E. 12th Ave., Deerfield Beach, 33441.
Tel: 954-427-2226; Email: principal.stambrose@gmail.com; Web: stambrosecs.org. Mrs. Lisa Dodge, Prin. Lay Teachers 14; Students 234.
Catechesis Religious Program—Email: stambrosere@gmail.com. Donna Gonzalez, D.R.E. Students 150.

2—OUR LADY OF MERCY (1974)
5201 N. Military Tr., Deerfield Beach, 33064.
Tel: 954-421-3246; Email: olmercy2004@att.net. Very Rev. Kenneth D. Whittaker, J.C.L., V.F.
Catechesis Religious Program—Students 52.

FORT LAUDERDALE, BROWARD CO.

1—ST. ANTHONY (1921)
901 N.E. 2nd St., Fort Lauderdale, 33301.
Tel: 954-463-4614; Fax: 954-527-5411; Email: churchoffice@stanthonyftl.org; Web: www.saintanthonyfl.org. Revs. Michael Grady; Kris Bartos, Parochial Vicar; Julio R. Solano, Parochial Vicar.
School—St. Anthony School, 820 N.E. Third St., Fort Lauderdale, 33301. Tel: 954-467-7747;
Fax: 954-467-9908; Email: t.maus@stanthonyftl.org; Web: www.saintanthonyschoolfl.org. Mrs. Terry Maus, Prin. Lay Teachers 32; Students 474.
Catechesis Religious Program—Tel: 954-467-7749. Mrs. Patricia Solenski, D.R.E. Students 165.

2—ST. BONAVENTURE aka St. Bonaventure Catholic Church (1985)
1301 S.W. 136th Ave., Davie, 33325-4300.
Tel: 954-476-5200; Fax: 954-424-9505; Email: stbonadmin@aol.com; Email: lkempinski@stbonaventurechurch.com; Email: smcrea@stbonaventurechurch.com; Web: www.stbonaventurechurch.com. Rev. Edmond Prendergast; Deacons Joseph M. Pearce; Domingo Vasquez; Nestor Cardenas.
School—St. Bonaventure School, (Grades PreK-8), Tel: 954-476-5200; Fax: 954-476-5203; Web: sbcs.weconnect.com. Lisa Kempinski, Prin. Lay Teachers 32; Students 661; Total Staff 67; Clergy / Religious Teachers 2.
Catechesis Religious Program—Tel: 954-476-5204; Email: smccrea@stbonaventurechurch.com. Susan McCrea, D.R.E. Students 863.

3—ST. CLEMENT (1954)
2975 N. Andrews Ave., Fort Lauderdale, 33311.
Tel: 954-563-1183; Fax: 954-564-6628; Email: stclement@ymail.com. Rev. Robes C. Charles.
Catechesis Religious Program—Tel: 954-563-2838. Sr. Anne Stinfil, D.R.E. Students 242.

4—DIVINE MERCY MISSION (1980) Merged with and sacramental records at Saint Clement Parish, Fort Lauderdale.

5—ST. HELEN (1968)
3033 N.W. 33rd Ave., Lauderdale Lakes, 33311.
Tel: 954-731-7314; Fax: 954-733-0023; Email: fatherlucien@sainthelen.net; Email: mchery@sainthelen.net; Web: www.sthelencatholicchurch.net. Rev. Lucien Eugene Pierre.
School—St. Helen School, (Grades PreK-8), 3340 W. Oakland Park Blvd., Fort Lauderdale, 33311.
Tel: 954-739-7094; Fax: 954-739-0797; Email: stascillo@sainthelen.net; Email: fbarrat@sainthelen.net; Web: www.sthelencatholicchurch.net. Stephanie Tascillo, Prin.; Farah Barrat, Vice Prin. Lay Teachers 15; Students 215.
Catechesis Religious Program—Email: hchamorro@sainthelen.net; Email: cdiaz@sainthelen.net. Mr. Hans Chamorro, D.R.E. Students 246.

6—ST. JEROME (1960)
2533 S.W. 9th Ave., Fort Lauderdale, 33315.
Tel: 954-525-4133; Email: church@stjfl.org. Rev. Luis Ardiel Rivero; Deacon Frank B. O'Gorman.
School—St. Jerome School, 2601 S.W. 9th Ave., Fort Lauderdale, 33315. Tel: 954-524-1990;
Fax: 954-524-7439; Email: office@stjfl.org; Email: school@stjfl.org; Web: www.stjfl.org. Mrs. Stephanie Murphy, Prin. Lay Teachers 20; Students 195.
Catechesis Religious Program—
Tel: 954-525-4133, Ext. 3040; Email: arojas@stjfl.org; Email: jrojas@stjfl.org. Ms. Alexandra Rojas, D.R.E.; Mrs. Julie Rojas, D.R.E. Students 90.

7—ST. JOHN THE BAPTIST CATHOLIC CHURCH (1969)
Tel: 954-771-8950; Fax: 954-771-4178; Email: church@stjohncc.org; Web: www.stjohncc.org. Rev. Msgr. Vincent T. Kelly; Rev. William H. Bowles, Parochial Vicar.
Catechesis Religious Program—Louise Cole-Reeser, D.R.E. Students 171.

8—OUR LADY QUEEN OF MARTYRS (1956)
2731 S.W. 11 Ct., Fort Lauderdale, 33312.
Tel: 954-583-8725; Fax: 954-583-9315; Email: regi1946@bellsouth.net. Rev. Flavio Montes.
School—Our Lady Queen of Martyrs School, 2785 S.W. 11th Ct., Fort Lauderdale, 33312.
Tel: 954-583-8112; Fax: 954-797-4984; Web: ourlqm.com. Ms. Althea Mossop, Prin. Lay Teachers 23; Students 285.
Catechesis Religious Program—Students 126.

9—ST. PIUS X (1959)
2500 N.E. 33rd Ave., Fort Lauderdale, 33305.
Tel: 954-564-1763; Fax: 954-568-2212; Email: office@stpiusxfl.org; Web: www.stpiusxfl.org. Rev. Biju Vells.
Catechesis Religious Program—

10—ST. SEBASTIAN (1959)
2000 S.E. 25th Ave., Fort Lauderdale, 33316.
Tel: 954-524-9344; Fax: 954-524-9347; Email: info@stsebastianfl.org; Web: www.stsebastianfl.org. Rev. Msgr. James F. Fetscher.
Catechesis Religious Program—Email: annie@stsebastianfl.org. Anne M. Gardner, D.R.E. Students 9.

HALLANDALE, BROWARD CO.

1—ST. CHARLES BORROMEO (1968) Merged with and sacramental records at Saint Matthew Parish, Hallandale Beach.

2—ST. MATTHEW (1959) [CEM]
542 Blue Heron Dr., Hallandale Beach, 33009.
Tel: 954-458-1590; Fax: 954-458-0612; Email: lois@saintmatthewcc.com; Email: fr_ayala@saintmatthewcc.com; Web: www.smatt.org. Rev. Robert M. Ayala.
Catechesis Religious Program—Email: Bworon12@gmail.com. Barbara Woroniecki, D.R.E. Students 93.

HALLANDALE BEACH, BROWARD CO., OUR LADY OF LA VANG VIETNAMESE CATHOLIC MISSION aka Our Lady

of La Vang
123 N.W. 6th Ave., Hallandale Beach, 33009.
Tel: 954-374-9100; Email: longknguyen14@gmail.com. Rev. Joseph Long Nguyen.
Catechesis Religious Program—Tel: 954-665-7572; Email: bnc7897@gmail.com. Kim Chung Nguyen, D.R.E. Students 220.

HOLLYWOOD, BROWARD CO.

1—ST. BERNADETTE (1959)
7450 Stirling Rd., Hollywood, 33024.
Tel: 954-432-5313; Tel: 954-432-7022;
Fax: 954-432-5344; Fax: 954-443-8030; Email: principal@stbcs.org; Email: dbuschman@stbernadettefl.com; Email: bagarcia19@gmail.com; Web: www.saintbernadettefl.org. Rev. Bryan A. Garcia.
School—St. Bernadette School, (Grades PreK-8), Tel: 954-432-7022; Email: principal@stbcs.org; Web: www.saintbernadettefl.org. Mrs. Maria Wagner, Prin. Clergy 1; Lay Teachers 18; Students 204.
Catechesis Religious Program—Tel: 954-432-6300; Email: sstettner@stbcs.org. Stacey Stettner, D.R.E. Students 77.

2—LITTLE FLOWER (1924)
1805 Pierce St., Hollywood, 33020. Tel: 954-922-3517; Fax: 954-922-6634; Email: littleflower_hwd@hotmail.com; Web: littleflowerhollywood.org. Very Rev. Thomas O'Dwyer, V.F.; Revs. Pierre Listo Charles, Parochial Vicar; Juan Antonio Tupiza, Parochial Vicar; Deacon William A. Watkins.
School—Little Flower School, 1843 Pierce St., Hollywood, 33020. Tel: 954-922-1217;
Fax: 954-927-8962; Email: lfshollywood@bellsouth.net; Web: www.littleflowerleopards.com. Mrs. Maureen McNulty, Prin. Deacons 1; Lay Teachers 15; Students 270.
Catechesis Religious Program—Rosalie Modzelewski, D.R.E. Students 106.

3—NATIVITY (1960) [CEM]
5220 Johnson St., Hollywood, 33021. Email: office@nativityhollywood.org; Web: www.nativityhollywood.org. Very Rev. David A. Zirilli, V.F.; Revs. Victor J. Babin, Parochial Vicar; Fernando Carmona, Parochial Vicar; Deacons Chandy Luka; Timothy Smith; Jorge Reyes.
School—Nativity School, (Grades PreK-8), 5200 Johnson St., Hollywood, 33021.
Tel: 954-987-3301, Ext. 221; Fax: 954-987-6368; Email: jbeane@nativitysch.com; Web: www.nativityknights.com. Mrs. Elena Ortiz, Prin.; Mrs. Judy Skehan, Vice Prin. Lay Teachers 43; Students 832.
Catechesis Religious Program—
Tel: 954-987-3300, Ext. 203; Email: melanie@nativityhollywood.org. Melanie Lerch, D.R.E. Students 302.

4—OUR LADY APARECIDA MISSION (1996) Merged with and sacramental records at Saint Vincent Parish, Margate.

KEY LARGO, MONROE CO., ST. JUSTIN MARTYR (1973)
105500 Overseas Hwy., Key Largo, 33037.
Tel: 305-451-1316; Fax: 305-451-4633; Email: parishsecretary@sjmkeylargo.org. Rev. Stephen J. Hilley.
Catechesis Religious Program—Email: nonnaz17@aol.com. Donna Roberts, D.R.E. Students 74.

KEY WEST, MONROE CO., ST. MARY STAR OF THE SEA BASILICA (1846)
1010 Windsor Ln., Key West, 33040.
Tel: 305-294-1018; Email: stmary@stmarykeywest.com; Web: www.stmarykeywest.com. Very Revs. John C. Baker, V.F.; Juan Rumin Dominguez, Parochial Vicar; Rev. Arthur Dennison, In Res., (Retired); Deacon Peter H. Batty.
School—The Basilica School of Saint Mary Star of the Sea, 700 Truman Ave., Key West, 33040.
Tel: 305-294-1031; Fax: 305-294-2095; Email: principal@basilicaschool.com; Web: www.basilicaschoolkeywest.com. Robert M. Wright, Prin.; Mrs. LaTonya White, Vice Prin. Lay Teachers 25; Sisters 4; Students 305.
Catechesis Religious Program—Tel: 305-295-0306. Mrs. Alexandra Chuquillangui, D.R.E. Students 127.
Convent—St. Mary, Star of the Sea Convent, Holy Spirit Sisters, 724 Truman Ave., Key West, 33040. Sisters 4.
Mission—Star of the Sea Outreach Mission, 5640 Mac Donald Ave., Key West, Monroe Co. 33040.
Tel: 305-292-3013; Email: thomasmcallahan@gmail.com. Thomas Callahan.

LAUDERDALE-BY-THE-SEA, BROWARD CO., ASSUMPTION CHURCH (1959)
2001 S. Ocean Blvd., Lauderdale-by-the-Sea, 33062.
Tel: 954-941-7647; Email: blessedassumption@att.net; Web: www.assumptionlauderdale.org. Very Rev. Michael J. Greer, V.F.
Catechesis Religious Program—Students 7.

LAUDERHILL, BROWARD CO., ST. GEORGE (1964) Merged with and sacramental records at Our Lady Queen of Martyrs Parish, Fort Lauderdale.

LIGHTHOUSE POINT, BROWARD CO., ST. PAUL THE APOSTLE (1968)
2700 N.E. 36th St., Lighthouse Point, 33064.
Tel: 954-943-9154; Tel: 954-943-9155;
Fax: 954-943-1954; Email: stpaultheapostlechurch@gmail.com; Web: stpaulslhp.com. Rev. Msgr. William Dever; Rev. Matthew Thomas, Parochial Vicar.
Catechesis Religious Program—Tel: 954-571-3852; Email: mckayj@nova.edu. Judith McKay, D.R.E. Students 67.

MARATHON, MONROE CO., SAN PABLO (1958)
550 122nd St. Ocean, Marathon, 33050.
Tel: 305-289-0636; Email: frperez@sanpablomarathon.org; Email: info@sanpabomarathon.org; Web: www.sanpablomarathon.org. Rev. Luis A. Perez.
Catechesis Religious Program—Tel: 305-393-1403; Email: islandsun@aol.com. Therese Walters, D.R.E. Students 32.

MARGATE, BROWARD CO., ST. VINCENT (1960)
6350 N.W. 18th St., Margate, 33063-2320.
Tel: 954-972-0434; Fax: 954-971-9411; Email: stvincent7@aol.com; Email: matteod1942@gmail.com; Web: www.stvincentcatholicchurchmargate.org. Revs. Matthew Didonè, C.S.; Estevao Atanasio, Parochial Vicar.
Catechesis Religious Program—Tel: 954-292-7698. Mrs. Melissa Darrosier, D.R.E. Students 318.
Mission—Our Lady Aparecida Mission.

MIRAMAR, BROWARD CO.

1—ST. BARTHOLOMEW (1962)
8005 Miramar Pkwy., Miramar, 33025.
Tel: 954-431-3600; Fax: 954-435-9591; Email: office@stbartholomew.com; Web: www.stbartholomew.com. Revs. Andrew Chan-A-Sue, Admin.; Esteker Elyse, S.M.M., (Haiti) Parochial Vicar; Deacons Michel du Chaussee; Montas Onelien.
School—St. Bartholomew School, 8003 Miramar Pkwy., Miramar, 33025. Tel: 954-431-5253;
Fax: 954-431-3385; Email: school@stbartholomew.com. Christine M. Gonzalez, Prin. Clergy 1; Lay Teachers 15; Students 189.
Catechesis Religious Program—Email: religiouseducation@stbartholomew.com. Mercedes Brown, D.R.E. Students 138.

2—SAINT JOHN XXIII CHURCH (2002)
16800 Miramar Pkwy., Miramar, 33027.
Tel: 954-392-5062; Fax: 954-392-5063; Email: popestjohn23@gmail.com; Web: www.john23parish.org. Very Rev. Ernest Biriruka, (Burundi) V.F.; Rev. Javier Barreto, Parochial Vicar; Deacons Victor Lopez; Mario Ganuza.
Catechesis Religious Program—Kathryn Cabrisas, D.R.E. Students 365.

3—ST. STEPHEN (1956)
Mailing Address: 6044 S.W. 19th St., Miramar, 33023. Tel: 954-987-1100; Fax: 954-966-9881; Email: pastor@ststephenparish.net. Revs. Patrick Charles; Angel Calderon, Parochial Vicar; Raul Perez, Parochial Vicar.
Catechesis Religious Program—Tel: 954-260-8169; Email: joanne_day@bellsouth.net. Joann Day, D.R.E. Students 223.

NORTH LAUDERDALE, BROWARD CO., OUR LADY QUEEN OF HEAVEN (1974)
1400 S. State Rd. 7, North Lauderdale, 33068.
Tel: 954-971-5400; Email: olqh@bellsouth.net. Rev. Kidney M. Saint Jean; Deacon Antonio Bobadilla.
Catechesis Religious Program—Students 200.

OAKLAND PARK, BROWARD CO., BLESSED SACRAMENT (1961)
1701 E. Oakland Park Blvd., Oakland Park, 33334.
Tel: 954-564-1010; Fax: 954-566-0301; Email: bscc1701@bellsouth.net; Web: BlessedSacramentrcc.org. Rev. Robert F. Tywoniak; Deacon Dan Blaha.
Catechesis Religious Program—Tel: 954-383-6752. Students 25.

PARKLAND, BROWARD CO., MARY HELP OF CHRISTIANS CHURCH (1989)
5980 University Dr., Parkland, 33067.
Tel: 954-323-8028; Email: alejandra.martinez@mhocrc.org. Revs. Ireneusz Ekiert; Jorge I. Puerta, Parochial Vicar; Deacons Charles Edel; Ricardo Longueira; Alejandra Martinez, Sec.
School—Mary Help of Christians Church School, 6000 University Dr., Parkland, 33067.
Tel: 954-323-8006; Fax: 954-323-8010; Email: panthers@mhocschool.org; Web: mhocschool.org. Dr. Alexandra Fernandez, Prin. Administrators 1; Lay Teachers 40; Preschool 134; Students 470.
Catechesis Religious Program—Tel: 954-323-8025; Email: issa.gaytan@mhocrc.org. Issa Gaytan, D.R.E. Students 458.

PEMBROKE PINES, BROWARD CO.

1—ST. BONIFACE aka St. Boniface Catholic Church (1971)
8330 Johnson St., Pembroke Pines, 33024.
Tel: 954-432-2750; Email: ehenchy@saintboniface.us; Web: www.saintboniface.us. Revs. Fernando Orejuela, A.I.C., (Colombia); Diego A. Florez, A.I.C., (Colombia) Parochial Vicar/D.R.E.; Ivan Carrillo Paris, Parochial Vicar; Deacon Khatchig Chirinian.
Catechesis Religious Program—Email: frdiego@saintboniface.us. Students 191.

2—ST. EDWARD (1995)
19000 Pines Blvd., Pembroke Pines, 33029.
Tel: 954-436-7944; Email: stedward1@stedward.net; Web: www.stedward.net. Revs. John P. Peloso; Albert Lahens Jr., Parochial Vicar; Deacon Carl R. Cramer.
Catechesis Religious Program—Tel: 954-436-9744; Email: camille@stedward.net. Camille Laurino, D.R.E. Students 459.

3—ST. MAXIMILIAN KOLBE (1983)
701 N. Hiatus Rd., Pembroke Pines, 33026.
Tel: 954-432-0202; Email: office@stmax.cc; Web: www.stmax.cc. Revs. Jeffrey McCormick; Yamil A. Miranda, Parochial Vicar.
School—St. Maximilian Kolbe Pre-School, (Grades PreK-K), Pre School (1.5 - 4 years old) 601 N. Hiatus Rd., Pembroke Pines, 33026. Tel: 954-885-7250;
Fax: 954-885-7252; Email: preschool@stmax.cc; Web: www.stmax.cc. Mrs. Jimena Hibbard, Dir. Lay Teachers 16; Students 77.
Catechesis Religious Program—Tel: 954-885-7260; Email: reled@stmax.cc. Maryann Hotchkiss, D.R.E. Students 551.

PLANTATION, BROWARD CO., ST. GREGORY (1959)
200 N. University Dr., Plantation, 33324.
Tel: 954-473-6261; Email: info@saintgreg.org. Revs. Michael Hoyer; Gary De Los Santos, Parochial Vicar; Aldonny Varela, Parochial Vicar; Eliseus Ezeuchenne, Parochial Vicar.
School—St. Gregory School, Tel: 954-473-8169; Email: info@saintgreg.org; Web: www.saintgreg.org. Mrs. Cari Canino, Prin.; Mrs. Sandra Falter, Admin. Clergy 1; Lay Teachers 46; Students 801.
Catechesis Religious Program—
Tel: 954-473-6261, Ext. 149; Email: avomvolakis@saintgreg.org. Antonio Vomvolakis Jr., D.R.E. Students 388.

POMPANO BEACH, BROWARD CO.

1—ST. COLEMAN (1959)
1200 S. Federal Hwy., Pompano Beach, 33062.
Tel: 954-942-3533; Email: churchacct@stcoleman.org; Web: www.stcoleman.org. Revs. Michael A. Garcia, Parochial Admin.; Gerald Morris.
School—St. Coleman School, (Grades PreK-8), 2250 S.E. 12th St., Pompano Beach, 33062.
Tel: 954-942-3500; Fax: 954-785-0603; Email: churchacct@stcoleman.org. Dr. Lori St. Thomas, Prin. Aides 7; Lay Teachers 44; Students 541.
Catechesis Religious Program—1285 S.E. 22nd Ave., Pompano Beach, 33062. Tel: 954-782-1461; Email: dre@stcoleman.org. William Harvelle, D.R.E. Students 166.

2—ST. ELIZABETH OF HUNGARY CATHOLIC CHURCH (1959)
3331 N.E. 10th St., Pompano Beach, 33064-5298.
Tel: 954-941-8117; Tel: 954-943-6801; Email: stelizabeth@bellsouth.net; Web: www.saintelizabethofhungary.org. Revs. Harry Loubriel; Fenly E. Saint-Jean, (Haiti) Parochial Vicar; Deacons Willie Harris Sr.; Blaise Augustin; Mrs. Alicia McDermott, Contact Person; Ms. Dennise Perez, Sec.
Catechesis Religious Program—Tel: 954-943-6801; Email: religoused.ste@att.net. Nadine Destine, D.R.E. Students 256.
Mission—St. Joseph, 1210 N.W. 6th Ave., Pompano Beach, 33060.

3—ST. GABRIEL (1967)
731 N. Ocean Blvd., Pompano Beach, 33062.
Tel: 954-943-3684; Email: st_gabriel@bellsouth.net. Rev. Liam T. Quinn.
Catechesis Religious Program—

4—ST. HENRY (1969) [CEM]
1500 S. Andrews Ave., Pompano Beach, 33069.
Tel: 954-785-2450; Email: amy@sainthenrys.org; Web: www.sainthenrys.org. Rev. Francis Akwue, C.S.Sp.
Catechesis Religious Program—Email: pastor@sainthenrys.org. Gus Maldonado, D.R.E. Students 89.

5—ST. JOSEPH MISSION (1981) Merged with and sacramental records at Saint Elizabeth of Hungary Parish, Pompano Beach.

6—OUR LADY OF CZESTOCHOWA MISSION (1997) (Polish)
2400 N.E. 12th St., Pompano Beach, 33062.
Tel: 954-545-3861; Fax: 954-532-1436; Email: polishchurch@bellsouth.net; Web: www.polishchurch.com. Rev. Stanislaw Rakiej, S.Chr.
Catechesis Religious Program—Students 48.

7—SAN ISIDRO (1970)
2310 Martin Luther King Blvd., Pompano Beach, 33069-1591. Tel: 954-971-8780, Ext. 201;
Fax: 954-972-3607; Email: fatherwilfredo@sanisidro.org; Email: gildakawano@sanisidro.org; Web: www.sanisidro.org. Revs. Wilfredo Contreras; Tomasz Parzynski, Parochial Vicar.

Catechesis Religious Program—Email: luzlopez@sanisidro.org. Luz Lopez, D.R.E. Students 134.

SOUTHWEST RANCHES, BROWARD CO., ST. MARK (1985) 5601 S. Flamingo Rd., Southwest Ranches, 33330. Tel: 954-434-3777; Email: info@stmarkparish.org; Web: www.stmarkparish.org. Revs. Jaime H. Acevedo; Juan A. Aviles, Parochial Vicar; Paul G. Karenga, Parochial Vicar; Deacons Jose Manuel Gordillo; Vincent Farinato; John Lorenzo.

School—St. Mark School, (Grades PreK-8), Tel: 954-434-3887; Email: principal@stmarklions.com; Web: www.stmarkparish.org. Teresita Wardlow, Prin. Lay Teachers 31; Students 550.

Catechesis Religious Program—Tel: 954-252-9899; Email: ReligionDirector@stmarkparish.org. Donna Villavisanis, D.R.E. Students 817.

SUNRISE, BROWARD CO.

1—ALL SAINTS (1982) 10900 W. Oakland Park Blvd., Sunrise, 33351. Tel: 954-742-2666; Fax: 956-741-7238; Email: info@allsaintsvillage.com; Web: www.allsaintsvillage.com. Rev. Randall Musselman; Deacon Joseph Maalouf, Parochial Vicar.

School—All Saints School, Tel: 954-742-4842; Fax: 954-742-4871; Email: info@allsaintsvillage.com. Mrs. Kristen Whiting, Prin. Clergy 3; Lay Teachers 12; Students 221.

Catechesis Religious Program—Tel: 954-742-7742. Dr. Jorge Diez, D.R.E. Students 342.

2—ST. BERNARD (1971) 8279 Sunset Strip, Sunrise, 33322. Tel: 954-741-7800 ; Fax: 954-742-4558; Email: stbernardoffice@gmail.com; Web: www.saintbernardchurch.net. Rev. Carlos Vega; Deacons Armando Martinez; Humberto Reyes.

Catechesis Religious Program—Email: saintbernardccd@gmail.com. Carolina Kleber, D.R.E. Students 60.

TAMARAC, BROWARD CO., ST. MALACHY (1973) 6200 John Horan Terr., Tamarac, 33321. Tel: 954-726-1237; Email: stmalachychurch@comcast.net; Web: www.stmalachy.church. Revs. Dominick O'Dwyer; Alfredo Rolon Ortiz, Parochial Vicar; Edoualdo Desmornes.

Catechesis Religious Program—Tel: 954-721-5337; Email: StMalachyDRE@outlook.com. Rita Fonteciella, D.R.E. Students 78.

TAVERNIER, MONROE CO., SAN PEDRO (1954) 89500 Overseas Hwy., Tavernier, 33070. Tel: 305-852-5372; Email: office@sanpedroparish.org; Web: www.sanpedroparish.org. P.O. Box 456, Tavernier, 33070. Rev. Franky Jean.

Catechesis Religious Program—Mrs. Amy Pope Brown, D.R.E. Students 69.

WEST HOLLYWOOD, BROWARD CO., ANNUNCIATION (1959) 3781 S.W. 39th St., West Park, 33023. Tel: 954-989-0606; Email: annchrch@bellsouth.net. Rev. Michael Quilligan; Deacon Mitchell C. Abdallah.

School—Annunciation School, (Grades PreK-8), 3751 S.W. 39th St., West Park, 33023. Tel: 954-989-8287; Web: www.annun.org. Jennifer Nicholson, Prin. Lay Teachers 16; Students 192.

Catechesis Religious Program—Email: mendez@annun.org; Email: mpatino@annun.org. Mrs. Margareth Patino, Dir.; Mrs. Debbie Mendez, D.R.E. Students 85.

WEST PARK, BROWARD CO., ST. PAUL CHUNG HA SANG KOREAN MISSION 3600 S.W. 32 Blvd., West Park, 33023. 143 S. Royal Cove Cir., Davie, 33325. Tel: 954-474-9091; Email: miamikoreanmission@gmail.com. Rev. Jeonghoo Cho, Parochial Admin.

WESTON, BROWARD CO., ST. KATHARINE DREXEL (2001) 2501 S. Post Rd., Weston, 33327. Tel: 954-389-5003; Email: mariselaz@skdrexel.org; Web: skdrexel.org. Most Rev. Enrique Delgado, Ph.D., D.D., V.G.; Rev. Pedro Durango Agudelo, Parochial Vicar; Deacon Thomas Dawson.

Catechesis Religious Program—Tel: 954-389-1229; Email: mariab@skdrexel.org. Maria Barni Hopkins, D.R.E.; Mrs. Nancy Wrightsman, Pastoral Min./Coord. Students 766.

Special Assignment:
Rev. Msgr.—
Castaneda, Oscar F., Chap., Jackson Memorial Hospital
Revs.—
Martin, Daniel P., Doctoral Studies, Catholic University of America
Nwankwo, Fidelis, C.S.Sp., Chap., Jackson Memorial Hospital
Pietraszko, Andrew A., Chap., Baptist Hospital
Rios, Juan Carlos, Faculty, St. Vincent de Paul Regional Seminary, Boynton Beach.

On Non-Archdiocesan Assignment:
Rev. Msgr.—
Carruthers, Michael
Revs.—
Alonso, Armando
Arriola, James
Barajas, Abel E.
Bohorquez, Jesus Alberto
Jimenez, Eduardo
Pena, Cesar E.
Zegeer, Eric D.

Retired:
Most Rev.—
Favalora, John C., D.D., S.T.L., M.Ed., (Retired)
Rev. Msgrs.—
Anderson, Andrew L., J.C.D., (Retired)
Cassidy, Martin J., (Retired)
Delaney, John W., (Retired)
Doyle, Seamus, (Retired)
Garcia, Pedro F., (Retired)
Glorie, John W., (Retired)
Hennessey, William J., (Retired)
Hernando, Jose Luis, (Retired)
Martin, Emilio, (Retired)
Parappally, James, (Retired)
Reynolds, James B., (Retired)
Vaughan, John J., (Retired)
Revs.—
Adu, Martin, (Retired)
Angelini, Joseph, (Retired)
Angulo, Raul, (Retired)
Baky, Isidore, (Retired)
Bastien, Emmanuel, (Retired)
Bello, Jorge Luis, (Retired)
Brohammer, Ronald, (Retired)
Cabrera, Sergio, (Retired)
Capdepon, Federico, V.F., (Retired)
Cardona, George, (Retired)
Carrillo, Sergio, (Retired)
Clements, Charles, (Retired)
Coucelo, Andres, (Retired)
Dennison, Arthur, (Retired)
Duffy, George, (Retired)
Elbert, William, (Retired)
Fenger, Guy, (Retired)
Fink, John, (Retired)
Fishwick, Joseph, (Retired)
Foudy, Thomas F., (Retired)
Garcia, Luis G., (Retired)
Gomez, Miguel, (Retired)
Gubbins, John, (Retired)
Holoubek, Roger, (Retired)
Honold, Thomas G., (Retired)
Huesca, Omar A., (Retired)
Kent, Daniel, (Retired)
Kish, Michael A., (Retired)
Lambert, Peter, (Retired)
Lleo, Pedro, (Retired)
Lynch, Michael, (Retired)
Lyons, Lawrence, (Retired)
Massi, Anthony, (Retired)
McCreanor, James, (Retired)
Medina, Rolando, (Retired)
Miyares, Carlos, (Retired)
Mulcahy, Sean, (Retired)
Mulderry, Anthony J., (Retired)
Mullane, Thomas, (Retired)
Muniz, William, (Retired)
Murnane, Patrick J., (Retired)
Noda, Jorge, (Retired)
Noguera, Ronald, (Retired)
O'Leary, John, (Retired)
O'Neill, Patrick, (Retired)
O'Sullivan, Sean, (Retired)
Paniagua, Jose L., (Spain) (Retired)
Pedroso, Rafael, (Retired)
Quijano, Jose Juan, (Retired)
Quinn, James A., (Retired)
Rausch, Dennis, (Retired)
Reeves, Mark Thomas, (Retired)
Rivero, Jordi S., (Retired)
Russell, David, (Retired)
Scheiding, Philip, (Retired)
Shannon, Brendan, (Retired)
Silio, Antonio R., (Retired)
Singleton, Jeremiah, (Retired)
Smith, David, (Retired)
Soulliere, Richard, (Retired)
Sullivan, Michael P., (Retired)
Valoret, Joseph, (Retired)
Wisniewski, Thomas, (Retired).

Permanent Deacons:
Abdallah, Mitchell C., Annunciation
Agustin, Blaise, St. Elizabeth of Hungary, Pompano Beach
Aleman, Jose, Blessed Trinity
Alfonso, Manuel, Immaculate Conception
Batty, Peter H., St. Mary Star of the Sea
Bertot, William, Gesu
Bestard, Fernando, St. Timothy
Binder, Robert, St. John Neumann
Blanco, Eduardo, St. Raymond
Blanco, Emilio, St. Benedict
Bobadilla, Antonio, Our Lady Queen of Heaven
Bonnick, Bernard, (Jamaica) St. Malachy
Bowen, David, St. Bartholomew
Buigas, Manuel, St. Timothy
Calvo-Forte, Rafael, St. Michael the Archangel
Cardenas, Nestor, St. Bonaventure
Carrieri, Carl, St. Maximilian Kolbe
Charur, Carlos Jr., St. Thomas the Apostle
Chirinian, Khatchig, St. Boniface
Chirinos, Jose, St. Augustine
Cramer, Carl R., St. Edward
Currier, Roger, Our Lady of the Lakes
Dawson, Thomas, St. Katharine Drexel
de los Reyes, Rafael, Apostolate of Divine Mercy
De Luca, Arnold J., St. Edward
Del Riego, Ernesto, St. Agatha
Desmornes, Jean E., St. Malachy
Diaz, Nelson, St. Timothy
Dinsmore, Robert B., St. Kevin
Douyon, Pierre, St. Maximilian Kolbe
Du-Chaussee, Michel, St. Bartholomew
Dugard, James, St. Louis
Dutra, Guillermo, Good Shepherd
Eagan, Thomas V., Epiphany
Eberling, Vincent Jr., San Isidro
Edel, Charles, Mary Help of Christians
Ermer, John T., St. Joseph
Farias, Edgardo, Archdiocesan Dir., Detention Ministry
Farinato, Vincent, St. Mark
Feliciano, Santos, St. Agatha
Fernandez, Marco, St. John Neumann
Ferrarone, William, St. Gabriel
Fleitas, Roberto, Little Flower, Coral Gables
Fleurimond, Alpha, Sacred Heart
Flores, Raul, St. Mary Cathedral
Fresneda, Michael, St. Kevin
Friel, John, St. Elizabeth Ann Seton
Ganuza, Mario, St. John XXIII
Garcia, Carlos, Our Lady of Lourdes
Garret, Bill, St. Justin
Gazitua, Ralph, St. John Neumann
Gibson, George, Christ the King
Gomez, Jose Felipe, St. John Neumann
Gonzalez, F. Humberto, Immaculate Conception
Gonzalez, Frank, St. Andrew
Gonzalez, Henri, St. John Neumann
Gonzalez, Juan, Our Lady of the Lakes
Gordillo, Jose Manuel, St. Mark
Grille, Ramon, Sacred Heart
Gutierrez, Roberto F., San Lazaro
Hanlon, Thomas F., St. Louis
Harris, Willy, St. Elizabeth of Hungary
Horton, William, St. Gregory
Inda, Javier, Blessed Trinity
Irrizarry, Jose, St. Francis de Sales
Jimenez, Manuel, Our Lady of Guadalupe
Joiner, Scott, St. Maximilian Kolbe
Kelly, Edgar, St. Brendan
Kirk, John, San Pablo
Labelle, George, St. Coleman
Lam, Alex S., St. Louis
Lamas, Carlos, San Lazaro
Lannon, Billy Jr., St. Brendan
Lee, Steven, Sts. Peter and Paul
Livingstone, Donald, Epiphany
Llorens, Julke, St. John the Apostle
Longueira, Ricardo, Mary Help of Christians
Lopez, Mario, St. Elizabeth Ann Seton
Lopez, Victor, St. John XXIII
Lorenzo, John, St. Mark
Luka, Chandy, Nativity
Magnuson, Robert, Basilica of St. Mary, Star of the Sea
Martinez, Armando, St. Bernard
Martinez, Eduardo, St. Henry
Martinez, Jose, Mother of Christ
Martins, Alberto, St. Vincent
McFarland, Clyde, St. Lawrence
McGuinn, Gerald, St. Ambrose
McLaughlin, Gregory, St. Paul the Apostle
Mendoza, Manuel, St. Maximilian Kolbe
Mieyal, Denis, St. Andrew
Millikin, Randy, St. Ambrose
Mindel, Albert, Our Lady of the Lakes
Moreno, Vicente, St. Catherine of Siena
Munter, Paul H., Epiphany
Naranjo, Jose M., Our Lady of Lourdes
Norat, Hector, St. Agatha
O'Gorman, Frank B., St. Jerome
O'Malley, Robert F. Jr., St. Richard
O'Neill, James, Our Lady of Mercy
Okragleski, John, Blessed Sacrament
Onuigbo, Valentine, Holy Family
Panellas, Eduardo, Our Lady of Divine Providence
Parlade, Miguel, Little Flower
Pearce, Joseph M., St. Bonaventure
Peremenis, John, St. Louis

Perez, Antonio, Corpus Christi
Perez, Manuel, St. Agatha
Perez, Marcos, Epiphany
Phang Sang, Louis, St. John Neumann
Pierce, John (Jack), St. Peter
Pimentel, Victor M., S.T.L., Archdiocesan Dir., Permanent Diaconate
Pineda, Roberto, St. Joseph
Plummer, Michael, Our Lady of Lourdes
Prieto, Jorge, Prince of Peace
Pulido, Carlos, St. Thomas the Apostle
Ramirez, Carlos, Our Lady of the Lakes
Rauseo, Ricardo, Our Lady of Lourdes
Reyes, Jeffrey J., St. Louis
Reyes, Jorge, Nativity
Roa, Benjamin, All Saints
Rodicio, Sergio, St. Mary Cathedral
Rodriguez, Ernesto, St. Michael the Archangel
Rodriguez, Santos, St. Martin de Porres
Rojo, Orlando, Mother of the Redeemer
Rosado, Jose, Mother of Christ
Rosales, Marco, St. Monica
Ruiz-Castaneda, Norman, Epiphany
Rynkiewicz, Stephen, St. Andrew
Santos, Raimundo, St. Catherine of Siena
Santos, Tony, St. Patrick
Smith, Eduardo, Epiphany
Smith, Timothy, Navitity
Sommovigo, Joseph, St. Malachy
Starzinski, Louis, St. Bernadette, Hollywood
Ulloa, Lazaro, Prince of Peace
Valle, Alfredo, St. John Bosco
Vasquez, Domingo, St. Bonaventure
Villa, Isidoro, Our Lady of Lourdes
Villena, Jose, St. Ann Mission
Watkins, William A., Little Flower
Westman, Mark, St. Louis
Yglesias, Robert, St. Louis
Zapatero, Adrian, St. Agnes
Zayas, Julio, Good Shepherd.

INSTITUTIONS LOCATED IN DIOCESE

[A] SEMINARIES, ARCHDIOCESAN

MIAMI. *St. John Vianney College Seminary, Inc.*, 2900 S.W. 87th Ave., Miami, 33165. Tel: 305-223-4561; Tel: 305-223-4562; Fax: 305-223-0650; Email: frsantos@sjvcs.edu; Email: mhualpa@sjvcs.edu; Web: www.sjvcs.edu. Rev. Matias A. Hualpa, Dean; Dr. Ramon J. Santos, Academic Dean; Revs. Robert Vallee, Assoc. Prof. Philosophy & Liturgy Dir.; Joseph Kottayil, Spiritual Dir.; Jorge Perales, Theology Teacher; Very Rev. Ferdinand Santos, (Philippines) Philosophy Prof.; Deacon Carlos Garcia, Dir., IT. Lay Teachers 15; Priests 6; Seminarians 75; Total Students 76.

[B] SEMINARIES, ARCHDIOCESAN MISSIONARY

HIALEAH. *The Redemptoris Mater Seminary Archdiocese of Miami, Inc.*, 1040 W. 29th St., Hialeah, 33012. Tel: 305-882-1728; Email: seminary@rmmiami.org; Web: www.rmmiami.org. Very Rev. Emanuele DeNigris, Rector; Revs. Ivan M. Rodriguez, Vicar; Antonio Vicente, (Brazil) Spiritual Dir: Religious Teachers 3; Seminarians 25.

[C] COLLEGES AND UNIVERSITIES

MIAMI. *Barry University* (1940) President's Office 11300 N.E. 2nd Ave., Miami, 33161.
Tel: 305-899-3010; Email: officeofthepresident@barry.edu; Web: www.barry.edu. Sr. Linda Bevilacqua, O.P., Ph.D., Pres.; Jennifer Boyd Pugh, M.S., SHRM-SCP, Vice Pres., Admin. Svcs. & Organizational Devel.; Univ. Title IX Coord.; Susan Rosenthal, M.B.A., Vice Pres. Business & Finance; Dr. Eileen McDonough, Assoc. Vice Pres. Mission and Student Engagement; Dr. Maria Luisa Alvarez, Assoc. Vice Pres. Student Affairs & Dean of Students; Revs. Cristobal Torres, O.P., M.S.W., M.Div., M.A., Univ. Chap.; Mark Wedig, O.P., Ph.D., Prof. Liturgical Theology/Assoc Dean, Graduate Studies; Jorge L. Presmanes, O.P., D.Min., Prof.; Yvette Koottungal, Vice Pres., Enrollment & Digital Strategies; CIO; Dr. Jill Farrell, Dean School of Educ.; Dr. John McFadden, Dean College of Nursing & Health Sciences; Dr. Phyllis Scott, Dean School of Social Work; Dr. Karen A. Callaghan, Dean, College of Arts & Sciences; Leticia M. Diaz, J.D., Ph.D., Dean, School of Law; Dr. Scott F. Smith, Vice Pres., Mission & Student Engagement; Dr. Christopher Starratt, Vice Provost; David Dudgeon Esq., General Counsel; Albert Armstrong, D.P.M., Dean, School of Podiatric Medicine; Andrea Keener, Ph.D., Dean, School of Professional & Career Educ.; Rev. Jose David Padilla, O.P., M.Div., M.A., S.T.L., Prof.; John D. Murray, Provost; Ms. Karen J. Stalnaker, M.A., P.T., Dir., Campus Ministry; Rev. George R. Boudreau, O.P., Visiting Assoc. Prof. of Theology; Dr. Victor Romano, Assoc. Vice Provost; Joan Phillips, Dean. Sisters of St. Dominic (Adrian, MI). Priests 5; Sisters 3; Students 7,352; Lay Faculty 713.

MIAMI GARDENS. *St. Thomas University, Inc.* (1961) (Coed) 16401 N.W. 37th Ave., Miami Gardens, 33054. Tel: 305-628-6000; Fax: 305-628-6703; Email: signup@stu.edu; Web: www.stu.edu. Faculty 90; Priests 2; Sisters 1; Students 5,557.
Administration: David Armstrong, Pres.; Terry O'Connor, Vice Pres. Admin, Treas. & CFO; Rev. Msgr. Terence Hogan, S.L.D., Vice Pres. Mission, Dean Theology & Ministry; Janine Laudisio, Vice Pres. Philanthropy & Communications; Alfredo Garcia, Acting Provost; Mr. J. Patrick Fitzgerald, Esq., Counsel; Marlen Mursuli, Dir. Communications; Claudia Herrera, Dir. Campus Ministry; Larry Treadwell, Interim Dir., Library; Rev. Alfred Cioffi, Assoc. Dean, Sch of Science & Technology; Sr. Ondina Cortes, R.M.I., Prof.; Rev. Msgr. Franklyn M. Casale, Pres. Emeritus.
Trustees and Members: Most Revs. Thomas G. Wenski, D.D., Archbishop; Enrique Delgado, Ph. D., D.D., V.G., Auxiliary Bishop; John J. Dooner, Chairman; Wini Amaturo; Rev. John Butler; Bob Dickinson; Michael Fay; Constance Fernandez; Paul Garcia; Gary Goldbloom; Ray Gonzalez; Joseph P. Lacher; Victor H. Mendelson; Dominick Miniaci; Mario Murgado; Alex Penelas; Marcos Perez; Peter Prieto; Jorge Rico; Lourdes Rivas; Robert Sanchez; Frances Sevilla-Sacasa; Maureen Shea; Mario Trueba; Gregory T. Swienton, Trustee Emeritus.

[D] HIGH SCHOOLS, ARCHDIOCESAN

MIAMI. *Archbishop Coleman F. Carroll High School, Inc.*, 10300 S.W. 167th Ave., Miami, 33196.
Tel: 305-388-6700; Fax: 305-388-4371; Email: principal@colemancarroll.org; Web: www.archbishopcolemancarroll.org. Sr. Margaret Ann, O.C.D., Prin. Lay Teachers 24; Priests 1; Carmelite Sisters of the Most Sacred Heart of Los Angeles 4; Students 272; Staff 18.

St. Brendan High School, Inc. (1975) 2950 S.W. 87th Ave., Miami, 33165. Tel: 305-223-5181;
Fax: 305-220-7434; Email: info@stbhs.org; Web: www.stbrendanhigh.org. Jose Rodelgo-Bueno, Ph. D., Prin.; Katrina Ramos, Finance & H.R. Dir.; Guillermo Ramos, Dir. Lay Teachers 84; Students 1,200.

Immaculata La Salle High School, Inc. (1958) 3601 S. Miami Ave., Miami, 33133. Tel: 305-854-2334;
Fax: 305-858-5971; Email: principal@ilsroyals.com; Web: www.ilsroyals.com. Sr. Kim Keraitis, F.M.A., Prin.; Mrs. Luisa Serratore, Asst. Prin.; Mrs. Marlen Medina, Fin. Admin.; Mrs. Monica Orelle, Dean, Faculty; Alishea Jurado, Dean, Innovation; Mrs. Colette Varese, Dean, Students; Catherine Campos, Dean, Technology; Gaston Arellano, Dir., Campus Operations. Lay Teachers 63; Sisters 4; Students 865.

Msgr. Edward Pace High School, Inc. (1961) 15600 Spartan Blvd., N.W. 32nd Ave., Miami, 33054.
Tel: 305-623-7223; Fax: 305-521-0185; Email: agarcia@pacehs.com; Web: www.pacehs.com. Mrs. Ana Garcia, Prin.; Anthony Walker, Dean of Students (Attendance/Discipline); Ramon Rodriguez, Dean; Valarie Lloyd, Dean of Students (Grades 9 & 12); Lillian Dubon, Dean of Faculty; Melanie Otero, Dean. Lay Teachers 55; Students 885.

Our Lady of Lourdes Academy, Inc. (1963) 5525 S.W. 84th St., Miami, 33143. Tel: 305-667-1623; Email: skathryn@bobcats.olla.org; Web: www.olla.org. Sr. Kathryn Donze, I.H.M., Prin. Lay Teachers 65; Students 840; Sisters (Servants of the Immaculate Heart of Mary) 3.

FORT LAUDERDALE. *Cardinal Gibbons High School, Inc.* (1961) 2900 N.E. 47th St., Fort Lauderdale, 33308. Tel: 954-491-2900; Fax: 954-772-1025; Email: cghs@cghsfl.org; Web: www.cghsfl.org. Paul D. Ott, Prin.; Lori Kubach, Vice Prin.; Oscar Cedano, Vice Prin.; Thomas Mahon, Vice Prin.; Revs. Luis A. Cruz, Sch.P., Teacher; John Callan, Sch.P., Teacher; Vinod Angadathu, Sch.P., Teacher. Religious Teachers 3; Lay Teachers 73; Students 1,145.

St. Thomas Aquinas High School, Inc. (1936) 2801 S.W. 12th St., Fort Lauderdale, 33312.
Tel: 954-581-0700; Fax: 954-581-8263; Email: denise.aloma@aquinas-sta.org; Web: www.aquinas-sta.org. Rev. Msgr. Vincent T. Kelly, Supervising Prin.; Dr. Denise Aloma, Prin.; Mrs. Margie Scott, Asst. Prin. & Dir., Student Activities; Dr. Robert Mulder, Asst. Prin.; Dr. Suzy Prieto, Asst. Prin.; Dr. Ian Robertson, Dept. Chair, Theology; Michael McCormack, Campus Minister; Jane Curry, Campus Minister; Mr. Rob Biasotti, Dean of Students; Adam Matthews, Guidance Dir.; Mr. Norm Kunkel, Librarian; Mr. George Smith, Dir. of Athletics. Lay Teachers 124; Priests 1; Students 2,109.

SOUTHWEST RANCHES. *Archbishop Edward A. McCarthy High School, Inc.* (1998) 5451 S. Flamingo Rd., Southwest Ranches, 33330.
Tel: 954-434-8820, Ext. 202; Fax: 954-680-4835; Email: maverick@mccarthyhigh.org; Email: cthomas@mccarthyhigh.org; Web: www.mccarthyhigh.org. Mr. Richard P. Jean, Prin.; Rev. Jean Jadotte, Chap. Lay Teachers 80; Priests 1; Students 1,600.

[E] HIGH SCHOOLS, PRIVATE

MIAMI. *Belen Jesuit Preparatory School, Inc.* (1854) 500 S.W. 127th Ave., Miami, 33184.
Tel: 305-223-8600; Fax: 305-227-2565; Email: communications@belenjesuit.org; Email: tmartinez@belenjesuit.org; Web: www.belenjesuit.org. Revs. Guillermo Garcia-Tunon, S.J., Pres.; Alberto Garcia, Supr.; Mr. Jose Roca, Prin.; Rev. Pedro A. Suarez, S.J., Spiritual Advisor/Care Svcs., Tel: 305-205-1017; Alina Alpizar, Librarian; Revs. Pedro Cartaya, S.J.; Lionel Lopez; Ernesto Fernandez Travieso, S.J.; Nelson Garcia, S.J.; Francisco J. Permuy, S.J.; Eduardo Barrios, S.J. Deacons 2; Lay Teachers 124; Priests 9; Sisters 2; Students 1,410. *Belen Alumni Association of Jesuit Schools from Cuba and Miami*, 500 S.W. 127th Ave., Miami, 33184. Tel: 786-621-4667; Email: alumni@belenjesuit.org. Carlos Bravo, Exec. Dir.; Rev. Francisco J. Permuy, S.J., Spiritual Counselor.

Our Lady of Belen Jesuit Foundation, Inc., 500 S.W. 127th Ave., Miami, 33184. Tel: 786-621-4043;
Fax: 786-621-4044; Email: aperezabreu@belenjesuit.org. Rev. Guillermo Garcia-Tunon, S.J., Pres.

Carrollton School of the Sacred Heart (1962) 3747 Main Hwy., Miami, 33133. Tel: 305-446-5673;
Fax: 305-529-6533; Email: okalkus@carrollton.org; Email: tcheleotis@carrollton.org; Web: www.carrollton.org. Olen Kalkus, Headmaster; Mr. Tom Cheleotis, CFO; Maritza Fernandez, Dean; Melinee Fernandez, Librarian
Convent of the Sacred Heart of Miami, Inc. Religious Teachers 1; Lay Teachers 100; Priests 1; Religious of the Sacred Heart 1; Students 850.

Christopher Columbus High School, 3000 S.W. 87 Ave., Miami, 33165. Tel: 305-223-5650;
Fax: 305-559-4306; Email: info@columbushs.com; Web: www.columbushs.com. Mr. David Pugh, Prin.; Bro. Kevin Handibode, F.M.S., Pres. Marist Brothers 12; Deacons 1; Lay Teachers 120; Students 1,700.

HOLLYWOOD. *Chaminade-Madonna College Preparatory* (1960) 500 Chaminade Dr., Hollywood, 33021-5800. Tel: 954-989-5150;
Fax: 954-983-4663; Email: info@cmlions.org; Web: www.cmlions.org. Judith Mucheck, Ph.D., Pres.; Rev. Robert Bouffier, S.M., Chap.; Raiza Echemendia, Asst. Head of School; Antonio Mari, Campus Min.; Michael Eaton, Dean of Students; Carlton Preston, Dir.; Lauren Broeckelmann, Dir., Student Life; Lucelia Oganezov, Dir.; Andre Torres, Athletic Dir.; Luigina Billisi, Dir., Admissions; Ron Belanger, Librarian. Marianist Brothers 1; Lay Teachers 34; Priests 1; Students 525.

[F] SCHOOLS, OTHER

MIAMI. *Archdiocese of Miami Catholic Virtual School*, (Grades 6-12), 15600 N.W. 32nd Ave., Miami Gardens, 33054. Tel: 305-508-5556;
Fax: 305-521-0185; Email: rbautista@adomvirtual.com. Rebeca Bautista, Prin. Lay Teachers 20; Students 98.

MIAMI GARDENS. *Marian Center School and Services, Inc.* aka Marian Center, (Grades 1-12), 15701 N.W. 37 Ave., Miami Gardens, 33054. Tel: 305-200-8927;
Fax: 305-200-8926; Email: lidia.valli@mariancenterschool.org; Web: www.mariancenterschool.org. Lidia Valli, Prin. The Marian Center is accredited by the Florida Catholic Conference as an ungraded school. Lay Teachers 8; Sisters 4; Students 48; Volunteers 4.

[G] SHELTERS

MIAMI. *Brother Keily Place, Inc.*, 27940 S. Dixie Hwy., Homestead, 33032. Tel: 305-374-1065, Ext. 317; Email: hfernandez@camillus.org. Rev. Raphael Mieszala, O.H., Vice Pres. Bed Capacity 61; Tot Asst. Annually 67; Total Staff 10.

Brother Mathias Barrett, Inc., 680 N.E. 52nd St., Miami, 33137. Tel: 815-472-3131; Email: judy@sjog-na.org. Bro. Justin Howson, Prov.

Brownsville Housing, Inc., 1603 N.W. 7th Ave., Miami, 33136. Tel: 305-374-1065, Ext. 220; Email: hfernandez@camillus.org. 4700 N.W. 32nd Ave., Miami, 33142. Rev. Raphael Mieszala, O.H., Vice

Pres. Bed Capacity 74; Tot Asst. Annually 85; Total Staff 1.

Camillus Health Concern, Inc. dba Good Shepherd Health Center (1984) 336 N.W. 5th St., Miami, 33128. Tel: 305-577-4840; Fax: 305-373-7431; Email: info@camillushealth.org; Web: www.CamillusHealth.org. Mr. John Dubois, Chm.; Mr. Francis Afram-Gyening, CEO; Mr. Felix Manlunas, Treasurer. Provides medical, dental, mental health and social services to persons who are homeless, mentally ill, &/or poor. Tot Asst. Annually 4,981; Total Staff 6.

Camillus House, Inc. (1960) 1603 N.W. 7th Ave., Miami, 33136. Tel: 305-374-1065; Fax: 866-682-5935; Email: hfernandez@camillus.org; Web: www.camillus.org. Hilda Fernandez, CEO; Rev. Raphael Mieszala, O.H., Vice. Pres. Provides services to the homeless: emergency services, substance abuse rehabilitation, transitional and permanent housing. Bed Capacity 395; Tot Asst. Annually 6,397; Total Staff 94.

Charity Unlimited Foundation, Inc., 1603 N.W. 7th Ave., Miami, 33136. Tel: 305-374-1065, Ext. 220; Email: hfernandez@camillus.org. Rev. Raphael Mieszala, O.H., Vice Pres.

Charity Unlimited of Florida, Inc. (1995) 1603 N.W. 7th Ave., Miami, 33136. Tel: 305-374-1065, Ext. 220; Fax: 866-682-5935; Email: raphaelbgs@yahoo.com. Rev. Raphael Mieszala, O.H., Vice Pres. Provides buildings and grounds for charitable works. Bed Capacity 167; Tot Asst. Annually 213; Total Staff 27.

Emmaus Place, Inc., 1603 N.W. 7th Ave., Miami, 33136. Tel: 305-374-1065; Email: raphaelbgs@yahoo.com; Email: hfernandez@camillus.org. 432 N.W. 4th Ave., Miami, 33128. Rev. Raphael Mieszala, O.H., Vice Pres. Bed Capacity 7; Tot Asst. Annually 10; Staff 1.

Gift of Hope, Missionaries of Charity (1981) 724 N.W. 17th St., Miami, 33136. Tel: 305-326-0032; Email: weberag@att.net. Sisters M. Ajaya, M.C.; Loretta, M.C.; Flora Del Carmen, M.C.; Marie Alberta; M. Agna; M. Theola.

Women's and Children's Shelter, 724 N.W. 17 St., Miami, 33136. Tel: 305-326-0032; Email: weberag@att.net. Sr. M. Mangala, Supr. Bed Capacity 24; Tot Asst. Annually 2,750; Total Staff 2; Total Women Assisted 2,500; Total Children Assisted 250.

Soup Kitchen (1981) 724 N.W. 17 St., Miami, 33136. Tel: 305-326-0032; Email: weberag@att.net. Sr. M. Ajaya, M.C., Supr. Tot Asst. Annually 100,000; Total Staff 1.

Good Shepherd Villas, Inc., 1603 N.W. 7th Ave., Miami, 33136. Tel: 305-374-1065, Ext. 220; Email: raphaelbgs@yahoo.com; Email: hfernandez@camillus.org. Rev. Raphael Mieszala, O.H., Vice Pres. Bed Capacity 14; Tot Asst. Annually 24; Total Staff 14.

Labre Place, Inc., 1603 N.W. 7th Ave., Miami, 33136. Tel: 305-374-1065; Email: hfernandez@camillus.org. 350 N.W. 4th St., Miami, 33128. Rev. Raphael Mieszala, O.H., Vice Pres. Bed Capacity 50; Tot Asst. Annually 51; Total Staff 1.

**New Camillus House Campus, Inc.*, 1603 N.W. 7th Ave., Miami, 33136. Tel: 305-374-1065; Email: raphaelbgs@yahoo.com; Email: hfernandez@camillus.org. Rev. Raphael Mieszala, O.H., Vice Pres.

Somerville Residence, Inc., 1603 N.W. 7th Ave., Miami, 33136. Tel: 305-374-1065; Email: raphaelbgs@yahoo.com; Email: hfernandez@camillus.org. 400 N.W. 3rd Ct., Miami, 33128. Rev. Raphael Mieszala, O.H., Vice Pres. Bed Capacity 35; Tot Asst. Annually 11; Total Staff 1.

[H] GENERAL HOSPITALS

MIAMI. **Mercy Hospital, a Campus of Plantation General Hospital* (1950) 3663 S. Miami Ave., Miami, 33133. Tel: 305-854-4400; Email: michael.garrido2@hcahealthcare.com; Fax: 305-285-5066; Web: www.mercymiami.com. Sisters Stephanie Flynn, S.S.J., Trustee; Elizabeth Anne Worley, S.S.J., Trustee; Kathleen Carr, S.S.J., Trustee; Revs. Pedro Toledo, Chap.; Julio Estada, Chap.; Jean Sterling Laurent, Chap.; Eric D. Zegeer, Chap.; Emilio Garreaud, Chap.; Sr. Sonia Mancuello, Chap. Sponsored by the Sisters of St. Joseph of St. Augustine, FL.Mercy Hospital, a campus of Plantation General, is owned and operated by HCA, a for-profit health system, in a manner compliant with the Ethical and Religious Directives and requirements of the Archbishop of Miami to fulfill the essential requirements to be recognized as a Catholic hospital. Plantation Hospital, associated with Mercy, is compliant with the ERDs although not recognized as a Catholic hospital. Bed Capacity 488; Priests 5; Sisters 1; Tot Asst. Annually 93,412; Total Staff 1,320.

St. John Bosco Clinic Inc., 3661 S. Miami Ave., Ste. 103, Miami, 33133. Tel: 305-635-1335; Tel: 305-854-0533; Email: berta.cabrera@ssjhealthfoundation.org. 730 N.W. 34th St., Miami, 33127. Berta Cabrera, M.S., Dir., Tel: 305-854-0533. Employees 8; Patients Asst Anual. 1,250; Units 4,879; Volunteers 44.

**SSJ Health Foundation, Inc.*, 3661 S. Miami Ave., Miami, 33133. Tel: 305-854-0533; Email: bertacabrera@mercyfoundationmiami.org; Web: ssjhealthfoundation.org. Berta Cabrera, M.S., Dir.; Sr. Elizabeth Anne Worley, S.S.J., Board Mem.

FORT LAUDERDALE. *Holy Cross Hospital, Inc.* (1955) 4725 N. Federal Hwy., Fort Lauderdale, 33308. Tel: 954-771-8000; Fax: 954-492-5741; Email: patrick.taylor@holy-cross.com; Web: www.holy-cross.com. Dr. Patrick Taylor, Pres. & CEO; Sr. Rita Levasseur, R.S.M., Vice Pres., Mission Integration; Ms. Barbara Ouellette, Dir. of Spiritual Care; Sisters Claudia Steger, O.S.F., Pastoral Assoc.; Marilyn Canning, R.S.M., Pastoral Assoc.; Revs. Stephen LaCanne, Chap.; James A. Quinn, Chap., (Retired); Gary Weismann, Chap. Bed Capacity 557; Sisters 3; Tot Asst. Annually 501,216; Total Staff 3,207.

Holy Cross Outpatient Services, Inc. (2014) 4725 N. Federal Hwy., Fort Lauderdale, 33308. Tel: 954-771-8000; Email: parick.taylor@holy-cross.com. Dr. Patrick Taylor, Admin. Bed Capacity 25; Tot Asst. Annually 672,101; Total Staff 934.

Holy Cross Primary Care, Inc., 4725 N. Federal Hwy., Fort Lauderdale, 33308. Tel: 954-771-8000; Fax: 954-492-5741; Email: kara.hoag@holy-cross.com; Web: holycross.com. Dr. Patrick Taylor, CEO. Total Staff 644; Patient Visits 508.

[I] MONASTERIES AND RESIDENCES OF PRIESTS AND BROTHERS

MIAMI. *Brothers of the Good Shepherd of Florida, Inc.* (1960) 680 N.E. 52nd St., Miami, 33137. Tel: 815-472-3131; Email: judy@sjog-na.org. Rev. Raphael Mieszala, O.H., Mission Integration Dir.

Christian Brothers, 471 N.E. 53rd St., Miami, 33137. Bros. Joseph Payne, C.F.C., Community Leader; John Corcoran, C.F.C.; Robert Koppes, C.F.C.; Michael LaFrance, C.F.C. Edmund Rice Christian Brothers of North America Total in Residence 4.

Dominican Fathers of Miami, Inc., 5909 N.W. 7th St., Miami, 33126. Tel: 305-264-0181, Ext. 25; Cell: 305-613-8265; Fax: 305-262-4685; Email: jpresmanes@barry.edu; Web: www.opsouth.org. Revs. Restituto Perez, O.P.; Mark Wedig, O.P., Ph. D.; Jorge L. Presmanes, O.P., D.Min.; Orlando Cardozo, O.P.; Cristobal Torres, O.P., M.S.W., M.Div., M.A.; Charles Gerard Austin, O.P., S.T.D., S.T.M.; Jose David Padilla, O.P., M.Div., M.A., S.T.L.; Eduardo Logiste, O.P., M.Div., M.A.; George R. Boudreau, O.P. Priests 9.

Marist Brothers of the Schools, Inc., 3000 S.W. 87th Ave., Miami, 33165. Tel: 305-221-0824, Ext. 22; Email: khandibode@columbushs.com. Bro. Kevin Handibode, F.M.S., Pres. Brothers 21.

Marist Residences. Community #1: 3000 S.W. 87th Ave., Miami, 33165. Tel: 305-221-0834. Bro. Herbert Baker, F.M.S., Dir. Community #2: 8230 S.W. 136th St., Palmetto Bay, 33158. Tel: 305-251-6484; Fax: 305-378-2081; Email: danielj.grogan@yahoo.com. Bro. Daniel J. Grogan, F.M.S., Dir. Community #3: 2790 S.W. 89th Ave., Miami, 33165. Tel: 305-223-5570; Email: frankfil@bellsouth.net. Bro. Charles Filiatrault, F.M.S., Dir. Community #4: 8415 S.W. 81st Ter., Miami, 33143. Tel: 305-274-5946; Email: mbrady@columbushs.com. Bro. Michael Brady, F.M.S., Dir.

Piarist Fathers, Province of the USA & Puerto Rico, 4605 Bayview Dr., Fort Lauderdale, 33308. Tel: 954-771-6525; Fax: 954-776-8060; Email: piaristfl@bellsouth.net; Web: www.piarist.info. Rev. John Callan, Sch.P., Prov. Asst.

Villa Javier, 12725 S.W. 6th St., Miami, 33184-1305. Tel: 787-621-4599; Fax: 305-554-0017; Email: pedrosj@yahoo.com; Web: www.belenjesuit.org. Rev. Alberto Garcia, Supr.; Most Rev. Luis Castillo, Former Bishop; Revs. Guillermo Garcia-Tunon, S.J., Pres. Belen Jesuit Preparatory School; Marcelino Garcia, S.J., Retreat Ministry; Francisco J. Permuy, S.J., Spiritual Counselor/Care Svcs.; Revs. Eduardo Barrios, S.J., Spiritual Counselor; Pedro Cartaya, S.J., Spiritual Dir. & Chap. Belen Alumni; Guillermo Arias, S.J., Spiritual Counselor at Manresa Retreat House, Email: boneiesu@msn.com; Pedro A. Suarez, S.J., Spiritual Counselor & Supr. Jesuit Community; Nelson Garcia, S.J., Counselor, Retreats; Ernesto Fernandez Travieso, S.J.; Lionel Lopez, Spiritual Counselor; Pedro Gonzalez-Llorente, S.J., Spiritual Counselor at Menresa Retreat House.

HOMESTEAD. *Congregation of the Holy Spirit Province of Nigeria South East, Inc.*, 3490 N.W. 191 St., Miami Gardens, 33056. Tel: 305-621-9846; Email: smuodiaju@yahoo.com. Revs. Francis Akwue, C.S. Sp., Dir.; Samuel Muodiaju, C.S.Sp., (Nigeria) Sec.

MIAMI GARDENS. *Discalced Carmelite Friars of Miami, Inc.*, 15710 N.W. 44 Ct., Miami Gardens, 33054-6017. Tel: 305-816-6468; Email: casadeoracionocd@gmail.com; Web: www.carmelitasdescalzosmiami.org. Rev. Lazaro De la Fe Gafas, O.C.D., Supr.; Bro. Jorge Llorentes, O.C.D., Sec.; Revs. Miguel Gil-Diaz; Jacinto Rosario

House of Prayer "Our Lady of Mount Carmel" Total in Residence 4.

[J] CONVENTS AND RESIDENCES FOR SISTERS

MIAMI. *Claretian Missionary Sisters of Florida, Inc.*, 7080 S.W. 99th Ave., Miami, 33173. Tel: 305-274-6148; Fax: 305-274-6148; Email: usdelegation@claretiansisters.org; Email: ondina@claretiansisters.org; Web: www.claretiansisters.org. Sr. Ondina Cortes, R.M.I., Supr. Sisters 12.

Daughters of Charity of St. Vincent de Paul (1971) (Santo Domingo, R.D.), Mision San Vicente de Paul. 500 N.W. 63rd Ave., Miami, 33126. Tel: 305-266-6485; Fax: 305-265-9671; Email: caridad@gate.net; Email: eperezpuelles@yahoo.com. Sr. Eva Perez Puelles, Dir. Asociacion Hijas de la Caridad de San Vicente de Paul del Estado de la Florida, Inc. Sisters 4.

Daughters of Charity of St. Vincent de Paul (1973) 3609 S. Miami Ave., Miami, 33133. Tel: 305-854-2404; Fax: 305-854-8022; Email: sorines@ermita.org. Sr. Ines Espinosa, Prioress. Sisters 3.

Daughters of St. Paul Convent (1959) 11117 S.W. 2nd St., Miami, 33174. Tel: 305-227-2125; Email: miami@paulinemedia.com; Web: www.pauline.org. Sr. Maria Teresa Meza, F.S.P., Supr. Sisters 5.

Handmaids of the Sacred Heart of Jesus A.C.J. (1975) Handmaids of the Sacred Heart of Jesus 1615 N.E. 108th St., Miami, 33161. Tel: 305-891-9161; Fax: 305-891-9161; Email: gjpetrone@msn.com; Web: www.acjusa.org. Sr. Gloria Petrone, Supr. Sisters 4.

Missionaries of Charity (1980) 727 N.W. 17th St., Miami, 33136. Tel: 305-545-5699; Tel: 305-326-0032; Email: weberag@att.net. Sisters M. Ajaya, M.C., Supr.; M. Immacula, M.C., Prov. Sisters 6.

**Siervas de los Corazones Traspasados de Jesus y Maria, Inc. (Servants of the Pierced Hearts of Jesus and Mary)* aka Convento Dos Corazones, Two Hearts Convent (Mother House), 3098 S.W. 14th St., Miami, 33145. Tel: 305-444-7437; Fax: 305-447-0341; Cell: 786-554-7970; Email: sisterana@piercedhearts.org; Web: www.piercedhearts.org; Web: www.corazones.org. Sr. Ana M. Lanzas, S.C.T.J.M., Dir. Religious Ministry to Persons. Novices 8; Postulants 8; Sisters 44.

St. Therese Convent aka Convento Santa Teresita, 2996 S.W. 14th St., Miami, 33145. Tel: 305-444-7437; Email: sisterana@piercedhearts.org; Web: www.piercedhearts.org; Web: www.corazones.org. Sr. Ana M. Lanzas, S.C.T.J.M., Dir.

Mother of Love Convent aka Convento San Pio, 3046 S.W. 14th St., Miami, 33145. Tel: 305-444-7437; Email: sisterana@piercedhearts.org; Web: www.piercedhearts.org; Web: www.corazones.org. Sr. Ana M. Lanzas, S.C.T.J.M., Dir.

Immaculate Convent aka Convento Inmaculada, 1420 S.W. 31st Ave., Miami, 33145. Email: sisterana@piercedhearts.org; Web: www.piercedhearts.org; Web: www.corazones.org. Sr. Ana M. Lanzas, S.C.T.J.M., Dir.

HIALEAH. *Discalced Carmelite Nuns, Inc.*, 4525 W. 2nd Ave., Hialeah, 33012. Tel: 305-558-7122; Fax: 305-558-1190; Email: madrescarmelitasmiami2001@gmail.com. Mother Cristina Galvan, O.C.D., Pres. Postulants 2; Professed Sisters 10.

Monastery of the Most Holy Trinity, (Discalced Carmelite Nuns) (2001) 4525 W. 2nd Ave., Hialeah, 33012. Tel: 305-558-7122; Fax: 305-558-1190; Email: madrescarmelitasmiami2001@gmail.com. Mother Alba Mery de Jesus, O.C.D., Prioress. Postulants 2; Professed Sisters 10.

Dominicas de la Inmaculada Concepcion, 571 W. 33rd Pl., Hialeah, 33012. Tel: 305-823-3282; Email: dominicasmiami@yahoo.com; Email: dominicasinmaculadamiami@gmail.com. Blanca Hernandez, O.P., Supr.; Sisters Maria Teresa Flores, O.P.; Enith Montero, O.P. Professed Sisters 3.

Servants of Jesus of Charity, Inc., 126 W. 45th St., Hialeah, 33012. Tel: 305-231-2063; Fax: 305-231-2063; Cell: 305-299-3793; Email: tostadodeanda.yolanda@yahoo.com.mx. Sr. Yolanda de Anda, Prioress, Prioress. Sisters 4.

HOMESTEAD. *Daughters of Mary, Mothers of Mercy (Nigeria), Inc.*, 18444 S.W. 293rd Ter., Homestead, 33030. Tel: 954-397-1770; Email: bernadettedike44@gmail.com. Sr. Chidi Nwanya, D.M.M.M., Supr., Tel: 305-846-1459; Email: egoigboagwula@yahoo.com. Sisters 4.

Mercy Convent, 1618 Polk St., Hollywood, 33020. Tel: 954-895-3005; Cell: 954-397-1770; Email: bernadettedike44@gmail.com; Web: www.dmmmsisters-usa.org. 9751 S.W. 15th St., Pembroke Pines, 33025. Sr. Bernadette Dike, Supr. Sisters 11.

MIAMI SHORES. *Franciscan Sisters of Allegany*, 54 N.W. 103 St., Miami, 33150. Tel: 305-914-4500; Email: lcardet@fsallegany.org; Web: alleganyfranciscans.org. Sr. Lucy Cardet, Contact Person. Sisters 4.

WESTCHESTER. *Congregation of the French-Cuban Dominican Sisters of Holy Rosary, Inc.*, 7920 S.W. 23rd St., Miami, 33155. Tel: 305-265-9759; Email: cecilia.alonso1416@gmail.com. Sr. Mary Cecilia Alonso, O.P., Pres., Treas. & Contact. Sisters 3.

[K] RETREAT HOUSES

PINECREST. *MorningStar Renewal Center, Inc.*, 7275 S.W. 124th St., Pinecrest, 33156-4649. Tel: 305-238-4367; Email: info@morningstarrenewal.org; Web: www.morningstarrenewal.org. Sue DeFerrari, M.A., M.S.W., Dir., Ministry. Tot Asst. Annually 11,650.

[L] SHRINES

MIAMI. *National Shrine of Our Lady of Charity*, 3609 S. Miami Ave., Miami, 33133-4205. Tel: 305-854-2404; Fax: 305-854-8022; Email: santuario@ermita.org; Web: www.ermita.org. Revs. Fernando Heria, J.C.L., Rector; Carlos J. Cespedes, (Cuba) Vicar; Francisco Garcia Fernandez, Vicar. Sisters 3; Annual Visitors 228,600; Hours of Reconciliation (weeky avg. of normal hrs. for confession) 20.

**Schoenstatt Movement of Florida, Inc.*, 22800 S.W. 187 Ave., Miami, 33170. Tel: 305-248-4800; Email: schoenstattmiami@gmail.com; Email: schoenstattusa@aol.com; Email: kasanza@aol.com; Web: www.schoenstattmiamiusa.org. Katuzhka Asanza, Treas., Tel: 954-961-4507.

[M] CENTERS

MIAMI. *Pauline Books & Media* (1959) 145 S.W. 107th Ave., Miami, 33174. Tel: 305-559-6715; Fax: 305-225-4189; Email: miami@paulinemedia.com; Web: www.pauline.org. Sr. Maria Teresa Meza, F.S.P., Supr. Total Staff 9.

Paulinas Spanish Distribution Center (1996) 145 S.W. 107th Ave., Miami, 33174. Tel: 305-225-2513; Tel: 800-872-5852; Fax: 305-225-4189; Email: paulinas@paulinemedia.com; Web: www.pauline.org Spanish. Sr. Maria Teresa Meza, F.S.P., Dir.

SEPI Evangelization and Education Foundation, Inc., 7700 S.W. 56th St., Miami, 33155. Tel: 305-279-2333; Fax: 305-279-0925; Email: info@sepi.us. Rev. Rafael Capo, Sch.P., Dir., Contact.

Southeast Regional Office for Hispanic Ministry, Inc., 7700 S.W. 56th St., Miami, 33155. Tel: 305-279-2333; Fax: 305-279-0925; Email: info@sepi.us; Web: www.sepi.us. Rev. Rafael Capo, Sch.P., Dir.; Lizette Arguello, Business Mgr.

Southeast Pastoral Institute aka SEPI, 7700 S.W. 56th St., Miami, 33155. Tel: 305-279-2333, Ext. 3; Email: info@sepi.us. Rev. Rafael Capo, Sch.P., Exec. Dir.; Lizette Arguello, Business Mgr.

COOPER CITY. *Ministry to the Deaf or Disabled - Schott Memorial Center Inc.*, 6591 S. Flamingo Rd., Cooper City, 33330. Tel: 954-434-3306; Fax: 954-434-3307; Email: iramirez@schottcommunities.org; Web: www.schottcommunities.org. Mrs. Ileana Ramirez-Cueli, Exec. Dir.; Mr. Pablo A. Cuadra, Dir. Religious Education (DRE); Mary Roukas, Dir. Progs. & Residences; Jerry Cohen, Dir. Annual Fund & Stewardship; Audrey Brown, Dir. Finance & Admin. Center for persons who are deaf or with a disability. Children 22; Residents 19; Estimated Number of Catholics 200; Total Assisted 320.

Schott Memorial Center Foundation, Inc., 6591 S. Flamingo Rd., Cooper City, 33330. Email: rgschott@comcast.net; Cell: 239-877-9883. Rev. Msgr. Roberto Garza, Exec.; Greg Schott, Exec.; Jose Rementeria, Exec.

[N] PERSONAL PRELATURE

MIAMI. *Prelature of the Holy Cross and Opus Dei*, 4415 S.W. 88th Ave., Miami, 33165. Tel: 305-551-7956; Fax: 305-551-7957; Email: vacg6556@gmail.com. Revs. Victor Cortes, Contact Person; Juan Velez, Chap.; Jay Alvarez. Priests 3.

[O] MISCELLANEOUS LISTINGS

MIAMI. *ACU Holdings, Inc.*, 12805 S.W. 6th St., Miami, 33184. Rev. Guillermo Garcia-Tunon, S.J., Dir.

ACU Properties, LLC, 12805 S.W. 6th St., Miami, 33184. Tel: 786-360-8004; Email: evieira@estovir.org; Email: acuinfo@estovir.org. Rev. Guillermo Garcia-Tunon, S.J., Dir.

Agrupacion Catolica Universitaria, Inc., 12805 S.W. 6th St., Miami, 33184. Tel: 786-360-8004; Email: evieira@estovir.org; Email: acuinfo@estovir.org; Web: www.estovir.org. Rev. Guillermo Garcia-Tunon, S.J., Dir.

Alumni Association of the Apostolate of Cuba (in Exile), Inc., P.O. Box 653851, Miami, 33165. Tel: 305-666-0376; Email: pvsalinero@hotmail.com. Lourdes Garriga, Pres.

Catholic Charities of Florida, Inc., 201 W. Park Ave., Tallahassee, 32301.

Claretian Missions, Inc., 7080 S.W. 99th Ave., Miami, 33173. Tel: 305-274-6148; Fax: 305-274-6148; Cell: 305-586-6100; Email: ondina@claretiansisters.org; Email: chiquirmi@gmail.com; Web: www.claretiansisters.org. Sr. Ondina Cortes, R.M.I., Pres.

Father Tino Foundation, 12725 S.W. 6th St., Miami, 33184. Cell: 305-972-9499; Email: cdlt1948@yahoo.com. Carlos de la Torre, CEO; Rev. Alberto Garcia, Dir.

Federacion de Institutos Pastorales, Inc., 7700 S.W. 56th St., Miami, 33155. Tel: 305-279-2333, Ext. 3; Fax: 305-279-0925; Email: Robert.Hurteau@lm.edu; Web: Fipusa.org. Robert Hurteau, Pres.; Alejandro Siller, Vice Pres.; Maruja Sedano, Sec.; William Becerra, Treas.; Nelly Lorenzo, Vocal.

Hurley Heritage Trust, 9401 Biscayne Blvd., Miami, 33138.

Jesus Maestro, Inc., 12805 S.W. 6th St., Miami, 33184. Tel: 786-360-8004; Email: admin@estovir.org; Web: www.estovir.org. Rev. Guillermo Garcia-Tunon, S.J., Dir.

Leadership Learning Center at St. John Bosco, Inc., 1366 N.W. First St., Miami, 33125. Tel: 305-649-4730; Fax: 305-649-4733; Email: sdelriego@sjbmiami.org; Web: www.leadershiplearningcenter.org. Susana Del Riego, Dir. Students 240.

**Maria Vision US, Inc.*, 430 Grand Bay Dr., Ste. 1201, Miami, 33149. Tel: 786-485-3026; Email: presidencia@mariavision.com; Web: mariavision.com. Emilio Burillo, Pres.; Rafael Burillo, Treas. A Christian Catholic Multimedia Network.

Peruvian Mission, Inc. (1994) (A Florida Not-for-Profit Corporation) 9401 Biscayne Blvd., P.O. Box 432745, Miami, 33143. Tel: 786-452-7826; Email: aprilis2@bellsouth.net. Maria Delia Salazar, Dir., Sec. & Contact Person. Board Members Most Revs. Javier del Rio Alba, Archbishop of Arequipa; Jose Luis del Palacio, Bishop of Callao; Luis Abilio Sebastiani Aguirre, S.M., Archbishop of Ayacucho, Founding Member; Pedro Barreto, S.J., Archbishop of Huancayo; Jorge Carrion, Bishop of Puno; Enrique Delgado, Ph.D., D.D., V.G., Auxiliary Bishop of Miami.

Stella Maris Seamen Center, Inc., Port of Miami, Miami, 33139. Tel: 305-531-1124; Email: parish@stpatrickmiamibeach.com. Rev. Roberto M. Cid, Dir.

Teresian Institute, (Rome, Italy), Teresian Institute of Florida, Inc. (1911) An International Association of the Faithful. 3400 S.W. 99 Ave., Miami, 33165. Tel: 305-554-0035; Tel: 513-559-9498; Cell: 305-299-0880; Email: marbona@fuse.net; Web: www.institucionteresiana.org. Maria Rosa Arbona, U.S. Delegate; Rachel Portell, Sec. Total in Residence 2; Total Staff 4.

Center of Activities, National Headquarters, Web: www.institucionteresiana.org; Tel: 954-962-5682; Fax: 954-962-5682.

Theatine Sisters of the Immaculate Conception, Co. aka Religiosas Teatinas de la Immaculada Concepcion, 12261 S.W. 6th St., Miami, 33184. Tel: 786-409-5212; Email: teatinasmia@att.net. Sr. Esther Samudio, Supr. Sisters 3.

Vida Humana Internacional (Hispanic Division of Human Life International), 45 S.W. 71st Ave., Miami, 33144. Tel: 305-260-0525; Fax: 305-260-0595; Email: vhi@vidahumana.org; Email: adriana@vidahumana.org; Web: www.vidahumana.org. Rev. Shenan Boquet, Pres.

MIAMI GARDENS. **Fundacion Ramon Pane, Inc.*, 1335 N.W. 179th Ter., Miami Gardens, 33169. Tel: 305-323-9257; Cell: 786-473-9027; Email: presidencia@fundacionpane.org; Email: regrzona@hotmail.com; Web: www.cristonautas.com. Bro. Ricardo Grzona, F.R.P., Pres.

CORAL GABLES. *Foundation Order of Malta, Inc.* (1993) A National Association, part of the Sovereign Military and Hospitaler, Order of St. John of Jerusalem, of Rhodes and of Malta. 299 Alhambra Cir., Ste. 321, Coral Gables, 33134. Tel: 786-888-6494; Fax: 305-285-0837; Email: juan.t.onaghten@ondlaw.com; Email: presidente@ordendemaltacuba.org; Web: www.ordendemaltacuba.org. Juan Jose Calvo, Pres.; Juan T. O'Naghten, Vice Pres.; Luis F. Parajon, Chancellor; Jose Joaquin Centurion, Dir.; John Harriman, Treas.

Cuban Association of the Order of Malta.

House of the Divine Will, Inc. dba Casa de la Divina Voluntad (1996) 5900 Leonardo St., Coral Gables, 33146-3332. Tel: 305-667-5714; Fax: 305-667-7173; Cell: 786-467-7319; Cell: 786-344-6527; Email: casadivinavoluntad@msn.com; Web: www.casadivinavoluntad.org. Rev. Carlos Antonio Massieu Avila, Pres. & Chm.; Mother Marianela Perez, Treas. & Contact Person.

CUTLER BAY. *Magnificat, Inc.*, 9822 S.W. 222 St., Cutler Bay, 33190. Tel: 305-753-8380; Fax: 305-772-3073; Email: mariabl003@gmail.com. Maria Luque, Coord.; Valli Leoni, Asst. Coord.; Judith Johnson, Treas.; Lisette Fernandez, Sec.; Desiree Leone, Historian.

HIALEAH. **Opus Caritatis Corp.*, 998 W. 65 St., Hialeah, 33012. Tel: 786-312-4234; Fax: 305-822-0563. Rev. Msgr. Oscar F. Castaneda, Dir.

HOMESTEAD. **Centro de Artes y Oficios De La Salle, Inc.*, Vocational Center, 13350 S.W. 314 St., Homestead, 33033-5617. Tel: 305-245-5810; Fax: 305-553-3032; Email: center@celasalleh.org; Web: www.celasalleh.org. Salvador Romo, Pres.; Bro. Daniel Aubin, F.S.C., Dir., Board, 4937 Willow Dr., Boca Raton, 33487. Tel: 561-314-2121; Grace Veloz, Sec.; Francisco Briz, Treas. Vocational Center for adults. Classes are free of charge. Also after school for children K-9. Staff 9; Total Assisted 226.

MIAMI SHORES. *Archdiocese of Miami Millennium Appeal, Inc.*, 9401 Biscayne Blvd., 33138. Tel: 305-757-6241; Fax: 305-758-5261; Email: eworley@theadom.org. Sr. Elizabeth Anne Worley, S.S.J., Chancellor.

Archdiocese of Miami Mission Services, Inc., 9401 Biscayne Blvd., 33138. Tel: 305-762-1284; Email: eworley@theadom.org. Sr. Elizabeth Anne Worley, S.S.J., Chancellor.

Archdiocese of Miami, Inc. (1958) 9401 Biscayne Blvd., 33138. Tel: 305-757-6241; Fax: 305-758-5261; Email: eworley@theadom.org. Most Rev. Thomas G. Wenski, D.D., Archbishop.

Asociacion Nacional de Diaconos Hispanos, Inc., 9401 Biscayne Blvd., 33138. Tel: (305) 762-1024; Email: vpimentel@theadom.org. Deacon Fernando Bestard, Pres., Tel: 305-762-6510; Tel: 305-271-9586.

Bahamas Mission of Florida, Inc., Archdiocese of Miami, 9401 Biscayne Blvd., 33138. Tel: 305-762-1284; Email: eworley@theadom.org. Sr. Elizabeth Anne Worley, S.S.J., Chancellor.

Colonial Heritage of Florida, LLC, 9401 Biscayne Blvd., 33138. Tel: 305-762-1284; Email: eworley@theadom.org. Sr. Elizabeth Anne Worley, S.S.J., Chancellor.

DOM, Inc., 9401 Biscayne Blvd., 33138. Tel: 305-762-1284; Fax: 305-758-5261; Email: eworley@theadom.org. Sr. Elizabeth Anne Worley, S.S.J., Chancellor.

Ecclesiastical Province of Miami, Inc., 9401 Biscayne Blvd., 33138. Tel: 305-762-1284; Email: eworley@theadom.org. Sr. Elizabeth Anne Worley, S.S.J., Chancellor.

Francis Realty Corporation, 9401 Biscayne Blvd., 33138. Tel: 305-762-1284; Fax: 305-758-5261; Email: eworley@theadom.org. Sr. Elizabeth Anne Worley, S.S.J., Chancellor.

P.O.M., Inc., 9401 Biscayne Blvd., 33138. Tel: 305-762-1284; Fax: 305-758-5261; Email: eworley@theadom.org. Sr. Elizabeth Anne Worley, S.S.J., Chancellor.

Provincial Realty Associates, Inc. (A Florida Not-for-Profit Corporation) 9401 Biscayne Blvd., 33138. Tel: 305-762-1284; Email: eworley@theadom.org. Sr. Elizabeth Anne Worley, S.S.J., Chancellor. Land Holding Corporation.

**Roman Catholic Archdiocese of Nassau Foundation, Inc.*, 110 Merrick Way, Ste. 3-B, Coral Gables, 33134. Tel: 305-443-9162, Ext. 17; Email: jpf@jpfitzlaw.com. Mr. Patrick Fitzgerald, Archdiocesan Attorney.

*THE ST. VINCENT DE PAUL SOCIETY, ARCHDIOCESAN COUNCIL OF MIAMI, INC., Mailing Address: 9401 Biscayne Blvd., 33138. Tel: 786-245-8624 SVDP Call Center Numbers; Tel: 888-866-3811 (Toll-Free). Mr. Frank Voehl, Pres.

St. Vincent De Paul Food Pantry, 14141 S.W. 26 St., Miami, 33175. Tel: 305-282-4253; Email: svpmoc@hotmail.com. Jim Worley, Vice Pres.

SUNRISE. *Magnificat Broward County, Florida Chapter, Inc.* (2013) 5344 N.W. 127th Ave., Coral Springs, 33076. Cell: 754-484-4459; Email: kathycorona212@yahoo.com. Kathy Corona, Coord., 5344 N.W. 117th Ave., Coral Springs, 33076. Tel: 954-635-7458; Juliana Findley, Treas., 8020 Clearly Blvd. Apt. #212, Plantation, 3324. Tel: 754-234-1847; Martha Roman, Historian; Rev.

John Fink, Spiritual Advisor, (Retired), 2441 S.W. 82nd Ave. #204, Davenport, 33324. Tel: 954-529-4269.

RELIGIOUS INSTITUTES OF MEN REPRESENTED IN THE ARCHDIOCESE

For further details refer to the corresponding bracketed number in the Religious Institutes of Men or Women section.

[0140]—*The Augustinians* (St. Thomas of Villanova Prov.)—O.S.A.
[0310]—*Congregation of Christian Brothers* (Eastern Prov.)—C.F.C.
[]—*Congregation of the Mission*—C.M.
[0260]—*Discalced Carmelite Friars*—O.C.D.
[]—*Franciscan Friars*—O.F.M.
[0650]—*Holy Ghost Fathers*—C.S.Sp.
[0690]—*Jesuit Fathers and Brothers* (Antilles)—S.J.
[0580]—*Hospitaller Brothers of St. John of God*—O.H.
[0770]—*The Marist Brothers* (Bayonne, N.J. & Poughkeepsie Provs.)—F.M.S.
[1210]—*Missionaries of St. Charles-Scalabrinians*—C.S.
[]—*Missionaries of the Company of Mary* (U.S. Prov.)—S.M.M.
[]—*Montfort Missionaries*—S.M.M.
[0430]—*Order of Preachers (Dominican)* (St. Joseph & Southern Provs.)—O.P.
[1310]—*Order of the Most Holy Trinity and of the Captives*—O.SS.T.
[1020]—*Pauline Fathers & Brothers*—S.S.P.
[1040]—*Piarist Fathers*—Sch.P.
[1260]—*Society of Christ*—S.Ch.
[0760]—*Society of Mary (Marianists)*—S.M.
[]—*Society of the Divine Savior*—S.D.S.

RELIGIOUS INSTITUTES OF WOMEN REPRESENTED IN THE ARCHDIOCESE

[0370]—*Carmelite Sisters of the Most Sacred Heart of Los Angeles*—O.C.D.
[0685]—*Claretian Missionary Sisters*—R.M.I.
[0760]—*Daughters of Charity of St. Vincent de Paul*—D.C.
[0850]—*Daughters of Mary Help of Christians*—F.M.A.
[]—*Daughters of Mary, Mother of Mercy (Nigeria)*—D.M.M.M.
[]—*Daughters of Our Lady of Visitation*—F.M.V.
[0950]—*Daughters of St. Paul*—F.S.P.
[0420]—*Discalced Carmelite Nuns*—O.C.D.
[1070-13]—*Dominican Sisters (Adrian)*—O.P.
[]—*Dominican Sisters of Our Lady of the Most Holy Rosary (Colombia)*—O.P.
[]—*Dominicas de la Inmaculada Concepcion (Ecuador).*
[1180]—*Franciscan Sisters of Allegany, New York*—O.S.F.
[1870]—*Handmaids of the Sacred Heart of Jesus*—A.C.J.
[]—*Holy Spirit Sisters*—H.S.S.
[]—*Marianitas* (Santa Mariana de Jesus Institute, Inc.)—R.M.
[2710]—*Missionaries of Charity*—M.C.
[]—*Oblate Missionaries of Mary Immaculate*—O.M.M.I.
[3040]—*Oblate Sisters of Providence*—O.S.P.
[]—*Our Lady of Good Counsel* (Canada), S.B.C.
[]—*Secular Institute of the Schoenstatt Sisters of Mary*—I.S.S.M.
[]—*Servants of Jesus of Charity*—S.de.J.
[]—*Servants of the Pierced Hearts of Jesus and Mary*—S.P.H.J.M.
[]—*Sisters of Jesus the Saviour* (Nigeria)—S.J.S.
[]—*Sisters of Notre Dame* Chardon, Ohio—S.N.D.
[3000]—*Sisters of Notre Dame de Namur (Baltimore, MA)*—S.N.D.deN.
[1630]—*Sisters of St. Francis of Penance and Christian Charity*—O.S.F.
[]—*Sisters of St. Joseph Benedict Cottolengo*—S.S.J.C.
[3900]—*Sisters of St. Joseph of St. Augustine, Florida*—S.S.J.
[]—*Sisters of St. Philip Neri Missionary Teachers*—R.F.
[2160]—*Sisters of the Immaculate Heart of Mary* (Spain)—I.H.M.
[2170]—*Sisters, Servants of the Immaculate Heart of Mary* (Immaculata, PA)—I.H.M.
[4020]—*Society of St. Teresa of Jesus*—S.T.J.
[4070]—*Society of the Sacred Heart*—R.S.C.J.
[]—*The Lovers of the Holy Cross of Ba Ria-Vietnam*—L.H.C.
[]—*Theatine Sisters of the Immaculate Conception (Religiosas Teatinas de la Inmaculada Concepcion)*—R.T.

SECULAR INSTITUTE OF MEN

[]—*Voluntas Dei Institute*—I.V. Dei.

SECULAR INSTITUTES OF WOMEN

[]—*Oblate Missionaries of Mary Immaculate*—O.M.M.I.
[]—*Secular Institute of the Schoenstatt Sisters of Mary*—I.S.S.M.

NECROLOGY

† Marin, Tomas M., Coral Gables, FL St. Augustine, Died Dec. 28, 2018
† Dalton, Bryan, Deerfield Beach, FL St. Ambrose, Died Nov. 30, 2018
† Garcia, Jorge, (Retired), Died Dec. 19, 2018
† Kubala, Daniel I., (Retired), Died Aug. 31, 2018
† Melley, James J., (Retired), Died Jul. 1, 2018
† O'Brien, Anthony, Tamarac, FL St. Malachy, Died May. 13, 2018
† Torres, Juan, (Retired), Died Oct. 23, 2018

An asterisk (*) denotes an organization that has established tax-exempt status directly with the IRS and is not covered by the USCCB Group Ruling.

Archdiocese for the Military Services, U.S.A.

Ordinariatus Castrensis

Most Reverend

FRANCIS X. ROQUE, D.D.

Retired Auxiliary Bishop for the Military Services; ordained September 19, 1953; appointed Titular Bishop of Bagai and Auxiliary Bishop to the Military Ordinariate March 29, 1983; consecrated May 10, 1983; retired August 15, 2004.

Most Reverend

RICHARD B. HIGGINS, S.T.L., D.D.

Auxiliary Bishop for the Military Services; ordained March 9, 1968; appointed Titular Bishop of Casae Calanae and Auxiliary Bishop of the Archdiocese for the Military Services May 7, 2004; ordained July 3, 2004.

Most Reverend

F. RICHARD SPENCER, M.A., D.D.

Auxiliary Bishop for the Military Services; ordained May 14, 1988; appointed Titular Bishop of Auzia and Auxiliary Bishop of the Archdiocese for the Military Services May 22, 2010; ordained September 8, 2010.

Most Reverend

TIMOTHY P. BROGLIO, J.C.D., S.T.B.

Archbishop for the Military Services; ordained May 19, 1977; appointed Titular Archbishop of Amiternum & Apostolic Nuncio to the Dominican Republic February 27, 2001; ordained a bishop March 19, 2001; appointed Archbishop for the Military Services November 19, 2007; installed January 25, 2008.

Chancery: Edwin Cardinal O'Brien Pastoral Center, 1025 Michigan Ave., N.E., P.O. Box 4469, Washington, DC 20017-0469. Tel: 202-719-3600; Fax: 202-269-9022.

Web: www.milarch.org

Email: info@milarch.org

Most Reverend

NEAL J. BUCKON

Auxiliary Bishop for the Military Services; ordained May 25, 1995; appointed Titular Bishop of Vissalsa and Auxiliary Bishop of the Archdiocese for the Military Services January 3, 2011; ordained February 22, 2011.

Most Reverend

JOSEPH L. COFFEY

Auxiliary Bishop for the Military Services; ordained May 18, 1996; appointed Titular Bishop of Arsacal and Auxiliary Bishop of the Archdiocese for the Military Services January 22, 2019; ordained March 25, 2019.

Most Reverend

WILLIAM J. MUHM

Auxiliary Bishop for the Military Services; ordained May 13, 1995; appointed Titular Bishop of Capsus and Auxiliary Bishop of the Archdiocese for the Military Services January 22, 2019; ordained March 25, 2019.

Established as the Archdiocese For The Military Services, U.S.A. (Ordinariatus Castrensis) March 25, 1985.

Serving U.S. Catholics of the Army, Navy, Air Force, Marine Corps, Coast Guard, Department of Veterans Affairs and those in Government Service outside the USA.

STATISTICAL OVERVIEW

Personnel	
Archbishops	1
Auxiliary Bishops	5
Retired Bishops	1
Permanent Deacons in Diocese	2
Vital Statistics	
Receptions into the Church:	
Infant Baptism Totals	1,244
Minor Baptism Totals	214
Adult Baptism Totals	159
Received into Full Communion	140
First Communions	1,575
Confirmations	1,244
Marriages:	
Catholic	156
Interfaith	74
Total Marriages	230

Former Military Vicars—His Eminence PATRICK CARDINAL HAYES, cons. Titular Bishop of Tagaste, Oct. 28, 1914; appt. "Bishop Ordinary of U.S. Army and Navy Chaplains," Nov. 24, 1917; appt. Archbishop of New York, March 10, 1919; created Cardinal, March 24, 1924; died Sept. 4, 1938; FRANCIS CARDINAL SPELLMAN, cons. Auxiliary Bishop of Boston, Sept. 8, 1932; appt. Archbishop of New York, April 15, 1939; appt. "Military Vicar for the Armed Forces of U.S.," Dec. 11, 1939; created Cardinal, Feb. 18, 1946; died Dec. 2, 1967; TERENCE CARDINAL COOKE, cons. Auxiliary Bishop of New York, Dec. 13, 1965; appt. Archbishop of New York, March 2, 1968; appt. "Military Vicar of U.S. Armed Forces," April 4, 1968; created Cardinal, April 28, 1969; died Oct. 6, 1983; Most Revs. JOSEPH T. RYAN, appt. first Archbishop of Anchorage, Feb. 7, 1966; cons. March 25, 1966; appt. Titular Archbishop of Gabi and Coadjutor (Archbishop) of the Military Ordinariate, Oct. 24, 1975; installed first Ordinary of the Archdiocese for the Military Services March, 25, 1985; retired May 13, 1991; died Oct. 9, 2000; JOSEPH T. DIMINO, D.D., appt. Auxiliary Bishop of Military Odinariate and Titular Bishop of Carini, March 29, 1983; cons. May 10, 1983; appt. second Ordinary for the Military Services, May 13, 1991; retired Aug. 12, 1997; died Nov. 25, 2014; His Eminence EDWIN F. O'BRIEN, ord. May 29, 1965; appt. Titular Bishop of Tizica and Auxiliary Bishop of New York Feb. 6, 1996; cons. March 25, 1996; appt. Coadjutor April 8, 1997; succeeded as Ordinary to the Military Services Aug. 12, 1997; appt. Archbishop of Baltimore July 12, 2007; created Cardinal Feb. 18, 2012; appt. Grand Master of the Equestrian Order of the Holy Sepulchre of Jerusalem, March 15, 2012.

Vicar General & Moderator of the Curia—Rev. Msgr. JOHN J. M. FOSTER, J.C.D.

Episcopal Vicars—

Episcopal Vicar for Installations in Europe and Asia—Most Rev. F. RICHARD SPENCER, M.A., D.D.

Episcopal Vicar for Installations in the Eastern Vicariate of the AMS—VACANT.

Episcopal Vicar for Installations in the Western Vicariate of the AMS—Most Rev. NEAL J. BUCKON, D.D.

Episcopal Vicar for Veteran Concerns—Most Rev. RICHARD B. HIGGINS, S.T.L., D.D.

Archdiocese Offices

Chancery—Mailing Address: Edwin Cardinal O'Brien Pastoral Center, P.O. Box 4469, Washington, 20017. Tel: 202-719-3600; Fax: 202-269-9022; Email: info@milarch.org; Web: www.milarch.org.

Chancellor—Rev. ROBERT R. CANNON, M.A., J.C.L., J.C.D. (Cand.).

Vice Chancellor & Archivist—Sr. HELEN SUMANDER, M.C.S.T.

Office of Evangelization—

Vice Chancellor for Evangelization—DR. MARK MOITOZA.

Director of Faith Formation—JOSE M. AMAYA.

Office of Vocations—

Director of Vocations—Rev. AIDAN ARTHUR H. LOGAN, O.C.S.O.

Assistant to the Archbishop—Sr. LISA MARIE DROVER, O.S.F.

Chief Financial Officer—MR. WILLIAM BIGGS.

Director of Advancement—MR. SALVADOR PEREZ.

Tribunal—

Judicial Vicar—Very Rev. CHRISTOPHER R. ARMSTRONG, S.T.D., J.C.D.

Judges—Revs. JAMES E. BAKER, J.C.L.; JOHN B. WARD, J.C.L.; MS. LINDA E. PRICE, J.C.L.; MS. DEBORAH BARTON, J.C.L.; MR. ED CONDON, J.C.D.; Rev. THOMAS J. PETRO, J.C.L.

Defenders of the Bond—Revs. G. PAUL HERBERT, J.C.L.; JORDAN F. HITE, T.O.R., J.C.L.; JOSEPH G. MULRONEY, J.C.L.; MS. ZABRINA DECKER, J.C.D.; MS. ELISA UGARTE, J.C.L.

Notary—MISS PATRICIA HUTCHISON, T.O. Carmelite.

General Counsel—MS. ELIZABETH TOMLIN, J.D.

Presbyteral Council—Most Revs. NEAL J. BUCKON, D.D.; RICHARD B. HIGGINS, S.T.L., D.D.; F. RICHARD SPENCER, M.A., D.D.; Rev. Msgr. JOHN J. M. FOSTER, J.C.D.; Very Rev. CHRISTOPHER R. ARMSTRONG, S.T.D., J.C.D.; Revs. AIDAN ARTHUR H. LOGAN, O.C.S.O.; GREGORY G. CAIAZZO; ROBERT R. CANNON, M.A., J.C.L., J.C.D. (Cand.); JOSEPH DEICHERT; WILLIAM KENNEDY; FRANCIS FOLEY; PAUL HURLEY; RICHARD NOVOTNY; R. PETER FRANCIS, IVDei; MATTHEW PAWLIKOWSKI.

Military Council of Catholic Women—Most Rev. NEAL J. BUCKON, D.D., Episcopal Moderator.

National Conference of Veterans Affairs Catholic Chaplains, Inc.—Most Rev. RICHARD B. HIGGINS, S.T.L., D.D., Episcopal Advisor.

Areas of Service

Armed Forces, Active Duty: The Archdiocese for the Military Services is responsible for the pastoral care of the Catholic men and women who serve on active duty in the U.S. Armed Forces. It is also responsible for the dependents of these persons. Included also are the cadets and resident personnel of the three military academies (the U.S. Military Academy at West Point, the U.S. Air Force Academy at Colorado Springs, the U.S. Naval Academy at Annapolis) and the U.S. Coast Guard Academy at New London. Pastoral care is provided by priest-chaplains on loan from their dioceses or religious communities to serve as chaplains for the Military and Department of Veterans Affairs. Members of the Marine Corps and Coast Guard are served by Navy Chaplains, Armed Forces, Reserves, National Guard: In addition to the personnel on active duty in the Armed Forces, there is a considerable reserve component. Some of these personnel serve a number of days each year on active duty with a branch of the service; some serve on extended tours of active duty; all are subject to recall to active duty in a national emergency. In addition to the reserve components of the Army, Air Force, Navy and Coast Guard, there are also the Air National Guard and the Army National Guard, which are organized on a state-by-state basis.

Department of Veterans Affairs: The Archdiocese for the Military Services is responsible for the spiritual care of Catholics at V.A. medical facilities. Chaplaincy services are provided by full- and part-time priests, many of whom are retired military chaplains. U.S. Government Civilian Employees outside the national borders: U.S. citizens in government service outside the national borders (and their family members living with them) are subjects of the Archdiocese for the Military Services. Civil Air Patrol: The Civil Air Patrol, as an auxiliary of the Air Force, is under the jurisdiction of the Archdiocese for the Military Services. The jurisdiction applies to its chaplains and members only when participating in exercises on a military installation.

UNITED STATES ARMY CHAPLAINS

Army Chaplains
Revs.—
Adunchezor, Christopher, (Nigeria)
Akeriwe, Raymond A., S.M.A.
Albano, Alwyn M., (Philippines)
Albertson, Eric J.
Amande, Lito D., (Philippines)
Anumata, Christopher C., (Nigeria)
Awotwi, Charles K.
Barkemeyer, John F.
Bolin, Kenneth M.
Brankatelli, Joseph R.
Bulinski, Marcin J.
Caballejo, Yuen Servanez
Camiring, Paul John, (Philippines)
Campbell, Joseph C.
Collins, James B.
Cotter, Stephen Duane
Dechenne, Jason
Doering, Christopher E.
Fleury, Joseph M., S.M.
Gabriel, John B., (India)
Gaskin, Grantley DaCosta
Goulet, Daniel R.
Gross, Gary L.
Halka, Frantisek A.
Halladay, Paul A.
Hernandez, Anselmo, L.C.
Hesseling, Jason E.
Hubbs, Timothy L.
Hurley, Paul K.
Iheke, Uche G., S.M.M.M.
Ijeoma, John Vianney, (Nigeria)
Irizarry, Alan M.
Jong, Lyndon A., (Philippines)
Kazarnowicz, Anthony S.
Kelly, Thomas N.
Kilumbu, Claudes, (Congo)
Kirk, David R.
Kondik, Curtis L.
Kopec, Krzysztof A.
Kopec, Rajmund
Kumai, Felix K., (Nigeria)
Lawrence, Andrew F.
Lea, Joseph P.
Lemor, Kiskama, C.S.Sp.
Lindsay, Michael P.
LosBanes, Hermes, (Philippines)
Madu, Ferdinand E., (Nigeria)
Magnuson, Sean R.
Manuel, Vincent, (India)
Manzano, Delfin F., (Philippines)
Martin, Edward
McDermott, Stephen C.
Mora Gomez, Guillermo Leon
Moras, Leo, (India)
Muda, Adam
Muli, Killian, (Kenya)
Munoz-Lasalle, Jesus M.
Napieralski, Maciej, (Poland)
Novitzky, Martin
Nwagbara, Anselm, (Nigeria)
Ochalek, Arkadiusz
Oforka, Francis I., (Nigeria)
Okoth, George, (Kenya)
Opara, Isaac, (Nigeria)
Panzer, Joel
Pawlikowski, Matthew
Peak, James
Pomposello, Peter A.
Ranada, Arnel O., (Philippines)
Reffner, Joseph
Rzasowski, Jerzy, (Poland)
Scibbior, Mikolaj L., (Poland)
Sherbourne, Gerald
Somera, Romelo B., (Philippines)
Tah, Philip P., (Nigeria)
Uwakwe, Uzoma E., (Nigeria)
Villanueva, Edgar, (Philippines)
Whitehead, Matthew
Whorton, Jeffrey T.
Willenberg, Lukasz J.
Wodecki, Jeremi C.
Wood, Tyson J.
Yebra, Bernardino S., (Philippines)
Zemczak, Pawel.

Army National Guard Chaplains
Very Rev.—
Allen, Richard J., E.V.
Revs.—
Ahern, Adam L., M.Div.
Alvarado de Jesus, Jose R.
Brownell, Patrick P.
Butera, Christopher S., M.Div., M.A.
Cavanaugh, Kevin P.
Constant, Van
Converse, Brian J.
Creagan, Michael
Fehn, Jerome W.
Friedley, Craig W.M.
Gion, Chad O.
Jaramillo, Peter, S.S.A.
Kane, Brian P., S.T.B., M.Div., M.A.
Lacey, Robert Edward
LaVoie, Raymond J.
Meier, Timothy, S.J.
Meinzen, David L.
Murphy, David F.
Paveglio, Jeffrey A.
Peek, Kevin T., B.A., M.Div.
Rhodes, Christopher S.
Sanchez, Angel
Sanchez-Munoz, Alejandro
Severson, David
Stodola, Francis
Tyhovych, Ivan
Vera Gonzalez, Julio Angel
Worster, John R.

Army Reserve Chaplains
Revs.—
Adams, Joseph M., O.S.B.
Anaya, Jose Angel Estrada
Aniekwe, Samuel O., (Nigeria)
Augustyn, Boguslaw Adam, C.Ss.R.
Axalan, Romeo J., (Philippines)
Behay, Vasyl S.
Bernas, Anthony N., (Philippines)
Carlson, Kenneth F., M.Div.
Cho, Minhyun
Corneille, Cecil C.
Dorsey, Christopher
Grice, Edward M.
Horning, Jay
Iwuala, Ishmael O.
Jimenez-Soto, Julio
Kanai, Charles, (Kenya)
Khomyn, Andriy
Kilcawley, Sean P.
Kokeram, Sudash Joseph
Kovalyshin, Severyn
Krische, James J.
Mandamuna, Denis M., C.F.I.C.
McKusky, Kristoffer T.
Molina, Bolivar G.
Morse, Jonathan K.
Moughalu, Adolphus
Nambatac, Alner U., (Philippines)
Ngwila, Filbert
Nzeabalu, Cosmas
Onyejiuwa, Dilio A., (Nigeria)
Opara, Christopher, (Nigeria)
Palanca, Mario S., (Philippines)
Palmer, Michael, C.S.C.
Pamula, Robert, (Poland)
Parappilly Xavier, Sojan
Ray, Brian
Scott, Alexander B.
Sigarara, Ione I., M.S.C.
Ubiparipovic, Sinisa
Ugwuanya, Valentine C.
Weberg, M. Paul, O.S.B.

UNITED STATES AIR FORCE CHAPLAINS

Air Force Chaplains
Revs.—
Amaliri, Paul Obi
Appiah, Kwaku John
Barna, Dariusz P., O.F.M.Cap.
Boyle, Ryan
Catungal, Mario T., O.C.D.
Covos, Ruben
De Guzman, Dennis
Deichert, Joseph
Deka, Robbie
Diaz, Dairo E.
Dumag, Peter
Enoh, Emmanuel
Foley, Thomas S.
Fonseca, Oscar D.
Gajda, Piotr J.
Gomez, Edwin A.
Guillory, Brad D.
Hamel, James A.
Hirten, Timothy J.
Hoang, Joseph
Idomele, Joseph O., (Nigeria)
Janko, Joshua, PSC 78 Box 7005, APO AP, 96326-0071. Yokota Air Base, Japan
Kagere, Guy, (Zambia)
Klingele, Brian
Knox, Sean Vincent
Kruse, David B.
Labacevic, Ihar
Lachica, Jose Nestor P., (Philippines)
Longe, James W.
Mbagwu, Brendan O., (Nigeria)
McGuire, David V.
Monagle, Robert J.
Navarrete, Jesus, (Spain)
Nguyen, Hoang Peter
Nguyen, Son, S.V.D.
Nwoga, Laserian
Ogwuegbu, Nelson, S.M.M.M.
Okorie, Onyema
Okwaraocha, Emmanuel, (Nigeria)
Onyejegbu, Cyriacus N.
Poole, Richard C.
Reid, Nicholas J.
Reutemann, John F. III
Rigonan, Antonio R., (Philippines)
Romero, Donald
Rosario, Mario S., (Philippines)
Szyda, Arkadiusz, (Poland)
Tenorio, Michael C., O.F.M.Cap.
Udechukwu, Bedemoore, (Nigeria)
Ugo, Charles Chidindu
Vit, William J. Jr.
Vo, Peter Son
Young, Andrew
Zygadlo, Mitchell.

Air National Guard Chaplains
Rev. Msgrs.—
Butler, Michael T.
Heiar, Donald Joseph Jr.
Very Revs.—
Dandurand, Michael G.
Rella, Francis J.
Revs.—
Bateman, John B.
Bergbower, Daniel J.
Bohorquez, Carlos M.
Bolger, Jesse L.
Brewer, Vincent
Cheney, James W.
Clement, Frederick, M.SS.CC.
Colarusso, Darin V.
Cunningham, Douglas D.
Donovan, Bernard Thomas
Duston, Thomas L.
Echert, John P., S.S.L.
Foster, Thomas J.
Fuller, Timothy M.
Garrison, Gary M.
Giamello, Anthony
Gomez-Baca, Walter
Gray, Samuel M.
Laible, Jeffrey G.
Love, John W., V.F.
Ludwig, Thomas
Martinez, Michael
McDaniel, Ryan
McDonough, John P.
McNamara, Brian J.
Medas, Michael B., M.S.W.
Mink, John J.
Nicolas, Jeffrey Scott
Pitstick, Rory K.
Stevens, Joshua R.
Thurber, David G. Jr.
Tirado, Ramon Orlando
Zalewski, Peter
Zimmer, Michael.

Air Force Reserve Chaplains
Rev. Msgrs.—
Padazinski, C. Michael, J.C.D.
Randall, Kevin S.
Revs.—
Ballou, Jeffrey A.
Blake, Lawrence R.
Bochnak, Zenon A.
Caggianelli, Gregg, D.Min.
King, Stuart
Mattina, Louis A.
McGrade, Kevin M.
McGregor, Mark D., S.J.
Nguyen, Hung Van, S.O.L.T.

Phan, John
Strzadala, Wieslaw P., S.D.S.
Sweeney, Daniel, S.J.
Thottankara, Raju, (India)
Torres, Ivan J.
Tran, Joseph
Travers, Patrick J., J.C.L., J.D.
Yanju, Henry M.

UNITED STATES NAVY CHAPLAINS

Navy Chaplains
Revs.—
Aguilera, Salvador
Amora, Eduardo B., (Philippines)
Appel, William A.
Barakeh, Imad N., B.S.O.
Bargola, Cerino O., (Philippines)
Beltran, Jacque
Benjamin, Matthew
Brackett, Matthew J.
Brunner, William J. III
Burchell, Jason C.
Caliba, Jude C., (Philippines)
Coffey, Joseph L.
Colvin, Andrew
Daigle, David A.
Dundon, Luke R.
Dwyer, Curtiss
Enriquez, Rean F., (Philippines)
Foley, Francis P.
Fullerton, Daniel J.
Garrett, Benton Lee
Hammond, David I.
Hinkle, James
Ianucci, Thomas
Johnson, Charles W.
Keener, Robert J.
Kennedy, William M.
Kersten, Jay J.
Lesher, Gregory L.
Maka, Tomasz
Marcelli, Michael
Mode, Daniel L.
Nguyen, Long
O'Flanagan, Thomas P.
Offor, Celsius, (Nigeria)
Reardon, Joseph D.
Riffle, Patrick J.
Shimotsu, John M.
Shuley, Keith J.
Sikorski, Leszek
Sweeney, Kevin
Thevenin, Donelson
Tiongson, Joselito S., (Philippines)
Tran, Tung T.
Ubalde, Ulysses L.
Weiss, Erich.

Navy Reserve Chaplains
Very Revs.—
Lavastida, Jose I., S.T.D., S.T.L., N.D.S., J.C.D.
Westcott, Matthew J., V.F.
Revs.—
Arnone, Leo F.
Cantrell, William
Coffiey, Christopher
Cricchio, Santo, O.F.M.Conv.
Cuddy, James M.
Davantes, Carlo B., (Philippines)
Fronk, Christopher S., S.J.
Gayton, John J., M.I.C.
Glassmire, David R.
Gorman, Edward M., O.P.
Guzman, Paul
Kelley, John E.
Kostka, Paul
LaBat, Sean J.
McKenzie, John H., O.S.B.
Neitzke, Ron P.
O'Brien, Sean
Okoli, Francis
Pham, Thomas T., C.Ss.R.
Reedy, Brian, S.J.
Romanello, Carmelo A.
Totton, Joseph.

DEPARTMENT OF VETERANS AFFAIRS HOSPITALS AND CHAPLAINS:
Rev. Msgr.—
Callahan, Kevin G.
Very Revs.—
Clements, Thomas P.
Jaeger, James P.
Revs.—
Abaneke, Aloysius, (Nigeria)
Abara, Lawrence N., (Retired)
Abrahams, John J.
Adejoh, Patrick O., (Nigeria)
Adu-Kwaning, Stephen, (Ghana)
Aduaka, Anthony
Akajiofor, Pius, (Nigeria)
Anthony, Joseph, (Retired)
Anyaeche, Jude, (Nigeria)
Archibong, Cosmas P., (Nigeria)
Aribe, Stephen, (Nigeria)
Audet, Phil
Axalan, Romeo J., (Philippines)
Barnes, Charles, S.J.
Bartoul, William, (Retired)
Bartsch, Kenneth W., O.F.M.Conv.
Bastian, James R.
Blangiardi, B. Jeffrey, S.J.
Blas, Mario W., (Philippines)
Boateng-Mensah, Samanhyia, (Ghana)
Brandow, Stephen J.
Brennan, George P., (Retired)
Brioso-Texidor, Luis
Brooks, Brian
Brown, Lewis
Bruggeman, Sidney B.
Burke, Paul A., J.C.L.
Byaruhanga, Frederick K., (Uganda)
Cadri, Diego, (Uganda)
Caffrey, Gerald, C.M.F.
Campos, Daniel
Cavey, Donald J.
Chacko, Joseph, (India)
Chembakassery, Vincent Lazar, (India)
Chevalier, Martin
Chigbo, Chijioke A., (Nigeria)
Chinnappan, Benjamin, (India)
Clapham, Bruce R.
Connolly, James M.T.
Conway, Edward, O.F.M.Cap.
Cuevas, Diego O.
D'Souza, Maurice, C.S.C.
Dalton, James E., O.S.F.S.
Damian, Rinaldo, (Retired)
David, Craig
de la Pena, Uldarico, (Philippines)
DeJesus, Alejandro, O.S.B.
Delgado, Lenin
Denig, Philip P., (Retired)
Devore, Daniel B.
DeWane, E. Thomas, O.Praem.
Diaz, Hector
Dumas, Terrence J.
Ejiofo, Lawrence, (Nigeria)
Eke, Raphael, (Nigeria)
Emeli, Edwin O., (Nigeria)
Eneh, Barry C., (Nigeria)
Eraly, Mathew, (India)
Estrada, Ignacio M., S.V.D.
Fallon, Marc F., C.S.C.
Fitzsimons, Patrick
Florido, Robert, (Philippines)
Foster, Thomas J.
Francis, Bijoy, O.Praem.
Francis, R. Peter, O.F.M.
Franco, Joseph E.
Fukes, Gary M.
Funke, Gerald John
Gardocki, Patrick M., O.F.M.
George, Jacob, (India)
Gicheru, Leonard M.
Gould, Lawrence, S.A.C.
Grasso, Joseph A., C.PP.S.
Gully, Bernard Leo
Hannigan, John T.
Hyde, Robert P. Jr., J.C.L.
Igwenwanne, Fidelis, (Nigeria)
Igwilo, Peter C., (Nigeria)
Iheaka, Emmanuel K., (Nigeria)
Ihuoma, Alphonsus, (Nigeria)
Ike, Anthony, (Nigeria)
Ilokaba, Damian O., (Nigeria)
Inke, Alexander, A.J.
Iorio, Peter J.
Iwuji, Paulinus, (Nigeria)
James, David John
Kaczmarek, James A.
Keenan, Basil M.
Kielkowski, Andrzej, S.D.S.
King, Stuart
Kirchhoefer, Thomas A.
Kloton, Michael J.
Knipe, Michael J., J.C.L.
Kopec, Edward
Kunisch, William II
Kunnalakattu, Peter Raphael
Kuss, Allen R.
LaBat, Sean J.
Lacroix, Charles L.
Laframboise, Ross
Langford, Terry L.
Lankford, Michael G.
Legarski, Anthony J.
Leonard, Matthew
Lindblad, Karl-Albert
Lipareli, Michael A.
Lopes, Richard A., O.F.M.Cap
Madu, Anthony, (Nigeria)
Malloy, Francis X.
Malone, Patrick
Mattox, Richard F.
McCord, Kent G.
Mena, Jose
Mensah, Isaac Ebo, (Ghana)
Mensah, Tony Kyere, (Ghana)
Mestas, Leonard J.
Miller, Abraham
Morse, Jonathan K.
Moster, James E.
Murphy, Patrick E.
Myers, Christopher P., S.O.L.T.
Neuzil, Lowell Greg
Njoku, Hippolytus C., S.M.M.M., (Nigeria)
Njoku, Innocent E., C.S.Sp
Ochu, Austin Charles, S.M.A.
Okeiyi, Emmanuel, C.C.C.E.
Olikkara, Joseph, M.S.T.
Onwumere, Leonard, J.P., (Nigeria)
Onyeabor, Ukachukwu S., (Nigeria)
Opara, Christopher, (Nigeria)
Parker, Theodore K.
Perez, Juan C.
Pesaresi, Thomas, M.M.
Piekarczyk, Marian A., S.D.S.
Rajayan, Antony W., (India)
Rath, Richard J.
Reeson, David G.
Reinders, David H.
Repko, Joseph, M.Div.
Rich, John A., M.M.
Roberts, Randall, O.F.M.
Roetzel, Robert E.
Roof, Francis M.
Rowgh, Matthew T.
Saavedra, Ramon, (Philippines)
Saldua, Max Ernesto M., (Philippines)
Santiago, Leoncio S.
Saunders, Douglas W.
Schill, Gerald F. (Damien)
Shortt, David J.
Sioleti, Andrew, i.v.dei.
Smith, Charles F., S.V.D.
Soto, Charles, O.F.M.
Soutus, Hugo
Steinbrunner, Jerome R., C.PP.S.
Steinmetz, Thomas P.
Stump, James M., O.F.M.Cap.
Tanto, Henry, S.M.M.A.
Taylor, Reynaldo S.
Teague, Bruce
Torrente, Lorenzo, (Retired)
Torres, Ivan J.
Trujillo, Ivan R.
Tufail, Augustine, (Pakistan)
Tumuhereze, Tarasisio, A.J.
Tyhovych, Ivan
Udoh, Chrysanthus F., M.S.P.
Ugobueze, John, (Nigeria)
Ugochukwu, Sebastian A., (Nigeria)
Uralikunnel, George V., (India)
Uwandu, Marcellinus U., (Nigeria)
Vacek, Carl E., T.O.R.
Van Alstyne, Donald J., M.I.C.
VanDoan, Vincent
Vistal, Felix
Vitaliano, Dominic J.
Weise, Thomas
Westfall, Joseph B.
Wood, Charles A.
Wydeven, John L.
Young, Dennis M.
Youssef, Clement Aziz, C.S.B.

CIVIL AIR PATROL:
Revs.—
Gonzalez y Perez, Belen
Harth, John M.
Hopper, Jeffrey G.
Killeen, William J., (Retired)
Mercieri, Dennis J.
Reiter, James E., (Canada)
Syracuse, Ross, O.F.M.Conv.

Auxiliary Priests-GS AND NON GS FULL TIME CONTRACT:
Rev. Msgrs.—
Cuddy, William F.
McManus, Gerald D., M.Div.
Metha, Ronald W., (Retired)
Rowan, Mark P.
Revs.—
Abas, Rolando, O.F.M.Conv.
Barrett, Miles
Berchmanz, Antony
Bernas, Antony N., (Philippines)
Berrera-Hernandez, Luis
Booth, Michael

Britanico, Rafael, (Philippines)
Brock, William, (Retired)
Bruno, Robert A., O.F.M.
Buhake, Longin, (Congo)
Castro, Dominic Joseph, M.Div.
Choung, ChoungYoungku, (South Korea)
Cleatus, Chitteth Biju
Coindreau, James M., L.C.
Di Renzo, Michael
Dowds, James, C.Ss.R.
Enyiaka, Canice
Fadallan, Elbert A.
Fey, Thomas J., (Retired)
Fimian, Kevin
Galinac, Robert, O.F.M.
Garcia-Chavez, Luis
Gaspar, Juan, O.M.I.
Gonzalez, George G.
Harbour, Linn S., (Retired)
Henry, Jeffrey F.
Hoar, Thomas, S.S.E.
Hoog, Eric R., C.Ss.R.
Ignacio, Simon, (Philippines)
Ivey, David
Karava, Norbert, O.F.M.Cap.
Kasule, Gerald, (Uganda)
Kinney, John M.
Kiwera, Thaddeus, S.O.L.T.
Langhans, Victor E., (Retired)
Madumere, Ignatius, O.P., (Nigeria)
Mahalic, Philip A.
McLaughlin, Peter
Morugudi, Bhaskar, (India)
Moss, Donald
Najera, Arthur Jr.
Nielson, Kenneth, O.S.B.
Nolan, Michael E., J.C.L.
Nwatarali, Linus, (Nigeria)
Okoro, Martin, (Nigeria)
Oloyede, Samuel, O.P.
Omana, Max B., (Philippines)
Omolo, Gilbert, C.P.
Pawlowski, Dariusz
Pimentel, Jose W., O.P.
Ramos, Alexander, (Philippines)
Raux, Redmond P.
Roldan, Jovy
Salonga, Juan S.
Shayo, Jude, A.J.
Smith, Lawrence C., S.J.
Stewart, Paul
Toledo, Nelson T., (Philippines)
Watts, Franklin, ((United Kingdom))
Waun, William
White, Robert.

DIOCESES WITH PRIESTS SERVING IN UNIFORM IN THE ARCHDIOCESE FOR THE MILITARY SERVICES

Agana, Guam.
Albany, NY.
Alexandria, LA.
Allentown, PA.
Altoona-Johnstown, PA.
Arecibo, Puerto Rico.
Arlington, VA.
Atlanta, GA.
Austin, TX.
Baker, OR.
Baltimore, MD.
Baton Rouge, LA.
Belleville, IL.
Biloxi, MS.
Birmingham, AL.
Bismarck, ND.
Boise, ID.
Boston, MA.
Bridgeport, CT.
Brooklyn, NY.
Brownsville, TX.
Buffalo NY.
Burlington, VT.
Camden, NJ.
Chair of St. Peter.
Charleston, SC.
Charlotte, NC.
Cheyenne, WY.
Chicago, IL.
Cincinnati, OH.
Cleveland, OH.
Columbus, OH.
Colorado Springs, CO.
Corpus Christi, TX.
Covington, KY.
Dallas, TX.
Davenport, IA.
Denver, CO.
Des Moines, IA.
Detroit, MI.
Dubuque, IA.
Duluth, MN.
El Paso, TX.
Eparchy of St. Maron of Brooklyn, NY.
Erie, PA.
Fargo, ND.
Fresno, CA.
Galveston-Houston, TX.
Gaylord, MI.
Grand Island, NE.
Green Bay, WI.
Harrisburg, PA.
Helena, MT.
Honolulu, HI.
Houma-Thibodaux, LA.
Indianapolis, IN.
Jefferson City, MO.
Joliet, IL.
Juneau, AK.
Kansas City in Kansas.
Kansas City-St. Joseph, MO.
Knoxville, TN.
Lafayette, IN.
Lafayette, LA.
Lansing, MI.
Las Vegas, NV.
Lexington, KY.
Lincoln, NE.
Louisville, KY.
Los Angeles, CA.
Lubbock, TX.
Madison, WI.
Manchester, NH.
Marquette, MI.
Memphis, TN.
Metuchen, NJ.
Miami, FL.
Milwaukee, WI.
Mobile, AL.
Newark, NJ.
Newton (Melkite Rite).
New Orleans, LA.
New York, NY.
Oakland, CA.
Ogdensburg, NY.
Oklahoma City, OK.
Omaha, NE.
Orange, CA.
Orlando, FL.
Owensboro, KY.
Palm Beach, FL.
Eparchy of Parma.
Eparchy of Passaic (Byzantine).
Paterson, NJ.
Pensacola-Tallahassee, FL.
Peoria, IL.
Philadelphia, PA.
Pittsburgh, PA.
Ponce, Puerto Rico.
Portland in Oregon.
Providence, RI.
Raleigh, NC.
Rapid City, SD.
Reno, NV.
Richmond, VA.
Rochester, NY.
Rockford, IL.
Rockville Centre, NY.
Saginaw, MI.
Salina, KS.
St. Augustine, FL.
St. Cloud, MN.
St. Louis, MO.
Eparchy of St. Nicholas in Chicago (Ukrainian).
St. Paul-Minneapolis, MN.
St. Petersburg, FL.
St. Thomas, Virgin Islands.
San Angelo, TX.
San Antonio, TX.
San Bernardino, CA.
San Diego, CA.
San Francisco, CA.
San Jose in California.
San Juan, Puerto Rico.
Santa Fe, NM.
Savannah, GA.
Scranton, PA.
Seattle, WA.
Shreveport, LA.
Sioux City, IA.
Sioux Falls, SD.
Spokane, WA.
Springfield-Cape Girardeau, MO.
Springfield in Illinois.
Springfield in Massachusetts.
Eparchy of Stamford (Ukrainian).
Steubenville, OH.
Exarchate of Syro-Malabar.
Syracuse, NY.
Toledo, OH.
Trenton, NJ.
Tucson, AZ.
Tulsa, OK.
Venice, FL.
Washington, D.C.
Wheeling-Charleston, WV.
Witchita, KS.
Wilmington, DE.
Worcester, MA.
Yakima, WA.
Youngstown, OH.

RELIGIOUS INSTITUTES WITH PRIESTS SERVING IN UNIFORM IN THE ARCHDIOCESE FOR THE MILITARY SERVICES

[]Apostles of Jesus A.J.
[]Basilian Fathers C.S.B.
[]Capuchin Franciscan Friars O.F.M.Cap.
[]Cistercians of the Strict Observance O.C.S.O.
[]Claretian Missionaries C.M.F.
[]Conventual Franciscans O.F.M.Conv.
[]Congregation of the Holy Cross C.S.C.
[]Congregation of Marians of the Immaculate Conception M.I.C.
[]Congregation of the Priest of the Sacred Heart S.C.J.
[]Discalced Carmelite Friars O.C.D.
[]Dominican Fathers O.P.
[]Dominican Fathers O.P. Nigeria.
[]Franciscan Fathers O.F.M.
[]Holy Ghost Fathers C.C.Cp.
[]Legionaries of Christ L.C.
[]Maryknoll Fathers M.M.
[]Missionaries of the Holy Apostles M.S.A.
[]Missionaries of the Sacred Heart M.S.C.
[]Missionary Father of La Salette M.S.
[]Norbertines.
[]Oblates of St. Francis de Sales O.S.F.S.
[]Order of St. Benedict O.S.B.
[]Pallottine Fathers S.A.C.
[]Paulist Fathers C.S.P.
[]Redemptorist Fathers C.SS.R.
[]Salesians of Don Bosco S.D.B.
[]Society of African Missions S.M.A.
[]Society of the Divine Savior S.D.S.
[]Society of the Divine Word.
[]Society of Jesus S.J.
[]Society of Our Lady of the Most Holy Trinity S.O.L.T.
[]Society of Mary S.M.
[]Society of the Precious Blood C.PP.S.
[]Sons of Mary Mother of Mercy S.M.M.M.
[]Third Order Regular of St. Francis T.O.R.
[]Vincentian Fathers.
[]Voluntas Dei Institute.

ASSOCIATIONS SUPPORTING THE MISSION OF THE ARCHDIOCESE

21st Century Centurions.
The Chaplains Aid Association.
National Conference of Veterans Affairs Catholic Chaplains, Inc.
Catholic War Veterans, USA, Inc., 441 N. Lee St., Alexandria, VA 22314-2301. Tel: 703-549-3622.
Military Council of Catholic Women (MCCW).
Father Capodanno Guild.

Archdiocese of Milwaukee

(Archidioecesis Milvauchiensis)

Most Reverend

JEROME E. LISTECKI

Archbishop of Milwaukee; ordained May 14, 1975; appointed Auxiliary Bishop of Chicago and Titular Bishop of Nara November 7, 2000; consecrated January 8, 2001; appointed Bishop of La Crosse December 29, 2004; installed March 1, 2005; appointed Archbishop of Milwaukee November 14, 2009; installed January 4, 2010. *Chancery Office: 3501 S. Lake Dr., P.O. Box 070912, Milwaukee, WI 53207-0912.* Tel: 414-769-3497.

Chancery Office: 3501 S. Lake Dr., P.O. Box 070912, Milwaukee, WI 53207-0912. Tel: 414-769-3340; Fax: 414-769-3408.

Web: www.archmil.org

Email: information@archmil.org

Most Reverend

REMBERT G. WEAKLAND, O.S.B., D.D.

Archbishop Emeritus of Milwaukee; ordained June 24, 1951; appointed Archbishop of Milwaukee September 20, 1977; consecrated and installed as Ninth Archbishop November 8, 1977; retired May 24, 2002.

Most Reverend

RICHARD J. SKLBA, D.D.

Auxiliary Bishop Emeritus of Milwaukee; ordained December 20, 1959; appointed Auxiliary Bishop of Milwaukee and Titular Bishop of Castro November 6, 1979; consecrated December 19, 1979; retired October 18, 2010. *Res.: 836 N. Broadway, Milwaukee, WI 53202-3608.* Tel: 414-962-3941. *All official communications should be addressed to: Chancery Office, 3501 S. Lake Dr., P.O. Box 070912, Milwaukee, WI 53207-0912.* Tel: 414-769-3594.

Most Reverend

JEFFREY R. HAINES

Auxiliary Bishop of Milwaukee; ordained May 17, 1985; appointed Titular Bishop of Thagamuta and Auxiliary Bishop of Milwaukee January 25, 2017; installed March 17, 2017. *Chancery Office: 3501 S. Lake Dr., P.O. Box 070912, Milwaukee, WI 53207-0912.* Tel: 414-769-3594.

Most Reverend

JAMES T. SCHUERMAN

Auxiliary Bishop of Milwaukee; ordained May 17, 1986; appointed Titular Bishop of Girba and Auxiliary Bishop of Milwaukee January 25, 2017; installed March 17, 2017. *Chancery Office: 3501 S. Lake Dr., P.O. Box 070912, Milwaukee, WI 53207-0912.* Tel: 414-769-3594.

Square Miles 4,758.

Established November 28, 1843; Created Archbishopric February 12, 1875.

Corporate Title: Archdiocese of Milwaukee.

Comprises the Counties of Dodge, Fond du Lac, Kenosha, Milwaukee, Ozaukee, Racine, Sheboygan, Walworth, Washington and Waukesha in the State of Wisconsin.

For legal titles of parishes and archdiocesan institutions, consult the Chancery Office.

STATISTICAL OVERVIEW

Personnel	
Archbishops	1
Retired Archbishops	1
Auxiliary Bishops	2
Retired Bishops	1
Retired Abbots	3
Priests: Diocesan Active in Diocese	127
Priests: Diocesan Active Outside Diocese	12
Priests: Diocesan in Foreign Missions	1
Priests: Retired, Sick or Absent	152
Number of Diocesan Priests	292
Religious Priests in Diocese	334
Total Priests in Diocese	626
Extern Priests in Diocese	60
Ordinations:	
Diocesan Priests	4
Religious Priests	5
Transitional Deacons	6
Permanent Deacons	7
Permanent Deacons in Diocese	176
Total Brothers	65
Total Sisters	1,173
Parishes	
Parishes	193
With Resident Pastor:	
Resident Diocesan Priests	86
Resident Religious Priests	28
Without Resident Pastor:	
Administered by Priests	70
Administered by Deacons	3
Administered by Lay People	6
New Parishes Created	1
Closed Parishes	3
Professional Ministry Personnel:	
Brothers	5
Sisters	22
Lay Ministers	760
Welfare	
Catholic Hospitals	11
Total Assisted	1,052,361
Health Care Centers	1
Total Assisted	420
Homes for the Aged	17
Total Assisted	3,726
Day Care Centers	2
Total Assisted	145
Specialized Homes	4
Total Assisted	1,052
Special Centers for Social Services	6
Total Assisted	236,879
Residential Care of Disabled	2
Total Assisted	164
Other Institutions	18
Total Assisted	28,258
Educational	
Seminaries, Diocesan	1
Students from This Diocese	37
Students from Other Diocese	13
Diocesan Students in Other Seminaries	4
Seminaries, Religious	2
Students Religious	39
Total Seminarians	80
Colleges and Universities	5
Total Students	19,100
High Schools, Diocesan and Parish	8
Total Students	3,986
High Schools, Private	7
Total Students	3,368
Elementary Schools, Diocesan and Parish	94
Total Students	24,534
Elementary Schools, Private	3
Total Students	1,147
Non-residential Schools for the Disabled	1
Total Students	30
Catechesis/Religious Education:	
High School Students	9,582
Elementary Students	24,914
Total Students under Catholic Instruction	86,741
Teachers in the Diocese:	
Priests	49
Scholastics	5
Sisters	19
Lay Teachers	3,732
Vital Statistics	
Receptions into the Church:	
Infant Baptism Totals	4,812
Minor Baptism Totals	347
Adult Baptism Totals	201
Received into Full Communion	262
First Communions	5,293
Confirmations	4,469
Marriages:	
Catholic	1,083
Interfaith	321
Total Marriages	1,404
Deaths	4,384
Total Catholic Population	543,155
Total Population	2,354,807

Former Bishops—Most Revs. JOHN MARTIN HENNI, D.D., cons. March 19, 1844; created Archbishop, Feb. 11, 1875; died Sept. 7, 1881; MICHAEL HEISS, D.D., cons. Bishop of La Crosse, Sept. 6, 1868; appt. Coadjutor of Milwaukee and Titular Archbishop of Adrianople, March 14, 1880; succeeded to Archbishop Henni in 1881; died March 26, 1890; FREDERICK XAVIER KATZER, D.D., cons. Sept. 21, 1886; Bishop of Green Bay; transferred to Milwaukee and raised to the Archiepiscopal Dignity, Jan. 30, 1891; died July 20, 1903; SEBASTIAN GEBHARD MESSMER, D.D., D.C.L., ord. July 23, 1871; cons. March 27, 1892; Bishop of Green Bay; transferred to Milwaukee and raised to the Archiepiscopal dignity Dec. 10, 1903; made assistant at the Pontifical Throne, Nov. 16, 1906; died Aug. 4, 1930; His Eminence SAMUEL ALPHONSUS STRITCH, D.D., ord. May 21, 1910; cons. Nov. 30, 1921; Bishop of Toledo; transferred to Milwaukee and raised to the Archiepiscopal dignity, Aug. 26, 1930; transferred to Chicago, Dec. 27, 1939; created Cardinal, Feb. 18, 1946; died May 27, 1958; Most Rev. MOSES E. KILEY, S.T.D., appt. Bishop of Trenton, Feb. 10, 1934; cons. March 17, 1934; appt. Archbishop of Milwaukee, Jan. 1, 1940; died April 15, 1953; His Eminence ALBERT G. MEYER, S.T.D., S.S.L., ord. July 11, 1926; cons. Bishop of Superior, April 11, 1946; appt. Archbishop of Milwaukee, July 21, 1953; transferred to Chicago, Sept. 24, 1958; created Cardinal, Dec. 14, 1959; died April 9, 1965; Most Revs. WILLIAM E. COUSINS, D.D., ord. April 23, 1927; appt. Titular Bishop of Forma and Auxiliary Bishop of Chicago Dec. 17, 1948; cons. March 7, 1949; appt. Bishop of Peoria, May 19, 1952; installed July 2, 1952; appt. Archbishop of Milwaukee, Dec. 18, 1958; installed Jan. 27, 1959; retired Sept. 20, 1977; died Sept. 14, 1988; REMBERT G. WEAKLAND, O.S.B., (Retired), ord. June 24, 1951; appt. Archbishop of Milwaukee, Sept. 20, 1977; cons. and installed as Ninth Archbishop, Nov. 8, 1977; retired May 24, 2002; His Eminence TIMOTHY M. DOLAN, ord. June 19, 1976; appt. Auxiliary Bishop of St. Louis June 19, 2001; installed Aug. 15, 2001; appt. Archbishop of

Milwaukee June 25, 2002; installed as Tenth Archbishop Aug. 28, 2002; appt. Archbishop of New York Feb. 23, 2009; elevated to Cardinal Feb. 18, 2012.

Chancery Office—3501 S. Lake Dr., P.O. Box 070912, Milwaukee, 53207-0912. Tel: 414-769-3300; Fax: 414-769-3408.

Vicars General—Most Revs. JEFFREY R. HAINES; JAMES T. SCHUERMAN; Very Revs. JAVIER BUSTOS-LOPEZ, S.T.D.; CURT J. FREDERICK, J.C.L., M.Div., (Retired); JEROME G. HERDA; JAMES E. LOBACZ; DAVID H. REITH.

Moderator of the Curia—Very Rev. CURT J. FREDERICK, J.C.L., M.Div., (Retired).

Chief of Staff—JEROME T. TOPCZEWSKI, Tel: 414-769-3590; Fax: 414-769-3430; Email: topczewskij@archmil.org.

Archdiocesan Consultors—Most Revs. JEFFREY R. HAINES; JAMES T. SCHUERMAN; RICHARD J. SKLBA, S.S.L., S.T.D., (Retired); Very Revs. CURT J. FREDERICK, J.C.L., M.Div., (Retired); JOHN D. HEMSING; JAMES E. LOBACZ; ROBERT J. WEIGHNER; Rev. Msgr. T. GEORGE GAJDOS, (Retired); Revs. DENNIS ACKERET, (Retired); MICHAEL BERTRAM, O.F.M.Cap.; RALPH C. GROSS, (Retired); Very Rev. PATRICK E. HEPPE; Revs. JOSEPH F. HORNACEK, (Retired); RICARDO MARTIN, J.C.L.

Archdiocesan Council of Priests—Most Rev. JEFFREY R. HAINES; Very Revs. CURT J. FREDERICK, J.C.L., M.Div., (Retired); JOHN D. HEMSING; JEROME G. HERDA; Rev. Msgr. T. GEORGE GAJDOS, (Retired); Revs. PETER J. BERGER; DENNIS ACKERET, (Retired); MICHAEL BERTRAM, O.F.M.Cap.; RALPH C. GROSS, (Retired); Very Rev. PATRICK E. HEPPE; Revs. JOSEPH F. HORNACEK, (Retired); ALAN F. JURKUS, (Retired); JUSTIN L. LOPINA; RICARDO MARTIN, J.C.L.; KEVIN MCMANAMAN; ROMANUS N. NWARU; ARULANANTHAN PONNAIYAN; EDWARD TLUCEK, O.F.M.; GARY WEGNER, O.F.M.Cap.

Archdiocesan Pastoral Council—JEANNE BITKERS; BARBIE BOEHME-DECHANT; Sr. DURSTYNE FARNAN, O.P.; NOEL FORTIER; HOPE JANUCHOWSKI-BALEYWAH; MARY ANN JOHNSON; MICHAEL KAROLEWICZ; Deacon PAUL KLINGSEISEN; Rev. JUSTIN L. LOPINA; MARY MARTONE; ELIZABETH MELENDEZ-JOP; ROBERT MEULER; DIANE NOWINSKI; Deacon DALE R. PACZKOWSKI; MIKE PREVITE; MADONNE RAUCH; VERN REHLINGER; DANNY RODRIQUEZ; DEBBIE RUCHALSKI; CARRIE SCHANEN; BARBARA SCHERRER, B.A., M.S.T.; CINDY SEMSKI; JEAN MARIE WEBER; MATTHEW WALLNER; Sr. JOMARIE ZIELKE, C.S.A.; DOUGLAS WILDES.

Archbishop's Executive Council—Most Revs. JEFFREY R. HAINES; JAMES T. SCHUERMAN; Very Revs. CURT J. FREDERICK, J.C.L., M.Div., (Retired); JEROME G. HERDA; BRAD BERGHOUSE; CHRIS BROWN; BARBARA ANNE CUSACK, J.C.D.; Deacon ANTON B. NICKOLAI; JEROME T. TOPCZEWSKI.

Office of the Archbishop

Chief of Staff—JEROME T. TOPCZEWSKI, Tel: 414-769-3590; Email: topczewskij@archmil.org.

Chief Operating Officer—BRAD BERGHOUSE, Tel: 414-769-3360; Email: berghouseb@archmil.org.

Moderator of the Curia—Very Rev. CURT J. FREDERICK, J.C.L., M.Div., (Retired), Tel: 414-758-2220; Email: frederickc@archmil.org.

Executive Secretary—GWEN FASTABEND, Tel: 414-769-3497; Email: fastabendg@archmil.org.

Auxiliary Bishops—Most Revs. JEFFREY R. HAINES, Tel: 414-769-3595; Email: bishophaines@archmil.org; JAMES T. SCHUERMAN, Tel: 414-769-3592; Email: bishopschuerman@archmil.org.

Administrative Assistant to Auxiliary Bishops—NANCY KERNS, Tel: 414-769-3594; Email: kernsn@archmil.org.

Bishop Emeritus—Most Rev. RICHARD J. SKLBA, S.S.L., S.T.D., (Retired), Tel: 414-769-3486.

Manager of Diocesan Events and Special Programs—JENNIFER OLIVA, Tel: 414-758-2213; Email: olivaj@archmil.org.

Schools Walk Coordinator—MARCY STONE, Tel: 414-69-3507; Email: stonem@archmil.org.

Chancery Office—Email: chancery@archmil.org.

Chancellor—BARBARA ANNE CUSACK, J.C.D., Tel: 414-769-3341; Email: cusackb@archmil.org.

Vice Chancellor—Rev. RICARDO MARTIN PINILLOS, J.C.L., Tel: 414-769-3307; Email: rmartin@archmil.org.

Canonical Consultant—REBECCA RUESCH, Tel: 414-769-3442; Email: rueschr@archmil.org.

Archivist—SHELLY TAYLOR, Tel: 414-769-3407; Email: taylors@archmil.org.

Associate Director of Archives—AMY NELSON, Tel: 414-769-3431; Email: nelsona@archmil.org.

Communications Office—Email: communication@archmil.org.

Director—AMY GRAU, Tel: 414-769-3461; Email: graua@archmil.org.

Associate Director—Tel: 414-769-3435. VACANT.

Associate Director for Creative Services—GINA RUPCIC, Tel: 414-769-3436; Email: rupcicg@archmil.org.

Graphic Designer for Creative Services—MEGHAN ENDTER, Tel: 414-769-3437; Email: endterm@archmil.org.

Communications Coordinator—HEIDI HEISTAD, Tel: 414-769-3494; Email: heistadh@archmil.org.

Schools Marketing Manager—CAROL RYBACK, Tel: 414-769-3453; Email: rybakc@archmil.org.

Hispanic Communications Coordinator—MARIA PRADO, Tel: 414-769-3504; Email: pradom@archmil.org.

Ecumenical and Interfaith Concerns—

Director—VACANT.

Financial Services—

Archdiocesan Treasurer/Chief Financial Officer—CHRIS BROWN, Tel: 414-769-3325; Email: brownc@archmil.org.

Diocesan Controller—MICHAEL FRIES, Tel: 414-769-3347; Email: friesm@archmil.org.

Diocesan Parish and School Financial Consulting, Director—KATHERINE ESTERLE, Tel: 414-769-3377; Email: esterlek@archmil.org.

Diocesan Parish and School Financial Consulting, Associate Director—DENISE MONTPAS, Tel: 414-769-3336; Email: montpasd@archmil.org.

Staff Accountants—JANICE O'CONNOR, Tel: 414-769-3314; Email: oconnorj@archmil.org; CAROL ABUYA, Tel: 414-769-3315; Email: abuyac@archmil.org.

Payroll Bookkeeper—BARBARA KISSH, Tel: 414-769-3318; Email: kisshb@archmil.org.

Accounts Payable Bookkeeper—VACANT.

Lay Pension and Life Insurance Coordinator—BRIDGET FISCHER, Tel: 414-769-3317; Email: fischerb@archmil.org.

Financial Services Support Coordinator—KIM KASTEN, Tel: 414-769-3326; Email: kastenk@archmil.org.

General Counsel—ANTON NICKOLAI, Tel: 414-769-3379; Email: nickolaia@archmil.org.

Building Services—JOE KALLENBERGER, Tel: 414-769-3491; Email: kallenbergerj@archmil.org.

Maintenance Coordinator—STEVE JUPP, Tel: 414-769-3566; Email: jupps@archmil.org.

Cemeteries and Mausoleums Director—7301 W. Nash St., Milwaukee, 53216. MARY THIEL, Tel: 414-438-4420; Email: mthiel@cfcmission.org.

Cemeteries and Mausoleums Spiritual Director—Rev. AURELIO H. PEREZ, Tel: 414-645-0611; Email: pereza@archmil.org.

Archdiocesan Marian Shrine—Tel: 414-640-5590. Deacon STEVEN F. PEMPER, Dir.

Human Resource Services—

Director of Personnel Services—RICHARD J. TANK, Tel: 414-769-3458; Email: tankr@archmil.org.

Central Offices and Agencies Director—SUSAN GORSKI, Tel: 414-769-3328; Email: gorskis@archmil.org.

Parish and School Personnel Director—CATHERINE GRYNIEWICZ, Tel: 414-769-3370; Email: gryniewiczc@archmil.org.

Human Resources & Benefits Administrator—MANDI BOTTOMLEY, Tel: 414-769-3540; Email: bottomleym@archmil.org.

Information Services—

Director and System Administrator—ALLAN RIES, Tel: 414-769-3332; Email: riesa@archmil.org.

Webmaster and Coordinator of Electronic Communications—MARK BARTHEL, Tel: 414-769-3454; Email: barthelm@archmil.org.

Information Systems Specialist—DALE KLEIN, Tel: 414-769-3440; Email: kleind@archmil.org.

Computer Systems Trainer/Help Desk—MARGARET ERHART, Tel: 414-769-3335; Email: erhartm@archmil.org.

Intercultural Ministries Office—

Director—EVA J. DIAZ, M.A.P.S., Tel: 414-769-3397; Email: diaze@archmil.org.

Associate for Hispanic Ministry—VACANT.

Associate Director for Intercultural Ministries—LETZBIA LAING-MARTINEZ, Tel: 414-769-3398; Email: laingmartinezl@archmil.org.

Vicar for Hispanic Ministry—Very Rev. JAVIER BUSTOS-LOPEZ, S.T.D., Tel: 262-542-2589; Email: bustosj@archmil.org.

Ministry to the Deaf and Hard of Hearing—Rev. CHRISTOPHER L. KLUSMAN, Email: klusmanc@archmil.org.

John Paul II Center for the New Evangelization—

Director—RICHARD HARTER, Tel: 414-758-2215; Email: harterr@archmil.org.

Catechesis and Youth Ministry Office Director—GARY POKORNY, M.Div., D.Min. (Cand.), Tel: 414-769-2242; Email: pokornyg@archmil.org.

Campus Ministry Director—PETE BURDS, Tel: 414-758-2219; Email: burdsp@archmil.org.

UW-Milwaukee Director—MARY MUELLER, Tel: 414-704-0619; Email: burnsm@archmil.org.

UW-Whitewater Associate Director—BRIAN ZANIN, Tel: 262-473-5555; Email: zaninb@uww.edu.

Associate Evangelization Director—MARGARET RHODY, Tel: 414-758-2218; Email: rhodym@archmil.org.

Marriage and Family Life Director—VACANT.

Marriage and Family Life Associate Director—EMILY BURDS, Dir., Tel: 414-758-2211; Email: burdse@archmil.org.

Dignity of the Human Person Director—ROBERT SHELLEDY, Tel: 414-758-2286; Email: shelledyr@archmil.org.

Sexual Abuse Prevention and Response Services, Victim Assistance Coordinator—MANDY BIBO, M.S., Tel: 414-758-2232; Email: mbibo@ccmke.org.

Sexual Abuse Prevention and Response Services, Safe Environment Coordinator—SUZANNE NICKOLAI, Tel: 414-769-3449; Email: nickolias@archmil.org.

Metropolitan Tribunal—

Judicial Vicar—Very Rev. PAUL B.R. HARTMANN, M.Div., J.C.L., Tel: 414-769-3304; Email: hartmannp@archmil.org.

Adjutant Judicial Vicar—Very Rev. MARK C. PAYNE, J.C.L., Tel: 414-769-3376; Email: paynem@archmil.org.

Tribunal Chancellor—MS. ZABRINA R. DECKER, J.C.D., Tel: 414-769-3302; Email: deckerz@archmil.org.

Office Manager—MR. MAURICE C. THOMPSON, B.B.A., Tel: 414-769-3301; Email: thompsonm@archmil.org.

Judges—Very Revs. PAUL B.R. HARTMANN, M.Div., J.C.L.; MARK C. PAYNE, J.C.L.; Rev. Msgr. THOMAS P. OLSZYK, J.C.L., (Retired); JESUS CABRERA, J.C.L.; Rev. BERNARD S. SIPPEL, M.Div., (Retired).

Judges for the Appellate Court—Very Revs. PAUL B.R. HARTMANN, M.Div., J.C.L.; MARK C. PAYNE, J.C.L.; Rev. Msgr. THOMAS P. OLSZYK, J.C.L., (Retired); Revs. JAMES E. CONNELL, J.C.D., (Retired); DENNIS C. KLEMME, J.C.D., (Retired); BERNARD S. SIPPEL, M.Div., (Retired).

Defender of the Bond—MS. ZABRINA R. DECKER, J.C.D.

Procurators and Advocates—STEPHEN J. HARVEY, M.Div.; MR. MAURICE C. THOMPSON, B.B.A.; ANDREW R.J. VAUGHN, M.A.

Promoter of Justice—Very Rev. PHILIP D. REIFENBERG, J.C.L.

Office for Marital Reconciliation-Separation—Very Rev. PAUL B.R. HARTMANN, M.Div., J.C.L.

Archdiocesan Court of Equity—Very Rev. PAUL B.R. HARTMANN, M.Div., J.C.L.; MS. ZABRINA R. DECKER, J.C.D.

Canonical Consultant—REBECCA RUESCH, Tel: 414-769-3442; Email: rueschr@archmil.org.

Canonical Notaries—MARY CHRISTINE ELLISON, B.A.; KAREY SIPOWICZ, B.S.; MR. MAURICE C. THOMPSON, B.B.A.

Office for Lay Ministry—

Director—SUSAN MCNEIL, Tel: 414-758-2214; Email: mcneils@archmil.org.

Office for Planning and Councils—

Director—MARK KEMMETER, Tel: 414-769-3352; Email: kemmeterm@archmil.org.

Ordained and Lay Ecclesial Ministry—

Vicar for Ordained, Lay Ecclesial Ministry—Very Rev. JEROME G. HERDA, Tel: 414-769-3490; Email: herdaj@archmil.org.

Vicar for Senior Priests—Very Rev. JAMES E. LOBACZ, Tel: 414-769-3496; Email: lobaczj@archmil.org.

Director of Priest and Lay Ecclesial Personnel, Placement—RICHARD J. TANK, Tel: 414-769-3458; Email: tankr@archmil.org.

Minister to Priests—VACANT.

Vocations Director—Rev. LUKE N. STRAND, Tel: 414-747-6489; Email: lstrand@sfs.edu.

Associate Director for Deacon Services—Deacon MICHAEL J. CHMIELEWSKI, Tel: 414-769-3409; Email: chmielewskim@archmil.org.

Director, Diaconate Formation—Deacon DALE T. NEES, Tel: 414-758-2212; Email: neesd@archmil.org.

Associate Director, Diaconate Formation—MANUEL MALDONADO, Tel: 414-758-2207; Email: maldonadom@archmil.org.

Coordinator for Continuing Formation of Clergy—Deacon ALFRED C. LAZAGA, Tel: 414-769-3489; Email: lazagaa@archmil.org.

Schools Office—

Superintendent—KATHLEEN A. CEPELKA, Ph.D., Tel: 414-758-2251; Email: cepelkak@archmil.org.

Associate Superintendents—SUSAN NELSON, Tel: 414-758-2263; Email: nelsons@archmil.org; JOHN

SOPER, Tel: 414-758-2262; Email: soperj@archmil.org; BRUCE VARICK, Tel: 414-758-2252; Email: varickb@archmil.org.

Stewardship and Development—

Development Director—ANDY GAERTNER, Tel: 414-769-3322; Email: gaertnera@archmil.org.

Catholic Stewardship Appeal Director—ROBERT BOHLMANN, Tel: 414-769-3320; Email: bohlmannr@archmil.org.

Major and Planned Giving Director—VACANT.

Parish Stewardship Director—BARBARA VITE, Tel: 414-769-3331; Email: viteb@archmil.org.

Schools Development Director—JENNY MENDENHALL, Tel: 414-769-3451; Email: mendenhallj@archmil.org.

Systems and Operations Director—MICHELE NABIH, Tel: 414-769-3323; Email: nabihm@archmil.org.

Synod Implementation—

Director—RANDY NOHL, Tel: 414-758-2216; Email: nohlr@archmil.org.

Associate Director—MICHELLE NEMER, Tel: 414-769-3354; Email: nemerm@archmil.org.

World Mission Ministries

Director—ANTOINETTE MENSAH, Tel: 414-758-2282; Email: mensaha@archmil.org.

Associate Director—VACANT, Tel: 414-758-2283.

Worship—

Coordinator—KIM MANDELKOW, Tel: 414-769-3359; Email: mandelkowk@archmil.org.

Catholic Charities—

Vicar—Very Rev. DAVID H. REITH, Tel: 414-769-3400; Email: dreith@ccmke.org.

Chief Operating Officer—RICARDO CISNEROS, Tel: 414-769-3400; Email: rcisneros@ccmke.org.

Chief Financial Officer—JASON FLANDERS, CPA, Tel: 414-769-3420; Email: jflanders@ccmke.org.

Director of Mission Advancement—JACKIE REKOWSKI, Tel: 414-769-3524; Email: jrekowski@ccmke.org.

Executive Assistant—VACANT.

Director of Adult Day Services—ANNETTE JANKOWSKI, Tel: 414-771-6063; Email: ajankowski@ccmke.org.

Director of Behavioral Health—MANDY BIBO, M.S., Tel: 414-771-2881; Email: mbibo@ccmke.org.

Director of Child Welfare Services—SARAH CHIDESTER, M.S.W., A.P.S.W., Tel: 414-771-6063; Email: schidester@ccmke.org.

Director of In-Home Support Services—CARLA ALEJO, Dir., Tel: 414-771-2881; Email: calejo@ccmke.org.

Director of Outreach and Case Management—SUSAN HOWLAND, Tel: 414-771-2881; Email: showland@ccmke.org.

Director of Legal Services for Immigrants—BARBARA GRAHAM, Tel: 414-643-8570; Email: bgraham@ccmke.org.

Director of Supported Parenting—SARAH MATSON, M.S., Tel: 262-547-2463; Email: smatson@ccmke.org.

Human Resources Manager—NATE BRAUN, Tel: 414-769-3415; Email: nbraun@ccmke.org.

Parish Relations Coordinator—SHARON BRUMER, Tel: 414-769-3543; Email: sbrumer@ccmke.org.

Catholic Herald—

Publisher—Most Rev. JEROME E. LISTECKI, Tel: 414-769-3497; Email: archbishoplistecki@archmil.org.

Associate Editor—LARRY HANSON, Tel: 414-769-3466; Email: hansonl@archmil.org.

CLERGY, PARISHES, MISSIONS AND PAROCHIAL SCHOOLS

CITY OF MILWAUKEE

(MILWAUKEE COUNTY)

1—CATHEDRAL OF ST. JOHN THE EVANGELIST (1847)
Mailing Address: 831 N. Van Buren St., 53202. Tel: 414-276-9814; Email: cathedral@stjohncathedral.org. Most Rev. Jeffrey R. Haines, Rector; Deacon Thomas N. Hunt.
Res.: 802 N. Jackson St., 53202.
Catechesis Religious Program—East Side Child & Youth Ministry, 1716 N. Humboldt Ave., 53202. Tel: 414-962-3776; Email: escym@sbcglobal.net. Ralph Stewart, D.R.E. Students 15.

2—ST. ADALBERT (1908) (Polish—Hispanic)
1923 W. Becher St., 53215. Tel: 414-645-0413; Email: stadalbert@archmil.org; Email: businessoffice@adalbertschool.org. Rev. Mauricio Fernandez-Boscan; Raquel Roque, Business Mgr.
School—St. Adalbert School, (Grades K-8), 1913 W. Becher St., 53215-2688. Tel: 414-645-5450; Fax: 414-645-5510; Email: info@adalbertschool.org. Dan Heding, Prin. Religious Teachers 1; Lay Teachers 24; Students 441.
Catechesis Religious Program—Email: srjaneth@adalbertschool.org. Sr. Janeth Vasconez, D.R.E. Students 187.

3—ST. AGNES, Closed. For sacramental records, contact Archdiocese of Milwaukee Archives Office, Tel: 414-769-3407.

4—ST. ALBERT, Closed. For sacramental records, contact Archdiocese of Milwaukee Archives Office, Tel: 414-769-3407.

5—ST. ALEXANDER (1926) (Polish), Closed. For sacramental records, contact St. John Paul II Parish, 3307 S. 10th St., Milwaukee, WI 53215-5116, 414-744-3695, Fax: 414-744-2874.

6—ALL SAINTS (1994)
4051 N. 25th St., 53209. Tel: 414-444-5610; Email: allsaintsmke@gmail.com; Web: allsaintsmke.org. 4060 N. 26th St., 53209-6695. Very Revs. Timothy L. Kitzke, Admin.; Robert X. Stiefvater, M.Div., Parochial Vicar; Rev. Alan D. Veik, O.F.M.Cap., Parochial Vicar; Deacon Edward Blaze.
Catechesis Religious Program—Email: ceciliasr2@yahoo.com. Cecilia Smith-Robertson, D.R.E. Students 59.

7—ST. ANNE, Closed. For sacramental records, contact Archdiocese of Milwaukee Archives Office, Tel: 414-769-3407.

8—ST. ANTHONY OF PADUA (1872)
1711 S. 9th St., 53204. Tel: 414-645-1455; Email: antonius@archmil.org; Web: www.stanthony-sthyacinth.org. Rev. Hugo Londono; Jaime Charuc, F.M.M.; Rev. Jose Angel Estrada Anaya; Deacons Carlos Cornejo; Rogelio Macias; Henry O. Reyes.
School—St. Anthony of Padua School, (Grades PreK-12), 1727 S. 9th St., 53204. Tel: 414-384-6612; Fax: 414-384-6613; Email: info@stanthonymilwaukee.org; Web: www.stanthonymilwaukee.org. Jose Vazquez, Pres.; Jennifer Lopez, Vice Pres., Academic Affairs. Religious Teachers 2; Lay Teachers 87; Students 1,741.
Catechesis Religious Program—Email: andac@stanthonymilwaukee.org. Sr. Maria del Carmen de Anda, R.M., D.R.E. Students 220.

9—ST. ANTHONY OF PADUA (1923) Closed. For sacramental records, contact St. Vincent Pallotti Parish, Milwaukee, Tel: 414-453-4225.

10—ST. AUGUSTINE OF HIPPO (1888)
2530 S. Howell Ave., 53207. Tel: 414-744-0808; Email: info@staugies.org; Web: www.staugies.org. Rev. Philip J. Schumaker, Admin.; Paul Weisenberger, Dir. Worship; Rebecca Scholz, Dir. Youth Min.
See St. Thomas Aquinas Academy located in the Institution section under Consolidated Elementary Schools.
Catechesis Religious Program—341 E. Norwich Ave., 53207. Email: Karen@secatholic.org; Email: rebecca@secatholic.org. Karen Bushman, D.R.E. (Elementary). Students 11.

11—ST. BARBARA, Closed. For sacramental records, contact Archdiocese of Milwaukee Archives Office, Tel: 414-769-3407.

12—BASILICA OF ST. JOSAPHAT (1888) (Polish)
2333 S. 6th St., 53215-3203. Tel: 414-645-5623; Fax: 414-645-2216; Email: sjbdome@archmil.org; Web: www.thebasilica.org. Revs. Lawrence Zurek, O.F.M. Conv., Admin.; John Clote, O.F.M. Conv.; Deacon Theodore Faust.
School—St. Josaphat Parish School, (Grades PreK-8), 801 W. Lincoln Ave., 53215-3222. Tel: 414-645-4378; Fax: 414-645-1978; Email: ksavasta@sjpsmke.org; Web: www.thebasilica.org. Kely Savasta, Prin. Lay Teachers 15; Students 232.
Endowments—Basilica of Saint Josaphat Endowment Fund—
Saint Josaphat Parish School Endowment Fund, Mailing Address: 2333 S. 6th St., 53215. Tel: 414-645-5623; Email: sjbdome@archmil.org.
Catechesis Religious Program—Basilica Parish Center, 2322 S. 7th St., 53215-3206. Email: dre@thebasilica.org. Jerry Krajewski, D.R.E. Students 65.

13—ST. BENEDICT THE MOOR (1908)
1015 N. 9th St., 53233. Tel: 414-271-0135; Email: stbensparish@thecapuchins.org; Web: www.stbensparishmilwaukee.org. Friar Michael Bertram, O.F.M.Cap; Rev. Jason Graves, O.F.M.Cap.; Deacon John I. Champagne.
Catechesis Religious Program—Students 2.

14—ST. BERNADETTE (1958)
8200 W. Denver Ave., 53223. Tel: 414-358-4600; Email: stbernadette@archmil.org; Web: www.stbweb.com. Rev. Gregory J. Greiten.
See Northwest Catholic School Association, Milwaukee under Consolidated Elementary Schools in the Institution section.
Catechesis Religious Program—8661 N. 76th Pl., 53223. Tel: 414-365-2020; Email: lmaples@stcatherinemke.org. Lorrie Maples, Dir., Christian Formation. Clustered with St. Catherine of Alexandria & Our Lady of Good Hope. Students 9.

15—BLESSED SACRAMENT (1927) (Polish)
3100 S. 41st St., 53215. Tel: 414-649-4720; Fax: 414-649-4727; Email: blsacrament@wi.rr.com; Web: www.blessedsacramentmke.org. Very Rev. Mark C. Payne, J.C.L.; Sr. Theresa Engel, O.S.F., Pastoral Coord.; Bro. James Scarpace, S.A.C., Pastoral Min.; Deacon Paul Klingseisen; Mr. Thomas Adamski, Business Mgr.
School—Blessed Sacrament School, 3126 S. 41st St., 53215. Tel: 414-649-4730; Fax: 414-649-4726; Email: vile.carlos@blessedsacramentmke.org; Web: www.blessedsacramentmke.org. Mrs. Carol Degen, Prin. Lay Teachers 14; Students 185.
Catechesis Religious Program—Email: michael.federman@blessedsacrmentmke.org. Michael Federman, D.R.E. Students 30.

16—BLESSED SAVIOR PARISH (2007)
8545 W. Villard Ave., 53225. Tel: 414-464-5033; Email: blessedsavior@archmil.org; Web: www.blessedsaviorparish.org. Rev. Romanus N. Nwaru.
School—Blessed Savior Catholic School, 8607 W. Villard Ave., 53225. Tel: 414-464-5033 (Main); Tel: 414-438-2745 (East Campus); Tel: 414-466-0470 (North Campus); Tel: 414-463-3878 (South Campus); Tel: 414-464-5775 (West Campus); Email: bodonnell@blessedsavior.org; Email: npope@blessedsavior.org; Email: mprudom@blessedsavior.org; Email: shelms@blessedsavior.org. Barbara O'Donnell, Prin., East Campus; Nadia Pope, Prin., North Campus; Megan Prudom, Prin., South Campus; Sarah Radiske, Prin. Clergy 1; Lay Teachers 42; Students 558.
Catechesis Religious Program— Shared program with St. Catherine Alexandria, Milwaukee & St. Agnes, Butler. Students 22.

17—BLESSED TRINITY, Closed. For sacramental records, contact St. Catherine Parish, Milwaukee, Tel: 414-445-5115.

18—BLESSED VIRGIN OF POMPEI, Closed. For sacramental records, contact Archdiocese of Milwaukee Archives Office, Tel: 414-769-3407.

19—ST. BONIFACE, Closed. For sacramental records, contact Archdiocese of Milwaukee Archives Office, Tel: 414-769-3407.

20—ST. CASIMIR (1894) (Polish—Spanish), Closed. For sacramental records, contact Our Lady of Divine Providence, Milwaukee, Tel: 414-264-0049.

21—ST. CATHERINE (1922)
5101 W. Center St., 53210. Tel: 414-445-5115; Email: secretary@saintcatherine.org. Rev. Lawrence J. Chapman; Deacon Ralph W. Kornburger Jr. In Res., Rev. Thomas Suriano, (Retired).
School—St. Catherine School, (Grades K-8), 2647 N. 51st St., 53210. Tel: 414-445-2846; Fax: 414-445-0448; Email: mparis@saintcatherine.org. Michelle Paris, Prin. Lay Teachers 18; Students 130.
Catechesis Religious Program—Email: eduncklee@saintsebs.org. Edward Duncklee, Dir. Faith Formation. Students 23.

22—ST. CATHERINE (Granville) (1855) [CEM]
8661 N. 76th Pl., 53223-2697. Tel: 414-365-2020; Fax: 414-365-2021; Email: dhintz@stcatherinemke.org; Web: www.stcatherinemke.org. Debra A. Hintz, Parish Dir.
See Northwest Catholic School Association, Milwaukee in the Institution Section under Consolidated Elementary Schools.
Catechesis Religious Program—Email: lmaples@stcatherinemke.org. Lorrie Maples, Dir. Christian Formation. Students 25.

23—ST. CHARLES BORROMEO (1960)
5571 S. Marilyn Ave., 53221. Tel: 414-281-8115; Fax: 414-281-8150; Email: info@scbmil.org; Web: www.scbmil.org. Revs. Brian T. Holbus; Norberto Sandoval.
School—St. Charles Borromeo School, (Grades PreK-8), 3100 W. Parnell Ave., 53221. Tel: 414-282-0767; Fax: 414-817-9605; Email: schoolinfo@scbmil.org. Courtney Albright, Prin. Lay Teachers 20; Students 222.
Catechesis Religious Program—
Tel: 414-281-8115, Ext. 24; Email: ckrol@scbmil.org; Web: www.scbmil.org. Students 115.

24—CONGREGATION OF THE BLESSED TRINITY (1991) Closed. For Sacramental records, contact St. Catherine Parish, Milwaukee, 414-445-5115.

25—CONGREGATION OF THE GREAT SPIRIT (1989) (Native American)
1000 W. Lapham Blvd., Milwauke, 53204. Tel: 414-672-6989; Email: siggenauk@wi.twcbc.com; Web: www.congregationofthegreatspirit.org/. 1050 W. Lapham Blvd., P.O. Box 4219, 53204. Rev. Edward J. Cook; Chris Serio, Business Mgr.; Mrs. Michelle Boyd, Treas.
Catechesis Religious Program—Students 14.

26—CORPUS CHRISTI (1958) Closed. For sacramental records, contact Blessed Savior, Milwaukee, Tel: 414-464-5033.

27—SS. CYRIL AND METHODIUS (1893)
2427 S. 15th St., 53215. Tel: 414-383-3973; Email: pastor@cmmk.org; Web: www.cmmk.org. Rev. Edward W. Traczyk, S.Ch.
Catechesis Religious Program—Students 31.

28—ST. ELIZABETH, Closed. For sacramental records, contact Archdiocese of Milwaukee Archives Office, Tel: 414-769-3407.

29—ST. EMERIC (1919) Closed. For sacramental records, contact Sacred Heart, Milwaukee, Tel: 414-774-9418.

30—ST. FLORIAN (1911) (German—Austrian)
1210 S. 45th St., 53214. Tel: 414-383-3565; Email: stflorian@archmil.org; Web: www.stflorian.org. Rev. Fred Alexander, O.C.D.
See Mary Queen of Saints Catholic Academy, West Allis under Consolidated Elementary Schools located in the Institution Section.
Catechesis Religious Program—Tel: 414-541-7515; Email: barb.strita@wi.rr.com. Barbara Krieger, D.R.E. Students 2.

31—ST. FRANCIS OF ASSISI (1870) (Hispanic—African American)
Mailing Address: 1927 Vel R. Phillips Ave., 53212.
Tel: 414-374-5750; Email: stfrancismil@gmail.com; Web: www.stfrancismil.org. Revs. Michael Bertram, O.F.M.Cap.; Jason Graves, O.F.M.Cap. In Res., Revs. Augustine Cops, O.F.M.Cap.; Perry McDonald, O.F.M.Cap.; Bro. Rob Roemer, O.F.M.Cap.
Res.: 327 W. Brown St., 53212.
Catechesis Religious Program—Tel: 414-374-5750; Fax: 414-374-5553. Students 7.

32—ST. GABRIEL (1913) (Lithuanian), Closed. For sacramental records, contact Archdiocese of Milwaukee Archives Office, Tel: 414-769-3407.

33—ST. GALL, Closed. For sacramental records, contact Archdiocese of Milwaukee Archives Office, Tel: 414-769-3407.

34—ST. GERARD (1925) Closed. For sacramental records, contact Archdiocese of Milwaukee Archives Office, Tel: 414-769-3407.

35—GESU PARISH (1893)
1210 W. Michigan St., 53233. Tel: 414-288-7101; Email: gesuparish@gmail.com; Web: www.gesuparish.org. P.O. Box 495, 53201. Revs. James P. Flaherty, S.J.; Mr. Matthew S. Walsh, S.J.
Catechesis Religious Program—Students 82.

36—ST. GREGORY THE GREAT (1955)
3160 S. 63rd St., 53219. Tel: 414-543-8292; Email: ppenkalski@stgregsmil.org; Web: www.stgregsmil.org. Rev. Thomas P. Demse.
Res.: 3129 S. 63rd St., 53219.
School—St. Gregory the Great School, 3132 S. 63rd St., 53219. Tel: 414-321-1350; Email: sfritz@stgregsmil.org; Web: www.stgregsmil.org. Mrs. Amy Schlegel, Prin. Lay Teachers 15; Students 260.
Catechesis Religious Program—Tel: 414-543-8292. Patti Penkalski, D.R.E. Students 79.

37—ST. HEDWIG (1871) (Polish), Closed. For sacramental records, contact Archdiocese of Milwaukee Archives Office, Tel: 414-769-3407.

38—ST. HELEN (1925) (Polish), Closed. For sacramental records, contact St. John Paul II Parish, 3307 S. 10th St., Milwaukee, WI 53215-5116, 414-744-3695, Fax: 414-744-2874.

39—HOLY ANGELS, Closed. For sacramental records, contact Archdiocese of Milwaukee Archives Office, Tel: 414-769-3407.

40—HOLY CROSS (1879) Closed. For sacramental records, contact St. Vincent Pallotti, Milwaukee, Tel: 414-453-4225.

41—HOLY REDEEMER, Closed. For sacramental records, contact Archdiocese of Milwaukee Archives Office, Tel: 414-769-3407.

42—HOLY ROSARY (1885) (Irish), Closed. For sacramental records, contact Archdiocese of Milwaukee Archives Office, Tel: 414-769-3407.

43—HOLY SPIRIT (1902) (German), Closed. For sacramental records, contact Archdiocese of Milwaukee Archives Office, Tel: 414-769-3407.

44—HOLY TRINITY-OUR LADY OF GUADALUPE (1849) (Hispanic), Closed. For sacramental records, contact Our Lady of Guadalupe, Milwaukee, Tel: 414-271-6181.

45—ST. HYACINTH (1883) (Polish—Hispanic)
1414 W. Becher St., 53215. Web: www.stanthony-sthyacinth.org. 1711 S. 9th St., 53204.
Tel: 414-645-1455; Fax: 414-645-1456; Email: sthyacinth@archmil.org. Rev. Hugo Londono; Jaime Charuc, F.M.M.; Rev. Jose Angel Estrada Anaya; Deacons Carlos Cornejo; Rogelio Macias; Henry O. Reyes.
Catechesis Religious Program—Email: andac@stanthonymilwaukee.org. Sr. Maria del Carmen de Anda, R.M., D.R.E. Students 63.

46—ST. IGNATIUS LOYOLA, Closed. For sacramental records, contact Archdiocese of Milwaukee Archives Office, Tel: 414-769-3407.

47—IMMACULATE CONCEPTION (1870)
1023 E. Russell Ave., 53207. Tel: 414-769-2480; Email: icbayview@gmail.com; Web: icbayview.wordpress.com. Mailing Address: 2530 S. Howell Ave., 53207. Rev. Philip J. Schumaker; Paul Weisenberger, Dir. Liturgy & Music.
See St. Thomas Aquinas Academy located in the Institution Section under Consolidated Elementary Schools.
Catechesis Religious Program—
Tel: 414-481-0777, Ext. 1117; Email: karen@secatholic.org; Email: rebecca@secatholic.org; Web: southeastcatholic.org. Karen Bushman, D.R.E. (Elem); Rebecca Scholz, Youth Min. Students 13.

48—ST. JOHN DE NEPOMUC, Closed. For sacramental records, contact Archdiocese of Milwaukee Archives Office, Tel: 414-769-3407.

49—ST. JOHN KANTY (1907) (Polish), Closed. For Sacramental records, contact St. John Paul II Parish, 3307 S. 10th St., Milwaukee, WI 53215-5116, 414-744-3695, Fax: 414-744-2874.

50—ST. JOHN PAUL II PARISH (2011)
3307 S. 10th St., 53215. Tel: 414-744-3695; Email: petrovicd@archmil.org; Web: www.sjpii-parish.org. Revs. Michael A. Ignaszak; Michael Wolfe.
School—St. John Kanty School, 2840 S. 10th St., 53215. Tel: 414-483-8780; Fax: 414-744-1846; Email: prncpl57@gmail.com. Beth Eichman, Prin. Lay Teachers 12; Students 125.
Catechesis Religious Program—Email: dahles@archmil.org. Roy Salinas, D.R.E. Students 293.

51—ST. JOSEPH, Closed. For sacramental records, contact St. Joseph, Wauwatosa, Tel: 414-771-4626.

52—ST. LAWRENCE (1888) Closed. For sacramental records, contact Archdiocese of Milwaukee Archives Office, Tel: 414-769-3407.

53—ST. LEO, Closed. For sacramental records, contact Archdiocese of Milwaukee Archives Office, Tel: 414-769-3407.

54—ST. MARGARET MARY (1955)
3970 N. 92nd St., 53222-2506. Tel: 414-461-6073; Email: mblinkhorn@stmmp.org; Web: stmmp.org. Rev. Patrick Nelson, S.D.S., Admin.; Deacon Frank Pemper, Tel: 414-461-6073.
School—St. Margaret Mary School, (Grades K-8), 3950 N. 92nd St., 53222-2587. Tel: 414-463-8760; Fax: 414-463-2373; Email: ncordova@stmms.org; Web: www.stmmp.org. Nilda Cordova, Prin. Lay Teachers 10; Students 160.
Catechesis Religious Program—Email: dliccione@stmmp.org. David Liccione, D.R.E. Students 35.

55—ST. MARTIN DE PORRES (1994) (African American)
128 W. Burleigh St., 53212-2046. Tel: 414-372-3090; Email: smdp@smdpmilw.com; Web: www.smdpmilwaukee.org. Very Rev. Timothy L. Kitzke, Admin.
Church: 3114 N. 2nd St., 53212-2046.
Catechesis Religious Program—Peggy Bowles, D.R.E. Students 8.

56—ST. MARY MAGDALEN (1925) (Korean)
1854 W. Windlake Ave., 53215. Tel: 414-810-1405; Email: stmarymagdalen@archmil.org. Rev. Su Young Ruy, M.S.C., (Korea, South).
Catechesis Religious Program—Students 4.

57—ST. MARY OF CZESTOCHOWA (1907) (Polish), Closed. For sacramental records, contact Our Lady of Divine Providence, Milwaukee, Tel: 414-264-0049.

58—MARY, QUEEN OF MARTYRS (2001) Closed. For sacramental records, contact Blessed Savior, Milwaukee, Tel: 414-464-5033.

59—ST. MATTHEW (1892) Closed. For sacramental records, contact Archdiocese of Milwaukee Archives Office, Tel: 414-769-3407.

60—ST. MATTHIAS (1850) [CEM]
9306 W. Beloit Rd., 53227. Tel: 414-321-0893; Email: jvandalen@stmatthias-milw.org. Revs. Charles H. Schramm, Supervising Assisting Priest, (Retired); David E. Cooper, Assisting Priest, (Retired); Jeffrey Van Dalen, Parish Dir.
School—St. Matthias School, 9300 W. Beloit Rd., 53227. Tel: 414-321-0894; Fax: 414-321-9228; Email: kearle@stmatthiasmilw.org. Karen Earle, Prin. Lay Teachers 18; Students 245.
Catechesis Religious Program—Email: tgallagher@stmatthias-milw.org. Thomas Gallagher, Coord., Christian Formation. Students 206.

61—ST. MICHAEL (1882)
1445 N. 24th St., 53205. Tel: 414-933-3143; Email: st.michaelsrectory@gmail.com. Revs. Rafael G. Rodriguez; Lawrence Michaphitak; Very Rev. Timothy L. Kitzke, Parish Admin.; Deacons Eugenio Ramirez-Murphy; Moualee Thao.
Catechesis Religious Program—Email: thepalice@gmail.com. Shanedra Johnson, Youth Dir. & Pastoral Assoc. Students 180.

62—MOTHER OF GOOD COUNSEL (1925)
6924 W. Lisbon Ave., 53210-1259. Tel: 414-442-7600; Email: mgc@mgcparish.org; Web: www.mgcparish.org. Rev. Reed Mungovan, S.D.S., Admin.; Deacons Dean J. Collins; Andrew Meuler.
School—Mother of Good Counsel School, 3001 N. 68th St., 53210-1299. Tel: 414-442-7600, Ext. 118; Email: shaw@mgcparish.org. Regina Shaw, Prin. Lay Teachers 16; Students 224.
Catechesis Religious Program—
Tel: 414-442-7600, Ext. 107; Email: mason@mgcparish.org. Mr. Richard Mason, D.R.E. Students 76.

63—MOTHER OF PERPETUAL HELP (1941) Closed. For sacramental records, contact Archdiocese of Milwaukee Archives Office, Tel: 414-769-3407.

64—ST. NICHOLAS, Closed. For sacramental records, contact Archdiocese of Milwaukee Archives Office, Tel: 414-769-3407.

65—OLD ST. MARY (1846) (Bavarian—German)
835 N. Milwaukee St., 53202-3605.
Tel: 414-271-6180; Email: riverad@archmil.org; Web: www.oldsaintmary.org. Very Rev. Timothy L. Kitzke; Rev. John J. Baumgardner; Terri Balash, Dir. Pastoral Care; James Piotrowski, Dir. Administrative Svcs.; Joseph P. Wittmann, M.T.S., Dir. Liturgy & Music; Andrew Musgrave, Dir. Social Justice Ministries. In Res., Most Rev. Richard J. Sklba, S.S.L., S.T.D., (Retired); Rev. Joseph J. Juknialis, (Retired).
Res.: 836 N. Broadway, 53202-3608.
Catechesis Religious Program—Email: gardinierk@archmil.org. Ken Gardinier, D.R.E. Students 28.

66—OUR LADY OF DIVINE PROVIDENCE (2003)
2600 N. Bremen St., 53212. Email: blackmerla@archmil.org; Web: www.ourladyofdivineprovidence.org. Mailing Address: 1716 N. Humboldt Ave., 53202. Tel: 414-264-0049. Very Rev. Timothy L. Kitzke; Rev. John J. Baumgardner; Terri Balash, Dir. Pastoral Care; James Piotrowski, Dir. Administrative Svcs.; Mary Robertson, Dir. Liturgy & Music; Andrew Musgrave, Dir. Social Justice Ministries; Chad Griesel, Dir.
Catechesis Religious Program—Tel: 414-962-3776; Email: escym@sbcglobal.net. Chad Griesel, Dir. Adult Faith Formation; Ralph Stewart, Dir. East Side Child & Youth Ministry. Students 7.

67—OUR LADY OF GOOD HOPE (1952)
7152 N. 41st St., 53209. Tel: 414-352-1148; Email: parish.office@olghparish.org; Web: www.olghparish.org. Rev. Gregory J. Greiten.
Catechesis Religious Program—8661 N. 76th Pl., 53223. Tel: 414-365-2020; Email: lmaples@stcatherinemke.org. Lorrie Maples, D.R.E. Students 6.

68—OUR LADY OF GUADALUPE PARISH (2000)
Mailing Address: 723 W. Washington St., 53204.
Tel: 414-645-7624; Email: guadalupe@archmil.org. Rev. Timothy Manatt, S.J.
Res.: 613 S. 4th St., 53204.
Catechesis Religious Program— Combined with St. Patrick, Milwaukee. Silvia Jiminez, C.R.E. Students 85.

69—OUR LADY OF LOURDES (1958)
3722 S. 58th St., 53220. Tel: 414-545-4316;
Fax: 414-541-2251; Email: olol@archmil.org; Web: www.ololmke.org. Rev. William C. Burkert, Assisting Priest, (Retired); Deacon John P. Monday; Nancie Chmielewski, Parish Dir.
Catechesis Religious Program—Tel: 414-541-9470. Steve Szymanski, D.R.E.; Taylor Baar, Youth Min. Students 133.

70—OUR LADY OF SORROWS (1955) Closed. For Sacramental records, contact Blessed Savior, Milwaukee, Tel: 414-464-5033.

71—OUR LADY QUEEN OF PEACE (1948)
3222 S. 29th St., 53215. Tel: 414-672-0313; Email: fkleczka@olqpmke.org; Email: lbarilla@olqpmke.org; Web: www.olqpmke.org. Rev. Javier Bustos.
School—Our Lady Queen of Peace School, 2733 W. Euclid Ave., 53215. Tel: 414-672-6660;
Fax: 414-672-2739; Tel: 414-672-0313; Email: fklecz@olqpmke.org; Email: jorlow@olqpstaff.org. Janet Orlowski, Prin. Lay Teachers 16; Students 166.
Catechesis Religious Program—Students 168.

72—ST. PATRICK (1876) [CEM]
723 W. Washington St., 53204. Tel: 414-645-7624; Email: stpats@archmil.org. Rev. Timothy Manatt, S.J.
Catechesis Religious Program— Combined with Our Lady of Guadalupe, Milwaukee. Silvia Jiminez, D.R.E. Students 90.

73—ST. PAUL (1920)
1720 E. Norwich Ave., 53207. Tel: 414-482-3510; Email: cheryl@saintpaulmke.com; Web: saintpaulmke.com. Rev. Arulananthan Ponnaiyan.
See St. Thomas Aquinas Academy located in the Institution Section under Consolidated Elementary Schools.
Catechesis Religious Program—Tel: 414-481-0777; Fax: 414-482-3025; Email: karen@secatholic.org. Karen Bushman, Dir., Elem. Formation; Rebecca Scholz, Youth Min. Students 16.

74—SS. PETER AND PAUL (1889) (German)
2490 N. Cramer St., 53211. Tel: 414-962-2443; Email: ssppmilw@archmil.org; Web: www.ssppmilw.

org. Mailing Address: 2491 N. Murray Ave., 53211. Very Rev. Timothy L. Kitzke, Co-Pastor; Rev. John J. Baumgardner, Co-Pastor.
See Catholic East Elementary, Milwaukee under Consolidated Elementary Schools located in the Institution section.
Catechesis Religious Program—East Side Child & Youth Ministry, Consolidated from the following parishes: SS. Peter & Paul, Our Lady of Divine Providence, Cathedral of St. John the Evangelist, and Three Holy Women. 1716 N. Humboldt Ave., 53211. Tel: 414-962-3776; Email: escym@sbcglobal.net. Ralph Stewart, Dir. Students 51.

75—ST. PHILIP NERI (1956) Closed. For sacramental records, contact Blessed Savior, Milwaukee, Tel: 414-464-5033.

76—PRINCE OF PEACE/PRINCIPE DE PAZ (1999)
Mailing Address: 1138 S. 25th St., 53204-1940. Rev. Dionicio Maximo Tzul, Admin.; Jenny Barrantes, Business Mgr.
Schools—Prince of Peace/Principe de Paz School - 25th Street Campus—(Grades K-3), 1114 S. 25th St., 53204. Tel: 414-383-2157; Fax: 414-383-7645; Email: blaszczykp@princeofpeaceschool.org; Web: www.princeofpeaceschool.org. Patricia Blaszczyk, Prin. Clergy 1; Lay Teachers 9; Students 200.
Prince of Peace/Principe de Paz School - 22nd Street Campus, 1646 S. 22nd St., 53204. Tel: 414-645-4922; Fax: 414-645-4940; Email: blaszczykp@princeofpeaceschool.org. Patricia Blaszczyk, Prin. Lay Teachers 42; Students 263.
Catechesis Religious Program—Email: vasconezj@princeofpeaceschool.org. Sr. Janeth Vasconez, D.R.E. Students 253.

77—ST. RAFAEL THE ARCHANGEL (1999) (Hispanic)
2059 S. 33rd St., 53215. Tel: 414-645-9172; Email: parish@strafael.org. Revs. Dionicio Maximo Tzul; Ermes Leon Aguirre, F.M.M., Pastoral Assoc.; Lisamarie Lukowski, Business Mgr.
School—St. Rafael the Archangel School, (Grades PreK-8), Tel: 414-645-1300; Email: abarbiaux@strafael.org; Web: www.strafael.org. Amy Barbiaux, Prin. Lay Teachers 27; Students 325.
Catechesis Religious Program—Jose Cruz, D.R.E. Students 244.

78—ST. RITA (1936) (Italian), Closed. For sacramental records, contact Archdiocese of Milwaukee Archives Office, Tel: 414-769-3407.

79—ST. ROMAN (1956) (Polish)
1710 W. Bolivar Ave., 53221. Tel: 414-282-9063; Email: pdeleon@stromans.com; Web: www.stromans.com. Revs. Brian T. Holbus; Norberto Sandoval; Deacon Jorge Zuniga.
School—St. Roman School, 1810 W. Bolivar Ave., 53221. Tel: 414-282-7970; Fax: 414-282-5140; Email: stromanschool@stromans.com. Susan Shawver, Prin. Lay Teachers 19; Students 292.
Catechesis Religious Program—Email: pdeleon@stromans.com. Students 133.

80—ST. ROSE (1888)
540 N. 31st St., 53208. Tel: 414-342-1778; Email: st.rosemilwaukee@gmail.com. Revs. Rafael G. Rodriguez; Lawrence Chakrit Micaphitak, C.Ss.R.; Very Rev. Timothy L. Kitzke, Admin.
See St. Rose Messmer, Milwaukee under Elementary Schools, Archdiocesan located in the Institution section.
Catechesis Religious Program—

81—SACRED HEART (1917) (Croatian)
917 N. 49th St., 53208. Tel: 414-774-9418; Fax: 414-774-7406; Email: sh.croatian@yahoo.com; Web: SacredHeartMilwaukee.org. Rev. Ivan Strmecki, O.F.M.
Catechesis Religious Program—Students 22.

82—ST. SEBASTIAN (1911)
5400 W. Washington Blvd., 53208. Tel: 414-453-1061; Email: saintsebs@saintsebs.org. Rev. Lawrence J. Chapman; Deacons Warren D. Braun, (Retired); James J. Peterson.
School—St. Sebastian School, 1747 N. 54th St., 53208. Tel: 414-453-5830; Email: saintsebs@saintsebs.org; Web: www.saintsebastianonline.net/school/. Heather Grams, Prin. Lay Teachers 27; Students 327.
St. Sebastian School Foundation, Inc.—Carole Poth, Admin.
Catechesis Religious Program—Email: edunckle@saintsebs.org. Edward Dunckle, D.R.E. Students 150.

83—ST. STANISLAUS (1866)
Mailing Address: 524 W. Historic Mitchell St., 53204. Tel: 414-226-5490; Email: ststanislaus@institute-christ-king.org; Web: www.institute-christ-king.org/milwaukee. Rev. Canon Benoit Jayr.
Catechesis Religious Program—Students 112.

84—ST. STEPHEN, MARTYR (1907) (Slovak), Closed. For sacramental records, contact Archdiocese of Milwaukee Archives Office, Tel: 414-769-3407.

85—ST. THERESE (1956)
Mailing Address: 9525 W. Bluemound Rd., 53226. Tel: 414-771-2500; Email: info@sttheresemke.org; Web: www.sttheresemke.org. Very Rev. Joseph Koyickal, S.A.C., Admin.; Heather Goeden, Business Mgr.; Mary Radspinner, Coord., Music & Accompanist.
Res.: 9427 W. Bluemound Rd., 53226.
Catechesis Religious Program—Students 48.

86—ST. THOMAS AQUINAS, Closed. For sacramental records, contact Archdiocese of Milwaukee Archives Office, Tel: 414-769-3407.

87—THREE HOLY WOMEN CATHOLIC PARISH (2000)
1716 N. Humboldt Ave., 53202-1697. Tel: 414-271-6577; Email: blackmerla@archmil.org; Web: www.threeholywomenparish.org. Very Rev. Timothy L. Kitzke; Rev. John J. Baumgardner; Chad Griesel, Dir.; Terri Balash, Dir. Pastoral Care; James Piotrowski, Business Mgr.; Mary Robertson, Dir. Liturgy & Music; Andrew Musgrave, Dir. Social Justice Ministries.
Catechesis Religious Program— (Collaborative) Tel: 414-962-3776; Email: escym@sbcglobal.net. Chad Griesel, Dir. Adult Faith Formation; Ralph Stewart, Dir. East Side Child & Youth Ministry. Students 36.

88—ST. VERONICA (1925)
Mailing Address: 353 E. Norwich St., 53207. Tel: 414-482-2920; Web: parishoffice@stvmke.org. Rev. Carmelo Giuffre.
See St. Thomas Aquinas Academy located in the Institution Section under Consolidated Elementary Schools.
Catechesis Religious Program—Tel: 414-481-0777; Email: karen@secatholic.org. Karen Bushman, D.R.E. & RCIA Coord. Students 91.

89—ST. VINCENT DE PAUL (1888) [CEM] (Polish)
2100 W. Mitchell St., 53204. Email: parishoffice@princeofpeaceschool.org. Mailing Address: 1138 S. 25th St., 53204-1940. Rev. Dionicio Maximo Tzul, Admin.; Jenny Barrantes, Business Mgr.
Catechesis Religious Program—Email: vasconezj@princeofpeaceschool.org. Sr. Janeth Vasconez, D.R.E.

90—ST. VINCENT PALLOTTI (1998)
Mailing Address: 201 N. 76th St., 53213. Tel: 414-453-5344; Email: lgabert@stvincentpallotti.org; Web: www.stvincentpallotti.org. Rev. Thomas Manjaly, S.A.C.
Res.: 5424 W. Bluemound Rd., 53208.
School—St. Vincent Pallotti Catholic School, (Grades K-8), 201 N. 76th St., 53213. Tel: 414-258-4165; Fax: 414-258-9844; Email: jjohnson@stvincentpallotti.org; Web: www.stvincentpallottischool.org. Mr. Jeffrey Johnson, Prin. Lay Teachers 13; Students 194.
Catechesis Religious Program—Tel: 414-453-5344. Jan Grosschadl, D.R.E. Students 17.

91—ST. WENCESLAUS (1883) (Hispanic), Closed. For sacramental records, contact Archdiocese of Milwaukee Archives Office, Tel: 414-769-3407.

OUTSIDE THE CITY OF MILWAUKEE

ADELL, SHEBOYGAN CO., ST. PATRICK (1853) (Irish), Closed. For sacramental records, contact Archdiocese of Milwaukee Archives Office, Tel: 414-769-3407.

ALLENTON, WASHINGTON CO.
1—ST. ANTHONY (1851) Closed. For sacramental records, contact Resurrection, Allenton, Tel: 262-629-5240.
2—RESURRECTION (1997) [CEM 3]
215 Main St., Allenton, 53002. Tel: 262-629-5240; Email: Alleluia1@frontier.com. Very Rev. Richard J. Stoffel; Rev. Davies Edassery, S.A.C.
Catechesis Religious Program—Tel: 262-629-1500; Email: resreled@frontier.com. Students 86.
3—SACRED HEART (1917) Closed. For sacramental records, contact Resurrection, Allenton, Tel: 262-629-5240.

ARMSTRONG, FOND DU LAC CO., OUR LADY OF ANGELS (1856) (Irish), Closed. For sacramental records, contact Good Shepherd, Eden, Tel: 920-477-3201.

ASHFORD, FOND DU LAC CO., ST. MARTIN (1847) [CEM] Closed. For sacramental records, contact St. Matthew, Campbellsport, Tel: 920-533-4441.

AUBURN, FOND DU LAC CO., ST. MATTHIAS (1863) (German), Closed. For sacramental records, contact Holy Trinity, Kewaskum, Tel: 262-626-2860.

BEAVER DAM, DODGE CO.
1—ST. KATHARINE DREXEL (2003) [CEM]
Mailing Address: 408 S. Spring St., Beaver Dam, 53916. Revs. Michael J. Erwin; Erick Cassiano-Amaya, F.M.M.
Church: 511 S. Spring St., Beaver Dam, 53916. Tel: 920-887-2082; Email: heinzenb@stkatharinedrexelbd.org; Web: stkatharinedrexelbd.org.
School—St. Katharine Drexel School, (Grades PreSchool-8), 503 S. Spring St., Beaver Dam, 53916. Tel: 920-885-5558; Fax: 920-885-7610; Email: haaseb@stkatharinedrexelbd.org; Web: www.skds.org. Barbara M. Haase, Prin.; Kimberly Lopas, Librarian. Lay Teachers 18; Students 206.
Catechesis Religious Program— Combined program (PreK - 11). Email: adsitk@stkatharinedrexelbd.org. Kristin Adsit, D.R.E.; John Pryme, D.R.E. Students 242.
2—ST. MICHAEL (1893) Closed. For sacramental records, contact St. Katharine Drexel, Beaver Dam, Tel: 920-887-2082.
3—ST. PATRICK (1860) Closed. For sacramental records, contact St. Katharine Drexel, Beaver Dam, Tel: 920-887-2082.
4—ST. PETER (1855) Closed. For sacramental records, contact St. Katharine Drexel, Beaver Dam, Tel: 920-887-2082.

BELGIUM, OZAUKEE CO., ST. MARY (1848) [CEM] (German—Luxembourg), Closed. For sacramental records, contact Divine Savior Parish, Fredonia, 262-692-9994.

BIG BEND, WAUKESHA CO., ST. JOSEPH (1872)
S89 W22650 Milwaukee Ave., Big Bend, 53103. Tel: 262-662-2832; Email: parish@stjoesbb.com; Web: www.stjoesbb.com. Rev. Kevin McManaman
St. Joseph's Congregation
School—St. Joseph Catholic School, (Grades K-8), Tel: 262-662-2737; Email: school@stjoesbb.com; Web: www.stjoesbb.com. Jeff Van Rixel, Prin. Lay Teachers 8; Students 116.
Catechesis Religious Program—Tel: 262-662-3317; Email: cfm@stjoesbb.com. Lorraine Labadie, D.R.E.; Annie Collins, D.R.E. Students 155.

BRANDON, FOND DU LAC CO., ST. BRENDAN (1921) [CEM] (German), Closed. For sacramental records, contact St. Joseph Parish, Waupun. Tel: 920-324-5400.

BRIGHTON, KENOSHA CO., ST. FRANCIS XAVIER (1838) [CEM] (German)
1704 240th Ave., Kansasville, 53139. Tel: 262-878-2267; Email: sfxsjb@archmil.org. Revs. Russell L. Arnett, Admin.; Jose Edapparakel Mathai, M.C.B.S.
Catechesis Religious Program— Combined with St. John the Baptist, Paris. Cynthia Cetera, D.R.E. (Gr. K-10); Katherine Peterson, D.R.E. (Grades K-10). Students 100.

BRISTOL, KENOSHA CO.
1—HOLY CROSS (2009)
18700 116th St., Bristol, 53104. Tel: 262-857-2068; Email: holycross@archmil.org; Web: www.holycrosscatholicchurch.net. Dr. Sandra J. Schmitt, Parish Dir.
Catechesis Religious Program—Tel: 262-857-9032; Email: holycross.christianformation@gmail.com. Darlene Lasch, D.R.E. Students 76.
2—ST. SCHOLASTICA (1945) [CEM] Closed. For sacramental records, contact Holy Cross, Bristol, Tel: 262-857-2068.

BROOKFIELD, WAUKESHA CO.
1—ST. DOMINIC (1866)
18255 W. Capitol Dr., Brookfield, 53045-1422. Tel: 262-781-3480; Fax: 262-781-3283; Email: info@stdominic.net; Web: www.stdominic.net. Revs. Dennis J. Saran, Admin.; Aaron Laskiewicz; Deacons Gregory H. Diciaula; Jim Mathias; Senior Deacon Larry LaFond; Mary Lestina, Pastoral Assoc.; Michael Ricci, Dir. Opers.; Paul Burzynski, Dir. Liturgy & Music; Karen Chaffee, Dir. Finance; Meg Picciolo, Dir. Mktg. & Communication; Molly Schmidt, Dir. Membership & Events.
Rectory—3760 Arroyo Rd., Brookfield, 53045-1422.
School—St. Dominic School, 18105 W. Capitol Dr., Brookfield, 53045-1425. Tel: 262-783-7565; Fax: 262-783-5947; Email: jill.fischer@stdominic.net; Email: school@stdominic.net; Web: www.stdominic.net/school. Mrs. Jill Fischer, Prin. Lay Teachers 28; Students 440.
Catechesis Religious Program—Andrew Schueller, Dir., Formation; Stacey Irvine, Dir. Child Ministry; Debbie Olla, Dir. Adult Min.; Sarah Daszczuk, Dir., Youth, Young Adult Min. & Evangelization. Students 452.
2—ST. JOHN VIANNEY (1956)
1755 N. Calhoun Rd., Brookfield, 53005-5036. Tel: 262-796-3940; Tel: 262-796-3944; Fax: 262-796-3958; Email: edwink@stjohnv.org; Web: www.stjohnv.org. Revs. Edwin M. Kornath; Nathaniel J. Miniatt; David Sanders, Dir. Liturgy & Music; Dr. Dennis D. Sylva, Ph.D., Dir. Adult & Family Ministry; Robb Lied, Dir. Admin. Svcs.; John Thompson, Dir. Human Concerns; Vincent La Tona, Assoc. Dir. Liturgy & Music.
School—St. John Vianney School, 17500 W. Gebhardt Rd., Brookfield, 53045-5096. Tel: 262-796-3942; Fax: 262-796-3953; Email: brians@stjohnv.org; Web: www.stjohnv.org. Brian Shimon, Prin. Religious Teachers 2; Lay Teachers 32; Students 325.
Catechesis Religious Program—Tel: 262-796-3944; Email: daveb@stjohnv.org. David Baudry, D.R.E. Students 485.
3—ST. LUKE (1956)
18000 W. Greenfield Ave., Brookfield, 53045. Tel: 262-782-0032; Email: stluke@stlukebrookfield.

org; Web: stlukebrookfield.org. Rev. Kenneth J. Augustine.
Catechesis Religious Program—Email: sfoster@stlukebrookfield.org. Suzanne Foster, D.R.E. Students 69.

BURLINGTON, RACINE CO.
1—ST. CHARLES (1908) [CEM]
440 Kendall St., Burlington, 53105.
Tel: 262-763-2260; Email: jmorrow@mystcharles.org; Web: www.mystcharles.org. 441 Conkey St., Burlington, 53105. Very Rev. James T. Volkert; Rev. Carlos Alberto Zapata.
School—St. Charles School, 449 Conkey St., Burlington, 53105. Tel: 262-763-2848;
Tel: 262-762-2637 (Grade School); Email: principalstcharles@wi.rr.com. Mary MacDonald, Prin. Lay Teachers 16; Students 144.
Catechesis Religious Program—
Tel: 262-763-2260, Ext. 204 (Grade School Rep.); Email: eschultz@mystcharles.org (High School Rep.); Email: eschultz@mystcharles.org. Margie Robers, D.R.E.; Elle Schultz, D.R.E.; Rita Van Schyndel, D.R.E. Students 264.

2—IMMACULATE CONCEPTION (1838) [CEM] (German)
108 McHenry St., Burlington, 53105. Very Rev. James T. Volkert; Rev. Carlos Alberto Zapata.
School—Immaculate Conception School dba St. Mary School, (Grades K-8), 225 W. State St., Burlington, 53105. Tel: 262-763-1515; Web: www.stmb.org. Loretta Jackson, Prin. Lay Teachers 25; Priests 2; Students 309.
Catechesis Religious Program—Email: mrobers@stmb.org. Margie Robers, D.R.E.; Elle Schultz, D.R.E.; Rita Van Schyndel, D.R.E. Students 264.

BUTLER, WAUKESHA CO., ST. AGNES (1915)
12801 W. Fairmount Ave., Butler, 53007.
Tel: 262-781-9521; Email: stagnes007@archmil.org; Web: stagnesparish.org. Rev. Mark J. Brandl; Deacon Raymond Waitrovich.
School—St. Agnes School, Tel: 262-781-4996; Email: nkuehne@stagnesparish.org; Web: www.stagnesparish.org. Nicole Kuehne, Prin. Lay Teachers 14; Students 146.
Catechesis Religious Program—Tel: 262-781-6998; Email: fellinm@stagnesparish.org. Michelle Fellin, D.R.E. Students 129.

BYRON, FOND DU LAC CO.
1—ST. JOHN (1847) Closed. For sacramental records, contact Sons of Zebedee: Saints James and John, Byron, Tel: 920-922-1167.
2—SONS OF ZEBEDEE: SAINTS JAMES AND JOHN (2000) [CEM]
Mailing Address: W5882 Church Rd., Fond du Lac, 54937-8602. Tel: 920-922-1167; Email: zebedee@excel.net. Rev. Michael C. Petersen.
Catechesis Religious Program— Twinned with St. Mary, Lomira. 699 Milwaukee St., Lomira, 53048. Tel: 920-269-4326; Email: lstaehlerdre@gmail.com. Lesa Staehler, D.R.E. Students 12.

CALEDONIA, RACINE CO., ST. LOUIS (1846) [CEM]
13207 County Rd. G, Caledonia, 53108-9531.
Tel: 262-835-4533; Fax: 262-835-0421; Email: stlouis@wi.rr.com; Web: www.stlouisparishwi.com. Rev. Yamid Blanco; Deacon Jim Zdeb.
Catechesis Religious Program—Colleen Rooney, Dir. Youth Faith Formation. Students 65.

CAMPBELLSPORT, FOND DU LAC CO., ST. MATTHEW (1864) [CEM 3]
P.O. Box 740, Campbellsport, 53010.
Tel: 920-533-4441; Email: werths@archmil.org; Web: www.stmatthewofcsport.org. 419 Mill St., Campbellsport, 53010. Rev. Mark R. Jones; Shawn Werth, Business Mgr. Includes St. Martin Chapel, Ashford & St. Kilian, St. Kilian.
School—St. Matthew School, 423 Mill St., P.O. Box 639, Campbellsport, 53010. Tel: 920-533-4103; Fax: 920-533-8078; Email: smslion@archmil.org; Web: www.stmattschoolcampbellsport.com. Joan Schlaefer, Prin. Lay Teachers 10; Students 118.
Catechesis Religious Program—Email: kboehm@sothparish.org. Katherine Boehm, D.R.E. Students 159.

CASCADE, SHEBOYGAN CO., ST. MARY-CASCADE (1852) Closed. For sacramental records, contact Archdiocese of Milwaukee Archives Office, Tel: 414-769-3407.

CEDARBURG, OZAUKEE CO.
1—DIVINE WORD (1970) Closed. For sacramental records, contact St. Francis Borgia, Cedarburg, Tel: 262-377-1070.
2—ST. FRANCIS BORGIA (1844) [CEM]
1375 Covered Bridge Rd., Cedarburg, 53012.
Tel: 262-377-1070; Email: parish@sfbchurch.org. Rev. Patrick J. Burns, Admin.; Deacon Mark Leonardelli.
School—St. Francis Borgia School, 1425 Covered Bridge Rd., Cedarburg, 53012. Tel: 262-377-2050; Fax: 262-377-4099; Email: office@sfbschool.org; Web: www.sfbschool.org. Kelly Swietlik, Prin. Lay Teachers 30; Students 322.
Catechesis Religious Program—Chris Crom, Child Min. Students 414.

CLYMAN, DODGE CO., ST. JOHN (1900) [CEM 2] (German—Irish) Also serves Holy Family, Reeseville & St. Columbkille, Elba.
417 Church St., Clyman, 53016. Mailing Address: 302 Prairie St., P.O. Box 277, Reeseville, 53579-0277. Tel: 920-927-3102; Email: triparish@charter.net; Web: www.triparishwi.com. Revs. Michael J. Erwin; Erick Cassiano-Amaya, F.M.M.
Catechesis Religious Program—Connie Caine, D.R.E., Tel: 920-210-1865; John Pryme, Youth Min. Students 8.

CUDAHY, MILWAUKEE CO.
1—ST. FREDERICK (1896) Closed. For sacramental records, contact Nativity of the Lord, Cudahy, Tel: 414-744-6622.
2—HOLY FAMILY (1900) Closed. For sacramental records, contact Nativity of the Lord, Cudahy, Tel: 414-744-6622.
3—ST. JOSEPH (1909) (Slovak—Moravian), Closed. For sacramental records, contact Nativity of the Lord, Cudahy, Tel: 414-744-6622.
4—NATIVITY OF THE LORD PARISH (2000) [JC]
3672 E. Plankinton Ave., Cudahy, 53110.
Tel: 414-744-6622; Fax: 414-483-4599; Email: parishoffice@nativitycudahy.org. Mailing Address: 4611 S. Kirkwood Ave., Cudahy, 53110. Web: www.nativitycudahy.org. Rev. Carmelo Giuffre.
See St. Thomas Aquinas Academy located in the Institution Section under Consolidated Elementary Schools.
Catechesis Religious Program—353 E. Norwich Ave., 53207. Tel: 414-481-0777, Ext. 1117; Email: karen@southeastcatholic.org. Karen Bushman. Students 9.

DACADA, SHEBOYGAN CO., ST. NICHOLAS (1848) (Luxembourgian), Closed. For sacramental records, contact Archdiocese of Milwaukee Archives Office, Tel: 414-769-3407.

DELAFIELD, WAUKESHA CO., ST. JOAN OF ARC (1923) [CEM]
120 Nashotah Rd., Nashotah, 53058.
Tel: 262-646-8078; Fax: 262-646-8079; Email: sj-office@scsjcluster.org; Web: www.sjarc.org. Rev. Michael D. Strachota.
School—St. Joan of Arc School, (Grades PreK-8), Tel: 262-646-5821; Email: school-office@scsjcluster.org. Mrs. Holly Cerveny, Prin. Religious Teachers 1; Lay Teachers 9; Students 74.
Catechesis Religious Program—Tel: 262-646-5979; Email: mreutebuch@scsjcluster.org. Mary Sue Reutebuch, Dir. Christian Formation K4-Grade 11. Students 179.

DELAVAN, WALWORTH CO., ST. ANDREW (1848) [CEM]
714 E. Walworth Ave., Delavan, 53115.
Tel: 262-728-5922; Email: stewardship@saspcatholics.org; Web: www.standrews-delavan.org. Revs. Oriol Regales; Josegerman Zapata-Ramirez; Deacon Philip O. Kilkenny; Sr. Monica Semper, Pastoral Min.; Becky Baker, Business Mgr.
School—St. Andrew School, 115 S. 17th St., Delavan, 53115. Tel: 262-728-6211; Fax: 262-728-3683; Email: school@standrewparishschool.com; Web: standrews-delavan.org. Randal Green, Prin. Lay Teachers 14; Students 154.
Catechesis Religious Program—Email: rayhenderson33@gmail.com. Jennifer Paul, D.R.E.; Ray Henderson, D.R.E. Students 188.

DOTYVILLE, FOND DU LAC CO., ST. MICHAEL (1853) (German), Closed. For sacramental records, contact Good Shepherd, Eden, Tel: 920-477-3201.

DOUSMAN, WAUKESHA CO., ST. BRUNO (1852) [CEM]
Tel: 262-965-2332; Email: stbruno@wi.rr.com. Rev. Daniel P. Volkert; Deacons Tom Filipiak; Joseph M. Senglaub; Steve Spiegelhoff, Business Mgr.; Mark Mrozek, Asst. Dir., Liturgy & Music.
Res.: 266 W. Ottawa Ave., Dousman, 53118.
School—St. Bruno School, 246 W. Ottawa Ave., Dousman, 53118. Tel: 262-965-2291; Email: stbruno@wi.rr.com. Ben Holzem, Prin. Clergy 1; Lay Teachers 13; Students 110.
Catechesis Religious Program—Email: aldgolden@gmail.com; Email: stbrunoyouth@wi.rr.com. Amy Golden, D.R.E. (Preschool-8); Mary Kral, Adult Ministry. Students 106.

EAGLE, WAUKESHA CO., ST. THERESA (1852) [CEM 2]
136 W. Waukesha Rd., Eagle, 53119-2026.
Tel: 262-594-5200; Email: hernkej@archmil.org. Rev. Loyola Amalraj.
Catechesis Religious Program—Tel: 262-592-3075; Email: tanell@archmil.org. Laurie Tanel, Christian Formation. Students 83.

EAST TROY, WALWORTH CO., ST. PETER (1854) [CEM] (Irish—German)
1975 Beulah Ave., East Troy, 53120.
Tel: 262-642-7225; Email: office@stpeterset.org; Web: stpeterset.org. Rev. Mark Molling.
School—St. Peter School, (Grades PreK-8), 3001 Elm St., East Troy, 53120. Tel: 262-642-5533; Fax: 262-642-5897; Email: mprudom@stpetersschoolet.org. Megan Prudom, Prin. Religious Teachers 1; Lay Teachers 10; Students 77.
Catechesis Religious Program—
Tel: 262-642-7225, Ext. 5; Email: religedsuz@gmail.com. Suzanne Kasper, D.R.E. Students 131.

EDEN, FOND DU LAC CO.
1—ST. MARY (1888) (Irish), Closed. For sacramental records, contact Good Shepherd, Eden, Tel: 920-477-3201.
2—SHEPHERD OF THE HILLS (GOOD SHEPHERD) (2001) [JC6]
W1562 Cty. B, Eden, 53019. Tel: 920-477-3201; Email: sgitter@sothparish.org; Web: www.sothparish.org. Rev. Mark R. Jones.
Res.: N4348 Mercury Ln., Eden, 53019.
School—Shepherd of the Hills (Good Shepherd) School, Tel: 920-477-3551; Email: aroyes@sothparish.org; Web: www.sothparish.org. Amy Royes, Prin. Lay Teachers 13; Students 110.
Catechesis Religious Program—Katherine Boehm, D.R.E. Students 142.
Mission—St. Michael Chapel, N3604 Scenic Dr., Cascade, Sheboygan Co. 53011. Tel: 920-477-3201; Fax: 920-477-3030.

ELBA, DODGE CO., ST. COLUMBKILLE (1856) [CEM] (Irish) Also serves Holy Family, Reeseville and St. John the Baptist, Clyman.
Mailing Address: P.O. Box 277, Reeseville, 53579-0277. Tel: 920-623-3989; Tel: 920-927-3102; Email: triparish@charter.net; Web: www.triparishwi.com. W10802 County Rd. TT, Columbus, 53925. Revs. Michael J. Erwin; Erick Cassiano-Amaya, F.M.M.
Catechesis Religious Program—Fax: 920-927-1970; Email: triparish@charter.net. Connie Caine, D.R.E.; John Pryme, Youth Min. Students 15.

ELDORADO, FOND DU LAC CO.
1—ST. MARY, Closed. For sacramental records, contact Our Risen Savior, Eldorado, Tel: 920-922-2412.
2—OUR RISEN SAVIOR (1998) [CEM 2] (Irish—German)
N6499 County Y, Eldorado, 54932. Tel: 920-921-9383 ; Email: pbvmoffice@yahoo.com. Rev. Ryan J. Pruess.
Catechesis Religious Program—Sue Stephani, C.R.E. Students 49.

ELKHART LAKE, SHEBOYGAN CO.
1—ST. GEORGE (1896) Closed. For sacramental records, contact St. Thomas Aquinas, Elkhart Lake, Tel: 920-876-2457.
2—ST. THOMAS AQUINAS (2001) [CEM 2] (Merger of St. George, Elkhart Lake and St. Fridolin, Glenbeulah.)
94 N. Lincoln St., Elkhart Lake, 53020-0396.
Tel: 920-876-2457; Email: st.thomas.aquinas@frontier.com; Web: StThomasAquinasEL.org. P.O. Box 396, Elkhart Lake, 53020-0396. Very Rev. Philip D. Reifenberg, J.C.L.
Catechesis Religious Program—Tel: 920-980-9591; Email: sta.ff@frontier.com. Lisa Gross, D.R.E. Students 66.

ELKHORN, WALWORTH CO., ST. PATRICK (1878) [CEM] (Irish—German)
107 W. Walworth St., Elkhorn, 53121.
Tel: 262-723-5565; Email: office@stpatrickselkhorn.org; Email: business@stpatrickelkhorn.org; Web: www.stpatrickselkhorn.org. Revs. Oriol Regales; Josegerman Zapata-Ramirez.
Catechesis Religious Program—Tel: 262-723-5565. Ray Henderson, D.R.E. Students 294.

ELM GROVE, WAUKESHA CO., ST. MARY'S VISITATION (1848) [CEM]
1260 Church St., Elm Grove, 53122.
Tel: 262-782-4575; Email: parish@stmaryeg.org; Web: stmaryeg.org. Revs. Peter J. Berger; John S. Gibson; Deacons Charles J. Kustner; Richard T. Piontek.
School—St. Mary's Visitation School, 13000 Juneau Blvd., Elm Grove, 53122. Tel: 262-782-7057; Fax: 262-782-3035; Email: info@stmaryeg.org; Web: www.stmaryeg.org. Mary Tretow, Prin. Lay Teachers 21; Students 283.
Catechesis Religious Program—Tel: 414-771-4626; Fax: 262-782-0677; Email: stmaryeg@stmaryeg.org. Students 166.

FARMINGTON, WASHINGTON CO., ST. JOHN OF GOD (1859) (Irish), Closed. For sacramental records, contact St. Michael, St. Michael, 53040, Tel: 262-334-5270.

FOND DU LAC, FOND DU LAC CO.
1—HOLY FAMILY (2000)
271 Fourth Street Way, Fond du Lac, 54937-7508.
Tel: 920-921-0580; Fax: 920-922-4866; Email: holyfam@hffdl.org; Web: www.hffdl.org. Revs. Ryan J. Pruess, Admin.; Fabian Rodas, F.M.M.; John Paul Mitchell; Thomas Naidu.
Catechesis Religious Program—Email: scarter@hffdl.org. Sabrina Carter, Christian Formation Coord. Students 722.
2—ST. JOSEPH (1871) Closed. For sacramental records through June 12, 1967, contact Archdiocese of Milwaukee Archives Office, Tel: 414-769-3407. For

records after June 12, 1967, contact Holy Family, Fond du Lac, Tel: 920-921-0580.
3—ST. LOUIS (1847) (French), Closed. For sacramental records through September 19, 1959, contact Archdiocese of Milwaukee Archives Office, Tel: 414-769-3407. For records after September 19, 1959, contact Holy Family, Fond du Lac, Tel: 920-921-0580.
4—ST. MARY (1866) (German), Closed. For sacramental records through 1975, contact Archdiocese of Milwaukee Archives Office, Tel: 414-769-3407. For records after 1975, contact Holy Family, Fond du Lac, Tel: 920-921-0580.
5—ST. PATRICK (1855) Closed. For sacramental records through September 18, 1960, contact Archdiocese of Milwaukee Archives Office, Tel: 414-769-3407. For records after September 18, 1960, contact Holy Family, Fond du Lac, Tel: 920-921-0580.
6—SACRED HEART (1957) (German), Closed. For sacramental records through November 1970, contact Archdiocese of Milwaukee Archives Office, Tel: 414-769-3407. For records after November 1970, contact Holy Family, Fond du Lac, Tel: 920-921-0580.

FONTANA, WALWORTH CO., ST. BENEDICT (1912) [JC]
137 Dewey Ave., Fontana, 53125-1239.
Tel: 262-275-2480; Fax: 262-275-6426; Email: office@stbensparish.org; Web: www.stbensparish.org. Revs. Mark J. Danczyk; Sergio Lizama, S.A.C.
Catechesis Religious Program—Tel: 262-275-2993; Email: msmith@stbensparish.org. Molly Smith, D.R.E. Students 153.

FOX LAKE, DODGE CO.
1—ANNUNCIATION (1998) [CEM 3]
305 W. Green St., Fox Lake, 53933-9472.
Tel: 920-928-3513; Email: annunciationparish305@gmail.com. Rev. John J. Radetski.
Catechesis Religious Program—Tel: 920-928-6022; Email: annunciationparishdre@gamil.com. Jennifer Crombie, D.R.E. Students 53.
2—ST. MARY (1850) (Irish), Closed. For sacramental records, contact Annunciation, Fox Lake, Tel: 920-928-3513.

FOX POINT, MILWAUKEE CO., ST. EUGENE (1957)
7600 N. Port Washington Rd., Fox Point, 53217.
Tel: 414-918-1100; Email: seoffice@stme.church; Web: steugenecongregation.org. Very Rev. Paul B.R. Hartmann, M.Div., J.C.L.; Rev. Andrew J.T. Linn; John Fritsch, Pastoral Assoc.; Monica Cardenas, Dir. Parish Stewardship Devel.
School—St. Eugene School, (Grades PreK-8),
Tel: 414-918-1120; Email: schooloffice@steugene.school; Web: www.steugene.school. Rebecca Jones, Prin. Lay Teachers 10; Students 164.
Catechesis Religious Program—Tel: 414-967-8780; Email: childministry@stme.church. Ms. Jeanette Lambrecht, D.R.E. (Child Ministry); Meaghan Turner, D.R.E. (Youth & Young Adult Ministry). Students 161.

FRANKLIN, MILWAUKEE CO.
1—ST. JAMES (1857) [CEM]
7219 S. 27th St., Franklin, 53132. Tel: 414-761-0480; Email: dhull@stjames-franklin.org; Web: www.stjames-franklin.org. Daniel L. Hull, Parish Dir.; Rev. Msgr. T. George Gajdos, Assisting Priest, (Retired); Revs. Bernard S. Sippel, M.Div., Assisting Priest, (Retired); Robert Betz, Assisting Priest, (Retired).
Catechesis Religious Program—Email: MaryJo@stjames-franklin.org. Mary Jo Hennemann, D.R.E. Students 132.
2—ST. MARTIN OF TOURS (1998) [CEM]
7963 S. 116th St., Franklin, 53132.
Tel: 414-425-1114; Fax: 414-425-2527; Email: parish@stmoftours.org; Web: www.stmoftours.org. Revs. Terence Langley, S.C.J., Admin.; Joseph Quang Tran, S.C.J.; Deacons Bruno Long H. Nguyen; Charles G. Schneider.
School—St. Martin of Tours School, 7933 S. 116th St., Franklin, 53132. Tel: 414-425-9200; Email: s.marino@stmoftours.org; Web: www.stmoftours.org. Robert Beckmann, Prin. Lay Teachers 15; Students 58.
Catechesis Religious Program—Email: mkreuser@stmoftours.org. Michelle Kreuser, D.R.E. Students 126.
3—SACRED HEARTS OF JESUS AND MARY (1858) Closed. For sacramental records, contact St. Martin of Tours, Franklin, Tel: 414-425-1114.

FREDONIA, OZAUKEE CO.
1—DIVINE SAVIOR CONGREGATION (2012)
305 Fredonia Ave., P.O. Box 250, Fredonia, 53021-0250. Tel: 262-692-9994; Email: divinesavior@archmil.org; Web: divinesavior.weconnect.com. Rev. Todd Budde.
School—Divine Savior School, Tel: 262-692-2141; Fax: 262-692-3085; Email: dscsoffice@dscsfredonia.org; Web: divinesavior.weconnect.com. Lynn Sauer, Prin. Lay Teachers 10; Students 92.
Catechesis Religious Program—Email: riesselmannt@archmil.org. Terri Riesselmann, D.R.E. Students 175.
2—HOLY ROSARY (2001) [CEM 4] Closed. For sacramental records, contact Divine Savior Parish, Fredonia, 262-692-9994.
3—ST. ROSE OF LIMA (1909) Closed. For sacramental records, contact Holy Rosary, Fredonia, Tel: 262-692-9994.

GENESEE DEPOT, WAUKESHA CO., ST. PAUL (1863) [CEM]
Mailing Address: S38 W31602 Hwy. D, P.O. Box 95, Genesee Depot, 53127. Tel: 262-968-3865;
Fax: 262-968-5546; Email: office@stpaulgenesee.net; Web: www.stpaulgenesee.net. Rev. Daniel P. Volkert, Admin.; Deacon Joseph M. Senglaub; Sherri Meyer, Dir. Admin. Svcs.; Peggy Kolonko, Dir. Liturgy & Music; Mrs. Nancy Bastian, Bookkeeper.
School—St. Paul School, Tel: 262-968-3175; Email: school@stpaulgenesee.net. Angela Gunderson, Prin. Lay Teachers 16; Students 92.
Catechesis Religious Program—Tel: 262-968-2276. Karen Farrell, Dir., Child & Family Min. Students 274.

GERMANTOWN, WASHINGTON CO., ST. BONIFACE (1845) [CEM]
W204 N11940 Goldendale Rd., Germantown, 53022.
Tel: 262-628-2040; Email: parish@stbonifacewi.org; Web: www.stbonifacewi.org. Rev. Michael J. Petrie.
School—St. Boniface School, W204 N11968 Goldendale Rd., Germantown, 53022.
Tel: 262-628-1955; Email: derlandson@stbonifacewi.org; Web: www.stbonifacewi.org. Diana Erlandson, Prin. Religious Teachers 1; Lay Teachers 14; Students 108.
Catechesis Religious Program—Tel: 262-628-8143; Email: jkascht@stbonifacewi.org. Kathryn Harvey, Youth Min. Students 252.

GLENBEULAH, SHEBOYGAN CO., ST. FRIDOLIN (1878) Closed. For sacramental records, contact St. Thomas Aquinas, Elkhart Lake, Tel: 920-876-2457.

GRAFTON, OZAUKEE CO., ST. JOSEPH (1849) [CEM]
Brenda Cline, Parish Dir.; Rev. Stephen J. Lampe, M.Div., S.S.L., S.T.D., Assisting Priest; Deacons Alfred C. Lazaga; Scott T. Wiese.
Pastoral Center—1619 Washington St., Grafton, 53024. Tel: 262-375-6500; Email: parish@stjosephgrafton.org; Web: www.stjosephgrafton.org.
School—St. Joseph School, (Grades PreK-8),
Tel: 262-375-6505; Email: jfrymark@stjosephgrafton.org. Brenda Cline, Dir. Lay Teachers 11; Students 160.
Catechesis Religious Program—Email: shanson@stjosephgrafton.org. Sheri Hanson, D.R.E. Students 342.

GREENDALE, MILWAUKEE CO., ST. ALPHONSUS (1938)
6060 W. Loomis Rd., Greendale, 53129. 5960 W. Loomis Rd., Greendale, 53129. Tel: 414-421-2442;
Fax: 414-421-8744; Email: stals@st-alphonsus.org; Web: www.st-alphonsus.org. Revs. Aaron J. Esch; Britto Raja Suresh; Deacons Theodore A. Gurzynski; James Leggett.
School—St. Alphonsus School, 6000 W. Loomis Rd., Greendale, 53129. Tel: 414-421-1760;
Fax: 414-433-0709; Email: school@st-alphonsus.org. Patrice Wadzinski, Prin. Lay Teachers 28; Students 435.
Catechesis Religious Program—Email: julie@st-alphonsus.org; Email: carol@st-alphonsus.org. Carol Fischer, D.R.E.; Julie Petri, Dir., Child Min. Students 486.

GREENFIELD, MILWAUKEE CO., ST. JOHN THE EVANGELIST (1916)
8500 W. Cold Spring Rd., Greenfield, 53228.
Tel: 414-321-1965; Fax: 414-321-4407; Email: rectory@stjohns-grfd.org; Web: www.stjohns-grfd.org. Rev. Michael F. Merkt.
School—St. John the Evangelist School, (Grades PreK-8), 8500 W. Cold Spring Rd., Greenfield, 53228.
Tel: 414-321-8540; Fax: 414-321-4450; Email: principal@sje.k12.wi.us. Mary Laidlaw Otto, Prin. Lay Teachers 15; Students 104.
Catechesis Religious Program—Tel: 414-321-8922; Email: arahill@stjohns-grfd.org. Austin Rahill, D.R.E. Students 106.

HALES CORNERS, MILWAUKEE CO., ST. MARY (1842) [CEM]
9520 W. Forest Home Ave., Hales Corners, 53130.
Tel: 414-425-2174; Email: foxl@stmaryhc.org; Web: www.stmaryhc.org. Rev. Brian G. Mason; Deacons John R. Burns; William Goulding.
School—St. Mary School, 9553 W. Edgerton Ave., Hales Corners, 53130. Tel: 414-425-3100;
Fax: 414-425-6270; Email: mroczenskim@stmaryhc.org. Maria Schram, Prin. Lay Teachers 36; Students 425.
Catechesis Religious Program—Email: kacalaj@stmaryhc.org. Jeff Kacala, D.R.E. Students 450.

HARTFORD, WASHINGTON CO., ST. KILIAN (1863) [CEM 4]
264 W. State St., Hartford, 53027. Mailing Address: 428 Forest St., Hartford, 53027. Tel: 262-673-4831; Email: parishoffice@stkiliancong.org. Rev. David W. La Plante.
School—St. Kilian School, (Grades PreK-8), 245 High St., Hartford, 53027. Tel: 262-673-3081;
Fax: 262-673-0412; Email: trimbergerj@stkiliancong.org; Web: www.stkiliancong.org/school. Jenny Trimberger, Prin. Lay Teachers 20; Students 97.
Catechesis Religious Program—
Tel: 262-673-4831, Ext. 406; Email: dre@stkiliancong.org. Dennis Vlasak, D.R.E., Tel: 262-673-4831, Ext. 407. Students 270.

HARTLAND, WAUKESHA CO., ST. CHARLES (1906) [CEM]
313 Circle Dr., Hartland, 53029-1824.
Tel: 262-367-0800; Email: parish@stcharleshartland.org; Web: www.stcharleshartland.com. Revs. Kenneth E. Omernick; Patrick Behling.
Res.: 521 Renson Rd., Hartland, 53029.
Tel: 262-367-9936.
School—St. Charles School, 526 Renson Rd., Hartland, 53029. Tel: 262-367-2040; Email: school@stcharleshartland.com; Web: www.stcharleshartland.com. Laura Anderson, Prin. Clergy 3; Lay Teachers 21; Students 298.
Catechesis Religious Program—Students 625.

HOLY CROSS, OZAUKEE CO., HOLY CROSS (1845) (Luxembourgian), Closed. For sacramental records, contact Holy Rosary, Fredonia, Tel: 262-692-9994.

HORICON, DODGE CO.
1—ST. MALACHY (1856) Closed. For sacramental records, contact Sacred Heart, Horicon, Tel: 920-485-0694.
2—SACRED HEART (2001) [CEM 2] (Clustered with St. Matthew, Neosho)
950 Washington St., Horicon, 53032.
Tel: 920-485-0694; Email: sheartchurch@sbcglobal.net; Web: www.sheart.org. P.O. Box 27, Horicon, 53032. Rev. Justin L. Lopina.
Catechesis Religious Program—Tel: 920-485-0694; Email: dresheart@sbcglobal.net. Margaret Sadoski, D.R.E.; William Thimm, Youth Min. Students 207.

HUBERTUS, WASHINGTON CO.
1—ST. GABRIEL (2002) [CEM] [JC3]
1200 St. Gabriel Way, Hubertus, 53033.
Tel: 262-628-1141; Email: stgabriel@stgabrielhubertus.org; Web: www.stgabrielhubertus.org. Rev. Timothy C. Bickel.
School—St. Gabriel School, (Grades PreK-8), 3733 Hubertus Rd., Hubertus, 53033. Tel: 262-628-1711;
Fax: 262-628-0280; Email: shamilton@sgabriel.org; Web: www.sgabriel.org. Steve Hamilton, Prin. Lay Teachers 14; Students 121.
Catechesis Religious Program—Email: dbraun@stgabrielhubertus.org. Dave Braun, D.R.E. Students 362.
2—ST. HUBERT (1846) Closed. For sacramental records before 1961, contact the Archdiocese of Milwaukee Archives, Tel: 414-769-3407. For sacramental records after 1960, contact St. Gabriel, Hubertus, Tel: 262-628-1141.
3—ST. MARY OF THE HILL (1924) [CEM] [JC] (German—Irish)
1515 Carmel Rd, Hubertus, 53033-9770.
Tel: 262-628-3606; Tel: 262-673-7505;
Fax: 262-673-7568; Email: secretary@stmaryhh.org; Web: www.stmaryhh.org. Rev. Bonaventure Lussier, O.C.D.
Res.: 1525 Carmel Rd., Hubertus, 53033.
Catechesis Religious Program—
Tel: 262-628-3606, Ext. 4; Email: dre@stmaryhh.org. Tammy Streitmatter, D.R.E. Students 81.

JOHNSBURG, FOND DU LAC CO., ST. JOHN THE BAPTIST (1840) [CEM]
N9288 County W, Malone, 53049. Tel: 920-795-4316; Email: st.johnthebaptist@frontier.com. Rev. Gary Wegner, O.F.M.Cap.
School—St. John the Baptist School,
Tel: 920-795-4222. Holyland Catholic School: St. John the Baptist, Johnsburg; St. Mary, Marytown; St.Isidore the Farmer, Mount Calvary Lay Teachers 8; Students 63.
Catechesis Religious Program— Program is shared with St Mary, Marytown, and St Isidore the Farmer, Mount Calvary.

JUNEAU, DODGE CO., IMMACULATE CONCEPTION (1875) Closed. For sacramental records, contact Sacred Heart, Horicon, Tel: 920-485-0694.

KANSASVILLE, RACINE CO., ST. MARY-DOVER (1869) [CEM]
23211 Church Rd., Kansasville, 53139-9518. Email: office@smd-srb.org. 3320 S. Colony Ave., Union Grove, 53182. Tel: 262-878-3476. Revs. Russell L. Arnett; Jose Edapparakel Mathai, M.C.B.S.; Sarah Gray, Business Mgr.; Maria Wargolet, Liturgy Dir.

KENOSHA, KENOSHA CO.
1—ST. ANTHONY (1910) [JC] (Slovak)
5100 22nd Ave., Kenosha, 53140. Mailing Address: 2223 51st St., Kenosha, 53140. Tel: 262-652-1844; Email: padua@twc.com. Rev. Todd Belardi.
2—ST. CASIMIR (1901) Closed. For sacramental

records, contact Archdiocese of Milwaukee Archives Office, Tel: 414-769-3407.

3—ST. ELIZABETH (2000) [CEM 2]
4801 8th Ave., Kenosha, 53140. Mailing Address: 4816 7th Ave., Kenosha, 53140. Tel: 262-657-1156; Email: office@stelizabethkenosha.org; Web: www.stelizabethkenosha.org. Rev. Sean Granger.
Res.: 4804 7th Ave., Kenosha, 53140.
Catechesis Religious Program—
Tel: 262-657-1156, Ext. 105. Students 37.

4—ST. GEORGE (1851) (German), Closed. For sacramental records, contact Archdiocese of Milwaukee Archives Office, Tel: 414-769-3407.

5—ST. JAMES (1845) [CEM 2]
5815 10th Ave., Kenosha, 53140. Tel: 262-657-1156; Email: office@stjameskenosha.org; Web: www.stjameskenosha.weconnect.com. Mailing Address: 4816 7th Ave., Kenosha, 53140. Rev. Sean Granger.
Catechesis Religious Program—Students 19.

6—ST. MARK (1924)
7117 14th Ave., Kenosha, 53143. Tel: 262-656-7373; Email: saintmark.kenosha@gmail.com; Web: stmark-kenosha.org. Rev. Carlos A. Florez.
See St. Joseph Catholic Academy, Inc., Kenosha under School Systems located in the Institution section.
Catechesis Religious Program—Email: stmarkfaithk8@gmail.com. Gema Soria, C.R.E., K-8. Students 290.
St. Mark Outreach Center—Tel: 262-656-7370; Email: stmark@archmil.org. Betty Regalado, Social Outreach Dir. Total Assisted 2,400.

7—ST. MARY (1929)
7307 40th Ave., Kenosha, 53142. Tel: 262-694-6018; Email: shejnal@stmarycatholic.org; Web: www.stmarycatholic.org. Rev. Roman Stikel; Deacons Ronald F. Lesjak; James S. Francois; Wilson A. Shierk.
School—All Saints Catholic School, 7400 39th Ave., Kenosha, 53142. Tel: 262-925-4000;
Fax: 262-925-0399. Dr. Jacqueline Lichter, Ph.D., Prin. Lay Teachers 27; Students 363.
Catechesis Religious Program—Sandy Slivon, Dir. Child & Early Adolescent Min.; Corinne Dillon, Dir., Youth Min. Students 343.

8—OUR LADY OF MOUNT CARMEL (1904) (Italian)
1919 54th St., Kenosha, 53140. Tel: 262-652-7660; Email: parishoffice@olmckenosha.org; Web: www.olmckenosha.org. Revs. Dwight Campbell; Robert T. McDermott.
School—Mt. Carmel Preschool, 5400 19th Ave., Kenosha, 53140. Tel: 262-653-1464. Lori Lux, Dir. Lay Teachers 6; Students 63.
Catechesis Religious Program— Twinned with St. Elizabeth, St. James and St. Therese, Kenosha. Email: religioused@olmckenosha.org. Delia Chiappetta, D.R.E.; Mariann Kramer, High School D.R.E. Students 63.

9—OUR LADY OF THE HOLY ROSARY (1904)
2224 45th St., Kenosha, 53140. Tel: 262-652-2771; Email: dcleveland@hrosarykenosha.org; Web: www.hrosarykenosha.org. Revs. Michael Callea, M.I.C., Admin.; Joseph Lappe, M.I.C.
Res.: 2224 30th Ave., Kenosha, 53140.
Catechesis Religious Program—Email: kathydelconte@gmail.com. Kathy DelConte, D.R.E. Students 131.

10—ST. PETER (1903)
2224 30th Ave., Kenosha, 53144. Tel: 262-551-9004; Tel: 262-551-9006; Email: stpeterskenosha@gmail.com. Revs. Ireneusz Chodakowski, M.I.C.; Joseph Lappe, M.I.C.; Deacon Terrance A. Maack.
Catechesis Religious Program—Students 51.

11—ST. THERESE (1953)
2020 91st St., Kenosha, 53143-6699.
Tel: 262-694-4695; Email: valang@tds.net. Revs. Dwight P. Campbell, Email: frcampbell@olmckenosha.org; Robert T. McDermott.
Res.: 1919 54th St., Kenosha, 53140.
Catechesis Religious Program—Tel: 262-694-0118. Students 21.

12—ST. THOMAS AQUINAS (1911) Closed. For sacramental records, contact Archdiocese of Milwaukee Archives Office, Tel: 414-769-3407.

KEWASKUM, WASHINGTON CO., HOLY TRINITY (1861) [CEM 2] [JC3] Rev. Jacob A. Strand, Admin.; Deacon Ralph E. Horner.
Res.: 331 Main St., P.O. Box 461, Kewaskum, 53040. Tel: 262-626-2860; Email: htkewaskum@alexssa.net; Web: www.kewaskumcatholicparishes.org/.
School—Holy Trinity School, 305 Main St., Kewaskum, 53040. Tel: 262-626-2603;
Fax: 262-626-8863; Email: crombiej@htschool.net; Web: www.htschool.net. Jennifer Crombie, Prin. Lay Teachers 15; Students 154.
Catechesis Religious Program— Combined program with St. Michael, St. Michael. Tel: 262-626-2650; Email: htsmreligioused@hotmail.com. Mary Breuer, D.R.E. (Grades K-11). Students 214.

KOHLER, SHEBOYGAN CO., ST. JOHN EVANGELIST (1927)
600 Green Tree Rd., Kohler, 53044.
Tel: 920-452-9623; Email: stjohnev@btsje.org; Web: www.btsje.org. Rev. Joseph Dominic, S.A.C., Admin.
Catechesis Religious Program—Email: nicole@btsje.org; Email: jen@btsje.org. Nicole Wittwer, D.R.E.; Jan Vallo, D.R.E. Students 130.

LAKE FIVE, WASHINGTON CO., ST. COLUMBA (1843) Closed. For sacramental records, contact St. Gabriel, Hubertus, Tel: 262-628-1141.

LAKE GENEVA, WALWORTH CO., ST. FRANCIS DE SALES (1842) [CEM]
148 W. Main St., Lake Geneva, 53147.
Tel: 262-248-8524; Email: parish@sfdslg.org; Web: www.sfdslg.org. Revs. Mark J. Danczyk; Sergio Lizama, S.A.C.
School—St. Francis de Sales School, 130 W. Main St., Lake Geneva, 53147. Tel: 262-248-2778;
Fax: 262-248-7860. Lay Teachers 11; Students 175.
Catechesis Religious Program—Tel: (262) 248-1152; Email: childministry@sfdslg.org. Lori Glass, D.R.E. Students 161.

LE ROY, DODGE CO., ST. ANDREW (1849) [CEM] Also serves St. Mary, Mayville & St. Theresa, Theresa.
W3081 County Rd. Y, Lomira, 53048.
Tel: 920-583-4125; Email: biersackt@archmil.org. Rev. Thomas E. Biersack.
Catechesis Religious Program—P.O. Box 22, Mayville, 53048. Email: ritgerk@archmil.org. Kathy Ritger, D.R.E. Students 50.

LIMA, SHEBOYGAN CO., ST. ROSE (1860) Closed. For sacramental records, contact Blessed Trinity, Sheboygan Falls, Tel: 920-467-4616.

LITTLE KOHLER, OZAUKEE CO., MOTHER OF SORROWS, Closed. For sacramental records, contact Holy Rosary, Fredonia, Tel: 262-692-9994.

LOMIRA, DODGE CO., ST. MARY (1870) [CEM] (German)
699 Milwaukee St., Lomira, 53048.
Tel: 920-269-4429; Email: StMaryLomira@gmail.com; Web: www.stmarylomira.org. Rev. Michael C. Petersen.
Catechesis Religious Program—Tel: 920-269-4326; Email: lstaehlerdre@gmail.com. Lesa Staehler, D.R.E. Students 68.

LOST LAKE, DODGE CO., ST. MARY (1893) Closed. For sacramental records, contact Annunciation, Fox Lake, Tel: 920-928-3513.

LYONS, WALWORTH CO.

1—ST. JOSEPH (1870) [CEM 2] (German)
1540 Mill St., Lyons, 53148-0060. Tel: 262-763-2050; Fax: 262-763-9377; Email: saintjoe@bizwi.rr.com; Web: www.st-josephsparish.org. Very Rev. James T. Volkert; Rev. Carlos Alberto Zapata.
Catechesis Religious Program— Tri-Parish Program with St. Charles & Immaculate Conception, Burlington Tel: 262-763-2260; Email: eschultz@mystcharles.org. Margie Robers, D.R.E.; Elle Schultz, D.R.E.; Rita Van Schyndel, D.R.E. Students 160.

2—ST. KILIAN, Closed. For sacramental records, contact St. Joseph, Lyons, Tel: 262-763-2050.

MAPLETON, WAUKESHA CO., ST. CATHERINE (1847) [CEM] (Irish) Rev. Michael D. Strachota.
Res.: W359 N8512 Brown St., Oconomowoc, 53066.
Tel: 920-474-7000; Fax: 920-474-4661; Email: stcath@stcathofalex.com; Web: scsjcluster.org.
Catechesis Religious Program—Fax: 920-474-4461; Email: mreutebuch@sjarc.org. Mary Sue Reutebuch, D.R.E. Students 148.

MARYTOWN, FOND DU LAC CO., ST. MARY (1849) [CEM] Mailing Address: N9288 County Rd. W, Malone, 53049. Tel: 920-795-4316; Email: st.johnthebaptist@frontier.com. N10232 County Rd. G, New Holstein, 53061. Rev. Gary Wegner, O.F.M.Cap.
Catechesis Religious Program— Program twinned with St. Isidore the Farmer, Mount Calvary.

MAYVILLE, DODGE CO., ST. MARY (1856) [CEM] Also serves St. Andrew, LeRoy & St. Theresa, Theresa.
302 S. German St., P.O. Box 22, Mayville, 53050-0022. Tel: 920-387-3130; Email: biersackt@archmil.org. Rev. Thomas E. Biersack.
Res.: W3081 Hwy. Y, Lomira, 53048.
School—St. Mary School, (Grades PreSchool-2), 28 Naber St., Mayville, 53050. Tel: 920-387-2920; Email: smsmayville@archmil.og. (PreK3-2) Clergy 1; Lay Teachers 6; Students 57.
Catechesis Religious Program—P.O. Box 22, Mayville, 53050. Email: ritgerk@archmil.org. Kathy Ritger, D.R.E. Students 160.

MENOMONEE FALLS, WAUKESHA CO.

1—ST. ANTHONY (1846) [CEM]
N74 W13604 Appleton Ave., Menomonee Falls, 53051. Tel: 262-251-5910; Email: dhyde@stanthony-parish.org; Email: wendellr@archmil.org; Web: www.stanthony-parish.org. Very Rev. Msgr. Ross A. Shecterle, Admin.; Rev. Richard Wendell.
Catechesis Religious Program—Email: jahying@hotmail.com. John Hying, Dir. Faith Formation. Students 178.

2—GOOD SHEPHERD (1957)
N88 W17658 Christman Rd., Menomonee Falls, 53051-2630. Tel: 262-255-2035; Email: goodshepherd@gdinet.com; Web: www.mygoodshepherd.org. Revs. Richard Hart, O.F.M.Cap., M.A., Assisting Priest; Martin Pable, O.F.M.Cap., Ph.D., Assisting Priest; Deacon Sanford Sites, Parish Dir.; Mark Steimle, Dir. Admin. Svcs.; Sr. Joann Julka, Liturgy Dir.; Jane Clare Ishiguro, Pastoral Assoc.
Catechesis Religious Program—Corinna Ramsey, Dir. Youth Ministry; Michael Crain, Dept. Dir. Christian Formation. Students 115.

3—ST. JAMES CONGREGATION (1847) [CEM]
W 220-N 6588 Town Line Rd., Menomonee Falls, 53051. Tel: 262-251-3944; Email: stjameschurch@bizwi.rr.com; Web: www.stjamesparish.com. Deacon Sanford Sites, Parish Dir.; Rev. Dennis J. Lewis, Assisting Priest, (Retired); Deacon Michael R. Rooney; Gerard Wolf, Pastoral Assoc.; Barbara Schuelke, Liturgy Dir.; Theresa Weber, Business Mgr.
Catechesis Religious Program—Tel: 262-253-2904; Email: devinesimons@archmil.org. Kristin Kebis, Child Min.; Bryan Ramsey, Youth Min.; Sue Devine-Simon, Dir. Christian Formation. Students 567.

4—ST. MARY PARISH (1905) [CEM]
N89 W16297 Cleveland Ave., Menomonee Falls, 53051. Tel: 262-251-0220; Email: info@stmaryparish.net; Web: stmaryparish.net. Very Rev. Msgr. Ross A. Shecterle; Rev. Richard Wendell; Deacon James P. Goetter; Steve Cosentino, Dir. Administrative Svcs.
School—St. Mary Parish School, N89 W16215 Cleveland Ave., Menomonee Falls, 53051.
Tel: 262-251-1050; Fax: 262-502-1671; Email: schooloffice@stmaryparishschool.org. Mrs. Linda Joyner, Prin. Lay Teachers 27; Students 387.
Catechesis Religious Program—Email: harveyC@stmaryparish.net. Students 249.

MEQUON, OZAUKEE CO.

1—ST. JAMES (1851) (German), Closed. For sacramental records, contact Lumen Christi, Mequon, Tel: 262-242-7967.

2—LUMEN CHRISTI (2005) [CEM]
2750 W. Mequon Rd., Mequon, 53092.
Tel: 262-242-7967; Fax: 262-242-7970; Email: lcmail@lumenchristiparish.org; Web: www.lumenchristiparish.org. Revs. Daniel J. Sanders; Matthew Jacob; Deacons Anthony Monfre; Joseph P. Wenzler; Dr. David W. Grambow.
School—Lumen Christi School (2005) (Grades PreK-8), 1300 N. St. James Ln., Mequon, 53092.
Tel: 262-242-7960; Fax: 262-512-8986; Email: lcschool@lumenchristiparish.org; Web: www.lumenchristiparish.org/school/. Mrs. Kelly Fyfe, Prin. Clergy 2; Lay Teachers 32; Students 306; Staff 5.
Catechesis Religious Program—Tel: 262-512-8985; Fax: 262-242-7977; Email: berschk@lumenchristiparish.org. Jon Metz, Dir. Catholic Formation. Students 521.

MITCHELL, SHEBOYGAN CO., ST. MICHAEL (1852) Closed. For sacramental records, contact Archdiocese of Milwaukee Archives Office, Tel: 414-769-3407.

MONCHES, WAUKESHA CO., ST. JOHN (1843) [CEM] Closed. For sacramental records, contact Blessed Teresa of Calcutta, North Lake, Tel: 262-966-3191.

MOUNT CALVARY, FOND DU LAC CO.

1—HOLY CROSS (1849) [CEM] Closed. For sacramental records contact St. Isidore, Mount Calvalry, Tel: 920-753-3311.

2—ST. ISIDORE THE FARMER PARISH (2010) [CEM 3]
308 S. Cty. Rd. W., P.O. Box 176, Mount Calvary, 53057-0716. Tel: 920-753-3311; Email: llemke@saintisidoreparish-wi.org. Revs. Gary Wegner, O.F.M.Cap.; Joseph Mattathil, O.F.M.Cap.
Catechesis Religious Program—Tel: 414-313-1435; Email: ablerk@archmil.org. Karen Abler, D.R.E. Students 115.

MUKWONAGO, WAUKESHA CO., ST. JAMES (1896)
830 E. Veterans Way, Mukwonago, 53149.
Tel: 262-363-7615; Fax: 262-363-2416; Email: parish@stjmuk.org; Web: www.stjamesmukwonago.org. Rev. Loyola Amalraj, Admin.; Renee Hitt, Parish Life Coord.
Catechesis Religious Program—
Tel: 262-363-7615, Ext. 121. Susan Bashynski, D.R.E. Students 362.

MUSKEGO, WAUKESHA CO., ST. LEONARD CONGREGATION (1957)
W173 S7743 Westwood Dr., Muskego, 53150-9160.
Tel: 262-679-1773; Email: parish@stleonards.org; Web: www.stleonards.org. Very Rev. Daniel R. Janasik; Deacons Rick J. Wirch; Larry L. Ramsey; Bridget Klawitter, Pastoral Assoc., Email: klawitterb@foursaints.org; Kathleen McGillis Drayna, Stewardship & Communs. Coord.; Karen Tenfel, Business Mgr.; Bryan Staedler, Music Min.
School—St. Leonard Congregation School, (Grades PreK-8), Tel: 262-679-0451; Fax: 262-679-8519; Email: school@stleonards.org; Web: www.stleonards.org. Lisa Ellis, Prin. Lay Teachers 17; Students 127.
Catechesis Religious Program—Tel: 262-679-0880; Email: lisa.jachimiec@stleonards.org. Lisa Jachimiec, D.R.E. Students 496.

NABOB, WASHINGTON CO., ST. MATTHIAS (1848) Closed.

For sacramental records, contact St. Lawrence, St. Lawrence, Tel: 262-644-5701.
NENNO, WASHINGTON CO.
1—ST. ANTHONY, Closed. For sacramental records, contact Resurrection, Allenton, Tel: 262-629-5240.
2—SS. PETER AND PAUL (1848) Closed. For sacramental records, contact Resurrection, Allenton, Tel: 262-629-5240.
NEOSHO, DODGE CO., ST. MATTHEW - NEOSHO (1857) [CEM] (German) Clustered with Sacred Heart, Horicon.
P.O. Box 27, Horicon, 53032. Tel: 920-485-0694; Email: sheartchurch@sbcglobal.net. Rev. Justin L. Lopina.
NEW BERLIN, WAUKESHA CO.
1—ST. ELIZABETH ANN SETON (1981)
12700 W. Howard Ave., New Berlin, 53151.
Tel: 262-782-6760; Email: office@mystelizabeth.com; Web: mystelizabeth.com. Rev. Joseph A. Aufdermauer; Deacons Jeffrey J. Copson; Richard Winkowski; Susan Switalski, Pastoral Min.; David Fennelly, Business Mgr.; Linda Noel Halverson, Music Min.
Catechesis Religious Program—Tel: 262-782-8982. Ann Ryan, Dir. Child Ministry; Mickey Holtz, Dir. Youth Ministry. Students 262.
2—HOLY APOSTLES (1855) [CEM]
16000 W. National Ave., New Berlin, 53151.
Tel: 262-786-7330; Email: jfredrickson@hanb.org; Web: www.hanb.org. Rev. Donald H. Thimm; Deacon Michael J. Chmielewski.
School—Holy Apostles School, 3875 S. 159 St., New Berlin, 53151. Tel: 262-786-7331; Email: klee@hanb.org; Web: www.hanbschool.org. Kristin Lee, Prin. Lay Teachers 27; Students 429.
Catechesis Religious Program—Tel: 262-754-0157; Email: dthimm@hanb.org. Teresa Tobin, Child & Family Ministry; Rachel Madden, D.R.E.; Sharon Baxter, D.R.E. Students 330.
NEW MUNSTER, KENOSHA CO., ST. ALPHONSUS (1849) [CEM] (German)
6301 344th Ave., P.O. Box 767, New Munster, 53152. Tel: 262-537-4370; Email: rectory@st-alphonsus.com; Web: staljohn.org. Rev. Arthur Wayne Mattox, Admin.
Catechesis Religious Program—Jan McRae, D.R.E. Students 139.
NEWBURG, WASHINGTON CO., HOLY TRINITY (1859) [CEM 3] (German)
521 Congress Dr., P.O. Box 16, Newburg, 53060-0016. Rev. Kevin J. Kowalske; Deacon Michael S. Koebel.
Catechesis Religious Program—Carol Altschwager, D.R.E.
Stations—St. Augustine— (1857) Co. Rd. Y, Trenton Twp., West Bend, 53095.
St. Peter (1855) Newark Dr., Farmington Twp., West Bend, 53090.
NORTH FOND DU LAC, FOND DU LAC CO., PRESENTATION OF THE BLESSED VIRGIN MARY (1902) [JC] (Irish—German)
701 Michigan Ave., North Fond du Lac, 54937.
Tel: 920-921-9383; Email: pbvmoffice@yahoo.com. Rev. Ryan J. Pruess, Admin.
Catechesis Religious Program—Sue Stephani, C.R.E. Students 60.
NORTH LAKE, WAUKESHA CO.
1—SAINT TERESA OF CALCUTTA (2006) [JC2]
W314N7462 State Rd. 83, Hartland, 53029. Mailing Address: P.O. Box 68, North Lake, 53064-0068.
Tel: 262-966-2191; Email: office@stteresaofcalcutta.org; Web: www.stteresaofcalcutta.org. Revs. Kenneth E. Omernick; Patrick Behling; Deacon Allen B. Olson.
Catechesis Religious Program—Tel: 262-966-2191; Email: jen@stteresaofcalcutta.org. Jennifer Ishizaki, D.R.E. Students 172.
2—ST. CLARE (1916) [CEM] Closed. For sacramental records, contact Blessed Teresa of Calcutta, North Lake 53064-0068.
OAK CREEK, MILWAUKEE CO.
1—ST. MATTHEW (1841) [CEM]
9303 S. Chicago Rd., Oak Creek, 53154.
Tel: 414-762-4200; Email: parish@stmattoc.org; Web: www.stmattoc.org. Rev. Patrick J. O'Loughlin.
School—St. Matthew School, (Grades PreK-8), 9329 S. Chicago Rd., Oak Creek, 53154. Tel: 414-762-6820 ; Email: school@stmattoc.org; Web: www.stmattoc.org. Kelly Stefanich, Prin. Religious Teachers 1; Lay Teachers 13; Students 179.
Catechesis Religious Program—Darlene Finn, Youth Min.; Karin Felske, Youth Min. Students 208.
2—ST. STEPHEN (1847) [CEM 2] (German)
Mailing Address: 1441 W. Oakwood Rd., Oak Creek, 53154. Tel: 414-762-0552; Email: secretary@saintstephenmil.org; Email: rkacalo@saintstephenmil.org; Web: www.saintstephenmil.org. Rev. Robert C. Kacalo; Deacon Stanley J. Lowe.
Catechesis Religious Program—Email: mheeren@saintstephenmil.org. Michelle Heeren, C.R.E. Students 168.
OAKFIELD, FOND DU LAC CO., ST. JAMES (1909) Closed. For sacramental records, contact Sons of Zebedee: Saints James and John, Byron, Tel: 920-583-4376.
OCONOMOWOC, WAUKESHA CO., ST. JEROME (1860) [CEM]
995 S. Silver Lake St., Oconomowoc, 53066.
Tel: 262-569-3020; Email: parish@stjerome.org; Web: www.stjerome.org. Rev. Thomas T. Brundage, M.Div., J.C.L.; Deacon John C. Mezydlo.
School—St. Jerome School, 1001 S. Silver Lake St., Oconomowoc, 53066. Tel: 262-569-3030;
Fax: 262-569-3023; Email: school@stjerome.org. Mrs. Mary Johnson, Prin. Lay Teachers 25; Students 234.
Catechesis Religious Program—Tel: 262-569-3025; Email: lffaa@stjerome.org. Students 316.
PARIS, KENOSHA CO., ST. JOHN THE BAPTIST (1859) [CEM]
1501 172nd Ave., Union Grove, 53182.
Tel: 262-859-2484; Email: sfxsjb@archmil.org. Mailing Address: 1704 240th Ave., Kansasville, 53139. Revs. Russell L. Arnett, Admin.; Jose Edapparakel Mathai, M.C.B.S.
School—All Saints Catholic School, Consolidated with St. Francis Xavier, Brighton 1481 172nd Ave., Union Grove, 53182. Tel: 262-864-3110;
Tel: 262-925-4000; Fax: 262-925-4030; Email: glauritsen@allsaintskenosha.org; Web: www.allsaintskenosha.org. Dr. Jacqueline Lichter, Ph.D., Prin. Lay Teachers 7; Students 69.
Catechesis Religious Program—Tel: 262-878-2267; Fax: 262-878-3683. Cynthia Cetera, D.R.E. (Grades K-8); Katherine Peterson, D.R.E. (Grades K-8). Students 100.
PELL LAKE, WALWORTH CO., ST. MARY (1928) [JC] Closed. For sacramental records, contact St. Francis de Sales, Lake Geneva, Tel: 262-248-8524/8525.
PEWAUKEE, WAUKESHA CO.
1—ST. ANTHONY ON THE LAKE (1918)
W 280 N 2101 Prospect Ave., Pewaukee, 53072.
Tel: 262-691-1173; Email: parish@stanthony.cc; Web: www.stanthony.cc. Rev. Anthony J. Zimmer; Dr. Kathie Amidei, Pastoral Assoc.; Ben Brzeski, Dir., Commun. & Stewardship.
School—St. Anthony on the Lake School,
Tel: 262-691-0460; Email: parish@stanthony.cc. Ellen Knippel, Prin. Lay Teachers 17; Students 221.
Catechesis Religious Program—Tel: 262-691-9170. Dr. Kathie Amidei, D.R.E.; Debbie Kusch, D.R.E.; Ann Fons, Dir. Youth Ministry; Cindi Petre, Dir. Youth Ministry. Students 579.
2—ST. MARY (1858) Closed. For sacramental records, contact Queen of Apostles, Pewaukee, Tel: 262-691-1535.
3—SS. PETER AND PAUL (1848) Closed. For sacramental records, contact Queen of Apostles, Pewaukee, Tel: 262-691-1535.
4—QUEEN OF APOSTLES (1997) [CEM 2]
N35 W23360 Capitol Dr., Pewaukee, 53072. Web: www.queenofapostles.net. Rev. Charles T. Hanel; Deacon Eugene A. Kempka.
Catechesis Religious Program—Email: bethp@queenofapostles.net. Beth Wexler, D.R.E. Students 172.
PLEASANT PRAIRIE, KENOSHA CO., CONGREGATION OF ST. ANNE (1998)
Mailing Address: 9091 Prairie Ridge Blvd., Pleasant Prairie, 53158-1934. Tel: 262-942-8300; Email: parishoffice@saint-anne.org; Web: www.saint-anne.org. Very Rev. Robert J. Weighner; Deacon Richard J. Stanula.
Catechesis Religious Program—Email: mmowry@saint-anne.org. Mary Mowry, D.R.E. Students 307.
PLYMOUTH, SHEBOYGAN CO., ST. JOHN THE BAPTIST (1861) [CEM]
115 Plymouth St., Plymouth, 53073.
Tel: 920-892-4006; Email: sjbparish@sjbplymouth.org; Web: www.sjbplymouth.org. Very Rev. Philip D. Reifenberg, J.C.L.; Lisa Schoneman, Business Mgr.
School—St. John the Baptist School, 116 Pleasant St., Plymouth, 53073. Tel: 920-893-5961;
Fax: 920-893-3160; Email: school@sjbplymouth.org. Amy Nelson, Prin. Religious Teachers 1; Lay Teachers 16; Students 157.
Catechesis Religious Program—Tel: 920-892-6015; Email: aalbers@sjbplymouth.org. Amy Albers, D.R.E. Students 295.
PORT WASHINGTON, OZAUKEE CO.
1—ST. JOHN XXIII (2016)
1800 N. Wisconsin St., Port Washington, 53074.
Tel: 262-284-4266; Fax: 262-284-4216; Email: parish@stjohn23rd.org; Web: www.st.john23rd.org. Rev. Patrick Wendt; Deacons Michael F. Burch, Pastoral Coord.; Thomas J. Surges; Kelly Lemens, Pastoral Assoc.
School—St. John XXIII Catholic School, 1802 N. Wisconsin St., Port Washington, 53074.
Tel: 262-284-2441 (PreK-4);
Tel: 262-284-2682 (Grades 5-8); Fax: 262-284-4216; Email: kklein@stjohn23rd.school; Email: jschueller@stjohn23rd.school; Email: savina@portcatholic.org; Web: stjohn23rd.school. Kristine Klein, Prin. Clergy 2; Lay Teachers 16; Students 182.
Catechesis Religious Program—Tel: 262-284-6472; Email: murred@stjohn23rd.org; Web: www.stjohn23rdyouth.org. Denise Murre, D.R.E. (Grades K-6); Maureen Rotramel, D.R.E. (Grades 7-12). Students 366.
2—ST. MARY (1853) [CEM] Closed. For sacramental records, contact St. John XXIII Parish, Port Washington. Tel: 262-284-4266.
Catechesis Religious Program— Consolidated with St. Peter of Alcantara, Port Washington and Immaculate Conception, Saukille.
Tel: 262-284-6472 (Child Ministry); Email: portchild@archmil.org; Email: portyouth@catholic.org. Denise Murre, D.R.E. (Grades K-6); Maureen Rotramel, D.R.E. (Grades 7-11), Tel: 262-284-2102. Students 183.
3—ST. PETER OF ALCANTARA, Closed. For sacramental records, contact St. John XXIII Parish, Port Washington. Tel: 262-284-4266.
RACINE, RACINE CO.
1—ST. CASIMIR (1913) (Lithuanian), Closed. For sacramental records, contact Archdiocese of Milwaukee Archives Office, Tel: 414-769-3407.
2—CRISTO REY (1980) (Hispanic), Closed. For sacramental records, please contact St. Patrick Parish, Racine. Tel: 262-632-8808; Fax: 262-637-1536.
3—ST. EDWARD (1919) [JC]
1401 Grove Ave., Racine, 53405. Tel: 262-636-8040; Email: parish@saintedwardracine.ogr; Web: www.saintedwardracine.org. Rev. Allen J. Bratkowski.
School—Our Lady of Grace Academy, 1435 Grove Ave., Racine, 53405. Fax: 262-636-8040, Ext. 1000; Email: mkrezinski@ologa.org. Erin O'Donnell, Prin. Lay Teachers 19; Students 206.
Catechesis Religious Program—
Tel: 262-636-8040, Ext. 1005. Students 26.
4—HOLY NAME (1884) (German), Closed. For sacramental records, contact Archdiocese of Milwaukee Archives Office, Tel: 414-769-3407.
5—HOLY TRINITY (1914) Closed. For sacramental records, contact Archdiocese of Milwaukee Archives Office, Tel: 414-769-3407.
6—ST. JOHN NEPOMUK (1896) [JC]
1903 Green St., Racine, 53402. Email: stjohnnepomuk@wi.rr.com. 700 English St., Racine, 53402. Tel: 262-634-5647. Rev. Steven K. Varghese, S.A.C.
See John Paul II Academy at Sacred Heart Congregation, Racine.
Catechesis Religious Program—1911 Green St., Racine, 53402. Tel: 630-965-9142; Email: oconnelld@archmil.org. Dan O'Connell, D.R.E. Students 18.
7—ST. JOSEPH (1875) [JC4]
1533 Erie St., Racine, 53402. Mailing Address: 1532 N. Wisconsin St., Racine, 53402. Tel: 262-633-8284; Email: info@st-joes.org. Rev. Steven K. Varghese, S.A.C.
School—St. Joseph School, (Grades PreK-8), 1525 Erie St., Racine, 53402. Tel: 262-633-2403; Email: jeanmaried@st-joes-school.org. Heidi Hernandez, Prin. Lay Teachers 16; Students 199.
Catechesis Religious Program—Email: faithformationsjsjn@gmail.com. Dan O'Connell, D.R.E. & Youth Min. Tri-Parish; Susan Gehrig, D.R.E. Students 53.
8—ST. LUCY (1958)
3101 Drexel Ave., Racine, 53403. Tel: 262-554-1801; Email: stlucy@archmil.org; Email: feiler@archmil.org; Web: www.stlucychurch.org. Revs. Javier Guativa; Nabil Mouannes; Deacon Eric M. Sewell.
School—St. Lucy Catholic School, (Grades PreK-8), 3035 Drexel Ave., Racine, 53403. Fax: 262-554-7618; Email: stlucyschool@archmil.org; Web: www.stlucysschool.com. Mrs. Amy Jarmuz-Kluth, Prin. Lay Teachers 15; Students 211.
Catechesis Religious Program—
Tel: 262-554-1801, Ext. 208; Email: kureks@archmil.org. Susi Kurek, D.R.E. Students 144.
9—ST. MARY BY THE LAKE (1852) [JC]
Mailing Address: 7605 Lakeshore Dr., Racine, 53404. Tel: 262-639-3616; Fax: 262-639-1999; Email: stmarybl@wi.twcbc.com; Web: www.stmarybythelake.org. Rev. Patrick J. O'Loughlin.
Catechesis Religious Program—Tel: 262-639-4493; Fax: 262-639-1999. Heather Warner, D.R.E. Students 55.
10—ST. PATRICK (1856) [JC4] Rev. Antony Primal Thomas; Deacons Leonides Rocha; Roberto Fuentes; Julio Lopez.
John the 23rd Educational Center—1100 Erie St., Racine, 53402. Sarah Oates, Dir. (After School Program). Served by Casa Benedicta Community, Racine (Christian Brothers of the Midwest). Students 120.
Catechesis Religious Program—Email:

cabrerag@archmil.org. Laura Gabriela Cabrera, D.R.E.; Eloy Contreras, Youth Coord. Students 393.
11—ST. PAUL THE APOSTLE (1965) [JC]
6400 Spring St., Racine, 53406. Tel: 262-886-0530; Email: mchuchara@stpaulracine.org. Rev. Yamid Blanco, Admin.; Deacons Keith A. Hansen; Dale T. Nees; Ronnie Quella, Music Dir.; Michael Chuchara, Dir.
Catechesis Religious Program—Tel: 262-886-0531; Email: awallschlaeger@stpaulracine.org. Audra Radke, D.R.E.; Leticia Gutierrez-Kenny, Youth Min. Students 173.
12—ST. RICHARD OF CHICHESTER (1998) [JC]
1503 Grand Ave., Racine, 53403. Rev. Allen J. Bratkowski; Deacon Howard J. Wirtz, Deacon Emeritus.
Res.: 1509 Grand Ave., Racine, 53403.
Tel: 262-637-8374; Email: info@strichard-parish.org; Web: www.strichard-parish.org.
Catechesis Religious Program—Email: jdclarke@tds.net. John Clarke, D.R.E. Students 36.
13—ST. RITA (1926) [CEM]
4339 Douglas Ave., Racine, 53402. Tel: 262-639-3223 ; Email: sritarac@archmil.org; Web: www.st-ritas.org. Revs. Richard T. O'Leary, O.S.A.; Fred Taggart, O.S.A., In Res.; David Cregan, O.S.A., In Res.
School—St. Rita School, 4433 Douglas Ave., Racine, 53402. Tel: 262-639-3333; Email: principal@st-ritas.org. Jennifer Petruska, Prin. Lay Teachers 13; Students 149.
Catechesis Religious Program—Tel: 262-639-6280; Email: StRitaReligiousEd@archmil.org. Rachel Kroes, D.R.E. Students 102.
14—ST. ROSE (1886) Closed. For sacramental records, contact Archdiocese of Milwaukee Archives Office, Tel: 414-769-3407.
15—SACRED HEART CONGREGATION (1916) [CEM 4] [JC12]
2201 Northwestern Ave., Racine, 53404.
Tel: 262-634-5526; Fax: 262-634-5767; Email: shracine@archmil.org; Web: www.sacredheartracine.com. Rev. Ricardo Martin, J.C.L.
School—John Paul II Academy, (Grades PreK-8), 2023 Northwestern Ave., Racine, 53404.
Tel: 262-637-2012; Fax: 262-637-5130; Email: gschumacher@johnpaulacademy.org; Email: office@johnpaulacademy.org; Web: jp2aracine.org. Mrs. Gloria Schumacher, Prin. Sacred Heart & St. John Nepomuk schools merged. Clergy 1; Lay Teachers 15; Students 220.
Catechesis Religious Program—Email: shracineformation@gmail.com. Students 39.
16—ST. STANISLAUS (1904) (Polish), Closed. For sacramental records, contact Archdiocese of Milwaukee Archives Office, Tel: 414-769-3407.
RANDOLPH, COLUMBIA CO., ST. GABRIEL, Closed. For sacramental records, contact Annunciation, Fox Lake, Tel: 920-928-3513.
RANDOM LAKE, SHEBOYGAN CO.
1—ST. MARY (1855) Closed. For sacramental records, contact Archdiocese of Milwaukee Archives Office, Tel: 414-769-3407.
2—OUR LADY OF THE LAKES (1998) [CEM 4]
Mailing Address: 230 Butler St., Random Lake, 53075-1710. Tel: 920-994-4380; Fax: 920-994-2605; Email: ourladyrlp@archmil.org; Web: www.ourladylakes.org. Rev. Todd Budde; Debbie Hamm, Pastoral Assoc.
Catechesis Religious Program—Linda Guokas, D.R.E. Students 89.
Chapels—St. Mary—300 Butler St., Random Lake, 53075.
St. Nicholas, W4274 Hwy. K, Random Lake, 53075.
St. Patrick, W4690 Hwy. A, Adell, 53001.
REESEVILLE, DODGE CO., HOLY FAMILY (1901) [CEM] (German—Irish) Also serves St. Columbkille, Elba and St. John the Baptist, Clyman.
302 Prairie St., P.O. Box 277, Reeseville, 53579-0277. Tel: 920-927-3102; Fax: 920-927-1970; Email: triparish@charter.net; Web: www.triparishwi.com. Revs. Michael J. Erwin; Erick Cassiano-Amaya, F.M.M.
Catechesis Religious Program—Connie Caine, D.R.E., Tel: 920-210-1865; John Pryme, Youth Min. Students 28.
RICHFIELD, WASHINGTON CO., ST. MARY (1854) (German), Closed. For sacramental records before 1967, contact Archdiocese of Milwaukee Archives Office, Tel: 414-769-3407. For sacramental records after 1966, contact St. Gabriel, Hubertus, Tel: 262-628-1141.
RIPON, FOND DU LAC CO.
1—ST. CATHERINE OF SIENA (2005) [CEM]
218 E. Blossom St., Ripon, 54971-1526.
Tel: 920-748-2325; Email: office@stcatofsiena.org; Web: www.stcatofsiena.org. Rev. Robert A. Fictum; Diane Nowinski, Business Mgr.
Catechesis Religious Program—Email: dianenowinski@stcatofsiena.org. Diane Nowinski, D.R.E. Students 77.
2—ST. PATRICK (1858) Closed. For sacramental records, contact St. Catherine of Siena, Ripon, Tel: 920-748-2345.
3—ST. WENCESLAUS (1896) (Polish), Closed. For sacramental records, contact St. Catherine of Siena, Ripon, Tel: 920-748-2345.
RUBICON, DODGE CO., ST. JOHN (1870) [CEM] [JC] (German) Also serves St. Kilian, Hartford.
W1170 Rome Rd., Rubicon, 53078. 428 Forest St., Hartford, 53027. Tel: 262-673-4831; Email: stjohnsrubicon@gmail.com; Email: parishoffice@stkiliancong.org. Rev. David W. La Plante.
Catechesis Religious Program—Tel: 262-673-4397; Email: thimmb@archmil.org. William Thimm, D.R.E. Students 78.
ST. CLOUD, FOND DU LAC CO., ST. CLOUD (1870) [CEM] (German), Closed. For sacramental records, contact St. Isidore, Mount Calvary, Tel: 920-753-3311.
ST. FRANCIS, MILWAUKEE CO., SACRED HEART OF JESUS (1868) [CEM]
3635 S. Kinnickinnic Ave., St. Francis, 53235.
Tel: 414-489-2806; Email: sue.edson@aol.com; Web: sacredheartofjesus.weconnect.com. Rev. Arulananthan Ponnaiyan, Admin.
See St. Thomas Aquinas Academy located in the Institution Section under Consolidated Elementary Schools.
Catechesis Religious Program— Combined program with Immaculate Conception, St. Augustine, St. Veronica, and St. Paul, Milwaukee and Nativity of the Lord, Cudahy. Tel: 414-481-0777, Ext. 117; Fax: 414-482-3025; Email: rebecca@secatholic.org. Students 6.
ST. GEORGE, SHEBOYGAN CO., ST. GEORGE (1860) Closed. For sacramental records, contact Blessed Trinity, Sheboygan Falls, Tel: 920-467-4616.
ST. JOE, FOND DU LAC CO., ST. JOSEPH (1858) [CEM] (German), Closed. For sacramental records, contact St. Isidore, Mount Calvary, Tel: 920-753-3311.
ST. KILIAN, FOND DU LAC CO., ST. KILIAN (1848) [CEM] Closed. For sacramental records, contact St. Matthew, Campbellsport, Tel: 920-533-4441.
ST. LAWRENCE, WASHINGTON CO., ST. LAWRENCE (1846) [CEM] (German)
4886 Hwy. 175, Hartford, 53027. Tel: 262-644-5701; Email: stlawrenceoffice@gmail.com; Email: stlawrencepastor@gmail.com; Web: www.stlawrence-parish.com. Rev. Davies Edassery, S.A.C., Admin.
Catechesis Religious Program—Tel: 262-644-0011; Email: stlawreled@gmail.com. Jacquelyn Haas, D.R.E. Students 136.
ST. MARTIN, MILWAUKEE CO., HOLY ASSUMPTION, Closed. For sacramental records through 1990, contact St. Mary, Hales Corners, Tel: 414-425-2174. For sacramental records after 1990, contact St. Martin of Tours, Franklin, Tel: 414-425-1114.
ST. MICHAEL, WASHINGTON CO., ST. MICHAEL (1846) [CEM] [JC2] (German—Irish)
8883 Forestview Rd., Kewaskum, 53040.
Tel: 262-334-5270; Email: stmickew@kmoraine.com. Rev. Jacob A. Strand, Admin.; Deacon Ralph E. Horner.
Res.: 331 Main St., Kewaskum, 53040.
Catechesis Religious Program—Tel: 262-626-2650; Email: htsmreligioused@hotmail.com. Mary Breuer, D.R.E. Twinned with Holy Trinity, Kewaskum. Students 212.
ST. PETER, FOND DU LAC CO., ST. PETER (1867) (German), Closed. For sacramental records through 1952, contact Archdiocese of Milwaukee Archives Office, Tel: 414-769-3407. For records after 1952, contact Holy Family, Fond du Lac, Tel: 920-921-0580.
SAUKVILLE, OZAUKEE CO., IMMACULATE CONCEPTION (1858) [CEM] Merged For sacramental records, contact St. John XXIII Parish, Port Washington. Tel: 262-284-4266.
SHARON, WALWORTH CO., ST. CATHERINE (1854) [CEM]
125 Pearl St., P.O. Box 393, Sharon, 53585.
Tel: 262-736-4615; Cell: 815-520-3190; Email: tmckenna@rockforddiocese.org. Deacon Thomas McKenna, Parish Dir.
Catechesis Religious Program— In collaboration with St. Andrews, Delavan. Students 19.
SHEBOYGAN, SHEBOYGAN CO.
1—ST. CLEMENT (1914) [JC]
707 N. 6th St., Sheboygan, 53081. Web: www.holynamestclement.org. Mailing Address: 807 Superior Ave., Sheboygan, 53081. Tel: 920-457-4629; Email: petriem@catholicnorth.org. Revs. Matthew Widder; Gideon K. Buya.
Res.: 522 New York Ave., Sheboygan, 53081.
Catechesis Religious Program—2133 N. 22nd St., Sheboygan, 53081. Tel: 920-458-5390; Email: morrisone@catholicnorth.org; Email: marshalld@catholicnorth.org. Edie Morrison, D.R.E.; Dianne Marshall, Youth Min. Collaborated with Holy Name of Jesus & St. Dominic to be Northside Catholic Faith Formation Students 148.
2—SS. CYRIL AND METHODIUS (1910) [CEM] (Slovenian)
822 New Jersey Ave., Sheboygan, 53081. Mailing Address: 1439 S. 12th St., Sheboygan, 53081.
Tel: 920-457-7110; Email: sscm@catholicsouthside.com; Web: www.catholicsouthside.com. Rev. Paul J. Fliss; Deacons Richard P. Gulig, Pastoral Min.; John R. Gavin, Pastoral Min.; Rochelle Ross, Pastoral Assoc.; Nancy Roerdink, Dir. Administrative Svcs.
Catechesis Religious Program—834 New Jersey Ave., Sheboygan, 53081. Email: Shackelfords@catholicsouthside.com. Samuel Shackelford, D.R.E. Students 24.
3—ST. DOMINIC (1927) [JC] (German—Dutch)
2133 N. 22nd St., Sheboygan, 53081.
Tel: 920-458-7070; Email: tewinklel@catholicnorth.org; Web: www.stdominic.us. Revs. Matthew Widder; Gideon K. Buya.
Catechesis Religious Program— Collaborates with St Clement, Holy Name of Jesus, Sheboygan Edie Morrison, D.R.E.; Dianne Marshall, Youth Min. Students 154.
4—HOLY NAME OF JESUS (1845) [JC] (German)
818 Huron Ave., Sheboygan, 53081. Email: petriem@catholicnorth.org. 807 Superior Ave., Sheboygan, 53081-3442. Tel: 920-458-7721, Ext. 101; Web: www.holynamestclement.org. Revs. Matthew Widder; Gideon K. Buya.
Catechesis Religious Program— Shared with St. Dominic & St. Clement. 2133 N. 22nd St., Sheboygan, 53081. Tel: 920-458-5390; Email: morrisone@catholicnorth.org; Email: marshalld@catholicnorth.org. Edie Morrison, D.R.E.; Dianne Marshall, Youth Min. Students 123.
5—IMMACULATE CONCEPTION (1903) [CEM] (Lithuanian)
1305 Humboldt Ave., Sheboygan, 53081.
Tel: 920-457-3967; Email: icparish@catholicsouthside.com; Web: www.catholicsouthside.com. Mailing Address: 1439 S. 12th St., Sheboygan, 53081. Rev. Paul J. Fliss; Deacons Richard P. Gulig, Pastoral Min.; John R. Gavin, Pastoral Min.; Rochelle Ross, Pastoral Assoc.; Nancy Roerdink, Dir. Administrative Svcs.
Child Care—Christ Child Academy, 2722 Henry St., Sheboygan, 53081. Tel: 920-459-2660; Email: christchildacademyoffice@gmail.com; Web: www.christchildacademy.com. Mark Ruedinger, Prin. Religious Teachers 1; Lay Teachers 11; Students 136.
Catechesis Religious Program—834 New Jersey Ave., Sheboygan, 53081. Tel: 920-457-8422; Email: shackelfords@catholicsouthside.com. Samuel Shackelford, D.R.E. Students 24.
6—ST. PETER CLAVER (1888) [CEM] (German)
1439 S. 12th St., Sheboygan, 53081.
Tel: 920-457-9408; Email: spc@catholicsouthside.com; Web: www.catholicsouthside.com. Rev. Paul J. Fliss; Deacons John R. Gavin, Pastoral Min.; Richard P. Gulig, Pastoral Min.; Nancy Roerdink, Dir. Administrative Svcs.; Rochelle Ross, Pastoral Assoc.
Child Care—Christ Child Academy, (Grades PreK-5), See Immaculate Conception for details. 2722 Henry St., Sheboygan, 53081. Tel: 920-459-2660; Fax: 920-457-5885; Email: christchildacademyoffice@gmail.com; Web: www.christchildacademy.com. Mark Ruedinger, Prin.
Catechesis Religious Program—822 New Jersey Ave., Sheboygan, 53081. Tel: 920-457-8422; Email: shackelfords@catholicsouthside.com. Samuel Shackelford, D.R.E. Students 42.
SHEBOYGAN FALLS, SHEBOYGAN CO.
1—BLESSED TRINITY (2001) [CEM] [JC3] (German) (Merger of St. Mary, Sheboygan Falls; St. Rose, Lima; and St. George, St. George.)
327 Giddings Ave., Sheboygan Falls, 53085-1598.
Tel: 920-467-4616; Email: sandy@btsje.org; Web: www.btsje.org. Rev. Joseph Dominic, S.A.C.
Catechesis Religious Program—Fax: lisa@btsje.org. Lisa Gross, D.R.E. Students 144.
2—ST. MARY (1896) (German), Closed. For sacramental records, contact Blessed Trinity, Sheboygan Falls, Tel: 920-467-4616.
SHOREWOOD, MILWAUKEE CO., ST. ROBERT OF NEWMINSTER (1912)
2200 E. Capitol Dr., Shorewood, 53211-2110.
Tel: 414-332-1164; Email: ddannecker@strobert.org; Web: www.strobert.org. 4019 N. Farwell Ave., Shorewood, 53211-2110. Revs. Raymond Guthrie, Admin.; Peter Patrick Kimani; Lisa Lesjak, Dir. School Advancement; Karen Raap, Business Mgr.
School—St. Robert of Newminster School, 2200 E. Capitol Dr., Shorewood, 53211.
Tel: 414-332-1164, Ext. 3018; Email: lbeckmann@strobert.org; Web: www.strobert.org/school. Lauren Beckmann, Prin. Lay Teachers 27; Students 278.
Catechesis Religious Program—
Tel: 414-332-1164, Ext. 3012; Email: jreisel@strobert.org. Jennifer Reisel, D.R.E.; Emily Schaefer, Youth Min. Students 98.
SLINGER, WASHINGTON CO., ST. PETER (1856) [CEM 2] (German)
200 E. Washington St., Slinger, 53086. Mailing

Address: 208 E. Washington St., Slinger, 53086. Tel: 262-644-8083; Email: st.peterslinger@archmil.org; Web: www.stpeterslinger.org. Very Rev. Richard J. Stoffel.
Res.: 214 E. Washington St., Slinger, 53086.
School—St. Peter School, (Grades PreK-5), 206 E. Washington St., Slinger, 53086. Email: schoolsecretary@stpeterslinger.org; Web: www.spcsslinger.org; Web: www.stpeterslinger.org. Cheryl Jaeger, Prin. & Marketing Dir. Religious Teachers 1; Lay Teachers 12; Students 106.
Catechesis Religious Program—Email: REsecretary@stpeterslinger.org. Paul Rogers, D.R.E.; Eileen Belongea, D.R.E. Students 365.

SOUTH MILWAUKEE, MILWAUKEE CO.
1—ST. ADALBERT (1898) Closed. For sacramental records, contact Divine Mercy, South Milwaukee, Tel: 414-762-6810.
2—DIVINE MERCY (2003) [JC]
695 College Ave., South Milwaukee, 53172. Tel: 414-762-6810; Email: dianneangst@divinemercysm.org; Email: dmparish@divinemercysm.org; Web: divinemercysm.org. Revs. Joseph Pradeep Sebastian, M.C.B.S.; Dennis G. Budka.
Child Care—Divine Mercy Early Childhood Center, Tel: 414-764-0283; Email: deefuchs@divinemercysm.org. Dee Fuchs, Dir. Students 6.
School—Divine Mercy School, Tel: 414-764-4360; Email: divinemercy@divinemercysm.org. Students 180; Teachers 15.
Catechesis Religious Program—Megan Moore, D.R.E.; Maggie Russell, Youth Min. Students 203.
3—ST. JOHN (1893) (Irish), Closed. For sacramental records, contact Divine Mercy, South Milwaukee, Tel: 414-762-6810.
4—ST. MARY (1893) Closed. For sacramental records, contact Divine Mercy, South Milwaukee, Tel: 414-762-6810.
5—ST. SYLVESTER (1962) (Polish—Irish), Closed. For sacramental records, contact Divine Mercy, South Milwaukee, Tel: 414-762-6810.

SPRINGVALE, COLUMBIA CO., ST. MARY (1858) [CEM] (Irish), Closed. For sacramental records, contact St. Joseph Parish, Waupun. Tel: 920-324-5400.

STURTEVANT, RACINE CO., ST. SEBASTIAN (1905)
3050 95th St., Sturtevant, 53177. Email: stseb@archmil.org; Web: stsebracine.org. 3126 95th St., Sturtevant, 53177. Tel: 262-886-4398. Revs. Javier Guativa; Nabil Mouannes; Deacon Eric M. Sewell.
Catechesis Religious Program— Twinned with St. Lucy, Racine. Tel: 262-554-1801; Email: antrime@archmil.org. Susi Kurek, D.R.E.; Eric Antrim, Youth Min. Students 23.

THERESA, DODGE CO., ST. THERESA (1849) [CEM]
102 Church St., St. Theresa, 53091. Mailing Address: P.O. Box 22, Mayville, 53050. Tel: 920-387-3130; Email: biersackt@archmil.org; Web: www.stsmaryandrewtheresa.weconnect.com. Rev. Thomas E. Biersack.
Catechesis Religious Program—
Tel: 920-387-2470, Ext. 336; Email: ritgerk@archmil.org. Kathy Ritger, D.R.E. Students 21.

THIENSVILLE, OZAUKEE CO., ST. CECILIA (1919) Closed. For sacramental records, contact Lumen Christi, Mequon, Tel: 262-242-7967.

THOMPSON, WASHINGTON CO., ST. PATRICK (Tn. Erin) (1855) (Irish), Closed. For sacramental records, contact St. Kilian, Hartford, Tel: 262-673-4831.

TWIN LAKES, KENOSHA CO., ST. JOHN THE EVANGELIST (1932) [CEM]
701 N. Lake Ave., Twin Lakes, 53181. Tel: 262-877-2557; Email: stjohnev@archmil.org; Web: www.staljohn.org. Rev. Arthur Wayne Mattox, Admin.
Catechesis Religious Program—Email: p_vos@st-alphonsus.com. Jan McRae, D.R.E., Grades K-5; Karen Olejniczak, D.R.E., Grades 6-11. Students 70.

UNION GROVE, RACINE CO., ST. ROBERT BELLARMINE (1965)
3320 S. Colony Ave., Union Grove, 53182. Tel: 262-878-3476; Email: office@smd-srb.org; Web: www.stmary-strobert.org. Revs. Russell L. Arnett; Jose Edapparakel Mathai, M.C.B.S.
Catechesis Religious Program—Email: jenkinsj@smd-srb.org. Dr. Jon Jenkins, D.R.E. Students 129.

WATERFORD, RACINE CO., ST. THOMAS AQUINAS (1851) [CEM]
305 S. First St., Waterford, 53185. Tel: 262-534-2255; Email: nhutchings@saintthomaswaterford.org. Rev. Edward Tlucek, O.F.M.; Deacons Carl A. Mahnke, (Retired); Jim Nickel; Michael Hoffman.
School—St. Thomas Aquinas School, Tel: 262-534-2265; Email: kshipley@saintthomaswaterford.org. Religious Teachers 1; Lay Teachers 12; Students 57.
Catechesis Religious Program—Students 430.

WAUKESHA, WAUKESHA CO.
1—ST. JOHN NEUMANN, CATHOLIC COMMUNITY OF WAUKESHA (1981)
Mailing Address: 2400 W. State Hwy. 59, Waukesha, 53189-6323. Tel: 262-549-0223; Email: sjn@ccwauk.org; Web: catholic4waukesha.org. Revs. Howard G. Haase; Harry Buzbuzian; Charles Wrobel; Jorge Perez; Deacons Gary J. Stephani; David L. Zimprich; Scott Campbell; Chuck Hankins; Jorge Benavente; Antonio Palacios; Aristeo Ortiz; John Shaughnessy, Pastoral Min.; Jim Baenan, Music Min.
Catechesis Religious Program—Tel: 262-547-6555; Email: mherran@ccwauk.org. Michelle Herran, D.R.E. Students 48.
2—ST. JOSEPH, CATHOLIC COMMUNITY OF WAUKESHA (1844) (Hispanic)
818 N. East Ave., Waukesha, 53186. Tel: 262-542-2589; Email: sJparish@ccwauk.org; Web: www.catholic4waukesha.org. Revs. Howard G. Haase; Harry Buzbuzian; Charles Wrobel; Jorge Perez; Deacons Jorge Benavente; Aristeo Ortiz; Antonio Palacios; David L. Zimprich; Gary J. Stephani; Chuck Hankins; Scott Campbell; John Shaughnessy, Pastoral Min.; Michael Thiele, Music Min.
Catechesis Religious Program—
Tel: 262-542-2589, Ext. 110. Michelle Herran, D.R.E.; Juana Avila Palacios, D.R.E., Hispanic. Students 108.
3—ST. MARY, CATHOLIC COMMUNITY OF WAUKESHA (1950)
225 S. Hartwell Ave., Waukesha, 53186-6400. Tel: 262-547-6555; Email: smparish@ccwauk.org; Web: catholic4waukesha.org. Revs. Howard G. Haase; Harry Buzbuzian; Charles Wrobel; Jorge Perez; Deacons David L. Zimprich; Chuck Hankins; Scott Campbell; Gary J. Stephani; Jorge Benavente; Aristeo Ortiz; Antonio Palacios; John Shaughnessy, Pastoral Min.; Scott Currier, Music Min.
School—St. Mary School, School is a campus of the Waukesha Catholic School System. 520 E. Newhall Ave., Waukesha, 53186. Tel: 262-896-2932; Fax: 262-896-2931; Web: www.waukeshacatholicschoolsystem.org.
Catechesis Religious Program—Email: mherran@ccwauk.org. Michelle Herran, D.R.E. Students 167.
4—ST. WILLIAM, CATHOLIC COMMUNITY OF WAUKESHA (1957) [JC]
440 N. Moreland Blvd., Waukesha, 53188. Tel: 262-547-2763; Email: swparish@ccwauk.org; Web: Catholic4waukesha.org. Revs. Howard G. Haase; Harry Buzbuzian; Charles Wrobel; Jorge Perez; Deacons Scott Campbell; Chuck Hawkins; Gary J. Stephani; David L. Zimprich; Jorge Benavente; Aristeo Ortiz; Antonio Palacios; John Shaughnessy, Pastoral Min.; Robert Gallagher, Liturgy Dir.
Catechesis Religious Program—
Tel: mherran@ccwauk.org. Michelle Herran, D.R.E. Students 293.

WAUPUN, FOND DU LAC CO., ST. JOSEPH (1866) [CEM] (Irish)
118 W. Main St., Waupun, 53963. Tel: 920-324-5400; Email: office@stjoeschurch.org; Web: www.stjoeschurch.org. Rev. John J. Radetski; Deacon Steven L. Hayes.
Catechesis Religious Program—
Tel: 920-324-5400, Ext. 25; Email: childfam@stjoeschurch.org. Sr. M. Gemma Therese Harvey, D.R.E. Students 66.

WAUWATOSA, MILWAUKEE CO.
1—ST. BERNARD OF CLAIRVAUX PARISH (1911) (Irish)
7474 Harwood Ave., Wauwatosa, 53213. Tel: 414-258-4320; Email: bulletin@stbernardparish.org; Web: www.stbernardparish.org. 1500 Wauwatosa Ave., Wauwatosa, 53213. Very Rev. Phillip A. Bogacki; Rev. Will Arnold.
Catechesis Religious Program—Students 42.
2—CHRIST KING (1939)
2604 N. Swan Blvd., Wauwatosa, 53226. Tel: 414-258-2604; Email: brownl@christkingparish.org; Email: bogackip@christkingparish.org; Web: www.christkingparish.org. Very Rev. Phillip A. Bogacki; Rev. Will Arnold; Deacon John A. Ebel.
School—Christ King School, 2646 N. Swan Blvd., Wauwatosa, 53226. Tel: 414-258-4160; Fax: 414-258-0916; Email: school@christkingschool.org; Web: www.christkingschool.org. Regina Brown, Prin. Clergy 2; Lay Teachers 30; Sisters 1; Students 366.
Catechesis Religious Program— Tri Parish Program. Email: daszczuks@christkingparish.org. Samantha El-Azem, D.R.E.; Sarah Daszczuks, Youth Min. Students 338.
3—ST. JOSEPH CONGREGATION (1855)
Mailing Address: 12130 W. Center St., Wauwatosa, 53222-4096. Tel: 414-771-4626; Email: brenda@stjoetosa.archmil.org; Web: www.stjoetosa.com. Rev. Dennis J. Wieland.
School—St. Joseph Congregation School, 2750 N. 122nd St., Wauwatosa, 53222. Fax: 414-771-5577, Ext. 119; Email: stjosephschool@archmil.org; Web: www.stjoetosa.com. Linda Cooney, Prin. Lay Teachers 16; Students 175.
Catechesis Religious Program—Students 145.
4—ST. JUDE THE APOSTLE (1928)
734 Glenview Ave., Wauwatosa, 53213. Tel: 414-258-8821; Fax: 414-258-7371; Email: dengelhart@stjudetheapostle.net; Web: www.stjudeparishwauwatosa.org. Rev. Charles Conley; Deacon Donald A. Borkowski; Crawford Wiley, Dir. Liturgy/Music; Gerald Stilp, Dir. Admin. Svcs.; Melinda Morris, Dir. Fin.
School—St. Jude the Apostle School, 800 Glenview Ave., Wauwatosa, 53213. Tel: 414-771-1520; Fax: 414-771-3748; Email: cladien@saintjudeschool.net. Catherine LaDien, Prin. Lay Teachers 31; Students 427.
Catechesis Religious Program—Email: gheun@stjudetheapostle.net. Gary Heun, D.R.E./Pastoral Assoc. Students 177.
5—ST. PIUS X PARISH COMMUNITY (1952)
75th & Wright St., Wauwatosa, 53213. Web: www.stpiusparish.org. Mailing Address: 2506 Wauwatosa Ave., Wauwatosa, 53213. Tel: 414-453-3875; Email: frpaul@stpiusparish.org. Rev. Paul Portland, S.D.S.
Catechesis Religious Program—Tel: 414-453-3199; Email: ablerb@archmil.org. Barbara Abler, D.R.E. & Youth Min. Students 88.

WAYNE, WASHINGTON CO., ST. BRIDGET, Closed. For sacramental records, contact Holy Trinity, Kewaskum, Tel: 262-626-2860.

WEST ALLIS, MILWAUKEE CO.
1—ST. ALOYSIUS GONZAGA (1920) Closed. For sacramental records, contact Mother of Perpetual Help, West Allis. Tel: 414-453-5192.
2—ST. AUGUSTINE CONGREGATION (1928) [CEM] (Croatian)
6768 W. Rogers St., West Allis, 53219-1344. Tel: 414-541-5207; Fax: 414-541-0273; Email: staugwa@att.net; Web: staugwa.org. Mailing Address: 6762 W. Rogers St., West Allis, 53219-1344. Rev. Lawrence Frankovich, O.F.M.
See Mary Queen of Saints Catholic Academy under Consolidated Elementary Schools located in the Institution section.
Catechesis Religious Program—St. Rita Parish, 2318 S. 61 St., West Allis, 53219. Tel: 414-541-7515; Email: barb.strita@wi.rr.com. Barbara Krieger, D.R.E.
3—HOLY ASSUMPTION (1902)
1526 S. 72nd St., West Allis, 53214. Tel: 414-774-3010; Email: haparish@archmil.org; Web: haparish.org. Revs. Gregory M. Spitz, Admin., (Retired); David Zampino.
Catechesis Religious Program—Barbara Krieger, D.R.E. Students 8.
4—IMMACULATE HEART OF MARY (1948) Closed. For sacramental records, contact Mother of Perpetual Help, West Allis. Tel: 414-453-5192.
5—ST. JOSEPH (1909) (Polish), Closed. For sacramental records, contact Archdiocese of Milwaukee Archives Office, Tel: 414-769-3407.
6—ST. MARY, HELP OF CHRISTIANS (1907) [CEM] (Slovenian), Closed. For sacramental records, contact Archdiocese of Milwaukee Archives Office, Tel: 414-769-3407.
7—MARY, QUEEN OF HEAVEN (1958) Closed. For sacramental records, contact Mother of Perpetual Help, West Allis. Tel: 414-453-5192.
8—MOTHER OF PERPETUAL HELP
1121 S. 116th St., West Allis, 53214. Tel: 414-453-5192; Email: office@mphwa.org; Web: www.mphwa.org. Revs. Jeffery A. Prasser; Thomas Vathappallil, M.C.B.S.; Deacons Walter Henry; Keith R. Marx.
Catechesis Religious Program—Email: becca@mphwa.com. Rebecca Bojarski, D.R.E. Students 98.
9—OUR LADY OF MT. CARMEL (1938) (Italian), Closed. For sacramental records, contact Archdiocese of Milwaukee Archives Office, Tel: 414-769-3407.
10—ST. RITA (1924)
2318 S. 61st St., West Allis, 53219. Tel: 414-541-7515; Fax: 414-541-7568; Email: stritaparishwa@wi.rr.com; Web: stritawestallis.org. Rev. Charles G. Zabler, Admin.; Barbara Krieger, Pastoral Assoc.; Kevin Bourassa, Pastoral Musician.
See Mary Queen of Saints Catholic Academy Association under Consolidated Elementary Schools located in the Institution section.
Catechesis Religious Program—Tel: 414-541-7515; Email: barb.strita@wi.rr.com. Barbara Krieger, D.R.E. Students 33.

WEST BEND, WASHINGTON CO.
1—ST. FRANCES CABRINI (1955)
1025 S. 7th Ave., West Bend, 53095. Tel: 262-338-2366; Email: jrude@wbparishes.org; Web: www.saintfrancescabrini.com. Revs. Nathan D. Reesman; Andrew Infanger; Deacons Michael S. Koebel; Ronald Schneider; Richard Doll, Business Mgr.
School—St. Frances Cabrini School, 529 Hawthorn Dr., West Bend, 53095. Tel: 262-334-7142;

Fax: 262-334-8168; Email: wwaech@wbparishes.org. William Waech, Prin. Lay Teachers 27; Students 269.
Catechesis Religious Program—Email: kschaitberger@wbparishes.org. Katherine Schaitberger, D.R.E. Students 266.
2—HOLY ANGELS (1852) [CEM]
138 N. 8th Ave., West Bend, 53095.
Tel: 262-334-3038; Email: vanderwielenb@hawb.org; Web: www.hawb.org. Very Rev. Patrick E. Heppe; Deacons Mark Jansen; David N. Young.
School—Holy Angels School, 230 N. 8th Ave., West Bend, 53095. Tel: 262-338-1148; Email: has@has.pvt.k12.wi.us; Web: www.has.pvt.k12.wi.us. Mike Sternig, Prin., Email: mst@has.pvt.k12.wi.us. Lay Teachers 29; Students 279.
Catechesis Religious Program—Tel: 262-334-9393; Email: berglandh@hawb.org. Hannah Bergland, D.R.E. Students 351.
3—IMMACULATE CONCEPTION (1857) [CEM 2]
406 Jefferson St., West Bend, 53090.
Tel: 262-338-5600; Email: rprim@wbparishes.org; Web: www.stmaryparishwb.org. Revs. Nathan D. Reesman; Andrew Infanger; Katie Schaitberger, Pastoral Assoc. & Dir. Catholic Formation; Elizabeth Habersetzer, Music Min.; Mary Hernikl, Pastoral Coord.
Catechesis Religious Program—Email: mabel@wbparishes.org. Mary Abel, D.R.E. Students 129.
WHITEFISH BAY, MILWAUKEE CO.
1—HOLY FAMILY (1949)
4825 N. Wildwood Ave., Whitefish Bay, 53217.
Tel: 414-332-9220; Email: holyfam@hfparish.org; Web: www.hfparish.org. Revs. Raymond Guthrie, Admin.; Peter Patrick Kimani.
School—Holy Family School, (Grades PreK-8), 4849 N. Wildwood Ave., Whitefish Bay, 53217.
Tel: 414-332-8175; Email: hfpschool@hfparishschool.org; Web: www.hfparish.org. Amy Kern, Prin. Lay Teachers 21; Students 176.
Catechesis Religious Program—Tel: 414-332-8156; Email: obergj@hfparish.org. Jennifer Oberg, D.R.E.; Emily Schaefer, Youth Min. Students 275.
2—ST. MONICA (1923)
5681 N. Santa Monic Blvd., Whitefish Bay, 53217.
Tel: 414-332-1576; Email: smoffice@stme.church; Web: www.st-monica.org. 160 E. Silver Spring Dr., Whitefish Bay, 53217. Very Rev. Paul B.R. Hartmann, M.Div., J.C.L.; Rev. Andrew J.T. Linn; Deacon Michael A. Bowen; Monica Cardenas, Dir.
School—St. Monica School, 5635 N. Santa Monica Blvd., Whitefish Bay, 53217. Tel: 414-332-3660;
Fax: 414-332-8649; Web: www.stmonica.school. Michael Landgraf, Prin., Email: mlandgraf@st-monica.org. Religious Teachers 2; Lay Teachers 28; Students 379.
Catechesis Religious Program—Tel: 414-964-8780; Email: jlambrecht@stme.church; Email: mturner@stme.church. Jeanette Lembrecht, Child Min.; Meaghan Turner, Youth Min. Students 435.
WHITEWATER, WALWORTH CO., ST. PATRICK (1853) [CEM]
1225 W. Main St., Whitewater, 53190-1620.
Tel: 262-473-3143; Email: stpatrickww@gmail.com; Web: stpatrickwhitewater.org. Rev. Mark J. Niehaus, J.S.P.
Catechesis Religious Program—Email: rupprechtr@archmil.org. Richard Rupprecht, Dir. Faith Formation. Students 144.
WILMOT, KENOSHA CO., HOLY NAME OF JESUS (1856) [CEM] Closed. For sacramental records, contact Holy Cross, Bristol 53104, Tel: 262-857-2068.
WIND LAKE, RACINE CO., ST. CLARE (1965)
7616 Fritz St., Wind Lake, 53185. Tel: 262-895-2729; Email: woody@tritchey.com. Rev. Edward Tlucek, O.F.M., Admin.; Deacon Richard J. Brown, Parish Dir.
Catechesis Religious Program—Tel: 262-895-2797; Email: stclareyouth@tds.net. Trista Minezes, D.R.E.; Maureen LeGros, Youth Min. Students 132.
WOODHULL, FOND DU LAC CO., ST. JOHN THE BAPTIST, Closed. For sacramental records, contact Our Risen Savior, Eldorado, Tel: 920-922-2412.
WOODLAND, DODGE CO., ST. MARY - WOODLAND, [CEM 2] (German), Closed. For sacramental records, contact Sacred Heart, Horicon. Tel: 920-485-0694.

Chaplains of Public Institutions

MILWAUKEE. *Milwaukee County House of Correction.* Attended by St. James, Franklin.
Milwaukee County Jail. Bro. Jerome Smith, O.F.M.Cap., Chap.
JUNEAU. *Dodge County Center.* Attended by Sacred Heart, Horicon.
KENOSHA. *Kenosha Hospital and Medical Center*, 6308 8th Ave., Kenosha, 53143-5082. Vacant.
WAUWATOSA. *Froedtert Memorial Lutheran Hospital*, 9200 W. Wisconsin Ave., 53226. Rev. Florent Kanga, S.A.C., (Cameroon) Chap.
WEST ALLIS. *Aurora West Allis Medical Center*, 8901 W. Lincoln Ave., West Allis, 53227.
Tel: 414-328-6000.
WOOD. *Veterans Administration Medical Center*, Wood, 53193. Tel: 414-384-2000. Rev. Dominic Vitaliano, Chap.

Special Assignment:
Very Revs.—
Hemsing, John D., Rector, St. Francis de Sales Seminary, 3257 S. Lake Dr., St. Francis, 53235
Herda, Jerome G., Ordained & Lay Ecclesiastical Ministry, P.O. Box 070912, 53207-0912
Knoebel, Thomas L., Ph.D., M.Div., Rector/Pres., Sacred Heart Seminary and School of Theology, 7335 S. Hwy. 100, P.O. Box 429, Hales Corners, 53130-0429
Lobacz, James E., Sr. Ministry; Master of Ceremonies/Logistics Coord. for Archbishop Listecki, P.O. Box 070912, 53207-0912
Revs.—
Avella, Steven M., Faculty, 3222 S. 29th St., 53215
Cirujeda, Pablo, 1505 Howard St., Racine, 53404
Ermatinger, Cliff O., 1858 N. Cambridge Ave., 53202
Gibson, John S., Catholic Memorial High School, 601 E. College Ave., Waukesha, 53186-5538
Hernandez, Enrique, Vocation Promoter, Vocation Office, Saint Francis de Sales Seminary, 3257 S. Lake Dr., St. Francis, 53235
Krawczyk, Brad A., Saint Francis de Sales Seminary, 3257 S. Lake Dr., St. Francis, 53235
Lampe, Stephen J., M.Div., S.S.L., S.T.D., Cardinal Stritch University, 6801 N. Yates Rd., 53217-3985. Tel: 414-410-4000, Ext. 4830. (Faculty)
O'Brien, Timothy J., Faculty, Marquette Univ., 8521 Kenyon Ave., Wauwatosa, 53226
Powers, Glenn E., Dir., Formation Svcs., St. Francis de Sales Seminary, 3257 S. Lake Dr., St. Francis, 53235. Tel: 414-747-6400
Strand, Luke N., Dir., Vocation Office; Vice Rector of Human Formation, Saint Francis de Sales Seminary, 3257 S. Lake Dr., St. Francis, 53235.

On Duty Outside the Archdiocese:
Revs.—
Camacho Porras, Juan, Apartado 53, Azua, Dominican Republic
Lee, Roy, P.O. Box 37058, Decatur, GA 30037-0587
Lightner, Michael F., St. Anthony, 1432 River St., Niagara, 54151
Malloy, Francis X., Bay Pines VA Medical Center, Bay Pines FL, 33744
Massingale, Bryan N., Faculty, Fordham University, 441 E. Fordham Rd., Bronx, NY 10458
Weiss, Erich, United States Navy, c/o Joe Weiss, 5356 Woodland Summit, West Bend, 53095
Witczak, Michael G., M.Div., S.L.D., Faculty, 620 Michigan Ave., N.E., Washington, DC 20064.

Study Leave:
Revs.—
Barnekow, Kevin, St. Mary Parish, 314 Duke St., Alexandria, VA 22314. Divine Mercy University, Arlington, VA
Burns, John B., Casa Santa Maria, Rome, Italy
LoCoco, John Christopher, Pontifical North American College, Rome, Italy
Nieto, Jose Mario, Catholic University of America, Washington, DC.

Sick Leave:
Very Rev.—
Eichenberger, Thomas P.
Revs.—
Moran, Michael F.
Shimek, Joseph J.
Stanosz, Paul A.

Retired:
Most Revs.—
Sklba, Richard J., S.S.L., S.T.D., (Retired)
Weakland, Rembert G., O.S.B., (Retired)
Rev. Msgrs.—
Gajdos, T. George, (Retired), 7350 S. Lovers Lane Rd., #234, Franklin, 53132
Olszyk, Thomas P., J.C.L., (Retired), 3257 S. Lake Dr., St. Francis, 53235
Very Revs.—
Frederick, Curt J., J.C.L., M.Div., (Retired), W240 N2389 A E. Pkwy Meadow Cir., Pewaukee, 53072
Gramza, Ronald, (Retired), 2201 Northwestern Ave., Racine, 53404
Kohler, William E., (Retired), 26047 W. Loomis Rd., Wind Lake, 53185-1457
Revs.—
Acker, Karl H., (Retired), 1400 W. Sonata Dr., #140, 53221
Ackeret, Dennis, (Retired), 2796 Thomas Dr., East Troy, 53120
Aiken, Richard J., (Retired), 2637 N. 53rd St., 53210
Amann, Steven J., (Retired), The Regency, 13750 W. National Ave., #1105, New Berlin, 53151
Artmann, Robert J., (Retired), 523 Kennedy Dr., Northglenn, CO 80234
Bales, Robert, (Retired), 125 University Dr., #117, West Bend, 53095
Barbian, Leonard M., (Retired), 6750 Parkedge Cir., Franklin, 53132
Barrett, Michael, (Retired), 9991 W. North Ave., #105, Wauwatosa, 53226
Baumgartner, John H., (Retired), 9339 W. Howard Ave., #221, 53228
Betz, Robert, (Retired), 3486 W. Sycamore St., Franklin, 53132
Bittner, Wayne W., (Retired), 306 N. Highland Ave., #327, Plymouth, 53073
Breitbach, Richard C., (Retired), 14140 Regis St., Brookfield, 53005
Briske, Larry, (Retired), 711 McLaine St., Escondido, CA 92027
Brittain, Gerald W., (Retired), 3674 S. Logan Ave., 53207
Brophy, John L., (Retired), 5101 Center St., 53210-2361
Burkert, William C., (Retired), 3147 S. 42nd St., 53215-4030
Carroll, Edward E., (Retired), 3524 7th Ave. Apt. 127, Kenosha, 53140
Cera, James B., (Retired), 9301 N. 76th St., 53223
Cerpich, Richard J., (Retired), 2532 S. 7th St., Sheboygan, 53081
Chycinski, Gregory A., (Retired), W7955 Creek Rd. #605, Delavan
Coerber, Joseph H., (Retired), W8272 Forest Ave., Eldorado, 54932-9631
Connell, James E., J.C.D., (Retired), 2462 N. Prospect Ave., #204, 53211
Cooper, David E., (Retired), 9410 W. Loomis Rd., #5, Franklin, 53132
Crewe, Ronald O., (Retired), 419 Shoreland Dr., Racine, 53402
Debski, Joseph E., (Retired), 2209 Browns Lake Dr. #105, Burlington, 53105
DeLeers, Stephen V., (Retired), 1742 N. Prospect Ave., #313, 53202
DeVries, Thomas D., (Retired), 5135 Diversey Blvd., Whitefish Bay, 53217
Diederichs, Carl E., (Retired), N10232 County Hwy. G, New Holstein, 53061
Dietzler, William J., (Retired), 4127 81st Pl., Kenosha, 53142
Dineen, Michael P., (Retired), 1016 North Ave., Sheboygan, 53083
Dirkx, Dennis A., (Retired), 406 Kames Cove, Slinger, 53086
Doda, Eugene J. Jr., (Retired), 1740 W. Meyer Ln., #8102, Oak Creek, 53154
Drenzek, Peter C., (Retired), S70 W17635 Muskego Dr., Muskego, 53150
Dulek, Lawrence V., (Retired), 8112 N. 38th St., Brown Deer, 53209
Ernster, James M., (Retired), 570 Hwy. D, Belgium, 53004
Eschweiler, Edward R., (Retired), 9405 W. Howard Ave., #369, Greenfield, 53228
Fait, Thomas G., (Retired), 117 Midwood Dr., Burlington, 53105-1322
Filut, David C., (Retired), W157 S7275 Quietwood Dr., Muskego, 53150
Fleischman, Richard J., (Retired), 4221 Cherrywood Ct., Sheboygan, 53081
Gloudeman, Robert J., (Retired), 10020 Whitnall Edge Dr. # D, Franklin, 53132
Gosma, Robert D., (Retired), W379 S4988 W. Pretty Lake Rd., Dousman, 53118
Gross, Ralph C., (Retired), 3940 S. Prairie Hill Ln., #105, Greenfield, 53228
Gurath, Guy G., (Retired), 211 Fredonia Ave., Fredonia, 53021
Haas, Joseph H., (Retired), P.O. Box 14363, West Allis, 53214-0363
Hammer, Michael J., (Retired), 709 E. Juneau Ave., #704, 53202
Heinze, Arthur G., (Retired), 9032 W. Elm Ct., Unit D, Franklin, 53132
Hessel, Gerald J., (Retired), 2001 41st St., Kenosha, 53140-5615
Hornacek, Joseph F., (Retired), 1355 Hillwood Blvd., Unit C, Pewaukee, 53072
Hudziak, Jerome M., Ph.D., (Retired), 10020 Whitnall Edge Dr., Unit C, Franklin, 53132

Huebner, Terrance J., (Retired), 1640 96th St., Unit 82, Sturtevant, 53177
Johnson, Howard J., (Retired), W6332 Lake Ellen Dr., Cascade, 53011
Juknialis, Joseph J., (Retired), 836 N. Broadway, 53202
Jurkus, Alan F., (Retired), 5435 Morningside Ln., 53221
Kasten, Edward F., (Retired), 7979 W. Glenbrook Rd., #6002, 53223
Keefe, Charles R., (Retired), 3231 W. Brown St., Phoenix, AZ 85051
Kern, John R., (Retired), 3340 N. 57th St., 53216
Key, William W., (Retired), 8811 W. Oklahoma Ave. #305, 53227
Kienzle, Jerome C., (Retired), 51 N.W. Columbia Dr., #202, Oak Harbor, WA 98277
Klemme, Dennis C., J.C.D., (Retired), W267 N2515 Meadowbrook Rd., Pewaukee, 53072
Klink, Anthony G., (Retired), 229 E. Washington St., Slinger, 53086
Knippel, Kenneth P., (Retired), 15205 Casey Cir., Brookfield, 53005-4149
Knoebel, Thomas L., Ph.D., M.Div., (Retired), 7569 W. Tuckaway Pines Cir., Franklin, 53132
Kotecki, Ronald E., (Retired), 3851 E. Hammond Ave., Cudahy, 53110
Le Mieux, Thomas A., (Retired), Juniper Ct., 3209 S. Lake Dr., #305, 53235
Lewis, Dennis J., (Retired), 3315 N. 51st Blvd., 53216
Lijewski, Thomas F., (Retired), N4348 Mercury Ln., Eden, 53019
Lippert, Paul R., (Retired), W175 N791 Wildwood Dr., A231, Menomonee Falls, 53051
Liska, Richard A., (Retired), 555 E. Quail Run, Oak Creek, 53154
Lisowski, Edward E., (Retired), P.O. Box 210182, 53221
Loehr, James P., (Retired), 739 Roosevelt Ave., Oconomowoc, 53066
Macoskie, Melvin H., (Retired), c/o Monica Waszak, 1019 Bay View Ct., Mukwonago, 53149
Marek, Dean V., (Retired), 7601 Settlers Ridge Ct., Henrico, VA 23231
Mateljan, Roy A., (Retired), 868 Americana Dr., Fond Du Lac, 54935-2954
Matt, Erwin H., (Retired), 3209 S. Lake Dr., St. Francis, 53235
McCarthy, Anthony T., (Retired), 7350 S. Lovers Lane Rd., #438, Franklin, 53132
Metz, Kenneth J., (Retired), 301 W. 8th St., Sanford, FL 32771
Mich, Kenneth A., (Retired), 111 11th St., #4AS, Racine, 53403
Michalski, Michael F., (Retired), 3373 S. 15th Pl., 53215
Mikalofsky, Hilarion A., Ch. Lt. Col., (Retired), 82 Edgewater Dr., Lakeside City, TX 76308
Mirsberger, Richard E., (Retired), 9995 W. North Ave. #353, Wauwatosa, 53226
Molter, Richard J., (Retired), 6545 Mariner Dr., #6, Racine, 53406
Mueller, Robert F., (Retired), St. Camillus Assisted Living, 10201 W. Wisconsin Ave., #15, Wauwatosa, 53226
Murphy, Daniel T., (Retired), Clement Manor, 9405 W. Howard Ave., #156, Greenfield, 53228
Newman, Michael T., J.C.L., (Retired), St. Catherine's Community, 3524 7th Ave., #205, Kenosha, 53140
Nowicki, Gary D., (Retired), 812 Hazelridge Rd. #203, Elkhorn, 53121-1245
Oswald, Norman R., (Retired), 7813 N. 60th St., #F, 53223
Pacheco-Sanchez, Luis, (Retired), P.O. Box 1856, 53201-1856
Pocernich, Eugene, (Retired), 2400 E. Bradford Ave. #702, 53211
Pulice, John J., (Retired), 2325 W. Jonathan Dr., Oak Creek, 53154
Raczynski, Paul L., (Retired), 1644 Rivergate Dr., Jacksonville, FL 32223
Rausch, John W., (Retired), Box 475, Eagle, 53119
Rebatzki, George M., (Retired), 17330 W. Birch Dr. #102, Brookfield, 53045
Repenshek, Jerome V., (Retired), 138 N. 8th Ave., West Bend, 53095-3201
Richetta, John J., (Retired), 4014 81st St., Kenosha, 53142
Richter, Robert J., (Retired), 2700 S. 19th St., Arlington, VA 22204
Robinson, Richard J., (Retired), 7350 S. Lovers Lane Rd., #440, Franklin, 53132
Roscioli, Dominic J., (Retired), 6863 S. 68th., Franklin, 53132
Savage, Roger A., (Retired), 7350 S. Lovers Lane Rd., #140, Franklin, 53132
Schlenker, Richard J., (Retired), Clement Manor, 9339 W. Howard Ave., #244, Greenfield, 53228
Schmidt, Donald, (Retired), Marquette Manor, 2409 10th Ave., Unit 10, South Milwaukee, 53172
Schmitz, John A., (Retired), Prairie Place, 479 E. Oshkosh St., Ripon, 54971
Schramm, Charles H., (Retired), 8767 Westlake Dr., Greendale, 53129
Schreiter, John P., (Retired), W3898 Lemonweir Ct., Mauston, 53948
Schubert, Herbert, (Retired), 5104 S. Hidden Dr., #21, Greenfield, 53221
Schwartz, Norman R., (Retired), 716 Manatee Bay Dr., Boynton Beach, FL 33435
Sepich, Lawrence, (Retired), 8638 Westlake Dr., Greendale, 53129
Simon, John L., (Retired), 214 Beaver St., P.O. Box 357, Beaver Dam, 53916
Sippel, Bernard S., M.Div., (Retired), 10300 W. Bluemound Rd., #220, Wauwatosa, 53226
Sippel, Edward F., (Retired), 519 W. 11th St., Fond du Lac, 54935
Skeris, Robert A., (Retired), 722 Dillingham Ave., Sheboygan, 53081
Slodowski, Bruno, (Retired), 26513 Marion Ct., Wind Lake, 53185
Sommer, Allan J., (Retired), Lighthouse, 2130 Continental Dr., West Bend, 53095. 995 Fairfield Ln., West Bend, 53090-9058
Spitz, Gregory M., (Retired), 4448 N. Lydell Ave. #409, Whitefish Bay, 53217
Stanfield, William L., (Retired), 9405 W. Howard Ave., #371, Greenfield, 53228
Stradinger, Stephen J., (Retired), 1515 92nd St. #94, Sturtevant, 53177
Surges, Robert F., (Retired), S76 W16851 Gregory Dr., Unit C, Muskego, 53150
Suriano, Thomas, (Retired), 5101 W. Center St., 53210-2361
Thielen, Jeffrey M., (Retired), 3134 Wood Rd., Unit 3, Racine, 53406-6202
Tikalsky, Russell F., (Retired), 1532 S 72nd St., West Allis, 53219
Tino, Robert F., (Retired), 16133 W. Parkview Rd.,, Surprise, AZ 85387-6319
Turner, Robert D., (Retired)
Van Abel, John W., (Retired), 235 Tamarack Dr., #8, Lake Mills, 53551
Van Beek, Alois, (Retired), N3256 Highland Rd., Oakfield, 53065
Van Beek, Dennis E., (Retired), P.O. Box 197, Kohler, 53044
Van Vlaenderen, Leonard S., (Retired), P.O. Box 100522, Cudahy, 53110
Venne, R. Thomas, (Retired), San Camillo, 10200 W. Bluemound Rd., #103, Wauwatosa, 53226
Verberg, Richard R., (Retired), 8565 W. Waterford Ave., #4, Greenfield, 53228
Vogel, Walter J., (Retired), 5960 W. Loomis Rd., Greendale, 53129
Vojtik, James P., (Retired), W228 S2376 Oriole Dr., Waukesha, 53186
Walker, Thomas J., (Retired), 3505 S.W. Dosch Rd., Portland, OR 97239. Tel: 414-769-3345
Wawrzyniakowski, Edward J., (Retired), N7594 Sandy Beach Rd., Fond du Lac, 54937
Weis, Denis P., (Retired), 9405 W. Howard Ave, #353, Greenfield, 53228-1400
Wester, Charles H., (Retired), St. Francis Terrace, 345 First St., #132, Fond Du Lac, 53019
Whalen, William, (Retired), W3327 Orchard Ave., Green Lake, 54941
Wild, Michael L., (Retired), 628 Shepherd Dr. #3, West Bend, 53090-8478
Winkler, Eugene, (Retired), 3939 S. 92nd St., #120, Greenfield, 53228
Witon, Russell F., (Retired), 11515 W. Cleveland Ave., # 303A, West Allis, 53227
Wittliff, Thomas F., (Retired), 2260 S. 4th St., 53207
Yockey, John G., (Retired), N43 W32907 Rasmus Rd., #D, Nashotah, 53058
Zerkel, Donald F., (Retired), P.O. Box 74, Newburg, 53060
Zinthefer, Neil G., (Retired), P.O. Box 740, Campbellsport, 53010-0740.

Permanent Deacons:
Backes, David J., (On Leave)
Banach, James D., St. Gregory the Great, Milwaukee
Banach, William A., (Retired)
Benavente, Jorge, St. Joseph, Waukesha
Blaze, Edward, All Saints, Milwaukee
Borkowski, Donald A., St. Jude the Apostle, Wauwatosa
Bowen, Michael A., St. Monica, Whitefish Bay
Braun, Warren D., (Retired)
Brown, Richard J., St. Clare, Wind Lake
Burch, Michael F., St. John XXIII, Port Washington
Burmeister, Dan, Our Lady of the Holy Rosary, Kenosha
Burns, John R., St. Mary, Hales Corners
Buth, Robert H., (Retired)
Buyck, Gerald W., (Out of Archdiocese)
Campbell, Scott, St. William, Waukesha; St. John Neumann, Waukesha
Cesarec, Michael E., (Retired)
Chalhoub, Robert, (Out of Archdiocese)
Champagne, John I., St. Benedict the Moor, Milwaukee
Chmielewski, Michael J., Holy Apostles, New Berlin
Chrisien, James, St. Boniface, Germantown
Clark, William, (Retired), Archdiocese of Chicago
Cody, Edward F., St. Katharine Drexel, Beaver Dam
Collins, Dean J., Mother of Good Counsel, Milwaukee
Copson, Jeffrey J., St. Elizabeth Ann Seton, New Berlin
Cornejo, Carlos, St. Anthony, Milwaukee
D'Alessio, John, St. Aloysius, West Allis
Deiters, James, (Out of Archdiocese)
Derks, Robert, St. Peter, Slinger
Diciaula, Gregory H., St. Dominic, Brookfield
Dieters, James, St. Benedict, Fontana
Dominguez, Alvaro, St. Francis de Sales, Lake Geneva
Doyle, James B., (Out of Archdiocese)
Ebel, John A., St. Bernard, Wauwatosa; Christ the King, Wauwatosa
Faust, Theodore, Basilica of St. Josaphat, Milwaukee
Ference, Dennis H., (Retired), Faust, Theodore J. Basilica of St. Josaphat, Milwaukee
Filipiak, Thomas P., St. Bruno, Dousman
Finley, Michael J., St. Anthony, Pewaukee
Foeckler, Allan J., St. Charles Borromeo, Milwaukee
Fogarty, Thomas, St. Paul, Milwaukee
Francois, James S., St. Mary, Kenosha
Fritsch, John J., St. Monica, Whitefish Bay; St. Eugene, Fox Point
Frye, Patrick H., (Out of Archdiocese)
Fuentes, Roberto, St. Patrick, Racine
Gaudioso, Carmelo, (Out of Archdiocese)
Gavin, John R., Immaculate Conception, Sheboygan; Ss. Cyril and Methodius, Sheboygan
Goetter, James P., St. Mary, Menomonee Falls; St. Anthony, Menomonee Falls
Gonzales, Jose U., St. Joseph, Wauwatosa
Gonzalez, Baleriano O., (Retired)
Goodman, Robert E., (Retired), (Out of Archdiocese)
Goulding, William, St. Mary, Hales Corners
Govek, Richard J., (Retired)
Dr. Grambow, David W., Lumen Christi, Mequon
Griffiths, Joseph J., (Out of Archdiocese)
Gulig, Richard P., St. Peter Claver, Sheboygan
Gundlach, Douglas P., St. Joseph, Racine
Gurzynski, Theodore A., St. Alphonsus, Greendale
Guzman, Armindo, (Out of Archdiocese)
Hankins, Chuck, St. William, Waukesha; St. John Neumann, Waukesha
Hanley, Thomas, (Retired), (Diocese of Green Bay)
Hansen, Keith A., St. Paul the Apostle, Racine
Hayes, Steven L., Annunciation, Fox Lake; St. Joseph, Waupun (Diocese of Madison)
Heideman, Willis, St. Mary, Mayville; St. Andrew, LeRoy
Henry, Walter, (Retired)
Hiller, Richard D., (Retired)
Hoffman, Michael D., St. Thomas Aquinas, Waterford
Horner, Ralph E., Holy Trinity, Kewaskum; St. Michael, St. Michaels
Huber, Paul, (Retired)
Hunt, Thomas N., Cathedral of St. John the Evangelist, Milwaukee
Iwan, Henry F., (Retired)
Jansen, Mark, Holy Angels, West Bend
Jens, William T., (Retired)
Kabara, Donald F., (Retired)
Kaczmarek, Raymond J., (Retired)
Kehrer, Daniel F., St. Elizabeth, Kenosha; St. James, Kenosha
Kempka, Eugene A., Queen of Apostles, Pewaukee
Kennedy, Claude V., (Retired), St. Charles Borromeo, Milwaukee
Kennedy, David L., (Out of Archdiocese)
Kilkenny, Philip O., St. Andrew, Delavan; St. Patrick, Elkhorn
Klingseisen, Paul, Blessed Sacrament, Milwaukee
Koebel, Michael S., St. Frances Cabrini, West Bend; Holy Trinity, Newburg
Kornburger, Ralph W. Jr., St. Catherine, Milwaukee
Kramer, Steven L., St. Matthew, Oak Creek (Diocese of Rockville Centre)
Kustner, Charles J., St. Mary, Elm Grove
La Fond, M. Larry Jr., (Retired)
LaPointe, Patrick J., St. Veronica, Milwaukee
Lauer, David A., (Personal Leave)
Lazaga, Alfred C., St. Joseph, Grafton
Lebron, Gregorio M., (Retired)

Leggett, A. James, St. Alphonsus, Greendale
Leonardelli, Mark, (Outside of Archdiocese)
Lesjak, Ronald F., St. Mary, Kenosha
Lopez, Julio, St. Patrick, Racine
Losiniecki, Thomas, (Retired)
Lowe, Stanley J., St. Stephen, Oak Creek
Lydolph, Donald J., (Retired)
Maack, Terrance A., St. Peter, Kenosha
Macias, Rogelio, St. Anthony, Milwaukee
Mahnke, Carl A., St. Thomas Aquinas, Waterford
Major, Troy, (Retired)
Malueg, Gerald D., Divine Savior, Fredonia; Our Lady of the Lakes, Random Lake
Martino, Anthony, (Outside of the Archdiocese)
Marx, Keith R., Immaculate Heart of Mary, West Allis
Matthias, James J., St. Dominic, Brookfield
McKenna, Thomas, St. Catherine, Sharon (Diocese of Rockford)
Meuler, Andrew, Mother of Good Counsel, Milwaukee
Mezydlo, John C., St. Jerome, Oconomowoc
Moczydlowski, Chester A., (Retired)
Monday, John P., Our Lady of Lourdes, Milwaukee
Monfre, Anthony, Lumen Christi, Mequon
Monzel, Paul S., (Retired)
Muller, John, (Retired), (Diocese of Crookston)
Munoz, Ricardo, Holy Family, Fond du Lac
Nawrocik, Zenon L., (Out of Archdiocese)
Nees, Dale T., St. Paul the Apostle, Racine
Nguyen, Bruno Long H., St. Martin of Tours, Franklin
Nickel, James, St. Thomas Aquinas, Waterford
Nickolai, Anton B., St. Charles, Immaculate Conception, Burlington; St. Joseph, Lyons
Niggemann, Richard D., Waukesha County Jail, Waukesha
Normann, Larry E., St. Joan of Arc, Delafield; St. Catherine, Mapleton
Nosacek, Gary J., Ss. Peter & Paul, Milwaukee
Olson, Allen B., Saint Teresa of Calcutta, North Lake
Ortiz, Aristeo, St. Joseph, Waukesha
Paczkowski, Dale R., Holy Family, Fond du Lac
Palacios, Antonio, St. Joseph, Waukesha
Pemper, Frank, St. Margaret Mary, Milwaukee
Pemper, Steven F., St. Augustine, West Allis; St. John the Evangelist, Greenfield
Pena, Luis, Office for Intercultural Ministry; Hispanic Ministry, Waukesha County
Peterson, James J., (Retired)
Petrie, Dennis J., St. Anthony on the Lake, Pewaukee
Petro, Greg D., St. Rita, Racine
Pettey, Lawrence C., (Retired)
Piontek, Richard T., St. Mary, Elm Grove; (Archdiocese of Chicago)
Pollak, David R., (Retired)
Ponec, Gerald R., Nativity of the Lord, Cudahy
Price, Gregory R., St. Peter, Easy Troy
Przedpelski, Steven J., Three Holy Women, Milwaukee; Our Lady of the Divine Providence, Milwaukee; Old St. Mary, Milwaukee; Ss. Peter and Paul, Milwaukee; Franciscan Peacemakers, Inc.
Ramirez-Murphy, Eugenio, St. Michael and St. Rose, Milwaukee
Ramsey, Larry L., St. Leonard, Muskego
Regan, Sylvester R., (Retired)
Reyes, Edwin, St. John Paul II, Milwaukee
Reyes, Henry O., St. Anthony, Milwaukee; St. Hyacinth, Milwaukee
Rocha, Leonides, (Retired)
Rodriguez, Virgilio, (Out of Archdiocese)
Rooney, Michael R., St. James, Menomonee Falls
Rosado, Salvador, (Retired), St. Michael, St. Rose, Milwaukee
Salazar, Roberto, (On Duty Outside of the Archdiocese)
Schieffer, Robert M., (Retired)
Schneider, Charles G., St. Martin of Tours, Franklin
Schneider, Ronald W., St. Francis Cabrini, West Bend; (Archdiocese of Washington, D.C.)
Schopper, Eugene E., (Retired)
Senglaub, Joseph M., St. Bruno, Dousman; St. Paul, Genesee Depot
Sewell, Eric M., St. Sebastian, Sturtevant; St. Lucy, Racine
Shierk, Wilson A., St. Mary, Kenosha
Sites, Sanford, Good Shepherd, Menomonee Falls; St. James, Menomonee Falls
Smallhoover, James A., (Retired)
Snyder, Gordon J., St. James, Mukwonago; St. Theresa, Eagle
Sommers, David, Deaf and Hard of Hearing Office, Archdiocese of Milwaukee
Stanula, Richard J., St. Anne, Pleasant Prairie
Starke, James J., St. Boniface, Germantown
Starns, Terry, (Out of Archdiocese)
Starr, Robert G., St. Mary of the Lake, Racine; (Archdiocese of Chicago)
Stephani, Gary J., St. John Neumann, Waukesha; St. William, Waukesha
Stodola, John, St. Matthew, Oak Creek
Surges, Thomas J., St. John XXIII, Port Washington
Thao, Moualee, St. Rose, Milwaukee
Villarreal, Hector, St. Patrick, Whitewater
Waitrovich, Raymond, (Retired)
Waldoch, Timothy, St. Gregory the Great, Milwaukee
Weber, C. Edward, (Retired)
Wells, Randal S., (Retired), St. Katharine Drexel, Beaver Dam
Wenzler, Joseph P., Lumen Christi, Mequon
Widmar, Willard M., St. Paul the Apostle, Racine
Wiese, Scott T., St. Joseph, Grafton
Winkowski, Richard, St. Elizabeth Ann Seton, New Berlin
Wirch, Rick J., St. Leonard, Muskego
Wirtz, Howard J., (Retired)
Wisniewski, Ralph, (Retired)
Wittak, Jay W., Wisconsin Veterans Home, Union Grove; (Diocese of Marquette)
Wodushek, Robert A., (Retired)
Young, David N., Holy Angels, West Bend
Zalewski, Leon J., St. John the Evangelist, Greenfield
Zdeb, James, St. Louis, Caledonia; (Archdiocese of Chicago)
Zimprich, David L., St. William, Waukesha; St. John Neumann, Waukesha
Zozakiewicz, Daniel T., (Retired)
Zuniga, Jorge, St. Roman, Milwaukee.

INSTITUTIONS LOCATED IN DIOCESE

[A] SEMINARIES, ARCHDIOCESAN

ST. FRANCIS. *Saint Francis de Sales Seminary*, 3257 S. Lake Dr., St. Francis, 53235. Tel: 414-747-6400; Fax: 414-747-6442; Email: dbrotz@sfs.edu; Web: www.sfs.edu. Very Rev. John D. Hemsing, Pres. & Rector; Revs. Glenn E. Powers, Dir., Pastoral Counseling; Luke N. Strand, Dir. Human Formation and Vice Rector; Mark Schrauth, Dir. Salzmann Library; Marijo Zielinski, Librarian; Rev. David E. Windsor, C.M., Psy.D., Dir. Admissions. Priests 6; Seminarians 54; Administration & Faculty 10.

[B] SEMINARIES, RELIGIOUS OR SCHOLASTICATES

FRANKLIN. *Sacred Heart Seminary and School of Theology* aka SHSST, P.O. Box 429, Hales Corners, 53130-0429. Tel: 414-425-8300; Fax: 414-529-6999; Email: cmcatee@shsst.edu; Web: www.shsst.edu. 7335 S. Hwy. 100, Franklin, 53132. Revs. Thomas L. Knoebel, Ph.D., M.Div., Pres. & Rector, (Retired); Zbigniew Morawiec, S.C.J., Vice Rector & Vice Pres. Human and Spiritual Formation; James Walters, S.C.J., M.S., M.Div., Dir. Hispanic Studies & Asst. Prof. Pastoral Studies; Dr. Patrick J. Russell, Ph.D., Vice Pres. for Intellectual Formation & Chief Academic Officer; Dr. Jeremy Blackwood, Dir. Admissions & Asst. Prof. in Systematic Studies; Mr. Michael Erato, Dir. Plant Opers.; Ms. Jennifer Bartholomew, Dir. Library & Academic Support Svcs.; Dr. James Stroud, Asst. Prof. Moral Theology; Julie O'Connor, Registrar & Academic Planning Officer; Dr. Robert Gotcher, Ph.D., Coord. of Mission Effectiveness; John Olesnavage, Vice Pres. Pastoral Formation & Dir. Human Formation; Christopher Lambert, Vice Pres. Finance & Bus. Svcs.; Christopher McAtee, Vice Pres. Inst. Dev. & External Affairs. Religious Teachers 6; Lay Teachers 14; Priests 4; Students 166.

Full-Time Faculty: Revs. George Mangiaracina, O.C.D., S.L.D., Asst. Prof. Systematic Studies; Michael Udoekpo, S.T.L., Assoc. Prof. Scripture Studies; Deacon Steven L. Kramer, Dir. Homiletics; Asst. Prof. Pastoral Studies; Dir. Recruitment; Dr. John Gallam, Ph.D., Prof., Systematic Studies; Dr. Steven Shippee, Ph.D., Prof., Systematic Studies; Mr. Brian Lee, Asst. Prof. Scripture Studies; Mr. Dominic Fendt, Instructor ESL Prog.; Ms. Kathleen M. Harty, M.R., M.A.L.S., Resource & Educ. Svcs. Librarian; Ms. Kelly Kornacki, Dir. ESL Prog., Email: kkornacki@shsst.edu; Dr. Charles Ludwick, Dir. Liturgical Music & Organist, Email: cludwick@shsst.edu; Rev. James Walters, S.C.J., Dir. Hispanic Studies; Mr. Michael F. Brummond, Asst. Prof. Systematic Studies; Paul Monson, Asst. Prof. Church History; Rev. Vien Nguyen, S.C.J., Asst. Prof. Scripture Studies.

Xaverian Missionary Fathers College Seminary, 4500 Xavier Dr., Franklin, 53132-9066. Tel: 414-421-0831; Fax: 414-421-9108; Email: xavmissionswi@hotmail.com; Web: www.xaviermissionaries.org. Revs. Alejandro Rodriguez Gomez, S.X., Rector; Aniello Salicone, S.X., (Italy) Vicar; Dominic Caldognetto, S.X., (Italy) Asst. Treas.; Giuseppe Matteucig, S.X., Vocation/Mission Ministry; Edgar Ruiz Leon, Language Studies; Dharmawan Adharius, Graduate Degree Studies. Religious Teachers 1; Priests 6.

MOUNT CALVARY. *St. Lawrence Seminary High School*, 301 Church St., Mount Calvary, 53057. Tel: 920-753-7500; Fax: 920-753-7507; Email: frzoy@stlawrence.edu; Web: www.stlawrence.edu. Rev. Zoilo Garibay, O.F.M.Cap., Rector; Bro. David Schwab, O.F.M.Cap., Bus. Mgr.; Rev. Oliver Bambenek, O.F.M.Cap., Librarian; Bros. Neal Plale, O.F.M.Cap.; John Willger, O.F.M.Cap., Teacher; Mr. David Bartel, Academic Dean & Prin.; Mr. Timothy Schroeder, Business Mgr.; Mr. Kevin Buelow, Dean, Students; Bro. Mark Romanowski, O.F.M.Cap., Spiritual Direction; Rev. Madalai Muthu Savariappan, O.F.M.Cap., Spiritual Direction; Bro. Mitchell Frantz, O.F.M.Cap., Spiritual Direction Supvr.; Revs. Alphonse Pushparaj, Spiritual Direction; Biju Varghese, O.F.M.Cap., Spiritual Direction. High School Seminary and Ministry Program Brothers 5; Religious Teachers 4; Lay Teachers 19; Priests 5; Students 158; Total Staff 75; Non-Teaching Lay Staff 46.

[C] COLLEGES AND UNIVERSITIES

MILWAUKEE. *Alverno College*, 3400 S. 43rd St., P.O. Box 343922, 53234-3922. Tel: 414-382-6000; Fax: 414-382-6066; Email: president.ac@alverno.edu; Web: www.alverno.edu. Donald Layden, Chm., Bd. of Trustees; Sr. Andrea Lee, Pres.; Robin Hansen, Vice Pres., Fin. & Admin.; Scott Zeman, Vice Pres., Academic Affairs; Larry Duerr, Library Dir. Religious Teachers 3; Faculty 99; Sisters 7; Students 2,083.

Cardinal Stritch University (1937) 6801 N. Yates Rd., 53217. Tel: 414-410-4000; Fax: 414-410-8506; Email: president@stritch.edu; Email: kghohl@stritch.edu; Web: www.stritch.edu. Kathleen A. Rinehart, Pres.; Thomas J. Congdon, Sr. Exec. Vice Pres., Fin. & Admin.; Tonya Mantilla, Vice Pres., University Advancement; Tracy A. Fischer, Vice Pres., Student Affairs; Sean T. Lansing, Vice Pres., Mission Integration; Daniel J. Scholz, Ph.D., Vice Pres., Academic Affairs. Sisters of St. Francis of Assisi. Religious Teachers 1; Lay Teachers 86; Sisters 6; Students 2,355; Total Staff 202.

**Marquette University* (1881) Office of Mktg. & Comm., Zilber 235, P.O. Box 1881, 53201-1881. Tel: 414-288-7452; Fax: 414-288-7197; Email: stacy.tuchel@mu.edu; Web: www.marquette.edu. Conducted under the auspices of the Society of Jesus.

Marquette University Students 11,491; Total Staff 1,516; Total Faculty 1,217; Jesuit Priests 17; Women Religious 4; Non-Jesuit Catholic Clergy 4; Non-Catholic Clergy 4.

Major University Officers: Dr. Michael R. Lovell, Pres.; Joel Pogodzinski, Sr. Vice Pres. & COO; Steven Frieder, Asst. to the Pres. & Corp. Secy.; Ms. Cynthia M. Bauer, Vice Pres. & Gen. Counsel; Ms. Rana Altenburg, Vice Pres. Public Affairs; Xavier Cole, Vice Pres. Student Affairs; Timothy McMahon, Vice. Pres., University Advancement; Rev. Frederick P. Zagone, S.J., Acting Vice Pres., Mission & Ministry; Dr. Gary Meyer, Senior Vice Provost for Faculty Affairs; Dr. Jeanne M. Hossenlopp, Vice Pres. Research & Innovation; Mr. David Murphy, Vice Pres., Mktg. & Comm.; John Baworowsky, Vice Provost; Bill Scholl, Vice Pres. & Dir. Athletics; Lora Strigens, Vice Pres. Planning & Facilities Mgmt.; Dr. John Su, Vice Provost; Jennifer Watson, Vice Provost; Dr. Douglas Woods, Vice Provost & Dean, Grad. School; Mary Sue Callan-Farley, Dir. Campus Min.

Deans: Dr. Richard Holz, Dean Helen Way Klinger College of Arts & Sciences; Dr. Brian Till, Dean, College of Business Admin.; Dr. James Kimo Ah Yun, Dean J. William and Mary Diederich College of Communication; Dr. William K. Lobb, Dean School of Dentistry; Dr. William Henk, Dean College of Educ.; Dr. Kristina Ropella, Opus Dean, Opus College of Engineering; Dr. William Cullinan, Dean College of Health Sciences; Mrs. Janice Welburn, Dean Univ. Libraries; Mr. Joseph D. Kearney, Dean Law School; Dr. Janet Krejci, Dean, College of Nursing.

Mount Mary University (1913) 2900 N. Menomonee River Pkwy., 53222-4545. Tel: 414-930-3000; Fax: 414-930-3710; Email: mmu-president@mtmary.edu; Web: www.mtmary.edu.

Christine Pharr, Pres. School Sisters of Notre Dame. Lay Teachers 70; Sisters 7; Students 1,349; Total Staff 402.

FOND DU LAC. *Marian University, Inc.* (1936) 45 S. National Ave., Fond du Lac, 54935.
Tel: 920-923-7600; Fax: 920-923-8087; Email: admissions@marianuniversity.edu; Web: www.marianuniversity.edu. Dr. Andrew Manion, Pres.; Kathryn Johnston, Dir. Libraries; Russell K. Mayer, Vice Pres. Academic Affairs; Sr. Edie Crews, Campus Min. Religious Teachers 2; Lay Teachers 99; Sisters of the Congregation of St. Agnes 2; Students 1,822; Total Staff 244.

[D] HIGH SCHOOLS, ARCHDIOCESAN AND PAROCHIAL

MILWAUKEE. *Pius XI Catholic High School* (1929) 135 N. 76th St., 53213. Tel: 414-290-7000;
Fax: 414-290-7001; Email: areilly@piusxi.org; Web: www.piusxi.org. John Herbert, Pres.; Mark Ostap, Prin. Religious Teachers 1; Lay Teachers 64; School Sisters of St. Francis 2; Students 758.

St. Thomas More High School, 2601 E. Morgan Ave., 53207. Tel: 414-481-8370; Fax: 414-481-3382; Email: ljanick@tmore.org; Email: mcintoshm@tmore.org; Web: www.tmore.org. Mary McIntosh, Pres.; Nicholas Kelly, Prin. (Coed) Lay Teachers 39; Students 513.

BURLINGTON. *Catholic Central High School* (1925) 148 McHenry St., Burlington, 53105. Tel: 262-763-1510 ; Fax: 262-763-1509; Email: bscholz@cchsnet.org; Web: www.catholiccentralhs.org. Bonnie Scholz, Prin.; Theresa Phillips, Dean of Students; Tom Aldrich, Athletic Dir. Lay Teachers 21; Students 240.

WAUKESHA. **Catholic Memorial High School of Waukesha, Inc.* (1949) 601 E. College Ave., Waukesha, 53186-5538. Tel: 262-542-7101;
Fax: 262-542-1633; Email: dbembenek@catholicmemorial.net; Web: www.catholicmemorial.net. Mrs. Donna Bembenek, Pres. Religious Teachers 1; Lay Teachers 48; Students 665.

[E] HIGH SCHOOLS, PRIVATE

MILWAUKEE. *Divine Savior Holy Angels High School, Inc.* (Girls) 4257 N. 100th St., 53222.
Tel: 414-462-3742; Fax: 414-466-0590; Email: officeofthepresident@dsha.k12.wi.us; Email: czosneks@dsha.info; Email: konieczny@dsha.info; Web: www.dsha.info. Katherine Konieczny, Pres.; Dan Quesnell, Prin.; Maria-Christina Thiele, Librarian. Sponsored by the Sisters of the Divine Savior. Religious Teachers 1; Lay Teachers 56; Priests 1; Students 696.

St. Joan Antida High School, Inc. (Girls) 1341 N. Cass St., 53202. Tel: 414-272-8423;
Fax: 414-272-3135; Email: MCoryell@saintjoanantida.org; Email: ELingen@saintjoanantida.org; Web: www.saintjoanantida.org. Marikris Coryell, Pres.; Elizabeth Lingen, Prin.; Sue Kosiboski, Librarian. Lay Teachers 14; Sisters of Charity of St. Joan Antida 3; Students 165.

Marquette University High School (Boys). 3401 W. Wisconsin Ave., 53208. Tel: 414-933-7220; Email: ap@muhs.edu; Web: www.muhs.edu. Rev. Michael J. Marco, S.J., Pres.; Jeff Monday, Prin.; Ms. Ann O'Hara, Librarian; Paul Farrell, Pastoral Min./Coord. (See separate listing for resident information). Lay Teachers 132; Priests 2; Students 981.

RACINE. *St. Catherine's High School* (1864) 1200 Park Ave., Racine, 53403. Tel: 262-632-2785;
Fax: 262-632-5144; Email: sgeertsen@racinedominicans.org; Web: www.saintcats.org. Betty Hunt, Prin.; Mr. Russell Tillmann, Asst. Prin. Part of Siena Catholic Schools of Racine, Inc.
St. Catherine's High School Corporation
The elected leadership of the Congregation of St. Catherine of Siena (most commonly known as the Racine Dominicans) are the members of this corporation with reserved powers. Religious Teachers 1; Lay Teachers 43; Students 625.

WEST MILWAUKEE. *Cristo Rey Jesuit Milwaukee High School, Inc.*, 1215 S. 45th St., West Milwaukee, 53214. Tel: 414-436-4600; Fax: 414-645-0046; Email: mtalavera@cristoreymilwaukee.org; Email: astith@cristoreymilwaukee.org; Web: www.cristoreymilwaukee.org. Mr. Andrew Stith, Pres., Tel: 414-288-7375; Luke Harrison, Prin. Religious Teachers 1; Lay Teachers 25; Students 393.

WHITEFISH BAY. *Dominican High School* (1956) 120 E. Silver Spring Dr., Whitefish Bay, 53217.
Tel: 414-332-1170; Fax: 414-332-4101; Email: lgiese@dominicanhighschool.com; Web: dominicanhighschool.com. Leanne M. Giese, Pres.; Edward Foy, Prin.; Vincent A. Murray, Dean Students; Mr. Nate Friday, Campus Min. Sponsored by Sinsinawa Dominicans. Religious Teachers 4; Lay Teachers 32; Dominican Sisters of the Congregation of the Most Holy Rosary, Sinsinawa, WI 1; Students 350.

[F] ELEMENTARY SCHOOLS, PRIVATE

MILWAUKEE. *St. Coletta Day School of Milwaukee* (1956) (Grades 3-12), 1740 N. 55th St., 53208.
Tel: 414-453-1850; Fax: 414-453-9449; Email: scdsmke@gmail.com; Web: www.scdsmke.org. William A. Koehn, Prin. & Admin. For Exceptional Children. Lay Teachers 3; Students 30; Paraprofessionals 3.

Nativity Jesuit Academy, Inc., 1515 S. 29th St., 53215-1912. Tel: 414-645-1060; Fax: 414-645-0505; Email: info@njms.org; Email: businessoffice@njms.org; Web: www.nativityjesuit.org. Susan Smith, Pres.; Vanessa Solis, Prin.; Chris Banach, Vice Prin., Email: banachc@njms.org; John Meuler, Vice Prin.; Jonathon Nowak, Dir., Operations; Kyle Dlabay, Dir., Advancement; Alex Eichelberger, Dir., Finance; Bro. Matt Wooters, Spiritual Advisor/Care Svcs. Wisconsin Province of the Society of Jesus. Lay Teachers 19; Students 235.

Notre Dame School of Milwaukee, Inc. (1996) 1418 S. Layton Blvd., 53215. Tel: 414-671-3000;
Fax: 414-671-6138; Email: plandry@notredamemke.com; Web: www.notredamemke.com. Patrick Landry, Pres.; David D'Anfonio, Prin., Middle School; Itzel Galindo, Prin., Primary School. Sponsored by: School Sisters of Notre Dame. Lay Teachers 24; Sisters 3; Students 456.

[G] CONSOLIDATED ELEMENTARY SCHOOLS

MILWAUKEE. *All Saints Catholic East School System, Inc.*, (Grades PreK-8), 2461 N. Murray Ave., 53211.
Tel: 414-964-1770; Fax: 414-964-6578; Email: jjones@catholiceast.org; Email: hesteves@catholiceast.org; Web: catholiceast.org. Most Rev. Jeffrey R. Haines, Bd. Chm.; Jennifer Jones, Prin. Sponsored by the following Milwaukee parishes: Cathedral of St. John the Evangelist; Our Lady of Divine Providence; Old St. Mary's; Ss. Peter and Paul; Three Holy Women Catholic Parish, and is also part of Seton Catholic Schools. Lay Teachers 21; Students 263.

Holy Wisdom Academy (2002) 3344 S 16th St., 53215. c/o St. John Paul II Congregation, 3307 S. 10th, 53215-5039. Tel: 414-744-3695;
Fax: 414-744-2874; Email: jar.principal.hwa@gmail.com. Revs. Michael A. Ignaszak, Contact; Michael Wolfe; Mrs. Julie Ann Robinson, Prin. Sponsored by St. John Paul II, Milwaukee. Lay Teachers 16; Sisters 1; Students 237.

Northwest Catholic School Association Formerly St. Bernadette, St. Catherine of Alexandria, and Our Lady of Good Hope Schools. Lower Campus: 7140 N. 41st St., 53209. Rev. Gregory J. Greiten, Admin.; Michelle Paris, Prin., Prin. (Lower Campus). Lay Teachers 20; Students 229.

St. Thomas Aquinas Academy, 341 E. Norwich St., 53207. Tel: 414-744-1214; Fax: 414-744-8340; Email: hedingd@staamke.org; Web: thomasaquinasacademy.com. Rev. Carmelo Giuffre, Pastor Designate; Dan Heding, Prin. Sponsored by St. Augustine, St. Paul, St. Veronica & Immaculate Conception, Milwaukee; Nativity of the Lord, Cudahy, and Sacred Heart of Jesus, St. Francis.Seton Catholic Schools, Inc. provides administrative services for the school. Lay Teachers 16; Students 222.

KENOSHA. *All Saints Catholic School of Kenosha, Inc.*, (Grades PreK-8), 7400-39 Ave., Kenosha, 53142.
Tel: 262-925-4000; Fax: 262-925-0399; Email: info@allsaintskenosha.org; Web: www.allsaintskenosha.org. Daniel Jorgensen, Prin. Religious Teachers 1; Lay Teachers 47; Students 587.

MALONE. *Holyland Catholic School* (1969) (Grades PreK-8), N9290 County Rd. W, Malone, 53049.
Tel: 920-795-4222; Fax: 920-795-4126; Email: dre@archmil.org; Email: holylandcatholic@gmail.com; Web: Holylandcatholicschool.com. Rev. Gary Wegner, O.F.M.Cap., Pastor; Rick Erickson, Ph.D., Admin. Members: St. John the Baptist, Johnsburg; St. Mary, Marytown; St. Isidore Parish, Mount Calvary. Lay Teachers 8; Students 68.

SHEBOYGAN. *St. Elizabeth Ann Seton Catholic School, Inc.*, 814 Superior Ave., Sheboygan, 53081.
Tel: 920-452-1571; Fax: 920-208-4371; Email: info@sheboyganseton.org; Web: www.sheboyganseton.org. Dr. Stephanie Nardi, Prin. School is supported by Holy Name of Jesus, St. Clement, and St. Dominic parishes, Sheboygan. Lay Teachers 9; Students 195; Total Staff 15.

WAUKESHA. *Waukesha Catholic School System, Inc.* (1990) (Grades PreK-8), 221 S. Hartwell Ave., Waukesha, 53186. Tel: 262-896-2929;
Fax: 262-896-2934; Email: lkovaleski@waukeshacatholic.org; Web: www.waukeshacatholic.org. Ms. Lisa Kovaleski, Prin.; Rev. Howard G. Haase, Pastor Liaison, Tel: 262-542-2589. Members: St. Joseph, St. Mary, St. John Neumann, St. William. Lay Teachers 33; Students 470.

WAUWATOSA. *Wauwatosa Catholic School*, (Grades PreK-8), 1500 Wauwatosa Ave., Wauwatosa, 53213. Tel: 414-258-9977; Email: businessmgr@wauwatosacatholic.org; Web: www.wauwatosacatholic.org. Lori Suarez, Prin. Lay Teachers 16; Students 209.

WEST ALLIS. *Mary Queen of Saints Catholic Academy* aka A Seton Catholic School (2004) (Grades PreK-8), 1435 S. 92nd St., West Allis, 53214.
Tel: 414-476-0751; Fax: 414-259-9285; Email: floodc@mqscateacher.org; Web: mqsca.org. Rev. Jeffery A. Prasser, Priest Designate. Sponsored by St. Florian, West Milwaukee; Holy Assumption, Mother of Perpetual Help, St. Augustine & St. Rita, West Allis. Lay Teachers 16; Students 214; Full-time Lay Teachers 1.

[H] SCHOOL SYSTEMS

MILWAUKEE. *Messmer Catholic Schools, Inc.*, 742 W. Capitol Dr., 53206. Jim Piatt, Pres.; Mike Bartels, Vice Pres. Religious Teachers 6; Lay Teachers 102; Elementary School Students 832; High School Students 598; Total Students 1,430.

**Messmer High School* (1926) 742 W. Capitol Dr., 53206. Tel: 414-264-5440; Fax: 414-264-0672; Email: generalinfo@messmerschools.org; Web: www.messmerschools.org. Jim Piatt, Pres.; Mike Bartels, Vice Pres.; Andrew Muszytowski, Assoc. Prin. Lay Teachers 59; Students 727.

Messmer Saint Mary (1999) 3027 N. Fratney St., 53212. Tel: 414-264-6070; Fax: 414-264-6430; Email: generalinfo@messmerschools.org; Web: www.messmerschools.org. Kendra Kuhnmuench, Prin. Lay Teachers 25; Students 435.

Messmer Saint Rose, 514 N. 31st St., 53208.
Tel: 414-933-6070; Fax: 414-933-3071; Email: generalinfo@messmerschools.org; Web: www.messmerschools.org. Kristin Merry, Prin. Lay Teachers 25; Students 460.

FOND DU LAC. *St. Mary's Springs Academy of Fond du Lac, WI*, (Grades PreK-12), Admin. Office: 255 County Rd. K, Fond du Lac, 54937.
Tel: 920-924-0993;
Tel: 920-921-4870, Ext. 8009 (Business Office);
Fax: 920-922-7849; Email: knett@smsacademy.org; Web: www.smsacademy.org. Kelly Norton, Pres.; Sharon Hoepfner, Librarian. Lay Teachers 67; Total Enrollment 886; High School Students 291; Elementary School Students 595.

Pre-School & Elementary, (Grades PreK-5), 255 County Rd. K, Fond du Lac, 54937.
Tel: 920-921-4870; Fax: 920-921-5908. Erin Flood, System Prin.; Steven Kelnhofer, Assoc. Prin. (PreK-5). Lay Teachers 35; Students 594.

Middle School & High School, (Grades 6-12), 255 County Rd. K, Fond du Lac, 54937.
Tel: 920-921-4870; Fax: 920-921-2786; Email: eflood@smsacademy.org. Erin Flood, System Prin.; Michael Kaszuba, Assoc. Prin. (6-12); Steven Kelnhofer, Assoc. Prin. (PreK-5). Lay Teachers 20; Students 288.

KENOSHA. *St. Joseph Catholic Academy, Inc.*, (Grades PreK-12), Upper Campus (6-12): 2401 69th St., Kenosha, 53143. Tel: 262-654-8651;
Fax: 262-654-1615; Email: rfreund@sjcawi.org; Web: www.sjcawi.org. Mr. Robert Freund, Pres., High School Prin.; Ms. Kerstin Santarelli, Prin., Elementary/Preschool; Matthew Rizzo, Prin., Middle School; Rev. Todd Belardi, Campus Min. & Chap. Lay Teachers 63; Priests 1; Sisters 1; Students 713; H.S. Students 255; Elem. Students 458.

RACINE. *Siena Catholic Schools of Racine, Inc.* (2017) 1200 Park Ave., Racine, 53403.

ST. FRANCIS. *Seton Catholic Schools, Inc.*, 3501 S. Lake Dr., St. Francis, 53235. Tel: 414-831-8400; Email: ddrees@setoncatholicschools.org; Web: www.setoncatholicschools.com. Donald Drees, Pres.; Cathy Cramer, CFO; Dr. Bill Hughes, Ph.D., Chief Academic Officer. Religious Teachers 160; Lay Teachers 226; Students 2,878.

[I] CHILD CARE CENTERS

MILWAUKEE. *St. Joseph Academy* (1999) (Grades PreK-8), 1600 W. Oklahoma Ave., 53215.
Tel: 414-645-5337; Fax: 414-935-6181; Email: tjones@sjamilwaukee.org; Email: sbrendan@sjamilwaukee.org; Web: www.sjamilwaukee.org. Tabia Jones, Pres.; Scott Hanson, Prin.; Sr. Mary Brendan Bogdan, C.S.S.F., Dir.; Julia Lazacki, Librarian & Media Specialist. Sponsored by the Congregation of the Sisters of St. Felix of Cantalice of the North American Province, Inc. (Felician Sisters). Children 88; Religious Teachers 5; Lay Teachers 52; Felician Sisters 5; Students 468.
Mission/Outreach: Sisters Mary Brendan Bogdan, C.S.S.F.; Mary Camille Bena, C.S.S.F., Receptionist; Mary Rosalie Disterhaft, C.S.S.F.,

Educational Tutor; Michelle Marie Konieczny, C.S.S.F., C.R.E.

SOUTH MILWAUKEE. *Franciscan Villa Child Day Center*, 3601 S. Chicago Ave., South Milwaukee, 53172. Tel: 414-570-5410; Fax: 414-764-0706; Email: ssuehring@chilivingcomm.org; Web: www.homeishere.org. Stacy Suehring, Dir. Part of Catholic Health Initiatives Living Communities. Children 57; Lay Teachers 11; Total Staff 12.

[J] GENERAL HOSPITALS

MILWAUKEE. *Ascension St. Francis Hospital, Inc.* (1946) 3237 S. 16th St., 53215. Tel: 414-647-5000; Fax: 414-647-5565; Email: timothy.waldoch@ascension.org; Web: healthcare.ascension.org. Travis Andersen, Regl. Pres., South Region; Deacon Timothy Waldoch, Chief Mission Integration Officer; Antonina Olszewski, Dir., Spiritual Svcs. Sponsored by Ascension Health Ministries (Ascension Sponsor), a public juridic person.

Formerly Wheaton Franciscan Healthcare - St. Francis, Inc. Bed Capacity 166; Tot Asst. Annually 16,852; Total Staff 741.

Ascension SE Wisconsin Hospital, Inc. (1927) St. Joseph Campus: 5000 W. Chambers St., 53210. Tel: 414-447-2000; Fax: 414-874-4393; Email: timothy.waldoch@ascension.org; Web: healthcare.ascension.org. Travis Andersen, Pres.; Deacon Timothy Waldoch, Chief Mission Integration Officer; Antonina Olszewski, Spiritual Care Dir. Sponsored by Ascension Health Ministries (Ascension Sponsor), a public juridic person.

Formerly Wheaton Franciscan, Inc. Bed Capacity 565; Tot Asst. Annually 32,195; Total Staff 1,576.

St. Joseph Campus, 5000 W. Chambers St., 53210. Tel: 414-447-2000; Email: timothy.waldoch@ascension.org. Elizabeth Ritter, Admin. Bed Capacity 420; Tot Asst. Annually 14,394; Total Staff 748.

Elmbrook Campus, 19333 W. North Ave., Brookfield, 53045. Tel: 262-785-2000; Fax: 262-785-2485; Email: timothy.waldoch@ascension.org. Sponsored by Ascension Health Ministries (Ascension Sponsor), a public juridic person. Bed Capacity 108; Tot Asst. Annually 10,177; Total Staff 472.

**Franklin Campus*, 10101 S. 27th St., Franklin, 53132. Tel; 414-325-8640; Fax: 414-325-4511; Email: karla.ashenhurst@ascension.org; Web: healthcare.ascension.org. Sponsored by Ascension Health Ministries (Ascension Sponsor) a public juridic person. Bed Capacity 44; Tot Asst. Annually 7,430; Total Staff 359.

Columbia St. Mary's Hospital Milwaukee, Inc. dba Ascension Columbia St. Mary's Hospital Milwaukee (1859) 2320 N. Lake Dr., 53211. Tel: 414-291-1000; Email: timothy.waldoch@ascension.org; Web: healthcare.ascension.org/. Travis Andersen, Regl. Pres., South Region; Deacon Timothy Waldoch, Chief Mission Integration Officer; Antonina Olszewski, Dir., Spiritual Svcs. Sponsored by Ascension Health Ministries (Ascension Sponsor) a public juridic person. Bed Capacity 308; Tot Asst. Annually 26,073; Total Staff 2,232.

Ministry Health Care, Inc. (1984) 400 W. River Woods Pkwy., Glendale, 53212. Tel: 414-465-3000; Fax: 414-465-3021; Email: timothy.waldoch@ascension.org; Web: healthcare.ascension.org/. Bernie Sherry, CEO; Deacon Timothy Waldoch, Chief Mission Integration Officer; Antonina Olszewski, Dir., Spiritual Svcs. Sponsored by Ascension Health Ministries (Ascension Sponsor), a public juridic person.

FOND DU LAC. *Agnesian Health Care, Inc.* dba St. Agnes Hospital, 430 E. Division St., Fond du Lac, 54935. Tel: 920-929-2300; Fax: 920-926-4306; Email: Steven.Little@ssmhealth.com; Email: Damond.Boatwright@ssmhealth.com; Web: www.agnesian.com. 10101 Woodfield Ln., St. Louis, MO 63132. Mr. Steven Little, Pres. & CEO. Bed Capacity 146; Sisters 4; Tot Asst. Annually 781,231; Total Staff 2,629.

MEQUON. *Columbia St. Mary's Hospital Ozaukee, Inc.* dba Ascension Columbia St. Mary's Hospital Ozaukee (1995) 13111 N. Port Washington Rd., Mequon, 53097-2416. Tel: 262-243-7300; Fax: 262-243-7416; Email: timothy.waldoch@ascension.org; Web: healthcare.ascension.org/. Travis Andersen, Regl. Pres., South Region; Deacon Timothy Waldoch, Chief Mission Integration Officer; Antonina Olszewski, Dir., Spiritual Svcs. Sponsored by Ascension Health Ministries (Ascension Sponsor) a public juridic person. Bed Capacity 120; Tot Asst. Annually 12,501; Total Staff 726.

RACINE. *Ascension All Saints Hospital, Inc.* (1974) 3801 Spring St., Racine, 53405. Tel: 262-687-4011; Fax: 262-687-8039; Email: timothy.waldoch@ascension.org; Web: healthcare.ascension.org. Travis Andersen, Regl. Pres., South Region; Deacon Timothy Waldoch, Chief Mission Integration Officer; Antonina Olszewski, Dir., Spiritual Svcs. Sponsored by Ascension Health Ministries (Ascension Sponsor), a public juridic person.

Formerly Wheaton Franciscan Healthcare - All Saints, Inc. Bed Capacity 571; Tot Asst. Annually 33,256; Total Staff 1,808.

SHEBOYGAN. *St. Nicholas Hospital* dba Prevea Health (1890) 3100 Superior Ave., Sheboygan, 53081. Tel: (920) 459-8300; Email: mary.salm@hshs.org; Email: Mark.Repenshek@hshs.org; Web: www.stnicholashospital.org. Justin Selle, Pres.; Mary Salm, Div. Dir. Spiritual Care; Mark Repenshek, Exec.

St. Nicholas Hospital of the Hospital Sisters of the Third Order of St. Francis. Bassinets 5; Bed Capacity 185; Tot Asst. Annually 79,677; Total Staff 424.

WAUPUN. *Waupun Memorial Hospital, Inc.*, 620 W. Brown St., Waupun, 53963. Tel: 920-324-5581; Fax: 920-324-2085; Email: Damond.Boatwright@ssmhealth.com; Web: www.agnesian.com. 10101 Woodfield Ln., St. Louis, MO 63132. Deann Thurmer, COO. Corporate Title: Waupun Memorial Hospital, Inc. Bed Capacity 25; Tot Asst. Annually 62,952; Total Staff 277.

[K] SPECIAL HOSPITALS AND SANATORIA

MILWAUKEE. *Sacred Heart Rehabilitation Institute, Inc.* dba Ascension Sacred Heart Rehabilitation Hospital (1955) Tel: 414-585-6750; Email: timothy.waldoch@ascension.org; Web: healthcare.ascension.org/. Travis Andersen, Regl. Pres., South Region; Deacon Timothy Waldoch, Chief Mission Integration Officer; Antonina Olszewski, Dir., Spiritual Svcs. Sponsored by Ascension Health Ministries (Ascension Sponsor), a juridic person. Bed Capacity 49; Tot Asst. Annually 420; Total Staff 63.

[L] PROTECTIVE INSTITUTIONS

MILWAUKEE. *St. Charles Youth and Family Services, Inc.* (1920) 151 S. 84th St., 53214. Tel: 414-476-3710; Fax: 414-778-5985; Email: scarpenter@stcharlesinc.org; Web: www.stcharlesinc.org. Ms. Cathy Connolly, Pres. Bed Capacity 45; Residents 136; Tot Asst. Annually 1,000; Total Staff 150.

Daystar, Inc., P.O. Box 2130, 53201-2130. Tel: 414-385-0334; Fax: 414-385-0336; Email: director@daystarinc.org; Web: www.daystarinc.org. Vicki Lipinski, Exec. Dir. Transitional living program for victims of domestic violence without children, for up to two years. Bed Capacity 10; Residents 10; Tot Asst. Annually 25; Total Staff 6.

MOUNT CALVARY. *Cristo Rey Ranch, Inc.*, 998 Calvary St., Mount Calvary, 53057. Tel: 920-753-1055; Tel: 920-753-3211; Fax: 920-753-3100; Email: boddenw@yahoo.com; Email: nunbetterfarm@hotmail.com. Sr. Stephen Bloesl, Prin. Sister Servants of Christ the KingProvides weekend respite services to families caring for emotionally/behaviorally challenged children and adolescents. Program emphasis on pet therapy. Some day and evening programs thru County Social Services Department. Bed Capacity 4; Tot Asst. Annually 12; Total Staff 1.

WAUWATOSA. *Carmelite Ministry of St. Teresa* (1917) 1214 Kavanaugh Pl., Wauwatosa, 53213. Tel: 414-258-4791; Email: carmeldcjnorth@gmail.com. Sisters Maria Goretti, D.C.J., Admin.; M. Rose Therese, Treas. Mission: to provide a Carmelite-inspired formation program for independent female adults with intellectual and developmental disabilities where they can live and mature in their physical, emotional, social and spiritual lives. Residents 15; Carmelite Sisters D.C.J. 4; Total Staff 2.

[M] HOMES FOR AGED AND NURSING HOMES

MILWAUKEE. *Alexian Village of Milwaukee, Inc.* (1980) 9301 N. 76th St., 53223. Tel: 414-355-9300; Fax; 414-357-5106; Email: Andrea.Ohman@ascension.org; Web: www.ascenionseniorliving.org. Andrea Ohman, CEO; Rev. Joel Szydlowski, O.F.M., Chap. Congregation of Alexian Brothers, Immaculate Conception ProvinceContinuing Care Retirement Community. Residents 491; Tot Asst. Annually 930; Total Staff 330; Units 457.

St. Ann Rest Home, 2020 S. Muskego Ave., 53204-3522. Tel: 414-383-2630; Fax: 414-383-0305; Email: srandrea@stannrh.org; Web: www.stannrh.org. Sr. Andrea K. Andrzejewska, Admin. Conducted by Dominican Sisters Immaculate Conception Province.

Dominican Sisters d/b/a St. Ann Rest Home. Bed Capacity 50; Residents 50; Sisters 7; Tot Asst. Annually 76; Total Staff 59.

St. Anne's Home for the Elderly, Milwaukee, Inc. aka St. Anne's Salvatorian Campus, 3800 N. 92nd St., 53222-2589. Tel: 414-463-7570; Fax: 414-463-2311; Email: lvogt@stannescampus.org; Email: ckinney@stannescampus.org; Web: www.stannessc.org. Ms. Lynn Vogt, Admin.; Revs. Arturo Ysmael, S.D.S., Dir. of Pastoral; Alan Wagner, S.D.S. Sisters of the Divine Savior. Total Staff 215; Nursing Home 50; Assisted Living Apartments 124.

**Milwaukee Catholic Home*, 2462 N. Prospect Ave., 53211-4462. Tel: 414-224-9700; Fax: 414-224-1666; Email: info@milwaukeecatholichome.org; Web: milwaukeecatholichome.org. David Fulcher, Exec. Dir.; Mr. Robert Frediani, Vice Pres. Corporate Title: Milwaukee Catholic Home, Inc. Tot Asst. Annually 381; Retirement Home Residents 120; Retirement Home Total Staff 67; Nursing Home Residents 122; Nursing Home Total Staff 200; Assisted Living 24.

Villa St. Francis, Inc. (1990) 1910 W. Ohio Ave., 53215. Tel: 414-649-2888; Fax: 414-649-2880; Email: tloduca@villastfrancis.org; Web: www.villastfrancis.org. Tony LoDuca, Pres. & CEO; Sisters Barbara Marie Brylka, C.S.S.F., Spiritual Care Svcs.; Mary Lorraine Vukovich, C.S.S.F., Accounting Assoc.; Mary Roberta Moser, C.S.S.F., Mission Integration; Susan Holbach, C.S.S.F., Receptionist. Sponsored by the Congregation of the Sisters of St. Felix of Cantalice of the North American Province, Inc. (Felician Sisters)Assisted Living Facility for the Elderly Bed Capacity 134; Felician Sisters 4; Tot Asst. Annually 160; Total Staff 51; Resident Apartments 129.

**Ascension Living-St. Francis Place* (1994) 3200 S. 20th St., 53215. Tel: 414-389-3200; Fax: 414-389-3300; Email: cynthia.gutschow@ascension.org. Vivian G. Dorn, Vice Pres. Opers., NHA; Ann Varner, Vice Pres., Mission Integration. Ascension Health Senior Care-Skilled Nursing Facility for Transitional & Extended Subacute Care. Bed Capacity 81; Patients Asst Anual. 497; Total Staff 90.

FOND DU LAC. *St. Francis Home* (1978) 33 Everett St., Fond du Lac, 54935. Tel: 920-923-7980; Fax: 920-923-7995; Email: douglas.trost@ssmhealth.com; Email: Damond.Boatwright@ssmhealth.com; Email: janel.konkel@ssmhealth.com. Douglas Trost, Pres. & CEO; Janel Konkel, Dir. A member of SSM Healthcare of WI. Bed Capacity 107; Sisters 2; Tot Asst. Annually 142; Total Staff 253.

St. Clare Terrace (1991) Tel: 920-923-7996; Fax: 920-923-7995. Residents 30; Total Staff 3; Independent Elderly Apartments 30.

St. Francis Terrace (1998) Tel: 920-923-7980; Fax: 920-923-7995. Residents 52; Total Staff 46; Assisted Living Units 55.

GREENFIELD. *Clement Manor Health Center*, 3939 S. 92nd St., Greenfield, 53228. Tel: 414-321-1800; Fax: 414-546-7357; Email: info@clementmanor.com; Web: www.clementmanor.com. Mr. Dennis Ferger, Pres. & CEO. Sponsored by School Sisters of St. Francis.Corporate Title: Clement Manor, Inc. A skilled care and transitional rehab care facility and Adult Day Care services. Residents 105; Tot Asst. Annually 200; Adult Day Care 45.

KENOSHA. *St. Joseph's Home and Rehabilitation Center*, 9244 29th Ave., Kenosha, 53143. Tel: 262-925-8125; Tel: 262-925-8102; Tel: 262-925-8104; Fax: 262-697-2065; Fax: 262-925-8131; Fax: 262-925-8137; Email: asi@stjosephshome.org; Email: donna@stjosephshome.org; Email: susie@stjosephshome.org; Web: stjosephshome.org. Sr. Mary Emmanuel Apanites, D.C.J., Admin.; Rev. Anthony Thundathil. Corporate Title: Carmelite Sisters of the Divine Heart of Jesus; St. Joseph's Villa, Independent Living Apts. Bed Capacity 73; Residents 52; Sisters 3; Tot Asst. Annually 52; Total Staff 95; Apartments 40.

MOUNT CALVARY. *Villa Loretto Nursing Home*, N8114 County WW, Mount Calvary, 53057. Tel: 920-753-3211; Fax: 920-753-3100; Email: jenna.floberg@ssmhealth.com; Web: agnesian.com. 10101 Woodfield Ln., St Louis, MO 63132. Douglas Trost, Pres. & CEO; Jenna Floberg, Dir. Corporate Title: Sister Servants of Christ the King, Inc. dba Villa Loretto. Member of SSM Healthcare of WI. Bed Capacity 50; Tot Asst. Annually 85; Total Staff 82; Sisters in Residence 4.

Villa Rosa, Inc., N8120 County WW, Mount Calvary, 53057. Tel: 920-753-3015; Fax: 920-753-2508; Email: jenna.floberg@ssmhealth.com; Web: agnesian.com. 10101 Woodfield Ln., St Louis, MO 63132. Douglas Trost, Pres. & CEO; Jenna Floberg, Dir. A member of SSM Healthcare of WI. Bed Capacity 20; Tot Asst. Annually 23; Total Staff 11.

RACINE. *Marian Housing Center, Inc.* (1985) 4105 Spring St., Racine, 53405. Tel: 262-633-5807; Fax: 262-633-9780; Tel: 303-830-3300; Email: mrankin@mercyhousing.org; Web: www.

mercyhousing.org. Melissa Clayton, Contact Person. Residents 40; Total Staff 3; Units 40.

St. Monica's Senior Living, 3920 N. Green Bay Rd., Racine, 53404. Tel: 262-639-5050; Fax: 262-639-5673; Email: lbaxter@stmonicasseniorliving.com; Web: www.stmonicasseniorliving.com. Loretta Baxter, R.N., M.B.A., Admin. Nonprofit Corp. Bed Capacity 110; Residents 117; Sisters of St. Rita 5; Tot Asst. Annually 148; Total Staff 110.

SOUTH MILWAUKEE. *Franciscan Villa of South Milwaukee, Inc.* (1966) 3601 S. Chicago Ave., South Milwaukee, 53172. Tel: 414-764-4100; Fax: 414-570-5301; Email: mgulock@chilivingcomm.org; Web: www.homeishere.org. Michael Gulock, Exec.; Jennifer Rowinski, Admin.; Ryan O'Rourke, Chap. Skilled Nursing and Assisted Living.; CHI Living Communities, a subsidiary of Catholic Health Initiatives Residents 150; Skilled Nursing Beds 150; Total Staff 250.

WAUWATOSA. *St. Camillus Health Center, Inc.*, 10101 W. Wisconsin Ave., Wauwatosa, 53226. Tel: 414-258-1814; Fax: 414-259-4987; Email: pedrotramontin@yahoo.com.br; Web: www.stcam.com. Very Rev. Pedro Tramontin, M.I.; Kevin Schwab, CEO; Revs. Leandro Blanco, M.I., Counselor; Agustin R. Orosa, M.I., Prov. Asst.; Brandon Luke, Admin. Ministers of the Sick (Order of St. Camillus)Skilled Nursing Home, Assisted Living, Home Care & Hospice. Bed Capacity 66; Patients Asst Anual. 150; Total Staff 225.

[N] PERSONAL PRELATURES

BROOKFIELD. *Prelature of the Holy Cross and Opus Dei Layton Study Center*, 12900 W. North Ave., Brookfield, 53005. Tel: 262-784-1523; Fax: 262-782-5183; Email: info@opusdei.org. Revs. Eduardo J. Castillo; John C. Kubeck.

[O] MONASTERIES AND RESIDENCES FOR PRIESTS AND BROTHERS

MILWAUKEE. *Alexian Brothers Community* (1980) Immaculate Conception Province 8000 Limerick Rd., 55223-1072. Bro. John Howard, C.F.A., Dir.

Arrupe House Jesuit Community, 831 N. 13th St., 53233-1706. Tel: 414-288-5855; Fax: 414-288-5852; Email: mwalsh@jesuits.org. Revs. Thomas G. Boedy, S.J.; Walter E. Boehme, S.J.; Patrick J. Burns, S.J.; Frederick E. Brenk, S.J.; Joseph B. Coelho; Robert M. Doran, S.J.; D. Thomas Hughson, S.J.; William T. Johnson, S.J.; James Dixon; Eugene F. Merz, S.J.; Robert F. O'Connor, S.J.; Philip J. Rossi, S.J.; Thomas P. Sweetser, S.J.; Matthew S. Walsh, S.J.; Michael Coffey, S.J.; Michael R. Kolb, S.J.; Philip Sutherland, S.J. Society of Jesus, Wisconsin Prov. Priests 16.

St. Conrad Friary, 3138 N. 2nd St., 53212. Tel: 414-372-3620; Email: kent-bauer@att.net. Bro. Kent Bauer, O.F.M.Cap., Admin.; Rev. Arlen Harris, O.F.M.Cap., Dir.; Bro. David Hirt, O.F.M.Cap., Dir.; Rev. Richard Hart, O.F.M.Cap., M.A., Local Vicar; Bro. Carl Schaefer, O.F.M.Cap.; Revs. Niles J. Kauffman, O.F.M.Cap., M.A.; Roche Gaspar, O.F.M.Cap. Capuchin Friars, Province of St. Joseph. Brothers 5; Priests 4; Total in Residence 9.

Jesuit Community at Marquette University, 1345 W. Wells St., 53233-1714. Tel: 414-288-5000; Fax: 414-288-1758; Email: Obrien.Jesuits@Marquette.edu; Web: www.marquette.edu/jesres. Revs. Michael J. Marco, S.J., Pres.; Robert A. Wild, S.J., Chancellor; Frederick P. Zagone, S.J., Vice Pres.; Joseph G. Mueller, S.J., Rector; James P. Flaherty, S.J.; Thomas S. Anderson, S.J.; Kent A. Beausoleil, S.J.; Ronald Bieganowski, S.J.; Grant S. Garinger, S.J.; John A. Schwantes, S.J.; Jeffrey T. LaBelle, S.J.; John D. Laurance, S.J.; Frank A. Majka, S.J.; Timothy Manatt, S.J.; D. Edward Mathie, S.J.; Donald R. Matthys, S.J.; T. Michael McNulty, S.J.; Thomas E. Schwarz, S.J.; Mr. Stephen J. Molvarec, S.J.; Revs. Nicholas Santos, S.J.; David G. Schultenover, S.J.; John S. Thiede, S.J.; Andrew J. Thon, S.J.; Michael J. Zeps, S.J.; William Blazek, S.J.; Christopher J. Krall, S.J.; Michael Maher, S.J.; Aaron Pidel, S.J.; James Bretzke, S.J.; Ryan Duns, S.J.; Tomas Garcia-Huidobo, S.J. Marquette Jesuit Associates, Inc. Priests 31; Scholastics 1.

Pallotti House, 5424 W. Bluemound Rd., 53208. Tel: 414-258-0653; Fax: 414-258-9314; Email: pallotti.milw@pallottines.org; Web: www.pallottines.org. Very Rev. Joseph Koyickal, S.A.C., Prov. Supr.; Revs. Joseph Dominic, S.A.C.; Davies Edassery, S.A.C., St. Lawrence & Resurrection, Hartford; Jose Eluvathingal, S.A.C., (India) Catholic Charities, Racine; Florent Kanga, S.A.C., (Cameroon) Chaplain-Froedtert Hospital; Sergio Lizama, S.A.C., St. Charles Borromeo, Burlington; Leon J. Martin, S.A.C., Vocation Promoter & Formation Dir., Pius XI HS Chaplain, Milwaukee; Bruce J. Schute, S.A.C.; Gregory P. Serwa, S.A.C.; Steven K. Varghese, S.A.C., St. Joseph & St. John Nepocene, Racine; Bro. James Scarpace, S.A.C., Consultor & Admin. of Pallotti House; Revs. Christudasan Kurisadima, S.A.C.; Thomas Manjaly, S.A.C. Residence of Fathers and Brothers and Offices of Mother of God Province of the Society of the Catholic Apostolate also, Provincial House. Brothers 1; Priests 18.

Serving Outside the Archdiocese of Milwaukee: Revs. George P. Nellikunnel, S.A.C., (India) St. John Vianney Parish, Sherman IL; James Palakudy, S.A.C., Holy Cross Parish, Auburn, IL; Joy A. Thachil, S.A.C., San Ramon Parish, Lubbock, TX.

Pere Marquette Jesuit Community, 726 N. 34th. St., 53208-3301. Tel: 414-342-7503; Email: rabert@jesuits.org. Revs. Richard P. Abert, S.J., Supr.; Brad Held, S. J., Treas.; Josemiguel Jaramillo; Robert J. Kroll, S.J.; Bros. Kenneth A. Homan, S.J.; Matthew Wooters; Mr. Thomas A. Bambrick, S.J. Society of Jesus, Wisconsin Province. Brothers 2; Priests 4; Scholastics 1.

Provincial Office - Discalced Carmelites (1947) 1233 S. 45th St., 53214-3693. Tel: 414-672-7212; Email: juderjp@gmail.com; Web: www.ocdwashprov.com. Sr. Beth Lyman, S.S.S.F., Prov. Admin. Asst. Brothers 22; Deacons 3; Novices 5; Postulants 8; Priests 45.

Discalced Carmelite Friars, Sacred Heart Monastery, 1233 S. 45th St., 53214. Fax: 414-645-7785; Email: wasj-prov.6@gmail.com. Rev. Ernest Unverdorben, O.C.D., Prior; Bro. Charles Gamen, O.C.D., (Kenya); Revs. Thomas Ochieng' Otang'a, O.C.D., (Kenya); Fred Alexander, O.C.D. Brothers 1; Priests 3.

Serving Abroad: Revs. Arnold Boehme, O.C.D., Supr., Iloilo City, Philippines; Dennis Geng, O.C.D., Treas., Nairobi, Kenya; Thomas Martin, O.C.D., Formation Team, Davao City, Philippines; Alan J. Rieger, O.C.D., Local Supr., Davao City, Philippines.

Priests of the Province Not Otherwise Listed: Revs. Daniel Chowning, O.C.D., 5th Gen. Definitor, Rome, Italy; Reginald Foster, O.C.D., Latinist, 3553 S. 41st St., #403, 53221. Milwaukee, WI; Eugene C. Wehner, O.C.D.; Francis Miller, O.C.D., (Retired); Kieran Kavanaugh, O.C.D., (Retired); Bros. Gilbert Tovares, O.C.D., (Retired); Martin Murphy, O.C.D., (Retired), Milwaukee, WI; Bonaventure Potter, O.C.D., (Retired), Milwaukee, WI; Sebastian Reale, O.C.D., Biddeford, ME.

Salvatorian Provincial Offices, 1735 N. Hi-Mount Blvd., 53208-1720. Tel: 414-258-1735; Fax: 414-258-1934; Email: sds@salvatorians.com; Web: salvatorians.com. Society of the Divine Savior.

Provincialate: Very Rev. Joseph C. Rodrigues, S.D.S., Prov.; Revs. John Tigatiga, S.D.S., Dir.; Peter Schuessler, S.D.S., M.A., Vicar Prov. & Dir. Formation; Scott Wallenfelsz, S.D.S., M.B.A., Consultor; Douglas Bailey, S.D.S., Consultor; Bro. Sean McLaughlin, S.D.S., M.A., Consultor.

Priests/Brothers at Residences Not Listed Elsewhere: Revs. Bruce Clanton, S.D.S., P.O. Box 574, Racine, 53401-0574. Tel: 262-880-5047; Arturo Ysmael, S.D.S.; Joe Jagodensky, S.D.S.; Robert Marsicek, S.D.S., (Retired); John Vianney Muweesi, S.D.S.; Neil Durham, S.D.S., (Retired).

Priests of the USA Province serving at the Generalate in Rome, Italy: Rev. Raul Gomez Ruiz, S.D.S., Ph.D., Gen. Sec.

Priests and Brothers Residing Outside the Archdiocese of Milwaukee: Revs. David Bergner, S.D.S., Youngstown; Thomas Bielawa, S.D.S., Venice; Keith Brennan, S.D.S., (Retired), Tucson; Michael Burns, S.D.S., Indianapolis; Peter Coffey, S.D.S., (Retired), Brooklyn; Richard Driscoll, S.D.S., Venice; Gary New, S.D.S., Birmingham; Michael Newman, S.D.S., (Retired), Sacramento; William Remmel, S.D.S., Tucson; Joseph Wambach, S.D.S., Phoenix; David Cooney, S.D.S., Nashville.; Chad Puthoff, S.D.S., Nashville.; William Kelly, S.D.S., Birmingham.; Very Rev. Jeffrey Wocken, S.D.S., M.A., Tucson; Rev. Joseph Lubrano, S.D.S., Birmingham.; Bros. Robert Broeg, S.D.S., Portland; Ervan Digman, S.D.S., Madison; Rev. Thomas Perrin, S.D.S., Birmingham.; Bro. Kilian Harrington, S.D.S., St. Cloud; Revs. Roman Mueller, S.D.S., Sacramento.; Salvatore Ragusa, S.D.S., Oakland.; John Pantuso, S.D.S., Tucson.; Thomas Tureman, S.D.S., Tucson.; Bros. Jeffrey St. George, S.D.S., Tucson.; George Maufort, S.D.S., Bismarck; Rev. Julian Guzman, S.D.S., NYC.; Bro. Roger Nelson, S.D.S., WDC; Revs. Richard Maloney, S.D.S., St. Petersburg.; Eliot Nitz, S.D.S., Washington, DC.; Patrick Nelson, S.D.S., Greenbay.; Roman Stadtmueller, S.D.S., Wilmington.; Glen Wilis, S, D,S., Washington, DC.; Michael Neeland, S.D.S.

Holy Apostles House of Formation, 1735 N. Hi Mount Blvd., 53208-1720. Tel: 414-258-1735; Email: sds@salvatorians.com. 937 N. 37th St., Milwauke, 53208-3104. Revs. Paul Portland, S.D.S., Dir. Candidates; James Weyker, S.D.S.; Bro. Van Todd, S.D.S.

Salvatorians - Jordan Hall, 7979 W. Glenbrook Rd., 53223-1055. Tel: 414-357-5152; Email: johau4@aol.com. Revs. Hugh G. Birdsall, S.D.S., M.A., M.S., 7100 W. Old Loomis Rd., Greendale, 53129-2761. Tel: 414-427-8352; Alan Wagner, S.D.S.; Dennis D. Thiessen, S.D.S., M.A., M.Div.; Michael Hoffman, S.D.S.; Michael Shay, S.D.S.; Robert Wicht, S.D.S.; Thomas Novak, S.D.S., (Retired); Loren Nys, S.D.S.; Andre Papineau, S.D.S., M.A.; Glen Sayers, S.D.S.; Donald Loskot, S.D.S.; Bros. George Armstrong, S.D.S., (Retired); Paul Bauer, S.D.S., (Retired); Peter Farnesi, S.D.S., (Retired); Regis Fust, S.D.S.; Edward Havlovic, S.D.S., (Retired); John Hauenstein, S.D.S., Coord.; Marvin Kluesner, S.D.S.; Joseph Kreutzer, S.D.S.; Thomas Meyer, S.D.S. Fathers & Brothers of the Society of the Divine Savior. Brothers 11; Priests 13.

St. Vincent Community, 145 S. 76th St., 53214. Tel: 414-476-2447; Email: leonjmartin@gmail.com; Web: www.pallottines.org. Revs. Leon J. Martin, S.A.C., Rector, Formation Dir. & Pius XI High School Chap.; Richard J. Lorenz, S.A.C. Priests 2.

BENET LAKE. *St. Benedict's Abbey* (1945) 12605 224th Ave., Benet Lake, 53102-1000. Tel: 262-396-4311; Fax: 262-396-4365; Email: patrick@conception.edu; Web: www.BenetLake.org. Very Rev. Patrick Caveglia, O.S.B., Prior; Rt. Rev. Edmund Boyce, O.S.B., Abbot. Brothers 1; Priests 2.

BURLINGTON. *Queen of Peace Friary*, 2281 Browns Lake Dr., Burlington, 53105. Tel: 262-763-3241; Fax: 262-763-3326; Email: paulreczek@aol.com. Revs. Thomas Wojciechowski, O.F.M., Guardian; Sante De Angelis, O.F.M.; Stan Janowski, O.F.M.; Linus E. Kopczewski, O.F.M.; James Krasman, O.F.M.; Ponciano Macabalo, O.F.M.; Vianney Sipulski, O.F.M.; DePaul Sobotka, O.F.M.; Melvin Wierzbicki, O.F.M.; Raymond Zsolczai; Bros. David Dodge, O.F.M.; Gregory Havel, O.F.M.; Michael May, O.F.M.; Joseph Krymkowski, O.F.M.; David Typek, O.F.M.; Revs. Bede Hepnar, O.F.M.; Myron Lowisz, O.F.M.; Bro. Joseph Molinari, O.F.M. Franciscan Friars of the Assumption B.V.M. Province.Retirement Home for Franciscan Friars Brothers 4; Priests 9.

EAST TROY. *Divine Word Missionaries* (1875) P.O. Box 107, East Troy, 53120-0107. Tel: 262-642-3300; Fax: 262-642-7754; Email: stanuroda@gmail.com. Revs. Stanley Uroda, S.V.D., Rector; Lucien Gaudreault, S.V.D.; Vincent Ohlinger, S.V.D.; Edward Peklo, S.V.D.; Walter Ostrowski, S.V.D.; Bros. Kevin Diederich, S.V.D.; Bernard Scherger, S.V.D. Society of the Divine Word. Brothers 2; Priests 5; Total in Residence 7.

FRANKLIN. *Dehon House* (1993) 10731 W. Rawson Ave., Franklin, 53132. Tel: 414-425-3768; Email: provsec@usprovince.org. Rev. William Pitcavage, S.C.J., Local Supr.; Bro. Matthew Miles, S.C.J. Priests of the Sacred Heart. Brothers 1; Priests 1.

Francis and Clare Friary (2002) 9230 W. Highland Park Ave., Franklin, 53132. Tel: 414-525-9253; Fax: 414-525-9289; Email: province@ofm-abvm.org; Web: www.franciscan-friars.org. *Provincial Offices of the Franciscan Friars, Assumption BVM Province, Inc.* (2002) Tel: 414-525-9253; Fax: 414-525-9289; Email: province@ofm-abvm.org; Web: www.franciscan-friars.org. Revs. James Gannon, O.F.M., Prov.; John Cella, O.F.M., J.C.D., M.Div., M.B.A., Dir., Franciscan Pilgrimage Programs, Inc. & Guardian; Carl Graczyk, O.F.M., Chap., St. Ann Rest House; Stephen E. Malkiewicz, O.F.M., M.A., Faculty, Sacred Heart Seminary, Hales Corner; Bro. Andrew J. Brophy, O.F.M., M.Ed., Sec. of the Province & Prov. Brusar; Revs. Leonard Stunek, O.F.M., Chap. Clement Manor; Joel Szydlowski, O.F.M., Chap.; Bro. Justin Kwietniewski, O.F.M., Chap.; Revs. Stan Janowski, O.F.M., Chap.; Jason Welle, O.F.M., Missionary; Bro. Didacus Weber, O.F.M., Office Asst.; Revs. Gregory Plata, O.F.M.; John Puodziunas, O.F.M.; William Stout, O.F.M. Brothers 3; Priests 11.

Priests of the Province serving abroad: Rev. Laurian Janicki, O.F.M., Missionary, Elgise de Saints Martyrs, Rue El Imam Ali, Marakkech-Gueliz, Morocco.

St. Francis Residence (1985) 12001 W. Woods Rd., Franklin, 53132. Tel: 414-425-6910; Email: provsec@usprovince.org. Revs. Dominic Peluse, S.C.J., Local Supr.; Charles Brown, S.C.J., Ph.D.; Bro. Andrew Lewandowski, S.C.J. Brothers 1; Priests 2.

St. Joseph's at Monastery Lake (1979) 7330 S. Lovers Lane Rd., Franklin, 53132-1849. Tel: 414-525-2457; Email: provsec@usprovince.org. Revs. Joseph Thien Dinh, S.C.J., D.Min., Supr.; Edward Kilianski, S.C.J., Prov.; Terence Langley, S.C.J.; Bros. Raymond Kozuch, S.C.J.; Frank Presto, S.C.J.,

M.B.A.; Revs. Vien Nguyen, S.C.J.; Joseph Quang Tran, S.C.J. Priests of the Sacred Heart. Brothers 2; Priests 6.

Sacred Heart at Monastery Lake (1989) 7330 S. Lovers Lane Rd., Franklin, 53132.
Tel: 414-425-5968; Tel: 414-425-5981;
Fax: 414-425-0268; Email: provtreas@usprovince.org; Web: www.sacredheartusa.org. Revs. Quang Nguyen, S.C.J., Ph.D., Local Supr.; James D. Brackin, S.C.J., M.Div., J.D.; Paul Casper, S.C.J.; Thomas Cassidy, S.C.J.; John Czyzynski, S.C.J., S.T.L., S.S.L.; Jan de Jong, S.C.J., S.T.D., S.T.L.; Mark Fortner, S.C.J., Ph.D.; Edward Griesemer, S.C.J.; John Klingler, S.C.J.; Anthony P. Russo, S.C.J.; James Schifano, S.C.J; James Schroeder, S.C.J., Ph.D.; Thomas Westhoven, S.C.J.; Charles Wonch, S.C.J.; Bros. Peter Mankins, S.C.J.; Brian Tompkins, S.C.J.; Leonard Zaworski, S.C.J.; Deacon David Nagel, S.C.J.; Revs. Gary Lantz, S.C,J.; Wayne Jenkins, S.C.J.; James Walters, S.C.J.; Nicholas Brown, S.J.C., (Retired); Bro. Clay Diaz, (Retired). Brothers 6; Deacons 1; Priests 18.

Attached to the Community But Living Elsewhere: Rev. Robert Naglich, S.C.J.; Bro. John Monek, S.C.J.

Sacred Heart at Monastery Lake, Inc., 7330 & 7350 S. Lovers Lane Rd., Franklin, 53132.
Tel: 414-425-3383; Email: provtreas@usprovince.org. Deacon David Nagel, S.C.J., Treas.

FRANKSVILLE. *Sacred Heart Novitiate*, 8409 3 Mile Rd., Franksville, 53126.

HALES CORNERS. *Priests of the Sacred Heart* (1933) 7373 S. Lovers Lane Rd., P.O. Box 289, Hales Corners, 53130-0289. Tel: 414-425-6910;
Fax: 414-425-2938; Email: provsec@usprovince.org; Web: www.sacredheartusa.org. Rev. Edward Kilianski, S.C.J., Prov. Supr.; Bro. Frank Presto, S.C.J., M.B.A., Prov. Sec.; Rev. Quang Nguyen, S.C.J., Ph.D., Vice Pres.; Deacon David Nagel, S.C.J., Dir. Missions and Prov. Treas.

Attached to the Province but Living Elsewhere: Rev. Bryan Benoit, S.C.J., P.O. Box 220, Dittmer, MO 63023. Tel: 636-285-1733.

Sacred Heart Monastery (1929) 7335 S. Lovers Ln. Rd., P.O. Box 566, Hales Corners, 53130.
Tel: 414-425-8300; Fax: 414-529-6988; Email: provsec@usprovince.org; Web: www.sacredheartusa.org. Bro. Duane Lemke, S.C.J., Admin.; Revs. Zbigniew Morawiec, S.C.J., Vice Pres.; Yvon Sheehy, S.C.J.; Edward Zemlik, S.C.J.; Robert Tucker, S.C.J.; Diego Diaz; Phong Hoang; Bro. Long Nguyen, S.C.J. Brothers 2; Priests 4; Scholastics 3.

HUBERTUS. *Basilica and National Shrine of Mary, Help of Christians at Holy Hill* (Shrine 1863) (Carmelite Friars 1906) Mailing Address: 1525 Carmel Rd., Hubertus, 53033. Tel: 262-628-1838;
Fax: 262-628-4294; Email: dabrickocd@aol.com; Email: rmitchell@holyhill.com; Web: www.holyhill.com. Revs. Jude Peters, O.C.D., Prov.; Donald Brick, O.C.D., Prior; Bonaventure Lussier, O.C.D., Sec.; Bro. Peter Mwabishi, O.C.D., Treas.; Revs. Celedonio Martinez Daimiel, O.C.D.; Cyril Guise, O.C.D., Dir. Devel.; Phillip Thomas, O.C.D., Novice Master; George Mangiaracina, O.C.D., S.L.D.; Michael-Joseph Paris, O.C.D.; John Grennon, O.C.D.; Elijah Martin, O.C.D.; Bros. Emmanuel Burke, O.C.D.; Vincent Deming, O.C.D., Novice; Joey Chee, Novice

Legal Title: Discalced Carmelite Friars of Holy Hill, Inc. Brothers 4; Priests 10. *Retreat Center*, 1525 Carmel Rd., Hubertus, 53033.
Tel: 262-628-1838, Ext. 127; Fax: 262-628-4294; Email: guesthouse@holyhill.com; Web: www.holyhill.com. Rev. Donald Brick, O.C.D., Prior
Discalced Carmelite Friars of Holy Hill, Inc.

MOUNT CALVARY. *St. Felix Friary*, N8477 County Rd. WW, Mount Calvary, 53057. Tel: 920-753-3111; Email: froliver@stlawrence.edu. Revs. Lester Bach, O.F.M.Cap.; Oliver Bambenek, O.F.M.Cap.; Ken Smits, O.F.M.Cap.; Adrian Staehler, O.F.M.Cap.; Michael Zuelke, O.F.M.Cap.; Bros. Leopold Gleissner, O.F.M.Cap.; Raymond Meier, O.F.M.Cap.; Isidore Herriges, O.F.M.Cap. Priests 5.

St. Lawrence Friary (1856) 301 Church St., Mount Calvary, 53057. Tel: 920-753-7550;
Fax: 920-753-7507; Email: brdave@stlawrence.edu; Email: brdaveschwab@juno.com; Web: stlawrence.edu. Revs. John Holly, O.F.M.Cap, Rector, Pres. & Teacher; Paul Craig, O.F.M.Cap.; Jerome Higgins, O.F.M.Cap., M.Ed., M.A.S., D.Min., (Retired); Elroy Pesch, O.F.M.Cap., (Retired); Zoilo Garibay, O.F.M.Cap., Rector; Bro. Mark Romanowski, O.F.M.Cap., Supvr.; Revs. Kenan Siegel, O.F.M.Cap., (Retired); Joachim Strupp, O.F.M.Cap., (Retired); Gary Wegner, O.F.M.Cap., Teacher & Pastor, St. Isidore the Farmer, Mt. Calvary; Larry Abler, O.F.M.Cap., Assisting Priest, St. Isidore the Farmer, Mt. Calvary; Bros. John Willger, O.F.M.Cap., Teacher; Jerome Campbell, O.F.M.Cap., Maintenance Personnel; Neal Plale, O.F.M.Cap., Teacher & Business Mgr.; David Schwab, O.F.M.Cap., Local Min.; Mitchell Frantz, O.F.M.Cap., Supvr.; Revs. Madalai Muthu, O.F.M.Cap., Teacher and Supvr.; Ed Hagman; Joseph Mattathil, O.F.M.Cap., Pastoral Assoc.; Alphonse Pushparaj, Teacher & Suprv.; Biju Varghese, O.F.M.Cap. Brothers 6; Priests 14.

RACINE. *Augustinian Novitiate*, 4339 Douglas Ave., Racine, 53402-2956. Tel: 262-681-3221;
Fax: 262-639-3602; Email: jdposa5@aol.com. Revs. Jerome G. Knies, O.S.A., Prior; James D. Paradis, O.S.A., Novice Dir.; James Wenzel, O.S.A.; Frederick H. Taggart, O.S.A., Treas.; Richard T. O'Leary, O.S.A., Pastor; William Donnelly, O.S.A., Pastoral Assoc. Novices 6; Priests 5.

TWIN LAKES. *La Salette Missionaries* (1967) 10330 336th Ave., P. O. Box 777, Twin Lakes, 53181.
Tel: 262-877-3111; Email: glebanowskit@aol.com; Web: www.lasaletteshrine.org. Revs. Andrew Zagorski, M.S., Dir.; Peter Stangricki, M.S., Assoc. Dir.; Bros. Anthony Sepanik, M.S., Music Min.; Adam Mateja, M.S. Brothers 2; Priests 1.

WAUWATOSA. *St. Camillus Community House*, 10233 W. Wisconsin Ave., Wauwatosa, 53226.
Tel: 414-481-3696; Email: pedrotramontin@yahoo.com.br. 10101 W. Wisconsin Ave., Wauwatosa, 53226. Very Rev. Pedro Tramontin, M.I., Pres.; Revs. Leandro Blanco, M.I., Treas.; Agustin R. Orosa, M.I., Prov. Asst.; Joseph L. Bisoffi, M.I.; Stephen Braddock, M.I.; John Gallagher, M.I.; Louis Lussier, M.I.; Very Rev. Richard O'Donnell, M.I.; Revs. Peter C. Opara, M.I.; Mathai Naveen Pallurathil, M.I.; Albert Schempp, M.I.; Jung Seo, M.I.; Bro. Mario Crivello, M.I. Brothers 1; Priests 12; Total in Residence 13.

St. Camillus Jesuit Community, 10201 W. Wisconsin Ave., Wauwatosa, 53226-3541. Tel: 414-259-6399;
Fax: 414-259-8614; Email: tmbrennan@jesuits.org; Email: dleonhardt@jesuits.org. Revs. Burnell B. Bisbee, S.J.; Thaddeus J. Burch, S.J.; Louis E. Busemeyer, S.J.; Thomas A. Caldwell, S.J.; Anthony L. Dagelen, S.J.; J. Patrick Donnelly, S.J.; Philip F. Dreckman, S.J.; Eugene M. Dutkiewicz, S.J.; Joseph F. Eagan, S.J.; Robert L. Faricy, S.J.; James E. Fitzgerald, S.J.; David H. Gau, S.J.; Gerald E. Goetz, S.J.; Jonathan Haschka, S.J., Supr.; John A. Hennessy, S.J.; Theodore J. Hottinger, S.J.; Theodore M. Kalamaja, S.J.; William J. Kelly, S.J.; William J. Kidd, S.J.; James J. King, S.J.; Michael D. Kurimay, S.J.; Douglas J. Leonhardt, S.J., Supr.; Jeffrey R. Loebl, S.J.; Patrick L. Murphy, S.J.; James J. O'Leary, S.J.; Joseph N. Pershe, S.J.; Nicholas F. Pope, S.J.; James H. Ryan, S.J.; Thomas N. Schloemer, S.J.; Paul B. Steinmetz, S.J.; James B. Warosh, S.J.; M. John Wymelenberg, S.J.; Kenneth J. Herian, S.J.; Terrence M. Brennan, S.J.; Patrick J. McAteer, S.J.; Francis A. Prokes, S.J.; Bro. Edward C. Gill, S.J.; Revs. Donald F. Rowe, S.J.; George R. Sullivan, S.J.; Joseph Bracken, S.J.; William Gerut; Revs. Leon Klimczyk, S.J.; William S. Kurz, S.J.; Richard Murphy, S.J.; Donald Rauscher, S.J.; Lawrence Reuter, S.J.; Bros. Robert Smith, S.J.; Michael Wilmot, S.J.; Revs. Kevin Kersten, S.J.; Charles L. Stang, S.J.; Edward Sthokal, S.J. Society of Jesus, Wisconsin Province. Brothers 3; Priests 48.

WEST ALLIS. *Missionary Congregation of the Blessed Sacrament, Inc., Zion Province*, 695 College Ave., South Milwaukee, 53172. Tel: 262-225-3357; Email: kaippallymcbs@gmail.com. Revs. Joseph Pradeep Sebastian, M.C.B.S., Contact Person; Jose Edapparakal Mathai, M.C.B.S., Business Mgr.; Joseph Chelakunnel, M.C.B.S., Member; Abraham Karott George, M.C.B.S., Member; Shibi Devasia Kattikulakattu, M.C.B.S., 126 Fort Couch Rd., Pittsburgh, PA 15241; Sebastian Madathummuriyil, M.C.B.S., Member; Jeeson Venattu Stephan, M.C.B.S., Member; Thomas Vathappallil, M.C.B.S., Member; Stephen Kanippillil, M.C.B.S.; Dominic Thomas, M.C.B.S.; Binu Sebastian, M.C.B.S.; Tijo Naduviledom, M.C.B.S. Priests 3.

[P] CONVENTS AND RESIDENCES FOR SISTERS

MILWAUKEE. *St. Clare Convent*, 3276 S. 16th St., 53215. Tel: 414-647-2437; Email: smverona@feliciansisters.org; Web: www.feliciansistersna.org. Sisters Susan Holbach, C.S.S.F.; Mary Roberta Moser, C.S.S.F., Local Minister. Felician Sisters. Sisters 3.

Dominican Sisters of the Perpetual Rosary (1897) 3980 W. Kimberly Ave., Greenfield, 53221.
Tel: 414-322-9744; Fax: 414-763-1768; Email: mjoannahastings@gmail.com; Web: www.dsopr.org. Sr. Joanna Hastings, O.P., Prioress. Cloistered Dominican Sisters of the Perpetual Rosary. Sisters 5.

St. Francis Convent, 3170 S. 17th St., 53215.
Tel: 414-643-6387; Email: mmkonieczny@feliciansisters.org. Sisters Michelle Marie Konieczny, C.S.S.F., Local Min.; Barbara Marie Brylka, C.S.S.F.; Mary Brendan Bogdan, C.S.S.F. Felician Sisters. Sisters 3.

School Sisters of St. Francis (1874) 1501 S. Layton Blvd., 53215. Tel: 414-808-3779;
Fax: 414-944-6060; Email: generalate@sssf.org; Web: www.sssf.org. Sisters Mary Diez, O.S.F., Pres.; Tresa Abraham Kizhakeparambil, 1st Vice Pres.; Barbara Kraemer, O.S.F., 2nd Vice Pres.; Lucy Kalapurackel, 3rd Vice Pres.; Catherine Ryan, O.S.F., Treas.

School Sisters of St. Francis, Inc. Sisters 683; Sisters Resident in Archdiocese of Milwaukee 259.

Mercedes Molina - Instituto Santa Mariana de Jesus, 1234 N. 24th Pl., 53205. Tel: 414-210-4700; Email: milwaukeemarianitas94@gmail.com. Sisters Gloria Piedad Garzon, Supr.; Maria del Carmen de Anda, R.M., Sec. Corporate Title: Mercedes Molina, Inc. Sisters 2.

Sacred Heart, 1545 S. Layton Blvd., 53215.
Tel: 414-383-9038; Fax: 414-647-4888; Email: ckelling@sssf.org; Web: www.sssf.org/unitedstates/sacredheart/htm. Cathleen Kelling, Exec. Dir.; Sr. Marcian Swanson, Facility Dir. Sponsored by the School Sisters of St. FrancisRetirement community providing independent, assisted living and skilled care svcs. for the School Sisters of St. Francis. Sisters 85.

San Damiano Convent (2000) 3159 S. 17th St., 53215. Tel: 414-489-9195; Fax: 414-483-5861; Email: smramona@fs-inc.net. Sr. Mary Ramona Dombrowski, C.S.S.F., Local Min. Sisters 2.

Sisters of Charity of St. Joan Antida Convent (Presentation), 1329 N. Cass St., 53202.
Tel: 414-276-4173; Email: present@scsja.org. Sr. Elizabeth A. Weber, S.C.S.J.A., Supr. Sisters 6.

Sisters of Charity of St. Joan Antida Convent (St. Charles Community), 3214 W. Parnell Ave., 53221.
Tel: 414-282-9627; Email: srmonica@scsja.org. Sr. Monica Fumo, S.C.S.J.A., Supr. Sisters 5.

Sisters of Charity of St. Joan Antida Regina Mundi Provincial House and Novitiate, 8560 N. 76th Pl., 53223. Tel: 414-354-9233; Fax: 414-355-6463; Email: sisters@scsja.org. Sr. Theresa Rozga, S.C.S.J.A., Prov. Sisters 6; Total in Community 23.

Sisters of the Divine Savior (1888) 4311 N. 100th St., 53222-1393. Tel: 414-466-0810; Fax: 414-466-4335; Email: admin-offmgr@salvatoriansisters.org; Web: sistersofthedivinesavior.org. Sisters Beverly Heitke, S.D.S., Prov.; Nelda Hernandez, S.D.S., Vicaress; Ellen Sinclair, S.D.S., Treas. Provincial Administration Sisters 44.

Provincial Team: Sisters Beverly Heitke, S.D.S., Prov. Leader; Ellen Sinclair, S.D.S., Vicaress & Treas.; Nelda Hernandez, S.D.S., Prov. Sec. Corporate Title: Sisters of the Divine Savior, Inc.

Salvatorian Sisters Residence (2001) 3810 N. 92nd St., 53222-2504. Tel: 414-760-7900;
Fax: 414-358-9906; Email: honishsds@att.net. Sr. Virginia Honish, S.D.S., Coord.

Sisters of the Sorrowful Mother, 7050 N. Braeburn Ln., 53209. Tel: 414-357-8940; Email: pegg@ssmfinance.org. 8858 N. 60 St., Brown Deer, 53223. Sr. Lois Bush, Contact Person. Sisters 2.

Sisters of the Sorrowful Mother, 444 W. Bradley, 53217. Tel: 414-357-8940; Email: pegg@ssmfinance.org. 8858 N. 60 St., Brown Deer, 53223. Sr. Lois Bush, Contact Person. Sisters 2.

United States Province, 1515 S. Layton Blvd., 53215.
Tel: 414-384-1515; Fax: 414-384-1950; Email: info@sssf.org; Web: www.sssf.org. Sisters Carol Rigali, O.S.F., Prov.; Marilyn Ketteler, O.S.F., Prov. Asst.; Deborah Fumagalli, O.S.F., Prov. Asst. School Sisters of St. FrancisCorporate Title: The School Sisters of St. Francis of St. Joseph's Convent, Milwaukee, Wisconsin, Inc. Sisters 713; Total in U.S. Province 378.

BURLINGTON. *Misioneras Franciscanas de la Juventud, Inc.*, 456 Kendall St., Burlington, 53105.
Tel: 414-502-0957; Email: pglg@yahoo.com. Sr. Lilia G. Paredes, M.F.J., Contact Person. Sisters 2.

Missionary Sisters of the Holy Family, 31144 Hunters Tr., Burlington, 53105. Tel: 262-514-2076; Email: barbarakacka@yahoo.com. Sr. Joanna Barbara Kacka, M.S.F., Supr. Sisters 5.

CEDAR GROVE. *Sacred Heart of the Lake Chalet*, 6378 Sauk Tr., Box 46A, Cedar Grove, 53013.
Tel: 262-285-5019; Tel: 920-652-0653; Email: smchristopher@feliciansisters.org. Sr. Mary Christopher Moore, C.S.S.F., Provincial Min. Recreation Home for Felician Sisters of Our Lady of Hope Province. Sisters 511.

DELAVAN. *Villa Celine*, 3127 S. Shore Dr., Delavan, 53115. Tel: 773-792-6363; Email: svawanzek@gmail.com. 7260 W. Peterson Ave., E-216, Chicago, IL 60631. Sr. Virginia Ann Wanzek, C.R., Prov. Supr. Summer Rest Home for Sisters of the Resurrection.

ELM GROVE. *Notre Dame of Elm Grove*, 13105 Watertown Plank Rd., Elm Grove, 53122-2291.
Tel: 262-782-1450; Fax: 262-782-2349; Email: drussart@ssndcp.org; Web: www.ssndcp.org. Mr.

Robert Frediani, Admin.; Dana Russart, Contact Person. The School Sisters of Notre Dame of the Central Pacific Province.S.S.N.D. Assisted Care, Independent Living. Total in Residence 105.

FOND DU LAC. *Nazareth Center-Nazareth Court* (1998) 375 Gillett St., Fond du Lac, 54935.
Tel: 920-923-7993; Fax: 920-926-6200; Email: janel.konkel@ssmhealth.com. Janel Konkel, Admin. Retirement Home of the Congregation of Sisters of St. Agnes.Retirement Home of the Congregation of Sisters of St. Agnes Sisters 49.

St. Agnes Convent (1858) Motherhouse 320 County Rd. K, Fond du Lac, 54937-8158. Tel: 920-907-2300 ; Fax: 920-923-3194; Email: jsteffes@csasisters.org; Web: www.csasisters.org. Sr. Jean Steffes, C.S.A., Gen. Supr.

Congregation of Sisters of St. Agnes of Fond du Lac, Wisconsin, Inc. Sisters 29; Total in Community 189.

MOUNT CALVARY. *Loretto Convent*, N8114 County WW, Mount Calvary, 53057. Tel: 920-753-1055;
Fax: 920-753-3100; Email: boddenw@yahoo.com; Web: www.cristoreyranch.org. Sr. Stephen Bloesl, Pres. General Motherhouse of Sister-Servants of Christ the King; Corporate Title: Congregation of Sister Servants of Christ the King, Inc. Sisters 4.

OCONOMOWOC. *St. Joseph Convent*, 2653 N. Mill Rd., Oconomowoc, 53066. Tel: 262-646-2707; Email: smchristopher@feliciansisters.org. Sr. Mary Christopher Moore, C.S.S.F., Prov. Sponsored by the Congregation of the Sisters of St. Felix of Cantalice of the United States of America, Inc.

PEWAUKEE. *Carmel of the Mother of God* (1940) W267 N2517 Carmelite Rd., Pewaukee, 53072-4528.
Tel: 262-691-0336; Fax: 262-695-0143; Email: pewaukeecarmel@aol.com; Web: www.pewaukeecarmel.com. Sr. Mary Agnes Kramer, O.C.D., Prioress; Rev. Dennis C. Klemme, J.C.D., Chap., (Retired). Discalced Carmelite Nuns of Milwaukee. Professed Sisters 6.

RACINE. *Convent of St. Catherine of Siena* (1903) 5635 Erie St., Racine, 53402-1900. Tel: 262-639-4100;
Fax: 262-639-9702; Email: sgeertsen@racinedominicans.org; Email: mmcmahon@racinedominicans.org; Web: www.racinedominicans.org. Sisters Maryann A. McMahon, O.P., Pres.; Kathleen Slesar, O.P., 1st Vice Pres.; Lisa Kane, O.P., 2nd Vice Pres. Motherhouse of the Sisters of St. Dominic (Congregation of St. Catherine of Siena).

Corporate Title: Sisters of St. Dominic Sisters 111.

Siena Center, 5635 Erie St., Racine, 53402-1900.
Tel: 262-639-4100; Fax: 262-639-9702; Email: sgeertsen@racinedominicans.org; Web: www.racinedominicans.org. Sisters Maryann A. McMahon, O.P., Pres.; Agnes Johnson. Sisters in Archdiocese 104; Total Religious in Community 123.

St. Rita's Convent, 4014 N. Green Bay Rd., Racine, 53404. Tel: 262-639-1766; Fax: 262-639-5673; Email: sr.angelica@sbcglobal.net; Web: sistersofstrita.org. Sr. Angelica Summer, O.S.A., Supr. Sisters 3.

ST. FRANCIS. *St. Francis Convent, Motherhouse of the Sisters of St. Francis of Assisi* (1849) 3221 S. Lake Dr., St. Francis, 53235-3702. Tel: 414-744-1160;
Fax: 414-744-7193; Email: administration@lakeosfs.org; Email: tergerson@lakeosfs.org; Web: www.lakeosfs.org. Sisters Diana De Bruin, O.S.F., Dir. of the Congregation; Marcia Lunz, O.S.F., Assoc. Dir.; Sylvia Anne Sheldon, O.S.F., Assoc. Dir. Corporate Title: The Sisters of St. Francis of Assisi, Milwaukee, Wis.

Corporate Title: The Sisters of St. Francis of Assisi, Milwaukee, Wis.

The Sisters of St. Francis of Assisi, Inc., The Ongoing Community Support Trust of the Sisters of St. Francis of Assisi, St. Francis Convent, Inc. Sisters 168.

WAUWATOSA. *Provincial Motherhouse of the Carmelite Sisters of the Divine Heart of Jesus* (1891) 1230 Kavanaugh Pl., Wauwatosa, 53213.
Tel: 414-453-4040; Fax: 414-453-5603; Email: carmeldcjnorth@gmail.com; Email: srrosetherese.stjo@gmail.com; Web: www.carmelitedcjnorth.org. Sisters M. Immaculata Osterhaus, D.C.J., Supr.; Maria Giuseppe, Prov. Corporate Title: Carmelite Sisters of the Divine Heart of Jesus, Milwaukee, Wisconsin. Sisters 11; Total Staff 138; Total Religious in Province 26; Total Assisted 140.

[Q] HERMITAGES

SLINGER. *Carmelite Hermit of the Trinity - CHT* (1982) 4270 Cedar Creek Rd., Slinger, 53086-9372. Email: jmjose3@frontier.net; Web: www.carmelitehermit.homestead.com. Rev. James M. Tambornino, S.O.L.T.; Sr. Joseph Marie, C.H.T., Foundress & Admin. Priests 1; Hermit Sisters (Professed) 1.

[R] RETREAT HOUSES

MILWAUKEE. *Casa Romero Renewal Center, Inc.* (2001) 423 W. Bruce St., 53204. Tel: 414-224-7564; Email: mcoffey@casaromerocenter.org; Web: www.casaromerocenter.org. Office: 1501 S. Layton Blvd. Ste. 221, 53215. Mr. Michael Coffey, Exec.; Rev. David M. Shields, S.J., Chap.

BENET LAKE. *St. Benedict's Retreat Center* (1945) 12605 224th Ave., Benet Lake, 53102-1000.
Tel: 262-396-4311; Fax: 262-396-4365; Email: benetlakeretreatcenter@gmail.com; Web: www.benetlake.org. Rev. Phillip Schoofs, Dir.; Tracie Young, Dir.

BRISTOL. *Mercy Retreat Center*, 12009 221st Ave., Bristol, 53104. Tel: 262-862-6648; Email: mvalenti@mercywmw.org. Sr. Margaret Brennan, R.S.M., Contact Person, Tel: 630-365-0828. Sisters of Mercy of the Americas West Midwest Community.

CUDAHY. *The Dwelling Place* (1986) 5839 S. Indiana Ave., Cudahy, 53110. Tel: 414-483-3062; Email: occam77@gmail.com. Mary Klotz, Team Member. Priests 1; Total in Residence 1; Total Staff 2.

ELKHORN. *St. Vincent Pallotti Center* Pallottine Fathers & Brothers, Inc. N. 6409 Bowers Rd., Elkhorn, 53121. Tel: 262-723-2108; Email: retreat@pallottines.org; Web: www.pallottines.org. Rev. John R. Scheer, S.A.C., Retreat Center Admin. Retreat and Christian Formation Center Lay Staff 2; Priests 1.

OCONOMOWOC. *The Redemptorist Retreat Center*, 1800 N. Timber Trail Ln., Oconomowoc, 53066-4897.
Tel: 262-567-6900; Fax: 262-567-0134; Email: sristow@redemptoristretreat.org; Web: www.redemptoristretreat.org. Rev. Edward Vella, C.Ss.R., Supr.; Bro. Gerard Patin, C.Ss.R., Dir.; Revs. Charles Beierwaltes, C.Ss.R.; Richard Mevissen, C.Ss.R.; Edward F. Monroe, C.Ss.R.; Richard Schiblin, C,Ss.R.; James White, C.Ss.R.; Bro. Michael Rhodes, C.Ss.R. Brothers 2; Priests 6; Total in Residence 8.

RACINE. *Siena Retreat Center, Inc.*, 5637 Erie St., Racine, 53402-1900. Tel: 262-898-2590;
Fax: 262-898-7332; Email: retreats@racinedominicans.org; Web: sienaretreatcenter.org. Claire Anderson, Contact Person.

WAUKESHA. *Schoenstatt Retreat Center*, W284 N698 Cherry Ln., Waukesha, 53188-9402.
Tel: 262-522-4300; Fax: 262-522-4301; Email: intlcenter@schsrsmary.org; Web: www.schoenstattwisconsin.org. Sr. M. Catherine Ditto, Dir. Sisters 14; Total Staff 2.

[S] SECULAR INSTITUTES

MILWAUKEE. *Secular Institute of the Schoenstatt Sisters of Mary* (1926) 5310 W. Wisconsin Ave., 53208-3061. Tel: 414-774-3536; Email: srellenmarie@schsrsmary.org. Sr. M. Joanna Buckley, Prov. Sisters 2.

WAUKESHA. *Secular Institute of Schoenstatt Fathers* (1965) Tel: 262-548-9061; Fax: 262-548-9061; Email: fr.mjniehaus@gmail.com; Web: www.schoenstatt-wisconsin.org. Revs. Mark J. Niehaus, J.S.P., Rector; Pushparaj Antonysamy. Priests 3.

Schoenstatt Fathers (1965) W284 N746 Cherry Ln., Waukesha, 53188. Tel: 262-548-9061;
Fax: 262-548-9061; Email: fr.mjniehaus@gmail.com. Revs. Mark J. Niehaus, J.S.P., Rector, Email: niehausm@archmil.org; Dietrich A. Haas, J.S.P.; Gerold M. Langsch, J.S.P.; Francisco Rojas, J.S.P.; Pushparaj Antonysamy. Priests 10; Total in Residence 4.

Attached to the house but living elsewhere: Revs. Patricio Rodriguez, J.S.P., Supr., (Austin,TX); Christian Christensen, J.S.P., (Austin, TX); Marcelo Aravena, J.S.P., (Austin, TX); Jesus Ferras, J.S.P., (Austin, TX); Johnson Nellissery, J.S.P., (Austin, TX); Hector R. Vega, C.C., J.S.P., (Austin, TX); Raimundo Costa.

Secular Institute of the Schoenstatt Sisters of Mary (1926) W284 N404 Cherry Ln., Waukesha, 53188-9416. Tel: 262-522-4200; Fax: 262-522-4201; Email: schoenstattsisters@schsrsmary.org; Web: www.schsrsmary.org. Sisters M. Joanna Buckley, Prov. Supr.; M. Gloriana Rivera, Prov. Asst. Sisters 50.

[T] ASSOCIATIONS OF THE FAITHFUL

BELOIT. *Franciscan Sisters of Our Lady* (1981) 2110 Bootmaker Dr., Beloit, 53511-2318.
Tel: (608) 368-7001. Sr. Timothy Geenen, F.S.O.L., Supr. Sisters 2.

FRANKLIN. *Franciscan Sisters of Saint Clare, Inc.* (1977) 7732 S. 51st St., Franklin, 53132.
Tel: 414-423-5277; Fax: 414-421-7869; Email: smcs@wi.rr.com; Web: fssclare.org. Sr. Mary Celine Stein, F.S.S.C., Supr. Non-Cloistered Contemplative Community. Lay Affiliates 10; Professed Sisters 2.

[U] MISSIONARY ACTIVITIES

MILWAUKEE. *Milwaukee Archdiocesan Office for World Mission* (1966) (Formerly Latin American Office) 3501 S. Lake Dr., P.O. Box 07912, 53207-0912.
Tel: 414-758-2280; Fax: 414-769-3408; Email: wmo@archmil.org; Web: www.archmil.org/offices/world-mission.htm. Antoinette Mensah, Dir. Educates and raises funds for worldwide mission. Promotes parish twinning between archdiocese and other countries.

Society for the Propagation of the Faith, Archdiocese of Milwaukee (1822) (Pontifical Mission Societies) P.O. Box 07912, 53207-0912. Tel: 414-758-2280;
Fax: 414-769-3408; Email: wmo@archmil.org; Web: www.archmil.org/offices/world-mission.htm. 3501 S. Lake Dr., St. Francis, 53235. Antoinette Mensah, Dir.

Society for the Propagation of the Faith, Missionary Childhood Association dba Society for the Propagation of the Faith, Archdiocese of Milwaukee (1822) (Pontifical Mission Societies) P.O. Box 07912, 53207-0912. Tel: 414-758-2280;
Fax: 414-769-3408; Email: wmo@archmil.org; Web: www.archmil.org/offices/world-mission.htm. 3501 S. Lake Dr., St. Francis, 53235. Antoinette Mensah, Dir.

BURLINGTON. *General Secretariat of the Franciscan Missions, Inc.*, P.O. Box 130, Waterford, 53185.
Tel: 262-534-5470; Fax: 262-534-4342; Email: info@franciscanmissions.org; Web: franciscanmissions.org. 940 N. Browns Lake Dr., Burlington, 53105. Bro. Andrew J. Brophy, O.F.M., M.Ed., Dir.; Revs. Sante De Angelis, O.F.M., Assoc. Dir.; Ponciano Macabalo, O.F.M. Missionaries 5,400.

RACINE. *Community of St. Paul, Inc.* (1994) 1505 Howard St., Racine, 53404. Tel: 262-634-2666; Email: racine@comsp.org; Web: www.comsp.org/en. Revs. Marti Colom, Pres.; Ricardo Martin, J.C.L., Vice Pres.; Javier Guativa, Treas.; Deacon Michael Wolfe, Sec.; Revs. Juan Manuel Camacho, Bd. Member; Esteve Redolad, Bd. Member; Ms. Dolors Puertolas, Bd. Member. Public Association of Christian Faithful, comprised of clergy and laity. Present in North and South America and Africa, the community fosters pastoral activities and human development initiatives, while promoting mission awareness internationally.

[V] SOCIETIES

MILWAUKEE. **Christ Child Society, Inc. - Milwaukee Chapter*, 4033 W. Good Hope Rd., 53209-2268.
Tel: 414-540-0489; Email: christchildmilwaukee@gmail.com; Web: www.christchildsociety.com. Katie Clark, Pres.; Mary Nichol, Treas.

Cursillos in Christianity, P.O. Box 341726, 53234-1726. Tel: 414-481-6449; Email: milwaukeecurcillos@gmail.com; Web: www.natl-cursillo.org/milwaukee. Gilberto Martinez, Dir.; Rev. Carlos Alberto Zapata, Spiritual Advisor/Care Svcs. Total Staff 7.

Legion of Mary, 6962 N. Raintree Dr., Unit D, 53223. Cell: 828-280-1438; Email: hudsoncolin@yahoo.com. Colin Hudson, Pres.

Priests' Purgatorial Society, 3501 S. Lake Dr., P.O. Box 070912, 53207-0912. Tel: 414-769-3340;
Fax: 414-769-3908; Email: cusackb@archmil.org; Web: archmil.org. Barbara Anne Cusack, J.C.D., Sec.

**St. Vincent de Paul Society of Milwaukee*, 9601 W. Silver Spring Dr., 53225-3301. Tel: 414-462-7837;
Fax: 414-462-5458; Email: council@svdpmilw.org. Deborah Duskey, Exec. Dir.

WEST ALLIS. *Milwaukee Archdiocesan Holy Name Union*, P.O. Box 270562, West Allis, 53227.
Tel: 262-784-3822; Fax: 414-546-4650; Email: stevenandbecky@sbcglobal.net. Mr. Steven R. Lazarczyk, Pres.; Rev. Edward Griesemer, S.C.J.

[W] NEWMAN CENTERS

MILWAUKEE. *Marquette University/Campus Ministry*, P.O. Box 1881 - AMU236, 53201-1881.
Tel: 414-288-6873; Fax: 414-288-3696; Email: ann.hilbert@marquette.edu; Web: www.marquette.edu/cm. Campus Ministry/AMU 236, 1442 W. Wisconsin Ave., 53233. Mary Sue Callan-Farley, Dir.; Gerald Fischer, Assoc. Dir.

Milwaukee Archdiocesan Campus Ministry, 3501 S. Lake Dr., P.O. Box 070912, 53207-0912.
Tel: 414-758-2219; Fax: 414-769-3408; Email: burdsp@archmil.org; Web: brewcitycatholic.com. Peter Burds, Dir.

Campus Ministry of the Archdiocese of Milwaukee

Catholic Campus Ministry - U.W. Whitewater, 344 N. Prairie St., Whitewater, 53190.
Tel: 262-473-5555; Fax: 262-473-5855; Email: zaninb@uww.edu. Brian Zanin, Dir. Campus Ministry.

Catholic Campus Ministry Newman Center - U.W. Milwaukee, 3001 N. Downer Ave., 53211.
Tel: 414-964-6640; Fax: 414-964-3608; Email: info@uwmcatholic.org. Mary Burns, College Mission Dir.

[X] MISCELLANEOUS

MILWAUKEE. *Adult Learning Center, Inc.*, 1916 N. 4th St., 53212. Tel: 414-263-5874; Fax: 414-431-2031; Email: jon@alcmke.org. Jon Gilgenbach, Interim Dir.; Sr. Callista Robinson, Asst. Admin. Students Assisted 80.

Agape Community Center of Milwaukee, Inc. (1989) 400 W. River Woods Pkwy., Glendale, 53212. Deacon Timothy Waldoch, Chief Mission Integration Officer. Corporate Sponsor: Ascension Health Ministries (Ascension Sponsor), a public juridic person.

St. Ann Center for Intergenerational Care, Inc., 2801 E. Morgan Ave., 53207. Tel: 414-977-5000; Fax: 414-977-5050; Email: jjansen@stanncenter.org; Web: www.stanncenter.org. Mr. John Jansen, Vice Pres., Grants, Community & Capital Dev. Day care center for both children and adults.

Apostleship of Prayer dba Pope's Worldwide Prayer Network, 1501 S. Layton Blvd., 53215-1924. Tel: 414-486-1152; Email: info@popesprayerusa.net; Web: www.popesprayerusa.net. Rev. William Blazek, S.J., Dir.

Archdiocesan Marian Shrine, P.O. Box 070912, 53207-0912. Tel: 414-769-3325; Email: brownc@archmil.org. Christopher Brown, Contact Person.

**Archdiocese of Milwaukee Catholic Community Foundation, Inc.*, 637 E. Erie St., 53202. Tel: 414-431-6402; Fax: 414-431-6407; Email: info@legaciesoffaith.org; Web: legaciesoffaith.org. Ms. Mary Ellen Markowski, Pres.

**Ascension Medical Group - Northern Wisconsin, Inc* (1999) 400 W. River Woods Pkwy., Glendale, 53212. Tel: 414-465-3000; Fax: 414-465-3021; Email: timothy.waldoch@ascension.org; Web: healthcare.ascension.org. Mary Beth McDonald, Pres.; Deacon Timothy Waldoch, Chief Mission Integration Officer; Antonina Olszewski, Dir., Spiritual Svcs. Sponsored by Ascension Health Ministries (Ascension Sponsor), a public juridic person.Formerly Ministry Medical Group, Inc.

**Ascension Medical Group - Southeast Wisconsin, Inc.* (1933) 400 W. River Woods Pkwy., 53212. Tel: 414-465-3000; Fax: 414-465-3001; Email: timothy.waldoch@ascension.org; Web: healthcare.ascension.org. Mary Beth McDonald, Pres.; Deacon Timothy Waldoch, Chief Mission Integration Officer. Sponsored by Ascension Health Ministries (Ascension Sponsor), a public juridic person.Formerly Wheaton Franciscan Medical Group, Inc.

**Ascension Wisconsin Laboratories, Inc.*, 3237 S. 16th St., 53215. Tel: 414-256-5570; Fax: 414-256-5572; Email: timothy.waldoch@ascension.org; Web: healthcare.ascension.org. Tracy Rogers, COO; Deacon Timothy Waldoch, Chief Mission Integration Officer. Sponsored by Ascension Health Ministries (Ascension Sponsor), a public juridic person.Formerly Wheaton Franciscan Laboratories, Inc.

Assisi Homes - Jefferson Court, Inc. (1993) 415 E. Knapp St., 53202. Tel: 414-271-5370; Fax: 414-271-5988; Web: www.mercyhousing.org; Email: mrankin@mercyhousing.org; Tel: 303-830-3300. Melissa Clayton, Contact Person. Bed Capacity 222; Tot Asst. Annually 222; Total Staff 9.

Capuchin Community Services (1968) 1702 W. Walnut St., 53205-1616. Tel: 414-933-1300; Tel: 414-271-0135; Email: ccs@thecapuchins.org; Web: www.capuchincommunityservices.org. P.O. Box 5830, 53205-0830. Bro. Rob Roemer, O.F.M.-Cap., Exec. Dir.; Rev. Robert Wotypka, O.F.M.-Cap., Pastoral Dir.; Bros. Carl Schaefer, O.F.M.Cap., Reception/Front Office; Jerome Smith, O.F.M.Cap., Social Worker. Serving the poor, the hungry and the homeless. Tot Asst. Annually 188,852. In Res. Revs. Francis Dombrowski, O.F.-M.Cap.; Alan D. Veik, O.F.M.Cap.

St. Catherine Residence, Inc. (1913) 1032 E. Knapp St., 53202. Tel: 414-272-8470; Fax: 414-272-7579; Email: mrankin@mercyhousing.org; Web: www.mercyhousing.org. Mark Angelini, Pres. Affordable housing serving women in transition and those who will benefit from an environment where women support, encourage, and network with each other. Includes a Right Start Program for first-time, single, pregnant women over the age of 17. Residents 164.

The Catholic Charismatic Renewal Office of Southeastern Wisconsin, Inc. (1980) 3501 South Lake Dr., P.O. Box 070637, 53207-0637. Tel: 414-482-1727; Email: ccr@archmil.org; Email: liaison.815@archmil.org; Web: www.ccrmilwaukee.com. Marianne Skrobiak, Liaison.

Magnificat-West Bend Chapter: Mary Mother of All Hearts, 3351 Town Line Rd., West Bend, 53095. Tel: 262-677-1192; Email: ccr@archmil.org. Terri Biertzer, Pres. & Coord.

Magnificat-Kenosha/Racine Chapter: Mary Servant of the Lord, 6322 61st Ave., Kenosha, 53142. Tel: 262-654-7287; Email: suelippert@outlook.com. Rose Nelson, Coord.

Catholic Charities Foundation, Inc., 3501 S. Lake Dr., P.O. Box 070912, 53207-0912. Tel: 414-769-3400; Fax: 414-769-3428; Email: rcisneros@ccmke.org; Email: jrekowski@ccmke.org; Web: www.ccmke.org. Very Rev. David H. Reith, Vicar for Catholic Charities; Ricardo Cisneros, COO; Jason Flanders, CPA, Dir. Fin. & Admin.

Catholic Charities of the Archdiocese of Milwaukee, Inc. (1920) 3501 S. Lake Dr., P.O. Box 070912, 53207-0912. Tel: 414-769-3400; Fax: 414-769-3428; Email: info@ccmke.org; Web: www.ccmke.org. Ricardo Cisneros, COO, Tel: 414-771-2881; Jason Flanders, CPA, Dir. Fin. & Admin.; Jackie Rekowski, Dir. Advancement; Annette Jankowski, Dir. Adult Day Svcs.; Susan Howland, Dir. Community Outreach, Tel: 414-771-2881; Very Rev. David H. Reith, Vicar for Catholic Charities; Barbara Graham, Dir. Legal Svcs. for Immigrants, Tel: 414-643-8570; Nate Braun, HR Mgr.; Sharon Brumer, Communications Mgr., Tel: 414-769-3543; Carla Alego, Dir. In-Home Support Svcs.; Sarah Chidester, M.S.W., A.P.S.W., Adoption & Pregnancy Support Supvr.; Mandy Bibo, M.S., Dir. Behavioral Health; Sarah Matson, M.S., Supported Parenting Supvr. Tot Asst. Annually 43,850; Total Staff 84.

St. Clare Management, Inc., 1545 S. Layton Blvd., 53215. Tel: 414-385-5330; Fax: 414-385-5333; Email: margaretk@stclaremgt.org; Email: christinem@stclaremgt.org; Web: www.stclaremgt.org. Margaret E. Kidder, Exec. Dir. Sponsored by the School Sisters of St. FrancisA HUD housing management corporation to ensure the quality of life, safety, and independence of undeserved, low income people with disabilities.

Clare Towers, Inc. dba Clare Towers, Clare Woods, Clare Heights, Clare Meadows, Clare Court & Clare Lakes, 1545 S. Layton Blvd., 53215. Tel: 414-385-5330; Fax: 414-385-5333; Email: margaretk@stclaremgt.org; Email: christinem@stclaremgt.org; Web: www.stclaremgt.org. Margaret E. Kidder, Exec. Dir. Sponsored by School Sisters of St. FrancisHUD subsidized housing for the physically disabled to live independently. Apartments six locations 140.

Dismas Ministry (2000) P.O. Box 070363, 53207. Tel: 414-486-2383; Fax: 414-486-2383; Email: dismas@dismasministry.org; Web: www.dismasministry.org. Ronald Zeilinger, Exec. Dir. A national Catholic outreach to inmates, victims, their families, those released from prison, and the community. Tot Asst. Annually 12,000.

Dominican Center for Women, Inc., 2470 W. Locust St., 53206-1134. Tel: 414-444-9930; Fax: 414-444-4041; Email: patriciaarogersop@dominican-center.org. Sr. Patricia Rogers, Dir. & Contact Person. Tot Asst. Annually 150.

Eastside Senior Services (1974) 2618 N. Hackett Ave., 53211. Tel: 414-210-5881; Fax: 414-961-0661; Email: essmilw@gmail.com. Jane Raymer, Dir. Sponsored by SS. Peter and Paul, Lake Park Lutheran Church, ELCA, St. Mark's Episcopal Church, Plymouth Church, United Church of Christ, Our Lady of Divine Providence, Three Holy Women, Immanuel Presbyterian, Cathedral of St. John the Evangelist and Old St. Mary's, Milwaukee.Corporate Title: Eastside Senior Services, Inc. - an Interfaith Outreach Program Tot Asst. Annually 352; Total Staff 1.

**Erica P. John Fund, Inc.*, 330 E. Kilbourn Ave., Ste. 1454, 53202-3144. Tel: 414-607-6040; Fax: 414-607-6045; Email: epjfund@epjfund.org. Paula N. John, Pres.

Faith in Our Future Trust, 3501 South Lake Dr., P.O. Box 070504, 53207-0504. Tel: 414-769-3334; Email: jmarek@archmil.org. Most Rev. Jerome E. Listecki, Trustee.

Franciscan Peacemakers, Inc., Milwaukee (1995) 128 W. Burleigh St., 53212. Tel: 414-559-5761; Tel: 414-562-4780; Email: sprzedpel@gmail.com; Web: www.franciscanpeacemakers.com. Deacon Steven J. Przedpelski, Dir. Tot Asst. Annually 350; Total Staff 7.

**St. Joan Antida High School Foundation, Ltd.*, 1341 N. Cass St., 53202. Tel: 414-354-9233; Fax: 414-355-6463; Email: kathy@scsja.org. 8560 N. 76th Pl., 53223. Sr. Kathleen M. Lundwall, S.C.-S.J.A., Contact Person.

Lay Salvatorians, Inc. (2003) 1735 N. Hi-Mount Blvd., 53208-1720. Tel: 520-207-1642; Email: jwhite45@cox.net. Rev. Scott Wallenfelsz, S.D.S., M.B.A., Dir. Finance & Contact Person.

Layton Blvd. West Neighbors, Inc aka LBWN, 1545 S. Layton Blvd., 53215. Tel: 414-383-9038; Tel: 414-585-8539; Email: info@lbwn.org; Web: www.lbwn.org. Brianna Sas-Pérez, Exec. Sponsored by School Sisters of St. FrancisA community development organization which stabilizes and revitalizes the quality of life on Milwaukee's south side by building partnerships that achieve shared responsibility for the neighborhood.

Mareda, 3501 S. Lake Dr., P.O. Box 070912, 53207-0912. Tel: 414-758-2242; Fax: 414-769-3408; Email: pokornyg@archmil.org; Web: www.mareda.org. Lety Gutierrez-Kenny, Chm. Archdiocese of Milwaukee, Office of Catechesis and Youth Ministry.

Milwaukee Achiever Literacy Services, Inc. (1983) 1545 S. Layton Blvd., Rm. 40, 53215. Tel: 414-308-1102; Fax: 414-463-9484; Email: hmccoy@milwaukeeachiever.org; Web: www.milwaukeeachiever.org. Dennis J. Purtell, Esq., Legal Counsel. Founded by the School Sisters of St. Francis; Sisters of St. Francis of Assisi; School Sisters of Notre Dame, Alverno College, Cardinal Stritch University & Mount Mary University.Purpose: To provide adult literacy education and workforce development to economically and educationally disadvantaged adults in the Greater Milwaukee area. Tot Asst. Annually 1,157; Total Staff 9.

Milwaukee Archdiocesan Council of Deacons (1975) 3501 S. Lake Dr., P.O. Box 070912, 53207-0912. Tel: 414-769-3409; Fax: 414-769-3580; Email: chmielewskim@archmil.org. Deacon Michael J. Chmielewski, Deacon. Advisory/Governing Board of Deacons.

P.O. Box 070912, 53207-0912. Tel: 414-769-3409; Fax: 414-769-3408. Deacon David L. Zimprich.

Milwaukee Archdiocesan Principals' Association (MAPA), P.O. Box 070912, 53207-0912. Tel: 414-758-2251; Fax: 414-769-3408; Email: cepelkak@archmil.org. Kathleen A. Cepelka, Ph. D., Supt. Catholic Schools. Archdiocese of Milwaukee, Office for Schools.

The Milwaukee Guild of the Catholic Medical Association, 2735 N. Hackett Ave., 53211. Tel: 414-962-4997; Fax: 414-319-3113; Email: nosacek@msn.com; Web: www.mgcma.org. Cynthia Jones-Nosacek, Pres.

National Association of Catholic Chaplains, 4915 S. Howell Ave., Ste. 501, 53207. Tel: 414-483-4898; Fax: 414-483-6712; Email: info@nacc.org. Mr. David A. Lichter, D.Min., Exec. Dir.

National Office of Post-Abortion Reconciliation and Healing, Inc. (1991) 3501 S. Lake Dr., P.O. Box 070477, 53207-0477. Tel: 414-483-4141; Tel: 800-593-2273; Fax: 414-483-7376; Email: noparh@yahoo.com; Web: www.menandabortion.info. Victoria M. Thorn, Exec. Dir. Total Staff 3; Total Assisted 4,500.

Pallottine Fathers and Brothers, Inc., Disability Trust, 5424 W. Bluemound Rd., 53208. Tel: 414-259-0688; Fax: 414-258-9314; Email: pallotti_milw@pallottines.org; Web: www.pallottines.org. Very Rev. Joseph Koyickal, S.A.C., Pres.

Pallottine Fathers and Brothers, Inc., Educational and Apostolic Ministry Trust, 5424 W. Bluemound Rd., 53208. Tel: 414-259-0688; Fax: 414-258-9314; Email: pallotti_milw@pallottines.org; Web: www.pallottines.org. Very Rev. Joseph Koyickal, S.A.C., Prov.

Salvatorian Institute of Philosophy and Theology, Inc. (1993) 1735 N. Hi-Mount Blvd., 53208-1720. Tel: 414-258-1735; Email: sds@salvatorians.com. Rev. Scott Wallenfelsz, S.D.S., M.B.A., Dir. Finance.

**Santa Fe Communications, Inc.* dba Heart of the Nation, 1126 S. 70th St., Ste. N601, 53214-3155. Tel: 414-475-4444; Fax: 414-475-3621; Web: www.HeartoftheNation.org. Bruno John, Pres.

Salvatorian Advocacy for Victims of Exploitation (S.A.V.E.), 4311 N. 100th St., 53222-1393. Tel: 414-466-0810; Fax: 414-466-4335; Email: heitkeb@salvatoriansisters.org. Sr. Beverly Heitke, S.D.S., Contact Person.

SASC, Inc., 3800 N. 92nd St., 53222-2589. Tel: 414-463-7570; Fax: 414-463-2311; Email: ckinney@stannescampus.org. Ms. Lynn Vogt, Admin. & Contact Person; Revs. Arturo Ysmael, S.D.S., Dir.; Alan Wagner, S.D.S., Chap. Studio Apartments 55.

Society of the Divine Savior Ongoing Community Support Trust, 1735 N. Hi Mount Blvd., 53208-1720. Tel: 414-258-1735; Fax: 414-258-1934; Email: sds@salvatorians.com; Web: salvatorians.com. Rev. Scott Wallenfelsz, S.D.S., M.B.A., Treas. *Ongoing Community Support Trust.*

St. Stephen's League (of the Archdiocesan Council of Deacons) P.O. Box 070912, 53207-0912. Tel: 414-769-3409; Fax: 414-769-3408; Email: chmielewskim@archmil.org. Deacon Michael J. Chmielewski, Deacon.

Telos, Inc. dba Telos, Inc., Clare Place & Clare Central, 1545 S. Layton Blvd., 53215. Tel: 414-385-5330; Fax: 414-385-5333; Email: margaretk@stclaremgt.org; Email: christinem@stclaremgt.org; Web: www.stclaremgt.

org. Margaret E. Kidder, Exec. Dir. Sponsored by the School Sisters of St. Francis.HUD subsidized housing for the physically disabled to live independently. Apartments at two locations 24.

Wheaton Franciscan Healthcare-Southeast Wisconsin, Inc. (1986) 400 W. River Woods Pkwy., 53212. Tel: 414-465-3111; Fax: 414-465-3001; Email: timothy.waldoch@ascension.org; Web: healthcare.ascension.org. Bernie Sherry, CEO; Deacon Timothy Waldoch, Chief Mission Integration Officer; Antonina Olszewski, Dir., Spiritual Care. Sponsored by Ascension Health Ministries (Ascension Sponsor), a public juridic person.

**Wheaton Franciscan Healthcare-Foundation for St. Francis and Franklin, Inc.*, 3237 S. 16th St., 53215. Tel: 414-647-5000; Email: timothy.waldoch@ascension.org; Web: healthcare.ascension.org/donate. Racheal Faulks, Interim Exec. Dir.; Deacon Timothy Waldoch, Chief Mission Integration Officer. Sponsored by Ascension Health Ministries (Ascension Sponsor), a public juridic person.

Wheaton Franciscan Home Health and Hospice, Inc. (1986) 3070 N. 51st St., Ste. 406, 53210-1661. Tel: (800) 304-7873; Email: jennifer.marshall@ahah.net; Web: www.ascensionathome.com. James D. Gresham, Pres.; Terri Rocole, Senior Vice Pres. Mission Svcs. Franciscan Sisters, Daughters of the Sacred Hearts of Jesus and Mary, Wheaton, IL. Tot Asst. Annually 7,150; Total Staff 200.

Wheaton Franciscan-St. Joseph Foundation, Inc. (1984) 5000 W. Chambers St., 53210. Tel: 414-447-2844; Fax: 414-874-4399; Email: timothy.waldoch@ascension.org; Web: https://healthcare.ascension.org/donate. Racheal Faulks, Interim Exec. Dir.; Deacon Timothy Waldoch, Chief Mission Integration Officer. Sponsored by Ascension Health Ministries (Ascension Sponsor), a public juridic person.

Wisconsin Catholic Media Apostolate, Inc. (1869) 3501 S. Lake Dr., P.O. Box 070913, 53207-0913. Tel: 414-769-3500; Email: catholicherald@archmil.org; Web: www.catholicherald.org. Amy Grau, Dir.; Larry Hanson, Editor.

BROOKFIELD. *Ascension Wisconsin Pharmacy, Inc.* (1987) 400 West River Woods Pkwy., 53212. Tel: (414) 465-3111; Email: timothy.waldoch@ascension.org; Web: healthcare.ascension.org. Tracy Rogers, COO; Deacon Timothy Waldoch, Chief Mission Integration Officer. Sponsored by Ascension Health Ministries (Ascension Sponsor), a public juridic person.Previous name was Wheaton Franciscan Healthcare Pharmacy Enterprises and Franciscan Woods, Inc.

St. Thomas More Lawyers Society of Wisconsin, c/o Atty. Greg Helding, 100 E. Wisconsin Ave., Ste 3300, 53202. Tel: 414-225-2779; Email: gthelding@michaelbest.com; Web: stmls-wi.blogspot.com. Gregory Helding, Pres.; Very Rev. Paul B.R. Hartmann, M.Div., J.C.L., Chap.

**Wheaton Franciscan Healthcare-Circle of Life Foundation, Inc.*, 13950 W. Capitol Dr., Brookfield, 53005. Tel: 414-535-6829; Email: timothy.waldoch@ascension.org; Web: healthcare.ascension.org/donate. Tracy Rogers, COO; Deacon Timothy Waldoch, Chief Mission Integration Officer. Sponsored by Ascension Health Ministries (Ascension Sponsor), a public juridic person.

**Wheaton Franciscan-Elmbrook Memorial Foundation, Inc.* (2001) 19333 W. North Ave., Brookfield, 53045-4198. Tel: 262-785-2000; Email: timothy.waldoch@ascension.org; Web: healthcare.ascension.org/donate. Racheal Faulks, Interim Exec. Dir.; Deacon Timothy Waldoch, Chief Mission Integration Officer. Sponsored by Ascension Health Ministries (Ascension Sponsor). a public juridic person.

BROWN DEER. *Sisters of the Sorrowful Mother Charitable Trust* (1990) 8858 N. 60th St., Brown Deer, 53223. Tel: 414-357-8940; Fax: 414-357-8950 ; Email: pegg@ssmfinance.org. Sr. Catherine Hanegan, Trustee. To help provide for the needs of the aged and infirm members of the Sisters of the Sorrowful Mother. Sisters 71.

Sisters of the Sorrowful Mother International Finance, Inc. (1976) 8858 N. 60th St., Brown Deer, 53223. Tel: 414-357-8940; Fax: 414-357-8950; Email: pegg@ssmfinance.org; Web: ssmgen.org. Sr. Catherine Hanegan, Chairperson. Sisters in the U.S. community 71.

Sisters of the Sorrowful Mother-Generalate, Inc. (1980) 8858 N. 60th St., Brown Deer, 53223. Tel: 414-357-8940; Fax: 414-357-8950; Email: pegg@ssmfinance.org; Web: www.ssmgen.org. Sr. Catherine Hanegan, Supr. Sisters 71.

CEDARBURG. *Works of Mercy Ministry, Inc.*, W63 N605 Hanover Ave., #468, Cedarburg, 53012. Tel: 414-305-3384; Fax: 414-769-3439; Email: aveik@thecapuchins.org. Bro. Alan D. Veik, O.F.M.Cap., Pres.; Rev. Donald H. Thimm, Sec. Tot Asst. Annually 3,000.

FOND DU LAC. **Agnesian HealthCare Foundation, Inc.*, 430 E. Division St., Fond du Lac, 54935. Tel: 920-926-5421; Email: Damond.Boatwright@ssmhealth.com. 10101 Woodfield Ln., St. Louis, MO 63132. Holly Brenner, Pres.

**Fond du Lac Area Catholic Education Foundation*, 255 County K, Fond du Lac, 54935. Tel: 920-921-4870. Dean Zakos, Pres.; Joseph Bird, Vice Pres.

Hazotte Ministries, Inc., 320 County Rd. K, Fond du Lac, 54937-8158. Tel: 920-907-2300; Fax: 920-923-3194; Email: jquinn@csasisters.org. Sr. Hertha Longo, C.S.A., Pres. Sponsored by the Congregation of Sisters of St. Agnes.

FRANKLIN. *Franciscan Pilgrimage Programs, Inc.* (1974) 9230 W. Highland Park Ave., P.O. Box 321490, Franklin, 53132-6231. Tel: 414-427-0570; Fax: 414-427-0590; Email: infofpp@thefranciscans.net; Web: www.franciscanpilgrimages.com. Rev. John Cella, O.F.M., J.C.D., M.Div., M.B.A., Dir. & CEO. Catholic Franciscan Pilgrimages for religious men and women, leaders in Franciscan based institutions, members of the Secular Franciscan Order and any others who desire to deepen or discover Franciscan values and spirituality.

GLENDALE. **Metro Physicians, Inc.*, 400 W. River Woods Pkwy, Glendale, 53212. Tel: 414-465-3000; Fax: 414-465-3582; Email: timothy.waldoch@ascension.org; Web: healthcare.ascension.org. Mary Beth McDonald, Pres.; Deacon Timothy Waldoch, Chief Mission Integration Officer.

GREENFIELD. *Clement Manor Retirement Community*, 9339 W. Howard, Greenfield, 53228. Tel: 414- 321-1800; Fax: 414-546-7357; Email: info@clementmanor.com; Web: www.clementmanor.com. Mr. Dennis Ferger, Pres. & CEO; Rev. William L. Stanfield, Chap., (Retired). Sponsored by the School Sisters of St. FrancisCorporate Title: Clement Manor, Inc. A health care organization providing a continuum of care including independent living and assisted living (Skilled care, transitional rehab care, and adult day care are provided at the Clement Manor Health Center). Residents 201.

Our Lady of the Angels, Inc., 3995 S. 92nd St., Greenfield, 53228. Tel: 414-810-0950; Fax: 414-810-1141; Email: kweber@olacommunity.org. Kathy Weber, Pastoral Min./Coord.

HALES CORNERS. *Congregation of the Priests of the Sacred Heart Support and Maintenance Trust* (1991) 7373 S. Lovers Lane Rd., P.O. Box 289, Hales Corners, 53130. Tel: 414-425-6910; Fax: 414-425-2938; Email: provtreas@poshusa.org; Web: www.sacredheartusa.org. Bro. Raymond Kozuch, S.C.J., Trustee & Chair; Revs. Quang Nguyen, S.C.J., Ph.D., Trustee; James Walters, S.C.J., M.S., M.Div., Trustee.

Development Office (1929) Sacred Heart Monastery-Priests of the Sacred Heart-Reign of the Sacred Heart, Inc. 6889 S. Lovers Lane Rd., P.O. Box 367, Hales Corners, 53130. Tel: 414-425-3383; Fax: 414-425-5719; Email: provtreas@usprovince.org; Web: www.poshusa.org. Deacon David Nagel, S.C.J., Exec. Dir. U.S. Province of the Priests of the Sacred Heart.

KENOSHA. *Assisi Homes - Kenosha, Inc.* (1994) Independent Housing for Low Income Elderly 1860 27th Ave., Kenosha, 53140. Tel: 262-551-9821; Fax: 262-551-9843; Tel: 303-830-3300; Email: mrankin@mercyhousing.org; Web: www.mercyhousing.org. Melissa Clayton, Contact Person. Bed Capacity 60; Tot Asst. Annually 60; Staff 2.

Assisi Homes - Saxony, Inc. (1994) Independent Housing for Low Income Elderly 1850 22nd Ave., Kenosha, 53140. Tel: 262-551-9005; Fax: 262-551-7586; Tel: 303-830-3300; Email: mrankin@mercyhousing.org; Web: www.mercyhousing.org. Melissa Clayton, Contact Person. Bed Capacity 224; Tot Asst. Annually 224; Total Staff 8.

Catholic Woman's Club of Kenosha, c/o Sherry Thomas, 3524 7th Ave., #127, Kenosha, 53140. Tel: 262-658-3357; Email: rthomas2031@wi.rr.com. Sherry Thomas, Pres.

St. Mark Outreach Center, 7117 14th Ave., Kenosha, 53143. Tel: 262-656-7370; Fax: 262-656-7375; Email: stmarkoutreachbetty@gmail.com; Web: www.stmark-kenosha.org. Rev. Carlos A. Florez; Betty Regalado, Coord. of Human Resources. Total Staff 1; Total Assisted 2,400.

RACINE. *Catherine Marian Housing, Inc.* (1989) 5635 Erie St., Racine, 53402. Tel: 262-633-9446; Fax: 262-633-9463; Email: sgeertsen@racinedominican.org; Web: www.racinedominicans.org. 806 Wisconsin Ave., Racine, 53403. Sisters Maryann A. McMahon, O.P.; Lisa Kane, O.P., Vice Pres.; Kathleen Slesar, O.P. Congregation of St. Catherine of Siena.
dba Bethany Apartments.

St. Catherine's High School Corporation (1972) 1200 Park Ave., Racine, 53403. Fax: 262-632-5144; Email: sgeertsen@racinedominicans.org; Web: www.saintcats.org. Patrick Diem, Board Pres. The elected leadership of the Congregation of St.Catherine of Siena (most commonly known as the Racine Dominicans) are the members of this corporation with reserved powers. Students 644.

St. Catherine's High School of Racine, Inc. (1957) 5635 Erie St., Racine, 53402-1900. Tel: 262-639-4100; Fax: 262-639-9702; Email: sgeertsen@racinedominicans.org. Sisters Maryann A. McMahon, O.P., Pres.; Lisa Kane, O.P., Vice Pres.; Kathleen Slesar, O.P., Sec.

Dominicans at Siena on the Lake, Inc., 5635 Erie St., Racine, 53402. Tel: 262-639-4100; Fax: 262-639-9702; Email: sgeertsen@racinedominicans.org. Sisters Maryann A. McMahon, O.P., Pres.; Lisa Kane, O.P., Vice Pres.; Kathleen Slesar, O.P., Sec.

Eco-Justice Center, Inc., 7133 Michna Rd., Racine, 53402. Tel: 262-639-4100; Fax: 262-639-9702; Email: sgeertsen@racinedominicans.org; Web: www.ecojusticecenter.org. Sisters Maryann A. McMahon, O.P.; Lisa Kane, O.P., Vice Pres.; Kathleen Slesar, O.P.

HOPES Center of Racine, Inc., 521 6th St., Racine, 53403. Tel: 262-898-2940; Fax: 262-898-1772; Email: smetzel@hopescenter.org. Scott Metzel, Exec. Dir.

NewBridges, Ltd., 1510 Villa St., Racine, 53403. Tel: 262-637-8374; Email: gpetro@strichardparish.org. Rev. Allen J. Bratkowski, Chm.

Racine Dominican Ministries, Inc. (1989) 5635 Erie St., Racine, 53402-1900. Tel: 262-639-4100; Fax: 262-639-9702; Email: sgeertsen@racinedominicans.org; Web: www.racinedominicans.org. Sisters Maryann A. McMahon, O.P., Pres.; Lisa Kane, O.P., Vice Pres.; Kathleen Slesar, O.P.

Senior Companion Program, Inc., 5111 Wright Ave., Racine, 53406. Tel: 262-639-4100; Fax: 262 639-9702; Email: sgeertsen@racinedominicans.org; Web: www.racinedominicans.org. 5635 Erie St., Racine, 53402. Sisters Maryann A. McMahon, O.P.; Lisa Kane, O.P., Vice Pres.; Kathleen Slesar, O.P.

Wheaton Franciscan Healthcare-All Saints Foundation, Inc. (1986) 1320 Wisconsin Ave., Racine, 53403. Tel: 262-687-2239; Fax: 262-687-2674; Email: timothy.waldoch@ascension.org; Web: healthcare.ascension.org/donate. Racheal Faulks, Interim Exec. Dir.; Deacon Timothy Waldoch, Chief Mission Integration Officer. Sponsored by Ascension Health Ministries (Ascension Sponsor), a public juridic person.

ST. FRANCIS. *Archdiocese of Milwaukee Cemeteries Perpetual Care Trust*, 3501 S. Lake Dr., St. Francis, 53235. Tel: 414-769-3325; Email: brownc@archmil.org. Most Rev. Jerome E. Listecki, Trustee.

Canticle and Juniper Courts Foundation, Inc., 3221 S. Lake Dr., St. Francis, 53235. Tel: 414-294-7301; Fax: 414-744-3395; Email: scott@lakeosfs.org. Rev. Scott Wallenfelsz, S.D.S., M.B.A., Contact Person.

Canticle Court, Inc. (1987) 3201 S. Lake Dr., St. Francis, 53235-3708. Tel: 414-744-5878; Fax: 414-744-7636; Email: jschmitt@lakeosfs.org; Email: tergerson@lakeosfs.org. Mr. John Schmitt, Pres. & CEO. Sponsored by the Sisters of St. Francis of AssisiAn apartment building sponsored by the Sisters of St. Francis of Assisi funded by HUD for low income elderly persons who can live independently. Tot Asst. Annually 48; Total in Residence 48; Total Staff 3; Units 48.

Foundation for Religious Retirement, Inc. (1987) 3221 S. Lake Dr., St. Francis, 53235. Tel: 414-294-7324; Fax: 414-744-7193; Email: jparrott@thefrr.org; Web: www.thefrr.org. Jan Parrott, Exec. Dir. To raise funds to assist in supporting retired women religious in the Milwaukee Archdiocese.

Juniper Court, Inc. (1993) 3209 S. Lake Dr., St. Francis, 53235-3712. Tel: 414-744-5878; Fax: 414-744-7636; Email: jschmitt@lakeosfs.org; Email: tergerson@lakeosfs.org. Mr. John Schmitt, Pres. & CEO. Sponsored by the Sisters of St. Francis of Assisi, St. Francis, WI.An apartment building for persons of low to moderate income who can live independently. Tot Asst. Annually 52; Total in Residence 52; Total Staff 3; Total Units 52.

Wisconsin Religious Collaborative, Inc., 3221 S. Lake Dr., St. Francis, 53235. Sr. Sylvia Anne Sheldon, O.S.F., Contact Person.

SHEBOYGAN. *The Sheboygan County Catholic Fund, Inc.*, 1439 S. 12th St., Sheboygan, 53081. Tel: 920-457-9408; Email: Fr.

paul@catholicsouthside.com. Very Rev. Philip D. Reifenberg, J.C.L., Pres.; Revs. Matthew Widder, Vice Pres.; Paul J. Fliss, Treas. A fund to provide youth and adult religious education programs within the county.

WAUWATOSA. *St. Camillus Health System, Inc.*, 10101 W. Wisconsin Ave., Wauwatosa, 53226.
Tel: 414-258-1814; Fax: 414-259-4987; Email: pedrotramontin@yahoo.com.br. Very Rev. Pedro Tramontin, M.I., Pres.; Revs. Agustin R. Orosa, M.I., Prov. Asst.; Leandro Blanco, M.I., Counselor. Management Corporation. Order of the Servants of the Sick (Order of St. Camillus). Total Staff 525; Total Assisted 150.

St. Camillus Ministries, Inc., 10101 W. Wisconsin Ave., Wauwatosa, 53226. Tel: 414-258-1814;
Fax: 414-259-4987; Email: pedrotramontin@yahoo.com.br. Very Rev. Pedro Tramontin, M.I., Pres.; Revs. Agustin R. Orosa, M.I., Prov. Asst.; Leandro Blanco, M.I., Counselor. St. Camillus Ministries, Inc. operates under the auspices of the Order of St. Camillus and sponsors all social concerns ministry of the Order. Total Staff 3.

Friends of Calvary Cemetery, Inc., 2515 N. 66th St., Wauwatosa, 53213. Tel: 414-778-1187;
Fax: 414-778-1187; Email: swerk@juno.com. Mr. Keith Schultz, Pres. Purpose: To raise funds in connection with the restoration of Calvary Chapel located at Calvary Cemetery, 5503 West Bluemound Rd., Milwaukee, WI and overseeing such restoration.

Order of St. Camillus Foundation, Inc., 10200 W. Bluemound Rd., Wauwatosa, 53226.
Tel: 414-259-8335; Fax: 414-259-4987; Web: stcam.com. Very Rev. Pedro Tramontin, M.I., Pres.; Mr. Steve Watson, Exec.

San Camillo, Inc., 10200 W. Blue Mound Rd., Wauwatosa, 53226. Tel: 414-259-6300;
Fax: 414-259-4590; Email: jleveritt@stcam.com; Web: www.stcam.com. Very Rev. Pedro Tramontin, M.I., Pres.; Kevin Schwab, CEO; Julie Leveritt, Admin.; Revs. Leandro Blanco, M.I., Counselor; Agustin R. Orosa, M.I., Counselor. Ministers of the Sick (Order of St. Camillus)Independent living facilities for older adults. Residents 442; Total Staff 125; Total Assisted 442.

Servants of Saint Camillus Disaster Relief Services, Inc. dba Camillian Disaster Services U.S.A. - CADIS USA, 10101 W. Wisconsin Ave., Wauwatosa, 53226. Tel: 414-259-7750;
Fax: 414-259-4989; Email: cadis_usa@cadisusa.org; Web: www.cadisusa.org. Very Rev. Pedro Tramontin, M.I., Pres.

WEST MILWAUKEE. *Cristo Rey Jesuit Corporate Work Study Program, Inc.*, 1215 S. 45th St., West Milwaukee, 53214. Tel: 414-436-4600;
Fax: 414-645-0046; Email: mtalavera@cristoreymilwaukee.org; Email: astith@cristoreymilwaukee.org; Email: jmazza@cristoreymilwaukee.org; Web: www.cristoreymilwaukee.org. Mr. Andrew Stith, Pres.; Joe Mazza, Dir.

[Y] CLOSED PARISHES

MILWAUKEE. *St. Agnes* For sacramental records, contact Archives, Archdiocese of Milwaukee, P.O. Box 070912, Milwaukee, 53207-0912. Tel: 414-769-3407; Fax: 414-769-3408.

St. Albert For sacramental records, contact Archives, Archdiocese of Milwaukee, P.O. Box 070912, Milwaukee, 53207-0912. Tel: 414-769-3407; Fax: 414-769-3408.

St. Alexander For sacramental records, contact St. John Paul II Parish, 3307 S. 10th St., Milwaukee, 53215-5116, Tel: 414-744-3695, Fax: 414-744-2874.

St. Anne For sacramental records, contact Archives, Archdiocese of Milwaukee, P.O. Box 070912, Milwaukee, 53207-0912. Tel: 414-769-3407; Fax: 414-769-3408.

St. Anthony of Padua For sacramental records, contact St. Vincent Pallotti, 7622 W. Stevenson St., Milwaukee, 53223. Tel: 414-453-5344; Fax: 414-453-4225.

St. Barbara For sacramental records, contact Archives, Archdiocese of Milwaukee, P.O. Box 070912, Milwaukee, 53207-0912. Tel: 414-769-3407; Fax: 414-769-3408.

Blessed Trinity For sacramental records, contact St. Catherine Parish, 5101 W. Center St., Milwaukee, 53210-2361. Tel: 414-445-5115, Fax: 414-445-5198.

Blessed Virgin of Pompei For sacramental records, contact Archives, Archdiocese of Milwaukee, P.O. Box 070912, Milwaukee, 53207-0912. Tel: 414-769-3407; Fax: 414-769-3408.

St. Boniface For sacramental records, contact Archives, Archdiocese of Milwaukee, P.O. Box 070912, Milwaukee, 53207-0912. Tel: 414-769-3407; Fax: 414-769-3408.

St. Casimir For sacramental records, contact Our Lady of Divine Providence, 3055 N. Fratney St., Milwaukee, 53212, Tel: 414-264-0049, Fax: 414-264-7177.

Corpus Christi For sacramental records, contact Blessed Savior, 8607 W. Villard Ave., Milwaukee, 53225. Tel: 414-464-5033; Fax: 414-464-0079.

St. Elizabeth For sacramental records, contact Archives, Archdiocese of Milwaukee, P.O. Box 070912, Milwaukee, 53207-0912. Tel: 414-769-3407; Fax: 414-769-3408.

St. Emeric For sacramental records, contact Sacred Heart, 917 N. 49th St., Milwaukee, 53208. Tel: 414-774-9418; Fax: 414-774-7406.

St. Gabriel For sacramental records, contact Archives, Archdiocese of Milwaukee, P.O. Box 070912, Milwaukee, 53207-0912. Tel: 414-769-3407; Fax: 414-769-3408.

St. Gall For sacramental records, contact Archives, Archdiocese of Milwaukee, P.O. Box 070912, Milwaukee, 53207-0912. Tel: 414-769-3407; Fax: 414-769-3408.

St. Gerard For sacramental records, contact Archives, Archdiocese of Milwaukee, P.O. Box 070912, Milwaukee, 53207-0912. Tel: 414-769-3407; Fax: 414-769-3408.

St. Hedwig For sacramental records, contact Archives, Archdiocese of Milwaukee, P.O. Box 070912, Milwaukee, 53207-0912. Tel: 414-769-3407, Fax: 414-769-3408.

St. Helen For sacramental records, contact St. John Paul II Parish, 3307 S. 10th St., Milwaukee, 53215-5116, Tel: 414-744-3695, Fax: 414744-2874.

Holy Angels For sacramental records, contact Archives, Archdiocese of Milwaukee, P.O. Box 070912, Milwaukee, 53207-0912. Tel: 414-769-3407; Fax: 414-769-3408.

Holy Cross For sacramental records, contact St. Vincent Pallotti, 7622 W. Stevenson St., Milwaukee. Tel: 414-453-5344; Fax: 414-453-4225.

Holy Redeemer For sacramental records, contact Archives, Archdiocese of Milwaukee, P.O. Box 070912, Milwaukee, 53207-0912. Tel: 414-769-3407; Fax: 414-769-3408.

Holy Rosary For sacramental records, contact Archives, Archdiocese of Milwaukee, P.O. Box 070912, Milwaukee, 5307-0912. Tel: 414-769-3407, Fax: 414-769-3408.

Holy Spirit For sacramental records, contact Archives, Archdiocese of Milwaukee, P.O. Box 070912, Milwaukee, 53207-0912. Tel: 414-769-3407; Fax: 414-769-3408.

Holy Trinity-Our Lady of Guadalupe For sacramental records, contact Our Lady of Guadalupe, 613 S. 4th St., Milwaukee. Tel: 414-271-6181; Fax: 414-278-6090.

St. Ignatius For sacramental records, contact Archives, Archdiocese of Milwaukee, P.O. Box 070912, Milwaukee, 53207-0912. Tel: 414-769-3407; Fax: 414-769-3408.

St. John de Nepomuc For sacramental records, contact Archives, Archdiocese of Milwaukee, P.O. Box 070912, Milwaukee, 53207-0912. Tel: 414-769-3407; Fax: 414-769-3408.

St. John Kanty For sacramental records, contact St. John Paul II Parish, 3307 S. 10th St., Milwaukee, 53215-5116, Tel: 414-744-3695, Fax: 414-744-2874.

St. Joseph For sacramental records, contact St. Joseph, 12130 Center St., Wauwatosa, 53222-4096. Tel: 414-771-4626; Fax: 414-771-4311.

St. Lawrence For sacramental records, contact Archives, Archdiocese of Milwaukee, P.O. Box 070912, Milwaukee, 53207-0912. Tel: 414-769-3407; Fax: 414-769-3408.

St. Leo For sacramental records, contact Archives, Archdiocese of Milwaukee, P.O. Box 070912, Milwaukee, 53207-0912. Tel: 414-769-3407; Fax: 414-769-3408.

St. Mary of Czestochowa For sacramental records, contact Our Lady of Divine Providence, 3055 N. Fratney St., Milwaukee, 53212. Tel: 414-264-0049, Fax: 414-264-7177.

Mary Queen of Martyrs For sacramental records, contact Blessed Savior, 8607 W. Villard Ave., Milwaukee, 53225. Tel: 414-464-5033; Fax: 414-464-0079.

St. Matthew For sacramental records, contact Archives, Archdiocese of Milwaukee, P.O. Box 070912, Milwaukee, 53207-0912. Tel: 414-769-3407; Fax: 414-769-3408.

St. Maximilian Kolbe For sacramental records, contact Ss. Cyril & Methodius Parish, 2427 S. 15th St., Milwaukee, WI 53215, 414-383-3973.

St. Michael For sacramental records, contact Good Shepherd, W762 Armstrong Rd., Campbellsport, 53010-1400. Tel: 920-477-3201 Fax: 920-477-3030.

Mother of Perpetual Help For sacramental records, contact Archives, Archdiocese of Milwaukee, P.O. Box 070912, Milwaukee, 53207-0912. Tel: 414-769-3407; Fax: 414-769-3408.

St. Nicholas For sacramental records, contact Archives, Archdiocese of Milwaukee, P.O. Box 070912, Milwaukee, 53207-0912. Tel: 414-769-3407; Fax: 414-769-3408.

Our Lady of Sorrows For sacramental records, contact Blessed Savior, 8607 W. Villard Ave., Milwaukee, 53225. Tel: 414-464-5033, Fax: 414-464-0079.

St. Philip Neri For sacramental records, contact Blessed Savior, 8607 W. Villard Ave., Milwaukee, 53225. Tel: 414-464-5033; Fax: 414-464-0079.

St. Rita For sacramental records, contact Archives, Archdiocese of Milwaukee, P.O. Box 070912, Milwaukee, 53207-0912. Tel: 414-769-3407, Fax: 414-769-3408.

St. Stephen Martyr For sacramental records, contact Archives, Archdiocese of Milwaukee, P.O. Box 070912, Milwaukee, 53207-0912. Tel: 414-769-3407; Fax: 414-769-3408.

St. Thomas Aquinas For sacramental records, contact Archives, Archdiocese of Milwaukee, P.O. Box 070912, Milwaukee, 53207-0912. Tel: 414-769-3407; Fax: 414-769-3408.

St. Wenceslaus For sacramental records, contact Archives, Archdiocese of Milwaukee, P.O. Box 070912, Milwaukee, 53207-0912. Tel: 414-769-3407, Fax: 414-769-3408.

ADELL. *St. Patrick* For sacramental records, contact Archives, Archdiocese of Milwaukee, P.O. Box 070912, Milwaukee, 53207-0912. Tel: 414-769-3407; Fax: 414-769-3408.

ALLENTON. *Sacred Heart* For sacramental records, contact Resurrection, P.O. Box 96, Allenton, 53002-0096. Tel: 262-629-5240.

ARMSTRONG. *Our Lady of Angels* For sacramental records, contact Good Shepherd, W1562 Cty. Rd. B, Eden, 53019. Tel: 920-477-3201; Fax: 920-477-3030.

ASHFORD. *St. Martin* For sacramental records, contact St. Matthew, 419 Mill St., P.O. Box 740, Campbellsport, WI 53010, Tel: 920-533-4441, Fax: 920-533-5280.

AUBURN. *St. Matthias* For sacramental records, contact Holy Trinity, 331 Main St., P.O. Box 461, Kewaskum, 53040. Tel: 262-626-2860, Fax: 262-626-2301.

BEAVER DAM. *St Michael* For sacramental records, contact St. Katharine Drexel, 131 W. Maple Ave., Beaver Dam, 53916. Tel: 920-887-2082, Fax: 920-885-7602.

St. Patrick For sacramental records, contact St. Katharine Drexel, 131 W. Maple Ave., Beaver Dam, 53916. Tel: 920-887-2082, Fax: 920-885-7602.

St. Peter For sacramental records, contact St. Katharine Drexel, 131 W. Maple Ave., Beaver Dam, 53916. Tel: 920-887-2082, Fax: 920-885-7602.

BRANDON. *St. Brendan* For sacramental records, contact St. Joseph, Waupun, 53963-1455. Tel. 920-324-5400.

BRISTOL. *St. Scholastica* For sacramental records, contact Holy Cross, 18700 116th St., Bristol, 53104. Tel: 262-857-2068.

BELGIUM. *St. Mary* For sacramental records, contact Divine Savior Parish, PO. Box 250, Fredonia, WI 53021-0250, 262-692-9994, Fax: 262-692-3085.

BYRON. *St. John* For sacramental records, contact Sons of Zebedee: Saints James and John, W5882 Church Rd., Fond du Lac, 54937-8602. Tel: 920-922-1167.

CASCADE. *St. Mary* For sacramental records, contact Archives, Archdiocese of Milwaukee, P.O. Box 070912, Milwaukee, 53207-0912. Tel: 414-769-3407, Fax: 414-769-3408.

CEDARBURG. *Divine Word* For sacramental records, contact St. Francis Borgia, 1375 Covered Bridge Rd., Cedarburg, 53012. Tel: 262-377-1070; Fax: 262-377-6898.

COLGATE. *St. Columba* For sacramental records, contact St. Francis Borgia Parish, 1375 Covered Bridge Rd., Cedarburg, 53012. Tel: 262-377-1070; Fax: 262-377-6898.

CUDAHY. *St. Frederick* For sacramental records, contact Nativity of the Lord, 4611 S. Kirkwood Ave., Cudahy, 53110. Tel: 414-744-6622.

Holy Family For sacramental records, contact Nativity of the Lord, 4611 S. Kirkwood Ave., Cudahy, 53110. Tel: 414-744-6622.

St. Joseph For sacramental records, contact Nativity of the Lord, 4611 S. Kirkwood Ave., Cudahy, 53110. Tel: 414-744-6622.

DACADA. *St. Nicholas* For sacramental records, contact Archives, Archdiocese of Milwaukee, P.O. Box 070912, Milwaukee, 53207-0912. Tel: 414-769-3407, Fax: 414-769-3408.

DOTYVILLE. *St. Michael* For sacramental records, contact Good Shepherd, W1562 County Rd. B, Eden, 53019. Tel: 920-477-3201; Fax: 920-477-3030.

EDEN. *St. Mary* For sacramental records, contact Good Shepherd, W1562 County Rd. B, Eden, 53019. Tel: 920-477-3201; Fax: 920-477-3030.

ELDORADO. *St. Mary* For sacramental records, contact

Our Risen Savior, W8272 Forest Ave. Rd., Eldorado, 54932-9801. Tel: 920-922-2412.

ELKHART LAKE. *St. George* For sacramental records, contact St. Thomas Aquinas, P.O. Box T, Elkhart Lake, 53020-0396. Tel: 920-876-2457.

FARMINGTON. *St. John of God* For sacramental records, contact St. Michael, 8877 Forestview Rd., Kewaskum, 53040. Tel: 262-334-5270; Fax: 262-334-5233.

FOND DU LAC. *Sacred Heart* For sacramental records, contact Archives, Archdiocese of Milwaukee, P.O. Box 070912, Milwaukee, WI 53207-0912, Tel: 414-769-3407, Fax: 414-769-3408.

St. Joseph For sacramental records, contact Archives, Archdiocese of Milwaukee, P.O. Box 070912, Milwaukee, WI 53207-0912, Tel: 414-769-3407, Fax: 414-769-3408.

St. Louis For sacramental records, contact Archives, Archdiocese of Milwaukee, P.O. Box 070912, Milwaukee, WI 53207-0912, Tel: 414-769-3407, Fax: 414-769-3408.

St. Mary For sacramental records, contact Archives, Archdiocese of Milwaukee, P.O. Box 070912, Milwaukee, WI 53207-0912, Tel: 414-769-3407, Fax: 414-769-3408.

St. Patrick For sacramental records, contact Archives, Archdiocese of Milwaukee, P.O. Box 070912, Milwaukee, WI 53207-0912, Tel: 414-769-3407, Fax: 414-769-3408.

FOX LAKE. *St. Mary* For sacramental records, contact Annunciation, 305 Green St., P.O. Box 85, Fox Lake, 53933-0085. Tel: 920-928-3513; Fax: 920-928-6334.

FRANKLIN. *Sacred Hearts of Jesus and Mary* For sacramental records, contact St. Martin of Tours, 7963 S. 116th St., Franklin, 53132. Tel: 414-425-1114; Fax: 414-425-2527.

FREDONIA. *Holy Rosary* For sacramental records, contact Divine Savior Parish, P.O. Box 250, Fredonia, WI 53021-0250, 262-692-9994, Fax: 262-692-3085.

St. Rose of Lima For sacramental records, contact Holy Rosary, 305 Fredonia Ave., P.O. Box 250, Fredonia, 53021-0250. Tel: 262-692-9994; Fax: 262-692-3085.

GLENBEULAH. *St. Fridolin* For sacramental records, contact St. Thomas Aquinas, P.O. Box T, Elkhart Lake, 53020-0396. Tel: 920-876-2457.

HOLY CROSS. *Holy Cross* For sacramental records, contact Holy Rosary, 305 Fredonia Ave., P.O. Box 250, Fredonia, 53021-0250. Tel: 262-692-9994; Fax: 262-692-3085.

HORICON. *St. Malachy* For sacramental records, contact Sacred Heart, 113 Valley St., Horicon, 53032. Tel: 920-485-0694.

HUBERTUS. *St. Hubert* For sacramental records after 1960, contact St. Gabriel, 1200 St. Gabriel Way, Hubertus, 53033-9794, Tel: 262-628-1141, Fax: 262-628-1911. For sacramental records prior to 1961, contact the Archdiocese of Milwaukee Archives, Tel: 414-769-3407.

JUNEAU. *Immaculate Conception* For sacramental records, contact Sacred Heart, 113 Valley St., Horicon, 53032. Tel: 920-485-0694.

KENOSHA. *St. Casmir* For sacramental records, contact the Archdiocese of Milwaukee Archives. Tel: 414-769-3407.

St. George For sacramental records, contact the Archdiocese of Milwaukee Archives. Tel: 414-769-3407.

St. Thomas Aquinas For sacramental records, contact Archdiocese of Milwaukee Archives, Tel: 414-769-3407.

LAKE FIVE. *St. Columba* For sacramental records, contact St. Gabriel, 1200 St. Gabriel Way, Hubertus 53033-9794. Tel: 262-628-1141, Fax: 262-628-1911.

LITTLE KOHLER. *Mother of Sorrows* For sacramental records, contact Holy Rosary, 305 Fredonia Ave., P.O. Box 250, Fredonia, 53021-0250. Tel: 262-692-9994; Fax: 262-692-3085.

LIMA. *St. Rose of Lima* For sacramental records, contact Blessed Trinity, 327 Giddings Ave., Sheboygan Falls, 53085. Tel: 920-467-4616; Fax: 920-467-4290.

LOST LAKE. *St. Mary* For sacramental records, contact Annunciation, 305 Green St., P.O. Box 85, Fox Lake, 53933-0085. Tel: 920-928-3513; Fax: 920-928-6334.

LYONS. *St. Kilian* For sacramental records, contact St. Joseph, 1540 Mill St., P.O. Box 60, Lyons, 53148-0060. Tel: 262-763-2050; Fax: 262-763-9377.

MEQUON. *St. James* For sacramental records, contact Lumen Christi, 11300 N. St. James Ln., 28W. Mequon, 53092, Tel: 262-242-7967; Fax: 262-242-7970.

MITCHELL. *St. Michael* For sacramental records, contact Archives, Archdiocese of Milwaukee, P.O. Box 070912, Milwaukee, 53207-0912. Tel: 414-769-3407, Fax: 414-769-3408.

MONCHES. *St. John* (1843) For sacramental records, contact Blessed Teresa of Calcutta, P.O. Box 68, North Lake, 53064-0068, Tel: 262-966-2191, Fax: 262-966-1829.

MOUNT CALVARY. *Holy Cross* For sacramental records, contact St. Isidore, Mount Calvary. Tel: 920-753-3311, Fax: 920-753-2130.

NABOB. *St. Matthias* For sacramental records, contact St. Lawrence, 4886 Hwy. 175, Hartford, 53027. Tel: 262-644-5701.

NENNO. *St. Anthony* For sacramental records, contact Resurrection, P.O. Box 96, Allenton, 53002-0096. Tel: 262-629-5240.

SS. Peter and Paul For sacramental records, contact Resurrection, P.O. Box 96, Allenton, 53002-0096. Tel: 262-629-5240.

NORTH LAKE. *St. Clare* For sacramental records, contact Blessed Teresa of Calcutta, P.O. Box 68, North Lake, 53064-0068, Tel: 262-966-2191, Fax: 262-966-1829.

OAKFIELD. *St. James* For sacramental records, contact Sons of Zebedee: Saints James and John, W5882 Church Rd., Fond du Lac, 54937-8602. Tel: 920-922-1167.

PELL LAKE. *St. Mary* For sacramental records, contact St. Francis de Sales, 148 W. Main St., Lake Geneva, 53147. Tel: 262-248-8524/8525; Fax: 262-248-5302.

PEWAUKEE. *St. Mary* For sacramental records, contact Queen of Apostles, W280 N2101 Hwy. SS, Pewaukee, 53072. Tel: 262-691-1535; Fax: 262-691-7376.

SS. Peter and Paul For sacramental records, contact Queen of Apostles, W280 N2101 Hwy. SS, Pewaukee, 53072. Tel: 262-691-1535; Fax: 262-691-7376.

RACINE. *St. Casimir* For sacramental records, contact Archives, Archdiocese of Milwaukee, P.O. Box 070912, Milwaukee, 53207-0912. Tel: 262-769-3407; Fax: 262-769-3408.

Cristo Rey For sacramental records, contact Archives, Archdiocese of Milwaukee, P.O. Box 070912, Milwaukee, 53207-0912. Tel: 262-769-3407; Fax: 262-769-3408.

Holy Name For sacramental records, contact Archives, Archdiocese of Milwaukee, P.O. Box 070912, Milwaukee, 53207-0912. Tel: 262-769-3407; Fax: 262-769-3408.

Holy Trinity For sacramental records, contact Archives, Archdiocese of Milwaukee, P.O. Box 070912, Milwaukee, 53207-0912. Tel: 262-769-3407; Fax: 262-769-3408.

St. Rose For sacramental records, contact Archives, Archdiocese of Milwaukee, P.O. Box 070912, Milwaukee, 53207-0912. Tel: 262-769-3407; Fax: 262-769-3408.

St. Stanislaus For sacramental records, contact Archives, Archdiocese of Milwaukee, P.O. Box 070912, Milwaukee, 53207-0912. Tel: 262-769-3407; Fax: 262-769-3408.

RANDOLPH. *St. Gabriel* For sacramental records, contact Annunciation, 305 Green St., P.O. Box 85, Fox Lake, 53933-0085. Tel: 920-928-3513; Fax: 920-928-6334.

St. Mary For sacramental records, contact Annunciation, 305 Green St., P.O. Box 85, Fox Lake, 53933-0085. Tel: 920-928-3513, Fax: 920-928-6334.

RANDOM LAKE. *St. Mary* For sacramental records, contact Archives, Archdiocese of Milwaukee, P.O. Box 070912, Milwaukee, 53207-0912. Tel: 262-769-3407; Fax: 262-769-3408.

RICHFIELD. *St. Mary* For sacramental records after 1966, contact St. Gabriel, Hubertus. For sacramental records before 1967, contact Archives, Archdiocese of Milwaukee, P.O. Box 070912, Milwaukee, 53207-0912. Tel: 414-769-3707; Fax: 414-769-3408.

RIPON. *St. Patrick* For sacramental records, contact St. Catherine of Siena, 218 Blossom St., Ripon, 54971-1560. Tel: 920-748-2345; Fax: 920-748-3760.

St. Wenceslaus For sacramental records, contact St. Catherine of Siena, 218 Blossom St., Ripon, 54971-1560, Tel: 920-748-2345; Fax: 920-748-3760.

ST. CLOUD. *St. Cloud* For sacramental records, contact St. Isidore, Mount Calvary. Tel: 920-753-3311; Fax: 920-753-2130.

ST. GEORGE. *St. George* For sacramental records, contact Blessed Trinity, 327 Giddings Ave., Sheboygan Falls, 53085. Tel: 920-467-4616; Fax: 920-467-4290.

ST. JOE. *St. Joseph* For sacramental records, contact St. Isidore, Mount Calvary. Tel: 920-753-3311; Fax: 920-753-2130.

ST. KILIAN. *St. Kilian* For sacramental records, contact St. Matthew Parish, 419 Mill St., P.O. Box 740, Campbellsport, 53010, Tel: 920-533-4441, Fax: 920-533-5280.

ST. MARTIN. *Holy Assumption* For sacramental records through 1990, contact St. Mary, 9520 W. Forest Home Ave., Hales Corners, 53130. Tel: 414-425-2174; Fax: 414-425-9432. For records after 1990, contact St. Martin of Tours, 7963 S. 116th St., Franklin, 53132. Tel: 414-425-1114; Fax: 414-425-1114.

ST. PETER. *St. Peter* For sacramental records prior to 1953, contact Archdiocese of Milwaukee Archives; Tel: 414-769-3407. For records after 1952, contact Holy Family, 271 Fourth St. Way, Fond du Lac, 54935, Tel: 920-921-0580.

SOUTH MILWAUKEE. *St. Adalbert* For sacramental records, contact Archives, Archdiocese of Milwaukee, P.O. Box 070912, Milwaukee, WI 53207-0912, Tel: 414-769-3407, Fax: 414-769-3408.

St. John For sacramental records, contact Archives, Archdiocese of Milwaukee, P.O. Box 070912, Milwaukee, WI 53207-0912, Tel: 414-769-3407, Fax: 414-769-3408.

St. Mary For sacramental records, contact Archives, Archdiocese of Milwaukee, P.O. Box 070912, Milwaukee, WI 53207-0912, Tel: 414-769-3407, Fax: 414-769-3408.

St. Sylvester For sacramental records, contact Archives, Archdiocese of Milwaukee, P.O. Box 070912, Milwaukee, WI 53207-0912, Tel: 414-769-3407, Fax: 414-769-3408.

SPRINGVALE. *St. Mary* For sacramental records, contact St. Joseph, Waupun, 53963-1455. Tel: 920-324-5400.

THIENSVILLE. *St. Cecilia* For sacramental records, contact Lumen Christi, 11300 N. St. James Ln., 28W, Mequon, 53092, Tel: 262-242-7967, Fax: 262-242-7970.

THOMPSON. *St. Patrick* For sacramental records, contact St. Kilian, 264 W. State St., Hartford, 53027. Tel: 262-673-4831.

WAYNE. *St. Bridget* For sacramental records, contact Holy Trinity, 331 Main St., P.O. Box 461, Kewaskum, 53040. Tel: 262-626-2860; Fax: 262-626-2301.

WEST ALLIS. *St. Aloysius* For sacramental records, contact Mother of Perpetual Help, 1121 S. 116th St., West Allis, 53214. Tel.: 414-453-5192.

Immaculate Heart of mary For sacramental records, contact Mother of Perpetual Help, 1121 S. 116th St., West Allis, 53214. Tel.: 414-453-5192.

St. Joseph For sacramental records, contact Archives, Archdiocese of Milwaukee, P.O. Box 070912, Milwaukee, 53207-0912. Tel: 414-769-3407; Fax: 414-769-3408.

St. Mary Help of Christians For sacramental records, contact Archives, Archdiocese of Milwaukee, P.O. Box 070912, Milwaukee, 53207-0912. Tel: 414-769-3407; Fax: 414-769-3408.

Mary, Queen of Heaven For sacramental records, contact Mother of Perpetual Help, 1121 S. 116th St., West Allis, 53214. Tel.: 414-453-5192.

Our Lady of Mount Carmel For sacramental records, contact Archives, Archdiocese of Milwaukee, P.O. Box 070912, Milwaukee, 53207-0912. Tel: 414-769-3407; Fax: 414-769-3408.

WILMOT. *Holy Name of Jesus* For sacramental records, contact Holy Cross, 18700 116th St., Bristol, 53104. Tel: 262-857-2068.

WOODHULL. *St. John the Baptist* For sacramental records, contact Our Risen Savior, W8272 Forest Ave. Rd., Eldorado, 54932-9801. Tel: 920-922-2412.

RELIGIOUS INSTITUTES OF MEN REPRESENTED IN THE ARCHDIOCESE

For further details refer to the corresponding bracketed number in the Religious Institutes of Men or Women section.

[0120]—*Alexian Brothers* (Immaculate Conception Prov.)—C.F.A.

[0140]—*The Augustinians* (Mother of Good Counsel Prov.)—O.S.A.

[0200]—*Benedictine Monks*—O.S.B.

[0330]—*Brothers of the Christian Schools* (Midwest Prov., Burr Ridge, IL)—F.S.C.

[0470]—*The Capuchin Friars* (Prov. of St. Joseph)—O.F.M.Cap.

[0740]—*Congregation of Marians of the Immaculate Conception*—M.I.C.

[1330]—*Congregation of the Mission*—C.M.

[1130]—*Congregation of the Priests of the Sacred Heart*—S.C.J.

[0480]—*Conventual Franciscans* (St. Bonaventure, Prov. of Our Lady of Consolation)—O.F.M.Conv.

[0260]—*Discalced Carmelite Friars* (Prov. of the Immaculate Heart of Mary)—O.C.D.

[0520]—*Franciscan Friars*—O.F.M.

[0305]—*Institute of Christ the King-Sovereign Priest*—I.C.R.S.S.

[0690]—*Jesuit Fathers and Brothers*—S.J.

[]—*Missionaries of Mary Immaculate* (India).

[0720]—*The Missionaries of Our Lady of La Salette* (Prov. of Mary, Queen of Peace)—M.S.

[1110]—*Missionaries of the Sacred Heart*—M.S.C.

[]—*Missionary Congregation of the Blessed Sacrament (India)*—M.C.B.S.

[]—*Missionary Fraternity of Mary (Guatemala)*—F.M.M.

[0430]—*Order of Preachers* (Province of St. Albert the Great)—O.P.
[0240]—*Order of St. Camillus-Camillian Fathers and Brothers*—M.I.
[1070]—*Redemptorist Fathers* (Denver Prov.)—C.Ss.R.
[0990]—*Society of the Catholic Apostolate* (Mater Dei Prov.)—S.A.C.
[1260]—*Society of Christ*—S.Ch.
[1200]—*Society of the Divine Savior* (American Prov.)—S.D.S.
[0420]—*Society of the Divine Word* (Northern Prov.)—S.V.D.
[0975]—*Society of Our Lady of the Most Holy Trinity*—S.O.L.T.
[1360]—*Xaverian Missionary Fathers*—S.X.

RELIGIOUS INSTITUTES OF WOMEN REPRESENTED IN THE ARCHDIOCESE

[0360]—*Carmelite Sisters of the Divine Heart of Jesus*—Carmel.D.C.J.
[]—*The Christian Sisters (Pious Union)*—C.S.
[]—*Congregation of Institutio Santa Mariana de Jesus.*
[3710]—*Congregation of the Sisters of Saint Agnes*—C.S.A.
[1780]—*Congregation of the Sisters of the Third Order of St. Francis of Perpetual Adoration* (Eastern Region)—F.S.P.A.
[0420]—*Discalced Carmelite Nuns*—O.C.D.
[1060]—*Dominican Contemplative Sisters*—O.P.
[1070-03]—*Dominican Sisters*—O.P.
[]—*Dominican Sisters* (Vietnam).
[1070-09]—*Dominican Sisters*—O.P.
[1070-27]—*Dominican Sisters*—O.P.
[1070-25]—*Dominican Sisters*—O.P.
[1170]—*Felician Sisters*—C.S.S.F.
[1310]—*Franciscan Sisters of Little Falls, MN*—O.S.F.
[1415]—*Franciscan Sisters of Mary*—F.S.M.
[]—*Franciscan Sisters of Our Lady (Pious Union)*—F.S.O.L.
[]—*Franciscan Sisters of St. Clare (Pious Union)*—F.S.S.C.
[1470]—*Franciscan Sisters of St. Joseph*—F.S.S.J.
[1240]—*Franciscan Sisters, Daughters of the Sacred Hearts of Jesus and Mary*—O.S.F.
[]—*Hermanus Misioneras Franciscanas de la Juventud*—H.M.F.S.
[]—*Hermitage of the Trinity.*
[1820]—*Hospital Sisters of the Third Order of St. Francis*—O.S.F.
[]—*Missionary Sisters of the Holy Family*—M.S.F.
[2970]—*School Sisters of Notre Dame*—S.S.N.D.
[1680]—*School Sisters of St. Francis*—O.S.F.
[]—*Secular Institute of Schoenstatt Sisters of Mary*—I.S.S.M.
[0600]—*Sisters of Charity of St. Joan Antida*—S.C.S.J.A.
[0430]—*Sisters of Charity of the Blessed Virgin Mary*—B.V.M.
[2575]—*Sisters of Mercy of the Americas*—R.S.M.
[1705]—*The Sisters of St. Francis of Assisi*—O.S.F.
[3930]—*Sisters of St. Joseph of the Third Order of St. Francis*—S.S.J.-T.O.S.F.
[4020]—*Sisters of St. Rita*—O.S.A.
[1030]—*Sisters of the Divine Savior*—S.D.S.
[4100]—*Sisters of the Sorrowful Mother (Third Order of St. Francis)*—S.S.M.
[3510]—*Sisters Servants of Christ the King*—S.S.C.K.

ARCHDIOCESAN CEMETERIES

MILWAUKEE. *St. Adalbert*, 3801 S. 6th S., 53221. Tel: 414-483-3663; Email: mthiel@cfcsmission.org

Calvary, 5503 W. Bluemound Rd., 53208. Tel: 414-438-4430; Email: mthiel@cfcsmission.org. 7301 W. Nash St.. Mary Thiel, Dir.

Holy Cross, Tel: 414-438-4420; Email: mthiel@cfcsmission.org. Mary Thiel, Dir.

Holy Trinity, 3564 S. 13th St., 53221. Tel: 414-483-3663; Email: mthiel@cfcsmission.org. 3801 S. 6th St., 53221. Mary Thiel, Dir.

Mount Olivet, 3801 W. Morgan Ave., 53221. Tel: 414-645-0611; Email: mthiel@cfcsmission.org. Mary Thiel, Dir.

FRANKLIN. *All Souls*, Ryan Rd., Franklin, 53132. Tel: 414-438-4420; Email: mthiel@cfcsmission.org. 7301 W. Nash St., 53216. Mary Thiel, Dir.

KENOSHA. *All Saints*, 3300 Springbrook Rd., Pleasant Prairie, 53158-5712. Tel: 262-694-2040; Email: mthiel@cfcsmission.org. Mary Thiel, Dir.

MEQUON. *Resurrection*, 215 Main St., P.O. Box 96, Allenton, 53002. Tel: 262-629-5240; Email: alleluia1@frontier.com. Very Rev. Richard J. Stoffel

WAUKESHA. *St. Joseph*, S22 W22890 Broadway, Waukesha, 53186. 501 S. Lake Dr., Saint Francis, 53235. Mary Thiel, Dir.

NON-ARCHDIOCESAN CEMETERIES

SHEBOYGAN. *Calvary Cemetery, Sheboygan, Wisconsin*, 902 North Ave., Sheboygan, 53083. Tel: 920-458-7721; Email: jljacobchick@gmail.com; Web: www.sheboygancalvarycemetery.com. 807 Superior Ave., Sheboygan, 53081. David Fischer, Contact Person

SOUTH MILWAUKEE. *Holy Sepulcher*, 675 College Ave., South Milwaukee, 53172-1252. Tel: 414-762-6800; Email: dmparish@divinemercysm.org. Gregg F. Apostoloff, Archdiocesan Dir.

TAYCHEEDAH. *St. Charles Cemetery*, W4287 Golf Course Dr. (cor. Cty UU), Taycheedah, 54935. Tel: 920-921-0580; Email: ellenk@hffdl.org. 271 4th St. Way, Fond Du Lac, 54937. Most Rev. Jerome E. Listecki, Pres.; Rev. Ryan J. Pruess, Vice Pres. Contact Holy Family Congregation, Fond du Lac, WI.

NECROLOGY

† Brady, James J., (Retired), Died Aug. 14, 2018
† Brahm, Harvey, (Retired), Died Mar. 1, 2018
† Fleischmann, George R., (Retired), Died May. 28, 2018
† Hentzner, John T., (Retired), Died May. 7, 2018
† Hmircik, Donald A., (Retired), Died Sep. 18, 2018
† Kazmierczak, Carl M., (Retired), Died May. 6, 2018
† Lamb, Matthew L., Ave Maria, FL, Died Jan. 12, 2018
† Lasecki, Daniel J., (Retired), Died Jun. 26, 2018
† Last, Carl A., (Retired), Died Jun. 30, 2018
† Massey, Robert E., (Retired), Died Nov. 18, 2018
† Michalski, Melvin E., (Retired), Died May. 20, 2018
† Paczesny, John R., (Retired), Died Sep. 16, 2018
† Safiejko, Edward M., (Retired), Died May. 10, 2018
† Schneider, Karl J., (Retired), Died Mar. 29, 2018

An asterisk (*) denotes an organization that has established tax-exempt status directly with the IRS and is not covered by the USCCB Group Ruling.

Archdiocese of Mobile

(Archidioecesis Mobiliensis)

Most Reverend

THOMAS J. RODI

Archbishop of Mobile; ordained May 20, 1978; appointed Bishop of Biloxi May 15, 2001; ordained and installed July 2, 2001; appointed Archbishop of Mobile April 2, 2008; installed June 6, 2008. *Chancery Office: 400 Government St., Mobile, AL 36602.* Tel: 251-434-1585; Email: archbishop@mobarch.org.

Most Reverend

OSCAR H. LIPSCOMB, D.D., PH.D.

Archbishop Emeritus of Mobile; ordained July 15, 1956; appointed July 29, 1980; consecrated November 16, 1980; retired April 2, 2008. *Res.: Sacred Heart, 1655 McGill Ave., Mobile, AL 36604.*

Chancery Office: 400 Government St., Mobile, AL 36602. Tel: 251-434-1585; Fax: 251-434-1588.

Email: chancery@mobarch.org

Square Miles 22,969.

Established as Vicariate-Apostolic of Alabama and the Floridas, 1825; Diocese of Mobile, May 15, 1829; Name changed to Diocese of Mobile-Birmingham, July 9, 1954; Redesignated, June 28, 1969. Raised to rank of Archdiocese November 16, 1980.

Comprises the lower 28 Counties of the State of Alabama, namely: Choctaw, Clarke, Wilcox, Dallas, Autauga, Elmore, Lee, Russell, Macon, Montgomery, Lowndes, Barbour, Bullock, Pike, Crenshaw, Butler, Monroe, Conecuh, Escambia, Covington, Coffee, Geneva, Dale, Henry, Houston, Washington, Baldwin and Mobile.

For legal titles of parishes and archdiocesan institutions consult the Chancery Office.

STATISTICAL OVERVIEW

Personnel	
Archbishops	1
Retired Archbishops	1
Priests: Diocesan Active in Diocese	57
Priests: Diocesan Active Outside Diocese	3
Priests: Retired, Sick or Absent	24
Number of Diocesan Priests	84
Religious Priests in Diocese	29
Total Priests in Diocese	113
Extern Priests in Diocese	10
Ordinations:	
Diocesan Priests	2
Transitional Deacons	1
Permanent Deacons	11
Permanent Deacons in Diocese	66
Total Brothers	7
Total Sisters	93
Parishes	
Parishes	76
With Resident Pastor:	
Resident Diocesan Priests	49
Resident Religious Priests	14
Without Resident Pastor:	
Administered by Priests	13
Missions	9
Pastoral Centers	2
Professional Ministry Personnel:	
Brothers	7
Sisters	24
Lay Ministers	114
Welfare	
Catholic Hospitals	1
Total Assisted	190,000
Health Care Centers	1
Total Assisted	80
Homes for the Aged	4
Total Assisted	440
Residential Care of Children	1
Total Assisted	90
Day Care Centers	6
Total Assisted	182
Special Centers for Social Services	9
Total Assisted	22,770
Residential Care of Disabled	1
Total Assisted	58
Educational	
Diocesan Students in Other Seminaries	17
Total Seminarians	17
Colleges and Universities	1
Total Students	1,501
High Schools, Diocesan and Parish	3
Total Students	1,624
Elementary Schools, Diocesan and Parish	17
Total Students	3,821
Elementary Schools, Private	2
Total Students	151
Catechesis/Religious Education:	
High School Students	913
Elementary Students	1,652
Total Students under Catholic Instruction	9,679
Teachers in the Diocese:	
Priests	1
Brothers	1
Sisters	6
Lay Teachers	532
Vital Statistics	
Receptions into the Church:	
Infant Baptism Totals	959
Minor Baptism Totals	136
Adult Baptism Totals	129
Received into Full Communion	243
First Communions	1,123
Confirmations	935
Marriages:	
Catholic	171
Interfaith	114
Total Marriages	285
Deaths	556
Total Catholic Population	87,912
Total Population	1,801,274

Former Prelates—Rt. Revs. MICHAEL PORTIER, D.D., ord. May 16, 1818; First Bishop; cons. Nov. 5, 1826; died May 14, 1859; JOHN QUINLAN, D.D., ord. Aug. 30, 1852; cons. Dec. 4, 1859; died March 9, 1883; DOMINIC MANUCY, D.D., ord. Aug. 15, 1850; appt. Vicar Apostolic of Brownsville and cons. Bishop of Dulma Dec. 8, 1874; transferred to Mobile March 9, 1884, but resigned in the same year; died at Mobile, Dec. 4, 1885; JEREMIAH O'SULLIVAN, D.D., ord. June 30, 1868; cons. Sept. 20, 1885; died Aug. 10, 1896; E. P. ALLEN, ord. Dec. 17, 1881; cons. May 16, 1897; died Oct. 21, 1926; Most Revs. THOMAS J. TOOLEN, D.D., ord. Sept. 27, 1910; cons. May 4, 1927; appt. Archbishop "ad personam," May 27, 1954; resigned Oct. 8, 1969; died Dec. 4, 1976; JOHN L. MAY, D.D., ord. May 3, 1947; appt. Titular Bishop of Tagarbala and Auxiliary Bishop of Chicago, June 21, 1967; cons. Aug. 24, 1967; transferred to Mobile, Oct. 8, 1969; installed Dec. 10, 1969; appt. to Saint Louis, Jan. 29, 1980; died March 24, 1994; OSCAR H. LIPSCOMB, D.D., Ph.D., (Retired), ord. July 15, 1956; appt. July 29, 1980; cons. Nov. 16, 1980; retired April 2, 2008.

Vicar General and Moderator of the Curia—Rev. Msgr. MICHAEL L. FARMER, S.T.L., V.G., 400 Government St., Mobile, 36602. Tel: 251-434-1585; Fax: 251-434-1588; Email: vicargeneral@mobarch.org.

Vicars Forane—Very Rev. JAMES F. ZOGHBY, V.F., Mobile Deanery, 6300 McKenna Dr., Mobile, 36608. Tel: 251-342-1852; Tel: 251-342-1852; Fax: 251-342-6313; Rev. Msgrs. WILLIAM J. SKONEKI, V.F., Montgomery Deanery, 1100 N. College St., Auburn, 36830. Tel: 334-887-5540; PATRICK J. GALLAGHER, V.F., Dothan Deanery, 2700 W. Main St., Dothan, 36301. Tel: 334-793-5802; Fax: 334-792-2816; Very Rev. PAUL G. ZOGHBY, V.F., Baldwin/Escambia Deanery, 601 W. Laurel, Foley, 36535. Tel: 251-943-4009; Fax: 251-943-4010.

Chancellor—Deacon RONNIE A. HATHORNE, Email: rhathorne@mobarch.org.

Archivist—MRS. KAREN J. HORTON, C.A.

Archives Office—14 S. Franklin St., Mobile, 36602. Tel: 251-415-3850; Fax: 251-434-1588; Email: archives@mobarch.org. *Mailing Address: 400 Government St., Mobile, 36602.*

Liaison with African-American Catholic Ministries—8432 Whitestone Pl., Semmes, 36575. Email: memmett@mobarch.org. Deacon MARCENE E. EMMETT.

Metropolitan Tribunal—14 S. Franklin St., Mobile, 36602-2409. Tel: 251-432-4609; Fax: 251-432-4647.

Judicial Vicar—Rev. Msgr. JAMES S. KEE, S.T.L., J.C.L., J.V.

Associate Judges—Deacon J. DOUGLAS SINCHAK, M.S., J.C.L.; Rev. Msgr. LEONARDO C. GUADALQUIVER, J.C.L.; MRS. KATHERINE S. WEBER, MS (Th), J.C.L.; Rev. DANIEL F. GOOD, J.C.L.

Defender of the Bond—MRS. MICHELE MCALOON, J.C.L.

Advocate—Rev. JOHNNY S. SAVOIE.

Notaries and Secretaries—MS. SHARON B. CUSIMANO; MRS. SARAH K. ARENDALL.

Assessor—MR. ROBERT D. BROOKS, J.D.

Archdiocesan Consultors—Rev. Msgrs. STEPHEN E. MARTIN; JAMES S. KEE, S.T.L., J.C.L., J.V.; Revs. JAMES J. CINK; MARK I. NESKE; ALEJANDRO E. VALLADARES, S.T.L.; Very Rev. JAMES F. ZOGHBY, V.F.; Rev. Msgr. MICHAEL L. FARMER, S.T.L., V.G.

Liaison With Religious - Sisters, Nuns & Brothers—Sr. CAROLYN OBERKIRCH, R.S.M., 101 Wimbledon Dr.

W., Mobile, 36608. Tel: 251-344-1377; Email: coberkirch@mercysc.org.

Archdiocesan Finance Council—356 Government St., P.O. Box 230, Mobile, 36601. Tel: 251-432-1548; Fax: 251-434-1547; Email: mmanry@mobarch.org.

Presbyteral Council—Most Rev. THOMAS J. RODI, Pres. Officers: Very Rev. PAUL G. ZOGHBY, V.F., Chm.; Rev. PATRICK R. DRISCOLL, Vice Chm.; Rev. Msgr. MICHAEL L. FARMER, S.T.L., V.G., Sec.

Elected Members—Group I: Rev. MATTHEW J. O'CONNOR. Group II: Rev. PATRICK R. DRISCOLL. Group III: Rev. STEPHEN G. VRAZEL.

Religious—Rev. KENNETH C. UGWU, S.S.J.

Jesuit—Rev. MARK S. MOSSA, S.J.

Priests' Personnel Committee—400 Government St., Mobile, 36602. Tel: 251-434-1585. Very Rev. PAUL G. ZOGHBY, V.F., Chm.

Archdiocesan Offices and Directors

Catholic Department of Education—352 Government St., Mobile, 36602. Tel: 251-438-4611; Fax: 251-438-4612; Web: mobarchschools.org.

Executive Director—MISS GWENDOLYN P. BYRD, Email: gbyrd@mobarch.org.

Office of Catholic Schools—MISS GWENDOLYN P. BYRD, Supt.; MRS. KAREN F. ABREO, Assoc. Supt. Academics, Email: kabreo@mobarch.org; MRS. VIRGINIA N. KOPPERSMITH, Assoc. Supt. Student Svcs., Email: gkoppersmith@mobarch.org; MRS. JEAN C. DEMPSEY, Dir. Devel., 352 Government St., Mobile, 36602. Tel: 251-438-4611; Email: jdempsey@mobarch.org.

Office of Youth and Young Adult Ministry—MR. ADAM J. GANUCHEAU, Dir., 352 Government St., Mobile, 36602. Tel: 251-433-4138; Fax: 251-432-4801; Email: aganucheau@mobarch.org; Web: www.archmobyouth.org.

Office of Evangelization and Family Life—Mailing Address: 352 Government St., Mobile, 36602. Tel: 251-433-6991; Web: mobilefaithformation.org. MR. PATRICK J. ARENSBERG, Dir., Email: parensberg@mobarch.org; MRS. JANET M. MASLINE, Assoc. Dir., Email: jmasline@mobarch.org.

Ecumenical and Interreligious Affairs—Rev. DAVID J. TOKARZ, Liaison, 1801 Cody Rd. S., Mobile, 36695. Tel: 251-633-6762; Fax: 251-633-7790; Email: dtokarz@mobarch.org.

Hispanic Ministry—Deacon HECTOR J. DONASTORG, Archdiocesan Dir., 406 Government St., Mobile, 36602. Tel: 251-690-6907; Rev. JOSE LUIS MESA, S.J., Spring Hill College, 4000 Dauphin St., Mobile, 36608. Tel: 352-316-1700.

Prison Ministry—Deacon STEPHEN A. TIDWELL, Archdiocesan Dir., St. Maurice Parish, 202 E. Jackson St., Brewton, 36427. Tel: 251-434-1577.

Catholic Foundation of the Archdiocese of Mobile—356 Government St., P.O. Box 230, Mobile, 36601. Tel: 251-434-1556; Fax: 251-434-1547; Email: sroh@mobarch.org. MRS. SHANNON D. ROH, Exec. Dir.

Catholic Publishing Co., Inc.—Publisher of the Archdiocesan Newspaper "The Catholic Week" *356 Government St., P.O. Box 349, Mobile, 36601.* MR. ROBERT W. HERBST, Editor, Tel: 251-434-1544; Email: rherbst@mobarch.org.

Catholic Social Services—Mailing Address: P.O. Box 161229, Mobile, 36616. Tel: 251-434-1550; Fax: 251-431-1549. *188 S. Florida St., Mobile, 36606.* MRS. MARILYN D. KING, Exec. Dir., Email: mdking@mobarch.org; Web: catholicsocialservices-mobile.com. Total Archdiocesan-wide Assisted Annually 22,770.

Adoption Services—188 S. Florida St., P.O. Box 161229, Mobile, 36616. Tel: 251-232-2531; Tel: 251-434-1550; Email: dschofield@mobarch.org. MRS. DREAMA SCHOFIELD, L.I.C.S.W., Dir.

Counseling—188 S. Florida St., Mobile, 36606. Tel: 251-434-1550; Fax: 251-434-1549. MRS. BUFFY L. MARSTON, Clinical Dir., Email: bmarston@mobarch.org. Total Assisted Annually: 844.

Disability Ministry and Services—188 S. Florida St., P.O. Box 161229, Mobile, 36616. Tel: 251-434-1550. VACANT, Prog. Mgr. Total assisted annually 168.

Disaster Preparedness/Response—188 S. Florida St., Mobile, 36606. Tel: 251-895-8417; Fax: 251-434-1549. MR. JOHN P. WILSON, Dir.

Catholic Deaf Ministry—MR. WILLIAM F. JONES, Tel: 251-454-9098.

Father Purcell Memorial Exceptional Children's Center— (1958) 2048 W. Fairview Ave., Montgomery, 36108. Tel: 334-834-5590; Fax: 334-834-5592. MS. BRENDA F. WITHERS, Admin.Patients Asst Anual. 58.

St. Teresa of Calcutta Senior Ministry—188 S. Florida St., Mobile, 36606. Tel: 251-434-1550; Fax: 251-434-1549. MRS. BRITTANY RAJ, L.M.S.W., Prog. Mgr., Email: braj@mobarch.org. Total Annually Assisted: 109.

Pregnancy Services—

2-B Choices for Women—188 S. Florida St., Mobile, 36606. Tel: 251-343-4636; Fax: 251-434-1549. MISS KATHRYN VRAZEL, Prog. Mgr., Email: kvrazel@mobarch.org. Total Assisted: 354.

To Be Options for Pregnant Women—23010 Hwy. 59 N., P.O. Box 870, Robertsdale, 36567. Tel: 251-923-3305; Fax: 251-947-4058; Web: www.toberobertsdale.com. MS. DEBORAH GOMILLION, Prog. Mgr., Total Assisted Annually 103. Total Assisted Annually: 103.

Refugee Resettlement—188 S. Florida St., Mobile, 36606. Tel: 251-432-2727; Fax: 251-432-2927. MR. JOSEPH K. BAYER, Prog. Mgr., Email: jbayer@mobarch.org. Total Assisted: 118.

Emergency Assistance Program—188 S. Florida St., Mobile, 36606. Tel: 251-434-1500; Fax: 251-434-1509. MRS. DREAMA SCHOFIELD, L.I.C.S.W., Prog. Mgr., Email: dschofield@mobarch.org. Total Assisted: 6,185.

Family Service Center of Bay Minette—2402 Hwy. 31 S., Ste. C, Bay Minette, 36507. Tel: 251-937-7858. MRS. BUFFY L. MARSTON, Dir., Email: fscbm@aol.com. Total Assisted 1,359.

Robertsdale Baldwin Office—23010 Hwy. 59 N., P.O. Box 870, Robertsdale, 36567. Tel: 251-947-2293; Fax: 251-947-4058. MRS. PHYLLIS BEAM, Email: pbeam@mobarch.org. Total Assisted Annually 2,654.

Clarke County Office—3309 College Ave., P.O. Box 85, Jackson, 36545. Tel: 251-246-0131; Fax: 251-246-0131. MRS. SHIELA L. SMITH, Dir., Email: cssclarke@mindspring.com. Total Assisted 2,777.

Dothan Office—557 W. Main St., Dothan, 36302. Tel: 334-793-3601; Fax: 334-702-0825. MRS. CELESTE KELLY, Dir., Email: ckellydothancss@gmail.com. Total Assisted Annually: 4,206.

Montgomery Office—4455 Narrow Lane Rd., Montgomery, 36116. Tel: 334-288-8890; Fax: 334-288-9322. Deacon RAYMOND M. GUERET, Dir., Email: director@cssalabama.org. Total Assisted: 3,533.

St. Margaret's Services—MRS. CAROL B. HERRON, Supvr., Email: herron@cssalabama.org. Total Assisted Annually 92.

Censor Librorum—Rev. Msgr. MICHAEL L. FARMER, S.T.L., V.G., 400 Government St., Mobile, 36602. Tel: 251-434-1586; Fax: 251-434-1588; Email: vicargeneral@mobarch.org.

Development Office—356 Government St., P.O. Box 230, Mobile, 36601. Tel: 251-438-9668; Fax: 251-434-1547. MRS. SHANNON D. ROH, Dir., Email: sroh@mobarch.org. Funding Office for charitable and other works of Archdiocese.; Encompasses: Catholic Charities Appeal Office, Development, Stewardship and Planned Giving.

Financial Services—356 Government St., P.O. Box 230, Mobile, 36601. Tel: 251-432-2737; Fax: 251-434-1547.

Executive Director—MS. MICHELE C. MANRY, Email: mmanry@mobarch.org.

Accounting Department—MR. D. ROSS PARRISH, CPA, Accounting Mgr., Email: rparrish@mobarch.org.

Personnel Administration and Benefits—MRS. VICKI A. STRICKLIN, Mgr., Email: vstricklin@mobarch.org.

Information Systems/Technology—MR. ANDREW M. PITTS, Mgr., Email: apitts@mobarch.org.

Real Estate, Property/Liability Insurance & Risk Management—MRS. LISA B. HANSEN, Dir., Email: lhansen@mobarch.org.

Facilities Management—MR. ROBIN M. ROCKSTALL, Mgr., Tel: 251-434-1534; Email: rrockstall@mobarch.org.

Catholic Cemeteries, Inc.—400 Government St., Mobile, 36602. Tel: 251-434-1557. MS. FRANKIE M. YOUNG, Admin., Email: fyoung@mobarch.org.

Encompasses:—

Catholic Cemetery of Mobile—1700 Dr. Martin Luther King, Jr. Ave., Mobile, 36617. Tel: 251-479-5305. *Mailing Address: P.O. Box 230, Mobile, 36601.* MR. J. TILMON BROWN, Dir.

St. Margaret Catholic Cemetery—829 Columbus St., Montgomery, 36104. Mailing Address: P.O. Box 230, Mobile, 36601. Tel: 251-434-1557. MS. FRANKIE M. YOUNG, Admin., Email: fyoung@mobarch.org.

Allen Memorial Home Corporation—400 Government St., Mobile, 36602.

Catholic Housing of Mobile, Inc.—Most Rev. THOMAS J. RODI, Pres.; Rev. Msgr. MICHAEL L. FARMER, S.T.L., V.G., Vice Pres., 400 Government St., Mobile, 36602. Tel: 251-434-1585. Nonprofit Corp. of the State of Alabama; Encompasses Cathedral Place Apartments.

Catholic Housing Authority of Montgomery, Inc.—3721 Wares Ferry Rd., Montgomery, 36109. MR. ZACK AZAR, Pres. Nonprofit Corp. of the State of Alabama; encompasses Seton Haven Apartments.

Cullen Center—18701 Scenic Hwy. 98, Fairhope, 36532. Mailing Address: P.O. Box 230, Mobile, 36601. Tel: 251-434-1540.

McGill Institute Charitable Trust—400 Government St., Mobile, 36602.

McGill-Toolen Foundation—Mailing Address: 1501 Old Shell Rd., Mobile, 36604. Tel: 251-445-2939; Fax: 251-433-8356. MRS. JENNA L. WOOD, Dir., Email: woodj@mcgill-toolen.org.

Pontifical Mission Societies of the United States— (Encompasses Propagation of the Faith, Holy Childhood Assoc., Missionary Co-op) *Mailing Address: 400 Government St., Mobile, 36602.* Rev. Msgr. MICHAEL L. FARMER, S.T.L., V.G., Dir.

Legal Services—MRS. LISA B. HANSEN, Gen. Counsel, 356 Government St., Mobile, 36602. Tel: 251-434-1540; Email: lhansen@mobarch.org.

Liturgical Commission—Rev. Msgr. MICHAEL L. FARMER, S.T.L., V.G., 400 Government St., Mobile, 36602. Tel: 251-434-1585; Fax: 251-434-1588; Email: vicargeneral@mobarch.org.

Apostleship of Prayer—Mailing Address: 400 Government St., Mobile, 36602. Email: vicargeneral@mobarch.org. Rev. Msgr. MICHAEL L. FARMER, S.T.L., V.G.

Apostleship of the Sea—Rev. LITO J. CAPEDING, Chap., 400 Government St., Mobile, 36602. Tel: 251-432-7339; Email: lcapeding@mobarch.org.

Archdiocesan Council of Catholic Women (ACCW)—168 Trent Rd., Enterprise, 36330. Tel: 334-308-2564. MRS. CONNIE SEYLER, Pres., Email: seylerconnie@yahoo.com.

Confraternity of Intercessors for Priests in the Heart of St. Joseph—219 Adams Ave., P.O. Box 114, Montgomery, 36101. Tel: 334-262-7304; Web: www.intercessorsforpriests.com. Rev. J. FRANCIS SOFIE, Dir.

Vietnamese Apostolate—

Vietnamese Community Council—Rev. CU MINH DUONG, Vicar Vietnamese Affairs, St. Monica Parish, 1131 Dauphin Island Pkwy., Mobile, 36605. Tel: 251-479-7360.

Permanent Diaconate Program—Deacon RONNIE A. HATHORNE, Dir., Mailing Address: P.O. Box 728, Mobile, 36601. Tel: 251-473-3761.

Office for the Protection of Minors and Adults—352 Government St., P.O. Box 230, Mobile, 36601. Tel: 251-434-1559 (Office); Email: childprotection@mobarch.org. MRS. VIRGINIA N. KOPPERSMITH, Dir.; MRS. LEANNE R. OBERKIRCH, Administrative Asst.

Vocations—Rev. VICTOR P. INGALLS, Dir., 400 Government St., Mobile, 36602. Tel: 251-415-3871; Fax: 251-434-1588; Email: vocations@mobarch.org; Web: www.mobilevocations.com.

CLERGY, PARISHES, MISSIONS AND PAROCHIAL SCHOOLS

CITY OF MOBILE

(MOBILE COUNTY)

1—CATHEDRAL-BASILICA OF THE IMMACULATE CONCEPTION (1704)

2 S. Claiborne St., 36602. Tel: 251-434-1565; Email: cathaom@bellsouth.net. 400 Government St., 36602. Most Rev. Thomas J. Rodi; Rev. Msgr. Michael L. Farmer, S.T.L., V.G., Rector; Rev. Victor P. Ingalls; Rev. Msgr. James F. Dorrill, Ph.D., In Res., (Retired); Deacon John J. Archer

Legal Name: Cathedral-Basilica of the Immaculate Conception Parish, Mobile

The Portier House—(Historic home of first bishop of Mobile) Parish Office: 307 Conti St., 36602. Web: www.mobilecathedral.org.

2—ST. CATHERINE OF SIENA (1913)

2605 Springhill Ave., 36607. Tel: 251-473-1415; Fax: 251-473-6307. Rev. Msgr. James S. Kee, S.T.L., J.C.L., J.V.; Deacon J. Douglas Sinchak, M.S., J.C.L.

Catechesis Religious Program—Students 13.

3—CORPUS CHRISTI PARISH, MOBILE (1958)

6300 McKenna Dr., 36608. Tel: 251-342-1852; Email: Church@CorpusChristiParish.com; Web: www.corpuschristiparish.com. Very Rev. James F. Zoghby, V.F.; Rev. John S. Boudreaux; Deacon Arthur W. Robbins.

School—Corpus Christi Parish School, (Grades PreK-8), Tel: 251-342-5474; Fax: 251-380-0325; Email: school@corpuschristiparish.com; Web: www.corpuschristiparish.com/school. Mrs. Kristy F. Martin, Prin.; Mrs. Sally S. McKenna, Asst. Prin.; Penny Mansfield, Librarian. Aides 14; Lay Teachers 29; Students 567.

Catechesis Religious Program—
Tel: 251-342-5474, Ext. 2; Fax: 251-380-0325. Diane M. Stoyka, D.R.E. Students 126.

4—ST. DOMINIC PARISH, MOBILE (1958)
4156 Burma Rd., 36693. Tel: 251-661-5130; Fax: 251-661-0469. Revs. Patrick Remmers Driscoll; Christopher G. Boutin; Deacons Wiley J. Christian; Robert E. Kirby; Aldon O. Ward.
School—St. Dominic Parish, Mobile School, (Grades PreK-8), 4160 Burma Rd., 36693. Tel: 251-661-5226; Fax: 251-660-2242. Mrs. Laurie S. Michener, Prin.; Mrs. Debra A. Peuschel, Asst. Prin. Lay Teachers 32; Students 504.
Catechesis Religious Program—Students 95.
Convent—Tel: 251-661-3229.

5—ST. FRANCIS XAVIER PARISH, MOBILE (1867) (African American)
2034 St. Stephens Rd., 36617. Tel: 251-473-4975; Fax: 251-473-0291. Rev. Dominic Oguama, M.S.P.
Catechesis Religious Program—Students 7.

6—HOLY FAMILY PARISH, MOBILE (1959)
1400 Joyce Rd., 36618. Tel: 251-344-0271; Email: holyfamilychu637@bellsouth.net. Rev. Mark I. Neske.

7—ST. IGNATIUS PARISH, MOBILE (Spring Hill) (1947)
3704 Springhill Ave., 36608. Tel: 251-342-9221; Fax: 251-341-1481; Email: church@stignatius.org. Revs. W. Bry Shields; James Singarayar, H.G.N.; Deacon William J. Harkins.
School—St. Ignatius Parish, Mobile School, (Grades PreK-8), 3650 Springhill Ave., 36608. Tel: 251-342-5442; Fax: 251-344-0944. Ms. Tori Y. Miller, Prin.; Ms. Elizabeth Collins, Asst. Prin.; Mrs. Dorothy Beattie, Librarian. Lay Teachers 35; Students 553.
Catechesis Religious Program—Students 182.
Child Care—Early Learning Center,
Tel: 251-445-6720; Fax: 251-345-1064. Catherine McPhillips, Dir. Lay Teachers 6; Students 36.

8—ST. JOAN OF ARC PARISH, MOBILE (1920)
1260 Elmira St., 36604. Tel: 251-432-3505. Rev. Msgr. G. Warren Wall; Rev. Cecil R. Spotswood, Parochial Vicar; Deacon Douglas M. McEnery; Bro. Celestine Algero, S.C., Ph.D., D.R.E.

9—ST. JOSEPH PARISH, MOBILE (1857) Closed. For inquiries for sacramental records please contact Cathedral Parish, Mobile.

10—ST. JOSEPH PARISH, MAYSVILLE (1944) (African American)
1703 Dublin St., 36605. Tel: 251-473-3761; Fax: 251-473-3768; Email: stjosephmaysville@josephite.com. Deacon Ronnie A. Hathorne; Rev. Bura Aloysius Koroba, S.S.J.
Res.: 1701 Dublin St., 36605. Tel: 251-473-0223.

11—LITTLE FLOWER PARISH, MOBILE (1928)
2053 Government St., 36606. Tel: 251-478-3381; Email: lfbulletin@littleflower.cc; Web: www.littleflowermobile.com. Revs. John G. Lynes; Andrew Jones, Parochial Vicar; Sr. Mary Joyce Bringer, C.S.J., Pastoral Assoc.; Deacons Ronald Martin; Curt A. Crider.
School—Little Flower Parish, Mobile School, (Grades PreK-8), 2103 Government St., 36606. Tel: 251-479-5761; Fax: 251-450-3696. Ms. Alesa Weiskopf, Prin. Lay Teachers 18; Students 157.
Catechesis Religious Program—Students 75.
Convent—411 Glenwood Ave., 36606. Tel: 251-378-5761; Email: smjbringer@littleflower.cc. Sisters 1.

12—ST. MARY PARISH, MOBILE (1867)
1453 Old Shell Rd., 36604. Tel: 251-432-8678; Fax: 251-432-1009; Email: mrnaman@stmarymobile.org; Web: www.stmarymobile.org. 106 Providence St., 36604. Rev. Msgr. G. Warren Wall; Rev. Cecil R. Spotswood, Parochial Vicar; Deacon Ernest J. Johnson.
School—St. Mary Parish, Mobile School, (Grades PreK-8), 107 N. Lafayette St., 36604. Tel: 251-433-9904; Fax: 251-438-9069. Mrs. Debbie D. Ollis, Prin.; Sue Lyon, Librarian. Lay Teachers 35; Students 545.
Catechesis Religious Program—Students 50.

13—ST. MATTHEW PARISH, MOBILE (1904)
906 Garrity St., 36605-4699. Tel: 251-432-4784; Fax: 251-434-0020; Email: stmat9t@comcast.net. Rev. Joseph M. Bolling; Deacon Joseph V. Connick.

14—ST. MONICA PARISH, MOBILE (1950)
1131 Dauphin Island Pkwy., 36605. Tel: 251-479-7360. Rev. Cu Minh Duong.

15—MOST PURE HEART OF MARY (1899) (African American)
304 Sengstak St., 36603. Tel: 251-432-3344; Fax: 251-432-1192. Rev. Kenneth C. Ugwu, S.S.J.; Deacon James D. Bryant.
School—Most Pure Heart of Mary, (Grades K-8), 310 Sengstak St., 36603. Tel: 251-432-5270; Fax: 251-432-5271; Email: jcrain@mobarch.org. Mrs. Jamie G. Crain, Prin.; Ms. Brandy Black, Librarian. Students 160.
Catechesis Religious Program—Tel: 251-487-8891. Latanya Brown, D.R.E. Students 18.

16—OUR LADY OF LOURDES PARISH, MOBILE (1941)
1621 Boykin Blvd., 36605. Tel: 251-479-9885; Fax: 251-479-9892; Email: ollparish@att.net. Deacon Edward G. Connick; Rev. Marcin Dudziak.
Catechesis Religious Program—Students 11.

17—OUR SAVIOR PARISH, MOBILE (1977)
1801 Cody Rd. S., 36695. Tel: 251-633-6762; Fax: 251-633-7790; Email: office@oursaviorparish.org. Rev. David J. Tokarz; Deacons Norman M. Gale; Jay Boyd; Francis Hoai N. Tran.
Child Care—Our Savior Preschool & Mother's Day Out, (PK3-4) Tel: 251-633-3017; Email: director@oursaviorpreschool.com. Mrs. Rita G. Langan, Dir.
Catechesis Religious Program—Students 141.

18—ST. PIUS X PARISH, MOBILE (1954)
217 S. Sage Ave., 36606. Tel: 251-471-2449; Email: spx@stpiustenth.com; Web: stpiustenth.com. Rev. Johnny S. Savoie.
School—St. Pius X Parish School, (Grades K-8), Tel: 251-473-5004; Fax: 251-473-5008; Email: office@stpiusxmobile.com. Mrs. Lauren K. Alvarez, Prin.; Ms. Diane Roberts, Librarian. Lay Teachers 20; Sisters 1; Students 240.
Catechesis Religious Program—Tel: 251-473-4381. Students 50.

19—PRINCE OF PEACE PARISH, MOBILE (1970) (African American)
454 Charleston St., 36603. Tel: 251-432-2364; Fax: 251-432-2372; Email: princeofpeace@bellsouth.net. Rev. John R. Basiimwa, F.M.H.; Deacon Marcene E. Emmett.
Catechesis Religious Program—Tel: 251-433-1494. Students 6.

20—ST. VINCENT DE PAUL PARISH, MOBILE (1971)
6625 Three Notch Rd., 36619. Tel: 251-661-3908; Fax: 251-665-4956; Email: svrazel@mobarch.org. Rev. Stephen G. Vrazel; Deacon Gary J. Vrazel.
Child Care—St. Vincent De Paul Daycare, (Infant to 3 yrs.) 6651 Three Notch Rd., 36619. Tel: 251-666-4066; Email: stvincentdc@mobarch.org. Mrs. Anitra K. Smith, Dir.
School—St. Vincent de Paul Parish, Mobile School, (Grades PreK-8), 4980 St. Vincent Dr., 36619. Tel: 251-666-8022; Fax: 251-666-1296; Web: www.svsschool.org. Mrs. Corinne T. Cuffle, Prin. Lay Teachers 10; Students 183.
Catechesis Religious Program—Tel: 251-661-3908. Students 52.

OUTSIDE THE CITY OF MOBILE

ANDALUSIA, COVINGTON CO., CHRIST THE KING (1933)
508 Sanford Rd., P.O. Drawer 1546, Andalusia, 36420. Tel: 334-222-4808; Email: christthekingandalusia@gmail.com. Rev. Bieu Van Nguyen; Deacon Robert D. Bailey.
Catechesis Religious Program—Students 48.

ATMORE, ESCAMBIA CO., ST. ROBERT BELLARMINE (1943)
600 S. Main St., Atmore, 36502-2825. Tel: 251-368-3615. Rev. Arulappan Jayaraj, H.G.N.
Catechesis Religious Program—Students 27.

AUBURN, LEE CO., ST. MICHAEL (1912)
1100 N. College St., Auburn, 36830. Tel: 334-887-5540; Fax: 334-887-5572; Email: stmichaels@charter.net; Web: www.stmichaelsauburn.com. Rev. Msgr. William J. Skoneki, V.F.; Rev. Gilbert T. Pierre, Parochial Vicar; Deacons Paul W. Brown; Hector J. Donastorg
Legal Title: St Michael the Archangel Parish, Auburn
Child Care—St. Michael Catholic Preschool, (PK3) Ms. Cynthia L. Wilton, Dir.
Catechesis Religious Program—Students 449.
Chaplaincy—115 Mitcham Ave., Auburn, 36830. Tel: 334-209-1711; Email: aucatholic@gmail.com; Web: www.aucatholic.org. Auburn Catholic Campus Ministry.

BAY MINETTE, BALDWIN CO., ST. AGATHA PARISH, BAY MINETTE (1951)
1001 Hand Ave., Bay Minette, 36507. Tel: 251-937-8600; Email: stagathabm@gmail.com. Rev. Joseph Chacko.

BAYOU LA BATRE, MOBILE CO., ST. MARGARET PARISH, BAYOU LA BATRE (1880) [CEM]
13790 S. Wintzell Ave., Bayou La Batre, 36509. Tel: 251-824-2415; Email: fleetblessing@gmail.com. P.O. Box 365, Bayou La Batre, 36509. Rev. Alwin P. Legaspi.

BELLE FONTAINE, MOBILE CO., ST. PHILIP NERI (1908)
9101 Dauphin Island Pkwy., Belle Fontaine, 36582. Tel: 251-973-2096; Email: saintphilipneri@bellsouth.net; Web: loweralabamacatholic.com. Deacon James L. Scott; Rev. Daniel F. Good, J.C.L.
Catechesis Religious Program—Students 41.

BON SECOUR, BALDWIN CO., OUR LADY OF BON SECOUR PARISH, (Mission of St. John the Baptist Parish, Magnolia Springs)
17266 County Rd. 49 S., Bon Secour, 36511. Mailing Address: P.O. Box 206, Magnolia Springs, 36555. Tel: 251-965-7719. Rev. Jesuraj Babu Arulraj, H.G.N.

BREWTON, ESCAMBIA CO., ST. MAURICE PARISH, BREWTON (1948)
202 E. Jackson St., P.O. Box 206, Brewton, 36427-0206. Tel: 251-867-5189. Rev. Patrick J. Madden; Deacon Stephen A. Tidwell.

BROMLEY, BALDWIN CO., ST. JOHN PARISH, (Mission of Shrine of the Holy Cross Parish, Daphne)
7488 Herman Sledge Rd., Bromley, 36507. Email: lcapeding@mobarch.org. Mailing Address: P.O. Box 1497, Daphne, 36526. Rev. Lito J. Capeding.

BUTLER, CHOCTAW CO., ST. JOHN THE EVANGELIST (1958)
401 E. Pushmataha St., Butler, 36904. Tel: 251-275-3665. P.O. Box 456, Grove Hill, 36451. Rev. Travis J. Burnett.

CAMDEN, WILCOX CO., ST. JOSEPH PARISH, (Mission of Annunciation Parish, Monroeville)
565 Whetstone St., Monroeville, 36460. Tel: 251-575-2644; Email: annuncat@frontiernet.net. Rev. Stephen C. Hellman.
Res.: 302 Whiskey Run Rd., Camden, 36726.

CHASTANG, MOBILE CO., ST. PETER THE APOSTLE (1860) [CEM]
16650 Hwy. 43, Chastang, 36560. Tel: 251-829-5134; Fax: 251-829-6874; Email: stpetertheapostle@wildblue.net. P.O. Box 456, Mount Vernon, 36560. Rev. Amal Raj Samy, Admin.
Catechesis Religious Program—Students 16.

CHATOM, WASHINGTON CO., ST. PAUL PARISH, Closed. (Mission of St. John Parish, Butler).

CHICKASAW, MOBILE CO., ST. THOMAS THE APOSTLE (1947)
251 N. Craft Hwy., Chickasaw, 36611. Tel: 251-456-7931; Fax: 251-452-9837. Very Rev. William Patrick Saucier; Deacons James H. Bullock; Charles P. Groves.
Parish Center—253 N. Craft Hwy., Chickasaw, 36611. Tel: 251-452-9837.

CITRONELLE, MOBILE CO., ST. THOMAS AQUINAS PARISH, CITRONELLE (1913) [CEM]
8025 State St., P.O. Box 61, Citronelle, 36522. Tel: 251-866-7505. Rev. John P. Coghlan.

CLIO, BARBOUR CO., OUR LADY OF GUADALUPE PARISH, (Mission of St. Joseph Parish, Holy Trinity)
1022 Brundidge St., Clio, 36017. Tel: 334-855-3148; Email: clioguadalupe@gmail.com. Mailing Address: 1444 Hwy. 165, Fort Mitchell, 36856. Rev. David A. Hamm, S.T.

DAPHNE, BALDWIN CO.

1—CHRIST THE KING PARISH, DAPHNE (1896) [CEM]
711 College Ave., Daphne, 36526. Tel: 251-626-2343; Email: office@ctkdaphne.org. Rev. Matthew J. O'Connor; Deacons Malcolm C. Zellner; Walter J. Crimmins; William A. Robinson; Rev. Baskar Anandan, H.G.N., Parochial Vicar.
School—Christ the King Parish, Daphne School, (Grades PreK-8), 1503 Main St., P.O. Box 1890, Daphne, 36526. Tel: 251-626-1692; Fax: 251-626-9976. Mr. Maxwell J. Crain, Prin.; Mrs. Lisa M. McDuff, Prin. Lay Teachers 30; Students 465.
Catechesis Religious Program—Tel: 251-626-5963. Sam Di Benedetto, D.R.E. Students 397.

2—SHRINE OF THE HOLY CROSS PARISH, DAPHNE (1948)
612 Main St., P.O. Box 1497, Daphne, 36526. Tel: 251-621-9793. Rev. Lito J. Capeding.

DAUPHIN ISLAND, MOBILE CO., ST. EDMUND-BY-THE-SEA PARISH, DAUPHIN ISLAND, [CEM]
823 Cadillac Ave., P.O. Box 6, Dauphin Island, 36528. Tel: 251-895-5454; Email: stedmundauphin@gmail.com. Rev. Msgr. Leonardo C. Guadalquiver, J.C.L.

DOTHAN, HOUSTON CO., ST. COLUMBA (1943)
2700 W. Main St., Dothan, 36301. Tel: 334-793-5802; Fax: 334-792-2816. Rev. Msgr. Patrick J. Gallagher, V.F.; Rev. Jose J. Paillacho, Parochial Vicar; Deacons Joseph D. Mueller; Richard L. Risher; Steven H. Sykes.
Catechesis Religious Program—Tel: 334-792-3065. Students 355.

ELBERTA, BALDWIN CO., ST. BARTHOLOMEW PARISH, ELBERTA (1911) [CEM] (German)
12795 Illinois St., Elberta, 36530. Tel: 251-986-8142. Rev. Msgr. Stephen E. Martin; Deacon Kenneth J. Kaiser.
School—St. Benedict, (Grades PreK-8), 12786 Illinois St., Elberta, 36530. Tel: 251-986-8143; Email: rkrehlingssbcs@gmail.com; Web: www.saintbenedict.net. Dr. Kathy McCool, Prin. Lay Teachers 15; Students 150.
Catechesis Religious Program—Students 35.

ENTERPRISE, COFFEE CO., ST. JOHN (1959)
123 Heath St., Enterprise, 36330. Tel: 334-347-6751; Email: stjohn007@centurytel.net. Deacons Karl L. Lukas; Alfonso M. Diaz-Rivera; Rev. Zachary L. Greenwell.
School—St. John Catholic Montessori School, 3-6

years Tel: 334-347-0413; Email: sjcmontessori@yahoo.com; Web: saintjohnmontessori.com. Sandra P. Pellissier, Dir.

EUFAULA, BARBOUR CO., HOLY REDEEMER (1859)
515 W. Broad St., Eufaula, 36027. Tel: 334-687-3716; Email: hredeemer2015@yahoo.com. Rev. David M. Shoemaker.
Catechesis Religious Program—Students 71.

FAIRFORD, WASHINGTON CO., OUR LADY OF SORROWS PARISH, (Mission of St. Peter the Apostle, Chastang)
Mailing Address: P.O. Box 456, Mount Vernon, 36560. Tel: 251-829-5134; Fax: 251-829-6874. 2157 Little Chestang Rd., Fairford, 36553. Rev. Amal Raj Samy, Admin.

FAIRHOPE, BALDWIN CO., ST. LAWRENCE PARISH, FAIRHOPE (1961)
370 S. Section St., Fairhope, 36532.
Tel: 251-928-5931; Fax: 251-928-5938; Email: office@stlawrencefairhope.com. Revs. Steven T. Williams; Selvam Arputharaj, Parochial Vicar; Deacon Francis A. Zieman.
Catechesis Religious Program—Students 185.
SACRED HEART CHAPEL (BATTLES WHARF), 18673 Scenic Hwy. 98, Fairhope, 36532. Scheduling & Sacramental Records: c/o St. Lawrence Parish, Fairhope, AL.

FOLEY, BALDWIN CO., ST. MARGARET QUEEN OF SCOTLAND (1951) [CEM]
601 W. Laurel Ave., Foley, 36535. Tel: 251-943-4009; Fax: 251-943-4010; Email: stmargaret@gulftel.com. Very Rev. Paul G. Zoghby, V.F.

GENEVA, GENEVA CO., ST. MARY PARISH, (Mission of St. John Parish, Enterprise)
100 S. Commerce St., Geneva, 36340.
Tel: 334-797-6920; Email: zgreenwell@mobarch.org. 123 Heath St., Enterprise, 36330. Rev. Zachary L. Greenwell.

GRAND BAY, MOBILE CO., ST. JOHN THE BAPTIST (1924)
12450 Hwy. 188, P.O. Box 417, Grand Bay, 36541.
Tel: 251-865-6902; Fax: 251-865-1412; Email: stjohngrandbay@gmail.com. Rev. Sherwin C. Monteron; Deacon William H. Graham.

GREENVILLE, BUTLER CO., ST. ELIZABETH (1894)
407 E. Walnut St., Greenville, 36037.
Tel: 334-382-6203. Rev. Bieu Van Nguyen; Deacon Robert D. Bailey.

GROVE HILL, CLARKE CO., SACRED HEART (1944)
19730 Hwy. 43, Grove Hill, 36451. Tel: 251-275-3665 ; Email: shcc@tds.net. P.O. Box 70, Grove Hill, 36451. Rev. Travis J. Burnett.
Missions—St. Joseph—1020 W. Front St., Thomasville, 36784.
Visitation, 135 W. Clinton St., Jackson, 36545.

GULF SHORES, BALDWIN CO., OUR LADY OF THE GULF (1952)
308 E. 22nd Ave., Gulf Shores, 36542.
Tel: 251-968-7062; Email: office@olgal.org; Web: www.olgal.org. Rev. David P. Carucci.
Catechesis Religious Program—Tel: 251-967-2537. Suzette Taylor, D.R.E. Students 58.

HERON BAY, MOBILE CO., ST. MICHAEL THE ARCHANGEL (1880)
15872 Heron Bay Loop Rd. E., Coden, 36523.
Tel: 251-973-2096; Web: LOWERALABAMACATHOLIC.COM. Mailing Address: 9101 Dauphin Island Pkwy., Theodore, 36582. Rev. Daniel F. Good, J.C.L.

HOLY TRINITY, RUSSELL CO., ST. JOSEPH (1925)
1444 Hwy. 165, Fort Mitchell, 36856.
Tel: 334-855-3148; Fax: 334-408-6005; Email: info@holytrinityal.org. Revs. David A. Hamm, S.T.; Marco Antonio Sanchez Mendoza, S.T., Parochial Vicar; Raul Vasquez, Parochial Vicar; John Clifton Marquis, S.T., In Res.
Blessed John XXIII Center—16 Sussex St., P.O. Box 117, Hurtsboro, 36860. Tel: 334-667-7770. Ms. Catherine Metzler, Dir.

JACKSON, CLARKE CO., VISITATION PARISH, (Mission of Sacred Heart Parish, Grove Hill)
135 W. Clinton St., Jackson, 36545.
Tel: 251-275-3665; Email: shcc@tds.net. Mailing Address: P.O. Box 70, Grove Hill, 36451. Rev. Travis J. Burnett.

LILLIAN, BALDWIN CO., ST. JOSEPH (1941) [JC]
34290 U.S. Hwy. 98, Lillian, 36549.
Tel: 251-962-3649; Fax: 251-962-4811; Email: stjoseph1@gulftel.com. Rev. Saleth Mariadoss, H.G.N.

MAGNOLIA SPRINGS, BALDWIN CO., ST. JOHN THE BAPTIST (1881) [CEM] [JC2]
10800 St. John's Ln., P.O. Box 206, Magnolia Springs, 36555. Tel: 251-965-7719;
Fax: 251-988-1113; Email: stjohnmagspg@gulftel.com. Rev. Jesuraj Babu Arulraj, H.G.N.

MON LUIS ISLAND, MOBILE CO., ST. ROSE OF LIMA PARISH, MON LUIS ISLAND (1853) [CEM]
2951 Durette Ave. (Mon Luis Island), Coden, 36523.
Tel: 251-973-2592; Email: stroseonmonluis@gmail.com; Web: www.stroseonmonluis.com. Rev. Msgr. Leonardo C. Guadalquiver, J.C.L.

MONROEVILLE, MONROE CO., ANNUNCIATION (1982)
565 Whetstone St., Monroeville, 36460.
Tel: 251-575-2644; Email: annuncat@frontiernet.net. Rev. Stephen C. Hellman.
Catechesis Religious Program—Students 28.
Mission—St. Joseph, 302 Whiskey Run Rd., Camden, Wilcox Co. 36726.

MONTGOMERY, MONTGOMERY CO.

1—ST. ANDREW KIM TAEGON (1910)
433 Clayton St., Montgomery, 36104.
Tel: 334-262-3241. Rev. Young-Il Ju.

2—ST. BEDE THE VENERABLE CATHOLIC CHURCH (1925)
3870 Atlanta Hwy., Montgomery, 36109.
Tel: 334-272-3463; Fax: 334-272-3492. Revs. Alejandro E. Valladares, S.T.L.; Nicholas J. Napolitano.
Child Care—St. Bede Catholic Children's Ministry, Infant-PK 3 3870 Atlanta Hwy., Montgomery, 36109. Tel: 334-277-8551; Email: astarrett@stbede.org. Mrs. Audra P. Starrett, Dir.
School—Montgomery Catholic Preparatory School - St. Bede Campus, (Grades PreK-6), 3850 Atlanta Hwy., Montgomery, 36109. Tel: 334-272-3033;
Fax: 334-272-9394; Web: montgomerycatholic.org. Ms. Laurie A. Gulley, Prin. Lay Teachers 20; Students 194.
Catechesis Religious Program—Family Night, Students 243.

3—THE CITY OF ST. JUDE PARISH, MONTGOMERY (1934) (African American)
2048 W. Fairview Ave., Montgomery, 36108.
Tel: 334-265-6791; Fax: 334-265-6750; Email: parish@cityofstjude.org; Web: www.cityofstjude.org. Rev. Daniel A. Owuor, F.M.H.; Deacons Clarence E. Darrington; Deo G. McMeans.

4—HOLY SPIRIT (1977)
8570 Vaughn Rd., Montgomery, 36117.
Tel: 334-277-5631; Fax: 334-272-1008; Email: office@holyspiritmgm.org; Web: www.holyspiritmgm.org. Revs. Wayne M. Youngman; Philip A. McKenna; Deacon Raymond M. Gueret.
School—Montgomery Catholic Preparatory School - Holy Spirit Campus, (Grades PreK-6), 8580 Vaughn Rd., Montgomery, 36117. Tel: 334-649-4404;
Fax: 334-649-4409; Web: www.montgomerycatholic.org. Mrs. Nancy H. Foley, Prin.
Catechesis Religious Program—Tel: 334-277-1989; Email: dre@holyspiritmgm.org. Students 296.

5—ST. JOHN THE BAPTIST (1908)
Mailing: 543 S. Union St., P.O. Box 95, Montgomery, 36101-0095. Tel: 334-288-2850. Rev. Msgr. Juan R. Celzo.

6—OUR LADY QUEEN OF MERCY (1954)
4421 Narrow Lane Rd., Montgomery, 36116.
Tel: 334-288-2850; Fax: 334-281-7884. P.O. Box 95, Montgomery, 36101. Rev. Msgr. Juan R. Celzo.
Catechesis Religious Program—Students 15.

7—ST. PETER (1834) [CEM]
219 Adams Ave., P.O. Box 114, Montgomery, 36101.
Tel: 334-262-7304; Fax: 334-262-9735; Email: secretary@stpetermontgomery.net; Web: www.stpetermontgomery.net. Rev. J. Francis Sofie; Deacon James R. Labadie.

8—RESURRECTION CATHOLIC CHURCH (1943)
2815 Forbes Rd., Montgomery, 36110.
Tel: 334-269-1770; Email: parish@rcmsouth.org; Web: www.rcmsouth.org. Rev. Manuel B. Williams, C.R.

MOUNT VERNON, MOBILE CO., ST. CECILIA PARISH, MT. VERNON (1929) [CEM]
1305 Military Rd., P.O. Box 847, Mount Vernon, 36560. Tel: 251-866-7505. Rev. John P. Coghlan.

OPELIKA, LEE CO., ST. MARY CHURCH (1910)
1000 4th Ave., Opelika, 36801. Tel: 334-749-8359; Email: stmarysopelika@gmail.com; Web: www.stmaryopelika.org. Rev. Bruce J. Krause, C.M.
Catechesis Religious Program—Students 96.

ORANGE BEACH, BALDWIN CO., ST. THOMAS BY THE SEA (1991)
Mailing Address: 26547 Perdido Beach Blvd., P.O. Box 1190, Orange Beach, 36561. Tel: 251-981-8132; Fax: 251-981-1981; Email: stthomas@gulftel.com; Web: www.stthomasbythesea.org. Rev. James E. Dane; Deacon Stephen R. Seymour.

ORRVILLE, DALLAS CO., IMMACULATE CONCEPTION (1919)
13663 Alabama Hwy. 22 W., P.O. Box 248, Orrville, 36767. Tel: 334-874-8931; Email: rmyhalyk@mobarch.org. Rev. Richard M. Myhalyk, S.S.E.

OZARK, DALE CO., ST. JOHN (1958) [JC]
475 Camilla Ave., P.O. Box 1008, Ozark, 36361-1008.
Tel: 334-774-6826; Fax: 334-774-8675; Email: stjozark@gmail.com. Rev. Frederick G. Boni; Deacon Joseph L. Pattberg.
Catechesis Religious Program—Students 45.

PHENIX CITY, RUSSELL CO., ST. PATRICK (1911)
1502 Broad St., Phenix City, 36868-0147.
Tel: 334-298-9025; Email: stpats123@gmail.com; Web: stpatsphenixcity.org. Rev. David A. Hamm, S.T., Admin.
Catechesis Religious Program—Students 37.

PLATEAU, MOBILE CO., OUR MOTHER OF MERCY PARISH, MOBILE (1926) (African American)
805 East St., P.O. Box 10306, Prichard, 36610.
Tel: 251-473-4975; Fax: 251-479-0291. Rev. Dominic Oguama, M.S.P.

PRATTVILLE, AUTAUGA CO., ST. JOSEPH CHURCH (1962)
511 N. Memorial Dr., Prattville, 36067.
Tel: 334-365-8680; Email: Secretary@StJosephPrattville.org; Web: www.StJosephPrattville.org. Rev. James N. Dean; Deacon Joseph T. Roy; Paul Gauthe, Sec.
Catechesis Religious Program—
Tel: 334-365-8680, Ext. 212. Students 207.

PRICHARD, MOBILE CO., ST. JAMES MAJOR (1925) (African American)
714 N. College St., Prichard, 36610.
Tel: 251-456-6842. Rev. Hyginus L. Boboh, S.S.J.
Catechesis Religious Program—Students 69.

ROBERTSDALE, BALDWIN CO., ST. PATRICK PARISH, ROBERTSDALE (1974)
23035 Hwy. 59 N., Robertsdale, 36567.
Tel: 251-947-5054; Web: www.stpatcatholic.com. P.O. Box 1367, Robertsdale, 36567. Rev. James N. Morrison; Deacon Charles J. Eick.
School—St. Patrick Parish, Robertsdale School, (Grades K-8), 23070 Hwy. 59 N., P.O. Box 609, Robertsdale, 36567. Tel: 251-947-7395; Web: www.school.stpatcatholic.com. Sr. Margaret Harte, P.B.V.M., Prin. Lay Teachers 13; Presentation Sisters 1; Students 180.
Catechesis Religious Program—Students 42.
Convent—P.O. Box 609, Robertsdale, 36567.
Tel: 251-947-7396.

SELMA, DALLAS CO., OUR LADY QUEEN OF PEACE (1862)
309 Washington St., Selma, 36703.
Tel: 334-874-8931. Rev. Richard M. Myhalyk, S.S.E.; Bro. Peter J. Stanfield, S.S.E., Pastoral Asst.
Res.: 1401 Broad St., Selma, 36701-4314.
Catechesis Religious Program—Gabe Norton, D.R.E. Students 20.

SEMMES, MOBILE CO., HOLY NAME OF JESUS PARISH, SEMMES (1977)
2275 Snow Rd. N., Semmes, 36575.
Tel: 251-649-4794; Email: office@hnjcatholic.com. Rev. Patrick J. Arensberg.
Catechesis Religious Program—Students 58.

TALLASSEE, ELMORE CO., ST. VINCENT DE PAUL (1955) [JC]
620 Gilmer Ave., Tallassee, 36078. Tel: 334-283-2169 ; Tel: 334-991-4471; Fax: 334-991-4050; Email: stvincent620@gmail.com; Web: stvincent-tallasssee.org. Rev. Mateusz K. Rudzik; Mrs. Jan Brienza, Sec.

THOMASVILLE, CLARKE CO., ST. JOSEPH PARISH, (Mission of Sacred Heart Parish, Grove Hill)
1020 W. Front St. N., Thomasville, Clarke Co. 36784.
Tel: 251-275-3665; Email: shcc@tds.net. Mailing Address: P.O. Box 70, Grove Hill, 36451. Rev. Travis J. Burnett.

TROY, PIKE CO., ST. MARTIN OF TOURS (1944)
725 Elba Hwy., Troy, 36079. Tel: 334-566-2630; Email: stmartintroyalabama@gmail.com. Rev. Michael Dennis Irwin; Deacon David R. Newell.
Catechesis Religious Program—Students 53.

TUSKEGEE INSTITUTE, MACON CO., ST. JOSEPH (1940)
2007 W. Montgomery Rd., Tuskegee Institute, 36088. Tel: 334-727-2710; Email: stjosephtuskegee@gmail.com; Web: stjosephtuskegee.org. Rev. Mateusz K. Rudzik; Deacon Stanley B. Maxwell.
School—St. Joseph School, (Grades PreK-8), 2009 W. Montgomery Rd., Tuskegee Institute, 36088.
Tel: 334-727-0620; Fax: 334-727-0642; Email: mreese@mobarch.org. Mrs. Margorie L. Reese, Prin. Lay Teachers 8; Students 64.

UNION SPRINGS, BULLOCK CO., ST. PIUS X PARISH, (Mission of Holy Redeemer Parish, Eufaula)
308 Kennon St., Union Springs, Bullock Co. 36089.
Tel: 334-687-3716. Mailing Address: 515 W. Broad St., Eufaula, 36027. Rev. David M. Shoemaker.

WEST MOUNT VERNON, MOBILE CO., ST. THERESA PARISH, WEST MOUNT VERNON
1875 Hwy. 96, West Mount Vernon, 36560.
Tel: 251-866-7505. Mailing Address: P.O. Box 61, Citronelle, 36522. Rev. John P. Coghlan.

WETUMPKA, ELMORE CO., OUR LADY OF GUADALUPE (2006)
545 White Rd., Wetumpka, 36092. Tel: 334-567-0047 . Mailing Address: P.O. Box 479, Elmore, 36025. Rev. Albert P. Kelly; Rev. Msgr. F. Charles Troncale, In Res., (Retired).

WHISTLER, MOBILE CO., ST. BRIDGET (1864)
3625 W. Main St., Whistler, 36612.
Tel: 251-457-6847. Very Rev. William Patrick Saucier; Rev. Eamon Miley, In Res.; Deacons James H. Bullock; Charles P. Groves.

Chaplains of Public Institutions

CLAYTON. *Ventress Correctional Institution*. Rev. David M. Shoemaker
515 W. Broad St., Eufaula, 36027. Tel: 334-687-3716; Fax: 334-687-3766.

DEATSVILLE. *Frank Lee Correctional Facility*, 5305 Ingram Rd., Deatsville, 36022. Tel: 334-290-3200. Rev. Michael J. Sreboth, Chap.

UNION SPRINGS. *Bullock County Correctional Facility*. Rev. David M. Shoemaker, Chap.
515 W. Broad St., Eufaula, 36027. Tel: 334-687-3716; Fax: 334-687-3766.

On Duty Outside the Archdiocese:
Revs.—
McManus, Dennis Douglas, Mount St. Mary Seminary, 16300 Old Emmitsburg Rd., Emmitsburg, MD 21727
Robinson, Jerome.

On Leave for Military Service:
Rev.—
Halladay, Paul A.

Special Assignment:
Revs.—
Miley, Eamon, Chap., 3625 W. Main St., Whistler, 36612
Sreboth, Michael J., Chap., Prison Ministry, 2048 W. Fairview Ave., Montgomery, 36108
Weishaar, Leo G., Chap., 6801 Airport Blvd., 36608. Tel: 251-633-1341.

Retired:
Rev. Msgrs.—
Cunningham, Peter J., (Retired)
Dorrill, James F., Ph.D., (Retired)
Hay, Theodore H., S.T.L., (Retired)
James, William R., (Retired)
Klepac, Kenneth J., J.C.L., (Retired)
Shields, Maurice L., (Retired)
Troncale, F. Charles, (Retired)
Revs.—
Bolling, Francis Joseph, (Retired)
Carlsen, James F., (Retired)
Coleman, James Montini, (Retired)
Conry, Austin, (Retired)
Cook, Adrian L., (Retired)
Folsom, William P. Jr., (Retired)
Harbour, Linn S., (Retired)
Holden, James T., (Retired)
Holleman, John L., (Retired)
Kadavil, Antony, (Retired)
Kieltyka, Robert, (Retired)
McCabe, Charles J., (Retired)
Milsted, Gordon N., (Retired)
Reskey, George A., (Retired)
Sindik, Matthew A., (Retired)
Weise, Thomas D., (Retired)
Zagorski, Jan A., (Retired).

Permanent Deacons:
Anderson, Terrence L.
Archer, John J.
Bailey, Robert D.
Bosarge, Vincent R.
Boyd, Jay
Brewer, Arnold L., (Retired)
Brown, Paul W.
Bryant, James D.
Bullock, James H.
Christian, Wiley J.
Connick, Edward G.
Connick, Joseph V.
Crimmins, Walter J.
Darrington, Clarence E.
Diaz-Rivera, Alfonso M.
Dolan, William R., (Retired)
Donastorg, Hector J.
Eick, Charles J.
Emmett, Marcene E.
Gale, Norman M.
Geri, Eugene A., (Retired)
Gottstine, Joseph G., (Retired)
Graham, William H.
Groves, Charles P.
Gueret, Raymond M.
Harkins, William J.
Hathorne, Ronnie A.
Haughery, John Read, (Retired)
Johnson, Ernest J.
Kaiser, Kenneth J.
Kenny, Charles H., (Retired)
Kirby, Robert E.
Labadie, James R.
Lee, Frank A., (Retired)
Lukas, Karl L.
Martin, Ronald
Maxwell, Stanley B.
McEnery, Douglas M.
McMeans, Deo G.
Moore, Alexander F., (Retired)
Mueller, Joseph D.
Newell, David R.
Pattberg, Joseph L.
Phung, Joseph H., (Retired)
Pouliot, Henry D., (Retired)
Risher, Richard L.
Robbins, Arthur W.
Robinson, William A.
Roy, Joseph T.
Scarboro, William, (Retired)
Scott, James L.
Seymour, Stephen R.
Sinchak, J. Douglas, M.S., J.C.L.
Sullivan, Richard M., (Retired)
Sykes, Steven H.
Tew, William L.
Tidwell, Stephen A.
Tran, Francis Hoai N.
Wadas, Eugene A., (Retired)
Ward, Aldon O.
Weatherford, Stephen K., (Retired)
Yeend, George W.
Zellner, Malcolm C.
Zieman, Francis A.

INSTITUTIONS LOCATED IN DIOCESE

[A] COLLEGES AND UNIVERSITIES

MOBILE. *Spring Hill College* (1830) 4000 Dauphin St., 36608. Tel: 251-380-4000; Fax: 251-460-2195; Email: mmossa@shc.edu; Web: www.shc.edu. Dr. Christopher Puto, Pres.; Revs. Gregory F. Lucey, S.J., Chancellor; Robert Poirier, S.J., Rector; Raphael V. D. Baylon, S.J.; Stephen F. Campbell, S.J.; Jose Luis Mesa, S.J.; Michael A. Williams, S.J.; Christopher J. Viscardi, S.J.; Bro. Ferrell Blank, S.J. Brothers 1; Lay Teachers 84; Priests 7; Students 1,501.

[B] HIGH SCHOOLS, ARCHDIOCESAN

MOBILE. *McGill-Toolen Catholic High School*, 1501 Old Shell Rd., 36604. Tel: 251-445-2900; Fax: 251-433-8356; Email: shieldsb@mcgill-toolen.org; Web: www.mcgill-toolen.org. Rev. W. Bry Shields, Pres.; Mrs. Michelle T. Haas, Prin. Brothers 3; Lay Teachers 87; Priests 1; Students 1,060.

Catholic Youth Organization, 11 N. Lafayette St., P.O. Box 6955, 36660. Tel: 251-441-0805. Mr. David A. Weems, Dir.

FAIRHOPE. *St. Michael Catholic High School*, (Grades 9-10), 11732 Higbee Rd., Fairhope, 36532. Tel: 251-459-0210; Email: fweber@mobarch.org; Web: www.stmichaelchs.org. Mr. Faustin N. Weber, Prin. Lay Teachers 14; Students 98.

MONTGOMERY. *Montgomery Catholic Preparatory School* (1873) (Grades PreK-12), 5350 Vaughn Rd., Montgomery, 36116. Tel: 334-272-7220; Fax: 334-272-2440; Email: aceasar@montgomerycatholic.org; Web: montgomerycatholic.org. Mrs. Anne O. Ceasar, Pres. (PreK-12); Anna Lee Ingalls, Dir., Devel. (K-12); Mr. Justin Castanza, Prin. (7-12); Ms. Mindy Walski, Librarian. Lay Teachers 92; Total Enrollment 777.

High School Campus (1873) 5350 Vaughn Rd., Montgomery, 36116. Mr. Justin Castanza, Prin.; Ms. Mindy Walski, Librarian. Students 338; Teachers 35.

Middle School Campus (2004) (Grades 7-8), 5350 Vaughn Rd., Montgomery, 36116. Tel: 334-272-2465; Fax: 334-272-2330; Email: jcastanza@montgomerycatholic.org. Mr. Justin Castanza, Prin. Students 143; Teachers 19.

[C] HIGH SCHOOLS AND ELEMENTARY SCHOOLS, PRIVATE

HOLY TRINITY. *St. Joseph Child Development Center*, (Grades PreK-4), 1444 Hwy. 165, Ft. Mitchell, 36856. Tel: 334-855-4675; Email: saintjosephcdc@gmail.com. Melisa Smith, Dir. Students 70; Teachers 9.

MONTGOMERY. *Resurrection Early Childhood Center and Resurrection Catholic School*, (Grades PreK-8), 2815 Forbes Dr., Montgomery, 36110. Tel: 334-265-4615; Fax: 334-265-4568; Email: tmilner@mobarch.org. Ms. Brenda Overby, Librarian; Mr. Tamarcus A. Milner, Prin. Lay Teachers 12; Students 125.

[D] CHILDREN'S HOMES

MOBILE. *St. Mary's Home, Mobile*, 4350 Moffat Rd., 36618. Tel: 251-344-7733; Fax: 251-344-9753; Email: sjoshi@stmaryshomemobile.org. Ms. Sabrina Joshi, Admin. Dependent Children 70.

[E] GENERAL HOSPITALS

MOBILE. *Gulf Coast Health System* (1986) 6801 Airport Blvd., P.O. Box 850429, 36608. Tel: 251-266-1660; Fax: 251-266-1679; Email: windy.taylor@ascension.org. Jason Alexander, Pres.; Beth McFadden Rouse. Bed Capacity 349; Tot Asst. Annually 150,000; Total Staff 2,227.

**Providence Building Corporation* (1985) P.O. Box 850429, 36685. Tel: 251-266-1600; Fax: 251-266-1679; Email: windy.taylor@ascension.org; Web: providencehospital.org. 6801 Airport Blvd., 36608. Todd S. Kennedy, Pres.

Providence Foundation (1985) 6701 Airport Blvd. B 227, P.O. Box 850429, 36608. Tel: 251-266-2050; Fax: 251-266-2052; Email: amelia.bell@ascension.org. Jeanie Wilkins, Chm. Bd.; Allison Meacham, Asst. Sec.; Lamar Reeves, Treas.

Providence Hospital (1854) 6801 Airport Blvd., P.O. Box 850429, 36685. Tel: 251-266-1600; Fax: 251-266-1679; Email: windy.taylor@ascension.org; Web: www.providencehospital.org. Todd S. Kennedy, Pres.; Rev. Leo G. Weishaar, Chap.; Lawrence Ford, Chm. Bd. Bed Capacity 349; Nurses 600; Patients Asst Anual. 150,000; Sisters 6; Tot Asst. Annually 190,000; Total Staff 2,227.

Seton Medical Management, Inc. (1986) 6801 Airport Blvd., P.O. Box 850429, 36608. Tel: 251-266-2661; Fax: 251-266-2664; Email: christopher.byrd@ascension.org. Bob Murphy, Chm. Bd.; Justin Labrato, Vice Chair; C. Susan Cornejo, Sec. & Treas. Nurses 45; Patients Asst Anual. 110,204; Tot Asst. Annually 115,500; Total Staff 140.

[F] SPECIAL HOSPITALS AND HOMES FOR THE AGED

MOBILE. *Little Sisters of the Poor, Home For the Aged, Inc.* (1901) Sacred Heart Residence, 1655 McGill Ave., 36604. Tel: 251-476-6335; Fax: 251-478-6519; Email: msmobile@littlesistersofthepoor.org; Web: www.littlesistersofthepoormobile.org. Rev. Mother Judith Mary Meredith, L.S.P., Supr.; Rev. Antony Kadavil, Chap., (Retired). Residents 85; Sisters 10. In Res. Most Rev. Oscar H. Lipscomb, D.D., Ph.D., (Retired), Archbishop Emeritus of Mobile; Rev. Msgrs. Peter J. Cunningham, (Retired); Kenneth J. Klepac, J.C.L., (Retired).

MOBILE. *Mercy Life of Alabama*, 2900 Springhill Ave., 36607. Tel: 251-287-8420; Email: dianeb@mercymedical.com; Web: www.mercylifeal.com. Diane Brown, Dir.

[G] HOUSING FOR THE ELDERLY

MOBILE. *Cathedral Place*, 351 Conti St., 36602. Tel: 251-434-1590; Fax: 251-434-1592; Email: marie.dismukes@royalmgmt.com; Web: www.royalmgmt.com. Marie Dismukes, Managing Agent; Marvin Dismukes, Mgr. Residents 184; Total Staff 7.

MONTGOMERY. *City of St. Jude Apartments*, 2048 W. Fairview Ave., Montgomery, 36108. Tel: 334-265-6791; Fax: 334-265-6750; Email: mdking@mobarch.org. Mrs. Marilyn D. King, Exec.

Seton Haven, 3721 Wares Ferry Rd., Montgomery, 36109. Tel: 334-272-4000; Fax: 334-272-1788; Email: setonhaven@bellsouth.net. Mr. Frank Gitschier, Pres.; Ms. A. Ann Alosi, Admin. Residents 120; Total Staff 13.

[H] MONASTERIES AND RESIDENCES OF PRIESTS AND BROTHERS

MOBILE. *Brothers of the Sacred Heart* (1821) 2609 Springhill Ave., 36607. Tel: 251-438-3812; Email: noprovince@hotmail.com. Bros. Lee Barker, S.C., M.Ed.; Celestine Algero, S.C., Ph.D.; Paul Mulligan, S.C., M.R.E. Brothers 3.

Jesuits of Mobile, Inc., 4000 Dauphin St., 36608. Tel: 251-460-2167; Fax: 251-460-2198; Email: shcsjcom@gmail.com; Web: kudzu.shc.edu/jesuits. Rev. R.V. Baylon, S.J.; Bro. Ferrell Blank, S.J.; Revs. Stephen F. Campbell, S.J.; Gregory F. Lucey, S.J.; Jose Luis Mesa, S.J.; Mark S. Mossa, S.J.; Christopher J. Viscardi, S.J.; Michael A. Williams, S.J. Priests 7; Total in Community 8.

SELMA. *Edmundite Fathers*, Edmundite Missions House, 1428 Broad St., Selma, 36701. Tel: 334-872-2359; Email: missionsdirector@edmunditemissions.org. Rev. Richard M. Myhalyk, S.S.E., Pastor; Bro. Peter J. Stanfield, S.S.E., Pastoral Assoc.

Fathers of St. Edmund Southern Missions, Inc.

[I] CONVENTS AND RESIDENCES OF SISTERS

MOBILE. *Convent of the Sisters of Mercy of the Americas South Central Community*, 101 Wimbledon Dr. W., 36608. Tel: 251-344-1377; Email: coberkirch@comcast.net; Web: www.mercysistersbalt.com. Sr. Carolyn Oberkirch, R.S.M., Admin. Sisters 11; Total Staff 14.

Other Residences:*Convent of the Sisters of Mercy of the Americas South Central Community*, 4301 Bit & Spur Rd., 36608. Tel: 251-343-3674; Email:

rahattonrsm@aol.com. Sr. Regina Hatton, R.S.M., Contact Person. Sisters 1. *Convent of the Sisters of Mercy of the Americas South Central Community*, 2902 Brierwood Dr., 36606. Tel: 251-470-5757; Email: coberkirch@comcast.net. Sisters 1. *Convent of the Sisters of Mercy of the Americas South Central Community*, 172 N. Lafayette St., 36604.
Tel: 251-432-3178; Email: seac99@hotmail.com. Sisters 1.

Monastery of Discalced Carmelite Nuns (1943) 716 Dauphin Island Pkwy., 36606. Mother Mary Cecile Nguyen, O.C.D., Prioress. Sisters 11; Solemnly Professed 9; Perpetually Professed Extern 2.

Visitation Monastery and Retreat House (1833) 2300 Spring Hill Ave., 36607. Tel: 251-473-2321;
Fax: 251-476-9761; Email: kcarlisle@mobarch.org; Web: www.VisitationMonasteryMobile.org. Rev. Mother Rose Marie Kinsella, V.H.M., Supr. Sisters 20; Total Staff 3.

HOLY TRINITY. *Blessed Trinity Shrine Retreat and Cenacle*, 107 Holy Trinity Rd., Fort Mitchell, 36856. Tel: 334-855-4474; Fax: 334-855-4525; Email: btsrmsbt@aol.com; Web: www.msbt.org/btsr. Sr. Sylvia Griglak, M.S.B.T., Contact Person. Sisters 6; Retreat House Capacity 40.

MARBURY. *Dominican Monastery of St. Jude (St. Jude Monastery)*, 143 County Rd. 20 E., Marbury, 36051. Tel: 205-755-1322; Fax: 205-755-9847; Email: stjudemonastery@aol.com; Web: www.MarburyDominicanNuns.org. Mother Mary of the Precious Blood, O.P., Prioress. Cloistered Dominican Nuns of Perpetual Adoration and Rosary. Postulants 1; Professed 1; Sisters 7; Solemnly Professed 6.

OZARK. *Sinsinawa Dominican Sisters*, 375 County Rd. 404, Ozark, 36360. Tel: 334-805-0384; Email: psmithop@troycable.net. Sr. Penny Smith, O.P. Sisters 1.

SELMA. *Sisters of St. Joseph of Rochester*, 2511 Summerfield Rd., Selma, 36701. Tel: 334-526-2536 ; Email: knavarra@ssjrochester.org; Web: www.ssjrochester.org. Sr. Kathleen Navarra, S.S.J. Sisters 2.

[J] NEWMAN CENTERS

MOBILE. *Sacred Heart of Jesus Catholic Student Center at University of South Alabama* (2003) Catholic Student Center, 6051 Old Shell Rd., 36608.
Tel: 251-343-3662; Email: csajags@gmail.com; Web: www.csajags.com. Rev. Norbert K. Jurek, Chap.; Ms. Emma Zanotelli, Campus Min.

Spring Hill College Campus Ministry, 4000 Dauphin St., 36608-1791. Tel: 251-380-3495;
Fax: 251-460-2174; Email: campusministry@shc.edu; Web: kudzu.shc.edu/campusministry. Revs. Mark S. Mossa, S.J., Dir.; R.V. Baylon, S.J. Priests 7; Students 1,200.

AUBURN. *Auburn University Campus Ministry*, 115 Mitcham Ave., Auburn, 36830. Tel: 334-209-1711; Email: rudiacatholic@gmail.com; Web: www.aucatholic.org. Mrs. Rudi A. DiPrima, Campus Min.

MONTGOMERY. *Auburn University Montgomery Campus Ministry*, Holy Spirit Parish, 8570 Vaughn Rd., Montgomery, 36117.
Tel: 334-277-5631; Email: wyoungman@mobarch.org. Rev. Wayne M. Youngman, Campus Min.

SELMA. *Marion Military Institute Campus Ministry*, 309 Washington St., Selma, 36703.
Tel: 334-874-8931; Email: rmyhalyk@mobarch.org. Rev. Richard M. Myhalyk, S.S.E. Students 25.

TROY. *Mother Teresa Catholic Newman Ministry at Troy University*, 725 Elba Hwy., Troy, 36079.
Tel: 334-566-2630; Email: dirwin@mobarch.org. Rev. Michael Dennis Irwin.

TUSKEGEE INSTITUTE. *Tuskegee University Newman Center*, 2007 Montgomery Rd., Tuskegee Institute, 36088. Tel: 334-421-1178. Rev. Mateusz K. Rudzik, Chap.; Mr. Cecil Davis, Student Liaison; Ms. Ceyla Davis, Student Liaison, Tel: 334-421-1178. Total Staff 2.

[K] MISCELLANEOUS LISTINGS

MOBILE. *Catholic High Schools Alumni Association of Mobile* (1979) 1501 Old Shell Rd., 36604.
Tel: 251-445-2913; Fax: 251-433-8356; Email: tolbertj@mcgill-toolen.org; Web: www.mcgill-toolen.org. Jennifer D. Tolbert, Dir.

Catholic Scouting - Boy Scouts, St. Vincent de Paul Parish, 5023 Camelot Dr., 36619.
Tel: 251-661-3908; Email: svrazel@mobarch.org. Rev. Stephen G. Vrazel, Chap.

Men of St. Joseph, 14 Midtown Park E., 36606.
Tel: 251-450-2823; Fax: 251-450-2788; Web: www.menofstjoseph.com. Todd Martin, Chm.

Mobile Provincial Conference of Bishops and Priests' Councils, Mailing Address: 400 Government St., 36602. Tel: 251-434-1587; Email: archbishop@mobarch.org. Most Rev. Thomas J. Rodi, Ordinary.

Saint Serra Club of Mobile, 711 Dauphin St., 36602.
Tel: 251-510-1910; Email: dbarnett31@hotmail.com. Danny Barnett, Dir.

FAIRHOPE. **Archangel Communications*, 399 S. Section St., P.O. Box 1526, Fairhope, 36533.
Tel: 251-928-2111; Fax: 251-929-2660; Email: office@archangelradio.org. Joseph M. Roszkowski, Pres.; Ellen Taylor, MOB, Exec. Dir., Archangel Radio.

Cursillo, 112 Fels Ave., Fairhope, 36532.
Tel: 251-379-6798; Email: tim.simmonds.bysh@statefarm.com. Deacon Richard L. Risher, Spiritual Dir.; Mr. Tim Simmonds, Lay Dir.

MONTGOMERY. *Resurrection Catholic Missions*, 2815 Forbes Rd., Montgomery, 36110. Tel: 334-263-4221 ; Fax: 334-263-4999. Rev. Manuel B. Williams, C.R., Missions Dir.

Seton Haven Management Corporation, 3721 Wares Ferry Rd., Montgomery, 36109. Tel: 334-272-4000; Email: setonhaven@bellsouth.net. James Bickerton, Pres.

SELMA. *Edmundite Guild* Society of St. Edmund, Inc. 1428 Broad St., Selma, 36701. Tel: 888-540-7722; Fax: 334-875-8189; Email: missionsdirector@edmunditemissions.org. Mr. Chad McEachern, Pres. & CEO.

Edmundite Missions aka Fathers of St. Edmund, Southern Missions, Inc., 1428 Broad St., Selma, 36701. Tel: 334-872-2359; Fax: 334-875-8189; Email: Chadm@edmunditemissions.org. Mr. Chad McEachern, Pres. & CEO; Ms. Alice Mims, Exec. Asst.; Mr. David Dalling, CFO.

RELIGIOUS INSTITUTES OF MEN REPRESENTED IN THE ARCHDIOCESE

For further details refer to the corresponding bracketed number in the Religious Institutes of Men or Women section.

[1100]—*Brothers of the Sacred Heart* (New Orleans Prov.)—S.C.
[1330]—*Congregation of the Mission* (Eastern Prov.)—C.M.
[1080]—*Congregation of the Resurrection* (Chicago Prov.)—C.R.
[]—*Franciscan Missionaries of Hope (The Lyke Community)*—F.M.H.
[0585]—*Heralds of the Good News*—H.G.N.
[0690]—*Jesuit Fathers and Brothers* (New Orleans Prov.)—S.J.
[0840]—*Missionary Servants of the Most Holy Trinity*—S.T.
[0854]—*Missionary Society of St. Paul of Nigeria*—M.S.P.
[0440]—*Society of Saint Edmund* (Selma, AL)—S.S.E.
[0700]—*St. Joseph's Society of the Sacred Heart* (Baltimore, MD)—S.S.J.

RELIGIOUS INSTITUTES OF WOMEN REPRESENTED IN THE ARCHDIOCESE

[0760]—*Daughters of Charity of St. Vincent de Paul*—D.C.
[0420]—*Discalced Carmelite Nuns*—O.C.D.
[1050]—*Dominican Contemplative Nuns*—O.P.
[1070-03]—*Dominican Sisters*—O.P.
[1855]—*Handmaids of the Holy Child Jesus*—H.H.C.J.
[2340]—*Little Sisters of the Poor*—L.S.P.
[2790]—*Missionary Servants of the Most Blessed Trinity*—M.S.B.T.
[]—*Sisters for Christian Community*—S.F.C.C.
[0500]—*Sisters of Charity of Nazareth* (Nazareth, KY)—S.C.N.
[2549]—*Sisters of Mercy*—R.S.M.
[2575]—*Sisters of Mercy of the Americas*—R.S.M.
[3830-14]—*Sisters of St. Joseph*—S.S.J.
[3840]—*Sisters of St. Joseph of Carondelet*—C.S.J.
[0260]—*Sisters of the Blessed Sacrament*—S.B.S.
[1950]—*Sisters of the Holy Family*—S.S.F.
[3330]—*Union of the Sisters of the Presentation of the Blessed Virgin Mary*—P.B.V.M.
[4190]—*Visitation Nuns*—V.H.M.

NECROLOGY

† Calleja, Guido, (Retired), Died Aug. 1, 2018
† Robinson, John C., (Retired), Died Sep. 28, 2018

An asterisk (*) denotes an organization that has established tax-exempt status directly with the IRS and is not covered by the USCCB Group Ruling.

Diocese of Monterey in California

(Montereyensis in California)

Most Reverend

DANIEL E. GARCIA, D.D.

Bishop of Monterey; ordained May 28, 1988; appointed Titular Bishop of Capsus and Auxiliary Bishop of Austin January 21, 2015; ordained March 3, 2015; appointed Fifth Bishop of Monterey November 27, 2018; installed January 29, 2019. Email: bishop@dioceseofmonterey.org.

Most Reverend

SYLVESTER D. RYAN, D.D.

Bishop Emeritus; ordained May 3, 1957; appointed Auxiliary Bishop of Los Angeles and Titular Bishop of Remesiana February 17, 1990; ordained Bishop May 31, 1990; appointed Third Bishop of Monterey January 28, 1992; installed March 19, 1992; retired December 19, 2006. *c/o Diocese of Monterey, 425 Church St., Monterey, CA 93940.* Tel: 831-373-4345; Email: bsrdom@aol.com.

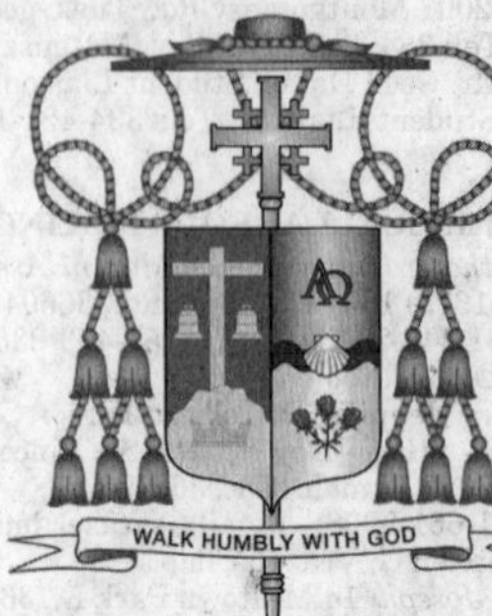

Pastoral Office: 425 Church St., Monterey, CA 93940. Tel: 831-373-4345; Fax: 831-373-1175. . *Mailing Address: P.O. Box 2048, Monterey, CA 93942-2048.*

Web: www.dioceseofmonterey.org

Email: diocese@dioceseofmonterey.org

ESTABLISHED DECEMBER 14, 1967.

Square Miles 21,916.

Comprises the Counties of Monterey, San Benito, San Luis Obispo and Santa Cruz in the State of California.

Legal Titles:
Diocese of Monterey in California.
The Roman Catholic Bishop of Monterey, California, a Corporation Sole.
Diocese of Monterey Parish & School Operating Corp.
The Bishop Harry A. Clinch Endowment Fund of the Diocese of Monterey.
Catholic Charities of the Diocese of Monterey (Corporation).
Ave Maria Convalescent Hospital, Inc.
St. Francis High School, Salesian College Preparatory.
Bishop Harry A. Clinch Trust Fund.
The Roman Catholic Bishop of Monterey Irrevocable Real Property Charitable Trust.
The Diocese of Monterey Parish & School Operating Corporation Irrevocable Real Property Charitable Trust.
Bishop Sylvester Ryan Tuition Opportunity Program Trust.
For legal titles of parishes and diocesan institutions, consult the Pastoral Office.

STATISTICAL OVERVIEW

Personnel	
Bishop	1
Retired Bishops	1
Priests: Diocesan Active in Diocese	62
Priests: Diocesan Active Outside Diocese	3
Priests: Retired, Sick or Absent	27
Number of Diocesan Priests	92
Religious Priests in Diocese	29
Total Priests in Diocese	121
Extern Priests in Diocese	3
Ordinations:	
Diocesan Priests	3
Transitional Deacons	4
Permanent Deacons in Diocese	28
Total Brothers	27
Total Sisters	81
Parishes	
Parishes	46
With Resident Pastor:	
Resident Diocesan Priests	40
Resident Religious Priests	5
Without Resident Pastor:	
Administered by Lay People	1
Missions	9
Welfare	
Catholic Hospitals	1
Total Assisted	151,523
Homes for the Aged	2
Total Assisted	302
Special Centers for Social Services	6
Total Assisted	18,000
Educational	
Diocesan Students in Other Seminaries	22
Total Seminarians	22
High Schools, Diocesan and Parish	2
Total Students	494
High Schools, Private	3
Total Students	980
Elementary Schools, Diocesan and Parish	11
Total Students	2,299
Elementary Schools, Private	3
Total Students	598
Catechesis/Religious Education:	
High School Students	3,810
Elementary Students	12,007
Total Students under Catholic Instruction	20,210
Teachers in the Diocese:	
Brothers	1
Sisters	6
Lay Teachers	398
Vital Statistics	
Receptions into the Church:	
Infant Baptism Totals	5,039
Minor Baptism Totals	482
Adult Baptism Totals	152
Received into Full Communion	232
First Communions	4,722
Confirmations	2,311
Marriages:	
Catholic	704
Interfaith	94
Total Marriages	798
Deaths	1,237
Total Catholic Population	164,331
Total Population	821,655

Former Prelates of the Diocese of Monterey—Most Revs. HARRY ANSELM CLINCH, D.D., ord. June 6, 1936; appt. Titular Bishop of Badiae and Auxiliary to the Bishop of Monterey-Fresno, Dec. 5, 1956; cons. Feb. 27, 1957; installed as first Bishop of Monterey in California, Dec. 14, 1967; retired Jan. 19, 1982; died March 8, 2003; THADDEUS SHUBSDA, D.D., ord. April 26, 1950; Titular Bishop of Trau and Auxiliary Bishop of Los Angeles; Episcopal Ordination; appt. Feb. 19, 1977; named Bishop of Monterey in California, June 1, 1982; installed as second Bishop of Monterey, July 1, 1982; died April 26, 1991; SYLVESTER D. RYAN, D.D., (Retired), ord. May 3, 1957; appt. Auxiliary Bishop of Los Angeles and Titular Bishop of Remesiana Feb. 17, 1990; ord. Bishop on May 31, 1990; appt. Third Bishop of Monterey Jan. 28, 1992; installed March 19, 1992; retired Dec. 19, 2006.; RICHARD J. GARCIA, D.D., ord. June 15, 1973; appt. Titular Bishop of Bapara and Auxiliary Bishop of Sacramento Nov. 25, 1997; ord. Jan. 28, 1998; appt. Fourth Bishop of Monterey Dec. 19, 2006; installed Jan. 30, 2007; died July 11, 2018.

Chancellor—425 Church St., Monterey, 93940. Mailing Address: P.O. Box 2048, Monterey, 93942-2048. Tel: 831-373-4345; Fax: 831-373-1175. Deacon HUGO PATINO, Email: hpatino@dioceseofmonterey.org.

Moderator of the Curia—425 Church St., Monterey, 93940. Mailing Address: P.O. Box 2048, Monterey, 93942-2048. Tel: 831-373-4345; Fax: 831-373-1175. Rev. PETER A. CRIVELLO, Email: pcrivello@dioceseofmonterey.org; BERNARDINE JOHNSON, Administrative Asst., Email: bjohnson@dioceseofmonterey.org.

Vicar for Clergy—St. Patrick's Church, 425 Church St., Monterey, 93940. Mailing Address: P.O. Box 2048, Monterey, 93942-2048. Tel: 831-373-4345; Fax: 831-373-1175. Rev. MIGUEL ANGEL GRAJEDA, V.C., Email: mgrajeda@dioceseofmonterey.org.

Vicar for Religious—Sr. GLORIA I. LOYA, P.B.V.M., 485 Church St., Monterey, 93940. Tel: 831-373-1335, Ext. 271; Email: srgiloya@dioceseofmonterey.org.

Vicar for Retired Priests—137 Sonoma St., Watsonville, 95076. Tel: 831-536-5177. Rev. PAUL R. VALDEZ, J.C.L., KCHS, (Retired), Email: prvprv007@yahoo.com.

Pastoral Office—425 Church St., Monterey, 93940. Mailing Address: P.O. Box 2048, Monterey, 93942-2048. Tel: 831-373-4345; Fax: 831-373-1175; Email: diocese@dioceseofmonterey.org. Administrative Assistants: LETICIA FLORES-MCPHERSON, Email: lmcpherson@dioceseofmonterey.org; ANALUISA CHAVEZ, Email: achavez@dioceseofmonterey.org; BERNARDINE JOHNSON, Email: bjohnson@dioceseofmonterey.org; ANGELICA GORDON, Email: agordon@dioceseofmonterey.org.

Pastoral Office, Ecclesiastical Notaries—DONA LOGEMAN ACUFF, Email: dacuff@dioceseofmonterey.org; ANALUISA CHAVEZ, Email: achavez@dioceseofmonterey.org; BERNARDINE JOHNSON, Email: bjohnson@dioceseofmonterey.org.

Vicars Forane—Very Revs. MICHAEL VOLK, V.U., Monterey Peninsula Vicariate; FREDY CALVARIO, V.F., Salinas Area Vicariate; PEDRO ESPINOZA, J.C.L., V.F., Santa Cruz County - Southern Vicariate; MARTIN CAIN, V.F., Santa Cruz County - Northern Vicariate; HEIBAR CASTANEDA, V.F., San Benito County Vicariate; ENRIQUE HERRERA, V.F., Salinas Valley Vicariate; RUSSELL D. BROWN, V.F., San Luis Obispo County, Southeast Vicariate; MARK STETZ, V.F., San Luis Obispo County, Southwest Vicariate.

Diocesan Consultors—Very Rev. RUSSELL D. BROWN, V.F., San Luis Obispo Southeast Vicariate; Rev. PETER A. CRIVELLO; Very Revs. ENRIQUE HERRERA, V.F., Salinas Valley Vicariate; FREDY CALVARIO, V.F., Salinas Area Vicariate; MARTIN CAIN, V.F., Santa Cruz County - Northern Vicariate; Rev. MIGUEL ANGEL GRAJEDA, V.C.; Very Revs. PEDRO ESPINOZA, J.C.L., V.F., Santa Cruz County

Southern Vicariate; MICHAEL VOLK, V.U.; HEIBAR CASTANEDA, V.F., San Benito County Vicariate; MARK STETZ, V.F., San Luis Obispo County Southwest Vicariate.

Diocesan Departments, Directors and Offices

Archives—Rev. CARL M.D. FARIA, Archivist; DONA LOGEMAN ACUFF, Archives Assoc., 580 Fremont St., Monterey, 93940. Mailing Address: P.O. Box 2048, Monterey, 93942-2048. Tel: 831-373-2127; Fax: 831-655-4809; Email: archives@dioceseofmonterey.org.

Office of Legal Counsel—425 Church St., Monterey, 93940. Mailing Address: P.O. Box 2048, Monterey, 93942-2048. Tel: 831-373-4345; Fax: 831-373-5765. SUSAN A. MAYER, Esq., Email: smayer@dioceseofmonterey.org; ANGELICA GORDON, Administrative Asst., Email: agordon@dioceseofmonterey.org.

Director of Finance—425 Church St., Monterey, 93940. CLANCY D'ANGELO, Email: cdangelo@dioceseofmonterey.org; MARIA GONZALEZ, Exec. Asst., Mailing Address: P.O. Box 2048, Monterey, 93942-2048. Email: mgonzalez@dioceseofmonterey.org.

Communication—ERIKA YANEZ, Dir. Media Rels., 485 Church St., Monterey, 93940. Tel: 831-373-4345; Fax: 831-373-5765; Email: eyanez@dioceseofmonterey.org.

Accounting Office—425 Church St., Monterey, 93940. Tel: 831-373-4346. CLANCY D'ANGELO, Dir. Finance, Email: cdangelo@dioceseofmonterey.org; KATHY ALDRETE, Controller, Email: kaldrete@dioceseofmonterey.org; TERI DAWN, Payroll & Banking Mgr., Email: tdawn@dioceseofmonterey.org; CLAUDIA ALFARO, Payroll Specialist, Email: calfaro@dioceseofmonterey.org; KAREN PRESTIGIACOMO, Accounts Payable, Email: kprestigiacomo@dioceseofmonterey.org; MARIA COTTRELL, Controller for Cemeteries, Email: mcottrell@dioceseofmonterey.org; JACKIE PEREZ, Accounting & Cemeteries Asst., Email: jperez@dioceseofmonterey.org.

Human Resources—425 Church St., Monterey, 93940. Mailing Address: P.O. Box 2048, Monterey, 93942-2048. Tel: 831-373-4345; Fax: 831-373-5765; Email: humanres@dioceseofmonterey.org. SUSAN A. MAYER, Esq., Dir.; STEFANIE OLSEN, Human Resources Assoc. Dir.; ANGELICA GORDON, Email: agordon@dioceseofmonterey.org.

California Missions—485 Church St., Monterey, 93940. Tel: 831-373-4345, Ext. 203; Fax: 831-373-3534. *Mailing Address: P.O. Box 2048, Monterey, 93942-2048.* JEWEL GENTRY, Coord., Email: jgentry@dioceseofmonterey.org.

Catholic Schools Department—KIMBERLY CHENG, Supt. Schools, Email: kcheng@dioceseofmonterey.org; MIRIAM (MIMI) SCHWERTFEGER, Administrative Asst., 485 Church St., Monterey, 93940. Tel: 831-373-1608; Email: mschwertfeger@dioceseofmonterey.org.

Catholic Funeral & Cemetery Services of Monterey—Administrative Office: 425 Church St., Monterey, 93940. Mailing Address: P.O. Box 2048, Monterey, 93942-2048. Tel: 831-373-4345; Fax: 831-373-2831. JARROD BOLLIGER, Dir., Email: jbolliger@cfcsmonterey.org; BERENICE ROSILLO, Assoc. Dir. Cemeteries, Email: brosillo@cfcsmonterey.org; MARY PAT ADAMS, Parish Outreach Mgr., Email: madams@cfcsmonterey.org.

Diocesan Tribunal—580 Fremont St., Monterey, 93940. Mailing Address: P.O. Box 350, Monterey, 93942-0350. Tel: 831-373-1833; Fax: 831-373-6761. CECILIA BRENNAN, M.A., M.C.L., J.C.L., Dir. Tribunal, Email: cbrennan@dioceseofmonterey.org; MARIA GONZALEZ, Tribunal Case Mgr., Email: mgonzalez@dioceseofmonterey.org.

Judicial Vicar—Rev. KENNETH J. LAVERONE, O.F.M., J.C.L.

Judges—Rev. KENNETH J. LAVERONE, O.F.M., J.C.L.; Very Rev. PEDRO ESPINOZA, J.C.L., V.F.; Rev. KELLY VENDEHEY, J.C.L.

Defenders of the Bond—Rev. PAUL R. VALDEZ, J.C.L., KCHS, (Retired); CECILIA BRENNAN, M.A., M.C.L., J.C.L.

Advocates—Revs. JOHN C. GRIFFIN; MICHAEL MARINI, (Retired); Deacon WARREN E. HOY.

Promoter of Justice—Rev. PAUL R. VALDEZ, J.C.L., KCHS, (Retired).

Notaries—DONA LOGEMAN ACUFF; MARIA GONZALES.

Divine Worship Department—Sr. BARBARA ANN LONG, O.P., Dir.; KAREN BENNETT, Administrative Asst., 210 High St., Santa Cruz, 95060. Tel: 831-423-4973; Fax: 831-427-2170; Email: worship@dioceseofmonterey.org.

Pastoral Response Coordinator—425 Church St., Monterey, 93940. Tel: 800-321-5220; Fax: 831-373-5765 (Confidential). *Mailing Address: P.O. Box 2048, Monterey, 93942-2048.* RIO CASTILLO, Email: rcastillo@dioceseofmonterey.org.

Pastoral Support & Planning—425 Church St., Monterey, 93940. Mailing Address: P.O. Box 2048, Monterey, 93942-2048. Tel: 831-373-4345; Fax: 831-373-1175. Rev. PETER A. CRIVELLO, Dir., Email: pcrivello@dioceseofmonterey.org; BERNARDINE JOHNSON, Administrative Asst., Email: bjohnson@dioceseofmonterey.org.

Protection of Children and Young People—485 Church St., Monterey, 93940. Deacon WARREN E. HOY, Dir., Tel: 831-645-2845; Fax: 831-373-3534; Email: whoy@dioceseofmonterey.org; ANN VENTURA, Administrative Asst., Tel: 831-645-2848; Fax: 831-373-3534; Email: aventura@dioceseofmonterey.org.

Clergy Life & Ministry—Very Rev. MARK STETZ, V.F., Santa Rosa Church, 1174 Main St., Cambria, 93428. Tel: 805-927-4816; Fax: 805-927-2880; Email: frmarksr@gmail.com.

Office of Development and Stewardship—485 Church St., Monterey, 93940. Mailing Address: P.O. Box 2048, Monterey, 93942-2048. Tel: 831-373-4345; Fax: 831-373-3534. VACANT, Dir.; PHYLLIS TOOTIE KLINE, Coord. Devel., Tel: 831-645-2812; Email: tkline@dioceseofmonterey.org; ADRIANA AQUINO-DIAZ, Administrative Asst., Tel: 831-645-2816; Email: aaquinodiaz@dioceseofmonterey.org.

Office of Faith Formation—425 Church St., Monterey, 93940. Mailing Address: P.O. Box 2048, Monterey, 93942-2048. Tel: 831-373-4345; Fax: 831-373-1175. Rev. PETER A. CRIVELLO, Dir., Email: pcrivello@dioceseofmonterey.org; BERNARDINE JOHNSON, Administrative Asst., Email: bjohnson@dioceseofmonterey.org.

Campus Ministry Department—Rev. PETER A. CRIVELLO, Dir., Email: pcrivello@diocsesofmonterey.org; BERNARDINE JOHNSON, Administrative Asst., 425 Church St., Monterey, 93940. Mailing Address: P.O. Box 2048, Monterey, 93942-2048. Tel: 831-373-4345; Fax: 831-373-1175; Email: bjohnson@dioceseofmonterey.org; Revs. JUSTIN E. BIANCHI, Dir. Campus Ministry, University of California - Santa Cruz, 285 Meder St., Santa Cruz, 95060. Tel: 831-423-9400; Fax: 831-423-8163; Email: newman.ucsc@dioceseofmonterey.org; Web: www.newmanite.org; THOMAS HALL, Dir. Campus Ministry, California State University at Monterey Bay (CSUMB), 485 Church St., Monterey, 93940. Tel: 831-373-1335, Ext. 248; Fax: 831-373-3534; Email: newman.csumb@dioceseofmonterey.org; GERALD ROBINSON, S.J., Dir. Campus Ministry, California State Polytechnic University & Cuesta College, San Luis Obispo, Email: frgerry@slonewman.org; LINDA GARCIA-INCHAUSTI, Dir. Admin., 1472 Foothill Blvd., San Luis Obispo, 93405. Tel: 805-543-4105; Fax: 831-543-5671; Email: linda@slonewman.org.

Catechetical Ministries Department—485 Church St., Monterey, 93940. Tel: 831-373-1335; Fax: 831-373-3554. TISH SCARGILL, Dir., Email: tscargill@dioceseofmonterey.org; OLGA FLORES, Administrative Asst., Tel: 831-373-1335; Fax: 831-373-3554; Email: oflores@dioceseofmonterey.org; TERRY BURROWS, Assoc. Dir. Catechesis, 751 Palm St., San Luis Obispo, 93401. Tel: 805-458-2006, Ext. 15; Fax: 805-781-8214; Email: tburrows@dioceseofmonterey.org.

Hispanic Ministry & Migrant Ministry Department—485 Church St., Monterey, 93940. Tel: 831-373-1335; Fax: 831-373-3534; Email: hispanicministry@dioceseofmonterey.org. SOCORRO LAGARDA-QUIOZ, M.A.P.M., Dir., Tel: 831-645-2835; Email: slagardaquioz@dioceseofmonterey.org; PETRA ROBLES, Administrative Asst./Migrant Ministry Coord., Tel: 831-645-2837; Email: probles@dioceseofmonterey.org.

Permanent Diaconate—Tel: 831-373-1335; Fax: 831-373-3534. Deacon DAVID FORD, Dir., Email: dford@dioceseofmonterey.org; ANN VENTURA, Administrative Asst., Email: formation@dioceseofmonterey; Email: aventura@dioceseofmonterey.org; Deacons ANDRES LARRAZA, Ph.D., Assoc. Dir. Deacon Formation for Hispanics, Tel: 831-645-2848; Email: alarraza@dioceseofmonterey.org; ED CALLAHAN, Assoc. Dir., Deacon Life & Ministry - South, Tel: 805-610-5298; Email: ecallahan237@gmail.com; DAVID LANSFORD, Assoc. Dir., Deacon Life & Ministry - North, Tel: 831-902-8969; Email: dnmlansford@gmail.com.

Family Life and Social Concerns—Deacon WARREN E. HOY, Dir., 485 Church St., Monterey, 93940. Tel: 831-645-2845; Fax: 831-373-3534; Email: whoy@dioceseofmonterey.org; ANN VENTURA, Administrative Asst., Tel: 831-645-2848; Fax: 831-373-3534; Email: aventura@dioceseofmonterey.org.

Respect Life—Rev. DEREK HUGHES, Dir., Holy Eucharist Church, 527 Corralitos Rd., Corralitos, 95076. Tel: 831-722-5490; Fax: 831-722-5421; Email: respectlife@dioceseofmonterey.org. Email: dhughes@dioceseofmonterey.org.

Restorative Justice—Deacon WARREN E. HOY, Dir., 485 Church St., Monterey, 93940. Tel: 831-645-2845; Fax: 831-373-3534; Email: whoy@dioceseofmonterey.org; ANN VENTURA, Administrative Asst., Tel: 831-645-2848; Fax: 831-373-3534; Email: aventura@dioceseofmonterey.org.

Youth and Young Adult Ministry—VACANT, 485 Church St., Monterey, 93940. Tel: 831-373-1335; Fax: 831-373-3351; Email: youth@dioceseofmonterey.org.

Scouting—ANN VENTURA, Coord. Scouting, Northern Diocese, 485 Church St., Monterey, 93940. Tel: 831-373-1335, Ext. 248; Fax: 831-373-3534; Email: aventura@dioceseofmonterey.org; Email: scouting@dioceseofmonterey.org; TRICIA VON DOHLEN, Coord. Scouting, Southern Diocese, 1002 Little Quail Pl., Paso Robles, 93446. Tel: 805-234-4463; Email: triciav@yahoo.com.

Vocations—425 Church St., Monterey, 93940. Mailing Address: P.O. Box 2048, Monterey, 93942-2048. Tel: 831-373-4345; Fax: 831-373-1175; Email: vocations@dioceseofmonterey.org. Rev. VICTOR OMMAR SOLIS, Dir.

Pontifical Mission SocietiesDiocese of Monterey: 425 Church St., Monterey, 93940. Tel: 831-373-4345; Fax: 831-373-1175. Mailing Address: P.O. Box 2048, Monterey, 93942-2048. Deacon HUGO PATINO, Coord., Email: hpatino@dioceseofmonterey.org.

St. Joseph's Conference Center—485 Church St., Monterey, 93940.

Catholic Charities of the Diocese of Monterey—ANA VENTURA PHARAS, Exec. Dir., Email: avphares@catholiccharitiescentralcoast.org; ALLEN GANADEN, Exec. Admin., Email: aganaden@catholiccharitiescentralcoast.org.

Administration, Family Supportive Services and Immigration—922 Hilby Ave., Ste. C, Seaside, 93955-5357. Tel: 831-393-3110; Fax: 831-393-3116.

Catholic Charities - Salinas Office—Buckley Hall, St. Mary of the Nativity, 1705 2nd Ave., Salinas, 93905. Immigration & Citizenship and Family Supportive Svcs.. Tel: 831-422-0602; Fax: 831-422-0759.

Catholic Charities - San Luis Obispo Office—3220 S. Higuera St., Ste. 303, San Luis Obispo, 93401. Tel: 805-541-9110; Fax: 805-541-9121. (Immigration & Citizenship and Family Supportive Svcs.).

Catholic Charities - Santa Cruz Office—610 Frederick St., Santa Cruz, 95062. Tel: 831-431-6939. (Tattoo Removal Program, Family Supportive Svcs.; Mental Health Counseling).

Catholic Charities - Watsonville Office—656 Main St., Watsonville, 95076. Tel: 831-722-2675; Fax: 831-722-9921. (Family Supportive Svcs.; Immigration & Citizenship Svcs. & Mental Health Counseling).

Campaign for Human Development—Deacon WARREN E. HOY, Dir., 485 Church St., Monterey, 93940. Tel: 831-373-1335; Fax: 831-373-3534; Email: whoy@dioceseofmonterey.org.

Catholic Relief Services—485 Church St., Monterey, 93940. Tel: 831-373-1335; Fax: 831-373-3534. TISH SCARGILL, Co Dir., Email: tscargill@dioceseofmonterey.org; Deacon WARREN E. HOY, Co Dir., Email: whoy@dioceseofmonterey.org.

Committees and Councils

Administrative Committee Priests' Pension Plan—Most Rev. DANIEL E. GARCIA, D.D.; Revs. EUGENIO ARAMBURO; JOSEPH L. OCCHIUTO, (Retired); GREGORY SANDMAN; ROBERT D. SULLIVAN; PAUL R. VALDEZ, J.C.L., KCHS, Chm., (Retired).

Ave Maria Board—Most Rev. DANIEL E. GARCIA, D.D.; THOMAS H. RIORDAN, Treas.; CLANCY D'ANGELO, Chm.; MRS. LOU LANGLEY, Vice Pres.; Sr. REGINA MTOWA, I.S.H.A, Sec.

Bishop Harry A. Clinch Endowment Fund, The Bishop Sylvester D. Ryan Continuing Education Fund—The Bishop Shubsda Memorial Seminary Endowment Burse and The Cemetery Endowment Burse Most Rev. DANIEL E. GARCIA, D.D.; LEAH DUNCAN; MAUREEN HALDERMAN; SUSAN A. MAYER, Esq., Ex Official; MICHAEL MORRIS; GENE ZANGER; THOMAS H. RIORDAN; LARRY SAGE; ROBERT SEMAS; CLANCY D'ANGELO, Dir. Finance; KATHY ALDRETE, Controller, (Staff).

Catholic Charities Board—Most Rev. DANIEL E. GARCIA, D.D.; CYNTHIA ZOLLER SILVER; MARIA ANDERSON; Very Rev. FREDY CALVARIO, V.F.; PAUL GUTIERREZ; JOSEPH GLUNZ SR.; LUMA WILLIAMS; Rev. JERRY MCCORMICK, (Retired), (Honorary); MELANIE NICORA; MARTINA O'SULLIVAN, M.S.W.; CHRISTOPHER PANETTA, Pres.; Deacon HUGO PATINO; LAURA SEGURA; LARRY SAGE, Treas. Staff: CLANCY D'ANGELO, Dir. Finance; KATHY ALDRETE, Controller, Catholic Charities; ANA VENTURA PHARAS, Exec. Dir.

Diocesan Consultors—Very Rev. RUSSELL D. BROWN, V.F.; Rev. PETER A. CRIVELLO; Very Rev. MARTIN CAIN, V.F., Santa Cruz County - Northern Vicariate; Rev. MIGUEL ANGEL GRAJEDA, V.C.; Very Revs. ENRIQUE HERRERA, V.F., Salinas Valley Vicariate; MICHAEL VOLK, V.U.; PEDRO ESPINOZA, J.C.L., V.F., Santa Cruz County - Southern Vicariate; HEIBAR CASTANEDA, V.F., San Benito County Vicariate; MARK STETZ, V.F., San Luis Obispo County, Southwest Vicariate.

Finance Council—Most Rev. DANIEL E. GARCIA, D.D.; DOUG ANDERSON; Rev. PETER A. CRIVELLO; WILLIAM DORLAND; DAVID HIGGINS; HARRY HOW; MARY HUBBELL, Chair; GARY PLUMMER; TOD SANCHEZ; MICHAEL SCANLON; MOSE THOMAS; ANN WIESER; CLANCY D'ANGELO, Dir. Finance; KATHY ALDRETE, Controller; SUSAN A. MAYER, Esq., Gen. Counsel.

Lay Employee Pension Plan Committee—CLANCY D'ANGELO; SUSAN A. MAYER, Esq.; TOD D. SANCHEZ.

Clergy Life and Ministry Board—Most Rev. DANIEL E. GARCIA, D.D.; Very Revs. MARK STETZ, V.F.; MARTIN CAIN, V.F.; BERNARDINE JOHNSON, Recording Sec.; Rev. ROBERT D. SULLIVAN.

Clergy Personnel Board—Most Rev. DANIEL E. GARCIA, D.D.; Rev. PETER A. CRIVELLO, Moderator of the Curia; Deacon HUGO PATINO, Chancellor; Sr. SHARON MCMILLAN, S.N.D.den.; Revs. PAUL P. MURPHY, Chm.; VICTOR OMMAR SOLIS; Deacon DAVID FORD; Revs. MIGUEL ANGEL GRAJEDA, V.C., Vicar for Clergy; GREGORY SANDMAN; BERNARDINE JOHNSON, Recording Sec.

Safety Committee—SUSAN A. MAYER, Esq.; CLANCY D'ANGELO; KIMBERLY CHENG; KAREN VICTORINO; Deacon WARREN E. HOY; TISH SCARGILL; MIRIAM (MIMI) SCHWERTFEGER, Recording Sec.

St. Francis Central Coast Catholic High School, Inc.—Most Rev. DANIEL E. GARCIA, D.D.; Rev. TED MONTEMAYOR, S.D.B.; Most Rev. SYLVESTER D. RYAN, D.D., Retired Bishop of Monterey, (Retired); MR. WILLIAM GOODMAN; CLANCY D'ANGELO; Rev. THO BUI, S.D.B.; LINA SILVA, Recording Sec.

Vocations Board—Most Rev. DANIEL E. GARCIA, D.D.; Revs. VICTOR OMMAR SOLIS; PETER A. CRIVELLO.

CLERGY, PARISHES, MISSIONS AND PAROCHIAL SCHOOLS

CITY OF MONTEREY

(MONTEREY COUNTY), CATHEDRAL OF SAN CARLOS BORROMEO (1770)
500 Church St., 93940. Tel: 831-373-2628; Fax: 831-373-0518; Web: www.sancarloscathedral.org. Revs. Jerry Maher; Efrain Medina, Parochial Vicar; Patrick Dooling, In Res., (Retired); Ron Shirley, In Res., (Retired); Mrs. Claudia Larraza, Pastoral Assoc.; Cindy Rybkowski, Business Mgr.
School—San Carlos School (1898) (Grades PreK-8), 450 Church St., 93940. Tel: 831-375-1324; Fax: 831-375-9736; Email: principal@sancarlosschool.org; Web: www.sancarlosschool.org. Teresa Bennett, Prin.; Mr. Timothy Krislyn, Vice Prin. Lay Teachers 18; Students 290; Total Staff 14.
Catechesis Religious Program—Tel: 831-373-2628; Fax: 831-373-0516. Cynthia Friesen, D.R.E. Sisters 1; Students 246; Lay Ministers 2.

OUTSIDE THE CITY OF MONTEREY

APTOS, SANTA CRUZ CO., RESURRECTION (1968)
7600 Soquel Dr., Aptos, 95003. Tel: 831-688-4300; Email: resurrectionparish@sbcglobal.net; Web: resurrection-aptos.org. P.O. Box 87, Aptos, 95001. Rev. Romeo Evangelista; Deacon Patrick Conway, Pastoral Assoc.
Please see Good Shepherd School under Inter-Diocesan School in the Institutions Located in the Diocese section.
Catechesis Religious Program—Email: darovick@att.net. Deborah Rovick, D.R.E. Students 137.

ARROYO GRANDE, SAN LUIS OBISPO CO., ST. PATRICK (1886)
501 Fair Oaks Ave., Arroyo Grande, 93421. Tel: 805-489-2680; Fax: 805-489-1316; Email: info@stpatsag.org; Web: www.stpatsag.org. P.O. Box 860, Arroyo Grande, 93421. Very Revs. Jose Alberto Vazquez-Martinez, V.F., 435 Church St., P.O. Box 2048, 93940-2048; Russell D. Brown, V.F., Parochial Vicar.
School—St. Patrick School (1963) (Grades PreK-8), 900 W. Branch St., Arroyo Grande, 93420. Tel: 805-489-1210; Fax: 805-489-7662; Email: mhalderman@stpatschoolag.com; Web: www.stpatschoolag.com. Maureen Halderman, Prin. Lay Teachers 20; Sisters of Mercy 1; Students 292; Total Staff 41; Religious Teachers 1; Clergy / Religious Teachers 1.
Catechesis Religious Program—
Tel: 805-489-2680, Ext. 33. Students 313.
Mission—St. Francis of Assisi, 17th & Beach, Oceano, San Luis Obispo Co. 93445.
Shamrock Thrift Shop—924 Grand Ave., Grover City, 93433. Tel: 805-481-0612; Email: thriftstore@stpatschoolag.com.

ATASCADERO, SAN LUIS OBISPO CO., ST. WILLIAM'S (1948) [JC]
6410 Santa Lucia Rd., Atascadero, 93422. Tel: 805-466-0849; Fax: 805-461-0743; Email: office@stwilliams.org; Web: www.stwilliams.org. Revs. Edwin Limpiado; Martel Ramos, In Res.
Catechesis Religious Program—Mr. Donald Brown Sr., D.R.E. Students 150.

BOULDER CREEK, SANTA CRUZ CO., ST. MICHAEL'S (1921)
13005 Pine St., Boulder Creek, 95006. Tel: 831-338-6112; Email: st.michaelschurch@sbcglobal.net. Rev. Robert Murrin.
Catechesis Religious Program—Judie D. Kolbmann, C.R.E. Students 12.

CAMBRIA, SAN LUIS OBISPO CO., SANTA ROSA (1961) [CEM]
1174 Main St., Cambria, 93428. Tel: 805-927-4816; Email: admin@santarosaparish.org. Very Rev. Mark Stetz, V.F.
Catechesis Religious Program—Tel: 805-924-1728; Email: faithformation@santarosaparish.org. Esther De Alba, D.R.E.; Sylvia Barker, Youth Min. Students 97.

CAPITOLA, SANTA CRUZ CO., ST. JOSEPH (1904) [JC]
435 Monterey Ave., Capitola, 95010. Tel: 831-475-8211, Ext. 40; Web: saint-josephs.church. Very Rev. Wayne Dawson; Socorro Wallace, Pastor's Asst.
Please see Good Shepherd School under Inter-Diocesan School in the Institutions Located in the Diocese section.
Catechesis Religious Program—Tel: 831-475-8211; Email: Shauna@stjoscap.org. Shauna Scott, Diocesan D.R.E. Students 148.

CARMEL VALLEY, MONTEREY CO., OUR LADY OF MT. CARMEL (1953)
9 El Caminito Rd., Carmel Valley, 93924. Tel: 831-659-2224; Email: olmc@ourladycarmelvalley.org. Rev. Dennis Gallo.
Catechesis Religious Program—Students 11.

CARMEL, MONTEREY CO., SAN CARLOS BORROMEO BASILICA (1771) [CEM] (Carmel Mission)
3080 Rio Rd., Carmel, 93923. Tel: 831-624-1271; Email: reception@carmelmission.org. Revs. Paul P. Murphy; Jhonnatan F. Carmona.
School—Junipero Serra School, (Grades 1-8), 3090 Rio Rd., Carmel, 93923. Tel: 831-624-8322; Fax: 831-624-8311; Email: bstewart@juniperoserra.org; Web: www.stjuniperoserraschool.org. Bruce J. Stewart, Prin. Lay Teachers 17; Students 150.
Catechesis Religious Program—
Tel: 831-624-1271, Ext. 216; Fax: 831-624-6840. Sanna Rosellen, D.R.E. Students 99.
Mission—St. Francis of the Redwoods, Hwy. 1, Big Sur, Monterey Co. 93920.
Chapel—Blessed Sacrament.

CASTROVILLE, MONTEREY CO., OUR LADY OF REFUGE (1869) [JC]
11140 Preston St., Castroville, 95012. Tel: 831-633-4015; Fax: 831-633-4653; Email: info@olorc.org; Web: www.olorc.org. Very Rev. Pedro Espinoza, J.C.L., V.F.
Res.: 14931 Charter Oak Blvd., Salinas, 93907.
Catechesis Religious Program—Tel: 831-633-4016. Sr. Christina Bortolotti, D.R.E. Students 462.

CAYUCOS, SAN LUIS OBISPO CO., ST. JOSEPH (1905)
360 Park Ave., Cayucos, 93430. Tel: 805-995-3243; Web: www.stjosephcayucos.org. P.O. Box 437, Cayucos, 93430. Rev. Msgr. Charles G. Fatooh, 395 Del Monte #147, 93940.
Catechesis Religious Program—

CORRALITOS, SANTA CRUZ CO., HOLY EUCHARIST (1969)
527 Corralitos Rd., Corralitos, 95076. Tel: 831-722-5490; Email: office.holyeucharistca@yahoo.com; Web: www.holyeucharistca@yahoo.com. Rev. Derek Hughes; Deacon Camerino Padilla.
Catechesis Religious Program—Email: maura.holyeucharistca@yahoo.com. Maura Motta, D.R.E. Students 166.

DAVENPORT, SANTA CRUZ CO., ST. VINCENT DE PAUL (1915)
123 Marine View Ave., P.O. Box 284, Davenport, 95017. Tel: 831-457-1868, Ext. 12. 544 West Cliff Dr., Santa Cruz, 95060. Rev. Steve Peterson, Admin.
Catechesis Religious Program—Josephine Gilbert, D.R.E. Students 8.

FELTON, SANTA CRUZ CO., ST. JOHN'S (1952)
120 Russell Ave., Felton, 95018. Tel: 831-335-4657; Email: contact@stjohnsfelton.org; Web: www.stjohnsfelton.org. P.O. Box M-1, Felton, 95018. Rev. Roy Margallo, O.S.A., Dominican Santa Cruz Hospital, 1555 Soquel Ave., Santa Cruz, 95065.
Catechesis Religious Program—Mary Sager, D.R.E. Students 9.

GONZALES, MONTEREY CO., ST. THEODORE (1892) [JC]
125 S. Center St., Gonzales, 93926. Tel: 831-675-3648; Email: sttheodripo@gmail.com. P.O. Box B, Gonzales, 93926. Revs. Hily Gonzales, Admin.; Hoang Phi Liem Nguyen, Parochial Vicar; Sr. Lourdina D. Souza, D.R.E.
Res.: 120 First St., P.O. Drawer B, Gonzales, 93926.
Catechesis Religious Program—
Tel: 831-675-3668, Ext. 7; Fax: 831-675-2974.
Mission—Chualar Mission, Scott & Grant Sts., Chualar, Monterey Co. 93925.

GREENFIELD, MONTEREY CO., HOLY TRINITY (1951) (Mexican—Italian)
27 S. El Camino Real, P.O. Box 276, Greenfield, 93927. Tel: 831-674-5428; Email: holytrinitychurch276@yahoo.com. Very Rev. Enrique Herrera, V.F.
Catechesis Religious Program—Tel: 831-674-3695. Gloria Aguilar, D.R.E. Students 591.

HOLLISTER, SAN BENITO CO
1—ST. BENEDICT, Merged with Sacred Heart, Hollister to form Sacred Heart/St. Benedict Catholic Community, Hollister.
2—SACRED HEART (1877) Merged with St. Benedict, Hollister to form Sacred Heart/St. Benedict Catholic Community, Hollister.
3—SACRED HEART/ST. BENEDICT CATHOLIC COMMUNITY (1877) [CEM]
680 College St., Hollister, 95023. Tel: 831-637-9212; Fax: 831-637-7299; Email: info@catholichollister.org; Web: www.catholichollister.org. Revs. Claudio Cabrera-Carranza, V.F.; Nguyen Dat, Parochial Vicar; German Rodriguez, Parochial Vicar; Hugues Beaugrand, In Res.; Very Rev. Heibar Castaneda, V.F., In Res.
Res.: 540 College St., Hollister, 95023.
School—Sacred Heart/St. Benedict Catholic Community School, (Grades PreK-8), 670 College St., Hollister, 95023. Tel: 831-637-4157; Fax: 831-637-4164; Email: rmckenna@sacredheartschool.org; Web: sacredheartschool.org. Rachel McKenna, Prin. Lay Teachers 20; Students 209.
Catechesis Religious Program—Nancy Lopez, D.R.E. Students 850.

JOLON, MONTEREY CO., MISSION SAN ANTONIO DE PADUA (1771)
End of Mission Rd., Jolon, 93928. Tel: 831-385-4478, Ext. 10; Email: office@missionsanantonio.net. P.O. Box 803, Jolon, 93928-0803. Joan Steele, Admin.

KING CITY, MONTEREY CO., ST. JOHN THE BAPTIST (1891) (Hispanic)
504 N. Third St., King City, 93930. Tel: 831-385-3377; Email: stjohnscc@att.net. Rev. Lucas Pantoja.
Catechesis Religious Program—Tel: 831-385-3464; Email: stjohnkingcm@gmail.com. Sr. Rosangela Filippini, I.M., D.R.E. Students 620.
Mission—St. Luke, Main St., San Lucas, Monterey Co. 93954.

LOS GATOS, SANTA CRUZ CO., CHRIST CHILD (1983)
23230 Summit Rd., Los Gatos, 95033. Tel: 408-353-2210; Web: www.christchild.org. Rev. Eugenio Aramburo.
Catechesis Religious Program—Tel: 408-353-9278. Mrs. Nanette Thomas, D.R.E. Students 15.

LOS OSOS, SAN LUIS OBISPO CO., ST. ELIZABETH ANN SETON (1984)
2050 Palisades Ave., Los Osos, 93402. Tel: 805-528-5319; Fax: 805-528-8893; Email: seaschurchlo@gmail.com; Web: www.seasparishlo.org. Rev. Joey R. Buena; Javier Soto Osorio, Business Mgr.
Catechesis Religious Program—Students 53.

MARINA, MONTEREY CO., ST. JUDE PARISH COMMUNITY (1963)
303 Hillcrest Ave., Marina, 93933-3599. Tel: 831-384-5434; Email: st_jude_marina_amy@sbcglobal.net. Rev. Jeronimo Marcelo.

Catechesis Religious Program—Tel: 831-384-8268. Esther Martinez, Rel. Educ. Coord. Students 178.

MORRO BAY, SAN LUIS OBISPO CO., ST. TIMOTHY (1950)
962 Piney Way, Morro Bay, 93442. Tel: 805-772-2840 ; Fax: 805-772-3184; Email: osainttims@yahoo.com; Web: www.sttimothymorrobay.org. Rev. Edward J. Holterhoff, Parochial Admin.
Catechesis Religious Program—Email: tlockwood.sttims@yahoo.com. Theresa Lockwood, D.R.E. Students 107.

NIPOMO, SAN LUIS OBISPO CO., ST. JOSEPH (1968)
298 S. Thompson, Nipomo, 93444. Tel: 805-922-1922; Email: office@stjonipomo.org; Web: www.stjonipomo.org. Revs. Miguel Rodriguez; Braulio Valencia, Vicar; Deacon Greg Barata.
Catechesis Religious Program—Tel: 805-929-1921. Students 461.

PACIFIC GROVE, MONTEREY CO., ST. ANGELA MERICI CHURCH (1928) [CEM]
362 Lighthouse Ave., Pacific Grove, 93950.
Tel: 831-655-4160. 146 8th St., Pacific Grove, 93950. Rev. Seamus O'Brien.
Res.: 161 9th St., Pacific Grove, 93950. Email: stangelachurch@stangelaamerici.org; Web: www.stangelamericipacificgrove.org.
School—St. Angela Preschool, 136 Eighth St., Pacific Grove, 93950. Tel: 831-372-3555; Fax: 831-440-7450; Email: office@stangelaspreschool.org. Mrs. Heather Diaz, Dir. Lay Teachers 8; Students 62.
Catechesis Religious Program—Jordan Lewis, D.R.E. Students 60.

PAJARO, MONTEREY CO., OUR LADY OF THE ASSUMPTION (1953) [CEM] (Hispanic)
100 Salinas Rd., Royal Oaks, 95076.
Tel: 831-722-1104; Email: info@ladyassumptionchurch.org. Revs. Victor M. Prado; Jesus Manuel Galvez, Parochial Vicar; Deacon Salvador Lopez.
Catechesis Religious Program—
Tel: 831-722-1104, Ext. 18; Email: Rosa@ladyassumptionchurch.org. Rosa Garcia, D.R.E. Students 397.

PASO ROBLES, SAN LUIS OBISPO CO., ST. ROSE OF LIMA CHURCH (1922) [CEM] [JC]
820 Creston Rd., Paso Robles, 93447.
Tel: 805-238-2218; Email: strose@saintrosechurch.org; Web: www.saintrosechurch.org. P.O. Box 790, Paso Robles, 93447. Revs. Rodolfo Contreras; Stephen Akers.
School—St. Rose of Lima Church School, (Grades PreK-8), 900 Tucker Ave., Paso Robles, 93446.
Tel: 805-238-0304; Fax: 805-238-7393; Email: srsoffice@saintrosecatholicschool.org; Web: www.saintrosecatholicschool.org. Mr. Trevor Knable, Prin. Lay Teachers 16; Students 197; Religious Teachers 1.
Catechesis Religious Program—Diana Mariscal, D.R.E.; Alejandra Mariscal, D.R.E. Students 363.

PISMO BEACH, SAN LUIS OBISPO CO., ST. PAUL THE APOSTLE (1929) [JC]
800 Bello St., Pismo Beach, 93449. Tel: 805-773-2219 ; Fax: 805-773-8617; Email: jcarazo2@gmail.com. Revs. Jacob Carazo; Allen Ramirez, O.F.M.Conv., Parochial Vicar; Alphonse Van Guilder, O.F.M.Conv., Parochial Vicar; Bro. Raphael Carl Drew, O.F.M.Conv., In Res.; Rev. John Farao, O.F.M.Conv., In Res.
Catechesis Religious Program—Tel: 805-773-3185. Ann Boulais, Diocesan D.R.E. Students 29.

SALINAS, MONTEREY CO.

1—CHRIST THE KING (1995) (Hispanic)
240 Calle Cebu, Salinas, 93901. Tel: 831-422-6543; Email: christtheking@dioceseofmonterey.org. Revs. Antonio Sanchez, Our Lady of the Assumption, 100 Salinas Rd., Watsonville, 95076; Aurelio Ortiz.
Religious Education Office—Tel: 831-422-6722.
Catechesis Religious Program—Email: chiw.nm0703@gmail.com. Patricia Chiw, D.R.E. Students 837.

2—MADONNA DEL SASSO (1960)
320 E. Laurel Dr., Salinas, 93906. Tel: 831-422-5323; Email: mdschurch@aol.com; Web: www.mdschurch.org. Revs. Gregory Sandman; Gabriel Okafor; Dan Derry, In Res.; Jose Aurelio Ortiz-Matiz, In Res.
School—Madonna Del Sasso School, (Grades 1-8), 20 Santa Teresa Way, Salinas, 93906.
Tel: 831-424-7813; Fax: 831-424-3359; Email: arivera@mdsschool.com; Web: mdsschool.com. Angel Rivera, Prin. Lay Teachers 11; Students 213.
Catechesis Religious Program—Tel: 831-422-6043; Email: ffmds@aol.com. Yolanda Irinco, D.R.E. Students 738.

3—ST. MARY OF THE NATIVITY (1947) (Hispanic)
424 Towt St., Salinas, 93905. Tel: 831-758-1669;
Fax: 831-758-4715. 1702 Second Ave., Salinas, 93905. Very Rev. Fredy Calvario, V.F.; Rev. Jason Simas, Vicar.
Catechesis Religious Program—Tel: 831-422-9964; Email: acardenas@stmarysalinas.org. Andrea Cardenas, D.R.E. Students 1,182.

4—SACRED HEART (1877) [JC]
22 Stone St., Salinas, 93901-2643. Tel: 831-424-1959; Email: scrhrtchurch@sbcglobal.net; Web: www.shsalinas.org. Revs. Manuel Recera; Rodrigo Paredes Cardona, Parochial Vicar; Deacons Rick Gutierrez; David Lansford.
School—Sacred Heart School, (Grades PreK-8), 123 W. Market St., Salinas, 93901. Tel: 831-771-1310; Fax: 831-771-1314; Email: crains@shschool.com; Web: www.shschool.com. Connie Rossi-Rains, Prin.; Jaynie MacDonald, Librarian. Lay Teachers 20; Sisters 1; Students 350; Total Staff 48; Religious Teachers 1.
Catechesis Religious Program—Mary Scattini, D.R.E. Students 526.

SAN JUAN BAUTISTA, SAN BENITO CO., SAN JUAN BAUTISTA (1797) [CEM] (Hispanic) (Old Mission)
406 Second St., San Juan Bautista, 95045.
Tel: 831-623-2127; Email: magda@oldmissionsjb.org; Web: www.oldmisionsjb.org. P.O. Box 400, San Juan Bautista, 95045. Rev. Alberto Cabrera.
Catechesis Religious Program—Tel: 831-623-4178; Email: elisa@oldmissionsjb.org. Mr. Elisa Hernandez, Coord. of Faith Formation. Students 115.

SAN LUIS OBISPO, SAN LUIS OBISPO CO.

1—NATIVITY OF OUR LADY (1964)
221 Daly Ave., San Luis Obispo, 93405-1099.
Tel: 805-544-2357; Email: parish@nativityslo.org; Web: NativitySLO.org. Very Rev. Matthew Pennington, V.F.; Deacon Tom O'Brien, Pastoral Assoc.; Susan Lindstrom, Hospital Min./ Bereavement Min.; Kayla Peracca, Bookkeeper; Helen Magee, Church Sec.
Catechesis Religious Program—Stephanie Purvis, D.R.E. (Children); Karen O'Brien, D.R.E. (Junior High); Katie Rose Cirillo, D.R.E. (High School). Students 66.

2—OLD MISSION CHURCH aka Mission San Luis Obispo de Tolosa (1772) (Old Mission)
751 Palm St., San Luis Obispo, 93401.
Tel: 805-781-8220, Ext. 13; Email: office@oldmissionslo.org; Web: www.missionsanluisobispo.org. Kelly M. Vandehey, J.C.L.; Revs. David Anthony Ramirez, Parochial Vicar; James Nisbet, In Res.; Deacons Jim Burrows; Charles M. Roeder.
Child Care—Preschool, 221 Daly St., San Luis Obispo, 93401. Tel: 805-549-8819; Email: sgray@omsslo.com; Web: www.oldmissionschool.com. Shirley Gray, Dir. Students 48; Clergy / Religious Teachers 3.
School—Old Mission Church School, (Grades PreK-8), 761 Broad St., San Luis Obispo, 93401.
Tel: 805-543-6019; Fax: 805-543-6246; Email: bjwoods@omsslo.com; Email: sgray@omsslo.com; Web: www.oldmissionschool.com. Shirley Gray, Prin. Lay Teachers 18; Students 234.
Catechesis Religious Program—Email: tburrows@oldmissionslo.org. Terry Burrows, D.R.E. Students 147.

SAN MIGUEL, SAN LUIS OBISPO CO., SAN MIGUEL (1797) [CEM] (Hispanic—Filipino) (Old Mission)
775 Mission St., San Miguel, 93451.
Tel: 805-467-2131; Email: info@missionsanmiguel.org. P.O. Box 69, San Miguel, 93451. Revs. Eleazar Díaz Gaytán, Apostolic Admin.; Dennis M. Peterson, In Res.
Catechesis Religious Program—Students 119.
Missions—Our Lady of Ransom—San Ardo, Monterey Co.
Our Lady of Guadalupe, Bradley, Monterey Co.

SANTA CRUZ, SANTA CRUZ CO.

1—HOLY CROSS (1791) [CEM 3] [JC2]
126 High St., Santa Cruz, 95060. Tel: 831-423-4182; Fax: 831-423-1043; Email: office@holycrosssantacruz.com; Web: www.holycrosssantacruz.com. 210 High St., Santa Cruz, 95060. Very Rev. Martin Cain, V.F.; Revs. Dat Dac Nguyen, Parochial Vicar; Constant Bossou, S.J., In Res.
School—Holy Cross School (1862) (Grades 1-8), 150 Emmet St., Santa Cruz, 95060. Tel: 831-423-4447; Fax: 831-423-0752; Email: admin@holycsc.org; Web: www.holycsc.org. Patty Patano, Prin. Lay Teachers 17; Adrian Dominican Sisters 1; Students 143; Total Staff 26; Religious Teachers 1; Clergy / Religious Teachers 1.
Catechesis Religious Program—Tel: 831-458-3041; Email: elizborgeshc@gmail.com; Email: faith@holycrosssantacruz.com. Elizabeth Borges-Yee, Youth Min.; Bobbie Herndon, D.R.E. (English); Claudia Manrique, D.R.E. (Spanish). Students 172.
Mission—Mision Galeria, 130 Emmet St., Santa Cruz, Santa Cruz Co. 95060. Tel: 831-426-5686.

2—STAR OF THE SEA (1947) [CEM]
515 Frederick St., Santa Cruz, 95062.
Tel: 831-429-1018; Email: nancy@ourladystar.org. Rev. Robert D. Sullivan, Sacramental Min.
Please see Good Shepherd School under Inter-Diocesan School in the Institutions Located in the Diocese section.
Catechesis Religious Program—Email: erika@ourladystar.org. Mrs. Erika Rivera, D.R.E. Students 295.
Chapel—Villa Maria del Mar, 2-1918 E. Cliff Dr., Santa Cruz, 95062. Tel: 831-475-1236.

SANTA MARGARITA, SAN LUIS OBISPO CO., SANTA MARGARITA DE CORTONA (1934) [JC]
22515 "H" St., P.O. Box 350, Santa Margarita, 93453. Tel: 805-438-5383; Email: decortona@aol.com. Rev. Robert Travis.
Catechesis Religious Program—Tel: 805-239-1597. Julie Smeltzer, D.R.E. Students 15.

SCOTTS VALLEY, SANTA CRUZ CO., SAN AGUSTIN (1969)
257 Glenwood Dr., Scotts Valley, 95066.
Tel: 831-438-3633; Fax: 831-438-0973; Email: info@sanagustin.church. Rev. John C. Griffin.
Catechesis Religious Program—Janet Gluch, D.R.E. Students 124.

SEASIDE, MONTEREY CO., ST. FRANCIS XAVIER (1950)
1475 LaSalle Ave., Seaside, 93955. Tel: 831-394-8546 ; Email: sbwasonga@gmail.com. Very Rev. Michael Volk, V.U.; Rev. Francisco J. Montes; Sr. Benedicta Wasonga, I.H.S.A., Parish Admin.
Catechesis Religious Program—Email: religiosued@stfxavier.org. Sr. Carmelita Heredia, S.A., D.R.E. Students 546.

SOLEDAD, MONTEREY CO., OUR LADY OF SOLITUDE (1933) [CEM] [JC] (Spanish)
235 Main St., Soledad, 93960. Tel: 831-678-2731;
Fax: 831-288-1026; Email: ourladyofsolitude@yahoo.com. Rev. Luiz Kendzierski; Deacon Ron Panziera.
Catechesis Religious Program—Tel: 831-678-1277;
Fax: 831-678-0111. Sr. Theresita Crasta, I.M., D.R.E. Students 875.
Mission—Nuestra Senora de la Soledad, 36641 Fort Romie Rd., Soledad, 93960. Tel: 831-678-2586. Rte. 1 Box 72, Soledad, Monterey Co. 93960.

SPRECKELS, MONTEREY CO., ST. JOSEPH (1969) [CEM]
Spreckels Blvd. & Railroad Ave., Spreckels, 93962.
Tel: 831-455-2249; Fax: 831-455-9357; Email: office@stjchurch.org; Web: stjchurch.org. P.O. Box 7158, Spreckels, 93962. Revs. Roy Shelly, M.A., Ph. D.; Victor Ommar Solis, Parochial Vicar.
1 Railroad Ave., Spreckels, 93962.
.
Catechesis Religious Program—Tel: 831-455-8720; Email: caragon@stjchurch.org. Carrie Aragon, D.R.E. Students 220.

TRES PINOS, SAN BENITO CO., IMMACULATE CONCEPTION (1892)
7290 Airline Hwy., P.O. Box 247, Tres Pinos, 95075.
Tel: 831-628-3216; Email: office@immaculateattrespinos.org; Web: www.immaculateattrespinos.org. Very Rev. Heibar Castaneda, V.F.
Catechesis Religious Program—Email: dre@immaculateattrespinos.org. Ivan Arevalo, D.R.E. Students 105.

WATSONVILLE, SANTA CRUZ CO.

1—OUR LADY HELP OF CHRISTIANS (1854) (Portuguese—Spanish)
2401 E. Lake Ave., Watsonville, 95076.
Tel: 831-722-2665; Email: olhcchurch@yahoo.com; Web: OLHCchurch.org. Revs. Joseph M. Paradayil, S.D.B.; Luis A. Oyarzo, S.D.B., In Res.
Catechesis Religious Program—Tel: 831-722-2392; Email: itapiafma@gmail.com; Email: feliciah18@gmail.com. Sr. Irene Tapia, D.R.E.; Felicia Hernandez, D.R.E. Students 280.

2—ST. PATRICK aka Saint Patrick's Parish (1861)
721 Main St., Watsonville, 95076. Tel: 831-724-1317; Email: office@spatricks.org. Revs. Miguel Angel Grajeda, V.C.; Phil Dumanacal, Parochial Vicar; Deacon Pedro Ramos.
Catechesis Religious Program—Tel: 831-724-2141; Email: confirmation@spatricks.org. Silvia Pineda, D.R.E. (English & Spanish); Emiko Torres, C.R.E. Students 1,165.

Shrines

SANTA CRUZ, SANTA CRUZ CO., SHRINE OF ST. JOSEPH GUARDIAN OF THE REDEEMER (1952) Revs. Paul McDonnell, O.S.J., Dir.; Steve Peterson; Bro. Mathew Chipp, O.S.J., Business Mgr.
Res.: 544 W. Cliff Dr., Santa Cruz, 95060-6147.
Tel: 831-457-1868; Cell: 831-239-5019;
Fax: 831-457-1317; Email: shrine@stjosephshrinesc.org; Email: provincial@osjoseph.org; Web: www.shrinestjoseph.com.
Guardian of the Redeemer Bookstore—
Tel: 831-471-1700.

Chaplains of Public Institutions

ATASCADERO. *Atascadero State Hospital*. Vacant.
SAN LUIS OBISPO. *California Men's Colony East*. Rev. John Farao, O.F.M.Conv., Chap.
California Men's Colony West. Rev. John Farao, O.F.M.Conv.

SOLEDAD. *Correctional Training Facility*. Rev. Ignacio Martinez, Chap.

Salinas Valley State Prison. Rev. Miguel Corona, Chap.

Special Assignment:

Revs.—

Bianchi, Justin E., Campus Ministry Santa Cruz, Newman Catholic Center, 285 Meder St., Santa Cruz, 95060. Tel: 831-423-9400

Castro, Dominic Joseph, M.Div., Chap., 1130 Fremont Blvd., #105-270, Seaside, 93955

Crivello, Peter A., Moderator of the Curia, Pastoral Office, 425 Church St., P.O. Box 2048, 93942-2048. Tel: 831-373-4345; Fax: 831-373-1175; Email: pcrivello@dioceseofmonterey.org

Deibel, David, 3609 Deibel Pl., P.O. Box 608, Indian River, MI 49749-0608. Tel: 331-238-7100

Faria, Carl M.D., P.O. Box 2048, 93942-2048. Tel: 831-373-2127; Fax: 831-655-4809

Grajeda, Miguel Angel, V.C., Vicar for Clergy, P.O. Box 2048, 93942-2048. Tel: 831-373-4345; Email: mgrajeda@dioceseofmonterey.org

Laverone, Kenneth J., O.F.M., J.C.L., Judicial Vicar, Diocesan Tribunal, 580 Fremont St., 93940. Tel: 831-373-1833; Fax: 831-373-6761. P.O. Box 350, 93942-0350

Miller, Michael J., St. Margaret Mary Church, 12686 Central Ave., Chino, 91710. Tel: 909-591-7400

Solis, Victor Ommar, Dir. of Vocations, P.O. Box 2048, 93942-2048. Tel: 831-373-4345; Fax: 831-373-1175

Deacon—

Patino, Hugo, Chancellor, P.O. Box 2048, 93942-2048. Tel: 831-373-4345; Email: hpatino@dioceseofmonterey.org.

On Leave:

Revs.—

Chavez, Jose, Contact Pastoral Office

Dauphine, Marc Rene, Contact Pastoral Office

Green, Ronald L., Contact Pastoral Office

Monfette, Edmond, Contact Pastoral Office.

Retired:

Most Rev.—

Ryan, Sylvester D., D.D., (Retired), c/o Diocese of Monterey, 425 Church St., 93940. Tel: 831-373-4345; Email: bsrdom@aol.com

Revs.—

Almendras, Joel P., (Retired)

Batchelder, George, (Retired), P.O. Box 4136, Santa Cruz, 95061

Carvajal, Raul H., (Retired)

Cicinato, Michael Jerome, (Retired), 135 Cuyama Ave., Shell Beach, 93449-1810

Cross, Michael L., (Retired), Dominican Oaks, 3400 Paul Sweet Rd., Apt. C-305, Santa Cruz, 95065. Tel: 831-621-2870

Dooling, Patrick, (Retired), 500 Church St., 93940

Gilbert, Dennis M., (Retired), 200 S. Lexington Dr., Apt. 814, Folsom, 95630-7027

Henry, James, V.F., (Retired), 1008 Putter Ave., Paso Robles, 93446. Tel: 805-489-1316

Hercek, Joseph R., V.F., (Retired), P.O. Box 2230, Atascadero, 93423

Kelly, Tom, (Retired), 1305 Craig Dr., Lompoc, 93436. Tel: 805-733-1901

Marini, Michael, (Retired), 518 King St., Santa Cruz, 95060. Tel: 831-457-8628

McCarthy, Scott, (Retired), 20 Hitchcock Rd., Salinas, 93901

McCormick, Jerry, (Retired), P.O. Box 51338, Pacific Grove, 93950. Tel: 831-372-8644

McDonald, Martin, (Retired), 2 Huband Mews, Stephens Ln., Dublin 2, Ireland. Cell: 011-35-387-969-0117

Nisbet, James Robert, (Retired), 668 Serrano Dr., San Luis Obispo, 93405-1760

Occhiuto, Joseph L., (Retired), 17503 Sugarmill Rd., Salinas, 93908

Ruiz, Rudy, (Retired), 850 Meridian Way, Apt. 34, San Jose, 95126

Schwarz, Robert, (Retired), 651 Sinex Ave., L-118, Pacific Grove, 93950. Tel: 831-657-4196

Shirley, Ronald, (Retired), 500 Church St., 93940

Valdez, Paul R., J.C.L., KCHS, (Retired), 133 Sonoma St., Watsonville, 95076. Tel: 831-536-5177

Vela, Fabian, (Retired), EGI-Bldg 1, Room 414, Looc. Maribago, Lapu-Lapu City, Cebu Philippines 6015.

Permanent Deacons:

Ashe, Bob, 1598 Stuart St., Cambria, 93428. Tel: 661-313-0648. (Santa Rosa, Cambria)

Avila, Jesse, 5 Creekbridge Cir., Salinas, 93906. (St. Jude's Catholic Church and Shrine, Marina)

Barata, Greg, 2535 Snowcone Place, Arroyo Grande, 93420. Tel: 805-481-9371. (St. Joseph's, Nipomo)

Burrows, Jim, 672 Howard St., San Luis Obispo, 93401. Tel: 805-543-9459 (Home)

Callahan, Ed, Assoc. Dir. Deacon Life & Ministry, South, 603 Turtle Creek, Paso Robles, 93446. Tel: 805-610-5298. (St. Rose of Lima, Paso Robles)

Conway, Patrick, 88 Mar Monte Ave., La Selva Beach, 95076. Tel: 831-840-3750 (Home). (Resurrection Church, Aptos

Dutra, Greg, 210 LaJoya Dr., Nipomo, 93444. Tel: 805-929-1235 (Home). (St. Patrick's, Arroyo Grande)

Espinoza, Manuel, 1813 Driftwood Dr., Paso Robles, 93447. Tel: 805-238-5588. (St. Rose of Lima, Paso Robles)

Figenshow, Carl, 22551 Murietta Rd., Salinas, 93908. Tel: 831-455-0377 (Home); Cell: 831-676-8169. (Madonna del Sasso, Salinas)

Gutierrez, Richard, P.O. Box 7254, Spreckels, 93962. Tel: 831-455-1640 (Home); Cell: 831-594-1836. (Sacred Heart Salinas & Prison Youth Ministry, Salinas)

Hoy, Warren E., Dir. Family Life, Soc. Concerns & Safe Environment Coord., 1168 Roosevelt St., 93940. Tel: 831-642-9821. (Carmel Mission, Carmel)

Lansford, David, Assoc. Dir., Deacon Life & Ministry, 105 Maple St., Salinas, 93901. Tel: 831-424-3803 (Home). (Sacred Heart, Salinas)

Larraza, Andres, Ph.D., Assoc. Dir., Hispanic Formation, P.O. Box 1568, 93942. Tel: 831-206-3121. (Our Lady of Refuge, Castroville)

Lopez, Salvador, 7 Jonathan St., Watsonville, 95076. Tel: 831-728-2312. (Our Lady of the Assumption, Pajaro)

Minton, Rick, 2490 Adobe Rd., Paso Robles, 93446. Tel: 805-239-3020 (Work)

O'Brien, Tom, 8340 Curbaril Ave., Atascadero, 93422. Tel: 831-345-0596

Padilla, Camerino, 148 Montebello Dr., Watsonville, 95076. Tel: 831-761-0182. (Holy Eucharist, Corralitos)

Panziera, Ron, P.O. Box 715, Soledad, 93960. Tel: 831-678-3180 (Home); Cell: 831-595-1992

Pasculli, Nicholas, Tel: 831-758-6425 (Work)

Patino, Hugo, Chancellor, 903 Jefferson St., 93940. Tel: 831-324-4725. (San Carlos Cathedral, Monterey)

Ramos, Pedro, 10 Crescent Dr., Watsonville, 95076. Tel: 831-763-2802. (St. Patrick, Watsonville)

Reichmuth, William (Bill), (Retired), 200 Iris Cyn Rd., Apt. LOZ, 93940. Tel: 831-316-9280 (Home); Cell: 831-233-9551

Roeder, Chuck, 6082 Pebble Beach Way, San Luis Obispo, 93401. Tel: 805-544-2707 (Home); Cell: 805-745-1718. (Old Mission, San Luis Obispo)

Rutledge, Clark, P.O. Box 1232, Morro Bay, 93443. Tel: 805-772-2993 (Home). (St. Timothy's, Morro Bay)

Seagren, Charles, 106 Spanish Bay, Aptos, 95003. Cell: 650-804-8985

Valenzuela, Jose, Tel: 831-262-0298. (Sacred Heart-St. Benedict's, Hollister)

Weber, Dan, 2225 W. Rivers Edge, St. George, UT 84770. Tel: 805-468-2489

Wilhelm, Greg, P.O. Box 2232, Jasper, OR 97438. Cell: 805-550-0739

Winston, Douglas, 12056 Aragon Springs Ave., Las Vegas, NV 89138. Cell: 831-595-1939

Wolverton, Van, (Retired), 1057 Carr Ave., Aromas, 95004. Tel: 831-726-9145

Zabala, Morton, (Retired), P.O. Box 141, Waianae, HI 96792. Cell: 808-229-7370.

INSTITUTIONS LOCATED IN DIOCESE

[A] HIGH SCHOOLS, PRIVATE

MONTEREY. *Santa Catalina Upper School* (1950) (Girls) 1500 Mark Thomas Dr., 93940-5291. Tel: 831-655-9300; Fax: 831-649-3056; Email: julie.edson@santacatalina.org; Web: www.santacatalina.org. Margaret K. Bradley, Headmaster; Julie Edson, Admin. Lay Teachers 37; Students 209.

SALINAS. *Christian Brothers Institute of California, Inc.* dba Palma School (1951) (Boys) 919 Iverson St., Salinas, 93901-1816. Tel: 831-422-6391; Fax: 831-422-5065; Email: dunne@palmaschool.org; Web: www.palmaschool.org. Bro. Patrick D. Dunne, C.F.C., Pres. & Community Leader; David J. Sullivan, Prin. Congregation of Christian Brothers. Brothers 1; Lay Teachers 28; Students 521; Total Staff 38; Boys (Jr. High) 135; Boys (Total) 386.

Congregation of Christian Brothers Residence, 263 West Acacia Street, Salinas, 93901. Tel: 831-299-1101. Bro. Patrick D. Dunne, C.F.C., Contact Person. Brothers 3.

WATSONVILLE. *St. Francis High School Salesian College Preparatory* (2001) 2400 E. Lake Ave., Watsonville, 95076. Tel: 831-724-5933; Fax: 831-724-5995; Email: lee@stfrancishigh.net; Web: www.stfrancishigh.net. Patrick Lee, Pres. & Prin. Joint High School between Diocese of Monterey and Salesians of St. John Bosco. Lay Teachers 20; Students 250.

[B] HIGH SCHOOLS, DIOCESAN

SALINAS. *Notre Dame High School*, 455 Palma Dr., Salinas, 93901. Tel: 831-751-1850; Fax: 831-757-5749; Email: businessmanager@notredamesalinas.org; Web: www.notredamesalinas.org. Kristi McLaughlin, Prin.; Corrie Cubillas, Bus. Mgr.; Jenn Oberg, Campus Min.; Alyssa Barnes, Contact Person. Religious Teachers 4; Girls 201; Lay Teachers 20; Sisters 1.

SAN LUIS OBISPO. *Mission College Preparatory Catholic High School*, 682 Palm St., San Luis Obispo, 93401. Tel: 805-543-2131; Fax: 805-543-4359; Email: info@missionprep.org; Web: www.missionprep.org. Michael Susank, Prin. Lay Teachers 24; Students 294; Total Staff 50.

[C] ELEMENTARY SCHOOLS, PRIVATE

MONTEREY. *Santa Catalina Lower School* (1950) (Grades PreK-8), (Coed) 1500 Mark Thomas Dr., 93940-5291. Tel: 831-655-9300; Fax: 831-649-3056; Email: christy.pollacci@santacatalina.org; Web: www.santacatalina.org. Margaret K. Bradley, Head of School; Christy Pollacci, Admin. Lay Teachers 35; Students 238.

CORRALITOS. *Salesian Elementary & Jr. High School: Mary Help of Christians Youth Center* (1978) (Grades K-8), 605 Enos Ln., Corralitos, 95076. Tel: 831-728-5518; Fax: 831-728-0273; Email: office@salesianschool.org; Web: salesianschool.org. Sr. Carmen Botello, F.M.A., Prin. Religious Teachers 4; Lay Teachers 11; Sisters 5; Students 121.

WATSONVILLE. *Moreland Notre Dame School* (1899) (Grades PreK-8), 133 Brennan St., Watsonville, 95076. Tel: 831-728-2051; Fax: 831-728-2052; Email: cmottau@mndschool.org; Web: www.mndschool.org. Mrs. Cathy Mottau, Prin.; Mrs. Jeannie Nunez, Admin. Asst. Religious Teachers 1; Lay Teachers 11; Students 241.

Our Lady Help of Christians Church Youth Ministry, 2401 E. Lake Ave., Watsonville, 95076. Tel: 831-722-2665; Fax: 831-722-8305; Email: olhcchurch@yahoo.com. Revs. Luis A. Oyarzo, S.D.B., Parochial Vicar; Joseph M. Paradayil, S.D.B., Pastor. Supports youth activities at parish summer camp and school level. Brothers 1; Religious Teachers 1; Priests 2; Students 100; Total Staff 7.

[D] INTER-DIOCESAN SCHOOL

SANTA CRUZ. *Good Shepherd School (Inter-Parish)*, (Grades PreK-8), 2727 Mattison Ln., Santa Cruz, 95062. Tel: 831-476-4000; Fax: 831-476-0948; Email: inbox@gsschool.org; Web: www.gsschool.org. Richard Determan, Prin. Serves the following parishes: Resurrection, Aptos; St. Joseph, Capitola; & Star of the Sea, Santa Cruz. Religious Teachers 1; Lay Teachers 10; Students 182.

[E] GENERAL HOSPITALS

SANTA CRUZ. *Dominican Hospital* dba of Dignity Health, 1555 Soquel Dr., Santa Cruz, 95065. Tel: 831-462-7700; Fax: 831-462-7555; Email: Robert.Sahagian@DignityHealth.org; Web: www.dominicanhospital.org. Dr. Nanette Mickiewicz, M.D., Pres. Sponsored by Sisters of St. Dominic, Congregation of the Most Holy Rosary, Adrian, MI. Bed Capacity 222; Sisters 8; Tot Asst. Annually 151,523; Total Staff 1,665.

[F] SPECIAL HOSPITALS AND SANATORIA ACUTE CARE HOSPITAL

MONTEREY. *Ave Maria Convalescent Hospital* dba Ave Maria Senior Living (1954) 1249 Josselyn Canyon Rd., 93940. Tel: 831-373-1216; Fax: 831-242-8980; Email: Lekpenyong@avemarias1.org; Web: www.avemariamonterey.com. Clancy D'Angelo, Pres.; Lovian Ekpenyong, Admin. Bed Capacity 45; Tot Asst. Annually 85; Total Staff 60; Skilled Nursing 31; Assisted Living 14.

[G] MONASTERIES AND RESIDENCES OF PRIESTS AND BROTHERS

MONTEREY. *Oratorian Community-Congregation of the Oratory of Pontifical Right*, 302 High St., P.O. Box

1688, 93942-1688. Tel: 831-373-0476;
Fax: 831-373-1718; Email: takorat@sbcglobal.net. Very Rev. Peter C. Sanders, Orat., Supr., Tel: 831-375-9769; Rev. Thomas A. Kieffer, Orat., Vicar & Sec., Tel: 831-372-1325. Priests 2.

ARROYO GRANDE. *St. Francis of Assisi Friary & Novitiate*, 1352 Dale Ave., Arroyo Grande, 93420-5913. Tel: 805-489-1012; Fax: 805-489-8303; Email: friarjwood@gmail.com. Revs. Alexander Cymerman, O.F.M.Conv., Sr. Friar; Masseo Gonzales, O.F.M.Conv., Province Ministry; Maurice Richard, O.F.M.Conv., Assoc. Dir. of Novices; Bro. Joseph Wood, OFM Conv, Guardian & Dir. Novices, (Retired). Brothers 1; Priests 3.

BIG SUR. *New Camaldoli Hermitage* (1958) 62475 Hwy. # 1, Big Sur, 93920-9533. Tel: 831-667-2456;
Fax: 831-667-0209; Email: prior@contemplation.com; Web: www.contemplation.com. Rev. Cyprian Consiglio, O.S.B.Cam., Prior; Very Rev. Raniero Hoffman, O.S.B.Cam.; Revs. Thomas Matus, O.S.B.Cam.; Zacchaeus Maria Naegele, O.S.B.Cam.; Isaiah Teichert, O.S.B.Cam.; Rev. Deacon Ignatius Tully, O.S.B.Cam.; Bros. Benedict Dell'Osa, O.S.B.Cam.; Michael Harrington, O.S.B.Cam.; David Meyers, O.S.B.Cam.; Joshua Monson, O.S.B.Cam. Professed Monks (including 6 Priests) 10.

SALINAS. *Palma Community of Edmund Rice Christian Brothers* (1951) 263 W. Acacia St., Salinas, 93901.
Tel: 831-229-1101; Fax: 831-422-5065; Email: dunne@palmaschool.org; Web: palmaschool.org. Bros. Patrick D. Dunne, C.F.C., Pres.; Donald Dominic Murray, C.F.C., Province Advancement; Charles Joachim Avendano, C.F.C., Retired. Congregation of Christian Brothers. Brothers 3.

SAN JUAN BAUTISTA. *Franciscan Friars*, 549 Mission Vineyard Rd., P.O. Box 970, San Juan Bautista, 95045-0970. Tel: 831-623-4234; Fax: 831-623-9046; Email: kwarner@scu.edu. Bros. Keith Warner, O.F.M., Supr.; Mateo Guerrero, O.F.M.; James D. Swan, O.F.M.; Rev. Kenneth J. Laverone, O.F.M., J.C.L.; Fr. Paul Botenhagen, O.F.M. Brothers 3; Priests 2.

SAN LUIS OBISPO. *Monastery of the Risen Christ*, P.O. Box 3931, San Luis Obispo, 93403.
Tel: 805-544-1810; Fax: 805-544-1810; Email: monasteryrc@gmail.com; Web: monasteryrisenchrist.com. Priests 2. *Monastery of the Risen Christ*, 2308 O'Connor Way, San Luis Obispo, 93405. Tel: 805-544-1810;
Fax: 805-544-1810; Email: monasteryrc@gmail.com; Web: monasteryrisenchrist.com. Revs. Daniel Manger, O.S.B.Cam., Prior; Stephen G. Coffey, O.S.B.Cam.

SANTA CRUZ. *Oblates of St. Joseph Provincial House and Shrine*, 544 W. Cliff Dr., Santa Cruz, 95060.
Tel: 831-457-1868; Fax: 831-457-1317; Email: provincial@osjoseph.org; Web: www.osjusa.org. Bro. Mathew Chipp, O.S.J., Bus. Mgr.; Revs. Paul McDonnell, O.S.J., Prov.; Steve Peterson, O.S.J., Asst. Shrine Dir.
Oblates of St. Joseph, Provincial House and Shrine of St. Joseph, Guardian of the RedeemerReligious Community, Tel: 831-471-1702. Brothers 1. *Provincial*, Tel: 831-457-1868. *Shrine of St. Joseph*,
Tel: 831-471-0442; Email: guardian@osjoseph.org. Brothers 1; Priests 2; Total in Residence 3.

WATSONVILLE. *Salesians of St. John Bosco*,
Tel: 831-722-2665; Fax: 831-722-8305; Email: olhcchurch@yahoo.com. Rev. Joseph M. Paradayil, S.D.B., Pastor; Bro. Michael Herbers, S.D.B., Camp Dir.; Rev. Luis A. Oyarzo, S.D.B., Pastoral Assoc. Brothers 1; Priests 2. *Saint Francis Salesian Community*, 2401 East Lake Ave., Watsonville, 95076-2670. Tel: 831-722-2665; Fax: 831-722-8305; Email: olhcchurch@yahoo.com; Web: www.donboscowest.org. Revs. Alberto Chavez, S.D.B., Dir.; Joseph M. Paradayil, S.D.B., Pastor; David Purdy, S.D.B.; Bro. Michael Herbers, S.D.B., Camp Dir.; Thomas Mass, Economer. Brothers 2; Priests 3.

[H] CONVENTS AND RESIDENCES FOR SISTERS

MONTEREY. *Franciscan Sisters of the Immaculate Conception and St. Joseph for the Dying*, 1249 Josselyn Canyon Rd., 93942-1977.
Tel: 831-373-1216; Fax: 831-373-2238; Email: counsel@dioceseofmonterey.org. Sr. Patricia M. Murtagh, I.M., Pres.; Thomas H. Riordan, CFO; Susan A. Mayer, Esq., Sec. Motherhouse of the Franciscan Sisters of the Immaculate Conception and St. Joseph for the Dying.

ARROYO GRANDE. *Sisters of Mercy*, Sisters of Mercy, Attn: Sr. Margaret Malone, 451 Woodland, Arroyo Grande, 93420. Tel: 805-489-8788;
Fax: 805-489-4367. Sr. Margaret Malone Sr., Member. Sisters 1.

CARMEL. *Carmelite Monastery of Our Lady and St. Therese* (1925) 27601 Hwy. 1, Carmel, 93923-9612.
Tel: 831-624-3043; Fax: 831-624-5495; Email: carmelitesofcarmelca@gmail.com; Web: www.carmelitesistersbythesea.org. Mother Teresita Flynn, O.C.D., Prioress. Professed Nuns 12.
Sisters of Notre Dame de Namur (1930) 27951 Hwy. 1, Carmel, 93923. Tel: 831-624-9416;
Fax: 831-624-4865; Email: carmelhop@sndden.org. Sr. Michelle Henault, S.N.D.de N., Member. Sisters 2.

CORRALITOS. *Daughters of Mary Help of Christians* (1872) 605 Enos Ln., Corralitos, 95076.
Tel: 831-728-4700; Fax: 831-728-5802; Email: fmasuocor@gmail.com. Sr. Carmen Botello, F.M.A., Supr. Sisters 6.

GONZALES. *Sisters of Charity of the Infant Mary Capitanio Convent*, 512 Fairview Dr., P.O. Box 178, Gonzales, 93926. Tel: 831-675-2975;
Fax: 831-675-2974; Email: sistersmb@att.net. Sisters Rosangela Filippini, I.M., Supr.; Lundin D'Souza, I.M., Asst. Catechetical Min., St. Theodore's Parish. Residents 7; Sisters 7.

SALINAS. *Sisters of Charity of the Infant Mary*, 15785 Alto Way, Salinas, 93907-9148. Tel: 831-663-3675;
Fax: 831-663-3749; Email: virgennina@aol.com. Sr. Patricia M. Murtagh, I.M., Supr. Sisters of Charity of the Infant Mary. Residents 5.
Sisters of Notre Dame de Namur, 56 Talbot St., Salinas, 93901. Tel: 831-424-4370; Email: bmatasci@aol.com. Sr. Barbara Matasci, S.N.D., Member, (Retired). Sisters 2.

SAN JUAN BAUTISTA. *Franciscan Sisters of the Atonement*, 408 Second St., P.O. Box 1094, San Juan Bautista, 95045-1094. Tel: 831-623-4267; Email: dfenzel30@yahoo.com. Sisters Dolores Fenzel, S.A., RCIA Coord.; Carmelita Heredia, S.A., DRE. Franciscan Sisters of the Atonement 2.

SOQUEL. *St. Clare's Retreat & Convent* (1950) 2381 Laurel Glen Rd., Soquel, 95073. Tel: 831-423-8093;
Fax: 831-423-1541; Email: stclaresretreatcenter@gmail.com; Web: www.stclaresretreat.com. Sisters Carol Ann Kos, O.S.F., Supr.; Mary Vincent Nguyen, O.S.F., Retreat Directress; Mary John Paul Marquez Floro, O.S.F, Sacristan; Christine Marie Chauvel, O.S.F., Asst.; Maria Gabriel Standfield, O.S.F. Sisters 5; Total in Residence 5.

[I] RETREAT HOUSES

APTOS. *Camp St. Francis*, 2320 Sumner Ave., Aptos, 95003. Tel: 831-684-1439; Fax: 831-662-2454; Email: campstfrancis@gmail.com. Bro. Michael Herbers, S.D.B., Dir. Summer Camp for Boys 8-13, Meeting Center for large groups and Retreat Center for large groups of youth and adults; conducted by Salesians of St. John Bosco.

SAN JUAN BAUTISTA. *St. Francis Retreat Center*, 549 Mission Vineyard Rd., P.O. Box 970, San Juan Bautista, 95045. Tel: 831-623-4234;
Fax: 831-623-9046; Email: info@stfrancisretreat.com; Web: www.stfrancisretreat.com. Rev. Kenneth J. Laverone, O.F.M., J.C.L., Dir.; Edward DeGroot, Bus. Mgr.; Bro. James D. Swan, O.F.M., Retreat Coord. Retreats for men, women, singles, married couples, A.A. and 12-step. Programs include Spiritual Growth, Ecumenical, Spanish & conducted by Franciscan Friars, Province of St. Barbara. Brothers 1; Priests 1; Total Staff 21.

SANTA CRUZ. *Villa Maria del Mar Retreat Center*, 21918 E. Cliff Dr., Santa Cruz, 95062.
Tel: 831-475-1236; Fax: 831-475-8867; Email: villamaria@snjmuson.org; Web: www.villamariadelmar.org. Sr. Cheryl Milner, S.N.J.M., Dir. Sisters of the Holy Names of Jesus and Mary, U.S.-Ontario Province Corp. Lay Staff 14; Sisters 4; Total Staff 18.

SOQUEL. *St. Clare's Retreat House* (1950) 2381 Laurel Glen Rd., Soquel, 95073. Tel: 831-423-8093; Email: st.clares.retreat.house.1959@gmail.com; Web: www.stclaresretreat.com. Sisters Carol Ann Kos, O.S.F., Supr.; Mary Vincent Nguyen, O.S.F., Retreat Dir.; Mary John Paul Marquez Floro, O.S.F, Sacristan; Christine Marie Chauvel, O.S.F., Asst.; Maria Gabriel Standfield, O.S.F. Franciscan Missionary Sisters of Our Lady of Sorrows 5; Total Staff 5.

[J] NEWMAN CHAPLAINS AND CENTERS

MONTEREY. *Department of Campus Ministry* (1970) 425 Church St., 93940. Tel: 831-373-4345;
Fax: 831-373-1175; Email: pcrivello@dioceseofmonterey.org; Web: www.dioceseofmonterey.org. Rev. Peter A. Crivello, Dir. Total Staff 6.
California State Polytechnic Institute/Cuesta College, Newman Catholic Center, 1472 Foothill Blvd., San Luis Obispo, 93405-1416.
Tel: 805-543-4105; Fax: 805-543-5671; Email: linda@slonewman.org; Web: slonewman.org. Rev. Gerald Robinson, S.J., Dir.; Linda Garcia-Inchausti, Admin.
Cabrillo College, 285 Meder Street, Santa Cruz, 95064. Tel: 831-479-6100; Fax: 831-423-8163; Email: newman.ucsc@dioceseofmonterey.org. Rev. Justin E. Bianchi, Dir.
University of California at Santa Cruz, 285 Meder St., Santa Cruz, 95060. Tel: 831-423-9400;
Fax: 831-423-8163; Email: newmanslug@aol.com; Web: www.newmanite.org. Rev. Justin E. Bianchi, Dir.
California State University of Monterey Bay, 485 Church St., 93940. Tel: 831-373-1335;
Fax: 831-373-3315; Email: newman.csumb@dioceseofmonterey.org. Rev. Peter A. Crivello, Contact Person.

[K] SENIOR RESIDENCES

SANTA CRUZ. *Dominican Oaks Corporation* (1988) 3400 Paul Sweet Rd., Santa Cruz, 95065.
Tel: 831-462-6257; Fax: 831-462-6742; Email: Deborah.Routley@DignityHealth.org; Web: www.dominicanoaks.com. Deborah Routley, Admin. Sponsored by Dominican Hospital, a dba of Dignity Health. Total in Residence 217; Total Staff 98.

[L] MISCELLANEOUS

MONTEREY. *Newman Institute for Historical and Religious Studies/Domus Patris Foundation*, Domus Patris Foundation, 302 High Street, P.O. Box 748, 93942. Tel: 831-373-0477; Email: takorat@sbcglobal.net. Rev. Thomas A. Kieffer, Orat., Admin.

SALINAS. *Magnificat the Monterey Bay Chapter*, 302 San Juan Grade Rd., Salinas, 93906.
Tel: 831-449-1069; Fax: 831-449-1069; Email: dlraras@pacbell.net. Dora Lee Raras, Coord.; Stella Marquez, Treas.; Diosefe Lantaca, Sec. A Ministry to Catholic Women.

WATSONVILLE. *St. Thomas More Society*, c/o 262 E. Lake Ave., Watsonville, 95076. Tel: 831-722-2456; Fax: 831-722-0414.

RELIGIOUS INSTITUTES OF MEN REPRESENTED IN THE DIOCESE

For further details refer to the corresponding bracketed number in the Religious Institutes of Men or Women section.

[]—*Camaldolese Monks*—O.S.B.Cam.
[]—*Cistercian Monks*—O.Cist.
[0950]—*Congregation of Oratory Pontifical Right*—Orat.
[]—*Congregation of Scalabrini*—C.S.
[0480]—*Conventual Franciscans*—O.F.M.Conv.
[0520]—*Franciscan Friars* (Santa Barbara Prov.)—O.F.M.
[0930]—*Oblates of St. Joseph* (Asti, Italy)—O.S.J.
[0200]—*Order of St. Benedict* (Monastery of the Risen Christ)—O.S.B.
[]—*Palma Community of Edmund Rice Christian Brothers.*
[1190]—*Salesians of Don Bosco (Turin, Italy)*—S.D.B.
[]—*Society of Jesus, Jesuits*—S.J.

RELIGIOUS INSTITUTES OF WOMEN REPRESENTED IN THE DIOCESE

[]—*Catechists Sisters of Jesus Crucified* (Mexico)—C.J.C.
[1070-13]—*Congregation of the Most Holy Rosary - Adrian Dominican Sisters*—O.P.
[0850]—*Daughters of Mary of Help of Christians - Salesian Sisters*—F.M.A.
[0420]—*Discalced Carmelite Nuns*—O.C.D.
[1070-04]—*Dominican Sisters of San Rafael*—O.P.
[1390]—*Franciscan Missionary Sisters of Our Lady of Sorrows*—O.S.F.
[]—*Franciscan Sisters* (Redwood City)—O.S.F.
[1190]—*Franciscan Sisters of the Atonement*—S.A.
[]—*Immaculate Heart of Mary*—I.H.M.
[]—*Immaculate Heart Sisters of Africa*—I.H.S.A.
[]—*School Sisters of Notre Dame*—S.S.N.D.
[]—*Sisters of Charity of the Infant Mary*—I.M.
[2549]—*Sisters of Mercy* (Irish American Prov.)—R.S.M.
[3000]—*Sisters of Notre Dame de Namur*—S.N.D.deN.
[3840]—*Sisters of St. Joseph of Carondelet*—C.S.J.
[]—*Sisters of the Holy Family*—S.H.F.
[1990]—*Sisters of the Holy Name of Jesus and Mary*—S.N.J.M.
[]—*Sisters of the Presentation* (San Francisco)—P.B.V.M.

DIOCESAN CEMETERIES

MONTEREY. *Diocesan Cemeteries Office*, 485 Church St., 93942-1048. Web: www.dioceseofmonterey.org/. Mailing Address: P.O. Box 2048, 93942-2048.
Tel: 831-373-4345, Ext. 276; Fax: 831-373-2831; Email: jbolliger@cfcsmission.org. Jarrod Bolliger, Dir.
San Carlos (Monterey), 792 Fremont Blvd., 93940.
Tel: 831-372-0327; Fax: 831-372-8726; Email: jbolliger@cfcsmission.org. Jarrod Bolliger, Dir.

CAMBRIA. *Old Santa Rosa (Cambria)*, 2353 Main St, San Luis Obispo, 93428. Tel: 805-541-0584;
Fax: 805-541-2127; Email: oldmissioncemetery@cfcsmonterey.org; Email: jbolliger@cfcsmission.org. Jarrod Bolliger, Dir.

HOLLISTER. *Sacred Heart/Calvary Cemetery*, 1100 Hillcrest Rd., Hollister, 95023. Tel: 831-637-0131; Fax: 831-637-2980; Email: calvarycemetery@cfcsmonterey.org; Email: jbolliger@cfcsmission.org. Mailing Address: P.O. Box 1166, Hollister, 95024. Jarrod Bolliger, Dir.

SALINAS. *Queen of Heaven Salinas*, 18200 Damian Way, Salinas, 93907. Tel: 831-449-5890; Fax: 831-449-6928; Email: queenofheavencemetery@cfcsmonterey.org; Email: jbolliger@cfcsmission.org. Jarrod Bolliger, Dir.

SAN LUIS OBISPO. *Old Mission San Luis Obispo*, 101 Bridge Street, San Luis Obispo, 93401. Tel: 805-541-0584; Fax: 805-541-2127; Email: oldmissioncemetery@cfcsmonterey.org; Email: jbolliger@cfcsmission.org. 751 Palm Street, San Luis Obispo, 93401. Jarrod Bolliger, Dir.

SANTA CRUZ. *Holy Cross Cemetery Santa Cruz*, 2271 7th Ave., Santa Cruz, 95062. Tel: 831-475-3222; Fax: 831-475-6132; Email: holycrosscemetery@cfcsmonterey.org; Email: jbolliger@cfcsmission.org. Jarrod Bolliger, Dir.

NECROLOGY

† Garcia, Richard J., Bishop of Monterey, Died Jul. 11, 2018

† Clark, Richard Dale, (Retired), Died Jan. 21, 2019

An asterisk (*) denotes an organization that has established tax-exempt status directly with the IRS and is not covered by the USCCB Group Ruling.

Diocese of Nashville

(Dioecesis Nashvillensis)

Most Reverend

JOSEPH M. SPALDING

Bishop of Nashville; ordained August 3, 1991; appointed Bishop of Nashville November 21, 2017; installed February 2, 2018. *Chancery Office, 2800 McGavock Pike, Nashville, TN 37214.*

Chancery Office: 2800 McGavock Pike, Nashville, TN 37214. Tel: 615-783-0765

Web: www.dioceseofnashville.com

ESTABLISHED JULY 28, 1837.

Square Miles 16,302.

Established Diocese of Nashville, comprising entire State of Tennessee, July 28, 1837; comprising Middle and East Tennessee, January 6, 1971, after the establishment of the Diocese of Memphis; comprising the following thirty eight Counties of Middle Tennessee, September 8, 1988, after the establishment of the Diocese of Knoxville: Bedford, Cannon, Cheatham, Clay, Coffee, Davidson, DeKalb, Dickson, Franklin, Giles, Grundy, Hickman, Houston, Humphreys, Jackson, Lawrence, Lewis, Lincoln, Macon, Marshall, Maury, Montgomery, Moore, Overton, Perry, Putnam, Robertson, Rutherford, Smith, Stewart, Sumner, Trousdale, VanBuren, Warren, Wayne, White, Williamson and Wilson.

Primary Patron: St. Joseph, Spouse of the Blessed Virgin Mary.

Secondary Patroness: Our Lady of Guadalupe.

For legal titles of parishes and diocesan institutions, consult the Chancery Office.

STATISTICAL OVERVIEW

Personnel	
Bishop	1
Priests: Diocesan Active in Diocese	50
Priests: Retired, Sick or Absent	13
Number of Diocesan Priests	63
Religious Priests in Diocese	19
Total Priests in Diocese	82
Extern Priests in Diocese	12
Ordinations:	
Diocesan Priests	3
Transitional Deacons	5
Permanent Deacons in Diocese	93
Total Sisters	12
Parishes	
Parishes	52
With Resident Pastor:	
Resident Diocesan Priests	34
Resident Religious Priests	10
Without Resident Pastor:	
Administered by Priests	8
Missions	3
Pastoral Centers	3
Professional Ministry Personnel:	
Sisters	2
Lay Ministers	64
Welfare	
Catholic Hospitals	5
Total Assisted	554,500
Health Care Centers	11
Total Assisted	80,000
Homes for the Aged	2
Total Assisted	230
Day Care Centers	2
Total Assisted	300
Special Centers for Social Services	6
Total Assisted	200,000
Educational	
Diocesan Students in Other Seminaries	28
Total Seminarians	28
Colleges and Universities	1
Total Students	200
High Schools, Diocesan and Parish	2
Total Students	1,493
High Schools, Private	1
Total Students	254
Elementary Schools, Diocesan and Parish	14
Total Students	3,302
Elementary Schools, Private	2
Total Students	657
Catechesis/Religious Education:	
High School Students	922
Elementary Students	6,366
Total Students under Catholic Instruction	13,222
Teachers in the Diocese:	
Priests	2
Sisters	22
Lay Teachers	487
Vital Statistics	
Receptions into the Church:	
Infant Baptism Totals	1,754
Minor Baptism Totals	240
Adult Baptism Totals	213
Received into Full Communion	303
First Communions	1,928
Confirmations	1,825
Marriages:	
Catholic	277
Interfaith	139
Total Marriages	416
Deaths	522
Total Catholic Population	76,140
Total Population	2,069,976

Former Bishops—Rt. Revs. RICHARD PIUS MILES, O.P., D.D., cons. Sept. 16, 1838; died Feb. 21, 1860; JAMES WHELAN, O.P., D.D., cons. May 8, 1859; resigned May, 1863; died Feb. 18, 1878; P. A. FEEHAN, cons. Nov. 1, 1865; created first Archbishop of Chicago, Sept. 10, 1880; died July 12, 1902; JOSEPH RADEMACHER, D.D., cons. June 24, 1883; transferred to Ft. Wayne, July 13, 1893; died Jan. 12, 1900; THOMAS S. BYRNE, D.D., cons. July 25, 1894; died Sept. 4, 1923; Most Revs. ALPHONSE J. SMITH, D.D., cons. March 25, 1924; died Dec. 16, 1935; WILLIAM L. ADRIAN, D.D., cons. April 16, 1936; died Feb. 13, 1972; JOSEPH A. DURICK, D.D., cons. March 24, 1955; retired April 8, 1975; died June 26, 1994; JAMES D. NIEDERGESES, D.D., cons. May 20, 1975; retired Oct. 13, 1992; died Nov. 16, 2007; EDWARD U. KMIEC, D.D., S.T.L., ord. Dec. 20, 1961; appt. Titular Bishop of Simidicca and Auxiliary Bishop of Trenton Aug. 26, 1982; cons. Nov. 3, 1982; appt. Bishop of Nashville Oct. 13, 1992; installed Dec. 3, 1992; appt. Bishop of Buffalo Aug. 12, 2004; DAVID R. CHOBY, ord. Sept. 6, 1974; appt. Bishop of Nashville Dec. 20, 2005; ord. Feb. 27, 2006; died June 3, 2017.

Vicars General—Very Revs. JOHN J.H. HAMMOND, J.C.L., V.G.; DEXTER S. BREWER, J.C.L., V.G., 2800 McGavock Pike, Nashville, 37214.

Deans—Revs. JOSEPH V. MCMAHON, Central Deanery; STEVE WOLF, Northwest Deanery; DAVIS CHACKALECKEL, M.S.F.S., South Deanery; DAN RECHIL, City Deanery; ERIC L. FOWLKES, Northeast Deanery.

Chancery Office—2800 McGavock Pike, Nashville, 37214. Tel: 615-783-0765. Office Hours: Mon.-Fri. 8-4:30All official business should be directed to this office.

Chancellor—Deacon HANS M. TOECKER.

Vice Chancellor—MR. BRIAN COOPER.

Executive Assistant to the Bishop—MRS. JENNY SCAGGS.

Accounting Systems—MR. WILLIAM J. WHALEN, CFO.

Diocesan Tribunal—2800 McGavock Pike, Nashville, 37214. Tel: 615-783-0765.

Judicial Vicar—Very Rev. JOHN J.H. HAMMOND, J.C.L., V.G.

Adjutant Judicial Vicar—Very Rev. DEXTER S. BREWER, J.C.L., V.G.

Director of Tribunal—MS. JANETTE BUCHANAN, J.C.L.

Defender of the Bond—MS. CHERRY HEAD CLARK, J.C.L.

Advocates—MRS. ERIN STRACENER; Deacon PHILIP JOHNSON.

Judges—Very Rev. DEXTER S. BREWER, J.C.L., V.G.; MS. JANETTE BUCHANAN, J.C.L.; Very Rev. JOHN J.H. HAMMOND, J.C.L., V.G.

Formal Case Instructor—MRS. VALERIE COOPER.

Formal Case Instructor—HEATHER MENDIOLA.

Auditors—All priests and deacons assigned in the Nashville and Knoxville dioceses.

Secretary-Notaries—HEATHER MENDIOLA; MRS. VALERIE COOPER.

Presbyteral Council—Revs. STEPHEN J. WOLF; MARK SAPPENFIELD; MICHAEL O. JOHNSTON, (Retired); THOMAS KALAM, C.M.I.; MARK BECKMAN; EDWARD F. STEINER III; J. PATRICK CONNOR, V.G., (Retired); PATRICK J. KIBBY; JOSEPH V. MCMAHON; JEAN BAPTISTE KYABUTA.

Diocesan Finance Board—MRS. ANGELA M. ROBINSON; Very Rev. DEXTER S. BREWER, J.C.L., V.G.; MR. CLARK BAKER; MR. JOHN SCHNEIDER; Deacon WILLIAM HILL; MR. JOHN GROMOS; MR. EDWARD STACK, Chair; MR. DAVID GLASCOE; MR. WILLIAM J. WHALEN; MR. PAT WATSON; Deacon HECTOR MARTINEZ; MR. DWAYNE DILLARD; MS. LISA DAVIS.

DIONASH—A Partnership acting as Nominee for marketable securities for the Diocese of Nashville.

Diocesan Offices and Directors

The following offices and agencies are located at the Chancery unless otherwise indicated.

Archives and Records—Deacon HANS M. TOECKER; VACANT, Archives Coord.

Campaign for Human Development—2806 McGavock Pike, Nashville, 37214. VACANT.

Campus Ministries—VACANT.

University Catholic—Rev. MICHAEL FYE, 2417 W. End Ave., Nashville, 37240. Tel: 615-322-0104.

MTSU-Murfreesboro—St. Rose of Lima Church, 1601 N. Tennessee Blvd., Murfreesboro, 37130. Tel: 615-893-1843. Rev. JOHN SIMS BAKER.

Austin Peay-Clarksville—Deacon TIMOTHY F. WINTERS, 709 Franklin St., Clarksville, 37040. Tel: 931-645-6275.

Tenn. Tech-Cookeville—MR. CLARK JAMESON; MRS. MARTHA JAMESON, St. Thomas Aquinas Church, 421 N. Washington Ave., Cookeville, 38501. Tel: 931-526-2575.

Fisk-Meharry-Tennessee State University Campus Ministries—MS. BARBARA KING, St. Vincent de Paul Church, 1700 Heiman St., Nashville, 37208. Tel: 615-320-0695.

Univ. of South-Sewanee—Good Shepherd Church, 2021 Decherd Blvd., Decherd, 37324. Tel: 931-967-0961. Rev. ANTHONY MUTUKU.

Catholic Charismatic Renewal—VACANT, Bishop's Liaison; MRS. TERESA SEIBERT, Assoc. Liaison.

Catholic Charities of Tennessee, Inc.—2806 McGavock

Pike, Nashville, 37214. Tel: 615-352-3087; Fax: 615-352-8591. VACANT.

Catholic Medical Association, Nashville Chapter—RACHEL KAISER, M.D., Pres., Email: rtkaiser@bellsouth.net; Web: www.cathmed.org.

Catholic Public Policy Commission of TN—JENNFIER MURPHY, Exec. Sec.

Catholic Relief Services—Deacon HANS M. TOECKER, Dir.

Catholic Charities of Tennessee Social Services—2806 McGavock Pike, Nashville, 37214. Tel: 615-352-3087. VACANT.

Catholic Youth Office and Search Program—MR. WILLIAM STALEY, 2800 McGavock Pike, Nashville, 37214. Tel: 615-383-6393.

Cemeteries—MR. WILLIAM J. WHALEN, CFO.

Censor Librorum—Rev. ANDREW BULSO.

Priest Benefit Foundation—Revs. PHILLIP A. HALLADAY; JUSTIN N. RAINES; Very Rev. DEXTER S. BREWER, J.C.L., V.G.; MR. WILLIAM J. WHALEN; TERRY ROBINSON, P.H.R.; Revs. ANDREW BULSO; JERRY STRANGE; STEVE WOLF; JOHN RAPHAEL.

Continuing Education of Priests—Rev. EDWARD F. STEINER III, Dir.

Cursillo—GARY GUINN, Lay Dir.; Deacon MARTIN DESCHENES, Assoc. Spiritual Advisor; JENNIE GUINN, Lay Dir.

Permanent Diaconate Office—Deacon TOM SAMORAY, Dir.

Diocesan Communications Director—RICK MUSSACHIO.

Diocesan Planning—Rev. STEPHEN A. KLASEK, Dir.

Hispanic Ministry—Rev. DAVID RAMIREZ, Dir.; MRS. ANABELL C. TREVINO, Asst. Dir.

Korean Catholic Community—2319 Lebanon Rd., Nashville, 37214. Tel: 615-727-1225; Email: altreteia@naver.com. Rev. S. BANG.

Holy Childhood Association—Deacon HANS M. TOECKER, Dir.

Human Resources—BILL STEJSKAL, Dir.

Lay Retirement Administrative Board—D. SCOTT DONNELLAN; CHRISTOPHER P. KELLY; MR. JOHN SCHNEIDER; Very Rev. DEXTER S. BREWER, J.C.L., V.G.; BILL STEJSKAL; MR. WILLIAM J. WHALEN; KATHY WRIGHT.

Liturgical Life—VACANT.

Ministry Formation—JOAN WATSON, Dir.; SHERI ISHAM, Office of Catechetical Formation, Catechetical Coord.; Deacon THOMAS SAMORAY, Engaged Couple Formation, Prog. Coord.

Newspaper—The Tennessee Register RICK MUSACCHIO, Editor in Chief.

Prison Ministry—Deacon JAMES BOOTH.

Pontifical Mission SocietiesDeacon HANS M. TOECKER, Dir.

Catholic Charities Refugee Services—KELLYE BRANSON, Dir., 2806 McGavock Pike, Nashville, 37214. Tel: 615-259-3567; Fax: 615-259-2851.

Schools Office—2800 McGavock Pike, Nashville, 37214. Tel: 615-383-6393. REBECCA HAMMEL, Supt.

Stewardship and Development—ASHLEY LINVILLE, Dir.; ANNA BETH GODFREY, Asst. Dir.

Victim Assistance Coordinator—Deacon HANS M. TOECKER, 2800 McGavock Pike, Nashville, 37214. Tel: 615-783-0765; Fax: 615-292-8411; Email: hans.toecker@dioceseofnashville.com.

Vietnamese Ministry—Rev. PETER DO QUANG CHAU, P.O. Box 55, Ashland City, 37015. Tel: 615-792-4255.

Vocations—Rev. AUSTIN GILSTRAP.

CLERGY, PARISHES, MISSIONS AND PAROCHIAL SCHOOLS

CITY OF NASHVILLE

(DAVIDSON COUNTY)

1—CATHEDRAL OF THE INCARNATION (1909)
2015 W. End Ave., 37203. Tel: 615-327-2330; Email: esteiner@cathedralnashville.org. Revs. Edward F. Steiner III; Benjamin Butler; Deacons Mark Faulkner; Thales Finchum; Joe Holzmer; James W. McKenzie; Jayd Neely, In Res.
Catechesis Religious Program—Robin Baskin, D.R.E. Students 153.

2—ST. ANN (1921)
5101 Charlotte Ave., 37209. Tel: 615-298-1782; Email: Nancy@stannnash.org. Rev. Michael Fye; Deacons John P. Casey; Jim Holzemer; Martin Mulloy, Pastoral Assoc. & D.R.E.
School—St. Ann School, (Grades K-8), Tel: 615-269-0568; Fax: 615-297-1383; Email: arumfola@stannnash.org. Anna Rumfola, Prin.; Judy Graham, Librarian. Lay Teachers 15; Students 145.
Catechesis Religious Program—Students 71.

3—ASSUMPTION (1859) Attended by
1227 Seventh Ave. N., 37208. Tel: 615-256-2729; Email: lcooper@assumptionchurchnashville.org. Rev. William M. Fitzgerald, O.Praem., Admin.
Catechesis Religious Program—Students 58.

4—CHRIST THE KING (1937)
3001 Belmont Blvd., 37212. Tel: 615-292-2884; Fax: 615-868-4900; Email: Nancy.Rohling@ctk.org. Very Rev. Dexter S. Brewer, J.C.L., V.G.; Rev. Ahn Phan; Deacons Andrew D. McKenzie; Robert H. True; David Lybarger; John G. Krenson; Brian Schulz.
School—Christ the King School, (Grades PreK-8), 3105 Belmont Blvd., 37212. Tel: 615-292-9465; Fax: 615-292-2477. Sherry Woodman, Prin.; Rai Lynn Wood, Librarian. Lay Teachers 24; Students 260.
Catechesis Religious Program—Students 256.

5—CHURCH OF THE MOST HOLY NAME (1857)
521 Woodland St., 37206. Tel: 615-254-8847; Email: holynamenashville@comcast.net. Rev. Theophilus Ebulueme; Deacon Robert L. Mahoney.
Catechesis Religious Program—Ms. Mary Evans, D.R.E. Students 52.

6—ST. EDWARD (1952)
188 Thompson Ln., 37211. Tel: 615-833-5520; Email: shouse@steward.org. Revs. Bede Price; Daniel J. Reehil; Deacons Brian Edwards; Gerard Ziemkiewicz.
School—St. Edward School, (Grades PreK-8), 190 Thompson Ln., 37211. Tel: 615-833-5770; Fax: 615-833-9739. Dr. Marsha Wharton, Prin. Lay Teachers 25; Students 323.
Catechesis Religious Program—Students 95.

7—ST. HENRY (1955)
6401 Harding Pike., 37205. Tel: 615-352-2259; Email: chale@sthenry.org. Revs. Mark Beckman; Andrew Bulso; Abraham M. Panthalanickal; Deacons Michael Catalano; Mark Deschenes; Gregory Meinhart.
School—St. Henry School, (Grades K-8), Tel: 615-352-1328; Fax: 615-356-9293. Sr. Maria Christi Greeve, O.P., Prin.; Dr. Kellye Bradley, Vice Prin.; Mrs. Kerry Connor, Librarian. Lay Teachers 37; Dominican Sisters of St. Cecilia Congregation 4; Students 591.
Catechesis Religious Program—Tel: 615-352-4586; Email: reled@sthenry.org. Beth Holzapfel, D.R.E. Students 254.

8—HOLY ROSARY (1954)
192 Graylynn Dr., 37214. Tel: 615-889-4065; Email: cynthia@holyrosary.edu. Rev. Daniel J. Steiner; Deacons Gilbert P. Huhlein; Wayne Gregory; Mark White; Mike Wilkins.
School—Holy Rosary School, (Grades PreK-8), Tel: 615-883-1108; Fax: 615-885-5100; Email: Rodgersp@holyrosary.edu. Peter Rodgers, Prin. Lay Teachers 24; Students 304.
Catechesis Religious Program—Students 54.

9—ST. MARY OF THE SEVEN SORROWS (1847)
Mailing Address: P.O. Box 190606, 37219. Tel: 615-256-1704; Email: office@stmarysdowntown.org. Rev. Jayd Neely.
Church: 330 Fifth Ave. N., 37219.
Catechesis Religious Program—Mr. Joe Augustine, D.R.E. Students 46.

10—ST. MARY VILLA CHAPEL (1982)
34 White Bridge Rd., 37205. Tel: 615-353-6181; Email: lyndsey.gower@maryqueenofangels.com. Rev. Mark Hunt, Chap.

11—ST. PATRICK (1890)
1219 2nd Ave. S., 37210. Tel: 615-256-6498; Email: secretary@stpatricksnashville.org; Web: stpatricksnashville.org. Rev. John Hammond.

12—ST. PIUS X (1958)
2800 Tucker Rd., 37218. Tel: 615-244-4093; Email: lcooper@stpiusnashville.org. Rev. Phillip A. Halladay, Admin.
School—St. Pius X Classical Academy, (Grades PreK-8), 2750 Tucker Rd., 37218. Tel: 615-255-2049; Fax: 615-255-2049; Email: stpiusXschool@yahoo.com. Lori Patton, Prin. Lay Teachers 10; Students 62.
Catechesis Religious Program—Cynthia Catignani, D.R.E., R.C.I.A.

13—ST. VINCENT DE PAUL (1932)
1700 Heiman St., 37208. Tel: 615-320-0695; Fax: 615-320-0698; Email: svdepnash@aol.com. Rev. Francis G. Appreh, Admin.; Deacons Henry Harrington Jr.; William Hill.
Catechesis Religious Program—Mary Hernandez, D.R.E. Students 25.

OUTSIDE THE CITY OF NASHVILLE

ANTIOCH, DAVIDSON CO.

1—ST. IGNATIUS OF ANTIOCH (1976)
601 Bell Rd., Antioch, 37013. Tel: 615-367-0085; Email: Mariabraswell@stignatiouscc.com. Rev. Titus Augustine, C.M.I.; Deacons Doug Shafer; Ron Shaw; Edgardo Jayme; Roberto Ochoa.
Catechesis Religious Program—Louise Gregory, D.R.E. Students 126.

2—OUR LADY OF GUADALUPE (2007)
3112 Nolensville Pike, Antioch, 37211. Tel: 615-333-8660; Email: deniagulo@gmail.com. Revs. Fernando Lopez; Ramon Ayala.
Catechesis Religious Program—Teresa Beltran, D.R.E.; Hernan Andrade, D.R.E. Students 324.

ASHLAND CITY, CHEATHAM CO., ST. MARTHA (1975)
3331 Bell St., Ashland City, 37015. Tel: 615-792-4255; Email: peterchaudo@gmail.com. P.O. Box 55, Ashland City, 37015. Rev. Peter Do Quang Chau.
Catechesis Religious Program—Juliana Watson, D.R.E. Students 76.

BRENTWOOD, WILLIAMSON CO., HOLY FAMILY (1989)
9100 Crockett Rd., Brentwood, 37027. Tel: 615-373-4696; Email: holyfamily@holyfamilycc.com. Revs. Joseph V. McMahon; Anthony Stewart; Deacons Ronald B. Deal Jr.; John Calzavara; James Booth.
Catechesis Religious Program—Tel: 615-373-4351. Catherine Birdwell, D.R.E. Students 1,100.

CENTERVILLE, HICKMAN CO., CHRIST THE REDEEMER (1983) Attended by Holy Trinity, Hohenwald.
Mailing Address: P.O. Box 323, Centerville, 37033. Tel: 931-796-3738; Email: mmsmbarr@bellsouth.net. Rev. Tien Tran.
Church: 1515 Woodland Dr., Centerville, 37033. Tel: 931-729-4669.
Catechesis Religious Program—Melanie Harris, D.R.E. Students 6.

CLARKSVILLE, MONTGOMERY CO., IMMACULATE CONCEPTION (1845)
709 Franklin St., Clarksville, 37040. Tel: 931-645-6275; Email: ICACCOUNTS@IMMACONCEPTION.ORG. Revs. Stephen J. Wolf; Richard Childress; Rodolfo Rivera; Deacons Dominick Azzara; Robert Berberich; Timothy Winters; Juan Garza, D.R.E.; Manuel Martinez.
School—Immaculate Conception School, (Grades K-8), 1901 Madison St., Clarksville, 37043. Tel: 931-645-1865; Fax: 931-645-1160; Email: icaaccounts@immaconception.org. Stephanie Stafford, Prin.; Rebecca Dean, Librarian. Lay Teachers 14; Students 155.
Catechesis Religious Program—Students 589.

COLUMBIA, MAURY CO., ST. CATHERINE (1843)
3019 Cayce Ln., Columbia, 38401. Tel: 931-388-3803; Fax: 931-381-8837; Email: frdavis@stcatherinecc.org; Email: tbailey@stcatherinecc.org; Web: www.stcatherinecc.org. Rev. Davis Chackaleckel, M.S.F.S.; Deacons Price Keller; Daniel McCulley; Raymond Seibold.
Catechesis Religious Program—Tel: 931-381-6784; Email: jsparkman@stcatherinecc.org. Jeanette Sparkman, D.R.E. Students 187.

COOKEVILLE, PUTNAM CO., ST. THOMAS AQUINAS (1951)
421 N. Washington Ave., Cookeville, 38501. Tel: 913-526-2575; Fax: 931-526-5869; Email: info@saintthomasaquinaschurch.com. Revs. Christiano Nunes de Silva; James Panackal.
Catechesis Religious Program—Tel: 931-526-4411. Valerie Richardson, D.R.E. Students 254.

DECHERD, FRANKLIN CO., GOOD SHEPHERD (1900)
2021 Decherd Blvd., Decherd, 37324. Tel: 931-967-0961; Email: info@goodshepherdtn.com. Rev. Anthony Mutuku; Deacon Philip Johnson, D.R.E.
Catechesis Religious Program—Students 30.
Mission—St. Margaret Mary, 9458 Old Alto Hwy., Alto, Franklin Co. 37324.

DICKSON, DICKSON CO., ST. CHRISTOPHER (1951)
713 W. College St., Dickson, 37055. Tel: 615-446-3927; Email: susan@stchristophercc.com. Rev. Justin N. Raines; Deacon James Tucker.
Catechesis Religious Program—Theresa Roberts, D.R.E.; Lidia Mota, D.R.E.; Kathy Tucker, D.R.E.; Amber Gonzales, D.R.E. Students 150.

DOVER, STEWART CO., ST. FRANCIS OF ASSISI (1982)
1489 Donelson Pkwy., Dover, 37058. Tel: 931-232-9422; Email: stfroa@gmail.com. P.O. Box 307, Dover, 37058-0307. Rev. David J. Gaffny, (Retired).
Catechesis Religious Program—Tel: 931-232-1924. Linda Allen, D.R.E. Students 40.

FAYETTEVILLE, LINCOLN CO., ST. ANTHONY (1983)
1900 Huntsville Hwy., Fayetteville, 37334. Tel: 931-433-6525; Fax: 931-433-6283; Email: stanthony@fpunet.com; Web: www.stanthonyfayetteville.org. Rev. George Panthananickal, C.M.I.
Catechesis Religious Program—Students 96.

FRANKLIN, WILLIAMSON CO.

1—ST. MATTHEW (1979)
535 Sneed Rd. W., Franklin, 37069.

Tel: 615-646-0378; Email: info@stmatthewtn.org; Web: www.stmatthewtn.org. Rev. Mark Sappenfield; Deacons Daniel Pyles Jr., Chap.; Bill Forte.
School—St. Matthew School, (Grades PreK-8), 533 Sneed Rd. W., Franklin, 37069. Tel: 615-662-4044; Fax: 615-662-6822. Tim Forbes, Prin.; Katie Hubbuch, Librarian. Lay Teachers 35; Students 417.
Catechesis Religious Program—Email: estracener@stmatthewtn.org. Mrs. Erin Stracener, D.R.E. Students 333.

2—ST. PHILIP (1843)
113 2nd Ave. S., Franklin, 37064. Tel: 615-794-8588; Fax: 615-794-3083; Email: Office@stphilipfranklin.com. Revs. Marneni Showraiah, O.F.M.; Gervan Menezes.
Catechesis Religious Program—Josh Medeiros, Youth Min.; Melissa Doyle, Pastoral Min./Coord.; Susan Skinner, Pastoral Min./Coord.; Ms. Julianne Staley, Pastoral Min./Coord. Students 714.

GALLATIN, SUMNER CO., ST. JOHN VIANNEY (1929)
449 N. Water St., Gallatin, 37066.
Tel: 615-452-2977, Ext. 10; Email: sjvcatholicchurch@gmail.com; Web: www.saintjohnvianneychurch.org. Rev. Stephen G. Gideon.
School—St. John Vianney School, (Grades PreK-8), 501 N. Water St., Gallatin, 37066. Tel: 615-230-7048; Fax: 615-206-9839; Email: frank.cronin@saintjohnvianney.org. Frank Cronin, Prin. Lay Teachers 10; Students 61.
Catechesis Religious Program—Students 204.

HENDERSONVILLE, SUMNER CO., OUR LADY OF THE LAKE (1969)
1729 Stop Thirty Rd., Hendersonville, 37075.
Tel: 615-824-3276; Fax: 615-824-7989; Email: office@ololcconline.com. Revs. Eric L. Fowlkes; Thomas Kalam, C.M.I.; Sr. Maria Edwards, R.S.M., Pastoral Assoc.; Deacons James F. Carr; John Lammers; Mike Rector.
Catechesis Religious Program—Cyndi Sabatino, D.R.E. Students 606.

HOHENWALD, LEWIS CO., HOLY TRINITY (1983)
610 Kimmins St., Hohenwald, 38462.
Tel: 931-796-3738; Email: office@holytrinityhohenwald.org. Rev. John O'Neill.
Catechesis Religious Program—Darie McCarthy, D.R.E. Students 25.

JOELTON, DAVIDSON CO., ST. LAWRENCE (1885) [CEM]
5655 Clarksville Hwy., Joelton, 37080.
Tel: 615-878-2127; Email: stlawrence@comcast.net. Rev. Joseph P. Edwidge Carre, Admin.; Deacon Rock Hasenberg.
Catechesis Religious Program—Students 3.

LAFAYETTE, MACON CO., HOLY FAMILY (1982)
901 Vinson Rd., Lafayette, 37083. Tel: 615-666-6466; Fax: 615-357-8108; Email: holyfamily@nctc.com. Deacon Jose G. Pineda; Rev. Victor Subb.
Catechesis Religious Program—Faye Fitzpatrick, D.R.E. Students 97.
Mission—Divine Savior, Celina, Clay Co.

LAWRENCEBURG, LAWRENCE CO., SACRED HEART (1870) [CEM]
222 Berger St., Lawerenceburg, 38464.
Tel: 931-762-3183; Email: shoffice@shlawrenceburg.org. P.O. Box 708, Lawrenceburg, 38464. Rev. Joseph Mundakal, C.M.I.
School—Sacred Heart School, (Grades K-8), 220 Berger St., Lawrenceburg, 38464. Tel: 931-762-6125; Fax: 931-244-7234; Email: rosemary.harris@shslburg.com; Web: www.shslburg.com. Rosemary Harris, Prin. Lay Teachers 6; Students 101.
Catechesis Religious Program—Students 10.

LEBANON, WILSON CO., ST. FRANCES CABRINI (1953)
300 S. Tarver Ave., Lebanon, 37087.
Tel: 615-444-0524; Email: info@sfctn.org. Rev. Michael O'Bryan; Deacons James A. Dixon; Hector Martinez; Paul Taylor.
Catechesis Religious Program—Ms. Jan Trahan, D.R.E. Students 238.

LEWISBURG, MARSHALL CO., ST. JOHN THE EVANGELIST (1982)
1061 S. Ellington, Lewisburg, 37091.
Tel: 931-359-5017; Email: stjohnchurch37091@att.net. Rev. Regimon Augustine, Admin.; Ms. Jenny Mckay, Contact Person.
Catechesis Religious Program—Students 92.

LORETTO, LAWRENCE CO., SACRED HEART (1872) [CEM]
305 Church St., Loretto, 38469. Tel: 931-853-4370; Email: office@sacredheartloretto.com. P.O. Box 86, Loretto, 38469. Rev. Paul Nguyen; Deacon Samuel Beckman.
School—Sacred Heart School, (Grades PreK-8), 307 Church St., Loretto, 38469. Tel: 931-853-4388; Fax: 931-853-4388; Email: tneese@shsloretto.com. Ms. Tina A. Neese, Prin. Lay Teachers 7; Students 92.
Catechesis Religious Program—Emily Evers, D.R.E. Students 10.

MADISON, DAVIDSON CO., ST. JOSEPH (1953)
1225 Gallatin Pike S., Madison, 37115.
Tel: 615-885-1071; Email: SJSecretary@sjsandchurch.com. Rev. Jean Baptiste; Deacons Gordon W. McBride Sr.; Theodore B. Welsh; Don Craighead.
School—St. Joseph School, (Grades PreK-8), Tel: 615-865-1491; Fax: 615-612-0228; Email: principal@stjosephnashville.org. C.J. Martin, Prin. Lay Teachers 28; Dominican Sisters of St. Cecilia Congregation 2; Students 315.
Catechesis Religious Program—Email: sturbo37066@yahoo.com. Sharyn Curbo, D.R.E. Students 116.

MANCHESTER, COFFEE CO., ST. MARK (2000)
2941 McMinnville Hwy., Manchester, 37355.
Tel: 931-723-4107; Email: saintmarkchurchmanchester@gmail.com; Web: www.facebook.com/saintmarkcatholicchurchmanchestertn. Rev. Stephen A. Klasek; Deacon Ronald F. Munn.
Res.: 304 W. Gizzard St., Tullahoma, 37388.
Catechesis Religious Program—Email: stpaulchurch@cafes.net. Students 95.

MCEWEN, HUMPHREYS CO., ST. PATRICK'S (1855) [CEM]
175 St. Patrick's St., McEwen, 37101.
Tel: 931-582-3633; Email: stpatsfinance@bellsouth.net. Rev. Zachaeus Munyao Kirangu, Admin.
School—St. Patrick's School, (Grades PreK-8), Tel: 931-582-3493; Fax: 931-582-6386. Sr. Mary Grace Watson, O.P., Prin.; Karen Martin, Librarian. Lay Teachers 6; Dominican Sisters of St. Cecilia Congregation 4; Students 108.
Catechesis Religious Program—Students 3.

MCMINNVILLE, WARREN CO., ST. CATHERINE (1958)
1024 Faulkner Spring Rd., McMinnville, 37110.
Tel: 931-473-4932; Email: stcatherines@blomand.net; Web: sites.google.com/view/st-catherines-catholic-church/. Ms. Jena Kagarise, Contact Person.
Catechesis Religious Program—Judy Davis, D.R.E.; Janice Saylors, D.R.E. Students 110.

MURFREESBORO, RUTHERFORD CO., ST. ROSE OF LIMA (1929)
1601 N. Tennessee Blvd., Murfreesboro, 37130.
Tel: 615-893-1843; Email: djackson@saintrose.org. Revs. John Sims Baker; Michael Baltrus, Parochial Vicar; Joseph Fessenden, Parochial Vicar; Deacons Thomas McGrane; Peter Semich; John D'Amico.
School—St. Rose of Lima School, (Grades K-8), Tel: 615-898-0555; Fax: 615-890-0977. Sr. Mary Patrick, O.P., Prin.; Holly Bruser, Librarian. Lay Teachers 24; Students 379; Clergy / Religious Teachers 4.
Catechesis Religious Program—Email: formation@saintrose.org. Michaela Miller, D.R.E. Students 150.

OLD HICKORY, WILSON CO., ST. STEPHEN (1942)
14544 Lebanon Rd., Old Hickory, 37138.
Tel: 615-754-2424; Fax: 615-754-0043; Email: ststephen@ssccohtn.org. Revs. Patrick J. Kibby; Emmanuel Dirichukwu; Deacons Hans Toecker; Fred Bourland; Robert A. Montini; Tom Samoray; Steve Molnar.
Catechesis Religious Program—Email: Greg.Karn@saintstephencommunity.com; Email: amaddyb@gmail.com; Email: music.dept@comcast.net. Greg Karn, D.R.E.; Angie Bosio, Life Teen; Scott Goudeau, RCIA Coord.; Connie Blevins, RCIC. Students 410.

PULASKI, GILES CO., IMMACULATE CONCEPTION (1941)
100 Chapel Rd., Pulaski, 38478. Tel: 931-363-5776; Email: iccpulaski@energize.net. Rev. George Panthananickal, C.M.I.; Deacon W. Michael Hume, Parish Coord.
Catechesis Religious Program—JoAnn Beam, D.R.E. Students 12.

SAINT JOSEPH, LAWRENCE CO., ST. JOSEPH (1872) Attended by Sacred Heart, Loretto.
502 American Blvd., St. Joseph, 38481.
Tel: 931-853-4370; Fax: 931-853-4373; Email: amy.sacred.heart@gmail.com. P.O. Box 86, Loretto, 38469. Rev. Luckas Arulappa, M.S.F.S.

SHELBYVILLE, BEDFORD CO., ST. WILLIAM OF MONTEVERGINE (1941)
719 N. Main St., Shelbyville, 37160.
Tel: 931-735-6004; Email: st.William.secretary@hotmail.com. Rev. Louis E. Rojas, S.A.C. Church: 500 S. Brittain, Shelbyville, 37160. Email: st.william931@gmail.com; Web: www.stwilliamshelbyville.org.
Catechesis Religious Program—Isabel Grajales, D.R.E. Students 190.

SMITHVILLE, DEKALB CO., ST. GREGORY (1982) Attended by St. Catherine, McMinnville.
712 W. Main St., Smithville, 37166.
Tel: 615-597-1970; Email: stgregorys2@dtccom.net. P.O. Box 712, Smithville, 37166. Ms. Arlene Hullet, Contact Person.
Catechesis Religious Program—Ana Jarvis, D.R.E. Students 63.

SMYRNA, RUTHERFORD CO., ST. LUKE (1982)
10682 Old Nashville Hwy., Smyrna, 37167.
Tel: 615-459-9672; Email: stluke123@comcast.net; Web: www.stlukesmyrnatn.com. Rev. Jacob Dio, M.S.F.S.; Deacons Simeon Panagatos; Ernie Gartung; Roger F. Huber.
Catechesis Religious Program—Email: denise.stluke123@comcast.net. Denise M. Leaver, D.R.E. Students 255.

SPARTA, WHITE CO., ST. ANDREW (1982)
829 Valley View Dr., Sparta, 38583.
Tel: 931-738-2140; Email: saccsec@blomand.net. Rev. John Day, Admin.
Catechesis Religious Program—Students 12.

SPRING HILL, MAURY CO., CHURCH OF THE NATIVITY (2008)
2001 Campbell Station Pkwy., Ste. C-7, Spring Hill, 37174. Tel: 615-302-4004; Email: parishoffice@nativitycatholic.net; Web: www.nativitycatholic.net. Rev. Gerard Strange; Deacons Timothy Conley; Conrad J. Donarski.
Catechesis Religious Program—Ms. Nancy Martinez, D.R.E. Students 346.

SPRINGFIELD, ROBERTSON CO., OUR LADY OF LOURDES (1946) [CEM]
103 Golf Club Ln., Springfield, 37172.
Tel: 615-384-6200; Email: 0iism@att.net. Rev. Anthony Lopez, Admin.; Deacon Michael Morris.
Catechesis Religious Program—Deacon Michael Morris, D.R.E. Students 116.
Mission—St. Michael, [CEM] Cedar Hill, Robertson Co.

TENNESSEE RIDGE, HOUSTON CO., ST. ELIZABETH ANN SETON (1977) Attended by St. Patrick, McEwen.
755 State Rte. 49, Tennessee Ridge, 37178.
Tel: 931-721-3769; Email: vbrown1234@aol.com. Rev. Zachaeus Munyao Kirangu, Admin.
Catechesis Religious Program—Students 23.

TULLAHOMA, COFFEE CO., ST. PAUL THE APOSTLE CATHOLIC CHURCH (1954)
304 W. Grizzard St., Tullahoma, 37388.
Tel: 931-455-3050; Email: stpaulchurch@cafes.net; Web: www.stpaulstullahoma.com. Rev. Stephen A. Klasek; Deacon Ronald F. Munn.
Catechesis Religious Program—Terri Daugherty, D.R.E. Students 15.

WAYNESBORO, WAYNE CO., ST. CECILIA (1982) Attended by Holy Trinity, Hohenwald.
50 Willowbrook Dr., Waynesboro, 38485.
Tel: 931-796-3738; Email: holytrinity67477@bellsouth.net. 610 Kimmins St., Hohenwald, 38462. Rev. John O'Neill.
Catechesis Religious Program—Students 1.

Graduate Studies:
Revs.—
Bolster, Rhodes
Wilgenbusch, Luke.

Unassigned:
Revs.—
Johansen, Eric
Sappenfield, John P.

Retired:
Revs.—
Breen, Joseph P., (Retired)
Campion, Owen F., (Retired)
Connor, J. Patrick, V.G., (Retired), 9126 Sawyer Brown Rd., 37221
Henrick, John C., (Retired)
Johnston, Michael O., (Retired)
Mallett, James K., (Retired), 728 Bacon Tr., #61, Chattanooga, 37412
McMurry, John E., S.S., (Retired)
Miller, James Norman, (Retired)
Stolowski, Stephen, (Retired).

Permanent Deacons:
Ambriz, Anselmo, St. Luke
Andrade, Hernan, Our Lady of Guadalupe
Ascencio, Luis, Our Lady of Guadalupe
Azzara, Dominic D., Immaculate Conception, Clarksville
Bainbridge, Frank, (Retired)
Beckman, Samuel C., Sacred Heart, Loretto
Berberich, Robert R., Immaculate Conception, Clarksville
Booth, W. James, Holy Family, Brentwood
Bougrat, Raphael, St. Philip, Franklin
Bourland, Fred, St. Stephen, Old Hickory
Brancheau, Paul, St. Philip, Franklin
Calzavara, John, St. Edward, Nashville
Carr, James F., Our Lady of the Lake, Hendersonville
Casey, Bernard J., (On Duty Outside the Diocese)
Casey, John P., St. Ann, Nashville
Catalano, Michael, St. Henry, Nashville
Cheasty, John C., (On Duty Outside the Diocese)
Conley, Timothy, Church of the Nativity
Cook, Thomas H., St. Patrick, Nashville
Craighead, Don, St. Joseph, Madison
D'Amico, John, St. Rose of Lima

Deal, Ronald B. Jr., Holy Family, Brentwood
Deschenes, Martin, St. Henry, Cursillo, Nashville
Desmond, Mark, St. Matthew, Franklin; (On Duty Outside the Diocese)
Dixon, James A., St. Francis Cabrini, Lebanon
Donarski, Conrad J., Church of the Nativity
Edwards, Brian, John Paul II High School, Hendersonville
Faulkner, Mark C., Cathedral of the Incarnation, Nashville
Finchum, Thales, Cathedral of the Incarnation, Nashville
Forte, William, St. Matthew
Francescon, Samuel A., (Retired)
Gartung, Ernest, St. Luke
Garza, Juan, Immaculate Conception, Clarksville
Graham, Robert L., (Retired)
Gregory, L. Wayne, Holy Rosary, Nashville
Guess, Harry, St. Vincent de Paul, Nashville
Hasenberg, Rock, St. Joseph, Madison
Hill, William, St. Vincent de Paul, Nashville
Holzemer, James, St. Ann
Holzmer, Joe, Cathedral
Huber, Roger F., St. Rose of Lima, Murfreesboro
Huhlein, Gilbert P., Holy Rosary, Nashville
Hume, W. Michael, Immaculate Conception, Springfield
Jayme, Edgardo, St. Edward, Nashville
Johnson, Philip, Good Shepherd
Keller, I. Price, St. Catherine, Columbia
Kopczynski, Michael R., Our Lady of the Lake, Hendersonville
Krenson, John G., Cathedral of the Incarnation, Nashville
Lammers, John, Our Lady of the Lake
Levinson, Ken, St. Pius X, Nashville
Lovell, David, (Unassigned)
Lybarger, David, Christ the King, Nashville
Mahoney, Robert L., Holy Name, Nashville
Martinez, Hector, St. Francis Cabrini
Martinez, Juan, Immaculate Conception, Clarksville
McBrayer, J. Harold Jr., (Retired)
McBride, Gordon W. Sr., St. Joseph, Madison
McCulley, Daniel, St. Catherine
McGrane, Thomas J., St. Rose Lima, Murfreesboro
McKenzie, Andrew D., Christ the King, Nashville
McKenzie, James W., Cathedral of the Incarnation, Nashville
Meinhart, Gregory, St. Henry, Nashville
Molnar, Stephen Jr., St. Stephen
Montini, Robert A., St. Stephen, Old Hickory
Morris, Michael, Our Lady of Lourdes
Mulloy, Martin, (Retired), St. Ann, Nashville
Munn, Ronald F., St. Mark, Manchester; St. Paul the Apostle, Tullahoma
Nardini, James, St. John Vianney, Galatin
Ochoa, Roberto, St. Ignatius, Nashville
Panagatos, Simeon W., St. Luke, Smyrna
Pineda, Jose G., Holy Family, Lafayette
Pyles, Daniel Jr., St. Matthew, Franklin
Randall, Ralph, (Retired)
Rector, Michael, Our Lady of the Lake
Samoray, Tom, St. Stephen, Old Hickory
Schulz, Brian, Christ the King
Seibold, Raymond, St. Catherine, Columbia
Semich, Peter, St. Rose of Lima, Murfreesboro
Shafer, L. Douglas, St. Ignatius of Antioch, Antioch
Shaw, Ronald, St. Ignatius, Antioch
Stanford, James E., (Retired)
Taylor, Paul, St. Francis Cabrini
Toecker, Hans M., St. Stephen, Old Hickory; Chancellor
True, Robert H., Christ the King, Nashville
Tucker, James, St. Christopher, Dickson
Walter, James, (On Duty Outside of Diocese)
Weaver, Matthew, (On Duty Outside of Diocese)
Weller, Richard, (Retired)
Welsh, Theodore B., St. Joseph, Madison
White, Mark, Holy Rosary, Nashville
Wilkins, Michael, Holy Rosary, Nashville
Winters, Timothy F., Immaculate Conception, Clarksville
Ziemkiewicz, Gerard, St. Edward, Nashville.

INSTITUTIONS LOCATED IN DIOCESE

[A] COLLEGES

NASHVILLE. *Aquinas College*, 4210 Harding Pike, 37205. Tel: 615-297-7545; Email: admissions@aquinascollege.edu; Web: www.aquinascollege.edu. Sr. Mary Grieffendorf, O.P., Pres.; Mother Anna Grace Neenan, O.P., Chm.; Gabriella Yi, Dir.; Sisters Thomas More Stepnowski, O.P., Provost & Vice Pres. Academics; Mary Evelyn Potts, O.P., Librarian. Dominican Sisters of St. Cecilia Congregation. Religious Teachers 2; Lay Teachers 9; Sisters 14; Students 83.

[B] HIGH SCHOOLS, DIOCESAN

NASHVILLE. *Father Ryan High School* (1925) Corporate Title: Father Ryan High School, Inc. 700 Norwood Dr., 37204. Tel: 615-383-4200; Fax: 615-383-9056; Email: mcintyrej@fatherryan.org; Web: www.fatherryan.org. Mr. James McIntyre, Pres.; Mr. Paul Davis, Prin.; Christi Foreman, Librarian; Rev. Delphinus Mutajuka, Chap. Religious Teachers 1; Lay Teachers 88; Students 912.

Father Ryan Board of Trust, Devel. & Alumni Office, 770 Norwood Dr., 37204. Tel: 615-383-4200.

HENDERSONVILLE. *Pope John Paul II High School, Inc.* (2002) 117 Caldwell Dr., Hendersonville, 37075. Tel: 615-822-2375; Fax: 615-822-6226; Email: info@jp2hs.org; Web: www.jp2hs.org. Michael Deely, Headmaster; Ms. Joan Lange, Librarian. Religious Teachers 1; Lay Teachers 54; Students 578.

[C] HIGH SCHOOLS, PRIVATE

NASHVILLE. *St. Cecilia Academy* (1860) The Dominican Campus, 4210 Harding Pike, 37205. Tel: 615-298-4525; Fax: 615-783-0561; Email: capriolic@stcecilia.edu; Web: www.stcecilia.edu. Sr. Anna Laura Karp, O.P., Prin.; Cheryl Carpenter, Librarian. Conducted by the St. Cecilia Congregation of Dominican Sisters.

St. Cecilia Academy. Religious Teachers 10; Lay Teachers 29; Students 267.

[D] ELEMENTARY SCHOOLS, PRIVATE

NASHVILLE. **St. Bernard Academy*, (Grades PreK-8), 2020 24th Ave. S., 37212-4202. Tel: 615-385-0440; Fax: 615-783-0241; Email: csabo@stbernard.org; Web: www.stbernardacademy.org. Carl Sabo, Prin.

Saint Bernard Academy Corporation. Lay Teachers 38; Students 349.

Overbrook School (1936) (Grades PreK-8), 4210 Harding Pike, 37205. Tel: 615-292-5134; Fax: 615-783-0560; Email: information@overbrook.edu; Web: www.overbrook.edu. Sr. Julia Marie, O.P., Prin. The St. Cecilia Congregation of Dominican Sisters. Religious Teachers 5; Lay Teachers 28; Students 308.

[E] CHILD-CARING INSTITUTIONS

NASHVILLE. **St. Bernard After School Program*, 2020 24th Ave. S., 37212. Tel: 615-298-1298; Fax: 615-783-0241; Email: csabo@stbernard.org. Suzanne Southworth, Dir. Students 60.

St. Mary Villa Child Development Center, 1700 Heiman St., 37208. Tel: 615-356-6336; Fax: 615-356-6421; Email: claire.givens@stmaryvilla.org. Claire Givens, Exec. Dir. Students 106; Total Staff 44.

St. Mary Villa, Inc., 1700 Heiman St., 37208. Tel: 615-356-6336; Fax: 615-356-6421; Email: yneal@stmaryvilla.org. Clarie Givens, Admin. Students 106.

[F] GENERAL HOSPITALS

NASHVILLE. *Saint Thomas Health Foundations* (1978) 4220 Harding Rd., 37205. Tel: 615-222-6800; Fax: 615-222-6159; Email: gfulcher@ascension.org; Web: www.sthealth.com/how-to-help/honor/saint-thomas-health-foundation. 102 Woodmont Blvd., Ste. 600, 37205. Greg Pope, Chief Mission Officer.

Saint Thomas Midtown Hospital, 2000 Church St., 37236. Tel: 615-284-5555; Fax: 615-284-1592; Email: gfulcher@ascension.org; Web: www.sthealth.com/locations/saint-thomas-midtown-hospital. Greg Pope, Chief Mission Officer; Rev. Eric Johansen, Chap.

Saint Thomas Midtown Hospital Bed Capacity 683; Tot Asst. Annually 196,327; Total Staff 1,988; Chaplains 3.

Saint Thomas Regional Hospitals, 4220 Harding Pike, 37205. Tel: 844-655-2111; Email: gfulcher@ascension.org. 102 Woodmont Blvd., Ste. 600, 37205. Greg Pope, Chief Mission Officer.

Saint Thomas West Hospital (1898) 4220 Harding Rd., 37205. Tel: 615-222-2111; Fax: 615-222-6502; Email: gfulcher@ascension.org; Web: www.sthealth.com/locations/saint-thomas-west-hospital. 102 Woodmont Blvd., Ste. 600, 37205. Greg Pope, Vice Pres. Mission; Rev. John Raphael, Chap. Ascension Health, St. Louis, MO.

Saint Thomas West Hospital Bed Capacity 541; Tot Asst. Annually 204,926; Total Staff 1,908; Chaplains 7.

St. Thomas Health Foundation, 102 Woodmont Blvd., Ste 600, 37205. Tel: 615-222-6800; Fax: 615-222-6159; Email: gfulcher@ascension.org. Greg Pope, Chief Mission Officer.

St. Thomas Network (1986) 4220 Harding Rd., 37205. Tel: 615-222-2111; Fax: 615-222-6502. 102 Woodmont Blvd., Ste. 600, 37205. Greg Pope, Chief Mission Officer

Saint Thomas Network (fka Saint Thomas Health Services Total Staff 3.

CENTERVILLE. *Saint Thomas Hickman Community Hospital*, 135 E. Swan St., Centerville, 37033-1466. Tel: 931-729-4271; Fax: 931-729-4612; Email: jack.keller@baptisthospital.com; Email: gfulcher@ascension.org; Web: www.sthealth.com/locations/saint-thomas-hickman-hospital. 102 Woodmont Blvd., Ste. 600, 37205. Greg Pope, Chief Mission Officer

Hickman Community Health Care Services, Inc. dba Hickman Community Hospital (fka Baptist Hickman Community Health Care Services, Inc. dba Baptist Hickman Community Hospital) Bed Capacity 25; Tot Asst. Annually 35,759; Total Staff 107.

MURFREESBORO. *Saint Thomas Rutherford Foundation*, 1700 Medical Center Pkwy., Murfreesboro, 37129. Tel: 615-396-4996; Fax: 615-396-4997; Email: gfulcher@ascension.org; Web: www.sthealth.com/how-to-help/honor/saint-thomas-rutherford-foundation. 102 Woodmont Blvd., Ste 600, 37205. Greg Pope, Chief Mission Officer

Saint Thomas Rutherford Foundation.

St. Thomas Rutherford Hospital, 1700 Medical Center Pkwy., Murfreesboro, 37129. Tel: 615-396-4101; Fax: 615-396-4119; Email: gfulcher@ascension.org; Web: www.sthealth.com/locations/saint-thomas-rutherford-hospital. 102 Woodmont Blvd., Ste. 600, 37205. Gordon B. Ferguson, CEO; Greg Pope, Chief Mission Officer

Middle Tennessee Medical Center, Inc. Bed Capacity 286; Tot Asst. Annually 116,451; Total Staff 8,392; Chaplains 2.

[G] HOMES FOR THE AGED

NASHVILLE. *Villa Maria Manor, Inc.*, 32 White Bridge Rd., 37205. Tel: 615-352-3084; Fax: 615-352-0553; Email: sclinton@VillaMariaManor.org. Mr. David Glascoe, Mng. Agent. Residents 230; Total Staff 10.

[H] CONVENTS AND RESIDENCES FOR SISTERS

NASHVILLE. *St. Cecilia Convent* Motherhouse and Novitiate of St. Cecilia Congregation of Dominican Sisters. 801 Dominican Dr., 37228-1905. Tel: 615-256-5486, Ext. 1312; Fax: 615-687-3512; Email: smsartain@op-tn.org; Web: www.nashvilledominican.org. Mother Ann Marie Karlovic, O.P., Prioress Gen.; Sr. Mary Raymond Thye, O.P., Prioress. Novices 16; Postulants 12; Sisters 303; Sisters in Residence 141.

Mercy Convent, 2629 Pennington Bend Rd., 37214. Tel: 615-885-1863; Fax: 615-885-4304; Email: bhiggins@mercysc.org. Sr. Beth Higgins, R.S.M., Coord.; Rev. Mark Hunt, Chap.

Sisters of Mercy of Nashville, TN, Inc. Sisters 22.

[I] CAMPS AND COMMUNITY CENTERS

FAIRVIEW. *Camp Marymount* Catholic summer camp for boys and girls. 1318 Fairview Blvd., Fairview, 37062. Tel: 615-799-0410; Fax: 615-799-2261; Email: info@campmarymount.com; Web: www.campmarymount.com. Tommy Hagey, Dir.

[J] RENEWAL CENTERS

DICKSON. *Bethany Retreat House*, 2002 Garners Creek Rd., Dickson, 37055. Tel: 615-446-2063; Tel: 615-878-0280 (Reservations); Email: bethanyretreat@op-tn.org. Sr. Mary Evelyn Potts, O.P., Coord. Owned and operated by St. Cecilia Congregation.

LIBERTY. *Carmel Center of Spirituality*, P.O. Box 117, Liberty, 37095. Tel: 615-536-5177; Email: bbean@atccom.net. Revs. Jo Joy Pacheril, C.M.I.; Roy Palatty, C.M.I.; Titus Augustine, C.M.I.; James Panackal, C.M.I., Dir.

[K] MISCELLANEOUS

NASHVILLE. *Catholic Community Foundation of Middle Tennessee, Inc.* (2011) 2800 McGavock Pike, 37214. Tel: 615-783-0278; Fax: 615-292-8411; Email: william.whalen@dioceseofnashville.com; Web: www.ccfmtn.org. Mr. William J. Whalen, Business Mgr.

Catholic Community Investment and Loan, Inc., 2800 McGavock Pike, 37214. Tel: 615-383-6393; Email: william.whalen@dioceseofnashville.com. Mr. William J. Whalen, Business Mgr.

Catholic Foundation of Tennessee, Inc., 2800 McGavock Pike, 37214. Fax: 615-783-0774; Email: William.Whalen@dioceseofnashville.com.

**Catholic Media Productions, Inc.*, 2800 McGavock Pike, 37214. Tel: 615-783-0754; Email: Tom.Samoray@dioceseofnashville.com; Web: www.webelieveshow.org. Deacon Tom Samoray, Admin.

Diocesan Properties, Inc. dba Marina Manor East Apartments, 2800 McGavock Pike, 37214. Tel: 615-383-6393; Fax: 615-292-8411; Email: william.whalen@dioceseofnashville.com. Mr. William J. Whalen, Sec. & Treas.

Dominican Campus, 4210 Harding Pike, 37205. Tel: 615-383-3230; Fax: 615-383-3196; Email: muehe@dominicancampus.org. Rev. John O'Neill.

Endowment for the Advancement of Catholic Schools, Trust aka Advancement for Catholic Education, 2800 McGavock Pike, 37214. Tel: 615-383-6393; Fax: 615-292-8411; Email: william.whalen@dioceseofnashville.com. Mr. William J. Whalen, Business Mgr.

FrassatiUSA Inc. aka University Catholic, P.O. Box 50571, 37205. Tel: 615-322-0104; Email: KathleenCordell@gmail.com. 2004 Terrace Pl, 37203. Rev. Michael Fye, Chap.

**St. Henry Property Development, Inc.* dba The Cloister, 30 White Bridge Rd., 37205. Tel: 615-760-4424; Email: david@maryqueenofangels.com. David Glacoe, Admin.

Ladies of Charity of Nashville, Inc., 2216 State St., 37203. Tel: 615-327-3453; Tel: 615-327-3430; Fax: 615-321-3312. Affiliated with the Ladies of Charity of the United States of America, LCUSA, and the Association of International Charities, AIC.

Ladies of Charity Welfare Agency, Inc. (1617) 2212 State St., 37203. Tel: 615-327-3430; Fax: 615-321-3312; Email: locwelfare@bellsouth.net. Mrs. Terri Puma, Exec. Dir. Tot Asst. Annually 4,215; Total Staff 123.

Mary, Queen of Angels. Inc. (1999) 34 White Bridge Rd., 37205. Tel: 615-760-4424; Email: david@maryqueenofangels.com; Web: www.maryqueenofangels.com. Mr. David Glascoe, CEO.

Mid-Tennessee Rural Outreach Association, 2800 McGavock Pike, 37214. Tel: 615-352-3087; Tel: 615-383-6393; Email: hans.toecker@dioceseofnashville.com. Deacon Hans Toecker, Chancellor
Mid-Tennessee Rural Outreach Association; Assumption-St. Vincent North Nashville Outreach Association.

Parish Twinning Program of the Americas, 309 Windemere Woods Dr., 37215. Tel: 615-298-3002; Fax: 615-298-2253; Email: parishprogram@aol.com; Web: www.parishprogram.org. Theresa Patterson, Exec. Dir.

Priests Eucharistic League, 2800 McGavock Pike, 37214. Tel: 615-383-6393; Email: hans.toecker@dioceseofnashville.com. Deacon Hans Toecker, Chancellor.

**Visitation Hospital Foundation*, 237 Old Hickory Blvd., Ste. 201, 37221. Tel: 615-673-3501; Email: lawills@visitationhospital.org; Email: tpatterson@visitationhospital.org; Web: www.visitationhospital.org. Theresa Patterson, Exec. Dir.; Mrs. Lee Anne Wills, Dir.

ASHLAND CITY. *Diocesan Council of Catholic Women*, 3384 Bell St., Ashland City, 37015. Tel: 615-476-6244; Email: ejbardet@comcast.net. Rev. Daniel J. Steiner, Dir.

RELIGIOUS INSTITUTES OF MEN REPRESENTED IN THE DIOCESE

For further details refer to the corresponding bracketed number in the Religious Institutes of Men or Women section.

[0275]—*Carmelites of Mary Immaculate*—C.M.I.
[0520]—*Franciscan Friars* (Prov. of Sacred Heart)—O.F.M.
[0570]—*Glenmary Home Missioners*—G.H.M.
[0690]—*Jesuit Fathers and Brothers*—S.J.
[]—*Missionaries of St. Francis de Sales* (Annecy, France)—M.S.F.S.
[1200]—*Society of the Divine Savior* (Milwaukee, WI)—S.D.S.

RELIGIOUS INSTITUTES OF WOMEN REPRESENTED IN THE DIOCESE

[0760]—*Daughters of Charity of St. Vincent de Paul* (East Central Prov., Evansville, IN)—D.C.
[1070-03]—*Dominican Sisters*—O.P.
[1070-07]—*Dominican Sisters*—O.P.
[1070-09]—*Dominican Sisters*—O.P.
[2575]—*Institute of the Sisters of Mercy of the Americas* (Baltimore, MD; Cincinnati, OH)—R.S.M.
[]—*Sacred Heart Congregation (India)*—S.H.
[1680]—*School Sisters of St. Francis*—O.S.F.
[]—*Sisters for Christian Community* (St. Louis)—S.F.C.C.
[0990]—*Sisters of Divine Providence* (St. Louis Prov.)—C.D.P.
[1705]—*Sisters of St. Francis of Assisi*—O.S.F.
[3270]—*Sisters of the Most Precious Blood*—C.PP.S.

DIOCESAN CEMETERIES

NASHVILLE. *Calvary Cemetery*, 1001 Lebanon Rd., 37210. Tel: 615-256-4590; Email: michael.wilkins@dioceseofnashville.com. Deacon Michael Wilkins, Admin.

NECROLOGY

† Niedergeses, W. Bernard, (Retired), Died Nov. 4, 2018

An asterisk (*) denotes an organization that has established tax-exempt status directly with the IRS and is not covered by the USCCB Group Ruling.

Archdiocese of Newark

(Archidioecesis Novarcensis)

His Eminence

JOSEPH CARDINAL TOBIN, C.SS.R.

Archbishop of Newark; ordained a priest of the Congregation of the Most Holy Redeemer June 1, 1978; Episcopal Ordination as Titular Archbishop of Obba October 9, 2010; installed Archbishop of Indianapolis December 3, 2012; appointed Archbishop of Newark November 7, 2016; Elevated to Cardinal November 19, 2016; installed Archbishop of Newark January 6, 2017. *Office: 171 Clifton Ave., P.O. Box 9500, Newark, NJ 07104-9500.*

Archdiocesan Center: 171 Clifton Ave., P.O. Box 9500, Newark, NJ 07104-9500. Tel: 973-497-4000; Fax: 973-497-4033.

Web: www.rcan.org

Email: webmaster@rcan.org

Most Reverend

JOHN J. MYERS, J.C.D., D.D.

Archbishop Emeritus of Newark; ordained December 17, 1966; appointed Coadjutor Bishop of Peoria July 14, 1987; Episcopal ordination September 3, 1987; succeeded to See of Peoria January 23, 1990; appointed Fifth Archbishop of Newark July 24, 2001; installed October 9, 2001; Pallium conferred June 29, 2002; retired November 7, 2016. *Res.: Cathedral Basilica of the Sacred Heart, 89 Ridge St., Newark, NJ 07104.* Tel: 973-484-4600; Fax: 973-497-4018.

Most Reverend

DOMINIC A. MARCONI, D.D.

Retired Auxiliary Bishop of Newark; ordained May 30, 1953; appointed Titular Bishop of Bure and Auxiliary Bishop of Newark May 3, 1976; Episcopal ordination June 25, 1976; retired July 1, 2002. *Res.: 71 Washington Ave., Chatham, NJ 07928-2014.* Tel: 973-635-8777; Fax: 973-635-8647.

Most Reverend

CHARLES J. MCDONNELL

Retired Auxiliary Bishop of Newark; ordained May 29, 1954; appointed Titular Bishop of Pocofelto and Auxiliary Bishop of Newark March 15, 1994; Episcopal ordination May 12, 1994; retired May 21, 2004. *Res.: 140 Shepherd Ln., Totowa, NJ 07512.* Tel: 973-904-0635.

Most Reverend

JOHN W. FLESEY, S.T.D., D.D.

Retired Auxiliary Bishop of Newark; ordained May 31, 1969; appointed Titular Bishop of Allegheny and Auxiliary Bishop of Newark May 21, 2004; Episcopal ordination August 4, 2004; retired October 16, 2017. *Res.: Most Blessed Sacrament, 787 Franklin Lake Rd., Franklin Lakes, NJ 07417.* Tel: 201-891-4200; Fax: 201-891-4243.

Most Reverend

MANUEL A. CRUZ

Auxiliary Bishop of Newark; ordained May 31, 1980; appointed Titular Bishop of Gaguari and Auxiliary Bishop of Newark May 19, 2008; Episcopal ordination September 8, 2008; installed September 8, 2008. *Res.: Cathedral Basilica of the Sacred Heart, 89 Ridge St., Newark, NJ 07104.* Tel: 973-497-4009.

Square Miles 513.

Diocese Established, 1853; Erected an Archdiocese, December 10, 1937.

Comprises Four Counties in the State of New Jersey, viz.: Bergen, Hudson, Essex and Union.

For legal titles of parishes and archdiocesan institutions, consult the Chancery Office.

STATISTICAL OVERVIEW

Personnel	
Cardinals	1
Retired Archbishops	1
Auxiliary Bishops	1
Retired Bishops	4
Abbots	1
Priests: Diocesan Active in Diocese	391
Priests: Diocesan Active Outside Diocese	27
Priests: Diocesan in Foreign Missions	15
Priests: Retired, Sick or Absent	169
Number of Diocesan Priests	602
Religious Priests in Diocese	130
Total Priests in Diocese	732
Extern Priests in Diocese	51
Ordinations:	
Diocesan Priests	9
Permanent Deacons in Diocese	144
Total Brothers	61
Total Sisters	708
Parishes	
Parishes	212
With Resident Pastor:	
Resident Diocesan Priests	177
Resident Religious Priests	22
Without Resident Pastor:	
Administered by Priests	13
Closed Parishes	2
Professional Ministry Personnel:	
Brothers	6
Sisters	65
Lay Ministers	479
Welfare	
Catholic Hospitals	3
Total Assisted	949,770
Health Care Centers	1
Total Assisted	11,077
Homes for the Aged	4
Total Assisted	741
Day Care Centers	4
Total Assisted	566
Specialized Homes	5
Total Assisted	719
Special Centers for Social Services	23
Total Assisted	71,952
Educational	
Seminaries, Diocesan	3
Students from This Diocese	54
Diocesan Students in Other Seminaries	3
Students Religious	24
Total Seminarians	81
Colleges and Universities	4
Total Students	20,661
High Schools, Diocesan and Parish	13
Total Students	6,270
High Schools, Private	14
Total Students	5,180
Elementary Schools, Diocesan and Parish	66
Total Students	11,974
Elementary Schools, Private	6
Total Students	1,118
Catechesis/Religious Education:	
High School Students	4,000
Elementary Students	61,874
Total Students under Catholic Instruction	111,158
Teachers in the Diocese:	
Priests	18
Brothers	23
Sisters	73
Lay Teachers	2,427
Vital Statistics	
Receptions into the Church:	
Infant Baptism Totals	10,894
Minor Baptism Totals	276
Adult Baptism Totals	309
Received into Full Communion	176
First Communions	9,619
Confirmations	8,190
Marriages:	
Catholic	1,645
Interfaith	232
Total Marriages	1,877
Deaths	8,229
Total Catholic Population	1,220,143
Total Population	2,965,397

Former Bishops—Most Revs. JAMES ROOSEVELT BAYLEY, D.D., cons. Oct. 30, 1853; promoted to the Archiepiscopal See of Baltimore, July 30, 1872; died Oct. 3, 1877; MICHAEL AUGUSTINE CORRIGAN, D.D., cons. May 4, 1873; promoted to the Archiepiscopal See of Petra, Oct. 1, 1880; succeeded to the Archiepiscopal See of New York, Oct. 10, 1885; died May 5, 1902; WINAND MICHAEL WIGGER, D.D., cons. Oct. 18, 1881; died Jan. 5, 1901; JOHN J. MYERS, J.C.D., D.D., (Retired), ord. Dec. 17, 1966; appt. Coadjutor Bishop of Peoria July 14, 1987; Episcopal ord. Sept. 3, 1987; succeeded to See of Peoria Jan. 23, 1990; appt. Fifth Archbishop of Newark July 24, 2001; installed Oct. 9, 2001; Pallium conferred June 29, 2002; retired Nov. 7, 2016.; JOHN JOSEPH O'CONNOR, D.D., ord. Dec. 22, 1877; cons. July 25, 1901; died May 20, 1927; THOMAS J. WALSH, S.T.D., J.C.D., ord. Jan. 27, 1900; appt. Bishop of Trenton, May 10, 1918; cons. July 25, 1918; made Assistant at the Pontifical Throne March 13, 1922; transferred to the See of Newark, March 2, 1928; appt. First Archbishop of Newark, Dec. 10, 1937; Pallium conferred, Dec. 18, 1937; installed April 27, 1938; died June 6, 1952; THOMAS A. BOLAND, S.T.D., LL.D., ord. Dec. 23, 1922; appt. Titular Bishop of Hirina and Auxiliary to the Archbishop of Newark, May 21, 1940; cons. July 25, 1940; transferred to Paterson, June 21, 1947; appt. Second Archbishop of Newark, Nov. 15, 1952; installed Jan. 14, 1953; Assistant at the Pontifical Throne, May 6, 1965; retired April 2, 1974; died March 16, 1979; PETER LEO GERETY, D.D., ord. June 29, 1939; appt. Coadjutor Bishop of Portland, March 4, 1966; cons. June 1, 1966; succeeded to See, Sept. 15, 1969; appt. Third Archbishop of Newark, April 2, 1974; installed June 28, 1974; retired June 1, 1986; died Sept. 20, 2016.; THEODORE E. MCCARRICK, Ph.D., ord. May 31, 1958; appt. Auxiliary Bishop of New York and Titular Bishop of Rusibisir, May 24, 1977; Episcopal ordination June 29, 1977; appt. First Bishop of Metuchen, Nov. 19, 1981; installed Jan. 31, 1982; appt. Fourth Archbishop of Newark, May 30, 1986; Pallium conferred June 29, 1986; installed July 25, 1986; appt. to See of Washington, D.C., Nov. 21, 2000; installed Jan. 3, 2001; created Cardinal Feb. 21, 2001; retired May 16, 2006; resigned from College of Cardinals July 27, 2018; dismissed from the clerical state Feb. 15, 2019.

Archdiocesan Officials

Archdiocesan Officials—Web: www.rcan.org.

Archdiocesan Archbishop—His Eminence JOSEPH CARDINAL TOBIN, C.Ss.R., D.D.

Chancellor—Sr. DONNA L. CIANGIO, O.P., Tel: 973-497-4128.

Assistant to the Archbishop for Public Affairs—Rev.

Msgr. CHRISTOPHER J. HYNES, Ed.S., Tel: 973-497-4107.

Vicar General and Moderator of the Curia—Rev. Msgr. THOMAS P. NYDEGGER, Ed.D., M.Div.

Archbishop Emeritus of Newark—Most Rev. JOHN J. MYERS, J.C.D., D.D., (Retired).

Auxiliary Bishop of Newark and Regional Bishop for Hudson County—VACANT.

Retired Auxiliary Bishop of Newark and Regional Bishop for Bergen County—Most Rev. JOHN W. FLESEY, S.T.D., D.D., (Retired).

Auxiliary Bishop of Newark, Regional Bishop for Union County and Rector of the Cathedral Basilica of the Sacred Heart—Most Rev. MANUEL A. CRUZ, D.D.

Director/Master of Ceremonies for Pontifical Liturgies—Rev. JOSEPH A. MANCINI, Tel: 973-497-4038.

Delegate for Religious—Tel: 973-497-4582. Sr. PATRICIA WORMANN, O.P.

Metropolitan Judicial Vicar—Rev. ROBERT G. MCBRIDE, J.C.L., J.V., Tel: 973-497-4145.

Adjutant Judicial Vicar—Rev. GIOVANNI RIZZO, M.Div., J.C.L., Tel: 973-497-4149.

Episcopal Vicar for Healthcare and Social Concerns—Rev. Msgr. RONALD J. ROZNIAK, V.E., V.G., P.A., Tel: 201-444-2000.

Superintendent of Schools/Secretariat for Education—DR. MARGARET A. DAMES, Tel: 973-497-4253.

Director for Family Life—Deacon JAMES DETURA, Tel: 973-497-4324.

Vicar for Pastoral Life—Tel: 973-497-4353. Very Rev. JOHN F. GORDON, V.F.

Vicar for Canonical Affairs—Tel: 973-497-4096. Rev. Msgr. PETER SMUTELOVIC, J.C.D.

Vicar for Priests—Tel: 973-497-4222. Very Rev. JOHN J. PALADINO.

Regional Vicar for Essex County—Rev. Msgr. ROBERT E. EMERY, J.C.L., M.A., V.E., E.V.

Chief Financial Officer—JOSEPH C. PESCATORE, K.C.H.S., CFO, Tel: 973-497-4560.

Minister for Priests—Rev. GABRIEL B. COSTA, Ph.D., Tel: 845-938-5625; Tel: 862-215-2333.

Episcopal Vicar for Hudson County—Rev. Msgr. GREGORY J. STUDERUS, V.F., V.E., E.V.

Director of Selection & Formation of Permanent Deacons—Rev. JAMES V. TETI, J.C.L., S.T.B., Tel: 201-261-6322.

Executive Director of Human Resources—Deacon JOHN J. MCKENNA, K.H.S., Vice chancellor.

Director of Vocations—Rev. EUGENIO P. DE LA RAMA, Tel: 973-313-6190.

Director of Communications and Public Relations—MR. JAMES GOODNESS, K.H.S., M.A., Vice Chancellor, Tel: 973-497-4186.

Executive Director of Parish Business Services—NANCY F. LYSTASH, L.H.S., Vice Chancellor.

Regional Bishops & Deans

Regional Bishops & Deans—Most Rev. JOHN W. FLESEY, S.T.D., D.D., Regl. Bishop for Bergen County, (Retired); Rev. Msgr. GREGORY J. STUDERUS, V.F., V.E., E.V., Regl./Episcopal Vicar for Hudson County; Most Rev. MANUEL A. CRUZ, D.D., Regl. Bishop for Union County.

BERGEN COUNTY

Northwest Bergen Region Deanery 1Very Rev. THOMAS P. LIPNICKI, V.F., Our Lady of Perpetual Help, 25 Purdue Ave., Oakland, 07436. Tel: 201-337-7596; Fax: 201-337-7810.

Northern Valley Bergen Deanery 2NVery Rev. MAREK B. WYSOCKI, V.F., St. Pius X, 268 Old Tappan Rd., Old Tappan, 07675. Tel: 201-664-0913; Fax: 201-664-1013.

Bergen Pascack Valley Deanery 2PVery Rev. SEAN A. MANSON, V.F., Our Lady Mother of the Church, 209 Woodcliff Ave., Woodcliff Lake, 07677. Tel: 201-391-2826; Fax: 201-391-7101.

Central Bergen Region Deanery 3Very Rev. MICHAEL J. SHEEHAN, V.F., St. Peter the Apostle, 445 Fifth Ave., River Edge, 07661. Tel: 201-261-3366; Fax: 201-261-0117.

Southwest Bergen Region Deanery 4Rev. Msgr. WILLIAM J. REILLY, V.F., Most Holy Name, 99 Marsellus Pl., Garfield, 07026. Tel: 973-340-0032; Fax: 973-340-1618.

South Central Bergen Deanery 5Very Rev. LARRY EVANS, V.F., St. Francis of Assisi, 114 Mt. Vernon St., Ridgefield Park, 07660. Tel: 201-641-6464; Fax: 201-641-2282.

Southeast Bergen Region Deanery 6Very Rev. STEVEN CONNER, V.F., Saint Matthew, 555 Prospect Ave., Ridgefield, 07657. Tel: 201-945-3500; Fax: 201-945-3796.

South Bergen Region Deanery 7Very Rev. MICHAEL J. KREDER, V.F., St. Mary Parish, 91 Home Ave., Rutherford, 07070. Tel: 201-438-2200; Fax: 201-438-1098.

HUDSON COUNTY

North Hudson Deanery 8Very Rev. CARLO B.M. FORTUNIO, (Italy) V.F., Holy Redeemer, 569 - 65th St., West New York, 07093. Tel: 201-868-9444; Fax: 201-868-5944.

Central Hudson Region Deanery 9Very Rev. ALEXANDER M. SANTORA, V.F., Our Lady of Grace/St. Joseph, 400 Willow Ave., Hoboken, 07030. Tel: 201-659-0369; Fax: 201-659-5833.

Jersey City North Region Deanery 10Very Rev. NIGEL R. MOHAMMED, Saint Anne, 3545 Kennedy Blvd., Jersey City, 07307. Tel: 201-360-0838; Fax: 201-721-5996.

Jersey City Downtown Deanery 11Very Rev. JERZY R. ZASLONA, V.F., Holy Rosary, 344 Sixth St., Jersey City, 07302. Tel: 201-795-0120; Fax: 201-795-3230.

Jersey City South Deanery 12Rev. JUANCHO D. DE LEON, St. Aloysius, 691 W. Side Ave., Jersey City, 07304. Tel: 201-433-6365; Fax: 201-451-6438.

Bayonne Deanery 13Rev. PETER G. WEHRLE, Blessed Miriam Demjanovich, 326 Avenue C, Bayonne, 07002. Tel: 201-437-4090; Fax: 201-437-0388.

West Hudson Region Deanery 14Rev. JOSEPH A. MANCINI, St. Stephen, 141 Washington Ave., Kearny, 07032. Tel: 201-998-3314; Fax: 201-998-4924.

ESSEX COUNTY

West Essex Deanery 15Rev. ROBERT G. LAFERRERA, Our Lady of the Blessed Sacrament, 28 Livingston Ave., Roseland, 07068. Tel: 973-226-7288; Fax: 973-226-4893.

North Essex Deanery 16Very Rev. JOHN F. GORDON, V.F., St. Thomas the Apostle, 60 Byrd Ave., Bloomfield, 07003. Tel: 973-338-9190; Fax: 973-338-4224.

Central Essex Deanery 17Very Rev. JEAN MAX OSIAS, V.F., Holy Spirit/Our Lady of Help of Christians, 17 North Clinton St., East Orange, 07017. Tel: 973-673-1077; Fax: 973-676-6494.

South Essex Deanery 18Very Rev. FRANK J. ROCCHI, V.F., Good Shepherd Parish, 954 Stuyvesant Ave., Irvington, 07111. Tel: 973-375-8568; Fax: 973-375-7040.

North Newark Essex Deanery 19Very Rev. JAN SASIN, V.F., St. Francis Xavier, 243 Abington Ave., W., Newark, 07107. Tel: 973-482-8410; Fax: 973-485-7471.

Essex Central Newark Deanery 20Very Rev. PHILIP J. WATERS, O.S.B., V.F., St. Mary of the Immaculate Conception, 528 Martin Luther King Blvd., Newark, 07102. Tel: 973-792-5793; Fax: 973-643-6922.

Ironbound Deanery 21Very Rev. CELSO LUIZ MARTINS JR., C.Ss.R., V.F., St. James, 142 Jefferson St., Newark, 07105. Tel: 973-344-8322; Fax: 973-344-6158.

UNION COUNTY

Union Northwest Deanery 22Very Rev. JOHN M. MCCRONE, V.F., St. Rose of Lima, 50 Short Hills Ave., Short Hills, 07078. Tel: 973-379-3912; Fax: 973-379-6157.

Union North Deanery 23Very Rev. JAMES F. SPERA, M.Div., V.F., Assumption, 113 Chiego Pl., Roselle Park, 07204. Tel: 908-245-1107; Fax: 908-245-2789.

Union County Southeast Deanery 24Very Rev. IRENEUSZ PIERZCHALA, V.F., St. Theresa of the Child Jesus, 131 E. Edgar Rd., Linden, 07036. Tel: 908-862-1116; Fax: 908-862-2930.

Elizabeth Deanery 25Very Rev. DIEUSEUL ADAIN, (Haiti) V.F., Our Lady of the Most Holy Rosary and St. Michael, 52 Smith St., Elizabeth, 07201. Tel: 908-354-2454; Fax: 908-354-3207.

Union County Southwest Deanery 26Very Rev. FRANK ROSE, M.Div., V.F., St. Bernard & St. Stanislaus, 368 Summit Ave., Plainfield, 07062. Tel: 908-756-3393; Fax: 908-756-3059.

Advisory Bodies

College of Consultors—Members: His Eminence JOSEPH CARDINAL TOBIN, C.Ss.R., D.D.; Most Revs. JOHN W. FLESEY, S.T.D., D.D.; MANUEL A. CRUZ, D.D.; Rev. Msgrs. THOMAS P. NYDEGGER, Ed.D., M.Div., Vicar Gen. & Moderator of the Curia; ROBERT E. EMERY, J.C.L., M.A., V.E., E.V.; GREGORY J. STUDERUS, V.F., V.E., E.V.; RONALD J. ROZNIAK, V.E., V.G., P.A., Sec.; RENATO GRASSELLI, S.T.L.; TIMOTHY J. SHUGRUE; Revs. JOHN R. JOB; JOSEPH A. D'AMICO; MICHAEL J. REARDON, S.D.V.; JOSEPH D. GIRONE, V.F.; DAVID CAIXEIRO SANTOS.

Council of Priests—His Eminence JOSEPH CARDINAL TOBIN, C.Ss.R., D.D., Pres. Ex Officio Members: Most Revs. MANUEL A. CRUZ, D.D., Auxiliary Bishop & Regl. Bishop for Union County; JOHN W. FLESEY, S.T.D., D.D., Auxiliary Bishop & Regl. Bishop Emeritus for Bergen County; Rev. Msgrs. THOMAS P. NYDEGGER, Ed.D., M.Div., Vicar Gen. & Moderator of the Curia; EDWARD G. BRADLEY, Minister for Retired Priests; PETER SMUTELOVIC, J.C.D., Vicar for Canonical Affairs; ROBERT E. EMERY, J.C.L., M.A., V.E., E.V., Regl. Vicar for Essex County; GREGORY J. STUDERUS, V.F., V.E., E.V., Regl. Vicar for Hudson County; ROBERT F. COLEMAN, J.C.D., Minister to Priest Community at Seton Hall Univ.; Very Rev. JOHN J. PALADINO, Vicar for Clergy.

Appointed/Elected—Rev. Msgrs. BEAUBRUN ARDOUIN; JOSEPH R. CHAPEL, S.T.D.; RENATO GRASSELLI, S.T.L.; TIMOTHY J. SHUGRUE; Revs. YUVAN ARBEY ALVAREZ; JOSEPH J. ASTARITA; ZENON BOCZEK, S.D.S.; STEPHEN A. CAREY; ESTERMINIO CHICA; JOSEPH A. D'AMICO; Very Rev. ANTONIO F. DA SILVA, V.F.; Revs. LAWRENCE J. FAMA; ERIC W. FUCHS; GEORGE D. GILLEN; JOSEPH D. GIRONE, V.F.; MICHAEL A. HANLY, (Retired); Very Rev. GERALD T. HAHN, V.F.; Revs. JOHN R. JOB; RICHARD P. KWIATKOWSKI; JOSEPH KATO KALEMA; JAMES V. PAGNOTTA; DANIEL RAYMOND PETERSON; FREDERICK A. PFEIFER; ANDREW M. PRACHAR; MAURO PRIMAVERA; THOMAS PATRICK QUINN; MICHAEL J. REARDON, S.D.V.; DANIEL R. RODRIGUEZ; DAVID D. SANTOS; DENIS S. SURBAN; THOMAS THOTTUNGAL.

Archdiocesan Finance Council—Members: Rev. Msgr. THOMAS P. NYDEGGER, Ed.D., M.Div., Vicar Gen. & Moderator of the Curia; HENRY J. AMOROSO, Esq., Vice Chm.; ROBERT C. BUTLER; CHARLES C. CARELLA, Esq.; ANTHONY J. DENICOLA; BRIAN D. MCAULEY; W. PETER MCBRIDE; JOSEPH MCSWEENEY; GERALD NOLAN; MS. DENISE ROVER, L.H.S.; Rev. Msgr. RONALD J. ROZNIAK, V.E., V.G., P.A.; MS. LIZA M. WALSH, L.H.S., Esq.; MR. PAUL H. SIMPSON; MS. ANNE EVANS ESTABROOK; MR. JOHN SWIFT.

Priest Personnel Policy Board—Very Rev. JOHN J. PALADINO, Archbishop's Liaison. Ex Officio Members: Rev. Msgr. EDWARD G. BRADLEY; Rev. STANLEY GOMES, M.Div.; Very Rev. JOHN M. MCCRONE, V.F. Members: Rev. Msgr. PAUL L. BOCHICCHIO, (Retired); Revs. LAWRENCE J. FAMA; PEDRO BISMARCK CHAU; Rev. Msgrs. C. ANTHONY ZICCARDI, S.T.L., S.S.L.; EDWARD J. CIUBA, (Retired); DONALD E. GUENTHER, (Retired).

Diaconate Executive Committee—Deacon JOSEPH YANDOLI, Chm.

New Energies - Archdiocesan Implementation Team (New Energies Parish Transition Project)—Rev. TIMOTHY G. GRAFF, Chm., Tel: 973-497-4318; Fax: 973-497-4316; NANCY BARCKETT, Office Mgr. & Sec., Tel: 973-497-4319. Members: Revs. KEVIN E. CARTER; JOHN E. WASSELL; JOSEPH A. D'AMICO; OSCAR MARTIN; PAUL A. CANNARITO; ROBERT WOLFEE, M.Div.; Deacon KENNETH DIPAOLA; Sr. LINDA KLAISS, S.S.J.; MRS. GLADYS POZZA; CAROL ORLANDO; MARK HOWARD. Consultants: NANCY F. LYSTASH, L.H.S.; JOSEPH C. PESCATORE, K.C.H.S.; STEVEN BELLOISE, K.H.S.

Archdiocesan Offices and Agencies

Office of the Archbishop—Fax: 973-497-4018.

Chancellor—Tel: 973-497-4128. Sr. DONNA L. CIANGIO, O.P.

Secretary to the Archbishop—Rev. JASON J. MAKAROW, Tel: 973-497-4005.

Assistant to the Archbishop for Public Affairs—Rev. Msgr. CHRISTOPHER J. HYNES, Ed.S., Tel: 973-497-4107.

Executive Assistant to the Archbishop—MRS. ROSEANN BIASI-VAZQUEZ, Tel: 973-497-4006; Tel: 973-497-4006.

Office of the Vicar General & Moderator of the Curia—Tel: 973-497-4002; Fax: 973-497-4018. Rev. Msgr. THOMAS P. NYDEGGER, Ed.D., M.Div., Tel: 973-497-4002; Fax: 973-497-4018.

Executive Assistant to the Vicar General—LEOCADIA MATUSZCZAK, M.B.A., Tel: 973-497-4003.

N.B. Dispensation requests or questions regarding canonical matters can be directed to Rev. Msgr. Frank Del Prete, 171 Clifton Ave., Newark, NJ 07104-0500.

Office of Child and Youth Protection—MR. JAMES GOODNESS, K.H.S., M.A., Coord. Review Bd., Tel: 973-497-4186; KAREN CLARK, Dir. Safe Environment Prog., Tel: 973-497-4254; Email: clarkkar@rcan.org.

Victims Assistance Coordinator—WENDY PIERSON, Tel: 201-407-3256; Fax: 973-497-4001.

Review Board/Safe Environment Coordinator—YOLANDA MILCZARSKI, Tel: 973-497-4012.

Advocate Publishing Corp.—Publisher of "New Jersey Catholic" (magazine of the Archdiocese of Newark); "The Catholic Advocate" (print and online newspaper of the Archdiocese of Newark); "New Jersey Catolico" (Spanish language newspaper); annual Directory & Almanac Tel: 973-497-4200 Main Office; Fax: 973-497-4192.

MARGE PEARSON-MCCUE, Dir. Advertising & Oper., Tel: 973-497-4201; Email: pearsoma@rcan.org; Rev. EDINSON E. RAMIREZ, Editor, New Jersey Catolico; KELLY MARSICANO, Assoc. Publisher, Editor, New Jersey Catholic; MS. MELISSA MCNALLY, Editor, The Catholic Advocate; MARK CHRISCO, Subscription Coord.; MS. MARILYN SMITH, Production Supvr.

Office of Banking and Investments—MATTHEW PHELAN, Dir., Tel: 973-497-4069; Fax: 973-497-4083; Email: phelanma@rcan.org.

Office of African American, African, and Caribbean Apostolate—Rev. EMEKA OKWUOSA, Coord., Tel: 973-497-4304.

Campus Ministry—Tel: 973-497-4305. Rev. JAMES N. CHERN, Dir.; LISA ABRUSIA, Office Asst.

Catechetical Office—MR. RONALD L. PIHOKKER, M.A., Dir., Tel: 973-497-4291; Email: pihokkro@rcan.org.

Central Office of Catholic Cemeteries—171 Clifton Ave., Newark, 07104. ANDREW P. SCHAFER, K.H.S., CCCE, Exec. Dir., Tel: 973-497-7975.

Mausoleum Office—Tel: 973-497-7988. ANDREW P. SCHAFER, K.H.S., Exec. Dir., Tel: 973-497-7975; Email: schafean@rcan.org.

Archdiocesan Cemeteries—COLONIA: St. Gertrude; MAHWAH: Maryrest; EAST HANOVER: Gate of Heaven; EAST ORANGE: Holy Sepulchre, St. Mary; FRANKLIN LAKES: Christ the King; JERSEY CITY: Holy Name, Saint Peter; NORTH ARLINGTON: Holy Cross; RIVER VALE: St. Andrew; TENAFLY: Mount Carmel.

Parochial Cemeteries—NEWARK: Mount Olivet; BELLEVILLE: St. Peter's; BLOOMFIELD: Mount Olivet; CLARK: St. Mary's; FORT LEE: Madonna; HACKENSACK: St. Joseph's; HOHOKUS: St. Luke's; LINDEN: Mount Calvary; LYNDHURST: St. Joseph's; ORANGE: St. John's; PLAINFIELD: St. Mary's; SHORT HILLS: St. Rose of Lima; SUMMIT: St. Teresa's; UPPER MONTCLAIR: Immaculate Conception; ELIZABHETH: St. Mary; LODI: St. Francis de Sales.

Office of Clergy Personnel—Tel: 973-497-4220; Fax: 973-497-4219. Very Rev. JOHN J. PALADINO, Exec. Dir., Tel: 973-497-4222; SIEGRID EVERS, Administrative Coord., Tel: 973-497-4220.

Adjunct Clergy Personnel—Fax: 973-497-4180. Rev. STANLEY GOMES, M.Div., Asst. to Exec. Dir., Tel: 973-497-4374; TERESA GRILLO, Administrative Asst., Tel: 973-497-4225; Fax: 973-497-4180.

Continuing Education and Formation of Priests—Very Rev. JOHN M. MCCRONE, V.F., Dir., Tel: 973-497-4218; TERESA GRILLO, Administrative Asst., Tel: 973-497-4225; Fax: 973-497-4180.

Office of the Permanent Diaconate—Rev. JAMES V. TETI, J.C.L., S.T.B., Dir. Selection & Deacon Formation, Annunciation, 50 W. Midland Ave., Paramus, 07652-2140. Tel: 201-261-6322; Deacon JOHN J. MCKENNA, K.H.S., Dir. Deacon Personnel & Vice Chancellor, Tel: 973-497-4125.

Ministry to Retired Priests—Rev. Msgr. EDWARD G. BRADLEY, Dir., Tel: 973-669-9561; Tel: 973-497-4224; KARIN WALTERS, Administrative Asst., Tel: 973-497-4226.

Office of Communications and Public Relations—MR. JAMES GOODNESS, K.H.S., M.A., Dir. & Vice Chancellor, Tel: 973-497-4186; Fax: 973-497-4185; Email: goodneja@rcan.org.

Office of Information Technology Services—ROBERT J. KENNELLY, K.H.S., Chief Technology Officer, Tel: 973-497-4161; Fax: 973-497-4277; Email: kennelro@rcan.org.

Office of Archdiocesan Counsel—Carella, Byrne, Cecchi, Olstein, Brody and Agnello, P.C., Archdiocesan Counsel. *5 Becker Farm Rd., Ste. 2, Roseland, 07068-1739.* Tel: 973-994-1700; Fax: 973-994-1744. CHARLES M. CARELLA, Esq.

Delegate for Religious—Sr. PATRICIA WORMANN, O.P., Delegate & Dir. Vocations for Rel. Life, Tel: 973-497-4582; Tel: 973-497-4368; Fax: 973-497-4228; Fax: 973-497-4369; KARIN WALTERS, Administrative Asst., Tel: 973-497-4226; Email: walterka@rcan.org.

Office of Development—MR. IVAN AROCHO, Acting Dir., Tel: 973-497-4332; Fax: 973-497-4031; Email: ivan.arocho@rcan.org; Web: www.rcan.org/development. Annual Appeal and General Inquiries: Tel: 973-497-4091; Tel: 973-497-4126.

Parish Stewardship and the Annual Appeal—ALLAN CABALLERO, Assoc. Dir., Tel: 973-497-4126; Email: allan.caballero@rcan.org.

Office of Evangelization—Fax: 973-497-4317. Very Rev. JOHN F. GORDON, V.F., Coord., Tel: 973-497-4353; Email: gordonjo@rcan.org; MAUREEN SRINIVASA, Ministry Assoc., Tel: 973-497-4137; Email: srinivma@rcan.org.

Family Life Ministries—Fax: 973-497-4317. Deacon JAMES DETURA, Dir. Family Life, Tel: 973-497-4324; NANCY DELLISANTI, Pre-Cana Reservations, Tel: 973-497-4328; Web: www.rcan.org/famlife/pre-cana.htm (Pre-Cana registration online).

Ministry to the Bereaved, Separated, Divorced, Widowed—Tel: 973-497-4327. LAUREN EGAN, Assoc. Dir., Email: eganlaur@rcan.org; VACANT, Chap., Widows, Widowers & Bereaved.

Hispanic Family Life Ministries—YAMILKA GENAO, Assoc. Dir., Tel: 973-497-4326.

Couples for Christ—Rev. ED JOCSON, Spiritual Dir., Tel: 973-985-1592; RODGER SANTOS, Area Dir., CFC, NJ, Tel: 848-459-8019; Email: rjusa@aol.com.

Focolare Movement—MARIAPOLIS LUMINOSA, 200 Cardinal Rd., Hyde Park, NY 12538. Tel: 973-726-6224. Local Coordinators: JIM MILWAY; MARY JANE MILWAY, Tel: 973-726-6224; Web: www.focolare.us; CECILIA FUENTES, Tel: 718-828-1969; J.P. SLEE, Tel: 212-388-9498.

Engaged Encounter Registration—LINDA ALEXANDER, Sec., Tel: 973-497-4323.

Worldwide Marriage Encounter—Tel: 800-823-5683; Web: www.wwme.org. Newark Ecclesial Team: PETER TORPIE; LYNNE TORPIE, Tel: 201-262-6037. Application Couple: MICHAEL TURCO; JANET TURCO, Tel: 973-427-7016.

Natural Family Planning—Coordinating Couple: JIM CHERREY; JILL CHERREY, Tel: 973-497-4325; Email: jillc@joyfilledmarriagenj.org.

Office of Divine Worship—Fax: 973-497-4314. Revs. THOMAS A. DENTE, K.H.S., Dir., Liturgical Formation Progs. & Resources, Tel: 973-497-4347; Email: dentetom@rcan.org; JOSEPH A. MANCINI, Dir. Pontifical Liturgies & Archdiocesan Ceremonies; ARMAND MANTIA, Dir. R.C.I.A., Tel: 973-497-4346; JOAN M. CONROY, Assoc. Dir., Office of Divine Worship, Tel: 973-497-4343; Fax: 973-497-4314; Email: conroyjo@rcan.org; Rev. Msgr. CHARLES W. GUSMER, S.T.D., V.E., Liturgical Consultant, (Retired), Tel: 908-464-7600; JOHN J. MILLER, Music Ministry, Tel: 973-484-2400; Email: millerjo@rcan.org; Rev. Msgr. RICHARD F. GRONCKI, Liturgical Consultant, (Retired), Tel: 973-484-4600; Tel: 973-497-4344; Email: gronckri@rcan.org; REGINA CHAMBERLAIN, Administrative/Liturgical Asst., Tel; 973-497-4345; Email: chambere@rcan.org; Rev. THOMAS B. IWANOWSKI, Liturgical Consultant. Book Orders: Tel: 973-497-4361.

Office of Finance—Fax: 973-497-4320. JOSEPH C. PESCATORE, K.C.H.S., CFO, Tel: 973-497-4560; Email: pescatjo@rcan.org; DANIELLE O'SULLIVAN, Exec. Administrative Asst., Tel: 973-497-4051; Fax: 973-497-4320; Email: osullida@rcan.org; STEPHANIE M. ALCUINO, Controller, Tel: 973-497-4716; Email: alcuinst@rcan.org; ARMILEE SITON, Asst. Controller, Tel: 973-497-4067; Email: armilee.siton@rcan.org.

Hispanic Apostolate—Most Rev. MANUEL A. CRUZ, D.D., Vicar, Tel: 973-497-4009; Deacon ASTERIO VELASCO, Coord., Tel: 973-497-4335; Email: velascas@rcan.org.

Department of Social Concerns—Rev. TIMOTHY G. GRAFF, Dir., Tel: 973-497-4318; Email: grafftim@rcan.org.

Public Policy Committee of the New Jersey Catholic Conference—Rev. TIMOTHY G. GRAFF, Social Concerns Rep.

Office of Human Resources—Fax: 973-497-4103. Deacon JOHN J. MCKENNA, K.H.S., Exec. Dir. & Vice Chancellor, Tel: 973-497-4125; Email: mckennjo@rcan.org; RAMONA FLORES, Dir. Human Resources, Tel: 973-497-4026; Email: floresra@rcan.org; DENNIS MILLER, Dir. Employee Benefits, Tel: 973-497-4095; Email: dennis.miller@rcan.org; MARIA JOYNER, Benefits Admin., Tel: 973-497-4089; Tel: 973-497-4092; Email: joynerma@rcan.org; ELENA SKINNER, Pension Supvr., Tel: 973-497-4089; Email: skinneel@rcan.org.

Office Services/Mailroom—
Tel: 973-497-4035 Mailroom. LUCIA LOPEZ, Oper. Supvr., Tel: 973-497-4045; Email: lopezluc@rcan.org; ELIZABETH RODRIGUEZ, Supvr. Mailroom, Tel: 973-497-4035; Email: rodrigel@rcan.org.

Metropolitan Tribunal—Special Delegate of the Archbishop for nuptial matters and N.B. Dispensation requests or questions regarding canonical matters can be directed to Rev. Msgr. Frank Del Prete, J.C.D. at 973-497-4148; 171 Clifton Ave., Newark, NJ 07104; Email: delprefr@rcan.org. Revs. ROBERT G. MCBRIDE, J.C.L., J.V., Judicial Vicar, Tel: 973-497-4145; Email: mcbridro@rcan.org; GIOVANNI RIZZO, M.Div., J.C.L., Adjutant Judicial Vicar, Tel: 973-497-4149.

Full-time Staff—Revs. GIOVANNI RIZZO, M.Div., J.C.L.; RAPHAEL LEE, J.C.L.; CARMINE RIZZI, M.Div., J.C.L.

Archdiocesan Judges—Revs. JOHN J. CRYAN, M.Div.; PAUL A. CANNARIATO; Very Rev. FRANK ROSE, M.Div., V.F.; Revs. ROBERT WOLFEE, M.Div.; RAPHAEL LEE, J.C.L.; ROBERT G. MCBRIDE, J.C.L., J.V.; GIOVANNI RIZZO, M.Div., J.C.L.

Defenders of the Bond—Rev. Msgrs. FRANK G. DEL PRETE, J.C.D., Promoter of Justice; MARK CONDON, J.C.L.; DR. CHRISTINA HIP-FLORES; Rev. CARMINE RIZZI, M.Div., J.C.L.

Part-time Staff/Advocates/Procurators—Revs. PAUL A. CANNARIATO; ROBERT WOLFEE, M.Div.; VINCENT D'AGOSTINO; LEANDRO NICOLAS TORRES MAS; Deacons JOHN J. MCKENNA, K.H.S.; JORGE A. MONTALVO; FRANCISCO E. NOH; DANIEL O'NEILL; RAJGOPAL K. SRINIVASA; MR. FRANK CASTENBADER; MARINA PERNA; Deacon LAURENCE BONNEMERE; Rev. JACK CRYAN; Deacons REYNALDO ESCALON; PEDRO HERRERA; Revs. MAURO PRIMAVERA; CESAR QUINONES; FRANCISCO J. RODRIGUEZ.

Notaries—SANDRA PERRINI; JOHN WALSH, Fax: 973-497-4138.

Secretarial Staff—ROSE MARIE FITZGERALD; NANCY I. NEGRON.

Multicultural Affairs—Fax: 973-497-4317. Rev. Msgr. WILLIAM J. REILLY, V.F., Coord., Tel: 973-497-4013; Very Rev. JOHN F. GORDON, V.F., Assoc. Coord., Tel: 973-497-4353.

Brazilian Apostolate—Saint James, 143 Madison St., Newark, 07105. Tel: 973-344-8322. Rev. CLEMENT M. KRUG, C.Ss.R., Coord.

Chinese Apostolate—VACANT.

Filipino Apostolate—St. Joseph of the Palisades, 6401 Palisade Ave., West New York, 07093. Rev. ERNESTO C. TIBAY, Coord.

Croatian Apostolate—Holy Redeemer, 6502 Jackson St., West New York, 07093. Rev. GIORDANO BELANICH, Coord.

Haitian Apostolate—Saint Leo, 103 Myrtle Ave., Irvington, 07111. Tel: 973-372-1272. Rev. Msgr. BEAUBRUN ARDOUIN, Coord.

Asian-Indian Apostolate—Saint Paul the Apostle, 14 Greenville Ave., Jersey City, 07305. Rev. THEESMAS PANKIRAJ, Coord., Tel: 201-433-8500.

Liaison to the Irish Community—Seton Hall Prep, 120 Northfield Ave., West Orange, 07052.
Tel: 973-325-6624. Rev. Msgr. MICHAEL E. KELLY, M.A.

Italian Apostolate—Our Lady of Mount Carmel Rectory, 259 Oliver St., Newark, 07105.
Tel: 973-589-2090. Rev. Msgr. JOSEPH F. AMBROSIO, V.F., Coord.

Korean Apostolate—St. Michael, 19 E. Central Blvd., Palisades Park, 07650. Rev. MINHYUN CHO, Coord., Tel: 973-763-1170.

Nigerian IBO Catholic Community—Blessed Sacrament/Saint Charles Borromeo, 15 Van Ness Pl., Newark, 07108. Tel: 973-824-6548. Rev. ERASMUS OKERE, Coord.

Polish/Slavic Apostolate—Rev. ANDRZEJ OSTASZEWSKI, Ph.D., Coord., St. Casimir, 164 Nichols St., Newark, 07105-2596. Tel: 973-344-2743.

Portuguese Apostolate—Our Lady of Fatima, 403 Spring St., Elizabeth, 07201. Tel: 908-355-3810. Rev. JOSEPH E.S. DOS SANTOS, Coord.

Vietnamese Apostolate—Saint Michael Rectory, 252 Ninth St., Jersey City, 07302. Tel: 201-434-8500. Rev. JOSEPH MINH NGUYEN, Coord.

Parish Business Services—NANCY F. LYSTASH, L.H.S., Exec. Dir. & Vice Chancellor, Tel: 973-497-4074; Fax: 973-497-4320; Email: lystasna@rcan.org; ARLENE WISNIOWSKI, Business Systems Analyst, Tel: 973-497-4306; Email: wisnioar@rcan.org.

Office of Parish Internal Audit—Fax: 973-497-4320. THERESE A. KROPP, Asst. Dir., Tel: 973-497-4073; Email: kroppter@rcan.org.

Office of School Business Services—DONNA QUINN, Dir., Tel: 973-497-4211; Email: quinndon@rcan.org; JULIAN FERREIRA, Coord. School Business Svcs., Tel: 973-497-4075; HEIDI KOPALA, Sr. Auditor Regl. & Parish High School Finances, Tel: 973-497-4078.

Office of Research and Planning—MARK HOWARD, Dir., Tel: 973-497-4024; Tel: 973-497-4024; Fax: 973-497-4029; Email: howard@rcan.org.

Ministry to People on the Move—

Apostleship of the Air—Newark International Airport Chaplaincy, P.O. Box 2220, Newark, 07114. Tel: 973-961-0260. Rev. DAVID J. BARATELLI, Ed.D., Chap.

Apostleship of the Sea—Newark International Airport Chaplaincy, Stella Maris Chapel, 114 Corbin St., Port Newark, 07101.
Tel: 973-589-7946. Rev. JOHN F. CORBETT, Dir.

Office of Property Management Administration—
Fax: 973-497-4362. STEVEN BELLOISE, K.H.S., Exec. Dir., Tel: 973-497-4118; Fax: 973-497-4362; Email: belloist@rcan.org; NASSAR SHABO, Dir. Con-

struction, Tel: 973-497-4120; Email: shabonas@rcan.org; Kevin Comp, Dir. Facility Operations, Tel: 973-497-4117; Email: compkevi@rcan.org; Teresa Dobbs-Robinson, Administrative Sec., Tel: 973-497-4110; Email: dobbster@rcan.org; Frank Valliciergo, Project Mgr., Tel: 973-497-4106; Email: vallicfr@rcan.org; Kathleen Dodds, Sec., Tel: 973-497-4250; Email: kathleen.dodds@rcan.org; Valentina Baldessarre, Ecclesiastical Project Mgr./Patrimony, Tel: 973-497-4116; Email: baldesva@rcan.org; Emet Huelgas, Real Estate Mgr., Hudson & Union Counties, Tel: 973-497-4082; Email: huelgaem@rcan.org; Joseph Lucia, Administrative Asst., Tel: 973-497-4121; Email: luciajos@rcan.org; Jennifer Negron, Project Asst., Tel: 973-497-4097; Email: jennifer.negron@rcan.org; Yves Auborg, Construction Project Mgr., Tel: 973-497-4112; Email: auboryv@rcan.org; Martha Rodriguez, Real Estate Mgr., Essex County, Tel: 973-497-4123; Email: rodrigma@rcan.org; Patricia Emory, Construction Admin., Tel: 973-497-4105; Email: emorypat@rcan.org; Marilyn Pena, Property Real Estate Project Mgr., Bergen County, Tel: 973-497-4136; Email: penamari@rcan.org; Ursula Rivera, Sustainable Energy Coord./ Real Estate Mgr., Tel: 973-497-4132; Email: riveraur@rcan.org; Curtis St. Louis, Asst. Construction Project Mgr., Tel: 973-497-4114; Email: stlouicu@rcan.org. Maintenance Help Desk: Tel: 973-497-4333.

Respect Life Office—Archdiocese of Newark, 171 Clifton Ave., Newark, 07104. Ms. Cheryl Riley, Dir., Tel: 973-497-4350; Email: rileyche@rcan.org; Patricia Decker, Assoc. Dir., Tel: 973-497-4348; Email: patricia.decker@rcan.org.

Risk Management, Insurance Services and Business Administration—Fax: 973-497-4313. Joseph A. Frank, Exec. Dir., Tel: 973-497-4041; Email: frankjoe@rcan.org; Donna M. Wrobel, Asst. Dir., Tel: 973-497-4044; Email: wrobeldo@rcan.org; Diannah P. Hedgebeth, Account Svc. Mgr., Tel: 973-497-4040.

Office of the Superintendent of Schools/Secretariat for Education—Tel: 973-497-4260; Fax: 973-497-4249. Dr. Margaret A. Dames, Supt. Schools/Sec. Catholic Education, Tel: 973-497-4253; Email: damesmar@rcan.org.

Assistant Superintendents for Secondary Schools—Mr. John O'Neil, M.A., Assoc. Supt. Secondary Schools.

Assistant Superintendents for Elementary Schools—Sisters Patricia Butler, S.C., M.A., Assoc. Supt. Elementary Admin., (Essex and Union Counties); Marie Gagliano, M.P.F., M.A., Asst. Supt., (Hudson and Bergen).

Assistant Superintendent of Curriculum, Instruction and Assessment—Ms. Barbara Dolan; June Butchko, Prog. Asst., Curriculum & Assessment, (Asst. to Barbara Dolan). Directors: Gloria Castucci, M.A., Early Childhood; Karen Mirrow-Drew, M.S.W., S.B.A., School Svcs.; Sr. Patricia Butler, S.C., M.A., Assoc. Supt. Elementary Schools; Mary McElroy, Esq., NJ Network of Catholic School Families; Ann Oro, K-12 Instructional Technology; Andrea Koenig-Feldman, Devel. & Event Planning Asst., Email: feldmaan@rcan.org; Eileen O'Neill, Coord. Special Educ. Svc.

Vicar for Pastoral Life—Fax: 973-497-4317. Very Rev. John F. Gordon, V.F., Vicar for Pastoral Life, Tel: 973-497-4353; Email: gordonjo@rcan.org; Marissa Espinosa, Administrative Asst., Tel: 973-497-4013.

Pastoral Ministries with Persons with Disabilities—Anne Masters, M.A., Dir., Tel: 973-497-4309; Email: anne.masters.@rcan.org.

Pastoral Ministry with the Deaf—Gina Maria Correia, Dir., St. John Church, 22 Mulberry St., Newark, 07102.

Vocations Office—Seton Hall Univ., Immaculate Conception Seminary, 400 S. Orange Ave., South Orange, 07079. Tel: 973-313-6190; Web: www.newpriestnj.org. Rev. Eugenio P. De La Rama, Dir.; Mr. Matthew Higgins, M.A., Assoc. Dir., Email: higginma@rcan.org.

Vocations Board—Revs. Eugenio P. De La Rama; John J. Chadwick, S.T.D.; Very Rev. Sean A. Manson, V.F.; Rev. Manuel Duenas; Mr. Matthew Higgins, M.A.; Revs. Robert K. Suszko, M.B.A., M.Div.; Michael G. Ward; Deacon Thomas Shubeck; Mrs. Tara Hart; Mr. John Mailley.

Youth and Young Adult Ministries—499 Belgrove Ave., Kearny, 07032. Tel: 201-998-0088; Fax: 201-299-0801; Web: www.newarkoym.com. Thomas G. Conboy, Dir., Tel: 201-998-0088, Ext. 4146; Email: conboyth@rcan.org; Rev. Timothy G. Graff, Archdiocesan Chap., Girl Scouts, Email: grafftim@rcan.org; Mrs. Geraldine Ricci-Menegolla, Office Mgr. & Exec. Sec., Tel: 201-998-0088, Ext. 4154; Email: ricciger@rcan.org; Rev. Eugene J. Field, Archdiocesan Chap., Boy Scouts; Mr. Rich Donovan, Assoc. Dir., Events, Camp, Athletics, & Scouting, Tel: 201-998-0088, Ext. 4150; Email: donovari@rcan.org; Mrs. Maria Santamaria, Finance Sec., Tel: 201-998-0088, Ext. 4144; Tel: 201-998-0088, Ext. 4144; Email: santamar@rcan.org; Brian Caldwell, Assoc. Dir. Retreats & Challenge Course, Tel: 201-998-0088, Ext. 4153; Email: caldwebr@rcan.org; Rev. Esterminio Chica, Assoc. Dir., Parish Outreach & Formation, Tel: 201-998-0088, Ext. 4147; Email: chicaest@rcan.org.

Catholic Scouting—

Boy Scouts/Girl Scouts/Catholic Committee on Scouting—499 Belgrove Dr., Kearny, 07032. Tel: 201-998-0088; Fax: 201-299-0801; Web: www.newarkoym.com. Mr. Rich Donovan, Assoc. Dir., Events, Camp, Athletics, & Scouting, Tel: 201-998-0088, Ext. 4150; Email: donovari@rcan.org; Revs. Timothy G. Graff, Archdiocesan Chap., Girl Scouts, Tel: 973-497-4341; Tel: 201-998-0088, Ext. 4144; Email: grafftim@rcan.org; Eugene J. Field, Archdiocesan Chap., Boy Scouts, Tel: 201-998-0088, Ext. 4144.

CYO Youth Retreat Center—499 Belgrove Dr., Kearny, 07032. Tel: 201-998-0088; Fax: 201-299-0801; Web: www.newarkoym.com. Thomas G. Conboy, Dir., Tel: 201-998-0088, Ext. 4140.

Catholic Charities of the Archdiocese of Newark—Administration—590 N. 7th St., Newark, 07107. Tel: 973-596-4100; Fax: 973-596-7950. Rev. Msgr. Robert J. Fuhrman, Chm. Bd. Trustees; Mr. John Westervelt, B.A., Pres. & CEO, Tel: 973-596-3984.

Catholic Charities of the Archdiocese of Newark—Main automated attendant number Tel: 973-596-4100. Joycelynn J. Murray, Exec. Asst. to CEO, 590 N. 7th St., Newark, 07107. Tel: 973-266-7989; Fax: 973-266-7950.

Mount Carmel Guild Behavioral Health System—Mr. John Westervelt, B.A., CEO, Tel: 973-596-3984; Ms. Elizabeth A. McClendon, A.C.S.W., L.C.S.W., Assoc. Exec. Dir., Tel: 973-266-7992; Fax: 973-266-7950.

Catholic Charities - Programs—

Children and Family Services Division—Lesley Moore, L.C.S.W., Div. Mgr., 249 Virginia Ave., Jersey City, 07304. Tel: 201-798-9957; Fax: 201-333-4425.

Children & Family Services Division Office—Vacant.

West Side Children's Counseling Center—249 Virginia Ave., Jersey City, 07304. To Access Services: Suzy Takvorian, Screener, Tel: 201-798-2165; Tel: 201-798-9900; Fax: 201-333-4211.

Intensive Family Support Services—Iskra Gomez, L.C.S.W., Prog. Mgr., 249 Virginia Ave., Jersey City, 07304. Tel: 201-798-9925; Fax: 201-333-4211.

Intensive In-Home Family Counseling—Susan Takvorian, Prog. Mgr., 249 Virginia Ave., Jersey City, 07304. Tel: 201-798-9921; Fax: 201-333-4211.

Family and Adoption Services—Patricia Chiarello, M.S.W., Prog. Mgr., 2201 Bergenline Ave., Union City, 07087. Tel: 201-246-7379; Fax: 201-991-3771.

Hudson Mobile Response and Stabilization Services (MRSS)—Patricia Valdivia, Prog. Mgr., 249 Virginia Ave., Jersey City, 07304. Tel: 201-798-7452; Fax: 201-333-4099.

Family Resource Center—Gilma Garcia, M.S.W., Prog. Mgr., 249 Virginia Ave., Jersey City, 07304. Tel: 201-798-9904; Tel: 201-798-9900; Fax: 201-333-4211.

Partners With Parents and Families—Patricia Chiarello, M.S.W., Prog. Mgr., 2201 Bergenline Ave., Union City, 07087. Tel: 201-246-7379; Fax: 201-991-3771.

Partnership for Children—37 Evergreen Pl., East Orange, 07018. Shelley Steinberg, L.C.S.W., Prog. Mgr., Tel: 973-266-7983; Fax: 973-266-7970.

Providence Place—249 Virginia Ave., Jersey City, 07304. Tel: 201-433-1832; Fax: 201-433-4980. Christina Acosta, Prog. Mgr.

Child Protective Services & In-Home Hispanic Family Services—Dawn Glasgow, L.C.S.W., Prog. Mgr., 505 South Ave. E., Cranford, 07016. Tel: 908-497-3946; Fax: 908-276-1067.

Connecting Youth—505 South Ave. E., Cranford, 07016. Tel: 908-497-3946; Fax: 908-276-1067. Dawn Glasgow, L.C.S.W., Prog. Mgr.

School Social Work Services—Shelley Steinberg, L.C.S.W., Prog. Mgr., 37 Evergreen Place, East Orange, 07018. Tel: 973-266-7983; Fax: 973-266-7970.

Strong Futures—Kathy Elias, Prog. Mgr., 511 Monastery Place, Union City, 07087. Tel: 201-864-2290; Fax: 201-770-1692.

Supportive Services for Veterans Families (SSVF), Essex County—481 Sanford Ave., Newark, 07106. Lakisha Stewart, Prog. Supvr., Tel: 973-399-1145; Tel: 201-452-3963; Fax: 973-399-1557.

SSVF, Bergen County—57 Pink St., Hackensack, 07801. Lorena Libreros, Case Mgr., Tel: 908-612-2491; Anna Rizzo, Case Mgr. Asst., Tel: 973-220-5749; Fax: 201-441-9423.

SSVF, Essex County—37 Evergreen Pl., East Orange, 07018. Karolyn Mora, Case Mgr., Tel: 973-399-1333; Brianna Williams, Case Mgr. Asst., Tel: 973-266-7958; Adria Goldenkranz, Outreach Worker, Tel: 973-266-7968; Taina Rodriguez, Outreach Worker, Tel: 973-266-7959; Fax: 973-399-1557.

SSVF Hudson County—285 Magnolia Ave., Jersey City, 07306. Briana Washington, Case Mgr., Tel: 201-395-5443; Tel: 201-395-5441; Anna Rizzo, Case Mgr. Asst., Tel: 201-395-5441; Fax: 201-239-9580.

SSVF Union County—505 South Ave., E., Cranford, 07016. Johnia Osias, Case Mgr., Tel: 908-497-3940; Maricarmen Richter, Case Mgr. Asst., Tel: 908-497-3938; Fax: 908-497-3958.

DCA Housing Counseling Program—505 South Ave. E., Cranford, 07016. Kerri Brown, M.S.W., Supvr., Tel: 862-229-4469; Cell: 908-603-0857; Emma Papiol-Izquierdo, Housing Counselor, 2201 Bergenline Ave., Union City, 07087. Cell: 973-902-3462; Fax: 201-617-1683; Shirley Hill, Prog. Asst., 505 South Ave. E., Cranford, 07016. Tel: 908-603-0858; Cell: 862-229-4468; Fax: 908-276-0549; Christine Opt Hof, CCUSA DCA Housing Counselor, 37 Evergreen Pl., East Orange, 07018. Cell: 973-902-7356 DCA; Tel: 973-266-7964 CCUSA; Marayah Costa, CCUSA Housing Counselor, 37 Evergreen Pl., East Orange, 07018. Tel: 973-266-7942; Cell: 862-233-3293; Fax: 973-676-0172; Denise Bustamante, Prog. Asst., 37 Evergreen Pl., East Orange, 07018. Tel: 862-229-4464; Cell: 973-266-7944; Fax: 973-676-0172.

Workforce Development Division—321 Central Ave., Newark, 07103. Sandra Fils, Div. Dir., Tel: 973-268-3162; Fax: 973-350-0790.

Workforce Development - SAIF—Sophia Davis, Prog. Mgr., 37 Evergreen Pl., East Orange, 07018. Tel: 973-266-7984; Fax: 973-266-7990; Reginald Holding Jr., Prog. Mgr. Middlesex/Union, Tel: 973-266-7993; Ivette Davis, Administrative Asst., Tel: 973-266-7946.

SAIF: Middlesex/Union—37 Evergreen Pl., East Orange, 07018. Reginald Holding Jr., Prog. Mgr., Tel: 973-266-7993. Intensive Case Managers: Rachid Taylor, Tel: 973-266-7999; A'Nijaah Hollaway, Tel: 973-266-7994; Shacha Dias, Tel: 973-266-7965; Fax: 973-266-7990.

Workforce Development - Boland Training Center—Sandra Fils, 321 Central Ave., Newark, 07103. Tel: 973-268-3162; Fax: 973-350-0790. Union City: 2201 Bergenline Ave., Union City, 07087. Tel: 201-325-4800; Fax: 201-601-0490; Daniella Hincapie, Prog. Mgr., Tel: 201-325-4800, Ext. 4806; Armando Rivera, Displaced Homemaker, Tel: 201-325-4800, Ext. 4836; Wendy García, Case Mgr. Refugee Prog., Tel: 201-325-4800, Ext. 4801; Mounir Samaran, ESL/GED Instructor, Tel: 201-325-4800, Ext. 4824; Laverne Butler, ESL Instructor, Tel: 201-325-4800, Ext. 4812; Luis Andrade, Office Technology Instructor, Tel: 201-325-4800.

Supported Employment Program—Harry Frazier, M.S.W., Prog. Mgr., Tel: 201-558-3789; Michelle Bravo, Vocational Counselor, Tel: 201-558-3793.

Housing Division—615 Grove St., Jersey City, 07310. Rose Howard, Div. Dir., Tel: 201-653-3366, Ext. 121301; Minerva Perez, Admin. Asst., Tel: 201-653-3366, Ext. 121304; Fax: 201-653-0370.

St. Lucy Single Person Shelter—(Men and Women) *619 Grove St., Jersey City, 07310.* Laurie Cherry, Acting Prog. Mgr., Tel: 201-656-7201; Fax: 201-653-0370.

PATH Outreach - Homeless Street Outreach PATH Train Stations—(Men and Women). *619 Grove St., Jersey City, 07310.* Rose Howard, Div. Dir., Tel: 201-653-3366, Ext. 121301; Fax: 201-656-0412.

Canaan House—(HIV/AIDS) (Permanent Housing for individuals & families with HIV/AIDS). Lance Kearny, Prog. Mgr., 389 Bergen Ave.,

Jersey City, 07304. Tel: 201-434-3939; Fax: 201-432-4223.

Franciska Residence—(HIV/AIDS) (Transitional Residence for single men). JAMES SMITH, Prog. Mgr., 615 Grove St., Jersey City, 07310. Tel: 201-653-3366, Ext. 302; Fax: 201-653-3070.

Hope House—(Emergency Shelter) (Women and Children). LILLYBETH RAMIREZ, Prog. Mgr., 246 Second St., Jersey City, 07302. Tel: 201-420-1220; Fax: 201-420-1825.

St. Jude Oasis—612, 614, 616, 618 & 620 Grove St., Jersey City, 07310. ROSE HOWARD, Div. Dir., Tel: 201-656-7201, Ext. 121205; Fax: 201-656-0412.

St. Rocco Emergency Family Shelter—(Women and Children). *368 S. 7th St., Newark, 07103.* MAKAGBE SWARAY, Prog. Mgr., Tel: 973-286-4175; Fax: 973-242-2864.

St. Bridget Residence—(AIDS/HIV) Support/ Outreach Center Transitional Housing & Emergency Shelter Good Shepherd (Permanent Housing for HIV/AIDS Men). *404 University Ave., Newark, 07102.* SHRONICA THOMPSON, Prog. Mgr., Tel: 973-799-0484, Ext. 202; Fax: 973-799-0486.

Hudson County, Visually Impaired Socialization Program—IVIS L. ALVAREZ, M.A., 2201 Bergenline Ave., Union City, 07087. Tel: 201-325-4811; Fax: 201-601-0490.

Hudson County Prevention, Information, and Education Services for Seniors (P.I.E.S. for Seniors)—505 South Ave. E., Cranford, 07016. Tel: 908-497-3953; Fax: 908-709-9580. ALICIA BOONE, Prog. Mgr.

Hudson County Jail (Men's Substance Abuse Progran & HIV Rapid Testing)—

Union County Jail (HIV Rapid Testing & Ryan White HIV Discharge Planning)—(Women's Substance Abuse Program, Ryan White HIV Discharge Planning Program & HIV Rapid Testing Program). ALICIA BOONE, Prog. Mgr., 505 South Ave. E., Cranford, 07016. Tel: 908-497-3953.

Bishop Francis Immigration Services—976 Broad St., Newark, 07102. KIERA LOBREGLIO, Mng. Attorney, Tel: 973-733-3516, Ext. 225; POLLIANN HARDEO, Staff Attorney, Tel: 973-733-3516, Ext. 205; MICHAEL YOUNKER, Staff Attorney, Tel: 973-733-3516, Ext. 207; JANELLE BAPTISTE, Staff Attorney, Tel: 973-733-3516, Ext. 229; PIERRE MOREAU, Immigration Counselor, Tel: 973-733-3516, Ext. 211; LILIANA VERGEL, Immigration Counselor, Tel: 973-733-3516, Ext. 210; THERESA TIBERI, Office Mgr., Tel: 973-733-3516, Ext. 203; OLGA PEREZ, Administrative Asst. & Receptionist, Tel: 973-733-3516, Ext. 201; VACANT, Immigration Case Mgr., Legal Orientation for Parent & Custodians Prog., Tel: 973-733-3516, Ext. 206; NANCY TORRES, Immigration Counselor, Safe Relief Support Prog., Tel: 973-733-3516, Ext. 209; LUIS VARGAS, Administrative Asst., Safe Relief Support Prog., Tel: 973-733-3516, Ext. 226; Tel: 973-733-3516, Ext. 200 (Main reception desk).

Community Access and Volunteer Services Division—SUSANA ARMAS, Div. Dir. & Dir. Volunteer Svcs., 37 Evergreen Pl., East Orange, 07018. Tel: 973-266-7978.

Emergency Food and Nutrition Network—505 South Ave. E., Cranford, 07016. Tel: 908-497-3903; Tel: 908-407-4012; Fax: 908-709-9580. CONSTANZA ROBLEDO, Dir.

New Day Community—37 Evergreen Pl., East Orange, 07018. VINCENT MCMAHON, Ed.D., Dir., Tel: 973-763-6430.

Parish Access Centers—Information and Referral Tel: 800-227-7413. PAMELA GRAHAM, B.S.W., C.S.W., Exec. Sec., Tel: 800-227-7413; Tel: 973-266-7967.

Parish Access Center - Essex County—37 Evergreen Pl., East Orange, 07018. Tel: 973-266-7991; Fax: 973-676-0712. KAREN CARINHA.

City of Newark: Rapid Re-Housing—MELANIE DANIELS, Tel: 973-266-7969 DCA HPP.

Parish Access Center - Hudson County—249 Virginia Ave., Jersey City, 07304. Tel: 201-798-9958; Fax: 201-333-4412. YANIL MENDONZA.

Parish Access Center - Union County—505 South Ave. E., Cranford, 07016. Tel: 908-497-3966; Fax: 908-276-7185. VACANT, Prog. Mgr.

Adult Protective Services—SUSAN HARRIGAN FOWLES, L.C.S.W., 505 South Ave. E., Cranford, 07016. Tel: 908-497-3932; Fax: 908-709-9580.

Bergen Care Management Program - Bergen Senior Center—TAMAR AULET, M.S.W., Prog. Mgr., 57 Pink St., Hackensack, 07801. Tel: 201-441-9428; Fax: 201-441-9423.

Mental Health Caregiver Program—505 South Ave. E., Cranford, 07016. MARGARET MCGROARY, Caregiver Clinician/Project Mgr., Tel: 908-497-4011; Fax: 908-709-9580.

Telephone Reassurance, Home Shopping Services, Hispanic Older Adult Information and Referral, Visually Impaired Seniors Program—GABRIELA RICHTER, 505 South Ave. E., Cranford, 07016. Tel: 908-497-3950; Fax: 908-709-9580; JACKLYN MILONAS, Sec., Tel: 908-497-4002; GLORIA LEPORE, Front Desk Receptionist, Tel: 908-497-3900.

Mount Carmel Guild Behavioral Health System—590 N. Seventh St., Newark, 07107. MR. JOHN WESTERVELT, B.A., CEO, Tel: 973-596-3984; Fax: 973-412-7710; Fax: 973-266-7950; MS. ELIZABETH A. MCCLENDON, A.C.S.W., L.C.S.W., Assoc. Exec. Dir., Tel: 973-266-7992; Fax: 973-266-7950; JOYCELYNN J. MURRAY, Exec. Asst. to CEO, Tel: 973-266-7942.

Behavioral Health Services—RIMA PATEL, Outpatient & Partial Care Clinical Team Leader, Essex County, 58 Freeman St., Newark, 07105. Tel: 973-596-3975; Cell: 973-727-2402; Fax: 973-639-6583; MARGERY A. GRIMM-DEFRANCO, L.R.C., Dir. Partial Care Svcs., 58 Freeman St., Newark, 07105. Tel: 973-596-3971; Cell: 973-396-6499; Fax: 973-598-4030; AHYLAZBETH GIANNANTONIO, Partial Clinical Team Leader, 2201 Bergenline Ave., Union City, 07087. Tel: 201-558-3726; Cell: 201-207-8853; Fax: 201-392-5048; CAROL COLEMAN, Outpatient & Partial Care Team Leader, 285 Magnolia Ave., Jersey City, 07306. Tel: 201-395-4812; Cell: 973-609-7826; Fax: 201-435-9580; DIANE RICHARDSON, Outpatient & Partial Care Team Leader, 108 Alden St., Cranford, 07016. Tel: 908-497-3990; Tel: 908-497-3982; Fax: 908-497-3989.

PACT (Program for Assertive Community Treatment)—269 Oliver St., Newark, 07105. Tel: 973-466-1348; Fax: 973-466-2715; Fax: 973-344-0026. RASHIDAH JENIOUS, Dir. PACT/ICMS.

ICMS-Essex (Integrated Case Management Services-Essex County)—ROGENA NAVARIN, Prog. Mgr., 273 Oliver St., Newark, 07105. Tel: 973-522-2125; Cell: 973-432-0718; Fax: 973-578-2818.

ICMS-Union (Integrated Case Management Services-Union County)—505 South Ave., E, Cranford, 07016. CHERYL TOLENTINO, Prog. Mgr., Tel: 908-497-3927; Tel: 908-497-3918; Fax: 908-709-9612; ROSALVA VILLARONGA, Administrative Specialist.

Residential Services—JENNIFER QUICK, Acting Prog. Dir., 39 Gifford Ave., Jersey City, 07304. Tel: 201-451-2217; Fax: 201-324-0378; CATHERINE MIGUEL, Team Leader, Union City Residential, 2606 New York Ave., Union City, 07087. Tel: 201-392-9019; Fax: 201-392-9019.

Patient Accounts—590 N. 7th St., Newark, 07107. MARY MEEHAN-CAIRNS, Dir. Patient Accounts, Tel: 973-596-4058; Cell: 201-755-7850; Fax: 973-482-1978.

Mount Carmel Guild Education—MR. JOHN WESTERVELT, B.A., CEO, Tel: 973-596-3984; JOYCELYNN J. MURRAY, Exec. Asst. to Mr. Westervelt, 590 N. 7th St., Newark, 07107. Tel: 973-266-7989; Fax: 973-266-7950.

Mount Carmel Guild Academy—100 Valley Way, West Orange, 07052. Tel: 973-325-4000; Fax: 973-669-8450. JAMES BADAVAS, Prin., Tel: 973-325-4400, Ext. 106; CATHERINE CRUZ, Vice Prin., Tel: 973-325-4400, Ext. 135; ROUSSEL SIMON, Vice Prin., Tel: 973-325-4400, Ext. 299; SARA RIVERA, Administrative Asst., Tel: 973-325-4400, Ext. 100.

Education Division—

Early Childhood Programs—(Child Study Team). *37 Evergreen Pl., East Orange, 07018.* SUSAN HARBACE, Dir.

Mount Carmel Guild Little Schoolhouse—SUSAN HARBACE, Prog. Dir., 103-110 Third St., Elizabeth, 07206. Tel: 908-282-4610; Fax: 908-353-0437; Fax: 908-353-5407.

Mount Carmel Guild Cares—DOROTHY CIMO, Mgr., 594 N. 7th St., Newark, 07104. Tel: 973-497-7714; Tel: 973-497-7715; Fax: 973-497-0891.

Domus Corporation—590 N. 7th St., Newark, 07107. Tel: 973-596-3984. MR. JOHN WESTERVELT, B.A., Pres. & Treas.; MS. ELIZABETH A. MCCLENDON, A.C.S.W., L.C.S.W., Vice Pres.; Bro. BENEDICT LOBALBO, F.M.S., Sec.; JOYCELYNN J. MURRAY, Exec. Asst. Properties managed by Domus Corp.: Sunrise House; Bramhall Apts.; Carmel House; Immaculate Conception Senior Residence; Holy Rosary Senior Residence; Kearny Senior Residence; St. Mary Senior Residence; The Apts. at St. Elizabeth; Myers Senior Residence; River Vale Senior Residence; Harrison Senior Residence and Northvale Senior Residence.

Commissions and Organizations

Bukas-Loob Sa Diyos Community (BLD) (Open to the Spirit of God)—Divine Mercy Parish, 232 Central Ave., Rahway, 07065. Tel: 973-856-8222; Fax: 845-818-3679; Email: secretariat@bldnewark.com; Web: www.bldnewark.com. Rev. Msgr. PAUL D. SCHETELICK, V.F., Spiritual Dir., (Retired), P.O. Box 499, Branchville, 07826. Cluster Shepherds: MANNY MANGALONZO; ARLENE MANGALONZO. District Council of Stewards: SAM OLASO; RORY OLASO; ERNEST SUN, Secretariat; NELLIE SUN, Secretariat; MANNY SAN LUIS; JOUY LUCERO; JUDY SAN LUIS; EMILY LUCERO; GERRY CANLAS; STELLA CANLAS; NONG BUSTOS; TRICIA BUSTOS.

Buklod Ng Pag-Ibig Foundation, USA, Inc. (Bond of Love)—285 Garfield Ave., Jersey City, 07305. Tel: 201-521-1019. Revs. CHRISTOPHER M. PANLILO; JOEMARIE M. PARCON, (Retired); ALEXANDER VER, (Philippines). Spiritual Directors: PANTALEON ESCOBAR JR.; FELY ESCOBAR; ROBINSON GUIAO; AMY GUIAO; TONY MABALOT; JULIET MABALOT; JOHN ALONZON. Founding & Council Elders: ELIZABETH ALONZO; RUBY VISAYA.

Charismatic Renewal—Very Rev. JOHN F. GORDON, V.F., Tel: 973-497-4353.

Archdiocesan Commission of Christian Unity—Revs. LUKE A. EDELEN, O.S.B., Chm., Tel: 973-643-4800; PHILIP F.A. LATRONICO, M.A., M.Div., Exec. Sec., Tel: 201-935-6492; Tel: 973-497-4338.

The Community of God's Love—70 W. Passaic Ave., Rutherford, 07070. STEVE BOYKEWICH, Dir., Tel: 201-405-2208; Rev. PHILIP F.A. LATRONICO, M.A., M.Div., Chap., Tel: 201-935-6492.

Cursillo Movement—25 Perdue Ave., Oakland, 07436. Very Rev. THOMAS P. LIPNICKI, V.F., Spiritual Dir., Tel: 201-337-7596; PAT FERRARA, Lay Dir., Tel: 973-227-2350; JOANNE RINKUS, Cursillo Sec., 504 River Renaissance, East Rutherford, 07073. Tel: 973-249-0049.

Archdiocesan Commission for Interreligious Affairs—Rev. PHILIP F.A. LATRONICO, M.A., M.Div., Chm., Tel: 201-935-6492.

Archdiocesan Commission on Justice and Peace—Rev. TIMOTHY G. GRAFF, Exec. Sec., Tel: 973-497-4341.

Archdiocesan Liturgical Commission—VACANT.

Archdiocesan Liturgies for the Archdiocese of Newark—Revs. JOSEPH A. SCARANGELLA, Assoc. Coord./ Master of Ceremonies; JOSEPH A. MANCINI, Dir., Master of Ceremonies for Pontifical Liturgies & Archdiocesan Ceremonies.

Commission for the Men's Apostolate—JOHN D'ALESSIO, Chm.

Pontifical Mission Societies—

Propagation of the Faith; Society of St. Peter the Apostle; Missionary Childhood Association; Missionary Union of Priests & Religious—Fax: 973-497-4371. Rev. Msgr. ROBERT J. FUHRMAN, Dir., Tel: 973-497-4372.

Archdiocesan Pro-Life Commission—171 Clifton Ave., Newark, 07104. JAMES SONDEY, Chm.

Renew International—1232 George St., Plainfield, 07062-1717. Tel: 908-769-5400; Fax: 908-769-5660; Email: renew@renewintl.org; Web: www.renewintl.org; Web: www.parishlife.com; Web: www.whycatholic.org; Web: www.campusrenew.org; Web: www.renewtot.org. Rev. Msgr. THOMAS A. KLEISSLER, Pres. Emeritus, (Retired); Sisters THERESA RICKARD, O.P., D.Min., Pres. & Exec. Dir.; HONORA NOLTY, O.P., Dir. Devel. & Asst. Dir.; PATRICIA WILEY, Human Resources & Information Technology; MARY BETH ORIA, Dir. Business Oper.; DEIRDRE TRABERT MALACREA, Dir. Mktg. & Communications; EARTHA JOHNSON, Mgr. Customer Svc. & Fulfillment; MILISSA ELSE, Dir. Pastoral Svc. Coord.; Deacon CHARLES PAOLINO, Mng. Editor.

Pastoral Services Team—Revs. JEREMIAH BROWNE; ALEJANDRO LOPEZ-CARDINALE; Sisters MAUREEN COLLEARY, F.S.P.; MARIE COOPER, S.J.C.; MARENID FABRE, O.P.; AINE HUGHES, H.C.; ELIZABETH O'DONNEL, O.P.; JANET SCHAEFFLER, O.P.; MANUEL HERNANDEZ; SOEURETTE FOUGERE; NICOLE JANAZZO; MR. GREG KREMER; JUAN RAMON CORDOVA; DR. LAURA ZANE KOLMAR; BRENDA MAIMAN; DR. MARIELA SARAVIA. Additional Staff: JENNIFER BOBER; SUSAN CAPURSO; MARTHA ANN HAGEDORN; REGINA CROWLEY; YVETTE HUTCHINS; CHARMAINE WOOLARD; MAGGIE CARPEN; Rev. STEPHEN J. CONNOR, M.Div.; MARY BETH HOWATH.

Archdiocesan Council of Catholic Women (N.C.C.W.)—Tel: 973-497-4356; Fax: 973-497-4317. D. JEAN SCHNEIDER, Pres., Email: d.jeansch@juno.com; MARY R. LOFTUS, Past Pres. & Recording Sec., 263 Concord Dr., Paramus, 07652. Tel: 201-265-2048; BEATRICE MAHR, Treas.; MARGARET HENDERSON, Second Vice Pres., Tel: 908-688-2228; FLORENCE HORGAN, First Vice Pres.

Archdiocesan Women's Commission—694 Cheyenne Dr., Franklin Lakes, 07417. PAMELA MUELLER-SWARTZEBERG, Chair; MAUREEN SRINIVASA, Vice Chair, Tel: 973-497-4137; LORETTA LOVELL, Administrative Asst., Tel: 973-497-4008. Members: ANN BURGMEYER; MARY ELAINE CONNELL; CHRISTINE FLAHERTY; HOLLY WRIGHT; MS. CHERYL RILEY; YAMILKA GENAO; CATHERINE L'INSALATA, M.A., C.S.W.; TRACY RICARDI.

Miscellaneous Organizations in the Archdiocese

Affirmative Action—5 Becker Farm Rd., Roseland, 07068. Tel: 973-994-1700. CHARLES M. CARELLA, Esq., Counselor at Law.

Archdiocesan / University Archives—Seton Hall University, Walsh Library, 400 S. Orange Ave., South Orange, 07079. Tel: 973-761-9476; Fax: 973-761-9550. Rev. Msgr. FRANCIS R. SEYMOUR, K.H.S., Archdiocesan Archivist, (Retired), Tel: 973-761-9126; Email: seymoufr@shu.edu; ALAN DELOZIER, University Archivist, Tel: 973-275-2378; Email: delozial@shu.edu; DR. JOHN BUSCHMAN, Dir. Special Collections & Dean Univ. Libraries, Tel: 973-761-9005; AMANDA MITA, Technician Svc. Head, Tel: 973-761-9271; Email: amanda.mita@shu.edu.

Censores Librorum—Rev. Msgr. ROBERT F. COLEMAN, J.C.D., Chm.; Revs. JOHN J. CHADWICK, S.T.D.; HONG-RAY PETER CHO, Ph.D., S.T.L.; CHRISTOPHER M. CICCARINO, S.T.L., S.T.D.; STEPHEN J. FICHTER, Ph.D., S.T.B.; TIMOTHY P. FORTIN, Ph.D; Revs. LAWRENCE FRIZZELL, D.Phil.; PABLO T. GADENZ, S.S.L., S.T.D.; Rev. Msgr. THOMAS G. GUARINO, S.T.D.; Rev. KRZYSZTOF K. MASLOWSKI, Ph.D., D.D., S.T.D.; Rev. Msgr. GERARD H. MCCARREN, S.T.D.; Revs. FREDERICK L. MILLER, S.T.D.; MARK FRANCIS O'MALLEY, D.Eccl.Hist.; LAWRENCE B. PORTER, Ph.D.; Rev. Msgr. JOSEPH R. REILLY, S.T.L., Ph.D.; ELLEN R. SCULLY, Ph.D.; Rev. ZACHARY SWANTEK, S.T.L.; DIANNE M. TRAFLET, J.D., S.T.D.; Rev. Msgr. ROBERT J. WISTER, D.Eccl. Hist; Rev. AURELIO YANEZ GOMEZ, S.T.D.; Rev. Msgr. C. ANTHONY ZICCARDI, S.T.L., S.S.L.

Holy Name Federation—1805 Penbrook Terr., Linden, 07036. Tel: 908-486-6363. NORMAN S. KARF, Dir., Essex-West Hudson County; VACANT, Hudson County Dir., Union County Dir.

Legion of Mary—

Archdiocese of Newark Commitium—Saint John, 94 Ridge St., Orange, 07050. Tel: 973-674-0110; Fax: 973-674-3965. Rev. JOSE M. PARCON, Spiritual Dir., Tel: 973-674-0110, Ext. 205; Email: stjohnora@comcast.net.

Our Lady of the Most Holy Eucharist Curia of Bergen County—Holy Name Hospital, 718 Teaneck Rd., Teaneck, 07666. Rev. JOHN T. MICHALCZAK, Spiritual Dir., (Retired), Tel: 973-617-6407.

Hispanic Curia of Essex and Union Counties—St. Leo, 103 Myrtle Ave., Irvington, 07111. Rev. CARLOS M. VIEGO, Spiritual Dir., Tel: 973-372-1272; Fax: 973-674-3965.

Hispanic Curia of Hudson County—St. Rocco / St. Bridget, 4206 Kennedy Blvd., Union City, 07087. Rev. JOSEPH D. GIRONE, V.F., Spiritual Dir., Tel: 201-945-4865.

Maria Immaculata Curia of Hudson County— VACANT, Spiritual Dir.

Our Lady Gate of Heaven Curia—St. Andrew Kim, 280 Parker Ave., Maplewood, 07040. Rev. MIN (JOSEPH) HYUN CHO, Spiritual Dir., Tel: 973-763-1170.

Mary Most Humble Curia (Korean)—St. Joseph Korean Catholic Church, 280 County Rd., Demarest, 07627. Rev. DIDACO YUNG SOO KIM, Spiritual Dir., Tel: 201-767-1954.

Throne of God's Wisdom Curia—St. Joseph Korean Catholic Church, 280 County Rd., Demarest, 07627. Rev. DIDACO YUNG SOO KIM, Spiritual Dir., Tel: 201-767-1954.

Our Lady of Love Curia—Church of the Madonna, 304 Main St., Fort Lee, 07024. Rev. PAUL KYUNG LEE, Spiritual Dir., Tel: 201-803-7557.

Our Lady Mother of God Curia (Korean)—Church of Korean Martyrs, 595 Saddle River Rd., Saddle Brook, 07663. Tel: 201-703-0080. Rev. HONGSHIK DON BOSCO PARK, Spiritual Dir.

Foundation of Mercy Curia—Church of the Madonna, 304 Main St., Fort Lee, 07024. Rev. PAUL KYUNG LEE, Spiritual Dir., Tel: 201-803-7557.

New Jersey Historical Records Commission—Rev. Msgr. FRANCIS R. SEYMOUR, K.H.S., Chm., (Retired); JOSEPH F. MAHONEY, Ph.D., Dir., Seton Hall University, Fahy Hall, 400 South Orange Ave., South Orange, 07079. Tel: 973-275-2773; ALAN DELOZIER, Exec. Dir.

Our Lady of Fatima First Saturday Family—(Ministry to the Disabled) Rev. Msgr. PAUL L. BOCHICCHIO, Chap., (Retired), Our Lady of Grace/St. Joseph, 400 Willow Ave., Hoboken, 07030. Tel: 201-659-0369; Rev. KEVIN E. CARTER, Chap., St. Margaret of Cortona, 31 Chamberlain Ave., Little Ferry, 07643. Tel: 201-641-2988.

Pastoral Association for Music & Liturgy—MR. ANDREW CYR.

Serra Clubs—JOSEPH PAGANO, Governor, District 22, 469 Teal Pl., Secaucus, 07094; PAUL C. TULLY, Past District Governor; ROSE MARIE DEEHAN, L.C.H.S., Sec.; JOSEPH SCIBETTA, K.H.S., Treas.; Rev. MATTHEW R. DOOLEY, Chap.

Serra Club of Bergen County—DR. MARY NORTON, Pres., 30 Canterbury Gardens, North Arlington, 07031. Tel: 201-998-9710; Email: nortonm@felician.edu; Rev. JOSEPH M. QUINLAN JR., Chap.

Serra Club of the Oranges—ROSE MARIE DEEHAN, L.C.H.S., Pres., 171 Vose Ave., Apt. 2K, South Orange, 07079. Tel: 973-762-6180; Email: rjdeehan@gmail.com; Rev. Msgr. THOMAS P. NYDEGGER, Ed.D., M.Div., Chap.

Serra Club of Union County West—139 Stoneridge Rd., New Providence, 07974. Tel: 908-464-4058. JOSEPH DUNN, Pres.

Serra Club of West Essex—THERESA O'BOYLE, Pres., 21 Pitcairn Dr., Roseland, 07068. Tel: 973-669-8001; Email: dtoboyle@hotmail.com.

Serra Club of North Essex—NEIL PAGANO, Pres., 39 Cole Rd., Fairfield, 07004. Tel: 973-227-4689; Email: epagano@comcast.net; Very Rev. JAMES M. MANOS, V.F., Chap.

Serra Club of Hudson County—MICHAEL BRUZZIO, Pres., 21 Garreston Ave., Totowa, 07512. Tel: 201-436-0263; Email: mabruz@verizon.net; Rev. PETER G. WEHRLE, Chap.

The Scholarship Fund for Inner City Children— Fax: 973-497-4282. DR. MICHELLE L. HARTMAN, CEO, Tel: 973-497-4287; Email: michelle.hartman@rcan.org; JASMIN ROMAN, C.S.F., Scholarship Prog. Mgr., Tel: 973-497-4280; Email: jasmin.roman@rcan.org; SEAN E. FLOOD, Dir. Devel., Tel: 973-497-4184; Email: sean.flood@rcan.org; BARBARA CORTES, Office Mgr., Tel: 973-497-4278; Email: barbara.cortes@rcan.org; WILLIAM LESZCZUK, Finance Mgr., Tel: 973-497-4340; VACANT, Devel. Assoc.

University Heights Property Co., Inc.— Tel: 973-690-3606; Fax: 973-690-3601.

Cathedral Affiliated Group at Orange, Inc.— Tel: 973-690-3606; Fax: 973-690-3601.

CLERGY, PARISHES, MISSIONS AND PAROCHIAL SCHOOLS

CITY OF NEWARK

1—CATHEDRAL BASILICA OF THE SACRED HEART (1898) Most Rev. Manuel A. Cruz, D.D., Rector; Revs. Joseph A. Mancini, Coord. & Master of Ceremonies for Archdiocesan Liturgies; Joseph A. Scarangella, Assoc. Coord. & Master of Ceremonies for Archdiocesan Liturgies; Deacons Thomas DeBenedictis; Guy W. Mier; Craig Stewart; John J. Miller, Dir. Music. In Res., Most Rev. John J. Myers, D.D., J.C.D.; Rev. Msgr. Michael A. Andreano, M.B.A., K.C.H.S., Vicar Gen. & Chancellor/Sec. to the Archbishop.
Res.: 89 Ridge St., 07104. Tel: 973-484-4600; Fax: 973-483-8253; Web: www.cathedralbasilica.org.
Catechesis Religious Program—Sr. Josefa Gonzalez, H.S.C.J., D.R.E.
Convent—Sacred Heart Convent
109 Parker St., 07104. Tel: 973-484-1516.

2—ST. ALOYSIUS (1877) Revs. Elky Reyes; Brian O. Gonzalez, Parochial Vicar.
Res.: 66 Fleming Ave., 07105. Tel: 973-344-4736; Email: aloysiuschurch@gmail.com; Web: saintaloysiusnewark.com.
Catechesis Religious Program—
56 Freeman St., 07105. Mr. Paulo Correia, D.R.E.; Mrs. Paula Correia, Family Ministry.

3—ST. ANN (1886) Merged with St. Rocco, Newark to form The Parish of the Transfiguration, Newark.

4—ST. ANTONINUS (1875) Rev. Joseph R. Meagher; Gerard Cleffi, Pastoral Assoc.
Res.: 337 South Orange Ave., 07103.
Tel: 973-623-0258; Fax: 973-623-0694; Email: st_antoninus@msn.com.
Catechesis Religious Program—Students 20.

5—ST. AUGUSTINE (1874) (German) Rev. Andres Codoner-Contell.
Church Office: P.O. Box 7126, 07107.
Tel: 973-622-7712; Email: saintcolumba@hotmail.com.
Convent—Sisters Missionaries of Charity
168 Sussex Ave., 07103. Tel: 973-483-0165. Sr. M. Regi Paul, M.C., Local Supr.
Soup Kitchen and Women's Shelter Queen of Peace—
170 Sussex Ave., 07103. Tel: 973-481-9056.
Catechesis Religious Program—Students 80.

6—ST. BENEDICT (1854) Revs. Elky Reyes, Admin.; Cesar Joan Quinones Diaz; Mr. Luis Lorenzo, Family Ministry; Nilsa Lorenzo, Family Ministry; Mr. Philip Mealy, Music Min.; Mr. Paulo Correia, Business Mgr. In Res.
Res.: 65 Barbara St., 07105. Tel: 973-589-7930; Fax: 973-589-3665; Email: saintbenedictnewark@gmail.com.
See Ironbound Catholic Academy, Newark under St. Casimir's, Newark for details.
Catechesis Religious Program—
Tel: 973-589-7930; Email: saintbenedictnewark@gmail.com. Marina Galindez, D.R.E.

7—BLESSED SACRAMENT-ST. CHARLES BORROMEO (1905) (African American) Rev. Msgr. Anselm I. Nwaorgu, Ph.D.; Revs. Albert Nzeh, Admin.; Longinus N. Ugwuegbulem, Parochial Vicar; Erasmus Okere, Parochial Vicar; Deacon Emeruwa Anyanwu.
Res.: 15 Van Ness Pl., 07108. Tel: 973-824-6548; Fax: 973-624-6030; Web: www.bssc.fatcow.com.
Catechesis Religious Program—
Email: bsscbchurch@yahoo.com; Web: www.bsscbchurch.com. Students 37.

8—ST. BRIDGET (1887) Merged with St. Patrick Pro-Cathedral. Records located at St. Patrick, Newark. Tel: 973-623-0497.

9—ST. CASIMIR (1908) (Polish)
164 Nichols St., 07105-2596. Tel: 973-344-2743; Email: stcasimirnewark@gmail.com; Web: www.stcnewark.com. Rev. Andrzej Ostaszewski, Ph.D.
School—Ironbound Catholic Academy (1910) (Grades K-8), Serves St. Benedict, St. Casimir, Immaculate Heart of Mary, St. James, and Our Lady of Mt. Carmel, Newark.
380 E. Kinney St., 07105. Tel: 973-589-0108; Fax: 973-589-0239; Email: ica@ironboundcatholic.org. Mrs. Egle Sausaitiene, Prin. Lay Teachers 17; Students 173.
Catechesis Religious Program—
Tel: 973-743-6285. Sr. Malgorzata Tomalka, M.Ch.R., D.R.E.; Maria Murano, D.R.E. Students 20.

10—ST. CHARLES BORROMEO (1910) Merged with Blessed Sacrament. Records located at Blessed Sacrament, Newark. Tel: 973-824-6548.

11—ST. COLUMBA (1869) (Hispanic) Revs. Andres Codoner-Contell; Jose Carlos Garzon-Pastrana, Parochial Vicar. In Res., Rev. Hector Larrea.
Res.: 25 Thomas St., 07114. Tel: 973-622-7712; Fax: 973-504-8075; Email: saintcolumba@hotmail.com; Web: www.stcolumbanewark.com.
Catechesis Religious Program—Irma Garcia, D.R.E. Students 160.
Convent— Sisters of Charity
7 South St., 07102. Tel: 973-622-7325.

12—HOLY TRINITY (1901) (Lithuanian), Merged with Epiphany, Newark. Sacramental records located at Holy Trinity - Epiphany, Newark.

13—HOLY TRINITY - EPIPHANY (1992) (Portuguese) Rev. Msgr. Joseph F. Ambrosio, V.F., Admin.; Rev. Ezio Antunes.
Rectory—Holy Trinity - Epiphany
207 Adams St., 07105. Tel: 973-491-9761; Fax: 973-344-5641.
Catechesis Religious Program—Students 125.

14—IMMACULATE CONCEPTION (1925) (Italian)
372 Woodside Ave., 07104. Mailing Address: 654 Summer Ave., 07104. Tel: 973-482-0619; Email: olgc_ic@yahoo.com; Web: www.gcic.newark.org. Revs. Jorge E. Acosta Pena, (Nicaragua); Marcos Sequeira, (Costa Rica) Parochial Vicar.

15—IMMACULATE HEART OF MARY (1926) (Spanish)
202 Lafayette St., 07105. Revs. Luis A. Vargas, T.O.R., (Peru); Lucio M. Nontol, T.O.R., (Peru) Parochial Vicar; Deacon Miguel Loperena.
Res.: 114 Prospect St., 07105. Tel: 973-589-8249; Fax: 973-589-1858; Email: heart.of.mary@verizon.net.
See Ironbound Catholic Academy, Newark under St. Casimir's, Newark for details.
Catechesis Religious Program—Students 125.

16—ST. JAMES (1854) (Brazilian—Portuguese)
142 Jefferson St., 07105. Tel: 973-344-8322; Fax: 973-344-6158; Email: saintjamesrc@outlook.com; Web: stjameschurchrc.com. Very Rev. Celso Luiz Martins Jr., C.Ss.R., V.F.; Revs. Clement M. Krug, C.Ss.R.; Gerard Oberle, C.Ss.R.
Rectory—
143 Madison St., 07105.
See Ironbound Catholic Academy, Newark under St. Casimir's, Newark for details.
Catechesis Religious Program—
Tel: 201-852-1157; Email: ludalmoro6@gmail.com. Sr. Luiza Dal Moro, M.S.C.S., D.R.E. Students 53.

17—ST. JOHN (1826) Rev. Pedro Bismarck Chau;

Deacon Thomas M. Smith. In Res., Rev. Thomas A. Orians, S.A.
Res.: 22 Mulberry St., P.O. Box 200147, 07102.
Tel: 973-623-0822; Email: info@njsoupkitchen.org; Web: www.njsoupkitchen.org.
Chapel—St. John Chapel
Gateway I, 07102.

18—St. Joseph (1850) Closed. Sacramental records located at the Archives, Walsh Library, Seton Hall University, South Orange. Tel: 973-761-9476; Fax: 973-761-9550.

19—St. Lucy (1891) (Italian) Rev. Msgr. Joseph J. Granato, Pastor Emeritus, (Retired); Rev. Paul Donohue, M.C.C.J.; Deacons Simplice Ahoua; Dennis F. LaScala.
Res.: 118 Seventh Ave., 07104. Tel: 973-803-4200; Fax: 973-482-6575; Email: stlucysnwk@yahoo.com; Web: www.saintlucy.net.
Catechesis Religious Program—
Tel: 973-803-4207; Fax: 973-482-6575. Omar Navarro, D.R.E. Students 155.

Comboni Missionaries of the Heart of Jesus (Verona Fathers)—

20—St. Mary Magdalene (1893) Closed. Sacramental records located at the Archives, Walsh Library, Seton Hall University, South Orange. Tel: 973-761-9476; Fax: 973-761-9550.

21—St. Mary of the Immaculate Conception (1842) (Newark Abbey Church) Rt. Rev. Melvin J. Valvano, O.S.B., Abbot; Very Rev. Philip J. Waters, O.S.B., V.F., Rector; Rev. Linus V. Edogwo, (Nigeria); Sr. Linda Klaiss, S.S.J., Pastoral Assoc. & D.R.E.; Mr. Ambrose Amoakoh, Pastoral Min.
Res.: 528 Martin Luther King, Jr. Blvd., 07102.
Tel: 973-792-5793; Fax: 973-643-6922; Email: pwaters@sbp.org; Web: www.smpnewark.org.
School—St. Mary of the Immaculate Conception School
Tel: 973-792-5749; Fax: 973-792-5702. Bro. Patrick Winbush, O.S.B., Prin. Joined to St. Benedict's Prep. Lay Teachers 16; Sisters of St. Joseph of Chestnut Hill 3; Students 200.
Catechesis Religious Program—
Tel: 973-792-5790; Fax: 973-643-6922. Students 95.

22—St. Michael (1878)
172 Broadway, 07104. Tel: 973-484-7100; Email: smc172broadway@yahoo.com; Web: www.saintmichaelparish.com. Revs. Michael J. Reardon, S.D.V.; Eric I. Ugochukwu, S.D.V., (Nigeria); Robinson Gonzalez Herrera, S.V.D.; Bro. Harold Hernandez, S.D.V., Sacristan; Deacons Daniel Ravelo; Restituto Quintana; Cecilio S. Polanco; Miguel Figueroa; Jose A. Negron.
Res.: 25 Crittenden St., 07104.
School—St. Michael School (1881) (Grades K-8),
27 Crittenden St., 07104. Tel: 973-482-7400;
Fax: 973-482-1833; Email: lindacerino@yahoo.com; Web: www.stmichaelnwkpenguins.com. Dr. Linda C. Cerino, Ed.D., Prin. Lay Teachers 14; Sisters of St. Martha 3; Students 314.
Child Care—Perpetual Help Day Nursery
170 Broad St., 07104. Tel: 973-484-3535;
Fax: 973-484-2526. Children 126; Lay Teachers 14; Vocationist Sisters 5.
Catechesis Religious Program—
Tel: 973-482-1109; Email: smc172broadway@yahoo.com. Students 374.

23—Our Lady of Fatima (1956) (Portuguese) Very Rev. Antonio F. da Silva, V.F.; Rev. Joseph E.S. Dos Santos, Parochial Vicar; Deacon Albino P. Marques.
Res.: 82 Congress St., 07105. Tel: 973-589-8433;
Fax: 973-589-2611.
See Ironbound Catholic Academy, Newark under St. Casimir's, Newark for details.
Child Care—Day Nursery
79 Jefferson St., 07105. Tel: 973-589-1639.
Catechesis Religious Program—Laura Martins, D.R.E. Students 4.

24—Our Lady of Good Counsel (1902)
654 Summer Ave., 07104. Tel: 973-482-1274; Email: parish@gcicnewark.org; Web: www.gcic.newark.org. Revs. Jorge E. Acosta Pena, (Nicaragua); Marcos Sequeira, (Costa Rica) Parochial Vicar.
Catechesis Religious Program—
Tel: 973-482-1275; Email: ms_villegas@yahoo.com. Mrs. Mariana Villegas, D.R.E.

25—Our Lady of Mt. Carmel (1889) (Italian) Rev. Msgr. Joseph F. Ambrosio, V.F.
Res.: 259 Oliver St., 07105. Tel: 973-589-2090;
Fax: 973-589-2662; Email: mtcarmel259@optonline.net; Web: www.ourladyofmtcarmelnewark.myownparish.com.
See Ironbound Catholic Academy, Newark under St. Casimir's, Newark for details.
Catechesis Religious Program—Regina Oliveira, D.R.E. Students 50.

26—Our Lady of the Rosary (1918) (Italian), Closed. For inquiries for parish records contact Our Lady of Mt. Carmel, Newark. Tel: 973-589-2090.

27—Parish of the Transfiguration (2005)
103 16th Ave., 07103. Revs. Josephat Kato Kalema, (Uganda) S.T.D.; Jose Wilson Bello; Deacon Justo Rodriguez.
Worship Sites—
St. Anne—
St. Rocco
Divine Mercy Center, 212 Hunterdon St., 07103.
Catechesis Religious Program—
Tel: 201-913-3862; Email: elaramirez4142@gmail.com. Ela Ramirez, D.R.E. Students 99.

28—St. Patrick Pro-Cathedral (1848)
Mailing Address: 91 Washington St., 07102.
Tel: 973-623-0497; Email: info@stppcnewark.org; Web: stppcnewark.com. Revs. Pedro Bismarck Chau; Juan Alexander Ortega, Parochial Vicar; Deacon Leonides Aponte.
Res.: 39 Bleeker St., 07102.
Catechesis Religious Program—Students 28.

29—St. Peter (1864) Closed. Sacramental records located at the Archives, Walsh Library, Seton Hall University, South Orange. Tel: 973-761-9476; Fax 973-761-9550.

30—St. Philip Neri (1887) Closed. Sacramental records located at the Archives, Walsh Library, Seton Hall University, South Orange. Tel: 973-761-9476; Fax 973-761-9550.

31—Queen of Angels (1930) (African American), Closed. Sacramental records are located at St. Augustine Parish, Newark. Tel: 973-482-1817.

32—St. Rocco (1899) Merged with St. Ann, Newark to form Parish of the Transfiguration, Newark.

33—St. Rose of Lima (1888)
11 Gray St., 07107. Tel: 973-482-0682; Email: fatherjoestrose@gmail.com. Revs. Joseph Kwiatkowski; Marco Hurtado-Olazo, Parochial Vicar; Deacon Pedro Herrera; Sr. Monica Alvarado, H.S.C.J., Pastoral Assoc.; Ms. Madge Wilson, Pastoral Outreach.
Catechesis Religious Program—Students 150.

34—Sacred Heart (Vailsburg) (1892) Closed. Sacramental records located at Archives, Walsh Library, Seton Hall University Archives, South Orange (Tel. 973-761-9476; Fax 973-761-9550).

35—Shrine of Divine Mercy St. Francis Xavier (1914) [JC] Rev. Cayetano Moncada Laguado; Very Revs. Jan Sasin, V.F., Parochial Vicar; Dieuseul Adain, (Haiti) V.F.
Res.: 243 Abington Ave., 07107-2598.
Tel: 973-482-8410; Fax: 973-485-7471; Email: fatherjanpastor@gmail.com.
School—Shrine of Divine Mercy St. Francis Xavier School (1924) (Grades PreK-8),
594 N. Seventh St., 07107. Tel: 973-482-9410;
Fax: 973-482-2466; Email: lisaperezst.francis@gmail.com. Sr. Lisa Perez, Prin. Lay Teachers 11; Students 161.
Catechesis Religious Program—Students 300.

36—St. Stanislaus (1889) (Polish) Revs. Marian Spanier, S.T.L.; Bogumil Chrusciel, (Retired).
Res.: 146 Irvine Turner Blvd., 07103.
Tel: 973-642-7961; Fax: 973-642-2295; Email: ststannk@optonline.net.
Catechesis Religious Program—

37—St. Stephen (1902) Closed. Sacramental records located at the Archives, Walsh Library, Seton Hall University Archives, South Orange. Tel: 973-761-9476; Fax: 973-761-9550.

38—St. Thomas Aquinas (1957) (Hispanic), Closed. For inquiries for sacramental records, please contact Blessed Sacrament Parish, Elizabeth. Tel: 908-352-0338.

OUTSIDE THE CITY OF NEWARK

Allendale, Bergen Co., Guardian Angel (1954)
320 Franklin Tpke., Allendale, 07401.
Tel: 201-327-4359; Fax: 201-327-6478; Email: gachurch@guardianangelchurch.org; Web: www.guardianangelchurch.org. Revs. Charles Pinyan; Donald P. Sheehan, In Res., (Retired); Deacon Reynaldo Escalon; Mr. Andrew Monticello, Music Min.; Mr. Alex Capicchioni, Youth Min.; Lori O'Reilly, Sec.
Catechesis Religious Program—Tel: 201-327-0352; Email: inayden@guardianangelchurch.org. Irene Nayden, D.R.E. Students 265.

Bayonne, Hudson Co.

1—St. Andrew (1914) Merged with St. Mary, Star of the Sea Church, Bayonne to form The Parish of the Blessed Miriam Teresa Demjanovich Church, Bayonne.

2—St. Henry (1889)
82 W. 29th St., Bayonne, 07002. Tel: 201-436-0857; Email: sthenryrc@optonline.net; Web: www.sthenryrc.org. Revs. Raul R. Gaviola; Alfie A. Pangilinan.
See All Saints Catholic Academy, Bayonne under Blessed Miriam Teresa Parish.
Catechesis Religious Program—Avenue C & 28 St., Bayonne, 07002.

3—Saint John Paul II Church (2016) Revs. Zenon Boczek, S.D.S.; Andrzej Kujawa, S.D.S.
Res.: 39 E. 22nd St., Bayonne, 07002.
Tel: 201-339-2070; Email: stjp2church@gmail.com; Web: www.johnpaul2parish.com.
Catechesis Religious Program—Debra Czerwienski, D.R.E. Students 140.

4—St. Joseph (1888) (Slovak), Merged with Our Lady of Mount Carmel, Bayonne; Assumption of the Blessed Virgin Mary, Bayonne & St. Michael's, Bayonne to form Saint John Paul II Church, Bayonne.

5—St. Mary Star of the Sea (1861) Merged with St. Andrew the Apostle Church, Bayonne to form The Parish of the Blessed Teresa Miriam Demjanovich Church, Bayonne.

6—St. Michael (1907) (Lithuanian), Merged with Our Lady of Mount Carmel, Bayonne; Assumption of the Blessed Virgin Mary, Bayonne & St. Joseph, Bayonne to form Saint John Paul II Church, Bayonne.

7—Our Lady of Mt. Carmel (1898) [CEM] (Polish), Merged with St. Joseph, Bayonne; Assumption of the Blessed Virgin Mary, Bayonne & St. Michael's, Bayonne to form Saint John Paul II Church, Bayonne.

8—Our Lady of the Assumption (1902) (Italian), Merged with Our Lady of Mount Carmel, Bayonne; St. Joseph, Bayonne & St. Michael's, Bayonne to form Saint John Paul II Church, Bayonne.

9—The Parish of Blessed Miriam Teresa Demjanovich Church (2016)
326 Avenue C, Bayonne, 07002. Tel: 201-437-4090;
Fax: 201-437-0388; Email: secretary@bmtparish.org; Email: pastor@bmtparish.org; Web: bmtparish.org. Revs. Peter G. Wehrle; Philip A. Sanders, Parochial Vicar.
Worship Sites—
St. Mary, Star of the Sea Church—326 Avenue C, Bayonne, 07002.
St. Andrew the Apostle Church, 10 W. 4th St., Bayonne, 07002.
School—All Saints Catholic Academy (2008) (Grades PreK-8), 19 W. 13th St., Bayonne, 07002.
Tel: 201-443-8384; Fax: 201-443-8387; Email: rfritzen@ascabayonne.org. Sr. Rita M. Fritzen, Prin. Clergy 1; Lay Teachers 33; Students 412.
Catechesis Religious Program—Email: ccd@bmtparish.org. Ms. Philomena Coco, D.R.E. Students 334.

10—St. Vincent de Paul (1894) Revs. Sergio O. Nadres, (Philippines); Hermes Diaz; Deacon Michael P. Missaggia. In Res., Revs. Carl J. Arico, (Retired); David Buckles.
Res.: 979 Ave. C, Bayonne, 07002. Tel: 201-436-2222; Fax: 201-437-5235.
See All Saints Catholic Academy, Bayonne under St. Mary Star of the Sea.
Catechesis Religious Program—Tel: 201-823-0184. Christina Smith, D.R.E. Students 150.

Belleville, Essex Co.

1—St. Anthony of Padua (1901) (Italian) Revs. Dave Thomas N. Sison; Robert S. Gajewski, Parochial Vicar; Deacon Louis Acocella, Ed.D.
Res.: 750 N. Seventh St., 07107. Tel: 973-481-1991; Fax: 973-481-1993.
Church: 63 Franklin St., Belleville, 07109.
Tel: 973-450-0936.
Catechesis Religious Program—25 N. 7th St., Belleville, 07109.

2—St. Peter (1837) [CEM] Revs. Ivan Sciberras, B.A., M.Div., Redemptoris Mater Seminary, 130 Chalan Seminariu, Yona, GU 96915; Wojciech B. Jaskowiak, Parochial Vicar, Redemptoris Mater Seminary, 130 Chalan Seminariu, Yona, GU 96915; Jakov Vidov; Deacons William Valladares; Julio Roig, (Retired). In Res., Revs. Giovanni Rizzo, M.Div., J.C.L.; Hector Larrea.
Res.: 155 William St., Belleville, 07109.
Tel: 973-751-2002; Fax: 973-751-6201.
School—St. Peter School (1854) (Grades PreK-8), 152 William St., Belleville, 07109. Tel: 973-759-3143;
Fax: 973-759-4160. Phyllis A. Sisco, Prin. Lay Teachers 16; Students 163.
Catechesis Religious Program—Tel: 973-751-4290. Mrs. Lisa Melillo, D.R.E. Students 193.
Retreat Center—149 William St., Belleville, 07109.
Tel: 973-751-2002, Ext. 121.

Bergenfield, Bergen Co., St. John the Evangelist (1905)
29 N. Washington Ave., Bergenfield, 07621.
Tel: 201-384-0101; Fax: 201-384-2055; Email: pastor@sjrc.org; Web: www.sjrc.org. Rev. Msgr. Richard J. Arnhols, M.Div.; Revs. Raymond R. Filipski; Gustavo A. Alfaro, SS. Peter & Paul Rooma Katoliku Kirik, Vene tn 18, Tallinn, Estonia 10123; Jonathan Perez; Jesus Mesias Ramos; Deacon James Detura.
School—Transfiguration Academy (2006) (Grades PreK-8), 10 Bradley Ave., Bergenfield, 07621.
Tel: 201-384-3627; Fax: 201-384-0293; Email: principal@transfigurationacademy.org; Web: www.transfigurationacademy.org. James V. Carlo, Prin. Lay Teachers 18; Students 212.
Catechesis Religious Program—15 N. Washington Ave., Bergenfield, 07621.

Berkeley Heights, Union Co., Church of the Little

FLOWER (1955)
290 Plainfield Ave., Berkeley Heights, 07922.
Tel: 908-464-1585; Fax: 908-464-6342; Email: rectory.lf@gmail.com; Web: www.littleflowerbh.org. Revs. Andrew M. Prachar; Matthew R. Dooley, Parochial Vicar; Rev. Msgr. William C. Harms, In Res., (Retired); Deacon James P. Stumbar; Margaret Manning, Pastoral Assoc.; Mrs. Sabina Opechowski, Business Mgr.; Liz Mancinelli, Dir. Music Ministry; Mr. Daniel Grossano, Youth Min.; Carolee Aresco, Office Mgr./Asst. to the Pastor.
Catechesis Religious Program—Tel: 908-464-1585; Email: religioused.lf@gmail.com. Teresa Johnson, C.R.E.; Eileen Baker, RCIA Coord. Students 375.

BLOOMFIELD, ESSEX CO.
1—CHURCH OF ST. THOMAS THE APOSTLE (1939) Revs. Charles J. Miller, V.F.; Antonio T. Sarento, Parochial Vicar; Deacons Thomas J. Coyle; Albert H. Tizzano; Brian Murphy; Mr. Robert Miller, Pastoral Assoc.; Timothy Dennin, Youth Min. In Res., Very Rev. John F. Gordon, V.F.
Res.: 60 Byrd Ave., Bloomfield, 07003.
Tel: 973-338-9190; Fax: 973-338-4224.
School—Church of St. Thomas the Apostle School (1939) (Grades PreK-8), 50 Byrd Ave., Bloomfield, 07003. Tel: 973-338-8505; Fax: 973-338-9565; Email: mpetrillo@stthomastheapostlenj.com. Michael Petrillo, Prin.; Ann Bialkowski, Librarian. Lay Teachers 18; Students 209.
Catechesis Religious Program—Tel: 973-338-7400. Tracey K. Hann, D.R.E. Students 450.
Convent—55 Day St., Bloomfield, 07003.
Tel: 973-338-9118; Fax: 973-338-6495.
2—SACRED HEART (1878) [CEM]
76 Broad St., Bloomfield, 07003. Tel: 973-748-1800; Email: info@shcbloomfield.org; Web: www.shcbloomfield.org. Revs. James T. Brown; Lukasz Stanislaw Rokita, Parochial Vicar; Gerald F. Greaves, In Res., (Retired); Deacons Guy W. Mier; Jerry S. Rossi.
Catechesis Religious Program—683 Bloomfield Ave., Bloomfield, 07003. Tel: 973-743-4061; Email: nancy@shcbloomfield.org. Nancy Plate, D.R.E.
3—ST. VALENTINE (1899) (Polish) Rev. Basil L. Lek; Deacons Joseph J. Malanga; Louis Rusignuolo. In Res., Rev. John J. Donohue, (Retired).
Res.: 125 N. Spring St., Bloomfield, 07003.
Tel: 973-743-0220; Fax: 973-743-2041.
Catechesis Religious Program—Tel: 973-743-6122. Josephine Sarno, D.R.E. Students 100.

BOGOTA, BERGEN CO., ST. JOSEPH (1929) Revs. Timothy G. Graff; Luis F. Diaz, Parochial Vicar.
Res.: 115 E. Fort Lee Rd., Bogota, 07603-1301.
Tel: 201-342-6300; Fax: 201-883-9392.
School—St. Joseph School (1925) 131 E. Fort Lee Rd., Bogota, 07603-1301. Tel: 201-487-8641;
Fax: 201-487-7405; Email: sscarano@stjosephbogota.org. Stella Scarano, Prin. Lay Teachers 21; Preschool 38; Students 200; Total Enrollment 238.
Catechesis Religious Program—Tel: 201-343-4316; Fax: 201-883-9302. Patricia Rodriguez, D.R.E. Students 297.

CALDWELL, ESSEX CO., ST. ALOYSIUS (1892) Rev. Msgr. Michael J. Desmond; Revs. Edinson E. Ramirez; Juan J. Esteban, Parochial Vicar; Joseph T. Wozniak, Music Min.
Res.: 219 Bloomfield Ave., Caldwell, 07006.
Tel: 973-226-0221; Fax: 973-226-2204; Email: info@stalscaldwell.org; Web: www.stalscaldwell.org.
School—Trinity Academy (1991) (Grades PreK-8), 235 Bloomfield Ave., Caldwell, 07006.
Tel: 973-226-3386; Fax: 973-226-6548; Email: info@trinityk8.com; Web: www.trinityk8.com. Ms. Linda Payonzeck, Prin. Lay Teachers 16; Preschool 73; Students K-8 150.
Catechesis Religious Program—Tel: 973-226-0209; Fax: 973-226-0923. Edward Karpinski, D.R.E. (Jr. High); Jacqueline A. Alworth, D.R.E. (Elementary); Sisters Justine Pinto, O.P., Social Concerns; Alice Uhl, O.P., RCIA Coord. Students 578.

CEDAR GROVE, ESSEX CO., ST. CATHERINE OF SIENA (1949) Rev. Msgrs. Robert H. Slipe; Charles W. Gusmer, S.T.D., V.E., Pastor Emeritus, (Retired); Revs. Stephen A. Kopacz, (Retired); Daniel Raymond Peterson, Parochial Vicar; Carol Orlando, Pastoral Assoc.
Res.: 339 Pompton Ave., Cedar Grove, 07009.
Tel: 973-239-7960; Fax: 973-239-1008; Email: stcatherine@scscedargrove.org.
School—St. Catherine of Siena School (1958) 39 E. Bradford Ave., Cedar Grove, 07009.
Tel: 973-239-6968; Email: c.kerwin@scs-school-cedargrovenj.org. Celine Kerwin, Prin. Lay Teachers 14; Students 255.
Catechesis Religious Program—Tel: 973-239-3332. Rosemary Couillou, D.R.E. Students 510.

CLARK, UNION CO., ST. AGNES (1961) Revs. Dennis J. Cohan, (Retired); Denis S. Surban.
Res.: 332 Madison Hill Rd., Clark, 07066.
Tel: 732-388-7852; Fax: 732-388-7064; Email: stagneschurch@comcast.net; Web: www.stagnesparish.com.
Catechesis Religious Program—Tel: 732-388-2560; Email: cff@stagnesparish.com. Jeanne Fox, D.R.E. Students 492.

CLIFFSIDE PARK, BERGEN CO., EPIPHANY (1916)
247 Knox Ave., Cliffside Park, 07010.
Tel: 201-943-7320; Email: epiphanycp@juno.com; Web: epiphanyrcchurch.org. Revs. Bruce E. Harger, Admin.; Boniface Anusiem, Parochial Vicar.
Catechesis Religious Program—263 Lafayette Ave., Cliffside Park, 07010. Donna Murtagh, D.R.E. Students 110.

CLOSTER, BERGEN CO., ST. MARY (1911) Rev. Paul A. Cannariato; Deacon James P. Tobin. In Res., Rev. Richard J. Mroz, (Retired).
Res.: 20 Legion Pl., Closter, 07624. Tel: 201-768-7565; Fax: 201-784-5814.
Catechesis Religious Program—Tel: 201-767-8247. Mary Jo Armen, D.R.E. Students 180.

CRANFORD, UNION CO., ST. MICHAEL (1872)
40 Alden St., Cranford, 07016. Tel: 908-276-0360;
Fax: 908-272-0273; Email: parishcenter@stmichaelscranford.org; Web: www.stmichaelscranford.org. Rev. Msgr. Timothy J. Shugrue; Revs. Thomas P. Quinn, Parochial Vicar; Sebastian Valencia Obando, Parochial Vicar.
School—St. Michael School (1929) (Grades PreK-8), 100 Alden St., Cranford, 07016. Tel: 908-276-9425;
Fax: 908-276-4371; Email: saint.michael@verizon.net; Web: www.smscranford.com. Sandy Miragliotta, Prin.; Maria Singer, Librarian. Lay Teachers 19; Students 230.
Catechesis Religious Program—Tel: 908-276-2050; Email: msilva@stmichaelscranford.org. Margaret Silva, D.R.E. Students 928.

CRESSKILL, BERGEN CO., ST. THERESE OF LISIEUX (1925)
120 Monroe Ave., Cresskill, 07626. Mailing Address: 200 Jefferson Ave., Cresskill, 07626.
Tel: 201-567-2528; Fax: 201-541-1269; Email: sttherese@stheresecresskill.org; Web: www.sttheresecresskill.org. Revs. Samuel Citero, O.-Carm.; Brian Henden, O.Carm., Parochial Vicar; Deacon Anthony Porcaro.
School—St. Therese of Lisieux School, (Grades PreK-8), 220 Jefferson Ave., Cresskill, 07626.
Tel: 201-568-4296; Fax: 201-568-3179; Email: gclark@academyofsttherese.com; Web: www.academyofsttherese.com. Glenn Clark, Prin. Lay Teachers 13; Students 154.
Catechesis Religious Program—Tel: 201-567-4781; Email: lpagnozzi@sttheresecresskill.org. Lois Pagnozzi, D.R.E. Students 379.

DEMAREST, BERGEN CO.
1—ST. JOSEPH (1931) (Korean), Merged with St. Joseph, Demarest to form the Parish of St. Joseph, Demarest.
2—ST. JOSEPH (1989) (Korean), Merged with St. Joseph, Demarest to form the Parish of St. Joseph, Demarest.
3—PARISH OF ST. JOSEPH (2008)
Res. & Mailing Address: 573 Piermont Rd., Demarest, 07627. Tel: 201-768-2371;
Tel: 201-767-3115 (Korean); Fax: 201-767-8874; Email: stjosephdemarest@gmail.com; Web: www.stjosephdemarest.com. Revs. Don Bosco Park; James Hooyeon Cho, Parochial Vicar; Thomas E. Pendrick, Parochial Vicar.
Catechesis Religious Program—Students 360.

DUMONT, BERGEN CO., ST. MARY (1914)
280 Washington Ave., Dumont, 07628.
Tel: 201-384-0557; Email: info@stmarysdumont.org. Revs. Stephen A. Carey; Michael C. Barone, Parochial Vicar; Deacon John Sylvester. In Res., Rev. Patrick W. Donohue, V.F., (Retired).
Catechesis Religious Program—Tel: 201-384-3062; Email: religioused@stmarysdumont.org. Dr. William J. Mascitello, D.R.E. Students 439.

EAST NEWARK, HUDSON CO., ST. ANTHONY (1901) (Italian), Merged and fully pastorally integrated into the Parish of Holy Cross, Harrison. For parish sacramental records, please contact Parish of Holy Cross, Harrison.

EAST ORANGE, ESSEX CO.
1—HOLY NAME OF JESUS (1910) Revs. William G. Cook, (Retired); Jude Caliba; Deacon Leo Woodruff.
Res.: 184 Midland Ave., East Orange, 07017.
Tel: 973-675-5901; Fax: 973-674-1767; Email: holynameeo@verizon.net.
Parish Center—200 Midland Ave., East Orange, 07017-1855. Tel: 973-675-4444; Fax: 973-674-1767.
Catechesis Religious Program—Students 35.
2—HOLY SPIRIT-OUR LADY HELP OF CHRISTIANS (1882) (African American—Haitian)
17 N. Clinton St., East Orange, 07017.
Tel: 973-673-1077; Fax: 973-676-6494. Very Rev. Jean Max Osias, V.F.
School—Our Lady Help of Christians (1883) (Grades PreK-8), 23 N. Clinton St., East Orange, 07017.
Tel: 973-677-1546; Fax: 973-677-3939; Email: phoganop@aol.com; Web: www.njolhc.org. Sr. Patricia Hogan, O.P., Prin. Lay Teachers 10; Students 205.
Catechesis Religious Program—Anita Hernandez, D.R.E., Email: hsolhc@verizon.net. Students 61.
3—SAINT JOSEPH PARISH (1916)
110 Telford St., East Orange, 07018.
Tel: 973-678-4030; Fax: 973-677-7875; Email: st.josepheo@verizon.net. Rev. Jose Manuel Abalon; Deacon Jerry Romero. In Res., Revs. Anthony Uwandu; Julius M. Eyyazo; Didam David Kazzahchiyang; John Opara.
School—Saint Joseph School, 115 Telford St., East Orange, 07018. Tel: 973-674-2326;
Fax: 973-674-7718; Email: kcavaness@stjosepheo.com. Ms. Karen Cavaness, Prin. Lay Teachers 14; Daughters of Mary, Mother of Mercy, D.M.M.M. 1; Students 264.
Catechesis Religious Program—Sr. Theresia Maria, D.R.E. Students 11.
4—OUR LADY OF ALL SOULS (1914) Closed. Sacramental records located at the Archives, Walsh Library, Seton Hall University, South Orange, Tel: 973-761-9476; Fax: 973-761-9550.
5—OUR LADY OF THE MOST BLESSED SACRAMENT (1916) Closed. Sacramental records located at the Archives, Walsh Library, Seton Hall University, South Orange. Tel: 973-761-9476; Fax: 973-761-9550.

EAST RUTHERFORD, BERGEN CO., ST. JOSEPH (1872) [CEM] Revs. Joseph J. Astarita; Arokiadoss Raji.
Res.: 120 Hoboken Rd., East Rutherford, 07073.
Tel: 201-939-0457; Email: stjosepher@aol.com.
Catechesis Religious Program—Tel: 201-939-3441. Students 242.

EDGEWATER, BERGEN CO., HOLY ROSARY (1906) Rev. George Ruane, M.A.; Deacons Robert E. Thomson; Michael A. Lydon.
Res.: 365 Undercliff Ave., Edgewater, 07020.
Tel: 201-945-6329 (Parish Center);
Fax: 201-945-6599; Email: holyrosary@aol.com; Web: www.edgewateronlin.com/holyrosarychurch.
See Christ the Teacher Interparochial School, under Madonna, Fort Lee.
Catechesis Religious Program—Linda Corona, D.R.E. Students 88.

ELIZABETH, UNION CO.
1—ST. ADALBERT (1905) (Polish), Merged with SS. Peter & Paul, Elizabeth to form Saint Adalbert/ Saints Peter & Paul Parish, Elizabeth.
2—SAINT ADALBERT AND SAINTS PETER & PAUL (Saints Peter & Paul, 1895; Saint Adalbert, 1905) [CEM] Revs. Krzysztof Szczotka, (Poland); John T. Michalczak, (Retired).
Res.: 250 E. Jersey St., Elizabeth, 07206.
Tel: 908-352-2791; Fax: 908-469-6199; Email: officestadalbert@gmail.com; Email: stadalbert1905@gmail.com.
Catechesis Religious Program—Students 14.
3—ST. ANTHONY OF PADUA (1895) (Italian) Revs. Oscar Martin; Juan Carlos Zapata, Parochial Vicar.
Res.: 853 Third Ave., Elizabeth, 07202.
Tel: 908-351-3300; Fax: 908-351-3609; Email: stanthonyofpaduaelizabeth@gmail.com.
School—Our Lady of Guadalupe Academy, (Grades PreK-8), 227 Centre St., Elizabeth, 07202.
Tel: 908-352-7419; Fax: 908-352-7062; Email: pcymbaluk@olgacademy.org. Patricia Cymbaluk, Prin. Lay Teachers 24; Benedictine Sisters 3; Students 144.
Catechesis Religious Program—Sr. M. Charitina Frabizio, S.C., D.R.E. Students 300.
Convent—Tel: 908-354-0825; Fax: 908-354-4451.
4—BLESSED SACRAMENT (1922)
1096 North Ave., Elizabeth, 07201.
Tel: 908-352-0338; Fax: 908-352-4553; Email: bseliz@optonline.net. Revs. Gerardo D. Gallo; Fredy Sanchez, Parochial Vicar. In Res., Rev. Alejandro Lopez-Cardinale.
See Our Lady of Guadalupe Academy under St. Anthony, Elizabeth.
Catechesis Religious Program—Ms. Susan Hernandez, D.R.E. (English); Lucia Solis, D.R.E. (Spanish). Students 133.
5—ST. GENEVIEVE (1920) Revs. George D. Gillen; Ronnie Nombre, (Philippines); Joseph Khai Vu, (Vietnam); Deacon Joseph Caporaso.
Res.: 200 Monmouth Rd., Elizabeth, 07208.
Tel: 908-351-4444; Fax: 908-351-5454; Email: stgens@optonline.net.
School—St. Genevieve School (1929) (Grades PreK-8), 209 Princeton Rd., Elizabeth, 07208.
Tel: 908-355-3355; Fax: 908-355-1460; Email: principal@saintgenevieveschool.com. Anika Logan, Prin. Lay Teachers 17; Students 138.
Catechesis Religious Program—Tel: 908-355-1584. Thedora Enojo, M.A., D.R.E. Students 151.
Convent—
6—ST. HEDWIG (1925) (Polish) Revs. Andrzej Zmarlicki; Kajetan Klein, Parochial Vicar.
Parish Office: 717 Polonia Ave., Elizabeth, 07202.
Tel: 908-352-1448; Fax: 908-352-8389.

Res.: 716 Clarkson Ave., Elizabeth, 07202.
Church: 600 Myrtle St., Elizabeth, 07202.
Religious Education Center—717 Polonia Ave., Elizabeth, 07202. Michele Yamakaitis, D.R.E. Students 45.

7—HOLY ROSARY (1886) Closed. For inquiries for sacramental records, please contact Our Lady of Most Holy Rosary/St. Michael, Elizabeth. Tel: 908-354-2454.

8—IMMACULATE CONCEPTION (1907) Revs. Jorge Chacon; Juan Carlos Vargas, Parochial Vicar. In Res., Rev. Brendan Quinn.
Pastoral Center: 417 Union Ave., Elizabeth, 07208.
Tel: 908-352-6662; Fax: 908-352-8484; Web: iconceptionparish.org.
Res.: 425 Union Ave., Elizabeth, 07208.
Tel: 908-352-6662.
Catechesis Religious Program—417 Union Ave., Elizabeth, 07208.

9—IMMACULATE HEART OF MARY (1947) (Hispanic), Merged with St. Patrick, Elizabeth to form Immaculate Heart of Mary and Saint Patrick, Elizabeth.

10—IMMACULATE HEART OF MARY AND SAINT PATRICK (1858) [CEM] (Hispanic) Rev. Fabio Roy De Jesus Brenes-Chaves; Deacon Nestor Charriez.
Res.: 215 Court St., Elizabeth, 07206.
Tel: 908-354-0023; Tel: 908-355-0807;
Fax: 908-355-0526.
Catechesis Religious Program—Students 198.

11—ST. JOSEPH (1911) (Slovak), Closed. Records at Holy Family, Linden. Tel: 908-862-1060.

12—ST. MARY OF THE ASSUMPTION (1844) [CEM] Revs. Manuel D. Rios; Duberley Salazar, Parochial Vicar. In Res., Rev. Msgr. Jeremias R. Rebanal, J.C.D., Ph. D., (Retired).
Res.: 155 Washington Ave., Elizabeth, 07202.
Tel: 908-352-5154;
Fax: stmaryoftheassumption@gmail.com.
High School—St. Mary of the Assumption High School, 237 S. Broad St., Elizabeth, 07202. David Evans, Prin. Lay Teachers 19; Students 184.
Child Care—Child Care Center, Tel: 908-355-8723. Anna Rojas, Dir. Students 39.
Catechesis Religious Program—Students 450.

13—OUR LADY OF FATIMA (1973) (Portuguese) Revs. Antonio Nuno Rocha; Adauto Alves, Parochial Vicar; Deacon Manuel Almeida; Margaret De Jesus, Music Min.
Res.: 403 Spring St., Elizabeth, 07201.
Tel: 908-355-3810; Email: olfatimachurch-elizabeth@live.com.
Catechesis Religious Program—Tel: 908-352-9713. Christina Simoes, D.R.E. Students 701.

14—OUR LADY OF MOST HOLY ROSARY/ST. MICHAEL (1886/1852) [JC] Rev. Jose Amante M. Abalon; Deacon Wilbert Alexandre.
Res.: 52 Smith St., Elizabeth, 07201.
Tel: 908-354-2454; Email: holyrsmc16@gmail.com.
Catechesis Religious Program—Students 269.

15—ST. PATRICK, Merged with Immaculate Heart of Mary, Elizabeth to form Immaculate Heart of Mary and Saint Patrick, Elizabeth.

16—SS. PETER AND PAUL (1895) (Lithuanian), Merged with St. Adalbert, Elizabeth to form Saint Adalbert/Saints Peter & Paul Parish, Elizabeth.

17—SACRED HEART (1871) Merged All records at Our Lady of Fatima Parish, Elizabeth. Tel: 908-355-3810.

ELMWOOD PARK, BERGEN CO., ST. LEO (1910) Revs. Reinerio Agaloos; Diego Navarro Rodriguez.
Res.: 324 Market St., Elmwood Park, 07407.
Tel: 201-796-3521; Fax: 201-703-8408; Web: www.stleosep.org.
School—St. Leo School (1912) (Grades PreK-8), 300 Market St., Elmwood Park, 07407. Tel: 201-796-5156 ; Fax: 201-796-2092; Email: eventola@stleosschool.org; Web: www.stleosschool.org. Ms. Elizabeth Ventola, Ed.D., Prin. Lay Teachers 21; Franciscan Sisters of Peace 1; Students 191; Clergy / Religious Teachers 1.
Catechesis Religious Program—William Schulenburg, Pastoral Assoc./Faith Formation. Students 143.
Convent—305 Miller Ave., Elmwood Park, 07407. Tel: 201-797-6993.

EMERSON, BERGEN CO., ASSUMPTION (1947)
29 Jefferson Ave., Emerson, 07630.
Tel: 201-262-1122; Email: church@assumptionacad.org; Web: www.assumption-emerson.org. Revs. Paul A. Cannariato; Christopher D. Isinta, Parochial Vicar; Eugene Joseph Bettinger, O.Carm., In Res.; Deacons John E. Hogan; Joseph J. Paulillo.
School—Assumption Early Childhood Center, (Grades PreK-K), 35 Jefferson Ave., Emerson, 07630. Tel: 201-262-0300; Fax: 201-262-5910; Email: sjurevich@assumptionacad.org. Ms. Susan Jurevich, Dir. Early Childhood Center. Lay Teachers 4; Students 80.
Catechesis Religious Program—Tel: 201-986-0970. Ms. Judi Agnew, D.R.E. Students 396.

ENGLEWOOD, BERGEN CO., ST. CECILIA (1866) [JC]
55 W. Demarest Ave., Englewood, 07631.
Tel: 201-568-0654; Fax: 201-568-0364; Email: st.cecilia55d@aol.com. Revs. Hilary Milton, O.Carm.; Thomas Jordan, O.Carm., Parochial Vicar; Ashley J. Harrington, O.Carm., Prior; Joseph P. O'Brien, O.-Carm., Dir. Carmelite Missions; Paul Schweizer, O.-Carm., In Res.; Michael Mulhall, O.Carm., In Res., (Retired); Sr. Thomas Marie, O.P., Pastoral Assoc.
Office of Concern—(Food Pantry) 85 W. Demarest Ave., Englewood, 07631. Tel: 201-568-1465;
Fax: 201-568-8004. George McKenna, Dir.
Catechesis Religious Program—Tel: 201-568-7882. Esther Lara, D.R.E. Students 200.

FAIR LAWN, BERGEN CO., ST. ANNE (1909) Revs. Joseph C. Doyle; Colin Adrian Kay; Deacon Richard M. McGarry. In Res.
Res.: 15-05 Saint Anne St., Fair Lawn, 07410.
Tel: 201-791-1616; Email: lhessman@stannefairlawnnj.org.
School—Saint Anne School (1949) (Grades PreK-8), 1-30 Summit Ave., Fair Lawn, 07410.
Tel: 201-796-3353; Fax: 201-796-9058; Email: the.principal@stannenj.com; Web: www.stannenj.com. Loretta Stachiotti, Prin. Lay Teachers 28; Students 292.
Catechesis Religious Program—Donna Stickna, D.R.E. Students 680.

FAIRFIELD, ESSEX CO., ST. THOMAS MORE (1962) Revs. Marek Chachlowski, (Poland); Ward P. Moore, Pastor Emeritus, (Retired); Juan Pablo Esteban, Parochial Vicar; Deacon P. Aidan King.
Res.: 210 Horseneck Rd., Fairfield, 07004.
Tel: 973-227-0055; Fax: 973-227-2495; Email: stmparish@verizon.net; Web: www.stmchurch.net.
Catechesis Religious Program—12 Hollywood Ave., Fairfield, 07004. Mr. Fred Giordano.

FAIRVIEW, BERGEN CO.

1—ST. JOHN THE BAPTIST (1873) Revs. Jose I. Gamba; Melvin Oseguera.
Res.: 239 Anderson Ave., Fairview, 07022.
Tel: 201-945-4865; Fax: 201-945-8171; Email: sjbhope2@verizon.net.
Catechesis Religious Program—Students 150.

2—OUR LADY OF GRACE (1913) (Italian)
395 Delano Pl., Fairview, 07022. Tel: 201-943-0904; Email: frpeter@nj.rr.com; Web: www.olgrc.org. Revs. Peter T. Sticco, S.A.C.; Francis M. Gaetano, S.A.C.; Luiz Quaini, S.A.C.
School—Our Lady of Grace School, (Grades PreSchool-8), (plus 2 & 3 yr. old program) 400 Kamena St., Fairview, 07022. Tel: 201-945-8300; Fax: 201-945-4580; Email: olgschool@olgfairview.org; Web: www.olgfairview.org. Mrs. Filomena D'Amico, Prin. Lay Teachers 24; Students 429.
Catechesis Religious Program—Tel: 201-945-1201. Students 180.
Convent—St. Vincent Pallotti, 545 Victory Ave., Ridgefield, 07657.

FORT LEE, BERGEN CO.

1—HOLY TRINITY (1906) Revs. Richard E. Cabezas; Edmundo Sombilon; Peter Baratta Jr., Music Min.
Res.: 2367 Lemoine Ave., Fort Lee, 07024-6269.
Tel: 201-947-1216; Fax: 201-947-1217.
School—Christ the Teacher Interparochial School, (Grades PreK-8), Tel: 201-944-0421;
Fax: 201-994-6293. Mrs. Katherine Murphy, Prin. Co-Sponsored. (See Madonna Parish, Fort Lee).
Catechesis Religious Program—Tel: 201-947-1216. Rosemarie Flood, C.B.S., D.R.E. Students 50.
Convent—

2—MADONNA (1858) [CEM] Revs. Bruce G. Janiga, M.A.; James Hooyeon; John Berchmans Antony, (India).
Res.: 340 Main St., Fort Lee, 07024.
Tel: 201-944-2727; Fax: 201-944-5986; Email: madonnachurch@verizon.net.
School—Christ the Teacher Interparochial School, (Grades PreK-8), 359 Whiteman St., Fort Lee, 07024. Tel: 201-944-0421; Fax: 201-944-6293; Email: flacinak@christtheteacherschool.org. Frances Lacinak, Prin. Lay Teachers 22; Students 266.
Catechesis Religious Program—Madonna Religious Education Center, Tel: 201-944-4261. Students 119.

FRANKLIN LAKES, BERGEN CO., MOST BLESSED SACRAMENT (1961)
787 Franklin Lake Rd., Franklin Lakes, 07417. Rev. John R. Job; Most Rev. John W. Flesey, S.T.D., D.D., In Res., (Retired); Sr. Rose Marie Kean, S.S.J., Pastoral Assoc.
Res.: 835 High Mountain Rd., Franklin Lakes, 07417. Tel: 201-485-7865.
School—Academy of the Most Blessed Sacrament (1963) (Grades PreK-8), 785 Franklin Lake Rd., Franklin Lakes, 07417. Tel: 201-891-4250;
Fax: 201-847-9227; Email: taltonjy@rcmbs.org; Web: www.ambs.org. Dr. Thomas Altonjy, Prin. Lay Teachers 24; Students 170.
Catechesis Religious Program—Tel: 201-891-8390; Email: kpastor@mbschurchnj.org. Krista Pastor, D.R.E. Students 670.
Convent—782 Franklin Lake Rd., Franklin Lakes, 07417. Tel: 201-891-1836.

GARFIELD, BERGEN CO.

1—MOST HOLY NAME (1911) (Hispanic) Rev. Msgr. William J. Reilly, V.F.; Ms. Maricela Quintana, Pastoral Assoc.; Ms. Dalia Serrano, Pastoral Assoc.
Res.: 99 Marsellus Pl., Garfield, 07026.
Tel: 973-340-0032; Fax: 973-340-1618.
Catechesis Religious Program—Students 270.

2—OUR LADY OF MT. VIRGIN (1901) (Italian) Revs. Peter J. Palmisano; Marco Vitrano. In Res., Rev. George M. Reilly, (Retired).
Res.: 188 MacArthur Ave., Garfield, 07026.
Tel: 973-772-2295; Fax: 973-478-4389.
Catechesis Religious Program—Mrs. Rose Todaro, D.R.E. Students 137.

3—OUR LADY OF SORROWS (1917) Closed. Records kept at: Our Lady of Mount Virgin Parish, 188 MacArthur Ave., Garfield, NJ 07026.

4—ST. STANISLAUS KOSTKA (1917) (Polish)
184 Ray St., Garfield, 07026. Tel: 973-772-7922; Email: ststankostka@optonline.net; Web: www.ststangarfield.org. Revs. Piotr Haldas, S.D.S.; Dawid Adamczak, S.D.S., Parochial Vicar; Andrzej Kujawa, S.D.S., Parochial Vicar.
Catechesis Religious Program—Tel: 973-772-7222. Ethel Kordosky, D.R.E. Students 265.

GARWOOD, UNION CO., ST. ANNE (1925) Rev. Msgr. Ronald J. Marczewski, V.F.
Res.: 325 Second Ave., Garwood, 07027.
Tel: 908-789-0280; Email: stannesec@comcast.net.
Catechesis Religious Program—
Tel: 908-789-0280, Ext. 10; Email: stannereled@comcast.net. Students 75.

GLEN ROCK, BERGEN CO., ST. CATHARINE (1953)
905 S. Maple Ave., Glen Rock, 07452.
Tel: 201-445-3703; Email: maryann@stcatharinechurch.org; Email: tsw48@hotmail.com; Web: www.stcatharinechurch.org. Revs. Thomas S. Wisniewski; Bogumil Misiuk, Parochial Vicar; Deacons Joseph Castoro; Leonard A. Minichino; James A. Mueller; John A. Sarno; George Carbone; Sally Trahan, Music Min./Organist; Megan Breitenbach, Youth Min.
School—Academy of Our Lady, (Grades PreK-8), 180 Rodney St., Glen Rock, 07452. Tel: 201-445-0622; Email: jnewman@academyofourlady.org; Web: www.academyofourlady.org. Mr. Patrick Martin, Ed.D., Prin. Lay Teachers 30; Students 334.
Catechesis Religious Program—Tel: 201-444-5690; Email: religiouseducation@stcatharinechurch.org. Maryann Facciolo, D.R.E.; Michelle Torpey, D.R.E. Students 717.

GUTTENBERG, HUDSON CO., ST. JOHN NEPOMUCENE (1910) (Slovak), Merged with Our Lady Help of Christians, West New York to form Holy Redeemer, West New York.

HACKENSACK, BERGEN CO.

1—ST. FRANCIS OF ASSISI (1917) (Italian—Hispanic)
50 Lodi St., Hackensack, 07601. Tel: 201-343-6243; Fax: 201-343-0854; Email: st.francisrcchurch@gmail.com; Web: stfrancisofassisihackensack.com. Revs. John Salvas, O.F.M.Cap.; Francisco Arredondo, O.F.-M.Cap., Admin.; Tulasi Babu Garapati, O.F.M.Cap., Parochial Vicar; Deacons Douglas Christmann; Angel Hernandez; Alejandro Polanco.
Catechesis Religious Program—Tel: 201-488-2614. Mr. Alex Collantes, D.R.E. Students 250.

2—HOLY TRINITY (1861) [CEM]
34 Maple Ave., Hackensack, 07601.
Tel: 201-343-5170; Email: churchholytrinity@yahoo.com; Web: www.holytrinity1861.org. Revs. Paul Prevosto; Jose Pablo Muralles, Parochial Vicar; Octavio Gonzalez, Parochial Vicar; Arokiaswamy Samson, Chap.; Lynn Behrlater, Pastoral Assoc.
Catechesis Religious Program—Tel: 201-343-5170; Email: julian@holytrinity1861.org. Mr. Julian Garcia, C.R.E. Students 400.

3—IMMACULATE CONCEPTION aka St. Mary's (1891)
49 Vreeland Ave., Hackensack, 07601.
Tel: 201-440-2798; Fax: 201-440-6756; Email: immcon@verizon.net; Web: www.icchackensack.com. Rev. Michael S.P. Trainor.

4—ST. JOSEPH (1909) (Polish) Rev. Wlodzimierz R. Las, S.D.S.
Res.: 460 Hudson St., Hackensack, 07601.
Tel: 201-440-3224; Fax: 201-641-8685.
School: See Padre Pio Academy under Church of St. Francis of Assisi, Hackensack.
Catechesis Religious Program—Marzanna Kopacz, D.R.E. (Polish). Students 130.

HARRINGTON PARK, BERGEN CO., OUR LADY OF VICTORIES (1910)
81 Lynn St., Harrington Park, 07640-1831.
Tel: 201-768-1706; Email: olvrectory.hp@gmail.com; Web: www.olvhp.org. Rev. Wojciech B. Jaskowiak, Admin.; Deacons Al McLaughlin; Tom Lagatol.
Catechesis Religious Program—155 The Parkway, Harrington Park, 07640-1820. Tel: 201-768-1400. Curtis Stella, Youth Min. Students 288.

Convent—145 The Parkway, Harrington Park, 07640-1820.

HARRISON, HUDSON CO.

1—HOLY CROSS (1865) Revs. John C. DeSousa, Admin.; Francisco J. Rodriguez, Parochial Vicar.
Res.: 16 Church Sq., Harrison, 07029.
Tel: 973-484-5678; Fax: 973-484-0906; Email: holycrossharrison@verizon.net; Web: www.holycross-stanthony.org.
Catechesis Religious Program—Students 250.
Convent—Carmelite Friars, 324 Jersey St., Harrison, 07029. Tel: 973-485-7233.

2—OUR LADY OF CZESTOCHOWA (1908) (Polish) Rev. Pawel Molewski. In Res., Rev. Msgr. Joseph P. Plunkett, (Retired).
Res.: 115 S. Third St., Harrison, 07029.
Tel: 973-483-2255; Fax: 973-483-4688; Email: rectory@olczestochowa.com; Web: www.olczestochowa.com.
Catechesis Religious Program—Marzena Zmude-Dudek, D.R.E. Students 65.

HASBROUCK HEIGHTS, BERGEN CO., CORPUS CHRISTI (1897) Revs. Patrick M. Mulewski; Raymond M. Holmes, (Retired); Juan Camilo Restrepo; Gabriel Angel Perdomo Jimenez; Deacons Vincent J. DeFedele; Paul Carris; Joanna Kowalska, Music Min.
Parish Offices & Center—218 Washington Pl., Hasbrouck Heights, 07604. Tel: 201-288-4844; Fax: 201-288-0237; Email: corchris@optonline.net.
School—Corpus Christi School (1928) (Grades PreK-8), 215 Kipp Ave., Hasbrouck Heights, 07604.
Tel: 201-288-0614; Fax: 201-288-5956; Email: epinto@corpuschristischool.net. Elizabeth A. Pinto, Prin. Lay Teachers 27; Students 400.
Catechesis Religious Program—
Tel: 201-288-4844, Ext. 142. Verna Paiotti, D.R.E. Students 553.

HAWORTH, BERGEN CO., SACRED HEART (1914)
102 Park St., Haworth, 07641. Tel: 201-387-0080; Fax: 201-439-1395; Email: parishoffice@sacredhearthaworth.com; Web: www.sacredhearthaworth.com. Revs. Robert Wolfee, M.Div.; Ashley J. Harrington, O.Carm., Weekend Asst.; John R. O'Connell, V.F., In Res., (Retired); Sr. Joanne Picciurro, Pastoral Assoc.; Alan Pitman, Youth Min.
Res.: 100 Park St., Haworth, 07641.
Tel: 201-387-0470.
Catechesis Religious Program—Tel: 201-387-0080; Email: sreginaccd@yahoo.com. Sr. Regina McTiernan, D.R.E. Students 250.

HILLSDALE, BERGEN CO., ST. JOHN THE BAPTIST (1925) Revs. John J. Korbelak; Tadeusz Jank, Parochial Vicar; Rev. Msgr. Philip D. Morris, S.T.D., Pastor Emeritus, (Retired); Deacons Albert J. Ganter; John A. Gray Jr.; Sr. Mary McFarland, O.P., Pastoral Assoc.; Jennifer Cannon, Business Mgr.; Catherine Wollyung, Pastoral Assoc. for Catechetics; Mr. Roberto Sabastiani, Music Min.
Res.: 69 Valley St., Hillsdale, 07642.
Tel: 201-664-3131; Fax: 201-664-0772; Web: www.stjohnhillsdale.com.
School—St. John Academy Interparochial (1955) (Grades PreK-8), 460 Hillsdale Ave., Hillsdale, 07642. Tel: 201-664-6364; Fax: 201-664-8096; Email: ssocha@sja-hillsdale.org. Suzanne Socha, Prin.; Deborah Fagnan, Librarian. Lay Teachers 20; Students 247.
Catechesis Religious Program—Faith Formation Center, 1 Valley St., Hillsdale, 07642.

HILLSIDE, UNION CO.

1—ST. CATHERINE OF SIENA (1912) Revs. Aurelio Yanez Gomez, (Colombia); Marco Hurtado-Olazo.
Res.: 19 King St., Hillside, 07205. Tel: 908-351-1515; Fax: 908-351-2139; Email: scatherineparish@aim.com; Web: stcatherinehillside.org.
Catechesis Religious Program—Elizabeth.

2—CHRIST THE KING (1948) Revs. Luke Duc Tran; Andrew J. Njoku, (Nigeria) (In Res.).
Res.: 411 Rutgers Ave., Hillside, 07205.
Tel: 908-686-0722; Fax: 908-686-2504; Email: christthekinghillside@yahoo.com; Web: www.christthekinghillsidenj.tk.
Catechesis Religious Program—Email: ginabejar@yahoo.com; Email: mcconloguejm@aol.com; Web: www.ctkre.org. Gina Bejar, C.R.E.; Jane McConlogue, C.R.E. Students 42; R.C.I.A. Program for Children 2.

HOBOKEN, HUDSON CO.

1—ST. ANN (1900) Rev. Remo DiSalvatore, O.F.M.Cap.
Res.: 704 Jefferson St., Hoboken, 07030.
Tel: 201-659-1114; Fax: 201-659-1416.
School—Hoboken Catholic Academy, (Grades PreK-8), 555 Seventh St., Hoboken, 07030.
Tel: 201-963-9535; Fax: 201-963-1256; Email: jcordova@hobokencatholic.org; Web: www.hobokencatholic.org. Matthew McGrath, Prin. Lay Teachers 25; Students 320.
Catechesis Religious Program—Barbara Migliori, D.R.E. Students 75.

2—ST. FRANCIS OF ASSISI (1888) (Italian)
308 Jefferson St., Hoboken, 07030. Tel: 201-659-1772; Fax: 201-222-7975; Email: stfrancis308@gmail.com. Rev. Christopher Panlilio; Rev. Msgr. Paul L. Bochicchio, In Res., (Retired); Rev. Bryan F.J. Adamcik, K.H.S., In Res.
Catechesis Religious Program—Email: ccdstfrancis@gmail.com. Eileen Carvalho, D.R.E. Students 107.

3—ST. JOSEPH (1871) Merged with Our Lady of Grace, Hoboken to form Our Lady of Grace and Saint Joseph Parish, Hoboken. For inquiries for parish records, contact Our Lady of Grace and Saint Joseph Parish.

4—OUR LADY OF GRACE (1851) Merged with St. Joseph's, Hoboken to form Our Lady of Grace and Saint Joseph Parish, Hoboken.

5—OUR LADY OF GRACE AND SAINT JOSEPH PARISH (1851) Very Rev. Alexander M. Santora, V.F.; Rev. Philip Micele, Parochial Vicar; Angela Maffei, Pastoral Assoc.
Rectory—400 Willow Ave., Hoboken, 07030.
Tel: 201-659-0369; Fax: 201-659-5833; Email: olgrace@optonline.com; Web: www.olghoboken.com.
See Hoboken Catholic Academy, Hoboken under St. Ann's, Hoboken for details.
Catechesis Religious Program—Students 75.

6—SS. PETER AND PAUL (1889) Rev. Msgr. Michael A. Andreano, M.B.A., K.C.H.S.
Res.: 404 Hudson St., Hoboken, 07030.
Tel: 201-659-2276; Email: info@spphoboken.com; Web: www.spphoboken.com.
See Hoboken Catholic Academy, Hoboken under St. Ann's, Hoboken for details.
Catechesis Religious Program—Students 165.

HO-HO-KUS, BERGEN CO., ST. LUKE (1864) [CEM] Very Rev. James M. Manos, V.F.; Deacons John McKeon; Andrew E. Saunders, M.A.; Barbara Weiss, Business Mgr.
Res.: 340 N. Franklin Tpke., Ho Ho Kus, 07423.
Tel: 201-444-0272; Fax: 201-652-7044; Web: www.churchofstluke.org; Email: admin@churchofstluke.org.
Catechesis Religious Program—Tel: 201-447-2779; Email: ccd@churchofstluke.org. Ms. Bridget Sarkowicz, D.R.E. Students 752.

IRVINGTON, ESSEX CO.

1—ASSUMPTION OF THE BLESSED VIRGIN MARY (1907) (Hungarian), Closed. Sacramental records located at the Archives, Walsh Library, Seton Hall University, South Orange. Tel: 973-596-9476; Fax: 973-761-9550.

2—GOOD SHEPHERD (2005) Very Rev. Frank J. Rocchi, V.F.
Res.: 954 Stuyvesant Ave., Irvington, 07111.
Tel: 973-375-8568; Email: gsirvington@comcast.net.
School—Good Shepherd Academy (2005) 285 Nesbit Ter., Irvington, 07111. Tel: 973-375-0659; Fax: 973-375-0766; Email: tscalea@gmail.com. Thomas Scalea, Prin. Lay Teachers 15; Students 172.
Catechesis Religious Program—Tel: 908-296-3511; Email: perryden@verizon.net. Denise Perry, D.R.E.

3—ST. LEO (1878) Rev. Msgr. Beaubrun Ardouin; Rev. Carlos M. Viego, Parochial Vicar; Deacon Nelson Ramirez. In Res., Rev. Stephen Aribe.
Res.: 103 Myrtle Ave., Irvington, 07111.
Tel: 973-372-1272; Fax: 973-416-8819; Email: saintleochurch@comcast.net.
See St. Leo's/Sacred Heart School, Irvington for details.
Catechesis Religious Program—Christian Nunes, D.R.E. Students 75.

4—ST. PAUL THE APOSTLE (1948) Merged with Immaculate Heart of Mary, Maplewood to form Good Shepherd, Irvington.

5—SACRED HEART OF JESUS (1925) (Polish)
537 Grove St., Irvington, 07111. Tel: 973-373-2232; Email: sacredheart07111@gmail.com. Rev. Tadeusz Trela.
Catechesis Religious Program—Aneta Jarosz, Youth Min. Students 58.

JERSEY CITY, HUDSON CO.

1—ST. AEDAN (1912) Revs. Vincent B. Sullivan, S.J., Admin.; John R. Hyatt, S.J., Parochial Vicar.
Res.: 800 Bergen Ave., Jersey City, 07306.
Tel: 201-433-6800; Fax: 201-433-1222; Web: www.staedanparish.org.
Catechesis Religious Program—Reina Osi, D.R.E. Students 70.

2—ST. ALOYSIUS (1897) Revs. Juancho D. De Leon; Edinson E. Ramirez, Parochial Vicar; Ralph D. Siendo, Parochial Vicar; Deacon Alfredo Zapata.
Res.: 691 West Side Ave., Jersey City, 07304.
Tel: 201-433-6365; Fax: 201-451-6438; Email: saintaloysius@verizon.net; Web: www.staloysiuschurch.com.
School—St. Aloysius School (1897) (Grades PreK-8), 721 West Side Ave., Jersey City, 07306.
Tel: 201-433-4270; Fax: 201-433-6916; Email: hoconnell@stalselem.org; Web: www.stalselm.org. Helen O'Connell, Co-Prin.; Michelle Bernatowicz, Co-Prin.; Rota Khoury, Librn. Lay Teachers 19; Students 278.
Catechesis Religious Program—Sr. Georgette A. Gavioli, S.S.J., D.R.E. Students 276.

3—ST. ANN (1910) (Lithuanian), Closed. Sacramental records located at the Archives, Walsh Library, Seton Hall University, South Orange. Tel: 201-761-9476; Fax: 201-761-9550.

4—ST. ANN (1911) (Polish) Rev. Kazimierz Kuczynski; Deacon John J. Karal.
Res.: 291 St. Pauls Ave., Jersey City, 07306-5008.
Tel: 201-656-4018; Fax: 201-656-0741.
Catechesis Religious Program—Students 15.
Mission—Jersey City, Hudson Co.. Tel: 201-656-0405.

5—ST. ANNE (1903) Very Rev. Nigel R. Mohammed.
Res.: 3545 John F. Kennedy Blvd., Jersey City, 07307. Tel: 201-360-0838; Fax: 201-721-5996; Email: st.annepray4us@gmail.com; Web: www.sahjerseycity.com.
Catechesis Religious Program—Students 115.

6—ST. ANTHONY OF PADUA (1884) (Polish) Rev. Joseph Urban.
Res.: 330 Sixth St., Jersey City, 07302.
Tel: 201-653-0343; Email: pastor433@verizon.net; Web: www.stanthonyjc.com.
Catechesis Religious Program—Students 41.

7—ASSUMPTION/ALL SAINTS (1896) Merged with St. Patrick, Jersey City to form St. Patrick and Assumption/All Saints Church, Jersey City.

8—ST. BONIFACE (1863) Merged with St. Bridget, St. Mary and St. Michael to form Parish of the Resurrection, June 1997. For inquiries for parish records call Tel: 201-434-8500.

9—ST. BRIDGET (1869) Merged with St. Boniface, St. Mary and St. Michael to form Parish of the Resurrection, June 1997. For inquiries for parish records call Tel: 201-434-8500.

10—CHRIST, THE KING (1930) (African American)
768 Ocean Ave., Jersey City, 07304.
Tel: 201-333-4862; Fax: 201-433-6352; Email: ctkjerseycity@gmail.com; Web: www.ChristtheKingJerseyCity.org. Revs. Esterminio Chica, Admin.; Robert Tooman, In Res., (Retired); Ms. Ann Warren, Business Mgr. & D.R.E.; Mr. Henry Rawls, Music Min.
Catechesis Religious Program—Students 26.

11—HOLY ROSARY (1885) (Italian)
344 Sixth St., Jersey City, 07302. Tel: 201-795-0120; Email: holyrosarychurch@gmail.com; Web: www.holyrosarychurch.com. Very Rev. Jerzy R. Zaslona, V.F.
Catechesis Religious Program—Tel: 201-795-0129. Christine Olasin, D.R.E. Students 40.

12—ST. JOHN THE BAPTIST (1884) Rev. Pedro Repollet, Parochial Vicar. In Res., Revs. Gregory V. Gebbia, O.F.M.; Robert J. Sandoz, O.F.M.
Res.: 3026 John F. Kennedy Blvd., Jersey City, 07306. Tel: 201-653-8814; Fax: 201-653-3771; Email: johns3026@comcast.net.
Catechesis Religious Program— Twinned with Our Lady of Mt. Carmel, Jersey City. 99 Broadway, Jersey City, 07306. JoAnne Oziemblo.

13—ST. JOSEPH (1856) Rev. James V. Pagnotta; Mrs. Roseann McLaughlin, Music Min.
Res.: 511 Pavonia Ave., Jersey City, 07306-1303.
Tel: 201-653-0392; Email: stjosephjc@yahoo.com; Web: www.stjosephjc.com.
Church: 272 Baldwin Ave., Jersey City, 07306.
School—St. Joseph School (1876) (Grades PreK-8), 509 Pavonia Ave., Jersey City, 07306.
Tel: 201-653-0128; Fax: 201-222-5324; Email: stjosephgrasch@yahoo.com. John Richards, Prin. Lay Teachers 13; Students 246.
Catechesis Religious Program—Tel: 201-659-5929; Email: stjosephreled@yahoo.com. Ms. Maria C. Pellecchia, D.R.E. & R.C.I.A. Students 124.

14—ST. LUCY (1884) Closed. For inquiries for parish records contact Parish of the Resurrection. Tel: 201-434-8500.

15—ST. MARY (1854) (Hispanic—Filipino), Merged with St. Boniface, St. Bridget and St. Michael to form Parish of the Resurrection, June 1997. For inquiries for parish records call Tel: 201-434-8500.

16—ST. MARY PARISH
209 Third St., Jersey City, 07302. Tel: 201-434-8500; Fax: 201-333-1816. Rev. Jose Helber Victoria.

17—ST. MICHAEL (1867) Merged with St. Boniface, St. Bridget and St. Mary to form Parish of the Resurrection, June 1997. For inquiries for parish records call Tel: 201-434-8500.

18—ST. MICHAEL PARISH (1867)
252 Ninth St., Jersey City, 07302. Tel: 201-653-7328; Fax: 201-333-1816; Email: st.michael.jerseycity@gmail.com. Rev. Thomas Patrick Quinn; Deacon Ralph M. Savo. In Res., Rev. Joseph Minh Nguyen.
Catechesis Religious Program—Linda Reagan, D.R.E. Students 31.

19—ST. NICHOLAS (1886) (German) Revs. Ordanico De La Pena; Alexander Ver, (Philippines); Jose deJesus

Rodriguez, Parochial Vicar; Deacons Robert A. Baker Sr., M.B.A., C.F.E.; Wilson Cordero; Clodualdo M. Leonida.
Res.: 122 Ferry St., Jersey City, 07307.
Tel: 201-659-5354; Fax: 201-798-6868; Web: www.saintnicholasparishjcnj.org.
School—St. Nicholas School (1886) (Grades PreK-8), 118 Ferry St., Jersey City, 07307. Tel: 201-659-5948; Email: principal@snsjc.com; Web: www.snsjc.com. Bernadette Miglin, Prin. Lay Teachers 11; Sisters of Christian Charity 3; Students 230.
Catechesis Religious Program—Tel: 201-659-5354. Debra Baker, Catechetical Coord.; Clarice Perdono, Catechetical Coord. (Spanish). Students 160.
Convent—Tel: 201-659-5644.

20—OUR LADY OF CZESTOCHOWA (1911) Revs. Bryan E. Page, Admin.; Gerald J. Sudol, In Res.; Mr. Jonathan Blevis, Pastoral Assoc.; Mr. Ben Rauch, Music Min.
Res.: 120 Sussex St., Jersey City, 07302.
Tel: 201-434-0798; Email: olcjc@olcjc.org; Web: www.olcjc.org.
School—Our Lady of Czestochowa School (1911) (Grades PreK-8), 248 Marin Blvd., Jersey City, 07302. Tel: 201-434-2405; Fax: 201-434-6068; Email: stefanellia@olcschool.org; Email: office@olcschool.org; Web: www.olcschool.org. Mrs. Anna Mae Stefanelli, Prin. Lay Teachers 43; Students 486.
Catechesis Religious Program—Students 30.

21—OUR LADY OF MERCY (1963) Revs. Marty Borbon Jacinto; Thomas B. Iwanowski, Parochial Vicar; Ranulfo D. Docabo, Parochial Vicar; Deacon Meynardo Espeleta, Pastoral Assoc.; Michael Rivera, Music Min.
Res.: 40 Sullivan Dr., Jersey City, 07305.
Tel: 201-434-7500; Email: olmjcnj@aol.com; Web: www.olmnj.org.
Catechesis Religious Program—
Tel: 201-434-7500, Ext. 12; Email: olmym@aol.com. Regina Matias-Villa, Faith Formation. Students 200.

22—OUR LADY OF MT. CARMEL (1905) (Italian) Rev. Pedro Repollet, Parochial Vicar.
Res.: 99 Broadway, Jersey City, 07306.
Tel: 201-435-7080; Fax: 201-432-4476; Email: mtcarmelschool@comcast.net.
Catechesis Religious Program—JoAnne Oziemblo, D.R.E. Students 76.

23—OUR LADY OF SORROWS (1914)
93-95 Clerk St., Jersey City, 07305.
Tel: 201-433-0626; Fax: 201-433-2928; Email: ols9395@comcast.net; Web: olsjc.com. Rev. Marty Borbon Jacinto, Admin.; Sisters Alice McCoy, O.P., Pastoral Assoc.; Elise Redmerski, O.P., Pastoral Assoc.
Res.: Our Lady of Mercy, 340 Winfield Ave., Jersey City, 07305.
Mary House Peace Center and Food Pantry—
Tel: 201-434-3175.
Catechesis Religious Program—Students 56.

24—OUR LADY OF VICTORIES (1917) Revs. Victor E. Paloma; Michael E. Gubernat, Parochial Vicar.
Res.: 2217 John F. Kennedy Blvd., Jersey City, 07304-1416. Tel: 201-433-4152; Fax: 201-433-0705; Email: olvictories1@aol.com; Web: www.olvictoriesjc.org.
Catechesis Religious Program—Students 85.

25—ST. PATRICK (1869) Merged with Assumption/All Saints, Jersey City to form St. Patrick and Assumption/All Saints Church, Jersey City.

26—ST. PATRICK AND ASSUMPTION/ALL SAINTS CHURCH, Rev. Marc-Arthur Francois, (Haiti); Deacon Jesus Reyes.
Res.: 492 Bramhall Ave., Jersey City, 07304.
Tel: 201-332-8600; Fax: 201-324-3919.
Convent—344 Pacific Ave., Jersey City, 07304.
Tel: 201-451-2765.
Catechesis Religious Program—Ann Marie Padilla, D.R.E. Students 60.

27—ST. PAUL OF THE CROSS (1868) Revs. George Joseph; Donato Cabardo, Parochial Vicar; Deacon Arnulfo Cuesta.
Res.: 156 Hancock Ave., Jersey City, 07307.
Tel: 201-798-7900; Email: stpaulcros@aol.com; Web: www.stpaulofthecrossjc.org.
Catechesis Religious Program—Students 156.

28—SAINT PAUL THE APOSTLE (1861)
Tel: 201-433-8500; Email: stpauljc@aol.com. Revs. Thomas Thottungal; Richard Thaddeus De Brasi, Parochial Vicar.
Res.: 14 Greenville Ave., Jersey City, 07305.
Tel: 201-433-8500; Fax: 201-433-9886; Email: stpauljc@aol.com.
Catechesis Religious Program—Tel: 201-435-8204. Virginia San Lorenzo, D.R.E. Students 110.

29—SACRED HEART (1905) Closed. Sacramental records located at the Archives, Walsh Library, Seton Hall University, South Orange. Tel: 973-761-9476; Fax: 973-761-9550.
School—Sacred Heart, (Grades K-8), 183 Bayview Ave., Jersey City, 07305. Tel: 201-332-7111; Fax: 201-332-7160; Email: office@sacredheartjc.org; Web: www.sacredheartjc.org. Sr. Frances Salemi, S.C., Prin. Clergy 1; Lay Teachers 11; Students 225.

KEARNY, HUDSON CO.

1—ST. CECILIA (1893)
120 Kearny Ave., Kearny, 07032. Tel: 201-991-1116; Email: jwassell@stceciliakearny.org; Web: www.stceciliakearny.org. Revs. John E. Wassell; Juan Carlos Velasquez-Ducayin; Rev. Msgr. Francis R. Seymour, K.H.S., In Res., (Retired); Rev. Richard J. Mroz, In Res., (Retired); Deacon Justo Aliaga.
Catechesis Religious Program—Mrs. Lilliana Soto-Cabrera, C.R.E. Students 275.

2—OUR LADY OF SORROWS (1915) (Lithuanian)
136 Davis Ave., Kearny, 07032. Tel: 201-998-4616; Email: office@olskearny.org; Web: www.olskearny.org. Revs. John E. Wassell, Admin.; Juan Carlos Velasquez-Ducayin, Parochial Vicar; Patrick R.C. Wilhelm, In Res., (Retired); Deacons Leonard J. Mackesy; John P. Sarnas; Donna Calcado, Sec.
Catechesis Religious Program—Email: dcalcado@olskearny.org. Lucille Muldoon, D.R.E. Students 51.

3—ST. STEPHEN (1904) Rev. Joseph A. Mancini; Deacon Earl W. White; Robert Maidhof, Music Min.; Deacon Robert C. Millea. In Res., Revs. Louis Pereira, (India); Richard J. Kelly.
Res.: 141 Washington Ave., Kearny, 07032.
Tel: 201-998-3314; Email: thechurchofsaintstephen@gmail.com; Web: www.ststephenkearny.com.
Catechesis Religious Program—
Tel: 201-998-3314, Ext. 338; Email: MarthaLaneDRE@gmail.com. Mrs. Martha Lane, D.R.E. Students 340.

KENILWORTH, UNION CO., ST. THERESA (1949) Very Rev. Joseph J. Bejgrowicz, V.F., K.H.S.; Revs. Michele Mario Pedroni, Parochial Vicar; Vincent D'Agostino, Parochial Vicar; Deacon Gino de la Rama. In Res., Rev. Msgr. Venantius M. Fernando, (Retired).
Res.: 541 Washington Ave., Kenilworth, 07033.
Tel: 908-272-4444; Fax: 908-272-4424; Email: sainttheresa@icatholiczone.com.
School—St. Theresa School, (Grades PreK-8), 540 Washington Ave., Kenilworth, 07033.
Tel: 908-276-7220; Fax: 908-709-1103; Email: lcaporaso@mysts.org. Deacon Joseph Caporaso, Prin. Clergy 1; Lay Teachers 13; Salesian Sisters 2; Students 203.
Catechesis Religious Program—Tel: 908-276-4881. Sr. Monique Huarte, F.M.A., Pastoral Min. Catechesis; Richard Donovan, Youth Min., Tel: 908-709-1930. Students 748.
Convent—112 W 23rd St., Kenilworth, 07033.
Tel: 908-276-5028.

LEONIA, BERGEN CO., ST. JOHN THE EVANGELIST (1912)
235 Harrison St., Leonia, 07605. Tel: 201-947-4545; Email: parishoffice@stjohnleonia.org; Web: www.stjohnleonia.org. Revs. Richard P. Kwiatkowski; Arlou Buslon, (Philippines); Deacons Brian Burke; Joseph Yandoli, Business Mgr.
Catechesis Religious Program—260 Harrison St., Leonia, 07605. Tel: 201-944-4346; Email: mtarabokija@stjohnleonia.org. Mirela Tarabokija, D.R.E.

LINDEN, UNION CO.

1—ST. ELIZABETH OF HUNGARY (1909)
220 E. Blancke St., Linden, 07036. 179 Hussa St., Linden, 07036. Tel: 908-486-2514; Fax: 908-486-1757; Email: sehplinden@gmail.com; Web: sainteonline.org. Revs. Ed Jocson; Jose M. Parcon, Parochial Vicar; Deacon John P. Bejgrowicz, (Retired); Raymond Bassford, Music Min.
Catechesis Religious Program—170 Hussa St., Linden, 07036.

2—HOLY FAMILY (Tremley Point) (1955) [CEM] (Slovak) Rev. Jozef Krajnak.
Res.: 210 Monroe St., Linden, 07036.
Tel: 908-862-1060; Fax: 908-862-9483; Email: hfamilyc@comcast.net.
Catechesis Religious Program—Anita Garcia, D.R.E. Students 36.

3—ST. JOHN THE APOSTLE (1948)
1805 Penbrook Ter., Linden, 07036.
Tel: 908-486-6363; Email: parish@sjanj.net; Web: www.sjanj.net. Revs. Robert G. McBride, J.C.L., J.V.; Nnaemeka A. Onyemaobi; Paul A. Passant, Redemptoris Mater House of Formation, 672 Passaic Ave., Kearny, 07032; Deacons Michael D. York; Edward A. Campanella; Timothy A. Kennedy.
School—St. John the Apostle School (1950) (Grades PreK-8), Valley Rd., Clark, 07066. Tel: 732-388-1360; Fax: 732-388-0775; Email: degan@sjanj.org; Web: www.sjanj.org. Dr. Deborah Egan, Prin. Lay Teachers 25; Students 433; Clergy / Religious Teachers 1.
Catechesis Religious Program—Tel: 732-388-1253; Email: myork@sjanj.net. Students 505.

4—ST. THERESA OF THE CHILD JESUS (1925) (Polish) (Archdiocesan Shrine of St. John Paul II) Very Rev. Ireneusz Pierzchala, V.F.; Revs. Tomasz Koszalka, Parochial Vicar; Tadeusz Mierzwa, Parochial Vicar; Zachary Swantek, S.T.L., Weekend Asst.
Res.: 122 Liberty St., Linden, 07036.
Tel: 908-862-1116; Email: sttheresalinden@gmail.com; Web: sttheresalinden.com.
Church: 131 E. Edgar Rd., Linden, 07036.
Catechesis Religious Program—705 Clinton St., Linden, 07036. Tel: 908-862-7551; Email: sirene0713@hotmail.com. Sr. Irene Lisowska, L.S.I.C., D.R.E. Students 350.

LITTLE FERRY, BERGEN CO., ST. MARGARET OF CORTONA (1912) Rev. Kevin E. Carter; Sr. Dorothy A. Donovan, S.S.J., Pastoral Assoc. In Res., Rev. Onyedika Michael Otuwurunne, Adjunct.
Res.: 31 Chamberlain Ave., Little Ferry, 07643-1898.
Tel: 201-641-2988; Fax: 201-641-0664; Email: smcortona1912@aol.com; Web: www.stmargaretlfnj.org.
Catechesis Religious Program—Tel: 201-641-3937. Students 210.

LIVINGSTON, ESSEX CO.

1—ST. PHILOMENA (1927)
386 S. Livingston Ave., Livingston, 07039.
Tel: 973-992-0994; Fax: 973-992-0970; Email: staff@stphilomena.org; Web: www.stphilomena.org. Rev. Msgr. Robert J. Fuhrman; Francisco Maria Cordeiro Mendonca, Parochial Vicar; Revs. Jacek J. Napora, Parochial Vicar; Mathew Eraly, (India) In Res.; Deacon John F. Smith.
School—Aquinas Academy (1952) (Grades PreK-8), 388 S. Livingston Ave., Livingston, 07039.
Tel: 973-992-1587; Fax: 973-992-4173; Email: jcohrs@aquinasacademynj.org. John Cohrs, Prin. Lay Teachers 25; Students 301.
Child Care—Aquinas Academy Pre-School,
Tel: 973-992-5181; Fax: 973-992-2652. Gloria Castucci, M.A., Dir. Aides 9; Lay Teachers 4; Students 67.
Catechesis Religious Program—Tel: 973-992-4466; Email: gruth2@verizon.net. Gary Ruth, D.R.E. Students 548.
Convent—392 S. Livingston Ave., Livingston, 07039.
Tel: 973-992-1581.

2—ST. RAPHAEL (1961) Revs. Gerald F. Greaves, (Retired); Peter M. Aquino, (Retired); Jose Erlito Ebron, (Philippines) Parochial Vicar; Yolanda Cifarelli, Pastoral Assoc.
Res.: 346 E. Mt. Pleasant Ave., Livingston, 07039.
Tel: 973-992-9490; Fax: 973-740-0236; Email: straphaelrcc@comcast.net.
Catechesis Religious Program—Ann Marie Gesualdo, Youth Min. Students 288.

LODI, BERGEN CO.

1—ST. FRANCIS DE SALES (1854) [CEM]
125 Union St., Lodi, 07644. Tel: 973-779-4330; Fax: 973-779-8842; Email: francisdesales@hotmail.com; Web: saintfrancisdeslodinj.org. Rev. Francisco J. Rodriguez; Deacon Cesar Chen; Sisters Martine M. Pijanowski, C.S.S.F., R.N., Pastoral Assoc.; Lois Parente, C.S.S.F., Business Mgr.; Mrs. Michelline Satkowski, Pastoral Min.; Mr. Paul Diverio, Music Min.; Mr. Alex Duran, Music Min.; Mrs. Francia Polanco, Music Min.; Mrs. Clarena Santamaria, Local Safe Environment Coord.; Mrs. Maria Camacho, Sec.; Ms. Yesenia Marte, Sec.
Catechesis Religious Program—Tel: 973-779-3949; Email: CCD@saintfrancisdesaleslidinj.org. Mrs. Judith Santlofer, D.R.E.; Ms. Karina Ramirez, D.R.E.; Ms. Rosa Maria De Leon, RCIA Coord. Students 174.
Convent—111 Union St., Lodi, 07644.
Tel: 973-773-4366.

2—ST. JOSEPH (1917) Revs. Teodoro Kalaw, C.R.M.; Anastacio Villaluz, C.R.M., Parochial Vicar; Deacon Jorge E. Ochoa.
Res.: 40 Spring St., Lodi, 07644. Tel: 973-779-0643; Fax: 973-471-1442; Email: stjosephparishlodi@gmail.com.
Catechesis Religious Program—Tel: 973-779-8275; Email: stjoelodiredre@yahoo.com. Jennifer DeCaux, D.R.E. Students 172.

LYNDHURST, BERGEN CO.

1—ST. MICHAEL THE ARCHANGEL (1912) (Polish) Rev. Stanley Kostrzomb. In Res., Revs. George F. Sharp, (Retired); John A. Quill, (Retired).
Res.: 624 Page Ave., Lyndhurst, 07071.
Tel: 201-939-1161; Email: fr.stanleyk@gmail.com.
Catechesis Religious Program—Tel: 201-460-9174; Email: applejpgr@verizon.net. Mr. Gene DeHaven, D.R.E.

2—OUR LADY OF MOUNT CARMEL (1966) (Italian) Rev. Nazareno Orlandi.
Res.: 197 Kingsland Ave., Lyndhurst, 07071.
Tel: 201-935-1177; Fax: 201-935-5675; Email: olmc1177@verizon.net.
Catechesis Religious Program—146 Copeland Ave., Lyndhurst, 07071.

3—SACRED HEART (1902) [CEM]
324 Ridge Rd., Lyndhurst, 07071. Tel: 201-438-1147; Fax: 201-507-5861; Email: sacredheartchurch@comcast.net; Web: www.

sacredheartlynd.org. Revs. Theesmas Pankiraj; Archibald L. Mabini, Parochial Vicar.
School—Sacred Heart School, (Grades PreK-8), 620 Valley Brook Ave., Lyndhurst, 07071.
Tel: 201-939-4277; Fax: 201-939-0534; Email: sacredheartlynd@hotmail.com. Linda Durocher, Prin.; Joann Hessian, Librarian. Lay Teachers 28; Students 390.
Catechesis Religious Program—Tel: 201-935-3094. Mrs. Margaret Dacchille, D.R.E. Students 220.

MAHWAH, BERGEN CO.
1—IMMACULATE CONCEPTION (1930) Rev. Manolo Punzalan, (Philippines).
Res.: 900 Darlington Ave., Mahwah, 07430.
Tel: 201-327-1276; Fax: 201-327-0185; Email: info@iccmahwah.org; Web: www.iccmahwah.org.
See St. Paul's Interparochial School, Ramsey under St. Paul's, Ramsey for details.
Catechesis Religious Program—Tel: 201-825-0333. Patrice Hess, Catechetical Associate. Students 213.
2—IMMACULATE HEART OF MARY (1915) (Polish)
47 Island Rd., Mahwah, 07430. Tel: 201-529-3517; Email: pastor@ihmcmahwah.org; Web: www.ihmcmahwah.org. Revs. Jacek Marchewka; Marcin Fuks.
See St. Paul's Interparochial School, Ramsey under St. Paul's, Ramsey for details.
Catechesis Religious Program—Tel: 201-529-2294; Email: religiouseducation@ihmcmahwah.org. Anne Laura, D.R.E. Students 260.

MAPLEWOOD, ESSEX CO.
1—ST. ANDREW KIM (1972) (Korean) Revs. Paul Kyung Lee; Sangkyun Kim, Parochial Vicar; Mr. Inhyon Park, Pastoral Assoc.
Res.: 280 Parker Ave., Maplewood, 07040.
Tel: 973-763-1170; Fax: 973-763-1169; Email: catholicmaplewood@yahoo.com; Web: www.ilovesak.org.
Catechesis Religious Program—Kwang Oh Chi, D.R.E.; Matthew Park, D.R.E. Students 75.
Convent—Tel: 973-762-1297; Email: maplewoodsisters@gmail.com.
2—IMMACULATE HEART OF MARY (1954) Merged with St. Paul the Apostle, Irvington to form Good Shepherd, Irvington. For inquiries for sacramental records, contact Good Shepherd, Irvington; Tel: 973-375-8568.
3—ST. JOSEPH (1914) Revs. James Worth; Manolo Punzalan, (Philippines); Deacon John J. Florio; Ms. Leslie Frost, Dir. Music. In Res., Revs. Thomas A. Dente, K.H.S.; Matthew R. Dooley.
Res.: 767 Prospect St., Maplewood, 07040.
Tel: 973-761-5933; Fax: 973-761-6705; Email: info@stjosephmaplewood.org; Web: www.stjosephmaplewood.org.
Catechesis Religious Program—Ms. Darlene Wade, D.R.E. Students 214.

MAYWOOD, BERGEN CO., OUR LADY QUEEN OF PEACE (1950) Revs. Lawrence J. Fama; Jonathan Yabiliyok, (Nigeria) In Res.; Deacon Joseph L. Mantineo; Steven Taylor, Music Min.
Res.: 400 Maywood Ave., Maywood, 07607.
Tel: 201-845-9566; Email: admin@olqp.org; Web: www.olqp-maywood.org.
School: See St. Peter Academy, River Edge under St. Peter the Apostle, River Edge for details.
Catechesis Religious Program—Tel: 201-845-9545; Email: reolqp@yahoo.com. Angela Connelly, D.R.E. Students 213.

MIDLAND PARK, BERGEN CO., CHURCH OF THE NATIVITY (1955) Rev. Edward George Klybus. In Res., Rev. Msgr. James A. Burke, (Retired).
Res.: 315 Prospect St., Midland Park, 07432.
Tel: 201-444-6362; Email: nativityparish.reception@gmail.com; Web: www.churchofthenativitynj.com.
Catechesis Religious Program—Tel: 201-447-1776. Ms. Olivia Harrington, D.R.E. Students 326.

MONTCLAIR, ESSEX CO.
1—IMMACULATE CONCEPTION (1864) [CEM] Closed. Records kept at: St. Teresa of Calcutta Parish, 30 N. Fullerton Ave., Montclair, NJ 07042.
2—OUR LADY OF MT. CARMEL (1907) (Italian), Closed. Records kept at: St. Teresa of Calcutta Parish, 30 N. Fullerton Ave., Montclair, NJ 07042.
3—ST. PETER CLAVER (1931) (Other) Rev. Zephyrin Kabengele Katompa, St. Roseline Church, 409 Edouard Herriot Escallion, Toulon, France 83200.
Res.: 56 Elmwood Ave., Montclair, 07042.
Tel: 973-783-4852; Email: peterclave@aol.com; Web: www.saintpeterclaverchurch.org.
Catechesis Religious Program—Sharon Huebner, D.R.E. Students 92.
4—SAINT TERESA OF CALCUTTA PARISH
1 Munn St., Montclair, 07042. Tel: 973-744-5650; Fax: 973-744-7939; Email: info@montclaircatholics.org; Web: montclaircatholics.org. Revs. Amilcar B. Prado; Samuel Monaco, Parochial Vicar; Thomas M. Cembor, In Res.; Frank J. Burla, In Res., (Retired); Louis M. Pambello, In Res. Immaculate Conception Church, Montclair and Our Lady of Mt. Carmel Church, Montclair merged to form St. Teresa of Calcutta Parish.
Worship Sites—
Immaculate Conception Church—30 N. Fullerton Ave., Montclair, 07042.
Our Lady of Mount Carmel Church, 94 Pine St., Montclair, 07042.
Catechesis Religious Program—
Tel: 973-744-5650, Ext. 118. Ms. Janet Natale, Parish Catechetical Leader.
Immaculate Conception Cemetery & Mausoleum—712 Grove St., Upper Montclair, 07043.
Tel: 973-744-5939; Fax: 973-744-5659.

MOONACHIE, BERGEN CO., ST. ANTHONY (1931) Closed. Sacramental records located at the Archives, Walsh Library, Seton Hall University, South Orange. Tel: 973-761-9476; Fax: 973-761-9550.

MOUNTAINSIDE, UNION CO., OUR LADY OF LOURDES (1958) Revs. Richard J. Carrington; William F. Benedetto, Parochial Vicar; Deacon Michael DeRoberts.
Res.: 300 Central Ave., Mountainside, 07092.
Tel: 908-232-1162; Fax: 908-232-0776; Email: office@ollmountainside.org; Web: www.ollmountainside.org.
Schools—Holy Trinity School (Westfield Campus)—(1991) (Grades PreK-8), 336 First St., Westfield, 07090. Tel: 908-233-0484; Fax: 908-233-6204; Email: office-wc@htisnj.com; Web: www.htisnj.com. Sr. Maureen Fichner, S.S.J., Prin. Lay Teachers 17; Students 305.
Holy Trinity School (Mountainside Campus), 304 Central Ave., Mountainside, 07092.
Tel: 908-233-1899; Fax: 908-233-2109. Mrs. Leslie Lewis, Prin.
Catechesis Religious Program—Tel: 908-233-1777. Fran Michetti, D.R.E.; Kevin Donahue, Youth Min. Students 396.

NEW MILFORD, BERGEN CO., ASCENSION (1953) Very Rev. David W. Milliken, V.F.
Res.: 256 Azalea Dr., New Milford, 07646.
Tel: 201-836-8961; Email: ascension@optonline.net; Web: www.churchoftheascension.com.
School—Transfiguration Academy, 10 Bradley Ave., Bergenfield, 07621. Tel: 201-834-3627;
Fax: 201-834-0293; Email: principal@transfigurationacademy.org; Web: www.transfigurationacademy.org. James V. Carlo, Prin. Lay Teachers 17; Students 216.
Catechesis Religious Program—1092 Carnation Dr., New Milford, 07646. Tel: 201-836-3085. Theresa Carbone, C.R.E. Students 154.

NEW PROVIDENCE, UNION CO., OUR LADY OF PEACE (1942)
111 South St., New Providence, 07974.
Tel: 908-464-7600; Fax: 908-508-1845; Email: secretary@olpnp.com; Web: www.olpnp.com. Revs. William A. Mahon; Johan D. Betancourt, Parochial Vicar; Deacon Charlie Boucher II.
School—The Academy of Our Lady of Peace, (Grades PreK-8), 99 South St., New Providence, 07974.
Tel: 908-464-8657; Fax: 908-464-3377; Email: principal@theacademyolp.org. Joel A. Castillo, Ed.S., Prin. Lay Teachers 17; Students 175; Librarian 1.
Catechesis Religious Program—Tel: 908-464-8156; Email: catoff@olpnp.com. Joanne Fezza, D.R.E.; Anne Mendez, D.R.E.
Convent—

NORTH ARLINGTON, BERGEN CO., QUEEN OF PEACE (1922) Rev. Edward M. Donovan; Rev. Msgr. Thomas G. Madden, Pastor Emeritus, (Retired); Revs. Scott Attanasio; Jeivi Miguel Hercules; Bro. Francis M. Farrell, F.M.S., Pastoral Assoc.; Sr. Anita Maria O'Dwyer, S.S.J., Pastoral Assoc.; Deacons William R. Benedetto, D.R.E.; William H. Myers.
Res.: 10 Franklin Pl., North Arlington, 07031.
Tel: 201-997-0700; Fax: 201-997-6214; Email: qpchurch@comcast.net; Web: www.qpcna.org.
School—Queen of Peace School (1925) (Grades PreK-8), 21 Church Pl., North Arlington, 07031.
Tel: 201-998-8222; Fax: 201-997-7930; Email: enaughton@qpgs.org; Web: www.qpgs.org. Mrs. Ellen Naughton, Prin. Lay Teachers 16; Students 280.
High School—Queen of Peace High School (1930) 191 Rutherford Pl., North Arlington, 07031.
Tel: 201-998-8227; Fax: 201-998-3040; Email: info@qphs.org; Web: www.qphs.org. John Tonero, Prin.; Don DePascale, Asst. Prin. Lay Teachers 26; Sisters 1; Students 293.
Catechesis Religious Program—Students 366.
Convent—Tel: 201-997-2141;
Tel: 201-991-0235 (La Salle Parish Center).

NORTH BERGEN, HUDSON CO.
1—ST. BRIGID (1900) Merged with St. Rocco's, Union City to form Saint Rocco/Saint Brigid, Union City. For inquiries see Saint Rocco/Saint Bridgid, Union City listing.
2—OUR LADY OF FATIMA (1963) Revs. Yuvan Arbey Alvarez; Francis Perry Azah.
Res.: 8016 Kennedy Blvd., North Bergen, 07047.
Tel: 201-869-7244; Fax: 201-869-0940; Email: office@ourladyoffatimanj.org; Web: www.ourladyoffatimanj.org.
Catechesis Religious Program—Tel: 201-869-0506. Silvia Velasquez, BSW, CSW, D.R.E. Students 219.
3—SACRED HEART (1917) (Polish)
Mailing Address: Box 9007, North Bergen, 07047. Revs. Eric W. Fuchs; Anthony G. Robak, (Retired).
Res.: 246 Hudson Pl., Cliffside Park, 07010.
Tel: 201-943-0305; Fax: 201-943-2676; Email: att33940@attglobal.net.
Catechesis Religious Program—Mr. Robert Francin Jr., D.R.E. Students 48.

NORTH CALDWELL, ESSEX CO., NOTRE DAME (1962) Revs. Thomas A. Dente, K.H.S.; Janusz Pigan; Sr. Carol Jaruszewski, R.S.M., Pastoral Assoc.
Res.: 359 Central Ave., North Caldwell, 07006.
Tel: 973-226-0979; Fax: 973-226-4118; Email: ndparishnc@verizon.net; Web: www.ndparishnc.com.
See Trinity Academy under St. Aloysius, Caldwell for details.
Catechesis Religious Program—Tel: 973-228-3338. William Schutte, D.R.E. Students 720.

NORTHVALE, BERGEN CO., ST. ANTHONY (1890) Very Rev. Gerald T. Hahn, V.F.
Res.: 199 Walnut St., Northvale, 07647.
Tel: 201-768-1177; Fax: 201-768-2522; Email: stanthonychurch@optonline.net.
Catechesis Religious Program—Tel: 201-768-5945. Debbie Pumilia, D.R.E. Students 227.

NORWOOD, BERGEN CO., IMMACULATE CONCEPTION (1921) Revs. Leo J. Butler; Franco Pinto, S.D.B.; Sr. Elizabeth Holler, S.C., Pastoral Min. to the Homebound & Infirm; Deacon James J. Puliatte; Mrs. Canice Cristofeletti, Business Mgr.; Ms. Louise Lucivero, Parish Sec.
Res.: 211 Summit St., Norwood, 07648.
Tel: 201-768-1600; Fax: 201-768-8006; Email: iccnorwood@verizon.net; Web: www.iccnorwood.org.
Catechesis Religious Program—Tel: 201-768-1771. Sr. Susanne Reynolds, S.S.J., D.R.E.; Mr. Michael Rooney, Sacramental Coord. Confirmation; Christina Benaquista, Coord. Jr. High Faith Formation & Dir. Music Ministry. Students 111.

NUTLEY, ESSEX CO.
1—HOLY FAMILY (1909) (Italian) Revs. Joseph A. Ferraro, K.H.S.; Mauro Primavera; Francesco Donnarumma; Sr. Eileen Hubbert, S.S.J., Pastoral Assoc.
Res.: 28 Brookline Ave., Nutley, 07110.
Tel: 973-667-0026; Fax: 973-661-1714.
School—Good Shepherd Academy, Elementary 24 Brookline Ave., Nutley, 07110. Tel: 973-667-2049; Fax: 973-661-9259; Email: principal@gsanutley.org. Sr. Jane Feltz, M.P.F., Prin. Clergy 2; Lay Teachers 19; Students 304.
Catechesis Religious Program—Tel: 973-667-6018. Sr. Ella Mae McDonald, M.P.F., D.R.E. Students 208.
Convent—60 Harrison St., Nutley, 07110.
Tel: 973-667-2050.
2—ST. MARY (1876) Revs. Richard J. Berbary, Email: frberbary@stmarysnutley.org; Thomas D. Nicastro Jr., Parochial Vicar.
Res.: 17 Msgr. Owens Pl., Nutley, 07110.
Tel: 973-235-1100; Fax: 973-661-0233; Email: info@stmarysnutley.org; Web: www.stmarysnutley.org.
See Good Shepherd Academy, Nutley under Holy Family, Nutley for details.
Catechesis Religious Program—Tel: 973-667-8239. Anthony Armando, D.R.E. & Youth Minister. Students 470.
3—OUR LADY OF MOUNT CARMEL (1925) (Polish) Revs. Paciano A. Barbieto; Kevin J. Schott, Parochial Vicar; Deacon Aldo P. Antola.
Res.: 120 Prospect St., Nutley, 07110.
Tel: 973-667-2580; Email: olmcnutley@optimum.net; Web: www.olmc-nutley.org.
See Good Shepherd Academy, Nutley under Holy Family, Nutley for details.
Catechesis Religious Program—Email: olmc.religion@optimum.net. Sr. Mary Rose Conforto, M.P.F., D.R.E. Students 110.
Convent—60 Harrison St., Nutley, 07110.
Tel: 973-667-2050.

OAKLAND, BERGEN CO., OUR LADY OF PERPETUAL HELP (1960)
25 Purdue Ave., Oakland, 07436. Tel: 201-337-7596; Fax: 201-337-7810; Email: parish@olphoakland.org; Email: music@olphoakland.org; Web: www.olphoakland.org. Very Rev. Thomas P. Lipnicki, V.F.; Joel Peters, Pastoral Assoc.; Michael Wada, Music Min.
Catechesis Religious Program—Tel: 201-337-5537; Email: reled@olphoakland.org; Email: youth@olphoakland.org. Michele Hans, P.C.L.; Brian Salvatore, Youth Min. Students 372.

OLD TAPPAN, BERGEN CO., ST. PIUS X (1954) Very Rev. Marek B. Wysocki, V.F.; Deacon John J. McKenna, K.H.S.; Agnes Kalinowski, Music Min.

Res.: 268 Old Tappan Rd., Old Tappan, 07675.
Tel: 201-664-0913; Email: stpiusot@optonline.net; Web: www.stpiusxoldtappan.org.
Catechesis Religious Program—Tel: 201-664-0927; Tel: spxpcl@optonline.net. Maria C. Charowsky, D.R.E. Students 410.

ORADELL, BERGEN CO., ST. JOSEPH (1903)
105 Harrison St., New Milford, 07646.
Tel: 201-261-0146; Email: office@sjcnj.org; Web: www.sjcnj.org. Rev. Msgr. David C. Hubba, M.A.; Revs. George M. Reilly, Pastor Emeritus, (Retired); Anthony Di Stefano; Roy B. Regaspi; Deacon Jorge A. Montalvo; Thomas Meli, Dir. Facilities.
School—St. Joseph School (1939) (Grades PreK-8), 305 Elm St., Oradell, 07649. Tel: 201-261-2388; Fax: 201-261-1570; Email: valentip@sjsusa.org. Paula Valenti, Prin. Lay Teachers 15; Students 200.
Catechesis Religious Program—Tel: 201-261-1144. Students 812.

ORANGE, ESSEX CO.
1—HOLY SPIRIT (1931) Closed. For inquiries for parish records contact Holy Spirit-Our Lady Help of Christians, East Orange. Tel: 201-673-1077.
2—ST. JOHN (1851) [CEM] (Hispanic) Very Rev. George Faour, V.F.; Rev. Msgr. Ricardo Gonzalez, Pastor Emeritus, (Retired); Rev. Peter West, Parochial Vicar.
Res.: 94 Ridge St., Orange, 07050. Tel: 973-674-0110; Fax: 973-674-3965; Email: stjohnora@comcast.net; Web: www.stjohnscatholicchurch.net.
Catechesis Religious Program—Saadatu Lynch, D.R.E. (English); Carlos Sposate, D.R.E. (English); Estela Rodas, D.R.E. (Spanish). Students 205.
Convents—Tel: 973-677-0379.
Daughters of Divine Love, 70 Ridge St., Orange, 07050. Tel: 973-673-1263.
3—OUR LADY OF MT. CARMEL (1896)
103 S. Center St., Orange, 07050. Tel: 973-674-2052; Email: secolmc@gmail.com; Web: olmcorange.com. Revs. Bernard Marie Guerin-Boutaud; Jesus Rodriguez, C.S.J., Parochial Vicar; Philippe-Joseph LeGallic, C.S.J., Campus Min.
4—OUR LADY OF THE VALLEY (1873)
510 Valley St., Orange, 07050. Tel: 973-674-7500; Email: olvgeneral@olvsalesianchurch.org; Web: www.olvsalesianchurch.org. Rev. Miguel Angel Suarez, S.B.D.
Catechesis Religious Program—Tel: 973-674-4272. Ms. Anna Samanamu, D.R.E.; Manuel Mendoza, RCIA Coord. Students 111.
5—ST. VENANTIUS (1886) Merged Sacramental records located at the Archives, Walsh Library, Seton Hall University, South Orange. Tel: 973-761-9126; Fax: 973-761-9550.

PALISADES PARK, BERGEN CO.
1—ST. MICHAEL (1912)
19 E. Central Blvd., Palisades Park, 07650.
Tel: 201-944-1061; Fax: 201-947-1798; Email: saintmichaelpp@aol.com; Web: www.stmichael-catholic.org. Revs. Minhyun Cho; Stanley M. Lobo, In Res., (Retired); Ernest G. Rush, In Res.; Sr. Joseph Clare Kim, Pastoral Assoc.
School—Notre Dame Academy (1991) (Grades PreK-8), 312 First St., Palisades Park, 07650.
Tel: 201-947-5262; Fax: 201-947-8319. Mr. Mark Valvano, Prin.
Catechesis Religious Program—Toni Fordyce, C.R.E. Students 70.
2—ST. NICHOLAS (1923) (Italian—Brazilian) Revs. Christogonus Iwunze, S.D.V.; Roberto da Silva, S.D.V., Parochial Vicar; Louis Caputo, S.D.V., Weekend Asst.; Deacon Thomas La Russa.
Res.: 442 E. Brinkerhoff Ave., Palisades Park, 07650.
Tel: 201-944-1154; Fax: 201-944-9510; Email: stnicholas07650@live.com; Web: stnicholasrcchurch.org.
See Notre Dame Interparochial Academy under St. Nicholas, St. Michael's & St. Matthews, Palisades Park for details.
Catechesis Religious Program—Tel: 201-944-1138. Students 73.

PARAMUS, BERGEN CO.
1—ANNUNCIATION (1953) Rev. James V. Teti, J.C.L., S.T.B.; Deacon William D. Joyce. In Res., Rev. Msgr. Richard F. Groncki, (Retired); Rev. Donald K. Hummel, D.Min.
Res.: 50 W. Midland Ave., Paramus, 07652-2140.
Tel: 201-261-6322; Fax: 201-261-6227; Email: info@annunciationchurch.org; Web: annunciationchurch.org.
Parish Center & Mailing Address: 49 Demarest Rd., Paramus, 07652-2109.
See Visitation Academy, Paramus under Our Lady of Visitation, Paramus for details.
Catechesis Religious Program—Tel: 201-261-4119. Mrs. Gladys Pozza, Pastoral Assoc. Faith Formation. Students 305.
2—CARMELITE CHAPEL OF ST. THERESE (1970) Rev. Eugene Joseph Bettinger, O.Carm., Dir.
Res.: 1095 Teaneck Rd., Teaneck, 07666.
Tel: 201-837-3354.
Chapel—Bergen Town Center, Chapel Doors #7 & #8, Rte. 4 E., Paramus, 07652. Tel: 201-845-6115; Fax: 201-837-3360.
3—OUR LADY OF THE VISITATION (1952) Revs. Eugene J. Field; Jose Monte De Oca; Deacons Peter R. Emr; Todd Rushing. In Res., Rev. Msgr. Paul D. Schetelick, V.F., (Retired).
Res.: 234 Farview Ave., Paramus, 07652.
Tel: 201-261-6080; Fax: 201-261-2995; Email: rectory@olvcommunity.org; Web: www.olvcommunity.org.
School—Visitation Academy (1991) (Grades PreK-8), 222 Farview Ave., Paramus, 07652.
Tel: 201-262-6067; Fax: 201-261-4613; Email: principal@visitationacademyparamus.org; Web: www.visitationacademyparamus.org. Kimberly A. Harrigan, Prin. Co-Sponsored. Lay Teachers 21; Students 292.
Catechesis Religious Program—Tel: 201-265-3812. Mrs. Barbara D'Arrigo, D.R.E.; Mr. Robert Leichte, Youth Min. Students 375.

PARK RIDGE, BERGEN CO., OUR LADY OF MERCY (1902) Revs. Charles P. Granstrand, V.F., (Retired); Robert T. Ulak; Patrick J. Seo, Parochial Vicar; Deacons Joseph S. Romano; Gary F. Tankard; Mr. John Rokoszak, Pastoral Assoc.
Res.: 2 Fremont Ave., Park Ridge, 07656.
Tel: 201-391-5315; Fax: 201-391-5614; Email: olm.church@gmail.com; Web: www.urolm.org.
School—Our Lady of Mercy Academy (1950) (Grades PreK-8), 25 Fremont Ave., Park Ridge, 07656.
Tel: 201-391-3838; Fax: 201-391-3080; Email: lmeehan@olmacademy.org. Laraine Meehan, Prin.; Karen Lawrence, Librarian. Lay Teachers 25; Students 337.
Catechesis Religious Program—50 Pascack Rd., Park Ridge, 07656. Fax: 201-391-4387.

PLAINFIELD, UNION CO.
1—ST. BERNARD (1921) Merged with St. Stanislaus Kostka to form The Parish of St. Bernard and St. Stanislaus, Plainfield.
2—ST. BERNARD OF CLAIRVAUX AND ST. STANISLAUS KOSTKA (2005) Very Rev. Frank Rose, M.Div., V.F.; Rev. Jan Krzystof Lebdowicz, (Poland).
Office & Rectory: 368 Sumner Ave., Plainfield, 07062. Tel: 908-756-3393; Fax: 908-756-3059; Email: office@bestchurch.net; Web: www.bestchurch.net.
Church: 1235 George St., Plainfield, 07062.
Catechesis Religious Program—Mrs. Linda Knowles-Mayers, D.R.E.; Karole Lechowski, Youth Min. Students 130.
3—ST. MARY (1851) [CEM] Revs. Manoel J. Oliveira; Pablo A. Martinez; Francesco Carraro, Parochial Vicar; Marco Pacciana, (Italy) Parochial Vicar; Jose A. Ortiz, Parochial Vicar; Deacon Pedro Nieves. In Res., Rev. Michael J. Feketie, (Retired).
Res.: 516 W. Sixth St., Plainfield, 07060.
Tel: 908-756-0085; Fax: 908-756-1658; Email: stmarysplainfield@msn.com; Web: stmarysplainfield.org.
Catechesis Religious Program—Students 920.
Convent—Missionaries of Charity, (Contemplative), 513 Liberty St., Plainfield, 07060. Tel: 908-754-1978. Sisters 14.
Cemetery—300 Berckman St., Plainfield, 07060.
4—ST. STANISLAUS KOSTKA (1919) Merged with St. Bernard to form St. Bernard of Clairvaux and St. Stanislaus Kostka, Plainfield.

RAHWAY, UNION CO.
1—DIVINE MERCY PARISH (2010) [CEM] Revs. Dennis J. Kaelin, (Retired); Peter Vo; Robert Lamirez; Oscar Ramirez Ruiz.
Res. & Office: 232 Central Ave., Rahway, 07065.
Tel: 732-388-0082; Email: stmaryschurchnj@comcast.net; Web: www.divinemercyparishnj.com.
See Sts. Mary & Elizabeth Academy, Linden under St. Elizabeth's, Linden for details.
Catechesis Religious Program—Tel: 732-382-0004; Fax: 732-382-4784; Email: frdenniskaelin@yahoo.com. Maryann Conroy, D.R.E. Students 217.
2—ST. MARK (1871) (German), Merged with St. Mary, Rahway to form Divine Mercy Parish, Rahway.
3—ST. MARY (1854) [CEM] Merged with St. Mark, Rahway to form Divine Mercy, Rahway.

RAMSEY, BERGEN CO., CHURCH OF ST. PAUL (1939)
Mailing Address: 193 Wyckoff Ave., Ramsey, 07446. Revs. John D. Gabriel, M.Div.; Sung Gye Hong, Parochial Vicar; Paul C. Houlis, Parochial Vicar; Deacon Thomas Patrick Flanagan; Mr. John Nunziata, Pastoral Assoc.; Mrs. Kristin Dabaghian, Dir. Music & Worship; Mr. John Weiss, Business Mgr.; Donna Schifano, Dir. Outreach.
Res.: 200 Wyckoff Ave., Ramsey, 07446.
Tel: 201-327-0976; Fax: 201-327-6197; Web: www.stpaulrcchurch.org.
School—Academy of St. Paul, (Grades PreK-8), 187 Wyckoff Ave., Ramsey, 07446. Tel: 201-327-1108; Fax: 201-236-1318; Email: gritchie@academyofstpaul.org. Gail Ritchie, Prin. Lay Teachers 17; Students 265.
Catechesis Religious Program—Tel: 201-327-8010. Mrs. Colleen Jagde, D.R.E.; Eric Erler, Youth Min. Students 1,108.

RIDGEFIELD, BERGEN CO., ST. MATTHEW (1899) Very Rev. Steven Conner, V.F.; Rev. William J. Halbing, Parochial Vicar; Deacon Joseph A. Dickson.
Res.: 555 Prospect Ave., Ridgefield, 07657.
Tel: 201-945-3500; Email: stmatthews@nj.rr.org; Web: stmatthewridgefield.org.
School—Notre Dame Academy (1991) (Grades PreK-8), 312 First St., Palisades Park, 07650.
Tel: 201-947-5262; Fax: 201-947-8319; Email: mvalvano@notredameint.org; Web: www.notredameint.org. Mr. Mark Valvano, Prin.; Mrs. Altamura, Librarian. Lay Teachers 28; Students 392.
Catechesis Religious Program—Students 162.

RIDGEFIELD PARK, BERGEN CO., ST. FRANCIS OF ASSISI (1890) Revs. Larry Evans II; Fernando E. Guillen; Bartley Baker.
Res.: 114 Mt. Vernon St., Ridgefield Park, 07660.
Tel: 201-641-6464; Email: pacosta@stfrancisrp.org; Web: www.stfrancisrp.org.
Catechesis Religious Program—Celeste Farrell, D.R.E. Students 372.

RIDGEWOOD, BERGEN CO., OUR LADY OF MOUNT CARMEL (1889) Rev. Msgr. Ronald J. Rozniak, V.E., V.G., P.A.; Revs. Kevin G. Waymel; Robert James Salm; Antonio N. Kuizon, (Philippines); Deacons Robert V. Thomann; Nicholas De Lucca; Roberto F. Liwanag; Mr. Peter Denio, Pastoral Assoc. for Faith Formation; Mr. Peter Sicko, Dir. Music Min.; Glen McCall, Dir. Youth Min. In Res., Rev. Mert Cordero.
Res.: 1 Passaic St., Ridgewood, 07450-4309.
Tel: 201-444-2000; Web: www.olmcridgewood.com; Email: pfrazza@olmcridgewood.com.
School—Academy of Our Lady, (Grades PreK-8), 180 Rodney St., Glen Rock, 07452. Tel: 201-445-0622; Email: jnewman@academyofourlady.org; Web: www.academyofourlady.org. James Newman, Prin. Clergy 2; Lay Teachers 23; Students 431.
Catechesis Religious Program—Tel: 201-444-0211; Fax: 201-444-4421. Ms. Cathy Hunt, D.R.E.; Kim Birdsall, Dir. Jr. High Youth Min.; Melissa Peters, Asst. Parish Catechetical Leader. Students 1,451.

RIVER EDGE, BERGEN CO., ST. PETER THE APOSTLE (1948) Very Rev. Michael J. Sheehan, V.F.; Revs. Camilo E. Cruz, Parochial Vicar; Chung Yeol Jung, Parochial Vicar; Deacons Edward Bowen; Andrew J. Golden; Paul Kazanecki.
Res.: 445 Fifth Ave., River Edge, 07661.
Tel: 201-261-3366; Email: reception@saint-peter.org; Web: www.saint-peter.org.
School—St. Peter Academy (1952) (Grades PreK-8), 431 Fifth Ave., River Edge, 07661. Tel: 201-261-3468; Fax: 201-261-4316; Email: jmccarthy@spare.org; Web: www.spare.org. Mr. James McCarthy, Prin. Aides 6; Lay Teachers 18; Students 186.
Catechesis Religious Program—Tel: 201-265-6019; Tel: 201-261-4316; Email: faithformation@saint-peter.org; Email: jmccarthy@spare.org. Mr. James McCarthy, D.R.E.; Eileen Hanrahan, D.R.E.

ROCHELLE PARK, BERGEN CO., SACRED HEART (1917)
12 Terrace Ave., Rochelle Park, 07662.
Tel: 201-843-1722; Email: jbecht@wearesacredheart.org; Web: www.wearesacredheart.org. Rev. Richard J. Kelly.
See Visitation Academy, Paramus under Our Lady of the Visitation for details.
Catechesis Religious Program—15 Forect Pl., Rochelle Park, 07662. Email: faithform@wearesacredheart.org. Students 198.

ROSELAND, ESSEX CO., OUR LADY OF THE BLESSED SACRAMENT (1955) Revs. Robert G. Laferrera; Antonio L. Ricarte, Parochial Vicar; Thomas F. Blind; Sr. Rie Crowley, S.S.J., Pastoral Assoc. (Sick & Homebound & Parish Outreach); Donald Pennell, Music Min.
Res.: 28 Livingston Ave., Roseland, 07068.
Tel: 973-226-7288; Fax: 973-226-4893; Email: olbs28@verizon.net; Web: www.olbs.org.
See Trinity Academy under St. Aloysius in Caldwell for details (Grade K-8).
Catechesis Religious Program—Tel: 973-226-5251; Fax: 973-403-8871. Catherine Gibbons, D.R.E. Students 414.

ROSELLE, UNION CO., ST. JOSEPH THE CARPENTER (1895) Revs. Krzysztof K. Maslowski, Ph.D., D.D., S.T.D.; Luis Mario Garcia, Parochial Vicar. Sisters of St. Joseph, Chestnut Hill.
Res.: 157 E. Fourth Ave., Roselle, 07203.
Tel: 908-241-1250; Email: parishoffice@stjosephroselle.org; Web: www.stjosephroselle.org.
School—St. Joseph the Carpenter School (1913) (Grades PreK-8), 140 E. Third Ave., Roselle, 07203.
Tel: 908-245-6560; Fax: 908-245-3342; Email: mullen@stjosephroselleschool.org; Web: www.stjosephsroselleschool.org. Mr. Patrick Mullen, Prin. Lay Teachers 23; Students 237.
Catechesis Religious Program—Students 105.

Convent—135 E. Fourth Ave., Roselle, 07203. Tel: 908-245-1594.

ROSELLE PARK, UNION CO., ASSUMPTION (1907)
113 Chiego Pl., Roselle Park, 07204.
Tel: 908-245-1107; Fax: 908-245-2789; Email: assumptionrp@yahoo.com; Web: www.assumptionrp.com. Very Rev. James F. Spera, M.Div., V.F.; Deacon David Farrell, Pastoral Assoc.
Catechesis Religious Program—110 Chiego Pl., Roselle Park, 07204. Tel: 908-245-6572. Ruth Anne Munroe, D.R.E. Students 240.

RUTHERFORD, BERGEN CO., ST. MARY (1908)
91 Home Ave., Rutherford, 07070. Email: rcansmr@aol.com; Web: www.stmaryrutherford.org. Very Rev. Michael J. Kreder, V.F.; Rev. Piotr Koziolkiewicz, Parochial Vicar; Deacon James J. Guida.
Res.: 98 Home Ave., Rutherford, 07070.
Tel: 201-438-2200; Fax: 201-438-1098; Email: rcansmr@aol.com; Web: www.stmaryrutherford.org.
School—The Academy at Saint Mary (1916) (Grades PreK-8), 72 Chestnut St., Rutherford, 07070.
Tel: 201-933-8410; Fax: 201-531-9020; Email: acastaneda@academyatsmes.org; Web: www.academyatsmes.org. Ana Maria Castaneda, Prin. Lay Teachers 14; Students 137.
High School—St. Mary High School (1928) 64 Chestnut St., Rutherford, 07070. Tel: 201-933-5220; Fax: 201-933-0834; Email: tbrunt@stmaryhs.org; Web: www.stmaryhs.org. Tara Brunt, Prin.; Dennis Hulse, Dean; Virginia Mitchell, Librarian; Marci Schrank, Vice Prin. Lay Teachers 24; Students 212.
Catechesis Religious Program—Tel: 201-438-2476. Betty Hatler, Parish Catechetical Leader. Students 460.

SADDLE BROOK, BERGEN CO.
1—CHURCH OF KOREAN MARTYRS (1986) (Korean) Revs. Hongshik Don Bosco Park, Admin.; Yeong Min Kim, Parochial Vicar; Deacon Francisco E. Noh.
Res.: 585 Saddle River Rd., Saddle Brook, 07663.
Tel: 201-703-0002; Fax: 201-703-7111; Email: martyrsnj@yahoo.com; Web: www.rcckm.org.
Catechesis Religious Program—Hyun Jim David Park, D.R.E. Students 191.
2—ST. PHILIP THE APOSTLE (1953) Revs. Theesmas Pankiraj; Matthew Fonseka, (Retired); John Z. Radwan.
Res.: 488 Saddle River Rd., Saddle Brook, 07663.
Tel: 201-843-1888; Fax: 201-368-9161; Email: ourparish@stphilipsb.org; Web: www.stphilipsb.org.
Catechesis Religious Program—Tel: 201-843-2240; Fax: 201-843-3150; Email: reled@stphilipsb.org; Web: reled-stphilipsb.org. Sr. Jadwiga Zaremba, D.R.E. Students 309.

SADDLE RIVER, BERGEN CO., ST. GABRIEL THE ARCHANGEL (1952)
88 E. Saddle River Rd., Saddle River, 07458. Mailing Address: 3 W. Church Rd., Saddle River, 07458.
Tel: 201-327-5663, Ext. 301; Email: office@stgabrielsr.org; Web: www.stgabrielchurch.org. Rev. Msgrs. Frank G. Del Prete, J.C.D.; Peter Smutelovic, J.C.D., In Res.
Catechesis Religious Program—Tel: 201-327-5663; Fax: 201-327-7063; Email: office@stgabrielsr.org. Patricia Pula, D.R.E.

SCOTCH PLAINS, UNION CO.
1—ST. BARTHOLOMEW (1948) Very Rev. John J. Paladino; Revs. David Caixeiro Santos, Parochial Vicar, Pontifical North American College, Vatican City, Italy 00120; Joseph Anthony Furnaguera; Deacons Robert Gurske; Don Hessemer; Paul Milan, Dir., Music. In Res., Rev. Michael A. Hanly, (Retired); Rev. Msgr. Donald E. Guenther, (Retired).
Res.: 2032 Westfield Ave., Scotch Plains, 07076.
Tel: 908-322-5192; Fax: 908-322-2598; Email: contact@stbartholomewchurch.org; Web: www.stbartholomewchurch.org.
School—St. Bartholomew Academy (1950) (Grades PreK-8), Tel: 908-322-4265; Email: principal@stbacademy.org. Sr. Elizabeth Calello, M.P.F., Prin. Religious Teachers Filippini 1; Lay Teachers 13; Students 206.
Catechesis Religious Program—Tel: 908-322-2359. Patricia Krema, Adult Faith Formation; Connie Boruch, D.R.E.; Jennifer Ryan, D.R.E. Students 976.
Convent—Tel: 908-322-5619.
2—IMMACULATE HEART OF MARY (1964)
1571 S. Martine Ave., Scotch Plains, 07076.
Tel: 908-889-2100; Email: office@ihmparish.net; Web: ihmparish.net. Revs. Michael G. Ward; Valentine C. Ugwuanya, Parochial Vicar.
Catechesis Religious Program—Mary Clinton, D.R.E. Students 420.

SECAUCUS, HUDSON CO., IMMACULATE CONCEPTION (1908)
1219 Paterson Plank Rd., Secaucus, 07094.
Tel: 201-863-4840; Email: iccofficemail@gmail.com. Revs. Victor P. Kennedy, V.F.; Rolando R. Yadao; Deacon Earle S. Connelly Jr.
Catechesis Religious Program—Tel: 201-520-0482; Email: iccdre@gmail.com. Linda Meyer, D.R.E.

SHORT HILLS, ESSEX CO., ST. ROSE OF LIMA (1852) [CEM] Very Rev. John M. McCrone, V.F.; Rev. Msgrs. Donald E. Guenther, Admin., (Retired); George R. Trabold, J.C.L.; Revs. M. Christen Beirne, Parochial Vicar; Alexander Orozco, Parochial Vicar; Thomas F. Blind, Parochial Vicar; Deacons Anthony Scalzo; Joseph M. Persinger; David J. Hughes.
Res.: 50 Short Hills Ave., Short Hills, 07078.
Tel: 973-379-3912; Fax: 973-379-6157; Email: jschultz@stroseshorthills.org; Web: www.stroseshorthills.org.
School—St. Rose of Lima School (1869) (Grades PreK-8), 52 Short Hills Ave., Short Hills, 07078.
Tel: 973-379-3973; Fax: 973-379-3722; Email: principal@srlacademy.org. Tina Underwood, Prin. Lay Teachers 19; Students 182.
Catechesis Religious Program—Tel: 973-376-1960; Fax: 973-376-3818. Michael Wojcik, D.R.E. Students 750.

SOUTH ORANGE, ESSEX CO., OUR LADY OF SORROWS (1887) Rev. Msgr. Robert E. Emery, J.C.L., M.A., V.E., E.V.; Revs. Richard Pfannenstiel; Danny Alexis Pabon, Parochial Vicar; Deacons John M. Inguaggiato; John M. Baltus; Rajgopal K. Srinivasa; Sr. Mary Selena McHugh, S.C.C., Pastoral Assoc.
Res.: 217 Prospect St., South Orange, 07079.
Tel: 973-763-5454; Fax: 973-763-9506; Email: ols217so@msn.com; Web: www.olschurch.com.
School—Our Lady of Sorrows School (1890) (Grades PreK-8), 172 Academy St., South Orange, 07079.
Tel: 973-763-5169; Fax: 973-378-9781; Email: principal@ourladyofsorrowsschool.org; Web: www.ourladyofsorrowsschool.org. Sr. Judy Foley, Prin.; Barbara McArthy, Media Specialist. Lay Teachers 15; Students 185.
Child Care—Day Care Nursery, Tel: 973-763-4040; Fax: 973-763-5151; Email: karlene@thenurseryatols.org. Karlene Snipe, Dir. Total Staff 18; Infants 12; Toddlers 12; Waddlers 12.
Catechesis Religious Program—
Tel: 973-763-5454, Ext. 235; Email: sorrowschurch@gmail.com. Joan Csedrik, D.R.E.; Christopher Kaiser, Youth Min. Students 380.

SPRINGFIELD, UNION CO., ST. JAMES (1923)
45 S. Springfield Ave., Springfield, 07081.
Tel: 973-375-6304; Fax: 973-376-0560; Email: jbarbone@msn.com; Email: jbarbone@aol.com; Web: www.saintjamesparish.org. Revs. Joseph F. Barbone; Jeong-Gyeong Kim, Parochial Vicar; Deacons Jerry Bongiovanni; Daniel O'Neill; Matt Wilson, Music Min.
School—St. James School, (Grades PreK-8), 41 S. Springfield Ave., Springfield, 07081-2301.
Tel: 973-376-5194; Fax: 973-376-5228; Email: sjschool@saintjamesparish.org. Ms. Caroline Ponterio. Lay Teachers 19; Students 200.
Catechesis Religious Program—Tel: 973-376-2061; Fax: 973-376-4079. Nancy Caputo, D.R.E.; Ann Marie Gesualdo, Youth Min. Students 377.

SUMMIT, UNION CO., SAINT TERESA OF AVILA (1863) [CEM]
306 Morris Ave., Summit, 07901. Tel: 908-277-3700; Email: info@stteresa.org; Web: st-teresa.org. Rev. Msgr. Robert S. Meyer Esq., S.T.L., J.D., J.C.L., V.F.; Deacon Kevin Reina.
School—St. Teresa Early Childhood Center, Email: cmonaco@stteresachurch.org. Mrs. Christine Monaco, Prin. Lay Teachers 6; Students 138.
Catechesis Religious Program—Tel: 908-273-6975; Fax: 908-273-1770. Brian Flanagan, Confirmation & Youth Min.; Timothy Margiotta, Youth Min.; Victtoria Cook, Youth Min. Preschool & Kindergarten Students 200; Students 1,118.
Cemetery & Mausoleum—140 Passaic Ave., Summit, 07901. Tel: 908-598-9426 (Cemetery);
Tel: 908-277-3741 (Mausoleum).

TEANECK, BERGEN CO., ST. ANASTASIA (1908) Rev. Herman Kinzler, O.Carm.; Deacons Kevin J. Regan; Roland O. Bianchi. In Res., Rev. Eugene Joseph Bettinger, O.Carm.
Res.: 1095 Teaneck Rd., Teaneck, 07666.
Tel: 201-837-3354; Fax: 201-837-3360; Email: secretary@saintanastasia.org; Web: www.saintanastasia.org.
Catechesis Religious Program—Tel: 201-837-3356. Sr. Adrienne Bradley, S.S.J., D.R.E. Students 225.
Convent—Tel: 201-837-3153.

TENAFLY, BERGEN CO., OUR LADY OF MOUNT CARMEL (1873)
10 County Rd., Tenafly, 07670. Tel: 201-568-0545; Fax: 201-568-3215; Email: rectory@olmc.us; Web: www.olmc.us. Revs. Daniel O'Neill, O.Carm.; Emmett Gavin, O.Carm., J.C.L., In Res.; Deacons Anthony Armstrong; Lex Ferrauiola; Michael Anthony Giuliano.
School—Our Lady of Mount Carmel School (1879) (Grades PreK-8), Tel: 201-567-6491;
Fax: 201-568-1402; Email: kkoval@academyolmc.org; Web: www.academyolmc.org. Kelly Koval, Prin. Lay Teachers 19; Students 272.
Catechesis Religious Program—Tel: 201-871-4662; Email: reled@olmc.us. Sr. Regina Chassar, S.S.J., D.R.E. Students 310.

UNION CITY, HUDSON CO.
1—ST. ANTHONY OF PADUA (1899) Revs. Jose Manuel de la Pena; Trinidad Jose Cuevas, Parochial Vicar; Yunior Almonte, Parochial Vicar.
Res.: 615 Eighth St., Union City, 07087.
Tel: 201-867-3818; Fax: 201-867-8859.
See Mother Seton Interparochial under Sts. Joseph and Michael, Union City.
Catechesis Religious Program—Luis Tobar, D.R.E. Students 208.
2—ST. AUGUSTINE (1886) Very Rev. Thomas J. Devine, O.A.R.; Revs. Jose Antonio Ciordia; Blas Montenegro, O.A.R.; Tonatiuh Espinosa, O.A.R.; Deacon Edward Donosso.
Res.: 3900 New York Ave., Union City, 07087.
Tel: 201-863-0233; Fax: 201-863-1344.
School—St. Augustine School (1891) (Grades PreK-8), 3920 New York Ave., Union City, 07087.
Tel: 201-865-5319; Fax: 201-865-2567; Email: lsharrock@optonline.net. Sr. Lillian Sharrock, S.C., Prin. Lay Teachers 13; Sisters of Charity 4; Students 189.
Catechesis Religious Program—Mr. David Pressey Waldburg, D.R.E.; Elkin Bustamente, D.R.E. Students 600.
Convent—342 39th St., Union City, 07087.
Tel: 201-348-0527.
3—HOLY FAMILY (1857) Very Rev. Thomas J. Devine, O.A.R.; Rev. Dionisio Gutierrez, O.A.R., (Spain) Parochial Vicar.
Res.: 530 35th St., Union City, 07087.
Tel: 201-867-6535; Fax: 201-867-1357.
Catechesis Religious Program—Milagros Villarreal, D.R.E. (English); Juana Alvarado, D.R.E. (Spanish). Students 60.
4—SS. JOSEPH AND MICHAEL (1887; 1851) Revs. Aro Nathan; Guillermo Mora, (Colombia) Parochial Vicar; Deacons Asterio Velasco; Ricardo L. Flores.
Res.: 1314 Central Ave., Union City, 07087.
Tel: 201-865-2325; Fax: 201-348-4412; Email: stsjoseph.michael@outlook.com.
School—Mother Seton Parochial, (Grades PreK-8), 1501 New York Ave., Union City, 07087.
Tel: 201-863-8433; Fax: 201-863-8145; Email: mothersetonoffice@yahoo.com. Mary P. McErlaine, Prin. Clergy 1; Lay Teachers 16; Students 252.
Catechesis Religious Program—Tel: 201-863-8145. Students 300.
5—SAINT ROCCO/SAINT BRIGID (1912)
4206 Kennedy Blvd., Union City, 07087.
Tel: 201- 863-1427; Tel: 201-863-0160;
Fax: 201-863-3877; Email: stroccounioncity@gmail.com; Web: www.stroccounioncity.org. Rev. Joseph D. Girone, V.F.; Luz V. Orejuela, Business Mgr.; Mrs. Carolyn Angelosante, Trustee; Mr. Keith Crichlow, Trustee.
Catechesis Religious Program—Teresita Ghabrial, C.R.E. & Formation Coord.; Rita Mendez, RCIA Coord. Students 117.

UNION, UNION CO.
1—HOLY SPIRIT (1963)
984 Suburban Rd., Union, 07083. Tel: 908-687-3327; Email: holyspiritchurch@comcast.net. Revs. Armand Mantia; Jose R. Valencia, Parochial Vicar; Deacons Kurt Landeck; Joseph J. Carlo.
Res.: 984 Suburban Rd., Union, 07083.
Tel: 908-687-3327; Email: holyspiritchurch@comcast.net.
School—Holy Spirit School, (Grades PreK-8), 970 Suburban Rd., Union, 07083. Tel: 908-687-8415;
Fax: 908-687-3996; Email: alaberti@holyspiritunionnj.org. Armand Lamberti, Prin. Lay Teachers 11; Students 170.
Catechesis Religious Program—984 Suburban Rd., Union, 07083.
2—SAINT MICHAEL THE ARCHANGEL (1928) Revs. Robert Wolfee, M.Div.; Emmanuel O. Agu, Parochial Vicar; Charles B. McDermott, Pastor Emeritus, (Retired); Camilo Lopez, Parochial Vicar.
Res.: 1212 Kelly St., Union, 07083. Tel: 908-688-1232 ; Fax: 908-810-1076; Email: stmichaelunion@comcast.net.
School—Saint Michael the Archangel School (1931) (Grades PreK-8), Tel: 908-688-1063; Email: ttelle@smsunion.org. Antoinette Telle, Prin. Lay Teachers 22; Students 359.
Catechesis Religious Program—Tel: 908-964-0965. Marilynn Dragone, C.R.E.; Philip Matrale, Youth Min., Tel: 908-686-3762. Students 350.

UPPER MONTCLAIR, ESSEX CO., ST. CASSIAN (1895)
187 Bellevue Ave., Upper Montclair, 07043.
Tel: 973-744-2850; Email: parishoffice@stcassianchurch.org; Web: www.stcassianchurch.org. Rev. Marc A. Vicari, M.Div.
Res.: 187 Lorraine Ave., Upper Montclair, 07043.
School—St. Cassian School, (Grades PreK-8), 190 Lorraine Ave., Upper Montclair, 07043.
Tel: 973-746-1636; Fax: 973-746-3271; Email: info@stcassianschool.org; Web: www.stcassianschool.

org. Maria A. Llanes, Prin. Clergy 1; Lay Teachers 13; Students 215.
Catechesis Religious Program—Tel: 973-744-2850; Email: rasammon@stcassianchurch.org. Regina Sammon, D.R.E. Students 263.

UPPER SADDLE RIVER, BERGEN CO., CHURCH OF THE PRESENTATION (1961) Revs. Robert B. Stagg; Jesus Carlo Leonardo Merino. In Res., Rev. Msgr. Edward J. Ciuba, (Retired).
Office: 271 W. Saddle River Rd., Upper Saddle River, 07458. Tel: 201-327-1313; Email: communications@churchofpresentation.org; Web: www.churchofpresentation.org.
Res.: 41 Riverview Ter., Upper Saddle River, 07458.
Catechesis Religious Program—Students 1,409.

VERONA, ESSEX CO., OUR LADY OF THE LAKE (1923)
32 Lakeside Ave., Verona, 07044. Tel: 973-239-5696; Fax: 973-239-7190; Email: ollrectory@gmail.com; Web: www.ollverona.org. Revs. Joseph A. D'Amico; Oliver D. Nilo, Parochial Vicar; Jerome S. Arthasseril, In Res., (Retired); William J. Melillo, M.A., M.Div., In Res., (Retired); Deacons David Strader; Ralph F. Powell; Paul Hui Ra-Se Pak.
Fr. Michael Hanly Pastoral Center—22 Lakeside Ave., Verona, 07044.
School—Our Lady of the Lake School (1924) (Grades PreK-8), 26 Lakeside Ave., Verona, 07044.
Tel: 973-239-1160; Email: info@myoll.org; Web: www.myoll.org. Benjamin Ronquillo, Prin. Lay Teachers 21; Students 238.
Catechesis Religious Program—Tel: 973-239-2950; Email: ursula_konrad@ollverona.org. Ursula Konrad, D.R.E.; Gina Butler, Youth Min. Students 950.

WALLINGTON, BERGEN CO., MOST SACRED HEART OF JESUS (1942) [CEM] (Polish)
127 Paterson Ave., Wallington, 07057.
Tel: 973-778-7405; Email: mostsacredheart@verizon.net; Web: www.mostsacredheart.org. Very Rev. Canon Felix R. Marciniak; Revs. Steven D. D'Andrea; Marcin Kuperski; Deacon Domenick DiBernardo; Sisters Emilia Zdeb, S.S.N.D., Pastoral Assoc.; Lisa Marie DiSabatino, C.S.S.F., Pastoral Assoc.
Catechesis Religious Program—Tel: 973-777-9505; Fax: 973-815-0176. Sr. Marie Victoria Bartkowski, D.R.E. Students 351.
Convent—27 Dankhoff Ave., Wallington, 07057.
Tel: 973-777-5124.

WASHINGTON TOWNSHIP, BERGEN CO., OUR LADY OF GOOD COUNSEL (1959)
668 Ridgewood Rd., Washington Township, 07676.
Tel: 201-664-6624; Email: olgcwt@aol.com; Web: www.olgcwt.org. Revs. Stephen J. Cinque; Raymond E. Rodrigue, Parochial Vicar; Stephen J. Toth, In Res.; Deacons Bruce Olsen, Pastoral Assoc.; Robert Glasner.
See Our Lady of Mercy Interparochial School, Park Ridge under Our Lady of Mercy, Park Ridge for details.
See St. John's Academy Interparochial, Hillsdale under St. John The Baptist, Hillsdale for details.
Catechesis Religious Program—Tel: 201-664-1679; Email: gagliostrot@gmail.com. Mrs. Teresa Dziob, D.R.E. Students 249.

WEEHAWKEN, HUDSON CO., ST. LAWRENCE (1887)
22 Hackensack Ave., Weehawken, 07086.
Tel: 201-863-6464; Email: coordinator@stlweehawken.com. Rev. Eric W. Fuchs, Admin.
Res.: Weehawken, 07086.
See Hoboken Catholic Academy, Hoboken under St. Ann's, Hoboken for details.
Catechesis Religious Program—Students 85.

WEST NEW YORK, HUDSON CO.
1—HOLY REDEEMER (2005) Very Rev. Carlo B.M. Fortunio, (Italy) V.F.; Revs. Giordano Belanich, Parochial Vicar; Angelo Pochelti, (Italy) In Res.; Deacon Jesus D. Aristy.
Office & Res.: 569 65th St., West New York, 07093.
Tel: 201-868-9444; Email: Holyredeemer569@gmail.com; Web: www.padrepiocenter.org.
Worship Sites—
Our Lady Help of Christians/St. Mary Church—West New York, 07093.
Our Lady of Libera Church, West New York, 07093.
St. John Nepomucene Church, Guttenberg, 07093.
Catechesis Religious Program—Ed Mendoza, D.R.E. & Business Admin.; Philip Dispensa, Coord., Protecting God's Children; Jaime Trelles, D.R.E.; Rosa Trelles, D.R.E., St. Mary's Worship Site; Sr. Ana Ruth Quilme, F.M.S.H., D.R.E., Spanish Our Lady of Libera Site. Students 395.
2—ST. JOSEPH OF THE PALISADES (1875) (Hispanic) Rev. Msgr. Gregory J. Studerus, V.F., V.E., E.V.; Revs. Gabriel G. Muteru; Nelson Oyola; Cesar A. Infante; Deacon Ernesto C. Tibay.
Res.: 6401 Palisade Ave., West New York, 07093.
Tel: 201-854-7006; Email: stjosephwny@optonline.net; Web: www.saintjosephpalisades.com.
School—Academy of St. Joseph of the Palisades (1872) (Grades PreK-8), 6408 Palisade Ave., West New York, 07093. Tel: 201-861-3227; Fax: 201-861-5744; Email: info@stjosephpalisadeselem.com; Web: www.stjosephpalisadeselem.com. Lauren Lytle, Prin. Lay Teachers 17; Students 246.
Catechesis Religious Program—Marco Guerrero, D.R.E. Students 550.
Chapel—Immaculate Heart of Mary, 7615 Broadway, North Bergen, 07047.
3—ST. MARY HELP OF CHRISTIANS (1895) Merged with St. John Nepomucene, Guttenberg to form Holy Redeemer, West New York.
4—OUR LADY OF LIBERA (1902) Merged with Holy Redeemer, West New York.

WEST ORANGE, ESSEX CO.
1—ST. JOSEPH (1931)
44 Benvenue Ave., West Orange, 07052.
Tel: 973-669-3221; Email: stjosephwestorange@hotmail.com; Web: www.stjoeswestorange.com. Rev. Dominick J. Lenoci; Deacon Richard O'Hara; Rev. James R. White, In Res.
Catechesis Religious Program—Tel: 973-669-8331. Pauline Alger, Pastoral Assoc. & D.R.E., Tel: 973-669-8331. Students 78.
2—ST. MARY
425 Northfield Ave., #19, West Orange, 07052.
Email: frdennismary@gmail.com. Rev. Dennis Culic.
School—St. Mary Academy, 425 Northfield Ave., #19, West Orange, 07052. Irene Manning, Prin. & D.R.E.
Catechesis Religious Program—
3—OUR LADY OF LOURDES (1914) Rev. James P. Ferry.
Res.: 1 Eagle Rock Ave., West Orange, 07052.
Tel: 973-325-0110; Fax: 973-325-9105; Email: ollwo@comcast.net; Web: www.lourdeswestorgange.com.
Catechesis Religious Program—Tel: 973-325-0029.
Convent—Tel: 973-325-0318; Fax: 973-325-0691.

WESTFIELD, UNION CO.
1—ST. HELEN (1968)
1600 Rahway Ave., Westfield, 07090.
Tel: 908-232-1214; Email: sthelen@sainthelen.org; Web: sainthelen.org. Revs. Michael A. Saporito; Gabriel J. Curtis, Parochial Vicar; Marilyn Ryan, Pastoral Assoc.; Aida Gabuzda, Parish Dir. Opers.; Carolyn Colonna, Business Mgr.; Adrian Soltys, Music Min.
See Holy Trinity Interparochial school, Westfield under Holy Trinity, Westfield for details.
Catechesis Religious Program—Tricia McGlynn, D.R.E.; Michael Fusco, D.R.E. & Youth Min.; Patricia Gardner, Youth Min. Students 1,621.
2—HOLY TRINITY (1872)
315 First St., Westfield, 07090. Tel: 908-232-8137; Email: htoffice@parishmail.com; Web: www.htrcc.org. Revs. Anthony J. Randazzo, V.F.; Alex D. Pinto, (India) (Retired), (In Res.); Deacons Thomas A. Pluta; Keith Gibbons.
Schools—Holy Trinity School—(Grades PreK-8), 336 First St., Westfield, 07090. Tel: 908-233-0484; Fax: 908-233-6204; Email: office-wc@htisnj.com; Web: www.htisnj.com. Mrs. Adele Ellis, Prin.; Sr. Maureen Fichner, S.S.J., Prin.
Holy Trinity School - Mountainside Campus, (Grades PreK-K), 304 Central Ave., Mountainside, 07092.
Tel: 908-233-1899; Fax: 908-654-6690. Mrs. Jacqueline Pantano, Prin. Lay Teachers 10; Students 82.
Catechesis Religious Program—Tel: 908-233-7455; Email: mlizzo.faithformation@verizon.net. Mrs. Marguerite Lizzo, D.R.E.; Patricia Martin, Youth Min. Students 667.

WESTWOOD, BERGEN CO., ST. ANDREW (1889) [CEM] Revs. Paciano A. Barbieto; Rafael I. Galvez-Pineda; Deacon Robert S. Pontillo; Alan Pitman, Youth Min.
Res.: 120 Washington Ave., Westwood, 07675.
Tel: 201-666-1100; Fax: 201-722-1432; Email: parishinfo@standrewcc.com; Web: www.standrewcc.com.
See St. John's Academy, Hillsdale under St. John the Baptist, Hillsdale for details.
Catechesis Religious Program—Tel: 201-664-6777; Email: reled@standrewcc.com. Mary Jean Conroy, D.R.E.; Carol Stalter, Asst. D.R.E. Students 1,005.

WOOD RIDGE, BERGEN CO., ASSUMPTION OF OUR BLESSED LADY (1926) Revs. Richard J. Mucowski, O.F.M., Ph.D.; Paul Keenan, O.F.M.; Robert Norton, O.F.M., Parochial Vicar; Deacon Francis P. Materia. In Res., Bro. Gary J. Maciag, O.F.M., M.F.A.
Res.: 143 First St., Wood Ridge, 07075.
Tel: 201-438-5555; Email: assumption143@yahoo.com; Web: www.assumptionwr.org.
Catechesis Religious Program—Hayes Center, 142 Second St., Wood Ridge, 07075. Tel: 201-933-6118; Email: arewrnj@yahoo.com. Donna Ryan, D.R.E.; Kristen Dziuba, Youth Min. & Dir. Music. Students 430.
Convent—450 Main Ave., Wood Ridge, 07075.

WOODCLIFF LAKE, BERGEN CO., OUR LADY MOTHER OF THE CHURCH (1967)
209 Woodcliff Ave., Woodcliff Lake, 07677.
Tel: 201-391-2826; Email: info@motherofthechurch.com; Web: www.motherofthechurch.org. Very Rev. Sean A. Manson, V.F.; Rev. Siffredus B. Rwechungura, Parochial Vicar, Archbishop's House, P.O. Box 167, Dar es Salaam, Tanzania East Africa; Rev. Msgr. Cajetan P. Salemi, Pastor Emeritus, (Retired); Deacon Stanley F. Fedison.
Rectory—130 Apple Ridge, Woodcliff Lake, 07677.
See St. John's Academy, Hillsdale under St. John the Baptist, Hillsdale for details.
Catechesis Religious Program—Tel: 201-391-7400. Patricia Keenaghan, D.R.E. Students 305.

WYCKOFF, BERGEN CO., ST. ELIZABETH (1902) Revs. Stephen J. Fichter, Ph.D., S.T.B.; Carlos Eduardo Briceno, Parochial Vicar; Vincent D'Agostino, Parochial Vicar; Deacon Andrew E. Saunders, M.A.
Res.: 700 Wyckoff Ave., Wyckoff, 07481.
Tel: 201-891-1122; Email: rectory@saintelizabeths.org; Web: www.saintelizabeths.org.
School—St. Elizabeth School, (Grades PreK-8), 700 Wyckoff Ave, Wyckoff, 07481. Tel: 201-891-1481; Fax: 201-891-8669; Email: admin@sainte-school.org; Web: www.sainte-school.org. Karen Lewis, Prin. Lay Teachers 16; Students 235.
Catechesis Religious Program—Tel: 201-891-3262; Fax: 201-891-3708; Email: jcamiolo@saintelizabeths.org. Jonathan Camiolo, D.R.E. Students 160.

Hospital Chaplaincy

NEWARK. *Office of Health Care Personnel*,
Tel: 973-877-2572. Most Rev. Manuel A. Cruz, D.D., Archdiocesan Dir., Hospital Chaplaincy, St. Michael Medical Center, 171 Clifton Ave., 07104. Tel: 973-497-4010.

Bergen County

ENGLEWOOD. *Englewood Hospital & Medical Center*, 350 Engle St., Englewood, 07631.
Tel: 201-894-3000. Vacant.

HACKENSACK. *Hackensack University Medical Center*, 30 Prospect St., Hackensack, 07601.
Tel: 201-996-2000; Tel: 201-996-2345. Revs. Francis Perry Azah, Chap. (Adjunct), German Coquillo Jr., C.R.M., Chap., John J. Prada, Chap., Arokiaswamy Samson, Chap. (Adjunct).

PARAMUS. *Bergen Regional Medical Center*, 230 E. Ridgewood Ave., Paramus, 07652.
Tel: 201-967-4177; Fax: 201-967-4277. Revs. German Coquillo Jr., C.R.M., Edito S. Gamallo, Chap., (Retired), Felix Antonio Castro Godinez, Chap. (Adjunct), John Opara, Chap. (Adjunct).

RIDGEWOOD. *Valley Hospital*, 223 N. Van Dien Ave., Ridgewood, 07450. Tel: 201-447-8150. Revs. Mert Cordero, Chap., Stephen J. Toth, Chap.

TEANECK. *Holy Name Medical Center*, 718 Teaneck Rd., Teaneck, 07666. Tel: 201-833-3000;
Tel: 201-833-3243 (Pastoral Care). Revs. Edward T. Veluz, Chap., Maciej Jan Zajac, Chap.

Essex County

NEWARK. *Beth Israel Medical Center*, 201 Lyons Ave., 07112. Tel: 973-926-7000;
Tel: 973-926-7178 (Pastoral Care). Vacant.
St. Michael Medical Center, 111 Central Ave., 07102.
Tel: 973-877-5467. Vacant.
University Hospital, 150 Bergen St., 07103.
Tel: 973-972-4300. Rev. Robert P. McLaughlin, Chap.

BELLEVILLE. *Clara Maass Medical Center*, One Clara Maass Dr., Belleville, 07109. Tel: 973-450-2000. Rev. Peter O. Iwuala, Chap.

EAST ORANGE. *Veterans Administration Hospital*, Tremont Ave. & Center St., East Orange, 07019.
Tel: 973-676-1000;
Tel: 973-972-5688 (Pastoral Care). Rev. Mathew Eraly, (India).

LIVINGSTON. *Saint Barnabas Medical Center*, 94 Old Short Hills Rd., Livingston, 07039.
Tel: 973-533-5015. Rev. Malachy E. Odoh, Chap. (Adjunct).

MONTCLAIR. *Mountainside Hospital*, One Bay Ave., Montclair, 07042. Tel: 973-429-6000;
Tel: 973-429-6047 (Pastoral Care). Rev. Thomas M. Cembor, Chap.

Hudson County

HOBOKEN. *Hoboken University Medical Center*, 308 Willow Ave., Hoboken, 07030. Tel: 201-418-1000.

JERSEY CITY. *Jersey City Medical Center*, 50 Baldwin Ave., Jersey City, 07304. Tel: 201-915-2000. Vacant.

Union County

ELIZABETH. *Trinitas Regional Medical Center*, 225 Williamson St., Elizabeth, 07202. Tel: 908-994-5000. Revs. Stephen Aribe, Chap., Brendan Quinn, Chap.

RAHWAY. *Rahway Hospital*, 865 Stone St., Rahway, 07065. Tel: 732-381-4200. Rev. Roberto A. Lamirez.

SUMMIT. *Overlook Hospital*, 99 Beauvoir Ave., Summit, 07902. Tel: 908-522-2000. Rev. Armando S. Crisostomo Jr., Chap.

Prison Ministry

NEWARK. *Office of Prison Ministry*, Our Lady of the Lake, 32 Lakeside Ave., Verona, 07044. Cell: 973-239-5696. Rev. Joseph A. D'Amico, Dir., Deacon Marcelo David, Asst. Dir.

Bergen County

HACKENSACK. *Bergen County Correctional Facility*, 160 S. River Rd., Hackensack, 07601. Tel: 201-527-3018. Rev. Onyedika Michael Otuwurunne, Chap., Mr. Anthony Terraboccio, Prison Min.

TETERBORO. *Bergen County Juvenile Detention Center*, 200 North St., Teterboro, 07608. Tel: 201-336-3905 . Vacant, Prison Min.

Essex County

NEWARK. *Delaney Hall Assessment Center*, 451 Doremus Ave., 07105. Tel: 973-274-0115. Rev. Paul J. Nolan, Chap., (Retired), Catherine Attara-Fink, Pastoral Staff, Sr. Antonelle Chunka, C.S.S.F., Prison Min., Thomas More Fink, Pastoral Staff.

Essex County Correctional Facility, 354 Doremus Ave., 07105. Tel: 973-621-5162. Vacant, Chap., Vacant, Prison Min.

Essex County Juvenile Detention Center, 208 Sussex Ave., 07103. Tel: 973-497-4720. Antoine Wilson, Pastoral Staff.

Essex County Logan Hall, 20 Toler Pl., 07104. Tel: 973-642-4249. Rev. Paul J. Nolan, Chap., (Retired).

Northern State Prison, 168 Frontage Rd., 07114. Tel: 973-465-0068, Ext. 4505. Deacon David Loman, Prison Min.

Hudson County

SECAUCUS. *Hudson County Juvenile Correctional Center*, 635 County Ave., Secaucus, 07094. Tel: 201-319-3750 (Promise/Outreach Ministry). Rev. Giordano Belanich, Chap., Sr. Antonelle Chunka, C.S.S.F., Prison Min., Bro. Thomas Corey, B.S.C.D., Prison Min.

SOUTH KEARNY. *Hudson County Correctional Center*, 35 Hackensack Ave., South Kearny, 07032. Tel: 973-558-7000. Revs. Joseph A. D'Amico, Chap., Eugene P. Squeo, J.D., Chap., (Retired), Deacons Marcello David, Prison Min., David Loman, Prison Min., Ms. Rosa Santana, Prison Min.

Talbot Hall Assessment Center, 100-140 Lincoln Hwy., South Kearny. Tel: 973-589-1114. Rev. Joseph A. D'Amico, Chap.

Union County

ELIZABETH. *Elizabeth Federal Detention Center*, 625 Evans St., Elizabeth, 07201. Tel: 908-352-3776. Rev. George F. Sharp, (Retired).

Union County Jail, 15 Elizabethtown Plaza, Elizabeth, 07207. Tel: 908-558-2636. Deacon Michael DeRoberts, Prison Min.

Special Assignment in the Archdiocese:
Rev. Msgr.—
Kleissler, Thomas A., Pastor Emeritus, (Retired), 7 Ryerson Ave., Caldwell, 07006
Revs.—
Dowd, William J., Chap., (Retired), 29 Madison Ave., Avenel, 07001. Tel: 973-226-1577
Sudol, Gerard J., Chap., 136 Brookline Ave., Nutley, 07110.

On Duty Outside the Archdiocese:
Very Revs.—
Gonzalez, Luis O., V.F., Our Lady of Divine Providence RC Mission, P.O. Box 340 Leeward Hwy., Providenciales, Turks and Caicos Islands
Krol, Miroslaw K., V.F., Orchard Lake Schools, 3535 Commerce Rd., Orchard Lake, MI 48324
Revs.—
Arata, Miguel A., Rooma Katoliku Kirik Kogudus, Veski TN 1-1A, EE2400, Tartu, Estonia
Basile, Gioacchino, St. Gabriel Parish, 26-26 98th St., East Elmhurst, NY 11369
Becerra, Robert L., Santa Clara Parish, P.O. Box 215, Santa Clara, NM 88026
Bornhauser, Emmanuel, 102 Rue Barbara, Montpellier, France 34080
Brosk, Steven J., 4 Liberty Pl., Sugarloaf, PA 18249
Caceres, Leonardo M., Notre Dame Le Rouet, 60 Boulevard de Louvain, Marseille, France 13008
Carranza, Fernando
Cho, Ray P., Casa Santa Maria, Via Dell'Umlita 30, Rome, Italy 00187
Ciriaco, Dominic G., Theological College, 401 Michigan Ave., NE, Washington, DC 20017
Dellagiovanna, Mariano N., St. Barnabas Rectory, 6300 Buist Ave., Philadelphia, PA 19142
Di Giovanni, Alfonso, SS. Peter and Paul, Rooma Katoliku Kirk, Vene tn 18, Tallinn, Estonia 10123
Donini, Leone, c/o Seminaire Redemptoris Mater, Sainte Mer, 3 Rue Jacques Lurent, La Seyne sur mer, France 83500
Fedele, Giuseppe, c/o St. James Roman Catholic Church, 1314 Newport St., Denver, CO 80220
Flor, Carlos, St. Thomas Aquinas Church, 97 South St., Jamaica Plain, MA 02130
Flora, Giandomenico M., St. Raphael Parish, 162 Oak St., Bridgeport, CT 06604
Forte, Anthony R., 825 Carolyn Dr., Chesapeake, VA 23320
Frade, Paulo, Av. Presidente Tancredo Neves, 447, Estacao, Itaquaquecetuba, SP CEP, Brazil 08571-000
Francesco, Richard G., Diocese of Helena, St. Mary Catholic Community, 1700 Missoula Ave., Helena, MT 59601
Gonzalez, Luis P., Calle Constructora Naval 7, 1 Derecha, 11100 San Fernando, Cadiz, Spain
Granyak, Esteban Nelson, Saint Charles Borromeo Rectory, 902 S. 20th St., Philadelphia, PA 19146
Guberovic, Zeljko J., Diocese of Gaylord, 611 W. North St., Gaylord, MI 49735-8349
Kimel, Alvin Jr., 6109 Saddle Ridge Rd., Roanoke, VA 24018
LaBranche, Raymond, Redemptoris Mater Seminary, 2215 rue Marie-Victorin, Quebec, Canada G1T 1J6
Lintz, Christoph, Holy Family Parish, A.M. Bienen Korb 2, Muenchen, Germany 81545
Luksza, Mariusz G., Diocese of Hamilton in Bermuda, P.O. Box HM 1191, Hamilton HM EX, Bermuda Islands
Markovic, Viktor, Rooma Katoliku Kirk Kogudas, Veski 1-A, Tartu, Estonia 51005
Marquez, Jose E., Mary, Queen of Peace, 120 S. 34th St., Billings, MT 59101-3715
Marroquin, Marco T., Our Lady of Divine Providence R.C. Mission, Leeward Hwy., P.O. Box 340, Providenciales, Turks and Caicos Islands
Martinez, Pablo A., Diocese of Gaylord, 611 W. North St., Gaylord, MI 49735
Morelli, Attilio, Diocese of Hamilton in Bermuda, P.O. Box HM 1191, Hamilton, Bermuda HM EX
O'Donoghue, Neil Xavier, Ph.D., Holy Redeemer Parochial House, Ard Easmuinn, Dundalk, Co. Louth Ireland
Ortiz-Garay, Jorge, St. Brigid Church, 409 Linden St., Brooklyn, NY 11237
Picone, Alfonso, (Italy) Sacred Heart Church, 37 Schuyler Ave., Stamford, CT 06902
Randl, Ewald, Pfarre St. Ruprecht, Kirchengasse 29 am Worthersee, Klagenfurt, Austria 9020
Rodriguez, Tobias, Remdemptoris Mater Missionary Seminary, 1300 S. Steele St., Denver, CO 80210
Roman, Julio I., Archdiocese of Asuncion, C. C. 654, Mariscal Lopez 130, Asuncion, Paraguay
Russo, Michael A., 125 Surf Way #309, Box 5166, Monterey, CA 93940
Sant, Ivan, Archdioces of St. Paul & Minneapolis, 226 Summit Ave., St. Paul, MN 55102
Silva, Raul, Queen of Angels Church, 1001 E. Oakland Ave., Austin, MN 55912
Skublics, Mat, 3530 Miskolc, Szechenyi, Istvan ut 2 Hungary
Tran, Joseph M. Duykim N., c/o Most Rev. Joseph Nguyen Van Yen, Bishop of Phat Diem, Toa Giam Muc, Kim Son, Ninh Binh Vietnam
Trujillo-Gonzalez, Francisco de Asis, IL. IL. Calle La Al-ondra, 8, El Puerto De Santa Maria, Cadiz, Spain 11500
Urnick, Charles B., St. John the Baptist, P.O. Box 31230, Laughlin, NV 89028
Velasquez, Rafael, Holy Cross Mission, P.O. Box 145, Grand Turks & Caicos Island, West Indies
Vilchez, Pedro E., P.O. Box 145, Grand Turk, Turks & Caicos Islands, British West Indies.

Military Chaplains:
Revs.—
Beale, Kenneth R., 10424 St. Tropez Pl., Tampa, FL 33615
Berchmanz, Anthony, 5970-B Mission Center Rd., San Diego, CA 92123
Fonseca, Oscar D., 1413 Beaumont St., Sheppard AFB, TX 76311
Hamel, James A., Col., 100 N. Santa Rosa St., Apt. 1005, San Antonio, TX 78207
Hanrahan, William P., P.O. Box 273, Seward, AK 99664-0273
Kokeram, Sudash Joseph, 8016 N. 46th St., Tampa, FL 33617
Kopec, Rajmund, Major, 1571 Churchhill Ct., Clarksville, TN 37042
Lesak, William P., 3519 Cranberry Ln., New Bern, NC 28562
Pawlikowski, Matthew, 1010 NW 82nd St., Lawton, OK 73505
Ubalde, Ulysses L., 2nd Mardiv 8th Marreg, Camp Lejeune, NC 28542
Uhde, Peter, Fort Huachuca, 103 Garrison Ave., Sierra Vista, AZ 85613.

Medical Leave:
Rev. Msgr.—
Figueiredo, Anthony J., S.T.D.
Revs.—
Importico, Paul D.
Larrea, Hector
McFadden, Brian F.
O'Malley, Mark Francis, Hist.Eccl.D.
Pambello, Louis M.
Plate, Brian G.

Administrative Leave:
Revs.—
Celis-Quintero, Marco A.
Njoku, Titus C.

Retired:
Most Revs.—
Myers, John J., J.C.D., D.D., (Retired)
Marconi, Dominic A., D.D., (Retired)
McDonnell, Charles J., D.D., (Retired)
Flesey, John W., S.T.D., D.D., (Retired)
Rev. Msgrs.—
Agan, Jose, (Retired), c/o Maria Bocanegra, 74 Beech St., Kearny, 07032
Antao, John S., (Retired), 65 Elmora Ave., Elizabeth, 07202
Bochicchio, Paul L., (Retired), St. Francis of Assisi Parish, 308 Jefferson St., Hoboken, 07030
Burke, James A., (Retired), 517 4th Ave., Avon By The Sea, 07717
Casale, Franklyn M., (Retired), 16500 Collins Ave., Apt. 1155, Sunny Isles Beach, FL 33160
Chabak, Robert M., V.F., (Retired), 302 6th Ave., Normandy Beach, 08739
Cheplic, Peter A., (Retired), 60 Home Ave., Rutherford, 07070
Chiang, Joseph, (Retired), 60 Home Ave., Rutherford, 07070
Ciuba, Edward J., (Retired), 271 W. Saddle River Rd., Saddle River, 07458
Eilert, Edward J., (Retired), 60 Home Ave., Rutherford, 07070. 60 Home Ave., Apt. 21, Rutherford, 07070
Fadrowski, William J., V.F., (Retired), Saint James Church, 184 S. Finely Ave., P.O. Box 310, Basking Ridge, 07920
Fernando, Venantius M., (Retired), 541 Washington Ave., Kenilworth, 07033
Gonzalez, Ricardo, (Retired), 166 Central Blvd., Brick, 08724
Granato, Joseph J., (Retired), 201 Clifton Ave., 07104
Groncki, Richard F., (Retired), 50 W. Midland Ave., Paramus, 07652
Guenther, Donald E., (Retired), 18 Pine Grove Rd., Manahawkin, 08050
Gusmer, Charles W., S.T.D., V.E., (Retired), 111 South St., New Providence, 07974
Harms, William C., (Retired), 290 Plainfield Ave., Berkeley Heights, 07922
Hendry, Owen J., (Retired), 3073 Eastwood Ter., The Villages, FL 32163
Herbster, Kenneth J., V.F., (Retired), 247 Bloomfield Ave., Apt. 11, North Caldwell, 07006
Ivory, Thomas P., S.T.D., (Retired), Rev. Msgr. James F. Kelley Residence, 247 Bloomfield Ave., Apt. 1, Caldwell, 07006
Kleissler, Thomas A., (Retired), 1 Commons Dr., Neptune, 07753. 7 Ryerson Ave., Caldwell, 07006
Kulig, Anthony J., K.H.S., M.A., (Retired), 400 So. Orange Ave., South Orange, 07079
Laferrera, John J., (Retired), 927 Montauk Dr., Forked River, 08731
LoBianco, Francis R., (Retired), 23 Wall St., Charlestown, MA 02129
Madden, Thomas G., (Retired), 60 Home Ave., Rutherford, 07070
Mahon, Dennis, (Retired), 123 Harbor Inn Rd., Bayville, 08721

Mahoney, Neil J., (Retired), 467 Springfield Ave., Summit, 07901
Masiello, Joseph P., V.F., (Retired), 150 Overlook Ave., Apt. 12B, Hackensack, 07601
McDade, Thomas J., (Retired), 34 Dickinson Ct., Red Bank, 07701
Miller, Lawrence J., (Retired), 66 W. 23rd St., Apt. A-1, Bayonne, 07002
Morris, Philip D., S.T.D., (Retired), 2700 S. Oakland Forest Dr., Apt. 103, Oakland Park, FL 33309-5640
Newland, Ronald A., (Retired), 21 Park End Ter., Rockaway Point, NY 11697-2303
O'Connor, John Philip, (Retired), Rev. Msgr. James F. Kelley Residence, 247 Bloomfield Ave., Apt. 4, Caldwell, 07006
O'Donnell, Hugh A., (Retired), 503 Gallows Hill Rd., Cranford, 07016
Papera, Lewis V., V.F., (Retired), 110 Del Dor Dr., Point Pleasant, 08742
Plunkett, Joseph P., (Retired), Our Lady of Czestochowa, 115 S. 3rd St., Harrison, 07029
Quill, John A., (Retired), Rev. Msgr. James F. Kelley Residence, 247 Bloomfield Ave., Apt. 8, Caldwell, 07006
Rebanal, Jeremias R., J.C.D., Ph.D., (Retired), 155 Washington Ave., Elizabeth, 07202
Schetelick, Paul D., V.F., (Retired), Our Lady of the Visitation, 234 N. Farview Ave., Paramus, 07652
Seymour, Francis R., K.H.S., (Retired), St. Cecilia Parish, 120 Kearny Ave., Kearny, 07032
Sheeran, Robert T., (Retired), Marin Catholic High School, 675 Sir Francis Drake Blvd., Kentfield, CA 94904
Strelecki, Richard T., (Retired), 411 W. Stimpson Ave., Linden, 07036. 60 Home Ave., Apt. 32, Rutherford, 7070. 411 W. Stimpson Ave., Linden, 07036. 60 Home Ave., Apt. 32, Rutherford, 07070
Templeton, Robert E., (Retired), 9252 Kennedy Blvd., Apt. 309, North Bergen, 07047
Tiboni, Vito, (Retired), 241 E. Kenney St., First Fl., 07105
Turro, James C., Ph.D., (Retired), Seton Hall University, 400 S. Orange Ave., South Orange, 07079
Zaccardo, Peter J., (Retired), 53 Seaview Ave., Brick, 08723

Revs.—
Aquino, Peter M., (Retired), P.O. Box 1087, Woodbridge, 07095
Arico, Carl J., (Retired), 979 Avenue C, Bayonne, 07002
Arthasseril, Jerome S., (Retired), 32 Lakeside Ave., Verona, 07044
Ashe, Kevin P., (Retired), 446 Adamston Rd., Brick, 08723
Ballance, Harvey, (Retired), 92 Edgemont Rd., Montclair, 07043
Baron, John B., Ph.D., (Retired), 2059 First Ave., Avalon, 08202
Barrow, Joseph A., (Retired), 404 Sumner St., East Boston, MA 02128-2218. 11620 W. Washington Blvd., Los Angeles, CA 90066
Bauman, John, (Retired), 393 Deuce Dr., Wall, 07719
Bejgrowicz, Joseph S., (Retired), St. Raphael Parish, 346 E. Mount Pleasant Ave., Livingston, 07039
Benedetto, James F., (Retired), 247 Bloomfield Ave., Caldwell, 07006. 247 Bloomfield Ave., Apt. 12, Caldwell, 07006
Bernas, Eugene, (Philippines) (Retired), 1392 Mansion Rd., Roxas City, Capiz Philippines 5800
Berner, Albert J., B.A., S.T.B., M.A., V.F., (Retired), 1 Seaview Ave., Brick, 08723
Blumenfeld, Donald E., Ph.D., (Retired), 42 Summer St., Emerson, 07630
Burke, Alfred J., (Retired), 113 Blake Cr., Brick, 08724
Burla, Frank J., (Retired), 30 N. Fullerton Ave., Montclair, 07042
Carlson, Richard D., (Retired), P.O. Box 471, Lavallette, 08735
Carroll, James J., (Retired), c/o Donald Campbell, 599 Avenue C, Bayonne, 07002
Celiano, Alfred V., Ph.D., (Retired), 400 South Orange Ave., South Orange, 07079
Chrusciel, Bogumil, (Retired), 22 Rockaway Pl., Parsippany, 07054
Ciba, Thomas J., M.P.A., (Retired), P.O. Box 54, Blakeslee, PA 18610
Cio, Robert J., (Retired), c/o Peggy Saulsgiver, 330 Lisa Ln., Oldsmar, FL 34677
Coda, Joseph F., (Retired), 60 Home Ave., Rutherford, 07070
Cohan, Dennis J., (Retired), 58 Plymouth Way, Barnegat, 08005
Collins, Neil J., (Retired), 60 Home Ave. Apt. 23, Rutherford, 07070
Cook, William G., (Retired), 41 Reverend Roberts Pl., Nutley, 07110
D'Emma, Gregory J., (Retired), 207 Hope Dr., Boiling Springs, PA 17007. 207 Hope Dr., Boiling Springs, PA 17007
Diurczak, Eugene, (Retired), 247 Bloomfield Ave., Apt. 2, Caldwell, 07006
Doherty, John R., (Retired), 362 Orient Way, Rutherford, 07070
Donohue, John J., (Retired), St. John Vianney Annex, 64 Home Ave., 2nd Fl., Rutherford, 07070
Donohue, Patrick W., V.F., (Retired), 280 Washington Ave., Dumont, 07628
Dowd, William J., (Retired), 724 Drum Point Rd., Brick, 08723-7548
Driscoll, William D., (Retired), 51 Monterey Ave., Teaneck, 07666
Evans, Ken, (Retired), St. John Vianney Residence, 60 Home Ave., Apt. 38, Rutherford, 07070
Farley, Leo O., (Retired), 247 Bloomfield Ave., Caldwell, 07006
Feketie, Michael J., (Retired), 516 W. 6th St., Plainfield, 07060
Fernando, Bernard, (Retired), 2808 Theresa Dr., Kissimmee, FL 34744
Finnerty, James J., (Retired), c/o James Neff, 18 Bowne Ave., Atlantic Highlands, 07716-2142. Tel: 732-872-2486
Fiorino, Dominic J., (Retired), c/o Angela Laucik, 16 Deer Trail Dr., Clarksburg, 08510
Fonseka, Matthew, (Retired), St. Philip the Apostle Convent, 426 Saddle River Rd., Saddle Brook, 07662
Fu, Joseph, (Retired), P.O. On Bldg., F/15 A 30 Mong Kok Rd., Mong Kok Kowloom, Hong Kong
Fuccile, Dominic G., (Retired), 520 W. Buena Ventura, Colorado Springs, CO 80907. 7 Lance Dr., Brick, 08723
Furrevig, Edward G., (Retired), 1694 Tilford Boulevard, Brick, 08724
Gamallo, Edito S., (Retired), c/o Bernardita G. Tangel, 438 Fairmount Ave., Chatham, 07928
German, Michael J., (Retired), 60 Home Ave., Apt. 1, Rutherford, 07070
Gniewyk, Eugene, (Retired), 340 N. Franklin Tpke., Ho Ho Kus, 07423
Gorospe, Paterno, (Retired), 2538 Market Ave., San Pablo, CA 94806
Granstrand, Charles P., V.F., (Retired), St. Rose of Lima Parish, 50 Short Hills Ave., Short Hills, 07078
Graziano, Gerard J., (Retired), 555 Prospect Ave., Ridgefield, 07657
Greaves, Gerald F., (Retired), 76 Broad St., Bloomfield, 07003
Guglielmo, Alan F., (Retired), c/o Deacon Earle S. Connelly, Immaculate Conception Church, 1219 Paterson Plank Rd., Secaucus, 07094
Gyure, William L., (Retired), P.O. Box 1106, Tombstone, AZ 85638
Hanly, Michael A., (Retired), 2032 Westfield Ave., Scotch Plains, 07076
Heinen, Francis A., (Retired), 247 Bloomfield Ave., Caldwell, 07006
Holian, John P., (Retired), McKeen Towers, 311 S. Flager Dr., Apt. 1104, West Palm Beach, FL 33401
Holmes, Raymond M., (Retired), St. John Vianney Residence, 60 Home Ave., Apt. 44, Rutherford, 07070
Horgan, Timothy J., (Retired), c/o Christine Lewis, 540 SE Onyx Dr., Lee's Summit, MO 64063
Idzik, George, (Retired), St. John Vianney Residence, 60 Home Ave., Apt. 24, Rutherford, 07070
Jones, Kenneth, (Retired), 985 Chapel Hill Rd., Whitingham, VT 05342
Kaelin, Dennis J., (Retired), 3416 Charmwood Ave., Spring Hill, FL 34609
Kopacz, Stephen A., (Retired), Rev. Msgr. James F. Kelley Residence, 247 Bloomfield Ave., Apt. 13, Caldwell, 07006
Kunnath, Matthew, (Retired), 43 Buckingham Rd., West Orange, 07052
Kunnath, Sebastian, (Retired), 7 Cannonball Ct., Allentown, 08501-1849. Tel: 609-208-2070
Kunze, Robert W., (Retired), 120 United States Ave., Gibbsboro, 08026. 12 Farrington Plaza, Somerset, 08873
Lavaroni, Rino, (Retired), Vicolo Cooperative #6, Remanzacco, Udine Italy
Lehman, Paul J., (Retired), Rev. Msgr. James F. Kelley Residence, 247 Bloomfield Ave., Apt. 5, Caldwell, 07006
Lionelli, Anthony J., (Retired), 32 Phillips Rd., Brick, 08724
Lobo, Stanley M., (Retired), 19 E. Central Blvd., Palisades Park, 07650. Tel: 404-909-8951
Maione, Francis T., (Retired), 16 B Walnut Rd., Manahawkin, 08050
Manning, Paul R., (Retired), 311 S. Flagler Dr., Apt. 1109, West Palm Beach, FL 33401
Marchand, Gerald A., (Retired), 1644 West End Dr., Point Pleasant Borough, 08742
Marcone, Eugene F., (Retired), 67 Claudia Ln., Manahawkin, 08050
Martin, John B., (Retired), 247 Bloomfield Ave., Apt. 10, Caldwell, 07006
McDermott, Charles B., (Retired), 2163 Kay Ave., Union, 07083
McKeon, Raymond T., (Retired), 14 Greenville Ave., Jersey City, 07305
McLaughlin, David S., (Retired), 19205 1st Ave. NE, Shoreline, WA 98155-2111
McNulty, Francis J., (Retired), 247 Bloomfield Ave., Apt. 4, Caldwell, 07006
Melillo, William J., M.A., M.Div., (Retired), 11 Beverly Rd., West Orange, 07052
Michalczak, John T., (Retired), 250 E. Jersey St., Elizabeth, 07206
Mohan, Bernard N., B.S., (Retired), 409 Earl Dr., Brick, 08723
Moore, Ward P., (Retired), 247 Bloomfield Ave., Apt. 7, Caldwell, 07006
Morley, John F., Ph.D., (Retired), 61 Hidden Lake Cir., Barnegat, 08005
Morris, John J., (Retired), Marian Manor, 5345 Marion Ln., Apt. 109, Virginia Beach, VA 23462
Morris, William T., (Retired), 100-A Sunrise Ct., Whiting, 08759. Tel: 732-762-8897
Mroz, Richard J., (Retired), St. Cecilia Parish, 120 Kearny Ave., Kearny, 07032
Murphy, Joseph H., (Retired), 175 Mount Nebo Rd., Milford, 08848
Navarro, Pedro, (Retired), 12 W. Concourse, Keyport, 07735
Nestor, Robert P., Ed.D., (Retired), 400 Seton Hall University, South Orange, 07079
Netta, John G., (Retired), P.O. Box 144, West Creek, 08092
Nguyen, Vinh Quang, (Retired), c/o Minhyen Tran, 68 Towers St., Jersey City, 07305
Nolan, Paul J., (Retired), 77 Lee Ct., Jersey City, 07305
Norton, Thomas, (Retired), 521 Piermont Ave., #424, River Vale, 07675
O'Brien, William, (Retired), 3436 Vicari Ave., Toms River, 08755
O'Connell, John R., V.F., (Retired), Sacred Heart Parish, 100 Park St., Haworth, 07641
Oddo, Peter A., (Retired), P.O. Box 11, Swartswood, 07877
Osbahr, Theodore W., V.F., (Retired), P.O. Box 417, Belvidere, 07823-0417
Petrillo, Thomas J., (Retired), 567 Garfield Ave., Toms River, 08753
Pinto, Alex D., (India) (Retired), Holy Trinity Parish, 315 First St., Westfield, 07090
Po, Fernando R., D.S.L., (Retired), 60-C Hontanosas Ext., Tagbilaran City (Bohol), Philippines 6300
Prindiville, Gerard T., (Retired), Redemptoris Mater Seminary, 106 Gurney Rd., Chester Hill, N.S.W., Australia 2162
Quinlan, Joseph M., (Retired), 18 Ellsworth Ct., Red Bank, 07701
Ransom, Donald B., (Retired), Allendale Community for Senior Living, 85 Harreton Rd., Rm. 291, Allendale, 07401
Redstone, James, (Retired), 161 Briar Mills Dr., Brick, 08724
Reed, William C., (Retired), 17 N. Clinton St., East Orange, 07017
Regula, Ronald R., (Retired), P.O. Box 2281, Bloomfield, 07003
Reiff, Dennis E., (Retired), St. Valentine Parish, 125 N. Spring St., Bloomfield, 07003
Reilly, George M., (Retired), 188 MacArthur Ave., Garfield, 07026
Reilly, James, (Retired), 60 Home Ave., Apt. 34, Rutherford, 07070
Reinbold, Charles, (Retired), 250 South St., Peekskill, NY 10566
Renard, John F., (Retired), 78 Seaview Ave., Brick, 08723
Revuelto, Manuel, (Retired), Calle Julio Romero de Torres, 5 Urbanizacion Casablanca Marbella, Malaga, Spain 29600
Reyes, Andres J., V.F., (Retired), 150 Overlook Ave., Apt. 10H, Hackensack, 07601. Tel: 201-214-9258
Robak, Anthony G., (Retired), c/o 144 Claremont Ave., Saddle Brook, 07663
Russo, Michael A., (Retired), 125 Surf Way #309, Monterey, CA 93940
Ryan, John P., (Retired), P.O. Box 3621 Hemlock Farms, Lords Valley, PA 18428
Salemi, Cajetan P., (Retired), 1600 16th Ave., Belmar, 07719
Saltarin, Jose C., (Retired), 734 Ten Eyck Ave., Lyndhurst, 07071. Tel: 201-636-2778
Sammarco, Bruno S., (Retired)
Schiller, Francis E., B.A., J.D., (Retired), 37 College Dr., Apt. 5H, Jersey City, 07305
Schreitmueller, Henry, (Retired), 8 Poinsettia Ct., Kinnelon, 07405

Schute, Arthur B., (Retired), 276 Orlando Blvd., Port Charlotte, FL 33954
Sharp, George F., (Retired), 624 Page Ave., Lyndhurst, 07071. Tel: 201-939-1161
Sheehan, Donald P., (Retired), 320 Franklin Tpke., Allendale, 07401
Sheeran, Robert, (Retired), 675 Sir Francis Drake Blvd., Kentfield, CA 94904
Spino, John J., (Retired), 116 New Jersey Ave., Point Pleasant Beach, 08742
Squeo, Eugene P., J.D., (Retired), 24 College Dr., Apt 2G, Jersey City, 07305. Tel: 201-207-0112
St. Amand, Kenneth J., (Retired), 85 Harreton Rd., Allendale, 07401
Szpiech, Edward P., (Retired), St. John Vianney Residence, 60 Home Ave., Rutherford, 07070
Theobald, Charles, (Retired), 602 Bloomfield Ave., Montclair, 07042
Tooman, Robert E., (Retired), Christ the King Parish, 768 Ocean Ave., Jersey City, 07304
Tortora, James F., Ph.D., (Retired), 2997 Aberdeen Rd., Union, 07083
Villanova, Richard A., (Retired), 2141 Locust Rd., Sea Girt, 08750
Vo, Peter Phong Cao, Mater Dei Retirement Home, 1900 Grand Ave., Carthage, MO 64836
Vu, Joseph Khai Dinh, (Retired), 2013 Fairway View Ln., Wylie, TX 75098
Whelan, James P., (Retired), 1712 Beverly St., Wall, 07719
Wilhelm, Patrick R.C., (Retired), 136 Davis Ave., Kearny, 07032
Wilson, William P., (Retired), Little Flower Manor, 200 S. Meade St., Wilkes-Barre, PA 18702
Zuber, Thaddeus F., (Retired), 60 Home Ave., Rutherford, 07070
Zubik, Rudolf, (Retired), 60 Home Ave., Apt. 24, Rutherford, 07070.

Permanent Deacons:
Acocella, Louis, Ed.D., St. Anthony, Newark
Ahoua, Simplice, St. Lucy, Newark
Alexandre, Wilbert, Holy Rosary & St. Michael, Elizabeth
Aliaga, Justo, St. Cecilia, Kearny
Almeida, Manuel, Our Lady of Fatima, Elizabeth
Anders, Joseph L., (Retired)
Antola, Aldo P., Our Lady of Mt. Carmel, Nutley
Anyanwu, Emeruwa, Blessed Sacrament/St. Charles Borromeo, Newark
Aponte, Leonides, St. Patrick Pro-Cathedral, Newark
Aristy, Jesus D., Our Lady of Libera, West New York
Baker, Robert A. Sr., M.B.A., C.F.E., St. Nicholas, Jersey City
Balestrieri, Anthony A., (Retired)
Baltus, John M., Our Lady of Sorrows, South Orange
Belluscio, Vincent Jr., (Retired)
Bendel, Arthur A., St. James, Springfield
Benedetto, William R., Queen of Peace, North Arlington
Besida, Dennis J., (Retired)
Bianchi, Roland O., St. Anastasia, Teaneck; Holy Name Medical Center, Teaneck
Bongiovanni, Jerome C., St. James, Springfield
Bonnemere, Laurence, St. Anastasia, Teaneck
Boucher, Charlie II, Our Lady of Peace, New Providence
Bowen, Edward J., St. Peter the Apostle, River Edge
Burke, Brian, St. John the Evangelist, Leonia
Campanella, Edward, St. John the Apostle, Linden
Campione, Frank J., (Retired)
Caporaso, Joseph, St. Anthony of Padua, Elizabeth; St. Genevieve, Elizabeth
Carbone, George, St. Catharine, Glen Rock
Carlo, Joseph J., Holy Spirit, Union
Carris, Paul, Corpus Christi, Hasbrouck Heights
Casanova, Eliot, Blessed Sacrament, Elizabeth
Castoro, Joseph, St. Catherine, Glen Rock
Cechony, Michael J., (Retired)
Charriez, Nestor, (Retired)
Christmann, Douglas, St. Francis of Assisi, Hackensack
Connelly, Earle S. Jr., Immaculate Conception, Secaucus
Coyle, Thomas J., St. Thomas, Bloomfield
Cuesta, Arnulfo, St. Paul of the Cross, Jersey City
Daniele, Paul R., (Retired)
David, Marcello, Saint Mary, Jersey City
DeBenedictis, Thomas, Cathedral Basilica of the Sacred Heart, Newark
DeFedele, Vincent J., Corpus Christi, Hasbrouck Heights
Degnon, Robert F., (Retired)
DeLucca, Nicholas J., Our Lady of Mt. Carmel, Ridgewood
DeRoberts, Michael, Our Lady of Lourdes, Mountainside
Detura, James, St. John the Evangelist, Bergenfield
Di Meo, John J., (Retired)
DiBernardo, Domenick, Most Sacred Heart of Jesus, Wallington
Dickson, Joseph A., St. Matthew, Ridgefield
DiPaola, Kenneth, Our Lady of Peace, New Providence
Donosso, Edward G., St. Augustine, Union City
Echevarria, Mario, St. Thomas Aquinas, Newark
Emr, Peter R., Our Lady of the Visitation, Paramus
Escalon, Reynaldo, Guardian Angel, Allendale
Espeleta, Meynardo, Our Lady of Mercy, Jersey City
Fargo, Nicholas C., (Retired), Our Lady of Mercy, Jersey City
Farrell, David, Assumption, Roselle Park
Fedison, Stanley F., Our Lady Mother of the Church, Woodcliff Lake
Fernandez, Jose R., (Retired)
Ferraiuola, Lex, Our Lady of Mt. Carmel, Tenafly
Figueroa, Miguel, St. Michael, Newark
Fischer, Robert, (Retired)
Flanagan, Thomas Patrick, St. Paul, Ramsey
Flores, Ricardo L., SS. Joseph & Michael, Union City
Florio, John J., St. Joseph, Maplewood
Ganter, Albert J., St. John the Baptist, Hillsdale
Gibbons, Keith, Holy Trinity, Westfield
Giuliano, Michael Anthony, Our Lady of Mount Carmel, Tenafly
Glasner, Robert, Our Lady of Good Counsel, Washington Township
Golden, Andrew J., St. Peter the Apostle, River Edge
Gonzalez, Frank, St. Paul the Apostle, Jersey City
Gonzalez, Pedro, Saint Mary, Jersey City
Gray, John A. Jr., St. John the Baptist, Hillsdale
Greydanus, Steven, St. John, Orange
Guida, James J., St. Mary, Rutherford
Gurske, Robert, St. Bartholomew, Scotch Plains
Haas, Henry W., (Retired)
Hall, Bruce J., (Retired)
Hernandez, Angel, St. Francis of Assisi, Hackensack
Herrera, Pedro, St. Mary of the Assumption, Elizabeth
Hessemer, Don, St. Bartholomew, Scotch Plains
Hodges, Richard G., (Retired)
Hoefling, Edward J., (Retired)
Hogan, John E., Church of the Assumption, Emerson
Hughes, David J., St. Rose of Lima, Short Hills
Inguaggiato, John M., Our Lady of Sorrows, South Orange
Joyce, William, Annunciation, Paramus
Jurjevic, Svetko, (Retired)
Karal, John J., St. Ann, Jersey City
Kazanecki, Paul, St. Peter the Apostle, River Edge
Kennedy, Timothy A., St. John the Apostle, Linden; Immaculate Heart of Mary, Scotch Plains
King, Patrick A., St. Thomas More, Fairfield
Kratchman, Robert M., (Retired)
LaFranca, Anthony, St. Joseph, Lodi
Lagatol, Thomas F., Our Lady of Victories, Harrington Park
Landeck, Kurt, Holy Spirit, Union
Langlois, Jose O., (Retired)
LaScala, Dennis F., St. Lucy, Newark
Leconte, Wilfrid, (Retired)
Leonida, Clodualdo M., St. Nicholas, Jersey City
Liguori, Anthony Jr., St. Elizabeth, Wyckoff
Liwanag, Robert, Our Lady of Mount Carmel, Ridgewood
Loman, David B., Our Lady of Mt. Carmel, Tenafly
Loperena, Miguel A., Immaculate Heart of Mary, Newark
Lopez, George, (Retired)
Lopez, Sixto, University Hospital, Newark
Lydon, Michael A., Holy Rosary, Edgewater
Lynch, John W., (Retired)
Mackesy, Leonard J., Our Lady of Sorrows, Kearny
Mantineo, Joseph L., Our Lady Queen of Peace, Maywood
Marchese, Stephen, (Retired), St. Joseph, Lodi
Maron, Edward J., (Retired)
Marques, Albino P., Our Lady of Fatima, Newark
Materia, Francis P., Assumption of Our Lady, Wood Ridge
Matthews, Michael E., (Retired)
McFadden, Edward, (Retired)
McGarry, Richard M., Saint Anne Parish, Fairlawn
McKenna, John J., K.H.S., St. Pius X, Old Tappan
McKeon, John W., St. Luke, Ho-Ho-Kus
McKnight, Keith, Christ the King, Jersey City
McLaughlin, Albert, Our Lady of Victories, Harrington Park
McQuade, Francis P., Our Lady of Sorrows, South Orange
Messina, Dominic S., (Retired)
Mier, Guy W., Cathedral Basilica of the Sacred Heart, Newark
Millea, Robert C., St. Stephen, Kearny
Minichino, Leonard A., St. Catharine, Glen Rock
Missaggia, Michael P., St. Vincent de Paul, Bayonne
Montalvo, Jorge A., St. Joseph, New Milford/Oradell
Montemurro, Michael V., (Retired)
Moore, Willie E. Jr., (Retired)
Mueller, James A., St. Catherine, Glen Rock
Murphy, Brian, St. Thomas the Apostle, Bloomfield
Myers, William, Queen of Peace, North Arlington
Negron, Jose A., St. Michael, Newark
Nieves, Pedro, St. Mary, Plainfield
Noh, Francisco E., Church of the Korean Martyrs, Saddle Brook
O'Hara, Richard, Seton Hall Preparatory School, West Orange; St. Joseph, West Orange
O'Neill, Daniel, St. James, Springfield
Ochoa, Jorge E., St. Joseph, Lodi
Pak, Paul Hui Ra-Se, Our Lady of the Lake, Verona
Park, Julio, (Retired)
Paulillo, Joseph J., Assumption Parish, Emerson
Peterson, Victor, (Retired)
Pluta, Thomas A., Holy Trinity, Westfield
Polanco, Alejandro, St. Francis of Assisi, Hackensack
Polanco, Cecilio S., St. Michael, Newark
Polanco, Leopoldo, (Retired)
Pons, Eduardo, Cathedral Basilica of the Sacred Heart, Newark
Pontillo, Robert, St. Andrew, Westwood
Pontoriero, Michael, St. Thomas More, Fairfield
Porcaro, Anthony, St. Therese of Lisieux, Cresskill
Powell, Ralph F., Our Lady of the Lake, Verona
Puliatte, James J., Immaculate Conception, Norwood
Quagliana, Pat, M.A., Ramapo College
Quintana, Restituto, (Retired)
Ramirez, Nelson, St. Leo, Irvington
Ravelo, Daniel, St. Michael, Newark
Regan, Kevin J., St. Anastasia, Teaneck
Rehse, Jeremiah K., (Retired)
Reina, Kevin, St. Teresa of Avila, Summit
Reyes-Aponte, Modesto, (Retired)
Rivera, Oscar E., (Retired)
Rodack, Stephen, (Retired)
Rodriguez, Jose A., (Retired)
Rodriguez, Justo, Parish of the Transfiguration, Newark
Rodriguez, Vicente, St. Francis Xavier, Newark
Roig, Julio, (Retired)
Romano, Joseph S., Our Lady of Mercy, Park Ridge
Romero, Jerry, St. Joseph, East Orange
Ronacher, Ronald, St. Mary, Nutley
Rossi, Jerry S., Sacred Heart, Bloomfield
Rushing, Todd, Our Lady of the Visitation, Paramus
Sarmiento, Cesar C., Our Lady of Sorrows, South Orange
Sarnas, John P., Our Lady of Sorrows, Kearny
Sarno, John A., St. Catherine, Glen Rock
Saunders, Andrew E., M.A., St. Luke, Ho-Ho-Kus
Savo, Ralph M., Saint Mary, Jersey City
Smith, John F., St. Philomena, Livingston
Smith, Thomas M., Catholic Charities, Newark
Srinivasa, Rajgopal K., St. Antoninus, Newark
Stewart, Craig, Cathedral Basilica, Newark
Strader, David, Our Lady of the Lake, Verona
Stumbar, James P., Little Flower, Berkeley Heights
Sylvester, John, St. Mary, Dumont
Tankard, Gary F., Ascension Church, New Milford; Our Lady of Mercy, Park Ridge
Thomson, Robert E., Holy Rosary, Edgewater
Tizzano, Albert H., St. Thomas the Apostle, Bloomfield
Trinidad, Reynaldo M., St. Mary, Nutley
Valladares, Guillermo, St. Peter, Belleville
Velasco, Asterio, SS. Joseph & Michael, Union City
Villeda, Ramon, (Retired)
Vrindten, Joseph G., (Retired)
Vuolo, Pasquale, (Retired)
White, Earl, St. Stephen, Kearny
Wiggins, Walter, Our Lady of Sorrows, South Orange
Woodruff, Leo A., Holy Name, East Orange; Holy Name of Jesus, East Orange
Yandoli, Joseph, St. John the Evangelist, Leonia
Yoon, David, Madonna, Fort Lee
York, Michael D., St. John the Apostle, Linden
Zapata, Alfredo, St. Aloysius, Jersey City
Zucaro, Andrew, Presentation, Upper Saddle River.

INSTITUTIONS LOCATED IN DIOCESE

[A] SEMINARIES, ARCHDIOCESAN

KEARNY. *Redemptoris Mater Archdiocesan Missionary Seminary* (1990) 672 Passaic Ave., Kearny, 07032. Tel: 201-997-3220; Fax: 201-997-5552; Email: rmnewark@gmail.com; Web: www.rmnewark.org. Rev. Msgr. Renato Grasselli, S.T.L., Rector; Revs. Manuel Duenas, Vice Rector; Zbigniew Kukielka, Prefect, Studies; Justino Cornejo-Castillero, Spiritual Dir.; Juan Alfredo Sanchez Leandro, Asst. Spiritual Dir. Priests 5; Students 37.

SOUTH ORANGE. *Immaculate Conception Seminary School of Theology*, Seton Hall University, 400 S. Orange Ave., South Orange, 07079. Tel: 973-761-9575; Fax: 973-761-9577; Email: theology@shu.edu; Web: theology.shu.edu. Rev. Msgr. Joseph R. Reilly, S.T.L., Ph.D., Rector/Dean. Total Enrollment 300.

Office of Administration: Rev. Msgr. Joseph R. Reilly, S.T.L., Ph.D., Rector/Dean; Revs. Robert K. Suszko, M.B.A., M.Div., Vice Rector & Business Mgr.; Christopher M. Ciccarino, S.T.L., S.T.D., Assoc. Dean, Seminary & Academic Studies; Dianne M. Traflet, J.D., S.T.D., Assoc. Dean, Graduate Studies & Admin. and Dean, Inst. for Christian Spirituality; Sr. Maria Pascuzzi, S.S.L., S.T.D., Assoc. Dean, Undergraduate Studies; Rev. Msgr. Gerard H. McCarren, S.T.D., Spiritual Dir.; Revs. William M. McDonald III, S.T.L., Assoc. Spiritual Dir.; Mariusz Koch, C.F.R., Assoc. Spiritual Dir.; Renato J. Bautista, M.Div., Dir. Formation; John J. Cryan, V.F., Dir. Pastoral Formation; Lawrence B. Porter, Ph.D., Dir. Seminary Library; Roberto Ortiz, S.T.L., Dir. Liturgy; Deacon Andrew E. Saunders, M.A., Dir., Center for Diaconal Formation; Ewa Bracko, M.B.A., Admin., Budgets & Financial Opers.; Michael F. Burt, Sr. Dir. Seminary Advancement; Eilish R. Harrington, Instl. Research Specialist; Diane M. Carr, M.A., Coord. Graduate & Intl. Svcs.; Maria McIlvaine, Coord. Events & Facilities Mgmnt.; Olivia Dinneen, L.C.S.W., Dir. Seminary Counseling; John D. Nowik, M.M., Dir. Music & Organist; Chandler Cohen, Seminary's ESL Svcs. Coord.; Deborah A. Kurus, Asst. to Rector/Dean & Vice Rector; Stella F. Wilkins, M.A., M.L.S., Librarian.

Priest Community, Administration & Faculty: Justin M. Anderson, Ph.D.; Revs. Renato J. Bautista, M.Div.; W. Jerome Bracken, C.P., Ph.D.; Hong-Ray Peter Cho, Ph.D., S.T.L.; Christopher M. Ciccarino, S.T.L., S.T.D.; John J. Cryan, V.F.; Timothy P. Fortin, Ph.D; Rev. Pablo T. Gadenz, S.S.L., S.T.D.; Gregory Y. Glazov, D.Phil. (Oxon.); Rev. Msgr. Thomas G. Guarino, S.T.D.; Eric M. Johnston, Ph.D.; Rev. Mariusz Koch, C.F.R.; Patrick R. Manning, Ph.D.; Rev. Msgr. Gerard H. McCarren, S.T.D.; Revs. William M. McDonald III, S.T.L.; Douglas J. Milewski, S.T.D.; Jeffrey L. Morrow, Ph.D.; Rev. Roberto Ortiz, S.T.L.; Sr. Maria Pascuzzi, S.S.L., S.T.D.; Revs. James P. Platania, S.S.L.; Lawrence B. Porter, Ph.D.; Rev. Msgr. Joseph R. Reilly, S.T.L., Ph.D.; Joseph P. Rice, Ph.D.; Ellen R. Scully, Ph.D.; Rev. Robert K. Suszko, M.B.A., M.Div.; Dianne M. Traflet, J.D., S.T.D.; Rev. Msgr. James C. Turro, Ph.D., (Retired); Víctor Velarde-Mayol, Ph.D., M.D.; Rev. Msgr. Robert J. Wister, D.Eccl.Hist.

*Darlington Fund*Lay Full-time Academic Faculty 9; Total Enrollment 321; Priest Full-time Academic Faculty 10; Priest Formation Faculty 11; Total Administration & Staff 26.

College Seminary of the Immaculate Conception (Saint Andrew's Hall) (1856) Seton Hall University, 400 S. Orange Ave., South Orange, 07079. Tel: 973-761-9420; Fax: 973-761-9421; Web: www.collegeseminary.shu.edu. Very Rev. John J. Chadwick, S.T.D., Rector; Revs. Duverney Bermudez, M.Div., M.A., Vice Rector; Frederick L. Miller, S.T.D., Spiritual Dir. Total Enrollment 40.

[B] COLLEGES AND UNIVERSITIES

CALDWELL. *Caldwell University*, Inst. Research Office, 120 Bloomfield Ave., Caldwell, 07006. Tel: 973-618-3000; Fax: 973-618-3300; Email: admissions@caldwell.edu; Web: www.caldwell.edu. Incorporated under the laws of the State of New Jersey with full power to confer degrees. Lay Teachers 199; Sisters 1; Sisters of St. Dominic of Caldwell 5; Students 2,208.

College Faculty: Nancy H. Blattner, Ph.D., Pres.; Dr. Barbara Chesler, Vice Pres., Academic Affairs; Ms. Nancy Becker, Exec. Dir. Jennings Library.

JERSEY CITY. *Saint Peter University*, 2641 Kennedy Blvd., Jersey City, 07306-5997. Tel: 201-761-6000; Fax: 201-451-0036; Email: lnieves@saintpeters.edu; Web: www.spc.edu. Eugene Cornacchia, Ph. D., Pres.; Rev. Michael Braden, S.J., Vice Pres. Mission & Ministry; Denton Stargel, Vice Pres. Office of Finance & Business; Dr. Marylou Yam, Vice Pres. Academic Affairs & Provost; Rev. Vincent B. Sullivan, S.J., Admin.; Mr. Lamberto Nieves, M.S., Dir. Inst. Research; Dr. Anna Cicirelli, Dean of Upper Classmen; Jeffrey Handler, Vice Pres. Enrollment Mgmt. & Mktg.; Ms. Virginia Bender, Ph.D., Special Asst. to Pres. for Inst. Planning; Dr. Velda Goldberg, Academic Dean; Mr. Ben Scholz, Dir. Enrollment, Research, & Technology; Ms. Irma Williams, Registrar & Exec. Dir. Enrollment Svcs.; Ms. Elizabeth Kane, Dean, School of Professional & Continuing Studies; Rev. Rocco C. Danzi, S.J., Dir. Campus Ministry; Mr. Terence Peavy, M.S., Ed., Vice Pres. Enrollment Mgmt. Mktg. Priests 22.

St. Aedan: St. Peter University Church, 800 Bergen Ave., Jersey City, 07306. Tel: 201-433-6800; Email: saintaedanjc@gmail.com. Rev. John R. Hyatt, S.J., Admin.

St. Peter University Jesuit Community, Gothic Towers, 50 Glenwood Ave., Jersey City, 07306-4606. Fax: 201-432-7397. Revs. Kenneth J. Boller, S.J.; Claudio Burgaleta, S.J.; John R. Hyatt, S.J. Lay Teachers 110; Priests 2; Students 2,986; Total Enrollment 3,800; Jesuit Priests in Faculty 3; Jesuit Priests in Staff 2.

LODI. *Felician University, A N.J. Nonprofit Corp.*, Lodi, 07644. Tel: 201-559-6000; Fax: 201-559-6188; Email: martink@felician.edu; Email: cachezs@felician.edu; Web: www.felician.edu. Brothers 1; Part-time Faculty 117; Full-time Faculty 85; Priests 2; Sisters 12; Total Enrollment 2,061.

Lodi Campus, (Grades Bachelors-Masters), 262 Main St., Lodi, 07644. Tel: 201-559-6000; Fax: 201-559-6188. Dr. Anne M. Prisco, Ph.D., Pres.; Edward H. Ogle, Ed.D., Vice. Pres. for Academic Affairs; Heidi Szymanski, Vice Pres. and CFO, Business & Finance; Francine Andrea, Vice Pres., Enrollment & Student Affairs; Reema Negi, Dir., Institutional Research; Mr. Robert H. Evans, Dean, School of Business; Dr. Rose Rudnitski, Dean, School of Education; Dr. Muriel M. Shore, Dean, School of Nursing; Rev. Richard J. Kelly, Dir. Campus Ministry; Edward Eichhorn, Vice Pres. Inst. Advancement; Dr. George Abaunza, Dean, School of Arts and Sciences; Gerard Shea, Acting Dir. Library.

SOUTH ORANGE. *Seton Hall University* (1856) 400 South Orange Ave., South Orange, 07079. Tel: 973-761-9000; Fax: 973-378-9812; Web: www.shu.edu. Amado Gabriel Esteban, Ph.D., Pres. Lay Teachers 467; Priests 47; Students 9,824.

Officers of University: Rev. Paul A. Holmes, S.T.D.; Rev. Msgr. Robert F. Coleman, J.C.D., Assoc. Vice Provost & Minister Comm.; Tracy Gottlieb, Ph.D., Vice Pres. Student Svcs.; Dennis Garbini, M.B.A., Vice Pres. for Admin.; Catherine Kiernan Esq., J.D., Vice Pres. & General Counsel; Mr. David J. Bohan, Vice Pres. for Univ. Advancement; Dr. Larry A. Robinson, Provost & Exec. Vice Pres.

Administrators: Gregory A. Burton, Ph.D., Assoc. Provost; Dean, Research & Graduate Studies; Alyssa McCloud, Ph.D., Vice Pres. Enrollment Mgmt.; Catherine Kiernan Esq., J.D., Vice Pres. & Gen. Council; John E. Buschman, D.L.S., Dean Univ. Libraries; Nicholas Snow, Interim Dir. Grants & Research; Patrick Lyons, Dir. University Athletics & Admin.; Rev. Brian X. Needles, S.T.L., Dir., Campus Min.; Rev. Msgr. Thomas P. Nydegger, Ed.D., M.Div., Adjunct Prof. of Pastoral Theology; Brigette A. Bryant, Assoc. Vice Pres., Devel.; Mr. Matthew Borowick, M.B.A., Assoc. Vice Pres., Alumni & Govt. Rels.; Ms. Mary Ann L. Hart, Assoc. Provost Finance & Admin.; Karen Van Norman, M.Ed., Assoc. Vice Pres. & Dean of Students.

College of Arts and Sciences Dr. Peter W. Shoemaker, Ph.D., Dean.

School of Business Joyce Strawser, Ph.D., Dean, Tel: 973-761-9013.

College of Education and Human Services Dr. Maureen Gilette, Ph.D., M.S.Ed., A.S.Ed., Dean.

College of Nursing Marie C. Foley, Ph.D., Dean, Tel: 973-761-9014.

School of Law, One Newark Center, 07102. Tel: 973-642-8750. Kathleen M. Boozang, J.D., L.L.M., Dean.

School of Theology Rev. Msgr. Joseph R. Reilly, S.T.L., Ph.D., Tel: 973-761-9016.

School of Health and Medical Science Brian B. Shulman, Ph.D., Dean, Tel: 973-761-2168.

School of Diplomacy and Intl. Rels. Ambassador Andrea Bartoli, Ph.D., Dean, Tel: 973-761-2515.

Priest Community: Rev. John F. Morley, Ph.D., (Retired); Rev. Msgrs. Robert F. Coleman, J.C.D.; Richard M. Liddy, Ph.D.; Dennis Mahon, (Retired); Robert T. Sheeran, S.T.D., (Retired); James C. Turro, Ph.D., (Retired); Robert J. Wister, D.Eccl.Hist; Revs. Renato J. Bautista, M.Div.; Duverney Bermudez, M.Div., M.A., Vice Rector, St. Andrew College Seminary; Donald E. Blumenfeld, Ph.D., (Retired), 42 Summer St., Emerson, 07630; Ian Boyd; Gerald Buonopane; W. Jerome Bracken, C.P., Ph.D.; Alfred V. Celiano, Ph.D., (Retired); Hong-Ray Peter Cho, Ph.D., S.T.L.; Christopher M. Ciccarino, S.T.L., S.T.D.; John J. Chadwick, S.T.D.; Gabriel B. Costa, Ph.D.; John D. Dennehy, Casa Santa Maria, Rome, Italy 00187; Nicholas G. Figurelli, B.S., M.A.; Lawrence E. Frizzell, D.Phil.; Pablo T. Gadenz, S.S.L., S.T.D.; Nicholas S. Gengaro, S.T.D.; Rev. Msgr. Thomas G. Guarino, S.T.D.; Rev. Paul A. Holmes, S.T.D., Vice Pres. & Interim Dean; Rev. Msgrs. Christopher J. Hynes, Ed.S., Adjunct Prof.; Anthony J. Kulig, K.H.S., M.A., (Retired); Rev. Joseph R. Laracy; Rev. Msgr. Gerard H. McCarren, S.T.D.; Revs. William McDonald; Frederick L. Miller, S.T.D.; Brian Keenan Muzas; Robert P. Nestor, Ed.D., (Retired); Lawrence B. Porter, Ph.D.; Rev. Msgr. John A. Radano, Villa Stritch, Via Della Nocetta 63, Rome, Italy 00164; Rev. John J. Ranieri, Ph.D.; Rev. Msgrs. Joseph R. Reilly, S.T.L., Ph.D.; Francis R. Seymour, K.H.S., (Retired); Rev. Robert K. Suszko, M.B.A., M.Div.; Rev. Msgr. C. Anthony Ziccardi, S.T.L., S.S.L. In Res. Revs. Douglas J. Milewski, S.T.D.; Roberto Ortiz, S.T.L.; Brian X. Needles, S.T.L.; John J. Cryan, M.Div.; James P. Platania, S.S.L.; Rev. Msgrs. Thomas P. Nydegger, Ed.D., M.Div.; John E. Doran, V.G., (Retired), Cathedral Basilica of the Sacred Heart, 89 Ridge St.

[C] HIGH SCHOOLS, PRIVATE

NEWARK. *Saint Benedict Preparatory School* (1868) (Grades K-12), 520 Dr. Martin Luther King Blvd., 07102-1314. Tel: 973-792-5700; Fax: 973-643-6922; Email: graybee@sbp.org; Web: www.sbp.org. Rev. Edwin D. Leahy, O.S.B., Headmaster; Paul E. Thornton, Assoc. Headmaster. Brothers 3; Lay Teachers 52; Sisters 3; Total Enrollment 492; Benedictine Monks of Newark Abbey 13.

Cristo Rey Newark High School, 239 Woodside Ave., 07104. Tel: 973-483-0033; Fax: 973-481-0693; Email: info@cristoreynewark.org; Web: cristoreynewark.org. Revs. Robert J. Sandoz, O.F.M., Pres.; Gregory V. Gebbia, O.F.M., Prin. Lay Teachers 32; Priests 2; Students 277.

Cristo Rey Newark Work Study Program, 239 Woodside Ave., 07104. Tel: 973-483-0033; Fax: 973-481-0693.

St. Vincent Academy (1869) (Girls) 228 W. Market St., 07103. Tel: 973-622-1613; Fax: 973-622-1128; Email: jfavata@svanj.org; Web: www.svanj.org. Sisters June Favata, Admin. Dir.; Margaret Killough, Fin. Dir.; Mary F. Nolan, Student Svcs. Dir.; Ms. Elizabeth Lyman, Librarian. Lay Teachers 25; Sisters 3; Students 248.

BAYONNE. *Marist High School* (1954) (Coed) 1241 Kennedy Blvd., Bayonne, 07002. Tel: 201-437-4545 ; Fax: 201-437-6013; Email: amiesnik@marist.org; Web: www.marist.org. Ms. Alice Miesnik, Head of School; Mr. Christopher Cassaro, Dean of Academics; Mr. Craig J. Carbone, Dean of Students; Bro. Robert Warren, F.M.S., Teacher; Ms. Miriam Eisenmenger, Dir. of School Counseling; Sr. Helen Moores, S.C., Dir. of Focus Ed.; Mr. Javaughn Mayers, I.T. Support; Ms. Tiffany McQueary, Chief Advancement Officer; Bro. Patrick McNamara, Teacher. Marist Brothers. Lay Teachers 23; Students 370.

CALDWELL. *Mount St. Dominic Academy* (Girls) 3 Ryerson Ave., Caldwell, 07006-6196. Tel: 973-226-0660; Fax: 973-226-2693; Email: mainoffice@msdacademy.org; Web: www.msdacademy.org. Sr. Frances Sullivan, O.P., Head of School; Linda Arndt, Academic Dean, Humanities; Pauline Condon, Dir. Admissions; Irena Telyan, Librarian. Sisters of St. Dominic of Caldwell. Girls 345; Lay Teachers 34; Sisters 3.

DEMAREST. *Academy of the Holy Angels* (Girls) 315 Hillside Ave., Demarest, 07627. Tel: 201-768-7822; Fax: 201-768-6933; Email: jmullooly@holyangels.org; Web: www.holyangels.org. Jean Mullooly, Dean Students; Andrea Beyer, Dean; Ms. Melinda Hanlon, Pres.; Catherine Korvin, Librarian; Francesca Puzio, Dean. Conducted by School Sisters of Notre Dame. Girls 559; Lay Teachers 78; Sisters 2.

ELIZABETH. *Benedictine Academy*, 840 N. Broad St., Elizabeth, 07208-2508. Tel: 908-352-0670; Fax: 908-352-9424; Web: www.benedictineacad.org; Email: principal@benedictineacad.org. Ashley Powell, Prin.; Sisters Sharon McHugh, O.S.B., Pres.; Mary Feehan, Prioress; Ms. Analisa Branco, Dir. Admissions; Jennifer Buckley, Dir. Guidance. Benedictine Sisters of Elizabeth, NJ.College Preparatory High School (Girls) Girls 140; Lay Teachers 22; Sisters 1; Total Staff 32.

JERSEY CITY. *Kenmare High School*, Tel: 201-451-1177;

Fax: 973-481-0693. Lay Teachers 5; Students 58; Total Staff 7.

St. Dominic Academy (Girls) 2572 John F. Kennedy Blvd., Jersey City, 07304. Tel: 201-434-5938; Fax: 201-434-2603; Email: sdegnan@stdominicacad.com; Web: www.stdominicacad.com. Sr. MaryLou Bauman, Dean Students & Dir., Guidance; Ms. Andrea Apruzzese, Dir. Admissions; Sharon Buge, Dir. Fin.; Sarah Degnan-Moje, Headmaster; M. Guendolyn Farrales, Academic Dean. Dominican Sisters of Caldwell. Lay Teachers 21; Sisters 1; Students 247; Total Staff 51.

St. Peter Preparatory School (1872) 144 Grand St., Jersey City, 07302. Tel: 201-547-6400; Fax: 201-547-2341; Email: deangeloj@spprep.org; Web: www.spprep.org. Mr. Philip F. McGovern Jr., Chm. Bd.; Rev. Kenneth J. Boller, S.J., Pres.; Mr. Christoplher Casazza, Chief Advancement Officer; Mr. James C. DeAngelo, Prin.; Mr. Robert D. Furlong, Vice Prin.; Mr. John Morris, Dean, Students; Mr. John Caulfield, Vice Pres. Fin.; Mr. James Horan, Vice Pres. Planning & Principal Giving; Mr. John Irvine, Dir. Admissions. Lay Teachers 78; Priests 5; Students 945.

Jesuit Community, 50 Glenwood Ave., Jersey City, 07302. Revs. Anthony J. Azzarto, S.J., Guidance & Alumni Chap.; John A. Mullin, S.J., Guidance Counselor; Robert V. O'Hare, S.J., Spiritual Dir. & Mathematics Teacher; Kenneth J. Boller, S.J.; Matthew J. Cassidy, S.J., History Teacher; Claudio Burgaleta, S.J., Rector; Mr. James C. DeAngelo, Prin.; William Reese, Librarian.

LODI. *Immaculate Conception High School* (1915) 258 S. Main St., Lodi, 07644. Tel: 973-773-2400; Fax: 973-614-0893; Email: jazzolino@ichslodi.org; Web: www.ichslodi.org. Mr. Joseph R. Azzolino, Pres. & Prin.; Jessica Fava-Cutrona, Dean; Marissa Hughes, Dir.; Renee Hyle Gitto, Dir.; Nicole Mineo, Dir. All girls Catholic high school. Girls 216; Lay Staff 17; Lay Teachers 21; Sisters 2.

MONTCLAIR. *Immaculate Conception High School* (Coed) 33 Cottage Pl., Montclair, 07042. Tel: 973-744-7445; Fax: 973-744-3926; Email: ichsmont@yahoo.com; Web: www.ichspride.org. Celia Honohan, Pres.; Michele Neves, Prin.; Sr. Ann Fay, S.C., Librarian. Lay Teachers 23; Students 210.

ORADELL. *Bergen Catholic High School* (1955) (Boys) 1040 Oradell Ave., Oradell, 07649. Tel: 201-261-1844; Fax: 201-599-9507; Email: drmahoney@bergencatholic.org; Web: www.bergencatholic.org. Brian Mahoney, Pres.; Timothy J. McElhinney, Prin.; Rev. Colin Adrian Kay, Chap. Congregation of Christian Brothers. Brothers 2; Lay Teachers 50; Students 631; Total Staff 72.

RAMSEY. *Don Bosco Preparatory High School* (1915) 492 N. Franklin Tpke., Ramsey, 07446. Tel: 201-327-8003; Fax: 201-327-3397; Email: rfazio@donboscoprep.org; Web: www.donboscoprep.org. Revs. James Heuser, S.D.B., Dir./Pres.; Matthew DeGance, S.D.B., B.S., PT, Coord. Youth Min.; John Janko, S.D.B., Facilities Mgr.; Michael Pender, Finance Admin.; Rev. Louis Konopelski, S.D.B., Math Teacher; Mr. Robert Fazio, Dean of Academics; Bro. Sasika Lokuhettige, S.B.D., Theology Teacher; Rev. James Mulloy, S.D.B., Theology Teacher; Bros. Alfred Flatoff, S.D.B., Staff Asst.; James Wiegand, S.D.B., Asst. Athletic Dir.; Thomas DeLucci, Guidance Dir.; Carmela Raiti, Vice Pres. Advancement; Bro. Travis Gunther, S.D.B., Art Instructor. Salesians of St. John Bosco. Lay Teachers 64; Students 860.

SUMMIT. *Oak Knoll School of the Holy Child Upper School* (1924) (Grades 7-12), (Girls) 44 Blackburn Rd., Summit, 07901. Tel: 908-522-8130; Fax: 908-522-8191; Email: timothy.saburn@oakknoll.org; Web: www.oakknoll.org. Mr. Timothy J. Saburn, Head of School; Jennifer Landis, US Div. Head; Mary Hoskins-Clark, Librarian. Conducted by the Sisters of the Holy Child Jesus. Lay Teachers 50; Students 262; Total Staff 30.

UPPER MONTCLAIR. *Lacordaire Academy*, (Grades PreK-12), 155 Lorraine Ave., Upper Montclair, 07043. Tel: 973-744-1156; Fax: 973-783-9521; Email: whambleton@lacordaire.net; Web: www.lacordaireacademy.com. William Hambleton, Head of School; Megan Mannato, Asst. Head of School. Sisters of St. Dominic. of Caldwell Lay Teachers 30; Sisters 1; Students 236; Total Staff 42.

WEST ORANGE. *Seton Hall Preparatory School*, 120 Northfield Ave., West Orange, 07052. Tel: 973-325-6651; Fax: 973-843-1504; Email: rharahan@shp.org; Web: www.shp.org. Rev. Msgrs. Michael E. Kelly, M.A., Pres.; Robert E. Harahan, S.T.D.; Headmaster & Dir., Priest Res.; Michael Gallo, Asst. Headmaster; Kevin McNulty, Asst. Headmaster; Mary Ann DeTrolio, Librarian; Revs. James R. White, Chap.; Zachary Swantek, S.T.L., Chap. Priests 4; Students 956; Lay Instructors 80.

Resident Faculty: Rev. Msgr. Edward G. Bradley; Rev. William J. Melillo, M.A., M.Div., (Retired).

[D] HIGH SCHOOLS, ARCHDIOCESAN

CLARK. *Mother Seton (Girls) Regional High School*, One Valley Rd., Clark, 07066. Tel: 732-382-1952; Fax: 732-382-4725; Email: missbarron@motherseton.org; Web: www.motherseton.org. Joan Barron, Dir.; Sr. Jacquelyn Balasia, S.C., Co-Prin.; Maureen Connell, Co-Prin.; Sr. Mary Anne Katlack, S.C., Campus Minister; Marge Barkan, Librarian. Sisters of Charity of St. Elizabeth. Girls 234; Lay Teachers 17; Sisters 2.

JERSEY CITY. *Hudson Catholic Regional High School*, 790 Bergen Ave., Jersey City, 07306. Tel: 201-332-5970; Fax: 201-332-6373; Email: rgaribell@hudsoncatholic.org; Web: www.hudsoncatholic.org. Richard Garibell, Pres. & Prin. Lay Teachers 30; Students 492; Total Staff 38.

MONTVALE. *St. Joseph Regional High School* (1962) (Boys) 40 Chestnut Ridge Rd., Montvale, 07645. Tel: 201-391-3300; Fax: 201-391-8073; Email: brunom@sjrnj.org; Web: www.saintjosephregional.org. Barry Donnelly, Pres.; Mr. Michael Bruno, Prin.; Michael Doherty, Vice Prin.; Margaret Sullivan, Media Specialist. Brothers 1; Lay Teachers 98; Students 500.

PARAMUS. *Paramus Catholic High School* (Coed) 425 Paramus Rd., Paramus, 07652. Tel: 201-445-4466; Fax: 201-445-6440; Email: jvail@paramus-catholic.org; Web: www.paramuscatholic.org. Declan Lynch, Vice Pres., Finance; William Brieden, Dean, Admissions; Stephanie Macaluso, Prin.; Jean Cousins, Librarian; Revs. Donald K. Hummel, D.Min., Chap.; Doroteo B. Layosa II, Chap.; Michael Freimuth, Dir., Opers., Email: mfreimuth@paramus-catholic.org; Michael Shea, Dean, Campus Ministry & Dir., Transportation; Sean Fallon, Dir., Technology; Lauren Daniell, Dean, Student Svcs.; Amy Shea, Dean, Studies; Danielle Moore, Vice Prin.; Jason Fortino, Dir., Alumni Rels.; Michael Dorrian, Dir. of Intl. Prog. Lay Teachers 100; Priests 2; Students 1,353; Total Staff 125.

ROSELLE. *Roselle Catholic High School* (Coed) 350 Raritan Rd., Roselle, 07203. Tel: 908-245-2350; Fax: 908-241-3869; Email: info@rosellecatholic.org; Web: www.rosellecatholic.org. Thomas C. Berrios, Prin. Marist Brothers. Lay Teachers 27; Students 341; Total Staff 45.

SCOTCH PLAINS. *Union Catholic Regional High School* (Coed) 1600 Martine Ave., Scotch Plains, 07076. Tel: 908-889-1600; Fax: 908-889-7867; Email: mainoffice@unioncatholic.org; Web: www.unioncatholic.org. Sr. Percylee Hart, R.S.M., Prin.; Ms. Karen Piasecki, Assoc. Prin.; Mrs. Noreen Andrews, Asst. Prin.; Dr. James Reagan Jr., Asst. Prin.; David Luciano, Dir. Lay Teachers 70; Sisters 3; Students 778; Total Staff 73.

SUMMIT. *Oratory Preparatory School* (1907) (Grades 7-12), 1 Beverly Rd., Summit, 07901. Tel: 908-273-1084; Fax: 908-273-5505; Email: mainoffice@oratoryprep.org; Web: www.oratoryprep.org. Mr. Robert Costello, Head of School; Rev. Salvatore DiStefano, Chap.; Mr. Owen McGowan, Assoc. Head of School; Elizabeth Acquardo, Dean; Jimmy Yoo, Technical Coord. Lay Teachers 63; Priests 1; Students 383; Total Staff 19.

WASHINGTON TOWNSHIP. *Immaculate Heart Academy* (Girls) 500 Van Emburgh Ave., Washington Township, 07676. Tel: 201-445-6800; Fax: 201-445-7416; Email: pmolloy@ihanj.com; Web: www.ihanj.com. Ms. Patricia Molloy, Pres.; Ms. Alice Rogers, Asst. Prin.; Jo-Ellen DeSanta, Asst. Prin. of Academics; Mr. Jason Schlereth, Prin. Girls 710; Lay Teachers 71; Sisters 2; Total Staff 92.

[E] ELEMENTARY SCHOOLS, PRIVATE

JERSEY CITY. *St. Joseph's School for the Blind*, 761 Summit Ave., Jersey City, 07307. Tel: 201-876-5432; Fax: 201-876-5431 (Admin.); Fax: 201-876-5430 (Ed.); Email: info@schoolfortheblind.org; Web: schoolfortheblind.org. David Feinhals, Exec. Dir.; Dr. Anthony Lentine Jr., Prin. Non-graded and graded school for blind, visually impaired, multi-disabled children; early intervention program, 5-day residential program, outreach services. Self-directed program for adults with special needs. Lay Teachers 19; Students 165; Total Staff 97.

LODI. *The Felician School for Exceptional Children* (1971) 260 S. Main St., Lodi, 07644. Tel: 973-777-5355; Fax: 973-777-0725; Email: fsecinlodi@aol.com; Web: www.fsec.org. Sr. Rosemarie Smiglewski, C.S.S.F., Dir.; Patricia Urgo, Prin. Children 73; Lay Teachers 16; Sisters 5; Total Staff 43.

Day Program, Tel: 973-777-5355, Ext. 12; Fax: 973-777-0725. Capacity 150.

SUMMIT. *Oak Knoll School of The Holy Child, Lower School* (1924) (Grades K-6), (Coed) 44 Blackburn Rd., Summit, 07901. Tel: 908-522-8120; Tel: 908-522-8100 (Main); Fax: 908-598-9757; Email: timothy.saburn@oakknoll.org; Web: www.oakknoll.org. Mr. Timothy J. Saburn, Head of School; Mrs. Christine Spies, Prin.; Megan Watkins, Dir. Student Svcs.; Elinor Takenaga, Librarian. Conducted by the Sisters of the Holy Child of Jesus. Lay Teachers 28; Students 259; Total Staff 30.

UNION CITY. *St. Francis Academy*, 1601 Central Ave., Union City, 07087. Tel: 201-863-4112; Fax: 201-601-5905; Email: lucy@stfrancisacademy.com; Web: www.stfrancisacademy.com. Sr. Mary Dora Sartino, O.S.F., Pres.; Ms. Deborah Savage, Prin., Email: principal@stfrancisacademy.com; Rose Farinola, Librarian. Missionary Franciscan Sisters of the Immaculate Conception. Lay Teachers 22; Sisters 1; Students 302.

[F] GENERAL HOSPITALS

NEWARK. *St. James Campus of Saint Michael Medical Center, Newark* Parent Corporation: Saint Michael's Medical Center, Inc. A member of Catholic Health East. 155 Jefferson St., 07105. Tel: 973-589-1300; Fax: 973-465-2861; Web: www.cathedralhealth.org. Bed Capacity 40.

Life at Saint Michael, Inc., 111 Central Ave., 07102-9880. Tel: 973-877-5350; Fax: 973-877-5672. Mr. David A. Ricci, Pres. & CEO.

Saint Michael Medical Center Parent Corporation: Catholic Health East. A member of Catholic Health East. 111 Central Ave., 07102-9880. Tel: 973-877-5000; Fax: 973-877-5672. Mr. David A. Ricci, Pres. & CEO; Dr. Claudia Komer, Pres. Medical Staff; Dr. Joseph DePasquale, Interim Chief Medical Officer; Rev. David S. McLaughlin, Chap., (Retired). Bed Capacity 358; Total Staff 1,407; Emergency Room 36,256; Outpatient 93,550; Inpatient 8,433.

Mount Carmel Guild Behavioral Health System, Inc., 590 N. 7th St., 07107. Tel: 973-266-7992; Fax: 973-596-4057; Web: www.ccannj.org. Ms. Elizabeth A. McClendon, A.C.S.W., L.C.S.W., Assoc. Exec. Dir.; Mr. John Westervelt, B.A., CEO, Tel: 973-596-3984. Behavioral Health Services in 3 counties. Bed Capacity 290; Patients Asst Anual. 11,077; Total Staff 200.

ELIZABETH. *Trinitas Regional Medical Center*, 225 Williamson St., Elizabeth, 07207. Tel: 908-994-5754; Fax: 908-994-5756; Web: www.trinitasrmc.com. Gary S. Horan, Pres. & CEO; William McHugh, M.D., Medical Dir., Chief Medical Officer; Rev. John T. Michalczak, Chap., (Retired); Sr. Mary Corrigan, S.C., Vice Pres. Mission Effectiveness; Revs. Brendan Quinn, Chap.; Stephen Aribe, Chap. Sisters of Charity of Saint Elizabeth and Elizabethtown Healthcare Foundation. Bassinets 11; Bed Capacity 553; Patients Asst Anual. 650,412; Sisters 9; Total Staff 2,749; Long Term Care Center Beds 120.

Trinitas Regional Medical Center, Williamson Street Campus, 225 Williamson St., Elizabeth, 07207. Tel: 908-994-5754.

Trinitas Regional Medical Center, New Point Campus, 655 E. Jersey St., Elizabeth, 07206. Tel: 908-994-5000.

**Marillac Corp.*, 240 Williamson St., Elizabeth, 07207. Tel: 908-994-5794; Fax: 908-994-5756. Gary S. Horan, Pres. & CEO.

TEANECK. *Holy Name Medical Center*, 718 Teaneck Rd., Teaneck, 07666. Tel: 201-833-3000; Fax: 201-833-3230; Email: n-bischoff@holyname.org; Web: www.holyname.org. Michael Maron, Pres. & CEO, Tel: 201-833-3000; Fax: 201-833-3230; Maureen Morosco, Chap.; Sr. Breda Boyle, C.S.J.P., Dir., Pastoral Care; Adam Jarrett, M.D., M.S., FACHE, Exec. Vice Pres. & CEO; Sheryl Slonim, D.N.P., R.N.-B.C., Exec. Vice Pres., Patient Care Svcs. & Chief Nursing Officer; Revs. Edwardo Veluz, Chap.; Maciej Jan Zajac, Chap. Sisters of St. Joseph of Peace. Bassinets 36; Bed Capacity 361; Tot Asst. Annually 99,372; Total Staff 3,229.

Holy Name EMS, 718 Teaneck Rd., Teaneck, 07666. Tel: 201-833-3248; Fax: 201-833-7213.

School of Nursing, Tel: 201-833-3002. Sisters 2.

Pastoral Care: Revs. Edwardo Veluz, Chap.; Maciej Jan Zajac, Chap.

[G] HOMES FOR AGED

CALDWELL. *St. Catherine of Siena, Inc.*, 7 Ryerson Ave., Caldwell, 07006. Tel: 973-226-1577; Fax: 973-226-5058; Email: dradtke@caldwellop.org; Web: www.caldwellop.org. Sisters Arlene Antczak, O.P., Prioress; Luella Ramm, O.P., Vicaress & Treas.; Patricia Stringer, O.P., Sec.; Elsie Bernauer, O.P., Councilor; Ms. Deirdre Radtke, Admin. Bed Capacity 30; Total of Sisters in Convent Living with Support Services 35; Total Staff 50.

CEDAR GROVE. *St. Vincent Nursing Home* (Div. of St. Joseph's Regional Medical Center) 315 E. Lindsley Rd., Cedar Grove, 07009. Tel: 973-754-4800; Fax: 973-812-4491. Deborah Quinn Martone, Admin.; Sr. Elizabeth Noonan, Chap. Conducted by Sisters of Charity of St. Elizabeth. Patients Asst Anual. 221; Sisters 2; Total Staff 190; Capacity: Long term care beds 151.

JERSEY CITY. *St. Ann Home for the Aged* dba Peace Care St. Ann's, 198 Old Bergen Rd., Jersey City, 07305. Tel: 201-433-0950; Fax: 201-433-6554; Email: jmerlyliranzo@peacecarenj.org; Web: www.peacecarenj.org. Janet Merly-Liranzo, LNA Admin.; Tiffany Romano, B.S.W., C.S.W., Admissions; James Barry, Pastoral Care. Bed Capacity 120; Sisters of St. Joseph of Peace 6; Tot Asst. Annually 1,920; Total Staff 204; Under Care (Male & Female) 120; Adult Medical Day Care Clients 50.

Margaret Anna Cusack Care Center, Inc. dba Peace Care St. Joseph's, 537 Pavonia Ave., Jersey City, 07306. Tel: 201-653-8300; Fax: 201-653-7705; Email: tsheehy@peacecarenj.org; Web: www.peacecarenj.org. Thomas P. Sheehy, Admin. Sponsored by the Sisters of St. Joseph of Peace.Skilled Nursing Facility for Men & Women. Bed Capacity 139; Sisters 4; Tot Asst. Annually 600; Total Staff 235.

[H] HOMES FOR THE BLIND

JERSEY CITY. *St. Joseph Home for the Blind* dba Peace Care St. Joseph's (1886) 537 Pavonia Ave., Jersey City, 07306. Tel: 201-653-8300; Fax: 201-653-7705; Email: tsheehy@peacecarenj.org; Web: www.peacecarenj.org. Thomas P. Sheehy, Admin. Sisters of St. Joseph of Peace.Skilled nursing facility for men and women. Bed Capacity 139; Sisters 4; Tot Asst. Annually 600; Total Staff 235.

[I] DAY NURSERIES

NEWARK. *Perpetual Help Day Nursery* (1967) 170 Broad St., 07104. Tel: 973-484-3535; Fax: 973-497-2526; Email: srmcriscinasdv@yahoo.com; Email: srmcriscina@yahoo.com. Sr. Christina Peteros, Prin. Vocationist Sisters. Children 141; Lay Teachers 15; Sisters 5; Total Staff 23.

ELIZABETH. **Benedictine Preschool*, 851 N. Broad St., Elizabeth, 07208. Tel: 908-352-8714; Fax: 908-352-6331; Email: benprek@msn.com; Web: www.benedictinepreschool.org. Michele Hopkins, Dir. Children 32; Students 32; Total Staff 8; Staff Members 3; Lay Faculty 8.

JERSEY CITY. *St. Elizabeth School & Child Care Center, Inc.*, 129 Garrison Ave., Jersey City, 07306. Tel: 201-795-1443; Fax: 201-795-4121; Email: st.stelizabethfsse@yahoo.com School E-mail. Sisters Anne Mankuzha, Supr.; Shelcy Catherine Kulangara, Prin. Franciscan Sisters of St. Elizabeth. Children 250; Sisters 10; Total Staff 36.

NUTLEY. *Holy Family Day Nursery and Convent*, 174 Franklin Ave., Nutley, 07110. Tel: 973-235-1170; Fax: 973-235-1940. Sr. Jycinth Valenciana, Supr.; Romilda Chiga, F.S.S.E., Prin. Franciscan Sisters of St. Elizabeth. Children 70; Sisters 9.

RAMSEY. *St. Joseph Pre-School*, 372 Wyckoff Ave., Ramsey, 07446. Tel: 201-825-8386; Fax: 201-825-8386 (Call First). Sr. Clare Arangassery, Prin. Franciscan Sisters of St. Elizabeth. Children 60; Sisters 5.

[J] PROTECTIVE INSTITUTIONS

NEWARK. *Missionaries of Charity, Queen of Peace Women's Shelter & Soup Kitchen* (1982) 168 Sussex Ave., 07103. Tel: 973-481-9056; Tel: 973-483-0165. Missionaries of Charity. Total Staff 6; Total Assisted (Shelter) 265; Total Assisted (Soup Kitchen) 26,502.

HOBOKEN. *Good Counsel, Inc.*, 411 Clinton St., Hoboken, 07030. Tel: 201-798-9059; Tel: 201-795-0637; Tel: 800-723-8331 (Hotline); Fax: 201-795-0809; Email: cbell@goodcounselhomes.org; Web: www.goodcounselhomes.org; Web: www.postabortionhelp.org. Mr. Mark Swartzberg, Chm. Bd. Dirs.; Christopher R. Bell, Pres. & Exec. Dir. Housing, counseling and referrals for single women who are pregnant or single mothers with children. Counseling for men and women experiencing post-abortion stress.

Good Counsel, Inc., P.O. Box 6068, Hoboken, 07030. Tel: 201-795-0637; Fax: 201-795-0809. Mr. Mark Swartzberg, Chm. Bd. Dirs.; Christopher R. Bell, Exec. Dir. Residences for single mothers and children. Post-abortion counseling and referrals through the Lumina Program. Bed Capacity 47; Tot Asst. Annually 195; Total Staff 70; Women & Children Assisted Annually 225; Total Hotline Assistance 3,200.

JERSEY CITY. *St. Joseph Home*, 81 York St., Jersey City, 07302. Tel: 201-413-9280; Fax: 201-451-0952. Ms. Gloria E. Acosta, M.S.W., Dir. Transitional housing for homeless women and children. Bed Capacity 60; Total Staff 12; Total Assisted 69.

The Nurturing Place, Tel: 201-413-1982; Fax: 201-413-1223. Sr. Barbara Moran, C.S.J.P., Dir., Tel: 201-413-1982. A developmental child care center for disadvantaged youngsters; homeless & economically deprived. Total Staff 14; Total Assisted 80.

[K] HOMES FOR WOMEN

JERSEY CITY. *St. Mary Residence*, 240 Washington St., Jersey City, 07302-3806. Tel: 201-432-6289; Fax: 201-451-0952. Sr. Harriet Hamilton, C.S.J.P., Admin., Dir. Sisters of St. Joseph of Peace.(Single working women of low income assisted; no children). Bed Capacity 42; Total Staff 9; Total Assisted 45.

[L] MONASTERIES AND RESIDENCES OF PRIESTS AND BROTHERS

NEWARK. *Franciscan Friars of the Renewal*, Most Blessed Sacrament Friary, 375 13th Ave., 07103. Tel: 973-622-6622; Fax: 973-624-8998; Web: www.newarkfriary.org. Revs. Francis Mary Roaldi, C.F.R., Supr.; Raphael Jacques Chilou, C.F.R.; Bro. John Joseph Brice, C.F.R.; Revs. Stephen Marie Dufrene, C.F.R., Vicar; Sebastian Kajko, C.F.R., Pastoral Assoc.; Bros. Andre Manders, C.F.R.; Thomas Joseph McGrinder, C.F.R.; Francois Marie Fontanie, C.F.R., Novice; Revs. Juniper Adams, C.F.R.; Mariusz Koch, C.F.R. Non-Professed 8.

Newark Abbey (1857) 528 Dr. Martin Luther King, Jr. Blvd., 07102. Mailing Address: 520 Dr. Martin Luther King, Jr. Blvd., 07102. Tel: 973-792-5700; Fax: 973-643-6922; Email: mvalvano@sbp.org; Web: www.newarkabbey.org. Rt. Rev. Melvin J. Valvano, O.S.B., Abbot; Very Rev. Augustine J. Curley, O.S.B., Prior; Revs. Francois Diabel, O.S.B.; Luke A. Edelen, O.S.B.; Francis Flood, O.S.B.; Albert T. Holtz, O.S.B., Novice Master; Edwin D. Leahy, O.S.B.; Maynard G. Nagengast, O.S.B.; Very Rev. Philip J. Waters, O.S.B., V.F.; Bros. Maximillian Buonocore, O.S.B.; Simon Clayton, O.S.B.; Mark Dilone, O.S.B.; Thomas Aquinas Hall, O.S.B.; Asiel Rodriguez, O.S.B.; Patrick Winbush, O.S.B., Subprior; Francis M. Woodruff, O.S.B.

Legal Title: Benedictine Abbey of Newark.

CALDWELL. *The Rev. Msgr. James F. Kelley Residence for Retired Priests*, 247 Bloomfield Ave., Caldwell, 07006. Tel: 973-364-1121; Fax: 973-364-9873. Mrs. Joan Stevens, Admin.; Rev. Msgr. Kenneth J. Herbster, V.F., (Retired); Revs. James F. Benedetto, Dir., (Retired); Eugene Diurczak, (Retired); Leo O. Farley, (Retired); Dominic J. Fiorino, (Retired); Francis A. Heinen, (Retired); John B. Martin, (Retired); Francis J. McNulty, (Retired); Ward P. Moore, (Retired); John A. Quill, (Retired).

JERSEY CITY. *Brothers of the Christian Schools* Hudson Catholic Brothers' Residence 790 Bergen Ave., Jersey City, 07306-4535. Tel: 201-332-5970; Tel: 201-332-0971 (House); Fax: 201-332-6373.

Jesuit Community of St. Peter Prep, Inc., 50 Glenwood Ave., Jersey City, 07306-4604. Tel: 201-432-7399; Fax: 201-432-7397; Email: mullinj@spprep.org. Revs. Kenneth J. Boller, S.J., Pres. St. Peter's Prep.; Anthony J. Azzarto, S.J., Alumni Chap. & Guidance Counselor; John A. Mullin, S.J., Guidance Counselor; Robert V. O'Hare, S.J., Math Teacher & Asst. for Ignatian Identity; Matthew J. Cassidy, S.J., History Teacher. Priests 5; Total in Residence 5.

Jesuits of Saint Peter College, Inc., 50 Glenwood Ave., Jersey City, 07306-4606. Tel: 201-432-7399; Fax: 201-432-7397; Email: cburgaleta@jesuits.org. Revs. Claudio Burgaleta, S.J., Supr.; Kenneth J. Boller, S.J., Pres., St. Peter's Prep; Matthew J. Cassidy, S.J., Teacher, St. Peter's Prep; Rocco C. Danzi, S.J., Vice Pres. Mission & Ministry, St. Peter's Univ.; Andrew Downing, S.J., Campus Min., St. Peter's Univ.; John R. Hyatt, S.J., Admin., St. Aedan's Church; Robert E. Kennedy, S.J., Prof. Emeritus, St. Peter's Univ.; Oscar G. Magnan, S.J., Prof., St. Peter's Univ.; Edmund W. Majewski, S.J., Prof., St. Peter's Univ.; John A. Mullin, S.J., Guidance Counselor, St. Peter's Prep; Robert V. O'Hare, S.J., Teacher, St. Peter's Prep; Joseph J. Papaj, S.J., Adjunct Prof., St. Peter's Univ.; David X. Stump, S.J., Asst to the Supr. Total in Residence 13; Total Staff 13.

MAHWAH. *Paulist Fathers - Paulist Press*, 997 MacArthur Blvd., Mahwah, 07430. Tel: 201-825-7300; Fax: 201-825-8345; Email: info@paulistpress.com; Web: www.paulistpress.com. Rev. Mark-David Janus, C.S.P., Pres. & Publisher.

MONTCLAIR. *Comboni Missionaries of the Heart of Jesus (Verona Fathers)*, P.O. Box 138, Montclair, 07042-0138. Tel: 973-744-8080; Fax: 973-744-8919; Email: luigizb@yahoo.com. 118 7th Ave., 07104. Fax: 973-482-6575. Revs. Provvido Crozzoletto, M.C.C.J.; John Michael Converset, M.C.C.J.; Paul Donohue, M.C.C.J.; John Paolo Pezzi, M.C.C.J. Total in Residence 5; Total Staff 1.

ORADELL. *Congregation of Christian Brothers*, Bergen Catholic Brothers' Residence, 1040 Oradell Ave., Oradell, 07649. Tel: 201-261-1844; Fax: 201-599-9507; Email: president@bergencatholic.org. Bro. Brian M. Walsh, C.F.C., Contact Person. Brothers 4.

ORANGE. *The Salesian Community* (1998) Don Bosco Residence, 518-B Valley St., Orange, 07050. Tel: 973-674-2400; Fax: 973-674-7051. Revs. Dominic Tran, S.D.B., M.A., Dir.; Javier Aracil, S.D.B.; James Berning, S.D.B.; Dennis Hartigan, S.D.B.; Steven Dumais, S.D.B., Pastor, O.L.O.V.; Vincent Paczkowski, S.D.B.; Derek Van Daniker, S.D.B.; Bros. Jhoni Chamorro, S.D.B.; Ronald Chauca, S.D.B.; Paul Garcia, S.D.B.; Branden Gordon, S.B.D.; Benito Guerrero, S.D.B.; Travis Gunther, S.D.B.; James Nguyen, S.B.D.; Wilgintz Polynice, S.D.B.; Juan Pablo Rubio, S.D.B.; Joshua Sciullo, S.B.D.; Simon Song; Raphael Vargas, S.D.B. Total in Residence 23; Total Staff 7.

RAMSEY. *Don Bosco Prep Salesian Residence* (1915) 492 N. Franklin Tpke., Ramsey, 07446-2811. Tel: 201-327-8100; Fax: 201-327-3397. Revs. James Heuser, S.D.B., Dir. & Pres.; James Cerbone, S.D.B.; Matthew DeGance, S.D.B., B.S., PT, Coord. Youth Ministry; John Janko, S.D.B., Facilities Mgr.; Louis Konopelski, S.D.B., Math Teacher; James Mulloy, S.D.B., Theology Teacher; Bros. Joseph Ackroyd, S.D.B., Bookstore Asst.; Alfred Flatoff, S.D.B., Staff Asst.; Sasika Lokuhettige, S.B.D., Theology Teacher; James Wiegand, S.D.B., (Retired); Travis Gunther, S.D.B., Art Instructor. Total in Residence 11.

ROSELLE. *Marist Brothers Residence*, 376 Raritan Rd., Roselle, 07203. Tel: 908-245-3574; Fax: 908-620-9507. Brothers 9.

RUTHERFORD. *St. John Vianney Residence for Retired Priests*, 60 Home Ave., Rutherford, 07070. Tel: 201-933-5155. Carol Hubba, Admin. Total in Residence 18; Total Staff 16. In Res. Rev. Msgrs. Peter A. Cheplic, (Retired); Joseph Chiang, (Retired); Edward J. Eilert, (Retired); Thomas G. Madden, (Retired); Richard T. Strelecki, (Retired); Revs. Sebastian Kunnath, (Retired); Joseph F. Coda, (Retired); Neil J. Collins, (Retired); Michael J. German, (Retired); Alan F. Guglielmo, (Retired); Jose C. Saltarin, (Retired); James J. Reilly, S.T.L., (Retired); Thaddeus F. Zuber, (Retired); Rudolf Zubik, (Retired); Stanley Gomes, M.Div., Dir.

SOUTH ORANGE. *Pallottine Fathers & Brothers*, 204 Raymond Ave., P.O. Box 979, South Orange, 07079-0979. Tel: 201-943-0972; Fax: 973-762-2939. Rev. Peter T. Sticco, S.A.C., Admin., Vicar Prov.

TENAFLY. *Society of African Missions, Provincialate, S.M.A. Fathers*, 23 Bliss Ave., Tenafly, 07670. Tel: 201-567-0450; Fax: 201-541-1280; Email: tenafly-superior@smafathers.org; Web: www.smafathers.org. Very Rev. Michael P. Moran, S.M.A., Prov. Supr.; Revs. John P. Brennan, S.M.A., Vice Prov.; Albert Cooney, S.M.A., (Retired); Julien Esse, S.M.A., Vocation Dir.; Edward Galvin, S.M.A., (Retired), (Retired); Anthony Korir, S.M.A., In Res.; Patrick Kroteh, S.M.A., In Res.; James J. McConnell, S.M.A., Prov. Councillor; Ranees Anbukumar Rayappan, S.M.A., House Supr.; Dermot Roache, S.M.A., Prov. Sec.; Theresa Hicks, In Res.

UNION CITY. *Augustinian Recollects, St. Nicholas of Tolentine Monastery* Prov. of St. Nicholas of Tolentine 3201 Central Ave., Union City, 07087. Tel: 201-433-7550; Fax: 201-422-7570; Email: nicholas@agustinosrecoletos.org. Rev. Francisco Sigulenza, O.A.R., Supr.

Capuchin Friars - Province of the Sacred Stigmata of St. Francis, Office of the Provincial Min., 319 36th St., P.O. Box 809, Union City, 07087. Tel: 201-865-0611; Fax: 201-866-7035; Email: stigmatanj@aol.com; Web: capuchinfriars.org. Revs. Remo DiSalvatore, O.F.M.Cap., Vicar Prov.; Robert Williams, O.F.M.Cap., Councilor; Bro. Rudolph Pieretti, O.F.M. Cap., Prov. Sec.; Margaret Milizzo, Exec. Asst. to the Prov. Min.; Revs. Francisco Arredondo, Councilor; Ronald Giannone, O.F.M.Cap., Councilor; Robert Perez, Councilor. Brothers 12; Priests 22.

VERONA. *The Salvatorian Fathers* (1881) (Polish Mission House) 23 Crestmont Rd., Verona, 07044. Tel: 973-746-8770; Tel: 973-433-7626; Fax: 973-746-8770; Fax: 973-433-7626; Email: veronasds@gmail.com; Web: www.veronasds.com. Revs. Zenon Boczek, S.D.S., Supr.; Pawel Dolinski, S.D.S.; Andrzej Kielkowski, S.D.S.; Jan J. Mysliwiec, S.D.S.; Damian Tomiczek, S.D.S.; Strzadala Wieslaw, S.D.S.; Bro. Marek Miazga.

WEST ORANGE. *Augustinian Recollects* Prov. Res., Monastery of St. Cloud 29 Ridgeway Ave., West

Orange, 07052. Tel: 973-731-0616, Ext. 12; Fax: 973-731-1033; Email: SAprovince@oar.cc; Web: www.augustinianrecollects.us. Revs. John Michael Rafferty, O.A.R., Prior Prov.; Frederic B. Abiera, O.A.R., Prov. Sec.; Fredric B. Abiera, O.A.R., Prov. Procurator. Priests 3.

[M] CONVENTS AND RESIDENCES FOR SISTERS

NEWARK. *Daughters of Mary Mother of Mercy (DMMM)*, 44 Monticello Ave., 07106. Tel: 862-902-7029.

Hermanas Misioneras del Corazon de Jesus (HMCJ), Sacred Heart Convent, 109 Parker St., 07104. Tel: 973-484-1516; Fax: 973-484-9701; Email: misionerascj@aol.com. Sr. Josefa Gonzalez, H.S.C.J., Supr. Parish Ministry. Sisters 4.

Missionaries of Charity - St. Augustine Convent (1981) 168 Sussex Ave., 07103. Tel: 973-483-0165. Sr. M. Assisi Jimenez, M.C., Supr. Sisters 6.

Missionary Sisters of the Most Blessed Sacrament and Mary Immaculate Day Care Center. 121 Congress St., 07105. Tel: 973-589-5794; Fax: 973-589-2474; Email: stisbeldehungria@yahoo.com; Email: nepo867@msn.com. Rev. Lucio M. Nontol, T.O.R., (Peru) Dir.

Sisters of St. Joseph of Chestnut Hill, Thea House (1992) 39 Bleeker St., 07102-1913. Tel: 973-622-7056; Email: ssjthea@gmail.com. Total in Residence 3.

Vocationist Sisters (1921) (Our Lady of Perpetual Help Center). Perpetual Help Day Nursery. 170 Broad St., 07104. Tel: 973-484-3535; Fax: 973-484-2526; Email: perhelp@yahoo.com. Sisters 5; Total Staff 23; Total Assisted 141.

CALDWELL. *Motherhouse of Sisters of St. Dominic*, 1 Ryerson Ave., Caldwell, 07006. Tel: 973-403-3331; Fax: 973-228-9611; Email: eivory@caldwellop.org; Web: www.caldwellop.org. Sr. Patrice Werner, O.P., Ph.D., Prioress. Sisters in Community 113; Sisters in Diocese 104.

DEMAREST. *Missionary Benedictine Sisters of Tutzing* (1997) 274 County Rd., Demarest, 07627. Tel: 201-767-3114; Fax: 201-767-8874. Sr. Ottilia Kim, O.S.B., Supr. Sisters 4.

ELIZABETH. *Holy Family Sisters of the Needy*, 1017-1019 Julia St., Elizabeth, 07201. Tel: 908-662-0996 ; Cell: 908-209-7436; Fax: 908-352-0546; Email: hfsnbeth2014@outlook.com; Web: holyfamilysistersoftheneedy.org. Mother Mary Michael Okafor, H.F.S.N., Supr. Gen.; Sisters Paschaline Uzochukwu, H.F.S.N., Regl. Supr./Local Supr. (Elizabeth Community); Stephena Dede, H.S.F.N., Local Supr. (Nevada Community), 135 Pascus Pl., Sparks, NV 89431. Sisters 8.

St. Walburga Monastery, 851 N. Broad St., Elizabeth, 07208-2593. Tel: 908-352-4278; Fax: 908-352-6331; Email: Bensisnj@aol.com; Web: www.catholic-forum.com/bensisnj. Benedictine Sisters of Elizabeth, NJ; Benedictine Academy; Benedictine Pre-School. Sisters in Archdiocese 30; Professed Sisters 29.

ENGLEWOOD CLIFFS. *St. Michael Villa*, 399 Hudson Ter., Englewood Cliffs, 07632. Tel: 201-871-1620; Fax: 201-871-7313. Sr. Bridget O'Shea, C.S.J.P., Admin.; Rev. James R. McDonald, C.Ss.R., Chap. Sisters of St. Joseph of Peace.Senior Sisters Residence and Infirmary for Eastern Region. Sisters 34; Total in Residence 34; Total Staff 61.

Sisters of St. Joseph of Peace, 399 Hudson Ter., Englewood Cliffs, 07632. Tel: 201-568-6348; Fax: 201-568-9880; Email: pweidner@csjp.org; Web: www.csjp.org/sjp. Sisters Sheila Lemieux, C.S.J.P., Congregation Leader; Margaret Shannon, C.S.J.P., Asst. Congregation Leader; Melinda McDonald, C.S.J.P., Conagregation Councillor; Susan Francois, C.S.J.P., Conagregation Councillor. Congregation of Sisters of St. Joseph of Peace. Eastern U.S. Offices for Sisters of St. Joseph of Peace. Sisters in Community 55.

St. Ann Home for the Aged dba Peace Care St. Ann's, 198 Old Bergen Rd., Jersey City, 07305. Tel: 201-433-0950; Email: jmerlyliranzo@peacecarenj.org. Janet Merly-Liranzo, Admin. Bed Capacity 120; Total Staff 250.

St. Ann Day Care, 198 Old Bergen Rd., Jersey City, 07305. Tel: 201-433-0950; Email: jmerlyliranzo@peacecarenj.org. Janet Merly-Liranzo, Admin. Employees 10; Clients 50.

St. Joseph School for the Blind: A New Jersey Nonprofit Corp., 761 Summit Ave., Jersey City, 07307. Tel: 201-876-5432; Fax: 201-876-5431; Email: dfeinhals@schoolfortheblind.org. David Feinhals, Admin. Lay Teachers 19; Students 165; Total Staff 97.

Holy Name Medical Center, 718 Teaneck Rd., Teaneck, 07666. Tel: 201-833-3000; Fax: 201-833-3230; Email: maron@mail.holyname.org; Web: www.holyname.org. Michael Maron, CEO. Bed Capacity 361; Tot Asst. Annually 389,487; Total Staff 2,504.

St. Joseph Home, 81 York St., Jersey City, 07302. Tel: 201-413-9280; Email: gacosta@yorkstreetproject.org. Ms. Gloria E. Acosta, M.S.W., Dir. Bed Capacity 60; Total Staff 16; Total Assisted 349.

St. Joseph Home for the Blind - Sisters of St. Joseph of Peace Sisters of St. Joseph of Peace Shalom Center, 399 Hudson Ter., Englewood Cliffs, 07632. Tel: 201-568-6348; Fax: 201-568-9880; Email: dfeinhals@schoolfortheblind.org.

Margaret Anna Cusack Care Center, Inc. dba Peace Care St. Joseph's, 537 Pavonia Ave., Jersey City, 07306. Tel: 201-653-8300; Tel: 201-963-4346; Fax: 201-653-7705; Email: tsheehy@peacecarenj.org; Web: www.peacecarenj.org. Thomas P. Sheehy, Admin. Bed Capacity 139; Sisters 4; Tot Asst. Annually 600; Total Staff 235.

St. Mary Residence, 240 Washington St., Jersey City, 07302. Tel: 201-432-6289; Email: gacosta@yorkstreetproject.org. Ms. Gloria E. Acosta, M.S.W., Dir. Tot Asst. Annually 44; Total Staff 11.

St. Michael Villa, 399 Hudson Ter., Englewood Cliffs, 07632. Tel: 201-871-1620; Email: mbuckstone@gmail.com. Merri Buckstone, Admin.

**Peace Care, Inc.*, 198 Old Bergen Rd., Jersey City, 07305. Tel: 201-433-0950; Fax: 888-560-5995; Email: mdonohue@peacecarenj.org; Web: www.peacecarenj.org. Mailing Address: 399 Hudson Ter., Englewood Cliffs, 07632. Ms. Maureen Donohue, CEO.

Peace Ministries, Inc., 399 Hudson Ter., Englewood Cliffs, 07632. Tel: 201-731-3325; Email: mdonohue@csjp.org. Ms. Maureen Donohue, Exec.

Nurturing Place Day Care Child Development Center. 81 York St., Jersey City, 07302. Tel: 201-413-1982; Email: vhayes@yorkstreetproject.org. Victoria Hayes, Dir. Students 70; Total Staff 16.

The York Street Project, 89 York St., Jersey City, 07302. Tel: 201-451-9838; Email: sbyrne@yorkstreetproject.org. Suzanne Byrne, Exec. Total Staff 11.

Stella Maris Retreat Center, 399 Hudson Ter., Englewood Cliffs, 07632. Tel: 201-568-6348.

WATERSPIRIT Ministry, 4 East River Rd., Rumson, 07760. Tel: 732-923-9788; Email: water@waterspirit.org. Sr. Suzanne Golas, C.S.J.P., Dir. Total Staff 4.

FORT LEE. *Holy Trinity Convent (Inter Community)*, 199 Myrtle Ave., Fort Lee, 07024. Tel: 201-944-2911. Dominican Sisters of Hope 1; Franciscan Sisters of St. Francis 2; Sisters of Charity 1.

IRVINGTON. *Immaculate Conception Convent*, St. Leo, 121 Myrtle Ave., Irvington, 07111. Tel: 973-757-2432. Augustinian Recollect Sisters (Cloistered) 11.

JERSEY CITY. *St. Nicholas Convent*, 115 Ferry St., Jersey City, 07307. Tel: 201-659-5644; Fax: 201-798-6868; Email: sjmaumand@yahoo.com. Sr. Joann Marie Aumand, S.C.C., Supr.

LODI. *Immaculate Conception Convent* (1913) 260 S. Main St., Lodi, 07644-2196. Tel: 973-473-7447; Fax: 973-473-7126; Email: sconniet@feliciansisters.org; Web: www.feliciansistersna.org. Sr. Constance Marie Tomyl, Prov. Sec. Convent of the Felician Sisters.

Congregation of the Sisters of Saint Felix Convent and Healthcare Center of the Felician Sisters. Sisters 75.

PLAINFIELD. *Contemplative Convent of the Missionaries of Charity*, 513 Liberty St., Plainfield, 07060. Tel: 908-754-1978. Sr. Mary Nazarene, M.C., Supr. Total in Residence 12.

RIDGEFIELD. *Pallottine Sisters - St. Vincent Pallotti Convent*, 545 Victory Ave., Ridgefield, 07657. Tel: 201-941-4552; Email: sralicemarie@gmail.com. Sisters 3.

SADDLE BROOK. *Miyazaki Caritas Sisters (Korea) - Caritas Sisters Convent*, 9 Jamros Ter., Saddle Brook, 07663. Tel: 201-703-0002; Fax: 201-703-7111.

SCOTCH PLAINS. *Union Catholic Convent* (1962) 1600 Martine Ave., Scotch Plains, 07076. Tel: 908-889-1600; Fax: 908-889-7867; Email: mainoffice@unioncatholic.org. Sr. Percylee Hart, R.S.M., Supr. Sisters of Mercy of Mid-Atlantic (R.S.M.) and Sisters of St. Joseph (S.S.J.). Sisters 5; Total in Residence 5.

SUMMIT. *Monastery of Our Lady of the Rosary* (1919) 543 Springfield Ave., Summit, 07901. Tel: 908-273-1228; Fax: 908-273-6511; Email: info@summitdominicans.org; Web: www.nunsopsummit.org. Sr. Mary Martin Jacobs, O.P., Prioress; Rev. Gregory Salomone, O.P., Chap.

Monastery of Our Lady of the Rosary, Dominican Nuns of the Perpetual Rosary Novices 1; Temporary Professed Sisters 1; Sisters 17; Professed Sisters 15.

TENAFLY. *Convent of Our Lady of the Angels*, 253 Knickerbocker Rd., Tenafly, 07670. Tel: 201-568-2171; Fax: 201-568-2352; Web: www.mficusa.org. Sr. Patricia Coyle, M.F.I.C., Local Min. Missionary Franciscan Sisters of the Immaculate Conception. Sisters 46.

UNION. *Sisters of St. Francis of the Providence of God*, 1137 Burnet Ave., Union, 07083. Tel: 908-206-1136 . Sisters 2.

UNION CITY. *Holy Rosary Convent* (1904) 1514 Central Ave., Union City, 07087. Tel: 201-617-4638; Email: holyrosaryconvent@verizon.net. Sisters of the Catholic Apostolate (Pallottines). Sisters 2.

[N] RETREAT HOUSES

KEARNY. *Archdiocesan Youth Retreat Center* Features: Newly renovated on six acres; centrally located in Kearny and accessible from the NJ Turnpike, Routes 21 & 280; can accommodate up to 400 guests for a day retreat and sleeps over 200 guests overnight; semi-private and dorm-style rooming can accommodate youth and/or adult groups; handicap accessible rooms available; multiple floors can accommodate multiple groups at one time; meeting rooms of various sizes can accommodate multiple groups at one time; walking outdoor rosary and prayer garden; separate dining hall; gymnasium; high and low ropes challenge course; two chapels; ample on-site parking for retreats or events. Programs: Already featured programs include Rejoice, leadership training, confirmation prep, youth day, overnight and weekend retreats, summer camp, Challenge Course, adult day overnight and weekend retreats, high school and elementary school retreats. 499 Belgrove Dr., Kearny, 07032. Tel: 201-998-0088; Fax: 201-299-0801; Web: www.newarkoym.com.

[O] CAMPUS MINISTRY

NEWARK. *The Newman Catholic Center at University Heights (Rutgers-Newark/NJIT/Essex)*, 91 Washington St., 07102. Tel: 973-624-1301; Fax: 973-623-1728; Email: NewmanCenter@optonline.net; Web: www.newmanclubnewark.org. Rev. Pedro Bismarck Chau, Dir. & Chap.; Patricia Decker, Office Asst., Tel: 973-497-4348; Joselina Castillo, Campus Min. Serving Essex County College, Rutgers University-Newark Campus, New Jersey Institute of Technology Total Staff 3.

HOBOKEN. *Stevens Institute of Technology*, Castle Point on Hudson, Hoboken, 07030-5991. Tel: 201-216-5000. Mr. Laurence Laurente, Campus Min.

JERSEY CITY. *New Jersey City University, Gilligan Student Union*, 2039 Kennedy Blvd., GSUB Rm. 316, Jersey City, 07305-1597. Tel: 201-200-2565 (Office); Tel: 973-792-5710 (Residence); Fax: 201-200-2329 (Office of Campus Life); Web: www.catholiccampusministry.org. Mr. Laurence Laurente, Campus Min. Total Staff 1.

MAHWAH. *Ramapo College* (1969) 505 Ramapo Valley Rd., Room SC207, Mahwah, 07430. Tel: 201-684-7251; Fax: 201-825-0276; Web: www.ramapo.edu/ministries/catholic-campus-ministry. Rev. Kevin Gugliotta, Chap. Students 6,008; Total Staff 1.

TEANECK. *Fairleigh Dickinson Univ.-Teaneck Campus*, 1000 River Rd., Teaneck, 07666. Tel: 201-692-2570 ; Fax: 201-692-2769. Breanna Silva, Campus Min. Total Staff 1.

UNION. *Kean University*, Catholic Campus Ministry, 1000 Morris Ave., Downs Hall 130, Union, 07083-7131. Tel: 908-737-4835. Jackie Oesmann, M.B.A., Campus Min.; Rev. William P. Sheridan, Dir., Campus Ministry.

UPPER MONTCLAIR. *Newman Catholic Center at Montclair State University*, 894 Valley Rd., Upper Montclair, 07043-2116. Tel: 973-746-2323; Fax: 973-783-3313; Email: chernjam@comcast.net; Web: www.msunewman.com. Rev. James N. Chern, Dir., Newman Catholic Ctr. & Chap. at Montclair State Univ.; Sean Grealy, Campus Min.; Mary Kominsky, Office Mgr. & Pastoral Assoc. Total Staff 3.

[P] SHRINES

KEARNY. *Eucharistic Shrine of the Adorable Face of Jesus*, 672 Passaic Ave., Kearny, 07032-1305. Tel: 201-997-1270; Fax: 201-997-5552; Email: eushrine@gmail.com. Rev. Msgr. Renato Grasselli, S.T.L., Shrine Dir.

[Q] MISCELLANEOUS LISTINGS

NEWARK. *CatholiCare, Inc.*, 171 Clifton Ave., P.O. Box 9500, 07104-0500. Tel: 973-497-4002; Fax: 973-497-4018.

Deacon St. Lawrence Welfare Fund, Office of Permanent Diaconate, 171 Clifton Ave., P.O. Box 9500, 07104-9500. Tel: 973-497-4125;

Fax: 973-497-4103; Email: mckennjo@rcan.org. Deacon John J. McKenna, K.H.S.

Diaconate Executive Committee, Archdiocesan Center, 171 Clifton Ave., P.O. Box 9500, 07104-9500. Tel: 973-497-4125; Fax: 973-497-4103; Email: mckennjo@rcan.org. Deacon John J. McKenna, K.H.S.

Saint James Care, Inc. A member of Catholic Health East. 155 Jefferson St., 07107. Alexander J. Hatala, Pres.

St. Mary Senior Residence, Inc., 590 N. 7th St., 07107. Tel: 973-596-3984; Fax: 973-412-7710. Mr. John Westervelt, B.A., Pres. & Treas.

St. Michael Foundation, Inc. Subsidiary of Saint Michael Medical Center. St. Michael Medical Center, 111 Central Ave., 07102.
Fax: 973-690-3601. Mr. David A. Ricci, Pres.; Michael F. Rems, Accounting Mgr.

New Jersey Caritas Corporation, Inc., 171 Clifton Ave., 07104. Tel: 973-497-4002; Fax: 973-497-4018.

Domus Corporation, Inc., 590 N. 7th St., 07107.
Tel: 973-596-3984; Fax: 973-424-9596.

Myers Senior Residence, Inc., 590 N. 7th St., 07107.
Tel: 973-596-3984; Fax: 973-412-7710.

Canaan House, Inc., 494 Broad St., 07102.
Tel: 973-596-5115; Fax: 973-424-9596.

Sunrise House, 185 Parkhurst St., 07114.
Tel: 973-624-9478; Fax: 973-424-9596.

Carmel House of Jersey City, Inc., 494 Broad St., 07102. Tel: 973-596-5115; Fax: 973-424-9596.

River Vale Senior Residence, Inc., 590 N. 7th St., 07107. Tel: 973-596-3984; Fax: 973-412-7710.

University Heights Property Company, Inc., 111 Central Ave., 07102. Tel: 973-690-3514;
Fax: 973-690-3605. Mr. Roosevel N. Nesmith Esq., Chm.; Mr. David A. Ricci, Pres.; Ronald J. Napiorski, Vice Pres. Finance.

ELIZABETH. *St. Joseph Social Service Center* (1986) 118 Division St., Elizabeth, 07201. Tel: 908-352-2989; Tel: 908-354-5456; Fax: 908-354-1433; Email: bmurphy@sjeliz.org; Web: www.sjeliz.org. Rev. Anthony J. Randazzo, V.F., Chap.; Ms. Bernadette Murphy, Dir. Tot Asst. Annually 5,000; Total Staff 13; Total Assisted 5,000.

ENGLEWOOD. *Carmelite Missions*, 55 W. Demarest Ave., Englewood, 07631. Tel: 201-568-0364, Ext. 25 ; Email: carmelitemissions@carmelitemissions.org; Web: www.carmelitemissions.org. Rev. Joseph P. O'Brien, O.Carm., Dir.

FAIRVIEW. *Pallottine Intra-Community Operating Corporation*, Mailing Address: P.O. Box 979, South Orange, 07079. Tel: 973-762-2926;
Fax: 973-762-2939. 395 Delano Pl., Fairview, 07022. Tel: 201-943-0972; Fax: 201-313-5616. Rev. Frank Donio, S.A.C.

JERSEY CITY. *St. Patrick and Assumption All Saints Foundation*, 511 Bramhall Ave., Jersey City, 07304. Tel: 201-521-0200; Fax: 201-521-0633; Email: jcfran@bellatlantic.net. Rev. Francis E. Schiller, B.A., J.D., Contact Person, (Retired).

St. Patrick Housing Corp., 492 Bramhall Ave., Jersey City, 07304. Tel: 201-401-4306;
Fax: 201-521-0100. Rev. Eugene P. Squeo, J.D., Pres., (Retired).

Trinity Child Care Center, 509 Bramhall Ave., Jersey City, 07304. Tel: 201-433-2701; Email: sonja@common-courtesies.com; Web: www.trinityccc.org. Sonja Garlin, Dir. Children 75.

KEARNY. *Family of Nazareth, Inc.* (1991) 672 Passaic Ave., Kearny, 07032. Tel: 201-997-3220;
Fax: 201-997-5552; Email: fnazareth@rmnewark.org. Fred Canlas, Pres.; Luis Abarca, Sec. A foundation to support the work of the Redemptoris Mater Missionary Seminary and for the new evangelization.

LINDEN. *Friends of St. John Paul II Be Not Afraid Center, Inc.*, 122 Liberty Ave., Linden, 07036.
Tel: 908-862-1116.

LODI. *Association of Franciscan Colleges and Universities, Inc.*, Email: afcu@felician.edu; Web: www.franciscancollegesuniversities.org. Bro. Gary J. Maciag, O.F.M., M.F.A., Exec. Dir.

**The Promise Outreach, Inc.* (1982) 260 S. Main St., Lodi, 07644. Tel: 973-460-3229; Fax: 973-473-7126; Email: smantonelle@feliciansisters.org; Web: home.catholicweb.com/thepromiseoutreachinc. Sr. Antonelle Chunka, C.S.S.F., Dir.; Bro. Thomas Corey, B.S.C.D., Co-Dir. Volunteers visit, correspond with, and provide opportunity for spirituality and other basic needs to teens and young adults in programs, correctional institutions and centers of rehabilitation. Support is also offered to their family and caretakers. Tot Asst. Annually 1,000; Total Staff 12.

MAHWAH. *Paulist Press*, 997 MacArthur Blvd., Mahwah, 07430. Tel: 201-825-7300;
Fax: 201-825-6921; Email: info@paulistpress.com; Email: bbyrns@paulistpress.com; Web: www.paulistpress.com. Rev. Mark-David Janus, C.S.P., Pres. & Publisher. Priests 1; Total Staff 40.

MONTCLAIR. *Tri-State Coalition for Responsible Investment*, 40 S. Fullerton Ave., Montclair, 07042. Tel: 973-509-8800; Fax: 973-509-8808; Email: mbgallagher@tricri.org; Web: www.tricri.org. Mary Beth Gallagher, Assoc. Dir.; Gina Falada, Prog. Assoc.

ORANGE. *Congregation of St. John, Inc.*, 103 S. Center St., Orange, 07050. Tel: 973-674-2052; Email: fr.bm@stjean.com.

Mee Joo Catholic Inc., 18 Cleveland St., Orange, 07050. Tel: 973-919-7124; Email: augpark@yahoo.com.

PLAINFIELD. **The Koinonia Academy*, 1040 Plainfield Ave., Plainfield, 07060. Tel: 908-668-9002;
Fax: 908-668-9883; Web: koinoniaacademy.org. Thomas J. Appert, Headmaster.

**The People of Hope* (1977) 1040 Plainfield Ave., St. Francis Bldg., Plainfield, 07060. Tel: 908-222-9722 ; Fax: 908-222-9755. David Touhill, Senior Coord. The People of Hope is a Catholic Charismatic Covenant community of prayer, family life, and evangelization. Officially recognized as a private association of the faithful in 2006 by Archbishop Myers, the People of Hope sponsors marriage and family retreats, youth, university, and young adult programs, Christian business seminars, and other evangelistic events. Its largest outreach is Koinonia Academy, a K-12 school, founded in 1984. The Community is organized to encourage individuals and families to dedicate their lives to God under the Lordship of Jesus Christ, to help in the renewal of the Catholic Church and to assist the spreading of the Gospel message of Jesus Christ locally and throughout the world. To be "a witness of an authentically Christian life, given over to God." (Pope Paul VI, Evangelii Nuntiandi, 1975).

RENEW International, 1232 George St., Plainfield, 07062-1717. Tel: 908-769-5400; Fax: 908-769-5660; Email: renew@renewintl.org; Web: www.renewintl.org; Web: www.bemywitness.org. Sr. Theresa Rickard, O.P., D.Min., Pres. & Exec. Dir.; Rev. Msgr. Thomas A. Kleissler, Pres. Emeritus, (Retired); Eartha Johnson, Mgr., Customer Svc., Sales & Fulfillment; Mr. Greg Kremer, Dir. Diocesan Sales & Svcs.; Rev. Alejandro Lopez-Cardinale, Coord. Hispanic Progs.; Sr. Honora Nolty, O.P., Asst. Dir. & Dir., Devel.; Mary Beth Oria, Dir., Finance & Business Opers.; Patricia Wiley, Dir., Human Resources & Information Technology; Jennifer Bober, Dir. of Marketing; Rev. Jeremiah Browne, Dir. RENEW Africa; Joanne Cahoon, D.Min.; Susan Capurso, Exec. Asst.; Sr. Maureen Colleary, F.S.P., Pastoral and Sales Consultant; Regina Crowley, Print Mgr.; Milissa Else, Dir. of Pastoral Services and Sales; Sr. Marenid Fabre, O.P.; John Fontana, Dir. Ignatian Business Chapters; Soeurette Fougere; Martha Ann Hagedorn, Customer Service Representative; Manuel Hernandez; Mary Beth Howath, Dev. Asst.; Yvette Hutchins, Asst. Mgr. of Finance and Accounting; Marissa Klapwald, Dir. of Dev.; Sisters Honora Nicholson; Elizabeth O'Donnell; Deacon Charles Paolino, Managing Editor; Mariann Salisbury, Major Gifts Consultant; Sr. Janet Schaeffler, O.P.
Pastoral Representatives Rev. Jeremiah Browne; Joanne Cahoon, D.Min.; Sisters Maureen Colleary, F.S.P.; Marie Cooper, S.J.C.; Aine Hughes, H.C.; Marenid Fabre, O.P.; Manuel Hernandez; Brenda Maiman; Sr. Marjorie McGregor, O.P.; Dr. Mariela Saravia.
Additional Staff: Jennifer Bober; Susan Capurso; Regina Crowley; Martha Ann Hagedorn; Yvette Hutchins; Deacon Charles Paolino; Charmaine Woolard.

RAMSEY. *Don Bosco Preparatory High School, Inc.*, 492 N. Franklin Turnpike, Ramsey, 07446.

RUTHERFORD. *The Community of God's Love* Catholic Charismatic Community 70 W. Passaic Ave., Rutherford, 07070. Tel: 201-935-0344;
Fax: 201-935-0111; Email: theCGL@aol.com; Web: thecgl.org. Rev. Philip F.A. Latronico, M.A., M.Div., Chap.; Doreen Cevasco, Dir.

SHORT HILLS. *Friends of the Newark Monastery, Inc.*, 9 Grosvenor Rd., Short Hills, 07078. Email: aluzarraga@shearman.com. Alberto Luzarraga, Pres. & Contact Person.

SOUTH ORANGE. *The Pallottines of South Orange, Inc.*, 204 Raymond Ave., South Orange, 07079-2305.
Tel: 973-763-5591; Fax: 973-762-2939. Rev. Peter T. Sticco, S.A.C., Supr.

Salesians of Don Bosco, Tel: 973-761-0201;
Fax: 973-763-9330; Email: ym@salesianym.com; Web: www.salesianym.com. Revs. Steve Ryan, S.D.B., Vocation Dir. & Prov. Councillor for Youth Ministry; P. Francis Pinto, S.D.B.; Dennis Donovan, S.D.B., Treas.

SUMMIT. *Association of the Monasteries of Nuns of the Order of Preachers in the United States of America*, 543 Springfield Ave., Summit, 07901-4400.
Tel: 650-322-1801; Fax: 650-322-6816; Email: prioress@summitdominicans.org; Email: christinemenlo@comcast.net. Sisters Maria Christine Behlow, O.P., Pres.; Mary Catharine Perry, O.P., Vice Pres., First Counselor; Marie Tersidis Lakimboria, O.P., First Counselor; Mary Rose Carlin, O.P., Sec. & Counselor; Mary Jeremiah Gillet, O.P., Counselor; Denise Marie Atkins, O.P., Treas.

Christ Child Society of Summit, New Jersey, Inc., P.O. Box 125, Summit, 07902-0125.
Tel: 908-598-1377; Email: ccssummit@gmail.com. Kathryn Colao, Bd. of Directors.

TEANECK. *Holy Name Medical Center Foundation*, 718 Teaneck Rd., Teaneck, 07666. Tel: 201-833-3187;
Fax: 201-833-3708; Email: foundation@mail.holyname.org; Web: www.holyname.org. Michael Maron, Pres. & CEO. Sisters of St. Joseph of Peace.

UNION. *Association of St. Philomena Helpers and Servants to the Suffering & the Poor* (1996) P.O. Box 393, Union, 07083-0393. Tel: 908-964-7653; Fax: 908-687-4209.

UNION CITY. *Cofradia Arquidiocesana de la Virgen de la Caridad del Cobre, Inc.*, 909 20th St., P.O. Box 682, Union City, 07087. Tel: 201-330-1352. Ana Theresa Serrand, Treas.

**New Jersey Friends of Mandeville, Inc.*, 526 Monastery Pl., Union City, 07087. Mr. Greg Hampson, CFO.

RELIGIOUS INSTITUTES OF MEN REPRESENTED IN THE ARCHDIOCESE

For further details refer to the corresponding bracketed number in the Religious Institutes of Men or Women section.

[0100]—*Adorno Fathers*—C.R.M.
[0200]—*Benedictine Monks* (Newark Abbey)—O.S.B.
[0330]—*Brothers of Christian Schools* (Baltimore Prov.; Long Island/New England Prov.; New York Prov.)—F.S.C.
[0470]—*The Capuchin Friars* (Prov. of the Stigmata)—O.F.M.Cap.
[0270]—*Carmelite Fathers & Brothers* (American Prov.)—O.Carm.
[0380]—*Comboni Missionaries of the Heart of Jesus (Verona)*—M.C.C.J.
[0310]—*Congregation of Christian Brothers*—C.F.C.
[]—*Congregation of Saint John.*
[0520]—*Franciscan Friars* (Prov. of Most Holy Name; Prov. of the Assumption)—O.F.M.
[0530]—*Franciscan Friars of the Atonement*—S.A.
[0535]—*Franciscan Friars of the Renewal*—C.F.R.
[0690]—*Jesuit Fathers and Brothers* (Prov. of New York)—S.J.
[0770]—*The Marist Brothers*—F.M.S.
[0840]—*Missionary Servants of the Most Holy Trinity*—S.T.
[0150]—*Order of the Augustinian Recollects* (Prov. of St. Augustine)—O.A.R.
[0150]—*Order of the Augustinian Recollects* (Prov. of St. Nicholas of Tolentine)—O.A.R.
[]—*Pallottine Fathers & Brothers*—S.A.C.
[1030]—*Paulist Fathers*—C.S.P.
[]—*Province of the Immaculate Conception.*
[1070]—*Redemptorist Fathers* (Byzantine Ukrainians)—C.Ss.R.
[1070]—*Redemptorist Fathers* (Prov. of Campo Grande, Brazil)—C.Ss.R.
[1190]—*Salesians of Don Bosco*—S.D.B.
[0110]—*Society of African Missions*—S.M.A.
[0990]—*Society of the Catholic Apostolate* (Prov. of the Immaculate Conception)—S.A.C.
[1200]—*Society of the Divine Savior*—S.D.S.
[1170]—*St. Patrick Missionary Society*—S.P.S.
[0560]—*Third Order Regular of Saint Francis* (U.S.A. Commissarate of the Spanish Prov.)—T.O.R.
[1340]—*Vocationist Fathers*—S.D.V.

RELIGIOUS INSTITUTES OF WOMEN REPRESENTED IN THE ARCHDIOCESE

[0230]—*Benedictine Sisters of Pontifical Jurisdiction-Newark* (Benedictine Sisters of Baltimore; Benedictine Sisters of Elizabeth)—O.S.B.
[1810]—*Bernardine Franciscan Sisters*—O.S.F.
[]—*Congregation of Caritas Sisters of Miyazaki* Korean Province.
[]—*Congregation of Kkottongnae Sisters of Jesus*—C.S.K.J.
[]—*Congregation of the Apostolic Sisters of Saint John*—C.S.J.
[]—*Daughters of Divine Love*—D.D.L.
[]—*Daughters of Mary*—D.M.
[0850]—*Daughters of Mary Help of Christians*—F.M.A.
[]—*Daughters of Mary, Mothers of Mercy* (Nigeria)—D.M.M.M.
[]—*Daughters of the Heart of Mary*—D.H.M.
[]—*Dominican Nuns of Perpetual Adoration and Perpetual Rosary*—O.P.
[1070-11]—*Dominican Sisters* (Sparkill, NY)—O.P.
[1070-15]—*Dominican Sisters* (Blauvelt, NY)—O.P.
[1070-18]—*Dominican Sisters* (Caldwell, NJ)—O.P.
[1070-06]—*Dominican Sisters of Hope* (Newburgh, NY)—O.P.
[1170]—*Felician Sisters*—C.S.S.F.
[1400]—*Franciscan Missionary Sister of the Sacred Heart*—F.M.S.C.

[1180]—*Franciscan Sisters of Allegany, New York*—O.S.F.
[1425]—*Franciscan Sisters of Peace*—F.S.P.
[1460]—*Franciscan Sisters of St. Elizabeth*—F.S.S.E.
[]—*Hermanas Missionaras del Corazon de Jesus* (Dominican Republic)—H.M.C.J.
[]—*Holy Family Sisters of the Needy*—H.F.S.N.
[]—*Little Servant Sisters of the Immaculate Conception*—L.S.I.C.
[2710]—*Missionaries of Charity* (Active and Contemplative)—M.C.
[0210]—*Missionary Benedictine Sisters of Tutzing* (Korean Mission)—O.S.B.
[1360]—*Missionary Franciscan Sisters of the Immaculate Conception*—M.F.I.C.
[2790]—*Missionary Servants of the Most Blessed Trinity*—M.S.B.T.
[3430]—*Religious Teachers Filippini*—M.P.F.
[2970]—*School Sisters of Notre Dame*—S.S.N.D.
[1700]—*School Sisters of the Third Order of St. Francis* (Bethlehem, PA)—O.S.F.
[0590]—*Sisters of Charity of Saint Elizabeth, Convent Station*—S.C.
[0660]—*Sisters of Christian Charity*—S.C.C.
[2575]—*Sisters of Mercy of the Americas* (New Jersey)—R.S.M.
[]—*Sisters of Our Lady of Perpetual Help*—S.O.L.P.H.
[]—*Sisters of Peace Pentecost.*
[3893]—*Sisters of Saint Joseph of Chestnut Hill, Philadelphia*—S.S.J.
[1650]—*Sisters of St. Francis of Philadelphia*—O.S.F.
[1660]—*Sisters of St. Francis of Providence of God*—O.S.F.
[]—*Sisters of St. Francis of the Neumann Communities*—O.S.F.
[3820]—*Sisters of St. John the Baptist*—C.S.J.B.
[3890]—*Sisters of St. Joseph of Peace*—C.S.J.P.
[3140]—*Sisters of the Catholic Apostolate (Pallottine)*—C.S.A.C.
[0970]—*Sisters of the Divine Compassion*—R.D.C.
[2183]—*Sisters of the Immaculate Heart of Mary, Mother of Christ*—I.H.M.
[]—*The Sisters of the Sacred Heart of Mary of Mirinae*—S.H.M.M.
[3320]—*Sisters of the Presentation of the Blessed Virgin Mary*—P.B.V.M.
[2160]—*Sisters, Servants of the Immaculate Heart of Mary (Scranton)*—I.H.M.
[4060]—*Society of the Holy Child Jesus*—S.H.C.J.
[4210]—*Vocationist Sisters*—S.D.V.

ARCHDIOCESAN CEMETERIES

Office of Catholic Cemeteries, Tel: 973-497-7981; Fax: 973-497-7984; Tel: 973-497-7981 (Cemeteries Office); Tel: 973-497-7988 (Mausoleum Office). Andrew P. Schafer, K.H.S., Exec. Dir., Tel: 973-497-7975.

COLONIA.
St. Gertrude
MAHWAH.
Maryrest
EAST HANOVER.
Gate of Heaven
EAST ORANGE.
Holy Sepulchre
St. Mary
FRANKLIN LAKES.
Christ the King
JERSEY CITY.
Holy Name
Saint Peter
NORTH ARLINGTON.
Holy Cross
RIVER VALE.
St. Andrew
TENAFLY.
Mount Carmel

PAROCHIAL CEMETERIES

NEWARK. *Mount Olivet*
BELLEVILLE. *St. Peter*
BLOOMFIELD. *Mount Olivet*
CLARK. *St. Mary*
FORT LEE. *Madonna*
HACKENSACK. *St. Joseph*
HOHOKUS. *St. Luke*
LINDEN. *Mount Calvary*
LYNDHURST. *St. Joseph*
ORANGE. *St. John*
PLAINFIELD. *St. Mary*
SHORT HILLS. *St. Rose of Lima*
SUMMIT. *St. Teresa*
UPPER MONTCLAIR. *Immaculate Conception*

NECROLOGY

† Arias, David, O.A.R., Retired Auxiliary Bishop of Newark., Died May. 9, 2019
† Gilchrist, John J., (Retired), Died Apr. 18, 2018
† Houghton, Francis J., (Retired), Died Oct. 31, 2018
† Linder, William J., (Retired), Died Jun. 8, 2018
† Basil, John E., (Retired), Died Jul. 20, 2018
† Comesanas, Raul E.L., (Retired), Died Oct. 23, 2018
† Langdon, Robert H., (Retired), Died Apr. 29, 2018
† Lester, John J., (Retired), Died Nov. 20, 2018
† Losarcos, Javier, (Retired), Died Nov. 8, 2018
† Mader, George L., (Retired), Died Jun. 19, 2018
† Moran, Michael J., (Retired), Died Nov. 25, 2018

An asterisk (*) denotes an organization that has established tax-exempt status directly with the IRS and is not covered by the USCCB Group Ruling.

Archdiocese of New Orleans

(Archidioecesis Novae Aureliae)

Most Reverend

GREGORY M. AYMOND, D.D.

Archbishop of New Orleans; ordained May 10, 1975; ordained Auxiliary Bishop of New Orleans January 10, 1997; appointed Coadjutor Bishop of Austin June 2, 2000; installed Bishop of Austin August 3, 2000; appointed Archbishop of New Orleans June 12, 2009; Pallium conferred by Pope Benedict XVI at the Vatican June 29, 2009; installed Archbishop of New Orleans August 20, 2009. *Archdiocesan Administration Building: 7887 Walmsley Ave., New Orleans, LA 70125-3496.* Tel: 504-861-9521.

Most Reverend

ALFRED C. HUGHES, S.T.D.

Former Archbishop of New Orleans; ordained December 15, 1957; appointed Auxiliary Bishop of Boston July 21, 1981; ordained Auxiliary Bishop of Boston September 14, 1981; appointed Bishop of Baton Rouge September 7, 1993; installed Bishop of Baton Rouge November 4, 1993; appointed Coadjutor Archbishop of New Orleans February 16, 2001; appointed Archbishop of New Orleans January 3, 2002; retired August 20, 2009. *Office: 7887 Walmsley Ave., New Orleans, LA 70125.* Tel: 504-861-9521.

Archdiocesan Administration Building: 7887 Walmsley Ave., New Orleans, LA 70125-3496. Tel: 504-861-9521; Fax: 504-866-2906.

Web: www.archdiocese-no.org

Most Reverend

FERNAND J. CHERI, III, O.F.M.

Auxiliary Bishop of New Orleans; ordained May 20, 1978; appointed Titular Bishop of Membressa and Auxiliary Bishop of New Orleans January 12, 2015; ordained March 23, 2015. *Office: 7887 Walmsley Ave., New Orleans, LA 70125-3496.*

Square Miles 4,208.

Established April 25, 1793; Archdiocese July 19, 1850.

Comprises the following Parishes of Louisiana: Orleans, St. Bernard, Plaquemines, Jefferson, St. Charles, St. John the Baptist, St. Tammany and Washington.

For legal titles of parishes and archdiocesan institutions, consult the Chancery Office.

STATISTICAL OVERVIEW

Personnel	
Archbishops	1
Retired Archbishops	1
Auxiliary Bishops	1
Abbots	1
Priests: Diocesan Active in Diocese	169
Priests: Diocesan Active Outside Diocese	4
Priests: Retired, Sick or Absent	55
Number of Diocesan Priests	228
Religious Priests in Diocese	124
Total Priests in Diocese	352
Extern Priests in Diocese	34
Ordinations:	
Diocesan Priests	4
Transitional Deacons	8
Permanent Deacons in Diocese	236
Total Brothers	56
Total Sisters	362
Parishes	
Parishes	112
With Resident Pastor:	
Resident Diocesan Priests	89
Resident Religious Priests	22
Without Resident Pastor:	
Administered by Priests	1
Missions	7
Pastoral Centers	2
Professional Ministry Personnel:	
Brothers	56
Sisters	362
Welfare	
Health Care Centers	10
Total Assisted	163,050
Homes for the Aged	25
Total Assisted	2,900
Residential Care of Children	1
Total Assisted	25
Day Care Centers	5
Total Assisted	525
Specialized Homes	3
Total Assisted	167
Special Centers for Social Services	415
Total Assisted	365,883
Residential Care of Disabled	6
Total Assisted	28
Other Institutions	1
Total Assisted	89
Educational	
Seminaries, Diocesan	2
Students from This Diocese	39
Students from Other Diocese	232
Seminaries, Religious	1
Students Religious	6
Total Seminarians	45
Colleges and Universities	3
Total Students	9,142
High Schools, Diocesan and Parish	9
Total Students	4,102
High Schools, Private	13
Total Students	8,517
Elementary Schools, Diocesan and Parish	48
Total Students	18,280
Elementary Schools, Private	8
Total Students	3,078
Non-residential Schools for the Disabled	1
Total Students	205
Catechesis/Religious Education:	
High School Students	2,906
Elementary Students	7,311
Total Students under Catholic Instruction	53,586
Teachers in the Diocese:	
Priests	44
Scholastics	3
Brothers	26
Sisters	31
Lay Teachers	3,586
Vital Statistics	
Receptions into the Church:	
Infant Baptism Totals	2,706
Minor Baptism Totals	903
Adult Baptism Totals	210
Received into Full Communion	480
First Communions	3,312
Confirmations	3,173
Marriages:	
Catholic	987
Interfaith	260
Total Marriages	1,247
Deaths	3,284
Total Catholic Population	520,411
Total Population	1,301,028

Former Bishops and Archbishops—Rt. Revs. LUIS PENALVER Y CARDENAS, D.D., cons. in 1793; transferred to Guatemala, in 1801; resigned in 1806; retired to Havana, Cuba; died in Havana, July 17, 1810; Under the administration of the Archbishop of Baltimore from 1805-1815.; FRANCIS PORRO, Bishop-elect; LOUIS WILLIAM DUBOURG, S.S., D.D., cons. Sept. 24, 1815; died Archbishop of Besancon, Dec. 1833; JOSEPH ROSATI, C.M., D.D., cons. March 25, 1824; Bishop of Tanagre and coadjutor; transferred to St. Louis, March 20, 1827; died Sept. 25, 1843; LEO DE NECKERE, C.M., D.D., cons. Aug. 4, 1829; died Sept. 4, 1833; Most Revs. ANTOINE BLANC, first Archbishop; cons. Nov. 22, 1835; Archbishop, July 19, 1850; died June 20, 1860; JEAN MARIE ODIN, C.M., D.D., cons. Bishop of Claudiopolis and Vicar-Apostolic of Texas, March 6, 1842; transferred to Galveston, 1847; promoted to New Orleans in 1861; died at Ambierle, France, May 25, 1870; NAPOLEON J. PERCHE, cons. Bishop of Abdera and coadjutor, March 21, 1870; promoted to the See of New Orleans, May 25, 1870; died Dec. 1883; F. X. LERAY, D.D., cons. Bishop of Natchitoches, April 22, 1877; appt. coadjutor of New Orleans, and Bishop of Janopolis, Oct. 23, 1879; promoted to the See of New Orleans, Dec., 1883; died at Chateaugiron, France, Sept. 23, 1887; FRANCIS JANSSENS, D.D., cons. Bishop of Natchez, MS, May 1, 1881; promoted to the Archiepiscopal See of New Orleans, Aug. 7, 1888; died June 9, 1897; PLACIDE LOUIS CHAPELLE, D.D., Apostolic Delegate Extraordinary for Cuba and Puerto Rico; Archbishop of New Orleans; appt. Bishop of Arabissus and Coadjutor of Santa Fe cum jure successionis, Aug. 21, 1891; cons. Nov. 1, 1891; promoted to the Titular Archiepiscopal See of Sebaste May 10, 1893; Archbishop of Santa Fe, Jan. 9, 1894; appt. to New Orleans, Dec. 1, 1897; died Aug. 9, 1905; JAMES H. BLENK, S.M., D.D., appt. Bishop of Puerto Rico, June 12, 1899; cons. July 2, 1899; promoted to the See of New Orleans, April 20, 1906; died April 20, 1917; JOHN W. SHAW, D.D., appt. Coadjutor Bishop of San Antonio, Feb. 7, 1910; cons. Titular Bishop of Castabala, April 14, 1910; succeeded to the See of San Antonio, March 11, 1911; made assistant at the Pontifical Throne, Sept., 1916; promoted to the See of New Orleans, Jan. 25, 1918; died Nov. 2, 1934; JOSEPH FRANCIS RUMMEL, D.D., ord. May 24, 1902; appt. Bishop of Omaha, March 30, 1928; cons. May 29,

1928; appt. Archbishop of New Orleans, March 9, 1935; died Nov. 8, 1964; His Eminence JOHN CARDINAL CODY, D.D., S.T.D., cons. July 2, 1947; promoted to Coadjutor cum jure successionis of New Orleans, Aug. 10, 1961; acceded to the See, Nov. 8, 1964; transferred to Chicago, June 16, 1965; created Cardinal, June 26, 1967; died April 25, 1982; Most Revs. PHILIP M. HANNAN, D.D., J.C.D., S.T.L., Archbishop of New Orleans; ord. Dec. 8, 1939; appt. Titular Bishop of Hieropolis and Auxiliary Bishop of Washington, June 16, 1956; cons. Aug. 28, 1956; promoted to Archbishop of New Orleans, Sept. 29, 1965; retired Feb. 14, 1989; died Sept. 29, 2011.; FRANCIS B. SCHULTE, D.D., Archbishop of New Orleans; ord. May 10, 1952; appt. Titular Bishop of Afufenia and Auxiliary Bishop of Philadelphia, June 27, 1981; appt. Sixth Bishop of Wheeling-Charleston, June 4, 1985; appt. Archbishop of New Orleans, Dec. 13, 1988; installed Feb. 14, 1989; Pallium conferred by Pope John Paul II at the Vatican, June 29, 1989; retired Jan. 3, 2002; died Jan. 17, 2016; ALFRED C. HUGHES, S.T.D., (Retired), ord. Dec. 15, 1957; appt. Auxiliary Bishop of Boston July 21, 1981; ord. Auxiliary Bishop of Boston Sept. 14, 1981; appt. Bishop of Baton Rouge Sept. 7, 1993; installed Bishop of Baton Rouge Nov. 4, 1993; appt. Coadjutor Archbishop of New Orleans Feb. 16, 2001; appt. Archbishop of New Orleans Jan. 3, 2002; retired June 12, 2009.

Vicars General—Most Rev. FERNAND J. CHERI III, O.F.M., V.G.; Very Rev. PATRICK J. WILLIAMS, M.Div., M.S., V.G.

Moderator of the Curia—VACANT.

Chancellor and Special Delegate for Dispensations and Permissions—Very Rev. PETER O. AKPOGHIRAN, J.C.D., J.C.L., 7887 Walmsley Ave., New Orleans, 70125-3496. Tel: 504-861-6256; Fax: 504-866-2906.

Vice Chancellor and Special Delegate for Dispensations and Permissions—Deacon A. DAVID WARRINER JR.

Archdiocesan Administration Building—7887 Walmsley Ave., New Orleans, 70125-3496. Tel: 504-861-9521; Fax: 504-866-2906. Office Hours: Mon.-Fri. 9-5.

Archdiocesan Consultors—Most Rev. FERNAND J. CHERI III, O.F.M., V.G.; Rev. Msgrs. L. EARL GAUTHREAUX, J.C.L.; FRANK J. GIROIR; Very Revs. PETER O. AKPOGHIRAN, J.C.D., J.C.L.; PATRICK J. WILLIAMS, M.Div., M.S., V.G.; Revs. RONALD L. CALKINS; JAMES J. JEANFREAU JR.; GERALD L. SEILER JR., M.Div., J.C.L.

Canonical Consultant to the Archbishop—Rev. VIEN THE NGUYEN, J.C.L., M.Div.

Deans—Very Rev. ANTHONY RIGOLI, O.M.I., V.F., Cathedral Deanery I; Rev. JOHN G. RESTREPO, O.P., V.F., City Park-Gentilly Deanery II; Rev. Msgr. JOHN CISEWSKI, V.F., Uptown Deanery III; Very Revs. LUIS F. RODRIGUEZ, V.F., East Jefferson Deanery IV; WALTER J. AUSTIN, V.F., St. John-St. Charles Deanery V; EMILE G. (BUDDY) NOEL, V.F., West Bank Deanery VI; JOHN F. TALAMO, V.F., Algiers-Plaquemines Deanery VII; OSWALD PIERRE-JULES JR., S.S.J., V.F., St. Bernard Deanery VIII; RODNEY P. BOURG, V.F., West St. Tammany-Washington Deanery IX; WAYNE C. PAYSSE, V.F., East St. Tammany-Washington Deanery X.

Archdiocesan Administrative Council—Most Rev. GREGORY M. AYMOND, Chm. Members of the Council: Most Rev. FERNAND J. CHERI III, O.F.M., V.G.; Very Rev. PATRICK J. WILLIAMS, M.Div., M.S., V.G.; Deacon A. DAVID WARRINER JR.; MR. JOHN SMESTAD JR.; JEFFREY J. ENTWISLE; MRS. WENDY VITTER; MS. KAREN HEIL.

Presbyteral Council of the Archdiocese of New Orleans—Most Rev. GREGORY M. AYMOND, Pres.

Archdiocesan Finance Council—Most Rev. GREGORY M. AYMOND, Chm.

Ministerial Council—
- *Archbishop*—Most Rev. GREGORY M. AYMOND, D.D.
- *Vicars General*—Most Rev. FERNAND J. CHERI III, O.F.M., V.G.; Very Rev. PATRICK J. WILLIAMS, M.Div., M.S., V.G.
- *Co Chairs*—Very Rev. PATRICK J. WILLIAMS, M.Div., M.S., V.G.; MR. JOHN SMESTAD JR.
- *Members*—Directors of archdiocesan ministries.

Censores Librorum—Very Rev. JOSE I. LAVASTIDA, S.T.D., S.T.L., N.D.S., J.C.D.; Revs. DENNIS J. HAYES III; STANLEY P. KLORES, M.A., M.Div., S.T.L., S.T.D.; Very Rev. PATRICK J. WILLIAMS, M.Div., M.S., V.G., Coord.

Louisiana Conference of Catholic Bishops—MR. ROBERT M. TASMAN, Exec. Dir., 2431 S. Acadian Thruway, Ste. 250, Baton Rouge, 70808-2365. Tel: 225-344-7120; Fax: 225-383-9591; Email: lccb@cox.net; Web: www.laccb.org.

Archdiocesan Offices

Accounting Office—MR. KENNETH JAYROE, Chief Administrative Officer, 7887 Walmsley Ave., New Orleans, 70125-3496. Tel: 504-861-6236; Fax: 504-861-6202; Email: kjayroe@archdiocese-no.org.

Archdiocese of New Orleans North Shore Pastoral Center—4465 Hwy. 290 E. Service Rd., Covington, 70433. Tel: 985-605-5840; Email: npastoralcenter@arch-no.org. MS. STEPHANIE DUPEPE, CCANO Coord., Northshore Svcs.

Archives and Records (Archdiocesan)—DR. EMILIE G. LEUMAS, C.A., C.R.M., 7887 Walmsley Ave., New Orleans, 70125-3496. Tel: 504-861-6241; Fax: 504-866-2906; Email: archives@arch-no.org.

The Bishop Perry Center—1941 Dauphine St., New Orleans, 70116-1609. Tel: 504-227-3272; Fax: 504-227-3271; Web: bpc.arch-no.org. VACANT.

Black Catholic Ministries—7887 Walmsley Ave., New Orleans, 70125-3496. Tel: 504-861-6207; Tel: 504-861-9521; Fax: 54-866-2906; Email: bcatholics@arch-no.org. Rev. DANIEL H. GREEN.

Building Office—MR. ANDRE L. VILLERE JR., Dir., 7887 Walmsley Ave., New Orleans, 70125-3496. Tel: 504-861-6210; Fax: 504-861-7652; Email: avillere@archdiocese-no.org.

Campus Ministry—VACANT, Archdiocesan Coord., Email: yam@arch-no.org.

Catholic Counseling Service—2814 S. Carrollton Ave., New Orleans, 70118. Tel: 504-861-6245; Fax: 504-227-3750; Email: ccs@arch-no.org. MR. JOEY PISTORIUS, M.A., P.L.C.P., N.C.C., Coord.

Catholic Cultural Heritage Center/Old Ursuline Convent—1100 Chartres St., New Orleans, 70116-2596. Mailing Address: 615 Pere Antoine Alley, New Orleans, 70116. Tel: 504-525-9585, Ext. 135; Fax: 504-525-9583; Email: cathedral@arch-no.org. Very Rev. PHILIP G. LANDRY, V.F., Dir.

Catholic Schools Office—7887 Walmsley Ave., New Orleans, 70125-3496. Tel: 504-866-7916; Fax: 504-861-6260; Email: superintendent@archdiocese.no.org. DR. RAENELL BILLIOT HOUSTON, Supt. Assoc. Superintendents: MRS. JANE BAKER; MR. MICHAEL BURAS II; MRS. CAROLE ELLIOT; MS. INGRID R. FIELDS; MRS. MARTHA M. MUNDINE; MRS. KATHERINE SHEA; MRS. KASEY WEBB, Dir. Blended Learning; MS. HELEN BRANLEY, C.P.A., C.G.M.A., Dir. Finance; MR. KEITH HANSON, Dir. Finance, Elementary Schools. Administrative Assistants: MS. MADELINE BORDELON; MS. SHANITRA CORLEY; MS. NICOLE JEFFERSON; MS. SUSAN WOLF.

Center of Jesus the Lord—Rev. GEORGE ROY, O.M.I., 1301 Louisiana Ave., New Orleans, 70115. Tel: 504-529-1636; Fax: 504-529-5003; Email: office@centerofjesusthelord.org.

Chancellor—Very Rev. PETER O. AKPOGHIRAN, J.C.D., J.C.L.

Charismatic Renewal—Liaisons: MR. AL MANSFIELD; MRS. PATTI MANSFIELD, 1901 Division St., Metairie, 70001-2716. Tel: 504-828-1368; Fax: 504-831-5810; Email: info@ccrno.org. Mailing Address: P.O. Box 7515, Metairie, 70010-7515.

Christian Formation—Very Rev. JOSE I. LAVASTIDA, S.T.D., S.T.L., N.D.S., J.C.D., Exec. Dir., 7887 Walmsley Ave., New Orleans, 70125-3496. Tel: 504-861-6228; Fax: 504-866-2906.

Clergy—Very Rev. PATRICK J. WILLIAMS, M.Div., M.S., V.G., Exec. Dir., 7887 Walmsley Ave., New Orleans, 70125-3496. Tel: 504-861-6268; Fax: 504-866-2906; Email: pwilliams@archdiocese-no.org.

Communications—MRS. SARAH COMISKEY MCDONALD, Dir., 1000 Howard Ave., Ste. 400, New Orleans, 70113. Tel: 504-596-3023; Fax: 504-596-3020; Email: communications@archdiocese-no.org.

Continuing Formation for Priests Committee—Rev. MARK S. RAPHAEL, Ph.D., Dir., Tel: 504-861-6269; Fax: 504-866-2906.

Cultural Heritage Office—DR. EMILIE G. LEUMAS, C.A., C.R.M., Dir., 7887 Walmsley Ave., New Orleans, 70125-3496. Tel: 504-527-5781; Fax: 504-527-5797; Email: archives@archdiocese-no.org.

CYO - Youth and Young Adult Ministry Office—2241 Mendez St., New Orleans, 70122. Tel: 504-836-0551; Fax: 504-836-0552. MR. TIMMY MCCAFFERY, Dir.
- *Camp Abbey Retreat Center and Camp Abbey Summer Program*—(conducted by the CYO/ Youth and Young Adult Ministry Office).

Deaf Apostolate—MRS. ARTHINE VICKS POWERS, Dir., Tel: 504-943-2456; Tel: 504-338-8808 (Video Phone); Email: gerarddeaf@arch-no.org.

Ecumenical Officer—Very Rev. EMILE G. (BUDDY) NOEL, V.F., 146 Fourth St., Westwego, 70094-4297. Tel: 504-341-9522; Fax: 504-341-5957; Email: frbuddy@olps.nocoxmail.com.

Evangelization—Very Rev. DAVID G. CARON, O.P., D.Min., Vicar of Evangelization, Tel: 504-267-9650; Fax: 504-566-9718; Email: dcaron@arch-no.org. 1000 Howard Ave., Ste. 913, New Orleans, 70113.

Family Life Apostolate—(See Marriage and Family Life).

Commission for Persons with Disabilities—MRS. JANET PESCE, 7887 Walmsley Ave., New Orleans, 70125-3496. Tel: 504-861-6243; Fax: 504-866-2906; Email: mfl@arch-no.org.

Filipino Catholic Ministry—DR. ADLAI DEPANO, Coord.; Rev. ROBUSTIANO D. MORGIA, Spiritual Advisor, 2361 Hwy. 18, Edgard, 70049-9101. Tel: 504-280-7370.

Financial and Administrative Services—JEFFREY J. ENTWISLE, CFO; MS. KATHLEEN HEBERT, COO; MR. KENNETH J. JAYROE III, CAO.

Healthcare Chaplaincy Coordinator—Deacon JEFFREY R. TULLY, Archdiocesan Coord., 1000 Howard Ave., Ste. 909, New Orleans, 70113. Tel: 504-227-3606; Email: jtully@arch-no.org.

Hispanic Apostolate—Rev. SERGIO SERRANO, O.P., 2525 Maine Ave., Metairie, 70003. Tel: 504-467-2550; Fax: 504-467-2552.

Human Resources—MS. KAREN HEIL, Dir., 1000 Howard Ave., Ste. 1200, New Orleans, 70113. Tel: 504-310-8792; Fax: 504-568-1699; Email: kheil@arch-no.org.

Information Technology—MR. JUSTIN GIBSON, Dir., 1000 Howard Ave., Ste. 700, New Orleans, 70113-1903. Tel: 504-596-3064; Fax: 504-566-9718; Email: it@arch-no.org.

Insurance Office—MS. CHERYL HARPER, Oper. Mgr., 1000 Howard Ave., Ste. 1202, New Orleans, 70113. Tel: 504-527-5760; Tel: 877-527-5760 (Toll Free); Fax: 504-527-5799; Email: charper@catholicmutual.org; MS. SUE FOSTER, Contracts/Risk Mgmt., Email: sfoster@catholicmutual.org.

Internal Audit/Special Assignments—MRS. ANGELA WILCOX, Sr. Internal Auditor, Tel: 504-861-6231; MS. CORINNE MARSH BARNES, Internal Auditor; MR. NICK SAYBE, Internal Auditor, 7887 Walmsley Ave., New Orleans, 70125-3496. Tel: 504-861-6203; Fax: 504-355-0077.

Legal Services—MRS. WENDY VITTER, Archdiocesan Legal Counsel, 7887 Walmsley Ave., New Orleans, 70125. Tel: 504-861-6277; CHARLES I. DENECHAUD III; OTTO SCHOENFELD; RICHARD BORDELON; TODD R. GENNARDO; RALPH J. AUCOIN, 1010 Common St., Ste. 3010, New Orleans, 70112. Tel: 504-522-4756; Fax: 504-568-0783.

Magnificat House—Vocation House of Discernment for Women, 2729 Lowerline St., New Orleans, 70125. Tel: 504-227-3203; Tel: 504-861-6281. Sr. GLORIA MURILLO, S.T.J., Mentor/Dir.

Marriage and Family Life—7887 Walmsley Ave., New Orleans, 70125-3496. Tel: 504-861-6243; Fax: 504-866-2906; Email: mfl@arch-no.org. MR. DAVID C. DAWSON JR., Dir.

Metropolitan Tribunal—Very Rev. PETER O. AKPOGHIRAN, J.C.D., J.C.L., Judicial Vicar, All rogatorial commissions should be sent to this address c/o:, 7887 Walmsley Ave., New Orleans, 70125-3496. Tel: 504-861-6291; Fax: 504-861-9525; Email: tribunal@archdiocese-no.org.
- *Court of First Instance*—
- *Court of Second Instance*—
- *Judges*—Very Rev. PETER O. AKPOGHIRAN, J.C.D., J.C.L.; Rev. Msgr. L. EARL GAUTHREAUX, J.C.L.; Very Rev. VINH DINH LUU, J.C.L.; Rev. GERALD L. SEILER JR., M.Div., J.C.L.; Rev. Msgr. ANDREW C. TAORMINA, J.D., (Retired).
- *Defenders of the Bond*—Deacon A. DAVID WARRINER JR.; MS. GERI M. WOODWARD.
- *Defender of the Bond for Matrimonial Causes and Promoter of Justice for Penal Causes*—Rev. GARRETT M. O'BRIEN, J.C.L.
- *Ecclesiastical Notaries*—MS. JANICE BUHLER; MS. OLIVIA GEORGE; MS. JANET URRUTIA.
- *Procurators and Advocates*—(Priests and Deacons of the Archdiocese).

Pastoral Planning and Ministries—MR. JOHN SMESTAD JR., Exec. Dir., 7887 Walmsley Ave., New Orleans, 70125-3496. Tel: 504-861-6294; Fax: 504-866-2906; Email: planningandministries@archdiocese-no.org.

Permanent Diaconate—Deacon RAPHAEL DUPLECHAIN JR., Dir., 7887 Walmsley Ave., New Orleans, 70125-3496. Tel: 504-861-6329; Fax: 504-866-2906.

Pontifical Mission Societies—Consists of four Pontifical Mission Aid Societies forming one institution with four branches - Society of the Propagation of the Faith, Missionary Childhood Association, Society of St. Peter the Apostle, Missionary Union. Rev. JAMES J. JEANFREAU JR., Dir., 1000 Howard Ave., Ste. 1213, New Orleans, 70113. Tel: 504-527-5771; Email: pof@arch-no.org; Web: www.archnomo.org.

Priest Personnel Office—Very Rev. PATRICK J. WILLIAMS, M.Div., M.S., V.G.

Property and Building Management—MRS. ELIZABETH F. LACOMBE, Dir., 1000 Howard Ave., Ste. 107, New Orleans, 70113-1903. Tel: 504-596-3070; Fax: 504-596-3073; Email: llacombe@archdiocese-no.org.

Property Records Office—MRS. EMILY MORRIS, 7887 Walmsley Ave., New Orleans, 70125-3496. Tel: 504-861-6323; Fax: 504-866-2906.

Racial Harmony Liaison—Liaison to the Committee for Implementation of the Pastoral Letter on Racial Harmony. *1000 Howard Ave., Ste. 109, New Orleans, 70113.* Tel: 504-861-6272;
Fax: 504-267-9759; Web: orh.arch-no.org. MR. WAYNE CASTILLO.

Religious—Sr. ELIZABETH FITZPATRICK, O.Carm., M.A., Exec. Dir., Liaison between the Archbishop and all religious congregations of sisters and brothers, with third orders and secular institutes, and with leadership conferences of women and men religious., 7887 Walmsley Ave., New Orleans, 70125-3496. Tel: 504-861-6281; Tel: 504-861-9521; Fax: 504-866-2906; Email: rpersonnel@archdiocese-no.org.

Religious Education Office—DR. ALICE HUGHES, M.R.E., Dir., 7887 Walmsley Ave., New Orleans, 70125. Tel: 504-861-6270; Fax: 504-861-6276.

Respect Life Office—MS. DEBBIE SHINSKIE, Dir., 1000 Howard Ave., 9th Fl., New Orleans, 70113. Tel: 504-286-1119; Email: respectlife@arch-no.org; Web: respectlife.arch-no.org.

Safe Environment Coordinator—Sr. MARY ELLEN WHEELAHAN, O.Carm., Coord., 7887 Walmsley Ave., New Orleans, 70125. Tel: 504-861-6278; Fax: 504-866-2906; Email: srmwheelahan@arch-no.org.

Victims Assistance Coordinator—Bro. STEPHEN SYNAN, F.M.S., 7887 Walmsley Ave., New Orleans, 70125-3496. Tel: 504-861-6253; Tel: 504-522-5019 (New Orleans Sex Abuse Hotline); Fax: 504-866-2906; Email: ssynan@arch-no.org.

Vicars General—Most Rev. FERNAND J. CHERI III, O.F.M., V.G.; Very Rev. PATRICK J. WILLIAMS, M.Div., M.S., V.G., 7887 Walmsley Ave., New Orleans, 70125. Tel: 504-861-6262; Fax: 504-861-6312.

Vietnamese Catholics Office—

Liaisons for the Vietnamese Community—Rev. NGHIEM VAN NGUYEN, 5069 Willowbrook Dr., P.O. Box 870607, New Orleans, 70187-0607. Tel: 504-254-5660; Fax: 504-254-9250; Very Rev. JOHN-NHAN TRAN, V.F., 1501 W. Causeway Approach, Mandeville, 70471-3047. Tel: 985-626-6977; Fax: 985-626-6971.

Vocation Office—Rev. KURT R. YOUNG, Dir., 7887 Walmsley Ave., New Orleans, 70125-3496. Tel: 504-861-6298; Fax: 504-866-2906.

Worship Office—7887 Walmsley Ave., New Orleans, 70125-3496. Tel: 504-861-6300; Fax: 504-866-2906; Email: worship@archdiocese-no.org. Rev. NILE C. GROSS, Dir.

Liturgical Commission—7887 Walmsley Ave., New Orleans, 70125-3496. Tel: 504-861-6300;
Fax: 504-866-2906; Email: worship@archdiocese-no.org. Rev. NILE C. GROSS, Coord.

Archdiocesan Agencies

Apostleship of the Sea—Deacon WAYNE A. LOBELL, Dir. & Port Min., Stella Maris Maritime Center, 14538 River Rd., Destrehan, 70047. Tel: 985-307-0601; Cell: 504-669-5709; Fax: 985-307-0967.

Catholic Charities Archdiocese of New Orleans—1000 Howard Ave., Ste. 200, New Orleans, 70113.
Tel: 504-523-3755; Fax: 504-523-2789; Email: ccano@ccano.org; Web: www.ccano.org. Sr. MARJORIE A. HEBERT, M.S.C., Pres. & CEO; MRS. CHERYL D. LABORDE, CFO; MR. ORVILLE DUGGAN, Chief Admin. Officer; MRS. MARIA PARDO HUETE, Dir. Institutional Advancement; MR. THOMAS M. COSTANZA, Div. Dir.; MS. CINDY DISTEFANO, Div. Dir.; MR. MARTIN GUTIERREZ, Div. Dir.; DR. ELMORE RIGAMER, Medical Dir. If additional information is needed, please contact the main office at 504-523-3755.

Catholic Foundation for the Archdiocese of New Orleans, Inc.—MR. CORY J. HOWAT, Exec. Dir., 1000 Howard Ave., Ste. 700, New Orleans, 70113-1903. Tel: 504-596-3045; Fax: 504-596-3068; Email: catholicfoundation@archdiocese-no.org.

Chateau de Notre Dame—Administrative Office: 1000 Howard Ave., 10th Fl., New Orleans, 70113.

Chief Executive Officer—MR. WAYNE PLAISANCE.

Chateau de Notre Dame Apartments—2820 Burdette St., New Orleans, 70125-2596. Tel: 504-866-2741; Fax: 504-866-2861. MS. SHERRI GUIDRY, Admin.

Chateau de Notre Dame Nursing Home—2832 Burdette St., New Orleans, 70125-2596.
Tel: 504-866-2741; Fax: 504-866-2861; Web: www.cdnd.org. MR. RONNIE BARRERA, Admin.; Rev. ALBERTO BERMUDEZ, Chap.

Chateau de Notre Dame Facilities Corporation—7887 Walmsley Ave., New Orleans, 70125.

Christopher Homes, Inc.—Deacon DENNIS F. ADAMS, Dir., 1000 Howard Ave., Ste. 100, New Orleans, 70113-1903. Tel: 504-596-3460; Fax: 504-596-3466; Email: dfadams@chi-ano.org; Web: www.christopherhomes.org.

Clarion Herald Newspaper—Newspaper of the Archdiocese of New Orleans. Published by Clarion Herald Publishing Co., Inc., "Clarion Herald" PETER P. FINNEY JR., Gen. Mgr. & Exec. Editor, 1000 Howard Ave., Ste. 400, New Orleans, 70113-1903. Tel: 504-596-3035; Fax: 504-596-3020; Email: clarionherald@clarionherald.org.

New Orleans Archdiocesan Cemeteries and New Orleans Cemeteries Trust—MS. SHERRI PEPPO, Dir., 1000 Howard Ave., Ste. 500, New Orleans, 70113-1903. Tel: 504-596-3050; Fax: 504-596-3055; Email: speppo@archdiocese-no.org.

Notre Dame Hospice—MR. WAYNE PLAISANCE, CEO, 1000 Howard Ave., 10th Fl., New Orleans, 70113. Tel: 504-227-3600; Fax: 504-227-3601; Email: wplaisance@archdiocese-no.org.

Project Lazarus—Residential Program for Persons with HIV/AIDS *Mailing Address: P.O. Box 3906, New Orleans, 70177-3906.* Tel: 504-949-3609;
Fax: 504-944-7944; Email: info@projectlazarus.net; Web: www.projectlazarus.net. MR. STEVE RIVERA, Exec. Dir.; MS. LILY HANNIGAN, Devel. Mgr.

School Food and Nutrition Services of New Orleans Inc.—MS. JANET SANDERSON, COO, 1000 Howard Ave., Ste. 300, New Orleans, 70113-1925. Tel: 504-596-3434; Fax: 504-596-3459; Fax: 504-596-6901; Email: jsanderson@schoolcafe.org.

**Second Harvest Food Bank of Greater New Orleans and Acadiana—700 Edwards Ave., New Orleans, 70123-2236.* Tel: 504-734-1322; Fax: 504-733-8336; Web: www.no-hunger.org.

Wynhoven Health Care Center—1050 Medical Center Blvd., Marrero, 70072-3170. Tel: 504-347-0777; Fax: 504-341-7240; Web: www.wynhoven.org. JANE FOCKLER, Admin.

Catholic Charities

Catholic Charities Archdiocese of New Orleans—1000 Howard Ave., Ste. 200, New Orleans, 70113.
Tel: 504-523-3755; Fax: 504-523-2789; Email: ccano@ccano.org; Web: www.ccano.org. Sr. MARJORIE A. HEBERT, M.S.C., Pres. & CEO; MRS. CHERYL D. LABORDE, CFO; MR. ORVILLE DUGGAN, Chief Admin. Officer; MRS. MARIA PARDO HUETE, Dir. Institutional Advancement; MR. THOMAS M. COSTANZA, Div. Dir.; MS. CINDY DISTEFANO, Div. Dir.; MR. MARTIN GUTIERREZ, Div. Dir.; DR. ELMORE RIGAMER, Medical Dir., If additional information is needed, please contact the main office at 504-523-3755.

Adult Day Health Care Center—

Greenwalt—RONNA (NIKI) GARNER, Admin., Tel: 504-392-0502.

Catholic Charities School-Based Counseling (CCSBC)—MS. SUSAN FENDLASON, Admin., Tel: 985-307-6882.

Ciara Independent Living—MS. BRITTANY SIMMONS, Prog. Coord., Tel: 504-524-8394.

Ciara Permanent Housing—MS. TROY YANCY, Case Mgr., Tel: 504-861-0643.

Cornerstone Builders—MR. RONNIE MOORE, Prog. Dir., Tel: 504-451-8351.

Counseling Solutions—(Counseling Services by appointment for individuals, couples, families and goups of all faiths in Jefferson, Orleans, St. Charles, St. John the Baptist and St. Tammany civil parishes. MR. MARK TALIANCICH, Ph.D., LPC-S, Clinical Dir., Tel: 504-310-6933.

Deaf Action Center of Greater New Orleans—MS. SHARI BERNIUS, Admin., Tel: 504-615-7122.

Disaster Relief—1000 Howard Ave., Ste. 200, New Orleans, 70113. Tel: 866-891-2210.

ESL Services—MS. JULIE WARD, Dir. Immigration & Refugee Svcs., Tel: 504-457-3462.

Food for Families/Food for Seniors—MR. TIMOTHY ROBERTSON, Exec. Dir., Tel: 504-245-7207.

Foster Grandparents—Tel: 504-310-6882. MRS. PRISCILLA MANTILLA, Prog. Dir.

Head Start Centers—Covenant House Early Head Start, Incarnate Word Head Start/Early Head Start, St. John the Baptist Head Start, St. Mary of the Angels Head Start/Early Head Start, St. Paul the Apostle Head Start/Early Head Start. MRS. RHONDA TAYLOR, Dir. Early Childhood Education, 8326 Apricot St., 2nd Fl., New Orleans, 70118. Tel: 504-861-6359.

Health Guardians—MR. BEN WORTHAM, L.M.S.W., Prog. Dir., Tel: 504-310-6908.

Homeless Services—(assists homeless individuals & families with case management and supportive housing) MR. MARTIN GUTIERREZ, Div. Dir., Tel: 504-310-6914.

Bethlehem Housing Services—

Bridges to Self-Sufficiency—MS. TRINNA STANFORD, Tel: 504-310-8788.

Immigration Services—(Provides free or low-cost legal immigration counseling and representation to families and individuals who are eligible for immigration benefits but cannot afford private attorneys. Specialized pro bono programs to provide legal representation and holistic case management support for survivors of domestic violence/abuse, unaccompanied children, survivors of trafficking and other crimes and those detained in immigration facilities. MS. JULIE WARD, Dir. Immigration & Refugee Svcs., Tel: 504-457-3462.

Isaiah 43—(Parenting and Mentoring Program) MS. KRISTINA GIBSON, Prog. Dir., Tel: 504-310-8772.

North Shore Branch Office—MS. STEPHANIE DUPEPE, Coord. North Shore Svcs., 4465 Hwy. 190 E. Service Rd., Covington, 70433-4957. Tel: 985-905-5847.

Office of Institutional Advancement—MRS. MARIA PARDO HUETE, Dir., Tel: 504-592-5688; MRS. LAUREN ZERINGUE, Grants Coord., Tel: 504-592-5680.

Archbishop Hannan Community Appeal (AHCA)—1000 Howard Ave., Ste. 200, New Orleans, 70113-1903. Tel: 504-592-5688.

Office of Justice and Peace—MR. KEVIN FITZPATRICK, Dir., Tel: 504-592-5692.

Catholic Campaign for Human Development (CCHD)—

Catholic Relief Services (CRS)—

PACE Greater New Orleans—(Program of All-inclusive Care for the Elderly) (An Affiliated Ministry)
Tel: 504-941-6050. ANTHONY DIAS, Exec. Dir., Shirley Landry Benson PACE Center, 4201 N. Rampart St., New Orleans, 70117. Hope Haven St. John Bosco PACE Center, 1131 Barataria Blvd., Marrero, 70072.

Padua Community Services—RONNA (NIKI) GARNER, Admin., 200 Beta St., Belle Chasse, 70037-1499. Tel: 504-392-0502.

Padua Community Homes—Ocean Avenue (West Bank-New Orleans), Sts. Mary & Elizabeth (Metairie), St. Rosalie (Gretna).

Padua House—(formerly known as Padua Pediatric Program).

Parish & Community Ministries—(Short-term Limited Case Management Services offered by appointment in various areas of the Archdiocese of New Orleans). . MS. VICKIE LELEU, Coord., Tel: 504-451-1889.

PHILMAT, Inc.—Sr. MARJORIE A. HEBERT, M.S.C., Pres., 1000 Howard Ave., Ste. 200, New Orleans, 70113. Tel: 504-596-3099.

Project SAVE—(Stopping Abuse through Victim Empowerment) MRS. ALLYSON TUTTLE, Admin., Tel: 504-310-6871.

Pro-Life Services—MRS. MICHELLE BLACK, Dir., 921 Aris Ave., Ste. B, Metairie, 70002. Tel: 504-885-1141.

ACCESS Pregnancy & Referral Centers—MRS. MICHELLE BLACK, Dir., Tel: 504-885-1141.

Adoption Services—MRS. DANNA P. COUSINS, M.S.W., L.C.S.W., Prog. Dir., Tel: 504-885-1141.

St. Vincent Maternity Clinic—MARGARET MURPHY, R.N., Nurse Mgr., Tel: 504-837-6346.

Refugee Services—Welcomes refugees who are resettled by the U.S. government to the GNO area with case management and services oriented to cover the basic needs of newly-arrived eligible clients and promote self-sufficiency. MS. JULIE WARD, Dir. Immigration & Refugee Svcs., Tel: 504-457-3462.

Spirit of Hope Disaster Response—MR. THOMAS M. COSTANZA, Division Dir., Tel: 504-596-3097.

Therapeutic Family Services—MS. SHACIDY HADLEY-BUSH, Admin., Tel: 504-310-6939.

Volunteer Department—MRS. SHANNON MURPHY, Dir., Tel: 504-310-6962.

Voyage House—c/o Catholic Charities, 1000 Howard Ave., Ste. 200, New Orleans, 70113-1942. MS. ALECIA BLANCHARD, Admin. & Prog. Dir., Tel: 504-269-3969. Independent permanent supportive housing for single women 39+ years of age who experience substance abuse and/or mental health issues and/or other non-immobilizing physical disabilities.

Workforce Development—MRS. SHAULA LOVERA, Dir. Integrated Workforce Svcs., Tel: 504-310-6998.

Archdiocesan Offices and Corporations

7887 Walmsley, Inc.—Mailing Address: Archdiocese of New Orleans, Dept. of Financial and Administrative Svcs., 7887 Walmsley Ave., New

Orleans, 70125. Tel: 802-922-9457. JEFFREY J. ENTWISLE, Dir. & Pres.

Archdiocese of New Orleans Indemnity, Inc.—Mailing Address: Archdiocese of New Orleans, Dept. of Financial and Administrative Svcs., 7887 Walmsley Ave., New Orleans, 70125. Tel: 802-922-9457. JEFFREY J. ENTWISLE, Dir. & Pres.

Bernard A. Grehan Trust—7887 Walmsley Ave., New Orleans, 70125-3496. Tel: 504-861-9521.

Catholic Charities Children's Day Care Centers Inc.—Registered Office, 1000 Howard Ave., Ste. 200, New Orleans, 70113-1903.

Christopher Inn—1000 Howard Ave., Ste. 100, New Orleans, 70113.

Mental Health Association Development Corporation—7887 Walmsley Ave., New Orleans, 70125-3496. Tel: 504-861-9521.

Our Lady of Wisdom Facility Corporation—7887 Walmsley Ave., New Orleans, 70125.

St. Mary's Catholic Orphan Boys' Asylum Board—Registered Office: 1000 Howard Ave., Ste. 200, New Orleans, 70113-1903.

St. Michael Special School—Registered Office: 7887 Walmsley Ave., New Orleans, 70125. Tel: 504-524-7285; Fax: 504-524-5883; Web: www.archdiocese-no.org/stmichael. *1522 Chippewa St., New Orleans, 70130.* MS. TISHNA SAUERHOFF, Dir. & Prin.

St. Elizabeth's Guild—Mailing Address: P.O. Box 8394, Metairie, 70011. MRS. KATHLEEN ROBERT, Pres.

St. Vincent's Infant and Maternity Guild—7045 Argonne Blvd., New Orleans, 70124. MRS. CINDY WOODERSON, Pres.

Hanmaum Korean Catholic Chapel—4812 W. Napoleon Ave., Metairie, 70001-2364. Tel: 504-888-8772; Fax: 504-888-2366. Rev. JONGKWON CHOI, (Korea, South) Chap.

Department of Religious

St. Gertrude's Retirement Center—

Catholic Organizations

Archconfraternity of St. Ann—4920 Loveland St., Metairie, 70006.

Beginning Experience—7887 Walmsley Ave., New Orleans, 70125. MS. RENELL PRAVATA, Pres.

Blue Army of Our Lady of Fatima—Rev. DENZIL M. PERERA, Spiritual Dir., (Retired), 1307 Louisiana Ave., New Orleans, 70115. Tel: 504-529-1636.

The Christ in Christmas Committee of New Orleans—123 Iroquois Dr., Abita Springs, 70420. Tel: 985-893-0169; Email: kcicno@bellsouth.net.

Community of John the Evangelist—MS. VIVIEN MICHALS, Contact, 2639 DeSoto St., New Orleans, 70119. Tel: 504-944-4000.

Confraternity of the Holy Face—1050 Robert Blvd., Slidell, 70458.

Council of Catholic School Cooperative Clubs—MRS. CINDY WOODERSON, (2018-2020 Term), 4025 Argonne Blvd., New Orleans, 70124. Email: cswoody1@cox.net; Web: www.ccscc.catholicweb.com.

The Cursillo Movement—MR. BILLY APP, Lay Dir., Mailing Address: P.O. Box 741745, New Orleans, 70174-1745. Tel: 504-464-0181, Ext. 111; Web: www.neworleanscursillo.org.

Engaged Encounter—Executive Couple: DERRICK SALVANT; TY SALVANT, Tel: 504-286-4650; Tel: 504-861-6243; Web: www.nocee.org.

Holy Name Societies—MR. JOSEPH SIMON, Pres.; MR. ANTHONY SMITH, Exec. Sec., Mailing Address: P.O. Box 6644, Metairie, 70009-6644. Tel: 504-282-5315.

Ladies of Charity of the Archdiocese—2028 Burdette St., Apt. 401, New Orleans, 70125. Tel: 504-810-1733.

Lay Carmelites of Our Lady of Mount Carmel—1437 Ave. C, Marrero, 70072.

Legatus of New Orleans—332 East Ave., Harahan, 70123. Tel: 504-343-2478; Web: www.legatus.org; Email: neworleans@legatus.org.

Legion of Mary—Mailing Address: Immaculata Regia of New Orleans, P.O. Box 50605, New Orleans, 70150-0605. Tel: 504-975-6930; Email: lalegionofmary@att.net. MR. RICHARD E. LAUNEY, Pres.

Magnificat, Ministry to Catholic Women—1629 Metairie Rd., Ste. 3, Metairie, 70005-3926. Tel: 504-828-6279; Email: magnificatcst@aol.com; Web: www.magnificat-ministry.org. MRS. DONNA ROSS, Coord. Central Svc. Team; Rev. Msgr. DAVID TOUPS, S.T.D., Spiritual Advisor.

Magnificat Chapters—

Metairie Chapter—MRS. MELANIE BAGLOW, Coord., 6208 Ithaca St., Metairie, 70003. Tel: 504-889-2431; Email: mkbaglow@cox.net.

Slidell Chapter—Very Rev. WAYNE C. PAYSSE, V.F., Spiritual Advisor; MS. DEBORAH CALLENS, 202 Robin St., Slidell, 70461-2049. Tel: 985-502-0349.

West Bank Chapter—Rev. Msgr. LANAUX J. RARESHIDE, Spiritual Advisor, (Retired).

West St. Tammany Chapter—MS. NICOLE JOHNSON, Coord., 3 Wood Duck Lane, Mandeville, 70471-3380. Tel: 985-635-9665; Email: nicolea707@gmail.com.

Marians of New Orleans—MRS. BOBBIE FAZENDE, (2018-2020 Term), 8736 Donnaway St., Metairie, 70003. Tel: 504-466-2295; Email: office@sleoh.com.

Maryknoll Mission Education Center (Promotion of Missionary Work)—MR. MATTHEW F. ROUSSO, Dir., 7730 Walmsley Ave., New Orleans, 70125. Tel: 504-866-8516.

Mary's Children—MRS. NORA LAMBERT, Pres., 631 St. Charles Ave., New Orleans, 70130-3411. Tel: 504-218-8739.

Mary's Helpers—MRS. GAYLE PONSETI, Admin., Mailing Address: P.O. Box 1853, Marrero, 70073-1853. Tel: 504-348-7729; Tel: 800-573-4130.

MIR Group—MR. ROBERT HALE, Pres., 1 Galleria Blvd., Ste. 744, Metairie, 70001-2081. Tel: 504-849-2570; Email: themirgroup@aol.com.

Missionaries of St. Therese—Rev. JAMES J. JEANFREAU JR., Spiritual Moderator, 1000 Howard Ave., Ste. 1213, New Orleans, 70113. Tel: 504-527-5771.

Naim Conference—MRS. PATRICIA KELLEY, Pres., Tel: 504-283-3270; Email: mfl@arch-no.org.

National Council of Catholic Men—7887 Walmsley Ave., New Orleans, 70125.

National Council of Catholic Women—VACANT.

**National T.E.C. Conference—1007 Airline Park Blvd., Metairie, 70003.*

Pax Christi New Orleans—Chairpersons: MR. TOM EGAN; MRS. JEANNIE EGAN, Mailing Address: P.O. Box 50304, New Orleans, 70150-0304. Tel: 504-522-3751; Email: jeanegan@tulane.edu.

People Program— (1974) 2240 Lakeshore Dr., New Orleans, 70122. Tel: 504-284-7678; Email: info@peopleprogram.org; Web: www.peopleprogram.org. MR. STEVE LENAHAN, Exec. Dir., Email: director@peopleprogram.org.

Westbank Program—6201 Stratford Pl., New Orleans, 70131. Tel: 504-394-5433.

Priests for Life—Rev. LANCE J. CAMPO, S.T.L., Coord.

Retrouvaille/Rediscovery—7887 Walmsley Ave., New Orleans, 70125-3496. Tel: 504-861-6243; Email: mfl@arch-no.org; Web: www.retrouvaille.org.

Rosary Congress Committee—Rev. JOHN G. RESTREPO, O.P., V.F., Spiritual Dir., 4640 Canal St., New Orleans, 70119. Tel: 504-488-2651; Web: www.rosarycongress.org.

St. Thomas More Catholic Lawyers Association—Rev. JOSEPH S. PALERMO JR., J.D., 444 Metairie Rd., Metairie, 70005. Tel: 504-834-0340, Ext. 3335; Fax: 504-837-8735.

St. Vincent de Paul Society—MR. ALAN DEMMA, Pres.; Deacon RUDOLPH J. RAYFIELD SR., Exec. Dir., Mailing Address: P.O. Box 792880, New Orleans, 70179. Tel: 504-940-5031, Ext. 10; Email: svdped@bellsouth.net; Web: www.svdpneworleans.org.

St. Vincent's Infant and Maternity Home Guild—MS. MARCY MAYEAUX, 4605 Henican Pl., Metairie, 70003.

Scouting—

Archdiocesan Liaison—MR. TIMMY MCCAFFERY, Dir. CYO/Youth & Young Adult Ministry Office, Email: tmccaffery@arch-no.org.

Catholic Committee on Boy Scouting—Deacon DANIEL FLYNN, Pastoral Min.; SUSAN GUIDRY, Chm., 251 Halsey Dr., Harahan, 70123-4401. Tel: 504-737-8370; Email: boyscouts@arch-no.org.

Catholic Committee on Girl Scouting—Deacon RICHARD BRADY, Pastoral Min., Tel: 504-885-3780; MS. JAIME MIXON, Chm., Email: girlscouts@arch-no.org.

Serra Clubs—

Serra Club of New Orleans—Rev. KURT R. YOUNG, Chap., 7887 Walmsley Ave., New Orleans, 70125-3496. Tel: 504-861-6298; Fax: 504-866-2906.

Serra Club of East Jefferson—Rev. Msgr. ROBERT D. MASSETT, Chap., 6425 W. Metairie Ave., Metairie, 70003-4327. Tel: 504-733-0922; MR. JOE DICHARRY, District Governor, Tel: 504-888-3958.

The Theresians International—MRS. SALLY DUPLANTIER, Pres., Crescent City, 6311 St. Bernard Ave., New Orleans, 70122. Tel: 504-288-1897.

Woman's New Life Center—MRS. ANGELA THOMAS, Esq., CEO, 3032 Ridgelake Dr., Ste. 101, Metairie, 70002. Tel: 504-496-0212; Fax: 504-831-3155; Email: info@womansnewlife.com; Web: www.womansnewlife.com.

CLERGY, PARISHES, MISSIONS AND PAROCHIAL SCHOOLS

CITY OF NEW ORLEANS

(ORLEANS CIVIL PARISH)

1—CATHEDRAL - BASILICA OF ST. LOUIS KING OF FRANCE (1720) (A Minor Basilica)
615 Pere Antoine Alley, 70116-3291.
Tel: 504-525-9585; Email: cathedral@arch-no.org. Very Rev. Philip G. Landry, V.F., Rector; Rev. Terence Hayden, (Ireland) In Res.; Deacons Ronald Guidry, Master of Ceremonies; Richard Brady; A. David Warriner Jr.
Mission—St. Mary's Roman Catholic Church, New Orleans, Louisiana, 1116 Chartres St., 70116.
Tel: 504-529-3040.

2—ALL SAINTS (1919) (African American)
1441 Teche St., 70114-5899. Tel: 504-361-8835; Email: allsaint.church@att.net; Web: allsaintschurchnola.org. Rev. Peter C. Weiss, S.S.J.; Deacon Larry L. Calvin.
Catechesis Religious Program—Students 34.

3—ST. ALPHONSUS (1847) (Irish)
2030 Constance St., 70130-5099. Tel: 504-522-6748. Revs. Richard Thibodeau, C.Ss.R.; Thomas T. Pham, C.Ss.R.; Allen Weinert, C.Ss.R., Parochial Vicar.
School—St. Alphonsus School, 2001 Constance St., 70130-5094. Tel: 504-523-6594. Sr. Monica Ellerbusch, R.S.M., Prin. Lay Teachers 12; Students 267.
Catechesis Religious Program—Students 57.

4—ST. ANDREW THE APOSTLE (1952)
3101 Eton St., 70131-5399. Tel: 504-393-2334; Fax: 504-392-0635; Email: info@standrewparish.net; Web: www.standrewparish.net. Very Rev. John F. Talamo, V.F.; Deacons Thomas Beyer; Edward Rapier Jr.; Mrs. Mary Ann Dallam, Sacramental Min.; Mr. Eddie Dallam, Sec.; Mrs. Sharon Kleefisch, Sec.
School—St. Andrew the Apostle School, 3131 Eton St., 70131. Tel: 504-394-4171; Fax: 504-391-3627; Email: info@sasno.org. Mr. Katherine Houin, Prin.; Mrs. Elizabeth Konecni, Headmaster. Lay Teachers 67; Sisters 2; Students 441; Clergy / Religious Teachers 1.
Catechesis Religious Program—Email: fharrison@standrewparish.net. Mrs. Francis Harrison, D.R.E. Students 35.

5—ANNUNCIATION (1844) Merged with St. Cecilia, St. Gerard, SS. Peter & Paul & St. Vincent de Paul to form Blessed Francis Xavier Seelos, New Orleans.

6—ST. ANTHONY OF PADUA (1915) Assumed parish territory of Sacred Heart of Jesus, New Orleans.
4640 Canal St., 70119-5808. Tel: 504-488-2651; Email: church@sapparish.org; Web: www.sapparish.org. Revs. John Dominic Sims, O.P.; Mariano D. Veliz, O.P., Parochial Vicar; Deacon Joseph M. Dardis.

7—ST. AUGUSTINE (1841) (African American)
1210 Gov. Nicholls St., 70116-2324.
Tel: 504-525-5934; Email: staugustine@archdiocese-no.org; Web: staugchurch.org. Rev. Emmanuel Mulenga, O.M.I.
Catechesis Religious Program—Students 10.

8—BLESSED FRANCIS XAVIER SEELOS (2001) [CEM]
3037 Dauphine St., 70117-6794. Tel: 504-943-5566; Email: pastor@bfs.nocoxmail.com. Very Rev. Jose I. Lavastida, S.T.D., S.T.L., N.D.S., J.C.D.; Deacon Jesse A. Watley.
Catechesis Religious Program—Ms. Arthine T. Vicks, D.R.E. & Deaf Ministry. Students 90.

9—BLESSED SACRAMENT (1915) (African American), Merged See Blessed Sacrament-St. Joan of Arc, New Orleans. For inquiries about sacramental records, contact Blessed Sacrament-St. Joan of Arc parish.

10—BLESSED SACRAMENT-ST. JOAN OF ARC (2008) Merger of Blessed Sacrament & St. Joan of Arc, New Orleans, worshipping at St. Joan of Arc Church, which was established in 1909.
8321 Burthe St., 70118-1195. Tel: 504-866-7330; Fax: 504-866-1319; Email: bssj@josephite.com; Web: www.josephite.com/parish/la/bssj. Revs. Charles Andrus, S.S.J.; Etido Jerome, S.S.J., In Res.
School—St. Joan of Arc School, 919 Cambronne St., 70118-1199. Tel: 504-861-2887; Fax: 504-866-9588; Email: stjoanno@archdiocese-no.org. Ms. Dionne Frost, Prin.
Catechesis Religious Program—Students 35.

11—BLESSED TRINITY (2008) Merger of St. Matthias, Our Lady of Lourdes and St. Monica, New Orleans, worshipping at St. Matthias Church, which was established in 1920.

4230 S. Broad St., 70125-3699. Mailing Address: 8321 Burthe St., 70118-1198. Tel: 504-822-3394; Fax: 504-822-3397; Email: boss@josephite.com. Rev. Daniel H. Green; Deacon Michael J. Taylor.
Catechesis Religious Program—Sadie White, D.R.E. Students 17.

12—ST. BRIGID (1977) Closed. See Mary Queen of Vietnam, New Orleans. For inquiries regarding sacramental records, contact Archives.

13—ST. CECILIA (1897) Merged with Annunciation, St. Gerard, SS. Peter & Paul & St. Vincent de Paul to form Blessed Francis Xavier Seelos, New Orleans.

14—CORPUS CHRISTI (1916) (African American), Merged See Corpus Christi-Epiphany. For inquiries regarding sacramental records, contact Corpus Christi-Epiphany parish.

15—CORPUS CHRISTI-EPIPHANY (2008) Merger of Corpus Christi & Epiphany, New Orleans, worshipping at Corpus Christi Church, which was established in 1916.
2022 St. Bernard Ave., 70116-1388.
Tel: 504-945-8931; Fax: 504-947-5347; Email: corpuschristiepiphanychurch@ccecno.org; Web: www.ccecno.org. Revs. Henry J. Davis, S.S.J.; David P. Begany, S.S.J., Parochial Vicar; Deacon Larry Lee Calvin.
Catechesis Religious Program—Students 46.

16—ST. DAVID (1937) (African American) Assumed territory of St. Maurice, New Orleans.
5617 St. Claude Ave., 70117-2533. Tel: 504-947-2853 ; Fax: 504-943-0577; Email: stdavid@arch-no.org. Very Rev. Oswald Pierre-Jules Jr., S.S.J., V.F.

17—ST. DOMINIC (1924)
775 Harrison Ave., 70124-3192. Tel: 504-482-4156. Revs. John G. Restrepo, O.P., V.F.; Scott Daniels, Parochial Vicar; Bro. Roger Shondel, O.P.; Rev. Richard Archer, O.P., In Res.; Very Rev. David G. Caron, O.P., In Res.; Rev. Dominic Colangelo, O.P., In Res.; Very Rev. Thomas M. Condon, O.P., In Res.; Revs. Eduardo Gabriel, O.P., In Res.; Philip Neri Powell, O.P., Ph.D., In Res.; David K. Seid, O.P., B.A., M.A., M.A.Th., M.A.Ph., In Res.; Marcelo Solorzano, O.P., In Res.; Deacons Jody J. Fortunato; John Pippenger.
School—St. Dominic School, 6326 Memphis St., 70124. Tel: 504-482-4123; Fax: 504-486-3870. Lay Teachers 51; Sisters 1; Students 447.
Catechesis Religious Program—6361 Memphis St., 70124. Students 103.

18—EPIPHANY (1948) (African American), Merged See Corpus Christi-Epiphany. For inquiries regarding sacramental records, contact Corpus Christi-Epiphany parish.

19—ST. FRANCES XAVIER CABRINI (1952) Merged with St. Raphael the Archangel & St. Thomas the Apostle, New Orleans to form Transfiguration of the Lord, New Orleans. For inquiries regarding sacramental records, contact the archives office.

20—ST. FRANCIS DE SALES (1870) (African American), Merged with Holy Ghost, New Orleans to form St. Katharine Drexel. For inquiries regarding sacramental records, contact St. Katharine Drexel parish.

21—ST. FRANCIS OF ASSISI (1890)
631 State St., 70118-5899. Tel: 504-891-4479; Email: sfa@stfrancisuptown.com; Web: www.stfrancisuptown.com. 611 State St., 70118. Rev. Michael J. Schneller; Deacons Wilbur A. Toups; Thomas M. Kratochvil.
Catechesis Religious Program—Email: cschott@stfrancisuptown.com. Christi Schott, D.R.E. Students 135.

22—ST. GABRIEL THE ARCHANGEL (1954) (African American)
4700 Pineda St., 70126-3599. Tel: 504-282-0296; Fax: 504-288-8585; Email: stgabriel@arch-no.org; Web: www.stgabe.net. Rev. Rodney Anthony Ricard; Deacon Uriel A. Durr.
Catechesis Religious Program—Students 46.

23—ST. GERARD (1971) Merged with Annunciation, St. Cecilia, SS. Peter & Paul & St. Vincent de Paul to form Blessed Francis Xavier Seelos, New Orleans.

24—GOOD SHEPHERD ROMAN CATHOLIC CHURCH, NEW ORLEANS, LOUISIANA (2008)
1025 Napoleon Ave., 70115-2898. Tel: 504-899-1378; Fax: 504-899-0480; Email: ststephenpar@archdiocese-no.org; Web: GoodShepherdParishNOLA.com. Rev. Msgr. Christopher Nalty; Rev. Douglas C. Brougher, In Res.; Deacon Richard B. Eason.
School—St. Stephen Catholic School, 1027 Napoleon Ave., 70115-2899. Tel: 504-891-1927; Fax: 504-891-1928; Email: ststephen@archdiocese-no.org. Ms. Rosie Kendrick, Prin.
Catechesis Religious Program—Phillip Bellini, D.R.E. Students 180.

25—ST. HENRY (1856) Merged with Our Lady of Good Counsel & St. Stephen, New Orleans to form Good Shepherd. For inquiries regarding sacramental records, contact Good Shepherd parish.

26—HOLY GHOST (1915) (African American), Merged See St. Katharine Drexel. For inquiries regarding sacramental records contact St. Katharine Drexel parish.

27—HOLY NAME OF JESUS (1892) Assumed parish territory of St. Thomas More, New Orleans.
6367 St. Charles Ave., 70118. Tel: 504-865-7430; Fax: 504-866-3391; Email: holyname@hnjchurch.org; Web: www.hnjchurch.org. 6220 LaSalle Pl., 70118. Revs. Ronald Boudreaux, Admin.; Stephen C. Rowntree, S.J., B.A., M.A., M.Div., M.Th., Parochial Vicar.
School—Holy Name of Jesus School, 6325 Cromwell Pl., 70118-6299. Tel: 504-861-1466; Fax: 504-861-1480. Jessica Dwyer, Prin. Lay Teachers 48; Students 493.
Catechesis Religious Program—Email: pmathes@hnjchurch.org. Patirica Mathes, D.R.E. Students 203.

28—HOLY NAME OF MARY (ALGIERS) (1848) [CEM 2]
400 Verret St., 70114-1098. Tel: 504-362-5511; Email: hnmary@nocoxmail.com. 500 Eliza St., 70114-1098. Rev. Michael Roberson; Deacon Dean D. Herrick
Holy Name of Mary Roman Catholic Church
Catechesis Religious Program—Students 34.

29—HOLY SPIRIT ROMAN CATHOLIC CHURCH, NEW ORLEANS, LOUISIANA (1972)
6201 Stratford Pl., 70131-7397. Tel: 504-394-5492; Email: holyspirit@archdiocese-no.org. Rev. James N. Bach; Deacon Daniel F. Reynolds; Pam Kamphuis, Music Ministry Coord.
Catechesis Religious Program—Jane Mix, D.R.E. Students 16.

30—HOLY TRINITY, Closed. For inquiries for parish records contact the chancery.

31—IMMACULATE CONCEPTION (1851)
130 Baronne St., 70112-2304. Tel: 504-529-1477; Email: icjcnolapastor@gmail.com; Web: www.jesuitchurch.net. Revs. Anthony F. McGinn, S.J., B.A., M.A.; David Paternostro.
Catechesis Religious Program—Students 17.

32—IMMACULATE HEART OF MARY (1954) Closed. See St. Maria Goretti. For inquiries regarding sacramental records, contact Archives.

33—INCARNATE WORD (1922) Closed. See Mater Dolorosa, New Orleans. For inquiries regarding sacramental records, contact Mater Dolorosa. Also known as St. Theresa of the Little Flower.

34—ST. JAMES MAJOR (1920)
3736 Gentilly Blvd., 70122-6199. Tel: 504-304-6750; Email: stjamesmajor@sjmc.nocoxmail.com; Web: saintjamesmajor.org. Rev. Michael M. Labre; Deacon Glenn J. Wiltz.
Catechesis Religious Program—Mrs. Evangeline Richard, D.R.E. Students 18.

35—ST. JOAN OF ARC (1909) Merged with Blessed Sacrament, New Orleans to form Blessed Sacrament-St. Joan of Arc parish. For inquiries regarding sacramental records, contact Blessed Sacrament-St. Joan of Arc parish.

36—ST. JOHN THE BAPTIST (1851) (Irish) Open for weddings, funerals and vigil mass only. Church under care of pastor of St. Patrick, New Orleans. For inquiries regarding sacramental records, contact Archives.
1139 Oretha Castle Haley Blvd., 70130-3757. 724 Camp St., 70130-3757. Tel: 504-525-4413; Fax: 504-568-1324; Email: stpatrick@archdiocese-no.org; Web: goldensteeple.com. Revs. Stanley P. Klores; Ian M. Bozant, Admin.; Deacon Chris J. DiGrado.
1137 Oretha Castle Haley Blvd., 70130.
Catechesis Religious Program—Email: stpatricksnola.rectory@gmail.com. Joseph Meisch, D.R.E.

37—ST. JOSEPH (1844)
1802 Tulane Ave., 70112-2246.
Tel: 504-522-3186, Ext. 141; Fax: 504-522-3171; Email: stjoseph@bellsouth.net. Rev. Thomas J. Stehlik, C.M.
(Legal Title: St. Joseph Roman Catholic)
Catechesis Religious Program—Students 15.

38—ST. JOSEPH ROMAN CATHOLIC CHURCH, ALGIERS, LOUISIANA
6450 Kathy Ct., 70131-7515. Mailing Address: 4410 Fields St., 70131. Tel: 504-347-4725; Fax: 540-340-2476; Email: stjosephalgiers@archdiocese-no.org. Rev. Joseph Thang Dinh Tran.

39—ST. JULIAN EYMARD (1952) Closed. Parish territory assigned to Holy Name of Mary, New Orleans. For inquiries regarding sacramental records, contact Holy Name of Mary parish.

40—ST. KATHARINE DREXEL (2008)
Church: 2015 Louisiana Ave., 70115. Office: 3325 Danneel St., 70115. Tel: 504-891-3172; Email: stkatherine@arch-no.org. Rev. Msgr. John Cisewski, V.F.
Catechesis Religious Program—Grace Lemieux, D.R.E. Students 32.

41—ST. LEO THE GREAT (1920) (African American), Merged with St. Raymond, New Orleans to form St. Raymond-St. Leo the Great. For inquiries regarding sacramental records, contact St. Raymond-St. Leo the Great.

42—ST. MARIA GORETTI (1965) Assumed parish territory of Immaculate Heart of Mary & St. Simon Peter, New Orleans. For inquiries about sacramental records for Immaculate Heart of Mary, St. Maria Goretti or St. Simon Peter, contact Archives Tel. 504-861-6241.
7300 Crowder Blvd., 70127-1599. Tel: 504-242-7554; Fax: 504-242-0755; Email: stmariagoretti@archdiocese-no.org. Rev. Msgr. L. Earl Gauthreaux, J.C.L.; Rev. Cyril Buyeera, Parochial Vicar; Deacon Terrel J. Broussard.
School—St. Maria Goretti School, Tel: 504-242-1313; Fax: 504-242-4126.
Catechesis Religious Program—Students 89.

43—ST. MARY OF THE ANGELS (1925) (African American)
3501 N. Miro St., 70117-5899. Tel: 504-945-3186; Email: frjoe@smaneworleans.org. Rev. Joseph Hund; Bros. Andrew Stetiler, O.F.M.; David Crank, O.F.M.; Jeoffre Duplessis, Music Min.
Catechesis Religious Program—Vanessa Matthews, D.R.E. & Youth Min. Students 28.

44—MARY, QUEEN OF VIETNAM ROMAN CATHOLIC CHURCH, NEW ORLEANS, LOUISIANA (1983) [JC] (Vietnamese) Assumed St. Nicholas of Myra & St. Brigid, New Orleans.
Mailing Address: P.O. Box 870607, 70187.
Tel: 504-254-5660. Rev. Nghiem Van Nguyen; Deacon Vinh V. Tran.
Res.: 5069 Willowbrook Dr., 70129-1047.
Catechesis Religious Program—Tel: 504-254-5247. Students 915.
Mission—Our Lady of La Vang, 6054 Vermillion Blvd., Orleans Civil Parish 70122-4296.
Tel: 504-283-0559; Fax: 504-286-1937. Rev. Anthony Hien Nguyen, Admin.
Chapel—Vietnamese Martyrs, 14400 Peltier Dr., New Orleans East, 70129-1713. Tel: 504-254-5660.
Shrine—Vietnamese Martyrs Shrine of the Archdiocese of New Orleans.

45—MATER DOLOROSA (1848) Assumed Incarnate Word, New Orleans & St. Theresa of the Child Jesus, also known as St. Theresa of the Little Flower.
8128 Plum St., 70118-2012. Tel: 504-866-3669; Email: materdolorosa@arch-no.org; Web: www.mdolorosa.com. Revs. Herbert J. Kiff Jr.; Francis Ferrie, In Res., (Retired); Maria Oppliger, Parish Admin.
Catechesis Religious Program—Email: conceicao_q@hotmail.com. Maria Oppliger, D.R.E. Students 67.

46—ST. MATTHIAS (1920) (African American), Merged with Our Lady of Lourdes & St. Monica, New Orleans to form Blessed Trinity. For inquiries regarding sacramental records, contact Blessed Trinity parish.

47—ST. MAURICE (1852) Closed. Assumed by St. David, New Orleans. For inquiries regarding sacramental records, contact Archives.

48—ST. MONICA (1924) [CEM] Merged with Our Lady of Lourdes & St. Matthias to form Blessed Trinity. For inquiries regarding sacramental records, contact Blessed Trinity parish.

49—ST. NICHOLAS OF MYRA (1971) [CEM] Closed. Became a mission of Resurrection of Our Lord in 2014. For inquiries regarding sacramental records, contact Archives.

50—OUR LADY OF GOOD COUNSEL (1887) Merged with St. Henry & St. Stephen. See Good Shepherd. For inquiries regarding sacramental records, contact Good Shepherd.

51—OUR LADY OF GUADALUPE (1826) (African American)
411 N. Rampart St., 70112. Tel: 504-525-1551; Email: judeshrine@aol.com. Very Rev. Anthony Rigoli, O.M.I., V.F.; Revs. Richard Sudlik, O.M.I., Parochial Vicar; Donald McMahon, O.M.I., In Res.
Legal Name: Our Lady of Guadalupe / International Shrine of St. Jude
Catechesis Religious Program—Tel: 504-522-8546. Students 66.
St. Jude Community Center—400 N. Rampart St., 70112-3594. Tel: 504-553-5790.

52—OUR LADY OF LOURDES (1905) (African American), Merged with St. Monica & St. Matthias, New Orleans to form Blessed Trinity worshipping at St. Matthias. For inquiries regarding sacramental records, contact Blessed Trinity parish.

53—OUR LADY OF THE ROSARY aka Holy Rosary (1907)
1322 Moss St., 70119-3132. Tel: 504-488-2659; Fax: 504-488-6741; Web: www.olr-nola.org. Rev. Jonathan P. Hemelt; Deacons James A. Bialas; Ronald J. Drez Jr.
Church: 3368 Esplanade Ave., 70119.
Catechesis Religious Program— Contact Parish office.

54—OUR LADY STAR OF THE SEA (1911) [CEM]
1835 St. Roch Ave., 70117-8199. Tel: 504-944-0166;

Email: olssno@arch-no.org. Rev. Anthony Ataamine Anala, S.V.D.; Deacon Brian A. Gabriel.
Catechesis Religious Program—Students 47.

55—ST. PATRICK (1833) (Irish)
724 Camp St., 70130-3757. Tel: 504-525-4413; Web: oldstpatricks.org. Revs. Stanley P. Klores, M.A., M.Div., S.T.L., S.T.D.; Ian M. Bozant, Admin.; Deacon Chris DiGrado. Assumed St. John the Baptist, New Orleans.
Catechesis Religious Program—Joseph Meisch, D.R.E.

56—ST. PAUL THE APOSTLE (1947) [CEM] (African American)
6828 Chef Menteur Hwy., 70126-5297.
Tel: 504-242-8820. Rev. Arockiam Arockiam, S.V.D.; Deacon Graylin J. Miller.
Catechesis Religious Program—Email: charityjoy4725@att.net. Jacqueline E. Mayo, D.R.E. Students 23.

57—SS. PETER AND PAUL (1848) Merged with Annunciation, St. Cecilia, St. Gerard & St. Vincent de Paul to form Blessed Francis Xavier Seelos, New Orleans.

58—ST. PETER CLAVER (1920) (African American)
1923 St. Philip St., 70116-2199. Tel: 504-822-8059; Email: pastor@spclaverchurch.org. Rev. John Asare-Dankwah, (Ghana); Deacons Allen Stevens; Lawrence C. Houston; Veronica Downs-Dorsey, Music Dir.
School—St. Peter Claver School, 1020 N. Prieur St., 70116-2194. Tel: 504-822-8191; Fax: 504-822-2692; Web: spclaver.eduk12.net. Deacon Lawrence C. Houston, Prin. Lay Teachers 23; Students 240.
Catechesis Religious Program—Alena Boucree, D.R.E.; Marinda Lee-Houston, Youth Min. Students 170.

59—ST. PHILIP THE APOSTLE (1949) (African American), Closed. Assigned to St. Mary of the Angels, New Orleans, under the care of Franciscans. Buildings are under the care of the Archdiocese of New Orleans. For inquiries regarding sacramental records, contact Archives.

60—ST. PIUS X (1953)
6666 Spanish Fort Blvd., 70124-4324.
Tel: 504-282-3332; Email: spxparish@arch-no.org. Very Rev. Patrick J. Williams, M.Div., M.S., V.G.; Deacons Christopher A. Bertucci; Gary T. Levy.
School—St. Pius X School, 6600 Spanish Fort Blvd., 70124-4399. Tel: 504-282-2811; Fax: 504-282-3043; Email: spxsch@archdiocese-no.org. Lay Teachers 30; Students 504.
Catechesis Religious Program—Students 120.

61—ST. RAPHAEL THE ARCHANGEL (1947) Merged with St. Frances Cabrini & St. Thomas the Apostle, New Orleans to form Transfiguration of the Lord New Orleans. For inquiries regarding sacramental records, contact Archives.

62—ST. RAYMOND (1927) (African American), Merged with St. Leo the Great, New Orleans to form St. Raymond-St. Leo the Great. For inquiries regarding sacramental records, contact St. Raymond-St. Leo the Great parish.

63—ST. RAYMOND-ST. LEO THE GREAT (2008) Merger of St. Leo the Great & St. Raymond, New Orleans, worshipping at St. Leo the Great Church, which was established in 1920.
2916 Paris Ave., 70119. Tel: 504-945-8750;
Fax: 504-309-1691; Email: crivera@archdiocese-no.org. Revs. Anthony M. Bozeman, S.S.J.; Victor H. Cohea, In Res.; Deacons Royal C. Shelton, Pastoral Assoc.; Troy Anthony Smith; Dwight Alexander.
School—St. Leo the Great School, 1501 Abundance St., 70119-2098. Tel: 504-943-1482;
Fax: 504-944-5895; Email: cmire@archdiocese-no.org. Mrs. Carmel Mire, Prin. Clergy 1; Lay Teachers 28; Students 266.
Catechesis Religious Program—Marlene Wilson, D.R.E. Students 265.

64—RESURRECTION OF OUR LORD ROMAN CATHOLIC CHURCH, NEW ORLEANS, LOUISIANA aka St. Nicholas of Myra Mission (1963)
9701 Hammond St., 70127-3519. Tel: 504-242-8669; Email: resurrectionchurch@archdiocese-no.org; Web: www.resurrectionofourlord.org. Revs. Geoffrey Omondi Muga, F.M.H.; Raphael Mbotela Kasele, F.M.H., Parochial Vicar.
School—Resurrection of Our Lord School, 4861 Rosalia Dr., 70127-3598. Tel: 504-243-2257;
Fax: 504-241-5532; Email: resurrection@archdiocese-no.org. Mrs. Vickie Helmstetter, Prin. Lay Teachers 50; Students 434.
Catechesis Religious Program—Students 23.
Mission—St. Nicholas of Myra, 21420 Chef Menteur Hwy., 70129.

65—ST. RITA CATHOLIC CHURCH (1921)
2729 Lowerline St., 70125-3599. Tel: 504-866-3621; Email: stritachurchno@archdiocese-no.org. Rev. Peter P. Finney III.
Admin. Res.: 2801 Pine St., 70125.
School—St. Rita Catholic School, 65 Fontainebleau Dr., 70125-3495. Tel: 504-866-1777;
Fax: 504-861-8512; Email: stritano@archdiocese-no.org. Mrs. Karen Henderson, Prin. Lay Teachers 11; Sisters 2; Students 215.
Catechesis Religious Program—Students 228.

66—ST. ROSE OF LIMA (1857) Closed. Assigned to Our Lady of the Rosary, New Orleans. Buildings are under the care of the Archdiocese of New Orleans. For inquiries regarding sacramental records, contact Archives.

67—SACRED HEART OF JESUS (1879) [CEM] Closed. Parish territory assigned to St. Anthony of Padua, New Orleans. For inquiries for sacramental records, contact the archives office.

68—ST. SIMON PETER (1986) Closed. Assigned to St. Maria Goretti, New Orleans. For inquiries regarding sacramental records, contact Archives.

69—ST. STEPHEN (1849) Merged with Our Lady of Good Counsel & St. Henry, New Orleans to form Good Shepherd. For inquiries regarding sacramental records, contact Good Shepherd parish.

70—ST. THERESA OF AVILA (1848) Special care to the Hispanic Community.
1404 Erato St., 70130-4387. Tel: 504-525-4226. Rev. Roman Burgos, T.O.R.
Catechesis Religious Program—Email: acartagena@arch-no.org. Alma Cartagena, D.R.E. Students 35.

71—ST. THERESA OF THE CHILD JESUS (1929) Closed. Parish territory entrusted to Incarnate Word, New Orleans. For inquiries regarding sacramental records, contact the archives office.

72—ST. THOMAS MORE (1970) Closed. Became a campus ministry center (Tulane Catholic Center) serving Tulane University. For inquiries regarding sacramental records, contact Holy Name of Jesus parish.

73—ST. THOMAS THE APOSTLE (1974) Merged Became a campus ministry center (UNO Newman Center) serving the University of New Orleans. For inquiries regarding sacramental records, contact Archives.

74—TRANSFIGURATION OF THE LORD (2008)
2212 Prentiss Ave., 70122. Tel: 504-302-7931;
Fax: 504-324-8102; Email: transfiguration@arch-no.org; Web: transfigurationnola.org. Very Rev. Paul H. Desrosiers, V.F.; Deacons Peter C. Rizzo; Lloyd E. Huck.

75—ST. VINCENT DE PAUL (1838) Merged with Annunciation, St. Cecilia, St. Gerard & SS. Peter & Paul to form Blessed Francis Xavier Seelos, New Orleans.

OUTSIDE THE CITY OF NEW ORLEANS

ABITA SPRINGS, ST. TAMMANY PARISH, ST. JANE DE CHANTAL (1887) [JC]
72040 Maple St., P.O. Box 1870, Abita Springs, 70420-1870. Tel: 985-892-1439; Email: dmarkey@arch-no.org; Web: saintjanedechantal.com. Revs. Kenneth Allen; Charles W. Dussouy, Parochial Vicar; Angel Antonio Diaz-Perez, O.P., In Res.; Deacons Donald E. Bourgeois; Mark C. Coudrain; Michael J. Talbot.
Res.: 22122 Main St., Abita Springs, 70420-1870.
Catechesis Religious Program—Tel: 985-893-3914. Christina Uhlich, D.R.E. Students 222.
Mission—St. Michael the Archangel, 81349 Hwy. 41, Bush, St. Tammany Parish. Tel: 985-886-1015;
Fax: 985-886-0302.

AMA, ST. CHARLES PARISH, ST. MARK ROMAN CATHOLIC CHURCH, AMA, LOUISIANA (1974)
10773 River Rd., Ama, 70031. Tel: 504-431-8505; Email: stmarkama@arch-no.org. Rev. Edward J. Lauden.
Catechesis Religious Program—Tel: 504-289-2900; Email: restmarkama@yahoo.com. Ms. Mary Loup, D.R.E. Students 39.

ARABI, ST. BERNARD PARISH

1—ST. LOUISE DE MARILLAC (1954) Closed. Assigned to Our Lady of Prompt Succor, Chalmette. For inquiries regarding sacramental records, contact Archives.

2—ST. ROBERT BELLARMINE (1964) Closed. Assigned to Our Lady of Prompt Succor, Chalmette. For inquiries regarding sacramental records, contact Archives.
Res.: 408 Cougar Dr., Arabi, 70032-2098.

AVONDALE, JEFFERSON PARISH

1—ASSUMPTION OF MARY ROMAN CATHOLIC CHURCH, AVONDALE, LOUISIANA
172 Andre Dung Lac Dr., Avondale, 70094. 533 S. Jamie Blvd., Avondale, 70094. Tel: 504-347-4725;
Fax: 504-340-2476; Email: assumptionofmary@archdiocese-no.org. Rev. Peter Hoai T. Nguyen.

2—ST. BONAVENTURE ROMAN CATHOLIC CHURCH, AVONDALE, LOUISIANA (1965)
329 S. Jamie Blvd., Avondale, 70094-2821.
Tel: 504-436-1279. Rev. Joseph Dau Van Nguyen.
Catechesis Religious Program—Tel: 504-436-0744. Tina Adams, D.R.E. Students 72.

BELLE CHASSE, PLAQUEMINES PARISH, OUR LADY OF PERPETUAL HELP (1928) [CEM]
8968 Hwy. 23, Belle Chasse, 70037-2296.
Tel: 504-394-0314; Email: churchoffice@olphbc.org. Rev. Kyle V. Dave; Deacon George E. Merritt Jr.
School—Our Lady of Perpetual Help School, 8970 Hwy. 23. Tel: 504-394-0757; Fax: 504-394-1627. Mrs. Kirsch Wilberg, Prin. Lay Teachers 14; Students 171.
Catechesis Religious Program—Email: cre@olphbc.org. Cecilia Merritt, C.R.E. Students 250.

BOGALUSA, WASHINGTON PARISH, ANNUNCIATION CATHOLIC CHURCH (1906) [JC3]
517 Avenue B, Bogalusa, 70427-3711.
Tel: 985-732-4280; Email: annchurch@att.net. Rev. Daniel E. Brouillette; Deacon Edward Francis Kelley.
School—Annunciation Catholic Church School, 511 Avenue C, Bogalusa, 70427-3797. Tel: 985-735-6643; Fax: 985-735-6119; Email: annunciationsch@archdiocese-no.org; Web: www.acsbogalusa.org. Mrs. Veda Matthews, Prin. Lay Teachers 14; Students 135.
Catechesis Religious Program—Students 47.

BRIDGE CITY, JEFFERSON PARISH, HOLY GUARDIAN ANGELS (1963) Closed. Mission of Our Lady of Prompt Succor, Westwego.

BURAS, PLAQUEMINES PARISH, OUR LADY OF GOOD HARBOR (1864) [CEM] Closed. Parish & mission territory assigned to St. Patrick, Port Sulphur. For inquiries regarding sacramental records, contact Archives.

CHALMETTE, ST. BERNARD PARISH

1—ST. MARK (1964) Closed. Assigned to Our Lady of Prompt Succor, Chalmette. For inquiries regarding sacramental records, contact Archives.

2—OUR LADY OF PROMPT SUCCOR (1951) Parish assumed territory of Prince of Peace, Chalmette, St. Bernard Parish; St. Louise de Marillac, Arabi, St. Bernard Parish; St. Mark, Chalmette, St. Bernard Parish; & St. Robert Bellarmine, Arabi, St. Bernard Parish.
2320 Paris Rd., Chalmette, 70043-5098.
Tel: 504-271-3441; Fax: 504-271-2927; Email: info@olps-chalmette.org. Revs. Marlon Mangubat; Salvador Galvez, Parochial Vicar; Deacon Lino G. Parulan.
School—Our Lady of Prompt Succor School, 2305 Fenelon St., Chalmette, 70043-4951.
Tel: 504-271-2953; Fax: 504-271-1490; Email: scoll8312@aol.com; Web: www.olpsschool.org. Mrs. Annette Accomando, Prin. Lay Teachers 31; Students 370.
Catechesis Religious Program—Tel: 504-271-1217. Terri Smith, C.R.E. Students 219.
Mission—Chapel of St. Lawrence, St. Bernard Parish Prison, Chalmette, St. Bernard Parish 70043.
Tel: 504-278-7645; Fax: 504-278-7785.

3—PRINCE OF PEACE (1977) Closed. See Our Lady of Prompt Succor, Chalmette. For inquiries regarding sacramental records, contact Archives.

COVINGTON, ST. TAMMANY PARISH

1—ST. BENEDICT ROMAN CATHOLIC CHURCH, COVINGTON, LOUISIANA (1970)
20370 Smith Rd., Covington, 70435.
Tel: 985-892-5202; Email: office@stbencov.org; Web: www.stbenedictchurchcovington.com/. Rev. Charles Benoit, O.S.B., M.A.Th.; Deacons Daniel P. Musso; Ellis Iverson.

2—MOST HOLY TRINITY ROMAN CATHOLIC CHURCH, LOUISIANA (2006)
501 Holy Trinity Dr., Covington, 70433.
Tel: 985-892-0642; Email: office@mhtcc.net. Very Rev. Rodney P. Bourg, V.F.; Rev. Dean L. Robins, In Res.; Deacons Thomas E. Caffery Jr.; Brian M. McKnight Sr.; Charles R. Swift; Kenneth J. Uhlich Jr.; Stephen W. Sperier.
Catechesis Religious Program—Email: amconstant@mhtcc.net. Anna Maria Constant, D.R.E. Students 278.

3—ST. PETER (1843)
125 E. 19th St., Covington, 70433-3195.
Tel: 985-892-2422; Email: rectory@stpeterparish.com. Rev. Otis W. Young Jr.; Colm Cahill; Deacons James Clyde Ardoin; Dennis F. Adams; John A. Jung; Virgil D. Roberts.
School—St. Peter School, Tel: 985-892-1831;
Fax: 985-898-2185; Email: stpetercov@stpetercov.org. Michael Kraus, Prin. Lay Teachers 48; Students 772.
Catechesis Religious Program—Tel: 985-893-2446; Email: ore@stpeterparish.com. Penny Flores, D.R.E. Students 223.

CROWN POINT, JEFFERSON PARISH, ST. PIUS X (1971) Closed. Mission of St. Anthony, Lafitte.

DES ALLEMANDS, ST. CHARLES PARISH, ST. GERTRUDE (1955) [CEM]
17292 La. Hwy. 631, Des Allemands, 70030.
Tel: 985-758-7542; Email: office@stgertrude.nocoxmail.com. Rev. John Ryan.
Catechesis Religious Program—Tel: 985-758-1332. Tina Montz, C.R.E. Students 88.

DESTREHAN, ST. CHARLES PARISH, ST. CHARLES BORROMEO (1723) [CEM] (German)
13396 River Rd., Destrehan, 70047-0428.

Tel: 985-764-6383; Email: rrodrigue@scbhumilitas.org; Web: www.scblittleredchurch.org. P.O. Box 428, Destrehan, 70047. Revs. Dominic Arcuri; Jude O. Emunemu, Parochial Vicar; Deacons Harry Schexnayder; Michael Stohlman; Jeffrey R. Tully.
School—St. Charles Borromeo School,
Tel: 985-764-9232; Fax: 985-764-3726. Lay Teachers 28; Preschool 100; Students 328.
Catechesis Religious Program—Students 260.

DIAMOND, PLAQUEMINES PARISH, ST. JUDE (1981) Closed. Parish territory entrusted to St. Patrick, Port Sulphur. For inquiries regarding sacramental records, contact Archives.

EDGARD, ST. JOHN THE BAPTIST PARISH, ST. JOHN THE BAPTIST (1770) [CEM] (African American)
2361 Hwy. 18, Edgard, 70049-9101.
Tel: 985-497-3412; Email: stjohn3412@bellsouth.net. Rev. Robustiano D. Morgia; Deacon Warren R. Pierre.
Catechesis Religious Program—Students 157.

FLORISSANT, ST. BERNARD PARISH, SAN PEDRO PESCADOR (1966) (Islenos), Closed. Parish territory assigned to St. Bernard, St. Bernard. For inquiries regarding sacramental records, contact St. Bernard parish.

FOLSOM, ST. TAMMANY PARISH, ST. JOHN THE BAPTIST (1921)
11345 St. John Church Rd., Folsom, 70437-7155.
Tel: 985-796-3806; Fax: 985-796-9554; Email: stjohnthebaptistfolsom@yahoo.com; Web: stjohnbaptistfolsom.org. Rev. Vincent Phan; Deacons Julius T. Zimmer; Jeffrey J. Stein.
Catechesis Religious Program—Tel: 985-796-5507. Students 107.

FRANKLINTON, WASHINGTON PARISH, HOLY FAMILY ROMAN CATHOLIC CHURCH, FRANKLINTON, LOUISIANA aka Holy Family Catholic Church (1982)
1220 14th Ave., Franklinton, 70438.
Tel: 985-839-4040; Fax: 985-839-2429; Email: holyfamilychurchfranklinton@yahoo.com; Web: www.holyfamilyfranklinton.org. Rev. Kyle J. Sanders.
Catechesis Religious Program—Tel: 985-839-2428. Students 64.

GARYVILLE, ST. JOHN THE BAPTIST PARISH, ST. HUBERT (1907)
176 Anthony Monica St., Garyville, 70051-0851.
Tel: 985-535-3312; Email: sthubert@rtconline.com. Rev. Ray A. Hymel; Deacon Garland J. Roussel Jr.
Catechesis Religious Program—Students 47.

GRETNA, JEFFERSON PARISH
1—ST. ANTHONY
924 Monroe St., Gretna, 70053. Tel: 504-368-6161; Fax: 504-362-7811; Email: stjosephgretna@bellsouth.net; Web: www.stjosephgretna.com. Rev. Gary P. Copping; Deacons Leonard E. Enger II; Gerard L. Labadot.
School—St. Anthony School, 900 Franklin Ave., Gretna, 70053-2224. Tel: 504-367-0689;
Fax: 504-361-9054. Miss Jo Anna Russo, Prin.
2—ST. CLETUS ROMAN CATHOLIC CHURCH, GRETNA, LOUISIANA (1965)
3600 Claire Ave., Gretna, 70053-7699.
Tel: 504-367-7951; Email: stcletuschurch@arch-no.org; Web: stcletuschurch.org. Rev. Tuan Anh Pham; Deacon Patrick L. Dempsey.
School—St. Cletus School, (Grades PreK-7),
Tel: 504-366-3538; Email: jgrabert@stcletuscolts.com; Email: stcletus@arch-no.org; Web: stcletus.com. Mrs. Jill Grabert, Prin. Lay Teachers 36; Students 360.
Catechesis Religious Program—Students 58.
3—ST. JOSEPH CHURCH AND SHRINE ON THE WESTBANK (1857)
610 Sixth St., Gretna, 70053-6098. Tel: 504-368-1313 ; Fax: 504-368-6841; Email: stjosephgretna@bellsouth.net; Web: www.stjosephgretna.com. Rev. Gary P. Copping; Deacons Leonard E. Enger II; Gerard L. Labadot.
Catechesis Religious Program—Students 35.

HAHNVILLE, ST. CHARLES PARISH, OUR LADY OF THE HOLY ROSARY (1877) [CEM]
1 Rectory Ln., Hahnville, 70057. Tel: 985-783-1199; Email: olrhahn@arch-no.org. Rev. Joel P. Cantones; Deacon David E. Caldero.
Catechesis Religious Program—Jacqueline Robert, D.R.E. Students 112.

HARAHAN, JEFFERSON PARISH, ST. RITA (1950)
7100 Jefferson Hwy., Harahan, 70123-4928.
Fax: 504-737-2921; Email: parish@stritaharahan.com. Revs. Steven V. Bruno; Kenneth Smith, Parochial Vicar; Deacons Danny Flynn; Gary J. Borne; Nolen J. LeBlanc.
Res.: 160 Imperial Woods Dr., Harahan, 70123-4998.
School—St. Rita School, 194 Ravan Ave., Harahan, 70123-4999. Tel: 504-737-0744; Fax: 504-738-2184. Mrs. Miriam Daniel, Prin. Lay Teachers 42; Students 421.
Catechesis Religious Program—Email: emaffe@arch-no.org. Students 59.

HARVEY, JEFFERSON PARISH
1—INFANT JESUS OF PRAGUE (1969) Closed. Mission of St. Martha, Harvey.
2—ST. JOHN BOSCO ROMAN CATHOLIC CHURCH, HARVEY, LOUISIANA (1983)
2114 Oakmere Dr., Harvey, 70058-2275.
Tel: 504-340-0444; Email: office@saintjohnboscochurch.org. Rev. Lawrence Urban, S.D.B.; Deacon Kevin M. Steel.
Catechesis Religious Program—Paul G. Haddican Jr., Youth Min.; Caroline Vuong, Youth Min.; Sarah Bui, Youth Min. Students 30.
3—ST. MARTHA ROMAN CATHOLIC CHURCH, HARVEY, LOUISIANA (1973)
2555 Apollo Dr., Harvey, 70058-5813.
Tel: 504-366-1604; Email: stmartha@arch-no.org. Rev. Lich Van Nguyen; Deacons Tyrell Manieri; Larry Murphy; Brian P. Soileau Sr.
Catechesis Religious Program—Tel: 504-366-4142. Students 88.
Mission—Infant Jesus of Prague, 700 Maple St., Harvey, Jefferson Parish 70058-4008.
Tel: 504-368-1397; Fax: 504-368-0662.
4—ST. ROSALIE (1949)
601 2nd Ave., Harvey, 70058-2728.
Tel: 504-340-1962; Email: jbourgeois@strosalieparish.com; Web: strosalieparish.com. 600 2nd Ave., Harvey, 70058-2728. Revs. Lawrence Urban, S.D.B.; George Hanna, S.D.B., Parochial Vicar.
School—St. Rosalie School, 617 Second Ave., Harvey, 70058-2798. Tel: 504-341-4342;
Fax: 504-347-0271. Mary C. Wenzel, Prin. Lay Teachers 60; Students 800.
Catechesis Religious Program—Guyann Murphy, D.R.E. Students 12.

JEFFERSON, JEFFERSON PARISH, ST. AGNES (1931)
3310 Jefferson Hwy., Jefferson, 70121-2699.
Tel: 504-833-3366; Tel: 504-833-4118;
Fax: 504-834-1532; Email: stagneschurch@nocoxmail.com; Web: www.stagnesjefferson.org. Rev. Bac-Hai Viet Tran; Deacons Piero Caserta; Frank G. DiFulco.
Catechesis Religious Program—Email: kellywilbert@aol.com. Kelly Wilbert, D.R.E. Students 101.

KENNER, JEFFERSON PARISH
1—DIVINE MERCY ROMAN CATHOLIC CHURCH, KENNER, LOUISIANA (2009) Merger of Nativity of Our Lord and St. Elizabeth Ann Seton, Kenner.
4337 Sal Lentini Pkwy., Kenner, 70065. Email: office@divinemercyparish.org; Web: www.divinemercyparish.org. Revs. David W. Dufour; Paul Clark, Parochial Vicar; Deacons Andrea Capaci; Noel W. Martinsen; Larry D. Oney; David E. Caldero.
School—St. Elizabeth Ann Seton, 4119 St. Elizabeth Dr., Kenner, 70065. Tel: 504-468-3524;
Fax: 504-469-6014; Web: www.seasparish.com/school. Joan Kathmann, Prin. Lay Teachers 29; Students 485.
2—ST. ELIZABETH ANN SETON (1981) Merged with Nativity of Our Lord, Kenner to form a new parish, Divine Mercy. For inquiries regarding sacramental records, contact Divine Mercy parish office.
3—ST. JEROME ROMAN CATHOLIC CHURCH, KENNER, LOUISIANA (1963)
2400 33rd St., Kenner, 70065-3899.
Tel: 504-443-3174; Fax: 504-443-5499; Email: stjeromepsh@archdiocese-no.org; Web: stjeromecatholic.org. Rev. Quentin E. Moody; Deacon Leo Tran.
Res.: 2402 33rd St., Kenner, 70065-3899.
Catechesis Religious Program—Gail Bordelon, D.R.E. Students 144.
4—NATIVITY OF OUR LORD (1977) Merged with St. Elizabeth Ann Seton, Kenner to form Divine Mercy parish. For inquiries regarding sacramental records, contact Divine Mercy parish.
5—OUR LADY OF PERPETUAL HELP (1869)
1908 Short St., Kenner, 70062-7599.
Tel: 504-464-0361; Email: secretary@olphla.org; Web: www.olphla.net. Revs. Richard M. Miles; Edward Owusu-Ansah, Parochial Vicar; Deacon Greg A. Gross.
Res.: 1912 Short St., Kenner, 70062-7599.
Tel: 504-464-0362.
School—Our Lady of Perpetual Help School, 531 Williams Blvd., Kenner, 70062-7598.
Tel: 504-464-0531; Fax: 504-464-0725; Email: olph@olphla.org; Web: www.olphla.org. Gina Mahl, Prin. Lay Teachers 22; Sisters 1; Students 216.
Catechesis Religious Program—Sr. Christella Emano, S.F.C.C., D.R.E. Students 55.

LA PLACE, ST. JOHN THE BAPTIST PARISH
1—ASCENSION OF OUR LORD ROMAN CATHOLIC CHURCH, LAPLACE, LOUISIANA (1979)
799 Fairway Dr., La Place, 70068-2007.
Tel: 985-652-2615; Email: aolparishoffice@gmail.com; Web: www.aolparish.org. Very Rev. Walter J. Austin, V.F.; Deacons Thomas J. St. Pierre; David W. Farinelli.
Church: 1900 Greenwood Dr., La Place, 70068.
School—Ascension of Our Lord Roman Catholic Church, LaPlace, Louisiana School, 1809 Greenwood Dr., La Place, 70068-2098. Tel: 985-652-4532;
Fax: 985-651-5151; Email: office@aolcrusaders.org; Web: www.aolcrusaders.org/. Mrs. Toni Ruiz, Prin. Lay Teachers 23; Students 252.
Catechesis Religious Program—Email: aolprep@gmail.com. Andree Gurdian, D.R.E. Students 58.
2—ST. JOAN OF ARC (1947) [JC]
529 W. 5th St., La Place, 70068. Tel: 985-652-9100; Email: office@sjachurch.com; Email: bookkeeper@sjachurch.com; Web: sjachurch.com. Revs. Patrick Collum, V.F.; Matthew D. Johnston, Parochial Vicar; Deacons Maurice V. Casadaban; Daniel F. Reynolds.
School—St. Joan of Arc School, 412 Fir St., La Place, 70068-4310. Tel: 985-652-6310; Fax: 985-652-6390; Web: www.sja-school.com. Mr. Jeffrey Montz, Prin. Lay Teachers 30; Students 375.
Catechesis Religious Program—Email: dre@sjachurch.com. Bro. Benedict Kelley, D.R.E. Students 75.
Convent—Daughters of Divine Providence, 386 Fir St., La Place, 70068-3941. Tel: 985-359-3163.

LACOMBE, ST. TAMMANY PARISH
1—ST. JOHN OF THE CROSS ROMAN CATHOLIC CHURCH, LACOMBE, LOUISIANA (1984)
61030 Brier Lake Dr., Lacombe, 70445-2911.
Tel: 985-882-3779; Fax: 985-882-9282; Email: sjc1286@bellsouth.net; Web: www.stjohnofthecrosslacombe.org. Very Rev. Gilmer J. Martin, V.F.; Deacons Ricky J. Suprean; Francis W. Drake; Donald R. St. Germain Jr.; Eugene P. Templet; Kathie Lusch, Sec.
Res.: 61051 Brier Lake Dr., Lacombe, 70445-2911. Web: stjohnofthecrosscatholicchurch.org.
Community Center—61038 Brier Lake Dr., Lacombe, 70445-2911. Tel: 985-882-6625.
Catechesis Religious Program—Lynn Suprean, D.R.E. Students 64.
2—SACRED HEART (1890)
28029 Main St., P.O. Box 1080, Lacombe, 70445-1080. Tel: 985-882-5229. Rev. Thomas Kilisara; Deacons William P. Curry Jr.; Steven L. Ferran.
Catechesis Religious Program—Tel: 985-882-8041. Students 117.

LAFITTE, JEFFERSON PARISH, ST. ANTHONY (1936) [CEM] Assumed parish territory of St. Pius X, Crown Point which became a mission of the parish.
2653 Jean Lafitte Blvd., Lafitte, 70067.
Tel: 504-689-4101. Rev. Luke Hungdung Nguyen; Deacon Edward Cain Jr.
Catechesis Religious Program—Tel: 504-689-0069. Ms. Wendy M. Houin, D.R.E. (Elementary); Ms. Paula Martin, D.R.E. (High School). Students 320.
Mission—St. Pius X, 8151 Barataria Blvd., Crown Point, 70072-9704.

LULING, ST. CHARLES PARISH
1—ST. ANTHONY OF PADUA (1961)
234 Angus Dr., Luling, 70070-4427.
Tel: 985-785-8885; Email: stanthonyluling@arch-no.org. Rev. Anthony Odiong; Deacon Michael A. Fabre Sr.
Catechesis Religious Program—Tel: 504-785-0050. Students 94.
2—HOLY FAMILY ROMAN CATHOLIC CHURCH, LULING, LOUISIANA (1980)
155 Holy Family Ln., Luling, 70070-6103.
Tel: 985-785-8585; Email: hlyfamilystaff@bellsouth.net. Rev. Stephen Dardis.
Catechesis Religious Program—Tel: 985-331-9100. Mrs. Fran M. Petit, C.R.E. (Elementary). Students 425.

MADISONVILLE, ST. TAMMANY PARISH, ST. ANSELM (1962)
306 St. Mary St., Madisonville, 70447.
Tel: 985-845-7342; Fax: 985-845-3076. Rev. Msgr. Frank J. Giroir; Rev. Travis J. Clark, Parochial Vicar; Deacons John Glover; Abner J. Guillory; Henry P. Wellmeyer; Edward R. Morris.
Catechesis Religious Program—Sheri Williams, D.R.E. Students 656.

MANDEVILLE, ST. TAMMANY PARISH
1—MARY, QUEEN OF PEACE ROMAN CATHOLIC CHURCH, MANDEVILLE, LOUISIANA (1988)
1501 W. Causeway Approach, Mandeville, 70471-3047. Tel: 985-626-6977; Email: mqop@maryqueenofpeace.org. Very Rev. John-Nhan Tran, V.F.; Rev. Jared Rodrigue, Parochial Vicar; Deacons John J. Finn; Edward Beckendorf; Timothy R. Jackson.
School—Mary, Queen of Peace Roman Catholic Church, Mandeville, Louisiana School, 1515 W. Causeway Approach, Mandeville, 70471.
Tel: 985-674-2466; Fax: 985-674-1441; Email: school@maryqueenofpeace.org; Web: www.mqpcs.org. Mrs. Sybil Skansi, Prin. Lay Teachers 50; Students 485.
Catechesis Religious Program—Tel: 985-674-9794. Jewell Bayhi, D.R.E. Students 214.

2—Our Lady of the Lake Roman Catholic Church (1850) [JC]
312 Lafitte St., Mandeville, 70448-5827.
Tel: 985-626-5671; Email: bonnie@ollparish.info. Very Rev. Mark Lomax, V.F.; Revs. Christopher P. Zavackis, Parochial Vicar; Charles L. Latour, O.P., In Res.; Deacons Jay C. Frantz; Steven R. Cohan; Andrew P. Raspino Sr., Email: apraspino@bellsouth.net; Owen P. Francis.
School—Our Lady of the Lake Roman Catholic Church School, 316 Lafitte St., Mandeville, 70448-5827. Tel: 985-626-5678; Fax: 985-626-4337; Email: pjohnson@ourladyofthelakeschool.org; Web: www.ourladyofthelakeschool.org. Frank Smith, Prin. Clergy 6; Lay Teachers 73; Students 697.
Catechesis Religious Program—
Tel: 985-626-5671, Ext. 114; Email: andrea@ollparish.info. Andrea LaBranche, C.R.E. Students 404.

Marrero, Jefferson Parish
1—St. Agnes Le Thi Thanh Roman Catholic Church, Marrero, Louisiana (1995) [JC] (Vietnamese) (Personal Parish for Southeast Asians)
6851 St. Le Thi Thanh St., Marrero, 70072-2556.
Tel: 504-347-4725; Email: stagnesltt@archdiocese-no.org. 1000 Westwood Dr., Marrero, 70072-2415. Rev. Peter Nam Van Tran.
*Catechesis Religious Program—*Students 921.
2—Immaculate Conception (1924)
4401 7th St., Marrero, 70072-2099.
Tel: 504-341-9516. Revs. James J. Jeanfreau Jr.; Pedro Prada, Parochial Vicar; Deacons Oscar Alegria; James H. Simmons; Janel Ockman, Music Dir.
School—Immaculate Conception School, 4520 6th St., Marrero, 70072-2098. Tel: 504-347-4409; Fax: 504-340-2895; Email: iconception@archdiocese-no.org; Web: icschargers.org. Mrs. Kim DiMarco, Prin. Clergy 7; Lay Teachers 46; Salesian Sisters 2; Students 628.
*Catechesis Religious Program—*Email: raaucoin@gmail.com. Rhoda Aucoin, D.R.E. Students 765.
3—St. Joachim Roman Catholic Church, Marrero, Louisiana (1985)
5505 Barataria Blvd., Marrero, 70072-6660.
Tel: 504-341-9226; Email: stjoachim@arch-no.org. Rev. G. Amaldoss; Deacon Quin Ortega.
*Catechesis Religious Program—*Students 75.
4—St. Joseph the Worker (1955)
455 Ames Blvd., Marrero, 70072-1599.
Tel: 504-347-8438; Email: frgene@archdiocese-no.org. Rev. Eugene F. Jacques; Deacon Charles E. Allen.
*Catechesis Religious Program—*Tel: 504-348-4784; Fax: 504-347-0852. Students 80.
5—The Visitation of Our Lady Roman Catholic Church, Marrero, Louisiana (1963)
3500 Ames Blvd., Marrero, 70072-5699.
Tel: 504-347-2203; Email: volchurch@vol.org. Revs. Colin V. Braud; Francis Nguyen, Parochial Vicar; Deacons James P. Rooney Jr.; James A. Venturella.
School—The Visitation of Our Lady Roman Catholic Church, Marrero, Louisiana School, 3520 Ames Blvd., Marrero, 70072-5698. Tel: 504-347-3377; Fax: 504-341-5378; Email: volschool@vol.org. Mrs. Carolyn Levet, Prin. Lay Teachers 32; Students 532.
*Catechesis Religious Program—*Tel: 504-341-8477. Jenny Doskey, D.R.E. Students 212.

Metairie, Jefferson Parish
1—St. Angela Merici Roman Catholic Church, Metairie, Louisiana (1964)
835 Melody Dr., Metairie, 70002.
Tel: 504-835-0324, Ext. 301; Fax: 504-834-9709; Email: parish@stangela.org; Web: www.stangela.org. 901 Beverly Garden Dr., Metairie, 70002. Revs. Clayton J. Charbonnet III; Patrick Carr, Parochial Vicar; Deacons Gilbert R. Schmidt; Nicholas Chetta; Raymond E. Heap; David P. Aaron.
Res.: 828 Melody Dr., Metairie, 70002.
School—St. Angela Merici Roman Catholic Church, Metairie, Louisiana School, Tel: 504-835-8491; Fax: 504-835-4463; Web: www.stangelaschool.org. Mrs. Paige Bennett, Prin. Lay Teachers 41; Students 370.
Catechesis Religious Program— (Combined with St. Clement of Rome) Tel: 504-835-0324, Ext. 306; Email: candice@stangela.org. Candice Schmidt, Catechetical Coord. Students 365.
2—St. Ann Roman Catholic Church and Shrine, Metairie, Louisiana (1971)
3601 Transcontinental, Metairie, 70006-4040.
Tel: 505-455-7071; Email: contact@stannchurchandshrine.org; Web: stannchurchandshrine.org. 4940 Meadowdale St., Metairie, 70006-4040. Revs. William O'Riordan, V.F.; Vincent Nguyen, Parochial Vicar; Deacons Philip E. Doolen; Thomas H. Fox.
School—St. Ann Roman Catholic Church and Shrine, Metairie, Louisiana School, (Grades PreK-7), 4921 Meadowdale St., Metairie, 70006-4098.
Tel: 504-455-8383; Fax: 504-455-9572; Email: stann@stannschool.org; Web: www.stannschool.org. Mrs. Susan Kropog, Prin. Lay Teachers 53; Students 828.
Catechesis Religious Program—
Tel: 504-455-7071, Ext. 225; Email: stannreled@bellsouth.net. David Wilson, D.R.E. Students 63.
3—St. Benilde Roman Catholic Church, Metairie, Louisiana (1964)
1901 Division St., Metairie, 70001-2798.
Tel: 504-834-4980; Email: stbenildechurch@cox.net; Web: www.stbenilde.org. Revs. Robert T. Cooper; H. L. Brignac, In Res., (Retired); Deacons Clifford S. Wright; Biaggio DiGiovanni; Stephen J. Gordon.
School—St. Benilde Roman Catholic Church, Metairie, Louisiana School, 1801 Division St., Metairie, 70001-2799. Tel: 504-833-9894; Fax: 504-834-4380; Email: stbenilde@stbenilde.com; Web: www.stbenilde.com. Mr. Thomas Huck, Prin. Clergy 11; Lay Teachers 23; Students 255.
*Catechesis Religious Program—*Students 289.
4—St. Catherine of Siena (1921)
105 Bonnabel Blvd., Metairie, 70005-3736.
Tel: 504-835-9343; Email: info@stcatherineparish.com. Revs. Timothy D. Hedrick; Garrett M. O'Brien, J.C.L.; Deacons Michael Coney; Don M. Richard; Paul G. Hauck.
School—St. Catherine of Siena School, 400 Codifer Blvd., Metairie, 70005-3797. Tel: 504-831-1166; Fax: 504-833-8982; Web: www.scsgators.org. Mrs. Kimberlie Haik Kilroy, Prin. Lay Teachers 88; Students 845.
*Catechesis Religious Program—*Email: malley@stcatherineparish.com. Michelle Alley, D.R.E. Students 196.
5—St. Christopher the Martyr (1947)
309 Manson Ave., Metairie, 70001-4898.
Tel: 504-837-8214. Revs. Frank Candalisa; Raymond Igbogidi, Parochial Vicar; Deacons Charles Duke; Gerald J. Martinez; Philip C. McManamon.
School—St. Christopher the Martyr School, (Grades Toddler-8), 3900 Derbigny St., Metairie, 70001-4999. Tel: 504-837-6871; Fax: 504-834-0522;
Tel: 504-837-5929; Email: arnochrist@archdiocese-no.org; Web: www.stchristopherschool.org. Ruth Meche, Prin.; Brittany Gradwohl, Admin. Lay Teachers 33; Students (PreK) 157; Students (K-8) 417.
*Catechesis Religious Program—*Students 159.
6—St. Clement of Rome Roman Catholic Church, Metairie, Louisiana (1965)
4317 Richland Ave., Metairie, 70002-3097.
Tel: 504-887-7821; Email: stclement@scrparish.org. Very Rev. Luis F. Rodriguez, V.F.; Rev. David Ducote, Parochial Vicar; Deacons Carlo Maniglia; Robert E. Pendzimaz; Mr. Martin Gutierrez.
School—St. Clement of Rome Roman Catholic Church, Metairie, Louisiana School, 3978 W. Esplanade Ave., Metairie, 70002-3099.
Tel: 504-888-0386; Fax: 504-885-8273; Email: pspeeg@scrschool.org. Patricia Speeg, Prin. Lay Teachers 33; Students 484.
*Catechesis Religious Program—*Students 124.
7—St. Edward the Confessor Roman Catholic Church, Metairie, Louisiana (1964)
4921 W. Metairie Ave., Metairie, 70001-4466.
Tel: 504-888-0703; Email: stedward@steddy.org. Revs. Gerald L. Seiler Jr., M.Div., J.C.L.; Kevin T. DeLerno; Deacons Steven J. Koehler; Timothy G. Meaut.
School—St. Edward the Confessor School, (Grades PreK-7), Tel: 504-888-6353. Dr. Thomas Becker, Prin. Lay Teachers 27; Students 416; Clergy / Religious Teachers 3.
*Catechesis Religious Program—*Trevor D. Huster, D.R.E. Students 51.
Chapel—Hanmaum Korean Catholic Chapel, 4812 W. Napoleon Ave., Metairie, 70001-2364.
Tel: 504-888-8772; Fax: 504-888-2366.
8—St. Francis Xavier (1924)
444 Metairie Rd., Metairie, 70005-4307.
Tel: 504-834-0340; Email: rachelnrylee@yahoo.com; Web: stfrancisxavier.com. Revs. Joseph S. Palermo Jr., J.D.; Thien Nguyen, Parochial Vicar; Deacons Robert D. Normand; Kevin J. Darrah; Virgil M. Wheeler III.
Res.: 105 Vincent Ave., Metairie, 70005.
School—St. Francis Xavier School, 215 Betz Pl., Metairie, 70005-4167. Tel: 504-833-1471; Fax: 504-833-1498. Barbara Martin, Prin. Lay Teachers 37; Students 455.
Catechesis Religious Program— St. Francis Xavier Parish School of Religion Tel: 504-834-0348. Students 76.
9—St. Lawrence the Martyr (1958) Closed. Parish territory assigned to Our Lady of Divine Providence, Metairie. For inquiries regarding sacramental records, contact Our Lady of Divine Providence parish.
10—St. Louis King of France (1947)
1609 Carrollton Ave., Metairie, 70005-1498.
Tel: 504-834-9977; Email: stlouisrectory@aol.com. Rev. Mark S. Raphael, Ph.D.; Deacon J. Glen Casanova.
School—St. Louis King of France School, 1600 Lake Ave., Metairie, 70005-1499. Tel: 504-833-8224; Fax: 504-838-9938; Email: info@slkfschool.com; Web: www.slkfschool.com. Pamela Schott, Prin. Clergy 2; Lay Teachers 80; Students 400.
*Catechesis Religious Program—*Students 35.
11—St. Mary Magdalen (1955)
6425 W. Metairie Ave., Metairie, 70003-4327.
Tel: 504-733-0922; Email: magdalen@smm.nocoxmail.com; Web: www.stmarymagdalenchurch.com. Rev. Christian W. DeLerno Jr.; Deacons James P. Heneghan; James C. LeBlanc.
School—St. Mary Magdalen School, 6421 W. Metairie Ave., Metairie, 70003-4395.
Tel: 504-733-1433; Fax: 504-736-0727; Email: stmarymag@archdiocese-no.org. Ms. Valerie Rodriguez, Prin. Lay Teachers 18; Students 250.
*Catechesis Religious Program—*Tel: 504-733-8980. Linda Earle, D.R.E.; Susie Sullivan, RCIA Coord. Students 67.
12—Our Lady of Divine Providence Roman Catholic Church, Metairie, Louisiana (1965) Assumed parish territory of St. Lawrence the Martyr, Metairie.
1000 N. Starrett Rd., Metairie, 70003-5899.
Tel: 504-466-4511; Email: oldpparish@archdiocese-no.org; Web: www.oldp.org. Rev. Michael J. Mitchell; Deacons Roberto Angeli; Daniel J. Cordes; Roberto J. Garcia; Deborah Federer, Music Min.
Res.: 1029 N. Atlanta St., Metairie, 70003-5899.
School—Our Lady of Divine Providence Roman Catholic Church, Metairie, Louisiana School, 917 N. Atlanta St., Metairie, 70003-5898. Tel: 504-466-0591; Fax: 504-466-0671; Email: oldp@archdiocese-no.org; Web: www.oldpschool.org. Mrs. Elvina DiBartolo, Prin. Lay Teachers 21; Students 222.
*Catechesis Religious Program—*Mrs. Mickie Morris, D.R.E. Students 167.
13—St. Philip Neri (1960)
6500 Kawanee Ave., Metairie, 70003-3298.
Tel: 504-887-5535; Email: hbugler@stphilipneriparish.org. Rev. Msgr. Henry J. Bugler, V.F.; Very Rev. Michael J. Kettenring, V.F., Parochial Vicar; Deacons John P. LeDoux; Thomas P. Lotz; Dennis J. Hickey; Mrs. Yvette F. Ecuyer, Business Mgr.
Child Care—St. Philip Neri Learning Center, (6 weeks to 2 yrs.) Tel: 504-887-2322; Email: lrobinette@stphilipneri.org. Lori Robinette, Dir.
St. Philip Neri CampTastic—(PreK3-7)
Tel: 504-421-9392; Email: cgrote@stphilipneri.org. Wendy Paladino, Dir.
School—St. Philip Neri School, 6600 Kawanee Ave., Metairie, 70003-3199. Tel: 504-887-5600; Fax: 504-456-6857; Web: www.stphilipneri.org. Dr. Carol Stack, Ph.D., Prin. Lay Teachers 50; Students 585; Nursery 125.
*Catechesis Religious Program—*Email: rkirsh59@gmail.com. Ruby Kirsch, Coord. Rel. Educ. Students 81.

Norco, St. Charles Parish, Sacred Heart of Jesus (1959)
401 Spruce St., Norco, 70079-2137.
Tel: 985-764-6503; Email: shn@archdiocese-no.org. Rev. Edmund Akordor; Deacon W. Gerard Gautrau.
School—Sacred Heart of Jesus School, 453 Spruce St., Norco, 70079. Tel: 985-764-9958;
Fax: 985-764-0041; Email: sacredhrtjesus@archdiocese-no.org; Web: sacredheartschoolnorco.org. Laura Delaneuville, Prin. Lay Teachers 14; Students 102.
*Catechesis Religious Program—*Email: c.s.larosa@gmail.com. Cristina Larosa, D.R.E. Students 147.

Paradis, St. Charles Parish, St. John the Baptist (1971)
P.O. Box 1498, Paradis, 70080. Rev. Joseph Duc Dzien.
*Catechesis Religious Program—*Tel: 985-758-1593. Students 80.

Pearl River, St. Tammany Parish, SS. Peter and Paul Roman Catholic Church, Pearl River, Louisiana (1970)
66192 St. Mary Dr., Pearl River, 70452-5705.
Tel: 985-863-2726; Email: info@sppcprla.com; Web: www.sppcprla.com. Rev. Jerry Daniels; Deacons John Patrick Downey; Richard W. Calkins.
*Catechesis Religious Program—*Students 148.

Pointe a la Hache, Plaquemines Parish, St. Thomas (1844) [CEM 2]
17605 Hwy. 15, Pointe A La Hache, 70082.
Tel: 504-682-5607; Tel: 504-278-4008; Email: stthomaschurchparish@gmail.com; Web: myparishstthomas.org. 6951 Hwy. 39, Braithwaite, 70040. Rev. Sampson Abdulai; Mrs. Joni Beshel, Sec.
*Catechesis Religious Program—*Students 55.
Mission—Assumption of the Blessed Virgin Mary Roman Catholic Church, Braithwaite, Louisiana, Fax: 504-682-5617.

PORT SULPHUR, PLAQUEMINES PARISH, ST. PATRICK (1870) [CEM] Assumed St. Jude, Diamond and Our Lady of Good Harbor, Buras and its missions, St. Ann, Empire and St. Anthony, Boothville-Venice.
28698 Hwy. 23, Port Sulphur, 70083-9623.
Tel: 504-564-6792; Email: stpatrickps@aol.com; Web: www.stpatrickportsulphur.com. Rev. Gerard P. Stapleton.
Catechesis Religious Program— Public School of Religion Students 98.
Mission—St. Ann, Empire, 70050.

RESERVE, ST. JOHN THE BAPTIST PARISH
1—OUR LADY OF GRACE ROMAN CATHOLIC CHURCH (1937) (African American)
780 Hwy. 44, P.O. Box 464, Reserve, 70084-0464.
Tel: 985-536-2613; Fax: 985-536-1819; Email: olgchurch@arch-no.org; Web: olgcommunity.com. Rev. Christopher C. Amadi, S.S.J.
Catechesis Religious Program—Tel: 985-536-2028. Myrtle Ann Lucas, D.R.E. Students 34.
2—ST. PETER (1864) [CEM]
1550 Hwy. 44, Reserve, 70084. Tel: 985-536-2887; Email: petesec@rtconline.com. P.O. Box 435, Reserve, 70084-0435. Rev. John J. Marse; Deacon Richard S. Abbondante.
School—St. Peter School, Tel: 985-536-4296; Fax: 985-536-4305. Mrs. Marie Comeaux, Prin. Lay Teachers 18; Students 202.
Catechesis Religious Program—Tel: 985-536-2886. Students 159.

RIVER RIDGE, JEFFERSON PARISH, ST. MATTHEW THE APOSTLE (1959)
10021 Jefferson Hwy., River Ridge, 70123-2498.
Tel: 504-737-4537; Email: church@stmatthew.nocoxmail.com. Revs. Joseph Man Tran; Sidney Speaks, Parochial Vicar; Deacons Wayne A. Lobell; Nathan F. Simoneaux Jr.; Jerry B. Clark Sr.
School—St. Matthew the Apostle School, Tel: 504-737-4604; Fax: 504-738-7985; Web: www.smaschool.net. Lay Teachers 31; Students 337.
Catechesis Religious Program—Students 92.

ST. BERNARD, ST. BERNARD PARISH, ST. BERNARD (1787) [CEM] Assumed parish territory of San Pedro Pescador, Florissant.
2805 Bayou Rd., St. Bernard, 70085.
Tel: 504-281-2267; Email: stbernard@arch-no.org. Rev. Hoang Minh Tuong; Deacon Norbert P. Billiot Jr.
Catechesis Religious Program—Sr. Anne Marie Khuong, F.M.S.R., D.R.E. Students 43.

SLIDELL, ST. TAMMANY PARISH
1—ST. GENEVIEVE ROMAN CATHOLIC CHURCH, SLIDELL, LOUISIANA (1968)
58203 Hwy. 433, Slidell, 70460. Mailing Address: 58025 St. Genevieve Ln., Slidell, 70460.
Tel: 985-643-3832; Email: stgenevieve@stgenevieve.us; Web: www.stgenevieve.us. Rev. Jose Roel G. Lungay; Deacons Daniel B. Haggerty; Daniel L. Dashner; Reginald J. Seymour, Email: rjcmore@bellsouth.net. Res. and Mailing Address: 58031 St. Genevieve Ln., Slidell, 70460.
Catechesis Religious Program—Ona New, C.R.E. Students 54.
2—ST. LUKE THE EVANGELIST ROMAN CATHOLIC CHURCH, SLIDELL, LOUISIANA (1982)
910 Cross Gates Blvd., Slidell, 70461-8414.
Tel: 985-641-6429; Email: office@stlukeslidell.org. Revs. Patrick B. Wattigny; Warren L. Cooper, Sacramental Asst.; Francis Offia, Parochial Vicar; Deacons Harold J. Burke; Ronald C. LeBlanc; Paul G. Augustin; William J. Faustermann Jr.
Catechesis Religious Program—Tel: 985-641-2570; Fax: 985-641-6570. Students 465.
3—ST. MARGARET MARY ROMAN CATHOLIC CHURCH, SLIDELL, LOUISIANA (1965)
1050 Robert Blvd., Slidell, 70458-2098.
Tel: 985-643-6124; Email: stmargaretmary@saintmm.org. Revs. Edward M. Grice; Alexander Guzman, Parochial Vicar; Deacons Gilbert F. Ganucheau Jr.; John C. Weber; Carlos A. Ramirez; Louis F. Bauer; Christopher M. Schneider Sr.; Roberto L. Zambrano.
School—St. Margaret Mary School, Tel: 985-643-4612; Fax: 985-643-4659. Mr. Bobby Ohler, Prin. Lay Teachers 36; Students 646.
Catechesis Religious Program—Tel: 985-649-3055. Students 397.
4—OUR LADY OF LOURDES (1890) [CEM]
400 Westchester Blvd., Slidell, 70458.
Tel: 985-643-4137; Email: mguidry@ollourdes.org. 3924 Berkley St., Slidell, 70458-5143. Very Rev. Wayne C. Paysse, V.F.; Rev. Cletus Orji; Deacons Charles B. Faler Jr.; Robert Dunbar; Warren L. Berault; Peter J. Miranda.
School—Our Lady of Lourdes School, 345 Westchester Pl., Slidell, 70458-5299.
Tel: 985-643-3230; Fax: 985-645-0648. Mr. Michael Buras II, Prin. Lay Teachers 25; Students 460.
Catechesis Religious Program—Email: jstains@ollourdes.org. Janet Stains, D.R.E. Students 267.

TERRYTOWN, JEFFERSON PARISH, CHRIST THE KING (1963)
535 Deerfield Rd., Terrytown, 70056-2899.
Tel: 504-361-1500; Email: ckchurch@bellsouth.net; Web: www.christkingterrytown.com. Rev. Michael Nam Hoang Nguyen; Deacons William B. Jarrell; Walfredo Corral; John J. Walker IV.
School—Christ the King School, 2106 Deerfield Rd., Terrytown, 70056-2899. Tel: 504-367-3601; Fax: 504-367-3679; Email: christkingsch@archdiocese-no.org; Web: www.archdiocese-no.org/ctk. Lay Teachers 22; Students 274.
Catechesis Religious Program—Students 92.

VIOLET, ST. BERNARD PARISH, OUR LADY OF LOURDES ROMAN CATHOLIC CHURCH, VIOLET, LOUISIANA (1916)
2621 Colonial Blvd., Violet, 70092. Tel: 504-682-7070 ; Fax: 504-282-2621; Email: oll@arch-no.org. Rev. Bryan J. Howard; Deacon Craig P. Taffaro Jr.
Catechesis Religious Program—Rhonda Serpas, D.R.E. Students 80.

WAGGAMAN, JEFFERSON PARISH, OUR LADY OF THE ANGELS ROMAN CATHOLIC CHURCH, WAGGAMAN, LOUISIANA (1978) [CEM]
6851 River Rd., Waggaman, 70094-2404.
Tel: 504-436-4459; Fax: 504-436-8465; Email: office@oloa.nocoxmail.com; Web: www.oloacatholicchurch.org. Rev. John M. Perino.
Catechesis Religious Program—Cheryl Carmouche, C.R.E. Students 52.

WESTWEGO, JEFFERSON PARISH, OUR LADY OF PROMPT SUCCOR (1920) [CEM]
146 Fourth St., Westwego, 70094-4297.
Tel: 504-341-9522; Email: olpssecretary@gmail.com; Web: www.olpsw.org. Very Rev. Emile G. (Buddy) Noel, V.F.; Deacon Jose A. Sierra.
School—Our Lady of Prompt Succor School, 531 Avenue A, Westwego, 70094-4294. Tel: 504-341-9505 ; Fax: 504-341-9508. Sr. Anna Bui, Prin. Lay Teachers 17; Sisters 5; Students 283.
Catechesis Religious Program—Email: smsyrri@aol.com. Greg Smith, D.R.E. Students 49.
Mission—Holy Guardian Angels Mission, 1701 Bridge City Ave., Bridge City, Jefferson Parish 70094. Web: www.hgaparish.org.

Non-Parochial Churches & Chapels

NEW ORLEANS, ORLEANS PARISH
1—CATHOLIC CULTURAL HERITAGE CENTER ST. MARY CHAPEL (1845) St. Mary Chapel/Shrine of St. Lazarus of Jerusalem is under the auspices of the rector of St. Louis Cathedral. It also functions as a museum (Catholic Cultural Heritage Center).
Mailing Address: 1100 Chartres St., 70116-2596.
Tel: 504-525-9585; Email: cathedral@arch-no.org. Very Rev. Philip G. Landry, V.F., Rector.
Church: 1116 Chartes St., 70116-2596.
Fax: 504-525-9583. Very Rev. Philip G. Landry, V.F., Rector.
2—CHAPEL OF THE VIETNAMESE MARTYRS (1978) (Vietnamese) Chapel within Mary Queen of Vietnam Parish, New Orleans.
Mailing Address: P.O. Box 870607, 70187-0607. Rev. Nghiem Van Nguyen. In Res., Rev. Joseph Nguyen Van Nguyen.
Church: 14400 Peltier Dr., 70129-1713.
Tel: 504-254-5660; Fax: 504-254-9250.
Catechesis Religious Program—Students 545.
3—ST. JOSEPH CHAPEL (2000)
Mailing Address: c/o Archdiocesan Cemeteries Office, 1000 Howard Ave, Ste. 500, 70113-1903.
Tel: 504-596-3050; Fax: 504-596-3055. St. Joseph Cemetery, 2220 Washington Ave., 70113-2647.
Tel: 504-488-4989; Tel: 504-488-5200.
4—ST. MARY'S ASSUMPTION (1858) (German)
2030 Constance St., 70130-5004. Tel: 504-522-0748; Fax: 504-523-3734; Email: stalphonsusoffice@parishmail.com. Revs. Richard Thibodeau, C.Ss.R.; Allen Weinert, C.Ss.R., Parochial Vicar.
Catechesis Religious Program—Students 67.
5—ST. MARY'S CHAPEL, Associated with St. Alphonsus Parish.
1516 Jackson Ave., 70130. Tel: 504-522-6748; Email: rthibs@aol.com. Revs. Richard Thibodeau, C.Ss.R.; Eugene Harrison, C.Ss.R.
6—NATIONAL SHRINE OF OUR LADY OF PROMPT SUCCOR (1926)
Mailing Address: 2734 Nashville Ave., 70115.
Tel: 504-866-0216; Tel: 504-866-0200; Email: shrineolps@gmail.com; Web: www.shrineofourladyofpromptsuccor.com. 2701 State St., 70118. Sr. Carolyn Brockland, O.S.U., Dir.
National Votive Shrine of Our Lady of Prompt Succor.
7—ST. ROCH CHAPEL
St. Roch Cemetery, 1725 St. Roch Ave., 70117-8223.
Tel: 504-304-0576; Tel: 504-482-5065. Mailing Address: c/o Archdiocesan Cemeteries Office, 1000 Howard Ave., Ste. 500, 70113. Tel: 504-596-3050; Fax: 504-596-3055.
8—ST. TAMMANY CATHOLIC CEMETERY
7887 Walmsley Ave., 70125.

MANDEVILLE, ST. TAMMANY PARISH, ST. DYMPHNA CATHOLIC CENTER AND CHAPEL (1971)
Northlake Behavioral Health System, 23515 Hwy. 190, Mandeville, 70470-3850. For information, please call the Healthcare Chaplaincy Office, Tel: 504-227-3606.

METAIRIE, JEFFERSON PARISH, HANMAUM KOREAN CATHOLIC CHAPEL (1990)
4812 W. Napoleon Ave., Metairie, 70001-2364.
Tel: 504-888-2366. Rev. Jongkwon Choi, (Korea, South) Chap.

Pilgrimage Shrines

NEW ORLEANS, ORLEANS PARISH
1—NATIONAL SHRINE OF BLESSED FRANCIS XAVIER SEELOS (2000) Within the boundaries of St. Alphonsus Parish.
919 Josephine St., 70130-5071. Tel: 504-525-2495; Fax: 504-581-9181; Web: www.seelos.org; Email: hgrile@seelos.org. Rev. Harry Grile, C.Ss.R., Dir.; Bro. Leo Patin, C.Ss.R., Asst. Dir.
2—NATIONAL SHRINE OF OUR LADY OF PROMPT SUCCOR (1926)
2701 State St., 70118. Tel: 504-866-0200;
Tel: 504-866-0216; Email: shrineolps@gmail.com; Web: www.shrineofourladyofpromptsuccor.com. Mailing Address: Ursuline Convent, 2734 Nashville Ave., 70115. Sr. Carolyn Brockland, O.S.U., Dir.
Legal Title: National Votive Shrine of Our Lady of Prompt Succor.
3—SHRINE OF ST. JUDE THADDEUS (1826) (African American)
411 N. Rampart St., 70112-3594. Tel: 504-525-1551; Fax: 504-525-1827; Email: judeshrine@aol.com. Very Rev. Anthony Rigoli, O.M.I., V.F. Shrine under the auspices of Our Lady of Guadalupe Parish.
Catechesis Religious Program—Tel: 504-522-8546. Students 55.
4—SHRINE OF ST. LAZARUS OF JERUSALEM
Mailing Address: 1100 Chartres St., 70116-2596.
Tel: 504-529-3040. Very Rev. Philip G. Landry, V.F., Rector. Shrine under auspices of St. Louis Cathedral rector.
Church: 1116 Chartres St., 70116-2596.

METAIRIE, JEFFERSON PARISH, ST. ANN NATIONAL SHRINE (1971) Rev. William O'Riordan, V.F.
Church: 4940 Meadowdale St., Metairie, 70006-4040.
Tel: 504-455-7071; Fax: 504-455-7076; Email: contact@stannchurchandshrine.org; Web: stannchurchandshrine.org.
Catechesis Religious Program—Students 82.

Non-Parochial Community

NEW ORLEANS, ORLEANS PARISH, ST. NICHOLAS OF MYRA BYZANTINE CATHOLIC MISSION (1976) Ruthenian Rite Church Jurisdiction.
2435 S. Carrollton Ave, 70118. Mailing Address: P.O. Box 1359, Gray, 70359-1359. Revs. Phillip J. Linden Jr., S.S.J.; Etido Jerome, S.S.J.; Deacon Gregory Haddad, Mission Admin.

Chaplains of Public Institutions.

Hospitals

NEW ORLEANS. *Chateau de Notre Dame Assisted Living*, 2820 Burdette St., 70125.
Tel: 504-866-2741. Rev. Alberto Bermudez.
Chateau de Notre Dame Nursing Home, 2832 Burdette St., 70125. Tel: 504-866-2741. Rev. Alberto Bermudez.
Children's Hospital, 200 Henry Clay Ave., 70118.
Tel: 504-899-9511. Rev. Randy P. Roux, Chap., Deacons Thomas P. Lotz, Pastoral Min., Glenn Wiltz Sr., Pastoral Min.
Kindred Hospital, 3601 Coliseum St., 70115-3687.
Tel: 504-899-1555; Fax: 504-899-1509. Deacon Frank G. DiFulco, Pastoral Min.
Lafon Nursing Facility of the Holy Family, 6900 Chef Menteur Hwy., 70126. Tel: 504-241-6285. Rev. Victor H. Cohea.
New Orleans East Hospital, 5620 Read Blvd., 70127.
Tel: 504-592-6600. Rev. Geoffrey Omondi Muga, F.M.H.
Ochsner Baptist Medical Center, 2700 Napoleon Ave., 70115-6996. Tel: 504-899-9311. Rev. Msgr. Henry H. Engelbrecht, Chap.
Our Lady of Wisdom Healthcare, 5600 General DeGaulle Dr., 70131. Tel: 504-394-5991.
Touro Infirmary, 1401 Foucher St., 70115-3593.
Tel: 504-897-7011; Tel: 504-899-1378. Rev. Douglas C. Brougher, Dir., Pastoral Care & Chap.
Tulane Medical Center, 1415 Tulane Ave., 70112.
Tel: 504-988-5263. Rev. Donald McMahon, O.M.I.
University Medical Center, 2000 Canal St., 70112.
Tel: 504-702-3000. Rev. Anton Ba Phan, Chap.

BOGALUSA. *Our Lady of the Angels Hospital*, 433 Plaza St., Bogalusa, 70427. Tel: 985-730-6706. Attended by Annunciation Parish.

CHALMETTE. *St. Bernard Parish Hospital*, 8050 W. Judge Perez Dr., Chalmette, 70043.
Tel: 504-826-9500. Attended by Our Lady of Prompt Succor Parish (Chalmette).

COVINGTON. *Lakeview Regional Medical Center*, 95 E. Fairway Dr., Covington, 70433. Tel: 504-867-3800. Rev. Dean L. Robins, Chap., Deacon Edward F. Kelley, Pastoral Min.
St. Tammany Hospital, 1202 S. Tyler St., Covington, 70433. Tel: 504-898-4000. Rev. Dean L. Robins, Chap.

GRETNA. *Ochsner Medical Center, West Bank*, 2500 Belle Chasse Hwy., Gretna, 70056-7127.
Tel: 504-392-3131. Rev. Terence Hayden, (Ireland), Deacon James P. Rooney Jr., Pastoral Min.

JEFFERSON. *Ochsner Foundation Hospital*, 1516 S. Clearview Pkwy., Jefferson, 70121-2484.
Tel: 504-842-3000. Rev. Thomas M. McCann III.

KENNER. *Ochsner-Kenner*, 180 W. Esplanade Ave., Kenner, 70065. Tel: 504-464-8065. Rev. Eduardo Gabriel, O.P.

LULING. *Ashton Manor Assisted Living & Memory Care*, 270 Ashton Plantation Blvd., Luling, 70070.
Tel: 985-785-8288. Rev. Edward J. Lauden, Deacon W. Gerard Gautrau.
St. Charles Parish Hospital, 1057 Paul Mallard Rd., Luling, 70070. Tel: 985-785-6242. Deacon Michael A. Fabre Sr.

MANDEVILLE. *Northlake Behavioral Health System*, 123515 Hwy. 190, Mandeville, 70470-3850.
Tel: 504-626-6317; Fax: 504-626-6658. Deacons Ronald C. LeBlanc, Dir. Pastoral Ministry, Ricky J. Suprean, Pastoral Min.

MARRERO. *West Jefferson General Hospital*, 4500 11th St., Marrero, 70072-3191. Tel: 504-347-5511. Revs. Francis Berner, Chap., Eduardo Gabriel, O.P., Deacons Robert Beaumont, Pastoral Min., Quin Ortega, Pastoral Min.
Wynhoven Health Care Center, 1050 Medical Center Blvd., Marrero, 70072-3170. Tel: 504-347-0777.

METAIRIE. *East Jefferson General Hospital*, 4200 Houma Blvd., Metairie, 70002-2970.
Tel: 504-454-4000. Rev. Bartholomew Chukwuman, Chap., Deacons Gary J. Borne, Pastoral Min., Glen Casanova, Pastoral Min., Raymond E. Heap, Pastoral Min., Steven J. Koehler, Pastoral Min.

RESERVE. *Southeast Louisiana War Veterans Home*, 4080 W. Airline Hwy., Reserve, 70084.
Tel: 985-479-4080. Deacon Garland Joseph Roussel Jr.

SLIDELL. *Ochsner-Slidell*, 100 Medical Center Dr., Slidell, 70461. Tel: 985-649-7070. Attended by St. Luke the Evangelist Parish.
Slidell Memorial Hospital, 1001 Gause Blvd., Slidell, 70458-2987. Tel: 985-643-2200. Attended by St. Margaret Mary, Slidell.

Colleges and Universities

NEW ORLEANS. *Delgado College*, 615 City Park Ave., 70119. Email: yam@arch-no.org.
Delgado Community College, School of Nursing, 1450 Claiborne Ave., 70112. Email: yam@arch-no.org.
Father Val McInnes, OP, Center for Catholic Life, Tulane University, 1037 Audubon St., 70118-5294.
Tel: 504-865-2304. Rev. Thomas (Christopher) Schaefgen, O.P., Dir., Ministry.
Louisiana State University Medical Center, 1542 Tulane Ave., 70112. Email: yam@arch-no.org.
Southern University in New Orleans, 6400 Press Dr., 70126. See UNO Newman Center.
University of New Orleans, UNO Newman Center, 2000 Lakeshore Dr., 70148-0001.
Tel: 504-288-6336. Rev. Dennis J. Hayes III, Chap., Mr. Christopher Lazarine, Dir.

Prisons

NEW ORLEANS. *Orleans Parish Criminal Sheriff's Office-Orleans Justice Center*, 2800 Gravier St., 70119. Tel: 504-826-7050. Rev. Terence Hayden, (Ireland) Chap.

ANGIE. *Rayburn Correctional Center*, 27268 Hwy. 21, Angie, 70426-3030. Tel: 985-848-5232. Deacon Michael J. Talbot, Pastoral Min.(Dedicated to Sen. Rayburn).

ANGOLA. *Louisiana State Penitentiary*.
17544 Tunica Trace, Angola, 70712.
Tel: 225-655-4411.

CHALMETTE. *St. Bernard Parish Prison*, St. Bernard Courthouse, Chalmette, 70043-4793.
Tel: 504-279-8823. Tony Fernandez, Chap.

COVINGTON. *St. Tammany Parish Prison*, 10 Cherokee Ln., Covington, 70433-2222. Tel: 985-892-8324. Deacons Timothy R. Jackson, Pastoral Min., Charles R. Swift, Pastoral Min.

EDGARD. *Nelson Coleman Correctional Center*, 2361 Hwy. 18, Edgard, 70049. Tel: 985-785-8189. Deacon Warren R. Pierre, Pastoral Min.

GRETNA. *Jefferson Parish Correctional Center*, P.O. Box 388, Gretna, 70054-0388.
Tel: 504-374-7700, Ext. 3109. Deacon William B. Jarrell, Pastoral Min.

HARVEY. *Rivarde Juvenile Detention Home*, 1525 Manhattan Blvd., Harvey, 70058-3405.
Tel: 504-392-2097. Deacons Tyrell Manieri, Pastoral Min., John J. Walker IV.

On Special Assignment:
Revs.—
Bermudez, Alberto, Chateau de Notre Dame Nursing Home & Apartments, New Orleans
Cooper, Warren L., St. Luke the Evangelist
Maestri, William F., M.Div., M.A.

On Duty Outside the Archdiocese:
Revs.—
Nguyen, Paul Van Tung
Nguyen, Vien The, J.C.L., M.Div.

On Medical Leave of Absence:
Rev.—
Mongeon, Peter M.

Retired:
Most Rev.—
Hughes, Alfred C., S.T.D., (Retired), 2901 S. Carrollton Ave., 70125
Rt. Rev.—
Regan, Patrick, O.S.B., A.A., B.A., M.A., S.T.D., (Retired), St. Joseph Abbey, 75376 River Rd., St. Benedict, 70457-9900
Rev. Msgrs.—
Becnel, Terry B., V.F., (Retired), 705 Gassen St., Luling, 70070
Bilinsky, William, (Retired), 84031 Pine Dr., Folsom, 70437
Doussan, Douglas A., (Retired), Archdiocese of New Orleans Retreat Center, 5500 St. Mary St., Metairie, 70006
Glasgow, T. Gaspard, (Retired), St. John Vianney Villa, 4701 Wichers Dr., Apt. B, Marrero, 70072
Hecker, Lawrence A., (Retired), 1419 Milan St., Apt. 101, 70115
Hill, Robert, (Retired), 3456 Cleary Ave., Apt. 305, Metairie, 70002
Luminais, J. Anthony, (Retired), P.O. Box 344, Hanceville, AL 35077-0344
Massett, Robert D., 4929 York St., Apt. 1112, Metairie, 70001
Rareshide, Lanaux J., (Retired), St. Anthony Mission, 924 Monroe St., Gretna, 70053
Roy, Allen J., (Retired), St. John Vianney Villa, 4701 Wichers Dr., Apt. H, Marrero, 70072
Taormina, Andrew C., J.D., (Retired)
Revs.—
Agudo, Teodoro, O.F.M.Cap., (Spain) (Retired)
Benson, Joseph A., (Retired), St. John Vianney Villa, 4701 Wichers Dr., Apt. A, Marrero, 70072
Blank, William A., (Retired), 148 Heltz St., Garyville, 70051
Braud, Ronald J., (Retired), 2820 Burdette St., Apt. 604, 70125
Brignac, H. L., (Retired), 1400 Haring Rd., La Place, 70068
Caluda, Charles J., (Retired), 3205 Bayou Rd., Saint Bernard, 70085
Carabello, Francis J., (Retired), 840 Oakwood Dr., Terrytown, 70056
Cavalier, Robert C., (Retired), 18072 St. Joseph's Way, Covington, 70435-5623
Dabria, Jerry J., (Retired), 3701 Behrman Pl., Rm. 203, 70114
deWater, Joseph M., (Retired), Riinsburgerweg 4W59A, Voorhut, The Netherlands 2215 RA
Dixon, James R., (Retired), St. Anthony Rectory, 901 N.E. 2nd St., Fort Lauderdale, FL 33301-1621
Fernandez, Luis J., (Retired), VA Medical Center, 6863 S.W. 16th St., Miami, FL 33155-1709
Ferrie, Francis, (Retired), 8128 Plum St., 70118-2012
Francis, Bernard C., (Retired), P.O. Box 546, Hahnville, 70057
Gannon, Patrick, (Retired), 614 7th St., Apt. L-101, Gretna, 70053-6143
Heffner, Carroll, (Retired), 3310 Jefferson Hwy., Jefferson, 70121
Highfill, Brian H., (Retired), 1271 Mound House St., Las Vegas, NV 89110-5900. (Retired Military)
Kieltyka, Robert, (Retired), 423 Cedarwood Dr., Mandeville, 70471
Lobo, Raul Venust, (Retired), St. John Vianney Villa, 4701 Wichers Dr., Apt. F, Marrero, 70072
McGough, William J., (Retired), 309 W. 9th Ave., Covington, 70433
McGrath, Joseph, O.F.M.
Meyer, Leo A., (Retired), 805 Rue Decatur, Metairie, 70005
Morgan, Brendan P., (Retired), P.O. Box 73128, Metairie, 70033
Nguyen, Dominic Duc Huyen, (Retired), 13434 Lourdes St., 70129
Nguyen, Viet Chau, S.S.S., (Retired)
O'Donnell, William J., J.C.L., (Retired), 80335 Hollowhill Rd., Bush, 70431
O'Neill, Michael F., (Retired), 629 Birkdale Cove, Niceville, FL 32578
Pentecost, Denver B., (Retired), 2305 St. Charles Ave., 70130
Perera, Denzil M., (Retired), Center of Jesus the Lord, 1307 Louisiana Ave., 70115
Pham, Bernardo Son, S.D.D., (Retired), 13401 N. Lemans St., 70129
Pham, Vincent Don, (Retired), 1008 Candlelight Ct., Marrero, 70072
Qui, Vincent, (Retired)
Rabe, David L., (Retired), 2233 St. Charles Ave., Apt. 105, 70130
Schott, James E., (Retired), 501 Lake Ave., Apt. 3A, Metairie, 70005
Terrebonne, Burnick J., (Retired), Wynhoven Apartments, 4600 10th St., Unit A, Marrero, 70072
Thomas, Curtis R., (Retired), 625 Olive St., Leavenworth, KS 66048
Tranchina, Joseph, (Retired), 2820 Burdette St., Apt. 519, 70125
Trutter, Carl B., O.P., (Retired), Our Lady of Wisdom Healthcare Center, 5600 General De Gaulle Dr., 70131
Vitte, Jules, (Retired), 62 Grande Rue, 25160 Malbuisson, France
Vu, J.B. Han, (Retired), 10421 Orangewood Ave., Garden Grove, CA 92840-1540.

Permanent Deacons:
Aaron, David P., St. Angela Merici, Metairie
Abbondante, Richard S., St. Peter, Reserve
Adams, Dennis F., Dir. Christopher Homes, Inc., St. Peter, Covington
Alexander, Dwight, St. Raymond & St. Leo the Great, New Orleans
Allen, Charles E., St. Joseph the Worker, Marrero
Angeli, Santiago Roberto, Our Lady of Divine Providence, Metairie
Ardoin, James Clyde, St. Peter, Covington
Armshaw, Cornelius, (Retired)
Attaway, Charles, (On Leave)
Augustin, Paul G., St. Luke the Evangelist, Slidell; Pastoral Min, Reconcile New Orleans/Cafe Reconcile
Balderas, Robert Sr., (Retired)
Bauer, Louis F., St. Margaret Mary, Slidell; Northlake Behavioral Health System
Beaumont, Robert G. Sr., (Retired)
Beckendorf, Edward, Mary Queen of Peace, Mandeville
Berault, Warren L., Our Lady of Lourdes, Slidell
Bertin, Raymond J., St. Ann Church and Shrine, Metairie
Bertucci, Christopher A., St. Pius X, New Orleans
Bialas, James A., Diaconate Advisory & Formation, Our Lady of the Rosary, New Orleans
Billiot, Norbert P. Jr., St. Bernard
Binney, Robert, (Retired)
Blanchard, John, (Retired)
Boe, Kenneth, (Retired - Active)
Borne, Gary J., St. Rita, Harahan
Bourgeois, Donald E., St. Jane de Chantal, Abita Springs
Brady, Richard, Perm. Diaconate Adv. & Formation, St. Louis Cathedral; Master of Ceremonies
Bresler, Patrick
Broussard, Terrel J., St. Maria Goretti; Diaconate Personnel Board
Burke, Harold J., St. Luke the Evangelist; Pastoral Min., Pope John Paul II High School; Pastoral Min., Northshore Regional Medical Center; Slidell
Caffery, Thomas E. Jr., (Retired-Active)
Caldero, David, Divine Mercy, Kenner; Our Lady of the Holy Rosary, Hahnville
Calkins, Richard W., Chap., SS. Peter & Paul, Pearl River; Perm. Diaconate Personnel Bd.
Calvin, Larry Lee, Corpus Christi-Epiphany, New Orleans
Campeaux, Barry G., (Retired-Active)
Campuzano, Luis A., (Retired - Active)
Capaci, Andrea, Divine Mercy, Kenner; Pastoral Min., Archbishop Chapelle High School

Carrillo, Cesar Cornelio, (Retired-Active)
Casadaban, Maurice V., St. Joan of Arc, LaPlace
Casanova, Joseph Glen, Pastoral Min., East Jefferson Hospital; St. Louis King of France, Metairie
Caserta, Piero, St. Agnes, Jefferson
Chetta, Nicholas, St. Angela Merici, Metairie
Cimino, Paul, (Retired-Active)
Clark, Jerry B. Sr., St. Matthew the Apostle, River Ridge; Stella Maris Port Ministry; Diaconate Advisory & Formation
Cohan, Steven R., Our Lady of the Lake, Mandeville
Coney, Michael, St. Catherine of Siena, Metairie
Cordes, Daniel J., Our Lady of Divine Providence; Diaconate Personnel Board
Corral, Walfredo, Christ the King, Terrytown
Coudrain, Mark C., St. Jane de Chantal, Abita Springs
Crago, Jere L.
Curry, William P. Jr., Sacred Heart, Lacombe
Daigle, Irving J., (Retired)
Dardis, Joseph M., St. Anthony of Padua, New Orleans
Darrah, Kevin J., St. Francis Xavier, Metairie
Dashner, Daniel L., St. Genevieve, Slidell
Deichmann, Richard, (Retired)
Dempsey, Patrick L., St. Cletus, Gretna
DiFulco, Frank G., St. Agnes, Jefferson; Pastoral Min., Kindred Hospital
DiGiovanni, Biaggio, St. Benilde, Metairie; Admin., Ozanam Inn, New Orleans
DiGrado, Chris, Master of Ceremonies, St. Patrick, New Orleans
Donnaud, Paul J., (Retired)
Doolen, Philip E., Pastoral Assoc., St. Ann Church & Shrine, Metairie
Dorsey, Dan, (Retired-Active)
Downey, John Patrick, SS Peter and Paul, Pearl River
Drake, Francis W., (Retired)
Drez, Ronald J. Jr., Our Lady of the Rosary, New Orleans
Duet, Ferris J. Jr., (On Leave)
Duffy, Peter E., J.D., (Retired)
Duke, Charles, (Retired-Active)
Dunbar, Robert, Our Lady of Lourdes, Slidell
Duplechain, Raphael Jr., Dir., Permanent Diaconate
Durr, Uriel Andrew, St. Gabriel the Archangel, New Orleans
Eason, Richard B., Good Shepherd, New Orleans
Enger, Leonard E. II, St. Joseph on the Westbank, Gretna; St. Anthony Mission, Gretna
Fabre, Michael A. Sr., St. Anthony of Padua, Luling
Faler, Charles B. Jr., (Retired)
Farinelli, David W., Clinical Supvr. & Counselor, Catholic Counseling Service
Fariss, Jeffrey, (Retired-Active)
Fasullo, Gerard Sr., St. Edward the Confessor, Metairie
Faustermann, William J. Jr., St. Luke the Evangelist, Slidell
Ferran, Steven L., Sacred Hearts, Lacombe; Asst. Dir., Permanent Diaconate; Diaconate Advisory & Formation; Diaconate Personnel Board
Ferretti, Anthony J., (Retired)
Finn, John Joseph, Mary Queen of Peace, Mandeville
Flynn, Dan, St. Rita, Harahan; Catholic Committee on Boy Scouting
Fonseca, Rodrigo Alonso, Center of Jesus the Lord, New Orleans
Fortunato, Jody J., St. Dominic, New Orleans
Foster, Oscar G. III, (On Duty Outside the Diocese)
Fox, Thomas H., St. Ann Church & Shrine; Pastoral Min., Holy Cross High School
Francis, Owen P., Our Lady of the Lake
Frantz, Jay C., Our Lady of the Lake Roman Catholic Church, Mandeville; Diaconate Personnel Board
Fray, Ralph, (Retired)
Gabriel, Brian A., Our Lady Star of the Sea, New Orleans
Ganucheau, Gilbert F. Jr., St. Margaret Mary, Slidell
Garcia, Roberto J., Our Lady of Divine Providence, Metairie
Garon, Henry A., (Retired)
Gautrau, W. Gerard, Sacred Heart of Jesus, Norco
Glapion, Lloyd St. Clair, (Retired)
Glover, John A., St. Anselm, Madisonville
Gordon, Stephen J., St. Benilde, Metairie
Gross, Greg Andrew Nicholas, Our Lady of Perpetual Help, Kenner; Pastoral Min., Ozanam Inn
Gubert, Norbert
Guidry, Ronald, Master of Ceremonies, St. Louis Cathedral, New Orleans
Guillory, Abner J., St. Anselm, Madisonville
Guitterez, Clayton J., (On Leave)
Guntherberg, Thomas James, (On Leave)
Haggerty, Daniel B., Dir. Pastoral Care, F.B.I. & Slidell Police Dept.; St. Genevieve, Slidell
Hamm, John David, (Retired - Active), (On Leave)
Hartman, Charles, (Retired)
Hauck, Paul G., St. Catherine of Siena, Metairie; Pastoral Min., Ozanam Inn
Heap, Raymond E., Pastoral Min., East Jefferson Hospital, Metairie; St. Angela Merici, Metairie
Heine, Charles, (Retired-Active)
Heneghan, James P., St. Margaret Mary, Slidell
Herrick, Dean D., Holy Name of Mary, Algiers
Hickey, Dennis J., St. Philip Neri, Metairie
Houston, Lawrence C., St. Peter Claver, New Orleans
Howard, John, (Retired)
Huck, Lloyd E., Transfiguration of the Lord, New Orleans
Iverson, Ellis, St. Benedict, Mandeville
Jackson, Timothy R., Mary Queen of Peace, Mandeville
Jarrell, William B., Christ the King, Terrytown; Pastoral Minister, Jefferson Parish Correctional Center
Johnson, David L., (On Duty Outside Diocese)
Johnson, Dwight J., (Retired)
Jung, John A., St. Peter, Covington
Kelley, Edward Francis, Annunciation, Bogalusa
Klause, Brian Joseph, (On Leave)
Koehler, Steven J., St. Edward the Confessor, Metairie; Pastoral Min., East Jefferson General Hospital; Diaconate Advisory & Formation
Kratchovil, Thomas M., St. Francis of Assisi, New Orleans
Labadot, Gerard L., St. Joseph Church & Shrine on the West Bank
Labranche, Frans Jr., J.D., (Retired-Active)
Landry, Coy, (Retired-Active)
LeBlanc, James C., St. Mary Magdalen, Metairie
LeBlanc, Nolen J., St. Rita, Harahan
LeBlanc, Ronald C., St. Luke the Evangelist, Slidell
LeDoux, John P., St. Philip Neri, Metairie
Levy, Gary T., St. Pius X, New Orleans
Lewis, Raymond, (Retired)
Lobell, Wayne A., St. Matthew the Apostle, River Ridge; Stella Maris Port Ministry; Diaconate Advisory & Formation
Lorenz, Fallon Herbert, (Retired-Active)
Lotz, Thomas P., St. Philip Neri, Metairie; Pastoral Min., Children's Hospital
Luke, Nelvin, (Retired - Active)
Madere, Kenneth P., (Active-Retired)
Manieri, Tyrell, St. Martha, Harvey; Infant Jesus of Prague Mission; Pastoral Min., Rivarde Juvenile Detention Center, Gretna; Diaconate Advisory & Formation
Maniglia, Carlo, St. Clement of Rome, Metairie; Pastoral Min., Orleans Parish Criminal Sheriff's Office / Community Correctional Center
Martinez, Gerald J., St. Christopher the Martyr
Martinsen, Noel W., Divine Mercy, Kenner
McKnight, Brian M. Sr., Divine Mercy, Kenner
McManamon, Philip C., St. Christopher the Martyr, Metairie
Meaut, Timothy G., St. Edward the Confessor, Metairie
Mendel, August B., (Retired)
Mendieta, Roberto, (Retired)
Merritt, George E. Jr., Our Lady of Perpetual Help, Belle Chasse
Miller, Graylin J., St. Paul the Apostle, New Orleans
Minor, Francis M., (On Duty Outside the Archdiocese)
Miranda, Peter J., Our Lady of Lourdes, Slidell
Morris, Edward R., St. Anselm, Madisonville
Murphy, Larry, St. Martha, Harvey; Infant Jesus of Prague Mission, Harvey
Musso, Daniel P., St. Benedict, Covington
Normand, Robert D., St. Francis Xavier, Metairie
Nuss, Henry, St. Mary Magdalen, Metairie
Oney, Larry D., Divine Mercy, Kenner
Ortega, Quin, Immaculate Conception, Marrero
Parulan, Lino G., Our Lady of Prompt Succor, Chalmette; Pastoral Min., Stella Maris Port Ministry
Pendzimaz, Robert E., St. Clement of Rome, Metairie
Perez, Jose D., (On Duty Outside Archdiocese)
Pierre, Warren R., St. John the Baptist, Edgard; Pastoral Min., Nelson Coleman Correctional Center, St. Charles Parish
Pippenger, John, St. Dominic, New Orleans
Prestenbach, Ozema J., Our Lady of the Angels, Waggaman
Ramirez, Carlos Alfredo, Hispanic Apostolate-Northshore
Raper, Edward S. Jr., St. Andrew the Apostle, New Orleans
Raspino, Andrew P. Sr., Our Lady of the Lake, Mandeville
Rayfield, Rudolph J. Sr., Our Lady of Guadalupe, New Orleans, Exec. Dir., Society of St. Vincent de Paul
Reynolds, Daniel F., Holy Spirit; Pastoral Min., Kindred Hospital, New Orleans
Richard, Don Michael, St. Catherine of Siena, Metairie
Richardson, Ray, (Retired)
Rivere, Raymond H., (Retired)
Rizzo, Peter C., Transfiguration of the Lord, New Orleans
Roberts, Virgil D., St. Peter, Covington
Robicheaux, Wilfred Jr., St. Joachim, Marrero; Mgr., St. John Vianney Villa
Rooney, James P. Jr., Visitation of Our Lady; Pastoral Min., Ochsner Medical Center, Westbank
Rosato, Joseph R., Tulane Catholic Center; Pastoral Min., Christ the Healer Prog.
Roussel, Garland Joseph Jr., St. Hubert, Garyville
Roussel, Theodore J., (Retired)
Scalise, Bertrand Jr., (On Duty Outside the Archdiocese)
Schexnayder, Harry, St. Charles Borromeo, Destrehan
Schmidt, Gilbert R., St. Angela Merici, Metairie; Master of Ceremonies
Schneider, Christopher M. Sr., St. Margaret Mary, Slidell
Seymour, Reginald John, St. Genevieve, Slidell; Master of Ceremonies
Shartle, George (Butch), Mary Queen of Peace, Mandeville
Shelton, Royal C., St. Raymond-St. Leo the Great, New Orleans
Sierra, Jose A., Our Lady of Prompt Succor, Westwego; Master of Ceremonies
Simmons, James H., Immaculate Conception, Marrero
Simoneaux, Nathan F. Jr., St. Matthew the Apostle, River Ridge; Diaconate Advisory & Formation
Smith, Charles J., (On Duty Outside Archdiocese)
Smith, Troy Anthony, St. Raymond-St. Leo the Great
Soileau, Brian P. Sr., St. Martha, Harvey; Infant Jesus of Prague Mission, Harvey
Sperier, Stephen W., Most Holy Trinity, Covington
St. Germain, Donald R. Jr., St. John of the Cross, Lacombe
St. Pierre, Thomas Joseph, Ascension of Our Lord, La Place
Stahl, Rudolph W., (On Duty Outside the Archdiocese)
Steel, Kevin M., St. John Bosco, Harvey
Stein, Jeffrey J., St. John the Baptist, Folsom
Stevens, Allen, Pastoral Assoc., St. Peter Claver, New Orleans
Stohlman, Michael H., St. Charles Borromeo, Destrehan
Suprean, Ricky J., St. John of the Cross, Lacombe; Pastoral Min., Northlake Behavioral Health System
Swift, Charles R., Most Holy Trinity, Covington
Taffaro, Craig P. Jr., Our Lady of Lourdes, Violet
Talbot, Michael J., St. Jane de Chantal Abita Springs; Pastoral Min., Dir. Pastoral Care, Rayburn Correctional Center, Angie; Diaconate Advisory & Formation
Taylor, Michael J., Blessed Trinity, New Orleans
Templet, Eugene P., SS. Peter & Paul, Pearl River; Diaconate Adv. & Formation
Toups, Wilbur A., St. Francis of Assisi, New Orleans
Tran, Leo, St. Jerome, Kenner
Tran, Vihn V., Mary Queen of Vietnam, New Orleans; Our Lady of LaVang Mission, New Orleans
Tully, Jeffrey R., St. Charles Borromeo, Destrehan; Healthcare Chaplaincy Coord.
Uhlich, Kenneth J. Jr., Most Holy Trinity, Covington
Venturella, James A., Visitation of Our Lady; Diaconate Advisory & Formation
Vincent, Daniel P., (On Duty Outside Archdiocese)
Vincent, Harold A., Dir. of Pastoral Care, Xavier University of Louisiana
Vincent, Leslie D., (Retired)
Walker, John J. IV, Christ the King, Terrytown; Pastoral Min., Rivarde Juvenile Detention Ctr.
Warriner, A. David Jr., Master of Ceremonies, St. Louis Cathedral; Coord., Court of Second Instance, Metropolitan Tribunal; Vice Chancellor; Delegate, Dispensations & Permissions; Defender of the Bond
Watley, Jesse A., Blessed Francis Xavier Seelos, New Orleans; Master of Ceremonies
Weber, John C., St. Margaret Mary, Slidell
Weil, Jay J. III, (On Leave)
Wellmeyer, Henry P., St. Anselm, Madisonville
Wheeler, Virgil M. III, St. Francis Xavier, Metaire
Whitehouse, Michael P., Our Lady of Lourdes, Slidell

Williams, Herman J., Pastoral Assoc., St. Joseph Church & Shrine, Gretna
Wiltz, Glenn J., St. James Major, New Orleans; Pastoral Min., Children's Hospital
Wright, Clifford S., St. Benilde, Metairie
Zambrano, Roberto L., St. Margaret Mary, Slidell
Zimmer, Julius T., St. John the Baptist, Folsom.

INSTITUTIONS LOCATED IN DIOCESE

[A] SEMINARIES, ARCHDIOCESAN

NEW ORLEANS. *Notre Dame Seminary Graduate School of Theology* (1923) 2901 S. Carrollton Ave., 70118-4391. Tel: 504-866-7426; Fax: 504-866-3119; Email: jhattier@nds.edu; Web: www.nds.edu. Laymen 12; Priests 13; Seminarians 135.

Administration: Very Rev. James A. Wehner, S.T.D., Pres. & Rector; Deborah Panepinto, Registrar; Max Tenney, Dir.; Revs. Joseph M. Krafft, M.A.D.M., M.Div., D.Min., Dir. Pastoral Field Education; Minh Phan, S.T.L., S.T.D., Dir. Pre-Theology & Theology; Deogratias O. Ekisa, S.T.L., S.T.D., Vice Rector & Dir. Human Formation; Dr. Rebecca Maloney, Ph.D., Assoc. Academic Dean & Dir. Institutional Effectiveness; Thomas Bender IV, M.L.I.S., Librarian; Travis Gehrkin, Dir. Facilities; Ms. Michelle W. Klein, Business Mgr.; Thomas J. Neal, M.A., M.Div., Ph. D., Academic Dean; James Jacobs, M.A., Ph.D., M.T.S., Assoc. Academic Dean & Chair of Phil.

Faculty: Most Rev. Alfred C. Hughes, S.T.D., (Retired); Jennifer E. Miller, S.T.D., Prof. Moral Theology; Rev. Msgr. Christopher Nalty, J.C.L., Prof. Canon Law; Michael J. Piazza, M.M., M.Ed., Dir. Sacred Music; Revs. David Kelly, M.S., Lic., Ph.D.; Mark S. Raphael, Ph.D., Prof. Historical Theology; Joseph S. Palermo Jr., J.D.; Jeffrey A. Montz, S.T.L., Prof. Spiritual Theology; Nile C. Gross, Prof. Sacred Liturgy; Mark Barker, Ph.D.; David Liberto, M.A., Ph.D.; Mr. Angelo Lupinetti, M.A.; Mr. Kevin Redmann, Ph.D. Candidate; Gregory Vall, Ph.D., Prof. Sacred Signature; Revs. Gerald L. Seiler Jr., M.Div., J.C.L., Canon Law; Philip Neri Powell, O.P., Ph.D., Homiletics; Jordan Haddad; Rev. Timothy D. Hedrick; Kim Navarro; Rev. Kurt R. Young.

ST. BENEDICT. *Saint Joseph Seminary College* (1890) 75376 River Rd., St. Benedict, 70457-9999. Tel: 985-867-2232; Fax: 504-867-2295; Email: rectorsec@sjasc.edu; Web: www.sjasc.edu. Very Rev. Gregory M. Boquet, O.S.B., M.A., Pres. & Rector; Rev. Matthew R. Clark, O.S.B., B.A., M.A., Vice Pres.; Mrs. Jennifer Whitehouse, CFO; Rev. Jonathan Wallis, M.Ed., M.Div., M.A., S.T.L., Dean; Rt. Rev. Justin Brown, O.S.B., Abbot; Caroline Bizot, Registrar; Cindy Markham; Brenton Addison, Dir. Health & Wellness; Jared Zeringue, Counselor; Scott Wallace, Dir. Institutional Advancement; Rev. Kenneth G. Davis, O.F.M. Conv., Spiritual Advisor/Care Svcs. Benedictine Monks. Conducted by Provinces of New Orleans and Mobile and Monks of St. Joseph's Abbey. Religious Teachers 1; Lay Teachers 24; Priests 11; Seminarians 137.

Faculty: Michael Barocco, B.A., M.Ed., Admin.; Daniel Burns, B.A., M.A., Ph.D.; David Arbo, B.A., M.S.; Revs. William J. Farge, S.J., B.A., M.A., S.T.L., Ph.D.; Augustine E. Foley, O.S.B., B.A., M.T.S., M.A., S.T.B.; Ms. Josette Beaulieu-Grace, B.A., M.A.; Dianna Laurent, B.A., M.A., Ph.D.; Gregory Williams, B.A., M.A.; Casey Edler, B.A., M.A.; Robert Calmes, B.S., M.A.; Cory Hayes, B.A., M.A., Ph.D.; Revs. David K. Seid, O.P., B.A., M.A., M.A.Th., M.A.Ph.; Damian Hinojosa, B.A., M.A., Ph.D., M.Div.; Jude Israel, O.S.B., B.S., M.Ed., M.A.; Ben Frederick, B.M.Ed., M.M.Ed.; Jude Lupinetti, B.A., M.A., Ph.D., M.Cert; Robert Berger; Geoffrey Bain; Aimee Barrios; Joseph Bass; Samuel Fontana; John E. Hebert, B.A., M.A., Ph.D.; Jennifer Heil; Bro. Emmanuel Labrise, O.S.B.; Michael Lane; Robert Schmidt; Timothy Silva.

Professional Lay Staff: Todd Russell, IT Dir. & Webmaster; Chad Harvey, IT Asst. Dir.; Andrea Boudreaux, Accts. Payable; Bonnie Bess Wood, Librarian; Jo Ann Montalbano, M.L.I.S., Asst. Librarian.

[B] SEMINARIES, RELIGIOUS OR SCHOLASTICATES

METAIRIE. *Congregation of the Mother Coredemptrix Formation House* (1991) 112 Lilac St., Metairie, 70005-1817. Tel: 504-835-9746; Fax: 504-835-9746. Brothers 5; Priests 1.

[C] DIOCESAN EDUCATIONAL INSTITUTIONS

NEW ORLEANS. *Magnificat House* Vocation House of Discernment for Women 2729 Lowerline St., 70125. Tel: 504-227-3203; Tel: 504-861-6281. Sr. Gloria Murillo, S.T.J., Dir.

[D] COLLEGES AND UNIVERSITIES

NEW ORLEANS. *Loyola University New Orleans* (1912) 6363 St. Charles Ave., 70118-6195.
Tel: 504-865-2011 (General);
Tel: 504-865-3847 (Pres. Office); Fax: 504-865-3851 ; Email: pres@loyno.edu; Web: www.loyno.edu. Tania Tetlow, Pres.; Revs. Gregory S. Waldrop, S.J., B.A., M.S., S.T.B., M.A., Rector; Theodore A. Dziak, S.J., Vice Pres.; Maria Calzada, Vice Pres., Email: calzada@loyno.edu; Revs. James C. Carter, S.J., Prof.; Lawrence Moore, S.J., Prof., Dean, College of Law; Peter S. Rogers, S.J., Prof.; Alfred C. Kammer, S.J., B.A., M.A., J.D., Prof., (New Orleans Society of Jesus); (New Orleans Province of the Society of Jesus); Robert S. Gerlich, S.J., Prof.; Edward Vacek, S.J., Prof.; Gregg Grovenburg, S.J., Campus Min. Religious Teachers 9; Lay Teachers 485; Priests 10; Sisters 2; Students 4,864.

University of Holy Cross, 4123 Woodland Dr., 70131-7399. Tel: 504-394-7744; Fax: 504-391-2421; Email: communications@uhcno.edu; Email: jpierce@uhcno.edu; Email: ktedesco@uhcno.edu; Web: uhcno.edu. David M. "Buck" Landry, Pres.; Arleen Wehle, Vice Pres. Fin. Mgmt. & Admin.; Diana Schaubhut, Librarian

Our Lady of Holy Cross College Religious Teachers 11; Lay Teachers 157; Priests 2; Congregation of the Sisters Marianites of Holy Cross 1; Students 1,227; Total Staff 71.

Xavier University of Louisiana (Coed) One Drexel Dr., 70125-1098. Tel: 504-520-7411; Email: apply@xula.edu; Web: www.xula.edu. Dr. C. Reynold Verret, Pres.; Rev. Etido Jerome, S.S.J., Univ. Chap.; Mrs. Lisa Lewis McClain, Assoc. Dir., Campus Ministry. Brothers 1; Religious Teachers 2; Lay Teachers 222; Priests 2; Sisters 4; Students 3,231.

[E] HIGH SCHOOLS, ARCHDIOCESAN

NEW ORLEANS. *Holy Rosary High School* (1996) (Grades 8-12), 2437 Jena St., 70115.
Tel: 504-482-7173; Fax: 504-482-7229; Email: contactus@holyrosarynola.org; Web: www.holyrosarynola.org. Cheryl Orillion, Prin.; Jan Del Corral, Librarian. Lay Teachers 16; Students 63.

COVINGTON. *Archbishop Hannan High School*, 71324 Hwy. 1077, Covington, 70433. Tel: 985-249-6363; Fax: 985-249-6370; Email: principal@hannanhigh.org; Web: www.hannanhigh.org. Rev. Charles L. Latour, O.P., Prin.; Donalyn Hassenboehler, Ph.D., Academic Dean; Nancy Baird, Ph.D., Asst. Prin.; Denis Schexnaydre, Dir. Finance & Facilities; Steven Shepherd, Dir. Institutional Advancement. Lay Teachers 54; Priests 1; Students 618.

St. Scholastica Academy, 122 S. Massachusetts St., Covington, 70433. Tel: 985-892-2540;
Fax: 985-893-5256; Email: claforge@ssacad.org; Web: www.ssacad.org. Dr. Cissy LaForge, B.S., M.Ed., Ph.D., Prin. Lay Teachers 40; Students 485.

LA PLACE. *St. Charles Catholic High School*, 100 Dominican Dr., La Place, 70068-3499.
Tel: 985-652-3809; Fax: 985-652-2609; Email: stcharlescath@archdiocese-no.org; Web: www.stcharlescatholic.org. Mr. Andrew C. Cupit, Prin.; Angie Louque, Librarian. Lay Teachers 34; Students 430.

MARRERO. *Academy of Our Lady* (2007) 5501 Westbank Exprwy., Marrero, 70072-2934. Tel: 504-341-6217; Fax: 504-341-6229; Email: ourlady@theacademyofourlady.org; Web: www.theacademyofourlady.org. Sr. Michelle Geiger, F.M.A., Prin.; Michelle Maher, Librarian. Girls 553; Lay Teachers 56; Sisters 2.

Archbishop Shaw High School, 1000 Salesian Ln., Marrero, 70072-3052. Tel: 504-340-6727;
Fax: 504-347-9883; Email: arnoshaw@archdiocese.org; Web: www.archbishopshaw.org. Rev. Louis J. Molinelli, S.D.B., Dir.; Mr. Mark Williams, Prin.; Mr. John Corb, Fin. Admin.; Rev/ Gregory Fishel, S.D.B., Campus Min.; Bro. Gerald Meegan, S.D.B., Youth Min.; Rev. Thomas McGahee, S.D.B., Email: mcgahee6@archbisopshaw.us; Mr. Bernard DeSantis III, Media Specialist. Salesians of St. John Bosco. Boys 461; Brothers 3; Religious Teachers 5; Lay Teachers 34; Priests 3.

METAIRIE. *Archbishop Chapelle High School*, 8800 Veterans Blvd., Metairie, 70003-5235.
Tel: 504-467-3105; Fax: 504-466-3191; Email: info@archbishopchapelle.org; Web: www.archbishopchapelle.org. Ms. Leila Benoit, Prin. Lay Teachers 50; Priests 1; Students 600.

Archbishop Rummel High School, 1901 Severn Ave., Metairie, 70001. Tel: 504-834-5592;
Fax: 504-832-4016; Email: info@rummelraiders.com; Web: www.rummelraiders.com. Mr. Marc Milano, Prin.; Douglas Neill, Vice Prin., Vice Prin. Boys 659; Lay Teachers 54.

Archbishop Rummel Alumni Association,
Fax: 504-834-5592; Web: www.rummelraiders.com. Douglas Tillman, Pres.

SLIDELL. *Pope John Paul II Catholic High School* (1980) 1901 Jaguar Dr., Slidell, 70461-9098.
Tel: 985-649-0914; Fax: 985-649-5494; Email: info@pjp.org; Web: www.pjp.org. Douglas Triche, Prin.; Michael Bourgeois, Campus Min.; Lise Bremond, Asst. Prin.; Sherri Dutreix, Advancement Dir.; Kaitlin Short, Counselor; Sal Vinterella, Counselor. Religious Teachers 3; Lay Teachers 25; Students 338.

[F] HIGH SCHOOLS, RELIGIOUS COMMUNITY SPONSORED

NEW ORLEANS. *Academy of the Sacred Heart "The Rosary"* (1887) 4521 St. Charles Ave., 70115-9990. Tel: 504-891-1943; Fax: 504-891-9939; Email: ash@ashrosary.org; Web: www.ashrosary.org. Sr. Melanie A. Guste, R.S.C.J., Ph.D., Headmistress; Julie Boyd, Prin.; Mrs. Josephine Schloegel, Librarian. Girls 220; Lay Teachers 29; Carmelites 1.

St. Augustine High School (1951) (Grades 6-12), 2600 A.P. Tureaud Ave., 70119-1299. Tel: 504-944-2424; Fax: 504-947-7712; Email: staug@purpleknights.com; Web: www.StAugNola.org. Sean Goodwin, Prin.; Rev. Henry J. Davis, S.S.J., Dir. of Religious Education; Kenneth St. Charles, CEO. Brothers 1; Religious Teachers 5; Lay Teachers 49; Sisters 1; Students 600.

Brother Martin High School (1869) (Grades 8-12), 4401 Elysian Fields Ave., 70122-3898.
Tel: 504-283-1561; Fax: 504-286-8462; Email: gmrando@cox.net; Email: lgreco@brothermartin.com; Web: brothermartin.com. Mr. John J. Devlin III; Mr. Gregory Rando, Pres.; Ryan Gallagher, Prin.; Keiren Aucoin, Librarian. Boys 1,125; Brothers of the Sacred Heart 3; Religious Teachers 1; Lay Teachers 108.

Cabrini High School (1959) (Grades 8-12), 1400 Moss St., 70119-2904. Tel: 504-482-1193;
Fax: 504-483-8671; Email: admin@cabrinihigh.com; Web: www.cabrinihigh.com. Mr. Jack Truxillo, Pres.; Mrs. Yvonne L. Hrapmann, Prin.; Vivian Coutin, Academic Asst. Prin.; Cristen Watters, Dean. Girls 400; Lay Teachers 41; Missionary Sisters of the Sacred Heart 1.

Cabrini High School, Inc., Tel: 504-482-1193;
Fax: 504-483-8673; Web: cabrinihigh.com. Mrs. Yvonne L. Hrapmann, Prin.; Sandra Granier, Librarian.

De La Salle High School (1949) (Grades 10-12), (Coed) 5300 St. Charles Ave., 70115-4999.
Tel: 504-895-5717; Fax: 504-895-1300; Email: mgiambelluca@delasallenola.com; Web: www.delasallenola.com. Mr. Michael A. Giambelluca, Pres.; Mr. Paul Kelly, Prin.; Mrs. Jessica Atwood, Admissions Dir. Lay Teachers 39; Students 596.

Holy Cross School (1879) (Grades 5-12), (Middle & High School Campus) 5500 Paris Ave., 70122-2659. Tel: 504-942-3100; Email: contacthc@holycrosstigers.com; Web: www.holycrosstigers.com. Sean Martin, Headmaster; Dr. Joseph H. Murry Jr., High School Prin.; Rev. David Ducote, Chap. Boys 980; Lay Teachers 73.

Jesuit High School (1847) (Boys) 4133 Banks St., 70119-6883. Tel: 504-486-6631; Fax: 504-483-3816; Email: principal@jesuitnola.org; Web: www.jesuitnola.org. Mr. Peter S. Kernion, Prin.; Revs. Christopher Fronk, Pres.; Kevin B. Dyer, S.J., Chap.; John Brown, S.J., Rector. Boys 1,371; Brothers 2; Religious Teachers 8; Lay Teachers 111; Priests 6.

St. Mary's Academy of the Holy Family, Mailing Address: 6905 Chef Menteur Blvd., 70126-5215.
Tel: 504-245-0318; Fax: 504-245-0422; Email: smaoffice@archdiocese-no.org; Web: www.smaneworleans.com. Sisters Clare of Assisi Pierre, S.S.F., Pres.; Jennie Jones, S.S.F., Prin.; Michelle Ochillo. Lay Teachers 44; Sisters 8; Teachers 52.

St. Mary's Dominican High School (1860) 7701 Walmsley Ave., 70125-3494. Tel: 504-865-9401;
Fax: 504-866-5958; Email: president@stmarysdominican.org; Web: www.stmarysdominican.org. Dr. Cynthia A. Thomas, Ed.D., Pres.; Susan Finney, Librarian; Mrs. Carolyn Favre, Prin. Brothers 1; Religious Teachers 2; Lay Teachers 74; Sisters 3; Students 8,898.

Mount Carmel Academy (1833) 7027 Milne Blvd., 70124-2395. Tel: 504-288-7626; Fax: 504-288-7629; Email: mca@mcacubs.org; Email: admissions@mcacubs.org; Web: www.mcacubs.com. Sr. Camille Anne Campbell, O.Carm., M.A., Pres.; Ms. Beth Ann Simno, Prin.; Mrs. Terri Rousey, Librarian; Rev. Paul Clark, Chap. Congregation of Our Lady of Mount Carmel. Girls 1,232; Lay Teachers 138; Sisters 2.

Ursuline Academy, (Grades 8-12), Secondary Dept. Day School College Prep. 2635 State St., 70118-6399. Tel: 504-861-9150; Fax: 504-861-7392; Email: admissions@uanola.org; Email: info@uanola.org; Web: www.uanola.org. Mrs. Karen McNay, Pres.; Mrs. Alice Bairnsfather, Prin. Girls 317; Lay Teachers 34.

COVINGTON. *The St. Paul's School* (1911) (Grades 8-12), Mailing Address: P.O. Box 928, Covington, 70434-0928. Tel: 985-892-3200; Fax: 985-892-4048; Email: stpauls@stpauls.com; Web: www.stpauls.com. 917 S. Jahncke Ave., Covington, 70433. Bro. Raymond Bulliard, F.S.C., Pres.; Mr. Trevor Watkins, A.F.S.C., Prin. Day School for Young Men Brothers of the Christian Schools of the San Francisco-New Orleans Province 15; Religious Teachers 3; Lay Teachers 60; Students 850.

[G] ELEMENTARY SCHOOLS, ARCHDIOCESAN

NEW ORLEANS. *Holy Rosary Academy*, (Grades PreK-7), 2437 Jena St., 70115. Tel: 504-482-7173; Fax: 504-482-7229; Email: contactus@holyrosarynola.org; Web: www.holyrosarynola.org. Cheryl Orillion, Prin.; Jan Del Corral, Librarian. Lay Teachers 14; Students 47.

METAIRIE. *St. Therese Academy*, 917 N. Atlanta St., Metairie, 70003-5898.

[H] ELEMENTARY SCHOOLS - CATHOLIC, OTHER

NEW ORLEANS. *St. Benedict the Moor School* (1998) (Grades PreK-4), 5010 Piety Dr., 70126. Tel: 504-288-2745; Fax: 504-282-9386; Email: stbenmoor@archdiocese-no.org. Drue Dumas, Prin. Lay Teachers 8; Students 84.

Good Shepherd Nativity School (2001) 1839 Agriculture St., 70119. Tel: 504-598-9399; Fax: 504-598-9346; Email: tmoran@thegoodshepherdschool.org; Web: www.thegoodshepherdschool.org. Mr. Thomas G. Moran, Pres.; Mr. Don Boucree, Dean; Luellen Howard, Librarian. Lay Teachers 12; Students 106; Total Staff 24.

Stuart Hall School for Boys, 2032 S. Carrollton Ave., 70118. Tel: 504-861-1954; Fax: 504-861-5389; Email: bhagan@stuarthall.org; Web: www.stuarthall.org. Mr. Kevin Avin, Headmaster; Dr. Bridget Hagan, Asst. Head of School; Nancy Dunphy, Librarian. Lay Teachers 42.

[I] ELEMENTARY SCHOOLS, RELIGIOUS COMMUNITY SPONSORED

NEW ORLEANS. *Academy of the Sacred Heart* (1887) (Grades Toddler-12), 4521 St. Charles Ave., 70115-4831. Tel: 504-891-1943; Fax: 504-891-9939; Email: communications@ashrosary.org; Web: www.ashrosary.org. Sr. Melanie A. Guste, R.S.C.J., Ph.D., Headmistress; Maria Schneider, Early Childhood Div. Head; Laurie Friedrichs, M.S. Div. Head; Julie Boyd, Upper School Division Head; Shara Hammet, Preschool&Lower School Division Head. Starts at age 1. Religious Teachers 4; Lay Teachers 126; Students 731.

Christian Brothers School, St. Anthony Campus, (Grades 5-7), 4600 Canal St., 70119-5893. Tel: 504-488-4426; Email: school@cbs-no.org; Web: www.cbs-no.org. Mr. Joey M. Scaffidi, Pres.; Mr. Richard Neider, Prin.; Mr. Michael Prat, Prin.; Bro. Michael Livaudais, Dir. Boys 595; Brothers 6; Clergy 2; Girls 225; Lay Teachers 20; Students 820.

Christian Brothers School, #8 Friedrichs Ave., City Park, 70119-5893. Tel: 504-486-6770; Email: school@cbs-no.org. Mr. Michael Prat, Prin.; Mr. Joey M. Scaffidi, Pres.

Holy Cross School, (Grades PreK-4), (Primary Campus) 5601 Elysian Fields Ave., 70122. Tel: 504-942-1850; Email: eyounis@holycrosstigers.com; Web: www.holycrosstigers.com. Sean Martin, Headmaster; Eric DesOrmeaux, Prin.; Rev. David Ducote, Chap. Lay Teachers 14; Students 133.

St. Mary's Academy, (Grades PreK-12), 6905 Chef Menteur Blvd., 70126. Tel: 504-245-0200; Fax: 504-245-0422; Email: smaoffice@archdiocese-no.org; Web: www.smaneworleans.com. Sisters Clare of Assisi Pierre, S.S.F., Pres.; Jennie Jones, S.S.F., Prin.; Michelle Ochillo, Librarian. Religious Teachers 9; Lay Teachers 38; Sisters 8; Students 602.

Ursuline Academy of New Orleans, (Grades Toddler-7), 2635 State St., 70118-6399. Tel: 504-861-9150; Fax: 504-861-9159; Email: admissions@uanola.org; Email: info@uanola.org; Web: www.uanola.org. Mrs. Karen McNay, Pres.; Shannon Culotta, Prin. Lay Teachers 28; Students 297.

[J] SPECIAL EDUCATION

NEW ORLEANS. *St. Michael Special School*, 1522 Chippewa St., 70130. Tel: 504-524-7285; Fax: 504-524-5883; Email: stmichspecial@archdiocese-no.org; Web: www.stmichaelspecialschool.com. Ms. Tishna Sauerhoff, Pres. & Prin. Lay Teachers 43; Students 205.

[K] DAY CARE CENTERS, CAMPS AND PRESCHOOLS

NEW ORLEANS. *Carmelite Ministries, Inc. Cub Corner Preschool* (1975) 420 Robt E. Lee Blvd., 70124. Tel: 504-286-8673; Fax: 504-286-8676; Email: cubcornerpreschoolwaitinglist@yahoo.com; Web: www.home.bellsouth.net/p/pwp-mountcarmel. Sr. Gwen Grillot, O.Carm., Exec. Dir.; Elizabeth Coe, Child Care Dir. Pre-School; (A Ministry of the Sisters of Mount Carmel). Lay Staff 29; Religious 3.

St. John Berchmans Child Development Center, 2710 Gentilly Blvd., 70122-3098. Tel: 504-309-8125; Fax: 504-267-4718; Email: stjohnberchmans1@gmail.com. Sr. Andria Donald, S.S.F., Prin.

Lafon Child Development Center (1965) (Not open at this time. Contact the Sisters of the Holy Family for information.) 7024 Chef Menteur Hwy., 70126-5295. Tel: 504-241-3088; Email: g48j@aol.com. Mailing Address: 6901 Chef Menteur Hwy., 70126-5215. Sr. Greta Jupiter, S.S.F., Contact Person.

Rosary Child Development Center (2000) 5100 Willowbrook Dr., 70129-1047. Tel: 504-254-1528; Fax: 504-254-1531; Email: rosarycdc@yahoo.com. Sr. Thu-Ha Nguyen, F.M.S.R., Dir. Total Staff 17; Children (Daily Average) 90.

[L] HOMES FOR CHILDREN AND YOUTH

NEW ORLEANS. *Boys Hope Girls Hope* (1980) Group Homes for Boys and Girls. 4128 Baudin St., 70119. Tel: 504-484-7744; Fax: 504-484-6120; Web: www.bhghnola.org. P.O. Box 19307, 70179. Chuck Roth, Exec. Dir. Bed Capacity 16; Boys 8; Girls 8; Tot Asst. Annually 29; Total Staff 12; College Students 9; Total Assisted 25.

**Covenant House New Orleans* (1987) Home for Runaway, Abused & Homeless Youth aged 16-21. 611 N. Rampart St., 70112-3540. Tel: 504-584-1102; Fax: 504-584-1171; Email: jkelly@covenanthouse.org; Web: covenanthouseno.org. Mr. James R. Kelly, Exec. Dir. Total Staff 60; Total Assisted 1,300.

[M] RESIDENCES, ADULT

NEW ORLEANS. *Ozanam Inn* Multi-purpose shelter for men, women and children 843 Camp St., 70130-3751. Tel: 504-523-1184; Fax: 504-523-1187; Web: www.ozanaminn.org. Clarence Adams, Exec. Dir.; Deacon Biaggio DiGiovanni, Asst. Admin. Sponsored by Society of St. Vincent de Paul. Bed Capacity 96; Total Staff 15; Total Assisted 36,420.

Project Lazarus (1986) Residential Program for Persons with HIV/AIDS P.O. Box 3906, 70177-3906. Tel: 504-949-3609; Fax: 504-944-7944; Email: info@projectlazarus.net; Web: www.projectlazarus.net. Mr. Steve Rivera, Exec. Bed Capacity 23; Tot Asst. Annually 65; Total in Residence 23; Total Staff 24.

[N] HOMES AND RESIDENCES FOR FAMILIES AND SENIOR CITIZENS

NEW ORLEANS. *Annunciation Inn, Inc.*, Mailing Address: 1000 Howard Ave., Ste. 100, 70113. Tel: 504-596-3460; Tel: 504-944-0512; Fax: 504-944-0575; Fax: 504-596-3466; Email: dhicks@chi-ano.org. 1220 Spain St., 70117. Deacon Dennis F. Adams, Exec. Dir.; Dechaun Hicks, Community Mgr.; Fr. Louis Arceneaux, C.M., Chap. Elderly Affordable Housing Units 106.

St. Anthony's Gardens, 7887 Walmsley Ave., 70125. Tel: 504-861-6252; Fax: 504-866-2906; Email: jentwisle@archdiocese-no.org. Jeff Entwisle, Sec.

The Apartments at Mater Dolorosa, Mailing Address: 1000 Howard Ave., Ste. 100, 70113. Tel: 504-596-3460; Tel: 504-865-7222; Fax: 504-596-3466; Fax: 504-861-9225; Email: dpertuit@chi-ano.org. 1226 S. Carrollton Ave., 70118. Deacon Dennis F. Adams, Exec. Dir.; Dagianna Pertuit, Community Mgr.; Rev. Anton Ba Phan, Chap. Elderly Affordable Housing Total Staff 3; Units 68.

Chateau de Notre Dame Residence and Nursing Home 2832 Burdette St., 70125-2596. Tel: 504-866-2741; Fax: 504-866-2861; Email: wplaisance@archdiocese-no.org; Web: cdnd.org. Mr. Wayne Plaisance, CEO. Lay Staff 210; Priests 1; Sisters 2; Residential Units 100; Nursing Beds 171.

Christopher Inn dba Christopher Inn Apts. Elderly Affordable Housing Mailing Address: 1000 Howard Ave., Ste. 100, 70113. Tel: 504-596-3460; Tel: 504-949-0312; Fax: 504-596-3466; Fax: 504-227-3349; Email: gmiller@chi-ano.org. 2110 Royal St., 70116. Deacons Dennis F. Adams, Exec. Dir.; Graylin Miller, Community Mgr. Residents 144; Total Staff 8.

Delille Inn (1987) Mailing Address: 1000 Howard Ave., Ste. 100, 70113. Tel: 504-245-8660; Fax: 504-245-8677; Tel: 504-596-3460; Fax: 504-596-3466; Email: asampia@chi-ano.org. 6924 Chef Menteur Hwy., 70126. Deacon Dennis F. Adams, Exec. Dir.; Sr. Agnes Sampia, Community Mgr. Elderly Affordable Housing Total in Residence 51.

St. John Berchman's Manor, Mailing Address: 1000 Howard Ave., Ste. 100, 70113. Tel: 504-596-3460; Tel: 504-943-9331; Fax: 504-596-3466; Fax: 504-943-9380; Email: dhicks@chi-ano.org. St. John Berchman's Manor, 3400 St. Anthony Ave., 70122. Rev. Anthony M. Bozeman, S.S.J., Chap.; Dechaun Hicks, Community Mgr.; Deacon Dennis F. Adams, Exec. Dir. Elderly Affordable Housing Total Staff 5; Units 149.

Lafon Nursing Facility of the Holy Family, 6900 Chef Menteur Blvd., 70126. Tel: 504-241-6285. Beverly Greenwood, Admin. Sisters of the Holy Family. Bed Capacity 155; Residents 75; Sisters 5; Total Staff 130.

St. Martin's Manor Elderly Affordable Housing 1501 N. Johnson St., 70116. Tel: 504-227-3390; Tel: 504-596-3460; Fax: 504-227-3389; Fax: 504-596-3466; Email: tgoodman@chi-ano.org. Mailing Address: 1000 Howard Ave., Ste. 100, 70113. Deacon Dennis F. Adams, Exec. Dir.; Tanisha Goodman, Community Mgr.; Rev. Henry J. Davis, S.S.J., Chap. Residential Units 140.

The Mental Health Association Development Corporation dba St. Martin House, Mailing Address: 1000 Howard Ave., Ste. 100, 70113. Deacon Dennis F. Adams, Exec. Dir.; Tanisha Goodman, Admin.; Rev. Henry J. Davis, S.S.J., Chap. Affordable Housing for the Mentally Ill Residential Units 12.

Nazareth II, Mailing Address: 1000 Howard Ave., Ste. 100, 70113. Tel: 504-596-3460; Tel: 504-246-9640; Fax: 504-596-3466; Fax: 504-245-4273; Email: smccrary@chi-ano.org. 9640 Hayne Blvd., 70127. Deacon Dennis F. Adams, Exec. Dir.; Shevelle McCrary, Community Mgr.; Rev. Anton Ba Phan, Chap. Elderly Affordable Housing Units 120.

Nazareth Manor dba Nazareth Inn, Mailing Address: 1000 Howard Ave., Ste. 100, 70113. Tel: 504-596-3460; Tel: 504-246-9630; Fax: 504-596-3466; Fax: 504-241-3069; Email: tpoche@chi-ano.org. Nazareth Manor, 9630 Hayne Blvd., 70127. Deacon Dennis F. Adams, Exec. Dir.; Teresa Poche, Community Mgr.; Rev. Anton Ba Phan, Chap. Elderly Affordable Housing Total Staff 12; Apartments 150.

Our Lady of Wisdom Healthcare Center (Inter-Community Health Care, Inc.) 5600 Gen. de Gaulle Dr., 70131. Tel: 504-394-5991; Fax: 504-304-5421; Email: lheisser@arch-no.org; Web: www.olwhealth.org. Ms. Lisa Heisser, Admin. Inter-community healthcare facility for Archdiocesan clergy and Religious Men: Order of Preachers, Society of Jesus, Society of Mary (Marists), Vincentian, Dominican Brothers, Christian Brothers and Brothers of the Sacred Heart; Religious Women: Sisters of St. Joseph of Medaille, Sisters of Mercy, Sisters of the Living Word, Dominican Sisters of Peace, Sisters of the Immaculate Conception, Marianites of the Holy Cross, Sisters of Mount Carmel, Order of Saint Clare (Poor Clares) and Daughters of Charity. Bed Capacity 138; Tot Asst. Annually 210; Total Staff 170.

Villa St. Maurice, Inc., 500 St. Maurice Ave., 70117. Tel: 504-596-3460; Tel: 504-267-9640; Fax: 504-596-3466; Fax: 504-267-9649; Email: tgoodman@chi-ano.org. Deacon Dennis F. Adams, Exec. Dir.; Tanisha Goodman, Community Mgr. Elderly Affordable Housing Residential Units 77.

LA PLACE. *Dubourg Home* dba Place DuBourg (1981) Elderly Affordable Housing. 201 Rue Dubourg, La Place, 70068. Tel: 985-652-1981; Tel: 504-596-3460 ; Fax: 985-651-6147; Fax: 504-596-3466; Email: lrichard@chi-ano.org. Deacon Dennis F. Adams, Exec.; Mrs. Lynn Williams, Community Mgr.; Rev. Albert Villosillo, Chap. Total Staff 6; Units 115.

MANDEVILLE. *Rouquette III* (1998) 4300 Hwy. 22, Mandeville, 70471. Tel: 985-635-0305; Tel: 504-596-3460; Fax: 985-626-5833; Fax: 504-596-3466; Email: edoran@chi-ano.org. Deacon Dennis F. Adams, Exec.; Elizabeth Doran, Community Mgr.; Rev. Warren L. Cooper, Chap. Elderly Affordable Housing Total Staff 3; Units 67.

St. Bernard III dba Rouquette IV, Mailing Address: 1000 Howard Ave., Ste. 100, 70113. Tel: 985-635-0305; Tel: 504-596-3460; Fax: 504-596-3466; Fax: 985-635-0306; Email: edoran@chi-ano.org. 4310 Hwy. 22, Mandeville, 70471. Deacon Dennis F. Adams, Exec. Dir.; Elizabeth Doran, Community Mgr.; Rev. Warren L.

Cooper, Chap. Elderly Affordable Housing Total Staff 3; Units 66.

St. Tammany Manor dba Rouquette Lodge (1979) St. Tammany Manor Elderly Affordable Housing 4300 Hwy. 22, Mandeville, 70471. Tel: 985-626-5217; Tel: 504-596-3460; Fax: 985-605-5930; Fax: 504-596-3466; Email: bschouest@chi-ano.org. Deacon Dennis F. Adams, Exec. Dir.; Brenda Schouest, Community Mgr.; Rev. Warren L. Cooper, Chap. Total Staff 21; Units 170.

MARRERO. *Monsignor Wynhoven Apartments, Inc.* Elderly Affordable Housing 4600-10th St., Marrero, 70072. Tel: 504-347-8442; Tel: 504-596-3460; Fax: 504-340-6076; Fax: 504-596-3466; Email: nphillips@chi-ano.org. Deacon Dennis F. Adams, Exec. Dir.; Nicholas Phillips, Community Mgr.; Fr. Albert Bergeron, Chap. Residents 351; Total Staff 15.

Wynhoven Health Care Center, 1050 Medical Center Blvd., Marrero, 70072-3170. Tel: 504-347-0777; Fax: 504-341-7240; Web: www.wynhoven.org. Michelle Matthew, Admin.; Mr. Wayne Plaisance, CEO. Bed Capacity 188; Tot Asst. Annually 255; Total Staff 207.

MERAUX. *St. Bernard Manor* Elderly Affordable Housing 2400 Archbishop Hannan Blvd., Meraux, 70075. Tel: 504-596-3460; Tel: 504-227-3380; Fax: 504-596-3466; Fax: 504-278-8982; Email: wrobertson@chi-ano.org. Mailing Address: 1000 Howard Ave., Ste. 100, 70113. Deacon Dennis F. Adams, Exec. Dir.; Wanda Robertson, Community Mgr. Total Staff 3; Residential Units 82.

METAIRIE. *St. Bernard II* dba Metairie IV Elderly Affordable Housing 4937 York St., Metairie, 70001. Tel: 504-267-9067; Tel: 504-596-3460; Fax: 504-596-3466; Fax: 504-267-9068; Email: mletellier@chi-ano.org. Mailing Address: 1000 Howard Ave., Ste. 100, 70113. Deacon Dennis F. Adams, Exec. Dir.; Marie Letellier, Community Mgr.; Rev. Msgr. Robert D. Massett, Chap. Units 82.

Metairie Manor Elderly Affordable Housing Mailing Address: 1000 Howard Ave., Ste. 100, 70113. Tel: 504-596-3460; Tel: 504-456-1467; Fax: 504-596-3466; Fax: 504-456-3181; Email: mletellier@chi-ano.org. 4929 York St., Metairie, 70001. Deacon Dennis F. Adams, Exec. Dir.; Marie Letellier, Community Mgr.; Rev. Msgr. Robert D. Massett, Chap. Residential Units 287.

Metairie III Elderly Affordable Housing 4929 York St., Metairie, 70001. Tel: 504-456-1467; Tel: 504-596-3460; Fax: 504-456-3181; Fax: 504-596-3466; Email: mletellier@chi-ano.org. Mailing Address: 1000 Howard Ave., Ste. 100, 70113. Deacon Dennis F. Adams, Exec. Dir.; Marie Letellier, Community Mgr.; Rev. Msgr. Robert D. Massett, Chap. Number of Units 82.

SLIDELL. *Villa Additions* dba St. Teresa's Villa Elderly Affordable Housing 1938 Gause Blvd. W., Slidell, 70460. Deacon Dennis F. Adams, Exec. Dir.; Ms. Sharline O'Brien, Community Mgr.; Rev. Raymond J. Guillot, Chap. Total Staff 3; Units 75.

[O] CATHOLIC HEALTH SERVICES

NEW ORLEANS. *Daughters of Charity Services of New Orleans*, 3201 S. Carrollton Ave., 70118-4307. Tel: 314-733-8000; Email: jimpicciche@ascension.org. Mailing Address: 101 S. Hanley Rd., Ste. 450, St. Louis, MO 63105. Joseph Impicciche, Exec. Total Staff 168.

Daughters of Charity Health Center - Gentilly, 100 Warrington Dr., 70122.

Daughters of Charity Neighborhood Health Partnership, 3201 S. Carrollton Ave., 70118. Tel: 504-482-2080; Fax: 504-483-6016; Email: alandrum@dcsno.org. Ms. Aziza Landrum, Dir. Community Care.

Daughters of Charity Foundation of New Orleans, P.O. Box 850258, 70185-0528. Tel: 504-212-9568; Fax: 504-483-6016. Michael G. Griffin, Pres. & CEO.

Daughters of Charity Services of New Orleans Foundation, 3201 S. Carrollton Ave., 70118. Tel: 504-482-2080; Fax: 504-482-2080. Michael G. Griffin, Pres. & CEO.

Daughters of Charity Services of New Orleans East, 3201 S. Carrollton Ave., 70112.

**Marillac Community Health Centers*, 3201 S. Carrollton Ave., 70118-4307. Tel: 504-207-3060, Ext. 2205; Fax: 504-483-6016. Michael G. Griffin, Pres. & CEO. Tot Asst. Annually 64,086; Total Staff 98.

Daughters of Charity Health Center - Metairie, 111 N. Causeway Blvd., Metairie, 70001. Tel: 504-482-0084.

Daughters of Charity Health Center - Carrollton, 3201 S. Carrollton Ave., 70118. Tel: 504-207-3060.

Daughters of Charity Health Center - Bywater/St. Cecilia, 1030 Lesseps St., 70117. Tel: 504-941-6041.

Daughters of Charity Health Center - New Orleans East, 5630 Read Blvd., 70127. Tel: 504-248-5357.

BOGALUSA. *Our Lady of the Angels Hospital, Inc.*, 433 Plaza St., Bogalusa, 70427. Tel: 985-730-6706; Fax: 985-730-6709; Email: rene.ragas@fmolhs.org; Web: www.oloah.org. Rene Ragas, Pres. Bed Capacity 90; Total Staff 405.

METAIRIE. *Mercy*, 110 Veterans Memorial Blvd., Ste. 425, Metairie, 70005. Tel: 504-838-8283; Fax: 877-472-2158; Email: Marynell.Ploch@Mercy.Net. Philip Wheeler, Sr. Vice Pres.-Gen. Counsel. FKA Mercy Family Center; Psychological and psychiatric evaluation, counseling and tutorial services.

1445 W. Causeway Approach, Mandeville, 70471. Tel: 985-727-7993; Fax: 985-727-7016; Email: douglas.walker@mercy.net. Elaine Moore, Pres.; Rex Menasco, Exec. Dir. Total Staff 34; Total Assisted 2,800.

[P] MONASTERIES AND RESIDENCES OF PRIESTS AND BROTHERS

NEW ORLEANS. *Brothers of the Sacred Heart of New Orleans, Inc.* (1821) Mailing Address: New Orleans Regional Office, New Orleans, 4600 Elysian Fields Ave., 70122-3826. Bro. Ivy LeBlanc, S.C., Treas., 1156 Park Ave., 70119. Tel: 504-488-1353.

New Orleans Residences: Bros. Ronald Hingle, S.C., Prov., 1156 City Park Ave., 70119; Robert Croteau, S.C., 1156 City Park Ave., 70122; Neal Golden, S.C., 4671 Painters St., 70122. Tel: 504-324-4508; William Boyles, S.C., 4671 Painters St., 70122. Tel: 504-324-4508; Neri Falgout, S.C.; Leo Labbe, S.C. *Brothers of the Sacred Heart Foundation, Inc.*, 4600 Elysian Fields Ave., 70122. Tel: 504-301-4758; Fax: 504-301-4843; Email: bileblancsc@gmail.com; Email: unitedstatesprovince@gmail.com. Bro. Ivy LeBlanc, S.C., Exec. Dir.

Congregation of the Mission Western Province (Vincentians) aka DePaul Residence, DePaul Residence, 812 Constantinople St., 70115-2726. Cell: 504-413-7413. Rev. Thomas J. Stehlik, C.M., Supr.; Fr. Louis Arceneaux, C.M.

Congregation of the Mission Western Province, Louisiana.

Dominican Friars, Southern Dominican Province of St. Martin de Porres (1979) Provincial Headquarters, 1421 N. Causeway Blvd., Ste. 200, Metairie, 70001-4144. Tel: 504-837-2129; Fax: 504-837-6604; Email: provincial@opsouth.org; Web: www.opsouth.org. Very Rev. Thomas M. Condon, O.P., Prov.; Rev. Friar Victor Laroche, O.P., Vicar; Revs. Francis Orozco, O.P., Promoter of Vocations; John Dominic Sims, O.P., Syndic. Priests in the Archdiocese 25; Brothers in the Archdiocese 2. *Dominican Vocation Sponsors*, 1421 N. Causeway Blvd., Ste. 200, Metairie, 70001-4144. Tel: 504-837-2129; Fax: 504-837-6604; Email; provincial@opsouth.org. Very Rev. Thomas M. Condon, O.P., Prov. *Southern Dominican Foundation*, 1421 N. Causeway Blvd., Ste. 200, Metairie, 70001-4144. Tel: 504-837-2129; Fax: 504-837-6604; Email: provincial@opsouth.org. Very Rev. Thomas M. Condon, O.P., Pres.; Revs. Juan Torres, O.P., Promoter of Devel.; Scott O'Brien, O.P., Vicar Prov. and Socius. *Southern Dominican Global Missions*, 4640 Canal St., 70119. Tel: 504-488-2652. Bro. Herman D. Johnson, O.P., Dir.

Jesuit Provincial Office (1907) U.S. Central and Southern Province, Society of Jesus 1010 Common St., Ste. 3010, 70112. Tel: 800-925-8894; Fax: 314-758-7164; Email: ucsprov@jesuits.org. Very Rev. Ronald A. Mercier, S.J., M.Div., S.T.L., M.A., Th.D., Prov.; Revs. J. Daniel Daly, M.Div., M.S., Ph.D., Treas.; John F. Armstrong, S.J., B.A., M.A., M.Div., Socius to the Prov.

Catholic Society of Religious and Literary Education

Priests of the Province Abroad: Revs. Charles B. Thibodeaux, S.J., M.Div., Casa Parroquial, Santa Rosa (Misiones), Paraguay. Tel: 595-858-221; Fax: 595-858-221; Edward G. Benya, S.J., B.S., S.T.L., Residencia Nossa Senhora de Fatima, Trac. Carlos Portes 171, Russas CE, Brazil 62-900-000; David H. Romero, S.J., B.A., M.A., Residencia Sao Jose de Anchieta, Rua Eneida Batista, 940 B, Cascata, Assis, Brazil; Patrick S. Madigan, S.J., B.A., M.A., S.T.L., Mount Street Jesuit Residence, 114 Mount St., London, United Kingdom W1K 3AH; Joseph A. Carola, S.J., B.A., M.Div., S.T.L., S.T.D., Pontifical Gregorian Univ., Piazza della Pilotta 4, Rome, Italy 00187. Tel: 39-06-6701-5226; Fax: 39-06-6701-5419; Michael S. Gallagher, S.J., B.A., M.A., J.D., M.Div., S.T.M., St. Peter Faber Residence, Rue Jacques-Dalphin 18 1227, Carouge, Switzerland; David A. Brown, S.J., B.S., M.A., M.Div., Ph.D., Castel Gandolfo Specola Vaticana, Vatican City. Tel: 39-06-698-63-242; Anthony J. Corcoran, S.J., B.A., M.A., S.T.L., Kyrgyztan Office of the Apostolic Admin. ul. Mayakovskogo 25, Bishkek, Kyrgyzstan 720040; James N. Caime, S.J., B.A., M.B.A., M.A., M.Div.; Jesus Rodriguez, S.J., B.A., M.A., M.Div., Ph.D., Curia of the Society of Jesus, Borgo Santo Spirito 4, Roma, Italy 00193; David L. Andrus, S.J., B.S., M.Div.; Brian M. Reedy, S.J., B.S., M.A., M.S., M.Div., S.T.L.; Very Rev. Mark Lewis, S.J., B.A., M.A., Ph. L., M.Div., Th.M., Ph.D., Pontifical Gregorian University, Piazza della Pilotta, 4, Rome, Italy 00187.

Josephite Fathers and Brothers, 2600 A.P. Tureaud, 70119. Tel: 504-944-2424. (See Separate Listing for School)*The Josephite Faculty House of St. Augustine High School*, 2600 A.P. Tureaud, 70119. Tel: 504-944-2424. Bro. Laurence E. Price, S.S.J.; Revs. Joseph M. Doyle, S.S.J.; Howard W. Byrd, S.S.J.; Bura Aloysius Koroba, S.S.J.; Anthony Okum, S.S.J.

Loyola Jesuit Community, 1575 Calhoun St., 70118-6153. Tel: 504-865-3866; Fax: 504-899-1355; Email: gwaldrop@jesuits.org. Revs. Gregory S. Waldrop, S.J., B.A., M.S., S.T.B., M.A., Rector; Robert S. Gerlich, S.J.; James C. Carter, S.J.; Theodore A. Dziak, S.J.; Gregg Grovenburg, S.J.; Alfred C. Kammer, S.J., B.A., M.A., J.D.; Donald Martin, S.J., M.A., Ph.D.; Lawrence Moore, S.J.; Leo A. Nicoll, S.J.; Peter S. Rogers, S.J.; Edward Vacek, S.J.; Randall S. Gibbens, S.J.

COVINGTON. *De La Salle Christian Brothers (NOSF, Inc.)*, 104 W. 11th Ave., Covington, 70433. Tel: 985-892-2004; Fax: 985-893-2673; Email: brdonald@dlsi.org. Bros. Donald Johanson, F.S.C., Prov.; James Joost, F.S.C., Auxiliary Prov.

Brothers of the Christian Schools of Lafayette - Retirement Trust (1988) 104 W. 11th Ave., Covington, 70433. Tel: 985-892-2004; Fax: 985-893-2673; Email: brdonald@dlsi.org; Email: joecef@aol.com; Email: tripp@cbnosf.org; Email: roviracpa@aol.com. Joseph Taranto, Chm.

St. La Salle Auxiliary (1921) 104 W. 11th Ave., Covington, 70501. Tel: 337-234-1973; Fax: 337-261-1014; Email: welkerlvw@aol.com. Bro. Louis Welker, Chm. The St. LaSalle Auxiliary is a development project of "De La Salle Christian Brothers," a nonprofit organization.

ST. BENEDICT. *St. Joseph Abbey* (1890) 75376 River Rd., St. Benedict, 70457. Tel: 985-892-1800; Fax: 985-867-2270; Email: abbotsecretary@sjasc.edu; Web: www.sjasc.edu. Rt. Rev. Justin Brown, O.S.B., Abbot; Revs. Ephrem Arcement, O.S.B., B.A., M.A., Ph.D.; Raphael Barousse, O.S.B.; Charles J. Benoit, O.S.B., M.A.Th., J.C.L.; Very Rev. Gregory M. Boquet, O.S.B., M.A.; Revs. Timothy J. Burnett, O.S.B.; Matthew R. Clark, O.S.B., B.A., M.A.; Jonathan M. DeFrange, O.S.B.; Sean B. Duggan, O.S.B., B.Mus., M.A.Th., M.F.A.; Augustine E. Foley, O.S.B., B.A., M.T.S., M.A., S.T.B.; Peter E. Hammett, O.S.B.; Jude Israel, O.S.B., B.S., M.Ed., M.A.; Michael Jung, O.S.B.; Aelred Kavanagh, O.S.B., M.T.S., S.T.M., S.T.D.; Killian Tolg, B.A., M.A.; Lawrence J. Phelps, O.S.B.; Scott J. Underwood, O.S.B., M.T.S., M.Ed. Brothers 9; Novices 3; Priests 18.

[Q] CONVENTS AND RESIDENCES FOR SISTERS

NEW ORLEANS. *Congregation of St. Joseph, C.S.J.*, 4030 Delgado Dr., 70119-3807. Tel: 504-486-7682; Email: pwarbritton@csjoseph.org; Web: www.csjoseph.org. Barbara Hughes, Contact Person. Sisters 2; Total Sisters in Archdiocese 10.

Congregation of St. Joseph Ministry Against the Death Penalty, 3009 Grand Rte. St. John, #6, 70119. Tel: 504-948-6557; Fax: 504-948-6558; Email: hprejean@sisterhelen.org; Web: www.prejean.org. Mrs. Elizabeth Ryan, Dir. Sisters 500.

Congregation of the Marianites of Holy Cross (1841) 21388 Smith Rd., Covington, 70435-6349. Tel: 985-893-5201; Fax: 985-893-5190; Email: chrispmsc@marianites.org; Web: www.marianites.org. Sr. Ann Lacour, M.S.C., Congregational Leader. Sisters 98.

Congregation of the Sisters of the Holy Faith, C.H.F., 1063 Moss St., 70119. Web: www.holyfaithsisters.net. Total Sisters in Archdiocese 4.

Daughters of Charity of St. Vincent de Paul, D.C., Sisters' Residence, 7817 S. Claiborne Ave., 70125. Tel: 504-861-4516; Email: sranthony@archdiocese-no.org. Mailing Address: 2820 Burdette St., Apt. 314, 70125. Sr. Anthony Barczykowski, D.C., Sister Servant. Total Sisters in Archdiocese 37.

Daughters of Our Lady of the Holy Rosary Queen of Peace Province (1967) 1492 Moss St., 70119-2904. Tel: 504-486-0039; Fax: 504-298-0566; Email: fmsrusaprovince@yahoo.com; Web: www.dongmancoi.org. Sr. M. John Vianney Vi Huyen Tran, F.M.S.R., Prov. Supr. Sisters 52; Total Sisters in Archdiocese 25.

Dominican Sisters (Cabra, Ireland) O.P., 3524 DeSaix Blvd., 70119. Tel: 504-267-7867; Email:

tlenehanop@gmail.com; Web: www.dominicansisters.com. Therese Lenehan, Treas.; Sisters Elizabeth Ferguson, O.P.; Lilianne Flavin, O.P. Sisters 3; Total Sisters in Archdiocese 3.

Dominican Sisters of Peace, 5660 Bancroft Dr., 70122. Tel: 504-283-1122; Fax: 504-283-1217; Email: srkatop@aol.com. Sr. Kathy Broussard, O.P., Coord. Sisters 4.

Franciscan Poor Clares (1885) 720 Henry Clay Ave., 70118-5891. Tel: 504-895-2019; Fax: 504-899-6218; Email: elizmortell@juno.com; Web: www.poorclarenuns.com. Sr. Elizabeth Mortell, O.S.C., Abbess. Nuns of the Order of St. Clare. Solemn Professed Nuns 7.

Missionary Sisters of the Sacred Heart (Cabrini) M.S.C., 3443 Esplanade Ave., Apt. 314, 70119. Tel: 504-377-7561.

Presentation Sisters of the Blessed Virgin Mary (1968) 1706 S. Saratoga St., 70113. Tel: 504-715-9798; Email: marylou@dubuquepresentations.org; Web: www.dubuquepresentations.org. Julie Marsh; Mary Lou Specha

Union of Sisters of the Presentation of the Blessed Virgin Mary (United States Prov.).

Society of the Sacred Heart (1800) 2545 Bayou Rd., 70119. Tel: 504-309-2828; Email: bkearney@rscj.org; Web: www.rscj.org. Sr. Bonnie K, Dir. Sisters 11. *Duchesne House, Bayou Rd Community*, 2545 Bayou Rd., 70119. Tel: 504-309-2828; Email: bkearney@rscj.org; Email: llieux@rscj.org. Sisters 2; Total Sisters in Archdiocese 14.

Duchesne House, Bayou Rd. Com., 2545 Bayou Rd., 70119. Tel: 504-309-2828; Email: bkearney@rscj.org; Email: llieux@rscj.org.

Corondelet Community, 4600 Carondelet St., 70115. Tel: 504-891-0412; Tel: 504-382-0782; Email: llieux@rscj.org.

Shannon House, 1500 State St., 70118. Tel: 504-510-4543; Email: mguste@rscj.org; Email: gparizek@rscj.org; Email: llieux@rscj.org.

Sophie Barat House, 1719 Napoleon Ave., 70115. Tel: 504-899-6027; Email: jmckinlay@rscj.org; Email: mchicoine@rscj.org; Email: llieux@rscj.org; Web: www.rscj.org. Sr. Jane McKinlay, R.S.C.J., Dir.

Servants of Mary, Ministers to the Sick, 5001 Perlita St., 70122-1999. Tel: 504-282-5549; Fax: 504-282-5550; Email: ssm2@cox.net; Web: sisterservantsofmary.com. Sr. Rosa Valadez, S.de. M., Supr. Total Home Nursing Sisters in Archdiocese 10.

Sisters of Mercy of the Americas, R.S.M., 6024 Freret St., 70118. Tel: 504-452-1302; Email: amagro@oppeace.org; Web: www.mercysc.org. 66 Fontainebleau Dr., 70125. Sr. Angeline Magro, O.P., B.A., M.A., Contact Person. Other local residences: 5660 Bancroft Dr., New Orleans LA 70122; 4925 Pike Dr., Metairie, 70003; 837 Short St., New Orleans, LA 70118; 2835 Broadway St., New Orleans, LA 70125; 2826 Broadway St., New Orleans, LA 70125

Sisters of Mercy of the Americas, South Central Community, Inc. Total Sisters in Archdiocese 20.

Sisters of the Blessed Sacrament, S.B.S., 4921 Dixon St., 70125. Tel: 225-751-7161.

*Raphael Convent. Trinity House. Umoja*Total Sisters in the Archdiocese 8.

Sisters of the Holy Family Motherhouse, S.S.F. (1842) 6901 Chef Menteur Hwy., 70126-5215. Tel: 504-241-3088; Fax: 504-244-0454; Email: g48j@aol.com; Web: www.sistersoftheholyfamily.org. Sr. Greta Jupiter, S.S.F., Congregational Leader. Sisters 79; Total Sisters in Archdiocese 70.

Ursuline Sisters of the Roman Union, O.S.U. (1727) 2734 Nashville Ave., 70115. Tel: 504-891-3665; Tel: 504-861-4686; Email: annb@osucentral.org. Sr. Ann Barrett, O.S.U., Prioress. Sisters 13; Total Sisters in Archdiocese 13.

ABITA SPRINGS. *Sisters of Benedict of Colorado, Inc.*, 102 Maria Ave., Abita Springs, 70420. Tel: 303-916-1991; Email: sean.conrad.osb@gmail.com. Sr. Shawn Conrad, O.S.B., Pres.

COVINGTON. *Carmelite Nuns, Discalced, O.C.D., Monastery of St. Joseph and St. Teresa* (1877) 73530 River Rd., Covington, 70435-2206. Tel: 985-898-0923; Fax: 985-871-9333; Email: covingtoncarmel@yahoo.com; Web: www.covingtoncarmel.org. Sr. Edith Turpin, O.C.D., Prioress. Professed Nuns 7.

Daughters of Divine Providence, F.D.P. (1832) 74684 Airport Rd., Covington, 70435-5621. Tel: 985-809-8854; Fax: 985-809-8854; Email: daughtersofdivineprovidence@gmail.com. Total Sisters in Archdiocese 3.

Teresian Sisters (Society of St. Teresa of Jesus), S.T.J., Provincial Office, 18080 St. Joseph's Way, Covington, 70435-5623. Tel: 985-893-1470; Fax: 985-893-2476; Email: stjsecretarysfs@yahoo.es; Web: www.teresians.us. Sr. Marina Aranzabal, Prov. Sisters 26.

HARVEY. *Salesian Sisters (Daughters of Mary Help of Christians) F.M.A.*, 608 1st Ave., Harvey, 70058-5980. Tel: 504-325-5980; Email: SECHarveyIC19@gmail.com; Web: www.salesiansisters.org. Sisters in Archdiocese 5.

LACOMBE. *Congregation of Our Lady of Mount Carmel, O.Carm.* (1833) Generalate, 62284 Fish Hatchery Rd., P.O. Box 476, Lacombe, 70445-0476. Tel: 985-882-7577; Tel: 504-524-2398; Fax: 504-524-5011; Email: admin@sistersofmountcarmel.org; Email: finance@sistersofmountcarmel.org. Sr. Lawrence Habetz, O.Carm., M.T.S., Pres. Sisters 80. *Mount Carmel Development Office*, 62284 Fish Hatchery Rd., P.O. Box 1160, Lacombe, 70445-1160. Tel: 985-882-7577; Tel: 504-524-2398; Fax: 504-524-5011; Email: development@sistersofmountcarmel.org. Sr. Lawrence Habetz, O.Carm., M.T.S., Pres.

Carmelite Ministries, Inc. / Cub Corner Preschool, Tel: 504-286-8673; Fax: 504-286-8676. Sr. Gwen Grillot, O.Carm., Exec. Dir. Total Enrollment 120; Total Staff 27.

Carmelite Spirituality Center (2004) 62292 Fish Hatchery Rd., P.O. Box 130, Lacombe, 70445-0130. Tel: 985-882-7579; Fax: 985-882-6563; Email: carmelcenter@bellsouth.net; Web: www.carmelitespirituality.org.

Carmelite NGO, 1725 General Taylor St., 70115. Tel: 504-458-3029; Fax: 504-864-7438; Email: jfremson@gmail.com; Web: carmelitengo.org.

METAIRIE. *Daughters of St. Paul Convent, F.S.P.*, Pauline Book & Media Center, 4403 Veterans Memorial Blvd., Metairie, 70006-5321. Tel: 504-887-7631; Fax: 504-887-1357; Email: metairie@paulinemedia.com. Total Sisters in Archdiocese 5.

Sisters of the Living Word, S.L.W., 4900 Park Dr., Metairie, 70001-3237. Tel: 504-455-5905; Email: srstump@steddy.org; Web: www.slw.org. Sr. Julia Stump, Contact Person. Sisters 1; Total Sisters in Archdiocese 4.

[R] RETREAT HOUSES

NEW ORLEANS. *Center of Jesus the Lord*, 1307 Louisiana Ave, 70115. Tel: 504-529-1636; Fax: 504-529-5003; Email: office@centerofjesusthelord.org; Web: www.centerofjesusthelord.org. Rev. George Roy, O.M.I. Total in Residence 3; Total Staff 5; Total Assisted 326.

Sophie Barat House, 1719 Napoleon Ave., 70115-4809. Tel: 504-899-6027; Fax: 504-899-6210; Email: jmckinlay@rscj.org. Sisters Jane McKinlay, R.S.C.J.; Annice Callahan; Anne Sturges; Judith Vollbrecht; Carol Burk, R.S.C.J. Total in Residence 5; Total Staff 8.

COVINGTON. *Camp Abbey Retreat Center*, 77002 KC Camp Rd., Covington, 70435. Tel: 985-327-7240; Fax: 985-809-3590; Email: campabbey@arch-no.org. William O'Regan IV, Contact Person; Denise Emmons, Contact Person.

LACOMBE. *Carmelite Spirituality Center*, 62292 Fish Hatchery Rd., P.O. Box 130, Lacombe, 70445-0130. Tel: 985-882-7579; Tel: 985-264-0314; Fax: 985-882-6563; Email: carmelcenter@bellsouth.net; Web: www.carmelitespirituality.org. Sisters Barbara Breaud, O.Carm., Exec. Dir.; Terry Falco, R.S.M., Program Dir.; Lena Collins, O.Carm., House Dir.

METAIRIE. *Archdiocesan Spirituality Center*, 2501 Maine Ave., Metairie, 70003-5446. Tel: 504-861-3254; Fax: 504-861-0584; Email: archspirctr@archdiocese-no.org. Sr. Dorothy Trosclair, O.P., Exec. Dir.

Archdiocese of New Orleans Retreat Center (Dedicated to Our Lady of the Cenacle) 5500 St. Mary St., Metairie, 70006. Tel: 504-887-1420; Fax: 504-887-6624; Email: retreats@arch-no.org. Dr. Paul Ceasar, Exec. Dir.

ST. BENEDICT. *Christian Life Center at St. Joseph Abbey*, 75376 River Rd., St. Benedict, 70457-9900. Tel: 985-892-3473; Fax: 985-892-3448. Deacon Mark C. Coudrain, Dir. Conducted by Benedictine Monks.

[S] MISCELLANEOUS

NEW ORLEANS. *Archbishop Francis B. Schulte Testamentary Trust*, 7887 Walmsley Ave., 70125.

Archdiocese of New Orleans Indemnity, Inc., Mailing Address: Archdiocese of New Orleans, Dept. of Financial and Administrative Svcs., 7887 Walmsley Ave., 70125. Teletype: 802-922-9457. Jeffrey J. Entwisle, Dir. & Pres.

Chateau de Notre Dame Facilities Corporation, 7887 Walmsley Ave., 70125. Tel: 504-861-2906.

Christian Brothers Foundation, 8 Friederichs Ave., 70124-4602. Tel: 504-488-2802; Fax: 504-486-1053; Email: foundation@cbs-no.org.

Domus Dei Clerical Society of Apostolic Life, U.S.A., Inc. aka Society of Domus Dei (SDD), 13401 Lemans St., 70129. Tel: 504-254-9429; Cell: 360-909-8516; Email: domusdeiusa@gmail.com; Web: www.nhachua.net. Revs. Francis Quyet Bui, S.D.D., Supr.; David Kim, S.D.D., Treas.; Ansgar Pham, S.D.D., Sec.; Son Pham; John Tran; Phong Nguyen; Dieu Tran; Bros. Khoan Nguyen; Thanh Vu; Bro Minh Tran.

Holy Trinity Drive Land Corporation, 7887 Walmsley Ave., 70125. Jeff Entwisle, Contact Person.

#iGIVECATHOLIC, 7887 Walmsley Ave., 70125.

Jesuit Seminary and Mission Fund, 1010 Common St., Ste. 3010, 70112. Tel: 800-925-8894; Fax: 314-758-7164; Email: ucsprov@jesuits.org; Web: www.jesuitscentralsouthern.org. Rev. J. Daniel Daly, M.Div., M.S., Ph.D., Treas.

**Lord, Teach Me To Pray, Inc.*, 11 Warbler St., 70124-4401. Tel: 504-439-5933 (Mrs. Carol Weiler); Tel: 504-717-8770 (Fr. Martin Gleeson, O.P.); Email: carolweiler@cox.net; Web: www.lordteachmetopray.com. Mrs. Carol Weiler, Dir.

MCA Foundation, 7027 Milne Blvd., 70124. Tel: 504-288-7626, Ext. 137; Fax: 504-288-7629; Email: mca@mcacubs.org; Web: www.mcacubs.com. Sr. Camille Anne Campbell, O.Carm., M.A., Pres.

**National T.E.C. Conference* aka TEC Conference, 2241 Mendez St., 70122. Tel: 504-227-3233; Email: office@tecconference.org; Email: billy@tecconference.org; Web: www.tecconference.org. William O'Regan IV, Dir.

Our Lady of Wisdom Facility Corporation, 7887 Walmsley Ave., 70125. Tel: 504-861-2906; Email: jentwisle@archdiocese-no.org.

The Patrons of the Vatican Museums in the South, Inc. (1985) 1137 Jefferson Ave., 70115. Tel: 504-895-6822; Email: fesmd2@gmail.com. Dr. Frank Schmidt, Pres.

Peace Center, 2837 Broadway St., 70125-2655. Tel: 504-267-3342; Email: srsueop@aol.com. Sr. Suzanne Brauer, O.P., Dir.

Pierre Toussaint Foundation of New Orleans, Inc. (1995) 2600 A.P. Tureaud Ave., 70119-1299. Tel: 944-2424. Kenneth St. Charles.

**Second Harvest Food Bank of Greater New Orleans and Acadiana* (1982) 700 Edwards Ave., 70123-2236. Tel: 504-734-1322; Fax: 504-733-8336; Web: www.no-hunger.org. Total Staff 86.

7887 Walmsley, Inc., Archdiocese of New Orleans, Dept. of Financial and Administrative Svcs., 7887 Walmsley Ave., 70125. Tel: 802-922-9457. Jeffrey J. Entwisle, Dir. & Pres.

Southern Dominican Global Missions, 4640 Canal St., 70119. Tel: 504-488-2652; Email: hjohnson@xula.edu. Bro. Herman D. Johnson, O.P., Dir.

Stella Roman Foundation, Inc., 1010 Common St., Ste. 3010, 70112. Tel: 504-522-4756; Fax: 504-568-0783; Email: rbordelon@denechaudlaw.com. Most Rev. Gregory M. Aymond, D.D.

St. Tammany Catholic Cemetery, 7887 Walmsley Ave., 70125. Jeff Entwisle, Contact Person.

**Willwoods Community* (1978) 3900 Howard Ave., 70125. Tel: 504-830-3700; Fax: 504-840-9838; Email: willwoods@willwoods.org; Web: www.willwoods.org. Ron Yager, COO.

ABITA SPRINGS. *The Christ in Christmas Committee of New Orleans*, 123 Iroquois Dr., Abita Springs, 70420. Tel: 985-893-0169; Email: kcicno@bellsouth.net. Stephen F. Hart, Chm.

COVINGTON. *Magnolia Lafayette, Inc.*, 104 W. 11th Ave., Covington, 70433. Tel: 985-892-2004; Email: brdonald@dlsi.org. Bros. Donald Johanson, F.S.C., Visitor; James Joost, F.S.C., Auxiliary Visitor.

METAIRIE. *Congar Institute for Ministry Development* aka Instituto Congar para el Desarrollo Pastoral, 1421 N. Causeway Blvd., Ste. 200, Metairie, 70001. Rev. Wayne A. Cavalier, O.P., Dir.

Equestrian Order of the Holy Sepulchre (of Jerusalem, Southeastern Lieutenancy of the U.S.) 2955 Ridgelake Dr., Ste. 205, Metairie, 70002. Tel: 504-832-0892; Fax: 504-832-1929; Email: office@sleohs.com. Raymond J. Garrity, Lieutenant.

International Dominican Foundation, U.S.A. (2002) One Galleria Blvd., Ste. 710-B, Metairie, 70001. Tel: 504-836-8180; Fax: 504-836-8180; Email: info@intldom.org; Web: www.internationaldominicanfoundation.org. Rev. Allen B. Moran, O.P., Pres.

124 Airline Drive, Inc., 4133 Banks St., 70119-6883. Tel: 504-486-6631; Fax: 504-483-3816. Rev. Christopher Fronk, Pres.

**WLAE-TV, Educational Broadcasting Foundation, Inc.*, Box 792497, 70179-2497. Tel: 504-830-3700; Fax: 504-840-9838; Email: info@wlae.com; Web: www.wlae.com. 1500 River Oaks Dr. W., Jefferson, 70123.

MONTZ. **Lyke Foundation*, 102 Ann Ct., Montz, 70068-8980. Tel: 985-287-0161; Web: www.

lykefoundation.org. Richard Cheri, Exec. Dir.; Kathleen Kennedy, Pres.; Andrew Lyke, Sec.; Most Rev. Fernand Cheri, O.F.M., Treas.

SECULAR INSTITUTES

ABITA SPRINGS. *Caritas* (1950) Administration Center, P.O. Box 308, Abita Springs, 70420-0308.
Tel: 985-892-4345; Email: caritas11r@aol.com. 1000 Howard Ave., Ste. 400, 70113.

RELIGIOUS INSTITUTES OF MEN REPRESENTED IN THE ARCHDIOCESE

For further details refer to the corresponding bracketed number in the Religious Institutes of Men or Women section.

[0200]—*Benedictine Monks*—O.S.B.
[0330]—*Brothers of the Christian Schools* (New Orleans Prov.)—F.S.C.
[1100]—*Brothers of the Sacred Heart* (Pascoag, RI)—S.C.
[0470]—*The Capuchin Friars*—O.F.M.Cap.
[]—*Congregation of Christian Brothers (Edmund Rice)*—C.F.C.
[1330]—*Congregation of the Mission of St. Vincent de Paul Fathers & Brothers* (Southern Prov.)—C.M.
[]—*Congregation of the Mother Coredemptrix*—C.M.C.
[0260]—*Discalced Carmelite Friars*—O.C.D.
[0520]—*Franciscan Friars*—O.F.M.
[0690]—*Jesuit Fathers and Brothers* (New Orleans)—S.J.
[0780]—*Marist Fathers and Brothers* (USA Prov.)—S.M.
[0910]—*Oblates of Mary Immaculate* (Southern American Prov.)—O.M.I.
[0430]—*Order of Preacher-Dominicans* (St Martin de Porres/Southern Prov.)—O.P.
[0610]—*Priests of the Congregation of Holy Cross* (Southern Prov.; Indiana Prov.)—C.S.C.
[1070]—*Redemptorist Fathers and Brothers* (New Orleans)—C.Ss.R.
[1190]—*Salesians of Don Bosco*—S.D.B.
[0440]—*Society of St. Edmund*—S.S.E.
[0420]—*Society of the Divine Word* (St. Augustine Prov.)—S.V.D.
[0700]—*St. Joseph's Society of the Sacred Heart* (Baltimore, MD)—S.S.J.

RELIGIOUS INSTITUTES OF WOMEN REPRESENTED IN THE ARCHDIOCESE

[0230]—*Benedictine Sisters of Pontifical Jurisdiction* (Colorado)—O.S.B.
[0400]—*Congregation of Our Lady of Mount Carmel*—O.Carm.
[1940]—*Congregation of Sisters of the Holy Faith*—C.H.F.
[2410]—*Congregation of the Marianites of Holy Cross*—M.S.C.
[3832]—*Congregation of the Sisters of St. Joseph*—C.S.J.
[1950]—*Congregation of the Sisters of the Holy Family*—S.S.F.
[]—*Congregation of the Sisters of the Sacred Heart of Jesus*—S.S.H.
[0800]—*Daughters of Divine Providence*—F.D.P.
[0850]—*Daughters of Mary Help of Christians*—F.M.A.
[0895]—*Daughters of Our Lady of the Holy Rosary*—F.M.S.R.
[0760]—*Daughters of St. Vincent de Paul*—D.C.
[0420]—*Discalced Carmelite Nuns*—O.C.D.
[1110]—*Dominican Sisters of Our Lady of the Rosary and of Saint Catherine of Siena, Cabra, Ireland*—O.P.
[1115]—*Dominican Sisters of Peace*—O.P.
[]—*Lovers of the Holy Cross Sisters at Cho Quan*—L.H.C.
[2860]—*Missionary Sisters of the Sacred Heart*—M.S.C.
[0950]—*Pious Society Daughters of St. Paul*—F.S.P.
[3760]—*Poor Clare Nuns, Order of St. Clare*—O.S.C.
[2970]—*School Sisters of Notre Dame* (Dallas & Mankato)—S.S.N.D.
[0660]—*Sisters of Christian Charity* (Wilmette, IL)—S.C.C.
[2575]—*Sisters of Mercy of the Americas* (Brooklyn; St. Louis)—R.S.M.
[2630]—*Sisters of Mercy of the Holy Cross*—S.C.S.C.
[1530]—*Sisters of St. Francis of the Congregation of Our Lady of Lourdes, Sylvania, Ohio*—O.S.F.
[0260]—*Sisters of the Blessed Sacrament for Indians and Colored People*—S.B.S.
[2120]—*Sisters of the Immaculate Conception*—C.I.C.
[2350]—*Sisters of the Living Word*—S.L.W.
[3600]—*Sisters Servants of Mary*—S.de.M.
[4020]—*Society of St. Teresa of Jesus*—S.T.J.
[4070]—*Society of the Sacred Heart*—R.S.C.J.
[3330]—*Union of the Sisters of the Presentation of the Blessed Virgin Mary*—P.B.V.M.
[4110]—*Ursuline Nuns*—O.S.U.

NECROLOGY

† Carmon, Dominic, s.v.d., Retired Auxiliary Bishop of New Orleans, Died Nov. 11, 2018
† Tomasovich, John A., (Retired), Died Mar. 2, 2017
† Adams, Harry Joseph, (Retired), Died Nov. 20, 2018
† Finn, John Patrick, (Retired), Died Aug. 25, 2018
† Pericone, Nicholas P., Metropolitan Tribunal; Mater Dolorosa, Died Mar. 10, 2018
† Serio, Anthony, (Retired), Died Jul. 26, 2018

An asterisk (*) denotes an organization that has established tax-exempt status directly with the IRS and is not covered by the USCCB Group Ruling.

Diocese of New Ulm

(Dioecesis Novae Ulmae)

Most Reverend

JOHN M. LEVOIR

Bishop of New Ulm; ordained May 30, 1981; appointed Bishop of New Ulm July 14, 2008; ordained September 15, 2008. *Office: 1421 Sixth St., N., New Ulm, MN 56073-2071.*

Diocesan Pastoral Center: 1421 Sixth St. N., New Ulm, MN 56073-2071. Tel: 507-359-2966; Fax: 507-354-0268.

Web: www.dnu.org

Email: dnu@dnu.org

ESTABLISHED NOVEMBER 18, 1957.

Square Miles 9,863.

Comprises the Counties of Big Stone, Brown, Chippewa, Kandiyohi, Lac Qui Parle, Lincoln, Lyon, McLeod, Meeker, Nicollet, Redwood, Renville, Sibley, Swift, and Yellow Medicine in the State of Minnesota.

For legal titles of parishes and diocesan institutions, consult the Diocesan Pastoral Center.

STATISTICAL OVERVIEW

Personnel	
Bishop	1
Priests: Diocesan Active in Diocese	31
Priests: Diocesan in Foreign Missions	1
Priests: Retired, Sick or Absent	24
Number of Diocesan Priests	56
Total Priests in Diocese	56
Extern Priests in Diocese	2
Ordinations:	
Permanent Deacons	6
Permanent Deacons in Diocese	20
Total Sisters	36
Parishes	
Parishes	68
With Resident Pastor:	
Resident Diocesan Priests	20
Resident Religious Priests	1
Without Resident Pastor:	
Administered by Priests	48
Missions	4
Closed Parishes	2
Professional Ministry Personnel:	
Sisters	2
Welfare	
Catholic Hospitals	1
Homes for the Aged	8
Special Centers for Social Services	4
Total Assisted	1,401
Educational	
Diocesan Students in Other Seminaries	9
Total Seminarians	9
High Schools, Diocesan and Parish	3
Total Students	251
Elementary Schools, Diocesan and Parish	15
Total Students	1,498
Catechesis/Religious Education:	
High School Students	1,744
Elementary Students	3,597
Total Students under Catholic Instruction	7,099
Teachers in the Diocese:	
Lay Teachers	158
Vital Statistics	
Receptions into the Church:	
Infant Baptism Totals	692
Minor Baptism Totals	21
Adult Baptism Totals	4
Received into Full Communion	50
First Communions	579
Confirmations	626
Marriages:	
Catholic	127
Interfaith	68
Total Marriages	195
Deaths	682
Total Catholic Population	51,838
Total Population	280,178

Former Bishops—Most Revs. ALPHONSE J. SCHLADWEILER, D.D., ord. June 9, 1929; appt. Nov. 28, 1957; cons. Jan. 29, 1958; installed Jan. 30, 1958; retired Dec. 23, 1975; died April 3, 1996; RAYMOND A. LUCKER, S.T.D., ord. June 7, 1952; appt. Titular Bishop of Meta and Auxiliary Bishop of St. Paul & Minneapolis July 12, 1971; cons. Sept. 8, 1971; appt. Bishop of New Ulm, Dec. 23, 1975; installed Feb. 19, 1976; retired Nov. 17, 2000; died Sept. 19, 2001; JOHN C. NIENSTEDT, ord. July 27, 1974; appt. Auxiliary Bishop of Detroit June 12, 1996; ord. July 9, 1996; appt. Bishop of New Ulm June 12, 2001; installed Aug. 6, 2001; appt. Coadjutor Archbishop of Saint Paul and Minneapolis April 24, 2007.

Diocesan Officials

Diocesan Pastoral Center—Most Rev. JOHN M. LEVOIR, 1421 6th Street North, New Ulm, 56073-2099. Tel: 507-359-2966; Fax: 507-354-0268.

Vicar General—Very Rev. Msgr. DOUGLAS L. GRAMS, J.C.L., 1421 6th St. N., New Ulm, 56073-2099. Tel: 507-359-2966; Fax: 507-354-0268.

Chancellor—Very Rev. Msgr. EUGENE L. LOZINSKI, J.C.L., 1421 6th St. N., New Ulm, 56073-2099. Tel: 507-359-2966, Ext. 315; Fax: 507-354-0268.

Vice Chancellor—Rev. JOHN G. BERGER, (Retired), P.O. Box 85, Green Isle, 55338-0085. Tel: 507-326-5111; Fax: 507-964-5209.

Diocesan Tribunal—

Judicial Vicar (Officialis)—Very Rev. MARK S. STEFFL, S.T.L., J.C.L.

Director—MR. ALDEAN B. HENDRICKSON, J.C.L., Diocesan Pastoral Center, 1421 6th St. N., New Ulm, 56073-2099. Tel: 507-359-2966, Ext. 329; Fax: 507-354-0268.

Associate Judges—Very Rev. Msgr. EUGENE L. LOZINSKI, J.C.L.; Rev. PAUL L. WOLF; Very Rev. Msgr. DOUGLAS L. GRAMS, J.C.L.; Rev. JOHN G. BERGER, (Retired); MR. ALDEAN B. HENDRICKSON, J.C.L.

Defender of the Bond—Rev. MARK S. MALLAK, S.T.L., J.C.L.

Promoter of Justice—Rev. MARK S. MALLAK, S.T.L., J.C.L.

Notary—MRS. PENNY FORST.

Diocesan Boards and Councils

Building Committee—Revs. GEORGE V. SCHMIT JR., Chm., Church of St. Mary, 220 S. 10th St., P.O. Box 500, Bird Island, 55310-0500. Tel: 320-365-3593; Fax: 320-365-3142; AARON T. JOHANNECK; Deacon STEVEN P. SPILMAN; MR. RAYMOND MARTIN; MR. RICHARD GREENE.

College of Consultors—Very Rev. Msgrs. DOUGLAS L. GRAMS, J.C.L.; EUGENE L. LOZINSKI, J.C.L.; Rev. STEVEN J. VERHELST; Very Rev. MARK S. STEFFL, S.T.L., J.C.L.; Revs. CRAIG A. TIMMERMAN; ANTHONY J. STUBEDA.

Priests' Council—Very Rev. Msgrs. DOUGLAS L. GRAMS, J.C.L.; EUGENE L. LOZINSKI, J.C.L.; Revs. SAMUEL F. PEREZ; PHILIP M. SCHOTZKO; RONALD V. HUBERTY; STEVEN J. VERHELST; MARK S. MALLAK, S.T.L., J.C.L.; Very Rev. MARK S. STEFFL, S.T.L., J.C.L.; Revs. CRAIG A. TIMMERMAN; ANTHONY J. STUBEDA; GERMAIN P. RADEMACHER, (Retired); JEFFREY P. HOREJSI.

Committee on Parishes—MR. THOMAS P. KEAVENY, (Diocesan Liaison); Rev. ANTHONY J. STUBEDA; Very Rev. Msgr. DOUGLAS L. GRAMS, J.C.L.; Revs. GEORGE V. SCHMIT JR.; ANTHONY R. HESSE; MR. KEN NOYES; MRS. RONDA MATHIOWETZ; Sr. MARY ANN KUHN, S.S.N.D.; MS. MARY NORDSTROM; Revs. DENNIS C. LABAT; ZACHARY D. PETERSON. On Call Member: MRS. KARLA CROSS, M.Ed.

Property Committee—MR. ANDY RHODE, Chm.; Rev. TODD J. PETERSEN; MR. TOM CLYNE; MR. WAYNE A. PELZEL; MR. PHILIP LIESCH; MR. BILL BRENNAN; MR. MICHAEL H. BOYLE; MR. THOMAS J. HOLZER, Staff Liaison.

Corporate Board—Most Rev. JOHN M. LEVOIR; Very Rev. Msgr. EUGENE L. LOZINSKI, J.C.L.; MR. MICHAEL H. BOYLE; Very Rev. Msgr. DOUGLAS L. GRAMS, J.C.L.; MR. STEVE GEHRKE.

Diocesan Pastoral Council—MR. BRENT SUNDVE, Chair. Members: MRS. JULIE TREINEN; MR. RANDY KRZMARZICK; MR. P. J. BOCK; MRS. KAREN FOX; MR. THOMAS J. HOLZER, Staff Liaison; MR. WES EDWARDS; MR. BRAD SCHLOESSER; MS. SUE IMKER; MS. BARB POPOWSKI; MS. DIANA M. MCCARNEY; Rev. JOSEPH A. STEINBEISSER; MRS. BETTY THOOFT.

Finance Council—MR. STEVE SCHREIBER; Very Rev. MARK S. STEFFL, S.T.L., J.C.L.; Deacon RICHARD J. CHRISTIANSEN; MS. MARY NORDSTROM; MR. THOMAS J. HOLZER, Staff Liaison; MS. AMY WAIBEL.

Diocesan Pastoral Center

Director of Operations & Finance—Human Resources. MR. THOMAS J. HOLZER, Diocesan Pastoral Center, 1421 6th St. N., New Ulm, 56073-2099. Tel: 507-359-2966, Ext. 309; Tel: 507-233-5309; Fax: 507-354-0268; Email: tomholzer@dnu.org.

Office of Pastoral Planning—MR. THOMAS P. KEAVENY, Dir., 1421 6th St. N., New Ulm, 56073-2099. Tel: 507-359-2966; Email: tkeaveny@dnu.org.

Human Resources Consultant—MR. LARRY VANDEN PLAS, Tel: 651-788-3572.

Communications—MS. CHRISTINE CLANCY, Communications Specialist, Tel: 507-359-2966, Ext. 332; Tel: 507-233-5332; Fax: 507-354-0268; Email: cclancy@dnu.org.

The "Prairie Catholic"—MS. CHRISTINE CLANCY, Editor, Diocesan Pastoral Center, 1421 6th St. N., New Ulm, 56073-2099. Tel: 507-359-2966, Ext. 332; Tel: 507-233-5332; Fax: 507-354-0268; Email: cclancy@dnu.org.

Office of Worship—Rev. AARON T. JOHANNECK, Dir., Tel: 507-359-2966, Ext. 320; Tel: 507-233-5320; Email: ajohanneck@dnu.org.

Worship Committee—JOHN RABAEY, Member At-Large; MS. MARGIE DEGROTE; MS. TESSA

PARISEK; MS. ELIZABETH STANDBERG; Rev. AARON T. JOHANNECK, Staff Liaison; Sr. ANNA MARY, A.C.J.; MS. DIANA M. MCCARNEY; MS. TRUDI HENDRICKSON; Rev. PAUL D. TIMMERMAN; THOMAS ANDREWS.

Renewal of Pentecost—Deacon MICHAEL THOENNES, Diocesan Liaison, 10875 Greer Cir., S.W., Howard Lake, 55349. Tel: 320-485-4344; Email: drmike@hutchtel.net.

Ecumenism and Interreligious Affairs—Rev. AARON T. JOHANNECK, Diocesan Pastoral Center, 1421 6th St. N., New Ulm, 56073. Tel: 507-359-2966, Ext. 320; Tel: 507-233-5320.

Office of Social Concerns—Deacon TIMOTHY P. DOLAN, Dir., Diocesan Pastoral Center, 1421 6th St. N., New Ulm, 56073-2099. Tel: 507-359-2966; Tel: 507-233-5338; Fax: 507-354-0268.

Social Concerns Committee—MR. PAUL HAYDEN; Deacon TIMOTHY P. DOLAN, Diocesan Pastoral Council Rep. & Dir. Social Concerns; MS. JUDY HOFFER; MR. RANDY KRZMARZICK. Ex Officio Member: MR. THOMAS P. KEAVENY.

Office of Catholic Charities—

Tel: 507-359-2966, Ext. 339; Tel: 507-233-5339; Tel: 866-670-5163; Fax: 507-354-0268. MR. THOMAS P. KEAVENY, M.S.W., L.I.C.S.W., Dir., Email: tkeaveny@dnu.org; MRS. PAULETTE KRAL, Administrative Coord., Email: pkral@dnu.org.

New Ulm Diocesan Office—Diocesan Pastoral Center, 1421 6th St. N., New Ulm, 56073.

Hutchinson Regional Office—101 Main St. S., Ste. 205, Hutchinson, 55350. MRS. SANDRA SAM RICKERTSEN, M.S., L.M.F.T., Outreach Counselor.

Marshall Regional Office—Campus Religious Center, 1418 State St., Marshall, 56258. MS. TAMI BEHNKE, L.S.W., M.S., L.P.C.C., Outreach Counselor.

Willmar Regional Office—713 12th St., S.W., Willmar, 56201-3099. Sr. LOIS L. BYRNE, P.B.V.M., M.S.W.-L.I.C.S.W., Outreach & Pregnancy Counselor, Project Rachel and Spiritual Direction. Catholic Charities Advisory Committee: MR. DICK EMBACHER; MRS. ELVIA PENA; MRS. STACEY LONGTIN; Revs. BRIAN L. MANDEL; GERALD S. MEIDL; Deacon JOHN A. HANSEN; MRS. JAMIE RIESER; MR. THOMAS P. KEAVENY, Staff Liaison; MS. JODY STOFFELS.

Family Life—Sr. CANDACE FIER, I.S.S.M., Dir., 1421 6th St. N., New Ulm, 56073-2099. Tel: 507-359-2966, Ext. 328; Tel: 507-233-5328; Email: cfier@dnu.org.

Retrouvaille—Tel: 800-470-2230.

Propagation of the Faith/Holy Childhood Association—Rev. PHILIP M. SCHOTZKO, 1421 6th St. N., New Ulm, 56073-2099. Tel: 507-359-2966; Fax: 507-354-0268.

Hispanic Ministry—VACANT.

Office of Personnel—

Priest Personnel—Rev. STEVEN J. VERHELST, Exec. Dir., 1421 6th St. N., New Ulm, 56073-2099. Tel: 507-359-2966; Fax: 507-354-0268.

Priest Personnel Board—Very Rev. Msgr. DOUGLAS L. GRAMS, J.C.L.; Revs. DENNIS C. LABAT; STEVEN J. VERHELST, Exec. Dir.; MATTHEW J. WIERING; RONALD V. HUBERTY.

Victim Assistance Coordinator—Sr. CANDACE FIER, I.S.S.M., Tel: 507-359-2966, Ext. 328; Tel: 507-233-5328; Fax: 507-354-0268; Email: cfier@dnu.org.

Bishop's Delegate in Matters Pertaining to Sexual Misconduct—Very Rev. Msgr. DOUGLAS L. GRAMS, J.C.L., 1421 6th St. N., New Ulm, 56073-2099. Tel: 507-359-2966; Fax: 507-354-0268.

Bishop's Delegate for the Permanent Diaconate—Very Rev. Msgr. EUGENE L. LOZINSKI, J.C.L., Tel: 507-794-4171; Fax: 507-794-5871.

Safe Environment Coordinator—MRS. KARLA CROSS, M.Ed., 1421 6th St. N., New Ulm, 56073. Tel: 507-359-2966; Fax: 507-354-0268; Email: kcross@dnu.org.

Office of Conciliation—MR. ALDEAN B. HENDRICKSON, J.C.L., Dir., 1421 6th St. N., New Ulm, 56073-2099. Tel: 507-359-2966; Fax: 507-354-0268.

Vocations Team—1421 6th St. N., New Ulm, 56073-2099. Fax: 507-354-0268. Most Rev. JOHN M. LEVOIR, Team Chm.; Revs. MATTHEW J. WIERING, Dir., Tel: 507-359-2966, Ext. 331; Email: fatherwiering@gmail.com; CRAIG A. TIMMERMAN, Asst. Dir., Tel: 507-359-2966; Email: fathercraig@gmail.com.

Continuing Education of Clergy—MRS. KARLA CROSS, M.Ed., Dir., Diocesan Pastoral Center, 1421 6th St. N., New Ulm, 56073-2099. Tel: 507-359-2966, Ext. 323; Fax: 507-354-0268.

Board of Trustees for Pension Plan for Priests—Most Rev. JOHN M. LEVOIR; Very Rev. Msgrs. DOUGLAS L. GRAMS, J.C.L.; EUGENE L. LOZINSKI, J.C.L.; Revs. ZACHARY D. PETERSON; KEITH R. SALISBURY; MR. DON GUGGEMOS JR.; MR. MICHAEL SCHWARTZ; MR. THOMAS J. HOLZER, Staff Liaison.

Vicar for Retired Priests—Rev. GERMAIN P. RADEMACHER, (Retired).

Organizations in the Diocese of New Ulm

Diocesan Council of Catholic Women—MRS. BETTY THOOFT, Pres., Mailing Address: P.O. Box 128, Tyler, 56178. Tel: 507-247-5269; MRS. RONDA MATHIOWETZ, Past Pres., 17786 County Rd. 8, Sleepy Eye, 56085. Tel: 507-360-9162; Very Rev. Msgr. EUGENE L. LOZINSKI, J.C.L., Diocesan Moderator.

Girl Scouts—MRS. MARY REITSMA, 4313 N.E. 15th St., Willmar, 56201. Tel: 320-235-3471.

Boy Scouts—Rev. ANDREW J. MICHELS, Chap., St. Mary, 636 1st Ave. N., Sleepy Eye, 56085-1004. Tel: 507-794-4171; Fax: 507-794-5871.

Marriage Encounter—304 10th Ave. W., P.O. Box 302, Lamberton, 56152. Tel: 507-829-8869. CRAIG WETTER; BARB WETTER.

Catholic Medical Association—508 S. German St., New Ulm, 56073. Tel: 507-276-3070. FRANI KNOWLES, M.D.

CLERGY, PARISHES, MISSIONS AND PAROCHIAL SCHOOLS

CITY OF NEW ULM

(BROWN COUNTY)

1—CATHEDRAL OF THE HOLY TRINITY (1856) [CEM] [JC] (Holy Cross Area Faith Community with St. Gregory the Great, Lafayette; St. George, West Newton Township; St. John the Baptist, Searles; St. Mary's, New Ulm.)
605 N. State St., 56073-1898. Tel: 507-354-4158; Email: cathedral@holycrossafc.org; Web: www.holycrossafc.org/cathedral-of-the-holy-trinity. Very Rev. Msgr. Douglas L. Grams, J.C.L., Rector; Revs. Garrett Ahlers; Gerald S. Meidl; Cornelius Ezeiloaku; Deacon Richard J. Christiansen.
See New Ulm Area Catholic Schools, New Ulm under New Ulm Area Catholic Schools located in the Institution section.
Catechesis Religious Program—Students 126.

2—ST. MARY (1911) [JC] (Holy Cross Area Faith Community with Cathedral of Holy Trinity, New Ulm; St. John the Baptist, Searles; St. George, West Newton Township; & St. Gregory the Great, Lafayette)
417 S. Minnesota St., 56073-2120. Tel: 507-233-9500; Fax: 507-354-8414; Email: stmary@holycrossafc.org; Web: www.holycrossafc.org/church-of-st-mary.html. Very Rev. Msgr. Douglas L. Grams, J.C.L.; Revs. Garrett Ahlers, Parochial Vicar; Bruno Santiago, Parochial Vicar; Gerald S. Meidl, Parochial Vicar.
See New Ulm Area Catholic Schools, New Ulm under New Ulm Area Catholic Schools located in the Institution section.
Catechesis Religious Program—Tel: 507-233-9511. Students 146.

OUTSIDE THE CITY OF NEW ULM

APPLETON, SWIFT CO., ST. JOHN (1880) [CEM 2] [JC2] (St. Isidore the Farmer Area Faith Community with Benson; DeGraff; Murdock; Clontarf; & Danvers)
350 S Edquist St, Appleton, 56208-1516.
Tel: 320-289-1146; Tel: 320-842-4271; Email: office@stisidorethefarmerafc.org; Email: stjccao@gmail.com; Web: stisidorethefarmerafc.org. 349 E. Reuss Ave., Appleton, 56208-1516. Rev. Jeremy G. Kucera.
Catechesis Religious Program—Tel: 320-842-4021. Students 85.

ARLINGTON, SIBLEY CO., ST. MARY (1864) [CEM] (Area Faith Community with Gaylord & Green Isle.)
504 7th Ave., N.W., P.O. Box 392, Arlington, 55307-0392. Tel: 507-964-5821; Email: stmararl@frontiernet.net; Web: stmichaelmarybrendan.com. Rev. Aaron T. Johanneck, Parochial Admin.; Deacon Timothy P. Dolan.
Catechesis Religious Program—Tel: 507-327-1899; Email: bethwalters06@gmail.com. Beth Walters, D.R.E. & Youth Min. Students 168.

BARRY, BIG STONE CO., ST. BARNABAS, Closed. For sacramental records contact Holy Rosary, Graceville.

BEARDSLEY, BIG STONE CO., ST. MARY (1884) [CEM] Merged into Graceville(Spirit of Life Area Faith Community with Graceville, Ortonville, Rosen and Madision)
518 S. Forest St., Beardsley, 56211-0299.
Tel: 320-748-7313; Email: holygraceville@gmail.com. Mailing Address: P.O. Box 7, Graceville, 56240. Rev. Brian W. Oestreich.
Catechesis Religious Program—Attend Holy Rosary's program.

BECHYN, RENVILLE CO., ST. MARY, Closed. For sacramental records contact St. Aloysius, Olivia.

BELGRADE, NICOLLET CO., ST. MICHAEL, Closed. For sacramental records contact St. Paul, Nicollet.

BENSON, SWIFT CO., ST. FRANCIS (1881) [CEM] (St. Isidore the Farmer area faith community with Clontarf; Danvers; De Graff; Murdock; & Appleton.
508 13th St. N., Benson, 56215-1228.
Tel: 320-842-4271; Email: office@stisidorethefarmerafc.org; Web: stisidorethefarmerafc.org. Rev. Jeremy G. Kucera.
Catechesis Religious Program—Ms. Cyndi Stifter, D.R.E. Students 113.

BIRCH COOLIE, RENVILLE CO., ST. PATRICK, Closed. For sacramental records contact Sacred Heart, Franklin. Earlier records located at St. John, Morton.

BIRD ISLAND, RENVILLE CO., ST. MARY (1879) [CEM] (Heart of Jesus area faith community with Hector; Olivia; & Renville.)
220 S. 10th St., P.O. Box 500, Bird Island, 55310-0500. Tel: 320-365-3593; Email: stmary@heartofjesusafc.org; Web: www.heartofjesusafc.org. Revs. Joseph A. Steinbeisser; George V. Schmit Jr., Senior Associate.
School—St. Mary School, (Grades K-8), 140 S. 10th St., P.O. Box 500, Bird Island, 55310-0500.
Tel: 320-365-3693; Email: stmary@heartofjesusafc.org; Web: www.stmarysschoolbirdisland.com. Mrs. Tracy Bertrand; Mrs. Tracy Bertrand Sigurdson, Prin.; Mrs. Julie Elfering, Librarian. Aides 2; Lay Teachers 12; Students 124.
Catechesis Religious Program—
Tel: 320-365-3593, Ext. 251; Email: martya@heartofjesusafc.org. Marty Athmann, D.R.E. Students 89.

CANBY, YELLOW MEDICINE CO., ST. PETER (1897) [CEM] (Good Teacher area faith community with St. Leo; Ghent; & Minneota.)
307 W. 4th St., Canby, 56220-1211.
Tel: 507-223-7304. Revs. Craig A. Timmerman; Keith R. Salisbury, Parochial Vicar; Zachary D. Peterson.
School—St. Peter School, (Grades PreK-6), 410 Ring Ave. N., Canby, 56220-1237. Tel: 507-223-7729; Fax: 507-223-7178; Email: lori.rangaard@schoolofstpeter.com; Web: www.schoolofstpeter.com. Mrs. Lori Rangaard, Prin.
Legal Title: School of St. Peter. Lay Teachers 6; Students 78.
Catechesis Religious Program—Nathan Jones, D.R.E. Students 195.

CLARA CITY, CHIPPEWA CO., ST. CLARA (1890) [CEM]
414 N. Main St., Clara City, 56222-0310. 512 Black Oak Ave, Montevideo, 56265. Rev. Paul D. Timmerman. (Holy Family area faith community with Granite Falls & Montevideo).
Catechesis Religious Program—Email: sacoordinator@holyfamilyarea.org. Christina Wangen, D.R.E. Students 343.

CLARKFIELD, YELLOW MEDICINE CO., ST. ISIDORE, Closed. For sacramental records contact St. Joseph, Montevideo.

CLEMENTS, REDWOOD CO., ST. JOSEPH (ORATORY) (1902) [CEM]
120 Ash Street, Clements, 56224. Tel: 507-794-4171; Email: stmichaels@redred.com. 613 W. 3rd St, P.O. Box 459, Morgan, 56266. Very Rev. Msgr. Eugene L. Lozinski, J.C.L.

CLONTARF, SWIFT CO., ST. MALACHY (1878) (St. Isidore the Farmer area faith community with Benson; Danvers; DeGraff; Murdock & Appleton)
Mailing Address: 508 13th St. N., Benson, 56215.
Tel: 320-842-4271; Fax: 320-843-2264; Email: office@stisidorethefarmerafc.org. 300 Armagh St. SW, Clontarf, 56226. Rev. Jeremy G. Kucera.
Catechesis Religious Program—Students 17.

COMFREY, BROWN CO., ST. PAUL (1900) [CEM] (Divine Mercy area faith community with Clements; Morgan; Leavenworth; & Sleepy Eye.)
209 N. Field St., Comfrey, 56019-0277.
Tel: 507-877-2361; Email: stpcomfrey@yahoo.com. P.O. Box 277, Comfrey, 56019-0277. Very Rev. Msgr. Eugene L. Lozinski, J.C.L.
Catechesis Religious Program—Tel: 507-877-2119. Linda Schwab, D.R.E. Students 35.

COTTONWOOD, LYON CO., ST. MARY (1902) [CEM] (Bread of Life area faith community with Green Valley & Marshall.)
255 W. 4th St. S., P.O. Box 228, Cottonwood, 56229-0228. Tel: 507-423-5220; Email: stmarys.cottonwood@yahoo.com; Web: www.holy-redeemer.com. Rev. Matthew J. Wiering.
Catechesis Religious Program—Alyson Bossuyt, D.R.E.; Mary Beth Sinclair, D.R.E. Students 37.

DANVERS, SWIFT CO., CHURCH OF THE VISITATION (ORATORY) (1885) [CEM] (St. Isidore the Farmer area faith community with Benson; Clontarf; De Graff;

Murdock & Appleton)
Mailing Address: 508 13th St. N., Benson, 56215.
Tel: 320-842-4271; Email: office@stisidorethefarmerafc.org; Web: stisidorethefarmerafc.org. 201 County Road 14, Danvers, 56231. Rev. Jeremy G. Kucera.

DARWIN, MEEKER CO., ST. JOHN (1861) [CEM] (Shepherd of Souls Area Faith Community with Forest City; Litchfield & Manannah)
106 N. 4th St., Darwin, 55324-6016.
Tel: 320-275-2915; Tel: 320-693-9496; Email: rectory@stjohnscatholic-darwin.com; Web: www.shepherdofsouls.org. Revs. Jeffrey P. Horejsi; Brian L. Mandel, Senior Assoc.; Deacon John A. Hansen.
Catechesis Religious Program—17260 US-12, Cokato, 55321. Tel: 320-286-2800; Email: dcnjohnhansen@gmail.com. Students 534.

DAWSON, LAC QUI PARLE CO., ST. JAMES (1898) [CEM]
10th & Locust, Dawson, 56232-0270.
Tel: 507-223-7304. Mailing Address: 307 4th St. W., Canby, 56220. Revs. Craig A. Timmerman, Admin.; Zachary D. Peterson; Keith R. Salisbury. (Good Teacher Area Faith Community Minneota, Ghent, Canby, St. Leo, & Dawson.)
Catechesis Religious Program—Christina Wangen, D.R.E. Students 74.

DE GRAFF, SWIFT CO., ST. BRIDGET (1876) [CEM] (St. Isidore the Farmer area faith community with Benson; Clontarf; Danvers; Murdock & Appleton)
Mailing Address & Res.: 508 13th St. N., Benson, 56215-1228. Tel: 320-842-4271; Fax: 320-843-2264; Email: office@stisidorethefarmerafc.org; Web: www.stisidorethefarmerafc.org. 501 3rd St. S., DeGraff, 56271. Rev. Jeremy G. Kucera.
Catechesis Religious Program—Students 27.

EDEN VALLEY, MEEKER CO., ST. PETER (1903) Closed. For inquiries for parish records contact Assumption Church, Eden Valley, Diocese of St. Cloud.

FAIRFAX, RENVILLE CO., ST. ANDREW (1871) [CEM] (All Saints Area faith community with Franklin; Gibbon; & Winthrop.)
15 S.E. First St., P.O. Box C, Fairfax, 55332-0903.
Tel: 507-426-7739; Email: ffgw@centurytel.net; Web: www.allsaintsafc.org. Rev. Bruno Santiago.
Catechesis Religious Program—Tel: 507-426-7742. Students 67.

FAXON TOWNSHIP, SIBLEY CO., ST. JOHN-ASSUMPTION (1859) [CEM 2] Clustered with Henderson & Jessenland.
26523 200th St., Belle Plaine, 56011.
Tel: 507-248-3550; Email: stjos@frontiernet.net. P.O. Box 427, Henderson, 56044. Rev. Samuel F. Perez.
Catechesis Religious Program—Students 84.

FOREST CITY, MEEKER CO., ST. GERTRUDE (1857) [CEM] (Shepherd of Souls Area Faith Community with Darwin, Litchfield & Manannah.) Merged with St. Philip, Litchfield.
31608 650th Ave., Litchfield, 55355-4110.
Tel: 320-693-3313; Email: stphilip@hutchtel.net; Web: www.shepherdofsouls.org. Revs. Jeffrey P. Horejsi; Brian L. Mandel, Perochial Vicar.

Catechesis Religious Program—Students 18.

FRANKLIN, RENVILLE CO., SACRED HEART (1898) [CEM 2] (All Saints Area Faith Community with Fairfax; Gibbon; & Winthrop.)
551 2nd Ave E, P.O. Box 175, Franklin, 55333-0175.
Tel: 507-426-7739; Email: ffgw@centurytel.net; Web: www.allsaintsafc.org. Rev. Bruno Santiago.
Res.: 15 S.E. First St., P.O. Box C, Fairfax, 55332-0903.
Church: E. Main St., Franklin, 55333-0175.
Catechesis Religious Program—Students 36.

GAYLORD, SIBLEY CO., ST. MICHAEL (1882) (Ss. Michael, Mary & Brendan Area Faith Community with Arlington & Green Isle.)
411 Court Ave., P.O. Box 357, Gaylord, 55334-0357.
Tel: 507-237-2851; Email: stmichaelchurchof@yahoo.com. Rev. Aaron T. Johanneck, Paroachial Admin.
Catechesis Religious Program—P.O. Box 357, Gaylord, 55334-0357. Beth Walters, D.R.E. Students 37.

GHENT, LYON CO., ST. ELOI (1883) [CEM] (Good Teacher Area Faith Community with Canby; St. Leo; & Minneota.)
409 N. Adams St., Minneota, 56264. Rev. Craig A. Timmerman.
Church: 306 W. McQuestion, Ghent, 56239-9750.
Tel: 507-428-3285; Email: cbuyssegoodteacherafc@gmail.com.
Catechesis Religious Program—Students 34.

GIBBON, SIBLEY CO., ST. WILLIBRORD (1886) [CEM] (All Saints Area Faith Community with Fairfax; Franklin; & Winthrop.)
1032 Ash Ave., P.O. Box 436, Gibbon, 55335-0436.
Tel: 507-426-7739; Email: ffgw@centurytel.net; Web: www.allsaintsafc.org. Rev. Bruno Santiago.
Catechesis Religious Program—Tel: 507-834-6659. Students 44.

GLENCOE, MCLEOD CO.
1—ST. GEORGE, Closed. For sacramental records, contact St. Pius X, Glencoe.
2—SS. PETER AND PAUL, Closed. For sacramental records, contact St. Pius X, Glencoe.
3—ST. PIUS X (1983) [CEM] (Saint John Paul II Area Faith Community with Silver Lake & Winsted)
1014 Knight Ave., N., Glencoe, 55336-2300.
Tel: 320-864-3214; Email: danh@stpiusxglencoe.org. Revs. Anthony J. Stubeda; Michael M. Doyle, Parochial Vicar; Paul A. Schumacher, Parochial Vicar.
Catechesis Religious Program—Tel: 320-864-5162. Students 113.

GRACEVILLE, BIG STONE CO., HOLY ROSARY (1878) Spirit of Life Area Faith Community with Beardsley, Ortonville, Rosen, and Madison.
511 Studdart Ave., Graceville, 56240-0007.
Tel: 320-748-7313; Email: holygraceville@gmail.com; Web: www.spiritoflifeafc.org. P.O. Box 7, Graceville, 56240-0007. Rev. Brian W. Oestreich; Deacon Art D. Abel, Tel: 320-748-7573 (Home).
412 W 3rd St., Madison, 56256. Tel: 507-829-6667; Email: b.oestreich@hotmail.com.
Catechesis Religious Program—517 Studdart Ave., Graceville, 56240. Tel: 320-748-7501. Students 112.

GRANITE FALLS, YELLOW MEDICINE CO., ST. ANDREW (1885) [CEM] (Holy Family Area Faith Community with Montevideo & Clara City)
1094 Granite St., Granite Falls, 56241-1355.
Tel: 320-269-5954; Email: secretary@holyfamilyarea.org (Call First); Web: www.holyfamilyarea.org. 512 Black Oak Ave., Montevideo, 56265. Rev. Paul D. Timmerman.
Res.: 452 11th Ave., Granite Falls, 56241.
Tel: 320-269-5954; Email: businessmanager@holyfamilyarea.org. Melinda Hedman, Contact Person.
Catechesis Religious Program—450 11th Ave., Granite Falls, 56241. Tel: 320-269-5954; Email: sacoordinator@holyfamilyarea.org. Christina Wangen, D.R.E. Students 73.

GREEN ISLE, SIBLEY CO., ST. BRENDAN (1854) [CEM] (Ss. Michael, Mary & Brendan Area Faith Community with Arlington & Gaylord.)
221 McGrann St. S., P.O. Box 85, Green Isle, 55338-0085. Tel: 507-326-5111; Email: stbrendan@frontiernet.net. Revs. Aaron T. Johanneck, Parochial Admin.; John G. Berger, In Res., (Retired).
Catechesis Religious Program—Students 23.

GREEN VALLEY, LYON CO., ST. CLOTILDE (1912) [CEM] (Bread of Life Area Faith Community with Cottonwood & Marshall.)
3272 270th Ave., Marshall, 56258. Tel: 507-531-7970 ; Email: ccboerboom@mvtvwireless.com; Web: www.stclotilde.com. Rev. Matthew J. Wiering.
Res.: 255 W. 4th, Cottonwood, 56229.
Catechesis Religious Program—Students 43.

GREENLEAF, MEEKER CO., ST. COLUMBAN, Closed. For inquiries for sacramental records contact St. Philip, Litchfield.

HECTOR, RENVILLE CO., CHURCH OF ST. JOHN (1878) [CEM] (Heart of Jesus Area Faith Community with Bird Island; Olivia; & Renville.)
301 Cedar Ave. E., Hector, 55342. Tel: 320-848-6437; Tel: 320-365-3593; Email: stjohn@heartofjesus.org. P.O. Box 500, Bird Island, 55310. Revs. Joseph A. Steinbeisser; George V. Schmit Jr.

HEGBERT, SWIFT CO., ST. AGNES, Closed. For sacramental records, contact St. John, Appleton.

HENDERSON, SIBLEY CO., ST. JOSEPH (1859) [CEM] Clustered with Faxon Township & Jessenland.
213 S. 6th St., P.O. Box 427, Henderson, 56044-0427.
Tel: 507-248-3550; Email: stjos@frontiernet.net. Rev. Samuel F. Perez.
Catechesis Religious Program—Students 45.

HOLLOWAY, SWIFT CO., ST. JOSEPH, Closed. For sacramental records, contact St. John, Appleton.

HUTCHINSON, MCLEOD CO., CHURCH OF ST. ANASTASIA (1866) [CEM] Area Faith Community with Stewart.
460 Lake St., S.W., Hutchinson, 55350-2349.
Tel: 320-587-6507; Fax: 320-234-6756; Email: stanastasia@stanastasia.net; Web: www.stanastasia.net. Rev. Paul L. Wolf.
Res.: 1016 Roe Ave., Hutchinson, 55350-2117.
School—Church of St. Anastasia School, (Grades PreK-6), 400 Lake St., S.W., Hutchinson, 55350.
Tel: 320-587-2490; Email: principal@stanastasia.net. Julie Shelby, Prin. Lay Teachers 10; Students 95.
Catechesis Religious Program—Tel: 320-587-2490; Email: religioused@stanastasia.net. Students 204.

IVANHOE, LINCOLN CO., SS. PETER & PAUL (1900) [CEM] (Christ the King Area Faith Community with Lake Benton; Tyler; & Wilno.)
111 N. Sherwood, P.O. Box 49, Ivanhoe, 56142-0049.
Tel: 507-694-1402; Email: bjthooft@frontiernet.net; Web: ChristtheKing AFC.com. Rev. Ronald V. Huberty.
Catechesis Religious Program—213 Linwood, P.O. Box 310, Tyler, 56178. Tel: 507-247-3464;
Fax: 507-247-3286. Kari Nilles, D.R.E. & Youth Min. Students 36.

JESSENLAND, SIBLEY CO., ST. THOMAS (ORATORY) (1855) [CEM]
31624 Scenic Byway Rd., Henderson, 56044-0427.
Tel: 507-248-3550; Email: stjos@frontiernet.net. P.O. Box 427, Henderson, 56044. Rev. Samuel F. Perez, (Henderson).

KANDIYOHI, KANDIYOHI CO., ST. PATRICK (1868) [CEM] Closed. For inquiries for parish records please contact St. Mary, Willmar.

LAFAYETTE, NICOLLET CO., ST. GREGORY THE GREAT (1942) [CEM] (Holy Cross Area Faith Community with Cathedral & St. Mary's, New Ulm; St. John's, Searles; & St. George, West Newton Township.)
440 6th St., P.O. Box 5, Lafayette, 56054.
Tel: 507-228-8298; Email: stgregory@holycrossafc.org; Web: www.holycrossafc.org/church-of-st-gregory-the-great. Very Rev. Msgr. Douglas L. Grams, J.C.L.; Revs. Garrett Ahlers, Parochial Vicar; Cornelius Ezeiloaku, Parochial Vicar; Gerald S. Meidl, Parochial Vicar.

LAKE BENTON, LINCOLN CO., ST. GENEVIEVE (1897) [CEM] (Christ the King Area Faith Community with Ivanhoe; Tyler; & Wilno.)
111 N. Sherwood, P.O. Box 49, Ivanhoe, 56142.
Tel: 507-247-3464; Email: bjthooft@frontiernet.net. 213 Linwood, P.O. Box 310, Tyler, 56178. Rev. Ronald V. Huberty.
Church: 119 S. Sherman St., Lake Benton, 56149.
Tel: 507-368-4232.
Catechesis Religious Program—203 Linwood St., Tyler, 56178. Kari Nilles, D.R.E. - Youth Min. Students 21.

LAKE LILLIAN, KANDIYOHI CO., ST. THOMAS MORE (1934) Closed. For inquiries for parish records please contact St. Mary, Willmar.

LAMBERTON, REDWOOD CO., ST. JOSEPH (1895) [CEM] (Area Faith Community with Sanborn, Springfield)
400 W. 2nd Ave., P.O. Box 458, Lamberton, 56152-0458. Tel: 507-752-7269; Email: stjoseph@centurylink.net. Rev. Philip M. Schotzko.
Catechesis Religious Program—Students 34.
ST. THOMAS, 301 E. Winona St., Sanborn, 56083.
Tel: 507-648-3754.

LEAVENWORTH, BROWN CO., CHURCH OF THE JAPANESE MARTYRS (1867) [CEM] (Divine Mercy Area Faith Community with Clements; Comfrey; Morgan; & Sleepy Eye.)
30881 County Rd. 24, Sleepy Eye, 56085-4361.
Tel: 507-794-6974; Email: jmartyrs@sleepyeyetel.net. Very Rev. Msgr. Eugene L. Lozinski, J.C.L.
Catechesis Religious Program—Rhonda Lux, D.R.E.; Lori Groebner, D.R.E. Students 26.

LESTER PRAIRIE, MCLEOD CO., ST. CONRAD, Closed. Incorporated but never organized. No sacramental records.

LITCHFIELD, MEEKER CO., ST. PHILIP (1859) [CEM] (Shepherd of Souls Area Faith Community with Manannah; Forest City; & Darwin)
821 E. 5th St., Litchfield, 55355-2223.
Tel: 320-693-3313; Email: stphilip@hutchtel.net; Web: www.shepherdofsouls.org. Revs. Jeffrey P. Horejsi; Brian L. Mandel.
School—St. Philip School, (Grades PreK-5), 225 E. 3rd St., Litchfield, 55355. Tel: 320-693-6283; Email: mkramer@thechurchofstphilip.org. Ms. Michelle Kramer, Prin. Lay Teachers 6; Students 56.
Catechesis Religious Program—Karen Kulzer, D.R.E. Students 182.

LUCAN, REDWOOD CO., OUR LADY OF VICTORY (1889) [CEM] (Light of the World Area Faith Community with Seaforth; Wabasso; & Wanda.)
P.O. Box 96, Lucan, 56255-0096. Tel: 507-747-2231; Email: ourlady@mnval.net; Web: www.lowafc.org. Rev. Anthony R. Hesse, (Wabassso).
Church: 303 Third St., Lucan, 56255.
Catechesis Religious Program—1052 Cedar St., P.O. Box 239, Wabasso, 56293. Ms. Sherry Plaetz, D.R.E. Students 7.

MADISON, LAC QUI PARLE CO., ST. MICHAEL (1884) [CEM] (Spirit of Life Area Faith Community with Graceville, Ortonville & Rosen)
412 3rd St. W., Madison, 56256-1494.
Tel: 320-598-3690; Email: stmichael1891@gmail.com; Web: spiritoflifeafc.org. Rev. Brian W. Oestreich.
Catechesis Religious Program—Students 32.

MANANNAH, MEEKER CO., CHURCH OF OUR LADY (1876) [CEM] (Shepherd of Souls Area Faith Community with Litchfield; Darwin & Forest City)
57482 CSAH 3, Grove City, 56243-9786.
Tel: 320-693-8900; Email: ourlady@meltel.net; Web: www.shepherdofsouls.org. Revs. Jeffrey P. Horejsi; Brian L. Mandel, Parochial Vicar.
Catechesis Religious Program—Email: sknisley@arvig.net. Shirley Knisley, C.R.E. Students 94.

MARSHALL, LYON CO., HOLY REDEEMER (1883) [CEM] (Bread of Life Area Faith Community with Cottonwood & Green Valley.)
Mailing Address: 503 W. Lyon St., Marshall, 56258-1311. Tel: 507-532-5711; Email: lnelson@holy-

redeemer.com; Web: www.holy-redeemer.com. Very Rev. Mark S. Steffl, S.T.L., J.C.L.
School—Holy Redeemer School, (Grades K-8), 501 S. Whitney, Marshall, 56258-1995. Tel: 507-532-6642; Fax: 507-532-2636. Johsua Langseth, Prin. Lay Teachers 24; Students 237.
Catechesis Religious Program—503 W. Lyon St., Marshall, 56258-1995. Tel: 507-532-3602; Email: ltimmerman@holy-redeemer.com; Email: danaweb@holy-redeemer.com. Lori Timmerman, D.R.E.; Dana Webskowski, Youth Min. Students 308.

MIDDLE LAKE, NICOLLET CO., ST. NICHOLAS, Closed. Incorporated but never organized. No sacramental records.

MILROY, REDWOOD CO., ST. MICHAEL (1904) [CEM] (Our Lady of the Prairie Area Faith Community with Tracy, St. Mary. and share priests with Marshall, MN)
200 Euclid Ave., Milroy, 56263. Tel: 507-336-2505; Fax: 507-336-2505; Email: stmichael@mnval.net. Very Rev. Mark S. Steffl, S.T.L., J.C.L.; Rev. Mark S. Mallak, S.T.L., J.C.L.
Res.: 400 Cedar St., Milroy, 56263.
Catechesis Religious Program—249 6th St., Tracy, 56175. Tel: 507-629-3667; Email: saintmaryre@iw.net. Ashley Benson, D.R.E. Students 52.

MINNEOTA, LYON CO., ST. EDWARD (1880) [CEM] (Good Teacher Area Faith Community with Canby; Ghent; & St. Leo.)
409 N. Adams St., Minneota, 56264-9801.
Tel: 507-872-6346; Email: cbuyssegoodteacherafc@gmail.com; Web: www.stedschurch.com. Rev. Craig A. Timmerman.
School—St. Edward School, (Grades PreK-8), 210 W. 4th St., Minneota, 56264. Tel: 507-872-6391; Email: jgarveysteds@hotmail.com; Web: stedwardcatholicschool.com. Jaci Garvy, Prin. Lay Teachers 8; Students 52.
Catechesis Religious Program—Students 195.

MONTEVIDEO, CHIPPEWA CO., ST. JOSEPH (1882) [CEM] (Holy Family Area Faith Community with Granite Falls, Clara City.)
512 Black Oak Ave., Montevideo, 56265-1874.
Tel: 320-269-5954; Email: secretary@holyfamilyarea.org; Web: www.holyfamilyarea.org. Rev. Paul D. Timmerman.
Res.: 521 Eureka Ave., Montevideo, 56265-1899.
Catechesis Religious Program—Christina Wangen, D.R.E. Students 775.

MORGAN, REDWOOD CO., ST. MICHAEL (1890) [CEM] (Divine Mercy Area Faith Community with Clements; Comfrey; Leavenworth; & Sleepy Eye.)
510 W. 3rd St., P.O. Box 459, Morgan, 56266-0459.
Tel: 507-249-3192; Email: stmichaels@redred.com. Very Rev. Msgr. Eugene L. Lozinski, J.C.L.
School—St. Michael School, (Grades PreK-6), 612 W. 3rd St., P.O. Box 459, Morgan, 56266-0459.
Tel: 507-249-3192; Fax: 507-249-2557; Email: stmichaels@redred.com; Web: www.divinemercyafc.prg. Jennifer Fischer, Prin. Lay Teachers 4; Students 34.
Catechesis Religious Program—Email: dre.st.michaels@gmail.com. Daniel Davis, D.R.E. Students 61.

MORTON, RENVILLE CO., ST. JOHN (1873) [CEM] Area Faith Community with Redwood Falls.
331 W. 3rd St., P.O. Box 88, Morton, 56270-0088.
Tel: 507-697-6120; Email: stjohnsmorton@mchsi.com. Very Rev. Mark S. Steffl, S.T.L., J.C.L.
Res. & Mailing Address: 341 W. 3rd St., P.O. Box 88, Morton, 56270-0088.
Catechesis Religious Program—Students 30.

MURDOCK, SWIFT CO., CHURCH OF THE SACRED HEART (1879) [CEM] (St. Isidore the Farmer Area Faith Community with Benson; Clontarf; Danvers; De Graff & Appleton)
201 Orleans, Murdock, 56271. Tel: 320-875-2451; Email: office@stisidorethefarmerafc.org; Email: lauraebowman@stisidorethefarmerafc.org; Web: www.stisidorethefarmerafc.org. P.O. Box 9, Murdock, 56271. Rev. Jeremy G. Kucera.
Catechesis Religious Program—508 13th Street North, Benson, 56215. Tel: 320-842-4271. Students 61.

NASSAU, LAC QUI PARLE CO., ST. JAMES (1902) [CEM] Closed. For inquiries for parish records contact the chancery.

NICOLLET, NICOLLET CO., ST. PAUL (1907) [CEM 4] (Apostles Peter & Paul Area Faith Community with St. Peter.)
Church & Mailing Address: 410 5th St., P.O. Box 248, Nicollet, 56074-0248. Tel: 507-232-3857; Email: stpaulccnicollet@gmail.com. Rev. Todd J. Petersen.

NORTH MANKATO, NICOLLET CO., HOLY ROSARY (1924)
525 Grant Ave., North Mankato, 56003-2939.
Tel: 507-387-6501; Email: hros2@hickorytech.net; Web: www.holyrosarynorthmankato.com. Rev. Paul H. van de Crommert.
Catechesis Religious Program—Catherine Neve, D.R.E. Students 254.

OLIVIA, RENVILLE CO., ST. ALOYSIUS (1888) [CEM 2] [JC] (Heart of Jesus Area Faith Community with Renville; Hector; & Bird Island.)
302 S. 10th St., Olivia, 56277-1288.
Tel: 320-523-2030; Email: staloysius@heartofjesusafc.org; Web: www.heartofjesusafc.org. Revs. Joseph A. Steinbeisser; George V. Schmit Jr., Parochial Vicar.

ORTONVILLE, BIG STONE CO., ST. JOHN (1879) Spirit of Life Area Faith Community with Madison, Rosen & Graceville.
421 Madison Ave., Ortonville, 56278-2713.
Tel: 320-839-2772; Web: www.spiritoflifeafc.org. Rev. Brian W. Oestreich; Deacon Paul W. Treinen.
Catechesis Religious Program—Tel: 320-305-3364; Email: joymcdolan@gmail.com. Joy Dolan, D.R.E. Students 120.

RAYMOND, KANDIYOHI CO., SACRED HEART, Closed. For sacramental records, contact St. Clara, Clara City.

REDWOOD FALLS, REDWOOD CO., ST. CATHERINE (1870) [CEM] Area Faith Community with Morton.
900 E. Flynn St., P.O. Box 383, Redwood Falls, 56283-0383. Tel: 507-644-2278; Email: stcath@mystcatherines.org. Very Rev. Mark S. Steffl, S.T.L., J.C.L.
Res.: 904 E. Flynn St., P.O. Box 383, Redwood Falls, 56283-0383.
Catechesis Religious Program—Students 212.

REGAL, KANDIYOHI CO., ST. ANTHONY (MISSION) (1933) [CEM] Closed. Records at Our Lady of the Lakes, Spicer.

RENVILLE, RENVILLE CO., HOLY REDEEMER (1891) [CEM] (Heart of Jesus Area Faith Community with Olivia; Bird Island; & Hector.)
106 3rd St. SE, Renville, 56284. Tel: 320-523-2030; Email: staloysius@heartofjesusafc.org; Email: holyredeemer@heartofjesusafc.org; Web: www.heartofjesusafc.org. 302 S. 10th St., Olivia, 56277. Revs. Joseph A. Steinbeisser; George V. Schmit Jr.

ROSEN, LAC QUI PARLE CO., ST. JOSEPH (1885) [CEM] Spirit of Life Area Faith Community with Ortonville, Graceville & Madison
1741 340th St., Bellingham, 56212.
Tel: 320-839-2772; Email: stjohnortonville@gmail.com; Web: www.spiritoflifeafc.org. 421 Madison Ave., Ortonville, 56278-2713. Rev. Brian W. Oestreich.
Catechesis Religious Program—Joy Dolan, D.R.E. Students 41.

ST. LEO, YELLOW MEDICINE CO., ST. LEO (1881) [CEM] (Good Teacher Area Faith Community with Canby; Ghent; & Minneota.)
307 4th St. W., Canby, 56220. Tel: 507-223-7304; Email: mary.knollenberg@schoolofstpeter.com. Revs. Craig A. Timmerman; Keith R. Salisbury, Parochial Vicar; Zachary D. Peterson.
Catechesis Religious Program—409 N Adams, Minneota, 56264. Tel: 507-259-8766; Email: ffdstmarys@gmail.com. Nathan Jones, D.R.E. Students 22.

SAINT PETER, NICOLLET CO.
1—CHURCH OF ST. PETER (1856) [CEM] (Apostles Peter & Paul Area Faith Community with Nicollet.)
1801 W. Broadway, St. Peter, 56082.
Tel: 507-931-1628; Fax: 507-931-2977; Email: office@churchofstpeter.org; Web: www.churchofstpeter.org. Rev. Todd J. Petersen.
School—John Ireland School, (Grades K-6),
Tel: 507-931-2810; Email: colleen.wenner@johnirelandschool.org; Web: www.churchofstpeter.org. Lay Teachers 11; Students 73.
2—IMMACULATE CONCEPTION, Closed. For sacramental records, contact St. Peter's, St. Peter.

SANBORN, REDWOOD CO., ST. THOMAS (ORATORY) (1902) (Vine and Branches Area Faith Community with Springfield & Lamberton.)
301 E. Winona St., P.O. Box 176, Sanborn, 56083-0176. Tel: 507-752-7269; Email: stjoseph@centurylink.net. Rev. Philip M. Schotzko.

SEAFORTH, REDWOOD CO., ST. MARY (1880) [CEM 2] [JC2] (Light of the World Area Faith Community with Wabasso; Lucan; & Wanda.)
P.O. Box 239, Wabasso, 56293-0239.
Tel: 507-342-5190 (Office); Fax: 507-342-5156; Email: stannesschool@wabassostannesschool.com; Web: lowafc.org. Rev. Anthony R. Hesse.
Catechesis Religious Program—Students 7.

SEARLES, BROWN CO., ST. JOHN THE BAPTIST (1905) [CEM] (Holy Cross Area Faith Community with Cathedral & St. Mary's, New Ulm; Lafayette; & West Newton Township.)
18241 First Ave. S., 56073-5171. Tel: 507-359-4244; Email: stjohn@holycrossafc.org. Very Rev. Msgr. Douglas L. Grams, J.C.L.; Revs. Garrett Ahlers, Parochial Vicar; Cornelius Ezeiloaku, Parochial Vicar; Gerald S. Meidl, Parochial Vicar.
See New Ulm Area Catholic Schools, New Ulm under New Ulm Area Catholic Schools located in the Institution section.

SILVER LAKE, MCLEOD CO.
1—ST. ADALBERT, Closed. For sacramental records, contact Holy Family, Silver Lake.
2—CHURCH OF THE HOLY FAMILY (1993) [CEM 4] (St. John Paul II Area Faith Community with Glencoe & Winsted)
720 Main St. W., Silver Lake, 55381-0326.
Tel: 320-327-2356; Email: office@holyfamilysilverlake.org; Web: www.holyfamilysilverlake.org. Revs. Anthony J. Stubeda; Michael M. Doyle, Parochial Vicar; Paul A. Schumacher, Parochial Vicar.
Catechesis Religious Program—Tel: 320-327-2931; Email: re@holyfamilysilverlake.org. Students 114.
3—ST. JOSEPH, Closed. For sacramental records, contact Holy Family, Silver Lake.

SLEEPY EYE, BROWN CO., ST. MARY (1876) [CEM] (Divine Mercy Area Faith Community with Comfrey; Leavenworth; & Morgan)
636 First Ave. N., Sleepy Eye, 56085-1004.
Tel: 507-794-4171; Email: saintmaryse@sleepyeyetel.net; Web: www.divinemercyafc.org. Very Rev. Msgr. Eugene L. Lozinski, J.C.L.; Rev. Andrew J. Michels, Senior Assoc.; Deacons Mark D. Kober, Tel: 507-794-4682; Michael J. McKeown.
School—St. Mary Elementary School, (Grades PreK-6), 104 St. Mary St. N.W., Sleepy Eye, 56085.
Tel: 507-794-6141; Web: www.sesmschool.com. Mary Gangelhoff, Prin. Lay Teachers 14; Students 146.
High School—St. Mary High School, (Grades 7-12), 104 St. Mary's St., N.W., Sleepy Eye, 56085.
Tel: 507-794-4121. Peter Roufs, Prin. Lay Teachers 16; Students 125.
Catechesis Religious Program—Tel: 507-794-7600; Fax: 507-794-5871. Shauna Molden, D.R.E. Students 112.

SPICER, KANDIYOHI CO., OUR LADY OF THE LAKES (1962) [CEM] (Jesus Our Living Water Area Faith Community with Willmar; Kandiyohi; & Lake Lillian.)
6680 153rd Ave., N.E., Spicer, 56288-9659.
Tel: 320-796-5664; Fax: 320-796-6310; Email: afcoffice@ourlivingwater.org; Web: www.ourlivingwater.org. Revs. Steven J. Verhelst; Jerome E. Paulson, J.C.L., Parochial Vicar.
Res.: 15525 69th St., N.E., Spicer, 56288-9659.
Catechesis Religious Program—Tel: 320-796-5664; Email: BarbGarding@OurLivingWater.org. Barb Garding, D.R.E. Students 198.

SPRINGFIELD, BROWN CO., ST. RAPHAEL (1874) [CEM] (Vine & Branches Area Faith Community with Lamberton & Sanborn.)
112 W. Van Dusen St., Springfield, 56087-1396.
Tel: 507-723-4137; Email: straphael@newulmtel.net; Web: www.vineandbranchesafc.org. 20 W Van Dusen St, Springfield, 56087. Rev. Philip M. Schotzko.
School—St. Raphael School, (Grades PreK-6),
Tel: 507-723-4135; Fax: 507-723-5409; Email: straysschooloffice@newulmtel.net; Email: straysprincipal@newulmtel.net; Web: vineandbranchesafc.org. Jennifer Fischer, Prin. Lay Teachers 7; Students 81.
Catechesis Religious Program—Tel: 507-723-4138; Email: straysfaithformation@gmail.com. Erin Hauth, D.R.E. Students 171.

STEWART, MCLEOD CO., CHURCH OF ST. BONIFACE (1877) [CEM]
551 Main St., P.O. Box 202, Stewart, 55385-0202.
Tel: 320-562-2344; Email: mmnavara@embarqmail.com. Rev. Paul L. Wolf. Area Faith Community with Hutchinson.
Catechesis Religious Program—Karen Maiers, D.R.E. Students 26.

SWAN LAKE, NICOLLET CO.
1—THE CHURCH OF THE VISITATION, Closed. For sacramental records, contact St. Paul, Nicollet.
2—VISITATION, Closed. For sacramental records, contact St. Paul, Nicollet.

TAUNTON, LYON CO., SS. CYRIL AND METHODIUS (1895) [CEM 2] Closed. For inquiries for parish records contact the chancery.

TRACY, LYON CO., ST. MARY (1885) [CEM] (Our Lady of the Prairie Area Faith Community with Walnut Grove & Milroy.)
249 6th St., Tracy, 56175-1114. Tel: 507-629-4075;
Tel: 507-629-3667; Email: stmary@iw.net; Web: www.stmarytracy.org; Web: www.ourladyoftheprairie-afc.org. Becky Lanoue, Contact Person.
Church: 285 6th St., Tracy, 56175.
School—St. Mary School, (Grades PreK-6), 225 6th. St., Tracy, 56175. Tel: 507-629-3270;
Fax: 507-629-3518; Email: lisa.dieter.sms@gmail.com; Web: www.stmarysschooltracy.org. Mrs. Lisa Dieter, Prin. Lay Teachers 6; Students 39.
Catechesis Religious Program—247 6th St., Tracy, 56175. Students 53.

TYLER, LINCOLN CO., ST. DIONYSIUS (1880) [CEM] (Christ the King Area Faith Community with Ivanhoe; Lake Benton; & Wilno.)
213 Linwood St, P.O. Box 310, Tyler, 56178-0310.
Tel: 507-247-3464; Email: bjthooft@frontiernet.net; Web: ChristtheKingAFC.com. Rev. Ronald V. Huberty.

Res.: 111 N. Sherwood, P.O. Box 49, Ivanhoe, 56142-0049.
Church: 203 Linwood St., P.O. Box 310, Tyler, 56178.
Catechesis Religious Program—Students 61.

VESTA, REDWOOD CO., HOLY NAME, Closed. For sacramental records, contact St. Catherine's, Redwood Falls.

WABASSO, REDWOOD CO., ST. ANNE (1900) [CEM] [JC] (Light of the World Area Faith Community with Lucan; Wanda; & Seaforth.)
1052 Cedar St., P.O. Box 239, Wabasso, 56293-0239. Tel: 507-342-5190; Email: stannesschool@wabassostannesschool.com; Web: lowafc.org. Rev. Anthony R. Hesse.
Church Address: 950 North St., Wabasso, 56293-0239.
School—St. Anne School, (Grades PreSchool-6), 1054 Cedar St., P.O. Box 239, Wabasso, 56293-0239. Tel: 507-342-5389; Email: stannesschool@wabassostanneschool.com; Web: wabassostanneschool.com. Mary Franta, Prin. Lay Teachers 8; Students 96.
Catechesis Religious Program—Tel: 507-342-5190. Students 125.

WALNUT GROVE, REDWOOD CO., ST. PAUL (1902) [CEM] (Our Lady of the Prairie Area Faith Community with Tracy & Milroy.)
Mailing Address: 600 3rd St., P.O. Box 236, Walnut Grove, 56180-0236. Tel: 507-859-2164;
Fax: 507-859-2375; Email: fatherbob@iw.net; Web: www.smstracy.org. Rev. Robert J. Mraz.
Catechesis Religious Program—249 6th St., Tracy, 56175. Tel: 507-629-3667; Email: saintmaryre@iw.net. Ashley Benson, D.R.E. Students 3.

WANDA, REDWOOD CO., ST. MATHIAS (1871) [CEM] (Light of the World Area Faith Community with Seaforth; Lucan; & Wabasso.)
Mailing Address: P.O. Box 239, Wabasso, 56293-0239. Tel: 507-342-5190; Email: stannesschool@wabassostannesschool.com; Web: lowafc.org. Rev. Anthony R. Hesse.
Church: 308 St. Mathias Blvd., Wanda, 56293.
Catechesis Religious Program—Students 1.

WATKINS, MEEKER CO., CHURCH OF ST. ANTHONY (1889) [CEM]
201 Central Ave. S., P.O. Box 409, Watkins, 55389-0409. Tel: 320-764-2755; Email: stanthony@meltel.net; Web: www.stanthonywatkins.com. Rev. Aaron Nett.
Catechesis Religious Program—Students 133.

WEST NEWTON TOWNSHIP, NICOLLET CO., ST. GEORGE (1858) [CEM] (Holy Cross Area Faith Community with Cathedral & St. Mary's, New Ulm; Lafayette; & Searles.)
63105 Fort Rd., 56073. Tel: 507-276-5461; Email: stgeorge@holycrossafc.org; Web: www.holycrossafc.org/church-of-st-george. 63128 388th Ln., 56073. Very Rev. Msgr. Douglas L. Grams, J.C.L.; Revs. Garrett Ahlers, Parochial Vicar; Cornelius Ezeiloaku, Parochial Vicar; Gerald S. Meidl, Parochial Vicar.

WILLMAR, KANDIYOHI CO., ST. MARY (1871) [CEM] (Jesus Our Living Water Area Faith Community with Spicer.)
713 12th St., S.W., Willmar, 56201-3099. Tel: 320-235-0118; Fax: 320-235-0153; Email: afcoffice@ourlivingwater.org; Web: www.ourlivingwater.org. Revs. Steven J. Verhelst; Jerome E. Paulson, J.C.L., Parochial Vicar.
Catechesis Religious Program—Tel: 320-235-0118; Email: ChristinePinto@OurLivingWater.org; Email: ErinWendt@OurLivingWater.org. Christine Pinto, D.R.E.; Erin Wendt, D.R.E. Students 385.

WILNO, LINCOLN CO., ST. JOHN CANTIUS (1883) [CEM] (Christ the King Area Faith Community with Ivanhoe; Lake Benton; & Tyler.)
3069 Kowno St., Ivanhoe, 56142-0049.
Tel: 507-694-1402; Email: bjthooft@frontiernet.net. P.O. Box 49, Ivanhoe, 56142-0049. Rev. Ronald V. Huberty.
Church: 111 N. Sherwood, Ivanhoe, 56142-0049.
Catechesis Religious Program—213 Linwood, P.O. Box 310, Tyler, 56178. Fax: 507-694-1548. Kari Nilles, D.R.E. & Youth Min. Students 78.

WINSTED, MCLEOD CO., HOLY TRINITY (1869) [CEM 2] (Blessed John Paul II Area Faith Community with Glencoe & Silver Lake)
111 Winsted Ave. W., P.O. Box 9, Winsted, 55395-0009. Tel: 320-485-2182; Email: pastor@stpiusxglencoe.org; Email: danh@stpiusxglencoe.org; Web: www.winstedholytrinity.org. Revs. Anthony J. Stubeda; Paul A. Schumacher; Michael M. Doyle; Deacon Michael Thoennes.
School—Holy Trinity Elementary School, (Grades PreK-6), 211 2nd St. N., Winsted, 55395-0038. Tel: 320-485-2182; Web: www.winstedholytrinity.org. Cathy Millerbernd, Prin. Clergy 2; Lay Teachers 10; Students 89.
High School—Holy Trinity High School, (Grades 7-12), 110 Winsted Ave., P.O. Box 38, Winsted, 55395-0038. Tel: 320-485-2182; Fax: 320-485-4283; Email: info@winsteadholytrinity.org; Web: www.winsteadholytrinity.org. Bonnita Jungels, Prin. Lay Teachers 8; Students 68.
Catechesis Religious Program—
Tel: 320-485-2182, Ext. 5633; Fax: 320-485-4283; Email: htre@tds.net. Students 166.

WINTHROP, SIBLEY CO., ST. FRANCIS DE SALES (1906) (All Saints Area Faith Community with Fairfax; Gibbon; & Franklin.)
510 N. Brown St., P.O. Box 447, Winthrop, 55396-0447. Tel: 507-426-7739; Email: ffgw@centurytel.net; Web: www.allsaintsafc.org. Rev. Bruno Santiago; Deacon Roger B. Osborne.
Catechesis Religious Program—Box C, Fairfax, 55332. Fax: 507-426-7742. Connie Serbus, D.R.E. Students 23.

Chaplains of Public Institutions

IVANHOE. *Divine Providence Hospital & Home.*
ST. PETER. *St. Peter Regional Treatment Center.* Rev. John G. Berger, Chap., (Retired).
WINSTED. *St. Mary's Care Center.*

On Special or Other Diocesan Assignment:
Very Rev. Msgrs.—
Grams, Douglas L., J.C.L.
Lozinski, Eugene L., J.C.L.
Very Rev.—
Steffl, Mark S., S.T.L., J.C.L.
Revs.—
Berger, John G., (Retired)
Johanneck, Aaron T.
Schotzko, Philip M.
Timmerman, Craig A.
Verhelst, Steven J.
Wiering, Matthew J.

On Duty Outside the Diocese:
Rev.—
Goggin, John T., Parroquia San Lucas Toliman, Depto. Solola, Guatemala 07013. Tel: 011-502-7722-0112; Fax: 011-502-7722-0112.

Retired:
Rev. Msgr.—
Richter, John A., (Retired), 702 3rd Ave., NW, Sleepy Eye, 50685
Revs.—
Barry, James D., (Retired), 9300 Collegeville Rd., Apt. 305, Bloomington, 55437. Tel: 952-846-0551
Behan, Harry P., (Retired), P.O. Box 35, Saint Peter, 56082-0035
Berger, John G., (Retired), P.O. Box 186, Green Isle, 55338. Tel: 507-326-5111
Bowles, William H., (Retired), 4595 Bayview Dr., Fort Lauderdale, FL 33308-5330
Breu, David L., (Retired), P.O. Box 127, Graceville, 56240
Brown, Eugene M., (Retired), 1320 Riverside Ln., Apt. 203, Mendota Heights, 55118-1754
Casey, Patrick L., (Retired), 525 Fairview Ave S., #439, Saint Paul, 55116-1669
Devorak, James, (Retired), 2048 Hamline Ave. N., Saint Paul, 55113
Fink, Frederick T., (Retired), 1219 Trisco Cove Dr., S.E., Osakis, 56360-4943
Goblirsch, Robert P., (Retired), 702 Third Ave.. Apt. 10, Sleepy Eye, 56085
Gross, Richard C., (Retired), Tel: 320-764-2856
Hackert, Eugene C., (Retired), 700 3rd Ave. N.W., Sleepy Eye, 56085. Tel: 507-794-2566
Hansen, Lawrence H., (Retired), 501 Plush Mill Rd., Apt. 428, Wallingford, PA 19086-6073. Tel: 484-469-4250
Nordick, Jack (John) A., (Retired), 3660 111th Ave., Ortonville, 56278-2801
Nosbush, Peter C., (Retired), 504 W. Franklin Ave., Apt. 1A, Minneapolis, 55405
Pearson, John A., (Retired), 14180 Broadmore Dr., Apt. 214, Baxter, 56425-8772
Plathe, Anthony H., (Retired), 1381 Mission Hills Blvd., Clearwater, FL 33759-2767. Tel: 727-417-2668
Rademacher, Germain P., (Retired), 60297 402nd Ln., 56073. Tel: 507-359-5157; Fax: 507-359-5157
Steiner, Bernard J., (Retired).

INSTITUTIONS LOCATED IN DIOCESE

[A] NEW ULM AREA CATHOLIC SCHOOLS

NEW ULM. *New Ulm Area Catholic Schools*, (Grades K-12), 514 N. Washington St., 56073-1897.
Tel: 507-354-2719; Fax: 507-354-7071; Email: e.fischer@nuacs.com; Web: www.nuacs.com. Very Rev. Msgr. Douglas L. Grams, J.C.L., Bd. Delegate & Canonical Admin. Consolidated: The two schools consolidated under the above title are as follows: St. Anthony Elementary School, New Ulm and Cathedral High School, New Ulm. Religious Teachers 4; Lay Teachers 31; Priests 1; Sisters 3; Students 409.
St. Anthony Elementary School, (Grades K-6), 514 N. Washington St., 56073. Tel: 507-354-2928;
Fax: 507-359-7029; Email: shelly.bauer@nuacs.com. Shelly Bauer, Prin., (Grades Pre K-6). Religious Teachers 1; Lay Teachers 17; Students 226.
Cathedral High School, 600 N. Washington St., 56073-1897. Tel: 507-354-4511; Fax: 507-354-5711; Email: alan.woitas@nuacs.com. William Schumacher, Prin.; JoAnne Griebel, Librarian. Religious Teachers 3; Lay Teachers 14; Students 183.

[B] GENERAL HOSPITALS

GRACEVILLE. *Graceville Health Center* DBA: Essentia Health Graceville, Essentia Health Holy Trinity Hospital, Essentia Health Graceville Clinic, Essentia Health Graceville Home, Essentia Health Graceville Home Health, Essentia Health Graceville Chokio Clinic, Grace Village. 115 W. 2nd St., P.O. Box 157, Graceville, 56240-0157.
Tel: 320-748-7223; Fax: 320-748-7225; Email: lori.rixe@essentiahealth.org. Lori Rixe, Catholic Values Chm. Bed Capacity 15; Total Staff 165; Clinic Visits 6,198; Home Health Visits 1,886.
Graceville Health Center DBA: Essentia Health Graceville Chokio Clinic. 101 S. Main St., Chokio, 56221. Tel: 320-324-7500; Fax: 320-324-7563; Email: kevin.gish@essentiahealth.org. John Costello, Bd. Chm.; Lori Rixe, Catholic Values Chm. Total Staff 3; Clinic Visits 673.

MARSHALL. **Avera Marshall*, 300 S. Bruce St., Marshall, 56258-1934. Tel: 507-532-9661. Mary Maertens, Pres. Sponsored by the Sisters of the Presentation of the BVM of Aberdeen, South Dakota, and the Benedictine Sisters of Sacred Heart Monastery, Yankton, SD Bed Capacity 25; Tot Asst. Annually 8,471; Total Staff 556.

[C] HOMES FOR AGED

GRACEVILLE. *Graceville Health Center* dba Essentia Health-Grace Home (SNF) and Grace Village (ALF), 116 W. 2nd St., P.O. Box 638, Graceville, 56240. Tel: 320-748-7261; Fax: 320-748-8238; Email: kevin.gish@essentiahealth.org. John Costello, Bd. Chm.; Lori Rixe, Catholic Values Chm. Total Staff 80; Grace Village Number of Rooms 16; GH Bed Capacity 45.

IVANHOE. *Divine Providence Apartments*, 312 E. George St., P.O. Box 136, Ivanhoe, 56142-0136.
Tel: 507-694-1414; Fax: 507-694-1191. Margaret Schmidt, Admin. Total Apartments 7.

NEW LONDON. *Benedictine Senior Living Community of New London*, 100 GlenOaks Dr., New London, 56273. Tel: 320-354-2231. Mr. James Ingersoll, Dir. Certified Beds 52; Assisted Living 12; Independent Living 35.

SAINT PETER. *Benedictine Living Community of St. Peter*, 1907 Klein St., St. Peter, 56082.
Tel: 507-934-8273; Fax: 507-934-8392; Web: www.bhshealth.org. Teresa Hildebrandt, Admin. Bed Capacity 79; Tot Asst. Annually 431; Total Staff 143; Long Term Care Beds 79.
Benedictine Senior Living Community of St. Peter, 1906 N. Sunrise Dr., St. Peter, 56082.
Tel: 507-934-8817; Fax: 507-934-0214. Teresa Hildebrandt, Admin. Bed Capacity 46; Total Staff 12.

SLEEPY EYE. *Divine Providence Community Home & Lake Villa Maria Senior Apts.*, 700 3rd Ave., N.W., Sleepy Eye, 56085-1099. Tel: 507-794-3011;
Tel: 507-794-5333 (Lake Villa); Fax: 507-794-3020; Email: divine@sleepyeyetel.net; Web: divineprovidencehome.org. Sr. Rhonda Brown, Supr.; Jayna Groebner, Admin. Daughters of St. Mary of Providence. Aged Residents 53; Bed Capacity 53; Sisters 3; Tot Asst. Annually 93; Total Staff 87; Lay Workers 87; Tenants 24.

WINSTED. *Benedictine Senior Living Community of Winsted* (1959) 551 4th St. N., Ste. 101, Winsted, 55395-0750. Tel: 320-485-2151; Fax: 320-485-4241; Email: talia.pletcher@bhshealth.org; Web: www.stmaryscarecenter.org. Talia Pletcher, Admin. Subsidiary of the Benedictine Health System. Bed Capacity 65; Tot Asst. Annually 166; Total Staff 163.

[D] RETREAT HOUSES

SLEEPY EYE. *Schoenstatt Sisters of Mary (Secular*

Institute) (1926) 27762 County Rd. 27, Sleepy Eye, 56085-9801. Tel: 507-794-7727; Email: schoenstattonthelake@schsrsmary.org. Sisters Rita-Marie Otto, Supr.; Marie Day, Movement Coord. Total Staff 7.

[E] MISCELLANEOUS

NEW ULM. *Friends of San Lucas*, 4679 Cambridge Dr., Eagan, 55122. Tel: 651-454-0981; Email: bill.peterson@sanlucasmission.org; Web: www.sanlucasmission.org. Bill Peterson, Dir.

Handmaids of the Heart of Jesus (ACJ), 515 N. State St., 56073. Tel: 507-276-9128; Web: www.handmaidsoftheheartofjesus.com. Mother Mary Clare Roufs, Supr.

GHENT. *Sisters of Maria Stella Matutina* (2014) 318 W. McQuestion St., Ghent, 56239. Tel: 507-428-3919. Sisters Mary Thomas Leary, Prov.; Aude Renard, Prioress.

RELIGIOUS INSTITUTES OF WOMEN REPRESENTED IN THE DIOCESE

For further details refer to the corresponding bracketed number in the Religious Institutes of Men or Women section.

[0940]—*Daughters of St. Mary of Providence* (Immaculate Conception Province, Chicago, IL)—D.S.M.P.

[1310]—*Franciscan Sisters of Little Falls, MN*—O.S.F.

[1870]—*Handmaids of the Heart of Jesus Sisters* (New Ulm, MN)—A.C.J.

[]—*Presentation of the Blessed Virgin Mary* (Fargo, ND)—P.B.V.M.

[]—*Schoenstatt Sisters of Mary* (Waukesha, WI).

[2970]—*School Sisters of Notre Dame* (Central Pacific Province, St. Louis, MO)—S.S.N.D.

[]—*Sisters of Mary Morning Star* (Ghent, MN).

[3830-03]—*Sisters of St. Joseph of Orange* (Orange, CA)—C.S.J.

[1720]—*Sisters of the Third Order Regular of St. Francis of the Congregation of Our Lady of Lourdes* (Rochester, MN)—O.S.F.

NECROLOGY

† Irrgang, Kenneth Edward, (Retired), Died May. 7, 2018

An asterisk (*) denotes an organization that has established tax-exempt status directly with the IRS and is not covered by the USCCB Group Ruling.

Archdiocese of New York

(Archidioecesis Neo-Eboracensis)

His Eminence

TIMOTHY MICHAEL CARDINAL DOLAN, PH.D.

Archbishop of New York; ordained June 19, 1976; appointed Auxiliary Bishop of St. Louis June 19, 2001; installed August 15, 2001; appointed Archbishop of Milwaukee June 25, 2002; installed as Tenth Archbishop August 28, 2002; appointed Archbishop of New York February 23, 2009; installed April 15, 2009; elevated to Cardinal February 18, 2012. *Office: 1011 First Ave., New York, NY 10022.*

Chancery: 1011 First Ave., New York, NY 10022. Tel: 212-371-1000; Fax: 212-813-9538.

Web: www.ny-archdiocese.org

Most Reverend

PETER J. BYRNE, D.D.

Auxiliary Bishop of New York; ordained December 1, 1984; appointed Titular Bishop of Cluain Iraird and Auxiliary Bishop of New York June 14, 2014; consecrated August 4, 2014. *Res.: Saint Kateri Residence, 24 Sloane Rd., Newburgh, NY 12550.*

Most Reverend

JOSU IRIONDO, D.D.

Retired Auxiliary Bishop of New York; ordained December 23, 1962; appointed Titular Bishop of Alton and Auxiliary Bishop of New York October 30, 2001; consecrated December 12, 2001; retired February 1, 2014. *Res.: Our Lady of Esperanza, 624 W. 156th St., New York, NY 10032.*

Most Reverend

JOHN J. JENIK, D.D.

Auxiliary Bishop of New York; ordained May 30, 1970; appointed Titular Bishop of Druas and Auxiliary Bishop of New York June 14, 2014; consecrated August 4, 2014. *Res.: Our Lady of Refuge, 290 E. 196 St., Bronx, NY 10458.* Tel: 718-367-4690.

Most Reverend

DOMINICK J. LAGONEGRO, D.D.

Retired Auxiliary Bishop of New York; ordained May 31, 1969; appointed Titular Bishop of Modrus and Auxiliary Bishop of New York October 30, 2001; consecrated December 12, 2001; retired July 2, 2018. *Res.: Saint Kateri Residence, 24 Sloane Rd., Newburgh, NY 12550.* Tel: 845-391-8819; Fax: 845-245-4423.

Most Reverend

JAMES F. MCCARTHY, D.D.

Retired Auxiliary Bishop of New York; ordained June 1, 1969; appointed Titular Bishop of Verrona and Auxiliary Bishop of New York May 11, 1999; consecrated June 29, 1999; retired June 15, 2002.

Most Reverend

JOHN J. O'HARA, D.D.

Auxiliary Bishop of New York; ordained December 1, 1984; appointed Titular Bishop of Ath Truim and Auxiliary Bishop of New York June 14, 2014; consecrated August 4, 2014. *Res.: St. Charles, 644 Clawson St., Staten Island, NY 10306.*

Most Reverend

GERALD T. WALSH, D.D.

Retired Auxiliary Bishop of New York; ordained May 27, 1967; appointed Auxiliary Bishop and Titular Bishop of Altiburus June 28, 2004; consecrated September 21, 2004; retired September 5, 2017. *Res.: St. Joseph's Seminary, 201 Seminary Ave., Yonkers, NY 10704.*

SEE ERECTED APRIL 8, 1808.

Square Miles 4,683.

Created an Archdiocese July 19, 1850.

Comprises the Boroughs of Manhattan, Bronx, and Richmond of the City of New York, and the Counties of Dutchess, Orange, Putnam, Rockland, Sullivan, Ulster and Westchester in the State of New York.

Legal Title: Archdiocese of New York.

STATISTICAL OVERVIEW

Personnel	
Cardinals	1
Auxiliary Bishops	3
Retired Bishops	4
Priests: Diocesan Active in Diocese	334
Priests: Diocesan Active Outside Diocese	32
Priests: Retired, Sick or Absent	186
Number of Diocesan Priests	552
Religious Priests in Diocese	576
Total Priests in Diocese	1,128
Extern Priests in Diocese	166
Ordinations:	
Diocesan Priests	5
Religious Priests	4
Transitional Deacons	10
Permanent Deacons	10
Permanent Deacons in Diocese	385
Total Brothers	283
Total Sisters	2,207
Parishes	
Parishes	288
With Resident Pastor:	
Resident Diocesan Priests	227
Resident Religious Priests	61
Closed Parishes	4
Professional Ministry Personnel:	
Brothers	37
Sisters	150
Lay Ministers	339
Welfare	
Catholic Hospitals	5
Total Assisted	37,500
Health Care Centers	7
Total Assisted	13,200
Homes for the Aged	7
Total Assisted	3,820
Residential Care of Children	32
Total Assisted	1,881
Day Care Centers	346
Total Assisted	4,550
Specialized Homes	29
Total Assisted	9,764
Special Centers for Social Services	101
Total Assisted	436,123
Residential Care of Disabled	111
Total Assisted	2,023
Other Institutions	2,134
Total Assisted	26,101
Educational	
Seminaries, Diocesan	1
Students from This Diocese	15
Students from Other Diocese	55
Diocesan Students in Other Seminaries	6
Seminaries, Religious	5
Students Religious	33
Total Seminarians	54
Colleges and Universities	9
Total Students	40,000
High Schools, Diocesan and Parish	8
Total Students	3,261
High Schools, Private	37
Total Students	19,424
Elementary Schools, Diocesan and Parish	133
Total Students	34,617
Elementary Schools, Private	22
Total Students	5,229
Non-residential Schools for the Disabled	8
Total Students	74
Catechesis/Religious Education:	
High School Students	3,916
Elementary Students	73,517
Total Students under Catholic Instruction	180,092
Teachers in the Diocese:	
Priests	31
Brothers	24
Sisters	81
Lay Teachers	5,533
Vital Statistics	
Receptions into the Church:	
Infant Baptism Totals	16,646
Minor Baptism Totals	1,848
Adult Baptism Totals	1,126
Received into Full Communion	882
First Communions	17,384
Confirmations	15,856
Marriages:	
Catholic	2,774
Interfaith	394
Total Marriages	3,168
Deaths	11,082
Total Catholic Population	2,807,298
Total Population	6,238,441

Succession of Prelates—Most Rev. R. LUKE CONCANEN, O.P., D.D., first Bishop; cons. April 24, 1808; died June 19, 1810; Rt. Revs. JOHN CONNOLLY, O.P., D.D., second Bishop; cons. Nov. 6, 1814; died Feb. 6, 1825; JOHN DUBOIS, S.S., D.D., third Bishop; cons. Oct. 29, 1826; died Dec. 20, 1842; Most Rev. JOHN HUGHES, D.D., cons. Titular Bishop of Basileopolis and coadjutor to the Bishop of New York, Jan. 7, 1838; succeeded to the See of New York, Dec. 20, 1842; created first Archbishop, July 19, 1850; died Jan. 3, 1864; His Eminence JOHN CARDINAL MCCLOSKEY, D.D., second Archbishop; cons. Titular Bishop of Axiere, and coadjutor to the Bishop of New York, March 10, 1844; translated to the See of Albany, May 21, 1847; promoted to the See of New York, May 6, 1864; created first U.S. Cardinal, Cardinal Priest of the Holy Roman Church, March 15, 1875 under the title of Sancta Maria Supra Minervam; died Oct. 10, 1885; Most Rev. MICHAEL AUGUSTINE CORRIGAN, D.D., third Archbishop; cons. Bishop of Newark, NJ May 4, 1873; promoted to the Archiepiscopal See of Petra and made coadjutor to His Eminence <sc>Cardinal McCloskey, Archbishop of New York, with the right of succession, Oct. 1, 1880; succeeded to the See of New York, Oct. 10, 1885; made Assistant at the Pontifical Throne, April 19, 1887; died May 5, 1902; His Eminence JOHN CARDINAL FARLEY, fourth Archbishop of New York; ord. June 11, 1870; cons. Titular Bishop of Zeugma and Auxiliary to the Archbishop of New York, Dec. 21, 1895; promoted to this See, Sept. 15, 1902; preconized June 22, 1903; made Assistant at the Pontifical Throne, Dec. 4, 1904; created Cardinal Priest of the Holy Roman Church under the Title of Sancta Maria Supra Minervam, Nov. 27, 1911; died Sept. 17, 1918; PATRICK CARDINAL HAYES, fifth Archbishop of New York; ord. Sept. 8, 1892; appt. Auxiliary to the Archbishop of New York, July 3, 1914; cons. Titular Bishop of Tagaste, Oct. 28, 1914; appt. Bishop Ordinary of U.S. Army and Navy Chaplains by the Holy See, Nov. 24, 1917; promoted to the See of New York, March 10, 1919; created Cardinal Priest of the Holy Roman Church under the title of Sancta Maria in Via, March 24, 1924; died Sept. 4, 1938; FRANCIS CARDINAL SPELLMAN, sixth Archbishop of New York; ord. May 14, 1916; appt. Auxiliary Bishop of Boston, July 30, 1932; cons. Sept. 8, 1932; appt. to the See of New York, April 15, 1939; appt. Military Vicar for the Armed Forces of the United States, Dec. 11,

1939; created and proclaimed Cardinal Priest under the title of SS. John and Paul in the Consistory, Feb. 18, 1946; died Dec. 2, 1967; TERENCE CARDINAL COOKE, seventh Archbishop of New York; ord. Dec. 1, 1945; appt. Auxiliary Bishop of New York, Sept. 15, 1965; cons. Dec. 13, 1965; appt. to the See of New York, March 8, 1968; installed and appt. Military Vicar of the United States Armed Forces, April 4, 1968; created and proclaimed Cardinal Priest under the title of SS. John and Paul in the Consistory, April 28, 1969; died Oct. 6, 1983; JOHN CARDINAL O'CONNOR, eighth Archbishop of New York; ord. Dec. 15, 1945; appt. Titular Bishop of Curzola and Auxiliary Bishop to the Military Vicar, April 24, 1979; cons. May 27, 1979; appt. Bishop of Scranton, May 10, 1983; installed June 29, 1983; appt. Archbishop of New York, Jan. 31, 1984; installed March 19, 1984; created Cardinal Priest, May 25, 1985; died May 3, 2000; EDWARD CARDINAL EGAN, J.C.D., D.D., ord. Dec. 15, 1957; appt. Titular Bishop of Allegheny and Auxiliary Bishop of New York April 1, 1985; cons. May 22, 1985; appt. Bishop of Bridgeport Nov. 8, 1988; installed Dec. 14, 1988; appt. Archbishop of New York May 11, 2000; installed June 19, 2000; elevated to Cardinal Feb. 21, 2001; retired Feb. 23, 2009; died March 5, 2015.

Vicar General / Chancellor—Rev. JOSEPH P. LAMORTE.

Retired Bishops—Most Revs. JAMES F. MCCARTHY, D.D., (Retired); JOSU IRIONDO, S.T.L., D.D., (Retired).

Deans

Central Harlem—Rev. GREGORY CHISHOLM, S.J., St. Charles Borromeo, 211 W. 141st St., New York, 10030. Tel: 212-281-2100.

Central Westchester—Rev. Msgr. DONALD M. DWYER, Resurrection, 910 Boston Post Rd., Rye, 10580. Tel: 914-967-0142.

Dutchess—Rev. Msgr. JAMES SULLIVAN, St. Martin de Porres, 118 Cedar Valley Rd., Poughkeepsie, 12603. Tel: 845-473-4222.

East Bronx—Rev. Msgr. JOHN K. GRAHAM, St. Frances de Chantal, 190 Hollywood Ave., Bronx, 10465. Tel: 718-792-5500.

East Manhattan—Rev. DONALD C. BAKER, St. Monica's, 413 E. 79th St., New York, 10075.

North Manhattan—Rev. EDWARD K. RUSSELL, Church of the Incarnation, 1290 St. Nicholas Ave., New York, 10033. Tel: 212-568-0091.

Northeast Bronx—Rev. BRENDAN A. FITZGERALD, St. Barnabas, 409 E. 241st St., Bronx, 10470. Tel: 718-324-1478.

Northern Westchester and Putnam—Rev. Msgr. JOSEPH GIANDURCO, St. Patrick's Church, 137 Moseman Rd., Yorktown Heights, 10598. Tel: 914-962-5050.

Northwest Bronx—VACANT.

Orange—Rev. DANIEL O'HARE, Holy Name of Mary and Assumption, 89 Union St., Montgomery, 12549. Tel: 845-457-5276.

Rockland—Rev. Msgr. EMMET R. NEVIN, Saint Aedan, 23 Reld Dr., Pearl River, 10965. Tel: 845-735-7405.

South Bronx—Rev. FRANCIS G. SKELLY, C.Ss.R., Immaculate Conception, 389 E. 150th St., Bronx, 10455. Tel: 718-292-6970.

South Manhattan—Rev. Msgr. KEVIN J. NELAN, Immaculate Conception, 414 E. 14th St., New York, 10009. Tel: 212-254-0200.

South Shore—Rev. ALFREDO MONTEIRO, Our Lady of Victory and Sacred Heart, 28 W. Sidney Ave., Mount Vernon, 10550. Tel: 917-668-5861.

Staten Island—Rev. Msgr. PETER G. FINN, M.Div., M.S., M.Ed., Blessed Sacrament, 30 Manor Rd., Staten Island, 10310. Tel: 718-442-1581.

Sullivan—Rev. EDWARD BADER, St. Aloysius, 30 Church St., Livingston Manor, 12758. Tel: 845-439-5625.

Ulster—Rev. GEORGE W. HOMMEL, St. Frances de Sales, 109 Main St., Phoenicia, 12464. Tel: 845-688-5617.

West Manhattan—Rev. Msgr. JOHN N. PADDACK, Notre Dame, 405 W. 114th St., New York, 10025. Tel: 212-866-1500.

Yonkers—Rev. ROBERT F. GRIPPO, Annunciation and Our Lady of Fatima, 470 Westchester Ave., Crestwood, 10707. Tel: 914-779-7345.

Vicar for Clergy—Rev. Msgr. EDMUND J. WHALEN, S.T.D.; Most Rev. GERALD T. WALSH, D.D., Emeritus, 1011 First Ave., New York, 10022. Tel: 212-371-1000, Ext. 2922.

Vicar for Religious—Sr. CATHERINE CLEARY, P.B.V.M., 1011 First Ave., New York, 10022. Tel: 212-371-1000, Ext. 2576.

Archbishopric of New York—1011 First Ave., New York, 10022.

Chancery—1011 First Ave., New York, 10022. Tel: 212-371-1000; Fax: 212-826-6020.

Vice-Chancellors—Rev. Msgr. DOUGLAS J. MATHERS, J.D., J.C.D.; Sr. EILEEN CLIFFORD, O.P.

Secretary to the Archbishop—Rev. JAMES FERREIRA.

Archbishop's Delegate for Healthcare—KARL P. ADLER, M.D.

Chief Financial Officer—MR. WILLIAM E. WHISTON.

General Counsel—JAMES P. MCCABE, J.D.

Canon 1742 Panel of Pastors—Rev. Msgrs. JOSEPH R. GIANDURCO, J.C.D.; JOHN K. GRAHAM; FRANCIS J. MCAREE, S.T.D.; Revs. ROBERT F. GRIPPO; WILLIAM B. COSGROVE; GEORGE W. HOMMEL; MICHAEL F. KEANE; THOMAS F. MADDEN; ROBERT F. MCKEON; EDWARD K. RUSSELL.

Archdiocesan Consultors—His Eminence TIMOTHY M. DOLAN, Ph.D.; Most Revs. DOMINICK LAGONEGRO, D.D.; GERALD T. WALSH, D.D.; JOHN J. JENIK, D.D.; Rev. Msgrs. GREGORY MUSTACIUOLO; EDWARD J. WEBER; WILLIAM J. BELFORD; Revs. GREGORY CHISHOLM, S.J.; LOUIS R. JEROME; JOHN M. LAGIOVANE; LAWRENCE D. FORD, O.F.M.; JOSEPH P. LAMORTE; ROBERT A. QUARATO; RICHARD VERAS, M.A.

Metropolitan Tribunal—Serving as: The Court of First Instance Archdiocese of New York The Court of Second Instance Province of New York/ Archdiocese for Military Services *1011 First Ave., New York, 10022.* Tel: 212-371-100, Ext. 3200; Tel: 646-794-3200; Email: tribunal@archny.org.

Judicial Vicar—Very Rev. RICHARD L. WELCH, C.Ss. R., J.C.D., M.R.E., M.Div.

Associate Judicial Vicar—Rev. ANTHONY OMENIHU, J.C.D.

Judges—Rev. ANTHONY OBIOMA OMENIHU, J.C.D.; Rev. Msgr. KENNETH J. SMITH, M.A., S.T.B.; Ms. SILVANA USANDIVARAS, J.C.L., L.L.M.; Rev. MICHAEL T. MARTINE, J.C.L.; Very Rev. RICHARD L. WELCH, C.Ss.R., J.C.D., M.R.E., M.Div.; Deacon JOHN LYTTLE, J.D., J.C.L.

Defenders of the Bond—Rev. ROBERT HOSPODAR, J.C.L.; Rev. Msgr. OSCAR A. AQUINO, J.C.D.; Rev. JAYARAJ PUTTI, J.C.L.

Promoter of Justice—Rev. ROBERT HOSPODAR, J.C.L.

Auditor—Rev. JAYARAJ PUTTI, J.C.L.

Moderator of the Tribunal Chancery—JANE ANN SARGIA.

Office Finance Administrator—CATHERINE CAMPISI.

Advocates—MS. MARIA BELARDO; MS. LYDIA MARTINEZ; MS. INGRID PENA.

Assistant to the Judicial Vicar, Special Cases—MARIA LUISA RIVERA.

Notaries—JANET ESTRADA; KIMBERLY BAEZ; GINA LEVEQUE; CARMEN RODRIGUEZ; ZACHARY QUIZA.

Students—Revs. NICHOLAS E. CALLAGHAN, J.C.L., J.C.D. (cand. Rome); BRIAN P. TAYLOR, J.C.L., J.C.D. (cand. Rome); MS. KATHERINE DEVORAK, J.C.L. (cand. Rome).

Censors Librorum—Rev. Msgrs. FRANCIS J. MCAREE, S.T.D.; PETER VACCARI, S.T.L.; Revs. MATTHEW S. ERNEST, S.T.D.; KEVIN O'REILLY, S.T.D.

Archdiocesan Offices and Directors

Adult Faith Formation—DANIEL FRASCELLA, Ph.D., Tel: 646-794-2577; Email: daniel.frascella@archny.org; ELIZABETH GUERARA, Dir. Oper., Tel: 646-794-2579; Email: elizabeth.guerara@archny.org.

ArchCare—MR. FRANCIS J. SERBAROLI, Chm., Tel: 212-801-2212; SCOTT LARUE, Pres. & CEO, 205 Lexington Ave., 3rd Fl., New York, 10016. Tel: 646-633-4700; KARL P. ADLER, M.D., Vice Chm., 1011 First Ave., New York, 10022. Tel: 212-371-1000, Ext. 2972.

Archives—201 Seminary Ave., Yonkers, 10704. KATE FEIGHERY, M.A.C.A., Dir., Tel: 914-476-6333; Email: archives@archny.org; ELIZABETH ALLEVA; EUGENE O'DRISCOLL, Asst. Archivist, Tel: 914-968-6200, Ext. 8357.

Black Ministry, Office of—Bro. TYRONE DAVIS, C.F.C., Dir., 1011 First Ave., New York, 10022. Tel: 212-371-1000, Ext. 2682.

Building Commission—St. Joseph's Seminary, 201 Seminary Ave., Yonkers, 10704. Tel: 914-476-1058. MR. RON ANGELO.

Consultants—MR. RON ANGELO; MR. JASON GAYNOR; MR. DAVID MINERVINI; MR. SCOTT ROBINSON; MS. JANE SCHWEDFEGER; MR. STEPHEN WOODLAND.

Catechetical Office—Sr. JOAN CURTIN, C.N.D., Tel: 212-371-1000, Ext. 2849; Email: sr.joan.curtin@archny.org.

Catholic Charismatic Center—(Centro Carismatico Catolico) Rev. JOSEPH ESPAILLAT II, M.Div., M.A., Center Dir., 826 E. 166th St., Bronx, 10460. Tel: 212-378-1734.

Catholic Charities—Rev. Msgr. KEVIN L. SULLIVAN, Exec. Dir., 1011 First Ave., New York, 10022. Tel: 212-371-1000. (Consult separate listing); Rev. ERIC CRUZ, Regl. Coord. CC Bronx Svcs., 402 E. 152nd St., Bronx, 10455. Tel: 718-292-9090.

Catholic Health Care Foundation of the Archdiocese of New York, Inc.—G. T. SWEENEY, Chm., 205 Lexington Ave., 3rd Fl., New York, 10016. Tel: 646-633-4700.

Catholic High School Association—1011 First Ave., New York, 10022. Tel: 646-794-2707. MR. MARCUS RYAN, Dir. Finance.

Catholic New York—(See Ecclesiastical Communications Corp.), JOHN WOODS, Editor; MR. JOSEPH ZWILLING, Assoc. Publisher, Tel: 646-794-3119.

Cemeteries—(The Trustees of St. Patrick's Cathedral in the City of New York, Inc.) MR. SCOTT HANLEY, Mng. Dir., 1011 First Ave., New York, 10022. Tel: 212-753-4883.

Central Services—Archdiocese of New York *1011 First Ave., New York, 10022.* Tel: 212-371-1000.

Charismatic Renewal Office—194 Gaylor Rd., Scarsdale, 10583. Tel: 914-725-1773; Fax: 914-725-5227. Rev. WILLIAM B. COSGROVE, Tel: 845-634-3641.

Communications Office (Bureau of Information for the Media)—MR. JOSEPH ZWILLING, Dir., Tel: 646-794-2997.

Conciliation and Arbitration, Office of—Rev. Msgr. DOUGLAS J. MATHERS, J.D., J.C.D., Dir., 1011 First Ave., New York, 10022. Tel: 212-371-1000, Ext. 2929.

Coordinator of Priest Retiree Affairs—Bishop Fearns Bldg.: St. Joseph Seminary, 201 Seminary Ave., Yonkers, 10704. Tel: 914-968-1252. MRS. MARY B. LYNCH, R.N.

Data Systems Center and Telecommunication Office—MR. ANDREW J. DONNELLY, Dir., 1011 First Ave., New York, 10022. Tel: 212-371-1000, Ext. 3385.

Development Office—Tel: 646-794-3300. BETTINA ALONSO, Exec. Dir., Email: bettina.alonso@archny.org. Cardinal's Appeal, Renew Rebuild Campaign, Alfred E. Smith Memorial Foundation, St. Patrick's Cathedral Restoration, Planned Giving.

Planned Giving—Tel: 646-794-3234. NANCY MATHIASEN, Planned Giving Mgr.

Ecclesiastical Assistance Corporation—1011 First Ave., New York, 10022. Tel: 212-371-1000.

Ecclesiastical Communications Corp.—1011 First Ave., New York, 10022. Tel: 212-371-1000. (See Catholic New York).

Ecclesiastical Maintenance Services, Inc.—

Ecclesiastical Properties Corporation—1011 First Ave., New York, 10022. Tel: 212-371-1011, Ext. 2069; Email: nicholas.canepa@archny.org.

Office of Ecumenical and Interreligious Affairs—Rev. BRIAN E. MCWEENEY, D.Min. (Prin.), M.S., 1011 First Ave., New York, 10022. Tel: 212-371-1000, Ext. 3074.

Educational Services of the Archdiocese of New York, Inc.—1011 First Ave., New York, 10022.

Education, Department of, Archdiocese of New York—1011 First Ave., New York, 10022. Tel: 212-371-1000, Ext. 2802. (Consult separate listing).

Family Life—KATHLEEN WITHER, D.Min., Dir., Tel: 212-371-1000, Ext. 3186; Email: dr.kathleen.wither@archny.org.

Hispanic Ministry, Office of—(Vicario, Ministerio Hispano), Most Rev. PETER J. BYRNE, Vicario; WANDA F. VASQUEZ, Dir., Tel: 212-371-1000, Ext. 2981; Rev. LORENZO ATO, Dir., 1011 First Ave., New York, 10022. Tel: 212-371-1000, Ext. 2994.

Hospital Apostolate, Office of the—205 Lexington Ave., 3rd Fl., New York, 10016. MR. JOHN SCHULTZ, Dir.

Human Resources—MR. DAVID CAULFIELD, Dir., 1011 First Ave., New York, 10022. Tel: 212-371-1000, Ext. 3052; Fax: 212-838-0637.

Information, Bureau of and Radio-T.V. Communications—(See Communications).

Inner City Scholarship Fund, Inc.—1011 First Ave., 18th Fl., New York, 10022. Tel: 212-753-8583. SUSAN GEORGE, Exec. Dir.

Institutional Commodity Services Corporation—THERESA CULLEN-SEIDEL, Exec. Dir., 1011 First Ave., New York, 10022. Tel: 646-794-2735.

Intercultural Institute—VACANT.

Insurance Division—MR. FRANK NAPOLITANO, Dir., Tel: 212-371-1000, Ext. 3024.

Internal Audit, Office of—BRUCE BIEGELEISEN, Dir., Tel: 212-371-1000, Ext. 2941; Email: bruce.biegeleisen@archny.org.

Inter-Parish Financing, Commission for—Rev. BRIAN P. MCCARTHY, Chm., 1011 First Ave., New York, 10022. Tel: 212-371-1000.

Italian Apostolate, Office of the—

Justice and Peace, Archdiocesan Office of—MR. GEORGE HORTON, Dir., 1011 First Ave., New York, 10022. Tel: 212-371-1000, Ext. 2480.

Legal Affairs, Office of—JAMES P. MCCABE, J.D., Gen. Counsel; RODERICK J. CASSIDY, J.D., Assoc. Gen. Counsel, 1011 First Ave., New York, 10022. Tel: 212-371-1000, Ext. 2440; Fax: 212-826-8795.

Office of Liturgy—Rev. MATTHEW S. ERNEST, S.T.D., St. Joseph's Seminary, 201 Seminary Ave., Yonkers, 10704. Tel: 914-968-6200, Ext. 8177; Email: liturgy@archny.org; Web: www.nyliturgy.org.

Parish Assistance Corporation—1011 First Ave., 16th Fl., New York, 10022. Tel: 646-794-3381.

Parish Fundraising—St. Joseph's Seminary, 201 Seminary Ave., Yonkers, 10704. Tel: 914-968-6200, Ext. 8386.

Partnership for Inner City Education—1011 First Ave., 18th Fl., New York, 10022. JILL KAFKA, Exec. Dir., Tel: 646-794-3338.

Partnership for Quality Education—1011 First Ave., New York, 10022. Tel: 212-753-8583. SUSAN GEORGE, Exec. Dir.

Parish Life Conference—Rev. Msgr. EDWARD J. WEBER, Tel: 212-371-1000, Ext. 2930.

Pastoral Planning, Office of—Most Rev. JOHN J. O'HARA, D.D., Vicar; EILEEN MULCAHY, Dir., 1011 First Ave., New York, 10022. Tel: 212-371-1000, Ext. 2732.

Pastoral Services, Archdiocese of New York—1011 First Ave., New York, 10022. Tel: 212-371-1000.

Pension Office, Archdiocesan—MR. DAVID CAULFIELD, Exec., 1011 First Ave., New York, 10022. Tel: 212-371-1000, Ext. 3052.

Permanent Diaconate Office (Oficina de Diaconos Permanente)—Tel: 914-367-8269. Deacons FRANCIS B. ORLANDO, Dir. Diaconate Formation; JAMES BELLO, Dir. Diaconate Ministry & Life.

Priest Personnel, Office of—Rev. Msgr. EDWARD J. WEBER, Dir., 1011 First Ave., New York, 10022. Tel: 212-371-1000, Ext. 2930; Fax: 212-826-8173.

Adjunct and International Clergy Office—St. Joseph's Seminary, 201 Seminary Ave., Yonkers, 10704. Tel: 914-968-6200, Ext. 8122. Rev. Msgr. EDWARD J. WEBER; THERESA JENSON, Administrative Asst.

Priest Personnel Board—Rev. Msgr. EDWARD J. WEBER.

Priest Wellness Office—St. Joseph's Seminary. Tel: 914-367-8245. Deacon STEVEN DEMARTINO, Coord.

Priest Retiree Affairs—MRS. MARY B. LYNCH, R.N., Bishop Fearns Bldg.: St. Joseph's Seminary, 201 Seminary Ave., Yonkers, 10704. Tel: 914-968-1252.

Priests Council of the Archdiocese of New York—His Eminence TIMOTHY M. DOLAN, Ph.D., Pres.; Revs. ARTHUR MASTROLIA, Chm.; FREDY O. PATINO, M.A., Vice Chm.

Prison Apostolate—Catholic State Prison Ministerial Association, 1011 First Ave., New York, 10022. Tel: 212-371-1000, Ext. 3065. Rev. Msgr. MARC J. FILACCHIONE, Dir.; Revs. GEORGE J. DASH, O.F.M.-Cap., Pres.; GAMINI E. FERNANDO, (Sri Lanka) Vice Pres.; AUGUSTINE GRAAP, O.Carm., Sec.; Deacon FRANK GOHL, Treas.

Respect Life—450 W. 51st St., New York, 10019. Tel: 646-689-2613; Tel: 646-476-0931; Web: archny.org/respect-life. Sisters VIRGINIA JOY, Dir., Email: sr.virginia.joy@archny.org; PIA JUDE, Email: pia.jude@archny.org.

Retirement Plan for Priests—VACANT, 1011 First Ave., New York, 10022. Tel: 212-371-1000, Ext. 2851; Tel: 212-371-1000, Ext. 2934.

Safe Environment Program—MR. EDWARD MECHMANN, Dir., Tel: 646-794-2807; Email: edward.mechmann@archny.org.

St. Joseph's Cursillo Center—Rev. RAMON A. LOPEZ, Dir., 620 Thieriot Ave., Bronx, 10473.

Schools, Superintendent of—1011 First Ave., New York, 10022. Deputy Superintendent: MR. MICHAEL DEEGAN, Interim Supt., Tel: 212-371-1000, Ext. 2802.

Cardinal's Appeal—MS. REGINA KING, 1011 First Ave., New York, 10022. Tel: 212-371-1000, Ext. 3305.

Trustees of St. Patrick's Cathedral in the City of New York, Inc.—Rev. Msgr. DENNIS P. KEANE, Ph.D., Exec. Dir., Cemeteries; MR. SCOTT HANLEY, Mng. Dir., Cemeteries.

Victim Assistance Coordinators—Sr. EILEEN CLIFFORD, O.P., Tel: 646-794-2949; Email: victimsassistance@archny.org.

Vocations, Archdiocesan Office for—St. Joseph's Seminary, 201 Seminary Ave., Yonkers, 10704. Tel: 914-968-1340. Rev. CHRISTOPHER ARGANO, Dir.

Youth Faith Formation—1011 First Ave., New York, 10022. Tel: 212-371-1000, Ext. 2821. ELA MILEWSKA, Exec. Dir., Email: ela.milewska@archny.org.

Youth Ministry, Office of—1011 First Ave., New York, 10022. Tel: 646-794-2853. CYNTHIA PSENCIK, Dir., Email: cynthia.psencik@archny.org.

CLERGY, PARISHES, MISSIONS AND PAROCHIAL SCHOOLS

NEW YORK CITY

BOROUGH OF MANHATTAN

1—CATHEDRAL OF ST. PATRICK St. Patrick's Cathedral (Old, 1809; New, 1879)
50-51 Street and Fifth Ave., 10022.
Tel: 212-753-2261; Web: saintpartrickscathedral.org. Rev. Msgr. Robert T. Ritchie, Rector; Revs. Andrew King, S.T.D. (Cand.), Master of Ceremonies & Parochial Vicar; Donald Haggerty, Parochial Vicar; Arthur A. Golino, Parochial Vicar; Damian O'Connell, S.J., Parochial Vicar; Deacons Edmundo Ramos; Anthony Gostkowski; Jeffrey Trexler.
Rectory—460 Madison Ave., 10022.
Tel: 212-753-2261; Email: spctrojas@saintpatrickscathedral.org.
Archbishop's Residence, Archbishop's Res.: 452 Madison Ave., 10022. Tel: 212-371-1000. His Eminence Timothy M. Dolan, Ph.D., Archbishop of N.Y.; Rev. Msgr. Edward J. Weber, Dir. Priest Personnel; Revs. Joseph P. LaMorte, Vicar; James Ferreira, Sec. to Archbishop.

2—ST. AGNES (1873) (Opus Dei) Revs. Michael Barrett; Robert A. Brisson; Anna Megan, Business Mgr.; Heitor A. Caballero, Music Dir. In Res., Most Rev. John J. O'Hara, D.D.
Res.: 143 E. 43rd St., 10017. Tel: 212-682-5722; Email: church@stagneschurchnyc.org.

3—ST. ALBERT (1916) Closed. Parochial records at Sacred Heart.

4—ALL SAINTS (1879) Records at Parish of St. Charles Borromeo and All Saints, 211 W. 141st St., New York. Rev. Gregory Chisholm, S.J. In Res., Rev. Evariste Ouedraogo.
Res.: 47 E. 129th St., 10035. Tel: 212-534-3535; Fax: 212-987-1930.

5—ST. ALOYSIUS (1899) (Jesuit) Revs. Victor O. Emumwen; Frederick J. Pellegrini, S.J.; Thomas P. Green, S.J.
Res.: 219 W. 132nd St., 10027. Tel: 212-234-2848.
Catechesis Religious Program—Students 20.

6—ST. ALPHONSUS (1847) Closed. Records at St. Anthony of Padua.

7—ST. AMBROSE (CHAPEL CENTRO MARIA) (1897) Closed. Records at Sacred Heart Church.

8—ST. ANDREW (1842) Administered from Parish of Our Lady of Victory and St. Andrew, 60 William St., New York. Rev. Myles P. Murphy, S.T.L.
Res.: 20 Cardinal Hayes Pl., 10007.
Tel: 212-962-3972; Tel: 212-962-3973;
Fax: 212-962-1012; Email: churchofsaintandrewnyc@verizon.net.
Stations—New York Presbyterian Lower Manhattan Hospital—170 William St., 10007. Tel: 212-312-5000.
St. Margaret's House, 49 Fulton St., 10007.
Tel: 212-766-8122.

9—PARISH OF ST. ANN AND ST. LUCY (1911) (PIME Missionaries) Rev. Vijay Marneni, P.I.M.E.
Res.: 312 E. 110th St., 10029. Tel: 646-461-1236.
Catechesis Religious Program—Students 210.
Chapel—St. Ann's Convent, 319 E. 109 St., 10029.

10—ST. ANN'S ROMAN CATHOLIC CHURCH (1852) Administered from and records located at Immaculate Conception, 414 E. 14th St., New York, NY 10009. Tel: 212-254-0200.
110 E. 12th St., 10003.

11—ANNUNCIATION (1853) (Hispanic) (Piarist Fathers) Revs. Emilio Sotomayer, Sch.P., (Spain); Felix Ganuza, Sch.P., (Spain).
Res.: 88 Convent Ave., 10027. Tel: 212-234-1919; Email: office@theannunciation.net.
Catechesis Religious Program—Students 285.

12—ST. ANTHONY OF PADUA (Org. 1859; Re-org. 1866) (Italian) (Franciscan) Rev. Mario Julian, O.F.M.
Res. & Chapel: 154 Sullivan St., 10012.
Tel: 212-777-2755.
Catechesis Religious Program—Sr. Annette Seiter, O.S.F., D.R.E. Students 64.

13—ASCENSION (1895)
Tel: 212-222-0666; Email: frkearney@ascensionchurchnyc.org; Web: www.ascensionchurchnyc.org. Rev. Daniel S. Kearney. In Res., Revs. Raymond M. Rafferty; Daniel LeBlanc, O.M.I.
Res.: 221 W. 107th St., 10025. Tel: 212-222-0666; Email: dkearney@ascensionchurchnyc.org.
Catechesis Religious Program—220 W. 108th St., 10025. Tel: 212-749-5938; Fax: 212-749-8658; Email: rklueber@ascensionchurchnyc.org; Web: ascensionchurchnyc.org. Students 294.
Chapel—Riverside Study Center, 330 Riverside Dr., 10025. Tel: 212-222-3285; Fax: 212-316-3629. (Opus Dei).

14—ASSUMPTION (1858) Closed. Records at Sacred Heart Church.

15—ST. BENEDICT THE MOOR (1883) Attended by Sacred Heart of Jesus, New York
Res.: 457 W. 51st St., 10019. Tel: 212-265-5020; Fax: 212-977-4116.

16—ST. BERNARD (1868) Closed. Records at Our Lady of Guadalupe-St. Bernard.

17—BLESSED SACRAMENT (1887)
Tel: 212-877-3111. Rev. John P. Duffell.
Res.: 152 W. 71st St., 10023. Tel: 212-877-3111; Email: jpduffell@aol.com.
Catechesis Religious Program—Students 200.
Chapels—Convent of Blessed Sacrament—133 W. 70th St., 10023.
St. Agnes' Home, 237 W. 74th St., 10023.
Tel: 212-874-9203.

18—ST. BONIFACE (1858) Closed. Records at Holy Family Church.

19—ST. BRIGID (1848; 1955) Rev. Lorenzo Ato.
Res.: 119 Avenue B, 10009. Tel: 646-476-5617.
Catechesis Religious Program—Students 245.

20—ST. CATHERINE OF GENOA (1887) Revs. Evaristus C. Ohuche; Dessier Predelus, (Haiti).
Res.: 506 W. 153rd St., 10031. Tel: 212-862-6130; Email: scgnyc@yahoo.com.
Catechesis Religious Program—Students 165.

21—ST. CATHERINE OF SIENA (1897) (Dominican) Administered from Parish of St. Vincent Ferrer and St. Catherine of Siena, 869 Lexington Ave, New York. Revs. Walter Cornelius Wagner, O.P., J.D., S.T.L.; Philip Innocent Smith, O.P., S.T.L., Parochial Vicar; Joseph Allen, O.P., Parochial Vicar; Jonah F. Pollock, O.P., Assoc. Dir. Dominican Friars Health Care Min. of New York; Sr. Margaret T. Oettinger, O.P., Hospital Chap. In Res., Rev. John Aquinas Farren, O.P., S.T.D.; Bro. Thomas Aquinas Dolan, O.P.; Rev. John Patrick McGuire, O.P.
Res.: 411 E. 68th St., 10065. Tel: 212-988-8300; Fax: 212-988-6918.

22—PARISH OF ST. CECILIA AND HOLY AGONY (1873) (Apostles of Jesus)
125 E. 105th St., 10029. Tel: 212-534-1350. Rev. Peter Mushi, A.J.; Deacon Jose M. Hernandez. In Res., Rev. Godfrey Awobi, A.J.
Catechesis Religious Program—Students 194.

23—CHAPEL OF THE RESURRECTION (1907) Mission of St. Charles Borromeo. Records at St. Charles Borromeo, 211 W. 141st St., New York, NY 10030 (212-281-2100).
276 W. 151st St., 10039.
Catechesis Religious Program—Mr. Francis Mendez, C.R.E.; Ms. Yolanda Torres, D.R.E. Students 30.
Mission—Chapel of the Resurrection, All sacraments are administered through St. Charles Church. Email: scbharlem211@gmail.com; Web: scbrchurch.org.

24—CHAPEL OF THE SACRED HEARTS OF JESUS AND MARY (1914) Administered from Parish of Our Saviour and St. Stephen/Our Lady of the Scapular, 59 Park Ave., New York.
142 E. 29th St., 10016. Rev. Robert J. Robbins, Admin.
Res.: 325 East 33rd Street, 10016. Tel: 212-213-6027; Fax: 212-213-9136.

25—PARISH OF ST. CHARLES BORROMEO AND ALL SAINTS (1888) Revs. Gregory Chisholm, S.J.; Thomas B. Fenlon, (Retired); Rev. Msgr. John T. Meehan, (Retired); Rev. Anthony Iroh; Deacons Rodney Beckford; Kenneth L. Radcliffe.
Res.: 211 W. 141st St., 10030. Tel: 212-281-2100; Fax: secretary@scbrchurch.org.
Catechesis Religious Program—Students 75.
Mission—Resurrection, 276 W. 151st St., New York Co. 10039. Tel: 212-690-7555; Fax: 212-690-6590.

26—ST. CLARE (1903) Closed. Records at St. Raphael's Church.

27—ST. CLEMENS MARY (1909) Closed. Records at Holy Cross Church, Manhattan.

28—ST. COLUMBA (1845) Administered from Parish of Guardian Angel and St. Columba, 193 Tenth Ave., New York. Rev. James H. Hauver; Rev. Msgr. Walter J. Niebrzydowski, (Retired); Elizabeth Foley, RCIA Coord.; David Strickland, Music Min. In Res., Revs. Tomas DelValle; Francis Okoli; Chrisanth Mugasha, A.J.
Res.: 343 W. 25th St., 10001. Tel: 212-807-8876; Fax: 212-989-6548; Email: saintcolumba@outlook.com.
Chapel—Sisters of Congregation of Notre Dame, 329 W. 25th St., 10001. Tel: 212-243-1760.

29—CORPUS CHRISTI (1906) Rev. Daniel O'Reilly, M.A., M.Div.
Res.: 529 W. 121st St., 10027. Tel: 212-666-9350; Email: corpus-christi-nyc@nyc.rr.com.
Catechesis Religious Program—Students 30.

30—ST. CYRIL (1916) (Slovenian) (Franciscan)

151 First Ave., #185, 10003. Rev. Krizolog Cimerman, O.F.M.
Res.: 62 St. Mark's Pl., 10003. Tel: 212-674-3442; Email: krizolog@yahoo.com; Web: www.slovenskacerkev-ny.si.

31—SS. CYRIL AND METHODIUS - ST. RAPHAEL (1913; 1886) (Croatian) (Franciscan) Revs. Nikola Pasalic, O.F.M.; Iliya Puyic, O.F.M.; Zegko Barbaric, O.F.M.
Res.: 502 W. 41st St., 10036. Tel: 212-563-3395; Email: info@croatianchurchnewyork.org.
Catechesis Religious Program—Students 105.

32—ST. ELIZABETH (1869) Revs. Ambiorix Rodriguez; Lorenzo Laboy, Parochial Vicar.
Res.: 268 Wadsworth Ave., 10033. Tel: 212-568-8803.
Catechesis Religious Program—Tel: 212-923-4900. Students 350.
Chapels—Sisters Residence—
Cabrini Chapel, 701 Ft. Washington Ave., 10040. Tel: 212-923-3536; Fax: 212-923-1871; Email: st.francescabrinishrine@verizon.net.
Isabella Geriatric Center—515 Audubon Ave., 10040. Tel: 212-342-9245.

33—ST. ELIZABETH OF HUNGARY (1891) (Slovak) Records at Parish of St. Monica, St. Elizabeth of Hungary, and St. Stephen of Hungary, 413 E. 79th St., New York. Rev. Donald C. Baker; Rev. Msgr. Patrick P. McCahill. In Res., Rev. James C. Sheehan.
Res.: 211 E. 83rd St., 10028-2854. Tel: 212-734-5747; Tel: 212-988-1903 (TTY); Tel: 646-755-3086 (VP); Fax: 212-988-1903; Email: MO65@archny.org; Web: www.stmonicanyc.org.

34—ST. EMERIC (1949) Records at St. Brigid, 119 Ave. B, New York. Rev. Lorenzo Ato, Admin.
Res.: 185 Avenue D, 10009. Tel: 212-228-4494; Fax: 212-375-1163.
Catechesis Religious Program—Students 139.

35—EPIPHANY (1868) Revs. Austin E. Titus; Arthur A. Golino, Parochial Vicar. In Res., Rev. Msgr. Thomas A. Modugno; Rev. Livinus Obianisi, (Nigeria) Hospital Chap.
Res.: 239 E. 21st St., 10010. Tel: 212-475-1966; Fax: 212-477-0537; Email: epiphanychurch239@gmail.com.
Catechesis Religious Program—Students 110.

36—ST. FRANCES CABRINI (1973) Administered from Parish of St. John Nepomucene, St. Frances Cabrini, and St. John the Martyr, New York.
411 E. 66th St., 10065. Revs. Richard Baker, M.L.M.; Antonio Ferrer; Martin Kertys, C.O.
Res.: 504 Main St., Roosevelt Island, 10044.
Tel: 212-734-4613 (office); Email: parishfin@eastrivercatholics.org; Web: www.eastrivercatholics.org.

37—ST. FRANCIS DE SALES (1894) Rev. Philip J. Kelly.
Res.: 135 E. 96th St., 10128. Tel: 212-289-0425; Email: fatherkelly@sfdsnyc.org; Web: sfdsnyc.org.
Catechesis Religious Program—Jayne Porcell, D.R.E.

38—ST. FRANCIS OF ASSISI (1844) (Franciscan. For priests and brothers not listed here, see St. Francis Monastery under Monasteries and Residences of Priests and Brothers.)
St. Francis of Assisi Friary, 135 W. 31st St., 10001. Tel: 212-736-8500; Email: areitz@stfrancisnyc.org. Revs. Andrew J. Reitz, O.F.M.; William Beaudin, O.F.M., Parochial Vicar; Michael Carnevale, O.F.M., Parochial Vicar; Joseph F. Cavoto, O.F.M., Parochial Vicar; Michael Kim, O.F.M., (South Korea) Parochial Vicar; Julian Jagudilla, O.F.M., Parochial Vicar; David McBriar, O.F.M., Parochial Vicar; Paul Lostritto, O.F.M., Parochial Vicar; Timothy J. Shreenan, O.F.M., Parochial Vicar; Brian E. Smail, O.F.M., Parochial Vicar. In Res., Revs. Stephen D. Mimnaugh, O.F.M.; Daniel T. Kenna, O.F.M.; Very Rev. Kevin J. Mullen, O.F.M., Min. Provincial; Revs. David Convertino, O.F.M.; Dennis M. Wilson, O.F.M., Prov. Treas.; Allan G. Von Kobs, O.F.M., Fin. Admin.; John M. Felice, O.F.M.; John J. McVean, O.F.M.; Thomas Walters, O.F.M.; Bros. Basil Valente, O.F.M., Vocation Dir.; Michael Harlan, O.F.M., Sec. of the Province; Timothy Miskowski, O.F.M., Assoc. Treas.; Ramoncito Razon, O.F.M.; Rev. Michael Reyes.
Res.: St. Francis of Assisi Friary, 129 W. 31st St., 10001. Tel: 212-736-8500; Email: information@stfrancisnyc.org.
Catechesis Religious Program—Students 30.

39—ST. FRANCIS XAVIER (1847) (Jesuit)
46 W. 16th St., 10011. Tel: 212-627-2100; Email: StFrancisXavier@sfxavier.org; Web: www.sfxavier.org. 55 W. 15th St., 10011. Rev. David Corrou, S.J.; John Uehlein, Dir. Music Min.
Catechesis Religious Program—Dr. Luz Marina Diaz, D.R.E. Students 102.

40—ST. GABRIEL (1867) Closed. Records at Church of Sacred Hearts of Jesus and Mary.

41—GOOD SHEPHERD (1912) (Capuchin Franciscans) Revs. Thomas Faiola, O.F.M.Cap.; Eduardo Diaz, O.F.M.Cap., Parochial Vicar; Deacons Rafael Then; Antonio Guzman. In Res., Revs. James R. Gavin, O.F.M.Cap.; Arlen Harris, O.F.M.Cap.
Res.: 608 Isham St., 10034. Tel: 212-567-1300; Email: GSC@goodshepherdNYC.ORG.
Catechesis Religious Program—Students 209.
Chapel—630 Isham St., 10034. Tel: 212-567-1600. (Private).

42—ST. GREGORY (1907) Administered from Parish of Holy Name of Jesus and St. Gregory the Great, 207 W. 96th St., New York. Rev. Lawrence D. Ford, O.F.M.; Rev. Msgr. Michael Crimmins; Rev. Luis Pulido.
Res.: 144 W. 90th St., 10024. Tel: 212-724-9766; Tel: 212-724-9767; Fax: 212-579-3380.
Catechesis Religious Program—Email: stgregnyc@aol.com. Students 41.

43—PARISH OF GUARDIAN ANGEL AND ST. COLUMBA (1888) Rev. James H. Hauver, Admin. In Res., Rev. Philip S. Phan.
Res.: 193 Tenth Ave., 10011-4709. Tel: 212-807-8876; Fax: saintcolumba@outlook.com.
Catechesis Religious Program—Students 20.

44—ST. HEDWIG (1934) Closed. Parochial records at St. Stanislaus Church.

45—HOLY AGONY (1930) (Spanish) Records at Parish of St. Cecilia and Holy Agony, 125 W. 105th St., New York. (Vincentian) Revs. Peter Mushi, A.J.; Godfrey Awobi, A.J.; Jesus Arellano, C.M.
Res.: 1834 Third Ave., 10029. Tel: 212-289-5589; Fax: 212-289-8321; Email: milagha2@verizon.net.

46—PARISH OF HOLY CROSS AND ST. JOHN THE BAPTIST (1852)
Tel: 212-246-4732; Email: t.tracy@christinthecity.nyc. Revs. Francis Gasparik, O.F.M.Cap.; Michael Marigliano, O.F.M.Cap.; Thomas Franks, O.F.M.-Cap., Guardian; John B. Riordan, O.F.M.Cap., Parochial Vicar; Mr. Edward Greene, LAMP Missionary.
Res.: 329 W. 42nd St., 10036. Tel: 212-246-4732; Fax: 212-307-5033.

47—HOLY FAMILY (1924)
Tel: 212-753-3401; Email: info@churchholyfamily.org. Revs. Gerald E. Murray; Joseph T. Chacko, Parochial Vicar. In Res., Revs. Gerard Messier, A.A.; Roger J. Landry.
Res.: 315 E. 47th St., 10017-2318. Tel: 212-753-3401; Fax: 212-753-3428; Email: info@churchholyfamily.org; Web: www.churchholyfamily.org.
Catechesis Religious Program—Email: e.rivera@churchholyfamily.org. Elizabeth Rivera, D.R.E. Students 100.

48—HOLY INNOCENTS (1866) Revs. James L. Miara; Louis M. Van Thanh. In Res., Rev. Oliver Chanama, (Nigeria).
Res.: 128 W. 37th St., 10018. Tel: 212-279-5861; Email: rectory@shrineofholyinnocents.org.
Catechesis Religious Program—Students 20.

49—PARISH OF HOLY NAME OF JESUS AND ST. GREGORY THE GREAT (1868) (Franciscan) Revs. Lawrence D. Ford, O.F.M.; Michael McDonnell, O.F.M.; Kevin Tortorelli, O.F.M.; Lawrence Hayes, O.F.M. In Res., Revs. Matthew A. Pravetz, O.F.M.; John J. Coughlin, O.F.M.; Deacon Andre Alexandre.
Res.: 207 W. 96th St., 10025. Tel: 212-749-0276; Email: holynamenyc@aol.com.
Catechesis Religious Program—
Tel: 212-749-0276, Ext. 116. Students 142.

50—HOLY ROSARY (1884) Records at Parish of St. Paul and Holy Rosary, 113 E. 117th St., New York. (Augustinian) Revs. Pablo Waldmann, I.V.E., (Argentina); Gilbert Luis R. Centina III, O.S.A.; Abel Alvarez, O.S.A., Parochial Vicar; Basilio S. Alava, O.S.A., Parochial Vicar.
Res.: 444 E. 119th St., 10035. Tel: 212-534-0740; Fax: 212-534-7572.
Catechesis Religious Program—Students 16.

51—HOLY TRINITY (1898) Rev. Msgr. Thomas P. Sandi. In Res., Revs. Gary M. Mead; Stephen M. Koeth, C.S.C.
Res.: 213 W. 82nd St., 10024. Tel: 753-300-2230; Email: trinitycatholicparish213@gmail.com; Web: www.htcny.org.
Catechesis Religious Program—Students 165.

52—ST. IGNATIUS LOYOLA (1851) (Jesuit) Revs. Dennis J. Yesalonia, S.J.; William J. Bergen, S.J.; Michael P. Hilbert, S.J.; Thomas H. Feely, S.J.; Teresa Marie Carino, Pastoral Assoc.; Ms. Carly-Anne Gannon, Pastoral Assoc.
Res.: 980 Park Ave., 10028. Tel: 212-288-3588; Email: church@stignatiusloyola.org.
School—Loyola School, (Independent Catholic)
Tel: 212-288-3522; Email: loyolaprincipal@adnyeducation.org. Adam Lewis, Prin. Lay Teachers 21; Students 205.
Catechesis Religious Program—Tel: 212-861-4764. Ms. Carly-Anne Gannon, D.R.E. Students 525.

53—IMMACULATE CONCEPTION (1855) Rev. Msgr. Kevin J. Nelan; Revs. Francis X. Buu; James D. Flanagan. In Res., Rev. Stephen Okeke.
Res.: 414 E. 14th St., 10009. Tel: 212-254-0200; Web: www.immaculateconception-nyc.org; Email: iccboss@aol.com.
Catechesis Religious Program—Students 100.

54—INCARNATION (1908) (Hispanic)
1290 St. Nicholas Ave., 10033. Tel: 212-927-7474; Email: IncarnationChurch_NY@outlook.com. Revs. Edward K. Russell; Franciso Tejada, Parochial Vicar; Aroldo Guerra, In Res., (Retired); Edwin Bonifacio, Parochial Vicar.
Catechesis Religious Program—Rafael Aledo, D.R.E. Students 370.

55—ST. JAMES (1827) Records at Parish of Transfiguration and St. James/St. Joseph, 29 Mott St., New York. Rev. Raymond J. Nobiletti, M.M.
Rectory—23 Oliver St., 10038. Tel: 212-233-0161; Fax: 212-964-0132.
Catechesis Religious Program—Elba Feliciano, D.R.E. Students 20.

56—ST. JEAN BAPTISTE (1882) (Blessed Sacrament Fathers & Brothers) Revs. John A. Kamas, S.S.S.; Ernest R. Falardeau, S.S.S.; Bernard J. Camire, S.S.S.; Jude Gregory Fernando, S.S.S.; Norman Pelletier, S.S.S.; James Hayes, S.S.S.
Res.: 184 E. 76th St., 10021. Tel: 212-288-5082; Email: sjbrcc@aol.com.
Catechesis Religious Program—
Tel: 212-288-5082, Ext. 30; Email: robinscott@yahoo.com. Joan Prenty, D.R.E. Students 68.
Chapel—Sisters' Convent, Tel: 212-472-1230 (Apt. A) ; Tel: 212-472-8821 (Apt. B); Fax: 212-396-2025; Web: www.cnd-m.com.

57—ST. JOACHIM (1888) (Italian), Closed. Parochial records are at Church of St. Joseph.

58—PARISH OF ST. JOHN NEPOMUCENE, ST. FRANCES CABRINI, AND ST. JOHN THE MARTYR (1895) (Slovak)
411 E. 66th St., 10065. Tel: 212-734-4613; Email: parishoffice@eastrivercatholics.org; Web: www.eastrivercatholics.org. Revs. Richard Baker, M.L.M.; Paul Pratap Reddy Gatia, Parochial Vicar.
Catechesis Religious Program—Students 30.
Chapel—Sisters' Convent, 320 E. 66th St., 10065. Tel: 212-737-0221.

59—ST. JOHN THE BAPTIST (1840) Administered from Parish of Holy Cross and St. John the Baptist, 329 W. 42nd St., New York. (Capuchin) Revs. Thomas Franks, O.F.M.Cap., Pastor & Guardian; John B. Riordan, O.F.M.Cap., Parochial Vicar. In Res., Bro. George McCloskey, O.F.M.Cap., Mission & Devel. & Communications Office.
Res.: 213 W. 30th St., 10001. Tel: 212-564-9070; Fax: 212-564-3964.

60—PARISH OF ST. JOHN THE EVANGELIST AND OUR LADY OF PEACE (1840) [CEM]
Tel: 212-753-8418; Email: churchofstjohn@cs.com. Rev. Msgr. Douglas J. Mathers, J.D., J.C.D.; Rev. Wilfred Y. Dodo, Parochial Vicar.
Res.: 348 E. 55th St., 10022. Tel: 212-753-8418; Email: churchofstjohn@cs.com.
Catechesis Religious Program—Students 3.

61—ST. JOHN THE MARTYR (1903) Records at Parish of St. John Nepomucene, St. Frances Cabrini, and St. John the Martyr, 411 E. 66th St., New York. Rev. Richard D. Baker.
Res.: 259 E. 71st St., 10021-4596. Tel: 212-744-4880; Tel: 212-744-4881; Fax: 212-628-6662; Email: saintjohnthemartyr@gmail.com.

62—ST. JOSEPH (1829) (Dominican) Revs. Michael Cuddy, O.P.; John Baptist Hoang, Parochial Vicar; Sebastian White, O.P., S.T.L., Chap. N.Y.U.
Res.: 371 Sixth Ave., 10014. Tel: 212-741-1274.
Catechesis Religious Program—Thomas Sabatelli, D.R.E. Students 126.

63—ST. JOSEPH (1924) Records at Parish of Transfiguration and St. James/St. Joseph, 29 Mott St., New York. (Scalabrinian) Rev. Raymond J. Nobiletti, M.M.
Res.: 5 Monroe St., 10002. Tel: 212-267-8376; Fax: 212-964-0132; Email: sjch5@aol.com; Web: www.stjosephnyc.org.
Convent—83 Madison St., 10002. Tel: 212-233-5670.

64—ST. JOSEPH CHURCH - YORKVILLE (1873) Rev. James Boniface Ramsey. In Res., Rev. Elias Mallon, S.A.
Res.: 404 E. 87th St., 10128. Tel: 212-289-6030; Email: info@stjosephsyorkville.org; Web: www.stjosephsyorkville.org.
Catechesis Religious Program—Tel: 212-861-4764; Fax: 212-734-3671. Regional. See St. Ignatius Loyola, New York.

65—ST. JOSEPH OF THE HOLY FAMILY (1860) Revs. David E. Nolan; Neil J. O'Connell, O.F.M., B.A., S.T.B., M.A., Ph.D.; Ransford Clarke.
Res.: 405 W. 125th St., 10027. Tel: 212-662-9125; Email: sjhfnyc@gmail.com.
Catechesis Religious Program—Students 90.
Convent—400 W. 126th St., 10027.

66—ST. JUDE (1949) Rev. Felix Antonio Reyes Alba, C.R.L.; Deacon Porfirio Rodriguez.
Res.: 439 W. 204th St., 10034. Tel: 212-569-3000; Email: churchofstjude@yahoo.com.
Catechesis Religious Program—Tel: 212-569-3002. Students 275.

67—ST. LEO (1880) Closed. Parochial records at St. Stephen's Church.

68—ST. LUCY (1900) Administered from Parish of St.

Ann and St. Lucy, 312 E. 110th St., New York. Rev. Vijay Marneni, P.I.M.E., Admin.
Res.: 344 E. 104th St., 10029. Tel: 212-534-1470.

69—ST. MALACHY'S (1902) (The Actors' Chapel) Rev. John Fraser. In Res., Rev. Msgr. Oscar A. Aquino, J.C.D.; Rev. Ernest Izummuo.
Res.: 239 W. 49th St., 10019. Tel: 212-489-1340; Email: parishoffice@actorschapel.org.
Encore Community Services—Tel: 646-726-4299; Fax: 212-757-0244; Web: www.encorecommunityservices.org. Sisters Elizabeth Hasselt, O.P., Exec. Dir.; Lillian McNamara, O.P., Dir.; Peggy Gearity, Controller.
Encore Community Center & Programs—
Tel: 212-581-2910.
Catechesis Religious Program—Students 47.

70—ST. MARK THE EVANGELIST (1907) (Holy Spirit Fathers) Rev. Jean Pierre Kapumet Tambwe, C.S. Sp.
Res.: 65 W. 138th St., 10037. Tel: 212-281-4931; Email: fr.jeanpierre.tambwe@archny.org.
Catechesis Religious Program—Students 16.
Chapel—St. Mark Convent, Tel: 212-283-5306.

71—ST. MARY (1826) Rev. Andrew O'Connor, Admin.
Res.: 28 Attorney St., 10002. Tel: 212-674-3266; Email: Info@Saintmarygrand.org.
Catechesis Religious Program—Students 126.

72—MARY HELP OF CHRISTIANS (1908) (Salesian) Records at: Immaculate Conception, 414 E. 14th St., New York, NY 10009 (212-254-0200)
Res.: 440 E. 12th St., 10009.

73—ST. MARY MAGDALEN (1873) (German), Closed. Parochial records at Immaculate Conception Church.

74—ST. MATTHEW (1902) Closed. Parochial records at Blessed Sacrament Church.

75—ST. MICHAEL (1857) Revs. George W. Rutter; Moses Mary Aprekie, Parochial Vicar.
Res.: 424 W. 34th St., 10001. Tel: 212-563-4087; Email: office@stmichaelnyc.org.
Catechesis Religious Program—Students 4.

76—ST. MICHAEL CHAPEL (1936) (Russian)
Tel: 212-226-2644; Email: ligreci@msn.com. Rev. Volodymyr Sibirnyy; Very Rev. Protodeacon Christopher LiGreci.
Church: 266 Mulberry St., 10012. Tel: 212-622-0799; Email: info@saintmichaels.nyc; Web: www.stmichaelruscath.org.

77—PARISH OF ST. MONICA, ST. ELIZABETH OF HUNGARY, AND ST. STEPHEN OF HUNGARY (1879) Revs. Donald C. Baker; Joseph A. Francis.
Res.: 413 E. 79th St., 10075. Tel: 212-288-6250; Email: frdcab@stmonicanyc.org.

78—MOST HOLY CRUCIFIX (1925) (Italian) Records at Basilica of St. Patrick's Old Cathedral, 263 Mulberry St., New York, NY 10012. Tel: 212-226-8075.
Res.: 378 Broome St., 10013. Tel: 212-226-2556.

79—PARISH OF MOST HOLY REDEEMER AND NATIVITY (1844) (Redemptorist)
Tel: 212-673-4224. Revs. Sean J. McGillicuddy, C.Ss. R.; James R. Cascione, C.Ss.R. In Res., Revs. Adam M. Koncik, C.Ss.R.; Robert Pagliari, C.Ss.R., B.A., M.A., Ph.D.; Charles Coury, C.Ss.R.
Res.: 173 E. Third St., 10009. Tel: 212-673-4224; Email: nilsaacevedo173@hotmail.com.
Catechesis Religious Program—Students 50.

80—MOST PRECIOUS BLOOD (1891) [CEM] (Italian) Administered from Parish of St. Patrick's Old Cathedral and Most Precious Blood, 263 Mulberry St., New York. (Franciscan) Rev. Msgr. Donald Sakano.
Res.: 109 Mulberry St., 10013. Tel: 212-226-6427; Fax: 212-226-1837.

81—NATIVITY (1842) Records at Parish of Most Holy Redeemer and Nativity, 173 Third St., New York. Rev. Sean J. McGillicuddy, C.Ss.R.
Res.: 141 Henry St., 10002. Tel: 212-674-8590; Fax: 212-674-8789.
Nativity Mission Center—204 Forsyth St., 10002.
Tel: 212-477-2472; Fax: 212-473-0538.

82—ST. NICHOLAS (1833) (German), Closed. Parochial records at Most Holy Redeemer Church.

83—NOTRE DAME (1910) Rev. Msgr. John N. Paddack; Rev. Michael K. Holleran, Parochial Vicar. In Res., Revs. Enrique Salvo; Louis-Xavier Ardillier.
Res.: 405 W. 114th St., 10025. Tel: 212-866-1500; Email: parish@ndparish.org; Web: www.ndparish.org.
Catechesis Religious Program—Students in French Program (E. 75th St.) 165; Students in English Program 35.
St. Luke's Hospital—Tel: 212-523-4000.
AMSTERDAM NURSING HOME, Tel: 212-316-7700.

84—OUR LADY OF ESPERANZA (1912) (Spanish) Rev. Ramon A. Lopez.
Res.: 624 W. 156th St., 10032. Tel: 212-283-4340.
Catechesis Religious Program—Students 186.

85—PARISH OF OUR LADY OF GOOD COUNSEL AND ST. THOMAS MORE (1886) Rev. Kevin V. Madigan. In Res., Rev. Msgr. Patrick P. McCahill.
Res.: 230 E. 90th St., 10128. Tel: 212-289-1742; Email: olgcrectory@gmail.com.
Catechesis Religious Program—Marcelle Devine, D.R.E. Students 85.

86—OUR LADY OF GRACE (Stanton St.) (1907) Closed. Parochial records at Church of the Nativity.

87—OUR LADY OF GUADALUPE AT ST. BERNARD'S (1869) Rev. Santiago Rubio, (Mexico).
Res.: 328 W. 14th St., 10014. Tel: 212-243-0265; Email: guadalupesanctuary@gmail.com.
Catechesis Religious Program—Students 150.
Mission—St. Veronica, 149 Christopher St., New York Co. 10014.

88—OUR LADY OF LORETO (1891) (Sicilian), Closed. For inquiries for parish records contact the chancery.

89—OUR LADY OF LOURDES (1901) Rev. Gilberto Angel-Neri; Deacon Pedro O'Brien; Hector Martinez, Music Dir. In Res., Rev. Lawrence E. Lucas.
Res.: 472 W. 142nd St., 10031. Tel: 212-862-4380.
Catechesis Religious Program—Pablo Ortega, D.R.E. Students 306.
Chapel—Convent of Our Lady of Lourdes, 463 W. 142nd St., 10031. Tel: 212-862-4380.

90—OUR LADY OF MT. CARMEL (1884) (Italian) (Pallottine) Rev. Marian Wierzchowski, S.A.C.
Res.: 448 E. 116th St., 10029-0614.
Tel: 212-534-0681; Fax: 646-568-2992.
Catechesis Religious Program—Students 44.
Convent—456 E. 116th St., 10029-0614.
Tel: 212-427-2381. Sisters of Charity 2.

91—OUR LADY OF PEACE (1918) (Italian) Records at Parish of St. John the Evangelist and Our Lady of Peace, New York.
348 E. 55th St., 10065. Tel: 212-753-8418; Email: churchofstjohn@cs.com. Rev. Bartholomew Daly, M.H.M.; Rev. Msgr. Douglas J. Mathers, J.D., J.C.D.; Deacon G. Thomas Harenchar. In Res., Rev. Andrew Bielak, (Poland).
Catechesis Religious Program—

92—OUR LADY OF PERPETUAL HELP (1887) Closed. For inquiries for parish records please see Our Lady of Peace.

93—OUR LADY OF POMPEII (1892) (Scalabrinian) Revs. Angelo Piodari, Admin.; Jonathan Loverita.
Res.: 25 Carmine St., 10014. Tel: 212-989-6805.
Catechesis Religious Program—Students 15.

94—OUR LADY OF SORROWS (1867) (Capuchin) Revs. Thomas McNamara, O.F.M.Cap.; Michele Vricella, O.F.M.Cap., Parochial Vicar; Bro. Robert Gerdin, O.F.M.Cap., Pastoral Assoc.; Deacon Wallace Zambrana. In Res., Rev. Michael Marigliano, O.F.M.Cap.; Bro. Mario Guerrero, O.F.M.Cap.
Res.: 213 Stanton St., 10002-1898. Tel: 212-673-0900; Email: oloschurch@yahoo.com; Web: www.olsweconnect.com.
Church: 103 Pitt St., 10002. Fax: 212-982-0166.
Catechesis Religious Program—
Tel: 212-673-0900, Ext. 306; Email: olsprep@yahoo.com. Yvette Rivera, D.R.E. Students 128.

95—OUR LADY OF THE MIRACULOUS MEDAL (1926) Closed. For inquiries for parish records, see Holy Agony, New York.

96—OUR LADY OF THE ROSARY (1883) Administered from Parish of St. Peter and Our Lady of the Rosary, 18 Vesey St., New York. Shrine of St. Elizabeth Ann Seton. Rev. Jarlath Quinn. In Res., Rev. Msgr. Leslie Ivers; Rev. Robert A. Jeffers, (Retired).
Res.: 7 State St., 10004. Tel: 212-269-6865;
Tel: 212-233-8355; Fax: 212-809-6850; Email: setonshrine05@netscape.com; Web: www.setonshrine.com.
Catechesis Religious Program—Maiwenn Jeffers-Bell, D.R.E.

97—PARISH OF OUR LADY OF VICTORY AND ST. ANDREW (1944)
60 William St., 10005. Tel: 212-422-5535; Email: parishmail@olvsta.org; Web: www.olvsta.org. Revs. Myles P. Murphy, S.T.L.; Edwin Ezeokeke, Parochial Vicar; Lino Gonsalves, In Res.

98—OUR LADY OF VILNIUS (1905) (Lithuanian), Closed. For inquiries for Sacramental records contact St. Anthony of Padua, 154 Sullivan St., New York, NY 10012.

99—OUR LADY QUEEN OF ANGELS (1886) Closed. Records at: Our Lady of Mt. Carmel, 448 E. 116th St., New York, NY 10029 (212-534-0681).

100—OUR LADY QUEEN OF MARTYRS (1927) Revs. Antonio Almonte; Jose Cruz Alverez; Deacons Narciso Hernandez; Luis Feliz; Delio Fernandez; Bienvenido Valdez.
Res.: 91 Arden St., 10040. Tel: 212-567-2637; Email: olqmchurchnyc@gmail.com.
Catechesis Religious Program—Students 270.

101—PARISH OF OUR SAVIOUR AND ST. STEPHEN/OUR LADY OF THE SCAPULAR (1955) Revs. Robert J. Robbins; Andrew E. Kurzyna, Parochial Vicar. In Res., Rev. Msgr. Kevin L. Sullivan.
Res.: 59 Park Ave., 10016.
Tel: 212-679-8166, Ext. 210; Email: info@oursaviournyc.org; Web: www.oursaviournyc.org.
Mission—St. Stephen and Our Lady of the Scapular, 142 E. 29th St., 10016.
Chapel—Chapel of the Sacred Hearts of Jesus and Mary, 325 E. 33rd St., 10016. Tel: 212-213-6027; Fax: 212-213-9136.

102—PARISH OF ST. PATRICK'S OLD CATHEDRAL AND MOST PRECIOUS BLOOD (1809) Rev. Msgr. Donald Sakano; Rev. Andrew Thi; Deacon Paul Vitale.
Res.: 263 Mulberry St., 10012. Tel: 212-226-8075; Email: pastor@oldcathedral.org; Web: www.oldcathedral.com.
Catechesis Religious Program—Students 50.
Chapel—St. Michael, [JC] 266 Mulberry St., 10012.
Tel: 212-226-2644; Fax: 212-226-1219.

103—PARISH OF ST. PAUL AND HOLY ROSARY (1834) (Institute of the Incarnate Word) Rev. Pablo Waldmann, I.V.E., (Argentina); Bro. Pablo Torre, I.V.E.
Res.: 113 E. 117th St., 10035. Tel: 212-534-4422; Email: par.newyork@ive.org; Web: www.stpaulchurchive.org.
Catechesis Religious Program—
Tel: 212-534-4422, Ext. 19; Email: ccdstpaul@servidoras.org. Students 335.
Convent— (Sisters of The Servants of the Lord and The Virgin of Matara) St. Paul Convent, 149 E. 117th St., 10035. Tel: 917-492-3668; Email: c.roseduchesne@servidoras.org; Web: www.ssvmusa.org.

104—ST. PAUL THE APOSTLE (1858) (Paulist. See also Paulist Fathers' Motherhouse under Monasteries located in the Institution section.)
Church of St. Paul the Apostle: 405 W. 59th St., 10019. Tel: 212-265-3495; Fax: 212-262-9239; Email: contact@stpaultheapostle.org; Web: www.stpaultheapostle.org. Revs. Joseph Ciccone; Matthew Berrios; Deacon Waldemar Sandoval.
Catechesis Religious Program—Students 150.
Chapel—Oblates of Jesus the Priest,
Tel: 212-265-3209; Fax: 212-265-4154.

105—PARISH OF SAINT PETER AND OUR LADY OF THE ROSARY (1785)
Mailing Address: 22 Barclay St., 10007. Revs. Jarlath Quinn; John Kwaku Brobbey, (Ghana); Louis Xavier Ardillier, (France).
Res.: 18 Vesey St., 10007. Tel: 212-233-8355; Email: info@spcolr.org; Web: www.spcolr.org.
Catechesis Religious Program—Maiwenn Jeffres-Bell, D.R.E. Students 186.
Chapel—St. Joseph's Chapel, 385 South End Ave., 10280.

106—ST. RAPHAEL (1886) Closed. See Sts. Cyril and Methodius.

107—ST. ROSE (1868) Closed. Parochial records at St. Mary Church.

108—ST. ROSE OF LIMA (1902) Revs. Ramon A. Lopez; Richard Marrano, Parochial Vicar; Jesus Ledezma, Parochial Vicar. In Res., Rev. Melchor Ferrer, S.D.B.
Res.: 510 W. 165th St., 10032. Tel: 212-568-0091.
Catechesis Religious Program—Sr. Ramona Liriano, D.R.E. Students 290.
Chapel—St. Rose of Lima Convent, 509 W. 164th St., 10032.

109—SACRED HEART OF JESUS (1876) Rev. Jose Gabriel Piedrahita.
Res.: 457 W. 51st, 10019. Tel: 212-208-1090; Email: info@shjnycparish.org.
Chapels—Centro Maria—539 W. 54th St., 10019.
Tel: 212-757-6989; Fax: 212-307-5687.
Convent of the Sisters of Life, 450 W. 51st St., 10019.
Tel: 212-397-1396; Fax: 212-397-1397.
Catechesis Religious Program—
Tel: 212-265-5020, Ext. 16. Students 108.

110—ST. SEBASTIAN (1915) Closed. Parochial records at Epiphany Church.

111—ST. STANISLAUS BISHOP AND MARTYR (1872) (Polish) (Pauline Fathers) Revs. Rafal D. Kandora, O.S.P.P.E.; Piotr D. Bednarski, O.S.P.P.E.
Res.: 101 E. Seventh St., 10009. Tel: 212-475-4576; Email: rectory@stanislauschurch.com.
Catechesis Religious Program—Students 103.

112—ST. STEPHEN (1848) Consolidated in 1990. See Our Lady of Scapular/St. Stephen for details.

113—ST. STEPHEN AND OUR LADY OF THE SCAPULAR (1848; 1869) Administered from Parish of Our Saviour and St. Stephen/Our Lady of the Scapular, 59 Park Ave., New York. Rev. Robert J. Robbins, Admin.
Res.: 142 E. 29th St., 10016. Tel: 212-683-1675;
Fax: 212-683-7921; Email: olsss142@aol.com; Web: www.churchofststephen.com.
Mission—Chapel of the Sacred Hearts of Jesus and Mary, 325 E. 33rd St., New York Co. 10016.
Tel: 212-213-6027; Fax: 212-213-9136.

114—ST. STEPHEN OF HUNGARY (1902) Records at Parish of St. Monica, St. Elizabeth of Hungary, and St. Stephen of Hungary, 413 E. 79th St., New York. (Franciscan) Rev. Donald C. Baker.
Res.: 414 E. 82nd St., 10028. Tel: 212-861-8500;
Fax: 212-535-9221; Web: www.stmonicanyc.org.
DEWITT NURSING HOME, 211 E. 79th St., 10021.
Tel: 212-879-1600.

115—ST. TERESA (1863) Revs. Alexis Bastidas,

(Venezuela); Joseph Guo Zhang Ruan; Deacon Patrick So.
Church & Res.: 141 Henry St., 10002.
Tel: 212-233-0233; Email: teresa141henry@hotmail.com.
Catechesis Religious Program—Students 96.
Mission—Church of the Nativity, 44 - 2nd Ave., 10003. Tel: 212-674-8590; Fax: 212-619-4530.

116—ST. THOMAS MORE (1950) Administered from Parish of Our Lady of Good Counsel and St. Thomas More, 230 E. 90th St., New York. Rev. Kevin V. Madigan.
Res.: 65 E. 89th St., 10128. Tel: 212-876-7718; Fax: 212-831-5756; Email: m106@archny.org; Web: www.thomasmorechurch.org.
Catechesis Religious Program—Students 238.

117—ST. THOMAS THE APOSTLE (1889) [CEM] (African American) Records at St. Joseph of the Holy Family, 405 W. 125th St., NY, NY 10027.
Res.: 262 W. 118th St., 10026. Tel: 212-662-2693; Fax: 212-662-4560.
Catechesis Religious Program—Students 127.

118—PARISH OF TRANSFIGURATION AND ST. JAMES/ST. JOSEPH (1827) (Chinese-English) Rev. Raymond J. Nobiletti, M.M.
Res.: 29 Mott St., 10013-5006. Tel: 212-962-5157; Email: info@transfigurationnyc.org; Web: www.transfigurationnyc.org.
School—Early Childhood Campus (1954) 10 Confucius Pl., 10002. Tel: 212-431-8769; Fax: 212-431-8917; Email: earlychildhood@transfigurationschoolnyc.org; Email: emily.tran@adnyeducation.org. Ms. Emily Eng, Prin. Lay Teachers 32; Students 150.
Catechesis Religious Program—Students 138.

119—ST. VINCENT DE PAUL (1841) (French), Closed. For inquiries for parish records contact the chancery.

120—PARISH OF ST. VINCENT FERRER AND ST. CATHERINE OF SIENA (1867) (Dominican) Revs. Walter Cornelius Wagner, O.P., J.D., S.T.L.; Philip Innocent Smith, O.P., S.T.L., Parochial Vicar; Joseph Allen, O.P., Parochial Vicar; Bro. John Damian McCarthy, O.P.
Res.: 869 Lexington Ave., 10065-6648.
Tel: 212-744-2080; Fax: parish@svsc.info.
Catechesis Religious Program—Students 118.
Chapels—Dominican Sisters of Our Lady of the Springs—152 E. 66th St., 10065. Tel: 212-744-2375; Fax: 212-249-5355.
Dominican Academy, 44 E. 68th St., 10065. Tel: 212-744-0195; Fax: 212-744-0375.

BOROUGH OF BRONX

1—ST. ADALBERT (1898) (Polish), Closed. For inquiries for parish records contact the chancery.

2—ST. ANGELA MERICI (1899) (Apostles of Jesus) Revs. Nestorio Agirembabazi, A.J.; John Stephen Ariko, A.J., Parochial Vicar; Deacon Felipe Sin-Garciga.
Res.: 917 Morris Ave., Bronx, 10451.
Tel: 718-293-0984; Email: saintangelamerici@yahoo.com.
Church: E. 163rd St., Bronx, 10451.
Catechesis Religious Program—Students 197.

3—ST. ANN (1927) All records at Parish of St. Brendan and St. Ann, 333 E. 206th St., Bronx. Revs. Raul G. Miguez, (Cuba); Francis P. Scanlon. In Res., Revs. Misael Bacleon, (Philippines); Andrew Ovienloba, (Nigeria).
Res.: 3519 Bainbridge Ave., Bronx, 10467.
Tel: 718-547-9350; Fax: 718-547-1718; Email: saintannchurch@aol.com.

4—PARISH OF ST. ANSELM AND ST. ROCH (1892) (Augustinian Recollects) Revs. Enrique Salvo, Admin.; Jose Antonio Rodrigalvarez, O.A.R.; Deacon Apolonio Mejia.
Res.: 685 Tinton Ave., Bronx, 10455.
Tel: 718-585-8666.
Catechesis Religious Program—
Tel: 718-585-8542. Students 240.

5—ST. ANTHONY (1908) Rev. Louis Anderson, Admin.
Res.: 1496 Commonwealth Ave., Bronx, 10460.
Tel: 718-931-4040.
Catechesis Religious Program—Mr. Oscar Aviles, D.R.E. Students 85.

6—ST. ANTHONY (1919) Records at Parish of St. Frances of Rome, St. Francis of Assisi, St. Anthony, and Our Lady of Grace, 4307 Barnes Ave., Bronx. Rev. Georginus Esiofor Ugwu, M.S.P.
Res.: 4307 Barnes Ave., Bronx, 10466.

7—ST. ANTHONY OF PADUA (1903) [CEM] (African American—Hispanic) Revs. Joseph Espaillat II, M.Div., M.A.; Eduardo Gomez-Rivera, Parochial Vicar; Shane Johnson, L.C., Parochial Vicar; Deacons Nelson Duran; Candido Padro Jr.
Res.: 832 E. 166th St., Bronx, 10459.
Tel: 718-542-7293; Email: info@sapbronx.com.
Catechesis Religious Program—Students 297.

8—ST. ATHANASIUS (1907)
878 Tiffany St., Bronx, 10459. Tel: 718-328-2558; Fax: 718-328-3121; Email: stathanasiuchurchbx@gmail.com; Web: www.stathanasiusbx.org. Rev. Jose Rivas.
Catechesis Religious Program—Juan A. Sotomayor Jr., C.R.E. Students 163.

9—ST. AUGUSTINE (1849) Merged with Our Lady of Victory, Bronx to form St. Augustine Our Lady of Victory, Bronx. Records are located at St. Augustine Our Lady of Victory.

10—ST. AUGUSTINE OUR LADY OF VICTORY (2012) Rev. George R. Stewart; Maria Peguero, Pastoral Assoc.; Sr. Dorothy Hall, O.P., Pastoral Assoc.; Rita Velez, Sec. In Res., Rev. Luke Ibeh, Chap. Bronx Lebanon Hosp.
Res.: 1512 Webster Ave., Bronx, 10457.
Tel: 718-583-4044; Email: saolvrectory@gmail.com.
Catechesis Religious Program—Mr. W. Giles Naedler, D.R.E.; Ms. Lourdes Reyes, C.R.E. Students 150.
Chapel—St. Augustine Chapel
1168 Franklin Ave., Bronx, 10456. Tel: 718-617-7581 ; Fax: 718-583-4764.

11—ST. BARNABAS (1910) (Irish—Italian) Revs. Brendan A. Fitzgerald; Jean-Pierre Seon; Paul John; Deacon Vincent Laurato.
Res.: 409 E. 241st St., Bronx, 10470.
Tel: 718-324-1478; Email: stbarnabasbronx@aol.com.
Catechesis Religious Program—
Tel: 718-324-0865. Students 490.
Chapel—St. Barnabas High School Chapel
Yonkers.

12—ST. BENEDICT (1923) Rev. Stephen P. Norton, M.Ed., M.Div.; Deacons A. Michael Salvatorelli; John Scott.
Res.: 2969 Otis Ave., Bronx, 10465-2198.
Tel: 718-829-1304; Email: stbenedict@optonline.net.
Catechesis Religious Program—
Tel: 718-829-1200. Students 388.
Chapel—St. John
1082 Edison Ave., Bronx, 10465.

13—BLESSED SACRAMENT (1927) Administered from Parish of Holy Family, Blessed Sacrament, and St. John Vianney, 2158 Watson Ave., Bronx. Rev. Peter Mushi, A.J.; Deacon Epi Portalatin.
Res.: 1170 Beach Ave., Bronx, 10472.
Tel: 718-892-3214; Fax: 718-892-3907; Email: blsacramentchurch@yahoo.com.

14—PARISH OF ST. BRENDAN AND ST. ANN (1908) Revs. Raul G. Miguez, (Cuba); Ambrose Madu; Rev. Msgr. Joachim B. Beaumont; Revs. Sancho Garrote; Sunny Mathew, (India) J.C.O.D.; Deacon Paul Hveem.
Res.: 333 E. 206th St., Bronx, 10467.
Tel: 718-547-6655; Email: stbrendanrectory@gmail.com.
Catechesis Religious Program—
Tel: 718-654-6424. Judith Cordero, D.R.E. Students 235.

15—CHRIST THE KING (1926) Rev. Sixto Quezada, (Dominican Republic).
Res.: 141 Marcy Pl., Bronx, 10452. Tel: 718-538-5546 .
Catechesis Religious Program—Students 287.

16—ST. CLARE OF ASSISI (1929) (Italian) Rev. John F. Palatucci, Admin.
Res.: 1918 Paulding Ave., Bronx, 10462.
Tel: 718-863-8974; Email: stclareofassisi@aol.com.
Church: 1027 Rhinelander Ave., Bronx, 10461.
Catechesis Religious Program—
Tel: 718-829-9624. Sr. Linda Giovanelly, P.V.M.I., D.R.E. Students 155.

17—ST. DOMINIC (1924) (Italian) Rev. Robert P. Badillo, M.Id, Ph.D.; Deacon Reynaldo Rosado.
Res.: Fernando Rielo Residence, 1739 Unionport Rd., Bronx, 10462. Tel: 718-863-3282; Fax: 718-792-4950; Email: ols731@optimum.net.
Catechesis Religious Program—
Our Lady of Solace, 1710 Unionport Rd., Bronx, 10462. Tel: 718-239-6926; Email: ols.sd.faith.formation@gmail.com. Leonardo Soliman, D.R.E. Students 141.

18—ST. FRANCES DE CHANTAL (1927) Rev. Msgr. John K. Graham; Rev. Dennis Iddamalgoda, O.M.I.
Res.: 190 Hollywood Ave., Bronx, 10465.
Tel: 718-792-5500; Email: sfdchantal@gmail.com; Web: www.sfdchantal.org.
Catechesis Religious Program—Ms. Christi Chiapetti. Students 123.
Convent—Convent of Sisters of Life
198 Hollywood Ave., Bronx, 10465.
Tel: 718-863-2264.

19—PARISH OF ST. FRANCES OF ROME, ST. FRANCIS OF ASSISI, ST. ANTHONY, AND OUR LADY OF GRACE (1898) Revs. Georginus Esiofor Ugwu, M.S.P.; Francis A. Oroffa, Parochial Vicar.
Res.: 4307 Barnes Ave., Bronx, 10466.
Tel: 718-324-5340; Fax: 718-324-5373.
Church: 761 E. 236th St., Bronx, 10466.
Catechesis Religious Program—Bro. Lucian Knaap, C.F.C., D.R.E. Students 98.
Missions—St. Anthony—
4505 Richardson Ave., Bronx, 10470.
St. Francis of Assisi
4330 Baychester Ave., Bronx, 10466.

20—ST. FRANCIS OF ASSISI (1928) Mission of Sacred Heart. Records at Sacred Heart, 1253 Shakespeare Ave., Bronx.
Mailing Address: P.O. Box 520013, Bronx, 10452. Fax: 718-731-6841. 1544 Shakespeare Ave., Bronx, 10452. Tel: 718-731-6840; Tel: 718-731-6841.

21—ST. FRANCIS OF ASSISI (1949) Administered from Parish of St. Frances of Rome, St. Francis of Assisi, St. Anthony, and Our Lady of Grace, Bronx.
4307 Barnes Ave., Bronx, 10466. Rev. Georginus Esiofor Ugwu, M.S.P.

22—ST. FRANCIS XAVIER (1928) Revs. Salvatore DeStefano; Matthew W. Reiman. In Res., Rev. Hippolytus Duru.
Res.: 1703 Lurting Ave., Bronx, 10461.
Tel: 718-892-3330; Fax: sfx1mpkny@aol.com.
Catechesis Religious Program—Students 100.
Chapel—St. Francis Xavier Convent, (San Damiano Convent Franciscan Sisters of the Renewal)
1661 Haight Ave., Bronx, 10461. Tel: 718-892-9466; Fax: 718-829-1488.

23—ST. GABRIEL (1939) Administered from Parish of St. Margaret of Cortona and St. Gabriel, 6000 Riverdale Ave., Bronx. Rev. Brian P. McCarthy; Deacon Eugene Burke, (Retired).
Res.: 3250 Arlington Ave., Bronx, 10463.
Tel: 718-548-4470; Tel: 718-548-4471;
Fax: 718-548-6451.
Church: 235th & Netherland Ave., Bronx, 10463.
Fax: 718-548-0444.
Catechesis Religious Program—
Tel: 718-548-6585. Mrs. Marie-Jeanne Gwertzman, D.R.E. Students 122.

24—ST. HELENA (1940) Revs. David B. Powers, Sch.P.; Richard S. Wyzykiewicz, Sch.P.; Nelson Henao, Sch. P., (Colombia).
Res.: 1315 Olmstead Ave., Bronx, 10462.
Tel: 718-892-3232; Email: sthelenarc@yahoo.com.
Catechesis Religious Program—
Tel: 718-892-3233. Students 149.

25—HOLY CROSS (1921) Rev. John J. Higgins; Deacon Luis J. Torres.
Res.: 620 Thieriot Ave., Bronx, 10473.
Tel: 718-893-5550; Email: holycross@holycrossbronx.org; Web: www.holycrossbronx.org.
Catechesis Religious Program—Deacon Jaime A. Bello, D.R.E. Students 192.

26—PARISH OF HOLY FAMILY, BLESSED SACRAMENT, AND ST. JOHN VIANNEY (1896) Revs. Joseph Mujaeropiro, A.J.; Omumuawuike Ambrose Madu, C.M.F., (Nigeria) Parochial Vicar; Deacon Dhoel Canals.
Res.: 2158 Watson Ave., Bronx, 10472.
Tel: 718-863-9156; Email: holyfamilychurchbx@gmail.com.
Catechesis Religious Program—
2169 Blackrock Ave., Bronx, 10472.
Tel: 718-822-8030. Students 125.
Chapel—Holy Family
2155 Blackrock Ave., Bronx, 10472.

27—PARISH OF HOLY ROSARY AND NATIVITY OF OUR BLESSED LADY (1925) Revs. Dennis T. Williams; Sebastian Pandarathikudiyil, V.C., (India) Parochial Vicar; Anthony J. Pleho, Nursing Home Chap.
Res.: 1510 Adee Ave., Bronx, 10469.
Tel: 718-379-4432.
Catechesis Religious Program—
Tel: 718-654-9381. Students 75.

28—HOLY SPIRIT (1901) Revs. Ricardo Fajardo, (Dominican Republic); Damian Ekete, (Nigeria).
Res.: 1940 University Ave., Bronx, 10453.
Tel: 718-583-0120; Email: holyspiritbx@yahoo.com.
Catechesis Religious Program—Students 160.

29—IMMACULATE CONCEPTION (1853) (German) (Redemptorist)
Tel: 718-292-6970; Email: immaculateconception389@gmail.com. Revs. Francis G. Skelly, C.Ss.R.; Charles P. McDonald, C.Ss.R.; Ngo Joseph; Robert Wojtek; Deacon Ako Walker.
Res.: 389 E. 150th St., Bronx, 10455.
Tel: 718-292-6970; Email: immaculateconception389@gmail.com.
Catechesis Religious Program—
Tel: 718-292-6970, Ext. 15; Email: garzamps@yahoo.com. Sr. Melissa Garza, D.R.E. Students 285.
Chapel—Sisters of Christian Charity
365 E. 150th St., Bronx, 10455. Tel: 718-585-8981.

30—IMMACULATE CONCEPTION (1903) (Capuchin) Revs. John Aurilia, O.F.M.Cap.; John LoSasso, O.F.M.Cap.; Bros. Walter Fitzpatrick, O.F.M.Cap., Pastoral Assoc.; Kevin O'Loughlin, O.F.M.Cap., Business Mgr.; Jesu Perez, O.F.M.Cap., Pastoral Assoc.; Jose Alfredo Avila de Santiago, O.F.M.Cap., Business Mgr.; Deacon Victor Tosi.
Capuchin Friary: 754 E. Gun Hill Rd., Bronx, 10467.
Tel: 718-653-2200; Email: immaculateconception.bronx@gmail.com; Web: www.iccbronxcapuchin.org.
Catechesis Religious Program—Roberta Lener, D.R.E.

31—ST. JEROME'S (1869) Rev. Javier Correa-Llano, I.V.E.
Res.: 230 Alexander Ave., Bronx, 10454.
Tel: 718-665-5533.
Catechesis Religious Program—Students 412.
32—ST. JOAN OF ARC (1949)
Tel: 718-842-2233; Email: pastorstjoanofarc@gmail.com. Rev. Paul J. LeBlanc; Deacons Ismael Camacho; Angel Alvarez.
Res.: 1372 Stratford Ave., Bronx, 10472.
Tel: 718-842-2233; Email: pastorstjoanofarc@gmail.com; Web: www.stjoanofarcbronx.org.
Catechesis Religious Program—Students 439.
33—ST. JOHN CHRYSOSTOM (1899) Revs. Eric Cruz; James Benavides.
Res.: 985 E. 167th St., Bronx, 10459.
Tel: 718-542-6164; Email: StJohnChry@aol.com.
Catechesis Religious Program—
Tel: 718-328-7723. Students 194.
34—ST JOHN NAM (1989) (Korean) Revs. Simon Nam; Andrew H. Lee, (Korea, South).
Res.: 3663 White Plains Rd., Bronx, 10467.
Tel: 718-231-2414.
Catechesis Religious Program—Students 36.
35—ST. JOHN VIANNEY, CURE OF ARS (1960) Records at Parish of Holy Family, Blessed Sacrament, and St. John Vianney, 2158 Watson Ave., Bronx. Rev. Peter Mushi, A.J.; Deacon Edwin Cruz.
Res.: 725 Castle Hill Ave., Bronx, 10473.
Tel: 718-863-4411; Fax: 718-863-1673.
36—PARISH OF ST. JOHN AND VISITATION (1886) Revs. Michael Kerrigan; Asdruval Antonio Astudillo Montalvan, (Ecuador); Deacon Miguel E. Granda. In Res., Rev. Msgr. Hugh F. McManus, Ph.D., (Retired).
Res.: 3021 Kingsbridge Ave., Bronx, 10463.
Tel: 718-548-1221; Email: stjohnvisitation@yahoo.com.
Catechesis Religious Program—
275 W. 230 St., Bronx, 10463.
Tel: 718-548-1221, Ext. 124. Students 275.
Convent—Religious of Jesus and Mary
3029 Godwin Ter., Bronx, 10463. Tel: 718-548-4902; Tel: 718-543-2454.
37—ST. JOSEPH (1873) Records at Parish of St. Simon Stock and St. Joseph, 2191 Valentine Ave., Bronx. Revs. Nelson Belizario, O.Carm.; Christopher J. Iannizzotto, O.Carm.
Res.: 1949 Bathgate Ave., Bronx, 10457.
Tel: 718-731-2504; Fax: 718-731-0478.
38—ST. LUCY (1927)
Tel: 718-882-0710; Fax: 718-882-8876; Email: stlucybronx@gmail.com; Web: stlucybronx.org. Revs. Nikolin Pergjini; Urbano Rodrigues, Parochial Vicar. In Res., Rev. Msgr. Frederick J. Becker.
Church: 833 Mace Ave., Bronx, 10467.
Tel: 718-882-0710; Email: stlucybronx@gmail.com; Web: stlucybronx.org.
Catechesis Religious Program—
Web: www.stlucysreligiouseducation.com. Ms. Isabel Salcedo, C.R.E. Students 318.
39—ST. LUKE (1897) Rev. Osiris Salcedo, S.D.B., (Dominican Republic).
Res.: 623 E. 138th St., Bronx, 10454.
Tel: 718-665-6677; Email: sanctuslucas@outlook.com.
Catechesis Religious Program—
Tel: 718-801-5512; Fax: 718-665-6677. Students 180.
Chapel—St. Luke Convent
621 E. 138th St., Bronx, 10454. Tel: 718-292-3016.
40—ST. MARGARET MARY (1923) Revs. Rudolph Francis Gonzalez; Jose Ambooken, Parochial Vicar; J. Oscar Munoz, Parochial Vicar.
Res.: 1914 Morris Ave., Bronx, 10453-5904.
Tel: 718-299-4233.
Catechesis Religious Program—Students 268.
41—PARISH OF ST. MARGARET OF CORTONA AND ST. GABRIEL (1887)
Tel: 718-549-8053; Email: smcchurch@optonline.net. Revs. Brian P. McCarthy; Julius M. Eyyazo; George C. Lodi; Willem Klaver.
Res.: 6000 Riverdale Ave., Bronx, 10471.
Tel: 718-548-4470; Email: info@stgabrielsinthebronx.org.
Catechesis Religious Program—
Tel: 718-884-9777. Students 272.
42—ST. MARTIN OF TOURS (1897) Revs. Cosme S. Fernandes; Francis Nampiaparambil Luke; Deacon Luis Velasquez.
Res.: 664 Grote St., Bronx, 10457. Tel: 718-295-0913; Email: stmartinoftoursparish@yahoo.com; Web: www.stmartinoftoursbronx.org.
Catechesis Religious Program—Sr. Georgina Maria, D.R.E. Students 125.
43—ST. MARY (1866) Records at: Our Lady of Grace, 3985 Bronxwood Ave., Bronx, NY 10466 (718-652-4817).
Church: White Plains Rd., Bronx, 10466-3932.
Catechesis Religious Program—
Tel: 718-231-2569. Students 100.
Chapel—Convent
3961 Carpenter Ave., Bronx, 10466.
Tel: 718-652-2873.
School Chapel—
E. 224th St., Bronx, 10466.
44—ST. MARY STAR OF THE SEA (1887) Administered from Parish of Our Lady of the Assumption and St. Mary Star of the Sea, 1634 Mahan Ave., Bronx. Rev. John M. Knapp. In Res., Rev. Augustus Onwubiko, (Nigeria).
Res.: 595 Minneford Ave., Bronx, 10464-1118.
Tel: 718-885-1440; Fax: 718-885-9498; Email: stmssci@gmail.com.
Church: 600 City Island Ave., Bronx, 10464.
Catechesis Religious Program—Sr. Bernadette Hannaway, O.S.U., D.R.E. Students 117.
Chapel—Daughters of Mary
176 Kilroe St., Bronx, 10464. Tel: 718-885-1842.
Ursuline Community—
596 Minnieford Ave., Bronx, 10464.
Tel: 718-885-2139.
Convent—Daughters of Mary Convent.
45—ST. MICHAEL (1969) Revs. Pat F. Rossi, Ph.D.; Benedict Paul, Ph.D., Parochial Vicar.
Res.: 765 Co-Op City Blvd., Bronx, 10475-1601.
Tel: 718-671-8050.
Catechesis Religious Program—Students 31.
46—NATIVITY OF OUR BLESSED LADY (1924) Records at Parish of Holy Rosary and Nativity of Our Blessed Lady, 1510 Adee Ave., Bronx. Rev. Dennis T. Williams.
Rectory—
1531 E. 233rd St., Bronx, 10466. Tel: 718-324-3531; Fax: 718-798-0628; Email: natychurch@aol.com.
Catechesis Religious Program—Students 25.
Convent—
1534 E. 233rd St., Bronx, 10466. Tel: 718-325-5355.
47—ST. NICHOLAS OF TOLENTINE (1906) (Augustinian) Revs. Luis A. Vera, O.S.A.; Joseph Tran; Jorge Luis Cleto, O.S.A. In Res., Revs. William J. Wallace, O.S.A.; Richard Nahman, O.S.A.; James L. MacDougall, O.S.A.
Res.: 2345 University Ave., Bronx, 10468.
Tel: 718-295-6800; Email: pastor@tolentinebronx.org.
Catechesis Religious Program—
Tel: 718-295-6800, Ext. 19. Mr. Jesus de La Rosa, Coord. Faith Formation. Students 296.
Convent—Convent of St. Nicholas of Tolentine
2341 University Ave., Bronx, 10468.
Tel: 718-367-3102.
48—OUR LADY OF ANGELS (1924) Revs. Thomas A. Lynch, Ph.D. (Cand.); Ricardo Garcia, Parochial Vicar; Deacons Wilson Martinez; Carlos Sanchez.
Res.: 2860 Webb Ave., Bronx, 10468.
Tel: 718-548-3005; Email: ourladyofangels@hotmail.com.
Church: 2860 Sedgwick Ave., Bronx, 10468.
Catechesis Religious Program—
Tel: 646-508-3699; Email: ourladyofangels/religiousedhotmail.com. Sr. Lorena Pallares, P.C., D.R.E. Students 200.
49—OUR LADY OF GRACE (1924) Records at St. Frances of Rome, St. Francis of Assisi, St. Anthony and Our Lady of Grace, 4307 Barnes Ave., Bronx. Revs. Georginus Esiofor Ugwu, M.S.P.; Felix Gonzalez, Parochial Vicar; Deacons W. Joseph Mulryan; Salvatore Mazzella. In Res., Rev. Charles Udokang.
Res.: 3985 Bronxwood Ave., Bronx, 10466.
Tel: 718-652-4817; Fax: 718-652-2996.
Catechesis Religious Program—Students 40.
50—OUR LADY OF MERCY (Fordham) (1852-1892) Rev. Jose Ambooken.
Res.: 2496 Marion Ave., Bronx, 10458.
Tel: 718-933-4400; Email: office@ourladyofmercyny.org; Web: www.ourladyofmercyny.org.
Catechesis Religious Program—Sr. Reyna Huerta, H.M.S.P., C.R.E. Students 403.
51—OUR LADY OF MT. CARMEL (1906) (Italian) Revs. Jonathan Morris; Urbano Rodrigues, Parochial Vicar.
Res.: 627 E. 187th St., Bronx, 10458.
Tel: 718-295-3770; Email: mtcarmelbx@aol.com; Web: www.ourladymtcarmelbx.org.
Catechesis Religious Program—
2380 Belmont Ave., Bronx, 10458. Tel: 718-295-7397; Fax: 718-295-7656. Sr. Edna Loquias, M.S.C., C.R.E. Students 216.
Convent—Suore Missionarie del Catechismo
2410 Hughes Ave., Bronx, 10458. Tel: 718-329-0390; Fax: 718-329-0390. Sisters 3.
52—OUR LADY OF PITY (1908) Records at Sts. Peter & Paul, 833 St. Ann's Ave., Bronx, NY 10456.
Res.: 276 E. 151st St., Bronx, 10451.
Tel: 718-665-3880.
53—OUR LADY OF REFUGE (1923) [JC] Most Rev. John J. Jenik.
Res.: 290 E. 196th St., Bronx, 10458.
Tel: 718-367-4690; Email: pastor@ourladyofrefuge.com; Web: www.ourladyofrefuge.com.
Catechesis Religious Program—
Tel: 718-367-3384. Students 200.
54—OUR LADY OF SOLACE (1903) Revs. Robert P. Badillo, M.Id, Ph.D.; Vasanthakumar Sebalamai.
Res.: 731 Morris Park Ave., Bronx, 10462.
Tel: 718-863-3282; Fax: 718-792-4950; Email: ols731@optimum.net.
Catechesis Religious Program—
1710 Unionport Rd., Bronx, 10462.
Tel: 718-239-6926; Email: ols.sd.faith.formation@gmail.com. Leonardo Soliman, D.R.E. Students 230.
55—PARISH OF OUR LADY OF THE ASSUMPTION - ST. MARY STAR OF THE SEA (1923) Revs. John M. Knapp; Augustus Onwubiko, (Nigeria); Sebastian Joseph Chirayath, S.D.B.; Deacon William J. Mueller.
Res.: 1634 Mahan Ave., Bronx, 10461.
Tel: 718-824-5454; Email: pastorolabx@yahoo.com; Web: olaparishbx.org; Web: stmarystaroftheseacityisland.com.
Catechesis Religious Program—
1617 Parkview Ave., Bronx, 10461.
Tel: 718-904-8464; Email: olareled@verizon.net. Diana Liccese, D.R.E. Students 112.
Chapel—Convent
1639 Parkview Ave., Bronx, 10461.
Tel: 718-829-7980.
56—OUR LADY OF VICTORY (1909) Merged with St. Augustine, Bronx to form St. Augustine Our Lady of Victory, Bronx.
57—OUR SAVIOUR (1912) (Yarumal Missionaries)
Tel: 718-295-9600; Email: oursavior4@hotmail.com; Web: churchoursaviour.org. Revs. Tulio E. Ramirez, M.X.Y., (Colombia); Ramiro Reyes, M.X.Y., In Res.; Juan Solorzano, M.X.Y., In Res.
Res.: 2317 Washington Ave., Bronx, 10458.
Tel: 718-561-8248; Email: imeyusa@aol.com.
Catechesis Religious Program—Students 115.
58—ST. PETER AND ST. PAUL (1897) Rev. Richard Mederich Marcelino Cisneros.
Res.: 833 St. Ann's Ave., Bronx, 10456.
Tel: 718-665-3924.
Catechesis Religious Program—Students 155.
59—SS. PHILIP AND JAMES (1949) Rev. Steven Masinde.
Res.: 1160 E. 213th St., Bronx, 10469.
Tel: 718-547-2203.
Catechesis Religious Program—Students 34.
Chapel—
1180 E. 214th St., Bronx, 10469.
60—ST. PHILIP NERI (1898) Revs. Jose A. Serrano; Marco Antonio Ortega, (Peru) Parochial Vicar. In Res., Rev. Arthur T. Welton.
Res.: 3025 Grand Concourse, Bronx, 10468.
Tel: 718-733-3200; Email: spnchurch@optimum.net.
Catechesis Religious Program—Students 250.
61—ST. PIUS V (1907) Records at Parish of St. Rita of Cascia and St. Pius V, Bronx.
448 College Ave., Bronx, 10451. Rev. Pablo Gonzalez.
Res.: 420 E. 145th St., Bronx, 10454.
Tel: 718-585-5900; Email: santaritabronx@gmail.com.
Catechesis Religious Program—Students 50.
62—ST. RAYMOND (1842) [CEM 2] Rev. James A. Cruz; Deacon Fernando Vazquez. In Res., Revs. William Brogan; Joseph Darbouze; Raphael Boansi; Elvin Rivera; Patrick K. Agbeko.
Res.: 1759 Castle Hill Ave., Bronx, 10462.
Tel: 718-792-4044; Email: straysoffice@yahoo.com.
Catechesis Religious Program—
Tel: 718-792-4044, Ext. 238. Sr. Adelina Garcia, P.C.I., D.R.E. Students 156.
Chapel—Brothers Residence
1754 Castle Hill Ave., Bronx, 10462.
Tel: 718-829-1417; Fax: 718-863-8392. Brothers of the Christian Schools 6.
63—ST. RITA OF CASCIA (1900) (Spanish), Merged with St Pius V, Bronx to form St. Rita of Cascia and St. Pius V, Bronx.
64—PARISH OF ST. RITA OF CASCIA AND ST. PIUS V
448 College Ave, Bronx, 10451. Tel: 718-585-5900; Fax: 718-585-5901; Email: santaritabronx@gmail.com; Web: www.santaritabronx.com. Rev. Pablo Gonzalez, Afmin.
Catechesis Religious Program—
452 College Ave., Bronx, 10451. Students 500.
65—ST. ROCH (1899) Records at Parish of St. Anselm and St. Roch, 685 Tinton Ave., Bronx. (Augustinian Recollects) Rev. Antonio Palacios, O.A.R.
Res.: 525 Wales Ave., Bronx, 10455.
Tel: 718-292-3833; Fax: 718-292-3834.
66—SACRED HEART (1875)
Tel: 718-293-2766; Email: receptionist@bronxaltar.org; Web: www.bronxaltar.org. Revs. Joseph E. Franco; Luis Olivares, (Dominican Republic); Deacons Alfonso Ramos; Juan Chaparro; Valentin Acabeo; Ralph Rios. In Res., Revs. Rufino Lecumberri; Isaac Mensah; Rev. Msgr. Kevin P. O'Brien, Ph.D.
Res.: 1253 Shakespeare Ave., Bronx, 10452.
Tel: 718-293-2766; Tel: 718-293-4288;
Fax: 718-293-1581; Email: pastor@bronxaltar.org; Email: parishman@bronxaltar.org; Web: www.bronxaltar.org.

Catechesis Religious Program—
Email: redirector@bronxaltar.org. Vera V. Galeas, D.R.E. Students 175.

67—SANTA MARIA (1926) (Idente Missionaries) Rev. Martin Esguerra, M.Id.
Res.: 2352 St. Raymond Ave., Bronx, 10462.
Tel: 718-828-2380; Email: b265@archny.org.
Catechesis Religious Program—Deacon Vincent Verlezza, Catechetical Leader. Students 100.
Chapel—*Santa Maria Convent*
1460 Zerega Ave., Bronx, 10462.

68—PARISH OF ST. SIMON STOCK AND ST. JOSEPH (1919) (Carmelite)
Tel: 718-367-1251; Fax: 718-933-8822; Email: stsimonstockchurch@gmail.com. Revs. Nelson Belizario, O.Carm.; Nicholas Blackwell, O.Carm., Parochial Vicar; Mark C. Zittle, In Res.; Roberto Perez, O.F.M. Cap., In Res.; Bro. Robert Chiulli, Teacher.
Res.: 2191 Valentine Ave., Bronx, 10457.
Tel: 718-367-1251.
Church: E. 182nd St. & Ryer Ave., Bronx, 10457.
Tel: 718-367-1251; Fax: 718-933-8822; Email: frnelson@stsimonstockschool.org; Web: saintsimonstockchurch.org.
Catechesis Religious Program—
Web: www.saintsimonstockchurch.org. Students 158.

69—ST. THERESA OF THE INFANT JESUS (1927) (Italian) Rev. Msgr. Thomas B. Derivan; Rev. Joseph Ligory, Parochial Vicar; Deacon Anthony P. Cassaneto.
Res.: 2855 St. Theresa Ave., Bronx, 10461.
Tel: 718-892-1900; Fax: rectorystc@aol.com.
Catechesis Religious Program—
Tel: 718-792-8434; Web: www.sttheresachurchbronx.org. Mrs. Marie McCarrick, D.R.E. Students 181.

70—ST. THOMAS AQUINAS (1890) Revs. Librado Godinez-Rivera, I.V.E.; Jeffrey Obniski, I.V.E., Parochial Vicar.
Res.: 1900 Crotona Pkwy., Bronx, 10460.
Tel: 718-589-5235; Email: sainttomasqns3@gmail.com; Web: stabronx.org.
Catechesis Religious Program—
Tel: 718-861-3638. Students 150.
Convent—
1899 Daly Ave., Bronx, 10460. (Closed).

71—ST. VALENTINE (1891) (Polish), Closed. For information for sacramental records, please contact Our Lady of Grace, Bronx.

72—VISITATION (1928) Records at Parish of St. John and Visitation, 3021 Kingsbridge Ave., Bronx. Rev. Michael Kerrigan; Rev. Msgr. Robert W. Larkin.
Res.: 160 Van Cortlandt Park S., Bronx, 10463.
Tel: 718-548-1455; Fax: 718-548-0289.

BOROUGH OF RICHMOND

STATEN ISLAND

1—PARISH OF ST. ADALBERT AND ST. ROCH (Elm Park) (1901) (Other) Rev. Albin Roby, Admin.
Res.: 602 Port Richmond Ave., Staten Island, 10302.
Tel: 718-442-4755; Email: strochs@si.rr.com.
Catechesis Religious Program—Students 136.

2—ST. ANN (1914)
Tel: 718-351-0270; Fax: 718-980-4731; Email: stannschurch@verizon.net; Web: www.stannschurchstatenisland.org. Rev. Joy Mampilly.
Res.: 101 Cromwell Ave., Staten Island, 10304.
Tel: 718-351-0270; Email: stannschurch@verizon.net.
Catechesis Religious Program—Mrs. Kathleen Daly, C.R.E. Students 185.

3—ST. ANTHONY OF PADUA (1908) Administered from Parish of Our Lady of Pity and St. Anthony of Padua, 1616 Richmond Ave., Staten Island.
24 Shelly Ave., Staten Island, 10314.
Tel: 718-761-6660; Fax: 718-761-1029. Rev. John J. Wroblewski.
Church: 4055 Victory Blvd., Staten Island, 10314.

4—ASSUMPTION/ST. PAUL (1922) Records at Parish of Sts. Peter and Paul and Assumption, 53 St. Mark's Pl., Staten Island. Rev. Michael W. Cichon.
Res.: 53 St. Mark's Pl., Staten Island, 10301.
Tel: 718-447-6362; Email: assumptionstpaulsi@gmail.com.
Catechesis Religious Program—Maria Magdalena Centeno, D.R.E. Students 135.

5—ST. BENEDICTA (1925) Closed. For inquiries for parish records contact Our Lady of Mount Carmel.

6—BLESSED SACRAMENT (1910) Rev. Msgrs. Peter G. Finn, M.Div., M.S., M.Ed.; Francis V. Boyle, Pastor Emeritus, (Retired); Revs. Francisco Lanzaderas; Roland Antony Raj, M.M.I., (India).
Res.: 30 Manor Rd., Staten Island, 10310.
Tel: 718-442-1581; Email: bldscrt@aol.com.
Church: Manor Rd. & Forest Ave., Staten Island, 10310.
Catechesis Religious Program—Tel: 718-448-0378. Students 458.

7—ST. CHARLES (1960) Revs. Louis R. Jerome; Stefan Chanas; Marius Fernando, (Sri Lanka); Deacons Lawrence Droge; Stephen Tobon.
Res.: 644 Clawson St., Staten Island, 10306.
Tel: 718-987-2670; Email: secretary@stcharlessi.org.
Catechesis Religious Program—Tel: 718-979-6800; Email: stcharlesccd@gmail.com. Students 401.

8—ST. CHRISTOPHER AND ST. MARGARET MARY (1926) Revs. Joseph M. McLafferty; Thomas A. DeSimone, Parochial Vicar; Deacon Patrick Graham. In Res., Rev. John P. DeLora, Chap.
Res.: 130 Midland Ave., Staten Island, 10306.
Tel: 718-351-2452; Email: jmtamcl@aol.com; Web: stcstmmsi.org.
Catechesis Religious Program—560 Lincoln Ave., Staten Island, 10306. Tel: 718-351-2119; Email: mmaryrectoryreled1@verizon.net. Barbara Regan, C.R.E. Students 118.

9—ST. CLARE (1921)
Tel: 718-984-7873; Email: rectory@stclaresi.com. Rev. Msgr. Richard J. Guastella; Revs. Patrick Amedeka; Brendan Gormley; Joseph Harrison; Deacon Richard T. Mitchell.
Res.: 110 Nelson Ave., Staten Island, 10308.
Tel: 718-984-7873; Email: rectory@stclaresi.com; Web: www.stclaresi.com.
Catechesis Religious Program—Tel: 718-948-4829. Seton Harney, C.R.E. Students 881.

10—ST. CLEMENT (1910) Rev. Jean-Paul Soler.
Res.: 207 Harbor Rd., Staten Island, 10303.
Tel: 718-442-1688.
Church: 126 Van Pelt Ave., Staten Island, 10303.
Catechesis Religious Program—Tel: 718-727-6442. Students 259.

11—HOLY CHILD (1966) Revs. Alan Travers; Wilfred Y. Dodo; Edwin H. Cipot, M.Div.; Sandra Pace, Music Min.
Res.: 4747 Amboy Rd., Staten Island, 10312.
Tel: 718-356-5890; Email: holychildprek@gmail.com.
Catechesis Religious Program—Tel: 718-356-5277; Fax: 718-227-0898. Marie Ferro, D.R.E. Students 1,153.

12—HOLY FAMILY (1966) [JC]
Mailing Address: 366 Watchogue Rd., Staten Island, 10314. Tel: 718-761-6671; Email: holyfamily@si.rr.com. Revs. Angelo J. Micciulla; Anthony Enyinmful, (Ghana).
Catechesis Religious Program—Students 205.

13—HOLY ROSARY (1927)
Tel: 718-727-3360; Web: www.hrosary.com. Revs. Michael T. Martine, J.C.L.; Bernal Stainwall; Rizalino P. Garcia, C.M.; Patrick Anthony, (Pakistan) Chap.; Deacon Rosario Tirella.
Res.: 80 Jerome Ave., Staten Island, 10305.
Tel: 718-727-3360; Email: rectory@hrosarychurch.com; Web: www.hrosarychurch.com.
Catechesis Religious Program—Tel: 718-273-6695. Jennifer Rizzuto, C.R.E. Students 200.

14—IMMACULATE CONCEPTION (1887) Administered from Parish of St. Joseph, Immaculate Conception and St. Mary, 171 St. Mary's Ave., Staten Island. Rev. Fredy Patino Montoya; Deacon Hector Espinal.
Res.: 463 Tompkins Ave., Staten Island, 10305.
Tel: 718-447-2165; Fax: 718-447-4835; Email: i303@archny.org.

15—ST. JOHN NEUMANN (1982) Revs. John S. Kostek; Robert W. Dillon; Patrick Anthony, (Pakistan) (In Res.).
Res.: 1380 Arthur Kill Rd., Staten Island, 10312.
Tel: 718-984-8535; Fax: 718-984-6948; Email: rectory@sjneumann.org.
Catechesis Religious Program—Tel: 718-966-7327. Students 192.

16—ST. JOHN THE BAPTIST DE LA SALLE (1900) Records at: Immaculate Conception, 463 Tompkins Ave., Staten Island, NY 10305. Tel: 718-816-0047.
Church: 76 Jackson St., Staten Island, 10304.
Mission—*Korean Catholic Apostolate of Staten Island*, 76 Jackson St., Staten Island, 10304.
Tel: 718-273-3311; Email: kcasi08@hanmail.net. Rev. Hyunsang Sung.

17—SAINT JOSEPH AND SAINT MARY IMMACULATE (1902) (Other) Rev. Fredy O. Patino, M.A.; Deacons Hector Espinal; Paul Kosinski.
Office: 463 Tompkins Ave., Staten Island, 10305.
Tel: 718-816-0047; Email: i303@archny.org.
Res.: 171 St. Mary's Ave., Staten Island, 10305.
Church: 466 Tompkins Ave., Staten Island, 10305.
Catechesis Religious Program—139 St. Mary's Ave, Staten Island, 10305. Email: reled463@gmail.com. Ms. Terry Ann Venturini, D.R.E.; Mrs. B. Nelly Corona, D.R.E. Students 324.

18—ST. JOSEPH-ST. THOMAS ST. JOHN NEUMANN PARISH (1848) [CEM] Revs. Robert W. Dillon; Rizalino P. Garcia, C.M.; Evangelio R. Suaybaguio; Neil A. Kelly.
Res.: 6097 Amboy Rd., Staten Island, 10309.
Tel: 718-356-0294; Fax: 718-948-3885; Email: sjstparish@gmail.com; Web: sjstparish.org.
Catechesis Religious Program—Tel: 718-984-1156. Elizabeth Brim, D.R.E. Students 1,428.

19—ST. MARGARET MARY (1926) Administered from Parish of St. Christopher and St. Margaret Mary, 130 Midland Ave., Staten Island. Rev. Joseph M. McLafferty, Admin.; Deacon Patrick Graham.
Res.: 560 Lincoln Ave., Staten Island, 10306.
Tel: 718-351-2612; Fax: 718-987-0446; Email: mmaryrectory@verizon.net.

20—ST. MARY (1852) [CEM] Closed. Administered from Parish of St. Joseph, Immaculate Conception and St. Mary, 171 St. Mary's Ave., Staten Island.
463 Tompkins Ave., Staten Island, 10305.

21—ST. MARY OF THE ASSUMPTION (1853) [CEM] Records are now at Parish of Our Lady of Mount Carmel-St. Benedicta and St. Mary of the Assumption, 1265 Castleton Ave., Staten Island. (Jesuit) Rev. Hernan Paredes Carrera, S.J.; Deacon James Stahlnecker.

22—ST. MICHAEL (1922) Rev. Richard Alejunas, S.D.B.
Res.: 207 Harbor Rd., Staten Island, 10303.
Tel: 718-442-1688; Fax: 718-442-4689.
Church: 211-213 Harbor Rd., Staten Island, 10303.
Catechesis Religious Program—Tel: 718-727-6442. Students 259.

23—OUR LADY HELP OF CHRISTIANS (1898)
Tel: 718-317-9772; Email: fr.frank.dias@olhcparish.org; Web: www.olhcparish.org. Revs. D. Francis Dias; R.D.J. Sylvester Ranasinghe, (Sri Lanka); Deacons John Singler; Richard Salhany.
Res.: 7396 Amboy Rd., Staten Island, 10307.
Tel: 718-317-9772; Email: fr.frank.dias@olhcparish.org.
Catechesis Religious Program—Students 470.

24—OUR LADY OF GOOD COUNSEL (1898) (Augustinian) Revs. Omumuawuike Madu; Anthony Sebamalai, (Sri Lanka) Parochial Vicar.
Rectory: 10 Austin Pl., Staten Island, 10304.
Tel: 718-447-1503; Email: ologc@verizon.net.
Catechesis Religious Program—Linda Affatato, D.R.E. Students 262.

25—PARISH OF OUR LADY OF MOUNT CARMEL-ST. BENEDICTA AND ST. MARY OF THE ASSUMPTION (1913) [CEM] Revs. Hernan Paredes Carrera, S.J.; Marc J. Roselli, S.J.
Res.: 1265 Castleton Ave., Staten Island, 10310.
Tel: 718-442-3411; Email: mountcarmelsi@verizon.net.
Catechesis Religious Program—Students 320.

26—PARISH OF OUR LADY OF PITY AND ST. ANTHONY OF PADUA (1923) Revs. John J. Wroblewski; Ruwandana Mendis; Deacon Michael Venditto.
Res.: 1616 Richmond Ave., Staten Island, 10314.
Tel: 718-761-5421; Email: jcallari@olpsare.com; Web: www.churchofourladyofpity.com.
Catechesis Religious Program—Sr. Marcia Vinje, D.R.E. Students 320.

27—OUR LADY STAR OF THE SEA (1916) Revs. Thomas P. Devery; Basil Akut, (Nigeria) Parochial Vicar; David Rider, Parochial Vicar; Mrs. Debra Emigholz, Business Mgr.
Res.: 5371 Amboy Rd., Huguenot Park, Staten Island, 10312. Tel: 718-984-0593; Email: deolss@si.rr.com; Web: www.olssparish.org.
Catechesis Religious Program—Tel: 718-984-1885. Camille Quaglia, D.R.E. Students 995.

28—OUR LADY, QUEEN OF PEACE (1922) Revs. Pancrose Kalist; Charles Achi; Joselin Pens Berkmans, M.M.I.
Res.: 90 Third St., Staten Island, 10306.
Tel: 718-351-1093; Email: pkalist58@yahoo.com.
Catechesis Religious Program—Tel: 718-979-0989. Students 265.
Mission—*Our Lady of Lourdes*, 130 Cedar Grove Ave., New Dorp Beach, Richmond Co. 10306.

29—ST. PATRICK (1862) Rev. Msgr. Jeffrey Conway; Rev. Joseph Victor Maynigo-Arenas, (Philippines).
Office: 3560 Richmond Rd., Staten Island, 10306.
Tel: 718-351-0044; Fax: 718-979-7637; Email: parishadmin@stpatrickssi.org; Web: stpatrickssi.org.
Res.: 53 St. Patrick's Pl., Staten Island, 10306.
Catechesis Religious Program—Tel: 718-979-1272; Email: religiousedstpatrickssi.org. Maria Giura, Ph.D., C.R.E. Students 177.

30—ST. PAUL (1924) Records at Parish of Sts. Peter and Paul and Assumption, 53 St. Mark's Pl., Staten Island.
53 St. Mark's Pl., Staten Island, 10301.
Tel: 718-727-2672; Email: assumptionstpaulsi@gmail.com. Rev. Michael W. Cichon.
Christian Brothers Residence—148 Cassidy Pl., Staten Island, 10301.

31—PARISH OF STS. PETER AND PAUL AND ASSUMPTION (1839) [CEM]
Tel: 718-727-2672; Email: assumptionstpaulsi@gmail.com; Web: stpetersi.com. Revs. Michael W. Cichon; Matthew Takyi-Asante, Parochial Vicar.
Res.: 53 St. Mark's Pl., Staten Island, 10301.
Tel: 718-727-2672; Email: assumptionstpaulsi@gmail.com; Web: stpetersi.com; Web: assumptionstpaul.com.
Catechesis Religious Program—Tel: 718-447-1290; Email: mcmalena068@gmail.com. Maria Magdalena Centeno, D.R.E. Students 128.

32—ST. RITA (1921) Revs. Eugene J. Carrella; Abraham A. Berko, (Ghana). In Res., Rev. Stephen G. Challman.
Res.: 281 Bradley Ave., Staten Island, 10314.
Tel: 718-698-3746; Email: mliss@stritachurch.net.
Catechesis Religious Program—Tel: 718-982-6948; Email: mgillespie@stritachurch.net. Mary Gillespie, C.R.E. Students 225.
Convent—Dominican Sisters, 61 Wellbrook Ave., Staten Island, 10314. Tel: 718-761-1171. (Roman Congregation of St. Dominic).
33—ST. ROCH (1922) Records at Parish of St. Adalbert and St. Roch, 337 Morningstar Rd., Staten Island. Revs. Albin Roby, Admin.; James A. Garisto.
Res.: 602 Port Richmond Ave., Staten Island, 10302.
Tel: 718-442-4755; Fax: 718-981-4455; Email: strochs@si.rr.com.
34—SACRED HEART (1875) Rev. Eric Rapaglia.
Res.: 981 Castleton Ave., Staten Island, 10310.
Tel: 718-442-0058; Email: frrapaglia@yahoo.com; Web: www.sacredheartsi.org.
Catechesis Religious Program—Tel: 718-448-1536; Fax: 718-448-1526. Students 240.
35—ST. STANISLAUS KOSTKA (1923) (Polish) Rev. Jacek Wozny.
Res.: 109 York Ave., Staten Island, 10301.
Tel: 718-447-3937; Email: jpwozny61@aol.com.
Catechesis Religious Program—Students 101.
36—ST. SYLVESTER (1921) Rev. Jacob Thumma, (India).
Res.: 854 Targee St., Staten Island, 10304-4517.
Tel: 718-727-4639; Email: stsylvesterschurch@yahoo.com.
Catechesis Religious Program—Tel: 718-420-1374. Students 81.
37—ST. TERESA (1926) Rev. Msgr. William J. Belford; Revs. Jean-Marie V. Uzabakiriho; John Kallattil, V.C.; Deacon Phillip J. Maroon.
Res.: 1634 Victory Blvd., Staten Island, 10314.
Tel: 718-442-5412; Email: parishmanager@saintteresasi.org.
Catechesis Religious Program—Tel: 718-981-2632; Fax: 718-981-0026. Students 351.
Chapel—St. Nicholas, La Bau Ave. & Northern Blvd., Staten Island, 10301.

OUTSIDE THE CITY OF NEW YORK

AMENIA, DUTCHESS CO., PARISH OF IMMACULATE CONCEPTION AND ST. ANTHONY (1868) [CEM] Rev. Robert K. Wilson. In Res., Deacon David Weinstein.
Res.: 4 Lavelle Rd., Box 109, Amenia, 12501.
Tel: 845-373-8193; Email: icspamen@optonline.net.
Catechesis Religious Program—Students 121.
ARDSLEY, WESTCHESTER CO., OUR LADY OF PERPETUAL HELP (1929) Administered from Parish of St. Matthew and Our Lady of Perpetual Help, 616 Warburton Ave., Hastings-on-Hudson. Rev. Robert P. Henry.
Res.: One Cross Rd., Ardsley, 10502.
Tel: 914-693-0030.
Catechesis Religious Program—Tel: 914-693-0037; Email: religioused@olphardsley.org. Students 300.
ARMONK, WESTCHESTER CO., ST. PATRICK (1966) Rev. Jeffrey R. Galens.
Res.: 29 Cox Ave., P.O. Box 6, Armonk, 10504.
Tel: 914-273-9724; Email: churchofstpat@optonline.net.
Catechesis Religious Program—Tel: 914-273-8226; Email: reled@stpatrickinarmonk.org. Allanna Hasselgren, C.R.E. Students 430.
BANGALL, DUTCHESS CO., IMMACULATE CONCEPTION (1919) [CEM] Records at Parish of St. Joseph and Immaculate Conception, 15 North Ave., P.O. Box 439, Millbrook. Rev. Msgr. Gerardo J. Colacicco, J.C.L.
Res.: 15 North Ave., P.O. Box 439, Millbrook, 12545.
Tel: 845-677-3422; Fax: 845-677-3423; Email: stjosephmillbrook@gmail.com.
BARRYTOWN, DUTCHESS CO., SACRED HEART, Closed. Parochial records at St. Christopher, Red Hook.
BEACON, DUTCHESS CO.
1—ST. JOACHIM, Merged with St. John the Evangelist, Beacon to form St. Joachim - St. John the Evangelist, Beacon.
2 Oak St., Beacon, 12508.
2—ST. JOACHIM - ST. JOHN THE EVANGELIST, Revs. Richard G. Smith; Wenceslaus Rodriguez, (India) Parochial Vicar; Deacon Martin Mayeski; Sr. Kathleen Marie, O.S.F., Pastoral Assoc.; Catherine Crocco, Music Min.
Res.: 2 Oak St., Beacon, 12508. Tel: 845-838-0915; Email: stsjoachimjohn@optonline.net.
Catechesis Religious Program—Tel: 845-831-6550. Albert Griffith, D.R.E. Students 360.
BEDFORD, WESTCHESTER CO., ST. PATRICK (1929) Revs. Joseph F. Bisignano; Joseph Domfeh-Boateng, (Ghana); Deacon Louis Santore.
Parish Office: 485 Old Post Rd., Bedford, 10506.
Tel: 914-234-3344; Email: patrick485@optonline.net.
Res.: 7 Pound Ridge Rd., Box 303, Bedford, 10506.
Tel: 914-234-3668; Fax: 914-234-9126.
Catechesis Religious Program—Tel: 914-234-3775; Fax: 914-234-0579. Mrs. Pat Perlstein, D.R.E.; Mrs. Karen Schmidt, D.R.E. Students 580.
BLAUVELT, ROCKLAND CO., ST. CATHARINE (1868) [CEM]
Tel: 845-359-0542; Email: saintcatharineschurch@gmail.com; Web: www.saintcatharines.org. Rev. Msgr. Francis J. McAree, S.T.D.; Rev. Abraham Vallayil, C.M.I.; Deacon John Jurasek.
Res.: 523 Western Hwy., Blauvelt, 10913.
Tel: 845-359-0542; Email: saintcatharineschurch@gmail.com; Web: www.saintcatharines.org.
Catechesis Religious Program—517 Western Hwy., Blauvelt, 10913. Tel: 845-359-4014; Email: stcatharineprep@optonline.net. Mrs. Audrey Angelini, C.R.E. Students 490.
BREWSTER, PUTNAM CO., ST. LAWRENCE O'TOOLE (1878) [CEM]
Tel: 845-279-2021; Email: stlotoole@comcast.net; Web: www.stlawrenceotoole.org. Rev. Richard Gill, Email: stlotoole@comcast.net; Deacons Mark Shkreli; Gregory Miller; Adhur Lekovic. Spanish Mass: 7:30PM Saturdays
Res.: 31 Prospect St., Brewster, 10509.
Tel: 845-279-2021; Email: frrichardgill@gmail.com.
Catechesis Religious Program—Tel: 845-279-6098; Fax: 845-279-8165. Theresa Scorca, D.R.E. Students 502.
BRIARCLIFF MANOR, WESTCHESTER CO., ST. THERESA (1926) Revs. John T. McLoughlin; John Edison Lourdhusamy.
Res.: 1394 Pleasantville Rd., Briarcliff Manor, 10510. Tel: 914-941-1646; Email: stchurch@optonline.net.
Catechesis Religious Program—Tel: 914-762-1050; Fax: 914-941-9483. Students 297.
Mission—Our Lady of the Wayside, 219 Saw Mill River Rd., Millwood, Westchester Co. 10546.
BRONXVILLE, WESTCHESTER CO., ST. JOSEPH (1922)
Tel: 914-337-1660. Rev. Peter McGeory; Deacon Bernard Moran. In Res., Revs. Dawson Ambosta, (India); Thomas Augustine Badgley.
Res.: 15 Cedar St., Bronxville, 10708.
Tel: 914-337-1660; Email: saintjosephsbronxville@gmail.com.
Catechesis Religious Program—28 Meadow Ave., Bronxville, 10708. Tel: 914-337-6383;
Fax: 914-779-8103. Mrs. Antoinette Gilligan, D.R.E. Students 830.
BUCHANAN, WESTCHESTER CO., PARISH OF ST. CHRISTOPHER AND ST. PATRICK (1929) Revs. George Oonnoonny, J.C.D., Ph.D.; Regimon Cherian, (India); Deacon Vincent Astarita. In Res., Rev. Matthew Ugwoji, (Africa).
Res.: 3094 Albany Post Rd., Buchanan, 10511.
Tel: 914-737-1046; Email: stchristopher3094@verizon.net.
Catechesis Religious Program—Tel: 914-737-1437; Email: lisaduffyquist@gmail.com. Lisa Quist, C.R.E. Students 287.
CALLICOON, SULLIVAN CO., HOLY CROSS (1870) [CEM] [JC2]
9719 Rte. 97, P.O. Box 246, Callicoon, 12723. Rev. Joseph Ray Sami, O.F.M.
Res.: 9711 Rte. 97, P.O. Box 246, Callicoon, 12723.
Tel: 845-887-5450; Email: holycrosscallicoonny@gmail.com.
Catechesis Religious Program—Students 20.
Mission—St. Patrick,, Long Eddy, 12760.
Chapel—Callicoon, Holy Cross Rectory.
CARMEL, PUTNAM CO., ST. JAMES THE APOSTLE (1913) Rev. Msgrs. Anthony D. Marchitelli; Joseph Martin; Deacons Arthur Weiner; Gerard Cartwright; Anthony Gruerio; Scott Bierbaum.
Res.: 14 Gleneida Ave., Carmel, 10512.
Tel: 845-225-2079.
Catechesis Religious Program—Tel: 845-225-6504. Students 1,100.
Missions—Our Lady of the Lake/Mt. Carmel—[JC] 1 Doherty Dr., Lake Carmel, Putnam Co. 10512.
Tel: 845-228-1235.
Chapel of Life, Carmel.
CHAPPAQUA, WESTCHESTER CO., ST. JOHN AND ST. MARY (1922) Rev. Msgr. Patrick Barry; Deacons Charles Devlin; Walter Brady; Mrs. Joan Corso Ferroni, Pastoral Assoc.
Res.: 15 St. John's Pl., Chappaqua, 10514.
Tel: 914-238-3260; Email: jcboutross@sjsmrcc.com; Web: www.sjsmrcc.com.
Catechesis Religious Program—30 Poillon Rd., Chappaqua, 10514. Tel: 914-238-3696; Email: kidsrelig@optimum.net. Students 664.
CHESTER, ORANGE CO., ST. COLUMBA (1875) [CEM] Rev. John S. Bonnici, S.T.D.
Res.: 27 High St., Chester, 10918. Tel: 845-469-2108.
Catechesis Religious Program—Tel: 845-469-9503. Students 260.
COLD SPRING, PUTNAM CO., OUR LADY OF LORETTO (1833)
Tel: 845-265-3718; Email: lorettochurch@gmail.com. Revs. Thomas P. Kiely; Anthony Yorke, (Ghana).
Res.: 24 Fair St., Cold Spring, 10516.
Tel: 845-265-3718; Email: lorettochurch@gmail.com.
Catechesis Religious Program—Tel: 845-265-2594; Email: ollfaithformation@gmail.com. Students 149.
Mission—St. Joseph's Chapel, Garrison, Putnam Co. 10524.
CONGERS, ROCKLAND CO., PARISH OF ST. PAUL AND ST. ANN (1896) [CEM] Revs. Vladimir Chripko, C.O.; Roman Dominic Palecko, C.O.; Arogya Raju, Parochial Vicar; Peter Bujdos, Parochial Vicar; Deacons Dominic Buonocore, Parish Mgr.; Luke Conroy, Sacramental Min.; Mark Czerwinski, RCIA Coord.; Gerald Fenton, Sacramental Min.
Res.: 82 Lake Rd. W., Congers, 10920.
Tel: 845-268-4464; Email: office@spasaparish.org.
Catechesis Religious Program—Tel: 845-268-5442. Marianna Dalsass, C.R.E.
Chapel—Sisters' Convent and School, Valley Cottage.
CORNWALL-ON-HUDSON, ORANGE CO., PARISH OF ST. THOMAS OF CANTERBURY AND ST. JOSEPH (1870) [CEM]
Tel: 845-534-2547; Fax: 845-534-1357; Email: office@stt-stj.com; Web: ststhomasjoseph.com. Revs. Rees W. Doughty; John Sah, Parochial Vicar; Deacons John V. Pelella; Anthony P. Ferraiuolo; Joseph Lieby; Leonard Farmer; John Hanley.
Res.: 340 Hudson St., Cornwall-on-Hudson, 12520.
Tel: 845-534-2547; Fax: 845-534-1357; Email: office@stt-stj.com; Web: ststhomasjoseph.com.
Catechesis Religious Program—Tel: 845-534-2547; Email: reled@sttstj.com. Annmarie O'Connor, D.R.E.; Mary Ellen Tiernan, Family Formation, RCIA. Students 508.
CORTLANDT MANOR, WESTCHESTER CO.
1—ST. COLUMBANUS (Van Cortlandtville) (1950) Rev. Pratap Reddy Gatla, M.H.M.; Rev. Msgr. Patrick J. Keenan, Pastor Emeritus; Deacon Christopher Mendoza.
Res.: 122 Oregon Rd., Cortlandt Manor, 10567.
Tel: 914-737-4705; Email: stcol122@optonline.net.
Catechesis Religious Program—Tel: 914-739-2441. Isabel Arroyo, D.R.E. Students 245.
Mission—North American Martyrs, 55 Oscawana Lake Rd., Putnam Valley, Putnam Co. 10579.
2—HOLY SPIRIT (1966) Revs. John A. DeBellis; Vernon P. Wickrematunge, (Sri Lanka) Parochial Vicar; Deacons Ray Parchen; Lawrence Candarelli.
Res.: 1969 Crompond Rd., Cortlandt Manor, 10567-4113. Tel: 914-737-2316; Email: holyspiritchurch1969@verizon.net.
Catechesis Religious Program—Tel: 914-734-9243; Email: re_holyspiritchurch1969@verizon.net. Elizabeth Kogler, D.R.E. Students 627.
Chapel—Cortlandt Manor.
CRESTWOOD, WESTCHESTER CO., PARISH OF ANNUNCIATION-OUR LADY OF FATIMA (1931) Rev. Robert F. Grippo; Deacons Ralph D. Longo; Michael J. Fox; Guy A. Pellegrini; Revs. Salvatore Riccardi, C.P.; Livinus Anweting; Kareem Smith. In Res., Rev. Christopher Argano.
Res.: 470 Westchester Ave., Crestwood, 10707.
Tel: 914-779-7345; Email: anna.caruso@annunciation-fatima.com.
Catechesis Religious Program—Tel: 914-779-2374. Mary Rose, C.R.E. Students 28.
CROTON-ON-HUDSON, WESTCHESTER CO., HOLY NAME OF MARY (1874) Revs. Brian C. Brennan; Nelson Couto, (India).
Res.: 114 Grand St., Croton-on-Hudson, 10520.
Tel: 914-271-4797; Fax: frbrennan@hnmchurch.org.
Catechesis Religious Program—Tel: 914-271-4254. Students 388.
Mission—Chapel of the Good Shepherd, Benedict Blvd. and Young Ave., Harmon, Westchester Co. 10520.
DOBBS FERRY, WESTCHESTER CO.
1—OUR LADY OF POMPEII (1922) (Italian) Merged with Sacred Heart to form Sacred Heart and Our Lady of Pompeii Parish, Dobbs Ferry. Administered from Parish of Sacred Heart and Our Lady of Pompeii, 18 Bellewood Ave., Dobbs Ferry. Rev. Timothy J. Scannell, Ph.D., Admin.
Rectory—18 Bellewood Ave., Dobbs Ferry, 10522.
2—PARISH OF SACRED HEART AND OUR LADY OF POMPEII (1862) Revs. Timothy J. Scannell, Ph.D.; Marialal Joseph, C.M.I., (India).
Res.: 18 Bellewood Ave., Dobbs Ferry, 10522.
Tel: 914-693-0119; Fax: 914-693-3408; Email: shrectory@aol.com; Web: www.sh-olp.weconnect.com.
Sacred Heart, Church: 417 Broadway (corner Broadway & Ashford Ave.), Dobbs Ferry, 10522.
Tel: 914-693-5541; Email: shrectory@aol.com.
Catechesis Religious Program—Tel: 914-479-1045; Email: reled09@aol.com. Mrs. Mary Perillo, D.R.E. Students 290.
DOVER PLAINS, DUTCHESS CO., ST. CHARLES BORROMEO (1859) [CEM] Rev. John F. Palatucci; Deacon James Lawlor, (Retired).

Res.: 83 Mill St., P.O. Box 9, Dover Plains, 12522. Tel: 845-877-9934; Email: scbsje@gmail.com.

EAST KINGSTON, ULSTER CO., ST. COLMAN (1904) Closed. Administered from Parish of St. Catherine Laboure and St. Colman, 200 Tuytenbridge Rd., Lake Katrine.

ELLENVILLE, ULSTER CO., ST. MARY AND ST. ANDREW (1850) Revs. Kenneth Riello; Y. Vijaya Shekar.
Res.: 137 S. Main St., Ellenville, 12428.
Tel: 845-647-6080; Email: u426@archny.org; Web: www.smsaparish.org.
Catechesis Religious Program—Bruce Santiago, C.R.E. Students 160.
Mission—Our Lady of Lourdes, Kerhonkson, Ulster Co. 12446.

ELMSFORD, WESTCHESTER CO., OUR LADY OF MT. CARMEL (1904)
Tel: 914-592-6789; Email: secraolmc@gmail.com; Web: olmcchurchelmsford.com. Rev. Robert J. Norris, Ph.D.; Rev. Msgr. Frederick J. Becker; Rev. Augustine Dada, In Res.; Deacon Daniel Moliterno.
Res.: 59 E. Main St., Elmsford, 10523.
Tel: 914-592-6789; Fax: 914-592-3898; Email: frbob@olmc.ws; Web: www.olmcchurchelmsford.com.
Catechesis Religious Program—Tel: 914-592-4280. Students 190.

FISHKILL, DUTCHESS CO., CHURCH OF ST. MARY, MOTHER OF THE CHURCH (1953) Revs. Joseph A. Blenkle; Thomas Colucci; Adolfo Occeno, (Philippines); Deacons Joseph R. Hafeman; Michael Decker; Rommel Pampolina; Paul L. Smith.
Res.: 103 Jackson St., P.O. Box 780, Fishkill, 12524-0499. Tel: 845-896-6400; Email: contactstmarys@gmail.com.
Catechesis Religious Program—100 Jackson St., P.O. Box 780, Fishkill, 12524. Tel: 845-896-6430; Fax: 845-896-6764. Kathy Hamilton, D.R.E. Students 610.

FLORIDA, ORANGE CO., ST. JOSEPH (1895) [CEM] (Polish) Rev. Frank Borkowski.
Res.: 14 Glenmere Ave., Florida, 10921.
Tel: 845-651-7792; Email: saintjoseph@optonline.net.
Catechesis Religious Program—19 Glenmere Ave., Florida, 10921. Tel: 845-651-4240. Students 283.
Mission—St. Stanislaus, 17 Pulaski Hwy., Pine Island, Orange Co. 10969. Tel: 845-258-4426.

FORESTBURGH, SULLIVAN CO., ST. THOMAS AQUINAS (1900) [CEM] Records at Parish of St. Anthony of Padua and St. Thomas Aquinas, 25 Beaver Brook Rd., Yulan. Rev. Joselin Pens Berkmans, M.M.I.; Deacon Paul A. Rausch.
Res. & Rectory: One Forestburgh Rd., Forestburgh, 12777. Tel: 845-791-7400.

GARDINER, ULSTER CO., ST. CHARLES BORROMEO (1883) [CEM] Rev. Matthew Yatkauskas.
Res.: 2212 Rte. 44/55, Gardiner, 12525.
Tel: 845-255-1374; Email: borromeogardiner@aol.com.
Catechesis Religious Program—Students 105.

GARNERVILLE, ROCKLAND CO., ST. GREGORY BARBARIGO (1961)
Tel: 845-947-1873; Email: sgbparish@verizon.net; Web: www.stgregorybarbarigo.org. Rev. Joseph P. LaMorte; Deacons George M. Albin Jr.; Roland F. Dowen; John J. Kelly.
Res.: 21 Cinder Rd., Garnerville, 10923.
Tel: 845-947-1873; Email: sgbparish@verizon.net; Web: www.stgregorybarbarigo.org.
Catechesis Religious Program—Tel: 845-429-8775; Email: sgbreled@verizon.net. Mr. Donald A. Ruzzi, C.R.E. Students 426.

GLASCO, ULSTER CO., ST. JOSEPH (1919) Administered from Parish of St. Mary of the Snow and St. Joseph, 36 Cedar St., Saugerties. Rev. Christopher H. Berean.

GOSHEN, ORANGE CO., ST. JOHN THE EVANGELIST (1837) [CEM]
71 Murray Ave., Goshen, 10924. Tel: 845-294-5328; Email: stjohnrc@frontiernet.net; Web: www.sjegoshen.org. Revs. George Hafemann; Anthony A. Amponsah, Parochial Vicar; Anthony Giacona, Parochial Vicar; Deacons William Castellane; James Faulkner.
Catechesis Religious Program—Tel: 845-294-6947; Email: religed@hotmail.com. Cathy Fife, D.R.E. Students 400.
Stations—Valley View Nursing and Rehabilitation Center—Goshen. Tel: 845-294-7971.
Campbell Hall Nursing Facility, Orange. Tel: 845-294-8154.

GREENWOOD LAKE, ORANGE CO., HOLY ROSARY (1954)
Tel: 845-477-8378; Email: holy_rosary_gwl@yahoo.com; Web: www.holyrosary-ny.org. Rev. Robert J. Sweeney.
Res.: 41 Windermere Ave., Greenwood Lake, 10925-2105. Tel: 845-477-8378; Email: holy_rosary_gwl@yahoo.com.
Catechesis Religious Program—Tel: 845-477-0906; Fax: 845-477-0906. Students 162.

HARRIMAN, ORANGE CO., ST. ANASTASIA (1899) [CEM] Revs. Michael F. Keane; Francisco Tejeda; Deacons Eugene E. Bormann; Brian O'Neill.
Res.: 21 N. Main St., Harriman, 10926.
Tel: 845-238-3844; Email: stanastasia@optonline.net.
Catechesis Religious Program—Tel: 845-782-5099. Students 497.

HARRISON, WESTCHESTER CO., ST. GREGORY THE GREAT (1911)
Tel: 914-835-0677; Email: stgreggreat@aol.com. Revs. Richard M. Guarnieri; James B. Teague; Soosairaj Michael.
Res.: 215 Halstead Ave., Harrison, 10528.
Tel: 914-835-0677; Email: stgreggreat@aol.com.
Catechesis Religious Program—94 Broadway, Harrison, 10528. Tel: 914-835-3685; Fax: 914-835-2070. Students 437.

HARTSDALE, WESTCHESTER CO.
1—CHURCH OF OUR LADY OF SHKODRA (1989) [CEM] (Albanian) Rev. Peter Popovich.
Res.: 361 W. Hartsdale Ave., Hartsdale, 10530.
Tel: 914-761-3523.
2—SACRED HEART (1926) Revs. Michael C. Moon, Admin.; Wenceslaus Rodrigues, (India).
Res.: 10 Lawton Ave., Hartsdale, 10530.
Tel: 914-949-0028; Email: shchartsdale@gmail.com.
Catechesis Religious Program—Tel: 914-428-5043; Fax: 914-428-5043; Email: sacredheart.re@aol.com. Students 215.
Convent—11 Lawton Ave., Hartsdale, 10530. Tel: 914-946-2581.

HASTINGS-ON-HUDSON, WESTCHESTER CO.
1—PARISH OF ST. MATTHEW AND OUR LADY OF PERPETUAL HELP (1892) Rev. Robert P. Henry.
Res.: 616 Warburton Ave., Hastings-on-Hudson, 10706. Tel: 914-478-2822; Email: office@stmolph.com.
Catechesis Religious Program—(Combined with Our Lady of Perpetual Help, Ardsley) Students 465.
2—ST. STANISLAUS KOSTKA (1912) (Polish) Records at: St. Matthew and Our Lady of Perpetual Help, 616 Warburton Ave., Hastings-on-Hudson, NY 10706 (914-478-2822).
Res.: 616 Warburton Ave., Hastings-on-Hudson, 10706.

HAVERSTRAW, ROCKLAND CO.
1—ST. MARY OF THE ASSUMPTION (1899) (Slovak) Merged into St. Peter and St. Mary of the Assumption. Records at Parish of St Peter and St. Mary of the Assumption, 115 Broadway, Haverstraw. Rev. Thomas F. Madden.
Res.: 115 Broadway, Haverstraw, 10927.
Tel: 845-429-2196; Email: pastor@stpeterstmary.us.
2—PARISH OF ST. PETER AND ST. MARY OF THE ASSUMPTION (1848) [CEM] [JC]
Tel: 845-429-2196; Email: pastor@stpeterstmary.us; Web: www.stpeterstmary.us. Revs. Thomas F. Madden; Osvaldo Hernandez.
Res.: 115 Broadway, Haverstraw, 10927.
Tel: 914-429-2196; Fax: 914-947-4564; Email: pastor@saintpeterschurch.us; Web: www.saintpeterschurch.us.
Catechesis Religious Program—21 Ridge St., Haverstraw, 10927. Tel: 914-429-8824; Fax: 845-429-2721. Milagros Cobb, D.R.E. Students 674.
Stations—Green Hills Home—Haverstraw. Tel: 914-429-8411.
Northern Riverview Health Care Center, Haverstraw. Tel: 914-429-5381.

HAWTHORNE, WESTCHESTER CO., HOLY ROSARY (1901) Tel: 914-769-0030; Email: hrc10532@gmail.com. Rev. Msgr. Edward M. Barry, V.F.
Res.: 170 Bradhurst, Hawthorne, 10532.
Tel: 914-769-0030; Email: hrc10532@gmail.com.
Catechesis Religious Program—
Tel: 914-769-0030, Ext. 23. Deacon Richard McLaughlin, D.R.E.

HIGHLAND FALLS, ORANGE CO., SACRED HEART OF JESUS (1870) [CEM] Rev. Joseph M. Tokarczyk.
Res.: 353 Main St., Highland Falls, 10928.
Tel: 845-446-2071; Email: sacredheartchurch@twcmetrobiz.com; Web: www.sacredheart-highlandfalls.org.
Catechesis Religious Program—Tel: 845-446-2674. Maryann Brigham, D.R.E. Students 127.
Mission—Blessed Sacrament, 794 Rte 9W, Fort Montgomery, Orange Co. 10922.

HIGHLAND MILLS, ORANGE CO., ST. PATRICK St. Patrick's Church (1957)
Tel: 845-928-6027; Tel: 845-928-6688; Email: margie.lynch@stpatrickny.org; Web: www.stpatrickny.org. Rev. Joseph J. Tyrrell; Deacon Paul Weireter.
Res.: 26 Hunter St., Highland Mills, 10930.
Tel: 845-928-6027; Tel: 845-928-6688;
Fax: 845-928-2982; Email: stpatssor@gmail.com; Email: frjoetyrrell@gmail.com; Email: margie.lynch@stpatrickny.org; Web: stpatrickny.org.
Catechesis Religious Program—Tel: 845-928-6688. Jennie Dabney, D.R.E. Students 640.

HIGHLAND, ULSTER CO., ST. AUGUSTINE (1899) Revs. John W. Lynch; Joseph Peh Akomeah, (Ghana); Deacons John Bellacicco; Frank S. Ottaviano.
Res.: 55 Main St., Highland, 12528.
Tel: 845-691-7673; Email: st.augustine1899@gmail.com.
Catechesis Religious Program—Students 290.

HOPEWELL JUNCTION, DUTCHESS CO.
1—ST. COLUMBA (1992)
Tel: 845-227-8380; Email: rectory@stcolumbaonline.org; Web: www.stcolumbaonline.org. Revs. Michael P. McLoughlin; Michael Connelly; Deacons William Alvarado; John Reilly; Warren Testa.
Res.: 835 Rte. 82, P.O. Box 428, Hopewell Junction, 12533. Tel: 845-227-8380; Email: rectory@stcolumbaonline.org; Web: www.stcolumbaonline.org.
Catechesis Religious Program—P.O. Box 368, Hopewell Jct., 12533. Tel: 845-221-4900; Email: smpappascr@parishmail.com. Sr. Marie Pappas, C.R., Ph.D. (Cand), D.R.E. Students 873.
2—ST. DENIS (1899) [CEM]
602 Beekman Rd., P.O. Box 10, Hopewell Junction, 12533. Revs. Robert D. Porpora; Patrick J. Dunne, Parochial Vicar; Deacons Walter Dauerer; Stanley Aviles; Enrico Messina; Robert Pelech; Frank Munoz.
Res. & Office: 598 Beekman Rd., P.O. Box 10, Hopewell Junction, 12533. Tel: 845-227-8382; Email: webmaster@stdenischurch.org.
Child Care—The Ark and The Dove Preschool:, 604 Beekman Rd., P.O. Box 1139, Hopewell Junction, 12533. Tel: 845-227-5232; Fax: 845-227-0435; Email: noah1@stdenischurch.org.
Catechesis Religious Program—Tel: 845-227-3949; Email: stdenisre@stdenischurch.org. Students 426.

HYDE PARK, DUTCHESS CO., REGINA COELI (1863) Revs. Michael Morris, M.A., M.Div.; Joseph A. Gaspar; Deacons Frank J. Gohl; Gerard Lindley; Mark O'Sullivan; Peter Dalmer; James R. Hayes.
Res.: 2 Harvey St., Hyde Park, 12538.
Tel: 845-229-2134; Email: frontdesk@reginacoelihp.org.
Catechesis Religious Program—Tel: 845-229-9139. Students 135.
Mission—St. Paul (1851) Mulford Ave., Staatsburg, Dutchess Co. 12580.

IRVINGTON, WESTCHESTER CO., IMMACULATE CONCEPTION (1873) Revs. Robert Ashman; Roy Chettaniyil, (India).
Res.: 16 N. Broadway, Irvington, 10533.
Tel: 914-591-7480; Email: immacon@optonline.net; Web: www.iccirvington.com.
Catechesis Religious Program—Tel: 914-591-7740; Email: ccdicc@optonline.net. Students 199.

JEFFERSONVILLE, SULLIVAN CO.
1—ST. GEORGE (1963) [CEM] Merged with St. Francis of Assisi to form St. George-St. Francis, Jeffersonville.
2—ST. GEORGE-ST. FRANCIS (1843; 1909) [CEM] Rev. Ignatius Vu.
Res.: 97 Schoolhouse Hill Rd., P.O. Box 672, Jeffersonville, 12748. Tel: 845-482-4640; Email: saintgeorgesaintfran@hvc.rr.com.
Catechesis Religious Program—Students 75.
Mission—St. Francis of Assisi, 4020 State Rte. 52, Youngsville, Sullivan Co. 12791.

KATONAH, WESTCHESTER CO., ST. MARY OF THE ASSUMPTION (1908)
Tel: 914-232-3356; Email: stmarysparish@yahoo.com. Revs. John J. Duff; Vincent Paul, Parochial Vicar; Aloysius Thumma, (India) S.T.D., Parochial Vicar; Deacon George Chiu.
Res.: 117 Valley Rd., Katonah, 10536.
Tel: 914-232-3356; Email: stmarysparish@yahoo.com.
Catechesis Religious Program—99 Valley Rd., Katonah, 10536. Tel: 914-232-4648. Students 460.
Mission—St. Matthias (1909) 107 Babbitt Rd., Bedford Hills, Westchester Co. 10507.

KINGSTON, ULSTER CO.
1—HOLY NAME OF JESUS (1884) Closed. Records at Parish of St. Mary/Holy Name of Jesus and St. Peter, 160 Broadway, Kingston.
2—IMMACULATE CONCEPTION (1896) [CEM] (Polish) Rev. Miroslaw Pawlaczyk, (Poland) Admin.
Res.: 467 Delaware Ave., Kingston, 12401.
Tel: 845-331-0846.
Catechesis Religious Program—Tel: 845-331-7352. Students 40.
3—ST. JOSEPH (1868) Revs. Uldarico de la Pena, (Philippines); George K. Nedumaruthumchalil, (India); Deacons Richard Frohmiller; Robert Winrow; John Peters; Joseph Doherty.
Res.: 242 Wall St., Kingston, 12401.
Tel: 845-338-1554; Email: sjcr242@earthlink.net.
Catechesis Religious Program—Tel: 845-339-4391; Fax: 845-339-5049. Students 215.
Mission—Msgr. O'Reilly Chapel, Zandhoeck Rd., Hurley, 12443.
4—PARISH OF ST. MARY/HOLY NAME OF JESUS AND ST. PETER (2015) [CEM] Rev. Robert J. Bubel. In Res.,

Rev. Daniel Machiki, (Nigeria) Chap., Kingston Hospital & Parochial Vicar.
Res.: 160 Broadway, Kingston, 12401.
Tel: 845-331-0301; Email: stmaryskingston@gmail.com.
Catechesis Religious Program—Students 115.
5—SAINT PETER THE APOSTLE (1858) [CEM] (German) Records at Parish of St. Mary/Holy Name of Jesus and St. Peter, 160 Broadway, Kingston. Rev. Robert J. Bubel.
Res.: 93 Wurts St., Kingston, 12401-6328.
Tel: 845-331-0436; Fax: 845-340-0807.
LAGRANGEVILLE, DUTCHESS CO., SAINT KATERI TEKAKWITHA (2002) Rev. Msgr. Desmond O'Connor; Rev. Michael Achanyi, Parochial Vicar; Deacons Andrew Daubman; Robert Horton; John McCormack.
Res.: 1925 Rte. 82, LaGrangeville, 12540.
Tel: 845-227-1710; Email: saintkateri@optonline.net.
Catechesis Religious Program—
Tel: 845-227-1710, Ext. 3; Fax: 845-227-1734; Email: sktfaithform@optonline.net. Students 971.
LAKE KATRINE, ULSTER CO., PARISH OF ST. CATHERINE LABOURE AND ST. COLMAN (1957)
Tel: 845-382-1133; Email: parish383ny@gmail.com; Web: www.parish383ny.weebly.com. Rev. Slawomir Ciszkowski, (Poland).
Res.: 200 Tuytenbridge Rd., P.O. Box 271, Lake Katrine, 12449. Tel: 845-382-1133;
Fax: parish383ny@gmail.com.
Catechesis Religious Program—Students 61.
LARCHMONT, WESTCHESTER CO.
1—ST. AUGUSTINE (1892) Rev. Msgrs. Thomas R. Kelly, Admin.; Walter F. Kenny, S.T.D., Pastor Emeritus, (Retired); Robert W. Larkin.
Res.: 18 Cherry Ave., Larchmont, 10538.
Tel: 914-834-1220.
Catechesis Religious Program—Email: srsuzanne@staugustineny.org. Sr. Suzanne Duzen, SS.C.M., D.R.E. Students 662.
2—SS. JOHN AND PAUL (1949) Rev. Msgr. Thomas F. Petrillo, Ed.D.; Revs. Dominique De Lafforest, (Belgium); Frank J. Prima, (France); Deacons James Brown; John Shea.
Res.: 280 Weaver St., Larchmont, 10538.
Tel: 914-834-5458.
Catechesis Religious Program—Tel: 914-834-4597; Fax: 914-834-7493. Students 400.
LIBERTY, SULLIVAN CO., ST. PETER (1894) [CEM] Rev. William A. Scafidi, M.Ss.A.; Deacon John Riley.
Res.: 264 N. Main St., Liberty, 12754.
Tel: 845-292-4525; Fax: srectory1@hvc.rr.com.
Catechesis Religious Program—Students 153.
LIVINGSTON MANOR, SULLIVAN CO., ST. ALOYSIUS (1899) [CEM] Rev. Edward Bader.
Res.: 22 Church St., Box 206, Livingston Manor, 12758. Tel: 845-439-5625; Email: st.aloysius@hotmail.com.
Missions—Sacred Heart— (1906) P.O. Box 206, De Bruce, Sullivan Co. 12758.
Gate of Heaven (1901) Highland Ave., Roscoe, Sullivan Co. 12776.
Catechesis Religious Program—Students 41.
MAHOPAC, PUTNAM CO., ST. JOHN THE EVANGELIST (1889) Revs. Philip J. Caruso, Admin.; Patrick J. McCarthy; Maximo Villanueva, (Philippines); Deacon John Scarfi.
Res.: 221 E. Lake Blvd., Mahopac, 10541.
Tel: 845-628-2006.
Catechesis Religious Program—Students 1,200.
Chapel—Convent of Religious of the Divine Compassion, Tel: 914-628-6497.
MAMARONECK, WESTCHESTER CO.
1—MOST HOLY TRINITY (1874) Records at Parish of St. Vito and Most Holy Trinity, 816 Underhill Ave., Mamaroneck. Rev. Msgr. James E. White; Revs. Robert P. Henry; Joseph Kahumburu, (Kenya); Deacon Augustine DiFiore.
Res.: 320 E. Boston Post Rd., Mamaroneck, 10543.
Tel: 914-698-5944; Fax: 914-698-5274; Email: mostholytrinityc@gmail.com.
2—PARISH OF ST. VITO AND MOST HOLY TRINITY (1911) (Italian) Rev. Msgr. James E. White; Deacon Augustine DiFiore, Email: awdifiore@optonline.net.
Res.: 816 Underhill Ave., Mamaroneck, 10543.
Tel: 914-698-2648; Email: stvitochurch@optonline.net; Web: www.stvitochurch.com.
Catechesis Religious Program—826 Underhill Ave., Mamaronek, 10543. Students 282.
MARLBORO, ULSTER CO., PARISH OF ST. MARY AND ST. JAMES (1900) [CEM] Rev. Thomas Dicks; Deacons Thomas Cornell; Vincent Porcelli; John T. Repke.
Res.: 71 Grand St., P.O. Box 730, Marlboro, 12542.
Tel: 845-236-4340; Fax: frtdicks1958@aol.com.
Catechesis Religious Program—Tel: 845-236-7791. Mrs. Anne Marie Coleman, C.R.E. Students 335.
Mission—Our Lady of Mercy, 977 River Rd., Newburgh/Roseton, Orange Co. 12550.
MAYBROOK, ORANGE CO., CHURCH OF THE ASSUMPTION (1907) Administered from Parish of Holy Name of Mary and Assumption, 89 Union St., Montgomery, NY. Rev. Daniel M. O'Hare; Deacon Edward M. Grosso.
Res.: 211 Homestead Ave., P.O. Box 320, Maybrook, 12543. Tel: 845-427-2046.
Catechesis Religious Program—Tel: 845-427-5318. Students 222.
MIDDLETOWN, ORANGE CO.
1—HOLY CROSS (1999) Rev. Michael G. Cedro.
Res.: 626 County Rte. 22, Middletown, 10940.
Tel: 845-355-4439; Email: Cedro2004@cs.com.
Catechesis Religious Program—Tel: 845-355-6255. Students 386.
Mission—Our Lady of the Scapular, 125 Main St., Unionville, Orange Co. 10988.
2—ST. JOSEPH (1865) [CEM] Revs. Dennis A. Nikolic; Sandro Rodriguez Leyton; Cruz Sanchez Mares; Deacons Richard Trapani; Albert Loeffler; Alexander Gapay; Michael Brescia. In Res., Rev. Donald Timone, (Retired).
Res.: 149 Cottage St., Middletown, 10940.
Tel: 845-343-6013.
Catechesis Religious Program—Tel: 845-343-4415. Angelica Frausto, C.R.E. Students 782.
3—OUR LADY OF MT. CARMEL (1912)
Tel: 845-343-4121; Email: ourladyofmtcarmel883@hotmail.com; Web: www.olmcmiddletown.org. Revs. Paul Denault, O.Carm.; Anthony Trung Nguyen, O.Carm., Parochial Vicar; Sean R. Harlow, O.Carm., Parochial Vicar; Deacon Edward Woods, Pastoral Assoc.
Res.: 90 Euclid Ave., P.O. Box 883, Middletown, 10940. Tel: 845-343-4121; Fax: 845-343-4433; Email: ourladyofmtcarmel883@hotmail.com; Web: www.olmcmiddletown.org.
Catechesis Religious Program—Tel: 845-342-1510; Email: olmcre90@gmail.com. Mrs. Nancy Miller, D.R.E. Students 478.
Missions—Our Lady of the Assumption—P.O. Box 527, Bloomingburg, Sullivan Co. 12721-0527.
Tel: 845-733-1477.
St. Paul, Rte. 17K, P.O. Box 222, Bullville, Orange Co. 10915. Tel: 845-361-3107.
MILLBROOK, DUTCHESS CO., PARISH OF ST. JOSEPH AND IMMACULATE CONCEPTION (1890) [CEM]
15 North Ave., Millbrook, 12545. Tel: 845-677-3422; Email: stjosephmillbrook@gmail.com; Web: www.stjosephmillbrookny.org. P.O. Box 439, Millbrook, 12545. Rev. Msgr. Gerardo J. Colacicco, J.C.L.
Catechesis Religious Program—Tel: 845-677-3273; Email: ccdstjosephmillbrook@gmail.com. Laura Warning, D.R.E. Students 161.
Stations—Green Briar Home—Millbrook.
Tel: 845-677-9997.
The Fountains, Millbrook. Tel: 845-677-8550.
MILTON, ULSTER CO., ST. JAMES (1874) Records at Parish of St. Mary and St. James, 71 Grand St., P.O. Box 730, Marlboro. Rev. Thomas Dicks.
Res.: 71 Grand St., P.O. Box 730, Marlboro, 12542.
MONROE, ORANGE CO., SACRED HEART CHURCH (1957) Revs. Thomas J. Byrnes; Anthony A. Amponsah; Raymond Nwegede; Deacons Peter Brockmann; Richard McCarthy, (Retired); Angelo Corsaro; Robert Duncan.
Res.: 26 Still Rd., Monroe, 10950. Tel: 845-782-8510; Fax: 845-782-3593; Email: info@sacredheartchurch.org; Web: www.sacredheartchurch.org.
Catechesis Religious Program—Tel: 845-782-7420; Fax: 845-782-5192. Sr. Rose O'Rourke, D.R.E. Students 916.
Convent—Still Rd., Monroe, 10950.
Mission—Sacred Heart Chapel, 151 Stage Rd., Monroe, 10950.
MONTGOMERY, ORANGE CO., PARISH OF HOLY NAME OF MARY - ASSUMPTION (1868) [CEM] Rev. Daniel M. O'Hare; Deacon Edward Grasso.
Res.: 89 Union St., Montgomery, 12549.
Tel: 845-457-5276; Email: hnm469@frontiernet.net.
Worship Site: Assumption, 211 Homestead Ave., Maybrook, 12543.
Catechesis Religious Program—Tel: 845-457-1738. Students 203.
MONTICELLO, SULLIVAN CO., ST. PETER (1874) [CEM] Revs. John Tran; John P. Sheehan. In Res., Rev. Stanislaus Ogbonna, C.S.Sp., (Nigeria).
Res.: 10 Liberty St., Monticello, 12701.
Tel: 845-794-5577; Email: s470@archny.org.
Catechesis Religious Program—Tel: 845-665-7345. Students 185.
Missions—St. Joseph—Mongaup Valley, Sullivan Co.
St. Anne, White Lake, Sullivan Co.
MT. KISCO, WESTCHESTER CO., ST. FRANCIS OF ASSISI (1868) [CEM] Revs. Steven E. Clark; Benjamin Obuor, Parochial Vicar; Deacon Isaac Marquez, Pastoral Assoc. In Res., Rev. Msgr. John J. Budwick, (Retired).
Res.: 2 Green St., Mt. Kisco, 10549.
Tel: 914-666-5986; Fax: 914-666-9390; Email: sanfrankisco@verizon.net; Web: sfamountkisco.org.
Catechesis Religious Program—16 Green St., Mount Kisco, 10549. Students 269.
MOUNT VERNON, WESTCHESTER CO.
1—PARISH OF ST. MARY-OUR LADY OF MT. CARMEL (1894)
Tel: 914-664-5855; Email: stmarymv@yahoo.com; Web: stmarys-ny.org. Rev. Francis P. Scanlon; Deacon Joseph Patrona.
Res.: 23 S. High St., Mount Vernon, 10550.
Tel: 914-664-5855.
Catechesis Religious Program—Students 181.
2—OUR LADY OF MT. CARMEL (1897) (Italian), Closed. For inquiries for parish records see Parish of St. Mary and Our Lady of Mt. Carmel, Mount Vernon.
3—PARISH OF OUR LADY OF VICTORY AND SACRED HEART (1871) Rev. Alfredo Monteiro.
Res.: 28 W. Sidney Ave., Mount Vernon, 10550.
Tel: 914-668-5861.
Catechesis Religious Program—Students 175.
4—PARISH OF STS. PETER AND PAUL AND ST. URSULA (1929) Rev. John F. Lauri, J.C.L. In Res., Rev. Francis Michaelsamy.
Res.: 129 Birch St., Mount Vernon, 10552.
Tel: 914-668-9815; Email: rectory@stspeterpaulandstursula.org.
Catechesis Religious Program—Tel: 914-668-9880. Students 106.
5—SACRED HEART (1872) Records at Parish of Our Lady of Victory and Sacred Heart, 28 W. Sidney Ave., Mount Vernon. Revs. Alfredo Monteiro; Andrew Florez.
Res.: 115 S. Fifth Ave., Mount Vernon, 10550.
Tel: 914-668-7440; Fax: 914-668-1177.
6—ST. URSULA (1908) Records at Parish of Sts. Peter and Paul and St. Ursula, 129 Birch St., Mount Vernon. Revs. John F. Lauri, J.C.L.; Francis Michaelsamy, (India); Deacons Thomas J. Abbamont; Carl Degenhardt.
Res.: 214 E. Lincoln Ave., Mount Vernon, 10552.
Tel: 914-668-0085; Fax: 914-668-4228.
Catechesis Religious Program—Tel: 914-699-7964. Ms. Mona Parkinson, C.R.E. Students 54.
NANUET, ROCKLAND CO., ST. ANTHONY (1897) [CEM] Revs. Joseph J. Deponai; Cresus Fernando; Ronelo Anung; Deacon John R. Maloney.
Res.: 36 W. Nyack Rd., Nanuet, 10954.
Tel: 845-623-2138; Email: stanthonys.church@verizon.net.
Catechesis Religious Program—Tel: 845-624-2230; Email: st.anthony.prep@gmail.com. Ursula Magee, C.R.E. Students 525.
Mission—St. Anthony Shrine Church, 38 W. Nyack Rd., Nanuet, Rockland Co. 10954.
NARROWSBURG, SULLIVAN CO., ST. FRANCIS XAVIER (1862) [CEM 2] (Franciscan) Rev. Dennis M. Dinan.
Res.: 151 Bridge St., Narrowsburg, 12764.
Tel: 845-252-6681; Email: sfxnarrowsburg@gmail.com.
Catechesis Religious Program—Students 27.
Mission—Our Lady of the Lake, Rte. 52, Lake Huntington, Sullivan Co. 12752. Web: www.ollhuntington.com.
NEW CITY, ROCKLAND CO., ST. AUGUSTINE (1957) Rev. William B. Cosgrove; Deacons James Suchy; Samir Mobarek.
Res.: 140 Maple Ave., New City, 10956.
Tel: 845-634-3641; Email: staug@optonline.net.
Catechesis Religious Program—Tel: 845-634-8462; Email: staugustinereo@gmail.com. Students 400.
NEW PALTZ, ULSTER CO., ST. JOSEPH (1894) (Capuchin Franciscans) Rev. Fr. Salvatore Cordaro, O.F.M.Cap.; Revs. Raphael Iannone, O.F.M.Cap.; Michael Ramos, O.F.M.Cap., Parochial Vicar.
Res.: 34 S. Chestnut St., New Paltz, 12561.
Tel: 845-255-5635; Email: salccapuchin@hotmail.com.
Catechesis Religious Program—Tel: 845-255-0237; Fax: 845-256-0687. Sr. Philomena Fleck, O.S.B., D.R.E. Students 350.
NEW ROCHELLE, WESTCHESTER CO.
1—BLESSED SACRAMENT (1848) [CEM 2] Revs. William J. Luciano; Biju Peter, C.M.I., Parochial Vicar; George Obeng-Yeboah-Asuamah, Parochial Vicar; Deacons Frank Orlando; Angel Camacho.
Res.: 15 Shea Pl., New Rochelle, 10801.
Tel: 914-632-3700; Email: 15shea@optonline.net.
Catechesis Religious Program—Tel: 914-235-7311. Students 235.
Chapel—Holy Family Chapel, College of New Rochelle, 29 Castle Pl., New Rochelle, 10805.
2—PARISH OF ST. GABRIEL AND ST. JOSEPH (1893) Rev. Edward P. O'Halloran, Email: churchofstgabriels@verizon.net.
Res.: 120 Division St., New Rochelle, 10801.
Tel: 914-632-0211; Email: churchstgabriel@optimum.net.
Catechesis Religious Program—Mrs. Maria Elena Marquez, D.R.E. Students 245.
3—HOLY FAMILY (1913)
Tel: 914-632-0673. Rev. Msgr. Dennis P. Keane, Ph. D.; Revs. Robert Verrigni, Parochial Vicar; Patrick N. Nsionu, (Nigeria) Parochial Vicar; Deacons Donald Gray; Raymond Hall.

Res.: 83 Clove Rd., New Rochelle, 10801.
Tel: 914-632-0673; Email: HolyFamilyNR@gmail.com.
Church: Mayflower Ave. & Mt. Joy Pl., New Rochelle, 10801.
Catechesis Religious Program—Tel: 914-636-6758. Sr. Connie Koch, O.P., Pastoral Asst. for Faith Formation. Students 351.
Chapels—Ursuline Sisters—1352 N. Ave., New Rochelle, 10804. Tel: 914-636-3456; Fax: 914-576-2620.
Iona Grammar and Preparatory Schools, 173 Stratton Rd., New Rochelle, 10804.
Tel: 914-633-7744; Tel: 914-632-2727; Fax: 914-235-6338.
Iona College, 715 N. Ave., New Rochelle, 10801.
Tel: 914-633-2000; Fax: 800-633-2329.
St. Joseph's Residence, St. Patrick Prov., 30 Montgomery Circle, New Rochelle, 10801.
Tel: 914-633-6851; Fax: 914-633-5579.
New Rochelle, St. Joseph Chapel, Tel: 914-632-6592; Fax: 914-533-4264.
Edmond Rice Hall, 33 Pryer Ter., New Rochelle, 10804. Tel: 914-636-6194; Fax: 914-636-0021.
Opus Dei, 99 Overlook Cir., New Rochelle, 10804.
Tel: 914-235-1201; Fax: 914-235-7805.

4—HOLY NAME OF JESUS (1929) Revs. Michael F. Challinor; Francis Maurice; Deacons Carmine DeMarco; Robert Gontcharuk.
Res.: 75 Lispenard Ave., New Rochelle, 10801.
Tel: 914-636-4856; Fax: 914-636-8474.
Church: Petersville Rd. and Halligan St., New Rochelle, 10801.
School—Holy Name of Jesus School (1954) (Regional) 70 Petersville Rd., New Rochelle, 10801.
Tel: 914-576-6672; Fax: 914-576-6676; Email: w493@adnyeducation.org; Web: www.holynamenewrochelle.com. Joanne Kelly, Prin. Lay Teachers 10; Students 166.
Catechesis Religious Program—Tel: 914-576-6038. Students 210.
Chapels—Sisters of Charity Convent—78 Petersville Rd., New Rochelle, 10801. Tel: 914-636-4354.
Salesian HS Chapel, 148 Main St., New Rochelle, 10801. Tel: 914-632-0248.
Salesian Provincial House Chapel, Tel: 914-636-4225.

5—ST. JOSEPH (1901) (Italian) Administered from Parish of St. Gabriel and St. Joseph, 120 Division St., New Rochelle. Rev. Edward P. O'Halloran; Rev. Msgr. John A. Ruvo, Senior Priest, (Retired).
Res.: 280 Washington Ave., New Rochelle, 10801.
Tel: 914-632-0675; Fax: 914-633-4264.
Catechesis Religious Program—St. Joseph School of Religion, 53 Sixth St., New Rochelle, 10801.
Tel: 914-632-3458; Email: stjoenr@aol.com. Antoinette Rossetti, D.R.E. Students 199.

NEW WINDSOR, ORANGE CO., ST. JOSEPH (1962) Administered from Parish of St. Thomas of Canterbury and St. Joseph, 10 Second St., Cornwall-on-Hudson. Rev. Rees W. Doughty; Deacons Joseph Lieby; Anthony Ferraiuolo; Leonard Farmer.
Res.: 4 St. Joseph Pl., New Windsor, 12553.
Tel: 845-561-8467; Fax: 845-562-3269; Email: stjosephschurch@hvc.rr.com.

NEWBURGH, ORANGE CO.
1—ST. FRANCIS OF ASSISI (1909) [CEM] (Polish), Merged with St. Francis of Assisi to form Sacred Heart Saint Francis Church, Newburgh.
2—ST. MARY (1875) Records at Parish of St. Patrick and St. Mary, 55 Grand St., Newburgh. Rev. Fernando A. Hernandez; Deacons John L. Seymour; William Castellane.
Res.: 180 South St., Newburgh, 12550.
Tel: 845-562-0862; Fax: 845-562-0876; Web: www.stmary.org.
3—PARISH OF ST. PATRICK AND ST. MARY (1836) [CEM 2] Revs. Fernando A. Hernandez; Bladi J. Socualaya; Patrick Bonner, J.C.D., Parochial Vicar; Deacons Donald Halter; William Castellane; Dennis White.
Res.: 55 Grand St., Newburgh, 12550.
Tel: 914-561-0885.
Catechesis Religious Program—Tel: 914-561-6470. Students 300.
Mission—Our Lady of the Lake, Lakeside & Rte. 52, Orange Lake, Orange Co. 12550. Tel: 914-561-9537.
4—ROMAN CATHOLIC CHURCH OF SACRED HEART AND SAINT FRANCIS OF ASSISI (1912) (Italian)
301 Ann St., Newburgh, 12550. Tel: 845-561-2264; Email: sacredheart.newburgh@verizon.net. Revs. William J. Damroth III; Bejoy Thomas Valliyil, C.M.I., (India); Deacon Peter Haight.
Catechesis Religious Program—Tel: 845-561-2589. Students 340.

NYACK, ROCKLAND CO., ST. ANN (1869) Administered from Parish of St. Paul and St. Ann, Congers.
82 Lake Rd., Congers, 10920. Revs. Vladimir Chripko, C.O.; Simon Gyanobeng; Fidelis Enzeani, (Nigeria); Deacons Thomas Luke Conroy; Charles DeGroat.
Res.: 16 Jefferson St., Nyack, 10960.
Tel: 845-268-4464; Email: office@spasaparish.org.
Catechesis Religious Program—Tel: 845-358-3758; Email: julielepore@verizon.net. Ms. Julie LePore, C.R.E. Students 190.
Convent—150 Third Ave., Nyack, 10960.

OBERNBURG, SULLIVAN CO., ST. MARY (1854) [CEM] Rev. George E. Baker.
Res.: 388 Obernburg Rd., P.O. Box 1, Obernburg, 12767. Tel: 845-482-5541.
Catechesis Religious Program—Students 10.

OSSINING, WESTCHESTER CO.
1—ST. ANN (1927) Revs. Edward G. Byrne; Alberto Espinal; Allan Delima; Deacon Jose DeJesus.
Res.: 25 Eastern Ave., Ossining, 10562.
Tel: 914-941-2556; Email: sarcc25ea@gmail.com.
Catechesis Religious Program—Tel: 914-941-2420. Students 740.
Convent—
2—ST. AUGUSTINE (1853) [CEM]
Mailing Address: 381 N. Highland Ave., Ossining, 10562. Revs. Brian T. McSweeney; Joseph A. Nahas; Deacons Steven DeMartino; Clifford Calanni; John A. Barbera.
Catechesis Religious Program—Students 250.

OTISVILLE, ORANGE CO., HOLY NAME OF JESUS (1969) [CEM]
Tel: 845-386-1320; Email: hnojotisville@frontiernet.net; Web: www.hnojotisville.com. Rev. Michael L. Palazzo.
Res.: 45 Highland Ave., P.O. Box 597, Otisville, 10963-0597. Tel: 845-386-1320; Email: hnojotisville@frontiernet.net; Web: www.hnojotisville.com.
Catechesis Religious Program—Tel: 845-386-2327; Email: hnojre@yahoo.com. Sr. Nancy Elizabeth Doran, S.S.C., D.R.E. Students 158.

PATTERSON, PUTNAM CO., SACRED HEART (1957)
Web: www.sacredheartpattersonny.org. Rev. Richard Gill.
Res.: 414 Haviland Dr., Patterson, 12563.
Tel: 845-279-4832.
Catechesis Religious Program—Mrs. Margaret Cairney, C.R.E. Students 160.

PAWLING, DUTCHESS CO., ST. JOHN THE EVANGELIST (1848) [CEM] Revs. John F. Palatucci; Sibi Thomas.
Res.: 39 E. Main St., Pawling, 12564.
Tel: 845-855-5488; Fax: scbsje@gmail.com.
Catechesis Religious Program—Tel: 845-855-9408. Students 266.

PEARL RIVER, ROCKLAND CO.
1—ST. AEDAN (1966) Rev. Msgr. Emmet R. Nevin; Rev. John F. Palatucci; Deacon James F. Maher.
Res.: 23 Reld Dr., Pearl River, 10965.
Tel: 845-735-7405; Email: staedan@optonline.net.
Catechesis Religious Program—Tel: 845-735-2036; Email: staedan3@verizon.net. Students 525.
2—ST. MARGARET OF ANTIOCH (1895)
Tel: 845-735-4746; Web: smparish.com. Revs. Eric P. Raaser; Ransford Clarke, Parochial Vicar.
Res.: 33 N. Magnolia St., Pearl River, 10965.
Tel: 845-735-4746; Email: info@smparish.com.
Catechesis Religious Program— PREP
Tel: 845-735-5489. Mrs. Brenda Lattuca, D.R.E. Students 700.

PEEKSKILL, WESTCHESTER CO., CHURCH OF THE ASSUMPTION (1859) [CEM]
Tel: 914-737-2071; Email: info@assumptionpeekskill.org; Email: pastor@assumptionpeekskill.org; Web: assumptionpeekskill.org. Esteban Sanchez, Admin.; Rev. Carlos Limongi, Parochial Vicar; Deacon Carlos H. Campoverde.
Res.: 131 Union Ave., Peekskill, 10566.
Tel: 914-737-2071; Email: manager@assumptionpeekskill.org.
Catechesis Religious Program—Tel: 914-737-2231; Fax: 914-737-1277. Mrs. Catherine Bischoff, Diocesan D.R.E. Students 685.

PELHAM, WESTCHESTER CO., ST. CATHARINE (1896) Administered from Parish of Our Lady of Perpetual Help and St. Catharine, 559 Pelham Manor Rd., Pelham Manor. Revs. Robert J. DeJulio; Trevor Nicholls, Parochial Vicar.
Res.: 25 Second Ave., Pelham, 10803.
Tel: 914-738-1491; Fax: 914-738-0398.
Catechesis Religious Program—Tel: 914-738-1332. Students 150.

PELHAM MANOR, WESTCHESTER CO., PARISH OF OUR LADY OF PERPETUAL HELP AND ST. CATHARINE (1954)
Tel: 914-738-1449; Fax: 914-738-9454; Email: Olph10803@msn.com; Web: www.olph-pelhammanor.org. Revs. Robert J. DeJulio; Ferdinand Madaki; Trevor Nicholls; Ernest Frimpong; Deacons Joseph McQuade; Paul Brisson; Michael Hall; John Catalano.
Res.: 559 Pelham Manor Rd., Pelham Manor, 10803.
Tel: 914-738-1449; Email: olph@msn.com.
Worship Site: St. Catherine, 25 Second Ave., Pelham, 10803. Tel: 914-738-1491.
Catechesis Religious Program—575 Fowler Ave, 25 Second Ave, Pelham, 10803. Tel: 914-738-0670; Email: olphccd0670@optonline.net; Web: www.olph-pelhammanor.org. Students 750.

PHOENICIA, ULSTER CO., ST. FRANCIS DE SALES (1902) [CEM]
Tel: 845-688-5617; Email: sfdchurch@hvc.rr.com. Revs. George W. Hommel, Admin.; Raphael Iannone, O.F.M.Cap. In Res., Rev. Raphael Iannone, O.F.M.-Cap.
Res.: 109 Main St., P.O. Box 25, Phoenicia, 12464.
Tel: 845-688-5617; Email: sfdchurch@hvc.rr.com.
Catechesis Religious Program—Gerry Nilsen, D.R.E. Students 8.

PIERMONT, ROCKLAND CO., ST. JOHN THE BAPTIST (1852) Rev. Thomas Kunnel, C.O., Admin.
Res.: 895 Piermont Ave., Piermont, 10968.
Tel: 845-359-0078; Email: admin@stjohnspiermont.org.
Catechesis Religious Program—Students 155.

PINE BUSH, ORANGE CO., THE INFANT SAVIOUR Infant Saviour Church (1951)
Tel: 845-744-2391; Email: infsavpb@hvc.rr.com; Web: infantsaviour.org. Rev. Niranjan Rodrigo; Deacons John Carr; Frank Rose.
Res.: 22 Holland Ave., Pine Bush, 12566.
Tel: 845-744-2391; Email: infsavpb@hvc.rr.com; Web: infantsaviour.org.
Catechesis Religious Program—Tel: 845-744-9944; Email: shintydre@gmail.com. Sr. Shinty Antony, D.R.E. Students 255.
Mission—Our Lady of the Valley, Walker Valley, Ulster Co. 12588.

PINE ISLAND, ORANGE CO., ST. STANISLAUS MISSION (1912) [CEM] (Polish) Mission of St. Joseph. Records at St. Joseph, 14 Glenmare Ave., Florida, NY 10921. Rev. Frank Borkowski.
Res.: 17 Pulaski Hwy., Pine Island, 10969.
Tel: 845-651-7792.

PINE PLAINS, DUTCHESS CO., ST. ANTHONY (1958) Administered from Parish of Immaculate Conception and St. Anthony, 4 Lavelle Rd., Box 109, Amenia. Rev. Robert K. Wilson.
Church: 68 Poplar Ave., Pine Plains, 12567-5531.
Tel: 518-398-7115; Fax: 518-398-9146; Email: stanthonys58@fairpoint.net.

PLATTEKILL, ULSTER CO., OUR LADY OF FATIMA (1960) Rev. Kevin M. Malick.
Res.: 1250 State Rt. 32, P.O. Box 700, Plattekill, 12568. Tel: 845-564-4972; Email: olfplattekill@aol.com; Web: olfplattekill.org.
Catechesis Religious Program—Students 161.

PLEASANT VALLEY, DUTCHESS CO., ST. STANISLAUS KOSTKA (1903)
1590 Main St., P.O. Box 558, Pleasant Valley, 12569.
Tel: 845-635-1700; Fax: 845-635-8675; Email: secretary.ststanislaus@gmail.com; Web: www.saintstanislaus.net. Rev. John J. Backes; Deacon John Dunn.
Catechesis Religious Program—Tel: 845-635-8611. Students 195.

PLEASANTVILLE, WESTCHESTER CO., HOLY INNOCENTS (1894) [CEM] (Dominican) Revs. Hugh Burns, O.P.; Frank I. Sutman, O.P.; Daniel G. Doherty, O.P.
Res.: 431 Bedford Rd., Pleasantville, 10570.
Tel: 914-769-0025; Email: office@hiparish.org.
Catechesis Religious Program—Tel: 914-769-3297; Email: mlamorgese@hiparish.org. Ms. Maria Lamorgese, D.R.E. Students 624.
Mission—Our Lady of Pompeii, Saratoga and Garrigan, Pleasantville, Westchester Co. 10570.

POCANTICO HILLS, WESTCHESTER CO., THE MAGDALENE (1894) Rev. John A. Vigilanti, J.C.L., Ph.D., Admin.
Res.: 525 Bedford Rd., Pocantico Hills, Sleepy Hollow, 10591-1216. Tel: 914-631-0529; Email: padrejav@gmail.com.
Catechesis Religious Program—Students 190.

PORT CHESTER, WESTCHESTER CO.
1—PARISH OF CORPUS CHRISTI AND OUR LADY OF THE ROSARY (1925) Merged with Parish of Our Lady of Mercy and Sacred Heart of Jesus to form parish of Saint John Bosco, Port Chester.
2—PARISH OF OUR LADY OF MERCY AND SACRED HEART OF JESUS (1854) [CEM] Merged with Parish of Corpus Christi and Our Lady of the Rosary to form Parish of Saint John Bosco, Port Chester.
3—PARISH OF ST. JOHN BOSCO (1904) Revs. Patrick Angelucci, S.D.B.; Tarcisio Dos Santos, S.D.B., (Brazil) Parochial Vicar; Peter Granzotto, S.D.B., Parochial Vicar; Joseph Vien Hoang, S.D.B., Parochial Vicar; Sr. Ana Maria Causa, S.A., Pastoral Assoc. In Res., Revs. Jorge Rodriguez, S.D.B.; John Grinsell, S.D.B.; David Moreno, S.D.B.; Lawrence Naskar, (India).
Church, Res. & Mailing Address: 260 Westchester Ave., Port Chester, 10573. Tel: 914-881-1400;
Tel: 914-514-4025; Email: mmassa@donboscopc.org.
Catechesis Religious Program—Irma Austin, C.R.E.
Chapel—Adoration Chapel, 23 Nicola Pl., Port Chester, 10573.
4—SACRED HEART OF JESUS (1917) Administered from Parish of Saint John Bosco, 260 Westchester Ave., Port Chester.

229 Willett Ave., Port Chester, 10573.
Tel: 914-939-1497; Fax: 914-937-6232. Rev. Michael F. Challinor.

PORT EWEN, ULSTER CO., PARISH OF PRESENTATION OF THE BLESSED VIRGIN MARY AND SACRED HEART (1874) Fr. Kelley Dr., Box 904, Port Ewen, 12466. Rev. Carl D. Johnson; Deacons John J. Larkin; Timothy Dean.
Presentation of the Blessed Virgin Mary—209 Hoyt St., Port Ewen, 12466. Tel: 845-331-0053; Fax: 845-331-3836; Email: presentationbvm@aol.com; Web: www.pbvmc.com.
Sacred Heart, 1055 Broadway, Box 200, Esopus, 12429. Tel: 845-384-6828; Fax: 845-384-6234; Email: genejgrohe@aol.com; Web: www.sacredheartesopus.org.
Catechesis Religious Program—Email: mmcre1@aol.com. Mrs. Michelle Metelski, C.R.E. Students 88.

PORT JERVIS, ORANGE CO.
1—IMMACULATE CONCEPTION (1851) [CEM] Revs. Matthew C. Newcomb; Ivan L. Csete, Sr. Priest in. Res.; Deacon Richard Marino.
Res.: 50 Ball St., Box 712, Port Jervis, 12771.
Tel: 845-856-8212; Fax: 845-858-8375; Email: stmarys-rectory@hvc.rr.com; Web: stmarysportjervis.com.
Catechesis Religious Program—Tel: 845-858-4208. Students 177.
2—MOST SACRED HEART (1899) [CEM] Records at: Immaculate Conception, P.O. Box 712, 50 Ball St., Port Jervis, NY 12771 (845-856-8212/5924)
Mailing Address: 12 McAllister St., P.O. Box 712, Port Jervis, 12771-0712. Fax: 845-858-8375; Email: office@stmarysportjervis.com; Web: stmarysportjervis.com.

POUGHKEEPSIE, DUTCHESS CO.
1—HOLY TRINITY (1921) Revs. Anthony Mizzi-Gill, Admin.; Jaccius Jean-Pierre, Parochial Vicar. In Res., Rev. Gamini E. Fernando, (Sri Lanka).
Res.: 775 Main St., Poughkeepsie, 12603.
Tel: 845-452-1863; Email: htpok@hvc.rr.com; Web: www.holytrinitypoughkeepsie.com.
Catechesis Religious Program—Tel: 845-471-5838; Fax: 845-471-0309; Email: htre@hvc.com. Mrs. Lisa P. Timm, D.R.E. Students 130.
2—ST. JOHN THE BAPTIST (1923) Records at: Our Lady of Mt. Carmel, 11 Mt. Carmel Pl., Poughkeepsie, NY 12601 (845-454-0340).
Res.: 1 Grand St., Poughkeepsie, 12601.
Tel: 845-454-0340; Fax: 845-486-8154.
3—ST. JOSEPH (1901) (Polish) Records at Parish of St. Mary and St. Joseph, 231 Church St., Poughkeepsie. (Society of Christ) Rev. Ronald P. Perez, Admin.
Res.: 9 Lafayette Pl., Poughkeepsie, 12601.
Tel: 845-452-2333; Fax: 845-452-6686; Web: www.stjosephpol.com.
Chapels—Poughkeepsie, Rectory—
Cemetery Chapel, 42 Evergreen Ave., Poughkeepsie, 12601.
4—ST. MARTIN DE PORRES (1962) [CEM]
Tel: 845-473-4222; Email: smdppok@optonline.net. Rev. Msgr. James P. Sullivan; Revs. Hartley Bancroft; Abraham K. George, M.C.B.S.; Deacons Franklin Hung, Pastoral Assoc.; Victor Salamone, Pastoral Assoc.; Michael Correale, Pastoral Assoc.; David Nash, Pastoral Assoc.; James Fiorio, Pastoral Assoc.
Res.: 118 Cedar Valley Rd., Poughkeepsie, 12603.
Tel: 845-473-4222; Email: smdpnorman@gmail.com; Email: smdppok@optonline.net.
Catechesis Religious Program—122 Cedar Valley Road, Poughkeepsie, 12603. Tel: 845-471-8728. Cynthia Fratto, D.R.E. Students 560.
5—PARISH OF ST. MARY AND ST. JOSEPH (1873) Revs. Ronald P. Perez, Admin.; Charles Heston Joseph. In Res., Rev. Msgr. John J. Brinn, M.A.
Res.: 231 Church St., Poughkeepsie, 12601-4200.
Tel: 845-452-8250; Fax: d526@archny.org.
Catechesis Religious Program—Tel: 845-471-4747; Fax: 845-471-4747. Sally Bellacicco, C.R.E. Students 206.
6—OUR LADY OF MT. CARMEL (1910) (Italian) Rev. John Francis Antony; Deacon George F. Cacchione; Claudia A. Coroban, Parish Mgr.
Res.: 11 Mt. Carmel Pl., Poughkeepsie, 12601.
Tel: 845-454-0340; Email: fr.antony@mtcarmelpok.org.
Catechesis Religious Program—Email: mtcfaithform@hvc.rr.com. Jane Bunt, D.R.E. Students 132.
7—ST. PETER (1837) [CEM] Rev. Patrick K. Curley.
Res.: 6 Father Cody Plaza, Hyde Park, Poughkeepsie, 12601. Tel: 845-452-8580; Email: stpetescemetery@gmail.com.
Catechesis Religious Program—
Tel: 845-452-8580, Ext. 205. Students 160.
Mission—Our Lady of the Rosary Chapel, 99 Inwood Ave., Poughkeepsie, 12601.
Chapels—Poughkeepsie, Convent of St. Peter—
Hyde Park, P.J. Kenedy Memorial Chapel of Our Lady of the Way, Culinary Institute of America, Albany Post Rd., Hyde Park, 12538. Rev. Marc K. Oliver, Chap.
Our Lady of the Holy Souls, St. Peter's Cemetery, 171 Salt Pt. Tpk., Poughkeepsie, 12603.

RED HOOK, DUTCHESS CO., PARISH OF ST. CHRISTOPHER AND ST. SYLVIA (1875) [CEM] Rev. Patrick F. Buckley; Rev. Msgr. Charles P. Coen, Pastor Emeritus; Rev. Xavier S. Santiago, (India) Parochial Vicar.
Res.: 7411 S. Broadway, Red Hook, 12571.
Tel: 845-758-3732; Email: rectory@stchrisredhook.org.
Catechesis Religious Program—30 Benner Rd., Red Hook, 12571. Tel: 845-758-5506. Ellen Farina, C.R.E. Students 293.

RHINEBECK, DUTCHESS CO., CHURCH OF THE GOOD SHEPHERD (1901) [CEM] Rev. Douglas Y. Crawford.
Res.: 3 Mulberry St., Rhinebeck, 12572.
Tel: 845-876-4583; Email: goodshep1@frontiernet.net.
Catechesis Religious Program—Tel: 845-876-7298; Email: gscp@frontier.com. Students 130.
Mission—St. Joseph, Church St., Rhinecliff, Dutchess Co. 12574.
RHINEBECK, FERNCLIFF NURSING HOME,
Tel: 845-876-2011; Fax: 845-876-4810.
RHINEBECK, SISTERS OF ST. URSULA, LINWOOD RETREAT HOUSE, Tel: 845-876-4178;
Fax: 845-876-6544.

ROSENDALE, ULSTER CO., ST. PETER (1855) [CEM] Revs. Edmund Burke; John Audu, (Nigeria).
Res.: 1017 Keator Ave., P.O. Box 471, Rosendale, 12472. Tel: 845-658-3117; Email: petrus1855@hotmail.com; Web: www.stpeterrosendale.org.
Catechesis Religious Program—Tel: 845-658-8911. Students 85.

RYE, WESTCHESTER CO., RESURRECTION (1880) Rev. Msgr. Donald M. Dwyer; Revs. Jon Tviet, Parochial Vicar; Epifanio Marcaida, (Philippines) Parochial Vicar.
Res.: 910 Boston Post Rd., Rye, 10580.
Tel: 914-967-0142; Email: Rectory910@msn.com.
Catechesis Religious Program—Tel: 914-925-2754; Fax: 914-925-2758; Email: resprep@optonline.net; Web: www.ryeprep.org. Students 1,105.

SAUGERTIES, ULSTER CO.
1—ST. JOHN THE EVANGELIST (1886)
915 Rte. 212, Saugerties, 12477. Tel: 845-246-9581. Rev. William F. Woodruff; Rev. Msgr. William E. Williams, Pastor Emeritus, (Retired); Deacon Robert Cranston.
Catechesis Religious Program—Students 87.
2—PARISH OF ST. MARY OF THE SNOW AND ST. JOSEPH (1833) [CEM]
Tel: 845-246-4913; Fax: 845-246-4996; Email: u533@archny.org; Web: stmaryofthesnow.org. Rev. Christopher H. Berean; Deacons Michael Sweeney, Music Min.; Donald Trees; Karl Pietkiewicz, (Retired); Arnie Hyland; Hank Smith.
Res.: 36 Cedar St., Saugerties, 12477.
Tel: 845-246-4913.
Catechesis Religious Program—Tel: 845-217-3333; Email: smssjreligioused@gmail.com; Web: stmaryofthesnow.org. Alison Belfance, Coord. Rel. Ed. Students 177.
Chapel—Saugerties, Parish Center.

SCARSDALE, WESTCHESTER CO.
1—IMMACULATE HEART OF MARY (1912) Rev. Msgr. John T. Ferry; Revs. Gerard F. Rafferty, S.S.L., Parochial Vicar; Rayappa Reddy Thumma, (India) Parochial Vicar; Deacons Ernest F. Salomone; Robert di Targiani, (Retired); Thomas Cusick.
Res.: 8 Carman Rd., Scarsdale, 10583.
Tel: 914-723-0276; Email: w534@archny.org; Web: www.ihm-parish.org.
Catechesis Religious Program—Tel: 914-723-7593; Fax: 914-723-7209; Email: ihmsor@aol.com; Web: www.ihmreled.org. Mrs. Diane Meade, D.R.E. Students 817.
2—ANNUNCIATION-OUR LADY OF FATIMA (1948) Administered from Parish of Annunciation and Our Lady of Fatima, 470 Westchester Ave., Crestwood. Rev. Robert F. Grippo.
Rectory Office & Res.: c/o 470 Westchester Ave., Tuckahoe, 10707. Tel: 914-779-7345; Web: www.annunciation-fatima.com.
Res.: 5 Strathmore Rd., Scarsdale, 10583.
Tel: 914-723-7421; Fax: 914-723-7229.
3—ST. PIUS X (1954) Revs. Francisco Sebastian Bacatan, A.M., (Philippines) Ph.D.; Jose C. Ramos, A.M., (Philippines); Romeo Ascan, A.M., (Philippines); Deacon Theodore A. Gaskin.
Res.: 91 Secor Rd., Scarsdale, 10583.
Tel: 914-725-2755; Email: fbacatan@yahoo.com.
Catechesis Religious Program—Tel: 914-472-5594; Fax: 914-725-2782; Email: stpiusxreled@yahoo.com. Students 225.

SHRUB OAK, WESTCHESTER CO., SAINT ELIZABETH ANN SETON (1963) Revs. Robert A. Quarato; Adolfo Novio; Deacons Michael Wilson; Richard Juliano.
Res.: 1377 E. Main St., Shrub Oak, 10588.
Tel: 914-528-3547; Email: seton@bestweb.net.
Catechesis Religious Program—Tel: 914-528-8553; Email: setonre@bestweb.net. Sara Koshofer, C.R.E. Students 1,220.

SLEEPY HOLLOW, WESTCHESTER CO.
1—HOLY CROSS (1921) (Slovak—Polish) Records at: St. Teresa of Avila, 130 Beekman Ave., Sleepy Hollow, NY 10591 (914-631-0720).
Res.: 118 Beekman Ave., Sleepy Hollow, 10591.
2—IMMACULATE CONCEPTION (1917) Rev. Dany Abi Akar.
Res.: 199 N. Broadway, Sleepy Hollow, 10591.
Tel: 914-631-0446.
Catechesis Religious Program—Students 6.
3—ST. TERESA OF AVILA (1853) Revs. Rumando Peralta Genao, C.R.L.; Felix Reyes, C.R.L.; Edison Navarro, C.R.L.
Res.: 130 Beekman Ave., Sleepy Hollow, 10591.
Tel: 914-631-0720; Email: StTeresa130@gmail.com.
Catechesis Religious Program—Tel: 914-631-1831.

SLOATSBURG, ROCKLAND CO., PARISH OF ST. JOAN OF ARC-OUR LADY OF MOUNT CARMEL (2016) (Other—Other) Rev. Joseph A. Emmanuel.
Res.: 32 Eagle Valley Rd., Sloatsburg, 10974.
Tel: 845-753-5239; Email: mtcarmeltuxedo@optonline.net.
Catechesis Religious Program—Tel: 845-753-5193. Students 94.

SOMERS, WESTCHESTER CO., ST. JOSEPH (1845) [CEM] Revs. John M. Lagiovane; Jude Aguwa, (Nigeria); Matthew MacDonald, S.A.; Deacons Generosa Sica; Larry Battersby.
Res.: 95 Plum Brook Rd., Somers, 10589.
Tel: 914-232-2910; Fax: jlagiovane@gmail.com.
Catechesis Religious Program—14 Croton Falls Rd., Croton Falls, 10519. Tel: 914-276-1067. Students 950.

SPRING VALLEY, ROCKLAND CO., ST. JOSEPH (1894)
Tel: 845-356-0311. Revs. Levelt Germain; Patrick Adekola, (Nigeria); Adaly Rosado, Parochial Vicar; Jaccius Jean-Pierre, Parochial Vicar; Deacons John Sadowski; Jose Pena.
Res.: 333 Sneden Pl. W., Spring Valley, 10977.
Tel: 845-356-0311; Email: church@stjosephspringvalley.org; Web: www.stjosephspringvalley.org.
Catechesis Religious Program—245 N. Main St., Spring Valley, 10977. Tel: 845-356-0054. Maureen Foley, D.R.E. Students 700.

STONY POINT, ROCKLAND CO., IMMACULATE CONCEPTION (1889)
Tel: 845-786-2742; Email: r547@archny.org. Rev. Herbert T. DeGaris; Deacon Philip Marino.
Res.: 26 John St., Stony Point, 10980.
Tel: 845-786-2742; Email: r547@archny.org; Web: www.immaculatestonypoint.org.
Catechesis Religious Program—School of Religion, Tel: 845-786-5298; Email: immaculate-prep@yahoo.com. Mrs. Ughetta Jilleba, D.R.E. Students 201.
Mission—Immaculate Conception - Cove Church, 5 Buckberg Rd., Tomkins Cove, Rockland Co. 10986.

SUFFERN, ROCKLAND CO., SACRED HEART (1868)
Tel: 845-357-0035; Email: shsuff@gmail.com; Web: www.sacredheartparish.org. Revs. Matthew J. Furey; Charles Achi, Parochial Vicar. In Res.
Res. & Office: 129 Lafayette Ave., Suffern, 10901.
Tel: 845-357-0035; Email: shsuff@gmail.com; Web: www.sacredheartparish.org.
Catechesis Religious Program—Tel: 845-357-6044; Email: sacredheartreligiouseducation@yahoo.com. Janis Batewell, C.R.E. Students 480.
Chapels—Good Samaritan Hospital—255 Lafayette Ave., Suffern, 10901. Tel: 845-368-5000.
Tagaste Monastery, 220 Lafayette Ave., Suffern, 10901. Tel: 845-357-0067; Fax: 845-369-0625.

TAPPAN, ROCKLAND CO., OUR LADY OF THE SACRED HEART (1952) Revs. Francis Conka, C.O.; Ravi K. Dasari, C.O., Parochial Vicar; George J. Torok, C.O., Weekend Assoc., (Retired); John F. Dwyer, Weekend Assoc., (Retired). In Res., Rev. Martin Kertys, C.O.
Res.: 120 King's Hwy., Tappan, 10983.
Tel: 845-359-1230; Email: secretary@olshtappan.com.
Catechesis Religious Program—Tel: 845-365-2141; Email: rc@olshtappan.com. Students 470.

TARRYTOWN, WESTCHESTER CO., TRANSFIGURATION (1896) (Carmelite) Revs. Emiel Abalahin, O.Carm.; Viet Dinh, O.Carm., Parochial Vicar; Daniel Moriarty, Music Dir. In Res., Rev. Francis F. Dixon, O.Carm.
Res.: 268 S. Broadway, Tarrytown, 10591.
Tel: 914-631-3737.
Catechesis Religious Program—Tel: 914-631-2380; Fax: 914-524-9352. Nancy Nelson, C.R.E. Students 193.

TIVOLI, DUTCHESS CO., ST. SYLVIA (1890) [CEM] Records at Parish of St. Christopher and St. Sylvia, 7411 S. Broadway, Red Hook. Revs. Patrick F. Buckley; H. Theriault, M.Div., Pastor Emeritus.
Res.: 104 Broadway, P.O. Box 95, Tivoli, 12583-0095.
Tel: 845-757-2442.

TUCKAHOE, WESTCHESTER CO.

1—ASSUMPTION (1911) (Italian) Administered from Parish of Immaculate Conception and Assumption, Tuckahoe.
53 Winterhill Rd., Tuckahoe, 10707.
Tel: 914-961-3643; Fax: 914-961-0283; Web: www.assumption-immaculate.org. Rev. Anthony D. Sorgie.
2—PARISH OF IMMACULATE CONCEPTION AND ASSUMPTION (1853) [CEM] Revs. Anthony D. Sorgie; Sean Connolly; Paul M. Waddell; Deacons Anthony Viola; Carl Degenhardt.
Res.: 53 Winterhill Rd., Tuckahoe, 10707.
Tel: 914-961-3643; Email: asorgie@aol.com.
Catechesis Religious Program—Tel: 914-961-1076; Email: ica.prep.office@gmail.com. Sr. Cora Lombardo, D.R.E. Students 538.

TUXEDO, ORANGE CO., OUR LADY OF MOUNT CARMEL (1895) Administered from Parish of St. Joan of Arc and Our Lady of Mount Carmel, 32 Eagle Valley Rd., Sloatsburg. Rev. Joseph A. Emmanuel.
Res.: 5 Tobin Way, P.O. Box 697, Tuxedo, 10987.
Tel: 845-351-5284; Fax: 845-351-2141; Email: mtcarmeltuxedo@optonline.net.

VALHALLA, WESTCHESTER CO., HOLY NAME OF JESUS (1896) Rev. Philip T. Persico.
Res.: Two Broadway, Valhalla, 10595.
Tel: 914-949-2323; Email: HNJValhallaNY@gmail.com.
Catechesis Religious Program—Tel: 914-949-1422; Email: hnjre@aol.com. Students 594.

VERPLANCK, WESTCHESTER CO., ST. PATRICK (1843) [CEM] Administered from Parish of St. Christopher and St. Patrick, 3094 Albany Post Rd., Buchanan. Rev. George Oonnoonny, J.C.D., Ph.D.
Res.: 240 11th St., P.O. Box 609, Verplanck, 10596.
Tel: 914-737-0635; Fax: 914-788-0584.

WALDEN, ORANGE CO., MOST PRECIOUS BLOOD (1894) Rev. Joseph Fallon.
Res.: 42 Walnut St., Walden, 12586.
Tel: 845-778-5719; Fax: 845-778-5659; Email: mpbparish@frontiernet.net; Web: mpbparish.com.
Catechesis Religious Program—Tel: 845-778-7081; Email: mpbreled@aol.com. Students 220.
Mission—St. Benedict, Wallkill, Ulster Co. 12589.

WAPPINGERS FALLS, DUTCHESS CO., ST. MARY (1850) [CEM]
Tel: 845-297-6261; Email: d555@archny.org. Revs. Daniel D'Alliessi; Emmanuel Anyansi, Parochial Vicar.
Res.: 11 Clinton St., Wappingers Falls, 12590.
Tel: 845-297-6261; Email: d555@archny.org; Web: stmarywappingers.org.
Catechesis Religious Program—Tel: 845-297-7586. Patricia Manuli, D.R.E. Students 270.

WARWICK, ORANGE CO., ST. STEPHEN (1865) [CEM] Revs. Jack Arlotta; Richard Marrano; Deacons Thomas MacDougall; Emmet Noonan; Daniel Byrne; John Tomasicchio.
Res.: 75 Sanfordville Rd., Warwick, 10990.
Tel: 845-986-4028; Email: o556@archny.org; Web: www.ststephenchurchwarwick.org.
Catechesis Religious Program—Tel: 845-986-2231; Email: reledoffice@gmail.com. Lydia vanDuynhoven, D.R.E. Students 655.

WASHINGTONVILLE, ORANGE CO., ST. MARY (1902) [CEM] Revs. Jeffrey J. Maurer; Paul Dmoch; Deacon Timothy D. Curran.
Res.: 2 Fr. Tierney Cir., Washingtonville, 10992.
Tel: 845-496-3730;
Fax: stmaryswashingtonville@gmail.com.
Catechesis Religious Program—Tel: 845-496-4101. Students 878.

WEST HARRISON, WESTCHESTER CO., ST. ANTHONY OF PADUA (1952) Revs. Christopher W. Monturo; George Kanshamba, (Zambia).
Res.: 85 Harrison St., West Harrison, 10604.
Tel: 914-948-1480; Email: admin@saintanthonyofpaduawh.org; Web: www.saintanthonyofpaduawh.org.
Catechesis Religious Program—45 Gainsborg Ave., West Harrison, 10604. Tel: 914-949-0212; Email: stanthonyreled@optonline.net. Jean Jackson, D.R.E. Students 370.

WESLEY HILLS, ROCKLAND CO., ST. BONIFACE (1966) Rev. Thadeus Aravindathu.
Res.: 5 Willow Tree Rd., Wesley Hills, 10952.
Tel: 845-354-7307; Email: r399@archny.org.

WEST HURLEY-WOODSTOCK, ULSTER CO., ST. JOHN (1860) Rev. George W. Hommel.
Res.: 12 Holly Hills Dr., Woodstock, 12498.
Tel: 914-679-7696; Email: rectory@sjwoodstock.org.
Catechesis Religious Program—Tel: 914-679-2869. Students 83.
Mission—St. Augustine, Watson Hollow Rd., West Shokan, Ulster Co. 12494. Tel: 914-657-2190.

WEST NYACK, ROCKLAND CO., ST. FRANCIS OF ASSISI (1964)
Tel: 845-634-4957; Fax: 845-639-6629; Email: stfrancisassisiparish@gmail.com; Web: www.stfrancis-assisi.org. Rev. Robert F. McKeon; Deacon Thomas Bennett; Sr. Patricia Hogan, O.P., Pastoral Assoc., Email: phogan10944@verizon.net; Tom Snowden, Music Min.
Res.: 128 Parrott Rd., West Nyack, 10994.
Tel: 845-634-4957; Email: stfrancisassisiparish@gmail.com; Web: stfrancis-assisi.org/sfa.
Catechesis Religious Program—Tel: 845-638-4215; Email: stfrancisprepoffice@gmail.com. Catherine Saladino, D.R.E.; James Russell, Youth Min. Students 1,087.

WEST POINT, ORANGE CO., CATHOLIC CHAPEL OF THE MOST HOLY TRINITY (1899) Most Holy Trinity is being served under the Archdiocese for Military Services. For inquiries for sacramental records before Jan. 1, 1999, please contact Sacred Heart, Highland Falls.
United States Military Academy, 699 Washington Rd., West Point, 10996. Tel: 845-938-8760; Fax: 845-938-8763. Rev. Kenneth W. Nielson.
Catechesis Religious Program—Tel: 845-938-8761. Joseph L. Lynch, D.R.E. Students 206.

WHITE PLAINS, WESTCHESTER CO.
1—ST. BERNARD (1926) Rev. Robert J. Morris.
Res.: 51 Prospect St., White Plains, 10606.
Tel: 914-949-2111; Email: rectory@stbernardswp.com.
Catechesis Religious Program—
Tel: 914-949-2111, Ext. 16. Students 380.
2—PARISH OF ST. JOHN THE EVANGELIST AND OUR LADY OF MOUNT CARMEL (1868) [CEM] Revs. Thomas Kallumady; Rubenus Cammayo, (Philippines). In Res., Rev. Chellan Joseph.
Res.: 148 Hamilton Ave., White Plains, 10601.
Tel: 914-949-0439; Tel: 914-948-5909;
Fax: 914-421-1202; Email: info@sjeolmc.org; Web: www.sjeolmc.org.
Catechesis Religious Program—Tel: 914-437-5144. Iris Flores, D.R.E. Students 192.
3—OUR LADY OF MOUNT CARMEL (1902) (Italian) Administered from Parish of St. John the Evangelist and Our Lady of Mount Carmel, White Plains.
148 Hamilton Ave., White Plains, 10601.
Tel: 914-948-5909; Tel: 914-949-0439;
Fax: 914-421-1202; Email: info@sjeolmc.org; Web: www.sjeolmc.org. Revs. Thomas Kallumady; Rubenus Cammayo, (Philippines) Parochial Vicar. In Res., Rev. Chellan Joseph.
Catechesis Religious Program—Iris Flores, D.R.E. Students 117.
4—OUR LADY OF SORROWS (1929) Revs. Philip J. Quealy; Paul Obiji.
Res.: 920 Mamaroneck Ave., White Plains, 10605.
Tel: 914-949-4148; Email: olscc@optonline.net; Web: www.olscc.com.
Catechesis Religious Program—Tel: 914-949-3896. Jennifer DeMilio, C.R.E. Students 341.

WOODBOURNE, SULLIVAN CO., IMMACULATE CONCEPTION (1957) [CEM] Rev. John J. Lynch.
Res.: 6317 Rte. 42, P.O. Box 66, Woodbourne, 12788.
Tel: 845-434-7643.
Catechesis Religious Program—Tel: 845-436-7370. Students 53.

WURTSBORO, SULLIVAN CO., ST. JOSEPH (1880) [CEM] Rev. Peter J. Madori. In Res., Rev. Matthias Ndulaka.
Res.: 180 Sullivan St., P.O. Box 277, Wurtsboro, 12790. Tel: 845-888-4522; Email: stjoswurts@frontiernet.net.
Catechesis Religious Program—Students 85.

YONKERS, WESTCHESTER CO.
1—ST. ANN (1947)
Tel: 914-965-1555; Fax: 914-965-0678; Email: stannsparishyonkers@gmail.com; Web: stannsyonkers.org. Revs. Andrew P. Carrozza; James K. Annor-Ohene, (Ghana).
Res.: 854 Midland Ave., Yonkers, 10704.
Tel: 914-965-1555; Fax: 914-965-0678; Email: stannsparishyonkers@gmail.com; Web: stannsyonkers.org.
Catechesis Religious Program—Email: michael.vicario@archny.org. Mr. Michael Vicario, D.R.E. Students 60.
2—ST. ANTHONY (Nepera Park) (1923) Rev. Arthur Mastrolia.
Res. & Church: 10 Squire Ave., Yonkers, 10703.
Tel: 914-965-2733; Web: stpaul82@aol.com.
Catechesis Religious Program—Tel: 914-965-5535. Students 250.
3—ST. ANTHONY (Willow St.) Closed. For inquiries for parish records contact Our Lady of Mt. Carmel, Yonkers.
4—ST. BARTHOLOMEW (1910) (Missionaries of St. Paul of Nigeria) Revs. Raphael Ezeh, M.S.P.; Anthony Mbanefo, M.S.P., Parochial Vicar; Deacon Robert A. Clemens.
Res.: 15 Palmer Rd., Yonkers, 10701.
Tel: 914-965-0566; Email: stbartschurch@aol.com.
Catechesis Religious Program—Tel: 914-476-6676. Students 198.
5—ST. CASIMIR (1899) (Polish) (Pauline) Revs. Tomasz P. Wilk, O.S.P.P.E.; Mark Kreis, O.S.P.P.E.
Res.: 239 Nepperhan Ave., Yonkers, 10701.
Tel: 914-963-1254; Email: office@casimirchurch.com; Web: www.casimirchurch.com.
Catechesis Religious Program—Students 45.
6—CHRIST THE KING (1927)
Tel: 914-963-7474; Email: ctkyonkers@gmail.com; Web: CTKYonkers.org. Revs. Robert J. Staar; Sebastian Mathew, C.M.I.
Res.: 740 N. Broadway, Yonkers, 10701.
Tel: 914-963-7474; Email: ctkrectory@optonline.net.
Catechesis Religious Program—Email: reledctk@optonline.net. Joan Brisson, D.R.E. Students 41.
7—ST. DENIS (1910) Records at Parish of St. Peter and St. Denis, 91 Ludlow St., Yonkers. Rev. Donald Kaufman, L.C.
Res.: 470 Van Cortlandt Park Ave., Yonkers, 10705.
Tel: 914-963-8468; Fax: 914-963-7354.
8—ST. EUGENE (1949)
707 Tuckahoe Rd., Yonkers, 10710.
Tel: 914-961-2590; Fax: 914-961-2881; Email: ginamastrangelo@csey.org; Email: fatherfernan@csey.org; Web: www.csey.org. Revs. Matthew F. Fernan; Anthony Gyamerah; Deacon John Duffy; Gina Mastrangelo, Business Mgr.
Parish Office: 31 Massitoa Rd., Yonkers, 10710.
Tel: 914-961-2590; Email: fatherfernan@csey.org; Web: www.csey.org.
Catechesis Religious Program—Email: ginamastrangelo@csey.org. Gina Mastrangelo, C.R.E. Students 155.
9—IMMACULATE CONCEPTION (1848) [CEM] (Spanish—Arabic) Rev. Msgr. Hugh J. Corrigan; Revs. Fares Hattar, (Jordan); Felino Reyes, (Dominican Republic).
Res.: 103 S. Broadway, Yonkers, 10701.
Tel: 914-963-0156; Email: Icmary103@gmail.com.
Catechesis Religious Program—Tel: 914-963-1053. Students 160.
Good Shepherd Arabic Community of St. Mary—Rev. Fares Hattar, (Jordan).
10—PARISH OF ST. JOHN THE BAPTIST AND MOST HOLY TRINITY (1903)
Tel: 914-963-1486; Email: stjohnsp@optonline.net. Rev. Msgr. J. Christopher Maloney; Revs. Joseph Mathew, (India); Daniel Ulloa, O.P., (Mexico); Deacons Martin J. Olivieri; Nicholas Ramoni.
Res.: 670 Yonkers Ave., Yonkers, 10704.
Tel: 914-963-1486; Email: stjohnsp@optonline.net.
Catechesis Religious Program—Tel: 914-965-2338. Sr. Mary Beth Read, O.S.U., B.A., M.S., D.R.E. Students 160.
Chapel—Convent, 176 Sweetfield Circle, Yonkers, 10704. Tel: 914-965-1837.
11—ST. JOSEPH PARISH (1871) [CEM] Rev. Joseph A. Francis, Temporary Admin.; Deacon Abraham Santiago.
Res.: 141 Ashburton Ave., Yonkers, 10701.
Tel: 914-963-0730; Email: stjosephchurch@optonline.net.
Catechesis Religious Program—Students 203.
12—ST. MARGARET OF HUNGARY (1928) Records at St. Joseph, 141 Ashburton Ave., Yonkers, NY 10701 (914-963-0730).
13—MOST HOLY TRINITY (1894) (Slovak) Records at Parish of St. John the Baptist and Most Holy Trinity, 670 Yonkers Ave., Yonkers. Rev. Msgr. J. Christopher Maloney; Rev. Susai Antony Devasagayam.
Res.: 18 Trinity Pl., Yonkers, 10701.
Tel: 914-963-0720; Fax: 914-709-0224.
Chapel—Franciscan Friars of the Renewal, 15 Trinity Pl., Yonkers, 10701. Tel: 914-476-7279; Fax: 914-476-5033. Rev. Richard Roemer, C.F.R.
14—OUR LADY OF FATIMA (1977) Rev. Osvaldo Franklin, J.C.D.
Legal Name: Our Lady of Fatima Portuguese Roman Catholic Church
Portuguese R.C. Center, 355 S. Broadway, Yonkers, 10705. Tel: 914-423-9688; Email: info@fatima-port-church.com; Web: www.fatima-port-church.com.
Catechesis Religious Program—Angelina Tome, D.R.E. Students 103.
15—OUR LADY OF MT. CARMEL (1913) (Other) (Pallottine) Rev. Marek Rudecki, S.A.C.; Deacons Alfred R. Impallomeni; Nick A. Mazzei Jr.
Res.: 70 Park Hill Ave., Yonkers, 10701.
Tel: 914-963-4766; Email: contact@olomc.church.
Catechesis Religious Program—Fax: 914-410-4101. Students 235.
16—OUR LADY OF THE ROSARY (1907) Records At: Immaculate Conception/St. Mary, 103 S. Broadway, Yonkers, NY 10701 (914-963-0156). Rev. Msgr. Hugh J. Corrigan, Temporary Admin.
Res.: 226 Warburton Ave., Yonkers, 10701.
17—ST. PAUL THE APOSTLE (1923) Revs. Leonard F. Villa; Michael D. Morrow; Sr. Eileen Treanor, P.B.V.M., Parish Ministry; Deacons Rudolfo Teng; Thomas J. Barbagallo.
Res.: 602 McLean Ave., Yonkers, 10705.
Tel: 914-963-7330; Email: stpaulyonkers@gmail.com.

Church: Lincoln Park, Yonkers, 10705.
Catechesis Religious Program—Sr. Eileen Treanor, P.B.V.M., D.R.E. Students 148.

18—Parish of St. Peter and St. Denis (1894) Revs. Donald Kaufman, L.C.; Jose Helio Cantu, L.C., Parochial Vicar; Eric Nielsen, Youth Min.; Deacon Pedro Irizarry.
Res.: 91 Ludlow St., Yonkers, 10705.
Tel: 914-963-0822; Email: spyonkers@gmail.com.
Catechesis Religious Program—Tel: 914-969-3813. Students 545.

19—Sacred Heart (1891) (Capuchin)
Tel: 914-963-4205; Fax: 914-476-4960; Email: sacredheartyonkers@gmail.com; Web: sacredheartyonkers.org. Revs. Matthew Janeczko, O.F.M.Cap.; John McHugh, O.F.M.Cap.; Bro. Roger Deguire, O.F.M.Cap., Pastoral Assoc.
*Legal Title: Roman Catholic Church of the Sacred Heart*In Res., Very Rev. Fr. Robert J. Abbatiello, O.F.-M.Cap.; Bro. John Shento, O.F.M.Cap.
Res.: 110 Shonnard Pl., Yonkers, 10703.
Office: 40 Convent Ave., Yonkers, 10703.
Tel: 914-963-4205; Email: sacredheartyonkers@gmail.com.
Catechesis Religious Program—Email: dmay@sacredheartyonkers.org. Deanne May, D.R.E. Students 170.
Convent—27 Convent Ave., Yonkers, 10703.

Yorktown Heights, Westchester Co., St. Patrick (1898)
Tel: 914-962-5050; Email: stpatsyorktown@optonline.net; Web: stpatricks-yorktown.org. Rev. Msgr. Joseph R. Giandurco, J.C.D.; Revs. Christian Amah, Parochial Vicar; John Wilson, Parochial Vicar; Deacon Richard Scheibe.
Res.: 137 Moseman Rd., Yorktown Heights, 10598.
Tel: 914-962-5050; Email: W583@archny.org; Web: stpatricks-yorktown.org.
Catechesis Religious Program—Tel: 914-962-5586; Fax: 914-962-3207. Students 1,107.

Youngsville, Sullivan Co., St. Francis of Assisi (1963) Merged with St. George, Jeffersonville to form St. George-St. Francis, Jeffersonville.

Yulan, Sullivan Co., Parish of St. Anthony of Padua and St. Thomas Aquinas (1907) [CEM] (Franciscan) Rev. Joselin Pens Berkmans, M.M.I.
Res.: Yulan, 12792. Tel: 845-557-8512; Email: churchofstanthony@gmail.com.
Catechesis Religious Program—Students 73.
Mission—Sacred Heart, Berme Church Rd., Pond Eddy, Sullivan Co. 12770.

Chaplains of Public Institutions.

Military Installations

New York. *National Catholic Community Service*, 487 Park Ave., 10022. (Cardinal Spellman Servicemen's Club).
New York City Veterans Administration Hospital, 406 First Ave., 10022. Revs. Pasquale V. Laghezza, SS.CC., Jose A. Salazar.

Bronx. *Veterans Administration Hospital*, 130 W. Kingsbridge Rd., Bronx, 10460. Rev. Paul F. O'Connor, O.S.B.

Montrose. *Franklin D. Roosevelt Hospital*. Vacant.

West Point. *Stewart Field*. Rev. Nash P. Geany.
U.S. Military Academy, West Point, 10966. Vacant.

Societies

New York. *Marine and Aviation Department*. Vacant.
New York Fire Department. Rev. Msgr. Marc J. Filacchione.
New York Police Department. Rev. Msgr. Joseph J. Zammit.
New York Postal Service.

Prisons

City. *Anna M. Kross Center*, 18-18 Hazen St., East Elmhurst, 11370. Tel: 718-546-3520. Rev. Thomas Mestriparampil.
Eric M. Taylor Center, 10-10 Hazen St., East Elmhurst, 11370. Tel: 718-546-5796. Rev. Oliver Chanama, (Nigeria).
George M. Motchan Detention Center, 15-15 Hazen St., East Elmhurst, 11370. Tel: 718-546-4543. Rev. Thomas Mestriparampil.
George Vierno Center, 09-09 Hazen St., East Elmhurst, 11370. Tel: 718-546-2241. Rev. Gonzalo Morocho, S.D.B., (Ecuador).
Manhattan Detention Center, 125 White St., 10013. Tel: 212-225-1367. Rev. John Mattimore, S.J., Deacon Miguel Granda.
North Infirmary Command, 15-00 Hazen St., East Elmhurst, 11370. Tel: 718-546-1256. Rev. Thomas Mestriparampil.
Otis Bantum Correctional Center, 16-00 Hazen St., East Elmhurst, 11370. Tel: 718-546-6618. Rev. Michael Koncik, C.Ss.R.
Robert N. Davoren Center, 11-11 Hazen St., East Elmhurst, 11370. Tel: 718-546-7223. Rev. Michael Koncik, C.Ss.R., Sr. Margaret McCabe, S.U.S.C.
Rose M. Singer Center, 19-19 Hazen St., East Elmhurst, 11370. Rev. David E. Nolan.
Vernon C. Bain Center, 1 Halleck, Bronx, 10474. Tel: 718-579-8385.

County. *Dutchess County Jail*, 150 N. Hamilton St., Poughkeepsie, 12601. Tel: 845-297-5706. Attended by St. Mary, Poughkeepsie, Tel: 845-452-8250.
Orange County Jail, 6 1/2 Station Rd., Goshen, 10924. Attended from St. John, Goshen. Tel: 845-294-5328.
Putnam County Jail, Carmel, 10512. Deacon Anthony GruerioAttended by St. James, Carmel. Tel: 845-225-2079.
Rockland County Jail, P.O. Box 86, New City, 10956. Rev. William B. Cosgrove, Deacon John MaloneyAttended by St. Anthony, Nanuet.
Sullivan County Jail. Rev. Stanislaus Ogbonna, C.S. Sp., (Nigeria)Attended by St. Peter, Monticello. Tel: 845-794-5577.
Ulster County Jail, Box 1800, Dept. 3150, Kingston, 12401. Tel: 845-338-1554. Deacon James Fiorio.
Westchester County Jail, Box 389, Valhalla, 10595. Tel: 914-347-6132. Revs. Jude Egbeji, Gonzalo Morocho, S.D.B., (Ecuador), Paul Tolve, I.V.Dei.

Federal. *Federal Correctional Institution*, 2 Mile Dr., Otisville, 10963. Tel: 845-386-5855, Ext. 291. Rev. Nigozi Osuji.
Metropolitan Correctional Center, 150 Park Row, 10007-1779. Tel: 212-240-9656, Ext. 6454; Tel: 646-836-6300.

State. *Bedford Hills Correctional Facility*, 247 Harris Rd., Bedford Hills, 10507-2499. Tel: 914-241-3100. Sr. Mary Anne Collins, O.P.
Downstate Correctional Facility, Box 445, Fishkill, 12524-0445. Tel: 845-831-6600, Ext. 4800. Rev. Arecio P. Dormido.
Eastern Correctional Facility, Napanoch, 12458-0338. Tel: 845-647-7400, Ext. 4812. Deacon Joseph Doherty.
Edgecombe Correctional Facility, 611 Edgecombe Ave., 10032-4398. Tel: 212-923-2575. Rev. Matthew Ugwoji, (Africa).
Fishkill Correctional Facility, Box 307, Beacon, 12508. Tel: 845-831-4800, Ext. 4860. Rev. George J. Dash, O.F.M.Cap., Deacon Frank Gohl.
Green Haven Correctional Facility, Stormville, 12582. Tel: 845-221-2711. Rev. Gamini E. Fernando, (Sri Lanka), Deacon Robert Buckner.
Lincoln Correctional Facility, 31-33 W. 110 St., 10026-4398. Tel: 212-860-9400, Ext. 4800.
Otisville Correctional Facility, Box 8, Otisville, 10963-0008. Tel: 845-386-1490, Ext. 4830. Rev. Augustine Graap, O.Carm., Deacon Eugene Bormann.
Shawangunk Correctional Facility, Box 750, Wallkill, 12589-0750. Tel: 845-895-2081. Rev. Frank Naccarato.
Sing Sing Correctional Facility, 354 Hunter St., Ossining, 10562-5442.
Tel: 914-941-0108, Ext. 2099. Rev. Matthew Ugwoji, (Africa).
Sullivan Correctional Facility, P.O. Box AG, Fallsburg, 12733-0116. Tel: 845-434-2080. Rev. Stanislaus Ogbonna, C.S.Sp., (Nigeria).
Taconic Correctional Facility, 250 Harris Rd., Bedford Hills, 10507-2498. Tel: 914-241-3010. Deacon Clifford Calanni.
Ulster Correctional Facility, Berne Rd., P.O. Box 800, Napanoch, 12458. Tel: 914-647-1670, Ext. 2004. Deacon James Faulkner.
Wallkill Correctional Facility, Box G, Wallkill, 12589-0286. Tel: 845-895-2021, Ext. 4800. Rev. Frank Naccarato.

Hospitals

Bronx. *St. Barnabas Hospital*, 3rd Ave. & 183rd St., Bronx, 10457. Tel: 718-960-9000;
Tel: 718-960-6280 (Chaplaincy). Rev. Francis Nampiaparambil Luke.
Bronx Psychiatric Center, Bronx. Tel: 718-931-0600. Vacant.
Bronx-Lebanon Hospital Center, Bronx.
Tel: 718-590-1800; Tel: 718-518-5059. Revs. Luke Ibeh, Izuna Okwonkwo.
Calvary Hospital, 1740 Eastychester Rd., Bronx, 10461. Tel: 718-518-2114. Rev. Msgr. John Farley, Revs. Jude Egbeji, Nicholas Ibe, Chux Okochi, Dir. Pastoral Svcs., Raymond G. Pierini, M.M., P/T Spiritual Counselor.
Jacobi Medical Center, 1400 Pelham Pkwy., S., Bronx, 10451. Tel: 718-918-5254. Revs. Hippolytus Duru, Chap., Sancho Garrote.
James F. Peters Medical Center, 130 W. Kingsbridge Rd., Bronx, 10468. Tel: 718-584-9000, Ext. 5622. Revs. Isaac Mensah, Tony K. Mensah.
Lincoln Medical and Mental Health Center, 234 E. 149th St., Bronx, 10451. Tel: 718-579-5000;
Tel: 718-579-5059. Rev. Nicholas UgochukwuServiced by the Holy Rosary, 444 E. 119th St. New York, NY 10035.
Montefiore Medical Center, Henry and Lucy Moses Division, 111 E. 210th St., Bronx, 10467.
Tel: 718-920-4997. Revs. Ferdinand Medaki, Livinus Obiansi, Roberto Perez, O.F.M. Cap.
Montefiore Medical Center - Wakefield Hospital, 600 E. 233rd St., Bronx, 10466. Tel: 718-920-9086. Rev. Msgr. Frederick J. Becker, Vice Pres. Pastoral Svcs.
Montefiore Westchester Square Medical Center, 2475 St. Raymond Ave., Bronx, 10461.
Tel: 718-828-2380. Serviced by Santa Maria Parish. Tel: 718-920-2408.
North Central Bronx Hospital, 3424 Kossuth Ave., Bronx, 10467. Tel: 718-519-5000. Revs. Hippolytus Duru, Sancho GarroteServiced by Jacobi Medical Center.

Bronxville. *New York Presbyterian, Lawrence Hospital*, 55 Palmer Ave., Bronxville, 10708.
Tel: 914-787-1000. Rev. Augustine Badgley.

Callicoon. *Catskill Regional Hospital, Grover M. Hermann Hospital*, 8881 NY-97, Callicoon, 12723.
Tel: 845-887-5530. Rev. Joseph Nahas, Jodi Goodman, Dir. Patient Advocate & Comm. Support Groups, Tel: 845-794-3300 ext. 2185Serviced by Holy Cross, Callicoon.

Carmel. *Putnam Hospital Center*, Carmel.
Tel: 845-279-5711. Serviced by St. James the Apostle, Carmel.

Castle Point. *V.A. Hudson Valley Healthcare*, Castle Point. Tel: 845-831-2000, Ext. 5453. Revs. Lino Blad, Lenin Delgado, Joseph Westfall.

Cornwall. *St. Luke's-Cornwall Hospital*, Cornwall.
Tel: 845-534-2547. Serviced by St. Thomas of Canterbury, Cornwall-on-Hudson.

Dobbs Ferry. *Dobbs Ferry Pavilion/St. John's Riverside Hospital*, 128 Ashford Ave., Dobbs Ferry, 10522. Tel: 914-693-0700. Serviced by Sacred Heart, Dobbs Ferry. Hospital.

Ellenville. *Ellenville Regional Hospital*, Rte. 209, Ellenville, 12428. Tel: 845-647-6080. Serviced by the Church of St. Mary & St. Andrew, Ellenville.

Harris. *Catskill Regional Hospital*, Harris.
Tel: 845-794-3300. Serviced by St. Peter, Monticello.

Harrison. *St. Vincent's Hospital Westchester*, 275 North St., Harrison, 10580. Tel: 914-967-6500. Rev. Lawrence Naskar, (India).

Kingston. *Health Alliance Hospital*, 150 Mary's Ave., Kingston, 12401. Tel: 845-338-2500. Rev. Louis Yaya, Sr. M. Dorothy Huggard, O.S.B.
Health Alliance Hospital, 396 Broadway, Kingston, 12401. Tel: 845-331-3131. Rev. Daniel Maichiki-Serviced by St. Mary, Kingston.

Manhattan. *Bellevue Hospital*, 1st Ave. & 27th St., 10016. Revs. Alexis C.P. Fernando, Francis Okoli.
Beth Israel Medical Center, First Ave. & 16th St., 10003. Tel: 212-420-2759, Ext. 3.
Gracie Square, 420 E. 76th St., 10021.
Tel: 212-988-4400. Serviced by St. Jean Baptiste, NYC.
Harlem Hospital, 506 Lenox Ave. & 136th St., 10037. Tel: 212-281-4931. Rev. Emmanuel OkpalauwaekweServiced by St. Mark.
Henry J. Carter Specialty Hospital, 1752 Park Ave., 10035. Tel: 646-686-0000. Rev. Andrew Bielak, (Poland).
Hospital for Special Surgery, 535 E. 70th St., 10021. Tel: 212-606-1757. Revs. David Adiletta, O.P., S.T.L., John M. Devaney, O.P., M.Div., Martin Farrell, O.P., Jonah F. Pollock, O.P., Sr. Margaret T. Oettinger, O.P.Serviced by Dominican Fathers.
Lenox Hill Hospital, 100 E. 77th St., 10075.
Tel: 212-439-2547. Serviced by St. Jean Baptiste.
Manhattan Eye, Ear & Throat Hospital, 210 E. 64th St., 10065. Tel: 212-838-9200. Serviced by St. Vincent Ferrer.
Memorial Sloan Kettering Cancer Center, 1275 York Ave., 10065. Tel: 212-639-5982. Revs. David Adiletta, O.P., S.T.L., John M. Devaney, O.P., M.Div., Martin Farrell, O.P., Jonah F. Pollock, O.P.Serviced by Dominican Fathers.
Metropolitan Hospital, 1901 First Ave., Rm. 216, 10029. Rev. Michael J. Sala, S.J.
The Mount Sinai Hospital, 1 Gustave L. Levy Pl., 10029-6575. Rev. James Hayes, S.S.S., Rev. Akram Javid.
Mt. Sinai St. Luke's-Roosevelt Hospital Center, 1111 Amsterdam Ave., Manhattan, 10025.
Tel: 212-523-4000.
Mount Sinai West. Revs. Thomas J. Holahan, C.S.P., Michael J. Kallock, C.S.P., (Retired).
St. Luke's Site. Serviced by Notre Dame, NYC.
New York Eye & Ear Infirmary, 310 E. 14th St., 10003. Tel: 212-673-3480. Serviced by Immaculate Conception, 414 E. 14th St., NY, NY 1009.
New York Presbyterian (Downtown Hospital), 170 William St., 10038. Tel: 212-312-5000;
Tel: 212-233-5300. Rev. Edward Kofi Owusu-

AnsahServiced by Our Lady of Victory-St. Andrew, NYC.
New York Presbyterian-Columbia Medical Center, 622 W. 168th St., 10032. Tel: 212-305-3101. Revs. Melchor Ferrer, S.D.B., Clement Umoenoh
Allen Pavilion-Columbia Presbyterian, 5141 Broadway, 10034. Tel: 212-305-3710. Rev. Arlen Harris, O.F.M.Cap.
New York Presbyterian Hospital, Manhattan. Tel: 212-746-4690. Revs. John M. Devaney, O.P., M.Div., James O'Connell, O.F.M., Jonah F. Pollock, O.P.
New York University Medical Center, 34th St. & 1st Ave., 10016. Tel: 212-263-7300. Revs. Martin Ene, Stephen Okeke
Hospital for Joint Disease. Revs. Martin Ene, Stephen OkekeServiced by NYU Pastoral Care Dept., 414 E. 14th St., NY, NY 10009, Tel: 212-254-0200.
Rockefeller University, Manhattan. Tel: 212-570-8000. Serviced by Dominican Friars Healthcare.
Terence Cardinal Cooke Health Care Center, Manhattan. Tel: 212-360-3993. Rev. Bart Amobi.
U.S.V.A. Medical Center, Manhattan. Tel: 212-686-7500. Revs. Andrew Sioleti, I.V.Dei., Evon Tyhovych.
MIDDLETOWN. *Orange Regional Medical Center*, 707 E. Main St., Middletown, 10940. Tel: 845-343-2424. Serviced by St. Joseph, Middletown.
MONTROSE. *FDR DVA Hospital*. Rev. Joseph Westfall, Lenny Delgado.
MOUNT KISCO. *Northern Westchester Hospital*, 380 Main St., Mount Kisco, 10549. Tel: 914-666-1200. VacantServiced by St. Francis of Assisi, Mt. Kisco.
MOUNT VERNON. *Mount Vernon Hospital*, 12 N. 7th Ave., Mount Vernon, 10550. Tel: 914-664-8000. Rev. Raymond Nwegede.
NEW HAMPTON. *Mid-Hudson Psychiatric Center*, Rte. 17M, New Hampton, 10958. Tel: 845-374-8700. Rev. Mark SchaarschmidtServiced by National Shrine of Our Lady of Mount Carmel, Middle Town.
NEW ROCHELLE. *Montefiore New Rochelle Hospital*, New Rochelle. Tel: 914-632-5000. Rev. Segundo PalaciosChaplain, contact hospital operator.
NEWBURGH. *St. Luke-Cornell Hospital*, Newburgh. Tel: 845-561-4400. Serviced by St. Patrick, Newburgh.
NORTH TARRYTOWN. *Phelps Memorial Hospital*, North Tarrytown. Tel: 914-631-0720. Rev. Ronald J. Lemmert.
NYACK. *Nyack Hospital*, Nyack. Tel: 845-358-6200. Rev. Joseph NarisettyServiced By St. Paul-St. Ann, Congers.
ORANGEBURG. *Rockland Psychiatric Center*, 140 Old Orangeburg Rd., Orangeburg, 10962. Serviced by area parishes.
PEEKSKILL. *Hudson Valley Hospital Center*, Peekskill. Tel: 914-737-9000. Rev. Vernon P. Wickrematunge, (Sri Lanka)Serviced by Holy Spirit, Cortlandt Manor.
PORT JERVIS. *Bon Secours Community Hospital*, Port Jervis. Tel: 845-856-5351. Revs. Charles Chukwuani, Dir., Vincent Odikanoro, Sr. Rosemary Corr, BCC, Chap.
POUGHKEEPSIE. *Vassar Brothers Hospital*, Poughkeepsie, 12601. Tel: 845-454-8500, Ext. 72470. Rev. Rick De La PenaServiced by St. Mary's Church, 231 Church St., Poughkeepsie, NY 12601, Telephone: 845-452-8250.
RHINEBECK. *Northern Dutchess Hospital*, Rhinebeck. Tel: 845-876-4583. Serviced by St. Christopher, Good Shepherd and Regina Coeli.
STATEN ISLAND. *Richmond University Medical Center*, 355 Bard Ave., Staten Island, 10310. Tel: 718-818-1234. Revs. Michael Arputham Arockiam, Wilfred Y. Dodo.
Richmond University Medical Center/Bayley Seton Campus, 75 Vanderbilt Ave., Staten Island, 10304. Tel: 718-354-6000.
Staten Island University Hospital North, 475 Seaview Ave., Staten Island, 10305. Tel: 718-226-2294. Revs. John P. DeLora, Percy Joseph Raj.
Staten Island University Hospital South, 375 Seguine Ave., Staten Island, 10309. Tel: 718-226-2294; Tel: 718-226-9435 (Pastoral Care). Revs. Patrick Anthony, (Pakistan), John P. DeLora, Percy Joseph Raj.
SUFFERN. *Good Samaritan Hospital*, 255 Lafayette Ave., Suffern, 10901. Tel: 845-368-5171. Revs. Hippolytus Duru, Clement Unoenoh.
VALHALLA. *Blythedale Children's Hospital*, 95 Bradhurst Ave., Valhalla, 10595. Tel: 914-592-7555. Supported by Holy Name of Jesus.
Westchester Medical Center, Valhalla. Tel: 914-493-7125. Revs. Peter Claver, Raymond NwegedeSupport coverage by The Magdalene Pocantico Hills, 525 Bedford Rd. Pocantico Hills, NY 10591.
WARWICK. *St. Anthony Community Hospital*, 15-19 Maple St., Warwick, 10990. Tel: 845-986-2276. Rev. Charles Chukwuani.
WEST HAVERSTRAW. *Helen Hayes Hospital*, West Haverstraw. Tel: 845-786-4000. Rev. Thomas ReukertServiced by Marion Shrine, Salesians.
WHITE PLAINS. *Burke Rehabilitation Center*, White Plains. Tel: 914-948-0050. Serviced by Our Lady of Sorrow, (914) 949-9819.
New York Presbyterian-Westchester Division, White Plains. Tel: 914-997-5999. Rev. Thomas Joseph, (India).
White Plains Hospital, Davis Ave. & Post Rd., White Plains, 10606. Tel: 914-539-2196. Rev. Thomas Joseph, (India)Serviced by St. Bernard, White Plains.
YONKERS. *St. John's Riverside Hospital*, Yonkers. Tel: 914-964-7300. Rev. Nicholas NwagwuPark Care Pavillion (formerly Yonkers General)Night Call-Christ the King, Yonkers, (914-963-7474). Serviced by St. Joseph's, Yonkers.

On Duty Outside the Archdiocese:
Most Rev.—
Brown, Charles, Apostolic Nuncio, Albania
Rev. Msgrs.—
Berardi, Ferdinando D., Casa Santa Maria, Rome
Irwin, Kevin W., Catholic University of America, Washington, DC
Revs.—
Serra, Dominic, Catholic University of America, Washington, DC 20261
Sweeney, Luke M., S.T.L., Holy See, Rome.

Graduate Studies:
Revs.—
Callaghan, Nicholas E., J.C.L., J.C.D. (cand. Rome), North American College, Rome
Graebe, Brian, North American College, Rome
Heasley, Peter A., North American College, Rome
Masi, Louis, North American College, Rome
Taylor, Brian P., J.C.L., J.C.D. (cand. Rome), North American College, Rome.

Military Chaplains:
Rev. Msgr.—
Hill, Philip W., Office of the Chief of Chaplains, 2700 Army Pentagon, Washington, DC
Revs.—
Collins, James B., N.Y. Army Nat. Guard
Lindblad, Karl-Albert, 2031 Nicklaus Dr., Suffolk, VA 23435. U.S.N.
O'Reilly, Edward M., (Retired)
Pomposello, Peter.

Unassigned:
Rev. Msgr.—
Harris, Wallace A.
Revs.—
Betances, Torres
Fennessey, Keith
Florez, Andrew
Jenik, John
Mandato, Kieran, 7437 Heatherfield Ln., Box 1799, Alexandria, VA 22315
Migueli, Peter
O'Leary, Michael J., (Ireland)
Paolicelli, Lawrence
Persico, Philip T.
Pliauplis, Christopher
Repenning, Robert B.
Taylor, Samuel.

Absent on Sick Leave:
Revs.—
Bidar, John
Bubel, Robert J.
Challman, Stephen G.
Howley, Vincent
Rodriguez, Carlos
Tran, Philip
Rev. Canon—
Pintabone, John A.

On Leave of Absence:
Revs.—
Altrui, Ronald P.
Fanning, John
Kang, Paul
Lemmert, Ronald D.
Mallorhous, Stephen.

Retired:
Most Rev.—
Iriondo, Josu, S.T.L., D.D., (Retired), Our Lady of Esperanza, New York City
Rev. Msgrs.—
Bergin, Thomas, (Retired)
Birkle, Walter A., (Retired), St. John the Baptist, 670 Yonkers Ave., Yonkers, 10704
Boyle, Francis V., (Retired), John Cardinal O'Connor Clergy Pavilion, 5655 Arlington Ave., Bronx, 10471
Brennan, Dermot R., (Retired), John Cardinal O'Connor Clergy Pavilion, 5655 Arlington Ave., Bronx, 10471
Byrne, Harry J., (Retired), Edward Cardinal Egan Pavilion, 5655 Arlington Ave., Bronx, 10471
Curran, Hugh D., (Retired), John Cardinal O'Connor Pavilion, Bronx
Franco, Hilary, (Retired), 2051 Oakwood Dr., Peekskill, 10566
Kenny, Walter F., S.T.D., (Retired), St. Augustine, 18 Cherry Ave., Larchmont, 10538
Loughman, Kenneth M., (Retired), Most Precious Blood, 42 Walnut St., Walden, 12586
McCabe, Robert J., (Retired)
McCarthy, John M., (Retired)
McCorry, Edward J., (Retired), 5 Daisy Ct., Suffern, 10901
McManus, Hugh F., Ph.D., (Retired)
McNamara, Patrick V., (Retired)
Moore, James R., (Retired)
O'Donnell, Edward D., (Retired)
O'Donnell, Peter C., (Retired), John Cardinal O'Connor Clergy Pavilion, 5655 Arlington Ave., Bronx, 10471
Penna, Joseph P., J.C.D., (Retired), John Cardinal O'Connor Clergy Pavilion, 5655 Arlington Ave., Bronx, 10471
Ruvo, John A., (Retired)
Shelley, Thomas J., (Retired), John Cardinal O'Connor Clergy Pavilion, 5655 Arlington Ave., Bronx, 10471. Fordham
Soares, Nicholas J., (Retired)
Stern, Robert L., (Retired), Edward Cardinal Egan Pavilion, Bronx
Straub, Edward F., (Retired)
Vinci, Guy, (Retired)
Revs.—
Bannan, Peter F., (Retired)
Beaumont, Joachim, (Retired)
Bellew, Francis, (Retired)
Borstelmann, James E., (Retired)
Carney, Patrick, (Retired)
Competente, Virgilio, (Retired)
Connolly, James P., (Retired)
Conte, James W., (Retired), 2156 Catalina Blvd., San Diego, CA 92107
Conti, John P., (Retired), 537 Third St., Brooklyn, 11215
Curley, Thomas J., (Retired)
D'Incecco, Alfred, (Retired)
Daly, Christopher H., (Retired), John Cardinal O'Connor Clergy Pavilion, 5655 Arlington Ave., Bronx, 10471
Darbouze, Joseph, (Retired)
Dibble, Michael, (Retired), 5 Corte de la Canada, Martinez, CA 94553
Dietz, Joseph, (Retired)
Dillon, Richard J., (Retired), University of Milan
DiNola, Leonard J., (Retired), Edward Cardinal Egan Pavilion, Bronx
DiSenso, Gerard, (Retired), John Cardinal O'Connor Clergy Pavilion, 5655 Arlington Ave., Bronx, 10471
Dwyer, John F., (Retired), Our Lady of the Sacred Heart, 120 Kings Hwy., Tappan, 10983
Fenlon, Thomas B., (Retired)
Gigante, Louis R., (Retired), P.O. Box 820, Philmont, 12565
Gomez, Edmundo, (Retired), St. Athanasius, Bronx. Incarnation Church
Guerra, Aroldo, (Retired)
Jeffers, Robert A., (Retired), John Cardinal O'Connor Clergy Pavilion, 5655 Arlington Ave., Bronx, 10471
Keenan, Patrick, (Retired)
Kelly, John, (Retired)
Kennedy, Robert T., J.U.D., J.D., (Retired), 400 Symphony Cir., Hunt Valley, MD 21030
Martin, William F., (Retired), Warren, VT 05674
McAndrew, Joseph P., (Retired), Edward Cardinal Egan Pavilion, Bronx
McDonagh, John, (Retired), Edward Cardinal Egan Pavilion, Bronx
McDonald, Bernard J., (Retired), Mt. Alverno, Warwick
McKenna, John J., (Retired), Edward Cardinal Egan Pavilion, Bronx
O'Meara, Joseph P., (Retired), Edward Cardinal Egan Pavilion, Bronx
O'Reilly, Edward M., (Retired), P.O. Box 5592, Hudson, FL 34674
O'Shaughnessy, James J., (Retired), Spellman High School, Bronx
Oliver, Marc, (Retired)

Pizzuto, Alfred, (Retired), Edward Cardinal Egan Pavilion, Bronx
Quinn, John L., (Retired), Fort Lauderdale, FL
Reardon, John F., (Retired), John Cardinal O'Connor Clergy Residence, 5655 Arlington Ave., Bronx, 10471
Scaramuzzo, Peter C., (Retired)
Seagraves, Richard, (Retired), John Cardinal O'Connor Clergy Residence, 5655 Arlington Ave., Bronx, 10471
Smarsh, Charles F., (Retired), University of Maryland
Walsh, Ronald J., (Retired), 87 Star Crest, Sand Lake, 12153
White, William A., (Retired)
Whitson, Robley E., (Retired), 73 W. Shore Rd., New Preston, CT 06777.

Permanent Deacons:
Abbamont, Thomas J., Holy Name of Jesus, Valhalla
Abels, Gregory, (Leave of Absence)
Abreu, Jose, St. Catherine of Genoa, New York
Acabeo, Valentin, St. Helena, Bronx
Ackerman, Henry, (Leave of Absence)
Adams, Douglas, St. Joan of Arc - Our Lady of Mt. Carmel, Sloatsburg
Aglietti, Richard, (Retired)
Albin, George M. Jr., St. Gregory Barbarigo, Garnersville
Alexandre, Andre, Parish of Holy Name of Jesus and St. Gregory the Great, Manhattan
Almanzar, Andres A., Puerto Rico
Alvarado, William, St. Columba, Hopewell Junction
Alvarez, Angel, St. Joan of Arc, Bronx
Arroyo, Santos, St. Lucy, Bronx
Astarita, Vincent, (Leave of Absence)
Aviles, Stanley, St. Denis, Hopewell Junction
Baffa, John, NC
Barbagallo, Thomas J., St. Paul the Apostle, Yonkers
Barbera, John, St. Augustine, Ossining
Barone, John, Saratoga Springs
Battersby, William L., St. Mary-Our Lady of Mt. Carmel, Mt. Vernon
Beckford, Rodney, St. Charles Borromeo-All Saints, Manhattan
Bellacicco, John A., St. Augustine, Highland
Bello, James, Holy Cross, Bronx
Bennett, Thomas, St. Francis of Assisi, West Nyack
Bernal, Enrique, Fort Mill, SC
Biasotti, John C., (Leave of Absence)
Bierbaum, Scott, St. James the Apostle, Carmel
Blake, George W., St. Martha, Sarasota, FL
Bormann, Eugene, St. Anastasia, Harriman
Borsavage, Charles T., St. James the Apostle-Our Lady of the Lake, Carmel, NY
Brady, Walter, St. John & St. Mary, Chappaqua
Brescia, Michael, SC
Briskey, Kenneth, Regina Coeli, Hyde Park
Brisson, Paul, O.L.P.H., Parish of Our Lady of Perpetual Help-St. Catharine, Pelham Manor
Brockmann, Peter, Sacred Heart, Monroe
Brown, James A., Parish of St. John-St. Paul, Larchmont
Buckner, Robert, St. Paul's Chapel-Greenhaven Correctional Facility
Buonocore, Dominic, St. Paul-St. Ann, Congers
Burke, Eugene F., (Medical Leave)
Burnett, Robert V., Antigua, WI
Burns, James T., (Medical Leave)
Byrne, Daniel, St. Stephen Martyr, Warwick
Byrne, Kevin, St. Monica, St. Elizabeth of Hungary, St. Stephen of Hungary, Manhattan
Calafiore, Michael R., Pennsylvania
Calanni, Clifford, St. Augustine, Ossining
Camacho, Angel, Medical Leave
Camacho, Ismael, St. Joan of Arc, Bronx
Camacho, Jose, St. Peter - St. Denis, Yonkers
Campoverde, Carlos H., Assumption, Peekskill
Candarelli, Lawrenoe, Holy Spirit, Cortlandt Manor
Carr, John, Infant Saviour, Pine Bush
Cartwright, Gerard, St. James the Apostle, Carmel
Carvajal, Rafael, Christ the King, Bronx
Cassaneto, Anthony P., Bridgeport
Castellane, William, St. John the Evangelist, Goshen
Catalano, John, Parish of Our Lady of Perpetual Help-St. Catharine, Pelham Manor
Chaparro, Juan, Sacred Heart, Bronx
Charbonneau, Andre, (Leave of Absence)
Charlesworth, Myles J., Our Lady of Lourdes Parish, Raleigh, NC
Chiu, George, St. Mary of the Assumption, Katonah
Cifuentes, Oscar, St. Joachim - St. John the Evangelist, Beacon
Cirone, Anthony, St. Kateri Tekakwitha, La Grangeville
Clemens, Robert A., St. Bartholomew, Yonkers
Conroy, Thomas Luke, St. Paul-St. Ann, Congers
Cookingham, Vincent, Port St. Lucie, FL
Coppola, George, Florida
Cornell, Thomas, (Extern), (Medical Leave)
Correale, Michael, St. Martin de Porres, Poughkeepsie
Corsaro, Angelo, Sacred Heart, Monroe
Cosme, Felix, Gainsville, GA
Cotto, Angel L., Caguas, Puerto Rico
Cowan, James, Our Lady of Good Counsel, Staten Island
Cranston, Robert, St. John the Evangelist, Saugerties
Crapanzano, John, Bluffton, SC
Cruz, Edwin J., Parish of Holy Family, Blessed Sacrament and St. John Vianney, Bronx
Cunningham, John, St. John the Baptist, Piermont
Curran, Timothy D., St. Mary, Washingtonville
Cusick, Thomas, PA
Czerwinski, Mark, St. Paul-St. Ann, Congers
Dalmer, Peter, Regina Coeli, Hyde Park
Darlestin, Leones J., (Leave of Absence)
Daubman, Andrew, St. Kateri Tekakwitha, La Grangeville
Dauerer, Walter P., St. Denis, Hopewell Junction
De Jesus, Jose L., St. Ann, Ossining
De Maio, Donald J., Naples, FL
De Marco, Carmine J., Holy Name of Jesus, New Rochelle
De Meis, John, Our Lady of Grace, Staten Island
De Vivo, Michael, York, PA
Dean, Timothy, Parish of Presentation of Blessed Virgin Mary and Sacred Heart, Port Ewen
Decker, Michael, St. Mary, Mother of the Church, Fishkill
Degenhardt, Carl, Parish of the Immaculate Conception and Assumption, Tuckahoe
DeGroat, Charles, Parish of St. Paul-St. Ann, Congers
DeMartino, Steven, St. Augustine, Ossining
Deschler, Bernard M., Rockaway Pt., Brooklyn, NY
Devlin, Charles, St. John-St. Mary, Chappaqua
Di Fiore, Augustine, Parish of St. Vito and Most Holy Trinity, Mamaroneck
di Targiani, Robert, (Medical Leave)
Dickson, Donald, (Leave of Absence)
Doherty, Joseph, St. Joseph, Kingston
Dowen, Roland F., St. Gregory Barbarigo Parish, Garnerville
Droge, Lawrence, St. Charles Borromeo, Staten Island
Duffy, John, St. Eugene, Yonkers
Duncan, Robert, Sacred Heart, Monroe
Dunn, John, St. Stanislaus, Pleasant Valley, NY
Duran, Nelson, St. Anthony of Padua, Bronx
Edgerton, John M., Tarpon Springs, FL
Espinal, Hector, Immaculate Conception, Staten Island
Esposito, Robert A., The Villages, FL
Estela, Jorge, Parish of St. Peter and St. Mary of the Assumption, Haverstraw
Fama, Arthur, St. Anthony of Padua, Redbank, NJ
Fanelli, Marc, St. Augustne, Highland
Farmer, Leonard, St. Joseph, New Windsor
Faulkner, James, St. John the Evangelist, Goshen
Feliz, Luis J., Our Lady Queen of Martyrs, Manhattan
Fenton, Gerald, St. Paul-St. Ann, Nyack
Fernandez, Delio, Our Lady Queen of Martyrs, Manhattan
Fernandez, Roberto, (Medical Leave)
Ferraiuolo, Anthony P., St. Joseph, New Windsor
Finnerty, Thomas, Our Lady of Queen of Peace, Staten Island
Fiorio, James, St. Martin de Porres, Poughkeepsie
Fox, Michael J., Parish of Annunciation and Our Lady of Fatima, Crestwood
Francis, James, Sts. Peter and Paul, Bronx
Frohbose, John M., (Medical Leave)
Frohmiller, Richard J., Florida
Gallagher, James, (Extern), Holy Child, Staten Island
Gapay, Alexander, St. Joseph, Middletown
Garcia, Rene, Immaculate Conception, Manhattan
Gaskin, Theodore A., (Medical Leave)
Gemio, Ivan, Corpus Christi-Our Lady of the Rosary, Port Chester
Gizzo, Michael, Parish of Corpus Christi and Our Lady of the Rosary, Port Chester
Gohl, Frank, Regina Coeli, Hyde Park
Gomas, Kelly, (Leave of Absence)
Gontcharuk, Robert, St. Augustine, Larchmont
Gorman, James, (Retired), Charlotte, NC
Gorzka, Stephen S., (Leave of Absence)
Grady, Paul, (Leave of Absence)
Graham, Patrick, St. Margaret Mary, SI
Granda, Miguel E., Parish of St. John and Visitation, Bronx
Gray, Donald, Holy Family, New Rochelle
Grosso, Edward, Parish of Holy Name of Mary and Assumption, Montgomery
Gruerio, Anthony G., St. James the Apostle, Carmel
Guzman, Antonio, Good Shepherd, Manhattan
Hafeman, Joseph R., (Medical Leave)
Haight, Peter R., St. Mother Teresa of Calcutta
Hall, Michael, OLPH and St. Catherine, Pelham Manor
Hall, Raymond, Holy Family, New Rochelle
Halter, Donald, St. Patrick, Newburgh
Hamilton, Eugene R., Parish of St. Peter and St. Mary of the Assumption, Haverstraw
Hanley, John, St. Thomas of Centerbury - St. Joseph, Cornwall on Hudson
Hayes, James R., (Medical Leave)
Hernandez, Jose M., Parish of St. Cecilia-Holy Agony, Manhattan
Hernandez, Narcisco, Our Lady Queen of Martyrs, Manhattan
Hodge, Michel, St. Charles Borromeo-Resurrection, Central Harlem
Hoey, John, St. Christopher-St. Sylvia, Trenton, NJ
Hogan, Dennis, Our Lady of Queen of Peace, Staten Island
Horton, Robert, St. Kateri Tekakwitha, La Grangeville
Horvath, Robert J., Sarasota, FL
Hung, Franklin, St. Martin de Porres, Poughkeepsie
Hveem, Paul, (Retired)
Hyland, Arnold, Parish of St. Mary of the Snow and St. Joseph, Saugerties
Idehen, Francis, St. Patrick-St. Mary, Newburgh
Impallomeni, Alfred R., Our Lady of Mount Carmel, Yonkers
Iovine, Frank, Our Lady of Fatima, Plattekill
Irizarry, Pedro, Parish of St. Peter and St. Denis, Yonkers
Jarmick, Robert E., Troy, NY
Jean-Gilles, Gabriel, Miami, FL
Jesselli, Stephen, (Leave of Absence)
Johnson, Robert Joseph, (Retired)
Jordan, Thomas, (Leave of Absence)
Juliano, Richard, Millville, DE
Jurasek, John, St. Catharine, Blauvelt
Kahn, Bernard, St. Mary, Washingtonville
Kawula, Lawrence, St. Teresa of Calcutta
Kazimir, Martin, (Retired), Albany, NY
Kelleher, John C., St. Catharine, Blauvelt
Kelly, John J., St. Gregory Barbarigo, Garnerville
Kenefick, Cecil, (Retired)
Knack, Lawrence F., St. Mary, Obernberg
Knight, Charles C., OH
Koch, George J., AZ
Konas, Dale, Port St. Lucie, FL
Kozinski, Paul, St. Mary, Staten Island
Larkin, John J., Parish of Presentation of the Blessed Virgin Mary and Sacred Heart, Port Ewen
Laurato, Vincent I., (Retired)
Le Blanc, Vincent F., Westchester Medical Center, West Harrison
Leasiolagi, Taulafoga, (Medical Leave)
Lekovic, Adhur, St. Lawrence O'Toole, Brewster
Li Greci, Christopher, St. Michael Chapel, Manhattan
Lieby, Joseph, St. Joseph, New Windsor
Liegey, Gabriel, St. Patrick, Fairfield, VT
Lindley, Gerard, Regina Coeli, Hyde Park
Locatelli, Carl, St. Paul, Bullville
Loeffler, Albert, St. Joseph, Middletown
Lopez, Francisco Javier, Florida
Lousa, Pedro, Palm Bay, FL
Lyons, Robert, (Extern), St. Christopher - St. Patrick Buchan
Lyttle, John, J.D., J.C.L., Holy Cross, Callicoon
Mac Dougall, Thomas, St. Stephen the Martyr, Warwick, NY
Maher, James, St. Aedans, Pearl River
Maldonado, Eusebio, (Retired)
Maloney, John R., St. Anthony, Nanuet
Man, Chi Sum, Parish of Transfiguration and St. James & Joseph, Manhattan
Mangino, Charles, (Leave of Absence)
Marino, Philip A., Immaculate Conception, Stony Point
Marino, Richard, Immaculate Conception & St. Mary, Port Jervis
Maroon, Phillip J., (Retired), St. Teresa of the Infant Jesus, Staten Island
Marquez, Jose, St. Francis of Assisi, Mt. Kisco
Martinez, Luis A., (Medical Leave)
Martinez, Wilson, Our Lady of Angels, Bronx
Masbad, Raymundo, St. Anthony, Nanuet
Maulucci, John, St. Francis of Rome, St. Francis of Assisi, St. Anthony & Our Lady of Grace, Bronx
Mayeski, Martin, St. Joachim & St. John the Evangelist, Beacon
Mazzei, Nicholas A., Our Lady of Mt. Carmel, Yonkers
Mazzella, Salvatore, Parish of St. Frances of Rome, St. Francis of Assisi, St. Anthony and Our Lady of Grace, Bronx
McCarthy, Richard, Sacred Heart, Monroe

McCormack, John, St. Kateri Tekakwitha, La Grangeville
McGarry, James, St. Catherine of Siena, Sebring, FL
McLaughlin, Richard, Holy Rosary, Hawthorne
McQuade, Joseph, Parish of Our Lady of Perpetual Help and St. Catherine, Pelham Manor
Meier, Anthony C., Raleigh, NC
Mendoza, Christopher, St. Columbanus, Cortlandt Manor
Mercado, Carlos V., (Retired)
Messina, Enrico, St. Denis, Hopewell Junction
Miller, Gregory, St. Lawrence O'Toole, Brewster
Mitchell, Richard F., St. Clare, Staten Island
Mobarek, Samir, St. Augustine, New City
Mojica, Jose, San Juan, Puerto Rico
Moliterno, Daniel, Our Lady of Mt. Carmel, Elmsford
Monegro, Juan, (Medical Leave)
Montealegre, Jorge, Our Lady of Mt. Carmel, Elmsford
Moran, Bernard, St. Joseph, Bronxville
Morillo, Felix M., Good Shepherd, Orlando, FL
Mueller, William J., Parish of Our Lady of the Assumption and St. Mary Star of the Sea, Bronx
Mulryan, W. Joseph, (Retired)
Munoz, Frank, St. Denis, Hopewell Junction
Munoz, Jose, Mt. Pocono, PA
Murphy, Daniel, (Retired)
Murphy, John G., (Retired)
Nash, David, St. Martin de Porres, Poughkeepsie
Nash, John J., (Retired)
Neppl, Thomas, St. Patrick & St. Mary, Newburgh
Nolasco, Rolando, Our Lady of Mercy, Bronx
Noonan, Emmet, (Retired)
Nunez, Acadio, (Leave of Absence)
O'Brien-Lambert, Pedro, Our Lady of Lourdes, Manhattan
O'Neill, Brian, St. Anastasia, Harriman
O'Sullivan, Mark, Regina Coeli, Hyde Park
O'Toole, Lawrence, Charlotte, NC
Ojeda, Jose, St. Francis of Rome, St. Francis of Assisi, St. Anthony and Our Lady of Grace, Bronx
Olivieri, Martin J., Parish of St. John the Baptist and Most Holy Trinity, Yonkers
Orlando, Francis B., Blessed Sacrament, New Rochelle
Ortíz, Louis, Ponce, Puerto Rico
Osgood, Kevin, Boca Raton, FL
Ottaviano, Frank S., Bedford, NH
Pacheco, Angel, St. Isaac Jogues Parish, Orlando, FL
Padro, Candido Jr., St. Anthony of Padua, Bronx
Padron, Jose R., (Leave of Absence)
Pampolina, Rommel, St. Mary, Mother of the Church, Fishkill
Pang, Robert, St. John the Baptist, Piermont
Parchen, Raymond, Holy Spirit, Cortlandt Manor
Patricola, Salvatore, O.F.M.Cap., Holy Cross-St. John the Baptist, New York
Patrona, Joseph, Parish of St. Mary and Our Lady of Mount Carmel, Mt. Vernon
Pelech, Robert, St. Denis, Hopewell Junction
Pelella, John V., Parish of St. Thomas of Canterbury and St. Joseph, Cornwall-on-Hudson
Pellegrin, Daniel, (Retired)
Pena, Jose, St. Joseph, Spring Valley
Pereira, Joaquim, Parish of St. Margaret of Cortona and St. Gabriel, Bronx
Peters, John, (Retired)
Pietkiewicz, Karl J., (Retired)
Piloco, Robert, Sacred Heart, Hartsdale
Pino, Victor M., (Unassigned)
Pipher, Jesse E., Our Lady Queen of Martyrs, Sarasota, FL
Pitula, George, Parish of St. Margaret of Cortona and St. Gabriel, Bronx
Porcel, Carlos M., Parish of Holy Family, Blessed Sacrement & St. John Vianney, Bronx
Porcelli, Vincent, Parish of St. Mary and St. James, Marlboro
Portalatin, Epimegnio, Parish of Holy Family, Blessed Sacrament and St. John Vianney, Bronx
Powers, John, St. Vincent Ferrer, Manhattan
Prendergast, Donald, St. Aloysius, Livingston Manor
Quadrino, James, Our Lady Star of the Sea, Staten Island
Quigley, Donald M., Parish of St. Margaret of Cortona and St. Gabriel, Bronx
Radcliffe, Kenneth L., St. Charles Borromeo & All Saints, Central Harlem
Ramoni, Nicholas, Parish of St. John the Baptist and Most Holy Trinity, Yonkers
Ramos, Alfonso, Sacred Heart, Bronx
Ramos, Edmundo A., St. Patrick's Cathedral, Manhattan
Ramos, Epifanio, Puerto Rico
Reilly, John P., St. Columba, Hopewell Junction
Reisinger, Scott, (Extern), Blessed Sacrament, New York
Rentkowski, Joseph, Parish of Our Lady of Pity-St. Anthony of Padua, Staten Island
Repke, Robert, Florida
Rettino, P. Robert, (Medical Leave)
Reynolds, Peter E., St. Columba, Chester
Ricci, Raymond, St. Christopher - St. Sylvia
Riley, John M., FL
Rios, Ralph, Sacred Heart, Bronx
Rivera, Andrew A., (Retired)
Rivera, José A., Aguas Buenas, Puerto Rico
Rizzo, Charles A., (Retired)
Rodgers, James, (Retired)
Rodrigues, Siriaco, (Extern), Immaculate Conception, Bronx
Rodriguez, Arnaldo, (Retired)
Rodriguez, Cristobal, (Medical Leave)
Rodriguez, Hector R., Orlando, FL
Rodríguez, Jacinto, Guayama, PR
Rodriguez, Porfirio, St. Jude, Manhattan
Rosado, Alejandro, (Retired)
Rosado, Odalis R., (Leave of Absence)
Rosado, Reynaldo, St. Dominic, Bronx
Rosado, Ricardo, (Retired)
Rose, Frank, Infant Saviour, Pine Bush
Rush, James J., Harrisburg, PA
Sadowski, John, St. Joseph, Spring Valley
Sakowicz, Albert, Albany, NY
Salamone, Victor A., St. Martin de Porres, Poughkeepsie
Salhany, Richard, Our Lady Help of Christians, Staten Island
Salvatorelli, A. Michael, St. Benedict, Bronx
Sanchez, Carlos, Our Lady of Angels, Bronx
Sanchez, Oscar, Puerto Rico
Sandoval, Waldemar, St. Paul the Apostle, Manhattan
Santiago, Abraham, St. Joseph, Yonkers
Santore, Louis, GA
Scarfi, John, St. John the Evangelist, Mahopac
Scheibe, Richard, St. Patrick, Yorktown Heights
Scott, John, St. Benedict, Bronx, NY
Sepulveda, Miguel A., Puerto Rico
Sequeira, Ronald, (Leave of Absence)
Serrano, Jose I., St. Jude, Marion Oaks, FL
Seymour, John L., (Retired)
Shea, John, SS. John and Paul, Larchmont
Shiel, Thomas P., (Retired)
Shkreli, Mark, St. Lawrence O'Toole, Brewster
Sica, Generosa, St. Joseph, Croton Falls
Sin-Garciga, Felipe, (Medical Leave)
Singler, John A., Our Lady Help of Christians, Staten Island
Slominski, Timothy, St. Augustine, Ossining
Smith, Eymard, St. Barnabas, Bronx
Smith, Henry, St. Mary of the Snow - St. Joseph, Saugerties
Smith, Paul L., St. Mary, Mother of the Church, Fishkill
So, Patrick, St. Teresa, Manhattan
Solanto, Joseph P., (Retired)
Stahlnecker, James J., (Retired)
Suarez, Israel, Guaynabo, Puerto Rico
Suchy, James, St. Augustine, New City
Sullivan, John D., (Retired)
Sweeney, Michael, St. Mary of the Snow - St. Joseph, Saugerties
Tayco, Renato, (Medical Leave)
Teng, Rudolph, St. Paul the Apostle, Yonkers
Testa, Warren, St. Columba, Hopewell Junction
Then, Rafael, Good Shepherd, Manhattan
Thompson, Alfred, (Medical Leave)
Tirella, Rosario J., Holy Rosary, Staten Island
Tobin, William D., (Medical Leave)
Tobon, Stephen, St. Charles Borromeo, Staten Island
Tomasicchio, John, St. Stephen Martyr, Warwick
Torres, Luis A., Mayaguez, Puerto Rico
Torres, Luis J., Holy Cross, Bronx
Tortorella, Thomas, St. Michael, Bronx
Trapani, Richard, St. Joseph, Middletown, NY
Trees, Donald F., Parish of St. Mary of the Snow and St. Joseph, Saugerties
Trexler, Jeffrey, (Extern), St. Patrick; Exec Dir. of Order of Malta
Ungco, Jose, St. Francis de Sales, Manhattan
Vaccaro, William N., Parish of Corpus Christi and Our Lady of the Rosary, Port Chester
Valdez, Bienvenido, Our Lady Queen of Martyrs, Manhattan
Vargas, Thomas A., (Leave of Absence)
Vasquez, Domingo, Sunrise, FL
Vazquez, Fernando, St. Frances de Chantal, Bronx
Vazquez, Francisco J., Newnan, GA
Velasquez, Jose Luis, St. Martin of Tours, Bronx
Velez, Randy, Cooperstown, NY
Venditto, Michael, Parish of Our Lady of Pity and St. Anthony of Padua, Staten Island
Verboys, Joseph, Palm Beach, FL
Verlezza, Vincent, Santa Maria, Bronx
Villanueva, Engracio G., St. Joseph-St. Thomas, Staten Island
Viola, Anthony, Immaculate Conception & Assumption, Tuckahoe
Vitale, Paul, (Extern), Parish of St. Patrick's Old Cathedral and Most Precious Blood, Manhattan
Weiner, Arthur, St. James the Apostle, Carmel
Weinstein, David, Immaculate Conception, Amenia
Weir, John E., (Medical Leave)
Weireter, Paul J., St. Patrick, Highland Mills
White, Dennis, Geneva, IL
Whiteman, Robert, J.D., Ed.D., Milwaukee, WI
Wilson, Michael, St. Elizabeth Ann Seton, Shrub Oak, NY
Wodzinski, Christopher, Blessed Sacrament, Staten Island
Woods, Edward J., Our Lady of Mt. Carmel, Middletown
Wright, Kevin, St. Teresa, Manhattan
Zambrana, Wallace, Our Lady of Sorrows, Manhattan
Zatarga, Michael, St. Joan of Arc, Boca Raton, FL.

INSTITUTIONS LOCATED IN DIOCESE

[A] SEMINARIES, ARCHDIOCESAN

YONKERS. *Cathedral Prep Program* (1963) 201 Seminary Ave., Yonkers, 10704. Tel: 914-968-1340; Fax: 914-968-6671; Email: cprep@archny.org; Web: www.nypriest.com. Priests 1.

St. Joseph's Seminary (1896) Archdiocesan Major Seminary, 201 Seminary Ave., Yonkers, 10704-1896. Tel: 914-968-6200; Fax: 914-376-2019; Email: sjs@archny.org; Web: www.ny-archdiocese.org/pastoral/seminary.cfm. Rev. Msgr. Peter Vaccari, S.T.L., Rector & Assoc. Prof. of Church; Revs. Thomas V. Berg, Ph.D., Dean of Admissions, Vice Rector & Prof. of Moral Theology; Charles Caccavale, S.T.D.; Peter J. Cameron, O.P.; William Cleary, S.T.D.; Rev. Msgr. Michael Curran, S.T.D., Dir. Assessment & Accreditation; Very Rev. William S. Elder, J.C.D.; Revs. Matthew S. Ernest, S.T.D., Dir. Office of Liturgy Archdiocese NY, Prof. & Dir Liturgy St. Joseph's Seminary; Kevin O'Reilly, S.T.D., Academic Dean; Luis Saldana, S.T.L., Dir., Spiritual Formation; Richard Veras, M.A., Dir., Pastoral Formation; Nicholas Zientarski, S.T.D., Dean of Seminarians; Michael Bruno, S.T.D. Brothers 1; Deacons 1; Lay Teachers 18; Students 91; Non-Resident Faculty: Priests 14.

Non-Resident Faculty: Rev. Msgr. Robert Batule, S.T.L.; Rev. Solanus Benfatti, C.F.R., S.T.L.; Mr. David Bonagura, M.A.; Rev. John S. Bonnici, S.T.D.; Larry Boone, Ph.D.; Rev. Michael Bruno, S.T.D.; Dr. Stephen Buglione, Ph.D., Psychology; Rev. Claudio Burgaleta, S.J., Ph.D., S.T.D.; Alexander Burke, Ph.D.; Ms. Jan Edmiston, Dir. Corrigan Library; Rev. Christopher Cullen, S.J., Ph.D.; Jennifer Donelson, D.M.A., Dir., Sacred Music; Ms. Marie Bridget Dundon, M.A.; Dr. Donna Eschenauer, Ph.D., Assoc. Dean M.A. Program; Daniel Frascella, Ph.D.; Dr. Richard Gallagher, M.D., Psychiatrist & Dir., Psychological Counseling Svcs.; Rev. Msgr. Richard Henning, S.T.D.; Dr. Michael Hoonhout, Ph.D.; Revs. Joseph W. Koterski, S.J., Ph.D.; Joseph T. Lienhard, S.J., Dr. Theol. Habil.; Dr. Anthony Marinelli, Ph.D.; Annabella Mosely; Revs. John O'Neill, Ph.D., D.Min.; Fredy O. Patino, M.A.; Eugen Pentiuc, M.A., Ph.D., Lic Th, Th.D.; Walter Petrovitz, Ph.D.; Rev. Gregory Rannazzisi, S.T.L.; Deacon Thomas Rich; Bro. Owen Sadlier, O.S.F., S.T.L.; Rev. Timothy J. Scannell, Ph.D.; Rev. Msgr. Robert Thelen, S.T.L.; Mr. Ryan Williams, Ph.D. (Cand.); Ms. Catherine Lamanna, Pastoral Spanish Instructor; Ana Varek, Pastoral Spanish Instructor.

[B] SEMINARIES, RELIGIOUS OR SCHOLASTICATES

BEACON. *St. Lawrence of Brindisi Friary*, Province of the Stigmata of St. Francis, 180 Sargent Ave., Beacon, 12508-3993. Tel: 845-831-0394; Tel: 845-838-0759 (Infirmary); Fax: 845-831-0918; Fax: 845-838-1352 (Infirmary). Revs. Pius Caccavalle, O.F.M.Cap.; Achilles Cassieri, O.F.M.Cap.; Sylvester Catallo, O.F.M.Cap.; Luke Guastella, O.F.M.Cap.; Peter Napoli, O.F.M.Cap.; Bros. Jack Boehm, O.F.M.Cap.; Julius Tkaczyk, O.F.M.Cap.; Revs. Stanley Kobel, O.F.M.Cap.; Santo Frapaul, O.F.M.Cap., Vicar; Praveen Boyapati, O.F.M.Cap., Guardian. (Friary and Infirmary) Brothers 2; Priests 9.

BRONX. *Ciszek Hall* Residence for Jesuit Scholastics

and Brothers engaged in Philosophy and Theology Studies at Fordham University. 2502 Belmont Ave., Bronx, 10458-6282. Tel: 718-817-9100;
Fax: 718-365-3166; Email: minister@ciszekhall.org. Rev. Joseph O'Keefe, S.J., Rector. Priests 3.

STATEN ISLAND. *Society of St. Paul*, 2187 Victory Blvd., Staten Island, 10314. Tel: 718-761-0047;
Fax: 718-761-0057; Email: provincialoffice@stpauls.us; Web: www.stpauls.us. Bros. Augustine Condon, S.S.P., Prov. Sec.; Lawrence H. Schubert, S.S.P., Bursar's Office; Zbigniew Gawron, S.S.P., Graphics Editor; Revs. Matthew Roehrig, S.S.P., Prov. Supr.; Sebastian Lee, S.S.P., Korean Apostolate; Tony Bautista, Prov.; Marco Bulgarelli, Admin.; Rev. Jeffrey Mickler, Youth Min. Brothers 20; Priests 7.

SUFFERN. *Tagaste Monastery* Major Seminary of the Province of St. Augustine of the Augustinian Recollect Fathers & Brothers 220 Lafayette Ave., Suffern, 10901. Tel: 845-357-0067;
Fax: 845-369-0625; Email: tagastesuffern@gmail.com; Web: www.tagastemonastery.org. Revs. John Oldfield, O.A.R., Sr. Religious; John Gruben, O.A.R., Prior; Fidel Hernandez, O.A.R. Deacons 1; Priests 4.

[C] COLLEGES AND UNIVERSITIES

NEW YORK. *College of Mount Saint Vincent* (Coed) Founded by the Sisters of Charity of Saint Vincent de Paul. Chartered by the University of the State of New York. 6301 Riverdale Ave., 10471-1093.
Tel: 718-405-3200; Fax: 718-549-2603; Email: carol.finegan@mountsaintvincent.edu; Web: www.mountsaintvincent.edu. Charles L. Flynn Jr., Ph. D., Pres.; Sarah Stevenson, Ph.D., Provost & Dean, Faculty; Madeline Melkonian, Sr. Vice Pres., Inst. Advancement and College Rels.; Dr. Patrick Valdez, Dean, Undergraduate College; Joseph Levis, Dir. of Library. Sisters 2; Total Enrollment 1,695; Lay Faculty 80.

Marymount Manhattan College Chartered by the Univ. of the State of NY. 221 E. 71st St., 10021.
Tel: 212-517-0400; Email: vdorgan@mmm.edu; Web: www.mmm.edu. Dr. Judson Shaver, Pres.; Dawn Webber, Vice Pres. Academic Affairs; Christy Gaiti, Vice Pres. Student Affairs (Acting); Paul Ciraulo, Vice Pres. Business & Financial Affairs; Mary Kay Demetry-Jeynes, Dean Courses for Adults; Jeanne Evans, Dir. College Rels. & Institutional Advancement; Sr. Virginia Dorgan, R.S.H.M., Campus Min. Sisters 3; Students 2,330.

BRONX. **Fordham University* (1841) Second campus and Branch campus at Lincoln Center, New York, NY 10023 and 400 Westchester Ave., West Harrison, NY 10528. Chartered by the Legislature of the State of New York. 441 E. Fordham Rd., Bronx, 10458. Tel: 718-817-1000;
Fax: 718-817-3050; Email: president@fordham.edu; Web: www.fordham.edu. Rev. Joseph M. McShane, S.J., Pres.; Dr. Stephen Freedman, Provost; Mr. Roger A. Milici Jr., Vice Pres., Devel. & Univ. Rels.; Rev. Michael C. McCarthy, S.J., Vice Pres. Mission Integration & Planning; Martha Hirst, Sr. Vice Pres., CFO & Treas.; Dr. Frank J. Sirianni, Vice Pres., Information Technology; Mr. Jeffrey L. Gray, Senior Vice Pres., Students Affairs; Dr. Brian Byrne, Vice Pres., Lincoln Center; Dr. Peter Stace, Vice Pres., Enrollment; Mr. Marco Valera, Vice Pres., Facilities Mgmt.; Mr. Thomas A. Dunne, Vice Pres., Admin.; Dr. John P. Harrington, Dean, Arts & Sciences Faculty; Dr. Eva Badowska, Dean, Graduate School of Arts & Sciences; Dr. Maura Mast, Dean, Fordham College at Rose Hill; Dr. Donna Rapaccioli, Dean, Gabelli School of Business & Dean, Busines Faculty; Dr. Virginia Roach, Dean, Graduate School of Educ.; Matthew Diller, J.D., Dean, School of Law; Dr. Debra M. McPhee, Dean, Graduate School of Social Svc.; Rev. Robert R. Grimes, S.J., Dean, Fordham College at Lincoln Center; Dr. Isabelle Frank, School, Professional Studies & Continuing Studies; Dr. C. Colt Anderson, Dean, Graduate School of Religion & Religious Educ.; Linda LoSchiavo, Dir. Univ. Library. Clergy 5; Priests 29; Sisters 5; Students 16,262; Total Enrollment 16,262; Total Staff 4,346.

Manhattan College (1853) 4513 Manhattan College Pkwy., Riverdale, 10471. Tel: 718-862-7200;
Tel: 800-622-9235; Fax: 718-862-8019; Email: admit@manhattan.edu; Web: www.manhattan.edu. Brennan O'Donnell, Ph.D., Pres.; William Clyde, Ph.D., Provost & Exec. Vice Pres., Academic Affairs; William Bisset, Ph.D., Vice Pres., Enrollment Mgmt.; Barbara Fabe, Vice Pres., Human Resources; Thomas Mauriello, Vice Pres., College Advancement; Andrew Ryan, Vice Pres., Facilities; Matthew McManness, Vice Pres., Finance & CFO; Richard Satterlee, Ph.D., Vice Pres., Student Life; Bro. Jack Curran, F.S.C., Ph.D., Vice Pres., Mission; Keith Brower, Ph.D., Dean, School of Liberal Arts; Salwa Ammar, Ph.D., Dean, School of Business; Karen Nicholson, Dean, School of Educ. & Health; Tim J. Ward, Ph.D., Dean, School of Engrg.; Constantine Theodosiou, Ph.D., Dean, School of Science; William H. Walters, Ph.D., Librarian. Founded in 1853 by the Brothers of the Christian Schools. Total Enrollment 3,664.

NEW ROCHELLE. **The College of New Rochelle* (1904) Founded in 1904 by the Religious of the Order of St. Ursula. Chartered by the Regents of the University of the State of New York. The College is composed of four schools: School of Arts and Sciences (Women); Graduate School; School of New Resources; School of Nursing (Coed). 29 Castle Pl., New Rochelle, 10805. Tel: 914-654-5000;
Fax: 914-654-5980; Email: info@cnr.edu; Web: www.cnr.edu. Dr. David Latimer, Pres.; Tiffani Blake, Dean, Students, Tel: 914-654-5862; Betty Roberts, Vice Pres., Finance & Administration; H. Michael Dreher, Dean, School of Nursing; Dr. Kristine Southard, Dean, School of New Resources, Tel: 914-654-5527; Ana Fontura, Dean, Gill Library; Rev. J. Joseph Flynn, O.F.M.Cap., Chap.; Jenny Rroji, Campus Min. Priests 1; Sisters 2; Students 3,363; Total Faculty & Staff 433.

Iona College (Coed) Education in the tradition of the Christian Brothers. Independent College 715 North Ave., New Rochelle, 10801.
Tel: 914-633-2000; Fax: 914-633-2018; Email: webmaster@iona.edu; Web: www.iona.edu. Dr. Joseph E. Nyre, Ph.D., Pres.; Ms. Mary Ellen Callaghan, Vice Pres., Chief of Staff & Board Sec.; Anne Marie Schettini-Lynch, S.V.P. Fin. & Admin.; Paul Sutera, S.V.P. Advancement & External Affairs; Denise Hopkins, Vice Provost Student Life; Dr. William Lamb, Dean School of Business; Mr. Richard Palladino, Dir. of Libraries; Ms. Kathleen McElroy, Legal Counsel; Dr. Darrell Wheeler, S.V.P. Academic Affairs; Dr. Joseph Stabile, Interim Dean School of Arts & Sciences. Brothers 7; Clergy 4; Lay Teachers 324; Priests 1; Sisters 1; Students 3,926.

NEWBURGH. *Mt. St. Mary College* (1954) (Coed) 330 Powell Ave., Newburgh, 12550. Tel: 845-561-0800;
Fax: 845-562-6762; Email: ryan.williams@msmc.edu; Web: www.msmc.edu. Jason Adsit, Pres.; Michael Olivette, Vice Pres.; Jannelle Haug, Registrar; Barbara Pertuzzelli, Library Dir.; Rev. Gregoire Fluet, Chap. Divisions: Arts & Letters; Education; Natural Sciences; Mathematics & Information Technology; Philosophy & Religious Studies; Social Sciences. Schools: Business & Nursing. Lay Teachers 79; Students 2,689.

ORANGEBURG. *Dominican College* (1952) Chartered by University of the State of New York. 470 Western Hwy., Orangeburg, 10962. Tel: 845-848-7800;
Fax: 845-359-2313; Email: admissions@dc.edu; Web: www.dc.edu. Sisters Mary Eileen O'Brien, O.P., Ph.D., Pres.; Kathleen Sullivan, O.P., Chancellor; Dr. Thomas Nowak, Vice Pres. Academic Affairs & Academic Dean; John Burke, Vice Pres. Student Devel. & Dean of Students; Anthony Cipolla, Vice Pres. Financial Affairs & Chief Fiscal Officer; Dorothy Filoramo, Vice Pres. Institutional Advancement; Brian Fernandes, Vice Pres. Enrollment Mgmt.; Mary McFadden, Registrar; Dr. Shao-Wei Wu, Institutional Research; Mr. Joseph Clinton, Athletics; Sr. Barbara McEneany, O.P., Campus Min.; Gina M. Shelton, MSLIS, Librarian. Lay Teachers 75; Sisters 6; Students 2,012.
Divisions: Daphne Estwick, Allied Health; Dr. Mark Meachem, C.D.R., Arts & Sciences; Dr. Clare Pennino, Business Admin.; Dr. Nancy Di Dona, Nursing; Dr. Christopher G. Libertini, Social Sciences; Dr. Diane DiSpagne, Educ. Teacher; Brian Fernandez, Interim Dir. Admissions; Stacy Salinas, Dir. Financial Aid.

SPARKILL. *St. Thomas Aquinas College*, Sparkill, 10976. Tel: 845-398-4000; Fax: 845-359-8136; Web: www.stac.edu. Sr. Margaret M. Fitzpatrick, S.C., Ed.D., Pres.; Dr. L. John Duvney, Vice Pres. Academic Affairs. Founded by Dominican Sisters of Sparkill in 1952. Senior coed college, chartered by Univ. of the State of New York. Sisters 2; Students 2,700; Lay Professors 65.

STATEN ISLAND. *St. John's University Staten Island Campus*, 300 Howard Ave., Staten Island, 10301.
Tel: 718-390-4545; Fax: 718-390-4520; Web: www.stjohns.edu. Very Rev. Donald J. Harrington, C.M., Pres.; Rev. Patrick J. Griffin, C.M., Exec. Vice Pres. Mission; Dr. Jerrold Ross, Academic Vice Pres. & Dean; Donna Narducci, Assoc. Dean & Dir. Peter J. Tobin College of Business; James O'Keefe, Assoc. Dean College of Professional Studies; Stephen Kuntz, Assoc. Dean, School of Education, Graduate Div.; Kimberly Palmieri, Asst. Dean, Office of Student Affairs; Kelly Rocca, Assoc. Dean, St. John's College; Mark Meng, Librarian. Vincentian Community. Students 2,215.

VALHALLA. **New York Medical College*, Administration Bldg., 40 Sunshine Cottage Rd., Valhalla, 10595.
Tel: 914-594-4600; Web: www.nymc.edu.

[D] DEPARTMENT OF EDUCATION

NEW YORK. *Department of Education, Superintendent of Schools Office*, 1011 First Ave., 10022.
Tel: 212-371-1000, Ext. 2800; Fax: 212-758-3018; Email: dr.timothy.mcniff@archny.org; Web: www.buildboldfutures.org. Dr. Timothy J. McNiff, Supt. of Schools; Mrs. Doreen DePaolis, Office Mgr.; Mr. Daniel Murphy, Chief of Staff.
Office of Finance, Tel: 212-371-1011, Ext. 2707;
Fax: 212-758-3018. Mr. Frank Napolitano, Exec. Dir.
Deputy Superintendent: Mr. Michael Deegan.
Associate Superintendents: Mr. Frank Viteritti, Assoc. Supt. Personnel; Paige Sanchez, Assoc. Supt. Mission Effectiveness; Steven Virgadamo, Assoc. Supt. Leadership; Michael Coppotelli, Assoc. Supt. Public Policy & Student Svcs.
Directors: Ms. Lucia DiJusto, Admin. Asst., Catechist Formation; Mrs. Oneeka Jordan, Dir., Student Information Svcs.; Sr. Alice Kirk, O.P., SIS Helpdesk; Mrs. Eileen Murtha, Special Educ.; Ms. Lillian Valentin, Data Collections; Mr. Nicholas Iacono, Communications & Public Rels.; Mrs. Joanne Walsh, Dir., Early Childhood Educ.; Stephen Marositz, Curriculum Devel. Assoc.
Regional Superintendents: Mrs. Noelle Beale, Regl. Supt., Central Westchester; Mrs. Cathleen Cassel, Regl. Supt., Rockland, Orange, Sullivan, Ulster Counties; Mrs. Mary Jane Daley, Regl. Supt., Dutchess, Northern Westchester, Putnam Counties; Mrs. Zoilita Herrera, Regl. Supt., Staten Island; Mrs. Linda Dougherty, Regl. Supt., (NE/E) Bronx; Mr. John Riley, Regl. Supt., (NW/S) Bronx; Mr. Damian Hermann, Regl. Supt., Manhattan.
University Apostolate - Campus Ministry, 1011 First Ave., 7th Flr., 10022. Tel: 646-794-3168. Christopher Oravetz, M.S., M.T.S., Dir.
Archdiocesan Drug Abuse Prevention Program, 2789 Schurz Ave., 10465. Tel: 718-904-1333;
Fax: 718-823-2177; Email: info@adapp.org; Web: www.adapp.org. Mrs. Christine Cavallucci, Dir.
Family Life/Respect Life Office, 1011 First Ave., 10022. Tel: 212-371-1000, Ext. 3185;
Fax: 212-371-3382. Kathleen Wither, D.Min., Dir.
Archdiocesan Catechetical Office, 1011 First Ave., 10022. Tel: 212-371-1000, Ext. 2849;
Fax: 212-980-1035. Sr. Joan Curtin, C.N.D., Archdiocesan Dir.; Estala D. Guevara, Asst. to Dir., Tel: 212-371-1000, Ext. 2859; Mrs. Nancy Doran, Dir. Catechist Formation, Tel: 212-371-1000, Ext. 2867; Sr. Teresita Morse, R.J.M., Dir. Formation of Catechetical Leaders, Tel: 212-371-1000, Ext. 2858; Mr. Oscar Cruz, Dir. Catechumenate/Family Catechesis, Tel: 212-371-1000, Ext. 2851; Ms. Maureen McKew, Dir. Communications/New York Catholic Bible School, Tel: 212-371-1000, Ext. 2855; Mr. James Connell, Webmaster, Tel: 212-371-1000, Ext. 2808; Sr. Zelide M. Ceccagno, M.S.C.S., Regl. Dir., Yonkers & Central & Southern Westchester County - Adult Media, 56 Dunston Ave., Yonkers, 10701; Ms. Jeannette Chishibanji, Regl. Dir., Bronx, 4505 Richardson Ave., Bronx, 10470; Sr. Mary Crucifix Pandullo, C.S.J.B., Regl. Dir., Staten Island, 203 Sand Ln., Staten Island, 10305; Mrs. Peg Hoblin, Regl. Dir., Northern Westchester, Rockland & Putnam Counties, 24 E. Main St., Stony Point, 10980. Tel: 845-624-3190 (Westchester/Putnam); Mrs. Linda Fitzsimmons, Regl. Dir., Dutchess & Ulster Counties, 26 S. Hamilton St., Poughkeepsie, 12601; Sisters Catherine Ryan, F.S.P., Regl. Dir., Manhattan, c/o St. Jude Church, 431 West 204 St., 10034; Kevin John Shields, O.P., Regl. Dir., Orange & Sullivan Counties, Blessed Kateri Tekakwitha Center, P.O. Box 1011, Liberty, 12754.
Department of Education Archdiocese of NY Child Nutrition Program, 1011 First Ave., 10128.
Tel: 212-371-1000, Ext. 2760; Fax: 212-421-3760. Mr. Thomas Smith, Child Nutrition Dir.
Center for Spiritual Development.
Instructional Television, 215 Seminary Ave., Yonkers, 10704. Tel: 914-968-7800;
Fax: 914-968-2075. Rev. Gary M. Mead, Admin. Dir.
High School: Full-time Sisters 86; Elementary School: Full-time Sisters 142; Full-time Brothers 10; Part-time Brothers 1; Full-time Order Priests 2; Part-time Order Priests 3; Full-time Lay Teachers 3,870; Part-time Lay Teachers 988; Total Parish Enrollment 76,387; Total Inter-Parish Enrollment 1,709; Total Private Enrollment 4,250; Part-time Sisters 51; Part-time Sisters 39; Full-time Brothers 37; Part-time Brothers 5; Full-time Order Priests 27; Part-time Order Priests 4; Full-time Diocesan Priests 26; Full-time Lay Teachers 2,304; Part-time Lay Teachers 191; Total Diocesan Enrollment 10,588; Total Parish Enrollment 4,664; Total Private Enrollment 12,359.
New York Catholic School Region of Manhattan
NEW YORK.
Catholic School Region of Manhattan, 1011 First

Ave., 12th Fl., 10022. Tel: 212-371-1000, Ext. 2006 ; Email: info@transfigurationschoolnyc.org. Rev. Peter Yuan, Admin.

Academy of St. Joseph, (Grades PreK-8), 111 Washington Pl., 10014. Tel: 212-243-5420; Fax: 212-414-4526; Email: josephvillage@adnyeducation.org; Web: www.academyofsaintjoseph.org. Ms. Angela M. Coombs, Head of School. Lay Teachers 11; Students 77.

Ascension School (1912) (Regional) 220 W. 108th St., 10025. Tel: 212-222-5161; Fax: 212-280-4690; Email: m003@adnyeducation.org; Web: www.ascensionschoolnyc.org. Ms. Donna Gabella, Prin. Lay Teachers 15; Students 292.

Blessed Sacrament School (1902) (Grades PreK-8), (Regional) 147-151 W. 70th St., 10023. Tel: 212-724-7561; Fax: 212-724-0735; Email: m010@adnyeducation.org; Web: www.blessedsacramentnyc.org. Ms. Caroline Sliney, Prin. Lay Teachers 17; Students 405.

Convent of the Sacred Heart, (Grades PreK-8), (Girls) 1 E. 91st St., 10128. Tel: 212-722-4745; Fax: 212-996-1784; Email: coshes@adnyeducation.org; Web: cshnyc.org. Dr. Joseph J. Ciancaglini, Head of School. Lay Teachers 116; Elementary School Students 491.

Corpus Christi School (1907) (Regional) 535 W. 121st St., 10027. Tel: 212-662-9344; Fax: 212-662-2725; Email: m004@adnyeducation.org; Web: www.ccschoolnyc.org. Matthew Bull, Prin. Lay Teachers 8; Students 174.

Good Shepherd School (1925) (Grades PreK-8), 620 Isham St., 10034. Tel: 212-567-5800; Fax: 212-567-5839; Email: m006@adnyeducation.org; Web: www.gsschoolnyc.org. Geraldine Lavery, Prin. Lay Teachers 14; Students 262.

Guardian Angel School (1911) (Grades PreK-8), (Regional) Tel: 212-989-8280; Email: m007@adnyeducation.org; Web: www.guardianangels.org. Christie Acosta-Perez, Prin. Lay Teachers 12; Students 181.

Immaculate Conception School (1864) (Grades PreK-8), 419 E. 13th St., 10009. Tel: 212-475-2590; Fax: 212-777-2818; Email: m016@adnyeducation.org; Web: www.immaculateconceptionschoolnyc.org. Mary Barry, Prin. Lay Teachers 12; Students 194.

Incarnation School (1910) (Grades PreK-8), (Regional) 570 W. 175th St., 10033. Tel: 212-795-1030; Fax: 212-795-1564; Email: ngreen@incarnationnyc.org; Email: m017@adnyeducation.org; Web: www.incarnationnyc.org. Nicholas Green, Prin. Lay Teachers 14; Students 305.

Marymount School of New York, (Grades PreK-8), (Independent Catholic) 1026 Fifth Ave., 10028. Tel: 212-744-4486; Fax: 212-744-0163; Email: marymtes@adnyeducation.org. Concepcion Alvar, B.S., M.A., Headmaster. Lay Teachers 47; Students 507.

Mt. Carmel - Holy Rosary School, (Grades PreK-8), (Partnership School) 371 Pleasant Ave., 10035. Tel: 212-876-7555; Fax: 212-876-0152; Email: m014@adnyeducation.org; Email: admin@mchrschool.org; Email: msmith@mchrschool.org; Web: www.mtcarmelholyrosary.org. Ms. Molly Smith, Prin. Lay Teachers 31; Students 228.

Our Lady of Lourdes School (1903) (Grades PreK-8), (Regional) 468 W. 143rd St., 10031. Tel: 212-926-5820; Fax: 212-491-6034; Email: m029@adnyeducation.org; Web: www.ollnyc.org. Ms. Suzanne Kaszynksi, Prin. Lay Teachers 11; Students 287.

Our Lady of Pompeii School (1930) (Grades PreK-8), 240 Bleecker St., 10014. Tel: 212-242-4147; Fax: 212-691-2361; Email: m034@adnyeducation.org; Web: www.ourladyofpompeii.nyc. Sr. Diane Mastroianni, A.S.C.J., Prin. Lay Teachers 10; Students 144; Clergy / Religious Teachers 2.

Our Lady Queen of Angels School (1886 and 1955) (Regional) 232 E. 112th St., 10029. Tel: 212-722-9277; Fax: 212-987-8837; Email: m024@adnyeducation.org. Ms. Stephanie Becker, Prin. Lay Teachers 12; Students 280.

Our Lady Queen of Martyrs School (1932) (Grades PreK-8), (Regional) 71 Arden St., 10040. Tel: 212-567-3190; Fax: 212-304-8587; Email: m035@adnyeducation.org; Web: www.olqmnyc.org. Andrew Woods, Prin. Lay Teachers 12; Students 272.

Sacred Heart of Jesus School (1892) (Regional) 456 W. 52nd St., 10019. Tel: 212-246-4784; Fax: 212-707-8382; Email: m043@adnyeducation.org; Web: www.shjsnyc.org. Ms. Caroline Sliney, Prin. Lay Teachers 9; Students 125.

St. Ann School (1926) (Grades PreK-8), (Regional) 314 E. 110th St., 10029. Tel: 212-722-1295; Fax: 212-722-8024; Email: m051@adnyeducation.org; Web: www.stannschoolnyc.org. Hope Mueller, Prin. Lay Teachers 12; Students 219.

St. Brigid School, (Grades PreK-8), (Regional) 185 E. Seventh St., 10009. Tel: 212-677-5210; Fax: 212-260-2262; Email: m055@adnyeducation.org; Web: stbrigidschoolny.com. Molly Carone, Prin. Lay Teachers 12; Students 150.

St. Charles Borromeo School (1904) (Grades PreK-8), (Regional) 214 W. 142 St., 10030. Tel: 212-368-6666; Fax: 212-281-1323; Email: m059@adnyeducation.org; Web: www.stcharlesborromeoschool.org. Dan Faas, Prin. Lay Teachers 15; Students 259.

St. Elizabeth School (1936) (Grades PreK-8), (Regional) 612 W. 187th St., 10033. Tel: 212-568-7291; Fax: 212-928-2515; Email: m064@adnyeducation.org; Web: www.saintelizabethschool.org. Mr. Jon Frega, Prin. Lay Teachers 15; Students 323.

St. Ignatius Loyola Day Nursery Early Childhood School 240 E. 84th St., 10028. Tel: 212-734-6427; Fax: 212-734-6972; Email: yesaloniad@saintignatiusloyola.org. Ms. Joy Blom, Prin. Lay Teachers 7; Students 56.

St. Ignatius Loyola School (1854) (Grades K-8), 48 E. 84th St., 10028. Tel: 212-861-3820; Fax: 212-879-8248; Email: m074@adnyeducation.org; Web: www.stignatiusloyola.org. Mary Larkin, Prin. Lay Teachers 20; Students 541.

St. Joseph Church - Yorkville School (1880) (Grades PreK-8), 420 E. 87th St., 10128. Tel: 212-289-3057; Fax: 212-289-7239; Email: m082@adnyeducation.org; Web: www.sjyorkville.org. Theresa Bernero, Prin. Lay Teachers 14; Students 346.

St. Mark the Evangelist School (1912) (Partnership) 55 W. 138th St., 10037. Tel: 212-283-4848; Fax: 212-926-0419; Email: m088@adnyeducation.org; Web: www.saintmarkschool.org. Dominic Fanelli, Prin. Lay Teachers 11; Students 260.

St. Paul School (1870) (Grades PreK-8), (Regional) 114 E. 118th St., 10035. Tel: 212-534-0619; Fax: 212-534-3990; Email: m095@adnyeducation.org; Web: www.stpaulschool.us. Dr. Joseph Muscente, Prin. Lay Teachers 13; Students 211; Clergy / Religious Teachers 2.

St. Rose of Lima School (1924) (Grades PreK-8), (Regional) 517 W. 164th St., 10032. Tel: 212-927-1619; Email: m099@adnyeducation.org; Web: www.stroseoflimanyc.org. Joseph DeBona, Prin. Lay Teachers 11; Students 151.

St. Stephen of Hungary School (1918) (Grades PreK-8), 408 E. 82nd St., 10028. Tel: 212-288-1989; Fax: 212-517-5877; Email: m103@adnyeducation.org; Web: www.saintstephenschool.org. Kelly Burke, Prin. Lay Teachers 20; Students 386.

The Epiphany School (1869) (Grades PreK-3), 234 E. 22nd St., 10010. Tel: 212-473-4128; Fax: 212-473-4392; Email: m005@adnyeducation.org; Web: www.theepiphanyschool.org. Kate McHugh, Prin. Lay Teachers 24; Students 384.

Transfiguration School - Lower School (1832) (Grades K-3), Tel: 212-964-8965; Email: m110@adnyeducation.org; Web: www.transfigurationschoolnyc.org. Dr. Patrick Taharally, Prin. Lay Teachers 23; Students 535.

Transfiguration School - Upper School, (Grades 4-8), 37 St. James Pl., 10038. Tel: 212-267-9289; Fax: 212-227-0065; Email: info@transfigurationschoolnyc.org. Dr. Patrick Taharally, Prin. (Lower & Upper Campuses). Lay Teachers 8; Students 236.

BEACON.

Catholic School Region of Dutchess, 60 Liberty St., Beacon, 12508. Tel: 845-831-3073. Mrs. Mary Jane Daley, Supt.

Holy Trinity School (1952) (Grades PreK-8), (Regional) 20 Springside Ave., Poughkeepsie, 12603. Tel: 845-471-0520; Fax: 845-471-0309; Email: d520@adnyschools.org; Web: www.holy-trinity-school.com. Kathleen Spina, Prin. Lay Teachers 12; Students 223.

St. Denis - St. Columba School, (Grades K-8), 849 Rte. 82, P.O. Box 368, Hopewell Junction, 12533. Tel: 845-227-7777; Email: d392@adnyeducation.org. Lay Teachers 11; Sisters 1; Students 211.

St. Martin de Porres School, (Grades PreK-8), 122 Cedar Valley Rd., Poughkeepsie, 12603. Tel: 845-452-4428; Fax: 845-452-9013; Email: d525@adnyeducation.org; Web: www.smdpschool.net. Mrs. Kathleen Leahy, Prin. Lay Teachers 12; Students 446.

St. Mary School (1890 and 1955) (Grades PreK-8), (Regional) Convent Ave., Wappingers Falls, 12590. Tel: 845-297-7500; Fax: 845-297-0886; Email: d555@adnyeducation.org; Web: www.stmarywappingers.org. Mr. Thomas J. Hamilton, Prin. Lay Teachers 10; Students 117.

St. Mary, Mother of the Church School (1955) (Regional) Tel: 845-896-9561; Email: d428@adnyeducation.org; Web: www.stmaryfishkill.org. Ms. Barbara Schwiebert, Prin. Lay Teachers 9; Students 230.

St. Peter School (1844) (Grades PreK-8), (Regional) 12 Fr. Cody Plaza, Poughkeepsie, 12601. Tel: 845-471-6600; Email: d527@adnyeducation.org; Web: www.stpeterschoolpoughkeepsie.com. Susan Troudt, Prin. Lay Teachers 14; Students 249.

The Ark and the Dove School, (Grades PreK-PreK), P.O. Box 1139, Hopewell Junction, 12533. Tel: 845-227-5232; Fax: 845-227-0435; Email: arkdove@adnyeducation.org. Sarah Smith, Prin. Early Childhood Lay Teachers 5; Students 71.

Catholic School Region of Northern Westchester-Putnam, 60 Liberty St., Beacon, 12508. Tel: 845-831-3073.

St. Ann's Peas & Karrots Program, (Grades PreK-K), 25 Eastern Ave., Ossining, 10562. Tel: 914-941-0312; Fax: 914-949-6044; Email: peaskarrots@adnyeducation.org. Ms. Cookie Colucci, Dir. Early Childhood Education Lay Teachers 3; Students 56.

St. Augustine School (1893) (Grades PreK-8), Tel: 914-941-3849; Email: w496@adnyeducation.org; Web: www.staugny.org. Sr. Mary Elizabeth Donoghue, Prin. Lay Teachers 21; Students 437.

St. Columbanus School, (Grades PreK-8), (Regional) Tel: 914-739-1200; Email: w552@adnyeducation.org; Web: www.st-columbanus.com. Carole Arbolino, Prin. Lay Teachers 10; Students 160.

Saint Elizabeth Ann Seton School, (Grades PreK-8), (Regional) 1375 E. Main St., Shrub Oak, 10588. Tel: 914-528-3563; Fax: 914-528-0341; Email: w592@adnyeducation.org; Web: www.seasschool.com. Brian Donohue, Prin. Lay Teachers 10; Students 145.

St. James the Apostle School (1954) (Grades PreK-8), Tel: 845-225-9365; Email: p610@adnyeducation.org; Web: www.edline.net/pages/St_James_the_school. Valerie Crocco, Prin. Lay Teachers 9; Students 145.

St. Patrick School (1956) (Grades PreK-8), (Regional) 483 Old Post Rd., Bedford, 10506. Tel: 914-234-7914; Email: w406@adnyschools.org; Web: www.stpatricksbedford.com. Mrs. Sharyn O'Leary, Prin. Lay Teachers 11; Sisters 1; Students 170.

St. Patrick School (1953) (Grades PreK-8), (Regional) 117 Moseman Rd., Yorktown Heights, 10598. Tel: 914-962-2211; Fax: 914-243-4814; Email: w583@adnyeducation.org; Web: www.stpatricks-yorktown.org. Ms. Rebecca Steck, Prin. Lay Teachers 11; Students 165.

BRONX.

Catholic School Region of Northeast-East Bronx, 2962 Harding Ave., Ste. 401, Bronx, 10465. Tel: 718-892-5359; Email: linda.doughty@archny.org. Mrs. Linda Dougherty, Supt.

Holy Cross School (1923 & 1955) (Grades PreK-8), 1846 Randall Ave., Bronx, 10473. Tel: 718-842-4492; Fax: 718-842-4052; Email: b202@adnyeducation.org; Web: www.holycrossbx.org. Ernie Zalamea, Prin. Lay Teachers 15; Students 363.

Holy Family School (1913) (Regional) 2169 Blackrock Ave., Bronx, 10472. Tel: 718-863-7280; Fax: 718-931-8690; Email: b203@adnyeducation.org; Web: www.hfsny.org. Claire LaTempa, Prin. Lay Teachers 13; Students 267.

Holy Rosary School (1927; 1955) (Grades PreK-8), (Regional) 1500 Arnow Ave., Bronx, 10469. Tel: 718-652-1838; Fax: 718-515-9872; Email: b204@adnyeducation.org; Web: www.holyrosaryschoolbronx.org. Mrs. Maryann Fusco, Prin. Lay Teachers 18; Students 420.

Immaculate Conception School, (Grades PreK-8), (Regional) 760 E. Gun Hill Rd., Bronx, 10467. Tel: 718-547-3346; Fax: 718-547-5505; Email: b207@adnyeducation.org; Web: www.schoolofimmaculateconception.org. Ms. Amy Rodriguez, Prin. Lay Teachers 14; Students 267.

Nativity of Our Blessed Lady School (1953) (Grades PreK-8), (Regional) 3893 Dyre Ave., Bronx, 10466. Tel: 718-324-2188; Fax: 718-324-1128; Email: b208@adnyeducation.org. Douglas Klice, Prin. Lay Teachers 12; Students 194.

Our Lady of Grace School, (Grades PreK-8), (Regional) 3981 Bronxwood Ave., Bronx, 10466. Tel: 718-547-9918; Fax: 718-547-7602; Email: b211@adnyeducation.org; Web: www.olgschoolbronx.com. Richard Helmrich, Prin. Lay Teachers 20; Students 439.

Our Lady of the Assumption School (1928) (Grades PreK-8), (Regional) 1617 Parkview Ave., Bronx, 10461. Tel: 718-829-1706; Fax: 718-931-2693; Email: b210@adnyeducation.org; Web: www.olassumptionbronx.org. John-Paul Barnaba, Prin. Lay Teachers 14; Students 235.

Santa Maria School (1951) (Grades PreK-8), (Regional) 1510 Zerega Ave., Bronx, 10462. Tel: 718-823-3636; Fax: 718-823-7008; Email: b265@adnyeducation.org; Web: https://santamariabronx.org/. Sr. Maureen Flynn,

A.S.C.J., Prin. Lay Teachers 24; Sisters Apostles of the Sacred Heart of Jesus 3; Students 463.

St. Benedict School (1923) (Grades PreK-8), (Regional) 1016 Edison Ave., Bronx, 10465. Tel: 718-829-9557; Fax: 718-319-1898; Email: b230@adnyeducation.org; Web: www.stbenedictschoolbx.org/. Mr. Oriento Vitiello, Prin. Lay Teachers 12; Students 321.

St. Clare of Assisi School (1951) (Grades PreK-8), (Regional) 1911 Hone Ave., Bronx, 10461. Tel: 718-892-4080; Fax: 718-239-1007; Email: b232@adnyschools.org; Web: www.stclareassisischool.org. Theresa Bivona, Prin. Lay Teachers 20; Students 466.

St. Frances de Chantal School (1929) (Grades PreK-8), (Regional) 2962 Harding Ave., Bronx, 10465. Tel: 718-892-5359; Fax: 718-892-6937; Email: b235@adnyeducation.org; Web: www.sfdchantal.org. Sr. Patricia Brito, R.J.M., Prin. Lay Teachers 16; Students 306.

St. Francis of Assisi School, (Grades PreK-8), (Regional) 4300 Baychester Ave., Bronx, 10466. Tel: 718-994-4650; Email: b268@adnyeducation.org; Web: www.sfabx.com. Mark Silva, Prin. Lay Teachers 14; Students 399.

St. Francis Xavier School (1930) (Grades PreK-8), (Regional) 1711 Haight Ave., Bronx, 10461. Tel: 718-863-0531; Fax: 718-319-1152; Email: b237@adnyeducation.org; Web: www.stfrancisxavierbx.com. Mrs. Angela Deegan, Prin. Lay Teachers 14; Students 286.

St. Helena School (1941) (Grades PreK-8), 2050 Benedict Ave., Bronx, 10462. Tel: 718-892-3234; Fax: 718-892-3924; Email: b239@adnyeducation.org; Web: www.sthelenaelementary.com. Richard Meller, Prin. Lay Teachers 15; Students 320.

St. Lucy School (1955) (Grades PreK-8), (Regional) 830 Mace Ave., Bronx, 10467. Tel: 718-882-2203; Fax: 718-547-8351; Email: b246@adnyeducation.org; Web: www.stlucys.org. Mrs. Jane Stefanini, Prin. Lay Teachers 20; Students 480.

St. Raymond School (1860) (Grades PreK-8), 2380 E. Tremont Ave., Bronx, 10462. Tel: 718-597-3232; Fax: 718-892-4449; Email: b258@adnyeducation.org; Web: www.straymondelementary.org. Eugene Scanlon, Prin. Lay Teachers 34; Sisters 4; Students 802.

St. Theresa School (1954) (Grades PreK-8), 2872 St. Theresa Ave., Bronx, 10461. Tel: 718-792-3688; Fax: 718-892-9441; Email: b262@adnyeducation.org; Web: www.sttheresaschoolbronx.org. Mrs. Josephine Fanelli, Prin. Lay Teachers 20; Students 471.

SS. Philip and James School (1953) (Grades PreK-8), (Regional) Tel: 718-882-4576; Email: b255@adnyeducation.org; Web: www.spjschoolbronx.org. Maria Cuomo, Prin. Lay Teachers 12; Students 220.

Villa Maria Academy (1887) (Grades PreK-8), 3335 Country Club Rd., Bronx, 10465. Tel: 718-824-3260; Fax: 718-824-7315; Email: villa@archny.org; Web: www.vma-ny.org. Sr. Teresa Barton, C.N.D., Prin. Congregation of Notre Dame. Lay Teachers 20; Sisters 3; Students 332.

Catholic School Region of the Northwest and South Bronx, 2962 Harding Ave., Bronx, 10465. Tel: 718-597-3134; Fax: 718-597-3678.

Christ the King School, (Grades PreK-8), (Regional) 1345 Grand Concourse, Bronx, 10452. Tel: 718-538-5959; Email: b201@adnyeducation.org. Mr. Steven Iuso, Prin. Lay Teachers 14; Students 282.

Immaculate Conception School (1854) (Grades PreK-8), (Partnership) 378 E. 151st St., Bronx, 10455. Tel: 718-585-4843; Fax: 718-585-6846; Email: b206@adnyeducation.org; Web: www.icsfamily.org. Sr. Patrice Owens, S.C.C., Prin. Lay Teachers 19; Sisters of Christian Charity 3; Students 510.

Our Lady of Mt. Carmel School (1925) (Grades PreK-8), (Regional) 2465-67 Bathgate, Bronx, 10458. Tel: 718-295-6080; Fax: 718-561-5205; Email: b213@adnyeducation.org; Web: wwwmtcarmelschoolbronx.org. Ms. Valerie Savino, Prin. Lay Teachers 17; Students 297.

Our Lady of Refuge School (1923) (Grades PreK-8), 2708 Briggs Ave., Bronx, 10458. Tel: 718-367-3081 ; Fax: 718-367-0741; Email: b215@adnyeducation.org; Web: www.olrbronx.com. Robert W. Billings, Prin. (Regional) Lay Teachers 10; Students 261.

Sacred Heart School (1926) (Grades PreK-8), (Partnership) 95 W. 168th St., Bronx, 10452. Tel: 718-293-4288; Fax: 718-293-4886; Email: b219@adnyeducation.org; Web: www.shhighbridge.org. Abigail Akano, Prin. Lay Teachers 27; Students 451.

St. Angela Merici School (1917) (Grades PreK-8), (Regional) 266 E. 163rd St., Bronx, 10451. Tel: 718-293-3365; Fax: 718-293-6617; Email: b221@adnyeducation.org; Web: www.saintangelamericischool.org. John Bellocchio, Prin. Lay Teachers 25; Students 457.

Preschool (1911) (Regional) 838 Brook Ave., Bronx, 10456. Tel: 718-665-2056. PreK3-PreK4.

St. Anselm School (1908) (Grades PreK-8), Tel: 718-993-9464; Email: b223@adnyeducation.org; Web: www.stanselmbx.org. Ms. Teresa M. Lopes, Prin. Lay Teachers 14; Students 261.

St. Athanasius School (1913) (Grades PreK-8), (Partnership) 830 Southern Blvd., Bronx, 10459. Tel: 718-542-5161; Fax: 718-542-7584; Email: b227@adnyschools.org; Web: www.stathanasiusbronx.org. Mrs. Jessica Aybar, Prin. Lay Teachers 11; Students 309.

St. Brendan School (1912) (Grades PreK-8), (Regional) 268 E. 207th St., Bronx, 10467. Tel: 718-653-2292; Fax: 718-653-3234; Email: b231@adnyeducation.org; Web: www.stbrendanschoolbronx.org. Miss Michele Pasquale, Prin. Lay Teachers 12; Students 380.

St. Gabriel School, (Grades PreK-8), (Regional) 590 W. 235th St., Bronx, 10463. Tel: 718-548-0444; Fax: 718-796-2638; Email: b23@adnyeducation.org; Web: www.saintgabrieldschoolbronx.org. Anthony Naccari, Prin. Lay Teachers 24; Students 263.

Saint Ignatius School, (Grades 6-8), 740 Manida St., Bronx, 10474-5420. Tel: 718-861-9084; Fax: 718-861-9096; Email: info@sis-nativity.org; Email: ignatiusacademy@adnyeducation.org; Web: www.sis-nativity.org. Richard Darrell, Prin. Lay Teachers 8; Students 79.

St. John School (1903) (Grades PreK-8), (Regional) 3143 Kingsbridge Ave., Bronx, 10463. Tel: 718-548-0255; Fax: 718-548-0864; Email: b242@adnyeducation.org; Web: www.stjohnschoolbronx.org. Melissa Moore, Prin. Lay Teachers 12; Students 252.

St. John Chrysostom School (1914) (Grades PreK-8), 1144 Hoe Ave., Bronx, 10459. Tel: 718-328-7226; Fax: 718-378-5368; Email: b243@adnyeducation.org; Web: www.sjcbronx.org. Sr. Mary Elizabeth Mooney, O.P., Prin. Lay Teachers 14; Sisters of St. Dominic (Sparkill, NY) 3; Students 319.

St. Joseph School (Regional) 1946 Bathgate Ave., Bronx, 10457. Tel: 718-583-9432; Fax: 718-299-0780; Email: info@saintjosephschoolbronx.org; Web: www.saintjosephschool.org. Ms. Carmen Lopez. Lay Teachers 11; Students 198.

St. Luke School (1910) (Grades PreK-8), (Regional) 608 E. 139th St., Bronx, 10454. Tel: 718-585-0380; Fax: 718-665-3407; Email: b247@adnyeducation.org; Web: www.stluke138.org. Tracey Coleman, Prin. Lay Teachers 11; Sisters of St. Dominic (Blauvelt) 1; Students 232.

St. Margaret Mary School (1923) (Grades PreK-8), 121 E. 177th St., Bronx, 10453-5901. Tel: 718-731-5905; Fax: 718-731-8924; Email: b249@adnyeducation.org; Web: www.stmargaretmaryschoo.net. Sr. Ann Bivona, Prin. Lay Teachers 12; Sisters of Mercy of the Americas 1; Students 235.

St. Margaret of Cortona School (1926) (Grades PreK-8), (Regional) 452 W. 260th St., Bronx, 10471. Tel: 718-549-8580; Fax: 718-884-3298; Email: b248@adnyeducation.org; Web: www.smcsriverdale.org. Mr. Hugh Keenan, Prin. Lay Teachers 13; Students 272.

St. Nicholas of Tolentine School (1907) (Grades K-8), (Regional) 2336 Andrews Ave., Bronx, 10468. Tel: 718-364-5110; Fax: 718-561-3964; Email: b253@adnyeducation.org; Web: www.sntschoolny.org. Lay Teachers 9; Students 152.

St. Philip Neri School (1913) (Grades PreK-8), (Regional) 3031 Grand Concourse, Bronx, 10468. Tel: 718-365-8806; Email: b256@adnyeducation.org; Web: www.school.stphilipneribronx.org. Ajai Beebe, Prin. Lay Teachers 15; Students 338.

St. Simon Stock School, (Grades PreK-8), (Regional) 2195 Valentine Ave., Bronx, 10457. Tel: 718-367-0453; Fax: 718-733-1441; Email: tbraswell@stsimonstockschool.org; Web: www.stsimonstockschool.org. Tara Braswell, Prin. Lay Teachers 13; Students 256.

St. Thomas Aquinas School (1907) (Grades PreK-8), (Regional) 1909 Daly Ave., Bronx, 10460. Tel: 718-893-7600; Fax: 718-378-5531; Email: b263@adnyeducation.org; Web: www.staschoolbx.org. Jessica Perez-Maldonado, Prin. Lay Teachers 11; Students 188.

FLORIDA.

Catholic School Region of Ulster-Sullivan-Orange, 19 Glenmere Ave., Florida, 10921. Tel: 845-508-6628; Fax: 845-508-6632.

Bishop Dunn Memorial School, (Grades PreK-8), 50 Gidney Ave., Newburgh, 12550. Tel: 845-569-3494; Fax: 845-569-3303; Email: bishdunn@adnyeducation.org; Web: www.bdms.org. Mrs. Nancy Benfer, Devel. Coord. & Asst. Prin. Dominican Sisters of Hope. Lay Teachers 11; Students 198.

Most Precious Blood School (Regional) 180 Ulster Ave., Walden, 12586. Tel: 845-778-3028; Fax: 845-778-3785; Email: mpbschool180@gmail.com; Email: or554@adnyeducation.org; Web: www.mpbschool.org. Woodrow Hallaway, Prin. Lay Teachers 11; Students 136.

Nora Cronin Presentation Academy, (Grades 5-8), 69 Bay View Terr., Newburgh, 12550-6004. Tel: 845-567-0708; Fax: 845-567-0709; Email: presentationacad@ncpany.org; Email: ncpa@adnyeducation.org; Web: www.noracroninpresentationacademy.org. Sr. Yliana Hernandez, P.B.V.M., Contact Person, Pres., Prin. Lay Teachers 3; Sisters 2; Students 59.

Our Lady of Mt. Carmel School (Regional) 205 Wawayanda Ave., Middletown, 10940. Tel: 845-343-8836; Fax: 845-342-1404. Jennifer Langford, Prin. Lay Teachers 11; Students 155.

Sacred Heart Church School (1964) (Grades PreK-8), (Regional) Tel: 845-783-0365; Email: or468@adnyeducation.org; Web: www.sacredheartmonroe.net. Catherine Muenkel, Prin. Lay Teachers 10; Students 201.

Sacred Heart School (1951) (Grades PreK-8), (Regional) 148 Windsor Hwy., New Windsor, 12553. Tel: 845-561-1433; Fax: 845-561-4383; Email: or486@adnyeducation.org; Web: www.shsnewburgh.org. Ms. Erin Contrady. Lay Teachers 9; Religious 1; Students 141.

St. John School, (Grades PreK-8), (Regional) 77 Murray Ave., Goshen, 10924. Tel: 845-294-6434; Fax: 845-294-7303; Email: sjsoffice@saintjohngoshen.org; Email: or433@adnyeducation.org; Web: www.saintjohngoshen.org. Mr. Dustyn Cormier, Prin. Lay Teachers 10; Students 151.

St. Stephen - St. Edward School, (Grades PreK-8), (Regional) Tel: 845-986-3533; Email: or556@adnyeducation.org; Web: ststephen-stedward.org. Bethany Negersmith, Prin. Lay Teachers 12; Students 171.

Kingston Catholic School (1867) (Grades PreK-8), (Regional) Web: www.kingstoncatholic.org. Jill Albert, Pres.; Jodi Vines, Vice Prin. Lay Teachers 10; Students 254.

Kingston Catholic Elementary School, (Grades PreK-4), 159 Broadway, Kingston, 12401. Tel: 845-331-9318; Fax: 845-331-2674; Email: ul452@adnyeducation.org.

Kingston Catholic Middle School (1869) (Grades 5-8), 235 Wall St., Kingston, 12401. Tel: 845-339-4390; Fax: 845-339-7994; Email: kcscommunication@kingstoncatholic.org.

NANUET.

Catholic School Region of Rockland, 32 W. Nyack Rd., Nanuet, 10954. Tel: 845-623-3504; Fax: 845-623-1550.

Sacred Heart School (1909) (Regional) 60 Washington Ave., Suffern, 10901. Tel: 845-357-1684; Fax: 845-357-0318; Email: rk539@adnyeducation.org; Web: www.sacredheartschoolsuffern.com. Mrs. Kathleen Grande, Prin. Lay Teachers 10; Students 269.

St. Anthony School (1953) (Grades PreK-8), (Regional) 34 W. Nyack Rd., Nanuet, 10954. Tel: 845-623-2311; Fax: 845-623-0055; Email: office@stanthonyschoolnanuet.org; Email: rk480@adnyeducation.org; Web: www.stanthonyschoolnanuet.org. Dr. Andrea Caputo, Prin. Lay Teachers 10; Sisters 3; Students 179.

St. Gregory Barbarigo School (Regional) 29 Cinder Rd., Garnerville, 10923. Tel: 845-947-1330; Fax: 845-947-4392; Email: rk431@adnyeducation.org; Web: www.stgregorybarbarigoschool.org. Mrs. Dana Spicer, Prin. Lay Teachers 10; Sisters of St. Dominic (Sparkill) 2; Students 205.

St. Margaret School (1953) (Grades PreK-8), (Regional) 34 N. Magnolia St., Pearl River, 10965. Tel: 845-735-2855; Fax: 845-735-0131; Email: rk499@adnyschools.org; Web: www.saintmargaretschool.com. Patricia Maldonado, Prin. Lay Teachers 11; Students 244.

St. Paul School, (Grades PreK-8), (Regional) 365 Kings Hwy., Valley Cottage, 10989. Tel: 914-268-6506; Fax: 914-268-1809; Email: rk417@adnyeducation.org; Web: www.saintpaulschoolvc.org. Rev. Michelle Pitot, Prin. Lay Teachers 11; Sisters 1; Students 209.

RYE.

Catholic School Region of Central Westchester, 86 Mayflower Avenue., New Rochelle, 10801. Tel: 914-481-5993. Mrs. Noelle Beale, Supt.

Annunciation School (1943) (Grades PreK-8), 465 Westchester Ave., Crestwood, 10707. Tel: 914-337-8760; Fax: 914-337-8878; Email: w419@adnyeducation.org; Web: www.school.annunciationcrestwood.com. Mrs. Rose Ragone, Prin. Lay Teachers 21; Sisters 2; Students 431.

Corpus Christi - Holy Rosary School (1959) (Grades

PreK-8), (Regional) 135 S. Regent St., Port Chester, 10573. Tel: 914-937-4407; Fax: 914-937-6904; Email: w513m@adnyeducation.org; Web: www.cchrs.org. Sr. Lise Parent, Pres.; Mrs. Deirdre McDermott, Prin. Lay Teachers 10; Sisters, Daughters of Mary Help of Christians 2; Students 239.

Holy Name of Mary Montessori School, (Grades PreK-K), Tel: 914-271-5182; Email: hnom@adnyeducation.org. Jeanne-Marie Gagnon, Dir. Early Childhood Lay Teachers 2; Students 26.

Immaculate Conception School (1913) (Grades PreK-8), (Regional) Tel: 914-961-3785; Email: w549@adnyeducation.org; Web: www.icschoolonline.org. Ms. Maureen J. Harten, Prin. Lay Teachers 13; Students 241.

Immaculate Heart of Mary School (1928) (Grades PreK-8), 201 Boulevard, Scarsdale, 10583. Tel: 914-723-5608; Fax: 914-723-8004; Email: w534@adnyeducation.org; Web: www.ihmscarsdale.org. Mrs. Teresa Sopot, Prin. Lay Teachers 12; Students 222.

Iona Grammar School, (Grades PreK-8), (Boys) 173 Stratton Rd., New Rochelle, 10804. Tel: 914-633-7744; Fax: 914-235-6338; Email: jblanco@ionagrammer.com; Web: www.ionagrammar.com. Mr. Joseph Blanco, Prin. Lay Teachers 10; Students 194.

Our Lady of Mt. Carmel School (1929) (Grades PreK-8), Tel: 914-592-7575; Email: w427@adnyeducation.org; Web: www.olmcelmsford.com. Sr. Mary Healy, Prin. Lay Teachers 11; Sisters 1; Students 172.

Our Lady of Perpetual Help School (1957) (Grades PreK-8), 575 Fowler Ave., Pelham Manor, 10803. Tel: 914-738-5158; Email: w502@adnyeducation.org. Paul Henshaw, Prin. Lay Teachers 10; Students 157.

Our Lady of Sorrows School (1957) (Grades K-8), 888 Mamaroneck Ave., White Plains, 10605. Tel: 914-761-0124; Fax: 914-761-0176; Email: w561@adnyeducation.org; Web: www.olsschoolwp.com. Sr. Marie Cecile, R.D.C., Prin. Lay Teachers 10; Students 206.

Our Lady of Victory School (1898) (Grades PreK-8), (Regional) 38 N. Fifth Ave., Mount Vernon, 10550. Tel: 914-667-4063; Fax: 914-665-3135; Email: w475@adnyeducation.org; Web: www.ourladyofvictoryschool.org. Helena Castilla-Byrne, Prin. Lay Teachers 15; Students 363.

Resurrection Grammar School (1906) (Grades PreK-8), 116 Milton Rd., Rye, 10580. Tel: 914-967-1218; Fax: 914-925-3511; Email: w532@adnyeducation.org; Web: www.resurrectionschool.com. Gina M. Fonte. Lay Teachers 21; Students 325.

Sacred Heart Grade School (1893) (Grades PreK-8), (Regional) Tel: 914-963-5318; Email: w571@adnyeducation.org; Web: www.shgsyonkers.org. Casimiro Cibelli, Prin. Lay Teachers 14; Students 333.

Sacred Heart School (1953) (Grades PreK-8), (Regional) 59 Wilson St., Hartsdale, 10530. Tel: 914-946-7242; Fax: 914-946-7323; Email: w437@adnyeducation.org; Web: www.shshartsdale.org. Christopher Siegfried, Prin. Lay Teachers 10; Students 184.

St. Ann School, (Grades PreK-8), (Regional) 40 Brewster Ave., Yonkers, 10701. Tel: 914-965-4333; Fax: 914-965-1778; Email: w572@adnyeducation.org; Web: www.stannschoolyonkers.org. Mr. Michael Vicario, Prin. Lay Teachers 11; Students 172.

St. Anthony School, (Grades PreK-8), (Regional) 1395 Nepperhan Ave., Yonkers, 10703. Tel: 914-476-8489; Fax: 914-965-7939; Email: w482@adnyeducation.org; Web: www.stanthonyschoolyonkers.org. Mrs. Elizabeth Carney, Prin. Lay Teachers 15; Students 278.

St. Barnabas School (1912) (Grades PreK-8), (Regional) 413 E. 241st St., Bronx, 10470. Tel: 718-324-1088; Fax: 718-324-2397; Email: B229@adnyschools.org; Web: www.stbarnabasschool.org. Jonathan Morano, Prin. Lay Teachers 17; Students 373.

St. Eugene School (1951) (Grades PreK-8), 707 Tuckahoe Rd., Yonkers, 10710. Tel: 914-779-2956; Fax: 914-779-7668; Email: w577@adnyeducation.org. Joan Fox, Prin. Lay Teachers 12; Students 204.

St. John the Baptist School (1954) (Grades PreK-8), Tel: 914-965-2356; Email: w578@adnyeducation.org; Web: www.sjbyonkers.org/sjbschool. Sr. Maryalice Reamer, Prin. Lay Teachers 9; Sisters 1; Students 304.

St. Joseph School (1951) (Grades K-8), 30 Meadow Ave., Bronxville, 10708. Tel: 914-337-0261; Fax: 914-395-1192; Email: w410@adnyeducation.org; Web: www.saintjosephbronxville.org. Mrs. Mary Ellen Sanchez, Prin. Lay Teachers 13; Students 216.

St. Paul the Apostle School (1949) (Grades PreK-8), (Regional) 77 Lee Ave., Yonkers, 10705. Tel: 914-965-2165; Fax: 914-965-5792; Email: w581@adnyeducation.org; Web: www.stpaultheapostleschoolyonkers.org. Grace Mallardi, Prin. Lay Teachers 10; Students 171.

St. Peter School (1894 and 1955) (Grades PreK-8), (Regional) 204 Hawthorne Ave., Yonkers, 10705. Tel: 914-963-2314; Fax: 914-966-8822; Email: w582@adnyeducation.org; Web: www.stpetersny.com. Sheila Alagia, Prin. Lay Teachers 12; Students 223.

SS. John and Paul School (1952) (Grades PreK-8), Tel: 914-834-6332; Email: w457@adnyeducation.org; Web: www.sjpschool.org. Fatima Carvalho-Gianni, Prin. Lay Teachers 19; Students 636.

The Little Disciple Learning Center, Inc., 348 S. Lexington Ave., White Plains, 10606. Tel: 914-949-2111; Email: littledisciple@adnyeducation.org. Jennifer Frias, Dir. Lay Teachers 6; Total Enrollment 81.

Transfiguration School (1949) (Grades PreK-8), (Regional) 40 Prospect Ave., Tarrytown, 10591. Tel: 914-631-3737; Fax: 914-631-6640; Email: w545@adnyeducatio.org; Web: www.transfigurationschool.org. Margaret Kazan. Lay Teachers 11; Students 169.

STATEN ISLAND.

Catholic School Region of Staten Island, 2820 Amboy Rd., Staten Island, 10306. Tel: 718-667-5350, Ext. 1006; Fax: 718-351-3427.

Academy of St. Dorothy (1932) (Grades PreK-8), 1305 Hylan Blvd., Staten Island, 10305. Tel: 718-351-0939; Fax: 718-351-0661; Email: dorothy@adnyeducation.org; Email: srsharon@adnyeducation.org; Web: www.ny02224597.schoolswire.net. Sr. Sharon A. McCarthy, S.S.D., Prin. Lay Teachers 10; Sisters of St. Dorothy 1; Students 240.

Blessed Sacrament School (1917) (Grades PreK-8), (Regional) 830 Delafield Ave., Staten Island, 10310. Tel: 718-442-3090; Fax: 718-442-9654; Email: si301@adnyeducation.org; Web: www.blessedsacramentsi.com. Mr. Joseph Cocozello, Prin. Lay Teachers 22; Sisters 1; Students 544.

Holy Child Pre-School, 747 Amboy Rd., Staten Island, 10312. Tel: 718-356-5159; Fax: 718-356-1933. JoAnn Gaal, Prin. Lay Teachers 7; Students 220.

Holy Rosary School (1955) (Grades PreK-8), (Regional) 100 Jerome Ave., Staten Island, 10305. Tel: 718-447-1195; Fax: 718-815-5862; Email: si302@adnyeducation.org; Web: www.holyrosaryschoolsi.org. Ann Major, Prin. Lay Teachers 15; Students 217.

Notre Dame Academy - Elementary School (1903) (Grades PreK-8), 78 Howard Ave., Staten Island, 10301. Tel: 718-273-9096; Fax: 718-273-1093; Email: ntdames@adnyeducation.org; Web: www.notredameacademy.org. Mrs. Rebecca Signorelli, Prin. Congregation of Notre Dame. Lay Teachers 13; Students 219.

Our Lady Help of Christians School (1910 and 1955) (Grades PreK-8), (Regional) 23 Summit St., Staten Island, 10307. Tel: 718-984-1360; Fax: 718-966-9356; Email: si305@adnyeducation.org; Web: www.olhcschoolsi.org. Mrs. Rosaria Mincher, Prin. Lay Teachers 10; Students 146.

Our Lady of Good Counsel School (1923) (Grades PreK-8), 42 Austin Pl., Staten Island, 10304. Tel: 718-447-7260; Fax: 718-447-8639; Email: si304@adnyschools.org; Web: www.goodcounselsch.org. Mrs. Tara Hynes, Prin. Lay Teachers 11; Students 300.

Our Lady of Mount Carmel - St. Benedicta School (Regional) 285 Clove Rd., Staten Island, 10310. Tel: 718-981-5131; Fax: 718-981-0027; Email: si306@adnyedu.org; Web: www.olmcsb.org. Stephen Sanchez, Prin. Lay Teachers 10; Students 170.

Our Lady, Queen of Peace School (1924) (Grades PreK-8), (Regional) 22 Steele Ave., Staten Island, 10306. Tel: 718-351-0370; Fax: 718-351-0950; Email: si307@adnyeducation.org; Web: www.olqpsi.com. Miss Margaret Annunziata, Prin. Lay Teachers 18; Students 349.

Our Lady Star of the Sea School (1959) (Grades PreK-8), 5411 Amboy Rd., Staten Island, 10312. Tel: 718-984-5750; Email: si309@adnyeducation.org; Web: www.oss-si.org. Jeanine Roland, Prin. Lay Teachers 21; Students 621.

Sacred Heart School (1875) (Grades PreK-8), (Regional) 301 N. Burgher Ave., Staten Island, 10310. Tel: 718-442-0347; Fax: 718-442-6978; Email: si310@adnyeducation.org; Web: sacredheartschoolsi.org. Ms. Celeste Catalano, Prin. Lay Teachers 13; Students 257.

St. Adalbert School (1905) (Grades PreK-8), (Regional) 355 Morningstar Rd., Staten Island, 10303. Tel: 718-442-2020; Fax: 718-447-2012; Email: si311@adnyeducation.org; Web: www.stadalbertschool.com. Diane Hesterhagen, Prin. Lay Teachers 11; Students 193.

St. Ann School (1955) (Grades PreK-8), (Regional) 125 Cromwell Ave., Staten Island, 10304. Tel: 718-351-4343; Email: si312@adnyeducation.org; Web: www.stannschoolstatenisland.com. Mrs. Bernadette Ficchi, Prin. Lay Teachers 12; Students 245.

St. Charles School, (Grades PreK-8), (Regional) 200 Penn Ave., Staten Island, 10306. Tel: 718-987-0200; Fax: 718-987-8158; Email: si314@adnyschools.org; Web: www.saintcharlesschoolsi.org. Mr. John Kiernan, Prin. Lay Teachers 22; Students 469.

St. Christopher School (1930) (Grades PreK-8), (Regional) 15 Lisbon Pl., Staten Island, 10306. Tel: 718-351-0902; Fax: 718-351-0975; Email: si315@adnyeducation.org; Web: www.stchristophersi.com. Catherine Falabella, Prin. Lay Teachers 12; Students 256.

St. Clare School, (Grades PreK-8), 151 Lindenwood Rd., Staten Island, 10308. Tel: 718-984-7091; Fax: 718-227-5052; Email: si316@adnyeducation.org; Web: www.stclaresi.com. Theresa Signorile, Prin. Lay Teachers 22; Students 671.

St. Joseph and St. Thomas School, (Grades PreK-8), 50 Maguire Ave., Staten Island, 10309. Tel: 718-356-3344; Fax: 718-227-9531; Email: si320@adnyeducation.org; Web: www.ststsjn.org/school. Mary Ellen Cilento, Prin. Lay Teachers 10; Students 163.

St. Joseph Hill Academy Elementary School (1919) (Grades PreK-8), 850 Hylan Blvd., Staten Island, 10305. Tel: 718-981-1187; Fax: 718-448-7016; Email: joshiles@adnyschools.org; Web: www.stjosephhill.org. Lawrence Hansen, Prin. Lay Teachers 16; Students 507.

St. Patrick School (1919) (Grades PreK-8), Tel: 718-979-8815; Fax: 718-979-9002; Email: schooloffice@stpatrickssi.org; Email: si325@adnyeducation.org; Web: www.school.stpatrickssi.org. Vincent Sadowski, Prin. Lay Teachers 16; Students 393.

St. Peter - St. Paul School, (Grades PreK-8), (Regional) 129 Clinton Ave., Staten Island, 10301. Tel: 718-447-1796; Fax: 718-447-4240; Email: si327@adnyeducation.org; Email: jolivera@stpeterstpaulschoolsi.org; Web: www.stpeterstpaulschoolsi.org. Mrs. Jennifer Olivera, Prin. Lay Teachers 13; Students 228.

St. Rita School (1922) (Grades PreK-8), (Regional) 30 Wellbrook Ave., Staten Island, 10314. Tel: 718-761-2504; Fax: 718-761-0014; Email: si328@adnyeducation.org; Web: www.stritaschoolsi.org. Nicole C. Fresca, Prin. Lay Teachers 12; Sisters 1; Students 209.

St. Teresa School (1955) (Grades PreK-8), (Regional) 1632 Victory Blvd., Staten Island, 10314. Tel: 718-448-9650; Tel: 718-447-6426; Email: si332@education.org; Web: www.stteresaschoolsi.org. Mrs. Rita Azzopardi, Prin. Lay Teachers 12; Students 238.

[E] HIGH SCHOOLS

NEW YORK. *All Hallows Institute* aka All Hallows High School (1909) (Boys) 111 E. 164th St., Bronx, 10452. Tel: 718-293-4545; Fax: 718-410-8298; Email: hallows@adnyeducation.org; Web: www.allhallows.org. Mr. Sean J. Sullivan, Prin.; Mr. Ronald Schutte, Pres. Congregation of Christian Sisters & Brothers 3; Lay Teachers 36; Students 574.

Aquinas High School (Girls) 685 E. 182nd St., Bronx, 10457. Tel: 718-367-2113; Fax: 718-295-5864; Email: aquinashs@adnyeducation.org; Web: www.aquinashs.org. Anna Parra, Pres.; Sr. Catherine Rose Quigley, O.P., Prin. Lay Teachers 16; Sisters 4; Students 286.

Cathedral High School (Girls) 350 E. 56th St., 10022. Tel: 212-688-1545; Fax: 212-754-2024; Email: cathedhs@adnyeducation.org; Web: www.cathedralhs.org. Ms. Maria Spagnuolo, Prin.; Mrs. Rosemary Eivers, Asst. Prin. Lay Teachers 38; Sisters 4; Students 539.

Convent of the Sacred Heart (Girls) One E. 91st St., 10128-0689. Tel: 212-722-4745; Fax: 212-996-1784; Email: coshhs@adnyeducation.org; Web: www.cshnyc.org. Dr. Joseph J. Ciancaglini, Head of School; Angela Carstensen, Librarian. Religious of the Sacred Heart. Lay Teachers 125; High School Students 236.

**Cristo Rey New York High School, Inc.* (2004) 112 E. 106th St., 10029. Tel: 212-996-7000; Fax: 212-427-7444; Email: cristorey@adnyeducation.org; Web: www.cristoreyny.org. Rev. Joseph P. Parkes, S.J., Pres.; William P. Ford III, Prin.; Catalina Gutierrez, Dir. Corp. Work Study Prog. Lay Teachers 125; Jesuit 1; Students 236.

Cristo Rey New York Corporate Work Study Program, Inc., 112 E. 106th St., 10029.

Tel: 212-996-7000; Fax: 212-427-7444; Email: wporcaro@cristoreyny.org; Web: www.cristoreyny.org. Catalina Gutierrez, Mng. & Sales Dir. Lay Teachers 57; Students 354.

Dominican Academy (Girls) 44 E. 68th St., 10065. Tel: 212-744-0195; Fax: 212-744-0375; Email: dominica@adnyeducation.org; Web: www.dominicanacademy.org. Sr. Margaret Ormond, O.P., Pres.; Nicole Grimes, Ph.D., Prin.; Murielle Louis, Librarian. Brothers 1; Lay Teachers 40; Dominican Sisters 5; Students 230.

St. Jean Baptiste High School, 173 E. 75th St., 10021. Tel: 212-288-1645; Fax: 212-288-6540; Email: bapt@adnyeducation.org; Web: www.stjean.org. Sr. Maria Cassano, C.N.D., Prin. (Girls High School) Lay Teachers 20; Sisters of the Congregation of Notre Dame 3; Students 349.

La Salle Academy (Boys) 215 E. 6th St., 10003. Tel: 212-475-8940; Fax: 212-529-3598; Email: lasalle@adnyeducation.org; Web: www.lasalleacademy.org. Catherine Guerriero, Pres.; Ms. Kerry Conroy, Prin., (Retired); Ms. Patricia Toney, Librarian. Brothers of The Christian Schools. Brothers 2; Lay Teachers 4; Students 341. In Res. Bros. William Johnson; Peter Nguyen, F.S.C.; Richard Galvin, F.S.C.; Anwar Martinez, F.S.C.

Loyola School (Coed) 980 Park Ave., 10028. Tel: 212-288-3522; Fax: 212-861-1021; Email: loyola@adnyeducation.org; Web: www.loyola-nyc.org. Mr. Robert Sheehy, Bd. Chm.; Tony Oroszlany, Pres.; Revs. Hernan Paredes Carrera, S.J.; Michael E. Sehler, S.J.; Adam Lewis, Prin. Society of Jesus. Lay Teachers 26; Priests 2; Students 208.

Marymount School, (Grades 9-12), 1026 Fifth Ave., 10028. Tel: 212-744-4486; Fax: 212-744-0163; Email: marymths@adnyeducation.org; Web: www.marymountnyc.org. Concepcion Alvar, B.S., M.A., Head of School; Carolyn Booth, Dir. Admissions; Alexis Bradford, Dir. Finance; Nora Gibson, Dir. School Affairs; Annah Jones, Head Librarian. Religious of the Sacred Heart of Mary. Lay Teachers 133; Sisters 2; Students 247.

Notre Dame School of Manhattan (1912) (Girls) 327 W. 13th St., 10014. Tel: 212-620-5575; Fax: 212-620-0432; Email: ntdamehs@adnyeducation.org; Web: www.cheznous.org. Ms. Jaclyn Brilliant, Prin.; Sr. Virginia O'Brien, Pres.; Ms. Andrea Catenaccio, Librarian. Lay Teachers 18; Sisters 1; Students 344.

Regis High School (1914) (Boys) 55 E. 84th St., 10028. Tel: 212-288-1100; Email: regishs@adnyeducation.org; Email: dallison@regis.org; Web: www.regis.org. Rev. Daniel K. Lahart, S.J., Pres.; Dr. Gary J. Tocchet, Prin.; Rev. Ian R. Gibbons, S.J., Asst. Prin.; Mr. Kyle Mullins, Dean, Students; Revs. Mark J Lane, C.O., Campus Min.; Anthony Andreassi, C.O.; Arthur C. Bender, S.J.; Mario M. Powell, S.J.; Mrs. Diane Del Priore, Librarian; Mr. Donald Allison, Vice Pres. Society of Jesus. Lay Teachers 40; Students 534.

Residence, Res.: 53 E. 83rd St., 10028. Tel: 212-288-1100; Fax: 212-794-1221; Email: fpellegrini@jesuits.org. Rev. Daniel K. Lahart, S.J., Pres.

St. Vincent Ferrer High School, 151 E. 65th St., 10065-6607. Tel: 212-535-4680; Fax: 212-988-3455; Email: vincferr@adnyeducation.org; Web: www.saintvincentferrer.com. Sr. Gail Morgan, O.P., Prin. Girls 500; Lay Teachers 27; Dominican Sisters of Our Lady of the Springs 5; Students 500; Clergy / Religious Teachers 1.

Xavier High School (Boys) 30 W. 16th St., 10011. Tel: 212-924-7900; Fax: 212-924-0303; Email: xavierhs@adnyeducation.org; Web: www.xavierhs.org. Mr. John R. Raslowsky II, Pres.; Mr. Michael LiVigni, Headmaster; Rev. John Replogle, S.J., Asst. to Pres. & Alumni Chap.; Mr. Luciano Lovallo, Dean, Academics; Ms. Lindsay Willert, Registrar; Revs. Ralph Rivera, S.J., School Chap.; Louis T. Garaventa, S.J., History & Religion Depts.; James J. Hederman, S.J., Religion Dept.; Tracy Tong, Librarian; Kevin Jacobsen, Dean, Faculty; Rev. Vincent L. Biagi, S.J., Dir., Engagement. Society of Jesus.(See listing for Xavier Jesuit Community for additional names of priests and brothers.) Lay Teachers 75; Students 1,067; Clergy / Religious Teachers 4.

BARDONIA. *Albertus Magnus*, 798 Rte. 304, Bardonia, 10954. Tel: 845-623-8842; Fax: 845-623-0009; Email: albertus@adnyeducation.org; Web: www.albertus.edu. Mr. Robert J. Gomprecht, Pres.; Mr. Christopher Power, Prin. Lay Teachers 33; Sisters of St. Dominic (Sparkill) 1; Students 498.

BRONX. *Academy of Mount St. Ursula* (1855) (Girls) 330 Bedford Park Blvd., Bronx, 10458. Tel: 718-364-5353; Fax: 718-364-2354; Email: mtstursu@adnyeducation.org; Web: www.amsu.org. Sr. Jean Marie Humphries, O.S.U., Ph.D., Prin. Lay Teachers 25; Sisters 3; Students 321.

St. Barnabas High School, 425 E. 240th St., Bronx, 10470. Tel: 718-325-8820; Email: barnabas@adnyeducation.org; Web: www.stbarnabashigh.com. Mrs. Theresa Napoli, Prin. Lay Teachers 14; Nuns 1; Students 218.

Cardinal Hayes High School (Boys). 650 Grand Concourse, Bronx, 10451. Tel: 718-292-6100; Fax: 718-292-9178; Email: hayes@adnyeducation.org; Web: www.cardinalhayes.org. Mr. William D. Lessa, Prin.; Rev. Joseph P. Tierney, M.Div., Pres. Brothers 3; Lay Teachers 54; Students 948. In Res. Faculty Bro. William Sherlog, C.F.C. In Res. Revs. Emmanuel Okpalauwaekwe; James Sheehan; Thomas Mestriparampil; Bro. Tyrone Davis, C.F.C.

Cardinal Spellman High School, One Cardinal Spellman Pl., Bronx, 10466. Tel: 718-881-8000; Fax: 718-515-6615; Email: dokeefe@cardinalspellman.org; Email: ehealy@cardinalspellman.org; Email: spellman1@adnyeducation.org; Web: www.cardinalspellman.org. Mr. Daniel O'Keefe, Pres./Prin.; Revs. John R. Kraljic, (Retired); John T. Monaghan; James J. O'Shaughnessy, (Retired); Peter R. Pilsner; Kathy Steves, Librarian; Maria Piri, Asst. Prin. & Dir. Giuidance; Elizabeth Healy, Vice Pres. Finance; Jennifer Rivera Velez, Vice Pres. Advancement; Collin Smith, Dean, Students; Delia Rivera, Dir. Annual Giving. Lay Teachers 78; Priests 4; Sisters 1; Students 1,363.

St. Catharine Academy (1889) (Girls) 2250 Williamsbridge Rd., Bronx, 10469-4891. Tel: 718-882-2882; Fax: 718-231-9099; Email: catherin@adnyeducation.org; Web: www.scahs.org. Sisters Ann M. Welch, R.S.M., Prin.; Patricia Wolf, R.S.M., Pres.; Christina Antico, Librarian. Lay Teachers 27; Sisters 4; Students 469.

Fordham Preparatory School (1841) (Boys) 441 E. Fordham Rd., Bronx, 10458. Tel: 718-367-7500; Fax: 718-367-7598; Email: fordhamprep@adnyeducation.org; Web: www.fordhamprep.org. Rev. Christopher Devron, S.J., Pres.; Dr. Joseph Petriello, Prin.; Mr. Dennis M. Ahern, Asst. Prin.; Mr. Steven Pettus, Dean of Students; Mrs. Maureen Martinez, Dir. Guidance; Rev. John M. Costello, S.J.; Brian Carney, Vice Pres. Mission & Identity; Revs. Stanley J. O'Konsky, S.J.; Charles D. Sullivan, S.J.; Raymond M. Sweitzer, S.J.; Mr. Michael Higgins, Treas. Lay Teachers 68; Priests 3; Students 1,009; Clergy / Religious Teachers 6.

Msgr. Scanlan High School (1949) (Coed) (Independent) 915 Hutchinson River Pkwy., Bronx, 10465. Tel: 718-430-0100; Fax: 718-892-8845; Email: scanlan@adnyeducation.org; Web: www.scanlanhs.edu. Dr. Peter Doran, Prin. Lay Teachers 27; Students 460.

Mount St. Michael Academy, (Grades 6-12), (Boys) 4300 Murdock Ave., Bronx, 10466. Tel: 718-515-6400; Fax: 718-994-7729; Email: mount@adnyschools.org; Web: www.mountstmichael.org. Mr. Peter Corritori, Pres. & CEO; Bro. Stephen Schlitte, F.M.S., Prin.; Sr. Joan Whittle, O.P., Librarian; Bro. Brian Poulin, F.M.S., Campus Min.; Nina Lokar, Campus Min.; Clare Brewster, Asst. Prin., Academics; Mr. James Burke, Asst. Prin., Discipline (Grades 6-9); Mr. Walter Stompfil, Asst. Prin., Discipline (Grades 9-12). Brothers 3; Lay Teachers 41; Students 747.

Preston High School (1947) (Girls) 2780 Schurz Ave., Bronx, 10465. Tel: 718-863-9134; Fax: 718-863-6125; Email: preston@adnyeducation.org; Web: www.prestonhs.org. Mrs. Jane Grendell, Prin.; Cynthia Chambers, Asst. Prin.; Sr. Loretta Marie Schollhamer, R.D.C., Librarian. Lay Teachers 32; Sisters of the Divine Compassion 1; Students 482.

St. Raymond High School (Girls) 1725 Castle Hill Ave., Bronx, 10462. Tel: 718-824-4220; Fax: 718-829-3571; Email: rayacad@adnyschools.org; Web: www.saintraymondacademy.org. Sr. Mary Ann D'Antonio, S.C., Prin. Lay Teachers 20; Sisters 2; Students 330.

St. Raymond High School for Boys (Boys) 2151 St. Raymond Ave., Bronx, 10462. Tel: 718-824-5050; Fax: 718-863-8808; Email: rayhsboy@adnyeducation.org; Web: www.straymondhighschool.org. Judy Carew, Prin. Brothers of the Christian Schools 2; Lay Teachers 36; Students 549.

GOSHEN. *John S. Burke Catholic High School*, 80 Fletcher St., Goshen, 10924. Tel: 845-294-5481; Fax: 845-294-0817; Email: jdolan@burkecatholic.org; Email: burke@adnyeducation.org; Web: www.burkecatholic.org. Mrs. Colette Austin, Asst. Prin., Academics; Mr. Kevin Canty, Asst. Prin., Student Affairs; Mrs. Audrey Clarke, Asst. Prin., P.P.S.; Mrs. Joanne Fitzpatrick, Procurator. Lay Teachers 25; Students 398.

HARTSDALE. *Maria Regina High School*, 500 W. Hartsdale Ave., Hartsdale, 10530. Tel: 914-761-3300; Fax: 914-761-0860; Email: mariareg@adnyeducation.org; Web: www.mariaregina.org. Rosemarie Decker, Prin.; Sr. Mary Krystyna Kobielus, C.R., Librarian. Sisters of the Resurrection. Lay Teachers 31; Sisters 3; Students 506.

HURLEY. *John A. Coleman Catholic High School* (1967) 430 Hurley Ave., Hurley, 12443. Tel: 845-338-2750 ; Fax: 845-388-0250; Email: office@colemancatholic.net; Email: coleman@adnyeducation.org; Web: www.colemancatholic.net. Mr. James Lyons, Prin.; Susan Bannon, Librarian. Lay Teachers 13; Sisters 1; Students 133.

MOUNT VERNON. **The Montfort Academy*, Lt. Col. David Petrillo, 125 E. Birch St., Mount Vernon, 10552. Tel: 914-699-7090; Fax: 914-699-7150; Email: montfort@adnyeducation.org; Email: office@themontfortacademy.org; Web: www.themontfortacademy.org. Lt. Col. David Petrillo, Ph.D., Headmaster. Lay Teachers 16; Students 130.

NEW ROCHELLE. *Iona Preparatory School* (1916) (Grades K-12), (All Boys) Upper School: 255 Wilmot Rd., New Rochelle, 10804. Tel: 914-632-0714; Tel: 914-633-7744; Fax: 914-632-9760; Fax: 914-235-6338; Email: ionaprep2@adnyeducation.org; Web: www.ionaprep.org. Bro. Thomas R. Leto, C.F.C., Pres.; Mrs. Barbara O'Meara, CFO; Mr. Mark Hogan, Chief Advancement Officer; Mrs. Barbara Robertson, Dir. Admissions - Upper School; Deidre Mone, Dir. Admissions - Lower School; Greg Quirolo, Dir., Counseling; Bros. Michael Binkley, C.F.C.; John H. Greenan, C.F.C.; William R. Harris, C.F.C.; Lucian Knaap, C.F.C.; Gerard Menezes, C.F.C.; Andrew Prendergast, C.F.C.; Anthony Reynolds, C.F.C.; Kevin J. Kiernan, C.F.C.; Kiernan Daly, Prin. Edmund Rice Christian Brothers North America. Brothers 7; Lay Teachers 53; Students 783.

Salesian High School, 148 Main St., New Rochelle, 10801. Tel: 914-632-0248; Fax: 914-632-5426; Email: salesian@adnyeducation.org; Web: www.salesianhigh.org. Rev. John J. Serio, S.D.B., Pres.-Prin.; Bro. Craig Spence, S.D.B.; Sr. Barbara Wright, O.P., Asst. Prin., Academics; Mr. Robert Molinaro, Dean of Students; Mr. Steven Sallustio, Dir. Admissions; Paul Zaccagnino, Librarian; Fr. Richard Rosin, Prin. Brothers 3; Lay Teachers 31; Priests 2; Sisters 2; Students 531.

The Ursuline School (1897) (Grades 6-12), (Girls) 1354 North Ave., New Rochelle, 10804. Tel: 914-636-3950; Fax: 914-636-3949; Email: ursuline@adnyeducation.org; Web: www.ursulinenewrochelle.org. Rosemary Beirne, Prin.; James Phelan, Treas.; Mrs. Eileen Davidson, Pres.; Mrs. Erin Johnston, Dir. Admissions; Catherine Fay McCarthy, Dir. Philanthropy; Kathy Freeman, Librarian. Lay Teachers 106; Sisters 4; Students 796; Clergy / Religious Teachers 4.

POUGHKEEPSIE. *Our Lady of Lourdes High School* (1954) 131 Boardman Rd., Poughkeepsie, 12603. Tel: 845-463-0400; Fax: 845-463-0174; Email: lourdes@adnyeducation.org; Web: www.ollchs.org. Catherine B. Merryman, Prin., Admissions; Mr. Michael Krieger, Asst. Prin., Academics; Mr. Charles Junjulas Jr., Campus Min.; Meghan Vilardo, Dir. Instruction & Curriculum; Lauren Prince, Dean of Women; Nicholas Fernandez, Dean of Men; Mrs. Judith Maher, Dir., Guidance; William Ficker, Faculty Coord. Lay Teachers 34; Sisters 1; Students 735.

RYE. *School of the Holy Child*, (Grades 5-12), (Girls) 2225 Westchester Ave., Rye, 10580. Tel: 914-967-5622; Fax: 914-967-6476; Email: holychild@adnyeducation.org; Web: www.holychildrye.org. Melissa Dan, Prin.; Monique Gordon, Librarian. Lay Teachers 46; Students 604.

SOMERS. *John F. Kennedy Catholic High School*, 54 Rte. 138, Somers, 10589. Tel: 914-232-5061; Fax: 914-232-3416; Email: jfkhs@adnyeducation.org; Web: www.kennedycatholic.org. Rev. Mark G. Vaillancourt, Ph.D., Pres. & Prin.; Sr. Barbara Heil, R.D.C., Dir. Admissions. Diocesan Priests, Sisters of the Divine Compassion. Lay Teachers 36; Priests 1; Students 667; Clergy / Religious Teachers 6.

STATEN ISLAND. *St. Joseph by the Sea, High School* (Coed) 5150 Hylan Blvd., Staten Island, 10312. Tel: 718-984-6500; Fax: 718-984-6503; Email: josbysea@adnyeducation.org. Rev. Michael P. Reilly, Prin. Lay Teachers 43; Priests 3; Students 1,152.

St. Joseph Hill Academy (Girls) 850 Hylan Blvd., Staten Island, 10305-2095. Tel: 718-447-1374; Fax: 718-447-3041; Email: joshill@adnyeducation.org; Web: stjhill.org. Stephanie Brodeur, Prin. Daughters of Divine Charity. Lay Teachers 23; Sisters 1; Students 407.

Monsignor Farrell High School, 2900 Amboy Rd., Staten Island, 10306. Tel: 718-987-2900;

Fax: 718-987-4241; Email: mainoffice@msgrfarrellhs.org; Email: farrell@adnyeducation.org; Web: www.msgrfarrellhs.org. Rev. Msgr. Edmund J. Whalen, S.T.D., Prin.; Kathleen Sparnroft, Librarian. Lay Teachers 43; Priests 1; Sisters 1; Students 880.

Moore Catholic High School, 100 Merrill Ave., Staten Island, 10314. Tel: 718-761-9200; Fax: 718-982-7779; Email: moorecats@adnyeducation.org; Web: www.moorechs.org. Gina De Santis, Prin.; Marie DeAngelo, Librarian. Lay Teachers 19; Priests 1; Daughters of Our Lady of the Garden 1; Students 342.

Notre Dame Academy High School, 134 Howard Ave., Staten Island, 10301. Tel: 718-447-8878; Fax: 718-447-2926; Email: kjaenicke@notredameacademy.org; Email: ntdameac@adnyeducation.org; Web: www.hs.notredameacademy.org. Sr. Patricia Corley, C.N.D., Pres.; Dr. Kathryn Jaenicke, Prin.; Christine Gullo, Librarian. Congregation of Notre Dame. Lay Teachers 25; Students 439.

St. Peter's Boys High School, 200 Clinton Ave., Staten Island, 10301. Tel: 718-447-1676; Fax: 718-447-4027; Email: mcosentino@stpetersboyshs.org; Email: stpeterb@adnyeducation.org; Web: www.stpetersboyshs.org. Michael Consentino, Prin. Brothers of the Christian Schools 3; Lay Teachers 24; Students 529.

WHITE PLAINS. *Archbishop Stepinac High School*, 950 Mamaroneck Ave., White Plains, 10605. Tel: 914-946-4800; Fax: 914-684-2591; Email: stepinac@adnyeducation.org; Web: www.stepinac.org. Rev. Thomas E. Collins, Pres., Email: tcollins@stepinac.org; Mr. Paul Carty, Prin.; Patrick Duffy, Librarian. Lay Teachers 55; Priests 2; Students 813.

YONKERS. *Sacred Heart High School*, 34 Convent Ave., Yonkers, 10703. Tel: 914-965-3114; Fax: 914-965-4510; Email: scrdhrt@adnyeducation.org; Web: www.sacredhearths.org. Karen Valenti-Dececco, Prin. Lay Teachers 17; Students 310.

[F] SPECIAL SCHOOLS

NEW YORK. *Grace Institute*, 40 Rector St., 14th Fl., 10006. Tel: 212-832-7605; Fax: 212-486-2869; Email: info@graceinstitute.org; Web: www.graceinstitute.org. Sisters of Charity, Mt. St. Vincent. Students 300; Teachers 5; Tot Asst. Annually 300; Total Staff 25.

Lavelle School for the Blind, 3830 Paulding Ave., 10469. Tel: 718-882-1212; Fax: 718-882-0005; Web: www.lavelleschool.org. Lorrie Nanry, Exec. Dir. Sisters of St. Dominic of Blauvelt. Capacity 150; Lay Teachers 27; Total Staff 110.

Seton Foundation for Learning, Inc. (1985) 315 Arlene St., Staten Island, 10314. Tel: 718-982-5084 ; Fax: 718-982-5114; Email: mhughes@sflschools.org; Web: www.sflschools.org. Rev. Msgr. Peter G. Finn, M.Div., M.S., M.Ed., Co-Chm.; Mary D. Hughes, M.A., J.D., Exec. Dir.; Mrs. Margaret Sacca, Dir.; Donna Jennings, M.S.Ed., Educational Dir.; Dr. Diane Taranto, Ph.D., Educational Dir. Lay Teachers 13; Total Enrollment 84; Assistants 17.

Bishop Patrick V. Ahern High School, 315 Arlene St., Staten Island, 10314. Tel: 718-982-5084; Fax: 718-982-5114; Email: mhughes@sflschools.org; Web: www.sflschools.org. Donna Jennings, M.S.Ed., Educational Dir.

Mother Franciska Elementary School, 850 Hyland Blvd., Staten Island, 10305. Tel: 718-876-0939; Fax: 718-816-6507; Email: seton@adnyeducation.org. Dr. Diane Taranto, Ph.D., Educational Dir. Lay Teachers 6; Students 34.

Joan Ann Kennedy Memorial Preschool, 850 Hylan Blvd., Staten Island, 10305. Tel: 718-876-0939; Fax: 718-816-6507; Email: mhughes@sflschools.org. Mrs. Margaret Sacca, Educational Dir. Lay Teachers 4; Students 26.

BRONX. *St. Joseph's School for the Deaf*, 1000 Hutchinson River Pkwy., Bronx, 10465. Tel: 718-828-9000; Fax: 718-239-7520; Email: DArles@sjsdny.org. Debra Arles, Exec. Dir.

IRVINGTON. *John Cardinal O'Connor School*, (Grades 2-8), 16 N. Broadway, Irvington, 10533. Tel: 914-591-9330; Email: jcoconnor@adnyeducation.org. Ms. Kristen O'Leary, Prin. Lay Teachers 5; Students 86.

MILLBROOK. *Cardinal Hayes School for Special Children* (1984) 3374 Franklin Ave., P.O. Box CH, Millbrook, 12545. Tel: 845-677-3251; Fax: 845-677-0356; Email: drussell@cardinalhayeshome.org; Web: www.hayesdayschool.org. Catherine Varano, CEO. Day school programs for multi-handicapped children. Capacity 60; Lay Teachers 10; Students 57; Total Enrollment 57.

YONKERS. *John A. Coleman School*, 300 Corporate Blvd., S., Yonkers, 10701. Tel: 914-5970-4054; Fax: 914-397-1765; Email: mtomkiel@colemanschool.org; Web: www.colemanschool.org. Ms. Maureen Tomkiel, Exec. Dir. Bed Capacity 144; Tot Asst. Annually 933.

[G] ELEMENTARY SCHOOLS, PRIVATE

STATEN ISLAND. *St. John Villa Academy Elementary School*, Mailing Address: 57 Cleveland Pl., Staten Island, 10305. Tel: 708-447-2668; Fax: 718-447-2079; Email: johnvles@adnyeducation.org; Web: www.sjva.org. James Smith, Prin. Lay Teachers 11; Sisters 1; Students 188.

[H] THE CATHOLIC CHARITIES OF THE ARCHDIOCESE OF NEW YORK

NEW YORK. *Catholic Charities Alliance*, 1011 First Ave., 10022. Tel: 212-371-1011, Ext. 2400; Email: msgr.kevin.sullivan@archny.org. Rev. Msgr. Kevin L. Sullivan, Pres.

Catholic Charities Community Services of Dutchess, Inc., 218 Church St., Poughkeepsie, 12601. Tel: 845-452-1400; Fax: 845-452-3336. Ms. Mary Marshall, Exec. Dir.

The Catholic Charities of the Archdiocese of New York, 1011 First Ave., 10022. Tel: 212-371-1000; Fax: 212-755-1526; Web: wwwcatholiccharitiesny.org. Rev. Msgr. Kevin L. Sullivan, Exec. Dir.; Ms. Talia Lockspeiser, Assoc. Exec. Dir.; Mr. Kenneth Dempsey, CFO; Mr. George B. Horton, Dir., Social & Community Devel.; Ms. Luz Taverez-Salazar, Dir., Government & Community Relations; William Miller, Chief Devel. Officer; Shannon Kelly, Catholic Charities Dir. Hudson Valley; Mr. Philip Dorian, Sr. Dir. Federation Advancement; Paul Costiglio, Dir., Communications.

The Ladies of Charity of the Catholic Charities of the Archdiocese of New York, 1011 First Ave., Room 1316B, 10022. Tel: 212-371-1000; Fax: 212-752-0719; Email: loc@archny.org. Mary Buckley Teatum, Pres.; Rev. Msgr. Peter G. Finn, M.Div., M.S., M.Ed., Spiritual Dir.

Catholic Charities Community Services, Archdiocese of New York, 1011 First Ave., 10022. Tel: 212-371-1000; Fax: 212-826-8795. Ms. Beatriz Diaz, Exec. Dir., Catholic Charities Community Svcs.; Ms. Denise Bauer, LCSW-R, Dir. Beacon of Hope Svcs. Div.; Mr. C. Mario Russell Esq., Dir. Immigrant Refugee Svcs.; Ms. Helen Lauffer, Assoc. Exec. Dir., CCCS; Mr. Edwin Broderick, Dir. CYO Div.; Ms. Joy Jasper, M.S., Dir. Human Resources; Mr. Eddie Silvero, Dir. Alianza Svcs.; Mr. Joseph Panepinto, Catholic Charities Dir. Staten Island; Ms. Dianna Johnson, Dir., Community Outreach Svcs.

Roman Catholic Fund for Children and Other Purposes, 1011 First Ave., 10022. Tel: 212-371-1000; Fax: 212-826-8795. Rev. Msgr. Kevin L. Sullivan.

Holy Name Centre for Homeless Men, Inc., 101 First Ave., 10022. Tel: 466-794-2492.

Providence Health Services, 1249 Fifth Ave., 10029. Karl Adler, Pres.

St. Michael's Home, c/o The Catholic Charities of the Archdiocese of New York, 1011 First Ave., 10022. Tel: 212-371-1000; Web: cathwww.org. Bernard E. Reidey, Vice Pres.

GOSHEN. *Catholic Charities Community Services of Orange and Sullivan County*, Administrative Offices: 27 Mathews St., Goshen, 10924. Tel: 845-294-5124; Fax: 845-294-1369. Dr. Dean Scher, COO, Exec. Dir.

Chemical Dependency Clinics:

Medically supervised, outpatient clinics for chemically dependent adults and their families.

27 Mathews St., Goshen, 10924. Tel: 845-294-5888; Fax: 845-294-1402.

305 North St., Middletown, 10940. Tel: 845-343-7675; Fax: 845-343-2501.

101 Carpenter Pl., Monroe, 10950. Tel: 845-782-0295; Fax: 845-782-5164.

280 Broadway, Newburgh, 12550. Tel: 845-562-8255 ; Fax: 845-562-4140.

Gateway Clinic, 280 Broadway, Newburgh, 12550. Tel: 845-569-0034; Fax: 845-569-0047.

17 Sussex St., Port Jervis, 12771. Tel: 845-856-6344; Fax: 845-856-4091.

8 Scofield St., Walden, 12586. Tel: 845-778-5628; Fax: 845-778-5168.

Housing Resource Center, 280 Broadway, Newburgh, 12550. Tel: 845-561-1665; Fax: 845-561-2825. Provides eviction prevention services as part of a collaborative effort among Catholic Charities Community Services of Orange County and the Orange County Department of Social Services.

Student Assistance Services, 305 North St., Middletown, 10940. Tel: 845-344-5565; Fax: 845-344-6982. Chemical dependency awareness, prevention, life skills education; Counseling, assessment, and referral services for students in Pine Bush School District.

Employee Assistance Program: Employee Assistance Programs for 45 corporations, businesses, governments, groups, etc. Provides confidential counseling assessment, and referral services for employees on a self-initiated or supervisor-recommended basis. Training programs and related consultative services provided.

305 North St., Middletown, 10940. Tel: 845-344-5565; Fax: 845-344-6982.

Community Outreach Services–Immigration Services: Provides services to immigrants in need of assistance.

305 North St., Middletown, 10940. Tel: 845-341-1978.

Community Outreach Services-Social Services: Provides information and referral, case management/service coordination, emergency assistance for rent, utilities, transportation, food and clothing (limited by available resources), entitlement assistance and advocacy. Also available to help parishes with CYO programs and to assess needs, evaluate existing service programs, recruit and train volunteers to meet parish needs and facilitate service to the parish.

305 North St., Middletown, 10940. Tel: 845-344-4242; Fax: 845-343-2501.

78 Mathews St., Goshen, 10924. Tel: 845-294-5124, Ext. 302; Fax: 845-294-1369. Offers free or low cost health insurance through Family Health Plus and Child Health Plus programs. Coverage includes: check-ups, prenatal care, screenings and preventive care, well-child visits, immunizations, lab tests, x-rays, hospitalization and emergency treatment. (Appointments are set up at various sites in Orange County).

[I] HOUSING

NEW YORK. *Catholic Charities Department of Housing, Housing Development Institute, Inc.*, 1011 First Ave., 10022. Tel: 212-371-1000. Rev. Msgr. Kevin L. Sullivan, Pres.

[J] MENTAL HEALTH SERVICES

NEW YORK. *Catholic Charities Community Services, Beacon of Hope*, 1011 First Ave., 6th Fl., 10022. Tel: 212-371-1000, Ext. 3608; Fax: 212-421-0021; Email: denise.bauer@archny.org; Web: www.catholiccharitiesny.org. Ms. Denise Bauer, LCSW-R, Dir., Beacon of Hope.

[K] IMMIGRANT AND REFUGEES SERVICES

NEW YORK. *Catholic Charities Immigrant Legal Services*, 80 Maiden Ln., 13th Fl., 10038. Tel: 212-419-3700; Fax: 212-751-3197; Email: Immigration.Services@archny.org; Web: www.catholiccharitiesny.org. Ms. Raluca Oncioiu, Dept. Dir.; Mr. C. Mario Rusell, Div. Dir. Immigrant & Refugee Services.

Refugee Resettlement, 80 Maiden Ln., 13th Fl., 10038. Tel: 212-419-3726; Fax: 212-688-4178. Kelly Agnew, Prog. Dir.

Project Irish Outreach, 990 McLean Ave., Yonkers, 10704. Tel: 914-237-5098; Fax: 917-237-5172.

New York State New American Hotline, 80 Maiden Ln., 13th Fl., 10038. Tel: 212-419-3737; Tel: 800-566-7636; Email: NewAmericans.Hotline@archny.org; Web: www.catholiccharitiesny.org. Ms. Raluca Oncioiu, Dir.; Stephanie Ortiz, Contact Person. Tot Asst. Annually 36,000; Total Staff 12.

[L] COMMUNITY OUTREACH SERVICES DIVISION

NEW YORK. *Catholic Charities Community Services, Community Outreach Services Division*, 1011 First Ave., 10022. Tel: 212-371-1000, Ext. 2010; Fax: 212-317-8719.

Case Management/Social Services:

Central Office, 1011 First Ave., 10022. Tel: 212-371-1000, Ext. 2035; Tel: 888-744-7900 (Catholic Charities Helpline).

Central Harlem - Lt. Joseph P. Kennedy Jr. Memorial Center, 34 W. 134th St., 10037. Tel: 212-862-6401; Fax: 212-862-6421.

Lower Manhattan - Our Lady of Sorrows, 213 Stanton St., 10002. Tel: 212-673-0900.

East Manhattan, St. Cecilia's Church, 125 E. 105th St., 10029. Tel: 212-348-0488; Fax: 212-876-1827.

Washington Hts., 4111 Broadway, 10033. Tel: 212-795-6860; Fax: 212-781-2935.

South Bronx, 402 E. 152nd St., Bronx, 10455. Tel: 718-292-1485; Fax: 718-742-9754.

Staten Island, 120 Anderson Ave., Staten Island, 10302. Tel: 718-448-5757; Fax: 718-448-6749.

Westchester County/Peekskill, Our Lady of the Rosary, 22 Don Bosco Pl., Port Chester, 10573. Tel: 914-939-0547; Fax: 914-965-4241.

Westchester County/Yonkers, 204 Hawthorne Ave.,

Yonkers, 10701. Tel: 914-476-2700; Fax: 914-965-4241.
Dutchess County, 218 Church St., Poughkeepsie, 12601. Tel: 845-454-3855; Fax: 845-452-3336.
Rockland County, 78 Hudson Ave., Haverstraw, 10927. Tel: 845-942-5791; Fax: 845-429-2938.
Sullivan County, 59 North St., Monticello, 12701. Tel: 845-791-6023; Fax: 845-791-7003.
Ulster County, 6 Adams St., Kingston, 12401. Tel: 845-340-9170; Fax: 845-340-9596.
Emergency Food Services, 34 W. 134th St., 10030. Tel: 212-862-6401; Fax: 212-862-6421.
Homelessness Prevention Services:
34 W. 134th St., 10030. Tel: 212-862-6401, Ext. 313.
2155 Blackrock Ave., Bronx, 10472. Tel: 718-414-1050; Fax: 718-414-1058.
4377 Bronx Blvd., 3rd Fl., Bronx, 10472. Tel: 347-414-1050.
Hudson Valley Regional Services:
Catholic Charities Community Services Hudson Valley Regional Services, Putnam Catholic Center, 175 Main St., Brewster, 10509. Tel: 845-279-5276. Ms. Mary Ellen Ros, Dir.
Regional Offices:
Dutchess, Poughkeepsie Catholic Center, 218 Church St., Poughkeepsie, 12601. Tel: 845-452-1400; Fax: 845-452-3336. Ms. Mary Marshall.
Westchester, 22 Don Bosco Pl., Port Chester, 10573. Tel: 914-939-0547; Fax: 914-965-4241.
Sullivan, 59 North St., Monticello, 12701. Tel: 845-791-6023; Fax: 845-791-7023. Rhetta Eason, Regl. Admin.
Ulster, 6 Adams St., Kingston, 12401. Tel: 845-340-9170; Fax: 845-340-9596. Thomas Kelly, Regl. Admin.
Putnam, 175 Main St., Brewster, 10509. Tel: 845-279-5276. John Scarfi, Parish Social Min.
Brewster, 175 Main St., Brewster, 10509. Tel: 845-279-5276; Fax: 845-278-2079; Email: lakisha.morris@archny.org. Frank Kortright, Dir.

[M] SOCIAL AND COMMUNITY DEVELOPMENT

NEW YORK. *Catholic Charities Department of Social and Community Development*, 1011 First Ave., Room 787, 10022. Tel: 212-371-1000, Ext. 2480; Fax: 212-319-0405. Mr. George B. Horton, Dir., Tel: 212-371-1000, Ext. 2475.
Offices and Staff:.
Justice and Peace Ministry Thomas Dobbins Jr., Coord., Tel: 212-371-1000, Ext. 2473.
Education Outreach Program Alison Hughes-Kelsick, Dir., Tel: 212-371-1000, Ext. 2450.
Association of New York Catholic Homes, 80 Maiden Ln., 13th Fl., 10038. Tel: 212-371-1000, Ext. 3167. Susan Albrecht, Dir.
Institute for Human Development, 80 Maiden Ln., 13th Fl., 10038. Tel: 212-371-1000, Ext. 2032. Melissa Pavone, Dir.
The Guild for Dorothy Day Mr. George B. Horton.
Deaf Apostolate Rev. Msgr. Patrick P. McCahill, Dir.

[N] SPECIAL SERVICES FOR THE ELDERLY/ HANDICAPPED

BEACON. *Metropolitan Association of Contemplative Communities, Inc.*, 89 Hiddenbrooke Dr., Beacon, 12508. Tel: 845-831-5572; Fax: 845-831-5579; Web: macc.catholic.org. Sr. Michaelene Devine, O.C.D., Contact Person.

[O] SERVICES TO THE DISABLED

NEW YORK. *Catholic Charities Community Services Beacon of Hope House Division*, Catholic Charities, 1011 First Ave., 10022. Tel: 212-371-1000; Fax: 212-421-0021; Email: denise.bauer@archny.org; Web: www.archny.org. Ms. Denise Bauer, LCSW-R, Division Dir.; Ms. Joy Jasper, M.S., Dir. Human Resources; Mr. Dennis Scimone, M.S.W., M.P.A., Assoc. Dir. of Residential Svcs.; Michele Miller, LCSW, Assoc. Dir. Quality Improvement, Staff Devel. & Compliance; Deborah Neal, M.S.W., Assoc. Dir. of Supported Housing & Operations.
Beacon of Hope House Bronx Congregate Services, 1400 Waters Pl., Bronx, 10461. Tel: 718-892-3494; Fax: 718-892-5507. Ms. Jacqueline Rosario-Perez, M.S.W., Dir. Bronx Congregate Progs.
Terence Cardinal Cooke Residence, 2467 Bathgate Ave., Bronx, 10458. Tel: 718-367-6990; Tel: 718-367-5405 (TTY); Fax: 718-365-2544. Penny Douglas-Clemmons, Prog. Supvr.
Beacon of Hope House Staten Island Supervised Programs, 777 Seaview Ave., Bldg. D, 2nd Fl., Staten Island, 10305. Tel: 718-980-1072; Fax: 718-980-1077. Mr. Dennis Scimone, M.S.W., M.P.A., Dir. Staten Island & Brooklyn Svcs.
Staten Island Apartment Programs, Tel: 718-979-6241; Fax: 718-979-6941. Jillian Maye, Prog. Mgr.
90-92 Hancock St., Staten Island, 10305. Tel: 718-979-6241; Fax: 718-979-6941.
Highbridge Neighborhood Supported Housing Program, 1484 Nelson Ave., Ste. A, Bronx, 10452. Tel: 718-503-8106; Fax: 718-503-7909. Sharon Bertie, Prog. Mgr.
Kingsborough Intensive Supported Apartment Program, 647 Vanderbilt Ave., Brooklyn, 11238. Tel: 718-398-4556; Fax: 718-398-4807.
Bronx Supported Housing, 2510 Westchester Ave., Ste. 210, Bronx, 10461. Tel: 718-239-5206; Fax: 718-239-5287. Michael Harris, Dir. Bronx Supported Housing.
New York Catholic Deaf Center, 65 E. 89th St., 10128. Tel: 212-988-8563; Tel: 646-755-3086 (Video Phone); Fax: 212-988-1903; Email: msgr.patrick.mccahill@archny.org; Web: www.deafcathnyc.org. Rev. Msgr. Patrick P. McCahill, Dir. Tot Asst. Annually 6,658; Total Staff 3.
BARRYVILLE. *New Hope Manor*, 35 Hillside Rd., Barryville, 12719. Tel: 845-557-8353; Fax: 845-557-6603; Email: newhopemnr@aol.com; Web: www.newhopemanor.org. Ms. Barrie Jacobsen, LCSW-R, Dir.; Bro. Charles Kinney, S.A., Bd. of Directors; Sr. Margaret Murphy, O.P., Bd. of Directors. See listing in the Miscellaneous section for further details. Bed Capacity 60; Tot Asst. Annually 100; Total Staff 60.
Staff: Sisters Maureen Conway, O.P., Dir. of Education, Housemother, Counselor & Teacher, (Retired); Patricia Conway, O.P., Housemother, Counselor & Teacher, (Retired). An all-female substance abuse treatment center.

[P] YOUTH SERVICES

NEW YORK. *Catholic Youth Organization of the Archdiocese of New York Inc.*, Executive Office, 1011 First Ave., 10022-4187. Tel: 212-371-1000; Fax: 212-826-3347. Chris Gallagher, Pres., CYO Bd.; Mr. Edwin Broderick, Exec. Dir.
Archdiocesan Committee on Scouting, Tel: 845-340-9170. Mr. Seth Peloso, Dir. Opers.; Anthony Badger, Dir., County Progs.
CYO Bronx County - CYO New York County, Tel: 212-371-1000; Fax: 212-826-3347. Mr. Anthony D'Angelo, County Dir.
CYO Staten Island County, Tel: 718-448-4949; Fax: 718-448-0576.
120 Anderson Ave., Staten Island, 10302. Tel: 718-448-4950; Fax: 718-448-0576. Michael Neely, County Dir.
120 Anderson Ave., Staten Island, 10302. Tel: 718-448-4949; Fax: 718-448-0576.
CYO Westchester/Putnam Offices, Tel: 845-623-2785; Fax: 845-624-0889. Frank Magaletta, County Dir.
9 Brookview Blvd., Chestnut Ridge, 10977. Tel: 845-623-2785; Fax: 845-624-0889.
1011 First Ave., 10022. Tel: 845-783-1254; Fax: 212-826-3347.
CYO Orange Office Mr. John Smith, Sports Coord.
P.O. Box 234, Highland Mills, 10930. Tel: 845-534-7700; Fax: 212-826-3347.
CYO Rockland Office, Tel: 845-620-1662. Thomas F. Collins, County Dir.
34 Graney Ct., Pearl River, 10965. Tel: 845-620-1662; Fax: 845-452-3336.
CYO Dutchess Office, Tel: 845-452-1400; Fax: 845-452-3336.
Catholic Center, 218 Church St., Poughkeepsie, 12601. Tel: 845-452-1400; Fax: 845-452-3336. Jill Dennin, Dutchess County Dir.
CYO Ulster, Tel: 845-340-9170; Fax: 845-340-9596.
59 Pearl St., Kingston, 12401. Tel: 845-340-9170; Fax: 845-340-9596. Walter Gaceta, County Dir.
BRONX. *St. Francis Youth Center, Inc.*, 427 E. 155th St., Bronx, 10455. Tel: 718-993-3405 (Friary); Tel: 718-402-6235 (Youth Center); Fax: 718-993-9997. Rev. Bonaventure Rummell, C.F.R., Dir.; Yvette Torres, Admin. Brothers 2; Clergy 3; Priests 1; Students 60.
GARRISON. *Capuchin Youth and Family Ministries*, 781 Rte. 9D, Garrison, 10524. Tel: 845-424-3609; Fax: 845-424-4403; Email: cyfm@cyfm.org; Web: www.cyfm.org. Thomas Brinkmann, Exec. Dir.; Revs. Fred Nickle, O.F.M.Cap., Chap.; Erik Lenhart, Chap. A ministry of the Capuchin Franciscan Province of St. Mary. Clergy 3.

[Q] INSTITUTIONS FOR DEPENDENT CHILDREN

NEW YORK. *Covenant House Under 21*, 460 W. 41st St., 10036-6801. Tel: 212-613-0300; Fax: 212-629-3756. Philip J. Andryc, Bd. Chair.; Mr. Creighton Drury, Exec. Dir. Runaway and Homeless Youth. Total Staff 278; Total Assisted 2,811.
Rights of Passage Transition Housing. Bed Capacity 160.
Crisis Center Emergency Shelter. Bed Capacity 226.
Vincent J. Fontana Center for Child Protection, 590 Ave. of the Americas, 10011. Tel: 212-660-1323; Fax: 212-660-1319. Total Staff 12; Children & Families 250.
BLAUVELT. *St. Dominic's Family Services, St. Dominic's Home* (1878) 500 Western Hwy., Blauvelt, 10913. Tel: 845-359-3400; Fax: 845-359-4253; Email: jkydon@sdomhome.org; Web: www.stdominicshome.org. Judith D. Kydon, Pres. & CEO.
Foster Care, 853 Longwood Ave., Ste. 202, Bronx, 10459. Tel: 917-645-9100; Fax: 917-645-9095; Web: www.stdominicshome.org.
St. Dominic's School, Blauvelt. Tel: 845-359-3400, Ext. 243; Fax: 845-359-5286; Web: www.stdominicshome.org. (Serves children and adolescents with emotional disabilities, K-12th grade.) Capacity 80.
Community Based Services/Waiver, 1 Fordham Plaza, Ste. 901, Bronx, 10458. Tel: 718-295-9112; Fax: 718-295-2104.
Community residences for developmentally disabled, Tel: 845-359-3400; Fax: 845-359-3673. Capacity 150.
Community residences for mentally ill, Tel: 845-359-3400; Fax: 845-359-7361. Capacity 36; Supported Housing Apartments 38.
TORCH (To Reach Children), 2340 Andrews Ave., Bronx, 10468. Tel: 718-365-7238; Fax: 718-584-3057; Web: www.stdominicshome.org.
Torch Annex, 2195 Valentine Ave., Bronx, 10457.
Friends of St. Dominic's Inc., 500 Western Hwy., Blauvelt, 10913. Tel: 845-359-3400; Fax: 845-398-0466; Email: smflood@sdfs.org; Web: www.stdominicshome.org. Sr. Margaret Flood, O.P., B.S.N., M.A., M.P.A., Pres. Tot Asst. Annually 2,500; Total Staff 4.
BRONX. *Saint Dominic's Home - Prevention Program (ASTAAN)* Parent Aide Counseling Advocacy Information and Referral. 2345 University Ave., Bronx, 10468. Tel: 718-584-4407; Fax: 718-584-4540; Email: kthompson@sdomhome.org; Web: www.stdominicshome.org/friends. Families 100; Families Served 200.
Little Angels Head Start Program, 529 Courtlandt Avenue, Bronx, 10451. Tel: 718-402-0081; Fax: 718-665-9161; Email: rgershenlowy@cmcs.org; Web: www.littleangelsheadstart.org. Statistical Information: Annunciation Capacity: 80, 80 Head Start Children Served, 72 UPK Children Served; Cardinal Spellman Capacity: 102, 95 Head start Children Served, 63 UPK Children Served; Concord Capacity: 108, 110 Head Start Children Served, 52 UPK Children Served; Holy Spirit Capacity: 37, 37 Head Start Children Served, 36 UPK Children Served; Msgr. Boyle Capacity: 220, 213 Head Start Children Served, 63 UPK Children Served; Queen of Martyrs Capacity: 79, 80 Head Start Children Served, 21 UPK Children Served; Sacred Heart Capacity: 113, 145 Children Served, 66 UPK Children Served; St. Anthony Capacity: 120, 180 Head Start Children Served, 63 UPK Children Served; St. Martin Capacity: 40, 71 Head Start Children Served; St. Rita's Capacity: 140, 157 Head Start Children Served, 63 UPK Children Served; St. Simon Capacity: 60, 70 Head Start Children Served; Tolentine Capacity: 165, 217 Head Start Children Served, 42 UPK Children Served. ACS Head Start Capacity 1,170; ACS UPK Capacity 694; ACF Head Start Capacity 372; ACF UPK Capacity 318; Staff 291.
NANUET. *St. Agatha Home of the New York Foundling Hospital* (Residential.) 135 Convent Rd., Nanuet, 10954. Tel: 845-623-3461. Sisters of Charity of St. Vincent de Paul of New York.Residence for adults with developmental disabilities.; Respite for caregivers of adults and children with developmental disabilities.; Group Home.
OSSINING. *Cardinal McCloskey Emergency Residential School* (1980) 155 N. Highland Ave., Ossining, 10562. Tel: 914-762-5302; Fax: 914-762-7844. Capacity 12; Total Staff 7; Total Assisted 45.
SPRING VALLEY. *Good Counsel, Inc.* (Homes for Women) 22 Linden Ave., Spring Valley, 10977. Tel: 845-356-0517; Tel: 800-723-8331 (Info & Referrals); Fax: 845-356-0406; Web: www.goodcounselhomes.org; Web: www.postabortionhelp.org. Mark Swartzberg, Chm.; Christopher Bell, Pres.; Nannette Morris, House Mgr. Bed Capacity 47; Tot Asst. Annually 225; Total Staff 70.
Good Counsel, Inc., 38 Wiman Pl., Staten Island, 10305. Tel: 718-650-6994; Tel: 800-723-8331 (Info. & Referrals); Fax: 718-650-6997; Web: www.goodcounselhomes.org; Web: www.postabortionhelp.org.
Good Counsel, Inc., 1157 Fulton Ave., Bronx, 10456. Tel: 718-312-3980, Ext. 10; Tel: 800-723-8331 (For Info & Referrals); Fax: 718-312-3991; Web: www.goodcounselhomes.org. Christopher Bell, Exec. Dir.
Good Counsel/Daystar Program, 205 E. Prospect

Ave., Mount Vernon, 10550. Tel: 914-925-9834; Tel: 800-723-8331 (Info. & Referrals); Web: www.goodcounselhomes.org; Web: www.postabortionhelp.org. Faye Armstrong, House Mgr.

WEST PARK. *St. Cabrini Home* (1890) Rte. 9W, P.O. Box 69, West Park, 12493. Tel: 212-375-0752; Tel: 732-547-5452; Fax: 646-602-2050; Email: mlefante@msshnyc.org.

VALHALLA. *Cardinal McCloskey Community Services* (1946) 115 Stevens Ave., Valhalla, 10595. Tel: 914-997-8000; Fax: 914-997-2166; Email: bfinnerty@cmcs.org; Web: www.cardinalmccloskeycommunityservices.org. Mrs. Beth Finnerty, Pres. & CEO. Statistical Information: Hayden House Capacity: 18, 32 Children Served; Horizons of Hope Capacity: 12, 86 Children Served; Tappan Group Home Capacity: 8, 12 Assisted; Foster Boarding Home, Therapeutic Foster Boarding Home, Westchester Treatment Family Foster Care Assisted: 404; Family Treatment Rehabilitation Services Total Assisted: 74 Families, 175 Children; Medically Fragile Preventive Program: 95 Families, 222 Children; East Harlem Family CNNX Total Assisted: 37 Families, 66 Children; Federal Head Start Total Assisted: 1037 Children; Family Day Care Capacity: 600, 902 Children Served; Day Care Centers Capacity: 64 Children Served; OPWDD Residence Capacity: 103, 103 Families Assisted; OPWDD Day Habilitation: 48 Consumers Assisted; OPWDD Case Management: 119 Consumers Assisted; OPWDD Family Support: 28 Consumers Assisted; Enhanced Supportive Employment: 29 Consumers Assisted; Medical and Clinical Services Total Assisted: 898; Drop-in-Center: 1371 Individuals Served; B2H: 322 Children Served; Youth Development Assisted: 41 Youths; Strategies for Success Assisted: 239 Individuals; Rockland Diagnostic: 7 Children Served; Total Assisted: 4870; Total Staff: 1055. Bed Capacity 16; Tot Asst. Annually 6,746; Total Staff 980.

[R] SPECIALIZED CHILD CARING HOMES

NEW YORK. **Good Shepherd Services*, 305 7th Ave., 9th Fl., 10001. Tel: 212-243-7070; Fax: 212-929-3412; Email: plomonaco@goodshepherds.org; Web: www.goodshepherds.org. Sr. Paulette LoMonaco, R.G.S., Exec. Dir. Provides foster care and adoption services and eight residential programs for at risk adolescents, a training program for social service workers and a comprehensive range of neighborhood family services to individuals and youth in the Bronx and in Brooklyn. These services include a range of educational support, counseling, after school program, community centers, community schools, crisis intervention, and advocacy services. Sisters 2; Total Staff 1,220; Total Assisted 30,365.

Kennedy Child Study Center (1958) 2212 3rd Ave., 2nd Fl., 10035. Tel: 212-988-9500; Fax: 888-493-6324; Email: info@kenchild.org; Web: www.kenchild.org. Jeanne Alter, Exec. Dir. Preschool Special Education 150.

Case Management Services, Tel: 212-988-9500; Fax: 888-493-6324. Family Support Services 20.

Bronx Site, 1028 E. 179th St., Bronx, 10460. Tel: 718-842-0200; Fax: 718-842-1328. Preschool Special Education 240.

Case Management Services, Tel: 718-842-0200; Fax: 718-842-1328. Family Support Services 40.

Catholic Charities of Staten Island (1871) 6581 Hylan Blvd., Staten Island, 10309. Tel: 718-317-2803; Tel: 718-984-1500; Fax: 718-317-2830; Email: info@mountloretto.org; Web: www.mountloretto.org. Vincent Ignizio, CEO

Catholic Charities of Staten Island

Intermediate Care Facility, Tel: 718-317-2825. Capacity 12.

Day Care Center & Universal Pre-K, Tel: 718-317-2849; Fax: 718-317-2802. Capacity 85.

Individual Residential Alternatives

Individual Residential Alternatives (I.R.A.), Tel: 718-317-2825; Fax: 718-317-2830. Capacity 36.

Day Habilitation Program, Tel: 718-317-2825; Fax: 718-317-2830. Capacity 8.

Residential & Day Care, Tel: 718-317-2825; Tel: 718-317-2803; Fax: 718-317-2830. Total Staff 182; Total Assisted 297.

New York Foundling Charitable Corp., 590 Avenue of the Americas, 10011. Tel: 212-633-9300; Web: www.nyfoundling.org. Mr. William Baccaglini, Asst. Treas.

New York Foundling Hospital, The, 590 Avenue of the Americas, 10011. Tel: 212-633-9300; Fax: 212-886-4086; Email: info@nyfoundling.org; Web: www.nyfoundling.org. Mr. William Baccaglini, Pres. & CEO.

MILLBROOK. *Cardinal Hayes Home for Children* (1941) Residential care for developmentally disabled children and young adults. St. Joseph Dr., P.O. Box CH, Millbrook, 12545. Tel: 845-677-6363; Fax: 845-677-6691; Email: cvarano@cardinalhayeshome.org; Email: mhurley@cardinalhayeshome.org; Web: www.cardinalhayeshome.org. Catherine Varano, Exec. Community Supervised Individualized Residential Alternative (IRA) 9; Franciscan Missionaries of Mary 3; Capacity of Residential Facilities: Millbrook Intermediate Care Facility 60; Community Intermediate Care Facilities 50.

RHINEBECK. *Astor Learning Center, The* The Astor Learning Center (ALC) is an intensive, highly structured, school-based treatment program operated by Astor Services for Children & Families. An interdisciplinary team of trained professionals provides educational services to emotionally disabled children ages 5 to 12. The Program utilizes a holistic approach for developing the social, emotional, and educational needs of our children through a nurturing and supportive environment. We currently serve both residential and day student populations. 6339 Mill St., P.O. Box 5005, Rhinebeck, 12572-5005. Tel: 845-871-1032; Fax: 845-876-2020; Web: www.astorservices.org. John J. Kegan, Prin. Capacity 75; Total Staff 50; Total Assisted 107.

Astor Services for Children & Families Residential Treatment Facility for severe emotionally disturbed-mentally ill boys and girls, ages 5-12. 6339 Mill St., P.O. Box 5005, Rhinebeck, 12572-5005. Tel: 845-871-1000; Fax: 845-876-2020; Email: jmcguirk@astorservices.org; Web: www.astorservices.org. James McGuirk, Ph.D., Exec. Dir. & CEO. Bed Capacity 20.

*Residential Treatment Center (Rhinebeck)*Bed Capacity 27; Therapeutic Foster Boarding Homes 30; Family-Based Treatment 10.

Counseling Centers: Poughkeepsie, Beacon, Bronx, Dover, Hyde Park, Ulster County - Kingston, Ellenville, New Paltz (Ages birth-18).

Day Treatment Programs (Ages 3-12) Capacity 397.

Astor Family Services Program, Bronx (Ages birth-18) Capacity 90.

*Head Start-Day Care Centers: Poughkeepsie, Beacon, Millerton, Wingdale, Wappingers Falls, Red Hook, Hyde Park*Capacity 418.

*Day Care Centers: Beacon, Wingdale*Capacity 50.

Special Class Integrated Services (Ages 3-5) Capacity 32.

*Early Head Start*Capacity 135; Total Staff 718; Total Assisted 5,515.

YONKERS. **Elizabeth Seton Pediatric Center* (1987) 300 Corporate Blvd., S., Yonkers, 10701. Tel: 914-294-6300; Fax: 914-294-6305; Email: ptursi@setonpediatric.org; Web: www.setonpediatric.org. Patricia A. Tursi, CEO. Sponsored by Sisters of Charity of St. Vincent de Paul of New York. Bed Capacity 137; Tot Asst. Annually 184; Total Staff 492.

[S] CHILDREN'S AGENCIES & PROTECTIVE INSTITUTIONS

NEW YORK. *Catholic Guardian Services* (1899) 1011 First Ave., 10th Fl., 10022. Tel: 212-371-1000; Fax: 212-935-7820; Email: clongley@catholicguardian.org. Mr. Craig Longley, Exec. Dir. Residences and family respite support programs for developmentally disabled adults and adolescents. Group home program for boys and girls, ages 13-21 years; foster and kinship family care and adoption for boys and girls, ages 0-21; provides regular and therapeutic foster homes for boys and girls ages 0-21; and specialized foster homes for children with behavioral issues, HIV/AIDS and special medical conditions; Child abuse and neglect prevention programs; Specialized group care programs for maternity and mother-child population, children with special needs, pregnancy and parenting support services; private adoption services; post-adoption services and after-care services for women with children; and shelter and family care for unaccompanied minors. Total Staff 1,200; Total Assisted 3,863.

LINCOLNDALE. *Lincoln Hall*, P.O. Box 600, Lincolndale, 10540. Tel: 914-248-7474; Fax: 914-248-8391; Email: info@lincolnhall.org. Jack Flavin, Exec. Dir. Capacity (Boys) 224; Total Staff 265; Total Assisted 1,600.

[T] CATHOLIC CHARITIES - CHILD CARING AGENCIES

OSSINING. *The Cardinal McCloskey Emergency Residential School*, 155 N. Highland Ave., Ossining, 10562. Tel: 914-762-5302; Fax: 914-762-7844; Email: jfedele@cardinalmccloskey.org. Teachers 4; Assistants 2.

RYE. *Catholic World Mission, Inc.* (1998) 815 Boston Post Rd., Rye, 10580. Tel: 770-828-4966; Fax: 770-828-4955; Email: eramirez@arcol.org; Web: www.catholicworldmission.org. Tot Asst. Annually 100,000; Total Staff 5.

[U] DAY NURSERIES

NEW YORK. *St. Benedict's Day Nursery, Day Care Center*, 21 W. 124th St., 10027. Tel: 212-423-5715; Fax: 212-423-5917; Email: st.benedictdaynursery@yahoo.com. Sr. Mary Ann Baichan, F.H.M., Prin.; Doris Moore, Office Admin. Children 50; Lay Teachers 2; Handmaids of the Most Pure Heart of Mary 2.

Providence Rest Child Day Care Center, Inc. (1991) (UPK District 8) 3310 Campbell Dr., 10465. Tel: 718-823-3588; Fax: 718-518-8930. Sr. Theresa Ann D'Onofrio, C.S.JB., Dir.; Tina Marie Robbinson-Lopez, Teacher. Sisters 1; Total Staff 7; Total Assisted 18.

San Jose Day Nursery, 432 W. 20th St., 10011. Tel: 212-929-0839; Email: sanjoseday@yahoo.com. Sisters Haydee Luisa Fernandez, Supr.; Trinidad Fernandez, Dir. Clergy 3; Students 55.

YONKERS. *Queen's Daughters Day Care Center, Inc.* (1903) 73 Buena Vista Ave., Yonkers, 10701. Tel: 914-969-4491; Fax: 914-969-4823; Email: qddcc@excite.com. Barbara Berrios, Dir. Children 125; Lay Teachers 12; Total Staff 20.

[V] GENERAL HOSPITALS

NEW YORK. *Saint Vincent Catholic Medical Centers of New York*, 5 Penn Plaza, 9th Fl., 10001. Tel: 212-356-4400; Email: jcoffey@svcmcny.org; Web: svcmc.org. Jennifer Coffey, Gen. Counsel. Bed Capacity 662; Tot Asst. Annually 300,000; Total Staff 4,545.

Bayley Seton Campus, 75 Vanderbilt Ave., Staten Island, 10304. Tel: 212-356-4792. Jennifer Coffey, Gen. Counsel.

Saint Vincent's Catholic Medical Centers Foundation, Inc., Saint Vincents Catholic Medical Centers of New York, 5 Penn Plaza, 9th Fl., 10001. Tel: 212-356-4400; Fax: 646-502-5565; Email: jcoffey@svcmcny.org. Jennifer Coffey, Gen. Counsel.

KINGSTON. *Benedictine Hospital* (1901) 105 Mary's Ave., Kingston, 12401. Tel: 845-338-2500; Fax: 845-334-3149; Web: www.hahv.org. Sisters Mary Feehan, O.S.B., Senior Vice Pres., Mission Effectiveness; Mary Dorothy Huggard, O.S.B., Dir., Pastoral Care. Capacity 150; Patients Asst Anual. 77,748; Sisters of St. Benedict (Federation of St. Scholastica) 3; Total Staff 727.

PORT JERVIS. *Bon Secours Community Hospital* (1915) Part of Bon Secours Charity Health System 160 E. Main St., Port Jervis, 12771. Tel: 845-858-7000; Fax: 845-858-7415; Email: jeff_reilly@bshsi.org; Web: http://bschs.bonsecours.com. Jeff Reilly, Sr. Vice Pres. Opers.; Clare Brady, SVP Mission. Sisters of Charity of St. ElizabethSisters of Bon Secours Capacity 168; Patients Asst Anual. 69,360; Total Staff 432; SNF Beds 46.

SUFFERN. *Good Samaritan Hospital* Part of Bon Secours Charity Health System 255 Lafayette Ave., Suffern, 10901. Tel: 845-368-5000; Fax: 845-368-5430; Web: http://bsch.bonsecours.com. Mary P. Leahy, M.D., CEO, Bon Secours Charity Health System; Sr. Susan Evelyn, R.S.M., Sr. Vice Pres. Mission. Sisters of Charity of St. ElizabethSisters of Bon Secours Bed Capacity 286; Patients Asst Anual. 276,181; Sisters of Charity of St. Elizabeth & Sisters of Bon Secours 1; Total Staff 1,796.

WARWICK. *St. Anthony Community Hospital* Part of Bon Secours Charity Health System 15-19 Maple Ave., Warwick, 10990. Tel: 845-986-2276; Fax: 845-986-2687; Web: http://bschs.bonsecours.com. Jeff Reilly, Senior Vice Pres. & Admin.; Clare Brady, SVP Mission. Sisters of Charity of St. ElizabethSisters of Bon Secours Capacity 62; Patients Asst Anual. 46,830; Total Staff 283.

YONKERS. *St. Joseph's Medical Center* (1888) 127 S. Broadway, Yonkers, 10701. Tel: 914-378-7000; Fax: 914-965-4838; Email: public.relations@saintjosephs.org; Web: saintjosephs.org. Mr. Michael J. Spicer, Pres.; Rev. Thomas Murphy, O.F.M.Cap.; Sr. Dolores Doyle, P.B.V.M., Dir., Pastoral Care. Bed Capacity 394; Patients Asst Anual. 340,407; Sisters of Charity of St. Vincent de Paul 7; Total Staff 1,411; Nursing Home Beds 200.

[W] SPECIAL HOSPITALS AND SANATORIA FOR INVALIDS

NEW YORK. *Calvary Hospital* (1889) For advanced cancer patients. 1740 Eastchester Rd., Bronx, 10461. Tel: 718-863-6900; Fax: 718-518-2674; Email: sgarry@calvaryhospital.org; Web: www.calvaryhospital.org. Frank A. Calamari, Pres. & CEO; Rev. Chux Okochi, Dir. Pastoral Svcs. Bed Capacity 200; Tot Asst. Annually 5,756; Total Staff 1,038; Pastoral Staff 27; Accommodations for 225.

Terence Cardinal Cooke Health Care Center, 1249 Fifth Ave., 10029. Tel: 212-360-1000;

Fax: 212-289-2739; Email: npollack@archcare.org; Web: www.archcare.org. Neil Pollack, Admin. Hospital for developmentally disabled. Bed Capacity 50.

Developmental Disabilities Clinic, 1249 Fifth Ave., 10029. Tel: 212-360-3703; Fax: 212-360-3842. Comprehensive Outpatient medical, therapeutic and educational services. On site and off site OMRDD Article 16 services. Patients Asst Anual. 44,000.

BRONX. *St. Eleanora's Home for Convalescents* (1901) Sisters of Charity Center, 6301 Riverdale Ave., Bronx, 10471-1046. Tel: 718-549-9200; Fax: 718-884-3013; Email: mobrien@scny.org; Web: scny.org. Sr. Margaret M. O'Brien, Treas. Tot Asst. Annually 100; Total Staff 8.

HARRISON. *St. Vincent's Hospital Westchester, a Division of Saint Joseph's Medical Center* (1879) 275 North St., Harrison, 10528. Tel: 914-967-6500; Fax: 914-925-5157; Web: www.svcmc.org. Bernadette Kingham-Bez. Psychiatric Hospital; Clergy Consultation Program; Inpatient and outpatient mental health and substance abuse services for adults, adolescents, children and their families. Sites in Harrison, Tuckahoe & White Plains. Services available in Spanish. Capacity 133; Sisters of Charity of St. Vincent de Paul 3; Inpatients Assisted Annually 2,891; All outpatient program admissions 165,000; Partial Hospital 50; Opiod Maintenance Treatment Program 43.

HAWTHORNE. *Rosary Hill Home* (1901) Free home for incurable cancer patients. 600 Linda Ave, Hawthorne, 10532. Tel: 914-769-0114; Fax: 914-769-3916; Email: srmthanh@gmail.com; Web: www.rosaryhillhome.org. Sisters Mary Edwin, O.P., Admin.; Mary Thanh, O.P., Supr.

The Servants of Relief for Incurable Cancer Bed Capacity 54; Capacity 54; Professed Sisters of St. Dominic 25; Tot Asst. Annually 122; Total Staff 45.

[X] ORDERS OF NURSING SISTERS

NEW YORK. *Little Sisters of the Assumption Family Health Service, Inc.* (1958) 333 E. 115th St., 10029. Tel: 646-672-5200; Fax: 212-348-8284. Reada Edelstein, Interim CEO.

BRONX. *Sisters, Servants of Mary, Ministers to the Sick* Mission: Private nursing in the homes. 3305 Country Club Rd., Bronx, 10465-1296. Tel: 718-829-0428; Fax: 718-829-2346; Email: superiorany@gmail.com; Web: sistersservantsofmary.org. Sr. Germana Contreras, S.deM., Mother Supr. Sisters 14.

OSSINING. **Dominican Sisters Family Health Service, Inc. (DSFHS) (Corporate Office/Administration)* (1974) 299 N. Highland Ave., Bldg. 7, Ossining, 10562-2327. Tel: 914-941-1710; Fax: 914-941-0518; Email: rscanga@dsfhs.org; Web: www.dsfhs.org. DSFHS is community-based, Joint Commission Accredited Certified Home Health Agency providing home nursing care, rehabilitation, social work, pastoral care, and other health related services in All of NYC's five boroughs, Westchester/Putnam, Rockland/Orange and Nassau/Suffolk Counties. Total Staff 775; Total Patients 11,586; Total Visits 235,131. Executive Officers Mary Zagajeski, M.S., R.N., Pres./CEO; John A. Salandra, CPA, FHFMA, CFO; Randolf P. Palmaira, COO`.

New York City Offices, Bronx Office, 279 Alexander Ave., Bronx, 10454. Tel: 718-665-6557; Fax: 718-292-9113. Mary Lou Harren-Matamoras, R.N., Regional Admin., NYC.

Hudson Valley Offices, Westchester Office, 299 N. Highland Ave., Bldg. 4, Ossining, 10562. Tel: 914-941-1710; Fax: 914-941-1556; Email: acrane@dsfhs.org. Ann Crane, R.N., Regional Admin., Hudson Valley.

Suffolk County Offices, Hampton Bay Office, 103-6 W. Montauk Hwy., Hampton Bays, 11946. Tel: 631-728-0181; Fax: 631-728-2943; Email: ptobin@dsfhs.org; Web: www.dsfhs.org. Patricia Tobin, Regl. Admin., Long Island. 2 Offices in Suffolk.

3237 Rte. 112, Bldg. 6, Medford, 11763. Tel: 631-736-1527; Fax: 631-736-1747.

**Family Home Health Care, Inc.* (Licensed Home Health Care Affiliate) (LHCSA) LHCSA - Westchester, 65 S. Broadway, Tarrytown, 10591. Tel: 914-631-7200; Fax: 914-631-2382; Email: sniman@dsfhs.org. Sharon Niman, R.N., Vice Pres. LCHSA Svcs.

Family Home Health Care, Inc. (Licensed Home Health Care Affiliate) (LHCSA) LHCSA - Suffolk, 3237 Rte. 112, Bldg. 6, Medford, 11763. Tel: 631-289-9560; Fax: 631-289-9562; Email: sniman@dsfhs.org. Sharon Niman, R.N., Vice Pres. LCHSA Svcs.

[Y] NURSING HOMES

NEW YORK. *Kateri Residence* (1981) Skilled Nursing Care/Residential Health Care Facility for the Elderly. 150 Riverside Dr., 10024-2201. Tel: 646-633-4700; Web: www.archcare.org.

Mary Manning Walsh Home, 1339 York Ave., 10021. Tel: 212-628-2800; Fax: 212-585-3896; Email: swilliam@archcare.org. Sr. Sean William O'Brien, O.Carm., Exec. Dir. Carmelite Sisters for the Aged and Infirm. Bed Capacity 362; Total Staff 480; Total Assisted 724.

Terence Cardinal Cooke Health Care Center Skilled Nursing Facility AIDS Program 1249 Fifth Ave., 10029. Tel: 212-360-1000; Fax: 212-289-2739; Email: npollack@archcare.net; Web: www.tcchcc.org. Skilled Nursing Facility; (See Special Hospitals Category for additional services offered from this Health Care Center.) Bed Capacity 523; Bed Capacity 156.

BRONX. *Bon Secours New York Health System, Inc.*, 2975 Independence Ave., Bronx, 10463-4699. Tel: 718-548-1700; Fax: 718-554-8826; Email: stephen_kazanjian@bshsi.org; Web: www.scherviercares.org. Carlos G. Beato, CEO; Charles Ignatius, Chap. & Dir., Pastoral Care

Frances Schervier Home and Hospital

Frances Schervier Housing Development Fund Corporation Bed Capacity 366; Tot Asst. Annually 1,050; Total Staff 458.

Jeanne Jugan Residence (1903) 2999 Schurz Ave., Bronx, 10465. Tel: 347-329-1800; Fax: 347-329-1815; Email: bxmothersuperior@littlesistersofthepoor.org; Web: www.littlesistersofthepoorbronx.org. Sr. Gertrude Maiorino, Pres. Bed Capacity 47; Skilled 30; Tot Asst. Annually 90; Total Staff 60; Day Share 16; Low Income Apartments 17.

St. Patrick's Home for the Aged and Infirm (1931) 66 Van Cortlandt Park S., Bronx, 10463. Tel: 718-519-2800; Fax: 718-304-1817; Email: www.admissions@stpatrickshome.org; Web: www.stpatrickshome.org/. Sr. M. Kevin Patricia, O.-Carm., Admin. Carmelite Sisters for the Aged and Infirm. Bed Capacity 264; Sisters 15; Tot Asst. Annually 429; Total Staff 350.

Providence Rest (1922) 3304 Waterbury Ave., Bronx, 10465. Tel: 718-931-3000; Fax: 718-514-8447; Email: prnh@providencerest.org; Web: www.providencerest.org. Sisters Seline Mary Flores, C.S.J.B., CEO; Loretta Marie Florio, C.S.J.B., Supr. Bed Capacity 200; Sisters of St. John the Baptist 19; Tot Asst. Annually 559; Total Staff 320.

St. Vincent de Paul Residence (1992) 900 Intervale Ave., Bronx, 10459. Tel: 917-645-9200; Fax: 718-589-7010; Email: fcianciotto@chcsnet.org; Web: www.svdpres.org. Mr. Frank Cianciotto, CEO.

DOBBS FERRY. *Cabrini of Westchester*, 115 Broadway, Dobbs Ferry, 10522. Tel: 914-693-6800; Fax: 914-693-1731; Email: sstrangio@cabrini-eldercare.org; Web: www.cabrini-eldercare.org. Patricia Krasnausky, Pres. & CEO; Rev. Edwin F.D. Robinson, O.F.M., Dir. Pastoral Care. Bed Capacity 304; Missionary Sisters of the Sacred Heart 6; Total Staff 425; Home Health Care 250; Adult Day Health Care 50.

MIDDLETOWN. *St. Teresa's Nursing Home*, 120 Highland Ave., Middletown, 10940. Tel: 845-342-1033; Fax: 845-344-5631; Email: mchaiken@chcsnet.org. Bed Capacity 98; Total Staff 122; Total Assisted 98.

RHINEBECK. *Ferncliff Nursing Home* (1973) 21 Ferncliff Dr., Rhinebeck, 12572. Tel: 845-876-2011; Fax: 845-876-4810. Sr. Sean Damien Flynn, O.-Carm., B.S., M.B.A., Admin. Member: Catholic Health Care System. Bed Capacity 328; Total Staff 450; Total Assisted 410.

STATEN ISLAND. *Carmel Richmond Healthcare and Rehabilitation Center* (1969) 88 Old Town Rd., Staten Island, 10304-4299. Tel: 718-979-5000; Fax: 718-979-8027. Sr. Maureen T. Murray, O.-Carm., Pres. & CEO. Carmelite Sisters for the Aged and Infirm. Bed Capacity 300; Tot Asst. Annually 330; Total Staff 350.

Friends of Carmel Richmond, Inc. (1981) Staten Island. Tel: 718-979-5000; Fax: 718-979-8027. Adult Daycare Program. Total Staff 350; Adult Day Healthcare Program Rehabilitation Unit 30; Total Assisted 330.

WARWICK. *Schervier Pavilion* Schervier Pavilion Part of Bon Secours Charity Health System. 22 Van Duzer Pl., Warwick, 10990. Tel: 845-987-5717; Fax: 845-986-1231; Web: bschs.bonsecours.com. Jeff Reilly, Senior Vice Pres. & Admin.; Clare Brady, Senior Vice Pres. Mission. Sisters of Charity of St. ElizabethSisters of Bon Secours Capacity 120.

[Z] ADULT RESIDENCES

NEW YORK. *St. Agnes' Residence*, 237 W. 74th St., 10023. Tel: 212-874-1361. Nancy Clifford, Admin. Franciscan Fathers of St. Francis Monastery.For students and working women. Daughters of Mary of the Immaculate Conception 2; Total Staff 6; Accommodations for 99; Total Assisted 104.

Centro Maria, Inc., 539 W. 54th St., 10019. Tel: 212-757-6989; Fax: 212-307-5687; Email: cenmariany@gmail.com; Web: www.religiosasmariainmaculada.org. Sr. Maryanne Fernandes, R.M.I., Local Supr. For young students and working women. Bed Capacity 86; Tot Asst. Annually 667; Religious of Mary Immaculate 8.

Cor Mariae, c/o 1011 First Ave., Rm. 1130, 10022. Tel: 212-371-1000, Ext. 2435. Residence for formerly homeless senior women.

The Dwelling Place of NY, Inc. (1977) For homeless women. 409 W. 40th St., 10018. Tel: 212-564-7887; Fax: 212-695-3642; Email: dpny409@aol.com; Web: www.thedwellingplaceofny.org. Sr. Joann Sambs, C.S.A., Admin. Bed Capacity 14; Tot Asst. Annually 1,500; Total Staff 11; Dinner Program (weekly) 50; Total Assisted 12,000.

El Carmelo Residence, 249 W. 14th St., 10011. Tel: 212-242-8224; Fax: 212-242-7233. Sr. Modesta Perez, Supr.

The Jeanne d'Arc Residence (1896) 253 W. 24th St., 10011. Tel: 212-989-5952; Fax: 212-337-3450; Email: jdaresidence@gmail.com. Ms. Eileen C. Piazza, Admin. Women. Lay Staff 13; Sisters of Divine Providence 5; Tot Asst. Annually 200; Accommodations for 139.

St. Joseph's Immigrant Home For students and working women. 425 W. 44th St., 10036-4402. Tel: 212-246-5363. Sr. Mary Celine, D.M., Admin. Daughters of Mary of the Immaculate Conception 2; Accommodations for 90.

Kolping Society of New York Men's Residence (Catholic Kolping Society New York, Inc.) (1888) 165 E. 88th St., 10128. Tel: 212-369-6647; Fax: 212-987-5652; Email: residence@kolpingny.org; Web: www.kolpingny.org. Katrina Dengler, Pres. Short-term residence for Christian young students and working young men. Bed Capacity 88; Tot Asst. Annually 350; Total Staff 10.

The Leo House (1889) 332 W. 23rd St., 10011. Tel: 212-929-1010; Fax: 212-366-6801. Mr. Frank Castro, Exec. Dir. Clergy, Sisters & Other Travelers. Bed Capacity 81; Total Staff 35.

St. Mary's Residence (1913) 225 E. 72nd St., 10021. Tel: 212-249-6850; Fax: 212-249-4336; Email: St. MarysRes72@aol.com. Sr. Almaisa Brito, F.D.C., Admin.; Mrs. Lisa Rodriguez, Dir. of Admissions. For students and young working women. Bed Capacity 152; Daughters of Divine Charity 4; Tot Asst. Annually 152; Total Staff 15.

Sacred Heart Residence, 432 W. 20th St., 10011. Tel: 212-929-5790; Fax: 212-924-0891; Email: sacredheartresidence@hotmail.com; Web: www.sacredheartresidence.com. Sr. Haydee Luisa Fernandez, Admin. Congregation of Mothers of the Helpless.Working or studying young ladies ages 19-29. Capacity 30; Total Staff 3.

Thorpe Family Residence, Inc. (1988) 2252 Crotona Ave., 10457. Tel: 718-933-7312; Fax: 718-933-7311; Email: mcallaghan@nazarethhousingnyc.org; Web: thorpeonline.org. Bernard Carr, Exec. Dir. Residents 65; Total Staff 10; Total Assisted 130.

BRONX. *Kolping-on-Concourse*, 2916 Grand Concourse, Bronx, 10458. Tel: 718-733-6119; Email: kolpingconcourse@yahoo.com; Web: www.kolpingny.org. Jose A. Aguiluz, Mgr. (Catholic Kolping Society New York, Inc.) Bed Capacity 96; Tot Asst. Annually 124; Total Staff 11.

DOBBS FERRY. *Cabrini Housing Development Fund Corporation*, c/o of St. Cabrini Nursing Home, Inc., 115 Broadway, Dobbs Ferry, 10522. Tel: 914-693-6800; Fax: 914-693-1731; Email: pkrasnausky@cabrini-eldercare.org; Web: www.cabrini-eldercare.org. Patricia Krasnausky, Pres.

GARRISON. *St. Christopher's Inn* (1908) 21 Franciscan Way, P.O. Box 150, Garrison, 10524-0150. Tel: 845-335-1000; Fax: 845-335-1017; Email: dpolanco@atonementfriars.org; Web: www.stchristophersinn-graymoor.org. Rev. Dennis Polanco, S.A., Pres. Atonement Friars.Temporary shelter for homeless men. Outpatient chemical dependency services & primary healthcare. Bed Capacity 180; Tot Asst. Annually 1,100; Total Staff 109; Volunteers 25; Total Assisted 1,100.

MONTROSE. *Kolping-on-Hudson* (Catholic Kolping Society New York, Inc.) 95 Montrose Point Rd., Montrose, 10548. Tel: 914-736-0117; Email: residence@kolpingny.org; Web: www.kolpingny.org. Katrina Dengler, Pres. Tot Asst. Annually 1,300; Total Staff 10.

MOUNT VERNON. *St. Theresa's Residence*, 30 S. 10th Ave., Mount Vernon, 10550. Tel: 914-664-5900; Fax: 914-664-6733. John Schroeder, Exec. Dir. Bed Capacity 12.

TARRYTOWN. **The Crotona Thorpe Housing Development Fund Corporation*, 48 Wilson Park Dr., Tarrytown, 10591. Tel: 845-359-6400; Fax: 845-359-6503. Sr. Irene Ellis, O.P., Pres.

[AA] CATHOLIC CAMPS

NEW YORK. *The Catholic Camp Association Inc.*, 1011 First Ave., 10022. Tel: 212-371-1000.

John V. Mara CYO Camps, Putnam Valley, 10579.

*Hill Camp*Capacity 120.

*Valley Camp*Capacity 120; Total in Residence 271; Total Staff 48; Total Assisted 147.

RYE. *RC Activities, Inc.* (1997) 815 Boston Post Rd., Rye, 10580. Tel: 770-828-4950; Email: eramirez@arcol.org. Rev. Frank Formolo, Contact Person. Clergy 300; Students 2,000.

[BB] COMMUNITY CENTERS

NEW YORK. *Archbishop Fulton J. Sheen Center, Inc.* (2014) 18 Bleecker St., 10012. Tel: 212-219-3132; Web: www.sheencenter.org. William Spencer Reilly, Exec. Dir.

Cardinal Spellman Center, Inc., 137 E. Second St., 10009. Tel: 212-677-6600; Fax: 212-995-8537. Community Centers foster and promote the positive development of children, youth, their families and other adults by providing or hosting various wholesome activities.

Casita Maria Inc. (1934) 928 Simpson St., 6th Fl., Bronx, 10459. Tel: 718-589-2230; Fax: 718-842-4622; Email: info@casitamaria.org; Web: www.casitamaria.org. Haydee Morales, Exec. Dir.; Mrs. Jacqueline Weld, Chm. Serves the Bronx, East Harlem, and greater New York City; Casita Maria serves over 5,000 individuals each year through arts, education, and community programs.

Casita Maria Inc., 928 Simpson St., Bronx, 10459. Tel: 718-589-2230; Fax: 718-589-5714.

Drew-Hamilton CYO Center, 220 W. 143rd St., 10030. Serves Central Harlem.

Lieut. Joseph P. Kennedy, Jr. Memorial Community Center, 34 W. 134th St., 10037.

Tel: 212-862-6401, Ext. 410; Fax: 212-862-6421. Deacon Rodney Beckford. Community Centers foster and promote the positive development of children, youth, their families and other adults by providing or hosting various wholesome activities.

Life Experience and Faith Sharing Associates, 1991A Lexington Ave., 10035. Tel: 212-987-0959; Fax: 212-987-0958; Email: kmay@scny-lefsa.com; Web: www.scny-lefsa.org. Karolina May, LEFSA Team Dir.; James Addison, LEFSA Team - Opers. Mgr. LEFSA - Ministry among people who are homeless and formerly homeless. Total Staff 8; Total Assisted 3,000.

Staten Island CYO Center Serves residents of Port Richmond and surrounding areas.

120 Anderson Ave., Port Richmond, Staten Island, 10302. Fax: 718-273-8361.

HAVERSTRAW. *Catholic Charities Community Services of Rockland, Inc.*, 78 Hudson Ave., Haverstraw, 10927. Tel: 845-942-5791; Fax: 845-429-2938; Email: martha.robles@archny.org. Martha Robles, Exec. Dir. Provides emergency services to those in need.

PORT CHESTER. *Don Bosco Community Center of Port Chester, Inc.*, Office of the Pres., 22 Don Bosco Pl., Port Chester, 10573. Tel: 914-939-0323, Ext. 11; Fax: 914-939-3490; Email: dbccportchester@yahoo.com; Web: www.donboscocenter.com.

YONKERS. *Casa Juan Diego, Inc.*, 97 Yonkers Ave., Yonkers, 10701. Tel: 914-963-0250; Fax: 914-476-5033. Rev. Agustino Miguel Torres, C.F.R., Exec. Dir.; Bro. Philip Allen, C.F.R., Dir. Services to the needy; especially Spanish Speaking immigrants, day laborers.

[CC] MONASTERIES AND RESIDENCES OF PRIESTS AND BROTHERS

NEW YORK. *All Saints Friary* (2002) 47 E. 129th St., 10035. Tel: 212-534-3535; Fax: 212-534-7832.

America; Residence and publication office of the America Press, 120 W. 60th St, 10023.

Tel: 917-444-5313; Email: americahouseguest@gmail.com. Revs. Matthew F. Malone, S.J., Editor-in-Chief; Robert C. Collins, S.J.; Vincent P. DeCola, S.J.; Daniel J. Gatti, S.J.; Roger D. Haight, S.J.; Philip G. Judge, S.J., Supr.; James J. Martin, S.J.; James J. Miracky, S.J.; Damian O'Connell, S.J.; Leo J. O'Donovan, S.J.; Joseph P. Parkes, S.J.; Michael E. Sehler, S.J.; John J. Hanwell, S.J.; Samuel Sawyer; Edward W. Schmidt, S.J.; Jeremy Zipple. Priests 15.

Atonement Friars, 138 Waverly Pl., 10014-3845. Tel: 212-243-4692; Fax: 212-675-6160; Email: info@atonementfriars.org; Web: www.atonementfriars.org. Bro. Gerard Hand, S.A., (Retired); Rev. Charles J. Sharon, S.A., 4th Gen. Councilor, Sec. Gen. & Assoc. Treas.; Very Rev. Brian F. Terry, S.A.

Brothers of the Christian Schools of Manhattan College, Inc., 4415 Post Rd., Bronx, 10471. Bros. Lawrence Goyette, Pres.; John Muller, F.S.C., Sec. Total in Residence 23; Total Staff 4.

Calasanzian Fathers (Piarists), 88 Convent Ave., 10027. Tel: 212-234-1919; Fax: 212-281-7205; Email: annunciationchurchnyc@yahoo.com. Revs. Baltazar Sanchez, Sch.P., (Mexico) Pastor; Jose M. Clavero, Sch.P., (Spain) Associate Pastor; Szymon Kurpios, Sch.P., (Poland) Parochial Vicar; Felix Ganuza, Sch.P., (Spain) Parochial Vicar.

St. Catherine of Siena Priory, 411 E. 68th St., 10021. Tel: 212-988-8300; Fax: 212-988-6918; Email: info@stcatherinenyc.org. Rev. Walter Cornelius Wagner, O.P., J.D., S.T.L., Prior; Bro. Ignatius Perkins, O.P., R.N., Ph.D., Dir., Dominican Friars Healthcare Ministry of NY; Revs. David Adiletta, O.P., S.T.L., Sec., The Missions; Jonah F. Pollock, O.P., Hospital Chap.; Jerome Zeiler, Parochial Vicar; Joseph Allen, O.P., Parochial Vicar; Bro. Thomas Aquinas Dolan, O.P.

St. Clare Friary, 440 W. 36th St., 10018-6326. Tel: 212-594-4108; Email: sground440@aol.com; Web: www.solidgroundministry.com. Rev. James Goode, O.F.M., Ph.D., Local Minister, Pastoral Dir., Solid Ground Ministry; Harold Williams Jr., Affiliate, Solid Ground Prog. Coord.; James P. Newson Jr., Affiliate Black Catholic Apostolate for Life Asst.; Florence Binns, Affiliate Asst. *Shrine of Saint Josephine Bakhita* In the Holy Mother of God Chapel Tel: 212-868-1847; Web: www.solidgroundministry.com. *Solid Ground Ministry: A Franciscan Ministry with African American Families* (1996) Tel: 212-868-1847; Email: sground440@aol.com; Web: www.solidgroundministry.com. *National Black Catholic Apostolate for Life* (1997) Tel: 212-594-4108; Email: tnbcalife@aol.com; Web: www.blackcatholicsforlife.org.

St. Crispin Friary (1987) 420 E. 156th St., Bronx, 10455. Tel: 718-665-2441; Fax: 718-292-2432; Email: cfrgensec@gmail.com; Web: www.franciscanfriars.com. Revs. James Mary Atkins, C.F.R.; Mark Ames, Pastoral Assoc.; Friars Patrick Crowley; Simon Dankoski, C.F.R.; Revs. Louis Marie Leonelli, C.F.R.; John-Mary Johannssen, Vicar; Fidelis Moscinski, C.F.R., Supr.; Fr. Maximilian Mary Stelmachowski, C.F.R. *Franciscan Friars of the Renewal* (1987) 421 E. 155th St., Bronx, 10455. Tel: 718-402-8255; Fax: 718-402-5556; Web: www.franciscanfriars.com. Bro. Peter Westall, C.F.R., Treas,; Rev. John Anthony Boughton, C.F.R., Vicar; Bros. John Joseph Brice, C.F.R., Admin.; Xavier Mariae Meiergerd, C.F.R.; Revs. Fidelis Moscinski, C.F.R., Admin.; John Paul Ouellette, Supr.; Bro. Maximilian Stelmachowski. Brothers 3; Priests 5.

St. Francis Monastery Foundation, Inc., 129 W. 31st St., 2nd Fl., 10001-3403. Tel: 212-736-8500; Email: hnp@hnp.org. Rev. Dennis M. Wilson, O.F.M., Treas.

Franciscan Friars, Holy Name Province, Holy Name Province Provincialate, 129 W. 31st St., 2nd Fl., 10001-3403. Tel: 646-473-0265; Fax: 800-420-1078; Email: admin@hnp.org; Web: www.hnp.org. Very Rev. Kevin J. Mullen, O.F.M., Pres. & Min. Prov.; Rev. Lawrence Hayes, O.F.M., Vicar Prov.; Bro. Michael Harlan, O.F.M., Prov. Sec.; Rev. Dennis M. Wilson, O.F.M., Prov. Treas.

The Order of Friars Minor of the Province of the Most Holy Name

Priests of the Province in Residences not listed elsewhere: Revs. Christopher B. Keenan, O.F.M., B.A., M.A., D.Min., Seton Hall University, 400 S. Orange Ave., South Orange, NJ 07079-2696. Tel: 973-761-9770; Fax: 973-275-2333; James R. O'Connell, O.F.M.; Benedict M. Taylor, O.F.M., Create Inc., 73 Lenox Ave., 10026. Tel: 212-663-1975; Fax: 212-663-1293.

Franciscan Province of the Immaculate Conception, 125 Thompson St., 10012. Tel: 212-674-4388; Fax: 212-533-8034. Revs. Robert M. Campagna, O.F.M., Min. Prov.; Patrick Boyle, O.F.M., Vicar Prov. & Prov. Sec.; James Goode, O.F.M., Ph.D., Promoter Missions; Bro. Vincent de Paul Ciaravino, O.F.M., Treas. Franciscan Province of the Immaculate Conception of New York City.

Friars Minor of the Order of St. Francis, Incorporated, New York, 1871 Brothers 23; Priests 94; Permanent Deacons 1; Bishops 4. *Franciscan Mission Associates*, 274-280 W. Lincoln Ave., Mount Vernon, 10550. Tel: 914-664-5604; Fax: 914-664-3017; Email: mbonnici@franciscanmissionassoc.org. Ms. Madeline Bonnici, Exec. Dir.; Rev. Pierre John Farrugia, O.F.M., Spiritual Asst. Secular Franciscans.

Priests of the Province Abroad: Rev. Antonio Riccio, O.F.M., Guardian.

Military Chaplains: Rev. Michael Travaglione, O.F.M., St. Joseph Friary, P.O. Box 63, Onset, MA 02558-0063.

Retired Military Chaplains: Rev. Charles Soto, O.F.M., (Retired), VAPHS, P.O. Box 12049, Pittsburgh, PA 15240. Tel: 740-424-9434.

Priests of the Province Residing Elsewhere: Revs. Lucius Annese, O.F.M., 73 Simpson Ave., Somerville, MA 02144. Tel: 212-995-6056; Roderick Crispo, O.F.M., Redemptoris Mater, 77 Boylston St., Chestnut Hill, MA 02467-2501; Simeon C. Distefano, O.F.M., Chap., 1339 York Ave., 10021. Tel: 212-628-2800; Stephen Galambos, O.F.M., 15200 Magnolia St., Apt. 53, Westminster, CA 92683. Tel: 507-454-8000; Ciro Iodice, O.F.M., 1111 Langley St., Fall River, MA 02720. Tel: 508-679-2105; Clement Procopio, O.F.M., 30188 Mulholland Hwy., Agoura Hills, CA 91301-3107. Tel: 928-639-4583; Roberto Siguere, O.F.M., Orfanato Valle De Los Angeles, Santa Catarina Pinola, Guatemala.

Residing in Canada: Revs. Celestino Canzio, O.F.M., Villa Colombo, 40 Playfair Ave., Toronto, ON Canada M6B 2P9. Tel: 416-787-0369; Fax: 416-256-4466; Michael D'Cruz, O.F.M., Immaculate Conception Friary, 2 Richardson Ave., Toronto, ON Canada M6M 3R4. Tel: 416-787-0369; Fax: 416-256-4466; Conrad Fernandes, O.F.M., St. Francis of Assisi Friary, 72 Mansfield Ave., Toronto, ON Canada M6J 282; Giacomo LaSelva, O.F.M., St. Jane Frances Friary, 2747 Jane St., North York, ON Canada M3L 2E8; Frederick Mazzarella, O.F.M., St. Alphonsus Parish, 540 St. Clair Ave., W, Toronto, ON Canada M6C 1A4; Amedeo Nardone, O.F.M., St. Jane Frances de Chantal Friary, 2747 Jane St., Downsview, ON Canada M3L 2E8. Tel: 416-741-1463; Fax: 416-741-1469; Peter Nguyen Van Quy, O.F.M.; Rohwin Pais, O.F.M., Immaculate Conception Friary, 2 Richardson Ave., Toronto, ON Canada M3M 3R4; Ralph Paonessa, O.F.M., Immaculate Conception Friary, 2 Richardson Ave., Toronto, ON Canada M6M 3R4; Joseph Powell, O.F.M.; James Wells, O.F.M.; Jimmy Zammit, O.F.M., St. Francis of Assisi Friary, 72 Mansfield Ave., Toronto, ON Canada M6J 282. *St. Francis Center for Religious*, 208501 Hwy. #9, Caledon, ON Canada L7K OA8. Tel: 519-941-1747; Fax: 519-941-6961. Bro. Philip Adamo, O.F.M.; Revs. Peter Furgiuele, O.F.M.; Pierre John Farrugia, O.F.M., St. Francis Centre, 208501 Hwy. 9, Caledon, ON Canada L7K OA8.

St. Peter Friary, 100 Bainbridge Ave., Woodbridge, ON Canada L4L-3Y1. Tel: 905-851-3600; Fax: 905-856-0171. Revs. Michael Corcione, O.F.M.; Claudio Moser, O.F.M.; Giacomo La Selva, O.F.M.

The Franciscan Vocation Ministry of Holy Name Province (1901) 129 W. 31st St., 2nd Fl., 10001-3403. Tel: 646-473-0265; Tel: 800-677-7788; Fax: 800-793-7649; Email: vocations@hnp.org; Web: www.vocation.org. Rev. Dennis M. Wilson, O.F.M., Treas.

St. Ignatius Loyola Residence (1866) 53 E. 83rd St., 10028. Tel: 212-606-3420; Fax: 212-606-3460; Email: fpellegrini@jesuits.org. Revs. Frederick J. Pellegrini, S.J., Rector; Arthur C. Bender, S.J.; William J. Bergen, S.J.; Thomas H. Feely, S.J.; Michael P. Hilbert, S.J.; Michael McFarland, S.J.; Daniel G. O'Hare, S.J.; Michael J. Sala, S.J.; Dennis J. Yesalonia, S.J.; Ronald Amiot; James Carr; Philip A. Florio, S.J.; Michael J. Garanzini, S.J.; Daniel K. Lahart, S.J.; Brett McLaughlin; Leo J. O'Donovan, S.J.; Mr. Leopold Stuebner; Rev. Eric Sundrup.

Immaculate Conception Friary, 754 E. Gun Hill Rd., 10467. Tel: 212-653-2200. Rev. John Aurilia, O.F.M.Cap. Capuchin Friars of the Province of the Stigmata of St. Francis. Brothers 4; Priests 2; Total Staff 20; Total Assisted 190.

Institute of the Incarnate Word, Inc., 113 E. 117th St., 10035. Tel: 301-853-2789; Fax: 301-559-1713; Email: prov.immaculate.conception@ive.org; Web: www.iveamerica.org. Rev. Alberto Barattero, I.V.E., Pres.

Jesuit Community at Fordham University (1846) 441 E. Fordham Rd., Spellman Hall, 10458.

Tel: 718-817-5350; Fax: 718-817-5717; Email: rsarro@fordham.edu. Rev. Thomas J. Scirghi, S.J., Rector/Supr., Jesuit Community at Cardinal Spellman Hall. Priests 31. *Cardinal Spellman Hall, Jesuit Community* (1995) Tel: 718-817-5350; Fax: 718-817-5717. Revs. Thomas J. Scirghi, S.J., Rector; Ronald E. Wozniak, S.J., Min. & Asst. to Rector; R. Bentley Anderson, S.J.; Alexander H.D. Asmara, S.J.; Peter N. Bwanali, S.J.; Martin Chase, S.J.; Christopher M. Cullen, S.J.; John D. Cunningham, S.J.; Leo Daly, S.J.; Christopher J. Devron, S.J., Pres., Fordham Prep.; Edward T. Dowling, S.J.; George W. Drance, S.J.; John T. Dzieglewicz, S.J.; Robert R. Grimes, S.J.; Brendan Horan, S.J.; Aloysius P. Kelley, S.J.; Joseph W. Koterski, S.J., Ph.D.; Joseph T. Lienhard, S.J.; Dan T. Mai, S.J.; David P. Marcotte, S.J.; Francis X. McAloon, S.J.; Michael C. McCarthy, S.J.; Thomas M. McCoog, S.J.; Paul D. McNelis, S.J.; Joseph M. McShane, S.J., Pres., Fordham Univ.; Stanley J. O'Konsky, S.J.; Patrick J. Ryan, S.J.; Jose Luis S. Salazar, S.J.; Richard P. Salmi, S.J.; John J. Shea, S.J.; Raymond M. Sweitzer, S.J.; Michael F. Suarez, S.J. Priests 32; Total in Residence 30.

St. Joseph's Friary (Franciscan Friars of the Renewal) (Postulancy) 523 W. 142nd St., 10031.
Tel: 212-234-9089;
Tel: 212-281-4355 (Vocations Office);
Fax: 212-234-8871; Web: www.franciscanfriars.com. Revs. Innocent Mariae Montgomery, C.F.R., Supr.; Emmanuel Mary Mansford, C.F.R., Local Servant & Vocation Dir.; Angelus Immaculata Montgomery, C.F.R., Vicar; Glenn Sudano, C.F.R., Rel Order Leader; Fr. Kolbe Immaculata Blashock, C.F.R.; Bros. Pier Giorgio Welch; Paschal Goode. Postulants 8.

Marist Residence, 226 E. 113th St., 10029.
Tel: 212-348-2702. Bros. Santos Garcia Garcia, F.M.S.; James McKnight, F.M.S.; Luis Vega, F.M.S.

Maryknoll House Catholic Foreign Mission Society. 121 E. 39th St., 10016. Tel: 212-697-4470;
Fax: 212-697-4472; Email: mklnyc@aol.com; Web: www.maryknoll.org. Rev. Francis T. McGourn, M.M., Dir.

Murray-Weigel Hall (A Jesuit Community at Murray-Weigel Hall and Kohlmann Hall), 515 E. Fordham Rd., 10458-5004. Tel: 718-430-4900;
Fax: 718-365-8650. Revs. Thomas E. Smith, S.J., Supr.; James J. Yannarell, S.J., Clinical Asst.; Joseph E. Billotti, S.J.; Bro. Sebastian A. Boccabella, S.J.; Revs. Pierce A. Brennan, S.J.; Raymond A. Bucko, S.J.; Bros. John J. Campbell, S.J.; Ralph Cilia, S.J.; Revs. John M. Costello, S.J.; Robert H. Cousineau, S.J.; John F. Curran, S.J.; James J. Curry, S.J.; James J. Dinneen, S.J.; Paul J. Dugan, S.J.; Gerard H. Ettlinger, S.J.; Mallick J. Fitzpatrick, S.J.; James French; Pasquale T. Giordano, S.J.; Damian Halligan; Richard J. Hoar, S.J.; John R. Keating, S.J.; Donald J. Keefe, S.J.; Donal MacVeigh; John Madden; Paul J. McCarthy, S.J.; Robert McCarty; Vincent McDonough; Robert A. McGuire, S.J.; William McKenna; Bro. Jerome P. Menkhaus, S.J.; Revs. Donald J. Moore, S.J.; Ugo R. Nacciarone, S.J.; Daniel J. O'Brien, S.J.; Thomas V. O'Connor, S.J.; Joseph A. O'Hare, S.J.; Thomas S. Prout, S.J.; William J. O'Malley, S.J.; William P. Poorten, S.J.; Richard J. Regan, S.J.; George Restrepo; Bro. Marco Rodriguez; Revs. James Roleke; John J. Ryan, S.J.; Thomas F. Sable, S.J.; Ramon A. Salomone, S.J.; Raymond A. Schroth, S.J.; Brendan T. Scott, S.J.; Thomas L. Sheridan, S.J.; Charles D. Sullivan, S.J.; Patrick J. Sullivan, S.J.; William M. Sullivan, S.J.; Andrew Szebenyi; Bro. Francis W. Turnbull, S.J.; Revs. William P. Walsh, S.J.; David F. White, S.J.; John F. Wrynn, S.J. Brothers 5; Priests 54. *Murray-Weigel Hall Jesuit Community* Revs. Pierce A. Brennan, S.J.; John M. Buckley, S.J.; Raymond A. Bucko, S.J.; John M. Costello, S.J.; Robert H. Cousineau, S.J.; John F. Curran, S.J.; James J. Dinneen, S.J.; Paul J. Dugan, S.J.; Mallick J. Fitzpatrick, S.J.; D. James French, S.J.; Richard J. Hoar, S.J.; John R. Keating, S.J.; Donald J. Keefe, S.J.; Edward C. Lynch, S.J.; Paul J. McCarthy, S.J.; Robert A. McGuire, S.J.; Donald J. Moore, S.J.; Thomas P. Murphy, S.J.; Edmund W. Nagle, S.J.; Daniel J. O'Brien, S.J.; Thomas V. O'Connor, S.J.; Joseph A. O'Hare, S.J.; William J. O'Malley, S.J.; William P. Poorten, S.J.; Thomas S. Prout, S.J.; Richard J. Regan, S.J.; H. James Roleke, S.J.; John J. Ryan, S.J.; Thomas F. Sable, S.J.; Brendan T. Scott, S.J.; Thomas L. Sheridan, S.J.; Thomas E. Smith, S.J., Supr.; William M. Sullivan, S.J.; Francis P. Valentino, S.J.; Jose M. Vilaplana, S.J., (Spain); Joseph E. Billotti, S.J.; Vincent M. Cooke, S.J.; James J. Curry, S.J.; Gerard H. Ettlinger, S.J.; Ugo R. Nacciarone, S.J.; Ramon A. Salomone, S.J.; Raymond A. Schroth, S.J.; William P. Walsh, S.J.; David F. White, S.J.; John F. Wrynn, S.J.; Bros. Ralph Cilia, S.J.; Jerome P. Menkhaus, S.J.; Francis W. Turnbull, S.J.
Brothers: Bro. John J. Campbell, S.J. *Kolhmann Hall Jesuit Community* Revs. James J. Fedigan, S.J.; Alfred L. Fiorino, S.J.; Daniel J. Fitzpatrick, S.J.; Richard D. Hunt, S.J.; Charles D. Sullivan, S.J.; Daniel J. Sullivan, S.J.; Vincent Fernandes; James Bony; James F. Joyce, S.J. The Kohlmann Hall Jesuit Community was formerly part of the Fordham Jesuit Community. It is now attached to Murray-Weigel Hall.

Our Lady of Consolation Residence,
Tel: 718-548-0888; Fax: 718-548-7824. 3103 Arlington Ave., Bronx, 10463-3305.
Tel: 718-548-0889; Tel: 718-548-0889;
Fax: 718-548-7824. Rev. Edward J. O'Neill, (Retired).

Padua Friary (1866) 151 Thompson St., 10012-3110.
Tel: 212-254-9553, Ext. 1100; Email: dpoirier2200@yahoo.com. Revs. Daniel B. Morey, O.F.M., Guardian; Fabian N. Grifone, O.F.M.; Bro. Vincent de Paul Ciaravino, O.F.M.; Revs. Francis A. Hanudel, O.F.M.; Capristran Polgar; Paul Rotondi, O.F.M., (Retired); Louis Troiano, O.F.M., (Retired); Bros. Paschal De Mattia, O.F.M., (Retired); Dominic Poirier, O.F.M., Vicar; Ronald Bolfeta, O.F.M.

Pallottine Fathers, Society of the Catholic Apostolate, 448 E. 116th St., 10029.
Tel: 212-534-0681; Fax: 212-534-0629. Revs. Terzo Vinci, S.A.C., Admin.; Christopher Salvatori, S.A.C., Assoc. Admin. Total Staff 15; Total Assisted 300.

Paulist Fathers - Generalate, 415 W. 59th St., 10019.
Tel: 212-757-8072; Fax: 212-757-8527; Email: admingenoffice@paulist.org; Web: www.paulist.org. Revs. Eric Andrews, C.S.P., Pres.; Frank Desiderio, C.S.P., M.A. Theology, M.A. Communication, First Consultor; John J. Behnke, C.S.P., Vice Pres.; Gregory Apparcel, C.S.P., Rector Rome; Bernard J. Campbell, C.S.P., Vice Rector Rome; Wilfrid Dewan, (Retired); David E. Farnum, C.S.P.; James A. Haley, C.S.P., (Retired); Joachim Lally, C.S.P., (Retired); Kenneth H. McGuire, C.S.P., (Retired); Robert P. Michele, C.S.P., (Retired); Ernest C. Mort, C.S.P., (Retired); Ryan Casey; Michael Hennessy; Charles J. Brunick, C.S.P., (Retired).

Paulist Fathers' Motherhouse, 415 W. 59th St., 10019. Tel: 212-265-3209; Fax: 212-265-4154; Email: johnbehenke@aol.com; Email: pfmotherhouse@aol.com; Web: www.paulist.org. 405 W. 59th Street, 10019. Revs. Eric Andrews, C.S.P., Pres.; John J. Behnke, C.S.P., Vice Pres.; Joesph Ciccone, C.S.P.; Donald Campbell, C.S.P., (Retired); William J. Cantwell, C.S.P., (Retired); John E. Collins, C.S.P., Preaching Apostolate; Kevin A. Devine, C.S.P., (Retired); James M. DiLuzio, C.S.P., Preaching Apostolate; David P. Dwyer, C.S.P., Dir. Busted Halo; John J. Foley, C.S.P.; Thomas J. Holahan, C.S.P., In Res.; Mark-David Janus, C.S.P., Pres. Paulist Press; Michael J. Kallock, C.S.P., Chap., (Retired); James B. Lloyd, C.S.P., (Retired); Kevin A. Lynch, C.S.P., Emeritus Publisher Paulist Press; Joseph F. Mahon, C.S.P., (Retired); James F. McQuade, C.S.P., In Res.; Edward S. Pietrucha, C.S.P., (Retired); Frank Sabbatte, C.S.P., Art Ministry; Jeremiah D. Sullivan, C.S.P., (Retired); Timothy P. Tighe, C.S.P., Preaching Apostolate, (Retired); Thomas F. Stransky, C.S.P., (Retired); Steven A. Bell, C.S.P., Preaching Apostolate; Matthew Berrios; Frank Desiderio, C.S.P., M.A. Theology, M.A. Communication, First Consultor; Paul Robinchaud, Archivist; Dat Tran, Dir. of Vocation. See also St. Paul the Apostle Parish.

Redemptorist Priests and Brothers, C.Ss.R. (1887) (Prov. of Baltimore) Redemptorist Residence, 323 E. 61st St., 10065-8204. Tel: 212-838-1324;
Fax: 212-838-4154.

Scalabrinian Missionaries, The Center for Migration Studies of New York, 307 E. 60th St., 10022.
Tel: 212-337-3080; Email: cms@cmsny.org; Web: www.cmsny.org. Rev. Moacir Balen, C.S., Prov. Supr. & Pres. Corporate Bd., Center for Migration Studies of New York; Donald Kerwin, Exec. Dir., Center for Migration Studies of New York.

Society of Jesus, New York Province aka New York Province of the Society of Jesus a.k.a. Jesuit Seminary and Mission Bureau, Inc. U.S.A. North East Province of the Society of Jesus. 39 E. 83rd St., 10028-0810. Tel: 212-774-5500;
Fax: 212-794-1036; Email: uneprovincial@jesuits.org; Web: www.jesuitseast.org. Rev. John J. Cecero, S.J., Prov.; Margaret Florentine, Asst. for Secondary & Presecondary Educ.; Revs. John J. Hanwell, S.J., Socius; James F. Keenan, S.J., Dir. Donor Relations; Michael McFarland, S.J., Province Treas., NYK, NEN & UNE; Mr. Nick Napolitano, Asst. Social Min. for NYK, NENE, MAR & UNE Provs.; Revs. James J. Miracky, S.J., Asst. for Higher Ed., NYK, NEN, UNE & MAR Provs.; Victor Salanga, S.J., Archivist; Dr. Jacqueline C. Perez, Asst. for Healthcare; Rev. Philip A. Florio, S.J., Asst. for Formation for the Maryland, NYK&UNE Provs. Operations have been transferred to the USA Northeast Province of the Society of Jesus.

Jesuit Provincial's Office (1540) 39 E. 83rd St., 10028. Tel: 212-774-5500; Fax: 212-794-1036; Email: uneprovincial@jesuits.org; Web: www.jesuitseast.org. Rev. John J. Cecero, S.J., Prov. Staff 29.

Priests of the Province Abroad: Rev. Keith F. Pecklers, S.J., Coll Bellarmino, Via del Seminario 120, 00186, Rome, Italy. Tel: 39-06-69527-6638; Fax: 39-06-6701-5413.

Priests of the Province in Residences Not Listed Elsewhere: Revs. Edward J. Mally, S.J., 1S 150 Spring Rd., Apt. 2E, Oakbrook Terrace, IL 60181. Tel: 630-833-0645; Fax: 708-756-6863; Walter J. Smith, S.J., 370 First Ave., Apt. 12C, 10010. Tel: 646-215-5347.

USA Northeast Province of the Society of Jesus, Inc., 39 E. 83rd St., 10028. Tel: 212-774-5500; Email: uneprovincial@jesuits.org; Web: www.jesuitseast.org. Rev. John J. Cecero, S.J., Prov. Tot in Congregation 477.

The Society of Jesus of New England, 39 E. 83rd St., 10028. Tel: 212-774-5500; Email: uneprovincial@jesuits.org. Rev. John J. Cecero, S.J., Prov.

St. Vincent de Paul Residence, 900 Intervale Ave., 10459. Tel: 718-589-6965; Fax: 718-589-7010; Email: svdpres@chcn.org; Web: www.svdpres.org. Total Staff 8; Total Assisted 3,120.

St. Vincent Ferrer Priory (1867) Dominican Friars Provincial House (Province of St. Joseph). 869 Lexington Ave., 10065-6648. Tel: 212-744-2080;
Fax: 212-327-3011. Revs. Gabriel Gillen, O.P., Dir.; Kenneth Letoile, O.P., Prov.; Very Rev. Darren Michael Pierre, O.P., S.T.L., M.S., Prior; Revs. Allen Moran, Subprior; Luke Hoyt, Parochial Vicar; Matthew Carroll, Mod.; John M. Devaney, O.P., M.Div., Chap.; Very Rev. William Alexander Holt, O.P., B.A., M.Div.; Revs. Sebastian White, O.P., S.T.L.; Peter John Cameron, O.P., M.F.A., S.T.L.; Ronald Eugene Henery, O.P, S.T.B.; John Aedan McKeon, O.P., S.T.B.; Bro. John Damian McCarthy, O.P.

Vincentian Fathers, 1834 Third Ave., 10029.
Tel: 212-289-5589; Fax: 212-289-8321; Email: milagha2@verizon.net. Revs. Victor Elia, C.M., Supr.; Candido Arrizurieta, C.M.; Jesus Arellano, C.M., Vicar

Padres Paules Community (Vincentians) Inc.

Xavier Jesuit Community, 30 W. 16th St., 10011.
Tel: 917-409-5580; Fax: 646-869-1018; Email: sjguests@gmail.com; Web: www.xavierhs.org. Revs. James P. Croghan, S.J., Rector; John J. Cecero, S.J.; Louis T. Garaventa, S.J.; James J. Hederman, S.J.; James F. Keenan, S.J., Admin.; James L. Pierce, S.J.; Mario M. Powell, S.J., Dir., Reach Prog.; John F. Replogle, S.J.; Mr. Michael Bartlett, Special Studies; Revs. Vincent L. Biagi, S.J., Alumni Relations; Mark Burke, Lecturer at Fordham Univ.; Daniel Corrou; Mr. Jose Dueno Gorbea, Regent America Media; Revs. Patrick Gilger, Special Studies; James Mayzik, Parochial Vicar; Hernan Paredes; Mr. Zachariah Presutti, THRIVE; Revs. Carlos Quijano, O.P.; Marc J. Roselli, S.J.; Robert VerEecke; John Wronski, Formation. (For list of faculty see the high school listing for Xavier High School)

Jesuit Residence, 326 W. 14th St., 10014.
Tel: 212-675-5685; Fax: 212-675-8573. Rev. Edward J. Quinnan, S.J., Admin.

BEACON. *St. Joachim Friary*, 61 Leonard St., Beacon, 12508. Tel: 845-838-0000; Email: frfred@cyfm.org; Web: www.cyfm.org. Revs. Thomas McNamara, O.F.M.Cap., Chap. at CYFM; Fred Nickle, O.F.M.Cap., Chap. & Vicar; Robert Phelps, O.F.M.Cap., Senior Friar; Bro. Carlos Hernandez, O.F.M.Cap., Guardian. Serving Capuchin Youth and Family Ministries, Garrison, NY.

BRONX. *Idente Missionaries - Santa Maria Residence*, 2352 St. Raymond Ave., Bronx, 10462.
Tel: 718-828-2380; Fax: 718-828-4296; Email: rpbadillo@gmail.com. Revs. Robert P. Badillo, M. Id, Ph.D., Prov. Supr.; Martin I. Esquerra, M.Id, D.Min.

John Cardinal O'Connor Residence, 5655 Arlington Ave., Bronx, 10471. Tel: 718-581-0070; Email: mail@jmcpllc.com. Rev. Msgrs. Francis V. Boyle, (Retired); Dermot R. Brennan, (Retired); Harry J. Byrne, (Retired); Peter C. O'Donnell, (Retired); Revs. Christopher H. Daly, (Retired); Gerard DiSenso, (Retired); Alfred Pizzuto, (Retired); John F. Reardon, (Retired).

Marist Brothers Champagnat Hall Community (1926) 2115 Pitman Ave., Bronx, 10466-1928.
Tel: 718-994-4227, Ext. 34; Tel: 917-292-2671;
Fax: 718-881-7888. Bros. James Adams, F.M.S., Dir.; Gerard Cormier, F.M.S.; Thomas Delaney, F.M.S.; Gerald Doherty, F.M.S.; Francis Klug, F.M.S.; Augustine Landry, F.M.S.; Joseph McAlister, F.M.S., Staff; Luke Reddington, F.M.S.; Julian Roy, F.M.S.; Joseph Scanlon, F.M.S.; Joseph Teston, F.M.S.

Our Lady of the Angels Friary (Franciscan Friars of the Renewal) 427 E. 155th St., Bronx, 10455.
Tel: 718-993-3405; Fax: 718-993-9997; Web: www.franciscanfriars.com. Revs. Bonaventure Rummell, C.F.R., Supr.; Pierre Toussaint Guiteau, Vicar; Luke Joseph Leighton, C.F.R.; Stanley Fortuna, C.F.R.; Solanus M. Benfatti, C.F.R., M.A., S.T.L.; John Anthony Boughton, C.F.R.; John Paul Ouellette, C.F.R.; Xavier Meiergerd; Friars Lawrence Johnson; John Scheibner; Peter Marie Westall, C.F.R.

Passionist Residence Riverdale, 5801 Palisade Ave. Ste 300, Bronx, 10471. Tel: 914-633-3130; Email: pfagan@cpprov.org; Web: www.thepassionists.org. Passionist Province Pastoral Center, 111 S. Ridge St., Ste. 300, Rye Brook, 10573. Fax: 914-881-9002. Rev. Paul R. Fagan, C.P.

Yarumal Mission Society, Inc. (1997) Office of the

Pres., 2317 Washington Ave., Bronx, 10458. Tel: 718-561-8248; Fax: 718-295-9607; Email: imeyusa@aol.com; Web: www.yarumal.org. Revs. David Guzman Perez, M.X.Y., Pres.; Tulio E. Ramirez, M.X.Y., (Colombia); Ramiro Reyes, M.X.Y.; Juan Solorzano, M.X.Y., Trustee.

CORNWALL. *Jogues Retreat Center*, P.O. Box 522, Cornwall, 12518-0522. Tel: 845-534-7570; Fax: 845-534-3276; Email: conroyp48@hotmail.com. Rev. Michael R. Hoag, S.J., Supr.

ESOPUS. *Marist Brothers F.M.S. (Province of U.S.A.)* (1942) 70-20 Juno St., Forest Hills, 11375. Tel: 845-384-6625; Fax: 845-384-6277; Email: brohen@aol.com. Bros. Patrick McNamara, Prov.; Daniel O'Riordan, F.M.S., Prov. Asst. Brothers 130.

GARRISON. *St. Christopher's Inn Friary*, 21 Franciscan Way, Box 150, Garrison, 10524-0150. Tel: 845-335-1000; Fax: 845-424-3786; Web: www.stchristophersinn-graymoor.org. Revs. John F. Kiesling, S.A., Guardian; John W. Coppinger, S.A., (Retired); William Drobach, S.A.; Robert Warren, S.A.; Bros. Benedict Terasawa, S.A.; Charles Kenney, S.A.; Joseph O'Gara, S.A.; John O'Hara, S.A. Total Staff 90; Total Assisted 1,200.

Franciscan Friars of the Atonement (1898) Graymoor, 40 Franciscan Way, P.O. Box 300, Garrison, 10524-0300. Tel: 845-424-3671; Tel: 845-424-3672; Tel: 845-424-3673; Fax: 845-424-2166; Email: csharon@atonementfriars.org; Web: www.atonementfriars.org. Revs. Martin Carter, S.A., (Retired); Joseph Di Mauro, S.A.; Bros. John Baptist Hildreth, S.A.; Daniel Houde, S.A.; Hugh MacIsaac, S.A., Guardian, St. Paul's Friary; Dominic McDonnell, S.A.; Theodore Novak, S.A.; Rev. Thomas Orians, S.A., Dir., Graymoor Spiritual Life Center; Bro. DePorres Poncia, S.A., (Retired); Revs. Emil Tomaskovic, S.A., Dir., Major Gifts/Planned Giving; Peter Taran, (Retired). *St. Francis of Assisi Novitiate*, Graymoor, 40 Franciscan Way, P.O. Box 300, Garrison, 10524-0300. Tel: 845-424-3671; Email: csharon@atonementfriars.org; Web: www.atonementfriars.org. Bros. Leo Hall, S.A., (Retired); Francis Papineau, S.A., (Retired). *St. Christopher's Inn*, Graymoor, P.O. Box 150, Garrison, 10524-0150. Tel: 845-424-3616; Fax: 845-424-3786. Revs. Charles Angell, S.A., (Retired); John W. Coppinger, S.A., (Retired); William Drobach, S.A., Pres. & CEO; Bro. Charles Kenney, S.A.; Rev. John F. Kiesling, S.A., Guardian, St. Christopher's Inn, St. Joan of Arc Parish, Toronto, ON Canada M6P 1B1. Tel: 416-762-1026; Fax: 416-762-4194; Bros. Joseph O'Gara, S.A., Healthcare Coord.; John O'Hara, S.A.; Benedict Terasawa, S.A., (Retired); Rev. Robert Warren, S.A. *Graymoor Ecumenical and Interreligious Institute*, 475 Riverside Dr., Rm. 1960, 10115-1999. Tel: 212-870-2330; Fax: 212-870-2001. Rev. James L. Loughran, S.A., Dir., Tel: 212-807-9694; Fax: 212-870-2001; Bro. Francis Papineau, S.A., (Retired). *Atonement Friars*, Atonement Friars, 138 Waverly Pl., 10014. Bro. Gerard Hand, S.A.; Rev. Wilfred Tyrrell, S.A.

Priests of the Province Serving Elsewhere: Revs. David Fitzgerald, S.A., Pastor, St. Andrew the Apostle, Apex, NC; Thomas Gumprecht, S.A., St. Andrew the Apostle, Apex, Inc.; Francis Eldridge, S.A., Pastor, St. Odilia's Parish, 522 Hooper Ave., Los Angeles, CA 90011. St. Odilia's Parish, Los Angeles, CA. *Chapel of Our Savior* Brockton, MA Tel: 508-583-8357; Fax: 508-586-5510. Bro. Thomas Banacki, S.A.; Revs. Gerald DiGiralamo, S.A., (Retired), 4 Buttercup Dr., Bohemia, 11716; Robert Langone, S.A., Retreat Dir.; Bros. Louis Marek, S.A.; Savio McNiece, S.A., Chapel of Our Savior, 475 Westgate Dr., Brockton, MA 02301.

Franciscan Friars of the Atonement, Minister General Office (1898) Graymoor, 40 Franciscan Way, P.O. Box 300, Garrison, 10524-0300. Tel: 845-424-2113; Fax: 845-424-2166; Email: ministergen@atonementfriars.org; Web: www.atonementfriars.org. Revs. William Drobach, S.A., Pres.; Christopher's Inn, Garrison; James Gardiner, S.A., Dir.; Franciscan Monastery of the Holy Land, Washington, DC; Damian MacPherson, S.A., (Canada) Dir.; St. Joan of Arc Parish; Thomas Orians, S.A., Dir.; Retreat House; Charles J. Sharon, S.A., Dir.; Treas.; 4th Gen. Counselor, Sec. Gen, Assoc. Treas.; Emil Tomaskovic, S.A., Dir.; St. Paul's Friary, Garrison, NY; Bro. Charles Kenney, S.A., Admin.; Christopher's Inn, Garrison; Rev. Joseph Hiramatsu, S.A., (Japan) Regl. Min.; Very Rev. Brian F. Terry, S.A., Supr.; Rev. James L. Loughran, S.A., Vicar Gen., 1st Gen. Councilor & Dir. G.E.I.I.; Bro. Louis Marek, S.A., Vicar; Chapel of Our Savior, Brockton, Massachusetts; Revs. Bernard Palka, S.A., 2nd Gen. Councilor; Daniel Callahan, S.A., 3rd Gen. Councilor/Pastor, Joan of Arc Parish; Patrick Cogan, S.A., St. Paul's Friary, Garrison, NY; Martin Carter, S.A., St. Paul's Friary, Garrison, NY, (Retired); Joseph Di Mauro, S.A., St. Paul's Friary, Garrison, NY; Bros. Leo Hall, S.A., St. Paul's Friary, Garrison, NY; Daniel Houde, S.A., St. Paul's Friary, Garrison, NY; John Baptist Hildreth, S.A., St. Paul's Friary, Garrison, NY; Rev. John Keane, S.A., St. Paul's Friary, Garrison, NY, (Retired); Bros. William Martyn, S.A., St. Paul's Friary, Garrison, NY; Dominic McDonnell, S.A., St. Paul's Friary, Garrison, NY; Theodore Novak, S.A., St. Paul's Friary, Garrison, NY; Rev. Daniel O'Shea, S.A., St. Paul's Friary, Garrison, NY, (Retired); Bro. DePorres Poncia, S.A., St. Paul's Friary, Garrison, NY; Rev. Peter Taran, St. Paul's Friary, Garrison, NY, (Retired); Bros. Joseph O'Gara, S.A., Christopher's Inn, Garrison; John O'Hara, S.A., Christopher's Inn, Garrison; Rev. Robert Warren, S.A., Christopher's Inn, Garrison; Bro. Gerard Hand, S.A., Waverly Place; Rev. Elias D. Mallon, S.A., St. Joseph's Yorkville, New York City; Bros. Alan LeMay, S.A., St. Joseph's Addiction Treatment & R.C., Saranac Lake; Thomas Banacki, S.A., Chapel of Our Savior, Brockton, Massachusetts; Revs. Gerald DiGiralamo, S.A., Chapel of Our Savior, Brockton, Massachusetts, (Retired); Dennis Polanco, S.A., Atonement Friars, Washington, DC; Bro. Timothy MacDonald, S.A., Atonement Friars, Washington, DC; Revs. Edward Gallagher, S.A., Rehoboth Beach, DE, (Retired); Robert Langone, S.A., Christ the Redeemer, Sterling, VA; Francis Eldridge, S.A., Christ the Redeemer, Sterling, VA; David Fitzgerald, S.A., St. Andrew the Apostle, Apex, NC; Bro. Ignatius Kobayashi, S.A., (Japan) Tsurumi-Ku, Yokohama Japan; Rev. Pacificus Von Essen, S.A., Tsurumi-Ku, Yokohama Japan, (Retired); Bros. Paschal Steen, T.S.A., Uihlein Living Center, Lake Placid, NY; Denis Burgelin, S.A., Wales & Kent & London, England; Revs. Robert Mercer, S.A., Wales & Kent & London, England, (Retired); Michael Seed, S.A., (England) Wales & Kent & London, England; Arthur Gouthro, S.A., St. Joseph the Worker, Richmond, BC, (Retired); David Poirier, S.A., St. Joseph the Worker, Richmond, BC; Matthew MacDonald, S.A., St. Joseph the Worker, Richmond, BC; Bro. Hugh MacIsaac, S.A., Vancouver, BC Canada; Rev. Edward Boes, S.A., Rome & Assisi, Italy; Bro. Gregory Lucrezia, S.A., Rome & Assisi, Italy; Revs. James F. Puglisi, S.A., Rome & Assisi, Italy; Kenneth Cienik, S.A., Rome & Assisi, Italy; Bro. Paolo Nicosia, S.A., Rome & Assisi, Italy; Rev. Charles Angell, S.A., Holy Name Community, Ringwood, NJ, (Retired).

Graymoor Ecumenical & Interreligious Institute, 475 Riverside Dr., Rm. 1960, 10115-1999. Tel: 212-870-2330; Fax: 212-870-2001; Email: lmnygeii@aol.com; Web: www.geii.org. (G.E.I.I.)

Friars of the Atonement, Inc.
St. Christopher's Inn, Inc.
Union That Nothing Be Lost, Inc.
Paul Wattson Human Resources Fund, Inc.
Friars of the Atonement (Canada), Inc.
Graymoor Village, Inc.

HARTSDALE. *Mill Hill Fathers Residence*, 222 W. Hartsdale Ave., Hartsdale, 10530-1667. Tel: 914-682-0645; Fax: 914-682-0862; Email: mhmnyoffice@aol.com; Web: www.millhillmissionaries.com. Revs. Terence J. Lee, M.H.M., Admin.; James Brian Coffey, M.H.M.; Bartholomew Daly, M.H.M.; Lester Lonergan, M.H.M., (Retired), 1415 Abbey Pl., Apt. 14, Charlotte, NC 28209; Peter Major, M.H.M.; Robert J. O'Neil, M.H.M., Society Rep.; Paul Pratrap, M.H.M.; Gregory P. Rice, M.H.M.; Willem Klaver.

MARYKNOLL. *M.M.A.F. Charitable Trust*, Treasury Office, P.O. Box 306, Maryknoll, 10545-0306. Tel: 914-941-7590; Fax: 914-941-3619; Email: rcallahan@maryknoll.org. Rev. Richard B. Callahan, M.M., Contact Person.

Maryknoll Fathers and Brothers, 55 Ryder Rd., Ossining, 10562. Tel: 914-941-7590; Fax: 914-944-3600; Email: mklcouncil@maryknoll.org; Web: www.maryknollsociety.org. P. O. Box 303, Maryknoll, 10545-0303. Revs. Raymond J. Finch, M.M., Supr. Gen. & Pres.; Joseph M. Everson III, M.M., Vicar Gen. & Vice Pres.; Russell Feldmeier, M.M., Asst. Gen. & Rector; Thomas J. O'Brien, M.M., Sec. Gen.; David A. Smith, M.M., Treas.; David E. La Buda, M.M., Asst. to C.F.O.; J. Edward Szendrey, M.M., Pastoral Min./Coord.; Edward J. McGovern, M.M., Supr.; Kevin J. Hanlon, M.M., Supr.; Most Rev. William J. McNaughton, M.M., (Retired); Revs. Daniel Ohmann, M.M.; Norbert Pacheco, M.M.; Thomas A. Peyton, M.M., (Retired); Richard J. Quinn, M.M., (Retired); Joseph Slaby, M.M.; Richard P. Smith, M.M., (Retired); Thomas A. Ahearn, M.M., (Retired); Richard Albertine, M.M.; John Cioppa, M.M., (Retired); Dennis W. Cleary, M.M.; Joseph B. Arsenault, M.M., (Retired); Paul J. Duffy, M.M.; Michael Gould, M.M., (Retired); Regis Ging, M.M.; Francis B. Higdon, M.M., (Retired); Richard Aylward, M.M., (Retired); Richard M. Baker, M.M., (Retired); Dale Barron, M.M.; Paul D. Belliveau, M.M., (Retired); Francis H. Beninati, M.M., (Retired); Patrick A. Bergin, M.M., (Retired); Leslie F. Blowers, M.M., (Retired); Francis J. Breen, M.M.; John Brinkman, M.M.; J. Ernest Brunelle, M.M., (Retired); Curtis R. Cadorette, M.M.; Richard B. Callahan, M.M.; John J. Casey, M.M.; Peter L. Chabot, M.M., (Retired); James P. Colligan, M.M., (Retired); James Conard, M.M.; Robert F. Crawford, M.M., (Retired); Robert F. Crohan, M.M., (Retired); Richard J. Czajkowski, M.M., (Retired); Edward V. Davis, M.M., (Retired); Donald J. Doherty, M.M., (Retired); Thomas Donnelly, M.M.; William Donnelly, M.M., (Retired); Joseph Donovan, M.M.; Edward M. Dougherty, M.M.; Michael A. Duggan, M.M.; Emile E. Dumas, M.M., (Retired); Thomas Dunleavy, M.M., (Retired); Arthur J. Dwyer, M.M., (Retired); Clarence A. Engler, M.M., (Retired); Philip N. Erbland, M.M., (Retired); John Felago, M.M.; Francis Felter, M.M.; Lawrence W. Flynn, M.M., (Retired); William B. Frazier, M.M.; Herbert T. Gappa, M.M., (Retired); Donald F. Glover, M.M., (Retired); John F. Gorski, M.M.; Fernand L. Gosselin, M.M., (Retired); Scott T. Harris, M.M., (Retired); Frederick J. Hegarty, M.M., (Retired); Joseph A. Heim, M.M., (Retired); James L. Hilgeman, M.M., (Retired); John P. Hudert, M.M., (Retired); Delos A. Humphrey Jr., M.M., (Retired); James H. Huvane, M.M.; Robert A. Jalbert, M.M.; John M. Kaserow, M.M., (Retired); John E. Keegan, M.M., (Retired); Martin P. Keegan, M.M., (Retired); Leo R. Kennedy, M.M, (Retired); Timothy O. Kilkelly, M.M.; Alfonso Kim, M.M.; Joseph W. Kowalczyk, M.M., (Retired); Ralph S. Kroes, M.M., (Retired); Joseph P. LaMar, M.M., (Retired); Daniel A. Lanza, M.M., (Retired); Peter M. Le Jacq, M.M.; James W. Lehr, M.M., (Retired); Lawrence J. Lewis, M.M.; Robert A. Lilly, M.M., (Retired); Robert J. Lloyd, M.M., (Retired); Martin J. Lowery, M.M.; Ernest C. Lukaschek, M.M.; William T. Madden, M.M., (Retired); John P. Martin, M.M., (Retired); Douglas E. May, M.M.; William D. McCarthy, M.M., (Retired); Gerard T. McCrane, M.M., (Retired); Lawrence F. McCulloch, M.M., (Retired); Thomas P. McDonnell, M.M., (Retired); J. Donald McGinnis, M.M., (Retired); Cuong H. Nguyen, M.M.; Francis S. Meccia, M.M., (Retired); Manuel J. Mejia, M.M., (Retired); Carl P. Meulemans, M.M., (Retired); Edward F. Moore, M.M., (Retired); John J. Moran, M.M.; Laurence T. Murphy, M.M., (Retired); Gerald J. Nagle, M.M., (Retired); Robert Nehrig, M.M.; Raymond J. Nobiletti, M.M.; Brendan M. O'Connell, M.M., (Retired); Richard T. Ouellette, M.M., (Retired); Gerald J. Persha, M.M., (Retired); Thomas E. Pesaresi, M.M.; David L. Pfeiffer, M.M.; Clyde Phillips, M.M.; Raymond G. Pierini, M.M.; Edward J. Quinn, M.M., (Retired); Robert J. Reiley, M.M., (Retired); John A. Rich, M.M., (Retired); Richard Rolewicz, M.M.; James R. Roy, M.M., (Retired); Peter L. Ruggere, M.M., (Retired); Thomas C. Saunders, M.M., (Retired); J. Lawrence Schanberger, M.M., (Retired); Steven S. Scherrer, M.M., (Retired); Leo B. Shea, M.M., (Retired); Edward D. Shellito, M.M.; John C. Sivalon, M.M.; Michael J. Snyder, M.M.; Romane St. Vil, M.M.; John J. Sullivan, M.M., (Retired); Kenneth J. Sullivan, M.M., (Retired); Donald F. Sybertz, M.M., (Retired); Eugene A. Theisen, M.M., (Retired); Eugene Toland, M.M.; Joseph W. Towle, M.M., (Retired); Joseph R. Veneroso, M.M., (Retired); John J. Vinsko, M.M., (Retired); Robert W. Vujs, M.M., (Retired); John Walsh, M.M.; Michael P. Walsh, M.M.; Gerald M. Wickenhauser, M.M., (Retired); Arthur H. Wille, M.M., (Retired); Peter A. Wu, M.M., (Retired); Elmer P. Wurth, M.M.; John F. Wymes, M.M., (Retired); Robert Wynne, M.M.; Maurice J. Zerr, M.M., (Retired); Michael O. Zunno, M.M., (Retired); Bros. John E. Argauer, M.M.; Frank Tenhoopen, M.M.; Francis Dolphin, M.M.; Luke R. Baldwin, M.M.; John J. Blazo, M.M.; Gordon M. Burns, M.M.; Robert A. Butsch, M.M., (Retired); Eugene E. Casper, M.M.; Brendan J. Corkery, M.M.; Kevin F. Dargan, M.M.; Goretti A. Zilli, M.M.; Wayne J. Fitzpatrick, M.M.; Vianney R. Flick, M.M.; Lawrence E. Kenning, M.M.; Anthony Lopez, M.M.; Victor E. Marshall, M.M.; Andrew E. Marsolek, M.M.; David E. McKenna, M.M.; Donald R. Miriani, M.M.; Frank J. Norris, M.M.; Albert F. Patrick, M.M.; DePorres Stilp, M.M.; Raymond C. Tetrault, M.M.

Maryknoll Fathers and Brothers Charitable Trust, P.O. Box 306, Maryknoll, 10545-0306. Tel: 914-941-7590, Ext. 2422; Fax: 914-944-3628; Web: www.maryknoll.org. Revs. Francis J. Breen, M.M., Trustee; Kevin J. Hanlon, M.M., Trustee; J. Edward Szendrey, M.M., Trustee; Bros. Brendan J.

Corkery, M.M., Trustee; Wayne J. Fitzpatrick, M.M., Trustee.

MIDDLETOWN. *St. Albert's Priory*, 72 Carmelite Dr., P.O. Box 908, Middletown, 10940-0908. Revs. Francis Amodio, O.Carm.; Raymond Bagdonis, O.-Carm.; Paul Feeley, O.Carm., (Retired); James Hess, O.Carm.; Philip F. Marani, O.Carm.; Thomas Zalewski, O.Carm., Prior; Bro. Michael Garraghan, O.Carm. *The National Shrine of Our Lady of Mount Carmel*, 70 Carmelite Dr., P.O. Box 2163, Middletown, 10940-2163. Tel: 845-343-1879; Fax: 845-343-1912.

Brandsma Priory, Carmelite Novitiate, 1 Carmelite Dr., P.O. Box 2127, Middletown, 10940-0439. Tel: 845-343-2959; Fax: 845-344-1808. Revs. Robert Traudt, O.Carm., Co-Dir. Novices; Paul Denault, O.Carm., Co-Dir. Novices. Carmelite Friars (North American Prov. of St. Elias and Most Pure Heart of Mary Province).

Carmelite Friars (North American Province of St. Elias) (1931) 68 Carmelite Dr., P.O. Box 3079, Middletown, 10940-0890. Tel: 845-344-2223; Tel: 845-344-2225 (Vocation phone); Tel: 845-344-2474; Fax: 845-344-2210; Email: wward@carmelites.com (Provincial Secretary); Email: vocations@carmelites.com (Vocation Secretary); Email: provincial@carmelites.com; Email: laycarmelitessel@carmelites.com; Web: www.carmelites.com. Very Rev. Michael Kissane, O.Carm., Prior Prov.; Revs. Paul Denault, O.-Carm., Prov. Procurator, Tel: 914-344-2224; Francis Amodio, O.Carm., Vocations Dir.; Stephan Tuu Le, O.Carm., Formation Dir., Vietnam; Bro. Paul Therese Hung Tran, O.Carm, Asst. Formation Dir.; Rev. Hasely King, O.Carm., Vocations Dir., Trinidad; Very Rev. Mario Esposito, O.Carm., Pre-Novice Dir.; Revs. Gregoire Fluet, Vocation Dir.; Vincent Nguyen, Formation and Vocation Dir.

Legal Title: The Missionary Society of Our Lady of Mt. Carmel of the State of New York; The Carmelite Fathers, Inc. of New York; Carmelite Fathers, Inc. of the Commonwealth of Massachusetts; Mt. Carmel Hermite; Order of Carmelites of Palm Beach, Inc.; National Shrine of Our Lady of Mt. Carmel, Inc. Office of Lay Carmelites, 70 Carmelite Dr., P.O. Box 3079, Middletown, 10940-0890. Tel: 845-344-2474; Fax: 845-344-2476; Email: jsoreth@frontiernet.net. Rev. Francis Amodio, O.Carm., Provincial Delegate Lay Carmelites.

MOUNT VERNON. *St. Bernardine of Siena Friary*, 25 Laurel Ave., Mount Vernon, 10552-1018. Tel: 914-699-1221; Fax: 914-668-6143. Rev. James Villa, O.F.M., Admin. & Guardian. Franciscan Friars, Province of Immaculate Conception. Priests 3. In Res. Revs. Andre Cirino, O.F.M.; Roderick Crispo, O.F.M.

Kolbe Friary, 274-280 W. Lincoln Ave., Mount Vernon, 10550. Tel: 914-664-7169. Bro. Angelo Monti, O.F.M., Guardian. Franciscan Friars, Province of the Immaculate Conception.

NEW PALTZ. *St. Joseph Friary*, 34 S. Chestnut St., New Paltz, 12561. Tel: 914-255-5635; Fax: 914-255-5679 . Rev. Fr. Salvatore Cordaro, O.F.M.Cap., Pastor; Revs. Raphael Iannone, O.F.M.Cap., Province Property Mgr.; Michael Ramos, O.F.M.Cap.; Bro. Timothy Aller, O.F.M.Cap., Counselor. Capuchin Franciscans, Province of St. Mary.

NEW ROCHELLE. *Edmund Rice Christian Brothers North America Congregation of Christian Brothers* (1906) 260 Wilmot Rd., New Rochelle, 10804. Tel: 914-636-6194; Fax: 914-636-0021; Email: cab@cbinstitute.org. Bro. Kevin M. Griffith, C.F.C., Prov. *Saint Joseph Residence, Inc.* (1986) 30 Montgomery Cir., New Rochelle, 10804. Tel: 914-633-6851; Fax: 914-633-5579; Email: jbm@atgnet.com. Bro. Vincent McNally, C.F.C., Pastoral Care Coord. Limited care facility for male religious. Total in Residence 20; Total Staff 5.

Saint Joseph Residence, Inc., 30 Montgomery Cir., New Rochelle, 10804-4413. Tel: 914-633-6851; Fax: 914-633-5579; Email: crhaynes@hotmail.com. Bros. Charles Haynes, Vice Pres. Finance; Kevin M. Griffith, C.F.C.; Thomas C. Higgins, Sec.; James B. Moffett, C.F.C., Vice Pres. Admin. Congregation of Christian Brothers.A facility of limited care for male religious. Total in Residence 20; Total Staff 5.

Salesian Cooperators of St. John Bosco, 148 E. Main St., P.O. Box 639, New Rochelle, 10802-0639. Rev. Thomas Dunne, S.D.B., Prov. Delegate; Mr. Michael Hahn, Prov. Coord.

Salesian Office of Youth & Young Adult Ministry, 148 E. Main St., New Rochelle, 10801. Tel: 914-636-4225; Fax: 914-636-4925; Email: ym@salesianym.com; Web: www.salesianym.com. PO Box 639, New Rochelle, 10802-0639. Rev. Abraham Feliciano, S.D.B., Provincial Delegate Youth Ministry.

Salesian Provincial House (1959) 148 Main St., P.O. Box 639, New Rochelle, 10802-0639. Tel: 914-636-4225; Fax: 914-636-0159; Email: sdbsue@aol.com; Web: www.salesians.org. Very Rev. Timothy Zak, S.D.B., Vice Prov.; Revs. Robert Bauer, S.D.B.; Anthony D'Angelo, S.D.B.; Dennis Donovan, S.D.B., Prov. Treas.; Mark Hyde, S.D.B.; Kenneth Shaw, S.D.B.; Bros. Bruno Busatto, S.D.B.; Andrew Lacombe, S.D.B.; Gerald Warner, S.D.B.; Revs. Abraham Feliciano, S.D.B., Youth Min.; William Ferruzzi, S.D.B., Teacher; John J. Serio, S.D.B., Prov. Asst.; Dominic Dahn Cong Tran, S.D.B., Vocation Ministry. Brothers 8; Priests 18.

PELHAM. *Marist Brothers* (1994) 2 Eden Ter., Poughkeepsie, 12601-4803. Tel: 845-471-8354. Bros. John Malich, F.M.S., Dir.; Kenneth V. Hogan, F.M.S.; John Nash, F.M.S.

Marist Brothers Community (1993) 26 First Ave., Pelham, 10803. Tel: 914-738-1218. Bros. James Devine, F.M.S.; James McKnight, F.M.S.; Dominick Pujia, F.M.S.; Leo Shea, F.M.S.

Marist Brothers-St. Benedict Community, 1082 Edison Ave., Bronx, 10465. Tel: 718-931-3744. Bros. Gerald Doherty, F.M.S., Dir.; Frederick Sambor, F.M.S., Dir.; Eugene Birmingham; Armand Lamagna, F.M.S.; Thomas Schady, F.M.S.

PELHAM MANOR. *St. Vincent Strambi Residence*, 190 Mt. Tom Rd., Pelham Manor, 10803-3309. Tel: 914-738-6138; Fax: 914-738-6136; Email: pfagan@cpprov.org; Email: edwardlbeck@aol.com. Revs. Paul R. Fagan, C.P., Supr.; James O'Shea, C.P., Prov.; Salvatore Enzo Del Brocco, C.P., 1st Consultor; Edward L. Beck, C.P.; Very Rev. Robert H. Joerger, C.P. The Passionists. Priests 5.

RYE. *Legionaries of Christ*, 815 Boston Post Rd., Rye, 10580. Tel: 301-580-3040; Email: sreilly@legionaries.org; Web: www.legionofchrist.org. Revs. Steven Reilly, L.C., Supr.; Donal O'Keeffe, L.C.; Jason Smith, L.C.; Michael Sliney, L.C.; Rev Stephen Dyas, L.C.; Revs. Mark Haydu, L.C.; David Barton.

RYE BROOK. *The Congregation of the Passion - St. Paul of the Cross Province* Passionists, Pastoral Center, 111 S. Ridge St., Ste. 300, Rye Brook, 10573. Tel: 914-633-3130; Tel: 914-908-6736; Tel: 914-908-6737; Fax: 914-881-9002; Web: www.thepassionists.org. Revs. James O'Shea, C.P., Prov.; St. Vincent Strambi Residence, Pelham, NY; Salvatore Enzo Del Brocco, C.P., Vice Prov.; James Price, C.P., 2nd Consultor; Outside the Archdiocese of NY; William Murphy, C.P., 3rd Consultor; Immaculate Conception Monastery, Jamaica, NY; Hugo Esparza-Perez, C.P., 4th Consultor; Serving in Haiti; Thomas Bonacci, C.P., Outside the Archdiocese of NY; Rob Carbonneau, C.P., Outside the Archdiocese of NY; John Cashman, C.P., Outside the Archdiocese of NY; Patrick Daugherty, C.P., Outside the Archdiocese of NY; Charles Dougherty, C.P., Outside the Archdiocese of NY; Francis Finnigan, C.P., Outside the Archdiocese of NY; Peter Grace, C.P., Outside the Archdiocese of NY; Justin Kerber, C.P., Outside the Archdiocese of NY; Edward Wolanski, C.P., Outside the Archdiocese of NY; William Maguire, C.P., Outside the Archdiocese of NY; Jerome McKenna, C.P., Outside the Archdiocese of NY; David Monaco, C.P., Outside the Archdiocese of NY; Lionel Pacheco, C.P., Outside the Archdiocese of NY; Dominic Papa, C.P., Outside the Archdiocese of NY; Gregory Paul, C.P., Outside the Archdiocese of NY; Claudio Piccinini, C.P., Outside the Archdiocese of NY; Salvatore Riccardi, C.P., Outside the Archdiocese of NY; Very Rev. Robin Ryan, C.P., Outside the Archdiocese of NY; Revs. Lawrence Rywalt, C.P., Outside the Archdiocese of NY; Jed Sumampong, C.P., Outside the Archdiocese of NY; Jerome Vereb, C.P., Outside the Archdiocese of NY; Theodore Vitali, C.P., Outside the Archdiocese of NY; James Barry, C.P., Immaculate Conception Monastery, Jamaica, NY; Thomas Brislin, C.P., Immaculate Conception Monastery, Jamaica, NY; Jerome Bracken, C.P., Immaculate Conception Monastery, Jamaica, NY; Paul Chenot, C.P., Immaculate Conception Monastery, Jamaica, NY; Lucian Clark, C.P., Immaculate Conception Monastery, Jamaica, NY; Alberto Cabrera, C.P., Immaculate Conception Monastery, Jamaica, NY; Rogie Castellano, C.P., Immaculate Conception Monastery, Jamaica, NY; Chris Cleary, C.P., Immaculate Conception Monastery, Jamaica, NY; Theophane Cooney, C.P., Immaculate Conception Monastery, Jamaica, NY; Neil Davin, C.P., Immaculate Conception Monastery, Jamaica, NY; John Douglas, C.P., Immaculate Conception Monastery, Jamaica, NY; Evans Fwamba, C.P., Immaculate Conception Monastery, Jamaica, NY; James R. Gillette, C.P., Immaculate Conception Monastery, Jamaica, NY; Michael Greene, C.P., Immaculate Conception Monastery, Jamaica, NY; Victor Hoagland, C.P., Immaculate Conception Monastery, Jamaica, NY; Joseph Jones, C.P., Immaculate Conception Monastery, Jamaica, NY; John Michael Lee, C.P., Immaculate Conception Monastery, Jamaica, NY; Miroslaw Lesiecki, C.P., Immaculate Conception Monastery, Jamaica, NY; Bonaventure Moccia, C.P., Immaculate Conception Monastery, Jamaica, NY; Gilbert Omolo, C.P., Immaculate Conception Monastery, Jamaica, NY; Kenan Peters, C.P., Immaculate Conception Monastery, Jamaica, NY; John Powers, C.P., Immaculate Conception Monastery, Jamaica, NY; Vincent Segotta, C.P., Immaculate Conception Monastery, Jamaica, NY; Paul Vaeth, C.P., Immaculate Conception Monastery, Jamaica, NY; Theodore Walsh, C.P., Immaculate Conception Monastery, Jamaica, NY; Vincent Youngberg, C.P., Immaculate Conception Monastery, Jamaica, NY; Paul Wierichs, C.P., Our Lady of Florida Spiritual Center, N. Palm Beach, FL:; Melvin Shorter, C.P., Our Lady of Florida Spiritual Center, N. Palm Beach, FL:; Brando Recana, C.P., St. Gabriel's Parish, Toronto, ON, Canada; John Muthengi, C.P., St. Gabriel's Parish, Toronto, ON, Canada; Stephen Dunn, C.P., Ministry in Canada; Paul Cusack, C.P., Ministry in Canada; Bernard McEachern, C.P., Ministry in Canada; Richard Frechette, C.P., Serving in Haiti; Richard Award, C.P., Jamaica, WI; Michael Rowe, C.P., Jamaica, WI; Very Rev. Robert H. Joerger, C.P., St. Vincent Strambi Residence, Pelham, NY; Revs. Paul R. Fagan, C.P., St. Vincent Strambi Residence, Pelham, NY; Richard Burke, C.P., St. Ann Monastery, Scranton, PA; Vincent Boney, C.P., St. Ann Monastery, Scranton, PA; Edward Buchheit, C.P., St. Ann Monastery, Scranton, PA; John Connor, C.P., St. Ann Monastery, Scranton, PA; Lee Havey, C.P., St. Ann Monastery, Scranton, PA; Earl Keating, C.P., St. Ann Monastery, Scranton, PA; Francis Landry, C.P., St. Ann Monastery, Scranton, PA; Thomas McCann, C.P., St. Ann Monastery, Scranton, PA; Paul Ruttle, C.P., St. Ann Monastery, Scranton, PA; David Cinquegrani, C.P., Holy Family Passionist Retreat Center, W. Hartford, CT; Terence Kristofak, C.P., Holy Family Passionist Retreat Center, W. Hartford, CT; Terence Skorka, C.P., Holy Family Passionist Retreat Center, W. Hartford, CT; Mark Ward, C.P., St. Paul of the Cross Monastery & Retreat Center, Pittsburgh, PA; Gerald Laba, C.P., St. Paul of the Cross Monastery & Retreat Center, Pittsburgh, PA; Timothy Fitzgerald, C.P., St. Paul of the Cross Monastery & Retreat Center, Pittsburgh, PA; Patrick Geinzer, C.P., St. Paul of the Cross Monastery & Retreat Center, Pittsburgh, PA; John McMillan, C.P., St. Paul of the Cross Monastery & Retreat Center, Pittsburgh, PA; Edwin Moran, C.P., St. Paul of the Cross Monastery & Retreat Center, Pittsburgh, PA; Richard Nalepa, C.P., St. Paul of the Cross Monastery & Retreat Center, Pittsburgh, PA; Michael J. Salvagna, C.P., St. Paul of the Cross Monastery & Retreat Center, Pittsburgh, PA; Joseph Sedley, C.P., St. Paul of the Cross Monastery & Retreat Center, Pittsburgh, PA; Junesh Xavier, C.P., St. Paul of the Cross Monastery & Retreat Center, Pittsburgh, PA; Donald Ware, C.P., St. Paul of the Cross Monastery & Retreat Center, Pittsburgh, PA; Javier Aviles Mercado; Edward L. Beck, C.P.; Curtis Kiddy; Luis Lopez Galarza; Ferdinand Mbuta Bitori; Jose Ramon Montanez Lopez; Gaston Nsongolo, C.P.; Sibi Padinjaredath, C.P.; Moises Rios Ruiz; Anibal Rodriguez; Carlos Rodriguez Hernandez; Bros. Terrence Scanlon, C.P., Outside the Archdiocese of NY; Leo DiFiore, C.P., Outside the Archdiocese of NY; James Johnson, C.P., Immaculate Conception Monastery, Jamaica, NY; Robert McKenna, C.P., Immaculate Conception Monastery, Jamaica, NY; August Parlavechio, C.P., Immaculate Conception Monastery, Jamaica, NY; Angelo Sena, C.P., Immaculate Conception Monastery, Jamaica, NY; Edward Hall, C.P., Our Lady of Florida Spiritual Center, N. Palm Beach, FL:; Augustine Paul Lowe, C.P., Our Lady of Florida Spiritual Center, N. Palm Beach, FL:; Michael Stomber, C.P., Jamaica, WI; Andre Mathieu, C.P., St. Ann Monastery, Scranton, PA; Joseph Rogers, C.P., St. Ann Monastery, Scranton, PA; Daniel Turner, C.P., St. Ann Monastery, Scranton, PA; Michael Moran, C.P., Holy Family Passionist Retreat Center, W. Hartford, CT; Jonathan Pabon Tirado; Mr. Daniel Allen, Postulant; Mr. Jonathan Ramos, Postulant; Mr. Luis Guivas Gerena; Mr. Cristian Martinez Montalvo

Legal Title: St. Paul's Benevolent Educational & Missionary Institute, Inc.

Passionist Volunteers International PVI, 111 S. Ridge St., Ste 302, Rye Brook, 10573. Tel: 202-210-5175; Web: passionistvolunteers.org. Rev. Lucian Clark, C.P., Founder; Mr. Ross Boyle, Dir.

STATEN ISLAND. *St. Francis Friary*, 500 Todt Hill Rd., Staten Island, 10304. Tel: 718-981-3131; Fax: 718-981-2742; Email: bjfarleo@aol.com. Revs. Brennan-Joseph Farleo, O.F.M.Conv., Guardian, Supr. & Preaching Min.; Philip Blaine, O.F.M.-Conv., Spiritual Center Dir.; Edward Costello, O.-F.M.Conv.; George Sabol, O.F.M. Conv. In Res. Bro. Joseph Freitag. *Friars Minor Conventual Im-*

maculate Conception Province Charitable Trust, Tel: 718-981-3131; Fax: 718-981-2742. Brothers 1; Priests 4.

WEST PARK. *Congregation of Christian Brothers*, Santa Maria-on-Hudson, P.O. Box 39, West Park, 12493. Tel: 845-384-3006; Fax: 845-750-6290. Bros. Richard E. Pigott, C.F.C.; Anthony Alex Cannon, C.F.C., Contact Person; John B. Chaney, C.F.C.; D. D. Crimmins, C.F.C.; J. Laurence Heathwood, C.F.C.; R.J. Lasik, C.F.C. Total in Residence 6.

WHITE PLAINS. *Capuchin Friars International, Inc.* (1984) St. Conrad Friary, 30 Gedney Park Dr., White Plains, 10605-3599. Tel: 303-586-1672; Fax: 303-477-6925; Email: mark.schenk@capuchins.org; Web: www.ofmcap.org. 3613 Wyandot St., Denver, CO 80211. Bro. Mark Schenk, O.F.M.Cap., Pres.; Revs. Victorius Pictorius, O.F.M.Cap., Vice Pres.; Alejandro Nunez, O.F.M.Cap., Treas.; Giampiero Gambaro, O.F.M.Cap., Sec.

Capuchin Friars of North America, 30 Gedney Park Dr., White Plains, 10605-3599. Tel: 914-761-3008; Tel: 920-960-5646; Fax: 914-948-6429; Email: harlan0253@gmail.com. Rev. Michael Sullivan, Pres.; Very Rev. Thomas Betz, O.F.M.Cap., Vice Pres.; Harlan Swift, Sec. & Treas.

St. Francis of Assisi Foundation, St. Conrad Friary, 30 Gedney Park Dr., White Plains, 10605-3599. Tel: 303-586-1672; Fax: 303-477-6925; Email: mark.schenk@capuchins.org. 3613 Wyandot St., Denver, CO 80211. Dr. Livio Camozzi, Pres.; Bro. Mark Schenk, O.F.M.Cap., Vice Pres.; Rev. Giampiero Gambaro, O.F.M.Cap., Treas.

The Province of St. Mary of the Capuchin Order (1882) 30 Gedney Park Dr., White Plains, 10605-3599. Tel: 914-761-3008; Fax: 914-948-6429; Email: fgasparik@capuchin.org; Web: www.capuchin.org. Revs. Francis Gasparik, O.F.M.Cap., Min. Prov.; Michael Marigliano, O.F.M.Cap., Vicar Prov.; Jerome McHugh, O.F.M.Cap., Sec.; Mr. David LeGare, Dir. Finance; Revs. Ramon Frias, O.F.M.Cap., Local Min.; John Mellitt, O.F.M.Cap., Sabbatical; John Rathschmidt, O.F.M.Cap., Retreats & Missions; Bro. Pius Blandino, O.F.M.-Cap., Plant Mgr.; Revs. Paul Engel, O.F.M.Cap., Dir. Downey Side; Joseph Flynn, O.F.M.Cap., Chap., College of New Rochelle; Bros. Carlos Hernandez, O.F.M.Cap., Treas.; Roger Deguire, O.F.-M.Cap., Archivist; Timothy Aller, O.F.M.Cap., Dir., Halfway House. Provincial Headquarters of the Province of St. Mary of the Capuchin Order.; (Nature of Apostolate: Provincial Administration, Parishes, College, Hospital & Prison Chaplains, Preaching, Recruitment). Total Staff 14.

YONKERS. *St. Clare Friary* Residence for Senior Friars. 110 Shonnard Pl., Yonkers, 10703. Tel: 914-423-2392. Revs. Michael Connolly; Senan Taylor, O.F.M.Cap., Guardian; Philip Bohan, O.F.-M.Cap., (Retired); John Clermont, O.F.M.Cap.; Andrew Drew, O.F.M.Cap., (Retired); Knute Kenlon, O.F.M.Cap.; Paul Minchak, O.F.M.Cap.; Louis Chiusano, O.F.M.Cap. Capuchin Franciscan Friars, Province of St. Mary. Total in Residence 11; Total Staff 3.

St. Leopold's Friary (Franciscan Friars of the Renewal) (House of Studies) 259 Nepperhan Ave., Yonkers, 10701-3461. Tel: 914-965-8143; Fax: 914-709-8986; Web: www.franciscanfriars.com. Revs. Luke Mary Fletcher, C.F.R., Supr.; Leo Joseph Fisher, C.F.R., Pastoral Assoc.; Pio Maria Hoffman, C.F.R., In Res.; Robert Lombardo, C.F.R., In Res.; Bros. Isaiah Marie Hofmann, C.F.R., Seminarian; Seraphim Pio Baalbaki, C.F.R., Seminarian; Michelangelo Best, C.F.R., Seminarian; Frantisek Chloupek, C.F.R., Seminarian; Elijah Perri, C.F.R., Seminarian; Oisin Martin, C.F.R.; Gabriel Monahan, C.F.R.; Malachy Napier, C.F.R.; Ignatius Pio Doherty, C.F.R.; Joseph Michael Fino, C.F.R.

[DD] CONVENTS AND RESIDENCES OF SISTERS

NEW YORK. *Academy of St. Dorothy* (1932) 1305 Hylan Blvd., Staten Island, 10305. Tel: 718-987-0677; Tel: 718-351-0939; Fax: 718-351-0661; Email: dorothy@adnyeducation.org; Email: cportu@gmail.com. Sr. Caridad Portu, S.S.D., Coord. Sisters of St. Dorothy. Sisters 5.

Convent of Our Lady of the Presentation (1775) 419 Woodrow Rd., 10312. Tel: 718-356-2121; Fax: 718-948-4115; Email: lorraine.hale1@verizon.net. Sr. Lorraine Hale, Congregation Leader. Motherhouse and Novitiate of the Sisters of the Presentation. Sisters 9.

Corpus Christi Monastery, 1230 Lafayette Ave., 10474-5399. Tel: 718-328-6996; Fax: 718-328-1974; Email: dominicannunsny@verizon.net. Sr. Maria Pia, Prioress. Solemnly Professed 10.

Franciscan Handmaids of the Most Pure Heart of Mary Generalate of the Franciscan Handmaids of Mary. 15 W. 124th St., 10027. Tel: 212-289-5655; Fax: 212-987-5447; Email: handmaidsofmary@aol.com; Web: www.passionforsocialjustice.com. Sisters Gertrude Lilly Ihenacho, F.H.M., Congregation Min. & Missionary Community Admin., Tel: 347-937-0112; Chala Marie Hill, F.H.M., Base Community Admin. Sisters 17.

Other Convents:

Most Pure Heart of Mary Convent, 63 Bayside Ln., Staten Island, 10309. Tel: 718-227-5575; Email: pfsocialjustice@yahoo.com. Sr. Rose Mary Onwuemene, F.H.M., Local Min. (Staten Island). *St. Edward Food Pantry*, 6581 Hylan Blvd., Staten Island, 10309. Tel: 718-984-1625; Fax: 718-996-0814. Sr. Rose Mary Onwuemene, F.H.M., Site Coord.

Handmaids of Mary Altar Bread Distribution Service, 6581 Hylan Blvd., Staten Island, 10309. Tel: 718-984-1625; Fax: 718-966-0814. Ms. Cyril Agap, Mgr. Associates 35.

St. Benedict Toddler Care Center (Day Care Center) 21 W. 124 St., 10027. Tel: 212-423-5715; Fax: 212-423-5917; Email: st.benedictdaynursery@verizon.net. Sr. Mary Ann Baichan, F.H.M., Dir.

Franciscan Missionaries of Mary, 3305 Wallace Ave., Bronx, 10467-6519. Tel: 718-547-4693; Fax: 718-325-5102; Email: nmfmm@aol.com; Web: www.fmmusa.org. Religious 3.

FMM Provincialate, 3305 Wallace Ave., Bronx, 10467-6519. Tel: 718-547-4693; Fax: 718-325-5102; Email: nmfmm@aol.com; Web: www.fmm.org; Web: www.fmmusa.org. Sr. Noreen Murray, Prov. Religious 3.

Holy Name of Jesus Convent, 204 W. 97th St., 10025-5620. Tel: 212-678-6901; Email: fmmny97@aol.com; Web: www.fmmusa.org. Sisters 6.

Our Lady of Millbrook Convent, Box K, Millbrook, 12545. Tel: 845-677-6739; Fax: 845-677-6530; Email: fmmch@aol.com; Web: www.fmmusa.org.

Franciscan Sisters of the Poor, 708 3rd Ave., Ste. 1920, 10017. Tel: 718-643-1945; Fax: 212-808-0096; Email: sfp@franciscansisters.org; Web: www.franciscansisters.org. Sr. Licia Mazzia, S.F.P., Congregation Min. Sisters 118.

Franciscan Sisters of the Poor Foundation, Inc., 708 Third Ave., Ste. 1920, 10017. Tel: 212-818-1987; Fax: 212-808-0096; Email: pfagan@franciscanfoundation.org; Web: www.franciscanfoundation.org. Sr. Licia Mazzia, S.F.P., Pres. Sisters 118.

Holy Family Provincialate (1921) 850 Hylan Blvd., Staten Island, 10305. Tel: 718-720-7365; Fax: 718-727-5701; Email: smcoffeltfdc@hotmail.com; Email: rgegic@aol.com; Email: holyfamilyprovince@aol.com; Web: www.daughtersofdivinecharity.org. Sr. Mary Coffelt, F.D.C., Prov. Provincialate of the Daughters of Divine Charity (Holy Family Province). Sisters 37; In Province 37.

International Presentation Association of the Sisters of the Presentation of the Blessed Virgin Mary, 1011 First Ave., Ste. 1313, 10022. Tel: 646-494-3093; Email: pbvmipa@msn.com; Web: internationalpresentationassociation.org. Elsa Muttathu, P.B.V.M., Contact Person & Main Rep.

Little Sisters of the Assumption, Territory Office, 475 E. 115th St., 1st Fl., 10029. Tel: 212-289-4014; Fax: 212-876-2075; Web: www.littlesisters.org. Sr. Annette Allain, L.S.A., Territory Coord. Sisters in Province 15.

Other residences in New York:*Little Sisters of the Assumption*, 475 E. 115th St., 10029. Tel: 212-369-2097.

Parish Visitors of Mary Immaculate (1920) 2151 Watson Ave., Bronx, 10472-5401. Tel: 718-823-0350; Fax: 718-823-0350. Sr. Mary Roberta White, P.V.M.I., Supr. Sisters 4.

Sisters of Charity Center, 6301 Riverdale Ave., 10471-1093. Tel: 718-549-9200; Fax: 718-884-3013; Email: emcgrory@scny.org; Web: www.scny.org. Sr. Jane Iannucelli, Pres.
The Sisters of Charity of Saint Vincent de Paul of New York
Sisters of Charity Center
Mount Saint Vincent on Hudson Sisters 236; Adult Baptisms 252; In Archdiocese 244.

Sisters of Charity Novitiate, 3 Haven Plaza, 4GH, 10009. Tel: 212-673-6707; Email: mmccormick@scny.org. Sr. Mary McCormick, Novice Dir.

Sisters of the Good Shepherd, 337 E. 17th St., 10003-3804. Tel: 212-475-4245; Fax: 212-777-9260.
Sisters of the Good Shepherd Province of New York Sisters 3.

Society of Helpers, 385 W. 263rd St., Bronx, 10471. Sr. Geraldine Finan, Supr. Sisters 2. *Society of the Sacred Heart, R.S.C.J.*, 501 W. 52nd St., #4E, 10019. Tel: 212-581-3894. Sr. Lydia Cho, Supr. Sisters 1. *Society of the Sacred Heart, R.S.C.J.*, 310 E. 120th St., 10035. Tel: 212-876-2895. Sisters 4.

Visitation Convent (Sisters of Life) 320 E. 66th St., 10065. Tel: 212-737-0221. Sisters 10.

BEACON. *Carmelite Monastery* (2000) 89 Hiddenbrooke Dr., Beacon, 12508-2230. Tel: 845-831-5572; Fax: 845-831-5579; Email: carmelitesbeacon@gmail.com; Web: www.carmelitesbeacon.org. Sr. Marjorie Robinson, O.C.D., Prioress. Sisters 15; Professed Nuns 15.

Mother of Perpetual Help Monastery, 89 Hiddenbrooke Dr., Beacon, 12508-2230. Tel: 845-831-3132; Fax: 845-831-5579; Email: rednunsny@gmail.com; Web: www.rednunsny.org. Sr. Moira Quinn, O.SS.R., Prioress. Redemptoristine Nuns. Sisters 6; Professed Sisters 6.

BLAUVELT. *Congregation of Sisters of St. Dominic of Blauvelt*, 496 Western Hwy., Blauvelt, 10913. Tel: 845-359-5600; Fax: 845-359-5773; Email: mconnolly@opblauvelt.org; Web: www.opblauvelt.org. Sr. Michaela Connolly, O.P., Prioress
The Sisters of St. Dominic of Blauvelt, New York Sisters 115.

BRONX. *Franciscan Sisters of the Renewal* (Franciscan Sisters of the Renewal) Convent of San Damiano, 1661 Haight Ave., Bronx, 10461. Tel: 718-863-8040; Tel: 718-829-9466; Fax: 718-863-8130; Web: www.franciscansisterscfr.com. Mother Lucille Cutrone, C.F.R., Community Servant; Sr. Francis O'Donnell, C.F.R., Novice Directress. (Motherhouse, Novitiate House, Convent of Damiano) Sisters 6.

Franciscan Sisters of the Renewal, 3537 Bainbridge Ave., Bronx, 10467. Tel: 718-547-9840; Tel: 718-828-4104; Web: www.franciscansisterscfr.com. Sisters Mary Pieta Geier, C.F.R., Local Servant; Clare Marie Matthiass, C.F.R., Vocation Dir. (Franciscans Sisters of the Renewal) Sisters 9.

Missionary Sisters of Our Lady of Perpetual Help, Inc. (1934) Office of the President, 389 E. 150th St., Bronx, 10455. Tel: 718-801-2461; Email: garzamps@yahoo.com. Sr. Melissa Garza, Supr.

Missionaries of Charity, Inc., 335 E. 145th St., Bronx, 10451. Tel: 718-292-0019; Fax: 718-292-2929. Sisters Maria Agnes, M.C., Regl. Supr.; M. Regi Paul, M.C., Supr. 406 W. 127th St., 10027. Tel: 212-222-7229. Sr. Marie Joel, M.C., Supr. 657 Washington St., 10014. Tel: 212-645-0587. Sr. Maria Bernadette, M.C., Supr.

Missionary Sisters of the Immaculate Heart of Mary (1897) District House 2550 Webb Ave., Apt. 7E, Bronx, 10468. Sr. Kathryn Vercelline, I.C.M., Dist. Treas.

Sisters of St. John the Baptist, Provincial Residence, 3308 Campbell Dr., Bronx, 10465-1358. Tel: 718-518-7820; Fax: 718-518-8930; Email: srmcecile@hotmail.com; Web: baptistines.org. Claudette Jasczynski Sr., Prov. Sisters 67; In Province 76; In Archdiocese 69.

Mt. St. John Convent, 150 Anderson Hill Rd., Purchase, 10577. Tel: 914-761-7965; Fax: 914-761-2315; Email: smdcsjb@hotmail.com. Sr. Mary Dulsky, Supr. (Retired Sisters' Residence) Sisters in Residence 24.

GARRISON. *Franciscan Sisters of the Atonement* (1898) St. Francis Convent - Graymoor, 41 Old Highland Tpke., Garrison, 10524. Tel: 845-424-3625; Fax: 845-424-3298; Web: www.graymoor.org. Sr. Mary Patricia Galvin, S.A., Min. Gen.
Franciscan Sisters of the Atonement, Inc. Sisters 98.

Mother Lurana House of Graymoor, 166 Old W. Point Rd., E., Garrison, 10524. Tel: 845-424-3184; Fax: 845-424-4137; Web: www.graymoor.org. Sr. Loretta Bezner, S.A., Admin. Franciscan Sisters of the Atonement.

Our Lady of the Atonement Retreat House, St Francis Convent, 41 Old Highland Tpke., Garrison, 10524. Tel: 845-424-3300; Fax: 845-230-8400; Email: retreathouse@graymoor.org; Web: www.graymoor.org. Sr. Eleanor White, S.A., Directress. Franciscan Sisters of the Atonement, Graymoor. Sisters 2.

HARTSDALE. *Institute of the Sisters of Mercy of the Americas, Mid-Atlantic Community*, 150 Ridge Rd., Hartsdale, 10530-2205. Tel: 914-328-3200; Fax: 914-328-3761; Web: www.mercymidatlantic.org. Sr. Patricia Vetrano, R.S.M., Pres. Sisters of Mercy.
The Sisters of Mercy, Inc. Sisters of Mercy of the Americas 927.

HAVERSTRAW. *Sisters of St. Francis of Peace* (1986) Congregation Center, 20 Ridge St., Haverstraw, 10927-1198. Tel: 845-942-2527; Fax: 845-429-8141; Email: hwacker@fspnet.org; Web: www.fspnet.org. Sr. Helen Wacker, F.S.P., Congregation Min. Sisters 49.

HAWTHORNE. *Motherhouse & Novitiate of the Sisters of St. Dominic, Congregation of St. Rose of Lima* (1900) 600 Linda Ave, Hawthorne, 10532. Tel: 914-769-5628; Fax: 914-769-0827; Web: www.hawthorne-dominicans.org. Mother Mary Francis, O.P., Supr. Gen.; Rev. Gregory Doherty, Chap.
Motherhouse and Dominican Sisters, Congregation of St. Rose of Lima. Sisters 47; Sisters in Community 45; In Archdiocese 31; Professed Sisters 43.

HIGHLAND MILLS. *Religious of Jesus and Mary* (1911) 15 Bethany Dr., Highland Mills, 10930-1003. Tel: 202-526-3203; Email: amagner@rjmusa.org. 821 Varnum St., NE, Washington, DC 20017-2144. Sr. Anne Magner
Legal Title: Convent of Jesus & Mary of Highland Mills, New York, Inc. Sisters 3.

HOPEWELL JUNCTION. *Oblates to the Blessed Trinity, St. Aloysius Novitiate*, 306 Beekman Rd., P.O. Box 98, Hopewell Junction, 12533. Tel: 845-226-5671; Fax: 845-226-5671; Email: jstab35097@aol.com; Web: www.oblatestotheblessedtrinity.org. Mother Gloria Castro, Supr. Gen. Professed Sisters 7.

LIBERTY. *Blessed Kateri Tekakwitha Religious Education Center*, 16 Frankie Ln., Box 1011, Liberty, 12754. Tel: 845-292-9100; Fax: 845-292-9100; Email: BKT4@verizon.net. Sr. Kevin John Shields, O.P., Dir. of Religious Education. Dominican Sisters. Sisters 1.

LIVINGSTON MANOR. *Monastic Sisters of Bethlehem and of the Assumption of the Virgin* (1951) 393 Our Lady of Lourdes Camp Rd., Livingston Manor, 12758. Tel: 845-439-4300; Fax: 845-439-3069. Sr. Amena Figeat, M.S.B.A.V., Supr. Total in Residence 15.

MARYKNOLL. *Maryknoll Communities, Inc.*, 77 Ryder Rd., P.O. Box 133, Maryknoll, 10545-0133. Tel: 914-941-7590; Fax: 914-944-3628; Email: rcallahan@maryknoll.org; Web: www.maryknoll.org.
Maryknoll Residential Care Skilled Nursing home for the Maryknoll sisters only. Maryknoll Sisters Center, Maryknoll, 10545-0311. Tel: 914-941-9230; Fax: 914-941-0213; Email: swaldstein@mksisters.org; Web: www.maryknoll.org. Sr. Patricia Edmiston, M.M., Admin. Bed Capacity 42; Sisters 33.
Maryknoll Sisters Charitable Trust, Treasury Office, P.O. Box 306, Maryknoll, 10545-0306. Tel: 914-941-7590; Fax: 914-944-3628; Email: rcallahan@maryknoll.org; Web: www.maryknoll.org. Rev. Richard B. Callahan, M.M., Trustee.
Maryknoll Sisters Contemplative Community Contemplative Community of the Maryknoll Sisters of St. Dominic. P.O. Box 311, Maryknoll, 10545-0311. Tel: 914-941-7575; Fax: 914-923-0733; Email: mkcontemplative@optimum.net. Sr. Grace Myerjack, M.M., Coord. Sisters 9.
Maryknoll Sisters of St. Dominic Inc. (1912) P.O. Box 311, Maryknoll, 10545-0311. Tel: 914-941-7575; Fax: 914-941-5535; Email: secretariat@mksisters.org; Web: www.maryknollsisters.org. Sr. Connie Krautkremer, M.M., Center-Rogers Coord. Sisters 394; Total in Residence 201; Professed Sisters 201.

MILLBROOK. *Franciscan Missionaries of Mary* (1941) P.O. Box K, Millbrook, 12545. Tel: 845-677-6739; Fax: 845-677-9530; Email: fmmch@aol.com; Web: fmmusa.org. Sisters Anne Turbini, F.M.M.; Martha Vu, F.M.M. Sisters 3.

MONROE. *Parish Visitors of Mary Immaculate* (1920) Marycrest Convent, 164 Quaker Hill Rd., P.O. Box 658, Monroe, 10949-0658. Sisters Carole Marie Troskowski, Dir.; Maria Iannotti, Supr. A contemplative-missionary community serving the Church by person-to-person evangelization through visiting parish families on behalf of their priests; religious education for children and adults not connected with the Catholic schools, giving spiritual counsel and serving as a liaison for social service needs of family members. Total in Community 59.
Queen of Apostles Convent Provincial Retirement Home and Provincialate of the Sisters of the Catholic Apostolate (Pallottine). 98 Harriman Heights Rd., Monroe, 10950. Tel: 845-492-5000; Fax: 845-492-5070; Email: qoaconvent@hotmail.com; Web: www.pallottinesisters.org. Sisters Ann Joachim Firneno, C.S.A.C., Prov.; Angela Marie Verdi, C.S.A.C., Supr.; Rev. Michael F. Keane, Chap. Sisters 27.

MONSEY. *St. Zita's Villa* Motherhouse and Novitiate of Sisters of Reparation of the Congregation of Mary. 50 Saddle River Rd., N., Monsey, 10952. Tel: 845-356-2011; Fax: 845-364-6520. Sr. Maureen Francis, S.R.C.M., Supr. Sisters 2.

NEW ROCHELLE. *Ursuline Bedford Park Convent* (1855) 1338 North Ave., New Rochelle, 10804. Tel: 914-636-3456; Fax: 914-636-2240; Email: finnertycait@hotmail.com. Sr. Kathleen Finnerty, Supr.
Ursuline Communities, Inc. (1997) 1338 North Ave., New Rochelle, 10804. Tel: 914-712-0060; Fax: 914-712-3134; Email: ursruepr@aol.com. Sr. Jane Finnerty, O.S.U., Prov.
Ursuline Convent of St. Teresa's, 39 Willow Dr., New Rochelle, 10805. Tel: 914-632-1199; Fax: 914-633-5281; Email: mtwosu@gmail.com. Maureen Welch, Supr.
Ursuline Convent of St. Teresa's, New York Sisters 18.
Ursuline Provincialate, 1338 North Ave., New Rochelle, 10804-2121. Tel: 914-712-0060; Fax: 914-712-3134; Email: ursruepr@aol.com. Sr. Jane Finnerty, O.S.U., Prov. Sisters in Province 82.
Ursuline Residence, Inc., 1338 North Ave., New Rochelle, 10804. Tel: 914-712-0060; Fax: 914-712-3134. Sr. Jane Finnerty, O.S.U., Prov.

NEW WINDSOR. *Sisters of the Presentation of the Blessed Virgin Mary, Inc.*, Mt. St. Joseph Administration Center, 84 Presentation Way, New Windsor, 12553. Tel: 845-564-0513; Fax: 845-567-0219; Email: pbvmadministration@hvc.rr.com; Web: sistersofthepresentation.org. Sr. Patricia Anastasio, P.B.V.M., Pres. Ministry in the field of academic education in parochial elementary and high schools; pastoral services; health care; social services. Sisters 104.

NEWBURGH. *Daughters of Mary Immaculate* (1898) Italian Apostolate in Sacred Heart Church. 15 Stori Rd., Newburgh, 12550. Tel: 845-565-5034. Sr. Alba Danese, F.M.I., Supr. Total Staff 2; Total Assisted 57.

NYACK. *Sisters of Our Lady of Christian Doctrine* aka Institute of Christian Doctrine Visitation House 110 Larchdale Ave., Nyack, 10960. Tel: 845-512-8669; Fax: 845-358-7663; Email: veromrcd@gmail.com; Web: www.sistersrcd.org. Sr. Mary Murray, O.P., Pres. Sisters 18.

OSSINING. *Dominican Sisters of Hope, Inc.* (1995) 299 N. Highland Ave., Bldg. 5, Ossining, 10562-2327. Tel: 914-941-4420; Fax: 914-941-1125; Email: lelcock@ophope.org; Web: www.ophope.org. Sr. Lorelle Elcock, O.P., Prioress. Sisters 148; Total in Community 148.
Dominicare, Inc. (2001) Office of the President, 299 N. Highland Ave., Bldg. 5, Ossining, 10562-2327. Tel: 914-941-4420; Fax: 914-941-1125; Email: lelcock@ophope.org; Web: www.ophope.org. Sr. Lorelle Elcock, O.P., Pres.
Sisters of St. Dominic Charitable Trust, 299 N. Highland Ave., Bldg. 5, Ossining, 10562. Tel: 914-941-4455; Fax: 914-502-0574; Email: hdowney@ophope.org. Hugh R. Downey, Trustee, Email: hdowney@ophope.org.

PEEKSKILL. *Mt. St. Francis, Motherhouse & Infirm of Franciscan Missionary Sisters of Sacred Heart* Canonical Name: Franciscan Missionary Sisters of the Sacred Heart. 250 South St., Peekskill, 10566. Tel: 914-737-5409; Fax: 914-736-9614; Email: slmfmsc@mail.com; Web: fmscusa.org. Sisters Laura Morgan, F.M.S.C., Prov. Supr.; Anne James Guerin, F.M.S.C., Vocations Contact, Tel: 914-737-3373
Missionary Sisters of the Third Order of St. Francis.

RHINEBECK. *Linwood Spiritual Center*, 50 Linwood Rd., Rhinebeck, 12572-2507. Tel: 845-876-4178; Fax: 845-876-1920; Email: lscoffice@st-ursula.org; Email: msteeley@st-ursula.org; Web: www.linwoodspiritualctr.org. Sr. Maureen Steeley, S.U., Dir. Spiritual Center. Society of St. Ursula.

SCARSDALE. *Blessed Sacrament Monastery*, 86 Dromore Rd., Scarsdale, 10583-1706. Tel: 914-722-1657; Fax: 914-722-1665; Email: obsny@optonline.net; Web: www.catholic.org/macc. Sr. Mary Francis Blackmore, O.S.S., Prioress. Sacramentine Nuns. Sisters 5.

SLOATSBURG. *St. Mary's Villa, Spiritual & Educational Center*, 150 Sisters Servants Ln., P.O. Box 9, Sloatsburg, 10974-0009. Tel: 845-753-5100; Fax: 845-753-1956; Email: ssminy@aol.com. Sr. Kathleen Hutsko, S.S.M.I., Prov. Sisters Servants of Mary Immaculate. Sisters 5.

SPARKILL. *Dominican Convent of Our Lady of the Rosary* (1876) Motherhouse and General Novitiate of Dominican Sisters of Congregation of Our Lady of the Rosary. 175 Rte. 340, Sparkill, 10976-1047. Tel: 845-359-4088; Fax: 845-359-4083; Email: ghogan@sparkill.org; Web: www.sparkill.org. Sr. Mary Murray, O.P., Pres.; Rev. George Torak, Chap. Sisters 263.

STATEN ISLAND. *Daughters of St. Paul, Pious Society* (1915) 236 Richmond Ter., Staten Island, 10301. Tel: 718-447-5071; Email: statenisland@pauline.org; Web: www.pauline.org. Sr. Sean Marie David Mayer, Supr. Missionary Sisters of the Communications Media. Sisters 5.
Pious Disciples of the Divine Master, Regional and Formation House, 60 Sunset Ave., Staten Island, 10314. Tel: 718-761-2323; Tel: 718-494-8597; Fax: 718-494-2123; Web: www.pddm.us. Sr. M. Josephine Fallon, P.D.D.M., Regl. Supr. Sisters 8.

SUFFERN. *Sisters of Life* (1991) Annunciation, 38 Montebello Rd., Suffern, 10901. Tel: 845-357-3547; Fax: 845-357-5040; Web: sistersoflife.org. Sr. Bethany Madonna Burwell, Vocations Dir.; Mother Agnes Mary Donovan, S.V., Supr. Gen.; Sr. Mary Elizabeth Wusinch, Vicar. Novices 19; Postulants 7; Sisters 100; In residence at motherhouse 32; Professed Sisters 81; Total in Community 107.
Sacred Heart of Jesus (Sisters of Life), 450 W. 51st St., 10019. Tel: 212-397-1396; Fax: 212-397-1397; Web: sistersoflife.org. Sisters Catherine Marie, S.V., Local Supr.; Mary Kolbe, S.V., Email: holyrespite@sistersoflife.org; Virginia Joy, Respect Life Office Dir.; Pia Jude, Asst. Respect Life Office Director; Maeve Nativitas, S.V., Asst. to Supr. Sisters 10.
St. Frances de Chantal (Sisters of Life), 198 Hollywood Ave., Bronx, 10465. Tel: 718-863-2264; Fax: 718-409-2033; Web: sistersoflife@sistersoflife.org. Sisters Mariae Agnus Dei, S.V., Supr.; Hosanna Immaculata, Asst. to Supr. Sisters 11.
Sisters of Life Center (Mission to Serve Pregnant Women), 257 E. 71st St., 10021. Tel: 877-777-1277; Tel: 212-737-0221; Email: visitation@sistersoflife.org. Sisters Magdalene Teresa, S.V., Supr.; Brigid Ancilla Marie, Asst. to Supr.; Amata Filia, S.V., Co-worker Mission Coord. Sisters 12.

TARRYTOWN. *Provincial Center, Religious Sacred Heart of Mary*, 50 Wilson Park Dr., Tarrytown, 10591-3023. Tel: 914-631-8872; Fax: 914-631-7803; Email: delourdes@rshmeap.org; Web: www.rshm.org. Sisters Catherine M. Patten, R.S.H.M., Prov. Supr.; Monica Walsh, R.S.H.M., Councillor; Catherine Vincie, R.S.H.M., Councillor; Mary Alice Young, R.S.H.M., Dir., Advancement; Mary Lou Bloomingdale, R.S.H.M., Archivist; Anna Maria Lionetti, R.S.H.M., Vocation Dir.
Sisters of the Sacred Heart of Mary Total Staff 16.

WAPPINGERS FALLS. *Monastery of St. Clare - Franciscan Poor Clare Nuns* (1915) 70 Nelson Ave., Wappingers Falls, 12590-1121. Tel: 845-297-1685; Fax: 845-297-7657; Email: claresny@gmail.com; Web: www.poorclaresny.com. Sr. Mary Michael Boisseau, O.S.C., Abbess
Franciscan Poor Clare Nuns Sisters 9.

WARWICK. *Mt. Alverno Center, Bon Secours Charity Health System*, 20 Grand St., Warwick, 10990. Tel: 845-986-2267; Fax: 845-986-9269; Web: http://bschs.bonsecours.com. Jeff Reilly, Senior Vice Pres. & Admin.; Clare Brady, Senior Vice Pres. Mission. Sisters of Charity of St. ElizabethSisters of Bon SecoursSt. Francis Center at the Knolls.; Part of Bon Secours Charity Health System.

WHITE PLAINS. *Convent of Our Lady of Good Counsel* Motherhouse of the Sisters of the Divine Compassion 52 N. Broadway, White Plains, 10603. Tel: 914-798-1300; Fax: 914-949-5169; Email: cwagner@divinecompassion.org; Web: divinecompassion.org. Sr. Laura Donovan, R.D.C., Prov. Sisters 20.
RDC Center for Counseling and Human Development, Inc. (1991) 52 N. Broadway, White Plains, 10603. Tel: 914-949-0504; Fax: 914-997-1979. Sr. Carol T. Wagner, R.D.C., Pres. To provide counseling services for laity, religious and clergy. Individual and group counseling are offered as well as marital and family therapy.

YONKERS. *The Congregation of The Daughters of Mary, Inc.*, 15 Trinity St., Yonkers, 10701. Tel: 914-207-6854; Fax: 914-207-6854; Email: dmcityisland@optimum.net. Sr. Agnes Jose, D.M., Sec. & Treas.

[EE] RETREAT HOUSES

BEACON. *St. Lawrence of Brindisi Friary*, 180 Sargent Ave., Beacon, 12508-3993.

BRONX. *St. Joseph's Center*, 275 W. 230th St., Bronx, 10463. Tel: 718-796-4340. Rev. Jose Luis Martinez, O.A.R., Dir.; Bro. Mario Alvarez, O.A.R., Admin. (Spanish Cursillo Center) Total in Residence 1; Total Staff 2.

ESOPUS. *Marist Brothers of Ulster County* (1994) Mid Hudson Valley Camp - Summer camp for disadvantaged children/Retreat house for youth. Winter youth retreat facility. P.O. Box 197, Esopus, 12429. Tel: 845-384-6620 (office); Fax: 845-384-6479; Email: maristbce@gmail.com; Web: www.maristretreathouse.com. Bro. Owen Ormsby, F.M.S., Dir. Total Staff 2.

HIGHLAND MILLS. *Bethany Spirituality Center, Inc.*, 15 Bethany Dr., Highland Mills, 10930. Tel: 202-526-3203; Email: amagner@rjmusa.org. 821 Varnum St., NE, Washington, DC 20017-2144. Mary C. Spanos, Dir.; Sr. Anne Magner. Religious of Jesus and Mary. Total in Residence 2.

LARCHMONT. *St. Francis Retreat, Inc.*, 1 Pryer Manor Rd., Larchmont, 10538. Tel: 718-402-8255; Fax: 718-665-2441. Fr. Patrick Crowley, Dir.
Trinity Retreat (Retreat Center for Clergy) 1 Pryer Manor Rd., Larchmont, 10538. Tel: 914-235-6839; Fax: 914-576-6540; Email: trinityret@aol.com. Rev. Eugene J. Fulton, Dir.

MIDDLETOWN. *National Shrine of Our Lady of Mount Carmel*, 70 Carmelite Dr., P.O. Box 2163, Middletown, 10940-2163. Tel: 845-343-1879; Fax: 845-343-1912; Email: cbezak@carmelites.com; Web: www.ourladyofmtcarmelshrine.com. Carol Bezak, Dir. Total Staff 3.

SLOATSBURG. *St. Mary's Villa*, 150 Sisters Servants Ln., P.O. Box 9, Sloatsburg, 10974-0009.

Tel: 845-753-5100; Fax: 845-753-1956; Email: ssminy@aol.com. Sr. Kathleen Hutsko, S.S.M.I., Prov. Sisters Servants of Mary Immaculate.Spiritual and Educational Center. (Retreats) Total in Residence 5; Total Staff 4.

STATEN ISLAND. *Mount Manresa Jesuit Retreat House* (1911) 239 Fingerboard Rd., Staten Island, 10305. Tel: 718-727-3844; Fax: 718-727-4881; Email: info@mountmanresa.org; Web: www.mountmanresa.org. Mr. Fred Herron, Interim Dir.; Ms. Arlene Volsario, Admin.; Revs. Thomas M. Gavin, S.J., Retreat Min.; Matthew F. Roche, S.J., Retreat Min.; Sr. Maureen Skelly, S.C., Retreat Min. Society of Jesus. Total in Residence 4; Total Staff 6.

STONY POINT. *Don Bosco Retreat Center and Marian Shrine* Founded 1947. 174 Filors Ln., Stony Point, 10980-2620. Tel: 845-947-2200; Fax: 845-947-2203; Email: directorssecretary@yahoo.com; Web: www.marianshrine.org. Revs. Richard J. Putnam, S.D.B., Retreat Team Coord.; Nesly Leonard, Youth Min.; Augustine Baek, S.D.B., RYC Korean Min.; Waclaw Swierzbiolek, S.D.B., Polish Min.; Thomas E. Ruekert, S.D.B., Retreat Team; Thomas Dunne, S.D.B., In Res.; Joseph Doran, S.D.B., In Res.; Javier Aracil, S.D.B., In Res.; Kenneth Shaw, S.D.B., In Res.; Very Rev. Steve Shafran, S.D.B., In Res.; Revs. Stephen M. Ryan, In Res.; James McKenna, S.D.B.; Bros. Donald Caldwell, Admin.; Charles Thenier, S.D.B., In Res.; Henry van der Velden, S.D.B.; Richard Pasiak, S.D.B. Total in Residence 16; Total Staff 20.

Marian Shrine (1947) 174 Filors Ln., Stony Point, 10980-2620. Tel: 845-947-2200; Fax: 845-947-2203; Web: www.marianshrine.org. Revs. James McKenna, S.D.B., Dir.; Nesly Leonard, Youth Min.; Joseph Doran, S.D.B., Chap.; Javier Aracil, S.D.B., In Res.; Stephen M. Ryan, In Res.; Very Rev. Steve Shafran, S.D.B., In Res.; Revs. Augustine Baek, S.D.B.; Kenneth Shaw, S.D.B., In Res.; Thomas E. Ruekert, S.D.B.; Thomas Dunne, S.D.B.; Waclaw Swierzbiolek, S.D.B.; Richard J. Putnam, S.D.B.; Bros. Donald Caldwell, S.D.B., Admin.; Charles Thenier, S.D.B., In Res.; Richard Pasaik, S.D.B.; Henry van der Velden, S.D.B. Total in Residence 16; Total Staff 20.

ULSTER PARK. *Redemptorist Community at Esopus*, 32 Peters Ln., Ulster Park, 12487. Tel: 845-340-1732; Fax: 845-340-1787. Revs. Thomas J. Travers, C.Ss. R.; Thomas (Martin) Deely, C.Ss.R.; Eugene J. Grohe, C.Ss.R. Redemptorist Fathers and Brothers.Rural parish and outreach program (Brazos Abiertos) for Hispanics/Latinos.

WAPPINGERS FALLS. *Mt. Alvernia Retreat House*, Wappingers Falls, 12590. Tel: 845-297-5706; Fax: 845-298-0309; Email: mtalverniarh@optonline.net. Revs. Roch Ciandella, O.F.M., Dir. Retreats; Thomas Garone, O.F.M., Assoc. Dir., Retreats, Guardian & Chap.; Armand Padula, O.F.M., Parochial Ministry; Romano S. Almagno, O.F.M., Retreat Staff; Brennan Egan, O.F.M., Retreat Staff.

WARWICK. *Franciscan Sisters of the Poor Convent*, 24 Grand St., Warwick, 10990. Tel: 845-986-6799; Email: warwickconvent@optonline.net. Sr. Margaret A. Ferri, S.F.P., Local Community Min. Franciscan Sisters of the Poor.

YONKERS. *Sisters of Mary Reparatrix*, 287 Hayward St., Yonkers, 10704. Tel: 914-376-3245; Fax: 914-423-5721. Sisters Judy Frasinetti, S.M.R.; Geraldine McCullagh, S.M.R. Sisters 2.

[FF] UNIVERSITY APOSTOLATES

NEW YORK. *University Apostolate*, 1011 First Ave., Fl. 7, 10022. Tel: 646-794-3168; Email: vincent.dasilva@archny.org. Vincent DaSilva, Dir.

Baruch College, 55 Lexington Ave., 10010. Tel: 646-312-4762; Web: www.baruch.cuny.edu. Sr. Kathleen Logan, O.P., Campus Min.

Bronx Community College, Loew Hall-Room 422, University Ave. & W. 181st St., Bronx, 10453. Tel: 718-289-5954; Web: www.bcc.cuny.edu. Sr. Barbara Ann Mueller, O.P., Campus Min.

City College of New York, Baskerville, 204, 137th St. & Convent Ave., 10031. Tel: 212-650-5866; Web: www.ccny.cuny.edu. Sr. Barbara Ann Mueller, O.P., Campus Min.

Columbia University, 110 Earl Hall, 10027. Tel: 212-854-5110; Web: www.columbia.edu. Revs. Daniel O'Reilly, M.A., M.Div., Dir. Campus Min.; Jonathan Morris, Asst. Dir. Campus Min.

Culinary Institute of America, 93 Wurts St., Kingston, 12401. Tel: 845-331-0436; Fax: 845-340-9596; Email: chaplainua@gmail.com; Web: www.ciachef.edu. Rev. Marc K. Oliver, Campus Min.

Dutchess Community College, 93 Wurts St., Kingston, 12401-4509. Tel: 845-331-0436; Web: www.cunydutchess.edu. Rev. Marc K. Oliver, Campus Min.

Vassar College, St. Raymond Ave., Poughkeepsie, 12604. Tel: 845-437-7000; Web: www.vassar.edu. Ms. Linda Tuttle, Campus Min.

Dominican College, 470 Western Hwy., Orangeburg, 10962. Tel: 845-848-7800; Email: henrietta.malzacher@dc.edu; Web: dc.edu. Sr. Barbara McEneany, O.P., Dir. Campus Min.

Fordham University at Rosehill, 441 E. Fordham Rd., Bronx, 10458. Tel: 718-817-4500; Fax: 718-817-4505; Email: currie@fordham.edu; Web: www.fordham.edu/cm. Rev. Philip A. Florio, S.J.; Sr. Regina DeVitto, C.N.D., Faith Formation; Randy Jerome, Retreats & CLC; Mr. Denis Kelly; Mr. Robert Minotti, Dir. Music; Lisandro Pena, Liturgy Coord.; Gil Severiano, Sec.; Rev. Erika Crawford, Interfaith Coord.

Fordham Lincoln Center, 113 W. 60th St., Lowenstein 217, 10023. Tel: 212-636-6267; Tel: 212-636-6268. Ms. Joan Cavanagh, Assoc. Dir.; Mr. Patrick Callaghan, Sec.

Herbert H. Lehman College, Student Life Bldg., 250 Bedford Park Blvd. W. (222E), Bronx, 10468. Tel: 718-960-4979; Web: www.lehman.cuny.edu. Sr. Barbara Ann Mueller, O.P., Campus Min.

Hostos Community College, 475 Grand Concourse (Rm. C371), Bronx, 10451. Tel: 718-518-6873 (Mon-Tues); Web: www.hostos.cuny.edu. Sr. Barbara Ann Mueller, O.P., Campus Min.

Hunter College, Newman Catholic Center, 695 Park Ave., Rm. 1317 E. Bldg., 10021. Tel: 212-772-4752 (Hunter); Web: www.hunter.cuny.edu. Sr. Barbara Ann Mueller, O.P., Campus Min.

Iona College, 715 North Ave., New Rochelle, 10801. Tel: 914-633-2632; Fax: 914-633-2363; Web: www.iona.edu. Mr. Carl Procario-Foley, Dir. Campus Min.; Rev. Francis F. Dixon, O.Carm., Campus Min.; Tiffany Di Nomi, Campus Min.; Jeanne McDermott, Campus Min.

Manhattan College, 4513 Manhattan College Pkwy., Bronx, 10471. Tel: 718-862-7972; Fax: 718-862-8073; Email: lois.harr@manhattan.edu; Web: www.manhattan.edu.

Campus Ministry and Social Action Lois Harr, M.A., Dir. Campus Min.; Rev. George H. Hill, M.Div., M.A., Chap., Tel: 718-862-7972; Mr. Kevin McCloskey, Campus Min.; Jennifer Edwards, M.A., Campus Min.

Manhattanville College, 2900 Purchase St., Purchase, 10577. Tel: 914-323-5150, Ext. 447; Fax: 914-694-2496. Rev. William Tyrrell, S.A., Campus Min.

Marist College, 3399 North Rd., Poughkeepsie, 12601. Tel: 845-575-3130; Tel: 845-575-3000, Ext. 2275; Fax: 845-575-3299; Email: francis.kelly@marist.edu. Rev. Richard LaMorte, Chap.; Bro. Frank Kelly, F.M.S., Campus Min.

Mt. St. Mary College, 330 Powell Ave., Newburg, 12550. Tel: 845-569-3517; Web: campusministry@msmc.edu; Web: www.msmc.edu. Rev. Gregoire Fluet, Chap.

College of Mt. St. Vincent, 6301 Riverdale Ave., Riverdale, 10471. Tel: 718-405-3200; Tel: 718-405-3215; Tel: 718-405-3216; Web: www.cmsv.edu. Sr. Theresa Capria, S.C.

College of New Rochelle, 29 Castle Pl., New Rochelle, 10805. Tel: 914-654-5052; Tel: 914-654-5867; Fax: 914-654-5958; Email: hwolf@cnr.edu; Web: www.cnr.edu. Helen Wolf, Dir.; Rev. John Joseph Flynn, O.F.M.Cap., Chap.

New York Maritime College, 6 Pennyfield Ave., Fort Schuyler, Bronx, 10465-4198. Tel: 718-409-7200; Web: www.sunymaritime.edu. Dr. Mary Ellen Keefe, Campus Min.

New York University, Catholic Center at NYU, 238 Thompson St., 10012. Tel: 212-995-3990; Email: contact@catholiccenternyu.org; Web: catholiccenternyu.org. Rev. Sebastian White, O.P., S.T.L., Chap.

Office: St. Joseph's Rectory, 371 - 6th Ave., 10014. Tel: 212-741-1274; Fax: 212-473-2971.

Pace University, One Pace Plaza, 20 Cardinal Hayes Pl., 10038. Tel: 212-962-3972; Web: www.pace.edu. Rev. John McGuire, O.P., Campus Min.

Rockland Community College, 145 College Rd., Suffern, 10901. Tel: 845-574-4531; Fax: 845-574-4552; Web: www.sunyrockland.edu. Mr. Michael Ver'Schneider, Campus Min.

St. John's University, 300 Howard Ave., Rm. B9, Staten Island, 10301. Tel: 718-390-4473; Web: www.stjohns.edu. Stephen DeBlasio, Dir. Campus Min., Tel: 718-390-4473; James Behan Jr., Campus Min.; Melissa Gibilaro, Campus Min.

St. Thomas Aquinas, 125 Rte. 340, Sparkill, 10976. Tel: 845-398-4062; Fax: 845-398-4061; Web: www.stac.edu. Sr. Madeleine Murphy, O.P., Campus Min.

SUNY Maritime - University Apostolate, 6 Pennyfield Ave., Bronx, 10465. Tel: 718-409-7200. Peter St. Lawrence, M.A., Campus Min.

SUNY/New Paltz, 75 S. Manheim Blvd., New Paltz, 12561. Tel: 845-691-7151; Web: www.newpaltz.edu. Mr. Henry Grimsland, Campus Min.

SUNY Purchase - Campus Ministry Program, 35 Anderson Hill Rd., Purchase, 10577. Peter St. Lawrence, M.A., Campus Min.

Wagner College & The College of Staten Island, One Campus Rd., Staten Island, 10301. Tel: 718-390-3461 (Wagner); Tel: 718-982-2652 (College of Staten Island); Web: www.wagner.edu; Web: www.csi.cuny.edu. Sr. Kathleen Logan, O.P., Campus Min.

[GG] MISCELLANEOUS

NEW YORK. *1011 First Avenue, Inc.*, 29 Cinder Rd., Garnerville, 10923. Tel: 458-947-1330; Email: sgbs29@aol.com; Web: www.stgregorybarbarigoschool.org/. Mrs. Dana Spicer, Prin.

Aged and Infirm Trust, 39 E. 83rd St., 10028. Tel: 212-774-5500; Email: unesocius@jesuits.org. Rev. John J. Cecero, S.J., Prov.

Alfred E. Smith Memorial Foundation, Inc., The (1946) 1011 First Ave., Ste. 1400, 10022-4134. Tel: 646-794-3331; Email: juliette.picciano@archny.org. Juliette Picciano, Contact Person.

America Media (1909) 1212 Ave. of the Americas 11th Fl., 10036. Tel: 212-581-4640; Fax: 212-399-3596; Email: america@americamedia.org; Web: www.americamedia.org. Rev. Matthew F. Malone, S.J., Pres. & Editor-in-Chief; Mr. William R. Kunkel, Chm. Bd. of Trustees.

American Committee on Italian Migration, Inc., 25 Carmine St., 10014. Tel: 212-247-7373; Fax: 212-265-5793; Email: acimny@aol.com; Web: www.aciminnigra.org. Rev. Matthew Didone, C.S., Natl. Exec. Sec. To insure fair immigration policy favoring reunion of families and cultural integration of Italian Americans. Total Staff 3.

St. Ansgar Scandinavian Catholic League (1910) 430 E. 20th St., Apt. MB, 10009. Tel: 212-675-0400; Fax: 201-433-3355; Email: viggor@rambusch.com; Web: www.saintansgars.org. Lennard Rambusch, Pres.; Catha Rambusch, Vice Pres. & Sec.; Rev. Philip Sandstrom, Chap.; Mr. Viggo B. Rambusch, Treas.

Apostleship of the Sea, Stella Maris Maritime Center for Seamen, Pier 52, 10019. Tel: 212-265-5020. Rev. Msgr. Kevin J. Nelan, Dir.

Apostolic Works Trust, 39 E. 83rd St., 10028. Tel: 212-774-5500; Email: uneprovincial@jesuits.org. Rev. John J. Cecero, S.J., Prov.

ArchCare Community Services, 205 Lexington Ave., 3rd Fl., 10016. Tel: 646-633-4700; Email: info@archcare.org; Web: www.archcare.org/community-resources. Scott LaRue, CEO.

Association of New York Catholic Homes, Inc., 1011 First Ave., 10022. Tel: 212-371-1000, Ext. 2939; Email: william.whiston@archny.org. Mr. William E. Whiston, Treas. & Contact Person.

Benefice Advantage, 205 Lexington Ave., 3rd Fl., 10016. Tel: 646-633-4422; Fax: 646-395-5902; Email: hpizarro@archcare.org; Email: mbryanmaher@archcare.org. Hugo Pizarro, Human Resources.

Cabrini Immigrant Services of New York City, Inc., 139 Henry St., 10002. Tel: 212-791-4590; Fax: 212-791-4592. Javier Ramirez-Baron, LMSW, Dir. & Contact Person.

Calvary Fund, Inc., 1740 Eastchester Rd., Bronx, 10461. Tel: 718-518-2077; Fax: 718-518-2477; Email: webmaster@calvaryhospital.org; Web: calvaryhospital.org. Frank A. Calamari, Pres.; Carlos M. Hernandez, Chm.

The Cardinal Cooke Guild, c/o St. Patrick's Church, 137 Moseman Rd., Yorktown Heights, 10598. Tel: 914-962-5050; Email: Cardinal.CookeGuild@archny.org; Web: www.terencecardinalcooke.org. Rev. Msgr. Joseph Giandurco. Official organization for the promotion of the Cause of Canonization of the Servant of God Terence Cardinal Cooke.Cause: Dr. Avv. Andrea Ambrosi, Roman Postulator; Rev. Msgr. Joseph R. Giandurco, J.C.D., Vice Postulator Coord.

Cardinal Cooke Memorial Foundation, 1011 First Ave., Rm. 1940, 10022. Tel: 212-371-1000; Fax: 212-813-9538.

The Cardinal Spellman Memorial Foundation, 1011 First Ave., 10022.

Cardinal's Fund for Children, 1011 First Ave., Rm. 1130, 10022.

Charismatic Renewal Office, 194 Gaylor Rd., Scarsdale, 10583. Tel: 914-925-1973; Fax: 914-925-5227. Rev. William B. Cosgrove.

Carmel Housing Development Fund Co., Inc., 1011 First Ave., 10022. Tel: 212-371-1000; Fax: 212-826-8795. Rev. Msgr. Kevin L. Sullivan, Pres.

Catholic Alumni Partnership, 1011 First Ave., 14th Fl., 10022. Tel: 646-794-3376.
Catholic Alumni Club of the Archdiocese of New York, 83 Christopher St., 10014. Tel: 212-243-6513 ; Email: marydplaza@yahoo.com; Web: www.caci.org/cac/newyorkcac.html. Marguerite Cronin, Pres.
Catholic Big Sisters and Big Brothers, 137 E. 2nd St., 2nd Fl., 10009. Tel: 212-475-3291; Fax: 212-475-0280; Email: director@cbsbb.org; Web: www.cbsbb.org. Total Assisted 1,029.
Catholic Charismatic Center (Centro Carismatico Catolico), 826 166th St., Bronx, 10460. Tel: 212-378-1734. Rev. Joseph Espaillat II, M.Div., M.A., Dir.
Catholic Daughters of the Americas and Its Courts, 10 W. 71st St., 10023. Tel: 212-877-3041; Fax: 212-724-5923; Email: cdofanatl1@aol.com; Web: www.catholicdaughters.org. Mary Impellizeri, Exec. Dir. & Contact Person; Helene Shepard, Natl. Regent.
Catholic Elementary School Association of New York, 1011 First Ave., 19th Fl., 10022. Tel: 212-371-1000 ; Fax: 212-758-3018; Email: superintendent@archny.org; Web: www.archny.org.
Catholic Health Care Foundation of the Archdiocese of New York, Inc., 205 Lexington Ave., 3rd Fl., 10016. Tel: 212-752-4735; Email: poconnor@archcare.org; Web: www.archcare.org. Mrs. Patricia O'Connor, Contact Person.
Catholic Health Care System, 205 Lexington Ave., 3rd Fl., 10016. Tel: 212-752-4735; Tel: 646-475-4839; Email: slarue@archcare.org; Web: www.archcare.org; Email: mbryanmaher@archcare.org. Karl P. Adler, M.D., Archbishop's Delegate for Health Care.
Catholic High School Association of New York (1928) 1011 First Ave., 19th Fl., 10022. Tel: 212-371-1000 ; Fax: 212-758-3018; Email: superintendent@archny.org; Web: www.archny.org.
Catholic High Schools' Athletic Association of the Archdiocese of New York, Fordham Preparatory School, 441 E. Fordham Rd., Bronx, 10458-5175. Tel: 347-334-1243; Email: pigottk@fordhamprep.org. Mr. Kevin Pigott, Pres.; Mr. Kevin Cullen, Vice Pres.; Mr. Chris Beal, Treas.; Bro. Paul Hannon; Mr. Wally Stampfel.
4300 Murdock Ave., Bronx, 10466. Tel: 718-325-6423. Mr. Richard Tricario, Pres.
Catholic Indemnity Insurance Company, c/o 1011 First Ave., 10022. Tel: 212-371-1000; Fax: 212-838-0841; Email: frank.napolitano@archny.org. Mr. Frank Napolitano, Sec.
Catholic Interracial Council of N.Y., The, 899 10th Ave., 10019. Tel: 212-237-8600. Gerard W. Lynch, Pres.
**Catholic League for Religious and Civil Rights*, 450 Seventh Ave., 34th Fl., 10123. Tel: 212-371-3191; Fax: 212-371-3394; Email: cl@catholicleague.org; Web: www.catholicleague.org. Dr. William A. Donohue, Pres.; Bernadette Brady-Egan, Vice Pres. Total Staff 12.
Catholic Medical Mission Board, Inc., 10 W. 17th St., 10011-5765. Tel: 212-242-7757; Fax: 212-807-9161; Fax: 212-242-0930; Email: info@cmmb.org; Web: www.cmmb.org. With over 100 years of service since 1912, CMMB (Catholic Medical Mission Board) is the leading U.S.-based Catholic charity focused exclusively on global healthcare. CMMBjs medical volunteer, donated medicines, HIV/AIDS, child survival and neglected tropical diseases programs and initiatives focus on making healthcare available to all. In 2013, with revenues of more than $530 million, CMMB worked in nearly 50 countries, serving the poorest of the poor. Specifically, Healing Help, CMMBjs medical donation program, delivered supplies valued at more than $497 million to 173 hospitals, clinics and other health facilities in 38 countries. MVP, CMMBjs medical volunteer program, deployed 68 long-term volunteers and facilitated the placement of an additional 1,595 short-term volunteers in 24 countries. CMMB is headquartered in New York City. Globally, it has offices in Haiti, Kenya, Peru, South Sudan, and Zambia.
Board of Directors: Chris Allen, FACHE, Bd. Chm.; John E. Celentano; Michael Doring Connelly, Chm.; Nicholas D'Agostino III; Sr. Patricia Eck, C.B.S.; Stephanie L. Ferguson, Ph.D., R.N., F.A.A.N.; Ed Giniat; JeanMarie C. Grisi; Clarion E. Johnson, M.D.; Sr. Rosemary Moynihan, S.C.; Maria Rosa Robinson, M.D., M.B.A.; Robert E. Robotti; Mary Colleen Scanlon, R.N., J.D., Sec.; Rev. J. Peter Schineller, S.J.; F. William Smullen III, Vice Chm.; Most Rev. Joseph M. Sullivan, D.D.; Bruce Wilkinson, Pres. & C.E.O., Catholic Medical Mission Board.
Legal Counsel: John A. Matthews Jr., Esq.
Catholic Near East Welfare Association (CNEWA) (1926) 1011 First Ave., 10022. Tel: 212-826-1480; Fax: 212-838-1344; Email: cnewa@cnewa.org; Web: www.cnewa.org. His Eminence Timothy M. Dolan, Ph.D., Chair & Treas.; Rev. Msgr. John E. Kozar, Pres.; Bro. Gerard Conforti, F.S.C., Chief Administration Officer.
Catholic Resources, Inc., 1339 York Ave., 10021. Tel: 646-475-4835; Email: kmcguire@chcsnet.org. Kathryn McGuire, Sr. Vice Pres.
Catholic Spiritual Family, The Work, Inc., 419 E. 13th St., 10009. Tel: 212-677-5680; Email: inc@theworkfso.org; Web: www.thework-fso.org. Sr. Maria Hugens, F.S.O., Treas.
**Catholic Voices USA*, 1011 First Ave., 10022.
The Catholic World Wide Web Corporation, 1011 First Ave., 10022. Tel: 212-371-1000; Email: bernard.reidy@archny.org; Web: www.archny.org. Bernard E. Reidy, Archbishop's Delegate for Admin. & Fin.
Centro Altagracia de Fe y Justicia, Inc. (Altagracia Center of Faith and Justice, Inc.), 39 E. 83rd St., 10028. Tel: 127-774-5505; Email: UNESocius@jesuits.org; Web: www.jesuitseast.org. Rev. John J. Cecero, S.J., Prov.
Centro Carismatico Catolico Hispano De La Arquidiocesis De Nueva York, 826 E. 166th St., Bronx, 10459. Tel: 718-378-1734; Fax: 718-378-1819; Email: centro826@aol.com; Web: www.centrocatolicocarismatico.com. Rev. Joseph Espaillat II, M.Div., M.A., Dir.
Chapel San Lorenzo Ruiz (Philippine Pastoral Center), 378 Broome St., 10013. Tel: 212-966-1019; Fax: 212-966-1034; Email: chapelofsanlorenzoruiz@gmail.com; Web: www.chapelofsanlorenzo.com. Rev. Erno Diaz, Dir.
Chinese Catholic Information Center, 86 Riverside Dr., 10024. Tel: 212-787-6969; Email: brotherli2000@yahoo.com. Rev. Phi Phu Ho, C.S.J.B., (Taiwan) Dir.; Peter Li. Total in Residence 5; Total Staff 4.
The Christophers (1945) 5 Hanover Sq., 22nd Fl., 10004. Tel: 212-759-4050; Fax: 212-838-5073; Email: mail@christophers.org; Web: www.christophers.org. Mary Ellen Robinson, Vice Pres./COO; Tony Rossi, Dir., Commun. & Editor-in-Chief. A multi-media organization reaching millions with the Gospel message. Total Staff 6.
CIF Catholic Corp., 1011 First Ave., 10022.
Committee for Mission Responsibility Society, Inc. The Propagation of the Faith 1011 First Ave., 10022. Tel: 212-371-1000, Ext. 2700; Fax: 212-371-7220; Email: pchirchirillo@aol.com.
Community of St. Egidio, U.S.A., Inc., 380 Lenox Ave., 6H, 10027. Tel: 212-663-1483; Fax: 212-663-1483; Email: santegidiousa@gmail.com; Web: www.santegidio.org. Paola Piscitelli, Pres.
Cor Mariae Development Fund Corporation, 1011 First Ave., 10022. Rev. Msgr. Kevin L. Sullivan, Pres. & Contact Person.
Cor Mariae Housing Development Fund, Inc., 1011 First Ave., 10022. Tel: 212-371-1000, Ext. 2400. Rev. Msgr. Kevin L. Sullivan, Pres.
Cornelia Connelly Center for Education, Holy Child Middle School, 220 E. 4th St., 10009. Tel: 212-982-2287; Fax: 212-982-0547; Email: hraftery@connellycenter.org; Email: holchimd@adnyeducation.org; Web: www.connellycenter.org. Shalonda Gutierrez-Neely, Prin. Lay Teachers 6; Students 89.
Courage International, Incorporated, St. Paul the Apostle, 415 W, 59th St., 10019. Tel: 212-265-3495, Ext. 291; Email: NYcourage@aol.com; Web: www.couragerc.org. Rev. James B. Lloyd, C.S.P., (Retired). Total Staff 4.
Deaf Catholic Center, 1011 First Ave., 10022. Tel: 212-988-8563. Rev. Msgr. Patrick P. McCahill, Dir.
Descubriendo El Siglo XXI, Inc. (Discovering XXI Century Inc.) (2001) Holy Cross Church, 329 W. 42nd St., 10036. Tel: 212-244-4778; Fax: 212-868-6997; Email: radiosigloxxi@aol.com; Web: www.descubriendoelsiglo21.org. Rev. Tomas Del Valle-Reyes, Pres.
The Dominican Foundation of Dominican Friars, Province of St. Joseph, Inc., 141 E. 65th St., 10065. Tel: 212-535-3664; Email: df@dominicanfriars.org; Web: www.dominicanfriars.org. Rev. Kevin Gabriel Gillen, O.P., Exec. Dir.
Dominican Mission Secretariat Rev. David Adiletta, O.P., S.T.L., Exec. Dir.
Dominican Friars Health Care Ministry of New York, Inc., 411 E. 68th St., 10065-6305. Tel: 212-988-8303; Email: info@dfhcmny.org. Revs. John M. Devaney, O.P., M.Div., Dir.; Jonah F. Pollock, O.P., Assoc. Dir.
Dominican Friars' Guilds, 141 E. 65th St., 10065. Tel: 212-535-3664; Email: df@dominicanfriars.org. Rev. Gabriel Gillen, O.P., Dir.
St. Jude Dominican Missions, 141 E. 65th St., 10065. Tel: 212-535-3664; Email: df@dominicanfriars.org. Rev. Kevin Gabriel Gillen, O.P., Dir.
Dominican Rosary Apostolate, 141 E. 65th St., 10065. Tel: 212-535-3664; Email: df@dominicanfriars.org. Rev. Gabriel Gillen, O.P., Dir.
Deserving Poor Boys Priesthood Association, 141 E. 65th St., 10065. Tel: 212-535-3664; Email: df@dominicanfriars.org. Rev. Gabriel Gillen, O.P., Dir.
St. Martin de Porres Guild, 141 E. 65th St., 10065. Tel: 212-535-3664; Email: df@dominicanfriars.org. Rev. Gabriel Gillen, O.P., Dir.
Dominican Shrine of St. Jude, Inc., St. Catherine of Siena Priory, 411 E. 68th St., 10065-6305. Tel: 212-249-6067; Fax: 212-988-8920; Email: kfrancekelly@dominicanshrineofsaintjude.org; Web: www.dominicanshrineofsaintjude.org. Rev. John Aquinas Farren, O.P., S.T.D., Admin. Dir.
**The Elizabeth Seton Housing Development Fund Corporation*, 1991 Lexington Ave., 10035. Tel: 212-348-1655; Fax: 212-348-1822; Email: epfeldmann@att.net. Sr. Elizabeth Vermaelon, Pres. Total Staff 3; Total Assisted 87.
Emmanuel Community Inc., 280 Weaver St., 10538. Web: www.emmanuelcommunity.com.
Felix Varela Foundation, Inc., The, 1011 First Ave., 10022. Tel: 718-229-8001, Ext. 677; Tel: 718-281-9677; Fax: 917-522-9707. Most Rev. Octavio Cisneros, Pres.
Focolare Movement-Manhattan, 7 Intellect Way, Hyde Park, 12538. Tel: 718-828-1969; Email: nyanadias@gmail.com; Web: www.focolare.org. J.P. Slee, Regl. Dir.
Formation Trust, 39 E. 83rd St., 10028. Tel: 212-774-5500; Email: UNESocius@jesuits.org. Rev. John J. Cecero, S.J., Prov.
Foundation of the Order of Friars Minor of the Province of the Most Holy Name, 129 W. 31st St., 2nd Fl., 10001-3403. Tel: 646-473-0265; Fax: 800-420-1078. Rev. Kevin Mullen, O.F.M., Pres.
Foundation Trust, 39 E. 83rd St., 10028. Tel: 212-774-5500; Email: UNESocius@jesuits.org. Rev. John J. Cecero, S.J., Prov.
St. Frances Cabrini Shrine, Inc., 701 Fort Washington Ave., 10040. Tel: 212-923-3536; Fax: 212-923-1871; Web: cabrinishrinenyc.com.
St. Francis Counseling Center, Inc., 135 W. 31st St., 10001. Tel: 212-736-8500; Fax: 212-736-8545; Web: www.stfrancisnyc.org. Total Staff 5; Therapy Hours 3,500.
Franciscan Bread for the Poor, Inc., The Order of Friars Minor of the Province of the Most Holy Name, 129 W. 31st St., 10001-3439. Tel: 646-473-0265; Fax: 646-420-1078; Email: admin@hnp.org. Rev. Dennis M. Wilson, O.F.M., Treas.
Franciscan Missionary Charities, Inc. (1997) 2101 Fifth Ave., Unit 1-S, 10035. Tel: 917-797-8890; Tel: 646-685-7788; Email: cowofm@gmail.com; Email: haemiw@msn.com. Revs. Ronald P. Stark, O.F.M., Pres.; Francis K. Kim, O.F.M., B.A., M.Div., Exec. Vice Pres.
Franciscan Missionary Union, Province of the Most Holy Name Headquarters 144 W. 32nd St., 10001-3202. Tel: 212-564-8799; Email: info@fmu.org; Web: www.fmunion.org. Rev. Dennis M. Wilson, O.F.M., Treas. The Franciscan Missionary Union ministers in Peru, Brazil, Japan, Taiwan and the home missions in the USA. Friar Missionaries 10.
Franciscan Sisters of the Poor Charitable Trust, 708 3rd Ave., Ste. 1920, 10017. Tel: 718-643-1945; Fax: 212-808-0096; Email: sfp@franciscansisters.org; Web: www.franciscansisters.org. Sr. Licia Mazzia, S.F.P., Congregational Min.
Franciscan Sisters of the Poor Communities, Inc., 708 3rd Ave, Ste. 1920, 10017. Tel: 718-643-1945; Fax: 212-808-0096; Email: sfp@franciscansisters.org; Web: www.franciscansisters.org. Sr. Licia Mazzia, S.F.P., Pres.
Franciscans International, Inc., 246 E. 46th St., #1F, 10017. Tel: 917-675-1075; Email: newyork@fiop.org; Web: www.franciscansinternational.org. Revs. Markus Heinze, O.F.M., Exec. Dir.; Odile Coirier, F.M.M., Liaison Officer.
Franciscans of Holy Name Province Benevolence Trust, Inc., 129 W. 31st St., 2nd Fl., 10001-3403. Tel: 646-473-0265; Fax: 800-420-1078; Email: admin@hnp.org; Web: hnp.org. Rev. Dennis M. Wilson, O.F.M., Treas.
Franciscans of Holy Name Province Sick, Aged and Retired Trust, 129 W. 31st St., 2nd Fl., 10001-3403. Tel: 646-473-0265; Fax: 800-420-1078. Rev. Kevin Mullen, O.F.M., Pres.
Franciscans of Holy Name Province Education and Formation Trust, 129 W. 31st St., 2nd Fl., 10001-3403. Tel: 646-473-0265; Fax: 800-420-1078; Email: admin@hnp.org; Web: www.hnp.org. Rev. Dennis M. Wilson, O.F.M., Treas.

The Fratecelli Corporation, 129 W. 31st St., 2nd Fl., 10001-3403. Tel: 646-473-0265; Fax: 800-420-1078; Email: admin@hnp.org. Rev. Dennis M. Wilson, O.F.M., Treas.

Friends of American Art in Religion, Inc., 143 E. 43rd St., 10017. Tel: 212-682-5722; Fax: 212-370-5791. Vacant, Pres.

The Good Shepherd Volunteers, Inc., 337 E. 17th St., 10003. Tel: 212-475-4245, Ext. 718; Fax: 212-979-8604; Email: gsv@goodshepherds.org; Web: www.gsvolunteers.org. Michele G. Gilfillan, M.A., Dir.

Guild of Catholic Lawyers, The (1928) 101 Park Ave., 30th Fl., 10178. Tel: 212-808-7847; Fax: 212-808-7897. Rev. George W. Rutler, Spiritual Dir.

Hispanic Catholic Charismatic Center of the Archdiocese of New York, 826 E. 166th St., Bronx, 10459. Tel: 718-378-1734; Fax: 718-378-1819; Email: centro826@aol.com; Web: wwwcentrocatolicocarismatico.com. Rev. Joseph Espaillat II, M.Div., M.A.

The Housing Fund of the Archdiocese of New York, 1011 First Ave., 10022. Tel: 212-371-1000. Rev. Msgr. Kevin L. Sullivan, Vice. Pres.

The Human Adventure Corp. Doing Business for Communion and Liberation and Fraternity of Communion and Liberation, USA. 125 Maiden Ln., 15th Fl., 10038. Tel: 212-337-3580; Fax: 212-337-3585; Email: cladministration@clhac.com; Web: www.clonline.us. Rev. Jose Medina, Exec. Dir.

Hungarian Catholic League of America, Inc., 414 E. 82 St., 10028. Tel: 212-327-2959; Fax: 212-535-9221. Rev. Msgr. William I. Varsanyi, P.A., Bd. Chm.; A. Petrak, Sec.

Incarnation Children's Center Fund, Inc. (1988) 142 Audubon Ave., 10032. Tel: 212-928-2590; Fax: 212-928-1500; Email: ccastro@incarnationchildrenscenter.org; Web: www.incarnationchildrenscenter.org. Carolyn Castro, Exec. Dir. Capacity 21.

Institute of the Helpers, 385 W. 263rd St., Bronx, 10471. Gudrun Bohle.

**The Jesuit Collaborative*, c/o New York Province of the Society of Jesus, 39 E. 83rd St., 10028-0810. Tel: 212-774-5505; Email: UNESocius@jesuits.org. Rev. John J. Cecero, S.J., Prov.

Jesuit Seminary and Mission Bureau, Inc., 39 E. 83rd St., 10028. Tel: 212-774-5500; Fax: 212-794-1036; Email: UNESocius@jesuits.org. Rev. John J. Cecero, S.J., Prin. See Jesuit Provincial's office.

Joint Perpetual Care Fund, Inc., 1011 First Ave., 19th Fl., 10022.

St. Joseph's Union of Staten Island, New York Inc., 108 Bedell St., Staten Island, 10309. Tel: 718-984-9296. Sr. Una McCormack, O.P., Treas.

LAMP Ministries, Inc. (1982) 2704 Schurz Ave., Bronx, 10465. Tel: 718-409-5062; Fax: 718-904-0048; Email: tscheuring@lampministries.org; Web: www.lampministries.org. Dr. Tom Scheuring, Ph.D., Co-Dir.; Dr. Lyn Scheuring, Ph.D., Co-Dir.; Marybeth Greene, Assoc. Dir.; Ed Greene, Assoc. Dir.

Language Institute, 1011 First Ave., 10022. Tel: 212-371-1000, Ext. 2982.

LaSalle New York City, Inc., 44 E. 2nd St., 10003. Tel: 212-475-8940; Fax: 212-529-3598; Web: www.lasalleacademy.org. Bros. Franc Byrnes, F.S.C., Chm.; Michael Farrell, F.S.C., Pres. Total Staff 45; Total Assisted 370.

The Lay Fraternity of St. Dominic, Inc., 141 E. 65th St., 10021-6618. Tel: 212-737-5757; Email: socius@opeast.org; Web: http://laydominicans.org/. Mrs. Cosette Heimann, Pres.

Legion of Mary, Office, 1011 First Ave., 10022. Tel: 212-752-7966; Email: ny.senatus@verizon.net; Web: legion-of-mary-ny.org. John Kinney, Pres.

**Life Athletes, Inc.*, 1011 First Ave., 10022. Tel: 574-237-9000; Email: chris@lifeathletes.org; Web: www.lifeathletes.org. Christopher J. Godfrey, Pres.

Light and Life Evangelization Program (Luz & Vida) St. Joseph's Cursillo Center, 523 W. 142nd St., 10031. Tel: 212-926-7433.

Little Sisters of the Assumption Family In Mission, Inc., 475 E. 115th St., 1st. Fl., 10029. Tel: 212-289-4014; Fax: 212-876-2075; Email: coordinator@lsafim.org; Web: www.lsafim.org. Sr. Annette Allain, L.S.A., Exec. Dir.

Lumen Dei, 340 W. 53rd St., 10019. Tel: 212-586-4447; Fax: 212-586-1640; Email: newyorkfem2@gmail.com; Web: www.lumendei.org. Rev. Wilberto Reyes-Garced, L.D., Regl. Supr. Priests of Lumen Dei 1; Sisters of Lumen Dei 5.

**The Malta Human Services Foundation*, 1011 First Ave., Rm. 1350, 10022. Tel: 212-371-1522. Deacon Jeffrey Trexler, Exec. Dir. & Contact Person.

Maria Droste Counseling Services, 171 Madison Ave., Ste. 400, 10016-5153. Tel: 212-889-4042; Fax: 212-889-3936; Email: n.selman@mdcsnyc.org; Web: www.mdcsnyc.org. Betsy Babinecz, LCSW, DCSW, BCD, Dir.
St. Germaine's Services.

The Migrant Center of New York, Inc. (2018) 135 W. 31st St., 10001. Rev. Julian Jagudilla, O.F.M., Dir.

Missionary Childhood Association (Holy Child Association) 1011 First Ave., 10022. Tel: 212-371-1000, Ext. 2700; Email: msgr.marc.filacchione@archny.org. Rev. Msgr. Marc J. Filacchione.

The Missionary Society of St. Paul the Apostle in the State of California, 415 W. 59th St., 10019. Tel: 212-757-8072; Fax: 212-757-8527; Email: admingenoffice@paulist.org. Rev. Gilbert S. Martinez, C.S.P., Pres.

**Monsignor Robert Fox Memorial Shelter Housing Development, Inc.*, Fox House, 111 E. 117th St., 10035. Tel: 212-534-6634; Fax: 212-427-8507; Email: foxshelter@aol.com. Sr. Florence Speth, S.C., Exec. Dir. Total Staff 17; Total Assisted 1,000.

National Federation for Life, 1011 First Ave., Rm. 1417, 10022.

National Office of the Devotees of Padre Pio, Inc., 1154 1st Ave., 10065. Tel: 212-838-6549. Mr. Mario Bruscki, Dir.

The National Shrines of St. Anthony and St. Jude, Inc., 144 W. 32nd St., 10001-3202. Tel: 212-564-8799; Tel: 646-473-0265; Fax: 212-736-8545; Fax: 800-420-1078; Email: hnp@hnp.org. Rev. Dennis M. Wilson, O.F.M., Treas.

**Nazareth Housing, Inc.* (1983) 519 E. 11th St., 10009. Tel: 212-777-1010; Fax: 347-396-3154; Web: www.nazarethhousingnyc.org.

New York Catholic Continuum Care, Inc. (NYCCC), 1011 First Ave., 11th Fl., 10022. Tel: 212-371-1011, Ext. 2462. Doug Sansted, Contact Person.

New York Catholic Foundation, Inc., 1011 First Ave., 19th Floor, 10022. Tel: 646-794-3289; Fax: 212-753-5980; Email: susan.george@archny.org; Web: archny.org. Rev. Msgr. Kevin P. O'Brien, Ph.D., Contact Person.

New York Society of the John Paul II Foundation, Inc. (1997) 101 E. 7th St., 10009. Tel: 718-383-9587 ; Email: polstarshop1@gmail.com. Mr. Michael Pajak, Pres., Tel: 718-383-9587.

North American College of Rome, Alumni Assoc. of, Msgr. Farrell High School, 2900 Amboy Rd., Staten Island, 10306. Tel: 718-987-2900; Fax: 718-987-4241. Rev. Msgr. Edmund J. Whalen, S.T.D.

Northeast Hispanic Catholic Center, 1011 First Ave., 10022. Tel: 212-751-7045; Fax: 212-753-5321; Email: nhcc1011@aol.com. Doris N. Valentin, Interim Exec. Dir.

**Paideia, Inc./New York Encounter*, Attorney St., 10002. Web: www.newyorkencounter.org. Olivetta Danese, Treas.

Parish Assistance Corporation, c/o 1011 First Ave., 10022. Tel: 646-794-3394; Email: paul.kefer@archny.org. Paul Kefer, Asst. Dir.

The Partnership for Inner-City Education, 1011 First Ave., 18th Fl., 10022. Tel: 646-794-3338; Fax: 212-688-2956; Email: jill.kafka@partnershipnyc.org. Jill Kafka, Exec. Dir.

Partnership for Quality Education, Inc., 1011 First Ave., 18th Fl., 10022. Tel: 646-794-3670; Fax: 212-371-6461. Lucson Andre, Controller.

St. Patrick's Cathedral Landmark Foundation, Inc., 1011 1st Ave., 17th Fl., 10022. Tel: 646-794-2790; Fax: 212-758-6925; Web: www.saintpatrickscathedral.org.

St. Patrick's International Inc., c/o Cullen & Dykman, 44 Wall St., 10005-2407. Tel: 212-732-2000; Fax: 212-742-8260; Email: burgeneral@spms.ie; Web: www.spms.org. Rev. Victor Dunne, S.P.S., Pres.

Patrons of the Arts in Vatican Museums, 1011 First Ave., 10022. Tel: 646-794-2925; Fax: 646-794-2025. Rev. George W. Rutler. Staff 2.

St. Paul's Guild, Inc., 1011 First Ave., Rm. 1940, 10022. Tel: 212-371-1000; Fax: 212-813-9538.

Pauline Books & Media, 115 E 29th St., 10016. Tel: 212-754-1110; Fax: 212-754-2268; Email: manhattan@paulinemedia.com; Web: www.pauline.org. Sisters Sean Marie David Mayer, Supr.; Neville Forchap, Business Mgr.
Pauline Books & Media Total Staff 5.

Paulist Religious Property Trust, 415 W. 59th St., 10019. Tel: 212-757-8072; Fax: 212-757-8527; Email: admingenoffice@paulist.org. Rev. Frank Desiderio, C.S.P., M.A. Theology, M.A. Communication, Trustee.

Pax Christi Metro New York (1983) 371 Sixth Ave., 10014. Rosemarie Pace, B.A., M.S., Ed.D., Dir. We are a regional chapter of Pax Christi USA, the national Catholic movement for peace.

Pontifical Mission Society Propagation of the Faith Propagation of the Faith, 1011 First Ave., 10022. Tel: 212-371-1000, Ext. 2700; Email: propagation@archny.org. Rev. Msgr. Marc J. Filacchione, Dir,.

Propagation of the Faith National Office, 70 W. 36th St., 10018. Tel: 212-563-8700. Rev. Andrew Small, O.M.I., Natl. Dir.

Regina Coeli Society First Friday Club for the Catholic Women of New York City Police Dept. P.O. Box 939, 10272-0604. Tel: 646-610-6169. Det. Gloria Felix, Pres.

Regis Fund Trust, 55 E. 84th St., 10028.

Regis High School Property Trust, 55 E. 84th St., 10028.

Religious Property Trust, 39 E. 83rd St., 10028. Tel: 212-774-5500; Email: UNESocius@jesuits.org. Rev. John J. Cecero, S.J., Prov.

St. Rose's Settlement, 1011 First Ave., Rm. 1940, 10022. Tel: 212-371-1000; Fax: 212-813-9538.

Scalabrini International Migration Network, 307 E. 60th St., 10022-1505. Tel: 212-913-0207; Fax: 212-207-3789; Email: contact@simm-global.org; Web: www.simm-global.org. Rev. Leonir Mario Chiarello, C.S., Exec. Dir.

Sisters of Charity of New York Charitable Trust (1988) 6301 Riverdale Ave., Bronx, 10471-1093. Tel: 718-549-9200; Fax: 718-884-3013; Email: emcgrory@scny.org; Web: www.scny.org. Sr. Eileen McGrory.

Sisters of Charity Center (1971) 6301 Riverdale Ave., Bronx, 10471-1093. Tel: 718-549-9200; Fax: 718-884-3013; Email: emcgrory@scny.org; Web: www.scny.org. Sr. Eileen McGrory.

The Society of St. Stephen USA, 125 Maiden Ln., Ste. 15E, 10038.

**Sovereign Military Hospitaller Order of Saint John of Jerusalem of Rhodes and of Malta* American Association, U.S.A. 1011 First Ave., Rm. 1350, 10022. Tel: 212-371-1522; Web: www.orderofmaltaamerican.org. Deacon Jeffrey Trexler, Exec. Dir. & Contact Person.

St. Thomas Aquinas Foundation National Headquarters (Order of Preachers, St. Joseph Prov.) 141 E. 65th St., 10065. Tel: 212-737-5757; Fax: 212-861-4216; Web: www.opeast.org. Very Revs. Kenneth R. Letoile, O.P., Pres.; Mark Padrez, O.P., Bd. Member; Thomas Condon, O.P., Bd. Member; James Marchionda, O.P., Bd. Member; Rev. Allen Moran, Treas.
St. Thomas Aquinas Foundation of the Dominican Fathers of the United States (STAF).

Thorpe Family Residence, Inc. (1988) 2252 Crotona Ave., Bronx, 10457. Tel: 212-982-7571; Fax: 347-396-3165. Total Staff 7; Total Assisted Families 16.

Trust for the Center for Migration Studies in New York, 307 E. 60th St., 4th Fl., 10022. Tel: 212-675-3993; Fax: 646-998-4625; Email: scbprovince@gmail.com; Web: www.cmsny.org. Rev. Moacir Balen, C.S.

Voluntas Dei USA, 244 Fifth Ave., Ste. P250, 10001. Tel: 212-726-2286; Email: anthonyciorra@gmail.com. Rev. Anthony J. Ciorra, District Dir.

**WorldPriest, Inc.*, 600 Third Ave., 2nd Fl., 10016. Tel: 646-355-4106; Email: info.worldpriest@gmail.com; Web: www.worldpriest.com. Marian Mulhall, CEO.

**Xavier Mission, Inc.*, 55 W. 15th St., 10011. Tel: 212-627-2100; Fax: 212-675-6997; Email: cagredo@xaviermission.org; Email: info@xaviermission.org; Web: www.xaviermission.org. Rev. Robert VerEecke, Pres.; Ms. Cassandra Agredo, Exec.

Xavier Society for the Blind (1900) 248 W 35th St Ste 1502, 10001. Tel: 212-473-7800; Fax: 212-473-7801 ; Email: info@xaviersocietyfortheblind.org; Web: www.xaviersocietyfortheblind.org. Malachy Fallon Jr., Dir.

BARRYVILLE. *New Hope Manor*, 35 Hillside Rd., Barryville, 12719. Tel: 845-557-8353; Fax: 845-557-6603; Email: newhopemnr@aol.com; Web: www.newhopemanor.org. Ms. Barrie Jacobsen, LCSW-R, Exec. Dir.; Sr. Margaret Murphy, O.P., Bd. Member; Bro. Charles Kinney, S.A., Bd. Member. A live-in therapeutic community for the substance abuse rehabilitation of women, pregnant women, and infants.

BEACON. *Carmelite Communion, Inc.* (2000) 89 Hiddenbrooke Dr., Beacon, 12508-2230. Tel: 845-831-5572; Fax: 845-831-5579; Email: carmelitesbeacon@gmail.com; Web: www.carmelitesbeacon.org. Sr. Marjorie Robinson, O.C.D., Prioress & Contact Person. Professed Sisters 15.

Metropolitan Association of Contemplative Communities, Inc. (1967) 89 Hiddenbrooke Dr., Beacon, 12508. Tel: 845-831-5572; Fax: 845-831-5579; Web: macc.catholic.org. Sr. Rita Donahue, O.C.D., Contact Person.

BRONX. *Abraham House, Inc.*, 340 Willis Ave., P.O. Box

305, Bronx, 10454. Tel: 718-292-9321; Fax: 718-292-5925; Email: abrooks@abrahamhouse.org. Robert Murphy, Pres. Total Staff 24; Volunteers 10; Total Assisted 6,000.

All-Africa Conference: Sister to Sister, Inc., 2715 Bainbridge Ave., Bronx, 10458.

American St. Boniface Society, Incorporated, 4011 Wickham Ave., Bronx, 10466-1352. Tel: 914-281-1371. Teri Powers, Exec. Dir.

St. Anthony Shelter for Renewal, 410 E. 156th St., Bronx, 10455. Tel: 718-993-5161; Fax: 718-993-4754. Rev. Louis Marie Leonelli, C.F.R., Dir. Bed Capacity 30.

Apostles of the Sacred Heart of Jesus of New York, Inc., 1651 Zerega Ave., Bronx, 10462.

Brooklyn Prep Alumni Association (1964) Xavier High School, 30 W. 16th St., 10011-6302. Tel: 212-924-7900; Email: brooklynprep@gmail.com; Web: www.brooklynprep.org. Rev. Daniel J. Fitzpatrick, S.J., Moderator & Contact Person. Membership 4,000.

Calvary Holding Company, Inc., 1740 Eastchester Rd., Bronx, 10461. Tel: 718-518-2251; Fax: 718-518-2674. Frank A. Calamari, Pres.; Thomas J. Fahey Jr., M.D., Chm.

Church of St. Philip Neri Holding Corp., 3025 Grand Concourse, Bronx, 10468.

Corazon Puro, 420 E. 156th St., P.O. Box 946, Bronx, 10455. Tel: 718-841-6575; Fax: 718-292-2432; Email: info@corazonpuro.org; Web: www.corazonpuro.org. Rev. Agustino Miguel Torres, C.F.R., Pres.; Odelis Bisono, Dir., Opers.

Focolare Movement, 179 Robinson Ave., Bronx, 10465. Tel: 718-828-1969; Email: focfny@gmail.com; Web: www.focolare.us. Ms. Endy Moraes, Contact Person.

Focolare Movement Formation Fund, 179 Robinson Ave., Bronx, 10465. Tel: 718-828-1969; Email: nyanadias@gmail.com; Web: www.focolare.org. Ana Dias, Contact Person.

Fordham Prep Formation Foundation Trust, 441 E. Fordham Rd., Bronx, 10458.

Foundation of Christ the Redeemer Institute Id of Christ the Redeemer, Idente Missionaries. 2352 St. Raymond Ave., Bronx, 10462. Tel: 718-828-2380; Fax: 718-828-4296; Email: rpbadillo@gmail.com. Revs. Robert P. Badillo, M.Id, Ph.D., Prov.; Martin Esguerra-Lopez, Rector.

**Francesco Productions Inc.* (2003) 420 E. 156th St., Bronx, 10455. Tel: 718-401-1589; Fax: 718-618-0334; Web: www.francescoproductions.com. Kim Yu, Volunteer Mng. Dir.; Rev. Stanley Fortuna, C.F.R., Founder.

Franciscan Mission Outreach, Inc., 420 E. 156th St., Bronx, 10455. Tel: 718-402-8255; Fax: 718-402-5556. Bro. John Joseph Brice, C.F.R., Contact Person. Priests 2; Total Staff 2.

Franciscan Renewal Ministries, Inc., 427 E. 155th St., Bronx, 10455. Tel: 718-402-8255. Bro. John Joseph Brice, C.F.R., Dir.

Holy Name Society Archdiocesan Union of New York, 1905 Tenbroeck Ave., Bronx, 10461-1833. Tel: 718-931-9239. Rev. James P. Connolly, Assoc. Dir., (Retired); Mr. Anthony J. Merolla, Exec. Sec.

St. Joseph's Center (1994) For the development of Lay Leaders, Cursillo Center, Marriage Encounter. (Spanish) 275 W. 230th St., Bronx, 10463. Tel: 718-796-4340; Fax: 718-796-4340. Rev. Jose Luis Martinez, O.A.R., Dir. Capacity 45; Total in Residence 2; Total Staff 4.

St. Joseph's Cursillo Center, 620 Thieriot Ave., Bronx, 10473. Rev. Ramon A. Lopez, Dir.

St. Joseph's School for the Deaf Childrens Fund, Inc., 1000 Hutchinson River Pkwy., Bronx, 10465. Tel: 718-828-9000; Fax: 718-792-6631; Email: darles@sjsdny.org. The Children's Fund assists St. Joseph's School for the Deaf in meeting the needs of the children and their educational experiences.

Saint Jutta Foundation, Inc. (1956) Murray-Weigal Hall, 515 E. Fordham Rd., Bronx, 10458-5029. Tel: 718-817-3671; Fax: 718-365-8650; Email: hegyi@fordham.edu.

The Land Trust of the Sisters of Charity at Mount St. Vincent, 6301 Riverdale Ave., Bronx, 10471-1093.

**Mercy Center, Inc.* (1990) 377 E. 145th St., Bronx, 10454-1006. Tel: 718-993-2789; Fax: 718-402-1594; Email: administration@mercycenterbronx.org; Web: www.mercycenterbronx.org. Stephen J. Stritch III, Dir. Parenting skills courses, business training, support groups, spirituality groups, & ESL. Sisters 4; Total Staff 21; Total Assisted 2,500.

Metro New York Christian Life Communities, Inc., Fordham Univ., Manresa House, 2540 Hughes Ave., Bronx, 10458. Tel: 718-817-5454; Fax: 718-817-5504; Email: metronyclc@yahoo.com; Web: www.fordham.edu/clc. Sr. Eileen Schulenburg, S.C., Moderator & Contact Person.

Nativity Mission Center, Inc. (1971) 740 Manida St., Bronx, 10474. Tel: 718-861-9084; Fax: 718-861-9096; Email: info@sis-nativity.org; Web: www.sis-nativity.org. Eavan O'Driscoll, Pres. & Contact Person.

The Saint Padre Pio Shelter Corporation, 427 E. 155th St., Bronx, 10455. Tel: 718-292-3713; Fax: 718-993-9997. Rev. Bonaventure Rummell, C.F.R., Dir. Total Assisted 18.

Park Avenue Thorpe, HDFC, 406 E. 184th St., Bronx, 10458. Tel: 718-295-2550; Fax: 718-295-2558.

Preston Center of Compassion, Inc. (2003) Office of the President, 2780 Schurz Ave., Bronx, 10465. Tel: 718-892-8977. Donna Santarpia, Pres.; Sr. Patricia Warner, R.D.C., Dir.

Rosalie Hall Maternity Services Division of Catholic Guaradian Society & Home Bureau, 420 Howe Ave., Bronx, 10473. Tel: 718-684-3855; Fax: 347-547-7920; Email: clongley@catholicguardian.org. Craig Longley, Exec. Dir. Residence for pregnant and parenting adolescent mothers with their children in foster care. Parenting Resource Center, offering evidence-based parenting skills training programs, concrete and case management services.

Siervas De Cristo Resucitado, Inc., 832 E. 166th St., Bronx, 10459. Tel: 718-991-9674; Email: siervas.scrny826@gmail.com. Sr. Alexandra Rosa, S.C.R., Dir.

**Tolentine-Zeiser Community Life Center, Inc.*, 2345 University Ave., Bronx, 10468. Tel: 718-933-6935; Fax: 718-733-1653. Total Staff 12; Total Assisted 172.

Youth Ministries for Peace & Justice, Inc. (1994) 1384 Stratford Ave., Bronx, 10472. Tel: 718-328-5622; Fax: 718-328-5630; Email: dshuffler@ympj.org; Web: www.ympj.org.

BRONXVILLE. *Polish Knights of Malta, Inc.* (1986) 3 Stoneleigh Plaza, #4-E, Bronxville, 10708. Tel: 914-793-4596; Email: witoldsulimirski@cs.com. Mr. Witold S. Sulimirski, Pres.

CORNWALL. *Contemplative Outreach, Ltd.*, 1 David Ln. Apt 7H, Yonkers, 10701. Tel: 914-423-4888; Email: office@coutreach.org; Web: www.contemplativeoutreach.org. Ms. Diane Harkin, Contact Person; Rt. Rev. Thomas Keating, O.C.S.O., Spiritual Dir.; Patricia Johnson, Admin. Tot Asst. Annually 1,000; Total Staff 7.

DOVER PLAINS. *RDC Loaves and Fishes, Inc.*, 52 Mill St., P.O. Box 665, Dover Plains, 12522. Tel: 845-877-9076; Fax: 888-316-4540; Web: roccenterofcompassion.org. Lori Vincent, Dir.

ESOPUS. *MBCE Mid Hudson Valley Camp, Inc.*, 1455 Broadway, Rte. 9W, P.O. Box 197, Esopus, 12429.

HARTSDALE. *Marian Woods, Inc.* (2001) 152 Ridge Rd., Hartsdale, 10530. Tel: 914-750-6000; Fax: 914-750-6100. Sr. Aileen Donovan, O.P., Exec. Dir.

Mercy Education Support Fund, Inc., 150 Ridge Rd., Hartsdale, 10530. Tel: 718-882-2882, Ext. 128; Fax: 718-231-9099; Email: srpwolf@optonline.net. Sr. Patricia Wolf, R.S.M., Pres. & Contact Person.

HAVERSTRAW. *Franciscan Sisters of Peace*, 20 Ridge St., Haverstraw, 10927-1198. Tel: 845-942-2527; Fax: 845-429-8141; Email: hwacker@fspnet.org; Web: www.fspnet.org. Sisters Dorothy DeYoung, Contact Person; Helen Wacker, F.S.P., Congregation Min. Sisters 49.

Ladycliff College Alumnae Association, Inc., c/o Franciscan Sisters of Peace, 20 Ridge St., Haverstraw, 10927-1198. Tel: 914-446-2973; Tel: 914-446-5921.

HAWTHORNE. *Blessed Margaret's Cancer Relief Fund, Inc.*, Rosary Hill Home, 600 Linda Ave., Hawthorne, 10532. Tel: 914-769-0923; Fax: 914-769-0710; Email: sistermaryjoseph@hawthorne-dominicans.org. Mother Mary Francis, O.P., Pres.

The Rose Hawthorne Guild, 600 Linda Ave., Hawthorne, 10532. Tel: 914-769-0114; Fax: 914-769-0827; Email: srmjoseph@gmail.com; Web: www.hawthorne-dominicans.org. Mother Mary Francis, O.P., Pres. & Contact Person.

HIGHLAND MILLS. *Thevenet Montessori School*, (Grades PreK-1), 21 Bethany Dr., Highland Mills, 10930. Tel: 845-928-6981; Fax: 845-928-3179; Email: thevenet02@optimum.net. Sr. Joan Faraone, R.J.M., Dir. Religious of Jesus and Mary. Lay Teachers 9; Sisters 3; Students 110.

HYDE PARK. *Focolare Movement, (Women's Branch) - National Center* (1943) Women's Branch 200 Cardinal Rd., Hyde Park, 12538. Tel: 845-229-0230 ; Email: nyanadias@gmail.com; Web: www.focolare.org. Ana Dias, Contact Person. Founded in Trent, Italy in 1943. International Headquarters are in Rome, Italy. Movement was approved in March 1962 with the aim of working toward the fulfillment of Christ's prayer for unity, that all may be one. More than four million people, in all walks of life, married and single, are committed in or connected with the Movement. Centers in over fifty countries. Call for additional information.

Focolare Movement (Men's Branch) - National Center (Men) 7 Intellect Way, Hyde Park, 12538. Tel: 845-229-0307; Email: czmlumi@optonline.net; Web: www.focolare.us. Hugh Moran.

Focolare Movement, Mariapolis Luminosa (Work of Mary), 200 Cardinal Rd., Hyde Park, 12538. Tel: 845-229-0230; Email: nyanadias@gmail.com; Web: www.focolare.org. Antonio Vallejo, Contact Person.

Focolare Movement, Women's Branch (East Coast) (Work of Mary), 257 Peace Ave., Hyde Park, 12538. Tel: 718-828-1969; Email: focfny@gmail.com; Web: www.focolare.org. Ana Dias, Dir.

Living City of the Focolare Movement, Inc., 202 Comforter Blvd., Hyde Park, 12538. Tel: 845-229-0496; Fax: 845-220-1770; Email: livingcity.ed@livingcitymagazine.com; Web: www.livingcitymagazine.com. Susanne Jenssen, Contact Person.

New City Press of the Focolare Movement, Inc., 202 Comforter Blvd., Hyde Park, 12538. Tel: 845-229-0335; Fax: 845-229-0351; Email: claude.blanc@newcitypress.com; Web: www.newcitypress.com. Mr. Claude Blanc, Dir.

LARCHMONT. *American Compassion Services, Inc.*, 280 Weaver St., Larchmont, 10538. Tel: 484-619-3824; Fax: 610-432-4382; Email: dleblond@fidescousa.org. Rosemary Leblond, Exec. Dir.

The Oratory of Divine Love, Inc., 1 Pryer Manor Rd., Larchmont, 10538. Tel: 914-643-3743; Email: ycleffi@aol.com; Web: www.oratoryofdivinelove.com. Rev. Benedict Joseph Groeschel, C.F.R., Ed. D., Pres.

Songcatchers, Inc., Mailing Address: 2005 Palmer Ave. #252, Larchmont, 10538. Email: songcatchers@gmail.com. Sr. Beth Dowd, O.S.U., Rel. Order Leader; Zane Myers, Dir. Program activities for elementary and middle school children, including Choir Camp, Concert Choir, and an After-School Music Program, Early Childhood Music Program. Young adults: volunteer staff of after-school program and camp.

Spiritual Development Office, 1 Pryer Manor Rd., Larchmont, 10538. Tel: 914-235-6939. Rev. Eugene J. Fulton, Dir.

LIVINGSTON MANOR. *The Monastic Family of Bethlehem* (1987) 393 Our Lady of Lourdes Camp Rd., Livingston Manor, 12758. Tel: 845-439-4300; Fax: 845-439-3069.

MARYKNOLL. *Maryknoll Fathers and Brothers Apostolic Trust*, P.O. Box 306, Maryknoll, 10545-0306. Tel: 914-941-7590; Fax: 914-944-3628; Web: www.maryknoll.org. Rev. David A. Smith, M.M., Contact Person.

Maryknoll Mission Association of the Faithful dba Maryknoll Lay Missioners (1994) P.O. Box 307, Maryknoll, 10545-0307. Tel: 914-762-6364; Fax: 914-944-3576; Email: info@mklm.org; Web: www.mklm.org. Marj Humphrey, Dir. Missions; Ted Miles, Exec. Purpose: Maryknoll Lay Missioners (MKLM) is a Catholic organization, comprising single men and women, couples and families, inspired by the mission of Jesus to live and work with poor communities in Africa, Asia and the Americas, responding to basic needs and helping to create a more just and compassionate world. MKLM applies skills and knowledge, raising the quality of life, and restoring hope, by making lasting improvements in the areas of justice and peace, education, health, pastoral care and sustainable development. MKLM recruits, trains and financially supports its missioners solely by public donation.

Legal Name: Maryknoll Mission Association of the Faithful

Maryknoll Lay Missioners Foundation, P.O. Box 307, Maryknoll, 10545-0307. Tel: 914-762-6364; Fax: 914-762-7031; Email: mboyle@mklm.org. Matt Boyle, Liaison.

Maryknoll Missionary Education Trust, P.O. Box 306 Ryder Rd., Maryknoll, 10545. Tel: 914-941-7590; Fax: 914-944-3628.

MOUNT VERNON. *St. Dymphna Devotion* (1961) 274-280 W. Lincoln Ave., P.O. Box 598, Mount Vernon, 10551-0598. Tel: 914-664-5604; Fax: 914-664-3017; Email: mbonnici@franciscanmissionassoc.org. Rev/ Robert M. Campagna, O.F.M., Prov.; Ms. Madeline Bonnici, Exec. Dir. Province of the Immaculate Conception.

Franciscan Mission Associates (1961) 274-280 W. Lincoln Ave., P.O. Box 598, Mount Vernon, 10550. Tel: 914-664-5604; Fax: 914-664-3017; Email: mbonnici@franciscanmissionassoc.org; Web: www.franciscanmissionassoc.org. Rev/ Robert M. Campagna, O.F.M., Prov.; Ms. Madeline Bonnici, Exec. Dir. Province of the Immaculate Conception.

NANUET. *Catholic School Region of Rockland Co.*, 32 W. Nyack Rd., Nanuet, 10954. Tel: 845-623-3504; Fax: 845-623-1550.

NEW ROCHELLE. *Christian Brothers Foundation* dba Edmund Rice Christian Brothers Foundation, 260 Wilmot Rd., New Rochelle, 10804. Tel: 914-636-1035; Fax: 914-636-0021; Email:

cab@cbinstitute.org. Bro. Kevin M. Griffith, C.F.C., Pres.

Marian Residence Fund (1997) 1338 North Ave., New Rochelle, 10804. Tel: 914-712-0060; Fax: 914-712-3134; Email: ursruepr@aol.com. Sr. Jane Finnerty, O.S.U., Prov.

OSU Charitable Trust (1997) 1338 North Ave., New Rochelle, 10804. Tel: 914-712-0060; Fax: 914-712-3134; Email: ursruepr@aol.com. Sr. Jane Finnerty, O.S.U., Prov.

Salesian Missions, Inc., 2 Lefevre Ln., New Rochelle, 10801. Tel: 914-633-8344; Fax: 914-633-7404; Web: www.salesianmissions.org. Rev. Mark Hyde, S.D.B., Dir.

Salesian Office of Vocations, 148 E. Main St., Box 639, New Rochelle, 10802-0639. Tel: 914-636-4225; Email: info@salesiansofdonbosco.org. Rev. Dominic Tran, S.D.B., M.A.

NEWBURGH. **Newburgh Ministry* (1983) 9 Johnston St., P.O. Box 1449, Newburgh, 12551. Tel: 845-561-0070; Fax: 845-561-5087. Michele McKeon, Chairperson, Bd. Dir.; Colin Jarvis, Exec. Dir.

Newburgh San Miguel Program dba Newburgh San Miguel Program, P.O. Box 284, Chappaqua, 10514. Tel: 845-561-2822; Fax: 845-561-0312; Email: connell.sanmiguel@gmail.com. Rev. Mark J. Connell, D.Min., Pres. & CEO; Catherine Joyce Wooters, Dir. Devel.

Our Lady of Comfort Women's Center, 91 Ann St., Newburgh, 12550. Tel: 845-561-6267; Fax: 914-565-0572. Nina Faulkner, Treas. Shelter for Women & Children.

PORT CHESTER. **Caritas of Port Chester, Inc.*, 19 Smith St., P.O. Box 682, Port Chester, 10573. Tel: 914-305-3967; Email: caritaspc@hotmail.com. Patricia Walsh Hart, Bd. Pres.

Don Bosco Workers, Inc., 22 Don Bosco Pl., Port Chester, 10573. Tel: 914-433-6666. Ann Heekin, Pres.

RHINEBECK. **The Children's Foundation of Astor*, 6339 Mill St., P.O. Box 5005, Rhinebeck, 12572-5005. Tel: 845-871-1117; Fax: 845-876-2020; Email: smoorhead@astorservices.org; Web: www.astorservices.org. Sonia Barnes-Moorhead, Exec. Vice Pres.

RIVERDALE. *Holy Innocents Foundation*, 5272 Post Rd., Riverdale, 10471. Fax: 718-548-4042; Email: ktoreilly@hotmail.com. Kevin T. O'Reilly, Pres.

RYE. *Alpha Omega Family Center, Inc.* (1993) 815 Boston Post Rd., Rye, 10580. Tel: 770-828-4950; Email: eramirez@arcol.org. Rev. Frank Formolo, Contact Person.

Arke, Inc., 815 Boston Post Rd., Rye, 10580. Tel: 770-828-4950; Email: fformolo@legionaries.org. Rev. Frank Formolo, Contact Person.

Catholic Net, Inc. (1997) 815 Boston Post Rd., Rye, 10580. Tel: 770-282-4950; Email: eramirez@arcol.org. Rev. Frank Formolo, Contact Person.

Consolidated Catholic Administrative Services, Inc. (1999) 815 Boston Post Rd., Rye, 10580. Tel: 770-828-4950; Fax: 770-828-4955; Email: eramirez@arcol.org. Rev. Frank Formolo, Contact Person.

Helping Hands Medical Missions, Inc. (1997) 815 Boston Post Rd., Rye, 10580. Tel: 972-253-1800; Fax: 972-253-1900; Email: eramirez@arcol.org; Web: hhmm.org/. Rev. Frank Formolo.

Legacy Growth, Inc., 815 Boston Post Rd., Rye, 10580. Tel: 203-795-2800; Fax: 203-281-6051; Email: eramirez@arcol.org. Rev. Frank Formolo.

Legion of Christ and Consecrated Regnum Christi Members Assistance Foundation (2002) 815 Boston Post Rd., Rye, 10580. Tel: 770-828-4950; Email: fformolo@legionaries.org. Rev. Frank Formolo, Contact Person.

Legion of Christ North America, Inc., 815 Boston Post Rd., Rye, 10580. Tel: 770-828-4950; Email: eramirez@arcol.org. Rev. Frank Formolo, Contact Person.

Legion of Christ, Incorporated (1978) 815 Boston Post Rd., Rye, 10580. Tel: 770-828-4950; Fax: 770-828-4595; Email: eramirez@arcol.org. Rev. Frank Formolo, Contact Person.

The Legion of Christ, Incorporated, 815 Boston Post Rd., Rye, 10580. Tel: 770-828-4950; Fax: 770-828-4955; Email: fformolo@legionaries.org; Web: legionariesofchrist.org. Rev. Frank Formolo, Admin.

Logos, Inc., 815 Boston Post Rd., Rye, 10580. Tel: 770-828-4950; Email: eramirez@arcol.org. Rev. Frank Formolo.

Mission Network Programs USA, Inc. (1997) 815 Boston Post Rd., Rye, 10580. Tel: 770-828-4950; Email: eramirez@arcol.org. Rev. Frank Formolo, Contact Person.

Nueva Primavera Inc., 815 Boston Post Rd., Rye, 10580. Tel: 770-828-4950; Email: eramirez@arcol.org. Rev. Frank Formolo, Contact Person.

Pastoral Support Services, Inc., 815 Boston Post Rd., Rye, 10580. Tel: 770-828-4950; Email: sbaldwin@regnumchristi.net. Ms. Sonia Baldwin, Sec.

Regina Apostolorum, Inc., 815 Boston Post Rd., Rye, 10580. Tel: 770-828-4950; Email: eramirez@arcol.org. Rev. Frank Formolo, Contact Person.

The Resurrection School Foundation, Inc., 910 Boston Post Rd., Rye, 10580. Tel: 914-925-2731; Fax: 914-925-2751; Email: admin.foundation@resurrectionschool.com; Web: www.resurrectionschool.com. Kathleen Callahan, Dir., Devel.

Rossotto, Inc., 815 Boston Post Rd., Rye, 10580. Tel: 770-828-4950; Email: eramirez@arcol.org. Rev. Frank Formolo.

RYE BROOK. **New Jersey Friends of Mandeville Inc.*, 111 S. Ridge St., Ste. 302, Rye Brook, 10573. Tel: 914-908-6737; Fax: 914-881-9002. Rev. James O'Shea, C.P., Pres.; Most Rev. Neil Tiedemann, C.P., Vice Pres.; Revs. David Monaco, C.P., Treas.; James Price, C.P., Sec.; William Murphy, C.P., Asst. Sec. & Asst. Treas.

Passionist Communications, Inc., 111 S. Ridge St., Ste. 303, PO Box 111, Rye Brook, 10573. Tel: 914-738-3344; Email: contact@TheSundayMass.org; Web: www.thesundaymass.org. Rev. Paul R. Fagan, C.P.; Mrs. Kathy Rego; Mr. Shahib Narine.

Passionist Communications Center, 111 S. Ridge St., Ste. 303, Rye Brook, 10573. Tel: 914-738-3344; Email: contact@TheSundayMass.org; Web: www.thesundaymass.org. Rev. Paul R. Fagan, C.P., Exec. Producer.

St. Paul's Benevolent, Educational and Missionary Institute, Inc., Passionist Province Center, 111 S. Ridge St., Ste. 300, Rye Brook, 10573. Tel: 914-633-3130; Fax: 914-881-9002; Email: provincialstpaul@cpprov.org; Web: www.thepassionists.org. Revs. James O'Shea, C.P., Prov.; Salvatore Enzo Del Brocco, C.P., Vice Prov.; James Price, C.P., 2nd Consultor; William Murphy, C.P., 3rd Consultor; Hugo Esparza-Perez, C.P., 4th Consultor; David Monaco, C.P., Treas.; Mr. Daniel Flynn, Dir. Healthcare & Social Svcs.; Ms. Anastasia Raven, Sec. Prov.; Mr. Ross Boyle, Dir. Passionist Volunteers Intl. & Vocation Team Coord. Legal Title for the Congregation of the Passion - St. Paul of the Cross Province Employees 8; Tot in Congregation 106; Volunteers 2.

SALT POINT. *Camp Veritas*, 1653 Salt Point Tpke., Salt Point, 12578. Tel: 845-266-5784; Email: ryan1@campveritas.com; Web: www.campveritas.com. Ryan Young, Bd. Chairperson.

SCARSDALE. *Catholic Charismatic Renewal Office*, 194 Gaylor Rd., Scarsdale, 10583. Tel: 914-725-1773; Fax: 914-725-5227; Email: charismny@optonline.net; Web: www.catholiccharismaticny.org. Rev. William B. Cosgrove, Co-Liaison. Tel: 845-634-3641; Fax: 845-639-6118; Email: frbill@optonline.net.

SLEEPY HOLLOW. *RSHM Life Center, Inc.* (1995) 32-34 Beekman Ave., Sleepy Hollow, 10591. Tel: 914-366-9710; Fax: 914-366-9713; Email: susan@rshmlifecenter.org; Web: www.rshmlifecenter.org. Sacred Heart of Mary. Children 450; Total Staff 16; Adults 1,150; Total Assisted 1,600.

SLOATSBURG. *St. Mary's Villa, Inc.*, 150 Sisters Servants Ln., P.O. Box 9, Sloatsburg, 10974-0009. Tel: 845-753-5100; Fax: 845-753-1956; Email: ssminy@aol.com. Sisters Kathleen Hutsko, S.S.M.I., Pres.; Cecelia Sworin, S.S.M.I., Sec.

The Blessed Josaphata Fund (2001) 9 Emmanuel Dr., P.O. Box 9, Sloatsburg, 10974-0009. Tel: 845-753-2840; Fax: 845-753-1956; Email: rmulcahey@sbcq.com; Email: ssminy@aol.com. Richard T. Mulcahey Jr., Esq., Contact Person; Sr. Kathleen Hutsko, S.S.M.I., Provincial Supr.

SPARKILL. *Hallel Institute* (1974) 175 Rte. 340, Sparkill, 10976-1047. Tel: 845-365-2277; Fax: 845-365-2279; Email: hallel@hallel.net; Web: hallel.net. Rev. George J. Torok, C.O., Pres., (Retired). Total in Residence 40; Total Staff 7.

New York Oratory of St. Philip Neri, Inc., 175 Rte. 340, Sparkill, 10976. Tel: 845-365-2277; Fax: 845-365-2279; Email: nyoratory@yahoo.com. Revs. George J. Torok, C.O., Provost, (Retired); Vladimir Chripko, C.O., Vice Provost & Treas.; Martin Kertys, C.O., Deputy; Frantisek Conka, C.O., Sec.; Roman Dominic Palecko, C.O., Member; Thomas Kunnel, C.O., Member.

One to One Learning, Inc. (1997) Office of the President, 175 Rte. 340, Sparkill, 10976. Tel: 845-512-8176; Fax: 845-512-8178; Email: clpangel59@gmail.com. Sr. Cecilia LaPietra, O.P., Executive Dir.

Sisters of St. Dominic of Sparkill Charitable Trust, 175 Rte. 340, Sparkill, 10976-1047. Tel: 845-358-4088; Fax: 845-359-4083; Web: www.sparkill.org.

STATEN ISLAND. **Catholic High School Football League of Metropolitan N.Y.*, St. Peter's Boys High School, 200 Clinton Ave., Staten Island, 10301. Tel: 718-447-1676. Mr. John Fodera, Prin.

Catholic School Region of Staten Island, 139 Windsor Rd., Staten Island, 10314. Tel: 718-447-1034.

Indian Knanaya Catholic Community of Greater NY, Inc., 94 Wilcox St., Staten Island, 10303. Tel: 914-494-7571; Fax: 914-494-9183; Email: ikcc@hotmail.com. Jose Chummar, Pres.

Korean Catholic Apostolate of Staten Island, Inc., 76 Jackson St., Staten Island, 10304. Tel: 718-273-3311; Fax: 718-273-3312; Email: kcasi08@hanmail.net. Hyunwoung Park, Contact Person.

Schoenstatt Sisters of Mary, Secular Institute, 337 Cary Ave., Staten Island, 10310-2041. Tel: 718-727-8005; Email: shrineny@schsrsmary.org. W284N404 Cherry Ln., Staten Island, 10310. Sr. Georgina Ramirez, Supr. Sisters 6.

**Sisters of Charity Housing Development, Corp.*, 150 Brielle Ave., Staten Island, 10314-6400. Tel: 718-477-6803; Fax: 718-477-1356; Email: dodged@optonline.net; Email: vanessa.reilly@si.rr.com; Web: www.sistersofcharityhousing.org. Sr. Donna Dodge, S.C., Exec. Dir.

SUFFERN. *Good Samaritan Foundation for Better Health, Inc.*, 255 Lafayette Ave., Suffern, 10901-4869. Tel: 845-368-5151; Fax: 845-368-5596; Email: stacey_kirschenbaum@bshsi.org; Web: www.bschsf.org. Sr. Mary Louise Moran, S.C., Pres.; Stacey Kirschenbaum, Dir. Fundraising arm of Good Samaritan Hospital, Suffern, NY.

TARRYTOWN. *Leviticus 25:23 Alternative Fund, Inc.* (1983) 220 While Plains Rd., Ste. 125, Tarrytown, 10591. Tel: 914-909-4381; Fax: 914-606-9006; Email: info@leviticusfund.org; Web: www.leviticusfund.org. Gregory Maher, Exec. Dir.; Sr. Margaret Murphy, O.P., Finance Officer; Maryann Sorese, Devel. & Communs. Officer; Sabine Werner, Lending Officer.

Religious of the Sacred Heart of Mary Charitable Trust, 50 Wilson Park Dr., Tarrytown, 10591. Tel: 914-631-2979; Fax: 914-332-4735; Email: bkenny1@mindspring.com. Sr. Bernadette Kenny, Contact Person.

THORNWOOD. *Youth and Family Encounter, Inc.* (1998) 590 Columbus Ave., Thornwood, 10594. Tel: 914-773-1368; Fax: 914-773-1438. Rev. Jose Felix Ortega, L.C., Contact Person.

TUCKAHOE. **Peace Through Divine Mercy, Inc.* (1988) 50 Columbus Ave., #410, Tuckahoe, 10707. Tel: 914-771-7717; Email: reginacleri@aol.com; Web: www.peacethroughmercy.com. Kathleen Keefe, Contact Person. Apostolate for priestly and family renewal.

UPPER NYACK. *Marydell Faith and Life Center*, 640 N. Midland Ave., Nyack, 10960. Tel: 845-358-5399; Email: marydellflc@gmail.com; Web: www.marydellsisters.com. Mrs. Maria Joy, Dir.

WEST PARK. *Sacred Heart Center for New Americans, Inc.*, 2085 Rte. 9W, West Park, 12493. Tel: 646-342-4177. Sr. Pietrina Raccuglia, M.S.C., Pres.

WHITE PLAINS. *Children's Rehabilitation Center, Inc.*, 317 North St., White Plains, 10605. Tel: 914-294-6128; Fax: 914-294-6181; Web: www.childrensrehabcenter.org. Carla Perruccio, CFO.

Company of St. Paul, 52 Davis Ave., White Plains, 10605. Tel: 914-946-1019; Fax: 914-946-1019; Email: jssandberg@optonline.net. Rev. Stuart Sandberg, Pres.

Concerts at the Chapel, Inc., White Plains Center of Compassion, 52 N. Broadway, White Plains, 10603. Tel: 914-798-1201; Web: www.divinecompassion.org. Paula Caracappa, Coord.

Deutschsprachige Katholische Gemeinde New York-German Speaking Catholic Congregation New York, 106 Greenacres Ave., White Plains, 10606. Tel: 914-831-3165. Rev. Peter Bleeser, Contact Person.

Religious of Divine Compassion Charitable Trust, 52 N. Broadway, White Plains, 10603. Tel: 914-798-1300; Fax: 914-949-5169; Email: cwagner@divinecompassion.org; Web: divinecompassion.org.

WOODBOURNE. *Heart's Home USA* (2003) 2299 Ulster Heights Rd., Woodbourne, 12788. Tel: 845-434-5076; Email: info@heartshomeusa.org; Web: www.heartshomeusa.org. Ms. Cecile Fourmeaux, Pres.

YONKERS. *St. Elizabeth Seton Children's Foundation Ltd.*, 300 Corporate Blvd., S., Yonkers, 10701. Tel: 914-294-6301; Fax: 914-226-3003.

Finian Sullivan Corporation, One Father Finian Sullivan Dr., Yonkers, 10703. Tel: 914-969-6159; Fax: 914-969-1503; Email: scorbett@hhmgmt.com. Peter Bassano, Esq., Contact Person.

Instructional T.V. Communications Center, 201 Seminary Ave., Yonkers, 10704. Tel: 914-968-7800; Web: www.itvny.org.

Jesus Caritas Fraternity, Inc., 4 Curran Ct., 1R,

Yonkers, 10710. Tel: 914-961-0050; Email: margebaker@secularinstitutes.org. Mary D. Christensen, Corresponding Sec.

Magnificat Foundation, Inc., P.O. Box 845, Yonkers, 10702. Tel: 914-502-1859; Fax: 914-969-6446; Web: www.magnificatfoundation.org.

[HH] PERSONAL PRELATURES

NEW YORK. *Prelature of the Holy Cross and Opus Dei* (1928) 139 E. 34th St., 10016. Tel: 646-742-2700; Fax: 646-742-2747; Email: newyork@opusdei.org; Web: www.opusdei.org. Rev. Msgrs. Thomas G. Bohlin, Ph.D., S.T.D., Regl. Vicar for the U.S.; Javier Garcia de Cardenas; Revs. Robert A. Brisson; James W. Albrecht; John C. Agnew; Jeffrey J. Langan; Jichael J. Barret; Timothy J. Uhen.

Prelature of the Holy Cross and Opus Dei, Tel: 914-235-0199; Fax: 914-637-9597. Revs. Bradley K. Arturi, J.C.D.; Michael J. Manz; Thomas J. Lamb.

99 Overlook Cir., New Rochelle, 10804. Tel: 914-235-6128. Revs. Malcolm M. Kennedy; Orestes Gonzalez.

Personal Prelature, Prelature of the Holy Cross and Opus Dei, 139 E. 34th St., 10016-4704. Tel: 212-222-3285; Fax: 212-316-3629; Email: info.us@opusdei.org; Web: www.opusdei.org. Rev. Msgr. Thomas G. Bohlin, Ph.D., S.T.D., Vicar.

[II] SECULAR INSTITUTES

NEW YORK. *Lay Women's Association / Secular Institute of the Missionaries of the Kingship of Christ*, 33 W. 60th St., Ste. 223, 10023. Tel: 917-327-0255; Email: suelarkin2@gmail.com; Web: www.simkc.org. Rev. Dominic Monti, O.F.M., Ecclesiastical Asst.

RELIGIOUS INSTITUTES OF MEN REPRESENTED IN THE ARCHDIOCESE

For further details refer to the corresponding bracketed number in the Religious Institutes of Men or Women section.

[0140]—*The Augustinians* (Prov. of St. Joseph)—O.S.A.
[0330]—*Brothers of the Christian Schools* (New York Prov.)—F.S.C.
[0400]—*Canons Regular of the Order of the Holy Cross* (Prov. of St. Odilia, Minneapolis, MN)—O.S.C.
[0470]—*The Capuchin Friars* (St. Mary Prov.)—O.F.M.Cap.
[0270]—*Carmelite Fathers & Brothers* (St. Elias Prov.)—O.Carm.
[0310]—*Congregation of Christian Brothers* (Eastern U.S.)—C.F.C.
[0220]—*Congregation of the Blessed Sacrament*—S.S.S.
[1210]—*Congregation of the Missionaries of St. Charles*—C.S.
[1000]—*Congregation of the Passion* (St. Paul Prov.)—C.P.
[0480]—*Conventual Franciscans* (Immaculate Conception Prov.)—O.F.M.Conv.
[0520]—*Franciscan Friars* (Provs. of Most Holy Name of Jesus, Immaculate Conception; Commissariats of Holy Cross, Holy Family)—O.F.M.
[0530]—*Franciscan Friars of the Atonement*—S.A.
[0690]—*Jesuit Fathers and Brothers* (New York Prov.)—S.J.
[]—*Little Brothers of the Gospel*.
[0770]—*The Marist Brothers*—F.M.S.
[0780]—*Marist Fathers* (Northeastern Prov.)—S.M.
[0800]—*Maryknoll*—M.M.
[0830]—*Mill Hill Missionaries*—M.H.M.
[0910]—*Oblates of Mary Immaculate* (Eastern Prov.)—O.M.I.
[0430]—*Order of Preachers-Dominicans* (St. Joseph Prov.)—O.P.
[0150]—*Order of the Augustinian Recollects*—O.A.R.
[1030]—*Paulist Fathers*—C.S.P.
[1040]—*Piarist Fathers*—Sch.P.
[1070]—*Redemptorist Fathers* (Baltimore Prov.)—C.SS.R.
[1190]—*Salesians of Don Bosco* (St. Philip Prov.)—S.D.B.
[1020]—*Society of St. Paul*—S.S.P.
[0990]—*Society of the Catholic Apostolate*—S.A.C.
[1280]—*Stigmatine Fathers and Brothers*—C.S.S.
[1300]—*Theatine Fathers*—C.R.
[0560]—*Third Order Regular of Saint Francis*—T.O.R.

RELIGIOUS INSTITUTES OF WOMEN REPRESENTED IN THE ARCHDIOCESE

[0130]—*Apostles of the Sacred Heart of Jesus*—A.S.C.J.
[0230]—*Benedictine Sisters of Pontifical Jurisdiction*—O.S.B.
[0330]—*Carmelite Sisters for the Aged and Infirm*—O.Carm.
[3710]—*Congregation of the Sisters of Saint Agnes*—C.S.A.
[0790]—*Daughters of Divine Charity* (St. Joseph Prov.)—F.D.C.
[0850]—*Daughters of Mary Help of Christians*—F.M.A.
[0860]—*Daughters of Mary of the Immaculate Conception*—D.M.
[0950]—*Daughters of St. Paul*—F.S.P.
[0810]—*Daughters of the Heart of Mary*—D.H.M.
[0420]—*Discalced Carmelite Nuns*—O.C.D.
[1050]—*Dominican Contemplative Nuns*—O.P.
[1070-03]—*Dominican Sisters*—O.P.
[1070-11]—*Dominican Sisters*—O.P.
[1070-05]—*Dominican Sisters*—O.P.
[1070-06]—*Dominican Sisters*—O.P.
[1070-13]—*Dominican Sisters*—O.P.
[1070-16]—*Dominican Sisters*—O.P.
[1070-23]—*Dominican Sisters*—O.P.
[1070-15]—*Dominican Sisters*—O.P.
[1115]—*Dominican Sisters of Peace*—O.P.
[1120]—*Dominican Sisters of the Roman Congregation*—O.P.
[1260]—*Franciscan Handmaids of the Most Pure Heart of Mary*—F.H.M.
[1370]—*Franciscan Missionaries of Mary*—F.M.M.
[1400]—*Franciscan Missionary Sisters of the Sacred Heart* (Peekskill, NY)—F.M.S.C.
[1180]—*Franciscan Sisters of Allegany, New York*—O.S.F.
[1425]—*Franciscan Sisters of Peace*—F.S.P.
[1190]—*Franciscan Sisters of the Atonement*—S.A.
[1440]—*Franciscan Sisters of the Poor*—S.F.P.
[]—*Franciscan Sisters of the Renewal*.
[2070]—*Holy Union Sisters*—S.U.S.C.
[]—*Idente Missionaries*—M.Id.
[3790]—*Institute of the Sisters of St. Dorothy*—S.S.D.
[2310]—*Little Sisters of the Assumption*—L.S.A.
[2340]—*Little Sisters of the Poor*—L.S.P.
[2470]—*Maryknoll Sisters of St. Dominic*—M.M.
[2680]—*Misericordia Sisters*—S.M.
[2710]—*Missionaries of Charity*—M.C.
[1360]—*Missionary Franciscan Sisters of the Immaculate Conception*—O.S.F.
[2900]—*Missionary Sisters of St. Charles Borromeo*—M.S.S.C.B.
[2750]—*Missionary Sisters of the Immaculate Heart of Mary*—I.C.M.
[2860]—*Missionary Sisters of the Sacred Heart*—M.S.C.
[2920]—*Mothers of the Helpless*—M.D.
[3030]—*Oblates of the Most Holy Redeemer*—O.SS.R.
[3760]—*Order of St. Clare*—O.S.C.
[2010]—*Order of the Most Holy Redeemer*—O.SS.R.
[3160]—*Parish Visitors of Mary Immaculate*—P.V.M.I.
[3450]—*Religious of Jesus-Mary*—R.J.M.
[3460]—*Religious of Mary Immaculate*—R.M.I.
[3465]—*Religious of the Sacred Heart of Mary* (Eastern North American Prov.)—R.S.H.M.
[3490]—*Sacramentine Nuns*—O.S.S.
[]—*Siervas de Cristo Resucitado*.
[0980]—*Sister Disciples of the Divine Master*—P.D.D.M.
[1830]—*Sister of the Good Shepherd*—R.G.S.
[3020]—*Sisters Oblates of the Blessed Trinity*—O.B.T.
[0650]—*Sisters of Charity of St. Vincent de Paul, New York*—S.C.
[0660]—*Sisters of Christian Charity*—S.C.C.
[2575]—*Sisters of Mercy of the Americas*—R.S.M.
[3080]—*Sisters of Our Lady of Christian Doctrine*—R.C.D.
[]—*Sisters of Life*.
[3830-05]—*Sisters of St. Joseph*—C.S.J.
[3890]—*Sisters of St. Joseph of Peace*—C.S.J.P.
[3140]—*Sisters of the Catholic Apostolate (Pallottine)*—C.S.A.C.
[2980]—*Sisters of the Congregation de Notre Dame*—C.N.D.
[0970]—*Sisters of the Divine Compassion*—R.D.C.
[1000]—*Sisters of the Divine Providence of Kentucky*—C.D.P.
[1990]—*Sisters of the Holy Names of Jesus & Mary*—S.N.J.M.
[3320]—*Sisters of the Presentation of the B.V.M.* (Aberdeen, SD)—P.B.V.M.
[3470]—*Sisters of the Reparation of the Congregation of Mary*—S.R.C.M.
[3480]—*Sisters of the Resurrection*—C.R.
[1490]—*Sisters of the Third Franciscan Order (Syracuse)*—O.S.F.
[3600]—*Sisters, Servants of Mary*—S.M.
[2160]—*Sisters, Servants of the Immaculate Heart Of Mary*—I.H.M.
[1890]—*Society of Helpers*—H.H.S.
[2460]—*Society of Mary Reparatrix*—S.M.R.
[4040]—*Society of St. Ursula*—S.U.
[4060]—*Society of the Holy Child Jesus*—S.H.C.J.
[4070]—*Society of the Sacred Heart*—R.S.C.J.
[4110]—*Ursuline Nuns*—O.S.U.

ARCHDIOCESAN CEMETERIES

AIRMONT. *Ascension Cemetery*
HAWTHORNE. *Gate of Heaven Cemetery*
STATEN ISLAND. *Resurrection Cemetery*
WOODSIDE. *Calvary Cemetery*

NECROLOGY

† Brucato, Robert A., Retired Auxiliary Bishop of New York, Died Nov. 7, 2018
† Bartley, Vincent, (Retired), Died Nov. 6, 2017
† Gilleece, Thomas E., Chappaqua, NY Church of St. John & St. Mary, Died Jun. 15, 2018
† Graham, Neil, (Retired), Died Apr. 20, 2018
† D'Angelo, Thomas, Died Jun. 21, 2018
† Doyle, Philip R., (Retired), Died Jun. 30, 2018
† Fussner, Donald T., (Retired), Died Jun. 10, 2018
† Leonard, Thomas, (Retired), Died Oct. 18, 2018
† Leone, Arthur, (Retired), Died Jul. 12, 2018
† Szivos, Charles S., Bronx, NY Church of St. Theresa of the Infant Jesus, Died Sep. 5, 2018

An asterisk (*) denotes an organization that has established tax-exempt status directly with the IRS and is not covered by the USCCB Group Ruling.

Diocese of Norwich

(Dioecesis Norvicensis)

Most Reverend

MICHAEL R. COTE, D.D.

Bishop of Norwich; ordained June 29, 1975; appointed Titular Bishop of Cebarades and Auxiliary Bishop of Portland May 9, 1995; ordained July 27, 1995; appointed Bishop of Norwich March 11, 2003; installed May 14, 2003. *Res.: 274 Broadway, Norwich, CT 06360.*

Chancery: 201 Broadway, Norwich, CT 06360. Tel: 860-887-9294; Fax: 860-886-1670.

Web: www.norwichdiocese.org

ESTABLISHED AUGUST 6, 1953.

Square Miles 1,978.

Corporate Title: The Norwich Roman Catholic Diocesan Corporation.

Comprises the Counties of Middlesex, New London, Tolland and Windham in the State of Connecticut and Fishers Island, a portion of Suffolk County in the State of New York.

For legal titles of parishes and diocesan institutions, consult the Chancery Office.

STATISTICAL OVERVIEW

Personnel	
Bishop	1
Priests: Diocesan Active in Diocese	54
Priests: Diocesan Active Outside Diocese	2
Priests: Diocesan in Foreign Missions	1
Priests: Retired, Sick or Absent	38
Number of Diocesan Priests	95
Religious Priests in Diocese	39
Total Priests in Diocese	134
Extern Priests in Diocese	7
Ordinations:	
Diocesan Priests	1
Permanent Deacons	3
Permanent Deacons in Diocese	50
Total Brothers	15
Total Sisters	144
Parishes	
Parishes	76
With Resident Pastor:	
Resident Diocesan Priests	65
Resident Religious Priests	4
Without Resident Pastor:	
Administered by Priests	3
Completely Vacant	4
Missions	2
Pastoral Centers	6
Professional Ministry Personnel:	
Sisters	20
Lay Ministers	46
Welfare	
Homes for the Aged	2
Total Assisted	428
Special Centers for Social Services	6
Total Assisted	14,776
Educational	
Diocesan Students in Other Seminaries	9
Seminaries, Religious	1
Students Religious	25
Total Seminarians	34
Colleges and Universities	1
Total Students	606
High Schools, Diocesan and Parish	3
Total Students	1,475
High Schools, Private	2
Total Students	1,544
Elementary Schools, Diocesan and Parish	11
Total Students	1,532
Catechesis/Religious Education:	
High School Students	1,495
Elementary Students	6,834
Total Students under Catholic Instruction	13,520
Teachers in the Diocese:	
Priests	1
Sisters	12
Lay Teachers	164
Vital Statistics	
Receptions into the Church:	
Infant Baptism Totals	1,114
Minor Baptism Totals	84
Adult Baptism Totals	54
Received into Full Communion	119
First Communions	1,253
Confirmations	1,406
Marriages:	
Catholic	273
Interfaith	50
Total Marriages	323
Deaths	1,875
Total Catholic Population	228,520
Total Population	700,499

Former Bishops—Most Revs. BERNARD J. FLANAGAN, D.D., J.C.D., ord. Dec. 8, 1931; cons. Nov. 30, 1953; installed Dec. 9, 1953; transferred to See of Worcester, Aug. 12, 1959; retired March 31, 1983; died Jan. 28, 1998; VINCENT J. HINES, D.D., J.C.D., ord. May 2, 1937; appt. Nov. 27, 1959; cons. March 17, 1960; retired June 17, 1975; died April 23, 1990; DANIEL P. REILLY, D.D., ord. May 30, 1953; appt. June 17, 1975; cons. Aug. 6, 1975; transferred to See of Worcester, Oct. 27, 1994; installed Dec. 8, 1994; retired March 9, 2004; DANIEL A. HART, D.D., ord. Feb. 2, 1953; cons. Auxiliary Bishop of Boston Oct. 18, 1976; appt. Sept. 12, 1995; installed Bishop of Norwich Nov. 1, 1995; retired March 11, 2003; died Jan. 14, 2008.

Office of the Bishop—Most Rev. MICHAEL R. COTE, D.D., Tel: 860-887-9294; Email: bpcote@norwichdiocese.net; MRS. ALICE PUDVAH, Administrative Asst., Tel: 860-887-9294, Ext. 234; Email: alice@norwichdiocese.net; Deacon JORGE ESCALONA, Master of Ceremonies.

The Chancery

Chancery—201 Broadway, Norwich, 06360. Tel: 860-887-9294; Fax: 860-886-1670.

Vicar General—Rev. Msgr. LESZEK T. JANIK, J.C.L., V.G., Tel: 860-887-9294, Ext. 231; Email: vicargeneral@norwichdiocese.net; MRS. TERRI ZAMPINI, Sec., Tel: 860-887-9294, Ext. 265; Email: financeterriz@norwichdiocese.net.

Chancellor—Rev. PETER J. LANGEVIN, Chancellor, Tel: 860-887-9294, Ext. 232; MRS. BECKY CADY, Sec., Tel: 860-887-9294, Ext. 235; Email: becky@norwichdiocese.net; MRS. REBECCA MCDOUGAL, Receptionist, Tel: 860-887-9294, Ext. 100.

Vice Chancellor—Rev. BRIAN J. ROMANOWSKI, J.C.L., Tel: 860-887-9294, Ext. 254; Email: ajudicialvicar@norwichdiocese.net.

Vicar for Clergy—Very Rev. DENNIS M. PERKINS, Tel: 860-887-9294, Ext. 258; Email: vicarclergy@norwichdiocese.net; Deacon MICHAEL L. PUSCAS, Dir. Permanent Deacon Personnel; MRS. REBECCA MCDOUGAL, Sec., Tel: 860-887-9294, Ext. 100; Email: rebecca@norwichdiocese.net.

Diaconate: Office of Permanent Deacon Personnel—The Chancery, 201 Broadway, Norwich, 06360-4458. Web: www.norwichdeacons.org. Deacon MICHAEL L. PUSCAS, Diocesan Dir., Permanent Deacon Personnel, Tel: 860-887-9294; Fax: 860-886-1670; Email: director@norwichdeacons.org; MRS. REBECCA MCDOUGAL, Sec., Tel: 860-887-9294, Ext. 100; Fax: 860-886-1670; Email: rebecca@norwichdiocese.net.

Diocesan Attorney—MICHAEL E. DRISCOLL ESQ., 22 Courthouse Sq., Norwich, 06360. Tel: 860-889-3321.

Diocesan Finance Office—Tel: 860-887-9294; Fax: 860-885-1512. NICOLE KRAMER, Internal Auditor, Tel: 860-887-9294, Ext. 241; MS. KAREN HUFFER, Diocesan Finance Officer; SUSAN GARDINER, Administrative Asst., Tel: 860-887-9294, Ext. 261; JANET WEST, Finance Analyst, Tel: 860-887-9294, Ext. 243; MS. BIANCA MUSCARELLA, Benefits Admin., Tel: 860-887-9294, Ext. 245; NICOLE KRAMER, Internal Auditor, Tel: 860-887-9294, Ext. 241; JENNIFER BEAUDOIN, Accounting Clerk, Tel: 860-887-9294, Ext. 242; MRS. TERRI ZAMPINI, Accounts Payable, Tel: 860-887-9294, Ext. 265; MS. ROBIN HOLTSCLAW, Risk Mgr. (CMRS), Tel: 800-331-2561; Fax: 860-726-9412.

College of Consultors—Rev. Msgrs. HENRY N. ARCHAMBAULT, P.A., J.C.D., (Retired); ANTHONY S. ROSAFORTE; MICHAEL T. DONOHUE, (Retired); LESZEK T. JANIK, J.C.L., V.G.; Very Revs. LAURENCE A.M. LAPOINTE; DENNIS M. PERKINS; TED F. TUMICKI, S.T.L., J.C.L., J.V.; Rev. ROBERT WASHABAUGH.

Presbyteral Council—Most Rev. MICHAEL R. COTE, D.D., Pres.; Very Rev. TED F. TUMICKI, S.T.L., J.C.L., J.V., Chm.; Rev. Msgr. LESZEK T. JANIK, J.C.L., V.G. Members: Rev. Msgrs. HENRY N. ARCHAMBAULT, P.A., J.C.D., (Retired); ANTHONY S. ROSAFORTE; JAMES P. CARINI, (Retired); Very Revs. RICHARD J. RICARD, Vice Chm.; LAURENCE A.M. LAPOINTE; DENNIS M. PERKINS; Rev. BRIAN J. CONVERSE; Very Rev. MARK L. CURESKY, O.F.M.Conv.; Revs. JOHN N. ANTONELLE; JOSEPH C. ASHE; GRZEGORZ P. BROZONOWICZ; Very Revs. DAVID P. CHOQUETTE; GREGORY P. GALVIN; Rev. PETER J. LANGEVIN; Very Rev. MICHAEL L. PHILLIPPINO; Revs. KEVIN M. REILLY; RUSSELL F. KENNEDY; GREGORY C. MULLANEY; WILLIAM J. OLESIK; BRIAN J. ROMANOWSKI, J.C.L., Sec.; ROBERT WASHABAUGH; EDWARD M. DEMPSEY, D.B.A.; JEFFREY R. ELLIS; JONATHAN J. FICARA; JOHN GALLAGHER, O.F.M.Cap.; MAREK MASNICKI; MARK D. O'DONNELL.

Deans—Very Revs. LAURENCE A.M. LAPOINTE, Willimantic; RICHARD J. RICARD, Vernon; Rev. Msgr. LESZEK T. JANIK, J.C.L., V.G., Norwich; Very Revs. DAVID CHOQUETTE, Putnam; GREGORY P. GALVIN, Old Saybrook; Rev. BRIAN J. CONVERSE, New London; Very Rev. JAN SWIDERSKI, S.D.B., Middletown.

Diocesan Pastoral Council—Most Rev. MICHAEL R. COTE, D.D., Chm.; Rev. Msgr. LESZEK T. JANIK, J.C.L., V.G.; Very Rev. TED F. TUMICKI, S.T.L., J.C.L., J.V.; Rev. WALTER M. NAGLE; MR. TODD POSTLER; Rev. PETER J. LANGEVIN; MRS. ESPERANZA NUGENT; MR. STEPHEN ST. JOHN; MR. ELBERT BURR; MS. LOIS DUPOINTE; MR. GEORGE GORTON; MS. SANDRA GRILLO; MRS. BARBARA LALIBERTE; MR. KEENAN MARR; MR. ROLAND

BOURDON; MR. MICHAEL MCMANUS; MR. ALEXANDER TADAY.

Diocesan Historian—Mount Saint Mary College, 330 Powell Ave., Newburgh, NY 12550. Tel: 845-869-3154. Rev. GREGOIRE J. FLUET, Ph.D., K.H.S.

The Tribunal

Diocesan Tribunal—

Judicial Vicar—Very Rev. TED F. TUMICKI, S.T.L., J.C.L., J.V.

Associate Judicial Vicar—Rev. GEORGE J. RICHARDS JR., J.C.L.

Adjutant Judicial Vicar—Rev. BRIAN J. ROMANOWSKI, J.C.L.

Defenders of the Bond—Revs. JOSEPH CASTALDI, J.C.L., (Retired); GEORGE J. RICHARDS JR., J.C.L.

Judges—Rev. Msgrs. HENRY N. ARCHAMBAULT, P.A., J.C.D., (Retired); LESZEK T. JANIK, J.C.L., V.G.; Revs. GEORGE J. RICHARDS JR., J.C.L.; BRIAN J. ROMANOWSKI, J.C.L.; Very Rev. TED F. TUMICKI, S.T.L., J.C.L., J.V.; Sr. ELISSA RINERE, C.P., J.C.D.

Auditor/Assessors—BEATRICE L. THEROUX, Consecrated Secular, D.H.S.; Sr. ELISSA RINERE, C.P., J.C.D.; Rev. Msgr. RICHARD P. LAROCQUE, (Retired); Rev. BRIAN J. ROMANOWSKI, J.C.L.; MS. JACQUELINE M. KELLER, M.A.

Advocates—MS. JACQUELINE M. KELLER, M.A.; MRS. ANN MARIE OSOWSKI.

Administrative Assistant of the Tribunal—MR. DAVID OSTAFIN, Ph.D.

Notaries—Rev. Msgr. THOMAS R. BRIDE, P.A., K.C.H.S., (Retired); Rev. GEORGE J. RICHARDS JR., J.C.L.; MS. JACQUELINE M. KELLER, M.A.; MRS. ALICE PUDVAH; MRS. ANN MARIE OSOWSKI; MR. DAVID OSTAFIN, Ph.D.

Diocesan Offices, Ministries and Societies

Advisory Ministry Evaluation Committee—(see Properties & Assets Committee).

Annual Catholic Appeal (ACA)—See Development, Diocesan Office.

Bishop's Liaison with Retired Clergy—Very Rev. DENNIS M. PERKINS, The Chancery, 201 Broadway, Norwich, 06360-4458. Tel: 860-887-9294, Ext. 258.

Bishop's Delegate for Safe Environments—Rev. BRIAN J. ROMANOWSKI, J.C.L.

Vicar for Consecrated Life—St. John Church, 5 St. John Court, Cromwell, 06416-2118. Tel: 860-635-5590. Very Rev. MARK L. CURESKY, O.F.M.Conv.

Delegate for Internal Investigations—MR. RICHARD WHEELER.

Diocesan Finance Council—Most Rev. MICHAEL R. COTE, D.D., Chm.; Rev. Msgr. LESZEK T. JANIK, J.C.L., V.G.; MR. PETER LAMALFA; MR. JOHN HOMISKI; MR. ANTHONY JOYCE; MR. WILLIAM MCGURK; MR. TERRENCE CAHILL; MR. PETER SIPPLES, Attorney; MS. MARY CONWAY.

Diocesan Panel of Pastors, Canon 1742—Rev. Msgr. ANTHONY S. ROSAFORTE; Very Revs. DENNIS M. PERKINS; RICHARD J. RICARD.

Diocesan Pastoral Council—See Chancery listing.

Board of Education—See School Office.

Board of Conciliation and Arbitration—Rev. BRIAN J. ROMANOWSKI, J.C.L., Exec. Dir.

Campaigns—

Campaign for Human Development—201 Broadway, Norwich, 06360-4480. Tel: 860-887-9294, Ext. 234. MRS. ALICE PUDVAH.

Catholic Relief Services—Rev. PETER J. LANGEVIN, Dir.; MRS. BECKY CADY, 201 Broadway, Norwich, 06360-4328. Tel: 860-887-9294, Ext. 235.

Campus Ministry—Very Rev. LAURENCE A.M. LAPOINTE, Diocesan Dir., Newman Hall, 290 Prospect St., Willimantic, 06226. Tel: 860-423-0856; Fax: 860-456-8083. (See separate category under Institutions for details).

Middletown—Wesleyan University, 171 Church St., Middletown, 06459-3625. Rev. WILLIAM WALLACE, O.S.A., J.D.

New London—Connecticut College, P.O. Box 5203, New London, 06320-5203. Tel: 860-439-2452; Fax: 860-439-2463. Revs. ROBERT WASHABAUGH, College Chap.; JONATHAN J. FICARA, Catholic Chap.

Storrs—University of Connecticut: St. Thomas Aquinas Chapel, 46 N. Eagleville Rd., Storrs, 06268-1710. Rev. JOHN N. ANTONELLE, Chap., Pastor/Campus Min.

Willimantic—Eastern Connecticut State University, Newman Hall, 290 Prospect St., Willimantic, 06226-2304. Tel: 860-423-0856; Fax: 860-456-8083. Very Rev. LAURENCE A.M. LAPOINTE, Campus Min.; Rev. JONATHAN J. FICARA.

Catechetical Ministry—See Faith Events, Office of.

Catholic Charities, Diocese of Norwich, Inc.—

Executive Director—331 Main St., Norwich, 06360. Tel: 860-889-8346; Fax: 860-889-2658. MR. EDWARD TESSMAN, Exec. Dir.

Adoption Services & Education, Immigration Services & Education, Pregnancy Services & Education—TRACY MARTONE, 331 Main St., Norwich, 06360. Tel: 860-889-8346.

Behavioral Health Clinics—Norwich: 331 Main St., Norwich, 06360. Tel: 860-889-8346. *New London: 28 Huntington St., New London, 06320.* Tel: 860-443-5328. *Middletown: 151 Broad St., Middletown, 06457.* Tel: 860-346-0060. SHAUNA GOODWIN, Lead Clinician, Email: shunagoodwin@ccsfn.org.

Resource Development Manager—331 Main St., Norwich, 06360. Tel: 860-889-8346. CHRISTINE JACKEL.

Emergency Basic Needs—TRACY MARTONE, Family & Community Svcs. Senior Mgr., Norwich: 331 Main St., Norwich, 06360. Tel: 860-889-8346; Fax: 860-889-2658. New London: 28 Huntington St., New London, 06320. Tel: 860-443-5328; Fax: 860-443-6013. Willimantic: 88 Jackson St., P.O. Box 54, Willimantic, 06226. Tel: 860-423-7065; Fax: 860-456-1096.

Intensive Case Management—TRACY MARTONE, Family & Community Svcs. Senior Mgr., Norwich Office: 331 Main St., Norwich, 06360. Tel: 860-889-8346; Fax: 860-889-2658. New London Office: 28 Huntington St., New London, 06320. Tel: 860-443-5328; Fax: 860-443-6013. Willimantic Office: 88 Jackson St., Willimantic, 06226. Tel: 860-423-7065.

Parenting Education Program—Norwich Office: 331 Main St., Norwich, 06360. Tel: 860-889-8346; Fax: 860-889-2658. TERRI FONTAINE, PEP Supvr. Classes held in Middletown, New London, Norwich, and Willimantic.

Temporary Assistance for Needy Families (TANF)—MARIEMGELIE RUIZ-LOMBARY, Case Mgr., 88 Jackson St., Willimantic, 06226. Tel: 860-423-7065; Fax: 860-456-1096.

Catholic Mutual Relief Society—Diocesan Property and Liability Insurance, MS. ROBIN HOLTSCLAW, Claims/Risk Mgr., Email: rholtsclaw@catholicmutual.org. Office for all claims: Catholic Mutual Group, 467 Bloomfield Ave., Bloomfield, 06002. Tel: 800-331-2561; Fax: 860-726-9412. National Office: Catholic Mutual Relief Society, 10843 Old Mill Rd., Omaha, NE 68154. Tel: 800-228-6108; Fax: 402-551-2943.

Catholic Youth Organization (CYO)—See Faith Events, Office of.

Cemetery Corporation and Subsidiaries, Diocesan Cemeteries—MR. JOSEPH M. MUSCARELLA, Dir. Diocesan Properties & Cemeteries; MS. JENNIFER FOWLER, Office Admin. Properties & Cemeteries, 815 Boswell Ave., Norwich, 06360-2536. Tel: 860-887-1019; Fax: 860-889-4804. (For details on individual cemeteries see separate listing); The following cemeteries are subsidiaries of the Norwich Diocesan Cemetery Corp.; MR. EDWARD COLBRIDGE, Foreman.

Moosup—All Hallows Cemetery, Green Hallow Rd., Moosup, 06354. Cemetery Office: 815 Boswell Ave., Norwich, 06360-2536. Tel: 860-887-1019.

New London—St. Mary Cemetery of New London Corp., 600 Jefferson Ave., New London, 06320-2412. Tel: 860-443-3465 (Office). Properties & Cemeteries Foreman: ROBERT MCDONALD.

Norwich—St. Mary & St. Joseph Cemetery Corp., 815 Boswell Ave., Norwich, 06360-2536. Tel: 860-887-1019.

Taftville—Sacred Heart Cemetery Corp., Harland Rd., Taftville, 06380. Cemetery Office, 815 Boswell Ave., Norwich, 06360-2536. Tel: 860-887-1019.

Uncasville—St. Patrick Cemetery, Depot Rd., Uncasville, 06382. Cemetery Office, 815 Boswell Ave., Norwich, 06360-2536. Tel: 860-887-1019.

Wauregan—Sacred Heart Cemetery, Wauregan Rd., Wauregan, 06387. Cemetery Office: 815 Boswell Ave., Norwich, 06360-2536. Tel: 860-887-1019.

Westbrook—Resurrection Cemetery Corp., Rte. 145, Westbrook, 06498. Tel: 860-399-6503 (Cemetery Office).

Censor of Books—Very Rev. LAURENCE A.M. LAPOINTE, St. Joseph Church, 99 Jackson St., Willimantic, 06226. Tel: 860-423-8439.

Communications, Office of—31 Perkins Ave., Norwich, 06360-3613. Tel: 860-887-3933; Fax: 860-859-1253; Web: www.norwichdiocese.org. MR. WAYNE GIGNAC, Email: wgignac@norwichdiocese.net; MS. MEREDITH MORRISON, Administrative Asst.

Four County Catholic—Official monthly newspaper of the Diocese of Norwich: (No July issue). *31 Perkins Ave., Norwich, 06360-3613.* Tel: 860-886-1281; Fax: 860-859-1253.

Publisher—Most Rev. MICHAEL R. COTE, D.D., Bishop of Norwich.

Executive Editor—MR. WAYNE GIGNAC.

Theological Advisor—Very Rev. TED F. TUMICKI, S.T.L., J.C.L., J.V.

Community Ministries—

Middletown—MS. ETHEL HIGGINS, Exec. Dir.; TERRY CARBONE, Housing Dir., St. Vincent de Paul, 617 Main St., P.O. Box 398, Middletown, 06457-0398. Tel: 860-344-0097; Fax: 860-343-0023; Web: www.svdmiddletown.org.

Norwich—JILLIAN CORBIN, Exec. Dir., Email: jcsvdpp@gmail.com; BONNIE YACKOVETSKY, Administrative Asst., St. Vincent de Paul Place, Norwich, Inc., 120 Cliff St., Norwich, 06360. Tel: 860-889-7374; Fax: 860-886-0178; Email: bysvdpp@gmail.com; Web: www.svdpp.org.

Connecticut Catholic Conference—MICHAEL CARROLL CULHANE, Exec. Dir.; Deacon DAVID REYNOLDS, Legislative Liaison, Connecticut Catholic Conference, 134 Farmington Ave., Hartford, 06105-3784. Tel: 860-524-7882; Fax: 860-525-0750; Email: ccc@ctcatholic.org; Web: www.ctcatholic.org.

Continuing Education and Formation Commission for the Clergy—Rev. GRZEGORZ P. BROZONOWICZ; Very Rev. DAVID P. CHOQUETTE; Revs. PETER B. LISZEWSKI; WALTER M. NAGLE; Very Rev. DENNIS M. PERKINS; Rev. JOHN N. ANTONELLE.

Council of Catholic Women—MRS. JUDITH K. PAPPAGALLO, Pres.; Rev. BRIAN MAXWELL, Diocesan Spiritual Advisor, St. Agnes Church, 22 Haigh Ave., Niantic, 06357. Tel: 860-739-9722. District Spiritual Advisors: Revs. JOHN N. ANTONELLE, Willimantic Deanery; STEPHEN S. GULINO, Norwich Deanery; DENNIS J. MERCIERI, New London Deanery; Very Rev. DAVID P. CHOQUETTE, Putnam Deanery; Revs. P. GRZEGORZ JEDNAKI, Rockville Deanery; JOSEPH F. DECOSTA, Shoreline Deanery; JAMES THAIKOOTTATHIL, S.T.L., J.C.D., Middletown Deanery.

Development, Diocesan Office of (DOD)—MRS. MARY ELLEN MAHONEY, Exec. Dir. & Devel. Mgr./Major Gifts, Tel: 860-886-1928, Ext. 14; Fax: 860-886-2651; Email: memahoney@norwichdiocese.net; Email: dod@norwichdiocese.net; SUSAN UNDERHILL, Campaign Mgr., Tel: 860-886-1928, Ext. 11; ROSELA PRECOPIO, Administrative Asst., 197 Broadway, Norwich, 06360-4407. Tel: 860-886-1928, Ext. 10.

Annual Catholic Appeal (ACA)—(See Development, Diocesan Office).

Stewardship Office—197 Broadway, Norwich, 06360. MRS. MARY ELLEN MAHONEY, Dir., Tel: 860-886-1928, Ext. 14; Email: dod@norwichdiocese.net; MRS. KATHY GAITO, Coord., Tel: 860-886-1928, Ext. 15; Email: kgaito@norwichdiocese.net.

The Catholic Foundation—MRS. MARY ELLEN MAHONEY, Dir., Tel: 860-886-1928, Ext. 14; Email: dod@norwichdiocese.net.

Catholic Family Services—199 Broadway, Norwich, 06360. Tel: 860-848-2237, Ext. 306. MRS. MARY-JO MCLAUGHLIN, Coord.

Deaf Ministry—199 Broadway, Norwich, 06360. Tel: 860-848-2237, Ext. 312. MRS. ANDREA HOISL, Coord.

One Heart Ministry—199 Broadway, Norwich, 06360. Tel: 860-848-2237, Ext. 312. MRS. ANDREA HOISL, Dir.

Office of Diocesan Properties & Cemeteries—MR. JOSEPH M. MUSCARELLA, Dir., 815 Boswell Ave., Norwich, 06360. Tel: 860-887-1019.

Disabilities-People with—See His Able People, Ministry of.

Ecumenism—

Ecumenical and Interreligious Affairs, Office of—Inquires should be made to: 201 Broadway, Norwich, 06360. Tel: 860-887-9294, Ext. 100. VACANT.

Evangelization & Catechumenate (RCIA), Office of—See Office of Faith Events.

Faith Events, Office of—199 Broadway, Norwich, 06360. Tel: 860-848-2237, Ext. 312; Fax: 860-848-2816; Email: faithevents@norwichdiocese.net. MRS. ANDREA HOISL, Dir.; MS. LIZA ROACH, Youth & Young Adult Min., Tel: 860-848-2237, Ext. 305; MRS. MARIANNE NICHOLAS, Administrative Asst., Tel: 860-848-2237, Ext. 304; Email: manicholas@norwichdiocese.net. Advisory Board: Deacon PETER L. GILL, Chm.; MRS. DIANE LETENDRE; MRS. KATHLEEN IRR; MR. TRAVIS MORAN; Deacon DAN D'AMELIO; MR. PETER SIMONCINI; Deacon WILLIAM H. MCGANN; MRS. BRIDGET THURSTON.

Diocesan Catholic Scouting— Tel: 860-848-2237, Ext. 311; Email: scouting@norwichdiocese.net. PAM PLASSE, Chair.

Faith Formation, Office for—See Office of Faith Events.

Four County Catholic—See Newspaper.

Haiti, Diocese of Norwich Outreach to, Inc.—a successor corporation of the two merged corporations, Haitian Ministries for the Diocese of Norwich and Hospice St. Joseph for the Diocese of Norwich. MR. DANIEL O'SULLIVAN, Dir. Administration & Prog., 815 Boswell Ave., Norwich, 06360. Tel: 860-887-1019; Email: osullivan@outreachtohaiti.org.

Chaplain and Director of Twinning in Haiti—Rev. FRANCIS ROULEAU.

His Able People, Ministry of—A ministry for persons with disabilities. *Inquiries should be made to: 199 Broadway, Norwich, 06360.* Tel: 860-848-2237, Ext. 312.

Hispanic Ministry—Mother MARY JUDE LAZARUS, S.C.M.C., Diocesan Dir., Hispanic Apostolate Office, 61 Club Rd., Windham, 06280-1007. Tel: 860-456-3349; Fax: 860-423-4157; Email: aposthispano@juno.com.

Hispanic Ministry Board—Rev. ROBERT WASHABAUGH; Very Rev. LAURENCE A.M. LAPOINTE; Revs. GEORGE J. RICHARDS JR., J.C.L.; L. HENRY AGUDELO; JUAN ANGEL AGUIRRE; Revs. JONATHAN J. FICARA; RUSSELL F. KENNEDY; MARK D. O'DONNELL; Sisters GLORIA SALDARRIAGA, R.O.D.A.; LEIDY CASTILLO, R.O.D.A.; Mother MARY JUDE LAZARUS, S.C.M.C.; Sr. XINIA RODRIGUEZ, R.O.D.A.; MRS. ZOILA DIAZ; MRS. MARIA TORRES; Deacon MARIO RAMOS; MR. VERTILIO RAMOS; MR. GEBERTH GAMBOA; MRS. ZULMA GAMBOA; MRS. IRIS FERNANDEZ; MR. DAVID FERNANDEZ.

Clinton—

St. Mary of the Visitation Church - Spanish Apostolate—Rev. MICHAEL C. GIANNITELLI, Pastor, 54 Grove St., Clinton, 06413-1999. Tel: 860-669-8512; Fax: 860-669-9052.

Middletown—

St. Francis of Assisi Church - Spanish Apostolate—10 Elm St., Middletown, 06457-4426. Tel: 860-347-4684; Fax: 860-347-7669. Rev. RUSSELL F. KENNEDY, Pastor; Deacon OCTAVIO FLORES; Sr. GLORIA SALDARRIAGA, R.O.D.A., Pastoral Assoc., Res.: 28 River Ave., Norwich, 06360. Tel: 860-886-6092.

New London—

St. Mary, Star of the Sea Church - Spanish Apostolate—10 Huntington St., New London, 06320-6198. Tel: 860-447-1431; Fax: 860-437-1889; Email: stmarysnl@aol.com. Sr. ZINIA RODRIGUES, R.O.D.A., Pastoral Assoc.; Revs. MARK D. O'DONNELL, Pastor; HENRY AGUDELO, Parochial Vicar; Deacon JESUS A. DIEZ-CANSECO, Tel: 860-443-2364.

Norwich—

St. Mary Church - Spanish Apostolate—Rev. ROBERT WASHABAUGH; Sr. LEIDY CASTILLO, R.O.D.A., Pastoral Assoc., 70 Central Ave., Norwich, 06360-4794. Tel: 860-887-2565.

Windham—

Iglesia del Sagrado Corazon de Jesus—61 Club Rd., Windham, 06280-1007. Very Rev. LAURENCE A.M. LAPOINTE, Pastor; JUAN ANGEL AGUIRRE, Parochial Vicar; Rev. JONATHAN J. FICARA, Parochial Vicar. Pastoral Associates: Sr. LEIDY CASTILLO, R.O.D.A.; Deacon FELIPE SILVA, 61 Club Rd., Windham, 06280-1007. Tel: 860-423-8617; Fax: 860-423-4157.

Holy Childhood—See Pontifical Association of the Holy Childhood.

Holy Name Societies—Address all mail to: *Holy Name Societies, 201 Broadway, Norwich, 06360-4328.* Tel: 860-887-9294.

Insurance—See Catholic Mutual Relief Society (C.M.R.S.).

Office of Internal Affairs—201 Broadway, Norwich, 06360-4480. Tel: 800-624-7407; Tel: 860-889-4455. MR. RICHARD WHEELER, Bishop's Delegate for Internal Investigations; MS. TRACY KNIGHT, Assistance Coord.

Justice & Peace—(see Office of Faith Events, 199 Broadway, Norwich, CT 06360. Tel. 860-848-2237, ext. 312.

Lawyers, Guild of Catholic—Mailing Address: 201 Broadway, Norwich, 06360-4328. Tel: 860-887-9294. MICHAEL E. DRISCOLL ESQ., Pres.; Rev. Msgr. HENRY N. ARCHAMBAULT, P.A., J.C.D., Chap., (Retired); MRS. TERRI ZAMPINI, Sec., Tel: 860-887-9294, Ext. 265.

Legion of Mary—St. Mary, Star of the Sea, 10 Huntington St., New London, 06320. Tel: 860-447-1431. Rev. VICTOR CHAKER, Diocesan Spiritual Dir., (Retired).

Marriage Encounter/Catholic Charities/Family Life Office—(See Catholic Charities & Family Services).

Mercy Xavier Fund—Bro. BRIAN DAVIS, C.F.X., Pres., 181 Randolph Rd., Middletown, 06457. Tel: 860-347-2343; Tel: 860-346-7735.

Newspaper—Official monthly newspaper of Diocese of Norwich–"Four County Catholic" *31 Perkins Ave., Norwich, 06360.* Tel: 860-886-1281. Most Rev. MICHAEL R. COTE, D.D., Publisher; Very Rev. TED F. TUMICKI, S.T.L., J.C.L., J.V., Theological Advisor.

Pastoral Planning, Office of—199 Broadway, Norwich, 06360. Tel: 860-848-2237, Ext. 203; Fax: 860-848-2816. VACANT. Advisory Board: Very Revs. DAVID CHOQUETTE; LAURENCE A.M. LAPOINTE; Revs. MARK D. O'DONNELL; JOHN N. ANTONELLE; ROLAND C. CLOUTIER, L.C.S.W., (Retired); PETER J. LANGEVIN; Deacon GERARD J. GAYNOR.

People with Disabilities—(See His Able People, Ministry of).

Planned Giving Office—See Development, Diocesan Office of.

Pontifical Association of the Holy Childhood—201 Broadway, Norwich, 860-887-9294. Tel: 860-887-9294. Rev. P. GRZEGORZ JEDNAKI.

Pontifical Society for the Propagation of the FaithSt. Philip the Apostle Church, 64 Pompey Hollow Rd., Ashford, 06278-1540. Tel: 860-429-2860; Email: stphilipstjude@gmail.com. Rev. P. GRZEGORZ JEDNAKI, Diocesan Dir.

Prison Ministry for Diocese of Norwich—199 Broadway, Norwich, 06360. Tel: 860-848-2237, Ext. 211; Fax: 860-848-2816; Email: prison@norwichdiocese.net. Deacon CHRISTOPHER DESKUS, Dir.

Brooklyn—

Brooklyn Correctional Institution—59 Hartford Rd., Brooklyn, 06234. Tel: 860-779-4568. Deacon CHRISTOPHER DESKUS, Chap.

Niantic—

York Correctional Institution—201 W. Main, Niantic, 06357. Tel: 860-691-6529. Rev. ZACHARIAS PUSHPANATHAN, Chap.

Somers—

Northern Correctional Institution—287 Bilton Rd., Somers, 06071. Tel: 860-763-8686. Deacon HENRY J. SZUMOWSKI, Chap.

Osborn Correctional Institution—100 Bilton Rd., Somers, 06071. Tel: 860-749-8391, Ext. 5476. Chaplains: Rev. ROBERT VUJS, M.M.; Deacons RAMON ROSADO; HENRY J. SZUMOWSKI.

Willard-Cybulski Correctional Institution—391 Shaker Rd., Enfield, 06082. Tel: 860-763-6100. Rev. ZACHARIAS PUSHPANATHAN, Chap.; Deacon MICHAEL TORRES.

Uncasville—

Corrigan-Radgowski Correctional Institution—986 Norwich-New London Tpke., Uncasville, 06382. Tel: 860-848-5034. Rev. ZACHARIAS PUSHPANATHAN, Chap.; Deacon CHRISTOPHER DESKUS, Chap.

Property and Assets Committee—MS. KAREN HUFFER; MR. JOSEPH M. MUSCARELLA; Deacon RENE N. BARBEAU JR.; MR. PETER A. HARDING; MS. ROBIN HOTLSCLAW.

Pro-Life Activities—Christ the King Church, 1 McCurdy Rd., Old Lyme, 06371-1629. Tel: 860-434-1669. Rev. WALTER M. NAGLE, Dir.

RCIA—See Evangelization & Catechumenate, Office of.

Religious—See Delegate for Consecrated Life.

Retirement—

Priests' Retirement Plan Board—Most Rev. MICHAEL R. COTE, D.D.; Very Rev. DENNIS M. PERKINS; Rev. Msgr. LESZEK T. JANIK, J.C.L., V.G.; Very Rev. RICHARD J. RICARD.

Safe Environments, Office of—199 Broadway, Norwich, 06360. Tel: 860-848-2237; Email: ose@norwichdiocese.net. Rev. BRIAN J. ROMANOWSKI, J.C.L., Bishop's Delegate; MRS. KAREN CAISE, Dir., Tel: 860-848-2237, Ext. 212; MRS. RANDY BOULEY, Tel: 860-848-2237, Ext. 212; Email: rbouley@norwichdiocese.net.

School Office, Diocesan—43 Perkins Ave., Norwich, 06360-4480. Tel: 860-887-4086; Fax: 860-887-9371; Web: www.norwichdso.org. MR. HENRY FIORE JR., Supt., Email: superintendentdso@norwichdiocese.net; Sr. BARBARA GOULD, R.S.M., Educ. Consultant, Email: asstsuperdso@norwichdiocese.net; MS. CAROL BENEVIDES.

Scouting—(See Faith Events, Office of).

Sick, Ministry to the—Sr. RITA JOHNSON, S.S.N.D., Dir., W.W. Backus Hospital, 326 Washington St., Norwich, 06360-2742. Tel: 860-889-8331, Ext. 2298. Res.: 7 Otis St., Norwich, 06360. Tel: 860-886-6948.

Soup Kitchen—(See Community Ministries, Saint Vincent de Paul Place). Email: svdpp@sbcglobal.net.

Spanish Speaking Apostolate—(See Hispanic Ministry).

Spiritual Renewal Services—Co-Directors: Rev. RAYMOND D. INTOVIGNE, Rectory: 156 Providence St., P.O. Box 208, Taftville, 06380. Tel: 860-887-3072; MRS. JUDITH HUGHES, Office, 11 Bath St., P.O. Box 6, Norwich, 06360-5836. Tel: 860-887-0702; Tel: 860-887-7667 Prayer Line; Fax: 860-859-1366; Email: srs1223@sbcglobal.net.

Victim Assistance Coordinator—Tel: 800-624-7407. MS. TRACY KNIGHT.

Vocation—Very Rev. GREGORY P. GALVIN, Dir.; MRS. TERRI ZAMPINI, Sec. to Dir., 201 Broadway, Norwich, 06360-4328. Tel: 860-887-9294, Ext. 265. Res.: St. Bridget of Kildare, 75 Moodus - Leesville Rd., P.O. Box 422, Moodus, 06469. Email: vocations@norwichdiocese.net; Email: sec.voc@norwichdiocese.net.

Seminarian Advisory Board—Very Revs. GREGORY P. GALVIN; DENNIS M. PERKINS; Rev. Msgr. LESZEK T. JANIK, J.C.L., V.G.; Revs. KEVIN M. REILLY; JAMES J. SUCHOLET; Very Rev. RICHARD J. RICARD; Rev. JOSEPH TITO.

Worship, Office of—199 Broadway, Norwich, 06360. Tel: 860-848-2237, Ext. 203; Fax: 860-848-2816. VACANT, Dir. Liturgical Commission: Deacon PETER L. GILL; MRS. NANCY MIGNAULT; MR. DOUGLAS GREEN; MS. CONNIE BUTLER; MR. HOWARD DRYE.

CLERGY, PARISHES, MISSIONS AND PAROCHIAL SCHOOLS

CITY OF NORWICH

(NEW LONDON COUNTY)

1—ST. PATRICK CATHEDRAL (1879)
213 Broadway, 06360-4307. Tel: 860-889-8441; Fax: 860-889-2978; Email: stpatricknorwich@sbcglobal.net; Web: stpatsnorwich.org. Rev. Msgr. Anthony S. Rosaforte, Rector; Revs. Peter J. Langevin, Parochial Vicar; Brian J. Romanowski, J.C.L., In Res.
School—St. Patrick Cathedral School, 211 Broadway, 06360. Tel: 860-889-4174; Web: www.st-patrickschoolnorwich.org; Fax: 860-889-0040; Email: info@st-patrickschoolnorwich.org. Mrs. Catherine Reed, Prin. Lay Teachers 16; Students 169.
Catechesis Religious Program—Students 128.

2—ST. JOSEPH (1904) (Polish) Yoked with SS Peter and Paul Norwich and St. Mary, Norwich.
120 Cliff St., 06360-5134. Tel: 860-887-1565; Email: stjosephnorwich@yahoo.com; Web: jnccfaith.org. Revs. Robert J. Washabaugh; Tomasz Albrecht, Parochial Vicar.
Catechesis Religious Program—Tel: 860-887-4565. Held at SS. Peter & Paul Church, 181 Elizabeth St., Norwich, CT 06360 (860-887-9857).

3—ST. MARY (1845) Yoked with SS Peter & Paul, Norwich and St. Joseph, Norwich.
70 Central Ave., 06360-4794. Tel: 860-887-2565; Email: secretary@stmarys1845.org. Revs. Robert J. Washabaugh; Tomasz Albrecht; Sisters Leidy Castillo, R.O.D.A., Pastoral Assoc. Hispanic Min.; Yannick Saieh, Pastoral Assoc. Haitian Ministry.
Catechesis Religious Program—Tel: 860-204-9875. Students 50.

4—SS. PETER AND PAUL (1938) Yoked with St. Joseph, Norwich, CT and St. Mary, Norwich, CT.
181 Elizabeth St., 06360-6199. Tel: 860-887-9857; Fax: 860-886-4728; Email: sspnorwich@yahoo.com; Web: jnccfaith.org. Revs. Robert Washabaugh; Tomasz Albrecht, Parochial Vicar.
Catechesis Religious Program—Students 59.

5—SACRED HEART (Norwichtown) (1902)
52 W. Town St., Norwichtown, 06360-2296. Tel: 860-887-1030; Fax: 860-887-6550; Email: sacredheart06360@gmail.com. Rev. Msgr. Leszek T. Janik; Deacon Wayne Sinclair.
Catechesis Religious Program—Tel: 860-887-1715. Eric von Tish, C.R.E. Students 25.
Mission—St. John, 190 Fitchville Rd., Bozrah, New London Co. 06334.

OUTSIDE THE CITY OF NORWICH

ASHFORD, WINDHAM CO., ST. PHILIP THE APOSTLE (1937) [CEM 2]
64 Pompey Hollow Rd., Ashford, 06278-1540. Tel: 860-429-2860; Fax: 860-487-5703; Email: stphilipstjude@gmail.com; Web: www.saintphilipsaintjude.org. Rev. P. Grzegorz Jednaki.
Catechesis Religious Program—Raymond Potter, D.R.E., Email: pottersowl@att.net. Students 45.

BALLOUVILLE, WINDHAM CO., ST. ANNE (1882) Closed. For inquiries for parish records contact St. Joseph, Dayville.

BALTIC, NEW LONDON CO., ST. MARY OF THE IMMACULATE CONCEPTION (1866) [CEM] Yoked with St. Joseph, Occum and Sacred Heart, Taftville.
70 W. Main St., Baltic, 06330-1348.
Tel: 860-822-6378; Email: saintjosephschool@att.net. Revs. Joseph Tito; Christopher J. Zmuda, Th.Psy.D., Parochial Vicar.
School—St. Joseph, 10 School Hill Rd., Baltic, 06330. Tel: 860-822-6141; Fax: 860-822-1479; Email: st33@snet.net. Sr. Mary Patrick Mulready, S.C.M.C., Prin. Clergy 1; Lay Teachers 7; Sisters of Charity of Our Lady, Mother of the Church 2; Students 56.
Catechesis Religious Program—Students 51.

BOLTON, TOLLAND CO., ST. MAURICE (1954)
32 Hebron Rd., Bolton, 06043-7606.
Tel: 860-643-4466; Fax: 860-643-8374; Email: saintmauricechurchbolton@gmail.com. Rev. Leon J. Susaimanickam, Admin.
Catechesis Religious Program—Students 36.

BROOKLYN, WINDHAM CO., OUR LADY OF LA SALETTE (1968)
Mailing Address: 21 Providence Rd., P.O. Box 211, Brooklyn, 06234-0211. Tel: 860-774-6275; Email: ourladybrooklyn@gmail.com. Rev. Ben Vinjoe, Admin.
Catechesis Religious Program—Tel: 401-529-8781; Email: elizabethnaultcosta@gmail.com. Elizabeth Costa, D.R.E. Students 33.
Mission—Our Lady of Lourdes, 41 Cedar Swamp Rd., Hampton, Windham Co. 06247.

CANTERBURY, WINDHAM CO., ST. AUGUSTINE (1978) Yoked with St. John the Apostle, Plainfield, All Hallows & Moosup
144 Westminster Rd., Canterbury, 06331-1417.
Tel: 860-564-3313; Email: secstaugus@gmail.com. Rev. Tadeusz Zadorozny, (Poland); Deacon Timothy M. Marshall.

CHESTER, MIDDLESEX CO., ST. JOSEPH (1885) [CEM] Yoked with Our Lady of Sorrows, Essex.
48 Middlesex Ave., Chester, 06412-1309.
Tel: 860-526-5495; Email: officeolos@comcast.net. Rev. Arul Rajan Peter; Deacon Lawrence Moneypenny.
Catechesis Religious Program—Tel: 860-526-2152. Students 118.

CLINTON, MIDDLESEX CO., ST. MARY CHURCH OF THE VISITATION (1934) [CEM]
54 Grove St., Clinton, 06413-1999. Tel: 860-669-8512 ; Fax: 860-669-9052; Email: godsquad@snet.net; Web: stmarysclinton.com. Rev. Michael C. Giannitelli.
Catechesis Religious Program—Tel: 860-669-7375. Peggy Abbott, C.R.E.; Margo Burke, Youth Min. Students 373.

COLCHESTER, NEW LONDON CO., ST. ANDREW (1860) [CEM 2] [JC2] Yoked with St. Francis of Assisi, Lebanon.
128 Norwich Ave., Colchester, 06415-1269.
Tel: 860-537-2355; Email: parishoffice@standrewofcolchester.org. Revs. Marek Masnicki; Richard D. Breton; Deacon Michael L. Puscas.
Catechesis Religious Program—Tel: 860-537-5415; Email: religioused@standrewofcolchester.org. Ron Kristofik, D.R.E. Students 329.

COLUMBIA, TOLLAND CO., ST. COLUMBA (1960) Yoked with Church of the Holy Family, Hebron.
328 Junction Rts. 66 and 87, P.O. Box 146, Columbia, 06237-0146. Very Rev. Michael L. Phillippino.
Catechesis Religious Program—Students 51.

COVENTRY, TOLLAND CO., ST. MARY (1877) [CEM] Yoked with St. Thomas Aquinas, Storrs.
1600 Main St., Coventry, 06238-0250.
Tel: 860-742-0681; Fax: 860-742-1318; Email: secretarystmarycoventry@gmail.com. Rev. John N. Antonelle.
Catechesis Religious Program—Tel: 860-742-0681; Email: secretarystmarycoventry@gmail.com. Students 172.

CROMWELL, MIDDLESEX CO., ST. JOHN (1882)
5 St. Johns Court, Cromwell, 06416-2118.
Tel: 860-635-5590; Fax: 860-635-5591; Email: pastormarkc@yahoo.com; Web: www.saintjohn-cromwell.org. Very Rev. Mark L. Curesky, O.F.M.-Conv.; Fr. Jerzy Auguscik, Parochial Vicar.
Catechesis Religious Program—Tel: 860-635-5156; Email: sjcffdre@gmail.com. Karen Romegialli, D.R.E. Students 86.

DANIELSON, WINDHAM CO., ST. JAMES (1869) [CEM]
12 Franklin St., Danielson, 06239. Tel: 860-774-3900 ; Email: stjames_parish@yahoo.com. Revs. John J. O'Neill, M.S.; Thomas G. Sickler, M.S., (Retired); John E. Welch, M.S., In Res., (Retired); Deacon Rene N. Barbeau Jr.
School—St. James School, (Grades PreK-8),
Tel: 860-774-3281; Fax: 860-779-2137; Email: c.benoit@stjamesdanielson.org; Email: l.joyal@stjamesdanielson.org; Web: www.stjamesdanielson.org. Deacon Rene N. Barbeau Jr., Head of School; Linda Joyal, Prin. Lay Teachers 15; Students 192.
Catechesis Religious Program—Tel: 860-774-8459. Students 230.

DAYVILLE, WINDHAM CO., ST. JOSEPH (1874) [CEM] Closed. For inquiries for parish records, contact St. James, Danielson.

DURHAM, MIDDLESEX CO., NOTRE DAME (1955) Yoked with St. Colman, Middlefield.
272 Main St., Durham, 06422-1611.
Tel: 860-349-3058; Email: scndchurches@comcast.net; Web: www.churchofnotredame.org. Rev. Jan Swiderski; Deacon Peter L. Gill.
Catechesis Religious Program—Tel: 860-349-3059; Email: drendc@comcast.net. Mrs. Kum Cha Soja, D.R.E. Students 248.

EAST HAMPTON, MIDDLESEX CO., ST. PATRICK (1879) [CEM] (Irish) Yoked with st. Bridget of Kildare, Moodus.
47 W. High St., East Hampton, 06424.
Tel: 860-267-6644; Fax: 860-267-7807; Email: stpatrick47@sbcglobal.net. Very Rev. Gregory P. Galvin; Sr. Dominic Joseph Valla, A.S.C.J., Pastoral Assoc.
Catechesis Religious Program—Students 329.

EAST LYME, NEW LONDON CO., ST. MATTHIAS (Flanders) (1939) Yoked with Saint Agnes, Niantic.
317 Chesterfield Rd., East Lyme, 06333.
Tel: 860-739-5208; Fax: 860-739-0524; Email: matthiasel@aol.com. Revs. Gregory C. Mullaney, Admin.; Brian Maxwell; Deacon Steven Reed
Saint Matthias Church Corporation
Res.: 186 Chesterfield Rd., P.O. Box 25, East Lyme, 06333-0025.
Catechesis Religious Program—Email: kathy@kathymirr.com; Email: gregg.r.d.kelly@pfizer.com; Email: holymartyrsyouthministry@gmail.com. Mrs. Kathleen Irr, D.R.E.; Gregg Kelly, D.R.E.; Rebecca Holmes, D.R.E. Students 224.

ELLINGTON, TOLLAND CO., ST. LUKE (1961)
141 Maple St., P.O. Box 246, Ellington, 06029-0246. Tel: 860-875-8552; Email: stluke_ellington@comcast.net. Revs. George Villamthanam, C.S.T.; Bijoy Joseph, Parochial Vicar; Deacons Harry Grospitch; Frank Hann.
Church: 139 Maple St., Ellington, 06029.
Catechesis Religious Program—Tel: 860-875-4951; Email: stlukedre@comcast.net. Mrs. Nancy Rudek, D.R.E. Students 233.

ESSEX, MIDDLESEX CO., OUR LADY OF SORROWS (1926) Yoked with St. Joseph Church, Chester.
14 Prospect St., Essex, 06426-1049.
Tel: 860-767-1284; Email: officeolos@comcast.net. Rev. Arul Rajan Peter; Deacon William Kaiser Jr.
Catechesis Religious Program—Tel: 860-767-1074. Students 172.

FISHERS ISLAND, SUFFOLK CO., OUR LADY OF GRACE (1902) Yoked with St. Joseph Church, New London and St. Mary Star of the Sea, New London.
P.O. Box 425, Fishers Island, NE 06390.
Tel: 631-788-7353; Fax: 631-788-7312; Email: olog@fishersisland.net; Email: sjc.secretary@yahoo.com. Revs. Mark D. O'Donnell, Canonical Pastor; Anthony J. DiMarco; Henry Agudelo.
Res.: 914 Montauk Ave., New London, 06320.
Catechesis Religious Program—Students 6.

GALES FERRY, NEW LONDON CO., OUR LADY OF LOURDES (1960)
1650 Rte. 12, Gales Ferry, 06335-1534.
Tel: 860-464-7251; Email: pastor@ololgf.org; Web: www.ololgf.org. Rev. Brian J. Converse; Deacon William H. McGann.
Catechesis Religious Program—Josephine Cometa, D.R.E. Students 150.

GROTON, NEW LONDON CO.

1—ST. MARY MOTHER OF THE REDEEMER (1964) Yoked with Sacred Heart Church, Groton.
69 Groton Long Point Rd., Groton, 06340.
Tel: 860-445-1446; Email: office@stmarysgroton.org. Rev. Dariusz K. Dudzik, J.C.L.; Deacons Paul Wallen; Douglas A. Hoffman.
Catechesis Religious Program—Tel: 860-448-0529. Mrs. Barbara Simoncini, D.R.E.; Mrs. Theresa Seals, D.R.E. Students 179.

2—SACRED HEART (1905) Yoked with St. Mary Mother of the Redeemer Church, Groton.
56 Sacred Heart Dr., Groton, 06340-4431.
Tel: 896-445-2905; Email: secretary@sacredheartgroton.org. Rev. Dariusz Dudzik, J.C.L.; Deacon Douglas A. Hoffman.
School—Sacred Heart School, (Grades PreK-8), 50 Sacred Heart Dr., Groton, 06340-4431.
Tel: 460-445-0611; Fax: 860-448-4999; Email: principal@sacredheartgroton.org; Web: sacredheartgroton.org. Dr. Gail Kingston, Prin. Aides 5; Lay Teachers 16; Students 168.
Catechesis Religious Program—
Tel: 860-445-2905, Ext. 12; Email: dre@sacredheartgroton.org. Mrs. Ann G. Crooks, D.R.E. Students 143.

HEBRON, TOLLAND CO., THE CHURCH OF THE HOLY FAMILY (1987) Yoked with St. Columba Church, Columbia.
Mailing Address: P.O. Box 146, Hebron, 06248-0146.
Tel: 860-228-0096; Fax: 860-228-1629; Email: parishadmin@comcast.net. Very Rev. Michael L. Phillippino; Nicole Bernier, Dir. Music; Dennis Chanski, Business Mgr.
Catechesis Religious Program—
Tel: 860-228-0096, Ext. 3. Ashley Dombrowski, C.R.E. Students 348.

HIGGANUM, MIDDLESEX CO., ST. PETER (1958) Yoked with St. Lawrence, Killingworth.
30 St. Peter Ln., P.O. Box 707, Higganum, 06441-0707. Tel: 860-345-8018; Fax: 860-345-4067; Email: stpeterhigganum@yahoo.com. Rev. Joseph F. DeCosta.
Catechesis Religious Program—Tel: 860-345-4992.

JEWETT CITY, NEW LONDON CO., ST. MARY (1872) [CEM 2] (Polish) Yoked with St. Catherine of Siena, Preston & SS. Thomas & Anne, Voluntown.
34 N. Main St., Jewett City, 06351-2012.
Tel: 860-376-2044; Email: saintmary.secretary@yahoo.com. Very Rev. Ted F. Tumicki, S.T.L., J.C.L., J.V.; Rev. Stephen S. Gulino; Deacons Paul R. Baillargeon; Bryan Jones.
Catechesis Religious Program—31 N. Main St., Jewett City, 06351. Fax: 860-376-5771. Students 104.

KILLINGWORTH, MIDDLESEX CO., ST. LAWRENCE (1978) Yoked with St. Peter, Higganum.
7 Hemlock Dr., Killingworth, 06419-2227.
Tel: 860-663-2576; Email: stlawrencec@yahoo.com; Web: www.stlawrencechurch.com. Revs. Joseph F. DeCosta; Martin J. Jones, Parochial Vicar; Deacons John A. Balchus; Robert Ferraro.
Catechesis Religious Program—Email: st.lawrencedre@yahoo.com. Mrs. Eileen Boulay, Business Mgr. Students 113.

LEBANON, NEW LONDON CO., ST. FRANCIS OF ASSISI (1945) Yoked with St. Andrew, Colchester.
67 W. Town St., Lebanon, 06249. Tel: 860-642-6711; Fax: 860-642-4032; Email: cheryl@stfrancisassisilebanonct.org. Revs. Marek Masnicki; Richard D. Breton Jr., Parochial Vicar; Deacon Michael L. Puscas.
Catechesis Religious Program—M. James Hay, D.R.E. Students 99.

MIDDLEFIELD, MIDDLESEX CO., ST. COLMAN (1886) Yoked with Notre Dame, Durham.
170 Hubbard St., P.O. Box 457, Middlefield, 06455-0457. Tel: 860-349-3058; Email: scndchurches@comcast.net; Web: www.churchofstcolman.org. Rev. Jan Swiderski; Deacon Peter L. Gill.
Catechesis Religious Program—Tel: 860-349-3059; Email: drendc@comcast.net. Mrs. Kum Cha Soja, D.R.E. Students 55.

MIDDLETOWN, MIDDLESEX CO.

1—ST. FRANCIS OF ASSISI (1903)
10 Elm St., Middletown, 06457-4427.
Tel: 860-347-4684; Email: office@saintfrancisofassisi.com. Revs. Russell F. Kennedy; George Busto, C.O., In Res.
Catechesis Religious Program—Students 24.

2—ST. JOHN (1843) [CEM] Yoked with St. Sebastian, Middletown.
19 John's Sq., Middletown, 06457-2201.
Tel: 860-347-5626; Fax: 860-638-3633; Email: stjohnsecretary@comcast.net; Web: www.saintjohnchurchmiddletown.com. Rev. James Thaikoottathil, S.T.L., J.C.D.
See Saint John Paul II School under Regional Schools Diocesan, Section D located in the Institution section.
Catechesis Religious Program—Mrs. Kathryn Connelly, D.R.E.; Sr. Ann Mack, R.S.M., D.R.E. Students 72.

3—ST. MARY OF CZESTOCHOWA (1903) [CEM] (Polish)
79 S. Main St., Middletown, 06457-3606.
Tel: 860-347-2365; Fax: 860-347-2110; Email: stmarymdtln@yahoo.com; Web: www.stmarymiddletown.com. Rev. Richard Sliwinski.
See Saint John Paul II School under Regional Schools Diocesan, Section D located in the Institution section.
Catechesis Religious Program—Email: saintmaryfaithformation@gmail.com. Susan Ferriaolo, D.R.E. Students 110.

4—ST. PIUS X (1957)
310 Westfield St., Middletown, 06457-2080.
Tel: 860-347-4441; Email: office@saintpius.org; Web: www.saintpius.org. Revs. John Gallagher, O.F.M.-Cap.; Scott Surrency, Parochial Vicar; Don Bosco Duquette, O.F.M.Cap., In Res., (Retired); James Hammer, O.F.M.Cap., In Res., (Retired); Raynold Thibodeau, O.F.M.Cap., In Res., (Retired).
Catechesis Religious Program—Tel: 860-346-9100; Email: c.butler@saintpius.org. Carol Butler, C.R.E.

(6th-Confirmation); Kimberly Molski, C.R.E. (PreK-5th). Students 443.

5—ST. SEBASTIAN (1930) [CEM] (Italian) Yoked with St. John, Middletown.
155 Washington St., Middletown, 06457-2800.
Tel: 860-347-2638; Fax: 860-347-6736; Email: church6892@att.net. Rev. James Thaikoottathil, S.T.L., J.C.D.
Catechesis Religious Program—Students 126.

MONTVILLE, NEW LONDON CO., ST. JOHN THE EVANGELIST (1881) [CEM] Yoked with Our Lady of Perpetual Help, Quaker Hill & Our Lady of the Lakes, Oakdale.
22 Maple Ave., Uncasville, 06382-2327. Revs. Robert F. Buongirno; James J. Sucholet; Deacon William T. Herrmann.
Catechesis Religious Program—Tel: 860-848-1409; Fax: 860-848-1258. Lorre Branstrom, D.R.E. Students 69.

MOODUS, MIDDLESEX CO., ST. BRIDGET OF KILDARE (1914) [CEM] Yoked with St. Patrick, East Hampton
75 Moodus-Leesville Rd., P.O. Box 422, Moodus, 06469-0422. Tel: 860-873-8623; Email: stbridgetofkildare@yahoo.com. Very Rev. Gregory P. Galvin; Rev. Francis Gilbert, Parochial Vicar.
Catechesis Religious Program—Students 169.

MOOSUP, WINDHAM CO., ALL-HALLOWS (1859) [CEM] Merged with Sacred Heart, Wauregan; yoked with St. John the Apostle, Plainfield & St. Augustine, Canterbury Rev. Tadeusz Zadorozny, (Poland).
Res.: 130 Prospect St., Moosup, 06354-1499.
Tel: 860-564-2668; Email: ahcmoosup@yahoo.com; Web: www.allhallowschurch.weebly.com.
Catechesis Religious Program—Tel: 860-230-0141. Lisa Stott, D.R.E. (Grades K-Confirmation). Students 86.

MYSTIC, NEW LONDON CO., ST. PATRICK (1870) [CEM]
32 E. Main St., Mystic, 06355. Tel: 860-536-1800; Email: secretary@saintpatrickmystic.org. Rev. Kevin M. Reilly.
Catechesis Religious Program—Tel: 860-536-6808; Fax: 860-572-1513. Kate Kappes, D.R.E. & Youth Min. Students 127.

NEW LONDON, NEW LONDON CO.

1—ST. JOSEPH (1907) Yoked with Our Lady of Grace, Fishers Island, NY and St. Mary Star of the Sea, New London.
37 Squire St., New London, 06320. Tel: 860-443-5393 ; Fax: 860-443-0113; Email: sjc.secretary@yahoo.com. Revs. Mark D. O'Donnell; Anthony J. DiMarco; Henry Agudelo; Deacon Gerard Gaynor Jr.
Res.: 914 Montauk Ave., New London, 06320.
School—St. Joseph School, Tel: 860-442-1720; Email: principal@sjsnl.org; Web: sjsnl.com. Lay Teachers 16; Students 130.
Catechesis Religious Program—Students 106.

2—ST. MARY, STAR OF THE SEA (1870) Yoked with St. Joseph, New London & Our Lady of Grace, Fishers Island, NY.
10 Huntington St., New London, 06320-6198.
Tel: 860-447-1431; Fax: 860-437-1889; Email: stbrendanthenavigator@gmail.com. Revs. Mark D. O'Donnell; L. Henry Agudelo, Parochial Vicar; Anthony J. DiMarco, Pastoral Assoc.; Deacons Mariano Ramos; Jesus A. Diez-Canseco.
Catechesis Religious Program—Sr. Yalile Ruiz, R.O.D.A., Pastoral Assoc. Students 87.

NIANTIC, NEW LONDON CO., ST. AGNES (1922) [JC] Yoked with St. Matthias, East Lyme.
22 Haigh Ave., Niantic, 06357-3129.
Tel: 860-739-9722; Fax: 860-691-2187; Web: saintagnescatholicchurch.com. Revs. Gregory C. Mullaney; Brian Maxwell, Parochial Vicar.
Catechesis Religious Program—Email: restagnes@outlook.com. Meghan Cambridge, D.R.E. Students 209.
Chapel—Crescent Beach, St. Francis Chapel (Summer), [JC] .

NORTH GROSVENORDALE, WINDHAM CO., ST. JOSEPH aka St. Joseph Church (1872) [CEM] Yoked with St. Stephen, Quinebaug, St. Mary, Putnam, & Most Holy Trinity, Pomfret
12 Main St., North Grosvenordale, 06255-0897.
Tel: 860-923-2361; Email: stjoseph18@sbcglobal.net; Web: www.stjosephng.weconnect.com. P.O. Box 897, North Grosvenordale, 06255-0897. Very Rev. David Choquette; Rev. Thomas Griffin, Parochial Vicar.
School—St. Joseph School, (Grades PreK-8), 26 Main St., North Grosvenordale, 06255-0137.
Tel: 860-923-2090. P.O. Box 137, North Grosvenordale, 06255-0137. Mr. David Sizemore, Prin. Clergy 2; Lay Teachers 16; Students 122; Clergy / Religious Teachers 2.

NORTH STONINGTON, NEW LONDON CO., ST. THOMAS MORE (1967) Yoked with St. Michael Church, Pawcatuck & St. Mary, Stonington.
87 Mystic Rd., North Stonington, 06359.
Tel: 860-535-1601; Email: smchurch01@snet.net. Very Rev. Dennis M. Perkins.
Catechesis Religious Program—Mrs. Crystal F. Wilcox, D.R.E.

OAKDALE, NEW LONDON CO., OUR LADY OF THE LAKES (1966) Yoked with Our Lady of Perpetual Help, Quaker Hill & St. John the Evangelist Church, Montville.
752 Norwich-Salem Tpke., Oakdale, 06370-1016.
Tel: 860-859-1575; Fax: 860-859-3273; Email: oll.oakdale@gmail.com. Revs. Robert F. Buongirno; James. J. Sucholet; Deacon William T. Herrmann.
Catechesis Religious Program—Tel: 860-859-8733; Email: faith.formation@att.net. Students 160.

OCCUM, NEW LONDON CO., ST. JOSEPH (1878) Yoked with St. Mary, Baltic and Sacred Heart, Taftville.
Mailing Address: P.O. Box 256, Versailles, 06383.
Tel: 860-887-3072; Email: st.josephrectory@comcast.net. Revs. Joseph Tito; Christopher J. Zmuda, Th. Psy.D., Pastoral Assoc.; Rev. Msgr. Henry N. Archambault, P.A., J.C.D., In Res., (Retired).
Res.: 11 Baltic Rd., Occum, 06383. Tel: 860-822-8020 ; Email: saintjosephschool@att.net.
Catechesis Religious Program—Tel: 860-822-6963. Students 8.
Saint Society Church—(Corporate Title: St. Joseph Church Society of Occum, CT, Inc.).

OLD LYME, NEW LONDON CO., CHRIST THE KING (1934)
1 McCurdy Rd., Old Lyme, 06371-1629. Revs. Joseph C. Ashe; Walter M. Nagle, Parochial Vicar; Mrs. Louise Young.
Catechesis Religious Program—Tel: 860-434-9873; Email: lyctkoldlyme@aol.com. Mrs. Louise Young, D.R.E. & Pastoral Assoc. Students 202.

OLD SAYBROOK, MIDDLESEX CO., ST. JOHN (1884) [CEM] Yoked with St. Mark Church, Westbrook.
161 Main St., Old Saybrook, 06475-2367. Revs. Grzegorz P. Brozonowicz; Martin S. Noe; Deacons Nicholas J. Iassogna Jr.; Thomas E. Rymut.
Res.: 222 McVeagh Rd., Westbrook, 06498.
Tel: 860-388-3787; Email: stjohnos@hotmail.com; Web: www.saintjohnstmark.org.
School—St. John School, (Grades PreK-8), 42 Maynard Rd., Old Saybrook, 06475.
Tel: 860-388-0849; Fax: 860-388-6265; Email: secretary@saintjohnschoolos.org; Email: principal@saintjohnschoolos.org; Web: www.saintjohnschoolos.org. Mother Elaine Moorcroft, S.C.M.C., Prin. Clergy 2; Lay Teachers 14; Sisters 2; Students 138; Clergy / Religious Teachers 2.
Catechesis Religious Program—Email: stjohnosccd@att.net. Lisa Collison, D.R.E. Students 186.

PAWCATUCK, NEW LONDON CO., ST. MICHAEL (1861) [CEM 2] Yoked with St. Thomas More Church, North Stonington & St. Mary Church, Stonington.
60 Liberty St., Pawcatuck, 06379. Tel: 860-599-5580; Web: www.stmichaelpawcatuck.com. Very Rev. Dennis M. Perkins.
School—St. Michael School, 63 Liberty St., Pawcatuck, 06379. Tel: 860-599-1084; Email: dmessina@stmichaelschoolct.com; Web: www.stmichaelschoolct.com. Lay Teachers 16; Students 118.
Catechesis Religious Program—Students 242.

PLAINFIELD, WINDHAM CO., ST. JOHN THE APOSTLE (1907) [CEM] Yoked with St. Augustine, Canterbury, All Hallows, Moosup.
15 Railroad Ave., Plainfield, 06374-1215.
Tel: 860-564-3313; Fax: 860-564-3314; Email: stjapostle@gmail.com; Web: stjapostle.weebly.com. 10 Railroad Ave., Plainfield, 06374. Rev. Tadeusz Zadorozny, (Poland); Deacon Leo N. Bernard.
Catechesis Religious Program—12 Railroad Ave., Plainfield, 06374. Students 60.

POMFRET, WINDHAM CO., MOST HOLY TRINITY (1886) Yoked with St. Mary Church, Putnam, St. Joseph, N. Grosvenor Dale & St. Stephen, Quinebaug.
568 Pomfret St., P.O. Box 235, Pomfret, 06258-0235. Tel: 860-928-5830; Email: mhtoffice@sbcglobal.net. Very Rev. David P. Choquette; Rev. Thomas Griffin, Parochial Vicar; Deacon Pierre M. Desilets.
Catechesis Religious Program—Email: robin.incera@yahoo.com. Robyn Incera, D.R.E. Students 22.

PORTLAND, MIDDLESEX CO., ST. MARY (1872) [CEM]
Mailing Address: 45 Freestone Ave., Portland, 06480. Tel: 860-342-2328; Fax: 860-342-1433; Email: stmaryportlandoffice@gmail.com. Rev. Paul Boudreau; Deacon Dana Garry.
Res.: 51 Freestone Ave., Portland, 06480.
Tel: 860-342-3028; Tel: 860-342-0308; Email: st.mary.rectory@sbcglobal.net; Web: stmaryportland.org.
Catechesis Religious Program—Tel: 860-342-2308; Email: stmarydre@gmail.com. Susan Ferriauolo, D.R.E. Students 304.

PRESTON, NEW LONDON CO., ST. CATHERINE OF SIENA (1975) Yoked with St. Mary, Jewett City & St. Thomas the Apostle, Voluntown.
243 Rte. 164, Preston, 06365-8726. Tel: 860-887-9966 ; Email: stcatherine.secretary@yahoo.com. Very Rev. Ted F. Tumicki, S.T.L., J.C.L., J.V.; Rev. Stephen S. Gulino; Deacon Paul R. Baillargeon.
Catechesis Religious Program—Email: nancy.stc@sbcglobal.net. Students 48.

PUTNAM, WINDHAM CO., ST. MARY CHURCH OF THE VISITATION (1866) [CEM] Yoked with Most Holy Trinity Church, Pomfret; St. Stephen, N. Grosvenordale & St. Stephen, Quinebaug.
218 Providence St., Putnam, 06260-1514.
Tel: 860-928-6535; Fax: 860-928-7246; Email: stmarychurchputnam@snet.net. P.O. Box 665, Putnam, 06260. Very Rev. David Choquette; Rev. Thomas Griffin, Parochial Vicar; Deacon Pierre M. Desilets.
Catechesis Religious Program—Email: jlindsaystmaryre@gmail.com. Janice Lindsay, D.R.E. Students 95.

QUAKER HILL, NEW LONDON CO., OUR LADY OF PERPETUAL HELP (1904) (Polish) Yoked with St. John the Evangelist, Montville & Our Lady of the Lakes, Oakdale.
63 Old Norwich Rd., P.O. Box 329, Quaker Hill, 06375-0329. Tel: 860-443-1875; Email: olphquakerhill@yahoo.com. Revs. Robert Buongirno; James. J. Sucholet; Deacon William T. Herrmann.
Catechesis Religious Program—59 Old Norwich Rd., Quaker Hill, 06375. Tel: 860-848-1409. Lorre Branstrom, D.R.E. Students 28.
Convent—Sisters of St. Joseph of Third Order of St. Francis, 59 Old Norwich Rd., P.O. Box 329, Quaker Hill, 06375.

QUINEBAUG, WINDHAM CO., ST. STEPHEN aka St. Stephen Church (1955) Yoked with St. Joseph, North Grosvenordale, St. Mary, Putnam, & Most Holy Trinity, Pomfret
130 Old Turnpike Rd., Quinebaug, 06262.
Tel: 860-923-2361; Email: stjoseph18@sbcglobal.net; Web: www.stjosephng.weconnect.com. P.O. Box 897, North Grosvenordale, 06255-0897. Very Rev. David Choquette; Rev. Thomas Griffin, Parochial Vicar.

ROCKVILLE, TOLLAND CO.

1—ST. BERNARD (1854) [CEM] Yoked with St. Matthew, Tolland.
25 St. Bernard's Ter., Rockville, 06066-3217.
Tel: 860-875-0753; Fax: 860-871-7460; Email: rectory@saintbernardchurch.org; Web: www.saintbernardchurch.org. Very Rev. Richard J. Ricard; Revs. William J. Olesik, Parochial Vicar; Jeffrey R. Ellis, Parochial Vicar; Deacons Michael Berstene; Ronald Freedman; Mr. Brian Kenny, Business Mgr.
School—St. Bernard School, 20 School St., P.O. Box 177, Rockville, 06066. Tel: 860-875-0753, Ext. 113; Fax: 860-872-2444; Email: sherry.y@saintbernardchurch.org; Web: www.saintbernardchurch.org. Sherry Yarusewicz, Dir. Preschool. Lay Teachers 2; Students 15.
Catechesis Religious Program—22 School St., Rockville, 06066. Kimberly Manganella, D.R.E. Students 293.
St. Bernard Cemetery Office—
Tel: 860-875-0753, Ext. 105; Email: cemetery@saintbernardchurch.org.

2—ST. JOSEPH (1905) [CEM] (Polish)
33 West St., Rockville, 06066-6154.
Tel: 860-871-1970; Fax: 860-872-0333; Email: info@stjosephct.org. Rev. Bogdan Olzacki, O.S.P.P.E.
Catechesis Religious Program—Students 98.

ROGERS, WINDHAM CO., ST. IGNATIUS (1939) Closed. For inquiries for parish records contact St. Joseph, Dayville.

SOMERSVILLE, TOLLAND CO., ALL SAINTS (1915)
25 School St., P.O. Box M, Somersville, 06072-0913.
Tel: 860-749-8625; Email: alstchurch@yahoo.com; Web: somersallsaints.church. Rev. Gerald S. Kirby.

STAFFORD SPRINGS, TOLLAND CO., ST. EDWARD (1869) [CEM]
6 Benton St., Stafford Springs, 06076-0433.
Tel: 860-684-2705; Fax: 860-684-0757; Email: stedwardparish@stedward-stafford.org; Web: www.stedward-stafford.org. Rev. Peter B. Liszewski.
Res.: 55 High St., Stafford Springs, 06076.
Mission—St. Joseph, (Summer Chapel) Closed, for records & inquiries contact St. Edward Church. 6 Benton St., Stafford Springs, Tolland Co. 06076.

STONINGTON, NEW LONDON CO., ST. MARY (1850) [CEM] Yoked with Saint Michael Church, Pawcatuck & St. Thomas More Church, North Stonington.
95 Main St., Stonington, 06378-1219.
Tel: 860-535-1700; Email: st.marychurchstonbor@comcast.net; Web: stmarychurch-stonington.weconnect.com. Very Rev. Dennis M. Perkins.
Catechesis Religious Program—Tel: 860-535-4252; Email: mwest012458@gmail.com. Matthew West, D.R.E. Students 96.

STORRS, TOLLAND CO., ST. THOMAS AQUINAS (1947) Yoked with St. Mary, Coventry.
46 N. Eagleville Rd., Storrs, 06268-1710.
Tel: 860-429-6436; Fax: 860-429-2809; Email: officemanagerstauconn@gmail.com; Web: stthomasaquinasuconn.org. Rev. John N. Antonelle;

Anthony Pandolfe, Music Dir.; Kathleen Dochter, Office Mgr.
Catechesis Religious Program—Tel: 860-429-6436; Fax: 860-429-2809; Email: religiousedsta@gmail.com. Beth Fiddler, D.R.E. Students 67.
TAFTVILLE, NEW LONDON CO., SACRED HEART (1883) Yoked with St. Mary, Baltic and St. Joseph, Occum.
156 Providence St., P.O. Box 208, Taftville, 06380.
Tel: 860-887-3072; Email: sacred.heart@sbcglobal.net. Revs. Joseph Tito; Christopher J. Zmuda, Th. Psy.D.; Raymond Introvigne, In Res., (Retired).
School—Sacred Heart School, 15 Hunters Ave., Taftville, 06380-0208. Tel: 860-887-1757; Fax: 860-889-7276; Email: principal@sacredhearttaftville.org; Web: www.sacredhearttaftville.org. Mother Mary Christina Van Beck, S.C.M.C., Prin. Lay Teachers 8; Sisters of Charity of Our Lady, Mother of the Church 3; Students 176.
Catechesis Religious Program—Students 56.
TOLLAND, TOLLAND CO., ST. MATTHEW (1964) Yoked with St. Bernard, Rockville
111 Tolland Green, Tolland, 06084.
Tel: 860-872-0200; Fax: 860-875-4413; Email: parishoffice@stmatthewct.org; Web: www.stmatthewct.org. Very Rev. Richard J. Ricard; Revs. William J. Olesik, Parochial Vicar; Jeffrey R. Ellis, Parochial Vicar; Deacons Ronald Freedman; Michael Berstene; Mr. Brian Kenny, Business Mgr.
Catechesis Religious Program—
Tel: 860-872-0200, Ext. 319; Email: cynde.yaconiello@stmatthewct.org. Mrs. Cynthia Yaconiello, C.R.E. (Grades K-6). Students 575.
VERNON, TOLLAND CO., SACRED HEART (1958) [JC] Closed. For inquiries for parish records contact St. Bernard, Rockville.
VOLUNTOWN, NEW LONDON CO., ST. THOMAS THE APOSTLE aka Ss. Thomas and Anne (1892) [CEM] Yoked with St. Mary, Jewett City & St. Catherine of Siena, Preston.
61 Preston City Rd., P.O. Box 99, Voluntown, 06384-0099. Tel: 860-376-8352. Very Rev. Ted F. Tumicki, S.T.L., J.C.L., J.V.; Rev. Stephen S. Gulino; Deacons Paul R. Baillargeon; Bryan Jones.
Catechesis Religious Program—49 Preston City Rd., Voluntown, 06384. Cathy Becotte, D.R.E. Students 32.
WATERFORD, NEW LONDON CO., ST. PAUL (1960) Yoked with St. Joseph, New London, St. Mary Star of the Sea, New London and Our Lady of Grace, Fishers Island.
170 Rope Ferry Rd., Waterford, 06385-2609.
Tel: 860-443-5587; Fax: 860-442-9308; Email: stpaulwtfd@yahoo.com; Web: www.stpaulchurchwaterfordct.org. Revs. Mark D. O'Donnell; Henry Agudelo, Parochial Vicar; Anthony J. DiMarco, Parochial Vicar.
Catechesis Religious Program—Tel: 860-443-3375. Mrs. Roseann Ward, D.R.E. Students 162.
WAUREGAN, WINDHAM CO., SACRED HEART (1889) [CEM] (French), Closed. For inquiries for parish records contact All Hallows, Moosup.
WEST WILLINGTON, TOLLAND CO., ST. JUDE (1981) Closed. For inquiries for parish records, contact St. Philip the Apostle, Ashford.
WESTBROOK, MIDDLESEX CO., ST. MARK (1962) Yoked with St. John Church, Old Saybrook.
222 McVeagh Rd., Westbrook, 06498-1512.
Tel: 860-399-9207; Tel: 860-399-6208; Web: www.stmarkstjohn.org. 161 Main St., Old Saybrook, 06475. Revs. Grzegorz P. Brozonowicz; Martin S. Noe, Parochial Vicar; Deacons Thomas E. Rymut; Nicholas J. Iassogna Jr.
Catechesis Religious Program—Tel: 860-399-6208; Email: re@stmarkct.org. Mrs. Patricia Moran, D.R.E. Students 150.
WILLIMANTIC, WINDHAM CO.
1—ST. JOSEPH (1859) [CEM] Yoked with Sagrado Corazon de Jesus, Windham, CT & St. Mary, Willimantic.
99 Jackson St., Willimantic, 06226-3077.
Tel: 860-423-8439; Fax: 860-423-6825; Email: stjosephwillimantic@gmail.com; Web: www.catholicwindham.org. Very Rev. Laurence A.M. LaPointe; Revs. Jonathan J. Ficara; Juan Angel Aguirre Palacio; Deacons Lawrence Goodwin; Felipe Silva.
School—St. Mary-St. Joseph, 35 Valley St., Willimantic, 06226. Tel: 860-423-8479; Fax: 860-423-8365. Miss Abby Demars, Prin.
Catechesis Religious Program—21 Valley St., Willimantic, 06226. Students 93.
2—ST. MARY (1903) (French) Yoked with St. Joseph, Willimantic & Sagrado Corazon De Jesus, Windham.
Church: 46 Valley St., Willimantic, 06226.
Tel: 860-423-5835; Fax: 860-423-9933; Email: stmaryparish06226@gmail.com; Web: www.catholicwindham.org. 80 Maple Ave., Willimantic, 06226-2733. Very Rev. Laurence A.M. LaPointe; Revs. Jonathan J. Ficara, Parochial Vicar; Juan Angel Aguirre Palacio, Parochial Vicar.
School—St. Mary-St. Joseph, (Grades PreK-8), 35 Valley St., Willimantic, 06226. Tel: 860-423-8479; Fax: 860-423-8365; Email: secretary@smsjschool.org; Email: principal@smsjschool.org; Web: www.smsjschool.org. Miss Abby Demars, Prin. Clergy 1; Lay Teachers 14; Sisters 1; Students 75.
Catechesis Religious Program—Tel: 860-423-8439; Email: stjosephwillimantic@gmail.com. Students 27.
Convent—Sisters of Charity of Our Lady, 88 Jackson St., Willimantic, 06226. Tel: 860-423-5122.
Faith Formulation—Tel: 860-423-9700.
WINDHAM, WINDHAM CO., SAGRADO CORAZON DE JESUS (1991) [JC] (Hispanic) Yoked with St. Joseph Church, Willimantic & St. Mary, Willimantic.
Mailing Address: 61 Club Rd., Windham, 06280-1007. Tel: 860-423-8617; Fax: 860-423-4157; Email: sagradocor@sbcglobal.net. Very Rev. Laurence A.M. LaPointe; Revs. Jonathan J. Ficara; Juan Angel Aguirre Palacio, D.R.E.; Sr. Leidy Castillo, R.O.D.A., Pastoral Assoc.; Deacons Felipe Silva; Lawrence Goodwin.
Catechesis Religious Program—Email: stjosephwillimantic@gmail.com. Students 145.

Chaplains of Public Institutions

NORWICH. *William W. Backus Hospital*, 06360.
Tel: 860-889-8331. Sr. Rita Johnson, S.S.N.D., Dir., Ministry to Sick.
GROTON. *U.S. Submarine Base-New London*, 1 Crystal Lake Rd., Box 13, Navsubase NLON, Groton, 06349-5013. Tel: 860-694-3232; Email: aaron.ames@navy.mil. Rev. Thomas F.X. Hoar, S.S.E., Chap.
MIDDLETOWN. *Connecticut Valley Hospital*, Eastern Dr., P.O. Box 351, Middletown, 06457.
Tel: 860-262-5900; Fax: 860-262-5900. Rev. Richard Okiria, Chap.
Middlesex Memorial Hospital, 28 Crescent St., Middletown, 06457-0822. Tel: 860-358-6725. Rev. George Busto, C.O., Chap.
NEW LONDON. *Lawrence and Memorial Hospitals*, 365 Montauk Ave., New London, 06320.
Tel: 860-442-0711, Ext. 2609. Rev. Dennis Mercieri, Chap.
U.S. Coast Guard Memorial Chapel, U.S. Coast Guard Academy, 15 Mohegan Ave., New London, 06320-4195. Tel: 860-444-8482; Fax: 960-701-6729; Email: michael.j.parisi@uscg.mil. Rev. Keith J. Shuley, Chap., C.D.R., C.H.C., U.S.N.

On Duty Outside the Diocese:
Rev. Msgr.—
Randall, Kevin S., 3339 Massachusetts Ave., N.W., Washington, DC 20008-3687
Revs.—
Fluet, Gregoire J., Ph.D., K.H.S.
Rouleau, Francis C.
Smith, Thomas J.

Absent on Leave:
Very Rev.—
LeBlanc, Charles L.
Revs.—
Angelo, Thomas M., Ch. Capt., 5415 Merritt Brown Rd., Panama City, FL 32404
Bolieau, Henry G.
Gwudz, John S.
Rweyemamu, Justinian B.
Schuh, Karl Christopher
Sennik, Thomas W.
Smith, Michael S.

Retired:
Rev. Msgrs.—
Archambault, Henry N., P.A., J.C.D., (Retired)
Bride, Thomas R., P.A., K.C.H.S., (Retired)
Carini, James P., (Retired)
Donohue, Michael T., (Retired)
LaRocque, Richard P., (Retired)
Malanowski, Thaddeus F., (Retired), Queen of the Clergy Residence, 274 Strawberry Hill Ave., #205, Stamford, 06902
Very Rev.—
Smith, Thomas J., V.F., (Retired)
Revs.—
Alaharasan, V. Antony, M.A., Ph.D., (Retired)
Archer, Arthur, (Retired)
Ashe, John F., (Retired)
Castaldi, Joseph, J.C.L., (Retired)
Chaker, Victor, (Retired)
Cloutier, Roland C., L.C.S.W., (Retired)
Flynn, William J., (Retired)
Gill, Michael J., (Retired)
Introvigne, Raymond, (Retired)
Irving, Alfred, (Retired)
Konopka, Edward M., (Retired)
Martin, Patrick A., (Retired)
McCorry, Patrick G., (Retired)
McGrail, Charles A., (Retired), 468 Main St., Apt. 218, Niantic, 06357
McKenna, Frank W., (Retired)
McNulty, William J., (Retired), 66 Brown St., Hamden, 06518
Naduvilekoot, Augustine, (Retired)
Ramen, Paul F., (Retired), 350 Pond Hill Rd., Moosup, 06354. Tel: 860-564-9767
Sequeira, Michael, (Retired)
Sickler, Thomas G., M.S., (Retired)
Szczapa, Stanley J., (Retired)
Wisneski, Edward, S.T.D., Ph.D., (Retired), 78 E. Ridge Rd., Middletown, 06457.

Permanent Deacons:
Abdalla, John, (Retired)
Bachand, Francis J., (Retired)
Baillargeon, Paul R., St. Mary, Jewett City; St. Catherine of Siena, Preston & St. Thomas the Apostle, Voluntown
Balchus, John A., St. Lawrence, Killingworth
Barbeau, Rene N. Jr., St. James, Danielson
Barlow, Robert C., (Retired)
Bernard, Leo N., (Retired)
Berstene, Michael C., St. Bernard, Rockville; St. Matthew, Tolland
Cannata, Nicholas J., (Retired)
Casey, Thomas J.
Cote, Albert J., (Retired)
Cyr, Warren
D'Amelio, Dan, St. Bridget, Moodus; St. Patrick, East Hampton
Desilets, Pierre M., St. Mary, Putnam; Most Holy Trinity, Pomfret
Deskus, Christopher, St. Philip, Ashford
Diez Conseco, Jesus A., St. Mary, Hispanic Apostolate, New London
Dolan, Dennis F.
Dombkowski, Anthony, (Retired)
Doyle, Dennis A. III
Escalona, Jorge, Bishop's Master of Ceremonies
Fecteau, Al R., (Retired)
Ferraro, Robert, St. Lawrence, Killingworth
Flores, Octavio, St. Francis, Middletown; Hispanic Ministry
Freedman, Ronald, St. Bernard, Rockville; St. Matthew, Tolland
Garry, Dana, St. Mary, Portland
Gaynor, Gerard J., (Retired)
Gill, Peter L., St. Colman, Middlefield; Notre Dame, Durham
Giuliano, Joseph, Cape Coral, FL
Goodwin, Lawrence M., St. Joseph, Williamantic; St. Margaret Mission, Scotland; Sagrado Corazon, Windham
Grospitch, Harry J., St. Luke, Ellington
Hann, Frank, St. Luke, Ellington
Hayes, Robert P., (Retired)
Herrmann, William, Our Lady of Lakes, Oakdale; St. John the Evangelist, Montville & Our Lady of Perpetual Help, Quaker Hill
Hoffman, Douglas A., St. Mary, Groton; Sacred Heart, Groton
Iassogna, Nicholas J. Jr., St. John, Old Saybrook.
Jolin, Joseph, North Fort Meyers, FL
Jones, Bryan, St. Mary, Jewett City; St. Catherine of Siena, Preston; St. Thomas & St. Anne, Voluntown
Kaiser, William Jr., Our Lady of Sorrows, Essex
King, Mark J., Charlotte, NC
Kitlinski, Ronald S., (Retired)
LaCasse, Roland J., (Retired)
LaPlante, Joseph A., Southwest Harbor, ME
LoCasto, Benedict, Church of the Holy Family, Hebron, St. Columba, Columbia, Immaculate Retreat House, Willimantic
Marshall, Timothy M., St. Augustine, Canterbury
McGann, William H., Our Lady of Lourdes, Gales Ferry
McMahon, James R. Sr., (Retired)
Melendez, Carlos, Port St. Lucie, FL
Moneypenny, Lawrence, St. Joseph, Chester
O'Reilly, Henry E., (Retired)
Osuba, Jose, Columbia
Pereira, Julias A., (Retired)
Phaneuf, Bernard A., St. Mary, Putnam
Puscas, Michael L., Diocesan Dir. Deacon Personnel, St. Francis of Assisi, Lebanon; St. Andrew, Colchester
Ramos, Mariano, St. Mary, New London
Reed, Steven W., St. Matthias, East Lyme
Rymut, Thomas E., St. Mark, Westbrook
Shaw, Gerald L., (Retired)
Silva, Felipe, Sagrado Corazon de Jesus, Windham; St. Joseph, Willimantic
Sinclair, Wayne, Sacred Heart, Norwichtown
Thompson, Kim, St. Thomas Aquinas, Storrs; St. Mary, Coventry
Tynan, Thomas M., Corrales, NM
Walker, Richard K., (Retired)

Wallen, Paul A., (Retired).

INSTITUTIONS LOCATED IN DIOCESE

[A] SEMINARIES, RELIGIOUS OR SCHOLASTICATES

CROMWELL. *Holy Apostles College and Seminary* (1956) 33 Prospect Hill Rd., Cromwell, 06416-2005.
Tel: 860-632-3010; Tel: 860-632-3012 (Admissions); Fax: 860-632-3030; Email: rector@holyapostles.edu; Email: afleck@holyapostles.edu; Web: www.holyapostles.edu. Very Rev. Douglas L. Mosey, C.S.B., Ph.D., Pres. & Rector; Mr. William J. Russell, CPA, D.F.O., Finance Officer; Sr. Mary Anne Linder, F.S.E., Dir. Field Educ.; Rev. David Zercie, M.S.A., Spiritual Advisor; Dr. Cynthia Toolin, Registrar; Revs. Anthony McLaughlin, Prof.; Jude Surowiec, O.F.M.Conv., Prof.; Clare Adamo, M.S.L.S., Library Dir.; Rev. Msgr. Albert Kuuire, Spiritual Advisor; Revs. Kermit Syren; Jeffrey Thompson, M.S.A.; Peter Kucer, M.S.A., S.T.D., Academic Dean. Brothers 1; Religious Teachers 8; Lay Teachers 10; Priests 21; Seminarians 50; Sisters 42; Students 585; College Division Lay Students 472.

[B] HIGH SCHOOLS, DIOCESAN

MIDDLETOWN. *Mercy High School* (1963) 1740 Randolph Rd., Middletown, 06457-5155.
Tel: 860-346-6659; Fax: 860-344-9887; Email: info@mercyhigh.com; Web: www.mercyhigh.com. Sr. Mary A. McCarthy, R.S.M., Pres.; Mr. Steven Brickey, Dean, Academics; Mrs. Melissa Bullock, Dean, Curriculum/Technology; Mrs. Virginia Sullivan, Dean, Students; Miss Ann Derbacher, Campus Min.; Mrs. Marie Leary, Dir. Communications; Mrs. Diane Santostefano, Dir. Admissions; Sr. Peggy O'Neill, R.S.M., Registrar; Jennifer Crutchfield, Librarian. Religious Teachers 3; Lay Teachers 45; Sisters 3; Students 450; Total Staff 48.

Xavier High School Corporation of Middletown (1963) 181 Randolph Rd., Middletown, 06457-5635. Tel: 860-346-7735; Fax: 860-346-6109; Email: deustis@xavierhighschool.org; Email: djaskot@xavierhighschool.org; Web: www.xavierhighschool.org. Mr. David Eustis, Headmaster; Mr. Brendan Donohue, Prin.; Mr. Nicholas Cerreta, Dean, Students; Mr. Andrew T. Gargano, Academic Dean; Mr. Peter Lyons, Dir. Faculty Formation. Brothers of St. Francis Xavier and Diocese of Norwich. Brothers 3; Religious Teachers 3; Lay Teachers 55; Students 692.

UNCASVILLE. *Saint Bernard School*, 1593 Norwich-New London Tpke., Uncasville, 06382-1399.
Tel: 860-848-1271; Fax: 860-848-1274; Email: info@saint-bernard.com; Web: www.saint-bernard.com. Donald Macrino, Headmaster, Tel: 860-848-1271, Ext. 146. Lay Teachers 32; Students 330.

Grades 6-12 School, (Grades 6-12),
Tel: 860-848-1271, Ext. 146 (Prin.); Email: info@saint-bernard.com. Donald Macrino, Headmaster. Lay Teachers 29; Students 334.

[C] HIGH SCHOOLS, PRIVATE

BALTIC. *Academy of the Holy Family* (1874) 54 W. Main St., P.O. Box 691, Baltic, 06330-0691.
Tel: 860-822-9272; Fax: 860-822-1318; Email: mothermdavid@ahfbaltic.org; Web: www.ahfbaltic.org. Mother Mary David Riquier, S.C.M.C., Prin. Sisters of Charity of Our Lady Mother of the Church. Religious Teachers 8; Lay Teachers 7; Sisters 8; Students 40.

THOMPSON. *Marianapolis Preparatory School*, 26 Chase Rd., P.O. Box 304, Thompson, 06277-0304.
Tel: 860-923-9565; Fax: 860-923-3730; Email: ddaniels@marianapolis.org; Web: www.marianapolis.org. Mr. Joseph C. Hanrahan, Headmaster; Douglas Daniels, CFO; Rev. Timothy Roth, M.I.C., Chap., Email: troth@marianapolis.org. Religious Teachers 4; Lay Teachers 51; Priests 1; Students 400.

Congregation of Marian Fathers of the Immaculate Conception of the B.V.M., 206 Chase Rd., P.O. Box 368, Thompson, 06277-0368. Tel: 860-923-2220; Fax: 860-923-6998; Email: aragon1948@yahoo.com; Email: troth@marianapolis.org; Email: bromic1@aol.com. Rev. Timothy J. Roth, M.I.C., Supr.; Bros. Brian Manian, M.I.C., First Councillor; Donald Schaefer, M.I.C., Treas. Total in Community 7.

[D] REGIONAL SCHOOL, DIOCESAN

MIDDLETOWN. *Saint John Paul II Regional School*, (Grades PreK-8), 87 S. Main St., Middletown, 06457-3606. Tel: 860-347-2978; Fax: 860-347-7267; Email: office@jpii.org; Web: jpii.org. Mr. Larry Fitzgerald, Prin. Lay Teachers 18; Students 180; Other 11.

[E] HOMES FOR AGED

WINDHAM. *St. Joseph Living Center* (1988) 14 Club Rd., Windham, 06280-1000. Tel: 860-456-1107; Fax: 860-450-7114; Email: info@sjlcct.org; Web: sjlivingcenter.org. Lynn M. Bellware, L.P.N., Admissions; Paula Haney, RPT; Michael Kilgannon, Medical Dir.; Valerie Oliver, R.N., DNS; Zachary Potter, ADNS; Ginny Person, Admin. Bed Capacity 120; Lay Staff 229; Sisters 4; Tot Asst. Annually 309; Total Staff 220; Volunteers 75.

[F] SPECIAL CARE FACILITIES

WILLIMANTIC. *Holy Family Home and Shelter, Inc.*, 88 Jackson St., P.O. Box 884, Willimantic, 06226-0884. Tel: 860-423-7719; Fax: 860-423-3770; Email: bonnie@holyfamilywillimantic.org; Web: www.holyfamilywillimantic.org. P.O. Box 884, Willimantic, 06226. Bonnie Reilein, Exec. Dir., Email: bonnie@holyfamilywillimantic.org. Bed Capacity 32; Tot Asst. Annually 160; Total Staff 16.

[G] MONASTERIES AND RESIDENCES OF PRIESTS AND BROTHERS

CROMWELL. *Society of the Missionaries of the Holy Apostles* (1956) 22 Prospect Hill Rd., Cromwell, 06416-2005. Tel: 860-316-5926; Cell: 860-202-8626; Email: pro.msa@gmail.com; Web: www.msausa.org. Very Revs. Luis Luna-Barrera, M.S.A., Rel. Order Leader; Edward Przygocki, M.S.A., Prov.; Revs. Charles Bak, M.S.A.; Edward C. Doherty, M.S.A.; Stanley Grove, M.S.A.; Peter Kucer, M.S.A., S.T.D.; John R. Lyons, M.S.A.; William McCarthy, M.S.A.; Vincent Salamoni, M.S.A.; Robert Sickler, M.S.A.; Thomas Simon, M.S.A.; David Zercie, M.S.A.; Bro. Jerome McCallum, Sec.; Rev. Jeffrey Thompson, M.S.A., Treas. Society of the Missionaries of the Holy Apostles.

Working Outside the Diocese: Revs. James Anderson, M.S.A.; Robert Anello, M.S.A.; Patrick Biegler, M.S.A.; J. Patrick Boyhan, M.S.A.; William Broome, M.S.A.; Dennis P. Connell, M.S.A.; James Downs, M.S.A.; Harold Dunn, M.S.A.; Addison Hallock, M.S.A.; Richard Hite, M.S.A.; Vincent Kilidjian, M.S.A.; Benedict Klucinec, M.S.A.; Laurence Preston, M.S.A.; Very Rev. Edward Przygocki, M.S.A.; Revs. Martin Rooney, M.S.A.; Pasquale Taliercio, M.S.A.

GRISWOLD. *Marian Friary of Our Lady of Guadalupe*, 199 Colonel Brown Rd., Griswold, 06351.
Tel: 860-376-6840; Email: ffi.griswold@gmail.com; Web: www.figuadalupe.com. Revs. Jacinto Chapin, Supr.; Dominic Savio Mary Murphy, F.I., Sec.; Friars Jude McFeeley, F.I.; Pasquale Gilbert. Brothers 6.

MIDDLETOWN. *Congregation of the Brothers of St. Francis Xavier*, 181 Randolph Rd., Middletown, 06457-5635. Tel: 860-346-8585; Fax: 860-346-6859; Email: deustis@xavierhighschool.org. Bros. Brian Davis, C.F.X., Dir.; James Eckert, C.F.X.; Philip Revell, C.F.X.; Thomas Ryan, C.F.X.; John Sullivan, C.F.X. Total in Residence 5.

THOMPSON. *Marians of the Immaculate Conception of the B.V.M.* (1673) 206 Thompson Rd., P.O. Box 368, Thompson, 06277-0368. Tel: 860-923-2220;
Tel: 860-634-7191; Fax: 860-923-6998; Email: aragon1948@yahoo.com; Email: troth@marianapolis.org; Email: bromicl@aol.com. Rev. Timothy Roth, M.I.C., Supr.; Bros. Donald Schaefer, M.I.C., Second Councilor & Treas.; Brian Manian, M.I.C., First Councilor. Total in Residence 7. In Res. Revs. Bernard Backiel, M.I.C.; Jerome Zalonis, M.I.C.

[H] CONVENTS AND RESIDENCES FOR SISTERS

NORWICH. *School Sisters Notre Dame*, 7 Otis St., 06360. Tel: 860-886-6948; Email: becky@norwichdiocese.net. Sr. Rita Johnson, S.S.N.D., Contact Person. Sisters 1.

BALTIC. *Sisters of Charity of Our Lady, Mother of the Church*, 54 W. Main St., P.O. Box 691, Baltic, 06330-0691. Tel: 860-822-8241; Fax: 860-822-9842; Email: sistermariejulie@gmail.com; Email: mothermdavid@gmail.com; Web: www.sistersofcharity.com. Mother Marie Julie Saegaert, S.C.M.C., Supr. Gen. Sisters of Charity of Our Lady, Mother of the Church.
Sisters of Charity of Our Lady, Mother of the Church Novices 3; Postulants 2; Professed 46; Sisters 52; Junior Professed 1.

HIGGANUM. *Apostles of the Sacred Heart of Jesus* (1894) Sacred Heart on the Lake, 529 Brainard Hill Rd., Higganum, 06441-4010. Tel: 860-345-4653;
Fax: 860-345-4469; Email: jhunihan@ascjus.org. Sr. Jerilyn Hunihan, Supr. Sisters 3; Total in Residence 3.

MIDDLETOWN. *Daughters of Our Lady of the Garden* (1829) Convent and Nursery School. 67 Round Hill Rd., Middletown, 06457-6119. Tel: 860-346-5765; Tel: 860-740-5169 (School); Fax: 860-346-6361; Email: juana.olmedo.fmh@gmail.com; Web: www.gianelliselc.org/ (School). Sr. Juana Olmedo, F.M.H., Supr. & Dir., Gianelli's Early Learning Center. Sisters 6; Total Staff 10.

Sisters of Mercy of the Americas, Northeast Community, 421 High St., Middletown, 06457.
Tel: 860-346-6619; Email: RTGarneau@aol.com. Sr. Rita Garneau, R.S.M., Contact Person. Other residences located in Middletown, Norwich & Portland Sisters 2.

PUTNAM. *Holy Spirit Provincial House*, 72 Church St., Putnam, 06260-1810. Tel: 860-928-0891;
Fax: 860-928-6496; Email: srpjdhs@yahoo.com; Email: dhsprovsec@gmail.com. Sr. Gertrude Lanouette, D.H.S., Prov.; Mr. Gary Spieker, Admin. Daughters of the Holy Spirit. Sisters 16.

Other Locations:*Notre Dame Convent*, 121 Hawkins St., Danielson, 06239. Tel: 860-412-9386; Email: lesleydhs@yahoo.com. Sr. Lesley Despathy, Contact Person. Sisters 3. *Provincialate Community*, 31 Ravine St., Putnam, 06260. Tel: 860-928-3882; Email: trudidhs@gmail.com. Sr. Gertrude Lanouette, D.H.S., Prov. Sisters 2. *All Hallows Convent*, 152 Prospect St., Moosup, 06354.
Tel: 860-564-5409; Email: tvanassedhs@att.net. Sr. Therese Vanasse, Contact Person. Sisters 4.
499 Church St., Putnam, 06260. Tel: 860-963-0311.

Immaculate Conception Convent, Spiritual Renewal Center, 600 Liberty Hwy., Putnam, 06260-2503.
Tel: 860-928-7955; Fax: 860-928-1930; Email: sesigne@gmail.com; Email: eugenia.luko@gmail.com; Web: immaculateconceptionsite.org. Sr. Igne Marijosius, M.V.S., Prov. Supr. Sisters of the Immaculate Conception of the Blessed Virgin Mary 4; Total in Residence 5; Total Staff 7.

Matulaitis Nursing Home Inc., 10 Thurber Rd., Putnam, 06260-2518. Tel: 860-928-7976;
Fax: 860-963-2378; Email: bclemens@matulaitisnh.org; Web: matulaitisnh.org. Rev. Izydor Sadowski, S.D.B., Chap.; Lisa Ryan, Admin. Sisters of the Immaculate Conception of the Blessed Virgin Mary. Residents 119; Sisters 1.

Provincialate Community of the Daughters of the Holy Spirit, 31 Ravine St., Putnam, 06260-1817. Email: trudidhs@gmail.com. Sisters Gertrude Lanouette, D.H.S., Prov., Tel: 860-928-7072; Marian St. Marie, D.H.S., Prov. Councillor, Tel: 860-928-3882. Sisters 2.

WILLIMANTIC. *Sisters of Charity of Our Lady, Mother of the Church*, St. Joseph Convent, 88 Jackson St., Willimantic, 06226. Tel: 860-423-5122; Email: aposthispano@gmail.com. Mother Mary Jude Lazarus, S.C.M.C., Supr. Sisters 3; Total in Residence 3.

[I] RETREAT HOUSES

MYSTIC. *St. Edmund's Retreat, Inc.*, 1 Enders Island, P.O. Box 399, Mystic, 06355-0399.
Tel: 860-536-0565; Fax: 860-572-7655; Email: cstclair@endersisland.com; Web: www.endersisland.com. Rev. Thomas F.X. Hoar, S.S.E., Pres.; Robert Goossens, Chm.; Mary Kathleen Careb, Vice Chair; Lynne Wilson, Treas.; Mrs. Claire St. Clair, Finance Mgr. Total in Residence 1; Total Staff 30.

[J] SECULAR INSTITUTES

WINDHAM. *Secular Branch of the Daughters of the Holy Spirit* (2003) 80 Tuckie Rd., Windham, 06280.
Tel: 860-456-9319; Tel: 860-456-2778; Email: conssecdhs@aol.com. Sally J. Tolles, D.H.S., J.D., J.C.L., Contact Person.

[K] CAMPUS MINISTRY

WILLIMANTIC. *Campus Ministry* Eastern Connecticut State University, Newman Hall. 290 Prospect St., Willimantic, 06226. Tel: 860-423-0856;
Fax: 860-456-8083; Email: lapointel@easternct.edu; Email: ficaraj@easternct.edu; Web: www.norwichdiocese.org. Very Rev. Laurence A.M. LaPointe, Diocesan Dir. Campus Ministry; Rev. Jonathan J. Ficara, Campus Min.

Wesleyan University-The University Ministry, Office of Religious & Spiritual Life, Wesleyan University, 171 Church St., Middletown, 06459-0029.
Tel: 860-685-2285; Fax: 860-685-2821; Email: wwallace@wesleyan.edu; Web: www.wesleyan.edu/chaplains. Rev. William Wallace, O.S.A., J.D., Chap.

Connecticut College, Harkness Chapel, 270 Mohegan Ave., New London, 06320-4196.
Tel: 860-439-2450; Fax: 860-439-2463; Email: rwashaba@conncoll.edu; Web: www.conncoll.edu/campus-life/religious-and-spiritual-life/catholic-

community/. Revs. Jonathan J. Ficara, Chap.; Robert Washabaugh, Chap.

University of Connecticut, St. Thomas Aquinas Chapel, 46 N. Eagleville Rd., Storrs, 06268-1710. Tel: 860-429-6436; Fax: 860-429-2809; Email: frjohnantonellesta@gmail.com; Web: www.stmary-stthomas.community. Rev. John N. Antonelle, Chap.

[L] MISCELLANEOUS

NORWICH. *The Annual Catholic Appeal of the Diocese of Norwich, Inc.*, 197 Broadway, 06360. Tel: 860-886-1928; Fax: 860-886-2651; Email: dodadm@norwichdiocese.net; Email: memahoney@norwichdiocese.net; Web: www.norwichdiocesedevelopment.org. Mrs. Mary Ellen Mahoney, Exec.

The Catholic Foundation of the Diocese of Norwich, Inc., 197 Broadway, 06360. Tel: 860-886-1928; Fax: 860-886-2651; Email: memahoney@norwichdiocese.net; Email: dodadm@norwichdiocese.net; Web: www.norwichdiocesedevelopment.org. Mrs. Mary Ellen Mahoney, Dir.

The Donor Advised Funds of the Diocese of Norwich, Inc., 201 Broadway, 06360. Tel: 860-887-9294; Fax: 860-886-1670; Email: financekarenh@norwichdiocese.net. Rev. Peter J. Langevin.

CROMWELL. *Basilian Fathers of Connecticut, Inc.* (1987) 33 Prospect Hill Rd., Cromwell, 06416. Tel: 860-632-3010; Fax: 860-632-3030; Email: rector@holyapostles.edu. Very Rev. Douglas L. Mosey, C.S.B., Ph.D., Pres. & Rector.

Marian Housing Corporation, 201 Broadway, 06360-4328. Tel: 860-632-1688; Fax: 860-632-1542; Email: manager.rook@gmail.com. Ms. Elizabeth Wytas, Contact Person.

DEEP RIVER. *Edmund Rice Charitable Foundation, Inc.*, 135 Kirtland St., Deep River, 06417. Tel: 860-343-1340; Fax: 860-343-1394; Email: potemrip@mtstjohn.org. Dr. Pamela Potemri, Dir.

Mount Saint John Foundation for Charitable Works, Inc., 135 Kirtland St., Deep River, 06417. Tel: 860-343-1300; Fax: 860-343-1394; Email: potemrip@mtstjohn.org. Dr. Pamela Potemri, Dir.

MIDDLETOWN. *Office of Advancement*, 1740 Randolph Rd., Middletown, 06457. Tel: 860-347-8957; Fax: 860-344-9887; Email: sdevany@mercyhigh.com; Web: www.mercyhigh.com. Susan Devany, Dir. Advancement; Barbara P. Miller, Dir. Alumnae.

Mercy-Xavier Fund Corporation, 181 Randolph Rd., Middletown, 06457. Tel: 860-346-7735; Fax: 860-346-6859; Email: deustis@xavierhighschool.org. Mr. David Eustis, Headmaster.

Xavier Advancement Office, 181 Randolph Rd., Middletown, 06457. Tel: 860-346-6109; Fax: 860-346-6859; Email: advancement@xavierhighschool.org; Web: www.xavierhighschool.org. Liz Whitty, Dir.; Greg Jaskot, Assoc. Dir. Total Staff 3.

MYSTIC. *St. Edmund's of Connecticut, Inc.*, 1 Enders Island, P.O. Box 399, Mystic, 06355-0399. Tel: 860-536-0565; Fax: 860-572-7655; Email: admin@endersisland.com; Web: www.endersisland.com. Most Rev. Michael R. Cote, D.D., Pres.; Revs. David Clay, Supr.; Thomas F.X. Hoar, S.S.E., Sec.; Most Rev. Thomas Tobin.

PUTNAM. *The Daughters of the Holy Spirit Charitable Trust* (1985) 72 Church St., Putnam, 06260-1810. Tel: 860-928-0891; Fax: 860-928-6496; Email: bmorrow@snet.net. Sr. Bonnie Morrow, Trustee & Contact Person.

WILLIMANTIC. *Saint Joseph Home for the Aged, Inc.* (1991) 88 Jackson St., Willimantic, 06226. Tel: 860-887-9294; Fax: 860-885-1512; Email: financekarenh@norwichdiocese.net. Ms. Karen Huffer, Contact Person.

WINDHAM. *Sagrado Corazon de Jesus, Inc. of Windham*, 61 Club Rd., Windham, 06280. Tel: 860-423-8617; Fax: 860-423-4157; Email: sagradocor@sbcglobal.net. Very Rev. Laurence A.M. LaPointe.

[M] CLOSED SCHOOLS

NORWICH. *Diocese of Norwich*, Tel: 860-887-9294; Email: rinere@norwichdiocese.net. Sr. Elissa Rinere, C.P., J.C.D., Chancellor.

St. Joseph, Norwich School: 120 Cliff St., Norwich CT 06360. Closed-for inquiries or records contact St. Joseph, Norwich.

St. Mary, Jewett City School: 54 Main St., Jewett City, CT 06351. Closed-for inquiries or records contact St. Mary Church, Jewett City.

St. John, Middletown School: 5 St. John Sq., Middletown, CT 06347. Closed-for inquiries or records contact St. John Church, Middletown.

St. Mary, Middletown School: 87 S. Main St., Middletown CT 06347. Closed-for inquiries or records contact St. Mary Church, Middletown.

St. Sebastian, Middletown School: 61 Durant Ter., Middletown, CT 06457. Closed-for inquiries or records contact St. Sebastian Church, Middletown.

All Hallows, Moosup School: Plainfield Catholic School, 120 Prospect St., Moosup, CT 06354. Closed-for inquiries or records contact St. John the Apostle, Plainfield.

St. John the Apostle, Plainfield School: Plainfield Catholic, 14 Railroad Ave., Plainfield, CT 06374. Closed-for inquiries or records contact St. John the Apostle, Plainfield.

St. Mary Church of the Visitation, Putnam School: 23 Marshall St., Putnam, CT 06260. Closed-for inquiries or records contact St. Mary Church of the Visitation, Putnam.

St. Bernard, Rockville School: 20 School St., Rockville, CT 06066. Closed-for inquiries or records contact St. Bernard Church, Rockville.

St. Joseph, Rockville School: 41 West St., Rockville, CT 06066. Closed-for inquiries or records contact St. Joseph Church, Rockville.

RELIGIOUS INSTITUTES OF MEN REPRESENTED IN THE DIOCESE

For further details refer to the corresponding bracketed number in the Religious Institutes of Men or Women section.

[1350]—*Brothers of St. Francis Xavier* (St. Joseph Prov.)—C.F.X.
[0470]—*The Capuchin Friars* (Prov. of St. Mary)—O.F.M. Cap.
[0740]—*Congregation of Marian Fathers of the Immaculate Conception of the B.V.M.*—M.I.C.
[]—*Congregation of Priests of St. Basil*—C.S.B.
[]—*Congregation of the Oratory of St. PhilipNeri*—C.O.
[]—*Congregation of St. Therese*—C.S.T.
[0480]—*Conventual Franciscans*—O.F.M.Conv.
[0533]—*Franciscan Friars of the Immaculate*—F. I.
[0720]—*The Missionaries of Our Lady of La Salette* (Prov. of Our Lady of the Americas)—M.S.
[]—*Order of St. Paul the First Hermit, Pauline Fathers*—O.S.P.P.E.
[]—*Order of Preachers*—O.P.
[1190]—*Salesians of Don Bosco*—S.D.B.
[]—*Salvatorian Fathers*—S.D.S.
[0440]—*Society of St. Edmund*—S.S.E.
[0590]—*Society of the Missionaries of the Holy Apostles*—M.S.A.

RELIGIOUS INSTITUTES OF WOMEN REPRESENTED IN THE DIOCESE

[0130]—*Apostles of the Sacred Heart of Jesus*—A.S.C.J.
[]—*Daughters of Our Lady of the Garden*—F.M.H.
[0820]—*Daughters of the Holy Spirit*—D.H.S.
[2970]—*School Sisters of Notre Dame*—S.S.N.D.
[]—*Sisters Oblates to Divine Love*—R.O.D.A.
[0530]—*Sisters of Charity of Our Lady, Mother of the Church*—S.C.M.C.
[3860]—*Sisters of St. Joseph of Cluny*—S.J.C.
[2575]—*Sisters of Mercy of the Americas*—R.S.M.
[]—*Sisters of the Cross and Passion*—C.P.
[2140]—*Sisters of the Poor of the Immaculate Conception of the Blessed Virgin Mary (Lithuanian)*—M.V.S.
[3320]—*Sisters of the Presentation of the B.V.M.*—P.B.V.M.

NECROLOGY

† Archambault, Richard L., Project Northeast, Putnam, Died Mar. 8, 2018

Diocese of Oakland

(Dioecesis Quercopolitana)

Most Reverend

MICHAEL C. BARBER, S.J.

Bishop of Oakland; ordained June 8, 1985; appointed Bishop of Oakland May 3, 2013; ordained and installed May 25, 2013. *Office: 2121 Harrison St., Ste. 100, Oakland, CA 94612-3788.* Tel: 510-267-8316; Fax: 510-839-6770.

Most Reverend

JOHN S. CUMMINS, D.D.

Retired Bishop of Oakland; ordained January 24, 1953; appointed Titular Bishop of Lambesi and Auxiliary Bishop of Sacramento February 26, 1974; consecrated May 16, 1974; appointed Bishop of Oakland May 3, 1977; installed June 30, 1977; retired September 30, 2003. *Office: 617 Prospect Ave., Oakland, CA 94610.* Tel: 510-832-5037.

Chancery Office: 2121 Harrison St., Ste. 100, Oakland, CA 94612-3788. Tel: 510-893-4711; Fax: 510-893-0945.

Email: chancellor@oakdiocese.org

Web: www.oakdiocese.org

ESTABLISHED JANUARY 13, 1962.

Square Miles 1,467.

Comprises two Counties in the State of California–viz., Alameda and Contra Costa.

Legal Title: The Roman Catholic Bishop of Oakland, a Corporation Sole.
For legal titles of parishes and diocesan institutions, consult the Chancery Office.

STATISTICAL OVERVIEW

Personnel	
Bishop	1
Retired Bishops	1
Priests: Diocesan Active in Diocese	100
Priests: Diocesan Active Outside Diocese	7
Priests: Diocesan in Foreign Missions	1
Priests: Retired, Sick or Absent	57
Number of Diocesan Priests	165
Religious Priests in Diocese	180
Total Priests in Diocese	345
Extern Priests in Diocese	37
Ordinations:	
Diocesan Priests	3
Transitional Deacons	1
Permanent Deacons in Diocese	110
Total Brothers	83
Total Sisters	372
Parishes	
Parishes	82
With Resident Pastor:	
Resident Diocesan Priests	45
Resident Religious Priests	9
Without Resident Pastor:	
Administered by Priests	28
Missions	1
Pastoral Centers	11
Professional Ministry Personnel:	
Brothers	1
Sisters	41
Lay Ministers	127
Welfare	
Health Care Centers	1
Total Assisted	3,545
Homes for the Aged	2
Total Assisted	280
Day Care Centers	1
Total Assisted	418
Specialized Homes	3
Total Assisted	4,410
Special Centers for Social Services	5
Total Assisted	738,389
Residential Care of Disabled	1
Total Assisted	915
Educational	
Diocesan Students in Other Seminaries	19
Seminaries, Religious	1
Students Religious	20
Total Seminarians	39
Colleges and Universities	2
Total Students	4,811
High Schools, Diocesan and Parish	2
Total Students	1,678
High Schools, Private	7
Total Students	3,951
Elementary Schools, Diocesan and Parish	39
Total Students	9,952
Elementary Schools, Private	2
Total Students	233
Catechesis/Religious Education:	
High School Students	6,336
Elementary Students	15,179
Total Students under Catholic Instruction	42,179
Teachers in the Diocese:	
Priests	21
Brothers	16
Sisters	18
Lay Teachers	1,790
Vital Statistics	
Receptions into the Church:	
Infant Baptism Totals	6,329
Minor Baptism Totals	510
Adult Baptism Totals	247
Received into Full Communion	251
First Communions	7,461
Confirmations	4,310
Marriages:	
Catholic	771
Interfaith	106
Total Marriages	877
Deaths	2,320
Total Catholic Population	384,605
Total Population	2,896,939

Former Bishops—Most Revs. FLOYD L. BEGIN, S.T.D., cons. May 1, 1947; appt. Bishop of Oakland on Feb. 21, 1962; died April 26, 1977; JOHN S. CUMMINS, D.D., (Retired), ord. January 24, 1953; appt. Titular Bishop of Lambesi and Auxiliary Bishop of Sacramento February 26, 1974; cons. May 16, 1974; appt. Bishop of Oakland May 3, 1977; installed June 30, 1977; retired Sept. 30, 2003; ALLEN HENRY VIGNERON, D.D., ord. July 27, 1975; appt. Auxiliary Bishop of Detroit and Titular Bishop of Sault Ste. Marie June 12, 1996; cons. July 9, 1996; appt. Coadjutor Bishop of Oakland Jan. 10, 2003; installed Feb. 26, 2003; succeeded to See Oct. 1, 2003; appt. Archbishop of Detroit Jan. 5, 2009; installed Jan. 28, 2009.; SALVATORE J. CORDILEONE, ord. July 9, 1982; appt. Auxiliary Bishop of San Diego and Titular Bishop of Natchesium July 5, 2002; ord. Aug. 21, 2002; appt. Bishop of Oakland March 23, 2009; installed May 5, 2009; appt. Archbishop of San Francisco July 27, 2012.

Chancery Office—2121 Harrison St., Ste. 100, Oakland, 94612-3788. Tel: 510-893-4711; Fax: 510-893-0945. Office Hours: 8:30 am-4:45 pm, except legal holidays.

Office of the Bishop—Most Rev. MICHAEL C. BARBER, S.J., Bishop; Rev. ALEXANDER Q. CASTILLO, Bishop's Sec. & Episcopal Master of Ceremonies, 2121 Harrison St., Ste. 100, Oakland, 94612-3788. Tel: 510-267-8316; Fax: 510-839-6770.

Vicar General—Very Rev. GEORGE E. MOCKEL.

Chancellor—MR. STEPHEN A. WILCOX.

Chief Financial Officer—MR. PAUL BONGIOVANNI.

Judicial Vicar—Very Rev. BICH N. NGUYEN, J.C.L.

Interim Director of Communications and Community Relations—MS. HELEN OSMAN.

Catholic Cathedral Corporation of the East Bay (CCCEB)—MR. PAUL BONGIOVANNI, Contact, 2121 Harrison St., Ste. 100, Oakland, 94612-3788. Tel: 510-267-8321; Fax: 510-839-7545; Email: pbongiovanni@oakdiocese.org. Officers: Very Rev. GEORGE E. MOCKEL, Pres.; MR. PAUL BONGIOVANNI, CFO/Treas.

Christ the Light Cathedral Corporation—MR. PAUL BONGIOVANNI, Contact, 2121 Harrison St., Ste. 100, Oakland, 94612-3788. Tel: 510-267-8321; Fax: 510-839-7545; Email: pbongiovanni@oakdiocese.org. Officers: Most Rev. MICHAEL C. BARBER, S.J., Pres.; MR. PAUL BONGIOVANNI, Treas.; MR. WILLIAM UTIC, Sec.

John Paul II High School, a California nonprofit religious corporation—Very Rev. GEORGE E. MOCKEL, Contact Person, 2121 Harrison St., Ste. 100, Oakland, 94612-3788. Tel: 510-267-8317; Fax: 510-893-0945; Email: gmockel@oakdiocese.org. Officers: MR. JOSEPH L. CONNELL, Ph.D., Pres.; Very Rev. GEORGE E. MOCKEL, Vice Pres.; MR. PAUL BONGIOVANNI, Treas.; Rev. LARRY E. YOUNG, Sec.

The Roman Catholic Welfare Corporation of Oakland—2121 Harrison St., Ste. 100, Oakland, 94612-3788. Tel: 510-893-4711. Officers: MS. KATHLEEN RADECKE, Pres.; MR. PAUL BONGIOVANNI, Sec./Treas.

Diocesan Consultors—Revs. GEORGE ALENGADAN; PAUL COLEMAN, (Ireland); Very Rev. GEORGE E. MOCKEL; Revs. KENNETH L. SALES; LARRY E. YOUNG; MARK WIESNER.

Diocesan Finance Council—MR. WILLIAM UTIC, Chm.; MR. DAVID L. ASH; MR. FRANK BALESTRERI; MR.

JOHN CALLAGY; Very Rev. GEORGE E. MOCKEL; MR. JOHN TARMAN.

Diocesan Review Board—MR. STEPHEN A. WILCOX, Victims Assistance Coord.; Rev. ROBERT J. MCCANN, R.S.C.J., J.C.L.; MRS. PENNY BEITLER; MRS. COLLEEN T. DAVIES, Esq.; MR. MICHAEL E. DELEHUNT, Esq.; MR. GEORGE FREUHAN.

Presbyteral Council—Revs. GEORGE ALENGADAN; MICHAEL T. CASTORI, S.J.; PAUL COLEMAN, (Ireland); PAUL R. VASSAR; RAMIRO FLORES; JOHN KASPER, O.S.F.S.; SERGIO LOPEZ, J.C.D.; ROBERT J. MCCANN, R.S.C.J., J.C.L., Chair; H. DAVID MENDOZA-VELA; Very Rev. BICH N. NGUYEN, J.C.L., Sec.; Revs. GERALD PEDRERA; RAYMOND SACCA, Vice Chair; KENNETH L. SALES; MARK WIESNER; LARRY E. YOUNG, Ex Officio; Very Rev. GEORGE E. MOCKEL. Ex Officio: Very Rev. GEORGE E. MOCKEL.

Diocesan Departments

Archivist/Records Management—MS. CARRIE MCCLISH, 2121 Harrison St., Ste. 100, Oakland, 94612-3788. Tel: 510-267-8318; Fax: 510-893-4734.

Bishop's Representative for the Eastern Catholic Churches—Rev. DAVID LINK, (Retired).

Canon Law Department—

Judicial Vicar & Director—2121 Harrison St., Ste. 100, Oakland, 94612-3788. Fax: 510-836-0611. Very Rev. BICH N. NGUYEN, J.C.L.

Adjutant Judicial Vicar—Rev. ROBERT J. MCCANN, R.S.C.J., J.C.L.

Promoter of Justice—Rev. SALVADOR MACIAS, J.C.L.

Defenders of the Bond—Revs. DAVID K. O'ROURKE, O.P.; TIMOTHY T. FERGUSON, J.C.L.

Judges—Very Rev. BICH N. NGUYEN, J.C.L.; Revs. ROBERT J. MCCANN, R.S.C.J., J.C.L.; HERMAN LEONG, J.C.L.; SERGIO LOPEZ, J.C.D.; DAVID E. STAAL, J.C.L., J.D.

Notaries of the Tribunal—NINA M. WOODCOCK; MARY O'SULLIVAN.

Auditors—MRS. CAROL IZO; Deacon JOHN KORTUEM; MARY MCMANUS; PATRICIA MOORE; TRIEU GENTRY; MR. MARCOS POZO; PATRICIA PARSON; Deacon LOC H. NGUYEN.

Court of Second Instance—Very Rev. BICH N. NGUYEN, J.C.L., Presiding Judge; MRS. CAROL IZO, Notary.

Censor—Rev. ROBERT J. MCCANN, R.S.C.J., J.C.L., 2121 Harrison St., Ste. 100, Oakland, 94612-3788. Tel: 510-267-8330.

Catholic Funeral and Cemetery Services—MR. ROBERT W. SEELIG, Exec. Dir., 4750 Willow Rd., Ste. 200, Pleasanton, 94588. Tel: 925-946-1440. ANTIOCH, Contra Costa County, Holy Cross Cemetery and Funeral Center; HAYWARD, Alameda County, Holy Sepulchre Cemetery and Funeral Center, Sorensen Chapel; LAFAYETTE, Contra Costa County, Queen of Heaven Cemetery and Funeral Center; LIVERMORE, Alameda County, St. Michael Cemetery and Funeral Center; OAKLAND, Alameda County, Cathedral of Christ the Light Mausoleum/St. Mary Cemetery and Funeral Center; Cooper Chapel; SAN PABLO, Contra Costa County, St. Joseph Cemetery and Funeral Center.

*Legal Title: The Roman Catholic Cemeteries of the Diocese of Oakland, a California nonprofit religious corporation, dba Catholic Funeral and Cemetery Services*Officers: MR. ROBERT W. SEELIG, Pres.; Very Rev. GEORGE E. MOCKEL, Vice Pres.; MR. PAUL BONGIOVANNI, Sec./Treas.

Catholic Youth Organization and Catholic Scouting—MR. BILL FORD, Dir., 2121 Harrison St., Ste. 100, Oakland, 94612-3788. Tel: 510-893-5154; Fax: 510-834-5498.

Diocesan Chaplain for Catholic Scouting—Rev. JAYSON J. LANDEZA.

Clergy Services—2121 Harrison St., Ste. 100, Oakland, 94612-3788. Tel: 510-267-8307. Rev. LARRY E. YOUNG, Vicar for Priests & Dir. Clergy Svcs.

Apostleship of the Sea—Rev. JOSEPH DUONG PHAN, Port Chap., 4001 Seventh St., Oakland, 94607. Tel: 510-444-7885.

Diaconate—2121 Harrison St., Ste. 100, Oakland, 94612-3788. Tel: 510-267-8305. Deacon TIMOTHY L. MOORE, Bishop's Rep. to Diaconate & Dir. Deacon Personnel.

Office of Permanent Deacon Formation—2121 Harrison St., Ste. 100, Oakland, 94612-3788. Tel: 510-267-8356. Deacon TIMOTHY L. MOORE, Dir.

Priest Personnel Board—Revs. GEORGE ALENGADAN; RAMIRO FLORES; JAMES V. MATTHEWS; KENNETH L. SALES; PAUL J. SCHMIDT, (Retired).

Ex Officio—Very Rev. GEORGE E. MOCKEL; Rev. LARRY E. YOUNG.

Priests' Ongoing Formation—2121 Harrison St., Ste. 100, Oakland, 94612-3788. Tel: 510-267-8364. Rev. KEVIN SCHINDLER-MCGRAW, O.F.M.Conv., Dir.

Vocations—2121 Harrison St., Ste. 100, Oakland, 94612-3788. Tel: 510-267-8356. Revs. WAYNE CAMPBELL, Dir. Vocations & Seminarians; ALEXANDER Q. CASTILLO, Co Dir. Seminarians.

Department of Diocesan Worship (Episcopal Master of Ceremonies)—Rev. ALEXANDER Q. CASTILLO, Dir.

Department of Faith Formation and Evangelization—2121 Harrison St., Ste. 100, Oakland, 94612-3788. Tel: 510-267-8357; Fax: 510-272-0738. Rev. ALEXANDER Q. CASTILLO, Dir.

Associate Director—VACANT.

Latino Ministry—MR. HECTOR D. MEDINA, Coord.

Marriage and Family Life Ministry—MRS. MIMI STREETT, Coord.

Life and Justice Ministry—CRISTINA HERNANDEZ, Coord.

Youth Ministry and Special Initiatives—MRS. PATTI COLLYER, Coord.

Special Religious Education (SPRED)—Web: www.oakdiocese.org/education/spred. MS. MICHELLE MARTINEZ-KILTY, Coord.

Ethnic Pastoral and Cultural Centers—Sr. FELICIA SARATI, C.S.J., Dir.

St. Joseph Center for the Deaf Catechetical and Faith Formation—Our Lady of Guadalupe Parish, 41933 Blacow Rd., Fremont, 94538-3365. Tel: 510-267-8348; Web: www.oakdiocese.org/sjcd. Rev. LARRY E. YOUNG, Contact, Email: lyoung@oakdiocese.org.

Diocesan Vicar for Religious—VACANT.

Ethnic Pastoral and Cultural Centers—

African American Community—MRS. JO ANN EVANS, 2858 Gonzaga Ave., Richmond, 94806. Tel: 510-223-9654.

Asian/Indian Community—MRS. BELLA COMELO, 2048 Juneau St., San Leandro, 94577. Tel: 510-357-0940.

Brazilian Community—MR. JOSE FREITAS, 1500 Elm St., El Cerrito, 94530. Tel: 510-232-4328.

Chinese Pastoral Center—Rev. PAUL FENG CHEN, Dir., 707 C St., Union City, 94587. Tel: 510-471-2609.

Eritrean Community—2611 E. 9th St., Oakland, 94601. Tel: 510-547-5948. Rev. GHEBRIEL WOLDAI, Bay Area Regl. Dir.

Ethiopian Community in Formation—MS. ELIZABETH GABRE-KRISTOS, 1239 Liberty St., #220, El Cerrito, 94530. Tel: 510-620-0594.

Fijian Community—MR. SAM DEO, 15207 Hardin St., San Leandro, 94579. Tel: 510-329-8621.

Indonesian Community—MR. IRWAN SIE, 246 Mission Tierra Pl., Fremont, 94539. Tel: 408-824-0052.

Kenyan Community—MR. BERNARD WANGO, 2643 Gibraltar Ln., Tracy, 95377. Tel: 209-834-6454.

Kmhmu/Laotian Pastoral Center—12490 San Pablo Ave., Richmond, 94805. Tel: 510-610-4466. MR. KAN SOURIYA.

Korean Pastoral Center—Revs. BARTHOLOMEW CHOI, Dir., St. Andrew Kim Korean Catholic Pastoral Center, 6226 Camden St., Oakland, 94605. Tel: 510-562-3843; JONG KWANG KIM, Dir., St. Paul Chong Korean Catholic Community in Tri-Valley, 425 Boulder Ct., #400, Pleasanton, 94566. Tel: 925-600-0177.

Nigerian-Igbo Community—Rev. JOHN OFFOR, (Nigeria) 2980 Senter Rd., San Jose, 94511. Tel: 510-731-8176.

Polish Pastoral Center—Deacon WITOLD CICHON, Dir., 4593 Ridgeline Dr., Antioch, 94531-9393. Tel: 925-779-1027.

Tongan Community—MRS. MELE TAUTUIAKI, 1633 87th Ave., Oakland, 94621-1511. Tel: 510-927-7131.

Vietnamese Pastoral Center—Sr. ROSALINE NGUYEN, L.H.C., 2121 Harrison St., Ste. 100, Oakland, 94612-3788. Tel: 510-628-2153.

Facilities, Planning and Services—MR. ALEX HERNANDEZ, Dir., Tel: 510-267-8355; Email: ahernandez@oakdiocese.org; MR. JAMES H. MCCANN, Assoc. Dir., 2121 Harrison St., Ste. 100, Oakland, 94612-3788. Tel: 510-267-8308; Fax: 510-839-7545; Email: jmccann@oakdiocese.org.

Design Review Board—Revs. FRED A. RICCIO; LARRY E. YOUNG; MR. PAUL BONGIOVANNI, Finance; MR. MICHAEL FORBES; MR. RAYMOND KUCA, AIA; MRS. LISA OBEREMPT, Finance; MR. ROBERT SILVA; MR. MARK ZALESKI; MR. ALEX HERNANDEZ; MR. JAMES H. MCCANN.

Financial Services—MR. PAUL BONGIOVANNI, CFO, Tel: 510-267-8321; Fax: 510-839-7545; Email: pbongiovanni@oakdiocese.org; MRS. HELEN V. GIUNTOLI, Controller, 2121 Harrison St., Ste. 100, Oakland, 94612-3788. Tel: 510-267-8336.

Human Resources—2121 Harrison St., Ste. 100, Oakland, 94612-3788. Tel: 510-267-8359. MR. GREGORY TOLER, Dir.

Safe Environment for Children—MS. DIANA BITZ, Prog. Coord., 2121 Harrison St., Ste. 100, Oakland, 94612-3788. Tel: 510-267-8315.

Newspaper: "The Catholic Voice"—MR. ALBERT C. PACCIORINI, Editor, 2121 Harrison St., Ste. 100, Oakland, 94612-3788. Tel: 510-419-1073; Web: www.catholicvoiceoakland.org.

El Heraldo Catolico—MR. ALBERT C. PACCIORINI, Editor, 2121 Harrison St., Ste. 100, Oakland, 94612-3788. Tel: 510-419-1073; Web: elheraldocatolico.org.

Office for Mission Advancement—MR. STEPHEN A. WILCOX, Exec. Dir. Mission Advancement, 2121 Harrison St., Ste. 100, Oakland, 94612-3788. Tel: 510-267-8334; Fax: 510-446-7429; Email: swilcox@oakdiocese.org; MR. GILES MILLER, Exec. Dir. Major Gifts/Planned Giving, Tel: 510-628-2156; Email: gmiller@oakdiocese.org; MS. FILOMENA SPERO, Exec. Dir. FACE (Family Aid-Catholic Education), Tel: 510-267-2169; Email: fspero@oakdiocese.org; MS. TERRI PORTER, Assoc. Dir. Office for Mission Advancement and FACE (Family Aid-Catholic Education), Tel: 510-267-8314; Email: tporter@oakdiocese.org.

Pastoral Planning—Very Rev. GEORGE E. MOCKEL, 2121 Harrison St., Ste. 100, Oakland, 94612-3788. Tel: 510-267-8317.

Diocesan Planning Board—MR. MARK BALES; Deacon REY ENCARNACION; MS. MARY FAIR; MR. MIKE HENDERSHOT; MS. JOANN MASS; MS. RITA MITCHELL. Ex Officio: Very Rev. GEORGE E. MOCKEL.

Propagation of the FaithVery Rev. GEORGE E. MOCKEL, Dir., 2121 Harrison St., Ste. 100, Oakland, 94612-3788. Tel: 510-267-8317. Legal Title: Oakland Society for the Propagation of the Faith.

Schools—2121 Harrison St., Oakland, 94612-3787. Tel: 510-628-2151. MS. KATHLEEN RADECKE, Supt.; MRS. LINDA BASMAN, WCEA Commissioner; MRS. MARGO TAMMEN, Fiscal Controller, Schools.

Organizations and Services—

Campaign for Human Development—433 Jefferson St., Oakland, 94607-3539. Tel: 510-768-3176. MR. MARC MCKIMMEY, Dir.

Catholic Charismatic Renewal—Revs. ROBERT MENDONCA, Diocesan Dir., English Speaking Charismatic Renewal, Tel: 925-828-2460; OLMAN SOLIS, Diocesan Dir. Hispanic Charismatic Renewal, Tel: 510-568-1080.

Catholic Relief Services—433 Jefferson St., Oakland, 94607-3539. Tel: 510-768-3176. MR. MARC MCKIMMEY, Dir.

Confraternity of Eucharistic Devotion (CEDDO)—MS. GLENDA DUBSKY, Mod.; MR. RICO BANSON, Asst. Mod.; MS. MAY PLATA, Sec.; Deacon ALBERTO DIZON, Treas.; Rev. BRANDON MACADAEG, Chap., Web: www.oakdiocese.org/ceddo.

Courage - Oakland Chapter—Chaplains: Revs. JOHN DIREEN, Tel: 510-374-2507; Email: johndireen@hotmail.com; FRANCISCO FIGUEROA-ESQUER, Tel: 510-932-1393; Email: fcofiguesquer@priest.com.

Cursillo Movement—Revs. LEO J. EDGERLY JR., Diocesan Spiritual Dir., Tel: 510-530-4343; GUSTAVO BARRIENTOS, (Guatemala) Spiritual Dir. for Spanish MCC (Cursillos in Christianity Movement), Tel: 510-782-2171.

Exorcist—Rev. KENNETH NOBREGA, 2121 Harrison St., Ste. 100, Oakland, 94612-3788. Tel: 510-843-2244; Email: fatherkennethnobrega@icloud.com.

Pontifical Association of the Holy Childhood—Very Rev. GEORGE E. MOCKEL, Dir., 2121 Harrison St., Ste. 100, Oakland, 94612-3788. Tel: 510-267-8317.

St. Peter the Apostle Society—Very Rev. GEORGE E. MOCKEL, Dir., 2121 Harrison St., Ste. 100, Oakland, 94612-3788. Tel: 510-267-8317.

CLERGY, PARISHES, MISSIONS AND PAROCHIAL SCHOOLS

CITY OF OAKLAND

(ALAMEDA COUNTY)

1—CATHEDRAL PARISH OF CHRIST THE LIGHT (2008)
2121 Harrison St., Ste. 130, 94612.
Tel: 510-832-5057; Email: cathedral@cpctl.net; Web: www.ctlcathedral.org. Rev. James V. Matthews, Rector; Very Rev. Bich N. Nguyen, J.C.L., Vice-Rector; Rev. Francsisco Diaz Diaz, Parochial Vicar; Deacon Eugene Stelly, (Retired); Rev. James Schexnayder, In Res., (Retired); Deacons Peter Ta; David Young.

Catechesis Religious Program—Email: amfulay@oakdiocese.org. Adrian Mison Fulay, D.R.E. Students 96.

2—ST. ANDREW-ST. JOSEPH (1965) (African American),

Merged into Cathedral Parish of Christ the Light, Oakland.
3—ST. ANTHONY (1871) Merged with Mary Help of Christians Church, Oakland to form St. Anthony-Mary Help of Christians, Oakland.
4—ST. ANTHONY-MARY HELP OF CHRISTIANS
1610 E. 15th St., 94606-4425. Tel: 510-534-2117; Fax: 510-534-2119; Email: office@stanthony-maryhelp.org. Mailing Address: 1520 E. 15th St., 94606. Revs. Juan Franco, Admin.; Mark Hoc Thai Kieu, O.Cist., (Vietnam) Parochial Vicar; Ghebriel Woldai, In Res.
Res.: 1535 16th Ave., 94606-4425.
Mary Help of Christians Church: 2611 E. 9th St., 94601.
School—St. Anthony School, (Grades K-8), 1500 E. 15th St., 94606. Tel: 510-534-3334; Fax: 510-534-3378; Email: mbravo@csdo.org; Web: stanthony-oakland.org. Marisol Preciado, Prin. Lay Teachers 7; Students 158.
Catechesis Religious Program—Email: juventudesperanza.sa@gmail.com. Iris Gutierrez, D.R.E.; Diana Mariscal, D.R.E.; Juan Pablo Meza, D.R.E.; Mai Nguyen, D.R.E.; Uyen Nguyen, D.R.E. Students 131.
5—ST. AUGUSTINE (1907)
400 Alcatraz Ave., 94609. Tel: 510-653-8631; Email: staugustinefrontdesk@gmail.com. Rev. Augustine Joseph, Parochial Admin.; Karen Glen, Ministries Coord.; April McNeely, Music Dir.; Linda Prara-Jenkins, Admin. Asst.
Catechesis Religious Program—
Tel: 510-653-8631, Ext. 103; Email: kglen.staugustine@gmail.com. Karen Glen, Ministry Coord. Students 26.
6—ST. BENEDICT (1930) (African American)
2245 82nd Ave., 94605-3407. Tel: 510-632-1847; Email: saintbenedictcrh@aol.com; Web: www.saintbenedictoakland.com. Revs. Jayson J. Landeza; Vincent Cotter, In Res., (Retired); Aris Pilapil Martin, S.V.D., In Res.; Deacon Ronald Tutson.
Catechesis Religious Program—Email: owanzo@yahoo.com. Students 16.
7—ST. BERNARD (1912) (Hispanic—African American)
1620-62nd Ave., 94621-4221. Tel: 510-632-3013; Fax: 510-632-5286; Email: st.bernard.church@sbcglobal.net. Rev. Stephen Ayisu, S.V.D.; Deacon Javier Fuentes.
Catechesis Religious Program—Students 121.
8—CATHEDRAL OF ST. FRANCIS DE SALES (1886) Merged with St. Mary, Immaculate Conception to form Cathedral Parish of Christ the Light.
9—ST. COLUMBA (1898) (African American)
6401 San Pablo Ave., 94608-1233. Tel: 510-654-7600; Email: stcolumba1898@gmail.com; Web: www.stcolumbao.com. Rev. Aidan McAleenan.
Catechesis Religious Program—Ms. Margaret Roncalli, Dir., Faith Formation. Students 52.
10—ST. CYRIL (1926) (Korean), Merged with St. Lawrence O'Toole, Oakland to form St. Lawrence O'Toole-St. Cyril of Jerusalem, Oakland. For parish records contact St. Lawrence O'Toole-St. Cyril of Jerusalem, Oakland.
11—DIVINE MERCY PARISH
3725 High St., 94619. Tel: 510-530-0761, Ext. 105; Email: slot.stpboffice@gmail.com; Web: www.divinemercyoak.org. Revs. Brandon Macadaeg, Admin.; Luis Lopez, Parochial Vicar.
Catechesis Religious Program—Email: bm.debrasmith@gmail.com. Students 128.
12—ST. ELIZABETH (1892) (Hispanic)
1500 34th Ave., 94601-3024. Tel: 510-536-1266; Email: stelizabethchurch@yahoo.com; Web: www.stelizabeth-church.org. Revs. Luis A. Guzman, O.F.M.; Nghia Phan, O.F.M., Parochial Vicar; Antonio Galindo-Carreon, O.F.M.
School—St. Elizabeth School, (Grades PreK-8), 1516 33rd Ave., 94601-3016. Tel: 510-532-7392; Fax: 510-532-0321; Email: lmullen@csdo.org; Web: www.stelizabeth.us. Mrs. Lynne Mullen, Prin. Lay Teachers 13; Students 238; Clergy / Religious Teachers 1.
Catechesis Religious Program—Olga Dueñas, D.R.E.; Elizabeth Medina, D.R.E.; Ms. Reyna Lupian, RCIA Coord. Students 332.
13—ST. JARLATH (1910)
2620 Pleasant St., 94602-2125. Tel: 510-532-2068; Email: sjarlath@sbcglobal.net; Web: www.stjarlath.org. Rev. Enrique Ballesteros, Admin.; Deacon Noe Gonzalez; Revs. Thomas Martin, (Australia) In Res.; Peter Buor Offeh, (Ghana) In Res.
Catechesis Religious Program—Email: raquesemail@gmail.com. Raquel Vasquez, D.R.E. Students 301.
14—ST. LAWRENCE O'TOOLE, Merged with St. Cyril, Oakland to form St. Lawrence O'Toole-St. Cyril of Jerusalem, Oakland.
15—ST. LAWRENCE O'TOOLE-ST. CYRIL OF JERUSALEM (1916) Merged with St. Paschal Parish to form Divine Mercy Parish.
16—ST. LEO THE GREAT (1911)
176 Ridgeway Ave., 94611-5122. Tel: 510-654-6177; Email: stleo@pacbell.net; Web: www.stleothegreat.org. Revs. Joseph T. Nguyen, Admin.; Bento Tamang, In Res.; Tegha Nji, In Res.; Deacon Dac Cao.
School—St. Leo the Great School, (Grades PreK-8), 4238 Howe St., 94611-4705. Tel: 510-654-7828; Fax: 510-654-4057; Email: ssimril@csdo.org; Web: www.stleothegreat.org. Sonya Simril, Prin. Lay Teachers 13; Students 239.
Catechesis Religious Program—Students 18.
17—ST. LOUIS BERTRAND (1908) (Hispanic—African American)
1410-100th Ave., 94603-2506. Tel: 510-568-1080; Fax: 510-632-8618; Email: parish@slboakland.com. Revs. Olman Solis; Salvador Macias, J.C.L., In Res.; Deacon Earl Johson.
Catechesis Religious Program—Sr. Martha Perez, O.P., D.R.E. Students 430.
18—ST. MARGARET MARY (1922)
1219 Excelsior Ave., 94610. Tel: 510-482-0596; Email: parishoffice@stmargaretm.org; Web: www.stmargmaryoak.org. Rev. Glenn A. Naguit, Admin.; Rev. Canon Olivier Meney, I.C.R.S.S., In Res.
Catechesis Religious Program—Email: luciaccdsmm@gmail.com. Lucia Wyborny, D.R.E. Students 84.
19—MARY HELP OF CHRISTIANS CHURCH (1915) (Spanish), Merged with St. Anthony, Oakland to form St. Anthony-Mary Help of Christians, Oakland.
20—ST. MARY, IMMACULATE CONCEPTION, Merged into the Cathedral Parish of Christ the Light, Oakland.
21—ST. MARY, IMMACULATE CONCEPTION-ST. FRANCIS DE SALES (1993) Merged into the Cathedral Parish of Christ the Light, Oakland.
22—OUR LADY OF LOURDES (1921)
2808 Lakeshore Ave., 94610. Tel: 510-451-1790; Email: lourdesoakland@icloud.com; Web: www.lourdesoakland.com. Revs. James V. Matthews, Parochial Admin.; Alexander Q. Castillo, In Res.; Wayne Campbell, In Res.; Label Carlson, Music & Liturgy Dir.; Carrie Schroeder, Co-Dir., Faith Formation & Ministries Support; Adrian Fulag, Co-Dir., Faith Formation & Ministries Support; Gwendolyn Erik, Office Mgr.
Catechesis Religious Program—Email: lourdesfaithformation@gmail.com. Keith Maczkiewicz, S.J., D.R.E. Students 35.
23—ST. PASCHAL BAYLON (1955) Merged with St. Lawrence O'Toole/St. Cyril Parish to form Divine Mercy Parish.
24—ST. PATRICK (1879) (African American—Hispanic)
1023 Peralta St., 94607-1927. Tel: 510-444-1081; Email: stpatricksecy@gmail.com. Rev. David Masikini, S.J., Admin.; Rosario Trujillo, Sec.
Catechesis Religious Program—Email: stpatrickdre1@aol.com. Nadia Fuentes, D.R.E. Students 72.
25—SACRED HEART (1876)
4025 Martin Luther King Jr. Way, 94609-2317. Tel: 510-655-9209; Fax: 510-652-1958; Email: shoakland@comcast.net; Web: www.sacredheartoak.com. Revs. William Mason, O.M.I.; Philip Singarayar, O.M.I., In Res.; Scott Hill, O.M.I., In Res.; John Mark Ettensohn, O.M.I., In Res.
Catechesis Religious Program—Students 5.
26—ST. THERESA OF THE INFANT JESUS (1925)
30 Mandalay Rd., 94618. Tel: 510-547-2777; Email: melody@sttheresaoakland.org; Web: www.sttheresaoakland.org. Revs. Robert J. McCann, R.S.C.J., J.C.L.; Luke Ssemakula, (Uganda) Parochial Vicar; Abraham Markos Addam, I.M.C., In Res.
Legal Name: St. Theresa of the Infant Jesus (The Little Flower)
School—St. Theresa of the Infant Jesus School, (Grades K-8), 4850 Clarewood Dr., 94618. Tel: 510-547-3146; Email: jkoneffklatt@csdo.org; Web: www.sttheresaschool.org. Judith KoneffKlatt, Prin. Lay Teachers 17; Students 234.
Catechesis Religious Program—
Tel: 510-547-2777, Ext. 39; Email: keri@sttheresaoakland.org. Keri Nims, D.R.E. Students 82.

OUTSIDE THE CITY OF OAKLAND

ALAMEDA, ALAMEDA CO.
1—ST. ALBERT (1976) Merged with St. Philip Neri, Alameda to form St. Philip Neri St. Albert the Great, Alameda.
2—ST. BARNABAS (1925)
1427 Sixth St., Alameda, 94501-3760. Tel: 510-522-8933; Fax: 510-522-8380; Email: sbparishoffice@comcast.net; Web: sbarnabas.weebly.com/. Revs. Dana P. Michaels, Admin.; Lawrence Ng, (Malaysia) In Res.
Catechesis Religious Program—Agatha Leong, D.R.E. Students 45.
3—ST. JOSEPH BASILICA (1885)
1109 Chestnut St., Alameda, 94501-4212. Tel: 510-522-0181; Email: parish@sjbalameda.org; Web: www.sjbalameda.org. Revs. George Alengadan; John Carillo, Parochial Vicar; Sunil Orathel, S.D.B., In Res.; Deacon Marty Leach.
School—St. Joseph Elementary School, (Grades K-8), 1910 San Antonio Ave., Alameda, 94501-4216. Tel: 510-522-4456; Fax: 510-522-2890; Email: myriarte@csdo.org; Email: cvanderveer@csdo.org; Email: cfoley@csdo.org; Web: www.stjosephalameda.org. Dr. Marquita Yriarte, Prin. Lay Teachers 14; Students 233.
Please see Saint Joseph Notre Dame High School under High Schools Parochial located in the Institution section.
Catechesis Religious Program—Tel: 510-995-9409; Email: afourre@sjbalameda.org. Ms. Anne Marie Fourre, Dir. Faith Formation. Students 246.
4—ST. PHILIP NERI (1925) Merged with St. Albert, Alameda to form St. Philip Neri St. Albert the Great, Alameda.
5—ST. PHILIP NERI-ST. ALBERT THE GREAT (2011)
3101 Van Buren St., Alameda, 94501-4840. Tel: 510-373-5200; Email: secretary@spnsa.org; Web: www.spnsa.org. Revs. Robert Kennady Chinnapan, M.F., (India); Anthony Madanu, M.F., (India) Parochial Vicar; Paul J. Schmidt, In Res., (Retired); James B. Pickett, In Res., (Retired).
School—St. Philip Neri-St. Albert the Great School, (Grades K-8), 1335 High St., Alameda, 94501-3165. Tel: 510-521-0787; Fax: 510-521-2418; Email: jmurray@csdo.org; Web: www.spnalameda.org. Jessica Murray, Prin. Lay Teachers 18; Students 253.
Catechesis Religious Program—Tel: 510-373-5218; Email: cff@spnsa.org. Diane Bustos, D.R.E. Students 95.

ANTIOCH, CONTRA COSTA CO.
1—ST. IGNATIUS OF ANTIOCH (1979) [CEM]
3351 Contra Loma Blvd., Antioch, 94509-5468. Tel: 925-778-0768; Email: st.ignatius@sbcglobal.net; Web: www.stignatiusofantioch.com. Rev. Robert K. Rien; Deacon Gary Hack.
Catechesis Religious Program—Tel: 925-778-1631; Email: francesrojek@aol.com. Frances Rojek, Dir. Faith Formation. Students 74.
2—MOST HOLY ROSARY (1874) [CEM] [JC] (Hispanic)
1313 A St., Antioch, 94509-2328. Tel: 925-757-4020, Ext. 10; Email: office@holyrosaryantioch.org; Web: www.holyrosaryantioch.org. Revs. Ramiro Flores; Jimmy Macalinao, Parochial Vicar; Deacon Charles Silvernale; Jorge Aragon, Business Mgr.; Tim McCain, Worship & Liturgy Dir.; Mrs. Jackie Hooke, Pastoral Assoc.; Jesus Tapia, Bookkeeper.
School—Most Holy Rosary School, (Grades PreK-8), 25 E. 15th St., Antioch, 94509. Tel: 925-757-1270; Fax: 925-757-9309; Email: administration@holyrosarycatholicschool.org; Web: www.holyrosarycatholicschool.org. Fely Fajardo, Prin. Lay Teachers 25; Students 393.
Catechesis Religious Program—Tel: 925-757-9515; Email: yolanda.garcia@holyrosaryantioch.org; Email: frbart@holyrosaryantioch.org; Email: lizette.suarez@holyrosaryantioch.org. Lizette Suarez, Dir. Youth Ministry; Ms. Yolanda Garcia, D.R.E., English; Sisters Angeles Gomez, D.R.E., Spanish; Olivia Gutierrez, D.R.E., Spanish. Students 601.

BAY POINT, CONTRA COSTA CO., OUR LADY, QUEEN OF THE WORLD (1962)
3155 Winterbrook Dr., Bay Point, 94565-3264. Tel: 925-458-4718; Email: rectory@olqw.org; Web: www.olqw.org. Rev. Peter Dung Duc Ngo; Deacon Loc H. Nguyen.
Catechesis Religious Program—Tel: 925-458-4574; Email: director@olqwre.com. Rene Asuncion, D.R.E. Students 190.

BERKELEY, ALAMEDA CO.
1—ST. AMBROSE (1909)
1145 Gilman St., Berkeley, 94706-2252. Tel: 510-525-2620; Email: stambrosechurch@comcast.net; Web: www.saintambroseberkeley.org. Rev. Alberto A. Perez, Admin.; Deacon Ralph Nagle.
Catechesis Religious Program—Bro. Damien Ho, D.R.E. Students 163.
2—HOLY SPIRIT PARISH/NEWMAN HALL (1967)
2700 Dwight Way, Berkeley, 94704-3113. Tel: 510-848-7812; Email: info@calnewman.org; Web: www.calnewman.org. Revs. Ivan Tou, C.S.P.; Paul Respond, C.S.P., Parochial Vicar; Stephen Bossi, Parochial VIcar. (Newman Center 1899).
Catechesis Religious Program—Email: faithformation@calnewman.org. Ms. Frances Rojek, D.R.E. Students 63.
3—ST. JOSEPH THE WORKER (1879)
1640 Addison St., Berkeley, 94703-1404. Tel: 510-843-2244; Email: info@stjosephtheworkerchurch.org; Web: www.stjosephtheworkerchurch.org. Revs. Kenneth Nobrega, Admin.; John Gribowich, In Res.; Deacon Jose Manuel Perez.
Catechesis Religious Program—Tel: 510-843-2244.
4—ST. MARY MAGDALEN (1923)
2005 Berryman St., Berkeley, 94709-1920.

Tel: 510-526-4811; Fax: 510-525-3638; Email: parish@marymagdalen.org; Web: marymagdalen.org. Revs. Nicholas Glisson; Laurent Okitakatshi, In Res.; Ioane Ono, In Res.
School—School of the Madeleine, (Grades K-8), 1225 Milvia St., Berkeley, 94709-1932. Tel: 510-526-4744; Fax: 510-526-5152; Email: mschweska@themadeleine.com; Web: www.themadeleine.com. Mr. Joseph Nagel, Prin. Lay Teachers 24; Students 324; Clergy / Religious Teachers 1.
Catechesis Religious Program—Email: hskinner@themadeleine.com. Heather Skinner, D.R.E. Students 32.

BRENTWOOD, CONTRA COSTA CO., IMMACULATE HEART OF MARY (1949) (Spanish—African American)
500 Fairview Ave., Brentwood, 94513-1742. Tel: 925-634-4154; Email: ihmchurch@ihmbrentwood.com; Web: www.ihmbrentwood.com. Revs. Quang Minh Dong; Arturo Bazan, Parochial Vicar; John Erick Villa, Parochial Vicar; Deacons John Kortuem; Ron Horan.
Rectory—1361 Downey Point Dr., Brentwood, 94513-1870.
Catechesis Religious Program—Email: lkortuem@ihmbrentwood.com. Linda Kortuem, D.R.E. Students 637.

BYRON, CONTRA COSTA CO., ST. ANNE (1916)
2800 Camino Diablo Rd., Byron, 94514. Tel: 925-634-6625; Fax: 925-634-4194; Email: office@stannechurchbyron.com; Web: www.stannechurchbyron.com. Mailing Address: P.O. Box 476, Byron, 94514-0476. Rev. Ronald G. Schmit.
Catechesis Religious Program—Tel: 925-634-6625, Ext. 224; Email: srbarbara@stannechurchbyron.com. Sr. Barbara Nixon, S.N.J.M., D.R.E. Students 288.

CASTRO VALLEY, ALAMEDA CO.

1—OUR LADY OF GRACE (1947)
3433 Somerset Ave., Castro Valley, 94546-3354. Tel: 510-537-0806; Email: parish@olgcv.org; Web: www.olgcv.org. Revs. Thomas J. Czeck, O.F.M.Conv.; Paul Fazio, O.F.M.Conv.; Thomas Hamilton, O.F.M.-Conv., In Res.; Francisco Nahoe, O.F.M.Conv., In Res.; Christopher Deitz, O.F.M.Conv., In Res.
Rectory—St. Maximilian Kolbe Friary, 19950 Anita Ave., Castro Valley, 94546.
School—Our Lady of Grace School, (Grades K-8), 19920 Anita Ave., Castro Valley, 94546. Tel: 510-581-3155; Fax: 510-581-1059; Email: sanderson@csdo.org; Web: www.olgschool.org. Susan Anderson, Prin. Lay Teachers 11; Students 216; Clergy / Religious Teachers 1.
Catechesis Religious Program—Tel: 510-582-9266; Email: olgcv@sbcglobal.net. Ms. Robyn Lang, D.R.E. Students 147.

2—TRANSFIGURATION (1961)
4000 E. Castro Valley Blvd., Castro Valley, 94552-4908. Tel: 510-538-7941; Email: transfig_office@sbcglobal.net; Web: www.transfigchurch.com. Revs. Mario L. Borges, Email: transfig_office@sbcglobal.net; Terence O'Malley, S.C.J., Admin.; Deacons Timothy Moore; Burton Rigley, (Retired); John Mignano.
Catechesis Religious Program—Tel: 510-537-1502. Patrice Ballinger, D.R.E. Students 298.

CONCORD, CONTRA COSTA CO.

1—ST. AGNES (1964)
3966 Chestnut Ave., Concord, 94519-1955. Tel: 925-689-0838; Email: marlene.stagnesparish@gmail.com; Web: www.stagnesparish.net. Rev. Johnson C. Abraham, (India); Deacons William Drobick, D.R.E.; Antonio Reyes, (Retired).
Res.: 3900 Chestnut Ave., Concord, 94519-1955.
School—St. Agnes School, (Grades PreK-8), 3886 Chestnut Ave., Concord, 94519-1907. Tel: 925-689-3990; Fax: 925-689-3455; Email: jlucia@csdo.org; Web: www.stagnesconcord.com. Jill Lucia, Prin. Lay Teachers 16; Students 282.
Catechesis Religious Program—Email: deaconbill3@gmail.com. Students 90.

2—ST. BONAVENTURE (1957)
5562 Clayton Rd., Concord, 94521. Tel: 925-672-5800; Email: cfairfield@stbonaventure.net; Web: www.stbonaventure.net. Revs. Mathew Vellankal, (India); David Lawrence, S.J., Parochial Vicar; Oscar Rojas, Parochial Vicar; Deacons Antonio Ambriz; William Gall; Christa L. Fairfield, Parish Life Dir.
Catechesis Religious Program—Email: rhalick@stbonaventure.net. Rosann Halick, D.R.E.; Eileen Limberg, D.R.E.; Gina Cattalini, Dir., Adult Faith Formation; Jacob Perry, Youth Min. Students 720.

3—ST. FRANCIS OF ASSISI (1984) (Formerly Most Precious Blood, 1955)
860 Oak Grove Rd., Concord, 94518-3461. Tel: 925-682-5447; Email: church@sfaconcord.org; Web: www.sfaconcord.com. Revs. Ismael Gutierrez; Rafal P. Duda, Parochial Vicar; Fernando Rubio-Boitel, In Res.; Deacons Charles Palomares; John Mazibrook; Fred Schaub, Business Mgr.
School—St. Francis of Assisi School, (Grades K-8), 866 Oak Grove Rd., Concord, 94518-3461. Tel: 925-682-5414; Fax: 925-682-5480; Email: jdelucchi@sfaconcord.org; Web: www.sfaconcord.org. Mrs. Patricia Calton, Prin. Lay Teachers 9; Students 272; Clergy / Religious Teachers 1.
Catechesis Religious Program—Email: youth@sfaconcord.org. Ms. Kathleen M. De Lemos, Youth Min. & Teen Sacraments; Mrs. Scarlett Salaverria, D.R.E.-Spanish; Mr. Nathan Cho, D.R.E.-English. Students 503.

4—QUEEN OF ALL SAINTS (1923) [CEM]
2390 Grant St., Concord, 94520. Tel: 925-825-0350; Email: qaschurch@yahoo.com; Web: www.qaschurch.org. Revs. Neal C. Clemens; Fabio Correa Correa, Parochial Vicar.
School—Queen of All Saints School, (Grades K-8), 2391 Grant St., Concord, 94520-2244. Tel: 925-685-8700; Fax: 925-685-2034; Email: jegray@csdo.org; Web: www.qasconcord.org. Lucia Prince, Prin. Lay Teachers 15; Students 244.
Catechesis Religious Program—Tel: 925-685-8707. Nancy Tomsic, D.R.E. Students 600.

CROCKETT, CONTRA COSTA CO., ST. ROSE OF LIMA (1912)
555 Third Ave., Crockett, 94525-1114. Tel: 510-787-2052; Email: strosecrockett@comcast.net. Rev. Leonardo Asuncion, (Philippines) Parochial Admin.
Catechesis Religious Program—Students 10.
Mission—St. Patrick, Prospect & Lake Canyon Rd., Port Costa, Contra Costa Co. 94569.

DANVILLE, CONTRA COSTA CO., ST. ISIDORE (1910)
445 La Gonda Way, Danville, 94526-2562. Tel: 925-837-2122; Email: office@sichurch.com; Web: www.sichurch.com. Mailing Address: 440 La Gonda Way, Danville, 94526-2562. Revs. Gerard K. Moran; Gerald Pedrera, Parochial Vicar.
School—St. Isidore School, (Grades K-8), 435 La Gonda Way, Danville, 94526. Tel: 925-837-2977; Fax: 925-837-2407; Email: mward@stisidore.org; Web: www.stisidore.org. Maria Ward, Prin. Lay Teachers 48; Students 629.
Catechesis Religious Program—Tel: 925-362-1900; Email: lford@sichurch.com; Email: kmachi@sichurch.com. Lyn Ford, D.R.E.; Mr. Keith Machi, Youth Min. Students 734.
Child Care—Kids Konnection, 432 La Gonda Way, Danville, 94526-2562. Tel: 925-820-7753. Before and after school child care.
Youth Ministry—Tel: 925-362-1904; Fax: 925-362-1929. Students 273.

DUBLIN, ALAMEDA CO., ST. RAYMOND (1961)
11555 Shannon Ave., Dublin, 94568-1376. Tel: 925-828-2460; Email: frontdesk@st-raymond-dublin.org; Web: www.st-raymond-dublin.org. Revs. Lawrence C. D'Anjou; Robert Mendonca, Parochial Vicar; Deacon Joe Sicat, (Retired).
School—St. Raymond School, (Grades K-8), 11557 Shannon Ave., Dublin, 94568. Tel: 925-828-4064; Fax: 925-828-2454; Email: cdeehan@csdo.org; Web: straymondschool.org. Catherine Deehan, Prin. Lay Teachers 18; Students 299.
Catechesis Religious Program—Tel: 925-574-7414; Email: office@st-raymond-dublin.org. Maggie Ringle, D.R.E. Students 560.

EL CERRITO, CONTRA COSTA CO.

1—ST. JEROME CHURCH (1941)
308 Carmel Ave., El Cerrito, 94530. Tel: 510-525-0876; Fax: 510-525-5227; Email: saintjeromechurch@comcast.net; Web: www.stjeromeec.org. Rev. Fernando J. Cortez.
Catechesis Religious Program—Email: theresaf@gmx.com. Theresa Fenzl, D.R.E. Students 57.

2—ST. JOHN THE BAPTIST (1925)
11150 San Pablo Ave., El Cerrito, 94530-2131. Tel: 510-232-5659; Email: stjohns@sjtbc.us; Web: stjohns@sjtbc.us. Revs. Thuong Hoai Nguyen; Joseph Tri Tran, Parochial Vicar; Thang Nhat Nguyen, In Res.; Deacons Loch Sekona, Baptism & Ministry Leader; Thomas McGowan, (Retired).
School—St. John the Baptist School, (Grades K-8), 11156 San Pablo Ave., El Cerrito, 94530-2131. Tel: 510-234-2244; Fax: 510-234-3726; Email: www.info@stjohnec.org; Web: www.stjohnec.org. Dina Trombettas, Prin. Lay Teachers 14; Students 205.
Catechesis Religious Program—Email: jcevans148@sbcglobal.net; Email: richard@sjtbc.us; Email: youthministry@sjtbc.us. Lynn Evans, D.R.E.; Christine Hickey, RCIA Coord.; Gina de la Torre, Youth Min. Students 38.

EL SOBRANTE, CONTRA COSTA CO., ST. CALLISTUS (1952)
3580 San Pablo Dam Rd., El Sobrante, 94803. Tel: 510-223-1153; Fax: 510-223-1137; Email: st.callistus@sbcglobal.net. Rev. James J. Thottapally.
Catechesis Religious Program—Tel: 510-222-0432; Email: bl.stcal@gmail.com. Beatriz Lopez, D.R.E. Students 61.

FREMONT, ALAMEDA CO.

1—CORPUS CHRISTI (1914)
37891 Second St., Fremont, 94536. Tel: 510-790-3207; Email: office@corpuschristifremont.org; Web: corpuschristifremont.org. Mailing Address: 37968 Third St., Fremont, 94536. Rev. H. David Mendoza-Vela, Admin.; Deacon Alfonso Perez.
Catechesis Religious Program—Tel: 510-790-3207, Ext. 103; Email: faithinformation@corpuschristifremont.org. Roberto De Leon, D.R.E. Students 152.

2—HOLY SPIRIT (1886) [CEM] [JC]
37588 Fremont Blvd., Fremont, 94536-3707. Tel: 510-797-1660; Email: info@holyspiritfremont.org; Web: www.holyspiritfremont.org. Revs. Kenneth L. Sales; Matthew Murray, Parochial Vicar; Weersak (Lee) Chompoochan, Parochial Vicar; Deacons Richard Yee, (Retired); Rigoberto Cabezas; Charles Glover; Stephen Lewellyn; Timothy Roberto.
School—Holy Spirit School, (Grades PreK-8), 3930 Parish Ave., Fremont, 94536. Tel: 510-793-3553; Fax: 510-793-2694; Email: hmarsh@csdo.org; Web: www.holyspiritfmt.com. Holly Marsh, Prin. Lay Teachers 23; Students 290; Clergy / Religious Teachers 1.
Catechesis Religious Program—37648 Fremont Blvd., Fremont, 94536. Tel: 510-366-4444; Email: dcnrigo@gmail.com. Students 515.

3—ST. JAMES THE APOSTLE (1972)
34700 Fremont Blvd., Fremont, 94555. Tel: 510-792-1962; Email: stjamesapostle@att.net. Rev. Anthony Vazhappilly, S.D.B., (India); Deacon Ernesto Dandan, Email: office@sjapostle.net.
Catechesis Religious Program—Sheila Reduta, D.R.E. Students 110.

4—ST. JOSEPH (OLD MISSION SAN JOSE) (1797) [CEM]
43148 Mission Blvd., Fremont, 94539. Tel: 510-656-2364; Email: stjomissj@aol.com; Web: saintjosephmsj.org. Mailing Address: P.O. Box 3276, Fremont, 94539. Rev. Msgr. Manuel C. Simas; Rev. Michael Nghia Pham, Parochial Vicar; Deacons Lance Vivet; Richard Bayless.
School—St. Joseph (Old Mission San Jose) School, (Grades K-8), 43222 Mission Blvd., Fremont, 94539-5827. Tel: 510-656-6525; Fax: 510-656-3608; Email: kmendoza@sjsmsj.org; Web: www.stjosephschoolfremont.org. Kelly Mendoza, Prin. Lay Teachers 18; Students 234.
Catechesis Religious Program—Tel: 510-657-0905. Sr. Bernadette Nguyen, L.H.C., D.R.E. Students 205.

5—ST. LEONARD (1959) Merged with Santa Paula, Fremont to form Our Lady of Guadalupe, Fremont.

6—OUR LADY OF GUADALUPE (2000)
41933 Blacow Rd., Fremont, 94538-3365. Tel: 510-657-4043; Email: secretary@olog.church; Web: www.olog.church. Revs. Joy Kumarthusseril, M.F., (India); Raju Palleti, M.F., (India) Parochial Vicar; Kuriakose Nadooparambil, M.F., (India) Chap.; Deacons Ovide Guesnon, (Retired); Steven Budnik Sr., Marriage Prep Coord.; Mrs. Jean Hui, Business Mgr.
Res.: 40382 Fremont Blvd., Fremont, 94538-3409.
School—Our Lady of Guadalupe School, (Grades K-8), 40374 Fremont Blvd., Fremont, 94538-3409. Tel: 510-657-1674; Fax: 510-657-3659; Email: sjtwellington@csdo.org; Web: www.guadalupe-school.com. Sr. Janice Therese Wellington, Prin. Lay Teachers 11; Students 217.
Catechesis Religious Program—Tel: 510-651-4966; Email: ologff@olog.church. Juan Jose Suarez, D.R.E. Students 480.

7—SANTA PAULA (1965) Merged with St. Leonard, Fremont to form Our Lady of Guadalupe, Fremont.

HAYWARD, ALAMEDA CO.

1—ALL SAINTS (1898) [CEM]
22824 Second St., Hayward, 94541-5217. Tel: 510-581-2570; Email: larechiga.allsaints@gmail.com; Web: allsaintshayward.org. Revs. Ramon Gomez; Michael T. Castori, S.J., Parochial Vicar; Deacons Rudi Fernandez; Jorge Angel; Lawrence Quinn.
School—All Saints School, (Grades K-8), 22870 Second St., Hayward, 94541. Tel: 510-582-1910; Fax: 510-582-0866; Email: jdiaz@csdo.org; Web: www.ascshayward.org. Jennifer Diaz, Prin. Lay Teachers 12; Students 231.
Catechesis Religious Program—Email: myallsaintshwd@yahoo.com. Students 294.

2—ST. BEDE (1955)
26950 Patrick Ave., Hayward, 94544-3851. Tel: 510-782-2171; Email: st.bedechurch@yahoo.com; Web: www.stbedechurchhay.org. Revs. Seamus J. Farrell; Gustavo Barrientos, (Guatemala) Parochial Vicar.
School—St. Bede School, (Grades K-8), 26910 Patrick Ave., Hayward, 94544-3851. Tel: 510-782-3444; Fax: 510-782-2243; Email: info@stbedeparish.org; Web: www.mystbede.com. Lisa Greco, D.R.E. Lay Teachers 13; Students 248.
Catechesis Religious Program—Tel: 510-782-4292. Thomas Booth, D.R.E.; Linda Montoya, Confirmation Coord. Students 575.

3—ST. CLEMENT (1951)
750 Calhoun St., Hayward, 94544-4202.
Tel: 510-582-7282; Email: stclementhayward@gmail.com; Web: www.saintclementchurch.org. Revs. Rolando Bartolay, Admin.; James Sullivan, Chap.; Benigno Vinluan, In Res.; Deacon Manuel Moya.
School—St. Clement School, (Grades K-8), 790 Calhoun St., Hayward, 94544-4202.
Tel: 510-538-5885; Fax: 510-538-1643; Email: scschoolboardinfo@gmail.com; Web: www.sclement.org. Erin Zajac, Prin. Lay Teachers 30; Students 282.
Catechesis Religious Program—Vanessa Alvarez, D.R.E. Students 334.
4—ST. JOACHIM (1950)
21250 Hesperian Blvd., Hayward, 94541-5809.
Tel: 510-783-2766; Email: stjoachimoffice@gmail.com; Web: stjoachim.net. Revs. Joseph Sebastian, S.V.D; Danh Pham.
School—St. Joachim School, (Grades PreK-8), 21250 Hesperian Blvd., Hayward, 94541-5809.
Tel: 510-783-3177; Email: aseishas@csdo.org; Web: www.stjoachimschool.org. Armond Seishas, Prin. Lay Teachers 17; Students 368.
Catechesis Religious Program—Tel: 510-785-1818; Email: glendaaragon@comcast.net. Glenda Aragon, D.R.E. Students 659.
LAFAYETTE, CONTRA COSTA CO., ST. PERPETUA (1952)
3454 Hamlin Rd., Lafayette, 94549-5019.
Tel: 925-283-0272; Email: office@stperpetua.org; Web: www.stperpetua.org. Revs. John Kasper, O.S.F.S., Admin.; Zacharias Thomas, (India) In Res.; Wendy Levich, Business Mgr.
School—St. Perpetua School, (Grades K-8), 3445 Hamlin Rd., Lafayette, 94549-5018.
Tel: 925-284-1640; Fax: 925-284-5676; Email: kgoodshaw@csdo.org; Web: www.stperpetua.org. Karen Goodshaw, Prin. Lay Teachers 23; Students 218.
Catechesis Religious Program—Kristine Kvochak, D.R.E. Students 380.
LIVERMORE, ALAMEDA CO.
1—ST. CHARLES BORROMEO (1964) [JC]
1315 Lomitas Ave., Livermore, 94550-6441. Email: office@stcharlesborromeo.org; Web: www.stcharlesborromeo.org. Rev. Mark Wiesner; Deacons Gilbert Pesqueira; David Cloyne; Ms. Karen Miller, Pastoral Assoc., Adult Faith Formation.
Catechesis Religious Program—Email: office@stperpetua.org. Kristine Kvochak, D.R.E. Students 341.
2—ST. MICHAEL (1878) [CEM] (Spanish)
458 Maple St., Livermore, 94550-3238.
Tel: 925-447-1585; Email: office@stmichaellivermore.com; Web: www.stmichaellivermore.com. Revs. Carl Tacuyan Arcosa; Alfonso Borgen, O.F.M.Conv., Parochial Vicar; David E. Staal, J.C.L., J.D., Weekend Assoc.; Deacons Robert Federle; William Archer; David Rezendes; Mr. Eric Hom, Business Mgr.; Ms. Debbie Pizzato, Liturgy Dir.; Janet Hancock, Music Min.; Ms. Jacqueline Garcia, Sec.
School—St. Michael School, (Grades K-8), 345 Church St., Livermore, 94550-3205.
Tel: 925-447-1888; Fax: 925-447-6720; Email: awilkie@csdo.org; Web: www.smsliv.org. Alison Wilkie, Prin. Lay Teachers 15; Students 181.
Catechesis Religious Program—Tel: 925-667-4097; Email: priscillastutzman@stmichaellivermore.com. Priscilla Stutzman, D.R.E. Students 437.
MARTINEZ, CONTRA COSTA CO., ST. CATHERINE OF SIENA (1873) [CEM]
606 Mellus St., Martinez, 94553-1707.
Tel: 925-228-2230; Email: stcathmtz@yahoo.com. Mailing Address: 1125 Ferry St., Martinez, 94553-1707. Rev. Anthony Le, Admin.; Deacons Alberto Dizon; David Holland.
Res.: 1100 Estudillo St., Martinez, 94553-1707.
Schools—St. Catherine of Siena School—(Grades PreK-8), 604 Mellus St., Martinez, 94553-1639.
Tel: 925-228-4140; Fax: 925-228-0697; Email: jgriswold@csdo.org; Web: www.stcath.net. Jessica Griswold, Prin. Lay Teachers 16; Students 131.
Pre-School and Transitional Kindergarten, 1125 Ferry St., Martinez, 94553. Tel: 925-229-2255; Fax: 925-229-2474; Email: dshapiro@csdo.org; Web: www.stcatherinemartinez.com. Doreen Shapiro. Lay Teachers 4; Students 39.
Catechesis Religious Program—
Tel: 925-228-2230, Ext. 30. Students 149.
MORAGA, CONTRA COSTA CO., ST. MONICA (1965)
1001 Camino Pablo, Moraga, 94556-1831.
Tel: 925-376-6900; Email: office@stmonicamoraga.com; Web: www.stmonicamoraga.com. Rev. Paul Coleman, (Ireland) Parochial Admin.
Catechesis Religious Program—Sr. Mary Teresa, D.R.E. Students 153.
NEWARK, ALAMEDA CO., ST. EDWARD (1920)
5788 Thornton Ave., Newark, 94560-3826.
Tel: 510-797-0241; Email: parishoffice@stedwardcatholic.church; Web: www.stedwardcatholic.com. Revs. Mark C. Amaral; Benedict Wonganant, Parochial Vicar; Deacons John Pietruszka, Transitional Deacon; Roger Wedl, (Retired).
School—St. Edward School, (Grades K-8), 5788 Thornton Ave., Newark, 94560-3826.
Tel: 510-793-7242; Email: cmonahan@csdo.org; Web: stedcs.org. Sr. Carolyn Monahan, Prin. Lay Teachers 14; Students 227; Clergy / Religious Teachers 1.
Catechesis Religious Program—Tel: 510-797-5588. Donalyn Deeds, D.R.E. Students 377.
OAKLEY, CONTRA COSTA CO., ST. ANTHONY (1925) [JC]
971 O'Hara Ave., Oakley, 94561-5785.
Tel: 925-625-2048; Fax: 925-625-4433; Email: Parish@stanthonyoakley.com; Web: www.stanthonyoakley.org. Revs. Rafael Hinojosa, Admin.; Giopre Prado, Parochial Vicar; Deacons Joseph Tovar, (Retired); Alan Layden, (Retired).
Catechesis Religious Program—Tel: 256-252-0489. Maricela Perez, Moderator; Emma Arcayena, Moderator; Michael Maeda, RCIA Coord. Students 465.
ORINDA, CONTRA COSTA CO., SANTA MARIA (1892)
40 Santa Maria Way, Orinda, 94563-2605.
Tel: 925-254-2426; Email: smoffice@smparish.org; Web: www.santamariaparish.org. Very Rev. George E. Mockel; Rev. Joseph Duong Nguyen, (Vietnam) In Res.; Deacons Rey Encarnacion, Sacramental Min.; James Pearce.
Catechesis Religious Program—Sr. Theresa Lan Do, L.H.C., D.R.E. Students 200.
Convent—50 Santa Maria Way, Orinda, 94563-2605.
PIEDMONT, ALAMEDA CO., CORPUS CHRISTI (1929)
322 St. James Dr., Piedmont, 94611-3627.
Tel: 510-530-4343; Email: judyhilgert@yahoo.com; Web: www.corpuschristipiedmont.org. Revs. Leo J. Edgerly Jr.; Basil DePinto, In Res., (Retired).
School—Corpus Christi School, (Grades K-8), One Estates Dr., Piedmont, 94611-3341.
Tel: 510-530-4056; Fax: 510-530-5926; Email: officesecretary@corpuschristischool.com; Web: www.corpuschristischool.com. Mrs. Kathleen Murphy, Prin. Lay Teachers 19; Students 260.
Catechesis Religious Program—Email: corpuschristisundayschool@gmail.com. Lori Arnold, D.R.E. Students 202.
PINOLE, CONTRA COSTA CO., ST. JOSEPH (1947)
837 Tennent Ave., Pinole, 94564-1711.
Tel: 510-471-7400; Email: contact.sjcpinole@gmail.com; Web: www.sjcpinole.org. Mailing Address: 2100 Pear St., Pinole, 94564-1711. Revs. Geoffrey Baraan; Francisco Figueroa-Esquer, Parochial Vicar; Deacons Benjamin Agustin; Leslie Miyashiro.
School—St. Joseph School, (Grades K-8), 1961 Plum St., Pinole, 94564-1711. Tel: 510-724-0242; Email: amarseille@csdo.org; Web: www.stjosephpinole.com. Arlene Marseille, Prin. Lay Teachers 15; Students 263.
Catechesis Religious Program—Carol Lujan, D.R.E. Students 311.
PITTSBURG, CONTRA COSTA CO.
1—GOOD SHEPHERD (1965)
3200 Harbor St., Pittsburg, 94565-5444.
Tel: 925-432-6404; Email: office@goodshepherdpittsburg.org; Web: www.goodshepherdpittsburg.org. Rev. Thi Hoang, Admin.; Deacon Gustavo Escruceria.
Catechesis Religious Program—
Tel: 925-432-6404, Ext. 11. Students 512.
2—ST. PETER, MARTYR OF VERONA (1914)
740 Black Diamond St., Pittsburg, 94565-2148.
Tel: 925-432-4771; Email: stpetermartyr@yahoo.com; Web: www.stpetermartyr.org. Revs. Jesus Hernandez Vidal; Rafael Chavez, Parochial Vicar.
School—St. Peter, Martyr of Verona School, (Grades PreK-8), 425 W. 4th St., Pittsburg, 94565-1968.
Tel: 925-439-1014; Fax: 925-439-1506; Email: jsiino@csdo.org; Web: www.stpetermartyrschool.org. Joseph Siino, Prin. Lay Teachers 8; Students 175.
Catechesis Religious Program—Tel: 925-595-6930. Emma OJeda, D.R.E. Students 478.
PLEASANT HILL, CONTRA COSTA CO., CHRIST THE KING (1951)
199 Brandon Rd., Pleasant Hill, 94523-3220.
Tel: 925-682-2486; Email: ctk.robin@gmail.com; Web: www.ctkph.org. Revs. Paulson Mundanmani; Mario Rizzo, Parochial Vicar; Brian Timoney, In Res., (Retired); Deacon John Ashmore.
School—Christ the King School, (Grades K-8), 195 Brandon Rd., Pleasant Hill, 94523.
Tel: 925-685-1109; Fax: 925-685-1289; Email: info@ctkschool.org; Web: www.ctkschool.org. Mr. Joseph Silveira, Prin. Lay Teachers 15; Students 314.
Catechesis Religious Program—Tel: 925-686-1017. Sr. Maureen Viani, S.N.J.M., D.R.E. Students 383.
PLEASANTON, ALAMEDA CO.
1—ST. AUGUSTINE (1901) Merged with St. Elizabeth Seton, Pleasanton to form The Catholic Community of Pleasanton.
2—THE CATHOLIC COMMUNITY OF PLEASANTON (1901) [CEM]
3999 Bernal, P.O. Box 817, Pleasanton, 94566-7264.
Tel: 925-846-4489, Ext. 2766; Email: omorineau@catholicsofpleasanton.org; Web: www.catholicsofpleasanton.org. Revs. Paul D. Minnihan, S.T.D.; Bernard Kwame Assenyoh, S.V.D., (Ghana) Parochial Vicar; Filiberto Barrera, Parochial Vicar; Deacons Richard Martin; Gary Wortham; Joseph Gourley.
Catechesis Religious Program—Tel: 925-846-3531. Henry Correa, D.R.E. Students 691.
3—ST. ELIZABETH SETON (1991) Merged with St. Augustine, Pleasanton to form The Catholic Community of Pleasanton.
POINT RICHMOND, CONTRA COSTA CO., OUR LADY OF MERCY (1902)
301 W. Richmond Ave., Point Richmond, 94801-3862.
Tel: 510-232-1843; Email: david@davidkorourke.com; Web: www.pointrichmondcatholic.org. Rev. David K. O'Rourke, O.P., Admin.
Catechesis Religious Program—Email: margaret123mm@msn.com. Margaret Morkowski, D.R.E. Students 28.
RICHMOND, CONTRA COSTA CO.
1—ST. CORNELIUS (1952) [CEM]
205-28th St., Richmond, 94804-3001.
Tel: 510-233-5901; Email: St.Cornelius33@yahoo.com. Revs. Sergio Mora; George E. Crespin, In Res., (Retired); Edmund Coppinger, In Res., (Retired); Raymond Ogbemure, (Nigeria) In Res.
School—St. Cornelius School, (Grades K-8), 201-28th St., Richmond, 94804-3001. Tel: 510-232-3326; Fax: 510-232-4071; Email: smoradi@csdo.org; Web: stcornelius-school.org. Ms. Sherri Moradi, Prin. Lay Teachers 12; Students 140.
Catechesis Religious Program—Patricia Ramirez, D.R.E. Students 599.
2—ST. DAVID OF WALES (1952)
5641 Esmond Ave., Richmond, 94805-1112.
Tel: 510-237-1531; Email: davidofwales@gmail.com; Web: stdavidofwales.church. Revs. John Direen; Michael Olawuni, In Res.
School—St. David of Wales School, (Grades PreK-8), 871 Sonoma St., Richmond, 94805-1122.
Tel: 510-232-2283; Fax: 510-231-0484; Email: jdeguzman@csdo.org; Web: www.stdavidschool.org. Jojo de Guzman, Prin. Lay Teachers 15; Students 183.
Catechesis Religious Program—Students 90.
3—ST. MARK (1912)
159 Harbour Way, Richmond, 94801-3553.
Tel: 510-234-5886; Email: parishoffice@stmarkrichmond.org; Web: www.stmarkrichmond.org. Rev. Ruben Morales-Morfin, Admin.
Catechesis Religious Program—
Tel: 510-234-5886, Ext. 222; Email: sanmarcos@comcast.net. Students 591.
RODEO, CONTRA COSTA CO., ST. PATRICK (1923)
825 Seventh St., Rodeo, 94572-1549.
Tel: 510-799-4406; Email: parishoffice@stpatrickrodeo.org; Web: www.stpatrickrodeo.org. Revs. Larry E. Young; Michael Figura Nufable, Parochial Vicar.
Res.: 902 Spruce Ct., Rodeo, 94572-1549.
School—St. Patrick School, (Grades PreK-8), 907 Seventh St., Rodeo, 94572-1549. Tel: 510-799-2506; Fax: 510-799-6781; Email: kstevens@csdo.org; Web: www.stpatrickschoolrodeo.org. Kelly Stevens, Prin. Lay Teachers 20; Students 365.
Catechesis Religious Program—Tel: 510-799-4434; Email: bfung@stpatrickrodeo.org. Beverly Fung, D.R.E. Students 285.
SAN LEANDRO, ALAMEDA CO.
1—ST. ALPHONSUS LIGUORI (1955) [CEM] Merged with Our Lady of Grace, Castro Valley. For parish records contact Our Lady of Grace, Castro Valley.
2—ASSUMPTION OF THE BLESSED VIRGIN MARY (1951)
1100 Fulton Ave., San Leandro, 94577-6210.
Tel: 510-352-1537; Email: slassumption@sbcglobal.net. Revs. Leonard Marrujo, Parochial Admin.; Christopher Berbena, Parochial Vicar.
School—Assumption of the Blessed Virgin Mary School, (Grades K-8), 1851 136th Ave., San Leandro, 94578-1661. Tel: 510-357-8772; Email: jpetersen@csdo.org; Web: www.assumptionschool-sl.org. Joseph Petersen, Prin. Lay Teachers 17; Students 200; Clergy / Religious Teachers 1.
Catechesis Religious Program—Maureen Moran, D.R.E. Students 60.
3—ST. FELICITAS (1952)
1662 Manor Blvd., San Leandro, 94579-1509.
Tel: 510-351-5244; Fax: 510-351-5730; Email: stfelicitaschurch@comcast.net; Web: www.stfelicitassl.org. Revs. Thomas Khue, Parochial Admin.; Edilberto S. Castanas, Parochial Vicar; Deacon Timothy Myers.
School—St. Felicitas School, (Grades PreK-8), 1650 Manor Blvd., San Leandro, 94579-1509.
Tel: 510-357-2530; Fax: 510-357-5358; Email: mjorgensen@csdo.org; Email: lzipp@csdo.org; Web: www.stfelicitas-school.org. Meghan Anne Jorgensen, Prin. Lay Teachers 16; Students 283; Clergy / Religious Teachers 1.

Catechesis Religious Program—Tel: 510-347-1282. Sandi Walton, D.R.E. Students 518.

4—ST. LEANDER (1864)
474 W. Estudillo Ave., San Leandro, 94577-3610. Tel: 510-895-5631; Email: stleander@sbcglobal.net; Web: www.stleanderchurch.org. Revs. Hugo Franca, (Brazil) Admin.; Kevin Schindler-McGraw, O.F.M.-Conv., Parochial Vicar; Michael Lacey, In Res., (Retired); Deacon Victor Silveira.
School—St. Leander School, (Grades PreK-8), 451 Davis St., San Leandro, 94577. Tel: 510-351-4144; Fax: 510-483-6060; Email: across@csdo.org; Web: www.stleanderschool.org. Amy Cross, Prin. Lay Teachers 16; Students 178.
Catechesis Religious Program—Anita Marquez, D.R.E. Students 180.

5—OUR LADY OF GOOD COUNSEL (1966) [JC]
2500 Bermuda Ave., San Leandro, 94577-6402. Tel: 510-614-2765; Tel: 510-969-7013; Email: linopoblete.olgc@yahoo.com; Email: olgc.finance@gmail.com; Web: www.olgcsanleandro.com. Rev. Jan Rudzewicz; Deacon Thomas Martin.
Rectory—14112 Azores Pl., San Leandro, 94577-6402.
Catechesis Religious Program—Students 43.

SAN LORENZO, ALAMEDA CO., ST. JOHN THE BAPTIST (1925)
16642 Ashland Ave., San Lorenzo, 94580-1736. Tel: 510-351-5050; Fax: 510-276-0397; Email: stjohnsrectory@gmail.com; Web: www.stjohnsparishslz.org. Revs. Sergio Lopez, J.C.D.; Joseph Tuan Anh Le, Parochial Vicar; Deacons Leonard J. Bettencourt, (Retired); Noe Tuason.
Res.: 264 E. Lewelling Blvd., San Lorenzo, 94580-1736.
School—St. John the Baptist School, (Grades PreK-8), 270 E. Lewelling Blvd., San Lorenzo, 94580-1736. Tel: 510-276-6632; Fax: 510-276-5645; Email: stjohncatholicschool@gmail.com; Web: stjohncatholicschool.org. Paige Child, Prin. Lay Teachers 24; Students 224.
Catechesis Religious Program—
Tel: 510-351-5050, Ext. 16. Students 224.

SAN PABLO, CONTRA COSTA CO., ST. PAUL (1864)
1845 Church Ln., San Pablo, 94806-3705. Tel: 510-232-5931; Fax: 510-232-1846; Email: info@stpaulchurchsanpablo.org; Web: www.stpaulchurchsanpablo.org. Revs. Lazaro Sandoval, O.F.M.Conv.; Tuan Nguyen, O.F.M.Conv., Parochial Vicar; Anthony Howard, O.F.M.Conv., Parochial Vicar; Deacon Arturo Jimenez; Bro. George Cherrie, O.F.M.Conv., Business Mgr.
School—St. Paul School, (Grades K-8), 1825 Church Ln., San Pablo, 94806. Tel: 510-233-3080; Fax: 510-231-8776; Email: nlenz-acuna@csdo.org; Web: www.st-paulschool.org. Natalie Lenz-Acuna, Prin. Lay Teachers 23; Students 213; Clergy / Religious Teachers 1.
Catechesis Religious Program—Email: carmennavarroccd@gmail.com. Carmen Navarro, D.R.E. Students 290.

SAN RAMON, CONTRA COSTA CO., ST. JOAN OF ARC (1979)
2601 San Ramon Valley Blvd., San Ramon, 94583-1630. Tel: 925-830-0600; Email: parishoffice@sjasr.org; Web: www.sjasr.org. Rev. Raymond Sacca; Deacons John Durden Jr.; Ruben Gomez.
Res.: 2421 Cuenca Dr., San Ramon, 94583.
Catechesis Religious Program—Tel: 925-830-4710; Email: mmachi@sjasr.org. Mary Machi, D.R.E. Students 782.

UNION CITY, ALAMEDA CO.

1—ST. ANNE (1973)
32223 Cabello St., Union City, 94587-0292. Tel: 510-471-7766, Ext. 50; Email: stanne@sbcglobal.net; Web: www.saintannecatholic.org. Revs. Rosendo R. Manalo Jr., Parochial Admin.; Augusto Tana Acob, (Philippines) Parochial VIcar; Deacons Benigno Calub, (Retired); Carlos Rabuy; Bernard Liwanag.
Catechesis Religious Program—Helen Rojas, D.R.E. Students 618.

2—HOLY FAMILY CATHOLIC ETHNIC MISSION (1933) Closed. For parish records contact St. Anne, Union City.

3—OUR LADY OF THE ROSARY (1951)
703 C St., Union City, 94587-2195. Tel: 510-471-2609 ; Fax: 510-471-4601; Email: admin@olrchurch.org; Web: www.olrchurch.org. Revs. Jesus Nieto-Ruiz; Paul Feng Chen, In Res.; Deacon Gustaaf Roemers, (Retired).
Catechesis Religious Program—Email: dmarquez@olrchurch.org. Donald Marquez, D.R.E. Students 361.

WALNUT CREEK, CONTRA COSTA CO.

1—ST. ANNE (1965)
1600 Rossmoor Pkwy., Walnut Creek, 94595-2507. Tel: 925-932-2324; Email: st_annes@comcast.net. Revs. Joseph Parekkatt; George Da Roza, S.S.C., In Res.

2—ST. JOHN VIANNEY (1965)
1650 Ygnacio Valley Rd., Walnut Creek, 94598-3123. Tel: 925-939-7911; Email: staff@sjvianney.org; Web: www.sjvianney.org. Rev. William D. Rosario, (India); Deacon Herb Casey.
Catechesis Religious Program—Ms. Elizabeth Rogers, D.R.E. Students 250.

3—ST. MARY (1941) [JC]
2051 Mt. Diablo Blvd., Walnut Creek, 94596. Tel: 925-891-8900; Fax: 925-934-1358; Web: www.st-mary.net. Revs. Fred Riccio; Dante Tamayo, Parochial Vicar; John R. Blaker, In Res.
Res.: 1201 Alpine Rd., Walnut Creek, 94596-4403.
School—St. Mary School, (Grades PreK-8), 1158 Bont Ln., Walnut Creek, 94596. Tel: 925-935-5054; Fax: 925-935-5063; Email: stmary@st-mary.net; Web: www.st-mary.net. Garrett Paid, Prin. Lay Teachers 22; Students 289.
Catechesis Religious Program—Tel: 925-891-8939; Email: maureen.stmary@gmail.com. Maureen Tiffany, D.R.E. Students 117.

4—ST. STEPHEN (1966)
1101 Keaveny Ct., Walnut Creek, 94597-2465. Tel: 925-274-1341; Email: saintstephenwc@gmail.com; Web: saintstephenparish.org. Rev. Paulson Mundanmani, Admin.

Chaplains of Public Institutions
Hospitals

OAKLAND.
Highland Hospital. Spiritual Care Services, Tel: 510-437-4431; Attended by St. Margaret Mary Parish, Tel: 510-428-0596.
Kaiser-Permanente Medical Center. Spiritual Care Services, Tel. 510-752-6281Attended by St. Leo the Great Parish, Tel: 510-654-6177; Cathedral Parish of Christ the Light, Tel: 510-832-5057; St. Augustine Parish, Tel:510-653-8631; St. Mary Magdalen Parish, Tel: 510-526-4811.
Summit Campus of the Alta Bates Summit Medical Center. Chaplaincy Services, Tel: 510-869-6784Attended by Sacred Heart Parish, Tel: 510-655-9209.
UCSF Benioff Children's Hospital. Chaplaincy Services Tel: 510-248-3885 Ext. 2676; Attended by Sacred Heart Parish, Tel: 510-655-9209.

ALAMEDA.
Alameda Hospital. Spiritual Care Services, Tel: 510-978-3869; Attended by St. Joseph Basilica, Tel: 510-522-0181.

ANTIOCH.
Kaiser Permanente Antioch Medical Center. Spiritual Care Services, Tel: 925-813-3270; Attended by St. Ignatius of Antioch Parish, Tel: 925-778-0768.
Sutter Delta Medical Center. Chaplaincy Services, Tel: 925-779-7237; Attended by Most Holy Rosary Parish, Tel: 925-778-0768.

BERKELEY.
Alta Bates Campus of the Alta Bates Summit Medical Center. Chaplaincy Services, Tel: 510-204-6730; Attended by St. Augustine Parish, Tel: 510-653-8631; Holy Spirit-Newman Hall Parish, Tel: 510-848-7812.
Herrick Campus of the Alpha Bates Summit Medical Center. Chaplaincy Services, Tel: 510-204-6730; Attended by St. Joseph the Worker Parish, Berkeley, Tel: 510-843-2244.

CASTRO VALLEY.
Eden Medical Center. Chaplaincy Services, Tel: 510-727-3119; Attended by Our Lady of Grace Parish, Tel: 510-537-0806.

CONCORD.
John Muir Medical Center. Concord CampusDept. of Spiritual Care, Tel: 925-674-2133.

FREMONT.
Kaiser Permanente Fremont Medical Center. Rev. Kuriakose Nadooparambil, M.F., (India) Chap.Tel. 510-344-8825. Attended by Our Lady of Guadalupe Parish, Tel: 510-657-4043; Holy Spirit Parish, Tel: 510-797-1660; St. Edward Parish, Tel: 510-797-0241; St. Joseph Parish, Tel: 510-656-2364.
Washington Hospital Healthcare System. Spiritual Care Services, Tel. 510-745-6569 Rev. Kuriakose Nadooparambil, M.F., (India) Chap., Tel: 510-344-8825Attended by Our Lady of Guadalupe Parish, Tel: 510-657-4043; Holy Spirit Parish, Tel: 510-797-1660; St. Edward Parish, 510-797-0241; St. Joseph Parish, 510-656-2364.

HAYWARD.
St. Rose Hospital. Attended by St. Bede Parish, Tel: 510-782-2171.

LIVERMORE.
Veterans' Affairs Palo Alto Health Care System Livermore Division. Chaplaincy Services, Tel: 925-373-4700; Attended by St. Michael Parish, Tel: 925-447-1585.
Valley Care Health System. Attended by St. Charles Borromeo Parish, Tel: 925-447-4549.

MARTINEZ.
Contra Costa Regional Medical Center. Spiritual Care Services, Tel: 925-370-5440 Rev. Padraig Greene, Chap., Tel: 925-323-9332Attended by St. Catherine of Siena Parish, Tel: 925-228-2230.
VA Administrative Skilled Nursing Center. Tel: 925-372-2000.

PLEASANTON.
Valley Care Medical Center. Attended by St. Augustine Parish, Tel: 925-846-4489.

RICHMOND.
Kaiser-Permanente Medical Center. Spiritual Care Services, Tel: 510-725-6281; Attended by St. David of Wales Parish, Tel: 510-237-1531; St. Mark Parish, Tel: 510-234-5886; St. Cornelius Parish, Tel: 510-233-5215.

SAN LEANDRO.
All Saints Subacute & Skilled Nursing. Attended by Assumption Parish, Tel: 510-352-1537.
Fairmont Hospital. Spiritual Care Services, Tel: 510-437-4431; Attended by Assumption Parish, Tel: 510-352-1537.
George Mark Children's House. (Hospice)Attended by Assumption Parish, Tel: 510-352-1537.
John George Psychiatric Hospital. Spiritual Care Services, Tel: 510-346-1335; Attended by Assumption Parish, Tel: 510-352-1537.
Kaiser Permanente Medical Center. Spiritual Care Services, Tel: 510-454-4716; Attended by Our Lady of Good Counsel Parish, Tel: 510-614-2765; St. Felicitas Parish, Tel: 510-351-5244.
Kindred Hospital. Attended by Assumption Parish, Tel: 510-352-1537.
San Leandro Hospital. Spiritual Care Services, Tel: 510-861-0510; Attended by St. Leander Parish, Tel: 510-895-5631.

SAN RAMON.
San Ramon Regional Medical Center. Attended by St. Joan of Arc Parish, Tel: 925-830-0600.

WALNUT CREEK.
Kaiser-Permanente Medical Center. Spiritual Care Services, Tel: 925-295-6945; Attended by St. Mary Parish, Tel: 925-891-8900. Rev. John R. Blaker, Chap.
Walnut Creek Campus of John Muir Medical Center. Pastoral Care Svcs., Tel: 925-947-5281 Attended by St. John Vianney Parish, Tel: 925-939-7911. Rev. John R. Blaker, Chap., Tel: 925-212-0042.

Prisons and Jails

OAKLAND.
Glenn E. Dyer Detention Facility. Richard Denoix, Tel: 925-367-5833Detention Ministry sponsored by, Cathedral Parish of Christ the Light, Sacred Heart Parish, St. Columba Parish & St. Patrick Parish, Oakland.

BYRON.
Orin Allen Youth Rehabilitation Facility. Ken Landoline, Tel: 925-513-3632Detention Ministry sponsored by, St. Anthony Parish, Oakley; Immaculate Heart of Mary Parish, Brentwood; Most Holy Rosary Parish, St. Ignatius Parish, Antioch & St. Anne Parish, Byron.

CLAYTON.
Marsh Creek Detention Facility. Kathleen Barrere, Tel: 925-674-9140Detention Ministry sponsored by, St. Bonaventure Parish, Queen of All Saints Parish, St. Agnes Parish & St. Francis of Assisi Parish, Concord.

DUBLIN.
Alameda County Santa Rita Jail. Richard Denoix, Tel: 925-367-5833Detention Ministry sponsored by, St. Joan of Arc Parish, San Ramon; St. Raymond Parish, Dublin; St. Isidore Parish, Danville.
Federal Prison Corrections Institution. Deacon Ruben Gomez, Tel: 925-901-0543Detention Ministry sponsored by, St. Joan of Arc Parish, San Ramon; St. Raymond Parish, Dublin & St. Isidore Parish, Danville.

MARTINEZ.
John A. Davis Juvenile Hall. Mr. Ed Chichon, Tel: 510-758-1469Detention Ministry sponsored by, St. Callistus Parish, El Sobrante; St. Joseph Parish, Pinole; St. Patrick Parish, Rodeo & St. Rose of Lima Parish, Crockett.
Martinez Detention Facility. Deacon Charles Silvernale, Tel: 925-754-1959Detention Ministry sponsored by, St. Catherine of Siena Parish, Martinez; Christ the King Parish, Pleasant Hill & St. Stephen Parish, Walnut Creek.

RICHMOND.
West County Detention. Jo Beth Strawn, Tel: 510-237-1531(formerly Richmond Jail)Detention Ministry sponsored by, St. Paul Parish, San Pablo; Our Lady of Mercy Parish, Point Richmond; St. Cornelius Parish & St. Mark Parish, Richmond.

SAN LEANDRO.
Juvenile Hall Facility. Mr. Byrne Sherwood, Tel: 925-283-0462Detention Ministry sponsored by, Our Lady of Good Counsel Parish, Church of the Assumption; St. Felicitas Parish & St. Leander Parish, San Leandro.

On Duty Outside the Diocese:
Revs.—
Kappler, Stephan
Leong, Herman
Nguyen, Hy, P.S.S.
Prochaska, John
Thurston, Anthony
Tompkins, Terry
Wydeven, John L.

On Leave:
Revs.—
Macias, Salvador, J.C.L.
Mendoza, Paul Christian
Nguyen, Peter Tu
Oliveira, Derrick K.

Military Chaplains:
Rev.—
Vo, Peter Son.

Retired:
Rev. Msgrs.—
Cardelli, Daniel E., (Retired)
Ferraro, Joseph, (Retired)
Valdivia, Antonio, (Retired)
Revs.—
Andrade, Bernardino, (Retired)
Atwood, Ronald E., (Retired)
Brown, Jerry W., (Retired)
Brylka, Vincent R., (Retired)
Charm, Robert, (Retired)
Chavez, Ricardo A., (Retired)
Cleu, Paul, (Retired)
Cotter, Vincent, (Retired)
Crespin, George E., (Retired)
Cunningham, Michael, (Retired)
DePinto, Basil, (Retired)
Des Rosiers, Denis A., (Retired)
Dinh, Tran Thuc, (Vietnam) (Retired)
Fernandes, John, (Retired)
Gagliardi, Richard, (Retired)
Johnson, Timothy K., (Retired)
Johnson, William B., (Retired)
Joyce, Brian T., (Retired)
LaBarbera, Robert, (Retired)
Lacey, Michael, (Retired)
Leon, Jose M., (Retired)
Lester, Thomas, (Retired)
Lima, John H., (Retired)
Mangini, Richard A., (Retired)
Marshall, William, (Retired)
Mayer, Walter W., (Retired)
Mifsud, Carmelo, (Retired)
Osuna, E. Donald, (Retired)
Pickett, James B., (Retired)
Poon, Stanislaus, (Retired)
Richter, Helmut W., (Retired)
Ruffing, Norman, (Retired)
Schexnayder, James, (Retired)
Schmidt, Paul J., (Retired)
Scott, Vincent J., (Retired)
Snyder, Alexander, (Retired)
Starbuck, James, (Retired)
Timoney, Brian, (Retired)
Vassar, Paul R., (Retired)
Zak, Stanislaw, (Retired)
Zamora, Clarence S. A., (Retired)
Zielezienski, Raymond, (Retired).

Permanent Deacons:
Agustin, Benjamin, St. Joseph, Pinole
Ambriz, Antonio, St. Bonaventure, Concord
Angel, Jorge, All Saints, Hayward
Archer, John, (Active Outside the Diocese)
Archer, William, St. Michael, Livermore
Ashmore, John, Christ the King, Pleasant Hill
Baptista, Antonio, (Retired), St. Leander, San Leandro
Bayless, Richard, St. Joseph, Old Mission San Jose, Fremont
Beltran, Juan, (Retired), St. Cornelius, Richmond
Bettencourt, Leonard, (Retired), St. John the Baptist, San Lorenzo
Bothe, William, (Retired), St. Stephen, Walnut Creek
Budnik, Steven Sr., Our Lady of Guadalupe, Fremont
Burns, Jeffrey, St. Lawrence O'Toole, Oakland; (Active Outside the Diocese)
Cabezas, Rigoberto, Holy Spirit, Fremont
Calub, Benigno, (Retired), St. Anne, Union City.
Cantlon, Michael, (Active Outside the Diocese)
Cao, Dac, St. Leo, Oakland
Casey, Herb, St. John Vianney, Walnut Creek
Cichon, Witold, Polish Pastoral Center, Union City
Cloyne, David, St. Charles Borromeo, Livermore
Clyde, Harry, (Active Outside the Diocese)
Dandan, Ernesto, St. James, Fremont
Davis, Dennis, (On Leave)
Dizon, Alberto, St. Catherine of Siena, Martinez
Drobick, William, St. Agnes, Concord
Dulka, Matthew, (Unassigned-Maryknoll)
Durden, John Jr., St. Joan of Arc, San Ramon
Ehling, Rex, (Retired)
Encarnacion, Rey, Santa Maria, Orinda
Escruceria, Gustavo, Good Shepard, Pittsburg
Evans, Garry, (Retired), Transfiguration, Castro Valley
Folger, Richard, (Retired), Our Lady of the Rosary, Union City
Freeman, Ernest, (Retired), St. Augustine, Pleasanton
Fuentes, Javier, St. Bernard, Oakland
Gall, William, St. Bonaventure, Concord
Glover, Chuck, Holy Spirit, Fremont
Gomez, Ruben, St. Joan of Arc, San Ramon
Gonsalves, Nelson, (Retired), Our Lady of Grace, Castro Valley
Gonzalez, Noe, St. Jarlath, Oakland
Gourley, Joseph, St. Augustine, Pleasanton
Grigg, Jerry, (Retired), Most Holy Rosary, Antioch
Guesnon, Ovide, (Retired), Our Lady of Guadalupe, Fremont
Hack, Gary, St. Ignatius, Antioch
Henderson, William, (Active Outside the Diocese)
Hernandez, Gabriel, (Retired), St. Anthony-Mary Help of Christians, Oakland.
Holland, David, St. Catherine of Siena, Martinez
Horan, Ronald, Immaculate Heart of Mary, Brentwood
Jee, John, (Retired)
Jimenez, Arturo, St. Paul, San Pablo
Johson, Earl, St. Louis Bertrand, Oakland
Kortuem, John, Immaculate Heart of Mary, Brentwood
Layden, Alan, (Retired), St. Anthony, Oakley
Leach, Marty, St. Joseph Basilica, Alameda
Lee, Stanley, (Retired), Filipino Pastoral Center, Oakland
Lewandowski, Daniel
Lewellyn, Stephen, Holy Spirit, Fremont
Liwanag, Bernard, St. Anne, Union City
Madrigal, Ysidro, (Retired), St. Paul, San Pablo
Martin, Richard, St. Augustine, Pleasanton
Martin, Thomas, Our Lady of Good Counsel, San Leandro
Mazibrook, John, St. Francis of Assisi, Concord
McGowan, Thomas, (Retired), St. John, El Cerrito
Mignano, John, Transfiguration, Castro Valley
Miyashiro, Leslie, St. Joseph, Pinole
Moore, Timothy, Transfiguration, Castro Valley
Moya, Manuel, St. Clement, Hayward
Myers, Timothy, St. Felicitas, San Leandro
Nagel, Ralph, St. Ambrose, Berkeley
Nguyen, John, (Retired)
Nguyen, Loc H., Our Lady Queen of the World, Bay Point
Oey, Hock Chuan, (Retired), St. Joan of Arc, San Ramon
Palomares, Charles, St. Francis of Assisi, Concord
Pearce, James, Santa Maria, Orinda
Perez, Alfonso, Corpus Christi, Fremont
Perez, Ernest, (Retired), St. Edward, Newark
Perez, Jose, St. Joseph the Worker, Berkeley
Pesqueira, Gilbert, St. Charles Borromeo, Livermore
Preza, Mariano, (Unassigned)
Quigley, Edward, (Retired)
Quinn, Lawrence, All Saints, Hayward
Rabuy, Carlos, St. Anne, Union City
Reyes, Antonio, (Retired), St. Agnes, Concord
Rezendes, David, St. Michael, Livermore
Rigley, Burton, (Retired), Transfiguration, Castro Valley
Rivilla, Luis, (Active Outside the Diocese)
Roberto, Timothy, Holy Spirit, Fremont
Roemers, Gustaaf, (Retired), Our Lady of the Rosary, Union City
Roque, Rolito C., (Retired), St. Edward, Newark
Sekona, Loch, St. John the Baptist, El Cerrito
Sicat, Joe, (Retired), St. Raymond Penafort, Dublin
Silva, Richard, (Retired)
Silveira, Victor, St. Leander, San Leandro
Silvernale, Charles, Most Holy Rosary, Antioch
Spano, Edward, (Active Outside the Diocese)
Stelly, Eugene, (Retired), Cathedral Parish of Christ the Light, Oakland
Ta, Peter, Cathedral Parish of Christ the Light, Oakland
Tovar, Joseph, (Retired), St. Anthony, Oakley
Tuason, Noe, (Retired), St. John the Baptist, San Lorenzo
Tutson, Ron, St. Benedict, Oakland
Vivet, Lance, St. Joseph, Fremont
Wedge, Ken, (Active Outside the Diocese)
Wedl, Roger, (Retired), St. Edward, Newark
Wong, Danny, Chinese Ministry Center, Oakland
Wortham, Gary, St. Augustine, Pleasanton
Yee, Richard, (Retired), Holy Spirit, Fremont
Young, David, Cathedral Parish of Christ the Light, Oakland.

INSTITUTIONS LOCATED IN DIOCESE

[A] SEMINARIES, RELIGIOUS OR SCHOLASTICATES

BERKELEY. *Dominican School of Philosophy and Theology* (St. Albert's College) 2301 Vine St., Berkeley, 94708-1816. Tel: 510-849-2030; Fax: 510-849-1372; Email: info@dspt.edu; Web: www.dspt.edu. Rev. Peter Rogers, O.P., Pres.; Ian Brooks, Vice Pres. Admin & CFO; Rev. Christopher J. Renz, O.P., Dean; Leslie Borquez, Registrar; Barbara Daniels, Dir.; Aaron Anderson, Dir.; Heidi McKenna, Dir.; Rodrigo Berrios, Admin.; Revs. Joseph Boenzi, S.D.B., Faculty; Michael J. Dodds, O.P., Faculty; Bro. Justin Gable, O.P., Faculty; Revs. Edward Krasevac, O.P., Faculty; Bryan Kromholtz, O.P., Faculty; Eugene Ludwig, O.F.M.-Cap., Faculty; Hilary Martin, O.P., Faculty; John Thomas Mellein, O.P., Faculty; Anselm Ramelow, O.P., Faculty; Augustine Thompson, O.P., Faculty; Sr. Marianne Farina, C.S.C., Faculty; Mrs. Jennifer Allen, Faculty; Dr. Margarita Vega, Ph.D., Faculty. Lay Teachers 2; Priests 12; Sisters 1; Students 45.

Jesuit School of Theology of Santa Clara University (Berkeley, California Campus), 1735 LeRoy Ave., Berkeley, 94709-1115. Tel: 510-549-5000; Email: jblattler@scu.edu; Web: www.scu.edu/jst. Rev. Kevin O'Brien, S.J., Dean; Alison Benders, Assoc. Dean; Patrick Coogan, Asst. Dean, Finance and Admin.; Paul Kircher, Asst. Dean, Students; Drew Roberts, Asst. Dean, Enrollment Mngmnt. & Mktg.; Jim Oberhausen, Registrar; Dianna Gallagher, Sr. Asst. to the Dean; Jasmine Allen, Admin. Asst. Finance & Admin.; Caroline Read, Mktg. & Communications Specialist; Mey Saechao, Academic Opers. Assoc.; Thanh Vo, Accounting Assoc.; Bro. Simon Kim, O.P., Dir.; Sr. Teresa Montes, Dir.; Rev. George R. Murphy, S.J., Dir.; Jim Siwicki, Dir. Renewal Program, A Sabbatical Experience; Amanda Kaminski, Dir. Academic Advising & Support Svcs.; Memphis Latchison, Sr. Assoc. Dir. Enrollment & Recruitment; Michelle Rey, Assoc. Dir. Major Gifts; Tanisha Sparks, Asst. Dir. Housing & Bldg. Opers.; Dr. Jerome P. Baggett, Prof.; Kate Barush, Prof.; Dr. Thomas Cattoi, Prof.; Revs. John C. Endres, S.J., Prof.; Eduardo C. Fernandez, S.J., Prof.; Dr. Lisa Fullam, Prof.; Revs. George E. Griener, S.J., Prof.; Christopher Hadley, S.J., Prof.; Dr. Gina Hens-Piazza, Prof.; Revs. Paul A. Janowiak, S.J., Prof.; Hung T. Pham, S.J., Prof.; Dr. Jean-Francois Racine, Prof.; Deborah Ross, Prof.; Julie Rubio, Prof.; Rev. Anh Q. Tran, S.J., Prof.; Pearl Barros, Adj. Faculty; Stephanie Dixon, Adj. Faculty; William Dohar, Adj. Faculty; Sisters Jane Ferdon, O.P., Adj. Faculty; Elizabeth Liebert, Adj. Faculty; Olga Louchakova, Adj. Faculty; John Mabry, Adj. Faculty; Sonny Manuel, Adj. Faculty; Rev. Robert J. McCann, R.S.C.J., J.C.L., Adj. Faculty; Sisters Mary McGann, R.S.C.J., Adj. Faculty; Julia Prinz, V.D.M.F., Adj. Faculty; Rev. George W. Quickley, S.J., Adj. Faculty; Ms. Clare Ronzani, Adj, Faculty; Shannon Vanderpol, Adj. Faculty; Bro. Keith Warner, Adj. Faculty; Rev. George Williams, S.J., Adj. Faculty; Dr. Bruce Lescher, Faculty Emeriti; Rev. William R. O'Neill, S.J., Faculty Emeriti; Sr. Sandra M. Schneiders, I.H.M., Faculty Emeriti. An Ecclesiastical Faculty of Theology under statutes approved by the Holy See; one of two theological centers of the U.S. Jesuit Conference, Society of Jesus; officially listed as a graduate school of Santa Clara University in the Diocese of San Jose; statistical reporting done through the Diocese of San Jose; member of the Graduate Theological Union (GTU), Berkeley. Faculty 20; Lay Teachers 9; Students 126; Clergy / Religious Teachers 11.

[B] COLLEGES AND UNIVERSITIES

OAKLAND. *Holy Names University* (1868) 3500 Mountain Blvd., 94619-1627. Tel: 510-436-1000; Fax: 510-436-1199; Email: tom@hnu.edu; Web: www.hnu.edu. Michael Groener, Pres.; Mr. Rob Kinnard, Vice Pres., Finance and Admin.; Mr. John Muccigrosso, Vice Pres., Academic Affairs; Mr. Alan Liebrecht, Vice Pres., Strategic Enrollment Management; Sr. Carol Sellman, S.N.J.M., Vice Pres., Mission Effectiveness; Mr. Luis Guerra, Vice Pres.; Mr. Kevin Gin, Vice Pres.; Ms. Laura

Lyndon, Vice Pres.; Mr. Stephen Sticka, Registrar; Rev. Salvatore Ragusa, S.D.S., Campus Min.; Ms. Jenny Girard Malley, Assoc. Pastor; Ms. Alison Mundy, Dir.; Ms. Sylvia Contreras, Librarian. Sponsorship: Sisters of the Holy Names of Jesus and Mary.Chartered 1868; Residence and Non-Residence Students.

Legal Titles: Sisters of the Holy Names of Jesus and Mary, A Corporation; Holy Names University, A Corporation. Clergy 2; Priests 1; Sisters 3; Students 930; Lay Professors 54; Clergy / Religious Teachers 2.

MORAGA. *Saint Mary's College of California* (1963) Coed. Resident and Non-Resident Students. 1928 St. Mary's Rd., Moraga, 94556-2715.
Tel: 925-631-4000; Email: cwolf@stmarys-ca.edu; Web: www.stmarys-ca.edu. 1928 St. Mary's Rd., PMB 4777, Moraga, 94575. James A. Donahue, Ph. D., Pres.; Margaret Kasimatis, Provost; Bros. Mel Anderson, F.S.C., Pres. Emeritus; Ronald Gallagher, F.S.C., Pres. Emeritus; Thomas Jones, F.S.C., Dir.; Chris Donnelly, F.S.C., Projects Mgr., Facilities; Martin Ash, F.S.C., Special Projects Coord., Alumni Engagement; Michael S. Avila, F.S.C., Prof.; Kenneth W. Cardwell, F.S.C., Prof.; Camillus Chavez, F.S.C., Ph.D., Prof.; Charles Hilken, F.S.C., Prof.; Mark McVann, F.S.C., Prof.; Michael Meister, F.S.C., Prof.; Michael Murphy, F.S.C., Prof.; Martin Yribaren, F.S.C., Prof.; Richard Lemberg, F.S.C., Librarian; Glenn Bolton, F.S.C., In Res.; Christopher Brady, F.S.C., In Res.; Bernard LoCoco, F.S.C., In Res.; Brenden Madden, F.S.C., In Res.; Patrick Moore, F.S.C., In Res.; Chris Patino, F.S.C., In Res.; Raphael Patton, F.S.C., In Res.; Stan Sobczyk, F.S.C., In Res.; Rev. David Gentry-Akin, F.S.C., Prof.; Bro. Hai Ho, O.-F.M.Cap., Campus Min.; Revs. Thomas McElligott, Campus Min., (Retired); John Morris, O.P., Campus Min. Brothers of the Christian Schools, District of San Francisco.

Saint Mary's College of California Clergy 4; Students 3,881; Brothers in Residence 22; Priests in Residence 3; Total Instructors 492; Clergy / Religious Teachers 9.

[C] HIGH SCHOOLS, DIOCESAN

OAKLAND. *Bishop O'Dowd High School* (1951) 9500 Stearns Ave., 94605-4720. Tel: 510-577-9100;
Fax: 510-638-3259; Email: sphelps@bishopodowd.org; Web: www.bishopodowd.org. James D. Childs, Pres.; Rev. James Sullivan, Chap.; Annette Counts, Librarian. Lay Teachers 95; Priests 1; Students 1,235.

[D] HIGH SCHOOLS, PAROCHIAL

ALAMEDA. *Saint Joseph Notre Dame High School*, 1011 Chestnut St., Alameda, 94501-4315.
Tel: 510-523-1526; Fax: 510-523-2181; Email: dlozano@sjnd.org; Email: kjennings@sjnd.org; Email: kventurini@sjnd.org; Web: www.sjnd.org. Kenneth Jennings, Prin.; Mallory Bickley, Librarian; Elizabeth Rochlin, Registrar. Lay Teachers 37; Students 450.

[E] HIGH SCHOOLS, PRIVATE

OAKLAND. *De La Salle Cristo Rey of East Bay, Inc.* (St. Elizabeth Campus) 1530 34th Ave., 94601.
Tel: 510-532-8947; Email: info@cristoreydelasalle.org; Web: www.cristoreydelasalle.org. Michael Anderer, Pres.; Ana Hernandez, Prin.; Damien McDuffie, Dir. Admissions & Community Engagement; John Coughlan, Dir. Corp. Work Study Prog.; Greg Young, Dir. Mission Advancement; Estelle Hunt, Dir. Finance & Opers. Sponsorship: Brothers of the Christian Schools. Lay Teachers 11; Students 64; Clergy / Religious Teachers 2.

Holy Names High School (1868) 4660 Harbord Dr., 94618-2211. Tel: 510-450-1110; Fax: 510-547-3111; Email: chubbard@hnhsoakland.org; Email: jcasella@hnhsoakland.org; Web: www.hnhsoakland.org. Constance Hubbard, Pres.; Kendra Carr, Prin. Sponsorship: Sisters of the Holy Names of Jesus and Mary. Lay Teachers 30; Students 138.

BERKELEY. *Saint Mary's College High School* (1863) Peralta Park, 1294 Albina Ave., Berkeley, 94706-2599. Tel: 510-526-9242; Fax: 510-559-6277; Email: jloughman@stmchs.org; Web: www.saintmaryschs.org. Mr. Lawrence Puck, Pres.; Dr. Peter Imperial, Prin.; Mr. Brian Thomas, Librarian. Sponsorship: Brothers of the Christian Schools. Brothers 2; Lay Teachers 52; Students 629; Clergy / Religious Teachers 2.

CONCORD. *Carondelet High School* (1965) 1133 Winton Dr., Concord, 94518-3527. Tel: 925-686-5353;
Fax: 925-671-9429; Email: chs@carondeleths.org; Web: www.carondeleths.org. Bonnie Cotter, Pres.; Kevin Cushing, Prin. Sponsorship: Sisters of St Joseph of Carondelet. Lay Teachers 99; Sisters 1; Students 803.

De La Salle High School of Concord, Inc. (1965) (Boys) 1130 Winton Dr., Concord, 94518-3528.
Tel: 925-288-8100; Fax: 925-686-3474; Email: silvam@dlshs.org; Web: www.dlshs.org. Mr. Mark DeMarco, Pres.; Dr. Heather Alumbaugh, Ph.D., Vice Pres. Academic Life; Mr. Mark Chiarucci, Vice Pres. Advancement; Mr. Jack Dyer, Vice Pres. Student Life; Mrs. Lynne Jones, Vice Pres. Finance; Mr. Leo Lopoz, Vice Pres. Athletics. Sponsorship: Brothers of the Christian Schools. Brothers 1; Lay Teachers 83; Priests 1; Students 1,041.

HAYWARD. *Moreau Catholic High School* (1965) 27170 Mission Blvd., Hayward, 94544. Tel: 510-881-4300; Fax: 510-581-5669; Email: tlee@moreaucatholic.org; Web: www.moreaucatholic.org. Terrence Lee, Pres.; Dr. Elizabeth Guneratne, Prin.; Jessica Simons, Librarian; Rev. Bruce Cecil, C.S.C, Chap. Sponsorship: Congregation of Holy Cross. Lay Teachers 80; Priests 1; Students 860; Clergy / Religious Teachers 10.

RICHMOND. *Salesian College Preparatory*, 2851 Salesian Ave., Richmond, 94804. Tel: 510-234-4433; Email: mflannery@salesian.com; Web: www.salesian.com. Stephen Pezzola, Pres.; Marylou Flannery, Prin.; Revs. John Itzaina, S.D.B., Dir.; Joe Nguyen, S.D.B., In Res.; John Puntino, S.D.B., In Res.; Robert Stein, S.D.B., In Res.; Bros. Jhoni Chamorro, S.D.B., In Res.; Patrick Maloney, S.D.B., In Res., (Retired); Jerry Weirich, S.D.B., In Res., (Retired). Sponsorship: Salesians of St. John Bosco. Lay Teachers 35; Priests 1; Students 424; Clergy / Religious Teachers 1.

[F] ELEMENTARY SCHOOLS, PRIVATE

CONCORD. **Wood Rose Academy*, (Grades PreK-8), 4347 Cowell Rd., Concord, 94518-1807.
Tel: 925-825-4644; Fax: 925-825-4645; Email: woodroseacad@sbcglobal.net; Email: aralday@woodroseacademy.org; Web: www.woodroseacademy.org. Mrs. Aracely Iniguez, Prin. Lay Teachers 20; Students 165.

[G] CATHOLIC CHARITIES OF THE DIOCESE OF OAKLAND

OAKLAND. *Catholic Charities of the Diocese of Oakland*, 433 Jefferson St., 94607-3539. Tel: 510-768-3100; Fax: 510-451-6998; Email: info@cceb.org; Web: www.cceb.org. Most Rev. Michael C. Barber, S.J., Pres.; John Espinoza, Chm., Bd. of Dirs.; Margaret Peterson, CEO; Sean Hanlon, CFO; Diana Pascual, Chief Admin. Officer; Christopher Martinez, Chief Prog. Officer, Tel: 510-768-3167; Tel: 888-277-8608 Legal Immigration Svcs. Toll Free; Mr. Stephen P. Mullin, Chief Devel. Officer; Mary Kuhn, Dir., Communication; Kathleen Manis Johnson, Dir., Grants; Kathryn Lee, Dir., Data Analytics & QA; Steve Wilcox, Diocesan Rep., Bd. of Dirs.; Mr. Chuck L. Fernandez, CEO, Sec.

Catholic Charities of the Diocese of Oakland, Inc. dba Catholic Charities of the East Bay. Tot Asst. Annually 24,688; Total Staff 75.

Oakland Service Center, 433 Jefferson St., 94607.
Tel: 510-768-3100; Fax: 510-451-6998; Email: info@cceb.org; Web: www.cceb.org. Mr. Chuck L. Fernandez, CEO; Margaret Peterson, CEO. Tot Asst. Annually 24,688; Total Staff 75.

Concord Service Center, 3540 Chestnut Ave., Concord, 94519. Tel: 925-825-3099;
Fax: 925-825-5503; Email: info@cceb.org. Mr. Chuck L. Fernandez, CEO; Margaret Peterson, CEO. Tot Asst. Annually 24,688; Total Staff 75.

West County Service Center, 217 Harbour Way, Richmond, 94801. Tel: 510-234-5110;
Fax: 510-237-6778; Email: info@cceb.org; Web: www.cceb.org. Margaret Peterson, CEO. Tot Asst. Annually 24,688; Total Staff 75.

[H] DAY NURSERIES

OAKLAND. **Saint Vincent's Day Home, Inc.* (1911) 1086 Eighth St., 94607-2616. Tel: 510-832-8324;
Fax: 510-832-5021; Email: info@svdh.org; Web: www.svdh.org. Kathleen Shaheed, Interim Exec. Dir. Purpose: Since 1911, Saint Vincent's Day Home's (SVDH) mission has been to serve and act on behalf of the needs, rights and well-being of all young children by offering educational and developmental services and resources to families struggling toward self-sufficiency. SVDH strives to achieve high-quality services while promoting excellence in the field of Child Development and Family Services.

Saint Vincent's Day Home, A Corporation Capacity 230; Students 198; Staff/Teachers 49; Total Assisted 418.

[I] ORGANIZATIONS FOR DEAF AND HARD OF HEARING

HAYWARD. *St. Joseph's Center for Deaf and Hard of Hearing*, 40374 Fremont Blvd., Hayward, 94538.
Tel: 510-267-8348; Tel: 510-250-2060; Email: lyoung@oakdiocese.org; Web: www.oakdiocese.org/sjcd. Mailing Address: 2121 Harrison St., Ste. 100, 94612-3788. Rev. Larry E. Young, Contact Person

St. Joseph's Center for the Deaf and Hard of Hearing, A Corporation. Tot Asst. Annually 1,700; Total Staff 1.

[J] RETIREMENT AND CARE FACILITIES

OAKLAND. *Bishop Begin Villa* (Retired Priests) 3418 E. 18th St., 94601-3004. Tel: 510-536-0719;
Fax: 510-261-4516; Email: natbrown@eldercarealliance.org. Revs. Vincent R. Brylka, (Retired); David Link, (Retired); Hilary Cooper; Alexander Snyder, (Retired); Stanislaw Zak, (Retired). Residents 5; Total Assisted 5.

Mercy Retirement and Care Center (1822) Affiliated with Elder Care Alliance. 3431 Foothill Blvd., 94601-3129. Tel: 510-534-8540; Fax: 510-261-7551; Email: natbrown@eldercarealliance.org; Web: www.mercyretirementcenter.org. Tamra M. Schmutzler, Exec. Dir. Sponsorship: Sisters of Mercy of the Americas - West Midwest Community.Residential care, assisted living & skilled nursing. Bed Capacity 107; Employees 175; Residents 105; Sisters of Mercy 1; Tot Asst. Annually 275; Brown Bag Grocery Distribution 6,055.

Bishop Begin Villa, Retirement Facility for Priests in the Oakland Diocese, 3431 Foothill Blvd., 94601-3129. Tel: 510-534-8540; Email: natbrown@eldercarealliance.org. Extensive community services.

Convalescent Hospital - Skilled Nursing Facility, 3431 Foothill Blvd., 94601. Tel: 510-534-8540;
Fax: 510-261-4516; Web: www.mercyretirementcenter.org. Bed Capacity 59; Residents 57.

[K] MONASTERIES AND RESIDENCES OF PRIESTS AND BROTHERS

OAKLAND. *Franciscan Friars of California (Province of St. Barbara)*, 1500 34th Ave., 94601-3091.
Tel: 510-536-1287; Fax: 510-536-3578; Email: main@sbofm.org; Web: www.sbfranciscans.org. Revs. Barry Brunsman, O.F.M.; Mel Bucher, O.F.M.; Eugene Burnett, O.F.M.; Rigoberto Calcoa-Rivas, O.F.M.; Ignatius DeGroot, O.F.M.; Patrick Evard, O.F.M.; Thomas Frost, O.F.M.; David Gaa, O.F.M.; Antonio Galindo-Carreon, O.F.M.; John Gibbons, O.F.M.; Luis Guzman, O.F.M.; William Haney, O.F.M.; Evan Arthur Howard, O.F.M., (Retired); Martin Ibarra, O.F.M.; Benedict Innes, O.F.M.; Richard Juzix, O.F.M.; Guglielmo Lauriola, O.F.M.; Nghia Phan, O.F.M.; Richard McManus, O.F.M.; Javier Reyes-Ruiz, O.F.M.; Louis Vitale, O.F.M.; Bros. Didacus Clavel, O.F.M.; David Cobian, O.F.M., M.Div.; Anthony Lavorin, O.F.M.; Hajime Okuhara, O.F.M.; Eric Pilarcik, O.F.M.; Freddy Rodriguez, O.F.M.; Brian Trawick, O.F.M.; Robert Valentine, O.F.M.; Victor Vega, O.F.M. Total in Community 30.

Franciscan Friars of California (Province of St. Barbara), Provincial Office, 1500-34th Ave., 94601-3092. Tel: 510-536-3722; Fax: 510-536-3970; Email: main@sbofm.org; Web: www.sbfranciscans.org. Revs. David Gaa, O.F.M., Prov.; Thomas West, O.F.M., Prov. Sec.; Martin Ibarra, O.F.M., Vice Prov.; Very Rev. Melvin A. Jurisich, O.F.M., Treas.; Bros. Eric Pilarcik, O.F.M., Dir., Vocations; Mark Schroeder, O.F.M., Dir., Franciscans for Justice; Brian Trawick, O.F.M., Admin.; Hajime Okuhara, O.F.M., Office Asst.; Mr. Stanley Raggio, COO; Ms. Reyna Lupian, Assoc. Treas.; Ms. Gerry Carbone, Sec. to the Treas.; Evelyn Torres, Accountant; Ms. Lara de Guzman, Admin.

Franciscan Friars of California Priests 4; Total Staff 13.

Jesuit Fathers and Brothers (1972) Murray Residence Community, 171 Santa Rosa Ave., 94610-1316. Tel: 510-655-8334; Fax: 510-655-4816; Email: tweston@jesuits.org. Revs. Thomas C. Weston, S.J., Supr.; John A. Baumann, S.J.; Stephen M. Kelly, S.J.; Lester E. Love, S.J.

Missionary Oblates of Mary Immaculate United States Province (1953) 290 Lenox Ave., 94610-4625. Tel: 510-452-1550; Fax: 510-893-1272; Email: lenoxmissionhouse@omiusa.org; Web: www.omiusa.org. Rev. Don Arel, O.M.I., Dir.

Missionary Oblates of Mary Immaculate United States Province Total in Residence 1; Total Staff 1.

Order of Preachers (Province of the Most Holy Name of Jesus - Western Dominican Province) (1914) 5877 Birch Ct., 94618-1626. Tel: 510-658-8722;
Fax: 510-658-1061; Email: wdp@opwest.org; Web: www.opwest.org. Rev. David Bello, O.P.; Bro. Bernhard Blankenhorn, O.P.; Revs. Michael Carey, O.P., Dir. Ongoing Formation; Timothy Conlan, O.P.; Roberto Corral, O.P.; Alejandro Crosthwaite, O.P., Prof.; Bartholomew de la Torre, O.P.; Peter Do, O.P.; Jude Eli, O.P., Dir. Western Dominican Preaching; Christopher Fadok, O.P., Prior Prov.; Peter Hannah, O.P.; Bro. Augustine Hilander, O.P., Promoter, Holy Name Society; Revs. Dennis Klein, O.P.; Bryan Kromholtz, O.P.; Francis Le, O.P.; Luke D. Buckles, O.P., Prof.; Stephen Maria Lopez, O.P., Acting Student Master; Isaiah Mary

Molano, O.P, Dir. Promoter Rosary Confraternity; James Moore, O.P., Vicar Prov., Advancement and Promoter, Mass Media & Arts; John Morris, O.P.; Very Rev. Mark C. Padrez, O.P., Prior; Revs. Thomas Raftery, O.P.; Christopher J. Renz, O.P., Dir.; Michael Rolland, O.P.; Anthony Rosevear, O.P.; Dismas Sayer, O.P., Dir. St. Jude Shrine; Richard Schenk, O.P.; Michael S. Sherwin, O.P., Prof.; Bro. Ambrose Sigman, O.P.; Revs. Daniel Syverstad, O.P.; Gregory T. Tatum, O.P., Serving in Rome; Martin Walsh, O.P., Dir. Vocations. Total in the Province 147.

Order of Preachers (Province of the Most Holy Name of Jesus - Western Dominican Province) (1932) St. Albert Priory, 5890 Birch Ct., 94618-1627. Tel: 510-596-1800; Fax: 510-596-1860; Email: frmaaop@opwest.org; Web: www.op.org/opwest/sap. Rev. Michael Augustine Amabisco, O.P., Prior; Very Rev. Mark C. Padrez, O.P., Prov.; Revs. Augustine Thompson, O.P., Subprior; James Moore, O.P., Vicar; Paul Conner, O.P.; Dominic DeDomenico, O.P.; Dominic DeMaio, O.P.; Christopher Fadok, O.P.; LaSalle Hallissey, O.P.; Augustine Hartman, O.P.; Thomas Hayes, O.P.; Bartholomew J. Hutcherson, O.P.; Bryan Kromholtz, O.P.; Joseph Quoc Quang Le, O.P.; Stephen Maria Lopez, O.P.; Hilary Martin, O.P.; Brendan McAnerney, O.P.; John Thomas Mellein, O.P.; Tuan Minh Nguyen, O.P.; Lawrence Ninh, O.P.; Sergius Propst, O.P.; Michael Sweeney, O.P.; Very Rev. Emmerich W. Vogt, O.P.; Rev. Antoninus Wall, O.P.; Bros. John Peter Anderson, O.P.; Karol Babis, O.P.; Antony Cherian, O.P.; Elias Ford, O.P.; Josh David Gatus, O.P.; Columban Mary Hall, O.P.; Matthew Heynen, O.P.; Cody Jorgensen, O.P.; Andrew Kang, O.P.; Gregory Liu, O.P.; Nathaniel Mayne, O.P.; Chrysostom Minjinke, O.P.; Andrezej Monka, O.P.; Paul Mullner, O.P.; Martin Maria Nguyen, O.P.; Phong Hoang Nguyen, O.P.; Scott Norgarrd, O.P.; Andrew Opsahl, O.P.; Patrick Rooney, O.P.; Joseph Selinger, O.P.; Paschal Strader, O.P.; Anthanasius Thompson, O.P.; Matthew Wanner, O.P.; John Winkowitsch, O.P. *Order of Preachers (Province of the Most Holy Name of Jesus - Western Dominican Province)*, Siena House, 5730 Presley Way, 94618-1633. Tel: (510) 654-8735; Email: wdp@opwest.org. Revs. Michael J. Dodds, O.P.; David K. O'Rourke, O.P.; Christopher J. Renz, O.P.; Peter Rogers, O.P.; Leo Tubbs, O.P.; Mark O'Leary, O.P. Priests 7.

Redemptorist Fathers (Denver Province), 8945 Golf Links Rd., P.O. Box 5007, 94605-4124. Tel: 510-653-6341; Email: brodanielhall@gmail.com. Bro. Daniel Hall, Dir.; Deacon Dennis Lee, C.Ss.R., In Res. Sponsorship: Redemptorist Society of California.
The Redemptorists of Oakland.

BERKELEY. *Incarnation Monastery, Camaldolese Benedictines* (1979) 1369 La Loma Ave., Berkeley, 94708-2031. Tel: 510-845-0601; Fax: 510-845-0601; Email: facolnaghi@aol.com; Web: www.contemplation.com. Revs. Andrew Colnaghi, O.S.B.Cam., Prior; Arthur Poulin, O.S.B.Cam., In Res.; Bros. Bede Heeley, O.S.B.Cam., In Res.; Ivan Nicoletto, O.S.B.Cam., In Res. Total in Residence 3.

Capuchin Franciscan Friars, House of Studies, 1534 Arch St., Berkeley, 94708-1829. Tel: 510-841-2229; Email: friarhung@yahoo.com; Web: www.olcapuchins.org. Revs. Hung Nguyen, O.F.M.Cap., Supr.; James Cleary, O.F.M.Cap., In Res.; Martin Haggins, O.F.M.Cap., In Res.; Michael O'Shea, O.F.M.Cap., In Res.; Ron Talbott, O.F.M.Cap., In Res.; Bros. Marvin Abella, O.F.M.Cap., In Res.; Nikolas Barth, O.F.M.Cap., In Res.; Austin Cambon, O.F.M.Cap., In Res.; Hai Ho, O.F.M.Cap., Chap.; Victor Taglianetti, O.F.M.Cap., In Res. Brothers 5; Priests 5. *Saint Conrad Friary*, 1534 Arch St., Berkeley, 94708-1829. Tel: 510-841-2229. Bros. Marvin Abella, O.F.M.Cap., (Postulant); Nikolas Barth, O.F.M.Cap.; Austin Cambon, O.F.M.Cap., (Postulant); Peter Ciolino, O.F.M.Cap.; Victor Taglianetti, O.F.M.Cap.

Jesuit Fathers and Brothers, Jesuit Community at Jesuit School of Theology, 1756 LeRoy Ave., Berkeley, 94709-1157. Tel: 510-225-6200; Fax: 510-280-6083; Email: jstrector@scu.edu; Web: www.jstjesuits.org. Revs. Martin T. Connell, S.J., Ph.D., Rector; Kevin O'Brien, S.J., Dean; Michael Agliardo, S.J., Dir.; George R. Murphy, S.J., Dir.; Michael Tyrrell, S.J., Treas.; David Masikini, S.J., Admin.; Javier Diaz y Diaz, S.J., Pastoral Assoc.; Michael T. Castori, S.J., Chap.; John C. Endres, S.J., Prof.; Eduardo C. Fernandez, S.J., Prof.; George E. Griener, S.J., Prof.; Christopher Hadley, S.J., Prof.; Paul A. Janowiak, S.J., Prof.; Hung T. Pham, S.J., Prof.; Anh Q. Tran, S.J., Prof.; Augustin Atsikin, S.J., (Togo) Student; Timothy Baghrmwin, S.J., Student; Bang Cao Do, S.J., Student; Santiago Garcia Pintos, S.J., Student; Robert Gbedolo Oke, S.J., Student; Aloysius Ming-te Hsu, S.J., Student; Josephat L. Kabutta, S.J., Student; Louis Leveil, S.J., (India) Student; Alex A. Llanera, S.J., Student; Benedict Mayaki, S.J., Student; Damas Missanga, S.J., Student; James Moro, S.J., Student; Peter Tang Van Nguyen, S.J., Student; Emile Nsengimana, S.J., Student; Nelson Nyamayaro, S.J., Student; Brent Otto, S.J., Student; Joseph Dinh Cu Pham, S.J., Student; Serge Rabotovao, S.J., Student; Perianayagam Seluvannan, S.J., Student; kyle K. Shinseki, S.J., Student; John T. Tanner, S.J., Student; Emmanuel L. Ugwejeh, S.J., Student; Cuong Duy Vu, S.J., Student; Jean Fleurys Zezika, S.J., Student
Jesuit Community at JST Brothers 2; Deacons 12; Priests 38; Scholastics 20; Total in Residence 70.

Priests of the Congregation of Holy Cross, Holy Cross Center, 2597 Virginia St., Berkeley, 94709-1108. Tel: 510-548-8515; Email: croninrc@earthlink.net. Revs. Harry Cronin, C.S.C., Dir.; Bruce Cecil, C.S.C, In Res.; Gregory Haake, C.S.C., In Res.; Aaron Michka, C.S.C., In Res. Residents 2.

Redemptorist Fathers (Denver Province), 8945 Golf Links Rd., P.O. Box 5007, 94605-4124. Tel: 510-635-6341; Email: brodanielhall@gmail.com. Bro. Daniel Hall, Dir.; Deacon Dennis Lee, C.Ss.R., In Res. Sponsorship: Redemptorist Society of California.
The Redemptorists of Berkeley.

Salesians of Don Bosco, Don Bosco Hall, 1831 Arch St., Berkeley, 94709-1309. Tel: 510-204-0800; Tel: 510-220-8064; Fax: 510-204-0800; Email: director@salesianstudies.org; Web: www.salesianstudies.org. Rev. Joseph Boenzi, S.D.B., Supr.; Bros. Joseph R. Lockwood, S.D.B., Treas.; Romualdo Orozco, C.J., Music Min.; Revs. Christopher Ford, S.D.B., In Res.; Jack F. Gibson, S.D.B., In Res.; Tri Minh (Matthew) Le, S.D.B., Member; Sang-chel Lee, S.D.B., In Res.; Adrian Mendoza, S.D.B., (Phillipines) In Res.; Jose Adao Rodrigues da Silva, S.D.B., Member; Moses Yoon, S.D.B., (Korea, South) In Res.; Bros. Gillianno Jose Mazzetto de Castro, S.D.B., Member; Vien Nguyen, S.D.B., In Res.; Gerardo Toscano, C.J., In Res. Total in Residence 14; Total Staff 4.

Society of the Precious Blood (Kansas City Province) (1985) 2800 Milvia St., Berkeley, 94703-2209. Tel: 816-522-9420; Email: JimUrbanic@aol.com. Rev. Jack McClure, C.PP.S. Priests 1.

CASTRO VALLEY. *Conventual Franciscans (Province of St. Joseph of Cupertino)*, St. Joseph of Cupertino Friary, 19697 Redwood Rd., Castro Valley, 94546-3456. Tel: 510-582-7333, Ext. 4; Fax: 510-582-7455; Email: ProvSec@franciscanfriars.org. Bro. James Reiter, O.F.M.Conv., Supr.; Revs. Victor P. Abegg, O.F.M.Conv., Prov.; John Heinz, O.F.M.Conv., Treas.; Alfonso Borgen, O.F.M.Conv., In Res.; Stephen King, O.F.M.Conv., In Res.; Bruce Lamb, O.F.M.Conv., In Res.; Kevin Schindler-McGraw, O.F.M.Conv., In Res.; Bros. Francisco Cabral, O.F.M.Conv., In Res.; Patrick Lytell, O.F.M.Conv., In Res.; Michael Paul, O.F.M.Conv., In Res.; Christopher Saindon, O.F.M.Conv., In Res. Brothers 5; Priests 5.

Conventual Franciscans (Province of St. Joseph Cupertino) Provincial Center, St. Joseph of Cupertino Friary, 19697 Redwood Rd., Castro Valley, 94546-3456. Tel: 510-582-7333; Email: VPAbegg@charter.net. Revs. Victor P. Abegg, O.F.M.Conv., Prov.; Jacob Carazo, O.F.M.Conv., Vicar; John Heinz, O.F.M.Conv., Treas.; Paul T. Gawlowski, O.F.M.Conv., Trustee; Thomas J. Czeck, O.F.M.Conv., Trustee; Bro. James Reiter, O.F.M.Conv., Sec. Brothers 1; Priests 5.

FREMONT. **Missionaries of Faith-India Inc.*, 41933 Blacow Rd., Fremont, 94538. Revs. Joy Kumarthusseril, M.F., (India) Supr.; Arogyaiah Bandanadam, M.F.; Robert Kennady Chinnapan, M.F., (India); Anthony Madanu, M.F., (India); Chacko Muthoottil, M.F.; Kuriakose Nadooparambil, M.F., (India); Raju Palleti, M.F., (India); Joseph Pathiyil, M.F., (India); JoJo Puthussery, M.F., (India); Sebastian Soosai, M.F. Clergy 10.

[L] CONVENTS AND RESIDENCES FOR SISTERS

OAKLAND. *Adrian Dominican Sisters (Congregation of the Most Holy Rosary)*, 3693 High St., 94619-2105. Tel: 510-530-2621; Email: mcastop@att.net. Sisters Marian Casteluccio; Eileen Johnson; Evelyn Montez; Cecilia Nguyen; Teresa Montes. Sisters 5.

Congregation of the Queen of the Holy Rosary (Dominican Sisters of Mission San Jose), St. Elizabeth Convent, 1555-34th Ave., 94601-3062. Tel: 510-532-8344; Fax: 510-533-2365; Web: www.msjdominicans.org. Sr. Karen Elizabeth Zavitz, Prioress. Sisters 9.

Sisters of Mercy of the Americas (West Midwest Community), Mercy Retirement and Care Center, 3431 Foothill Blvd., 94601-3129. Tel: 510-534-8540; Fax: 510-261-7551; Email: tschmutzler@eldercarealliance.org; Web: www.mercyretirementcenter.org. Tamra M. Schmutzler, Exec. Sisters 1.

Sisters of St. Joseph of Carondelet, 720 N. Gate Rd., Walnut Creek, 94598. Tel: 310-889-2100; Email: jawright@csjla.org; Web: www.csjla.org. Sr. Patricia Nelson, C.S.J., Supr. Sisters 10. *Christ the King Community*, 3095 Diablo View Rd., Pleasant Hill, 94523-4535. Tel: 925-280-1562; Email: jcgallagher@csjla.org. Sisters Joanne Gallagher, C.S.J., In Res.; Carmel Garcia, C.S.J., In Res.; Anna Marie Gillet, C.S.J., In Res. Sisters 3. *St. Anthony Community*, 2809 Bayview Dr., Alameda, 94501-6347. Tel: 310-889-2100; Email: jawright@csjla.org. Sisters Barbara Flannery, C.S.J., In Res.; Maureen Lyons, C.S.J., In Res. Sisters 2.

Kwanza House, 2203 Colonial Ct., Walnut Creek, 94598-1125. Tel: 310-889-2100; Email: jawright@csjla.org. Sr. Patricia Nelson, C.S.J., In Res. Sisters 1.

Via del Sol Community, 720 N. Gate Rd., Walnut Creek, 94598. Tel: 925-287-9611; Email: aboshea442@gmail.com. Sr. Ann Bernard O'Shea, C.S.J., In Res. Sisters 1.

Sisters of the Presentation of the Blessed Virgin Mary (1854) 1055 47th st. c, Emeryville, 94608. Tel: 510-655-8132; Email: marilynmedau026@gmail.com. Sr. Marilyn Medau, P.B.V.M. Sisters 1.

BERKELEY. *Franciscan Sisters of Little Falls, MN*, 2341 Prince St., Berkeley, 94705-1938. Tel: 510-848-5721; Email: akroll@fslf.org. Sr. Adeline Kroll. Sisters 1.

BRENTWOOD. *Religious Missionary Sisters of the Blessed Sacrament and Mary Immaculate*, 636 - 3rd St., Brentwood, 94513-1357. Tel: 925-513-8154; Fax: 925-516-4847; Email: grande815@msn.com. Sisters Guadalupe Grande, M.S.S., Supr.; Isle Gonzalez, M.S.S., In Res.; Maria C. Ortiz, M.S.S., In Res. Sisters 3.

CONCORD. *Quinhon Missionary Sisters of the Holy Cross*, 1685 Humphrey Dr., Concord, 94519-2810. Tel: 925-674-9639; Email: magdalenaduong@yahoo.com. Sr. Magdalena Oanh Duong, L.H.C., Provincial. Sisters 28.

Concord Convent, 1727 Humphrey Dr., Concord, 94519. Tel: 925-676-9320; Email: rnguyen@oakdiocese.org. Sr. Rosaline Lieu Nguyen, L.H.C., Supr., 1727 Humphrey Dr., Concord, 94519. *Aspirant House*, 50 Santa Maria Way, Orinda, 94563-2605. Tel: 925-253-0831; Email: BanDieuHanh.QNTSHK@gmail.com. Sr. Mary Margaret Phan, L.H.C., Dir.

St. Felicitas Convent, 1604 Manor Dr., San Leandro, 94579. Tel: 510-351-5577; Email: plhhoang@yahoo.com. Paulina Hang Hoang, L.H.C., Supr.

Sisters of St. Joseph of the Third Order of St. Francis, 2301 Mt. Diablo St., Concord, 94520-2213. Tel: 925-825-2091; Fax: 925-825-2439; Email: marygrace@eastbayservicesdd.org. Sr. Marygrace Puchac, Contact Person. Sisters 1.

EL CERRITO. *Sisters of Mercy of Ireland (U.S. Province)*, 11154 San Pablo Ave., El Cerrito, 94530-2131. Tel: 510-233-6769; Email: amaherrsm@gmail.com. Rosaline O'Connor Sr., Prov. Sisters 3.

Sisters of Sacred Hearts of Jesus and Mary, 1607 Liberty St., El Cerrito, 94530. Tel: 510-234-2702; Web: sacredheartsjm.org. Sr. Kathleen Laverty, Contact Person. Sisters 1.

EMERYVILLE. *Sisters of St. Francis of Penance and Christian Charity* (1835) Casa Guadalupe, 1231 40th St., Apt. 332, Emeryville, 94608. Tel: 510-655-5944; Tel: 510-601-8132; Tel: 510-614-2224; Tel: 510-532-2207; Email: mariaelenam@franciscanway.org; Email: marylitell@franciscanway.org; Email: lorsav@att.net; Email: ggmartinez@att.net; Web: www.franciscanway.org. Sr. Mary Litell, O.S.F., In. Res. Sisters 5.

FREMONT. *Congregation of the Queen of the Holy Rosary (Dominican Sisters of Mission San Jose)* (1876) 43326 Mission Cir., Fremont, 94539-5898. Tel: 510-657-2468; Fax: 510-657-1734; Email: pauline@msjdominicans.org; Web: www.msjdominicans.org. Sr. Cecilia Canales, O.P., Congregational Prioress. Generalate Motherhouse and Novitiate of the Dominican Sisters of Mission San Jose, Congregation of The Queen of the Holy Rosary. Sisters 154; Motherhouse Communities 63; St. Elizabeth Community 9; St. Edward Community 5.

Queen of Peace Community, Tel: 510-657-2468; Fax: 510-657-1734. Sr. Mary Liam Brock, O.P., Community Prioress.

Rosary Community, Tel: 510-657-2468; Fax: 510-657-1734. Sr. Mary Susanna Vasquez, O.P., Community Prioress.

St. Martin Community, Tel: 510-657-2468; Fax: 510-657-1734. Sr. Annunciata Auletta, O.P., Community Prioress.

Our Lady of the Angels Community (1977) Tel: 510-657-2468; Fax: 510-657-1734. Sr. Eva Beehner, O.P., Community Prioress, Email: eva@msjdominicans.org.

St. Edward Convent (1969) 37088 Arden St., Newark, 94560-3702. Tel: 510-793-9447; Email: ingrid@msjdominicans.org. Sr. Ingrid Clemmensen, O.P., Prioress. Sisters 4.

St. Elizabeth Convent, 1555-34th Ave., 94601-3062. Tel: 510-532-8344; Fax: 510-533-2365; Email: smls@msjdominicans.org. Sisters La Salette Fuselier, Community Prioress; Maura Cho, S.O.L.P.H., Bible Apostolate, Catechism. Sisters 10; (SOLPH) 1.

Sisters of the Holy Family, 211 Avenida Palmdale, P.O. Box 3248, Fremont, 94539-0324. Tel: 510-624-4596; Fax: 510-933-7595; Email: congsecy@holyfamilysisters.org; Web: www.holyfamilysisters.org. Sr. Caritas Foster, S.H.F., Pres. Sisters 59.

HAYWARD. *Dominican Sisters of Oakford*, Bethany House, 24237 Soto Rd., #$, Hayward, 94544. Tel: 510-652-0986; Email: bethanyop@gmail.com; Web: www.oakforddomnicans.org. Sr. Mary de Crus Nolan, O.P., Prioress. Sisters 1.

HERCULES. *Congregation of the Mother of Carmel* (1866) 142 Weiss Ct., Hercules, 94547-3750. Tel: 510-724-4178; Tel: 510-965-2147; Email: weisscarmel@gmail.com. Sr. Asha Kooliyadan, Supr. Sisters 3.

KENSINGTON. *Carmel of Jesus, Mary and Joseph of Kensington, California*, 68 Rincon Rd., Kensington, 94707. Tel: 510-267-8330; Email: chancellor@oakdiocese.org; Web: www.carmelofkensington.org. Mother Sylvia Gemma, O.C.D., Prioress. Sisters 6.

NEWARK. *Congregation of the Queen of the Holy Rosary (Dominican Sisters of Mission San Jose)*, 37088 Arden St., Newark, 94560-3702. Tel: 510-793-9447; Email: ingrid@msjdominicans.org. Sr. Ingrid Clemmensen, O.P., Prioress. Sisters 4.

SAN LEANDRO. *Dominican Sisters of Oakford*, 980 Woodland Ave., San Leandro, 94577. Tel: 510-638-0665; Email: oakfordusa@hotmail.com; Web: www.oakforddominicans.org. Sr. Mary de Crus Nolan, O.P., Prioress. Sisters 4.

Our Lady of Oakford Regional Office, 980 Woodland Ave., San Leandro, 94577. Tel: 510-638-2822; Email: oakfordusa@hotmail.com; Web: www.oakforddominicans.org. Sr. Mary de Crus Nolan, O.P., US Area Councillor. Sisters 5.

Missionary Sisters of the Society of Mary, 1515 Boxwood Ave., San Leandro, 94579-1303. Tel: 510-357-7816; Email: johnpaul01@aol.com; Web: www.maristsmsm.org. 1515 Boxwood Ave, San Leandro, 94579. Sisters John Paul Chao, S.M.S.M., Contact Person; Cletus Boyd, S.M.S.M., Coord. Sisters 3.

[M] PASTORAL CENTERS

OAKLAND. *Holy Redeemer Center*, 8945 Golf Links Rd., 94605-4124. Tel: 510-635-6341; Email: brodanielhall@gmail.com. Mailing Address: P.O. Box 5007, 94605-0007. Bro. Daniel Hall, Dir.; Deacon Dennis Lee, C.Ss.R., Dir. Spiritual hospitality center.

DANVILLE. *San Damiano Retreat* (1961) Retreat House for men, women and married couples. Franciscan Retreat House, 710 Highland Dr., Danville, 94526-3704. Tel: 925-837-9141; Fax: 925-837-0522; Email: Lisab@sandamiano.org; Web: www.sandamiano.org. Peter Wise, Dir.; Friars William Shaughnessy, O.F.M., In Res.; Stephen Cain, O.F.M., In Res.; Bro. Dennis Duffy, O.F.M., In Res.; Revs. Philip Garcia, O.F.M., In Res.; Josef Prochnow, O.F.M., In Res. Total in Residence 6; Total Staff 25.

LAFAYETTE. *Diocesan Youth Retreat Center*, 1977 Reliez Valley Rd., Lafayette, 94549. Tel: 925-934-5802; Fax: 925-934-0642; Email: youthretreat12@gmail.com; Web: www.oakdiocese.org/youth-and-young-adults/youth-retreat-center. 2121 Harrison St., Ste. 100, 94612-3788. Tim O'Hara, Business Mgr. Total Staff 1.

[N] NEWMAN CENTERS

OAKLAND. *Holy Names University Campus Ministry* (1868) 3500 Mountain Blvd., 94619-1627. Tel: 510-436-1002; Fax: 510-436-1199; Email: ragusa@hnu.edu; Web: www.hnu.edu. Rev. Salvatore Ragusa, S.D.S., Co-Dir. Campus Ministry/Chap., Tel: 510-436-1002; Email: ragusa@hnu.edu; Jenny Girard Malley, M.A., Co-Dir.

MORAGA. *St. Mary's College Mission and Ministry Center*, 1928 Saint Marys Rd., P.O. Box 4777, Moraga, 94575-4777. Tel: 925-631-4366; Email: cao6@stmarys-ca.edu; Web: https://www.stmarys-ca.edu/mission-ministry-center. Rev. Hai Ho, O.F.M.Cap., Chap.; Bros. Christopher Brady, F.S.C., Chap.; Camillus Chavez, F.S.C., Ph.D., Meditation Coord.; Karin L. McClelland, M.A., Dir., Mission & Ministry Center; Nick van Santen, M.Div., Asst. Dir.; Quang Luu, Asst. Dir.; Carrie Davis, Ed.M., Asst. Dir.; Colleen O'Healy Da Silva, M.A., Chapel Coord. & Admin. Asst.

[O] PERSONAL PRELATURES

BERKELEY. *Opus Dei*, Garber House, 1827 Oxford St., Berkeley, 94709-1800. Tel: 510-548-2819; Fax: 510-644-3898; Email: edwardmaristany@gmail.com. Revs. Edward Maristany, Chap.; Torlach Delargy. Prelature of the Holy Cross and Opus Dei.

[P] MISCELLANEOUS LISTINGS

OAKLAND. *Adventus, a California nonprofit public benefit corporation*, 2121 Harrison St., Ste. 100, 94612-3788. Tel: 510-267-8321; Fax: 510-839-7545; Email: pbongiovanni@oakdiocese.org. Mr. Paul Bongiovanni, Pres.; Mr. James H. McCann, Vice Pres.; John J. Ryan, Sec. Purpose: To support the mission of the Roman Catholic Diocese of Oakland.

The Benilde Religious & Charitable Trust, c/o Plageman, Lund and Cannon LLP, One Kaiser Plaza, Ste. 1440, 94612-3500. Tel: 510-899-6100; Fax: 510-899-6101; Email: ecannon@plagemanlund.com; Web: www.plagemanlund.com. Elizabeth Cannon, Contact Person. Charitable trust fund to benefit the educational activities of the Brothers of the Christian Schools of San Francisco.

**Catholic Management Services (CMS)*, 4750 Willow Rd., Ste. 200, Pleasanton, 94588. Email: ambaatz@cfcsmission.org. Mr. Robert W. Seelig, CEO; Mr. Paul Bongiovanni, Bd. Dirs.; Mr. Ronald Gies, Bd. Dirs.; Very Rev. George E. Mockel, Bd. Dirs.

Catholic Church Support Services dba Catholic Management Services.

De La Salle Cristo Rey High School of East Bay Work Study Corporation, 1530 34th Ave., 94601. Tel: 510-532-8947; Email: info@cristoreydelasalle.org; Web: www.cristoreydelasalle.org. Michael Anderer, Pres.; John Coughlan, Dir. Brothers of the Christian Schools Clergy 2; Lay Staff 4; Students 64.

Dominican Community Support Charitable Trust, 5877 Birch Ct., 94618-1626. Tel: 510-658-8722; Fax: 510-658-1061; Email: pvilla@opwest.org. Very Rev. Michael Fones, O.P., Socius; Rev. Christopher Fadok, O.P., Prior Provincial.

Dominican Sisters Vision of Hope (2000) 1555 34th Ave., 94601-3062. Tel: 510-533-5768; Fax: 510-533-2365; Email: amagovern@msjdominicans.org; Email: karene@msjdominicans.org; Web: www.visionofhope.org. Ms. Ann Magovern, Exec. Dir.

**Faith in Action* (1972) 171 Santa Rosa Ave., 94610-1316. Tel: 510-655-2801; Fax: 510-655-4816; Email: jbaumann@faithinaction.org; Web: www.faithinaction.org. Rev. John A. Baumann, S.J., Founder & Dir. Special Projects; Mr. Ronald White, Chm.

Franciscan Charities, Inc., 1500 34th Ave., 94601-3024. Tel: 510-536-3772; Fax: 510-536-3970; Email: main@sbofm.com. Rev. David Gaa, O.F.M., Pres.

Italian Catholic Federation (1924) 8393 Capwell Dr., Ste. 110, 94621-2117. Tel: 510-633-9058; Tel: 888-423-1924; Fax: 510-633-9758; Email: info@icf.org; Web: www.icf.org. Rev. Msgr. Daniel E. Cardelli, Diocesan Chap. & Spiritual Dir., (Retired).

**Next Step Learning Center, Inc.*, 2222 Curtis St., 94607. Tel: 510-251-1731; Fax: 510-271-3656; Email: LStringer@nextsteplc.org; Web: www.nextsteplc.org. Evelyn Ashcroft, Pres.; Lisa Stringer, Exec. Dir.

**Oakland Elizabeth House* (1991) 6423 Colby St., 94618-1309. Tel: 510-658-1380; Fax: 510-658-3160; Email: oakehouse@oakehouse.org; Web: www.oakehouse.org. Jackie Yancy, Exec. Dir. Purpose: 18-month transitional housing program for women and children. Tot Asst. Annually 22.

**Pan De Vida Retreat*, 2121 Harrison St., Ste. 100, 94612-3788.

**Providence House, LP* (1991) Rent-subsidized housing for persons with physical disabilities including persons with AIDS. Providence House, 540 - 23rd St., 94612-1718. Tel: 510-444-0839; Fax: 510-465-5420; Web: www.providencesupportivehousing.org. Sr. Dorthy Peterson, F.C.J., Acting Dir. Number Served Annually 54; Units 40.

Province of Saint Barbara Fraternal Care Trust, 1500 34th Ave., 94601. Tel: 510-536-3722; Email: fct@sbofm.org. Very Rev. Melvin A. Jurisich, O.F.M., Pres.; Rev. David Gaa, O.F.M., Prov.; Very Rev. John Hardin, O.F.M., Trustee; Mr. Edward J. Dantzig, Trustee; Mr. Stephen Ethridge, Trustee.

Redemptorist Vice Province Initiative (Closed) 8945 Golf Links Rd., P.O. Box 5007, 94605.

Religious Communities Impact Fund, Inc., 462 Elwood Ave., Ste. 2, 94610. Tel: 510-836-7556; Fax: 510-836-7556; Email: joltl@sbcglobal.net; Web: www.rcif.org. Sr. Corinne Florek, O.P., Dir. & Contact Person.

BERKELEY. *Inter-Friendship House Association, Friendship Center*, 1646 Addison St., Berkeley, 94703-1404. Tel: 415-308-2647; Email: ujeanlee@gmail.com; Web: www.fuyou-berkeley.org. Eugene Lee, Chm.

Multicultural Institute (1991) 1920 Seventh St., Berkeley, 94710-2011. Tel: 510-848-4075; Web: www.mionline.org. Rev. Rigoberto Caloca-Rivas, O.F.M., Ph.D., Exec.; Les Guliasi, Pres.; Jacqueline De Anda, Vice Pres.; Vice Weisser, Treas.; Charlotte F. TerKeurst, Sec. Tot Asst. Annually 3,360.

US-China Catholic Association (Formerly United States Catholic China Bureau) 1646 Addison St., Berkeley, 94703. Tel: 510-900-2015; Email: staff@uscatholicchina.org; Email: director@uscatholicchina.org; Web: www.uscatholicchina.org. Rev. Michael Agliardo, S.J., Dir.

CONCORD. *East Bay Services to the Developmentally Disabled* (1984) 1870 Adobe St., Concord, 94520. Tel: 925-825-2091; Fax: 925-825-2439; Email: marygrace@eastbayservicesdd.org. Sr. Marygrace Puchac, Exec. Tot Asst. Annually 915; Total Staff 70; Nonresident Assisted 850; Resident Assisted 65.

DANVILLE. *Catholic Professional & Business Breakfast Club of the Diocese of Oakland* aka Catholics@Work, 440 LaGonda Way, Danville, 94526. Tel: 925-525-0272; Email: info@catholicsatwork.com; Web: www.catholicsatwork.com. Mailing Address: 2485 Holly Oak Dr., Danville, 94506-2043. Rev. Paulson Mundanmani, Chap.; David R. Manion, Pres.; Mr. Thomas Loarie, Chm.; Rob Aceto, Treas.; Lynn Fischer, Communs.

FREMONT. *Dominican Sisters of Mission San Jose Foundation (A Nonprofit Corp.)*, 43326 Mission Cir., Fremont, 94539-5898. Tel: 510-933-6310; Fax: 510-933-6389; Email: clare.e.fischer@gmail.com; Email: fischer_clare@hotmail.com; Web: www.msjdominicans.org. Janice Caldwell, Pres.; Jennie Canales-Green, Treas.; Sr. Francis Clare Fischer, O.P., Admin.

Pia Backes Support Trust, 43326 Mission Ciir., Fremont, 94539-5898. Tel: 510-657-2468; Fax: 510-683-0712; Email: tan@msjdominicans.org. Sr. Mary Liam Brock, O.P., Pres.

LAFAYETTE. *Magnificat S.O.T.I. - Walnut Creek Chapter*, P.O. Box 4626, Walnut Creek, 94596. Tel: 925-788-7762; Web: www.magnificat-ministry.net/ca-walnut-creek. Maribel Serrano, Coord.

PITTSBURG. **District Council of Contra Costa County Society of St. Vincent de Paul*, 2210 Gladstone Dr., Pittsburg, 94565.

RELIGIOUS INSTITUTES OF MEN REPRESENTED IN THE DIOCESE

For further details refer to the corresponding bracketed number in the Religious Institutes of Men or Women section.

[]—*Augustinians* (Province of Nigeria)—O.S.A.
[0330]—*Brothers of the Christian Schools* (Prov. of San Francisco, New Orleans)—F.S.C.
[0200]—*Camaldolese Benedictine Congregation* (US Foundation)—O.S.B.Cam.
[0470]—*The Capuchin Franciscan Friars* (Our Lady of Angels, Western America Province)—O.F.M.Cap.
[0270]—*Carmelite Fathers and Brothers* (Province of the Most Pure Heart of Mary)—O.Carm.
[0605]—*Congregation of the Holy Spirit*—C.S.S.P.
[]—*Congregation of the Immaculate Heart of Mary, Province of Asia*—C.I.C.M.
[1130]—*Congregation of the Priests of the Sacred Heart*—S.C.J.
[]—*Consolata Missionaries, Ethiopia*—I.M.C.
[]—*Fraternity of St. Peter*—F.S.S.P.
[0480]—*Conventual Franciscans* (Province of St. Joseph of Cupertino)—O.F.M.Conv.
[0520]—*Franciscan Friars* (Prov. of St. Barbara)—O.F.M.
[0305]—*Institute of Christ the King Sovereign Priest*—I.C.
[0690]—*Jesuit Fathers and Brothers* (California Province)—S.J.
[]—*Missionaries of Faith* (India, Inc.)—M.F.
[]—*MIssionaries of the Nativity of Mary*—M.N.M.
[0975]—*Missionhurst Society of Our Lady of the Most Holy Trinity*—S.O.L.T.
[0910]—*Oblates of Mary Immaculate* (US Prov. - Pacific Area)—O.M.I.
[0920]—*Oblates of St. Francis de Sales*—O.S.F.S.
[0430]—*Order of Preachers* (Prov. of the Most Holy Name of Jesus, Western Dominican Prov.)—O.P.
[1030]—*Paulist Fathers*—C.S.P.
[0610]—*Priests of the Congregation of Holy Cross* (United States Province)—C.S.C.
[1070]—*Redemptorist Fathers* (Denver Prov.)—C.SS.R.

[1190]—*Salesians of Don Bosco* (San Francisco Prov.)—S.D.B.
[0420]—*Society of the Divine Word* (Western Province)—S.V.D.
[1060]—*Society of the Precious Blood* (Prov. of the Cincinnati)—C.PP.S.
[0370]—*Society of St. Columban*—S.S.C.

RELIGIOUS INSTITUTES OF WOMEN REPRESENTED IN THE DIOCESE

[]—*Congregation of Mother of Carmel*—C.M.C.
[1070-04]—*Congregation of the Most Holy Name (Dominican Sisters of San Rafael)*—O.P.
[1070-13]—*Congregation of the Most Holy Rosary* (Adrian Dominican Sisters)—O.P.
[1070-12]—*Congregation of the Queen of the Holy Rosary* (Dominican Sisters of Mission San Jose)—O.P.
[1920]—*Congregation of the Sisters of the Holy Cross*—C.S.C.
[0420]—*Discalced Carmelite Nuns*—O.C.D.
[1070-20]—*Dominican Sisters* Tacoma, WA.
[1070-30]—*Dominican Sisters of Oakford*—O.P.
[]—*Dominican Sisters of the Christian Doctrine*—O.P.
[1310]—*Franciscan Sisters of Little Falls, Minnesota*—O.S.F.
[2420]—*Marist Missionary Sisters*—S.M.S.M.
[2470]—*Maryknoll Sisters of St. Dominic*—M.M.
[2710]—*Missionaries of Charity*—M.C.
[]—*Quinhon Missionary Sisters of the Holy Cross*—L.H.C.
[2780]—*Religious Missionary Sisters of the Blessed Sacrament and Mary Immaculate*—M.S.S.S.
[1070-03]—*Sinsinawa Dominican Congregation of the Most Holy Rosary*—O.P.
[0480]—*Sisters of Charity of Leavenworth*—S.C.L.
[2549]—*Sisters of Mercy of Ireland* (U.S. Prov.)—R.S.M.
[2575]—*Sisters of Mercy of the Americas West Midwest Community* (Regional Community of Burlingame, CA)—S.M.
[3000]—*Sisters of Notre Dame de Namur* (California Prov.)—S.N.D.deN.
[]—*Sisters of Our Lady of Perpetual Help*—S.O.L.P.H.
[1650]—*Sisters of St. Francis of Philadelphia*—O.S.F.
[1630]—*Sisters of St. Francis of Penance and Christian Charity*—O.S.F.
[3840]—*Sisters of St. Joseph of Carondelet* (Prov. of Los Angeles)—C.S.J.
[3830-03]—*Sisters of St. Joseph of Orange*—C.S.J.
[3930]—*Sisters of St. Joseph of the Third Order of St. Francis*—S.S.J.-T.O.S.F.
[1960]—*Sisters of the Holy Family*—S.H.F.
[1990]—*Sisters of the Holy Names of Jesus and Mary* (U.S. - Ontario Prov.)—S.N.J.M.
[3320]—*Sisters of the Presentation of the B.V.M.* (San Francisco, CA)—P.B.V.M.
[3680]—*Sisters of the Sacred Hearts of Jesus and Mary*—S.H.J.M.
[2150]—*Sisters, Servants of the Immaculate Heart of Mary*—I.H.M.
[4070]—*Society of the Sacred Heart*—R.S.C.J.
[4048]—*Society of Sisters Faithful Companions of Jesus*—F.C.J.

NECROLOGY

† Danielson, Daniel E., (Retired), Died Jan. 5, 2019
† Goodwin, Patrick, (Retired), Died Jan. 7, 2019
† McGee, James J., (Retired), Died Jun. 14, 2018
† Ng, Thomas, (Retired), Died Jul. 31, 2018

An asterisk (*) denotes an organization that has established tax-exempt status directly with the IRS and is not covered by the USCCB Group Ruling.

Diocese of Ogdensburg

(Dioecesis Ogdensburgensis)

Most Reverend

TERRY R. LAVALLEY

Bishop of Ogdensburg; ordained September 24, 1988; appointed Bishop of Ogdensburg February 23, 2010; installed April 30, 2010. *Mailing Address: P.O. Box 369, Ogdensburg, NY 13669.*

Square Miles 12,036.

Erected by His Holiness Pius IX, February 16, 1872.

Incorporated by a special act of the Legislature of the State of New York, April 10, 1945, with the title: The Roman Catholic Diocese of Ogdensburg, New York.

Comprises that part of Herkimer and Hamilton Counties north of the northern line of the townships of Ohio and Russia as existing in 1872 with the entire Counties of Lewis, Jefferson, St. Lawrence, Franklin, Clinton and Essex in the State of New York.

For legal titles of parishes and diocesan institutions, consult the Chancery Office.

Chancery Office: P.O. Box 369, Ogdensburg, NY 13669. Tel: 315-393-2920; Fax: 866-314-7296.

Web: www.rcdony.org

STATISTICAL OVERVIEW

Personnel	
Bishop	1
Priests: Diocesan Active in Diocese	50
Priests: Diocesan in Foreign Missions	1
Priests: Retired, Sick or Absent	36
Number of Diocesan Priests	87
Religious Priests in Diocese	8
Total Priests in Diocese	95
Extern Priests in Diocese	5
Permanent Deacons in Diocese	87
Total Brothers	3
Total Sisters	79
Parishes	
Parishes	91
With Resident Pastor:	
Resident Diocesan Priests	87
Resident Religious Priests	2
Without Resident Pastor:	
Administered by Priests	2
Missions	5
Closed Parishes	4
Professional Ministry Personnel:	
Brothers	2
Sisters	25
Lay Ministers	87
Welfare	
Homes for the Aged	1
Total Assisted	146
Special Centers for Social Services	7
Total Assisted	13,000
Educational	
Diocesan Students in Other Seminaries	10
Total Seminarians	10
High Schools, Diocesan and Parish	2
Total Students	210
Elementary Schools, Diocesan and Parish	10
Total Students	1,382
Catechesis/Religious Education:	
High School Students	452
Elementary Students	2,286
Total Students under Catholic Instruction	4,340
Teachers in the Diocese:	
Sisters	10
Lay Teachers	198
Vital Statistics	
Receptions into the Church:	
Infant Baptism Totals	610
Minor Baptism Totals	37
Adult Baptism Totals	29
Received into Full Communion	35
First Communions	562
Confirmations	545
Marriages:	
Catholic	147
Interfaith	44
Total Marriages	191
Deaths	1,511
Total Catholic Population	86,182
Total Population	427,209

Former Bishops—Rt. Revs. EDGAR P. WADHAMS, D.D., ord. Jan. 15, 1850; cons. May 5, 1872; died Dec. 5, 1891; HENRY GABRIELS, D.D., ord. Sept. 21, 1861; cons. May 5, 1892; died April 23, 1921; Most Revs. JOSEPH H. CONROY, D.D., LL.D., ord. June 11, 1881; cons. May 1, 1912; succeeded to the See, Nov. 21, 1921; died March 20, 1939; FRANCIS J. MONAGHAN, S.T.D., LL.D., ord. May 29, 1915; cons. June 29, 1936; succeeded to the See, March 20, 1939; died Nov. 13, 1942; BRYAN J. MCENTEGART, D.D., LL.D., ord. Sept. 8, 1917; cons. Aug. 3, 1943; transferred to Titular See of Aradi, Aug. 19, 1953; appt. June 26, 1953; to Rectorship of Catholic University of America, Washington, D.C.; appt. Bishop of Brooklyn, April 16, 1957; installed June 13, 1957; appt. Archbishop, April 15, 1966; retired and appt. Titular Archbishop of Gabii, July 17, 1968; died Sept. 30, 1968; WALTER P. KELLENBERG, D.D., ord. June 2, 1928; cons. Oct. 5, 1953; appt. to Ogdensburg, Jan. 19, 1954; transferred to See of Rockville Centre, April 16, 1957; installed May 27, 1957; died Jan. 11, 1986; JAMES J. NAVAGH, D.D., ord. Dec. 21, 1929; cons. Sept. 24, 1952; appt. to Ogdensburg, May 8, 1957; transferred to Paterson, Feb. 12, 1963; died in Rome, Oct. 2, 1965; LEO R. SMITH, D.D., ord. Dec. 21, 1929; appt. Auxiliary Bishop of Buffalo, July 9, 1952; cons. Sept. 24, 1952; appt. Bishop of Ogdensburg, Feb. 12, 1963; died in Rome Oct. 9, 1963; THOMAS A. DONNELLAN, D.D., ord. June 3, 1939; appt. March 4, 1964; cons. April 9, 1964; appt. to Atlanta, May 29, 1968; transferred to Archdiocese of Atlanta, July 16, 1968; died in Atlanta, Oct. 15, 1987; STANISLAUS J. BRZANA, S.T.D., LL.D, ord. June 7, 1941; appt. Titular Bishop of Cufruta and Auxiliary of Buffalo, May 24, 1964; cons. June 29, 1964; transferred to Ogdensburg, Oct. 22, 1968; retired Nov. 11, 1993; died March 1, 1997; PAUL S. LOVERDE, D.D., S.T.L., J.C.L., ord. Dec. 18, 1965; appt. Titular Bishop of Ottabia and Auxiliary Bishop of Hartford, Feb. 3, 1988; cons. April 12, 1988; transferred to Ogdensburg, Nov. 11, 1993; installed Jan. 17, 1994; appt. Bishop of Arlington, Jan. 25, 1999; installed March 25, 1999; GERALD M. BARBARITO, D.D., J.C.L., ord. Jan. 31, 1976; appt. Titular Bishop of Gisipa and Auxiliary Bishop of Brooklyn June 28, 1994; cons. Aug. 22, 1994; transferred to Ogdensburg Oct. 26, 1999; installed Jan. 7, 2000; appt. Bishop of Palm Beach July 1, 2003; installed Aug. 28, 2003; ROBERT J. CUNNINGHAM, D.D., J.C.L., ord. May 24, 1969; appt. Bishop of Ogdensburg March 9, 2004; ord. and installed May 18, 2004; appt. Bishop of Syracuse April 21, 2009; installed May 26, 2009.

Diocesan Facilities

Spratt Memorial Building—604 Washington St., P.O. Box 369, Ogdensburg, 13669.

Bishop Stanislaus J. Brzana Diocesan Pastoral Center—622 Washington St., P.O. Box 369, Ogdensburg, 13669.

Bishop Paul S. Loverde Center for Education and Formation—100 Elizabeth St., P.O. Box 369, Ogdensburg, 13669. Office Hours: Mon.-Fri. 8:15-4; Summer Hours: 8:45-4.

Unless otherwise noted, mail and phone numbers: Roman Catholic Diocese of Ogdensburg, Bishop Stanislaus J. Brzana Diocesan Pastoral Center, 622 Washington St., P.O. Box 369, Ogdensburg, NY 13669. Tel: 315-393-2920; Fax: 866-314-7296.

Office of the Bishop—Most Rev. TERRY R. LAVALLEY, D.D., J.C.L.

Vicar General—Rev. JOSEPH MORGAN, V.G., Tel: 315-393-3930.

Consultative Bodies

Deans—Adirondack: Rev. JOHN R. YONKOVIG, V.F. Clinton: Rev. Msgr. DENNIS J. DUPREY, V.F. Essex: Rev. ALBERT J. HAUSER, V.F. Franklin: Rev. THOMAS E. KORNMEYER, V.F. Hamilton-Herkimer: Rev. SONY G. PULICKAL, V.F. Jefferson: Rev. ARTHUR J. LABAFF, V.F. Lewis: Rev. JAMES W. SEYMOUR, V.F. St. Lawrence: Rev. Msgr. JOHN R. MURPHY, V.F., B.A., S.T.L., M.A.

Diocesan Consultors—Rev. JOSEPH MORGAN, V.G.; Rev. Msgrs. C. JOHN MCAVOY, (Retired); ROBERT H. AUCOIN, S.T.L., M.Ed.; Revs. DONALD A. ROBINSON; JONAS RAPHAEL TANDAYU, M.S.C.; RAYMOND J. MOREAU; JOHN M. DEMO; KEVIN J. O'BRIEN; DOUGLAS J. LUCIA, J.C.L.

Council of Consecrated Life—Sisters ANNUNCIATA COLLINS, S.S.J., Pres.; JANET PETERS, R.S.M., Vice Pres.; NORMA BRYANT, Sec.; ELIZABETH MENARD, O.P., Treas.

Committee on Assignments—Revs. JOSEPH MORGAN, V.G.; KEVIN J. O'BRIEN; DOUGLAS J. LUCIA, J.C.L.; CHRISTOPHER C. CARRARA; Deacon JAMES CROWLEY; Revs. JOHN M. DEMO; JOSEPH W. GIROUX; DOUGLAS G. COMSTOCK; ARTHUR J. LABAFF, V.F.; STEPHEN ROCKER.

Diocesan Offices

Bishop's Office Secretary—Fax: 866-393-7642. MS. RENEE GRIZZUTO.

Episcopal Vicar for Pastoral Services and Moderator of the Curia—Rev. KEVIN J. O'BRIEN.

Chancellor—Deacon JAMES CROWLEY.

Director - Office of Public Information—Deacon JAMES CROWLEY.

Director - Office of Cemeteries—Deacon JAMES CROWLEY.

Diocesan Receptionist/Administrative Assistant—MARY JO ROCKER.

Director - Office of Communications—MRS. DARCY FARGO.

Development Office—Planned Giving. MR. SCOTT LALONE, Exec. Dir.; MRS. VALERIE MATHEWS, Asst. Dir.

Bishops' Fund Appeal & Stewardship Office—MRS. VALERIE MATHEWS, Dir.

The Foundation of the Roman Catholic Diocese of Ogdensburg, New York—MR. SCOTT LALONE, Exec. Dir.

Fiscal Officer—MR. MICHAEL J. TOOLEY, Fax: 866-314-7296.

Parish Administrative Services Coordinator—MR. CINDY GRANGER.

Human Resources Director—MS. KIMBERLY SNOVER.

Insurance Claims and Risk Management Department—MR. JACK CARTER, Mgr., Tel: 315-393-0441; Fax: 866-519-6423; MS. RITA REYNOLDS, Claims Svc. Representative, Fax: 866-519-6423.

Episcopal Vicar for Pastoral Personnel—Rev. CHRISTOPHER C. CARRARA.

Bishop's Delegate for Religious—Sr. BERNADETTE MARIE COLLINS, S.S.J.

Bishop's Delegate to Pastoral Ministers—Deacon JAMES CROWLEY.

Permanent Diaconate Program—415 Hamilton St., Ogdensburg, 13669. Tel: 315-393-6592. Deacons JOHN L. WHITE, Dir., Email: jwhite@rcdony.org; JOHN J. DROLLETTE, Asst. Dir., Email: jdrollette@rcdony.org.

Safe Environment—MR. JOHN MORRISON, Dir. & Charter Compliance Coord.

Vocations Office—MS. CATHERINE RUSSELL, Coord.; Rev. DOUGLAS J. LUCIA, J.C.L., Dir. Vocations & Seminarians.

Episcopal Vicar for Worship and Priestly Formation—Rev. DOUGLAS J. LUCIA, J.C.L.

Department of Worship—Rev. BRYAN D. STITT, S.T.L., Dir.

Family Life—Deacon JAMES D. CROWLEY, Chancellor.

Family Life Department and Pre-Cana—MR. STEPHEN TARTAGLIA, Dir.

Natural Family Planning Services—MR. ANGELO PIETROPAOLI; MRS. SUZANNE PIETROPAOLI, 36 First St., Malone, 12953. Tel: 518-483-0459.

Respect Life Office—175 Lake St., Saranac Lake, 12983. Tel: 518-524-0774. MR. JOHN MINER; COLLEEN MINER.

Marriage Enrichment and Preparation—Deacon HENRY LEADER; MRS. DANYA LEADER, 11 Valley Dr., Gouverneur, 13642. Tel: 315-287-2874.

Episcopal Vicar for Education and the New Evangelization—St. Mary's Church, 8408 S. Main St., Evans Mills, 13637. Tel: 315-629-4678; Email: raucoin@rcdony.org. Rev. Msgr. ROBERT H. AUCOIN, S.T.L., M.Ed.

Department of Education—Sr. ELLEN ROSE COUGHLIN, S.S.J., Supt.; MRS. KAREN DONAHUE, Asst. Supt.

Watertown Catechetical Office—1 Sterling Pl., Watertown, 13601. Tel: 315-782-0030; Email: specialreligioused@yahoo.com; Web: www.specreled.org. Sisters NOEL CHABANEL, S.S.J., Outreach Coord.; DIANE MARIE ULSAMER, S.S.J., Coord.

Department of Christian Formation—Sr. ELLEN ROSE COUGHLIN, S.S.J., Dir.

Eastern Regional Center—MS. PAM BALLENTINE, Dir., 4917 S. Catherine St., Plattsburgh, 12901. Tel: 518-563-2022; Fax: 518-563-2138.

Western Regional Center—MS. CATHERINE RUSSEL, Dir., 320 W. Lynde St., Watertown, 13601. Tel: 315-782-3620; Fax: 315-782-2009.

Formation for Ministry—MS. CATHERINE RUSSEL, Dir.

Office of Youth Ministry—MR. THOMAS SEMERARO, Dir.

Catholic Scouting—Rev. BRYAN D. STITT, S.T.L., Diocesan Liaison.

Office of Evangelization—MS. MARIKA DONDERS, Dir.

Hispanic Ministry—St. Paul's Church, 208 LeRay St., Black River, 13612. Tel: 315-773-5672. Rev. ROBERT L. DECKER, Dir.

Campus Ministry—Deacon RICHARD L. BURNS, Diocesan Coord., 652 Hatch Rd., Potsdam, 13676. Canton: MRS. AMANDA CONKLIN. Jefferson Community College: Sr. JULIANA RAYMOND, S.S.J., Campus Office: Gregor 5-112, 1220 Coffeen St., Watertown, 13601. North Country Community: Rev. PATRICK A. RATIGAN. Paul Smith's College: Rev. PATRICK A. RATIGAN. Plattsburgh: MS. MARY SKILLAN. Potsdam: MR. TYLER STARKEY. Wanakena: Rev. SHANE M. LYNCH; MR. PETER O'SHEA.

Newspaper—The North Country Catholic MRS. CHRISTINE WARD, Editorial Asst., Mailing Address: P.O. Box 326, Ogdensburg, 13669. Tel: 866-314-7296; MRS. DARCY FARGO, Editor.

Judicial Vicar and Vicar for Canonical Affairs—Rev. DOUGLAS J. LUCIA, J.C.L.

Moderator of the Tribunal—MRS. ELAINE SEYMOUR.

Adjutant Judicial Vicars—Rev. Msgr. HARRY K. SNOW, M.A.Th., J.C.L., V.F., (Retired); Revs. PHILIP T. ALLEN; GARRY B. GIROUX, J.C.L.

Promoter of Justice—Rev. Msgr. JOHN R. MURPHY, V.F., B.A., S.T.L., M.A.

Defenders of the Bond—Revs. RAYMOND J. MOREAU; JOSEPH A. MORGAN; ALAN D. SHNOB; JOHN R. YONKOVIG, V.F.; CATHERINE J. FRIEDERICHS, B.A., J.C.L.

Judges—Rev. GILBERT B. MENARD, (Retired); Rev. Msgr. ROBERT H. AUCOIN, S.T.L., M.Ed.; Revs. L. WILLIAM GORDON, (Retired); CLYDE A. LEWIS; F. JAMES SHURTELEFF, (Retired).

Notary—GIDGET L. KIMBLE.

Advocates—MRS. ELAINE SEYMOUR; Rev. Msgr. DENNIS J. DUPREY, V.F.; Revs. DOUGLAS A. DECKER; GARVIN J. DEMARAIS, (Retired); ALBERT J. HAUSER, V.F.; ALAN J. LAMICA.

Pontifical Mission SocietiesSr. MARY ELLEN BRETT, S.S.J., Dir., Society for The Propagation of the Faith; Missionary Childhood Association; Society of St. Peter the Apostle; Missionary Union of Clergy and Religious; Missionary Projects of the Diocese of Ogdensburg.

Office of Planning—Rev. CHRISTOPHER C. CARRARA, Dir.

Other Diocesan Offices and Directors

Diocesan Archivist—(see Chancellor's Office).

Apostleship of Prayer—Rev. ALBERT J. HAUSER, V.F., Dir., Mailing Address: 12 St. Patrick Pl., Port Henry, 12974.

Building Commission—MR. MICHAEL J. TOOLEY, Mailing Address: P.O. Box 369, Ogdensburg, 13669.

Catholic Charities—Deacon PATRICK J. DONAHUE, Diocesan Dir., Wadhams Hall, 6866 State Hwy. 37, Ogdensburg, 13669. Tel: 315-393-2255; Fax: 315-393-2402. Ogdensburg Office: Deacon PATRICK J. DONAHUE, Area Dir. Watertown Office: Deacon PATRICK J. DONAHUE, Area Dir., 145 Clinton St., Watertown, 13301. Tel: 315-788-4330; Fax: 315-786-0539. Malone Office: JOELLE LAMICA, Area Dir., 6 Cedar St., GS Food Pantry, 57 Rennie St., Malone, 12953. Tel: 518-483-1460; Fax: 518-483-1478. Tupper Lake Office - Foster Grandparent Program and Franklin County RSVP Program: VIVIAN SMITH, 80 Park St., Ste. 2, P.O. Box 701, Tupper Lake, 12986. Tel: 518-359-7688; Fax: 518-359-3927.

RSVP of Clinton County—46 Flynn Ave., Plattsburgh, 12901. Tel: 518-566-0944; Fax: 518-566-0945. KATE GARDNER.

RSVP of Essex County—KATE GARDNER, 38 Park Pl., Ste. 3, Port Henry, 12974. Tel: 518-546-3565.

RSVP of Hamilton County—VIVIAN SMITH, 1245 Main St., Long Lake, 12847. Tel: 518-624-6788.

Seaway House—CAROL WHITCOMBE, Dir., 212 Caroline St., Ogdensburg, 13669. Tel: 315-393-3133.

Catholic Relief Services—Mailing Address: 6866 State Hwy. 37, Ogdensburg, 13669. Tel: 315-393-2255; Fax: 315-393-2402. Deacon PATRICK J. DONAHUE.

Censor Librorum—VACANT.

Charismatic Renewal—VACANT.

Committee for the Continuing Education of Clergy—1347 State Rte. 11, Brushton, 12916. Revs. RAYMOND J. MOREAU, Chm.; MARTIN E. CLINE; ADRIAN GALLAGHER; ALAN J. LAMICA; KRIS C. LAUZON; SHANE M. LYNCH; HOWARD J. VENETTE; CHRISTOPHER C. CARRARA.

Ecumenical Commission—5312 Kamryn Rd., Lowville, 13367. Deacon THOMAS J. YOUSEY.

Legion of Mary—VACANT.

Priests' Eucharistic League—Rev. ALBERT J. HAUSER, V.F., Dir., Catholic Community of Moriah, 12 St. Patrick's Pl., Port Henry, 12974. Tel: 518-846-7254; Fax: 518-375-3624.

St. Vincent de Paul Society—VACANT.

Young Adult Ministry—MS. MARIKA DONDERS.

CLERGY, PARISHES, MISSIONS AND PAROCHIAL SCHOOLS

CITY OF OGDENSBURG

(ST. LAWRENCE COUNTY), ST. MARY'S CATHEDRAL (1748) [CEM]

415 Hamilton St., 13669. Tel: 315-393-3930; Tel: 315-393-5050; Email: secretary@smcogd.org; Web: www.smcoqd.org; Web: www.ogdensburgcatholics.org. Mailing Address: 125 Ford Ave., 13669. Revs. Joseph A. Morgan, Rector; Justin Thomas, Parochial Vicar; F. James Shurteleff, Pastor Emeritus, (Retired); Vicente F. Jazmines, In Res.; Deacons Francis F. Bateman; David J. Sandburg; Anthony J. Pastizzo; James D. Crowley; David D. Demers; Mark A. LaLonde, Pastoral Associate; William P. O'Brien; John L. White; Sr. Bernadette Marie Collins, S.S.J., Pastoral Assoc.

Outreach Center—214 Morris St., 13669-1714. Tel: 315-393-6579.

Notre Dame Church, (Worship Site) 119 Ford Ave., 13669.

Catechesis Religious Program—315 Gate St., 13669. Tel: 315-393-0165; Fax: 315-393-0499. Students 163.

OUTSIDE CITY OF OGDENSBURG

ADAMS, JEFFERSON CO., ST. CECILIA (1870) [CEM]

Mailing Address: 17 Grove St., Adams, 13605.

Tel: 315-232-2392; Email: adamscatholic@yahoo.com; Web: www.stceciliaandqoh.org. Rev. Martin E. Cline; Deacon Lawrence R. Ambeau.

Catechesis Religious Program—Students 117.

Mission—Queen of Heaven, 8900 NYS Rte. 3, Henderson, Jefferson Co. 13650.

ALEXANDRIA BAY, JEFFERSON CO., ROMAN CATHOLIC COMMUNITY OF ALEXANDRIA (1000 Islands) (1885) [CEM]

17 Rock St., Alexandria Bay, 13607.

Tel: 315-482-2670; Email: pastor@stcyrils.org; Web: www.stcyrils.org. Rev. Douglas G. Comstock; Deacons Bernard E. Slate; Joel E. Walentuk.

St. Cyril Church—(Worship Site) 28 Walton St., Alexandria Bay, 13607.

St. Francis Xavier Church, (Worship Site) 28685 Butterfield Lake Rd., Redwood, 13679.

Catechesis Religious Program—Trina Henry, D.R.E., Email: thenry2252@gmail.com. Students 38.

ALTONA, CLINTON CO., HOLY ANGELS (1865) [CEM] (Irish—French Canadian)

522 Devils Den Rd., Altona, 12910.

Tel: 518-236-5632; Email: sasj3062@primelink1.net; Web: www.annandangels.org. Mailing Address: 24 Town Hall Rd., Mooers Forks, 12959. Rev. Adrian Gallagher.

Catechesis Religious Program—Rte. 11, Ellenburg Center, 12933. Tel: 518-593-2774. Deacon Dennis Monty, D.R.E. Students 106.

AU SABLE FORKS, CLINTON CO.

1—CATHOLIC COMMUNITY OF HOLY NAME AND ST. MATTHEW

10 Church Ln., P.O. Box 719, Au Sable Forks, 12912. Tel: 518-647-8225; Email: ccofhnandsm@gmail.com. Rev. Kris C. Lauzon; Deacons John J. Ryan, (Retired); John D. Lucero.

Church of the Holy Name, 14203 Rte. 9N, P.O. Box 719, Au Sable Forks, 12912.

Catechesis Religious Program—14207 NYS Rte. 9N, Au Sable Forks, 12912. Tel: 518-647-8444; Email: hnandsmreligion@gmail.com. Students 30.

Mission—St. Margaret, 9 Church St., Wilmington, 12912.

ST. MATTHEW ORATORY, 781 Silver Lake Rd., Black Brook, 12912.

2—HOLY NAME (1848) [CEM] Merged with St. Matthew, Black Brook to form Catholic Community of Holy Name and St. Matthew, Au Sable Forks.

BLACK BROOK, CLINTON CO., ST. MATTHEW (1848) [CEM] Merged Now a Oratory site of Catholic Community of Holy Name and St. Matthew.

BLACK RIVER, JEFFERSON CO., ST. PAUL (1901)

210 LeRay St., Black River, 13612. Tel: 315-773-5672 ; Email: sp.sr6@outlook.com. Mailing Address: 208 LeRay St., Black River, 13612. Rev. Robert L. Decker; Deacon William S. Raven; Tarra Benson, Sec.

Catechesis Religious Program—Students 17.

BOMBAY, FRANKLIN CO., ST. JOSEPH (1912) [CEM]

22 County Rte. 4, Bombay, 12914. Tel: 518-358-2500; Email: smsjoffice@gmail.com; Web: www.smsjcatholics.com. Mailing Address: P.O. Box 499, Fort Covington, 12937. Rev. Thomas E. Kornmeyer, V.F.; Deacons Brian T. Dwyer, Pastoral Associate; Garry N. Burnell.

Catechesis Religious Program—Students 8.

BRASHER FALLS, ST. LAWRENCE CO., ST. PATRICK (1830) [CEM] (Irish—French)

836 State Hwy. 11C, Brasher Falls, 13613-0208.

Tel: 315-389-5401; Tel: 315-389-4066 (Parish Center) ; Email: parish@twcny.rr.com. Mailing Address: P.O. Box 208, Brasher Falls, 13613-0208. Rev. Garry B. Giroux, J.C.L.

St. Lawrence's Church, (Worship Site) 47 Church St., North Lawrence, 12967.

Catechesis Religious Program—Christine Leahy, D.R.E. Students 25.

BROWNVILLE, JEFFERSON CO., ROMAN CATHOLIC COMMUNITY OF BROWNVILLE AND DEXTER (1874) (Irish—Italian)

119 W. Main St., P.O. Box 99, Brownville, 13615.

Tel: 315-782-1143; Email: icses@twcny.rr.com; Web: immaculateconceptionbrownville.org. Rev. J. Michael Gaffney, V.F.

Immaculate Conception, (Worship Site) 214 W. Main St., Brownville, 13615.

Catechesis Religious Program—Tel: 315-788-7240. Mrs. Christina M. Corey, D.R.E. Students 141.

BRUSHTON, FRANKLIN CO., ST. MARY'S CHURCH (1870) [CEM]

1347 State Rte. 11, Brushton, 12916-0249.

Tel: 518-529-7433; Email: office@stmarysbrushton.org; Web: www.staugustinesandstmarys.org. Rev. Raymond J. Moreau.

Catechesis Religious Program—Judy King, D.R.E. (Shared with St. Augustine, North Bangor) Students 32.

BURKE, FRANKLIN CO., ST. GEORGE (1874) [CEM] Merged with St. Patrick, Chateaugay to form Catholic Community of Burke and Chateaugay.

CADYVILLE, CLINTON CO., ST. JAMES CHURCH (1854) [CEM]

27 Church Rd., Cadyville, 12918. Tel: 518-561-5039; Email: jackie@stalexanders.org; Web: www.stjamescadyville.org. Mailing Address: P.O. Box 159, Morrisonville, 12962. Rev. Scott R. Seymour; Deacon Michael J. Howley.

Res.: 26 Church Rd., Cadyville, 12918-0117.

Catechesis Religious Program—Sr. Deepali Bankar, S.C.C., D.R.E. Students 18.

CANTON, ST. LAWRENCE CO., ST. MARY (1868) [CEM]

66 Court St., Canton, 13617. Tel: 315-386-2543; Email: catholicrectory@twcny.rr.com; Web: www.cantoncatholics.com. Mailing Address: 68 Court St., Canton, 13617. Rev. Bryan D. Stitt, S.T.L.; Paul J. Schrems, Pastoral Assoc.; Deacon James M. Snell.

School—St. Mary's School, (Grades PreK-6), 2 Powers St., Canton, 13617. Tel: 315-386-3572; Email: smsoffice@twcny.rr.com; Web: www.stmaryscantonny.com. Michele Meyers, Prin. Lay Teachers 10; Students 72.

Catechesis Religious Program—Email: cantoncatholics@gmail.com. Jamie J. Burns, D.R.E. Students 64.

ST. PAUL ORATORY, 10193 Pink Schoolhouse Rd., Canton, St. Lawrence Co. 13617.

CAPE VINCENT, JEFFERSON CO.

1—THE CATHOLIC COMMUNITY OF CAPE VINCENT, ROSIERE AND CHAUMONT

Mailing Address: 139 N. Kanady St., Cape Vincent, 13618. Tel: 315-654-2662; Email: cvrchparish3@gmail.com; Email: misprojser2@gmail.com; Web: www.cvrchparish.org. Mailing Address: P.O. Box 288, Cape Vincent, 13618. Revs. Raymond Diesbourg, M.S.C.; Pierre Aubin, M.S.C., Pastor Emeritus.

All Saints Church—(Worship Site) 27396 Madison St., Chaumont.

St. Vincent de Paul Church, (Worship Site) 31385 Co. Rte. 4, Rosiere.

St. Vincent of Paul Church, (Worship Site) 1626 Kanady St., Cape Vincent, 13618.

Catechesis Religious Program—Joanne McCarthy-Cap, D.R.E., Tel: 315-778-8359; Julie Sharlow, D.R.E. All Saints, Tel: 315-767-8788. Students 49.

2—ST. VINCENT OF PAUL (1832) [CEM 2] Merged with St. Vincent de Paul, Rosiere & All Saints, Chaumont to form The Catholic Community of Cape Vincent, Rosiere and Chaumont, Cape Vincent.

CARTHAGE, JEFFERSON CO., ST. JAMES MINOR (1818) [CEM 2] [JC]

327 West St., Carthage, 13619. Tel: 315-493-3224; Email: stjames@twcny.rr.com; Web: www.catholicsofcarthagecopenhagen.org. Rev. Donald A. Robinson; Deacon Richard J. Staab, Pastoral Assoc.; Sr. Annunciata Collins, S.S.J., Pastoral Assoc.

The Society of St. Jame's Church Carthage

School—Augustinian Academy, (Grades PreK-8), 317 West St., Carthage, 13619. Tel: 315-493-1301; Fax: 315-493-0632; Email: mmargrey@augustinianacademy.org; Web: www.c-augustinian.org. Mary Ann Margrey, Prin. Clergy / Religious Teachers 1; Lay Teachers 15; Sisters of St. Joseph 2; Students 150.

Catechesis Religious Program—Students 30.

Convent—Tel: 315-493-1672.

CHAMPLAIN, CLINTON CO., ST. MARY (1861) [CEM 2]

90 Church St., Champlain, 12919. Tel: 518-298-8244; Email: churchofstmary@yahoo.com; Web: www.stmaryschamplain.org. Mailing Address: P.O. Box 368, 86 Church St., Champlain, 12919. Rev. Clyde A. Lewis; Sr. Jessintha Xavier, Pastoral Assoc.

Catechesis Religious Program—Tel: 518-298-8614. Patricia Gladd, D.R.E. Students 36.

CHASM FALLS, FRANKLIN CO., ST. HELEN (1881) [CEM] Merged into St. Andre Bessette Parish, Malone.

CHATEAUGAY, FRANKLIN CO., CATHOLIC COMMUNITY OF BURKE AND CHATEAUGAY (1848) [CEM]

132 W. Main St., P.O. Box 908, Chateaugay, 12920-0908. Tel: 518-497-6673; Email: ccbcparish@yahoo.com; Web: www.ccbcparish.com. Rev. Thomas E. Kornmeyer, V.F.; Deacon Brian T. Dwyer.

St. Patrick's Church—(Worship Site) 132 W. Main St., Chateaugay, 12920.

St. George's Church, (Worship Site) 797 Depot St., Burke, 12917.

Catechesis Religious Program—Students 73.

CHAUMONT, JEFFERSON CO., ALL SAINTS (1922) Merged with St. Vincent de Paul, Cape Vincent & St. Vincent de Paul, Rosiere to form The Catholic Community of Cape Vincent, Rosiere and Chaumont, Cape Vincent.

CHAZY, CLINTON CO., SACRED HEART (1898) [CEM 2]

27 Church St., P.O. Box 459, Chazy, 12921. Tel: 518-846-7650; Fax: 518-846-7655; Email: sacredheart@westelcom.com; Web: www.chazysacredheart.org. Rev. Theodore A. Crosby.

Catechesis Religious Program—Noreen N. Barcomb, D.R.E. Students 89.

CLAYTON, JEFFERSON CO., ST. MARY'S OF CLAYTON (1838) [CEM 2]

521 James St., Clayton, 13624. Tel: 315-686-3398; Email: reception@stmarysclayton.org; Web: www.stmarysclayton.org. Rev. Arthur J. LaBaff, V.F.; Deacons Gary A. Frank; Bruce Wayne Daugherty; Neil J. Fuller.

Catechesis Religious Program—Tel: 315-686-2638; Email: religioused@stmarysclayton.org. Students 40.

COLTON, ST. LAWRENCE CO., ST. PATRICK (1864) [CEM] [JC]

4897 State Hwy. 56, Colton, 13625.

Tel: 315-262-2871, Ext. 2; Email: stpatoffice@gmail.com; Web: stmarystpatrick.net. Mailing Address: P.O. Box 315, Colton, 13625. Rev. Stephen Rocker; Deacon Richard L. Burns.

Catechesis Religious Program—Elizabeth Tarbox, Faith Formation. Students 13.

ST. PAUL ORATORY, 3871 State Hwy. 56, South Colton, 12953.

CONSTABLE, FRANKLIN CO., THE CATHOLIC COMMUNITY OF CONSTABLE, WESTVILLE AND TROUT RIVER (1872) [CEM]

1197 State Rte. 122, P.O. Box 78, Constable, 12926.

Tel: 518-483-2775 (Rectory);

Tel: 518-483-0486 (Parish Office); Email: officecwtr@gmail.com; Web: www.cwtrcatholics.org. Rev. Thomas E. Kornmeyer, V.F.; Deacons Garry N. Burnell; Brian T. Dwyer.

St. Francis of Assisi Church—(Worship Site) 5 Poplar St., P.O. Box 78, Constable, 12926.

Our Lady of Fatima Church, (Worship Site) 4328 State Rte. 37, Westville.

Catechesis Religious Program—Students 30.

CONSTABLEVILLE, LEWIS CO., ST. MARY (1820) [CEM] [JC3]

5905 James St., P.O. Box 382, Constableville, 13325. Tel: 315-394-2556; Email: stmarys1@frontier.com. Rev. Lawrence E. Marullo; Deacon James W. Chaufty.

Rectory—St. Mary's Rectory, 3200 N. Main St., Constableville, 13325.

Catechesis Religious Program—Students 6.

COPENHAGEN, LEWIS CO., ST. MARY (1901) [CEM 2] (Irish—French)

9790 NYS Rte. 12, P.O. Box 12, Copenhagen, 13626-0012. Tel: 315-688-2683; Email: srectory2@twcny.rr.com; Web: www.catholicsofcarthagecopenhagen.org. Rev. Donald A. Robinson; Sr. Mary Ellen Brett, S.S.J., Pastoral Assoc.; Deacon Richard J. Staab.

Catechesis Religious Program—Sr. Mary Ellen, D.R.E. Students 20.

CROGHAN, LEWIS CO., ST. STEPHEN (1869) [CEM] [JC3]

9748 State Rte. 812, P.O. Box 38, Croghan, 13327-0038. Tel: 315-346-6958; Email: fststephens@twcny.rr.com; Web: www.ststephenscroghan.rcdony.org. Rev. Donald J. Manfred; Deacon Michael J. Allan.

Catechesis Religious Program—Tel: 315-346-6963. Eileen Greenwood, Catechetical Leader. Students 118.

ST. VINCENT DE PAUL ORATORY, 9551 Erie Canal Rd., Belfort, 13327.

ST. PETER ORATORY, 6466 Tillman Rd., Lowville, 13367.

CROWN POINT, ESSEX CO., SACRED HEART OF JESUS (1874) [CEM]

2673 Main St., Crown Point, 12928.

Tel: 518-546-7254; Email: stpatsph@nycap.rr.com; Web: www.catholiccommunityofmoriah.com. Mailing Address: P.O. Box 479, Crown Point, 12928. Rev. Albert J. Hauser, V.F.

Catechesis Religious Program—Students 5.

DANNEMORA, CLINTON CO., ST. JOSEPH (1853) [CEM 2]

179 Smith St., Dannemora, 12929-0418.

Tel: 518-492-7118; Fax: 518-492-7742; Email: office@stjosephsdannemora.com. Mailing Address: P.O. Box 418, Dannemora, 12929. Rev. John M. Demo; Deacon Edward L. Mazuchowski.

Catechesis Religious Program—Tel: 518-492-2524; Email: llelynch@aol.com. Lynn Lynch, C.R.E. Students 80.

DEFERIET, JEFFERSON CO., ST. RITA (1900)

31 Riverside Dr., Deferiet, 13628. Tel: 315-773-5672; Email: sp.sr6@outlook.com. Mailing Address: 208 LeRay St., Black River, 13612. Rev. Robert L. Decker.

Res.: 208 Leray St., Black River, 13612.

Tel: 315-773-5672; Email: Sp.Sr6@outlook.com.

EDWARDS, ST. LAWRENCE CO., SACRED HEART (1894)

20 Trout Lake St., Edwards, 13642.

Tel: 315-287-0114; Email: sjcshc@twc.com; Web: oswegatchiecatholics.org. Mailing Address: 164 E Main St, Gouverneur, 13642. Rev. Shane M. Lynch; Deacons Philip F. Giardino; Peter J. Lawless; Henry Leader; Lawrence C. Morse.

Catechesis Religious Program—Mary Anne Lawless, D.R.E.

ELIZABETHTOWN, ESSEX CO., ST. ELIZABETH (1881) [CEM]

7478 Court St, Elizabethtown, PA 12932.

Tel: 518-873-6760; Email: rccowe@gmail.com; Web: www.wewe4.org. Mailing Address: P.O. Box 368, 8434 NYS Rte. 9N, Elizabethtown, 12932. Rev. Francis J. Flynn; Deacon Paul M. White.

Catechesis Religious Program—Students 30.

ELLENBURG, CLINTON CO., ST. EDMUND (1869) [JC2]

5526 Rte. 11, Ellenburg Center, 12934.

Tel: 518-594-3907; Email: cathcommsbse@gmail.com. Rev. Todd E. Thibault, Admin.

Catechesis Religious Program—Mona LaBombard, D.R.E. Students 65.

IMMACULATE HEART OF MARY ORATORY, 560 State Rte. 189, Churubusco, 12923.

ESSEX, ESSEX CO., ST. JOSEPH, [CEM] [JC] Merged with St. Philip of Jesus, Willsboro to form Catholic Community of St. Philip of Jesus and St. Joseph of Willsboro.

EVANS MILLS, JEFFERSON CO., ST. MARY (1847) [CEM]

8408 S. Main St., Evans Mills, 13637.

Tel: 315-629-4678; Email: office@ircatholics.org; Web: ircatholics.org. Rev. Msgr. Robert H. Aucoin, S.T.L., M.Ed.; Deacon Patrick J. Donahue.

Catechesis Religious Program—Noel Voos, D.R.E. Students 15.

Missions—St. Joseph—1 Garden Rd., Philadelphia, 13673.

St. Teresa of Avila, 318 Main St., Theresa, Jefferson Co. 13691.

FORT COVINGTON, FRANKLIN CO., ST. MARY (1837) [CEM 2]

2549 Chateaugay St., Fort Covington, 12937.

Tel: 518-358-2500; Email: smsjoffice@gmail.com; Web: www.smsjcatholics.com. Mailing Address: P.O. Box 499, 3 Burns-Holden Rd., Fort Covington, 12937. Rev. Thomas E. Kornmeyer, V.F.; Deacons Brian T. Dwyer, Pastoral Assoc.; Garry N. Burnell.

Res.: 1197 State Rte. 122, Constable, 12926.

Tel: 518-483-2775.

Catechesis Religious Program—Tel: 518-358-2500. Jocelyn Kelly, D.R.E. Students 46.

GLENFIELD, LEWIS CO., ST. MARY (1919) [CEM]

6106 Blue St., Glenfield, 13343. Tel: 315-376-6662; Email: stpeters@centralny.twcbc.com. Mailing Address: 5457 Shady Ave., Lowville, 13367. Rev. James W. Seymour, V.F.; Deacons Ronnie Gingerich; Ronald J. Pominville; Kenneth A. Seymour; Thomas J. Yousey.

Catechesis Religious Program—Mrs. Deborah Mullin, D.R.E. Students 17.

ST. THOMAS ORATORY, 5229 Grieg Rd., Greig, 13345.

GOUVERNEUR, ST. LAWRENCE CO., ST. JAMES (1875) [CEM 2]

164 E. Main St., Gouverneur, 13642.

Tel: 315-287-0114; Email: sjcshc@twc.com; Web: oswegatchiecatholics.org. Rev. Shane M. Lynch; Deacons Henry Leader; Lawrence C. Morse; Philip F. Giardino.

Rectory—St. James Rectory, 14 Sterling St., Gouverneur, 13642.

School—St. James School, (Grades PreK-6), 20 S. Gordon St., Gouverneur, 13642. Tel: 315-287-0130; Fax: 315-287-0111; Email: principal@stjamesk-6.org; Web: www.stjamesk-6.org. Michele Lallier, Prin. Lay Teachers 10; Students 100.

Catechesis Religious Program—Stacey Cannell, D.R.E.

HAMMOND, ST. LAWRENCE CO., ST. PETER (1905) [CEM] (French—Irish), Merged with The Roman Catholic Community of Morristown, Hammond & Rossie. Now a worship site.

HARRISVILLE, LEWIS CO., ST. FRANCIS SOLANUS (1879) [CEM] (French—Irish)

143555 Maple St., Harrisville, 13648.

Tel: 315-543-2421; Email: solanus@verizon.net. Mailing Address: 14361 Maple St., P.O. Box 208, Harrisville, 13648. Rev. Donald J. Manfred.

Catechesis Religious Program—Students 28.

ST. HENRY ORATORY, 44063 NYS Rte. 3, Natural Bridge, 13665.

HEUVELTON, ST. LAWRENCE CO., ST. RAPHAEL'S (1880)

3 Clinton St., Heuvelton, 13654. Tel: 315-344-2383; Email: saintraphael@twcny.rr.com. Mailing Address: 5 Clinton St., P.O. Box 377, Heuvelton, 13654. Rev. Kevin J. O'Brien; Sr. Bernadette Marie Collins, S.S.J., Pastoral Assoc.; Deacon Richard L. Van Kirk.

Catechesis Religious Program—Carolyn Pierce, D.R.E. Students 52.

HOGANSBURG, FRANKLIN CO., ST. PATRICK (1834) [CEM] [JC] (Irish), Closed. For inquiries for parish records contact the chancery.

HOPKINTON, ST. LAWRENCE CO., CHURCH OF THE HOLY CROSS (1877) [CEM]

2807 State Hwy. 11B, Hopkinton, 12965.

Tel: 518-856-9456; Email: ahfish20@gmail.com. Mailing Address: P.O. Box 288, St. Regis Falls, 12980. Rev. Alfred H. Fish.

Catechesis Religious Program—
HOUSEVILLE, LEWIS CO., ST. HEDWIG (1922) (Polish)
5432 State Rte. 26, Turin, 13473. Tel: 315-376-6662; Email: stpeters@centralny.twcbc.com. Mailing Address: 5457 Shady Ave., Lowville, 13367-1615. Rev. James W. Seymour, V.F.; Deacons Ronnie Gingerich; Ronald J. Pominville; Kenneth A. Seymour; Thomas J. Yousey.
*Catechesis Religious Program—*Mrs. Deborah Mullin, Dir.
INDIAN LAKE, HAMILTON CO.
1—ST. MARY'S, Merged with St. Paul's Blue Mountain to form St. Mary's and St. Paul's Parish, Indian Lake.
2—ST. MARY'S AND ST. PAUL'S PARISH (1958) [CEM]
6335 NYS Rte. 30, Indian Lake, 12842.
Tel: 518-648-5422; Email: smil@frontiernet.net. Mailing Address: P.O. Box 332, Indian Lake, 12842. Rev. Philip T. Allen.
Res.: 6333 NYS Rte. 28, Indian Lake, 12842.
St. Mary's Church—(Worship Site) 6335 NYS Rte. 30, Indian Lake, 12842.
St. Paul's Church, (Worship Site) 3426 NYS Rte. 28, Blue Mountain Lake, 12812.
*Catechesis Religious Program—*Jennifer Zahray, D.R.E. Students 12.
INLET, HAMILTON CO., ST. ANTHONY OF PADUA (1929)
183 N. Rte. 28, Inlet, 13360. Mailing Address: P.O. Box 236, Old Forge, 13420. Tel: 315-369-3554; Fax: 315-390-4343; Email: stbartholomews@frontier.com; Web: fultonchaincatholic.rcdony.org. Rev. Msgr. John R. Murphy, V.F., B.A., S.T.L., M.A.; Deacon Timothy D. Foley.
Catechesis Religious Program—
ST. WILLIAM ORATORY, County Rte. 2, Raquette Lake, 13436.
KEENE, ESSEX CO., ST. BRENDAN (1868)
25 Church St., Keene, 12942. Tel: 518-523-2200; Email: stagnesch@roadrunner.com; Web: stagneslakeplacid.com. Mailing Address: 169 Hillcrest Ave., Lake Placid, 12946. Rev. John R. Yonkovig, V.F.; Deacon John A. Fehlner.
Rectory—St. Brenden's Rectory.
Catechesis Religious Program—
KEESEVILLE, CLINTON AND ESSEX COS.
1—CHURCH OF THE IMMACULATE CONCEPTION (1835) [CEM] (Irish—French), Consolidated with St. John the Baptist, Keeseville to form The Roman Catholic Community of Keeseville.
2—THE ROMAN CATHOLIC COMMUNITY OF KEESEVILLE (1853) [CEM 2] (French—Irish)
1804 Main St., Keeseville, 12944-3745.
Tel: 518-834-7100; Email: rcckparish@charter.net. Rev. Kris C. Lauzon; Deacons John D. Lucero; John J. Ryan.
Res.: 1806 Main St. Ste. 3, Keeseville, 12944-3745.
Church of the Immaculate Conception— (1835) (Worship Site) 1660 Front St., Rte. 9, Keeseville, 12944.
St. John the Baptist Church (1853) (Worship Site) 1803 Main St., Rte. 22, Keeseville, 12944.
*Catechesis Religious Program—*Tel: 518-578-5632. Susan Crowningshield, D.R.E.
LAFARGEVILLE, JEFFERSON CO., ST. JOHN THE EVANGELIST (1848) [CEM]
35923 NYS Rte. 180, LaFargeville, 13656.
Tel: 315-686-3398; Email: reception@stmarysclayton.org; Web: www.stmarysclayton.org. Mailing Address: 521 James St., Clayton, 13624. Rev. Arthur J. LaBaff, V.F.; Deacons Bruce Wayne Daugherty; Gary A. Frank; Neil Fuller.
*Catechesis Religious Program—*Students 12.
LAKE PLACID, ESSEX CO., ST. AGNES (1896) [CEM]
2338 Saranac Ave., Lake Placid, 12946.
Tel: 518-523-2200; Email: stagnesch@roadrunner.com; Web: stagneslakeplacid.com. Mailing Address: 169 Hillcrest Ave., Lake Placid, 12946. Rev. John R. Yonkovig, V.F.; Deacon John A. Fehlner.
School—St. Agnes School, (Grades PreK-3), 2322 Saranac Ave., Lake Placid, 12946. Tel: 518-523-3771; Email: admin@stagneslp.org; Email: info@stagneslp.org; Web: www.stagneslp.org. Catherine Bemis, Prin. Lay Teachers 15; Students 105.
*Catechesis Religious Program—*Mrs. Marcia Bugbee, Dir. Christian Formation. Students 86.
LAKE PLEASANT, HAMILTON CO., ST. JAMES MAJOR (1924)
2567 State Rte. 8, Lake Pleasant, 12108.
Tel: 518-548-6275; Email: sjcsac@frontiernet.net. Mailing Address: 2781 State Rte. 8, P.O. Box 214, Speculator, 12164. Rev. Sony G. Pulickal, V.F.
*Catechesis Religious Program—*Students 37.
LISBON, ST. LAWRENCE CO., SS. PHILIP AND JAMES (1872)
6892 County Rt. 10, P.O. Box 175, Lisbon, 13658.
Tel: 315-344-2383; Email: saintraphael@twcny.rr.com. Mailing Address: 5 Clinton St., P.O. Box 377, Heuvelton, 13654. Rev. Kevin J. O'Brien; Deacon Richard L. Van Kirk.
*Catechesis Religious Program—*Tel: 315-393-2920. Mrs. Christine Ward, D.R.E. Students 56.
LONG LAKE, HAMILTON CO., ST. HENRY (1899) [JC]
1187 Main St., Long Lake, 12847. Tel: 518-582-3671; Email: stetherese@frontiernet.net; Web: www.sthenryll.com. Mailing Address: 18 Adams Ln., Newcomb, 12852-1701. Rev. Peter M. Berg.
LOUISVILLE, ST. LAWRENCE CO., ST. LAWRENCE (1930) [CEM] Merged with Sacred Heart, Massena to form Church of Sacred Heart and St. Lawrence, Massena.
LOWVILLE, LEWIS CO., ST. PETER (1870)
5449 Shady Ave., Lowville, 13367. Tel: 315-376-6662 ; Email: stpeters@centralny.twcbc.com; Web: stpeterslowville.org. Mailing Address: 5457 Shady Ave., Lowville, 13367. Rev. James W. Seymour, V.F.; Deacons Ronnie Gingerich; Ronald J. Pominville; Kenneth A. Seymour; Thomas J. Yousey.
Res.: 5441 Shady Ave., Lowville, 13367.
*Catechesis Religious Program—*Mrs. Deborah Mullin, D.R.E. Students 121.
LYON MOUNTAIN, CLINTON CO., ST. BERNARD (1875) [CEM] [JC]
10 Church Pond Rd., Lyon Mountain, 12952.
Tel: 518-594-3907; Email: cathcommsbse@gmail.com. 5526 State Rte. 11, Ellenburg Center, 12934. Rev. Todd E. Thibault, Admin.; Deacon Francis C. Siskavich.
*Catechesis Religious Program—*Students 8.
Mission—St. Michael, [CEM 2] Standish, Clinton Co.
MADRID, ST. LAWRENCE CO., ST. JOHN THE BAPTIST (1869) [CEM]
29 North St., Madrid, 13660. Tel: 315-322-5661; Email: stmarys@twcny.rr.com. Mailing Address: P.O. Box 68, Madrid, 13660. Rev. Douglas J. Lucia, J.C.L.; Deacon Daniel B. McGrath
Legal Name: Church of St. John the Baptist Madrid.
MALONE, FRANKLIN CO.
1—ST. ANDRE BESSETTE ROMAN CATHOLIC PARISH
306 W. Main St., Malone, 12953. Tel: 518-483-1300; Fax: 518-483-1307; Email: office@standres.org; Web: www.standres.org. Mailing Address: P.O. Box 547, Malone, 12953. Revs. Joseph W. Giroux; Michael Jablonski, Parochial Vicar; Deacons Bryan J. Bashaw; Brent A. Charland; Nicholas J. Haas.
Notre Dame Church—(Worship Site) 11 Church Pl., Malone, 12953.
St. Helen Church, (Worship Site) 755 County Hwy. 41, Malone, 12953.
School—Holy Family School, (Grades PreK-8), Joint venture St. Andre Bessette and 5 other rural parishes. 12 Homestead Pk., P.O. Box 109, Malone, 12953. Tel: 518-483-4443; Fax: 518-481-6762; Email: hfsprincipal@hfsmalone.org; Web: hfsmalone.org. Marianne Jadlos, Prin. Lay Teachers 14; Students 86.
*Catechesis Religious Program—*Students 204.
ST. JOHN BOSCO ORATORY, 57 Rennie St., Malone, 12953.
2—ST. JOHN BOSCO (1935) [CEM] Consolidated into St. Andre Bessette R.C. Parish, Malone.
3—ST. JOSEPH'S (1849) [CEM 2] (Irish), Consolidated into St. Andre Bessette Parish, Malone.
4—NOTRE DAME (1868) Consolidated into St. Andre Bessette, Malone.
MASSENA, ST. LAWRENCE CO.
1—CHURCH OF SACRED HEART AND ST. LAWRENCE, Merged with St. Mary's & St. Joseph's, Massena to form St. Peter's Parish, Massena.
2—ST. JOSEPH (1947) [JC] Merged with St. Mary's to form The Catholic Community of St. Mary's & St. Joseph's.
3—ST. MARY (1913) [JC] Merged with St. Joseph's to form The Catholic Community of St. Mary's, St. Joseph's & Sacred Heart, Massena.
4—CATHOLIC COMMUNITY OF ST. MARY'S & ST. JOSEPH'S, Merged with Church of Sacred Heart and St. Lawrence, Massena to form St. Peter's Parish, Massena.
5—ST. PETER'S PARISH (1874) [CEM]
212 Main St., Massena, 13662. Pager: 315-769-2469; Tel: 315-764-0239; Email: pastor@massenacatholics.com; Web: massenacatholics.com. P.O. Box 329, Massena, 13662. Revs. Mark R. Reilly; Tojo Chacko, H.G.N., Parochial Vicar; Scott A. Belina, Parochial Vicar; Deacon Thomas E. Proulx; Julia LaShomb, Pastoral Assoc.
Res.: 105 Cornell Ave., P.O. Box 609, Massena, 13662.
St. Lawrence's Church—(Worship Site) 30 Willard Rd., Louisville.
Sacred Heart Church, (Worship Site) 212 Main St., Massena, 13662.
St. Mary's Church, (Worship Site) 9 Sycamore St., P.O. Box 609, Massena, 13662.
School—Trinity Catholic School, (Grades PreK-6), 188 Main St., Massena, 13662. Tel: 315-769-5911; Fax: 315-769-1185; Email: principa@twcny.rr.com; Web: www.trinitycatholicschool.net. Kathy Behrens, Prin.; Candace O'Neill, Contact Person. Clergy 3; Lay Teachers 15; Sisters 1; Students 176.
*Catechesis Religious Program—*Dianne Pomainville, D.R.E., Email: dpomainville@massenacatholics.com. Students 133.
*Convent—*188 Main St., P.O. Box 91, Massena, 13662. Tel: 315-769-6238.
ST. JOSEPH ORATORY, 22 Bayley Rd., Massena.
6—SACRED HEART, Merged with St. Lawrence, Louisville to form Church of Sacred Heart and St. Lawrence, Massena.
MINEVILLE, ESSEX CO., THE CHURCH OF ALL SAINTS (1872) [CEM] Merged with St. Patrick's, Port Henry to form Catholic Community of Moriah, Port Henry.
MOOERS FORKS, CLINTON CO., ST. ANN (1860) [CEM] (French-Canadian)
3066 Rte. 11, Mooers Forks, 12959.
Tel: 518-236-5632; Email: sasj3062@primelink1.net; Web: annandangels.org. 24 Town Hall Rd., Mooers Forks, 12959. Rev. Adrian Gallagher; Deacon Dennis Monty.
Res.: 3062 Rte. 11, P.O. Box 89, Mooers Forks, 12959.
*Catechesis Religious Program—*Tel: 518-593-2774. Students 25.
MORRISONVILLE, CLINTON CO., THE ROMAN CATHOLIC COMMUNITY OF ST. ALEXANDER AND ST. JOSEPH (1897) [CEM]
1 Church St., P.O. Box 159, Morrisonville, 12962.
Tel: 518-561-5039; Fax: 518-561-5040; Email: jackie@stalexanders.org. Revs. Scott R. Seymour; L. William Gordon, In Res., (Retired); Deacon Michael J. Howley.
*Rectory—*5 Church St., P.O. Box 159, Morrisonville, 12962.
*Catechesis Religious Program—*Sr. Deepali Bankar, S.C.C., Faith Formation. Students 72.
MORRISTOWN, ST. LAWRENCE CO., THE ROMAN CATHOLIC COMMUNITY OF MORRISTOWN, HAMMOND AND ROSSIE (1941)
P.O. Box 216, Morristown, 13664. Tel: 315-375-6571; Email: stjohns@centralny.twcbc.com; Web: stjohnpeterpatrick.com. Rev. Christopher C. Carrara; Sr. Shirley Anne Brown, S.S.J., Pastoral Assoc.; Deacons Patrick Lyons; Thomas Kilian.
St. Patrick's Church—(Worship Site) 1219 County Rte. 3, Hammond, 13646.
St. Peter's Church, (Worship Site) 47 Main St., Hammond, 13646.
St. John the Evangelist Church, (Worship Site) 506 Gouverneur St., P.O. Box 216, Morristown, 13664.
*Catechesis Religious Program—*Students 24.
NEWCOMB, ESSEX CO., ST. THERESE (1950) [CEM]
14 Adams Ln., Newcomb, 12852-1701.
Tel: 518-582-3671; Email: stetherese@frontiernet.net; Web: www.sttheresenewcomb.com. Mailing Address: 18 Adams Ln., Newcomb, 12852-1701. Rev. Peter M. Berg.
NORFOLK, ST. LAWRENCE CO.
1—PARISH OF THE VISITATION AND ST. RAYMOND (2015) [CEM]
3 Morris St., P.O Box 637, Norfolk, 13667.
Tel: 315-384-4242; Email: visitationchurch@centralny.twcbc.com; Web: norfolknorwoodraymondville.org. Revs. Garry B. Giroux, J.C.L.; Andrew J. Amyot, In Res., (Retired); Deacons Lawrence A. Connelly; John A. Levison; Philip J. Regan.
Res.: 2 Park Ave., Norwood, 13668.
Tel: 315-353-7303.
Church of the Visitation—(Worship Site) 1 Morris St., Norfolk, 13667.
St. Raymond's Church, (Worship Site) 8828 State Hwy. 56, Raymondville, 13678.
*Catechesis Religious Program—*Carol O'B. Gonthier, D.R.E. Students 41.
2—VISITATION OF THE B.V.M. (1880) [CEM] Merged with St. Raymond, Raymondville to form Parish of the Visitation and St. Raymond, Norfolk.
NORTH BANGOR, FRANKLIN CO., ST. AUGUSTINE (1887) [CEM]
2472 State Rte. 11, North Bangor, 12966.
Tel: 518-483-6674; Email: staugustine6674@gmail.com; Web: staugustinesandstmarys.org. Rev. Raymond J. Moreau
Legal Name: The Roman Catholic Church of St. Augustine in North Bangor, NY
Res.: 1347 Washington St., Brushton, 12916.
*Catechesis Religious Program—*2172 State Rte. 11, North Bangor, 12966. Mr. Troy Deno, D.R.E. Students 31.
NORWOOD, ST. LAWRENCE CO., ST. ANDREW (1876) [CEM]
4 Park Ave., Norwood, 13668. Tel: 315-353-7303; Email: pvsrsasec@gmail.com. Mailing Address: P.O. Box 637, Norfolk, 13667. Rev. Garry B. Giroux, J.C.L.; Deacons Lawrence A. Connelly; John A. Levison; Philip J. Regan.
Res.: 2 Park Ave., Norwood, 13668.
OLD FORGE, HERKIMER CO., ST. BARTHOLOMEW (1897)
103 Crosby Blvd., Old Forge, 13420.
Tel: 315-369-3554; Email: stbartholomews@frontier.com. Mailing Address: P.O. Box 236, Old Forge, 13420. Rev. Msgr. John R. Murphy, V.F., B.A., S.T.L., M.A.; Deacon Timothy D. Foley.
Res.: 189 Park Ave., Old Forge, 13420.

Catechesis Religious Program—Students 31.

OLMSTEDVILLE, ESSEX CO., ST. JOSEPH (1871) [CEM 2] 635 Church Rd., Olmstedville, 12857. Tel: 518-251-2565; Tel: 518-648-5422; Fax: 518-648-0323; Email: smil@frontiernet.net; Web: www.stjosephsolmstedville.org. Mailing Address: P.O. Box 332, Indian Lake, 12842. Rev. Philip T. Allen.

Rectory—6333 N.Y.S. Rte. 28/30, Box 322, Indian Lake, 12842.

Catechesis Religious Program—Diane McNally, D.R.E. Students 5.

ST. MARY ORATORY, 479 O'Neil Rd., Olmstedville, 12857.

PERU, CLINTON CO., ST. AUGUSTINE (1883) [CEM] 3029 Main St., Peru, 12972. Tel: 518-643-2435; Email: info@peruparish.org; Email: janice@peruparish.org; Web: www.peruparish.org. Revs. Alan D. Shnob; Richard D. Demers, In Res.; Deacon George Grady Benson.

Res.: 3035 Main St., Peru, 12972. Tel: 518-643-6759.

Catechesis Religious Program—3030 Main St., Peru, 12972. Tel: 518-643-2435, Ext. 101. Students 114.

ST. PATRICK ORATORY, [CEM 2] 51 Patent Rd., Peru, Clinton Co. 12972.

PLATTSBURGH, CLINTON CO.

1—ST. JOHN THE BAPTIST (1873) Merged with Newman Parish, John XXIII College Community to form The Roman Catholic Church of St. John the Baptist, Plattsburgh.

2—ST. JOSEPH (Treadwells Mill) (1935) Merged with St. Alexander, Morrisonville to form The Roman Catholic Community of St. Alexander and St. Joseph. (Closed worship site).

3—NEWMAN PARISH, JOHN XXIII COLLEGE COMMUNITY (1970) Merged with St. John the Baptist, Plattsburgh to form The Roman Catholic Church of St. John the Baptist, Plattsburgh.

4—OUR LADY OF VICTORY (1907) 4919 S. Catherine St., Plattsburgh, 12901. Tel: 518-561-1842; Email: office@olvc.org; Web: www.olvc.org. Rev. William G. Reamer; Deacon Jack M. Lukasiewicz

Notre Dame des Victoires of Plattsburgh.

5—ST. PETER (1853) [CEM] 114 Cornelia St., Plattsburgh, 12901. Tel: 518-563-1692; Email: spchurch1692@primelink1.net; Web: www.saintpeterschurch.org. Rev. Msgr. Dennis J. Duprey, V.F.; Rev. Eduardo Pesigan III, Parochial Vicar; Rev. Msgr. Joseph G. Aubin, In Res., (Retired); Sr. Jackie Sellappan, Pastoral Assoc.; Deacons Mark Bennett, Pastoral Assoc.; Frank A. Bushey Jr.; John J. Drollette; Tyrone A. Rabideau; Randal J. Smith; Brian D. Neureuther, Confirmation Coord.

See Seton Academy Elementary School, Plattsburgh under Elementary Schools, Private in the Institution Section.

Catechesis Religious Program—Tel: 518-563-3278. Anita Soltero, D.R.E.; Ms. Mary Skillan, LifeTeen Dir.; Starr Burke, Confirmation Coord.; Courtney Khristiansen, Edge Dir. Students 125.

6—THE ROMAN CATHOLIC CHURCH OF ST. JOHN THE BAPTIST (1837) [CEM 3] (Irish) 7 Margaret St., Plattsburgh, 12901. Tel: 518-563-0730; Fax: 518-563-0754; Email: office@broadstreetcatholics.org; Web: www.broadstreetcatholics.org. Revs. Kevin D. McEwan; (Bill) Guy F. Edwards, Parochial Vicar; Norman C. Cote, In Res., (Retired); Deacons John A. Cogan; Leonard L. Patrie; Brian D. Neureuther; Dave Clark; Sr. Jackie Sellappan, Pastoral Associate.

St. John the Baptist Church—(Worship Site) 18 Broad St., Plattsburgh.

St. John XXIII Newman Center Campus Minsitry, (Worship Site) 90 Broad St., Plattsburgh.

See Seton Academy Elementary School, Plattsburgh under Elementary Schools, Private in the Institution Section.

Catechesis Religious Program—Ms. Mary Skillan, D.R.E. Students 89.

ST. MARY OF THE LAKE ORATORY, 1202 Cumberland Head Rd., Plattsburgh, 12901.

PORT HENRY, ESSEX CO., CATHOLIC COMMUNITY OF MORIAH (1854) [CEM] (Irish) 12 St. Patrick's Pl., Port Henry, 12974. Tel: 518-546-7254; Email: stpatsph@nycap.rr.com; Web: www.catholiccommunityofmoriah.com. Rev. Albert J. Hauser, V.F.

Church of All Saints—(Worship Site) 35 Bartlett Pond Rd., Mineville, 12956.

St. Patrick's Church, (Worship Site) 12 St. Patrick's Pl., Port Henry, 12974.

Catechesis Religious Program—

PORT LEYDEN, LEWIS CO., ST. MARTIN (1879) [CEM] 7108 North St., P.O. Box 431, Port Leyden, 13433. Tel: 315-348-6104; Email: stmartins@frontiernet.net. Rev. Lawrence E. Marullo; Deacon James W. Chaufty.

Catechesis Religious Program—Students 15.

Mission—St. John, 5838 McAlpine St., Lyons Falls, Lewis Co. 13368. Tel: 315-348-6599.

POTSDAM, ST. LAWRENCE CO., ST. MARY (1841) [CEM] 20 Lawrence Ave., Potsdam, 13676. Tel: 315-265-9680; Email: smpotsdamoffice@gmail.com; Web: stmarystpatrick.net. Mailing Address: 17 Lawrence Ave., Potsdam, 13676. Rev. Stephen Rocker; Deacon Richard L. Burns.

Catechesis Religious Program—Email: menslow@stmarystpatrick.net. Serving SUNY Potsdam and Clarkson Univerities. Students 30.

RAYMONDVILLE, ST. LAWRENCE CO., ST. RAYMOND (1920) Merged with Visitation of the B.V.M., Norfolk to form Parish of the Visitation and St. Raymond, Norfolk.

REDFORD, CLINTON CO., CHURCH OF THE ASSUMPTION (1853) [CEM] 78 Clinton St., Redford, 12978. Tel: 518-293-5169; Fax: 518-293-5168; Email: carousel1850@charter.net. Rev. John M. Demo; Deacon Edward L. Mazuchowski.

Catechesis Religious Program—Bonnie Allen, C.R.E. Students 38.

REDWOOD, JEFFERSON CO., ST. FRANCIS XAVIER (1848) [CEM] Consolidated Worship site of Catholic Community of Alexandria.

ROSIERE, JEFFERSON CO., ST. VINCENT DE PAUL (1871) [CEM] Merged with St. Vincent de Paul, Cape Vincent & All Saints, Chaumont to form The Catholic Community of Cape Vincent, Rosiere and Chaumont, Cape Vincent.

ROUSES POINT, CLINTON CO., ST. PATRICK (1857) [CEM] [JC] (Irish) 140 Lake St., Rouses Point, 12979. Tel: 518-297-7361 ; Email: stpats@twcny.rr.com; Web: www.stpatricksrpny.org. Mailing Address: P.O. Box 217, 138 Lake St., Rouses Point, 12979. Sr. Jessintha Xavier, Pastoral Assoc.; Rev. Clyde A. Lewis; Deacon Noel A. Hinerth; Jo Anne Ryan, Business Mgr.

Catechesis Religious Program—9 Liberty St., P.O. Box 217, Rouses Point, 12979. Tel: 518-297-3504. Josie Maskell, D.R.E. Students 44.

ST. JOSEPH ORATORY, 74 Mason Rd., Champlain, 12919. Rev. Norman C. Cote, Pastor Emeritus, (Retired).

SAINT REGIS FALLS, FRANKLIN CO., ST. ANN (1883) [CEM] 77 N. Main St., P.O. Box 288, St. Regis Falls, 12980. Tel: 518-856-9456; Email: ahfish20@gmail.com. Rev. Alfred H. Fish

Legal Name: St. Ann's Church St. Regis Falls, New York

Catechesis Religious Program—Students 2.

ST. PETER ORATORY, NYS Rte. 458 & Center St., St. Regis Falls, 12980.

SARANAC LAKE, FRANKLIN CO., ST. BERNARD'S CHURCH (1888) [CEM] [JC] 27 St. Bernard St., Saranac Lake, 12983. Tel: 518-891-4616; Fax: 518-891-4619; Email: office@stbernards.church; Web: stbernards.church. Revs. Patrick A. Ratigan; Alex Guimpol, Parochial Vicar; Sr. Carol Kraeger, S.S.J., Pastoral Assoc.; Deacon Joseph Szwed.

St. Paul Church—(Worship Site) 1640 State Rte. 3, Bloomingdale, 12913.

Church of the Assumption, (Worship Site) 826 State Rte. 86, Gabriels, 12939.

School—St. Bernard School, (Grades K-5), 63 River St., Saranac Lake, 12983. Tel: 518-891-2830; Email: principal@stbernardsschool.org; Web: www.stbernards.org. Raymond Dora, Prin. Lay Teachers 6; Students 85.

Catechesis Religious Program—Pius X Center, Email: prep@stbernards.church. Mrs. Michelle Law, D.R.E. Students 50.

ST. JOHN IN THE WILDERNESS ORATORY, 6148 State Rte. 30, Lake Clear, 12945.

ST. PAUL ORATORY, 1640 State Rte. 3, Bloomingdale, 12913.

SCHROON LAKE, ESSEX CO., OUR LADY OF LOURDES (1883) [CEM] 1114 U.S. Rte. 9, Schroon Lake, 12870. Tel: 518-532-7100; Email: ollsjcoffice@verizon.net; Web: www.ollschroonlake.org. Mailing Address: P.O. Box 368, Schroon Lake, 12870. Rev. Howard J. Venette.

Res.: 22 Father Joques Pl., Ticonderoga, 12883.

Catechesis Religious Program—Linda Lowe, D.R.E. Students 17.

HOLY NAMES OF JESUS AND MARY ORATORY, [CEM] 3008 U.S. Rte. 9, North Hudson, 12855.

STAR LAKE, ST. LAWRENCE CO., ST. HUBERT (1893) [JC] (French—Irish) 1046 Oswegatchie Trail Rd., Star Lake, 13690. Tel: 315-848-3612; Email: st.huberts.church@gmail.com. Rev. Shane M. Lynch; Deacons Philip F. Giardino; Henry Leader; Lawrence C. Morse.

Catechesis Religious Program—Students 6.

TICONDEROGA, ESSEX CO., ST. MARY (1852) [CEM] 18 Father Jogues Pl., Ticonderoga, 12883. Tel: 518-585-7144; Fax: 518-585-3632; Email: stmarysti@bridgepoint1.com; Web: www.stmarysti.org. Mailing Address: 22 Father Jogues Pl., Ticonderoga, 12883. Rev. Howard J. Venette; Deacon Elliott A. Shaw.

Res.: 22 Father Jogues Pl., Ticonderoga, 12883. Tel: 518-585-7144; Email: stmarysti@bridgepoint1.com; Web: stmarysti.org.

School—St. Mary School, (Grades PreK-8), 64 Amherst Ave., Ticonderoga, 12883. Tel: 518-585-7433; Fax: 518-558-1433; Email: sschoo3@nycap.rr.com; Web: stmarysschoolticonderoga.org. Sr. Sharon Anne Dalton, S.S.J., Prin. Lay Teachers 11; Sisters 2; Students 103.

Catechesis Religious Program—Tel: 518-597-3924. Students 108.

TUPPER LAKE, FRANKLIN CO.

1—ST. ALPHONSUS - HOLY NAME OF JESUS (1890) [CEM] Holy Ghost Parish Center, 40 Marion St., Tupper Lake, 12986. Tel: 518-359-3405; Email: office@tupperlakecatholics.org; Web: www.tupperlakecathlolics.org. Rev. Douglas A. Decker; Deacons James T. Ellis; Gerald H. Savage.

Res.: 114 Main St., Tupper Lake, 12986.

St. Alphonsus Church—(Worship Site) 48 Wawbeek Ave., Tupper Lake, 12986.

Holy Name, (Worship Site) 115 Main St., Tupper Lake, 12986.

Catechesis Religious Program— Combined with Holy Name of Jesus, Tupper Lake.

2—HOLY NAME OF JESUS (Faust) (1904) [CEM] Merged with St. Alphonsus, Tupper Lake to form St. Alphonsus-Holy Name of Jesus, Tupper Lake.

WADDINGTON, ST. LAWRENCE CO., ST. MARY (1826) [CEM 3] 34 Oak St., P.O. Box 187, Waddington, 13694. Tel: 315-388-4466; Fax: 315-388-4722; Email: stmarys@twcny.rr.com. Rev. Douglas J. Lucia, J.C.L.; Deacon Daniel B. McGrath

Legal Name: St. Mary's, Waddington

Catechesis Religious Program—Msgr. Arquett Parish Center, Tel: 315-388-4423. Students 60.

WATERTOWN, JEFFERSON CO.

1—ST. ANTHONY (1913) [JC] (Italian) Linked with St. Patrick's 850 Arsenal St., Watertown, 13601. Tel: 315-782-1190; Email: info@sawatn.org; Web: catholicwatertown.org. Rev. Christopher J. Looby; Deacons John R. Murray, V.F., B.A., S.T.L., M.A.; Guy Javarone.

Catechesis Religious Program—Students 52.

2—HOLY FAMILY (1895) 129 Winthrop St., Watertown, 13601. Tel: 315-782-2468; Email: hfchurch@twcny.rr.com; Web: www.holyfamilywatertown.org. Rev. Steven M. Murray; Rev. Msgr. Paul E. Whitmore, In Res., (Retired); Rev. Leo A. Wiley, In Res., (Retired); Deacons Edward R. Miller; Michael J. Allan; Patrick J. Bates, Pastoral Assoc.; Sr. Angelica Rebello, S.C.C., Pastoral Assoc.

Catechesis Religious Program—Holy Family Religious Education Office, Sterling Pl., Watertown, 13601. Tel: 315-782-6750; Email: holyfamilyre@yahoo.com. Students 161.

3—OUR LADY OF THE SACRED HEART (1876) [CEM] 320 W. Lynde St., Watertown, 13601. Tel: 315-782-1474; Email: olshparish13601@gmail.com; Web: www.olshparish.org. Rev. Jonas Raphael Tandayu, M.S.C.; Sr. Constance Marie Sylver, S.S.J., Pastoral Assoc.; Deacons William Michael Johnston; John J. Trombly.

Catechesis Religious Program—Sr. Constance Marie Sylver, S.S.J., D.R.E.

4—ST. PATRICK (1854) [CEM] (Linked with St. Anthony) 123 S. Massey St., Watertown, 13601-3201. Tel: 315-782-1190; Email: info@spwatn.org; Web: www.spwatn.org. Rev. Christopher J. Looby; Deacons Guy Javarone; Kevin T. Mastellon.

Catechesis Religious Program—Mrs. Elizabeth Bamann, D.R.E. Students 54.

WELLS, HAMILTON CO., ST. ANN'S (1890) [CEM] 1303 State Rte. 30, Wells, 12190. Tel: 518-548-6275; Email: sjcsac@frontiernet.net. Mailing Address: P.O. Box 214, Speculator, 12164. Rev. Sony G. Pulickal, V.F.

WEST CHAZY, CLINTON CO., ST. JOSEPH (1884) [CEM] 56 W. Church St., West Chazy, 12992. Tel: 518-493-4521; Email: stjosephs@westelcom.com. Mailing Address: P.O. Box 224, West Chazy, 12992. Rev. Theodore A. Crosby.

Res.: 60 W. Church St., West Chazy, 12992.

Catechesis Religious Program—Email: stjosephsfaithformation101@gmail.com. Susan M. Corneau, D.R.E. Students 34.

WEST LEYDEN, LEWIS CO., ST. MARY'S NATIVITY (1900) [CEM] 1183 State Rte. 26, West Leyden, 13489. Tel: 315-397-2556; Email: stmarys1@frontier.com. Mailing Address: P.O. Box 382, Constableville,

13325. Rev. Lawrence E. Marullo; Deacon James W. Chaufty.
Res.: 3200 N. Main St., Constableville, 13325.
Catechesis Religious Program—Students 4.

WESTPORT, ESSEX CO., ST. PHILIP NERI (1879) [CEM]
6603 Main St., Westport, 12993. Tel: 518-873-6760; Email: rccowe@gmail.com; Web: www.wewe4.org. Mailing Address: P.O. Box 368, Elizabethtown, 12932. Rev. Francis J. Flynn; Deacon Paul M. White.
Res.: 8434 NYS Rte. 9N, Elizabethtown, 12932.
Catechesis Religious Program—Students 17.

WILLSBORO, ESSEX CO.
1—CATHOLIC COMMUNITY OF ST. PHILIP OF JESUS AND ST. JOSEPH OF WILLSBORO, NEW YORK, [CEM]
3748 Main St., Willsboro, 12996. Tel: 518-963-4524; Email: rccowe@gmail.com; Web: www.wewe4.org. Mailing Address: P.O. Box 607, Willsboro, 12996. Rev. Francis J. Flynn.
Res.: 8434 NYS 9 N., P.O. Box 368, Elizabethtown, 12932.
St. Joseph Church—(Worship Site) 2891 Essex Rd., Essex, 12996.
St. Philip of Jesus Church, (Worship Site) 3748 Main St., Willsboro, 12996.
Catechesis Religious Program—3746 Main St., Willsboro, 12996. Tel: 518-536-2642; Email: whitefam@westelcom.com. Deacon Paul M. White, Faith formation. Students 16.
2—ST. PHILIP OF JESUS (1909) [CEM] Merged with St. Joseph, Essex to form Catholic Community of St. Philip of Jesus and St. Joseph of Willsboro.

WITHERBEE, ESSEX CO., ST. MICHAEL (1911) Closed. For inquiries for parish records contact the chancery.

Chaplains of Public Institutions.

Military and Medical

OGDENSBURG. *St. Lawrence Psychiatric Center*, St. Lawrence Psychiatric Center, 1 Chimney Point Dr., 13669. Tel: 315-541-2001; Fax: 315-541-2088; Email: Vicente.Jazmines@omh.ny.gov. Rev. Vicente F. Jazmines, Chap.

FORT DRUM. *U.S. Army Headquarters Fort Drum*,
Tel: 315-772-5591; Fax: 315-772-6725. Revs. Daniel Goulet, Chap., Maciej Napieralski, Chap., Mikolaj L. Scibior, Chap., Deacon Richard J. Staab, DRE.

PLATTSBURGH. *University of Vermont Health Network*, 75 Beekman St., Plattsburgh, 12901.
Tel: 518-561-2000. Revs. Eduardo Pesigan III, Asst. Chap., William G. Reamer, Chap.

SARANAC LAKE. *Adirondack Health*, P.O. Box 471, Saranac Lake, 12983. Tel: 518-8914141. Rev. Steve Kovacevich, Dir. Pastoral Care.

TUPPER LAKE. *Sunmount Developmental Center*, 2445 State Rte. 30, Tupper Lake, 12986.
Tel: 518-359-3311; Email: laura.lavalley@opwdd.ny.gov; Web: www.opwdd.ny.gov. Rev. Paul J. Kelly, Chap., (Retired)
Sunmount DDSO Developmental Disabilities State Operations Office.
Sunmount DDSO Developmental Disabilities State Operations Office. Vacant.

WATERTOWN. *Samaritan Medical Center*, 830 Washington St., Watertown, 13601.
Tel: 315-785-4000; Fax: 315-785-4195. Sr. Maria Flavia D'Costa, SCC.

Prisons

OGDENSBURG. *Ogdensburg Correctional Facility*, One Correction Way, 13669.
Tel: 315-393-0281, Ext. 4815.
Riverview Correctional Facility, 1110 Tibbits Dr., Box 158, 13669. Tel: 315-393-8400, Ext. 4820. Deacon William Michael Johnston.

ALTONA. *Altona Correctional Facility*, P.O. Box 125, Altona, 12910. Tel: 518-236-7841;
Fax: 518-236-6235. Rev. Alan J. Lamica, Ms. Tamara Murphy.

CAPE VINCENT. *Cape Vincent Correctional Facility*, Cape Vincent, 13618. Tel: 315-654-4100, Ext. 548. Mr. Donald Wilder.

DANNEMORA. *Clinton Correctional Facility*, 1156 Cook St., P.O. Box 798, Dannemora, 12929-0798.
Tel: 518-492-2511, Ext. 4800. Deacon Frank A. Bushey Jr.

GOUVENEUR. *Gouverneur Corrrectional Facility*, 112 Scotch Settlement Rd., Gouverneur, 13642.
Tel: 315-287-7351. Deacon Lawrence C. Morse.

MALONE. *Barehill Correctional Facility*, 181 Brand Rd., Caller Box 20, Malone, 12953.
Tel: 518-483-8411, Ext. 4810. Rev. Alan J. Lamica.
Franklin Correctional Facility, P.O. Box 10, Malone, 12953-9720. Tel: 518-483-6040, Ext. 4805. Rev. Alan J. Lamica, Deacon Bryan J. Bashaw.
Upstate Correctional Facility, P.O. Box 2000, Malone, 12953. Tel: 518-483-6997, Ext. 4800. Rev. Alan J. Lamica, Mr. Seth Conklin.

MORIAH. *Moriah Shock Incarceration Correctional Facility*, 75 Burnhart Ln., P.O. Box 999, Mineville, 12956-0999. Tel: 518-942-7561. Deacon Elliott Shaw.

RAY BROOK. *Adirondack Correctional Facility*, 196 Ray Brook Rd., Box 110, Ray Brook, 12977-0110.
Tel: 518-891-1343, Ext. 4805. Vacant.
Federal Correctional Institution, Tel: 518-897-4000. Rev. Steve Kovacevich.

WATERTOWN. *Watertown Correctional Facility*, 23147 Swan Rd., Watertown, 13601.
Tel: 315-782-7490, Ext. 4800. Mr. Donald Wilder.

On Duty Outside the Diocese:
Rev.—
Chapin, Daniel L., Maryknoll Assoc., (Retired), Padres De Maryknoll, Casilla 131, Cochabamba, Bolivia.

Leave of Absence:
Rev.—
Menard, Bernard D., 2679 State Rte. 11, Mooers, 12958.

Absent on Sick Leave, Disabled:
Rev.—
Demers, Richard D., 3035 State Rte. 22, Peru, 12972.

Retired:
Rev. Msgrs.—
Aubin, Joseph G., (Retired), 114A Cornelia St, Plattsburgh, 12901
Deno, Lawrence M., (Retired), P.O. Box 549, Chazy, 12921
McAvoy, C. John, (Retired), 51 Willow Way, Apt. 19, Saranac Lake, 12983
Poissant, Leeward J., (Retired), 16 Glen Dr., Apt. 4, Plattsburgh, 12901
Riani, Peter R., V.F., S.T.D., M.Ed., (Retired), 10 Gilliland Lane, Willsboro, 12996
Snow, Harry K., M.A.Th., J.C.L., V.F., (Retired), 950 Linden St., 13369. St. Joseph's Home
Whitmore, Paul E., (Retired), 129 Winthrop St., Watertown, 13601

Revs.—
Amyot, Andrew J., (Retired), P.O. Box 637, Norfolk, 13667
Canaan, Timothy G., (Retired), Watertown
Cerank, Gerald A., (Retired), 2344 Melrose Dr., North Port, FL 34289
Chapin, Daniel L., Maryknoll Assoc., (Retired), Padres De Maryknoll, Casilla 131, Cochabamba
Cote, Norman C., (Retired), 7 Margaret St., Plattsburgh, 12901
Demarais, Garvin J., (Retired), P.O. Box 1741, Plattsburgh, 12901
Downs, John L., (Retired), 8828 State Hwy. 56, Massena, 13662
Elliott, Joseph W., V.F., (Retired), 32 S. Church St., Apt. 23, Brasher Falls, 13613
Gordon, L. William, (Retired), P.O. Box 159, Morrisonville, 12962. St. Alexander's, Morrisonville, NY
Hart, Rolland A., (Retired), 99 Allen Brook Ln., Williston, VT 05495
Helfrich, Peter G., (Retired), 34 Milrace Dr., East Rochester, 14445
Keefe, Daniel T., (Retired), Pine Harbour, 15 NH St., Plattsburgh, 12901
Kelly, Paul J., (Retired), 180 Correy's Rd., Tupper Lake, 12986
Kennehan, John P., (Retired), 55 Cty. Rte. 50, Brasher Falls, 13613
Kramberg, Donald F., (Retired), 8040 Rowland Ave., #B146, Philadelphia, PA 19136
Lamitie, Robert O., (Retired), 1836 Walden Pond Rd., Box 35 C, Fort Pierce, FL 34645
Looby, John J., V.F., (Retired), P.O. Box 78, Constable, 12926
McGuinness, J. Roger, (Retired), 94 Maryland Rd., Plattsburgh, 12903
Menard, Gilbert B., (Retired), 104 Bea's Way, Apt. 118, Plattsburgh, 12901
Muench, William G., (Retired), P.O. Box 664, Sackets Harbor, 13685
O'Reilly, Patrick J., (Retired), Cty. Kilminchy, Ireland
Patterson, Terrence R., (Retired), 18 Flow Dr., Potsdam, 13676. Tel: 315-265-2986
Sestito, Joseph N., (Retired), 100 Van Tassal Ln., Rome, 13440
Shurteleff, F. James, (Retired), 415 Hamilton St., 13669
Sturtz, Richard S., V.F., (Retired), St. Mary's Cathedral, 415 Hamilton St., 13669
Wertman, Raymond, (Retired), 2292 Costa Rican Dr., Apt. 56, Clearwater, FL 33763
Wiley, Leo A., (Retired), 129 Winthrop St., Watertown, 13601.

Permanent Deacons:
Allen, Michael J., 241 Michigan Ave., Watertown, 13669
Ambeau, Lawrence R., 11590 Ayles Rd., Adams, 13605
Bashaw, Bryan J., 4 Shova Rd., Malone, 12953
Bateman, Francis F., (Retired), 916 Jay St., 13669
Bennett, Mark E., Spiritual Life Dir., 95 Brinkerhoff St., Plattsburgh, 12901
Benson, George Grady, 137 Jabez Allen Rd., Peru, 12972
Brousseau, Frederick A., 15 Cygnet Cir., Slingerlands, 12159
Burns, Richard L., 652 Hatch Rd., Potsdam, 13676
Bushey, Frank A. Jr., 7 Addoms St., Plattsburgh, 12901
Charland, Brent A., 2672 State Rte. 11B, North Bangor, 12966
Chaufty, James W., P.O. Box 43, Port Leyden, 13433
Cheney, Jerome A., (Retired), 45 Willow Way, #10, Saranac Lake, 12983
Clark, David L., 10 Moreau Way, Plattsburgh, 12903
Cogan, John A., 108 Sunrise Dr., Plattsburgh, 12901
Connelly, Lawrence A., P.O. Box 22, Norfolk, 13667
Connor, Marvin M., 459 Irish Settlement Rd., Plattsburgh, 12901
Crosby, Patrick, Clayton
Crowley, James D., 9148 State Hwy. 37, 13669
Daugherty, Bruce Wayne, 36084 County Rte. 4, Clayton, 13624
Debiec, Larry R., 512 Box Turtle Ct., Myrtle Beach, SC 29588
Defayette, Gerald R., (Retired), 39 Oak St., Apt. 411, Plattsburgh, 12901
Demers, David D., 432 Oak St., 13669
Diehl, Robert F., (Retired), 4121 Hearthside Dr., Apt. 104, Wilmington, NC 28412
Donahue, Patrick J., P.O. Box 463, Chaumont, 13622
Drollette, John J., 44 Addoms St., Plattsburgh, 12901
Ellis, James T., 58 Broad St., Tupper Lake, 12986
Fehlner, John A., P.O. Box 552, Keene Valley, 12943
Foley, Timothy D., P.O. Box 696, Old Forge, 13420
Frank, Gary A., 16841 Hilltop Ln., Clayton, 13624
Fuller, Neil J., 1304 County Rte. 5, Clayton, 13624
Giardino, Philip F., 1070 Oswegatchie Tr. Rd., Star Lake, WI 13690
Gillen, James, 55 Hatch Knoll Rd., Jonesboro, ME 04648
Gilner, Gerard, (Retired), P.O. Box 166, Indian Lake, 12842
Gingerich, Ronnie, St. Peter's Church, 5449 Shady Ave., Lowville, 13367
Haas, Nicholas J., 36 Constable St., Malone, 12953
Hinerth, Noel A., 19 Lakeview Ave., Rouses Point, 12979
Howley, Michael J., 24 Lynde St., Plattsburgh, 12901
Hunneyman, Norman L., P.O. Box 82, Sackets Harbor, 13685
Javarone, Guy, 22558 Cook Rd., Watertown, 13601
Johnston, William Michael, P.O. Box 6125, Watertown, 13601
Kilian, Thomas F., 308 Hamilton St., 13669
King, Robert A., (Retired), 1200 Lakeshore Dr., Cuba, MO 65453
LaLonde, Mark A., 603 E. South St., 13669
Lawless, Peter J., 2002 County Rte. 24, Edwards, 13635
Lazlo, Ivantis, P.O. Box 309, Keeseville, 12944
Levison, John A., 10 Pleasant St., Norwood, 13668
Looby, Phillip M., (Retired), P.O. Box 286, Harrisville, 13648
Lukasiewicz, Jack M., 357 Cemetery Rd., Plattsburgh, 12901
Lyons, Patrick, 14 Briggs Dr., 13669
Mader, Frederick J., (Retired), 203 Neil St., Saranac Lake, 12983
Mastellon, Kevin T., 149 Flower Ave. W., Watertown, 13601
Mazuchowski, Edward L., 177 Gene LeFevre Rd., Cadyville, 12918
McGrath, Daniel B., P.O. Box 26, Madrid, 13660
Miller, Edward R., 15148 U.S. Rte. 11, Adams Center, 13606
Monty, Dennis, 48 Monty Rd., Altona, 12910
Morse, Lawrence C., St. James Church, 164 E. Main St., Gouverneur, 13642
Murray, John R., V.F., B.A., S.T.L., M.A., 302 Rivershore Dr., Clayton, 13624
Neureuther, Brian D., 11 Carriagehouse Ln., West Chazy, 12992
O'Brien, William P., 1416 Jay St., 13669
Oberst, Frederick R., 455 S. Suncoast Blvd., Crystal River, FL 34429
Pastizzo, Anthony J., 5717 State Hwy. 812, 13669

Patrie, Leonard L., 76 Fort Brown Dr., #201, Plattsburgh, 12903
Proulx, Thomas E., 21 Douglas Rd., Massena, 13662
Rabideau, Tyrone, 139 Beekman St., Plattsburgh, 12901
Raven, William S., P.O. Box 515, Black River, 13612
Regan, Philip J., P.O. Box 113, Norwood, 13668
Sandburg, David J., 9535 State Hwy. 37, 13669
Savage, Gerald H., 36 Broad St., Tupper Lake, 12986
Sharrow, Thomas D., 137 Fabian Dr., Schenectady, 12306
Siskavich, Francis C., P.O. Box 185, Lyon Mountain, 12952
Slate, Bernard E., 41743 State Rte. 180, Clayton, 13624
Smith, Randal J., 39 Sandra Ave., Plattsburgh, 12901
Snell, James M., 5689 State Hwy. 56, Potsdam, 13676
Staab, Richard J., 22 Stone St., West Carthage, 13619
Ste.-Marie, Ronald M., (Retired), 406 N. Washington St., Herkimer, 13350
Szwed, Joseph, 157 Kiwassa Rd., Saranac Lake, 12983
Trombly, John J., 678 Grant St., Watertown, 13601
Van Kirk, Richard L., 594 E. Rd., Heuvelton, 13654
Walentuk, Joel E., 19622 Peel Dock Rd., Wellesley Island, 13640
Warner, Richard C. Sr., 7853 Firecracker Tr., Fountain, CO 80817
White, Paul M., 150 Redmond Rd., Westport, 12993
Yarchuk, Andrew, (Retired), 87 N. Clinton Ave, Ste. 1, Rochester, 14604
Yousey, Thomas J., 5312 Kamryn Rd., Lowville, 13367.

INSTITUTIONS LOCATED IN DIOCESE

[A] INTERPAROCHIAL SCHOOLS

PLATTSBURGH. *Seton Catholic School*, (Grades PreK-12), 206 New York Rd., Plattsburgh, 12903.
Tel: 518-561-4031; Fax: 518-563-1193; Email: mforbes@setonknights.org; Web: www.setonknights.org. Ms. Mary Forbes, Prin.; Sharon Bainbridge, Librarian. Lay Teachers 36; Students 304; Clergy / Religious Teachers 1.

WATERTOWN. *Immaculate Heart Central School*, (Grades PreK-12), 1316 Ives St., Watertown, 13601. Tel: 315-788-4672; Fax: 315-788-4447; Email: lynise.lassiter@ichschool.org; Web: www.ihcschool.org. Mrs. Lynise Barker-Lassiter, Prin.; Mrs. Kari Conklin, Vice Prin.; Geoffrey Andrews, Vice Prin.; Teresa Lucas, Business Mgr.; Christin Filippelli, Enrollment Dir.; Amanda McIlroy, Mktg. & Commun. Dir. Lay Teachers 49; Students 442; Clergy / Religious Teachers 2.

Immaculate Heart Central Primary Campus, (Grades PreK-3), 122 Winthrop St., Watertown, 13601. Tel: 315-788-7011; Email: kari.conklin@ihcschool.org. Mrs. Kari Conklin, Vice Prin.

Immaculate Heart Central Intermediate Campus, (Grades 4-6), 733 S. Massey St., Watertown, 13601. Tel: 315-788-3935; Email: annette.connolly@ihcschool.org.

Immaculate Heart Central Junior / Senior High Campus, (Grades 7-12); 1316 Ives St., Watertown, 13601. Tel: 315-788-4670. Lay Teachers 27; Sisters 2; Students 250.

[B] CONFERENCE AND RETREAT CENTER

OGDENSBURG. *Wadhams Hall*, 6866 State Hwy. 37, 13669-4420. Tel: 315-393-4231; Fax: 315-393-4249; Email: inquiry@wadhams.edu; Web: www.wadhams.edu. Mr. Jeffrey Ward, A.A.S., Business Mgr. Total Staff 4.

[C] MONASTERIES AND RESIDENCES OF PRIESTS AND BROTHERSD

SARANAC LAKE. *St. Joseph's Friary*, 5 Franklin Ave., Saranac Lake, 12983. Tel: 518-891-2395;
Tel: 518-891-3801, Ext. 1244; Email: lemay@sjrcrehab.org. Bros. Alan Lemay, S.A., Prog. Asst.; Paschal Steen, T.S.A., Maintenance. Total in Residence 2.

WATERTOWN. *Missionaries of the Sacred Heart*, 668 Thompson St., Watertown, 13601.
Tel: 315-782-3480; Fax: 315-782-0473; Email: VTFMSC@neo.it.com. Revs. Jonas Raphael Tandayu, M.S.C., Supr.; Raymond Deisbourg, M.S.C., Pastor; Herman Pongantung, M.S.C., Assoc. Pastor; Pierre Aubin, M.S.C., Pastor Emeritus; Vincent T. Freeh, M.S.C., Pastor Emeritus; David DeLuca, M.S.C., In Res.

[D] CONVENTS AND RESIDENCES FOR SISTERS

OGDENSBURG. *Sisters of St. Joseph*, 251 Proctor Ave., 13669. Tel: 315-393-6511. Sisters Bernadette Marie Collins, S.S.J., Rel. Order Leader; Julie Adams, S.S.J., Member. Sisters 2; Total in Residence 2.

CARTHAGE. *St. James Convent, Sisters of St. Joseph*, Sisters of St. Joseph, 317 West St., Carthage, 13619. Tel: 315-493-1672; Email: smacollinsssj@yahoo.com. Sr. Annunciata Collins, S.S.J., Pastoral Assoc. Sisters 1; Total in Residence 1; Total Staff 1.

ELLENBURG CENTER. *Our Lady of the Adirondacks Inc. House of Prayer* (1972) 7270 Star Rd., Rte. 190, Ellenburg Center, 12934-2501. Tel: 518-594-3253; Email: olaprayerhouse@gmail.com; Web: www.ourladyoftheadirondackshouseofprayer.com. Rev. (Bill) Guy F. Edwards, Interim Spiritual Dir. Our Lady of the Adirondacks Community Total Staff 1; Membership 86.

Our Lady of the Adirondacks Community (1990) Email: olaprayerhouse@gmail.com; Web: www.ourladyoftheadirondackshouseofprayer.catholicweb.com. Jack Downs, Spiritual Dir., Tel: 315-384-4143.

Our Lady of the Adirondacks Prayer Association (1972) Tel: 518-594-3253; Email: olaprayerhouse@gmail.com; Web: www.ourladyoftheadirondackhouseofprayer.catholicweb.com.

LAKE PLACID. *St. Margaret Convent*, 185 Old Military Rd., Lake Placid, 12946. Tel: 518-523-2929;
Fax: 518-523-5449; Email: mokeefe@mercymidatlantic.org. Sr. M. Camillus O'Keefe, R.S.M., B.A., B.S., Supr. Sisters of Mercy. Sisters 3.

MASSENA. *Sacred Heart Convent*, 212 Main St., Massena, 13662. P.O. Box 91, Massena, 13662.
Tel: 315-769-6238; Email: srdorisosm@gmail.com. Sisters Doris Durant, O.S.M., Contact Person; Cincy Sullivan, B.V.M., Dir., Meals on Wheels. Sisters 2; Total in Residence 2.

PLATTSBURGH. *Sisters of Charity of St. Louis* (1910) 4907 S. Catherine St., Apt. 203, Plattsburgh, 12901. Tel: 518-802-0331; Email: srbernadetted@gmail.com. Sr. Bernadette Ducharme, S.C.S.L., Supr. Founded in France in 1803. First foundation in the United States in 1910.Generalate: 5169 Avenue MacDonald, Montreal QC H3X 2V9 Canada Sisters 3; Professed Sisters 481.

Sisters of Mercy, 101 Bea's Way, Apt. 102, Plattsburgh, 12901. Tel: 518-561-9689; Email: srbrianmarie@gmail.com. Sr. Brian Marie Latour, R.S.M., Semi-Retired. Sisters of Mercy Sisters of Mercy 1.

SARANAC LAKE. *Sisters of Mercy of the Americas* (1831) 35 Trudeau Rd., Saranac Lake, 12983-5635.
Tel: 518-891-3234; Email: srmcarolyn@roadrunner.com. Sr. Mary Madden. Sisters 1.

TICONDEROGA. *St. Mary's Convent, Sisters of St. Joseph* (1959) 145 Lake George Ave., Ticonderoga, 12883.
Tel: 518-585-6547; Fax: 518-558-1433; Email: sschoo3@nycap.rr.com. Sr. Sharon Anne Dalton, S.S.J. Sisters 2; Total in Residence 2.

TUPPER LAKE. *Dominican Sisters of Hope, Ossining* (1995) 1202 Cumberland Head Rd., Plattsburgh, 12901. Tel: 518-359-9632; Email: elizmenard40@gmail.com. Sr. Elizabeth Menard, O.P., Contact Person. Sisters 3.

WATERTOWN. *Precious Blood Monastery, Sister Adorers of the Precious Blood*, 400 Pratt St., Watertown, 13601. Tel: 315-788-1669; Fax: 315-779-9046; Email: smarilyn@twcny.rr.com; Web: sisterspreciousblood.org. Sr. Marilyn McGillan, A.P.B., Supr. Sisters 6; Total in Residence 6.

Sisters of St. Joseph Motherhouse (1880) 1425 Washington St., Watertown, 13601-4533.
Tel: 315-782-3460; Fax: 315-788-2794; Email: smelyngssj@yahoo.com; Web: www.ssjwatertown.org. Sisters Mary Eamon Lyng, S.S.J., Major Supr.; Jennifer Votraw, S.S.J., Supr.; Mr. Randy Belina, Motherhouse Admin. Sisters 33; Total in Residence 33; Total Staff 36.

[E] INCORPORATED CEMETERIES

BRASHER FALLS. *St. Patrick's Cemetery Association of Brasher Falls, N.Y.*, County Rte. 50, Brasher Falls, 13613. Tel: 315-389-5401; Email: parish@twcny.rr.com. Mailing Address: P.O. Box 208, Brasher Falls, 13613. Michael Hoag, Contact Person

CARTHAGE. *St. James Cemetery Corporation*, 500-576 S James St, Carthage, 13619. Tel: 315-493-3224; Email: stjames@twcny.rr.com. Mailing Address: 327 West St., Carthage, 13619. Rev. Donald A. Robinson, Contact Person

CROGHAN. *St. Stephen's Cemetery Association, Inc.*, 6979 Belfort Rd., Croghan, 13327.
Tel: 315-346-6958; Fax: 315-346-1200; Email: cschnee3@twcny.rr.com. P.O. Box 38, Croghan, 13327. Rev. Donald J. Manfred, Contact Person

MALONE. *St. Joseph's Cemetery of Malone, N.Y., Inc.*, Fort Covington St., Malone, 12953.
Tel: 518-483-1300; Fax: 518-483-1307; Email: office@standres.org; Web: www.standres.org. P.O. Box 547, Malone, 12953. Rev. Joseph W. Giroux, Contact Person

Notre Dame Cemetery of Malone, N.Y., Inc., 306 W. Main St., Malone, 12953. Tel: 518-483-1300;
Fax: 518-483-1307; Email: office@standres.org; Web: www.standres.org. Mailing Address: P.O. Box 547, Malone, 12953. Rev. Joseph W. Giroux, Contact Person

PLATTSBURGH. *Mount Carmel Cemetery*, 1202-1204 Cumberland Head Rd., Plattsburgh, 12901.
Tel: 518-563-0730; Fax: 518-563-0754; Email: office@broadstreetcatholis.org. Mailing Address: St. John the Baptist Church, 7 Margaret St., Plattsburgh, 12901. Rev. Timothy Canaan, Contact Person

WATERTOWN. *Calvary Cemetery Association of Watertown, N.Y.*, 320 W. Lynde St., Watertown, 13601. Tel: 315-782-1474; Fax: 315-782-4939; Email: jonas.tandayu@gmail.com. Rev. Jonas Raphael Tandayu, M.S.C., Contact Person

[F] MISCELLANEOUS LISTINGS

OGDENSBURG. *St. Joseph's Foundation, Inc.*, 950 Linden St., 13669. Tel: 315-394-0463;
Fax: 315-393-3847; Email: csteele@stjh.org; Web: www.stjh.org. Colleen Steele, Admin. Bed Capacity 84.

The Pontifical Mission Societies of the Diocese of Ogdensburg, New York, Inc., 622 Washington St., P.O. Box 369, 13669. Tel: 315-393-2920;
Fax: 866-314-7296; Email: mryan@rcdony.org; Web: www.rcdony.org/missionoffice. Sr. Mary Ellen Brett, S.S.J., Dir.

CHAUMONT. *Mission Project Service*, 27396 Madison St., P.O. Box 100, Chaumont, 13622.
Tel: 315-300-4233; Email: misprojser2@gmail.com; Web: www.missionprojectservice.org. Rev. Pierre Aubin, M.S.C., Dir.; Beverly Hennigan, Volunteer.

HOGANSBURG. ST. REGIS MISSION (Akwesasne) Reservation and parish on both sides of U.S.-Canadian border P.O. Box 429, Hogansburg, 13655. Tel: 613-575-2066; Email: st.regis.1752@gmail.com; Web: www.stregismission.org. Rev. Jerome Bose Pastores; Sr. Mary Christine Taylor, Pastoral Assoc. Priests 1.

Roman Catholic Community Center, Inc. (Kateri Tekakwitha Center), 597 State Route 37, Hogansburg, 13655. Tel: 518-358-2680; Email: st.regis.1752@gmail.com.
Dr. Rosealma McDonald, D.R.E.; Vicki Phillips, C.R.E.

LAKE PLACID. *Mercy Care for the Adirondacks, Inc.*, 185 Old Military Rd., Lake Placid, 12946.
Tel: 518-523-5580; Fax: 518-523-5449; Email: dbeal@adkmercy.org; Web: www.adkmercy.org. Donna Beal, Exec. Dir., Email: dbeal@adkmercy.org.

SARANAC LAKE. *Guggenheim Center for Religious Programs*, 1468 County Rte. 18, P.O. Box 664, Saranac Lake, 12983. Tel: 518-891-0809 (Lodge);
Tel: 518-891-3323 (Dorm); Email: bennett5@roadrunner.com. Mr. Ralph Bennett, Dir., Tel: 518-327-3545.

WATERTOWN. *Sacred Heart Foundation* (1967) 668 Thompson St., Watertown, 13601.
Tel: 315-782-3344; Email: mail@sacredheartfoundation.com; Web: www.sacredheartfoundation.com. Sabrina Rizzo, Business Mgr.

The Federation of Sisters of the Precious Blood, Inc. (1969) 400 Pratt St., Watertown, 13601.
Tel: 315-788-1669; Fax: 315-779-9046; Email: srm1@twcny.rr.com; Email: smarilyn@twcny.rr.com. Sisters Marilyn McGillan, A.P.B., Supr.; Joan Milot, A.P.B., Pres. Sisters 36.

RELIGIOUS INSTITUTES OF MEN REPRESENTED IN THE DIOCESE

For further details refer to the corresponding bracketed number in the Religious Institutes of Men or Women section.

[0320]—*Brothers of Christian Instruction* (Alfred, ME)—F.I.C.
[0530]—*Franciscan Friars of the Atonement* (Saranac Lake, NY)—S.A.
[1110]—*Missionaries of the Sacred Heart* (Watertown, NY)—M.S.C.

RELIGIOUS INSTITUTES OF WOMEN REPRESENTED IN THE DIOCESE

[]—*Congregation of the Sisters of the Cross of Chavanod, India* (Watertown, NY).

[0750]—*Daughters of the Charity of the Sacred Heart of Jesus* (Plattsburgh, NY)—F.C.S.C.J.
[1070-03]—*Dominican Sisters*—O.P.
[1105]—*Dominican Sisters of Hope* (Plattsburgh, NY)—O.P.
[1190]—*Franciscan Sisters of the Atonement* (Lisbon, Morrisonville, NY)—S.A.
[2575]—*Institute of the Sisters of Mercy of the Americas* (New York, Lake Placid, Plattsburgh, Saranac Lake, Watertown, NY)—R.S.M.
[3580]—*Servants of Mary (Servite Sisters)* (Massena, NY)—O.S.M.
[0110]—*Sisters of the Precious Blood* (Watertown, NY)—A.P.B.
[0620]—*Sisters of Charity of St. Louis* (Plattsburgh, NY)—S.C.S.L.
[3830-12]—*Sisters of St. Joseph of Watertown* (Bombay, Carthage, Copenhagen, Hammond, Lake Clear, Massena, Ogdensburg, Plattsburgh, Ticonderoga, Watertown, NY)—S.S.J.
[4110]—*Ursuline Nuns*—O.S.U.

An asterisk (*) denotes an organization that has established tax-exempt status directly with the IRS and is not covered by the USCCB Group Ruling.

Archdiocese of Oklahoma City

(Archidioecesis Oklahomapolitana)

Most Reverend

PAUL S. COAKLEY

Archbishop of Oklahoma City; ordained May 21, 1983; appointed Bishop of Salina October 21, 2004; installed December 28, 2004; appointed Archbishop of Oklahoma City December 16, 2010; installed February 11, 2011. *Catholic Pastoral Center: 7501 Northwest Expwy., P.O. Box 32180, Oklahoma City, OK 73123.*

Catholic Pastoral Center: 7501 Northwest Expwy., P.O. Box 32180, Oklahoma City, OK 73123. Tel: 405-721-5651; Fax: 405-721-5210.

Most Reverend

EUSEBIUS J. BELTRAN, D.D.

Archbishop Emeritus of Oklahoma City; ordained May 14, 1960; appointed Bishop of Tulsa February 28, 1978; installed April 20, 1978; appointed Archbishop of Oklahoma City November 24, 1992; installed January 22, 1993; retired December 16, 2010. *Res.: P.O. Box 32180, Oklahoma City, OK 73123.*

ESTABLISHED FEBRUARY 6, 1973.

Square Miles 42,470.

Erected into a Vicariate Apostolic by Brief of May 29, 1891. Erected into the Diocese of Oklahoma with the See in Oklahoma City by a Brief of Pope Pius X, August 17, 1905. Name changed to Diocese of Oklahoma City and Tulsa by Bull of Pope Pius XI, November 14, 1930. Erected into Archdiocese of Oklahoma City by a Bull of Pope Paul VI, December 13, 1972. The Province includes the Dioceses of Tulsa and Little Rock.

Comprises the following 46 Counties: Alfalfa, Beaver, Beckham, Blaine, Caddo, Canadian, Carter, Cimarron, Cleveland, Comanche, Cotton, Custer, Dewey, Ellis, Garfield, Garvin, Grady, Grant, Greer, Harmon, Harper, Jackson, Jefferson, Johnston, Kay, Kingfisher, Kiowa, Lincoln, Logan, Love, McClain, Major, Marshall, Murray, Noble, Oklahoma, Pontotoc, Pottawatomie, Roger Mills, Seminole, Stephens, Texas, Tillman, Washita, Woods and Woodward.

For legal titles of parishes and archdiocesan institutions, consult the Pastoral Office.

STATISTICAL OVERVIEW

Personnel	
Archbishops	1
Retired Archbishops	1
Abbots	1
Retired Abbots	2
Priests: Diocesan Active in Diocese	52
Priests: Retired, Sick or Absent	20
Number of Diocesan Priests	72
Religious Priests in Diocese	26
Total Priests in Diocese	98
Extern Priests in Diocese	28
Ordinations:	
Diocesan Priests	1
Transitional Deacons	5
Permanent Deacons in Diocese	110
Total Brothers	8
Total Sisters	69
Parishes	
Parishes	63
With Resident Pastor:	
Resident Diocesan Priests	58
Resident Religious Priests	5
Without Resident Pastor:	
Administered by Priests	1
Missions	46
Closed Parishes	1
Professional Ministry Personnel:	
Brothers	2
Sisters	17
Lay Ministers	107
Welfare	
Catholic Hospitals	13
Total Assisted	984,984
Homes for the Aged	9
Total Assisted	588
Specialized Homes	1
Total Assisted	70
Educational	
High Schools, Diocesan and Parish	3
Total Students	1,215
Elementary Schools, Diocesan and Parish	19
Total Students	3,826
Non-residential Schools for the Disabled	1
Total Students	31
Catechesis/Religious Education:	
High School Students	3,800
Elementary Students	10,200
Total Students under Catholic Instruction	19,072
Teachers in the Diocese:	
Sisters	2
Lay Teachers	523
Vital Statistics	
Receptions into the Church:	
Infant Baptism Totals	2,114
Minor Baptism Totals	328
Adult Baptism Totals	289
Received into Full Communion	490
First Communions	2,595
Confirmations	1,838
Marriages:	
Catholic	455
Interfaith	160
Total Marriages	615
Deaths	796
Total Catholic Population	226,408
Total Population	2,830,103

Former Bishops—Rt. Rev. THEOPHILE MEERSCHAERT, D.D., ord. Dec. 23, 1871; appt. first Vicar-Apostolic of Indian Territory and Titular Bishop of Sidyma by Bulls of June 2, 1891; cons. in Natchez, Sept. 8, 1891; appt. first Bishop of Oklahoma, Aug. 23, 1905; made assistant at the pontifical throne, Nov. 30, 1916; died Feb. 21, 1924; Most Revs. FRANCIS C. KELLEY, D.D., LL.D., Ph.D., Litt.D., Bishop of Oklahoma City & Tulsa; ord. Aug. 24, 1893; appt. Bishop of Oklahoma, June 25, 1924; cons. Holy Name Cathedral, Chicago, IL, Oct. 2, 1924; died Feb. 1, 1948; EUGENE J. MCGUINNESS, D.D., Bishop of Oklahoma City & Tulsa; ord. May 22, 1915; cons. Bishop of Raleigh, Dec. 21, 1937; appt. Coadjutor, Oklahoma City and Tulsa "cum jure successionis," Nov. 11, 1944; installed Jan. 10, 1945; succeeded to the See, Feb. 1, 1948; died Dec. 27, 1957; VICTOR J. REED, D.D., Bishop of Oklahoma City & Tulsa; ord. Dec. 21, 1929; cons. March 5, 1958; died Sept. 8, 1971; JOHN R. QUINN, D.D., ord. July 19, 1953; appt. Auxiliary Bishop of San Diego and Titular Bishop of Thisiduo, Oct. 21, 1967; Episcopal ordination, Dec. 12, 1967; transferred to Oklahoma City and Tulsa, Nov. 18, 1971; appt. as Archbishop of the Archdiocese of Oklahoma City, Dec. 13, 1972; installed as Archbishop of Oklahoma City, Feb. 6, 1973; transferred to Archbishop of San Francisco, April 26, 1977; CHARLES A. SALATKA, D.D., ord. Feb. 24, 1945; appt. Titular Bishop of Cariana and Auxiliary of Grand Rapids Dec. 9, 1961; cons. March 6, 1962; appt. Bishop of Marquette Jan. 10, 1968; installed March 25, 1968; appt. Archbishop of Oklahoma City Sept. 27, 1977; installed Dec. 15, 1977; retired Nov. 24, 1992; died March 17, 2003; EUSEBIUS J. BELTRAN, ord. May 14, 1960; appt. Bishop of Tulsa Feb. 28, 1978; installed April 20, 1978; appt. Archbishop of Oklahoma City Nov. 24, 1992; installed Jan. 22, 1993; retired Dec. 16, 2010.

Moderator of the Curia and Vicar General—Rev. WILLIAM L. NOVAK, V.G., Mailing Address: 1901 N.W. 18th, Oklahoma City, 73106.

Regional Vicars—Region I-A South: Rev. JOHN R. METZINGER, 3214 N. Lake Ave., Oklahoma City, 73118. Region I-B South: Rev. ROBERT T. WOOD, Mailing Address: 3939 W. Tecumseh Rd., Norman, 73072. Region II-A North: Rev. TIMOTHY D. LUSCHEN, 5024 N. Grove, Oklahoma City, 73122. Region II-B North: Rev. JOSEPH PATRICK SCHWARZ, Mailing Address: 632 N. Kickapoo, Shawnee, 74801. Region III: Rev. THOMAS R. DOWDELL, 101 E St., S.W., Ardmore, 73401. Region IV: Rev. PHILIP M. SEETON, 1010 N.W. 82nd St., Lawton, 73505-4103. Region V: Rev. THOMAS S. PUDOTA, Mailing Address: P.O. Box 1295, Clinton, 73601. Region VI: Rev. MICHAEL WHEELAHAN, Mailing Address: P.O. Box 731, Guymon, 73942-0731. Region VII: Rev. JOSEPH M. IRWIN, 110 N. Madison, Enid, 73701. Region VIII: Rev. CARSON KRITTENBRINK, 408 S. 8th St., Ponca City, 74601-6414. Region IX: Rev. MARK MASON, 208 S. Evans, El Reno, 73036.

Catholic Pastoral Center—7501 Northwest Expwy., P.O. Box 32180, Oklahoma City, 73123. Tel: 405-721-5651; Fax: 405-721-5210. Office Hours: Mon.-Fri. 8:30-4:30.

Chancellor—MICHAEL A. SCAPERLANDA, Esq.

Vicar for Priests—Rev. JOSEPH M. IRWIN.

Archdiocesan Tribunal of Oklahoma City—Mailing Address: P.O. Box 32180, Oklahoma City, 73123. Tel: 405-721-5651.

Judicial Vicar—Rev. RICHARD D. STANSBERRY JR., M.A., M.Div., J.C.L.

Associate Judges—Rev. CHRISTOPHER T. BRASHEARS, J.C.L.; Sr. KATHRYN OLSEN, I.H.M., J.C.L.

Defenders of the Bond—Revs. FRANCIS T. NGUYEN, J.C.L.; JAMES A. GOINS, J.D.

Notaries—MRS. MARY MILLS; MS. CAROL DAVITO.

Interdiocesan Tribunal of Second Instance for the Province of Oklahoma City—Mailing Address: P.O. Box 32180, Oklahoma City, 73123. Tel: 405-721-5651.

Judicial Vicar—Rev. BILL H. PRUETT, J.C.L.

Judges—Rev. Msgr. SCOTT L. MARCZUK, J.C.L.; Rev. PIUS AJUNWA IWU, J.C.L.; MR. GEORGE RIGAZZI, J.C.L.

Defender of the Bond—Rev. PETER QUANG LE, J.C.L.

Notaries—MRS. EDITH MIRANDA; Rev. ANDREW HART; MRS. FRANCES GEISBAUER.

Consultors Archdiocesan—Revs. RAYMOND K.

ACKERMAN; TIMOTHY D. LUSCHEN; JOHN R. METZINGER; WILLIAM L. NOVAK, V.G.; JOACHIM SPEXARTH, O.S.B.

Council of Priests Archdiocesan—Revs. JOHN PETER SWAMINATHAN; GILBERTO MOYA HURTADO; THOMAS S. PUDOTA, Vice Chm.; OBY J. ZUNMAS; JOSEPH A. JACOBI; PETER JANDACZEK; RAYMOND K. ACKERMAN, Chm.; WILLIAM L. NOVAK, V.G., Moderator of the Curia & Vicar Gen.; BILL H. PRUETT, J.C.L.; SCOTT A. BOECKMAN; MARK E. MASON, Sec. & Treas.

Personnel Committee—Revs. SCOTT A. BOECKMAN; JOSEPH M. IRWIN; TIMOTHY D. LUSCHEN; WILLIAM L. NOVAK, V.G.; JOHN R. METZINGER; ROBERT T. WOOD.

Priests' Nurse—MS. MARY DIANE STELTENKAMP, R.N., Mailing Address: 7501 N.W. Expressway, P.O. Box 32180, Oklahoma City, 73123. Tel: 405-709-2731.

Archdiocesan Offices and Directors

Secretariat for Evangelization and Catechesis—P.O. Box 32180, Oklahoma City, 73123. Tel: 405-721-5651. JIM BECKMAN, Exec. Dir.

Office of Human Resources—NANCY LARGENT, Dir., P.O. Box 32180, Oklahoma City, 73123. Tel: 405-709-2721; Fax: 405-709-2808.

Secretariat for Stewardship and Development—MR. PETER DE KERATRY, Exec. Dir., 7501 N.W. Expwy., P.O. Box 32180, Oklahoma City, 73123. Tel: 405-709-7245.

Annual Catholic Appeal—MR. PETER DE KERATRY, Exec. Dir., 7501 N.W. Expwy., P.O. Box 32180, Oklahoma City, 73123. Tel: 405-709-7245.

Archdiocese of Oklahoma City Educational Trust Fund—Sr. CATHERINE POWERS, C.N.D., Dir., 7501 N.W. Expwy., P.O. Box 32180, Oklahoma City, 73123.

Catholic Charities of the Archdiocese of Oklahoma City, Inc.—MR. PATRICK J. RAGLOW, Exec. Dir., 1232 N. Classen Blvd., Oklahoma City, 73106. Tel: 405-523-3000; Fax: 405-523-3030.

Archdiocesan Finance Council—Most Rev. PAUL S. COAKLEY; Revs. RICHARD D. STANSBERRY JR., M.A., M.Div., J.C.L.; WILLIAM L. NOVAK, V.G., Ex Officio, Moderator of the Curia & Vicar Gen.; MR. MICHAEL MILLIGAN, Chm.; MR. STEVE BROWN; MR. JOE FLECKINGER; MR. RALPH FREDRICKSON; MR. GARY MCCLANAHAN; MRS. AMY SINE; MR. DAVID JOHNSON, CFO, Mailing Address: Business Office, P.O. Box 32180, Oklahoma City, 73123. Tel: 405-721-5651.

Building Committee—Mailing Address: P.O. Box 32180, Oklahoma City, 73123. Tel: 405-721-5651. Rev. WILLIAM L. NOVAK, V.G., Moderator of the Curia & Vicar Gen.

Catholic Foundation of Oklahoma, Inc.—7501 Northwest Expwy., P.O. Box 32180, Oklahoma City, 73123. Tel: 405-721-5651. NANCY KOONS, Exec. Dir.

Catholic Lawyers Guild—Mailing Address: P.O. Box 32180, Oklahoma City, 73123. MICHAEL A. SCAPERLANDA, Esq.

Catholic Physicians Guild—Rev. DANIEL MCCAFFREY, Chap., Mailing Address: P.O. Box 32180, Oklahoma City, 73123. Tel: 405-942-4084.

Catholic Social Services—MR. PATRICK J. RAGLOW, Exec. Dir., 1232 N. Classen Blvd., Oklahoma City, 73106. Tel: 405-523-3000; Fax: 405-523-3030.

American Indian Catholic Outreach—Deacon ROY DON CALLISON, Coord., Tel: 918-822-3255; Email: rcallison@archokc.org; Email: nativeamerican@archokc.org.

Communications, Archdiocesan Department of—MRS. DIANE CLAY, Dir. Communications, Mailing Address: P.O. Box 32180, Oklahoma City, 73123. Tel: 405-721-1810, Ext. 120; Tel: 405-721-5651.

Council of Catholic Women, Archdiocesan—Rev. BILL H. PRUETT, J.C.L.

Ecumenical and Interreligious Affairs, Office for Archdiocesan Dir.—Deacon WILLIAM W. GORDEN.

Catholic Schools, Office of—MRS. DIANE FLOYD, Supt., P.O. Box 32180, Oklahoma City, 73123. Tel: 405-709-2721; Tel: 405-721-5651.

Christian Leadership Development, Office of—P.O. Box 32180, Oklahoma City, 73123. Tel: 405-721-5651. JASON FUGIKAWA, Ph.D., Dir.

Parish Leadership Engagement, Office of—P.O. Box 32180, Oklahoma City, 73123. Tel: 405-709-2721. VACANT.

Clergy Education—Mailing Address: P.O. Box 32180, Oklahoma City, 73123. Tel: 405-721-5651.

Safe Environment Coordinator—Sr. CATHERINE POWERS, C.N.D., Mailing Address: Archdiocese of Oklahoma City, P.O. Box 32180, Oklahoma City, 73123. Tel: 405-709-2750; Fax: 405-721-5210.

Victim Assistance Coordinator—MRS. JENNIFER GOODRICH, Mailing Address: P.O. Box 32180, Oklahoma City, 73123. Tel: 405-721-5651, Ext. 150; Email: jgoodrich@archokc.org.

Marriage and Family Life Ministry, Office of—Mailing Address: P.O. Box 32180, Oklahoma City, 73123. Tel: 405-721-5651. ALEX SCHIMPF, Ph.D., Dir.

Blessed Stanley Rother Cause—Mailing Address: P.O. Box 32180, Oklahoma City, 73123. Tel: 405-721-5651. Deacon NORMAN MEJSTRIK, Dir.

Hispanic Ministry and Cultural Diversity, Office of—Mailing Address: P.O. Box 32180, Oklahoma City, 73123. Tel: 405-709-2751. PEDRO A. MORENO GARCIA, Dir.

Justice and Human Development, Commission for—VACANT.

Library—Mailing Address: P.O. Box 32180, Oklahoma City, 73123. Tel: 405-721-5651. ROSE MARY STORY, Librarian.

Master of Ceremonies—Revs. ROBERT T. WOOD; STEPHEN V. HAMILTON, S.T.L., Asst.

Newspaper—The Sooner Catholic *Mailing Address: P.O. Box 32180, Oklahoma City, 73123.* Tel: 405-721-1810, Ext. 120. MRS. DIANE CLAY, Editor, Email: dclay@archokc.org.

Permanent Diaconate—Mailing Address: P.O. Box 32180, Oklahoma City, 73123. Tel: 405-721-5651. Deacon NORMAN MEJSTRIK, Dir.

Priests' Medical Fund—Rev. WILLIAM L. NOVAK, V.G., Moderator of the Curia & Vicar Gen., Mailing Address: P.O. Box 32180, Oklahoma City, 73123. Tel: 405-721-5651.

Priests' Retirement Trust Fund—Most Rev. PAUL S. COAKLEY; Revs. EDWARD T. MENASCO, Mailing Address: 211 N. Cherokee St., Hennessey, 73742; MICHAEL L. CHAPMAN, B.A., (Retired), 317 N. Blackwelder, Oklahoma City, 73106.

Prison Ministry—Deacon JAMES E. SMITH, Coord.

Propagation of the Faith, Holy Childhood Assoc., Missionary Cooperation PlanVACANT, P.O. Box 32180, Oklahoma City, 73123. Tel: 405-721-5651.

Rural Life—VACANT.

Scouting—Rev. CHARLES R. MURPHY, B.S., M.Ed., M.Div., (Retired), P.O. Box 32180, Oklahoma City, 73123. Tel: 405-282-4239.

St. Ann's Home, Inc.—MRS. SANDRA WINFIELD, Interim Dir., 9400 St. Ann Dr., Oklahoma City, 73162. Tel: 405-728-7888.

St. Francis de Sales Seminary (Legal Title)—Most Rev. PAUL S. COAKLEY; MR. DAVID JOHNSON, Treas., Mailing Address: P.O. Box 32180, Oklahoma City, 73123.

Vocations and Seminarians—Revs. BRIAN E. BUETTNER, Dir. Vocations; JOSEPH M. IRWIN, Dir. Seminarians.

Worship and Spiritual Life, Office of—Rev. STEPHEN J. BIRD, Dir.

Youth, Young Adult and Campus Evangelization and Discipleship, Office of—Mailing Address: P.O. Box 32180, Oklahoma City, 73123. Tel: 405-709-2743; Tel: 405-721-5651. JOSEPH CIPRIANO, Dir.

CLERGY, PARISHES, MISSIONS AND PAROCHIAL SCHOOLS

OKLAHOMA CITY

(OKLAHOMA COUNTY)

1—CATHEDRAL OF OUR LADY OF PERPETUAL HELP (1919) [JC]
3214 Lake Ave., 73118. Tel: 405-525-2349; Email: mail@cathedralokc.org; Web: www.cathedralokc.org. Revs. John R. Metzinger; Thanh Van Nguyen; Deacons William Enos; De Forest W. Hearn.
School—Bishop John Carroll Cathedral School, 1100 N.W. 32, 73118. Mr. Tim McFadden, Prin. Clergy 2; Lay Teachers 15; Students 215.
Catechesis Religious Program—
Tel: 405-525-2349, Ext. 140. Students 296.

2—ST. ANDREW DUNG-LAC (1994) [JC] (Vietnamese)
3115 S. W. 59th St., 73189. Tel: 405-681-2665; Web: www.saintandrewdunglacokc.org. P.O. Box 891584, 73119. Rev. Gregory Nguyen; Deacons Ty V. Nguyen; Kha Nguyen; Ms. Hue Nguyen, Sec.
Catechesis Religious Program—Students 358.

3—ST. CHARLES BORROMEO (1954) [JC]
5024 N. Grove Ave., 73122. Tel: 405-789-2595; Email: secretary@stcharlesokc.org; Web: www.stcharlesokc.org. Revs. Timothy D. Luschen; Macario Martinez-Arjona; Deacons Chet Bartlett; Bill Gorden; Bill King; Marc LeWand; Thomas Phan.
School—St. Charles Borromeo School, (Grades PreK-8), 5000 N. Grove St., 73122. Tel: 405-789-0224; Fax: 405-789-3583; Email: office@scbokc.org. Mr. Todd Gungoll, Prin. Clergy 1; Lay Teachers 20; Students 164; Clergy / Religious Teachers 1.
Catechesis Religious Program—Students 784.

4—CHRIST THE KING (1949) [JC]
8005 Dorset Dr., 73120-4713. Tel: 405-842-1481; Fax: 405-843-0539; Email: jayne@ckokc.org; Web: www.ckokc.org. P.O. Box 20508, 73156-0508. Rev. Richard D. Stansberry Jr., M.A., M.Div., J.C.L.; Deacons Richard L. Boothe III; James E. Smith.
Rectory—1900 Elmhurst Ave., 73120.
Tel: 405-841-6680.
School—Christ the King School, 1905 Elmhurst, 73120-4719. Tel: 405-843-3909; Fax: 405-843-6519; Email: helen@ckokc.org; Web: www.ckschool.com. Mrs. Amy Feighny, Interim Elementary Prin. Clergy 1; Lay Teachers 50; Students 525; Clergy / Religious Teachers 1.
Catechesis Religious Program—Email: jenni@ckokc.org. Mrs. Jennifer Butch, D.R.E. Students 260.

5—CHURCH OF THE EPIPHANY OF THE LORD (1976)
7336 W. Britton Rd., 73132. Tel: 405-722-2110; Fax: 405-722-6719; Email: epiphany@epiphanyokc.com; Web: www.EpiphanyOKC.com. Revs. Stephen J. Bird; Prabhakar Kalivela; Deacons Richard Fahy, Tel: 405-722-2110; Robert Heskamp, Tel: 405-722-2110; Jenny Fenner, Pastoral Assoc., Tel: 405-722-2110, Ext. 123; Mrs. Judy Reilly, Pastoral Assoc., Tel: 405-722-2110, Ext. 125; Bob Waldrop, Music Min., Tel: 405-722-2110, Ext. 115; Tracy Russo, Youth Min.
Catechesis Religious Program—Tel: 405-722-0051; Email: redirector@epiphanyokc.com. Mrs. Mandy Brown, D.R.E.; Tracy Russo, Youth Min. Students 282.

6—CORPUS CHRISTI (1924) [JC] (African American), See separate listing.
1616 N. Kelley Ave., 73117. Tel: 405-236-4301; Fax: 405-235-2122; Email: corpuschristichurch@cox.net; Web: corpuschristichurchok.org. Mailing Address: 1005 N.E. 15th St., 73117. Rev. Daniel G. Grover; Mr. Benton Jones, Business Mgr.; Ms. Sarah Merchant, D.R.E.
Mission—St. Robert Bellarmine, 121 N.W. 1st St., P.O. Box 280, Jones, 73049. Tel: 405-399-1727.

7—ST. EUGENE'S (1958) [JC]
2400 W. Hefner Rd., 73120.
Tel: 405-751-7115, Ext. 113; Email: MANAGER@STEUGENES.ORG; Web: www.steugenes.org. Revs. Donald J. Wolf; John J. Mejia Munoz; John Peter Swaminathan; Deacons Adolfo Aleman; Robert Blakely; Terrence Givens; Thomas O. Goldsworthy.
Res.: 10716 Greystone Ave., 73120.
School—St. Eugene's School, 2400 W. Hefner Rd., 73156. Tel: 405-751-0067; Email: principal@steugeneschool.org; Web: www.steugeneschool.org. Ms. Molly Goldsworthy, Prin. Clergy 4; Lay Teachers 28; Students 310.
Catechesis Religious Program—Students 664.

8—ST. FRANCIS OF ASSISI (1925) [JC]
1901 N.W. 18th St., 73106. Revs. William L. Novak, V.G.; Linh N. Bui; Ms. Jill Jacoby, Business Mgr,; Mr. Akvez Barkoskie IV, Music Min.; Ms. Lynn Cochran, Sec.
School—Rosary Catholic School, 1919 N.W. 18th St., 73106. Tel: 405-525-9272; Fax: 405-525-5643; Email: principal@rosaryschool.com; Web: www.rosaryschool.com. Mrs. Christy Harris, Prin. Lay Teachers 28; Students 240.
Catechesis Religious Program—Email: teresa-schumacher@att.net. Teresa Schumacher, D.R.E. Students 161.

9—HOLY ANGELS (1924) [JC] (Hispanic)
317 N. Blackwelder St., 73106. Tel: 405-232-6572; Fax: 405-235-8334; Email: holyangelsokc@outlook.com; Web: www.holyangelsokc.org. Rev. Russell L. Hewes; Deacon Armando L. Cruz-Rodz; Sr. Maria Perez, Faith Formation Dir.; Mr. Jose Marull, Business Mgr.
Convent—Carmelite Missionaries of St. Teresa, 1522 N.W. Third St., 73106. Tel: 405-231-1935.
Catechesis Religious Program—Students 731.

10—IMMACULATE CONCEPTION (1892) Closed. For inquiries for parish records contact the chancery.

11—ST. JAMES THE GREATER (1954)
4201 S. McKinley, 73109. Tel: 405-636-6801; Email: office@stjamesokc.com; Web: www.stjames-catholic.org. Revs. Bill H. Pruett, J.C.L.; Cristobal De Loera; Deacons Marti Gulikers, Business Mgr.; Fernando Hernandez.
Res.: 4308 S. Blackwelder, 73119. Tel: 405-636-6802; Fax: 405-636-6807; Web: www.stjamesokc.com.
School—St. James the Greater School, 1224 S.W. 41st St., 73109. Tel: 405-636-6810;
Fax: 405-636-6818; Email: avazquez@stjames-catholic.org. Alicia Vazquez, Prin. Lay Teachers 15; Students 205.
Catechesis Religious Program—Tel: 405-636-6840. Students 510.

12—ST. JOSEPH (1889) [JC] (Old Cathedral)
307 N.W. 4th St., 73102. Tel: 405-235-4565; Email:

office@sjocokc.org. P.O. Box 408, 73101. Rev. M. Price Oswalt.
Catechesis Religious Program—Students 229.

13—KOREAN MARTYRS (1996) (Korean)
2600 S.W. 74th St., 73159. Tel: 405-681-6464. Rev. J. Sung Yi.
Res.: 7517 S. Linn Ave., 73159. Tel: 405-688-5585; Fax: 405-688-5586.
Catechesis Religious Program—Students 7.

14—OUR LADY OF MOUNT CARMEL AND ST. THERESE LITTLE FLOWER (1921) [JC]
Mailing Address: 1125 S. Walker Ave., 73109-1341. Tel: 405-235-2037; Fax: 405-235-7023; Email: lfcokc@gmail.com. Revs. Jorge L. Cabrera, O.C.D., Supr. & Pastor; Jesus Sancho, O.C.D., Vicar; John Suenram, O.C.D., In Res.
Catechesis Religious Program—Students 511.

15—ST. PATRICK CHURCH (1950)
2121 N. Portland, 73107. Tel: 405-946-4441; Email: info@stpatrickokc.com; Web: www.stpatrickokc.com. Rev. Thomas McSherry; Deacon Duane Fischer.
Catechesis Religious Program—Students 333.

16—SACRED HEART (1911) [JC]
2706 S. Shartel Ave., 73109. Tel: 405-634-2458; Email: parish@sacredheartokc.org; Web: Sacredheartokc.org. Revs. Gilberto Moya Hurtado; Jose Graciano Reyes; Miguel Ayuso.
School—Sacred Heart School, 2700 S. Shartel Ave., 73109. Tel: 405-634-5673; Fax: 405-634-7011; Email: principal@sacredheartokc.org; Web: www.sacredheartokc.org. Adriana Garza, Prin. Clergy 1; Lay Teachers 15; Students 194.
Catechesis Religious Program—Tel: 405-634-6448; Fax: 405-456-6015; Email: catequista@sacredheartokc.org. Liliana Duron, D.R.E.

OUTSIDE OKLAHOMA CITY

ADA, PONTOTOC CO., ST. JOSEPH (1902)
1300 E. Beverly St., Ada, 74820. Tel: 580-332-4811; Fax: 580-436-1226; Web: www.stjosephada.com. P.O. Box 1585, Ada, 74820. Rev. Aaron J. Foshee; Deacon Dennis D. Fine; Ms. Allison Krause, Dir. of Christian Formation; Ms. Laura Miller, Office Mgr.; Ms. Rosalina Aglialoro-Hoyle, Office Mgr.
Catechesis Religious Program—Students 120.
Mission—St. Francis Xavier, 1313 E. 7th St., Sulphur, Murray Co. 73086. Tel: 580-622-3070.

ALTUS, JACKSON CO., PRINCE OF PEACE (1964)
1500 Falcon Rd., Altus, 73521. Tel: 580-482-3363; Email: secretary@popaltus.org; Web: www.princeofpeacealtus.org. Rev. Cory D. Stanley; Deacon Eulis Mobley; Ms. Judy Cosway, Music Min.
Mission—St. Helen Church, 507 E. Highview, Frederick, 73542. Tel: 580-335-3298; Fax: 580-335-3953; Email: sthelenchurch@pldi.net.
Catechesis Religious Program—Email: dre@popaltus.org. Alice Newman, D.R.E.

ALVA, WOODS CO., SACRED HEART (1897) [CEM]
627 12th St., Alva, 73717. Tel: 580-327-0339; Email: office@sacredheartalva.org. Rev. Balraj Sagili Jesudas.
Missions—Our Mother of Mercy—1325 Main St., Waynoka, Woods Co. 73860.
St. Cornelius (1895) 404 S. Massachusetts, Cherokee, Alfalfa Co. 73728.
Catechesis Religious Program—Students 53.

ANADARKO, CADDO CO., ST. PATRICK'S (1892) [JC5] (Native American)
1115 W. Petree Rd., Box 628, Anadarko, 73005. Tel: 405-247-5255; Email: stpats@sbcglobal.net. Rev. Joseph Nettem.
Missions—Our Lady of the Most Holy Rosary—Binger.
St. Richard, Hwy. 9, Carnegie, Caddo Co. 73015.
Catechesis Religious Program—Students 52.

ARDMORE, CARTER CO., ST. MARY (1898) [CEM]
101 E St., S.W., Ardmore, 73401. Tel: 580-223-0231; Fax: 580-226-2129; Email: stmaryardmore@hotmail.com; Web: www.stmaryardmoreok.org. Rev. Kevin J. Ratterman; Deacon Juan Jimenez, Dir. Hispanic Min./ Parish Life; Ms. Natalia Fuentes, Sec.
Res.: 112 F St., S.W., Ardmore, 73401.
Catechesis Religious Program—Ms. Julie Hunnicutt, D.R.E. Students 270.

BETHANY, OKLAHOMA CO., LATIN MASS COMMUNITY, See separate listing. See St. Damien of Molokai Chapel, Edmond.

BLACKWELL, KAY CO., ST. JOSEPH'S (1901)
324 W. Bridge, P.O. Box 578, Blackwell, 74631. Tel: 580-363-0441. Rev. Benjamin Lwin.
Catechesis Religious Program—Tel: 580-363-0441; Fax: 580-363-0441. Students 19.

CHANDLER, LINCOLN CO., OUR LADY OF SORROWS (1894) [CEM]
409 Price Ave., Chandler, 74834. Tel: 405-258-1239; Email: olschandler@att.net; Web: www.ourladyofsorrowschandler.org. P.O. Box 543, Chandler, 74834. Rev. James J. Mickus.
Mission—St. Louis, Hwy. 99 & Eighth Ave., Stroud, Lincoln Co. 74079.
Catechesis Religious Program—Email: ourladyofsorrowsdre@gmail.com. Ann Grim, D.R.E. Students 42.

CHICKASHA, GRADY CO., HOLY NAME (1895) [CEM]
210 S. 7th St., Chickasha, 73018. Tel: 405-224-6068; Email: secretary@holynamechickasha.org; Web: www.holynamechickasha.org. P.O. Box 748, Chickasha, 73023. Rev. Michael Wheelahan.
Catechesis Religious Program—Tel: 405-224-6068; Fax: 405-224-0168. Rosa Munoz, D.R.E. Students 155.
Mission—St. Peter Church, E. Second & Quapah, Lindsay, Garvin Co. 73052.

CLINTON, CUSTER CO., ST. MARY'S (1944)
1218 Knox, P.O. Box 1295, Clinton, 73601. Tel: 580-323-0345; Email: k.hubbard@stmarysclintonok.org; Web: www.stmarysclintonok.org. Rev. Thomas S. Pudota; Kimber Hubbard, Office Mgr.
Mission—St. Anne, 522 E. 3rd, Cordell, Washita Co. 73632. Kimber Hubbard, Contact Person.
Catechesis Religious Program—Email: k.moreno@stmarysclintonok.org. Kristine Moreno, D.R.E. Students 253.

DEL CITY, OKLAHOMA CO., ST. PAUL, APOSTLE (1956) [JC]
3901 S. Sunnylane Rd., Del City, 73115. Fax: 405-677-4873; Email: stpaulch@coxinet.net; Web: stpaulscatholic.org. Rev. Joseph Sundar Raju Pudota; Deacon John J. Page; Ms. Darla Bralley, Exec.; Ms. Michelle Hill-Lile, Music Min.
Catechesis Religious Program—Email: kdanner@coxinet.net. Kristen Danner, D.R.E. Students 61.

DUNCAN, STEPHENS CO., ASSUMPTION (1902) [CEM]
711 W. Hickory Ave., Duncan, 73533. Tel: 580-255-0590; Email: pneal@assumptionduncanok.com; Web: www.AssumptionDuncanOK.com. Revs. Peter Jandaczek; Joseph David; Deacons James Conway; Manuel G. Garcia; Mark Gildon; Mrs. Maria Martinez, D.R.E.
Missions—Immaculate Conception—Fourth & Comanche, Marlow, Stephens Co. 73055. Tel: 580-658-2365.
St. Patrick Church, 3rd & Ohio, Walters, Cotton Co. 73572.
San Jose, 1117 Lincoln Ave., Ryan, Jefferson Co. 73565.
Catechesis Religious Program—Mrs. Maria Martinez, D.R.E. Students 130.

EDMOND, OKLAHOMA CO.

1—ST. DAMIEN OF MOLOKAI CHURCH (2010)
8455 N.W. 234th Sorghum Mill, Edmond, 73025. Tel: 405-330-9968; Email: leperpriestokc@gmail.com; Web: saintdamiens.org. Revs. Christopher Pelster, F.S.S.P., Chap.; Simon Zurita, F.S.S.P.
Catechesis Religious Program—Students 102.

2—ST. JOHN THE BAPTIST (1889)
900 S. Littler Ave., Edmond, 73034. Tel: 405-340-0691; Email: parish_office@stjohn-catholic.org; Web: www.stjohn-catholic.org. P.O. Box 510, Edmond, 73083-0510. Revs. Raymond K. Ackerman; Anthony Raj Ram; Jennifer Dolf, Business Mgr.; Marsha Hoegger, Office Mgr.; Amy Dennis, Dir. of Outreach.
School—St. Elizabeth Ann Seton School, 925 South Blvd., Edmond, 73034-4710. Tel: 405-348-5364; Fax: 405-340-9627; Email: seas@stjohn-catholic.org; Web: www.stelizabethedmond.org. Mrs. Laura Gallagher, Prin. Clergy 4; Lay Teachers 35; Students 360.
Catechesis Religious Program—Tel: 405-340-9871; Fax: 405-340-3260; Web: www.stjohn-catholic.org/re.htm. Students 757.

3—ST. MONICA (1993) [CEM]
2001 N. Western, Edmond, 73012. Tel: 405-359-2700; Fax: 405-341-0023; Email: stmonica@stmonica-edmond.org; Web: www.stmonica-edmond.org. Revs. Stephen V. Hamilton, S.T.L.; Balireddy Ponnapati.
Res.: 1121 N.W. 199th St., Edmond, 73012. Tel: 405-330-2699; Fax: 405-330-2699.
Catechesis Religious Program—Students 282.

EL RENO, CANADIAN CO., SACRED HEART (1890) [CEM]
208 S. Evans Ave., El Reno, 73036-3636. Tel: 405-262-1405; Email: pastor@sacredheartelreno.com; Web: www.sacredheartelreno.com. Rev. Lance A. Warren.
School—Sacred Heart School aka Sacred Heart Catholic School-El Reno, (Grades PreK-8), 210 S. Evans, El Reno, 73036. Tel: 405-262-2284; Fax: 405-262-3818; Email: sacredheart@coxinet.net. Shannon Statton, Prin. Lay Teachers 15; Students 156.
Catechesis Religious Program—Tel: 405-262-2273. Students 173.

ELGIN, COMANCHE CO., ST. ANN (1914) [CEM] (German)
8492 St. Hwy. 17, P.O. Box 10, Elgin, 73538. Tel: 580-492-5914; Email: stann@tds.net; Web: www.triparishok.com. Rev. Rayanna Narisetti; Ms. Karen Jacobi, Sec.
Missions—Our Lady of Perpetual Help—220 N. A St., Sterling, Comanche Co. 73567.
Mother of Sorrows, 521 E. Wallace, Apache, Caddo Co. 73006.
Catechesis Religious Program—Students 68.

ELK CITY, BECKHAM CO., ST. MATTHEW'S (1970) [CEM] [JC4] (German)
3001 E. Hwy. 66, Elk City, 73644-9607. Tel: 580-225-0066; Fax: 580-225-3522; Email: stmatthew@cableone.net; Web: www.stmatthew.weconnect.com. Rev. Philip Louis; Deacon Paul Albert; Kathy Noble, Music Min.; Mr. Tim Crowley, Maintenance Coord.; Ms. Joyce Twyman, Sec.
Res.: 2900 E. Highway 66, Elk City, 73644. Tel: 580-225-3980.
Mission—Queen of All Saints, 914 N. 5th St., Sayre, Beckham Co. 73662. Tel: 580-928-2385. Deacon Sherman McKaskle.
Catechesis Religious Program—Email: stmatthewre@outlook.com. Mr. Jacob Farni, D.R.E. Students 205.

ENID, GARFIELD CO.

1—ST. FRANCIS XAVIER (1893) [CEM] [JC]
110 N. Madison, Enid, 73701. Tel: 580-237-0812; Email: xavier_enid@yahoo.com; Web: www.stfrancisenid.com. P.O. Box 3527, Enid, 73702-3527. Revs. Mark E. Mason; Kelly Edwards; Deacons Anthony Crispo; Val Ross; Ms. Lillian Highfill, Sec.
School—St. Joseph Catholic School, (Grades PreK-5), 110 N. Madison, Enid, 73701. Tel: 580-242-4449; Email: school@stjosephschoolenid.com; Web: stjosephschoolenid.com. Wade Laffey, Prin. Clergy 2; Lay Teachers 12; Students 99.
Catechesis Religious Program—Ms. Miriam Day, D.R.E. Students 445.
Missions—St. Gregory the Great—1924 W. Willow Rd., Enid, Garfield Co. 73703. Tel: 580-233-4589; Fax: 580-233-4590; Email: stgregorys@sbcglobal.net.
St. Michael, [CEM] Goltry.

2—ST. GREGORY THE GREAT (1971) See separate listing. Now a mission of St. Francis Xavier, Enid.

GUTHRIE, LOGAN CO., ST. MARY'S (1889) [CEM]
411 N. Elm, Guthrie, 73044. Tel: 405-282-4239, Ext. 4; Email: office@stmaryguthrie.com; Web: www.stmaryguthrie.com. P.O. Box 1556, Guthrie, 73044. Rev. James A. Wickersham; Deacon James S. Fourcade.
Res.: 604 E. Warner Ave., Guthrie, 73044.
School—St. Mary's School, (Grades PreK-8), 502 E. Warner Ave., Guthrie, 73044. Tel: 405-282-2071; Fax: 405-282-2924; Email: principal@stmaryguthrie.com. Mrs. Jacque Cook, Prin. Lay Teachers 11; Students 148.
Mission—St. Margaret Mary, 700 N. Grand, Crescent, 73028. P.O. Box 632, Crescent, Logan Co. 73028.
Catechesis Religious Program—Tel: 405-282-4239, Ext. 5; Email: dniles@stmaryguthrie.com. Debra Niles, D.R.E. Students 30.

GUYMON, TEXAS CO., ST. PETER'S (1906) [CEM] (Hispanic)
1220 N. Quinn St., P.O. Box 731, Guymon, 73942. Tel: 580-338-7212; Email: sec@panhandlecatholic.org; Web: www.panhandlecatholic.org. Revs. Christopher T. Brashears, J.C.L.; John Paul Lewis, Parochial Vicar; Raul Sanchez, Parochial Vicar; Deacons Joe Cruz; Luis De La Garza; Simon Guerra; German Rodriguez; Charles F. Romero; Joel Salcedo.
Missions—St. Frances Cabrini—101 Ave. C, Beaver, Beaver Co. 73932.
Sacred Heart, 106 N. Albright, P.O. Box 468, Hooker, Texas Co. 73945.
Good Shepherd, S. Ellis at Second, P.O. Box 966, Boise City, Cimarron Co. 73933. Email: fmwheel54@gmail.com.

HARRAH, OKLAHOMA CO., ST. TERESA OF AVILA (1907) (Polish)
1576 Tim Holt Dr., Harrah, 73045. Tel: 405-454-2819; Email: staharray@gmail.com; Web: www.stteresaharrah.org. Rev. Prakash Madineni; Ms. Jocelyn Payne, Sec.
Catechesis Religious Program—Tel: 405-454-9440. Students 150.
Mission—Saint Vincent de Paul Church, 123 S. 9th St., McLoud, 74851. Tel: 405-964-5606; Fax: 405-964-5606; Email: stvincentmcloud@gmail.com.

HENNESSEY, KINGFISHER CO., ST. JOSEPH'S (1890) [CEM] (Hispanic)
211 N. Cherokee St., Hennessey, 73742. Tel: 405-853-2158; Email: stjoseph@pldi.net. Rev. Edward T. Menasco; Deacon Jeffrey Kelly.
Mission—St. Joseph, 101 First St., P.O. Box 117, Bison, Garfield Co. 73720.
Catechesis Religious Program—Tel: 405-853-2158. Students 105.

HITCHCOCK, BLAINE CO., SACRED HEART MISSION, Closed. For inquiries for parish records contact St. Anthony of Padua Church, Okeene.

KINGFISHER, KINGFISHER CO., SS. PETER AND PAUL (1896) [CEM]
309 S. Main, Kingfisher, 73750. Tel: 405-375-4581; Email: secretary@stspeterandpaul.org; Web: www.stspeterandpaul.org. Rev. Francis T. Nguyen, J.C.L.; Deacon Terrence R. Rice; Ms. Stacy Pine, Sec.
Res.: 410 S. 6th St., Kingfisher, 73750.
School—SS. Peter and Paul School, 309 S. Main, Kingfisher, 73750. Tel: 405-375-4616; Email: secretary@stspeterandpaul.org; Web: stspeterandpaul.org. Steven Lykes, Prin. Clergy 1; Lay Teachers 6; Students 65.
Catechesis Religious Program—Ms. Sandy Murray, D.R.E. Students 126.
Mission—St. Rose of Lima, 900 N. Clarence Nash Blvd., Watonga, Blaine Co. 73772.

KONAWA, POTTAWATOMIE CO., SACRED HEART (1876) [CEM]
47943 Abbey Rd., Konawa, 74849. Tel: 580-925-2145. Rev. Adrian Vorderlandwehr, O.S.B.
Mission—St. Mary, Wanette, Pottawatomie Co.
Catechesis Religious Program—Students 18.

LAWTON, COMANCHE CO.
1—BLESSED SACRAMENT (1902)
12 S.W. 7th St., Lawton, 73501. Tel: 580-355-2054; Fax: 580-355-2055; Email: office@lawtoncatholic.com; Email: secretary@lawtoncatholic.com; Web: www.lawtoncatholic.com. P.O. Box 2546, Lawton, 73502. Revs. Brian E. Buettner; Vic Luong, Parochial Vicar; Deacons Bill Adamson; Robert L. Quinnett Jr.
School—St. Mary's, (Grades PreK-8), 611 S.W. A Ave., Lawton, 73501. Tel: 580-355-5288; Fax: 580-355-4336; Email: knights@stmarys-ok.org; Web: www.stmarys-ok.org. Mr. Stan Melby, Prin. Lay Teachers 17; Students 125.
Catechesis Religious Program—Tel: 580-353-8182; Email: re@lawtoncatholic.com. Mrs. Alicia Brierton, D.R.E. Students 142.
2—HOLY FAMILY (1959) (Formerly St. Barbara)
1010 N.W. 82nd St., Lawton, 73505.
Tel: 580-536-6351; Fax: 580-536-6352; Email: mromaka@holyfamilylawton.org; Email: pseeton@holyfamilylawton.org; Web: www.holyfamilylawton.org. Rev. Philip M. Seeton; Deacons Michael J. Romaka, Admin.; David B. Bunch; Wuse Cara; Jim Coe, Email: jcoe@holyfamilylawton.org; James Hankins; Anthony Layton.
Catechesis Religious Program—Tel: 580-536-6355; Email: vgable@holyfamilylawton.org. Vicki Gable, D.R.E. Students 221.

LEXINGTON, CLEVELAND CO., ST. JOHN THE BAPTIST, Closed. For parish records contact Our Lady of Victory, Purcell.

LOYAL, KINGFISHER CO., ST. JOSEPH MISSION, Closed. For inquiries for parish records contact Sts. Peter & Paul Church, Kingfisher.

MADILL, MARSHALL CO., HOLY CROSS CHURCH (1948)
14 W. Francis St., Madill, 73446-3234.
Tel: 580-795-3721; Fax: 888-696-2593; Email: hcccmadill@hotmail.com; Web: www.holycrossmadill.org. P.O. Box 791, Madill, 73446-0791. Rev. Oby J. Zunmas.
Mission—Good Shepherd, 200 N.W. 8th, P.O. Box 127, Marietta, 73448. Tel: 580-276-9604.
Catechesis Religious Program—
Tel: 903-312-5956 (Good Shepherd); Email: robbieroberts0123@gmail.com (Holy Cross); Email: csteinbock.dre@yahoo.com (Good Shepherd). Roberta Roberts, D.R.E. (Holy Cross); Carol Steinbock, D.R.E. (Good Shepherd). Students 303.

MANGUM, GREER CO., SACRED HEART (1896)
409 N. Byers, Mangum, 73554. Tel: 580-782-2657; Tel: 580-782-3363; Fax: 580-782-3297; Email: choo.choo@sbcglobal.net. Mailing Address: P.O. Box 310, Mangum, 73554. Rev. Arokiasamy Andarias; Cathy Dock, Contact Person.
Missions—Sts. Peter and Paul—328 S. Randlett St., Hobart, Kiewa Co. 73651. Tel: 580-682-3011; Fax: 580-726-3486; Email: arudkins8@gmail.com; Web: www.stspeter-paul.com. Amy Rudkins, Contact Person.
Our Lady of Guadalupe, 524 E. Chestnut, Hollis, Harmon Co. 73550. Tel: 580-471-3087; Email: clark48luce44@outlook.com. Anna Maria Aguilar, Contact Person.
Catechesis Religious Program—Tel: 580-450-8451; Email: kgelnar@yahoo.com. Kathy Gelnar, D.R.E. Students 46.

MCLOUD, POTTOWATOMIE CO., ST. VINCENT DE PAUL (1904) Merged Now a mission of St. Teresa of Avila, Harrah.

MEDFORD, GRANT CO., ST. MARY'S (1940) [CEM 3]
214 W. Cherokee, Medford, 73759-0360.
Tel: 580-395-2148. P.O. Box 360, Medford, 73759-0360. Rev. Carl William Janocha.
Missions—St. Mary's Assumption—Main & Birch, Wakita, Grant Co. 73771.
St. Joseph's, S. Hwy. 81, Pond Creek, Grant Co. 73766.
Catechesis Religious Program—Tel: 580-395-2290; Fax: 580-395-2064. Students 26.

MIDWEST CITY, OKLAHOMA CO., ST. PHILIP NERI (Midwest City) (1946) [CEM]
1107 Felix Pl., Midwest City, 73110-5331.
Tel: 405-737-4476; Email: parish@stphilipnerimwc.org; Web: www.stphilipnerimwc.org. Rev. Timothy M. Fuller.
Rectory—301 Wilson Dr., Midwest City, 73110-5346. Email: frfuller@stphilipnerimwc.org.
School—St. Philip Neri School, 1121 Felix Pl., Midwest City, 73110-5331. Tel: 405-737-4496; Fax: 405-732-7823; Email: btener@spnok.org; Web: https://www.stphilipnerischool.com/. Mrs. Brenda Tener, Prin. Lay Teachers 16; Students 174.
Catechesis Religious Program—
Tel: 405-737-4476, Ext. 108; Email: dre@stphilipnerimwc.org. Laurann Donahue, D.R.E. Students 36.

MOORE, CLEVELAND CO., ST. ANDREW THE APOSTLE CATHOLIC CHURCH (1962) [CEM]
800 N.W. Fifth St., Moore, 73160. Tel: 405-799-3334; Web: www.standrewmoore.com. Rev. John W. Feehily; Deacons George Fombe; Clyde Grover; Angus Watford; Ms. Jane Mitchell, Admin. Asst.
Catechesis Religious Program—Tel: 405-754-5303; Email: mhochla@standrewmoore.com; Email: agrover@standrewmoore.com. Tomasita Tran, Children's Faith Formation Coord.; Dina Jones-Griggs, Youth Min.; Brooke Beasley, Youth Min. Students 254.

MUSTANG, CANADIAN CO., HOLY SPIRIT CATHOLIC CHURCH (1983)
1100 N. Sara Rd., P.O. Box 246, Mustang, 73064.
Tel: 405-376-9435; Email: parish@holyspiritmustang.org; Web: www.holyspiritmustang.org. Rev. Joseph A. Jacobi; Deacons Paul D. Lewis, Pastoral Assoc.; William A. Hough; Ms. Elizabeth Hough, Music Min.
Catechesis Religious Program—Tel: 405-376-5633; Email: aduty@holyspiritmustang.org. Annamarie Duty, D.R.E.; Ms. Geri Hough, D.R.E. Students 305.

NEWKIRK, KAY CO., ST. FRANCIS OF ASSISI (1894) See separate listing. Now a mission of Church of St. Mary, Ponca City.

NICOMA PARK, OKLAHOMA CO., OUR LADY OF FATIMA (1949) Closed. For inquiries for parish record contact St. Philip Neri, Midwest City.

NORMAN, CLEVELAND CO.
1—ST. JOSEPH'S (1896) [CEM]
421 E. Acres St., Norman, 73070. Tel: 405-321-8080; Fax: 405-321-4360; Email: randy.hearn@stjosephsok.org; Web: www.stjosephsok.org. P.O. Box 1227, Norman, 73071. Revs. Joseph M. Irwin; Thomas Nallapatti; Deacons Angelo A. Lombardo; Richard Montedoro; Larry Sousa.
Res.: 422 E. Tonhawa, P.O. Box 1227, Norman, 73070.
Church: 211 N. Porter, Norman, 73071.
Catechesis Religious Program—Students 425.
2—ST. MARK THE EVANGELIST (1991)
Mailing Address: 3939 W. Tecumseh Rd., Norman, 73072-1708. Tel: 405-366-7676; Fax: 405-366-7842; Web: www.saintmarknorman.org. Rev. Robert T. Wood; Deacon Charles L. Allen.
Res.: 3701 Castlerock Rd., Norman, 73072.
Tel: 405-701-2793.
Catechesis Religious Program—Students 250.
3—ST. THOMAS MORE UNIVERSITY PARISH (1979) [JC]
100 Stinson St., Norman, 73072. Tel: 405-321-0990; Fax: 405-321-0964; Email: stmuniversityparish@gmail.com; Web: stm-ou.org. Rev. James A. Goins, J.D.; Deacons Steve Lewis; John D. Pigott; Brigid Brink, Business Mgr.; Mr. Clint Hardesty, Campus Min.; Nolan Reilly, Music Min.; Cathy Irwin, D.R.E.
Res.: 1501 Lincoln Ave., Norman, 73072.

OKARCHE, KINGFISHER CO., HOLY TRINITY (1893) [CEM]
211 W. Missouri, Okarche, 73762-0185.
Tel: 405-263-7930; Email: info@holytrinityok.org; Web: www.holytrinityok.org. P.O. Box 185, Okarche, 73762-0185. Rev. Gerard MacAulay, Admin., (Retired); Deacon Max Schwarz.
School—Holy Trinity School, 2nd and Missouri, Box 485, Okarche, 73762. Tel: 405-263-4422; Fax: 405-263-9753; Email: lschaefer@holytrinityok.org; Email: slykes@holytrinityok.org. Steven Lykes, Prin. Lay Teachers 16; Students 96.
Catechesis Religious Program—Tel: 405-263-7475; Email: bgmueggenborg@gmail.com. Bonnye Mueggenborg, D.R.E. Students 99.
Mission—Immaculate Heart of Mary, 107 Freehome, Calumet, Canadian Co. 73014.

OKEENE, BLAINE CO., ST. ANTHONY'S (1901) [CEM]
211 S. 5th, Okeene, 73763. Tel: 580-822-3544. P.O. Box 767, Okeene, 73763. Rev. Jaroslaw P. Topolewski; Deacons Michael Buchanan; Paul Reinart.
Rectory—220 E. Grant, Okeene, 73763.
Tel: 580-822-3511.
Missions—St. Thomas—P.O. Box 624, Seiling, Dewey Co. 73663. Tel: 580-922-4376.
St. Ann, 424 S. 6th, P.O. Box 55, Fairview, Major Co. 73737. Tel: 580-227-2270.
Catechesis Religious Program—Tel: 580-822-3507. Students 25.

PAULS VALLEY, GARVIN CO., ST. CATHERINE OF SIENA (1949) [JC] See separate listing. Now a mission of Our Lady of Victory, Purcell.

PERRY, NOBLE CO., ST. ROSE OF LIMA (1893) [CEM]
421 9th St., Perry, 73077. Tel: 580-336-9300; Email: stroseperry@sbcglobal.net; Web: www.stroseperry.com. P.O. Box 603, Perry, 73077-0603. Rev. Bala Raju Pudota.
Mission—Sacred Heart, Broadway & Lowe, Billings, Noble Co. 74630.
Catechesis Religious Program—Students 37.

PONCA CITY, KAY CO., ST. MARY'S CATHOLIC CHURCH (1893) [CEM] [JC]
408 S. 8th St., Ponca City, 74601. Tel: 580-765-7794; Email: office@stmarypc.com; Web: www.stmarypc.com. Revs. Carson Krittenbrink; Deva Undralla; Deacon Richard Robinson
Legal Title: St. Mary's Catholic Church
School—St. Mary, 415 S. 7th, Ponca City, 74601.
Tel: 580-765-4387; Fax: 580-765-1352; Email: info@smsponcacity.org; Web: www.stmaryspsok.com. Marilyn Nash, Prin. Clergy 1; Lay Teachers 17; Students 121.
Catechesis Religious Program—Tel: 580-382-6010; Email: drestmarys@gmail.com. Bridgit Coleman, D.R.E. Students 158.
Mission—St. Francis of Assisi, 610 W 9th St., P.O. Box 11, Newkirk, 74647. Email: Father.Krittenbrink@gmail.com.

PRAGUE, LINCOLN CO., ST. WENCESLAUS, NATIONAL SHRINE OF THE INFANT JESUS OF PRAGUE (1899) [CEM] (Czech)
304 Jim Thorpe Blvd., Prague, 74864.
Tel: 405-567-3080; Email: infantofpragueshrine@gmail.com; Web: www.shrineofinfantjesus.com. P.O. Box 488, Prague, 74864. Rev. Long N. Phan.
Mission—St. Michael, 217 S. Koonce, P.O. Box 684, Meeker, Lincoln Co. 74855. Tel: 405-567-3404; Email: longphanngoc@yahoo.com.
Catechesis Religious Program—Students 27.

PURCELL, MCCLAIN CO., OUR LADY OF VICTORY (1886) [CEM] (Hispanic)
307 W. Jefferson St., Purcell, 73080.
Tel: 405-527-3077. P.O. Box 1280, Purcell, 73080. Revs. James Chamberlain, Admin.; Nerio A. Espinoza; Deacons Jose Ortiz; John Warren.
Catechesis Religious Program—Students 160.

SEMINOLE, SEMINOLE CO., IMMACULATE CONCEPTION (1928) See separate listing. Now a mission of St. Benedict, Shawnee.

SHAWNEE, POTTAWATOMIE CO., ST. BENEDICT (1895) [CEM]
632 N. Kickapoo, Shawnee, 74801. Tel: 405-275-0001 ; Email: parishoffice@stbenedictchurch.net; Web: www.stbenedictchurch.net. Revs. Joseph Patrick Schwarz; Balaswamy Mandagiri; Deacons David Schrupp; William T. Thurman; Roy Don Callison.
Catechesis Religious Program—Tel: 405-275-5399. Students 165.
Mission—Immaculate Conception, 811 W. Wrangler Blvd., P.O. Box 164, Seminole, 74818-0164. Tel: 405-382-3602; Fax: 405-382-3602.
Chapel—St. Joseph Chapel, 702 S. Seminole, Wewoka, 74884.

SULPHUR, MURRAY CO., ST. FRANCIS XAVIER (1974) See separate listing. Became a mission of St. Joseph, Ada.

TONKAWA, KAY CO., ST. JOSEPH'S (1909) [JC]
320 W. North St., P.O. Box 525, Tonkawa, 74653.
Tel: 580-628-2416; Fax: 580-761-6937; Email: stjosephtonkawa@att.net. Rev. Benjamin Lwin.
Res.: 315 W. Blackwell Ave., Blackwell, 74631-0578. Tel: 580-363-0441.
Catechesis Religious Program—Students 38.

UNION CITY, CANADIAN CO., ST. JOSEPH'S (1893) [CEM]
403 N. Kate Boevers St., P.O. Box 100, Union City, 73090. Tel: 405-483-5329; Email: lloydmenz@gmail.com. Rev. Lance A. Warren; Deacon Lloyd Menz, Pastoral Assoc.
Catechesis Religious Program—Tel: 405-381-2569. Ms. Kim Warren, D.R.E. Students 60.

WEATHERFORD, CUSTER CO., ST. EUGENE'S (1960) [CEM 3]
704 N. Bryan, Weatherford, 73096.
Tel: 580-772-3209; Email: ste_secretary@att.net. Rev. Christopher H. Tran; Deacon Joseph Dubey, (Retired).
Missions—Blessed Sacrament—520 N. Oklahoma, Thomas, Custer Co. 73669.
Sacred Heart, 204 N. Clark Ave., Hinton, Caddo Co. 73047.
Catechesis Religious Program—Students 24.

WOODWARD, WOODWARD CO., ST. PETER'S (1905) (German)
2020 Oklahoma Ave., Woodward, 73801.

Tel: 580-256-5305; Fax: 580-256-5840; Web: stpeternwok.org. Rev. Joseph H. Arledge.

Missions—Sacred Heart—301 N. Main, Mooreland, Woodward Co. 73852.

Holy Name, 600 S. Main, Shattuck, Ellis Co. 73858.

St. Joseph, 325 S.W. 2nd, Buffalo, Harper Co. 73834.

Catechesis Religious Program—Tel: 580-256-2966; Email: stpeterdre@sbcglobal.net. Mrs. Tamara Rosales, D.R.E. Students 179.

YUKON, CANADIAN CO., ST. JOHN NEPOMUK (1889) 600 Garth Brooks Blvd., Yukon, 73099. Tel: 405-354-2743; Fax: 405-354-2773; Web: www.sjnok.org. P.O. Box 850249, Yukon, 73085-0249. Revs. Rex A. Arnold; Joseph Duggempudi; Deacons Clifford W. Fitzmorris; John Teague.

School—St. John Nepomuk School, (Grades PreK-8), 600 Garth Brooks Blvd., Yukon, 73099. Tel: 405-354-2509; Fax: 405-354-8192; Email: principal@sjnok.org; Web: www.sjnok.org/school. Mrs. Natalie Johnson, Prin. Lay Teachers 18; Students 203.

Catechesis Religious Program—Email: dre@sjnok.org. Mariavis Fitzmorris, D.R.E. Students 306.

Special Assignment:

Revs.—

McCaffrey, Daniel, Natural Family Planning Outreach, 3366 N.W. Expressway, Bldg. D, #630, 73112

Menasco, Edward T., Diaconate Program, P.O. Box 32180, 73123

Ram, Anthony Raj., Chap., St. Anthony Hospital, 1000 N. Lee St., P.O. Box 205, 73101.

Absent on Sick Leave:

Rev.—

Grimes, Price D. Jr., P.O. Box 32180, 73123. Tel: 405-720-9871.

Retired:

Revs.—

Beckman, Richard J., (Retired)
Boyer, Thomas J., (Retired)
Chapman, Michael L., B.A., (Retired)
Gallatin, Paul H., (Retired)
Greiner, James A., (Retired)
Hoang, Dominic Hung, (Retired)
Leven, Marvin F., (Retired)
MacAulay, Gerard, (Retired)
Michalcka, John J., (Retired)
Moore, Wilbur E., (Retired)
Murphy, Charles R., B.S., M.Ed., M.Div., (Retired)
Roberson, Henry, (Retired)
Ross, Joseph R., (Retired), Tel:
Walters, Graham.

Permanent Deacons:

Adamson, Bill, (Retired)
Albert, Paul, St. Matthew, Elk City
Aleman, Adolfo, St. Eugene, Oklahoma City
Allen, Charles L., St. James, Oklahoma City
Bartlett, Chet, St. Charles Borromeo, Oklahoma City
Bawden, William, St. Eugene, Oklahoma City
Best, David, (Retired)
Biles, Thomas E., St. Ann, Elgin
Black, James, Tinker AFB, MWC
Blakely, Robert, St. Eugene, Oklahoma City
Boothe, Richard L. III, Christ the King, Oklahoma City
Buchanan, Michael, St. Anthony, Okeene
Bunch, David B., Holy Family, Lawton
Butler, Chestney, St. Mary, Ardmore
Callison, Roy Don, St. Benedict, Shawnee
Cara, Wuse, Holy Family, Lawton
Coe, James, Holy Family, Lawton
Collier, E. Charles, (Retired)
Conway, James, Immaculate Conception, Marlow
Crispo, Anthony, St. Francis Xavier, Enid
Cruz, Joseph M., St. Peter, Guymon
Cruz-Rodz, Armando L., Holy Angels, Oklahoma City
Cumby, Dunn, Corpus Christi, Oklahoma City
De La Garza, Luis, St. Peter, Guymon
Doherty, James, (Retired), St. John the Baptist, Edmond
Dubey, Joseph, (Retired), St. Eugene, Weatherford
Duclos, Edward, St. Joseph Old Cathedral, Oklahoma City
Enos, William, Our Lady's Cathedral, Oklahoma City
Fahy, Richard, Epiphany of the Lord, Oklahoma City
Fine, Dennis D., St. Joseph, Ada
Fischer, Duane, St. Patrick, Oklahoma City
Fitzmorris, Clifford W., St. John Nepomuk, Yukon
Fombe, George, St. Andrew, Moore
Forgue, Joseph, (Retired), St. Francis of Assisi, Oklahoma City
Forsythe, Roy L., St. John the Baptist, Edmond
Fourcade, James S., St. Mary, Guthrie
Frazier, Dennis, Hospital Pastoral Care, Oklahoma City
Gabrish, Patrick, (Retired), St. Joseph, Norman
Garcia, Manuel G., Assumption, Duncan
Gildon, Mark, Immaculate Conception, Marlow
Givens, Terrence, St. Eugene, Oklahoma City
Goldsworthy, Thomas O., St. Eugene, Oklahoma City
Gorden, William W., St. Charles, Oklahoma City
Grover, Clyde, St. Andrew, Moore
Guerra, Simon, St. Peter, Guymon
Gulikers, Marti, St. James, Oklahoma City
Hankins, James, Holy Family, Lawton
Harned, John, Christ the King, Oklahoma City
Hearn, De Forest W., Our Lady's Cathedral, Oklahoma City
Hearn, Randy, St. John the Baptist, Edmond
Hernandez, Fernando, St. James, Oklahoma City
Hernandez, Santos, (Retired)
Heskamp, Robert, Epiphany of the Lord, Oklahoma City
Highsmith, Robert, St. Mary, Ardmore
Hollier, J. Bernie, Corpus Christi, Oklahoma City
Hough, William A., Holy Spirit, Mustang
Jacobson, Byron R., St. Mark, Norman
Jimenez, Juan, St. Mary, Ardmore
Keene, James, Immaculate Conception Church, Oklahoma City
Kelly, Jeffrey, St. Joseph Church, Hennessey
Kenny, Philip, St. Peter, Woodward
King, William, St. Charles, Oklahoma City
Layton, Anthony, Holy Family, Lawton
Le, Anthony, Our Lady's Cathedral, Oklahoma City
Leal, George, Sacred Heart Church, Oklahoma City
LeWand, Mark, (Retired)
Lewis, Paul D., Holy Spirit, Mustang
Lewis, Steve, St. Thomas More, Norman
Lombardi, Daniel, St. John Nepomuk, Yukon
Lombardo, Angelo A., St. Joseph Church, Norman
Lopez, Alfonso, Holy Angels Church, Oklahoma City
Maldonado, Pedro, (Retired), St. Mary, Clinton
Maloney, Kevin, St. Francis Xavier, Enid
McKaskle, Sherman, Queen of All Saints, Sayre
Means, Gary, (Retired)
Mejstrik, Norman, St. Philip Neri, Midwest City
Menz, Lloyd, St. Joseph, Union City
Mobley, Eulis, Prince of Peace, Altus
Montedoro, Richard, St. Joseph, Norman
Nguyen, Kha, St. Andrew Dung Lac, Oklahoma City
Nguyen, Manh San, (Retired)
Nguyen, Ty V., St. Andrew Dung Lac, Oklahoma City
Ninh, Sang, (Retired)
Ontiveros, Santiago, St. Peter, Woodward
Orellana, Gus, Holy Cross, Madill
Ortiz, Jose, Our Lady of Victory, Purcell
Page, John J., St. Paul the Apostle, Del City
Painter, Richard, St. Philip, Midwest City
Pereira, Jorge, St. Monica, Edmond
Peterson, Gary, St. John the Baptist, Edmond
Phan, Thomas, St. Charles, Oklahoma City
Pigott, John, St. Thomas More, Norman
Quinnett, Robert L. Jr., Blessed Sacrament, Lawton
Rakosky, Gerald, (Retired)
Randolph, Alejandro, St. Joseph Old Cathedral, Oklahoma City
Reinart, Paul, St. Anthony, Okeene
Rice, Terrence R., Sts. Peter & Paul, Kingfisher
Robinson, Richard, St. Mary, Ponca City
Rodriguez, Emilio, St. Peter, Guymon
Romaka, Michael J., Holy Family, Lawton
Romero, Charles F., St. Peter, Guymon
Ross, Val, St. Francis Xavier, Enid
Salcedo, Cruz, St. Peter, Guymon
Schrupp, David, St. Benedict, Shawnee
Schwarz, Max, Holy Trinity, Okarche
Smith, James E., Christ the King, Oklahoma City
Sousa, Lawrence, St. Joseph, Norman
Teague, John, St. John Nepomuk, Yukon
Thibodeau, Richard R., St. Robert Bellermine, Jones
Thurman, William T., St. Benedict, Shawnee
Vance, Herbert Reeves, Chap., VA & OK Medical Complex
Warnke, Jim E., (Retired)
Warren, John, Our Lady of Victory Church, Purcell
Washko, Richard, (Retired)
Watford, Angus, St. Andrew, Moore
Willard, Jeff, St. Joseph, Norman
Wooden, Rusty, (Retired)
Young, James G., (Retired).

INSTITUTIONS LOCATED IN DIOCESE

[A] HIGH SCHOOLS, ARCHDIOCESAN

OKLAHOMA CITY. *Bishop McGuinness Catholic High School* (1950) (Coed) 801 N.W. 50th St., 73118. Tel: 405-842-6638; Fax: 405-848-9550; Email: advancement@bmchs.org; Web: bmchs.org. Mr. David Morton, Pres. & Prin.; Rev. Daniel G. Grover; Kelly Allen, Campus Min.; Ms. Anne Hathcoat, Admin.; Dr. Andrew Worthington, Admin.; Robert Epps Jr., Admin. Religious Teachers 1; Lay Teachers 70; Priest/Chaplain 1; Sisters 1; Students 704; Total Staff 100.

Cristo Rey Oklahoma City Catholic High School, 900 N. Portland, 73107. Tel: 405-945-9100; Email: info@CristoReyOKC.org; Email: admissions@CristoReyOKC.org; Web: www.CristoReyOKC.org. Renee Porter, Pres./CEO; R. Cody Yocom, Prin.; Regina Birchum, Work Study Dir.; Lauren Johnson, Admissions Dir. Religious Teachers 2; Lay Teachers 7; Students 123.

Mount St. Mary High School (1903) (Coed) 2801 S. Shartel Ave., 73109. Tel: 405-631-8865; Fax: 405-631-9209; Email: jstiles@mountstmary.org (LC); Web: mountstmary.org. Rev. Cristobal De Loera, Chap.; Mrs. Talita DeNegri, Prin.; Mr. Brian Boeckman, Chm., Rel. Studies Dept.; Miss. Krystle Pierce, Librarian. Sisters of Mercy of the Americas, Archdiocese of Oklahoma City. Lay Teachers 46; Priests 1; Students 388.

[B] ELEMENTARY SCHOOLS, ARCHDIOCESAN

OKLAHOMA CITY. *Good Shepherd Catholic School* aka Good Shepherd Catholic School at Mercy, 13404 N. Meridian, 73120. Tel: 405-752-2264; Fax: 405-752-4638; Email: gscs@goodshepherdcs.org. Diane Floyd, Supt., Schools; Patricia Filer, Dir., Princ. Special needs. Lay Teachers 37; Preschool 15; Students 31; Elementary Students 16.

NORMAN. *All Saints Catholic School, Inc.* (1996) (Grades PreK-8), 4001 36th Ave., N.W., Norman, 73072. Tel: 405-447-4600; Fax: 405-447-7227; Email: info@allsaintsnorman.org; Web: www.allsaintsnorman.org. Dana Wade, Prin.; Teryle Dionisio, Librarian. Lay Teachers 30; Students 395; Total Staff 40.

[C] GENERAL HOSPITALS

OKLAHOMA CITY. *St. Anthony Hospital* dba SSM Health St. Anthony Hospital, 1000 N. Lee St., P.O. Box 205, 73101. Tel: 405-272-7000; Fax: 405-272-6477; Email: ramona.carey@ssmhealth.com; Web: www.saintsok.com. Tammy Powell, Pres.; Rev. George Parackal, Chap. A member of SSM Health Care. Bed Capacity 773; Patients Asst Anual. 368,330; Tot Asst. Annually 356,778; Total Staff 3,309.

Bone and Joint Hospital at St. Anthony, 1111 N. Dewey, 73101. Tel: 405-979-8000; Fax: 405-979-8001; Email: ramona.carey@ssmhealth.com. Tammy Powell, Pres. A member of SSM Health Care. Bed Capacity 85; Patients Asst Anual. 7,649; Total Staff 226.

Saint Anthony South Hospital dba SSM Health Saint Anthony South Hospital, P.O. Box 205, 73101. Tel: 405-713-5751; Fax: 405-680-4149; Email: ramona.carey@ssmhealth.com. Tammy Powell, Pres. A member of SSM Health Care. Bed Capacity 126; Total Staff 200.

Mercy Hospital Oklahoma City, Inc. Owned and operated by Mercy Health Oklahoma Communities, Inc. 4300 W. Memorial Rd., 73120. Tel: 405-755-1515; Fax: 405-752-3811; Email: Marynell.Ploch@Mercy.Net; Web: www.mercy.net. Jim R. Gebhart, Pres. Bed Capacity 374; Priests 2; Sisters 2; Tot Asst. Annually 294,375; Total Staff 3,107.

ARDMORE. *Mercy Hospital Ardmore, Inc.*, 1011 14th Ave., N.W., Ardmore, 73401. Tel: 580-220-6611; Fax: 580-220-6580; Email: Marynell.Ploch@Mercy.Net; Web: www.mercy.net. Vi Le, Counsel. Bed Capacity 190; Sisters 1; Tot Asst. Annually 129,328; Total Staff 731.

EL RENO. *Mercy Hospital El Reno, Inc.*, 2115 Parkview Dr., El Reno, 73036. Tel: 405-262-2640; Fax: 405-422-2521; Email: Marynell.Ploch@Mercy.Net. Doug Danker, Pres. Tot Asst. Annually 24,916; Total Staff 109; Total Beds 48.

GUTHRIE. *Mercy Hospital Logan County, Inc.*, 200 S. Academy, Guthrie, 73044. Tel: 405-282-6700; Fax: 405-282-6790; Email: Marynell.Ploch@Mercy.Net; Web: www.mercy.net. Joshua Tucker, Admin. Bed Capacity 25; Tot Asst. Annually 37,936; Total Staff 165.

HEALDTON. *Mercy Hospital Healdton, Inc.*, 3462 Hospital Rd., Healdton, 73438. Tel: 580-229-0701; Fax: 580-229-0691; Email: Marynell.Ploch@Mercy.Net. Jeremy Jones, Admin. Bed Capacity 22; Total Staff 43; Total Assisted 9,200.

KINGFISHER. *Mercy Hospital Kingfisher, Inc.*, 1000 Kingfisher Hospital Dr., Kingfisher, 73750. Tel: 405-375-3141; Fax: 405-375-7997; Email:

Marynell.Ploch@Mercy.Net; Web: www.mercy.net. Brian Denton, Admin.

SHAWNEE. *St. Anthony Shawnee Hospital* dba SSM Health St. Anthony Shawnee Hospital, 1102 W. MacArthur St., Shawnee, 74804-1743.
Tel: 405-878-8110; Fax: 405-878-8101; Email: ramona.carey@ssmhealth.com. Charles Skillings, Pres., Tel: 405-878-8110; Fax: 405-878-8101. Bed Capacity 96; Tot Asst. Annually 124,363 Total Staff 771 Basic Info Changes Detected Organization Contact Info Data Identical People; Total Staff 771.

TISHOMINGO. *Mercy Hospital Tishomingo, Inc.*, 1000 S. Byrd St., Tishomingo, 73460. Tel: 580-371-2327; Fax: 580-371-2889; Email: Marynell.Ploch@Mercy.Net. Gary Sharum, Admin. Bed Capacity 25; Tot Asst. Annually 5,088; Total Staff 41.

WATONGA. *Mercy Hospital Watonga, Inc.*, 500 N. Clarence Nash Blvd., Watonga, 73772.
Tel: 580-623-7211; Fax: 580-623-7405; Email: Marynell.Ploch@Mercy.Net; Web: www.mercy.net. Bobby Stitt, Admin. Bed Capacity 25; Tot Asst. Annually 3,000; Total Staff 75.

[D] SPECIAL CARE FACILITIES

OKLAHOMA CITY. *St. Ann's Home, Inc.* (1950) 9400 St. Ann's Dr., 73162. Tel: 405-728-7888;
Fax: 405-728-1302; Email: administrator@stannshomeokc.com. Mrs. Barbie Harter, Admin. Bed Capacity 120; Priests 2; Sisters 2; Tot Asst. Annually 302; Total Staff 122; Total Assisted 110.

[E] ECUMENICAL CENTERS

OKLAHOMA CITY. *Catholic Pastoral Center*, 7501 Northwest Expwy., 73132. Tel: 405-721-5651;
Fax: 405-721-5210; Email: tmaxwell@archokc.org; Web: www.archokc.org. Mr. Thomas Maxwell, Dir. of Facility; Shari Conrady, Assoc. Dir. Used for Archdiocesan Chancery; ecumenical activities; retreat-meeting center for ecumenical and non-profit organizations; and retired priests' residence.

[F] HOMES FOR THE AGED

OKLAHOMA CITY. *Saint Ann Retirement Center, Inc.*, 7501 W. Britton Rd., 73132. Tel: 405-721-0747;
Fax: 405-721-0492; Email: djohnson@archokc.org. Mr. David J. Johnson, Business Mgr. Total Staff 59; Total Independent 130; Total Assisted 50.

Trinity Gardens Apartments, 1232 N. Classen Blvd., 73106. Tel: 405-523-3000; Fax: 405-523-3015; Email: praglow@ccaokc.org; Email: jmoon@ccaokc.org. Mr. Patrick J. Raglow, Sec.-Treas. 58 low income apartments for senior citizens. Tot Asst. Annually 62; Total Staff 2.

Catholic Charity, Catholic Charities, 3825 N.W. 19th St., 73107. Tel: 405-523-3000;
Fax: 405-523-3030; Email: jmoon@ccaokc.org; Web: www.catholiccharitiesok.org. Jane Moon, Contact Person. Residents 67; Tot Asst. Annually 70.

Villa Isenbart, Inc. (1970) c/o Catholic Charities, 1232 Classen Blvd., 73106. Tel: 405-523-3000;
Fax: 405-523-3015; Email: praglow@ccaokc.org; Email: jmoon@ccaokc.org; Web: ccaokc.org. Mr. Patrick J. Raglow. 40 Apartment Residences for Low-Income Elderly. Tot Asst. Annually 44; Total Staff 2.
3801 N.W. 19th St., 73107. Tel: 405-947-4143;
Fax: 405-947-4199. Mr. Patrick J. Raglow, Dir. Residents 46.

EL RENO. *Saint Katharine Drexel Retirement Center, Inc.*, 301 W. Wade, El Reno, 73036.
Tel: 405-262-2920 (Legal Counsel);
Fax: 405-295-1950; Email: director@skdelreno.org; Web: skdelreno.org. Kim Bowles, Exec. Bed Capacity 74; Tot Asst. Annually 80; Total Staff 50; Apartments 49; Specialized Care Rooms 16.

PONCA CITY. *St. Mary's Housing Foundation*, 408 S. 8th St., Ponca City, 74602. Tel: 580-765-7794;
Fax: 580-765-1327; Email: stmarysponcacity@sbcglobal.net. Rev. Carson Krittenbrink, Pres. Senior Citizens Residences 6.

Via Christi Village Ponca City, Inc. (1985) Subsidiary of Via Christi Villages Inc.; Senior Care, Subsidiary of Ascension Health. 1601 Academy Rd., Ponca City, 74604.
Tel: 580-762-0927; Fax: 580-762-0933; Email: william.otjen@ascension.org; Web: www.viachristi.org/villages. Will Otjen III, Dir. (Formerly The Retirement Community Devel. Corp.); Continuum of care for the aged. Bed Capacity 163; Residents 120; Total Staff 132; Long Term 68; Total Assisted 69.

[G] MONASTERIES AND RESIDENCES OF PRIESTS AND BROTHERS

OKLAHOMA CITY. *Monastery of Our Lady of Mount Carmel and Little Flower*, 1125 S. Walker Ave., 73109. Tel: 405-446-0937; Fax: 405-235-7023; Email: mariamc0217@yahoo.com.mx. 526 S.E. 10th St., 73109. Order of Discalced Carmelites (Oklahoma Province).Little Flower Clinic: Free medical service for the poor. Tot Asst. Annually 1,800.

SHAWNEE. *St. Gregory's Abbey* (1875) Order of St. Benedict, including University, Novitiate, and Mabee-Gerrer Museum of Art. 1900 W. MacArthur Dr., Shawnee, 74804. Tel: 405-878-5491;
Fax: 405-878-5189; Email: abbot@monksok.org; Web: www.monksok.org. Rt. Rev. Lawrence R. Stasyszen, O.S.B., S.T.D., Abbot; Very Rev. Boniface T. Copelin, O.S.B., Prior; Rev. Joachim Spexarth, O.S.B., Subprior; Rt. Revs. Martin Lugo, O.S.B., Novice Master; Adrian R. Vorderlandwehr, O.S.B., CPA, Treas., Email: adrian74864@yahoo.com; Revs. Nicholas K. Ast, O.S.B.; Charles J. Buckley, O.S.B., Ph.D.; Brendan J. Helbing, O.S.B.; Manuel Magallanes, O.S.B.; Eugene C. Marshall, O.S.B.; Patrick McCool, O.S.B.; Simeon Z. Spitz, O.S.B.; Paul J. Zahler, O.S.B., Ph.D.; Bros. Benet S. Exton, O.S.B.; Isidore D. Harden, O.S.B.; George A. Hubl, O.S.B.; Kevin E. McGuire, O.S.B.; Dominic J. Ramirez, O.S.B.; Andrew C. Raple, O.S.B.; Damian S. Whalen, O.S.B., Ph.D.; Peter M. Shults, O.S.B.
Benedictine Fathers of Sacred Heart Mission, Inc. Brothers 8; Priests 13. *Saint Gregory's Abbey Benefit Trust*, 1900 W. MacArthur St., Shawnee, 74804-2404. Tel: 405-878-5463; Fax: 405-878-5189; Email: abbot@monksok.org. Rt. Rev. Lawrence R. Stasyszen, O.S.B., S.T.D., Trustee & Contact Person; Rev. Joachim Spexarth, O.S.B., Trustee; Very Rev. Boniface T. Copelin, O.S.B., Trustee.

[H] CONVENTS AND RESIDENCES FOR SISTERS

OKLAHOMA CITY. *Carmelite Sisters of St. Therese of the Infant Jesus Motherhouse* (1917) 7501 W. Britton Rd., #140, 73132. Tel: 405-837-7068; Email: srbarbarajoseph@gmail.com; Web: www.oksister.com. Sr. Barbara Joseph Foley, C.S.T., Supr. Sisters in Community 13; Resident Sisters 12.

Medical Sisters of St. Joseph, Little Flower Province, c/o 7217 N.W. 121st. St., 73162. Tel: 405-721-4390; Fax: 405-721-4390; Email: oklittleflower@yahoo.com. Sisters Rosemilla Michael, Supr.; Sona Mathai, M.S.J. Sisters 4.

Sisters of Mercy of the Americas (1831) Retirement Center for Sisters of Mercy of Oklahoma. 4300 W. Memorial Rd., 73120. Tel: 405-755-1515;
Fax: 405-936-5498; Email: peggy.lindgren@mercy.net; Web: www.mercy.net. Ms. Peggy Lindgren, Coord. Sisters 11; Staff 13.

PIEDMONT. *Carmel of St. Joseph* (1939) 2370 Morgan Rd. N.E., Piedmont, 73078-9123. Tel: 405-373-1735 ; Fax: 405-373-1732; Email: dcn@okcarmel.org; Web: www.okcarmel.org. Sr. Donna Ross, O.C.D., Prioress. Discalced Carmelite Nuns (Cloistered). Sisters 9; Professed Sisters 9.

[I] CAMPUS MINISTRY & NEWMAN CENTERS

NORMAN. *Campus Ministry for the Archdiocese of Oklahoma City*, 100 E. Stinson, Norman, 73072.
Tel: 405-321-0990; Fax: 405-321-0964; Email: mscaperlanda@archokc.org. Rev. James A. Goins, J.D., Pastor & Dir.

East Central State University, 1300 E. Beverly St., P.O. Box 1585, Ada, 74820. Tel: 580-332-4811;
Fax: 580-436-1226; Email: st_joseph3933@sbcglobal.net. Rev. Russell L. Hewes.

Northwestern Oklahoma State College, 627 12th St., Alva, 73717. Tel: 580-327-0339; Fax: 580-327-0710 ; Email: office@sacredheartalva.org.

University of Science & Arts of Oklahoma, 1610 S 19th St, P.O. Box 748, Chickasha, 73023.
Tel: 405-224-6068; Fax: 405-224-0168; Email: rmunoz@holynamechickasha.org. Rosa Munoz, Dir. of Religious Education; Rev. Krupavara Prasad Rao.

University of Central Oklahoma, 321 E. Clegern, Edmond, 73034. Tel: 405-340-6300;
Fax: 405-340-5715; Email: erinsnow11@gmail.com. Rev. Raymond K. Ackerman.

Oklahoma Panhandle State University, 505 W. 2nd St., P.O. Box 277, Goodwell, 73942.
Tel: 580-338-7212; Fax: 580-338-8746; Email: stpeterguymon10@gmail.com. Rev. Michael Wheelahan.

Cameron University, 1010 N.W. 82nd, Lawton, 73506. Tel: 580-536-6351; Email: pseeton@holyfamilylawton.org; Web: holyfamilylawtonoffice.org. Rev. Philip M. Seeton.

Northern Oklahoma College, 320 W North St, P.O. Box 525, Tonkawa, 74653. Tel: 580-628-2416;
Tel: 580-765-7794; Fax: 580-531-2607; Email: father.krittenbrink@yahoo.com. Rev. Larok Obwona Martin, F.C., (Uganda).

Southwestern Oklahoma State University, 704 N. Bryan St., P.O. Box 407, Weatherford, 73096.
Tel: 580-772-3209; Fax: 580-772-3541; Email: ste_secretary@att.net. Rev. Christopher H. Tran.

[J] MISCELLANEOUS

OKLAHOMA CITY. *St. Anthony Hospital Foundation, Inc., Oklahoma City, Oklahoma* Member of SSM Health 601 N.W. 11 St., 73103. Tel: 405-272-7070;
Fax: 405-270-7607; Email: saintsfoundation@ssmhc.com; Web: www.givetosaints.com. Sherry Rhodes, Vice Pres.

Bishop McGuinness Catholic High School Building Trust (2003) 9211 Lake Hefner Pkwy. Ste. 200, 73120. Tel: 405-936-0990; Fax: 405-748-4111; Email: dgeason@telepath.com. Douglas G. Eason, Contact Person.

Catholic Conference of Oklahoma, 1232 N. Classen Blvd., 73106. Tel: 888-514-1135; Email: brett@okcatholic.org; Web: www.okcatholic.org. Brett Farley, Exec. Dir.

Catholic Schools Opportunity Scholarship Fund, Inc., 7501 N.W. Expwy., P.O. Box 32180, 73123.
Tel: 405-721-4115; Email: bsemtner@archokc.org. Nancy Koons, Dir.

Mercy Health Foundation of Oklahoma, 13321 N. Meridian Rd., Ste. 206, 73120. Tel: 405-486-8773;
Fax: 405-936-5790; Email: Marynell.Ploch@Mercy.Net. Vi Le, Reg Gen Counsel.

Mercy Health Foundation Oklahoma City, 13321 N. Meridian, Ste. 206, 73120. Tel: 405-486-8773;
Fax: 405-936-5790; Email: Marynell.Ploch@Mercy.Net. Vi Le, Reg Gen Counsel.

Sister BJ's Pantry, Inc., 7501 W. Britton Rd., #140, 73132. Email: srbarbarajoseph@gmail.com; Web: srbjpantry.com. Sr. Barbara Joseph Foley, C.S.T., Pres. & Contact Person. An apostolate of the Oklahoma Carmelite Sisters of St. Therese of the Infant Jesus, Oklahoma City, OK.

SSM Health Care of Oklahoma, Inc. (For staff listings please see St. Anthony Hospital located under General Hospitals) 1000 N. Lee, 73102.
Tel: 405-272-7000; Fax: 405-272-6477; Email: ramona.carey@ssmhealth.com. P.O. Box 205, 73101. Joe Hodges, Regl. Pres. Hospital Operations Oklahoma, 1000 N. Lee Ave., 73102. Tel: 405-272-7345; Fax: 405-272-6477.

The Catholic Benefits Association (2013) 695 Jerry St., Ste. 306, Castle Rock, CO 80104.
Tel: 303-688-3822; Email: dougwilson@catholicbenefitsassociation.org; Web: www.catholicbenefitsassociation.com. Mr. Douglas G. Wilson Jr., CEO.

ADA. *Mercy Health Foundation Ada*, 430 N. Monte Vista St., Ada, 74820. Tel: 314-628-3608; Email: Marynell.Ploch@Mercy.Net. Vi Le, Reg Gen Counsel.

Mercy Hospital Ada, Inc., 430 N. Monte Vista St., Ada, 74820. Tel: 580-332-2323; Fax: 580-421-6054; Email: Marynell.Ploch@Mercy.Net. Vi Le, Reg Gen Counsel.

ARDMORE. *Mercy Health Foundation, Ardmore*, 1011 Fourteenth Ave., N.W., Ardmore, 73401.
Tel: 580-220-6712; Fax: 580-220-6170; Email: andre.more@mercy.net. Vi Le, Counsel.

LAWTON. *Columbia Square, Inc.* dba Villanova Apartments, 1232 Classen Blvd., 73106.
Tel: 405-523-3000; Tel: 580-248-2550;
Fax: 580-248-3001; Email: praglow@ccaokc.org; Email: jmoon@ccaokc.org; Web: ccaokc.org. Mr. Patrick J. Raglow, Pres. Total Assisted 230.
305 N.W. 4th St., Lawton, 73507. Tel: 580-248-2550 ; Fax: 580-248-3001. Mr. Patrick J. Raglow, Sponsor.

OKARCHE. **Center of Family Love*, 635 W. Texas, P.O. 245, Okarche, 73762. Tel: 405-263-4658; Email: info@cflinc.org; Web: centeroffamilylove.org. Debbie Espinosa, Dir.

PRAGUE. *National Shrine of the Infant Jesus of Prague*, St. Wenceslaus Church, 304 Jim Thorpe Blvd., P.O. Box 488, Prague, 74864. Tel: 405-567-3080;
Fax: 405-567-0364; Email: infantofpragueshrine@gmail.com; Web: www.shrineofinfantjesus.com. Rev. Long N. Phan, Admin. Novena to the Infant Jesus of Prague takes place the 17th through 25th of each month. Pilgrimages take place on Sunday prior to the 25th of the month.

RELIGIOUS INSTITUTES OF MEN REPRESENTED IN THE ARCHDIOCESE

For further details refer to the corresponding bracketed number in the Religious Institutes of Men or Women section.

[0200]—*Benedictine Monks*—O.S.B.
[0260]—*Discalced Carmelite Friars* (Oklahoma Prov.)—O.C.D.
[0690]—*Jesuit Fathers* (Missouri Prov.)—S.J.

RELIGIOUS INSTITUTES OF WOMEN REPRESENTED IN THE ARCHDIOCESE

[0100]—*Adorers of the Blood of Christ*—A.S.C.
[0380]—*Carmelite Sisters of St. Therese of the Infant Jesus*—C.S.T.
[0390]—*Congregation of Missionary Carmelites of St. Therese* (Houston, TX)—C.M.S.T.
[0895]—*Daughters of Our Lady of the Holy Rosary* (New Orleans, LA)—F.M.S.R.

[0420]—*Discalced Carmelite Nuns*—O.C.D.
[1070-13]—*Dominican Sisters* (Adrian, MI)—O.P.
[1070-06]—*Dominican Sisters* (Newburgh, NY)—O.P.
[1070-03]—*Dominican Sisters* (Sinsinawa, WI)—O.P.
[1070]—*Dominican Sisters of Hope* (Ossining, NY)—O.P.
[1900]—*Eucharistic Missionaries of St. Theresa* (Mexico)—M.E.S.T.
[1415]—*Franciscan Sisters of Mary*—F.S.M.
[]—*Hermanas Catequistas Guadalupanas*—H.C.G.
[2500]—*Medical Sisters of St. Joseph*—M.S.J.
[1680]—*School Sisters of St. Francis*—S.S.S.F.
[2980]—*Sisters of Congregation de Notre Dame*—C.N.D.
[2575]—*Sisters of Mercy of the Americas*—R.S.M.
[3360]—*Sisters of Providence of St. Mary-of-the-Woods*—S.P.
[3840]—*Sisters of St. Joseph of Carondelet*—C.S.J.
[2150]—*Sisters, Servants of the Immaculate Heart of Mary*—I.H.M.

CEMETERIES

OKLAHOMA CITY. *Resurrection Memorial Cemetery, Inc.*, 7500 W. Britton Rd., 73132. Tel: 405-721-4191 ; Fax: 405-721-3238; Email: cristford@aol.com; Web: www.resurrectionmemorialcemetery.com. Brandon Seid, Dir.

NECROLOGY

† Hayden, Grove Renier, (Retired), Died Feb. 9, 2018
† Pupius, George, (Retired), Died Nov. 23, 2018

An asterisk (*) denotes an organization that has established tax-exempt status directly with the IRS and is not covered by the USCCB Group Ruling.

Archdiocese of Omaha

(Archidioecesis Omahensis)

Most Reverend

GEORGE J. LUCAS

Archbishop of Omaha; ordained on May 24, 1975; appointed Bishop of the Diocese of Springfield in Illinois on October 19, 1999; ordained a Bishop and installed December 14, 1999; appointed Archbishop of Omaha June 3, 2009; installed July 22, 2009. *Chancery Office: 100 N. 62nd St., Omaha, NE 68132-2795.*

Most Reverend

ELDEN FRANCIS CURTISS

Retired Archbishop of Omaha; ordained May 24, 1958; appointed Bishop of Helena March 4, 1976; consecrated April 28, 1976; appointed Archbishop of Omaha May 4, 1993; installed June 25, 1993; retired June 3, 2009. *Chancery Office: 100 N. 62nd St., Omaha, NE 68132-2795.*

GRACE AND MERCY

Chancery Office: 100 N. 62nd St., Omaha, NE 68132-2795. Tel: 402-558-3100; Fax: 402-558-3026.

Web: www.archomaha.org

Email: contact@archomaha.org

ESTABLISHED AS A VICARIATE-APOSTOLIC JANUARY 6, 1857.

Square Miles 14,051.

Erected a Diocese October 2, 1885; Archdiocese October 10, 1945.

Comprises the Counties of Boyd, Holt, Merrick, Nance, Boone, Antelope, Knox, Pierce, Madison, Platte, Colfax, Stanton, Wayne, Cedar, Dixon, Dakota, Thurston, Cuming, Dodge, Burt, Washington, Douglas and Sarpy in the State of Nebraska.

For legal titles of parishes and archdiocesan institutions, consult the Chancery Office.

STATISTICAL OVERVIEW

Personnel	
Archbishops	1
Retired Archbishops	1
Abbots	1
Retired Abbots	2
Priests: Diocesan Active in Diocese	125
Priests: Diocesan Active Outside Diocese	7
Priests: Retired, Sick or Absent	45
Number of Diocesan Priests	177
Religious Priests in Diocese	60
Total Priests in Diocese	237
Extern Priests in Diocese	13
Ordinations:	
Diocesan Priests	3
Transitional Deacons	1
Permanent Deacons in Diocese	239
Total Brothers	20
Total Sisters	243
Parishes	
Parishes	124
With Resident Pastor:	
Resident Diocesan Priests	87
Resident Religious Priests	2
Without Resident Pastor:	
Administered by Priests	33
Administered by Deacons	2
Missions	15
Closed Parishes	1
Professional Ministry Personnel:	
Brothers	1
Sisters	34
Lay Ministers	322
Welfare	
Catholic Hospitals	6
Total Assisted	318,947
Homes for the Aged	5
Total Assisted	358
Day Care Centers	17
Total Assisted	28,848
Specialized Homes	4
Total Assisted	3,820
Special Centers for Social Services	5
Total Assisted	59,525
Educational	
Diocesan Students in Other Seminaries	23
Total Seminarians	23
Colleges and Universities	2
Total Students	10,078
High Schools, Diocesan and Parish	12
Total Students	2,756
High Schools, Private	5
Total Students	2,643
Elementary Schools, Diocesan and Parish	43
Total Students	11,730
Elementary Schools, Private	10
Total Students	2,441
Non-residential Schools for the Disabled	2
Total Students	71
Catechesis/Religious Education:	
High School Students	2,529
Elementary Students	13,705
Total Students under Catholic Instruction	45,976
Teachers in the Diocese:	
Priests	27
Brothers	5
Sisters	9
Lay Teachers	1,363
Vital Statistics	
Receptions into the Church:	
Infant Baptism Totals	3,365
Minor Baptism Totals	314
Adult Baptism Totals	128
Received into Full Communion	551
First Communions	3,748
Confirmations	3,764
Marriages:	
Catholic	651
Interfaith	332
Total Marriages	983
Deaths	1,776
Total Catholic Population	240,184
Total Population	1,002,959

Former Bishops—Rt. Revs. JAMES O'GORMAN, O.C.S.O., D.D., ord. Dec. 21, 1843; Vicar-Apostolic and Titular Bishop of Raphanea; cons. May 8, 1859; died July 4, 1874; JAMES O'CONNOR, D.D., ord. March 25, 1848; Vicar-Apostolic and Titular Bishop of Dibona; cons. Aug. 20, 1876; appt. first Bishop of Omaha, Oct. 2, 1885; died May 27, 1890; RICHARD SCANNELL, D.D., ord. Feb. 26, 1871; cons. Bishop of Concordia, Nov. 30, 1887; transferred to Omaha, Jan. 30, 1891; died Jan. 8, 1916; Most Revs. JEREMIAH J. HARTY, D.D., ord. April 28, 1878; cons. Archbishop of Manila, P.I., Aug. 15, 1903; transferred to Omaha, May 16, 1916; died Oct. 29, 1927; FRANCIS J. L. BECKMAN, S.T.D., D.D., Bishop of Lincoln and Apostolic Administrator of Omaha from June 1, 1926 to July 4, 1928; JOSEPH FRANCIS RUMMEL, D.D., Bishop of Omaha; appt. March 30, 1928; cons. May 29, 1928; installed July 4, 1928; transferred to the Archdiocese of New Orleans, March 9, 1935; died Nov. 8, 1964; JAMES H. RYAN, D.D., appt. Titular Bishop of Modra, Aug. 15, 1933; cons. Oct. 25, 1933; transferred to See of Omaha, Aug. 3, 1935; installed Nov. 21, 1935; installed to Archepiscopal dignity, Oct. 10, 1945; died Nov. 23, 1947; GERALD T. BERGAN, D.D., ord. Oct. 28, 1915; appt. Bishop of Des Moines, March 24, 1934; cons. June 13, 1934; promoted to Omaha, Feb. 7, 1948; retired June 18, 1969; made Titular Archbishop of Tacarata; died July 12, 1972; DANIEL E. SHEEHAN, D.D., J.C.D., ord. May 23, 1942; appt. Titular Bishop of Capsu and Auxiliary, Jan. 4, 1964; cons. March 19, 1964; succeeded to See, June 11, 1969; retired May 14, 1992; died Oct. 24, 2000; ELDEN FRANCIS CURTISS, ord. May 24, 1958; appt. Bishop of Helena March 4, 1976; cons. April 28, 1976; appt. Archbishop of Omaha May 4, 1993; installed June 25, 1993; retired June 3, 2009.

Vicar General—Very Rev. MICHAEL W. GREWE, V.G.

Chancery Office—100 N. 62nd St., Omaha, 68132-2795. Tel: 402-558-3100; Fax: 402-558-3026; Email: contact@archomaha.org. Office Hours: Mon.-Fri. 8:30-5.

Chancellor—Deacon TIMOTHY F. MCNEIL, J.C.L.

Vice Chancellor—ELIZABETH A. SONDAG, J.C.L.

Finance Director (canonical)—MR. JAMES J. STOLZE.

Metropolitan Tribunal—100 N. 62nd St., Omaha, 68132.

Judicial Vicar and Vicar for Clergy—Very Rev. SCOTT A. HASTINGS, J.C.L., J.V.

Judges—Rev. RYAN P. LEWIS, J.C.L., S.T.L.; Deacons ROBERT J. OVERKAMP, J.C.L.; RONALD R. RYAN, J.C.L.; Rev. JOSEPH C. TAPHORN, J.C.L.; ELIZABETH A. SONDAG, J.C.L.

Promoter of Justice—Deacon TIMOTHY F. MCNEIL, J.C.L.

Defenders of the Bond—Revs. DALE M. NAU, J.C.L.; MICHAEL F. GUTGSELL, J.C.L.; JAMES R. DE ANDA, J.C.L.

Appeal Court—The Missouri Appellate Tribunal is the Appeal Court for Omaha.

College of Consultors—Very Rev. MICHAEL W. GREWE, V.G.; Revs. MARK T. BERAN; ROSS C. BURKHALTER; HAROLD J. BUSE; DANIEL J. KAMPSCHNEIDER; DAVID M. KORTH; JOSEPH C. TAPHORN, J.C.L.; DAMIAN J. ZUERLEIN.

Deans—Revs. DAVID G. REESON, Sub.S.; HAROLD J. BUSE, U.S.C.; DAVID M. KORTH, U.N.E.; THOMAS E. BAUWENS, U.W.C.; DAMIAN J. ZUERLEIN, U.S.E.; FRANK J. BAUMERT, Sub.N; JAMES E. KEITER, R.N.C.; ROSS C. BURKHALTER, R.S.W.; KEITH D. REZAC, R.S.E.; DANIEL R. ANDREWS, R.C.; BERNARD G. STARMAN, R.N.W.; ANDREW L. SOHM, R.N.E.

Finance Council—Most Rev. GEORGE J. LUCAS; Very Rev. MICHAEL W. GREWE, V.G.; MR. JAMES J. STOLZE; PAT LACY; MR. RICK WITT; Rev. DAMIAN J. ZUERLEIN; LARRY KRITENBRINK; JIM CZYZ; MICHAEL

LAWLER; BRETT FREVERT; Deacon TIMOTHY F. MCNEIL, J.C.L.

Archdiocesan Offices and Directors

Cemeteries—Very Rev. MICHAEL W. GREWE, V.G., Dir.

Censor Librorum—Rev. MATTHEW J. GUTOWSKI.

Omaha Priests Retirement Plan and Trust, The—Most Rev. GEORGE J. LUCAS; Revs. HAROLD J. BUSE; FRANK W. LORDEMANN, (Retired); STEVE PATTERSON; MR. JAMES KINEEN; MR. JAMES J. STOLZE; MICHAEL A. INTRIERI.

Ecumenical Officer—Rev. RYAN P. LEWIS, J.C.L., S.T.L.

Worship Office—Bro. WILLIAM J. WOEGER, F.S.C., Dir.

Council of Catholic Women, Archdiocesan—Rev. ANDREW L. SOHM, Spiritual Advisor, P.O. Box 898, Ponca, 68770. Tel: 402-755-2773.

Diaconate Program—Deacon JAMES KEATING, Ph.D., Dir., 100 N. 62nd St., Omaha, 68132. Tel: 402-558-3100.

Catholic Schools Office—Mercy Hall, 3300 N. 60th St., Omaha, 68104. Tel: 402-557-5600. MICHAEL W. ASHTON, Ed.D.

Office of Evangelization & Catechesis—Mercy Hall, 3300 N. 60th St., Omaha, 68104. JAMES M. JANSEN, M.T.S.

Administrative Services Office—MR. JAMES J. STOLZE, Dir., 100 N. 62nd St., Omaha, 68132. Tel: 402-558-3100; Fax: 402-561-1210.

Information Technology Office—MR. SHAWN M. BAAS, Dir., Nazareth Hall, 3300 N. 60th St., Omaha, 68104. Tel: 402-557-5500; Fax: 402-827-3793.

Stewardship & Development Office—SHANNAN BROMMER, Dir., Mercy Hall, 3300 N. 60th St., Omaha, 68104. Tel: 402-557-5650; Fax: 402-551-3426.

Center for Family Life Formation—Nazareth Hall, 3300 N. 60th St., Omaha, 68104. Tel: 402-551-9003; Tel: 888-800-8352; Fax: 402-551-3050; Email: flo@archomaha.org. CRAIG T. DYKE, Dir. Areas of Ministry. Areas of Ministry: Hispanic Marriage and Family Life, Marriage and Family Life, Courage & Encourage, Fertility Awareness, Respect Life Apostolate, Bereavement, Human Sexuality Formation, & Baptism Preparation.

Human Resources—Deacon STEPHEN J. LUNA, Dir., 100 N. 62nd St., Omaha, 68132. Tel: 402-558-3100; Fax: 402-558-3026.

Newspaper—The Catholic Voice *Mercy Hall, 3300 N. 60th St., Omaha, 68104.* Tel: 402-558-6611; Fax: 402-558-6614. DAN J. ROSSINI, Editor.

Pastoral Services—Nazareth Hall, 3300 N. 60th St., Omaha, 68104. Tel: 402-558-3100; Fax: 402-551-3050. Rev. JEFFREY P. LORIG, Dir.

Propagation of the FaithDeacon OMAR GUTIERREZ, Mgr., 100 N. 62nd St., Omaha, 68132. Tel: 402-558-3100; Fax: 402-551-4212.

Priests' Council—

Officers—Revs. RICHARD J. REISER, Pres.; ANDREW L. SOHM, Vice Pres.; GREGORY P. CARL, Sec.; DAMIAN J. ZUERLEIN, Treas.

Special Group Representatives—Revs. GREGORY P. CARL; GARY L. OSTRANDER, (Retired); DAMIEN WEE.

Religious Order Representative—Rev. THOMAS J. SHANAHAN, S.J.

Deans—Revs. HAROLD J. BUSE, (USC); DAMIAN J. ZUERLEIN, (USE); DAVID M. KORTH, (UNE); JAMES E. KEITER, (RNC); ROSS C. BURKHALTER, (RSW); BERNARD G. STARMAN, (R.N.W.); KEITH D. REZAC, (RSE); ANDREW L. SOHM, (RNE); DANIEL R. ANDREWS, (RC); DAVID G. REESON, (Sub. S.); FRANK J. BAUMERT, (Sub.N.); THOMAS E. BAUWENS, (UWC).

Archbishop's Appointee—Rev. MICHAEL P. ECKLEY.

Ex Officio—Very Revs. MICHAEL W. GREWE, V.G., Vicar Gen.; SCOTT A. HASTINGS, J.C.L., J.V., Vicar for Clergy; Rev. JEFFREY P. LORIG, Dir. Pastoral Svcs.

St. Cecilia Institute for Sacred Liturgy, Music and the Arts—Bro. WILLIAM J. WOEGER, F.S.C., Dir., 3900 Webster St., Omaha, 68131. Tel: 402-553-5524; Fax: 402-551-2306.

Omaha. Archdiocesan Deposit and Loan Fund, Inc.—A pool of funds from archdiocesan parishes providing low interest loans for capital improvements and new construction by archdiocesan parishes. This nonprofit religious, charitable and educational corporation, whose president is the Archdiocese of Omaha, is duly constituted under the laws of the State of Nebraska. MR. JAMES J. STOLZE, Finance Dir., 100 N. 62nd St., Omaha, 68132. Tel: 402-558-3100; Fax: 402-561-1210.

Omaha. Archdiocesan Retreat and Conference Center—Located in renovated Sheehan Center; overnight, day and weekend accommodations for teens, young adults and adult groups, large and small meeting space, chapel and food service area. *St. Joseph's Hall, 3330 N. 60th St., Omaha, 68104.* Tel: 402-558-1442; Fax: 402-551-1482. JO ANN M. EVON, Mgr.

Servant Minister—Rev. MICHAEL P. ECKLEY.

Victim Outreach and Prevention—MARY BETH HANUS, Mgr., Mercy Hall, 3300 N. 60th St., Omaha, 68104. Tel: 402-827-3798; Tel: 888-808-9055; Email: mbhanus@archomaha.org.

Vocations Office—Rev. ANDREW J. ROZA, 100 N. 62nd St., Omaha, 68132. Tel: 402-558-3100; Fax: 402-554-0783; Email: ajroza@archomaha.org; Web: www.archomaha.org/vocations.

CLERGY, PARISHES, MISSIONS AND PAROCHIAL SCHOOLS

CITY OF OMAHA

(DOUGLAS COUNTY)

1—ST. CECILIA CATHEDRAL (1888)
701 N. 40th St., 68131-1826. Tel: 402-551-2313; Email: stceciliacathedral@stceciliacathedral.org; Web: stceciliacathedral.org. Very Rev. Michael W. Grewe, V.G.; Revs. James M. Buckley; Jeffrey P. Lorig, In Res.; Deacon Jim Tardy, D.R.E.
School—St. Cecilia Cathedral School, (Grades PreK-8), 3869 Webster St, 68131-1826. Tel: 402-556-6655; Email: admin@stcecilia.net; Web: stcecilia.net. Lay Teachers 24; Students 330.
Catechesis Religious Program—St. Cecilia Faith Formation Program, Email: mwgrewe@archomaha.org. Students 150.

2—ST. ADALBERT (1919) Merged with Our Lady of Lourdes, Omaha to form Our Lady of Lourdes - St. Adalbert Church of Omaha.

3—ST. AGNES (1889) (Irish—Spanish), Merged with Our Lady of Guadalupe, Omaha to form Our Lady of Guadalupe - St. Agnes Parish, Omaha.

4—ST. ANDREW KIM TAEGON CATHOLIC COMMUNITY (2009)
2617 S. 31st St., 68105. Tel: 402-345-1621; Email: saewoh@yahoo.com; Web: ch.cathlic.or.kr/omaha. Rev. Paul Saewan Oh.

5—ST. ANN (1917) (Italian—Hispanic), Closed. For inquiries for parish records contact St. Peter, Omaha.

6—ST. ANTHONY (1907) (Lithuanian), Merged with with SS. Peter and Paul, Omaha. For inquiries for parish records please see SS. Peter and Paul, Omaha.

7—ASSUMPTION OF THE BLESSED VIRGIN MARY-OUR LADY OF GUADALUPE CHURCH OF OMAHA (2014)
4930 S. 23rd St., 68107. Tel: 402-731-2196; Email: office@assumptionguadalupechurch.org; Web: assumptionguadalupechurch.org. Revs. Carl J. Zoucha; Rafael R. Majano; Deacons Luis Valadez; Martin Franco; John J. Digilio.
Rectory—Our Lady of Guadalupe, 2310 "O" St., 68107. Tel: 402-731-2196.
Catechesis Religious Program—Email: mcervantes@archomaha.org; Tel: 402-731-2709. Marcela Cervantes, D.R.E. Students 654.

8—ASSUMPTION, B.V.M. (1894) (Czech), Merged with Our Lady of Guadalupe-St. Agnes Parish, Omaha to form Assumption of the Blessed Virgin Mary-Our Lady of Guadalupe Church Church of Omaha.

9—ST. BENEDICT THE MOOR (1919)
2423 Grant St., 68111. Tel: 402-348-0631; Email: stbenedictomaha@gmail.com. Rev. Vitalis E. Anyanike; Deacon Ernie Spicer; Mrs. Patricia Bass, Business Mgr.
Catechesis Religious Program—Tel: 402-672-8884; Email: willamidder@yahoo.com. Willa Midder, D.R.E. Students 17.

10—ST. BERNARD (1905)
3601 N. 65 St., 68104. Tel: 402-551-0269; Email: stbernardchurch@hotmail.com. Rev. Daniel L. Wittrock; Deacons Charles Baughman, (Retired); Edwin Osterhaus; Paul Dreismeier; Timothy F. McNeil, J.C.L.; Charles Sheik.
School—St. Bernard School, (Grades PreK-8), 3604 N. 65th St., 68104. Tel: 402-553-4993; Fax: 402-551-4939; Email: stbernardchurch@hotmail.com. Lisa DuVall, Prin. Lay Teachers 12; Students 175.
Catechesis Religious Program—Katie Galloway, D.R.E. Students 25.

11—BLESSED SACRAMENT (1919) Merged with St. Philip Neri Church of Omaha to form St. Philip Neri-Blessed Sacrament Church of Omaha.

12—ST. BRIDGET (1887) (Irish), Merged with St. Rose Church of Omaha to form St. Bridget-St. Rose Church of Omaha.

13—ST. BRIDGET-ST. ROSE CHURCH OF OMAHA (1888)
4112 S. 26th St., 68107. Tel: 402-733-8811; Email: 2southoparishes@gmail.com. Rev. William Safranek.
Catechesis Religious Program—Tel: 402-672-6216; Email: 2catholic.parishes@gmail.com. Julie Welch, D.R.E. Students 65.

14—CHRIST THE KING (1953)
654 S. 86th St., 68114. Tel: 402-391-3606; Email: ctkparish@ctkomaha.org; Email: odomb@ctkomaha.org; Web: www.ctkomaha.org. Revs. Damien J. Cook; Benjamin Boyd; Deacons Jon Fulcher; Randy Park; Mrs. Ashley Johnson, Sec.
School—Christ the King School, (Grades PreSchool-8), 831 S. 88th St., 68114. Tel: 402-391-0977; Fax: 402-391-2418; Email: ctkschool@ctkomaha.org. Christopher Segrell, Prin. Lay Teachers 26; Students 352.
Catechesis Religious Program—Email: maldonadop@ctkomaha.org. Christina Sanchez, D.R.E. Students 103.

15—ST. ELIZABETH ANN (1981)
5419 N. 114th St., 68164. Tel: 402-493-2186; Email: seas@stelizabethann.org. Rev. Frank J. Baumert; Deacons Jack Finney; Martin Crowley; Dennis Connor; John Dagerman; Duane Karmazin; David Klein; Richard Niedergeses.
See St. James-Seton School, Omaha under Elementary Schools, Interparochial located in the Institution section.
Catechesis Religious Program—4720 N. 90th St., 68134. Tel: 402-572-0369; Fax: 402-572-0347; Email: jkusek9212@yahoo.com. Ms. Jo Kusek, D.R.E. Students 107.

16—ST. FRANCES CABRINI (1856)
1248 S. 10th St., 68108. Tel: 402-934-7706; Email: stfrancescabrinicatholicchurch@gmail.com; Email: djzuerlein@archomaha.org; Web: stcabriniomaha.org. Rev. Damian Zuerlein.
Catechesis Religious Program—Email: klreiser@hotmail.com. Karen Avila, D.R.E. Students 27.
See All Saints Catholic School, Omaha under Elementary Schools, Interparochial located in the Institution section.

17—ST. FRANCIS ASSISI, (Polish—Spanish)
4521 S. 32 St., 68107. Tel: 402-733-8811; Email: st.roseomaha@cox.net. 4112 S. 26th St., 68107. Rev. William J. Safranek.
Catechesis Religious Program—Email: 2catholic.parishes@gmail.com. Students 55.

18—HOLY CROSS (1920)
4810 Woolworth Ave., 68106. Tel: 402-553-7500; Fax: 402-553-7735; Email: misskatie@holycrossomaha.org. 4803 William St., 68106. Revs. Carl A. Salanitro; Anthony Ike, In Res.; Deacons Thomas Burton; George Elster; Timothy A. Mulcahy; Nickolas Rasmussen.
Catechesis Religious Program—Email: ehansen@holycrossomaha.org. Elizabeth Hansen, D.R.E. Students 43.

19—HOLY FAMILY (1876)
1715 Izard St., 68102. Tel: 402-345-1062; Email: holyfamily.omaha@cox.net. Deacon Albert W. Aulner Jr., Pastoral Coord.

20—HOLY GHOST (1918)
5219 S. 53rd St., 68117. Tel: 402-731-3176; Email: parishsecretary@holyghostomaha.org. Revs. William E. Sanderson; Ryan P. Lewis, J.C.L., S.T.L., In Res.; Deacons Tom Schulte; Paul Eubanks; Al Aulner.
Catechesis Religious Program—5302 S. 52nd St., 68117. Mitzi Taylor, D.R.E. Students 86.

21—HOLY NAME (1917)
3014 N. 45th St., 68104. Tel: 402-451-6622, Ext. 204; Email: PARISH@HOLYNAMEOMAHA.ORG; Web: www.holynameomaha.org. Revs. Vitalis E. Anyanike; Matthew J. Niggemeyer; Christopher N. Onuoha, In Res.
Catechesis Religious Program—Tel: 402-451-6622, Ext. 203; Email: religioused@holynameomaha.org. Ana Millan, D.R.E. Students 215.

22—IMMACULATE CONCEPTION, B.V.M. (1897) (Latin Rite)
2708 S. 24th St., 68108. Tel: 402-342-1074; Fax: 402-505-7616; Email: office@latinmassomaha.org; Email: pastor@latinmassomaha.org; Email: assistant@latinmassomaha.org; Web: www.latinmassomaha.org. Revs. John P. Rickert, F.S.S.P.; Christopher Fitzpatrick.
See Consortium, Omaha under Elementary Schools, Interparochial located in the Institution section.
Catechesis Religious Program—Email: assistant@latinmassomaha.org. Students 72.

23—ST. JAMES (1963)
9025 Larimore Ave., 68134. Tel: 402-572-0499. Revs. Thomas W. Weisbecker; Marcus E. Knecht; Deacons Jerry Gau; Stan Kurtz; Pat Lenz; Richard Hopkins;

Randy Grosse; Gregg Drvol; Steven Nelson; Lyle Simmons.
See St. James-Seton School, Omaha under Elementary Schools, Interparochial located in the Institution section.
Catechesis Religious Program—4720 N. 90th St., 68134. Tel: 402-572-0369; Fax: 402-572-0347; Email: jkusek9212@yahoo.com. Ms. Jo Kusek, D.R.E. Students 196.

24—ST. JOAN OF ARC (1955)
3122 S. 74th St., 68124. Tel: 402-393-2005, Ext. 4; Email: church@sjaomaha.org. Rev. Gregory Benkowski; Deacons Ronald R. Ryan; Tim Leininger.
School—St. Joan of Arc School, (Grades K-8), 7430 Hascall St., 68124. Tel: 402-393-2314;
Fax: 402-393-4405. Kayleen Wallace, Prin. Lay Teachers 13; Students 99; Clergy / Religious Teachers 1.
Catechesis Religious Program—Tel: 402-393-2315; Email: religioused@sjaomaha.org. Jennifer Muckey, D.R.E. Students 32.

25—ST. JOHN'S AT CREIGHTON UNIVERSITY PARISH - OMAHA (1897)
2500 California Pl., 68178. Tel: 402-280-3031; Email: stjohns@creighton.edu; Web: www.stjohns-creighton.org. Revs. Lorn J. Snow, S.J.; Philip R. Amidon, S.J.
Catechesis Religious Program—Jonathan Chiacchere, D.R.E. Students 50.

26—ST. JOHN PAUL II NEWMAN CENTER, INC.
1221 S. 71st St., 68106. Tel: 402-557-5575; Email: info@jpiiomaha.org. Revs. Joseph C. Taphorn, J.C.L.; Andrew J. Roza; Deacon James Keating, Ph.D.; Ms. Katie Winkler, Campus Min.; Ms. Lauren Hankes, Resident Mgr.; Mrs. Renee Hendricks, Business Mgr.

27—ST. JOHN VIANNEY (1974)
5801 Oak Hills Dr., 68137. Tel: 402-895-0808; Email: mjohnson@sjvomaha.org; Web: www.sjvomaha.org. Rev. Richard J. Reiser; Deacons Frank Telich; Harold Sawtelle; Joseph Choi; Thomas H. Frankenfield; Chris Hanson; Ron Horner.
Catechesis Religious Program—Tel: 402-895-0896; Fax: 402-932-1336. John Gencarelli. Students 371.

28—ST. JOSEPH aka St. Joseph Catholic Church (1887) (German—Hispanic)
1723 S. 17th St., 68108. Tel: 402-342-1618;
Fax: 402-342-2640. Rev. William D. Bond.
See All Saints Catholic School, Omaha under Elementary Schools, Interparochial located in the Institution section.
Catechesis Religious Program—Email: wdbond@archomaha.org. Elizabeth Trejo, D.R.E. Students 485.

29—ST. LEO (1978)
1920 N. 102nd St., 68114. Tel: 402-397-0407;
Fax: 402-397-2887; Email: dina_turco@stleo.net; Web: www.stleo.net. Revs. Craig J. Loecker; Jerome V. Dillon; Deacons George Knockenhauer; Trung Nguyen; Norman Tierney; James Shipman; Kevin Fuller.
Res.: 1724 N. 102nd Ave., 68114.
See St. Pius X-St. Leo School, Omaha under Elementary Schools, Interparochial located in the Institution section.
Catechesis Religious Program—
Tel: 402-397-0407, Ext. 206; Email: jen@stleo.net. Jennifer Fuller, D.R.E. Students 250.

30—ST. MARGARET MARY (1919)
6116 Dodge St., 68132-2114. Tel: 402-558-2255;
Fax: 402-551-6644; Email: parish@smmomaha.org; Web: www.smmomaha.org. Revs. Gregory P. Baxter, S.T.L.; Vincent Sunguti.
School—St. Margaret Mary School, (Grades K-8), 123 N. 61st St., 68132. Tel: 402-551-6663;
Fax: 402-551-5631; Email: pgrennan@smmomaha.org; Web: www.smmomaha.org/school. Maureen Berg, Prin. Lay Teachers 27; Students 551.
Catechesis Religious Program—123 N. 61st St., 68132. Tel: 402-558-9119; Fax: 402-551-5631. China Weil, D.R.E. Students 68.

31—ST. MARY (1901)
3529 Q St., 68107. Tel: 402-731-0204; Email: plgolka@archomaha.org. Mailing Address: 5912 S. 36th St., 68107. Rev. Frank E. Jindra.

32—ST. MARY MAGDALENE (1868)
109 S. 19th St., 68102. Tel: 402-342-4807; Email: smmomaha@msn.com. Revs. Rodney T. Adams; Andrew Ekpenyong, In Res.; Richard Ehusani, In Res.
See All Saints Catholic School, Omaha under Elementary Schools, Interparochial located in the Institution section.

33—MARY OUR QUEEN (1963)
3535 S. 119th St., 68144. Tel: 402-333-8662; Email: moq@maryourqueenchurch.com. Revs. Robert K. English; Augustine Gama; Deacons Paul Rooney; Steve Floersch; Robert Hamilton; Thomas H. Frankenfield.
Church: 3405 S. 118th St., 68144.
School—Mary Our Queen School, (Grades PreSchool-8), 3405 S. 119th St., 68144. Tel: 402-333-8663;
Fax: 402-334-3948; Web: www.moqschool.org. Maureen Hoy, Prin. Lay Teachers 36; Students 541.
Catechesis Religious Program—
Tel: 402-333-8231, Ext. 1208; Email: bjeastridge@schools.archomaha.org. Barb Eastridge, D.R.E. Students 388.

34—MOTHER OF PERPETUAL HELP (1975) (Church of the Deaf)
5215 Seward St., 68104. Tel: 402-558-3100; Email: tfmcneil@archomaha.org. Deacon Timothy F. McNeil, J.C.L., Pastoral Coord., Tel: 402-493-7220.

35—OUR LADY OF FATIMA CATHOLIC COMMUNITY
709 S. 28th St., 68105-1511. Tel: 515-822-6743; Email: tamnangcmc@yahoo.com. Rev. Tam Nguyen.

36—OUR LADY OF GUADALUPE (1927) (Spanish), Merged with St. Agnes, Omaha to form Our Lady of Guadalupe - St. Agnes Parish, Omaha.

37—OUR LADY OF GUADALUPE - ST. AGNES PARISH, Merged with Assumption, BVM, Omaha to form Assumption of the Blessed Virgin Mary-Our Lady of Guadalupe Church of Omaha.

38—OUR LADY OF LOURDES (1917) Merged with St. Adalbert, Omaha to form Our Lady of Lourdes - St. Adalbert Church of Omaha.

39—OUR LADY OF LOURDES-ST. ADALBERT PARISH (2014)
2110 S. 32nd Ave., 68105. Tel: 402-346-0900; Email: jlpietramale@archomaha.org; Web: ollomaha.com. Rev. John L. Pietramale; Deacons Ken Kalkowski; Frank Hilt.
Catechesis Religious Program—2124 S. 32nd Ave., 68105. Elaine Heaston, D.R.E. Students 32.

40—ST. PATRICK (1883) Merged with St. Frances Cabrini, Omaha. For inquiries for parish records please see St. Frances Cabrini, Omaha.

41—ST. PATRICK (ELKHORN) (1868) [CEM]
20500 West Maple Rd., Elkhorn, 68022.
Tel: 402-289-4289; Email: parish@stpatselkhorn.org; Web: www.stpatselkhorn.org. Revs. Thomas M. Fangman; Patrick Moser; Gary L. Ostrander, In Res., (Retired), St. Patrick Parish, 20755 Appaloosa St., Elkhorn, 68022; Deacons John Jacobs; Daniel E. Perchal; James Ricketts; Bud Simmonds.
Res.: 20755 Appaloosa Dr., Elkhorn, 68022.
School—St. Patrick School, (Grades PreK-8),
Tel: 402-289-5407; Email: klandenberger@stpatselkhorn.org. Mrs. Kami Landenberger, Prin. Lay Teachers 38; Students 825.
Catechesis Religious Program—Tel: 402-289-4947; Email: mmcmahon@stpatselkhorn.org. Mary F. McMahon, D.R.E. Students 900.

42—ST. PETER (1887)
709 S. 28th St., 68105-1511. Tel: 402-341-4560; Email: secretary@stpeterchurch.net; Web: www.stpeterchurch.net. Revs. John P. Broheimer; James R. de Anda, J.C.L.; Deacons John Zak; Gregorio Elizalde; Omar Gutierrez.
Catechesis Religious Program—
Tel: 402-341-4560, Ext. 113; Email: secretary@stpeterchurch.net. Brandon Harvey, D.R.E. Students 183.

43—STS. PETER AND PAUL CHURCH OF OMAHA (1917) (Croatian)
5912 S. 36th St., 68107. Tel: 402-731-4578. Rev. Frank E. Jindra.
Worship Site: St. Anthony, 5401 S. 33rd St., 68107.
Catechesis Religious Program—3619 X St., 68107.
Tel: 402-733-3344; Email: dlrodriguez@archomaha.org. Denise Rodriguez, Dir. Students 110.

44—ST. PHILIP NERI (1904) Merged with Blessed Sacrament, Omaha to form St. Philip Neri-Blessed Sacrament Church of Omaha.

45—ST. PHILIP NERI-BLESSED SACRAMENT PARISH OF OMAHA (2014)
8200 N. 30th St., 68112. Tel: 402-455-1289; Email: marieatspn@yahoo.com. Rev. Mario D. Rapose; Deacon Fred Hendricks.
School—St. Philip Neri-Blessed Sacrament Parish of Omaha School, (Grades PreK-8), 8202 N. 31st St., 68112. Tel: 402-315-3500; Fax: 402-453-3620; Email: mrsimerly@schools.archomaha.org. Mary Simerly, Prin.; Christine Clayton, Librarian. Lay Teachers 12; Students 145; Clergy / Religious Teachers 1.
Catechesis Religious Program—Email: emilybazer@gmail.com. Emily Bazer, D.R.E. Students 23.

46—ST. PIUS X (1954)
6905 Blondo St., 68104. Tel: 402-558-8446;
Fax: 402-558-4986; Email: rectory@stpiusxomaha.org; Web: www.stpiusxomaha.org. Rev. Joseph M. Wray; Michel N'Do, In Res.
See St. Pius X-St. Leo School, Omaha under Elementary Schools, Interparochial located in the Institution section.
Catechesis Religious Program—Tel: 402-558-1898. Colleen Ciciulla, D.R.E. Students 50.

47—ST. RICHARD (1963) Closed. For inquiries for parish records, please contact Holy Name Parish, Omaha.

48—ST. ROBERT BELLARMINE (1966)
11802 Pacific St., 68154. Tel: 402-333-8989; Web: www.stroberts.com. Revs. Steven J. Stillmunks; Mark J. McKercher; Deacons Michael Fletcher; Joseph Laird.
School—St. Robert Bellarmine School, (Grades K-8), 11900 Pacific St., 68154. Tel: 402-334-1929;
Fax: 402-333-7188; Email: ssuiter@stroberts.com. Sandra Suiter, Prin. Lay Teachers 29; Students 585.
Catechesis Religious Program—Tel: 402-333-1959; Email: kvazquez@stroberts.com. Kate Vazquez, D.R.E. Students 230.

49—ST. ROSE (1919) Merged with St. Bridget, Omaha to form St. Bridget-St. Rose Church of Omaha.

50—SACRED HEART (1890)
2204 Binney St., 68110. Tel: 402-451-5755; Email: info@sacredheartchurchomaha.org; Web: sacredheartchurchomaha.org. Mailing Address: 2207 Wirt St., 68110. Rev. David M. Korth; Deacons John Vrbka; James Chambers; Richard Crotty.
Res.: 2218 Binney St., 68110. Tel: 402-451-7897; Email: dmkorth@archomaha.org.
Catechesis Religious Program—2207 Wirt St., 68110. Tel: 402-451-5755; Fax: 402-451-1731. Sue Vavak, D.R.E. Students 103.

51—ST. STANISLAUS (1919) (Polish)
4002 J St., 68107. Tel: 402-731-4152; Email: prvasquez@archomaha.org. Rev. William E. Sanderson; Deacons Daniel Saniuk; James Staroski; Patricia Vasquez, Business Mgr.

52—ST. STEPHEN THE MARTYR (1989)
16701 S St., 68135. Tel: 402-896-9675; Email: e.abbott@stephen.org; Web: www.stephen.org. Revs. David D. Belt; Padraic Stack; Deacons Ernest Abbott Jr., Dir.; Dennis Dethlefs, Pastoral Min.; C. Martin Warwick; Jerry Kozney; Wes Kreun.
Res.: 17456 Orchard Ave., 68135. Email: stephenmartyr@stephen.org.
School—St. Stephen the Martyr School, (Grades PreSchool-8), Tel: 402-896-0754; Email: r.williby@stephen.org. Lay Teachers 36; Students 706.
Catechesis Religious Program—Tel: 402-896-5683; Email: m.maguire@stephen.org. Mary Maguire, D.R.E. Students 769.

53—ST. THERESE OF THE CHILD JESUS (1918) Closed. For inquiries for parish records please see Sacred Heart, Omaha.

54—ST. THOMAS MORE (1958)
4804 Grover St., 68106. Tel: 402-556-1456; Email: nfhunke@archomaha.org; Web: stmomaha.org. Rev. Norman F. Hunke.
Catechesis Religious Program—3515 S. 48th Ave., 68106. Cell: 402-990-2957; Fax: 402-551-9507; Email: tgunia11@gmail.com; Web: stmomaha.org. Theresa Gunia, D.R.E. Students 47.

55—ST. VINCENT DE PAUL (1991)
14330 Eagle Run Dr., 68164. Tel: 402-496-7988; Email: parishoffice@svdpomaha.org; Web: www.svdpomaha.org. Revs. Daniel J. Kampschneider; Eliot Schwer; Deacons David Bang; William J. Barnes; Gary J. Hennessey; Richard Jizba; Jay Reilly; Jenni Vankat, Pastoral Min. & Adult Formation; Kathy Mayer, Liturgy Dir.; TJ Ernst, Dir.; Nicole Florez, Pastoral Min./Coord.; Jennifer Veit, Pastoral Min./Coord.
Res.: 14217 Eagle Run Dr., 68164.
School—St. Vincent de Paul School, (Grades PreSchool-8), Tel: 402-492-2111; Email: schooladminstaff@svdpomaha.org; Web: www.svdpomaha.org. Dr. Barbara Marchese, Prin.; Lisa Nelson, Asst. Prin.; Diane Warneke, Asst. Prin. Lay Teachers 70; Students 873.
Catechesis Religious Program—Tel: 402-493-1642; Email: mcmahanj@svdpomaha.org. Jennifer McMahan, D.R.E. Students 474.

56—ST. WENCESLAUS (1877) (Czech)
15353 Pacific St., 68154. Tel: 402-330-0304;
Fax: 402-330-1476; Email: online@stwenceslaus.org; Web: www.stwenceslaus.org. Revs. Thomas E. Bauwens; Taylor Leffler; Ronald S. Wasikowski; Deacons Mark Capoun; Donald Cowles; Joe Kulus; Michael J. DeSelm; William Carter Jr.; Bradford Schaefer; Jack Miller.
Res.: 1516 S. 152nd Ave. Cir., 68144.
School—St. Wenceslaus School, (Grades PreK-8), 15353 Pacific St., 68154. Tel: 402-330-4356;
Fax: 402-884-4417; Email: hubenw@stwenceslaus.org; Email: schumachers@stwenceslaus.org; Web: www.stwenceslaus.org/school. William Huben, Prin.; Patricia Ahlgren, Asst. Prin.; Steve Schumacher, Asst. Prin. Lay Teachers 43; Students 895; Clergy / Religious Teachers 1.
Catechesis Religious Program—Tel: 402-330-1889. Julie Lukasiewicz, Faith Form. Dir. for Elementary Students; Olivier Coutant, Faith Form. Dir. for Elementary Students. Students 405.

2—WEST PAPILLION CATHOLIC COMMUNITY
100 N. 62nd St., 68132. Tel: 402-558-3100;
Fax: 402-558-3026. Mr. James J. Stolze, Sec.

OUTSIDE THE CITY OF OMAHA

ALBION, BOONE CO., ST. MICHAEL (1877) [CEM]
524 W. Church St., Albion, 68620. Tel: 402-395-2332;

Email: jlporter@archomaha.org. Rev. Mark A. Tomasiewicz.
School—St. Michael School, (Grades PreK-8), 520 W. Church St., Albion, 68620. Tel: 402-395-2926; Email: lschumac@stmichael.esu7.org; Web: www.stmichael.esu7.org. Mrs. Lisa Schumacher, Prin. Clergy 1; Lay Teachers 11; Students 129; Clergy / Religious Teachers 1.
Catechesis Religious Program—Lisa Wagner, D.R.E. Students 144.

ALOYS, CUMING CO., ST. ALOYSIUS (1891) [CEM] (German)
700 Hwy. 32, West Point, 68788. Tel: 402-372-2188; Email: wpstmary@gmail.com; Web: wpstmary.com. 343 N. Monitor St., West Point, 68788. Rev. Steven D. Emanuel.

ATKINSON, HOLT CO., ST. JOSEPH (1886) [CEM]
104 S. Tuller St., P.O. Box 220, Atkinson, 68713. Tel: 402-925-2122; Email: stjoechurchatkinson@gmail.com. Rev. James M. Weeder.
School—St. Joseph School, (Grades PreK-8), 102 N. Tuller St., Atkinson, 68713. Tel: 402-925-2104. Erin Jelinek, Teacher Facilitator. Lay Teachers 5; K-8 Students 59.
Catechesis Religious Program—Debra Liewer, D.R.E. Students 73.

BANCROFT, CUMING CO., HOLY CROSS (1884) [CEM] (German)
100 Park St., Bancroft, 68004. Tel: 402-687-2102; Email: fmfuston@archomaha.org; Web: www.stjoseph-holycross.com. P.O. Box 524, Lyons, 68038. Rev. Paul R. Ortmeier.
Catechesis Religious Program—Charlee Weborg, D.R.E. Students 15.

BATTLE CREEK, MADISON CO., ST. PATRICK'S (1875) [CEM]
107 N. Third St., P.O. Box 40, Battle Creek, 68715. Tel: 402-675-6345; Tel: 402-675-2485. Rev. Michael B. Malloy; Deacons Tom Hughes; Melvin Schaecher.
Catechesis Religious Program—Tel: 402-675-6345. Teresa Wilkinson, D.R.E. Students 129.
Mission—St. Francis de Sales Mission of Battle Creek, 82990 543rd Ave., Schoolcraft, 68715.

BEEMER, CUMING CO., HOLY CROSS (1913) [CEM]
517 Fraisier St. N., P.O. Box 212, Beemer, 68716. Tel: 402-528-3475. Rev. Vincent Sunguti.
Catechesis Religious Program—Email: stjo68791@gmail.com. Renae Carlson, D.R.E. Students 3.

BELLEVUE, SARPY CO.
1—ST. BERNADETTE (1963)
7600 S. 42nd St., Bellevue, 68147. Tel: 402-731-4694; Email: tristenriha@gmail.com. Revs. Harold J. Buse; Paul L. Vasquez, In Res.; Deacons Ron Casart; Pete Digilio, (Retired); Sebastian Enzolera, D.R.E.
Catechesis Religious Program—
Tel: 402-731-4694, Ext. 305. Students 42.

2—ST. MARY (1921)
811 W. 23rd Ave., Bellevue, 68005. Tel: 402-291-1350 ; Email: rectory@stmarysbellevue.com; Web: www.stmarysbellevue.com. Revs. Lydell T. Lape; Roger Kalscheuer; Deacons Ted Menzel; Chuck L'Archevesque; Andy Foray; John Huck; John Wacha; Lee Mayhan; Gary Bash; Jeff Braxton.
School—St. Mary School, (Grades PreK-8), 903 W. Mission Ave., Bellevue, 68005. Tel: 402-291-1694; Fax: 402-291-9667; Email: trish.wallinger@stmarysbellevue.com; Web: www.stmarysschoolbellevue.com. Trish Wallinger, Prin.; Jenny Schafer, Librarian. Lay Teachers 14; Students 205.
Catechesis Religious Program—Tel: 402-291-7222; Email: etomaso@stmarysbellevue.com. Elizabeth Tomaso, D.R.E. Students 186.

3—ST. MATTHEW THE EVANGELIST CHURCH OF BELLEVUE (1996)
12210 S. 36th St., Bellevue, 68123. Tel: 402-292-7418 ; Email: plbanks@archomaha.org. Rev. Leo A. Rigatuso; Deacons Mark White, D.R.E.; Edward J. Bevan; Tom Deall.
Res.: 3605 Looking Glass Dr., Bellevue, 68123. Tel: 402-932-3748; Email: stmatthew.bel@archomaha.org.
School—St. Matthew School, (Grades PreSchool-8), 12210 S. 36th St., Ste. B, Bellevue, 68123. Tel: 402-291-2030; Email: staff.stmatthewtheevangelist.oma@schools.archomaha.org; Web: www.stmatthewbellevuene.org. Angie Palmer, Prin. Lay Teachers 15; Students 161.
Catechesis Religious Program—Email: mhwhite@archomaha.org. Students 85.

BLAIR, WASHINGTON CO., ST. FRANCIS BORGIA (1865) [CEM]
2005 Davis Dr., Blair, 68008. Tel: 402-426-3823; Email: office@stfrancisborgia.org; Web: stfrancisborgia.org. Rev. James J. Netusil; Kelly Petersen, Sec.
Res.: 795 Southfork Rd., Blair, 68008.
Catechesis Religious Program—Sinead Chaffee, D.R.E. Students 229.

BLOOMFIELD, KNOX CO., ST. ANDREW (1892) [JC]
305 S. McNamara St., Bloomfield, 68718. Tel: 402-388-4814; Email: strosecrofton@gpcom.net. 1316 W. 5th St., Crofton, 68730. Rev. Timothy Podraza; Deacon Steve Archbold.
Catechesis Religious Program—Tel: 402-373-2696. Barb Jackson, D.R.E. Students 54.

BOW VALLEY, CEDAR CO., SS. PETER AND PAUL, Merged with Sacred Heart, Wynot; Ss. Philip and James, St. James and Immaculate Conception, St. Helena to form Holy Family Church of Cedar County, Hartington.

BOYS TOWN, DOUGLAS CO., IMMACULATE CONCEPTION B.V.M. (1936)
13943 Dowd Dr., Boys Town, 68010. Tel: 531-355-1037; Email: denise.wharton@boystown.org; Email: laura.buddenberg@boystown.org; Email: kimm.dilocker@boystown.org. Rev. Steven Boes; Rev. Msgr. James E. Gilg, In Res., (Retired); Rev. Frank W. Lordemann, In Res., (Retired); Laura Buddenberg, Dir. Pastoral Affairs; Denise Wharton, Catholic Ministry Coord.
Parish Center: 13900 Dowd Dr., Boys Town, 68010.
Catechesis Religious Program—The Catholic Center, 13702 Dowd Dr., Boys Town, 68010.

BUTTE, BOYD CO, SACRED HEART PARISH OF BOYD COUNTY (2007) [JC4]
921 Gale St., P.O. Box 8, Butte, 68722. Tel: 402-775-0067. Rev. Douglas P. Scheinost.
Assumption BVM Church—417 S. 4th St., Lynch, 68746.
St. Mary Church, 304 E. South St., Spencer, 68777.
Ss. Peter and Paul Church, 921 Gales St., Butte, 68722.
Catechesis Religious Program—Email: dpscheinost@archomaha.org. Charlotte Mitchell, D.R.E. Students 67.

CEDAR RAPIDS, BOONE CO., ST. ANTHONY (1884) [CEM]
508 W. Main St., P.O. Box 56, Cedar Rapids, 68627. Tel: 308-358-0773; Email: rjsteffensmeier@archomaha.org. Rev. Ralph J. Steffensmeier.
Catechesis Religious Program—Students 42.

CENTRAL CITY, MERRICK CO., ST. MICHAEL (1910)
2402 20th Ave., Central City, 68826. Cell: 402-659-8132; Email: frfulton@hotmail.com. Rev. David L. Fulton; Deacons Richard Larson; Donald Placke.
Catechesis Religious Program—Tel: 308-946-2855; Email: dlfulton@archomaha.org. Students 57.

CLARKS, MERRICK CO., ST. PETER (1918) [CEM]
302 N. Dixon St., Clarks, 68628. Tel: 402-659-8132; Email: frfulton@hotmail.com. Mailing Address: 315 N. Esther St., P.O. Box 368, Fullerton, 68638. Rev. David L. Fulton.
Catechesis Religious Program—Tel: 308-548-2745. Students 41.

CLARKSON, COLFAX CO.
1—SS. CYRIL AND METHODIUS (1901) [CEM] (Czech)
120 Cherry St., P.O. Box 457, Clarkson, 68629. Tel: 402-892-3464; Email: thecathchurches@gmail.com; Web: sites.google.com/site/sscyrilmethodiusclarkson. Rev. Rodney Kneifl.
School—St. John Neumann, 420 Cherry St., Clarkson, 68629. Tel: 402-892-3474. Ann Prokopec, Teacher Facilitator. Lay Teachers 5; Students 24.
Catechesis Religious Program—Email: frkneifl@aol.com. Aaron Fehringer, Co-D.R.E.; Kimberly Fehringer, Co-D.R.E.; Kaitlin Reick, Co-D.R.E. Students 49.

2—HOLY TRINITY (1878) [CEM] (Czech)
1733 Road 12, Clarkson, 68629. Tel: 402-892-3126; Email: cmyosten@archomaha.org. Rev. Stanley T. Schmit.
Res.: 320 S. Second St., Howells, 68641. Tel: 402-986-1627.

COLERIDGE, CEDAR CO., ST. MICHAEL (1886) [CEM] (German—Irish)
315 S. Madison, Coleridge, 68727. Tel: 402-256-3019; Tel: 402-256-3303; Email: stmam3303@yahoo.com. Mailing Address: 408 Elm St., P.O. Box 828, Laurel, 68745-0828. Rev. David F. Liewer.

COLUMBUS, PLATTE CO.
1—ST. ANTHONY (1913)
562 17th Ave., Columbus, 68601. Tel: 402-564-3313; Email: stanthonysc@neb.rr.com. Rev. Ross C. Burkhalter; Deacons Michael Placzek; Kelly McGowan; Mark Boeding.
School—St. Anthony School, (Grades PreSchool-6), 1719 6th St., Columbus, 68601. Tel: 402-564-4767; Fax: 402-564-5530; Email: asokol@sta.esu7.org; Web: sites.google.com/a/sta.esu7.org/stanthonysschool. Amy Sokol, Prin. Clergy 1; Lay Teachers 12; Students 186; Clergy / Religious Teachers 1.
Catechesis Religious Program—Lori Olson, D.R.E. Students 114.

2—ST. BONAVENTURE (1877) [CEM]
1565 18th Ave., Columbus, 68601. Tel: 402-564-7151; Fax: 402-562-6025; Web: www.stboncc.com. Revs. Michael J. Swanton; Matthew Capadano, In Res.; Deacons Daniel Keiter; Lawrence Mielak; James Naughtin; Arthur Spenner.
School—St. Bonaventure School, (Grades K-6), Tel: 402-564-7153; Email: czoucha@stb.esu7.org. Cheryl Zoucha, Prin. Lay Teachers 15; Students 165.
Catechesis Religious Program—Email: crambour@stboncc.com. Cheryl Rambour, D.R.E. Students 335.

3—ST. ISIDORE (1963) [JC]
3921 20th St., Columbus, 68601. Tel: 402-564-8993; Email: isidore@megavison.com. Rev. Joseph A. Miksch.
School—St. Isidore School, (Grades PreSchool-6), 3821 20th St., Columbus, 68601. Tel: 402-564-2604; Email: lstarostka@sti.esu7.org; Web: www.sti.esu7.org. Amy Evans, Prin. Clergy 19; Lay Teachers 24; Students 215; Clergy / Religious Teachers 1.
Catechesis Religious Program—Email: isidore@megavision.com. Mary Miksch, D.R.E. Students 182.

CREIGHTON, KNOX CO., ST. LUDGER (1885) [CEM] (German—Czech)
410 Bryant Ave., Creighton, 68729-2917. Tel: 402-358-3501; Email: tgragert@ludgercatholic.org; Web: ludgercatholic.org. Rev. Jeremy J. Hans.
Res.: 904 Lake Ave., Creighton, 68729-2917.
School—St. Ludger School, (Grades PreSchool-6), Tel: 402-358-3501; Email: tgragert@ludgercatholic.org. Miranda Hornback, Teacher Facilitator. Lay Teachers 4; Students 48.
Catechesis Religious Program—Tel: 402-358-3501. Linda Asher, D.R.E.; Darla Frisch, D.R.E. Students 74.
Mission—St. Ignatius Mission of Creighton, 407 S. Franklin St., Brunswick, 68720.

CROFTON, KNOX CO., ST. ROSE OF LIMA (1906) [CEM]
1316 W. Fifth St., Crofton, 68730. Tel: 402-388-4814. Rev. Timothy Podraza; Deacon Frank Fillaus.
School—St. Rose School, (Grades PreK-8), 1302 W. 5th St., Crofton, 68730. Tel: 402-388-4393; Fax: 402-388-4393; Email: jdfiscus@schools.archomaha.org; Web: stroseoflimaschoolcrofton.weebly.com. Mrs. Jennifer Fiscus, Prin. Lay Teachers 10; Students 133.
Catechesis Religious Program—Terry Mueller, D.R.E., (Grades 1-8). Students 102.

DELOIT TOWNSHIP, HOLT CO., ST. JOHN THE BAPTIST aka Rural St. John's (1910) [CEM 2]
50898 848 Rd., (Deloit Twp.), Clearwater, 68726. Tel: 402-626-7605; Fax: 402-685-3103; Email: parish@cppnebraska.org. Mailing Address: P.O Box 37, Ewing, 68735. Rev. John M. Norman; Mrs. Helen Larson, Sec.
Legal Title: St. John's Church of Deloit (Nebraska Non-Profit Corporation).

DODGE, DODGE CO., ST. WENCESLAUS (1883) [CEM 2] [JC] (Czech)
743 Second St., Dodge, 68633. Tel: 402-693-2235. Rev. Andy Phan.
School—St. Wenceslaus School, (Grades PreK-6), 212 N. Linden St., Dodge, 68633. Tel: 402-693-2819; Fax: 402-693-2347; Email: stwschool@gpcom.net. Danielle Klosen, Head Teacher. Lay Teachers 4; Students 44; Clergy / Religious Teachers 4.
Catechesis Religious Program—Email: clortmeier@archomaha.org. Students 26.
Mission—Sacred Heart Mission of Dodge (1874) [CEM] County Rd. 17, Olean, 68633. Email: rudynovak@hotmail.com.

DUNCAN, PLATTE CO., ST. STANISLAUS, [CEM]
Mailing Address: P.O. Box 155, Platte Center, 68653-0155. Tel: 402-246-2255; Email: stsjms@gmail.com. Rev. Walter Jong-A-Kiem.
Church: 1120 8th St., Duncan, 68634. Tel: 402-897-2625.
Catechesis Religious Program—Theresa Wenske, D.R.E. Students 26.

ELGIN, ANTELOPE CO., ST. BONIFACE (1902) [CEM] (German)
301 S. 2nd St., P.O. Box B, Elgin, 68636-0433. Tel: 402-843-2345; Fax: 402-843-2253; Email: stboniface.elg@archomaha.org. Rev. Kevin W. Vogel; Deacons Dennis Wiehn; Bill Camp.
School—St. Boniface School, (Grades PreK-6), 303 Remington St., Elgin, 68636-0433. Tel: 402-843-5325 ; Email: bgetzfred@pjcrusaders.org. Betty Getzfred, Prin. Lay Teachers 7; Students 81.
Catechesis Religious Program—205 Remington St., Elgin, 68636. Cheryl Veik, Family Formation Coord. Students 14.

EMERSON, DAKOTA CO., SACRED HEART (1886) [CEM]
601 N. Main St., P.O. Box 250, Emerson, 68733. Tel: 402-695-2342; Email: catholic@inebraska.com. Rev. Gerald Leise Jr.
Catechesis Religious Program—676 N. Main St., Emerson, 68733. Melissa Twohig, D.R.E. Students 55.
Mission—St. Mary Mission of Emerson, [CEM 2] 211 Iowas St., Hubbard, 68741.

EWING, HOLT CO., ST. PETER DE ALCANTARA aka St. Peter Church (1885) [CEM]

220 W. U.S. Hwy. 275, Ewing, 68735-2019.
Tel: 402-626-7605; Fax: 402-685-3103; Email: parish@cppnebraska.org; Web: stpeterewing.org. P.O. Box 37, Ewing, 68735-0037. Rev. John M. Norman; Mrs. Helen Larson
Legal Title: St. Peter's de Alcantara Church of Ewing (Nebraska Non-Profit Corporation)
Catechesis Religious Program—Students 120.
Mission—Mission of St. Theresa of Avila, Clearwater, NE (1886) 509 Nebraska St., Clearwater, 68726.
Legal Title: St. Theresa's Church of Clearwater (Nebraska Non-Profit Corporation).

FORDYCE, CEDAR CO., ALL SAINTS CHURCH OF NORTHEAST NEBRASKA (1909) [CEM] (German)
311 Omaha St., P.O. Box 170, Fordyce, 68736.
Tel: 402-357-3506; Email: jekeiter@archomaha.org; Web: www.stbonifaceparish.org. Rev. James E. Keiter; Deacons Marcus Potts; Brian Heine; Rodney Wiebelhaus; Clarence Jansen.
St. Boniface Church—55768 894 Rd., Menominee, 68736.
St. John the Baptist Church.
St. Joseph Church, 88870 554 Ave., Constance, 68730.
See West Catholic Elementary, Fordyce under Elementary Schools, Interparochial located in the Institution section.
Catechesis Religious Program—Students 121.

FORT CALHOUN, WASHINGTON CO., ST. JOHN THE BAPTIST (1883)
215 N. 13th St., P.O. Box 148, Fort Calhoun, 68023.
Tel: 402-468-5348; Fax: 402-468-4619; Email: sjcc@abbnebraska.com. Rev. Stephen J. Gutgsell, Admin.; Deacons Paul M. Cerio, D.R.E.; Gerald Mapes.
Catechesis Religious Program—Tel: 402-468-5659; Email: deaconpaulc@gmail.com. Students 124.

FREMONT, DODGE CO., ST. PATRICK (1858) [CEM]
3400 E. 16th St., Fremont, 68025. Tel: 402-721-6611; Fax: 402-727-8167; Email: stpats@stpatsfremont.org; Web: www.stpatsfremont.org. 422 E. Fourth St., Fremont, 68025. Revs. Walter L. Nolte; Nicholas A. Mishek; Damien Wee, Chap.; Deacons Edward Gentrup; Vic Henry; Dan Mueller; Joe Uhlik; David A. Probst; Craig Steel; Thomas Silva; Alberto Martinez.
School—Archbishop Bergan Elementary School, (Grades PreK-6), 1515 N. Johnson Rd., Fremont, 68025. Tel: 402-721-9766; Fax: 402-721-1180. Dan Koenig, Prin. Lay Teachers 14; Students 250; Clergy / Religious Teachers 2; Part-time 5.
High School—Archbishop Bergan High School,
Tel: 402-721-9683; Fax: 402-721-5366; Email: dan.koenig@berganknights.org; Web: www.berganknights.org. Dan Koenig, Prin. Lay Teachers 11; Students 73; Clergy / Religious Teachers 2.
School—Archbishop Bergan Middle School, (Grades 7-8), Dan Koenig, Prin. Lay Teachers 5; Students 49; Clergy / Religious Teachers 2.
Catechesis Religious Program—
Tel: 402-721-6611, Ext. 15. Lori Kisby, D.R.E. Students 226.

FULLERTON, NANCE CO., ST. PETER (1913) [CEM] (Polish)
315 N. Esther, P.O. Box 368, Fullerton, 68638.
Tel: 402-659-8132; Email: frfulton@hotmail.com. Rev. David L. Fulton.
Catechesis Religious Program—Tel: 308-536-2574. Students 78.

GENOA, NANCE CO., ST. ROSE OF LIMA (1900) [JC]
116 N. Elm St., Genoa, 68640-0490.
Tel: 308-773-2282; Email: saintslppr@gmail.com. Mailing Address: P.O. Box 490, Genoa, 68640. Rev. William D. L'Heureux.
Catechesis Religious Program—Students 91.

GRETNA, SARPY CO.
1—ST. CHARLES BORROMEO (2005)
7790 S. 192nd St., Gretna, 68028. Tel: 402-916-9730; Fax: 402-916-9740; Email: parish@scbccomaha.org; Web: www.stcharlesomaha.org. Rev. Jeffery S. Loseke.
Catechesis Religious Program—Jackie Schuler, D.R.E. Students 319.
2—ST. PATRICK (1858) [CEM] (Irish)
508 W. Angus St., Gretna, 68028. Tel: 402-332-4444; Email: stpatrick.gre@archomaha.org. Revs. Matthew J. Gutowski; Patrick C. Harrison, J.C.L., In Res.; Deacons Larry Heck; Steve Grandinetti; Joseph Hartnett.
Res.: 214 N. Cherokee Dr., Gretna, 68028.
Catechesis Religious Program—Tel: 402-332-3454; Email: smfagan@archomaha.org. Shane Fagan, D.R.E. Students 768.

HARTINGTON, CEDAR CO., HOLY TRINITY (1886) [CEM] [JC] (German—Irish)
404 S. Broadway, Hartington, 68739.
Tel: 402-254-6559; Email: holytrinity@hartel.net; Web: www.holytrinityhartington.com. P.O. Box 278, Hartington, 68739. Rev. Owen W. Korte.
School—Holy Trinity School, (Grades PreSchool-6), 502 S. Broadway, Hartington, 68739.
Tel: 402-254-6496. Lay Teachers 12; Students 153.
Catechesis Religious Program—Students 60.

HOOPER, DODGE CO., ST. ROSE OF LIMA (1885) [CEM 2]
405 Elk St., P.O. Box 443, Hooper, 68031.
Tel: 402-654-3449; Email: Parishroselaw@gmail.com. Rev. Damien Wee.
Catechesis Religious Program—Students 25.
Mission—St. Lawrence Mission of Hooper, [CEM] 910 Grant St., Scribner, 68057.

HOWELLS, COLFAX CO.
1—ST. JOHN NEPOMUCENE (1893) [CEM]
320 S. 2nd St., Howells, 68641. Tel: 402-986-1653; Email: cfcoday@archomaha.org. 614 Center St., Howells, 68641. Rev. Stanley T. Schmit.
Res.: 324 S. 2nd St., Howells, 68641.
Tel: 402-986-0890.
See Howells Community Catholic School, Howells under Elementary Schools, Interparochial located in the Institution section.
Catechesis Religious Program—Renae Vogel, D.R.E. Students 22.
2—SS. PETER AND PAUL (1890) [CEM] (German)
112 N. 6th St., Howells, 68641. Tel: 402-986-1653. 614 Center St., Howells, 68641. Rev. Stanley T. Schmit.
Res.: 324 S. 2nd St., Howells, 68641.
Tel: 402-986-0890; Email: cfcoday@archomaha.org.
See Howells Community Catholic School, Howells under Elementary Schools, Interparochial located in the Institution section.
Catechesis Religious Program—Renae Vogel, D.R.E. Students 45.

HUMPHREY, PLATTE CO., ST. FRANCIS (1883) [CEM] [JC2]
203 S. 5th, P.O. Box 116, Humphrey, 68642.
Tel: 402-923-0913. Revs. Patrick A. McLaughlin; Wayne Pavela, In Res.
School—St. Francis School, (Grades K-12), 300 S. 7th St., P.O. Box 277, Humphrey, 68642.
Tel: 402-923-0611; Email: jdunn@hsfschool.org; Web: www.humphreystfrancis.com. Mrs. Jennifer Dunn, Prin. Lay Teachers 20; Students 196; Clergy / Religious Teachers 2.
Catechesis Religious Program—Email: pamclaughlin@archomaha.org. Mrs. Lori Classen, Dir. Students 41.

JACKSON, DAKOTA CO., ST. PATRICK (1856) [CEM]
203 E. Elk St., Jackson, 68743. Tel: 402-755-2773; Email: cstwohig@archomaha.org; Email: alsohm@archomaha.org. P.O. Box 87, Ponca, 68770. Rev. Andrew L. Sohm.
Catechesis Religious Program—Email: megsevereide@gmail.com. Mrs. Megan Severeide, D.R.E. Students 53.

KRAKOW, NANCE CO., SS. PETER AND PAUL (1893) [CEM] (Polish)
52121 S. 380 Ave., Genoa, 68640. Tel: 308-773-2282; Email: saintslppr@gmail.com. P.O. Box 490, Silver Creek, 68640. Rev. William D. L'Heureux.
116 N. Elm St., Genoa, 68640. Res.: 407 Vine St., P.O. Box 332, Silver Creek, 68663.
Catechesis Religious Program—Students 14.

LAUREL, CEDAR CO., ST. MARY (1894)
406 Elm St., P.O. Box 828, Laurel, 68745.
Tel: 402-256-3303; Tel: 402-256-3019; Email: stmam3303@yahoo.com. Rev. David F. Liewer.
Catechesis Religious Program—408 Elm St., Laurel, 68745. Donna Kraft, D.R.E. Students 58.
Mission—St. Anne Mission of Laurel, [CEM] 510 Browning St., Dixon, Dixon Co. 68732.

LEIGH, COLFAX CO., ST. MARY (1900) [CEM]
220 W. Third St., P.O. Box 385, Leigh, 68643.
Tel: 402-487-2666; Email: thecathchurches@gmail.com; Web: sites.google.com/site/stmaryleigh. Rev. Rodney Kneifl.
Catechesis Religious Program—Students 51.

LINDSAY, PLATTE CO., HOLY FAMILY (1895) [CEM]
103 E. 3rd St., P.O. Box 68, Lindsay, 68644.
Tel: 402-428-2455; Email: lhfp@lhf.esu7.org. Rev. James F. Novotny.
School—Holy Family School, (Grades PreK-8), 301 Pine St., P.O. Box 158, Lindsay, 68644.
Tel: 402-428-3455; Email: lhfp@lhf.esu7.org. Lay Teachers 9; Students 102; Clergy / Religious Teachers 1.
High School—Holy Family High School, (Grades 9-12), Tel: 402-428-3215. Lay Teachers 6; Students 26; Clergy / Religious Teachers 1.
Catechesis Religious Program—Students 16.

LYNCH, BOYD CO., ASSUMPTION B.V.M. (1892) [CEM]
Merged with Ss. Peter and Paul, Butte and St. Mary, Spencer to form Sacred Heart Parish of Boyd Co.

LYONS, BURT CO., ST. JOSEPH (1884) [JC]
430 Lincoln St., P.O. Box 524, Lyons, 68038.
Tel: 402-687-2102; Web: www.stjoseph-holycross.com. Rev. Paul R. Ortmeier.
Catechesis Religious Program—Jane Olson, D.R.E.; Mark Olson, D.R.E. Students 48.

MADISON, MADISON CO., ST. LEONARD OF PORT MAURICE (1885) [CEM]
504 S. Nebraska St., P.O. Box 368, Madison, 68748.
Tel: 402-454-3529; Email: jmjurgens@archomaha.org. Rev. Gregory P. Carl; Deacon Lawrence F. Throener.
School—St. Leonard of Port Maurice School, (Grades PreK-6), Tel: 402-454-3525. Lisa Jackson, Teacher Facilitator. Lay Teachers 4; Students 33.
Catechesis Religious Program—Email: stleonardparish@gmail.com. Rebecca Leyva, D.R.E.; Erin Reeves, D.R.E.; Mary Throener, D.R.E. Students 82.

MENOMINEE, CEDAR CO., ST. BONIFACE (1882) [CEM] (German), Closed. For inquiries for parish records contact the chancery.

MONTEREY, CUMING CO., ST. BONIFACE (1905) [CEM] (German)
450 12th Rd., Monterey, 68788. Tel: 402-372-2188; Email: wpstmary@yahoo.com; Web: wpstmary.com. 343 N. Monitor St., West Point, 68788. Rev. Steven D. Emanuel, Admin.

NELIGH, ANTELOPE CO., ST. FRANCIS OF ASSISI CATHOLIC CHURCH (1900)
702 W. 11th St., P.O. Box 259, Neligh, 68756.
Tel: 402-887-4521; Email: stfranciscc@frontiernet.net. Rev. Patrick K. Nields.
Catechesis Religious Program—Amy Baker, D.R.E. Students 90.

NEWCASTLE, DIXON CO., ST. PETER (1873) [CEM]
403 Annie St., Newcastle, 68757. Tel: 402-755-2773; Email: cstwohig@archomaha.org. Mailing Address: P.O. Box 898, Ponca, 68770. Rev. Andrew L. Sohm; Deacon Dennis Knudsen.
Res.: 405 Annie St., P.O. Box 127, Newcastle, 68757.
Tel: 402-355-2620; Email: alsohm@archomaha.org.
Catechesis Religious Program—Email: alsohm@archomaha.org. Denise Kneifl, D.R.E. Students 42.

NORFOLK, MADISON CO., SACRED HEART CHURCH OF NORFOLK (1881) [JC] (German)
204 S. 5th St., Norfolk, 68701. Tel: 402-371-2621; Fax: 402-371-0403; Email: parishoffice@sacredheartnorfolk.com; Web: www.sacredheartnorfolk.com. Revs. Daniel R. Andrews; Scott A. Schilmoeller; Deacons Jim Doolittle; Leon Gentrup; Theodore Coler; Robert Viergutz; John Mines; Terry Price; Patrick Roche.
Res.: 202 S. Fifth St., Norfolk, 68701.
Tel: 402-371-2621; Fax: 402-371-0403; Web: www.sacredheartnorfolk.com.
Sacred Heart Church—200 S. 5th St., Norfolk, 68701.
St. Mary's Catholic Church, 2300 W. Madison Ave., Norfolk, 68701.
School—Norfolk Catholic Elementary School (1925) (Grades PreK-6), 2301 W. Madison Ave., Norfolk, 68701. Tel: 402-371-4584 (Pre-School-6);
Fax: 402-379-8129 (Pre-School-6). Dr. Don Ridder, Ed.D., Pres.; William Lafleur, Prin. (Preschool - 6); Renee Gilsdorf, Librarian. Aides 5; Lay Staff 8; Lay Teachers 18; Priests 2; Students 366.
High School—Norfolk Catholic High School (1925) (Grades 7-12), 2300 W. Madison Ave., Norfolk, 68701. Tel: 402-371-2784 (7-12);
Fax: 402-379-2929 (7-12). Amy Wattier, Prin. Aides 5; Lay Staff 10; Lay Teachers 23; Priests 2; Students 241.
Catechesis Religious Program—Jessica Wilkerson, D.R.E.; Philip Zimmerman, Adult Formation. Students 395.

NORTH BEND, DODGE CO., ST. CHARLES BORROMEO (1892) [JC]
831 Locust St., P.O. Box 457, North Bend, 68649.
Tel: 402-652-8484; Email: pastor.stcharles.neb@archomaha.org; Web: www.parishesonline.com/find/st-charles-borromeo-church-68649. Rev. Keith D. Rezac.
Catechesis Religious Program—Tel: 402-652-8437; Email: pastor.stcharles.nbe@archomaha.org. Carol Emmanuel, D.R.E.; Kelli Emmanuel, D.R.E.; Margaret Iossi, D.R.E. Students 129.

O'NEILL, HOLT CO., ST. PATRICK (1877)
330 E Benton, O'Neill, 68763. Tel: 402-336-1602; Email: bgstarman@archomaha.org; Web: www.stpatoneill.org. 301 E. Adams, O'Neill, 68763. Revs. Bernard G. Starman; Joseph R. Sund.
School—St. Mary's Catholic School of O'Neill, (Grades PreK-12), 300 N. 4th St., O'Neill, 68763.
Tel: 402-336-4455; Tel: 402-336-2664;
Fax: 402-336-1281; Fax: 402-336-2055; Email: chavranek@smcards.org; Web: www.stmarysoneill.org. Cody Havranek, Prin. Lay Teachers 28; Students 190; Clergy / Religious Teachers 2.
Catechesis Religious Program—Stephanie Nemec, Coord. of Evangelization & Catechesis. Students 103.
Mission—St. Joseph Mission of O'Neill, 85632 Ivy Ave., Amelia, 68711. Tel: 402-482-5283.

OSMOND, PIERCE CO., ST. MARY OF THE SEVEN DOLORS (1904) [CEM]
208 E. 5th St., P.O. Box 397, Osmond, 68765.
Tel: 402-748-3433; Email: cconley_stmarys@abbnebraska.com. Rev. Timothy W. Forget.

School—St. Mary of the Seven Dolors School, (Grades PreK-8), 302 E. 5th St., P.O. Box 427, Osmond, 68765. Tel: 402-748-3433 (Tel & Fax); Email: tiffanyguenther@gmail.com; Web: stmaryofthesevendolors.com. Tiffany Guenther, Teacher Facilitator; Camille Gerkins, Sec. Lay Teachers 5; Students 55; Clergy / Religious Teachers 1.

Catechesis Religious Program—Email: lisamschmit@gmail.com. Lisa Schmit, D.R.E. Students 66.

PAPILLION, SARPY CO., ST. COLUMBKILLE (1897)
200 E. 6th St., Papillion, 68046. Tel: 402-339-3285; Email: cmmcartney@saincolumbkille.org. Revs. David G. Reeson; Thomas A. Greisen; Deacons Eldon Lauber; Frank Mascarello; Robert J. Overkamp, J.C.L.; William Hill; Russ Perry; Duane Thome; Steve Jordan; Bob Stier; Eric VandeBerg; Brian Thomas; David Krueger; Bud Tharp; David Graef.

School—St. Columbkille School, (Grades K-8), 224 E. 5th St., Papillion, 68046. Tel: 402-339-8706; Fax: 402-592-4147; Email: bredburn@saintcolumbkilleschool.org. Brandi Redburn, Prin.; Sarah Foreman, Asst. Prin. Lay Teachers 25; Students 513.

Catechesis Religious Program—Tel: 402-339-0990; Fax: 402-592-4753; Email: llong@saintcolumbkille.org. Lori Long, D.R.E. Students 535.

PENDER, THURSTON CO., ST. JOHN (1889) [JC]
108 N. 5th, P.O. Box 96, Pender, 68047.
Tel: 402-385-3258; Email: catholic@inebraska.com. Rev. Gerald Leise Jr.

Catechesis Religious Program—Joanne Puckett, D.R.E. Students 52.

PETERSBURG, BOONE CO., ST. JOHN THE BAPTIST (1896) [CEM]
201 N. 4th St., Petersburg, 68652. Tel: 402-386-5580; Email: jhoefer@archomaha.org. P.O. Box 608, Petersburg, 68652-0608. Rev. Mark A. Tomasiewicz; Deacon John Starman.
Res.: 524 W. Church St., Albion, 68620.

Catechesis Religious Program—Lisa Wagner, D.R.E. Students 14.

PIERCE, PIERCE CO., ST. JOSEPH (1905) [CEM] (German)
118 W. Willow St., Pierce, 68767. Tel: 402-329-4200; Email: parishoffice@stjosephpierce.org. Rev. Marc Lim.

PLAINVIEW, PIERCE CO., ST. PAUL (1912) [CEM]
203 E. Park Ave., P.O. Box 387, Plainview, 68769.
Tel: 402-329-4200; Email: parishoffice@stjosephpierce.org. Mailing Address: 118 W. Willow St., Pierce, 68767. Rev. Marc Lim.

PLATTE CENTER, PLATTE CO., ST. JOSEPH (1884) [CEM] [JC] (German—Irish)
155 A St., P.O. Box 155, Platte Center, 68653-0155.
Tel: 402-246-2255; Email: stsjms@gmail.com. Rev. Walter Jong-A-Kiem.

Catechesis Religious Program—Tel: 402-246-5700. Angela Dolezal, D.R.E. Students 33.

PONCA, DIXON CO., ST. JOSEPH (1890) [CEM]
420 W. Second St., Ponca, 68770. Tel: 402-755-2773; Email: cstwohig@archomaha.org. P.O. Box 898, Ponca, 68770. Rev. Andrew L. Sohm.
Res.: 405 Annie St., Newcastle, 68757.
Tel: 402-355-2620.

Catechesis Religious Program—Email: alsohm@archomaha.org. Stacey Jackson, D.R.E. Students 73.

RAEVILLE, BOONE CO., ST. BONAVENTURE (1882) [CEM] (German)
2305 SR Rd., Raeville, 68636. Tel: 402-843-2345; Email: stbonaventure.rae@archomaha.org. P.O. Box B, Elgin, 68636. Fax: 402-843-2253. Rev. Kevin W. Vogel.

Catechesis Religious Program—Students 6.

RALSTON, DOUGLAS CO., ST. GERALD (1957)
9602 Q St, Ralston, 68127. Tel: 402-331-1955; Email: office@stgerald.org; Web: www.stgerald.org. 7859 Lakeview St., Ralston, 68127. Revs. Mark J. Nolte; Michael B. Voithofer; Cheryl Bolin, Sec.

School—St. Gerald School, (Grades PreK-8), Tel: 402-331-4223; Email: ckeenan@stgerald.org. Ms. Christy Keenan, Prin. Clergy 3; Lay Teachers 24; Students 377; Clergy / Religious Teachers 1.

Catechesis Religious Program—
Tel: 402-331-1955, Ext. 25; Email: dltrue@stgerald.org. Deb True, D.R.E. Students 163.

RANDOLPH, CEDAR CO., ST. JANE FRANCES DE CHANTAL (1892) [CEM] (German)
402 N. Bridge St., Randolph, 68771.
Tel: 402-337-0644; Fax: 402-337-1433. Rev. Timothy W. Forget; Deacon Doug Tunink.

Catechesis Religious Program—610 E. Jackson St., Randolph, 68771. Tel: 402-337-0341. Sandy Thies, D.R.E. Students 95.

ST. CHARLES, CUMING CO., ST. ANTHONY (1862) [CEM] (German)
449 15th Rd., Lot #1, St. Charles, 68788.
Tel: 402-372-2188; Email: wpstmary@yahoo.com; Web: wpstmary.com. 343 N. Monitor St., West Point, 68788. Rev. Steven D. Emanuel.

ST. EDWARD, BOONE CO., ST. EDWARD (1888) [CEM]
Tel: 402-678-2642; Email: stedward@gpcom.net. Rev. William D. L'Heureux; Deacon Harlan Long.
Res.: 805 Washington St., P.O. Box A, St. Edward, 68660-0136. Tel: 402-678-2642; Email: stedward@gpcom.net.

Catechesis Religious Program—Tel: 402-678-2880; Email: acruise@hotmail.com. Anita Cruise, D.R.E. (Elementary); Erica Werts, D.R.E. (Jr.-Sr. High). Students 66.

ST. HELENA, CEDAR CO., IMMACULATE CONCEPTION, Merged with Ss. Philip & James, St. James; Ss. Peter & Paul, Bow Valley & Sacred Heart, Wynot to form Holy Family Church of Cedar County.

ST. JAMES, CEDAR CO., SS. PHILIP AND JAMES, Merged with Immaculate Conception, St. Helena; Ss. Peter and Paul, Bow Valley and Sacred Heart, Wynot to form Holy Family Church of Cedar County.

SCHUYLER, COLFAX CO.

1—ST. AUGUSTINE (1878) (Irish—German), Merged with St. Mary, Schuyler to form Divine Mercy, Schuyler.

2—DIVINE MERCY
308 W. 10 St., Schuyler, 68661. Tel: 402-352-3540; Email: godshouse@isp.com. Revs. Gerald E. Gonderinger; Jairo Congote; Deacons Paul Doerneman; Danny Hastings.

Catechesis Religious Program—320 W. 10th St., Schuyler, 68661. Tel: 402-352-2149; Email: godshouse@isps.com. Renee Blum, D.R.E. Students 469.

3—ST. MARY (1914) Merged with St. Augustine, Schuyler to form Divine Mercy, Schuyler.

SILVER CREEK, MERRICK CO., ST. LAWRENCE (1902) [CEM] (Polish)
407 Vine St., Silver Creek, 68663. Tel: 308-773-2282; Email: saintslppr@gmail.com. P.O. Box 332, Silver Creek, 68663. Rev. William D. L'Heureux.

Catechesis Religious Program—Students 25.

SNYDER, DODGE CO., ST. LEO (1889) [CEM]
304 Ash St., Snyder, 68664. Tel: 402-652-8484; Email: stleo.sny@archomaha.org; Web: www.parishesonline.com/find/st-charles-borromeo-church-68649. P.O. Box 188, Snyder, 68664. Rev. Keith D. Rezac.

SOUTH SIOUX CITY, DAKOTA CO., ST. MICHAEL (1898) [CEM]
1405 1st Ave., South Sioux City, 68776.
Tel: 402-494-5423; Fax: 402-412-2902; Email: smsparish@gmail.com; Web: St. Michael'sChurchSSC@stmichaelscatholicchurchssc. Mailing Address: 1315 1st Ave., South Sioux City, 68776. Revs. S. Anthony Weidner; Michael P. Keating.

School—St. Michael School, (Grades PreK-8), Tel: 402-494-1526; Email: dnswilli2632@msn.com; Email: jeannie.mahaney@smcsssc.com; Web: www.stmichaels.schoolinsites.com. Mrs. Sandy Williams, Prin. Lay Teachers 12; Students 172; Clergy / Religious Teachers 2.

Catechesis Religious Program—Sr. Blanca Trinanes, D.R.E. (English); Maria Gomez, D.R.E. (Spanish). (English) 256; (Spanish) 213.

SPENCER, BOYD CO., ST. MARY (1892) [CEM 2] Merged with Ss. Peter and Paul, Butte and Assumption B.V.M., Lynch to form Sacred Heart Parish of Boyd Co.

SPRINGFIELD, SARPY CO., ST. JOSEPH (1980) [JC]
102 S. Ninth St., Springfield, 68059.
Tel: 402-253-2949; Fax: 402-253-8000; Email: mfgutgsell@archomaha.org. Rev. Michael F. Gutgsell, J.C.L.

Catechesis Religious Program—Email: shuntwork@msn.com. Sherry Huntwork, D.R.E. Students 22.

STANTON, STANTON CO., ST. PETER (1893) [JC]
1504 Ivy St., Stanton, 68779. Tel: 402-439-2147; Email: stpeters@stanton.net. P.O. Box 557, Stanton, 68779. Rev. Gerald A. Connealy.

Catechesis Religious Program—Tel: 402-439-2149. Tamy Bohac, D.R.E.; Stephanie Wurdinger, D.R.E. Students 133.

STUART, HOLT CO., ST. BONIFACE (1899) [CEM]
106 E. Fourth, P.O. Box 190, Stuart, 68780.
Tel: 402-924-3262; Email: stbonifacestuart@gmail.com. Rev. James M. Weeder.

Catechesis Religious Program—Jan Kunz, D.R.E. Students 87.

TARNOV, PLATTE CO., ST. MICHAEL (1884) [CEM] (Polish)
309 3rd St., Tarnov, 68642. Tel: 402-246-2255; Email: stsjms@gmail.com. P.O. Box 255, Platte Center, 68653. Rev. Walter Jong-A-Kiem.

Catechesis Religious Program—Tel: 402-923-1308; Email: rbrand1@megavision.com. Michelle Brandl, D.R.E. Students 41.

TEKAMAH, BURT CO., ST. PATRICK (1889) [JC]
3480 Hwy. 32, Tekamah, 68061-1542.
Tel: 402-374-1692; Email: frkjsp@gmail.com; Web: www.stpatstekamah.com. 1323 R St., Tekamah, 68061-1542. Rev. Kevin J. Joyce.

Catechesis Religious Program—Tel: 402-870-2158. Ashley Olson, D.R.E. Students 105.

Mission—Holy Family, [CEM] 703 Fourth Ave., Decatur, 68020.

TILDEN, MADISON CO., OUR LADY OF MT. CARMEL (1887) [CEM]
300 E. 2nd St., P.O. Box 458, Tilden, 68781.
Tel: 402-368-7710; Email: olmctilden@frontiernet.org. Rev. Patrick K. Nields.
Res.: 302 E. 2nd St., Tilden, 68781. Web: www.olmctilden.org.

Catechesis Religious Program—Tel: 402-368-2954; Email: olmctilden@frontiernet.net. Corinne Frey, D.R.E. Students 44.

VALLEY, DOUGLAS CO., ST. JOHN (1917)
307 E. Meigs, Valley, 68064. Tel: 402-359-5783; Fax: 402-359-5217; Email: stjohn@stjohnvalleyne.com; Web: www.stjohnvalleyne.com. Rev. Lloyd A. Gnirk.
Res.: 209 E. Sunset, Valley, 68064.

Catechesis Religious Program—Email: molly@stjohnvalleyne.com. Molly Zach, D.R.E. Students 169.

VERDIGRE, KNOX CO., ST. WENCESLAUS (1884) [CEM] (Czech—Bohemian)
211 4th Ave., Verdigre, 68783-0009.
Tel: 402-668-2331; Email: stwencoffice@gpcom.net; Web: www.saintsww.org. 409 S. Third St., P.O. Box 9, Verdigre, 68783-0009. Rev. Kizito R. Okhuoya.

Catechesis Religious Program—Jean Pavelka, D.R.E. Students 51.

Mission—St. William Mission of Verdigre, 262 Buckeye Rd., Niobrara, 68760.

WALTHILL, THURSTON CO., ST. JOSEPH (1912) (Native American)
501 Main St., Walthill, 68067. Tel: 402-878-2402; Email: newsstaugustine@archomaha.org; Web: staugustinemission.org. Mailing Address: P.O. Box 766, Winnebago, 68071-0766. Revs. Daniel L. Wittrock; Mark T. Beran; Mark M. Bridgman; Deacon Donald Blackbird Jr.

Mission—Our Lady of Fatima Mission of Walthill, Elk St., Macy, 68039.

WAYNE, WAYNE CO., ST. MARY (1881)
412 E. 8th St., Wayne, 68787. Tel: 402-375-2000; Email: parish@stmaryswayne.org. Rev. Jeffrey J. Mollner.

School—St. Mary's Catholic School, (Grades PreK-6), 420 E. 7th St., Wayne, 68787. Tel: 402-375-2337. Lay Teachers 4; Students 53.

Catechesis Religious Program—Students 128.

WEST POINT, CUMING CO., ASSUMPTION B.V.M. (1875) [CEM]
343 N. Monitor St., West Point, 68788.
Tel: 402-372-2188; Email: wpstmary@yahoo.com; Web: wpstmary.com. Rev. Steven D. Emanuel; Deacons Vincent Maly; Kenneth Batenhorst; David Baumert; Francis Meiergerd.

School—Guardian Angel Central Catholic, (Grades PreK-6), 408 E. Walnut St., West Point, NY 68788. Tel: 402-372-5328; Email: dmeister@gaccbluejays.org; Web: www.gaccbluejays.org. Mrs. Kate Hagemann, Prin. Lay Teachers 20; Students 254; Clergy / Religious Teachers 1.

Catechesis Religious Program—Email: spknobbe@gmail.com. Patti Knobbe, D.R.E. Students 79.

WINNEBAGO, THURSTON CO.

1—ST. AUGUSTINE CATHOLIC CHURCH (1909) [CEM] (Native American) (Indian Mission)
1 Mission Rd. S., P.O. Box 766, Winnebago, 68071.
Tel: 402-878-2402; Email: newsstaugustine@archomaha.org; Web: staugustinemission.org. Revs. Mark T. Beran; Mark M. Bridgman.

School—St. Augustine Indian Mission School, (Grades K-8), Tel: 402-878-2291; Fax: 402-878-2760; Email: dnblackbird@archomaha.org. Rev. Mark T. Beran, Dir.; Deacon Donald Blackbird Jr., Prin. Lay Teachers 13; Students 107; Clergy / Religious Teachers 1.

Mission—St. Cornelius Mission of Winnebago, 410 N. Third St., Homer, 68030.

Catechesis Religious Program—Email: mtberan@archomaha.org. Students 14.

2—OUR LADY OF FATIMA OF MACY, Closed. This is a mission of St. Joseph, Walthill.

WISNER, CUMING CO., ST. JOSEPH (1879) [CEM] [JC] (Irish—German)
1318 Ave. G West, Wisner, 68791. Tel: 402-529-3891. P.O. Box 623, Wisner, 68791. Rev. Vincent Sunguti, Admin.

Catechesis Religious Program—Mrs. Sarah Jacobs, D.R.E.; Mrs. Capri McGuire, D.R.E. Students 95.

WYNOT, CEDAR CO.

1—HOLY FAMILY PARISH OF CEDAR COUNTY (2000) [JC4] (German)
Paul St. and Valley View Dr., Bow Valley, 68739.
Tel: 402-254-3311; Tel: 402-357-2465; Email:

holyfamily@gpcom.net. Rev. Eric S. Olsen; Deacon Shane Kleinschmitt, D.R.E.

Immaculate Conception Church—St. Helena and 9th Sts., St. Helena, 68774.

Sacred Heart Church, W. 8th St. & Emerson Ave., Wynot, 68792.

Ss. Peter and Paul Church, Paul St. & Valley View Dr., Bow Valley, 68739.

Catechesis Religious Program—Wynot Public School: 709 St. James Ave., Wynot, 68792. Tel: 402-254-6980 . Students 107.

2—SACRED HEART, Merged see Holy Family of Cedar County.

On Duty Outside the Archdiocese:
Revs.—
Broudou, Joseph G., Order of St. Augustine, Our Lady of Good Counsel Province, Chicago, IL; Community of the Beatitudes, Denver, CO
Hoesing, Paul C., Kenrick-Glennon Seminary, St. Louis, MO
LaPlante, David W., Archdiocese of Milwaukee
O'Donnell, Ralph B., Secretariat for Clergy; Consecrated Life & Vocations of the USCCB
Parrinello, Frank P., Diocese of Tulsa
Perez, Oscar A., (Venezuela) Archdiocese of Miami.

Special Assignment:
Revs.—
Gabuzda, Richard J., Exec. Dir. I.P.F.
Melchior, Gerald P., Mass Supply
Sodoro, Carl F., Chap., CHI Health Bergan Mercy.

Military Chaplains:
Rev.—
DeGuzman, Dennis U., Army National Guard; U.S.A.F.

Leave of Absence:
Rev.—
Mendoza, Jose, (Venezuela).

Retired:
Rev. Msgrs.—
Furlong, Thomas D., (Retired), 7323 Shirley St., #116, 68124
Gilg, James E., (Retired), 14100 Crawford St., Boys Town, 68010
Newman, Nelson A., (Retired), 2015 24th St., Central City, 68826
Nienaber, Robert H., (Retired), 7323 Shirley St. #312, 68124
Whelan, Bill S., (Retired), 7323 Shirley St. #101, 68124
Wiese, Melvern A., (Retired), 320 E. Decatur St., West Point, 68788
Wolbach, Richard A., (Retired), 7323 Shirley St., #311, 68124
Revs.—
Albenesius, Paul M., (Retired), P.O. Box 151, Jackson, 68743
Bartek, William C., (Retired), 7323 Shirley St. #204, 68124
Battiato, Ronald A., (Retired), 2952 Bluff Rd., Cedar Bluffs, 68015
Benliro, Fernando C., (Retired), 9620 W. Russell Rd. #1105, Las Vegas, NV 89148
Cleary, Donald M., (Retired), 19217 Costanzo Plz., 1B, Elkhorn, 68022
Conley, Martin P., (Retired), 7323 Shirley St. #315, 68124
Dvorak, Franklin A., (Retired), 7323 Shirley St., #111, 68124
Finch, Joseph E., (Retired)
Fitzgerald, William J., (Retired), 4800 N. 68th St., Unit 133, Scottsdale, AZ 85251
Fitzpatrick, Michael R., (Retired), 7323 Shirley St., #308, 68124. 7323 Shirley St. #308, 68124
Hanneman, Dennis A., (Retired), 7323 Shirley St., #310, 68124
Kramper, James V., (Retired), P.O. Box 898, Ponca, 68770
Lordemann, Frank W., (Retired), 14100 Crawford St., Boys Town, 68010
McCaslin, John O., (Retired), 3636 California St., #415, 68131
McCaslin, R. Patrick, (Retired), 9215 Laurel Plaza, 68134
McCluskey, James F., (Retired), 311 E. 7th St., Apt. 106, Wayne, 68787
McKamy, Eldon J., (Retired), 7323 Shirley St., #103, 68124
Ostrander, Gary L., (Retired), St. Patrick Parish, 20755 Appaloosa St., Elkhorn, 68022
Peschel, Roland A., (Retired), 7323 Shirley St. #210, 68124
Peter, Valentine J., S.T.D., J.C.D., (Retired), 900 N. 90th St., Apt. 497, 68114
Preisinger, Robert F., (Retired), 1729 N. 177th Plz., 68118
Printy, Michael G., (Retired), 600 Brookstone Meadows Plz., #1402A, 68022
Richling, Theodore L., (Retired), 6809 N. 68th Plz., Rm. 271-A, 68152
Schlautman, Wayne W., (Retired), 6809 N. 68th Plz., #158, 68152
Schmitz, Michael D., (Retired), Avera Majestic Bluffs, 200 Benedictine Ln., Yankton, SD 57078
Schwartz, Hugh F., (Retired), 7323 Shirley St., #205, 68124
Schwertley, James F., (Retired), 17475 Frances St., 201, 68130
Shane, Donald W., (Retired), 11117 Jones St., 68154
Soltys, Daniel F., (Retired), 7323 Shirley St., #301, 68124
Spenner, Jerome I., (Retired), 7323 Shirley St., #203, 68124
Steffes, LuVerne W., (Retired), 208 N. Carberry, P.O. Box 494, Atkinson, 68713
Stevens, Clifford J., (Retired), 3636 California St., #201, 68131
Stortz, Donald L., (Retired), 626 N. 44th St., 68131
Swanson, Charles F., (Retired), 7323 Shirley St., #213, 68124
Tiegs, James R., (Retired), 7323 Shirley St., #102, 68124
Vavrina, Kenneth P., (Retired), 7323 Shirley St., #314, 68124
Whiteing, Richard J., (Retired), 2708 N. 109th Ct., Apt. 205, 68164.

Permanent Deacons:
Abbott, Ernest Jr.
Abboud, Fred
Adams, Chuck
Anderson, Andy
Anderson, Dennis
Archbold, Steve
Aulner, Al
Bang, David
Barbour, Frank, (On Duty Outside the Diocese)
Barnes, William J.
Bartman, Frank
Bash, Gary
Batenhorst, Kenneth F.
Baumert, David
Bevan, Edward J.
Blackbird, Donald Jr.
Blanton, Dan, (On Duty Outside the Diocese)
Bloomingdale, Tim
Boeding, Mark
Boettger, Kent, (On Duty Outside the Diocese)
Broz, Ken
Burbach, Bernie
Burton, Thomas
Butterfield, George, (On Duty Outside the Diocese)
Camp, William J.
Capoun, Mark
Capoun, Marvin
Carl, Robert J.
Carter, William Jr.
Casart, Ronald
Cerio, Paul M.
Chambers, James
Chapman, Robert
Choi, Joseph
Christensen, Dave
Clausen, Donald
Coler, Theodore
Connor, Dennis
Conrad, James J. Jr.
Conzett, Michael
Cowles, Donald
Crotty, Richard
Crowley, Martin
Dagerman, John
Dahlseid, John, (On Duty Outside the Diocese)
DeSelm, Michael J.
Dethlefs, Dennis
DiGiacomo, Yano
Digilio, John J.
Digilio, Peter
Dineen, Lonnie
Doerneman, Paul
Dohmen, Louis
Doolittle, James
Dreismeier, Paul
Drvol, Gregg
Elizalde, Gregorio
Elster, George
Enzolera, Sebastian
Eubanks, Paul
Ficenic, Terry
Filips, Roger
Fillaus, Frank
Finney, Jack
Fischman, David
Fisher, Ed
Fitzgerald, Thomas
Fletcher, Michael
Floersch, Steve
Foray, Andrew
Franco, Martin
Frankenfield, Thomas H.
French, Gary
Fulcher, Jon
Fuller, Andrew
Fuller, Kevin
Gau, Jerome
Gentrup, Edward
Gentrup, Leon
Goldsmith, Edwin G., (On Duty Outside the Diocese)
Graef, David
Grandinetti, Steve
Gross, Patrick
Grosse, Randy
Gurney, David
Gutierrez, Omar
Guzman, Luis
Hamilton, Robert
Hanson, Chris
Hartnett, Joseph
Hastings, Danny
Heck, Lawrence
Heine, Brian
Hendricks, Fred
Hennessey, Gary
Henry, Victor R.
Hesson, Ronald W.
Hill, William H. Jr.
Hills, Lyle
Hilt, Frank
Hopkins, Richard
Howard, Timothy
Huck, John
Hughes, Thomas J.
Hunke, Melvin, (On Duty Outside the Diocese)
Jackman, Raymond
Jansen, Clarence
Jizba, Richard
Jordan, Steve
Joyce, Kevin
Kaiser, Roland, (On Duty Outside the Diocese)
Kalkowski, Kenneth
Karmazin, Duane
Keating, James, Ph.D.
Keiter, Daniel
Keller, Daniel G.
Kelly, Brendan
Kersenbrock, Maurice
Klein, David
Kleinschmitt, Shane
Knockenhauer, George F.
Knudsen, Dennis
Kober, Mark, (On Duty Outside the Diocese)
Konsel, John
Koziel, Timothy J.
Kozney, Jerry
Kramper, Jim, (On Duty Outside the Diocese)
Kreun, Wesley
Krieski, Timothy, (On Duty Outside the Diocese)
Kronschnabel, John
Krueger, David
Kulus, Joe
Kurtz, Stanley
L'Archevesque, Charles
Laird, Joseph
Larson, Rick
Lauber, Eldon
Leick, Mike
Leininger, Tim
Lenz, Doug
Lenz, Patrick
Long, Harlan
Lukowski, Ray
Luna, Stephen J.
Maly, Vince
Mapes, Gerald
Marsh, Douglas
Martinez, Alberto
Mascarello, Frank
Mayhan, Leo II
McGowan, Kelly
McNeil, Timothy F., J.C.L.
Medeiros, David
Meiergerd, Francis
Menzel, Ted
Metzinger, Roger, (On Duty Outside the Diocese)
Mielak, Lawrence
Miller, Jack
Mines, John
Morello, Carl
Mruz, Lawrence F.
Mueller, Daniel D.
Mueting, Richard, (On Duty Outside the Diocese)
Mulcahy, Timothy A.
Nardini, James, (On Duty Outside the Diocese)
Narducci, Warren, (On Duty Outside the Diocese)

Naughtin, James
Nelson, Steven
Nguyen, Trung
Niedergeses, Richard
Olsenholler, Jeffery, (On Duty Outside the Diocese)
Osterhaus, Edwin
Overkamp, Robert J., J.C.L.
Park, Loren
Pavlik, Keith
Perchal, Daniel E.
Perry, Russ
Pickett, Robert
Placke, Donald
Placzek, Michael
Potts, Marcus
Powers, Paul, (On Duty Outside the Diocese)
Preister, Tim
Pribnow, Otto
Pribnow, Roger D.
Price, Terry
Probst, David A.
Rasmussen, Nickolas
Reed, Wayne
Reese, Mike, (On Duty Outside the Diocese)
Reilly, James L.
Reynolds, Mike
Ricketts, James
Rooney, Paul
Ryan, Ronald R.
Sachau, Kent E.
Sampier, Larry D.
Sanders, Thomas, (On Duty Outside the Diocese)
Saniuk, Daniel
Sawtelle, Harold
Schaecher, Melvin
Schaefer, Bradford
Schimonitz, Eugene
Schindel, James
Schlautman, William
Schulte, Thomas
Schultz, Charles J., (On Duty Outside the Diocese)
Schumacher, Allan
Seamann, Donald M., (On Duty Outside the Diocese)
Sheik, Charles
Shipman, James
Silva, Thomas
Simmonds, Bud
Simmons, Lyle
Small, John
Smith, Marty
Spenner, Arthur
Spicer, Ernest
St. Arnold, Skip
Starman, John
Staroski, Jim
Steel, Craig
Steffen, Paul
Stier, Robert A.
Sukup, Charles, (On Duty Outside the Diocese)
Tardy, Jim
Telich, Frank
Tharp, Bud
Thoene, Sylvan
Thomas, Brian
Thome, Duane
Throener, Lawrence F.
Tierney, Norman
True, John
Tunink, Douglas G.
Uhlik, Joseph R.
Valadez, Luis
VandeBerg, Eric
Viergutz, Robert
Villalobos, Benjamin Jr.
Villemure, Arthur, (On Duty Outside the Diocese)
Vrbka, John
Wacha, John
Warwick, Marty
Watson, James
Weeder, Paul
Weskirchen, Charles, (On Duty Outside the Diocese)
White, Mark
Wiebelhaus, Rodney
Wiehn, Dennis
Wolbach, Matthew
Wolverton, Allen
Young, William
Zak, John J. Jr.
Zurek, Jeffrey.

INSTITUTIONS LOCATED IN DIOCESE

[A] COLLEGES AND UNIVERSITIES

OMAHA. *College of Saint Mary* (1923) 7000 Mercy Rd., 68106. Tel: 402-399-2400; Fax: 402-399-2342; Email: enroll@csm.edu; Web: www.csm.edu. Dr. Maryanne Stevens, Pres.; Sara Kottich, Exec. Vice Pres. Opers. & Planning; Terri Campbell, Vice Pres. Alumnae & Donor Rels.; Sara Hanson, Vice Pres. Enrollment Svcs.; Tara Knudson Carl, Vice Pres. Student Devel.; Dr. John Healy, Vice Pres. Academic Affairs; Nate Neufind, Vice Pres. Strategic Mktg. & Commun.; Brigdette Renbarger, Vice Pres. Fin. & Admin. Svcs.; Marian Standeven, Vice Pres. Mission Integration. Lay Teachers 74; Sisters 5; Students 1,168.

**Creighton University* (1878) 2500 California Plaza, 68178. Tel: 402-280-2770; Fax: 402-280-2727; Email: president@creighton.edu; Web: www.creighton.edu. Rev. Daniel S. Hendrickson, S.J., Ph.D., Pres. & Contact; A. James Bothmer, Uni. Librarian. Lay Teachers 994; Priests 35; Students 8,910; Total Enrollment 8,910; Total Staff 1,281; Clergy / Religious Teachers 8.

The University is comprised of the following schools:

College of Arts and Sciences, 2500 California Plaza, 68178. Tel: 402-280-2431; Fax: 402-280-4729; Email: ccasdean@creighton.edu; Web: www.creighton.edu. Dr. Bridget Keegan, Dean, College Arts and Sciences. Students 2,845; Clergy / Religious Teachers 7.

Heider College of Business, 2500 California Plaza, 68178. Tel: 402-280-2852; Fax: 402-280-2172; Email: president@creighton.edu; Web: www.creighton.edu. Students 1,536; Clergy / Religious Teachers 1.

Graduate School and University College / Summer Sessions, 2500 California Plaza, 68178. Tel: 402-280-2424; Tel: 402-280-2870; Fax: 402-280-2423; Fax: 402-280-5762; Web: www.creighton.edu. Dr. Gail Jensen, Ph.D., Dean, Graduate School. Students 1,769; Clergy / Religious Teachers 2.

School of Law, 2500 California Plaza, 68178. Tel: 402-280-2874; Fax: 402-280-3161; Web: www.creighton.edu. Mr. Michael Kelly, Interim Dean. Students 287; Clergy / Religious Teachers 1.

School of Dentistry, 2500 California Plaza, 68178. Tel: 402-280-5061; Fax: 402-280-5094. Dr. Mark A. Latta, D.M.D., M.S., Dean, School of Dentistry; Dr. Thomas Murray, Interim Provost. Students 377; Clergy / Religious Teachers 1.

School of Medicine, 2500 California Plaza, 68178. Tel: 402-280-2600; Fax: 402-280-4027; Web: www.creighton.edu. Dr. Robert Dunlay, M.D., Dean, School of Medicine. Students 630; Clergy / Religious Teachers 5.

School of Nursing, 2500 California Plaza, 68178. Tel: 402-280-2004; Fax: 402-280-2045; Web: www.creighton.edu. Dr. Catherine Todero, Ph.D., R.N., F.A.A.N., Dean, School of Nursing.

School of Pharmacy and Health Professions, 2500 California Plaza, 68178. Tel: 402-280-1828; Fax: 402-280-5738. Dr. Amy Wilson, Interim Dean. Students 1,163; Clergy / Religious Teachers 1.

[B] NEWMAN CENTERS

OMAHA. *St. John Paul II Newman Center, Inc.*, 1221 S. 71st St., 68106. Tel: 402-557-5575, Ext. 3028; Email: info@jpiiomaha.org; Web: www.jpiiomaha.org. Rev. Joseph C. Taphorn, J.C.L., Pastor; Ms. Katie Winkler, Campus Min.; Mrs. Cathy Pacholski, Stewardship & Devel.; Ms. Lauren Hankes, Resident Mgr.; Mrs. Renee Hendricks, Business Mgr.

[C] HIGH SCHOOLS, ARCHDIOCESAN

OMAHA. *Roncalli Catholic High School of Omaha* (1964) 6401 Sorensen Pkwy., 68152. Tel: 402-571-7670; Fax: 402-571-3216; Email: businessoffice@roncallicatholic.org; Email: aoconnor@roncallicatholic.org; Web: www.roncallicatholic.org. Ann O'Connor, Pres.; Timothy Orr, Prin.; Mr. James Meister, Activities Dir. & Asst. Prin.; Revs. Lloyd A. Gnirk, Pres. Emeritus, Email: elgn52@cox.net; Matthew J. Niggemeyer, Chap. Lay Teachers 26; Priests 1; Students 370; Total Staff 50.

V.J. & Angela Skutt Catholic High School (1993) 3131 S. 156th St., 68130-1907. Tel: 402-333-0818; Fax: 402-333-1790; Email: jeremymoore@skuttcatholic.com; Web: www.skuttcatholic.com. Jeremy Moore, Pres.; Rob Meyers, Prin.; Michael Bailey, Asst. Prin.; Rev. Patrick C. Harrison, J.C.L., Chap. Lay Teachers 58; Priests 1; Students 740; Total Staff 80.

BELLEVUE. *Daniel J. Gross Catholic High School*, 7700 S. 43rd St., Bellevue, 68147. Tel: 402-734-2000; Fax: 402-734-4270; Email: dao@gcgmail.org; Web: www.grosscatholic.org. Rev. Ryan P. Lewis, J.C.L., S.T.L., Chap., Campus Min.; Dr. Dorothy Ostrowski, Pres. & Contact. Lay Teachers 32; Priests 1; Students 405; Total Staff 57.

COLUMBUS. *Scotus Central Catholic High School*, (Grades 7-12), 1554 18th Ave., Columbus, 68601. Tel: 402-564-7165; Fax: 402-564-6004; Email: johnoutka@scotuscc.org; Email: jschueth@scotuscc.org; Web: www.scotuscc.org. Jeff Ohnoutka, Pres.; Merlin Lahm, Asst. Prin.; Rev. Mathew Capadano, Chap. & Teacher; Mrs. Cathy Podliska, Librarian. Lay Teachers 27; Priests 1; Students 349; Clergy / Religious Teachers 4.

ELGIN. *Pope John XXIII Central Catholic High School at Elgin*, 303 Remington St., P.O. Box 179, Elgin, 68636. Tel: 402-843-5325; Fax: 402-843-2297; Email: bgetzfred@pjcrusaders.org. Betty Getzfred, Prin.; Rev. Kevin W. Vogel, Pres.; Lauren Borer, Librarian. Lay Teachers 10; School Sisters of St. Francis 1; Students 54; Clergy / Religious Teachers 1.

HARTINGTON. *Cedar Catholic High School* (1964) 401 S. Broadway, P.O. Box 15, Hartington, 68739-0015. Tel: 402-254-3906; Fax: 402-254-3976; Email: cuttecht@cedarcatholic.org; Web: www.cedarcatholic.org. Mr. Christopher Uttecht, Prin.; Rev. Owen W. Korte, Pres.; Rob Bengston, Guidance Counselor. Administrators 1; Lay Teachers 18; Priests 3; Students 180; Total Staff 22; Clergy / Religious Teachers 3.

WEST POINT. *Guardian Angels Central Catholic*, 419 E. Decatur, West Point, 68788. Tel: 402-372-5326; Fax: 402-372-5327; Email: dmeister@gaccbluejays.org; Web: www.gaccbluejays.org. Rev. Steven Emanuel, Pres.; Mrs. Kate Hageman, Prin. Lay Teachers 13; Priests 3; Students 167; Clergy / Religious Teachers 3.

[D] HIGH SCHOOLS, PRIVATE

OMAHA. *Creighton Preparatory School*, 7400 Western Ave., 68114. Tel: 402-393-1190; Fax: 402-393-0260; Web: www.creightonprep.creighton.edu. Rev. Thomas W. Neitzke, S.J., Pres.; James Bopp, Prin.; Revs. Kevin C. Schneider, S.J., Dir. Adult Spirituality; James A. Sinnerud, S.J.; Robert J. Tillman, S.J., Counselor; Dan Kennedy, Student Activities Dir.; Mrs. Diane Sands, Librarian. Lay Teachers 78; Priests 4; Students 1,010; Clergy / Religious Teachers 2.

Duchesne Academy of the Sacred Heart (1881) 3601 Burt St., 68131. Tel: 402-558-3800; Fax: 402-558-0051; Email: mbrudney@duchesneacademy.org; Web: www.duchesneacademy.org. Meg Brudney, Head of School & Contact; Dr. Laura Hickman, Prin. Girls 330; Lay Teachers 36; Students 330.

Marian High School, 7400 Military Ave., 68134. Tel: 402-571-2618, Ext. 1212; Fax: 402-571-2978; Email: mhiggins@omahamarian.org; Web: marianhighschool.net. Mary Higgins, Pres.; Susie Sullivan, Prin.; Rochelle Rohlfs, Asst. Prin. & Athletic Dir.; Deacon Kevin Fuller, Adult Faith Formation Coord.; Molly Raabe, Librarian. Servants of Mary. Girls 704; Lay Teachers 50; Students 704; Clergy / Religious Teachers 2.

Marian High School Endowment Trust.

Marian High School Scholarship Endowment Trust.

Mercy High School (1955) 1501 S. 48th St., 68106. Tel: 402-553-9424; Fax: 402-553-0394; Email: hannond@mercyhigh.org; Web: www.mercyhigh.org. Sr. Delores Hannon, R.S.M., Pres. & Contact; Kristi Wessling, Prin. Girls 362; Lay Teachers 36; Sisters of Mercy of the Americas 1; Students 362; Clergy / Religious Teachers 1.

ELKHORN. *Mount Michael Benedictine School*, 22520 Mt. Michael Rd., Elkhorn, 68022-3400. Tel: 402-289-2541; Fax: 442-289-4539; Email: dpeters@mountmichael.org; Web: www.mountmichael.com. Rt. Rev. Michael Liebl, O.S.B., Abbot; Dr. David Peters, Ed.D., Head of School; Revs. John Hagemann, O.S.B., Campus Min.; Daniel Lenz, O.S.B., Instructor; Louis L. Sojka, O.S.B., Business Mgr.; Stephen J. Plank, O.S.B., Instructor; Bros. August Schaefer, O.S.B., Theology Instructor; Luke Clinton, Librarian. Brothers 3; Lay Teachers 22; Priests 5; Sisters 1; Students 237; Clergy / Religious Teachers 9.

[E] ELEMENTARY SCHOOLS, INTER-PAROCHIAL

OMAHA. *St. James-Seton School*, (Grades PreK-8), 4720 N. 90th St., 68134. Tel: 402-572-0339; Fax: 402-572-0347; Email: wkell@sjsomaha.org; Web: sjsomaha.org. William Kelly, Prin. & Contact. Lay Teachers 33; Students 510; Total Staff 63.

St. Pius X-St. Leo School (1956) (Grades PreK-8), 6905 Blondo St., 68104. Tel: 402-551-6667; Fax: 402-551-8123; Email: cory.sepich@spsl.net; Web: www.spsl.net. Cory Sepich, Prin.; Mrs. Christy Vogel, Librarian. (Two-parish school) Lay Teachers 51; Students 697.

FORDYCE. *West Catholic Elementary*, (Grades PreK-6), 303 Omaha St., P.O. Box 167, Fordyce, 68736-0167. Tel: 402-357-3507; Fax: 402-357-3551; Email: jekeiter@archomaha.org. Mary Jean Klug, Teacher Facilitator; Dianne Becker, Librarian; Krista Heithold; Joni Stevens, Business Mgr.; Callie Sokol, Teacher; Minette Paltz, Teacher. Serving parishes in Constance, Fordyce & Menominee Lay Teachers 3; Students 13; Clergy / Religious Teachers 1.

HARTINGTON. *East Catholic Elementary*, (Grades PreK-6), Serving parishes in Bow Valley, St. Helena & Wynot. 108 W. 889th Rd., Hartington, 68739-6079. Tel: 402-254-2146; Fax: 402-254-3758; Email: mjklug@schools.archomaha.org; Email: mvpinkelman@schools.archomaha.org. Mary Jean Klug, Teacher Facilitator. Lay Teachers 5; Students 51.

HOWELLS. *Howells Community Catholic School*, (Grades 1-6), 114 N. 6th St., Howells, 68641. Tel: 402-986-1689; Fax: 402-986-1689; Email: office@hccs.esu7.org. Carol Vogel, Head Teacher. Serving parishes in Howells, Olean, Heun, Aloys & Tabor Clergy 1; Lay Teachers 5; Students 45; Clergy / Religious Teachers 1.

[F] ELEMENTARY SCHOOLS, PRIVATE

OMAHA. *CUES School System*, (Grades PreK-8), 2207 Wirt St., 68110. Tel: 402-451-5755; Email: john@cuesschools.org; Web: www.cuesschools.org. Rev. David M. Korth, Pres. Lay Teachers 45; Priests 1; Students 558; Clergy / Religious Teachers 1.

All Saints Catholic School, (Grades PreK-8), 1335 S. 10th St., 68108. Tel: 402-346-5757; Fax: 402-346-8794; Email: terri@allsaintscs.org; Web: allsaintscs.org/. Lay Teachers 12; Priests 1; Students 162.

Holy Name School, (Grades PreK-8), 2901 Fontenelle Blvd., 68104. Tel: 402-451-5403; Email: tmurray@hnsomaha.org; Web: holynameschoolomaha.org. Clergy 2; Lay Teachers 19; Priests 1; Students 249.

Sacred Heart School, (Grades K-8), 2205 Binney St., 68110. Tel: 402-451-5858. Lay Teachers 14; Priests 1; Students 147.

Jesuit Academy (1996) (Grades 4-8), 2311 N. 22nd St., 68110. Tel: 402-346-4464; Fax: 402-341-1817; Web: www.jesuitacademy.org. Mike Masek, Pres.; Mr. Troy Wharton, Prin. Lay Teachers 10; Students 76; Total Staff 21; Clergy / Religious Teachers 1.

Omaha Catholic School Consortium, (Grades PreK-8), 4501 S. 41 St., 68107. Tel: 402-590-2810; Fax: 402-590-2811; Web: www.omahacsc.org. Mrs. Chris Nelson, Exec. Lay Teachers 116; Students 1,807.

Holy Cross School Building, (Grades PreK-8), 1502 S. 48th St., 68106-2599. Tel: 402-551-3773; Fax: 402-556-1896; Email: tmann@omahacsc.org; Web: www.holycrossomaha.com. Tawnya Mann, Prin. Lay Teachers 29; Students 410.

Our Lady of Lourdes School Building, (Grades PreK-8), 2124 S. 32nd Ave., 68105-3198. Tel: 402-341-5604; Fax: 402-341-9957; Email: mjfiedler@omahacsc.org; Web: www.ollomaha.com. Megan Fielder, Prin. Lay Teachers 19; Students 315.

St. Bernadette School, (Grades PreSchool-8), 7600 S. 42nd St., 68147-1702. Tel: 402-731-3033; Fax: 402-731-8735; Email: lschultz@stbernadetteschool.net; Web: www.stbernadetteschool.net. Lynn Schultz, Prin. Lay Teachers 16; Students 273.

Ss. Peter & Paul Building, (Grades PreK-8), 3619 X St., 68107-3247. Tel: 402-731-4713; Fax: 402-731-2633; Email: abauer@sppsaints.org; Web: www.sppomaha.org. Andrew Bauer, Prin. Lay Teachers 23; Students 298.

St. Thomas More School Building, (Grades PreSchool-8), 3515 S. 48th Ave., 68106-4532. Tel: 402-551-9504; Fax: 402-551-9507; Email: gdavis@omahacsc.org; Web: www.stmbengals.org. Gary Davis, Prin. Lay Teachers 24; Students 425.

[G] SPECIAL EDUCATION

OMAHA. *Madonna School & Community-Based Services*, 6402 N. 71st Plaza, 68104. Tel: 402-556-1883; Fax: 402-556-7332; Web: www.madonnaschool.org. Mr. Jonathan Burt, Pres.; Jay Dunlap, Pres. Serving special needs students. Administrators 6; Lay Teachers 6; Students 36; Para Teachers 7.

Life Skills Transition Program, 6402 N. 71st Plaza, 68104. Tel: 402-556-1883; Fax: 402-556-7332; Email: dlcochran@cox.net. Diane Cochran, Dir.

Madonna Employment Services, 6402 N. 71st Plaza, 68104. Tel: 402-556-1883; Fax: 402-556-7332; Email: dlcochran@cox.net. Diane Cochran, Dir.

Madonna Community-Based Services, 9205 Bedford, 68134. Tel: 402-551-5441; Fax: 402-551-6910; Email: rmoses@mshop.omhcoxmail.com. Robin Moses, Dir. Workshop for physical and mental disabilities. Total Enrollment 35; Total Staff 10.

[H] GENERAL HOSPITALS

OMAHA. **Alegent Creighton Health*, 12809 W. Dodge Rd., 68154. Tel: 402-343-4343; Email: info@alegent.org. Cliff Robertson, CEO; Kevin Miller, Pres.; Kevin Beckmann, Pres.; Colleen Leise, Divsn. Mgr., Pastoral Care. Includes CHI Health Lakeside Hospital, CHI Health Midlands Hospital & CHI Health Plainview Hospital. Bed Capacity 402; Tot Asst. Annually 64,809; Total Staff 1,112.

**Alegent Health - Bergan Mercy Health System* (1910) 7500 Mercy Rd., 68124. Tel: 402-398-6060; Fax: 402-398-6920; Email: info@alegent.org. Kevin Nokels, Pres.; Colleen Leise, Divsn. Mgr., Pastoral Care; Rev. Carl F. Sodoro, Chap. Affiliate of Catholic Health Initiatives. Bed Capacity 335; Tot Asst. Annually 71,765; Total Staff 2,153.

**CHI Health Foundation*, 12809 W. Dodge Rd., 68154. Tel: 402-343-4550; Email: info@alegent.org. Kathy Bertolini, Divsn. Vice Pres., Philanthropy. Bed Capacity 400; Tot Asst. Annually 118,345; Total Staff 1,552.

**Alegent Health - Immanuel Medical Center*, 6901 N. 67th St., 68122. Tel: 402-572-2121; Email: info@alegent.org. Ann Schumacher, Pres.; Colleen Leise, Divsn. Mgr., Pastoral Care; Julia Knezetic, Chap. Bed Capacity 262; Tot Asst. Annually 38,941; Total Staff 1,177.

O'NEILL. *Avera St. Anthony's Hospital* (1952) 300 N. 2nd St., O'Neill, 68763. Tel: 402-336-2611; Fax: 402-336-5135; Email: todd.consbruck@avera.org; Web: www.avera.org/st-anthonys. Todd Consbruck, Pres. & CEO. Sponsored by Sisters of the Presentation of the B.V.M. of Aberdeen, SD & Benedictine Sisters of Sacred Heart Monastery, Yankton, SDAttended by St. Patrick Church. Bed Capacity 25; Tot Asst. Annually 33,138; Total Staff 252.

SCHUYLER. **Alegent Health - Memorial Hospital, Schuyler*, 104 W. 17th St., Schuyler, 68661. Tel: 402-352-2441; Email: info@alegent.org. Connie Peters, Pres. Bed Capacity 10; Tot Asst. Annually 2,741; Total Staff 59.

WEST POINT. *Franciscan Care Services, Inc.* dba St. Francis Memorial Hospital, 430 N. Monitor St., West Point, 68788-1595. Tel: 402-372-2404; Fax: 402-372-2360; Email: jwordekemper@fcswp.org; Web: www.fcswp.org. Jerry Wordekemper, CEO & Contact; Mary Jo "Mitch" Shemek, Chap. Franciscan Sisters of Christian Charity. Bed Capacity 25; Sisters 2; Tot Asst. Annually 114,299; Total Staff 265.

[I] NURSING AND CONVALESCENT HOMES

OMAHA. *Mercy Villa*, 1845 S. 72nd St., 68124. Tel: 402-391-6224; Fax: 402-390-8691; Email: mhilton@mercywmw.org. Terese Holm, R.N., M.S.N., Dir. Retirement Home for the Sisters of Mercy of the Americas for the West Midwest Community. Bed Capacity 33; Sisters 23; Tot Asst. Annually 40; Total Staff 44.

New Cassel Retirement Center, 900 N. 90th St., 68114. Tel: 402-393-2277; Fax: 402-393-3784; Email: info@newcassel.org; Web: www.newcassel.org. Julie Sebastian, Pres. & CEO. School Sisters of St. Francis. Tot Asst. Annually 225.

WEST POINT. .

[J] FAMILY SERVICE CENTERS

OMAHA. *Catholic Charities*, Daniel E. Sheehan Center, 3300 N. 60th St., 68104. Tel: 402-554-0520; Fax: 402-554-0365; Email: catholiccharities@ccomaha.org; Web: www.ccomaha.org. Mr. Gregg Wilson, Exec. Dir. Tot Asst. Annually 75,000; Total Staff 47.

Catholic Charities, Inc. Satellite Offices and Services:

Domestic Violence Services - The Shelter, c/o Daniel E. Sheehan Center, 3300 N. 60th St., 68104. Tel: 402-558-5700; Fax: 402-829-9208; Web: ccomaha.org. Mr. Gregg Wilson, Exec. Dir.; Joan Huss, L.M.H.P., L.A.D.C., Sr. Dir., Program Svcs. Dir., Behavioral Health Svcs. Services: 24-hour crisis line; advocacy; emergency shelter. Tot Asst. Annually 1,512; Total Staff 6.

Juan Diego Center, 5211 S. 31st St., 68107. Tel: 402-731-5413; Fax: 402-731-5865; Email: JuanDiegoCenter@ccomaha.org; Web: ccomaha.org. Jessica Bernal, Prog. Dir. Immigration Legal Assistance; Ana Barrios, Dir., Emergency and Supportive Food Svcs.; Guadalupe Millan, Dir. Microbusiness & Asset Devel. Services: Microbusiness and Asset Development, Emergency and Supportive Food Services, Immigration Legal Services, Latina Resource Center, Family Strengthening. Tot Asst. Annually 44,633; Total Staff 11.

St. Martin DePorres Center, 2111 Emmet St., 68110. Tel: 402-453-6363; Fax: 402-934-5313; Email: StMartinDePorresCenter@ccomaha.org. Ana Barrios, Dir. Emergency & Supportive Food Svcs.; Sue Malloy, Dir. Family Svcs.; Rita Heaston-Clark, Events & Projects Coord. Senior services; Food Assistance; Microbusiness Training. Tot Asst. Annually 11,881; Total Staff 2.

Sheehan Center, 3300 N. 60th St., 68104. Tel: 402-554-0520; Fax: 402-554-0365; Email: catholiccharities@ccomaha.org; Web: ccomaha.org. Mr. Gregg Wilson, Exec. Dir.; Theresa Swoboda, Vice Pres. Program Svcs.; Kathleen Berg, Vice Pres. Community Relations; Aaron Davis, Vice Pres. Ops.; Joan Huss, L.M.H.P., L.A.D.C., Sr. Dir. Program Svcs./Dir. Behavioral Health Svcs.; Dave Vankat, Sr. Dir. Community Relations; Ginny Czechut, Dir. Mktg. & Communications; Sue Malloy, Dir. Family Svcs.; Carly Bush, Controller. Services: Adoption services and support; Mental health/substance abuse assessments: Outpatient mental health treatment; Pregnancy counseling and support; Mentoring Moms program. Tot Asst. Annually 1,134; Total Staff 28.

[K] MONASTERIES AND RESIDENCES OF PRIESTS AND BROTHERS

OMAHA. *Jesuit Community at Creighton University*, 2500 California Plaza, 68178. Tel: 402-280-2776; Fax: 402-280-5590; Email: gomeara@jesuits.org. Revs. Philip R. Amidon, S.J.; Andrew Alexander, S.J.; Charles R. Baumann, S.J.; Hubert G. Boschert, S.J.; Gregory I. Carlson, S.J.; James F. Clifton, S.J.; Donald A. Doll, S.J.; Thomas Doyle, S.J., Spiritual Advisor/Care Svcs.; Robert J. Dufford, S.J.; Michael J. Flecky, S.J.; Lawrence D. Gillick, S.J.; Kevin Embach, Prof.; Kevin FitzGerald, S.J., Prof.; M. Dennis Hamm, S.J.; Daniel S. Hendrickson, S.J., Ph.D.; Charles T. Kestermeier, S.J.; Ashok Kujur, S.J., Doctoral Studies; David Matzko, S.J., Spiritual Advisor/Care Svcs.; John D. Mace, S.J.; Thomas Merkel, S.J.; Peter P. Nguyen, S.J.; Ugo Nweke, S.J., Grad. Student; Benjamin R. Osborne, S.J.; Gregory J. O'Meara, S.J., Rector; James Pribek, S.J., Prof.; Luis Rodriguez, S.J.; M. Ross Romero, S.J.; Martin Renzo Rosales, S.J.; Thomas J. Shanahan, S.J.; John F. Shea, S.J.; Thomas A. Simonds, S.J.; Lorn J. Snow, S.J.; Bros. Timothy R. Breen, S.J., Athletics Dept.; Arthur Deline, S.J., Grad. Student; Patrick J. Douglas, S.J., Vocations; James F. Heidrick, S.J., Univ. Maintenance; Gerald E. Peltz, S.J., Min.

Jesuit Community at Creighton University Brothers 4; Priests 31.

ELKHORN. *Mount Michael Benedictine Abbey* (1954) 22520 Mount Michael Rd., Elkhorn, 68022-3400. Tel: 402-289-2541; Fax: 402-289-4539; Email: mliebl@mountmichael.org; Web: www.mountmichael.org. Rt. Revs. Theodore Wolff, O.S.B.; Michael Liebl, O.S.B., Abbot; Raphael Walsh, O.S.B.; Revs. Nathanael Foshage, O.S.B.; Eugene McReynolds, O.S.B.; John Hagemann, O.S.B., Prior; Daniel Lenz, O.S.B.; Louis L. Sojka, O.S.B., Contact Person; Stephen J. Plank, O.S.B.; Bro. Jerome Kmiecik, O.S.B., Subprior. Mount Michael Benedictine Abbey Priests 9; Total Staff 60; Professed Brothers 11; Total Assisted 250.

ST. COLUMBANS. *Missionary Society of St. Columban*, P.O. Box 10, St. Columbans, 68056. Tel: 402-291-1920; Fax: 402-291-8693; Email: directorusa@columban.org; Email: usregionaloffice@columban.org; Web: www.columban.org. Revs. John Burger, S.S.C., Regl. Dir.; Gerald Saenz, S.S.C., Vice Dir.; John Valentine Kyne, S.S.C., House Superior; John Brannigan, S.S.C.; Diego Cabrera, S.S.C.; Arturo Aguilar, S.S.C.; William Brunner, S.S.C.; John Buckley, S.S.C.; Salvatore Caputo, S.S.C., (Retired); Francis Carroll, S.S.C.; Robert Clark, S.S.C.; David Clay; John Comiskey, S.S.C.; Peter Cronin, S.S.C.; Thomas Cusack, S.S.C.; George DaRoza, S.S.C.; Michael Donnelly, S.S.C.; Gerard Dunne, S.S.C.; James Dwyer, S.S.C.; Victor Gaboury, S.S.C., (Retired); Thomas Glennon, S.S.C.; Francis Grady, S.S.C., (Retired); Otto Imholte, S.S.C.; Donald Kelley, S.S.C., (Retired); Ronald Kelso, S.S.C.; Charles Lintz, S.S.C.; John Marley, S.S.C.; Vincent McCarthy, S.S.C., (Retired); Daniel McGinn, S.S.C.; Mark Mengel, S.S.C.; John Moran, S.S.C.; William Morton, S.S.C.; Kevin Mullins, S.S.C.; Robert Mosher, S.S.C.; Dennis O'Mara, S.S.C.; Charles O'Rourke, S.S.C., (Omaha, NE); Gerard O'Shaughnessy, S.S.C.; Brendan O'Sullivan, S.S.C.; Richard Pankratz, S.S.C.; Thomas Reynolds, S.S.C.; Francis Royer, S.S.C., (Retired); William Schmitt, S.S.C.; Thomas Shaughnessy, S.S.C., (Omaha, NE); John Smith, S.S.C.; James Stanley; Richard Steinhiber, S.S.C., (Omaha, NE); Alban Sueper, S.S.C., (Retired); William Sullivan, S.S.C.; William Sweeney, S.S.C.; Albert Utzig, S.S.C.; Thomas Walsh, S.S.C., (Retired); John Wanaurny, S.S.C.; Gerald Wilmsen, S.S.C., (Retired); Vincent Youngkamp,

S.S.C.; Rosalia Basada, Lay Missionary; Sainiana Tamatawale, Lay Missionary. Regional Headquarters and Administration Offices of the Columban Fathers in the United States

Corporate Title: Missionary Society of St. Columban Priests 54; Total in Community 10.

SCHUYLER. *Benedictine Mission House - Christ the King Priory*, 1123 Rd. I, P.O. Box 528, Schuyler, 68661-0528. Tel: 402-352-2177; Fax: 402-352-2176; Email: monastery@missionmonks.org; Web: www.missionmonks.org. Revs. Joel Macul, O.S.B., Prior; Volker Futter, O.S.B., Subprior; Thomas Aquinas Leitner, O.S.B.; Paul L. Kasun, O.S.B.; Adam Patras, O.S.B.; Thomas Andrew Hillenbrand, O.S.B. Brothers 4; Priests 6.

[L] CONVENTS AND RESIDENCES FOR SISTERS

OMAHA. *Franciscan Monastery of St. Clare* (1878) 22625 Edgewater Rd., 68022-3504. Cell: 402-350-6335; Tel: 402-558-4916; Fax: 402-558-5046; Email: srtheresina@omahapoorclare.org; Web: www.omahapoorclare.org. Sr. Theresina R. Santiago, O.S.C., Abbess. Poor Clares (Second Order of St. Francis)Poor Clare Nuns (Second Order of St. Francis) Sisters 13.

Motherhouse of the Servants of Mary, Convent of Our Lady of Sorrows, 7400 Military Ave., 68134. Tel: 402-571-2547; Fax: 402-573-6055; Email: secretary@osms.org; Web: www.osms.org. Sisters Mary Gehringer, O.S.M., Prioress & Contact; Jackie Ryan, O.S.M., Asst. Prioress. Sisters 67.

Provincial Motherhouse and Novitiate of the Notre Dame Sisters (1853) 3501 State St., 68112. Tel: 402-455-2994; Fax: 402-455-3974; Email: notredamesisters@notredamesisters.org; Web: www.notredamesisters.org. Sr. Margaret Hickey, N.D., Prov. Pres. Sisters 36.

Sisters of Mercy of the Americas West Midwest Community, Inc. (2008) 7262 Mercy Rd., 68124-2389. Tel: 402-393-8225; Fax: 402-393-8145; Email: sistersofmercy@mercywmw.org; Web: www.sistersofmercy.org/west-midwest. Sisters Susan Sanders, R.S.M., Pres.; Ana María Pineda, Vice Pres.; Margaret Mary Hinz, R.S.M., Leadership Team; Margaret Maloney, Leadership Team; Maria Klosowski, R.S.M., Leadership Team; Rebecca Vandenbosch, CFO. Sisters 531; Associates 605.

Knowles Mercy Spirituality Center, 2304 Campanile Rd., Waterloo, 68069. Tel: 402-393-8225; Fax: 402-393-8145; Email: sistersofmercy@mercywmw.org; Web: www.kmscenter.org. Overnight Capacity 15; Daytime Capacity 60; Staff 6.

BELLEVUE. *Sisters of the Good Shepherd (R.G.S.)*, 602B Fort Crook Rd. S., Bellevue, 68005. Tel: 402-551-2966; Fax: 402-291-1375; Email: ellen.dolan@stmarysbellevue.com; Web: www.goodshepherdsisters.org. Sr. Ellen Dolan, R.G.S., RCIA Coord. Sisters 1.

NORFOLK. *Immaculata Monastery* (1923) 300 N. 18th St., Norfolk, 68701-3622. Tel: 402-371-3438; Fax: 402-371-0127; Email: rtoffosb@gmail.com; Web: www.mbsmissionaries.org. Sr. Roseann Ocken, O.S.B., Prioress

Missionary Benedictine Sisters Sisters 37; Personnel 16.

[M] SECULAR INSTITUTES

OMAHA. *Cor Unum Family Inc.*, 7323 Shirley St., #101, 68124. Tel: 402-933-9812; Email: bwhelan333@gmailcom. Rev. Msgr. Bill S. Whelan, Contact Person, (Retired).

ELKHORN. *The Institute of the Apostolic Oblates, Inc.* (1947) 11002 N. 204th St., Elkhorn, 68022. Tel: 402-289-1938; Email: prosanctity@gmail.com; Web: www.prosanctity.org. Teresa Monaghen, Local Mod., Omaha, Tel: 402-289-2670; Jessica L. Kary, Natl. Pro Sanctity Dir., Natl. Admin., Local Mod. Ecclesial organization: Promotes apostolates of holiness; teaches, supports and guides people seeking to deepen their spiritual life.

DBA Pro Sanctity Movement.

[N] FOUNDATIONS AND TRUST FUNDS

OMAHA. *The Institute for Priestly Formation Foundation*, 2500 California Plaza, 68178-0207. Tel: 402-280-3528; Fax: 402-280-3529; Email: ptpogge@creighton.edu. Mr. P. Thomas Pogge, Exec. Dir.

Latino Catholic Scholarship Fund of Omaha, Mercy Hall, 3300 N. 60th St., 68104-3402. Tel: 402-557-5650; Fax: 402-551-3426; Email: smbrommer@archomaha.org; Web: www.archomaha.com. Shannan M. Brommer, Contact Person. Receives and distributes funds as financial aid to Latino students attending inner-city Catholic schools within the Archdiocese of Omaha.

Marian High School Endowment Trust, 7400 Military Ave., 68134. Tel: 402-571-2618; Fax: 402-571-1952; Email: mhiggins@omahamarian.org. Mary Higgins, Pres., Email: mhiggins@omahamarian.org; Susie Sullivan, Prin.

Marian High School Scholarship Endowment Trust, 7400 Military Ave., 68134. Tel: 402-571-2618; Fax: 402-571-1952; Email: mhiggins@omahamarian.org. Mary Higgins, Pres.; Susie Sullivan, Prin.

McAuley Ministry Fund (1995) 7262 Mercy Rd., 68124-2389. Tel: 402-393-8225; Fax: 402-393-8145; Email: sistersofmercy@mercywmw.org. Sr. Susan Sanders, R.S.M., Pres.; Rebecca Vandenbosch, CFO. (Provides support to the mission of the Sisters of Mercy of the Americas West Midwest Community Inc.).

The Omaha Archdiocesan Educational Foundation, Inc., Tel: 402-557-5650. Most Rev. George J. Lucas, Pres.

The Office of Stewardship and Development, Mercy Hall, 3300 N. 60th St., 68104-0130. Tel: 402-557-5650; Fax: 402-551-3426; Email: smbrommer@archomaha.org. Shannan Brommer, Dir.

Archbishop Sheehan Adult Education Endowment Trust.

All Saints Catholic School Educational Endowment Trust.

Black Students Catholic Educational Endowment Trust.

Black Students Catholic Scholarship Trust Fund.

Music in Catholic Schools Endowment Trust.

Roncalli Catholic High School Educational Endowment Trust.

Roncalli Catholic High School Scholarship Endowment Trust.

Religious Education Evangelization Commission Endowment Trust.

The Catholic Voice Educational Endowment Trust.

The Omaha Archdiocesan Parish Foundation, Inc.

St. Michael Church Endowment Trust, Albion.

St. Michael Church Educational Endowment Trust, Albion.

St. Aloysius Parish Endowment Trust, Aloys.

St. Aloysius Parish Educational Endowment Trust, Aloys.

St. Joseph Parish Endowment Trust, Amelia.

St. Joseph Parish Educational Endowment Trust, Amelia.

St. Joseph Parish Endowment Trust, Atkinson.

St. Joseph Church Educational Endowment Trust, Atkinson.

Holy Cross Parish Endowment Trust, Bancroft.

Holy Cross Parish Educational Endowment Trust, Bancroft.

St. Patrick Parish Endowment Trust, Battle Creek.

St. Patrick Parish Educational Endowment Trust, Battle Creek.

Holy Cross Parish Endowment Trust, Beemer, 68716.

Holy Cross Parish Educational Endowment Trust, Beemer.

St. Mary Church Endowment Trust, Bellevue.

St. Mary Church Educational Endowment Trust, Bellevue.

St. Matthew the Evangelist Parish Endowment Trust, Bellevue.

St. Francis Borgia Parish Endowment Trust, Blair.

St. Francis Borgia Parish Educational Endowment Trust, Blair.

St. Andrew Parish Endowment Trust, Bloomfield.

St. Andrew Parish Educational Endowment Trust, Bloomfield.

SS. Peter and Paul Parish Endowment Trust, Bow Valley.

SS. Peter and Paul Parish Educational Endowment Trust, Bow Valley.

East Catholic Elementary School Educational Endowment Trust, Bow Valley.

St. Ignatius Parish Endowment Trust, Brunswick.

St. Ignatius Parish Educational Endowment Trust, Brunswick.

SS. Peter and Paul Parish Endowment Trust, Butte.

SS. Peter and Paul Parish Educational Endowment Trust, Butte.

St. Anthony Parish Endowment Trust, Cedar Rapids.

St. Anthony Parish Educational Endowment Trust, Cedar Rapids.

St. Michael Catholic Church Parish Endowment Trust, Central City.

St. Michael Parish Educational Endowment Trust, Central City.

St. Peter Parish Endowment Trust, Clarks.

St. Peter Parish Educational Endowment Trust, Clarks.

SS. Cyril and Methodius Parish Endowment Trust, Clarkson.

SS. Cyril and Methodius Parish Educational Endowment Trust, Clarkson.

Holy Trinity Church of Colfax, County Parish and Cemetery Endowment Trust Fund, Clarkson.

St. Theresa of Avila Parish Endowment Trust, Clearwater.

St. Theresa of Avila Parish Educational Endowment Trust, Clearwater.

St. Theresa Church of Clearwater Cemetery Endowment Trust Fund, Clearwater.

St. Michael Parish Endowment Trust, Coleridge.

St. Michael Parish Educational Endowment Trust, Coleridge.

St. Anthony Parish Endowment Trust, Columbus.

St. Anthony Parish Educational Endowment Trust, Columbus.

St. Anthony Elementary School Endowment Trust, Columbus.

St. Bonaventure Church Endowment Trust, Columbus.

St. Isidore Church Endowment Trust, Columbus.

St. Isidore Parish Educational Endowment Trust, Columbus.

St. Isidore Elementary School Endowment Trust, Columbus.

Scotus Central Catholic High School Endowment Trust, Columbus.

St. Joseph Parish Endowment Trust, Constance.

St. Joseph Parish Educational Endowment Trust, Constance.

St. Ludger Parish Endowment Trust, Creighton.

St. Ludger Parish Educational Endowment Trust, Creighton.

St. Joseph Church of Constance Endowment Trust Fund, Crofton.

St. Rose Church Cemetery Endowment Trust Fund, Crofton.

St. Rose of Lima Parish Endowment Trust, Crofton.

St. Rose of Lima Parish Educational Endowment Trust, Crofton.

Holy Family Parish Endowment Trust, Decatur.

Holy Family Parish Educational Endowment Trust, Decatur.

St. Anne Parish Endowment Trust, Dixon.

St. Anne Parish Educational Endowment Trust, Dixon.

St. Anne Church of Dixon Cemetery Endowment Trust Fund, Dixon.

St. Wenceslaus Parish Endowment Trust, Dodge.

St. Wenceslaus Church Educational Endowment Trust, Dodge.

St. Stanislaus Parish Endowment Trust, Duncan.

St. Stanislaus Parish Educational Endowment Trust, Duncan.

St. Boniface Parish Endowment Trust, Elgin.

St. Boniface Parish Educational Endowment Trust, Elgin.

St. Boniface School Endowment Trust, Elgin.

Pope John XXIII Central Catholic High School Endowment Trust, Elgin.

St. Patrick Parish Endowment Trust, Elkhorn.

St. Patrick School Endowment Trust, Elkhorn.

St. Patrick School Tuition Assistance Endowment Trust, Elkhorn.

St. Patrick's Church of Elkhorn Cemetery Endowment Trust Fund, Elkhorn.

Mt. Michael Foundation, Inc., Elkhorn.

Sacred Heart Parish Endowment Trust, Emerson.

Sacred Heart Parish Educational Endowment Trust, Emerson.

St. Peter de Alcantara Parish Endowment Trust, Ewing.

St. Peter de Alcantara Parish Educational Endowment Trust, Ewing.

St. Theresa Church of Clearwater Cemetery Endowment Trust Fund, Ewing.

St. John the Baptist Parish Endowment Trust, Fordyce.

St. John the Baptist Parish Educational Endowment Trust, Fordyce.

West Catholic Educational Endowment Trust, Fordyce.

St. John the Baptist Parish Endowment Trust, Fort Calhoun.

St. John the Baptist Church Educational Endowment Trust, Fort Calhoun.

St. Patrick Catholic Church Endowment Trust, Fremont.

St. Patrick Parish Educational Endowment Trust, Fremont.

Archbishop Bergan Jr./Sr. Catholic High School Educational Endowment Trust, Fremont.

St. Peter Catholic Church Endowment Trust, Fullerton.

St. Peter Parish Educational Endowment Trust, Fullerton.

St. Rose of Lima Parish Endowment Trust, Genoa.

St. Rose of Lima Parish Educational Endowment Trust, Genoa.

St. Patrick Parish Endowment Trust, Gretna.

St. Patrick Parish Educational Endowment Trust, Gretna.

Holy Trinity Parish Endowment Trust, Hartington.

Holy Trinity Parish Educational Endowment Trust, Hartington.
Holy Trinity Grade School Endowment Trust, Hartington.
Cedar Catholic High School Educational Endowment Trust, Hartington.
Holy Trinity Parish Endowment Trust, Heun.
Holy Trinity Parish Educational Endowment Trust, Heun.
Holy Trinity Parish of Colfax County Parish and Cemetery Endowment Trust Fund, Heun.
St. Cornelius Parish Endowment Trust, Homer.
St. Cornelius Parish Educational Endowment Trust, Homer.
St. Rose of Lima Parish Endowment Trust, Hooper.
St. Rose of Lima Parish Educational Endowment Trust, Hooper.
St. John Nepomucene Parish Endowment Trust, Howells.
St. John Nepomucene Parish Educational Endowment Trust, Howells.
SS. Peter and Paul Parish Endowment Trust, Howells.
SS. Peter and Paul Parish Educational Endowment Trust, Howells.
SS. Peter and Paul Catholic Church Endowment for Howells Community Catholic School, Howells.
St. Mary Parish Endowment Trust, Hubbard.
St. Mary Parish Educational Endowment Trust, Hubbard.
St. Francis Parish Endowment Trust, Humphrey.
St. Francis Parish Educational Endowment Trust, Humphrey.
St. Francis Church of Humphrey Cemetery Endowment Trust Fund, Humphrey.
St. Patrick Parish Endowment Trust, Jackson.
St. Patrick Parish Educational Endowment Trust, Jackson.
SS. Peter and Paul Parish Endowment Trust, Krakow.
SS. Peter and Paul Parish Educational Endowment Trust, Krakow.
St. Anne Church of Dixon Cemetery Endowment Trust Fund, Laurel.
St. Mary Parish Endowment Trust, Laurel.
St. Mary Parish Educational Endowment Trust, Laurel.
St. Mary Parish Endowment Trust, Leigh.
St. Mary Parish Cemetery Endowment Trust, Leigh.
Holy Family Parish Endowment Trust, Lindsay.
Holy Family Parish Educational Endowment Trust, Lindsay.
Assumption Parish Endowment Trust, Lynch.
Assumption Parish Educational Endowment Trust, Lynch.
Assumption Parish Cemetery Endowment Trust, Lynch.
St. Joseph Parish Endowment Trust, Lyons.
St. Joseph Parish Educational Endowment Trust, Lyons.
Our Lady of Fatima Parish Endowment Trust, Macy.
Our Lady of Fatima Parish Educational Endowment Trust, Macy.
St. Leonard Parish Endowment Trust, Madison.
St. Leonard Parish Educational Endowment Trust, Madison.
St. Boniface Parish Endowment Trust, Menominee.
St. Boniface Parish Educational Endowment Trust, Menominee.
St. Boniface's Church Cemetery Endowment Fund, Menominee.
St. Boniface Parish Endowment Trust, Monterey.
St. Boniface Parish Educational Endowment Trust, Monterey.
Sacred Heart Parish Endowment Trust, Naper.
Sacred Heart Parish Educational Endowment Trust, Naper.
St. Francis of Assisi Parish Endowment Trust, Neligh.
St. Francis of Assisi Parish Educational Endowment Trust, Neligh.
St. Peter Parish Endowment Trust, Newcastle.
St. Peter Parish Educational Endówment Trust, Newcastle.
St. William Parish Endowment Trust, Niobrara.
St. William Parish Educational Endowment Trust, Niobrara.
Sacred Heart Parish Endowment Trust, Norfolk.
Sacred Heart Parish Religious Education Endowment Trust, Norfolk.
Sacred Heart Elementary School Educational Endowment Trust, Norfolk.
Norfolk Catholic High School Educational Endowment Trust, Norfolk.
St. Charles Borromeo Parish Endowment Trust, North Bend.
St. Charles Borromeo Parish Educational Endowment Trust, North Bend.
Sacred Heart Parish Endowment Trust, Olean.
Sacred Parish Educational Endowment Trust, Olean.
Church of the Assumption Endowment Trust.
Blessed Sacrament Parish Endowment Trust.
Blessed Sacrament School Educational Endowment Trust.
Christ the King Parish Endowment Trust.
Christ the King Educational Endowment Trust.
Holy Cross Parish Endowment Trust.
Holy Family Parish Endowment Trust.
Holy Family Parish Educational Trust.
Holy Ghost Parish Endowment Trust.
Holy Ghost Parish Educational Endowment Trust.
Holy Name Parish Endowment Trust.
Holy Name Parish Educational Endowment Trust.
Immaculate Conception Parish Endowment Trust.
Immaculate Conception Parish Educational Endowment Trust.
Mary Our Queen Educational Endowment Trust.
Mary Our Queen Parish Endowment Trust.
Mother of Perpetual Help Parish Endowment Trust.
Mother of Perpetual Help Parish Educational Endowment Trust.
Our Lady of Fatima Parish Endowment Trust.
Our Lady of Fatima Parish Educational Endowment Trust.
Our Lady of Guadalupe Parish Endowment Trust.
Our Lady of Guadalupe Educational Endowment Trust.
Our Lady of Lourdes Parish Endowment Trust.
Our Lady of Lourdes Parish Educational Endowment Trust.
Our Lady of Lourdes School Educational Endowment Trust.
Sacred Heart Parish Endowment Trust.
Sacred Heart Parish Educational Endowment Trust.
St. Adalbert Parish Endowment Trust.
St. Anthony Parish Endowment Trust.
St. Benedict Parish Endowment Trust.
St. Benedict Parish Educational Endowment Trust.
St. Bernadette Parish Endowment Trust.
St. Bernadette Parish Educational Endowment Trust.
St. Bernard Parish Memorial Endowment Trust.
St. Bernard Parish Religious Education Endowment Trust.
St. Bridget Parish Endowment Trust.
St. Bridget Parish Educational Endowment Trust.
St. Cecilia Cathedral Endowment Trust.
St. Elizabeth Ann Parish Endowment Trust.
St. Elizabeth Ann Parish Educational Endowment Trust.
St. Francis of Assisi Church of South Omaha Endowment Trust.
St. Francis of Assisi Church of South Omaha Educational Endowment Trust.
St. Frances Cabrini Parish Endowment Trust.
St. Frances Cabrini Parish Educational Endowment Trust.
St. James Parish Endowment Trust.
St. James Parish Educational Endowment Trust.
St. James/Seton School Educational Endowment Fund.
St. Joan of Arc Parish Endowment Trust.
St. Joan of Arc Parish Educational Endowment Trust.
St. Joan of Arc Grade School Educational Endowment Trust.
St. John Parish Endowment Trust.
St. John Parish Educational Endowment Trust.
St. John Vianney Church of Millard Parish Endowment Trust.
St. John Vianney Parish Educational Endowment Trust.
St. Joseph Parish Endowment Trust.
St. Joseph Parish Educational Endowment Trust.
St. Leo Parish Endowment Trust.
St. Leo Parish Educational Endowment Trust.
St. Margaret Mary Parish Endowment Trust.
St. Margaret Mary Parish Educational Endowment Trust.
St. Margaret Mary School Educational Endowment Trust.
St. Mary's Church of Tabor Parish and Cemetery Endowment Trust Fund, Dodge.
St. Mary Parish Endowment Trust.
St. Mary Parish Educational Endowment Trust.
St. Mary Elementary School Endowment Trust.
St. Patrick Parish Endowment Trust.
St. Peter Parish Endowment Trust.
St. Peter Parish Educational Endowment Trust.
SS. Peter and Paul Church Endowment Trust.
SS. Peter and Paul Parish Educational Endowment Trust.
SS. Peter and Paul Elementary School Educational Endowment Trust.
St. Philip Neri Church Endowment Trust.
St. Philip Neri Parish Educational Endowment Trust.
St. Pius X Parish Endowment Trust.
St. Pius X Parish Educational Endowment Trust.
St. Pius X/St. Leo School Educational Endowment Trust.
St. Robert Bellarmine Parish Endowment Trust.
St. Rose Parish Endowment Trust.
St. Rose Parish Educational Endowment Trust.
St. Stanislaus Parish Endowment Trust.
St. Stanislaus Parish Educational Endowment Trust.
St. Stephen the Martyr Parish Endowment Trust.
St. Stephen the Martyr Parish Educational Endowment Trust.
St. Stephen the Martyr Elementary School Educational Endowment Trust.
Teachers' Salary Endowment Trust Fund of St. Stephen Church of Omaha.
St. Thomas More Parish Endowment Trust.
St. Thomas More Parish Educational Endowment Trust.
St. Thomas More School Educational Endowment Trust.
St. Vincent de Paul Parish Endowment Trust.
St. Vincent de Paul Parish Educational Endowment Trust.
St. Wenceslaus Parish Endowment Trust.
St. Wenceslaus Parish Educational Endowment Trust.
St. Patrick Foundation, Inc., O'Neill.
St. Mary School Foundation, Inc., O'Neill.
St. Patrick Parish Educational Endowment Trust, O'Neill.
St. Mary of the Seven Dolors Parish Endowment Trust, Osmond.
St. Columbkille Parish Endowment Trust, Papillion.
St. Columbkille Educational Endowment Trust, Papillion.
St. John the Baptist Parish Endowment Trust, Pender.
St. John the Baptist Parish Educational Endowment Trust, Pender.
St. John the Baptist Parish Endowment Trust, Petersburg.
St. John the Baptist Parish Educational Endowment Trust, Petersburg.
St. John the Baptist Center Maintenance Endowment Trust, Petersburg.
St. John the Baptist Church of Petersburg Cemetery Endowment Trust, Petersburg.
St. Joseph Parish Endowment Trust, Pierce.
St. Joseph Parish Educational Endowment Trust, Pierce.
St. Paul Parish Endowment Trust, Plainview.
St. Paul Parish Educational Endowment Trust, Plainview.
St. Joseph Parish Endowment Trust, Platte Center.
St. Joseph Parish Educational Endowment Trust, Platte Center.
St. Joseph Parish Endowment Trust, Ponca.
St. Joseph Parish Educational Endowment Trust, Ponca.
St. Mary Parish Endowment Trust, Primrose.
St. Mary Parish Educational Endowment Trust, Primrose.
St. Bonaventure Parish Endowment Trust, Raeville.
St. Bonaventure Parish/Pope John XXIII High School Educational Endowment Trust, Raeville.
St. Gerald Parish Endowment Trust, Ralston.
St. Gerald Parish Educational Endowment Trust, Ralston.
St. Gerald School Educational Endowment Trust, Ralston.
St. Frances de Chantal Parish Endowment Trust, Randolph.
St. Frances de Chantal Parish Educational Endowment Trust, Randolph.
St. Frances de Chantal of Randolph Cemetery Endowment Trust Fund, Randolph.
St. Anthony Parish Endowment Trust, St. Charles.
St. Anthony Parish Educational Endowment Trust, St. Charles.
St. Edward Parish Endowment Trust, St. Edward.
St. Edward Parish Educational Endowment Trust, St. Edward.
St. Edward's Church of St. Edward Cemetery Endowment Trust Fund, St. Edward.
Immaculate Conception Parish Endowment Trust, St. Helena.
Immaculate Conception Parish Educational Endowment Trust, St. Helena.
SS. Philip and James Parish Endowment Trust, St. James.
SS. Philip and James Parish Educational Endowment Trust, St. James.
St. John Parish Endowment Trust, St. John.
St. Francis de Sales Parish Endowment Trust, Schoolcraft.
St. Augustine Parish Endowment Trust, Schuyler.
St. Augustine Parish Educational Endowment Trust, Schuyler.
St. Mary Parish Endowment Trust, Schuyler.

St. Mary Parish Educational Endowment Trust, Schuyler.
St. Lawrence Parish Endowment Trust, Scribner.
St. Lawrence Parish Educational Endowment Trust, Scribner.
St. Lawrence Parish Endowment Trust, Silver Creek.
St. Lawrence Parish Educational Endowment Trust, Silver Creek.
St. Lawrence Church of Silver Creek Cemetery Endowment Trust Fund, Silver Creek.
St. Leo Parish Endowment Trust, Snyder.
St. Leo Parish Educational Endowment Trust, Snyder.
St. Michael Parish Endowment Trust, South Sioux City.
St. Michael Educational Endowment Trust, South Sioux City.
St. Mary Catholic Church Endowment Trust, Spencer.
St. Mary Parish Educational Endowment Trust, Spencer.
St. Mary Cemetery Endowment Trust, Spencer.
St. Joseph Parish Endowment Trust, Springfield.
St. Joseph Parish Educational Endowment Trust, Springfield.
St. Peter Parish Endowment Trust, Stanton.
St. Peter Parish Educational Endowment Trust, Stanton.
St. Boniface Parish Endowment Trust, Stuart.
St. Boniface Elementary School Endowment Trust, Stuart.
St. Mary Parish Endowment Trust, Tabor.
St. Mary Parish Educational Endowment Trust, Tabor.
St. Michael Parish Endowment Trust, Tarnov.
St. Michael Parish Educational Endowment Trust, Tarnov.
St. Patrick Parish Endowment Trust, Tekamah.
St. Patrick Parish Educational Endowment Trust, Tekamah.
Our Lady of Mt. Carmel Parish Endowment Trust, Tilden.
Our Lady of Mt. Carmel Parish Educational Endowment Trust, Tilden.
St. John the Evangelist Parish Endowment Trust, Valley.
St. John the Evangelist Parish Educational Endowment Trust, Valley.
St. Wenceslaus Church Parish Endowment Trust, Verdigre.
St. Wenceslaus Parish Educational Endowment Trust, Verdigre.
St. Joseph Parish Endowment Trust, Walthill.
St. Joseph Parish Educational Endowment Trust, Walthill.
St. Mary Parish Endowment Trust, Wayne.
St. Mary Parish Educational Endowment Trust, Wayne.
Church of the Assumption of the B.V.M. Parish Endowment Trust, West Point.
Church of the Assumption of the B.V.M. Parish Educational Endowment Trust, West Point.
Guardian Angels Grade School Educational Endowment Trust, West Point.
West Point Central Catholic High School Educational Endowment Trust, West Point.
West Point Central Catholic High School Activity Center Endowment Trust, West Point.
St. Augustine Indian Mission Endowment Trust, Winnebago.
St. Augustine Indian Mission Educational Endowment Trust, Winnebago.
St. Augustine Indian Mission Tuition Relief Educational Endowment Trust, Winnebago.
FEATHERS, Winnebago.
St. Joseph Parish Endowment Trust, Wisner.
St. Joseph Parish Educational Endowment Trust, Wisner.
Sacred Heart Parish Endowment Trust, Wynot.
Sacred Heart Parish Educational Endowment Trust, Wynot.

New Cassel Foundation, 900 N. 90th St., 68114-2704. Tel: 402-390-5317; Fax: 402-393-3784; Email: cpetrich@newcassel.org; Email: mnaumann@newcassel.org; Web: www.newcassel.org. Cindy Petrich, Foundation Pres. A nonprofit religious, charitable and educational corporation, duly constituted under the laws of the State of Nebraska, to provide support and benefit for the New Cassel Retirement Center and the Franciscan Centre.

Perpetual Care Endowment Trust Fund of Catholic Cemeteries of the Archdiocese of Omaha, 7710 W. Center Rd., 68124-3199. Tel: 402-391-3711; Fax: 402-391-0321; Email: dgkeller@catholiccem.com; Web: www.catholiccem.com. Deacon Daniel G. Keller, Dir.

Saint Robert Bellarmine Parish Foundation (2015) 11802 Pacific St., 68154. Tel: 402-333-8989; Email: business@stroberts.com. Rev. Steven J. Stillmunks, Contact Person.

ELKHORN. *Mount Michael Foundation*, 22520 Mount Michael Rd., Elkhorn, 68022-3400. Tel: 402-289-2541; Fax: 402-289-4539; Email: business@mountmichael.org. Rt. Rev. Michael Liebl, O.S.B., Abbot; Rev. Louis L. Sojka, O.S.B., Business Mgr.

FORDYCE. *Cemetery Endowment for St. Boniface Church*, 311 Omaha St., Box 170, Fordyce, 68736. Tel: 402-357-3506; Fax: 402-357-3551; Email: jekeiter@archomaha.org; Web: www.stbonifaceparish.org. Rev. James E. Keiter, Contact Person.

GRETNA. *St. Patrick's Church of Gretna Cemetery Endowment Trust Fund* (2015) 508 W. Angus St., Gretna, 68028. Tel: 402-332-4444; Email: mjgutowski@archomaha.org. Rev. Matthew J. Gutowski, Contact Person.

NORFOLK. *Missionary Benedictine Sisters Foundation*, 300 N. 18th St., Norfolk, 68701-3622. Tel: 402-371-3438; Fax: 402-371-0127; Email: rtoffosb@gmail.com. Sr. Rita Marie Tofflemire, Contact Person.

PONCA. *St. Joseph's Church of Ponca South Creek Cemetery Endowment Fund*, 421 W 2nd St, P.O. Box 898, Ponca, 68770. Tel: 402-755-2773; Email: smrohde@archomaha.org. Rev. Andrew L. Sohm, Contact Person.

RAEVILLE. *St. Bonaventure's Church of Raeville Cemetery Endowment Trust Fund*, 301 S. 2nd St., P.O. Box B, Elgin, 68636. Tel: 402-843-2345; Email: stbonaventure.rae@archomaha.org. Rev. Kevin W. Vogel, Contact Person.

SCHUYLER. *St. Benedict Center Endowment Fund* (2000) 1126 Rd. "I", P.O. Box 528, Schuyler, 68661-0528. Tel: 402-352-8819; Fax: 402-352-8884; Email: retreats@stbenedictcenter.com; Web: www.stbenedictcenter.com. Rev. Joel Macul, O.S.B., Prior. An endowment for the purpose of providing for the support and benefit of development, maintenance and supplemental funding of programs and services of St. Benedict Center and the receipt and management of gifts and bequests to the same center. The nonprofit, charitable an educational corporation is duly constituted under the laws of the State of Nebraska.

St. Benedict Center A nonprofit, ecumenical retreat and conference center, founded by the Missionary Benedictines of Christ the King Priory, Schuyler, NE. As Benedictines we share our hospitality and spirituality with those who search for personal and spiritual growth. We welcome individuals and groups of all Christian denominations, as they seek God in a peaceful and quiet setting. We provide an atmosphere that is conducive to prayer, rest and renewal for laity, clergy and religious. 1126 Rd. I, P.O. Box 528, Schuyler, 68661-0528. Tel: 402-352-8819; Fax: 402-352-8884; Email: retreats@stbenedictcenter.com; Web: www.stbenedictcenter.com. Rev. Joel Macul, O.S.B., Prior.

Benedictine Mission House Endowment Trust, 1123 Rd. "I", P.O. Box 528, Schuyler, 68661-0528. Tel: 402-352-2177; Email: monastery@missionmonks.org; Web: www.missionmonks.org. Bro. Tobias Dammert, O.S.B., Contact Person & Treas.

ST. COLUMBANS. *Columban Fathers Regional Administration*, 1902 N. Calhoun St., P.O. Box 10, St. Columbans, 68056-0010. Tel: 402-291-1920; Fax: 402-291-8693; Email: deminger@columban.org; Web: www.columban.org. Dan Eminger, Treas.

St. Columban's Central Administration, 1902 N. Calhoun St., P.O. Box 10, St. Columbans, 68056-0010. Dan Eminger, Treas.

St. Columban's Medical and Retirement, Tel: 402-291-1920; Fax: 402-291-4984.

St. Columban's Gift Annuity Trust, Tel: 402-291-1920; Fax: 402-291-4984.

St. Columban's Education Trust, Tel: 402-291-1920; Fax: 402-291-4984.

St. Columban's Priests Health Program Trust, Tel: 402-291-1920; Fax: 402-291-4984.

St. Columban's Retirement Fund Trust, Tel: 402-291-1920; Fax: 402-291-4984.

St. Columban's Masses in Trust, Tel: 402-291-1920; Fax: 402-291-4984.

St. Columban's Donors / Personal Trust, Tel: 402-291-1920; Fax: 402-291-4984.

St. Columban's Regional Trust, Tel: 402-291-1920; Fax: 402-291-4984.

St. Columban's Burse Estate Trust, Tel: 402-291-1920; Fax: 402-291-4984.

St. Columban's Gift Annuity Trust California, Tel: 402-291-1920; Fax: 402-291-4984.

[O] MISCELLANEOUS

OMAHA. *Ablaze Ministries, Inc.*, 5318 S. 107th Ave., 68127. Tel: 402-301-3226; Email: ablazeworshipministry@gmail.com; Email: 3persons1god@gmail.com; Web: www.ablazeworship.org. Rev. Michael B. Voithofer, Pres.

Bethlehem House (2002) 2301 S. 15th St., 68108. Tel: 402-509-9224; Fax: 402-505-9016; Email: info@bethlehemhouseomaha.org; Web: www.bethlehemhouseomaha.org. Holly Sak, Exec. Dir. Provides support to wopmen who are pregnant and in crisis, enabling them to choose life for their children in a family environment both during and after pregnancy. Tot Asst. Annually 225; Staff 16.

C.M.G. Agency, Inc., 10843 Old Mill Rd., 68154-2600. Tel: 402-514-2400; Fax: 402-551-2943; Email: ppeterson@catholicmutual.org. Paul Peterson, Contact & Sec. An insurance agency supporting the religious and business activities of the Catholic Mutual Relief Society of America and The Catholic Relief Insurance Company of America.

Cathedral Arts Project, Inc., 3900 Webster St., 68132. Tel: 402-558-3100, Ext. 3007; Fax: 402-558-1325; Email: wjwoeger@archomaha.org; Web: www.cathedralartsproject.org. Bro. William J. Woeger, F.S.C., Exec. Dir. & Contact.

Catholic Cemeteries of the Archdiocese of Omaha Comprised of five cemeteries: Calvary, Resurrection, Holy Sepulchre, St. Mary, St. Mary Magdalene. 7710 W. Center Rd., 68124-3199. Tel: 402-391-3711; Fax: 402-391-0321; Email: dgkeller@catholiccem.com; Web: www.catholiccem.com. Deacon Daniel G. Keller, Dir.

**Catholic Charities Foundation*, 3300 N. 60th, 68104-3402. Tel: 402-554-0520; Fax: 402-829-9268; Email: catholiccharities@ccomaha.org; Web: www.ccomaha.org. Mr. Gregg Wilson, Exec. Dir. Tot Asst. Annually 75,000; Total Staff 50.

Catholic Jail and Prison Ministry (1998) 100 N. 62nd St., 68132. Tel: 402-342-7142; Email: jpmcord@archomaha.org. Deacon Albert W. Aulner Jr., Jail/Prison Ministry Coord. & Office of Missions & Justice. Coordinates Catholic jail & prison ministry in the Archdiocese.

Catholic Mutual of Canada, 10843 Old Mill Rd., 68154-2600. Tel: 402-514-2402; Email: mintrieri@catholicmutual.org. Michael A. Intrieri, Contact Person & Pres. To support the religious and business activities of the Catholic Mutual Relief Society of America and its subsidiary Catholic Relief Insurance Company of America.

Catholic Relief Insurance Company II, 10843 Old Mill Rd., 68154. Tel: 402-514-2400; Email: ppeterson@catholicmutual.org; Web: www.catholicmutual.org. Paul Peterson, Sec.

Catholic Umbrella Pool (1987) 10843 Old Mill Rd., 68154-2600. Tel: 402-514-2402; Fax: 402-551-2943; Email: mintrieri@catholicmutual.org. Michael A. Intrieri, Admin.

Christ Child Society of Omaha (1906) 1248 S. 10th St., 68108. Tel: 402-342-4566; Email: jekeiter@archomaha.org; Web: www.christchildomaha.org. Rev. James E. Keiter, Pres.; Abby Blair, Admin. Asst. For programming, see Catholic Charities.

Christian Family Movement (CFM), 3514 N. 63rd St., 68104. Tel: 402-558-1710; Email: esost@cox.net. Deacon Edwin Osterhaus, Contact; Sheila Osterhaus, Contact.

Christians Encounter Christ aka CEC, 13324 Meredith Ave., 68164. Tel: 402-960-1020; Email: corathelen@gmail.com; Web: www.cecomaha.org. P.O. Box 27581, 68127. Cora Thelen, Contact Person. CEC is an retreat opportunity for every Catholic or Christian who wishes to strengthen and ignite their faith! CEC is a combined effort of laity and clergy offering a personal encounter with Jesus over a 2 1/2 day weekend experience, beginning on Friday evening and ending on Sunday night. It is open to persons of all faiths. You are strengthened spiritually as you live and study with priests and laity with talks, discussion, prayer, and song.

The Community of IPF Priests, Inc. aka The IPF Priests of St. Joseph, 3833 Webster St., 68131. Tel: 402-546-6384; Email: rgabuzda@creighton.edu; Web: www.priestlyformation.org. Rev. Richard J. Gabuzda, Mod.

CUP Re, Inc., CUP Re, Inc., 10843 Old Mill Rd., 68154. Tel: 405-514-2402; Email: mintrieri@catholicmutual.org; Web: www.catholicumbrellapool.org. Michael A. Intrieri, Admin.

**Discerning Hearts*, 2117 S. 166th St., 68130. Tel: 402-215-5288; Email: kris@discerninghearts.com; Web: www.discerninghearts.com. Mrs. Kris McGregor, Dir. Non-profit apostolate dedicated to evangelization and spiritual formation through new media.

FOCCUS, Inc. USA (1986) Nazareth Hall, 3300 N. 60th St., 68104. Tel: 402-827-3735; Tel: 877-883-5422 (Toll free); Fax: 402-827-3732; Email: foccus@foccusinc.com; Web: www.foccusinc.com. Mike Koley, Dir. A marriage ministry offering research-based marriage preparation and marriage enrichment inventories, materials, and services supporting family life around the world.

Heart of Mary Publishing Company, Incorporated aka Heart of Mary Ministry, Incorporated (1991) 2216 Poppleton Ave., 68108-3436. Tel: 402-342-9265; Tel: 402-342-1032; Fax: 402-342-9094; Email: srmarylucy@aol.com; Web: www.heartofmaryministry.com. Sr. Mary Lucy Astuto, D.E.F., M.S., Pres.

IXIM, Spirit of Solidarity, 1248 S. 10th St., 68108. Tel: 402-934-7706; Email: mjzimmer@archomaha.org; Email: djzuerlein@archomaha.org; Web: archomaha.org/ministries/missions/ixim. Rev. Damian J. Zuerlein, Contact Person.

St. James Manor, Inc., 3102 N. 60th St., 68104. Tel: 402-551-4243; Fax: 402-558-8013; Email: catholiccharities@ccomaha.org. Mr. Gregg Wilson, Exec. Dir.

Latina Resource Center, Juan Diego Center, 5211 S. 31st St., 68107. Teletype: 402-939-4625; Email: AnaMB@ccomaha.org. Ana Barrios, Program Dir. Provides culturally and language supported community based services for Latinas. Tot Asst. Annually 1,788; Total Staff 1.

Legion of Mary, 709 S. 28th St., 68105. Tel: 402-341-4560; Email: fatherbroheimer@gmail.com. Rev. John P. Broheimer, Spiritual Dir.

Life Assistance Services (1979) 7262 Mercy Rd., 68124-2389. Tel: 402-393-8225; Fax: 402-393-8145; Email: sistersofmercy@mercywmw.org. Sr. Susan Sanders, R.S.M., Pres.; Rebecca Vandenbosch, CFO.

Magnificat-Omaha N.E. Chapter, Inc. aka Magnificat-Omaha, 1420 S. 126th St., 68144. Tel: 402-333-7704; Email: kdwyer1111@gmail.com; Email: magnificatomaha@gmail.com; Web: www.magnificatomaha.org. Karen Dwyer, Pres.

**Maria Regina Cleri*, P.O. Box 540657, 68154. Tel: 402-672-8624; Email: vicherout@gmail.com; Web: www.prayingforourpriests.org. Vicki Herout, Contact Person.

**Marianna, Inc.*, 100 N. 62 St., 68132. Tel: 402-371-2621; Email: drandrews@archomaha.org. 204 S. 5th St., Norfolk, 68701. Revs. Daniel R. Andrews, Pres.; Ron Battiato, Vice Pres.; Christopher Kubat, Treas.; Matthew Vandewalle, Sec.

The Most AMYable Roman Catholic Lending Library, Inc. (2001) 5404 William St., 68106-2355. Tel: 402-553-1837; Email: rogjud@yahoo.com. Roger Elliott, Pres.; Judy Elliott, Vice Pres. Purpose: a nonprofit religious, charitable and educational corporation is duly constituted under the laws of the State of Nebraska and operated by a Board of Directors for the purpose of collecting and lending orthodox Catholic books and magazines, videos and audiotapes, compact and video discs, prayer petitions and Rosary Decade Group.

New Covenant Center: Education for Justice and Peace (1982) 900 N. 90th St., #153, 68114. Tel: 402-390-5336; Email: omahaavp@gmail.com. Sr. Maureen Connolly, S.S.S.F., M.Div., M.A., B.A., Prog. Coord.

**Notre Dame Housing, Inc.* (1996) 3439 State St., 68112-1709. Tel: 402-451-4477; Fax: 402-451-7421; Email: mrobinson@ndhinc.org; Web: www.ndhinc.org. Michael Robinson, M.S., Exec. Dir. Purpose: To provide housing for elderly and persons of low-income or otherwise unable to afford market rate housing.

Notre Dame Living Center, Inc. (1996) 3501 State St., 68112-1709. Tel: 402-451-4477; Fax: 402-451-7421; Email: mrobinson@ndhinc.org; Web: www.ndhinc.org. Michael Robinson, M.S., Exec. Dir. Purpose: Provides affordable housing to the elderly, particularly those of low-income status.

One Heart One Fire Ministries, Inc., 5525 L St., Ste. 103, 68117. Tel: 402-681-6871; Email: ohofministries@gmail.com; Web: www.oneheartonefire.org. Jason Fett, Pres.; Machelle Krajewski, Sec.

Pope Paul VI Institute for the Study of Human Reproduction (1982) 6901 Mercy Rd., 68106. Tel: 402-390-6600; Fax: 402-390-9851; Email: thomaswhilgersmd@popepaulvi.com; Web: www.popepaulvi.com. Thomas W. Hilgers, M.D., Dir.

**Sancta Familia Medical Associates Inc.*, 10506 Burt Cir., 68114-2094.

TEC, Archdiocese of Omaha Office of Evangelization & Catechesis, Nazareth Hall, 3300 N. 60th St., 68104. Tel: 402-557-5610; Fax: 402-554-8402; Web: www.archomaha.org. Ms. Jodi Phillips, Contact Person.

BOYS TOWN. **Father Flanagan League Society of Devotion*, 14057 Flanagan Blvd., Boys Town, 68010. Tel: 402-498-3056; Email: stevewolf@cox.net; Web: www.fatherflanagan.org. Steven R. Wolf, Pres.

ELKHORN. *Equestrian Order of the Holy Sepulchre of Jerusalem, Northern Lieutenancy*, 2500 California Plaza, 68178. Tel: 402-280-3528; Tel: 402-639-4923 ; Email: ptpogge.eohsj@gmail.com. Thomas Pogge, Lt.

GRETNA. *Holy Family Shrine*, 23132 Pflug Rd., Gretna, 68028. Tel: 402-332-4565; Web: www.hfsgretna.org. Mailing Address: P.O. Box 507, Gretna, 68028. Bridget Chatterson, Office Mgr. A place of pilgrimage, prayer and resource for the public and private prayer. This nonprofit religious, charitable and educational corporation is duly constituted under the laws of the State of Nebraska and operated by a Board of Trustees.

LA VISTA. **Mercy Housing Midwest*, 7241 Edna Ct., La Vista, 68128. Tel: 303-830-3300. 1600 Broadway, Ste. 2000, Denver, CO 80202. Joe Rosenblum.

LYNCH. *Niobrara Valley House of Renewal*, 515 S. Fourth St, Lynch, 68746. Tel: 402-569-3433; Email: henderson@threeriver.net. Rev. Douglas P. Scheinost, Pastor.

OAKDALE. *Tintern Retreat and Resource Center*, 52619 843 Rd., Oakdale, 68761. Tel: 402-776-2188; Email: tintern670@gmail.com; Web: www.tintern.homestead.com. Cheryl Veik, Contact Person.

PLATTE CENTER. *Servants of the Heart of the Father*, 408 1st St., P.O. Box 218, Platte Center, 68653. Tel: 402-910-7111; Fax: 402-246-9232; Email: sothotf1@aol.com; Web: www.sothotf.wildapricot.org. Rev. Rodney V. Kneifl, Contact Person.

SCHUYLER. *El Puente Immigration Legal Services*, 1123 Rd. I, Schuyler, 68661. Tel: 402-352-3644; Fax: 402-352-3768; Email: JessicaB@ccomaha.org; Web: www.ccomaha.org. Jessica Bernal, Program Dir. Tot Asst. Annually 89; Total Staff 1.

TEKAMAH. *His Global Love, Inc.*, 1323 R St., Tekamah, 68061.

WEST POINT. *St. Joseph's Elder Services, Inc.*, 540 E. Washington St., West Point, 68788. Tel: 402-372-1118, Ext. 520; Email: ddeemer@sjeswp.org. Mr. David Deemer, Admin.; Sr. Joy Rose, Sacramental Min.

St. Joseph's Hillside Villa, 540 E. Washington St., West Point, 68788. Tel: 402-372-1118; Email: ddeemer@sjeswp.org. Mr. David Deemer, Admin.; Sr. Joy Rose, Sacramental Min.

St. Joseph's Retirement Community (1905) 320 E. Decatur, West Point, 68788. Tel: 402-372-3477; Fax: 402-372-6600; Email: ddeemer@sjeswp.org; Web: www.sjeswp.org. Mr. David Deemer, Admin. Bed Capacity 63; Tot Asst. Annually 48; Total Staff 42.

[P] PUBLIC ASSOCIATIONS OF THE CHRISTIAN FAITHFUL

OMAHA. *Christian Life Community-North Central Region (CLC)* (1998) 2500 California Plaza, 68178. Tel: 402-301-3417 (Rouse); Tel: 402-215-4773 (Berry); Fax: 402-280-5590; Email: mbr614@cox.net; Email: jgbclc4221@gmail.com. J. Berry, Co-Coord. CLC N. Central Region; Maryanne Rouse, Co-Coord. CLC N. Central Region. A public association of the Christian faithful of Pontifical Right providing spiritual support and guidance in the Jesuit tradition of the Spiritual Exercises.

Franciscan Sisters of Joy, 8141 Farnam Dr., #403, 68178. Tel: 515-822-6743; Email: jmueller@creighton.edu. Sr. Joan Mueller, O.S.C., Ph.D., Clare Sister.

Institute for Priestly Formation, 2500 California Plaza, 68178. Tel: 402-546-6384; Fax: 402-280-3529; Email: ipf@creighton.edu; Web: www.priestlyformation.org. Rev. Richard J. Gabuzda, Exec. Dir. Purpose: To offer programs and support for the integration of theological study, spiritual growth and direction, and retreat experiences for diocesan seminarians and priests.

[Q] PRIVATE ASSOCIATIONS OF THE FAITHFUL

OMAHA. *Daughters of the Eternal Father* (2002) 2216 Poppleton Ave., 68108-3436. Tel: 402-342-1032; Fax: 402-342-9094; Email: srmarylucy@aol.com; Web: www.omahadef.org. Sr. Mary Lucy Astuto, D.E.F., M.S., Foundress.

Seraphic Sisters of the Eucharist, St. Peter Catholic Church, 705 S. 28th St., 68105. Tel: 402-346-6845; Fax: 402-341-6483; Email: hermanasseraficas@gmail.com. Sisters Clara Maria Acosta-Millan, S.S.E., Supr.; Lourdes Candida-Cano, Asst.

RELIGIOUS INSTITUTES OF MEN REPRESENTED IN THE ARCHDIOCESE

For further details refer to the corresponding bracketed number in the Religious Institutes of Men or Women section.

[0200]—*Benedictine Monks*—O.S.B.
[0330]—*Brothers of the Christian Schools* (St. Louis, MO)—F.S.C.
[0690]—*Jesuit Fathers and Brothers* (Wisconsin Prov.)—S.J.
[1065]—*Priestly Fraternity of St. Peter*—F.S.S.P.
[0370]—*Society of St. Columban*—S.S.C.

RELIGIOUS INSTITUTES OF WOMEN REPRESENTED IN THE ARCHDIOCESE

[0230]—*Benedictine Sisters of Pontifical Jurisdiction*—O.S.B.
[1070-03]—*Dominican Sisters*—O.P.
[1230]—*Franciscan Sisters of Christian Charity*—O.S.F.
[1430]—*Franciscan Sisters of Our Lady of Perpetual Help*—O.S.F.
[2575]—*Institute of the Sisters of Mercy of the Americas*—R.S.M.
[0210]—*Missionary Benedictine Sisters*—O.S.B.
[2690]—*Missionary Catechists of Divine Providence.*
[2960]—*Notre Dame Sisters*—N.D.
[3760]—*Order of St. Clare*—O.S.C.
[2970]—*School Sisters of Notre Dame.*
[1680]—*School Sisters of St. Francis* (Our Lady of Angels Prov.)—O.S.F.
[3580]—*Servants of Mary*—O.S.M.
[0430]—*Sisters of Charity of the Blessed Virgin Mary*—C.S.J.
[1630]—*Sisters of St. Francis of Peace and Christian Charity* (Denver Prov.)—O.S.F.
[1640]—*Sisters of St. Francis of Perpetual Adoration* (Colorado Springs, CO)—O.S.F.
[1830]—*Sisters of the Good Shepherd*—R.G.S.
[3270]—*Sisters of the Most Precious Blood* (O'Fallon, MO)—C.PP.S.
[3320]—*Sisters of the Presentation of the B.V.M.*—P.B.V.M.
[4070]—*Society of the Sacred Heart*—R.S.C.J.

ARCHDIOCESAN CEMETERIES

OMAHA. *Calvary*, 7710 W. Center Rd., 68124. Tel: 402-391-3711. Very Rev. Michael W. Grewe, V.G., Exec. Dir.; Deacon Daniel G. Keller, Dir.

Holy Sepulchre, 4912 Leavenworth St., 68106. Tel: 402-391-3711. Very Rev. Michael W. Grewe, V.G., Exec. Dir.; Deacon Daniel G. Keller, Dir.

St. Mary, 3353 Q St., 68107. Tel: 402-391-3711. Catholic Cemeteries of the Archdiocese of Omaha: 7710 W. Center Rd., 68124. Very Rev. Michael W. Grewe, V.G., Exec. Dir.; Deacon Daniel G. Keller, Dir.

St. Mary Magdalene, 5226 S. 46 St., 68117. Tel: 402-391-3711. Catholic Cemeteries of the Archdiocese of Omaha, 7710 W. Center Rd., 68124. Very Rev. Michael W. Grewe, V.G., Exec.; Deacon Daniel G. Keller, Dir.

Resurrection, 7800 W. Center Rd., 68114. Tel: 402-391-3711. Catholic Cemeteries of the Archdiocese of Omaha: 7710 W. Center Rd., 68124. Very Rev. Michael W. Grewe, V.G., Exec. Dir.; Deacon Daniel G. Keller, Dir.

NECROLOGY

† Hall, Douglas C., (Retired), Died Nov. 25, 2018
† Meyer, Emmett F., (Retired), Died Dec. 3, 2018
† Schmitz, Robert A., (Retired), Died Mar. 18, 2018

An asterisk (*) denotes an organization that has established tax-exempt status directly with the IRS and is not covered by the USCCB Group Ruling.

Diocese of Orange in California

(Arausicanae in California)

Most Reverend

TOD DAVID BROWN, D.D.

Retired Bishop of Orange; ordained May 1, 1963; appointed Bishop of Boise December 27, 1988; Episcopal Ordination April 3, 1989; appointed Bishop of Orange June 29, 1998; installed September 3, 1998; retired December 10, 2012. *Office: Pastoral Center, 13280 Chapman Ave., Garden Grove, CA 92840. Res.: 200 W. LaVeta Ave., Orange, CA 92866.*

Most Reverend

TIMOTHY EDWARD FREYER, D.D.

Auxiliary Bishop of Orange; ordained June 10, 1989; appointed Auxiliary Bishop of Orange and Titular Bishop of Strathearn November 17, 2016; installed January 17, 2017. *Office: Pastoral Center, 13280 Chapman Ave., Garden Grove, CA 92840.*

Most Reverend

KEVIN WILLIAM VANN, J.C.D., D.D.

Bishop of Orange; ordained May 30, 1981; appointed Coadjutor Bishop of Fort Worth May 17, 2005; succeeded July 12, 2005; ordained July 13, 2005; appointed Bishop of Orange September 21, 2012; installed December 10, 2012. *Office: Pastoral Center, 13280 Chapman Ave., Garden Grove, CA 92840.*

Chancellor's Office: 13280 Chapman Ave., Garden Grove, CA 92840. Tel: 714-282-3000; Fax: 714-282-4202.

Web: www.rcbo.org

Email: gdenomie@rcbo.org

Most Reverend

THANH THAI NGUYEN, D.D.

Auxiliary Bishop of Orange; ordained May 11, 1991; appointed Auxiliary Bishop of Orange and Titular Bishop of Acalissus October 6, 2017; installed December 19, 2017. *Office: Pastoral Center, 13280 Chapman Ave., Garden Grove, CA 92840.*

ESTABLISHED JUNE 18, 1976.

Square Miles 782.

Comprises the County of Orange in the State of California.

Diocesan Patron: Our Lady of Guadalupe.

Legal Titles: (Prot. No. CD 528-76)
The Roman Catholic Bishop of Orange, a Corporation Sole.
Diocese of Orange Education and Welfare Corporation.
Catholic Charities of Orange.
For legal titles of parishes and diocesan institutions, consult the Diocesan Pastoral Service Office

STATISTICAL OVERVIEW

Personnel	
Bishop	1
Auxiliary Bishops	2
Retired Bishops	1
Abbots	1
Priests: Diocesan Active in Diocese	124
Priests: Diocesan Active Outside Diocese	8
Priests: Retired, Sick or Absent	52
Number of Diocesan Priests	184
Religious Priests in Diocese	88
Total Priests in Diocese	272
Extern Priests in Diocese	30
Ordinations:	
Diocesan Priests	2
Religious Priests	1
Transitional Deacons	6
Permanent Deacons in Diocese	140
Total Brothers	9
Total Sisters	290
Parishes	
Parishes	57
With Resident Pastor:	
Resident Diocesan Priests	42
Resident Religious Priests	6
Without Resident Pastor:	
Administered by Priests	9
Missions	5
Pastoral Centers	5
Professional Ministry Personnel:	
Brothers	9
Sisters	29
Lay Ministers	332
Welfare	
Catholic Hospitals	3
Total Assisted	1,000,000
Health Care Centers	5
Total Assisted	40,423
Homes for the Aged	1
Total Assisted	60
Day Care Centers	2
Total Assisted	485
Specialized Homes	5
Total Assisted	635
Special Centers for Social Services	11
Total Assisted	3,980,599
Other Institutions	2
Total Assisted	192
Educational	
Diocesan Students in Other Seminaries	31
Students Religious	3
Total Seminarians	34
High Schools, Diocesan and Parish	3
Total Students	4,177
High Schools, Private	4
Total Students	2,226
Elementary Schools, Diocesan and Parish	31
Total Students	9,819
Elementary Schools, Private	3
Total Students	1,079
Catechesis/Religious Education:	
High School Students	15,099
Elementary Students	26,093
Total Students under Catholic Instruction	58,527
Teachers in the Diocese:	
Priests	6
Brothers	12
Sisters	16
Lay Teachers	1,606
Vital Statistics	
Receptions into the Church:	
Infant Baptism Totals	9,575
Minor Baptism Totals	676
Adult Baptism Totals	563
Received into Full Communion	1,172
First Communions	9,835
Confirmations	6,749
Marriages:	
Catholic	1,715
Interfaith	393
Total Marriages	2,108
Deaths	3,095
Total Catholic Population	1,302,831
Total Population	3,190,400

Former Bishops—Most Revs. WILLIAM R. JOHNSON, appt. Titular Bishop of Biera and Auxiliary Bishop of Los Angeles, Feb. 9, 1971; cons. March 25, 1971; installed as first Bishop of Orange, June 18, 1976; died July 28, 1986; NORMAN F. MCFARLAND, D.D., J.C.D., ord. June 15, 1946; appt. Titular Bishop of Bida and Auxiliary of San Francisco, June 5, 1970; cons. Sept. 8, 1970; appt. Apostolic Administrator, Dec. 6, 1974; appt. Bishop of Reno-Las Vegas, Feb. 10, 1976; installed March 31, 1976; appt. Bishop of Orange, Dec. 29, 1986; installed Feb. 24, 1987; retired June 30, 1998; died April 16, 2010.; TOD DAVID BROWN, (Retired), ord. May 1, 1963; appt. Bishop of Boise Dec. 27, 1988; Episcopal Ord. April 3, 1989; appt. Bishop of Orange June 29, 1998; installed Sept. 3, 1998; retired Sept. 21, 2012.

Vicar General—Rev. Msgr. STEPHEN S. DOKTORCZYK, J.C.D., Office: Pastoral Center.

Chancellor—DR. PIA DE SOLENNI, SThD.

Moderator of the Curia—Rev. Msgr. STEPHEN S. DOKTORCZYK, J.C.D.

Master of Ceremonies—Rev. THANH-TAI P. NGUYEN, Office: Pastoral Center.

Secretary to the Bishop—Rev. THANH-TAI P. NGUYEN, Office: Pastoral Center.

Vice Chancellor/Director of Priest Personnel—Rev. DANIEL B. READER, Office: Pastoral Center.

Vicar for Religious Communities—VACANT.

Episcopal Vicar/Rector of Future Cathedral—Rev. CHRISTOPHER SMITH, 13280 Chapman Ave., Garden Grove, 92840.

Episcopal Vicar for Priests—Rev. PATRICK N. RUDOLPH, Office: Pastoral Center.

Episcopal Vicar for Special Projects—Rev. Msgr. MICHAEL HEHER, P.A.

Vicar for Faith Formation—VACANT.

Diocesan Pastoral Service Office—13280 Chapman Ave., Garden Grove, 92840. Tel: 714-282-3000; Fax: 714-282-3029. Office Hours: Mon.-Fri. 8-5.

Office of Canonical Services—13280 Chapman Ave., Garden Grove, 92840. Tel: 714-282-3080; Fax: 714-282-3087; Email: marriagetribunal@rcbo.org.

Judicial Vicar—Very Rev. E. SCOTT BORGMAN, J.C.D.

Adjutant Judicial Vicars—Rev. JOHN E. CARONAN, O.Praem.

Promoter of Justice—Rev. SY UY NGUYEN, J.C.L.; Rev. Msgr. DOUGLAS J. COOK, J.C.L.

Judges—Rev. JACK K. SEWELL, J.C.L., (Retired); FERNANDO ENGEL, J.C.L.; MS. PEGGY JEAN PAOLI, J.C.L.; Rev. Msgr. STEPHEN S. DOKTORCZYK, J.C.D.; Rev. SY UY NGUYEN.

Defenders of the Bond—Rev. JOHN CARONAN, O.Praem., J.C.L.; Rev. Msgr. TUAN JOSEPH PHAM, J.C.L.

Diocesan Tribunal Advocates—Deacons THOMAS MCGUINE; CARL SWANSON; MINH CONG TONG; MRS. PAULA LYNN; MS. CHARLENE DUMITRU; MRS. DENISE TERAN.

Ecclesiastical Notaries—MRS. LINDA BRAUN; MRS. PAULA LYNN; MRS. DENISE TERAN; MS. SUSAN STANKIS; MR. STEPHEN SHON; MRS. KIM BUI.

Archivist—VACANT.

Newman Apostolate—Mailing Address: P.O. Box 523, Garden Grove, 92842. Tel: 949-856-0211. Revs. JOHN FRANCIS VU, S.J., UCI; RAFAEL LUEVANO, Ph. D., Chapman Univ.; AARON GALVIZO, A.M., Cal State Fullerton.

Diocesan Pastoral Council—VACANT.

Parish Councils and Parish Development— Fax: 714-282-3029. Office: Pastoral Center.

Diaconate—Deacon FRANK CHAVEZ, 13280 Chapman Ave., Garden Grove, 92840. Tel: 714-282-3037.

Director of Priests' Personnel—Rev. DANIEL B. READER.

Clergy Personnel Board—Most Rev. KEVIN W. VANN, J.C.D., D.D.; Rev. Msgr. STEPHEN S. DOKTORCZYK, J.C.D.; Revs. GEORGE P. BLAIS; DANIEL B. READER; ENRIQUE SERA, Chm.; DUY T. LE; MIGUEL A. HERNANDEZ; VINCENT PHAM; Rev. Msgr. JOHN URELL; Rev. PAUL THAI TRINH.

Oversight Review Board—RON LOWENBERG, Chm.; Rev. Msgr. STEPHEN S. DOKTORCZYK, J.C.D.; Rev. BRUCE PATTERSON; JAMES BURNS; JOSEPH M. CERVANTES, Ph.D., ABPP; WILLIAM J. COLLINS, M.D.; Sr. KATHLEEN MARIE PUGHE, C.S.J.; DARLYNE PETTINICHIO; Honorable MICHAEL BRENNER, (Retired); DIANE GOMEZ-VALENZUELA, M.S.W.; TIM PETROPULOS; JACKIE GOMEZ-WHITELEY. Staff: MARIANNE BUNGCAG; Deacon MICHAEL STOCK; Rev. DANIEL B. READER.

Communications—TRACEY KINCAID, Dir., Tel: 714-282-3075. Office: Pastoral Center.

Marketing—MR. HANK EVERS, Dir., Tel: 714-282-3079. Office: Pastoral Center.

Orange Diocesan Council of Catholic Women—Most Rev. TIMOTHY E. FREYER, D.D., Moderator; MRS. PENELOPE HECKER, Pres.

General Counsel—Deacon MICHAEL STOCK, Office: Pastoral Center.

Primary Counsel—Sheppard, Mullin, Richter & Hampton, LLP, 650 Town Center Dr., 4th Fl., Costa Mesa, 92626-1993. ALAN MARTIN, Esq.

Priests' Relief—Rev. PATRICK N. RUDOLPH, Office: Pastoral Center.

Council of Priests—Most Revs. KEVIN W. VANN, J.C.D., D.D.; THOMAS THANH THAI NGUYEN, D.D.; Rev. Msgrs. STEPHEN S. DOKTORCZYK, J.C.D.; THEODORE OLSON, (Retired); MICHAEL HEHER, P.A.; Rev. JOHN FRANCIS, S.J., V.U.; Very Rev. E. SCOTT BORGMAN, J.C.D.; Revs. BRUCE PATTERSON; KHOI PHAN; JOHN E. JANZE; STEVEN SALLOT; EDWARD L. POETTGEN JR.; DANIEL B. READER; ANTONIO LOPEZ-FLORES; DANIEL BARICA, O.F.M.; THOMAS PAUL K. NAVAL; MIGUEL A. HERNANDEZ; PHILIP T. SMITH; BILL T. CAO; JAMES C. RIES.

Observer—Deacon FRANK CHAVEZ; DR. PIA DE SOLENNI, SThD; Deacon MICHAEL STOCK.

College of Consultors—Most Revs. KEVIN W. VANN, J.C.D., D.D.; TIMOTHY E. FREYER, D.D., Auxiliary Bishop; THOMAS THANH TAI NGUYEN, D.D., Auxiliary Bishop; Rev. EDWARD L. POETTGEN JR.; Rev. Msgrs. STEPHEN S. DOKTORCZYK, J.C.D.; MICHAEL HEHER, P.A.; THEODORE OLSON, (Retired); Revs. STEVEN SALLOT; JOHN E. JANZE; THOMAS PAUL K. NAVAL.

Vicars Forane (Deans)—Revs. PHILIP T. SMITH; BRUCE PATTERSON; EDWARD L. POETTGEN JR.; JOSEPH LUAN NGUYEN; MICHAEL P. HANIFIN; JOHN E. JANZE; KENNETH SCHMIDT; CHRYSOSTOM BAER, O.Praem.

Pastoral Care—(of families in all stages) MRS. LINDA JI, Dir., Tel: 714-282-4203. Office: Pastoral Center.

Propagation of the FaithMARISSA CORNEJO, Coord.; Office: Pastoral Center.

Council for Religious—VACANT, Dir.; Sisters JANE RUDOLPH, O.P.; JOSEFA HA, L.H.C.; ELVIRA RIOS, O.D.N.; ROSA ELBA MENDIA, O.S.F.; PAULETTE DETERS, C.S.J.; RITA PAUL, M.C.; JOAN PATTEN, A.O.; PAULA SAWHILL, S.D.S.H.; MARIA TERESA SALCEDO, M.E.S.S.T.

Diocesan Consultative Schools Board—Office: Pastoral Center.Membership: Most Revs. KEVIN W. VANN, J.C.D., D.D.; THANH THAI NGUYEN; MRS. SALLY TODD, Ex Officio; MR. GORDON SCHMITT; MRS. CINDY BOBRUK, Ex Officio; MS. DEB MCGRATH, Ex Officio; MR. ANDREW J. SULICK; Rev. TUYEN NGUYEN; Sr. JUDITH DUGAN, C.S.J.; MR. DAVE BIGLEY; MR. DAMIEN JORDAN; DIANNE SCHAUTSCHICK; MR. ERNIE GARCIA; MR. JOYCE ARMEN; MRS. NANCI DE LA ROSA-RICCO, Recording Sec.; MR. TUAN D. NGUYEN; RALPH GURGIS; MR. SCOTT GOTREAU, Ex Officio; MR. HANK EVERS, Ex Officio; MRS. ANGELINE TRUDELL; Sr. JOHNELLEN TURNER, O.P.; MS. ADELA SOLIS; DR. ERIN BARISANO; MS. GABRIELLA KARINA.

Vocations Office—Rev. JOHN W. MONEYPENNY, Dir., Office: Pastoral Center.

Catholic Campaign for Human Development—Local Board: Deacon JIM MERLE, Chm.; MRS. JUDY DONCKELS; DR. RUBEN BARRON; Deacons RICHARD DOUBLEDEE; NICHOLAS OH; MRS. REBECCA TAMONDONG; MRS. ELLIE WESTENHAVER; MISS CENIA MARTINES; MRS. HELEN MENDOZA; Deacon NICK SHERG.

Diocesan Offices and Directors

Apostleship of Prayer—VACANT.

Archivist—Rev. WILLIAM F. KREKELBERG, Emeritus, (Retired), 31522 Camino Capistrano, San Juan Capistrano, 92675-0691.

Boy Scouts/Girl Scouts—Deacon NICK SHERG, Diocesan Chap., Office: St. Martin de Porres, 19767 Yorba Linda Blvd., Yorba Linda, 92886. Tel: 714-970-2771, Ext. 134.

Liturgical Commission—Deacon FRANK CHAVEZ, Ex Officio; MRS. LESA TRUXAW, Ex Officio; Rev. VINCENT PHAM; Most Rev. THANH THAI NGUYEN; Rev. QUANG VINH CHU; MRS. MERCY ELSINGER; MRS. MARY KAY LAMARRE; DR. JOHN ROMERI; Rev. PATRICK A. MOSES.

Design and Renovation Committee—Rev. Msgr. J. MICHAEL MCKIERNAN; MRS. LESA TRUXAW, Chm.; MR. PAUL NGUYEN.

Real Estate Advisory Board—Most Rev. KEVIN W. VANN, J.C.D., D.D.; Rev. EDWARD L. POETTGEN JR.; MR. ARTHUR BIRTCHER; MR. LOU ODDO; MS. SHARON HENNESSEY, Chair; MR. RAND SPERRY; ELIZABETH JENSEN, CFO. Staff: MR. JOE NOVOA, Construction Mgr.; SANDY HULL, Real Estate Portfolio Mgr.; Deacon MICHAEL STOCK, Episcopal Dir. Oper.

Diocesan Construction Advisory Board—Most Rev. KEVIN W. VANN, J.C.D., D.D.; JACK W. FLEMING; Rev. KENNETH A. SCHMIT; MR. ARTHUR BIRTCHER, Chm.; MR. EDWARD REYNOLDS; MR. RICHARD HEIM; MS. TRUDY MAZZARELLA; MR. DUC BUI; MR. JOHN V. MARKEL. Staff: MR. JOE NOVOA, Dir. Construction; ELIZABETH JENSEN, CFO; KELLY LIND; MRS. VENEE WONG.

Diocesan Finance Council—Most Revs. KEVIN W. VANN, J.C.D., D.D.; TIMOTHY E. FREYER, D.D.; THANH THAI NGUYEN; Rev. Msgr. LAWRENCE J. BAIRD, P.A.; Rev. STEVEN SALLOT; MS. MAUREEN FLANAGAN, C.F.A., Chm.; Sr. MARY BERNADETTE MCNULTY, C.S.J.; MR. THOMAS GREELEY, Vice Chair; Revs. ANTONIO LOPEZ-FLORES; BRENDAN MANSON; MS. ANNETTE WALKER, Chair; GABRIEL FERRUCCI; DR. DON MILLER; MR. JIM REED; MR. TOM CROAL. Staff: ELIZABETH JENSEN, CFO; SEAN M. CONNOLLY; Rev. Msgr. STEPHEN S. DOKTORCZYK, J.C.D.; TOM BURNHAM; Deacon MICHAEL STOCK.

Director of Finance—ELIZABETH JENSEN, CFO, Tel: 714-282-4209. Office: Pastoral Center; SEAN M. CONNOLLY, Controller, Tel: 714-282-3011. Office: Pastoral Center.

Catholic Charities of Orange—TERESA SMITH, M.S.W., L.C.S.W., Exec. Dir., 1820 E. 16th St., Santa Ana, 92701. Tel: 714-347-9605; Fax: 714-542-3020.

Cemeteries—MR. MICHAEL WESNER, Dir., Tel: 714-282-3101. Office: Pastoral Center.

Ministry to Priests—Rev. PATRICK N. RUDOLPH, Vicar for Priests, Tel: 714-282-3053. Office: Pastoral Center.

Cursillo Movement—Deacons DOUG COOK, Exec. Spiritual Dir.; RAMON LEON, Spiritual Dir., Hispanic Cursillo; Rev. SY UY NGUYEN, J.C.L., Spiritual Dir., Vietnamese Cursillo, 19767 Yorba Linda Blvd., Yorba Linda, 92886.

Catholic Deaf Center—NANCY LOPEZ, Dir., 13280 Chapman Ave., Garden Grove, 92840. Tel: 714-547-0824 (Voice); Teletype: 714-547-7103; Fax: 714-547-7195; Email: nlopez@rcbo.org; Web: www.rcbo.org.

Detention Ministry/Restorative Justice—MR. FRED LAPUZZA, Dir., 1820 W. Orangewood Ave., Ste. 101, Orange, 92868. Tel: 714-634-9909; Fax: 714-634-9910.

Institute of Pastoral Ministry—MRS. OLIVIA CORNEJO, Dir., Office: Pastoral Center.

Ecumenical and Interreligious Affairs—Rev. QUAN DINH TRAN, J.D., Episcopal Vicar; Deacon CHRISTOPHER CIRAULO; Rev. EDWARD BECKER; MR. ROBERT MATTHEWS; MR. JOHN HARTMANN; KATHY CIRAULO; Deacon TOM CONCITIS; MR. MIKE MULLARD; MS. MARY SUSA; MR. MIKE CERRO; Rev. JOHN MONESTERO; MR. ANTHONY VULTAGGIO, Chm.; MR. GREG KELLEY; MRS. NANCI DE LA ROSA-RICCO.

Natural Family Planning—MRS. LINDA JI, Dir., Pastoral Center.

Engaged Encounter—TIM DONOVAN; SARAH DONOVAN, Tel: 714-455-9175; Email: donoclan1@aol.com.

Marriage Encounter - English—JOE CRUZ; TERI CRUZ, Tel: 714-873-5136; Email: cruzclan2@cox.net.

Marriage Encounter - Spanish - Encuentro Matrimonial Mundial—ALFONSO CEDILLO; ENEDINA CEDILLO, Tel: 714-925-2316; Email: acedillofam@yahoo.com.

Vietnamese Community Couples Retreat—MR. JOHN XUNG LE; MRS. MARIE LE, Tel: 714-538-5161.

The Family of Nazareth—MR. JOHN XUNG LE; MRS. MARIE LE, Tel: 714-538-5161; Email: johnle11@cox.net.

Retrouvaille - English—MIKE CLAY; LORI CLAY, Tel: 714-488-1864; Email: claycru@roadrunner.com.

Office of Hispanic Ministry—Deacon GUILLERMO TORRES, Dir., Office: Pastoral Center.

Holy Childhood—MARISSA CORNEJO, Coord.; Office: Pastoral Center.

Catholic Relief Services—MR. GREG WALGENBACK, Tel: 714-282-3100. Office: Pastoral Center.

Mental Health Ministry—DR. LOUISE DUNN, Tel: 714-620-8810; Email: ldunn@newhopenow.org.

Risk Management and Insurance Services—MARY JO MARSHALL, Analyst, Office: Pastoral Center.

Legion of Mary—

English—Orange County Comitium: NATALIE TUNG, Pres., Tel: 714-696-9149; Email: natalie.nguyen81@gmail.com. North Orange County English Curia: EUGENIA UKPO, Pres., Tel: 714-956-7662; Email: onwukpo@yahoo.com. Orange County Spanish: GUDULIA SALAS FLORES, Pres., Tel: 714-574-6393; Email: guduliasala55@gmail.com.

Vietnamese—Orange County: MICHAEL THUC VU, Pres., Tel: 714-852-1797; Email: thuctuyetvu@yahoo.com.

Korean—Southeast Orange County: SUKOK (ROSA) PARK, Pres., Tel: 949-285-7092; Email: sopark318@yahoo.com. North Orange County: FRANCISCO WOO, Pres., Tel: 714-318-7907; Email: westgate.usa@gmail.com. South Orange County: KU (GABRIEL) HAK YON, Pres., Tel: 714-394-0655; Email: yonkyuhag@gmail.com. Chinese Ministry: TONY CHENG, Pres., Tel: 949-230-0188; Email: tony_+_cheng@yahoo.com; PAUL YUNG, Vice Pres., Tel: 949-878-0180; Email: yungpaul180@gmail.com.

Worship—MRS. LESA TRUXAW, Dir., Office: Pastoral Center; Office: Pastoral Center; Office: Pastoral Center.

Life, Justice and Peace—GREG WALGENBACH, Dir., Office: Pastoral Center.

Catecumenate—MRS. LESA TRUXAW, Dir.

Victim Assistance Coordinator—MRS. SYLVIA PALDA, Tel: 800-364-3064; Email: palda.sylvia@gmail.com.

CLERGY, PARISHES, MISSIONS AND PAROCHIAL SCHOOLS

CITY OF ORANGE

1—CATHEDRAL OF THE HOLY FAMILY (1921)
566 S. Glassell St., Orange, 92866. Tel: 714-639-2900 ; Email: parish@hfcathedral.org; Web: www.hfcathedral.org. Revs. Patrick A. Moses, Rector; Rudolph Alumam, Parochial Vicar; Mark Aaron Riomalos, A.M., Parochial Vicar; Deacons Edward Bonnarens; Carlos Euyoque, (Retired); Pedro Cardenas.
School—Cathedral of the Holy Family School, (Grades PreSchool-8),
530 S. Glassell St., Orange, 92866. Tel: 714-538-6012 ; Fax: 714-633-5892. Margaret Harlow, Prin.; Elena Castillo, Librarian. Lay Teachers 33; Students 486.
Catechesis Religious Program—
Tel: 714-639-2900, Ext. 235; Fax: 714-516-9949. Students 350.

2—LA PURISIMA (1964) Revs. William Barman; Martin Hiep Nguyen, Parochial Vicar; Sergio Ramos, Parochial Vicar; Deacons Anthony Bube; Ricardo Barraza; Timothy O'Donoghue; David Tran; Miguel Espinoza; Miguel Sanchez.
Res.: 11712 N. Hewes, Orange, 92869. Tel: 714-633-5800; Email: maria.e@lapurisima.net; Email: office@lapurisima.net.
School—La Purisima School, (Grades PreK-8),
Tel: 714-633-5411; Fax: 714-633-1588; Email: rramirez@lpcs.net; Email: vserrano@lpcs.net; Web: www.lpcs.net. Ms. Rosa Ramirez, Prin. Lay Teachers 23; Students 150.
Catechesis Religious Program—
Tel: 714-633-5344. Claudia Zuniga Pham, Youth Min. & Confirmation Coord.; Valeria Tovar, Youth Min. & Confirmation Coord. Students 1,138.

3—ST. NORBERT (1963)

300 E. Taft Ave., Orange, 92865. Tel: 714-637-4360; Fax: 714-637-4311; Email: info@stnorbertchurch.org; Web: www.stnorbertchurch.org. Revs. Bruce Patterson; John Duy Nguyen, Parochial Vicar; Fredy Mancilla, Parochial Vicar; Deacons Joseph Esparza; Juan Espinoza; David Blake. In Res., Rev. James Barrand.
School—St. Norbert School, (Grades PreSchool-8), Tel: 714-637-6822; Fax: 714-637-1604; Email: jciccoianni@saintnorbertschool.org; Web: www.saintnorbertschool.org. Joseph Ciccoianni, Prin. Clergy 1; Lay Teachers 14; Students 311.
Catechesis Religious Program—
Tel: 714-998-1070. Robin Mayes, D.R.E.; Ms. Charlene Dumitru, Adult Faith Formation Dir.; Katie Mahoney, Dir. Youth Min.; April Curtin, Asst. Dir. Youth Faith Formation. Students 814.

ORANGE COUNTY OUTSIDE THE CITY

ALISO VIEJO, CORPUS CHRISTI (1999) [CEM]
27231 Aliso Viejo Pkwy., Aliso Viejo, 92656.
Tel: 949-389-9008; Fax: 949-831-6540; Email: corpuschristi@corpuschristialisoviejo.org; Web: www.avcatholics.org. Rev. Timothy Ramaekers.
Catechesis Religious Program—Students 266.

ANAHEIM
1—ST. ANTHONY CLARET (1955)
1450 E. La Palma Ave., Anaheim, 92805.
Tel: 714-776-0270; Fax: 714-776-6022; Email: sac@stanthonymaryclaret.org; Web: www.stanthonymaryclaret.org. Revs. Bill T. Cao, Admin.; Carlos Leon, Parochial Vicar; Thomas Tran, S.V.D., Parochial Vicar; Deacons August Mones; Salvador Sanchez.
Catechesis Religious Program—Tel: 714-778-1399; Fax: 714-956-2701. Margarita Navarro, D.R.E.; Ana Orozco, D.R.E. (Confirmation/ Youth Ministry); Socorro Valles, R.C.I.A. Students 1,169.

2—ST. BONIFACE (1860) Revs. Edward L. Poettgen Jr.; Leonel M. Vargas, Parochial Vicar; Danh Ngoc Trinh, Parochial Vicar.
Res.: 120 N. Janss St., Anaheim, 92805.
Tel: 714-956-3110; Email: stboniface120@aol.com; Web: stbonifaceonline.org.
Catechesis Religious Program—Tel: 714-772-3060; Fax: 714-399-0568; Email: fguzman@saint-boniface.org. Students 1,400.

3—ST. JUSTIN MARTYR (1958) Revs. Joseph Robillard; Manuel Lopez, Parochial Vicar; Nicolas Toan Nguyen, Parochial Vicar; Deacons Jose Ferreras; Kalini Folau; Ramon Leon; Rev. John Monestero, In Res.; Rev. Msgr. Kerry Beaulieu, In Res., (Retired).
Res. & Church: 2050 W. Ball Rd., Anaheim, 92804.
Tel: 714-774-2595; Fax: 714-774-9849; Email: lsardagna@saintjustin.org.
School—St. Justin Martyr School, (Grades PreK-8), 2030 W. Ball Rd., Anaheim, 92804.
Tel: 714-772-4902; Fax: 714-772-2092; Email: info@sjm-k8.com; Web: www.sjm-k8.com. Jan Balsis, Prin.; Alvaro Mendoza, Contact Person. Lay Teachers 12; Students 200.
Catechesis Religious Program—
Tel: 714-535-6111 (English & Spanish). Students 741.
Mission—Sacred Heart, 10852 Harcourt Ave., Anaheim, Orange Co. 92804.

4—SAN ANTONIO DE PADUA DEL CANON CHURCH (1977)
5800 E. Santa Ana Canyon Rd., Anaheim, 92807.
Tel: 714-974-1416; Fax: 714-974-9630; Email: admin@sanantoniochurch.org; Web: sanantoniochurch.org. Revs. John Neneman; Wayne Adajar, Parochial Vicar; Deacons Russell Millspaugh; Doug Cook; Paul Amorino.
See St. Francis of Assisi School, Yorba Linda under Multi-Parish Schools located in the Institution section.
Catechesis Religious Program—Tel: 714-974-2053; Email: pweller@sanantoniochurch.org. Patricia Weller, D.R.E. Students 688.

BREA, ST. ANGELA MERICI (1962) Revs. David Klunk, Admin.; Francis Ng, Parochial Vicar; Deacons Benjamin Flores; Michael Shaffer.
Res.: 585 Walnut St., Brea, 92821. Tel: 714-529-8121; Email: sue.stangela@gmail.com.
Church: Walnut and Fir, Brea, 92821.
School—St. Angela Merici School, (Grades PreK-8), 575 S. Walnut Ave., Brea, 92821. Tel: 714-529-6372; Fax: 714-529-7755. Nancy Windisch, Prin. Lay Teachers 16; Religious 1; Students 283.
Catechesis Religious Program—Tel: 714-529-2311. Students 564.

BUENA PARK, ST. PIUS V (1948) Revs. Paw Lwin; Juvy Crisomoto, A.M., Parochial Vicar; Deacon Richard Torres.
Res.: 7691 Orangethorpe Ave., Buena Park, 90621.
Tel: 714-522-2193; Email: admin@stpiusvbp.org; Web: www.stpiusvbp.org.
School—St. Pius V School, (Grades PreK-8), 7681 Orangethorpe Ave., Buena Park, 90621.
Tel: 714-522-5313; Fax: 714-522-1767; Web: stpius5school.net. Joan Bravo, Prin. Lay Teachers 18; Students 345.
Catechesis Religious Program—Tel: 714-522-3971; Email: sre@stpius5.org. Students 620.

CAPISTRANO BEACH, SAN FELIPE DE JESUS (1950) (Hispanic), See separate listing. See St. Edward the Confessor, Dana Point.

COSTA MESA
1—ST. JOACHIM (1947)
Mailing Address: 1964 Orange Ave., Costa Mesa, 92627. Revs. Michael P. Hanifin; Douglas A. Zavala, Parochial Vicar.
Res.: 1943 Orange Ave., Costa Mesa, 92627.
Tel: 949-574-7400; Fax: 949-574-7407; Email: teresa@stjccm.org; Web: stjccm.org.
School—St. Joachim School, (Grades PreSchool-8).
Catechesis Religious Program—Students 784.

2—ST. JOHN THE BAPTIST (1960) Revs. Augustine R. Puchner, O.Praem.; Andrew P. Tran, O.Praem., Parochial Vicar; Godfrey E. Bushmaker, O.Praem., Parochial Vicar; Claude A. Williams, O.Praem., Parochial Vicar; Michael U. Perea, O.Praem., Parochial Vicar; Patrick D. Foutts, O.Praem., In Res.; Damien V. Giap, O.Praem., In Res.
Res.: 1015 Baker St., Costa Mesa, 92626.
Tel: 714-540-2214; Email: info@sjboc.org; Web: www.sjboc.org.
School—St. John the Baptist School, (Grades PreK-8), 1021 Baker St., Costa Mesa, 92626.
Tel: 714-557-5060; Fax: 714-557-9263; Web: www.sjbschool.net. Paula Viles, Prin.; Jeff Urbaniec, Vice Prin. Lay Teachers 24; Students 511.
Catechesis Religious Program—Tel: 714-546-4102. Isabel Cacho, D.R.E.; Sisters Hoa Hoang, L.H.C., D.R.E. (Vietnamese); Bertha Rafael, M.C., D.R.E. (Spanish). Students 711.

CYPRESS, ST. IRENAEUS (1961) Rev. Binh T. Nguyen, Admin.; Deacons Jerry Pyne; Del Davis; Jose Pulido; Bruce Sago; Revs. Frederick Atentar, A.M., In Res.; William Brewer Goldin, In Res.
Res.: 5201 Evergreen Ave., Cypress, 90630.
Tel: 714-826-0760; Email: tkulassia@sticypress.org.
School—St. Irenaeus School, (Grades PreK-8), 9201 Grindlay St., Cypress, 90630. Tel: 714-827-4500; Fax: 714-827-2930; Email: office@stischoolcypress.org. Monica Hayden, Prin. Lay Teachers 20; Students 357.
Catechesis Religious Program—Tel: 714-826-1140; Email: rbradley@sticypress.org. Students 775.

DANA POINT, ST. EDWARD THE CONFESSOR (1969)
Mailing Address: 33926 Calle La Primavera, Dana Point, 92629. Revs. Brendan Manson; Armando Virrey, Parochial Vicar; Deacons Al Scaduto; Victor Samano, (Retired).
Res.: 24451 Alta Vista Dr., Dana Point, 92629.
Tel: 949-496-1307; Email: secretary@stedward.com.
School—St. Edward the Confessor School, (Grades PreSchool-8), 33866 Calle La Primavera, Dana Point, 92629. Tel: 949-496-1241; Fax: 949-496-1819. Dr. Catherine Muzzy, Prin. Lay Teachers 41; Students 752.
Catechesis Religious Program—Tel: 949-496-6011. Students 868.
Chapel—San Felipe de Jesus, 26010 Domingo Ave., Capistrano Beach, 92624.

FOUNTAIN VALLEY, HOLY SPIRIT (1972)
Mailing Address: 17270 Ward St., Fountain Valley, 92708. Revs. Joseph Thuong Tran, Admin.; Thomas De Nguyen, Parochial Vicar; Very Rev. Saul Alba-Infante, Parochial Vicar; Deacons Guillermo Torres; Phillip Goodman; Paul Manh Van Mai.
Res.: 16806 Mt. Olsen Cir., Fountain Valley, 92708.
Tel: 714-963-1811; Email: office@hsccfv.org; Web: holyspiritfv.org.
Catechesis Religious Program—Tel: 714-963-7871; Email: faithformation@hsccfv.org. Sr. Annuncia Thu Mai, L.H.C., D.R.E. Students 1,000.

FULLERTON
1—ST. JULIANA FALCONIERI (1965)
1316 N. Acacia Ave., Fullerton, 92831.
Tel: 714-879-1965; Fax: 714-526-6673; Email: info@stjulianachurch.org; Web: www.stjulianachurch.org. Revs. Michael M. Pontarelli, O.S.M.; Luke M. Stano, O.S.M., Parochial Vicar; Deacons Chuck Doidge; Peter Lauder.
School—St. Juliana Falconieri School, (Grades PreK-8), 1320 N. Acacia Ave., Fullerton, 92831.
Tel: 714-871-2829; Fax: 714-871-8465; Email: info@stjulianaschool.org; Web: www.stjulianaschool.org. Manuel Gonzalez, Prin. Lay Teachers 29; Students 306.
Catechesis Religious Program—Michael McHenry, Dir. Faith Formation. Students 348.

2—ST. MARY'S (1912) Revs. Enrique Sera; Hector Bedoya, Parochial Vicar; David Otto, Parochial Vicar; Deacons Carlos Gonzalez; Manuel Chavira; Erialdo Ramirez.
Res.: 400 W. Commonwealth Ave., Fullerton, 92832.
Tel: 714-525-2500; Fax: 714-525-3837; Email: secretary@saintmarysfullerton.org; Web: saintmarysfullerton.org.
Catechesis Religious Program—Students 339.

3—ST. PHILIP BENIZI (1958) Rev. Dennis Kriz, O.S.M.; Deacons Richard Glaudini; Richard Doubledee; Antonio Luna; Roger Vandervest; Marybell Bravo, Business Mgr.; Revs. Gerald M. Horan, O.S.M., In Res.; Joseph Arputhasamy, In Res.; Viblanc Steephen, O.S.M., In Res.; Bruce Klikunas, In Res.
Res. & Parish Office: 235 S. Pine Dr., Fullerton, 92833. Tel: 714-871-3610; Email: philipbenizi@aol.com.
Catechesis Religious Program—Tel: 714-870-0561; Email: spbfaithformation@gmail.com. Bro. Arnaldo M. Sanchez, O.S.M., Dir. Faith Formation. Students 330.

GARDEN GROVE
1—CHRIST CATHEDRAL PARISH (1961) Revs. Christopher H. Smith, Rector; Mario Juarez, Parochial Vicar; Quan Dinh Tran, J.D., Parochial Vicar; Christopher Pham, Parochial Vicar; Deacons Joseph Khiet Nguyen; Frank Chavez; Cruz Pleitez. In Res., Rev. Daniel B. Reader.
Church & Res.: 13280 Chapman Ave., 92840.
Tel: 714-971-2141; Email: gthomsen@christcathedralparish.org.
Catechesis Religious Program—Tel: 714-971-2091. Sr. Theresa Trang Nguyen, L.H.C., Dir. Faith Formation. Students 1,603.

2—ST. COLUMBAN (1953)
10801 Stanford Ave., 92840. Tel: 714-534-1174; Fax: 714-534-1937; Email: bphillips@saintcolumbanchurch.org; Web: saintcolumbanchurch.org. Rev. Msgr. Tuan Joseph Pham, J.C.L.; Revs. Phuong Nguyen, Parochial Vicar; Joseph Ngu Cong Truong, Parochial Vicar; Bridget Phillips, Business Mgr.
School—St. Columban School, (Grades PreSchool-8), 10855 Stanford Ave., 92840. Tel: 714-534-3947; Email: office@saintcolumbanschool.com; Web: www.saintcolumbanschool.com. Barbara Barreda, Prin. Clergy 1; Lay Teachers 18; Students 298.
Catechesis Religious Program—Tel: 714-537-2015. Sr. Brid O'Shea, R.S.C., RCIA Coord. Students 1,098.

HUNTINGTON BEACH
1—ST. BONAVENTURE (1965) Revs. Joseph Knerr; Timothy Donovan, Parochial Vicar; Martin Duc Tran, Parochial Vicar; Deacons Jim Andersen; Vincent Tran; Joseph Sullivan; John Davies.
Res.: 16400 Springdale St., Huntington Beach, 92649. Tel: 714-846-3359; Email: pastorsec@stbonaventure.org.
School—St. Bonaventure School, (Grades PreK-8), 16390 Springdale St., Huntington Beach, 92649.
Tel: 714-846-2472; Fax: 714-840-0498; Email: office@stbonaventureschool.org; Web: www.stbonaventureschool.org. 16377 Bradbury Ln., Huntington Beach, 92647. Janice Callender, Prin.; Mrs. Kim White, Vice Prin.; Mrs. Colleen Hoffmann, Business Mgr.; Mrs. Cathy Smith, Registrar; Kathi Vogel, Librarian. Lay Teachers 29; Students 500.
Catechesis Religious Program—Tel: 714-846-1187; Email: Debbie@stbonaventure.org. Debbie Doke, D.R.E. Students 747.

2—ST. MARY'S BY THE SEA (1912) Rev. Quang Vinh Chu.
Res.: 321 10th St., Huntington Beach, 92648.
Tel: 714-536-6913; Email: stmarys.hb@gmail.com.
Catechesis Religious Program—Students 60.

3—STS. SIMON & JUDE (1912) Rev. Daniel Barica, O.F.M.; Deacons Stephen Byars; Vincent Nguyen, Parochial Vicar; Colleen Murray, Pastoral Admin.; Mark Purcell, Pastoral Assoc. Liturgy & Music; Mrs. Shirl Giacomi, Pastoral Assoc.
Res.: 20444 Magnolia St., Huntington Beach, 92646.
Tel: 714-962-3333; Email: ssj@ssj.org.
School—Sts. Simon & Jude School, (Grades K-8), 20400 Magnolia St., Huntington Beach, 92646.
Tel: 714-962-4451; Fax: 714-968-1329; Email: school@ssjschool.org; Web: www.ssj.org/school/. Mrs. Crystal Pinkofsky, Prin. Lay Teachers 30; Students 422.
Catechesis Religious Program—Mrs. Shirl Giacomi, D.R.E. Students 414.

4—ST. VINCENT DE PAUL (1977)
8345 Talbert Ave., Huntington Beach, 92646.
Tel: 714-842-3000; Email: svdp@svdphb.org; Web: svdphb.org. Revs. Jerome T. Karcher; Gaston Mendiola Arroyo, Parochial Vicar; Deacons Gerard Wallace; Angelo Giambrone.
Catechesis Religious Program—Email: reled@svdphb.org. Students 639.

IRVINE
1—ST. ELIZABETH ANN SETON (1976) Rev. Thomas Pado; Deacon Steve Greco.
Res.: 9 Hillgate, Irvine, 92612-3265.
Tel: 949-854-1000, Ext. 221; Email: malu@seasirvine.org; Email: hector@seasirvine.org; Email: tompado@seasirvine.org; Web: www.seasirvine.org.
Catechesis Religious Program—James Abowd, D.R.E. Students 152.
Mission—Queen of Life Chapel, 2532 Dupont Dr., Irvine, 92612. Tel: 949-474-7368; Fax: 781-207-0713; Email: tbush@bushfirm.com.

2—ST. JOHN NEUMANN (1978)
5101 Alton Pkwy., Irvine, 92604-8605.
Tel: 949-559-4006; Email: alex.rivas@sjnirvine.org; Email: jocelyn.lacson@sjnirvine.org; Web: www.sjnirvine.org. Rev. Msgr. Colm Conlon; Revs. Jeffrey A. Droessler; Michael Khong, Parochial Vicar.
Catechesis Religious Program—Tel: 949-786-6105; Fax: 949-786-6102; Email: religioused@sjnirvine.org. Deacon Charles Boyer, D.R.E./ R.C.I.A.; Samantha Leveugle, Dir. Youth Min.; Rebecca LaBriola, D.R.E. Students 408.

3—ST. THOMAS MORE (1996) [CEM] Revs. John E. Janze; Paul Thai Trinh, Parochial Vicar; Deacons Tin Nguyen; Tony Patronite; Stan Necikowski; Theresa Nault, Office & Business Mgr.
Res.: 51 Marketplace, Irvine, 92602.
Tel: 949-551-8601; Email: stephanie@stmirvine.org; Email: theresa@stmirvine.org; Web: www.stmirvine.org.
Rectory—Rectory: 4112 Escudero, Irvine, 92602.
Catechesis Religious Program—Barbara Catiller, Dir. Adult Faith Formation. Students 800.

LA HABRA, OUR LADY OF GUADALUPE (1947)
900 W. La Habra Blvd., La Habra, 90631.
Tel: 562-691-0533; Email: dvonr@olglahabra.org; Email: ebecker@olglahabra.org; Web: www.olglahabra.org. Revs. Edward Becker; Ruben Ruiz, Parochial Vicar; Randy Guillen, Parochial Vicar.
School—Our Lady of Guadalupe School, (Grades PreK-8), Tel: 562-697-9726; Fax: 562-905-0095; Email: mlooney@olgvikings.org. Francine Kubasek, Prin.; Martina Looney, Business Mgr. Lay Teachers 12; Students 160.
Catechesis Religious Program—Stephanie Ruiz, D.R.E. Students 247.

LADERA RANCH, HOLY TRINITY (2005)
1600 Corporate Dr., Ladera Ranch, 92694.
Tel: 949-218-3131; Fax: 949-388-1311; Email: frreynold@holytrinityladera.org; Web: www.holytrinityladera.org. Revs. Reynold Furrell; John Duy Nguyen, Parochial Vicar; Alonso Rosado, Dir.; Deacon Randall McMahon; Casey McKinley, Music & Media Dir.; Angela Johnson, Business Mgr., Email: ajohnson@holytrinityladera.org; Patti Wieckert, RCIA Coordiantor; Andrew Watson, Youth Min.
See Serra Catholic School under Multi-Parish Schools located in the Institution section.
Catechesis Religious Program—Paula Baytien, Coord. Faith Formation; Andrew Watson, Youth Min.; Chentel Tabbada, Youth Min.; Patti Wieckert, RCIA Coord. Students 1,030.

LAGUNA BEACH, ST. CATHERINE OF SIENA (1923) Rev. Kenneth A. Schmit.
Res.: 1042 Temple Ter., Laguna Beach, 92651.
Tel: 949-494-9701; Email: lisa@stcathchurch.org.
School—St. Catherine of Siena School, (Grades PreK-8), 30516 S. Coast Hwy., Laguna Beach, 92651. Tel: 949-494-7339; Fax: 949-376-5752; Email: tsmith@stcathschool.org; Web: www.stcathschool.org. Mike Letourneau, Prin.; Ellen Kravitz, Librarian. Lay Teachers 19; Students 149.
Catechesis Religious Program—Students 108.

LAGUNA NIGUEL, ST. TIMOTHY (1980) Rev. Msgr. John Urell; Rev. Vincent Hung Pham, Parochial Vicar; Deacon Kenneth Hobbs; Rev. Craig M. Butters, In Res.
Rectory—29182 Via San Sebastian, Laguna Niguel, 92677.
Church: 29102 Crown Valley Pkwy., Laguna Niguel, 92677. Tel: 949-249-4091; Email: info@st-timsrc.org; Web: www.st-timsrc.org.
Catechesis Religious Program—Tel: 949-495-4126; Email: mwallace@st-timsrc.org. Students 260.

LAGUNA WOODS, ST. NICHOLAS (1965) Revs. George P. Blais, Admin.; Quyen Truong, Parochial Vicar; Deacons Wayne Thompson; Chau Tran; Gerardo DeSantos.
Res.: 24252 El Toro Rd., Laguna Woods, 92637.
Tel: 949-837-1090; Email: cwolski@stnicholaschurch.org.
Catechesis Religious Program—Tel: 949-837-7676. Students 370.

LAKE FOREST, SANTIAGO DE COMPOSTELA (1979) Revs. Thomas Paul K. Naval; Stephen Lesniewski; Deacons Ricardo Barraza; Daniel Diesel; Rev. John Block, In Res., (Retired).
Res.: 21682 Lake Forest Dr., Lake Forest, 92630.
Tel: 949-951-8599; Email: communications@sdccatholic.org.
See Serra Catholic School, Rancho Santa Margarita under Multi-Parish Schools located in the Institution section.
Catechesis Religious Program—Gloria Fetta, D.R.E.; Lyanamar Medina, D.R.E. (Formacion en la Fe); Joanne Lambert, D.R.E. (Confirmation); Tom Haas, R.C.I.A. (Adult Faith Formation). Students 453.

LOS ALAMITOS, ST. HEDWIG (1960)
11482 Los Alamitos Blvd., Los Alamitos, 90720.
Tel: 562-296-9000; Email: info@sainthedwigparish.org; Web: www.sainthedwigparish.org. Revs. Christopher Heath; David Gruver, Parochial Vicar; Daniel Wilder, Parochial Vicar; Deacons Gary Mucho; Larry Hurst; Henry Eagar. In Res., Rev. Joseph Droessler.
School—St. Hedwig School, (Grades K-8), 3591 Orangewood Ave., Los Alamitos, 90720.
Tel: 562-296-9060; Fax: 562-296-9089; Email: bfinn@sainthedwigparish.org. Erin Rucker, Prin. Lay Teachers 25; Students 358.

MISSION VIEJO, ST. KILIAN (1970)
26872 Estanciero Dr., Mission Viejo, 92691.
Tel: 949-586-4440; Email: office@stkilianchurch.org; Web: stkilianchurch.org. Rev. Angelos Sebastian, Admin.; Rev. Msgr. Tuan Joseph Pham, J.C.L., Parochial Vicar; Deacons Bob Kelleher; Mark Martin.
See Serra Catholic School, Rancho Santa Margarita under Multi-Parish Schools located in the Institution section.
Catechesis Religious Program—Tel: 949-586-4550; Email: skre@stkilianchurch.org. Cindy Hurley, D.R.E. Students 275.

NEWPORT BEACH
1—OUR LADY OF MOUNT CARMEL (1923)
1441 W. Balboa Blvd., Newport Beach, 92661-1163.
Tel: 949-673-3775; Email: rhallas@olmc.net; Web: olmc.net. Rev. Douglas Cook, J.C.L.; Deacon Stephen Mutz; Very Rev. E. Scott Borgman, J.C.D., In Res.; Rev. Sean Condon, (Ireland) In Res., (Retired).
Catechesis Religious Program—Tel: 949-673-2719. John Bruscia, D.R.E. (CRP); Mr. Greg Kelley, D.R.E. (Adult Education). Students 214.
Chapel—St. John Vianney, 314 Marine Ave., Balboa Island, 92662-1206. Tel: 949-432-5494, Ext. 1; Email: jbobier@sjvchapel.net.

2—OUR LADY QUEEN OF ANGELS (1961) Revs. Brandon Dang, Parochial Vicar; Charles Tran, Parochial Vicar; Anthony Hien Vu, Parochial Vicar; Deacon Charles Boyer; Rev. Msgr. Wilbur Davis, In Res., (Retired).
Res.: 2046 Mar Vista Dr., Newport Beach, 92660.
Tel: 949-644-0200; Fax: 949-644-6213; Web: inquiry@olqa.org.
School—Our Lady Queen of Angels School, (Grades K-8), Tel: 949-644-1166; Fax: 949-644-6213; Email: eryan@olqa.org; Web: www.olqaschool.org. Mrs. Julie Tipton, Prin. Lay Teachers 31; Students 405.
Catechesis Religious Program—Tel: 949-219-1497; Fax: 949-644-1349. Students 465.

PLACENTIA, ST. JOSEPH (1953) Revs. Miguel A. Hernandez, Admin.; Martin Phuoc Bui, Parochial Vicar; Rev. Msgr. Donald Romito, (In Res.), (Retired); Rev. Eamon O'Gorman, (Retired); Deacons Jim Merle; Ken Kleckner; Jorge Ramirez.
Res.: 717 N. Bradford Ave., Placentia, 92870-4514.
Tel: 714-528-1487; Email: jrodriguez@stjosephplacentia.org; Web: stjosephplacentia.org.
School—St. Joseph School, (Grades PreSchool-8), 801 N. Bradford Ave., Placentia, 92870-4515.
Tel: 714-528-1794; Fax: 714-528-0668; Web: www.sjsplacentia.org. Jo Ann Telles, Prin. Lay Teachers 15; Students 201.
Catechesis Religious Program—Summer Pongetti, Faith Formation Coord.; Eloisa Ramirez, Spanish Faith Formation Coord. Students 642.
Mission—Santa Teresita, 636 Van Buren Ave., Atwood, Orange Co. 92811.

RANCHO SANTA MARGARITA, SAN FRANCISCO SOLANO CHURCH (1989) Revs. Duy T. Le, Admin.; Aristotle G. Quan, Parochial Vicar; Deacon Carl Swanson.
Res.: 22082 Antonio Pkwy., Rancho Santa Margarita, 92688-1993. Tel: 949-589-7767; Email: information@sfsolano.org; Web: www.sfsolano.org.
See Serra Catholic School, Rancho Santa Margarita under Multi-Parish Schools located in the Institution section.
Catechesis Religious Program—Tel: 949-589-1709; Fax: 949-589-2840. Students 597.

SAN CLEMENTE, OUR LADY OF FATIMA (1947)
Mailing Address: 105 N. La Esperanza, San Clemente, 92672. Tel: 949-492-4101;
Fax: 949-492-4856; Email: Fatima@olfchurch.net; Web: www.olfchurch.net. Revs. James C. Ries; Salvador Landa, Parochial Vicar.
Res.: 406 Avenida Granada, San Clemente, 92672.
School—Our Lady of Fatima School, (Grades PreK-8), Tel: 949-492-7320; Fax: 949-492-3793; Email: jwilliams@olfschool.net; Web: www.olfschool.net. Joanne Williams, Prin. Students 170.
Catechesis Religious Program—Students 341.

SAN JUAN CAPISTRANO, MISSION BASILICA - SAN JUAN CAPISTRANO (1776) [CEM] Rev. Msgr. J. Michael McKiernan, Rector/Pastor; Rev. Domingo Romero, O.F.M., Parochial Vicar; Deacon Gary Griffin; Rev. Arthur Holquin, In Res., (Retired)
Historic Mission San Juan Capistrano
Res.: 31520 Camino Capistrano, San Juan Capistrano, 92675. Tel: 949-234-1360; Email: missionbasilicaparish@missionparish.org; Web: www.missionparish.org.
School—Mission Basilica - San Juan Capistrano School, (Grades PreSchool-8), 31641 El Camino Real, San Juan Capistrano, 92675. Tel: 949-234-1385; Fax: 949-243-1397; Email: ddauria@mbssjc.org; Web: www.missionbasilicaschool.org. Alycia Beresford, Prin. Lay Teachers 18; Students 275.
Catechesis Religious Program—Email: dflores@missionparish.org. Dulce Flores, D.R.E. Students 470.

SANTA ANA
1—ST. ANNE (1923) (Hispanic) Revs. Antonio Lopez-Flores; Luis G. Segura, O.F.M., Parochial Vicar; Deacons Francisco Martinez; Michael Mendiola; Salvador Del Real.
Res.: 109 W. Borchard Ave., P.O. Box 2425, Santa Ana, 92707. Tel: 714-835-7434; Tel: 714-835-7435; Fax: 714-975-8343; Email: stannecc@gmail.com; Web: www.saparish.org.
School—St. Anne School, (Grades PreSchool-8), 1324 S. Main St., Santa Ana, 92707. Tel: 714-542-9328; Fax: 714-542-3431. Sr. Teresa Lynch, C.S.J., Prin. Lay Teachers 22; Sisters 2; Students 231.
Catechesis Religious Program—Tel: 714-542-1213. Angelica Gutierrez, D.R.E. Students 490.

2—ST. BARBARA CATHOLIC CHURCH (1962) Revs. Ramon Cisneros, Parochial Vicar; Joseph Thai Nguyen, Parochial Vicar; Deacon Hao Nguyen, Pastoral Min./ Coord.; Revs. Joseph Tuan Pham; Anthony Hien Vu, Parochial Vicar; Deacons Joseph Anh Nguyen; Carlos Navarro.
Res.: 730 S. Euclid St., Santa Ana, 92704.
Tel: 714-775-7733; Tel: 714-775-9464;
Fax: 714-775-9467; Email: kbui@st-barbarachurch.org; Email: tta@st-barbarachurch.org; Email: anguyen@stbarbara.com; Web: www.saintbarbarachurch.org.
School—St. Barbara Catholic School, (Grades K-8), 5306 W. McFadden Ave., Santa Ana, 92704.
Tel: 714-775-9477; Fax: 714-775-9468; Email: sbs@stbarbara.com; Web: www.stbarbara.com. Mrs. Melissa Baroldi, Prin. Clergy 2; Lay Teachers 15; Students 289.
Catechesis Religious Program—Tel: 714-775-9475. Sr. Grace Duc Le, L.H.C., D.R.E. Students 1,392.

3—CHRIST OUR SAVIOR CATHOLIC PARISH (2005)
2000 W. Alton Ave, Santa Ana, 92704.
Tel: 714-444-1500; Email: parishoffice@coscp.org; Web: coscp.org. Rev. Steven Correz; Deacons Luis Gallardo; Francisco Martinez; Joe Garza; Revs. Kiet A. Ta, In Res.; Rudolph J. Preciado, In Res., (Retired).
Catechesis Religious Program—Mr. Luis Ramirez, Dir. Parish. Students 289.

4—ST. GEORGE (CHALDEAN CATHOLIC)
Mailing Address: 4807 W. McFadden, Santa Ana, 92704. Tel: 714-531-7760. Rev. Zuhair G. Toma.

5—IMMACULATE HEART OF MARY (1960) Revs. Gregory Marquez, Admin.; Mauro Trujillo, Parochial Vicar; Armando Virrey, Parochial Vicar; Joseph Luan Nguyen, Parochial Vicar; Deacons Adolfo Ramirez; Rigoberto Maldonado, Email: deaconrigo@gmail.com; Biviano Cordero. In Res., Rev. Ignatius Lau, (Retired).
Res.: 1100 S. Center St., Santa Ana, 92704.
Tel: 714-751-5335; Fax: 714-662-0130; Email: ihminfo@ihmsantaana.org.
School—School of Our Lady, (Grades K-8), 2204 W. McFadden, Santa Ana, 92704. Tel: 714-545-8185; Fax: 714-545-2362; Email: solis@schoolofourlady.org; Web: www.schoolofourlady.org. Ms. Adela Solis, Prin. Lay Teachers 11; Students 208.
Catechesis Religious Program—Tel: 714-546-5186. Students 1,657.

6—ST. JOSEPH (1887) Revs. Efrain Flores; David Otto, Parochial Vicar; Deacons Alfredo Rios; Certuro Giminez.
Res.: 727 Minter St., Santa Ana, 92701.
Tel: 714-542-4411; Email: receptionist@stjosephsa.org.
School—St. Joseph School, (Grades PreK-8), 608 Civic Center Dr. E., Santa Ana, 92701.
Tel: 714-542-2704; Fax: 714-542-2132; Email: stjoeprincipal@gmail.com; Web: www.stjoesa.org. Brad Snyder, Prin. Lay Teachers 11; Students 233.
Catechesis Religious Program—Delfina Diaz, D.R.E. Students 538.

7—OUR LADY OF GUADALUPE (1938) (Hispanic) Revs. Marlon Beof, O.A.R.; Jose Antonio Arias, O.A.R., Parochial Vicar; Jorge Mateos, O.A.R., Parochial Vicar; Deacons Miguel Gonzalez; Domingo Garza.
Res.: 1322 E. Third St., Santa Ana, 92701.
Tel: 714-836-4142; Email: ourladyg3@gmail.com.
Catechesis Religious Program—Tel: 714-973-0279. Imelda Bernal, D.R.E. Students 1,061.

8—OUR LADY OF GUADALUPE, DELHI (1927) (Hispanic) Rev. David Vuelvas-Arias.
Res.: 541 E. Central Ave., Santa Ana, 92707.
Tel: 714-540-0902; Email: garriaga@olgdelhi.org.
Catechesis Religious Program—Students 596.

9—OUR LADY OF LA VANG (2006) Revs. Joseph Luan Nguyen; Timothy Nguyen, Parochial Vicar; Deacon Adolfo Villapando.
Res.: 288 S. Harbor Blvd., Santa Ana, 92704.
Tel: 714-775-6200; Cell: 714-622-9268; Email:

parish@ourladyoflavang.org; Email: dphan@ourladyoflavang.org.
Catechesis Religious Program—Students 587.

10—OUR LADY OF THE PILLAR (1965) (Hispanic) Revs. Francisco Sandval, O.A.R.; Jose Luis Martinez, O.A.R., Parochial Vicar; Gabino Perez, O.A.R., Parochial Vicar; Thomas Devine, O.A.R., Parochial Vicar; Frank Wilder, O.A.R., Parochial Vicar; Deacons Luis Gallardo; Ulyses Feliciano, O.A.R.
Res.: 1622 W. 6th St., Santa Ana, 92703.
Tel: 714-543-1700; Fax: 714-543-9640; Email: elpilar@usa.com.
Catechesis Religious Program—Tel: 714-542-4684. Students 1,303.

SEAL BEACH

1—ST. ANNE CHURCH (1921) Rev. Msgr. Michael Heher, P.A.; Revs. Robert S. Vidal, Pastor Emeritus, (Retired); Benjamin Tran, Parochial Vicar; Deacon Peter Nguyen.
Res.: 340 Tenth St., Seal Beach, 90740.
Tel: 562-431-0721; Email: office@stannesealbeach.org; Web: www.stannesealbeach.org.
Catechesis Religious Program—
Tel: 562-431-0721, Ext. 16. Amy Papageorges, D.R.E. Students 207.

2—HOLY FAMILY (1969) Revs. Juan Caboboy; James Hartnett, Pastor Emeritus, (Retired); Venancio Amidar, Parochial Vicar.
Res.: 13900 Church Pl., Seal Beach, 90740.
Tel: 562-430-8170; Email: holyfamily.sb@verizon.net; Email: cvenegas@holyfamilysb.com; Email: bgormly@holyfamilysb.com; Web: www.holyfamilysb.com.

STANTON, ST. POLYCARP (1961)
8100 Chapman Ave., Stanton, 90680.
Tel: 714-893-2766; Fax: 714-898-6675; Email: dvella@stpolycarp.org; Web: www.stpolycarp.org.
Revs. Michael St. Paul; Miguel Angel Carabez, Parochial Vicar; Tuan John Nguyen, Parochial Vicar; Deacons Larry Leone; Ramiro Lopez; Jose Campos; Tri Kim Do; Rev. Msgr. Steve Doktorczyk, J.C.D., In Res.
School—St. Polycarp School, (Grades PreK-8), 8182 Chapman Ave., Stanton, 90680. Tel: 714-893-8882; Fax: 714-897-3357; Email: info@stpolycarpschool.org; Web: stpolycarpschool.org. Alison Daley, Prin.; Mary Flock, Prin. Religious Teachers 2; Lay Teachers 7; Students 116.

TUSTIN, ST. CECILIA (1957) (Spanish—Vietnamese) Revs. Bao Q. Thai; Ismael Silva, Parochial Vicar; Nicolaus Duy Thai, Parochial Vicar; Deacons Don Ngo; Rafael Romero; William Weeks.
Res.: 1301 Sycamore, Tustin, 92780.
Tel: 714-544-3250; Fax: 714-838-1996; Email: bthai@stceciliak8.org.
School—St. Cecilia School, (Grades PreSchool-8), 1311 Sycamore, Tustin, 92780. Tel: 714-544-1533; Fax: 714-544-0643; Email: school@stceciliak8.org; Web: MoreThanSchool.org. Mrs. Mary Alvarado, Prin.; Diane Smit, Librarian. Clergy 1; Lay Teachers 20; Students 310.
Catechesis Religious Program—Tel: 714-838-4466. Sr. Catherine Nguyen, L.H.C., D.R.E. Students 760.

WESTMINSTER, BLESSED SACRAMENT (1947) Revs. Tuyen Van Nguyen; Khoi Phan, Parochial Vicar; Jaime Hernandez, Parochial Vicar; Deacons Matt Calabrese; Miguel Sanchez; Arturo Gimenez.
Res.: 14072 S. Olive St., Westminster, 92683.
Tel: 714-892-4489; Email: office@bsc-od.org; Web: blessedsacramentchurch.com.
School—Blessed Sacrament School, (Grades PreSchool-8), 14146 S. Olive St., Westminster, 92683. Tel: 714-893-7701; Fax: 714-891-7186; Email: zpollock@bsscatholic.org; Web: www.bsscatholic.org. Gloria Castillo, Prin. Lay Teachers 17; Students 294.
Catechesis Religious Program—Tel: 714-897-2142. Deacon Hao Nguyen, Coord. Faith Formation. Students 1,142.

YORBA LINDA

1—ST. MARTIN DE PORRES (1970)
Mailing Address: 19767 Yorba Linda Blvd., Yorba Linda, 92886. Tel: 714-970-2771; Email: stmartin@smdpyl.org. Revs. Sy Uy Nguyen, J.C.L.; Hoa Tran, Parochial Vicar; Deacons Denis F. Zaun, Parish Dir.; Mark Murphy, Contact Person; Nick Sherg, Contact Person.
Res.: 19742 Lombardy Ln., Yorba Linda, 92886.
See St. Francis of Assisi School, Yorba Linda under Multi-Parish Schools located in the Institution section.
Catechesis Religious Program—Tel: 714-970-2771; Email: stephend@smdpyl.org. Rev. Stephen Duffin, D.R.E. Students 419.

2—SANTA CLARA DE ASIS (2001)
Mailing Address & Office: 22005 Avenida de la Paz, Yorba Linda, 92887. Tel: 714-970-7885;
Fax: 714-970-2618; Email: office@scdayl.org; Web: www.scdayl.org. Rev. Fred K. Bailey.
See St. Francis of Assisi School, Yorba Linda under Multi-Parish Schools located in the Institution section.
Catechesis Religious Program—Emily Bent, D.R.E.; Mary Chavez, RCIA Coord.; Kirsten King, Youth Min. Students 265.

Chaplains of Public Institutions

ORANGE. *UCI Medical Center*, 101 The City Dr. S., Orange, 92868. Tel: 714-634-5678. (Served by Christ Cathedral Parish)
13280 Chapman Ave., 92840. Tel: 714-971-2141.

COSTA MESA. *Fairview Developmental Center*, 2501 Harbor, Costa Mesa, 92626. Tel: 714-957-5242; Email: Gerard.Fay@fdc.dds.ca.gov. Cheryl Bright, Exec. Dir., Tel: 714-957-5105, Mr. Gerard Fay, Chap.

SANTA ANA. *All Adult and Juvenile Jail Facilities*, 1820 W. Orangewood Ave.; Ste. 101, Orange, 92868. Tel: 714-634-9909; Fax: 714-634-9910. Deacon Martin Ruiz, Hispanic Ministry, Mr. Fred LaPuzza, Dir., Sandra Negrete.

Special Assignment:
Rev. Msgr.—
Doktorczyk, Steve, J.C.D.
Revs.—
Baca, Alfred
Di Raimondo, Dominic, M.Ss.P., Dir., 7734 Santiago Canyon Rd., Orange, 92869
Luevano, Rafael, Ph.D.
Moneypenny, John W.
Navarro-Sanchez, Juan
Nguyen, Thanh-Tai P.
Reader, Daniel B.
Rudolph, Patrick N.
Smith, Christopher
Yang, Guo Yu (Joseph).

On Duty Outside the Diocese:
Revs.—
Capone, Robert
Kim, Simon Cheng ban
LeVecke, John R.
Sun Kim, Simon Chung
Vu, Paul Hoa Duy, J.C.L.
Weling, John B.

Military Chaplains:
Revs.—
Hoang, Joseph Duc Quang
Shimotsu, John M.
Sweeney, Kevin.

Absent on Sick Leave:
Revs.—
Justice, Joseph Charles
Monestero, John.

Graduate Studies:
Rev.—
Ho, Viet Peter, J.C.L.

Administrative Leave:
Revs.—
Escobedo, Gilberto
Henson, Jerome
Kim, Alex
Munoz, Matthew
Vu, Long Ngoc.

Retired:
Most Rev.—
Brown, Tod David, (Retired)
Rev. Msgrs.—
Beaulieu, Kerry, (Retired)
Caceres, Alonso, (Retired)
Campbell, John G., J.C.L., (Retired)
Davis, Wilbur, (Retired)
McGowan, Anthony, (Retired)
McLaughlin, William, (Retired)
Olson, Theodore, (Retired)
Romito, Donald, (Retired)
Revs.—
Bradley, John A., (Retired)
Buckman, Frank, (Retired)
Conlon, Columbanus, (Retired)
Dale, John Douglas, (Retired)
Delahunty, Richard A., (Retired)
Dunning, James Patrick, (Retired)
Fry, James Q., (Retired)
Glynn, Seamus A., (Retired)
Hartnett, James, (Retired)
Hoan, Michael Mai Khai, (Retired)
Holquin, Arthur, (Retired)
Hopcus, Daniel R., (Retired)
Kennedy, Richard C., (Retired)
Kolberg, Lawrence Floyd, (Retired)
Krekelberg, William F., (Retired)
Lau, Ignatius, (Retired)
Lavery, Bruce Dean, (Retired)
Lyons, Denis, (Retired)
MacCarthy, Justin H., Pastor Emeritus, (Retired)
Nettekoven, Joseph M., Pastor Emeritus, (Retired)
O'Gorman, Eamon T., (Retired)
Preciado, Rudolph, (Retired)
Rebamontan, Marito F., (Retired)
Sewell, Jack K., J.C.L., (Retired)
Skonezny, Raymond, (Retired)
Stone, Robert L., Pastor Emeritus, (Retired)
Vidal, Robert S., (Retired)
Zapata, Antonio Jesus, (Retired).

Permanent Deacons:
Amorino, Paul, San Antonio de Padua, Anaheim Hills
Andersen, James, St. Bonaventure, Huntington Beach
Barraza, Ricardo, Santiago de Compostela, Lake Forest
Bartolic, Patrick, St. John Vianney, Balboa Island
Blake, David, St. Norbert, Orange
Boyer, Charles, St. John Neuman, Irvine
Bube, Anthony, La Purisima, Orange
Byars, Stephen, Sts. Simon and Jude, Huntington Beach
Calabrese, Matt, Blessed Sacrament, Westminster
Campos, Jose, St. Polycarp, Stanton
Canlas, Fred, St. Joachim, Costa Mesa
Chavez, Frank, Christ Cathedral Parish, Garden Grove
Chavez, Jose Manuel, Our Lady of Guadalupe, La Habra
Chavira, Manuel, St. Mary, Fullerton
Cho, Paul, Holy Spirit, Fountain Valley
Chu, Binh
Chung, Peter, St. Thomas Korean Center, Anaheim
Concitis, Thomas, St. Mary by the Sea, Huntington Beach
Cook, Douglas, San Antonio de Padua, Anaheim Hills
Cordero, Biviano, Immaculate Heart of Mary, Santa Ana
Dao, Jerry, Holy Family, Seal Beach
Davies, John, St. Bonaventure, Huntington Beach
Davis, Del, St. Irenaeus, Cypress
Del Real, Salvador, St. Anne, Santa Ana
DeSantos, Gerardo, St. Nicholas, Laguna Woods
Diesel, Daniel, Santiago de Compostela, Lake Forest
Do, Tri Kim, St. Polycarp, Stanton
Doidge, Chuck, St. Juliana Falconieri, Fullerton
Doubledee, Richard, St. Philip Benizi, Fullerton
Eagar, Henry, St. Hedwig, Los Alamitos
Erdag, John, St. John Neumann, Irvine
Esparza, Joseph, St. Norbert, Orange
Espinoza, Juan, St. Norbert, Orange
Espinoza, Miguel, La Purisima, Orange
Euyoque, Carlos, Holy Family Cathedral, Orange
Ferreras, Jose, St. Justin Martyr, Anaheim
Flores, Benjamin, St. Angela Merici, Brea
Folau, Kalini, Tongan Community
Ford, Scott
Gallardo, Luis, Our Lady of the Pillar, Santa Ana
Garza, Domingo, Our Lady of Guadalupe, Santa Ana
Garza, Joe, Christ Our Savior, Santa Ana
Giambrone, Angelo, St. Vincent de Paul, Huntington Beach
Glaudini, Richard, St. Philip Benizi, Fullerton
Gonzalez, Carlos, St. Mary, Fullerton
Gonzalez, Miguel, Our Lady of Guadalupe, Santa Ana
Goodman, Phillip, Holy Spirit, Fountain Valley
Greco, Steve, Elizabeth Ann Seton, Irvine
Hernandez, Alfredo, St. Boniface, Anaheim
Hobbs, Kenneth, St. Timothy, Laguna Niguel
Hurst, Larry, St. Hedwig, Los Alamitos
Kelleher, Robert, Mission Hospital, Mission Viejo
Kim, Peter, Our Lady of Peace Korean Center
Kleckner, Ken, St. Joseph, Placentia
Lauder, Peter, St. Juliana Falconieri, Fullerton
Lee, Moon Chul, Korean Martyrs Catholic Center
Leon, Ramon, St. Justin Martyr, Anaheim
Leone, Larry, St. Polycarp, Stanton
Leuta, Tupuola Filipo, St. Joseph Medical Center
Liu, Louis, Chinese Catholic Community
Lopez, Ramiro, St. Polycarp, Stanton
Luna, Antonio, St. Philip Benizi, Fullerton
Maldonado, Rigoberto, Immaculate Heart of Mary, Santa Ana
Marin, Reynaldo, Our Lady of Guadalupe, La Habra
Martin, Mark, St. Kilian, Mission Viejo
Martinez, Francisco, St. Anne, Santa Ana
McGuine, Thomas, Holy Family Cathedral, Orange
McMahon, Randall, Holy Trinity, Ladera Ranch
Mendiola, Michael, St. Anne, Santa Ana
Merle, Jim, St. Joseph, Placentia
Millspaugh, Russell, San Antonio de Padua, Anaheim Hills
Mones, August, St. Anthony Claret, Anaheim

Mucho, Richard "Gary", St. Hedwig, Los Alamitos
Murphy, Mark, St. Martin de Porres, Yorba Linda
Mutz, Stephen, Our Lady of Mt. Carmel, Newport Beach
Necikowski, Stan, St. Thomas More, Irvine
Ngo, Dong Dinh, St. Cecilia, Tustin
Nguyen, Anh Phuong, St. Barbara, Santa Ana
Nguyen, Hao, St. Barbara, Santa Ana
Nguyen, Joseph Khiet, Christ Cathedral, Garden Grove
Nguyen, Peter, St. Anne, Seal Beach
Nguyen, Tin, St. Thomas More, Irvine
Nguyen, Tuan, St. Columban, Garden Grove
Nguyen, Tuyen, Redemptorist Vietnamese Center, Long Beach
O'Donoghue, Timothy, La Purisima, Orange
Oh, Nicholas, Korean Martyrs Catholic Center
Patronite, Tony, St. Thomas More, Irvine
Pleitez, Cruz, Christ Cathedral Parish, Garden Grove
Pulido, Jose, St. Irenaeus, Cypress
Pyne, Gerald, St. Irenaeus, Cypress
Ramirez, Adolfo, Immaculate Heart of Mary, Santa Ana
Ramirez, Humberto, Mission Basilica, San Juan Capistrano
Ramirez, Jorge, St. Joseph, Placentia
Reynoso, Jose Luis, St. Boniface, Anaheim
Rios, Alfredo, St. Joseph, Santa Ana
Rodriguez, Fidel, St. Pius V, Buena Park
Rodriguez, Jose Luis, Our Lady of Guadalupe, La Habra
Romero, Rafael, St. Cecilia, Tustin
Ruiz, Martin
Salgado, Eddie
Sanchez, Miguel, Blessed Sacrament, Westminster
Sanchez, Salvador, St. Anthony Claret, Anaheim
Scaduto, Al, Our Lady of Fatima, San Clemente
Shaffer, Michael, St. Angela Merici, Brea
Sherg, Nick, St. Martin de Porres, Yorba Linda
Sire, David
Song, Thomas, St. Thomas Korean Center, Anaheim
Stadel, Gerhard P., Holy Family Cathedral, Orange
Stock, Michael, St. Edward the Confessor, Dana Point
Sun, Leonard, Chinese Catholic Community
Swanson, Carl, San Francisco Solano, Rancho Santa Margarita
Thompson, Wayne, St. Nicholas, Laguna Woods
Tong, Minh, St. Boniface, Anaheim
Torres, Guillermo, St. Columban, Garden Grove
Torres, Richard, St. Pius V, Buena Park
Tran, Chau, St. Nicholas, Laguna Woods
Tran, David, La Purisima, Orange
Truong, Danny, St. Columban, Garden Grove
Vandervest, Roger, St. Philip Benizi, Fullerton
Villalpando, Adolfo, Our Lady of LaVang, Santa Ana
Wallace, Gerard, St. Vincent de Paul, Huntington Beach
Weeks, William, St. Cecilia, Tustin
Zaun, Denis, St. Martin de Porres, Yorba Linda.

INSTITUTIONS LOCATED IN DIOCESE

[A] SEMINARIES AND SCHOLASTICATES FOR RELIGIOUS

MIDWAY CITY. *Brothers of St. Patrick*, 7820 Bolsa Ave., Midway City, 92655. Tel: 714-897-8181; Email: brjoseph@patricianbrothers.com; Web: www.brothersofstpatrick.com. Bros. Aquinas Cassin, F.S.P., Supr.; Philip Shepler, F.S.P., Rel. Order Leader; Anoop Joseph, Member. Conducted by the Brothers of St. Patrick. Brothers 4; Students 2.

SILVERADO. *St. Michael's Norbertine Postulancy, Novitiate and Juniorate* (1959) 19292 El Toro Rd., Silverado, 92676. Tel: 949-858-0222; Fax: 949-858-4583; Email: admin@stmichaelsabbey.com; Web: www.stmichaelsabbey.com. Rt. Rev. Eugene J. Hayes, O.Praem., Abbot; Revs. Thomas W. Nelson, O.-Praem., Dir. Formation; Ambrose Criste, O.-Praem., Novice Master, Junior Master, Postulant Dir.; Very Rev. Hugh C. Barbour, O.Praem., Prof. Philosophy; Revs. Sebastian A. Walshe, O.Praem., Prof. Philosophy; Maximilian C. Okapal, O.Praem., Prof.; Chrysostom Anthony Baer, O.Praem, Prof. Latin, Philosophy. Conducted by the Norbertine Fathers.For listing of other Norbertine priests working in the Diocese, refer to St. Michael College Prep High School. Clergy 6; Students 34.

[B] COLLEGES AND UNIVERSITIES

ORANGE. *St. Joseph College, Orange* Branch Campus of University of San Francisco; St. Joseph Library. 480 S. Batavia St., Orange, 92868.
Tel: 714-633-8121; Fax: 714-744-3166; Email: sr.ellen.jordan@csjorange.org. Sisters Ellen Jordan, Council Adjunct Sec.; Christine Hilliard, C.S.J., Librarian. Lay Staff 7; Sisters 2.

[C] HIGH SCHOOLS, DIOCESAN

FULLERTON. *Rosary Academy* (Girls) 1340 N. Acacia Ave., Fullerton, 92831. Tel: 714-879-6302; Fax: 714-879-0853; Email: admissions@rosaryacademy.org; Web: www.rosaryacademy.org. Shawna Pautsch, Head of School. (Rosary High School) Lay Teachers 26; Priests 1; Students 371; Total Staff 60.

RANCHO SANTA MARGARITA. *Santa Margarita Catholic High School*, 22062 Antonio Pkwy., Rancho Santa Margarita, 92688. Tel: 949-766-6000;
Tel: 949-766-6004; Fax: 949-766-6005; Email: hassenc@smhs.org; Email: information@smhs.org; Web: www.smhs.org. Mr. Andrew J. Sulick, Pres.; Mr. Raymond R. Dunne, Prin. & Contact Person; Revs. Craig M. Butters; Mark Jon Cruz, A.M., Chap.; Maricar Laudato, Librarian. Religious Teachers 1; Lay Teachers 110; Priests 2; Students 1,673.

SANTA ANA. *Mater Dei High School* (1950) (Coed) 1202 W. Edinger Ave., Santa Ana, 92707-2191.
Tel: 714-754-7711; Fax: 714-754-1880; Email: admissions@materdei.org; Web: www.materdei.org. Ms. Frances Clare, Prin. & Contact; Mr. Patrick Murphy, Pres.; Rev. Kiet A. Ta, Rector/Chap.; Audrey Coburn, Asst. Prin., Personnel & Faculty Svcs.; Geri Campeau, Asst. Prin., Academic Svcs.; Lee Gaeta, Asst. Prin., Student Svcs. Religious Teachers 17; Lay Teachers 100; Students 2,135.

[D] HIGH SCHOOLS, PRIVATE

ANAHEIM. *Cornelia Connelly School of the Holy Child* (1961) (Girls) 2323 W. Broadway, Anaheim, 92804. Tel: 714-776-1717; Fax: 714-776-2534; Email: cornelia@connellyhs.org; Web: www.connellyhs.org. Mrs. Cheri Wood, Head of School; Dr. Cathleen Rauterkus, Asst. Head of School; Heather Daugherty, Librarian. Society of the Holy Child Jesus. Lay Teachers 20; Students 150; Total Staff 37.

Servite High School, A California Corporation, 1952 W. La Palma, Anaheim, 92801. Tel: 714-774-7575; Fax: 714-774-1404; Email: administration@servitehs.org; Web: www.servitehs.org. Randall Adams, Pres.; Mr. Michael P. Brennan, Prin., Email: mbrennan@servitehs.org; Mrs. Olga Hofreiter, Asst. Prin. Academic Affairs; Rev. Viblanc Steephen, O.S.M., Chap. Servite Friars. Brothers 1; Lay Teachers 53; Priests 2; Students 799.

SAN JUAN CAPISTRANO. *JSerra Catholic High School*, 26351 Junipero Serra Rd., San Juan Capistrano, 92675. Tel: 949-493-9307; Fax: 949-493-9308; Email: info@jserra.org; Web: www.jserra.org. Richard Meyer, Headmaster; Mr. Eric Stroupe, Head Admin.; Patrick Reidy, Head Faith Formation; Jeanne Swedo, Librarian. Lay Teachers 57; Priests 3; Sisters 2; Students 1,224.

SILVERADO. *St. Michael's Preparatory School* (Boarding school for boys) 19292 El Toro Rd., Silverado, 92676-9710. Tel: 949-858-0222; Fax: 949-858-7365; Email: admissions@stmichaelsprep.org; Web: www.stmichaelsprep.org. Revs. Alan Benander, O.-Praem., Dean, Students; Andrew Bartus, O.-Praem., History Teacher; Brendan R. Hankins, O.Praem., English Teacher; John Henry Hanson, O.Praem., English Teacher; James G. Smith, O.-Praem., Treas.; Maximilian C. Okapal, O.Praem., College Counselor; Justin S. Ramos, O.Praem., Latin Teacher; Sebastian Walshe, O.Praem., Philosophy Teacher; Joachim Aldaba, O.Praem., Dean; Vianney Ceja, Dean. Lay Teachers 8; Priests 10; Seminarians 4; Students 64; Total Staff 22.

[E] ELEMENTARY SCHOOLS AND DAY NURSERIES, PRIVATE

ANAHEIM. *St. Catherine's Academy* (1889) (Grades K-8), 215 N. Harbor Blvd., Anaheim, 92805.
Tel: 714-772-1363; Fax: 714-772-3004; Email: admissions@stcatherinesacademy.org; Web: stcatherinesacademy.org. Sr. Johnellen Turner, O.P., Admin./Prin.; Virginia Byard, Librarian
St. Catherine's Military Academy, a Corp. Lay Teachers 16; Students 145; Dominican Sisters of Mission San Jose 10.

GARDEN GROVE. *Christ Cathedral Academy*, (Grades PreK-8), 13280 Chapman Ave., 92840.
Tel: 714-663-2330; Email: kmcguire@ccaorange.com. Kathy McGuire, Prin.; Ashley-Rose Cameron, Vice Prin. Lay Teachers 33; Students 364.

SANTA ANA. *Santa Clara Day Nursery and Kindergarten*, 1021 N. Newhope, Santa Ana, 92703. Tel: 714-554-8850; Fax: 714-554-5886; Email: rocioalcantar532@yahoo.com. Sisters Rocio Alcantar, M.C., Contact; Maria Socorro Miranda, Prin. Poor Clare Missionary Sisters (M.C.). Children 95; Sisters 13; Total Staff 13.

TUSTIN. *Saint Jeanne de Lestonnac School* (1961) (Grades PreSchool-8), 16791 E. Main, Tustin, 92780. Tel: 714-542-4271; Fax: 714-542-0644; Email: srcduran@sjdlschool.com; Web: www.sjdlschool.com. Sr. Cecilia Duran, O.D.N., Prin.; Catherine Zimmerman, Librarian. Religious Teachers 2; Lay Teachers 30; Students 335.

[F] MULTI-PARISH SCHOOLS

RANCHO SANTA MARGARITA. *St. Junipero Serra Catholic School* (1995) (Grades PreK-8), 23652 Antonio Pkwy., Rancho Santa Margarita, 92688-1993. Tel: 949-888-1990; Fax: 949-888-1994; Email: serra@serraschool.org; Email: communications@serraschool.org; Web: www.serraschool.org. Mrs. Angeline Trudell, Pres.; Mrs. Carol Reiss, Prin., Preschool & Grades TK - 2; Mrs. Julie Tipton, Prin., Grades 3 - 8. (Parishes: Holy Trinity, St. Kilian, San Francisco Solano & Santiago de Compostela) Clergy 4; Religious Teachers 1; Lay Teachers 71; Students 1,040.

YORBA LINDA. *St. Francis of Assisi Catholic School* (1998) (Grades PreK-8), 5330 East Side Cir., Yorba Linda, 92887. Tel: 714-695-3700;
Fax: 714-695-3704; Email: office@sfayl.org; Web: www.sfayl.org. Thomas Waszak, Pres.; Jeannette C. Lambert, Prin. (Parishes: Santa Clara de Asis, San Antonio de Padua & St. Martin) Lay Teachers 30; Students 525.

[G] GENERAL HOSPITALS

ORANGE. *St. Joseph Hospital of Orange* (1929) 1100 W. Stewart Dr., Orange, 92868. Tel: 714-771-8000; Fax: 714-744-8137; Email: SJO-Feedback@stjoe.org. Steve Moreau, Pres. & CEO; Jeremy Zoch, Exec. Vice Pres. & COO; Linda Simon, Vice Pres. Mission Integration; Rev. Patrick Okonkwo. Nurses 1,000; Beds 525; Other Employees 3,800; Inpatients 22,442; Outpatients 272,510.

FULLERTON. *St. Jude Medical Center* (1957) 101 E. Valencia Mesa Dr., Fullerton, 92835-3875.
Tel: 714-992-3000; Fax: 714-992-3029; Email: sisterclaudette.desforges@stjoe.org; Web: www.stjudemedicalcenter.org. Revs. Timothy Freyer, Chap.; Sal Landa, Chap.; Judy Eugenio, Chap.; Sr. Josepha Ha, C.H.C., Chap.; Bill Boylan, Chap.; Luis Dicares, Chap.; Revs. Clement Oyafemi, Chap.; David Robinson, Chap.; Arul Irudayaraj, S.V.D., Chap. Bed Capacity 384; Nurses 656; Total Staff 3,126; Total Assisted Inpatient & Outpatient 1,000,000.

LAGUNA BEACH. *Mission Hospital Laguna Beach (MHLB)*, 31872 Coast Hwy., Laguna Beach, 92651. Tel: 949-499-1311; Fax: 949-499-5789; Email: richard.afable@stjoe.org; Web: www.mission4health.com. Richard Afable, M.D., Pres. St. Joseph Health System. Bed Capacity 178; Tot Asst. Annually 52,072; Total Staff 372.

MISSION VIEJO. *Mission Hospital Regional Medical Center (MHMV)*, 27700 Medical Center Rd., Mission Viejo, 92691. Tel: 949-364-1400;
Fax: 949-364-2056; Email: richard.afable@stjoe.org; Web: www.mission4health.com. Richard Afable, M.D., Interim Pres. & CEO; Cynthia H. Mueller, Vice Pres., Mission Integration. St. Joseph Health. Bed Capacity 345; Tot Asst. Annually 235,486; Total Staff 2,369; Patients Assisted: Inpatient Days 67,964; Outpatients 167,522.

[H] SPECIAL SERVICES

ORANGE. *Loyola Institute for Spirituality*, 434 S. Batavia St., Orange, 92868. Tel: 714-997-9587; Email: office@loyolainstitute.org; Web: www.loyolainstitute.org. Lori Stanley, Exec. Dir.; Rev. David C. Robinson, S.J., Assoc. Dir.; Bro. Charles Jackson, S.J., Assoc. Dir.; Rev. Eduardo A. Samaniego, S.J., Assoc. Dir.; Sr. Jeanne Fallon, C.S.J., Assoc. Dir.; Mr. Carlos E. Obando, Assoc. Dir. Total Staff 9.

ANAHEIM. *St. Thomas Korean Catholic Center*, 412 N. Crescent Way, Anaheim, 92801. Tel: 714-772-3995; Fax: 714-772-3636; Email: stthomas@stkcc.org; Web: www.stkcc.org. Rev. Benedict Yang, Dir.; Deacons Peter Chung; Thomas Song.

IRVINE. *Our Lady of Peace Korean Catholic Center*, 14010 Remington, Irvine, 92620-5703.
Tel: 949-654-5239; Fax: 949-654-5230; Email: irvinekcc@gmail.com. Rev. Alex H. Ha, Dir.

SANTA ANA. *St. Francis Home for the Aged* (1944) 1718 W. 6th St., Santa Ana, 92703. Tel: 714-542-0381; Fax: 714-542-4654; Email: stfrancishome@sbcglobal.net; Web: www.st-francis-home.org. Sr. Veronica Villalpando, O.S.F., Admin. & Contact Person. Franciscan Sisters of the Immaculate Conception, Inc. Bed Capacity 75; Sisters 11; Total Staff 20; Total Assisted 60.

Vietnamese Catholic Center, 1538 N. Century Blvd., Santa Ana, 92703. Tel: 714-554-4211;
Tel: 714-554-5565; Fax: 714-265-1161; Email:

hiepthong2013@gmail.com; Web: www.vncatholic.net. Rev. Kiem Van Tran, Coord. Total in Residence 2; Total Staff 4.

SILVERADO. *St. Michael's Summer Camp* Boys aged 7-12 years. St. Michael's Abbey, 19292 El Toro Rd., Silverado, 92676-9701. Tel: 949-858-0222, Ext. 261; Fax: 949-858-4583; Email: admin@stmichellesabbey.com; Web: www.stmichaelsabbey.com. Rev. Joachim Aldaba, O.-Praem. Capacity 120; Clergy 20; Students 100; Total in Residence 95; Total Staff 25.

WESTMINSTER. *Korean Martyrs Catholic Center*, 7655 Trask Ave., Westminster, 92683.
Tel: 714-897-6510; Fax: 714-897-0832; Email: natalia@kmccoc.org; Web: www.kmccoc.org. Rev. Eugene Lee, Dir. Total Staff 10.

YORBA LINDA. *Pope John Paul II Polish Center*, 3999 Rose Dr., Yorba Linda, 92886. Tel: 714-996-8161; Fax: 714-996-8161; Email: Polishcenter@sbcglobal.net; Web: www.polishcenter.org. Rev. Zbigniew Fraszczak, S.V.D., Dir. Total Staff 4.

[I] MONASTERIES AND RESIDENCES OF PRIESTS AND BROTHERS

ANAHEIM. *Manresa Jesuit Residence*, 401 W. Leonora St., Anaheim, 92805-2634. Tel: 714-991-7798; Email: office@loyolainstitute.org; Web: loyolainstitute.org. Rev. Felix N.W. Just, S.J., Exec. Dir., Loyola Institute for Spirituality; Bro. Charles Jackson, S.J., Assoc. Dir.; Revs. David C. Robinson, S.J., Assoc. Dir.; John Francis Vu, S.J., Email: jvu@calprov.org; Robert W. Stephan, S.J.

Servite Fathers and Brothers Servite Friars Servite Priory, 1922 W. La Palma Ave., Anaheim, 92801-3544. Tel: 714-774-8869; Fax: 714-774-6792; Email: gmh.osm@gmail.com; Web: www.servite.org. 8562 Links Rd., Buena Park, 90621-1603. Revs. Joseph Arputhasamy; Steephen Viblanc. *Servite High School*, 1952 W. La Palma Ave., Anaheim, 92801-3595. Tel: 714-774-7575;
Fax: 714-774-1401; Web: www.servitehs.org.

FULLERTON. *Servite Fathers and Brothers*, St. Juliana Falconieri, 1316 N. Acacia, Fullerton, 92831.
Tel: 714-879-1963; Fax: 714-526-6673; Email: info@stjulianachurch.org; Web: www.stjulianachurch.org. Rev. Michael M. Pontarelli, O.S.M., Contact Person. Total in Residence 2; Total Staff 2. *St. Philip Benizi*, 5210 Somerset Street, Buena Park, 90621-1456. Tel: 714-871-3613; Email: gmh.osm@gmail.com. Revs. Gerald M. Horan, O.S.M., Prioir; Dennis Kriz, O.S.M., Pastor; David Gallegos, O.S.M., Parochial Vicar; Joseph Arputhasamy, Campus Min.; Steephen Viblanc, Campus Min.; Bruce Klikunas, Member; Bros. Arnaldo Sanchez, O.S.M., D.R.E.; Christopher M. Moran, O.S.M., (Retired).

HUNTINGTON BEACH. *Franciscan Friars*, Sts. Simon & Jude, 20444 Magnolia St., Huntington Beach, 92646. Tel: 714-962-3333; Fax: 714-965-6456; Email: ssj@ssj.org; Web: www.ssj.org. Rev. Rusty Shaughnessy, O.F.M., Contact Person. Religious 1.

MIDWAY CITY. *Brothers of St. Patrick, St. Patrick's Novitiate*, 7820 Bolsa Ave., Midway City, 92655.
Tel: 714-897-8181; Fax: 714-898-9020; Email: brjoseph@sjsplacentia.org. Bros. Aquinas Cassin, F.S.P., Supr. (Retired); Joseph Anoop, F.S.P.; Kevin Minihan, F.S.P.; Matthew Regan, F.S.P., (Retired).

SANTA ANA. *Augustinian Recollects*, Our Lady of Guadalupe, 1322 E. 3rd St., Santa Ana, 92701-5104. Tel: 714-836-4142; Fax: 714-836-7417. Rev. Marlon Beof, O.A.R., Pastor & Contact Person. *Our Lady of the Pillar*, 1622 W. 6th St., Santa Ana, 92703. Tel: 714-543-1700; Fax: 714-543-9640; Email: elpilar@usa.com. Revs. Eliseo Gonzales, Pastor; Felizardo J. Daganta, O.A.R., Parochial Vicar; Alfredo de Dios, O.A.R., Parochial Vicar; Jose Luis Martinez, O.A.R., Parochial Vicar; Gabino Perez, O.A.R., Parochial Vicar.

SILVERADO. *Norbertine Fathers of Orange Inc.* (1959) For detailed information regarding St. Michael's Abbey and St. Michael's College Preparatory High School, please refer to Seminaries and Scholasticates for Religious and High Schools, Private in the Institutions section. St. Michael's Abbey (O.Praem.), 19292 El Toro Rd., Silverado, 92676-9710. Tel: 949-858-0222; Fax: 949-858-0225; Email: admin@stmichaelsabbey.com; Web: www.stmichaelsabbey.com. Revs. Martin Benzoni, O.-Praem.; Pio Vottola; Thomas W. Nelson, O.Praem.; Augustine R. Puchner, O.Praem.; Very Rev. Hugh C. Barbour, O.Praem.; Revs. Gregory M. Dick, O.-Praem.; Gabriel D. Stack, O.Praem.; Godfrey E. Bushmaker, O.Praem.; Jerome M. Molokie, O.-Praem.; Justin S. Ramos, O.Praem.; James G. Smith, O.Praem., Subprior; Charles W. Willingham, O.Praem.; Stephen M. Boyle, O.Praem.; Leo J. Celano, O.Praem.; Patrick D. Foutts, O.Praem.; Francis M. Gloudeman, O.Praem.; Alphonsus B. Hermes, O.Praem.; Robert S. Hodges, O.Praem.; Joseph K. Horn, O.Praem.; Bernard M. Johnson, O.Praem.; Luke S. Laslavich, O.Praem.; Pascal B. Nguyen, O.Praem.; Michael U. Perea, O.Praem.; Theodore R. Smith, O.Praem.; Victor S. Szczurek, O.Praem.; Rt. Rev. Eugene J. Hayes, O.Praem., Abbot; Revs. Norbert J. Wood, O.Praem.; John Caronan, O.Praem., J.C.L.; Hildebrand J. Garceau, O.-Praem.; Chrysostom Anthony Baer, O.Praem, Prior; Sebastian A. Walshe, O.Praem.; Charbel R. Grbavac, O.Praem.; John Henry Hanson, O.-Praem.; Adrian Sanchez, O.Praem.; Ambrose Criste, O.Praem.; Andrew P. Tran, O.Praem.; Brendan R. Hankins, O.Praem.; Benedict M. Solomon, O.Praem.; Claude A. Williams, O.Praem.; William M. Fitzgerald, O.Praem.; Damien V. Giap, O.Praem.; Maximilian C. Okapal, O.Praem.; Nathaniel P. Drogin, O.Praem.; Alan V. Benander, O.-Praem.; Raymond Perez, O.Praem.; Joachim Aldaba, O.Praem.; Vianney Ceja; Miguel Batres, O.Praem.; David Gonzalez, O.Praem.; Joseph Hsieh, O.Praem.; Nicholas M. Tacito, O.Praem. Postulants 8; Priests 51; Clerics 31.

Norbertine Fathers of Orange, Inc., 27977 Silverado Canyon Rd., Silverado, 92676. Tel: 949-858-0222; Email: info@stmichaelsabbey.com. Ralaine Young, Contact Person.

[J] CONVENTS AND RESIDENCES FOR SISTERS

ORANGE. *Sisters of St. Joseph of Orange Motherhouse Community*, 440 S. Batavia, Orange, 92868.
Tel: 714-633-8121; Email: sr.ellen.jordan@csjorange.org; Web: www.csjorange.org. Sisters Jayne Helmlinger, Rel. Order Leader; Cecilia Magladry, C.S.J., Rel. Order Leader. Administrators 5; Sisters 14.

CSJ Education Network, Tel: 714-633-8121; Email: ballen@csjorange.org. Bret Allen, Dir.

CSJ Justice Center, Tel: 714-633-8121, Ext. 7716; Email: mperales@csjorange.org. Maria Elena Perales, Dir.

Emmaus Ministries, 434 S. Batavia St., Orange, 92868. Tel: 714-744-3175, Ext. 7430;
Tel: 714-633-8121, Ext. 4429; Email: jdeslisle@csjorange.org; Email: chilliard@csjorange.org. Sisters Jane DesLisle, C.S.J., Dir.; Christine Hilliard, C.S.J., Dir. Sisters of St. Joseph of Orange.

*Casa Esperanza Community*Sisters 2.
*Greengrove Community*Sisters 2.
*Nazareth Community*Sisters 4.
*Palmyra Community*Sisters 2.
*Regina Residence Community*Sisters 48.
*St. Joseph Hospital Community*Sisters 7.
*Valencia Community*Sisters 3.
*Westwood Community*Sisters 3.

Union of Sisters of the Presentation of the Blessed Virgin Mary, 343 E. Chestnut, Orange, 92867.
Tel: 714-283-2496; Email: pbvmorange@aol.com; Web: pbvmunion.org. Sr. Breda Christopher, P.B.V.M., Contact Person. Sisters 2.

ANAHEIM. *Dominicans, Mission San Jose* dba St. Catherine Academy, St. Catherine's Academy, 215 N. Harbor Blvd., Anaheim, 92805-2596.
Tel: 714-772-1363; Fax: 714-772-3004; Email: sca@msjdominicans.org; Web: www.stcatherinesacademy.com. Sr. Imelda Pellettieri, Prioress. Sisters 9.

BREA. *Sisters of St. Clare*, 446 S. Poplar Ave., Brea, 92821-6649. Tel: 714-256-1278; Email: sshrewsbury@sbdiocese.org. Sr. Anne Otter, Contact Person. Sisters 4. *Convent*, St. Clare's Garden, 449 S. Pine Ave., Brea, 92821-6649.
Tel: 714-257-1113; Fax: 714-257-1068. Sr. Eymard Flood, O.S.C., Contact Person.

BUENA PARK. *Sisters of Our Lady of Perpetual Help* (1932) 6751 Western Ave., Buena Park, 90621.
Tel: 714-521-1345; Tel: 714-321-4271;
Fax: 714-521-7611; Email: miyelucia@gmail.com. Sr. Anselmo Kim, S.O.L.P.H., Pres. & Contact. Sisters 6.

COSTA MESA. *Sisters of Mercy of Ireland* (1959) St. John the Baptist Convent, 2960 Mendoza Dr., Costa Mesa, 92626. Tel: 714-545-2116;
Fax: 714-557-9263; Email: mvianney@sjbschool.net. Sr. Mary Vianney, S.M., Prin. & Contact Person. Sisters 5.

Sisters of St. Joseph of Orange (1946) Sr. Kathleen Marie, C.S.J., Prin. Sisters 1.

CYPRESS. *Union of the Sisters of the Presentation of the Blessed Virgin Mary*, 5151 Evergreen Ave., Cypress, 90630. Tel: 714-527-4844; Email: pbvmcypress@gmail.com. Sr. Annette Figueiredo, Admin. Sisters 10.

DANA POINT. *Sisters of St. Joseph of Orange* (1912) Sisters Martha Ann Fitzpatrick, C.S.J., Contact Person & Vice Pres., Mission Hospital, Mission Viejo; Mary Beth Inghas, Sabbatical; Thuy Tran, C.S.J., Mission Srvcs. Coord. Sisters 3.

FULLERTON. *Sisters of St. Joseph of Orange* Sr. Judith Fergus, Contact Person. Sisters 3.

GARDEN GROVE. *Eucharistic Missionaries of the Most Holy Trinity*, 11892 E. Lampson Ave., 92840.
Tel: 714-530-5727; Email: Srteresa@sticypress.org. Sr. Maria Teresa Salceda, M.E.S.S.T., Local Supr. Sisters 4.

Religious Sisters of Charity, St. Columban Convent, 12555 Westlake St., 92840. Tel: 714-534-1003;
Fax: 714-636-3529; Email: bmoran131@gmail.com. Sr. Bernadette Moran, Contact Person. Sisters 4.

HUNTINGTON BEACH. *Sisters of the Presentation of the Blessed Virgin Mary*, St. Bonaventure Convent, 16441 Bradbury Ln., Huntington Beach, 92647.
Tel: 714-846-6212; Email: presentation.HB@gmail.com; Web: www.pbvmunion.org. Sr. Mary Dunlea, P.B.V.M., Contact Person. Sisters 5.

SANTA ANA. *Franciscan Missionary Sisters of the Immaculate Conception* (1944) 1718 W. 6th St., Santa Ana, 92703. Tel: 714-542-0381;
Tel: 714-542-8352; Fax: 714-542-4654; Email: stfrancishome@sbcglobal.net; Web: www.st-francis-home.org. Sr. Maria de Luz Acosta, O.S.F., Rel. Order Leader. Sisters 11; Total Staff 21; Total Assisted 60.

Poor Clare Missionary Sisters of the Blessed Sacrament, 1019 N. Newhope St., Santa Ana, 92703-1534. Tel: 714-554-8850; Fax: 714-554-5886; Email: srsguzman@yahoo.com; Web: www.misionerasclarisas.com. Sr. Rocio Alcantar, M.C., Contact Person. Sisters 14.

Sisters of St. Joseph of Carondelet, 8681 Katella Avenue, Stanton, 90680. Tel: 714-825-4501; Cell: 714-300-4901; Email: srbeakelly@yahoo.com. Sr. Theresa Kuale, C.S.J., Prov. Sisters 1. *St. Joseph.*

Sisters of St. Joseph of Orange, Mailing Address: 440 S. Batavia St., Orange, 92868. Sisters Jane Hemlinger, Gen. Supr.; Cecilia Magladry, C.S.J., Rel. Order Leader. Sisters 110.

Taller San Jose, 801 N. Broadway, Santa Ana, 92707. Tel: 714-543-5105; Fax: 714-543-5032; Email: ssmith@tallersanjose.org. Shawna Smith, Exec. Dir. Sisters 4.

Sisters of the Company of Mary, St. Anne Convent, 1339 S. Broadway, Santa Ana, 92707.
Tel: 714-558-1340; Fax: 714-547-8110; Email: leticiasalazar@mac.com. Sr. Elvira Rios, O.D.N., Sec. Sisters 5.

Sisters of the Lovers of the Holy Cross, 1401 S. Sycamore St., Santa Ana, 92707. Tel: 714-973-1951; Fax: 714-667-0711; Email: srthuhong@lhcla.org; Web: www.lhcla.org. Sr. Dao Thu Hong Dao, L.H.C., Contact Person. Sisters 10. *Convent*, 920 N. Bewley St., Santa Ana, 92703.
Tel: 714-554-9385; Fax: 714-554-5925; Email: grace_duc@yahoo.com; Web: www.lhcla.org. Sr. Grace Duc Le, L.H.C., Contact Person. Sisters 15.

Society Devoted to the Sacred Heart, 2927 S. Greenville St., Santa Ana, 92704.
Tel: 714-557-4538; Fax: 714-668-9780; Email: sisterdebra7@yahoo.com; Web: www.sacredheartsisters.com. Sr. Debra Flander, S.D.S.H., Contact Person. Sisters 6. *Sacred Heart Convent*, 2911 S. Greenville St., Santa Ana, 92704.
Tel: 714-751-6335; Fax: 714-546-0873. Sisters 6.

SILVERADO. *Rosarian Dominicans* (1972) St. Michael's Convent, 19292 El Toro Rd., Silverado, 92676.
Tel: 949-858-0487; Email: stmicdominican@yahoo.com. Sr. Rosalia Cajilig, Supr. Sisters 8.

TUSTIN. *Adrian Dominicans*, St. Jeanne de Lestonnac Convent, 16791 E. Main St., Tustin, 92780.
Tel: 714-720-3693; Fax: 714-542-0644; Email: srterry@sjdlschool.com; Web: www.sjdlschool.com. Sr. Teresa Estrada, O.P., Contact Person. Sisters 2.

Sisters of the Company of Mary, Our Lady (1607) 16791 E. Main St., Tustin, 92780-4034.
Tel: 714-541-3125; Fax: 714-547-8110; Email: elviraodn@yahoo.com; Web: www.lestonnac.org. Sr. Elvira Rios, O.D.N., Sec. & Contact Person. Sisters 9.

Lestonnac Retreat Center: (1961) Tel: 714-541-3125; Fax: 714-547-8110.

Lestonnac Residence: (1980) Tel: 714-541-3125; Fax: 714-547-8110.

[K] CATHOLIC CHARITIES

SANTA ANA. *Catholic Charities of Orange County, Inc.* (1976) 1820 E. 16th St., Santa Ana, 92701.
Tel: 714-347-9680; Fax: 714-427-4585; Email: tsmith@ccoc.org; Web: www.ccoc.org. Teresa Smith, M.S.W., L.C.S.W., Exec. Dir. Total Staff 35; Total Assisted 165,674.

Re-creation Camp (Special Needs) Orange, CA. Weekend getaway and ACE camp. 1820 E. 16th St., Santa Ana, 92701. Tel: 714-347-9627;
Fax: 714-427-4585; Email: mdibb@ccoc.org; Web: www.recreationcampoc.com. Teresa Smith, M.S.W., L.C.S.W., Dir.

Casa Santa Maria, 7551 Orangethorpe Ave., Buena Park, 90621. Tel: 714-523-1734; Fax: 714-543-2123. Ofelia Aranda, Svc. Coord. Independent senior housing living project.

Counseling Services, 1800 E. 17th St., Santa Ana, 92701. Tel: 714-347-9674; Fax: 714-542-3541.

Cantlay Food Center, 3631 W. Warner St., Santa Ana, 92704. Tel: 714-668-1130; Fax: 714-957-2523. Michael Tijerino, Prog. Coord.

Immigration Services, 1820 E. 16th St., Santa Ana, 92701. Tel: 714-347-9664; Fax: 714-542-3541. Dee-Dee Gullo, M.S.W., L.C.S.W., H.P.M., Dir. Immigration Svcs.

[L] RETREAT HOUSES

ORANGE. *House of Prayer for Priests* (1983) 7734 E. Santiago Canyon Rd., Orange, 92869. Tel: 714-639-9740; Email: domenico1410@hotmial.com. Revs. Domenico Di Raimondo, Dir.; Robert J. Spitzer, S.J., Ph.D., M.Div., M.A., B.A., Th. M., Tel: 949-528-3223. Total in Residence 2; Total Staff 1; Total Assisted 1,500. In Res. Rev. Patrick B. Philbin, S.M., (Retired).

FULLERTON. *Pro Sanctity Spirituality Center, Retreat House* (1979) 205 S. Pine Dr., Fullerton, 92833. Tel: 714-449-0511; Email: caprosanctity@prosanctity.org; Web: caprosanctity.org. Sr. Joan Patten, A.O., Dir. Capacity 25.

Pro Sanctity Movement (1947) Fullerton. Tel: 714-956-1020. Sr. Joan Patten, A.O., Dir.

LA HABRA. *Villa Maria House of Prayer* (1978) 1252 N. Citrus Dr., La Habra, 90631-2652. Tel: 562-691-5838. Sr. Margaret Lucille, C.S.G., Contact Person. Sisters of St. Joseph of Carondelet. Sisters 2.

SANTA ANA. *Heart of Jesus Retreat Center*, 2927 S. Greenville St., Santa Ana, 92704. Tel: 714-557-4538; Fax: 714-668-9780; Email: heartofjesusrc@sbcglobal.net. Sr. Gabrielle Vogl, S.D.S.H., Dir. Society Devoted to the Sacred Heart Total Staff 7.

[M] NEWMAN CENTERS

ORANGE. *Chapman University*, 1 University Dr., Orange, 92866. Tel: 714-532-6098; Fax: 714-532-6078; Email: frluevano@oc.rcbo.org. Rev. Rafael Luevano, Ph.D., Catholic Chap., Assoc. Prof.

FULLERTON. *California State University Fullerton, Titan Catholic Newman Club* (1966) St. Juliana Falconieri, 1316 N. Acacia Ave., Fullerton, 92831-1202. Tel: 714-353-5001; Fax: 714-526-6673; Email: csufcatholicnewman@gmail.com. Rev. Mark Jon Cruz, A.M., Chap., Dir., Treas., Titan Catholic Newman Club, Tel: 714-353-5001.

IRVINE. *University Catholic Community at UCI*, 9 Hillgate, Irvine, 92612. Tel: 949-861-3445; Email: francisttvu@gmail.com; Web: ucicatholic.weebly.com. P.O. Box 523, 92842. Rev. John Francis Vu, S.J., Dir. Campus Ministry & Chap.

[N] SECULAR INSTITUTES

FULLERTON. *Institute of the Apostolic Oblates, Inc. (House of Professed Apostolic Oblates)* (1950) 2125 W. Walnut Ave., Fullerton, 92833. Tel: 714-449-0511; Email: caprosanctity@prosanctity.org. Renee Jarecki, Admin.; Joan Patten, Mod. House of Formation for Professed Apostolic Oblates. Secular Institute of the Apostolic Oblates, Inc.

[O] MISCELLANEOUS LISTINGS

ORANGE. *American Federation Pueri Cantores*, 1188 N. Tustin St., Orange, 92867. Tel: 714-633-7554; Fax: 714-516-1531; Email: info@pcchoirs.org; Web: www.pcchoirs.org. Jan Schmidt, Exec.

Christ Catholic Cathedral Corporation, 13280 Chapman Ave., 92840. Tel: 714-282-3076; Fax: 714-282-3029; Email: bmilligan@rcbo.org. Rev. Christopher H. Smith, CEO.

Christ Catholic Cathedral Facilities Corporation, 13280 Chapman Ave., Tower of Hope, 11th Floor, 92840. Tel: 714-282-3076; Fax: 714-282-3029; Email: bmilligan@rcbo.org. Mr. Rand Sperry, Chm.

St. Joseph Health Ministry, 500 S. Main St., Ste. 1000, Orange, 92868. Tel: 714-347-7778; Tel: 714-347-7586; Fax: 714-347-7501.

St. Joseph Health System, 500 S. Main St., Ste. 1000, Orange, 92868. Tel: 714-347-7500; Fax: 714-347-7663; Web: www.stjhs.org. William Noce, Bd. Chm.; Ms. Deborah Proctor, Pres. & CEO.

St. Joseph Health System Foundation, 500 S. Main St., Ste. 1000, Orange, 92868. Tel: 714-347-7500; Fax: 714-347-7663. Gabriela Robles, Dir., Community Outreach.

St. Jude Hospital Yorba Linda aka St. Joseph Heritage Healthcare, St. Joseph Health System, 500 S. Main St., Orange, 92868-4515. Tel: 714-347-7579; Fax: 714-347-7590. C. R. Burke.

Sisters of St. Joseph Healthcare Foundation, 480 S. Batavia St., Orange, 92868. Tel: 714-633-8121; Fax: 714-744-3135; Email: rfox@csjorange.org; Web: www.csjorange.org. Sr. Regina Fox, S.S.N.D., Exec. Dir.

FULLERTON. *St. Jude Memorial Foundation*, 1440 N. Harbor Blvd. Ste. 200, P.O. Box 4138, Fullerton, 92835. Tel: 714-992-3033; Fax: 714-446-5430; Email: dale.katsuyama@stjoe.org. Dale Katsuyama, Contact Person.

Western Catholic Educational Association, 101 Kraemer Blvd., Ste. 115, Placentia, 92870. Tel: 714-447-9834; Fax: 714-447-9846; Email: jdritschel@westwcea.org; Web: westwcea.org. Nancy Coonis, Exec. Dir.

GARDEN GROVE. **The Orange Catholic Foundation* (2000) 13280 Chapman Ave., 92840. Tel: 714-282-3021; Fax: 714-282-3136; Email: cbobruk@orangecatholicfoundation.org; Web: www.orangecatholicfoundation.org. Cynthia Bobruk, Exec. Dir. & Pres.

IRVINE. *Magis Institute*, Christ Cathedral Tower, 13280 Chapman Ave., 9th Fl., 92840. Tel: 949-271-2727; Email: spitzer@magiscenter.com; Web: magiscenter.com. Rev. Robert J. Spitzer, S.J., Ph.D., M.Div., M.A., B.A., Th. M., Pres.

**Second Harvest Food Bank of Orange County, Inc.*, 8014 Marine Way, Irvine, 92618. Tel: 949-653-2900; Fax: 949-653-9155; Email: jfoley@feedoc.org; Web: feedoc.org. Joyce Foley, CFO.

LAGUNA WOODS. **St. Michael's Abbey Foundation*, 19292 El Toro Rd., Silverado, 92676-9710. Tel: 949-858-0222; Email: admin@stmichaelsabbey.com; Web: www.stmichaelsabbey.com. Rt. Rev. Eugene J. Hayes, O.Praem., Abbot.

SAN JUAN CAPISTRANO. *Catholic Divorce Ministry*, 29122 Rancho Viejo Rd., Ste. 112, San Juan Capistrano, 92675-1020. Tel: 855-727-2269; Email: office@nacsdc.org; Web: www.nacsdc.org. Mrs. Suzanne Carr, Office Mgr.; Ms. Regina Stalock, Treas. Board Members Most Rev. Kevin W. Vann, J.C.D., D.D., Episcopal Mod.; Revs. Bill Cleary, Priest Consultant; Albert A. Grosskopf, S.J.; Gregory Mills, Exec. Dir.; Suzanne M. Carr, Pres.; Kelly A. Klaus, Vice Pres.; Laurie Njoku, Mem. at Large & Sec.; Regina Staloch, Treas.; Stephen Tartaglia; Maria Rodrigues; Susan Strain; Angela Falgoust; Julie Ayzeen, Mem. at Large; Maria Luna Orth, Mem. at Large.

SANTA ANA. **Council of Orange County - Society of St. Vincent de Paul*, 1505 E. 17th St., Ste. 109, Santa Ana, 92705. Tel: 714-542-0448; Fax: 714-426-8004.

RELIGIOUS INSTITUTES OF MEN REPRESENTED IN THE DIOCESE

For further details refer to the corresponding bracketed number in the Religious Institutes of Men or Women section.

[]—*Alagard Ni Maria*—A.M.
[0150]—*Augustinian Recollects*—O.A.R.
[]—*Brothers of St. Patrick*—F.S.P.
[0520]—*Franciscan Fathers*—O.F.M.
[0690]—*Jesuit Fathers and Brothers*—S.J.
[]—*Legionnaires of Christ*—L.C.
[0900]—*Norbertine Fathers*—O.Praem.
[1240]—*Servite Fathers and Brothers*—O.S.M.

RELIGIOUS INSTITUTES OF WOMEN REPRESENTED IN THE DIOCESE

[]—*Congregation of Servants of Jesus, The High Priest*—S.J.P.
[3832]—*Congregation of the Sisters of St. Joseph*—C.S.J.
[1070-13]—*Dominican Sisters* (Adrian, MI)—O.P.
[]—*Dominican Sisters* (Mission San Jose)—O.P.
[]—*Eucharistic Missionaries of the Most Holy Trinity*—M.E.S.S.T.
[]—*Family of Mary of the Visitation*—F.M.V.
[1350]—*Franciscan Missionary Sisters of the Immaculate Conception*—O.S.F.
[]—*Franciscans* (Philadelphia)—O.S.F.
[2390]—*Lovers of the Holy Cross Sisters*—L.H.C.
[2490]—*Medical Missionary Sisters*—M.M.S.
[2840]—*Poor Clare Missionaries of Blessed Sacrament*—M.C.
[3280]—*Presentation Sisters of Blessed Virgin Mary*—P.B.V.M.
[3400]—*Religious Sisters of Charity*—R.S.C.
[2575]—*Religious Sisters of Mercy of the Americas*—R.S.M.
[]—*Religious Sisters of the Sacred Heart of Mary*—R.S.H.M.
[]—*Rosarian Dominican Sisters*—O.P.
[]—*School Sisters of Notre Dame*—S.S.N.D.
[1680]—*School Sisters of St. Francis*—S.S.S.F.
[]—*Sisters for Christian Community*—S.F.C.C.
[]—*Sisters of Mercy*—S.M.
[]—*Sisters of Our Lady of Perpetual Help*—S.O.L.P.H.
[3770]—*Sisters of St. Clare*—O.S.C.
[3830-03]—*Sisters of St. Joseph* (Orange)—C.S.J.
[3840]—*Sisters of St. Joseph of Carondelet*—C.S.J.
[0700]—*Sisters of the Company of Mary*—O.D.N.
[]—*Sisters of the Good Shepherd*—R.G.S.
[4050]—*Sisters of the Society Devoted to the Sacred Heart*—S.D.S.H.
[]—*Sisters, Servants of the Immaculate Heart of Mary*—I.H.M.
[4060]—*Society of the Holy Child Jesus*—S.H.C.J.

DIOCESAN CEMETERIES

ORANGE. *Holy Sepulcher*, 7845 Santiago Canyon Rd., Orange, 92869. Tel: 714-532-6551; Fax: 714-288-8441; Email: holysepulcher@rcbo.org. Rene Acebal, Cemetery Mgr.

ANAHEIM. *Holy Cross Cemetery*, Mailing Address: c/o Holy Sepulcher, 7845 Santiago Cyn, Orange, 92869. Email: racebal@rcbo.org. Rene Acebal, Mgr.

HUNTINGTON BEACH. *Good Shepherd Cemetery and Mausoleum*, 8301 Talbert Ave., Huntington Beach, 92646. Tel: 714-847-8546; Fax: 714-842-9979; Email: goodshepherd@rcbo.org. Guadalupe Ramirez, Mgr.

LAKE FOREST. *Ascension*, 24754 Trabuco Rd., Lake Forest, 92630. Tel: 949-837-1331; Fax: 949-837-9013; Email: ascension@rcbo.org. Kevin M. Haynes, Mgr.

NECROLOGY

† Ruhl, John Edward, (Retired), Died Apr. 17, 2018

An asterisk (*) denotes an organization that has established tax-exempt status directly with the IRS and is not covered by the USCCB Group Ruling.

Diocese of Orlando

(Dioecesis Orlandensis)

Most Reverend

JOHN G. NOONAN

Bishop of Orlando; ordained September 23, 1983; appointed Auxiliary Bishop of Miami June 21, 2005; ordained Titular Bishop of Bonusta and Auxiliary Bishop of the Archdiocese of Miami August 24, 2005; appointed Bishop of Orlando October 23, 2010; installed as Fifth Bishop of the Diocese of Orlando December 16, 2010. *Chancery: 50 E. Robinson St., Orlando, FL 32801.* Tel: 407-246-4800. *Mailing Address: P.O. Box 1800, Orlando, FL 32802.*

Chancery: 50 E. Robinson St., Orlando, FL 32801. Mailing Address: P.O. Box 1800, Orlando, FL 32802. Tel: 407-246-4800; Fax: 407-246-4942.

Web: www.orlandodiocese.org

Email: cbrinati@orlandodiocese.org

ESTABLISHED JUNE 18, 1968.

Square Miles 9,611.

Comprises the Counties of Brevard, Lake, Marion, Orange, Osceola, Polk, Seminole, Sumter and Volusia in the State of Florida.

For legal titles of parishes and diocesan institutions, consult the Chancery.

STATISTICAL OVERVIEW

Personnel	
Bishop	1
Priests: Diocesan Active in Diocese	88
Priests: Diocesan Active Outside Diocese	5
Priests: Retired, Sick or Absent	44
Number of Diocesan Priests	137
Religious Priests in Diocese	46
Total Priests in Diocese	183
Extern Priests in Diocese	20
Ordinations:	
Diocesan Priests	3
Transitional Deacons	1
Permanent Deacons	8
Permanent Deacons in Diocese	122
Total Brothers	7
Total Sisters	58
Parishes	
Parishes	79
With Resident Pastor:	
Resident Diocesan Priests	43
Resident Religious Priests	12
Without Resident Pastor:	
Administered by Priests	24
Missions	12
Professional Ministry Personnel:	
Brothers	2
Sisters	22
Lay Ministers	342
Welfare	
Health Care Centers	3
Total Assisted	3,767
Homes for the Aged	3
Total Assisted	170
Day Care Centers	10
Total Assisted	321
Special Centers for Social Services	13
Total Assisted	77,500
Residential Care of Disabled	1
Total Assisted	207
Educational	
Diocesan Students in Other Seminaries	22
Total Seminarians	22
High Schools, Diocesan and Parish	5
Total Students	3,234
Elementary Schools, Diocesan and Parish	31
Total Students	11,056
Non-residential Schools for the Disabled	1
Total Students	73
Catechesis/Religious Education:	
High School Students	3,621
Elementary Students	14,768
Total Students under Catholic Instruction	32,774
Teachers in the Diocese:	
Priests	1
Brothers	1
Sisters	10
Lay Teachers	1,147
Vital Statistics	
Receptions into the Church:	
Infant Baptism Totals	4,302
Minor Baptism Totals	549
Adult Baptism Totals	269
Received into Full Communion	393
First Communions	5,290
Confirmations	4,391
Marriages:	
Catholic	800
Interfaith	233
Total Marriages	1,033
Deaths	3,597
Total Catholic Population	360,725
Total Population	4,803,686

Former Bishops—Most Revs. WILLIAM D. BORDERS, D.D., ord. May 18, 1940; appt. Bishop of Orlando, May 2, 1968; cons. June 14, 1968; transferred to Baltimore, March 25, 1974 as Archbishop; died April 19, 2010.; THOMAS J. GRADY, D.D., ord. April 23, 1938; appt. Second Bishop of Orlando, Nov. 9, 1974; installed Dec. 16, 1974; retired May 25, 1990; died April 21, 2002; NORBERT L. DORSEY, C.P., D.D., S.T.D., ord. April 28, 1956; appt. Titular Bishop of Mactaris and Auxiliary Bishop of Miami Jan. 10, 1986; cons. March 19, 1986; appt. Bishop of Orlando March 20, 1990; installed as Third Bishop of Orlando May 25, 1990; retired Nov. 13, 2004; died Feb. 21, 2013.; THOMAS G. WENSKI, ord. May 15, 1976; appt. Titular Bishop of Kearney and Auxiliary Bishop of Miami June 24, 1997; cons. Sept. 3, 1997; appt. Coadjutor Bishop of Orlando July 1, 2003; installed Aug. 22, 2003; appt. Fourth Bishop of Orlando Nov. 13, 2004; appt. Archbishop of Miami April 20, 2010.

Chancery—50 E. Robinson St., Orlando, 32801. Tel: 407-246-4800; Fax: 407-246-4942; Email: cbrinati@orlandodiocese.org; Web: www.orlandodiocese.org. *Mailing Address: P.O. Box 1800, Orlando, 32802.*

Vicar General—Very Rev. RICHARD WALSH, P.O. Box 1800, Orlando, 32802. Tel: 407-647-3392; Email: frwalsh@stmargaretmary.org.

Vicar General and Chancellor for Canonical Affairs—Very Rev. JOHN GIEL, V.G., J.C.L., P.O. Box 1800, Orlando, 32802. Tel: 407-246-4846; Email: jgiel@orlandodiocese.org.

Chief Operating Officer/Chancellor—CAROL BRINATI, Mailing Address: P.O. Box 1800, Orlando, 32802-1800. Tel: 407-246-4800; Email: cbrinati@orlandodiocese.org.

Presbyteral Council—

President—Most Rev. JOHN NOONAN, Diocese of Orlando.

Ex Officio Members—Very Revs. RICHARD W. TROUT, V.F., (South Central Dean); JOHN GIEL, V.G., J.C.L., Vicar Gen. & Chancellor for Canonical Affairs; IVAN OLMO, V.F., (Southern Dean); TIM DALY, V.F., (Eastern Dean); STEPHEN D. PARKES, V.F., (North Central Dean); CHARLES VIVIANO, V.F., (Western Dean); EDWARD WATERS, V.F., (Northern Dean); RICHARD WALSH, Vicar Gen.; MIGUEL A. GONZALEZ, Vicar for Priests; PAUL HENRY, Vicar for Priests; EDWARD MCCARTHY, S.T.L., D.Min., (Retired).

Representative by Age—Rev. MARTIN NGUYEN, (25-45); Rev. Msgr. JUANITO FIGURA, (46-64); Very Rev. RICHARD WALSH, (65 & over).

Representative - Secular Priests Not Incardinated—Rev. STEPHEN OGONWA, (Nigeria).

Representative - Religious Priests—Rev. MATTHEW VETTATH, S.D.V.

Representative - Retired Priests—Very Rev. EDWARD MCCARTHY, S.T.L., D.Min., (Retired).

Appointed Member—Rev. DAVID P. VIVERO JR.

Chief Financial Officer—KEVIN CASEY, Mailing Address: P.O. Box 1800, Orlando, 32802.

Tribunal—50 E. Robinson St., Orlando, 32801. Tel: 407-246-4850.

Judicial Vicar—Very Rev. FERNANDO GIL, J.D., J.C.D., 50 E. Robinson St., Orlando, 32801. Tel: 407-246-4854.

Adjunct Judicial Vicar—Rev. JOSEPH V. BELLERIVE, (France) J.C.D.

Promoters of Justice—Sr. LUCY VAZQUEZ, O.P., J.C.D.; Very Rev. JOHN GIEL, V.G., J.C.L.

Defenders of the Bond—Rev. JOSE BAUTISTA, (Colombia) J.C.L.; Sr. LUCY VAZQUEZ, O.P., J.C.D.

Judges—Revs. JOSEPH V. BELLERIVE, (France) J.C.D.; CROMWELL CABRISOS, J.C.L., (Retired); MICHAEL BURKE, J.C.L.; PEDRO POLACHE; Very Rev. FERNANDO GIL, J.D., J.C.D.

Regional Advocates—Sisters LUCY VAZQUEZ, O.P., J.C.D.; PATRICIA O'MALLEY, S.N.D.deN., Tel: 386-668-1426; ANN MARIE BENZINGER; GIGI SANTIAGO; CAROLINA BRETON; ISABEL MENJURA.

Deans—Very Revs. EDWARD WATERS, V.F., Northern Deanery; RICHARD W. TROUT, V.F., Central Deanery South; STEPHEN D. PARKES, V.F., Central Deanery North; TIM DALY, V.F., Eastern Deanery; IVAN OLMO, V.F., Southern Deanery; CHARLES VIVIANO, V.F., Western Deanery.

Vicars for Clergy—Very Revs. PAUL J. HENRY; MIGUEL A. GONZALEZ.

Vicar for Senior Priests—Very Rev. EDWARD MCCARTHY, S.T.L., D.Min., (Retired).

Vicar for Religious—Very Rev. DR. BENJAMIN A. BERINTI, C.PP.S., D.Min.

Moderator for Religious Women—Mailing Address: P.O. Box 1800, Orlando, 32802. Sr. CATHERINE NOECKER, O.S.F.

Vicar for Priestly Life and Ministry—Very Rev. RICHARD W. TROUT, P.O. Box 1800, Orlando, 32802. Tel: 407-246-4875.

Priests' Personnel Board—P.O. Box 1800, Orlando, 32802. Tel: 407-246-4875. Very Rev. RICHARD W. TROUT, V.F., Pres.

Diocesan Offices

Censor of Books—Rev. JEREMIAH L. PAYNE; Very Rev. ESAU GARCIA, V.F., Mailing Address: P.O. Box 1800, Orlando, 32802. Tel: 407-246-4814.

Victim Assistance Coordinator—Mailing Address: P.O. Box 1800, Orlando, 32802. Tel: 407-246-7179; Email: vac@orlandodiocese.org.

Secretariat for Communications

Secretary for Communications & Senior Director—JENNIFER DROW, Mailing Address: P.O. Box 1800, Orlando, 32802. Tel: 407-246-4811; Email: jdrow@orlandodiocese.org.

Archivist and Librarian—MS. RENAE BENNETT, Mailing Address: P.O. Box 1800, Orlando, 32802. Tel: 407-246-4920; Email: rbennett@orlandodiocese.org.

Faith Fit Radio—KATHERIN LAGUNA, Tel: 407-246-4924.

Newspaper: The Florida Catholic—MARJORIE DURANTE, Mailing Address: P.O. Box 1800, Orlando, 32802. Tel: 407-246-4810; Email: mdurante@orlandodiocese.org.

Secretariat for Discipleship & Stewardship

Catholic Foundation of Central Florida—KIMBERLEE RILEY, Pres., Mailing Address: P.O. Box 4905, Orlando, 32802. Tel: 407-246-7194; Email: kriley@cfocf.org.

Secretariat for Ecclesiastical Properties

Secretary of Ecclesiastical Property & Senior Director—Mailing Address: P.O. Box 1800, Orlando, 32802. Tel: 407-246-4870. SCOTT FERGERSON, Email: sfergerson@orlandodiocese.org.

Catholic Cemeteries—DAVID BRANSON, Email: dbranson@orlandodiocese.org.

Secretariat for Education

Secretary of Education & Superintendent of School—HENRY FORTIER, Mailing Address: P.O. Box 1800, Orlando, 32802. Tel: 407-246-4904; Email: hfortier@orlandodiocese.org.

Diocesan School Board—Very Rev. TIMOTHY P. LABO, V.F., Chm. Bd., Mailing Address: P.O. Box 1800, Orlando, 32802. Tel: 407-246-4904; Fax: 407-246-4940.

Mission Office, Sister Diocese of San Juan de la Maguana—SR. BERNADETTE MACKAY, O.S.U., Dir., Mailing Address: P.O. Box 1800, Orlando, 32802. Tel: 407-246-4890; Fax: 407-246-4892.

San Pedro Spiritual Development Center—RANDALL PINNER, Dir.

Secretariat for Financial Services

Secretary of Financial Services and CFO—KEVIN CASEY, P.O. Box 1800, Orlando, 32802. Tel: 407-246-4831; Email: kcasey@orlandodiocese.org.

Comptroller—ROGER BARNES, Mailing Address: P.O. Box 1800, Orlando, 32802. Tel: 407-246-4832; Email: rbarnes@orlandodiocese.org.

Diocesan Finance Committee—Mailing Address: P.O. Box 1800, Orlando, 32802. CESAR CALVET, Chm.

Information Technology—JACK PAIGE, Sr. Dir., Mailing Address: P.O. Box 1800, Orlando, 32802. Tel: 407-246-4839; Email: jpaige@orlandodiocese.org.

Risk Management—TRACY DANN, Mgr., Mailing Address: P.O. Box 1800, Orlando, 32802. Tel: 407-246-4877; Email: tdann@orlandodiocese.org.

Secretariat for Human Dignity & Solidarity

Secretary of Human Dignity & Solidarity—GARY TESTER, Mailing Address: 1819 N. Semoran Blvd., Orlando, 32807. Tel: 407-658-1818, Ext. 1040; Email: gtester@cflcc.org.

Catholic Charities of Central Florida, Inc.—GARY TESTER, Exec. Dir., Administration/Main Office: 1819 N. Semoran Blvd., Orlando, 32807-3598. Tel: 407-658-1818; Tel: 888-658-2828; Fax: 407-657-5648; Email: cathchar@cflcc.org; Web: www.cflcc.org.

Family Stability Program—HEATHER KNOOP, Dir.

Volusia County—Tel: 407-658-1818; Tel: 888-658-2828; Fax: 407-657-5648.

Lake County—Tel: 407-388-0245; Tel: 888-658-2828 (Toll Free); Fax: 407-657-5648.

Brevard County (North)—Tel: 407-658-1818; Tel: 888-658-2828 (Toll Free); Fax: 407-657-5648 (Diocese of Orlando).

Polk County (West)—801 S. Florida, Lakeland, 33801. Tel: 407-658-1818; Tel: 888-658-2828 (Toll Free); Fax: 407-657-5648.

Polk County (East)—197 W. Central Ave., Winter Haven, 33880. Tel: 407-658-1818; Tel: 888-658-2828 (Toll Free); Fax: 407-657-5648.

Immigration Legal Services—1771 N. Semoran Blvd., Orlando, 32807-3598. Tel: 407-658-0110; Fax: 407-249-5669. VANESSA MCCARTHY, Supervising Attorney.

Comprehensive Refugee Services—DEBORAH CRUZ, Prog. Dir., 1771 N. Semoran Blvd., Orlando, 32807-3598. Tel: 407-658-0110; Fax: 407-249-5699 (Diocese of Orlando).

Pathways to Care & Step 2—JENNIFER STEPHENSON CROUCH, Sr. Dir. Health Care Svcs., 450 Plumosa Ave., Casselberry, 32707. Tel: 407-388-0245; Tel: 888-658-2828; Fax: 407-657-5648.

Office of Advocacy and Justice—DEBORAH STAFFORD SHEARER, Dir., 1819 N. Semoran Blvd., Orlando, 32807. Tel: 407-658-1818; Tel: 888-658-2828 (Toll Free); Fax: 407-657-5648.

Bishop Grady Villas—KEVIN JOHNSON, Exec. Dir., 401 Bishop Grady Court, Saint Cloud, 34769. Tel: 407-892-6078; Fax: 407-892-3081; Web: www.bishopgradyvillas.org.

Farmworker Ministry—

Centro Guadalupano Mission—2150 Bomber Rd., Wahneta, 33880. Tel: 863-299-3854; Fax: 863-299-8247. Rev. LUIS OSORIO.

Farmworker Ministry, (Centro Campesino), Inc. Auburndale—EVA GARCIA, Co Dir., Mailing Address: 318 W. Bridges Ave., Auburndale, 33823. Tel: 847-967-9583; Email: centrocampesino@cs.com; Web: www.farmworkerministry.org.

Tourism Ministry—Basilica of the National Shrine of Mary, Queen of the Universe, 8300 Vineland Ave., Orlando, 32821. Tel: 407-239-6600. Very Rev. PAUL HENRY, Rector.

Airport Ministry, Orlando International Airport—Rev. ROBERT F. SUSANN, M.S., Airport Chap., Tel: 407-947-5453.

Secretariat for Human Resources

Secretary of Human Resources & Senior Director—THERESA SIMON, Mailing Address: P.O. Box 1800, Orlando, 32802. Tel: 407-246-4830; Email: tsimon@orlandodiocese.org.

Health and Welfare Insurance Committee—RYAN BURROWS, Chm., Mailing Address: P.O. Box 1800, Orlando, 32802. Tel: 407-246-4835.

Secretariat for Laity, Family and Life

Secretary for Laity, Family and Life—DENNIS JOHNSON JR., Mailing Address: P.O. Box 1800, Orlando, 32802. Tel: 407-546-4913; Email: djohnsonjr@orlandodiocese.org.

Diocesan Liaison of Ecumenism and Interreligious Dialogue—Mailing Address: P.O. Box 1800, Orlando, 32802. Tel: 407-422-2005. Rev. MATTHEW HAWKINS.

Multi-Cultural Ministries—

African Ministry—Rev. EMMANUEL AKALUE.

Portuguese/Brazilian Ministry—Rev. CARLOS ANKLAN, C.S.

Filipino Ministry—Rev. Msgr. JUANITO FIGURA.

Haitian Ministry—Rev. JEAN GAETAN BOURSIQUOT.

Hispanic Ministry—Rev. JOSE MUNOZ.

Korean Ministry—Rev. KIM JONGJOO.

Polish Ministry—Rev. ANDRZEJ JURKIEWICZ.

Vietnamese Ministry—Rev. CHAU J. NGUYEN.

Adult Ministry—TOMAS EVANS, Dir., Tel: 407-246-4926; Tel: 407-246-4912; Email: tevans@orlandodiocese.org.

Family Ministry—LYNDA MONCKTON, Dir., Tel: 407-246-4910; Email: lmonckton@orlandodiocese.org.

Youth Ministry—CARLOS BERNARD, Dir., Tel: 407-246-4881; Email: cbernard@orlandodiocese.org.

Propagation of the FaithMailing Address: P.O. Box 1800, Orlando, 32802. Tel: 407-246-4865. SHEILA HENRY.

Catholic Campus Ministry at Bethune Cookman University—Very Rev. TIM DALY, V.F., c/o Basilica of St. Paul, 317 Mullaly St., Daytona Beach, 32114. Tel: 386-226-6581; Tel: 386-252-5422.

Catholic Campus Ministry at Embry-Riddle Aeronautical University—Very Rev. TIM DALY, V.F., Interfaith Chapel, 600 S. Clyde Morris Blvd., Daytona Beach, 32114-3900. Tel: 386-226-6580; Fax: 386-226-7370.

Catholic Campus Ministry at Florida Institute of Technology—150 W. University Blvd., Melbourne, 32901-6988. Tel: 321-674-8045; Fax: 321-674-8938. Rev. MICHAEL NEELAND, S.D.S.

Catholic Campus Ministry at Florida Southern College—Very Rev. TIMOTHY P. LABO, V.F., c/o St. Joseph Catholic Church, 210 W. Lemon St., Lakeland, 33815. Tel: 863-686-9546.

Catholic Campus Ministry at Rollins College—Very Rev. RICHARD WALSH, 526 Park Ave., N., Winter Park, 32789. Tel: 407-647-3392; Fax: 407-647-4492.

Catholic Campus Ministry at Stetson University—359 W. New York Ave., DeLand, 32720. Tel: 386-822-6000; Fax: 386-822-6034. Rev. GILBERT MEDINA.

Catholic Campus Ministry at the University of Central Florida—Bro. ADAM NERI, B.H., Dir. Campus Ministry, 3925 Lockwood Blvd., Oviedo, 32765. Tel: 407-392-0834; Email: info@ccmknights.com; Web: www.cmknights.com.

Secretariat for Leadership and Parish Life

Secretary for Leadership & Parish Life—Mailing Address: P.O. Box 1800, Orlando, 32802. Tel: 407-246-4878. Deacon JOSEPH GASSMAN, Email: jgassman@orlandodiocese.org.

Permanent Diaconate—Mailing Address: P.O. Box 1800, Orlando, 32802. Tel: 407-246-4878. DAVID CAMOUS, Dir. Permanent Diaconate; Deacon PAUL VOLKERSON, Assoc. Dir. Externs & Administration.

Vocations—Mailing Address: P.O. Box 1800, Orlando, 32802. Tel: 407-246-4875; Fax: 407-246-4937. Rev. JOSH SWALLOWS, Dir.

Senior Priests—Very Rev. EDWARD MCCARTHY, S.T.L., D.Min., Vicar for Senior Priests, (Retired), Mailing Address: P.O. Box 1800, Orlando, 32802. Tel: 407-246-4845.

International Priests—Mailing Address: P.O. Box 1800, Orlando, 32802. Tel: 407-246-4815. Very Rev. MIGUEL A. GONZALEZ.

Liturgy—MR. BRUCE CROTEAU, Dir., Mailing Address: P.O. Box 1800, Orlando, 32802. Tel: 407-246-4861.

Liturgical Music—Mailing Address: P.O. Box 1800, Orlando, 32802. Tel: 407-246-4862. ADAM BRAKEL, Dir.

Ministry to the Incarcerated—Mailing Address: P.O. Box 1800, Orlando, 32802. Tel: 407-246-4878. Deacon RICHARD DODD, Prison Ministry Coord., Email: jgassman@orlandodiocese.org.

Other Diocesan Organizations

Diocesan Council of Catholic Women—Very Rev. MIGUEL A. GONZALEZ, Spiritual Dir.

CLERGY, PARISHES, MISSIONS AND PAROCHIAL SCHOOLS

CITY OF ORLANDO

(ORANGE COUNTY)

1—ST. JAMES CATHEDRAL (1881)

215 N. Orange Ave., 32801. Tel: 407-422-2005; Email: info@stjamesorlando.org; Web: www.stjamesorlando.org. Very Rev. Miguel A. Gonzalez, Rector; Revs. Christopher Dorsey; Martin Nguyen; Matthew Hawkins; Deacons David L. Gray; Patrick Kenneth McAvoy; Carlos Sola.

School—St. James Cathedral School, 505 E. Ridgewood St., 32803. Tel: 407-841-4432; Fax: 407-648-4603; Email: stjcs@stjcs.com; Web: www.stjcs.com. Mrs. Dawn Helwig, Prin. Lay Teachers 36; Students 506.

Catechesis Religious Program—Email: rjones@stjamesorlando.org. Renee Jones, D.R.E. Students 654.

Mission—St. Ignatius Kim Korean Mission, 1518 E. Muriel St., Orange Co. 32806.

2—ST. ANDREW (1957)

801 N. Hastings St., 32808. Tel: 407-293-0730; Tel: 407-985-1876; Email: standrewchurch@standrew-orlando.org; Web: www.standrew-orlando.org. Rev. Anthony Leo Hodges; Deacons Rafael Hernandez; Larry Herbert; Armand Carpentier.

Res.: 430 Cinnamon Bark Ln., 32835.

School—St. Andrew School, 877 Hastings St., 32808. Tel: 407-295-4230; Fax: 407-290-0959; Email: admissions@standrewcatholicschool.org; Web: www.standrewcatholicschool.org. Lay Teachers 22; Students 355.

Catechesis Religious Program—Email: mzayas@standrew-orlando.org. Martha Lushman-Zayas, D.R.E. Students 202.

3—BLESSED TRINITY (1965)

4545 Anderson Rd., 32812. Tel: 407-277-1702; Email: info@blessedtrinityorlando.org. Revs. Roland Nadeau, M.S.; William Slight, M.S.; Robert F. Susann, M.S., In Res.

Catechesis Religious Program—Email: lmurgia@blessedtrinityorlando.org. Louis A. Murgia, D.R.E. Students 259.

4—ST. CHARLES BORROMEO (1954)

4001 Edgewater Dr., 32804. Tel: 407-293-9556; Fax: 407-293-9213; Email: stcharleschurch@stcharlesorlando.com; Web: www.stcharlesorlando.org. Revs. Ralph DuWell; Hector Vazquez Saad, Parochial Vicar; Deacons Paul Volkerson; Alvin Bedneau; Wenceslao Cruz.

School—St. Charles Borromeo School, 4005 Edgewater Dr., 32804. Tel: 407-293-7691; Fax: 407-295-9839; Email: nnadeau@scbcs.net; Web:

www.stcharlesschoolorlando.org. Nathan Nadeau, Prin. Lay Teachers 20; Students 325.
Child Care—Preschool, Students 40.
Catechesis Religious Program—
Tel: 407-293-9556, Ext. 121; Email: srmarie@stcharlesorlando.org. Sr. Marie Skebe, D.R.E. Students 184.

5—GOOD SHEPHERD (1956)
Mailing Address: 5900 Oleander Dr., 32807.
Tel: 407-277-3939; Fax: 407-273-5148; Email: nsantana@gs.church. Revs. James Henault, M.S.; Frank Cooney, M.S.; Bino Francis; Deacons John T. Crotty; Jorge Garcia; Felix Morillo; Gerard Hampstead; Hector R. Rodriguez.
Res.: 567 Hewett Dr., 32807.
School—Good Shepherd School, (Grades PreK-8), 5902 Oleander Dr., 32807. Tel: 407-277-3973;
Fax: 407-277-2605; Email: jhartmann@goodshepherd.org; Web: www.goodshepherd.org. Lay Teachers 31; Students 515.
Child Care—Good Shepherd Early Childhood Educational Ctr., Tel: 407-277-3973, Ext. 105; Email: dahearn@goodshepherd.org. Lay Teachers 3; Students 19.
Catechesis Religious Program—
Tel: 407-277-3939, Ext. 212; Email: lmediavilla@gs.church. Laura Mediavilla, C.R.E. Students 422.

6—HOLY CROSS (1992)
12600 Marsfield Ave., 32837. Tel: 407-438-0990; Fax: 407-438-4090; Web: holycrossorlando.org. Very Rev. Esau Garcia, V.F.; Deacon Celso Diaz.

7—HOLY FAMILY (1975) [JC]
5125 S. Apopka-Vineland Rd., 32819.
Tel: 407-876-2211; Email: hfoffice@hfcchurch.com; Web: www.holyfamilyorlando.org. Very Rev. John Giel, V.G., J.C.L.; Revs. Benjamin Lehnertz, Parochial Vicar; Raul Caga, Parochial Vicar; Deacons Charles Mallon; Richard Dodd; Robert J. Pleus; Spencer Silvers; Carl Lawrence Brockman; Richard Chabot.
School—Holy Family School, 5129 S. Apopka-Vineland Rd., 32819. Tel: 407-876-9344;
Fax: 407-876-8775; Email: sisterdorothy@hfcschool.com; Web: www.hfcschool.com. Sr. Dorothy Sayers, M.P.F., Prin. Lay Teachers 28; Sisters 1; Students 682; Clergy / Religious Teachers 1.
Catechesis Religious Program—Tel: 407-876-6331; Email: ncarbone@holyfamilyorlando.com. Nora Carbone, D.R.E. Students 667.

8—ST. ISAAC JOGUES (1987)
4301 S. Chickasaw Tr., 32829. Tel: 407-249-0906; Fax: 407-273-3236; Email: stisaac@st-isaac.org; Web: st-isaac.org. Rev. Jose Munoz.
Catechesis Religious Program—Email: mbaker@st-isaac.org. Mike Baker, D.R.E. Students 1,412.

9—ST. JOHN VIANNEY (1959)
6200 S. Orange Blossom Tr., 32809.
Tel: 407-855-5391; Email: twalden@sjvorlando.org. Revs. Thomas R. Walden; Carlos Cabán, Parochial Vicar; Sebastian Mpango, Parochial Vicar.
Res.: 1625 Dewayne Dr., 32809. Email: rsobolewski@sjvorlando.org.
School—St. John Vianney School, Tel: 407-855-4660; Email: sjvs@sjvs.org. Miss Mary Catherine Marshall, Prin. Lay Teachers 29; Students 519.
Catechesis Religious Program—
Tel: 407-855-5391, Ext. 234; Email: tshannon@sjvorlando.org. Tina Shannon, D.R.E. Students 531.

10—ST. JOSEPH (1962) (Polish—Filipino)
1501 N. Alafaya Tr., 32828. Tel: 407-275-0841; Web: www.stjosephorlando.org. Revs. Steven Pavignano, Admin.; Luis Aponte-Merced, Parochial Vicar.
Catechesis Religious Program—Email: eheinsen@stjosephorlando.org. Edith Heinsen, D.R.E. Students 780.

11—ST. MAXIMILIAN KOLBE (2006)
1501 N. Alafaya Tr., 32828. Tel: 407-275-0841;
Fax: 407-482-4484; Web: stjosephorlando.org. Revs. Steven Pavignano, Admin.; Luis Aponte-Merced, Parochial Vicar.

12—ST. PHILIP PHAN VAN MINH CATHOLIC CHURCH (2004)
15 W. Par St., 32804. Tel: 407-896-4210; Email: office@philipminhparish.org; Web: philipminhparish.org. 297 W. Par St., 32804. Revs. Chau J. Nguyen; Trong Lam; Deacon Nuoc Van Dang, Marriage Prep. Coord.
Catechesis Religious Program—Tel: 407-894-6001; Email: snowdream2@yahoo.com. Sr. Marie Nguyen, D.R.E. Students 365.

OUTSIDE THE CITY OF ORLANDO

ALTAMONTE SPRINGS, SEMINOLE CO.

1—ANNUNCIATION (1982)
1020 Montgomery Rd., Altamonte Springs, 32714.
Tel: 407-869-9472; Fax: 407-869-4661; Email: noreilly@annunciationorlando.org; Web: www.annunciationorlando.org. Very Rev. Stephen D. Parkes, V.F.; Revs. Stephen A. Baumann; Alvin Erni.
School—Annunciation Catholic Academy, (Grades K-8), Tel: 407-774-2801; Email: kahlep@annunciationacademy.org; Web: annunciationacademy.org. Patricia Kahle, Prin. Clergy 1; Lay Teachers 30; Students 506.
Catechesis Religious Program—Tel: 407-215-7649; Email: lwirth@annunciationorlando.org. Lois Wirth, D.R.E. Students 611.

2—ST. MARY MAGDALEN (1959)
861 Maitland Ave., Altamonte Springs, 32701.
Tel: 407-831-1212; Email: office@stmarymagdalen.org; Web: www.stmarymagdalen.org. Revs. Charles I. Mitchell; Frank Lobo; Patrick G. Patton, (Retired); Michael Burke, J.C.L.; Deacons Jerry Kelly, (Retired); Marshall Ashby Gibbs, (Retired); Juan Cruz; Greg Nelsen; Bill O'Brien; Anthony Medina.
School—St. Mary Magdalen School, 869 Maitland Ave., Altamonte Springs, 32701. Tel: 407-339-7301;
Fax: 407-339-9556; Email: stmarymagdalen@smmschool.org; Web: www.smmschool.org. Mrs. Lorianne Rotz, Prin. Lay Teachers 26; Students 447.
Child Care—Early Learning Center, 710 Spring Lake Rd., Altamonte Springs, 32701.
Tel: 407-831-3740; Email: esteiner@smmschool.org. Elisa Steiner, Dir. Students 169.
Catechesis Religious Program—Tel: 407-265-2303; Email: larannw@stmarymagdalen.org. Larann Wilson, D.R.E. Students 387.

APOPKA, ORANGE CO., ST. FRANCIS OF ASSISI (1966)
834 S. Orange Blossom Tr., Apopka, 32703-6560.
Tel: 407-886-4602; Web: www.stfrancisapopka.org. Revs. Stephen Ehiahuruike, S.D.V.; Mathew Vettath Joseph, Parochial Vicar; Deacons Luis Alvira; Frank Diaz; Ruthven Jackie; James G. Shelley; Jesus Davila.
Catechesis Religious Program—Email: mhettler@stfrancisapopka.org. Margaret Hettler, D.R.E. Students 1,008.
Mission—Notre Dame de Fatima d'Orlando, 7401 Mott Ave., 32810. Mailing Address: P.O. Box 1800, 32802.

BAREFOOT BAY, BREVARD CO., ST. LUKE (1986) [JC]
5055 Micco Rd., Barefoot Bay, 32976.
Tel: 772-664-9310; Email: barbara@stlukebarefootbay.org. Rev. Robert W. Mitchell.
Catechesis Religious Program—Email: janefrancesugenti@yahoo.com. Jane Derenthal, D.R.E. Students 10.

BARTOW, POLK CO., ST. THOMAS AQUINAS (1956)
1305 E. Mann Rd., Bartow, 33830. Tel: 863-533-8578; Email: gloria121@verizon.net. Rev. Eugene Grytner, S.D.S.; Deacon Mark M. King.
Catechesis Religious Program—Email: clhorange@aol.com. Carol Polkowski, D.R.E. Students 46.
Mission—St. Elizabeth Ann Seton, 101 Edgewood Dr., Fort Meade, 33841.

BELLEVIEW, MARION CO., ST. THERESA (1951)
11528 S. U.S. Hwy. 301, Belleview, 34420-4430.
Tel: 352-245-2458; Email: operations1@mystcc.org; Web: www.mystcc.org. Rev. Thomas Connery; Rev. Msgr. James Lichtenthal; Deacon Antonio Torres.
Catechesis Religious Program—Tel: 352-245-5300; Email: religioused@mystcc.org. Students 50.

BUSHNELL, SUMTER CO., ST. LAWRENCE (1981)
Office & Mailing Address: 320 E. Dade Ave., Bushnell, 33513. Tel: 352-793-7788;
Fax: 352-793-4787; Email: church@stlawrencebushnell.org. Rev. Waldemar Maciag, (Poland) Parochial Admin.
Res.: 223 E. Vermont Ave., Bushnell, 33513.
Catechesis Religious Program—Email: anafav75@hotmail. Ana Garcia, D.R.E. Students 80.

CANDLER, MARION CO., IMMACULATE HEART OF MARY (1983)
Mailing Address: P.O. Box 310, Candler, 32111.
Tel: 352-687-4031; Fax: 352-687-1811; Email: office@ihmcatholicchurch.com; Web: ihmcatholicchurch.com. 10670 SE Maricamp Rd., Ocala, 34472. Rev. Stephen Ogonwa, (Nigeria).
Catechesis Religious Program—Tel: 352-653-0045; Email: dre@ihmcatholicchurch.com. Barbara Atkinson, D.R.E. Students 26.

CASSELBERRY, SEMINOLE CO., ST. AUGUSTINE (1969)
375 N. Sunset Dr., Casselberry, 32707.
Tel: 407-695-3262; Email: frontdesk@saintaugustinecc.org; Web: www.staugustinecc.org. Rev. Tomas Hurtado; Deacons Pedro Laboy; Felix Montanez; Antero Santos.
Rectory—
Catechesis Religious Program—Email: ff@saintaugustinecc.org. Marilyn Napoletano, D.R.E. Students 224.

CELEBRATION, OSCEOLA CO., CORPUS CHRISTI (2005)
Mailing Address: 1050 Celebration Ave., Celebration, 34747. Tel: 321-939-1491;
Fax: 321-939-1494; Email: brad@celebrationcatholic.org; Web: www.celebrationcatholic.org. Very Rev. Richard W. Trout; Deacons Robert D. Gaudioso; Stephen Knych; Lawrence Migliorato.
Catechesis Religious Program—Email: audrey@celebrationcatholic.org. Audrey Knych, D.R.E. Students 377.

CLERMONT, LAKE CO.

1—BLESSED SACRAMENT (1961)
720 12th St., Clermont, 34711. Tel: 352-394-3562;
Fax: 352-241-0062; Email: communications@mybscc.org; Web: www.mybscc.org. Very Rev. Robert E. Webster; Revs. Jose Augusto Cadavid; Roy V. Eco; Deacons Rafael Gonzalez; Fred Grant; Luis Roman; John Riley.
Res.: 1675 Grandiflora Ave., Clermont, 34711. Email: office@mybscc.org.
Catechesis Religious Program—
Tel: 352-394-3562, Ext. 120; Email: cstalnaker@mybscc.org. Chris Stalnaker, D.R.E. Students 447.
Mission—Mission Outreach - Santo Toribio Romo, 1043 E. Myers Blvd., Mascotte, 34753.

2—ST. FAUSTINA CATHOLIC CHURCH (2006)
1714 U.S. Hwy. 27, Ste. 23, Clermont, 34714.
Tel: 352-515-9297. P.O. Box 135576, Clermont, 34713-5576. Rev. Ramon Bolatete.
Catechesis Religious Program—Tel: 352-702-4735; Email: mmariniello@stfaustina.org. Marylu Mariniello, D.R.E. Students 92.

COCOA BEACH, BREVARD CO., CHURCH OF OUR SAVIOUR (1956)
5301 N. Atlantic Ave., Cocoa Beach, 32931.
Tel: 321-783-4554; Email: oursaviourchurch@cfl.rr.com; Web: www.oursavioursparish.org. Rev. Percival P. DeVera.
School—Church of Our Saviour School, (Grades PreK-8), Tel: 321-783-2330; Email: jbailey@oursaviourschool.org; Web: www.oursaviourschool.org. Janet Peddecord, Prin. Lay Teachers 15; Students 154.
Catechesis Religious Program—Email: mborer@oursavioursparish.org. Marita Borer, D.R.E. Students 133.

COCOA, BREVARD CO., BLESSED SACRAMENT (1967)
5135 N. U.S. Hwy. 1, Cocoa, 32927.
Tel: 321-632-6333; Email: secretary@blessedsacramentcocoa.org; Web: www.blessedsacramentcocoa.org. Rev. Marek Sarniewicz, S.D.S., Parochial Admin.; Deacons Nick Varsalona; William Shelden.
Catechesis Religious Program—Email: dwegner@blessedsacramentcocoa.org. Darlene Wegner, D.R.E. Students 62.

DAYTONA BEACH, VOLUSIA CO.

1—BASILICA OF SAINT PAUL (1881)
317 Mullally St., Daytona Beach, 32114.
Tel: 386-252-5422; Email: info@basilicaofsaintpaul.com; Web: www.basilicaofsaintpaul.com. Revs. Timothy P. Daly; Edwin Cardona; Deacon Rick Ferranti.
School—Basilica of St. Paul School,
Tel: 386-252-7915; Web: www.stpaulpanthers.org. Ron Pagano, Prin. Lay Teachers 20; Students 195.
Catechesis Religious Program—Email: dsmith@basilicaofsaintpaul.com. Dawn Smith, D.R.E. Students 65.

2—OUR LADY OF LOURDES (1953)
201 University Blvd., Daytona Beach, 32118.
Tel: 386-255-0433; Email: office@ourladyoflourdesdaytona.com; Web: www.ourladyoflourdesdaytona.com. Rev. Philip J. Egitto.
School—Our Lady of Lourdes School aka Lourdes Academy, (Grades PreK-8), 1014 N. Halifax Ave., Daytona Beach, 32118. Tel: 386-252-0391; Email: sdole@lourdesacademy.net; Web: lourdesacademydaytona.net. Lay Teachers 14; Students 225.
Catechesis Religious Program—Email: nmatthew@ourladyoflourdesdaytona.com. Nelson Matthew, D.R.E. Students 284.

DELAND, VOLUSIA CO., ST. PETER CHURCH (1883)
359 New York Ave., DeLand, 32720.
Tel: 386-822-6000; Fax: 386-822-6034; Email: office@stpeterdeland.org; Web: stpeterdeland.org. Rev. Gilbert Medina; Deacons Robert LaPlante; Gerard Smith; Heriberto Toledo; Kurt Slafkovsky; Esteban Ortizo.
School—St. Peter's Church School, 421 W. New York Ave., DeLand, 32720. Tel: 386-822-6010; Email: prandlov@stpeter-deland.org; Web: www.stpeter-deland.org. Rev. Thomas Connery, Admin. Lay Teachers 25; Students 273.
Catechesis Religious Program—Email: srowell@stpeterdeland.org. Shelby Rowell, D.R.E. Students 340.
Mission—San Jose Mission, 165 Emporia Rd., Pierson, Volusia Co. 32180-2784.

DEBARY, VOLUSIA CO., ST. ANN'S (1961)
26 Dogwood Tr., Debary, 32713. Tel: 386-668-8270; Email: office@stannsdebary.org; Web: stannsdebary.org. P.O. Box 530218, DeBary, 32753-0218. Rev. Andrzej Jurkiewicz.
Res.: 10 Larkspur Ln., DeBary, 32713.

Catechesis Religious Program—Email: ljufko@stannsdebary.org. Lenny Jufko, D.R.E. Students 121.

DELTONA, VOLUSIA CO.

1—ST. CLARE (1989) (Anglo—Hispanic)
2961 Day Rd., Deltona, 32738. Tel: 386-789-9990; Fax: 386-789-2430; Email: lydiam@stclarefl.org; Email: frcarlos@stclarefl.org; Email: monica@stclarefl.org; Web: stclarefl.org. Rev. Hector Vazquez.
Catechesis Religious Program—Email: Lydia@stclarefl.org. Dr. Lydia Navarro, D.R.E. Students 133.

2—OUR LADY OF THE LAKES (1970)
1310 Maximilian St., Deltona, 32725.
Tel: 386-574-2131; Email: olladmin@ourladyofthelakes.org; Web: www.ourladyofthelakes.org. Revs. Francisco Aquino, (Philippines) Parish Admin.; Frank Cerio, Parochial Vicar; Deacons Luis Baez; Hector Isaza.
Catechesis Religious Program—Email: ollfaithform@ourladyofthelakes.org. Dolores Brophy, Dir. Evangelization. Students 154.

DUNNELLON, MARION CO., ST. JOHN THE BAPTIST (1976)
7525 S. US Hwy. 41, Dunnellon, 34432.
Tel: 352-489-3166; Web: www.stjohncc.com. Rev. Jean Hugues Desir; Deacons Eric Makoid; Santos N. Santiago.
Res.: 7545 S. Hwy. 41, Dunnellon, 34432.
Catechesis Religious Program—Email: claire@stjohncc.com. Claire Hamilton, D.R.E. Students 72.

EUSTIS, LAKE CO., ST. MARY OF THE LAKES (1912)
218 Ocklawaha Ave., Eustis, 32726-4840.
Tel: 352-483-3500; Web: www.stmaryofthelakesparish.org. Rev. Carlos Bedoya.
Catechesis Religious Program—Email: jackie@stmaryofthelakesparish.org. Jackie Smart, D.R.E. Students 146.

HAINES CITY, POLK CO., ST. ANN (1969) [JC] (Anglo—Hispanic) (Formerly Transfiguration)
1311 E. Robinson Dr., P.O. Box 1285, Haines City, 33845. Tel: 863-422-4370; Fax: 863-421-2522; Web: www.stannhc.org. Rev. Alfonso Cely, O.P.; Deacons Jose Ramos; Hector Colon; Richard Demers; Orestes Hernandez.
Catechesis Religious Program—Tel: 863-438-2700; Email: srjosie@stannhc.org. Sr. Josie Canevari, D.R.E. Students 404.

INDIALANTIC, BREVARD CO., HOLY NAME OF JESUS (1959)
3050 Hwy. A1A, Indialantic, 32903.
Tel: 321-773-2783; Fax: 321-777-0929; Email: hnjparish@hnj.org; Web: www.hnj.org. Revs. Scott M. Circe; Francis Amponsah, Parochial Vicar; Peter Cordeno, Parochial Vicar; Rev. Msgr. David Page, Pastor Emeritus, (Retired); Deacons John Farrell; Michael Nussear; Vincent Trunzo; Edward Struttmann.
School—Holy Name of Jesus School, (Grades PreSchool-8), 3060 Hwy. A1A, Indialantic, 32903.
Tel: 321-773-1630; Fax: 321-773-7148; Email: hnj@hnj.org; Email: kfalk@hnj.org; Email: klaird@hnj.org. Kathleen Falk, Prin. Lay Teachers 23; Students 235.
Catechesis Religious Program—
Tel: 321-773-2783, Ext. 120. Debbie Weir Khan, D.R.E. Students 408.

KISSIMMEE, OSCEOLA CO.

1—ST. CATHERINE OF SIENA (2000)
2750 E. Osceola Pkwy., Kissimmee, 34743.
Tel: 407-344-9607; Fax: 407-344-9160; Email: info@stcatherineofsienacc.org; Web: www.stcatherineofsienacc.org. P.O. Box 450698, Kissimmee, 34745. Revs. Jose Bautista, (Colombia) J.C.L.; Nazaire Massillon, (Haiti) Parochial Vicar; Deacons Juan R. Vargas; Angel R. Morales; Esteban Cruz; Pablo Laguna; Wilfrid Tilus.

2—HOLY REDEEMER (1912)
1603 N. Thacker Ave., Kissimmee, 34741.
Tel: 407-847-2500; Fax: 407-847-9687; Email: frjorge@hredeemer.org; Web: www.hredeemer.org. Revs. Jorge Torres; Archie Faustino; Juan Osorno, Parochial Vicar; Deacons Tommy Tate; Eliezer Maldonado; Susano Neris; Juan Contreras; William Contreras; Ramon Smith.
School—Holy Redeemer School (1993) (Grades PreK-8), 1800 W. Columbia Ave., Kissimmee, 34741.
Tel: 407-870-9055; Fax: 407-870-2214; Email: gdelorbe@hrcschool.com; Web: www.hrcschool.com. Gloria Del Orbe, Prin. Lay Teachers 30; Students 417.
Catechesis Religious Program—Students 363.

3—ST. ROSE OF LIMA (1994)
3880 Pleasant Hill Rd., Kissimmee, 34746.
Tel: 407-932-5004; Email: info@srlcc.org; Web: www.srlcc.org. 3860 Pleasant Hill Rd., Kissimmee, 34746. Revs. Mariano Catura, Admin.; Aland Jean, C.I.C.M.; Mrs. Eva Barajas, Sec.; Mrs. Bethzaida Varela, Sec.; Mr. Alfredo Mejia, Custodian.
Catechesis Religious Program—Email: Jcontreras@srlcc.org. Deacon Juan Contreras, D.R.E. Students 264.

LADY LAKE, LAKE CO., ST. TIMOTHY (1985)
1351 Paige Pl., Lady Lake, 32159. Tel: 352-753-0989; Fax: 352-753-9602; Email: bulletin@sttimothycc.com; Web: www.sttimothycc.com. Very Rev. Edward Waters, V.F.; Revs. Paul Chemplamparampil Joseph, C.M.I.; Leo Perera, Hospital Ministry; Robert Fucheck, Pastor Emeritus, (Retired); Gerard Cunningham, (Retired); Peter Mitchell, (Retired); Gerald Shovelton, (Retired); Deacons John Bellacicco, (Retired); Dick Bigelow, (Retired); John Sullivan, (Retired); Richard R. Kaseta, (Retired); Ronald L'Huillier, (Retired); George Mattison, (Reitred); Robert Turbitt, (Retired); Robert Basye; Kevin Mukri.
Catechesis Religious Program—Email: rlaseter@sttimothycc.com. Robert Laseter, D.R.E. Students 115.

LAKE WALES, POLK CO., HOLY SPIRIT (1927)
644 S. 9th St., Lake Wales, 33853. Tel: 863-676-1556; Email: jessica.c@holyspiritlakewales.org. Rev. David Vargas, Admin.; Deacon Samuel Ralph Knight.
Res.: 1020 Sunset Dr., Lake Wales, 33853. Email: dvargas@holyspiritlakewales.org; Email: jessica.c@holyspiritlakewales.org.
Catechesis Religious Program—Email: Terri.s@holyspiritlakewales.org. Theresa Seitz, D.R.E. Students 259.

LAKELAND, POLK CO.

1—ST. ANTHONY CATHOLIC CHURCH (1982)
820 Marcum Rd., Lakeland, 33809-4306.
Tel: 863-858-8047; Email: businessmanager@saintacc.com; Web: www.saintacc.com. Revs. Luis Salazar; Gabriel Kamienski, S.D.S., Parochial Vicar; Deacon James Wade.
School—St. Anthony Catholic Church School, (Grades PreK-8), 924 Marcum Rd., Lakeland, 33809.
Tel: 863-858-0671; Fax: 863-858-0876; Email: jpeddecord@saintacs.com; Web: www.saintacs.com. Patricia Becker, Prin.; Janet Peddecord, Prin. Lay Teachers 15; Students 250.
*
Endowment—St. Anthony's Catholic School Endowment Fund, Inc., Mr. Freddie Sosa, Chm.
Catechesis Religious Program—Email: dre@saintacc.com. Laura Rector, D.R.E. Students 91.

2—CHURCH OF THE RESURRECTION (1963)
333 Terrace Way, Lakeland, 33813-1109.
Tel: 863-646-3556; Email: cviviano@churchoftheres.net; Web: www.churchoftheres.net. Very Rev. Charles Viviano, V.F.; Rev. Jose Vanegas, Parochial Vicar; Deacons Edgardo Cruz; James Spindler; Jean Pierre Espinoza.
School—Resurrection Catholic School (1990) (Grades PreK-8), 3720 Old Hwy. 37, Lakeland, 33813.
Tel: 863-644-3931; Fax: 863-648-0625; Email: office@rcslakeland.org; Email: dschwope@rcslakeland.org; Web: www.rcslakeland.org. Mrs. Deborah Schwope, Prin. Lay Teachers 28; Students 450.
Catechesis Religious Program—
Tel: 863-646-3556, Ext. 113; Email: mjimenez@churchoftheres.net. Maria Virgen Jimenez, D.R.E. Students 646.

3—ST. JOHN NEUMANN (1988)
501 E. Carter Rd., Lakeland, 33813.
Tel: 863-647-3400; Email: mailbox@sjncc.org; Web: www.sjncc.org. Revs. Jaroslaw Sztybel; Alvaro Jimenez, Parochial Vicar; Deacon George Ferraioli.
Res.: 601 E. Carter Rd., Lakeland, 33813.
Ministry Center—Ministry Center: 603 E. Carter Rd., Lakeland, 33813.
Catechesis Religious Program—Email: Jsztybel@sjncc.org. Students 160.

4—ST. JOSEPH'S (1898) [JC]
118 W. Lemon St., Lakeland, 33815.
Tel: 863-213-5280; Email: alofaro@stjosephlakeland.org; Web: stjosephlakeland.org. Very Rev. Timothy P. Labo, V.F.; Rev. Julius Lopez, Parochial Vicar.
School—St. Joseph's School, (Grades PreK-8), 310 Frank Lloyd Wright Way, Lakeland, 33803.
Tel: 863-686-6415; Fax: 863-687-8074; Email: jbruchey@sjalakeland.org; Web: www.sjalakeland.org. Jessica Bruchey, Prin.
Legal Title: St. Joseph Academy. Lay Teachers 22; Students 245.
Catechesis Religious Program—Email: salamm@stjosephlakeland.org. Samera Alamm, D.R.E. Students 204.

LEESBURG, LAKE CO., ST. PAUL CATHOLIC COMMUNITY (1954)
1330 Sunshine Ave., Leesburg, 34748.
Tel: 352-787-6354, Ext. 228. Revs. Mark R. Wajda, Parochial Admin.; Mark Librizzi, Parochial Vicar; Gianni Agostinelli, Spanish Ministry; Deacons Michael Francis McGinnity; Sam Damiano; Michael Balchus.
School—St. Paul Catholic Community School, 1320 Sunshine Ave., Leesburg, 34748. Tel: 352-787-4657; Fax: 352-787-0324; Email: ocornelio@saintpaulschool.com; Email: jgehrsitz@saintpaulschool.com; Web: saintpaulschool.com. Rev. Mark R. Wajda, Admin. Lay Teachers 19; Students 226; Clergy / Religious Teachers 1.
Catechesis Religious Program—Email: jfalanga@ccstpaul.com. Jeff Falanga, D.R.E. Students 85.
St. Paul's Thrift Shop—1321 Sunshine Ave., Leesburg, 34748.
St. Paul's Gift Shop—Tel: 352-365-6804.

LONGWOOD, SEMINOLE CO., CHURCH OF THE NATIVITY (1960)
3255 N. Ronald Reagan Blvd., Longwood, 32750.
Tel: 407-322-3961; Fax: 407-322-3981; Email: info@nativity.org; Web: www.nativity.org. Rev. Augustine Clark; Deacons David Baker; John Mire Gravois; Walt A. Skinner.
Catechesis Religious Program—Email: jelder@nativity.org. Jo Ann Elder, D.R.E. Students 499.

MELBOURNE BEACH, BREVARD CO., IMMACULATE CONCEPTION (1978)
3780 S. Hwy. A1A, Melbourne Beach, 32951.
Tel: 321-725-0552; Email: office@icparishmb.org; Web: www.icparishmb.org. Very Rev. Dr. Benjamin A. Berinti, C.PP.S., D.Min.; Rev. Peter A. Sagorski, Pastor Emeritus, (Retired); Deacons Howard Pettengill Jr.; Michael J. Biennas.
Catechesis Religious Program—Email: dweirkhan@icparishmb.org. Debbie Weir-Khan, D.R.E. Students 44.

MELBOURNE, BREVARD CO.

1—ASCENSION (1959)
2950 N. Harbor City Blvd., Melbourne, 32935-6259.
Tel: 321-254-1595; Fax: 321-255-3490; Email: mrusso@ascensioncatholicsch.org; Web: www.ascensioncatholic.net. Revs. Edmund J. Tobin; Richard Fitzgerald; Deacons William Terneus Sr.; Dr. Sergio Colon; Tom Stauffacher; Christopher Meehan.
School—Ascension School, (Grades PreK-8), c/o Ascension Parish, 3000 N. Harbor City Blvd., Melbourne, 32935-6259. Tel: 321-254-1595; Email: abrady@ascensioncatholicsch.org; Web: www.ascensioncatholicsch.org. Lay Teachers 35; Students 469.
Catechesis Religious Program—Email: dre@ascensioncatholicsch.org. Betsy Glasenapp, D.R.E. Students 379.

2—OUR LADY OF LOURDES (1931) (Hispanic)
1710 S. Hickory St., Melbourne, 32901-4517.
Tel: 321-723-3636; Web: www.ollmlb.org. 1626 Oak St., Melbourne, 32901-4517. Rev. Karl Bergin; Deacons Arcelio Perez; Gary Hessen; Daniel Powers.
School—Our Lady of Lourdes School, (Grades PreK-8), 420 E. Fee Ave., Melbourne, 32901.
Tel: 321-723-3631; Fax: 321-723-7408; Email: school@ollmelbourne.org; Email: office@ollmelbourne.org; Web: www.ollmelbourne.org. Mrs. Donna Witherspoon, Prin. Lay Teachers 23; Students 249.
Catechesis Religious Program—Email: pattytaylor@ollmlb.org. Patty Taylor, D.R.E. Students 139.

MERRITT ISLAND, BREVARD CO., DIVINE MERCY CATHOLIC COMMUNITY (1964)
1940 N. Courtenay Pkwy., Merritt Island, 32953.
Tel: 321-452-5955; Web: divinemercychurch.org. Rev. Matthew Mello.
School—Divine Mercy Catholic Community School, Tel: 321-452-0263; Email: parkerd@dmccs.org. Clergy 4; Lay Teachers 20; Students 150; Clergy / Religious Teachers 4.
Catechesis Religious Program—Email: maryfrances@divinemercychurch.org. Mary-Frances Coburn, D.R.E. Students 150.

MIMS, BREVARD CO., HOLY SPIRIT (1967)
2309 Holder Rd., Mims, 32754-2103.
Tel: 321-269-2282; Email: info@holyspiritmims.com; Web: holyspiritmims.com. 2399 Holder Rd., Mims, 32754. Rev. Andrzej Wojtan.
Catechesis Religious Program—Tel: 321-269-7785; Email: faithformation@holyspiritmims.com. Christopher McCormick, D.R.E. Students 103.

MOUNT DORA, ORANGE CO., ST. PATRICK'S (1973) [CEM] (Hispanic)
6803 Old Hwy. 441 S., Mount Dora, 32757.
Tel: 352-383-8556; Fax: 352-383-8443; Email: mbaugh@stpatrickmtdora.org; Email: aarruda@stpatrickmtdora.org; Web: www.stpatrickmtdora.org. Revs. Charles J. Deeney, O.M.I.; Nelson Javier, T.O.R., Parochial Vicar; Gianni Agostinelli; Deacons Jose Rodriguez; Paul Gaucher; Charles Lee.
Res.: 1323 Olympia Ave., Mount Dora, 32757.
Catechesis Religious Program—
Tel: 352-383-8556, Ext. 34; Email: srjudy@stpatrickmtdora.org. Sr. M. Judith Waldt, M.H.S.H., D.R.E. Students 283.

NEW SMYRNA BEACH, VOLUSIA CO.

1—OUR LADY STAR OF THE SEA (1973)
4000 S. Atlantic Ave., New Smyrna Beach, 32169.

Tel: 386-427-4530; Web: www.ourladystar.com. Rev. J. Patrick Quinn, T.O.R.
Catechesis Religious Program—
Tel: 386-427-4530, Ext. 11; Email: ministry@ourladystar.com. Sarah Schmidt, D.R.E. Students 49.
2—SACRED HEART (1926)
998 Father Donlon Dr., New Smyrna Beach, 32168.
Tel: 386-428-6426; Email: sacredheart@sacredheartnsb.com; Web: www.sacredheartnsb.com. P.O. Box 729, New Smyrna Beach, 32170. Revs. Thomas Burke, C.Ss.R., Email: fetom@sacredheartnsb.com; Edward J. Gray, C.Ss.R.; Francis Nelson, C.Ss.R.; George N. Rosario, C.Ss.R.; Aldrin Nunes, C.Ss.R.; Deacons Lou Bartos; Steve Cooley.
School—Sacred Heart School, 1003 Turnbull St., New Smyrna Beach, 32168. Tel: 386-428-4732;
Fax: 386-428-4087; Email: sniswonger@sacredheartcatholic.com; Web: shseagles.org. Lay Teachers 28; Students 254.
Catechesis Religious Program—Tel: 386-410-5957; Email: mbilodeau@sacredheartcatholic.com. Maria Bilodeau, C.R.E. Students 50.
Mission—St. Gerard, 3171 S. Ridgewood Ave., Edgewater, Volusia Co. 32141.
OCALA, MARION CO.
1—BLESSED TRINITY (1922)
5 S.E. 17th St., Ocala, 34471. Tel: 352-629-8092; Email: mail@blessedtrinity.org; Web: blessedtrinity.org. Revs. Patrick J. Sheedy; Zbigniew Stradomski; Raul Adrian Valdez; Michael O'Keeffe, In Res.; Deacons Heriberto Berrios; Stephen Floyd; James Maubach; James G. Schwartz.
School—Blessed Trinity School, (Grades K-8),
Tel: 352-622-5808; Email: mlosito@btschool.org; Email: childner@btschool.org; Web: btschool.org. Megan Losito, Prin. Lay Teachers 35; Students 609.
Catechesis Religious Program—Email: jburzotta@blessedtrinity.org. Jenny Burzotta, D.R.E. Students 235.
Missions—Christ the King—14045 N. U.S. Hwy. 301, P.O. Box 129, Citra, 32113.
Guadalupe Catholic Mission, 11153 W. Hwy. 40, Ocala, 34482.
2—ST. JUDE CATHOLIC COMMUNITY (1983)
443 Marion Oaks Dr., Ocala, 34473-3203.
Tel: 352-347-0154; Fax: 352-347-5211; Web: www.judeparish.org. Rev. Barthelemy Garcon, S.M.M.; Deacons Santos N. Santiago; Jose I. Serrano; Edward C. Wilson; Edward Mazuchowski.
Catechesis Religious Program—Email: religioused@stjudeparish.org. Linda Jones, C.R.E. Students 30.
3—OUR LADY OF THE SPRINGS (1982)
4047 N.E. 21st St., Ocala, 34470. Tel: 352-236-2230. Revs. Justin Vakko Kannamparabil, O.C.D., Parochial Admin.; Francis Joseph, Parochial Vicar; Deacon John Warren Howell; Mr. John Sherman, Music Min.
Catechesis Religious Program—Email: dhiggins@ourladyofthesprings.org. Deborah Higgins, D.R.E. Students 20.
Missions—St. Joseph of the Forest—17301 E. Hwy. 40, Silver Springs, Marion Co. 34488.
Tel: 352-625-4222; Email: jlammers6@gmail.com.
St. Hubert of the Forest, Mailing Address: P.O. Box 715, Astor, 32102.
4—QUEEN OF PEACE (1986)
6455 S.W. State Rd. 200, Ocala, 34476.
Tel: 352-854-2181; Fax: 352-854-7840; Email: qopparishoffice@queenofpeaceocala.com; Web: www.ocalaqueenofpeace.com. Revs. Patrick J. O'Doherty; Paul Thomas.
Catechesis Religious Program—Students 20.
ORMOND BEACH, VOLUSIA CO.
1—ST. BRENDAN (1960)
1000 Ocean Shore Blvd., 136 Banyan Dr., Ormond Beach, 32176. Tel: 386-441-1505; Email: cnewman@stbrendanchurchormond.org. Revs. Thomas G. Barrett; James T. Queen, In Res., (Retired); Deacons Fred D'Angelo; Gene Mastragelo; John Harvey.
School—St. Brendan School, Tel: 386-441-1331; Email: pgorrasi@stbrendanormond.org. Mr. Philip Gorrasi, Prin. Lay Teachers 26; Students 230.
Catechesis Religious Program—Email: vorlando@stbrendanchurchormond.org. Valeta Orlando, D.R.E. Students 90.
2—PRINCE OF PEACE (1966)
600 S. Nova Rd., Ormond Beach, 32174.
Tel: 386-672-5272; Email: admin@princeofpeaceormond.com. Revs. Bill Zamborsky; Titus Kachinda; Deacons Bruce Gesinski; Richard Van Glahn.
Catechesis Religious Program—Email: dod@princeofpeaceormond.com; Email: youth@princeofpeaceormond.com. Rigo Vega, D.R.E. Students 247.
OVIEDO, SEMINOLE CO., MOST PRECIOUS BLOOD CATHOLIC CHURCH (2005)
Mailing Address: 113 Lockwood Blvd., Oviedo, 32765. Tel: 407-365-3231; Fax: 407-365-3313; Email: info@oviedocatholic.org; Web: www.oviedocatholic.org. Revs. David Scotchie; George A. Nursey, Ph.D., Parochial Vicar.
Catechesis Religious Program—Email: jmolloy@oviedocatholic.org. John Molloy, D.R.E. Students 778.
PALM BAY, BREVARD CO.
1—ST. JOSEPH (1914) [CEM]
5330 Babcock St., N.E., Palm Bay, 32905.
Tel: 321-727-1565; Email: Frjeremiah@st-joe.org. Revs. Jeremiah L. Payne; Vilaire Philius, Parochial Vicar; Deacons Alfred P. Somma; Michael Patrick Mintern; James D. Stokes; Frank Falotico; Joseph Moran.
School—St. Joseph School, 5320 Babcock St., N.E., Palm Bay, 32905. Tel: 321-723-8866;
Fax: 321-727-1181; Email: stokesc@st-joe.org. Lay Teachers 17; Students 202.
Catechesis Religious Program—Email: Alegriaa@st-joe.org. Analisa Alegria, D.R.E. Students 164.
2—OUR LADY OF GRACE (1989)
300 Malabar Rd. S.E., Palm Bay, 32907-3005.
Tel: 321-725-3066; Email: olg@ourladyofgracechurch.com; Web: www.ourladyofgracechurch.com. Revs. Emmanuel Akalue; Vilaire Philius; Deacons William T. Wanca Sr., Pastoral Assoc.; Jack H. Rhine; Kevin Crawford; Thomas Flavell.
Res.: 949 Haas St., Palm Bay, 32907.
Catechesis Religious Program—Email: twood@ourladyofgracechurch.com. Theresa Wood, D.R.E. Teachers 183.
PORT ORANGE, VOLUSIA CO.
1—EPIPHANY (1962)
201 Lafayette St., Port Orange, 32127.
Tel: 386-767-6111; Web: epiphanypo.com. Very Rev. John Bosco Maison.
Catechesis Religious Program—Email: faithformation@catholicchurchofepiphany.com. Andy Baker, D.R.E. Students 181.
2—OUR LADY OF HOPE (1981) [CEM]
4675 S. Clyde Morris Blvd., Port Orange, 32129-4064. Tel: 386-788-6144; Email: admin@ladyofhope.org. P.O. Box 290216, Port Orange, 32129. Revs. Christopher Hoffmann, V.F.; Bernard Kiratu; Deacons Dave Sekel, Spiritual Advisor/Care Svcs.; Michael Samuel Pettit, Coord. for Human Trafficking Task Force; Michael Rosolino, Altar Server Coord./Young Adult; Michael Willems.
ROCKLEDGE, BREVARD CO., ST. MARY CATHOLIC CHURCH (1917) [JC]
75 Barton Ave., Rockledge, 32955. Tel: 321-636-6834;
Fax: 321-632-4301; Email: srauch@stmarysrockledge.org; Web: www.stmarysrockledge.org. Very Rev. Ivan Olmo, V.F.; Rev. Blake Britton; Deacon Michael J. Murphy.
School—St. Mary Catholic Church School, 1152 Seminole Dr., Rockledge, 32955. Tel: 321-636-4208; Fax: 321-636-0591; Email: info@stmarys-school.org; Web: www.stmarys-school.org. Sandra Basinger, Prin. Lay Teachers 18; Students 243.
Catechesis Religious Program—Tel: 321-636-6834; Email: staylor@stmarysrockledge.org. Sharon Taylor, D.R.E. Students 58.
SAINT CLOUD, OSCEOLA CO., ST. THOMAS AQUINAS CHURCH (1968)
700 Brown Chapel Rd., St. Cloud, 34769.
Tel: 407-957-4495; Email: sjefferson@stacatholic.org; Web: www.stacatholic.org. Revs. Kent A. Walker; Fidel Rodriguez, Parochial Vicar; Deacons John V. Del Guidice; Ernesto Nunez.
Res.: 721 Brown Chapel Rd., St. Cloud, 34769.
School—St. Thomas Aquinas Church School, (Grades K-8), 800 Brown Chapel Rd., St. Cloud, 34769. Tel: 407-957-1772; Fax: 407-957-8700; Web: stacschool.com. Nick Pavgouzas; Margie Smith, Business Mgr. Lay Teachers 27; Students 320.
Catechesis Religious Program—Email: jfey@stacatholic.org. Joe Fey, D.R.E. Students 422.
SANFORD, SEMINOLE CO., ALL SOULS (1911) [CEM]
301 W. 8th St., Sanford, 32771. Tel: 407-322-3795; Email: office@allsoulssanford.org. Revs. David P. Vivero Jr.; Ken Metz; Very Rev. Edward McCarthy, S.T.L., D.Min., (Retired).
Res.: 902 S. Oak Ave., Sanford, 32771.
Tel: 407-322-3795, Ext. 310; Email: mcosta@allsoulssanford.org; Web: www.allsoulssanford.org.
School—All Souls School, 810 S. Oak Ave., Sanford, 32771. Tel: 407-322-7090; Fax: 407-321-7255; Email: office@allsoulscatholicschool.org; Web: allsoulscatholicschool.org. Lay Teachers 17; Students 221.
Catechesis Religious Program—3201 W. 1st St., Sanford, 32771. Ms. Ann Cammarata, Sec. Students 310.
SUMMERFIELD, MARION CO., ST. MARK THE EVANGELIST (2005)
7081 S.E. Hwy. 42, Summerfield, 34491.
Tel: 352-347-9317; Fax: 352-347-9749; Email: reception@stmarkrcc.com; Web: www.stmarkrcc.com; Web: catherine.nocera@stmarkrcc.com. Revs. Mariusz Dymek, O.S.P.P.E.; Dominik Libiszewski, Parochial Vicar; Deacons Roger Gallagher; Robert A. Esposito; John Rumplasch; Charles Cimmino; Don Curtis, Business Mgr.; Roger Grenier, Music Min.; Catherine Nocera, Office Mgr.
Catechesis Religious Program— Twinned with St. Timothy's. Email: deaconjohnr1@aol.com. Deacon John A. Rumplasch, D.R.E.
TITUSVILLE, BREVARD CO., ST. TERESA (1958)
203 Ojibway Ave., Titusville, 32780.
Tel: 321-268-3441; Fax: 321-268-3270; Email: marge@stteresach.org; Web: www.saintteresatitusville.org. Revs. Krzysztof Bugno, S.D.S.; Ryszard Zgorzclak; Deacon Donald Boland.
School—St. Teresa School, 207 Ojibway Ave., Titusville, 32780. Tel: 321-267-1643;
Fax: 321-268-5124; Email: jzackel@steresa-titusville.org; Web: www.stteresa-titusville.org. Jacqueline Zackel, Prin. Lay Teachers 17; Students 135.
Catechesis Religious Program—Tel: 321-268-0440; Email: vshoemaker@stteresa-titusville.org. Vicky Shoemaker, D.R.E. Students 107.
Convent—Sisters of Notre Dame, Chardon, Ohio, 1735 Harrison #130, Titusville, 32780.
Tel: 321-264-4274.
VIERA, BREVARD CO., ST. JOHN THE EVANGELIST (2001)
5655 Stadium Pkwy., Viera, 32940.
Tel: 321-637-9650; Fax: 321-637-9651; Email: office@stjohnviera.org; Web: www.stjohnviera.org. Revs. John Britto Antony, C.S.C.; John Riley, Parochial Vicar; Deacons Tom Tagye; Donathan L. Durden; Dr. Michael J. McElwee; Heidi Pranzoni, Dir.
Catechesis Religious Program—Email: rbirmingham@stjohnviera.org. Robert Birmingham, D.R.E.; Jim Mascarenhas, Youth Min. Students 467.
WILDWOOD, SUMTER CO.
1—SAN PEDRO DE JESUS MALDONADO MISSION (2006)
210 Wonders St., Wildwood, 34785.
Tel: 352-787-9208; Email: giagox@gmail.com. 1330 Sunshine Ave., Leesburg, 34748. Rev. Gianni Agostinelli, Admin.
Catechesis Religious Program—Cecilia Montavlo, D.R.E. Students 102.
2—ST. VINCENT DE PAUL (2005)
5323 E. CR 462, Wildwood, 34785. Tel: 352-330-0220; Fax: 352-748-6106; Email: stvincentchurch@sumtercatholic.org; Web: www.sumtercatholic.org. Very Rev. Peter Puntal, V.F.; Rev. John E. McCracken, Parochial Vicar, (Retired); Deacons John Claude Curtin, Ph.D.; Walter Price; Dana McCarthy; Byron Anthony Otradovec, Sr. Deacon; Frank J. Campione, Sr. Deacon; Daniel James Pallo; Richard F. Radford, Sr. Deacon; Daniel G. Miller Sr.; Gregory Bruce Senholzi; Richard Stevens; Rossini Alcos.
Catechesis Religious Program—Tel: 352-643-7017; Email: faithformation@sumtercatholic.org. Frank Webber, Dir. Faith Formation. Students 271.
WINTER GARDEN, ORANGE CO., RESURRECTION CATHOLIC CHURCH (1967)
1211 Winter Garden Vineland Rd., Winter Garden, 34787-4338. Tel: 407-656-3113; Email: parish@resurrectionwg.org; Web: www.resurrectionwg.org. Revs. Carlos Anklan, C.S.; Vincenzo Ronchi, C.S., Parochial Vicar; Deacons Fred Molina; Jack Martin; Jose Navco; Carlos Conselho; Vincent Beckles.
Res.: 358 Floral Ave., Winter Garden, 34787-4338.
Catechesis Religious Program—Email: srpatsipan@resurrectionwg.org. Sr. Patricia Sipan, S.N.D., Faith Formation Dir. & RCIA. Students 800.
WINTER HAVEN, POLK CO.
1—ST. JOSEPH'S (1923)
532 Ave. M N.W., Winter Haven, 33881.
Tel: 863-294-3144; Email: ewaterman@stjosephwh.org; Web: www.stjosephwh.org. Revs. Jimson Varghese; Rony Parakkal, Parochial Vicar; Deacon Francisco Hernandez.
School—St. Joseph's School, (Grades PreK-8), 535 Ave. M, N.W., Winter Haven, 33881.
Tel: 863-293-3311; Fax: 863-299-7894; Email: thaas@stjosephwhschool.org; Web: www.stjosephwhschool.org. Mrs. Tammi Haas, Prin. Lay Teachers 27; Students 411.
Catechesis Religious Program—Email: broach@stjosephwh.org. Becky Roach, D.R.E. Students 346.
2—ST. MATTHEW (1973) [CEM 2]
1991 Overlook Dr., Winter Haven, 33884.
Tel: 863-324-3040; Email: info@saintmcc.com; Web: saintmcc.com. Rev. Nicholas J. O'Brien.
Res.: 558 Cody Caleb Dr., Winter Haven, 33884.
Catechesis Religious Program—Email: rmonteverde@saintmcc.com. Richard Monteverde, D.R.E. Students 508.
Mission—Our Lady of Guadalupe, 2150 Bomber Rd., Wahneta, Polk Co. 33880.
WINTER PARK, ORANGE CO., ST. MARGARET MARY

(1947)
526 N. Park Ave., Winter Park, 32789.
Tel: 407-647-3392; Email: debbie@stmargaretmary.org; Email: concetta@stmargaretmary.org. Very Rev. Richard Walsh; Revs. Shenoy Thomas, Parochial Vicar; James Tharakan, Parochial Vicar; Deacons Robert Kreps; Nemesio Gubatan; Bill Timmes; Thomas Cuff.
School—St. Margaret Mary School, 142 E. Swoope Ave., Winter Park, 32789. Tel: 407-644-7537; Fax: 407-644-7357; Email: walshk@smmknight.org; Web: www.smmknight.org. Kathleen Walsh, Prin. Lay Teachers 46; Students 539.
Catechesis Religious Program—Email: kristie@stmargaretmary.org. Kristie Altman, D.R.E. Students 1,127.

WINTER PARK, SEMINOLE CO., SAINTS PETER AND PAUL (1967)
5300 Old Howell Branch Rd., Winter Park, 32792.
Tel: 407-657-6114; Email: mail@stspp.net; Web: www.stspp.net. Rev. Derk Schudde; Rev. Msgr. Juanito Figura, Parochial Vicar; Bro. Paul Santoro, Pastoral Assoc.; Deacons Al Castellana; Norman Levesque; Donald M. Warner; Scott Lindeman; German Romero; Mark Fry.
Catechesis Religious Program—Tel: 407-636-4295; Email: paula.wright@stspp.net. Paula Wright, D.R.E. Students 460.

WINTER SPRINGS, SEMINOLE CO., ST. STEPHEN (1985)
575 Tuskawilla Rd., Winter Springs, 32708.
Tel: 407-699-5683; Fax: 407-542-0396; Email: ststephen@st-stephen.com; Web: st-stephen.com. Rev. John J. Bluett; Deacon James Ferruzzi.
Catechesis Religious Program—Email: caryld@st-stephen.com. Caryl M. DeGrandi, D.R.E. Students 699.

Shrines

BASILICA OF THE NATIONAL SHRINE OF MARY QUEEN OF THE UNIVERSE (1986)
8300 Vineland Ave., 32821. Tel: 407-239-6600; Email: shrine@maryqueenoftheuniverse.org; Web: maryqueenoftheuniverse.org. Very Rev. Paul J. Henry; Revs. Julian Bednarz; Barry Dowd; Gina Schwiegerath, Dir. Opers.; William Picher, Dir. Music; Vincent Castellano, Dir. Liturgy; Ludovico Carbone, Controller.

Special Assignment:
Revs.—
Gohring, William, Fire Dept. & Hospital Chap.
Nguyen, Andrew Chien, Hospital Chap.

On Duty Outside the Diocese:
Revs.—
Barrera, Luis
Buckley, Dominic
Olds, Steven, S.T.D.
Welle, Anthony
Zapata, Pedro.

Retired:
Rev. Msgrs.—
Ennis, William, (Retired)
Fernandez, Manuel, (Retired)
Gimeno, Fabian G., (Retired)
Harte, F. Joseph, (Retired)
Page, David, (Retired)
Very Rev.—
McCarthy, Edward, S.T.L., D.Min., (Retired)
Revs.—
Baybay, Felicito S., (Retired)
Bluett, Anthony, (Retired)
Bonar, Clyde A., (Retired)
Brown, Robert W., (Retired)
Buck, Frank, (Retired)
Cabrisos, Cromwell, J.C.L., (Retired)
Cooney, Sean K., (Retired)
Farrell, Michael A., (Retired)
Finley, William, (Retired)
Fucheck, Robert, (Retired)
Giglio, Michael E., V.F., (Retired)
Hanley, William, (Retired)
Henry, Peter J., (Retired)
Heslin, Sean, V.F., (Retired)
Hoeffner, Robert J., (Retired)
King, Nicholas, (Retired)
Kurber, Robert, (Retired)
Londono, Hugo, (Retired)
Mainardi, Donald G., (Retired)
Mallick, Andrew, (Retired)
Markunas, Robert, (Retired)
McMackin, Thomas P., (Retired)
Mitchell, Peter, (Retired)
Murray, John, (Retired)
Neumann, William J., (Retired)
O'Leary, Raymond J., (Retired)
Oser, Ronald E., (Retired)
Pinchock, Joseph, (Retired)
Roberts, Joseph, (Retired)
Rojas, Tito Nels, J.C.L., (Retired)
Ruse, Fred R., (Retired)
Ryan, John J., (Retired)
Sagorski, Peter A., (Retired)
Salazar, Franklin, (Retired)
Smith, Francis, (Retired)
Stahl, Allen M., (Retired), U.S. Military
Traupman, Robert, (Retired)
Wawrzycki, Andrew, (Retired)
Zammit, Francis X., (Retired).

Permanent Deacons:
Andrew, Donald, Resurrection Catholic Church, Lakeland
Avellan, Jamie, Holy Cross, Orlando
Baez, Luis, Our Lady of the Lakes, Deltona
Bartos, Lou
Beauton, Richard William, Our Lady of Lourdes, Melbourne
Beltran, Miguel A., St. Lawrence, Bushnell
Berrios, Heriberto, Blessed Trinity, Ocala
Biennas, Michael, Immaculate Conception, Melbourne Beach
Boland, Donald, St. Teresa, Titusville
Bom Conselho, Carlos, Prince of Peace, Ormond Beach
Breaud, Thomas P., St. John Vianney, Orlando
Brockman, Carl Lawrence, Holy Family, Orlando
Carpentier, Armand, St. Andrew, Orlando
Castellana, Al, Sts. Peter & Paul, Winter Park
Chabot, Richard, Holy Family, Orlando
Cimmino, Charles, St. Mark the Evangelist, Summerfield
Dr. Colon, Sergio, Ascension, Melbourne
Contreras, Juan, St. Rose of Lima, Kissimmee
Crawford, Kevin, Our Lady of Grace, Palm Bay
Crotty, John, Good Shepherd, Orlando
Cruz, Edgardo, Resurrection, Lakeland
Cruz, Juan, St. Mary Magdalen, Altamonte Springs
Cuff, Thomas, St. Margaret Mary, Winter Park
D'Angelo, Fred, St. Brendan, Ormond Beach
Dang, Nuoc Van, St. Joseph, Winter Haven
Diaz, Frank, St. Francis of Assisi, Apopka
Dodd, Richard, Holy Family, Orlando
Dwyer, Bruce, Diocese of Richmond
Espinoza, Alan, St. Isaac Jogues, Orlando
Farrell, John, Holy Name of Jesus, Indialantic
Ferraiolo, George, St. John Neumann, Lakeland
Ferranti, Richard L., Basilica of St. Paul, Daytona Beach
Ferriola, Constantino, Nativity, Longwood
Ferruzzi, James, St. Stephen Catholic Community, Winter Springs
Flavell, Thomas, Our Lady of Grace, Palm Bay
Floyd, Stephen, Blessed Trinity, Ocala
Foy, Charles, Holy Name of Jesus, Indialantic
Fry, Mark, Sts. Peter and Paul, Winter Park
Garcia, Jorge, Most Precious Blood, Oviedo
Garcia, Jose, Blessed Trinity, Orlando
Gassman, Joseph, Annunciation, Altamonte Springs
Gesinski, Bruce, Prince of Peace, Ormond Beach
Gibbs, Marshall Ashby, St. Mary Magdalen, Altamonte Springs
Gravois, John Mire, Nativity, Longwood
Gray, David L., Cathedral of St. James, Orlando
Gubatan, Nemesio, St. Margaret Mary, Winter Park
Hempstead, Gerard, Good Shepherd, Orlando
Herbert, Laurence Matthew, St. Francis of Assisi, Apopka; St. Andrew, Orlando
Hessen, Gerald, St. Joseph, Palm Bay
Isaza, Hector, Our Lady of the Lakes, Deltona
Jackie, Ruthven, St. Francis of Assisi, Apopka
Johnson, Stephen, Durango, CO
Kelly, Gerard H., St. Mary Magdalen, Altamonte Springs
King, Mark M., St. Thomas Aquinas, Bartow
Knight, Samuel Ralph, Holy Spirit, Lake Wales
Knych, Stephen, Corpus Christi, Celebration
Kreps, Robert P., St. Margaret Mary, Winter Park
Laboy, Pedro, St. Augustine, Casselberry
Laguna-Villegas, Pablo, St. Catherine of Siena, Kissimee
Lammers, John, St. Joseph of the Forest Mission, Silver Springs
LaPlante, Robert, St. Peter, DeLand
Levesque, Norman, Saints Peter and Paul, Winter Park
Libersat, Henry, St. Mary Magdalen, Altamonte Springs
Lindeman, Scott, Sts. Peter and Paul, Winter Park
Martin, John, Resurrection, Winter Garden
Martinez, Antonio, St. John Neumann, Lakeland
Martinez, Carlos, Holy Cross, Orlando
Mattison, George, St. Timothy, Lady Lake
McAvoy, Patrick Kenneth, St. James Cathedral, Orlando
Dr. McElwee, Michael J., St. John the Evangelist, Viera
Medina, Anthony, St. Mary Magdalen, Altamonte Springs
Meehan, Christopher, Ascension, Melbourne
Mintern, Michael Patrick, St. Joseph, Palm Bay
Montanez, Felix, St. Augustine, Casselberry
Moran, Joseph, St. Joseph, Palm Bay
Muller, Hugh, Diocese of Venice
Murello, Andrew Frank, St. Mary, Rockledge
Nelsen, Gregory, St. Mary Magdalen, Altamonte Springs
Nichols, Claude Jr., St. Sebastian, Owensboro, KY
Nussear, Michael, Holy Name of Jesus, Indialantic
O'Brien, William, St. Mary Magdalen, Altamonte Springs
Pagan, Miguel A., Blessed Trinity, Orlando
Perez, Arcelio, Our Lady of Lourdes, Melbourne
Pettengill, Howard Jr., Immaculate Conception, Melbourne Beach
Pettit, Michael Samuel, Our Lady of Hope, Port Orange
Pleus, Robert J., Holy Family, Orlando
Ramos, Jose Vidal, St. Rose of Lima, Kissimmee
Rhine, Jack H., Our Lady of Grace, Palm Bay
Rojas, Wilmar, St. Maximilian Kolbe, Orlando
Romero, German, Sts. Peter & Paul, Winter Park
Rosolino, Michael, Our Lady of Hope, Port Orange
Rumplasch, John A., St. Mark the Evangelist, Summerfield
Santiago, Santos N., St. Jude, Ocala
Schwartz, James G., Blessed Trinity, Ocala
Shelden, William, Blessed Sacrament, Cocoa
Shelley, James G., St. Francis of Assisi. Apopka
Silvers, Spencer, Holy Family, Orlando
Skinner, Walt A., Nativity Catholic Church, Longwood
Slafkovsky, Kurt, St. Peter, DeLand
Smith, Gerard F., St. Peter, DeLand
Spindler, James, Resurrection, Lakeland
Stauffacher, Thomas, Ascension, Melbourne
Stokes, James D., St. Joseph, Palm Bay
Struttmann, Edward, Holy Name of Jesus, Indialantic
Tagye, Thomas A., St. John the Evangelist, Viera
Tate, Tommy L., Holy Redeemer, Kissimmee
Terneus, William Sr., Ascension, Melbourne
Tilus, Wilfrid, St. Catherine of Siena, Kissimmee
Timmes, William, St. Margaret Mary, Winter Park
Toledo, Heriberto, St. Peter, DeLand
Torres, Antonio, St. Theresa, Belleview
Torres, Gilberto, Our Lady of the Lakes, Deltona
Treadwell, Byron, Diocese of St. Augustine, St. Michael
Trunzo, Vincent, Holy Name of Jesus, Indialantic
Volkerson, Paul, St. Charles Borromeo, Orlando
Wanca, William T. Sr., Our Lady of Grace, Palm Bay
Warner, Donald M., Sts. Peter & Paul, Winter Park
Wendell, David, Archdiocese of Atlanta, St. Augustine
Williams, Michael, Our Lady of Hope, Port Orange.

INSTITUTIONS LOCATED IN DIOCESE

[A] HIGH SCHOOLS, DIOCESAN AND PAROCHIAL

ORLANDO. *Bishop Moore Catholic High School Inc.* (1954) 3901 Edgewater Dr., 32804.
Tel: 407-293-7561; Fax: 407-296-8135; Email: doylet@bishopmoore.org; Web: www.bishopmoore.org. Thomas Doyle, Pres.; Scott Brogan, Prin.; Yvonne Toro, Vice Prin.; Charlotte Funston, Vice Prin.; Kristy Beiden, Dean, Women; Matt Gorden, Dean, Men; Daniel Boyd, Dir. Campus Ministry; Carol Guthrie, Dir. of Academic Support; Dr. Sally Caradona, Dir.; Mrs. Joan Wheeler, Dir.; Marvin Snyder, Dir.; Mike Malatesta, Atheletic Dir.; Maria Scarabino, Dir. Instruction; Lisa Sojourner, Dir. Pastoral Care; Missy Vananda, Dir. Guidance; David Manchon, Admissions; Sr. Kristy Bergman, Campus Ministry; Peter Dionne, Campus Min.; Ms. Amanda Livermore, Campus Min. Mission Trips; Revs. Anthony Aarons, T.O.R., Chap.; Ralph DuWell; Deacon Ruthven Jackie, Rel. Teacher. Lay Teachers 91; Students 1,443; Total Staff 42; Guidance Counselors 5; Clergy / Religious Teachers 3.

DAYTONA BEACH. *Father Lopez Catholic High School, Inc.*, 3918 LPGA Blvd., Daytona Beach, 32124.
Tel: 386-253-5213; Fax: 386-252-6101; Email: plamorte@fatherlopez.org; Email: lsvajko@fatherlopez.org; Web: www.fatherlopez.org. Mr. Pasquale "Pat" Lamorte, Pres.; Mrs. Leigh Svajko, Prin. Lay Teachers 30; Students 414; Total Staff 55.

LAKELAND. *Santa Fe Catholic High School, Inc.* (1960) 3110 Highway 92 E., Lakeland, 33801.
Tel: 863-665-4188; Fax: 863-665-4151; Email:

mfranzino@santafecatholic.org; Web: www.santafecatholic.org. Matthew Franzino, Pres. & Prin. Lay Teachers 25; Students 311.

MELBOURNE. *Central Catholic High School, Inc.* aka Melbourne Central Catholic High School, 154 E. Florida Ave., Melbourne, 32901. Tel: 321-727-0793; Fax: 321-952-0798; Email: burkem@melbournecc.org; Web: melbournecc.org. Michael Burke, Pres.; Ernie Herrington, Prin.; Rev. Karl Bergin, Chap.; Janet Keany, Librarian. Lay Teachers 35; Priests 1; Students 540; Clergy / Religious Teachers 1.

OCALA. *Trinity Catholic High School, Inc.* (2000) 2600 S.W. 42nd St., Ocala, 34471. Tel: 352-622-9025; Fax: 352-861-8164; Email: lpereira@tchs.us; Web: www.trinitycatholichs.org. Mr. Lou Pereira, Pres.; Dr. Erika Wikstrom, Prin.; Rev. Patrick J. Sheedy, School Pastor. Lay Teachers 32; Students 510.

[B] SPECIAL SCHOOLS

ORLANDO. *Morning Star Catholic School* (1960) 930 Leigh Ave., 32804-2299. Tel: 407-295-3077; Fax: 407-522-1700; Email: cooneys@morningstarorlando.org; Email: saless@morningstarorlando.org; Web: www.morningstarorlando.org. Thomas Doyle, Pres.; Sandra Cooney, Prin.; Dr. Alicia Abbey, Vice Prin. School for Special Needs Students from age 5 until 26 Clergy 1; Lay Teachers 9; Students 70.

[C] HOUSING ACCOMMODATIONS FOR THE ELDERLY

ORLANDO. *St. Joseph's Garden Courts, Inc.*, 1515 N. Alafaya Trail, 32828. Tel: 407-382-0808; Fax: 407-382-0812; Email: stjosephgardenctmgr@spm.net. Rev. Kent A. Walker, Member. Residents 80; Total Staff 4; Apartments 79.

Monsignor Bishop Manor, Inc., 815 Borders Cir., Ste. 144, 32808. Tel: 407-293-3339; Fax: 407-751-4393; Email: JGreauxmills@carteretmgmt.com. Mrs. Josephine Greaux-Mills, Business Mgr. Total in Residence 340; Total Staff 5.

DAYTONA BEACH. *Casa San Pablo*, 401 N. Ridgewood Ave., Daytona Beach, 32114. Tel: 386-253-2828; Fax: 386-253-0842; Email: casasanpablomgr@spm.net. Barbara D. Mitchell, Admin. Total in Residence 64; Total Staff 7.

MELBOURNE. *Ascension Manor* (1995) 2960 Pineapple Ave., Melbourne, 32935. Tel: 321-757-9828; Fax: 321-752-9437; Email: ascensionmanor@carteretmgmt.com. Josephine Stratford, Mgr. Total in Residence 79; Total Staff 9.

OCALA. *Trinity Villas, Inc.*, 3728 N.E. 8th Pl., Ocala, 34470-1093. Tel: 352-694-5507; Fax: 352-694-1434; Email: dcrawford@trinityvilla.cfcoxmail.com. Debra Crawford, Mgr. Total in Residence 98; Total Staff 5.

ORMOND BEACH. *Prince of Peace Housing, Inc.* dba Prince of Peace Villas (1996) 664 S. Nova Rd., Ormond Beach, 32174. Tel: 386-673-5080; Fax: 386-673-2008; Email: tbowen@carteretmgmt.com. Tammy Bowen, Mgr. Total in Residence 70; Total Staff 5.

PORT ORANGE. *Epiphany Manor* (1989) 4792 S. Ridgewood Ave., Port Orange, 32127. Tel: 386-767-2556; Fax: 386-761-0490; Email: rperoldo@carteretmgmt.com. Robin Peroldo, Mgr. Total Staff 5; Total Residence 72; Apartment Units 72.

SAINT CLOUD. *St. Anthony Garden Court*, 444 Hamilton Park Cir., St. Cloud, 34769. Tel: 321-805-4733; Fax: 321-805-4732; Email: stanthonygardenctmgr@spm.net. Rev. Kent A. Walker. Elderly 70; Apartments 51.

WINTER HAVEN. *Episcopal Catholic Apartments* (1974) 500 Ave. L, N.W., Winter Haven, 33881. Tel: 863-299-4481; Fax: 863-299-5719; Email: episcopalcatholicmgr@spm.net. Haley Alam, Admin. Tot Asst. Annually 97; Total Staff 12; Apartments 199.

[D] FAMILY CARE FACILITIES

SAINT CLOUD. *Bishop Grady Villas* (2004) 401 Bishop Grady Ct., St. Cloud, 34769. Tel: 407-892-6078; Fax: 407-892-3081; Email: kjohnson@bishopgradyvillas.org; Web: www.bishopgradyvillas.org. Kevin Johnson, Exec. Dir. Bed Capacity 48; Tot Asst. Annually 207; Full-time Equivalents 62.

[E] RETREAT CENTERS

WINTER PARK. *San Pedro Spiritual Development Center*, 2400 Dike Rd., Winter Park, 32792. Tel: 407-671-6322; Fax: 407-671-3992; Email: info@sanpedrocenter.org; Web: www.sanpedrocenter.org. Revs. John Vianney Cunningham, T.O.R., Sacramental Min.; Blase Romano, T.O.R., Sacramental Min.; Bro. Thomas Corrigan, In Res.; Mr. Charles Pinner, Admin. Total in Residence 3; Total Staff 15.

[F] MONASTERIES AND RESIDENCES OF PRIESTS AND BROTHERS

COCOA BEACH. *Congregation of Holy Cross, United States Province*, 325 Arthur Ave., Cocoa Beach, 32931-4005. Tel: 321-799-8383; Fax: 321-783-6312. Very Rev. R. Bradley Beaupre, C.S.C., V.F., Supr.; Revs. Fred Serraino, C.S.C., Asst. Supr., (Retired); Joseph J. Long, C.S.C.; Louis A. Manzo, C.S.C., (Retired); James Murphy, C.S.C., (Retired); Laurence Olszewski, C.S.C.; William R. Persia, C.S.C.; Thomas J. Shea, C.S.C.; Lawrence Jerge. Priests 9; Total Staff 4.

DELAND. *Augustinian Monks of the Primitive Observance*, Mother of the Good Shepherd Monastery, 2075 Mercers Fernery Rd., Deland, 32720. Tel: 386-736-4321; Email: monks@augustinianmonks.com; Web: www.augustinianmonks.com. Rev. A.M. Seamus, O.S.A.-Prim., Abbot.

NEW SMYRNA BEACH. *St. Alphonsus Villa-Redemptorist Fathers and Brothers*, 318 N. Riverside Dr., New Smyrna Beach, 32168. P.O. Box 548, New Smyrna Beach, 32170-0548. Tel: 386-428-6481; Email: cssrsecretary@gmail.com. Very Rev. Glenn D. Parker, C.Ss.R., Rector; Most Rev. Edward J. Gilbert, C.Ss.R., Former Bishop; Deacon Darrel Cevasco, C.Ss.R., Admin.; Revs. Karl Aschmann, C.Ss.R., (Retired), P.O. Box 548, New Smyrna Beach, 32170; Carlyle Blake, C.Ss.R., (Retired); Eugene Daigle, C.Ss.R., (Retired); William Spillane, C.Ss.R.; Bro. Leonard Samuel. Total in Residence 10; Total Staff 10.

Redemptorist Fathers of the Vice Province of Richmond, 313 Hillman St., New Smyrna Beach, 32168. Tel: 386-427-3094; Fax: 386-423-1270; Email: vpofrichmond@aol.com. P.O. Box 1529, New Smyrna Beach, 32170-1529. Ms. Luz Rodriguez, Business Mgr. Merged with the Province of Baltimore Redemptorists
Redemptorists Fathers of Florida, Inc.; Redemptorists Fathers of South Carolina, Inc.; Redemptorists Fathers of North Carolina, Inc.; Redemptorists Fathers of Virginia, Inc.; Redemptorists Fathers of Georgia, Inc.

Villa Madonna Friary, 4385 Saxon Dr., New Smyrna Beach, 32169. Tel: 386-427-4660; Email: seraphintor@aol.com. Very Revs. Seraphin J. Conley, T.O.R., (Retired), Email: seraphintor@aol.com; A. Giles Schinelli, T.O.R.
Franciscan Friars TOR.

WINTER PARK. *Franciscan Friars, T.O.R., San Pedro Friary*, 2400 Dike Rd., Winter Park, 32792. Tel: 407-671-6322; Fax: 407-671-3992; Email: info@sanpedrocenter.org; Web: www.sanpedrocenter.org. Friar John Vianney Cunningham, T.O.R., Sacramental Min.; Rev. Blase Romano, T.O.R., Sacramental Min.; Bro. Thomas Corrigan, In Res. For detailed information of staff and residences in this diocese, please see Retreat Centers in the Institution section. Priests 2; Total in Residence 3.

[G] CAMPUS MINISTRY

ORLANDO. *Catholic Campus Ministry at Embry-Riddle Aeronautical University* (1926) Center for Faith & Spirituality, 600 S. Clyde Morris Blvd., Daytona Beach, 32114-3900. Tel: 386-226-6580; Fax: 386-226-7370; Email: dbcsu@erau.edu. Rev. Timothy P. Daly, Campus Min.

Campus Ministry / Newman Center, Chaplain's Office, 600 S. Clyde Morris Blvd., Daytona Beach, 32114-3900. Tel: 386-226-6581; Fax: 386-226-7370 ; Email: dalyt@erau.edu. Rev. Timothy P. Daly, Catholic Chaplain.

DELAND. *Catholic Campus Ministry at Stetson University*, 359 W. New York Ave., Deland, 32720. Tel: 386-822-6000; Fax: 386-822-6034; Web: www.stpeterdeland.org. Rev. Gilbert Medina, Campus Min. Total Staff 2.

LAKELAND. *Florida Southern College Newman Center*, c/o St. Joseph, 118 W. Lemon St., Campus Ministry/Newman Center, Lakeland, 33815. Tel: 863-213-5280; Fax: 863-686-9546; Web: www.stjosephlakeland.org. Very Rev. Timothy P. Labo, V.F.; Rev. Julius Lopez, Parochial Vicar. Total in Residence 1; Total Staff 1.

MELBOURNE. *Catholic Campus Ministry at Florida Institute of Technology* (1958) Florida Institute of Technology, 150 W. University Blvd., Melbourne, 32901-6988. Tel: 321-674-8045; Fax: 321-674-8938; Email: dbailey@fit.edu; Email: ljaime@fit.edu; Email: mneeland@fit.edu; Web: www.fit.edu. Revs. Michael Neeland, S.D.S., Campus Min.; Douglas S. Bailey, S.D.S., Prov. Asst.; Deacon Thomas Stauffacher, Spiritual Adviser / Care Services; Lyan Jaime, Admin. Asst. Total Staff 3.

OVIEDO. *Catholic Campus Ministry at the University of Central Florida*, The Catholic Center at Northview, 3925 Lockwood Blvd., Oviedo, 32765. Tel: 407-392-0824; Email: info@ccmknights.com; Web: www.ccmknights.com. Bros. John McCabe, Campus Min.; Adam Neri, B.H., Dir. Adult Enrollment 500.

WINTER PARK. *Catholic Campus Ministry at Rollins College*, Rollins College c/o Dr. Joan Davison, 1000 Holt Ave., Box 2762, Winter Park, 32789. Tel: 407-647-3392; Tel: 407-646-2551; Fax: 407-647-4492; Email: jdavison@rollins.edu; Email: ddavison@rollins.edu; Web: stmargaretmary.org. Very Rev. Richard Walsh, Campus Min.

[H] MISCELLANEOUS

ORLANDO. **Catholic Volunteers in Florida, Inc.*, 50 E. Robinson St., 32801. Tel: 407-426-7771; Fax: 407-426-7774; Email: volunteer@cvif.org; Web: www.cvif.org. P.O. Box 536476, 32853-6476. Elizabeth Buckley, Exec. Dir.; Valarie Amica, Prog. Dir. National recruitment for placement of full-time volunteers in one-year service assignments in Florida. Co-sponsored by Florida's bishops, Sisters of St. Joseph of St. Augustine, and New Hope Charities. The Episcopal Advisor is Bishop John G. Noonan. Total Staff 3; Lay Volunteers 18.

The Florida Catholic Serving the Dioceses of Orlando, Palm Beach & Venice. 50 E. Robinson St., 32801. Tel: 888-275-9953. Mailing Address: P.O. Box 4993, 32802. Tel: 407-373-0075; Fax: 407-373-0087; Email: aborowski@thefloridacatholic.org; Web: www.thefloridacatholic.org. Ann B. Slade, Assoc. Publisher.

LAKELAND. **Resurrection Catholic School Endowment Fund, Inc.*, 3720 Old Road 37, Lakeland, 33813. Tel: 863-644-3931; Email: dschwope@rcslakeland.org; Web: www.rcslakeland.org. Mrs. Deborah Schwope, Prin.; Very Rev. Charles Viviano, V.F.

RELIGIOUS INSTITUTES OF MEN REPRESENTED IN THE DIOCESE

For further details refer to the corresponding bracketed number in the Religious Institutes of Men or Women section.

[0140]—*Augustinian Monks of the Primitive Observance Priests*—O.S.A. Prim.
[]—*Brotherhood of Hope*—B.H.
[0600]—*Congregation of Holy Cross*—C.S.C.
[0275]—*Congregation of the Carmelites of Mary Immaculate*—C.M.I.
[1210]—*Congregation of the Missionaries of St. Charles (Scalabrians)*—C.S.
[1070]—*Congregation of the Most Holy Redeemer (Redemptorists)*—C.Ss.R.
[0720]—*Missionaries of Our Lady of LaSalette*—M.S.
[0870]—*Missionaries of the Company of Mary (Montfort Missionaries)*—S.M.M.
[1060]—*Missionaries of the Precious Blood*—C.PP.S.
[0910]—*Missionary Oblates of Mary Immaculate*—O.M.I.
[0860]—*Missionhurst Congregation of the Immaculate Heart of Mary*—C.I.C.M.
[0260]—*Order of Discalced Carmelites*—O.C.D.
[0520]—*Order of Friars Minor*—O.F.M.
[0140]—*Order of St. Augustine*—O.S.A.
[1010]—*Order of St. Paul the First Hermit (Pauline Fathers)*—O.S.P.P.E.
[1190]—*Salesians of Don Bosco*—S.D.B.
[1340]—*Society of Divine Vocations*—S.D.V.
[1200]—*Society of the Divine Savior (Salvatorians)*—S.D.S.
[0560]—*Third Order Regular of Saint Francis*—T.O.R.

RELIGIOUS INSTITUTES OF WOMEN REPRESENTED IN THE DIOCESE

[0990]—*Congregation of the Sisters of Divine Providence*—C.D.P.
[3840]—*Congregation of the Sisters of St. Joseph of Carondelet*—C.S.J.
[0810]—*Daughters of the Heart of Mary*—D.H.M.
[1070-13]—*Dominican Sisters of Adrian, MI*—O.P.
[1115]—*Dominican Sisters of Peace (Dominicans)*—O.P.
[1230]—*Franciscan Sisters of Christian Charity*—O.S.F.
[2720]—*Mission Helpers of the Sacred Heart*—M.H.S.H.
[]—*Missionary Catechist Sisters (Hermanas Misioneras Catequistas)*—M.C.S.
[]—*Religious Sisters Filippini*—M.F.P.
[]—*Servants of the Pierced Hearts of Jesus and Mary*—S.C.T.J.M.
[1070-03]—*Sinsinawa Dominican Sisters*—O.P.
[]—*Sisters for Christian Community*—S.F.C.C.
[2187]—*Sisters of Incarnation-Consecration-Mission*—I.C.M.
[]—*Sisters of Mercy* (Ireland)—R.S.M.
[2990]—*Sisters of Notre Dame*—S.N.D.
[3000]—*Sisters of Notre Dame de Namur*—S.N.D.deN.
[3340]—*Sisters of Providence*—S.P.
[1650]—*Sisters of St. Francis of Philadelphia*—O.S.F.
[1805]—*Sisters of St. Francis of the Neumann Communities*—O.S.F.
[3890]—*Sisters of St. Joseph of Peace*—C.S.J.P.

[1990]—*Sisters of the Holy Names of Jesus and Mary*—S.N.J.M.
[]—*Sisters of the Immaculate Heart of Mary Reparatrix*—I.H.M.R.
[]—*Society of Sisters for the Church*—S.S.C.
[]—*Ursuline Sisters of the Eastern Province*—O.S.U.

NECROLOGY

† Sheedy, Valentine, (Retired), Died Jul. 14, 2018
† Benitez, Eduardo, (Retired), Died Apr. 21, 2018
† Hamilton, Edward A., (Retired), Died Apr. 6, 2018
† Ross, Kenneth, (Retired), Died Nov. 10, 2018

An asterisk (*) denotes an organization that has established tax-exempt status directly with the IRS and is not covered by the USCCB Group Ruling.

Diocese of Owensboro

(Dioecesis Owensburgensis)

Most Reverend

WILLIAM F. MEDLEY

Bishop of Owensboro; ordained May 22, 1982; appointed Bishop of Owensboro December 15, 2009; ordained February 10, 2010. *Mailing Address: 600 Locust St., Owensboro, KY 42301.*

McRaith Catholic Center: 600 Locust St., Owensboro, KY 42301. Tel: 270-683-1545; Fax: 270-683-6883.

Web: www.owensborodiocese.org

Email: kevin.kauffeld@pastoral.org

CREATED DECEMBER 9, 1937.

Square Miles 12,502.

Erected February 23, 1938.

Comprises the following thirty-two Counties in the western part of the State of Kentucky: Allen, Ballard, Breckinridge, Butler, Caldwell, Calloway, Carlisle, Christian, Crittenden, Daviess, Edmonson, Fulton, Graves, Grayson, Hancock, Henderson, Hickman, Hopkins, Livingston, Logan, Lyon, McCracken, McLean, Marshall, Muhlenberg, Ohio, Simpson, Todd, Trigg, Union, Warren and Webster.

For legal titles of parishes and diocesan institutions, consult the Catholic Pastoral Center.

STATISTICAL OVERVIEW

Personnel	
Bishop	1
Priests: Diocesan Active in Diocese	54
Priests: Diocesan Active Outside Diocese	4
Priests: Retired, Sick or Absent	11
Number of Diocesan Priests	69
Religious Priests in Diocese	9
Total Priests in Diocese	78
Extern Priests in Diocese	8
Permanent Deacons in Diocese	39
Total Sisters	170
Parishes	
Parishes	78
With Resident Pastor:	
Resident Diocesan Priests	46
Resident Religious Priests	4
Without Resident Pastor:	
Administered by Priests	28
Professional Ministry Personnel:	
Sisters	15
Lay Ministers	108
Welfare	
Catholic Hospitals	1
Total Assisted	254,516
Homes for the Aged	2
Total Assisted	218
Day Care Centers	1
Total Assisted	100
Specialized Homes	1
Total Assisted	20
Special Centers for Social Services	3
Total Assisted	11,138
Educational	
Colleges and Universities	1
Total Students	1,242
High Schools, Diocesan and Parish	3
Total Students	607
Elementary Schools, Diocesan and Parish	14
Total Students	2,504
Catechesis/Religious Education:	
High School Students	145
Elementary Students	1,511
Total Students under Catholic Instruction	6,009
Teachers in the Diocese:	
Priests	2
Sisters	8
Lay Teachers	322
Vital Statistics	
Receptions into the Church:	
Infant Baptism Totals	709
Minor Baptism Totals	95
Adult Baptism Totals	89
Received into Full Communion	131
First Communions	889
Confirmations	881
Marriages:	
Catholic	188
Interfaith	90
Total Marriages	278
Deaths	530
Total Catholic Population	51,043
Total Population	886,477

Former Bishops—Most Revs. FRANCIS R. COTTON, D.D., First Bishop of Owensboro; ord. June 17, 1920; appt. Dec. 16, 1937; cons. Feb. 24, 1938; died Sept. 25, 1960; HENRY J. SOENNEKER, D.D., Second Bishop of Owensboro; ord. May 26, 1934; appt. March 10, 1961; cons. April 26, 1961; installed May 9, 1961; retired June 17, 1982; died Sept. 24, 1987; JOHN J. MCRAITH, ord. Feb. 21, 1960; appt. Oct. 23, 1982; cons. Dec. 15, 1982; retired Jan. 5, 2009; died March 19, 2017.

McRaith Catholic Center—600 Locust St., Owensboro, 42301. Tel: 270-683-1545; Fax: 270-683-6883. Refer all official business to this address.

Vicar General—Very Rev. J. PATRICK REYNOLDS, J.C.L., Our Lady of Lourdes, 4029 Frederica St., Owensboro, 42301-7459. Tel: 270-684-5369.

Vicar of Clergy—Rev. JASON MCCLURE, Mailing Address: 600 Locust St., Owensboro, 42301.

Chancellor—MR. KEVIN KAUFFELD.

Vice Chancellor—MS. MARTHA HAGAN.

Administrative Assistant to the Bishop—MS. MARTHA HAGAN.

Archivist—HEIDI TAYLOR-CAUDILL.

Diocesan Tribunal—

Judicial Vicar—Very Rev. PATRICK COONEY, O.S.B., J.C.L.

Promoter of Justice—Very Rev. J. PATRICK REYNOLDS, J.C.L.

Adjutant Judicial Vicar—VACANT.

Defender of the Bond—Very Rev. J. PATRICK REYNOLDS, J.C.L.

Judges—Revs. JOSEPH M. MILLS, J.C.L., (Retired); JOHN R. VAUGHAN, J.C.D.; Very Rev. J. MICHAEL CLARK, J.C.L.

Judicial Assistant—MS. EMILY DANCHISIN.

Advocates—Priests and pastoral ministers of the diocese.

Director/Auditor and Case Promoter—MS. LOUANNE PAYNE.

Notaries—MRS. MARY ANN KURZ; MS. SANDY MORRIS; MS. JENNY SHELTON.

Peritus—MR. MICHAEL FLAHERTY, M.A.; MR. DONALD L. PREUSS, L.M.F.T.

Diocesan Boards and Councils

Diocesan Pastoral Council—(consists of all Parish Council Chairpersons).

Consultors—Revs. EMMANUEL UDOH; RANDY HOWARD; JOHN M. THOMAS; DARRELL VENTERS; RICHARD C. MEREDITH; Very Rev. J. PATRICK REYNOLDS, J.C.L.; Rev. JASON WAYNE MCCLURE.

Deans—Revs. DANIEL C. DILLARD; LARRY MCBRIDE; TONY JONES; ROBERT DRURY; JOSHUA A. MCCARTY; GREGORY G. TRAWICK, J.C.L.; BRIAN J. ROBY; SUNEESH MATHEW, H.G.N.; ALBERT BREMER.

Age Group Six Representative—Rev. RICHARD M. POWERS.

Priests' Council—Revs. DANIEL C. DILLARD; LARRY MCBRIDE; TONY JONES; ROBERT DRURY; JOSHUA A. MCCARTY; GREGORY G. TRAWICK, J.C.L.; BRIAN J. ROBY; SUNEESH MATHEW, H.G.N.; ALBERT BREMER; EMMANUEL UDOH; RANDY HOWARD; JOHN M. THOMAS; DARRELL VENTERS; RICHARD C. MEREDITH; Very Rev. J. PATRICK REYNOLDS, J.C.L.; Revs. JASON WAYNE MCCLURE; RICHARD M. POWERS.

Pastoral Office for Administration—MR. RAYMOND PURK, CFO; KIM HAIRE, Controller.

Pastoral Office for Stewardship—MR. KEVIN KAUFFELD, Dir.

Diocesan Finance Council—MS. JANET BERRY; Sisters BARBARA JEAN HEAD, O.S.U.; SARAH MURPHY FORD; MR. CHARLES KAMUF; MR. JOSEPH HANCOCK, Consultor; MR. BOB OGLE; Very Rev. J. PATRICK REYNOLDS, J.C.L.; MR. JT FULKERSON; Rev. JERRY RINEY; VICKI STOGSDILL; MS. REBECCA SCHWARTZ; MR. BRIAN WRIGHT.

Pastoral Office for Education—

Superintendent of Schools—MS. ANN FLAHERTY.

Assistant Superintendent of Schools—MR. DAVID KESSLER.

Director of Office for Faith Formation—VACANT.

Committee for Education—MR. JOE BLAND; MR. PATRICK CAIRNEY; Rev. ROBERT DRURY; MS. STEPHANIE FREY; MS. TINA KASEY; MS. ANGIE KRAMPE; MR. JAMES P. MATTINGLY; Rev. JOHN R. VAUGHAN, J.C.D.; MR. BEN WARRELL.

Director of Ecumenism—Rev. ANDREW GARNER.

Youth & Young Adult Ministry—MR. CHARLIE HARDESTY, Dir.

Gasper River Catholic Youth Camp and Retreat Center—MR. BEN WARRELL, Dir.

Director of Communications for the Diocese of Owensboro—Western Kentucky Catholic MS. TINA KASEY.

Editor and Coordinator Diocesan Publications—MS. ELIZABETH WONG-BARNSTEAD.

Media Specialist for the Diocese—MS. LAURA CLARKE.

Co-Coordinator of Worship—Rev. BRANDON WILLIAMS; MS. LAUREN JOHNSON.

Diocesan Liturgical Committee—Rev. CARL MCCARTHY; MS. PATTY BROWN; MR. MICHAEL BOGDAN; Rev. BRANDON WILLIAMS; MS. LAUREN JOHNSON; Rev. JOHN M. THOMAS; Sr. ALICIA COOMES, O.S.U.

Pastoral Office for Spiritual Life—Mount St. Joseph, 8001 Cummings Rd., Maple Mount, 42356. Tel: 270-229-0200; Fax: 270-229-0279. Sr. MARY MATTHIAS WARD, O.S.U., Dir.

Cursillo—Rev. TOM BUCKMAN, St. Pius X, 3418 Hwy. 144, Owensboro, 42303. Tel: 270-684-4745; Ms. FELICIA ELLIOTT, Lay Dir.

Catholic Charities—Tel: 270-852-8343. RICHARD MURPHY, Dr. Programs & Prog. Devel. Board Members: Rev. ED BRADLEY, Ex Officio; Sr. JOSEPH ANGELA BOONE, O.S.U., Ex Officio; DR. FRED LITKE; TIM HAMMOND; MARLA BERTSCHINGER; VANCE WEBB;

DEBBIE WEBB; IGNATIUS C. PAYNE JR.; NICK NICHOLS; LISA PRENDERGAST; VERONICA WILHITE; PAUL MONSOUR.
Catholic Campaign for Human Development—RICHARD MURPHY, Dir.
Catholic Relief Service—RICHARD MURPHY, Dir.
Pastoral Office for Social Concerns—RICHARD MURPHY, Dir.
Social Concerns Committee—RICHARD MURPHY; MR. JOE ABEL; MS. RANNI DILLARD; MR. MICHAEL BASILE; BRANDON SWAGGART; NOLA COURTNEY; ED HUFF; JOHN BLANKENDAAL.
Office for Safe Environment for the Protection of Children and Young People—MS. MOLLY THOMPSON, Coord.
Respect Life Office—RICHARD MURPHY.
African-American Office—VERONICA WILHITE, Dir.
Hispanic Office—Deacon CHRIS GUTIERREZ, Dir.
Office for Youth and Young Adult Ministry for Hispanics—VACANT.
Justice for Immigrants—VACANT.
Pastoral Office of Family Life—MR. DANNY MAY, Dir.
Family Life Committee—MR. DANNY MAY; AMANDA REFFITT; JOHN MCCARTY; CAROLYN MCCARTY; MARTHA WINN; SARAH RICE; AUSTIN RICE; AARON CARRICO; STEPHANIE CARRICO; SUZANNE PADGETT; Rev. MICHAEL WILLIAMS.
Natural Family Planning—Billings Ovulation Method: MICHELLE ROBERTS, Owensboro; MARTHA WINN, Bowling Green; JENNY RUSH, Hopkinsville; LYNDA HUTTON, Paducah; RONI MUDD, Leitchfield.
Society for the Propagation of the Faith—Rev. RAY CLARK.
Vicar of Clergy—Rev. JASON MCCLURE.
Priest Personnel Committee—Very Rev. J. PATRICK REYNOLDS, J.C.L., Vicar Gen. & Ex Officio; Revs. RYAN HARPOLE; THOMAS J. BUCKMAN; JOHN M. THOMAS; BRUCE MCCARTY; JOHN R. VAUGHAN, J.C.D.; JASON WAYNE MCCLURE, Vicar for Clergy & Ex Officio.
Vocations Office—Rev. JASON WAYNE MCCLURE, Dir.; DR. FRED LITKE, Assoc. Dir., Catholic Pastoral Center, 600 Locust St., Owensboro, 42301-2130. Tel: 270-683-1545; Fax: 270-683-6883.
Ongoing Formation of Priests—Rev. ANTHONY J. SHONIS.
**Roman Catholic Diocese of Owensboro Charitable Trust Fund, Inc.*—MR. RAYMOND PURK; Most Rev. WILLIAM F. MEDLEY; MR. KEVIN KAUFFELD.

Organizations

St. Vincent de Paul Society—IGNATIUS C. PAYNE JR., Diocesan Council Pres., 3880 Bordeaux Loop, S., Owensboro, 42303. Tel: 270-683-6525.
Scouting Activities—Rev. KENNETH J. MIKULCIK, J.C.L., Chap., 600 Locust St., Owensboro, 42301. Tel: 270-683-1545.
Holy Childhood Association—Rev. RAY CLARK.
Teens Encounter Christ—Rev. DANIEL C. DILLARD.
Legion of Mary—VACANT.
Serra Club—Rev. RAY CLARK, Chap.
Owensboro Chapter—MR. ERNIE TALIAFERRO, Pres., Tel: 270-683-1545.
Mercy Health Partners - Lourdes, Inc.—1530 Lone Oak Rd., P.O. Box 7100, Paducah, 42002-7100. Tel: 270-444-2444; Fax: 270-444-2980. MICHAEL YUNGMANN, Pres. & CEO.
Victim Assistance Coordinator—MS. LOUANNE PAYNE, Tel: 270-852-8369; Email: louanne.payne@pastoral.org.
Birthright—TERRI LAHUGH, Dir., 512 W. 7th St., Owensboro, 42301. Tel: 270-683-1103; Email: birthright839@bellsouth.net. Hours: Mon.-Fri. 9am-noon.
Daughters of Isabella—Rev. Msgr. BERNARD POWERS, State Chap., (Retired); ANN NEWBY, State Regent, Tel: 270-685-4001; JUANITA STINOGEL, Owensboro Circle #241 Regent, Tel: 270-683-4192; MARTHA FLOYD, Paducah Circle #258 St. Francis de Sales, Tel: 270-443-1640.

CLERGY, PARISHES, MISSIONS AND PAROCHIAL SCHOOLS

CITY OF OWENSBORO

(DAVIESS COUNTY)

1—ST. STEPHEN CATHEDRAL (1839)
614 Locust St., 42301. Tel: 270-683-6525; Fax: 270-683-3621; Email: cathedral.info@pastoral.org; Web: ststephencathedral.org. Revs. Jerry Riney, Rector; Sinoj Pynadath, Parochial Vicar; Crissy Stevenson, Youth Min.; Donna Tarantino, Dir. of Ministries & Volunteers; Mrs. Donna Murphy, RCIA Coord.; Mr. James Wells, Music Min.; Eddy McFarland, Business Mgr.; Beni Howell, Sec.
Chapel—Blessed Sacrament, [CEM] 602 Sycamore St., 42301. Tel: 270-926-4741; Email: blessedsac602@gmail.com; Web: www.blessedsacramentchapel.org. 610 Locust St., 42301-2130. Sr. Jeannette Fennewald, S.S.N.D., Pastoral Assoc. Families 84.

2—BLESSED MOTHER (1948)
601 E. 23rd St., 42303. Tel: 270-683-8444; Email: bmcbusiness1@outlook.com. Very Rev. J. Michael Clark, J.C.L.; Deacon Bill Bach; Patty Woerter, Liturgy & Music; Mary Colburn, Business Mgr. & Admin.; Cyndi Vaughan, Office Asst.
Res.: 515 E. 22nd St., 42303.
Catechesis Religious Program—Nicholas Hardesty, D.R.E.; Christina Banard, Youth Min. Students 71.

3—THE IMMACULATE (1954)
2516 Christie Pl., 42301. Tel: 270-683-0689; Email: sbelcher@immaculateparish.org; Web: Immaculateparish.org. Rev. John R. Vaughan, J.C.D.; Susan Belcher, Sec.
Res.: 2601 Christie Pl., 42301.
Catechesis Religious Program—Email: dwillis@immaculateparish.org. Diane Willis, D.F.F., D.R.E. Students 84.

4—SS. JOSEPH AND PAUL (1887)
609 E. 4th St., 42303. Tel: 270-683-5641; Fax: 270-685-4766; Email: aprilsjpc@owens.twcbc.com; Email: debbiesjpc@owens.twcbc.com; Web: www.stjpc.org. Revs. Jean Rene Kalombo; Basilio Az Cuc.
Catechesis Religious Program—423 Clay St., 42303. Students 117.
Mission—Good Samaritan Home, 1601 Pearl St., Daviess Co. 42303.

5—OUR LADY OF LOURDES (1959)
4029 Frederica St., 42301. Tel: 270-684-5369; Email: hbennett@lourdescatholicchurch.com. Very Rev. J. Patrick Reynolds, J.C.L.
Catechesis Religious Program—Email: jbennett@lourdescatholicchurch. Jessica Bennett, D.R.E. Students 77.
Child Care—Our Lady of Lourdes Day Care, 4005 Frederica St., 42301. Children 69.

6—ST. PIUS TENTH PARISH (1957)
3418 Hwy. 144, 42303. Tel: 270-684-4745; Email: frtom@stpiustenthparish.org; Web: www.stpiustentparish.org. Rev. Tom Buckman; Deacon Nick Nichols; Michelle Roberts, Business Mgr.
Res.: 3512 E. Sixth St., 42303.
Catechesis Religious Program—Vicki Conder, D.R.E.; Joe Wathen, D.R.E.; Matt Knight, Youth Min. Students 19.
Child Care—St. Pius Tenth Day Care, Tel: 270-684-7456. Children 83.

7—PRECIOUS BLOOD (1960)
3306 Fenmore St., 42301. Tel: 270-684-6888; Email: pblandford77@gmail.com. Rev. Suneesh Mathew Kulathanapatikal, H.G.N., (India).
Catechesis Religious Program—Email: rosanne31843@gmail.com. Sr. Rosanne Spalding, O.S.U., D.R.E. Students 36.

8—ST. RAPHAEL (1842) [CEM] Closed. Records at Diocesan Archives, 600 Locust St., Owensboro, Tel: 270-683-1545. St. Raphael Cemetery, est. 1847, became interparochial when church burned in 1983.

OUTSIDE THE CITY OF OWENSBORO

AURORA, MARSHALL CO., ST. HENRY (1967) [CEM]
16097 U.S. Hwy. 68 E., Hardin, 42048. Tel: 270-474-8058; Fax: 270-474-9567; Email: stchrch@bellsouth.net; Web: sainthenryparish.net. Rev. Gregory G. Trawick, J.C.L.; Deacon Randall Potempa.
Catechesis Religious Program—Peggy Potempa, D.R.E. Students 11.

AXTEL, BRECKINRIDGE CO., ST. ANTHONY (1812) [CEM]
1654 S. Hwy. 79, Hardinsburg, 40143. Tel: 270-257-2132; Email: sallyyountsac@att.net. Rev. Roy Anthony Stevenson; Deacon Michael Wiedemer.
Catechesis Religious Program—Mrs. Gale Hinton, D.R.E. Students 60.

BARDWELL, CARLISLE CO., ST. CHARLES (1891) [CEM]
6922 State Rte. 408, Bardwell, 42023. Tel: 270-642-2586; Email: sghayden@wk.net. Rev. Chrispin Oneko, (Kenya).
Catechesis Religious Program—Students 19.

BEAVER DAM, OHIO CO., HOLY REDEEMER (1962)
13th & Madison Sts., P.O. Box 106, Beaver Dam, 42320. Email: holyredeemercath@bellsouth.net. Rev. Julio Barrera.
Catechesis Religious Program—Students 67.

BIG CLIFTY, GRAYSON CO., ST. MARY, Closed. Records kept at St. Paul's Church, 1821 St. Paul Rd., Leitchfield, KY 42754. Tel: 270-242-7436.

BOWLING GREEN, WARREN CO.

1—HOLY SPIRIT (1970)
4754 Smallhouse Rd., Bowling Green, 42104-4141. Tel: 270-842-7777; Email: jmthomas@holyspiritcatholic.org; Email: Lori@holyspiritcatholic.org; Web: www.holyspiritcatholic.org. Revs. John M. Thomas; Jude Okeoma, Parochial Vicar; John Paul Mang, Parochial Vicar; Deacon Matthew Keyser; Lori Lewis, Pastoral Assoc.
Catechesis Religious Program—Students 872.

2—ST. JOSEPH (1859)
434 Church Ave., Bowling Green, 42101. Tel: 270-842-2525; Email: ryan.harpole@pastoral.org; Web: www.stjosephbg.org. Revs. Ryan Harpole; Gary Clark.
Res.: 401 Church Ave., Bowling Green, 42101.
Catechesis Religious Program—Students 240.

BROWN'S VALLEY, DAVIESS CO., ST. ANTHONY (1902) [CEM]
261 St. Anthony Rd., Utica, 42376. Tel: 270-733-4341 ; Email: stabv@bellsouth.net. Rev. Mark A. Buckner; Deacon Tim Nugent.
Catechesis Religious Program—Tammy Nugent, D.R.E. Students 49.

CADIZ, TRIGG CO., ST. STEPHEN (1966)
1698 Canton Rd., Cadiz, 42211. Tel: 270-522-3801; Fax: 270-522-3901; Email: ststephencath387@bellsouth.net; Web: ststephencc.com. Rev. Gregory G. Trawick, J.C.L.; Deacon Randall Potempa.
Catechesis Religious Program—Ms. April Washer, C.R.E. Students 23.

CALHOUN, MCLEAN CO., ST. SEBASTIAN (1871) [CEM]
180 State Rte. 136 W., Calhoun, 42327-9521. Tel: 270-273-3185; Email: stsebch@bellsouth.net. Rev. John Ighacho, (Kenya).
Res.: 445 Main St., Calhoun, 42327-9521.
Catechesis Religious Program—Students 35.

CALVERT CITY, MARSHALL CO., ST. PIUS TENTH (1954)
777 Fifth Ave., P.O. Box 495, Calvert City, 42029. Tel: 270-395-4727; Email: stpiusx@stpiusx.us. Rev. Brian A. Johnson.
Res.: 723 Fifth Ave., Calvert City, 42029.
Catechesis Religious Program—Email: crecalvertcity@gmail.com. Paula Schmidt, D.R.E. Students 46.

CENTRAL CITY, MUHLENBERG CO., ST. JOSEPH (1886)
109 S. Third St., Central City, 42330. Tel: 270-754-1164; Email: accounting@stjosephcc.org. Rev. Joshua A. McCarty; Deacon Donald Adams.
Res.: 113 S. Third St., Central City, 42330. Web: www.stjosephcc.org.
Catechesis Religious Program—Students 33.

CLARKSON, GRAYSON CO., ST. ELIZABETH OF HUNGARY (1906) [CEM]
306 Clifty Ave., P.O. Box 273, Clarkson, 42726. Tel: 270-242-4414; Email: saintelizabethclarkson@windstream.net. Rev. Steve Hohman.
Res.: 1821 St. Paul Rd., Leitchfield, 42754.
Catechesis Religious Program—Students 26.

CLINTON, HICKMAN CO., ST. JUDE (1982)
308 Mayfield Rd., Clinton, 42031. Tel: 270-653-6869; Email: jjhobbs@windstream.net. Rev. Robert Drury.
Catechesis Religious Program—Students 4.

CLOVERPORT, BRECKINRIDGE CO., ST. ROSE (1857) [CEM]
118 Chestnut St., Cloverport, 40111. Tel: 270-788-6422. Rev. Dan Kreutzer.
Catechesis Religious Program—Students 26.

CURDSVILLE, DAVIESS CO., ST. ELIZABETH
Mailing Address: 6143 First St., P.O. Box 9-A, Curdsville, 42334. Tel: 270-229-4134; Email: selizabethcville@gmail.com. Judy Schadler, Contact Person.

DAWSON SPRINGS, HOPKINS CO., RESURRECTION
530 Industrial Park Rd., Dawson Springs, 42408. Tel: 270-797-8665; Tel: 270-383-4743; Email: immaculatecc@bellsouth.net; Email: frdavidkennedy@aol.com. Rev. David Kennedy; Deacon Michael Marsili.
Catechesis Religious Program—Students 11.

EARLINGTON, HOPKINS CO., IMMACULATE CONCEPTION (1847)
112 S. Day St., Earlington, 42410. Tel: 270-383-4743; Email: kfct@umich.edu. Rev. David Kennedy; Deacon Michael Marsili.
Catechesis Religious Program—Students 3.

EDDYVILLE, LYON CO., ST. MARK CHURCH (1990)
302 Peachtree Ln., Eddyville, 42038. Tel: 270-388-2133; Email: kfct@umich.edu; Web: stmarkeddyville.weconnect.com. Rev. Jojy Joseph, H.G.N., (India); Deacon Paul Bachi.
Res.: 300 Peachtree Ln., Eddyville, 42038.
Catechesis Religious Program—Students 8.

FANCY FARM, GRAVES CO., ST. JEROME (1836) [CEM]
P.O. Box 38, Fancy Farm, 42039. Tel: 270-623-8181; Email: stjerome@wk.net; Web: www.stjeromefancyfarm.com. Rev. Darrell Venters.
Catechesis Religious Program—Students 202.

FANCY FARM, HICKMAN CO., ST. DENIS (1914) [CEM]
2758 Hwy. 1748 W., Fancy Farm, 42039. Tel: 270-642-2586; Email: jldenise@bellsouth.net.

Mailing Address: 6922 State Rte. 408, Bardwell, 42023. Rev. Chrispin Oneko, (Kenya).
Catechesis Religious Program—Students 17.

FORDSVILLE, OHIO CO., ST. JOHN THE BAPTIST (1893)
67 Smith St., P.O. Box 127, Fordsville, 42343.
Tel: 270-276-3619; Email: roby042569@gmail.com; Email: HaganD4001@gmail.com. Rev. Brian Roby.

FRANKLIN, SIMPSON CO., ST. MARY (1880) [CEM]
403 N. Main St., Franklin, 42134. Tel: 270-586-4515; Web: www.stmarysfranklin.cc. P.O. Box 388, Franklin, 42135. Rev. Daniel C. Dillard.
Res.: 408 N. College St., P.O. Box 388, Franklin, 42135-0388.
Catechesis Religious Program—Email: carole.j.ritter@gmail.com. Carole Ritter, D.R.E. Students 42.

FULTON, FULTON CO., ST. EDWARD (1932)
504 Eddings St., Fulton, 42041. Tel: 270-472-2742; Email: stedwardky@bellsouth.net. Rev. Robert Drury.
Catechesis Religious Program—Students 18.

GRAND RIVERS, LIVINGSTON CO., ST. ANTHONY OF PADUA (1986)
1518 J.H. O'Bryan Ave., P.O. Box 447, Grand Rivers, 42045. Tel: 270-508-2428; Email: stpiusx@stpiusx.us; Web: www.stanthonygrandrivers.org. Rev. Brian Johnson.
Catechesis Religious Program—Students 3.

GRAYSON SPRINGS, GRAYSON CO., ST. AUGUSTINE (1815) [CEM]
c/o St. Anthony Church, 1256 St. Anthony Church Rd., Clarkson, 42726. Tel: 270-242-4791; Email: stanthony1256@windstream.net. Rev. Babu Kulathumkal, H.G.N., (India); Deacon William Grant.
Catechesis Religious Program—Students 6.

GUTHRIE, TODD CO., ST. FRANCIS OF ASSISI CATHOLIC CHURCH (2016)
7600 Russellville Rd., P.O. Box 297, Guthrie, 42234.
Tel: 270-265-5263; Email: stfrancisofassis@outlook.com. Revs. Albert Bremer, Sacramental Min.; Ken Mikulcik, Sacramental Min.; Deacon Heriberto Rodriguez, Parish Life Coord.

HARDINSBURG, BRECKINRIDGE CO., ST. ROMUALD (1811) [CEM]
394 N. Hwy. 259, Hardinsburg, 40143.
Tel: 270-756-2356; Email: stromuald@bbtel.com. Rev. Anthony Jones; Deacon Tony Anthony.
Catechesis Religious Program—Students 85.

HAWESVILLE, HANCOCK CO., IMMACULATE CONCEPTION (1871) [CEM]
240 Court Sq., P.O. Box 219, Hawesville, 42348.
Tel: 270-927-8419; Email: bmonetathchi@aol.com. Rev. Terry Devine.
Res.: 190 Judith Lynn, P.O. Box 219, Hawesville, 42348. Tel: 270-927-8419; Email: bmonetathchi@aol.com; Web: icscchurch.org.
Catechesis Religious Program—Students 49.

HENDERSON, HENDERSON CO., HOLY NAME OF JESUS (1886) [CEM]
511 Second St., Henderson, 42420. Tel: 270-826-2096 ; Fax: 270-827-1494; Email: holyname@holynameparish.net; Web: www.holynameparish.net. Revs. Larry McBride; Maury D. Riney, Parochial Vicar; Anthony J. Shonis, Parochial Vicar; Deacons Richard Beaven; John Prough; Jaime Tiu; Joseph Loeffler.
School—Holy Name of Jesus School, (Grades PreK-8), 628 Second St., Henderson, 42420.
Tel: 270-827-3425; Fax: 270-827-4027; Email: jeadens@holynameschool.org; Web: www.holynameschool.org. Julie Eadens, Pres.; Scottie Koonce, Prin. Lay Teachers 27; Ursuline Sisters 1; Students 413.
Catechesis Religious Program—Email: rwheeler@holynameparish.net; Email: jeadens@holynameschool.org. Julie Eadens, Pres.; Ms. Rose Wheeler, D.R.E. Students 499.

HENSHAW, UNION CO., ST. AMBROSE (1832) [CEM]
P.O. Box 256, Sturgis, 42459. Tel: 270-333-1832; Email: stambrosercc@gmail.com. Rev. Ryan Harpole; Sr. Alicia Coomes, O.S.U., Pastoral Assoc.
Church: 5194 S.R. 270 W., Morganfield, 42437.
Catechesis Religious Program—Tel: 270-333-2806. Students 5.

HICKMAN, FULTON CO., SACRED HEART (1853)
411 Moulton St., Hickman, 42050-1327.
Tel: 270-236-2071; Email: ltbjr@ken-tennwireless.com. Rev. Robert Drury; Butch Busby, Contact Person, Email: sheart@zitomedia.net.
Catechesis Religious Program—1203 Lattus Rd., Hickman, 42050.

HOPKINSVILLE, CHRISTIAN CO., SS. PETER AND PAUL (1872)
902 E. Ninth St., Hopkinsville, 42240.
Tel: 270-885-8522. Revs. Richard C. Meredith; Michael Charles Ajigo Abiero; Deacons Timothy D. Barnes; William E. Sweet; Roberto Cruz; Timothy Schlueter.
School—SS. Peter and Paul School, (Grades PreK-8), Tel: 270-886-0172; Email: kwyatt@stsppschool.org. Katherine Wyatt, Prin.; Jennifer Groves, Sec. Lay Teachers 12; Students 125.
Catechesis Religious Program—Email: ljdowns@stsppchurch.org. Libby Downs, D.R.E. Students 100.

IRVINGTON, BRECKINRIDGE CO., HOLY GUARDIAN ANGELS (1898) [CEM]
301 W. High St., P.O. Box 155, Irvington, 40146.
Tel: 270-547-6422; Email: dan.krentzer@pastoral.org. Rev. Dan Kreutzer.
Catechesis Religious Program—Email: pmillay@gmail.com. Peter Millay, D.R.E. Students 31.

KNOTTSVILLE, DAVIESS CO., ST. WILLIAM (1887) [CEM]
9515 Hwy. 144, Philpot, 42366. Tel: 270-281-4802; Email: connie.lemmons@yahoo.com. Rev. Augusty Valomchalil.
Res.: 6007 St. Lawrence Rd., Philpot, 42366.
School—Mary Carrico Catholic School, (Grades PreK-8), Tel: 270-281-5526; Email: marthawarrenmccs144@yahoo.com. Clergy 1; Lay Teachers 6; Students 80.
Catechesis Religious Program—Nancy Greenwell, D.R.E. Students 109.

LACENTER, BALLARD CO., ST. MARY (1907) [CEM]
P.O. Box 570, LaCenter, 42056. Tel: 270-665-5551; Email: stmcc@brtc.net. Rev. Emmanuel Udoh.
Church: 624 Broadway, P.O. Box 570, LaCenter, 42056. Tel: 270-665-5654.
Catechesis Religious Program—Theresa Wilkins, D.R.E. Students 4.

LEITCHFIELD, GRAYSON CO., ST. JOSEPH, [CEM]
204 N. Main St., Leitchfield, 42754.
Tel: 270-259-3028; Email: stjoseph1840@yahoo.com; Web: stjosephch.org. Rev. Tony Bickett.
Catechesis Religious Program—Students 50.

LEWISPORT, HANCOCK CO., ST. COLUMBA (1850) [CEM]
815 Pell St., P.O. Box 358, Lewisport, 42351.
Tel: 270-295-3682; Email: bmonetathchi@aol.com. Rev. Terry Devine.
Res.: 190 Judith Lynn, P.O. Box 219, Hawesville, 42348. Tel: 270-927-8419; Web: icscchurch.org.
Catechesis Religious Program—Students 28.

LIVERMORE, MCLEAN CO., ST. CHARLES BORROMEO (1917)
180 Hwy. 136 W., Calhoun, 42327. Tel: 270-273-3185 ; Email: stsebch@bellsouth.net. Rev. John Ighacho, (Kenya).
Church: 506 Hill Ave., Livermore, 42352. Web: www.ccofmc.org.
Res./Rectory: 445 Main St., Calhoun, 42327.
Catechesis Religious Program—Students 18.

MADISONVILLE, HOPKINS CO., CHRIST THE KING (1969)
1600 Kingsway Dr., Madisonville, 42431.
Tel: 270-821-5494; Email: office.ctk@madisonville.org. Rev. Carl McCarthy; Patricia L. Brown, Pastoral Assoc.
School—Christ the King School, (Grades PreK-8), 1500 Kingsway Dr., Madisonville, 42431.
Tel: 270-821-8271; Fax: 270-825-9394; Email: office@ctksmadinsolville.com. Beth Herrmann, Prin. Lay Teachers 10; Students 123.
Catechesis Religious Program—Students 60.
Child Care—Preschool, Tel: 270-821-3954. Students 41.

MARION, CRITTENDEN CO., ST. WILLIAM (1962) [CEM]
860 S. Main St., Marion, 42064. Rev. Ryan Harpole.
Res.: 1317 N. Main, Sturgis, 42459.
Catechesis Religious Program—Students 14.

MAYFIELD, GRAVES CO., ST. JOSEPH (1887) [CEM]
702 W. Broadway St., Mayfield, 42066.
Tel: 270-247-2843; Web: stjosephmayfield.com. Rev. Eric D. Riley; Sr. Eloisa Solano, Pastoral Assoc.; Deacon Michael Clapp, Pastoral Assoc.
Catechesis Religious Program—Christie Scarbrough, Business Mgr.; Wanda Shelby, C.R.E. Students 182.

MCQUADY, BRECKINRIDGE CO., ST. MARY-OF-THE-WOODS (1870) [CEM 2]
1654 Hwy. 79 S., Hardinsburg, 40143.
Tel: 270-257-2132; Email: sallyyountsac@att.net. Rev. Roy Anthony Stevenson; Deacon Michael Wiedemer.
Church: 4711 Hwy. 105 S., Mc Quady, 40153.
Catechesis Religious Program—Email: galehinton@att.net. Mrs. Gale Hinton, C.R.E. Students 14.

MORGANFIELD, UNION CO.
1—ST. ANN (1877) [CEM]
304 Church St., Morganfield, 42437-1609.
Tel: 270-389-2287; Tel: 270-389-2292; Email: st304@bellsouth.net. Rev. Freddie Byrd.
Catechesis Religious Program—Email: stann304@bellsouth.net. Students 7.
2—SACRED HEART (1812) [CEM]
674 State Rte. 141 N., Morganfield, 42437.
Tel: 270-389-4224; Email: stpeter.sacredheart@gmail.com. 201 E. Market St., Waverly, 42462. Rev. Dave Johnson.
Catechesis Religious Program—Students 2.

MORGANTOWN, BUTLER CO., HOLY TRINITY (1958)
766 Logansport Rd., P.O. Box 222, Morgantown, 42261. Tel: 270-526-3723; Email: holyredeemercath@bellsouth.net. Rev. Julio Barrera.
Res.: 117 13th Rd., P.O. Box 106, Beaver Dam, 42320. Tel: 270-526-3723; Email: holyredeemercath@bellsouth.net.
Catechesis Religious Program—

MURRAY, CALLOWAY CO., ST. LEO (1933)
401 N 12th St., Murray, 42071. Tel: 270-753-2810; Web: www.stleoky.org. Revs. Brandon Williams; Eugene T. Batungbacal, C.Ss.R., Newman House Chap; Deacons Joseph R. Ohnemus; Victor Fromm.
Res.: 1304 Wells Blvd., Murray, 42071.
Catechesis Religious Program—Tel: 270-753-3876; Email: brandon.williams@pastoral.org. Students 94.

OAK GROVE, CHRISTIAN CO., ST. MICHAEL THE ARCHANGEL (1995)
448 State Line Rd., P.O. Box 505, Oak Grove, 42262.
Tel: 270-640-9850; Email: julian.ibemere@pastoral.org. Rev. Julian Ibemere, (Nigeria); Deacons Jack Cheasty; Tom Torson.
Catechesis Religious Program—Students 92.

PADUCAH, MCCRACKEN CO.
1—ST. FRANCIS DE SALES (1848) [CEM]
116 S. Sixth St., Paducah, 42001. Tel: 270-442-1923; Fax: 270-443-4616; Email: office@parishsfds.com; Web: www.parishsfds.com. Rev. Bruce McCarty.
Catechesis Religious Program—Ging Smith, D.R.E. Students 53.
2—ST. JOHN THE EVANGELIST (1839)
6705 Old U.S. Hwy. 45 S., Paducah, 42003.
Tel: 270-554-3810; Fax: 270-534-9163; Email: hwurth@comcast.net; Web: www.stjohnspaducah.com. Rev. Bruce Fogle.
Catechesis Religious Program—Paducah Faith Formation, 377 Highland Blvd., Paducah, 42003. Students 20.
3—ROSARY CHAPEL (1947)
711 Ohio St., P.O. Box 1481, Paducah, 42003.
Tel: 270-444-6383; Email: rosary@bellsouth.net. Rev. Stan Puryear.
Catechesis Religious Program—
4—ST. THOMAS MORE (1944) [CEM]
5645 Blandville Rd., Paducah, 42001-8722.
Tel: 270-534-9000; Email: jill@stmore.org. Revs. Brad Whistle; Albert Bremer; James Hess, Liturgy & Music Dir.; Sr. Celia Sanchez, Hispanic Ministry; Deacon Terry Larbes; Steve DuPerrieu, Office Mgr.
Catechesis Religious Program—Faith Formation, 1241 Elmdale Rd., Paducah, 42003. Students 113.

PEONIA, GRAYSON CO., ST. ANTHONY (1822) [CEM]
1256 St. Anthony Rd., Clarkson, 42726.
Tel: 270-242-4791; Email: stanthony1256@windstream.net. Rev. Babu Kulathumkal, H.G.N., (India); Deacon William Grant.
Catechesis Religious Program—Students 19.

PHILPOT, DAVIESS CO., ST. LAWRENCE (1821) [CEM]
6119 St. Lawrence Rd., Philpot, 42366.
Tel: 270-281-4802; Email: connie.lemmons@yahoo.com. 9515 State Rte. 144, St. William Catholic Church, Philpot, 42366. Rev. Augusty Valomchalil.
Res.: 6007 St. Lawrence Rd., Philpot, 42366. Email: stl_stw@yahoo.com; Email: connie.lemmons@yahoo.com.
Catechesis Religious Program—Nancy Greenwell, D.R.E. Students 15.

PRINCETON, CALDWELL CO., ST. PAUL (1874) [CEM]
813 S. Jefferson, Princeton, 42445. Tel: 270-365-6786 ; Email: jojy.joseph@pastoral.org. Rev. Jojy Joseph, H.G.N., (India).
Catechesis Religious Program—Students 11.

PROVIDENCE, WEBSTER CO., HOLY CROSS
112 S. Day St., Earlington, 42410. Tel: 270-383-4743; Email: david.kennedy@pastoral.org. Rev. David Kennedy; Deacon Michael Marsili.
Church: 730 North Highway 41A, Providence, 42450.
Catechesis Religious Program—Students 1.

REED, HENDERSON CO., ST. AUGUSTINE (1896) [CEM]
16777 Hwy. 60 E., Reed, 42451. Tel: 270-764-1983; Email: jegin.puthenpurackal@pastoral.org; Email: rmurphee@hotmail.com. Rev. Jegin Puthenpurackal, H.G.N., (India).
Res.: 81 Church St., 42301.
Catechesis Religious Program—Students 26.

ROME, DAVIESS CO., ST. MARTIN (1885)
5856 Kentucky 81, 42301. Tel: 270-685-0339; Email: stmartinrome@gmail.com. Rev. Patrick M. Bittel.
Catechesis Religious Program—

RUSSELLVILLE, LOGAN CO., SACRED HEART (1873)
296 W. 6th St., Russellville, 42276.
Tel: 270-726-6963; Email: email@sacredheartrussellville.org; Web: sacredheartrussellville.org. Rev. Ken Mikulcik.
Catechesis Religious Program—Melanie Abney, D.R.E. Students 70.

ST. JOSEPH, DAVIESS CO., ST. ALPHONSUS (1854) [CEM]
7925 State Rte. 500, 42301. Tel: 270-229-4164; Email: st.alphonsus@att.net. Rev. Anthoni Ottagan, H.G.N.
Res.: 7950 Cummings Rd., 42301.
Catechesis Religious Program—Email: vivian.bowles@maplemount.org. Sr. Vivian Marie Bowles, O.S.U., Ed.D., D.R.E. Students 62.

ST. PAUL, GRAYSON CO., ST. PAUL (1810) [CEM]

1821 St. Paul Rd., Leitchfield, 42754. Tel: 270-242-7436; Email: stpaulgrayson@windstream.net. Rev. Steve Hohman.
School—St. Paul School, (Grades PreSchool-8), 1812 St. Paul Rd., Leitchfield, 42754. Tel: 270-242-7483; Fax: 270-242-7483; Email: stpaulschool@mediacombb.net. Chris Reed, Prin.; Ms. Gina Sims, Sec. Clergy 2; Lay Teachers 6; Students 55.
Catechesis Religious Program—Students 44.

SCOTTSVILLE, ALLEN CO., CHRIST THE KING (1964)
298 Bluegrass Dr., P.O. Box 463, Scottsville, 42164. Tel: 270-237-4404; Email: christtheking298@gmail.com; Web: ctkscottsville.org. Rev. Daniel C. Dillard; Henriette Whitehead, Office Admin.
Catechesis Religious Program—Beth Gripp, D.R.E. Students 23.

SEBREE, WEBSTER CO., ST. MICHAEL (1977)
P.O. Box 705, Sebree, 42455. Tel: 270-835-2584; Email: carmelo.jimenez@pastoral.org. Rev. Jose Carmelo Jimenez, (Mexico); Deacon Chris Gutierrez, Pastoral Min./Coord.; Patti Gutierrez, Pastoral Assoc.; Bayardo Solorza, Pastoral Assoc.
Office: 57 Watkins Sebree Rd., P.O. Box 705, Sebree, 42455. Email: info@smsebree.org; Web: www.smsebree.org.
Catechesis Religious Program—Students 52.

SORGHO, DAVIESS CO., ST. MARY MAGDALENE (1907) [JC]
7232 Kentucky 56, 42301. Tel: 270-771-4436; Email: patti.bartley@stmarymagd.org; Web: stmarymagd.org. Rev. Shaiju Thomas Madhavappallil, H.G.N., (India).
Catechesis Religious Program—Email: debihopkins7@hotmail.com. Debi Hopkins, D.R.E. Students 72.

STANLEY, DAVIESS CO., ST. PETER OF ALCANTARA (1873) [CEM 2]
81 Church St., 42301. Tel: 270-764-1983; Email: office@stpeterofalcantara.com. Rev. Jegin Puthenpurackal, H.G.N., (India).
Catechesis Religious Program—Students 38.

STURGIS, UNION CO., ST. FRANCIS BORGIA (1952)
Mailing Address: P.O. Box 256, Sturgis, 42459. Rev. Ryan Harpole; Sr. Alicia Coomes.
Church: 1317 N. Main St., Sturgis, 42459. Tel: 270-333-2806; Email: saintfrancisborgia@yahoo.com.
Catechesis Religious Program—Students 24.

SUNFISH, EDMONSON CO., ST. JOHN THE EVANGELIST (1830) [CEM]
430 St. John Church Rd., Sunfish, 42210. Tel: 270-259-3028; Email: ftonyb57@ymail.com; Email: befitzhugh@windstream.net; Web: stjohnch.org. Rev. Tony Bickett.
Catechesis Religious Program—Students 1.

UNIONTOWN, UNION CO., ST. AGNES (1859) [CEM]
504 Mulberry St., Uniontown, 42461. Tel: 270-822-4416; Email: khumphrey32887@gmail.com; Email: randyhoward1962@gmail.com; Email: sonyagough2016@gmail.com; Web: www.stagnesuniontown.com. Rev. Randy Howard.
Res.: 407 Fifth St., Uniontown, 42461.
Church: 413 Fifth St., Uniontown, 42461.
Catechesis Religious Program—Sonya Gough, D.R.E. Students 30.

WAVERLY, UNION CO., ST. PETER (1909) [CEM]
201 E. Market St., Waverly, 42462. Tel: 270-389-4224; Email: stpeter.sacredheart@gmail.com. Rev. Dave Johnson.
Catechesis Religious Program—Students 14.

WAX, GRAYSON CO., ST. BENEDICT (1830) [CEM]
1256 St. Anthony Church Rd., Clarkson, 42726. Tel: 270-242-4824; Email: stanthony1256@windstream.net; Web: triparishcatholic.com. Rev. Babu Kulathumkal, H.G.N., (India); Deacon William Grant.
Catechesis Religious Program—Ms. Karen Meredith, C.R.E. Students 10.

WHITESVILLE, DAVIESS CO., ST. MARY OF THE WOODS (1845) [CEM]
10534 Main Cross, Whitesville, 42378. Tel: 270-233-4196; Email: debbie.aud4211@gmail.com; Web: www.stmaryofthewoodswhitesville.org. P.O. Box 1, Whitesville, 42378. Revs. Brian Roby; James (Jamie) Dennis.
Res.: 10503 Franklin St., Whitesville, 42378.
School—St. Mary of the Woods School, (Grades PreSchool-8), Tel: 270-233-5253; Email: emily.hernandez@stmarywoods.com. Emily Hernandez, Prin. Lay Teachers 13; Students 206.
Catechesis Religious Program—Email: choward522@gmail.com. Carrie Howard, D.R.E. Students 90.

Non-Parochial Assignments:
Revs.—
Cash, Richard, Chap., Carmel Home and Owensboro Health Regional Hospital
Clark, Ray, Chap., Prison Ministry
Hostetter, Larry, S.T.D., Pres., 717 Frederica St., 42301.

On Duty Outside the Diocese:
Revs.—
Enoh, Uwem, Air Force Chaplain, Atlus, OK
Garner, Andrew, Holy Family Church, 900 Winchester Ave., Ashland, 41101
Roof, Frank, 1493 Augusta Ln., Atwater, CA 95301. 1201 Northwest 16th St., Miami, FL 33125.

Absent on Leave:
Revs.—
Ausenbaugh, J. Andrew
Baker, Gerald H.
Hayes, Gary
Karl, Kevin
Meredith, John R.
Payne, Gary
Ulrich, Steve
Weider, Henry.

Retired:
Very Rev. Msgr.—
Hancock, George, (Retired), 2501 1/2 Old Hartford Rd., Apt. 6, 42303
Rev. Msgr.—
Powers, Bernard, (Retired), 6143 1st St., 42301
Revs.—
Bradley, J. Edward, (Retired)
Clemons, Delma, (Retired)
Mills, Joseph M., J.C.L., (Retired), 2501 Old Hartford Rd., 42303
Powers, Aloysius, (Retired), 2501 1/2 Old Hartford Rd., Apt. 6, 42303
Powers, Richard, (Retired), 10500 McIntyre Rd., 42301.

INSTITUTIONS LOCATED IN DIOCESE

[A] COLLEGES AND UNIVERSITIES

OWENSBORO. *Brescia University*, 717 Frederica St., 42301. Tel: 270-685-3131; Fax: 270-686-6422; Email: stephanie.clary@brescia.edu; Web: www.brescia.edu. Revs. Larry Hostetter, S.T.D., Pres.; J. Raymond Goetz, Faculty, Theology; Sisters Cheryl Clemons, O.S.U., Ph.D., Vice Pres. Academic Affairs & Academic Dean; Helena Fischer, O.S.U., Registrar; Barbara Jean Head, O.S.U., Controller; Betsy Moyer, O.S.U., Data Mgr., School of Educ.; Pam Mueller, O.S.U., Spiritual Advisor / Care Svcs.; Judith Riney, O.S.U., Dir. Library Svcs. Administrators 6; Clergy 4; Lay Teachers 52; Priests 2; Sisters 6; Students 1,020; Clergy / Religious Teachers 4.

[B] HIGH SCHOOLS, INTER-PAROCHIAL

OWENSBORO. *Owensboro Catholic High School*, 1524 W. Parrish Ave., 42301. Tel: 270-684-3215; Fax: 270-684-7050; Email: gates.settle@owensborocatholic.org; Web: www.owensborocatholic.org/schools/ochs. Mr. Gates Settle, Prin.; Ms. Sherry Orth, Rel. Dept. Chair; Mr. Tim Riley, Dean of Students; Mr. Keith Osborne, Devel. Dir.; Ms. Marilyn Pace, Librarian. Lay Teachers 41; Priests 1; Students 440; Clergy / Religious Teachers 1.

PADUCAH. *St. Mary High School*, 1243 Elmdale Rd., Paducah, 42003. Tel: 270-442-1681, Ext. 226; Fax: 270-442-7920; Email: dshelton@smss.org; Web: www.smss.org. Douglas Shelton, Prin.; Rhonda Webb, Librarian. Lay Teachers 15; Students 84.

WHITESVILLE. *Trinity High School*, 10510 Main Cross St., Whitesville, 42378. Tel: 270-233-5533; Fax: 270-233-5927; Email: emily.hernandez@stmarywoods.com; Web: www.trinityhs.com. Emily Hernandez, Prin. Lay Teachers 10; Students 89; Clergy / Religious Teachers 1.

[C] ELEMENTARY SCHOOLS, INTER-PAROCHIAL

OWENSBORO. *Owensboro Catholic Elementary 4-6 Campus*, (Grades 4-6), 525 E. 23rd St., 42303. Tel: 270-683-6989; Fax: 270-684-5956; Email: tracy.conkright@owensborocatholic.org. Ms. Tracy Conkright, Prin.; Theresa Sauer, Librarian. Lay Teachers 16; Students 290.
Owensboro Catholic Elementary K-3 Campus, (Grades K-3), 4017 Frederica St., 42301. Tel: 270-684-7583; Fax: 270-684-4938; Email: lori.whitehouse@owensborocatholic.org; Web: www.owensborocatholic.org. Ms. Lori Whitehouse, Prin.; Sherry Durham, Librarian. Lay Teachers 24; Students 376.
Owensboro Catholic Middle School, (Grades 7-8), 2540 Christie Pl., 42301. Tel: 270-683-0480; Fax: 270-683-0495; Email: david.kessler@owensborocatholic.org; Web: www.owensborocatholic.org. Ms. Sara Guth, Prin.; Ms. Lily McDivitt, Sec. Lay Teachers 17; Students 195.

BOWLING GREEN. *St. Joseph Interparochial School*, (Grades PreSchool-8), 416 Church Ave., Bowling Green, 42101-1887. Tel: 270-842-1235; Fax: 270-842-9072; Email: rschwartz@stjosephschoolbg.org; Web: stjosephschoolbg.org. Rodney Schwartz, Prin.; Joella Scheidegger, Librarian; Ms. Shanna Garland, Sec. Lay Teachers 26; Students 326.

HARDINSBURG. *St. Romuald School*, (Grades PreK-8), 408 N. Hwy. 259, Hardinsburg, 40143. Tel: 270-756-5504; Fax: 270-756-2099; Email: srissecretary@hotmail.com. Mr. Rob Cox, Prin.; Jennifer Moorman, Librarian. Lay Teachers 13; Students 243.

MORGANFIELD. *John Paul II Catholic School*, (Grades PreK-8), 307 S. Church St., Morganfield, 42437. Tel: 270-389-1898; Email: bhendrickson@johnpauliicatholicschool.org; Web: www.johnpauliicatholicschool.org; Web: www.johnpauliicatholicschool.org. Rev. Randy Howard, Parochial Vicar; Beth Hendrickson, Prin.; Renee French, Librarian. Lay Teachers 14; Students 218.

PADUCAH. *St. Mary Elementary*, (Grades PreK-5), 377 Highland Blvd., Paducah, 42003. Tel: 270-442-1681; Fax: 270-538-9057; Email: lclark@smss.org; Web: www.smss.org. Lisa Clark, Prin.; Eleanor Spry, Dir. Lay Teachers 15; Students 180.
St. Mary Middle School, (Grades 6-8), 1243 Elmdale Rd., Paducah, 42003. Tel: 270-442-1681; Fax: 270-442-7920; Email: jsmith@smss.org; Web: www.smss.org. Douglas Shelton, Prin.; Rhonda Webb, Librarian. Lay Teachers 8; Students 82.

[D] GENERAL HOSPITALS

PADUCAH. **Dublin Manor, Inc.* Apartments for the Elderly 665 McAuley Dr., Apt. 105, Paducah, 42003. Tel: 270-441-0026; Fax: 270-442-9499; Email: ltalley@mercyhousing.org. L. Talley, Dir.
McAuley Manor, Inc., 665 McAuley Dr., Apt. 105, Paducah, 42003. Tel: 270-444-7144; Fax: 270-415-9165; Email: ltalley@mercyhousing.org. L. Talley, Dir. Housing for Elderly.
Mercy Health Lourdes, Inc., 1530 Lone Oak Rd., Paducah, 42003. Tel: 270-444-2444; Fax: 270-444-2980; Email: cdobrzynski@mercy.com; Web: www.mercy.com/paducah. Michael Yungmann, CEO; Cynthia Dobrzynski, Vice Pres.
Legal Title: Mercy Health Lourdes Hospital LLC Bed Capacity 359; Tot Asst. Annually 254,516; Total Staff 1,545.
Lourdes Foundation, Inc., 1530 Lone Oak Rd., Paducah, 42002-7100. Tel: 270-444-3990; Fax: 270-444-2732; Email: lourdesfoundation@mercy.com; Web: foundation.mercy.com/paducah. Cynthia Dobrzynski, Admin.
Mercy Regional Emergency Medical System, 3551 Coleman Rd., Paducah, 42001. Tel: 270-443-6529; Fax: 270-444-9128.
Mercy Regional Emergency Medical System.
**Mercy Manor, Inc.*, 665 McAuley Dr., Apt. 105, Paducah, 42003. Tel: 270-415-9166; Fax: 270-415-9165; Email: ltalley@mercyhousing.org. L. Talley, Dir. Apartments for Elderly.

[E] HOMES FOR AGED

OWENSBORO. *Carmel Home*, 2501 Old Hartford Rd., 42303. Tel: 270-683-0227; Fax: 270-685-3406; Email: srmfrancisteresa@yahoo.com; Email: sr.mariacarmelita@yahoo.com. Rev. Richard Cash, Chap.; Sr. Maria Carmelita, Admin. Carmelite Sisters of the Divine Heart of Jesus. Bed Capacity 115; Residents 115; Sisters 5; Tot Asst. Annually 150; Total Staff 105.

KNOTTSVILLE. *Bishop Soenneker Home* Residential Care of the Handicapped/Disabled Elderly. 9545 State Rte. 144, Philpot, 42366. Tel: 270-281-4881; Fax: 270-281-5804; Email: angie.beyke@pastoral.org. Angie Beyke, Admin. Residents 53; Tot Asst. Annually 68; Total Staff 30.

[F] MONASTERIES AND RESIDENCES OF PRIESTS AND BROTHERS

AUBURN. *Fathers of Mercy*, 806 Shaker Museum Rd., Auburn, 42206. Tel: 270-542-4146, Ext. 4; Fax: 270-542-4147; Email: business@fathersofmercy.com; Web: www.fathersofmercy.com. Very Rev. David Wilton, C.P.M., Supr.; Revs. Joel Rogers, C.P.M., Prior; Wade Menezes, C.P.M., Vicar; Ricardo Pineda, C.P.M., Treas.; Allan Cravalho, Sec.; Joseph Aytona, C.P.M., Councilor; Anthony M. Stephens, C.P.M., Councilor; John Agapito, C.P.M., In Res.; Ben Cameron, C.P.M., In Res.; William Casey, C.P.M., In Res.; James P. Costigan, C.P.M., In

Res.; Kenneth Geraci, C.P.M., In Res.; Louis Guardiola, C.P.M., In Res.; Thomas Sullivan, C.P.M., In Res. Deacons 1; Novices 2; Priests 29; Seminarians 6; Tot in Congregation 37.

[G] CONVENTS AND RESIDENCES FOR SISTERS

OWENSBORO. *The Glenmary Center*, P.O. Box 22264, 42304-2264. Tel: 270-686-8401; Fax: 270-686-8759; Email: srdarlene@glenmarysisters.org; Web: www.glenmarysisters.org. Sr. Darlene Presley, Pres. Home Mission Sisters of America, Inc. aka Glenmary Sisters. Sisters 8.

*Service to the Home Missions*Tot Asst. Annually 10,000; Total Staff 9.

MAPLE MOUNT. *Ursuline Sisters of Mount Saint Joseph*, 8001 Cummings Rd., Maple Mount, 42356. Tel: 270-229-4103; Fax: 270-229-4953; Email: leadershipcouncil@maplemount.org; Web: www.ursulinesmsj.org. Sisters Amelia Stenger, O.S.U., M.A., M.A., Congregational Leader; Judith Riney, O.S.U., Treas. Motherhouse and Convent of the Ursuline Nuns of the Congregation of Paris.

St. Joseph's Female Ursuline Academy, Inc. Sisters 113.

WHITESVILLE. *Passionist Nuns / St. Joseph's Monastery*, 8564 Crisp Rd., Whitesville, 42378-9782. Tel: 270-233-4571; Fax: 270-233-4572; Email: nunsp@passionistnuns.org; Web: www.passionistnuns.org. Sr. John Mary Read, C.P., Supr. Religious of the Passion of Jesus Christ, (Passionist Nuns, Cloistered Contemplative). Postulants 1; Sisters 13; Junior Professed 4; Affiliate 1; Perpetually Professed 9; Aspirant 1.

[H] RETREAT CENTERS

BOWLING GREEN. *Gasper River Catholic Youth Camp & Retreat Center* (A diocesan-owned entity) 2695 Jackson Bridge Rd., Bowling Green, 42101. Tel: 270-781-2466; Email: ben.warrell@pastoral.org; Email: gasperriver@hotmail.com; Web: www.gasperriverretreatcenter.org. Mr. Ben Warrell, Dir.

MAPLE MOUNT. *Mount Saint Joseph Conference and Retreat Center*, 8001 Cummings Rd., Maple Mount, 42356. Tel: 270-229-0200; Fax: 270-229-0279; Email: msj.center@maplemount.org; Web: www.ursulines.org. Sr. Mary Matthias Ward, O.S.U., Dir.

[I] NEWMAN CENTERS

BOWLING GREEN. *St. Thomas Aquinas Catholic Campus Center at Western Kentucky University*, St. Thomas Aquinas Chapel, 1403 College St., P.O. Box 10170, Bowling Green, 42102-4770. Tel: 270-843-3638; Email: mew_62@hotmail.com; Web: www.wkucatholiccenter.com. Rev. Michael E. Williams, Dir. Students 1,651.

MURRAY. *Murray State University Newman House*, 401 N. 12th St., Murray, 42071. Tel: 270-767-6616; Email: freugene@stleoky.org; Web: catholicracersmsu.org. 220 N. 13th St., Murray, 42071. Rev. Eugene T. Batungbacal, C.Ss.R., Chap. Students 200.

[J] MISCELLANEOUS LISTINGS

OWENSBORO. *St. Benedict Joseph's Homeless Shelter*, 1001 W. 7th St., 42301. 600 Locust St., 42301. Tel: 270-541-1003; Tel: 270-315-4419; Fax: 270-215-0037; Email: stbenedicts42301@roadrunner.com; Web: stbenedictsowenboro.org. Mr. Harry Pedigo Jr., Dir.

Carmelite Sisters of the Divine Heart of Jesus of Kentucky Corporation, 2501 Old Hartford Rd., 42303. Tel: 270-683-0227; Email: carmelhomeinfo@yahoo.com; Web: www.carmelhomeky.com. Sr. M. Francis Teresa Scully, Carmel., D.C.J., Supr.

Cathedral Preschool, 600 Locust St., 42301. Tel: 270-926-1652; Fax: 270-683-3621; Email: pam.weafer@pastoral.org. Pam Weafer, Dir. Students 100; Clergy / Religious Teachers 6.

The Catholic Foundation of Western Kentucky, 600 Locust St., 42301. Tel: 270-683-1545; Fax: 270-683-6883; Email: kevin.kauffeld@pastoral.org; Web: www.owensborodiocese.org. Mr. Kevin Kauffeld, Chancellor.

**Catholic Men's Conference of Western KY*, 600 Locust St., 42301. Tel: 270-683-1545; Web: kycatholic.com. Mr. Raymond Purk, Dir.

Centro Latino, 524 Locust St., 42301. Tel: 270-683-2541; Fax: 270-684-5819; Email: ocentrolatino@aol.com. Sr. Fran Wilhelm, Dir. Tot Asst. Annually 10,669; Total Staff 4.

**Daniel Pitino Shelter, Inc.*, 501 Walnut St., 42301. Tel: 270-688-9000; Fax: 270-688-0093; Email: dpsjim@hotmail.com; Web: www.pitinoshelter.org. Thad Gunderson, Dir. Provides soup kitchen seven days a week, homeless shelter for 65 residents, education facilities. Employees 11; Tot Asst. Annually 469; Volunteers 200.

St. Gerard Life Home, 600 Locust St., 42301. Tel: 270-852-8328; Fax: 270-683-6883; Email: stgerard@pastoral.org. Sr. Anthonia Asayoma, O.S.F., Dir.; Ms. Susan Gesser, Dir. Birthmother housing and pregnancy outreach.

**Glenmary Sisters Charitable Trust*, P.O. Box 22264, 42304. Tel: 270-686-8401; Fax: 270-686-8759; Email: finance@glenmarysisters.org. John Kurtz, Chm.

Interparish Deposit Loan Fund Corp., 600 Locust St., 42301-2130. Tel: 270-683-1545; Fax: 270-683-6883; Email: ray.purk@pastoral.org; Web: www.owensborodiocese.org. Mr. Raymond Purk, Contact Person.

Owensboro Catholic Consolidated School System, 1524 W. Parrish Ave., 42301. Tel: 270-686-8896; Fax: 270-686-8997; Email: keith.osborne@owensborocatholic.org; Web: www.owensborocatholic.org. Very Rev. J. Patrick Reynolds, J.C.L., Vicar.

The Owensboro Catholic League, Inc., 3152 Pleasant Valley Rd., 42303.

**The Roman Catholic Diocese of Owensboro Kentucky Charitable Trust Fund, Inc.*, 600 Locust St., 42301. Tel: 270-683-1545; Fax: 270-683-6883; Email: ray.purk@pastoral.org; Web: www.owensborodiocese.org. Mr. Raymond Purk, C.F.O.

BOWLING GREEN. *Diocesan Shrine of Mary Mother of the Church and Model of all Christians*, St. Joseph, 434 Church Ave., Bowling Green, 42101. Tel: 270-842-2525; Fax: 270-843-9624. Very Rev. D. Andrew Garner, Rector.

PADUCAH. *St. Mary School System*, 1243 Elmdale Rd., Paducah, 42003. Tel: 270-442-1681, Ext. 273; Fax: 270-538-9058; Email: espry@smss.org; Web: www.smss.org. Lisa Clark, Prin.; Douglas Shelton, Prin.; Eleanor Spry, Dir.

St. Mary School System Benefit Fund, 1243 Elmdale Rd., Paducah, 42003. Tel: 270-442-1681, Ext. 273; Fax: 270-548-0958; Email: espry@smss.org; Web: www.smss.org. Eleanor Spry, Contact Person.

PRINCETON. *Heralds of Good News of St. Paul, Inc.*, 81 Church St., 42301. Tel: 270-764-1983; Email: jegin.puthenpurackal@pastoral.org. Rev. Jegin Puthenpurackal, H.G.N., (India) Sec.

RELIGIOUS INSTITUTES OF MEN REPRESENTED IN THE DIOCESE

For further details refer to the corresponding bracketed number in the Religious Institutes of Men or Women section.

[0820]—*Congregation of the Fathers of Mercy*—C.P.M.
[0570]—*Glenmary Home Missioners* (Glendale OH)—G.H.M.
[0585]—*Heralds of Good News* (India)—H.G.N.
[1120]—*Missionaries of the Sacred Hearts of Jesus and Mary*—M.S.S.C.C.
[0200]—*Order of Saint Benedict*—O.S.B.

RELIGIOUS INSTITUTES OF WOMEN REPRESENTED IN THE DIOCESE

[0360]—*Carmelite Sisters of the Divine Heart of Jesus*—Carmel D.C.J.
[0885]—*Daughters of Mary, Mother of Mercy*—D.M.M.M.
[]—*Dominican Congregation of St. Catherine of Siena*.
[]—*Dominican Sisters of Saint Rose of Lima* (Vietnam).
[]—*Franciscan Sisters of the Immaculate Conception, Inc.*—O.S.F.
[2080]—*Home Mission Sisters of America*—G.H.M.S.
[]—*Missionary Sisters of the Blessed Virgin Mary, Queen of the World*.
[]—*Missioneras del Sagrado Corazon de Jesus Ad Gentes*—M.A.G.
[3170]—*Religious of the Passion of Jesus Christ*—C.P.
[]—*School Sisters of Notre Dame*—S.S.N.D.
[2260]—*Sisters of the Lamb of God*—A.D.
[1760]—*Sisters of the Third Order of St. Francis of Penance and Charity* (Tiffin, OH)—O.S.F.
[1720]—*Sisters of the Third Order Regular of St. Francis of the Congregation of Our Lady of Lourdes* (Rochester, MN)—O.S.F.
[4120]—*Ursuline Nuns, of the Congregation of Paris*—O.S.U.

INTERPAROCHIAL CEMETERIES

OWENSBORO. *Mater Dolorosa*, 1860 W. 9th St., 42301. 5404 Hwy. 54, 42303. Tel: 270-926-8097; Fax: 270-926-8038; Email: cliff.russell@pastoral.org. Mr. Cliff Russell, Dir.; Mr. Alan Sims, Business Mgr. Staff 4

St. Raphael Cemetery (1847) 6025 Hayden Bridge Rd., 42301. McRaith Catholic Center, 600 Locust St., 42301-2130. Tel: 270-683-1545; Fax: 270-683-6883; Email: martha.hagan@pastoral.org. Mr. Kevin Kauffeld, Chancellor

Resurrection aka Owensboro Catholic Cemeteries, 5404 Hwy. 54, 42303. Tel: 270-926-8097; Fax: 270-926-8038; Email: cliff.russell@pastoral.org; Email: alan.sims@pastoral.org. Mr. Cliff Russell, Dir.; Mr. Alan Sims, Business Mgr.; Mrs. Vicki Jones, Office Mgr.

BOWLING GREEN. *St. Joseph Cemetery Foundation, Inc.*, St. Joseph Cemetery Foundation, P.O. Box 10334, Bowling Green, 42102. Tel: 270-842-2525 (St. Joseph Parish); Tel: 270-842-7777 (Holy Spirit Parish). 930 Saint Joseph Ln., Bowling Green, 42103. Email: kathleen@stjosephbg.org; Web: www.stjosephbg.org/cemetery.htm. Mr. Steve Dieball, Chief Oper. Mgr.

PADUCAH. *Mt. Carmel Cemetery, Inc.* (1893) P.O. Box 7346, Paducah, 42002. 4149 Old Mayfield Rd., Paducah, 42003. Tel: 270-534-5540; Tel: 270-331-1006; Email: mt.carmelcemetery@outlook.com; Web: www.mtcarmelcemeterypaducah.org. Rev. Brad Whistle *Mt. Carmel Cemetery, Inc.*

NECROLOGY

† Piskula, Louis, (Retired), Died Oct. 11, 2018
† Powell, Paul Pike, (Retired), Died Apr. 26, 2018

An asterisk (*) denotes an organization that has established tax-exempt status directly with the IRS and is not covered by the USCCB Group Ruling.

Diocese of Palm Beach

(Dioecesis Litoris Palmensis)

VERITATEM FACIENTES IN CARITATE

Most Reverend

GERALD M. BARBARITO

Bishop of Palm Beach; ordained January 31, 1976; appointed Auxiliary Bishop of Brooklyn June 28, 1994; installed August 22, 1994; appointed Bishop of Ogdensburg October 26, 1999; appointed Bishop of Palm Beach July 1, 2003; installed August 28, 2003. *Office: 9995 N. Military Tr., Palm Beach Gardens, FL 33410.*

The Pastoral Center Office: 9995 N. Military Tr., Palm Beach Gardens, FL 33410. Tel: 561-775-9500; Fax: 561-775-9556. . *Mailing Address: P.O. Box 109650, Palm Beach Gardens, FL 33410-9650.*

Web: diocesepb.org

Email: info@diocesepb.org

ESTABLISHED OCTOBER 24, 1984.

Square Miles 5,115.

Comprises the Counties of Palm Beach, Martin, Indian River, Okeechobee and St. Lucie in the State of Florida.

Legal Corporate Title: The Diocese of Palm Beach.

For legal titles of parishes and diocesan institutions, consult the Chancery.

STATISTICAL OVERVIEW

Personnel

Bishop	1
Retired Bishops	1
Priests: Diocesan Active in Diocese	80
Priests: Diocesan Active Outside Diocese	1
Priests: Retired, Sick or Absent	31
Number of Diocesan Priests	112
Religious Priests in Diocese	30
Total Priests in Diocese	142
Extern Priests in Diocese	2
Ordinations:	
Diocesan Priests	2
Permanent Deacons	2
Permanent Deacons in Diocese	102
Total Brothers	4
Total Sisters	78

Parishes

Parishes	50
With Resident Pastor:	
Resident Diocesan Priests	44
Resident Religious Priests	6
Missions	3
Pastoral Centers	1

Professional Ministry Personnel:	
Brothers	3
Sisters	75
Lay Ministers	170

Welfare

Special Centers for Social Services	11
Total Assisted	17,478

Educational

Seminaries, Diocesan	1
Students from This Diocese	4
Students from Other Diocese	111
Diocesan Students in Other Seminaries	6
Total Seminarians	10
High Schools, Diocesan and Parish	3
Total Students	1,270
Elementary Schools, Diocesan and Parish	14
Total Students	4,221
Elementary Schools, Private	2
Total Students	520
Catechesis/Religious Education:	
High School Students	3,054
Elementary Students	8,354
Total Students under Catholic Instruction	17,429
Teachers in the Diocese:	
Priests	2
Brothers	2
Sisters	5
Lay Teachers	569

Vital Statistics

Receptions into the Church:	
Infant Baptism Totals	2,913
Minor Baptism Totals	404
Adult Baptism Totals	240
Received into Full Communion	456
First Communions	3,402
Confirmations	2,757
Marriages:	
Catholic	591
Interfaith	111
Total Marriages	702
Deaths	2,122
Total Catholic Population	233,741
Total Population	2,140,567

Former Bishops—Most Revs. THOMAS V. DAILY, D.D., ord. Jan. 10, 1952; appt. Titular Bishop of Bladia and Auxiliary Bishop of Boston, Dec. 31, 1974; cons. Feb. 11, 1975; appt. first Bishop of Palm Beach, July 17, 1984; installed Oct. 24, 1984; transferred to Bishop of Brooklyn, Feb. 20, 1990; died May 15, 2017; J. KEITH SYMONS, D.D., ord. May 18, 1958; appt. Auxiliary Bishop of St. Petersburg, Jan. 16, 1981; cons. March 19, 1981; appt. second Bishop of Pensacola-Tallahassee, Sept. 29, 1983; installed Nov. 8, 1983; appt. second Bishop of Palm Beach, June 2, 1990; installed July 31, 1990; resigned June 2, 1998; ANTHONY J. O'CONNELL, D.D., ord. March 30, 1963; appt. Bishop of Knoxville, May 27, 1988; ord. and installed Sept. 8, 1988; appt. Bishop of Palm Beach Nov. 6, 1998; resigned March 8, 2002; died May 4, 2012.; SEAN P. O'MALLEY, O.F.M.Cap., Ph.D., ord. Aug. 29, 1970; appt. Coadjutor May 30, 1984; appt. Bishop of St. Thomas, Virgin Islands; ord. Aug. 2, 1984; installed Oct. 16, 1985; appt. Bishop of Fall River June 16, 1992; installed Aug. 11, 1992; appt. Bishop of Palm Beach Sept. 3, 2002; installed Oct. 19, 2002; appt. Archbishop of Boston July 1, 2003; installed July 30, 2003.

The Pastoral Center—Mailing Address: P.O. Box 109650, Palm Beach Gardens, 33410-9650. Tel: 561-775-9500; Fax: 561-775-9556. *9995 N. Military Tr., Palm Beach Gardens, 33410.*

Vicar General—Very Rev. CHARLES E. NOTABARTOLO, V.G.

Moderator of Curia—Very Rev. CHARLES E. NOTABARTOLO, V.G.

Episcopal Secretary—Rev. BRIAN KING.

Executive Secretary to Bishop—MRS. ANNETTE RUSSELL.

Chancellor—Very Rev. ALBERT A. DELLO RUSSO, J.C.L.

Administrative Assistant to the Vicar General and Chancellor—MRS. MERKE BARONI.

Administrative Assistant to the Chancellor—MRS. BEATRIZ URREA.

Coordinator of Archives and Records—MRS. MERKE BARONI.

Matrimonial Tribunal—

Judicial Vicar—Rt. Rev. Archimandrite GLEN J. POTHIER, J.C.L., D.Th., J.V.

Judges—Rev. Msgr. THOMAS J. KLINZING, J.C.L.; Rt. Rev. Archimandrite GLEN J. POTHIER, J.C.L., D.Th., J.V.; Very Rev. ALBERT A. DELLO RUSSO, J.C.L.; Rev. REMIGIUSZ BLASZKOWSKI, J.C.D.

Defender of the Bond—Rev. FRANCISCO J. OSORIO, J.C.L.

Assessors—Rev. MICHAEL W. EDWARDS, P.E., (Retired); Very Rev. KEVIN C. NELSON, M.A., M.Div., V.F.

Promoter of Justice—Rev. FRANCISCO J. OSORIO, J.C.L.

Notaries—MRS. LORRAINE SABATELLA, B.A.; MR. SANDI MARTINEZ, M.A.; MRS. DEBORAH DUXBURY, B.A.; MS. ALICE RIVERA.

Director of the Tribunal—MR. SANDI MARTINEZ, M.A.

Case Directors & Secretaries—MR. SANDI MARTINEZ, M.A.; MRS. DEBORAH DUXBURY, B.A.; MS. ALICE RIVERA.

Advocates—Deacon MARTIN SERRAES; Very Rev. KEVIN C. NELSON, M.A., M.Div., V.F.; Deacon JOHN BEAUDOIN.

Vicars Forane—Very Revs. KEVIN C. NELSON, M.A., M.Div., V.F., Northern Deanery; NESTOR RODRIGUEZ, V.F., Central Deanery; Rev. Msgr. MICHAEL D. MCGRAW, V.F., Southern Deanery; Very Rev. THOMAS R. LAFRENIERE, V.F., Cathedral Deanery.

Vocations—Rev. BRIAN LEHNERT, Dir., Tel: 561-775-9555.

Religious—Very Rev. MICHAEL DRISCOLL, O.Carm., Episcopal Delegate; Sr. JOAN DAWSON, O.S.F., Episcopal Delegate, Tel: 561-775-9554.

Diaconate—Tel: 561-775-9540. Deacon MARTIN SERRAES, Episcopal Delegate; Rev. ROBERT L. POPE JR., Dir. Formation.

Episcopal Delegate for Retired Priests—Rev. MICHAEL W. EDWARDS, P.E., (Retired).

Finance Officer—MR. VITO GENDUSA, Tel: 561-775-9500.

Consultative Bodies

Consultors—Rev. Msgr. THOMAS J. KLINZING, J.C.L.; Very Revs. CHARLES E. NOTABARTOLO, V.G.; NESTOR RODRIGUEZ, V.F.; THOMAS E. BARRETT; Rt. Rev. Archimandrite GLEN J. POTHIER, J.C.L., D.Th., J.V.; Revs. MICHAEL W. EDWARDS, P.E., (Retired); RICHARD MURPHY; ALFREDO HERNANDEZ; ELIFETE ST. FORT.

Presbyteral Council—Ex Officio: Very Rev. CHARLES E. NOTABARTOLO, V.G.; Rt. Rev. Archimandrite GLEN J. POTHIER, J.C.L., D.Th., J.V.; Very Revs. KEVIN C. NELSON, M.A., M.Div., V.F., Northern Deanery; THOMAS R. LAFRENIERE, V.F., Cathedral Deanery; NESTOR RODRIGUEZ, V.F., Central Deanery; Rev. Msgr. MICHAEL D. MCGRAW, V.F., Southern Deanery; Rev. RICHARD MURPHY. Elected Members: Rev. SEAMUS MURTAGH; Very Rev. THOMAS E. BARRETT; Revs. JULIAN P. HARRIS; BRIAN LEHNERT; SON LINH

HOANG; Very Rev. PAUL WIERICHS, C.P.; Revs. ELIFETE ST. FORT; DUCASSE FRANCOIS; GAVIN J. BADWAY.

Diocesan Offices

Building, Construction, Real Estate Office—Rev. RICHARD MURPHY, Episcopal Delegate, Tel: 561-775-9514; MICHAEL LOCKWOOD, Dir., Tel: 561-775-9523; DESTINY CALITTO, Tel: 561-775-9514.

Campus Ministry at Florida Atlantic University—Rev. BRIAN LEHNERT.

Catholic Charities Administrative Offices—MR. FRANCISCO CHEVERE, Exec. Dir., Tel: 561-775-9573; MR. ALEX STEVENS, Assoc. Dir., Tel: 561-360-3321.

Cemetery: Our Lady Queen of Peace—10941 Southern Blvd., West Palm Beach, 33411. Rev. ZBIGNIEW A. RUDNICKI, Dir.; MR. THOMAS JORDAN, Admin., Tel: 561-793-0711.

Communications—MRS. JENNIFER TREFELNER, Dir., Tel: 561-775-9529; Email: jtrefelner@diocesepb.org; VACANT, Florida Catholic Editor.

Development—MR. BRIAN DOYLE, Dir., Tel: 561-775-9519; Email: bdoyle@diocesepb.org; MR. DAVID WALSH, Assoc. Dir., Tel: 561-775-9590; Fax: 561-799-9527; Email: dwalsh@diocesepb.org; KELLY GARVIS, Admin. Asst., Tel: 561-775-9520.

Education—

Schools Office—MR. GARY GELO, Supt., Tel: 561-775-9546; Email: ggelo@diocesepb.org; MR. JOHN F. CLARKE, Asst. Supt.; LOUISE GALGANO, Admin. Asst., Tel: 561-775-9547; LISA GAYNES, Cert/In-Service Coord., Tel: 561-775-9509.

Office of Catechetical Leadership, Youth Ministry Formation and Young Adult—MR. ANTHONY MARCHICA, Dir., Tel: 561-775-9548; MRS. NATALIE LAFLEUR, Asst. Dir. Catechesis, Tel: 561-775-9549; KATHRYN SULLIVAN, Coord., Youth & Young Adults and Inclusion Ministries, Tel: 561-775-9559.

School of Christian Formation (English & Spanish)—Rev. DUVAN BERMUDEZ, Dir., Tel: 561-775-9506; MRS. ANGELICA AGUILERA, Admin. Asst., Tel: 561-775-9544.

Employee Services—(see also Insurance Services) MRS. ANA JAROSZ, Dir., Tel: 561-775-9525; GRETCHEN WOOD, Human Resources Asst., Tel: 561-775-9503.

Family Life/Marriage—Tel: 561-775-9557. MRS. CATHERINE LOH, Dir.; Deacon LOUIS ROMERO, Marriage Prep. Coord.

Finance—MRS. KAREN LENTZ, Controller, Tel: 561-775-9571.

Haitian Ministry—Rev. YVES GEFFRARD, Episcopal Delegate, Tel: 561-466-9617.

Hispanic Ministry—Rev. DUVAN BERMUDEZ, Dir., Tel: 561-775-9506; MRS. ANGELICA AGUILERA, Admin. Asst., Tel: 561-775-9544.

Information Technology—MIKE IRISH, Dir., Tel: 561-775-9504; ADAM PIECZARKA, IT Support Specialist, Tel: 561-775-9578; CARLOS MESA, IT Network Support Technician, Tel: 561-775-9542; MICHAEL WINNINGHAM, IT Workstation Support Technician, Tel: 561-775-9505.

Insurance Services—(see also Employee Services) MRS. ANA JAROSZ, Dir., Tel: 561-775-9525; SANDY MAULDEN, Benefits Asst., Tel: 561-775-9574.

Internal Services—MS. MARIAN LOYND, Dir.; MR. BRYAN GILL, Tel: 561-630-2694.

Liturgy—Rev. BRIAN KING, Dir.; MRS. JEANNE CLARK, Coord., Tel: 561-775-9539.

Permanent Diaconate/Diaconate Formation Program—Deacon MARTIN SERRAES, Episcopal Delegate, Tel: 561-775-9540; Rev. ROBERT L. POPE JR., Dir. Formation; MRS. LINA SALCEDO, Admin. Asst., Tel: 561-775-9540.

Propagation of the Faith & Missionary Cooperative PlanRev. MICHAEL W. EDWARDS, P.E., Dir., (Retired); MRS. BETTY MCKINLEY, Sec., Tel: 561-775-9598.

Real Estate—Rev. RICHARD MURPHY, Episcopal Delegate, Tel: 561-775-9514.

Religious Men and Women—Episcopal Delegate: Very Rev. MICHAEL DRISCOLL, O.Carm.; Sr. JOAN DAWSON, O.S.F.

Safe Environments—

Safe Environment Coordinator—Very Rev. ALBERT A. DELLO RUSSO, J.C.L.

Victim Assistance Coordinator—MRS. LORRAINE SABATELLA, B.A., Tel: 561-801-0999.

Administrator of Background Screening—MRS. KATHY CASEY, Tel: 561-775-9530.

Administrator of Education and Training Programs—MRS. LISA LINNELL, Tel: 561-775-9593.

Seminarians—Rev. BRIAN LEHNERT, Dir., Tel: 561-775-9555; MRS. CONSUELO MINUTOLI, Admin. Asst., Tel: 561-775-9552.

Vocations—Rev. BRIAN LEHNERT, Dir., Tel: 561-775-9555; MRS. CONSUELO MINUTOLI, Admin. Asst., Tel: 561-775-9552.

Young Adult Ministry—MR. ANTHONY MARCHICA, Dir., Tel: 561-775-9548.

Catholic Charities Services and Offices

Executive Director—MR. FRANCISCO CHEVERE, Tel: 561-775-9573.

Associate Director—Tel: 561-360-3321. MR. ALEX STEVENS.

Chief of Finance and Associate Director—LAURA STEVENSON, Tel: 561-345-2027.

Accounting Manager—Tel: 561-775-9577. MR. PETER HERRMANN.

Human Resources Director—THERESA MAIA, Dir., Tel: 561-775-9589.

Fund Development and Marketing Director—JANELLE HOFFMAN, Tel: 561-630-2695.

Marketing and Fundraising Manager—
Tel: 561-775-9567. MRS. COURTNEY TELLIER.

Catholic Charities Administrative Offices—9995 N. Military Trail, Palm Beach Gardens, 33410-9650. Tel: 561-775-9560; Fax: 561-625-5906. *Mailing Address: P.O. Box 109650, Palm Beach Gardens, 33410-9650.*

Anti-Human Trafficking Program - Catholic Charities—St. Francis Center, 100 W. 20th St., Riviera Beach, 33404. Tel: 561-345-2000;
Tel: 1-888-373-7888 (Hotline); Email: aht@ccdpb.org.

Counseling Services—

Counseling—NICOLE LOONEY, Dir. Clinical Svcs.

Riviera Beach—Catholic Charities St. Francis Center, 100 W. 20th St., Riviera Beach, 33404.
Tel: 844-848-6777.

Stuart—St. Joseph Center, 1300 S.E. 10th St., Stuart, 34996. Tel: 844-848-6777;
Fax: 772-220-9894.

Palm Beach—St. Edward Catholic Church, 144 N. County Rd., Palm Beach, 33480-3916.
Tel: 844-848-6777; Fax: 561-514-3528.

Boca Raton—St. Joan of Arc Catholic Church, 298 S.W. 3rd St., Boca Raton, 33432.
Tel: 844-848-6777; Fax: 561-368-6420.

Pahokee—St. Mary Ctr., 1200 E. Main St., Pahokee, 33476. Tel: 844-848-6777.

Disaster Relief & Recovery Program—Catholic Charities: 2001 Broadway Ave., Ste. 200, Riviera Beach, 33404. St. Joseph's Center, 1300 S.E. 10th St., Stuart, 34996. St. Mary's Center, 1200 E. Main St., Pahokee, 33476. Tel: 561-360-3324;
Fax: 561-863-5379; Email: disasterrecovery@ccdpb.org.

Elder Services—

Elder Affairs—Catholic Charities St. Francis Center, 100 W. 20th St., Riviera Beach, 33404. AMY FARIELLO-HANSEN, Prog. Admin., Tel: 561-345-2001; Fax: 561-863-5379.

Health Related Services—

Interfaith Health & Wellness/Wellness Ministry—Catholic Charities St. Francis Center, 100 W. 20th St., Riviera Beach, 33404. Tel: 561-345-2006; Email: wellness@ccdpb.org. *Catholic Charities St. Mary Center, 1200 E. Main St., Pahokee, 33476.* Tel: 561-924-5677. *Notre Dame Mission, 217 N. U.S. Hwy. 1, Fort Pierce, 34950.*
Tel: 772-466-9617. BERNADETTE MACY, Prog. Coord.

Immigration Services—

Immigration Legal Services—Catholic Charities: St. Francis Center, 100 W. 20th St., Riviera Beach, 33404. Tel: 561-345-2003; Fax: 561-202-2310. *Catholic Charities: St. Mary Center, 1200 E. Main St., Pahokee, 33476.* Tel: 561-924-5677. *1300 S.E. 10th St., Stuart, 34995.*
Tel: 772-463-0445; Fax: 772-872-0311. TIMOTHY KEOHANE, Attorney/Prog. Dir.

Hunger, Homeless and Outreach—Catholic Charities St. Francis Center, 100 W. 20th St., Riviera Beach, 33404. Tel: 561-345-2000. *St. Mary Center, 100 E. Main St., Pahokee, 33476.* Tel: 561-924-5677. MRS. ROCIO LOPEZ, Prog. Admin.

Pregnancy Services—

Birthline/Lifeline—212 E. Boynton Beach Blvd., Boynton Beach, 33435. Tel: 561-738-2060. *3115 45th St., West Palm Beach, 33407.*
Tel: 561-345-2037; Fax: 561-842-9303. *St. Mary Center, 1200 E. Main St., Pahokee, 33476.*
Tel: 561-924-5677. KATHERINE BOWERS, Prog. Dir.

Refugee Services—

Refugee, Resettlement and Human Trafficking—Catholic Charities St. Francis Center, 100 W. 20th St., Riviera Beach, 33404. Tel: 561-345-2002; Fax: 561-863-1680. SANDRA PEREZ, Prog. Admin.

Prison Ministry—Catholic Charities St. Francis Center, 100 W. 20th St., Riviera Beach, 33404.
Tel: 561-360-3326. Deacon GREGORY QUINN, Dir.

Respite Program—1300 S.E. 10th St., Stuart, 34996.
Tel: 772-283-0541. ANN SODDERS, R.N., Respite Nurse Coord.

Transitional Housing—

Samaritan Center—3650 41st St., Vero Beach, 32967. Tel: 772-770-3039; Fax: 772-567-0812. RENEE BIRELEY, Prog. Admin.

Respect Life Ministry—Catholic Charities St. Francis Center, 100 W. 20th St., Riviera Beach, 33404.
Tel: 561-360-3330. DEANNA HERBST-HOOSAC, Prog. Admin.

Project Rachel - Post Abortion Healing—SUSAN POLO, Coord., Tel: 561-360-3325; Cell: 561-531-3008 (call or text).

Catholic Relief Services—Catholic Charities St. Francis Center, 100 W. 20th St., Riviera Beach, 33404. Tel: 561-360-3327. ELENA M. GARCIA, Ministry Dir.

Parish Social Ministry—Catholic Charities St. Francis Center, 100 W. 20th St., Riviera Beach, 33404.
Tel: 561-360-3327. ELENA M. GARCIA, Ministry Dir.

Volunteer Services—Catholic Charities St. Francis Ctr., 100 W. 20th St., Riviera Beach, 33404.
Tel: 561-345-2005. NICOLE KILEY, Volunteer Coord.; CAROL RODRIGUEZ, PQI Compliance Admin.

Organizations and Movements

Charismatic Movement—

English—VACANT.

Spanish—Tel: 561-793-8544. Rev. FRANCISCO J. OSORIO, J.C.L.

Christ Child Society—

Boca Raton—AGNES GREGORY, Tel: 551-289-2371; Email: agnesgreg@aol.com.

North Palm Beach—ANNE KROHA, Tel: 231-526-0291; Email: annekroha@msn.com.

Stuart—LIZ MCINTYRE, Pres., Tel: 772-463-0405; Email: barbaralangella@optonline.net.

Con El, Healthcare Ministry to the Third World—DOROTHY MARTIN, Tel: 561-659-2822.

Council of Catholic Women—Rev. CLEMENS HAMMERSCHMITT, Spiritual Advisor, Tel: 561-966-8878; Email: frclemh@bellsouth.net; TAMMY FARR, Pres., Tel: 772-801-9772.

Cursillo Movement—

English—Tel: 561-747-9330. Deacon JOSEPH O'CONNELL, Spiritual Advisor, Tel: 561-798-0751; MR. RON CRESCENZO, Lay Dir., Tel: 561-758-9364.

Spanish—Tel: 561-964-4168. Sr. MARGARITA GOMEZ, R.M.I., S.T.L., D.Min., Spiritual Advisor; ALICIA M. FERNANDEZ, Lay Dir.

Damas Catolicas en Acion—Very Rev. NESTOR RODRIGUEZ, V.F., Spiritual Moderator.

Knights of Columbus—Very Rev. Canon THOMAS J. SKINDELESKI, Tel: 561-276-6892.

Legion of Mary, Palm Beach Curia—Rev. DANIS RIDORE, Spiritual Moderator, Tel: 561-276-6892; MRS. JILL KOZOL, Pres., Tel: 561-629-5200.

CLERGY, PARISHES, MISSIONS AND PAROCHIAL SCHOOLS

CITY OF PALM BEACH GARDENS

(PALM BEACH GARDENS), CATHEDRAL OF ST. IGNATIUS LOYOLA (1984) Very Rev. Thomas E. Barrett, Rector; Revs. J. Scott Adams, Parochial Vicar; Jose Crucet, Parochial Vicar.

Res.: 9999 N. Military Tr., 33410.

Tel: 561-622-2565, Ext. 1; Email: office@cathedralpb.com; Web: www.cathedralpb.com.

See All Saints Catholic School, Jupiter under Interparochial Schools located in the Institution section.

Catechesis Religious Program—Email: daitken@cathedralpb.com. Dee Aitken, D.R.E. Students 198.

OUTSIDE THE CITY OF PALM BEACH GARDENS

BELLE GLADE, PALM BEACH CO., ST. PHILIP BENIZI (1961) Revs. Matthew DeGance; Manuel Alvarez, S.D.B., Parochial Vicar; Jean Wilgintz Polynice, S.B.D., Parochial Vicar; Joseph Santa-Bibiana, S.D.B., Pastor Emeritus.

Res.: 710 S. Main St., Belle Glade, 33430-4202.

Tel: 561-996-3870; Email: philip710@comcast.net.

Catechesis Religious Program—Julissa Camacho, D.R.E.; Francisca Esparza, D.R.E. Students 393.

BOCA RATON, PALM BEACH CO.

1—ASCENSION (1968)

7250 N. Federal Hwy., Boca Raton, 33487.
Tel: 561-997-5486; Email: ascension@accboca.net; Email: admin-asst@accboca.net. Revs. Gavin J. Badway; Charles Hawkins, Pastor Emeritus, (Retired); Carl Hellwig, Parochial Vicar; Deacons Lon Phillips; Bruce Turnbull.
Catechesis Religious Program—Students 133.

2—ST. JOAN OF ARC (1956) Rev. Msgr. Michael D. McGraw, V.F.; Revs. Dominic Toan Tran, Parochial Vicar; Martin Dunne III, Parochial Vicar; Deacon William Watzek.
Res.: 370 S.W. 3rd St., Boca Raton, 33432.
Tel: 561-392-0007; Email: info_church@stjoan.org; Web: www.stjoan.org.
School—St. Joan of Arc School, (Grades 1-8), 501 S.W. 3rd Ave., Boca Raton, 33432. Tel: 561-392-7974; Fax: 561-368-6671; Email: roberts_caroline@stjoan.org; Web: www.stjoan.org. Sr. Caroline Roberts, Prin. Lay Teachers 36; Sisters 1; Students 565.
Catechesis Religious Program—Tel: 561-952-2870; Tel: 561-392-7974; Email: davidson_rosa@stjoan.org; Email: roberts_caroline@stjoan.org. Rosa Davidson, D.R.E.; Sr. Caroline Roberts, Prin. Students 564.
Convent—500 S.W. 4th Ave., Boca Raton, 33432.

3—ST. JOHN THE EVANGELIST (1992) Rev. Michael O'Flaherty.
Res.: 10300 Yamato Rd., Boca Raton, 33498.
Tel: 561-488-1373; Email: stjohnbocaraton@bellsouth.net.
Catechesis Religious Program—Email: religiousedstjohn@gmail.com. Margaret Ciccone, D.R.E. Students 216.

4—ST. JUDE (1979) Revs. John F. Horan, O.Carm.; Christopher Iannizzotto, Parochial Vicar; Joseph Nguyen Do, Parochial Vicar. In Res., Very Rev. Michael Driscoll, O.Carm.
Church: 21689 Toledo Rd., Boca Raton, 33433.
Tel: 561-392-8172; Fax: 561-362-0845; Email: info@stjudeboca.org; Web: www.stjudeboca.org.
Rectory & Priory: 2235 S.W. 16th Pl., Boca Raton, 33486-8560.
School—St. Jude School, (Grades 1-8), Saint Jude Catholic School, 21689 Toledo Road, Boca Raton, 33433. Tel: 561-392-9160; Email: duganda@saintjudeschool.org. Miss. Debbie Armstrong, Prin. & Preschool Dir. Lay Teachers 31; Students 394; Parish or Independent 1.
Catechesis Religious Program—Tel: 561-314-1057; Fax: 561-362-0845; Email: melanie@stjude.org. Students 465.

5—OUR LADY OF LOURDES (1977) Revs. Eduardo Medina; Francis Reardon, Pastor Emeritus, (Retired).
Res.: 22094 Lyons Rd., Boca Raton, 33428.
Tel: 561-483-2440; Email: secretary@lourdesboca.org.
Catechesis Religious Program—
Tel: 561-483-2440, Ext. 1429; Fax: 561-558-1434; Email: dre@lourdesboca.org. Students 427.

BOYNTON BEACH, PALM BEACH CO.

1—ST. MARK (1952)
730 N.E. 6th Ave., Boyton Beach, 33435. Revs. Daniel G. Fink, O.F.M.Conv.; Richard T. Florek, O.F.M.-Conv., Parochial Vicar; Joseph Dorniak, Parochial Vicar; Sr. Mary Joan Millecan, Contact Person, St. Mark Pastoral Care; Rev. Germain Kopaczynski, O.-F.M.Conv., In Res.
Res.: 643 St. Mark Pl., Boynton Beach, 33435.
Tel: 561-734-9330; Fax: 561-735-3463; Email: p.schultz@gostmark.com.
St. Mark Pastoral Care—730 N.E. 6th Ave., Boynton Beach, 33435. Tel: 561-735-3530.
Catechesis Religious Program—Email: mgaretano@gostmark.com. Margaret Castor, D.R.E. Students 171.

2—ST. THOMAS MORE (1972) Revs. Julian P. Harris; Alex J. Vargas, Parochial Vicar; Deacon Silvio Menendez.
Res.: 10935 S. Military Tr., Boynton Beach, 33436.
Tel: 561-737-3095; Web: chiefofstaff@stmbb.org.
School—Thomas More Academy for Early Childhood Learning, Tel: 561-737-3770; Email: academydirector@stmbb.org; Email: schooloffice@stmbb.org. Anne Marie Fischer, Dir. Lay Teachers 14; Students 100.
Catechesis Religious Program—Dorothy Kaiser, D.R.E. Students 308.

DELRAY BEACH, PALM BEACH CO.

1—EMMANUEL (1983)
15700 S. Military Tr., Delray Beach, 33484.
Tel: 561-496-2480; Email: ssahu@diocesepb.org; Email: secretary@emmanuelcatholic.church. Revs. Timothy Sockol, Pastor Emeritus, (Retired); Gaudioso Zamora, Admin.
Catechesis Religious Program—Students 105.

2—OUR LADY OF PERPETUAL HELP MISSION (1987) Rev. Roland Desormeaux, C.S.
Church & Res.: 510 S.W. Eighth Ave., Delray Beach, 33444-2448. Tel: 561-276-4880; Email: perpetualchurch@att.net.
Catechesis Religious Program—Students 92.

3—OUR LADY QUEEN OF PEACE (1963) Rev. Manuel Galvan Vargas, C.S. In Res., Rev. Alexander Dalpiaz, C.S.
Res.: 9600 W. Atlantic Ave., Delray Beach, 33446.
Tel: 561-499-6234, Ext. 0; Email: conchya@bellsouth.net.
Catechesis Religious Program—Students 232.

4—ST. VINCENT FERRER (1941) Very Rev. Canon Thomas J. Skindeleski; Deacons Frank Iovine; Gregory Osgood; Robert Laquerre, Business Mgr. In Res., Rev. Danis Ridore.
Res.: 840 George Bush Blvd., Delray Beach, 33483.
Tel: 561-276-6892; Fax: 561-276-8068; Email: office@stvincentferrer.com; Web: www.stvincentferrer.com.
School—St. Vincent Ferrer School, (Grades PreK-8), 810 George Bush Blvd., Delray Beach, 33483.
Tel: 561-278-3868; Fax: 561-279-9508; Email: vikki.delgado@stvfschool.org; Web: www.stvfschool.org. Mrs. M. Vikki Delgado, Prin. Religious Teachers 1; Lay Teachers 30; Little Servant Sisters of the Immaculate Conception 2; Students 357.
Catechesis Religious Program—Email: religioused@stvincentferrer.com. Students 127.

FELLSMERE, INDIAN RIVER CO., OUR LADY OF GUADALUPE MISSION (1991)
Tel: 772-571-9875; Email: office@olgmission.com. Revs. Sabas Ntimia Mallya, A.L.C.P., (Tanzania) Priest in Charge; John Morrissey.
Catechesis Religious Program—Students 252.
Mission—Rte. 512, P.O. Box 9, Fellsmere, Indian River Co. 32948.

FORT PIERCE, ST. LUCIE CO.

1—ST. ANASTASIA (1911)
407 S. 33rd St., Fort Pierce, 34947.
Tel: 772-461-2233; Email: annulments@stanastasiachurch.org; Web: www.stanastasiachurch.org. Revs. Richard E. George II; Jaime Dorado, (Colombia) Admin.; Daniel Daza-Jaller, Parochial Vicar.
School—St. Anastasia School, (Grades K-8), 401 S. 33 St., Fort Pierce, 34947. Tel: 772-461-2232; Fax: 772-468-2037; Email: info@stanna.org; Web: www.saintanastasiaschool.org. Dr. Kevin Hoeffner, Prin. Lay Teachers 36; Students 515.
Catechesis Religious Program—Email: sacraments@stanastasiachurch.org. Students 434.
Mission—San Juan Diego Hispanic Center, 401 S. 30th St., P.O. Box 1197, Fort Pierce, 34947.
Tel: 772-468-0806; Email: sanjuandiegohm129@outlook.com.
Catechesis Religious Program—
Tel: 772-216-7397; Email: tlezama@att.net. Teresa Velazquez Lezama, D.R.E. Students 92.

2—ST. MARK THE EVANGELIST (1972) Revs. Robert L. Pope Jr., Admin.; Edwin Edezath, O.C.D., Parochial Vicar; Michael J. McNally, M.Div., M.Th., M.A., Ph. D., Pastor Emeritus, (Retired).
Res.: 1924 Zephyr Ave., Fort Pierce, 34982.
Tel: 772-461-8150; Email: stmarkssecretary@bellsouth.com.
Catechesis Religious Program—Email: drestmark@bellsouth.net. Students 51.

3—NOTRE DAME MISSION (1995) Rev. Yves Geffrard.
Res.: 217 N. U.S. Hwy. #1, Fort Pierce, 34950.
Tel: 561-466-9617; Fax: 561-466-7075; Email: notredamecatholicmission@hotmail.com; Web: notredamecc.com.
Catechesis Religious Program—Tel: 772-335-9540. Students 24.

HIGHLAND BEACH, PALM BEACH CO., ST. LUCY (1968)
3510 S. Ocean Blvd., Highland Beach, 33487.
Tel: 561-278-1280; Email: stlucys@bellsouth.net; Web: www.stlucycommunity.com. Rev. Daniel B. Horgan, Ph.D.
Catechesis Religious Program—Students 12.

HOBE SOUND, MARTIN CO., ST. CHRISTOPHER (1960) Very Rev. Aidan Hynes, V.F.
Res.: 12001 S.E. Federal Hwy., Hobe Sound, 33455.
Tel: 772-546-5150; Email: office@stchrishs.com; Web: stchrishs.com.
See All Saints Catholic School, Jupiter under Interparochial Schools located in the Institution section.
Catechesis Religious Program—Students 175.

INDIANTOWN, MARTIN CO., HOLY CROSS (1960)
Mailing Address: 15939 S.W. 150th St., P.O. Box 999, Indiantown, 34956. Tel: 772-597-2798; Fax: 772-597-2741; Email: holcros1@itspeed.net; Email: holycross351@hotmail.com; Web: holycrossindiantown.org. Revs. Francisco J. Osorio, J.C.L.; Juan de la Calle, Pastor Emeritus; Raciel Trevino, Parochial Vicar.
Res.: 15670 Famel Blvd., Indiantown, 34956.
Catechesis Religious Program—Email: chontaduro73@hotmail.com. Juan Carlos lasso, D.R.E. Students 115.

JENSEN BEACH, MARTIN CO., ST. MARTIN DE PORRES (1973) Rev. James Molgano.
Res.: 2555 N.E. Savanna Rd., Jensen Beach, 34957.
Tel: 772-334-4214; Email: info@stmartindp.com; Web: www.stmartindp.com.
Catechesis Religious Program—Tel: 772-334-4492; Email: religioused@stmartindp.com. Students 37.

JUPITER, PALM BEACH CO., ST. PETER (1987) Revs. Donald T. Finney; Jean Wesner Boulin, Parochial Vicar; Wesler Hilaire, Parochial Vicar; Deacons Stephen McMahon; Donald Battison; Stephen Scienzo; Jean Serge Dube; John Collins; John Bartalini; Dave Licata.
Res.: 1701 Indian Creek Pkwy., Jupiter, 33458.
Tel: 561-575-0837; Email: parish@stpetercatholicchurch.com; Email: father.don@stpetercatholicchurch.com; Web: stpetercatholicchurch.com.
See All Saints Catholic School, Jupiter under Interparochial Schools located in the Institution section.
Catechesis Religious Program—Email: becky.miklos@stpetercatholicchurch.com. Students 540.

LAKE WORTH, PALM BEACH CO.

1—ST. MATTHEW (1992) Revs. Clemens Hammerschmitt; Leonard Dim, Parochial Vicar.
Res. & Mailing: 6090 Hypoluxo Rd., Lake Worth, 33463-7312. Tel: 561-966-8878; Email: frclemh@bellsouth.net.
Catechesis Religious Program—Tel: 561-966-1538. Students 237.

2—SACRED HEART (1916)
425 N. M St., Lake Worth, 33460. Tel: 561-582-4736; Email: rectory@sacredheartfamily.com; Web: sacredheartfamily.com. Revs. Quesnel Delvard; Nobert Jean-Pierre, (Haiti) Parochial Vicar.
School—Sacred Heart School, (Grades K-8), 410 N. M St., Lake Worth, 33460. Tel: 561-582-2242; Fax: 561-547-9699; Email: tamposic@sacredheartfamily.com; Web: www.sacredheartschoollakeworth.com. Candace Tamposi, Prin. Lay Teachers 32; Students 230.
Catechesis Religious Program—
Tel: 561-584-4156, Ext. 200. Students 231.

LANTANA, PALM BEACH CO., HOLY SPIRIT (1964) Revs. Elifete St. Fort; Ronald Schulz, Pastor Emeritus, (Retired).
Res. and Mailing: 1000 Lantana Rd., P.O. Box 3978, Lantana, 33465. Tel: 561-585-5970; Email: hspiritlantana@gmail.com.
Catechesis Religious Program—Students 146.

NORTH PALM BEACH, PALM BEACH CO.

1—ST. CLARE (1960) Revs. William D. O'Shea; Mark Mlay, A.L.C.P., (Tanzania) Parochial Vicar.
Res.: 821 Prosperity Farms Rd., North Palm Beach, 33408. Tel: 561-622-7477; Email: stclare821@aol.com.
School—St. Clare School, (Grades PreK-8),
Tel: 561-622-7171; Email: info@stclarecatholicschool.org; Web: stclareschool.com. Mrs. Rita Kissel, Prin. Lay Teachers 32; Students 325.
Catechesis Religious Program—Tel: 561-420-2311; Email: sbernardin@stclarecatholicschool.org. Sara Bernardin, D.R.E. Students 84.

2—ST. PAUL OF THE CROSS (1970) Very Rev. Thomas R. LaFreniere, V.F.; Deacons Frank Bandy; Gregory Quinn; Rev. Nadeem Yaqoob, In Res.
Res.: 10970 Jack Nicklaus Dr., North Palm Beach, 33408. Tel: 561-626-1873; Fax: 561-626-4383; Email: office@paulcross.org; Email: pattiwengierski@paulcross.org; Web: paulcross.org.
See All Saints Catholic School, Jupiter under Interparochial Schools located in the Institution section.
Catechesis Religious Program—Email: kate.devine@paulcross.org. Students 107.

OKEECHOBEE, OKEECHOBEE CO., SACRED HEART (1964)
Mailing Address: P.O. Box 716, Okeechobee, 34973. Rev. Yves Francois.
Res.: 901 S.W. 6th St., Okeechobee, 34974.
Tel: 863-763-3727; Fax: 863-763-9334; Email: sacredheart901@outlook.com.
Catechesis Religious Program—Tel: 863-763-2745. Students 420.

PAHOKEE, PALM BEACH CO., ST. MARY (1933) Rev. Juan Raul Cardenas.
Res.: 1200 E. Main St., Pahokee, 33476.
Tel: 561-924-7305; Email: office@stmaryofpahokee.com; Web: www.stmarysofpahokee.com.
Catechesis Religious Program—Tel: 561-342-8038. Students 141.

PALM BEACH, PALM BEACH CO., ST. EDWARD (1926) Rev. Msgr. Thomas J. Klinzing, J.C.L.
Res.: 144 N. County Rd., Palm Beach, 33480.
Tel: 561-832-0400; Email: stedwardch@aol.com.
Catechesis Religious Program—Students 77.

PALM BEACH GARDENS, PALM BEACH CO., ST. PATRICK (1987) Revs. Aidan Lacy; Brian Flanagan, Pastor Emeritus, (Retired); John D'Mello, Parochial Vicar; Mr. Mark Chiarello, Business Mgr.
Res.: 13591 Prosperity Farms Rd., 33410.
Tel: 561-626-8626; Email: mark@stpatrickchurch.org; Web: www.stpatrickchurch.org.
Rectory—2549 Hope Ln. W., 33410.

See All Saints Catholic School, Jupiter under Interparochial Schools located in the Institution section.
Catechesis Religious Program—Students 280.
PALM CITY, MARTIN CO., HOLY REDEEMER (1983)
1454 S. W. Mapp Rd, Palm City, 34990. Rev. Martin B. Mulqueen; Margaret Castor, D.R.E.
PALM SPRINGS, PALM BEACH CO., ST. LUKE (1961) Revs. Andrew Brierley; Edgar Mazariegos, Parochial Vicar.
Res.: 2892 S. Congress Ave., Palm Springs, 33461.
Tel: 561-965-8980; Email: frandrew@stlukeparish.com.
School—St. Luke School, (Grades 1-8), St. Luke Catholic School, 2892 S. Congress Ave., Palm Springs, 33461. Tel: 561-965-8190; Email: diana.flores@stlukeparish.com; Web: www.stlukepalmsprings.org/. Mrs. Diann Bacchus, Prin. Lay Teachers 17; Students 215.
Catechesis Religious Program—Email: sully@stlukeparish.com. Robert Sullivan, D.R.E. Students 700.
PORT ST. LUCIE, ST. LUCIE CO.
1—ST. BERNADETTE (2001)
350 N.W. California Blvd., Port St. Lucie, 34986.
Tel: 772-336-9956; Email: parish@stbernadetteslw.org; Web: www.stbernadetteslw.org. Revs. Victor A. Ulto; Antony Lopez, O.C.D.; Deacon Martin Ervin.
Catechesis Religious Program—Email: eric@stbernadetteslw.org. Mr. Eric Seibenick, D.R.E. Students 228.
2—ST. ELIZABETH ANN SETON (1993) Revs. Son Linh Hoang; Andre Dumarsais Pierre-Louis.
Church: 930 S.W. Tunis Ave., Port St. Lucie, 34953-3351. Tel: 772-336-0282; Email: seton@steasparish.org; Web: seascatholicparish.org.
Catechesis Religious Program—Tel: 772-336-0393; Email: donna@steasparish.org. Donna Caiazzo, D.R.E. Students 257.
3—HOLY FAMILY (1987)
Mailing Address: 2330 Mariposa Ave., Port St. Lucie, 34952. Tel: 772-335-2385; Fax: 772-335-2517; Email: holyfamilycat868@bellsouth.net; Web: holyfamilyccpsl.com. Revs. Tri Tang Pham; Thomas F. Cauley Jr., Pastor Emeritus, (Retired); Tomasz Bochnak, Parochial Vicar; Michael Cairnes, Parochial Vicar.
Catechesis Religious Program—Tel: 772-337-4313. Students 240.
4—ST. LUCIE (1961)
425 S.W. Irving St., Port St. Lucie, 34983.
Tel: 772-878-1215; Email: adeluca@stlucie.cc; Email: drecco@stlucie.cc; Web: www.stlucie.cc. 280 S.W. Prima Vista, Port St. Lucie, 34983. Rev. Mark Szanyi, O.F.M.Conv.; Rev. Msgr. James M. Burke, Pastor Emeritus, (Retired); Revs. Peter C. Dolan, Pastor Emeritus, (Retired); Paul Gabriel, O.F.M.Conv.; Daniel Pal, O.F.M.Conv., Parochial Vicar; Curt Kreml, O.F.M.Conv., Parochial Vicar; Deacons Carlos Melendez; Dale Konas; Vincent Cookingham; Normand Etienne.
Catechesis Religious Program—290 S.W. Prima Vista, Port Saint Lucie, 34983. Email: adraper@stlucie.cc. Andrea Draper, D.R.E. Students 300.
RIVIERA BEACH, PALM BEACH CO., ST. FRANCIS OF ASSISI (1948) Rev. Peter Truong.
Res.: 200 W. 20th St., Riviera Beach, 33404-6160.
Tel: 561-842-2482; Email: chathuongsfa@gmail.com.
Catechesis Religious Program—Students 10.
ROYAL PALM BEACH, PALM BEACH CO., OUR LADY QUEEN OF THE APOSTLES (1988) Revs. Zbigniew A. Rudnicki; Laurent Assenga, A.L.C.P., Parochial Vicar; Brian Campbell, Parochial Vicar; Deacons Robert Laquerre; Rodney Brimlow.
Res.: 100 Crestwood Blvd. S., Royal Palm Beach, 33411. Tel: 561-798-5661; Email: info@olqa.cc; Web: www.olqa.cc.
Catechesis Religious Program—Email: lauras@olqa.cc. Laura Schroeder, D.R.E. Students 252.
SEBASTIAN, INDIAN RIVER CO., ST. SEBASTIAN (1981)
Mailing Address: 13075 U.S. Hwy. 1, Sebastian, 32958. Tel: 772-589-5790; Fax: 772-388-0084; Email: office@stsebastian.com; Email: rectory@stsebastian.com; Web: www.stsebastian.com. Revs. John Morrissey; Sabas Mallya, A.L.C.P., Parochial Vicar; Deacons Patrick Moynihan; Arnold Goodman, Liturgy Dir.; Steven Guess, RCIA Coord.; John Dunlop.
Catechesis Religious Program—Tel: 772-589-4147; Email: debbie@stsebastian.com. Debbie Bova, D.R.E. Students 32.
STUART, MARTIN CO.
1—ST. ANDREW (1999) Rev. John A. Barrow.
Church & Mailing: 2100 S.E. Cove Rd., Stuart, 34997. Tel: 772-781-4415; Fax: 772-781-2906; Email: admin@saintandrewcatholic.org; Web: saintandrewcatholic.org.
Catechesis Religious Program—Students 119.
2—ST. JOSEPH (1916) Revs. Noel McGrath, (Ireland); John Minde, A.L.C.P., Parochial Vicar.
Res.: 1200 E. 10th St., Stuart, 34996.
Tel: 772-287-2727, Ext. 102; Email: maritam@sjcflorida.org; Web: sjcflorida.org.
School—St. Joseph School, (Grades PreK-8),
Tel: 772-287-6975; Email: tsprauer@sjscf.org; Web: sjcschargers.com. Mrs. Tina Sprauer, Sec. Clergy 2; Lay Teachers 30; Students 265; Parish or Independent 1.
Catechesis Religious Program—Email: srjadwiga@sjcflorida.org. Sr. Jadwiga Drapala, CACh, D.R.E. Students 90.
TEQUESTA, PALM BEACH CO., ST. JUDE (1962)
Mailing Address: 204 N US Hwy One, P.O. Box 3726, Tequesta, 33469. Tel: 561-746-7974; Email: info@stjudechurch.net; Web: www.stjudecatholicchurch.net. Very Rev. Charles E. Notabartolo, V.G.; Rev. Frank D'Amato, Parochial Vicar. In Res., Very Rev. Albert A. Dello Russo, J.C.L.
See All Saints Catholic School, Jupiter under Interparochial Schools located in the Institution section.
Catechesis Religious Program—Tel: 561-748-8805; Email: deaconles@stjudechurch.net; Email: ymdirector@stjudechurch.net. Deacon Lester Loh, D.R.E.; Frank Faranda, D.R.E. Students 186.
VERO BEACH, INDIAN RIVER CO.
1—ST. HELEN (1919)
2085 Tallahassee Ave., P.O. Box 2927, Vero Beach, 32961. Tel: 772-567-5129; Email: sthelenchurch@hotmail.com; Web: sthelenvero.org. Very Rev. Kevin C. Nelson, M.A., M.Div., V.F.; Revs. Michael W. Edwards, P.E., Pastor Emeritus, (Retired); Pierre-Soul Estefont, Parochial Vicar; Benedict Redito, Parochial Vicar.
School—St. Helen School, (Grades 1-8), 2050 Vero Beach Ave., Vero Beach, 32960. Tel: 772-567-5457; Fax: 772-567-4823; Email: s.harpring@sthelenschoolvero.org; Web: www.sthelenschoolvero.org. 2025 20th Ave., Vero Beach, 32960. Lisa Bell, Prin. Lay Teachers 24; Students 274.
Catechesis Religious Program—2025 20th Ave., Vero Beach, 32960. Students 299.
2—HOLY CROSS (1981) Rev. Richard Murphy.
Res.: 500 Iris Ln., Vero Beach, 32963.
Tel: 772-231-0671; Email: dtrue@holycrossverobeach.org; Web: www.holycrossverobeach.org.
Catechesis Religious Program—Email: lhumenik@holycrossverobeach.org. Lori Humenik, D.R.E. Students 140.
3—ST. JOHN OF THE CROSS (1989)
7550 26th St., Vero Beach, 32966. Revs. John J. Pasquini; Michael Massaro, C.S.C., Parochial Vicar; Chamindra Williams; Michael J. Martin, C.S.P.; Deacons Gary Gallagher; Charles Mallory; Joseph Verboys; Dennis Beauregard; Robert Borchert.
Res.: 7590 26th St., Vero Beach, 32966.
Tel: 772-563-0057; Email: stjohnofthecross@bellsouth.net; Web: stjotc.org.
Catechesis Religious Program—Students 23.
WELLINGTON, PALM BEACH CO.
1—ST. RITA (1980) Rev. Donald Munro. In Res., Rev. Duvan Bermudez.
Res.: 13645 Paddock Dr., Wellington, 33414.
Tel: 561-793-8544; Email: saintrita@bellsouth.net; Web: www.saintrita.com.
2—ST. THERESE DE LISIEUX (2000)
Mailing Address: 11800 Lake Worth Rd., Wellington, 33449. Rev. David C. Downey; Deacons Alfred C. Payne; Robert Rodriguez; Pedro DelValle.
Rectory—3760 Cypress Edge Dr., Lake Worth, 33467. Tel: 561-784-0689; Email: bookkeeper@sttherese-church.org; Web: sttheresechurch.org.
Catechesis Religious Program—Students 320.
WEST PALM BEACH, PALM BEACH CO.
1—ST. ANN (1895)
310 N. Olive Ave., West Palm Beach, 33401.
Tel: 561-832-3757; Email: saintannchurch1@msn.com. Very Rev. Nestor Rodriguez, V.F.; Revs. James Murtagh, Pastor Emeritus, (Retired); Dennis Gonzales, Parochial Vicar.
Our Lady Faith Haitian Center—Tel: 561-223-2762.
School—St. Ann School, (Grades 1-8), 324 N. Olive Ave., West Palm Beach, 33401. Tel: 561-832-3676; Fax: 561-832-1791; Email: cpagano@saswpb.org; Web: www.stannwpb.org. Mrs. Susan Demes, Prin. Clergy 1; Lay Teachers 25; Students 268.
Catechesis Religious Program—Email: ReligiousEd@stannchurch.net. Veronica Matias, D.R.E. Students 64.
St. Ann Place Outreach to the Homeless—2107 N. Dixie Hwy., West Palm Beach, 33407.
Tel: 561-805-7708. John Pescosolido, Dir.
2—HOLY NAME OF JESUS (1954) Revs. Antony Pulikal, O.C.D.; George Kodiyanthara, O.C.D., Parochial Vicar; Antony Madathiparambil, Parochial Vicar; Deacons Edgar Caceres; Jack Hamilton; Peter Mazzella.
Res.: 345 S. Military Tr., West Palm Beach, 33415.
Tel: 561-683-3555; Email: hnjchurch@aol.com.
Catechesis Religious Program—
Tel: 561-683-3555, Ext. 111; Email: jriveccio@myhnj.org. Josephine Riveccio, D.R.E. Students 269.
3—ST. JOHN FISHER (1963) Revs. Mario Castaneda; Marco Tulio DeLeon, Parochial Vicar.
Res.: 4001 N. Shore Dr., West Palm Beach, 33407.
Tel: 561-842-1224; Email: stjohnfisher4001@aol.com; Web: stjohnfisherwpb.com.
Catechesis Religious Program—Students 80.
4—ST. JULIANA (1949)
4510 S. Dixie Hwy., West Palm Beach, 33405. 4500 S. Dixie Hwy., West Palm Beach, 33405.
Tel: 561-833-9745; Fax: 561-833-4992; Email: dulcemaria@stjulianacatholicchurch.com; Web: www.stjulianacatholicchurch.com. Revs. Ducasse Francois; Wisman Simeon, Parochial Vicar; Pierre-Michel Alabre, I.V., Parochial Vicar.
School—St. Juliana School, 4355 S. Olive Ave, West Palm Beach, 33405. Tel: 561-655-1922;
Fax: 561-655-8552; Email: info@saintjuliana.org; Web: www.saintjuliana.org. Marikay Kervi, Prin. Lay Teachers 25; Students 350.
Catechesis Religious Program—326 Pine Ter., West Palm Beach, 33405. Tel: 561-833-1278. Students 304.
5—MARY IMMACULATE (1974)
390 Sequoia Dr. S., West Palm Beach, 33409.
Tel: 561-686-8128; Email: nflores@miwpb.com; Web: www.miwpb.com. Rev. Tomasz Makowski.
Catechesis Religious Program—Tel: 561-530-8003; Email: miwpb@miwpb.com. Kendall Castay, D.R.E. Students 112.

Released from Diocesan Assignment:
Revs.—
Hernandez, Alfredo, St. Vincent de Paul Regional Seminary
O'Flanagan, Thomas P., US Navy Chap.

Retired:
Rev. Msgrs.—
Burke, James M., (Retired)
McMahon, John, (Retired)
Revs.—
Block, John G., (Retired)
Calle, Juan de la, (Retired)
Cauley, Thomas F. Jr., (Retired)
Devereaux, Martin C., (Retired)
Dolan, Peter C., (Retired)
Duffy, Hugh, (Retired)
Edwards, Michael W., P.E., (Retired)
Flanagan, Brian, (Retired)
Guerin, Louis T., M.Div., (Retired)
Guinan, Frank, (Retired)
Hawkins, Edward
Kasparek, John A., (Retired)
Kuczborski, Joseph, (Retired)
MacGabhann, Kevin, (Retired)
McNally, Michael J., M.Div., M.Th., M.A., Ph.D., (Retired)
Mericantante, John J., (Retired)
Murtagh, James, (Retired)
O'Loughlin, Frank, (Retired)
O'Toole, Timothy, (Retired)
Reardon, Francis, (Retired)
Schulz, Ronald, (Retired)
Skehan, John A., (Retired)
Sockol, Timothy, (Retired)
Szpieg, Edmund L., (Retired)
Torres, Adrian, (Retired)
Van Nguyen, Peter, (Retired)
Venezia, Arthur, (Retired)
Vengayil, Thomas, V.F., (Retired).

Permanent Deacons:
Aceto, Igino
Bandy, Frank
Bartalini, John
Bartlett, Matthew
Battison, Donald
Battista, Donald
Beaudoin, John
Beauregard, Dennis
Beres, Ronald
Blake, Richard
Bloom, David
Borchert, Robert
Bott, Gerald
Brimlow, Rodney
Caceres, Edgar
Collins, John
Condon, Laurence
Cookingham, Vincent
Crary, Lawrence
Creelman, Wayne
Cunningham, John
Cuseo, Anthony
DelValle, Pedro
DiMauro, Joseph

Dingee, Richard
Dove, Steven
Draughton, Woodworth
Dube, Jean Serge
Dunlop, John
Ervin, Martin
Etienne, Normand
Farinas, Henry
Ferguson, William
Gallagher, Gary
Garamella, Robert
Gluhosky, Frank
Golden, Robert
Goodman, Arnold
Guardiario, Jose
Guess, Steven
Hamilton, Jack
Hankle, David
Hernandez, Ivan
Hoppe, Daniel
Horton, Gregory
Iovine, Frank
Konas, Dale
Laquerre, Robert
Levenson, Lee
Licata, David
Lizardi, Mark
Loh, Lester
Lyles, Richard
Mallory, Charles
Mares, Jose Antonio
Mazzella, Peter
McBride, Peter
McMahon, Stephen
Melendez, Carlos
Meyer, James
Miller, Michael
Mostler, John
Moynihan, Patrick
Munoz, Miguel
Nowak, Nick
Ortiz, Jose
Osgood, Kevin
Palermo, Gerard
Parrilli, James
Payne, Alfred C.
Phillips, Lon
Piasecki, Stanley
Plucinski, Andrew
Pollock, Joseph
Prestera, Michael
Quinn, Gregory
Rich, William
Rios, Oscar H.
Rivera, Angel
Rodriguez, Miguel
Rodriguez, Robert
Romero, Louis
Romero, Luis
Sandigo, Martin
Scienzo, Stephen
Serraes, Martin
Sherman, Gregory
Siegel, Lawrence
Sullivan, John
Topper, Wayne
Torres, Joseph
Turnbull, Bruce
Venezia, Richard
Verboys, Joseph
Vianale, Kenneth
Watzek, William
Weir, Charles
White, George
Zanotelli, David
Zapata, Jaime
Zatarga, Michael.

INSTITUTIONS LOCATED IN DIOCESE

[A] SEMINARIES, RELIGIOUS OR SCHOLASTICATES

BOYNTON BEACH. *St. Vincent de Paul Regional Seminary*, 10701 S. Military Tr., Boynton Beach, 33436. Tel: 561-732-4424; Fax: 561-737-2205; Email: hgarcia@svdp.edu; Web: www.svdp.edu. Mother Mary Roberta Connors, F.S.E., Dir. Ongoing Formation; Sr. Paula Jean Miller, F.S.E., Faculty; Rev. Higinio Rosolen, I.V.E., S.S.L., Faculty; Troy A. Stefano, Faculty; Rev. Msgr. David L. Toups, Rector; Dr. Antonio Lopez, Ph.D., Faculty; Mr. Art Quinn, B.A., M.A., M.S., Ed.S., Library Dir.; Revs. Arthur J. Proulx, V.F., Dean Spiritual Formation; Alfredo Hernandez, Academic Dean; Dr. Carol Razza, Ed.D., Faculty; Mr. Keith Parker, Campus Admin.; Dr. Joyce Martinez, B.A., M.Ed., Ed.D., Dir. Language; Revs. William L. Burton, O.F.M., Faculty; Remigiusz Blaszkowski, Dean of Human Formation; Juan Carlos Rios, Dean; Brian Bufford, Faculty; Gregg Caggianelli, D.Min., Dean of Pastoral Formation; Rev. Msgr. Stephen C. Bosso, Faculty; Revs. Nicholas Cachia, (Malta) S.T.D., Dir.; John Horn, S.J., Faculty; Daniel Ter Melaba, (Nigeria) Dir. of Field Educ.; Steven Olds, S.T.D., Dir. of Non-Res. Students; Dr. Mary Froehle, Ph.D., Dir.; Mrs. Shirley Luttio, Faculty; Revs. John A. Cippel, Priest in Res.; Llane Briese, Prof.; Mario Cardone, Prof.; Sr. Bernardone Rock, Music Min.; Alicia Rueff, Registrar. Clergy 12; Faculty 19; Seminarians 111; Sisters 3; Students 34.

Seminary Formation Council, LLC, 10701 S. Military Tr., Boynton Beach, 33436.
Tel: 561-732-4424; Email: jhorn@svdp.edu; Email: dtoups@svdp.edu. Rev. John Horn, S.J., Dir.; Rev. Msgr. David L. Toups, S.T.D., Treas.

[B] HIGH SCHOOLS, DIOCESAN AND PAROCHIAL

BOCA RATON. *Saint John Paul II Academy*, 4001 N. Military Tr., Boca Raton, 33431. Tel: 561-314-2100 ; Fax: 561-989-8582; Email: pjphs@pjpii.org; Web: www.sjpii.net. Bro. Daniel Aubin, F.S.C., Pres.; Edward Bernot, Librarian; Jennifer Mulhall, Asst. Prin. Academics; Sheila Garcia, Campus Min. Lay Teachers 34; Students 405.

FORT PIERCE. *John Carroll High School, Inc.* (1962) 3402 Delaware Ave., Fort Pierce, 34947-6116.
Tel: 772-464-5200; Fax: 772-464-5233; Email: jcchs@johncarrollhigh.com; Web: www.johncarrollhigh.com. Very Rev. Thomas E. Barrett, Pres.; Corey Heroux, Prin. Lay Teachers 32; Priests 1; Students 385.

WEST PALM BEACH. *Cardinal Newman High School, Inc.*, 512 Spencer Dr., West Palm Beach, 33409-3616. Tel: 561-683-6266; Fax: 561-683-7307; Email: chiggins@cardinalnewman.com; Web: www.cardinalnewman.com. Rev. David W. Carr, Pres.; Dr. Christine Higgins, Prin.; Ms. Theresa Fretterd, Vice Prin.; Ms. Susan Stephenson, Vice Prin. Lay Teachers 38; Priests 1; Students 477.

[C] INTERPAROCHIAL SCHOOLS

JUPITER. *All Saints Catholic School*, 1759 Indian Creek Pkwy., Jupiter, 33458. Tel: 561-748-8994;
Fax: 561-748-8979; Email: ascs@allsaintsjupiter.org; Web: www.allsaintsjupiter.org. Mrs. Jill Broz, Prin. Clergy 1; Lay Teachers 36; Students 497.

[D] SCHOOLS, PRIVATE

INDIANTOWN. *Hope Rural School*, (Grades PreK-5), 15929 S.W. 150th St., Indiantown, 34956.
Tel: 772-597-2203; Fax: 772-597-2259; Email: info@hoperuralschool.org; Web: www.hoperuralschool.org. Sisters Martha Rohde, O.P., Prin.; Elizabeth Dunn, O.P., Dir. Lay Teachers 12; Sisters 2; Students 142.

WEST PALM BEACH. *Holy Cross Catholic Preschool & Center*, 930 Southern Blvd., West Palm Beach, 33405. Tel: 561-366-8026; Fax: 561-366-8577; Email: director@holycrosscpc.org; Web: www.holcrosscpc.org. Ana M. Fundora, Exec. Dir. Clergy 1; Lay Teachers 19; Sisters 1; Students 95.

**Rosarian Academy*, (Grades 8-12), 807 N. Flagler Dr., West Palm Beach, 33401. Tel: 561-832-5131; Fax: 561-820-8750; Email: info@rosarian.org; Web: www.rosarian.org. Mrs. Linda Trethewey, Headmaster. Sisters of St. Dominic (Adrian, MI). Lay Teachers 47; Students 380.

[E] HOMES FOR AGED

WEST PALM BEACH. *Lourdes-Noreen McKeen Residence for Geriatric Care*, 315 Flagler Dr. S., West Palm Beach, 33401. Tel: 561-655-8544;
Fax: 561-650-8952; Email: srjeanette@lnmr.org; Web: www.lnmr.org. Sr. Jeanette Lindsay, O.-Carm., Admin.

[F] PERSONAL PRELATURES

DELRAY BEACH. *Prelature of the Holy Cross and Opus Dei*, 4409 Frances Dr., Delray Beach, 33445.
Tel: 561-498-1249; Email: vacg6556@gmail.com. Revs. Victor Cortes, Chap.; Joseph Landauer, Chap.; Eduardo Castillo, Chap.

[G] MONASTERIES AND RESIDENCES OF PRIESTS AND BROTHERS

NORTH PALM BEACH. *Our Lady of Florida Spiritual Center*, 1300 U.S. Hwy. No. 1, North Palm Beach, 33408. Tel: 561-626-1300; Fax: 561-627-3956; Email: lbrown@cpprov.org; Web: www.ourladyofflorida.org. Very Rev. Paul Wierichs, C.P., Rector; Bros. Augustine Lowe, C.P.; Edward Hall, C.P.; Rev. Melvin Shorter, C.P.; Very Rev. Edward Wolanski, C.P.; Rev. Francis Finnigan, C.P. Brothers 2; Priests 3.

VERO BEACH. *Paulist Fathers Residence*, 1225 20th Ave., Vero Beach, 32960. Tel: 772-532-4445; Email: phuesing@paulist.org. Revs. Paul Huesing, Supr.; Marcos Zamora, C.S.P.; James M. Brucz, C.S.P.; Michael J. Martin, C.S.P.; Richard Sparks.

[H] CONVENTS AND RESIDENCES FOR SISTERS

DELRAY BEACH. *Christ the King Monastery of St. Clare* (Solemn Vows, Papal Enclosure) 3900 Sherwood Blvd., Delray Beach, 33445-5655.
Tel: 561-498-3294; Fax: 561-498-2281; Email: ctkm.delray@juno.com. Sr. Leanna Chrostowski, O.S.C., Abbess. Cloistered Sisters 8.

STUART. *Congregation of the Sisters of the Most Holy Soul of Christ*, 1042 E. 9th St., Stuart, 34996.
Tel: 772-286-5720; Email: sisterscach@yahoo.com; Web: sistersofthemostholysoulofchrist.com. Sr. Anita Gabarczyk, C.A.C.H., Supr.

WEST PALM BEACH. *Adrian Dominican Sisters, Florida Mission Chapter*, 810 N. Olive Ave., West Palm Beach, 33401-3710. Tel: 561-832-6521;
Fax: 561-832-0365; Email: macaulfield@adriandominicans.org; Web: www.adriandominicans.org. Sr. Patricia Siemen, Prioress. Sisters 20.

Congregation of the Sisters of the Holy Cross, 2335 Edgewater Dr., West Palm Beach, 33406.
Tel: 561-434-7593; Email: sbrennan@cscsisters.org. Sr. Suzanne Brennan, Treas. Sisters 2.

[I] RETREAT HOUSES

NORTH PALM BEACH. *Our Lady of Florida Spiritual Center*, 1300 U.S. Hwy. No. 1, North Palm Beach, 33408. Tel: 561-626-1300; Fax: 561-627-3956; Email: lbrown@cpprov.org; Web: www.ourladyofflorida.org. Very Rev. Paul Wierichs, C.P., Rector; Revs. Francis Finnigan, C.P., Dir.; Edward Wolinkski, C.P., Dir.; Damian Towey, C.P., J.C.D., Assoc. Retreat Dir.; Bros. Augustine Lowe, C.P., Assoc. Retreat Dir.; Edward Hall, C.P., Assoc. Retreat Dir.; Rev. Melvin Shorter, C.P., Assoc. Retreat Dir.

[J] MISCELLANEOUS LISTINGS

PALM BEACH GARDENS. *Catholic Charities Foundation of the Diocese of Palm Beach, Inc.*, 9995 N. Military Tr., PO Box 109650, 33410. Tel: 561-775-9560; Email: catholiccharities@ccdpb.org. Mr. Francisco Chevere, Dir.

Catholic Charities of the Diocese of Palm Beach, Inc., P.O. Box 109650, 34410-9650. Email: catholiccharities@ccdpb.org. 9995 N. Military Tr., 34410. Tel: 561-775-9560; Fax: 561-625-5906. Francisco Chevere, Dir. Tot Asst. Annually 10,000; Total Staff 80.

Con El, Inc., P.O. Box 109650, 33410-9650.
Tel: 561-775-9500; Email: mbaroni@diocesepb.org. Dorothy Martin, Contact Person.

Diocesan Council of Catholic Women, c/o P.O. Box 109650, 33410. Cell: 561-523-8525; Email: tammyccwfarr@gmail.com; Web: pbdccw.org. 810 W Palm St., Lantana, 33462. Tammy Farr, Pres.; Rev. Clemens Hammerschmitt, Diocesan Advisor.

Diocese of Palm Beach, Inc., 9995 N. Military Trl., 33410-9650. Tel: 561-775-9500; Email: vgendusa@diocesepb.org. P.O. Box 109650, 33410-9650. Mr. Vito Gendusa, CFO.

Diocese of Palm Beach Burse Fund Trust.

Diocese of Palm Beach Endowment Trust.

Diocese of Palm Beach Health Plan Trust Very Rev. Charles E. Notabartolo, V.G., Chm.

Diocese of Palm Beach Pension Plan Trust Very Rev. Charles E. Notabartolo, V.G., Chm.

Diocese of Palm Beach Savings Fund Trust, 9995 N. Military Trl., P.O. Box 109650, 33410-9650.
Tel: 561-775-9500; Email: vgendusa@diocesepb.org. Mr. Vito Gendusa, CFO.

Diocesan Property & Liability Insurance Committee Rev. Richard Murphy, Chm.

The Florida Catholic of Palm Beach, Inc., Diocese of Palm Beach, P.O. Box 109650, 33410-9650.
Tel: 561-775-9500; Email: jtrefelner@diocesepb.org.

Helping Hands Scholarship Fund, Diocese of Palm Beach, P.O. Box 109650, 33410-9650.
Tel: 561-775-9547; Email: ggelo@diocesepb.org. Mr. Gary Gelo, Supt.

Vose Properties, Inc., 9995 N. Military Trail, 33410.
Tel: 561-775-9500; Email: vgendusa@diocesepb.org. P.O. Box 109650, Palm Beach, 33410. Mr. Vito Gendusa, CFO.

BOCA RATON. *Christ Child Society of Boca Raton*, P.O. Box 811025, Boca Raton, 33481-1025.
Tel: 561-289-2371; Fax: 561-482-3087; Email: agnesgreg@aol.com. Agnes Gregory, Pres.

**Cross Catholic Outreach*, 2700 N. Military Tr., Ste. 240, P.O. Box 273908, Boca Raton, 33427-3908.
Tel: 800-914-2420, Ext. 174; Fax: 561-288-4397; Email: jmiceli-bogash@crosscatholic.org; Web:

www.crosscatholic.org. Mr. James J. Cavnar, Pres.; David Adams, Vice Pres.; Michele Sagarino, Vice Pres.; Brian Schutt, Vice Pres.; Wade Crow, Vice Pres.

Friends of Newman, Inc., P.O. Box 27-3894, Boca Raton, 33427. Christopher Fluehr, Pres.

BOYNTON BEACH. *St. Vincent de Paul Regional Seminary Endowment Trust*, 10701 S. Military Tr., Boynton Beach, 33436. Tel: 561-732-4424; Email: dtoups@svdp.edu. Rev. Msgr. David L. Toups, S.T.D., Rector.

GREENACRES. *Villa Madonna*, 4809 Lake Worth Rd., Greenacres, 33463-3455. Tel: 561-963-1900; Fax: 561-963-1476; Email: villamadonnamgr@spm.net. Maddie Familia, Resident Mgr.

JENSEN BEACH. *Villa Assumpta, Inc.*, 2539 N.E. Mission Dr., 9-8, Jensen Beach, 34957. Tel: 561-334-0009; Fax: 561-334-2168; Email: villaassumptamgr@spm.net. Janice Foci, Resident Mgr.

NORTH PALM BEACH. *Christ Child Society of Palm Beach*, P.O. Box 14441, North Palm Beach, 33408. Tel: 231-526-0291; Email: annekroha@msn.com. Anne Kroha, Pres.

PORT ST. LUCIE. **Adorer Missionary Sisters of the Poor*, 1381 S.E. Airoso Blvd., Port Saint Lucie, 34983. Tel: 561-810-1963; Email: info@adorermissionaries.org; Web: adorermissionarysistersofthepoor.org. P.O. Box 19895, West Palm Beach, 33416. Rev. Mark Mlay, A.L.C.P.; (Tanzania) Dir.; Sr. Mary Jennifer Wandia, Dir.

Villa Seton, Inc., 3300 S.W. Chartwell St., Port St. Lucie, 34953. Tel: 772-344-6969; Fax: 772-344-7822; Email: villasetonmgr@spm.net. Janice Foci, Resident Mgr.

RIVIERA BEACH. *Villa Franciscan, Inc.*, 2101 Avenue F, Riviera Beach, 33404. Tel: 561-840-0444; Fax: 561-840-9444; Email: villafranciscanmgr@spm.net; Web: villafranciscan.catholicweb.com. Lillie Hill, Admin.

STUART. *Christ Child Society of Stuart*, P.O. Box 2007, Stuart, 34995. Tel: 772-463-0405; Email: barbaralangella@optonline.net. Liz McIntyre, Pres.

**Mary's Shelter of the Treasure Coast*, 1033 S.E. 14th St., Stuart, 34996. Tel: 772-223-5000; Fax: 772-223-0150; Email: gina@marysshelertc.org. Gina Thompson, Dir.

VERO BEACH. **St. Sebastian Conference of St. Vincent de Paul Society, Inc.*, 5480 85th St., Vero Beach, 32967-5544. Tel: 772-589-3338; Email: manager@svdp-sebastian.org; Web: www.svdp-sebastian.org. Mr. John Murphy Jr., Pres.

**St. Vincent de Paul Society of Indian River County, Incorporated*, 1745 14th Ave., Vero Beach, 32960. Tel: 772-567-6774; Email: svdpvero@att.net. Frank Skully, Pres.

WEST PALM BEACH. *Magnificat Palm Beach Center, Inc.*, 804 N. Olive Ave., Fl. 2, West Palm Beach, 33401. Tel: 561-659-7009; Email: magnificatwpb@comcast.net; Web: www.magnificat-ministry.net/chapters/chapter-state-f-k/fl-palm-beach/. Peggy Rowe-Linn, Coord.; Catherine Dorsey, Asst. Coord.; Cynthia A. Sheldon, Treas.; Jaimee Perez, Historian; Deanna Bartalini, Sec.

Villa Regina, 2660 Haverhill Rd. N., West Palm Beach, 33417. Tel: 561-478-3900; Fax: 561-478-9787; Email: villareginamgr@spm.net. Monica Alvarez, Admin.

RELIGIOUS INSTITUTES OF MEN REPRESENTED IN THE DIOCESE

For further details refer to the corresponding bracketed number in the Religious Institutes of Men or Women section.

[]—*Apostolic Life Community of Priests in the Opus Spiritus Sancti* (Tanzania)—A.L.C.P.
[]—*Brothers of the Christian Schools*—F.S.C.
[0030]—*Congregation of St. Paul*—C.S.P.
[0610]—*Congregation of the Holy Cross*—C.S.C.
[1000]—*Congregation of the Passion*—C.P.
[0260]—*Discalced Carmelite Friars*—O.C.D.
[0520]—*Franciscan Friars* (Holy Name Prov.)—O.F.M.
[0480]—*Franciscans Friars, Conventual*—O.F.M.Conv.
[0685]—*Institute of the Incarnate Word*—I.V.E.
[1210]—*Missionaries of St. Charles Borromeo*—C.S.
[0270]—*Order of Carmelites*—O.Carm.
[1040]—*Piarist Fathers*—Sch.P.
[1070]—*Redemptorist Fathers*—C.Ss.R.
[1190]—*Salesians of Don Bosco*—S.D.B.
[0690]—*Society of Jesus*—S.J.

RELIGIOUS INSTITUTES OF WOMEN REPRESENTED IN THE DIOCESE

[0330]—*Carmelite Sisters for the Aged and Infirm*—O.Carm.
[0685]—*Claretian Missionary Sisters*—R.M.I.
[1930]—*Congregation of the Sisters of the Holy Cross*—C.S.C.
[1070-03]—*Dominican Sisters* (Sinsinawa, WI)—O.P.
[1070-13]—*Dominican Sisters* (Adrian, MI)—O.P.
[1070-15]—*Dominican Sisters of Blauvelt* (New York)—O.P.
[1180]—*Franciscan Sisters of Allegany, NY*—O.S.F.
[1250]—*Franciscan Sisters of the Eucharist*—F.S.E.
[]—*Hermitage of the Diocese of Palm Beach.*
[2300]—*Little Servant Sisters of the Immaculate Conception*—L.C.I.S.
[2490]—*Medical Mission Sisters*—M.M.S.
[3760]—*Order of St. Clare*—O.S.C.
[3465]—*Religious of the Sacred Heart of Mary*—R.S.H.M.
[2970]—*School Sisters of Notre Dame*—S.S.N.D.
[]—*Sisters for Christian Community*—S.F.C.C.
[0590]—*Sisters of Charity of St. Elizabeth* (Convent Station, NJ)—S.C.
[2110]—*Sisters of the Humility of Mary*—H.M.
[2520]—*Sisters of Mercy* (Dublin, Ireland)—R.S.M.
[2575]—*Sisters of Mercy of the Americas* (NY, PA, Pacific West Community, Northeast Regional Community)—R.S.M.
[1630]—*Sisters of St. Francis of Penance and Christian Charity*—O.S.F.
[0260]—*The Sisters of the Blessed Sacrament*—S.B.S.
[]—*Sisters of the Most Holy Soul of Christ the Lord*—C.A.C.H.
[]—*United States Association of Consecrated Virgins*—U.S.A.C.V.

DIOCESAN CEMETERIES

ROYAL PALM BEACH. *Our Lady Queen of Peace Catholic Cemetery, Inc.*, 10941 Southern Blvd., Royal Palm Beach, 33411. Tel: 561-793-0711; Fax: 561-793-0182; Email: info@ourqueen.org; Email: reception@ourqueen.org; Web: www.ourqueen.org. Rev. Zbigniew A. Rudnicki, Dir.; Mr. Thomas Jordan, Admin.

NECROLOGY

† Grace, Gerald, (Retired), Died Aug. 10, 2018

An asterisk (*) denotes an organization that has established tax-exempt status directly with the IRS and is not covered by the USCCB Group Ruling.

Diocese of Paterson

(Dioecesis Patersonensis)

Most Reverend

ARTHUR J. SERRATELLI

Bishop of Paterson; ordained December 20, 1968; appointed Titular Bishop of Enera and Auxiliary Bishop of Newark July 3, 2000; Episcopal ordination September 8, 2000; appointed Bishop of Paterson June 1, 2004.

ESTABLISHED DECEMBER 9, 1937.

Square Miles 1,214.

Comprises the Counties of Passaic, Morris and Sussex in the State of New Jersey.

For legal titles of parishes and diocesan institutions, consult the Chancery Office.

Diocesan Center: 777 Valley Rd., Clifton, NJ 07013. Tel: 973-777-8818; Fax: 973-777-8976.

Web: www.patersondiocese.org

STATISTICAL OVERVIEW

Personnel	
Bishop	1
Abbots	2
Retired Abbots	3
Priests: Diocesan Active in Diocese	153
Priests: Diocesan Active Outside Diocese	11
Priests: Retired, Sick or Absent	111
Number of Diocesan Priests	275
Religious Priests in Diocese	98
Total Priests in Diocese	373
Extern Priests in Diocese	10
Ordinations:	
Diocesan Priests	9
Permanent Deacons in Diocese	195
Total Brothers	46
Total Sisters	591
Parishes	
Parishes	107
With Resident Pastor:	
Resident Diocesan Priests	91
Resident Religious Priests	7
Without Resident Pastor:	
Administered by Priests	10
Pastoral Centers	6
Closed Parishes	1
Professional Ministry Personnel:	
Brothers	4
Sisters	25
Lay Ministers	108
Welfare	
Catholic Hospitals	1
Total Assisted	315,000
Homes for the Aged	8
Total Assisted	440
Day Care Centers	6
Total Assisted	900
Specialized Homes	1
Total Assisted	6,313
Special Centers for Social Services	8
Residential Care of Disabled	12
Total Assisted	75
Educational	
Seminaries, Diocesan	1
Students from This Diocese	10
Diocesan Students in Other Seminaries	33
Seminaries, Religious	2
Students Religious	5
Total Seminarians	48
Colleges and Universities	2
Total Students	1,291
High Schools, Diocesan and Parish	3
Total Students	1,742
High Schools, Private	4
Total Students	1,139
Elementary Schools, Diocesan and Parish	20
Total Students	4,644
Elementary Schools, Private	3
Total Students	479
Catechesis/Religious Education:	
High School Students	6,400
Elementary Students	20,100
Total Students under Catholic Instruction	35,843
Teachers in the Diocese:	
Priests	6
Brothers	5
Sisters	46
Lay Teachers	814
Vital Statistics	
Receptions into the Church:	
Infant Baptism Totals	4,855
Minor Baptism Totals	185
Adult Baptism Totals	79
Received into Full Communion	196
First Communions	4,812
Confirmations	3,998
Marriages:	
Catholic	754
Interfaith	157
Total Marriages	911
Deaths	3,000
Total Catholic Population	430,000
Total Population	1,153,982

Former Bishops—Most Revs. THOMAS H. MCLAUGHLIN, S.T.D., LL.D., cons. July 25, 1935; transferred to Paterson, Dec. 16, 1937; died March 17, 1947; THOMAS A. BOLAND, S.T.D., LL.D., cons. July 25, 1940; transferred to Paterson, June 21, 1947; transferred to Newark as Archbishop, Nov. 15, 1952; died March 16, 1979; JAMES A. MCNULTY, D.D., appt. Auxiliary Bishop of Newark, Aug. 2, 1947; cons. Oct. 7, 1947; appt. Bishop of Paterson, April 9, 1953; transferred to Diocese of Buffalo, Feb. 12, 1963; died Sept. 4, 1972; JAMES J. NAVAGH, D.D., cons. Sept. 24, 1952; appt. Bishop of Ogdensburg, May 8, 1957; transferred to Bishop of Paterson, Feb. 12, 1963; died Oct. 2, 1965; LAWRENCE B. CASEY, D.D., appt. Auxiliary Bishop of Rochester, Feb. 10, 1953; cons. May 5, 1953; appt. Bishop of Paterson, March 9, 1966; died June 15, 1977; FRANK J. RODIMER, D.D., J.C.D., ord. May 19, 1951; appt. Bishop of Paterson Dec. 13, 1977; ord. and installed Feb. 28, 1978; retired June 1, 2004; died Dec. 6, 2018.

Vicar General and Moderator of the Curia—Rev. Msgr. JAMES T. MAHONEY, Ph.D., V.G.

Vicar General—Rev. MICHAEL J. PARISI, V.G.

Coordinator for Special Projects—MR. THOMAS A. BARRETT.

Chief Financial Officer—MR. PATRICK BRENNAN.

Episcopal Vicars—

Education—Rev. STANLEY C. BARRON.

Evangelization—Rev. PAUL S. MANNING.

Special Diocesan Initiatives—Rev. Msgr. GENO SYLVA, S.T.D.

Deans—Revs. A. STEFAN LAS, Passaic; LEONARDO JARAMILLO, Clifton; DANIEL P. O'MULLANE, Northeastern Morris; BRANDO IBARRA, Paterson; DAVID MCDONNELL, Sussex; J. PATRICK RYAN, D.Min., Mid-Passaic; MICHAEL J. DRURY, Southwestern Morris; THOMAS REKIEL, Southeastern Morris; MATTHEW J. TWIGGS, Western Morris; Rev. Msgr. HERBERT K. TILLYER, P.A., M.Ch.A., Eastern Morris; Revs. RICHARD BAY, Northern Morris; GREGORZ GOLBA, Northern Passaic.

Chancellor/Delegate for Religious—Sr. JOAN DANIEL HEALY, S.C.C.

Vice Chancellors—Revs. MARC A. MANCINI, J.C.L.; STEPHEN PRISK; Sr. CATHERINE MCDONNELL, O.P., (for Planning).

Archivist—Rev. Msgr. RAYMOND J. KUPKE, Ph.D.

Priest Secretary to the Bishop—Rev. STEPHEN PRISK.

Secretary to the Bishop—MRS. BARBARA FIERRO.

Secretary to the Vicar General and Chancellor—MRS. ARLINE PERRO.

Secretary to the Vice Chancellors—MRS. KERRY TIMONEY.

Diocesan Counsel—MR. KENNETH F. MULLANEY JR., ESQ.

Censor Librorum—Revs. KEVIN CORCORAN; LEMMUEL CAMACHO.

Diocesan Tribunal—

Judicial Vicar—Rev. Msgr. EDWARD J. KURTYKA, P.A., J.C.D.

Adjutant Judicial Vicar—Rev. Msgr. JOSEPH T. ANGINOLI, J.C.L.

Advocates—Revs. JOHN T. CONNOLLY, M.Div.; MICHAEL RODAK; PHILIP-MICHAEL TANGORRA; MATEUSZ JASNIEWICZ.

Auditors—Revs. JOHN P. HANLEY, (Retired); MANUEL GUEVARA; Deacon HENRY HYLE.

Defenders of the Bond—Rev. Msgrs. T. MARK CONDON, J.C.L., S.T.L.; GEORGE F. HUNDT, J.C.L.

Canonical Advisor—Rev. Msgr. JOSEPH J. GOODE, M.Ch.A., (Retired).

Associate Judges—Rev. MARC A. MANCINI, J.C.L.; Rev. Msgr. JOHN J. CARROLL, Ed.D.; Rev. EMMETT J. GAVIN, O.Carm., J.D., J.C.L.; Rev. Msgrs. JOHN E. HART; HERBERT K. TILLYER, P.A., M.Ch.A.

Administrative Assistants and Notaries—MRS. SHAWN VACCA; MRS. MARY BETH LEONHARD.

Consulting Psychologists and Experts—Rev. RICHARD MUCOWSKI, O.F.M., Ph.D.; MR. JOSEPH DE CHRISTOFANO, L.C.S.W.; MRS. MARY DE CHRISTOFANO, M.S.W., L.C.S.W.; Rev. EDWARD J. LAMBRO, Ph.D., C.C.M.H.C., (Retired).

Minister to Priests—Rev. DAVID MCDONNELL.

Delegate for Polish Seminarians and Clergy—Rev. DARIUSZ K. KAMINSKI.

Vocations Office—*737 Valley Rd., Clifton, 07013.* Tel: 973-777-2955; Fax: 973-777-4597. Rev. EDGAR O. RIVERA, Dir. Assistant Vocation Directors: Revs. VIDAL GONZALES; DAVID MONTELEONE.

Vocations Board—Revs. HERNAN ARIAS; SIGMUND PEPLOWSKI; T. KEVIN CORCORAN; MARC A. MANCINI, J.C.L.; EDWARD RAMA; CHRISTOPHER S. BARKHAUSEN.

Consultative Bodies—

Presbyteral Council—Rev. Msgr. JOHN E. HART, Chm.; Revs. DAVID MCDONNELL, Vice Chm.; BRIAN P. QUINN; JOSEPH BOYKOW; Rev. Msgr. MARTIN MCDONNELL, (Retired); Revs. PAWEL TOMCZYK; A. STEFAN LAS; Rev. Msgr. T. MARK CONDON, J.C.L., S.T.L.; Rev. RICHARD V. TARTAGLIA; Rev. Msgrs. JAMES T. MAHONEY, Ph. D., V.G.; GEORGE F. HUNDT, J.C.L.; Revs. JHON EDISSON MADRID; LEO ANTONY, S.D.V.

College of Consultors—Rev. Msgr. JOHN E. HART,

Chm.; Revs. DAVID McDONNELL, Vice Chm.; BRIAN P. QUINN; RICHARD V. TARTAGLIA; JARED J. BROGAN; Rev. Msgr. T. MARK CONDON, J.C.L., S.T.L.; Rev. JHON EDISSON MADRID; Rev. Msgr. JAMES T. MAHONEY, Ph.D., V.G.; Rev. JOSEPH BOYKOW; Rev. Msgr. MARTIN McDONNELL, (Retired); Rev. PAWEL TOMCZYK.

College of Deans—Rev. DAVID McDONNELL, Chm.

Finance Council—MR. HERBERT THOMAS, Chm.; Sr. JOAN DANIEL HEALY, S.C.C.; MR. THOMAS A. BARRETT; MS. JANE BROWN; MR. PATRICK BRENNAN; MR. JOHN COX; MR. STEPHEN TILTON; MR. MICHAEL NEWMAN; MR. RAFAEL CUELLAR; MR. RONALD COHEN; Rev. Msgr. JAMES T. MAHONEY, Ph.D., V.G.; MR. TIMOTHY SHEA.

Theological Commission—Rev. Msgrs. JOHN E. HART; T. MARK CONDON, J.C.L., S.T.L.; Sr. KATHLEEN FLANAGAN, S.C., Ph.D.; DR. JAMES INCARDONA, Ph.D.; Rev. ALEKSY KOWALSKI, Ph. D.; Rev. Msgr. RAYMOND J. KUPKE, Ph.D.; Rev. ANTHONY J. MASTROENI, S.T.D., J.D.; Rev. Msgr. HERBERT K. TILLYER, P.A., M.Ch.A.; DR. DIANNE TRAFLET, J.D., S.T.D.

Pastoral Council—MRS. ELIZABETH HELDAK, Chm.

Liturgical Commission—Rev. Msgr. T. MARK CONDON, J.C.L., S.T.L., Chm.

Hispanic Commission—MR. ALVARO CAMARGO, Pres.

Black Catholic Ministries Commission—MRS. RUTH LAWSON, Chm.

Education Council—MS. SOLIDAD ANSELMI, Chair.

Diocesan Secretariats

Communications Secretariat—Mailing Address: 775 Valley Rd., P.O. Box 1887, Clifton, 07015. Tel: 973-278-3202; Fax: 973-279-2265. MR. RICHARD A. SOKERKA, Exec. Sec. & Dir. Communications; MR. JOSEPH CECE, Webmaster, Email: cecej@infonetdev.com.

Diocesan Newspaper, "The Beacon"— Tel: 973-279-8845. MR. RICHARD A. SOKERKA, Editor & Gen. Mgr.; MR. MICHAEL WOJCIK, News Editor.

Secretariat for Evangelization—777 Valley Rd., Clifton, 07013. Tel: 973-777-8818. Rev. PAUL S. MANNING, Vicar for Evangelization & Exec. Dir.; MR. BRIAN HONSBERGER, Asst. Dir. Catechesis.

Office of Family Life—ENIOLA HONSBERGER, Dir.

Respect Life—DR. MARY MAZZARELLA, Consultant.

Office of Director of Catechesis—MS. IVANNIA VEGA-MCTIGHE.

Office of Worship and Spirituality—Rev. Msgr. T. MARK CONDON, J.C.L., S.T.L., Dir.

Diocesan Chapter, National Pastoral Musicians—MR. PRESTON DIBBLE.

Diocesan Director of Music—MR. PRESTON DIBBLE.

Young Adult Ministry—(23-35) MR. DANIEL FERRARI, Coord.

Catholic Scouting—

Boy Scouting—Rev. CHRISTOPHER S. BARKHAUSEN, Chap.

Girl Scouting—Rev. FRANK P. AGRESTI, Chap.

Related Organizations—

Catholic Deaf Society—

Charismatic Renewal—Rev. NICHOLAS BOZZA, Liaison, Tel: 973-347-0032.

English Cursillos—MR. MIKE WILSON, Lay Dir.; Rev. RAYMOND ORAMA, Spiritual Advisor.

Spanish Cursillos—LUIS SALERNA, Lay Dir.; WILLIAM TORRES; Rev. BRANDO IBARRA, Spiritual Advisor.

Secretariat for Pastoral Administration—775 Valley Rd., Clifton, 07013. Tel: 973-777-2955.

Clergy Personnel Office—Rev. Msgr. JOHN E. HART, Dir.; MRS. ROSEMARY J. DONNELLY, Administrative Asst.

Personnel Board—Rev. Msgrs. JOHN E. HART; T. MARK CONDON, J.C.L., S.T.L.; GEORGE F. HUNDT, J.C.L.; Revs. PETER S. GLABIK; LEONARDO JARAMILLO; DANIEL P. O'MULLANE; BRIAN SULLIVAN.

Deacon Internship Program—Revs. DARIUSZ K. KAMINSKI; HERNAN ARIAS.

Mission Office—777 Valley Rd., Clifton, 07013. Tel: 973-777-8818, Ext. 256; Email: mburdeos@patersondiocese.org; Web: chancery@rcdop.org; Web: www@rcdop.org. Rev. STANLEY C. BARRON, Assoc. Dir.

Office of the Permanent Diaconate—205 Madison Ave., Madison, 07940. Tel: 973-443-9300; Fax: 973-443-4140; Fax: 973-777-8976. Deacon PETER CISTARO, Dir.

Victim Assistance Coordinator—MS. PEGGY ZANELLO, Tel: 973-879-1489.

Division of Finance and Budget—777 Valley Rd., Clifton, 07013. Tel: 973-777-8818. MR. THOMAS A. BARRETT, Coord. Special Projects & Svcs.

Division of Finance and Budget—MR. PATRICK BRENNAN, CFO; MS. JOLANTA LONDENE, Controller; MR. TIMOTHY POTTER, Dir. Devel.; MS. JANE SUDOL, Mgr. Devel. Oper.

Diocesan Cemeteries Office—58 McLean Blvd., Paterson, 07513. Tel: 973-279-2900. Rev. PETER VB. WELLS, Dir.; MR. JOHN M. CAVANAUGH, Asst. Dir.

Office of Business Administration—Deacon ROBERT AYERS, Dir. Property Admin.; REBECA RUIZ, Diocesan Architect.

Office of Human Resources—MR. BILL RAFFERTY, Chief Human Resources; MRS. VIRGINIA EMAUS, Benefits Admin.; MR. RICHARD ZICCARDI, Risk Mgr.

Youth Protection—MRS. JOAN VALK, Dir. Human Resources; MR. ERIC WILSUSEN, Dir. Youth Protection.

School Division—777 Valley Rd., Clifton, 07013. Tel: 973-777-8818. Rev. STANLEY C. BARRON, Vicar for Educ.; MRS. MARY BAIER, Supt.; MRS. DEBBIE DUANE, Assoc. Supt.; MS. MARY WRENN, Dir. Technology Educ.

Secretariat for Catholic Charities—777 Valley Rd., Clifton, 07013. Tel: 973-777-8818; Fax: 973-523-6183. MR. THOMAS A. BARRETT, Acting Pres., Tel: 973-777-8818, Ext. 278; Rev. EDWARD J. LAMBRO, Ph.D., C.C.M.H.C., Dir. Devel. & Public Rels., (Retired), Tel: 973-777-8818, Ext. 294; RUTH SAGINARIO, Administrative Asst., Tel: 973-777-8818, Ext. 257.

Hispanic Information Center—186 Gregory Ave., Passaic, 07055. Tel: 973-779-7022. MS. DELIA ROSARIO, Site Dir.

Catholic Family and Community Services—24 De Grasse St., Paterson, 07505. MS. CHRISTINE BARTON, Exec. Dir., Tel: ; MR. ROBERT JACOB, Assoc. Dir. & CFO, Tel: 973-279-7100, Ext. 26; MR. DARRIN MALONEY, Asst. Exec. Dir. & Dir. Legal Svcs., Tel: 973-279-7100, Ext. 40.

Friendship Corner II—186 Butler St., Paterson, 07505. Tel: 973-405-6711. MS. GLORIA BODKER, Dir.

Partnership for Social Services—48 Wyker Rd., Franklin, 07416. Tel: 973-827-4702.

Senior Community Support Programs—KATHY TALMADGE, Dir.

Father English Multi-Purpose Community Center—435 Main St., Paterson, 07501. Tel: 973-279-7100. MS. DELIA ROSARIO, Site Dir.

Early Learning Programs—MR. JOSEPH MURRAY, Dir.

El Mundo de Colores—44 Ward St., Paterson, 07505. Tel: 973-523-0919. MS. LAURA ZARIFE, Dir.

Community and Emergency Support Services—MR. ARIEL ALONSO, Dir.

Pastoral Ministry and Volunteers—Sr. MAUREEN SULLIVAN, Dir.

Youth Risk Reduction—MS. DELIA ROSARIO, Dir.

Early Intervention Service Coordination—LISA O'CONNOR, Dir.

Early Intervention Targeted Evaluation and Case Management—DANIELLE CUSKEY, Dir.

Senior Day Program—LYNN GAFFNEY, Dir.

Veterans Services—MELISSA SCHABER, Dir.

Emergency Food and Clothing Programs—MR. CARLOS ROLDAN, Dir.

Hope House—(Catholic Social Services of Morris County, Inc.) *19-21 Belmont Ave., Dover, 07801.* Tel: 973-361-5555. MS. LEE ANN CIANCI, Site Dir.

Department for Persons with Disabilities—1 Catholic Charities Way, P.O. Box 2539, Oak Ridge, 07438. Tel: 973-406-1100. MS. JOANNA MILLER, Exec. Dir.; PATRICIA BARRETT, Pastoral Care Coord.; MR. ROCCO ZAPPILE, CFO; MR. CHRISTOPHER BRANCATO, Dir. Devel.

Group Homes—

Murray House—86 Allwood Place, Clifton, 07015. Tel: 973-470-5694. MS. TANIA ALESSIO, Dir.

Barnet House—52 Lenox Ave., Pompton Lakes, 07442. Tel: 973-409-2764. ASHLEY HIDALGO, Dir.

Finnegan House—1049 Weldon Rd., Oak Ridge, 07438. Tel: 973-697-1246. MS. LYNNE ROCKSTROH, Dir.

Columbus House—1048 Weldon Rd., Oak Ridge, 07438. Tel: 973-697-1644. MR. JAMES CERNY, Dir.

Fitzpatrick House—215 Mountain Ave., Pompton Lakes, 07442. Tel: 973-248-1569. TYLER ARTRESS, Dir.

Wehrlen House—18 Bisset Dr., West Milford, 07480. Tel: 973-208-1883. MS. CLARA LIST, Dir.

Gruenert Employment Center—725 Rte. 15 S., Lake Hopatcong, 07849. Tel: 973-663-9102. MS. CAROLINA NELSON, Dir.

Basile Apartment—Brittany Chase, Wayne, 07470. Tel: 973-409-2767. MR. GEOFFREY ONDIMU.

Giuliano House—1091 Weldon Rd., Oak Ridge, 07438. KELLY O'CAISIDE, Dir.

Greunert Center Special Needs—725 Rte. 15, Lake Hopatcong, 07849. Tel: 973-663-9102. MS. REBECCA DANN, Dir.

Support Coordination—1 Catholic Charities Way, Oak Ridge, 07438. MS. KRISTEN BULAS, Dir.

Calabrese House—829 Littleton Rd., Parsippany, 07054. Tel: 973-299-8360. LORI EVANS, Dir.

Wallace House—447 Glen Rd., Sparta, 07871. Tel: 973-276-3470. MS. KIM WALTER, Dir.

Keleher Apartments—124 Barrister Dr., Butler, 07405. Tel: 973-409-2761. MS. ISABEL MARTE, Dir.

Straight and Narrow, Inc.—508 Straight St., Paterson, 07503. Tel: 973-345-6000. DR. SAM PIROZZI, Exec. Dir.; DR. HAYMAN RAMBARAN, M.D., Medical Dir.; MS. RUTH JEAN-MARIE, Dir., Men's Residential Svcs.; Rev. PAUL BARBOUTZ, Dir. Pastoral Care Unit; MS. NANCY NAKHLE, Dir. Admissions; DR. ANNA DE MOLLI, Dir. Children's Daycare; MR. SHAWN T. MULLINS, Dir., Intoxicated Driver Resource Ctr.; MS. DONNA PUGLIA, Outpatient & Opioid Svcs., 508 Straight St., Paterson, 07503.

Migrant Ministry—Community of Our Lady of Guadalupe, 18 Church St., Ste. 222-224, Newton, 07860. Tel: 908-647-0280. Rev. ALEX LONDONO, Dir., Tel: 908-246-5939; LUIS ARIAS, Asst. Dir., Tel: 973-818-0075.

Affiliated Organizations—

Apostleship of Prayer—Rev. Msgr. CHRISTOPHER C. DILELLA, Dir.

Legion of Mary—MRS. LUCY LEONE, Pres., 63 Monroe St., Passaic, 07055. Tel: 973-779-0427.

Priests Eucharistic League—Rev. Msgr. CHRISTOPHER C. DILELLA, Dir.

Diocesan Pilgrimage Office—1911 Union Valley Rd., Hewitt, 07421. Tel: 973-728-8162. Rev. MICHAEL RODAK, Dir.

CLERGY, PARISHES, MISSIONS AND PAROCHIAL SCHOOLS

CITY OF PATERSON

(PASSAIC COUNTY)

1—CATHEDRAL OF ST. JOHN THE BAPTIST (1820) [CEM] Rev. Eugene R. Sylva, Rector; Rev. Msgr. Mark J. Giordani, Pastor Emeritus, (Retired); Revs. Leonardo Lopez, Parochial Vicar; Luis Alberto Hernandez, Parochial Vicar; Deacons Jose Pomales; Guido Pedraza; Luis Gil; German Vargas.
Res.: 381 Grand St., Paterson, 07505.
Tel: 973-345-4070; Fax: 973-345-7831.
Catechesis Religious Program—Students 275.

2—ST. AGNES (1883) Rev. Enrique Corona; Deacon Gilberto Vazquez.
Res.: 681 Main St., Paterson, 07503.
Tel: 973-279-0250; Email: stagnesrcchurch@netzero.net.
Catechesis Religious Program—Students 128.

3—ST. ANTHONY'S (1909) (Italian)
138 Beech St., Paterson, 07501. Tel: 973-742-9695; Email: stanthonypaterson1@yahoo.com; Web: stanthonypaterson.com. Rev. Eider Reyes.
Catechesis Religious Program—Email: st.anthonysccd@hotmail.com. Escari Tucker, D.R.E. Students 56.

4—BLESSED SACRAMENT (1911) (Italian)
224 E. 18th St., Paterson, 07524. Tel: 973-523-5002; Tel: 973-523-5003; Email: frrayorama@optonline.net; Email: francia.genao@yahoo.com. Rev. Raymond Orama.
Catechesis Religious Program—Email: shegegreand@verizon.net. Shella Marc, D.R.E. Students 32.

5—ST. BONAVENTURE (1877)
174 Ramsey St., Paterson, 07501. Tel: 973-279-1016; Fax: 973-279-2507; Email: parishoffice@stbonspaterson.org; Web: www.stbonspaterson.org. Revs. Daniel P. Grigassy, O.F.M.; Francis M. McHugh, O.F.M., Parochial Vicar; Deacons Joseph Balough; Anthony Fierro.
Catechesis Religious Program—Email: tgallo1130@yahoo.com. Teresa Gallo-Tomcho, D.R.E. Students 172.

6—ST. GEORGE (1897) Merged with Saint Brendan, Clifton to form Saint Brendan and Saint George, Clifton.

7—ST. GERARD MAJELLA (1962) Revs. Leo Antony, S.D.V., Admin.; Robert Vass, S.D.V., Parochial Vicar; Benny Chittilappilly, S.D.V., Parochial Vicar; James Butts, S.D.V.
Res.: 501 W. Broadway, Paterson, 07522.
Tel: 973-595-8446; Fax: 973-790-0778.

School—St. Gerard Majella School (1965) 10 Carrelton Dr., Paterson, 07522. Tel: 973-595-5640; Fax: 973-595-5475. Lay Teachers 9; Sisters 1; Students 223.
Catechesis Religious Program—Students 73.
8—ST. JOSEPH'S (1867)
399 Market St., Paterson, 07501. Tel: 973-278-0030; Email: rzadcaj@juno.com. Rev. Janusz Rzadca.
Catechesis Religious Program—Students 130.
9—ST. MARY'S (1873) (Auxilium Christianorum) Rev. Brando Ibarra; Deacons Antonio Salierno; Juan Carlos Carnero.
Res.: 410 Union Ave., Paterson, 07502.
Tel: 973-790-8651; Fax: 973-790-8534.
Catechesis Religious Program—Students 97.
10—ST. MICHAEL THE ARCHANGEL (1903) (Italian) Rev. Enrique Corona.
Res.: 70 Cianci St., Paterson, 07501-1831.
Tel: 973-523-8413; Email: st-michaelschurch@yahoo.com.
Catechesis Religious Program— Combined with St. Gerard, Majella Students 57.
11—OUR LADY OF LOURDES (1882) Revs. Raimundo Rivera, Admin.; Hector Melendez, Parochial Vicar; Deacon Raul Pamplona.
Res.: 440 River St., Paterson, 07524-1902.
Tel: 973-742-2142; Email: olvjude@gmail.com.
Catechesis Religious Program—Students 90.
12—OUR LADY OF POMPEI (1916) (Italian) Rev. Frank P. Agresti.
Res.: 70 Murray Ave., Paterson, 07501.
Tel: 973-742-1969; Email: ourladyofpompeii@aol.com.
Catechesis Religious Program—Students 60.
13—OUR LADY OF VICTORIES (1882) Revs. Raimundo Rivera, Admin.; Hector Melendez, Parochial Vicar; Deacon Maximo Paulino.
Res.: 100 Fair St., Paterson, 07501.
Tel: 973-279-0487; Tel: 973-279-0527;
Fax: 973-977-8506; Email: olvjude@verizon.net; Web: www.olvjude.org.
Catechesis Religious Program—Students 117.
14—ST. STEPHEN'S (1903) (Polish)
86 Martin St., Paterson, 07501. Tel: 973-742-2822; Fax: 973-742-1679. Rev. Dariusz K. Kaminski.
Catechesis Religious Program—Students 35.
15—ST. THERESE (1926)
80 13th Ave., Paterson, 07504. Tel: 973-881-0400; Fax: 973-881-7638. Rev. Luciano Cruz, (Retired); Deacon Luis Ramirez.
Catechesis Religious Program—Students 174.

OUTSIDE THE CITY OF PATERSON

ANDOVER, SUSSEX CO., GOOD SHEPHERD (1979) [CEM] Revs. Timothy Dowling; Michal J. Szwarc, Parochial Vicar; Deacons Thomas Sullivan; Keith Harris; Mrs. Sharon Matuza, Pastoral Assoc.
Office: Rte. 517 (48 Tranquility Rd.), P.O. Box 464, Andover, 07821. Tel: 973-786-6631;
Tel: 973-786-5520 (Res.); Tel: 973-786-5811 (CEM); Fax: 973-786-5233.
Catechesis Religious Program—Students 403.
BOONTON, MORRIS CO.
1—SS. CYRIL AND METHODIUS (1907) [CEM] (Slovak)
215 Hill St., Boonton, 07005. Tel: 973-334-0139; Email: stcyrilboonton@yahoo.com; Web: www.stscm.org. 910 Birch St., Boonton, 07005. Revs. Daniel P. O'Mullane, Admin.; Artur P. Zaba, Parochial Vicar.
2—OUR LADY OF MOUNT CARMEL (1847) [CEM]
910 Birch St., Boonton, 07005. Tel: 973-334-1017; Fax: 973-335-1833; Email: admin@olmcboonton.org; Web: www.olmcboonton.org. Revs. Daniel P. O'Mullane; Artur P. Zaba, Parochial Vicar.
School—Our Lady of Mount Carmel School (1868) (Grades PreK-8), 205 Oak St., Boonton, 07005.
Tel: 973-334-2777; Fax: school@olmcboonton.org; Web: www.olmc.academy. Lay Teachers 12; Students 120.
Catechesis Religious Program—Students 170.
BRANCHVILLE, SUSSEX CO., OUR LADY QUEEN OF PEACE (1951)
209 U.S. Hwy. 206, Branchville, 07826.
Tel: 973-948-3185; Email: office@olqpbranchville.org; Web: www.OLQPBranchville.org. Rev. Edward Rama.
Catechesis Religious Program—Email: reled@olqpbranchville.org. Diana Rimshnick, D.R.E. Students 115.
BUDD LAKE, MORRIS CO., ST. JUDE (1946) Rev. Jesus Antonio Gaviria; Deacons Anthony C. Siino; John M. Sanker.
Res.: 17 Mt. Olive Rd., Budd Lake, 07828.
Tel: 973-691-1561; Fax: 973-691-9060; Web: www.stjudeparish.org.
Catechesis Religious Program—Students 455.
BUTLER, MORRIS CO., ST. ANTHONY (1878) [CEM]
65 Bartholdi Ave., Butler, 07405. Tel: 973-838-0031; Email: bleck@saopp.org; Email: office@saopp.org; Web: www.saopp.org. Revs. Joseph Juracek, O.F.M.; Kevin Daly.
Catechesis Religious Program—Email: ascollante@saopp.org. Annette Miller, D.R.E. Students 230.
Parish House—71 Bartholdi Ave., Butler, 07405.
Tel: 973-838-8585.
CEDAR KNOLLS, MORRIS CO., NOTRE DAME OF MT. CARMEL (1917) Revs. Patrick G. O'Donovan; Jhon Edisson Madrid, Parochial Vicar; Deacons Joseph Harris; Victor Lupi; Ronald Forino; Alfredo Fanelli; Jean Pankow, Pastoral Assoc.
Office: 75 Ridgedale Ave., Cedar Knolls, 07927.
Tel: 973-538-1358; Email: parishsecretary@ndcarmel.com.
Res.: 13 Halko Dr., Cedar Knolls, 07927.
Catechesis Religious Program—Students 820.
CHATHAM TOWNSHIP, MORRIS CO., CORPUS CHRISTI (1966) Rev. T. Kevin Corcoran; Rev. Msgr. James T. Mahoney, Ph.D., V.G., Pastor Emeritus; Rev. Lemmuel Camacho, Parochial Vicar.
Res.: 234 Southern Blvd., Chatham, 07928.
Tel: 973-635-0070; Fax: 973-635-5518; Email: jmahoney@corpuschristi.org; Web: www.corpuschristi.org.
Catechesis Religious Program—Students 694.
CHATHAM, MORRIS CO., ST. PATRICK'S (1874)
85 Washington Ave., Chatham, 07928.
Tel: 973-635-0625; Web: www.st-pats.org. 41 Oliver St., Chatham, 07928. Revs. Robert J. Mitchell; Kamil Kiszka, Parochial Vicar; Deacons Joseph A. Wisneski; Mark Nixon.
School—St. Patrick's School (1872) 45 Chatham St., Chatham, 07928. Tel: 973-635-4623;
Fax: 973-635-2311. Lay Teachers 25; Students 259.
Catechesis Religious Program—Students 860.
CHESTER, MORRIS CO., ST. LAWRENCE THE MARTYR (1950)
375 Main St., Chester, 07930. Tel: 908-879-5371;
Tel: 908-879-6714; Email: parish@stlchester.org; Web: www.stlchester.org. P.O. Box 730, Chester, 07930. Revs. Nicholas Bozza; Yohan Serrano, Parochial Vicar; Deacon William DiVizio.
Catechesis Religious Program—Tel: 908-879-6714; Email: fft@stlchester.org. Kathy Galdi, D.R.E. Students 477.
CLIFTON, PASSAIC CO.
1—ST. ANDREW THE APOSTLE aka Diocese of Paterson (Allwood) (1938)
400 Mt. Prospect Ave., 07012.
Tel: 973-779-6873, Ext. 20; Email: barbarahsac@optonline.net; Web: www.StAndrewsClifton.org. Rev. Richard Kilcomons; Deacon Richard J. Goglia.
Catechesis Religious Program—Students 208.
2—ST. BRENDAN, Merged with Saint George, Paterson to form Saint Brendan and Saint George, Clifton.
3—SAINT BRENDAN AND SAINT GEORGE, Rev. Junior Flores. In Res., Revs. Jhon Edisson Madrid; Michael A. Burke.
Res.: 154 E. First St., 07011. Tel: 973-772-1115; Fax: 973-772-0497; Web: www.st-brendan.org.
School—Saint Brendan and Saint George School (1946) Tel: 973-772-1149; Fax: 973-772-5547. Lay Teachers 15; Students 306.
Catechesis Religious Program—Tel: 973-772-6775. Students 97.
4—ST. CLARE (1913) Revs. Peter S. Glabik; Thomas J. Fitzgerald.
Res.: 69 Allwood Rd., 07014. Tel: 973-777-9313; Email: office@saintclarenj.com; Email: finance@saintclarenj.com; Web: www.saintclarenj.com.
Catechesis Religious Program—Students 126.
5—SS. CYRIL AND METHODIUS (1913) (Slovak) Revs. John T. Connolly, M.Div.; Hector Melendez; Deacon Eugenio Morales.
Res.: 218 Ackerman Ave., 07011. Tel: 973-546-4390; Fax: 973-546-1252; Email: sscm100@gmail.com; Email: sscmchurch@gmail.com.
Catechesis Religious Program—Students 18.
6—ST. JOHN KANTY (1930) (Polish) Revs. Waclaw Sokolowski, O.F.M.Conv.; Boguslaw Czerniakowski, O.F.M.Conv.; Deacon Robert Altilio. In Res., Rev. Edward Handy, O.F.M.Conv.
Res.: 49 Speer Ave., 07013. Tel: 973-779-0564;
Tel: 973-779-4102 (Office); Fax: 973-773-0857; Web: www.saintjohnkanty.org.
Catechesis Religious Program—Students 146.
7—ST. PAUL (1914) Rev. Leonardo Jaramillo; Deacons Joseph Puskas; Hector Casillas.
Res.: 124 Union Ave., 07011. Tel: 973-546-2746;
Tel: 973-772-0117; Fax: 973-340-2083.
Catechesis Religious Program—92 Washington Ave., 07011. Students 123.
8—ST. PHILIP THE APOSTLE (1943)
797 Valley Rd., 07013. Tel: 973-779-6200; Email: bsalzer@stphilip.org; Web: www.stphilip.org. Revs. Joseph J. Garbarino; Joseph Boykow, Parochial Vicar; Mateusz Jasniewicz, Parochial Vicar; Deacons Nicholas Veliky; Robert G. Ayers. In Res., Rev. Msgr. P. Kevin Flanagan, (Retired).
School—St. Philip Preparatory School (1954) (Grades PreK-8), Tel: 973-779-4700; Email: principalzito@gmail.com; Web: saintphilipprep.com. Mrs. Barbara Zito, Prin. Lay Teachers 31; Students 476; Religious Teachers 1.
Catechesis Religious Program—Tel: 973-779-1439; Email: dpannullo@atphilip.org. Mrs. Denise Pannullo, D.R.E. Students 338.
9—SACRED HEART (1897) (Italian) Revs. John T. Connolly, M.Div.; Andrew T. Perretta, Parochial Vicar, (Retired). In Res., Revs. Robert W. Wisnefski; John Perricone.
Res.: 145 Randolph Ave., 07011. Tel: 973-546-6012; Fax: 973-546-1814; Email: church@sacredheartclifton.com.
Catechesis Religious Program—Students 74.
CONVENT STATION, MORRIS CO., ST. THOMAS MORE (1966)
4 Convent Rd., Morristown, 07960.
Tel: 973-267-5330; Email: info@stmnj.org; Web: www.stmnj.org. Mailing Address: P.O. Box 286, Convent Station, 07961. Rev. Thomas H. Fallone.
Catechesis Religious Program—Tel: 973-267-5585. Students 27.
DENVILLE, MORRIS CO., ST. MARY'S (1926) Revs. Martin G. Glynn; Richard V. Tartaglia, Parochial Vicar; Deacons Michael Allgaier; John Flynn; James Rizos.
Res.: 15 Myers Ave., Denville, 07834.
Tel: 973-627-0269; Email: dott@stmarys-denville.org; Web: www.stmarys-denville.org.
School—St. Mary's School (1954) Tel: 973-627-2606; Fax: 973-627-9316.
Catechesis Religious Program—Tel: 973-627-8276; Email: ccd@stmarys-denville.org. Mrs. PJ Miller, D.R.E. Students 606.
DOVER, MORRIS CO.
1—ST. MARY'S (1845) [CEM]
425 W. Blackwell St., Dover, 07801.
Tel: 973-366-0184; Email: info@stmarysdover.org; Web: www.stmarysdover.org. Rev. Derek Anderson, S.O.L.T.; Deacons Thomas P. Beirne; Stuart A. Hartnett; Steven Serafin, Pastoral Assoc. & D.R.E.; Alexandra Cernick, Youth Min.; Andrea Henry, Sec.
Catechesis Religious Program—Email: formation@stmarysdover.org. Students 46.
2—OUR LADY QUEEN OF THE MOST HOLY ROSARY (1959) (Hispanic), Merged with Sacred Heart, Dover to form Sacred Heart and Our Lady Queen of the Most Holy Rosary, Dover.
3—SACRED HEART CHURCH, Merged with Our Lady Queen of the Most Holy Rosary, Dover to form Sacred Heart and Our Lady Queen of the Most Holy Rosary, Dover.
4—SACRED HEART CHURCH AND OUR LADY QUEEN OF THE MOST HOLY ROSARY (1904)
4 Richards Ave., Dover, 07801. Tel: 973-366-0060; Email: phyle@sacredheart-dover.com; Web: www.sacredheart-dover.com. Revs. Brendan J. Murray; Nelson Betancur, Parochial Vicar; Rafael Ciro, Parochial Vicar; Carmen Buono, In Res., (Retired).
Catechesis Religious Program—Email: coordreled@sacredheart-dover.com. Ms. Sonia Castro, D.R.E. Students 125.
EAST HANOVER, MORRIS CO., ST. ROSE OF LIMA (1957)
312 Ridgedale Ave., East Hanover, 07936.
Tel: 973-887-5572; Fax: 973-884-0476; Web: saintroseoflimachurch.org. Revs. Owen B. Moran; Maciej Kranc, Parochial Vicar; Deacon Vincent Leo Jr.
Catechesis Religious Program—Tel: 973-887-0357. Students 455.
FLANDERS, MORRIS CO., ST. ELIZABETH ANN SETON (1985)
61 Main St., Flanders, 07836. Tel: 973-927-1629; Email: office@stelizabethschurch.org. Rev. Stanley C. Barron; Deacons Dennis King; Frank Puglia.
Catechesis Religious Program—Tel: 973-927-7077; Fax: 973-927-0093. Students 492.
FLORHAM PARK, MORRIS CO., HOLY FAMILY (1951)
35 Orchard Rd., Florham Park, 07932.
Tel: 973-377-1817; Email: rectory@holyfamilyfp.org. 1 Lloyd Ave., Florham Park, 07932. Revs. Thomas Rekiel; Krzysztof P. Liwarski, Parochial Vicar; Frederick Walters, (Retired); Deacon Peter Fiore; Mrs. Virginia Akhoury, Pastoral Assoc.
School—Holy Family School (1954) 17 Lloyd Ave., Florham Park, 07932. Tel: 973-377-4181;
Fax: 973-377-0273. Mary Smith, Dir. Lay Teachers 15; Students 106.
Catechesis Religious Program—Tel: 973-377-3101; Email: hfreducation@gmail.com. Anne Giedlinski, D.R.E. Students 479.
FRANKLIN, SUSSEX CO., IMMACULATE CONCEPTION (1867) [CEM] Rev. Boguslaw Kobus.
Res.: 75 Church St., Franklin, 07416.
Tel: 973-827-9575; Fax: 973-827-7375; Email: icchurch@ptd.net; Web: iccfranklin.org.
Catechesis Religious Program—Tel: 973-827-9501; Email: church@icrschool.com. Students 133.
GREEN POND, MORRIS CO., ST. SIMON THE APOSTLE (Rockaway Twp.) (1942)
1010 Green Pond Rd., Green Pond, 07435.
Tel: 973-697-4699; Fax: 973-697-1784; Email:

saintsimon@optonline.net; Web: www.stsimonapostle.org. Rev. Richard Bay; Deacon Kevin McKeever.
Catechesis Religious Program—Tel: 973-697-4699. Mrs. Connie Catania, D.R.E. Students 56.

HARDYSTON, SUSSEX CO., ST. JUDE THE APOSTLE (1966) 4 Beaver Run Rd., Hardyston, 07419.
Tel: 973-827-8030; Email: stjudehamburg@embarqmail.com. Rev. Michael Rodak.
Catechesis Religious Program—Tel: 973-827-2280. Students 225.

HASKELL, PASSAIC CO., ST. FRANCIS OF ASSISI (1905) Rev. Gregorz Golba, Admin.; Deacon Jose Rivera.
Res.: 868 Ringwood Ave., Haskell, 07420.
Tel: 973-835-0480; Fax: 973-835-3277; Email: stfrancis@optonline.net; Web: stfrancishaskell.org.
Catechesis Religious Program—Tel: 973-835-1946. Students 200.

HAWTHORNE, PASSAIC CO., ST. ANTHONY'S (1908) Rev. Msgr. Raymond J. Kupke, Ph.D.; Rev. Sylwester Pierzak, Parochial Vicar; Deacon Gerald Fadlalla.
Res.: 276 Diamond Bridge Ave., Hawthorne, 07506.
Tel: 973-427-1478; Email: info@stanthony-hawthorne.org; Web: www.stanthony-hawthorne.org.
School—St. Anthony's School (1912) 270 Diamond Bridge Ave., Hawthorne, 07506. Tel: 973-423-1818; Fax: 973-423-6065; Email: stanthony@nac.net. Sr. Colleen Clair, Prin. Lay Teachers 12; Sisters 1; Students 226; Religious Teachers 1.
Catechesis Religious Program—270 Diamond Bridge Ave., Hawthorne, 07506. Tel: 973-427-7873; Email: religiouseducation.stanthony@gmail.com. Sr. Betty Ann Martinez, F.M.A., D.R.E. Students 504.

HEWITT, PASSAIC CO., OUR LADY QUEEN OF PEACE (1921)
1911 Union Valley Rd., Hewitt, 07421-3056.
Tel: 973-728-8162; Fax: 973-728-4650; Email: olqpnj@gmail.com; Email: reception@olqpnj.org; Web: www.olqpnj.org. Rev. Kamil Stachowiak; Deacons Charles Roche; David Cedrone.
Catechesis Religious Program—
Tel: 973-728-8162, Ext. 308; Email: janet.scheil@olqpnj.org. Janet Scheil, D.R.E. Students 168.

HIGHLAND LAKES, SUSSEX CO., OUR LADY OF FATIMA (1954)
Mailing Address: 184 Breakneck Rd., P.O. Box 242, Highland Lakes, 07422. Tel: 973-764-4457;
Fax: 973-764-4504; Email: olfatima@warwick.net; Web: olfatimaparish.net. Rev. Ricardo Ortega, Admin.; Deacon William Aquino.
Catechesis Religious Program—Tel: 973-764-7277. Students 205.

HOPATCONG, SUSSEX CO., ST. JUDE'S (1931) Rev. Kamil Peter Wierzbicki, Admin.; Deacon Thomas Friel.
Res.: 40 Maxim Dr., Hopatcong, 07843.
Tel: 973-398-6377; Fax: 973-398-0121; Email: reled@stjudehopatcong.org; Web: www.stjudehopatcong.org.
Catechesis Religious Program—Students 107.

KINNELON, MORRIS CO., OUR LADY OF THE MAGNIFICAT (1961) [CEM] Rev. Steven Shadwell; Rev. Msgr. John J. Carroll, Ed.D., Pastor Emeritus; Rev. Lukasz Iwanczuk, Parochial Vicar.
Res.: 2 Miller Rd., Kinnelon, 07405.
Tel: 973-838-6838; Email: secy@olmchurch.org; Web: olmchurch.org.
Catechesis Religious Program—Email: dre@olmchurch.org. Mrs. Mary Ramsden, D.R.E. Students 450.

LAKE HOPATCONG, MORRIS CO., OUR LADY STAR OF THE SEA (Jefferson Twp.) (1910) Rev. P. Christopher Muldoon; Deacon Alberto R. Totino.
Res.: 237 Espanong Rd., P.O. Box 337, Lake Hopatcong, 07849. Tel: 973-663-0212, Ext. 16; Email: olsos@optonline.net; Web: www.olsoslh.org.
Catechesis Religious Program—204 Espanong Rd., Lake Hopatcong, 07849. Tel: 973-663-0124; Email: jhedrick@olsoslh.org. Josephine Hedrick, D.R.E. Students 352.

LINCOLN PARK, MORRIS CO., ST. JOSEPH'S (1922) Rev. Thomas P. Mangieri; Deacons Stephen J. Marabeti; Joseph Parlapiano.
Res.: 216 Comly Rd., Lincoln Park, 07035.
Tel: 973-696-4411, Ext. 101; Email: stjoelp@optonline.net.
Catechesis Religious Program—Students 230.

LITTLE FALLS, PASSAIC CO., OUR LADY OF THE HOLY ANGELS (1883)
473 Main St., Little Falls, 07424. Tel: 973-256-5200; Email: contact@holyangelscommunity.org; Web: www.holyangelsrc.org. 465 Main St., Little Falls, 07424. Rev. Msgr. T. Mark Condon, J.C.L., S.T.L.; Rev. Giovanni Rodriguez, Parochial Vicar; Deacon Joseph Sisco.
Catechesis Religious Program—465 Main St., Little Falls, 07424. Email: pfiliaci@gmail.com. Ms. Trish Filiaci, D.R.E. Students 465.

LONG VALLEY, MORRIS CO.
1—ST. LUKE (1982) Rev. Michael J. Drury.
Res.: P.O. Box 416, Long Valley, 07853.
Tel: 908-876-3515; Fax: 908-876-5277.
Church: 265 W. Mill Rd., Long Valley, 07853.
Catechesis Religious Program—Students 602.
2—ST. MARK THE EVANGELIST (1986)
Mailing Address: 24 Ann Rd., Long Valley, 07853.
Tel: 908-850-0652; Fax: 908-850-0648; Email: frjoe.stm@comcast.net. Revs. Marcin Michalowski, Admin.; Slawomir Tomaszewski, Parochial Vicar; Javier Bareno, Parochial Vicar; Deacons Nicholas Ardito; James Jones.
Office: 59 Spring Ln., Long Valley, 07853.
Res.: 2 E. Springtown Rd., Long Valley, 07853.
Catechesis Religious Program—Students 279.

MADISON, MORRIS CO., ST. VINCENT MARTYR (1805) [CEM]
26 Green Village Rd., Madison, 07940.
Tel: 973-377-4000; Fax: 973-377-8242. Rev. Msgr. George F. Hundt, J.C.L.; Rev. Darwin J. Lastra, Parochial Vicar; Deacon Robert Morton; Jan Figenshu, Pastoral Assoc.
School—St. Vincent Martyr School (1848) .
Catechesis Religious Program—Tel: 973-966-1771. Students 834.

MCAFEE, SUSSEX CO., ST. FRANCIS DE SALES (1963)
614 County Rte. 517, Vernon, 07462.
Tel: 973-827-3248; Fax: 973-827-7534; Email: office@stfrancisvernon.org; Web: www.stfrancisvernon.org. Mailing Address: P.O. Box 785, McAfee, 07428. Rev. Christopher S. Barkhausen, Admin.; Deacon Dennis Gil.
Catechesis Religious Program—Email: melory@st.francisvernon.org. Melory Weber, Youth Min.; Jane Kunzweiler, Youth Min. Students 348.

MENDHAM, MORRIS CO., ST. JOSEPH'S (1853) [CEM]
8 W. Main St., Mendham, 07945. Tel: 973-543-5950; Fax: 973-543-6025; Email: jcronin@stjoesmendham.org; Web: www.stjoesmendham.org. 6 New St., Mendham, 07945. Rev. Msgr. Joseph T. Anginoli, J.C.L.
School—St. Joseph School (1963) (Grades K-8), Tel: 973-543-7474; Email: CWitczak@sjsMendham.org; Web: www.sjsmendham.org. Lay Teachers 20; Students 146.
Catechesis Religious Program—Email: atracy@stjoesmendham.org. Annette Tracy, D.R.E. Students 474.

MONTAGUE, SUSSEX CO., ST. JAMES THE GREATER (1943) Rev. Wayne F. Varga; Deacon Wayne Von Doehren; Mrs. Patricia Hope, Pastoral Assoc.
Res.: 75 River Rd., Montague, 07827.
Tel: 973-948-2296; Email: stjamesthomas@aol.com.
Catechesis Religious Program—122 C.R. 645, Sandyston, 07826. Tel: 973-948-7004. Mrs. Mary Flexer, D.R.E. Students 11.

MONTVILLE, MORRIS CO., ST. PIUS X (1959)
24 Changebridge Rd., Montville, 07045.
Tel: 973-335-2894; Email: office@st-pius-x.org. Revs. Mark Olenowski; Dominik Bakowski, Parochial Vicar.
School—St. Pius X School (1963) .
Catechesis Religious Program—Peter Keenen O'Brien, D.R.E. Students 760.

MORRIS PLAINS, MORRIS CO., ST. VIRGILIUS (1881)
250 Speedwell Ave., Morris Plains, 07950.
Tel: 973-538-1418; Fax: 973-538-2992; Email: parishoffice@stvirgil.org; Web: www.stvirgil.org. Revs. Lancelot Reis; Daniel Chajkowski, Parochial Vicar; Deacons Merle Sisler; Rich Pinto.
Catechesis Religious Program—Students 426.

MORRISTOWN, MORRIS CO.
1—ASSUMPTION OF THE BLESSED VIRGIN MARY (1848) [CEM] Rev. Msgr. John E. Hart; Rev. Lukasz Wnuk, Parochial Vicar; Deacons P. Michael Hanly; Brian D. Beyerl; John Brandi; Elliott Stein; Rev. Dennis J. Crowley, (Retired).
Res.: 91 Maple Ave., Morristown, 07960.
Tel: 973-539-2141; Email: assumption@assumptionparish.org; Web: assumptionparish.org.
School—Assumption of the Blessed Virgin Mary School (1850) (Grades PreK-8), 63 MacCulloch Ave., Morristown, 07960. Tel: 973-538-0590;
Fax: 973-984-3632; Email: pdechiaro@assumptionnj.org; Web: www.assumptionnj.org/. Sr. Merris Larkin, Prin. Lay Teachers 45; Sisters of Charity 1; Students 500; Religious Teachers 1.
Catechesis Religious Program—Tel: 732-675-6389; Email: linda.macios@assumptionparish.org. Ms. Linda Macios, D.R.E. Students 650.
2—ST. MARGARET OF SCOTLAND (1885) Revs. Hernan Arias; Jesus Peralta, Parochial Vicar; Yasid Salas, Parochial Vicar; Deacons Tim Holden; Ken Rado.
Office: 12 Columba St., Morristown, 07960.
Res.: 6 Sussex Ave., Morristown, 07960.
Tel: 973-538-0874; Fax: 973-538-4581; Email: stmargaretchurchmorristown@gmail.com.
Catechesis Religious Program—Students 241.

MOUNT ARLINGTON, MORRIS CO., OUR LADY OF THE LAKE (1888) Revs. Paul Barboutz, Admin.; Hugh P. Murphy, Pastor Emeritus.
Res.: One Park Ave., Mount Arlington, 07856.
Tel: 973-398-0240; Email: ollmtarlington@aol.com.
Catechesis Religious Program—Tel: 973-770-0291. Students 285.

MOUNT HOPE, MORRIS CO., ST. BERNARD'S (1855) Rev. Alfred J. Lampron, Admin.
Res.: 446 Mt. Hope Rd., Wharton, 07885-2814.
Tel: 973-627-0066; Email: stbernardsmth@verizon.net.
Catechesis Religious Program—Students 4.

MOUNTAIN LAKES, MORRIS CO., ST. CATHERINE OF SIENA (1956) Rev. Jared J. Brogan, Admin.
Res.: 10 N. Pocono Rd., Mountain Lakes, 07046.
Tel: 973-334-7131; Email: jbrogan@stcatherine-ml.org.
Catechesis Religious Program—Tel: 973-334-5257. Students 487.

NETCONG, MORRIS CO., ST. MICHAEL'S (1873) [CEM] Revs. Michael Lee; Henry Pinto, Parochial Vicar; Deacons Joseph Keenan; Stuart Murphy; Richard F. Bias.
Res.: 4 Church St., Netcong, 07857.
Tel: 973-347-0032; Fax: 973-347-1560.
Catechesis Religious Program—Tel: 973-347-1465. Students 210.

NEW VERNON, MORRIS CO., CHRIST THE KING (1956)
16 Blue Mill Rd., New Vernon, 07976.
Tel: 973-539-4955, Ext. 10; Email: frbriansullivan@me.com; Web: www.churchofchristtheking.org. P.O. Box 368, New Vernon, 07976. Revs. Brian Sullivan; Marcin Kania, Parochial Vicar.

NEWTON, SUSSEX CO., ST. JOSEPH (1854) [CEM]
24 Halsted St., Newton, 07860. Tel: 973-383-1985; Email: parishoffice@stjosephnewton.org. 22 Halsted St., Newton, 07860-2003. Deacons Gerald Hanifan, (Retired); Thomas Zayac; Rev. ST Sutton, J.C.L.
Res.: 17 Elm St., Newton, 07860.
Catechesis Religious Program—Tel: 973-383-8413. Students 266.

OAK RIDGE, MORRIS CO., ST. THOMAS, THE APOSTLE (1949) [CEM]
5635 Berkshire Valley Rd., Oak Ridge, 07438.
Tel: 973-208-0090; Fax: 973-208-0092; Web: www.stthomasjohn.org. Rev. Matthew J. Twiggs, Admin.; Deacon Milton Smiler.
Catechesis Religious Program—Tel: 973-208-0096; Fax: 973-383-8495. Students 125.

OGDENSBURG, SUSSEX CO., ST. THOMAS OF AQUIN (1881) [CEM]
53 Kennedy Ave., Ogdensburg, 07439.
Tel: 973-827-3190; Email: stthomasofaquin@embarqmail.com; Web: www.stthomasofaquin.org. Rev. John P. Pilipie; Deacons Edward Reading; Dominic Zampella.
Catechesis Religious Program—Ms. Brigette Hanley, D.R.E. Students 71.

PARSIPPANY, MORRIS CO.
1—ST. ANN (1982)
781 Smith Rd., Parsippany, 07054.
Tel: 973-884-1986; Fax: 973-884-0940; Email: stann@saint-ann.net; Web: www.saint-ann.net. Rev. David Pickens; Deacons Alfred Frank; Leonard Deo; Sr. Frances Sanzo, S.S.C., Pastoral Assoc.; Mrs. Ginny Bissig, Pastoral Assoc.; Mr. Louis Castano, Music Min.
Catechesis Religious Program—Students 199.
2—ST. CHRISTOPHER (1944) Revs. Joseph G. Buffardi; Michal Falgowski, Parochial Vicar; Deacons Henry Rohrman; Richard A. Gaydo; Alan Lucibello.
Res.: 1050 Littleton Rd., Parsippany, 07054.
Tel: 973-539-7050; Fax: 973-539-3601.
See separate listing under Elementary Schools, Diocesan in the Institution section.
Catechesis Religious Program—Tel: 973-539-6208. Students 450.
3—ST. PETER THE APOSTLE (1938) Rev. Msgr. Herbert K. Tillyer, P.A., M.Ch.A.; Rev. Krzystof Slimak, Parochial Vicar; Deacons Louis Chiocco; Robert A. Lang; Joseph Marsicovete; Peter Cistaro. In Res., Rev. Msgr. Christopher C. DiLella, (Retired).
Res.: 179 Baldwin Rd., Parsippany, 07054.
Tel: 973-334-2090; Fax: 973-334-5397; Email: stpeterpar@optonline.net; Web: saintpetertheapostle.org.
See separate listing under Elementary Schools, Diocesan in the Institution section.
Catechesis Religious Program—189 Baldwin Rd., Parsippany, 07054. Students 424.

PASSAIC, PASSAIC CO.
1—ST. ANTHONY OF PADUA (1917) (Italian) Revs. Hernan Cely, Admin.; Duberney Villamizar.
Res.: 95 Myrtle Ave., Passaic, 07055.
Tel: 973-777-4793; Fax: 973-779-6864; Web: www.stanthonypassaic.org.
Catechesis Religious Program—Students 289.
2—ASSUMPTION OF THE BLESSED VIRGIN MARY (1891) (Slovak) Revs. Jorge I. Rodriguez; Jorge Castano, Parochial Vicar.
Res.: 63 Monroe St., Passaic, 07055.
Tel: 973-779-0427.

Catechesis Religious Program—Students 70.
3—HOLY ROSARY (1918) (Polish) (Shrine of Saint John Paul II) Revs. A. Stefan Las; Michal Dykalski.
Res.: 6 Wall St., Passaic, 07055. Tel: 973-473-1578; Email: shrinejp2passaic@gmail.com; Web: www.holyrosarypassaic.org.
Catechesis Religious Program—Students 657.
4—HOLY TRINITY (1900) (German) Rev. Antonio Rodriguez.
Res.: 226 Harrison St., Passaic, 07055.
Tel: 973-778-9763; Fax: 973-778-7582.
Catechesis Religious Program—Students 600.
5—ST. JOSEPH'S (1892) (Polish) Very Rev. Canon Stanley Lesniowski; Rev. Jakub Grzybowski, Parochial Vicar.
Res.: 7 Parker Ave., Passaic, 07055.
Tel: 973-473-2822; Fax: 973-473-2855.
Catechesis Religious Program—Students 216.
6—ST. NICHOLAS (1868) [CEM] Revs. Jorge I. Rodriguez; Jorge Castano, Parochial Vicar.
Res.: c/o St. Mary, 63 Monroe St., Passaic, 07055.
Tel: 973-779-7867; Fax: 973-472-5033; Email: stnicholasrc@prodigy.net.
Catechesis Religious Program—
7—OUR LADY OF FATIMA (1954) (Hispanic) Rev. Rolands Uribe, Admin.
Res.: 32 Exchange Pl., Passaic, 07055.
Tel: 973-472-0815; Fax: 973-472-0250.
Catechesis Religious Program—Students 136.
8—OUR LADY OF MT. CARMEL (1902) (Italian) Revs. Brian Tomlinson, O.F.M.Cap.; Edward Henning, O.F.M.Cap.
Res.: 10 St. Francis Way, Passaic, 07055.
Tel: 973-473-0246; Fax: 973-473-3404; Email: ladyofmtcarmel@verizon.net; Web: ladyofmtcarmel.org.
Catechesis Religious Program—Students 7.
9—ST. STEPHEN'S (1902) (Magyar)
223 Third St., Passaic, 07055. Tel: 973-779-0332; Fax: 973-778-4263. Rev. Laszlo Balogh, Admin.
Catechesis Religious Program—Students 5.
PEQUANNOCK, MORRIS CO.
1—HOLY SPIRIT (1949) Rev. David Monteleone, Admin.; Deacons Michael Scruggs; Gary Zack. In Res., Rev. Jose Bocanegra.
Res.: 318 Newark-Pompton Tpke., Pequannock, 07440. Tel: 973-696-1234; Fax: 973-305-9390; Email: info@holyspiritchurchnj.org.
School—Holy Spirit School (1956) 330 Newark-Pompton Tpke., Pequannock, 07440.
Tel: 973-835-5680; Fax: 973-835-1757. Lay Teachers 22; Maestre Pie Filippini (Religious Teachers Filippini) 1; Students 245.
Catechesis Religious Program—Students 153.
Convent—Tel: 973-694-2111.
2—OUR LADY OF FATIMA CHAPEL (TRIDENTINE) (1994) Revs. Matthew McNeely, F.S.S.P., Admin.; Karl Marsolle, F.S.S.P.; Robert Boyd.
Res.: 32 W. Franklin Ave., Pequannock, 07440.
Tel: 973-694-6727; Web: www.olfchapel.org.
School—Kolbe Immaculata School, 18 First St., Pequannock, 07440. Tel: 973-694-1034;
Fax: 973-694-1304. Jayne Bayne, Prin. Lay Teachers 6; Students 40.
Catechesis Religious Program—Students 39.
POMPTON LAKES, PASSAIC CO., OUR LADY OF THE ASSUMPTION (1906) Revs. Gonzalo Torres, O.F.M.; Richard Husted, O.F.M., Parochial Vicar; Barry Langley, Parochial Vicar; Deacons Thomas Kimak; Hal Clark.
Parish Office—17 Pompton Ave., Pompton Lakes, 07442. Tel: 973-835-0374; Email: smc@stmarys-pompton.org.
St. Mary's Friary: 37 Pompton Ave., Pompton Lakes, 07442.
School—Our Lady of the Assumption School (1951) (Grades PreK-8), 25 Pompton Ave., Pompton Lakes, 07442. Tel: 973-835-2010; Email: clasalle@smspompton.org; Email: msmith@smspompton.org; Web: www.stmarys-pompton.org. Carol LaSalle, Prin. Students 250.
Catechesis Religious Program—Tel: 973-835-7750; Email: maryan@smarys-pompton.org. Mary Ann Werner, D.R.E. Students 1,378.
POMPTON PLAINS, MORRIS CO., OUR LADY OF GOOD COUNSEL (1962) Rev. Peter J. Clarke; Deacons Herb D. Coyne; Carmen Restaino. In Res.
Res.: 155 W. Pkwy., Pompton Plains, 07444.
Tel: 973-839-2447; Fax: 973-839-9492.
Catechesis Religious Program—Tel: 973-839-3311; Fax: 973-839-5202. Students 520.
PROSPECT PARK, PASSAIC CO., ST. PAUL'S (1924) Rev. Msgr. Edward J. Kurtyka, P.A., J.C.D. In Res., Rev. James Moss, (Retired).
Res.: 286 Haledon Ave., Prospect Park, 07508.
Tel: 973-790-8169.
Catechesis Religious Program—Tel: 973-790-8135. Students 43.
RANDOLPH, MORRIS CO.
1—ST. MATTHEW THE APOSTLE (1988) Rev. Brian P. Quinn; Deacons Edward Keegan; Richard A. Brady.
Res.: 335 Dover-Chester Rd., Randolph, 07869.
Tel: 973-584-1101; Email: terry.shaw@stmatthewsrandolph.org; Web: www.stmatthewsrandolph.org.
Catechesis Religious Program—Tel: 832-251-4129; Email: moira.dziomba@stmatthewsrandolph.org. Mrs. Moira Dziomba, D.R.E. Students 460.
2—RESURRECTION (1978)
651 Millbrook Ave., Randolph, 07869.
Tel: 973-895-4224; Email: info@resurrectionparishnj.org; Web: www.resurrectionparishnj.org. Rev. John F. Tarantino, Admin.; Deacons Roger Lacouture; Raymond Latour; Richard Reck.
RINGWOOD, PASSAIC CO., ST. CATHERINE OF BOLOGNA (1917) Revs. Pawel F. Szurek; Michal Rybinski.
Res.: 112 Erskine Rd., Ringwood, 07456.
Tel: 973-962-7032, Ext. 7; Email: business@stcatherineofbologna.org.
School—St. Catherine of Bologna School (1948)
Tel: 973-962-7131; Fax: 973-962-0585; Email: office@stcbschool.org. Sr. Theresa Firenze, Prin. Lay Teachers 14; Students 164; Religious Teachers 2.
Catechesis Religious Program—Students 289.
ROCKAWAY, MORRIS CO.
1—ST. CECILIA'S (1869) [CEM] Revs. Sigmund A. Peplowski; Cerilo Javinez, Parochial Vicar; Mateusz Darlak, Parochial Vicar; Deacon Paul D. Willson.
Res.: 70 Church St., Rockaway, 07866.
Tel: 973-627-0313; Email: stcec@optonline.net; Web: www.st-cecilia-org.
Catechesis Religious Program—Email: stcecilia.faithformation@gmail.com. Mr. James Clancy, Dir. Faith Formation. Students 429.
Convent—100 Church St., Rockaway, 07866.
Tel: 973-627-6533.
2—SACRED HEART (1923) (Slovak) Rev. Pawel Bala, Admin. In Res., Rev. Stephen Sniscak.
Res.: 63 E. Main St., Rockaway, 07866.
Tel: 973-627-0422; Email: shrectory@gmail.com; Web: www.sacredheartrockaway.org.
Catechesis Religious Program—Students 25.
ROCKAWAY TOWNSHIP, MORRIS CO., ST. CLEMENT, POPE AND MARTYR (1964)
154 Mt. Pleasant Ave., Dover, 07801.
Tel: 973-366-7095; Fax: 973-366-6083; Email: parishoffice@stclement-rtwp.org; Web: www.stclement-rtwp.org. Rev. L. Richard Hardy; Deacon Henry Hyle.
Catechesis Religious Program—Tel: 973-366-7547; Email: dreparish@stclement-rtwp.org. Susan Drew, D.R.E. Students 251.
SANDYSTON, SUSSEX CO., ST. THOMAS THE APOSTLE (1941)
210 Rte. 206 N., Sandyston, 07826.
Tel: 973-948-2296; Fax: 973-948-2296; Email: stjamesthomas@aol.com. Rev. Wayne F. Varga; Deacon Wayne Von Doehren; Mrs. Patricia Hope, Pastoral Assoc.
Catechesis Religious Program—122 C.R. 645, Sandyston, 07826. Tel: 973-948-7004. Mrs. Mary Flexer, D.R.E. Students 97.
SCHOOLEY'S MOUNTAIN, MORRIS CO., OUR LADY OF THE MOUNTAIN (1954) [CEM] Revs. Marcin Michalowski, Admin.; Slawomir Tomaszewski, Parochial Vicar; Deacons Nicholas Ardito; James Jones; Thomas P. Gibbons; Robert C. Head.
Res.: 2 E. Springtown Rd., Long Valley, 07853.
Tel: 908-876-4395; Fax: 908-876-3744.
Catechesis Religious Program—Tel: 908-876-4003. Students 663.
SPARTA, SUSSEX CO.
1—SAINT KATERI TEKAKWITHA (1988) Revs. Vidal Gonzalez Jr.; Wilder A. Londono, (In Res.); Deacons Andrew Calandriello; Charles Mathias; Barry O'Brien; Glen P. Murphy. In Res.
Office: 427 Stanhope Rd., Sparta, 07871.
Tel: 973-729-1682; Fax: 973-729-0702; Email: office@saintkateri.org; Web: www.saintkateri.org.
Res.: 11 Cherry Tree Ln., Sparta, 07871.
Tel: 973-729-2892.
Catechesis Religious Program—Tel: 973-729-0489. Students 466.
2—OUR LADY OF THE LAKE (1935) Revs. David McDonnell; Marcin Bradtke, Parochial Vicar; Deacon James McGovern.
Res.: 294 Sparta Ave., Sparta, 07871.
Tel: 973-729-6107; Web: www.ourladyofthelake.org.
School—Our Lady of the Lake School (1954) (School operated by The Catholic Academy of Sussex County Inc.) Tel: 973-729-9174; Fax: 973-729-0318. Patty Kleber, Prin. Lay Teachers 32; Students 483.
Catechesis Religious Program—Students 550.
STIRLING, MORRIS CO., ST. VINCENT DE PAUL (1886) [CEM]
250 Bebout Ave., Stirling, 07980. Tel: 908-647-0118; Email: parish@stvincentschurch.org; Web: stvincentschurch.org. Rev. A. Richard Carton; Deacon Peter J. O'Neill.
Catechesis Religious Program—Tel: 908-647-0421; Fax: 908-647-3878. Students 420.
STOCKHOLM, SUSSEX CO., ST. JOHN VIANNEY (1958) Rev. Matthew J. Twiggs; Deacons James Camarrano; Kevin L. Combs.
Res.: c/o St. Thomas, 5655 Berkshire Valley Rd., Oak Ridge, 07438. Tel: 973-697-6550; Fax: 973-208-0092; Web: www.ststhomasjohn.org.
Catechesis Religious Program—Tel: 973-208-0096. Students 207.
SUCCASUNNA, MORRIS CO., ST. THERESE (1957)
7 Hunter St., Succasunna, 07876. Tel: 973-584-8271; Email: sttheresoffice@optonline.net. Revs. Marc A. Mancini, J.C.L.; Dulibber Gonzalez, Parochial Vicar; Jose Miguel Jimenez, Parochial Vicar; Deacons Bruce Olsen; Jose Padron.
School—St. Therese School (1963) 135 Main St., Succasunna, 07876. Tel: 973-584-0812;
Fax: 973-584-2029. Lay Teachers 10; Students 160.
Catechesis Religious Program—Tel: 973-584-9444; Fax: 973-584-9492. Students 660.
SUSSEX, SUSSEX CO., ST. MONICA (1881) Rev. Jan Wodziak; Carol Bezak, Pastoral Assoc.
Res.: 33 Unionville Ave., Sussex, 07461.
Tel: 973-875-4521; Fax: 973-875-7538.
Catechesis Religious Program—Students 50.
SWARTSWOOD, SUSSEX CO., OUR LADY OF MT. CARMEL (1951)
Mailing Address: P.O. Box 124, Swartswood, 07877.
Tel: 973-383-3566; Fax: 973-383-3831. Rev. Abuchi Nwosu, Admin.; Deacon Anthony P. Barile Jr.
Catechesis Religious Program—Tel: 973-579-2355. Students 131.
TOTOWA BOROUGH, PASSAIC CO., ST. JAMES OF THE MARCHES (1926) Rev. Yojaneider Garcia, Admin.
Res.: 32 St. James Pl., Totowa, 07512.
Tel: 973-790-0288; Email: stjameschurch@optonline.net.
Catechesis Religious Program—31 St. James Pl., Totowa, 07512. Students 208.
WAYNE, PASSAIC CO.
1—ANNUNCIATION (1963)
45 Urban Club Rd., Wayne, 07470. Tel: 973-694-5700; Fax: 973-694-5706; Email: trish23@optonline.net; Web: www.abvm-wayne.org. Rev. Brian Ditullio, Admin.; Deacon Joseph C. Crowley Jr.
Catechesis Religious Program—Tel: 973-694-0787. Students 133.
2—HOLY CROSS (1925)
Holy Cross Way & Van Duyne Ave., Wayne, 07470.
Tel: 973-694-4585; Email: VonBreton@aol.com. 630 Valley Rd., Wayne, 07470. Revs. Peter VB. Wells; Peter Filipkowski, Parochial Vicar, (Retired).
Catechesis Religious Program— Combined with Our Lady of the Valley, Wayne.
3—IMMACULATE HEART OF MARY (1956)
580 Ratzer Rd., Wayne, 07470. Tel: 973-694-3400; Email: ihmchurch@aol.com. Revs. Michael J. Parisi, V.G.; Jader Avila, Parochial Vicar; Daniel A. Kelly, Pastor Emeritus, (Retired).
School—Immaculate Heart of Mary School (1958) (Grades PreK-8), Tel: 973-694-1225; Email: ihm.wayne@gmail.com; Web: www.ihmwaynenj.org. Lay Teachers 15; Students 180.
Catechesis Religious Program—Tel: 973-694-4891. Students 390.
4—OUR LADY OF CONSOLATION (1963) Rev. Michael D. Lombardo. In Res., Rev. Philip-Michael Tangorra.
Res.: 1799 Hamburg Tpke., Wayne, 07470.
Tel: 973-839-3444; Fax: 973-839-9695.
Catechesis Religious Program—Students 291.
5—OUR LADY OF THE VALLEY (1960) Revs. Peter VB. Wells; Peter Filipkowski, Parochial Vicar, (Retired); Deacon Vincent Cocilovo. In Res., Rev. Michael Lee.
Office: 630 Valley Rd., Wayne, 07470.
Tel: 973-694-4585; Email: secretary@olvwayne.org.
Res.: 614 Valley Rd., Wayne, 07470. Web: www.olvwayne.org.
Catechesis Religious Program—Students 437.
WEST MILFORD TOWNSHIP, PASSAIC CO., ST. JOSEPH (1765) Rev. Aleksander Bialas, Admin.; Deacons Benjamin LoParo; Harry White.
Res.: 454 Germantown Rd., West Milford, 07480.
Tel: 973-697-6100; Fax: 973-697-3716; Web: www.stjoseph-nj.org.
Catechesis Religious Program—Tel: 973-208-0636. Students 325.
WHIPPANY, MORRIS CO., OUR LADY OF MERCY (1854) [CEM]
9 Parsippany Rd., Whippany, 07981.
Tel: 973-887-0050; Email: olmchwhip@aol.com; Web: ourladyofmercyparish.com. Rev. Roberto Amador, Admin.; Deacon Vincent LoBello.

Chaplains of Public Institutions
Hospitals

PATERSON.
St. Joseph Hospital, 703 Main St., Paterson, 07503.
Tel: 973-754-2000; Tel: 973-754-2060 (Office). Revs. David Ahiahornu, (Ghana) Chap., Francis Enrico Conde, Chap., Patrick Okafor, (Nigeria) Chap., Jesus Peralta, Chap., Mr. William McDonald, Pres. & CEO.

Preakness Hospital, P.O. Box V, Paterson, 07509. Tel: 973-278-6800.
DOVER.
Dover General Hospital, Jardine St., Dover, 07801. Tel: 973-939-3000.
MORRIS PLAINS.
Greystone Park Psychiatric Hospital, Morris Plains, 07950. Tel: 973-538-1800.
MORRISTOWN.
Morristown Memorial Hospital, 100 Madison Ave., Morristown, 07960. Tel: 973-540-5307. Revs. Jeider S. Barraza, Chap., Zbigniew Kluba, Sisters Teresa Chiappa, S.S.C., Jo Mascera, S.S.C.
NEWTON.
Newton Memorial Hospital, 175 High St., Newton, 07860. Tel: 973-383-2121. Rev. Jude S. Salus, O.S.B., Chap, Vacant.
POMPTON PLAINS.
Chilton Memorial Hospital, Pompton Plains, 07444. Tel: 973-831-5000. Revs. Andrew T. Perretta, Chap., (Retired), Robert W. Wisnefski, Deacons Edward Jaroszewski, Gil Leifer, Larry White.
TOTOWA.
North Jersey Developmental Center.
WAYNE.
St. Joseph's Wayne Hospital, Hamburg Tpke., Wayne, 07470. Tel: 973-942-6900.

Correctional Facilities

PATERSON.
Passaic County Jail. Vacant.
MORRISTOWN.
Morris County Jail. Rev. Hernan Arias, Coord. Prison Ministry.
NEWTON.
Sussex County Jail. Vacant.

Colleges

NEWTON.
Sussex County Community College.
RANDOLPH.
County College of Morris. Vacant, Campus Min.
WAYNE.
William Paterson College. Rev. Paul Tomczyk, Chap.

Special Assignment:
Rev. Msgr.—
Mahoney, James T., Ph.D., V.G., P.O. Box 70, Chatham, 07928
Rev.—
Prisk, Stephen.

On Duty Outside the Diocese:
Rev. Msgr.—
Vitillo, Robert J., Geneva, Switzerland
Revs.—
Farias, Joseph G., Fairfield, CT
Gajewski, Mariusz, Catholic University, Lublin, Poland
Grzybowski, Jakub, Orchard Lake, MI
Mastroeni, Anthony J., S.T.D., J.D.
Nowak, Przemyslaw, Orchard Lake, MI
Reading, Edward, Ortley Beach, NJ.

Graduate Studies:
.Revs.—
Burns, Andrew, Rome
Guevara, Manuel, Salamanca, Spain
Jamarillo, Cesar, Rome
Tangora, Philip-Michael, Washington.

Military Chaplains:
Rev.—
Muda, Adam.

Unassigned:
Revs.—
Barrera, Gabriel
Biegun, Marek.

Absent on Leave:
Revs.—
Bocanegra, Jose
Briganti, Philip
Castillo, Ruben Dario, (Colombia)
Jurjewicz, Hubert, Ph.D.
Long, David P., S.T.L., J.C.L.
Lopez, Jose
Mabango, Ashiono Anthony
Nurek, Marcin
Ruiz, Edgar
Scott, James C.
Treglio, Vincent
Walka, Marcin.

Retired:
Rev. Msgrs.—
Bihr, Louis J., (Retired), 2018 Ridley Ter., The Villages, FL 32162
Boland, Eugene, (Retired), 315 Lindsley Rd., Cedar Grove, 07009
Boland, John V., (Retired), 185 Tarrington Rd., Hamburg, 07149
Carroll, Robert B., (Retired), 133 Spencer Rd., Dingmans Ferry, PA 18328
Carvajal, Felipe N., (Retired), 30 Park Ave., Garfield, 07026
Cassidy, Charles C., (Retired), 15 Sea Girt Ln., Waretown, 08758
Ciampaglio, Joseph M., (Retired), 32 Greenways Ln., Lakewood, 08701
Conway, Michael, (Retired), 2510 S.W. 81st Ave., Apt. 308, Davie, FL 33328
Cusack, John J., (Retired), 4219 E. Shadow Branch Dr., Tucson, AZ 85756
Diachak, Robert M., (Retired), 11 Meadow Ln., P.O. Box 745, Chester, 07930
DiLella, Christopher C., (Retired), 179 Baldwin Rd., Parsippany, 07054
Doody, Peter J., (Retired), 5204 Lilac Ct., Lansdale, PA 19446
Dudak, George A., (Retired), Main St., Chester, 07930
Duffy, Francis J., (Retired), 107 Hawthorne Ave., Hawthorne, 07506
Ferrito, Joseph L., (Retired), 118 Main St., Succasunna, 07876
Fitzpatrick, John E., (Retired), 4 Lakeview Dr., Hamburg, 07419
Flanagan, P. Kevin, (Retired), 67 Lakeview Dr., Hamburg, 07419
Giordani, Mark J., (Retired), P.O. Box 67, Totowa, 07512
Goode, Joseph J., M.Ch.A., (Retired), 22 Heritage Ln., Hamburg, 07914
Introini, Elso C., (Retired), 34 San Carlos St., Toms River, 08757
Knauer, Paul F., (Retired), 133 Spencer Rd., Dingmans Ferry, PA 18328
Lasch, Kenneth E., J.C.D., (Retired), 706 Park View, Pompton Plains, 07444
Madden, Brendan P., (Retired), 118 Main St., Succasunna, 07876
McBride, Peter A., (Retired), 174 Glenelly Rd., Plumbridge, Omagh, County Tyrone, Northern Ireland BT798LL
McCarthy, William, (Retired), 3 Winding Wood Dr., Sayreville, 08872
McDonnell, Martin, (Retired), 8 Heiman Dr., Hopatcong, 07843
McHugh, Peter J., (Retired), P.O. Box 745, Chester, 07930
Naughton, William M., (Retired), 124 Weinmanns Blvd., Apt. 2, Wayne, 07470
O'Rorke, James H., (Retired), 41 Spruce Hill Ct., Hamburg, 07419
Rocco, Remigio G., (Retired), 101 Larch Ct., Dingmans Ferry, PA 18328
Rusconi, Richard A., (Retired), 612A Devonshire Ln., Manchester Township, 08759
Scott, Patrick J., (Retired), 400 Mt. Prospect Ave., 07012
Stober, William P., (Retired), 20 Sea Point Dr., Point Pleasant, 08742
Varettoni, Julian B., (Retired), 486 Rt. 46, Hackettstown, 07840
Wehrlen, John B., (Retired), 22 Morning Glory Ct., Toms River, 08755
Revs.—
Bradley, Charles, (Retired), 4017 Whitehall Way, Alpharetta, GA 30004
Buono, Carmen, (Retired), 4 Richards Ave., Dover, 07801
Catoir, John T., J.C.D., (Retired), 605 Autumn Gate Dr., Cary, NC 27518
Collins, William B., (Retired), Lisheenvala, Claregalway, County Galway, Ireland
Connell, John Andrew, (Retired), Main St., Chester, 07930
Coutinho, Absalom, (Retired), 1010 Warwick Ct., Sun City, FL 33573
Cramer, William N., (Retired), 47 Franklin Pl., Morris Plains, 07950
Crowley, Dennis J., (Retired), 91 Maple Ave., Morristown, 07960
Cruz, Luciano, (Retired), 11 Meadow Ln., P.O. Box 745, Chester, 07930
Davey, Edward M., (Retired), Main St., Chester, 07930
Davis, Joseph P., (Retired), Nazareth Village. Main St., Chester, 07930
DeMattia, John A., (Retired), 9 Pocono Rd., Denville, 07834
Dillon, Edward J., (Retired), 25 Wilmer St., Apt. E4-2, Madison, 07940
Drogon, Greg, (Retired), P.O. Box 3465, Toms River, 08756
Duggan, Paul O'Donnell, (Retired), 256 Fienna Pl., St. Augustine, FL 32085
Filipkowski, Peter, (Retired), 41 Mill Rd., Whiting, 08759
Gothie, George J., (Retired), Main St., Chester, 07930
Gutierrez, Gilberto, (Retired), Carrera 12, #16-25, Quindio, Barcelona Colombia
Hanley, John P., (Retired), 10 Zendzin Ave., Woodland Park, 07424
Holterhoff, Edward G., (Retired), 972 Piney Way, Morro Bay, CA 93443
Iovino, Paul, (Retired), 23 Mission Way, Barnegat, 08005
Kelly, Daniel A., (Retired), 480 Ratzer Rd., Wayne, 07470
Klein, John J., (Retired), 11 Meadow Ln., Box 635, Chester, 07930
Krajewski, Paul A., (Retired), 118 Main St., Succasunna, 07876
Lambro, Edward J., Ph.D., C.C.M.H.C., (Retired), 26 Quartz Ln., Paterson, 07501
Lugo, Joseph W., (Retired), 78 Chestnut St., Bridgewater, 08807
McGrath, Thomas, (Retired), 93 Springtown Rd., Washington, 07882
McHugh, Dennis, (Retired), Knock, County Mayo, Ireland
McLoughlin, Brendan, (Retired), 25 Orchard St., Denville, 07834
Mooney, William J., (Retired), P.O. Box 89, Basking Ridge, 07920
Moss, James, (Retired), 286 Haledon Ave., Prospect Park, 07508
Murphy, Daniel J., (Retired), 7 Sunny Lawn Ln., Lakewood, 08701
Murphy, Joseph E., (Retired), Main St., Box 635, Chester, 07930
Nix, Albert P., (Retired), P.O. Box 564, Sparta, 07871
O'Connor, John H., (Retired), 6 Condict St., Morris Plains, 07950
O'Grady, Frank, (Retired), 9016 Piwey Branch Rd., Silver Spring, MD 20903
O'Kielty, James P., (Retired), Main St., Chester, 07930
Orlandi, Joseph J., (Retired), Contrada Risand 27, Subiaco, Italy 00028
Panagia, Sal J., (Retired), 35 Echo Pl., Elmwood Park, 07407
Pavlick, Raymond A., (Retired), 38 Oakland Ave., Walden, NY 12586
Perretta, Andrew T., (Retired), 145 Randolph Ave., 07011
Perricone, Charles A., (Retired), 6176 King's Gate Cir., Delray Beach, FL 33484
Pisarcik, John G., (Retired), 302 Regent St., Dover, DE 19904-3392
Rainforth, Thomas G., (Retired), 36 Waterfall Ct., Bloomingdale, 07403
Rento, Richard G., (Retired), 33 Murray Ln., Lavalette, 08735
Savitt, Alan F., (Retired), 19 Nino Ct., 07013
Scolamiero, Dominic A., (Retired), 12 Rubin Ln., Ocean, 07712
Scurti, Louis J., (Retired), P.O. Box 7994, Haledon, 07508
Sordillo, Ronald, (Retired), Main St., Chester, 07930
Stephenson, Alphonse J., (Retired), P.O. Box 215, Bay Head, 08742
Stepien, Allen F., (Retired), 5 New Briar Ln., 07012
Termyna, James J., (Retired), 9 Pocono Rd., Apt. C-101, Denville, 07834
Tyburski, Zbigniew, (Retired), 81 Pondfield Rd., Bronxville, NY 10708
Velasquez, Bernardo, (Retired), CRA 83, #46-44, La Floresta, Medellin, Columbia
Waller, Charles J., (Retired), 200 Hospital Plaza, Apt. 310, Paterson, 07503
Weber, Frank W., (Retired), 118 Main St., Succasunna, 07876.

Permanent Deacons:
Acevedo, Pedro, (Retired)
Allgaier, Michael, St. Mary, Denville
Altilio, Robert M., St. John Kanty, Clifton
Aquino, William, Our Lady of Fatima, Highland Lakes
Ardito, Nicholas, Diocese of Scranton, PA
Ayers, Robert, St. Philip the Apostle, Clifton
Balough, Joseph, St. Bonaventure, Paterson
Bandel, Arthur, St. Luke, Long Valley
Barile, Anthony P. Jr., Our Lady of Mount Carmel, Swartswood
Beirne, Thomas P., St. Mary, Dover
Bernardine, Anthony E., (Retired)
Beyerl, Brian D., Assumption, Morristown
Bianchi, Roland, Archdiocese of Newark
Bias, Richard F., St. Michael, Netcong
Biersbach, Raymond, Archdiocese of Seattle
Boscia, Edward F., St. Jude, Hamburg
Brady, Richard A., St. Matthew, Randolph
Brandi, John, Assumption of the Blessed Virgin Mary, Morristown

Brudzynski, Richard, (Retired)
Butkus, James A., Diocese of Charleston, SC
Calandriello, Andrew, St. Kateri Tekakwitha, Sparta
Callahan, Jack, (Retired)
Cammarano, James, St. John Vianney, Stockholm
Carnero, Juan Carlos, St. Mary, Paterson
Casamento, Peter, Diocese of Charleston, SC
Casillas, Hector, St. Paul, Clifton
Castellanos, Hector, Our Lady of Fatima, Passaic
Cedrone, David, Our Lady Queen of Peace, West Milford
Chimileski, Raymond J., St. Luke, Long Valley
Chiocco, Louis, St. Peter the Apostle, Parsippany
Cistaro, Peter, St. Peter the Apostle, Parsippany
Clark, Hal G., St. Mary, Pompton Lakes
Cleary, Kevin, St. Luke, Long Valley
Cocilovo, Vincent, Our Lady of the Valley, Wayne
Combs, Kevin L., St. John Vianney, Stockholm
Cortes, Jesus, Puerto Rico
Coyne, Herb D., Our Lady of Good Counsel, Pompton Plains
Crowley, Joseph C. Jr., (Retired)
Cruz, Pedro, (Leave of Absence)
Curcio, Anthony Jr., Our Lady of the Lake, Sparta
D'Amico, Larry, (Suspended)
Dachisen, Harry, Retired
DaSilva, Joao, Morristown Memorial Hospital
Davila, Jesus, Puerto Rico
Davis, Robert T., (Retired)
de Mena, Henry, Notre Dame, Cedar Knolls
Delgado, Alberto, (Retired)
Deo, Leonard, St. Ann, Parsippany
DiLorenzo, Anthony, Diocese of Venice, FL
DiVizio, William, St. Lawrence the Martyr, Chester
Dolan, Eugene P., (Leave of Absence)
Drury, Brian, Diocese of Scranton, PA
Duarte, Hildebrando A., Diocese of Trenton, NJ
Dugger, John, Archdiocese of Newark
Elliott, James, St. Catherine of Bologna, Ringwood
Espinal, Candelario, Our Lady of Lourdes, Paterson
Fadalla, Gerald J., St. Anthony, Hawthorne
Fanelli, Alfredo, Notre Dame of Mt. Carmel, Cedar Knolls
Ferry, Daniel F., Diocese of Richmond, VA
Fierro, Anthony O., St. Bonaventure, Paterson
Fiore, Peter M., Holy Family, Florham Park
Flynn, Jack, St. Mary, Denville
Forino, Ronald, Notre Dame of Mount Carmel, Cedar Knolls
Forshay, George W., Diocese of Trenton
Frank, Alfred E., St. Ann, Parsippany
Friel, Thomas, St. Jude, Hopatcong
Gallo, Henry, (Retired)
Galvin, Daniel, Immaculate Heart of Mary, Wayne
Gaydo, Richard A., St. Christopher, Parsippany
Gibbons, Thomas P., Our Lady of the Mountain, Schooley's Mountain
Gil, Dennis, St. Francis de Sales, McAfee
Gil, Luis, St. John the Baptist, Paterson
Goglia, Richard J., St. Andrew, Clifton
Hackett, Jim, (Unassigned)
Hanifen, Gerald B., (Retired)
Hanly, P. Michael, Assumption, Morristown
Harenchar, Thomas G., Archdiocese of New York
Harris, Joseph, Notre Dame, Cedar Knolls
Harris, Keith, Good Shepherd, Andover
Hartnett, Stuart A., St. Mary, Dover
Head, Robert C., Our Lady of the Mountain, Schooley's Mountain
Healy, Thomas F. Jr., St. Luke, Long Valley
Holden, Timothy M., St. Margaret, Morristown
Hyle, Henry, St. Clement, Rockaway Township
Jones, James, Our Lady of the Mountain, Schooleys Mountain; St. Mark the Evangelist, Long Valley
Keegan, Edward, St. Matthew, Randolph
Keenan, Joseph, St. Michael, Netcong
Kimak, Thomas J., St. Mary, Pompton Lakes
King, Dennis, St. Elizabeth Ann Seton, Flanders
Kronyak, Thomas, (Retired)
Kucinski, Al, (Leave of Absence)
Lacouture, Roger, (Retired)
Lang, Robert A., St. Peter the Apostle, Parsippany
Latour, Raymond, Resurrection, Randolph
Leary, Gerard, (Retired)
Leo, Vincent Jr., St. Rose of Lima, East Hanover
Liotard, Paul, (Retired)
Lo Paro, Ben, St. Joseph, West Milford
LoBello, Vincent, Our Lady of Mercy, Whippany
Lucibello, Allan J., St. Christopher, Parsippany
Lupi, Victor, Notre Dame, Cedar Knolls
Madreperla, Steven A., (Retired)
Malecki, Michael J., Archdiocese of Baltimore, MD
Mallory, Charles, Florida
Mann, Patrick, (Retired)
Marabeti, Stephen J., St. Joseph Church, Lincoln Park
Maron, Edward, Archdiocese of Newark
Marsicovete, Joseph, St. Peter the Apostle, Parsippany
Mather, Brian F., (Retired)
Mathias, Charles T., (Retired)
Mazzaccoli, Sylvester A., (Retired)
McGovern, James, Our Lady of the Lake, Sparta
McKeever, Kevin, St. Simon the Apostle, Green Pond
McMahon, Matthew, (On Leave)
Michalski, Richard, (Retired)
Morales, Eugenio, SS. Cyril and Methodius, Clifton
Morton, Robert, St. Vincent Martyr, Madison
Muller, Edward J., (Retired)
Munoz, Mario, (Retired)
Murphy, Glen P., St. Kateri Tekakwitha, Sparta
Murphy, Stuart, St. Michael, Netcong
Natafalusy, Stephen P., (Retired)
Nixon, Mark G., St. Patrick, Chatham
Nolan, Richard, (Retired)
O'Brien, Barry, St. Kateri Tekakwitha, Sparta
O'Leary, Donald, (Sick Leave)
O'Neill, Peter J., St. Vincent de Paul, Stirling
Ochner, Ronald, (Retired)
Olsen, Bruce, St. Therese, Succasunna
Owens, Frank, (Retired)
Padron, Jose, St. Therese, Succasunna
Pamplona, Raul, Our Lady of Lourdes, Paterson
Parlapiano, Joseph J., St. Joseph, Lincoln Park
Paulino, Maximo, Our Lady of Victories, Paterson
Pearson, William, (Retired)
Pedraza, Guido, St. John the Baptist, Paterson
Pilek, John F., (Leave of Absence)
Pinto, Richard, St. Virgil, Morris Plains
Pomales, Jose, St. John Cathedral, Paterson
Pringle, Robert H., (Retired)
Puglia, Frank, St. Elizabeth Ann Seton, Flanders
Puleo, Paul A., (Retired)
Puskas, Joseph, St. Paul, Clifton
Quinn, Joseph, Notre Dame of Mt. Carmel, Cedar Knolls
Rado, Kenneth, St. Margaret, Morristown
Ramirez, Edward, (Retired)
Ramirez, Luis, St. Therese, Paterson
Reading, Edward J., St. Thomas of Aquin, Ogdensburg
Reck, Richard, Resurrection, Randolph
Restaino, Carmen, Our Lady of Good Counsel, Pompton Plains
Richardson, Joseph, (Retired)
Rivera, Jose M., St. Francis of Assisi, Haskell
Rizos, James, St. Mary, Denville
Roche, Charles, Our Lady Queen of Peace, Hewitt
Romano, Ron, (Leave of Absence)
Salierno, Anthony, (Retired)
Sanchez, Armando, Archdiocese of Lima, Peru
Sanker, John M., St. Jude, Budd Lake
Santiago, Manuel, (Retired)
Santos, Robert F., (Retired)
Schenker, Jerome, Diocese of Richmond, VA
Scrone, Daniel, Diocese of St. Augustine, FL
Scruggs, Michael K., Holy Spirit, Pequannock
Sheehan, Patrick, Diocese of Charleston, SC
Siino, Anthony C., St. Jude, Budd Lake
Silva, Percy, (Retired)
Simeone, Enio, (Retired)
Sisco, Joseph, Our Lady of Holy Angels, Little Falls
Sisler, Merle F., St. Virgil, Morris Plains
Sisson, Stanley, (Retired)
Smilek, Milton, St. Thomas the Apostle, Oak Ridge
Stein, Elliott, Assumption of the Blessed Virgin Mary, Morristown
Sullivan, Thomas, Good Shepherd, Andover
Taylor, John F., (Retired)
Thiuri, Phillipe, (Retired)
Totino, Alberto R., Our Lady Star of the Sea, Lake Hopatcong
Trinidad, Jose M., (Leave of Absence)
Van Glahn, Richard, Resurrection, Randolph
Vargas, German, Cathedral of St. John the Baptist, Paterson
Varsalona, Nicholas, Florida
Vazquez, Gilberto, St. Agnes, Paterson
Veliky, Nicholas, St. Philip the Apostle, Clifton
Vesota, Robert, (Retired)
Von Doehren, Wayne, St. James, Montague; St. Thomas, Hainesville
Walker, John, (Leave of Absence)
Wallace, Michael J., (Retired)
Ward, William, (Retired)
Whelan, Edward, Diocese of Richmond
White, Harry, St. Joseph, West Milford
Willson, Paul D., St. Cecelia, Rockaway
Wisneski, Joseph A., St. Patrick, Chatham
Wisniewski, Paul M., (Leave of Absence)
Zack, Gary, Holy Spirit, Pequannock
Zampella, Dominic, St. Thomas of Aquin, Ogdensburg
Zayac, Thomas, St. Joseph, Newton
Zimmerle, John, (Retired).

INSTITUTIONS LOCATED IN DIOCESE

[A] SEMINARIES, RELIGIOUS OR SCHOLASTICATES

BOONTON. *Domus Bartimaeus* (Diocesan House of Discernment) 913 Birch St., Boonton, 07005. Tel: 973-588-7814; Fax: 973-588-7814. Rev. Edgar O. Rivera, Dir. Seminarians 12.

[B] COLLEGES AND UNIVERSITIES

DENVILLE. *Assumption College for Sisters*, 200A Morris Ave., Denville, 07834. Tel: 973-957-0188; Fax: 973-957-0190; Email: president@acs350.org; Web: acs350.org. Sisters Jean Wedemeier, S.C.C., Tech. Consultant; Joseph Spring, S.C.C., Pres.; Teresa Bruno, S.C., Academic Dean; Ms. Barbara Kelly-Vegona, Registrar; Patricia McGrady, Treas. Conducted by Sisters of Christian Charity. (Full-time, paid) 1; Religious 3; Students 65; Clergy / Religious Teachers 8.

MORRISTOWN. *College of Saint Elizabeth*, 2 Convent Rd., Morristown, 07960-6989. Tel: 973-290-4000; Tel: 973-290-4475; Fax: 973-290-4485; Web: www.cse.edu. Rev. Msgr. Thomas J. McDade, Prof. Education/Chap., (Retired); Dr. Helen Streubert, Pres.; Katherine Buck, Vice Pres. Student Life; Mr. Neil Buckley, Vice Pres. Finance & Admin. and Treas.; Mr. Gree Tondi, Comptroller; Dr. Monique Guillory, Vice Pres. & Dean Academic Affairs; Mr. Alex Scott, Dean, Vice Pres., Enrollment Mgmt.; Jacqueline Weiskopff, Dir. Fin. Aid; Amira Unver, Librarian. Sisters of Charity of St. Elizabeth.Full-time Admin. and Faculty: Lay Teachers 44; Priests 1; Religious 3; Students 1,247.

[C] HIGH SCHOOLS, DIOCESAN

DENVILLE. *Morris Catholic High School*, Denville, 07834. Tel: 973-627-6674; Fax: 973-627-4351; Email: mchs@morriscatholic.org; Web: www.morriscatholic.org. Rev. Peter J. Clarke, Pres.; Robert Loia, Prin.; Dr. Jeanne Gradone, Dir. Student Svcs.; Rev. Carmen Buono, Chap., (Retired). Lay Teachers 38; Priests 1; Sisters 1; Students 398.

WAYNE. *De Paul Catholic High School*, 1512 Alps Rd., Wayne, 07470. Tel: 973-694-3702; Fax: 973-633-5381; Email: fr.peterclarke@dpchs.org; Web: depaulcatholic.org. Rev. Julio Barrios, Chap.; Joseph M. Tweed, Pres. Lay Teachers 48; Sisters 1; Students 550.

[D] HIGH SCHOOLS, PRIVATE

CONVENT STATION. *Academy of St. Elizabeth*, Convent Station, 07961. Tel: 973-290-5200; Fax: 973-290-5232. Sr. Gloria O'Brien, S.C., Prin. Sisters of Charity. Lay Teachers 25; Sisters 3; Students 225.

MORRISTOWN. *Delbarton School*, 230 Mendham Rd., Morristown, 07960. Tel: 973-538-3231; Fax: 973-538-8836; Email: headmaster@delbarton.org; Web: www.delbarton.org. Bro. Paul J. Diveny, O.S.B., Headmaster; Mr. Charles Ruebling, Asst. Headmaster; Mrs. Anne Leckie, Dean of Faculty; Dr. David Donovan, Dir. Admissions; Mr. David Hajduk, Dir. Campus Min. Day School for Boys. (Grades 7-12)

The Order of St. Benedict of New Jersey DBA Delbarton School Students 587; Monks 6; Laymen 83.

Villa Walsh Academy, Morristown, 07960. Tel: 973-538-3680; Fax: 973-538-6733; Email: villawalsh@aol.com; Web: www.villawalsh.org. Sr. Patricia Pompa, M.P.F., Prin. College Preparatory for girls (Grades 7-12). Conducted by Religious Teachers Filippini Lay Teachers 35; Sisters 4; Students 240.

NORTH HALEDON. *Mary Help of Christians Academy* aka Mary Help of Christians Academy, Inc., 659-723 Belmont Ave., North Haledon, 07508. Tel: 973-790-6200; Fax: 973-790-6125; Email: headofschool@maryhelp.org; Web: www.maryhelp.org. Sr. Marisa DeRose, Admin. Daughters of Mary Help of Christians (Salesian Sisters). Lay Teachers 27; Sisters 12; Students 159; Clergy / Religious Teachers 3.

[E] ELEMENTARY SCHOOLS, DIOCESAN

PARSIPPANY. *All Saints Academy*, 189 Baldwin Rd., Parsippany, 07054. Tel: 973-334-4704; Fax: 973-334-0622. Ms. Judy Berg, Prin. Lay Teachers 18; Sisters 2; Students 245.

TOTOWA. *Academy of Saint James of the Marches*, 400 Totowa Rd., Totowa, 07512. Tel: 973-956-8824; Fax: 976-956-9430; Email: office@academyofstjames.org; Web: academyofstjames.org. Ms. Leslie Dreps, Prin.; Blanca Hopper, Admin. Asst. Serves St. James of the Marches, Totowa Lay Teachers 11; Sisters 3;

Students 208; Religious Teachers 3; Clergy / Religious Teachers 3.

[F] PRIVATE PRESCHOOL

FLORHAM PARK. *Magic Kingdom Day Nursery*, 88 Brooklake Rd., Florham Park, 07932.
Tel: 973-966-9762; Fax: 973-377-3994; Email: magickingdom2008@yahoo.com; Web: www.magickingdomnurseryschool.com. Sr. Perpetua Da Conceicao, S.D.V., Prin. Vocationist Sisters. Lay Teachers 6; Sisters 7; Students 65.

NEWTON. *Camp Auxilium/The Auxilium School* aka Camp Auxilium Salesian Sisters, 14 Old Swartswood Rd., Newton, 07860.
Tel: 973-383-2621; Fax: 973-383-3214; Email: schooloffice@campauxilium.org; Web: www.campauxilium.org. Sr. Isabel Garza, F.M.A., Dir. Salesian Sisters.Operated by Salesian Sisters.
Legal Title: Camp Auxilium Salesian Sisters Children 250; Sisters 3.

PARSIPPANY. *St. Elizabeth Nursery and Montessori School, Inc.*, 499 Park Rd., Parsippany, 07054.
Tel: 973-540-0721; Fax: 973-540-9186; Email: elizabethsaint@yahoo.con; Web: www.stelizabethschool.com. Mother Lilly Perapaddan, F.S.S.E., Delegate General; Sr. Cathy Lynn Cummings, F.S.S.E., Prin. Lay Staff 16; Sisters 16; Students 350.

[G] EVANGELIZATION CENTERS

MADISON. *St. Paul Inside The Walls: The Catholic Center for Evangelization at Bayley-Ellard*, 205 Madison Ave., Madison, 07940. Tel: 973-377-1004; Fax: 973-377-1952; Web: insidethewalls.org. Rev. Paul S. Manning, Exec. Dir. & Vicar, Evangelization; Ms. Ivannia Vega-McTighe, Dir. Office of Catechesis; Assoc. Coord. Catechesis & Hispanic Min.; Revs. Pawel Tomczyk, Faculty; Christopher S. Barkhausen, Chap. Youth Min.; Jeider S. Barraza, Chap. Youth Min.; Artur P. Zaba, Chap. Youth Min.; Yojaneider Garcia, Chap. Hispanic Youth Min.; Darwin J. Lastra, Chap. Hispanic Youth Min.; Jesus Peralta, Chap. Hispanic Youth Min.; Deacons Guido Pedraza, Coord. Hispanic Min.; Eric Munoz, Coord. Campus Min.; Mr. Brian Honsberger, Asst. Dir., Evangelization; Mr. Daniel Ferrari, Outreach to Young Adults; Deacon Peter Cistaro, Dir., Diaconate Office; Eniola Honsberger, Dir. Family Life Office; Dr. Mary Mazzarella, Dir., Respect Life Office; Karl Schlegel, Music Min.; Jerilynn Ann Prokop, Office Mgr., Coord. of Hospitality.

[H] RETREAT HOUSES & HOUSES OF PRAYER

BRANCHVILLE. *Sanctuary of Mary-Our Lady of the Holy Spirit* aka Vocationist Fathers, 252 Wantage Ave., Branchville, 07826. Tel: 973-722-7142; Email: frlouissdv@gmail.com; Web: vocationist.org. Rev. Louis Caputo, S.D.V., Dir.

CHESTER. *Hermits of Bethlehem in the Heart of Jesus*, 82 Pleasant Hill Rd., Chester, 07930.
Tel: 908-879-7059; Fax: 908-879-7059. Revs. Mariusz Koch, C.F.R., Delegate; Eugene C. Romano, Desert Father; Raphael Joseph Peres. Priests 2; Sisters 4.

FLORHAM PARK. *Vocationist Fathers Retreat Center*, 90 Brooklake Rd., Florham Park, 07932.
Tel: 973-966-6262; Fax: 973-845-2996; Email: info@vocationist.org; Web: www.vocationist.org. Revs. Louis Caputo, S.D.V., Dir.; Hermogenes Sargado, S.D.V., Vice Rector.

MENDHAM. *Villa Pauline*, Mendham, 07945.
Tel: 973-543-9058; Email: bus.manager@scceast.org. Retreat House for Men & Women Sisters of Christian Charity 5.

MORRISTOWN. *Loyola Jesuit Center*, 161 James St., Morristown, 07960. Tel: 973-539-0740;
Fax: 973-898-9839; Email: retreathouse@loyola.org; Web: www.loyola.org. Revs. William Rakowicz, S.J., Supr.; Kirk R. Reynolds, S.J.; Steven Pugliese, S.J.; Leo Manglaviti, S.J. Society of Jesus. Priests 4.

St. Mary's Abbey Retreat Center, 230 Mendham Rd., Morristown, 07960. Tel: 973-538-5235, Ext. 2100; Fax: 973-538-7109; Email: retreatcenter@delbarton.org; Web: saintmarysabbey.org/retreat-center. Bro. Joseph Voltaggio, O.S.B., Dir.
The Order of St. Benedict of New Jersey DBA St. Mary's Abbey Retreat Center.

NEWTON. *Sacred Heart Retreat Center* aka Sacred Heart Center, 20 Old Swartswood Rd., Newton, 07860. Tel: 973-383-2620; Fax: 973-383-3083; Email: shretreatcenter@gmail.com; Email: secsecretary19@gmail.com; Web: sacredheartspiritualitycenter.org. Sr. Theresa Kelly, F.M.A., Dir.
Legal Title: Missionary Society of the Salesian Sisters Novices 5; Sisters 5.

STIRLING. *Trinity House at the Shrine of St. Joseph*, 1292 Long Hill Rd., Stirling, 07980.
Tel: 908-647-0208; Email: religious@stshrine.org; Web: stshrine.org. 1050 Long Hill Rd., Stirling, 07980. Rev. Dennis Berry, S.T., Dir.

[I] GENERAL HOSPITALS

PATERSON. *St. Joseph's Hospital and Medical Center*, 703 Main St., Paterson, 07503. Tel: 973-754-2000; Fax: 973-754-3273. Mr. William McDonald, Pres. & CEO; Sr. Maryanne Campeotto, S.C., Vice Pres., Mission; Revs. Martin Rooney, Dir. Mission Svcs.; Paul Barboutz, Chap.; Pros Pael, Chap.; Eric Ugochukwu, S.D.V., Chap. Bed Capacity 1,000; Patients Asst Anual. 315,607; Sisters of Charity of St. Elizabeth 35.

[J] HOMES FOR AGED

PATERSON. *St. Joseph Rest Home for Aged Women* Conducted by Daughters of Charity of the Most Precious Blood 52 Preakness Ave., Paterson, 07522. Tel: 973-956-1921; Fax: 973-956-1582; Email: josephinefcpps@gmail.com. 46 Preakness Ave., Paterson, 07522. Sr. Regi Karumakkel, D.C.P.B., Supr. Residents 18.

DENVILLE. *St. Francis Health Resort, Inc.*, 122-126 Diamond Spring Rd., Denville, 07834.
Tel: 973-627-5000; Fax: 973-627-6389; Email: sr.johnicethone@primehealthcare.com; Web: www.saintfrancisres.com. Sr. M. Johnice Thone, S.S.M., Exec. Dir. Senior Living Community Bed Capacity 100; Guests 150; Sisters of the Sorrowful Mother 4; Apartments 66.

TOTOWA. *St. Joseph's Home for the Elderly*, 140 Shepherd Ln., Totowa, 07512. Tel: 973-942-0300; Fax: 973-942-7201; Email: info@littlesistersofthepoor.org. Sr. Mary Thomas D'Mello, L.S.P., Pres./Supr.; Rev. Sean McDonnell, Chap. Conducted by Little Sisters of the Poor. Residents 110; Sisters 13.

[K] RESIDENCES FOR WOMEN

WAYNE. *Bethany Residence*, 738 Rte. 23, Wayne, 07470. Tel: 973-628-8109. Cora Ladung, Admin. Residents 12.

[L] MONASTERIES AND RESIDENCES OF PRIESTS AND BROTHERS

PATERSON. *Saint Michael's Friary*, 190 Butler St., Paterson, 07524. Tel: 973-345-7082;
Fax: 973-345-7081; Email: stmichaelcfr@gmail.com; Web: franciscanfriars.com. Bro. Shawn O'Conner, Supr.; Revs. Gabriel Bakkar, Pastoral Assoc.; Herald Brock, Pastoral Assoc.; Terry Messer, C.F.R.; Paulus Tautz, C.F.R.; Agustino Miguel Torres, C.F.R.; Bros. Francisco Griego; Gerard Kanapes, C.F.R.; Matthew Schumacher. Franciscan Friars of the Renewal.

BUTLER. *St. Anthony Friary*, 63 Bartholdi Ave., Butler, 07405. Tel: 973-838-4080; Fax: 973-492-5483; Email: hnp@hnp.org. Revs. Bernard R. Creighton, O.F.M., Vicar; Kevin M. Cronin, O.F.M.; Thomas R. Hartle, O.F.M.; Francis K. Kim, O.F.M.; Daniel J. Lanahan, O.F.M.; Claude T. Lenehan, O.F.M.; Jeremiah V. McGinley, O.F.M.; Bartholomew R. McMahon, O.F.M.; Gerald R. Mudd, O.F.M.; John J. Pierce, O.F.M.; Edwin F.D. Robinson, O.F.M.; Paul G. Sinnema, O.F.M.; Bros. Peter X. Ahlheim, O.F.M.; Thomas J. Cole, O.F.M.; Octavio A. Duran, O.F.M.; Robert M. Frazzetta, O.F.M., Guardian; Charles F. Gilmartin, O.F.M.; Paul J. Chelus, O.F.M.; Vianney J. Justin, O.F.M.; Robert J. Lentz, O.F.M.; Rev. Brice Leavins, O.F.M. Order of Friars Minor. Brothers 8; Priests 16. *Franciscan Ministry of the Word*, Tel: 973-838-4093; Web: www.franmow.org. Rev. Kevin M. Cronin, O.F.M.

CLIFTON. *Holy Face of Jesus Monastery*, 1697 State Hwy. 3, P.O. Box 691, 07012. Tel: 973-778-1177;
Fax: 973-778-3809; Email: holyface@worldnet.att.net. Revs. Bernard Schinn, O.S.B., Supr.; Louis-Marie Navaratne, O.S.B. Sylvestrine Benedictine Monks. Priests 2.

FLORHAM PARK. *Father Justin Vocationary* aka Vocationist Fathers, 90 Brooklake Rd., Florham Park, 07932. Tel: 973-966-6262; Fax: 973-845-2996 ; Email: info@vocationist.org; Web: www.vocationistfathers.org. Revs. Louis Caputo, S.D.V., Supr.; Hermogenes Sargado, S.D.V., Vice Rector.

MORRISTOWN. *St. Mary's Abbey*, 230 Mendham Rd., Morristown, 07960. Tel: 973-538-3235;
Fax: 973-538-7109; Email: osbmonks@delbarton.org; Web: www.saintmarysabbey.org. Rt. Revs. Richard F. Cronin, O.S.B., Abbot; Brian H. Clarke, O.S.B., Abbot Emeritus; Giles P. Hayes, O.S.B., Abbot Emeritus; Gerard P. Lair, O.S.B., Abbot Emeritus; Very Rev. Jerome Borski, O.S.B., Prior; Revs. Benet W. Caffrey, O.S.B.; Justin Capato, O.S.B.; Gabriel M. Coless, O.S.B.; Edward Seton Fittin, O.S.B.; Donal R. Fox, O.S.B.; Simon P. Gallagher, O.S.B.; John E. Hesketh, O.S.B.; Beatus T. Lucey, O.S.B.; Jude S. Salus, O.S.B.; James O'Donnell, O.S.B.; Hilary O'Leary, O.S.B., Novice Master; Rembert F. Reilly, O.S.B.; Anthony G. Sargent, O.S.B.; Andrew T. Smith, O.S.B., Subprior; Michael Tidd, O.S.B., Treas.; Basil Wallace, O.S.B.; Benedict M. Worry, O.S.B.; Bros. Paul J. Diveny, O.S.B.; Tarcisius Hoang-Hoa, O.S.B.; Jonathan M. Hunt, O.S.B.; James Konchalski, O.S.B.; Kieran M. Shiek, O.S.B.; Demetrius M. Thomas, O.S.B.; Joseph Voltaggio, O.S.B.; Revs. Elias R. Lorenzo, O.S.B., Abbot Pres., American Cassinese Congregation; Karl J. Roesch, O.S.B.
The Order of St. Benedict of New Jersey DBA St. Mary's Abbey Brothers 5; Novices 1; Postulants 1; Priests 23.
Resident Outside the Abbey: Rev. Timothy J. Brennan, O.S.B.

NEWTON. *St. Paul's Abbey*, 289 U.S. Hwy. 206 S., P.O. Box 7, Newton, 07860-0007. Tel: 973-383-2470;
Fax: 973-383-5782; Email: osbnewton@catholic.or.kr. Rt. Revs. Justin E. Dzikowicz, O.S.B., Abbot; Joel P. Macul, O.S.B., Abbot Emeritus; Very Rev. Samuel Kim, O.S.B., Prior. Order of St. Benedict, Congregation of St. Ottilien.(Formerly the Little Flower Monastery); Monastery established March 15, 1924; elevated on an abbey June 9, 1947. Priests 2; Lay Monks 10.
Priests Residing Outside the Monastery:, P.O. Box 213, Lushoto, Tanzania. Tel: 255-2726-40210;
Fax: 255-2726-40212. Rt. Rev. Justin E. Dzikowicz, O.S.B., Namibia; Revs. Peter W. Blue, O.S.B., Inkamana Abbey, P/Bag X9333, Vryheid, 3100, South Africa. Tel: 27-34-982-2577; Damian J. Milliken, O.S.B., P.O. Box 213, Lushoto. Tel: 255-2726-40210; Fax: 255-2726-40212. (Tanzania).

OAK RIDGE-MILTON. *St. Stanislaus B. M. Friary*, 2 Manor Dr., Oak Ridge-Milton, 07438.
Tel: 973-697-7757; Email: jkrzyskow@yahoo.com. Deacon Jerzy P. Krzyskow. Capuchin Fathers. Brothers 1.

RINGWOOD. *Holy Name Friary, Inc.*, 2 Morris Rd., Ringwood, 07456. Tel: 973-962-7200;
Fax: 973-962-9766; Email: hnfringwood@netscape.net. Bro. Richard McFeeley, O.F.M., Guardian; Rev. Charles Angell, S.A.; Most Rev. Capistran F. Heim, O.F.M., Bishop Prelate Emeritus of Itaituba, Brazil; Revs. Edward Dillan, O.F.M.; Charles Finnigan, O.F.M.; Clement Comesky, O.F.M.; Martin Bednar, O.F.M.; Bonaventure Hayes, O.F.M.; John J. Kull, O.F.M.; Leonard Lencewicz, O.F.M.; Myron McCormick, O.F.M.; Alexander Di Lella, O.F.M.; Philip O'Shea, O.F.M.; Blaise Reinhardt, O.F.M.; Bede Fitzpatrick, O.F.M.; Philip Romano, O.F.M.-Cap.; William Scully, O.F.M.; Conrad Harkins, O.F.M.; Reginald Reddy, O.F.M.; Bros. Romuald Chinetsky, O.F.M.; Justus Frazier, O.F.M.; William Herbst, O.F.M.; Lawrence Stumpo, O.F.M.; Ennis Thomas, O.F.M.; Frank B. Waywood, O.F.M.; Xavier de la Huerta, O.F.M.; Revs. Bernardine C. Kessing, O.F.M.; Richard Trezza, O.F.M. Brothers 5; Priests 25.

STIRLING. *Shrine of St. Joseph*, 1050 Long Hill Rd., Stirling, 07980. Tel: 908-647-0208;
Fax: 908-647-5770; Email: religious@stshrine.org; Web: stshrine.org. Revs. Gustavo Baloco, S.T.; Dennis Berry, S.T., Dir.; Bro. Joseph Dudek, S.T.; Rev. Ralph Frisch, S.T.; Ms. Peggy Lunsmann, Assoc. Dir.; Revs. Charles Piatt, S.T.; Conrad Schmitt, S.T.; Aro Varnabas, S.T. Brothers 1; Priests 6; Sisters 7.

WAYNE. *Xaverian Missionary Fathers*, Provincial House, 12 Helene Ct., Wayne, 07470-2813.
Tel: 973-942-2975; Fax: 973-942-5012; Email: wayne@xaverianmissionaries.org; Email: usasxprocure@hotmail.com; Web: www.xaverianmissionaries.org. Revs. Mark Marangone, S.X., Prov.; Michael Davitti, S.X., Rector; Frank B. Grappoli, S.X., Member.
Mission Assignments: Makeni, Sierra Leone: Rev. Luigi Brioni, S.X.
Belem, Brazil: Rev. Danilo Lago, S.X.
Parma, Italy: Revs. Mauro Loda, S.X.; Dario Maso, S.X.
Cameroon: Rev. Fernandes de Araujo Herondi, S.X.
Jakarta, Indonesia: Rev. Franco Qualizza, S.X.
Santa Cruz, Mexico: Revs. Dan Boschetto, S.X.; Ramon Cerratos, S.X.; Pablo Nieves, S.X.
Taiwan: Revs. Edi Foschiatto, S.X.; Martino Roia, S.X.; Joe Vignato, S.X.
Japan: Revs. Renato Filippini, S.X.; Frank Sottocornola, S.X.
Guadalajara, Mexico: Rev. Horacio Perez, S.X.

[M] CONVENTS AND RESIDENCES FOR SISTERS

PATERSON. *Daughters of Charity of the Most Precious Blood*, 46 Preakness Ave., Paterson, 07522.
Tel: 973-956-1921; Fax: 973-956-1582; Email: josephinefcpps@gmail.com. Sr. Regi Karumakkel, D.C.P.B., Supr. Sisters 10.
Missionary Sisters of the Immaculate Conception USA Unit, 25 Orchard Rd., Ste. 104, Denville, 07834. Tel: 973-279-3790; Email: jrsmic@optonline.net. Sr. Joanne Riggs, S.M.I.C., Prov. Sisters 14.

BOONTON. *Society of the Sisters of the Church*, 24 Deer Hill Ct., Boonton, 07005. Tel: 973-299-8365; Fax: 973-884-0940; Email: SRBW@ssoc.org; Web: www.ssoc.org. Sr. Frances Sanzo, S.S.C., Coord. Sisters 12.

CHESTER. *Carmel of the Immaculate Heart of Mary*, 80 Pleasant Hill Rd., Chester, 07930-2135. Tel: 908-879-4990; Tel: 908-879-0887; Fax: 908-879-0884; Email: hermcarm@gti.net. Sr. Theresa Margaret, O.Carm., Prioress. Hermits of Our Lady of Mt. Carmel Sisters 4.

CONVENT STATION. *Motherhouse of the Sisters of Charity of St. Elizabeth*, P.O. Box 476, Convent Station, 07961-0476. Tel: 973-290-5000; Fax: 973-290-5335; Email: escharity@aol.com; Web: www.scnj.org. Sr. Rosemary Moynihan, S.C., Gen. Supr. Professed Sisters 65.

DENVILLE. *Missionary Sisters of the Immaculate Conception USA Unit*, Our Lady of Sorrows Convent, 9 Pocono Rd., 1st Fl., Denville, 07834. Tel: 973-357-1915; Email: jrsmic@optonline.net. Sr. Joanne Riggs, S.M.I.C., Prov. Sisters 10.

Missionary Sisters of the Immaculate Conception-USA Unit, 25 Orchard St., Ste. 104, Denville, 07834. Tel: 973-279-3790; Email: smic@optonline.net. Sr. Joanne Riggs, S.M.I.C., Prov. Sisters 14.

Our Lady of Sorrows Convent, Sisters of Sorrowful Mother, 9 Pocono Rd., Denville, 07834. Tel: (973) 627-5000; Email: Sr. JohniceThone@primehealthcare.com. Sr. Lois Bush, Contact Person. Sisters 5.

FLORHAM PARK. *Sister Joanna House of Formation*, 88 Brooklake Rd., Florham Park, 07932. Tel: 973-966-9762; Fax: 973-377-3994; Email: vocationist@yahoo.com; Web: vocationist-sisters.org. Sisters Perpetua Da Conceicao, S.D.V., Supr. & Prin.; Romiloa Borges, S.D.V., Delegate. Sisters 11.

GLADSTONE. *Mt. St. John Convent*, 22 St. John's Dr., P.O. Box 711, Gladstone, 07934. Tel: 908-234-0640; Email: baptistines@worldnet.att.net; Web: www.baptistines.home.att.net. Sr. Angelita Vazzano, C.S.J.B., Admin. Sisters of St. John the Baptist. Sisters 3.

HALEDON. *St. Joseph Provincial Center*, 655 Belmont Ave., Haledon, 07508. Tel: 973-790-7966; Fax: 973-790-5054; Email: SECHaledonSJ19@gmail.com. Sr. Teresa Gutierrez, F.M.A., Supr. Provincialate of Daughters of Mary Help of Christians

St. Joseph Provincial Center Sisters 38.

MENDHAM. *Mallinckrodt Convent-Motherhouse and Novitiate of the Sisters of Christian Charity*, 350 Bernardsville Rd., Mendham, 07945. Tel: 973-543-6528; Fax: 973-543-9459; Email: secretary@scceast.org; Web: scceast.org. Sr. Mary Edward Spohrer, S.C.C., Prov. Supr. Daughters of the Blessed Virgin Mary of the Immaculate Conception. Novices 4; Postulants 2; Sisters 40.

MORRISTOWN. *St. Lucy Provincialate of the Religious Teachers Filippini, Novitiate, Villa Walsh Academy*, 455 Western Ave., Morristown, 07960-4912. Tel: 973-538-2886; Fax: 973-538-6107; Email: atizzano@hotmail.com; Web: www.filippiniusa.org. Sisters Ascenza Tizzano, M.P.F., Prov.; Alice Ivanyo, M.P.F., Supr.; Elaine Bebyn, M.P.F., Dir. Formation

Pontifical Institute of the Religious Teachers Filippini Postulants 1; Sisters 170.

St. Joseph Infirmary Hall, 455 Western Ave., Morristown, 07960. Tel: 973-538-2886, Ext. 276; Fax: 973-538-1827.

Monastery Discalced Carmelite Nuns of the Most Blessed Virgin Mary of Mt. Carmel, 189 Madison Ave., Morristown, 07960. Tel: 973-539-0773. Mother Therese Katulski, O.C.D., Prioress. Novices 4; Professed Nuns 14.

NEWTON. *Sacred Heart Novitiate* aka Salesian Sisters, 20 Swartswood Rd., Newton, 07860. Tel: 973-383-2620; Fax: 973-383-3083; Email: SECNewtonSH19@gmail.com; Email: secsecretary19@gmail.com. Sr. Karen Dunn, F.M.A., Supr. Novices 5; Sisters 5.

PARSIPPANY. *St. Francis of Assisi Novitiate-Franciscan Sisters of St. Elizabeth*, 499 Park Rd., Parsippany, 07054. Tel: 973-539-3857; Fax: 973-539-3347; Email: sr-cathylynn@yahoo.com; Web: www.franciscansisters.com. Mother Lilly Perapaddan, F.S.S.E., Delegate Gen. Perpetually Professed Sisters 44; Temporarily Professed Sisters 5.

STIRLING. *Holy Trinity Convent*, 1026 Long Hill Rd., Stirling, 07980. Tel: 908-647-6584. Sr. Sophia Kozikowska, Supr. Servants of Jesus 7.

WOODLAND PARK. *Missionary Sisters of the Immaculate Conception of the Mother of God*, Generalate, 47 Garden Ave., Woodland Park, 07424. Tel: 973-279-3480; Fax: 973-279-2991; Email: smicgen@optonline.net. Sr. Maria do Livramento Oliveira, S.M.I.C., Coord. Gen. Sisters 4.

The Society of Sisters for the Church, 396 Rifle Camp Rd., Woodland Park, 07424. Tel: 973-809-0746 (Pres.); Tel: 973-345-1816 (Res. Sister-2nd Fl.); Web: www.ssc-usa.org. Sr. Eleanor Ustach, Pres. Sisters 25.

[N] NEWMAN CENTERS

HALEDON. *William Paterson University of New Jersey*, 219 Pompton Rd., Haledon, 07508. Tel: 973-720-3524; Tel: 973-595-6184; Fax: 973-595-5312; Email: frhubert@jesuscampus.net; Web: www.jesuscampus.net. Rev. Paul Tomczyk, Dir. Jesus Christ, Prince of Peace Chapel Catholic Campus Ministry Center.

MADISON. *Drew University Catholic Campus Ministry*, St. Paul Inside the Walls, 205 Madison Ave., Madison, 07940. Tel: 973-408-3027. Brian Honsberger, Campus Min.

[O] MISCELLANEOUS LISTINGS

PATERSON. *St. Anthony's Guild*, P.O. Box 2948, Paterson, 07510. Tel: 212-564-8799; Email: frdavid@thefranciscans.org; Web: www.stanthonysguild.org. Rev. David I. Convertino, O.F.M., Dir. Membership organization supports the work of The Franciscan Friars of Holy Name Province.

The Association of the Marian Apostolate of Mercy, Inc., 701 Runnymede Dr., Wayne, 07470. Tel: 973-956-5969; Fax: 973-956-5969; Email: marianoutreach@gmail.com. Sr. Maria Elizabeth Whilifer, Pres.; Judith A. Bonnesen, Treas.; Rev. John Gordon.

Cor Jesu Mission Fund Inc, 40 Franek Rd., Hardyston, 07419. Tel: 973-220-6995; Email: mastroeni@juno.com. Rev. Anthony J. Mastroeni, S.T.D., J.D., Pres.; Sr. Jane Teresa Culligan, S.C., Vice Pres.; Mother Mary Taylor, R.S.C.J., Treas.

Martin de Porres Village Corporation, 1 Green St., Paterson, 07501. Tel: 973-881-8022; Fax: 973-881-0149. Rev. Msgr. Herbert K. Tillyer, P.A., M.Ch.A., Pres. Sponsoring Martin De Porres, Vill.

Sr. Merita Learning Center, Martin De Porres Village, 1 Green St., Paterson, 07501. Tel: 973-881-7115; Fax: 973-881-0748. Sr. Christina Schoen, F.S.P., Dir.

Province of the Immaculate Conception of the Missionary Sisters of the Immaculate Conception 1996 Trust Fund, 25 Orchard St., Suite 104, Denville, 07834. Tel: 973-279-3790; Fax: 973-742-8231; Email: smic@optonline.net. Sr. Kathryn Conti, S.M.I.C., Trustee.

Riese Corporation, c/o R.P. Marzulli Co., 264 Belleville Ave., Bloomfield, 07003. Tel: 973-743-2300; Fax: 973-743-8021. Rev. Msgr. Herbert K. Tillyer, P.A., M.Ch.A., Pres. Sponsoring Governor Paterson Towers, Maurice Brick Residence, Brestel Residence, William F. Hinchcliffe Pavilion, Ralph J. Diverio Residence, Murray M. Bisgaier Residence, William Levine Residence.

BUTLER. *Order of Friars Minor of the Province of the Most Holy Name* aka Franciscan Friars-Holy Name Province (NJ), Inc., 63 Bartholdi Ave., Butler, 07405-1462. Tel: 646-473-0265; Fax: 973-492-5483; Email: hnp@hnp.org. Very Rev. Kevin J. Mullen, O.F.M., Prov. Min., Tel: 973-838-4080; Fax: 973-492-5483.

CHESTER. *Nazareth Village* Retirement residence for diocesan priests. 11 Meadow Ln., Box 635, Chester, 07930. Tel: 908-879-6991; Fax: 908-879-7461; Email: nazarethvillage@hotmail.com; Web: www.nazarethvillage.net. Rev. Msgr. Raymond M. Lopatesky, Dir. In Res. Rev. Msgrs. Robert M. Diachak, (Retired); George A. Dudak, (Retired); Brendan P. Madden, (Retired); Peter A. McBride, (Retired); Peter J. McHugh, (Retired); Revs. John T. Catoir, J.C.D., (Retired); John Andrew Connell, (Retired); Edward M. Davey, (Retired); Joseph P. Davis, (Retired); George J. Gothie, (Retired); John J. Klein, (Retired); Joseph E. Murphy, (Retired); James P. O'Kielty; Ronald Sordillo, (Retired); Frank W. Weber, (Retired).

CLIFTON. *Saint Brendan School, Inc.*, 777 Valley Rd., 07013. Tel: 973-777-8818, Ext. 276. Rev. Jhon Edisson Madrid, Prin.

Casa Guadalupe House of Discernment for women contemplating religious life. 737 Valley Rd., 07013. Tel: 973-737-1466; Tel: 201-951-2857; Email: holly@casaguadalupe.net; Email: avemaria53@gmail.com; Web: www.casaguadalupe.net. Ms. Holly Wright, Dir.; Rev. Agustino Miguel Torres, C.F.R., Spiritual Dir.

Casa Guadalupe, Inc. Women 10.

Catholic Charities of the Roman Catholic Diocese of Paterson, Inc., 777 Valley Rd., 07013.

Catholic Foundation of the Diocese of Paterson, Inc., 777 Valley Rd., 07013. Tel: (973) 777-8818; Email: kmullaney@patersondiocese.org. Rev. Msgr. T. Mark Condon, J.C.L., S.T.L., Pres.; Revs. Hernan Arias, Vice Pres.; T. Kevin Corcoran, Sec. & Treas.

Consortium of Catholic Schools of the Roman Catholic Diocese of Paterson, Inc., Catholic Academy of Passaic County, 777 Valley Rd., 07013. Tel: 973-777-8818, Ext. 276; Fax: 866-214-6613; Email: patrickpeace@patersondiocese.org. Most Rev. Arthur J. Serratelli, S.T.D., S.S.L., D.D., Pres.; Rev. Msgr. James T. Mahoney, Ph.D., V.G., Vice Pres.; Mr. Patrick Peace, Dir.; Sr. Mary Edward Spohrer, S.C.C., Sec. & Treas.

Diocese of Paterson Catholic Cemetery Perpetual Care Trust, 777 Valley Rd., 07013. Tel: 973-777-8818, Ext. 240; Fax: 973-777-8822; Email: kmullaney@patersondiocese.org. Mr. Kenneth F. Mullaney Jr., Esq., Contact Person.

Diocese of Paterson Catholic Education Trust, 777 Valley Rd., 07013. Most Rev. Arthur J. Serratelli, S.T.D., S.S.L., D.D., Trustee.

Diocese of Paterson Mission Fund, Inc., 777 Valley Rd., 07013. Rev. Msgr. T. Mark Condon, J.C.L., S.T.L., Pres.; Revs. Hernan Arias, Vice Pres.; T. Kevin Corcoran, Sec. & Treas.

Saint Gerard Majella School, Inc., 777 Valley Rd., 07013. Tel: 973-777-8818, Ext. 276.

St. Joseph's Fund, 777 Valley Rd., 07013. Most Rev. Arthur J. Serratelli, S.T.D., S.S.L., D.D., Pres.; Rev. Msgr. T. Mark Condon, J.C.L., S.T.L., Vice Pres.; Rev. Hernan Arias, Sec. & Treas.; Mr. Kenneth F. Mullaney Jr., Esq., Registered Agent.

Paterson Diocese Central Investment & Lending Agency, Inc., 777 Valley Rd., 07013. Tel: 973-777-8818; Email: kmullaney@patersondiocese.org. Most Rev. Arthur J. Serratelli, S.T.D., S.S.L., D.D., Pres.; Rev. Msgr. James T. Mahoney, Ph.D., V.G., Vice Pres.; Mr. Kenneth F. Mullaney Jr., Esq., Registered Agent.

CONVENT STATION. *Seton Ministries, Inc.*, Convent of Saint Elizabeth, Sisters of Charity, 2 Convent Rd., Convent Station, 07960. Tel: 973-290-5450; Fax: 973-290-5335; Email: rmoynihan@scnj.org; Web: www.scnj.org. Sisters of Charity, P.O. Box 476, Convent Station, 07961-0476. Sr. Rosemary Moynihan, S.C., Pres.

DENVILLE. *Morris Catholic High School, Inc.*, 200 Morris Ave., Denville, 07834. Most Rev. Arthur J. Serratelli, S.T.D., S.S.L., D.D., Pres.; Rev. Msgr. James T. Mahoney, Ph.D., V.G., Vice Pres.; Michael St. Pierre, Registered Agent.

MENDHAM. *Sisters of Christian Charity United, Inc.*, Mallinckrodt Convent, 350 Bernardsville Rd., Mendham, 07945. Tel: 973-543-6528, Ext. 250; Email: smed@scceast.org. Sisters Mary Edward Spohrer, S.C.C., Pres.; DeSales Tonero, S.C.C., Sec.-Treas.

MORRISTOWN. *College of St. Elizabeth, Center for Theological and Spiritual Development*, 2 Convent Rd., Morristown, 07960. Tel: 973-290-4354, Ext. 4491; Fax: 973-290-4312; Email: ibaratte@cse.edu; Web: www.cse.edu/center.

PASSAIC. *St. Jude Media Ministries*, 63 Monroe St., Passaic, 07055. Tel: 908-879-1460; Fax: 908-879-7461; Email: jcatoir@aol.com; Web: www.messengerofjoy.com. Rev. John T. Catoir, J.C.D., Dir., (Retired).

Passaic Neighborhood Center for Women, 153 Washington Pl., Passaic, 07055-5119. Tel: 973-470-0844; Email: sam@patersondiocese.org; Web: www.ncwpassaic.org. Sr. Ann Marie Paul, S.C.C., Dir. Jointly sponsored by the Diocese of Paterson and 15 congregations of religious women.(Jointly sponsored by the Diocese of Paterson & 15 congregations of religious women).

POMPTON LAKES. *Pathways Counseling Center, Inc.*, 16 Pompton Ave., Pompton Lakes, 07442. Tel: 973-835-6337; Fax: 973-616-4688; Email: drhall@pathwayscounseling.org; Web: www.pathwayscounseling.org. Dr. Pamela Hall, Clinic Dir.

RINGWOOD. *NCPC, Inc.*, 112 Erskine Rd., Ringwood, 07456. Tel: 973-962-7032. Most Rev. Arthur J. Serratelli, S.T.D., S.S.L., D.D., Pres.

ROCKAWAY. *Divine Mercy Academy, Inc.*, 87 Halsey Ave., Rockaway, 07866. Tel: (973) 627-6003; Email: principal@dmarockaway.org; Web: dmarockaway.org. Mrs. Elizabeth Cassidy, Sec.; Rev. Mateusz Darlak, Deacon; Janet Maulbeck, Bus. Mgr.; Mrs. Ann Mitchell, Prin. Lay Teachers 14; Students 213; Religious Teachers 3.

SPARTA. *The Catholic Academy of Sussex County, Inc.*, 28 Andover Rd., Sparta, 07871. Tel: 973-729-6125; Email: johnfernandes@popejohn.org. Most Rev. Arthur J. Serratelli, S.T.D., S.S.L., D.D., Pres.; Rev. Msgr. James T. Mahoney, Ph.D., V.G., Pres.; Sr. Mary Edward Spohrer, S.C.C., Sec. & Treas.; Rev. Msgr. Kieran A. McHugh, Dir. The Academy operates Pope John XXIII H.S.; Rev. George Brown School; Pope John XXIII Middle School; Camp Auxilium Center.

Pope John XXIII Middle School, Inc., 28 Andover Rd., Sparta, 07871. Tel: (973) 729-1967; Email: johnfernandes@popejohn.org. Most Rev. Arthur J. Serratelli, S.T.D., S.S.L., D.D., Pres.; Rev. Msgr.

James T. Mahoney, Ph.D., V.G., Vice Pres.; Sr. Joan Daniel Healy, S.C.C., Sec.; Mr. Kenneth F. Mullaney Jr., Esq., Registered Agent. Lay Teachers 19; Students 243.

Pope John XXIII Regional High School, Inc., 28 Andover Rd., Sparta, 07871. Tel: 973-729-6125; Email: johnfernandes@popejohn.org. Most Rev. Arthur J. Serratelli, S.T.D., S.S.L., D.D., Pres.; Rev. Msgr. James T. Mahoney, Ph.D., V.G., Vice Pres.; Sr. Mary Edward Spohrer, S.C.C., Sec. & Treas.; Rev. Msgr. Kieran A. McHugh, Registered Agent.

WAYNE. *DePaul Catholic Diocesan High School, Inc.*, 1512 Alps Rd., Wayne, 07470. Tel: 973-694-3702; Tel: 973-694-3702; Email: weirk@dpchs.org; Email: bekkerk@dpchs.org. Most Rev. Arthur J. Serratelli, S.T.D., S.S.L., D.D., Pres.; Rev. Msgr. James T. Mahoney, Ph.D., V.G., Vice Pres.; Sr. Mary Edward Spohrer, S.C.C., Sec. & Treas.

Siena Village, 1000 Siena Village, Wayne, 07470. Tel: 973-696-2811; Fax: 973-696-2721; Email: aldors@aol.com. Sr. Alice Matthew, O.P., Dir.

RELIGIOUS INSTITUTES OF MEN REPRESENTED IN THE DIOCESE

For further details refer to the corresponding bracketed number in the Religious Institutes of Men or Women section.

[0200]—*Benedictine Monks* (St. Mary, St. Paul Abbeys; Holy Face of Jesus Monastery)—O.S.B.
[0470]—*The Capuchin Friars*—O.F.M.Cap.
[0480]—*Conventual Franciscans*—O.F.M.Conv.
[0520]—*Franciscan Friars* (Holy Name Prov.)—O.F.M.
[]—*Franciscans of the Renewal*—C.F.R.
[0690]—*Jesuit Fathers and Brothers* (New York Prov.)—S.J.
[0840]—*Missionary Servants of the Most Holy Trinity* (Silver Spring, MD)—S.T.
[]—*Priestly Fraternity of the Renewal*—F.S.S.P.
[]—*Society of Our Lady of the Holy Trinity*—S.O.L.T.
[1340]—*Vocationist Fathers*—S.D.V.
[1360]—*Xaverian Missionary Fathers* (Wayne)—S.X.

RELIGIOUS INSTITUTES OF WOMEN REPRESENTED IN THE DIOCESE

[0740]—*Daughters of Charity of the Most Precious Blood*—D.C.P.B.
[0850]—*Daughters of Mary Help of Christians*—F.M.A.
[]—*Daughters of the Most Pure Heart of the Most Holy Virgin Mary* (Passaic).
[0420]—*Discalced Carmelite Nuns*—O.C.D.
[1070-06]—*Dominican Sisters*—O.P.
[1070-18]—*Dominican Sisters*—O.P.
[1400]—*Franciscan Missionary Sisters of the Sacred Heart* (Peekskill)—F.M.S.C.
[]—*Hermits of Our Lady of Mt. Carmel*—H.O.Carm.
[2340]—*Little Sisters of the Poor*—L.S.P.
[2760]—*Missionary Sisters of the Immaculate Conception of the Mother of God*—S.M.I.C.
[3430]—*Religious Teachers Filippini*—M.P.F.
[1700]—*School Sisters of the Third Order of St. Francis*—O.S.F.
[3560]—*Servants of Jesus* (Stirling)—S.J.
[0590]—*Sisters of Charity of Saint Elizabeth, Convent Station*—S.C.
[0660]—*Sisters of Christian Charity*—S.C.C.
[3820]—*Sisters of St. John the Baptist*—C.S.J.B.
[3830]—*Sisters of St. Joseph* (Chestnut Hill, PA)—C.S.J.
[3890]—*Sisters of St. Joseph of Peace*—C.S.J.P.
[3320]—*Sisters of the Presentation of the B.V.M.*—P.B.V.M.
[4100]—*Sisters of the Sorrowful Mother (Third Order of St. Francis)*—S.S.M.
[]—*The Society of the Sisters of the Church* (Passaic).
[4210]—*Vocationist Sisters*—S.D.V.

NECROLOGY

† Rodimer, Frank J., Retired Bishop of Paterson, Died Dec. 6, 2018
† Carey, Leo P., (Retired), Died Nov. 15, 2018
† Demkovich, John J., (Retired), Died Aug. 1, 2018
† Russo, Charles J., (Retired), Died May. 15, 2018
† Heekin, John M., (Retired), Died Jul. 1, 2018
† Sella, Donald J., (Retired), Died Nov. 4, 2018

An asterisk (*) denotes an organization that has established tax-exempt status directly with the IRS and is not covered by the USCCB Group Ruling.

Diocese of Pensacola-Tallahassee

(Dioecesis Pensacolensis-Tallaseiensis)

Most Reverend

WILLIAM A. WACK, C.S.C.

Bishop of Pensacola-Tallahassee; ordained April 9, 1994; appointed Bishop of Pensacola-Tallahassee May 29, 2017; ordained August 22, 2017. *Office: 11 North B St., Pensacola, FL 32502.* Tel: 850-435-3500.

Most Reverend

JOHN H. RICARD, S.S.J.

Bishop Emeritus of Pensacola-Tallahassee; ordained May 25, 1968; ordained Auxiliary Bishop of Baltimore July 2, 1984; appointed Bishop of Pensacola-Tallahassee January 21, 1997.

ESTABLISHED NOVEMBER 6, 1975.

Square Miles 14,044.

Comprises the following Counties: Bay, Calhoun, Escambia, Franklin, Gadsden, Gulf, Holmes, Jackson, Jefferson, Leon, Liberty, Madison, Okaloosa, Santa Rosa, Taylor, Wakulla, Walton and Washington Counties.

For legal titles of parishes and diocesan institutions, consult the Pastoral Center.

Monsignor James Amos Pastoral Center: 11 North B St., Pensacola, FL 32502. Tel: 850-435-3500; Fax: 850-436-6424. *. Mailing Address: P.O. Drawer 13284, Pensacola, FL 32591.*

Web: www.ptdiocese.org

Email: chancellor@ptdiocese.org

STATISTICAL OVERVIEW

Personnel	
Bishop	1
Retired Bishops	1
Priests: Diocesan Active in Diocese	53
Priests: Diocesan Active Outside Diocese	7
Priests: Retired, Sick or Absent	12
Number of Diocesan Priests	72
Religious Priests in Diocese	10
Total Priests in Diocese	82
Extern Priests in Diocese	19
Ordinations:	
Diocesan Priests	1
Transitional Deacons	1
Permanent Deacons in Diocese	71
Total Brothers	11
Total Sisters	19
Parishes	
Parishes	50
With Resident Pastor:	
Resident Diocesan Priests	42
Resident Religious Priests	2
Without Resident Pastor:	
Administered by Priests	6
Missions	8
Professional Ministry Personnel:	
Brothers	4
Sisters	8
Lay Ministers	85
Welfare	
Catholic Hospitals	1
Total Assisted	1,044,400
Homes for the Aged	3
Total Assisted	829
Special Centers for Social Services	4
Total Assisted	52,285
Other Institutions	1
Total Assisted	34
Educational	
Diocesan Students in Other Seminaries	8
Total Seminarians	8
High Schools, Diocesan and Parish	2
Total Students	795
Elementary Schools, Diocesan and Parish	7
Total Students	2,104
Catechesis/Religious Education:	
High School Students	731
Elementary Students	3,189
Total Students under Catholic Instruction	6,827
Teachers in the Diocese:	
Priests	2
Sisters	2
Lay Teachers	240
Vital Statistics	
Receptions into the Church:	
Infant Baptism Totals	703
Minor Baptism Totals	100
Adult Baptism Totals	103
Received into Full Communion	215
First Communions	994
Confirmations	920
Marriages:	
Catholic	156
Interfaith	71
Total Marriages	227
Deaths	522
Total Catholic Population	67,458
Total Population	1,500,427

Former Bishops—Most Revs. RENE H. GRACIDA, D.D., ord. May 23, 1959; appt. Titular Bishop of Masuccaba and Auxiliary of Miami, Dec. 6, 1971; cons. Jan. 25, 1972; appt. first Bishop of Pensacola-Tallahassee, Oct. 1, 1975; installed Nov. 6, 1975; transferred to Bishop of Corpus Christi, May 19, 1983; J. KEITH SYMONS, D.D., Bishop of Pensacola-Tallahassee; ord. May 18, 1958; Titular Bishop of Siguritanus and Auxiliary of St. Petersburg; appt. Jan. 16, 1981; cons. March 19, 1981; Bishop of Pensacola-Tallahassee; appt. Sept. 29, 1983; installed Nov. 8, 1983; transferred to Bishop of Palm Beach, June 2, 1990; JOHN M. SMITH, J.C.D., D.D., Bishop of Pensacola-Tallahassee; ord. May 27, 1961; Titular Bishop of Tre Taverne and Auxiliary of Newark; appt. Dec. 1, 1987; cons. Jan. 25, 1988; Bishop of Pensacola-Tallahassee; appt. June 25, 1991; installed July 31, 1991; transferred to Coadjutor Bishop of Trenton, Nov. 21, 1995; appt. Bishop of Trenton July 1, 1997; retired Dec. 1, 2010; died Jan. 22, 2019.; JOHN H. RICARD, S.S.J., (Retired), ord. May 25, 1968; ord. Auxiliary Bishop of Baltimore July 2, 1984; appt. Bishop of Pensacola-Tallahassee Jan. 21, 1997; retired March 11, 2011.; GREGORY L. PARKES, ord. June 26, 1999; appt. Bishop of Pensacola-Tallahassee March 20, 2012; ord. Bishop June 5, 2012; appt. Bishop of St. Petersburg Nov. 28, 2016; installed Jan. 4, 2017.

Monsignor James Amos Pastoral Center—11 North B St., Pensacola, 32502. Tel: 850-435-3500; Fax: 850-436-6424. *Mailing Address: P.O. Drawer 13284, Pensacola, 32591.*

Chancellor—Rev. Msgr. MICHAEL V. REED, J.C.L.

Child and Youth Protection—Rev. Msgr. MICHAEL V. REED, J.C.L., V.F.; MRS. CLAUDIA WOLF, Diocesan Investigator, Pastoral Center, 11 N. B St., Pensacola, 32502. Mailing Address: P.O. Box 13284, Pensacola, 32591.

Vicar for Priests—VACANT.

Vicar for Permanent Deacons—Very Rev. JOSEPH P. CALLIPARE.

Delegate for Religious—Sr. MARGARET KUNTZ, A.S.C.J.

Vicars Forane—Rev. Msgr. MICHAEL V. REED, J.C.L., V.F., Western Vicariate Forane; Very Revs. STEPHEN A. VOYT, V.F., West Central Vicariate Forane; TED SOSNOWSKI, V.F., East Central Vicariate Forane; MICHAEL FOLEY, V.F., Eastern Vicariate Forane.

Vicar General—Rev. Msgr. LUKE HUNT, V.G.

Diocesan Tribunal—Mailing Address: P.O. Drawer 13284, Pensacola, 32591. Tel: 850-436-6454; Fax: 850-435-3549. Direct all matters regarding Marriage Dispensations and questions to Tribunal Office.

Interim Judicial Vicar—Rev. T. JOSEPH FOWLER, J.C.L., J.V.

Judge—Rev. T. JOSEPH FOWLER, J.C.L., J.V.

Promoter of Justice—Rev. Msgr. MICHAEL V. REED, J.C.L.

Defender of the Bond—Rev. EUGENE D. CASSERLY, M.Ch.A.

College of Consultors—Very Rev. MICHAEL FOLEY, V.F.; Rev. Msgr. MICHAEL W. TUGWELL, (Retired); Rev. PETER ZALEWSKI; Rev. Msgrs. MICHAEL V. REED, J.C.L.; LUKE HUNT, V.G.

Administrative Council—

Council of Priests—

Presider—Most Rev. WILLIAM ALBERT WACK, C.S.C., Bishop of Pensacola-Tallahassee.

Ex Officio Members—Rev. Msgrs. LUKE HUNT, V.G.; MICHAEL V. REED, J.C.L., V.F., Chancellor.

Elected by Deanery—Rev. KEVIN MCQUONE, Pres., East Central; Very Rev. JAMES PAUL VALENZUELA; Rev. MATTHEW CAMERON WORTHEN, West; Very Rev. STEPHEN A. VOYT, V.F., West Central; Rev. SHANE STEVENS, Eastern.

Members at Large—Revs. DUSTIN FEDDON; WILLIAM PHILIP GANCI.

Members Appointed—Very Rev. JOHN B. CAYER; Revs. HANK LECH; PAUL T. WHITE.

Council of Sisters—Sr. MARGARET KUNTZ, A.S.C.J., Pres.

Priests' Pension Plan, Board for—Very Revs. JOSEPH P. CALLIPARE; STEPHEN A. VOYT, V.F.; Revs. THOMAS S. COLLINS; THOMAS GUIDO; JOHN F. KELLY. Consultants: ROBERT EMMANUEL ESQ.; Rev. Msgrs. LUKE HUNT, V.G.; MICHAEL V. REED, J.C.L., V.F.

Priest Personnel Board—Rev. Msgrs. MICHAEL V. REED, J.C.L., V.F.; LUKE HUNT, V.G.; Very Revs. MICHAEL FOLEY, V.F.; TED SOSNOWSKI, V.F.; Rev. PETER ZALEWSKI.

Diocesan Commissions, Departments, and Offices

Director, Ministry to Priests—Rev. MICHAEL J. NIXON.

Apostleship of the Sea, Office of the—Very Rev. JOSEPH P. CALLIPARE.

Archivist—CARLISLE SEMMES, Ed.D., Mailing Address: P.O. Box 13284, Pensacola, 32591. Tel: 850-435-3500.

Commission for African American Catholics—GABRIEL M. BROWN, Chm., Mailing Address: P.O. Drawer 13284, Pensacola, 32591. Tel: 850-435-3500.

Campus Ministry—MR. CHRIS BENZINGER, Dir. Mission & Evangelization, Mailing Address: P.O. Drawer 13284, Pensacola, 32591. Tel: 850-435-3525. Catholic Student Union at Florida State University: Bro. CLINTON REED IV, Dir., Mailing Address: Catholic Student Union at Co-Cathedral of St. Thomas More, 900 W. Tennessee St., Tallahassee, 32304. Tel: 850-222-9630. Florida Agricultural & Mechanical University (FAMU): Rev. ANDERSON DE SOUZA, S.V.D., Dir. & Chap., St. Eugene Chapel, 701 Gamble St., Tallahassee, 32310. Tel: 850-222-6482.

Catholic Campus Ministry at University of West Florida—Rev. JAMES L. GREBE, Nativity of Our Lord Parish, 9945 Hillview Dr., Pensacola, 32514. Tel: 850-477-3221. Brotherhood of Hope: Bro. CLINTON REED IV, 2302 Mission Rd., Tallahassee, 32304. Franciscan Sisters, T.O.R. of Penance of the Sorrowful Mother: Sisters DELLA MARIE DOYLE, T.O.R.; ELIANA DAY, T.O.R., 811 Miccosukee Rd., Tallahassee, 32308.

Catholic Women, Diocesan Council of—MARY SAUVAGEAU, Pres.; Revs. RICHARD DAWSON, Chap.; ROBERT JOHNSON, Spiritual Advisor, West Central Deanery; WILLIAM P. BROWN, J.C.L., Spiritual Advisor, East Central Deanery.

Catholic Charities of Northwest Florida—Mailing Address: 11 North B St., Pensacola, 32502. Tel: 850-435-3516; Email: kneem@cc.ptdiocese.org. MR. MATTHEW KNEE, Pres. & Exec. Dir.

Pensacola Office (West Deanery)—Mailing Address: 1815 N. 6th Ave., Pensacola, 32503. Tel: 850-436-8754; Fax: 850-436-6439; Email: wisee@cc.ptdiocese.org. MS. EVA WISE, Asst. Exec. Dir.

Fort Walton Beach (West-Central Deanery)—Mailing Address: 11 1st St., S.E., Fort Walton Beach, 32548. Tel: 850-244-2825; Fax: 850-664-9146; Email: wisee@cc.ptdiocese.org. MS. EVA WISE, Asst. Exec. Dir.

Panama City Office (East Central Deanery)—Mailing Address: 3128 E. 11th St., Panama City, 32401. Tel: 850-382-1528; Fax: 850-763-2969; Email: wisee@cc.ptdiocese.org. MS. EVA WISE, Asst. Exec. Dir.

Tallahassee Office (East Deanery)—Mailing Address: 1380 Blountstown Hwy., Tallahassee, 32316. Tel: 850-222-2180; Fax: 850-681-6963; Email: wisee@cc.ptdiocese.org. MS. EVA WISE, Asst. Exec. Dir.

Fox Trace Housing, Inc.—Pensacola, 32502.

Charismatic Renewal, Diocesan Commission for—Rev. NICHOLAS SCHUMM; SUE MCALLISTER, 11 N. B St., Pensacola, 32502. Email: ptdccr@gmail.com.

Cursillo Movement—Rev. CRAIG SMITH, Spiritual Dir.; Deacon ROBERT MACKO, Spiritual Dir.; JEANETTE ASSELIN, Diocesan Lay Dir., Email: jaslin44@hughes.net.

Ecumenical & Interreligious Affairs, Office of—VACANT, Dir.

Finance, Department of—Mailing Address: P.O. Drawer 13284, Pensacola, 32591. Tel: 850-435-3500. VACANT, CFO.

Human Resources—ROBIN JONES.

Insurance—JEAN ORI.

Internal Review—BILL BECK.

Real Estate / Construction—ROBERT BENNETT.

Information Technology—CELESTE DURAND.

Accounting—PAULA BEAUCHAMP.

Cemetery, Office of—Holy Cross Cemetery, 1300 E. Hayes St., Pensacola, 32503. Tel: 850-432-0878; Fax: 850-434-9032. *Calvary Cemetery, 11 North B St., Pensacola, 32502.*

Diocesan Director of Catholic Cemeteries—11 North B St., Pensacola, 32503. VACANT.

Finance, Diocesan Commission for—WILLIAM WACK, C.S.C.; ROBERT EMMANUEL ESQ., Pres.; Rev. Msgrs. LUKE HUNT, V.G., Sec.; MICHAEL V. REED, J.C.L.; Rev. DOUGLAS G. HALSEMA; SUSAN DAVIS; ERIC NICKELSEN; DR. WILLIAM SIMMONS; KATHY CROWLEY; MR. JOHN GODLEWSKI, Mailing Address: P.O. Drawer 13284, Pensacola, 32591. Tel: 850-435-3500.

Independent Review Board—Mailing Address: P.O. Drawer 13284, Pensacola, 32591. Tel: 850-435-3500; Fax: 850-436-6424. Rev. DOUGLAS G. HALSEMA; MRS. STEPHANIE GARNETT; MRS. ANGELA GUILLAUME; DR. ANITA NUSBAUM; ROBERT EMMANUEL ESQ.; MRS. SHELLY REYNOLDS CLABAUGH; MR. PAUL JANSEN.

Knights of Columbus—Rev. JOHN F. KELLY, Diocesan Chap., Mailing Address: 6464 Gulf Breeze Pkwy., Gulf Breeze, 32563.

Lay Formation Institute—Mailing Address: 11 N. B St., Pensacola, 32502. Tel: 850-435-3549. Sr. MARGARET KUNTZ, A.S.C.J.

Legion of Mary—Rev. HECTOR R.G. PEREZ, S.T.D., Diocesan Spiritual Dir., 900 W. Garden St., Pensacola, 32502. Tel: 850-432-9362.

Worship, Office of—Rev. MICHAEL J. FLYNN, Dir.

Office for Faith Formation—Sr. MARGARET KUNTZ, A.S.C.J., Email: kuntzm@ptdiocese.org.

Office for Youth Ministry—LISA KURNIK, Scouting, Email: kurnikl@ptdiocese.org.

Office for Family Life & Marriage—CHEZ FILIPPINI.

Campaign for Human Development, Office of—Deacon RAYMOND AGUADO, 11 North B St., Pensacola, 32502. Tel: 850-435-3520.

Advocacy & Justice—Deacon RAYMOND AGUADO, 11 North B St., Pensacola, 32502. Tel: 850-435-3520.

Hispanic Ministry, Office for—Rev. ALVERO GONZALES, Dir., Mailing Address: P.O. Drawer 13284, Pensacola, 32591. Tel: 850-435-3500; Fax: 850-435-6424.

Orders & Ministries, Commission for—Mailing Address: P.O. Drawer 13284, Pensacola, 32591. Tel: 850-435-3500; Fax: 850-436-6424. Rev. Msgr. MICHAEL W. TUGWELL, (Retired); Rev. THOMAS J. GUIDO; Rev. Msgrs. JOHN V. O'SULLIVAN; MICHAEL V. REED, J.C.L.

Office of the Permanent Diaconate and Permanent Deacon Formation—Very Rev. JOSEPH P. CALLIPARE, Vicar for Permanent Deacons, 11 North B St., Pensacola, 32502. Tel: 850-435-3552; Fax: 850-435-3565; Email: calliparej@ptdiocese.org.

Permanent Deacon Formation Team—Very Rev. JOSEPH P. CALLIPARE, Dir.; Revs. DOUGLAS G. HALSEMA, Spiritual Formation; PAUL T. WHITE, Liturgical Formation; Deacons TIMOTHY M. WARNER, Esq., Pastoral Formation; C. LOUIS FETE, Pastoral Formation.

Permanent Deacon Formation Board—Committee for Admissions and Scrutinies Very Rev. JOSEPH P. CALLIPARE, Chm.; MS. CAROLINE BUSH; Rev. DOUGLAS G. HALSEMA; Deacons C. LOUIS FETE; JOSEPH JACOBS; WILLIAM WHIBBS; TIMOTHY M. WARNER, Esq.; Rev. PAUL T. WHITE.

Permanent Deacon Deanery Representatives—Deacons MIGUEL NOLLA, West Central; C. LOUIS FETE, Eastern; STEVEN SNIGG, East Central; THOMAS GORDON, Western; JOHN SHIN, At-Large; STEPHEN WULF, Western.

Priestly Formation—11 N. B St., Pensacola, 32502. VACANT.

Propagation of the Faith, Office ofRev. T. JOSEPH FOWLER, J.C.L., J.V.

Respect Life Committee—Deacons RAYMOND AGUADO; MARK SCHNEIDER, Chm., Email: maslas1@embarqmail.com.

Catholic Schools—MICHAEL JUHAS, Supt. Schools; DONNA BASS, Asst. to Supt. Schools & Teacher Certification, Mailing Address: P.O. Drawer 13284, Pensacola, 32591. Tel: 850-435-3500; Fax: 850-436-6424; Email: ptschools@ptdiocese.org.

Holy Childhood Association—MICHAEL JUHAS, Dir.

Catholic Youth Sports League—TONY HOWARD, Dir.

Office of Mission & Evangelization, Director—MR. CHRIS BENZINGER.

Communications—The Catholic Compass SHARMANE ADAMS.

Seminarian Candidate Review Board—Mailing Address: P.O. Drawer 13284, Pensacola, 32591. Tel: 850-435-3500. Revs. MICHAEL J. FLYNN; DOUGLAS G. HALSEMA; Deacon RAYMOND AGUADO; Sr. KIERSTIN MARTIN, A.S.C.J.; MRS. PENNY GORECKI; MR. LARRY VALLIA.

Vocations & Seminarians, Office of—Rev. TIMOTHY MICHAEL HOLEDA II, Dir. Associate Directors: Revs. TIMOTHY MICHAEL HOLEDA II; MICHAEL J. NIXON; MATTHEW CAMERON WORTHEN; MICHELE JOHNSTON, Staff, Mailing Address: P.O. Drawer 13284, Pensacola, 32591. Tel: 850-435-3552.

Serra Club—Pensacola: Rev. MATTHEW CAMERON WORTHEN, Chap.; MICHAEL BRADY, Pres. Tallahassee: CHRIS KROLL, Pres.

Stewardship & Development, Office of—JOHN KENNEDY, Dir.

Victim Assistance Coordinators—LOUIS MAKAROWSKI, Ph.D., P.A., Tel: 850-477-7181; DR. JAMES GAGNON, M.S.W., L.C.S.W., Tel: 850-877-0205.

CLERGY, PARISHES, MISSIONS AND PAROCHIAL SCHOOLS

GREATER PENSACOLA

(ESCAMBIA COUNTY)

1—CATHEDRAL OF THE SACRED HEART (1905)
Mailing Address: 1212 E. Moreno St., 32503.
Tel: 850-438-3131; Fax: 850-436-6428; Email: office@shc.ptdiocese.org; Web: shc.ptdiocese.org. Very Rev. James Paul Valenzuela, Rector; Rev. Michael Flynn, Parochial Vicar; Deacons John Parnham; Paul Graaff.
Res.: 1101 E. Mallory St., 32503.
School—Sacred Heart Cathedral School, (Grades K-8), 1603 N. 12th Ave., 32503. Tel: 850-436-6440; Fax: 850-436-6444; Email: esnow@shcs.ptdiocese.org. Elizabeth Snow, Prin. Clergy 1; Lay Teachers 23; Students 318.
Catechesis Religious Program—Students 100.

2—ST. ANNE (Brownsville) (1953) Closed. For inquiries for sacramental records, please see the Cathedral of the Sacred Heart, Pensacola.

3—ST. ANNE'S (Bellview) (1964)
5200 Saufley Field Rd., 32526-1626.
Tel: 850-456-5966; Email: office@stannebv.org; Web: www.saintannebellview.org. Rev. George Sammut.
Catechesis Religious Program—Louise Browne, D.R.E. Students 83.

4—ST. ANTHONY OF PADUA (1941) (African American)
1804 N. Davis Hwy., 32503. Tel: 850-982-0456; Email: valenzuelaj@shc.ptdiocese.org; Web: www.ptdiocese.org. Mailing Address: 1212 E. Moreno St., 32503. Very Rev. James Paul Valenzuela; Rev. Michael J. Flynn; Deacons John Parnham; Paul Graaff.
Catechesis Religious Program— Twinned with The Cathedral of the Sacred Heart. Community Center, 1804 N. Davis Hwy., 32503. Students 6.

5—BASILICA OF ST. MICHAEL THE ARCHANGEL (1781)
19 N Palafox St., 32502. Tel: 850-438-4985;
Fax: 850-433-9758; Email: office@stmichael.ptdiocese.org; Web: stmichael.ptdiocese.org. P.O. Box 12423, 32591. Very Rev. Joseph P. Callipare, Rector; Deacon Stephen Wulf, Marriage Coord.
Catechesis Religious Program—Students 10.

6—HOLY SPIRIT (1976)
10650 Gulf Beach Hwy., 32507. Tel: 850-492-0837;
Fax: 850-492-4968; Email: office@hs.ptdiocese.org; Web: www.holyspiritperdido.com. Rev. Thomas S. Collins; Deacon Robert Gregerson, (Atlanta).

7—ST. JOHN THE EVANGELIST (1851) [CEM]
303 S. Navy Blvd., 32507. Tel: 850-455-0356; Web: www.stjohnpensacoal.com. Rev. John J. Licari; Deacons Gerard Williamson; Donald Krehely.
Rectory—156 Yucatan Dr., 32506.
School—St. John the Evangelist School, (Grades PreK-8), 325 S. Navy Blvd., 32507. Tel: 850-456-5218 ; Fax: 850-456-5956; Email: williamsa@sjsw.ptdiocese.org; Web: www.stjohnpensacola.com. Mrs. Ann Williams, Prin. Clergy 2; Lay Teachers 15; Religious 1; Students 245.
Catechesis Religious Program—Students 75.

8—ST. JOSEPH (1891) [CEM]
140 W. Government St., 32502. Tel: 850-436-6461;
Fax: 850-436-6462; Email: stjoepnsoffice@gmail.com; Web: www.stjoepns.org. P.O. Box 13566, 32591. Rev. Chuck R. Collins.
Res.: 141 W. Intendencia St., 32502.
Catechesis Religious Program—Students 13.

9—LITTLE FLOWER (1945)
6495 Lillian Hwy., 32506. Tel: 850-455-5641;
Fax: 850-455-4508; Email: office@ptlittleflower.org; Web: www.ptlittleflower.org. Revs. Matthew Cameron Worthen; Alberic Lazerna, Parochial Vicar; Deacons Reymond Castellano; Thomas Gordon.
School—Little Flower School, (Grades PreK-8), Tel: 850-455-4851; Email: avarias@pensacolalfs.org. Aleli Varias, Prin. Clergy 1; Lay Teachers 45; Students 196.

10—ST. MARY (1941)
401 Van Pelt Ln., 32505. Tel: 850-478-2797;
Fax: 850-478-2739; Email: secretary@stmarypensacola.org; Web: stmarypensacola.org. Rev. Dominic Phan Sa; Deacon Ken McClure.

Catechesis Religious Program—Students 38.
11—NATIVITY OF OUR LORD (1969)
9945 Hillview Dr., 32514-5702. Tel: 850-477-3221; Email: admin@nativityofourlordcc.org; Web: www.nativityofourlordcc.org. Rev. James L. Grebe; Deacon Dennis Dobransky.
Catechesis Religious Program—Email: faith@nativityofourlordcc.org. Students 78.
12—OUR LADY QUEEN OF MARTYRS (1977) (Vietnamese)
3295 S. Barrancas Ave., 32507. Cell: 850-324-5856; Email: ourladyqueenofmartyrs@gmail.com; Web: nuvuongcacthanhtudaopensacola.com. Rev. Peter Nguyen, S.D.D.
Catechesis Religious Program—Thoa Nguyen, D.R.E.; Binh Pham, D.R.E. Students 9.
13—ST. PAUL (1963)
3131 Hyde Park Rd., 32503. Tel: 850-434-2551; Fax: 850-436-6449; Email: kirkr@stpaulcatholic.net; Web: www.stpaulcatholic.net. Mailing Address: 1700 Conway Dr., 32503. Revs. Craig Steven Smith; Jack Campbell, Parochial Vicar; Joseph Fowler, In Res.; Deacon William Whibbs.
School—St. Paul School, 3121 Hyde Park Rd., 32503. Tel: 850-436-6435; Fax: 850-436-6437; Email: school@stpaulcatholic.net. Mrs. Lara Schuler, Prin. Clergy 1; Lay Teachers 31; Students 378.
Catechesis Religious Program—
Tel: 850-434-2551, Ext. 102. Students 50.
14—ST. STEPHEN (1922) (Diocesan Shrine of Our Lady of Fatima)
900 W. Garden St., 32502. Tel: 850-432-9362; Email: fhrgp3@cox.net; Email: ststephenrectory@cox.net; Web: www.latinmasspensacola.com. Rev. Hector R.G. Perez, S.T.D.
Catechesis Religious Program—Students 30.
15—ST. THOMAS MORE (1954)
510 Bayshore Dr., 32507. Tel: 850-456-2543; Fax: 850-455-5203; Email: office@stm.ptdiocese.org; Web: www.stthomasmore.ptdiocese.org. Revs. Nicholas Schumm; Eugene D. Casserly, In Res., (Retired).
Catechesis Religious Program—Students 22.

CITY OF TALLAHASSEE

(LEON COUNTY)
1—CO-CATHEDRAL OF ST. THOMAS MORE (1968)
900 W. Tennessee St., Tallahassee, 32304. Tel: 850-222-9630; Fax: 850-222-6430; Email: office@cocathedral.com; Web: www.cocathedral.com. Very Rev. John B. Cayer, Rector; Rev. Timothy Michael Holeda II; Deacon Andrew Grosmaire.
832 W. Tennessee St., Tallahassee, 32304.
For a complete listing, see John Paul II Catholic High School located under High Schools, Diocesan in the Institution section.
Catechesis Religious Program—Students 122.
2—BLESSED SACRAMENT (1845)
654 Miccosukee Rd., Tallahassee, 32308. Tel: 850-222-1321; Email: blessedsacramentcatholicchurch@gmail.com; Web: bsctlh.com. 624 Miccosukee Rd., Tallahassee, 32308. Revs. Peter Zalewski; Matthew Busch; Joseph Anthu Raj; Bernard Jakubco, M.S.C., In Res.; Deacons C. Louis Fete; Patrick Dallet; Michael Nixon.
School—Trinity Catholic, (Grades PreK-8), 706 E. Brevard St., Tallahassee, 32308. Tel: 850-222-0444; Fax: 850-224-5067; Email: bridgest@trinityknights.org; Web: trinityknights.org. Mr. James Thomas Bridges, Prin. Lay Teachers 32; Students 430.
For a complete listing, see John Paul II Catholic High School located under High Schools, Diocesan in the Institution section.
ST. JOHN NEUMANN RETREAT CENTER, 685 Miccosukee Rd., Tallahassee, 32308.
Tel: 850-224-2971; Email: dasha@neumancenter.org; Web: www.neumanncenteroftallahassee.com. Mr. Dasha Nixon, Dir.
3—GOOD SHEPHERD (1973)
4665 Thomasville Rd., Tallahassee, 32309-2512. Tel: 850-893-1837; Email: goodshepherd@gsparishtlh.org; Email: haynesj@gsparishtlh.org. Very Rev. Michael Foley, V.F.; Revs. J. Thomas Dillon, Email: dillonj@clergy.ptdiocese.org; Arockiaraj Kunipaku Selvaraj, (India); Deacons Gerald Haynes, Admin.; Edward Melvin III; Thomas McBrearty; Mark Schneider.
For a complete listing, see John Paul II Catholic High School located under High Schools, Diocesan in the Institution section.
Catechesis Religious Program—Students 656.
4—ST. LOUIS (1979)
St. Louis Catholic Church: 3640 Fred George Rd., Tallahassee, 32303. Tel: 850-262-8156; Email: stlouischurch@embarqmail.com; Web: www.stlouiscatholicchurch.org. Rev. Shane Stevens; Deacons Nelson Madera, Ph.D.; Robert Macko; Joseph Jacobs.
Res.: 4151 Miraflores Ln., Tallahassee, 32303. Tel: 850-262-8156; Email: stlouischurch@embarqmail.com; Web: stlouis.ptdiocese.org.
Catechesis Religious Program—Elizabeth Angulo, D.R.E. Students 35.
Mission—St. Augustine Yu Korean Mission, 708 Hazel Dr., Fort Walton Beach, 32547-2002. Rev. Jungki Chun.

OUTSIDE THE CITIES OF PENSACOLA AND TALLAHASSEE

APALACHICOLA, FRANKLIN CO., ST. PATRICK (1851) [JC]
27 6th St., P.O. Box 550, Apalachicola, 32329.
Tel: 850-653-9453; Tel: 850-653-2100;
Fax: 850-653-4528; Web: stpatcath@fairpoint.net; Web: stpatricksmass.com. Rev. Roger Latosynski.
Catechesis Religious Program—Students 15.
BAYOU GEORGE, BAY CO., OUR LADY OF THE ROSARY
5622 Julie Dr., Panama City, 32404.
Tel: 850-769-5067; Email: ourladyoftherosarypc@gmail.com; Web: www.rosary.ptdiocese.org. Rev. W. P. Brown; Mrs. Debby Wuest; Mrs. Arlene Hall, Music Min.; Mr. John Koerner, IT Technician.
Catechesis Religious Program—Kerry Kolmetz, D.R.E. Students 14.
Mission—Our Lady Queen of Peace, P.O. Box 213, Fountain, Bay Co. 32438. Tel: 850-722-0466; Fax: 850-722-0466; Email: deak0744@mchs.com.
BLOUNTSTOWN, CALHOUN CO., ST. FRANCIS OF ASSISI (1972) [CEM]
16498 S.W. Gaskin St., Blountstown, 32424.
Tel: 850-674-4482; Fax: 850-674-4483; Email: office@sfa.ptdiocese.org. Rev. Richard Schamber.
Catechesis Religious Program—Students 51.
BONIFAY, HOLMES CO., BLESSED TRINITY (1979)
2331 Hwy. 177A, Bonifay, 32425. Tel: 850-547-3735; Fax: 850-547-7477; Email: btbonifay@embarqmail.com. Rev. Richard Dawson.
CANTONMENT, ESCAMBIA CO., ST. JUDE THADDEUS (1945) [CEM] [JC]
303 Rocky Ave., Cantonment, 32533.
Tel: 850-968-6189; Email: office@stjude.ptdiocese.org. Rev. George Thekku; Deacons Thomas Simard; Bradley M. Seabrook, (Retired); McBurnett J. Smith Jr.
Mission—St. Elizabeth of Hungary, 303 Rocky Ave., Cantonment, Escambia Co. 32533. Tel: 850-587-2550.
Catechesis Religious Program—Students 23.
CHATTAHOOCHEE, GADSDEN CO., HOLY CROSS CATHOLIC CHURCH (1979)
4034 Memorial Blue Star Hwy., Chattahoochee, 32324. Tel: 850-674-4482; Email: office@sfa.ptdiocese.org. 16498 S.W. Gaskin St., Blountstown, 32424. Rev. Richard Schamber. Clustered with St. Francis of Assisi Catholic Church, Blountstown.
CHIPLEY, WASHINGTON CO., ST. JOSEPH THE WORKER (1968) [CEM]
Mailing Address: 1664 Main St., P.O. Box 266, Chipley, 32428. Tel: 850-638-7654; Email: stjoe@chipley.ptdiocese.org; Web: www.STJosephTheWorker.ptdiocese.org. Rev. William Philip Ganci.
Res.: 3008 4th St., Marianna, 32446.
Catechesis Religious Program—Students 12.
CRAWFORDVILLE, WAKULLA CO., ST. ELIZABETH ANN SETON (1975) [CEM]
3609 Coastal Hwy., Crawfordville, 32327.
Tel: 850-745-8395; Web: www.catholicchurchwakulla.org. Rev. Dustin Feddon.
Catechesis Religious Program—Students 63.
CRESTVIEW, OKALOOSA CO., OUR LADY OF VICTORY (1954)
550 Adams Dr., Crestview, 32536. Tel: 850-682-4622; Fax: 850-689-0335; Email: olvadmin@ptdiocese.org. Rev. Roy C. Marien.
Catechesis Religious Program—Students 255.
DE FUNIAK SPRINGS, WALTON CO., ST. MARGARET (1931)
247 U.S. Hwy. 331 N., P.O. Box 590, De Funiak Springs, 32433. Tel: 850-892-9247;
Fax: 850-892-2065; Email: stmargaret@embarqmail.com; Web: www.stmargaret.ptdiocese.org. Rev. Richard Dawson; Deacon Walter D. Harris.
Catechesis Religious Program—Students 64.
DESTIN, OKALOOSA CO., CORPUS CHRISTI (1977)
307 Beach Dr., Destin, 32541. Tel: 850-654-5422; Email: corpusdomini@outlook.com; Web: ccdestin.com. Rev. Viet Huynh.
Catechesis Religious Program—Students 100.
FORT WALTON BEACH, OKALOOSA CO., ST. MARY CHURCH (1914)
110 St. Mary Ave., S.W., Fort Walton Beach, 32548-6645. Tel: 850-243-3742; Email: office@saintmary.life; Web: www.saintmary.life. Rev. Douglas G. Halsema; Deacons Daniel M. McAuliffe, J.C.L.; Michael Brown; Michael Symons; Wayne Walker.
School—St. Mary Church School, (Grades K-8), 110 Robinwood Dr., S.W., Fort Walton Beach, 32548.
Tel: 850-243-8913; Fax: 850-243-7895; Email: office@saintmaryschool.net. Ms. Amy Akins, Prin.; Mrs. Anne Neiger, Librarian. Lay Teachers 25; Students 312.
FOUNTAIN, BAY CO., OUR LADY QUEEN OF PEACE MISSION
Mailing Address: 5622 Julie Dr., Panama City, 32404. Tel: 850-722-0466; Fax: 850-722-0466; Email: brownw@clergy.ptdiocese.org. Rev. William P. Brown, J.C.L.
Church: 18005 Lazy Ln., Fountain, 32438.
Catechesis Religious Program—
FREEPORT, WALTON CO., CHRIST THE KING MISSION (1984)
Mailing Address: c/o St. Rita, 16250 US Highway 331 S., Freeport, 32439. Tel: 850-267-2558; Email: office@saintritaparish.org. Rev. Michael Hartley, Admin.; Deacon Dave Casey.
Church: 15542 U.S. Hwy. 3315, Freeport, 32439.
Catechesis Religious Program—Students 6.
GULF BREEZE, SANTA ROSA CO.
1—ST. ANN (1948)
100 Daniel Dr., Gulf Breeze, 32561.
Tel: 850-932-2859; Fax: 850-934-2804; Email: kathyb@stanngulfbreeze.org; Web: www.stanngulfbreeze.org. P.O. Drawer 1057, Gulf Breeze, 32562. Rev. Msgr. Luke Hunt, V.G.; Rev. Thomas Kennell; Deacon Ray Aquado.
School—St. Ann Discovery School, Tel: 850-932-9330. Lay Teachers 36; Students 140.
Catechesis Religious Program—Rona Skelton, D.R.E. Students 282.
Mission—Our Lady of the Assumption, Pensacola Beach. 920 Via de Luna, P.O. Box 1057, Gulf Breeze, Santa Rosa Co. 32561. Tel: 850-934-0222; Fax: 850-934-6020.
2—SAINT SYLVESTER (1979)
6464 Gulf Breeze Pkwy., Gulf Breeze, 32563.
Tel: 850-939-3020; Email: saintsylv@stsylv.org. Revs. John F. Kelly; Alvaro Pio Gonzalez, (Colombia); Deacon Charles Sukup.
Rectory—7083 Brighton Oaks Blvd., Navarre, 32566.
Catechesis Religious Program—Students 330.
LANARK VILLAGE, FRANKLIN CO., SACRED HEART OF JESUS (1956)
2653 Hwy. 98 E., Carrabelle, 32323.
Tel: 850-697-3669. P.O. Box 729, Lanark Village, 32323. Rev. Dustin Feddon; Deacon David Harris.
MADISON, MADISON CO., ST. VINCENT DE PAUL (1905)
186 N.W. Sumter St., Madison, 32340-2048.
Tel: 850-973-2428; Email: saintvdp@gmail.com. Rev. Dominic Dat Tran.
Catechesis Religious Program—Ruth Dominics, D.R.E. Students 10.
MARIANNA, JACKSON CO., ST. ANNE (1947) [CEM] [JC]
3009 5th St., Marianna, 32446. Tel: 850-482-3734; Email: stanne@stannemar.ptdiocese.org; Web: www.stannemarianna.com. Rev. William Philip Ganci.
Catechesis Religious Program—Christine Kerr, D.R.E. Students 32.
MARY ESTHER, OKALOOSA CO., ST. PETER (1975)
100 Francis St., Mary Esther, 32569.
Tel: 850-581-2556; Email: office@stpeter.ptdiocese.org. Rev. Paul T. White; Deacon David P. Robinson.
MEXICO BEACH, BAY CO., OUR LADY OF GUADALUPE MISSION (1980) Closed. For inquiries for parish records contact the chancery.
MILTON, SANTA ROSA CO., ST. ROSE OF LIMA (1957) [JC]
6451 Park Ave., Milton, 32570. Tel: 850-623-3600; Email: lewisk@srl.ptdiocese.org. Rev. Msgr. Michael V. Reed, J.C.L., V.F.; Rev. Hank Lech; Deacons Thomas Kennell; Chris Christopher; Jeffrey Massey.
Res.: 5965 Sleepy Hollow, Milton, 32570.
Catechesis Religious Program—Kate Lewis, D.R.E. Students 263.
MIRAMAR BEACH, WALTON CO., CHURCH OF THE RESURRECTION (1981)
259 Miramar Beach Dr., Miramar Beach, 32550.
Tel: 850-837-0357; Email: admin@resurrectionbythebeach.org. Rev. Thomas J. Guido.
Rectory—399 Hideaway Bay Dr., Miramar Beach, 32550.
Catechesis Religious Program—Students 56.
MONTICELLO, JEFFERSON CO., ST. MARGARET (1917)
1565 E Washington Hwy., Monticello, 32344.
Tel: 850-997-3622; Email: saintmarg@gmail.com. c/o 186 NW Sumter St., Madison, 32340. Rev. Dominic Dat Tran.
Church: U.S. Hwy. 90 E., Monticello, 32344.
Catechesis Religious Program—Ms. Carol Miller, D.R.E. Students 11.
NICEVILLE, OKALOOSA CO.
1—CHRIST OUR REDEEMER (1989)
1028 White Point Rd., Niceville, 32578.
Tel: 850-897-7797; Fax: 850-897-2422; Email: coraccount@gmail.com; Email: corpastor@gmail.com; Web: www.corcatholic.org. Rev. Robert Johnson; Deacons Joaquin Trevino; James Murray; William E. Schaal; Miguel Nolla; Sarah Dieterich, Music Min.; Norely Soto, Youth Min.
Res.: 1167 Muirfield Way, Niceville, 32578.
Catechesis Religious Program—Lisa Hall, D.R.E. Students 175.
2—HOLY NAME OF JESUS (1960)

Holy Name of Jesus Catholic Church: 1200 Valparaiso Blvd., Niceville, 32578. Tel: 850-678-7813 ; Tel: 850-678-6790; Tel: 850-678-7861; Fax: 850-678-5775; Email: holyname@holynamechurch.org; Web: www.holynamechurch.org. Very Rev. Stephen A. Voyt, V.F.; Deacons Gary McBride, Admin.; Louis Marini; James Cox; Thomas Fraites; John Shin; Thomas Dwyer.

PANAMA CITY BEACH, BAY CO., ST. BERNADETTE (1956) 1214 Moylan Rd., Panama City Beach, 32407. Tel: 850-234-3266; Fax: 850-233-1177; Email: stbernadette@knology.net; Web: www.stbernadette.com. Very Rev. Ted Sosnowski, V.F.; Juli Roock, Admin.; Deacon Dale Johnson.

Child Care—Child Development Center, Tel: 850-230-0009; Email: stbernadette@knology.net; Web: www.stbcda.com. Juli Roock, Dir. Students 141; Total Staff 28.

Catechesis Religious Program—Ivan Velazquez, D.R.E.; Stephanie Robertson, D.R.E. Students 77.

ST. BERNADETTE JOHN LEE OUTREACH CENTER (2003) 1329 Moylan Rd., Panama City Beach, 32407. Tel: 850-234-3266; Email: stbernadette@knology.net. Juli Roock, Contact Person. Tot Asst. Annually 136; Total Staff 1.

PANAMA CITY, BAY CO.

1—ST. DOMINIC (1890) 3308 E. 15th St., Panama City, 32405-7414. Tel: 850-785-4574; Web: www.saintdominicpc.com. Revs. Michael J. Nixon; Anthony Tin Nguyen; Luke Farabaugh; Joseph Pinchock, In Res., (Retired); Deacons Steven Snigg; Michael Theobald.

Catechesis Religious Program—Sr. Jean O'Connor, D.R.E. Students 265.

2—ST. JOHN THE EVANGELIST (1945) 1008 Fortune Ave., Panama City, 32401. Tel: 850-763-1821; Email: saintjohnpc@saintjohnpc.org; Web: www.saintjohnpc.org. Rev. Kevin McQuone; Deacons Timothy M. Warner, Esq.; Earl C. Mirus.

School—St. John the Evangelist School, (Grades PreK-8), 1005 Fortune Ave., Panama City, 32401. Tel: 850-763-1775; Fax: 850-784-4461; Email: vicki.parks@sjseagles.org; Web: www.stjohncatholicschool.com. Clergy 1; Lay Teachers 16; Students 145.

Catechesis Religious Program—Email: charlotte.dickey@saintjohnpc.org. Students 78.

3—SS. PETER & PAUL PARISH (1980) [JC] (Vietnamese) Mailing Address: 1003 E. Ave., Panama City, 32401. Tel: 985-518-2641; Email: antontin@hotmail.com. Rev. Anthony Tin Nguyen.

Res.: 3308 E. 15th St., Panama City, 32405.

Catechesis Religious Program—Students 51.

PENSACOLA BEACH, ESCAMBIA CO., OUR LADY OF THE ASSUMPTION MISSION (1979) 100 Via De Luna Dr., Pensacola Beach, 32561. Tel: 850-934-0222; Fax: 850-934-6020; Email: kathyb@stanngulfbreeze.org; Web: www.stanngulfbreeze.org. P.O. Box 1057, Gulf Breeze, 32562. Rev. Msgr. Luke Hunt, V.G.; Rev. Thomas Kennell. See St. Ann, Gulf Breeze.

Church: 920 Via de Luna, Pensacola Beach, 32561.

Catechesis Religious Program—Students 8.

PERRY, TAYLOR CO., IMMACULATE CONCEPTION (1914) 2750 S. Byron Butler Pkwy., Perry, 32348. Tel: 850-584-3169; Email: immac@fairpoint.net. Rev. Philip Fortin.

Catechesis Religious Program—Students 5.

PORT ST. JOE, GULF CO., ST. JOSEPH (1925) 2001 Monument Ave., Port St. Joe, 32456. Tel: 850-227-1417; Email: office@stjosephpsj.org; Web: www.stjosephpsj.org. P.O. Box 820, Port Saint Joe, 32457. Rev. Christian Winkeljohn.

Res.: 2006 Monument Ave., Port St. Joe, 32457-0820.

Catechesis Religious Program—Students 42.

Mission—San Blas Catholic Mission, 7524 Capesan Blas Rd., Port St. Joe, Gulf Co. 32456.

QUINCY, GADSDEN CO., ST. THOMAS THE APOSTLE (1957) 27 N. Shadow St., P.O. Box 549, Quincy, 32351. Tel: 850-627-2350. Rev. Michael Somers, S.V.D.

Catechesis Religious Program—Students 161.

HISPANIC MINISTRY OFFICE OF ST. THOMAS, Religious Education Office. Fax: 850-627-6755.

SANTA ROSA BEACH, WALTON CO., ST. RITA (1982) 137 Moll St., Santa Rosa Beach, 32459. Tel: 850-267-2558; Fax: 850-267-3711; Email: saintritacatholic.church@mchsi.com; Web: saintritaparish.org. Revs. Michael Hartley, Admin.; Christian Plancher; Deacon David Casey.

Res.: 33 Seagull Ct., Santa Rosa Beach, 32459.

Catechesis Religious Program—Jenna Danos, D.R.E. Students 114.

Mission—Christ the King Catholic Mission, Freeport, Walton Co.

SUNNY HILLS, WASHINGTON CO., ST. THERESA (1972) 2071 Sunny Hills Blvd., Chipley, 32428. Cell: 850-332-3188; Web: www.sttheresa.ptdiocese.org. Rev. Paul Moody, Admin.

Res.: 2056 Sunny Hills Blvd., Sunny Hills, 32428.

Catechesis Religious Program—

WEWAHITCHKA, GULF CO., ST. LAWRENCE MISSION, Closed. For inquiries for parish records contact the chancery.

WOODVILLE, LEON CO., ST. STEPHEN THE PROTOMARTYR (1979) 1997 Natural Bridge Road, P.O. Box 208, Woodville, 32362. Tel: 850-421-9094; Web: www.ststephenprotomartyr.ptdiocese.org. Rev. Peter Zalewski, Admin.

Catechesis Religious Program—Students 4.

Chaplains of Public Institutions

PENSACOLA. *Saufley Field Federal Prison Camp.* Deacon Thomas Simard.

TALLAHASSEE. *Federal Correctional Institution.* Rev. Dai Viet Mai, I.C.

CHATTAHOOCHEE. *Florida State Hospital.* Rev. Richard Schamber.

CHIPLEY. *Washington Correctional Institution.* Rev. William Philip Ganci.

CRAWFORDVILLE. *Wakulla Correctional Institution.* Deacons C. Louis Fete, Marcus Hepburn, Santiago Molino, Madera Nelson.

CRESTVIEW. *Okaloosa Correctional Facility.* Deacons James Cox, Timothy Taylor.

JAY. *Barrydale Workcamp.* Deacon John M. Bartoszewicz.

MARIANNA. *Florida Correctional Institutions.* Rev. William Philip Ganci.

MILTON. *Blackwater Correctional Institution.* Rev. Msgr. Michael V. Reed, J.C.L., V.F., Robert Blake, Mrs. Joan Moore.

Santa Rosa Correctional Institution. Rev. Hank Lech, Mr. Joey Davis, Mr. Bruce Donatelli, Mrs. Jan Shiplett.

SNEADS. *Apalachee Correctional Institution.*

WEWAHITCHKA. *Gulf Coast Institution.* Rev. Christian Winkeljohn.

On Duty Outside the Diocese:

Rev. Msgr.—

Bosso, Stephen C., 10701 E. Military Tr., Boynton Beach, 33436. St. Vincent de Paul Regional Seminary, Boynton Beach, FL

Revs.—

Krzywicki, Lance P., Chap., ILVA, 1, 07029, Tempio Paosania, Italy
LeBlanc, Christopher, Archdiocese of Chicago
Olson, Stephen, Studying Outside Diocese (Canada)
Ssemakula, Yozefu B.
Stewart, Paul.

Military Chaplains:

Rev. Msgr.—

Reed, Michael V., J.C.L., V.F., Naval Air Station Whiting Field, Milton, 32570

Revs.—

Buhake, Longin, Tyndall AFB
Knox, Sean Vincent
Lech, Hank, Naval Air Station Whiting Field
McGuire, David, Hurlburt Field Chapel
McLaughlin, Peter, Naval Air Station Pensacola.

Retired:

Rev. Msgrs.—

Cassidy, John, (Retired)
Crawford, C. Slade, (Retired)
Mooney, Michael P., (Retired)
O'Sullivan, John V., (Retired)
Tugwell, Michael W., (Retired)

Revs.—

Casserly, Eugene D., (Retired)
Foley, Patrick, (Retired)
Joseph, William, (Retired)
Lambert, James J., (Retired)
Morris, Robert F., (Retired)
O'Shea, David T., (Retired).

Permanent Deacons:

Aguado, Raymond, St. Ann, Gulf Breeze
Barrows, Stanley, (Retired Outside of Diocese)
Bartoszewicz, John M., (Retired)
Brown, Michael, St. Mary, Fort Walton Beach
Casey, David R., (Retired), St. Rita, Santa Rosa Beach
Castellano, Reymond, Little Flower, Pensacola
Christopher, Chris, St. Rose of Lima, Milton
Cox, James, (Retired), Holy Name of Jesus, Niceville
Dallet, Patrick, Blessed Sacrament, Tallahassee
Dobransky, Dennis, Nativity of Our Lord, Pensacola
Dwyer, Thomas, Holy Name of Jesus, Niceville (Archdiocese of Washington, DC) (Extern)
Fete, C. Louis, Blessed Sacrament, Tallahassee
Fraites, Thomas J., Holy Name of Jesus, Niceville
Gallagher, Roger, (On Duty Outside Diocese)
Gordon, Thomas, Little Flower, Pensacola
Graaff, Paul, Cathedral of the Sacred Heart, Pensacola
Gregerson, Robert, Holy Spirit, Pensacola (Archdiocese of Atlanta) (Extern)
Grosmaire, Andrew, Co-Cathedral of St. Thomas More, Tallahassee
Harris, Walter D., St. Margaret, Defuniak Springs
Haynes, Gerald, Good Shepherd, Tallahassee
Howell, John, (On Duty Outside Diocese)
Jacobs, Joseph, St. Louis, Tallahassee
Johnson, Dale R., (Retired), St. Bernadette, Panama City Beach
Kennell, Thomas H., St. Rose of Lima, Milton
Krehely, Donald, (Retired), St. John the Evangelist, Pensacola
Krueger, Lloyd, (Retired Outside Diocese)
L'Huillier, Ron, (Retired Outside Diocese)
Landry, Alduce, (Retired Outside of Diocese)
Leblanc, Robert, (Retired)
Lee, Charles, (On Duty Outside Diocese)
Lurton, Richard, Nativity of Our Lord, Pensacola
Macko, Robert, St. Louis, Tallahassee
Madera, Nelson I., (Retired), St. Louis, Tallahassee
Marini, Louis, (Retired)
Massey, Jeffrey, St. Rose of Lima, Milton
McAuliffe, Daniel, St. Mary, Ft. Walton Beach
McBrearty, Thomas, Good Shepherd, Tallahassee
McBride, Gary, Holy Name of Jesus, Niceville
McClure, Kenneth, St. Mary, Pensacola
Melvin, Edward III, Good Shepherd, Tallahassee
Mirus, Earl C., St. John the Evangelist, Panama City
Molina, Santiago, St. Eugene Chapel, Tallahassee
Murphy, Michael, (On Duty Outside Diocese)
Murray, James, Christ Our Redeemer, Niceville
Nixon, Michael, Blessed Sacrament, Tallahassee
Nolla, Miguel, Christ Our Redeemer, Niceville
Parnham, John, Cathedral of the Sacred Heart, Pensacola
Renick, John, M.D., (Retired Outside of Diocese)
Rezmer, Matthew, (Retired)
Robinson, David P., (Retired), St. Peter, Mary Esther
Rose, Joseph, (Retired Outside Diocese)
Schaal, William E., (Retired), Christ Our Redeemer, Blue Water Bay
Schneider, Mark, Good Shepherd, Tallahassee
Scott, John, (On Duty Outside Diocese)
Seabrook, Bradley M., (Retired)
Shin, John, Holy Name of Jesus, Niceville
Simard, Thomas, St. Jude; St. Elizabeth, Cantonment
Smith, McBurnett J. Jr., St. Jude, Cantonment; (Archdiocese of Washington DC) (Extern)
Snigg, Steven, St. Dominic, Panama City
Sukup, Charles, St. Sylvester, Gulf Breeze (Archdiocese of Omaha)(Extern)
Symons, Michael, St. Mary, Fort Walton Beach
Taylor, Timothy, (Archdiocese of Miami) (Extern) Prison Ministry
Theobald, Michael, St. Dominic, Panama City
Trevino, Joaquin D., (Retired)
Walker, Wayne, St. Mary, Fort Walton Beach
Warner, Timothy M., Esq., St. John the Evangelist, Panama City
Whibbs, William, St. Paul, Pensacola
Williamson, Gerard, (Retired)
Wulf, Stephen, Basilica of St. Michael the Archangel, Pensacola
Zmuda, Henry, (On Duty Outside the Diocese).

INSTITUTIONS LOCATED IN DIOCESE

[A] HIGH SCHOOLS, DIOCESAN

PENSACOLA. *Pensacola Catholic High School*, 3043 W. Scott St., 32505. Tel: 850-436-6400; Fax: 850-436-6405; Email: kmartin@pensacolachs.org; Web: www.pensacolachs.org. Sr. Kierstin Martin, A.S.C.J., Prin.; Rev. Joseph Fowler, Chap.; Jennifer Buer, Librarian. Lay Teachers 51; Sisters 1; Students 645; Total Staff 69; Clergy / Religious Teachers 1.

TALLAHASSEE. *St. John Paul II Catholic High School* (2001) 5100 Terrebone Dr., Tallahassee, 32311-7848. Tel: 850-201-5744; Fax: 850-205-3299; Email: jsheppard@jpiichs.org; Web: www.jpiichs.org. Greg Monroe, Prin.; Rev. Roy C. Marien, Pres. Lay Teachers 18; Students 155; Total Staff 8.

[B] GENERAL HOSPITALS

PENSACOLA. *The Mother Seton Guild of Sacred Heart Hospital, Inc.*, 5151 N. 9th Ave., 32504.

Tel: 850-416-7883; Email: cholmes1@ascension.org. Mr. Harold Knowles, Pres.

Sacred Heart Foundation, Inc. (1984) 2200 Airport Boul. Fl. 2, 32504. Tel: 850-416-4660; Fax: 850-416-4664; Email: carol.carlan@acsension.org; Web: foundation.sacred-heart.org. P.O. Box 2700, 32513-2700. Mr. Michael Johnson, Chm. Total Staff 8.

Sacred Heart Health System, Inc. DBA: Sacred Heart Hospital of Pensacola; Sacred Heart Hospital on the Emerald Coast; Sacred Heart Hospital on the Gulf. 5151 N. Ninth Ave., 32504. Tel: 850-416-7000 ; Web: sacred-heart.org. Thomas VanOsdol, CEO; Tracie Loftis, Chief Mission Officer. Bed Capacity 669; Tot Asst. Annually 1,042,355; Total Staff 3,235.

Sacred Heart Health Ventures, Inc., 5151 N. Ninth Ave., 32504. Tel: 850-416-6500; Fax: 850-416-6119; Email: tracie.loftis@ascension.org. Susan Davis, Pres. Tot Asst. Annually 2,045.

[C] HOMES FOR AGED

PENSACOLA. *Haven of Our Lady of Peace, Inc.* (2000) 1900 Summit Blvd., 32503. Tel: 850-436-5900; Fax: 850-436-5959; Email: miperez@ascension.org. Martha Perez, N. H. Admin. Bed Capacity 120; Tot Asst. Annually 712; Total Staff 210.

[D] APARTMENTS FOR THE ELDERLY AND HANDICAPPED

TALLAHASSEE. *Casa Calderon, Inc.*, 800 W. Virginia St., Tallahassee, 32304. Tel: 850-222-4026; Fax: 850-222-4026. Rev. John Cayer, Pres.; Ms. Barbara Caesar, Mgr. Total Staff 6; Total Assisted 111.

[E] MONASTERIES AND RESIDENCES FOR PRIESTS AND BROTHERS

TALLAHASSEE. *Brotherhood of Hope*, 900 W. Tennessee St., Tallahassee, 32304. Tel: 850-580-3553; Email: brother@brohope.net; Web: www.brotherhoodofhope.org. Bros. Raul Bunsa, B.H., Superior; Theodore Psemeneki, Rel. Order Leader; Clinton Reed IV, Campus Mininister; Ray Morris, B.H., Campus Minister; Brant Haglund, Campus Minister.

[F] CONVENT AND RESIDENCES FOR SISTERS

SUNNY HILLS. *Vestiarki Sisters of Jesus (Poland)* (1882) 3919 Vistula Dr., Sunny Hills, 32428. Tel: 850-773-3302; Email: vestiarki@att.net. Sr. Natalia Kwiateck, Supr. Sisters 6; Total Assisted 4.

[G] HOMELESS SHELTERS

PANAMA CITY. *St. Barnabas House*, 2943 E 11th St., Panama City, 32401. Tel: 850-624-0668; Fax: 850-763-2969; Email: langand@cc.ptdiocese.org. c/o Catholic Charities, 3128 E. 11th St., Panama City, 32401. Ms. Diane Langan, Contact Person. Bed Capacity 14; Tot Asst. Annually 34; Total in Residence 2; Total Staff 2.

[H] MISCELLANEOUS

PENSACOLA. *The Catholic Foundation of Northwest Florida, Inc.*, 11 N. B St., 32502. Tel: 850-435-3500 ; Fax: 850-435-3568; Email: kennedyj@ptdiocese.org; Web: www.ptdiocese.org. John Godlewski, Dir. Fin.

Joseph House LLC, 11 North B St., 32502.

TALLAHASSEE. *Florida Catholic Conference* (1969) Office: 201 W. Park Ave., Tallahassee, 32301-7760. Tel: 850-205-6820; Fax: 850-205-6849; Email: flacathconf@flacathconf.org; Web: www.flaccb.org. Mr. Michael Sheedy, Exec. Dir.

Magnificat of Tallahassee, Inc. (Mary, Mother of Mercy and Hope Chapter) 1232 Blockford Ct. W., Tallahassee, 32317. Tel: 850-321-8174; Email: terrylshine@gmail.com; Email: magnificattallahassee@gmail.com. Terry Shine, Pres. & Coord.

Martyrs of La Florida Missions, Incorporated, 1230 Archangel Way, Tallahassee, 32317-9636. Tel: 850-445-1326; Email: Secretary@MartyrsOfLaFloridaMissions.org. P.O. Box 12062, Tallahassee, 32317-2062. Mr. Michael Sheedy, Pres.; Heather Jordan, Sec.

PANAMA CITY. *St. Dominic Media Production Center*, 3308 E. 15th St., Panama City, 32405. Tel: 850-914-0072; Email: catholicinamerica.manager@gmail.com. Rev. Michael J. Nixon, Dir.

RELIGIOUS INSTITUTES OF MEN REPRESENTED IN THE DIOCESE

For further details refer to the corresponding bracketed number in the Religious Institutes of Men or Women section.

[]—*Brothers of Hope* (Benedictine - St. Meinrad, IN).
[0585]—*Heralds of the Good News*—H.G.N.
[]—*Missionaries of the Sacred Heart*—M.S.C.
[0870]—*Montfort Missionaries*—S.M.M.
[0200]—*Order of St. Benedict*—O.S.B.
[0610]—*Priests of Congregation of Holy Cross*—C.S.C.
[]—*Society of the Divine Word*—S.V.D.

RELIGIOUS INSTITUTES OF WOMEN REPRESENTED IN THE DIOCESE

[0130]—*Apostles of the Sacred Heart of Jesus*—A.S.C.J.
[1070-03]—*Dominican Sisters - Sinsinawa*—O.P.
[]—*Franciscan Sisters of Penance of the Sorrowful Mother*—T.O.R.
[]—*Lovers of the Holy Cross of Thu Thiem*—L.H.C.
[]—*Missionaries of Divine Love*—M.D.L.
[1650]—*Sisters of St. Francis of Philadelphia*—O.S.F.
[]—*Vestiarki Sisters of Jesus* (Poland)—V.S.J.

An asterisk (*) denotes an organization that has established tax-exempt status directly with the IRS and is not covered by the USCCB Group Ruling.

Diocese of Peoria

(Dioecesis Peoriensis)

Most Reverend

DANIEL R. JENKY, C.S.C.

Bishop of Peoria; ordained April 6, 1974; appointed Auxiliary Bishop of Fort Wayne-South Bend and Titular Bishop of Amantia October 21, 1997; consecrated December 16, 1997; appointed Bishop of Peoria February 12, 2002; installed April 10, 2002. *Office: 419 N.E. Madison Ave., Peoria, IL 61603.*

Chancery: 419 N.E. Madison Ave., Peoria, IL 61603. Tel: 309-671-1550; Fax: 309-671-1576.

ESTABLISHED 1877.

Square Miles 16,933.

A cross-section of Illinois, bounded on the north by the Counties of Whiteside, Lee, De Kalb, Grundy and Iroquois, and on the east by Kendall, Grundy, Kankakee and Ford, and on the south by Adams, Brown, Cass, Menard, Sangamon, Macon, Moultrie, Douglas and Edgar; comprising the Counties of Bureau, Champaign, Dewitt, Fulton, Hancock, Henderson, Henry, Knox, La Salle, Livingston, Logan, Marshall, Mason, McDonough, McLean, Mercer, Peoria, Piatt, Putnam, Rock Island, Schuyler, Stark, Tazewell, Vermilion, Warren and Woodford.

For legal titles of parishes and diocesan institutions, consult the Chancery.

STATISTICAL OVERVIEW

Personnel	
Bishop	1
Abbots	1
Priests: Diocesan Active in Diocese	111
Priests: Diocesan Active Outside Diocese	8
Priests: Retired, Sick or Absent	50
Number of Diocesan Priests	169
Religious Priests in Diocese	24
Total Priests in Diocese	193
Extern Priests in Diocese	10
Ordinations:	
Diocesan Priests	2
Transitional Deacons	1
Permanent Deacons in Diocese	155
Total Brothers	10
Total Sisters	163
Parishes	
Parishes	157
With Resident Pastor:	
Resident Diocesan Priests	134
Resident Religious Priests	13
Without Resident Pastor:	
Administered by Priests	10
Pastoral Centers	7
Closed Parishes	3

Professional Ministry Personnel:	
Brothers	4
Sisters	26
Lay Ministers	115
Welfare	
Catholic Hospitals	13
Total Assisted	6,749,581
Homes for the Aged	2
Total Assisted	144
Day Care Centers	1
Total Assisted	104
Special Centers for Social Services	1
Total Assisted	8,930
Educational	
Diocesan Students in Other Seminaries	19
Total Seminarians	19
Colleges and Universities	1
Total Students	350
High Schools, Diocesan and Parish	5
Total Students	2,091
High Schools, Private	1
Total Students	320
Elementary Schools, Diocesan and Parish	37
Total Students	8,427

Catechesis/Religious Education:	
High School Students	110
Elementary Students	1,896
Total Students under Catholic Instruction	13,213
Teachers in the Diocese:	
Priests	7
Brothers	2
Sisters	30
Lay Teachers	776
Vital Statistics	
Receptions into the Church:	
Infant Baptism Totals	1,700
Minor Baptism Totals	99
Adult Baptism Totals	181
Received into Full Communion	257
First Communions	2,031
Confirmations	2,567
Marriages:	
Catholic	391
Interfaith	206
Total Marriages	597
Deaths	1,777
Total Catholic Population	139,835
Total Population	1,492,335

Former Bishops—Most Revs. JOHN LANCASTER SPALDING, D.D., cons. May 1, 1877; resigned Sept. 11, 1908; Titular Archbishop of Scitopolis; appt. Oct. 14, 1908; died Aug. 25, 1916; EDMUND M. DUNNE, D.D., ord. June 24, 1887; cons. Sept. 1, 1909; died Oct. 17, 1929; JOSEPH H. SCHLARMAN, Ph.D., J.C.D., ord. June 29, 1904; cons. June 17, 1930; named Assistant at Papal Throne, Nov. 16, 1950; Archbishop ad personam; appt. June 27, 1951; died Nov. 10, 1951; WILLIAM E. COUSINS, D.D., ord. April 23, 1927; Titular Bishop of Forma and Auxiliary Bishop of Chicago; appt. Dec. 17, 1948; cons. March 7, 1949; Bishop of Peoria; appt. May 21, 1952; Archbishop of Milwaukee; appt. Dec. 17, 1958; died Sept. 14, 1988; JOHN B. FRANZ, D.D., ord. June 13, 1920; Bishop of Dodge City; appt. May 29, 1951; cons. Aug. 29, 1951; transferred to Peoria, Aug. 8, 1959; installed Nov. 4, 1959; retired June 1, 1971; died July 3, 1992; EDWARD W. O'ROURKE, D.D., ord. May 28, 1944; Bishop of Peoria; appt. May 24, 1971; cons. July 15, 1971; retired Jan. 23, 1990; died Sept. 29, 1999; JOHN J. MYERS, J.C.D., ord. Dec. 17, 1966; appt. Coadjutor Bishop of Peoria July 7, 1987; ord. Sept. 3, 1987; succeeded to Bishop of Peoria, Jan. 23, 1990; appt. Archbishop of Newark July 24, 2001; installed Oct. 9, 2001.

Bishop's Office—419 N.E. Madison Ave., Peoria, 61603. Tel: 309-671-1550; Fax: 309-671-1576. Please direct all calls for the Bishop's Office to this numberOffice Hours: Mon.-Fri. 8:30-4:30.

Vicar General—Rev. Msgr. JAMES E. KRUSE, J.C.L., V.G., Mailing Address: Spalding Pastoral Center, 419 N.E. Madison Ave., Peoria, 61603. Tel: 309-671-1550; Fax: 309-671-1576.

Chancellor—MS. PATRICIA GIBSON, J.C.L., J.D., Spalding Pastoral Center, 419 N.E. Madison Ave., Peoria, 61603. Tel: 309-671-1550; Fax: 309-671-1576.

Director of the Curia—MS. PATRICIA GIBSON, J.C.L., J.D., Spalding Pastoral Center, 419 N.E. Madison Ave., Peoria, 61603. Tel: 309-671-1550; Fax: 309-671-1576.

Development—Spalding Pastoral Center, 419 N.E. Madison Ave., Peoria, 61603. Tel: 309-671-1550; Fax: 309-671-1595. DEBBIE BENZ.

Directors of Finance—MR. RUSS COURTER, Parish & School Dir.; MR. MIKE BUCKLEY, Diocesan Dir., Spalding Pastoral Center, 419 N.E. Madison Ave., Peoria, 61603. Tel: 309-671-1550; Fax: 309-671-1597.

Legal Department—MS. PATRICIA GIBSON, J.C.L., J.D., Spalding Pastoral Center, 419 N.E. Madison Ave., Peoria, 61603-3720. Tel: 309-671-1550; Fax: 309-671-1576.

Diocesan Tribunal—Spalding Pastoral Center, 419 N.E. Madison Ave., Peoria, 61603.
Tel: 309-671-1550; Fax: 309-677-6798.
Judicial Vicar—Rev. Msgr. JAMES E. KRUSE, J.C.L., V.G.
Adjutant Judicial Vicar—Rev. Msgr. JASON A. GRAY, J.C.D.
Defender of the Bond—Rev. Msgr. ERIC S. POWELL.
Promoter of Justice—Rev. Msgr. ERIC S. POWELL.
Judges—MS. ADELA MARIA KIM, J.C.L.; Rev. Msgrs. JASON A. GRAY, J.C.D.; JAMES E. KRUSE, J.C.L., V.G.

Advocates—MRS. LINDA THOMAS; LIZ HEATWOLE.

Notaries—MRS. DEBRA WILLIAMS; DEBRA ANNE HILL.

Diocesan College of Consultors—Rev. Msgr. PAUL E. SHOWALTER, P.A., Vicar Gen., (Retired); Rev. GREGORY NELSON; Rev. Msgr. JAMES E. KRUSE, J.C.L., V.G.; Rev. PATRICK HENEHAN; Rev. Msgr. THOMAS MACK; Rev. STEPHEN A. WILLARD; Rev. Msgr. STANLEY L. DEPTULA, Spalding Pastoral Center, 419 N.E. Madison Ave., Peoria, 61603. Tel: 309-671-1550; Fax: 309-671-1576.

Vicariates and Vicars—Revs. DUSTIN P. SCHULTZ, Bloomington-Lincoln; JOEL PHELPS, Champaign; BOWAN M. SCHMITT, Danville; SCOTT ENGELBRECHT, Kewanee; GARY W. BLAKE, La Salle; Rev. Msgr. MARK J. MERDIAN, Rock Island; Rev. ANTHONY J. TROSLEY, Macomb; Rev. Msgrs. THOMAS MACK, Galesburg; PHILIP HALFACRE, Ottawa; Revs. MICHAEL J. ANDREJEK, Pekin; PATRICK HENEHAN, Peoria; DAVID SABEL, Pontiac.

Diocesan Offices and Directors

Finance Council (Canon 492)—Most Rev. DANIEL R. JENKY, C.S.C.; Rev. Msgrs. PAUL E. SHOWALTER, P.A., (Retired); JAMES E. KRUSE, J.C.L., V.G.; Sr. DIANE MARIE MCGREW, O.S.F.; Rev. ROBERT D. SPILMAN, (Retired); MR. VERNON WEGERER; MR. JOHN BANNON; MS. PATRICIA GIBSON, J.C.L., J.D.; MR. MIKE BUCKLEY; MR. RUSS COURTER; MR. DANIEL REYNOLDS; MR. ROBERT BRADY; MS. RITA KRESS, Spalding Pastoral Center, 419 N.E. Madison Ave., Peoria, 61603. Tel: 309-671-1550; Fax: 309-671-1595.

Liturgy, Churches and Chapels—419 N.E. Madison Ave., Peoria, 61603. Tel: 309-671-1550; Fax: 309-671-1573. MR. PHILIP LEE.

Catholic Cemeteries—Deacon ROBERT W. MYERS SR., Spalding Pastoral Center, 419 N.E. Madison Ave., Peoria, 61603. Tel: 309-671-1550; Fax: 309-671-1595.

Catholic Education Office—DR. SHARON WEISS, Supt., Catholic Schools, Spalding Pastoral Center, 419 N.E. Madison Ave., Peoria, 61603. Tel: 309-671-1550; Fax: 309-671-1595. Associate Superintendent: MR. KENNETH (JERRY) SANDERSON.

Respect Life & Human Dignity—419 N.E. Madison Ave., Peoria, 61603. CECILIA SONE.

Catholic Relief Services—419 N.E. Madison Ave., Peoria, 61603. Tel: 309-671-1550;

Fax: 309-671-1576. Rev. Msgr. JAMES E. KRUSE, J.C.L., V.G.

Catholic Women, Council of—Rev. Msgr. DALE L. WELLMAN, Moderator, 1608 13th St., Moline, 61265. Tel: 309-762-2362.

Censor Librorum—Rev. Msgr. PHILIP HALFACRE, St. Michael the Archangel Church, 801 Lundy St., Streator, 61364.

Clergymen's Aid, Inc.—Most Rev. DANIEL R. JENKY, C.S.C., Trustee & Ex Officio; Rev. Msgrs. PAUL E. SHOWALTER, P.A., Trustee & Ex Officio, (Retired); JAMES E. KRUSE, J.C.L., V.G.; Revs. PAUL CARLSON; PATRICK FIXSEN; Rev. Msgr. TIMOTHY NOLAN; Revs. JACOB ROSE; JOHNDAMASENI ZILIMU, Ph.D.; JEFFREY D. STIRNIMAN; JOEL PHELPS, 419 N.E. Madison Ave., Peoria, 61603. Tel: 309-671-1550; Fax: 309-671-1595.

Commission for Ecumenism—Rev. Msgr. JAMES E. KRUSE, J.C.L., V.G., 419 N.E. Madison Ave., Peoria, 61603. Tel: 309-671-1550.

Communications, Diocesan Office of—VACANT, 419 N.E. Madison, Peoria, 61603. Tel: 309-671-1550; Fax: 309-671-1595.

Cursillo Program—Spalding Renewal Center, 401 N.E. Madison Ave., Peoria, 61603. Tel: 309-676-5587. Deacon RICK MILLER, Diocesan Dir.

Diocesan Office of Development and Stewardship—Spalding Pastoral Center, 419 N.E. Madison Ave., Peoria, 61603. Tel: 309-671-1550; Fax: 309-671-1595. DEBBIE BENZ.

Diocesan Evangelization and Faith Formation—419 N.E. Madison Ave., Peoria, 61603. Sr. ANA PIA CORDUA, S.C.T.J.M.

Diocesan Office of Finance—MR. MIKE BUCKLEY, Diocesan Dir.; MR. RUSS COURTER, Parish & School Dir., Finance Office: Spalding Pastoral Center, 419 N.E. Madison Ave., Peoria, 61603. Tel: 309-671-1550; Fax: 309-671-1597.

Diocesan Hispanic Ministry Office—Spalding Pastoral Center, 419 N.E. Madison Ave., Peoria, 61603. Tel: 309-671-1550. Sr. ISABEL ROMERO, S.C.T.J.M., Dir.

Diocesan Office of Human Resources—KAREN SMALL, Dir., Spalding Pastoral Center, 419 N.E. Madison Ave., Peoria, 61603. Tel: 309-671-1550; Fax: 309-671-1583.

Diocesan Pastoral Council—Spalding Pastoral Center, 419 N.E. Madison Ave., Peoria, 61603. Tel: 309-671-1550; Fax: 309-671-1576. Rev. Msgr. JAMES E. KRUSE, J.C.L., V.G.

Diocesan Personnel Board—Spalding Pastoral Center, 419 N.E. Madison Ave., Peoria, 61603. Tel: 309-671-1550; Fax: 309-671-1576. Rev. Msgr. JAMES E. KRUSE, J.C.L., V.G.

Diocesan Director of Music—Tel: 309-671-1550. JON KROEPEL.

Divine Worship, Office of—Rev. Msgr. STANLEY L. DEPTULA, 419 N.E. Madison Ave., Peoria, 61603. Tel: 309-671-1550; Fax: 309-671-1573.

Holy Childhood Association—419 N.E. Madison Ave., Peoria, 61603. Tel: 309-671-1550. Rev. Msgr. JAMES E. KRUSE, J.C.L., V.G.

Office of Victims Assistance—419 N.E. Madison Ave., Peoria, 61603. Tel: 309-677-7082; Fax: 309-671-1576.

Office of Safe Environment—419 N.E. Madison Ave., Peoria, 61603. Tel: 309-671-1550. MR. KENNETH (JERRY) SANDERSON, Dir.

Newspaper-"The Catholic Post"—MR. THOMAS DERMODY, Editor-in-Chief, 419 N.E. Madison Ave., Peoria, 61603. Tel: 309-671-1550; Fax: 309-671-1579.

Nurses, Council of—VACANT.

Permanent Diaconate, Office of—Rev. Msgr. TIMOTHY NOLAN, Spalding Pastoral Center, 419 N.E. Madison Ave., Peoria, 61603. Tel: 309-671-1550; Fax: 309-671-1581.

Priests' Eucharistic League—Spalding Pastoral Center, 419 N.E. Madison Ave., Peoria, 61603. Tel: 309-671-1550; Fax: 309-671-1576. Rev. Msgr. JAMES E. KRUSE, J.C.L., V.G.

Propagation of the Faith419 N.E. Madison Ave., Peoria, 61603. Tel: 309-671-1550; Fax: 309-671-1576. Rev. Msgr. JAMES E. KRUSE, J.C.L., V.G.

Priests' Purgatorial Society—Spalding Pastoral Center, 419 N.E. Madison Ave., Peoria, 61603. Tel: 309-671-1550; Fax: 309-671-1576. Rev. Msgr. JAMES E. KRUSE, J.C.L., V.G.

Rural Life Conference—Rev. Msgr. THOMAS MACK, Dir., 210 W. Broadway, Monmouth, 61462.

Presbyteral Council—Rev. Msgr. PHILIP HALFACRE, Pres., Spalding Pastoral Center, 419 N.E. Madison, Peoria, 61603. Tel: 309-671-1550; Fax: 309-671-1576.

Catholic Charities—Sr. ANA PIA CORDUA, S.C.T.J.M., Exec. Dir., Senior Services, 711 N. Main St., Bloomington, 61701. Tel: 309-397-0822; Fax: 309-829-2243. Faith in Action, 803 W. Leander, Clinton, 61727. Tel: 217-935-2241. Guardian Angel Outreach, 405 Illinois St., Streator, 61364. Tel: 815-672-4567.

TEC—Deacon JAMES F. HEATWOLE, Spiritual Dir.; Rev. KYLE LUCAS, Spiritual Advisor, Spalding Renewal Center, 401 N.E. Madison Ave., Peoria, 61603. Tel: 309-676-4001; Fax: 309-676-4022; Email: tecinfo@peoriacursillotec.com.

Vocations Office—Revs. PATRICK HENEHAN, Formation; TIMOTHY HEPNER, Recruitment, Spalding Pastoral Center, 419 N.E. Madison Ave., Peoria, 61603. Tel: 309-671-1550; Fax: 309-671-1581.

Christ Child Society of Central Illinois—415 N.E. Monroe, Peoria, 61603. Tel: 309-637-1713; Email: christchildsociety@gmail.com.

Christ Child Society of the Quad Cities—Mailing Address: P.O. Box 6184, Rock Island, 61201. Email: ccsqc@yahoo.com. SHELLY HUISKAMP.

CLERGY, PARISHES, MISSIONS AND PAROCHIAL SCHOOLS

CITY OF PEORIA

(PEORIA COUNTY)

1—ST. MARY'S CATHEDRAL (1846) (Linked Parishes: St. Bernard, Peoria, Sacred Heart, Peoria & St. Joseph, Peoria)
607 N.E. Madison Ave., 61603. Tel: 309-673-6317. 504 Fulton St., 61602. Most Rev. Daniel R. Jenky, C.S.C.; Revs. Alexander Millar, Rector; James Pankiewicz, Parochial Vicar; Deacon Toby Tyler.
Catechesis Religious Program—Students 207.

2—ST. ANN (1994)
Mailing Address: 1010 S. Louisa St., 61605.
Tel: 309-674-5072; Fax: 309-655-1566; Email: stann_parish@comcast.net. Rev. Donald F. Roszkowski, Admin.; Deacons William Sloman; Stephen Cenek; Bruce Steiner; Sr. Judith Croegaert, O.S.B., Pastoral Assoc.
Catechesis Religious Program—Students 71.

3—ST. BERNARD'S (1903) (Linked Parishes: St. Mary Cathedral, Peoria, Sacred Heart, Peoria, & St. Joseph, Peoria)
509 E. Kansas Ave., 61603. Tel: 309-673-6317; Fax: 309-673-6300; Email: b.stbernards@comcast.net. 504 Fulton St., 61602. Revs. Alexander Millar; James Pankiewicz, Parochial Vicar.
Catechesis Religious Program—(Linked Parishes: St. Peter's & St. Mary's Cathedral) Students 17.

4—ST. BONIFACE'S (1881) (German), Closed. For inquiries for parish records contact St. Ann, Peoria.

5—ST. CECILIA'S, Closed. For Sacramental records write St. Philomena, 3300 N. Twelve Oaks Dr., Peoria, IL 61604.

6—HOLY FAMILY (1956)
3720 N. Sterling Ave., 61615.
Tel: 309-688-3427, Ext. 200; Email: parish.office@peoriaholyfamily.com. Revs. Paul Langevin; Giles Gilbert, Parochial Vicar; Anthony Labedis, O.-F.M.Conv., In Res.; Deacon Joseph Lahood.
School—Holy Family School, 2329 W. Reservoir, 61615. Tel: 309-688-2931; Fax: 309-681-5687; Email: dre@peoriahfs.com. Mrs. Anastacia Gianessi, Prin. Clergy 1; Lay Teachers 25; Students 180.
Catechesis Religious Program—Amy Coulter, D.R.E. Students 11.

7—ST. JOHN'S (1890) (Irish), Closed. For inquiries for parish records contact St. Ann, Peoria.

8—ST. JOSEPH (1976) (Linked Parishes: Sacred Heart, Peoria, St. Mary Cathedral, Peoria & St. Bernard, Peoria)
504 Fulton St., 61602. Tel: 309-676-0726;
Fax: 309-673-6330; Email: b.stbernards@comcast.net; Web: catholicpeoria.com. Revs. Alexander Millar, Admin.; James Pankiewicz.
Church: 103 Richard Pryor Pl., 61605.
Child Care—Southside Catholic Child Care Center, 1010 W. Johnson, 61605.

9—ST. JUDE (1975) [CEM]
10811 N. Knoxville Ave., 61615.
Tel: 309-243-7811, Ext. 2200; Email: stjude@stjudecatholic.com; Web: www.stjudechurchpeoria.org. Revs. Patrick Henehan; Andru O'Brien, Parochial Vicar; Deacons Thomas Rapach; Roger Hunter.
Catechesis Religious Program—
Tel: 309-243-7811, Ext. 2212; Email: disbell@stjudecatholic.com. Drew Isbell, D.R.E. Students 365.
Convent—Dominican Sisters of Mary, Mother of the Eucharist, 10809 N. Knoxville Ave., 61615. Sisters 6.

10—ST. MARK'S aka St. Mark Roman Catholic Parish (1891)
1113 W. Bradley Ave., 61606-1722.
Tel: 309-673-1263; Fax: 309-637-1484; Email: stmark@saint-mark.net. Rev. Msgr. Brian Brownsey; Rev. Richard Nguta, Parochial Vicar; Deacons John Skender; James F. Heatwole.
School—St. Mark's School, 711 N. Underhill, 61606.
Tel: 309-676-7131; Fax: 309-677-8060; Email: ndillon@saint-mark.net; Web: www.school.saint-mark.net. Dr. Noreen Dillon, Prin. Clergy 3; Lay Teachers 18; Students 179.
Catechesis Religious Program—Tel: 309-497-2838; Email: tmischler@saint-mark.net. Theresa Mischler, D.R.E. Students 48.

11—ST. PETER'S (1897) Closed. For inquiries for parish records, contact St. Bernard Parish, Peoria.

12—ST. PHILOMENA (1945) [JC]
1000 N Albany Ave., 61604-1419. Tel: 309-682-8642; Email: parish@stphils.com; Web: www.stphils.com. Revs. David P. Richardson; Kyle Lucas, In Res.; Deacon Michael C. Schallmoser.
Res.: 3312 N. Twelve Oaks Dr., 61604.
School—St. Philomena School, 3216 N. Emery Ave., 61604. Tel: 309-685-1208; Fax: 309-681-5676; Email: school@stphils.com; Web: www.stphils.com. Mrs. Jodi Peine, Prin.; Mr. Jack Dippold, Asst. Prin. Lay Teachers 28; Students 455.
Catechesis Religious Program—Ms. Jenny Witt, D.R.E. Students 470.

13—SACRED HEART (1879) (German) (Linked parishes: St. Joseph, Peoria, St. Mary Cathedral, Peoria & Sacred Heart, Peoria)
504 Fulton St., 61602. Tel: 309-673-6317; Email: b.stbernards@comcast.net. Revs. Alexander Millar, Admin.; James Pankiewicz.

14—ST. THOMAS (1937)
904 E. Lake Ave., Peoria Heights, 61616.
Tel: 309-688-3446, Ext. 1300; Email: parishoffice@stthomas-church.net; Web: www.stthomaspeoria.org. Rev. Msgr. Jason A. Gray, J.C.D.; Rev. Paul V. Stark, S.J., Parochial Vicar; Deacons Francis L. Eaton; Mark T. Kelsch; John R. Nelson; Edmund Mallow.
School—St. Thomas the Apostle School, (Grades PreSchool-8), 4229 N. Monroe, Peoria Heights, 61616. Tel: 309-685-2533; Fax: 309-681-7262; Email: office@stthomas-school.net; Web: school.stthomaspeoria.org. Mrs. Maureen Bentley, Prin. Lay Teachers 30; Students 417.
Catechesis Religious Program—Students 69.

15—ST. VINCENT DE PAUL (1962)
6001 N. University St., 61614. Tel: 309-691-3602; Email: svdppeoria@hotmail.com. Revs. Stephen A. Willard; Thomas Taylor; Deacons Robert W. Myers Sr.; Thomas DeBernardis.
School—St. Vincent De Paul School,
Tel: 309-691-5012; Email: svdpoffice@svdpvikings.com; Web: www.svdpvikings.com. Patsy Santen, Prin. Lay Teachers 24; Students 372.
Catechesis Religious Program—Email: shogan@svdpvikings.com. Sarah Hogan, D.R.E. Students 70.

OUTSIDE THE CITY OF PEORIA

ABINGDON, KNOX CO., SACRED HEART (1924) (Linked Parishes: St. Patrick, Galesburg & Corpus Christi, Galesburg)
506 N. Main St., Abingdon, 61410. Tel: 309-343-8256; Email: adorecc7@gmail.com. Rev. William T. Miller.
Catechesis Religious Program—Students 4.

ALEDO, MERCER CO., ST. CATHERINE'S CHURCH (1914) [CEM] (Linked Parishes: St. Anthony, Matherville & St. John, Viola)
106 N.E. Fourth, Aledo, 61231. Tel: 309-582-7500; Email: lcstc@hotmail.com. Rev. John Thieryoung.
Catechesis Religious Program—Students 28.
Linked Parish: St. Anthony, Matherville—
Linked Parish: St. John, Viola.

ALEXIS, WARREN CO., ST. THERESA'S (1877) [CEM] (Swedish), Closed. Sacramental records located at Immaculate Conception, Monmouth.

ANDALUSIA, ROCK ISLAND CO., ST. PATRICK CHURCH (1974)
9619 140th St. W., Taylor Ridge, 61284. P.O. Box 249, Andalusia, 61232. Rev. Charles Klamut.
Catechesis Religious Program—Students 60.

ANNAWAN, HENRY CO., SACRED HEART (1893) [CEM] (Linked Parish: St. Anthony, Annawan)
305 W. South Ave., Annawan, 61234.
Tel: 309-936-7900; Email: office@stanthonysatkinson.org. P.O. Box 210, Atkinson, 61235. Deacon Nicholas Simon, Sacramental Min.; Rev. S. Stephen Engelbrecht; Deacon Marshall Plumley, Sacramental Min.
Res.: 204 W. Main St., Atkinson, 61235.
Catechesis Religious Program—Students 26.
Linked Parish: St. Anthony, Annawan, 61234.

ARLINGTON, BUREAU CO., ST. PATRICK'S (1864) [CEM] (Linked Parishes: Holy Trinity, Cherry & St. Thomas More, Dalzell)
P.O. Box 159, Cherry, 61317. Tel: 815-894-2006; Email: holytsp@gmail.com; Web: www.bureaucatholic.org. Rev. Patrick Fixsen.
Res.: 302 Chestnut St., Dalzell, 61320.

ATKINSON, HENRY CO., ST. ANTHONY'S (1870) [CEM] (Belgian) (Linked Parish: Sacred Heart, Annawan)
204 W. Main St., P.O. Box 210, Atkinson, 61235-0210. Tel: 309-936-7900; Email: office@stanthonysatkinson.org. Rev. S. Stephen Engelbrecht; Deacons Marshall Plumley, Sacramental Min.; Nicholas Simon, Sacramental Min., Email: nicksimon@juno.com.
Catechesis Religious Program—Students 23.

BARTONVILLE, PEORIA CO., ST. ANTHONY (1969)
2525 S. Skyway Rd., Bartonville, 61607-1458. Tel: 309-697-0645; Web: www.stanthonybartonville.com. Rev. David C. Heinz; Deacon Louis Tomlianovich.
Catechesis Religious Program—Tel: 309-697-0627; Email: kcampbell@stanthonybartonville.com. Karen Campbell, D.R.E. Students 80.

BEMENT, PIATT CO., ST. MICHAEL (1891) (Linked Parish: St. Philomena, Monticello)
332 S. Macon, Bement, 61813. Tel: 217-762-2566; Fax: 217-762-8666; Email: St.PhilomenaChurch@yahoo.com; Web: stphilomenaonline.org. 1301 N. Market St., Monticello, 61856. Rev. Bruce Lopez; Deacon Gene Triplett.
Catechesis Religious Program—Students 4.

BENSON, WOODFORD CO., ST. JOHN (1873) [CEM] (Linked Parish: St. Mary's El Paso)
209 Jefferson St., Benson, 61516. Tel: 309-527-4555; Email: stmaryselpaso@fairpoint.net. P.O. Box 197, El Paso, 61738. Rev. Robert Rayson.
Catechesis Religious Program—Michelle Boland, C.R.E. Students 17.

BLACKSTONE, LIVINGSTON CO., ST. BERNARD, Closed. For inquiries for sacramental records contact St. Michael the Archangel, Streator.

BLOOMINGTON, MCLEAN CO.

1—HOLY TRINITY (1853) [CEM] (Linked Parishes: St. Patrick, Bloomington; St. Patrick, Wapella)
711 N. Main St., Bloomington, 61701. Tel: 309-829-2197; Email: office@holytrinitybloomington.org; Web: www.holytrinitybloomington.org. Revs. Jeffrey D. Stirniman, Admin.; Geoffrey Horton, Parochial Vicar; Deacons Brendan Carolan; James Gore; Robert Hermes; Michael A. Marvin; Joe Knapp; Albert Lundy; Todd Weber.
Catechesis Religious Program—Mr. Kevin O'Connell, Dir. of Discipleship; Mrs. Catalina Drew, RCIA Coord. Students 112.

2—ST. MARY'S (1867) [CEM] (German)
527 W. Jackson St., Bloomington, 61701. Tel: 309-827-8526; Email: stmarysparish@frontier.com; Web: www.stmarysbloomington.org. Revs. Gregory Nelson; John Pham; Timothy Hepner, In Res.; Deacons Jose Montenegro; Loren Keim; Antonio Herrera.
School—St. Mary's School, 603 W. Jackson St., Bloomington, 61701. Tel: 309-828-5954; Web: www.stmarysschool.net. Lay Teachers 21; Students 134.
Catechesis Religious Program—Students 135.

3—ST. PATRICK (1892) [JC] (Linked Parishes: Holy Trinity, Bloomington; St. Patrick, Wapella)
1209 W. Locust St., Bloomington, 61701. Tel: 309-829-1344; Email: office@historicsaintpatrick.org; Web: www.historicsaintpatrick.org. Revs. Jeffrey D. Stirniman, Admin.; Geoffrey Horton, Parochial Vicar; Deacons Todd Weber; Robert Hermes; Joe Knapp; Albert Lundy; Michael A. Marvin.
Catechesis Religious Program—Students 26.

4—ST. PATRICK CHURCH OF MERNA (1890) [CEM] (Linked Parish: St. Mary, Downs)
1000 N. Towanda Barnes Rd., Bloomington, 61705. Tel: 309-662-7361; Email: office@stpatrickmerna.org; Web: stpatrickmerna.org. Revs. Dustin P. Schultz; Michael Pica; Deacons Gayle E. Cryulik; Michael Pool.
Catechesis Religious Program—Students 595.

BRADFORD, STARK CO., ST. JOHN THE BAPTIST (1876) [CEM] (Linked Parish: St. Dominic, Wyoming)
218 First St., Bradford, 61421. Tel: 309-897-4081; Email: stdominicwy@hotmail.com. Rev. John Cyr.
Catechesis Religious Program—Students 9.

BRIMFIELD, PEORIA CO., ST. JOSEPH'S (1852) [CEM] (Irish) (Linked Parish: St. James, Williamsfield)
314 West Clay, Brimfield, 61517. Tel: 309-446-3275; Email: parishoffice@stjosephbrimfield.org. Mailing Address: P.O. Box 199, Brimfield, 61517. Rev. John M. Verrier.
Catechesis Religious Program—Students 39.
Linked Parish: St. James, Williamsfield, Knox Co. 61489.

BUDD, LIVINGSTON CO., ST. BERNARD'S, Closed. For parish records contact Church of the St. Michael the Archangel, Streator.

BUSHNELL, MCDONOUGH CO., ST. BERNARD (1877) (Linked Parish: St. Augustine, St. Augustine)
376 W. Hail St., Bushnell, 61422. Tel: 309-772-2333; Email: st.bbushnell@gmail.com. Rev. Patrick O'Neal.
Catechesis Religious Program—Students 15.

CAMP GROVE, MARSHALL CO., ST. PATRICK (1866) [CEM] (Irish), Closed. Sacramental records located at St. Dominic, Wyoming.

CAMPUS, LIVINGSTON CO., SACRED HEART (1882) [CEM] (Irish), Merged with St. Patrick, Dwight. Sacramental records are located at St. Patrick, Dwight.

CANTON, FULTON CO., ST. MARY'S (1862) [CEM 2] (Merged with: St. Michael, St. David)
159 E. Chestnut St., Canton, 61520. Tel: 309-647-1473; Email: st.marys1@hotmail.com. 139 E. Chestnut St., Canton, 61520. Rev. Daniel Ebker.
Catechesis Religious Program—Tel: 309-647-1476. Students 73.
Linked Parish: St. Michael Parish, 528 4th St., Saint David, 61563. Merged into St. Mary's, Canton, IL.

CARTHAGE, HANCOCK CO., IMMACULATE CONCEPTION (1860) [CEM] (Linked Parishes: Sacred Heart, Dallas City, St. Mary, Hamilton, Sacred Heart Warsaw and Sts. Peter & Paul, Nauvoo)
125 N. Fayette St., Carthage, 62354. Tel: 217-453-2428; Tel: 217-357-3087; Email: info@hancockcountycatholic.org; Web: www.HancockCountyCatholic.org. Revs. Anthony J. Trosley; Thomas R. Szydlik.
Catechesis Religious Program—Carrie Carroll, D.R.E. Students 56.

CHAMPAIGN, CHAMPAIGN CO.

1—HOLY CROSS (1912)
405 W. Clark St., Champaign, 61820. Tel: 217-352-8748; Email: office@holycrosscatholic.org. Revs. Joseph P. Donton; Remigius Ntahondi, Parochial Vicar; Deacons Edward Mohrbacher; Michael Smith.
School—Holy Cross School, 410 W. White St., Champaign, 61820. Tel: 217-356-9521; Fax: 217-356-1745; Email: meyersm@holycrosselem.org; Web: www.holycrosselem.org. Joseph McDaniel, Prin. Lay Teachers 26; Students 292.
Catechesis Religious Program—Tel: 217-352-8748; Fax: 217-366-2929. Cindy Howie, D.R.E. Students 34.

2—ST. JOHN'S CATHOLIC CHAPEL (1918) (For Catholic Students at the University of Illinois)
604 E. Armory Ave., Champaign, 61820. Tel: 217-344-1266; Email: info@sjcnc.org; Web: www.sjcnc.org. Revs. Robert Lampitt; Chase Hilgenbrinck.
Newman Hall, 604 E. Armory Ave., Champaign, 61820. Tel: 217-344-1266; Email: info@sjcnc.org; Web: www.sjcnc.org.
Legal Title: Newman Foundation. Bed Capacity 586.

3—ST. MARY'S (1854) [CEM]
612 E. Park St., Champaign, 61820. Tel: 217-352-8364; Fax: 217-352-6859; Email: stmary@stmary-cu.org. Rev. Fredi Gomeztorres.
Catechesis Religious Program—Students 138.

4—ST. MATTHEW (1965) (Linked Parish: St. Boniface, Seymour)
1303 Lincolnshire Dr., Champaign, 61821. Tel: 217-359-4224; Web: stmatt.net. Rev. Msgr. Stanley L. Deptula; Revs. Eric Bolek; Lee Brokaw.
School—St. Matthew School, 1307 Linconshire Dr., Champaign, 61821. Tel: 217-359-4114; Fax: 217-359-8319; Email: mbiggs@stmatt.net; Web: stmatt.net. Michelle Biggs, Prin. Lay Teachers 24; Students 385; Clergy / Religious Teachers 3.
Catechesis Religious Program—Email: jtaylor@stmatt.net. Joseph Taylor, D.R.E. Students 170.
Convent—Sisters of St. Francis of the Martyr St. George, 1719 Robert Dr., Champaign, 61821.

CHATSWORTH, LIVINGSTON CO., SS. PETER AND PAUL (1877) [CEM] (German—Irish), Closed. Sacramental records are located at St. Andrew Church, Fairbury.

CHENOA, MCLEAN CO., ST. JOSEPH'S (1859) [CEM] (Linked Parishes: St. Mary, Lexington & St. Joseph, Colfax)
225 W. Owsley, Chenoa, 61726. Tel: 815-945-2561; Tel: 815-844-7683; Email: stmaryspontiac@mchsi.com. 119 E. Howard St., P.O. Box 374, Pontiac, 61764. Rev. David Sable.
Catechesis Religious Program—Students 87.
Linked Parish: St. Mary, 201 Lee St., Lexington, McLean Co. 61753.

CHERRY, BUREAU CO., HOLY TRINITY (1904) [CEM] (Linked Parishes: St. Patrick, Arlington & St. Thomas More, Dalzell)
212 S. Main, P.O. Box 159, Cherry, 61317. Tel: 815-894-2006; Email: holytsp@gmail.com; Web: www.bureaucatholic.org. Rev. Patrick Fixsen.
Catechesis Religious Program—Email: juliehtc@outlook.com. Julie Hollinger, D.R.E. Students 82.

CHILLICOTHE, PEORIA CO., ST. EDWARD (1900) [CEM]
1216 N. 6th St., Chillicothe, 61523. Tel: 309-274-3809; Email: info@sainted.org. Rev. Msgr. Michael C. Bliss; Deacons John W. Merdian; Bob Pomazal; Gregory Serangeli.
School—St. Edward School, 1221 N. Fifth St., Chillicothe, 61523. Tel: 309-274-2994; Fax: 309-274-4141. Mr. Mike Domico, Prin. Lay Teachers 13; Students 97.
Catechesis Religious Program—Students 65.

CLINTON, DE WITT CO., ST. JOHN THE BAPTIST CATHOLIC CHURCH (1879) (Linked Parishes: Sacred Heart, Farmer City & St. John the Evangelist, Bellflower)
502 N. Monroe St., Clinton, 61727. Tel: 217-935-3727 ; Email: stjohnsclinton@yahoo.com; Web: www.clintonstjohns.org. Rev. James P. Henning, O.F.M.-Conv.; Deacons Patrick J. Comfort; Scott Whitehouse.
Res.: 612 N. Plum, Farmer City, 61842.
Catechesis Religious Program—Sue Neuschwanger, D.R.E. Students 31.

COAL VALLEY, ROCK ISLAND CO., ST. MARIA GORETTI (1972) (Linked Parish: Our Lady of Peace, Orion)
220 E. 22nd Ave., P.O. Box 159, Coal Valley, 61240. Tel: 309-799-3414; Email: smg@smgcv.org; Web: smgcv.org. Rev. Anthony M. Ego; Deacon Thomas C. Gainey.
Catechesis Religious Program—Email: smgdre@aol.com. Jammie Jamieson, D.R.E. Students 22.

COLFAX, MCLEAN CO., ST. JOSEPH'S (1850) (Linked Parishes: St. Joseph, Chenoa & St. Mary, Lexington)
107 W. North, P.O. Box 169, Colfax, 61728. Tel: 815-945-2561; Email: bcdc79@mchsi.com. Rev. David Sabel.
Catechesis Religious Program—Students 7.

COLONA, HENRY CO., ST. PATRICK'S (1941)
201 First St., Colona, 61241. Tel: 309-792-3854; Email: stpatcolona1954@gmail.com. Rev. Peter Zorjan; Deacons Al Angelo, Sacramental Min.; Aaron Hoste, Sacramental Min.; Matthew Levy, Sacramental Min.
Catechesis Religious Program—Rose Roe, C.R.E. Students 29.

CREVE COEUR, TAZEWELL CO., SACRE COEUR (1954) Closed. Sacramental records are located at St. Joseph Church, Pekin, IL.

CULLOM, LIVINGSTON CO., ST. JOHN'S (1881) [CEM]
113 W. Van Alstyne St., P.O. Box 376, Cullom, 60929. Tel: 815-844-7683; Email: stmaryspontiac@mchsi.com. Revs. David Sabel, Admin.; William Keebler; Adam Cesarek, Parochial Vicar; Deacon R.J. Wallace.
Res.: 119 E. Howard, Pontiac, 61764.
Catechesis Religious Program—

DALZELL, BUREAU CO., ST. THOMAS MORE (1934) (Italian) (Linked Parishes: St. Patrick, Arlington & Holy Trinity, Cherry)
302 Chestnut, Dalzell, 61320. Tel: 815-663-6201; Email: holytsp@gmail.com; Web: www.bureaucatholic.org. Rev. Patrick Fixsen.
Catechesis Religious Program—

DANVILLE, VERMILION CO.

1—HOLY FAMILY (1978) [CEM]
444 E. Main St., Danville, 61832. Tel: 217-431-5100; Email: office@holyfamilydanville.net; Web: holyfamilydanville.net. Rev. Steven P. Loftus.
Catechesis Religious Program—Students 60.

2—ST. PAUL'S (1910)
1303 N. Walnut St., Danville, 61832. Tel: 217-442-5313; Email: cindyharden@stpauldanville.org; Web: stpauldanville.org. Rev. Bowan M. Schmitt.
School—St. Paul's School, 2112 N. Vermilion St., Danville, 61832. Tel: 217-442-2725; Fax: 217-442-0293. Mrs. Gail Lewis, Prin. Lay Teachers 31; Students 352.
Catechesis Religious Program—Email: jennifermartindill@stpauldanville.org. Jennifer Martindill, D.R.E. Students 25.

DELAVAN, TAZEWELL CO., ST. MARY'S (1867) [CEM] (Linked Parish: St. Joseph, Hopedale)
505 E. 4th St., P.O. Box 769, Delavan, 61734. Tel: 309-244-8516; Email: secretary.stmary@mchsi.com; Web: stmarydelavan.org. Rev. Msgr. Timothy Nolan.
Catechesis Religious Program—Students 41.
Linked Parish: St. Joseph's, Hopedale, Tazewell Co.

DEPUE, BUREAU CO., ST. MARY'S (1908) [CEM] (Linked Parish: St. Mary, Tiskilwa)
312 Park St., P.O. Box 19, DePue, 61322. Tel: 815-447-2552; Email: frcreegan@netscape.net. Rev. Kevin G. Creegan.
Catechesis Religious Program—Students 64.
Linked Parish: St. Mary, Tiskilwa, 61368.

DOWNS, MCLEAN CO., ST. MARY'S (1910) (Linked Parish: St. Patrick of Merna, Bloomington)
108 E. Washington St., P.O. Box 66, Downs, 61736. Tel: 309-662-7361; Email: officestmarydowns@gmail.com; Web: stmarysdowns.org. Revs. Dustin P.

Schultz; Michael Pica, Parochial Vicar; Deacon Gary D. Koerner.
Catechesis Religious Program—Students 75.

DUNLAP, PEORIA CO., ST. CLEMENT'S, Closed. For inquiries for parish records contact St. Jude, 10811 N. Knoxville, Peoria, IL 61615.

DWIGHT, LIVINGSTON CO., ST. PATRICK'S (1862) [CEM] (Irish) (Linked Parish: Sacred Heart, Campus)
Mailing Address: 114 W. Mazon Ave., Dwight, 60420. Tel: 815-584-3522; Email: stpatsdwight@att.net. Rev. Chris G. Haake.
Res.: 126 W. Mazon Ave., Dwight, 60420.
Sacred Heart.
Catechesis Religious Program—Tel: 815-584-3110; Email: st.patricks.dwight.dre@gmail.com. Mrs. Andrea Pugh, D.R.E. Students 42.

EAGLE TOWNSHIP, LA SALLE CO., ANNUNCIATION OF BLESSED VIRGIN MARY (1869) [CEM] (Irish), Closed. Merged into Parish of Sts. Peter & Paul, Leonore.

EARLVILLE, LA SALLE CO., ST. THERESA PARISH (1904) [CEM 2] (Linked Parishes: St. Patrick's, Seneca; St. Joseph, Marseilles; St. Patrick's, Ransom & St. Mary's, Grand Ridge)
221 W. Union St., Earlville, 60518. Tel: 815-246-4321 ; Email: parishgroup3@gmail.com; Web: www.st-theresa-earlville.com. Revs. Ghislain Inai; Odilon Amenyaglo, Parochial Vicar; Augustin Kassa, S.M.A., Parochial Vicar; Deacon Michael Evers.
Catechesis Religious Program—Students 34.

EAST MOLINE, ROCK ISLAND CO.

1—ST. ANNE (1919) (Linked Parishes: St. Mary, Moline)
555 18th Ave., East Moline, 61244.
Tel: 309-755-5071; Fax: 309-755-5343; Email: Office@saintanne-em.org; Web: www.saintanne-em.org. Rev. Antonio Dittmer.
School—Our Lady of Grace Catholic Academy, 603 18th Ave., East Moline, 61244. Tel: 309-755-9771; Fax: 309-755-7407; Email: office@olgca.org; Web: www.olgca.org. Joan Leonard, Prin. Lay Teachers 13; Students 169.
Catechesis Religious Program—Tel: 309-752-1878; Email: amy.rel.ed@gmail.com. Amy Virnig, D.R.E. Students 155.

2—ST. MARY'S (1907) (English—Spanish) (Linked Parish: St. Mary, Moline)
412 10th St., Moline, 61265. Tel: 309-764-1562; Fax: 309-764-0317; Email: stmarysmolineil@hotmail.com. Rev. Antonio Dittmer.
School—Our Lady of Grace Catholic Academy, 602 17th Ave., East Moline, 61244. Tel: 309-755-9771.
Catechesis Religious Program—Tel: 309-269-3754; Email: talenself@gmail.com. Lisa Forgie, D.R.E. Students 213.

EAST PEORIA, TAZEWELL CO., ST. MONICA CHURCH (1898) (Linked Parish: St. Patrick, Washington)
303 Campanile Dr., East Peoria, 61611.
Tel: 309-694-2061; Email: stmonica@hotmail.com. Revs. John Steffen; Binh K. Tran, Parochial Vicar; Deacons Charles Robbins; Stephen Racki III.
Catechesis Religious Program—Email: kharkn1161@gmail.com. Laurie Harkness, D.R.E. Students 21.

EL PASO, WOODFORD CO., ST. MARY'S (1863) [CEM 2]
79 W. Third St., P.O. Box 197, El Paso, 61738.
Tel: 309-527-4555; Email: stmaryselpaso@fairpoint.net. Rev. Robert Rayson.
Catechesis Religious Program—Tel: 309-527-3958. Kisha Craig, D.R.E. Students 93.

ELKHART, LOGAN CO., ST. PATRICK (1856) (Linked Parishes: St. Mary, Atlanta, St. Thomas Aquinas, Mount Pulaski & Holy Family, Lincoln)
Mailing Address: 316 S. Logan St., Lincoln, 62656. Tel: 217-732-4019; Email: frlaible@logancountycatholic.org. Revs. Jeffrey G. Laible; Edward U. Ohm, Parochial Vicar; Deacon Wendell Lowry III.
Catechesis Religious Program—Students 12.
Linked Parish: St. Thomas Aquinas, Mount Pulaski.
Catechesis Religious Program—Students 16.

ELMWOOD, PEORIA CO., ST. PATRICK'S (1870) [CEM] (Irish) (Linked Parish: St. Mary's Kickapoo)
802 W. Main St., Elmwood, 61529. Tel: 309-742-4921 ; Fax: 309-742-4921; Email: stpatrickcc@gmail.com. Rev. Joseph Dondanville.
Catechesis Religious Program—Students 66.

EUREKA, WOODFORD CO., ST. LUKE (1982) [JC] (Linked Parish: St. Joseph, Roanoke)
904 E. Reagan Dr., P.O. Box 226, Eureka, 61530.
Tel: 309-467-4855; Web: www.stsJLJ.com. Rev. Eugene A. Radosevich; Deacon Michael Harris.
Catechesis Religious Program—Michele Gadbois, D.R.E. Students 48.

FAIRBURY, LIVINGSTON CO., ST. ANDREW (2013) [CEM]
110 E. Ash, Fairbury, 61739. Tel: 815-692-2555; Email: standrewparish@outlook.com; Web: www.fairburycatholic.org. Rev. Scott Archer.
Catechesis Religious Program—Students 42.

FARMER CITY, DE WITT CO., SACRED HEART (1899) [CEM] (Linked Parishes: St. John, Clinton)
612 N. Plum St., Farmer City, 61842.
Tel: 309-928-3855, Ext. 12; Email: shchurch612@frontier.com; Web: sacredheartfc.org. 502 N. Monroe St., Clinton, 61727. Rev. James P. Henning, O.F.M.Conv.; Deacon Scott Whitehouse.
Catechesis Religious Program—Students 35.
Linked Parish: St. John, Bellflower.

FARMINGTON, FULTON CO., ST. MATTHEW'S (1904) Linked to the Parish of St. Mary in Canton
156 E. Vernon St., Farmington, 61531.
Tel: 309-647-1473; Email: st.marys1@hotmail.com. 139 E. Chestnut St., Canton, 61520. Rev. Daniel Ebker; Deacon Gary Schultz.
Catechesis Religious Program—

GALESBURG, KNOX CO.

1—CORPUS CHRISTI (1885) [CEM] (Linked Parishes: Sacred Heart, Abingdon & St. Patrick, Galesburg)
273 S. Prairie St., Galesburg, 61401.
Tel: 309-343-8256; Email: adorecc7@gmail.com. Rev. William T. Miller.
School—Costa Catholic Academy, 2726 Costa Dr., Galesburg, 61401. Tel: 309-344-3151; Fax: 309-344-1594. Mrs. Jackie Nieukirk, Prin. Operates with Immaculate Heart and St. Patrick. Lay Teachers 18; Students 260.
Catechesis Religious Program—

2—IMMACULATE HEART OF MARY (1956)
2401 N. Broad St., Galesburg, 61401-1203.
Tel: 309-344-3108; Fax: 309-344-1205; Email: ihm@grics.net. Revs. William T. Miller; Jacob Rose, Parochial Vicar; Deacon Rod Gray.
See Costa Catholic Academy, Galesburg under Corpus Christi, Galesburg for details.
Catechesis Religious Program—Laura Junk, D.R.E. Students 68.

3—ST. PATRICK'S (1863) [JC] (Linked Parishes: Sacred Heart, Abingdon & Corpus Christi, Galesburg)
858 S. Academy St., Galesburg, 61401.
Tel: 309-343-9874; Fax: 309-343-9944; Email: stpatrickschurch@outlook.com; Web: galesburgcatholic.com. Revs. William T. Miller; Jacob Rose, Parochial Vicar; Deacon James D. Haneghan.
See Costa Catholic School, Galesburg under Corpus Christi, Galesburg for details.
Catechesis Religious Program—

GALVA, HENRY CO., ST. JOHN'S (1882) [CEM] (Swedish) (Linked Parishes: St. John Vianney, Cambridge & St. John, Woodhull)
212 N.E. 1st St., Galva, 61434. Tel: 309-932-2409; Email: stjohngalva2@gmail.com. P.O. Box 249, Woodhull, 61490. Rev. John R. Burns; Deacon John V. Holevoet.
Catechesis Religious Program—Students 44.

GENESEO, HENRY CO., ST. MALACHY'S (1866)
595 E. Ogden Ave., Geneseo, 61254.
Tel: 309-944-5393; Email: church@saintmalachy.org. Rev. Michael G. Pakula; Deacons Mike Sigwalt, RCIA Coord.; Harley Chaffee; Thomas Wachtel; Larry Honzel; Robert O'Rourke; Arthur Ries.
Res.: 551 E. Ogden Ave., Geneseo, 61254.
School—St. Malachy's School, 595 E. Ogden Ave., Geneseo, 61254. Tel: 309-944-3230; Email: hfrancque@stmalgeneseo.org; Web: www.saintmalachy.org. Mrs. Heather Francque, Prin. Lay Teachers 7; Students 103.
Catechesis Religious Program—Tel: 309-944-5393. Leigh Boorn, Faith Formation Leader. Students 220.

GEORGETOWN, VERMILION CO., ST. ISAAC JOGUES (1942) (Linked Parish: St. Mary, Westville)
231 N. State St., Westville, 61883. Tel: 217-267-3334 ; Tel: 217-662-8726 (St. Issac Jogues); Email: stisaac61846@att.net. 109 W. 7th St., Georgetown, 61846. Rev. Timothy J. Sauppe.
Catechesis Religious Program—Students 1.

GERMANTOWN HILLS, WOODFORD CO., ST. MARY OF LOURDES (1839) [CEM] (Linked Parish: St. Mary, Metamora)
424 Lourdes Church Rd., Germantown Hills, 61548.
Tel: 309-383-4460; Web: www.stmarylourdes.org. Revs. Greg Jozefiak; Vien Van Do, Parochial Vicar; Deacons Robert Heiple; William Read; Larry DeCapp.
Catechesis Religious Program—Email: igrebner@stmarylourdes.org. Ms. Ileen Grebner, D.R.E. Students 156.

GRANVILLE, PUTNAM CO., SACRED HEART OF JESUS (1908) [CEM] (Italian) (Linked Parish: St. Patrick, Hennepin)
311 Hennepin St., P.O. Box 217, Granville, 61326.
Tel: 815-339-2138; Email: shgsph@gmail.com. Rev. Patrick DeMeulemeester.
Catechesis Religious Program—Students 61.

HAVANA, MASON CO., ST. PATRICK'S (1865) [CEM] (Linked Parish: Immaculate Conception, Manito & St. Mary, Lewistown)
545 S. Orange St., Havana, 62644. Tel: 309-740-1495 ; Email: 3forthetrinity@gmail.com. Rev. David Whiteside; Deacon Jon Dosher.
Catechesis Religious Program—Students 71.
Linked Parish: Immaculate Conception, 505 S Adams St, Manito, 61546. Tel: 309-241-6600; Email: sondag@grics.net. Deacon Robert Sondag.

HENNEPIN, PUTNAM CO., ST. PATRICK'S (1865) [CEM] (Linked Parish: Sacred Heart, Granville)
Mailing Address: 311 Hennepin St., P.O. Box 217, Granville, 61326. 920 Dore Dr., Hennepin, 61327.
Tel: 815-339-2138; Fax: 815-339-2880; Email: shgsph@gmail.com. Rev. Patrick DeMeulemeester.
Catechesis Religious Program—Students 27.

HENRY, MARSHALL CO.

1—ST. JOHN XXIII (2014) [CEM 2] (Linked Parish: Immaculate Conception, Lacon)
401 South St., P.O. Box 75, Henry, 61537.
Tel: 309-246-5145; Email: iccc@grics.net. 405 N. High St., Lacon, 61540. Revs. John Bosco Mujuni; Harold F. Schmitt, In Res.
Parish Office: 415 N. High St., Lacon, 61540.
Catechesis Religious Program—Christy Beall, D.R.E. Students 60.

2—ST. JOSEPH'S (1878) [CEM 2] Closed. Sacramental records are located at St. John XXIII Church, Henry, IL.

HOOPESTON, VERMILION CO., ST. ANTHONY CHURCH (1877)
423 S. Third St., Hoopeston, 60942.
Tel: 217-283-6211; Email: stanthony423@gmail.com. 501 S. 3rd St., Hoopeston, 60942. Rev. Patrick O'Neal.
Catechesis Religious Program—Email: drestanthony@gmail.com. Students 55.

HOOPPOLE, HENRY CO., ST. MARY'S, Closed. Sacramental records are located at Sacred Heart Church, Annawan.

IVESDALE, CHAMPAIGN CO., ST. JOSEPH'S (1863) [CEM] (Irish) (Linked Parish: St. Patrick, Tolono) Rev. Fredi Gomeztorres; Deacon James Brewer.
Church: 201 Fifth St., P.O. Box 175, Ivesdale, 61851.
Tel: 217-485-1129; Email: officeofstp@gmail.com.
Catechesis Religious Program—James Brewer, D.R.E. Students 35.

KEWANEE, HENRY CO.

1—ST. FRANCIS OF ASSISI (1906) Closed. Sacramental records are located at St. John Paul II, Kewanee.

2—SAINT JOHN PAUL II PARISH (1855) [CEM 2]
406 W. Central Blvd., Kewanee, 61443-2010.
Tel: 309-852-4549; Email: office@saintjohnpaulii-kewanee.org; Web: saintjohnpaulii-kewanee.org. Rev. Johndamaseni Zilimu, Ph.D.
School—Visitation Catholic School, 107 S. Lexington, Kewanee, 61443. Tel: 309-856-7451; Fax: 309-852-4259. Sheila Cromien, Prin. Lay Teachers 12; Students 125.
Catechesis Religious Program—Email: abryan1999.ar@gmail.com; Email: office@saintjohnpaulii-kewanee.org. Mrs. Angela Ryan, D.R.E.; Mrs. Mary Ebert, RCIA Coord. Students 81.

KICKAPOO, (EDWARDS) PEORIA CO., ST. MARY OF KICKAPOO (1837)
9910 W. Knox St., Kickapoo (Edwards), 61528.
Tel: 309-691-2030; Email: stmarys@stmaryskickapoo.org. Rev. Joseph Dondanville; Deacon Thomas L. Mueller.
School—St. Mary of Kickapoo School, Tel: 309-691-3015. Rick Pantages, Prin. Lay Teachers 9; Students 87.
Catechesis Religious Program—Students 60.

LA SALLE, LA SALLE CO.

1—ST. HYACINTH (1875) [CEM] (Linked Parishes: St. Patrick, LaSalle & Shrine of the Holy Rosary, LaSalle)
927 10th St., La Salle, 61301. Tel: 815-223-0641; Email: office@lasallecatholic.org. Mailing Address: 725 4th St., LaSalle, 61301. Rev. Paul Carlson.
School—Trinity Catholic Academy, (Grades PreK-8), 650 Fourth St., La Salle, 61301. Tel: 815-223-8523; Fax: 815-223-5366. Deb Myers, Prin.
Legal Title: St Patrick. Lay Teachers 9; Students 177.
Catechesis Religious Program— Combined with St. Patrick Church, La Salle. Students 148.

2—ST. PATRICK (1838) [CEM] (Irish) (Linked Parishes: St. Hyacinth, LaSalle & Shrine of the Holy Rosary, LaSalle)
725 Fourth St., La Salle, 61301. Tel: 815-223-0641; Email: office@lasallecatholic.org. Rev. Paul Carlson.
Catechesis Religious Program—Email: dmyers@lasallecatholic.org. Deb Myers, D.R.E. Students 195.

3—RESURRECTION (1979) Closed. All sacramental records are located at St. Hyacinth, LaSalle.

4—SHRINE OF QUEEN OF THE HOLY ROSARY (1925) [JC] (Italian) (Linked Parishes: St. Hyacinth, LaSalle & St. Patrick, LaSalle)
529 4th St., La Salle, 61301. Tel: 815-223-0641; Email: office@lasallecatholic.org. 725 4th St., LaSalle, 61301. Revs. Paul Carlson; Jacob Valle, Parochial Vicar.
Catechesis Religious Program—Attend at Resurrection, La Salle.

LACON, MARSHALL CO., IMMACULATE CONCEPTION (1853) [CEM] (Linked Parish: St. John XXIII, Henry)

415 N. High St., Lacon, 61540. Rev. John Bosco Mujuni. In Res., Rev. Ronald Enderlin.
Church: 418 N. Center St., Lacon, 61540.
Catechesis Religious Program—Katie Bogner, D.R.E. & Youth Min. Students 30.

LADD, BUREAU CO., ST. BENEDICT'S (1893) Closed. All sacramental records requests can be sent to Holy Trinity Church, Cherry.

LEONORE, LA SALLE CO., SS. PETER AND PAUL'S (1860) [CEM] (German)
Mailing Address: 513 S. Shabbona St., Streator, 61364. Tel: 815-672-2474; Email: parishoffice@stmichael-streator.org. Rev. Msgr. Philip Halfacre; Deacon Robb Caputo.
Res.: 957 N. 17th Rd., Tonica, 61370.
Catechesis Religious Program—Students 2.

LEWISTOWN, FULTON CO., ST. MARY PARISH (1865) [CEM] (Linked Parish: St. Patrick, Havana & Immaculate Conception, Manito)
705 N. Broadway St., Lewistown, 61542.
Tel: 309-740-1495; Email: 3forthetrinity@gmail.com; Web: 3forthetrinity.com. 545 S Orange St, Havana, 62644. Rev. David Whiteside.
Catechesis Religious Program—

LINCOLN, LOGAN CO., HOLY FAMILY (1857) [CEM 2] (Linked Parishes: St. Patrick, Elkhart, St. Thomas, Mt. Pulaski & St. Mary's, Atlanta)
316 S. Logan St., Lincoln, 62656. Tel: 217-732-4019; Web: www.logancountycatholic.org. Revs. Jeffrey G. Laible; Edward U. Ohm; Deacon Wendell Lowry III.
School—Carroll Catholic School, (Grades PreSchool-8), 111 Fourth St., Lincoln, 62656. Tel: 217-732-7518; Fax: 217-651-8419; Email: dwelch@carrollcatholicschool.com; Web: www.carrollcatholic.com. Mr. David Welch, Prin. Lay Teachers 10; Students 141.
Catechesis Religious Program—Holy Family Religious Education Center, Tel: 217-735-3520. Students 69.
Linked Parish: St. Mary's.

LORETTO, LIVINGSTON CO., ST. MARY'S (1873) (German), Closed. For inquiries contact St. Patrick, Dwight.

LOSTANT, LA SALLE CO., ST. JOHN THE BAPTIST'S (1862) [CEM] (Linked Parishes: St. Patrick, Minock, St. Ann, Toluca & St. Mary, Wenona)
301 S. Sheridan St., Lostant, 61334.
Tel: 815-853-4558; Fax: 815-853-0111; Email: smary1876@mchsi.com. Mailing Address: 207 W. Third St. S., Wenona, 61377. Revs. Patrick Greenough; Stephen McKinley, O.F.M.Conv., In Res.; David Huebner, O.F.M.Conv., Parochial Vicar; Bro. Juniper Kriss, Pastoral Assoc.
Catechesis Religious Program—Tel: 815-252-3913. Dawn Rippel, D.R.E. Students 10.

MACOMB, MCDONOUGH CO., ST. PAUL'S (1854) [CEM]
309 W. Jackson, Macomb, 61455. Tel: 309-833-2496; Email: churchoffice@stpaulmacomb.com. Rev. Adam Stimpson; Deacons Lawrence Adams, D.R.E.; Tony Ensenberger.
School—St. Paul's School, (Grades PreK-6), 322 W. Washington St., Macomb, 61455. Tel: 309-833-2470; Fax: 309-833-2470; Email: office@stpaulmacomb.com; Web: www.stpaulmacomb.com/church. Laura Cody, Prin. Lay Teachers 8; Preschool 46; Students (K-6) 115.
Catechesis Religious Program—Students 155.

MAHOMET, CHAMPAIGN CO., OUR LADY OF THE LAKE (1981)
501 W. State St., Mahomet, 61853. Tel: 217-586-5153 ; Email: ololoffice@mchsi.com. P.O. Box 109, Mahomet, 61853. Rev. Joseph T. Hogan; Deacons Edward Mueller; John Leonard; Anthony Nickrent.
Res.: 703 N. Craig Dr., Mahomet, 61853.
Catechesis Religious Program—Tel: 217-840-6283. Mr. Roger L. Phelps, D.R.E. Students 228.

MARSEILLES, LA SALLE CO., ST. JOSEPH'S (1881) (Linked Parish: St. Patrick's, Seneca; St. Mary's, Grand Ridge; St. Theresa, Earlville; St. Patrick, Ransom)
200 Broadway St., Marseilles, 61341.
Tel: 815-795-2240; Email: stjoetorino@gmail.com. Revs. Ghislain Inai; Odilon Amenyaglo, Parochial Vicar; Augustin Kassa, S.M.A., Parochial Vicar; Deacon Ron Wackerlin.
Catechesis Religious Program—Tel: 815-795-2251. Students 45.

MATHERVILLE, MERCER CO., ST. ANTHONY'S CHURCH (1916) [CEM 2] (Linked Parishes: St. John, Viola & St. Catherine, Aledo)
1386 252nd St., Matherville, 61263.
Tel: 309-582-7500; Email: lcstc@hotmail.com. c/o St. Catherine Church, 106 N.E. 4th St., Aledo, 61231. Rev. John Thieryoung.
Catechesis Religious Program—Students 47.
Linked Parish: St. John, Viola, 61486.

MENDOTA, LA SALLE CO., HOLY CROSS (1863) [CEM] (Linked Parishes: Sts. Peter & Paul, Peterstown)
1010 Jefferson St., Mendota, 61342.
Tel: 815-538-6151. Rev. Peter A. Pilon; Deacons Hector Diaz; Jose Lopez; Raymond Fischer.
School—Holy Cross School, 1008 Jefferson St., Mendota, 61342. Tel: 815-539-7003; Fax: 815-539-9082. Mrs. Anita Kobilsek, Prin. Lay Teachers 12; Students 157.
Catechesis Religious Program—Email: briancorriganhcdre@gmail.com. Brian Corrigan, D.R.E. Students 240.

METAMORA, WOODFORD CO., ST. MARY'S (1864) [CEM] (German) (Linked Parish: St. Mary of Lourdes, Metamora)
415 W. Chatham St., P.O. Box 319, Metamora, 61548. Tel: 309-367-4407; Email: deb.adams@saintmarysmetamora.org. Revs. Greg Jozefiak; Vien Van Do, Parochial Vicar; Deacon Joseph Lowry.
School—St. Mary's School, Tel: 309-367-2528; Fax: 309-367-2169. Jim Dansart, Prin. Lay Teachers 14; Students 119.
Catechesis Religious Program—Email: ccd@mtco.com. Dan Fandel, D.R.E. Students 92.
Linked Parish: St. Mary of Lourdes, Metamora, 61548.

MILAN, ROCK ISLAND CO., ST. AMBROSE (1924)
312 First St., Milan, 61264-2501. Tel: 309-787-4593; Email: stambrosemilan@gmail.com. Rev. Charles Klamut.
Catechesis Religious Program—Students 134.

MINONK, WOODFORD CO., ST. PATRICK'S (1878) [CEM] (Linked Parishes: St. John the Baptist, Lostant, St. Anne, Toluca & St. Mary, Wenona)
420 E. Sixth St., Minonk, 61760. Tel: 815-853-4558; Email: smary1867@mchsi.com. 207 W. Third St., S., Wenona, 61377. Revs. Patrick Greenough; David Huebner, O.F.M.Conv., Parochial Vicar; Bro. Juniper Kriss, Pastoral Assoc.; Rev. Stephen McKinley, O.F.M.Conv., In Res.
Catechesis Religious Program—Tel: 309-824-6709. Melissa Meierhofer, D.R.E. Students 6.

MOLINE, ROCK ISLAND CO.
1—CHRIST THE KING (1967)
3209 60th St., Moline, 61265. Tel: 309-762-4634; Email: ctkenter@ctkmoline.com. Revs. Donald L. Levitt; Jean de Dieu Ahorloo, S.M.A., Parochial Vicar.
Catechesis Religious Program—
Tel: 309-762-4634, Ext. 206; Email: boudreau_beth@yahoo.com. Beth Boudreau, D.R.E. (PreK-6 & Junior High). Students 220.

2—ST. MARY'S (1875) [CEM] (Linked Parish: St. Mary, East Moline) Rev. Antonio Dittmer; Deacon Russ W. Swim.
Res.: 412 10th St., Moline, 61265. Tel: 309-764-1562; Fax: 309-764-0317; Email: stmarysmolineil@hotmail.com; Web: www.parishesonline.com.
Catechesis Religious Program—Meaghan Terry, D.R.E. Students 195.

3—SACRED HEART (1906) (Belgian)
1608 13th St., Moline, 61265.
Tel: 309-762-2362, Ext. 211; Email: desutter@sacredheartmoline.org; Email: shchurch@sacredheartmoline.org. Revs. Mark A. DeSutter; Matthew Cole, S.M.A., Parochial Vicar; Sr. Kathleen Mullin, Pastoral Assoc.; Deacon Patrick Murphy
Legal Title: Sacred Heart Roman Catholic Congregation of Moline Illinois.
School—Seton Catholic School, (Grades PreK-8), 1320 16th Ave., Moline, 61265. Tel: 309-757-5500; Fax: 309-762-0545. Lay Teachers 31; Sisters 1; Students 556.
Catechesis Religious Program—Email: ivygoes2church@sacredheartmoline.org. Ivy Padula, D.R.E.; Debbie Patronagio, D.R.E. Students 125.

MONMOUTH, WARREN CO., IMMACULATE CONCEPTION (1864) [CEM] (Linked Parish: St. Patrick, Raritan)
200 W. Broadway, Monmouth, 61462.
Tel: 309-734-7533; Email: mpinedo@immaculate-conception.net. Rev. Msgr. Thomas E. Mack; Rev. Thomas Otto, Parochial Vicar; Deacons William Clark; Thomas Mann; Joseph McCleary.
School—Immaculate Conception School, 115 North B St., Monmouth, 61462. Tel: 309-734-6037; Fax: 309-734-6082; Email: icstrojans@gmail.com; Web: www.immaculate-conception.net. Randy Frakes, Prin. Lay Teachers 12; Students 172.
Catechesis Religious Program—Rita Selby, D.R.E. Students 75.

MONTICELLO, PIATT CO., ST. PHILOMENA (1888) (Linked Parish: St. Michael, Bemont)
1301 N. Market St., Monticello, 61856.
Tel: 217-762-2566; Fax: 217-762-8666; Email: St.PhilomenaChurch@yahoo.com; Web: stphilomenaonline.org. Rev. Bruce Lopez; Deacon Gene Triplett.
Catechesis Religious Program—Kari Higgins, D.R.E. Students 147.

MORTON, TAZEWELL CO., BLESSED SACRAMENT (1957)
1020 S. First Ave., Morton, 61550. Tel: 309-266-9721 ; Email: blessedparish@bscmorton.org; Web: bscmorton.org. Rev. Msgr. Gerald T. Ward; Deacons Rick Miller; David Steeples; Kevin Zeeb; Michael Harris.
Res.: 217 E. Greenwood St., Morton, 61550.
School—Blessed Sacrament School, 1018 S. First Ave., Morton, 61550. Tel: 309-263-8442; Email: blessedschool@bssmorton.org. Mr. Michael Birdoes, Prin. Lay Teachers 17; Students 245.
Catechesis Religious Program—Email: rbarbour@bscmorton.org. Rick Barbour, D.R.E. Students 72.

NAUVOO, HANCOCK CO., SS. PETER AND PAUL (1848) [CEM 2] (German) (Linked Parishes: Sacred Heart, Dallas City, St. Mary, Hamilton, Sacred Heart, Warsaw & Immaculate Conception, Carthage)
190 N. Wells St., P.O. Box 147, Nauvoo, 62354.
Tel: 217-453-2428; Fax: 217-453-2427; Email: info@hancockcountycatholic.org; Web: www.HancockCountyCatholic.org. Revs. Anthony J. Trosley; Thomas R. Szydlik.
School—SS. Peter and Paul School,
Tel: 217-453-2511; Email: principal@stspeterpaul.org. Lisa Gray, Prin. Lay Teachers 7; Students 91.
Catechesis Religious Program—Students 17.
Linked Parish: Sacred Heart, Dallas City, 62330.

NORMAL, MCLEAN CO., EPIPHANY (1966) [JC]
1000 E. College Ave., Normal, 61761.
Tel: 309-452-2585; Email: office@epiphanyparish.com; Web: www.epiphanyparish.com. Rev. Msgr. Eric S. Powell; Deacons Mark Cleary; Michael An.
Res.: 1006 E. College Ave., Normal, 61761.
School—Epiphany School, 1002 E. College Ave., Normal, 61761. Tel: 309-452-3268;
Fax: 309-454-8087; Email: mary.brownfield@epiphanyschools.org; Web: epiphanyschools.org. Michael Lootens, Prin. Lay Teachers 23; Students 355.
Catechesis Religious Program—Mary Ellen Kiley, C.R.E. Students 234.

ODELL, LIVINGSTON CO., ST. PAUL'S (1873) [CEM 2] (Irish) (Linked Parishes: St. Patrick, Dwight, IL)
200 S. West St., Odell, 60460. Tel: 815-584-3522. 114 W. Mazon Ave., Dwight, 60420. Rev. Chris G. Haake.
School—St. Paul's School, P.O. Box 374, Pontiac, 61764. Tel: 815-998-2194; Email: stmaryspontiac@mchsi.com. Mr. Richard Morehouse, Pres. Lay Teachers 5; Students 54.
Catechesis Religious Program—

OGLESBY, LA SALLE CO., HOLY FAMILY (1953)
311 N. Woodland Ave., Oglesby, 61348.
Tel: 815-883-8233; Email: holyfamilyrec1@comcast.net. Rev. Gary W. Blake; Deacon Michael Timmerman.
School—Holy Family School, (Grades PreK-8), 336 Alice Ave., Oglesby, 61348. Tel: 815-883-8916;
Fax: 815-883-8943; Email: holyfamilyschool@comcast.net. Mrs. Jyll Jasiek, Prin. Lay Teachers 12; Students 183.
Catechesis Religious Program—Mrs. Lynn Quick, D.R.E. Students 56.

OHIO, BUREAU CO., IMMACULATE CONCEPTION CHURCH (1875) [CEM] (Irish) (Linked Parish: St. John, Walnut)
101 N. Main St., Ohio, 61349. Tel: 815-379-2602. P.O. Box 358, Walnut, 61376. Rev. Thomas Shaw.
Res.: c/o St. John's, 204 N. Main St., Walnut, 61376-0370.
Catechesis Religious Program—Students 10.

ORION, HENRY CO., MARY, OUR LADY OF PEACE (1960) (Linked Parish: St. Marla Goretti, Coal Valley)
1410 10th St., P.O. Box 175, Orion, 61273-0175.
Tel: 309-526-8422; Fax: 309-526-8469; Email: maryourladyofpeace@gmail.com. Rev. Anthony M. Ego; Deacon Thomas C. Gainey.
Catechesis Religious Program—Email: dremolop@gmail.com. Emily Dochterman, D.R.E. Students 95.

OTTAWA, LA SALLE CO.
1—ST. COLUMBA (1844) [CEM] (Irish) (Linked Parish: St. Francis of Assisi, St. Patrick, Ottawa, IL)
122 W. Washington St., Ottawa, 61350.
Tel: 815-433-0700; Email: ottawacatholiccommunity@gmail.com. Revs. David M. Kipfer; Bruno Byomuhangi, Parochial Vicar; Corey Krengiel, Parochial Vicar.
School—Marquette Academy, (Grades PreK-12), 1110 LaSalle St., 1000 Paul St., Ottawa, 61350.
Tel: 815-433-1199; Tel: 815-433-0125;
Fax: 815-433-1219; Fax: 815-433-2632; Email: mmann@marquetteacademy.net; Email: mmcconnaughhay@marquetteacademy.net; Web: www.marquetteacademy.net. Mrs. Brooke Rick, Prin. Clergy 6; Lay Teachers 27; Students 396.
Catechesis Religious Program—Students 173.

2—ST. FRANCIS OF ASSISI (1858) [CEM] (Linked Parish: St. Patrick, Ottawa)
820 Sanger St., Ottawa, 61350. Tel: 815-433-0700; Email: ottawacatholiccommunity@gmail.com. Mailing Address: 122 W. Washington St., Ottawa, 61350. Revs. David M. Kipfer; Bruno Byomuhangi, Parochial Vicar; Corey Krengiel, Parochial Vicar.

Catechesis Religious Program—Mrs. Rhonda Coveyou, D.R.E. Students 62.
3—St. Mary's (1927) Closed. Sacramental records are located at St. Francis of Assisi, Ottawa.
4—St. Patrick's (1893) (Irish) (Linked Parish: St. Francis of Assisi, Ottawa, St. Columba, Ottawa)
726 W. Jefferson St., Ottawa, 61350.
Tel: 815-433-0700; Email: ottawacatholiccommunity@gmail.com. 122 W. Washington St, Ottawa, 61350. Revs. David M. Kipfer; Corey Krengiel, Parochial Vicar; Bruno Byomuhangi, Parochial Vicar; Deacon Michael Driscoll.
Catechesis Religious Program—Joanne Sheridan, D.R.E. Students 74.
Pekin, Tazewell Co., St. Joseph Catholic Church (1863) [CEM 2]
303 S. Seventh St., Pekin, 61554. Tel: 309-347-6108; Email: stjoseph@stjosephpekin.org; Web: www.stjosephpekin.org. Rev. Michael J. Andrejek; Deacons Charles Murray; Mark Wilder; Ernie Whited; Tim Blanchard; Mark Scamp.
School—300 S. Sixth St., Pekin, 61554.
Tel: 309-347-7194; Fax: 309-347-7196. Shannon Rogers, Prin. Lay Teachers 18; Students 134.
Catechesis Religious Program—Email: amcmahan@stjosephpekin.org. Anna McMahan, D.R.E. Students 125.
Penfield, Champaign Co., St. Lawrence's (1898) [CEM] (Linked Parish: St. Charles Borromeo, Homer) Rev. Michael L. Menner.
Res.: P.O. Box 49, Penfield, 61862. Tel: 217-595-5560 ; Tel: 217-595-5620 (Office).
Catechesis Religious Program—Students 20.
Linked Parish: St. Charles Borromeo, Homer, 61849.
Peru, La Salle Co.
1—St. Joseph's (1854) [CEM]
829 Schuyler St., Peru, 61354. Tel: 815-223-0718; Email: parishoffice@stjoeperu.org. 1925 5th St., Peru, 61354. Rev. Harold L. Datzman, O.S.B.
Catechesis Religious Program—Kristi Bejster, D.R.E. Students 75.
2—St. Mary (1867) (Irish) (Linked Parish: St. Valentine, Peru)
1325 Sixth St., Peru, 61354. Tel: 815-223-0315; Email: stvalsperu@att.net. Mailing Address: 1109 Pulaski St., Peru, 61354. Rev. Msgr. Richard Soseman, M.A., J.C.L.
See Peru Catholic School System, Peru under St. Joseph's, Peru for details.
Catechesis Religious Program—Students 3.
3—St. Valentine (1891) [CEM] (Polish) (Linked Parish: St. Mary, Peru)
1109 Pulaski St., Peru, 61354. Tel: 815-223-0315; Email: stvalsperu@att.net. Rev. Msgr. Richard Soseman, M.A., J.C.L.
See Peru Catholic School System, Peru under St. Joseph's, Peru for details.
Catechesis Religious Program—Students 16.
Pesotum, Champaign Co.
1—St. Joseph (1904) [CEM] (German), Closed. Sacramental records are located at St. Mary Philo, Pesotum.
2—St. Mary (1875) [CEM] (Linked Parish: St. Thomas, Philo)
1247 City Rd. 200N, Pesotum, 61863.
Tel: 217-684-5107; Email: kthorson@stthomasphilo.org. P.O. Box 266, Philo, 61864. Rev. Keith A. Walder.
Catechesis Religious Program—Tel: 217-369-8453; Email: ddkoby@aol.com. Deacon Donald P. Koeberlein, D.R.E.
Peterstown, La Salle Co., SS. Peter and Paul (1872) [CEM] (Linked Parishes: Holy Cross, Mendota)
3864 E. 1st Rd., Mendota, 61342. Tel: 815-538-6151. 1010 Jefferson St., Mendota, 61342. Rev. Peter A. Pilon.
Philo, Champaign Co., St. Thomas (1869) [CEM] (Linked Parish: St. Mary, Pesotum)
310 E. Madison, P.O. Box 266, Philo, 61864.
Tel: 217-684-5107; Email: kthorson@stthomasphilo.org; Web: www.stthomasphilo.org. Rev. Keith A. Walder.
School—St. Thomas School, 311 E. Madison, Philo, 61864. Tel: 217-684-2309; Email: ldoughan@stthomasphilo.org; Web: www.stthomasphilo.org. Clergy 1; Lay Teachers 14; Students 150.
Catechesis Religious Program—Tel: 217-369-8453; Email: ddkoby@aol.com. Deacon Donald P. Koeberlein, D.R.E. Combined with Immaculate Conception Mission and St. Mary, Pesotum. Students 90.
Pontiac, Livingston Co., St. Mary's (1877) [CEM] (Linked Parishes: St. Joseph, Flanagan, St. John, Cullom, Sts. Peter & Paul, Chatsworth)
119 E. Howard St., P.O. Box 374, Pontiac, 61764.
Tel: 815-844-7683; Web: www.stmaryspontiacil.org. Revs. David Sabel; Adam Cesarek; William Keebler.
School—St. Mary's School, 414 N. Main St., Pontiac, 61764. Tel: 815-844-6585; Fax: 815-844-6987; Email: hatzer.kim@stmaryspontiac.org; Web: www.stmaryspontiac.org. Mr. Richard Morehouse, Prin. Lay Teachers 12; Students 151.
Catechesis Religious Program—Students 68.
Linked Parish: St. Joseph, Flanagan, 61740.
Princeton, Bureau Co., St. Louis (1865)
616 S. Gosse Blvd., Princeton, 61356.
Tel: 815-879-0181; Email: stlparishoffice@gmail.com; Web: stlouisprinceton.org. Rev. Daniel Gifford.
Catechesis Religious Program—Julia Mead, D.R.E. Students 20.
Princeville, Peoria Co., St. Mary of the Woods (1867) [CEM]
119 Saint Mary St., Princeville, 61559-9244.
Tel: 309-385-2578; Email: smowmo@frontier.com. Revs. Patrick Henehan; Andru O'Brien, Parochial Vicar; Deacon Frederick J. Kruse.
Catechesis Religious Program—Email: smowccd@yahoo.com. Students 76.
Ransom, La Salle Co., St. Patrick's (1883) [CEM] (Linked Parish: St. Joseph, Marseilles)
200 Broadway St., Marseilles, 61341.
Tel: 815-795-2240; Email: stjoetorino@gmail.com. Revs. Ghislain Inai; Odilon Amenyaglo, Parochial Vicar; Augustin Kassa, S.M.A., Parochial Vicar; Deacon Ron Wackerlin.
Catechesis Religious Program—Students 28.
Rantoul, Champaign Co., St. Malachy (1888) [CEM] (Linked Parish: St. Elizabeth, Thomasboro)
340 E. Belle Ave., Ste. 1, Rantoul, 61866.
Tel: 217-892-2044; Email: donnaa@stmal.pvt.k12.il.us; Web: sms217.org. Rev. Joel Phelps
Legal Title: St. Malachy R.C. Congregation.
School—61866. Tel: 217-892-2011;
Fax: 217-892-5780. Mrs. Anastacia Gianessi, Prin. Lay Teachers 12; Sisters 1; Students 113.
Catechesis Religious Program—Fax: 217-892-2011; Email: srp@stmal.pvt.k12.il.us. Sr. Paulette Joerger, D.R.E. Students 99.
Convent—Dominican Sisters (Springfield), 304 E. Belle Ave., Rantoul, 61866.
Rapids City, Rock Island Co., St. John the Baptist (1857) [CEM] (Linked Parish: St. Mary, Hampton)
1416 3rd Ave., P.O. Box 250, Rapids City, 61278-0250. Tel: 309-496-2414; Email: stjohnsrc@mchsi.com; Web: stjohnstmaryqc.org. Rev. Glenn Harris; Deacon Robert DePauw.
Catechesis Religious Program—Rose Roe, D.R.E. Students 97.
Linked Parish: St. Mary, Hampton, 61256.
Raritan, Henderson Co., Church of St. Patrick (1876) (Irish) (Linked Parish: St. Patrick's, Seneca; St. Joseph's, Marseilles; St. Mary's, Grand Ridge; St. Theresa, Earlville)
110 Wallace St., Ransom, 60470. Tel: 815-795-2240; Email: stjoetorino@gmail.com. Mailing Address: 200 W. Broadway, Monmouth, 61341. Revs. Ghislain Inai; Odilon Amenyaglo, Parochial Vicar; Augustin Kassa, S.M.A., Parochial Vicar; Deacon Ron Wackerlin.
Catechesis Religious Program—Students 28.
Roanoke, Woodford Co., St. Joseph (1874) (Linked Parish: St. Luke, Eureka)
508 W. Randolph, Roanoke, 61561.
Tel: 309-923-3031; Email: saintjandj@yahoo.com; Web: www.stsJLJ.com. 904 E. Reagan Dr., P.O. Box 226, Eureka, 61530. Rev. Eugene A. Radosevich; Deacon Michael Harris.
Catechesis Religious Program—Michelle Boland, C.R.E. Students 32.
Rock Island, Rock Island Co.
1—St. Joseph's (1876) Closed. All sacramental records are located at St. Pius X, Rock Island.
2—St. Mary (1851) (German) (Linked Parish: Sacred Heart, Rock Island)
2810 5th Ave., Rock Island, 61201. Tel: 309-788-3322 ; Email: stmaryri@gmail.com. Rev. Anthony Co.
Rectory—2208 4th Ave., Rock Island, 61201-8904.
Catechesis Religious Program—Students 25.
3—St. Pius X (1955)
2502 29th Ave., Rock Island, 61201.
Tel: 309-793-7373; Email: parishoffice@stpiusri.org. Rev. Msgr. Mark J. Merdian; Revs. Jeremy Freehill, Parochial Vicar; Matthew Hoelscher, In Res.; Deacons Timothy Granet; Paul Martin; Joseph Dockery-Jackson.
See Jordan Catholic School of Rock Island, Inc., Rock Island under Elementary Schools, Inter-Parochial located in the Institution section.
Catechesis Religious Program—Students 85.
4—Sacred Heart (1900) (Linked Parish: St. Mary, Rock Island)
2810 5th Ave., Rock Island, 61201. Tel: 309-794-0660 ; Email: shrec@sacredheartri.com. Rev. Anthony Co.
Res.: St. Mary's Church, 2208 4th Ave., Rock Island, 61201.
See Jordan Catholic School of Rock Island, Inc., Rock Island under Elementary Schools, Inter-Parochial located in the Institution section.
Catechesis Religious Program—
Rushville, Schuyler Co., St. Rose (1870) [JC]
319 N. Franklin St., Rushville, 62681-0292.
Tel: 309-833-2496; Email: churchoffice@stpaulmacomb.com. 309 W. Jackson St., Macomb, 61455. Revs. Adam Stimpson; Matthew Deptula, Parochial Vicar.
Catechesis Religious Program—Students 17.
Rutland, La Salle Co., Sacred Heart (1895) [CEM] (Irish), Closed. Sacramental records are located at Sacred Heart Church, Wenona.
St. Augustine, Knox Co., St. Augustine (1863) [CEM] (Linked Parish: St. Bernard, Bushnell)
Mailing Address: c/o 376 W. Hail, Bushnell, 61422.
Tel: 309-772-2333; Email: st.bbushnell@gmail.com. 103 State Rt.e 41, Abingdon, 61474. Rev. Patrick O'Neal.
Catechesis Religious Program—Students 6.
Seneca, La Salle Co., St. Patrick's (1856) [CEM] (Linked Parish: St. Joseph's, Marseilles; St. Mary's, Grand Ridge; St. Patrick's, Ransom; St. Theresa, Earlville)
176 W. Union St., Seneca, 61360. Tel: 815-357-6239; Email: parishgroup3@gmail.com; Web: www.senecastpatricks.com. Revs. Ghislain Inai; Odilon Amenyaglo, Parochial Vicar; Augustin Kassa, S.M.A., Parochial Vicar; Deacon Ron Wackerlin.
Catechesis Religious Program—Tel: 815-357-8509. Students 151.
Linked Parish: St. Mary's, Grand Ridge, 61235.
Seymour, Champaign Co., St. Boniface (1878) [CEM] (Linked Parish: St. Matthew, Champaign)
416 County Rd., 1100 N., Seymour, 61875.
Tel: 217-863-2190. Rev. Msgr. Stanley L. Deptula; Revs. Eric Bolek; Lee Brokaw, Parochial Vicar.
Catechesis Religious Program—Students 5.
Sheffield, Bureau Co., St. Patrick's (1854) [CEM]
231 W. Atkinson St., P.O. Box 514, Sheffield, 61361-0038. Tel: 815-454-8062; Email: stpatssheffield@mediacombb.net; Web: stpatssheffield.org. Rev. Mark O. Miller.
Catechesis Religious Program—Amy Wright, D.R.E. Students 22.
Silvis, Rock Island Co., Our Lady of Guadalupe (1927) (Linked Parish: St. Patrick, Colona)
800-17th St., Silvis, 61282. Tel: 309-792-3867; Email: olgsilvissec@gmail.com. Rev. Peter Zorjan.
Res.: 201 1st St., Colona, 61241.
Catechesis Religious Program—Email: stpatcolona1954@gmail.com. Rose Roe, D.R.E. Students 0.
Spring Valley, Bureau Co.
1—St. Anne's, Closed. For sacramental records contact Nativity of Our Lord Church, Spring Valley.
2—Immaculate Conception (1884) [CEM] Closed. For sacramental records contact Nativity of Our Lord Church, Spring Valley.
3—Nativity of Our Lord Church (2013)
510 Richard A. Mautino Dr., P.O. Box 150, Spring Valley, 61362. Tel: 815-663-3731. Rev. Scott Potthoff, Admin.
Catechesis Religious Program—206 N. Greenwood St., Spring Valley, 61362. Students 74.
4—SS. Peter and Paul's (1891) [CEM] (Polish), Closed. For sacramental records contact Nativity of Our Lord Church, Spring Valley.
Streator, La Salle Co.
1—St. Anthony of Padua (1881) [CEM] Closed. Sacramental records are located at St. Michael the Archangel Church, Streator, IL.
2—St. Casimir (1916) [CEM] (Polish), Closed. Sacramental records are located at St. Michael the Archangel Church, Streator. IL.
3—Immaculate Conception (1868) [CEM] Closed. Sacramental records are located at St. Michael the Archangel Church, Streator, IL.
4—St. Michael the Archangel Parish (2010) Linked Parish: Sts. Peter and Paul, Leonore, IL
513 S. Shabbona St., Streator, 61364.
Tel: 815-672-2474; Email: parishoffice@stmichaelstreator.org. Rev. Msgr. Philip Halfacre; Rev. Ryan Mattingly
Legal Titles:St. Stephen, St. Anthony of Padua, St. Casimir, Immaculate Conception.
School—St. Michael the Archangel School, (Grades PreK-8), 410 S. Park St., Streator, 61364.
Tel: 815-672-3847; Fax: 815-673-3590. Mrs. Ashley Davis, Prin. Students 189; Teachers 14.
Catechesis Religious Program—Bart Hipes, D.R.E. Students 195.
5—St. Stephen's (1884) [CEM 2] (Slovak), Closed. Sacramental records are located at St. Michael the Archangel Church, Streator, IL.
Thomasboro, Champaign Co., St. Elizabeth of Hungary (1893) [CEM] (Linked Parish: St. Malachy, Rantoul)
100 Church St., P.O. Box 307, Thomasboro, 61878.
Tel: 217-643-3395. Rev. Joel Phelps.
Tiskilwa, Bureau Co., St. Mary (1881) [CEM] (Linked Parish: St. Mary, Depue)
121 W. Main St., P.O. Box 271, Tiskilwa, 61368.
Tel: 815-646-4451; Email: Frcreegan@netscape.net. Rev. Kevin G. Creegan.
Tolono, Champaign Co., St. Patrick (1859) [CEM]

(Linked Parish: St. Joseph, Ivesdale)
212 E. Washington St., P.O. Box K, Tolono, 61880.
Tel: 217-485-1129; Email: officeofstp@gmail.com; Web: www.stpatricktolono.com. Rev. Fredi Gomez-torres.
Catechesis Religious Program—Students 25.

TOLUCA, MARSHALL CO., ST. ANN PARISH (1895) [CEM] (Italian) (Linked Parishes: St. John the Baptist, Lostant, St. Patrick, Minonk & St. Mary, Wenona)
311 W. Santa Fe Ave., Toluca, 61369.
Tel: 815-853-4558; Fax: 815-853-0111; Email: smary1867@mchsi.com. 207 W. Third St. S., Wenona, 61377. Revs. Patrick Greenough; David Huebner, O.F.M.Conv., Parochial Vicar; Bro. Juniper Kriss, Pastoral Assoc.; Rev. Stephen McKinley, O.F.-M.Conv., In Res.
Catechesis Religious Program—Tel: 815-252-3913. Dawn Rippel, D.R.E. Students 100.

URBANA, CHAMPAIGN CO., ST. PATRICK'S (1901)
708 W. Main St., Urbana, 61801. Tel: 217-367-2665; Email: secretary@stpaturbana.org. Rev. Luke A. Spannagel; Deacon Clifford Maduzia; Jim Urban, Pastoral Assoc.
Catechesis Religious Program—Jon McCoy, D.R.E. Students 160.

UTICA, LA SALLE CO., ST. MARY (1858) [CEM]
303 S. Division St., P.O. Box 159, Utica, 61373.
Tel: 815-667-4677; Email: office@stmaryutica.org; Web: stmarysutica.org. Rev. Michael J. Driscoll, O.S.F.
Catechesis Religious Program—Amy Weber, D.R.E. Students 46.

WALNUT, BUREAU CO., ST. JOHN THE EVANGELIST (1912) (Linked Parish: Immaculate Conception, Ohio.)
204 N. Main St., Walnut, 61376-0370.
Tel: 815-379-2602. P.O. Box 370, Walnut, 61376. Rev. Thomas Shaw.
Catechesis Religious Program—Students 14.

WAPELLA, DE WITT CO., ST. PATRICK CHURCH (1858) [CEM]
308 S. Locust St., P.O. Box 116, Wapella, 61777.
Tel: 217-935-8510; Email: stpatrickwapella@yahoo.com; Web: www.saintpatrickwapella.org. Revs. Jeffrey D. Stirniman; Geoffrey Horton, Parochial Vicar; Deacons Robert Hermes; Joe Knapp; Albert Lundy; Michael A. Marvin; Todd Weber.
Catechesis Religious Program—Students 41.

WARSAW, HANCOCK CO., SACRED HEART (1874) [CEM] (German) (Linked Parishes: Immaculate Conception, Carthage, Sacred Heart, Dallas City & Sts. Peter & Paul, Nauvoo)
245 S. 9th St., P.O. Box 93, Warsaw, 62379.
Tel: 217-256-3657; Tel: 217-453-2428; Email: info@hancockcountycatholic.org; Web: www.HancockCountyCatholic.org. Revs. Anthony J. Trosley; Thomas R. Szydlik, Parochial Vicar.
Catechesis Religious Program—Students 7.
Linked Parish: St. Mary, 560 Lakeview Ave., Hamilton, 62341.

WASHBURN, WOODFORD CO., ST. ELIZABETH, [CEM] Closed. Sacramental records are located at St. Mary Church, Metamora.

WASHINGTON, TAZEWELL CO., ST. PATRICK'S (1941) (Linked Parish: St. Monica, East Peoria)
705 E. Jefferson, Washington, 61571.
Tel: 309-444-3524; Email: churchoffice@stpatswashington.com; Web: stpatswashington.com. Revs. Jonathan Steffen; Binh K. Tran, Parochial Vicar; Deacons Paul Neakrase; Joe Venzon.
School—100 N. Harvey, Washington, 61571.
Tel: 309-444-4345; Fax: 309-444-7100; Email: schooloffice@stpatswashington.com. Mrs. Doreen Shipman, Prin. Lay Teachers 20; Students 239.
Catechesis Religious Program—Email: prattl@stpatswashington.com. Linda Pratt, D.R.E. Students 198.

WEDRON, LA SALLE CO., ST. JOSEPH'S (1947)
P.O. Box 60, Wedron, 60557. Tel: 815-792-2622. Rev. John G. Waugh.
Res.: 3609 E. 2351 Rd., Serena, 60549.
Catechesis Religious Program—Students 19.

WENONA, MARSHALL CO., ST. MARY'S (1867) [CEM] (Linked Parishes: St. John the Baptist, Lostant, St. Patrick, Minonk & St. Anne, Toluca)
207 W. Third St. S., Wenona, 61377.
Tel: 815-853-4558; Email: smary1867@mchsi.com. Revs. Patrick Greenough; David Huebner, O.F.M.-Conv., Parochial Vicar; Bro. Juniper Kriss, Pastoral Assoc.; Rev. Stephen McKinley, O.F.M.Conv., In Res.; Deacon Charles Zulz.
Catechesis Religious Program—Tel: 815-252-3913. Dawn Rippel, D.R.E. Students 20.

WESTVILLE, VERMILION CO.
1—ST. MARY'S (1903) [CEM] (Linked Parish: St. Isaac Jogues, Georgetown)
231 N. State St., Westville, 61883. Tel: 217-267-3334; Email: stmary1903@gmail.com. Rev. Timothy J. Sauppe.
Catechesis Religious Program—Email: lbdeath5@gmail.com. Laura DeAth, D.R.E. Students 16.
2—SS. PETER AND PAUL, Closed. For inquiries for parish records contact St. Mary's, Westville.

WOODHULL, HENRY CO., ST. JOHN'S (1889) [CEM 2] (Swedish) (Linked Parishes: St. John Vianney, Cambridge & St. John, Galva)
390 E. Highway Ave., P.O. Box 249, Woodhull, 61490. Tel: 309-334-2180; Email: stjohnchurch@divcominc.net. Rev. John R. Burns; Deacon Joseph O'Tool.
Catechesis Religious Program—Students 24.
Linked Parish: St. John Vianney, 313 S. West St., Cambridge, 61238. Tel: 309-937-3304; Email: stjohnvianney3@gmail.com; Web: www.threestjohns.com.

WYOMING, STARK CO., ST. DOMINIC'S (1881) [CEM 2] (Linked Parish: St. John the Baptist, Bradford)
303 N. Galena Ave., Wyoming, 61491.
Tel: 309-695-4031; Email: stdominicwy@hotmail.com. Rev. John Cyr.
Catechesis Religious Program—Mary Groter, D.R.E. Students 5.

Chaplains of Public Institutions

DANVILLE. *Veterans' Administration Hospital*, Danville. Tel: 217-442-8000.
DWIGHT. *Dwight Correctional Center*, Dwight. Tel: 815-584-3522. Attended from St. Patrick's, Dwight.
LINCOLN. *Logan Correctional Center*, Lincoln. Tel: 217-947-2714; Tel: 309-244-8516. Rev. Jeffrey G. Laible, Holy Family Parish, Lincoln.
PONTIAC. *Illinois State Penitentiary*. Attended from St. Paul, Odell.
Res.: 811 Hill St., Pontiac, 61704. Tel: 815-842-1150.
SHERIDAN. *Illinois Industrial School for Boys*. Rev. John G. Waugh, Chap.

On Duty Outside the Diocese:
Rev. Msgrs.—
Rohlfs, Steven P., S.T.D., V.G., St. Paul Seminary, St. Paul, MN
Swetland, Stuart W., S.T.D., Pres., Donnelly College, Kansas City, KS
Revs.—
Campbell, Dwight, Our Lady of Mount Carmel Parish, Kenosha, WI
Caster, Gary C., Chap., Williams College, Williamstown, MA
Hochstatter, Theodore, East Africa
Kopec, Edward S., Zablocki VA Medical Center, Milwaukee, WI
Myers, James E., 32 Middlefield Rd., Menlo Park, CA 94025
Vitaliano, Dominic J., Veteran's Administration, WI; (Military).

Retired:
Rev. Msgrs.—
Beebe, Charles J., P.A., (Retired), 6500 N. Allen Rd, Unit 63, 61614
Hallin, Albert W., P.A., (Retired), 17 E. University Pl., Champaign, 61820
Ham, Jerome, (Retired), 6335 N. Hoyne Ave., Chicago, 60659
Pizzamiglio, Ernest E., (Retired), 550 E. Carl Sandburg Dr., Apt. 114, Galesburg, 61401
Prendergast, John J., (Retired), 3415 N. Sheridan Rd., 61604
Pricco, Richard A., (Retired), 1125 N. Marquette, LaSalle, 61301
Ramer, James K., (Retired), 4723 8th St., #11107, East Moline, 61244
Showalter, Paul E., P.A., (Retired), 509 E. Kansas St., 61603. Vicar General Emeritius
Swaner, James J., (Retired), 263 W. Johnson St., P.O. Box 218, Utica, 61373
Watson, William A., (Retired), 313 W. Hamilton St., Odell, 60460
Wellman, Dale, (Retired), 24600 94th Avenue N., Port Byron, 61275
Very Rev. Canon—
Flattery, John J., (Retired), 20967 Walnut Hill Rd., Danville, 61834
Revs.—
Anderson, Joseph W., (Retired), 545 W. Paseo del Canto, Green Valley, AZ 85614
Barclift, Richard L., (Retired), 110 19th St., Ste. 205, Rock Island, 61201
Bresnahan, Richard F., (Retired), 2435 - 29th St., Moline, 61265
Carney, Edward, (Retired), 1295 Millpoint Rd., East Peoria, 61611
Collins, Patrick, (Retired), 609 Campbell Rd., P.O. Box 221, Douglas, MI 49406
Dodd, Ronald, (Retired), 120 N. Deerfield Rd, Pontiac, 61764
Enderlin, R. E., (Retired), 14 Sycamore Bay, Lacon, 61540
Harkrader, Edward O., (Retired), 545 S. Fifth St., Princeton, 61356
Henderson, Donald, (Retired), 1011 W. Bellhaven, 61614
Henseler, J. Thomas, (Retired), 3900 N. Stable Court, Unit 111, 61614
Hoffman, Robert, (Retired), 343 Hickory Ct., Oakwood, 61858
Kelly, Thomas F., (Retired), W6881 W. Lake Shore Dr., Elkhorn, WI 53121
Kretz, James C., (Retired), 2705 Westbrook Dr., Bloomington, 61705
LoPresti, Carl, (Retired), 530 S. 4th St., Fairbury, 61726
Mai-Chi-Than, Joseph M., (Retired), 904 Switchgrass Ln., Champaign, 61822
Maloy, Dale, (Retired), 1709 Char-Lu Dr., Mendota, 61342
Meismer, Paul J., (Retired), 12580 E. 1545th St., Granville, 61326
Meyer, Gerald J., (Retired), 108 W. Sunset Rd., Mt. Prospect, 60056
O'Riley, Dennis H., (Retired), 225 E. Autumn, Oakwood, 61858
Remm, George F., (Retired), P.O. Box 6136, Champaign, 61826
Riordan, Patrick M., (Retired), 364 Bedi Ave., Galesburg, 61401
Roche, David, (Retired), 413 E Second St., Minonk, 61760
Royer, Thomas J., (Retired), P.O. Box 17225, Urbana, 61803
Schaab, R. Michael, (Retired), 3262 E. Senachwine Valley Rd., Putnam, 61560
Schladen, Robert, (Retired), 16309 E. Cherokee Rd., Cuba, 61427
Spilman, Robert D., (Retired), 204 N. Hawthorne Ave., P.O. Box 217, Granville, 61326
Verdun, Gerald J., (Retired), 215 E. Washington St., #616, Pontiac, 61764.

Permanent Deacons:
Adams, John L., St. Paul's, Macomb
An, Yi-Ning Michael, Epiphany, Normal
Angelo, Alfredo W. Jr., St. Patrick, Colona
Blanchard, Timothy, St. Joseph, Pekin
Bradford, Bruce, Sacred Heart, Peoria
Breeden, Charles, St. Maria Goretti, Coal Valley
Brewer, James, St. Joseph, Ivesdale
Briggs, James W., St. Anne's, East Moline
Buczko, Stanley, (Working Outside the Diocese)
Burton, John, St. Joseph's, Brimfield and St. James, Williamsfield
Buyck, Jerry, Christ the King, Moline
Carolan, Brendan, Holy Trinity, Bloomington
Cenek, Stephen, St. Ann, Peoria
Chaffee, Harley, St. Malachy, Genesco
Clark, William H., Immaculate Conception, Monmouth and St. Theresa's Alexis.
Cleary, Mark, Epiphany, Normal
Comfort, Patrick J., (Working Outside the Diocese)
Crummer, Michael P., Corpus Christi, Galesbury
Cryulik, Gayle E., St. Patrick of Merna, Bloomington
DeBernardis, Thomas, St. Vincent de Paul, Peoria
DeCapp, Larry, St. Mary of Lourdes, Metamora
DeVooght, Dennis, (Working Outside the Diocese)
Dockery-Jackson, Joseph, St. Pius X, Rock Island
Dosher, Jon, St. Patrick, Havana
Eaton, Francis, St. Thomas, Peoria Heights
Efinger, Donald L., (Working Outside the Diocese)
Ensenberger, Tony, St. Paul, Macomb
Filzen, Bernard R., (Retired)
Fischer, Raymond, Holy Cross, Mendota
Gainey, Thomas C., Orion & Coal Valley
Gillian, Dennis J., St. Anthony, Spring Valley
Gore, James, Holy Trinity, Bloomington
Granet, Timothy, St. Pius X, Rock Island
Gratkowski, Daniel, (Working Outside the Diocese)
Gray, Rodney, Immaculate Heart of Mary, Galesburg
Gray, William, Dir. of Rural Life, Sts. Peter and Paul, Nauvoo
Guerrero, Gabriel, St. Hyacinth, LaSalle
Hammond, Richard G., St. Anthony, Bartonville
Haneghan, James, St. Patrick, Galesburg
Heatwole, James F., St. Mark, Peoria
Heipel, Robert, St. Mary of Lourdes, Metamora
Herdrich, Harold (Tony), Sacred Heart, Dallas City
Hermes, Robert, Holy Trinity, Bloomington
Herrera, Antonio, St. Mary, Bloomington
Holevoet, John V., St. John, Woodhull; St. John, Galva
Honzel, Larry, St. Malachy, Geneseo
Hoste, Aaron, St. Patrick, Colona
Hunter, Roger, St. Jude, Peoria
Jagiella, Thomas L., St. Joseph, Peru
Keim, Loren, St. Mary, Bloomington

Kelsch, Mark T., St. Thomas, Peoria Heights
Kettering, Jack M., St. Pius X, Rock Island
Kim, Byung-Joon (Paul), (Working Outside the Diocese)
Koeberlein, Donald P., Pesotum, Philo, Bongard
Koerner, Gary D., St. Mary, Downs
Kovachevich, Victor, St. Patrick of Merna, Bloomington
Kruse, Frederick J., Dir. King's House, Henry, IL
La Hood, Joseph, Holy Family, Peoria; Prison Ministry
Lalande, John II, (Working Outside the Diocese)
Landry, John, (Retired)
Leonard, John, St. John's, Bellflower; Sacred Heart, Farmer City
Levy, Matthew, Our Lady of Guadalupe, Silvis
Lopez, Jose, Holy Cross, Mendota
Lowry, Joseph, St. Mary of Lourdes, Metamora
Maduzia, Clifford, St. Patrick, Urbana
Martin, Paul, St. Pius X, Rock Island
Marvin, Michael A., Holy Trinity, Bloomington
Maubach, James, (Working Outside the Diocese)
Merdian, John W., St. Edward, Chillicothe
Meyer, William, Immaculate Conception, Manito; St. Patrick, Havana
Miller, Rick, Blessed Sacrament, Morton
Mock, John, (Retired)
Mohrbacher, Edward, Holy Cross, Champaign
Montenegro, Jose, St. Mary, Bloomington
Mueller, Edward, Our Lady of the Lake, Mahomet
Mueller, Thomas L., Holy Family, Peoria
Murphy, John P., St. Louis, Princeton; St. Mary's, Tiskilwa
Murphy, John R., Immaculate Conception, Lacon
Murphy, Patrick, Sacred Heart, Moline
Murray, Charles, St. Joseph, Pekin
Myers, Robert Sr., St. Vincent de Paul, Peoria; Executive Dir. Catholic Cemetery Assn. of Peoria
Neakrase, Paul, St. Patrick, Washington
Nelson, John R., St. Thomas, Peoria Heights
O'Rourke, Robert, St. Malachy, Geneseo
O'Tool, Joseph, St. John, Woodhull
Pinheiro, Edwin, (On Leave of Absence)
Pogioli, Martin, St. Joseph, Pekin
Pomazal, Robert, Vice Chancellor, St. Edward, Chillicothe
Pool, Michael, St. Patrick of Merna, Bloomington
Racki, Stephen III, St. Patrick of Merna, Bloomington
Randazzo, Frank G.
Rapach, Thomas, St. Jude's, Peoria
Read, William, Diocese Dir., Cursillo-Tec; St. Mary's of Lourdes, Metamora; St. Monica, Eat Peoria
Reaktenwalt, Craig, St. Ann, Peoria
Ries, Arthur, St. Malachy, Geneseo
Robbins, Charles, St. Monica, East Peoria
Rodriguez, Robert, Corpus Christi, Galesburg
Sandoval, Henry, (On Leave of Absence)
Schallmoser, Michael C., St. Philomena, Peoria
Schultz, Gary, St. Matthew, Farmington
Scott, William S., St. Matthew, Champaign
Serangeli, Gregory
Simon, Nicholas, St. Anthony, Atkinson
Sims, Fred, (Working Outside the Diocese)
Skender, John, St. Mark, Peoria
Sloman, William, St. Francis Medical Center & St. Ann, Peoria
Sondag, Robert, Immaculate Conception, Manito
Stalsburg, Terry, Benson, Roanoke
Steeples, David, Blessed Sacrament, Morton
Steiner, Bruce, St. Ann, Peoria
Swim, Russ, St. Mary, Moline
Taylor, Samuel W., St. Mary, Canton
Tomlianovich, Louis A., St. Anthony's, Bartonville
Triplett, Gene, St. Philomena, Monticello; St. Michael, Bement
Tyler, Raymond Toby, Cathedral of St. Mary of the Immaculate Conception, Peoria
Van Meltebeck, Martin, St. Mary, Kewanee
Van Wassenhove, Raymond, (Retired)
Vargas, Ausencio, Hispanic Ministry, St. Mary's Cathedral
Venzon, Joseph, St. Patrick, Washington
Vogelbaugh, Bob, Sacred Heart, Moline
Wachtel, Thomas, St. Malachy, Geneseo
Wagner, George, St. Mary's, Pontiac; St. John, Cullom; St. Joseph, Flanagan
Wallace, Ray, St. Mary's, Pontiac; St. John, Cullom; St. Joseph, Flanagan
Whited, Ernie, St. Joseph, Pekin
Whitehouse, Scott, Sacred Heart, Farmer City
Wilder, Mark, St. Joseph, Pekin
Zeeb, Kevin, Blessed Sacrament, Morton
Zimmerman, Richard, St. Peter, Peoria
Zulz, Charles, St. Mary's, Wenona; St. Patrick's Minonk; St. John's, Lostant.

INSTITUTIONS LOCATED IN DIOCESE

[A] SEMINARIES, RELIGIOUS OR SCHOLASTICATES

PERU. *St. Bede Abbey* (1891) St. Bede Abbey, 24 W. U.S. Hwy. 6, Peru, 61354. Tel: 815-223-3140; Fax: 815-223-8580; Email: frphilip@st-bede.com; Web: stbedeabbey.org. Bro. Markus Dicosola, Member. Benedictine Fathers and Brothers.

Benedictine Society of St. Bede Brothers 6; Priests 7; Students 1.

Staff: Rt. Rev. Philip D. Davey, O.S.B., Abbot; Revs. Michael Calhoun, Prior; Dominic M. Garramone, O.S.B., Subprior & CFO; Harold L. Datzman, O.S.B.; Patrick A. Fennell, O.S.B.; Gregory Jarzombek, O.S.B.; Ronald L. Margherio, O.S.B.; Samuel D. Pusateri, O.S.B.; Bros. David Freeman, O.S.B.; Nathaniel Grossman, O.S.B.; George J. Matsuoka, O.S.B., (Retired); Luke E. McLachlan, O.S.B.; Robert Pondant, O.S.B. The Benedictine Society of St. Bede.

[B] HIGH SCHOOLS, DIOCESAN AND INTER-PAROCHIAL

PEORIA. *Peoria Notre Dame High School*, 5105 N. Sheridan, 61614. Tel: 309-691-8741; Fax: 309-691-0875; Email: l.simmons@pndhs.org; Web: peorianotredame.com. Mr. Randy Simmons, Prin.; Mr. Tim Speck, Dean; Mrs. Theresa Geers, Business Mgr. Religious Teachers 1; Lay Teachers 63; Priests 1; Sisters 4; Students 760.

Peoria Notre Dame Scholarship Trust, 5105 N. Sheridan Rd., 61614. Tel: 309-691-8741; Email: t.geers@pndhs.org. Mr. Randy Simmons, Prin.; Mrs. Theresa Geers, Business Mgr.

Peoria Notre Dame High School Foundation, Peoria Notre Dame High School, 5105 N. Sheridan Rd., 61614. Tel: 309-691-8741; Email: t.geers@pndhs.org. Most Rev. Daniel R. Jenky, C.S.C., Contact Person.

BLOOMINGTON. *Central Catholic High School*, 1201 Airport Rd., Bloomington, 61704-2534. Tel: 309-661-7000; Fax: 309-661-7010; Email: sfoster@blmcchs.org; Web: www.blmcchs.org. Sean Foster, Prin. Religious Teachers 1; Lay Teachers 25; Priests 1; Students 325.

CHAMPAIGN. *High School of St. Thomas More*, 3901 N. Mattis Ave., Champaign, 61822. Tel: 217-352-7210; Fax: 217-352-7213; Email: jschreder@hs-stm.org; Web: www.hs-stm.org. Mr. Jason Schreder, Prin.; Rev. Matthew Hoelscher, Chap. Religious Teachers 3; Lay Teachers 27; Priests 1; Students 294.

DANVILLE. *Schlarman Academy*, 2112 N. Vermilion St., Danville, 61832. Tel: 217-442-2725; Fax: 217-442-0293; Email: mcroy@schlarman.com; Web: www.schlarmanacademy.com. Mark Janesky, Prin.; Rev. Bowan M. Schmitt, Chap. Lay Teachers 26; Students 323.

OTTAWA. *Marquette Academy of Ottawa, Inc.*, 1000 Paul St., Ottawa, 61350. Tel: 815-433-0125; Fax: 815-433-2632; Email: brick@marquetteacademy.net; Web: marquetteacademy.net. Mrs. Brooke Rick, Prin. Religious Teachers 3; Lay Teachers 35; Priests 5; Students 407.

ROCK ISLAND. *Alleman High School* (1949) 1103 40th St., Rock Island, 61201. Tel: 309-786-7793; Fax: 309-786-7834; Email: alleman@allemanhighschool.org; Web: www.allemanhighschool.org. Mr. David Hobin, Prin.; Revs. Daniel J. Mirabelli, C.S.V., Dir. of Devel.; Jeremy Freehill, Chap.; Nancy Morris, Librarian. Religious Teachers 1; Lay Teachers 24; Sisters 3; Students 428.

[C] HIGH SCHOOLS, PRIVATE

PERU. *St. Bede Academy* (1890) 24 W. U.S. Hwy. 6, Peru, 61354-2903. Tel: 815-223-3140; Fax: 815-223-8580; Email: mamershon@st-bede.com; Web: www.st-bede.com. Benedictine Fathers and Brothers. Religious Teachers 2; Lay Teachers 25; Benedictine Priests 2; Students 272.

Administration: Dr. Ted Struck, Supt.; Revs. Ronald L. Margherio, O.S.B., Chap.; Dominic M. Garramone, O.S.B., CFO, Religion Teacher; Mrs. Michelle Mershon, Prin.; Mrs. Theresa Bernabei, Dir. Guidance; Mrs. Eve Postula, Treas. & Business Mgr. Benedictine Fathers and Brothers.

[D] ELEMENTARY SCHOOLS INTER-PAROCHIAL

BLOOMINGTON. *Corpus Christi Catholic School of Bloomington Inc.*, (Grades PreK-8), 1909 E. Lincoln St., Bloomington, 61701. Tel: 309-662-3712; Fax: 309-663-9115; Email: jclark@corpuschristisaints.org; Email: awilson@corpuschristisaints.org; Web: www.corpuschristisaints.org. Mrs. Judy Clark, Prin.; Adrienne Wilson, Prin. Religious Teachers 1; Lay Teachers 54; Students 476.

EAST MOLINE. *Our Lady of Grace Catholic Academy*, 603 18th Ave., East Moline, 61244. Tel: 309-755-9771; Fax: 309-755-7407; Email: office@olgca.org; Web: www.olgca.org. Scott Turnipseed, Prin.; Carolyn DeBruine, Librarian, Email: cdebruine@olgca.org. Lay Teachers 12; Sisters 1; Students 150.

LA SALLE. *Trinity Catholic Academy*, 650 Fourth St., La Salle, 61301. Tel: 815-223-8523; Fax: 815-223-7450; Email: trinitycatholic@insightbb.com; Web: www.asd.com. Mr. Jerald Carls, Prin.; Kathy Brayton, Librarian, Email: kaybray557@yahoo.com. Lay Teachers 14; Students 189.

MOLINE. *Seton Catholic School*, (Grades PreSchool-8), 1320-16th & 17th Ave., Moline, 61265. Tel: 309-757-5500; Tel: 309-764-5418; Fax: 309-762-0545; Fax: 309-277-0015; Email: jbarrett@setonschool.com; Web: www.setonschool.com. Mrs. Jane Barrett, Prin. Lay Teachers 33; Sisters 1; Students 496.

ROCK ISLAND. *Jordan Catholic School of Rock Island, Inc.*, (Grades PreK-8), Directs the Elementary School System for the Rock Island-Milan area, operating facilities at St. Pius X. Parishes in Rock Island. 2901-24th St., Rock Island, 61201. Tel: 309-793-7366; Fax: 309-793-7361; Email: jsmithers@jordanschool.com; Email: karmetta@jordanschool.com; Web: www.jordanschool.com. Mr. Jacob Smithers, Prin. Religious Teachers 1; Lay Teachers 25; Students 388.

Commission on Education for Jordan Catholic School, P.O. Box 3490, Rock Island, 61204-3490. Tel: 309-793-7350; Fax: 309-793-7361; Email: jsmithers@jordanschool.com. Rev. Msgr. Mark J. Merdian.

[E] CATHOLIC CHARITIES OF THE DIOCESE PEORIA

PEORIA. *Catholic Charities of the Diocese of Peoria*, 419 N.E. Madison Ave., 61603. Tel: 309-636-8000; Fax: 309-674-1664; Email: sranapia@ccdop.org; Web: www.ccdop.org. Sr. Ana Pia Cordua, S.C.T.J.-M., Exec. Dir. Child Care, Food Pantry, Baby Pantry, Furniture Bank, Soup Kitchen, Senior Counseling Services, Senior Support Services, Family and Community Outreach Tot Asst. Annually 8,809; Total Staff 8; Other Staff 1; Total Assisted 8,808.

Catholic Charities Branch Offices

Guardian Angel Outreach, 405 Illinois St., Streator, 61364. Tel: 815-672-4567; Email: sranapia@ccdop.org. Sr. Ana Pia Cordua, S.C.T.J.M., Exec. Tot Asst. Annually 121; Total Staff 1.

[F] DAY CARE CENTERS

WEST PEORIA. *Jesu Children's Enrichment Centers*, 2903 Heading Ave., West Peoria, 61604. Tel: 309-636-8905; Fax: 309-671-8905; Email: jesu@rng3.com. 1717 W. Candletree Dr., Ste. C, 61614. Wendy Pettett, Business Mgr. Capacity 104; Students 90; Total Staff 13.

[G] GENERAL HOSPITALS

PEORIA. *OSF HealthCare Saint Francis Medical Center*, 1175 St. Francis Ln., East Peoria, 61611. Tel: 309-655-2000; Email: robert.brandfass@osfhealthcare.org. Robert G. Anderson, Pres.; Rev. Msgr. Michael C. Bliss, Dir., Pastoral Care. Sponsored and owned by the Sisters of the Third Order of St. Francis. Bed Capacity 629; Tot Asst. Annually 812,087; Total Staff 5,924; Sisters of the Third Order of St. Francis 5.

OSF Healthcare System (1880) 800 N.E. Glen Oak Ave., 61603-3200. Tel: 309-655-2850; Fax: 309-655-6869; Email: robert.brandfass@osfhealthcare.org; Web: www.osfhealthcare.org. Robert Sehring, CEO. Sponsored and owned by the Sisters of the Third Order of St. Francis. Bed Capacity 1,874; Tot Asst. Annually 3,731,666; Total Staff 18,884.

**OSF Multi Specialty Group*, 800 N.E. Glen Oak Ave., 61603. Tel: 309-655-2850; Email: robert.brandfass@osfhealthcare.org. Jeffry Tillery, Pres. Tot Asst. Annually 785,210; Total Staff 3,903.

BLOOMINGTON. *OSF HealthCare St. Joseph Medical Center*, 2200 E. Washington, Bloomington, 61701. Tel: 309-662-3311; Fax: 309-662-7143; Email: robert.brandfass@osfhealthcare.org; Web: osfhealthcare.org. Lynn Fulton, Pres.; Rev. Rogers Byambaasa, A.J., Chap. Sponsored and owned by the Sisters of the Third Order of St. Francis. Bed Capacity 149; Tot Asst. Annually 261,049; Total Staff 938.

DANVILLE. *OSF HealthCare Sacred Heart Medical Center*, 812 N. Logan, Danville, 61832. Tel: 217-443-5000; Fax: 217-443-1965; Email:

Teresa.Gaffney@presencehealth.org; Web: www.presencehealth.org/usmc. Jared C. Rogers, M.D., Pres. & CEO; Rev. Deusdedit Byomuhangi, Spiritual Care Mgr.; Philip Jackson, Chap.; Andrew Martin, Chap.; Timothy Shaw, Chap.; Ron Ziemer, Chap.

Presence Central and Suburban Hospitals Network d/b/a Presence United Samaritans Medical Center. Bed Capacity 174; Priests 1; Tot Asst. Annually 84,474; Total Staff 576.

GALESBURG. *OSF HealthCare St. Mary Medical Center,* 3333 N. Seminary St., Galesburg, 61401-1299. Tel: 309-344-3161; Fax: 309-344-9498; Email: robert.brandfass@osfhealthcare.org; Web: osfhealthcare.org. Jennifer Junis, Pres.; Rev. Deus-Dedit B. Byabato, Chap.; Deacon David Steeples, Dir., Pastoral Care. Bed Capacity 81; Tot Asst. Annually 193,742; Total Staff 587.

The Galesburg St. Mary Medical Center Foundation, 3333 N. Seminary St., Galesburg, 61401. 530 N.E. Glen Oak Ave., 61637. Tel: 877-574-5678; Email: robert.brandfass@osfhealthcare.org. Thomas Hammerton, Pres.

KEWANEE. *OSF HealthCare Saint Luke Medical Center,* 1501 W. South St., P.O. Box 747, Kewanee, 61443. Tel: 309-852-7500; Email: robert.brandfass@osfhealthcare.org. Jackie Kernan, Pres. Bed Capacity 25; Tot Asst. Annually 95,509; Total Staff 226.

MONMOUTH. *OSF HealthCare Holy Family Medical Center,* 1000 W. Harlem Ave., Monmouth, 61462-1099. Tel: 309-734-3141; Fax: 309-734-3029; Email: robert.brandfass@osfhealthcare.org. Patricia Luker, Pres. & CEO; Rev. Thomas Otto, Chap. Bed Capacity 23; Tot Asst. Annually 80,598; Total Staff 269.

OTTAWA. **OSF HealthCare Saint Elizabeth Medical Center,* 1100 E. Norris Dr., Ottawa, 61350. Tel: 815-433-3100; Email: robert.brandfass@osfhealthcare.org; Web: www.ottawaregional.org. Mr. Kenneth Beutke, Pres.; Rev. Michael J. Driscoll, O.S.F., Dir. Pastoral Care. Sponsored by The Sisters of the Third Order of St. Francis.Owned by Ottawa Regional Hospital & Healthcare Center. Bed Capacity 97; Tot Asst. Annually 169,572; Total Staff 750.

PONTIAC. *OSF HealthCare Saint James-John W. Albrecht Medical Center,* 2500 W. Reynolds, Pontiac, 61764. Tel: 815-842-2828; Fax: 815-842-4912; Email: robert.brandfass@osfhealthcare.org; Web: osfhealthcare.org. Bradley V. Solberg, Pres.; Deacon George Wagner, Dir., Pastoral Care. Sponsored and owned by the Sisters of the Third Order of St. Francis. Bed Capacity 42; Capacity 42; Tot Asst. Annually 175,699; Total Staff 341.

SPRING VALLEY. *St. Margaret's Hospital,* 600 E. First St., Spring Valley, 61362. Tel: 815-664-5311; Fax: 815-664-1335; Email: administration@aboutsmh.org; Web: www.aboutsmh.org. Timothy Muntz, Pres. & CEO; Deacon John Murphy, Pastoral Care Dir. Bed Capacity 44; Sisters of Mary of the Presentation 2; Tot Asst. Annually 323,733; Total Staff 777.

STREATOR. *St. Mary's Hospital,* 111 Spring St., Streator, 61364. Tel: 815-673-2311; Fax: 815-673-4590; Email: robert.brandfass@osfhealthcare.org; Web: www.osfhealthcare.org/streator. Ken Beutke, Pres. Hospital Sisters Third Order of St. Francis.St. Mary's Hospital no longer exists as an in-patient facility. The facility which was St. Mary's Hospital is now operated as an outpatient facility by OSF Saint Elizabeth Medical Center. Total Staff 220.

URBANA. *OSF HealthCare Heart of Mary Medical Center,* 1400 W. Park St., Urbana, 61801. Tel: 217-337-2000; Fax: 217-337-4541; Email: robert.brandfass@osfhealthcare.org; Web: www.osfhealthcare.org. Jared C. Rogers, M.D., Pres. & CEO; Vera Duncanson, Spiritual Care Mgr.; Rev. Peter Dyck, Chap.; Ginny Conron, Chap.; Robert Frank, Chap.; Kristin Godlin, Chap.; Patricia Justice, Chap.; Carolyn Mullally, Chap.; Dorey Riegel, Chap.; Jason Schiller, Chap.

Presence Central and Suburban Hospitals Network d/b/a Presence Covenant Medical Center Bed Capacity 210; Tot Asst. Annually 116,840; Total Staff 767.

[H] SPECIAL HOSPITALS AND SANATORIA

LACON. *St. Joseph Nursing Home,* 401 Ninth St., Lacon, 61540. Tel: 309-246-2175; Fax: 309-246-3609; Email: jjamison@stjosephnursinghome-lacon.com; Web: www.stjosephnursinghome-lacon.com. Timothy Wukey, Admin. Daughters of St. Francis of Assisi. Bed Capacity 93; Total Staff 135; Total Assisted 110.

[I] HOMES FOR AGED

PEORIA. *St. Augustine Manor,* 1301 N.E. Glendale Ave., 61603. Tel: 309-674-7069; Fax: 309-494-6547; Email: staugustinemanor@yahoo.com. Jill Briney, Residential Mgr. Bed Capacity 55; Residents 34; Tot Asst. Annually 34; Total Staff 6.

[J] MONASTERIES AND RESIDENCES FOR PRIESTS AND BROTHERS

PRINCEVILLE. *Congregation of St. John,* 11223 W. Legion Hall Rd., Princeville, 61559. Tel: 309-385-1193; Fax: 872-267-1897; Email: monastery.princeville@stjean.com; Web: csjohn.org. Rev. Benedict Paston-Bedingfeld, Prior. Deacons 1; Novices 2; Priests 3; Professed Brothers 2; Oblate Brothers 2.

[K] CONVENTS AND RESIDENCES FOR SISTERS

PEORIA. *St. Francis Medical Center Convent,* Mailing Address: St. Francis Medical Center, 1175 St. Francis Ln., East Peoria, 61611. Tel: 309-655-2083 ; Tel: 309-655-4840; Email: robert.brandfass@osfhealthcare.org; Web: franciscansisterspeoria.org. Sr. Agnes Joseph Williams, O.S.F., Dir. Formation. The Sisters of the Third Order of St. Francis 5.

Franciscan Apostolic Sisters, 600 N.E. Monroe St., 61603. Sr. Lourdes de Leon, Contact Person. Sisters 7.

Immaculate Conception Convent (1891) 2408 W. Heading Ave., 61604-5096. Tel: 309-674-6168; Fax: 309-674-2006; Email: kamourisse@gmail.com; Web: westpeoriasisters.org. Sr. Kathleen Mornisse, Pres. Motherhouse of the Sisters of St. Francis of the Immaculate Conception. Sisters 29; Professed Sisters 28.

Missionaries of Charity Convent (1991) 506 Hancock St., 61603. Tel: 309-495-9490 Convent; Email: scadiz7@hotmail.com. Sisters M. Jonathan, M.C., Regl. Supr.; M. Julian Paul, M.C., Supr. Sisters 4.

The Poor Clares, Tel: 309-682-3182; Fax: 309-682-3182; Web: www.poorclaresjoliet.org. Sisters 4.

Our Lady of the Angels Convent, 3432 W. Baskin Ridge, 61604. Tel: 309-682-3182; Fax: 309-682-3182.

EAST PEORIA. **Motherhouse, The Sisters of the Third Order of St. Francis,* 1175 Saint Francis Ln., East Peoria, 61611-1299. Tel: 309-699-7215; Email: robert.brandfass@osfhealthcare.org; Web: www.franciscansisterspeoria.org. Sr. Judith Ann Duvall, O.S.F., Major Supr. Sisters 20.

Mt. Alverno Novitiate, 1175 Saint Francis Ln., East Peoria, 61611-1299. Tel: 309-699-9313; Email: robert.brandfass@osfhealthcare.org; Web: www.franciscansisterspeoria.org. Rev. Msgr. Rick J. Oberch, Chap. Novitiate of The Sisters of the Third Order of St. Francis.Members of the Novitiate are currently residing at St. Francis Medical Center Convent. Sisters 20.

LACON. *St. Joseph Motherhouse and Novitiate,* 507 N. Prairie St., Lacon, 61540. Tel: 309-246-2175; Fax: 309-246-2708; Email: dsfcongregation@gmail.com; Web: www.laconfranciscans.org. Sr. Loretta Matas, D.S.F., Provincial Supr. Congregation of the Daughters of St. Francis of Assisi. Sisters 9; Sisters in Community (Professed) 11.

PEORIA HEIGHTS. *Franciscan Sisters of John the Baptist,* 1209 E. Lake Ave., Peoria Heights, 61616. Tel: 309-688-3500; Email: fsjbpeoria@yahoo.com; Web: www.sistersofjohnthebaptist.org. Mother M. Vaclava Ballon, F.S.J.B., Supr. Professed Sisters 6.

PRINCEVILLE. *Apostolic Sisters of St. John,* 10809 W. Legion Hall Rd., Princeville, 61559. Tel: 309-243-1488; Email: sr.ap.princeville@stjean.com; Web: www.apostolicsistersofsaintjohn.com. Sr. Anne of Jesus, C.S.J., Prioress. Sisters 6.

Sisters of St. John (1999) 11227 W. Legion Hall Rd., Princeville, 61559. Tel: 309-385-2550; Fax: 309-385-2550; Email: srs.princeville@gmail.com. Sr. Marie Francois, S.J., Supr. Sisters 8.

ROCK ISLAND. *St. Mary Monastery* (1874) 2200 88th Ave. W., Rock Island, 61201-7649. Tel: 309-283-2100; Fax: 309-283-2200; Email: smcgrath@smmsisters.org; Web: www.smmsisters.org. Sr. Sandra Brunenn, O.S.B., Prioress. Benedictine Sisters. Sisters in Community 34.

Benet House Retreat Center, Tel: 309-283-2108; Fax: 309-283-2200; Email: retreats@smmsisters.org; Web: www.smmsisters.org. Sr. Roberta Bussan, O.S.B., Dir.

WEST PEORIA. *Mother of Peace Home* (1970) 2408 W. Heading Ave., West Peoria, 61604. Tel: 309-673-4657; Fax: 309-674-2006; Email: iccmoph@yahoo.com; Web: osfsisterswpeoria.org. Sr. Linda Burkitt, Admin. Sisters 2; Total in Residence 2; Total Staff 8.

Servants of the Pierced Hearts of Jesus and Mary, 2327 W. Heading Ave., West Peoria, 61604. Cell: 309-642-4350; Email: srisabel@piercedhearts.org; Web: www.piercedhearts.org. Sr. Teresa Urioste, S.C.T.J.M., Supr. & Coord. Sisters 3.

[L] NEWMAN CENTERS

PEORIA. *Newman Foundation at Bradley University & Illinois Central College,* 1116 W. College Ave., 61606-1728. Tel: 309-674-0208 (Office); Fax: 309-497-3759; Email: stjosephnewman@gmail.com; Web: ncbu.org. Mr. Samuel Mangieri III, Campus Min. Total in Residence 3; Total Staff 2; Total Assisted 3,471.

CHAMPAIGN. *Newman Foundation at the University of IL* dba St. John's Catholic Newman Center, 604 E. Armory Ave., Champaign, 61820. Tel: 217-344-1266; Fax: 217-344-4957; Email: frlampitt@gmail.com; Web: www.sjcnc.org. Revs. Robert Lampitt, Chap.; Chase Hilgenbrinck, Asst. Chap. Total in Residence 2; Total Staff 21; Newman Center Residents 587; Newman Center Pastoral Staff 13; Newman Hall Staff 8.

EUREKA. *Salve Regina Newman Foundation,* Eureka College, 108 E. College Ave., Eureka, 61530. Tel: 309-467-2646; Email: cdopsrnc@gmail.com; Web: www.cdopsrnc.com. Rev. Eugene A. Radosevich, Chap.

MACOMB. *St. Francis of Assisi Newman Center* (1945) 1401 W. University Dr., Macomb, 61455. Tel: 309-837-3989; Email: wiucatholic@gmail.com; Web: www.wiucatholic.org. Rev. Adam Stimpson, Chap.; Jonathan Day, Ph.D., Dir.

MONMOUTH. *St. Augustine Newman Club,* Monmouth College, 502 N. 6th St., Monmouth, 61462. Tel: 309-734-7533; Email: fathertomotto@gmail.com. Mailing: 200 W. Broadway, Monmouth, 61462. Rev. Thomas Otto, Chap.

NORMAL. *St. John Paul II Catholic Newman Center, St. Robert Bellarmine Chapel,* 501 S. Main St., Normal, 61761. Tel: 309-452-5046; Fax: 309-452-3845; Email: srsilvia@stjpnc.org; Web: www.isucatholic.org. Sr. Silvia Tarafa, S.C.-T.J.M., Dir. Total Staff 6.

ROCK ISLAND. *Augustana College Catholic Campus Ministry,* Mailing: 419 N.E. Madison Ave., 61603. Tel: 309-671-1550; Email: dcnsondag@cdop.org. Deacon Robert Sondag, Contact Person.

[M] PERSONAL PRELATURES

URBANA. *Opus Dei* Prelature of the Holy Cross and Opus Dei Lincoln Green University Center, 715 W. Michigan Ave., Urbana, 61801. Email: gbcole123@gmail.com.

[N] MISCELLANEOUS

PEORIA. *Archbishop Fulton J. Sheen Foundation* (1996) 419 N.E. Madison, 61603. Tel: 309-671-1550; Fax: 309-671-1573; Email: info@sheencause.org; Web: www.archbishopsheencause.org. Rev. Msgr. Stanley L. Deptula, Exec. Dir.; Most Rev. Daniel R. Jenky, C.S.C., Pres.

Family Resource Center, 415 N.E. Monroe Ave., 61603. Tel: 309-839-2287; Email: csone@ccdop.org. Cecilia Sone, Dir.

Franciscan Spirituality and Resource Center, 2408 W. Heading Ave., 61604. Tel: 309-674-6168; Fax: 309-674-2006; Email: srdiane2408@gmail.com; Web: westpeoriasisters.org. Sisters Betty Jean Haverback, O.S.F., Contact Person; Diane VandeVoorde, O.S.F., Contact Person.

Jordan Catholic School of Rock Island, Inc., 419 N.E. Madison Ave., 61603. Tel: 309-671-1550; Email: cberkshier@cdop.org. Most Rev. Daniel R. Jenky, C.S.C., Contact Person.

Nazareth House, NFP, 419 N.E. Madison Ave., 61603. Tel: 309-671-1550; Email: cberkshier@cdop.org. Most Rev. Daniel R. Jenky, C.S.C., Contact Person.

Notre Dame High School of Peoria, Inc., 5105 N. Sheridan Rd., 61614. Tel: 309-691-8741; Fax: 309-691-0875; Email: r.simmons@pndhs.org; Email: t.geers@pndhs.org; Web: peorianotredame.com. Mr. Randy Simmons, Prin.; Mrs. Theresa Geers, Business Mgr.

Seton Catholic School of Moline, Inc., 419 N.E. Madison Ave., 61603. Tel: 309-671-1550; Email: cberkshier@cdop.org. Most Rev. Daniel R. Jenky, C.S.C., Contact Person.

STM Boosters, Inc., 3901 N. Mattis Ave., Champaign, 61822. Tel: 217-352-7210; Fax: 217-352-7213; Email: iblomberg@hs-stm.org. Mr. Ian Blomberg, Contact Person.

St. Vincent De Paul Society, 419 N.E. Madison Ave., 61603. Tel: 309-671-1550; Fax: 309-671-1576; Email: msgr_kruse@cdop.org. Rev. Msgr. James E. Kruse, J.C.L., V.G., Contact Person. Diocesan Council and Particular Council of Peoria.

ALEDO. *Family of Mary,* 1331 230th St., Aledo, 61231. Tel: 309-372-4654; Email: swhite.triumph@gmail.com; Email: scott_triumph@yahoo.com. Mr. Scott White, Pres.

BLOOMINGTON. *Central Catholic High School of Bloomington, Inc.* (1898) Mailing Address: 1201 Airport Rd., Bloomington, 61704. Tel: 309-661-7000; Fax: 309-661-7010; Email: sfoster@blmcchs.org. Sean Foster, Prin.

CHAMPAIGN. *Presence Home Care*, 1501 Interstate Dr., Champaign, 61822. Tel: 217-355-4120; Fax: 217-355-4121; Email: robert.brandfass@osfhealthcare.org; Web: www.osfhealthcare.org. A.J. Querciagrossa, Admin. Operated by OSF HealthCare System.

The High School of St. Thomas More of Champaign, Inc., 3901 N. Mattis, Champaign, 61822. Tel: 217-352-7210; Fax: 217-352-7213; Email: jschreder@hs-stm.org; Web: www.hs-stm.org. Mr. Jason Schreder, Prin.; Tracy Neitzel, Vice Prin.; Rev. Eric Bolek, Chap.

DANVILLE. *Schlarman Academy of Danville, Inc.* (1946) 2112 N. Vermilion, Danville, 61832. Tel: 217-442-2725; Fax: 217-442-0293; Email: mjanesky@schlarman.com; Web: www.schlarmanacademy.com. Mark Janesky, Prin.

LACON. *St. Francis of Assisi Fund, NFP*, 507 N. Prairie St., Lacon, 61540-1152. Tel: 309-246-2175; Fax: 309-246-2708; Email: dsfcongregation@gmail.com; Web: www.laconfranciscans.org. Sr. Loretta Matas, D.S.F., Pres.

Religious Sisters Aid, NFP, 507 N. Prairie St., Lacon, 61540-1152. Tel: 309-246-2175; Fax: 309-246-2708; Email: dsfcongregation@gmail.com; Web: laconfranciscans.org. Sr. Loretta Matas, D.S.F., Pres.

MOLINE. *The Order of the Legion of Little Souls of the Merciful Heart of Jesus*, 428 39th St., Moline, 61265. Tel: 309-797-8491; Email: teresahuyten@hotmail.com; Email: thuyten@yahoo.com; Web: www.littlesouls.org. Teresa I. Huyten, Dir.; Revs. Michael L. Menner, Diocesan Chap.; John R. Burns, Natl. Chap., Email: frjrburns@hotmail.com.

NORMAL. *Homes of Hope, Inc.*, 705 E. Lincoln St., Ste. 313, Normal, 61761. Tel: 309-862-0607; Fax: 309-452-7131; Email: homesofhope1@frontier.com. Maureen McIntosh, Dir. Bed Capacity 22; Tot Asst. Annually 22; Total Staff 37.

ROCK ISLAND. *Alleman High School of Rock Island, Inc.*, 1103 40th St., Rock Island, 61201. Tel: 309-786-7793; Fax: 309-786-7834; Email: allemanhs@mchsi.com; Web: www.allemanhighschool.org. Mr. David Hobin, Prin.

RELIGIOUS INSTITUTES OF MEN REPRESENTED IN THE DIOCESE

For further details refer to the corresponding bracketed number in the Religious Institutes of Men or Women section.

[]—*Apostles of Jesus - Peoria Community*.
[0200]—*Benedictine Monks* (St. Bede Abbey)—O.S.B.
[1320]—*Clerics of St. Viator*—C.S.V.
[]—*Congregation of St. John*—C.S.J.
[0480]—*Conventual Franciscans*—O.F.M.Conv.
[0520]—*Franciscan Friars* (Prov. of St. John the Baptist)—O.F.M.
[0720]—*The Missionaries of Our Lady of La Salette*—M.S.

RELIGIOUS INSTITUTES OF WOMEN REPRESENTED IN THE DIOCESE

[]—*Apostolic Sisters of St. John*.
[]—*Apostolic Sisters of the Community of St. John*.
[0230]—*Benedictine Sisters of Pontifical Jurisdiction*—O.S.B.
[0920]—*Congregation of the Daughters of St. Francis of Assisi, (American Prov.)*—D.S.F.
[2100]—*Congregation of the Humility of Mary*—C.H.M.
[1920]—*Congregation of the Sisters of the Holy Cross*—C.S.C.
[1730]—*Congregation of the Sisters of the Third Order of St. Francis, Oldenburg, IN*—O.S.F.
[1710]—*Congregation of the Third Order of St. Francis of Mary Immaculate, Joliet, IL*—O.S.F.
[0760]—*Daughters of Charity of St. Vincent de Paul*—D.C.
[1070-03]—*Dominican Sisters*—O.P.
[1070-10]—*Dominican Sisters*—O.P.
[]—*Dominican Sisters of Mary, Mother of the Eucharist*.
[]—*Franciscan Apostolic Sisters*.
[]—*Franciscan Sisters of John the Baptist*.
[1450]—*Franciscan Sisters of the Sacred Heart*—O.S.F.
[1770]—*Hospital Sisters of the Third Order of St. Francis*—O.S.F.
[2575]—*Institute of the Sisters of Mercy of the Americas*—R.S.M.
[2710]—*Missionaries of Charity*—M.C.
[3230]—*Poor Handmaids of Jesus Christ*—P.H.J.C.
[2970]—*School Sisters of Notre Dame*—S.S.N.D.
[1680]—*School Sisters of St. Francis*—O.S.F.
[3520]—*Servants of the Holy Heart of Mary*—S.S.C.M.
[]—*Servants of the Pierced Hearts of Jesus and Mary* (Miami, FL).
[0430]—*Sisters of Charity of the Blessed Virgin Mary*—B.V.M.
[0660]—*Sisters of Christian Charity*—S.C.C.
[2450]—*Sisters of Mary of the Presentation*—S.M.P.
[3360]—*Sisters of Providence of Saint Mary-of-the-Woods, Indiana*—S.P.
[1540]—*Sisters of Saint Francis, Clinton, Iowa*—O.S.F.
[1705]—*The Sisters of St. Francis of Assisi*—O.S.F.
[1580]—*Sisters of St. Francis of the Immaculate Conception*—O.S.F.
[3840]—*Sisters of St. Joseph of Carondelet*—C.S.J.
[]—*Sisters of the Community of St. John*.
[]—*Sisters of the Holy Cross*—C.S.C.
[]—*Sisters of the Sacred Heart and of the Poor* (Mexico).
[1820]—*Sisters of the Third Order of St. Francis (East Peoria, Illinois)*—O.S.F.
[]—*Sisters of the Visitation*.

CEMETERIES/CEMETERY ASSOCIATIONS

PEORIA. *Catholic Cemetery Association of Peoria, IL*, 7519 N. Allen, 61614. Tel: 309-691-5889; Fax: 309-690-4737; Email: info@ccapeo.org; Web: www.ccapeo.org. Deacon Robert Myers Sr., Dir. Operates St. Mary's Cemetery, St. Joseph's Cemetery and Resurrection Cemetery in Peoria.

BLOOMINGTON. *Bloomington-Normal Catholic Cemetery Association*, 711 N. Main St., Bloomington, 61701. Tel: 309-829-3019; Tel: 309-807-0338; Email: erinehimer@holytrinitybloomington.org. Steve Lyons, Dir.; Rev. Jeffrey D. Stirniman, Admin.

DANVILLE. *Resurrection Catholic Cemetery Association of Danville, IL*, 444 E. Main, Danville, 61832. Tel: 217-431-5114; Email: cemetery@holyfamilydanville.net. 813 Wendt Ave., Danville, 61832. Mike O'Kane, Trustee.

FARMER CITY. *St. Joseph Cemetery Association of Farmer City, IL*, 612 N. Plum St., Farmer City, 61842. 502 N. Monroe St., Clinton, 61727. Tel: 309-928-3855; Email: shchurch612@frontier.com. Vanessa Ophorst, Bookkeeper.

GALESBURG. *St. Joseph's Cemetery Association of Galesburg, IL*, 2315 Monmouth Blvd., Galesburg, 61401. 273 S. Prairie St., Galesburg, 61401. Tel: 309-342-8256; Tel: 309-342-1913; Email: kemlars@gmail.com; Email: adorecc7@gmail.com. Rev. William T. Miller, Admin.

PEKIN. *Catholic Cemetery Association of Pekin, IL*, 5th St. & Hanna Dr., Pekin, 61554. 303 S. 7th St., Pekin, 61554. Tel: 309-347-6108; Email: catholiccemeteries@stjosephpekin.org; Email: stjoseph@stjosephpekin.org. Rev. Michael J. Andrejek.

ROCK ISLAND. *Calvary Cemetery Association of Rock Island, IL*, 2901 12th St., Rock Island, 61201. Tel: 309-788-6197; Fax: 309-788-6734; Email: info@calvarycemetaryri.com; Web: www.calvarycemetaryri.com. Greg Vogele, Supt.

NECROLOGY

† Ketcham, Gregory K., Bloomington, IL, St Patrick Church of Merna, Died Feb. 8, 2018
† Brajkovich, Thomas R., (Retired), Died Jul. 5, 2018
† DeBisschop, James P., Coal Valley, IL St. Maria Goretti, Died Apr. 1, 2018
† King, James E., Died Oct. 12, 2018
† Mullen, Richard, (Retired), Died Mar. 23, 2018

An asterisk (*) denotes an organization that has established tax-exempt status directly with the IRS and is not covered by the USCCB Group Ruling.

The Personal Ordinariate of the Chair of Saint Peter

Most Reverend

STEVEN J. LOPES

Ordinary of The Chair of St. Peter; ordained June 23, 2001; appointed first Bishop of the Personal Ordinariate of the Chair of St. Peter November 24, 2015; ordained Bishop February 2, 2016.

ESTABLISHED JANUARY 1, 2012.

Ordinariate Office: 7730 Westview Dr., Houston, TX 77055. Tel: 713-609-9292; Fax: 713-957-5046. *Mailing Address: P.O. Box 55206, Houston, TX 77255.*

Email: office@ordinariate.net

Web: www.ordinariate.net

STATISTICAL OVERVIEW

Personnel	
Bishop	1
Priests: Diocesan Active in Diocese	37
Priests: Diocesan Active Outside Diocese	14
Priests: Retired, Sick or Absent	19
Number of Diocesan Priests	70
Total Priests in Diocese	70
Ordinations:	
Diocesan Priests	7
Transitional Deacons	2
Permanent Deacons	1
Permanent Deacons in Diocese	10
Total Sisters	5
Parishes	
Parishes	42
With Resident Pastor:	
Resident Diocesan Priests	38
Without Resident Pastor:	
Administered by Lay People	3
Completely Vacant	1
Missions	2
New Parishes Created	3
Professional Ministry Personnel:	
Sisters	5
Lay Ministers	18
Welfare	
Day Care Centers	1
Total Assisted	20
Educational	
Diocesan Students in Other Seminaries	7
Total Seminarians	7
Elementary Schools, Diocesan and Parish	1
Total Students	400
Catechesis/Religious Education:	
High School Students	130
Elementary Students	270
Total Students under Catholic Instruction	807
Teachers in the Diocese:	
Lay Teachers	45
Vital Statistics	
Receptions into the Church:	
Infant Baptism Totals	102
Minor Baptism Totals	18
Adult Baptism Totals	10
Received into Full Communion	62
First Communions	175
Confirmations	222
Marriages:	
Catholic	37
Interfaith	7
Total Marriages	44
Deaths	32
Total Catholic Population	6,000

Curial Officials

Bishop—Most Rev. STEVEN J. LOPES.

Chancellor/Executive Assistant to the Bishop—MS. LAUREL MILLER, Tel: 346-247-2201; Email: office@ordinariate.net.

Vicar General—Very Rev. TIMOTHY P. PERKINS, Tel: 346-247-2201; Email: vg@ordinariate.net.

Director of Vocations and Clergy Formation— Tel: 346-247-2205; Email: vocations@ordinariate.net. Rev. RICHARD D. KRAMER, (Retired).

Development Support ServicesTel: 346-247-2209; Email: devsupport@ordinariate.net. AMATA VERITAS, O.P.

Business Manager—Tel: 346-247-2218; Email: ag.stockstill@ordinariate.net. A.G. STOCKSTILL.

Director of Child and Youth Protection—MRS. LYNN SCHMIDT, Tel: 907-317-6257; Email: safeenvironment@ordinariate.net.

Officer for Child and Youth Protection-Canada—Email: safeenvironmentcanada@ordinariate.net. MRS. SHAUNA LOVE.

Vice Chancellor—Tel: 713-683-9407. Deacon MARK STOCKSTILL.

Notaries—MS. MARGARET PICHON; MS. LAUREL MILLER.

Ordinariate Legal Counsel—MR. MARK CHOPKO, Stradley, Ronan, Stevens and Young, LLP.

Ordinariate Web Page—Web: www.ordinariate.net.

Dean for Canada—Very Rev. CARL REID, (Retired).

CLERGY, PARISHES, MISSIONS AND PAROCHIAL SCHOOLS

STATE OF TEXAS

HOUSTON, HARRIS CO., THE CATHEDRAL OF OUR LADY OF WALSINGHAM (1984)
7809 Shadyvilla Ln., 77055-5011. Tel: 713-683-9407; Fax: 713-683-1518; Email: office@olwcatholic.org; Web: www.olwcatholic.org. Very Rev. Charles A. Hough IV, Rector; Rev. Justin Fletcher, Parochial Vicar; Deacons James Barnett; Mark Stockstill; Mark Baker.
Shrine—The American Shrine of Our Lady of Walsingham.

ARLINGTON, TARRANT CO., CHURCH OF ST. MARY THE VIRGIN (1994)
1408 N. Davis Dr., Arlington, 76012.
Tel: 817-460-2278; Email: office@stmarythevirgin.org; Web: www.stmaryarl@sbcglobal.net. Revs. Prentice Dean; Thomas Kennedy.

CLEBURNE, JOHNSON CO., ST. JOHN VIANNEY CATHOLIC CHURCH (2012)
501 N. Nolan River Rd., Cleburne, 76033.
Tel: 817-894-4266; Email: frchris@swbell.net; Web: www.st.johnvianneycleburne.com. 2020 W. Kilpatrick, Cleburne, 76033. Rev. Christopher Stainbrook, Admin.

DENISON, GRAYSON CO., ST. MICHAEL AND ALL ANGELS CATHOLIC CHURCH (2014)
101 E. Texas St., Denison, 75020. Tel: 903-821-7511; Email: Fr.Randall@yahoo.com. Rev. Randall Fogle, Parochial Vicar, (Retired).

FORT WORTH, TARRANT CO., SAINT TIMOTHY (2012)
c/o St. Mary of the Assumption Catholic Church, 800 W. Loop 820 S., Fort Worth, 76108.
Tel: 817-923-1911; Email: office@ordinariate.net; Web: www.sttimothyfortworth.org. Rev. Thomas Kennedy, Admin.

KATY, HARRIS CO., ST. MARGARET OF SCOTLAND CATHOLIC COMMUNITY (2015)
1800 Grand Pkwy., Katy, 77449. Tel: 281-693-1000; Tel: 701-429-0952; Email: drstevesellers@gmail.com; Web: www.stmargaretchurchhouston.org. Revs. Steven Sellers; Jonathan Michican, Parochial Vicar.

SAN ANTONIO, BEXAR CO., OUR LADY OF THE ATONEMENT CATHOLIC CHURCH (1983)
Tel: 210-695-2940; Email: FrLewis@AtonementOnline.com; Web: church.atonementonline.com. Very Rev. Mark W. Lewis; Revs. Christopher G. Phillips, Pastor Emeritus; Jeffery Wade Moore, Parochial Vicar; Deacons Michael D'Agostino; Michael Noble.
School—The Atonement Academy, (Grades PreK-12), Tel: 210-695-2240; Email: jmarkovetz@atonementonline.com. John Markovetz, Headmaster.

STATE OF ALABAMA

MOBILE, MOBILE CO., SOCIETY OF SAINT GREGORY THE GREAT (2012)
1413 Old Shell Rd., Mobile, AL 36604.
Tel: 252-402-0162; Email: info@stgregorymobile.org; Web: www.stgregorymobile.org. Mailing Address: 1001 Hillcrest Ln., Mobile, AL 36693. Andrew Pitts, Contact Person.

STATE OF ARIZONA

PAYSON, GILA CO., THE CATHOLIC CHURCH OF HOLY NATIVITY (1983; 2012 as a Catholic parish)
1414 N. Easy St., Payson, AZ 85541.
Tel: 928-478-6988; Email: fr.vieira.holynativity@gmail.com; Web: www.holynativitypayson.com. Rev. Joseph Vieira, Parochial Vicar.

STATE OF CALIFORNIA

CARLSBAD, SAN DIEGO CO., ST. AUGUSTINE OF CANTERBURY (2010)
Mailing Address: P.O. Box 2027, Carlsbad, CA 92019. Tel: 714-649-9800; Email: pastor@staugustineofcanterbury.org; Web: www.staugustineofcanterbury.org. 5555 Del Mar Heights Rd., San Diego, CA 92130. Rev. Glenn Baaten, Parochial Admin.

IRVINE, ORANGE CO., BLESSED JOHN HENRY NEWMAN CATHOLIC CHURCH

2646 Dupont Dr. -163, Irvine, CA 92612.
Tel: 949-474-1980; Email: socalordinariate@gmail.com; Web: www.newmanonline.org. Rev. Andrew Bartus, Admin.

STATE OF FLORIDA

ORLANDO, ORANGE CO., INCARNATION CATHOLIC CHURCH (2012) [CEM]
1515 Edgewater Dr., Orlando, FL 32804.
Tel: 407-843-2886; Fax: 407-423-0951; Email: incarnation@theparish.org; Web: www.theparish.org. Revs. William P. Holiday; Jason McCrimmon, Parochial Vicar.
Child Care—St. Vincent's Academy Preschool,
Tel: 407-843-1997; Fax: 407-423-0951; Web: www.stvincentsacademy.org. Julieann Campese, Dir.
Mission—St. John Fisher Mission.

ST. AUGUSTINE, ST. JOHNS CO., ST. JAMES CATHOLIC COMMUNITY (2015)
86 M L King Ave, St. Augustine, FL 32084.
Tel: 904-460-0635; Email: marniclaus@aol.com; Email: phil.mayer@gmail.com; Web: philmayer.wixsite.com/stjames. 3725 Lilly Rd., Jacksonville, FL 32207. Revs. Nicholas A. Marziani, Pastor Emeritus, (Retired); Philip Mayer, Parochial Vicar.

STATE OF GEORGIA

ATHENS, CLARKE CO., ST. AELRED CATHOLIC COMMUNITY (2017)
958 Epps Bridge Pkwy., Athens, GA 30605.
Tel: 346-247-2201; Email: office@ordinariate.net; Web: saintaelreds@gmail.com.

STATE OF KENTUCKY

LOUISVILLE, JEFFERSON CO., COMMUNITY OF OUR LADY AND SAINT JOHN (2017)
639 S. Shelby St., Louisville, KY 40202. Cell: 502-544-7879; Email: jonathan@ourladyandstjohn.org. Rev. Jonathan Erdman, Parochial Vicar.

STATE OF MARYLAND

BALTIMORE, ANNE ARUNDEL CO., MOUNT CALVARY CHURCH (1842)
816 Eutaw St., Baltimore, MD 21201.
Tel: 410-728-6140; Fax: 410-728-6720; Email: albert.scharbach@mountcalvary.com; Web: www.mountcalvary.com. Rev. Albert Scharbach, (Retired).

BLADENSBURG, PRINCE GEORGES CO., SAINT LUKE
1315 8th St., N.W., Washington, DC 20001.
Tel: 202-999-9934; Email: stlukesdcordinariate@gmail.com. Rev. John Vidal.

CATONSVILLE, BALTIMORE CO., ST. TIMOTHY CATHOLIC COMMUNITY (2014)
30 Melvin Ave., Catonsville, MD 21228.
Tel: 443-920-9104; Email: frworgul@yahool.com; Web: sttimsmd.weebly.com. 583 Frederick Rd., Ste. 6A, Catonsville, MD 21228. Rev. John Worgul, Parochial Vicar.

TOWSON, BALTIMORE CO., CHRIST THE KING CHURCH (1996; 2012 as a Catholic Parish)
1102 Hart Rd., Towson, MD 21286-1631.
Tel: 410-321-0711; Email: edmeeks10@gmail.com; Web: www.ctktowson.org. Rev. Edward Meeks, Email: emeeks@comcast.net; Deacon Melvin Reick.

STATE OF MASSACHUSETTS

MELROSE, MIDDLESEX CO., CHURCH OF SAINT GREGORY THE GREAT (2012)
137 Seven Star Rd., Groveland, MA 01834.
Tel: 617-860-2987; Email: office@saintgregoryordinariate.org. Kevin McDermott, Contact Person.

STATE OF MINNESOTA

SAINT LOUIS PARK, HENNEPIN CO., ST. BEDE THE VENERABLE (2016)
5900 W. Lake St., Saint Louis Park, MN 55416.
Tel: 612-564-3271; Email: office@thevenerablebede.org; Web: thevenerablebede.org.

STATE OF MISSOURI

KANSAS CITY, JACKSON CO., OUR LADY OF HOPE ORDINARIATE COMMUNITY (2016)
2552 Gillham Rd., Kansas City, MO 64108.
Tel: 816-421-2112; Web: www.ourladyofhopekc.com. Rev. W. Ed Wills, Parochial Vicar.

REPUBLIC, GREENE CO., SAINT GEORGE CATHOLIC CHURCH (2016)
645 S. Assisi Way, Republic, MO 65738.
Tel: 417-732-2018; Email: stgeorgechurchrepublic@gmail.com; Web: www.saint-george-church.net/. Rev. Chori Seraiah.

STATE OF NEBRASKA

OMAHA, DOUGLAS CO., ST. BARNABAS CHURCH OF THE PERSONAL ORDINARIATE OF THE CHAIR OF ST. PETER
129 N. 40th, Omaha, NE 68131. Tel: 402-558-4633; Email: office@ordinariate.net; Web: www.saintbarnabas.net. 4124 Davenport St., Omaha, NE 68131. Rev. Jason Catania.

STATE OF NEW YORK

HENRIETTA, MONROE CO., FELLOWSHIP OF SAINT ALBAN
2732 Culver Rd., Rochester, NY 14622.
Tel: 585-484-1827; Email: rochester.ordinariate@gmail.com; Web: www.stalbanfellowship.org. 2732 Culver Rd, Henrietta, NY 14422. Rev. Evan Simington, Parochial Vicar.

STATE OF NORTH CAROLINA

JACKSONVILLE, ONSLOW CO., OUR LADY OF GOOD COUNSEL COMMUNITY
1911-A Lejeune Blvd., Jacksonville, NC 28546.
Tel: 910-449-7500; Email: william.waun@gmail.com. Mailing Address: 816 Welton Cir., Jacksonville, NC 28546-2605. Rev. William Waun, Pastoral Admin., Tel: 910-378-9022.

STATE OF PENNSYLVANIA

PHILADELPHIA, PHILADELPHIA CO., ST. JOHN THE BAPTIST (2015) (2010 as St. Michael's.)
502 Ford St., Bridgeport, PA 19405.
Tel: 215-247-1092; Email: davidousley@verizon.net; Web: www.ordinariatephiladelphia.org. Rev. David A. Ousley.
Catechesis Religious Program—Students 23.

SCRANTON, LACKAWANNA CO., ST. THOMAS MORE CATHOLIC CHURCH (2012)
116 Theodore St., Scranton, PA 18508.
Tel: 570-343-0634; Email: contact@stmscranton.org; Web: www.stmscranton.org. 1625 North Main Ave., Scranton, PA 18508. Rev. Eric Bergman.

STATE OF SOUTH CAROLINA

CHARLESTON, CHARLESTON CO., CORPUS CHRISTI CATHOLIC COMMUNITY (2013)
P.O. Box 430, Charleston, SC 29402.
Tel: 843-722-7696; Tel: 832-531-6855; Email: psa@charlestonordinariate.org; Web: corpuschristicsp.org. 89 Hasell St., Charleston, SC 29402. Rev. Patrick Allen, (Retired).

GREENVILLE, GREENVILLE CO., SAINT ANSELM, Closed. St. Anselm's in Greenville, SC closed on December 5, 2017.

Military Services:
Revs.—
Bayles, Aaron
Bolin, Kenneth M., Chap.
Cantrell, William
Ray, Brian, Chap.
Reffner, Joseph
Sherbourne, Gerald
Whitehead, Matthew.

Serving with Permission Outside the Diocese:
Very Rev.—
Kenyon, Lee
Revs.—
Duncan, Jonathan
Gonzalez y Perez, Belen
Rojas, Richard.

Serving Outside the U.S.:
Revs.—
Beahen, Sean-Patrick, St. John Evangelist, Calgary, AB
Bengry, Robert-Charles.

Retired:
Very Rev. Msgr.—
Wilkinson, Peter, (Retired), Victoria, BC, Canada
Rev. Msgr.—
Gipson, Laurence A., (Retired), Mobile, AL
Very Rev.—
Hough, Charles A. III, (Retired), Houston, TX; Katy, TX
Revs.—
Blick, W. Scott, (Retired), Katy, TX
Cannaday, Mark, (Retired), Bourne, TX
Cornelius, John, (Retired), Fort Worth, TX
Davids, Peter, (Retired), Houston, TX
Liias, Jurgen, (Retired), Boston, MA
Malins, Donald, (Retired), Victoria, BC, Canada
Ortiz-Guzman, George, (Retired), San Diego, CA
Phillips, Christopher, (Retired), San Antonio, TX
Scheiblhofer, Robert, (Retired), Omaha, NE
Switzer, Peter, (Retired), Victoria, BC, Canada
Toledo, Pedro, (Retired)
Venuti, Matthew A., (Retired), Mobile, AL
Wolfe, Ken, (Retired), Marana, TX
Wright, John, (Retired), Calgary, AB, Canada.

Permanent Deacons:
Baker, Mark
Barnett, James
Brittain, Clark
D'Agostino, Michael
Davis, Joshua
Hodil, David
McKellar, Scott
Noble, Michael
Reick, Melvin
Stockstill, Mark
Tipton, Gregory.

INSTITUTIONS LOCATED IN DIOCESE

NECROLOGY

† Andrews, Lowell E., (Retired), Died Oct. 3, 2018
† Birch, Michael, (Retired), Died Nov. 26, 2016
† Lindsey, Lucien D., (Retired), Died Mar. 14, 2018

An asterisk (*) denotes an organization that has established tax-exempt status directly with the IRS and is not covered by the USCCB Group Ruling.

Archdiocese of Philadelphia

(Archidioecesis Philadelphiensis)

His Eminence

CARDINAL JUSTIN RIGALI

Archbishop Emeritus of Philadelphia; ordained a priest April 25, 1961; appointed Archbishop and President of the Pontifical Ecclesiastical Academy June 8, 1985; Episcopal ordination September 14, 1985; appointed Archbishop of St. Louis January 25, 1994; installed March 15, 1994; appointed Archbishop of Philadelphia July 15, 2003; installed October 7, 2003; created Cardinal Priest October 21, 2003; retired July 19, 2011. *Office: 928 Westmoreland Blvd., TN 37919.*

Most Reverend

ROBERT P. MAGINNIS, D.D.

Auxiliary Bishop Emeritus of Philadelphia; ordained May 13, 1961; appointed Auxiliary Bishop of Philadelphia and Titular Bishop of Siminia January 24, 1996; consecrated March 11, 1996; retired June 8, 2010. *Res.: St. Edmond Home for Children, 320 S. Roberts Rd., Rosemont, PA 19010.*

Most Reverend

MICHAEL J. FITZGERALD

Auxiliary Bishop of Philadelphia; ordained May 17, 1980; appointed Auxiliary Bishop of Philadelphia and Titular Bishop of Tamallula June 22, 2010; consecrated August 6, 2010. *Office: 222 N. 17th St., Rm. 530, Philadelphia, PA 19103-1299.* Tel: 215-965-8280; Fax: 215-965-8283.

Most Reverend

CHARLES J. CHAPUT, O.F.M. CAP.

Archbishop of Philadelphia; ordained August 29, 1970; appointed Bishop of Rapid City April 11, 1988; Episcopal ordination July 26, 1988; appointed Archbishop of Denver February 18, 1997; installed April 7, 1997; appointed Archbishop of Philadelphia July 19, 2011; installed September 8, 2011. *Office: 222 N. 17th St., Philadelphia, PA 19103-1299.*

The Chancery: 222 N. 17th St., Philadelphia, PA 19103-1299. Tel: 215-587-4538; Fax: 215-587-3907.

Web: www.archphila.org

Email: chancery@archphila.org

Most Reverend

JOHN J. MCINTYRE

Auxiliary Bishop of Philadelphia; ordained May 16, 1992; appointed Auxiliary Bishop of Philadelphia and Titular Bishop of Bononia June 8, 2010; consecrated August 6, 2010. *Office: 222 N. 17th St., Rm. 830, Philadelphia, PA 19103-1299.* Tel: 215-965-8190; Fax: 215-965-8193.

Most Reverend

TIMOTHY C. SENIOR

Auxiliary Bishop of Philadelphia; ordained May 18, 1985; appointed Auxiliary Bishop of Philadelphia and Titular Bishop of Floriana June 8, 2009; ordained July 31, 2009; appointed Rector of Saint Charles Borromeo Seminary July 1, 2012. *Res.: Saint Charles Borromeo Seminary, 100 E. Wynnewood Rd., Wynnewood, PA 19096.* Tel: 610-785-6200; Fax: 610-667-7635; Email: bsenior@scs.edu.

Most Reverend

EDWARD M. DELIMAN

Auxiliary Bishop of Philadelphia; ordained May 19, 1973; appointed Auxiliary Bishop of Philadelphia and Titular Bishop of Sufes May 31, 2016; installed August 18, 2016. *St. Charles Borromeo, 1731 Hulmeville Rd., Bensalem, PA 19020.* Tel: 215-638-3625; Fax: 215-245-8578.

DIOCESE ESTABLISHED APRIL 8, 1808.

Square Miles 2,202.

Erected an Archdiocese February 12, 1875.

Comprises all the City and County of Philadelphia, and the Counties of Bucks, Chester, Delaware and Montgomery in the State of Pennsylvania.

Patrons of the Diocese: I. Immaculate Conception B.V.M., December 8; II. Saints Peter and Paul, Apostles, June 29. This Archdiocese was solemnly consecrated to the Sacred Heart of Jesus on the Feast of Saint Teresa of Avila, October 15, 1873. On May 23, 1952, the Archdiocese of Philadelphia was solemnly consecrated to the Immaculate Heart of Mary at the Shrine of Our Lady of Fatima, Portugal.

For legal titles of parishes and archdiocesan institutions, consult The Chancery.

STATISTICAL OVERVIEW

Personnel	
Retired Cardinals	1
Archbishops	1
Auxiliary Bishops	4
Retired Bishops	1
Abbots	1
Priests: Diocesan Active in Diocese	312
Priests: Diocesan Active Outside Diocese	19
Priests: Retired, Sick or Absent	131
Number of Diocesan Priests	462
Religious Priests in Diocese	286
Total Priests in Diocese	748
Extern Priests in Diocese	52
Ordinations:	
Diocesan Priests	6
Transitional Deacons	7
Permanent Deacons	16
Permanent Deacons in Diocese	300
Total Brothers	64
Total Sisters	2,138
Parishes	
Parishes	217
With Resident Pastor:	
Resident Diocesan Priests	191
Resident Religious Priests	20
Without Resident Pastor:	
Administered by Priests	6
Missions	1
Pastoral Centers	13
New Parishes Created	1
Professional Ministry Personnel:	
Brothers	6
Sisters	1,601
Lay Ministers	212
Welfare	
Catholic Hospitals	5
Total Assisted	669,812
Health Care Centers	1
Total Assisted	588
Homes for the Aged	9
Total Assisted	4,097
Residential Care of Children	2
Total Assisted	900
Day Care Centers	1
Total Assisted	73
Specialized Homes	7
Total Assisted	7,733
Special Centers for Social Services	8
Total Assisted	201,556
Residential Care of Disabled	631
Total Assisted	1,956
Other Institutions	38
Total Assisted	728,785
Educational	
Seminaries, Diocesan	2
Students from This Diocese	74
Students from Other Diocese	87
Diocesan Students in Other Seminaries	1
Seminaries, Religious	3
Students Religious	10
Total Seminarians	85
Colleges and Universities	11
Total Students	35,885
High Schools, Diocesan and Parish	17
Total Students	11,683
High Schools, Private	17
Total Students	6,851
Elementary Schools, Diocesan and Parish	105
Total Students	36,239
Elementary Schools, Private	19
Total Students	3,090
Non-residential Schools for the Disabled	4
Total Students	171
Catechesis/Religious Education:	
High School Students	1,106
Elementary Students	41,957
Total Students under Catholic Instruction	137,067
Teachers in the Diocese:	
Priests	46
Brothers	8
Sisters	245
Lay Teachers	7,623
Vital Statistics	
Receptions into the Church:	
Infant Baptism Totals	10,224
Minor Baptism Totals	696
Adult Baptism Totals	301
Received into Full Communion	296
First Communions	10,234
Confirmations	10,416
Marriages:	
Catholic	2,259
Interfaith	860
Total Marriages	3,119
Deaths	9,427
Total Catholic Population	1,292,704
Total Population	4,119,268

Former Bishops—Most Revs. MICHAEL FRANCIS EGAN, O.F.M., D.D., cons. Oct. 28, 1810; died July 22, 1814; HENRY CONWELL, D.D., cons. Sept. 24, 1820; died April 22, 1842; FRANCIS PATRICK KENRICK, D.D., cons. June 6, 1830; transferred to Baltimore in 1851; died July 8, 1863; Saint JOHN

NEPOMUCENE NEUMANN, C.Ss.R., D.D., cons. March 28, 1852; died Jan. 5, 1860; Canonized June 19, 1977.

Former Archbishops—Most Revs. JAMES FREDERIC WOOD, D.D., cons. coadjutor, cum iure successionis, April 26, 1857; Bishop of Philadelphia, Jan. 5, 1860; appt. Archbishop Feb. 12, 1875; Sacred Pallium, June 17, 1875; died June 20, 1883; PATRICK JOHN RYAN, D.D., cons. April 14, 1872; Bishop of Tricomia and Coadjutor with right of succession to the Archbishop of St. Louis; appt. Titular Archbishop of Salamis, Jan. 6, 1884; Archbishop of Philadelphia, June 8, 1884; died Feb. 11, 1911; EDMOND FRANCIS PRENDERGAST, D.D., cons. Feb. 24, 1897, Titular Bishop of Scillio; Auxiliary Bishop of Philadelphia; Archbishop of Philadelphia, May 27, 1911; died Feb. 26, 1918; His Eminence DENNIS CARDINAL DOUGHERTY, D.D., appt. Bishop of Nueva Segovia, P.I., April 7, 1903; cons. June 14, 1903; transferred to Jaro, P.I., April 19, 1908; transferred to Buffalo Nov. 30, 1915; transferred to Philadelphia April 30, 1918; installed as Archbishop of Philadelphia July 10, 1918; Pallium conferred May 6, 1919; created Cardinal Priest, March 7, 1921; died May 31, 1951; JOHN CARDINAL O'HARA, C.S.C., appt. Military Delegate of Armed Forces and Titular Bishop of Mylasa Dec. 11, 1939; cons. Jan. 15, 1940; transferred to Buffalo March 10, 1945; transferred to Philadelphia Nov. 28, 1951; installed as Archbishop of Philadelphia Jan. 9, 1952; Pallium conferred Jan. 12, 1953; created Cardinal Priest Dec. 15, 1958; died Aug. 28, 1960; JOHN CARDINAL KROL, D.D., J.C.D., ord. Feb. 20, 1937; appt. Titular Bishop of Cadi and Auxiliary Bishop of Cleveland July 11, 1953; cons. Sept. 2, 1953; appt. Archbishop of Philadelphia Feb. 11, 1961; created Cardinal Priest June 26, 1967; retired Feb. 11, 1988; died March 3, 1996; ANTHONY CARDINAL BEVILACQUA, D.D., M.A., J.C.D., J.D., ord. June 11, 1949; appt. Auxiliary Bishop of Brooklyn Oct. 7, 1980; cons. Nov. 24, 1980; appt. Bishop of Pittsburgh Oct. 7, 1983; installed Dec. 12, 1983; installed Archbishop of Philadelphia Feb. 11, 1988; Created Cardinal Priest June 28, 1991; retired July 15, 2003; died Jan. 31, 2012.; CARDINAL JUSTIN RIGALI, (Retired), ord. a priest April 25, 1961; appt. Archbishop and President of the Pontifical Ecclesiastical Academy June 8, 1985; episcopal ord. Sept. 14, 1985; appt. Archbishop of St. Louis Jan. 25, 1994; installed March 15, 1994; appt. Archbishop of Philadelphia July 15, 2003; installed Oct. 7, 2003; Created Cardinal Priest Oct. 21, 2003; retired July 19, 2011.

Vicars General—Most Revs. TIMOTHY C. SENIOR, D.D., M.S.W., M.B.A.; JOHN J. MCINTYRE, D.D.; MICHAEL J. FITZGERALD, D.D., J.C.D., J.D.; EDWARD M. DELIMAN, D.D.; Rev. Msgr. DANIEL J. KUTYS, M.Div., V.G.

Office of the Archbishop—222 N. 17th St., Philadelphia, 19103-1299. Tel: 215-587-0506. Most Rev. CHARLES J. CHAPUT, O.F.M.Cap., Archbishop of Philadelphia; FRANCIS X. MAIER, Sr. Advisor; Rev. THOMAS A. VIVIANO, M.A., M.Div., Sec. to the Archbishop.

Office of the Moderator of the Curia—Rev. Msgrs. DANIEL J. KUTYS, M.Div., V.G., Tel: 215-587-4507; Fax: 215-587-4545; GERARD C. MESURE, J.D., J.C.D., M.A., Coord. Archdiocesan Planning Initiatives, Tel: 215-587-5663; MR. TIMOTHY O'SHAUGHNESSY, C.F.O.

Deans—Rev. Msgrs. JOSEPH M. CORLEY, M.S., M.Div., Deanery 1 - Eastern Delaware County, Blessed Virgin Mary Rectory, 1101 Main St., Darby, 19023-1407. Tel: 610-583-2128; HANS A.L. BROUWERS, M.A., M.Div., Deanery 2 - Western Delaware County, St. Katharine of Siena Rectory, 104 S. Aberdeen Ave., Wayne, 19087. Tel: 610-688-4584; Rev. MICHAEL J. FITZPATRICK, M.S., M.Div., Deanery 3 - Western Chester County, Saint Peter Rectory, 2835 Manor Rd., West Brandywine, 19320. Tel: 610-380-9045; Rev. Msgrs. THOMAS M. MULLIN, S.S.L., M.A., M.Div., Deanery 4 - Northern Chester County, St. Elizabeth Rectory, 115 Saint Elizabeth Dr., Chester Springs, 19425. Tel: 610-321-1200; JOSEPH J. NICOLO, M.Div., Deanery 5 - Western Montgomery County, Saint Helena Rectory, 1489 DeKalb Pike, Blue Bell, 19422. Tel: 610-275-7711; Rev. MARTIN T. CIOPPI, Ed.D., M.A., M.Div., Deanery 6 - Main Line, Bridgeport and Roxborough, Mother of Divine Providence Rectory, 333 Allendale Rd., King of Prussia, 19406-1640. Tel: 610-265-4178; Rev. Msgr. CHARLES P. VANCE, M.Div., Deanery 7 - Eastern Montgomery County and Northwest Philadelphia, St. Philip Neri Rectory, 437 Ridge Pike, Lafayette Hill, 19444. Tel: 610-828-5717; Rev. JOSEPH J. KELLEY, M.A., M.Div., Deanery 8 - South Philadelphia, Northern Liberties, Saint Monica Rectory, 2422 S. 17th St., Philadelphia, 19145. Tel: 215-334-4170; Tel: 215-334-4171; Rev. Msgrs. FEDERICO A. BRITTO, M.Div., M.A., Deanery 9 - West Philadelphia, Center City, St. Cyprian Rectory, 525 Cobbs Creek Pkwy., Philadelphia, 19143. Tel: 215-747-3250; JOHN C. MARINE, M.Div., Deanery 10 - Central and Upper Bucks County, St. Bede the Venerable Rectory, 1071 Holland Rd., Holland, 18966-2399. Tel: 215-357-5720; Revs. JOHN F. BABOWITCH, M.Div., Deanery 11 - Upper Northeast Philadelphia/Lower Bucks County, Our Lady of Calvary Rectory, 11024 Knights Rd., Philadelphia, 19154-4295. Tel: 215-637-7515; EFREN V. ESMILLA, M.Div., Deanery 12 - Lower Northeast Philadelphia, Our Lady of Hope Rectory, 5200 N. Broad St., Philadelphia, 19141. Tel: 215-329-8100.

Information Line, Archdiocesan—Tel: 215-587-3600.

The Chancery—Rev. Msgr. GERARD C. MESURE, J.D., J.C.D., M.A., Chancellor. Vice Chancellor: *222 N. 17th St., Philadelphia, 19103-1299.* Tel: 215-587-4538; Fax: 215-587-3907. Rev. SEAN P. BRANSFIELD, J.C.L., M.A., M.Div.

Catholic Historical Research Center of the Archdiocese of Philadelphia—6740 Roosevelt Blvd., Philadelphia, 19149. Tel: 215-904-8149, Ext. 1001; Web: www.chrc-phila.org. LESLIE O'NEILL, Dir. Archives.

Department for Media Affairs—

Office for Communications—KENNETH A. GAVIN, Dir., Tel: 215-587-3747; Fax: 215-587-3875.

CatholicPhilly.com—MATTHEW GAMBINO, Dir. & Gen. Mgr., Tel: 215-587-3509; Fax: 215-587-3979.

Metropolitan Tribunal—222 N. 17th St., Philadelphia, 19103-1299. Tel: 215-587-3750; Fax: 215-587-0508. Communications should be sent to the above address.

Judicial Vicar—Rev. Msgr. PAUL A. DIGIROLAMO, J.C.D., M.A., M.Div.

Assistant Judicial Vicar—Rev. EDUARDO G. MONTERO, J.C.L., M.Div.

Archdiocesan Judges—Revs. SEAN P. BRANSFIELD, J.C.L., M.A., M.Div.; JOSEPH C. DIECKHAUS, J.C.L., M.Div.; Rev. Msgr. JAMES J. GRAHAM, J.C.D., M.Div.; Sr. CARLOTTA BARTONE, S.H.C.J., J.C.L.

Promoter of Justice—Rev. Msgr. GERARD C. MESURE, J.D., J.C.D., M.A.

Defenders of the Bond—Rev. Msgrs. GERARD C. MESURE, J.D., J.C.D., M.A.; ROBERT J. POWELL, D.M.A, M.A., M.Div.; Rev. DOMINIC ISHAQ, J.C.D.; MR. SEAN T. DOYLE, J.C.L.

Approved Advocates—Revs. JOSEPH W. BONGARD, M.A., M.Div.; JOSEPH E. HOWARTH, M.A.L.S.; Rev. Msgr. JOSEPH J. NICOLO, M.Div.; Deacon JOHN M. BETZAL; MR. AUSTIN CHUKINAS, M.Div.

Ecclesiastical Notary—MRS. JANICE A. MARGERUM.

Office for Child and Youth Protection—LESLIE J. DAVILA, M.S., Dir., Tel: 215-587-3880; Fax: 215-587-3711.

Office for Consecrated Life—

Delegate for Consecrated Life—Office: 222 N. 17th St., Philadelphia, 19103-1299. Tel: 215-587-3795; Fax: 215-587-3790. Sr. GABRIELLE MARY BRACCIO, R.S.M.

Office for Divine Worship—Rev. GERALD DENNIS GILL, M.Div., S.L.L., Dir., Tel: 215-587-3537; Fax: 215-587-3561; Email: fr.dgill@archphila.org.

Director of Liturgical Music—Tel: 215-587-3696.

Office for General Counsel—SUZANNE HUESTON, Gen. Counsel, Tel: 215-587-0511; Fax: 215-587-0512.

Office for Insurance Services—MARGARET TOLAND, Insurance & Risk Mgr., Tel: 215-587-2494.

Office for Information Technology—LEE MYERS, Chief Information Officer, Tel: 267-663-0031.

Office for Parish Service and Support—MR. MARC A. FISHER, Dir., Tel: 215-587-3995; Fax: 215-587-2430.

Office for Financial Services—

All addresses are 222 N. 17th St., Philadelphia, PA 19103.

Chief Financial Officer—MR. TIMOTHY O'SHAUGHNESSY, Tel: 215-587-4510.

Controller—MR. PETER YECCO, Tel: 215-587-3943.

Investment Services—MR. ROBERT J. GUNN, Dir., Tel: 215-587-3969; Fax: 215-587-3939.

Office of Investigations—ALBERT J. TOCZYDLOWSKI, Esq., Dir., Tel: 215-587-3763; Fax: 215-587-0591.

Collections—Annual Catholic Charities Appeal, Annual St. Charles Borromeo Seminary Appeal, Stewards of St. John Neumann, Benefit for Aging/Infirm; Priests of Archdiocese. *Contact: Office of the Moderator of the Curia.* Tel: 215-587-4507.

Secretariat for Catholic Education

All addresses are: 222 N. 17th St., Philadelphia, PA 19103-1299 unless otherwise indicated.

Office of Catholic EducationTel: 215-587-3700; Fax: 215-587-5644; Email: ocathsch@archphila.org.

Secretary for Elementary SchoolsDR. ANDREW MCLAUGHLIN, Tel: 215-587-3585.

Superintendent for Secondary SchoolsSr. MAUREEN L. MCDERMOTT, I.H.M., Ph.D., Tel: 215-587-3736.

Deputy Secretary for Government RelationsMR. JASON BUDD, Tel: 215-587-3709.

Deputy Secretary for Institutional AdvancementMRS. REGINA DIGUILIO, Tel: 215-587-5664.

Deputy Secretary for Enrollment ManagementMR. NICK REGINA, Tel: 215-587-3759.

Director of International ProgramsMS. JANET DOLLARD, Tel: 215-587-3789.

Director of Government ProgramsDR. EILEEN SCHWEYER, Tel: 215-587-3919.

Director of Special EducationMRS. KATHLEEN A. GOULD, Tel: 215-587-3975.

Director of Urban EducationDR. ANTHONY IRVIN.

Assistant Superintendents for Secondary SchoolsDR. PATRICIA RIGBY, Tel: 215-587-3707; MRS. NANCY KURTZ, Tel: 215-587-3601.

Human Resources Manager of Secondary SchoolsMR. JAMES MOLNAR, Tel: 215-587-3976.

Director for K to 12 TechnologyMR. WILLIAM BRANNICK, Tel: 215-587-3710.

Assistant Superintendent for Curriculum Instruction and AssessmentSr. EDWARD WILLIAM QUINN, I.H.M., Tel: 215-587-3744.

Assistant Superintendents of Elementary SchoolsMRS. BERNADETTE DOUGHERTY, Tel: 215-587-3743; MR. MICAH SUMNER, Tel: 215-965-4616.

Director of GovernanceMS. BETHANNE KILLIAN, Tel: 215-587-3586.

Director of CYO AthleticsMR. MATT HASHER, Tel: 215-587-3716.

Executive Director of AthleticsMR. STEPHEN HAUG, Tel: 215-587-0514.

Senior Director of Enrollment ManagementMR. STEVE CLEMENT, Tel: 215-587-3972.

Director of Hispanic OutreachMS. NANCY SANCHEZ, Tel: 215-965-1738.

Associate Director of Educational TechnologyMRS. ALISSA DEVITO.

Associate Director of Information TechnologyMR. STEVE PAGANO.

System AdministratorVACANT.

Junior System AdministratorMRS. JILL LADD.

Senior Network TechniciansMR. ALBERT ROSSANA; MR. ANDREW CICCAGLIONE; MRS. JAMYE BYRNES.

Project ManagerMRS. ELIZABETH (PITEK) TORRE.

Technology Integration Coaches, PreK-12MR. AARON HEINTZ; MS. ANNABEL DOTZMAN.

Educational Financial ServicesMR. DAVID J. MAGEE, Ed.D., CFO, Tel: 215-587-3755; Fax: 215-587-3525; MAUREEN FISHER, M.B.A., Asst. CFO; MR. LOUIS GIULIANO, M.B.A., Ed.D., Asst. CFO.

Office for Catechetical FormationMRS. ANN MENNA, Deputy Sec. Catechetical Formation & Dir. Elementary and Secondary Rel. Educ., Tel: 215-587-3720; Fax: 215-965-1749; Rev. MATTHEW W. GUCKIN, M.A., M.Div., Dir. Catholic Mission & Identity, Secondary & Collegiate Education, St. Margaret Rectory, 208 N. Narberth Ave., Narberth, 19072-1806. Tel: 215-587-3714.

Secretariat for Catholic Human Services

All addresses are: 222 N. 17th St., Philadelphia, PA 19103 unless otherwise indicated.

Secretary for Catholic Human Services—JAMES AMATO, L.S.W., Sec., Tel: 215-587-3908; FRANZ FRUEHWALD, M.B.A., CFO, Tel: 267-663-5357; LEE MYERS, Chief Information Officer; EDWARD J. LIS, M.A., M.Div., Dir. Catholic Mission Effectiveness & Coord. Catholic Campaign for Human Devel., Tel: 215-965-1710; ANNE H. AYELLA, Dir. Catholic Relief Svcs., Tel: 215-895-3470; JOHN M. WAGNER, Deputy Sec. for Catholic Housing & Community Svcs.

Catholic Charities of the Archdiocese of Philadelphia—JAMES AMATO, L.S.W., Sec. Catholic Human Svcs.; GARY MILLER, Divisional Controller, Tel: 215-587-3892; AMY STONER, L.S.W., A.C.S.W., Dir. Community-Based Svcs. Div. & Dir. Housing & Homeless Svcs., Tel: 215-587-3590; DR. JAMES BLACK, Dir., Youth Svcs., 227 N. 18th St., Philadelphia, 19103. Tel: 215-665-8777; FRANCIS E. SWIACKI JR., M.S.W., Dir. Developmental Programs Div., Administrative Office, 20 E. Cleveland Ave., Norwood, 19074. Tel: 484-475-2469.

Catholic Services—JAMES AMATO, L.S.W., Sec. Catholic Human Svcs. & Archdiocesan Coord. Health Care Affairs, Tel: 215-587-3908; JOHN M.

WAGNER, Deputy Sec., Tel: 215-587-3663; HEATHER HUOT, Tel: 215-587-3663.

Information Technology Services (ITS) Division—Tel: 267-663-0031. LEE MYERS, CIO.

Director of Information Systems—MICHAEL LEIDEN, Assoc. CIO, Tel: 215-854-7061.

Director of IT Operations Associate CIO—DAVE FIEDLER, Tel: 267-663-0032.

Nutritional Development Services—Tel: 215-895-3470. LIZANNE E. HAGEDORN, Dir.

Office of Community Development—JOHN M. WAGNER, Deputy Sec., Tel: 215-587-3589.

For detailed information please see Catholic Social Services of the Archdiocese of Philadelphia in the Institution Section.

Secretariat For Evangelization

All addresses are: 222 N. 17th St., Philadelphia, PA 19103-1299. Fax: 215-587-3561, unless otherwise indicated.

Office for Black Catholics—Tel: 215-587-3541. Rev. RICHARD N. OWENS, O.F.M.Cap., Dir.

Secretariat for Evangelization—Most Rev. JOHN J. MCINTYRE, D.D., Auxiliary Bishop of Philadelphia, Tel: 215-965-8190; Fax: 215-965-8193.

Office for Hispanic Catholics—Most Rev. EDWARD M. DELIMAN, D.D., Auxiliary Bishop of Philadelphia; KATHIA ARANGO, Dir., Tel: 215-667-2823.

Hispanic Catholic Institute—BLANCA HERRERA, Coord., Tel: 215-667-2824; Fax: 215-667-2825.

Office for Pastoral Care for Migrants and Refugees—MATTHEW DAVIS, Dir., Tel: 215-587-3540.

Francophone African Community—Rev. RENE AGAINGLO, St. Cyprian Church, 525 Cobbs Creek Pkwy., Philadelphia, 19143. Tel: 215-747-3250.

Ghanaian Community—St. Ignatius of Loyola Church, 636 N. 43rd St., Philadelphia, 19104. Tel: 215-357-5905. Rev. LINUS D. NANGWELE, Contact Person.

Nigerian Igbo Community—St. Martin of Tours Church, 5450 Roosevelt Blvd., Philadelphia, 19124. Tel: 215-535-2962. Rev. LIVINUS C. UGOCHUKWU.

Other African Communities—Sr. FLORENCE ENECHUKWU, Tel: 610-525-3313.

Apostleship of the Sea—Apostleship of the Sea, 475 N. Fifth St., Philadelphia, 19123. Tel: 215-940-9900; Tel: 215-587-3540. Rev. RENNY ABRAHAM KATTEL, Chap. Coord.

Brazilian Apostolate—St. Martin of tours Rectory, 5450 Roosevelt Blvd., Philadelphia, 19124. Tel: 215-634-1133. Rev. JOSE LUIS QUIEMADO, C.Ss.R., Chap.

Chinese Apostolate—Rev. JOHN DAYA, O.F.M.Cap., Chap./Coord., Holy Redeemer Chinese Catholic Church, 915 Vine St., Philadelphia, 19107. Tel: 215-992-0999.

Filipino Apostolate—Rev. EFREN V. ESMILLA, M.Div., Chap., Our Lady of Hope Rectory, 5200 N. Broad St., Philadelphia, 19141. Tel: 215-329-8100; Sr. GERTRUDE BORRES, R.A., Coord.

French Apostolate—MATHILDE RUYANT-LUCQ, Lay Coord., Corr Chapel, Villanova Univ., Villanova, 19085. Tel: 610-527-1016.

Haitian Apostolate—St. William, 6200 Rising Sun Ave., Philadelphia, 19111. Tel: 215-745-1389. Rev. EUGENE R. ALMONOR, O.M.I., Chap./Coord.

Indian Apostolate, Syro Malankara Rite—Rev. SAJI GEORGE MUKKOOT, Chap./Coord., St. Jude Syro-Malankara Catholic Church, 244-258 W. Cheltenham Ave., Philadelphia, 19126. Tel: 215-673-8127.

Indian Apostolate - Knanayan Community of St. John Neumann—Rev. RENNY ABRAHAM KATTEL, Chap./Coord., St. Albert the Great, 212 Welsh Rd., Huntingdon Valley, 19006. Tel: 215-947-3500.

Indian Apostolate - St. Thomas Syro-Malabar Catholic Church—608 Welsh Rd., Philadelphia, 19115. Tel: 215-808-4052. Rev. VINOD MADATHIPARAMBIL, Pastor.

Indian Apostolate, Latin Rite—Rev. SHAJI SILVA, Chap./Coord., Tel: 215-855-1311.

Indonesian Apostolate—Tel: 215-587-3540. Rev. KURNIAWAN DIPTURA, C.M., Chap., St. Thomas Aquinas Church, 1719 Morris St., Philadelphia, 19145. Tel: 215-464-4008.

Korean Apostolate—Revs. JOHN JEUNG DAE WOUNG, Pastor, Holy Angels Rectory, 7000 Old York Rd., Philadelphia, 19126. Tel: 215-548-5535; JOHN SANG YONG LEE, Chap./Coord., Holy Mary Korean Catholic Church, 100 Media Line Rd., Newtown Square, 19073. Tel: 610-259-2240.

Pakistani Apostolate—Rev. TARIQ ISAAC, St. William Rectory, 6200 Rising Sun Ave., Philadelphia, 19111. Tel: 215-745-1389.

Polish Apostolate—St. John Cantius Rectory, 4415 Almond St., Philadelphia, 19137. Tel: 215-535-6667. Revs. JOSEPH J. ZINGARO, Chap.; KONSTANTY PRUSZYNSKI, Chap.

Portuguese Apostolate—Resurrection of Our Lord Church, 2000 Shelmire Rd., Philadelphia, 19152. Tel: 215-518-9083. Rev. JOSE LUIS QUIEMADO, C.Ss.R.

Vietnamese Apostolate—Rev. Msgr. JOSEPH T. TRINH, Ed.D., M.Div., Chap./Coord., St. Helena Rectory, 6161 N. 5th St., Philadelphia, 19120. Tel: 215-424-1300.

Office for Life and Family—STEVEN BOZZA, M.A., Dir., Tel: 215-587-5661; Web: www.phillycatholiclife.org.

Respect Life, Natural Family Planning, Marriage and Family, Life Affirming Choices, Marriage Preparation Ministry—Tel: 215-587-0510. Deacon PATRICK J. KENNEDY, Coord., Marriage Prep.

Office for Persons With Disabilities and the Deaf Apostolate—Sr. KATHLEEN SCHIPANI, I.H.M., M.Ed., M.A., Dir., Tel: 215-587-3530; Tel: 267-507-1215 (VP); Web: www.opdarchphilly.org.

Deaf Apostolate—Web: www.deafcatholicphilly.org. For information on Mass schedule visit our web-site.Chaplains: Rev. Msgr. PAUL V. DOUGHERTY, M.Div., M.A., St. Margaret Rectory, 208 N. Narberth Ave., Narberth, 19072-1806. Tel: 610-664-3770; Fax: 215-664-5001; Rev. SEAN A. LOOMIS, 222 N. 17th St., Philadelphia, 19103. Tel: 215-587-3913; Fax: 215-587-3561.

Office for the New Evangelization—MEGHAN COKELEY, Dir., Tel: 215-587-5630. Evangelization, Adult Faith Formation, Lay Associations, Parish Services Directors, Catholic Women's Conference; Men's/Women's Formation; Unbound Ministry.

Pontifical Mission SocietiesSociety for the Propagation of the Faith, Missionary Childhood Association, St. Peter Apostle. Rev. Msgr. ARTHUR E. RODGERS, Ph. D., Dir., (Retired); MICHELE MEIERS, Asst. Dir., Tel: 215-587-3944; ALIXANDRA HOLDEN, Mission Educ. Coord., Tel: 215-587-3945.

Secretariat For Clergy

All addresses are: 222 N. 17th St., Philadelphia, PA 19103-1299 unless otherwise indicated.

Office for Clergy—Rev. Msgrs. DANIEL J. SULLIVAN, M.Div.; GERARD C. MESURE, J.D., J.C.D., M.A.; Rev. SEAN P. BRANSFIELD, J.C.L., M.A., M.Div., Asst. to Vicar for Clergy.

Department Retired Clergy—Rev. Msgr. JOSEPH M. CORLEY, M.S., M.Div.

Permanent Diaconate Department—Deacon MICHAEL PASCARELLA JR., M.A., M.S., Assoc. to Vicar for Clergy.

St. Charles Borromeo Seminary—Most Rev. TIMOTHY C. SENIOR, D.D., M.S.W., M.B.A., Rector, 100 E. Wynnewood Rd., Wynnewood, 19096. Tel: 610-667-3394; Rev. JOSEPH T. SHENOSKY, S.T.D., M.A., M.Div., Vice Rector, St. Charles Borromeo Seminary, 100 E. Wynnewood Rd., Wynnewood, 19096.

Vocation Office for Diocesan Priesthood—Rev. STEPHEN P. DELACY, M.A., M.Div., St. Charles Borromeo Seminary, 100 E. Wynnewood Rd., Wynnewood, 19096. Tel: 610-667-5778.

Liaison for the Office for Catholic Cemeteries—MR. ROBERT WHOMSLEY, Tel: 215-895-3459.

Human Resources Office—MAUREEN GALLAGHER, Dir., Tel: 215-587-3910; Fax: 215-587-3572.

Office for General Services—MR. ROBERT WHOMSLEY, Dir., Tel: 215-895-3459; Fax: 215-965-7553.

Office for Ecclesiastical Exchange—Tel: 215-587-3996; Fax: 215-587-2481.

Office for Real Estate/Property Services—Deacon THOMAS M. CROKE, Dir., Tel: 215-587-3560; Fax: 215-587-0599.

Archdiocesan Offices, Boards, Commissions and Committees

All addresses are: 222 N. 17th St., Philadelphia, PA 19103-1299 unless otherwise indicated.

Board of Trustees of Lay Employees Retirement Plan—Most Rev. CHARLES J. CHAPUT, O.F.M.Cap., Chm.; MR. JAMES J. BOCK JR., Vice Chm.

Diocesan Priests' Compensation and Benefits Committee—Rev. Msgr. DANIEL J. SULLIVAN, M.Div., Chm.; Revs. EDWARD H. BELL, M.Div.; ANDREW C. BROWNHOLTZ, M.Div.; KENNETH C. BRABAZON, M.A., M.Div.; WILLIAM J. CHIRIACO, M.Div.; WILLIAM B. DOONER, M.Div., (Retired); Rev. Msgr. WILLIAM C. KAUFMAN, M.Div.

Building Committee—Rev. Msgr. ROBERT C. VOGAN, M.Div., Chm., (Drawings of building plans are reviewed by this committee).

Censores Librorum—Rev. Msgr. J. BRIAN BRANSFIELD, M.Div., M.A., S.T.L.; Rev. ROBERT A. PESARCHICK, M.A., S.T.L., S.T.D.; Rev. Msgr. JOSEPH G. PRIOR, M.Div., M.A., S.S.L., S.T.D.; Rev. JOSEPH T. SHENOSKY, S.T.D., M.A., M.Div.

College of Consultors—Most Revs. TIMOTHY C. SENIOR, D.D., M.S.W., M.B.A.; JOHN J. MCINTYRE, D.D.; MICHAEL J. FITZGERALD, D.D., J.C.D., J.D.; EDWARD M. DELIMAN, D.D.; Rev. Msgrs. DANIEL J. SULLIVAN, M.Div.; DANIEL J. KUTYS, M.Div., V.G., Consultant; JOSEPH M. CORLEY, M.S., M.Div.; ROBERT C. VOGAN, M.Div.; THOMAS M. MULLIN, S.S.L., M.A., M.Div.; GERARD C. MESURE, J.D., J.C.D., M.A.; JOHN C. MARINE, M.Div.; MICHAEL T. MCCULKEN, M.Div.; CHARLES P. VANCE, M.Div.

Council of Priests—Most Rev. CHARLES J. CHAPUT, O.F.M.Cap. Ex Officio: Most Revs. TIMOTHY C. SENIOR, D.D., M.S.W., M.B.A.; JOHN J. MCINTYRE, D.D.; MICHAEL J. FITZGERALD, D.D., J.C.D., J.D.; EDWARD M. DELIMAN, D.D.; Rev. Msgrs. DANIEL J. KUTYS, M.Div., V.G.; DANIEL J. SULLIVAN, M.Div.; MICHAEL T. MCCULKEN, M.Div. Deans: Rev. Msgrs. JOSEPH M. CORLEY, M.S., M.Div., Deanery 1; HANS A.L. BROUWERS, M.A., M.Div., Deanery 2; Rev. MICHAEL J. FITZPATRICK, M.S., M.Div., Deanery 3; Rev. Msgrs. THOMAS M. MULLIN, S.S.L., M.A., M.Div., Deanery 4; JOSEPH J. NICOLO, M.Div., Deanery 5; Rev. MARTIN T. CIOPPI, Ed.D., M.A., M.Div., Deanery 6; Rev. Msgr. CHARLES P. VANCE, M.Div., Deanery 7; Rev. JOSEPH J. KELLEY, M.A., M.Div., Deanery 8; Rev. Msgrs. FEDERICO A. BRITTO, M.Div., M.A., Deanery 9; JOHN C. MARINE, M.Div., Deanery 10; Revs. JOHN F. BABOWITCH, M.Div., Deanery 11; EFREN V. ESMILLA, M.Div., Deanery 12. By Election: Revs. SEAN P. ENGLISH, M.A., M.Div.; JOSEPH W. BONGARD, M.A., M.Div.; WILLIAM F. WATERS, O.S.A. By Appointment: Rev. Msgrs. GERARD C. MESURE, J.D., J.C.D., M.A.; ROBERT C. VOGAN, M.Div.

Educational Fund—Office of the Chief Financial Officer. Tel: 215-587-3943.

Legion of Mary—

Parish Sites and Boundaries, Commission for—Rev. Msgr. JAMES D. BEISEL, M.A., M.Div., Chm.

Pastors Review Board—Rev. JOHN F. BABOWITCH, M.Div.; Rev. Msgr. FEDERICO A. BRITTO, M.Div., M.A.; Rev. MARTIN T. CIOPPI, Ed.D., M.A., M.Div.

Pennsylvania Catholic Conference—(Harrisburg)Board of Governors: Most Rev. CHARLES J. CHAPUT, O.F.M.Cap. Administrative Board: Rev. Msgr. DANIEL J. KUTYS, M.Div., V.G. Department on Communications: KENNETH A. GAVIN. Education Department: MR. JASON BUDD. Social Concerns: JAMES AMATO, L.S.W.

CLERGY, PARISHES, MISSIONS AND PAROCHIAL SCHOOLS

CITY OF PHILADELPHIA

(PHILADELPHIA COUNTY)

1—CATHEDRAL BASILICA OF SS. PETER AND PAUL (1846)
1723 Race St., 19103. Tel: 215-561-1313;
Tel: 215-561-1314; Fax: 215-561-1580; Web: www.cathedralphila.org. Revs. Gerald Dennis Gill, M.Div., S.L.L.; Kenneth C. Brabazon, M.A., M.Div., Parochial Vicar; Louis J. Kolenkiewicz, M.Div., Parochial Vicar; Rev. Msgr. Louis A. D'Addezio, M.A., In Res., (Retired); Rev. Isaac Haywiser, In Res.; Deacon Epifanio DeJesus; Charlene Angelini, Liturgical Music Dir.
Catechesis Religious Program—Patricia Smith, C.R.E. Students 40.

2—ST. ADALBERT (1904) (Polish)
2645 E. Allegheny Ave., 19134. Tel: 215-739-3500;
Fax: 215-739-5706; Email: info@stadalbert.org; Web: www.stadalbert.org. Rev. Jan Palkowski.
See Our Lady of Port Richmond Regional School, Philadelphia under Regional Parish Schools located in the Institution Section.

3—ST. AGATHA-ST. JAMES (1976)
3720 Chestnut St., 19104. Rev. Carlos F. Keen, Admin.; Bros. Jose Ambrozic, Supr.; Michael Gokie, In Res.; Remigo Morales Bermudez Buse, In Res.; Leonardo Negrini, In Res.; Patrick Travers, In Res.
Res.: 3728 Chestnut St., 19104. Tel: 267-787-5000; Fax: 267-353-8335; Web: saintsaj.org.

4—ST. AGNES-ST. JOHN NEPOMUCENE (1907) (Slovak)
Consolidated January 1, 1980.
Res.: 319 Brown St., 19123. Tel: 215-627-0340; Email: stagsjo319brown@verizon.net.

5—ALL SAINTS (BRIDESBURG) (1860-2013) [CEM]
Closed. Formerly located at Buckius and E. Thompson Sts. Spiritual records are kept at St. John Cantius Church. Tel: 215-535-6667.

6—ALL SAINTS CHAPEL, Closed. (1877-1977) Formerly located at Philadelphia General Hospital, 700 Civic Center Blvd. Spiritual records are kept at St. Agatha-St. James Church. Tel: 267-787-5000; Fax: 215-386-5899.

7—ST. ALOYSIUS (1894-2003) (German), Closed.

Formerly located at 26th & Tasker Sts. Spiritual records are kept at St. Gabriel Church, Tel: 215-463-4060.
8—ST. ALPHONSUS (1852-1972) Closed. Formerly located at 1400 S. Fourth St. Spiritual records are kept at Sacred Heart of Jesus Church. Tel: 215-465-4050; 465-4051.
9—ST. AMBROSE (1923)
405 E. Roosevelt Blvd., 19120. Tel: 215-329-7900; Tel: 215-329-7901; Fax: 215-329-9206. Rev. James N. Catagnus.
Church: C St. & Roosevelt Blvd., 19120.
Catechesis Religious Program—Tel: 215-439-3671. Students 74.
10—ST. ANDREW (1924) (Lithuanian)
1913 Wallace St., 19130. Tel: 215-765-2322; Fax: 215-765-0124. Rev. Peter M. Burkauskas.
Worship Site: St. Casimir Church, 324 Wharton St., 19147. Tel: 215-468-2052; Fax: 215-468-0354.
11—ST. ANNE (1845) [CEM]
2328 E. Lehigh Ave., 19125. Tel: 215-739-4590. Rev. Mardean E. Miller.
Catechesis Religious Program—2330 E. Tucker St., 19125. Students 36.
12—ANNUNCIATION B.V.M. (1860)
1511 S. 10th St., 19147. Tel: 215-334-0160; Email: annunciation5@comcast.net; Web: www.annunciationbvmchurch.org. Revs. Nicholas Martorano, O.S.A.; Robert Terranova, Parochial Vicar.
Catechesis Religious Program—Students 50.
13—ST. ANSELM (1962)
12670 Dunks Ferry Rd., 19154. Tel: 215-637-3525; Email: father.chiriaco@stanselmparish.com. Revs. William J. Chiriaco, M.Div.; Thomas Murphy, Parochial Vicar; Jonathan J. Dalin, In Res.; Deacons Dennis P. Warner; Gerald J. Whartenby.
School—St. Anselm School, 12650 Dunks Ferry Rd., 19154. Tel: 215-632-1133; Fax: 215-632-3264. Mrs. Geraldine Murphy, Prin. Lay Teachers 16; Students 294.
Catechesis Religious Program—Email: apolselli@stanselmparish.com. Anthony Polselli, D.R.E. Students 195.
14—ST. ANTHONY OF PADUA (1886-1999) Closed. Formerly located at 2321 Fitzwater St. Spiritual records are kept at St. Charles Borromeo Church. Tel: 215-735-0600.
15—ASCENSION OF OUR LORD (1899-2012) Closed. Formerly located at 725 E. Westmoreland St. Spiritual records are kept at Holy Innocents Church. Tel: 215-743-2600.
16—ASSUMPTION B.V.M., Closed. (1848-1995) Formerly located at 1131 Spring Garden St. Spiritual records are kept at St. John the Evangelist Church. Tel: 215-563-4145.
17—ST. ATHANASIUS (1928)
2050 E. Walnut Ln., 19138. Tel: 215-548-2700; Email: rectory@stathanasiuschurch.us; Web: www.stathanasiuschurch.us. Revs. Joseph F. Okonski; Saji George Mukkoot, In Res.; Anayo Nna, C.Ss.R., (Nigeria) In Res.; Deacon James L. Mahoney.
School—St. Athanasius School, (Grades PreK-8), 7105 Limekiln Pike, 19138. Tel: 215-424-5045; Fax: 215-927-6615; Email: secretary@saschool.org; Web: www.saschool.org. Andrea Tomaino, Prin. Lay Teachers 13; Students 266; Religious Teachers 3.
Catechesis Religious Program—Judith L. Travis, D.R.E. Students 30.
18—ST. AUGUSTINE (1796) First foundation of Augustinian Order in U.S.A.
243 N. Lawrence St., 19106-1195. Tel: 215-627-1838; Email: staugustineparish09@gmail.com; Web: www.st-augustinechurch.com. Revs. William F. Waters, O.S.A.; James D. Paradis, O.S.A., Prior; James R. Keating, O.S.A., In Res.; Paul F. Morrisey, O.S.A., In Res.; Mr. Jacob Marquart III, Parish Svcs. Dir.
See St. Mary Interparochial School, Philadelphia under Regional Parish Schools located in the Institution section.
Catechesis Religious Program—Students 7.
19—ST. BARBARA (1921)
5359 Lebanon Ave., 19131. Tel: 215-473-1044; Fax: 215-473-5252; Email: saintbarbara5359@aol.com. Rev. Msgr. Wilfred J. Pashley.
Catechesis Religious Program—Students 10.
Convent—5336 Diamond St., 19131. Tel: 215-477-3839.
20—ST. BARNABAS (1919)
6300 Buist Ave., 19142-3098. Tel: 215-726-1119; Email: stbarnabasparish@comcast.net. Revs. Carlos A. Benitez, Admin.; Miguel Bravo, Parochial Vicar; Deacon John J. Kreczkevich.
St. Barnabas Catholic School. For further information see Independence Mission Schools in the Institution section.
Catechesis Religious Program—Students 9.
Convent—6328 Buist Ave., 19142-3097. Tel: 215-729-1572; Fax: 215-729-2315.
21—ST. BARTHOLOMEW (1919)
5600 Jackson St., 19124. Tel: 215-831-1224; Tel: 215-831-1225; Fax: 215-831-0467; Email: stbartrectory@yahoo.com; Web: stbartsparish.org. Rev. John J. LaRosa; Deacon Gerard J. McPhillips.
Catechesis Religious Program—Students 45.
22—ST. BENEDICT (1922-2013) Closed. Formerly located at Chelten Ave. and Garnet St. Spiritual records are kept at St. Athanasius Church, Philadelphia. Tel: 215-548-2700. Worship site for St. Athanasius Church.
23—ST. BERNARD (1927)
7341 Cottage St., 19136. Tel: 215-333-0446; Fax: 215-333-3215. Revs. Joseph N. Accardi, M.Div.; Robert Ngageno, In Res.; Deacon Richard F. Hunter.
Catechesis Religious Program—Students 50.
24—ST. BONAVENTURE (1889-1993) Closed. Formerly located at 9th & Cambria Sts. Spiritual records are kept at St. Veronica Church. Tel: 215-228-4878.
25—ST. BONIFACE (1865-2006) Closed. Formerly located at 174 W. Diamond St. Spiritual records are kept at Visitation B.V.M. Church. Tel: 215-634-1133.
26—ST. BRENDAN (1925-1934) Closed. Formerly located at 507 Manheim St. Spiritual records are kept at St. Vincent de Paul Church. Tel: 215-438-2925.
27—ST. BRIDGET (1853)
3667 Midvale Ave., 19129. Tel: 215-844-4126; Fax: 215-842-2536; Email: pastor@stbridgeteastfalls.org. Revs. Robert T. Feeney; Stephen P. DeLacy, M.A., M.Div., In Res.
Catechesis Religious Program—Students 31.
Convent—3665 Midvale Ave., 19129.
28—ST. CALLISTUS (1921-2013) Closed. Formerly located at 6700 Lansdowne Ave. Spiritual records are kept at Our Lady of Lourdes Parish, Philadelphia. Tel: 215-473-1669.
29—ST. CARTHAGE (1915-2000) Closed. Formerly located at 525 Cobbs Creek Pkwy. Spiritual records are kept at St. Cyprian Church. Tel: 215-747-3250.
30—ST. CASIMIR (1893-2011) (Lithuanian), Closed. Formerly located at 324-328 Wharton St. Spiritual records are kept at St. Andrew Church. Tel: 215-765-2322. Worship site of St. Andrew Church.
31—ST. CATHERINE OF SIENA (1910-1972) Closed. Formerly located at 436 W. Penn St. Spiritual records are kept at St. Vincent de Paul Church. Tel: 215-438-2925.
32—ST. CECILIA (1911)
535 Rhawn St., 19111. Tel: 215-725-1240; Email: parish@stceciliafc.org. Revs. Charles E. Bonner; Robert F. Lucas, Parochial Vicar; Deacon Patrick J. Diamond.
School—St. Cecilia School, 525 Rhawn St., 19111. Tel: 215-725-8588; Fax: 215-725-0247. Lay Teachers 32; Sisters of the Immaculate Heart of Mary 7; Students 720.
Catechesis Religious Program—Tel: 215-725-2821. Students 123.
33—CHAPEL OF OUR LADY OF THE MIRACULOUS MEDAL (LA MILAGROSA) (1912-2013) (Spanish), Closed. Formerly located at 1903 Spring Garden St. Spiritual records are kept at the Cathedral Basilica of SS. Peter & Paul, Philadelphia. Tel: 215-561-1313.
34—ST. CHARLES BORROMEO (1868)
902 S. 20th St., 19146. Tel: 215-735-0600; Fax: 215-735-6630. Rev. Esteban Granyak; Deacon William C. Mayes.
Church: 20th & Christian Sts., 19146.
Catechesis Religious Program—Tel: 215-735-6898; Fax: 215-732-6253. Students 10.
35—CHRIST THE KING (1963)
3252 Chesterfield Rd., 19114. Tel: 215-632-1144; Fax: 215-632-4933; Email: ctk@christthekingparish.net; Web: www.christthekingparish.net. Rev. James A. Callahan.
School—Christ the King School, (Grades PreK-8), 3205 Chesterfield Rd., 19114. Tel: 215-632-1375; Tel: 215-637-3838; Tel: 215-632-1144; Email: ctk@christthekingparish.net; Web: www.christthekingschool.net. Lay Teachers 16; Sisters of St. Joseph 1; Students 250; Religious Teachers 1.
Catechesis Religious Program—Tel: 215-632-2144. Students 86.
36—ST. CHRISTOPHER (1950)
13301 Proctor Rd., 19116. Tel: 215-673-5177; Email: info@stchrisparish.org; Web: www.stchrisparish.org. Rev. Msgr. Joseph P. Garvin, M.S.W., M.Div.; Revs. Sean P. English, M.A., M.Div., Parochial Vicar; Dennis O'Donnell, In Res.; Deacons Eugene J. McNally III; James O'Neill.
School—St. Christopher School, 13305 Proctor Rd., 19116. Tel: 215-673-5787; Fax: 215-673-8511; Web: www.stchrisstrong.org. Lay Teachers 26; Students 513.
Catechesis Religious Program—Email: Deaconjim@stchrisparish.org. Students 169.
37—ST. CLEMENT (1865-2004) Closed. Formerly located at 2220 S. 71st. St. Spiritual records are kept at Divine Mercy Parish. Tel: 215-727-8300.
38—ST. COLUMBA (1895-1993) Closed. Formerly located at 2340 W. Lehigh Ave. Spiritual records are kept at St. Martin de Porres Church. Tel: 215-228-8330; 228-8331.
39—CORPUS CHRISTI, Closed. (1912-1987) Formerly located at 29th & Allegheny Ave. Spiritual records are kept at St. Martin de Porres Church. Tel: 215-228-8330; 228-8331.
40—ST. CYPRIAN (2000) Rev. Msgr. Federico A. Britto, M.Div., M.A.; Revs. Rene Againglo, Parochial Vicar; John D. Hand, Parochial Vicar; David Fisher, In Res.; Deacons Richard G. Nightingale; Anthony O. Willoughby.
Res.: 525 Cobbs Creek Pkwy., 19143. Tel: 215-747-3250; Fax: 215-747-2372; Web: www.saintcyprian.net.
Catechesis Religious Program—Students 70.
41—DIVINE MERCY PARISH (2004)
6667 Chester Ave., 19142-1397. Tel: 215-727-8300; Fax: 215-727-5932; Email: divinemercyparish@comcast.net; Web: divinemercyrc.com. Revs. Peter N. Quinn; Son Ho, In Res.
School—St. Barnabas Independence Mission School, 64th and Buist Ave., 19142. Tel: 215-729-3603. Sr. Margaret McCullough, I.H.M., Prin. For further information see Independence Mission Schools in the Institution section.
Catechesis Religious Program—Christina Pilling, C.R.E. Students 30.
42—ST. DOMINIC (1849) [CEM]
8504 Frankford Ave., 19136. Tel: 215-624-5502; Tel: 215-624-5503; Fax: 215-333-1750; Email: stdominicphila@hotmail.com; Web: stdominicphilapa.e-paluch.com. Revs. Edward T. Kearns; Charles C. Garst, O.S.F.S., Parochial Vicar; Jacob John, In Res.; Deacon Mark A. Salvatore.
School—St. Dominic School, 8512 Frankford Ave., 19136. Tel: 215-333-6703; Fax: 215-333-9930. Sr. Shaun Thomas, I.H.M., Prin. Lay Teachers 23; Sisters, Servants of the Immaculate Heart of Mary 5; Students 415.
Catechesis Religious Program—Tel: 215-624-5301. Students 70.
43—ST. DONATO (1910-2013) (Italian), Closed. Formerly located at 65th and Callowhill Sts. Spiritual records are kept at Our Lady of Lourdes Church, Philadelphia. Tel: 215-473-1669. Worship site for Our Lady of Lourdes Church.
44—ST. EDMOND (1912-2014) Closed. Formerly located at 2130 S. 21st St. Spiritual records are kept at St. Monica Church, Philadelphia. Tel: 215-334-4170. Worship site for St. Monica Church, Philadelphia.
45—ST. EDWARD THE CONFESSOR (1865-1993) Closed. Formerly located at 8th and York Sts. Spiritual records are kept at Visitation B.V.M. Church. Tel: 215-634-1133.
46—ST. ELIZABETH (1872-1993) Closed. Formerly located at 23rd and Berks Sts. Spiritual records are kept at St. Martin De Porres Church. Tel: 215-228-8330; 228-8331.
47—EPIPHANY OF OUR LORD (1889)
1121 Jackson St., 19148. Tel: 215-334-1035; Fax: 215-334-7885. Rev. James R. Casey; Deacon Olindo Mennilli.
School—Our Lady of Hope Regional Catholic School, 1248 Jackson St., 19148. Tel: 215-467-5385; Fax: 215-336-5103. Patricia Cody, Prin. Lay Teachers 19; Students 310.
Catechesis Religious Program—Marge Jarman, C.R.E. Students 105.
48—ST. FRANCIS DE SALES (1890)
4625 Springfield Ave., 19143. Tel: 215-222-5819; Email: karenh@saintfrancisdesales.net; Web: www.saintfrancisdesales.net. Rev. Msgr. Joseph J. Anderlonis, S.T.D.; Rev. Benjamin Nwanonenyi, In Res.; Rev. Msgr. George L. Strausser, M.Div., In Res.; Karen Genzano Hand, Business Mgr.
School—St. Francis de Sales School, 917 S. 47th St., 19143. Tel: 215-387-1749; Fax: 215-387-6605. Sr. Mary McNulty, I.H.M., Prin. Lay Teachers 20; Sisters, Servants of the Immaculate Heart of Mary 6; Students 520.
Catechesis Religious Program—Email: sralicedaly@comcast.net. Sr. Alice Marie Daly, I.H.M., D.R.E. Students 44.
Convent—912 S. 47th St., 19143. Tel: 215-727-3929; Email: ihm912@comcast.net; Email: schristinelamb@desalesschool.net.
49—ST. FRANCIS OF ASSISI (1899-2012) Closed. Formerly located at 4821 Greene St. Spiritual records are kept at St. Vincent de Paul Church. Tel: 215-438-2925.
50—ST. FRANCIS XAVIER (1839)
2319 Green St., 19130. Tel: 215-765-4568; Fax: 215-765-4049; Email: sfx7840@msn.com. Revs. Paul C. Convery, C.O.; Brian R. Gaffney, C.O., Parochial Vicar; Very Rev. Georges G. Thiers, C.O., In Res.; Deacon Vincent J. Thompson.
School—St. Francis Xavier School, (Grades PreK-8), 641 N. 24th St., 19130. Tel: 215-763-6564; Fax: 215-236-2818; Email: APFranX032@aol.com; Web: sfxschool.com. Dolores Butler, Prin. Lay Teachers 16; Students 206.
Catechesis Religious Program—Students 29.

*Oratory*2321 Green St., 19130.
51—ST. GABRIEL (1895)
2917 Dickinson St., 19146. Tel: 215-463-4060; Email: myangel1134@aol.com. Rev. Carl Braschoss, O.-Praem.; Rt. Rev. Richard J. Antonucci, O.Praem., In Res.; Rev. James C. Rodia, O.Praem., In Res.
School—St. Gabriel Independence Mission School, Tel: 215-468-7230; Fax: 215-468-2554. Sr. Noreen James Friel, I.H.M., Prin. Lay Teachers 16; Sisters 1; Students 200.
Catechesis Religious Program—Email: roseadamsihm@gmail.com. Sr. Rose Marie Adams, I.H.M., D.R.E. Students 25.
Convent—2916 Dickinson St.. Tel: 215-334-2620.
52—ST. GEORGE (1902) (Lithuanian)
3580 Salmon St., 19134. Tel: 215-739-3102;
Fax: 215-739-7217. Rev. James P. Olson, M.Div., M.A., S.T.L., Admin.; Deacon Ralph J. Shirley.
School—St. George School, 2700 E. Venango St., 19134. Tel: 215-634-8803. Lay Teachers 10; Students 162.
Convent—3570 Salmon St., 19134. Tel: 215-739-0472.
53—GESU (1868-1993) Closed. Formerly located at 18th & Stiles Sts. Spiritual records are kept at St. Malachy Church. Tel: 215-763-1305.
54—GOOD SHEPHERD (1925-2004) Closed. Formerly located at 67th St. and Chester Ave. Spiritual records are kept at Divine Mercy Parish. Tel: 215-727-8300.
55—ST. GREGORY (1895-1981) Closed. Formerly located at 52nd & Warren Sts. Spiritual records are kept at St. Barbara Church. Tel: 215-473-1044.
56—ST. HEDWIG (1907-2000) (Polish), Closed. Formerly located at 24th & Brown Sts. Spiritual records are kept at St. Francis Xavier Church, Tel: 215-765-4568.
57—ST. HELENA (1924)
6161 N. Fifth St., 19120-1422. Tel: 215-424-1300; Email: JTMTrinh@aol.com; Web: sainthelenaparish.net. Rev. Msgr. Joseph T. Trinh, Ed.D., M.Div.; Revs. Peter J. Welsh, Parochial Vicar; Edward A. Pelczar, In Res., (Retired); Albert Gardy Villarson, O.M.I., In Res.; Deacons Victor M. Pomales; Victor I. Seda; Huan C. Tran.
School—St. Helena School, 6101 N. Fifth St., 19120. Tel: 215-549-2947; Fax: 215-549-5947. Lay Teachers 25; Sisters of St. Joseph 1; Students 557.
Catechesis Religious Program—Email: sophiessj@aol.com. Sr. Sophie Yondura, S.S.J., D.Min., D.R.E. Students 75.
58—ST. HENRY (1916-1993) (German), Closed. Formerly located at 4400 N. 5th St. Spiritual records are kept at St. Helena Church. Tel: 215-424-1300.
59—HOLY ANGELS (1906) (Korean)
7000 Old York Rd., 19126. Tel: 215-927-1662;
Fax: 215-224-6615. Revs. John Jeung Dae Woung, Admin.; Chan Kim, Parochial Vicar; John Sang Yong Lee, Parochial Vicar.
Catechesis Religious Program—Martin Shin, C.R.E. Students 200.
60—HOLY CHILD (1909-1993) Closed. Formerly located at 5200 N. Broad St. Spiritual records are kept at Our Lady of Hope Church. Tel: 215-329-8100; 329-8164.
61—HOLY CROSS (1890)
6440 Greene St., 19119. Tel: 215-438-2921;
Fax: 215-848-7953. Revs. William E. Grogan; Rayford E. Emmons, Parochial Vicar; Deacon Edward M. Purnell.
School—Holy Cross School, 144 E. Mt. Airy Ave., 19119. Tel: 215-242-0414; Fax: 215-242-0414. Lay Teachers 14; Students 175.
Catechesis Religious Program—Students 18.
Convent—148 E. Mt. Airy Ave., 19119.
Tel: 215-247-0262.
62—HOLY FAMILY (1885)
234 Hermitage St., 19127. Tel: 215-482-0450;
Fax: 215-482-7531; Email: holyfamily234@verizon.net; Web: www.holyfamilyphilly.org. Rev. Msgr. Patrick E. Sweeney; Deacon James M. Browne.
Catechesis Religious Program—Holy Family Prep, 242 Hermitage St., 19127. Email: holyfamilyprep@verizon.net. Catherine Kelley, D.R.E. Students 24.
63—HOLY INNOCENTS (1927)
1337 E. Hunting Park Ave., 19124.
Tel: 215-743-2600; Fax: 215-743-8041; Email: holyinnocents@comcast.net. Revs. Thomas M. Higgins, M.Div.; Vincent Tung The Pham, Parochial Vicar; Angelo J. Hernandez, Parochial Vicar; Deacon Andres A. Carrillo.
See Holy Innocents Area Catholic School, Philadelphia under Regional Parish Schools located in the Institution section.
Catechesis Religious Program—Tel: 215-743-5909. Students 400.
64—HOLY NAME OF JESUS (Fishtown) (1904)
701 E. Gaul St., 19125-2896. Tel: 215-739-3960;
Fax: 215-739-7597; Web: www.holyname-fishtown.org. Rev. Alfred E. Bradley, C.Ss.R., Admin.
School—Holy Name of Jesus School, 1612 E. Berks St., 19125. Tel: 215-423-8834; Fax: 215-426-4675; Email: aplauren06@nni.com; Web: userweb.nni.com/aplauren06. Lay Teachers 13; Students 219.
Catechesis Religious Program—Students 15.
65—HOLY REDEEMER (1941) (Chinese) Mission Chapel of the Church of St. John the Evangelist.
915 Vine St., 19107. Tel: 215-922-0999; Email: contact@stjohnsphilly.org. Rev. John Daya, O.F.M.-Cap., Coord. Chinese Apostolate.
School—Holy Redeemer School, (Grades 1-8), Tel: 215-922-0999; Fax: 215-922-6674; Web: www.holyredeemer.cc. Lay Teachers 12; Students 290.
Catechesis Religious Program—Students 88.
Parish House—916 Wood St., 19107.
Tel: 215-592-7552.
66—HOLY SPIRIT (1964-2014) Closed. Formerly located at 1845 Hartranft St. Spiritual records are kept at St. Richard Church, Philadelphia. Tel: 215-468-4777; 215-468-4778. Worship site for St. Richard Church.
67—HOLY TRINITY, [CEM] (German), Closed. (1788-2009) Formerly located at 6th & Spruce Sts. Spiritual records are kept at Old St. Mary's Church, Philadelphia. Tel: 215-923-7930. Worship site of Old St. Mary's Church.
68—ST. HUBERT (1924-1940) Closed. Formerly located at Torresdale and Cottman Aves. Spiritual records are kept at St. Bernard Church, Philadelphia. Tel: 215-333-0446.
69—ST. HUGH OF CLUNY (1922-2013) Closed. Formerly located at N.W. corner of Howard and Tioga Sts. Spiritual records are kept at St. Veronica Church, Philadelphia. Tel: 215-228-4878.
70—ST. IGNATIUS OF LOYOLA (1893)
636 N. 43rd St., 19104. Tel: 215-386-5065;
Fax: 215-386-2832; Email: oms-si@yahoo.com. Rev. Msgr. Federico A. Britto, M.Div., M.A., Admin.
School—Our Mother of Sorrows-St. Ignatius School, 617 N. 43rd St., 19104. Tel: 215-222-3626; Email: info@omssiphila.org; Web: omssiphila.org. Sr. Owen Patricia Bonner, S.S.J., Prin. Lay Teachers 14; Students 248; Religious Teachers 1.
Catechesis Religious Program—Mrs. Jennifer Simmons, D.R.E. Students 6.
Chaplaincy—St. Ignatius Nursing Home.
Tel: 215-349-8800; Fax: 215-222-3078.
71—IMMACULATE CONCEPTION (1869-2011) Closed. Formerly located at 1020 N. Front St. Spiritual Records are kept at St. Michael Church, Philadelphia. Tel: 215-739-2358. Worship site of St. Michael Church.
72—IMMACULATE CONCEPTION (1902-2012) Closed. Formerly located at 1020 E. Price St. Spiritual records are kept at St. Vincent de Paul Church. Tel: 215-438-2925.
73—IMMACULATE HEART OF MARY (1952)
819 E. Cathedral Rd., 19128. Tel: 215-483-1000;
Fax: 215-483-1732; Email: ihmparish@comcast.net; Web: www.ihmphila.org. Revs. Edward J. Casey, M.Div.; Joseph Bongard, In Res.; Samuel A. Verruni, M.Div., Parochial Vicar; Deacon Salvatore R. Bianco.
School—Immaculate Heart of Mary School, 815 E. Cathedral Rd., 19128. Tel: 215-482-2029;
Fax: 215-482-1075. Lay Teachers 26; Students 468.
Catechesis Religious Program—Tel: 215-483-4266. Students 85.
74—INCARNATION OF OUR LORD (1900-2013) Closed. Formerly located at 5th St. and Lindley Ave. Spiritual records are kept at St. Helena Church, Philadelphia. Tel: 215-424-1300.
75—SAINT IRENAEUS (1966-2004) Closed. Formerly located at 2728 S. 73rd St. Spiritual records are kept at Divine Mercy Parish. Tel: 215-727-8300. Worship Site of Divine Mercy Parish.
76—ST. JAMES (1850-1976) Closed. Formerly located at 38th and Chestnut Sts. Spiritual records are kept at St. Agatha-St. James Parish, Philadelphia. Tel: 267-787-5000.
77—ST. JEROME (1955)
8100 Colfax St., 19136. Tel: 215-333-4461;
Fax: 215-333-6791; Email: parish@stjeromechurchphila.org; Web: www.stjeromeparish.com. Revs. Michael J. Reilly; Richard E. Rudy; Michael J. Ryan, In Res.
School—St. Jerome School, (Grades PreK-8), 3031 Stamford St., 19136. Tel: 215-624-0637;
Fax: 215-624-5711; Email: principalstjerome@gmail.com; Web: sjsphila.org. Susan Gallagher, Prin. Lay Teachers 22; Students 360.
Catechesis Religious Program—Students 53.
78—ST. JOACHIM (1845-2013) [CEM] Closed. Formerly located at Church St. between Griscom and Penn Sts. Spiritual records are kept at Holy Innocents Church, Philadelphia. Tel: 215-743-2600.
79—ST. JOAN OF ARC (1919-2013) Closed. Formerly located at Frankford Ave. and Atlantic St. Spiritual records are kept at Holy Innocents Church, Philadelphia. Tel: 215-743-2600.
80—ST. JOHN CANTIUS (1892)
4415 Almond St., 19137. Tel: 215-535-6667;
Fax: 215-535-7107; Email: rectory@stjohncantiusparish.org; Web: www.stjohncantiusparish.org. Revs. Joseph J. Zingaro; Konstanty J. Pruszynski, Parochial Vicar.
See Blessed Trinity Regional Catholic School, Philadelphia under Regional Parish Schools located in the Institution section.
Catechesis Religious Program—Students 240.
81—ST. JOHN NEPOMUCENE (1902-1980) (Slovak), Closed. Formerly located at 9th and Wharton Sts., Philadelphia. Spiritual records are kept at St. Agnes-St. John Nepomucene Church, Philadelphia. Tel: 215-627-0340.
82—ST. JOHN THE BAPTIST (1831) [CEM]
146 Rector St., 19127. Tel: 215-482-4600;
Fax: 215-482-2976; Email: sjbphila@stjohnmanayunk.org; Email: dre@stjohnmanayunk.org; Web: www.stjohnmanayunk.org. Rev. Msgr. Kevin C. Lawrence, M.Div.; Revs. James J. McGuinn; Christopher D. Lucas, In Res.
Catechesis Religious Program—Students 85.
83—ST. JOHN THE EVANGELIST (1830) [CEM]
21 S. 13th St., 19107. Tel: 215-563-4145; Web: www.stjohnsphilly.com. Revs. John Daya, O.F.M.Cap.; John Paul Kuzma, O.F.M.Cap., Parochial Vicar; Rafael Anguiano-Rodriguez, O.F.M.Cap., In Res.; Benjamin F. Madden, O.F.M.Cap., In Res.; Richard N. Owens, O.F.M.Cap., In Res.; Benjamin R. Regotti, O.F.M.Cap., In Res.; Allan Wasiecko, In Res.; Roger White, O.F.M.Cap., In Res.
See St. Mary Interparochial School, Philadelphia under Regional Parish Schools located in the Institution section.
Mission—Holy Redeemer Chinese Church, 915 Vine St., 19107. Tel: 215-922-0999; Fax: 215-922-6674.
84—ST. JOSAPHAT (1898-2012) (Polish), Closed. Formerly located at 124 Cotton St. Spiritual records are kept at St. John the Baptist Church, Philadelphia. Tel: 215-482-4600. Worship Site of St. John the Baptist Church, Philadelphia.
85—ST. KATHERINE OF SIENA (1922)
St. Katherine of Siena Parish, 9700 Frankford Ave., 19114-2896. Tel: 215-637-7548; Email: skschurch@skschurch.com. Revs. Paul M. Kennedy, M.A., M.Div.; William B. Lange, M.Div., Parochial Vicar; Ronald J. Ferrier, M.A., In Res., (Retired); Deacons James J. Duffy; Robert H. Hall; Carol Buchsbaum, Business Mgr.
School—St. Katherine of Siena School, (Grades PreK-8), 9738 Frankford Ave., 19114.
Tel: 215-637-2181; Fax: 215-637-4867; Web: www.sksgradeschool.com. Regina A. Tanghe, Prin. Lay Teachers 26; Sisters of the Holy Family of Nazareth 1; Sisters, Servants of the Immaculate Heart of Mary 1; Students 615.
Catechesis Religious Program—Tel: 215-637-1464; Email: prep@skschurch.com. Students 85.
86—KING OF PEACE (1926-2004) (Italian), Closed. Formerly located at 26th and Wharton Sts. Spiritual records are kept at St. Gabriel Church, Philadelphia. Tel: 215-463-4060.
87—ST. LADISLAUS (1906-2003) (Polish), Closed. Formerly located at 1648 W. Hunting Park Ave. Spiritual records are kept at St. John the Baptist Church. Tel: 215-482-4600.
88—ST. LAURENTIUS (1882-2013) (Polish), Closed. Formerly located at Memphis and E. Berks Sts. Spiritual records are kept at Holy Name of Jesus Church, Philadelphia. Tel: 215-739-3960. Worship site of Holy Name of Jesus Church.
89—ST. LEO (1884-2013) Closed. Formerly located at Keystone and Unruh Sts. Spiritual records are kept at Our Lady of Consolation Church, Philadelphia. Tel: 215-333-0442. Worship site of Our Lady of Consolation Church.
90—ST. LUCY (1927-2012) (Italian), Closed. Formerly located at 140 Green Ln. Spiritual records are kept at Holy Family Church, Philadelphia. Tel: 215-482-0450. Worship Site of Holy Family Church, Philadelphia.
91—ST. LUDWIG (1891-1975) (German), Closed. Formerly located at 28th & Master Sts. Spiritual records are kept at St. Francis Xavier Church, Philadelphia. Tel: 215-765-4568.
92—ST. MADELEINE SOPHIE (1925-2013) Closed. Formerly located at Greene and Upsal Sts. Spiritual records are kept at Holy Cross Parish, Philadelphia. Tel: 215-438-2921.
93—ST. MALACHY (1850)
1429 N. 11th St., 19122. Tel: 215-763-1305;
Fax: 215-763-2023; Email: s.williams@saintmalachychurch.com; Email: pastor@saintmalachychurch.com; Web: saintmalachychurch.com. Rev. Thomas P. Kletzel, M.Div.
Catechesis Religious Program—Students 29.
94—SAINT MARTHA (1966)
11301 Academy Rd., 19154-3304. Tel: 610-275-1750;
Fax: 610-275-0480; Email: unitedinthesacredheart@aol.com; Web: stmarthachurch.com. Rev. Alexander Masluk; Rev.

Msgr. Andrew J. Golias, S.T.D., S.T.L., Parochial Vicar; Deacon Stephen A. Guckin.
School—St. Martha School, 11321 Academy Rd., 19154-3304. Tel: 215-632-0320; Fax: 215-632-5546. Lay Teachers 15; Students 279.
Catechesis Religious Program—Students 80.
95—ST. MARTIN DE PORRES (1993)
2340 W. Lehigh Ave., 19132. Tel: 215-228-8330; Fax: 215-221-6516; Email: SMDP2340@hotmail.com. Rev. Stephen D. Thorne, M.A., M.Div.
School—St. Martin De Porres School, 23rd St. & Lehigh Ave., 19132. Tel: 215-223-6872; Fax: 215-223-4126. Lay Teachers 30; Sisters of St. Joseph 5; Students 480.
Catechesis Religious Program—Students 30.
96—ST. MARTIN OF TOURS (1923)
5450 Roosevelt Blvd., 19124.
Tel: 215-535-2962, Ext. 403; Web: www.smtparish.org. Revs. Michael S. Olivere, M.Div., Admin.; Michael G. Mullan, Parochial Vicar; Livinus C. Ugochukwu, Parochial Vicar; Jose Luis Queimado, C.Ss.R., Brazilian Apostolate.
School—St. Martin of Tours Mission School, 5701 Loretto Ave., 19124. Fax: 215-533-1579. Lay Teachers 39; Sisters of the Immaculate Heart of Mary 10; Students 575.
Catechesis Religious Program—Fax: 215-535-3091; Email: ccd@smtparish.org. Students 159.
97—ST. MARY MAGDALEN DE PAZZI (1852-2000) (Italian), Closed. Formerly located at 712 Montrose St. Spiritual records are kept at St. Paul Church, Philadelphia. Tel: 215-923-0355. Worship site of St. Paul Church.
98—ST. MARY OF CZESTOCHOWA (1927-2000) (Polish), Closed. Formerly located at 59th St. and Elmwood Ave. Spiritual records are kept at St. Barnabas Church, Philadelphia. Tel: 215-726-1119; 1120.
99—ST. MARY OF THE ASSUMPTION (1849-2012) [CEM] (German), Closed. Formerly located at 172 Conarroe St. Spiritual records are kept at St. John the Baptist Church, Philadelphia. Tel: 215-482-4600.
100—ST. MARY OF THE ETERNAL (1911-1976) (Italian), Closed. Formerly located at 2222 W. Clearfield St. Spiritual records are kept at St. Martin de Porres Church, Philadelphia. Tel: 215-228-8330.
101—MATER DOLOROSA (1911-2013) (Italian), Closed. Formerly located at Paul and Ruan Sts. Spiritual records are kept at Holy Innocents Church, Philadelphia. Tel: 215-743-2600.
102—MATERNITY B.V.M. (1870)
9220 Old Bustleton Ave., 19115-4686.
Tel: 215-673-8127; Fax: 215-673-6597; Email: church@maternitybvm.net; Web: www.maternitybvmchurch.net. Revs. Paul S. Quinter; Michael J. Saban, Parochial Vicar; Joseph Sundaram, Parochial Vicar; Deacons Joseph W. Bernauer Jr.; Charles R. Lindsay.
School—Maternity B.V.M. School, 9322 Bustleton Ave., 19115. Tel: 215-673-0235; Fax: 215-671-1347. Mary Zawisza, Prin.; Carol Sims, Librarian. Lay Teachers 22; Students 503.
Catechesis Religious Program—Tel: 215-673-4010. Sr. Mary Beth Geraghty, R.S.M., D.R.E. Students 113.
Convent—Tel: 215-673-8118.
103—ST. MATTHEW (1927)
3000 Cottman Ave., 19149. Tel: 215-333-0585; Fax: 215-333-0757; Web: www.stmattsparish.com. Revs. Patrick J. Welsh, S.L.L., M.A., M.Div., S.T.B.; Brandon Artman, Parochial Vicar; Steven J. Marinucci, Parochial Vicar; Steven P. Wetzel, O.S.F.S., In Res.; Deacon Robert C. Burns.
School—St. Matthew School, 3040 Cottman Ave., 19149. Tel: 215-333-3142. Lay Teachers 33; Sisters, Servants of the Immaculate Heart of Mary 6; Students 741.
Catechesis Religious Program—Students 100.
Convent—Tel: 215-333-8214.
104—ST. MICHAEL (1831) [CEM]
1445 N. Second St., 19122. Tel: 215-739-2358; Fax: 215-739-5766; Web: icstmichael19122.wordpress.com. Rev. Arturo Chagala, Admin.
Catechesis Religious Program—Students 18.
105—ST. MICHAEL MISSION (1923-1958) Closed. Formerly located at Red Lion and Knights Rds. Spiritual records are kept at Our Lady of Calvary Church. Tel: 215-637-7515.
106—ST. MICHAEL OF THE SAINTS (1924-1982) (Italian), Closed. Formerly located at 4811 Germantown Ave. Spiritual records kept at St. Vincent de Paul Church. Tel: 215-438-2925.
107—ST. MONICA (1895)
2422 S. 17th St., 19145. Tel: 215-334-4170; Email: josephkelley56@gmail.com; Web: www.saintmonicaparish.net. Revs. Joseph J. Kelley, M.A., M.Div.; John E. Calabro, Parochial Vicar; Dennis J. Witalec, In Res., (Retired); Deacons Leonard D. DeMasi; James J. Stewart.
Schools—Junior School—1720 Ritner Ave., 19145. Tel: 215-334-3777; Fax: 215-389-0355.
Senior School, 2500 S. 16th St., 19145. Tel: 215-467-5338; Fax: 215-467-4599. Lay Teachers 23; Servants of the Immaculate Heart of Mary 7; Students 458.
Catechesis Religious Program—Tel: 215-334-1659; Fax: 215-389-0355. Students 250.
108—MOST BLESSED SACRAMENT (1901-2008) Closed. Formerly located at 56th St. & Chester Ave. Spiritual records are kept at St. Francis de Sales Church, Philadelphia. Tel: 215-222-5819.
109—MOST PRECIOUS BLOOD OF OUR LORD (1907-1993) Closed. Formerly located at 28th & Diamond Sts. Spiritual records are kept at St. Martin De Porres Church. Tel: 215-228-8330.
110—MOTHER OF DIVINE GRACE (1926) (Italian)
2918 E. Thompson St., 19134. Tel: 215-739-0353; Fax: 215-739-9910. Rev. James P. Olson, M.Div., M.A., S.T.L.; Deacon Ralph J. Shirley.
School—Mother of Divine Grace School, 2612 E. Monmouth St., 19134. Tel: 215-426-7325; Fax: 215-426-0753. Lay Teachers 10; Students 178.
Catechesis Religious Program— Twinned with Nativity of the Blessed Virgin Mary, Belgrade and Allegheny Aves. Students 5.
111—NATIVITY OF THE BLESSED VIRGIN MARY (1882)
2535 E. Allegheny Ave., 19134. Tel: 215-739-2735; Web: www.Nativitybvmphila.org. Revs. James P. Olson, M.Div., M.A., S.T.L.; James P. Gorman, Parochial Vicar; Deacon Ralph J. Shirley.
Catechesis Religious Program—Students 53.
112—ST. NICHOLAS OF TOLENTINE (1912) (Italian)
910 Watkins St., 19148. Tel: 215-463-1326; Email: stnicks910@verizon.net; Web: www.stnicksphila.com. Revs. Nicholas Martorano, O.S.A.; Robert Terranova, Parochial Vicar; Denis G. Wilde, O.S.A., In Res.
Church: Ninth St. below Morris St., 19148.
School—St. Anthony of Padua Regional Catholic School, 913 Pierce St., 19148. Tel: 215-468-0353; Fax: 215-334-9661. Lay Teachers 15; Religious 2; Religious Sisters Filippini 2; Students 220.
Catechesis Religious Program—Fax: 215-334-4255. Students 95.
113—OLD ST. JOSEPH'S (1733)
321 Willings Aly., 19106. Tel: 215-923-1733; Email: office@oldstjoseph.org; Web: www.oldstjoseph.org. Revs. Walter Modrys; Edward T. O'Donnell, S.J., Parochial Vicar; Bro. Robert J. Carson, S.J., In Res.; Rev. Edward C.A. Dougherty, S.J., In Res., (Retired). See St. Mary Interparochial School, Philadelphia under Regional Parish Schools located in the Institution section.
Catechesis Religious Program—St. Mary's Interparochial School, 500 Locust St., 19106. Christine Szczepanowski, C.R.E. Students 76.
114—OLD ST. MARY'S (1763) [CEM]
252 S. Fourth St., 19106. Tel: 215-923-7930; Web: www.oldstmary1763.com. Rev. Msgr. Paul A. DiGirolamo, J.C.D., M.A., M.Div.
See St. Mary Interparochial School, Philadelphia under Regional Parish Schools located in the Institution section.
Catechesis Religious Program—Students 15.
115—OUR LADY HELP OF CHRISTIANS (1885-2016) (German), Closed. Formerly located at E. Allegheny Ave. & Gaul St. Spiritual records are kept at Nativity B.V.M. Church, Philadelphia. Tel: 215-739-2735.
Res.: 2535 E. Allegheny Ave., 19134.
See Our Lady of Port Richmond Regional School, Philadelphia under Regional Parish Schools located in the Institution Section.
116—OUR LADY OF ANGELS (1907-2006) (Italian), Closed. Formerly located at 4970 Master St. Spiritual records are kept at Our Lady of Lourdes Church, Philadelphia. Tel: 215-473-1669.
117—OUR LADY OF CALVARY (1958)
11024 Knights Rd., 19154. Tel: 215-637-7515; Fax: 215-637-7517; Web: www.ourladyofcalvary.org. Revs. John F. Babowitch, M.Div.; William S. Kirk, Parochial Vicar; Deacons John P. Teson; Michael J. Bell.
School—Our Lady of Calvary School, (Grades PreK-8), 11023 Kipling Ln., 19154. Tel: 215-637-1648; Fax: 215-637-3810. Sr. Mildred Chesnavage, C.S.F., Prin. Lay Teachers 39; Sisters of the Holy Family of Nazareth 6; Students 912.
Catechesis Religious Program—Students 229.
118—OUR LADY OF CONSOLATION (1917)
7056 Tulip St., 19135. Tel: 215-333-0442; Tel: 215-333-5774; Fax: 215-333-2884; Web: www.olctacony.org. Rev. Joseph L. Farrell, M.Div.
Catechesis Religious Program—Students 50.
119—OUR LADY OF GOOD COUNSEL (1898-1932) Closed. Formerly located at 816 Christian St. Spiritual records are kept at St. Paul Church, Philadelphia. Tel: 215-923-0355.
120—OUR LADY OF HOPE (1993)
5200 N. Broad St., 19141-1628. Tel: 215-329-8100; Tel: 215-329-8164; Fax: 215-324-4660; Web: www.olhphila.org. Rev. Efren V. Esmilla, M.Div.; Deacons Felipe Hernandez; Homer A. Panganiban.
Catechesis Religious Program—Students 40.
121—OUR LADY OF LORETO (1932-2000) (Italian), Closed. Formerly located at 6214 Grays Ave. Spiritual records are kept at St. Barnabas Church. Tel: 215-726-1119.
122—OUR LADY OF LOURDES (1894)
6300 Woodbine Ave., 19151. Tel: 215-473-1669; Email: frmrock.oll@verizon.net; Web: www.ourladylourdes.org. 1941 Wynnewood Rd., 19151. Revs. Michael R. Rock, O.de.M.; Scottston F. Brentwood, O.de.M.
Res.: 6315 Lancaster Ave., 19151. Tel: 215-473-2874; Fax: 215-473-2878.
Catechesis Religious Program—Email: brianmurray12@yahoo.com. Mr. Brian Murray, D.R.E. Students 29.
123—OUR LADY OF MERCY (1889-1984) Closed. Formerly located at Broad St. & Susquehanna Ave. Spiritual records are kept at St. Malachy Church. Tel: 215-763-1305.
124—OUR LADY OF MT. CARMEL (1896)
2319 S. Third St., 19148. Tel: 215-334-7766; Email: olmc-phila@verizon.net; Web: www.ourladymountcarmel.net. Revs. Francis J. Cauterucci; Chanlis Chacko, Parochial Vicar.
Catechesis Religious Program—Students 108.
Convent—251 Ritner St., 19148. Tel: 215-334-6800.
125—OUR LADY OF POMPEII (1914-1993) (Italian), Closed. Formerly located at 6th St. & Erie Ave. Spiritual records are kept at St. Veronica Church, Philadelphia. Tel: 215-228-4878.
126—OUR LADY OF RANSOM (1954) Closed. Spiritual records are kept at Resurrection of Our Lord Church. Tel: 215-745-3211. Worship site for Resurrection of Our Lord Church.
See Resurrection Regional Catholic School, Philadelphia under Regional Parish Schools located in the Institution section.
127—OUR LADY OF THE BLESSED SACRAMENT (1910-1972) Closed. Formerly located at 712 N. Broad St. Spiritual records are kept at the Cathedral Basilica of SS. Peter and Paul, Philadelphia. Tel: 215-561-1313.
128—OUR LADY OF THE BLESSED SACRAMENT (2005-2013) Closed. Formerly located at 345 N. 63rd St. Spiritual records are kept at St. Cyprian Parish, Philadelphia. Tel: 215-747-3250.
129—OUR LADY OF THE HOLY ROSARY (1928-1977) (Italian), Closed. Formerly located at 528 E. Haines St. Spiritual records are kept at St. Vincent de Paul Church, Philadelphia. Tel: 215-438-2925.
130—OUR LADY OF THE HOLY SOULS (1909-1993) Closed. Formerly located at 19th & Tioga Sts. Spiritual records are kept at Our Lady of Hope Church, Philadelphia. Tel: 215-329-8100.
131—OUR LADY OF THE ROSARY (1886-2005) Closed. Formerly located at 345 N. 63rd St. Spiritual records are kept at St. Cyprian Church, Philadelphia. Tel: 215-747-3250.
132—OUR LADY OF VICTORY (1899-2005) Closed. Formerly located at 5412 Vine St. Spiritual records are kept at St. Cyprian Church, Philadelphia. Tel: 215-747-3250.
133—OUR MOTHER OF CONSOLATION (1855)
9 E. Chestnut Hill Ave., 19118. Tel: 215-247-0430; Email: bbazzoli@omcparish.com; Web: omcparish.com. Revs. Robert L. Bazzoli, O.S.F.S.; John J. McGinley, O.S.F.S., In Res.; Robert G. Mulligan, O.S.F.S., In Res.; Deacon Joseph L. Nines.
School—Our Mother of Consolation School, (Grades PreK-8), 17 E. Chestnut Hill Ave., 19118.
Tel: 215-247-1060; Fax: 215-247-0506; Email: tschmidt@omcparish.com; Web: school.omcparish.com. Theresa Schmidt, Prin. Lay Teachers 17; Students 231.
Catechesis Religious Program—Email: CKONOPELSKI@OMCPARISH.COM. Sr. Christine Konopelski, S.S.J., Pastoral Assoc. Faith Formation. Students 4.
Convent—23 E. Chestnut Hill Ave., 19118.
Tel: 215-247-0552.
134—OUR MOTHER OF SORROWS (1852-2013) Closed. Formerly located at 48th St. and Lancaster Ave. Spiritual records are kept at St. Ignatius of Loyola Parish, Philadelphia. Tel: 215-386-5065.
135—ST. PATRICK (1839)
242 S. 20th St., 19103. Tel: 215-735-9900; Email: stpatricksparish@aol.com; Web: www.stpatrickphilly.org. Friars George Schommer; Timothy Danaher, Parochial Vicar; Giles Dimock, In Res.; Edmund McCullough, In Res.; Loretta Colucci, Business Mgr.
School—St. Mary Interparochial School, 5th & Locust Sts., 19106. Tel: 215-923-7522; Email: schooloffice@saintmarys.us; Web: www.saintmarys.us.
See St. Mary Interparochial School, Philadelphia under Regional Parish Schools located in the Institution section.
Catechesis Religious Program—Students 25.
136—ST. PAUL (1843)

808 S. Hutchinson St., 19147. Tel: 215-923-0355; Fax: 215-923-1803. Rev. John J. Large.
Worship Site: St. Mary Magdalen de Pazzi Church, 712 Montrose St., 19147.
Catechesis Religious Program—Tel: 215-923-0355; Fax: 215-923-1803. Students 140.

137—ST. PETER CLAVER (1889-1985) Closed. Formerly located at 12th & Lombard Sts. Spiritual records are kept at St. John the Evangelist Church, Philadelphia. Tel: 215-563-4145.

138—ST. PETER THE APOSTLE (1842) [CEM]
1019 N. Fifth St., 19123. Tel: 215-627-2386; Fax: 215-627-2366; Email: stpetersoffice@comcast.net; Web: stjohnneumann.org/parish. Revs. Richard S. Bennett, C.Ss.R.; Gerard Chylko, C.Ss.R., Parochial Vicar; Blas Caceres, C.Ss.R., Parochial Vicar; Anthony Michalik, C.Ss.R., Parochial Vicar; Peter Linh Ba Quoc Nguyen, C.Ss.R., Parochial Vicar; Gerard J. Brinkman, C.Ss.R., In Res.; Raymond Collins, C.Ss.R., In Res.; Donald C. Miniscalco, C.Ss.R., In Res.; Peter Jittapol Plangklang, In Res.; Deacons Jose Miguel Betancourt; Juan F. Ramos.
School—St. Peter the Apostle School, 1009 N. Fifth St., 19123. Tel: 215-922-5958; Fax: 215-922-1015. Sr. Rose Federici, S.S.N.D. Lay Teachers 10; School Sisters of Notre Dame 1; Students 208.
Catechesis Religious Program—Students 40.
Convent—1005 N. 5th St., 19123. Tel: 215-627-3954.
Shrine—St. John Neumann, Tel: 215-627-3080; Fax: 215-627-3296. Deborah Binder, Asst. Dir.

139—ST. PHILIP NERI (1840)
218 Queen St., 19147. Tel: 215-468-1922; Email: stphilipneri@comcast.net; Web: queenvillagecatholic.com. Rev. Edward P. Kuczynski, M.Div.

140—ST. RAPHAEL (1904-1989) Closed. Formerly located at 86th St. & Tinicum Ave. Spiritual records are kept at Divine Mercy Parish, Philadelphia. Tel: 215-727-8300.

141—ST. RAYMOND OF PENAFORT (1941)
1350 Vernon Rd., 19150. Tel: 215-549-3760; Fax: 215-549-1271; Email: pastor@saintraymond.net; Web: www.saintraymond.net. Rev. Christopher M. Walsh; Deacon William C. Bradley.
School—St. Raymond of Penafort School, (Grades PreK-8), 7940 Williams Ave., 19150. Tel: 215-548-1919; Fax: 215-548-1925; Email: pwright@straymondphila.org; Web: straymondphila.independencemissionschools.org. Lay Teachers 16; Students 275.
Catechesis Religious Program—Students 35.

142—RESURRECTION OF OUR LORD (1928)
2000 Shelmire Ave., 19152. Tel: 215-745-3211; Email: secretaries@resrrectphila.org; Web: www.resurrectphila.org. Revs. James R. DeGrassa; Jose Luis Queimado, C.Ss.R., Portugese Apostolate; Deacons Joao A. Ferreira, Portugese Apostolate; Dennis J. Friel; John J. Knesis.
Our Lady of Ransom.
School—Resurrection of Our Lord School, 2020 Shelmire Ave., 19152. Tel: 215-742-1127; Fax: 215-742-0947; Email: resurrectionschool@yahoo.com; Web: www.resurrectschool.org. Mrs. Joan Stulz, Prin. Lay Teachers 25; Students 450.
Catechesis Religious Program— Tel: 215-742-1127, Ext. 120. Karen Fitzgerald, D.R.E. Students 70.

143—ST. RICHARD (1924)
3010 S. 18th St., 19145. Tel: 215-468-4777; Fax: 215-468-3161; Web: www.strichardchurch.org. Revs. John R. Weber, M.A., M.Div.; James C. Rodia, O.Praem., Parochial Vicar.
See St. Pio Regional Catholic School, Philadelphia under Regional Parish Schools located in the Institution section.
Catechesis Religious Program—Email: dre@strichardchurch.org. Maryellen Carroll, D.R.E. Students 195.
Worship Site: Holy Spirit Church, 1845 Hartranft St., 19145.

144—ST. RITA OF CASCIA (1907-2016) Spiritual records are kept at Annunciation B.V.M. Church, Philadelphia. Tel: 215-334-0159. Site of the National Shrine of St. Rita of Cascia.
1166 S. Broad St., 19146. Tel: 215-546-8333; Fax: 215-732-3510; Email: ritashrine@aol.com; Web: www.saintritashrine.org. Revs. Daniel McLaughlin, O.S.A., In Res.; William A. Recchuti, O.S.A, In Res.; James T. Spenard, O.S.A., In Res.
Shrine—The National Shrine of St. Rita of Cascia.

145—ST. ROSE OF LIMA (1921-2013) Closed. Formerly located at 1535 N. 59th St. Spiritual records are kept at St. Barbara Church, Philadelphia. Tel: 215-473-1044.

146—SACRED HEART (1913-1977) (Hungarian), Closed. Formerly located at Mascher & Master Sts. Spiritual records are kept at St. Michael Church, Philadelphia. Tel: 215-739-2358.

147—SACRED HEART OF JESUS (1871)
1404 S. Third St., 19147-6099. Tel: 215-465-4050; Fax: 215-465-0400; Email: sacredheart310@comcast.net; Web: www.sacredheartchurchsp.com. Rev. James C. Otto.
See Our Lady of Hope Regional Catholic School, Philadelphia under Regional Parish Schools located in the Institution section.
Catechesis Religious Program—John Paul Kasperowizc, D.R.E. Students 75.

148—ST. STANISLAUS (1891-2006) (Polish), Closed. Formerly located at 240 Fitzwater St. Spiritual records are kept at St. Philip Neri Church, Philadelphia. Tel: 215-468-1922. Worship site for St. Philip Neri Parish.

149—STELLA MARIS (1954)
2901 S. 10th St., 19148. Tel: 215-465-2336; Fax: 215-465-1061; Email: stellamarisparish@comcast.net; Web: www.stellamarisphila.com. Revs. John R. DiOrio, M.A., M.Div.; James T. McCabe, Parochial Vicar.
Catechesis Religious Program—Tel: 215-465-2335. Mrs. Marie Milano, D.R.E. Students 68.
Convent—2929 S. 10th St., 19148. Tel: 215-462-1111.

150—ST. STEPHEN (1843-1993) Closed. Formerly located at Broad & Butler Sts. Spiritual records are kept at Our Lady of Hope Church, Philadelphia. Tel: 215-329-8100.

151—ST. TERESA OF AVILA (1853-1972) Closed. Formerly located at Broad & Catherine Sts. Spiritual records are kept at Annunciation B.V.M. Church, Philadelphia. Tel: 215-334-0159.

152—ST. THERESE OF THE CHILD JESUS (1925-2013) Closed. Formerly located on Upsal St. between Ardleigh and Anderson Sts. Spiritual records are kept at Holy Cross Church, Philadelphia. Tel: 215-438-2921. Worship site of Holy Cross Church.

153—ST. THOMAS AQUINAS (1885)
1719 Morris St., 19145. Tel: 215-334-2312; Email: staquinasparish@gmail.com. Rev. Msgr. Hugh Joseph Shields, M.Div.; Revs. Dominic Tran Minh Duc, M.Div., Parochial Vicar; Kurniawan Diputra, C.M., In Res.; Deacon Cristobal Chavac.
See St. Thomas Aquinas under Independence Mission Schools in the Institutions section.
Catechesis Religious Program—Joanne Gledhill, D.R.E. Students 560.
Aquinas Center—1700 Fernon St., 19145. Tel: 267-928-4048; Web: www.staquinas.com. Dr. Bethany Welch, Dir.

154—ST. TIMOTHY (1928)
3001 Levick St., 19149. Tel: 215-624-6188; Fax: 215-624-1316; Email: rectory@st-tims.org; Web: www.st-tims.org. Revs. Michael S. Olivere, M.Div.; William J. Monahan, Parochial Vicar; Charles J. Noone, M.A., In Res., (Retired); Deacon Edward F. Hanley.
See Blessed Trinity Regional Catholic School, Philadelphia under Regional Parish Schools located in the Institution section.
Catechesis Religious Program— Tel: 215-338-9797, Ext. 123; Email: ckirschman@st-tims.org. Students 70.
Convent—3033 Levick St., 19149. Tel: 215-624-8333.

155—TRANSFIGURATION OF OUR LORD (1905-2000) Closed. Formerly located at 5533 Cedar Ave. Spiritual records are kept at St. Cyprian Church, Philadelphia. Tel: 215-747-3250.

156—ST. VERONICA (1872)
533 W. Tioga St., 19140. Tel: 215-228-4878; Tel: 215-225-5677; Fax: 215-228-0381; Email: stveronica.rcc@gmail.com; Web: www.saintveronicaparish.org. Revs. Joseph B. LoJacono, I.V.E.; Mario Avila, Parochial Vicar; Daniel C. Vitz, I.V.E., Parochial Vicar; Deacons Jose Luis Lozada, Pastoral Min./Coord.; Alexander Reyes, I.V.E., Pastoral Min./Coord.
School—St. Veronica School, 3521 N. 6th St., 19140. Tel: 215-225-1575; Fax: 215-225-2595. Sr. Eileen Buchanan, I.H.M., Prin. Lay Teachers 8; Sisters, Servants of the Immaculate Heart of Mary 3; Students 172.
Catechesis Religious Program—Tel: 267-836-9056; Email: stveronica@servidoras.org. Sr. Mother Mary Incarnation Creeden, S.S.V.M., D.R.E. Students 170.
Convents—Sisters, Servants of the Immaculate Heart of Mary—3521 N. Sixth St., 19140. Tel: 215-223-9107. Sr. Francis Mary Murray, I.H.M., Supr.
Katharine Drexel Sisters, Servants of the Lord and the Virgin of Matara, 632 W. Erie Ave., 19140. Tel: 215-225-9888.

157—ST. VINCENT DE PAUL (1851)
109 E. Price St., 19144. Tel: 215-438-2925; Email: secretary@saint-vincent-church.org; Web: www.saint-vincent-church.org. Revs. Sylvester Peterka, C.M.; Joseph Ita-Sam, Parochial Vicar; Bindel-Mary Nnabuife, Parochial Vicar; Bro. Alfred J. Smith, C.M., Pastoral Min./Coord.; Rev. Joseph V. Cummings, C.M., In Res.; Ms. Valerie Lee-Jeter, Music Min.; Mr. Darin Williams, Music Min.
St. Vincent De Paul Youth and Young Adult Center—49 W. Logan St., 19144. Tel: 215-842-3668. Sr. Sharon Horace, D.C., Co-Dir.
Catechesis Religious Program—Students 55.

158—VISITATION B.V.M. (1874)
2625 B St., 19125. Tel: 215-634-1133; Email: visitationchurch@visitationbvm.com; Web: www.visitationbvm.net. Revs. John Olenick, C.Ss.R.; Thomas McCluskey, C.Ss.R., Parochial Vicar; Joseph Hung Duc Tran, C.Ss.R., Parochial Vicar; Jose Luis Queimado, C.Ss.R., In Res.; Anthony T. Russo, C.Ss.R., In Res.
School—Visitation B.V.M. School, (Grades PreK-8), 300 E. Lehigh Ave., 19125. Tel: 215-634-7280; Fax: 215-634-4062; Email: contact@vizobvm.org; Web: www.vizobvm.org. Edward Coleman, Prin. Lay Teachers 19; Sisters of St. Joseph 3; Students 424.
Catechesis Religious Program—Email: nrivera@communitycenteratvis.org. Ms. Norma Rivera, D.R.E.; David Serrano, D.R.E. Students 243.
Cardinal Bevilacqua Community Center—2646 Kensington Ave., 19125. Tel: 215-426-9422; Fax: 215-426-9426. Sr. Elizabeth Scanlon, R.S.M., Dir.

159—ST. WILLIAM (1920)
6200 Rising Sun Ave., 19111. Tel: 215-745-1389; Email: office@churchofstwilliam.com; Web: www.churchofstwilliam.org. Revs. Alfonso J. Concha, M.Div.; Tariq Isaac, Parochial Vicar; Eugene R. Almonor, O.M.I., In Res.; Augusto M. Concha, In Res., (Retired); Deacons Felipe Cruz; William J. Moser.
Catechesis Religious Program—Tel: 215-745-0921. Sr. Bernadette Taraschi, I.H.M., D.R.E. Students 101.
Convent—6226 Rising Sun Ave., 19111. Tel: 215-745-3513.

OUTSIDE THE CITY OF PHILADELPHIA

ABINGTON, MONTGOMERY CO., OUR LADY HELP OF CHRISTIANS (1953)
1500 Marian Rd., Abington, 19001. Tel: 215-886-3456; Email: secretary@olhc-parish.org; Web: www.olhc-parish.org. Rev. Anthony W. Janton; Deacons John J. Nucero; Joseph T. Rooney; Mrs. Pamela McAfee, Business Mgr.
See Queen of Angels Regional Catholic School, Willow Grove under Regional Parish Schools located in the Institution section.
Catechesis Religious Program—Tel: 215-887-3466. Mrs. Jennifer Bellantoni, Diocesan D.R.E.; Dianne Donohue. Students 167.

AMBLER, MONTGOMERY CO.

1—ST. ANTHONY OF PADUA (1886) [CEM]
259 Forest Ave., Ambler, 19002-5903. Tel: 215-646-4742; Fax: 215-646-4864; Email: mchenry@saintanthonyparish.org; Email: pastor@saintanthonyparish.org; Web: www.saintanthonyparish.org. Rev. Msgr. Stephen P. McHenry, Ph.D., M.A., M.Div.; Rev. Stephen H. Paolino, Parochial Vicar; Deacons Edward M. Cuff; Kevin Gentilcore.
School—St. Anthony Preschool and Childcare, 260 Forest Ave., First Fl., Ambler, 19002. Tel: 215-646-6150; Fax: 215-465-5254. Students 61.
See Our Lady of Mercy Regional Catholic School, Maple Glen under Regional Parish Schools located in the Institution section.
Catechesis Religious Program—260 Forest Ave., Second Fl., Ambler, 19002. Students 313.

2—ST. JOSEPH (1920)
16 S. Spring Garden St., Ambler, 19002-4797. Tel: 215-646-0494; Fax: 215-643-6389. Revs. Eugene M. Tully; Charles J. McElroy, M.S., In Res., (Retired); Deacon Mark J. Kuhn.
Catechesis Religious Program—Students 109.

ARDMORE, MONTGOMERY CO., ST. COLMAN (1907)
11 Simpson Rd., Ardmore, 19003. Tel: 610-642-0545; Email: stcolmanchurch@gmail.com; Web: stcolmanardmore.com. Revs. John J. Ames, S.T.D., M.A., M.Div.; Ferdinand Buccafurni, In Res., (Retired); Deacon John J. Rodgers.
See SS. Colman-John Neumann School, Bryn Mawr under Regional Parish Schools located in the Institution section.
Catechesis Religious Program—Cathy Dernoncourt, D.R.E. Students 46.

ARDSLEY, MONTGOMERY CO., QUEEN OF PEACE (1954)
820 North Hills Ave., Ardsley, 19038. Tel: 215-887-1838; Fax: 215-887-8328; Email: queenofpeaceparish@comcast.net; Web: www.qofpeacechurch.org. Rev. Lawrence F. Crehan, M.Div.; Deacon Raymond Jacobucci; Joseph Costello, Business Mgr.
See Good Shepherd Catholic Regional School, Ardsley, under Regional Parish Schools located in the Institution Section.
Catechesis Religious Program—Tel: 215-886-3014. Mrs. Anne Florian, D.R.E. Students 240.
Convent—825 North Hills Ave., Ardsley, 19038. Tel: 215-887-4785.

ASTON, DELAWARE CO., ST. JOSEPH (1947)
3255 Concord Rd., Aston, 19014. Tel: 610-497-3340; Fax: 610-497-3383; Email: stjoseph256@comcast.net;

Web: www.stjosephaston.org. Rev. Msgr. Robert C. Vogan, M.Div.; Rev. Michael J. Pawelko, Parochial Vicar; Deacon John M. Betzal.
See Holy Family Regional Catholic School, Aston under Regional Parish Schools in the Institution section.
Catechesis Religious Program—Tel: 610-494-4358; Email: cmaugeri@stjoseph.org. Ms. Catherine Maugeri, D.R.E. Students 295.

AVONDALE, CHESTER CO.

1—ST. GABRIEL OF THE SORROWFUL MOTHER (1988)
Mailing Address: 8910 Gap Newport Pike, P.O. Box 709, Avondale, 19311. Tel: 610-268-0296;
Fax: 610-268-5022; Email: stgabriel@kennett.net; Web: www.stgabrielavondalepa.org. Rev. Anthony J. DiGuglielmo, J.C.L., M.Div.
Catechesis Religious Program—Email: reldd@kennett.net. Mrs. Donna DiUbaldo, D.R.E. Students 78.

2—ST. ROCCO (2010)
9016 Gap Newport Pike, P.O. Box 1019, Avondale, 19311. Tel: 610-268-3365; Fax: 610-268-5064; Email: Info@StRoccoChurch.org; Web: www.StRoccoChurch.org. Rev. Msgr. Francis J. Depman; Rev. Andres Arambula Garcia.
Church: 313 Sunny Dell Rd., Avondale, 19311.
Convent—Sisters, Servants of the Lord and the Virgin of Matara, 420 Auburn Rd., Avondale, 19311. Tel: 610-268-0675.
Mission—Santa Maria, Madre de Dios, 29 Gap Newport Pike, P.O. Box 1019, Avondale, 19311.
Tel: 610-268-1515; Email: mail@missionsantamaria.org; Web: www.missionsantamaria.org.

BALA CYNWYD, MONTGOMERY CO., ST. MATTHIAS (1906)
128 Bryn Mawr Ave., Bala Cynwyd, 19004-3013.
Tel: 610-664-0207; Web: www.saintmatthias.org. Rev. Msgr. Gerard C. Mesure, J.D., J.C.D., M.A.; Revs. Sean P. Bransfield, J.C.L., M.A., M.Div., Parochial Vicar; John Arthur McGinnis, In Res., (Retired); Deacon Michael J. Kubiak.
Catechesis Religious Program—Tel: 610-664-1942. Students 103.

BENSALEM, BUCKS CO.

1—ST. CHARLES BORROMEO (1903)
1731 Hulmeville Rd., Bensalem, 19020.
Tel: 215-638-3625; Fax: 215-245-8578; Email: st.charles@stcharlesbensalem.org; Web: www.stcharlesbensalem.org. Rev. Philip M. Forlano, M.A.; Deacons Adolfo Crespo; Louis Quaglia; Raymond N. Scipioni.
School—St. Charles Borromeo School, (Grades PreK-8), 1704 Bristol Pike, Bensalem, 19020.
Tel: 215-639-3456; Fax: 215-639-0496; Web: stcharlesbensalem.org.
Convent—1080 Kings Ave., Bensalem, 19020.
Tel: 215-639-0113. Sisters Servants of the Immaculate Heart of Mary 8.

2—ST. ELIZABETH ANN SETON (1976-2014) Closed. Spiritual records are kept at St. Thomas Aquinas Church, Croydon. Tel: 215-788-2989. Worship site of St. Thomas Aquinas Church.

3—ST. EPHREM (1966) [CEM]
5400 Hulmeville Rd., Bensalem, 19020.
Tel: 215-245-1698; Fax: 215-245-4787. Rev. Msgr. Kenneth P. McAteer, M.Div.; Rev. Stephen F. Katziner, Parochial Vicar; Deacons Edward J. Dymek Jr.; James P. DeBow.
School—St. Ephrem School, 5340 Hulmeville Rd., Bensalem, 19020. Tel: 215-639-9488;
Fax: 215-639-0206. Lay Teachers 25; Sisters, Servants of the Immaculate Heart of Mary 3; Students 454.
Catechesis Religious Program—Tel: 215-639-4895. Students 193.
Convent—5300 Hulmeville Rd., Bensalem, 19020. Tel: 215-638-1024.

4—OUR LADY OF FATIMA (1954-2014) Closed. 2913 Street Rd., Bensalem. Spiritual records are kept at St. Charles Borromeo Church, Bensalem. Tel:215-638-3625. Worship site for St. Charles Borromeo Church, Bensalem.

BERWYN, CHESTER CO., ST. MONICA (1897) [CEM]
635 First Ave., Berwyn, 19312. Tel: 610-644-0110;
Fax: 610-695-0850; Web: www.saintmonicachurch.org. Rev. Charles Zlock, M.A., M.Div.
Catechesis Religious Program—Tel: 610-647-4757. Mary Pizzano, D.R.E. Students 205.

BOOTHWYN, DELAWARE CO., ST. JOHN FISHER (1971)
4225 Chichester Ave., Boothwyn, 19061.
Tel: 610-485-0441; Email: contact@sjf71.org; Web: www.stjohnfisherchurch.com. Rev. Robert B. McDermott, M.Div.; Deacon Daniel Bingnear.
See Holy Family Regional Catholic School, Aston under Regional Parish Schools located in the Institution section.
Catechesis Religious Program—Tel: 610-485-0581. Students 165.

BRIDGEPORT, MONTGOMERY CO.

1—ST. AUGUSTINE (1892-2014) [CEM] Closed. Formerly located at 464 Ford St. Spiritual records are kept at Sacred Heart Church, Swedesburg. Tel: 610-275-1750.

2—OUR LADY OF MT. CARMEL (1924-2014) (Italian), Closed. Formerly located at 502 Ford St. Spiritual records are kept at Sacred Heart Church, Swedesburg. Tel: 610-275-1750.

3—OUR MOTHER OF SORROWS (1926-2001) (Slovak), Closed. Formerly located at 421 Coates St. Spiritual records are kept at Sacred Heart Church, Swedesburg. Tel: 610-275-1750.

BRISTOL, BUCKS CO.

1—ST. ANN (1906-2014) (Italian), Closed. 357 Dorrance St. Spiritual records are kept at St. Mark Church, Bristol. Tel: 215-788-2493. Worship site of St. Mark Church, Bristol.

2—ST. MARK (1844) [CEM]
1025 Radcliffe St., Bristol, 19007. Tel: 215-788-2493; Fax: 215-785-4121; Email: office@saintmarkchurch.net; Web: www.saintmarkchurch.net. Revs. Dennis M. Mooney; Daniel J. Arechabala, Parochial Vicar; Deacon Richard S. Malamut.
School—St. Mark School, 1024 Radcliffe St., Bristol, 19007. Tel: 215-785-0973; Fax: 215-781-0268. Mrs. Marie Sanson, Prin. Lay Teachers 12; Students 212.
Catechesis Religious Program—Tel: 215-788-2319. Mary Leonhauser, C.R.E. Students 156.

BROOKHAVEN, DELAWARE CO., OUR LADY OF CHARITY (1952)
231 Upland Rd., Brookhaven, 19015.
Tel: 610-872-6192; Fax: 610-872-1120. Revs. James A. Lyons, M.Div.; Richard C. Williams, In Res., (Retired).
Catechesis Religious Program—`. Tel: 484-924-9141. Students 101.

BROOMALL, DELAWARE CO., ST. PIUS X (1955)
220 Lawrence Rd., Broomall, 19008.
Tel: 610-353-4880; Email: stpiusxbusinessoffice@comcast.net. Rev. Msgr. William C. Kaufman, M.Div.; Rev. Eric Banecker, Parochial Vicar; Rev. Msgr. John J. Jagodzinski, M.A., In Res., (Retired); Deacon Francis X. Phillips.
School—St. Pius X School, 204 Lawrence Rd., Broomall, 19008. Tel: 610-356-7222;
Fax: 610-356-5380. Lay Teachers 22; Sisters, Servants of the Immaculate Heart of Mary 5; Students 421.
Catechesis Religious Program—Tel: 610-353-6950; Fax: 610-356-1084. Students 300.

BRYN MAWR, DELAWARE CO., ST. JOHN NEUMANN (1964)
380 Highland Ln., Bryn Mawr, 19010.
Tel: 610-525-3100; Fax: 610-525-6363; Email: mainoffice@sjnparish.org; Web: sjnparish.org. Rev. Msgr. Michael J. Matz; Rev. Robert J. Chapman, In Res., (Retired); Deacon David B. Schaffer, M.A., M.S.; Sr. Carol Kelly, S.S.J., Dir. Parish Svcs.
See SS. Colman-John Neumann School, Byrn Mawr under Regional Parish Schools located in the Institution section.
Catechesis Religious Program—Students 125.

BRYN MAWR, MONTGOMERY CO., OUR MOTHER OF GOOD COUNSEL (1885)
31 Pennswood Rd., Bryn Mawr, 19010.
Tel: 610-525-0147; Fax: 610-525-0157; Email: omgc@omgcparish.net; Web: www.omgcparish.org. Revs. Liam T. O'Doherty, O.S.A.; John F. Deary, O.S.A., Parochial Vicar; Bro. William C. Harkin, O.S.A.
Catechesis Religious Program—Email: kcarey@omgcparish.net. Karen Carey, D.R.E. Students 109.

BUCKINGHAM, BUCKS CO., OUR LADY OF GUADALUPE (2000)
5194 Cold Spring Creamery Rd., Doylestown, 18902.
Tel: 267-247-5374; Email: olguadbulletin@gmail.com; Web: www.olguadalupe.org. Rev. Msgr. Joseph P. Gentili, S.T.D., M.Div.; Rev. Robert A. Ianelli, Parochial Vicar; Deacon Robert F. Brady.
Res.: 3243 Ash Mill Rd., Doylestown, 18902.
Catechesis Religious Program—Email: jwalters@olguadalupe.org. Jessica Walters, D.R.E. Students 450.

CENTER SQUARE, MONTGOMERY CO., ST. HELENA (1919)
1489 DeKalb Pike, Blue Bell, 19422.
Tel: 610-275-7711; Web: www.sainthelenacentersquare.net. Rev. Msgr. Joseph J. Nicolo, M.Div.; Revs. Lawrence F. Kozak, M.Div., Parochial Vicar; Robert M. Gross, Parochial Vicar; Deacons A. Kenneth Belanger; Francis M. Cavaliere.
School—St. Helena School, 1499 DeKalb Pike, Blue Bell, 19422. Tel: 610-279-3345; Fax: 610-279-3272; Web: www.sainthelenaschool.org. Lay Teachers 29; Sisters of Mercy 1; Students 557.
Catechesis Religious Program—Tel: 610-279-3870. Students 271.

CHADDS FORD, DELAWARE CO., ST. CORNELIUS (1963)
160 Ridge Rd., Chadds Ford, 19317.
Tel: 610-459-2502; Email: stcorn1@comcast.net; Web: www.saintcornelius.org. Rev. Msgr. David E. Diamond, M.Div., M.A., Ph.D.; Deacons Harry J. Morris; John J. Todor.
School—St. Cornelius School, Tel: 610-459-8663; Fax: 610-459-7728. Students 235.
Catechesis Religious Program—Email: dperrystcorneliusprep@gmail.com. Dawn Perry, D.R.E.

CHALFONT, BUCKS CO., ST. JUDE (1962)
321 W. Butler Ave., Chalfont, 18914-2329.
Tel: 215-822-0179; Email: office@stjudechalfont.org; Web: www.stjudechalfont.org. Rev. Msgr. Francis W. Beach, M.Div.; Rev. Jeffrey M. Rott, M.Div., Parochial Vicar; Deacons Michael J. Cushing; Timothy P. Lynch; John T. Riordan.
School—St. Jude School, 323 W. Butler Ave., Chalfont, 18914-2329. Tel: 215-822-9225;
Fax: 215-822-0722; Email: semrsm@stjudeschool.com; Web: www.stjudeschool.com. Sr. Elizabeth Marley, R.S.M., Prin. Lay Teachers 21; Sisters 1; Students 365.
Catechesis Religious Program—Tel: 215-822-7553; Email: prep@stjudeschool.com. Angela McClellan, Dir., Faith Formation. Students 350.

CHELTENHAM, MONTGOMERY CO.

1—ST. JOSEPH (1953)
7631 Waters Rd., Cheltenham, 19012-1318.
Tel: 215-635-5533; Fax: 215-635-4578; Email: wshpresentation@aol.com; Email: wshstjos2000@gmail.com. Rev. William S. Harrison; Deacon William A. Cella.
Catechesis Religious Program—Students 37.

2—PRESENTATION OF BLESSED VIRGIN MARY (1890) (Twinned with St. Joseph Parish in Cheltenham)
100 Old Soldiers Rd., Cheltenham, 19012.
Tel: 215-379-1364; Email: wshpresentation@aol.com. Rev. William S. Harrison; Deacon William A. Cella.
School—Presentation of Blessed Virgin Mary School, 105 Old Soldiers Rd., Cheltenham, 19012.
Tel: 215-379-3798; Fax: 215-379-4430; Web: www.presentationbvm.org/school. Lay Teachers 15; Students 250.
Catechesis Religious Program—Tel: 215-379-2054; Email: presentationbvm@gmail.com. Students 340.
Convent—107 Old Soldiers Rd., Cheltenham, 19012. Tel: 215-379-8343.

CHESTER, DELAWARE CO.

1—ST. ANTHONY OF PADUA (1908-1993) (Italian), Closed. Formerly located at 308 W. 3rd St. Spiritual records are kept at St. Katharine Drexel Church, Chester. Tel: 610-872-3731.

2—ST. HEDWIG (1902-1993) (Polish), Closed. Formerly located at 4th & Hayes Sts. Spiritual records are kept at Sacred Heart Church, Clifton Heights. Tel: 610-623-0409.

3—IMMACULATE HEART OF MARY (1873-1993) Closed. Formerly located at 2nd & Norris Sts. Spiritual records are kept at St. Katharine Drexel Church, Chester. Tel: 610-872-3731.

4—ST. KATHARINE DREXEL (1993)
1920 Providence Ave., Chester, 19013.
Tel: 610-872-3731; Fax: 610-872-0545; Email: info@stkatharinedrexelparish.org; Web: www.stkatharinedrexelparish.org. Rev. Thomas P. Whittingham, M.A., M.Div.; Deacon John J. Pileggi
Legal Title: Blessed Katharine Drexel
Catechesis Religious Program—Jose Martin, D.R.E. Students 30.
Convent—1902 Providence Ave., Chester, 19013. Tel: 610-876-4916.
Saint Katharine Drexel Evangelization Center—226 Norris St., Chester, 19013. Tel: 610-872-3140; Fax: 610-872-0545.

5—ST. MICHAEL (1842-1993) Closed. Formerly located at 7th St. & Avenue of the States. Spiritual records are kept at St. Katharine Drexel Church, Chester. Tel: 610-872-3731.

6—OUR LADY OF VILNA (1924-1972) (Lithuanian), Closed. Formerly located at 4th & Madison Sts. Spiritual records are kept at St. Katharine Drexel, Chester. Tel: 215-872-3731.

7—RESURRECTION OF OUR LORD (1911-1993) Closed. Formerly located at 9th St. & Highland Ave. Spiritual records are kept at St. Katharine Drexel Church, Chester. Tel: 610-872-3731.

8—ST. ROBERT (1922-1993) Closed. Formerly located at 20th St. & Providence Ave. Spiritual records are kept at St. Katharine Drexel Church, Chester. Tel: 610-872-3731.

CLIFTON HEIGHTS, DELAWARE CO., SACRED HEART (1910) (Polish)
316 E. Broadway, Clifton Heights, 19018.
Tel: 610-623-0409; Email: sacredheartchurch@rcn.com; Web: sacredheart-cliftonheights.net. Rev. Msgr. George A. Majoros, M.S., M.Div.; Rev. Joseph S. Zaleski, In Res.
Catechesis Religious Program—
Mission—St. Hedwig Chapel, 4th & Hayes Sts., Chester, Delaware Co. 19013.

COATESVILLE, CHESTER CO.

1—ST. CECILIA (1869-2012) [CEM] Closed. Formerly located at 99 N. 6th Ave. Spiritual records are kept at Our Lady of the Rosary Church, Coatesville. Tel: 610-384-1415.

2—St. Joseph (1924)
404 Charles St., Coatesville, 19320.
Tel: 610-384-0360; Fax: 484-288-8030; Email: sjrectory@comcast.net; Web: www.stjosephcoatesville.org. Revs. Eder Estrada, F.M.; Antonio Gutierrez, Parochial Vicar.
See Pope John Paul II Regional Catholic Elementary School, West Brandywine under Regional Parish Schools located in the Institution section.
Catechesis Religious Program—Students 54.
3—Our Lady of the Rosary (1917)
80 S. 17th Ave., Coatesville, 19320.
Tel: 610-384-1415; Email: Fatherb@olrcc. Rev. Thomas J. Brennan; Deacon Frederick H. Kerr.
See Pope John Paul II Regional Catholic Elementary School, West Brandywine under Regional Parish Schools located in the Institution section.
Catechesis Religious Program—Students 125.
4—St. Stanislaus Kostka (1907-2012) [CEM] (Polish), Closed. Formerly located at 201 W. Lincoln Hwy. Spiritual records are kept at St. Joseph Church, Coatesville. Tel: 610-384-0360. Worship site for St. Joseph Parish.
Collegeville, Montgomery Co., St. Eleanor (1911)
647 Locust St., Collegeville, 19426.
Tel: 610-489-1647; Email: church@steleanor.com; Web: www.steleanor.com. Rev. Msgr. Michael T. McCulken, M.Div.; Rev. Jason E. Buck, Parochial Vicar; Rev. Msgr. Thomas A. Murray, In Res., (Retired); Deacons John A. Hasson; Edward T. Hinson.
School—Holy Cross Regional Catholic School, (Grades PreK-8), 701 Locust St., Collegeville, 19426. Tel: 610-489-9434, Ext. 2225; Fax: 610-489-6137; Email: thealy@hcrc.school; Web: www.hcrc.school. Lay Teachers 29; Students 539.
Catechesis Religious Program—
Tel: 610-489-4677, Ext. 2233; Email: religiousedsteleanor.com. Students 805.
Collingdale, Delaware Co., St. Joseph (1916)
500 Woodlawn Ave., Collingdale, 19023.
Tel: 610-583-4530; Fax: 610-583-7730; Email: stjoe.col@rcn.com; Web: www.saintjoseph-collingdale.com. Rev. Thomas M. Sodano; Rev. Msgr. Charles E. McGroarty, M.A., S.T.L., In Res., (Retired); Rev. John D. Gabin, M.S.W., M.Div., In Res.; Deacons Patrick J. Kelly; Thomas L. Taylor.
Catechesis Religious Program—Tel: 610-586-1520. Mary Carney, Dir. Faith Formation. Students 52.
Conshohocken, Montgomery Co.
1—SS. Cosmas and Damian (1912-2014) (Italian), Closed. Formerly located at 209 W. Fifth Ave., Conshohocken. Spiritual records are kept at St. Matthew Church, Conshohocken. Tel: 610-828-0424.
2—St. Mary (1905-2014) [CEM] (Polish), Closed. Formerly located at 140 W. Hector St., Conshohocken. Spiritual records are kept at St. Matthew Church, Conshohocken. Tel: 610-828-0424.
3—St. Mary Roman Catholic Church (2018)
140 Hector St., Conshohocken, 19428.
Tel: 610-717-3972; Email: st.marylatinmass@gmail.com. Rev. Carl Grismondi.
4—St. Matthew (1851) [CEM] [JC2]
219 Fayette St., Conshohocken, 19428.
Tel: 610-828-0424; Fax: 610-825-5168. Rev. J. Thomas Heron; Rev. Msgr. Thomas J. Owens, M.A., M.Div., In Res., (Retired); Rev. James J. McKeaney, M.Div., In Res., (Retired); Deacon Joseph C. Carr.
St. Matthew Parish Center, 205 Fayette St., Conshohocken, 19428.
Child Care—St. Matthew Daycare and Early Childhood Center, 210 Harry St., Conshohocken, 19428. Tel: 610-828-5191.
Catechesis Religious Program—Email: stmatthewdre@verizon.net; Web: www.stmatthewchurch.com. Students 201.
Croydon, Bucks Co., St. Thomas Aquinas (1922)
601 Bristol Pike, Croydon, 19021-5496.
Tel: 215-788-2989; Fax: 215-788-7626; Email: sta712014@gmail.com; Web: www.staq.org. Rev. David A. Fernandes; Deacon John J. Gallagher.
Catechesis Religious Program—Students 45.
Darby, Delaware Co., Blessed Virgin Mary (1913)
1101 Main St., Darby, 19023. Tel: 610-583-2128; Email: bvmrectory2@rcn.com; Email: bvmrectory@rcn.com; Web: www.bvm-darby.com. Rev. Msgr. Joseph M. Corley, M.S., M.Div.; Rev. Edward J. Kennedy, In Res.
School—Blessed Virgin Mary School, 47 MacDade Blvd., Darby, 19023. Tel: 610-586-0638;
Fax: 610-586-1582. Lay Teachers 14; Sisters, Servants of the Immaculate Heart of Mary 3; Students 200.
Catechesis Religious Program—Students 28.
Downingtown, Chester Co., St. Joseph (1851) [CEM]
334 Manor Ave., Downingtown, 19335.
Tel: 610-269-5890; Email: reception@stjosephrc.org. 332 Manor Ave., Downingtown, 19335. Revs. Stephen F. Leva; Anthony T. Rossi, Parochial Vicar; John E. Donia, In Res.; Francis J. Mulranen, M.Div., In Res.; Deacons James E. Bogdan; Edward R. Schiappa.
School—St. Joseph School, 340 Manor Ave., Downingtown, 19335. Tel: 610-269-8999;
Fax: 610-269-2252. Lay Teachers 29; Sisters, Servants of the Immaculate Heart of Mary 4; Students 575.
Catechesis Religious Program—Tel: 610-873-8798; Fax: 610-873-5466; Email: prep@stjosephrc.org. Mrs. Kathryn Thomas, D.R.E. Students 741.
Convent—336 Manor Ave., Downingtown, 19335. Tel: 484-593-4352.
Doylestown, Bucks Co., Our Lady of Mount Carmel (1850) [CEM]
235 E. State St., Doylestown, 18901.
Tel: 215-348-4190; Fax: 215-348-3104; Web: www.ourladymtcarmel.org. Rev. Msgr. Charles H. Hagan; Revs. Harold B. McKale, Parochial Vicar; Paschal U. Onunwa, (Nigeria) Parochial Vicar; Deacons George Corwell; James J. Fowkes.
School—Our Lady of Mount Carmel School, 225 E. Ashland St., Doylestown, 18901. Tel: 215-348-5907; Fax: 215-348-5671. Lay Teachers 25; Sisters of St. Francis of Philadelphia 1; Students 317.
Catechesis Religious Program—Tel: 215-345-7089; Fax: 215-345-4216. Cindy Balceniuk, D.R.E. Students 1,010.
Convent—209 E. State St., Doylestown, 18901. Tel: 215-348-4663.
Drexel Hill, Delaware Co.
1—St. Andrew (1916)
3500 School Ln., Drexel Hill, 19026.
Tel: 610-259-1169; Email: info@standrewdh.com; Web: www.standrewdh.com. Rev. Msgr. Albin J. Grous; Revs. Girard J. Cusatis, In Res., (Retired); John P. Masson, In Res.
School—St. Andrew School, 529 Mason Ave., Drexel Hill, 19026. Tel: 610-259-5145; Fax: 610-284-6956. Helen McLean, Prin.; Karen Tomasetti, Vice Prin. Lay Teachers 24; Sisters of St. Joseph 1; Students 425.
Catechesis Religious Program—Students 120.
Convent—535 Mason Ave., Drexel Hill, 19026. Tel: 610-259-6130.
2—St. Bernadette (1947)
1035 Turner Ave., Drexel Hill, 19026.
Tel: 610-789-7676; Fax: 610-789-9539; Web: www.stbl.org. Revs. Christopher J. Papa; Hugh J. Dougherty, M.Div., In Res., (Retired); Deacon Thomas P. Fitzpatrick.
School—St. Bernadette School, 1001 Turner Ave., Drexel Hill, 19026. Tel: 610-789-7676, Ext. 202. Lay Teachers 17; Students 336.
Catechesis Religious Program—
Tel: 610-789-7676, Ext. 202. Mary Kate Murphy, Dir., Faith Formation. Students 244.
3—St. Charles Borromeo (1849) [CEM]
3422 Dennison Ave., Drexel Hill, 19026.
Tel: 610-623-3800; Fax: 610-284-9583; Email: rectory@scbdh.org; Web: scbdh.org. Rev. Msgr. George A. Majoros, M.S., M.Div.; Revs. Edward C. Kelly, In Res.; Joseph S. Zaleski, In Res.; Deacon John H. Farrell.
Catechesis Religious Program—Tel: 610-259-4389. Students 100.
4—St. Dorothy (1947)
4910 Township Line Rd., Drexel Hill, 19026.
Tel: 610-789-7788; Email: jdougherty@stdots.org; Email: momalley@stdots.org. Rev. Michael D. Murphy; Rev. Msgr. Daniel J. Kutys, M.Div., V.G., In Res.; Deacons John P. Donnelly; Joseph P. McGonigal.
School—St. Dorothy School, (Grades K-8), 1225 Burmont Rd., Drexel Hill, 19026. Tel: 610-789-4100; Fax: 610-789-2008; Web: www.stdots.org. Karen Tomasetti, Prin. Lay Teachers 25; Students 401.
Catechesis Religious Program—Tel: 610-853-1499; Email: lquirk@stdots.org. Sr. Alice Grey, R.S.M., D.R.E. Students 235.
Convent—1201 Burmont Rd., Drexel Hill, 19026. Tel: 610-789-4112.
East Goshen, Chester Co., SS. Peter and Paul (1967)
1325 Boot Rd., West Chester, 19380.
Tel: 610-692-2216; Email: pafox@sspeterandpaulrc.org; Web: www.sspeterandpaulrc.org. Revs. Angelo R. Citino; Matthew D. Brody, Parochial Vicar; Deacons Robert F. Pierce; Patrick M. Stokely.
School—SS. Peter and Paul School, (Grades PreK-8), 1327 Boot Rd., West Chester, 19380-5901.
Tel: 610-696-1000; Fax: 484-631-0181; Email: school@sspeterandpaulrc.org. Mrs. Margaret Egan, Prin.; Dorothy Conway, Librarian. Lay Teachers 25; Students 431.
Catechesis Religious Program—
Tel: 610-692-2116, Ext. 235; Email: mdelassandro@sspeterandpaulrc.org. Michele D'Alessandro, D.R.E. Students 355.
East Lansdowne, Delaware Co., St. Cyril of Alexandria (1928-2013) Closed. Formerly located at 153 Penn Blvd. Spiritual records are kept at St. Philomena Church, Lansdowne. Tel: 610-622-2420. Worship Site of St. Philomena Church, Lansdowne.
East Norriton, Montgomery Co., St. Paul (1963)
2007 New Hope St., East Norriton, 19401.
Tel: 610-279-6725; Email: stpaulparish.eastnorriton@gmail.com; Web: stpaulcatholicchurcheastnorriton.net. Rev. Harry E. McCreedy; Sr. Rosellen Bracken, R.S.M., Spiritual Advisor/Care Svcs.; Deacon Matthew J. Hrobak; Mary Rose Edmonds, Business Mgr.
See Holy Rosary Regional Catholic School, Plymouth Meeting under Regional Parish Schools located in the Institution section.
Catechesis Religious Program—Mrs. Meg Farrell, D.R.E. Students 71.
Eddystone, Delaware Co., St. Rose of Lima (1890)
1901 Chester Pike, Eddystone, 19022.
Tel: 610-876-6170; Email: stroselimaparish@gmail.com; Web: www.stroseoflimaparish.net. Revs. Albert J. Santorsola, Parochial Admin.; Gerald D. Canavan, M.Div., Pastor Emeritus, (Retired); Deacons Anthony J. DiIenno; Frederick M. Ryan; Lawrence P. Schnepp.
See St. James Regional Catholic School, Ridley Park under Regional Schools located in the Institution section.
Catechesis Religious Program—Students 35.
Elkins Park, Montgomery Co., St. James (1923)
8320 Brookside Rd., Elkins Park, 19027.
Tel: 215-635-6210; Fax: 215-635-3346; Email: stjameselkinspark@comcast.net; Web: www.stjamesparish.net. Rev. Edward A. Windhaus, M.A., M.Div.
Catechesis Religious Program—Students 52.
Essington, Delaware Co., St. Margaret Mary Alacoque (1921-2014) Closed. 500 Wanamaer Ave., Essington. Spiritual records are kept at St. Gabriel Church, Norwood. Tel: 610-586-1225. Worship site of St. Gabriel Church, Norwood.
Exton, Chester Co., SS. Philip and James (1959)
107 N. Ship Rd., Exton, 19341. Tel: 610-363-6536; Fax: 610-524-7359; Web: www.sspj.net. Revs. Joseph C. Dieckhaus, J.C.L., M.Div.; Quan N. Tran, M.Div., In Res.; Deacon Charles W. Polley Jr.
School—SS. Philip and James School, (Grades PreK-8), 721 E. Lincoln Hwy., Exton, 19341.
Tel: 610-363-6530; Fax: 610-363-6495; Email: steresa@sspj.net; Web: school.sspj.net. Sr. Teresa A. Ballisty, I.H.M., Prin. Lay Teachers 17; Sisters, Servants of the Immaculate Heart of Mary 3; Students 201.
Catechesis Religious Program—Tel: 610-363-1307. Sisters Mary Ann Spaetti, I.H.M., D.R.E.; Eunice Marie Timony, I.H.M., D.R.E. Students 449.
Convent—105 N. Ship Rd., Exton, 19341. Tel: 610-363-2263.
Fairless Hills, Bucks Co., St. Frances Cabrini (1953)
325 S. Oxford Valley Rd., Fairless Hills, 19030.
Tel: 215-946-4040; Email: parish@saintfrancescabrini.net; Web: www.saintfrancescabrini.net. Rev. Msgr. Michael P. McCormac; Deacon Mace M. Mazzoni.
See Holy Family Regional Catholic School, Levittown, under Regional Parish Schools located in the Institution Section.
Catechesis Religious Program—Email: jeanemadden@gmail.com. Jean Madden, D.R.E. Students 201.
Fallsington, Bucks Co., St. Joseph the Worker (1956-2014) Closed. Formerly located at 9164 New Falls Rd., Fallsington. Spiritual records are kept at St. Frances Cabrini Church, Fairless Hills. Tel: 215-946-4040.
Feasterville, Bucks Co., Assumption B.V.M. (1950)
Revs. Michael J. Davis, M.Div.; Renny Abraham Kattel, In Res.; John J. Kelly, In Res.; Deacons Robert J. Stewart; Eric M. Umile; Sr. Diane Wolf, S.S.J., Pastoral Min./Coord.
Res.: 1900 Meadowbrook Rd., Feasterville, 19053.
Tel: 215-357-1221; Email: frmike42@comcast.net; Web: www.abvmfeasterville.org.
See St. Katharine Drexel Regional Catholic School, Holland under Regional Parish Schools located in the Institution section.
Catechesis Religious Program—Tel: 215-357-3445. Mrs. Joyce Boag-Leyrer, D.R.E. Students 240.
Flourtown, Montgomery Co., St. Genevieve (1953)
1225 Bethlehem Pike, Flourtown, 19031.
Tel: 215-836-2828; Email: rectory@stgensparish.com; Web: www.stgensparish.com. Rev. Kevin T. Mulligan; Deacon Michael G. Conroy.
School—St. Genevieve School, 1237 Bethlehem Pike, Flourtown, 19031. Tel: 215-836-5644;
Fax: 215-836-0159; Web: www.stgens.com. Lay Teachers 21; Sisters of St. Joseph 2; Students 272.
Catechesis Religious Program—Tel: 215-233-8934. Students 225.
Gladwyne, Montgomery Co., St. John Baptist Vianney (1927)
350 Conshohocken State Rd., Gladwyne, 19035.

Tel: 610-642-0938; Fax: 610-642-1432; Email: MLeuzzi@SJVGladwyne.com; Email: info@sjvgladwyne.com; Web: www.sjvgladwyne.com. 1110 Vaughan Ln., Gladwyne, 19035. Rev. Msgr. Donald E. Leighton.
Catechesis Religious Program—
Tel: 610-642-0938, Ext. 20; Email: MMonroe@SJVGladwyne.com; Web: www.sjvgladwyne.com/docs/religious_edu.html. Mrs. MaryAnne Monroe, C.R.E. Students 120.

GLEN MILLS, DELAWARE CO., ST. THOMAS THE APOSTLE (1729) [CEM]
430 Valleybrook Rd., Glen Mills, 19342.
Tel: 610-459-2224; Fax: 610-459-2677. Rev. Francis P. Groarke; Deacon Anthony J. Cincotta; Sr. Nicoletta Maria, R.S.M., Pastoral Ministry.
School—St. Thomas the Apostle School,
Tel: 610-459-8134; Fax: 610-459-8120. Lay Teachers 28; Students 430.
Catechesis Religious Program—Tel: 610-459-3477. Mary Sassani, D.R.E. Students 313.
Chaplaincies—Delaware County Prison; Brinton Manor; Riddle Hospital; Glen Mills Assisted Living; Maris Grove Continuing Care Community.

GLENOLDEN, DELAWARE CO., ST. GEORGE (1923)
22 E. Cooke Ave., Glenolden, 19036-1497.
Tel: 610-237-1633; Email: st.georgesec@rcn.com; Web: www.stgeorgeparish.org. Revs. Leo P. Oswald; Ignatius Marneni, In Res., (Retired).
Catechesis Religious Program—Tel: 484-425-7390. Rita Levase, C.R.E. Students 56.
Convent—11 E. Lamont Ave., Glenolden, 19036-1497. Tel: 484-318-5092.

GLENSIDE, MONTGOMERY CO., ST. LUKE THE EVANGELIST (1905)
2316 Fairhill Ave., Glenside, 19038.
Tel: 215-572-0128; Fax: 215-572-0482; Email: stlukerc@aol.com; Web: www.stlukerc.org. Rev. Joseph D. Brandt; Deacons Thomas M. Croke; John K. Hunter, Business Mgr.; Kevin J. Potter.
School—St. Luke Catholic School, (Grades PreK-8), 2336 Fairhill Ave., Glenside, 19038.
Tel: 215-884-0443; Fax: 215-884-4607; Email: office@saintlukeschool.org. Alicia Farren, Prin. Lay Teachers 28; Students 323.
Catechesis Religious Program—2316 Fairhill Ave., Glenside, 19038. Tel: 215-572-0128, Ext. 25; Email: prep@stlukerc.org. Mrs. Maria Hughes, D.R.E. Students 262.
Convent—2324 Fairhill Ave., Glenside, 19038. Tel: 215-884-0225.

HATBORO, MONTGOMERY CO., ST. JOHN BOSCO (1953)
235 E. County Line Rd., Hatboro, 19040. Web: www.saintjohnbosco.org. Revs. Gary J. Kramer; Mark J. Hunt, S.T.L., S.T.D., In Res.
Parish Office Center—215 E. County Line Rd., Hatboro, 19040-1244. Tel: 215-672-7280; Fax: 215-672-1105.
Catechesis Religious Program—Tel: 267-803-0774; Email: cflack@saintjohnbosco.org. Students 320.

HATFIELD, MONTGOMERY CO., ST. MARIA GORETTI (1953)
1601 Derstine Rd., Hatfield, 19440.
Tel: 215-721-0199; Email: cheryl.ryan@stmariagoretti.net. Rev. John C. Nguyen, M.A., M.Div.; Deacons Phuong Nguyen; Peter L. Niche.
Catechesis Religious Program—2980 Cowpath Rd., Hatfield, 19440. Tel: 215-721-6559. Meg Szewczak, D.R.E. Students 420.

HAVERTOWN, DELAWARE CO.
1—ANNUNCIATION B.V.M. (1927)
410 Sagamore Rd., Havertown, 19083. Revs. James M. Cox; Sean A. Loomis, Parochial Vicar; Tadeusz Pacholczyk, Ph.D., In Res.; Deacon Robert V. McElwee.
See Cardinal John Foley Regional Catholic School, Havertown under Regional Parish Schools located in the Institution section.
Catechesis Religious Program—Tel: 610-449-9858. Students 276.
Convent—421 Brookline Blvd., Havertown, 19083. Tel: 610-449-4065.

2—ST. DENIS (1825) [CEM]
2401 St. Denis Ln., Havertown, 19083.
Tel: 610-446-0200; Fax: 610-446-4638; Web: www.stdenishavertown.org. Revs. Kevin J. Gallagher, M.Div.; James J. Cardosi, Parochial Vicar; Rev. Msgr. Bernard J. Trinity, In Res., (Retired); Deacon Francis J. Connors.
See Cardinal John Foley Regional Catholic School, Havertown under Regional Parish Schools located in the Institution section.
Catechesis Religious Program—Tel: 610-449-7892; Fax: 610-446-5705. Sr. Rose Caritas, I.H.M., D.R.E. Students 315.
Convent—Tel: 610-446-1263.

HILLTOWN, BUCKS CO., OUR LADY OF THE SACRED HEART (1919) [CEM]
9 Broad St., Hilltown, 18927. Tel: 215-822-9224; Fax: 215-712-0278; Web: www.olsh-hilltown.com. Rev. John D. Schiele; Deacon Vincent G. Ceneviva.
Catechesis Religious Program—Tel: 215-822-9020. Students 525.

HOLLAND, BUCKS CO., ST. BEDE THE VENERABLE (1965)
1071 Holland Rd., Holland, 18966. Tel: 215-357-5720 ; Fax: 215-396-0704; Web: www.st-bede.org. Rev. Msgr. John C. Marine, M.Div.; Revs. Thomas D. O'Donald; Matthew J. Tralies.
See St. Katharine Drexel Regional Catholic School, Holland under Regional Parish Schools located in the Institution section.
Catechesis Religious Program—1053 Holland Rd., Holland, 18966. Tel: 215-357-2130;
Fax: 215-357-0232. Carole Obrokta, D.R.E. Students 550.

HORSHAM, MONTGOMERY CO., ST. CATHERINE OF SIENA (1963)
321 Witmer Rd., Horsham, 19044. Tel: 215-672-2881; Fax: 215-674-1025; Email: Pastor@stcatherineschurch.org; Web: stcatherineschurch.org. Revs. Joseph F. Rymdeika; Paul J. O'Donnell, M.Div., In Res.; Deacons Mario G. Mirabelli; Timothy Urbanski.
See Our Lady of Mercy Regional Catholic School, Maple Glen under Regional Parish Schools located in the Institution section.
Catechesis Religious Program—Tel: 215-674-8549; Email: Religioused@stcatherineschurch.org. Mrs. Regina Osborne, D.R.E. Students 351.

HUNTINGDON VALLEY, MONTGOMERY CO., ST. ALBERT THE GREAT (1962)
212 Welsh Rd., Huntingdon Valley, 19006.
Tel: 215-947-3500; Web: saintalthegreat.org. Rev. Msgr. Joseph P. Duncan, M.Div.; Revs. Quy Pham, Parochial Vicar; Anthony J. Cossavella, M.Div., In Res.; Alexander R. Gibbs, M.A., M.Div., In Res.; Deacon Edward J. Morris; Mrs. Christine Regan, Dir.; Mrs. Cheryl Lemma, Music Min.; Mrs. Alice Pesce, Business Mgr.
School—St. Albert the Great School,
Tel: 215-947-2332; Fax: 215-938-9360. Cynthia Koons, Prin.; Mr. John Schrenk, Prin. Lay Teachers 27; Students 492.
Catechesis Religious Program—Tel: 215-947-3641; Email: DRE@SATG1.org. Dennis Mueller, D.R.E. Students 270.

JAMISON, BUCKS CO., ST. CYRIL OF JERUSALEM (1965)
1410 Almshouse Rd., Jamison, 18929.
Tel: 215-343-1288; Email: ctomassoni01@gmail.com; Email: cmdunn12@gmail.com. Rev. Msgr. Robert J. Powell, D.M.A, M.A., M.Div.; Rev. Timothy J. Buckley; Deacons Joseph T. Owen; Joseph F. Windish.
Catechesis Religious Program—Tel: 215-343-3139; Email: Deaconjoe@saint-cyril.com. Daniel Rackers, Youth Min.

JENKINTOWN, MONTGOMERY CO., IMMACULATE CONCEPTION (1866)
604 West Ave., Jenkintown, 19046.
Tel: 215-884-4022; Fax: 215-277-1562. Revs. Joseph E. Howarth, M.A.L.S.; Charles J. Sullivan, In Res., (Retired); Deacon Alvin Clay.
See St. Joseph the Protector Regional Catholic School, Glenside under Regional Parish Schools located in the Institution section.
Catechesis Religious Program—Ms. Marie McGuigan, D.R.E. Students 163.

KENNETT SQUARE, CHESTER CO., ST. PATRICK (1869) [CEM]
St. Patrick Church Office: 205 Lafayette St., Kennett Square, 19348. Tel: 610-444-4364; Email: stpatrickkennett@gmail.com; Web: www.stpatrickkennettsquare.org. Revs. Christopher B. Rogers, M.A.; Andres Arambula Garcia, In Res.; Deacons James K. Madonna; James J. Elliott.
Res.: 218 Meredith St., Kennett Square, 19348.
Tel: 610-444-2128; Email: stpatkennett@verizon.net.
Catechesis Religious Program—Tel: 610-444-2214. Marianne Kane, D.R.E. Students 217.

KIMBERTON, CHESTER CO., ST. BASIL THE GREAT (1965)
2300 Kimberton Rd., P.O. Box 637, Kimberton, 19442-0637. Tel: 610-933-2110; Email: basilpastor1965@gmail.com; Web: www.stbasils.org. Rev. Gary T. Pacitti.
See Holy Family School, Phoenixville under Regional Parish Schools located in the Institution section.
Catechesis Religious Program—Tel: 610-935-1261; Fax: 610-422-2570; Email: dre@stbasil.org. James King, B.A., M.A., D.R.E.
Convent—Sisters of St. Francis Residence,
Tel: 610-933-2345.

KING OF PRUSSIA, MONTGOMERY CO., MOTHER OF DIVINE PROVIDENCE (1954)
333 Allendale Rd., King of Prussia, 19406-1640.
Tel: 610-265-4178; Email: mdpinfo@mdpparish.com; Web: mdpparish.com. Rev. Martin T. Cioppi, Ed.D., M.A., M.Div.; Deacons Mark H. Dillon; Gregory J. Maskarinec.
See Mother Teresa Regional Catholic School, King of Prussia under Regional Parish Schools located in the Institution section.

LAFAYETTE HILL, MONTGOMERY CO., ST. PHILIP NERI (1945)
437 Ridge Pike, Lafayette Hill, 19444.
Tel: 610-834-1975; Fax: 610-834-0392; Email: mcpastorius@comcast.net; Web: www.saintphilipnerichurch.com. Rev. Msgr. Charles P. Vance, M.Div.; Revs. Anthony R. Hangholt, Parochial Vicar; William B. Dooner, M.Div., In Res., (Retired); Deacon Robert G. Flynn; Mr. Michael Pastorius, Business Mgr.
School—St. Philip Neri School, (Grades PreK-8), 3015 Chestnut St., Lafayette Hill, 19444.
Tel: 610-828-3082; Fax: 610-828-2943; Email: venezialee@spnschool.org; Web: www.spnschool.org. Elizabeth Veneziale, Prin. Lay Teachers 35; Students 510.
Catechesis Religious Program—Tel: 610-834-9868; Email: spnprep@spnschool.org. Mrs. Sharon Otto, D.R.E. Students 257.
Convent—Tel: 610-828-2866. Sisters 11.

LANSDALE, MONTGOMERY CO., ST. STANISLAUS (1876) [CEM]
51 Lansdale Ave., Lansdale, 19446.
Tel: 215-855-3133; Email: ststan@comcast.net; Web: www.ststanislaus.com. Rev. Msgr. Joseph A. Tracy, S.T.D., M.S.W., M.A., M.Div.; Revs. Charles J. Ravert, Parochial Vicar; Zachary W. Navit, M.A., M.Div., In Res.; Deacons Anthony J. Bellitto Jr.; Charles G. Lewis; Juan E. Valentin.
School—Mater Dei Catholic School, (Grades PreK-8), 493 E. Main St., Lansdale, 19446-2898.
Tel: 215-368-0995; Fax: 215-393-4869; Email: gsamanns@materdeicatholic.com; Web: materdeicatholic.com. Diane E. McCaughan, Prin. Lay Teachers 32; Students 490.
Catechesis Religious Program—Tel: 215-855-9893; Email: ststansprep@yahoo.com. Leona Russell, C.R.E. Students 525.

LANSDOWNE, DELAWARE CO., ST. PHILOMENA (1898)
41 E. Baltimore Ave., Lansdowne, 19050.
Tel: 610-622-2420; Fax: 610-622-1215; Email: stphilomenaparish@rcn.com; Web: www.stphilspa.com. Revs. Paul J. Castellani; Ukachukwu Onyeabor, In Res.
Catechesis Religious Program—Students 28.

LENNI, DELAWARE CO., ST. FRANCIS DE SALES (1894) [CEM]
35 New Rd., P.O. Box 97, Lenni, 19052.
Tel: 610-459-2203; Fax: 610-459-5029; Web: www.sfdschurch.org. Rev. Alan J. Okon Jr.; Deacon Paul A. Quinn; Sr. Betty Kirk, O.S.F., Dir. Parish Svcs.
Catechesis Religious Program—Tel: 610-459-0554. Students 130.
Convent—28 New Rd., Aston, 19014.
Tel: 610-459-2501.
Stations—Fair Acres Geriatric Center—Lima.
Tel: 610-891-5600.
Granite Farms Est., Media. Tel: 610-358-3440.
Riddle Village, Media. Tel: 610-891-3777.
The Residence at Glen Riddle, Media.
Tel: 610-358-9933.
Riddle Hospital, Media. Tel: 610-566-9400.
Penn State Lima Campus, Media. Tel: 610-892-1350.
Williamson School, Media. Tel: 610-566-1776.

LEVITTOWN, BUCKS CO.
1—IMMACULATE CONCEPTION B.V.M. (1954-2014) Closed. Formerly located at 5201 Bristol Emile Rd., Levittown. Spiritual records are kept at Queen of the Universe Church, Levittown. Tel: 215-945-8750.

2—ST. MICHAEL THE ARCHANGEL (1953)
66 Levittown Pkwy., Levittown, 19054.
Tel: 215-945-1166; Fax: 215-945-6988; Email: church@stmichaellvt.org; Web: www.stmichaellvt.org. Rev. Michael C. DiIorio; Deacon John K. Murray, D.R.E.
School—St. Michael the Archangel School, 130 Levittown Pkwy., Levittown, 19054.
Tel: 215-943-0222; Fax: 215-943-9068; Web: www.sma-pa.org. Lay Teachers 14; Students 213.
Catechesis Religious Program—Tel: 215-547-2518; Email: PREP@stmichaellvt.org. Students 225.
Chapel—Our Lady of the Angels.

3—QUEEN OF THE UNIVERSE (1955)
2443 Trenton Rd., Levittown, 19056.
Tel: 215-945-8750; Fax: 215-945-0413; Web: www.quparish.com. Revs. John F. Wackerman; Daniel J. Arechabala, Parochial Vicar; John F. Bednarik, O.F.-M.Cap., Parochial Vicar; Deacon John K. Murray.
Parish Center—2505 Trenton Rd., Levittown, Bucks Co. 19056. Tel: 215-945-0215.
See Holy Family Regional Catholic School, Levittown, under Regional Parish Schools located in the Institution Section.
Catechesis Religious Program—Tel: 215-945-2704; Email: quparishprep@gmail.com. Students 325.

LIMERICK, MONTGOMERY CO., SAINT TERESA OF CALCUTTA (2006)
256 Swamp Pike, Schwenksville, 19473.
Tel: 610-287-2525; Fax: 610-287-7565; Web: www.blteresacalcutta.org. Revs. Paul C. Brandt, M.Div.; John J. Pidgeon, M.Div., In Res.; Deacons Louis F.

Hoelzle, St. Teresa of Calcutta Church, Schwenksville; David M. Kubczak, St. Teresa of Calcutta Church, Limerick; Thomas G. Phillips Jr.
Res.: 284 Swamp Pike, Schwenksville, 19473.
School—St. Teresa of Calcutta School, (Grades PreK-8), Tel: 610-287-2500; Fax: 610-287-2543. Anita M. Dixon, Prin.
Catechesis Religious Program—Students 750.

LINFIELD, MONTGOMERY CO., ST. CLARE (1963-2006) Closed. Formerly located at 1228 Main St., Linfield. Spiritual records are kept at Saint Teresa of Calcutta Church, Limerick. Tel: 610-287-2525.

LINWOOD, DELAWARE CO., HOLY SAVIOUR (1914-2013) Closed. Formerly located at E. Ridge Rd. at Rt. 452. Spiritual records are kept at St. John Fisher Church, Boothwyn. Tel: 610-485-0441.

MALVERN, CHESTER CO., ST. PATRICK (1915)
108 Woodland Ave., Malvern, 19355.
Tel: 610-647-2345; Fax: 610-647-4997; Web: www.stpatrickmalvern.org. Revs. Christopher Redcay; Mark J. Cavara, In Res.; Andrew Labatorio, In Res.; Deacon Louis Libbi.
School—St. Patrick School, 115 Channing Ave., Malvern, 19355. Tel: 610-644-5797;
Fax: 610-647-0535. Students 331.
Catechesis Religious Program—118 Woodland Ave., Malvern, 19355. Tel: 610-296-8899;
Fax: 610-296-8384. Students 450.

MANOA, DELAWARE CO., SACRED HEART (1927)
105 Wilson Ave., Havertown, 19083.
Tel: 610-449-3000; Email: shpmckee@comcast.net. Revs. Henry J. McKee; Michael G. Speziale, In Res.; Deacons John J. Suplee; William V. Williams.
School—Sacred Heart School, 109 N. Manoa Rd., Havertown, 19083. Tel: 610-446-9198;
Fax: 610-446-4861. Lay Teachers 14; Sisters, Servants of the Immaculate Heart of Mary 1; Students 219.
Catechesis Religious Program—Sr. Kathryn Benham, I.H.M., D.R.E. Students 320.
Convent—Tel: 610-446-3694.

MAPLE GLEN, MONTGOMERY CO., ST. ALPHONSUS (1963)
33 Conwell Dr., Maple Glen, 19002.
Tel: 215-646-4600; Fax: 215-646-0180; Email: rectory@stalphonsusparish.org; Web: stalphonsusparish.org. Rev. Brian P. Hennessy, J.C.L., M.A., M.Div.; Deacons John J. Mischler; James Toth.
School—Our Lady of Mercy Regional Catholic School, (Grades K-8), 29 Conwell Dr., Maple Glen, 19002. Tel: 215-646-0150; Fax: 215-646-7150. John C. McGrath, M.Ed., Prin. Lay Teachers 30; Students 407.
Catechesis Religious Program—Tel: 215-643-7938; Email: mgordan@stalphonsusparish.org. Michele Gordon, D.R.E. Students 302.

MARCUS HOOK, DELAWARE CO., IMMACULATE CONCEPTION (1917-2013) (Italian), Closed. Formerly located at 21 W. 8th St. Spiritual records are kept at St. John Fisher Church, Boothwyn. Tel: 610-485-0441.

MEDIA, DELAWARE CO.
1—ST. MARY MAGDALEN (1963)
2400 N. Providence Rd., Media, 19063.
Tel: 610-566-8821; Email: info@stmarymagdalen.net; Web: www.stmarymagdalen.net. Rev. Msgr. Ralph J. Chieffo; Rev. Brian A. Izzo, M.A., M.Div., Parochial Vicar; Rev. Msgr. Joseph T. Marino, M.Div., M.A., In Res.; Deacons E. Peter Zurbach; James A. DiFerdinand.
School—St. Mary Magdalen School, 2430 N. Providence Rd., Media, 19063. Tel: 610-565-1822;
Fax: 610-627-9670; Email: smsoffice@comcast.net. Lay Teachers 27; Students 367.
Catechesis Religious Program—Tel: 610-565-5782; Email: sistermj@stmarymagdalen.net. Students 150.
2—NATIVITY OF THE BLESSED VIRGIN MARY (1868) [CEM]
30 E. Franklin St., Media, 19063. Tel: 610-566-0185;
Fax: 610-566-2873; Email: nativitybvm@comcast.net; Web: www.nativity-bvm.org. Rev. Edward H. Bell, M.Div.; Rev. Msgr. Joseph P. McGeown, M.A., In Res., (Retired); Rev. John E. Mulgrew, M.A., In Res., (Retired); Deacon William G. Kussmaul.
See Mother of Providence Regional Catholic School, Wallingford under Regional Parish Schools located in the Institution section.

MILMONT PARK, DELAWARE CO., OUR LADY OF PEACE (1922)
501 Belmont Ave., Milmont Park, 19033-3308.
Tel: 610-532-8081; Tel: 610-532-8082;
Fax: 610-532-7402. Revs. Joseph P. Devlin, M.A., M.Div.; Dominic Ishaq, J.C.D., Parochial Vicar; Gerald D. Canavan, M.Div., In Res., (Retired); Deacons James A. Basilio; John J. Ellis; Michael J. McAndrews. Spiritual records kept at Resurrection of Our Lord Church, Philadelphia.
Catechesis Religious Program—Students 145.

MORRISVILLE, BUCKS CO.
1—HOLY TRINITY (1900) [CEM]
201 N. Pennsylvania Ave., Morrisville, 19067.
Tel: 215-295-3045; Email: holytrinityrcc@aol.com; Web: www.holytrinitymorrisville.org. Rev. John C. Eckert; Deacon Warren C. Leonard.
School—Holy Trinity School, (Grades PreK-8), Osborne Ave. & Stockham Ave., Morrisville, 19067.
Tel: 215-295-6900; Fax: 215-337-9079; Email: Teachlit25@aol.com. Mrs. Elaine McDowell, Prin. Lay Teachers 12; Students 250.
Catechesis Religious Program—Tel: 215-295-3079; Email: Holytrinitycre@aol.com. Mrs. Kathleen Gnida, D.R.E. Students 100.
2—ST. JOHN THE EVANGELIST (1964)
752 Big Oak Rd., Morrisville, 19067.
Tel: 215-295-4102; Email: SJEoffices@stjohnpa.org. Rev. Timothy F. O'Sullivan; Deacon Jonathan P. Hess, D.R.E.
Catechesis Religious Program—Tel: 215-295-9239; Email: prepdirector@stjohnpa.org.

MORTON, DELAWARE CO., OUR LADY OF PERPETUAL HELP (1907)
2130 Franklin Ave., Morton, 19070.
Tel: 610-543-1046; Email: OLPH0101@Comcast.net; Web: www.olphmorton.org. Rev. Msgr. John M. Savinski, M.Div., M.A.; Rev. Richard J. Smith, Parochial Vicar; Deacon Ronald F. Kelley.
School—Our Lady of Angels Regional School, (Grades PreK-8), Tel: 610-543-8350;
Fax: 610-544-3203. Lay Teachers 27; Sisters of St. Francis of Philadelphia 2; Students 395.
Catechesis Religious Program—Tel: 610-543-5448; Email: OLPHPrep@Gmail.com. Mrs. Michele Hundermark, D.R.E. Students 260.
Convent—Tel: 610-543-0186; Email: OLPHCC@Comcast.net.

NARBERTH, MONTGOMERY CO., ST. MARGARET (1900)
208 N. Narberth Ave., Narberth, 19072.
Tel: 610-664-3770; Email: office@saintmarg.org; Web: wwwsaintmarg.org. Rev. Msgr. Paul V. Dougherty, M.Div., M.A.; Rev. Matthew W. Guckin, M.A., M.Div., In Res.
School—St. Margaret School, 227 N. Narberth Ave., Narberth, 19072. Tel: 610-664-2640;
Fax: 610-664-4677; Email: office@smsnarberth.org; Web: www.smsnarberth.org. Lay Teachers 17; Students 308.
Catechesis Religious Program—
Tel: 610-664-3370, Ext. 16. Students 206.

NEW HOPE, BUCKS CO., ST. MARTIN OF TOURS (1885) [CEM]
1 Riverstone Cir., New Hope, 18938.
Tel: 215-862-5472; Fax: 215-862-1829; Email: frkindon@stmartinoftours.org; Email: info@saintmartinoftour.org; Web: www.stmartinoftours.org. Rev. W. Frederick Kindon.

NEWTOWN, BUCKS CO., ST. ANDREW (1880) [CEM]
81 Swamp Rd., Newtown, 18940. Tel: 215-968-2262;
Fax: 215-579-9344; Web: standrewnewtown.com. Rev. Msgr. Michael C. Picard, M.A.; Revs. Kyle Adamczyk, Parochial Vicar; Marc F. Capizzi, M.A., M.Div., Parochial Vicar; John F. McBride, In Res., (Retired); Deacons Edward E. Duess; John J. Pfeifer.
School—St. Andrew School, 51 Wrights Rd., Newtown, 18940. Tel: 215-968-2685;
Fax: 215-968-4795.
Child Care—Preschool, Lay Teachers 42; Students 817.
Catechesis Religious Program—Tel: 215-968-6929. Students 1,050.

NEWTOWN SQUARE, DELAWARE CO.
1—ST. ANASTASIA (1912)
3301 W. Chester Pike, Newtown Square, 19073.
Tel: 610-356-1613; Email: thaggerty@saintannies.org; Email: llawler@saintannies.org; Email: pastoralcouncil@saintannies.org; Email: mbarrar@saintannies.org; Web: saintanastasia.net. Revs. Michael A. Colagreco; Daniel J. Dwyer, Parochial Vicar; Sr. Mary Barrar, RCIA Coord.; Deacon Thaddeus C. Raczkowski; Mrs. Linda Lawler, Sec.
School—St. Anastasia School, 3309 W. Chester Pike, Newtown Square, 19073. Tel: 610-356-6225;
Fax: 610-356-5748; Web: www.saintannies.org. Beth Dotle, Prin.; Marlene Louden, Librarian. Lay Teachers 42; Students 610.
Catechesis Religious Program—Tel: 610-356-5069. Mrs. Theresa Haggerty, D.R.E. Students 373.
Convent—3305 W. Chester Pike, Newtown Square, 19073. Tel: 484-422-8861.
2—HOLY MARY KOREAN CATHOLIC CHURCH
100 Media Line Rd., Newtown Square, 19073.
Tel: 610-325-2240; Web: www.slachurch.com. Rev. John Sang Yong Lee, Parochial Admin.

NORRISTOWN, MONTGOMERY CO.
1—ST. FRANCIS OF ASSISI (1923)
600 Hamilton St., Norristown, 19401.
Tel: 610-272-0402; Fax: 610-272-1794; Email: sfarectory@yahoo.com; Web: www.stfrancisnorristown.com. Rev. James E. Goerner; Deacon James Mahar.
School—St. Francis of Assisi School, 601-A Buttonwood Sts., Norristown, 19401.
Tel: 610-272-0501; Fax: 610-272-8011; Email: btigue@sfacatholic.org; Web: sfa.ocephila.org. Lay Teachers 14; Students 222.
Catechesis Religious Program—Email: sfa600prep@gmail.com. Students 140.
2—HOLY SAVIOUR (1903) (Italian)
407 E. Main St., Norristown, 19401. Web: www.holysaviour.com; Tel: 610-275-0958; Email: msgrsangermano@holysaviour.com. Rev. Msgr. Charles L. Sangermano, M.Div.; Rev. Francis J. Sabatini, In Res., (Retired).
See Holy Rosary Regional Catholic School, Plymouth Meeting under Regional Parish Schools in Institution section.
Catechesis Religious Program—Students 110.
Mission—Our Lady of Mount Carmel, 460 Fairfield Rd., Plymouth Meeting, Montgomery Co. 19462.
Tel: 610-277-7739.
3—ST. PATRICK (1835) [CEM]
703 Green St., Norristown, 19401. Tel: 610-272-1408; Email: stpatnorris@comcast.net; Web: www.stpatrickchurch.com. Rev. Augustus C. Puleo, M.Div., M.A., M.S., Ph.D.; Christopher Lawrence, Business Mgr.
Res.: 714 DeKalb St., Norristown, 19401.
Catechesis Religious Program—Religious Educ. Bldg., 703 Green St., Norristown, 19401.
Tel: 610-272-4500. Sr. Marie Horstmann, I.H.M., D.R.E. Students 400.
Convent—Missionaries of Charity, 630 DeKalb St., Norristown, 19401. Tel: 610-277-5962.
4—ST. TERESA OF AVILA (1918)
1260 S. Trooper Rd., Norristown, 19403-3659.
Tel: 610-666-5820; Fax: 610-666-7511; Email: starectory@verizon.net; Web: www.stteresaofavilaparish.com. Rev. J. Jerome Wild, S.T.L., M.A., M.Div.; Deacons David J. Matour; Francis C. Lally.
Catechesis Religious Program—Tel: 610-666-0167. Rev. Erin Gaunter, C.R.E. Students 130.
5—ST. TITUS (1962)
3006 Keenwood Rd., East Norriton, 19403.
Tel: 610-279-4990; Fax: 610-279-8640; Web: www.sttitus.org. Rev. Leonard A. Lewandowski; Deacon Claude B. Granese.
See Holy Rosary Regional Catholic School, Plymouth Meeting under Regional Parish Schools located in the Institution section.
Catechesis Religious Program—Tel: 610-306-3438. Mrs. Claire Boyle, C.R.E. Students 54.
6—VISITATION B.V.M. (1954)
196 N. Trooper Rd., Norristown, 19403.
Tel: 610-539-5572; Email: visibulletin@gmail.com; Web: www.visitationbvm.org. Revs. Terence P. Weik; Brian T. Connolly, Parochial Vicar; Deacons Vincent M. Drewicz; Patrick J. Mandracchia.
School—Visitation B.V.M. School, 190 N. Trooper Rd., Norristown, 19403. Tel: 610-539-6080;
Fax: 610-630-7946. Lay Teachers 37; Sisters of the Holy Family of Nazareth 2; Students 628.
Catechesis Religious Program—Tel: 610-539-6211; Email: sister.diane@visitationbvmschool.org. Sr. Diane Marie, C.S.F.N., D.R.E. Students 410.
Convent—Tel: 610-539-5558.

NORTH WALES, MONTGOMERY CO.
1—MARY, MOTHER OF THE REDEEMER (1987)
1325 Upper State Rd., North Wales, 19454.
Tel: 215-362-7400; Tel: 215-362-8966;
Fax: 215-362-4127; Web: mmredeemer.org. Rev. Msgr. John T. Conway; Revs. William J. Teverzczuk, Parochial Vicar; Daniel J. Arechabala, Parochial Vicar; Patrick J. Muka; Deacons Paul A. Logan; John M. Travaline; Lou Tonelli, Business Mgr.; Gail Toto, Dir., Parish Svcs.
School—Mary, Mother of the Redeemer School, 1321 Upper State Rd., North Wales, 19454.
Tel: 215-412-7101; Fax: 215-412-7197. Mrs. Denise Judge, Prin. Students 621.
Catechesis Religious Program—Tel: 215-412-2251;
Fax: 215-412-7197. Nancy Franks, D.R.E. Students 440.
2—ST. ROSE OF LIMA (1919)
428 S. Main St., North Wales, 19454-3224. Rev. Msgr. James J. Graham, J.C.D., M.Div.; Deacon Robert P. Gohde.
Parish Center—425 S. Pennsylvania Ave., North Wales, 19454-3498. Tel: 215-699-4617;
Fax: 215-699-4452.
See Mater Dei Catholic School, Lansdale under Regional Parish Schools located in the Institution section.
Catechesis Religious Program—Tel: 215-699-4434. Joanne M. Tragesser, D.R.E. Students 171.

NORWOOD, DELAWARE CO., ST. GABRIEL (1891)
233 Mohawk Ave., Norwood, 19074.
Tel: 610-586-1225; Email: office@stgabrielnorwood.org. Rev. Anthony F. Orth; Deacon Albert J. Murphy.
See St. James Regional Catholic School, Ridley Park under Regional Parish Schools located in the Institution section.
Catechesis Religious Program—Tel: 610-532-5057;

Email: religiousedu@stgabrielnorwood.org. Students 300.

ORELAND, MONTGOMERY CO., HOLY MARTYRS (1949)
120 Allison Rd., Oreland, 19075. Tel: 215-884-8575; Email: holymartyrssecretary@gmail.com; Email: holymartyrschurch@gmail.com; Web: www.holymartyrschurch.net. Rev. Jason V. Kulczynski; Deacon Christopher C. Roberts.
Catechesis Religious Program—
Tel: 215-884-8575, Ext. 111; Email: holymartyrsreligioused@gmail.com. Students 92.

OTTSVILLE, BUCKS CO., ST. JOHN THE BAPTIST (1743) [CEM]
4050 Durham Rd., Ottsville, 18942.
Tel: 610-847-5521; Fax: 610-847-5522; Web: www.stjohnsottsville.org. Revs. Simione R. Volavola, M.S.C.; Anthony Ripp, M.S.C., Parochial Vicar; Deacon Ernest D'Angelo.
School—St. John the Baptist School, 4040 Durham Rd., Ottsville, 18942. Tel: 610-847-5523;
Fax: 610-847-8549; Email: principal@stjohnsottsville.org. Lay Teachers 15; Students 76.
Catechesis Religious Program—Students 155.

OXFORD, CHESTER CO., SACRED HEART (1914)
203 Church Rd., Oxford, 19363. Tel: 610-932-5040; Email: info@sacredheart.us; Web: sacredheartchurchoxford.org. Rev. Michael F. Hennelly, M.Div., M.S.; Deacon Justin J. Watkins.
School—Sacred Heart School, Tel: 610-932-3633;
Fax: 610-932-6051. Mr. Steven Brunner, Prin.
Catechesis Religious Program—Email: lisa.ledger@sacredheart.us. Mrs. Lisa Ledger, D.R.E. Students 169.

PAOLI, CHESTER CO., ST. NORBERT (1956)
50 Leopard Rd., Paoli, 19301. Tel: 610-644-1655; Web: parish.stnorbert.org. Revs. Steven J. Albero, O.Praem.; Arul Amalraj Selvanayagam, Parochial Vicar; Deacons John P. Lozano; Stephen J. Martino.
School—St. Norbert School, Greenlawn & Leopard Rds., Paoli, 19301. Tel: 610-644-1670;
Fax: 610-644-0201. Lay Teachers 24; Students 240.
Catechesis Religious Program—
Tel: 610-644-1670, Ext. 122. Students 462.

PARKESBURG, CHESTER CO., OUR LADY OF CONSOLATION (1853) [CEM]
603 W. Second Ave., Parkesburg, 19365.
Tel: 610-857-3510; Fax: 610-857-2353; Web: www.olcchurch.org. Rev. Victor J. Eschbach; Deacon Eugene Favinger.
Catechesis Religious Program—Tel: 610-857-1003. Delores Cain, D.R.E. Students 200.
Mission—St. Malachy (1838) [CEM] 76 St. Malachy Rd., Cochranville, Chester Co. 19330.
Tel: 610-857-3510; Fax: 610-857-2353.

PENN VALLEY, MONTGOMERY CO., ST. JUSTIN MARTYR (1964-2009) Closed. Formerly located at 1222 Hagysford Rd., Narberth. Spiritual records are kept at St. John Baptist Vianney, Gladwyne. Tel: 610-642-0938.

PENNDEL, BUCKS CO., OUR LADY OF GRACE (1908) [CEM]
225 Bellevue Ave., Penndel, 19047.
Tel: 215-757-7700; Fax: 215-757-5377; Email: parish@olg1.org; Web: www.olgparishpenndel.org. Parish Service Center: 338 Hulmeville Ave., Penndel, 19047. Rev. Msgr. Joseph G. Prior, M.Div., M.A., S.S.L., S.T.D.; Revs. William B. Dooner, M.Div., Pastor Emeritus, (Retired); Manuel Flores, Parochial Vicar; George E. Pereia, In Res.; Raju Pilla, In Res.; Sr. Mary Ellen Diehl, Parish Life Coord.; Deacon Dominic A. Garritano; Ms. Maddie Applebee, Youth Min.; Mrs. Catherine Galie, Music Min.; Paul Harvitz, Business Mgr.
School—Our Lady of Grace School, 300 Hulmeville Ave., Penndel, 19047. Tel: 215-757-5287;
Fax: 215-757-6199; Web: www.olgschoolpenndel.org. Mrs. Denise Lewis, Prin. Lay Teachers 17; Students 260.
Catechesis Religious Program—Tel: 215-757-5530; Email: dre@olg1.org. Mrs. Christine Flack, D.R.E. Students 350.

PENNSBURG, MONTGOMERY CO., ST. PHILIP NERI (1919) [CEM]
1325 Klinerd Rd., Pennsburg, 18073.
Tel: 215-679-9275; Email: ofcmgr@spnparish.org. Rev. Robert A. Roncase; Deacons Michael J. Franks Sr.; Patrick J. Kennedy.
St. Philip Neri Catholic Family Life Center—26 E. Sixth St., East Greenville, 18041. Tel: 215-679-2237;
Fax: 215-679-8370; Web: www.catholicfamilylifecenter.com.
Catechesis Religious Program—Tel: 215-679-7839. Students 183.

PHOENIXVILLE, CHESTER CO.
1—ST. ANN (1905) [CEM]
502 S. Main St., Phoenixville, 19460.
Tel: 610-933-3732; Email: stannphx@comcast.net; Web: www.churchofsaintann.org. Rev. John J. Newns; Deacons Daniel T. Giblin; Mark R. Szewczak.
See Holy Family School, Phoenixville under Regional Parish Schools located in the Institution section.
Catechesis Religious Program—Tel: 610-755-1077; Fax: 610-935-7958; Email: youthstann@comcast.net. Students 298.
2—HOLY TRINITY (1903-2012) [CEM] (Polish), Closed. 217 Dayton St. Spiritual records are kept at St. Mary of the Assumption Church, Phoenixville. Tel: 610-933-2526. Worship Site of St. Mary of the Assumption, Phoenixville.
3—ST. MARY OF THE ASSUMPTION (1840) [CEM 2]
212 Dayton St., Phoenixville, 19460.
Tel: 610-933-2526; Tel: 610-933-3311;
Fax: 610-935-1706; Email: ParishOffice@StMaryAssumption.org; Web: www.stmaryassumption.org. Rev. John S. Hutter; Deacon Jeffrey S. Hanna.
See Holy Family School, Phoenixville under Regional Parish Schools located in the Institution section.
Catechesis Religious Program—Students 124.
4—SACRED HEART (1900-2012) [CEM] (Slovak), Closed. Formerly located at 148 Church St. Spiritual records are kept at St. Ann. Church, Phoenixville. Tel: 610-933-3732. Worship Site of St. Ann. Church, Phoenixville.

PLYMOUTH MEETING, MONTGOMERY CO., EPIPHANY OF OUR LORD (1957)
3050 Walton Rd., Plymouth Meeting, 19462-2361.
Tel: 610-828-8634; Fax: 610-828-1802; Email: epiphanych@comcast.net; Web: www.epiphanyofourlord.com. Revs. Joseph J. Quindlen; John J. Nordeman, M.A., M.Div., In Res.; Deacons Michael Pascarella Jr., M.A., M.S.; Emil J. Wernert.
School—Holy Rosary Regional Catholic School, 3040 Walton Rd., Plymouth Meeting, 19462-2361.
Tel: 610-825-0160; Fax: 610-825-0460; Web: www.holyrosaryregional.com. Mrs. Lisa Hoban, Prin. Lay Teachers 25; Students 315.
Catechesis Religious Program—Tel: 215-367-5853; Fax: 610-825-0460; Email: rep@eol.comcastbiz.net. Stephanie Quigley, C.R.E.; Gail Toto, Youth Min., Tel: 215-367-5854; Fax: 215-367-5855. Students 40.

POTTSTOWN, MONTGOMERY CO.
1—ST. ALOYSIUS (1856) [CEM 2]
214 N. Hanover St., Pottstown, 19464. Rev. Joseph L. Maloney, M.Div.; Deacon George S. Harmansky; Emily Pufnoch, Librarian.
Parish Office: 223 Beech St., Pottstown, 19464.
Tel: 610-326-5877; Fax: 610-326-0901.
Res.: 176 N. Hanover St., Pottstown, 19464. Web: saintaloysius.net.
School—St. Aloysius School, (Grades PreK-8), 844 N. Keim St., Pottstown, 19464. Tel: 610-326-6167;
Fax: 610-970-9960; Email: kbruce@saintaloysius.net; Web: www.saintaloysius.net. Kathleen Bruce, Prin. Lay Teachers 18; Students 240.
Catechesis Religious Program—
Tel: 610-326-5877, Ext. 434. Students 173.
2—HOLY TRINITY (1899-2004) (Slovak), Closed. 366 South St., Pottstown. Spiritual records are kept at St. Aloysius Church, Pottstown. Tel: 610-326-5877. Worship site of St. Aloysius Church, Pottstown.
3—ST. PETER (1924-2006) (Polish), Closed. Formerly located at 1128 South St. Spiritual records are kept at SaintTeresa of Calcutta Church, Limerick. Tel: 610-287-2525.

PRIMOS, DELAWARE CO., ST. EUGENE (1955)
200 S. Oak Ave., Primos, 19018. Tel: 610-626-2866; Email: steugene55@rcn.com. Rev. Joseph M. McDermott, M.Div.; Deacon James V. Walsh.
School—St. Eugene School, (Grades K-8), 110 S. Oak Ave., Primos, 19018. Tel: 610-622-2909;
Fax: 610-622-6358; Email: dthompson@sainteugeneschool.org; Web: sainteugeneschool.org. Mrs. Diana Thompson, Prin. Lay Teachers 12; Students 195.
Catechesis Religious Program—Students 101.

QUAKERTOWN, BUCKS CO., ST. ISIDORE (1886) [CEM]
603 W. Broad St., Quakertown, 18951.
Tel: 215-536-4389; Email: izzyparoff@comcast.net; Email: stisidorechurch@comcast.net; Web: www.stisidores.org. Rev. Frederick J. Riegler; Deacons David C. Mitchell; Patrick J. O'Donnell; Michael P. Nungesser.
Res.: 2545 W. Pumping Station Rd., Quakertown, 18951.
School—St. Isidore School, Tel: 215-536-6052;
Fax: 215-536-8647. Lay Teachers 18; Students 258.
Catechesis Religious Program—Tel: 215-536-6498; Email: izprepoff@comcast.net. Nicole Hallowell, D.R.E. Students 341.

RICHBORO, BUCKS CO., ST. VINCENT DE PAUL (1968)
654 Hatboro Rd., Richboro, 18954-1039.
Tel: 215-357-5905; Fax: 215-953-8190; Email: revjjmcl@nni.net; Web: www.svdp-richboro.org. Revs. Joseph J. McLaughlin; Linus D. Nangwele, Parochial Vicar; Deacons John M. Golaszewski; Richard G. Napoli.
Catechesis Religious Program—Tel: 215-322-1932. Elaine Potalivo, D.R.E. Students 378.
Convent—Sisters of St. Joseph, 624 Hatboro Rd., Richboro, 18954-1039. Tel: 215-942-9152.

RIDLEY PARK, DELAWARE CO., ST. MADELINE (1908)
110 Park St., Ridley Park, 19078. Tel: 610-532-6880; Fax: 610-532-6653. Rev. John B. Flanagan; Deacon Michael J. Alexander.
Church: Penn St. & Morton Ave., Ridley Park, 19078.
See St. James Regional Catholic School, Ridley Park under Regional Parish Schools located in the Institution section.
Catechesis Religious Program—Tel: 610-583-6120. Students 230.

RIEGELSVILLE, BUCKS CO., ST. LAWRENCE (1974) [JC]
345 Elmwood Ln., Riegelsville, 18077.
Tel: 610-749-2684; Email: saintlawrence@verizon.net. Rev. Walter J. Benn.
Catechesis Religious Program—Students 27.

ROSLYN, MONTGOMERY CO., ST. JOHN OF THE CROSS (1953-2014) Closed. Formerly located at 2741 Woodland Rd., Roslyn. Spiritual records are kept at Queen of Peace Church, Ardsley. Tel: 215-887-1838.

ROYERSFORD, MONTGOMERY CO., SACRED HEART (1973)
838 Walnut St., P.O. Box 64, Royersford, 19468.
Tel: 610-948-5915, Ext. 2; Tel: 610-948-4087;
Fax: 610-948-0573; Web: www.sacredheartroyersford.org. Revs. Tadeusz Gorka; John J. Sibel, Ph.D., M.Div., In Res., (Retired).
Catechesis Religious Program—Patricia Fauls, C.R.E. Students 135.

RYDAL, MONTGOMERY CO., ST. HILARY OF POITIERS (1962)
820 Susquehanna Rd., Rydal, 19046.
Tel: 215-884-3252; Fax: 215-884-5342; Email: sthilaryrydal@comcast.net. Revs. Kevin P. Murray; Laurence J. Gleason, M.A., M.Div., In Res.; Deacon John K. Hunter.
School—St. Hilary of Poitiers School, (Grades PreK-8), 920 Susquehanna Rd., Rydal, 19046.
Tel: 215-887-4520; Fax: 215-887-6337. Eileen Fagan, Prin.; Diane Sawyer, Librarian. Students 260.
Catechesis Religious Program—Students 120.

SCHWENKSVILLE, MONTGOMERY CO., ST. MARY (1926)
40 Spring Mount Rd., Schwenksville, 19473.
Tel: 610-287-8156; Fax: 610-287-4226; Email: solzinski@churchofsaintmary.org; Web: www.churchofsaintmary.org. Revs. Louis P. Bellopede; Brian M. Kean, In Res.; Deacon Donald O. Nichols.
School—St. Mary School, Tel: 610-287-7757. Lay Teachers 22; Students 296.
Catechesis Religious Program—
Tel: 610-287-4517, Ext. 244. Students 298.

SECANE, DELAWARE CO., OUR LADY OF FATIMA (1952)
1 Fatima Dr., Secane, 19018. Tel: 610-532-5800;
Fax: 610-532-6937; Web: www.olfsecane.org. Revs. Roland D. Slobogin, M.Div.; Thomas P. Gillin, M.S., Parochial Vicar; Michael J. Lonergan, J.D., M.A., M.Div., In Res., (Retired); Deacon Gary W. Guy.
See Our Lady of Angels Regional Catholic School, Morton under Regional Parish Schools located in the Institution section.
Catechesis Religious Program—
Tel: 610-586-3633, Ext. 287. Students 122.
Convent—5 Fatima Dr., Secane, 19018.
Tel: 610-532-1190.

SELLERSVILLE, BUCKS CO., ST. AGNES (1919) [CEM]
445 N. Main St., Sellersville, 18960.
Tel: 215-257-2128, Ext. 10; Web: www.stagneschurch.org. Rev. Jeffrey M. Stecz; Deacons R. Lyle Benner; Harry Tucker; Raymond H. Thuel.
Catechesis Religious Program—Tel: 215-257-1811; Fax: 215-257-0525; Email: stagnesprep@gmail.com; Web: www.stagnesprep.org. Students 239.

SHARON HILL, DELAWARE CO., HOLY SPIRIT (1892-2014) Closed. Formerly located at 1028 School St., Sharon Hill. Spiritual records are kept at St. George Church, Glenolden. Tel: 610-237-1633.

SOUTH COVENTRY, CHESTER CO., ST. THOMAS MORE (1968)
2101 Pottstown Pike, Pottstown, 19465.
Tel: 610-469-9304; Fax: 610-469-9315. Revs. Edward E. Brady; Hugh J. Dougherty, M.Div., (Retired).
Catechesis Religious Program—Tel: 610-469-9302. Students 557.

SOUTHAMPTON, BUCKS CO., OUR LADY OF GOOD COUNSEL (1923)
611 Knowles Ave., Southampton, 18966-4198.
Tel: 215-357-1300; Email: tcoffice@olgc.org; Web: www.olgc.org. Revs. Robert G. Suskey; John J. Kilgallon, M.Div., In Res.
School—Our Lady of Good Counsel School,
Tel: 215-357-1300, Ext. 117. Mr. Frank Mokriski, Prin. Lay Teachers 20; Students 341.
Catechesis Religious Program—
Tel: 215-357-1300, Ext. 107. Students 361.

SPRING CITY, CHESTER CO., ST. JOSEPH (1919)
3640 Schuylkill Rd., Spring City, 19475.
Tel: 610-948-7760; Fax: 610-948-8509; Email: st.joes@comcast.net; Web: www.stjosephspringcity.com. Rev. Charles R. O'Hara.
Catechesis Religious Program—Tel: 610-850-4228;

Email: stjosephprep@comcast.net. Andrea Jackowski, D.R.E. Students 203.

SPRINGFIELD, DELAWARE CO.

1—ST. FRANCIS OF ASSISI (1923)
136 Saxer Ave., Springfield, 19064.
Tel: 610-543-0848; Web: www.sfaparish.org. Revs. Anthony J. Costa, M.Div., M.A., S.T.L., S.T.D.; Joseph J. Meehan, M.S., In Res., (Retired); Deacon William T. Baxter.
School—St. Francis of Assisi School, 112 Saxer Ave., Springfield, 19064. Tel: 610-543-0546;
Fax: 610-544-9431. Lay Teachers 15; Students 293.
Catechesis Religious Program—Students 430.

2—HOLY CROSS (1948)
651 E. Springfield Rd., Springfield, 19064-3336.
Tel: 610-626-3321; Email: contactus@holycrosscatholics.org. Rev. Eugene C. Wilson; Deacons Joseph N. Gousie Sr.; Kevin Harrington; Kelly Meliti, D.R.E.
School—Holy Cross School, (Grades PreK-8), 240 N. Bishop Ave., Springfield, 19064. Tel: 610-626-1709;
Fax: 610-626-1859; Email: mward@hcscrusaders.com; Web: www.hcscrusaders.com. Lay Teachers 15; Students 237.
Catechesis Religious Program—Tel: 610-626-1057;
Fax: 610-626-8057. Students 180.
Convent—Tel: 610-626-2492.

3—ST. KEVIN (1955)
200 W. Sproul Rd., Springfield, 19064-2016.
Tel: 610-544-8777; Tel: 610-544-8778;
Fax: 610-544-7832. Rev. John C. Moloney.
Catechesis Religious Program—Students 212.
Convent—Tel: 610-544-4535.

STOWE, MONTGOMERY CO., ST. GABRIEL OF THE SORROWFUL MOTHER (1929)
127 E. Howard St., Stowe, 19464-6707.
Tel: 610-326-5127; Email: contact@sgsm62.org. Rev. Gregory J. Hickey, M.A.
Res.: 421 Jefferson St., Stowe, 19464-6736.
Tel: 610-327-2248.
Catechesis Religious Program—Tel: 610-327-5376; Email: mboyer@sgsm61.org. Maria Boyer, D.R.E. Students 25.

STRAFFORD, CHESTER CO., OUR LADY OF THE ASSUMPTION (1908) [CEM] (Italian)
35 Old Eagle School Rd., Strafford, 19087.
Tel: 610-688-1178; Email: rwesterfer@olastrafford.org. Rev. Gerald P. Carey, M.Div.; Rev. Msgr. Richard Malone, M.A., J.C.L., S.T.D., In Res., (Retired); Rev. Martin E. Woodeshick, In Res.; Deacon John P. Rose.
Child Care—Preschool, 135 Fairfield Ln., Strafford, 19087. Tel: 610-688-5277; Fax: 610-688-4540. Students 98.
Catechesis Religious Program—Tel: 610-688-6590; Email: kfitzpatrick@olastrafford.org. Sr. Kathleen Fitzpatrick, I.H.M., D.R.E. Students 141.

SWARTHMORE, DELAWARE CO., NOTRE DAME DE LOURDES (1959-2014) Closed. 1000 Fairview Rd., Swarthmore. Spiritual records are kept at Our Lady of Peace Church, Milmont Park. Tel: 610-532-8081. Worship site of Our Lady of Peace Church, Milmont Park.

SWEDESBURG, MONTGOMERY CO., SACRED HEART (1907) [CEM] (Polish) Rev. Thomas A. Nasta.
Res.: 120 Jefferson St., Swedesburg, 19405.
Tel: 610-275-1750; Fax: 610-275-0480; Email: unitedinthesacredheart@aol.com; Web: unitedinthesacredheart.com.
Catechesis Religious Program—Students 60.
Convent—635 E. Fourth St., Swedesburg, 19405.
Tel: 610-239-1785. Sr. Ryszarda Wittbrodt, Supr. Sisters Servants of the Most Sacred Heart.

UPPER DARBY, DELAWARE CO.

1—ST. ALICE (1922-2013) Closed. Formerly located at Copley Rd. and Walnut St. Spiritual records are kept at St. Laurence Church, Upper Darby. Tel: 610-449-0600.

2—ST. LAURENCE (1917)
30 St. Laurence Rd., Upper Darby, 19082.
Tel: 610-449-0600; Tel: 610-449-0601;
Fax: 610-449-4299. Revs. Sean F. O'Neill; Joseph C. McCaffrey, M.B.A., M.Div., In Res.; Quan M. Trinh, M.A., M.Div., In Res.; Deacons Samuel Ortiz; Mark Wallace.
School—St. Laurence School, 8245 W. Chester Pike, Highland Park, 19082. Tel: 610-789-2670;
Fax: 484-452-6271; Web: www.saintlaurencedelco.org. Lay Teachers 30; Sisters, Servants of the Immaculate Heart of Mary 11; Students 359.
Catechesis Religious Program—
Tel: 610-449-0600, Ext. 215. Rita Marian, I.H.M., C.R.E. Students 95.
Convent—Tel: 610-449-7042.
H.O.P.E. Program—Tel: 610-449-0600, Ext. 16;
Fax: 610-449-4299.

UPPER GWYNEDD, MONTGOMERY CO., CORPUS CHRISTI (1964)
900 Sumneytown Pike, Lansdale, 19446.
Tel: 215-855-1311; Fax: 215-855-3631; Web: corpuschristilansdale.org. Rev. Msgr. Thomas P. Flanigan, Ed.D.; Revs. Dennis Z. Fedak, Parochial Vicar; Shaji Silva, Parochial Vicar; Deacons B. Stephen Currie; Francis E. Langsdorf; William W. Evans; Sr. Mary Carroll McCaffrey, S.S.J., Parish Outreach.
School—Corpus Christi School, 920 Sumneytown Pike, Lansdale, 19446. Tel: 215-368-0582;
Fax: 215-361-5927; Email: ccsprin@fast.net. Lay Teachers 32; Students 539.
Catechesis Religious Program—Tel: 215-362-2292. Trish Keen, D.R.E. Students 522.

UPPER UWCHLAN, CHESTER CO., SAINT ELIZABETH (2000)
100 Saint Elizabeth Dr., Chester Springs, 19425.
Tel: 610-321-1200; Email: steuucc@stelizabethparish.org; Web: www.stelizabethparish.org. Rev. Msgr. Thomas M. Mullin, S.S.L., M.A., M.Div.; Rev. John P. Stokely, Parochial Vicar; Deacons James T. McAvoy; Barry R. Midwood; Kevin T. Mead.
Res.: 115 St. Elizabeth Dr., Chester Springs, 19425.
Tel: 610-321-9616.
School—St. Elizabeth School, 120 Saint Elizabeth Dr., P.O. Box 780, Uwchlan, 19480-0780.
Tel: 610-646-6540; Fax: 610-646-6541; Email: dgreco@stelizabethparish.org. Dr. Diane Greco, Ed. D., Prin. Students 365.
Catechesis Religious Program—Tel: 610-646-6545; Email: religiousred@stelizabethparish.org. Students 650.

VILLANOVA, DELAWARE CO., ST. THOMAS OF VILLANOVA PARISH (1848)
1229 E. Lancaster Ave., Rosemont, 19010.
Tel: 610-525-4801, Ext. 210; Web: www.stthomasofvillanova.org. Revs. Joseph A. Genito, O.S.A.; Michael Hughes, O.S.A., Parochial Vicar; Allan Fitzgerald, O.S.A., In Res.; Deacon Donald P. DiCarlo Jr.
Res.: 1242 Montrose Ave., Rosemont, 19010.
Child Care—St. Thomas of Villanova Preschool, 1236 Montrose Ave., Rosemont, 19010.
Tel: 610-525-7554; Fax: 610-525-6041.
Catechesis Religious Program—Students 308.

WALLINGFORD, DELAWARE CO., ST. JOHN CHRYSOSTOM (1952)
617 S. Providence Rd., Wallingford, 19086.
Tel: 610-874-3418; Email: phoffice@sjcparish.org; Web: www.sjcparish.org. Rev. Edward J. Hallinan; Deacons John R. Bowie; Raymond Vadino.
School—Mother of Providence Regional Catholic School, 607 S. Providence Rd., Wallingford, 19086.
Tel: 610-876-7110; Fax: 610-876-5923; Web: www.mpregional.org. Lay Teachers 21; Students 253.
Catechesis Religious Program—Email: mpizzano@sjcparish.org. Mary Pizzano, D.R.E. Students 405.

WARMINSTER, BUCKS CO., NATIVITY OF OUR LORD (1956)
625 W. Street Rd., Warminster, 18974.
Tel: 215-675-1925. Revs. Joseph G. Watson, M.Div., M.A.; Addisalem T. Mekonnen, Parochial Vicar; David M. Friel, M.A., M.Div., In Res.
School—Nativity of Our Lord School, (Grades PreK-8), 585 W. Street Rd., Warminster, 18974.
Tel: 215-675-2820; Fax: 215-675-9413; Email: rmaddaloni@noolp.org. Lay Teachers 28; Students 493.
Catechesis Religious Program—Tel: 215-672-5316;
Fax: 215-675-9413. Students 215.
Convent—605 W. Street Rd., Warminster, 18974.
Tel: 215-672-0147.

WARRINGTON, BUCKS CO.

1—ST. JOSEPH (1922)
1795 Columbia Ave., Warrington, 18976.
Tel: 215-672-3020; Fax: 215-672-3114; Web: www.saintjosephchurch.us. Rev. Joseph C. Bordonaro, D.Min.
See St. Joseph-St. Robert Bellarmine School, Warrington under Regional Parish Schools located in the Institution section.
Catechesis Religious Program—Tel: 215-672-9990. Mrs. Cathy Cain, D.R.E. Students 177.

2—ST. ROBERT BELLARMINE (1968)
856 Euclid Ave., Warrington, 18976.
Tel: 215-343-0315; Email: strobertsecretary@verizon.net; Web: www.saintrobertwarrington.org. Rev. Msgr. James D. Beisel, M.A., M.Div.; Rev. Matthew Biedrzycki, Parochial Vicar; Deacon George E. Morris Jr.
School - See St. Joseph-St. Robert Bellarmine School, Warrington under Regional Parish Schools located in the Institution section.
Catechesis Religious Program—850 Euclid Ave., Warrington, 18976. Tel: 215-343-9433; Email: donnaheeneydre@gmail.com. Donna Heeney, D.R.E. Students 350.

WAYNE, CHESTER CO., ST. ISAAC JOGUES (1970)
50 W. Walker Rd., Wayne, 19087. Tel: 610-687-3366;
Fax: 610-293-9529; Email: rectory@stisaac.org; Web: www.stisaac.org. Rev. Stephen A. Moerman; Deacon Daniel E. Mazurek.
Catechesis Religious Program—Tel: 610-687-2481; Email: sijccd@gmail.com. Louis M. Valenti, D.R.E. Students 195.
Youth Ministry—Tel: 610-254-9106; Email: sijyouth@gmail.com.

WAYNE, DELAWARE CO., ST. KATHARINE OF SIENA (1893)
104 S. Aberdeen Ave., Wayne, 19087.
Tel: 610-688-4584; Fax: 610-688-7951; Web: www.sksparish.org. Rev. Msgrs. Hans A.L. Brouwers, M.A., M.Div.; Michael J. Carroll, M.A., In Res., (Retired); Mrs. Colleen Maguire, Dir. Parish Life Min.
School—St. Katharine of Siena School, (Grades K-8), 116 S. Aberdeen Ave., Wayne, 19087.
Tel: 610-688-5451; Fax: 610-688-6796. Frank Tosti, Prin. Lay Teachers 30; Students 390.
Catechesis Religious Program—Tel: 610-688-7890; Email: religioused@sksparish.org. Sr. Mary Elizabeth Karalis, S.S.J., D.R.E. Students 278.
Convent—235 Windermere Ave., Wayne, 19087.
Tel: 610-688-0655; Email: srkathleen@sksparish.org. Sisters 5.

WEST BRANDYWINE, CHESTER CO., ST. PETER (1963)
2835 Manor Rd., West Brandywine, 19320.
Tel: 610-380-9045; Email: stpeterchesco@comcast.net; Web: saintpeterchurch.net. Revs. Michael J. Fitzpatrick, M.S., M.Div.; Emmanuel K. Iheaka, In Res.; Deacon H.W. Todd Smith.
Res.: 284 Vincent Dr., Honey Brook, 19344.
See Pope John Paul II Regional Catholic Elementary School, West Brandywine under Regional Parish Schools located in the Institution section.
Parish Religious Education Program—2875 Manor Rd., West Brandywine. Tel: 610-384-3145. Patrice A. Peterson, D.R.E. Students 478.

WEST CHESTER, CHESTER CO.

1—ST. AGNES (1793) [CEM]
233 W. Gay St., West Chester, 19380.
Tel: 610-692-2990; Fax: 610-692-9623; Email: info@saintagnesparish.org; Web: saintagnesparish.org. Revs. William G. Donovan, M.Div., Ph.L., Ph.D.; Wilfred Emeh, Parochial Vicar; David A. Waters, Parochial Vicar; Deacons Dwight Johnson; Thomas E. Shurer.
School—St. Agnes School, 211 W. Gay St., West Chester, 19380. Tel: 610-696-1260;
Fax: 610-436-9631. Lay Teachers 30; Sisters, Servants of the Immaculate Heart of Mary 1; Students 360.
Catechesis Religious Program—207 W. Gay St., West Chester, 19380. Tel: 610-436-4640;
Fax: 610-719-1961. Students 590.
Convent—205 W. Gay St., West Chester, 19380.
Tel: 610-692-9430.

2—ST. MAXIMILIAN KOLBE (1986)
15 E. Pleasant Grove Rd., West Chester, 19382.
Tel: 610-399-6936; Email: saintmax@comcast.net; Web: www.stmax.org. Rev. Msgr. Robert J. Carroll, M.Div.; Revs. Matthew Windle, Parochial Vicar; Thomas J. Gardner, M.Div., In Res.; Deacons William L. Hickey; Alfred Mauriello.
School—St. Maximilian Kolbe School, (Grades PreK-8), 300 Daly Dr., West Chester, 19382.
Tel: 610-399-8400; Fax: 610-399-4684. Monica Malseed, Prin.
Catechesis Religious Program—Tel: 610-399-9642; Email: smk-prep@stmax.org. Mrs. Roberta Dainton, D.R.E.

3—SS. SIMON AND JUDE (1961) Revs. Michael J. Gerlach; James R. DeGrassa; Rt. Rev. Ronald J. Rossi, O.Praem., Senior Priest; Mr. Ronald B. Avellino, Business Mgr.; Deacons James T. Owens; Joseph A. Ruggiero; C. William Shearer.
Res.: 8 Cavanaugh Ct., West Chester, 19382.
Tel: 610-696-3624; Fax: 610-696-3971; Email: rectory@simonandjude.org; Web: www.simonandjude.org.
School—SS. Simon and Jude School, (Grades PreK-8), 6 Cavanaugh Ct., West Chester, 19382.
Tel: 610-696-5249; Fax: 610-696-4682; Email: ssjschool@simonandjude.org; Web: school.simonandjude.org. Sr. Regina Elinich, I.H.M., Prin. Lay Teachers 27; Sisters, Servants of the Immaculate Heart of Mary 4; Students 366.
Catechesis Religious Program—Tel: 610-692-3118. Sisters Barbara Jude Gentry, I.H.M., D.R.E.; Mary Beth Coyle, Coord. Evangelization & Adult Faith Formation. Students 440.
Convent—Tel: 610-692-4394.

WEST CONSHOHOCKEN, MONTGOMERY CO., ST. GERTRUDE (1888-2014) Closed. Formerly located at 209 Merion Ave., Conshohocken. Spiritual records are kept at St. Matthew Church, Conshohocken. Tel: 610-828-0424.

WEST GROVE, CHESTER CO., ASSUMPTION B.V.M. (1873) [CEM]
300 State Rd., West Grove, 19390. Tel: 610-869-2722;
Email: abvm@comcast.net; Web: www.assumptionbvmwestgrove.org. Rev. Scott D. Brockson, M.A., M.Div.; Rev. Msgr. Francis J. Depman, In

Res.; Deacons Ronald L. Lewis; Thomas Hannan; Michael DeGrasse; Rose Mary Edwards, Operations Mgr.
School—Assumption B.V.M. School, 290 State Rd., West Grove, 19390. Tel: 610-869-9576; Fax: 610-869-4049; Email: assumptionwestgrove@comcast.net. Danielle White, Prin. Lay Teachers 16; Students 184.
Catechesis Religious Program—Tel: 610-869-8575. Teresa Leszczynski, C.R.E. Students 412.

WILLOW GROVE, MONTGOMERY CO., ST. DAVID (1919)
316 N. Easton Rd., Willow Grove, 19090.
Tel: 215-657-0252; Email: stdavidparish@comcast.net. Revs. Richard P. Connors, M.Div.; Timothy M. Judge, M.Div., In Res.; Deacon Christopher J. Mars.
School—Queen of Angels Regional Catholic School, (Grades PreK-8), 401 N. Easton Rd., Willow Grove, 19090. Tel: 215-659-6393; Fax: 215-659-6377; Email: qoaschool@qoaschool.org; Web: www.qoaschool.org. Sr. Margaret Rose Adams, I.H.M., Prin. Lay Teachers 17; Sisters, Servants of the Immaculate Heart of Mary 3; Students 278; Religious Teachers 2.
Catechesis Religious Program—Tel: 215-659-4059. Students 298.
Convent—400 N. Easton Rd., Willow Grove, 19090. Tel: 215-659-0445.

WYNDMOOR, MONTGOMERY CO., SEVEN DOLORS (1916-2003) Closed. Formerly located at 1200 E. Willow Grove Ave. Spiritual records are kept at St. Genevieve Church, Flourtown. Tel: 215-836-2828.

WYNNEWOOD, MONTGOMERY CO., PRESENTATION B.V.M. (1954)
204 Haverford Rd., Wynnewood, 19096.
Tel: 610-642-8341; Email: parishcenter@presbvm.org; Web: www.presbvm.org. Rev. Eduardo G. Montero, J.C.L., M.Div.; Deacon Ernest W. Angiolillo.
Parish Center: 240 Haverford Rd., Wynnewood, 19096. Tel: 610-642-2919.
Catechesis Religious Program—Students 92.

YARDLEY, BUCKS CO., ST. IGNATIUS OF ANTIOCH (1920) [CEM] [JC]
999 Reading Ave., Yardley, 19067. Tel: 215-493-3377 ; Fax: 215-493-0450; Email: contact@stignatius.church; Web: www.stignatius.church. Rev. Andrew C. Brownholtz, M.Div.; Deacon Michael L. Cibenko.
School—St. Ignatius of Antioch School, 995 Reading Ave., Yardley, 19067. Tel: 215-493-3867; Fax: 267-573-3550; Web: www.sischool.org. Lay Staff 34; Students 269.
Catechesis Religious Program—Tel: 215-493-5204; Fax: 215-493-0956. Students 457.

YEADON, DELAWARE CO., ST. LOUIS (1928-2013) Closed. W. Cobbs Creek Pkwy. Spiritual records are kept at Blessed Virgin Mary Church, Darby. Tel: 610-583-2128. Worship site for Blessed Virgin Mary Church, Darby.

Chaplains of Public Institutions

PHILADELPHIA. *Philadelphia Federal Detention Center*, 700 Arch St., 19106. Tel: 215-521-4000. Rev. Benjamin R. Regotti, O.F.M.Cap.
Philadelphia Prison System, 8001 State Rd., 19136. Tel: 215-276-2288. Rev. Philip A. White Jr., O.F.M.Cap.
Veterans Administration Medical Center, University & Woodland Aves., 19104. Tel: 215-823-5800, Ext. 2776. Rev. Ukachukwu Onyeabor.

COATESVILLE. *Veterans Administration Medical Center*, Coatesville, 19320. Tel: 215-384-7711, Ext. 190. Revs. Semanhyia Boateng-Mensah, Emmanuel K. Iheaka.

GRATERFORD. *Graterford State Correctional Institution*, Graterford, 19426. Tel: 215-489-4151. Rev. John J. Pidgeon, M.Div.

NORRISTOWN. *Norristown State Hospital*, Norristown, 19401. Tel: 215-270-1104. Vacant.

SPRING CITY. *Southeastern Pennsylvania Veterans Center*, Spring City, 19475. Tel: 215-948-2400. Rev. John J. Sibel, Ph.D., M.Div., Chap., (Retired).

On Special or Other Archdiocesan Assignment:
Most Revs.—
Deliman, Edward M., D.D., 357 Dorrance St., Bristol, 19020
Fitzgerald, Michael J., D.D., J.C.D., J.D., 222 N. 17th St., 19103
McIntyre, John J., D.D., 222 N. 17th St., 19103
Senior, Timothy C., D.D., M.S.W., M.B.A., 100 E. Wynnewood Rd., Wynnewood, 19096
Rev. Msgrs.—
Britto, Federico A., M.Div., M.A., Dean, Deanery 9, St. Cyprian Rectory, 525 Cobbs Creek Pkwy., 19143
Brouwers, Hans A.L., M.A., M.Div., Dean, Deanery 2, St. Katharine of Siena Rectory, 104 S. Aberdeen Ave., Wayne, 19087
Corley, Joseph M., M.S., M.Div., Dean, Deanery 1, Blessed Virgin Mary Rectory, 1101 Main St., Darby, 19023
DiGirolamo, Paul A., J.C.D., M.A., M.Div., Judicial Vicar, Metropolitan Tribunal, Old St. Mary's Rectory, 252 S. Fourth St., 19106
Dougherty, Paul V., M.Div., M.A., Chap., Apostolate to Deaf Persons, St. Margaret Rectory, 208 N. Narberth Ave., Narberth, 19072
Kutys, Daniel J., M.Div., V.G., Mod., Curia, St. Dorothy Rectory, 4910 Township Line Rd., Drexel Hill, 19026
Logrip, Joseph L., M.A., M.Div., Chap., Camilla Hall, P.O. Box 100, Immaculata, 19345
Marine, John C., M.Div., Dean, Deanery 10, St. Bede The Venerable Rectory, 1071 Holland Rd., Holland, 18966
McCulken, Michael T., M.Div., Episcopal Vicar, St. Eleanor Rectory, 647 Locust St., Collegeville, 19426
Mesure, Gerard C., J.D., J.C.D., M.A., Chancellor, Office of the Chancellor, St. Matthias Rectory, 128 Bryn Mawr Ave., Bala Cynwyd, 19004
Mullin, Thomas M., S.S.L., M.A., M.Div., Dean, Deanery 4, St. Elizabeth Rectory, 115 Saint Elizabeth Dr., Chester Springs, 19425
Nicolo, Joseph J., M.Div., Dean, Deanery 5, St. Helena Rectory, 1489 DeKalb Pike, Blue Bell, 19422
Rodgers, Arthur E., Ph.D., Dir., Society for the Propagation of the Faith, (Retired), 1901 John F. Kennedy Blvd., Unit 2817, 19103
Strausser, George L., M.Div., Chap., Univ. City Hospitals, St. Francis De Sales Rectory, 4625 Springfield Ave., 19143
Sullivan, Daniel J., M.Div., Vicar for Clergy, Sisters of Mercy Convent, 515 Montgomery Ave., Merion Station, 19066
Trinh, Joseph T., Ed.D., M.Div., Coord., Vietnamese Apostolate, St. Helena Rectory, 6161 N. 5th St., 19120
Vance, Charles P., M.Div., Dean, Deanery 7, St. Philip Neri Rectory, 437 Ridge Pike, Lafayette Hill, 19444
Revs.—
Babowitch, John F., M.Div., Dean, Deanery 11, Our Lady of Calvary Rectory, 11024 Knights Rd., 19154
Bransfield, Sean P., J.C.L., M.A., M.Div., Vice Chancellor, St. Matthias Rectory, 128 Bryn Mawr Ave., Bala Cynwyd, 19004
Cioppi, Martin T., Ed.D., M.A., M.Div., Dean, Deanery 6, Mother of Divine Providence Rectory, 333 Allendale Rd., King of Prussia, 19406
Cossavella, Anthony J., M.Div., Chap., Saint John Neumann Center for Rehabilitation & Healthcare, St. Albert Rectory, 212 Welsh Rd., Huntingdon Valley, 19006
Dean, William E., M.Div., Chap., Camilla Hall, Camilla Hall, P.O. Box 100, Immaculata, 19345
DeLacy, Stephen P., M.A., M.Div., Dir., Vocation Office Diocesan Priesthood, St. Bridget Rectory, 3667 Midvale Ave., 19129-1712
Esmilla, Efren V., M.Div., Deanery 12, Our Lady of Hope Rectory, 5200 N. Broad St., 19141-1628. Chaplain, Filipino Apostolate
Fitzpatrick, Michael J., M.S., M.Div., Dean, Deanery 3, St. Peter Rectory, 2835 Manor Rd., West Brandywine, 19320
Gabin, John D., M.S.W., M.Div., Chap., St. Francis Center for Rehabilitation & Healthcare, 500 Woodlawn Ave., Collingdale, 19023
Gardner, Thomas J., M.Div., Newman Chap., West Chester University, St. Maximilian Kolbe Rectory, 15 E. Pleasant Grove Rd., West Chester, 19382
Gill, Gerald Dennis, M.Div., S.L.L., Dir., Office for Worship, Cathedral Basilica SS. Peter and Paul, 1723 Race St., 19103
Gleason, Joseph F., M.Div., M.S., M.A., Chap., Lankenau and Bryn Mawr Hospitals, 100 E. Wynnewood Rd., Wynnewood, 19096
Gleason, Laurence J., M.A., M.Div., Chap., Holy Redeemer Health Systems, St. Hilary of Poitiers Rectory, 820 Susquehanna Rd., Rydal, 19046
Guckin, Matthew W., M.A., M.Div., Dir., Catholic Mission & Identity Secondary & Collegiate Educ., St. Patrick Margaret Rectory, 208 N. Narberth Ave., Narberth, 19072
Hunt, Mark J., S.T.L., S.T.D., Prof., Holy Family Univ. - Newtown Campus, St. John Bosco Rectory, 235 E. County Line Rd., Hatboro, 19040
Ishaq, Dominic, J.C.D., Office of the Metropolitan Tribunal, Our Lady of Peace Rectory, 501 Belmont Ave., Milmont Park, 19033
Janicki, Carl F., Dir. Campus Ministry, Cabrini College, Saint Genevieve Rectory, 1225 Bethlehem Pike, Flourtown, 19031
Judge, Timothy M., M.Div., Chap., Holy Redeemer Health Systems, St. David Rectory, 316 N. Easton Rd., Willow Grove, 19090
Kelley, Joseph J., M.A., M.Div., Dean, Deanery 8, St. Monica Rectory, 2422 S. 17th St., 19145
Lowe, Philip J., Ed.D., Faculty - Neumann College, SS. Simon and Jude Rectory, 8 Cavanaugh Ct., West Chester, 19382
Mahoney, Shaun L., S.T.D., M.Div., Newman Chap., Temple Univ., Catholic Center for Young Adults, 244 Fitzwater St., 19147
McCabe, Kevin P., M.A., M.Div., Chap., Immaculata University, 1145 King Rd., Immaculata, 19345
McKay, Douglas M., Chap., Our House of Ministries, 1439 S. 29th St., 19146
Montero, Eduardo G., J.C.L., M.Div., Asst. Judicial Vicar, Office Metropolitan Tribunal, Presentation B.V.M. Rectory, 204 Haverford Rd., Wynnewood, 19096
Moriconi, Christopher C., M.A., M.Div., Admin. Sec., Office of the Archbishop, 100 E. Wynnewood Rd., Wynnewood, 19096
Mulranen, Francis J., M.Div., Chap., St. Martha Center for Rehabilitation & Healthcare, St. Joseph Rectory, 460 Manor Ave., Downingtown, 19335
Murphy, William S., Coord., Mother of Mary House, Kensington, 709-711 E. Allegheny Ave., 19134
Navit, Zachary W., M.A., M.Div., Chap., Our Lady of Guadalupe Rectory, 5175 Cold Spring Creamery Rd., Doylestown, 18902. St. Stanislaus Rectory, 51 Lansdale Ave., Lansdale, 19446. St. Mary Center for Rehabilitation & Healthcare
O'Donnell, Dennis J.W., Ph.D., Dir., Holy Redeemer Wellness Center, Saint Christopher Rectory, 13301 Proctor Rd., 19116
Pesarchick, Robert A., M.A., S.T.L., S.T.D., Vice Pres. for Academic Affairs, Systematic Theology, St. Charles Borromeo Seminary Overbrook, 100 E. Wynnewood Rd., Wynnewood, 19096
Pidgeon, John J., M.Div., Chap., Graterford Correctional Institute, St. Teresa of Calcutta, 256 Swamp Pike, Schwenksville, 19473
Sullivan, James F., M.Div., Chap., Holy Family Home, 5300 Chester Ave., 19143
Szparagowski, George J., M.Div., Dean of Men, College Division, St. Charles Borromeo Seminary, St. Charles Borromeo Seminary, Overbrook, 100 E. Wynnewood Rd., Wynnewood, 19096
Thorne, Stephen D., M.A., M.Div., Newman Chap., Neumann University, St. Martin de Porres Rectory, 2340 W. Lehigh Ave., 19132
Trinh, Quan M., M.A., M.Div., Chap., Vietnamese Apostolate, Delaware County, St. Laurence Rectory, 30 St. Laurence Rd., Upper Darby, 19082.

On Duty Outside the Archdiocese:
Rev. Msgrs.—
Bransfield, J. Brian, M.Div., M.A., S.T.L., U.S.C.C.B. Secretariat of Evangelization and Catechesis, 3211 4th St., N.E., Washington, DC 20017
McManus, Gerald D., M.Div., U.S. Air Force, 1835 Harmony Heights Ln., Rapid City, SD 57702
Revs.—
Bochanski, Philip G., C.O., M.A., M.Div., Assoc. Dir., St. Catherine of Siena Church, 2220 Shelton Rd., Trumbull, CT 06611. Courage International
Burns, Vincent P., Glenmary Home Missioners, P.O. Box 465618, Cincinnati, OH 45246
DiMaria, Peter J., M.Div., Saint Meinrad Seminary and School of Theology, 200 Hill Dr., Saint Meinrad, IN 47577
Funk, Peter C., (Retired), Diocese of Beaumont, 9920 N. Major Dr., Beaumont, TX 77713
Hamill, Gregory J., M.A., M.Div., Abbey of the Genesee, 3258 River Rd., Piffard, NY 14533
Kelly, Michael J., M.A., Dir. of Spiritual Formation, Pontifical College Josephinum, 7625 N. High, St., Columbus, OH 43235. Pontifical College Josephinum, 7625 N. High St., Columbus, OH 43235
Lee, Jaehwa John, M.S., M.Div., Diocese of Cheju, Hwabuk Catholic Church, Chungpungnam 8 Gil 14, Jeju Shi, Jeju Do, Seoul, Korea, South
Marczewski, Robert, S.T.L., M.Div., Thomas Aquinas College, 10000 Ojai Rd., Santa Paula, CA 93060
McGoldrick, Kevin B., M.A., M.Div., Chap., Saint Cecilia Academy and Overbrook School, 4210 Harding Pike, Nashville, TN 37205
Oliver, James M., J.C.D., Congregation for the Clergy, Rome, Italy.

Military Chaplains:
Revs.—
Coffey, Joseph L.
Foley, Francis P.
Lea, Joseph P.
McDermott, Stephen C.

Graduate Studies:
Revs.—
Friel, David M., M.A., M.Div., Catholic Univ. of America, Washington D.C., Curley Hall,

Washington, D.C., 20064. Catholic University of America, Curley Hall, Washington, DC 20064
Gibbs, Alexander R., M.A., M.Div., Gregorian University, 4 Piazza della Pilotta, Rome, Italy 00187
McFadden, Richard K., Casa Santa Maria, Via Dell'Umilta, 30, Rome, Italy
Viviano, Thomas A., M.A., M.Div., Pontificial University of St. Thomas (Angelicum), 1 Largo Angelicum, Rome, Italy 00184.

Absent On Sick Leave:
Revs.—
Kunigonis, Mark S.
Morabito, Vincent R., M.Div.

Absent On Leave:.

Retired:
Rev. Msgrs.—
Benz, David H., M.Div., (Retired), 2615 N.E. 3rd Ct., #304, Boynton Beach, FL 33435
Bolger, Richard T., M.A., M.Div., (Retired), Regina Coeli Residence for Priests, 685 York Rd., Warminster, 18974
Breslin, John E., (Retired), Saint Joseph's Manor, 1616 Huntingdon Pike, Meadowbrook, 19046
Carbine, Francis A., M.A., (Retired), Villa St. Joseph, 1436 Lansdowne Ave., Darby, 19023-1218
Carroll, Michael J., M.A., (Retired), Saint Katherine of Siena Rectory, 104 S. Aberdeen Ave., Wayne, 19087
Conahan, John J., (Retired), Osprey Point #13, 1731 U.S. Rte. 9 S., Ocean View, NJ 08230
Connelly, James E., S.T.L., H.E.D., (Retired), Villa St. Joseph, 1436 Lansdowne Ave., Danvers, MA 1923-1218
Cribben, Philip J., M.S., (Retired), 219 Sugartown Rd., R-301, Wayne, 19087
Curran, Paul F., Ph.D., M.A., (Retired), St. Joseph's Manor, 1616 Huntingdon Pike, Meadowbook, 19046
D'Addezio, Louis A., M.A., (Retired), Cathedral Basilica SS. Peter & Paul, 1723 Race St., 19103
Dreger, Francis X., (Retired), 2700 W. Brigantine Ave., Brigantine, NJ 08203
Flood, J. Michael, M.Div., (Retired), Regina Coeli Residence for Priests, 685 York Rd., Warminster, 18974
Graf, John W., M.Div., (Retired), 481 Robbins St., 19111
Grudowski, Robert J., (Retired), Holy Redeemer Lafayette, 8560 Verree Rd., Room 673, 19111
Jagodzinski, John J., M.A., (Retired), Saint Pius X Rectory, 220 Lawrence Rd., Broomall, 19008
Malone, Richard, M.A., J.C.L., S.T.D., (Retired), Our Lady of Assumption Rectory, 35 Old Eagle School Rd., Strafford, 19087
McBride, James P., (Retired), 10 E. Maple St., Tresckow, 18254
McCoy, James P., M.A., (Retired), Regina Coeli Residence for Priests, 685 York Rd., Warminster, 18974
McDonough, James T., M.S.W., L.L.D., (Retired), Villa St. Joseph, 1436 Lansdowne Ave., Darby, 19023-1218. Tel: 215-587-3944
McGeown, Joseph P., M.A., (Retired), Nativity B.V.M. Rectory, 30 E. Franklin St., Media, 19063
McGroarty, Charles E., M.A., S.T.L., (Retired), St. Joseph Rectory, 500 Woodlawn Ave., Collingdale, 19023
Mortimer, James E., M.Ed., (Retired), Villa Saint Joseph, 1436 Lansdowne Ave., Darby, 19023-1218
Murray, Ignatius L., (Retired), Villa St. Joseph, 1436 Lansdowne Ave., Darby, 19023-1218
Murray, Joseph W., M.A., (Retired), Regina Nursing Center, 550 E. Fornance St., Norristown, 19401
Murray, Thomas A., (Retired), St. Eleanor Rectory, 647 Locust St., Collegeville, 19426-2541
O'Brien, John F., (Retired), Villa Saint Joseph, 1436 Landsdowne Ave., Darby, 19023-1298
O'Donnell, William J. J., M.A., (Retired), Regina Coeli Residence for Priests, 685 York Rd., Warminster, 18974
Owens, Thomas J., M.A., M.Div., (Retired), St. Matthew Rectory, 219 Fayette St., Conshohocken, 19428
Ricci, Philip C., (Retired), P.O. Box 371, Conshohocken, 19428
Rodgers, Arthur E., Ph.D., (Retired), 1901 John F. Kennedy Blvd., Unit 2817, 19103
Schmidt, Francis X., (Retired), Villa Saint Joseph, 1436 Lansdowne Ave., Darby, 19023-1218
Trinity, Bernard J., (Retired), Saint Denis Rectory, 2401 Saint Denis Ln., Havertown, 19083
Revs.—
Amalfitano, Joseph A., (Retired), Sunrise of Newtown Sq., 333 S. Newtown St. Rd., Newtown Square, 19073
Bartos, Francis J., (Retired), Villa Saint Joseph, 1436 Lansdowne Ave., Darby, 19023-1298
Benonis, Richard R., (Retired), St. Margaret of Scotland Rectory, P.O. Box 1359, Maggie Valley, NC 28751
Boyle, Dennis P., (Retired), 8580 Verree Rd., Rm. 349, 19111
Bradley, John J., (Retired), Villa St. Joseph, 1436 Lansdowne Ave., Darby, 19023-1218
Buccafurni, Ferdinand, (Retired), St. Colman Rectory, 11 Simpson Rd., Ardmore, 19003-2812
Burke, Edward P., Ed.D., M.Div., M.A., (Retired), Villa St. Joseph, 1436 Lansdowne Ave., Darby, 19023-1218
Canavan, Gerald D., M.Div., (Retired), 501 Belmont Ave., Milmont Park, 19033
Chapman, Robert J., (Retired), St. John Neumann Rectory, 380 Highland Ln., Bryn Mawr, 19010
Chiaravalle, Dominic M., (Retired), Villa St. Joseph, 1436 Lansdowne Ave., Darby, 19023-1218
Collins, John P., M.Div., M.A., (Retired), St. Charles Borromeo Seminary, 100 E. Wynnewood Rd., Wynnewood, 19096
Concha, Augusto M., (Retired), St. William Rectory, 6200 Rising Sun Ave., 19111
Cornely, Francis J., (Retired), Regina Coeli Residence for Priests, 685 York Rd., Warminster, 18974
Crowe, George W., (Retired), Saint John Vianney Center, 151 Woodbine Rd., Downingtown, 19335
Cusatis, Girard J., (Retired), St. Andrew Rectory, 3500 School Ln., Drexel Hill, 19026
Dieckhaus, Anthony W., (Retired), 8580 Verree Rd. Apt. 212, 19111
DiGregorio, Joseph L., (Retired), 600 Sheridan Blvd., Brigantine, NJ 08203
Donnelly, William P., (Retired), Villa St. Joseph, 1436 Landsdowne Ave., Darby, 19023-1298
Dooner, William B., M.Div., (Retired), St. Philip Neri Rectory, 437 Ridge Pike, Lafayette Hill, 19444
Dougherty, Daniel J., (Retired), 2514 Parke Ln., Broomall, 19008-244
Dougherty, Hugh J., M.Div., (Retired), St. Bernadette Rectory, 1035 Turner Ave., Drexel Hill, 19026
Duffy, Thomas J., (Retired), Regina Coeli Residence for Priests, 685 York Rd., Warminster, 18974
Endres, James F., M.Div., (Retired), 155 Lakewood Dr., Dingmans Ferry, 18328
Farley, Bernard C., (Retired), 4000 Gypsy Ln., Apt. 238, 19129
Farry, John J., M.Div., (Retired), Village of Buckingham Springs, 63 Wild Briar Ct., New Hope, 18938
Ferrier, Ronald J., M.A., (Retired), St. Katherine of Siena Rectory, 9700 Frankford Ct., 19114-2896
Foley, Peter J., M.A., (Retired), Villa Saint Joseph, 1436 Lansdowne Ave., Darby, 19023-1218
Franey, John A., (Retired), P.O. Box 336, Perryville, MD 21903
Funk, Peter C., (Retired), 9920 N. Major Dr., Beaumont, TX 77713-7618
Furey, Thomas J., M.Div., (Retired), Villa St. Joseph, 1436 Lansdowne Ave., Darby, 19023-1218
Gallagher, Francis M., M.A., (Retired), 7 Greystone Rd., Ambler, 19002-5209
Genuardi, Gasper A., (Retired), 12 Dogwood Knoll, Lansdale, 19446
Gormley, James W., (Retired), Villa St. Joseph, 1436 Lansdowne Ave., Darby, 19023-1298
Grant, James A., J.C.L., (Retired), Villa Saint Joseph, 1436 Lansdowne Ave., Darby, 19023-1218
Harkins, John M., M.A., (Retired), Villa St. Joseph, 1436 Lansdowne Ave., Darby, 19023-1218
Himsworth, Raymond J., (Retired), 3218 Waterstreet Rd., Collegeville, 19426
Hutchins, H. James, (Retired), P.O. Box 264, Pomona, NJ 08240-0264
Jablonski, Edward J., M.Div., (Retired), 1621 Interlachen Rd., 265-H, Seal Beach, CA 90740
Jung, Joseph B., (Retired), Villa Saint Joseph, 1436 Lansdowne Ave., Darby, 19023-1298
Kelly, Edward J., (Retired), Regina Coeli Residence for Priests, 685 York Rd., Warminster, 18974
Kelly, Francis E., (Retired), 4972 Skippack Pike, P.O. Box 259, Creamery, 19430-0259
Kelly, James J., (Retired), Normandy Farms Estates, 1204 Twin Silo Dr., Apt. 204, Blue Bell, 19422
Kennedy, Charles J., M.Div., (Retired), Divine Word Missionaries, 101 Park St., P.O. Box 357, Bordentown, NJ 08505
Kilgallon, John J., M.Div., Our Lady of Good Counsel Rectory, 611 Knowles Ave., Southampton, 18966-4198
Kloda, Marshall J., M.Div., (Retired), Villa St. Joseph, 1436 Lansdowne Ave., Darby, 19023-1218
Locke, James E., (Retired), 31 Ocean Rd., Ocean City, NJ 08226
Lonergan, Michael J., J.D., M.A., M.Div., (Retired), Our Lady Fatima Rectory, 1 Fatima Dr., Secane, 19018-4640
Lyons, John T., (Retired), St. Genevieve Rectory, 1225 Bethlehem Pke., Flourtown, 19031-1902
Machain, David B., (Retired), Holy Redeemer Lafayette, 8580 Verree Rd. Apt. 348, 19111
Maisano, Richard J., M.A., M.Div., (Retired), 1118 Alexander Ave., Drexel Hill, 19026
Maloney, Wilfred F., (Retired), 1007 Fownes Ave., Brigantine, NJ 08203
Marneni, Ignatius, (Retired), St. George Rectory, 22 E. Cooke Ave., Glenolden, 19036-1497
McAndrews, Richard J., M.A., (Retired), Villa Saint Joseph, 1436 Lansdowne Ave., Darby, 19023-1218
McBride, John F., (Retired), St. Andrew Rectory, 81 Swamp Rd., Newtown, 18940
McCloskey, Joseph W., (Retired), Villa St. Joseph, 1436 Lansdowne Ave., Darby, 19023-1298
McElroy, Charles J., M.S., (Retired), St. Joseph Rectory, 16 S. Spring Garden St., Ambler, 19002-4797
McFadden, John R., (Retired), 100 Markham Way, P.O. Box 1383, Albrightsville, 18210
McKeaney, James J., M.Div., (Retired), St. Matthew Rectory, 219 Fayette St., Conshohocken, 19428
McKee, Francis X., (Retired), Villa St. Joseph, 1436 Lansdowne Ave., Darby, 19023-1218
McNamara, Donald P., (Retired), 2035 Arrowhead Tr., Coatesville, 19320
McNamee, John P., (Retired), The Philadelphian, 2401 Pennsylvania Ave., Apt. 17B27, 19130
Meehan, Joseph J., M.S., (Retired), St. Francis of Assisi Rectory, 136 Saxer Ave., Springfield, 19064-2333
Mulgrew, John E., M.A., (Retired), Nativity B.V.M. Rectory, 30 E. Franklin St., Media, 19063
Mulligan, James J., M.A., S.T.L., (Retired), Villa St. Joseph, 1436 Lansdowne Ave., Darby, 19023-1218
Noone, Charles J., M.A., (Retired), St. Timothy Rectory, 3001 Levick St., 19149
Obrimski, Paul, (Retired), Cathedral Village, 600 E. Cathedral Rd., 19128
Oulds, John V., (Retired), Villa St. Joseph, 1436 Lansdowne Ave., Darby, 19023-1218
Pelczar, Edward A., (Retired), Saint Helena Rectory, 6161 N. 5th St., 19120-1422
Peterson, Leonard N., M.A., (Retired), 5 Oaks Ct., Mays Landing, NJ 08330
Pronesti, Salvatore J., M.Ed, (Retired), 28 N. Frontenac Ave., Margate City, NJ 08402
Putz, Kenneth G., (Retired), Villa St. Joseph, 1436 Lansdowne Ave., Darby, 19023-1218
Riccio, Salvatore M., (Retired), 241 London Ct., Egg Harbor Township, NJ 08234
Ronan, Gerald C., M.S.W., M.A., M.Div., (Retired), Villa Saint Joseph, 1436 Lansdowne Ave., Darby, 19023-1218
Ryan, Michael J., M.S., M.Div., (Retired), St. Jerome Rectory, 8100 Colfax St., 19136-1801
Rzonca, Michael W., M.Div., (Retired), 16 Nathan Way, P.O. Box 929, Albrightsville, 18210-0929
Sabatini, Francis J., (Retired), Holy Saviour Rectory, 407 E. Main St., Norristown, 19401-5119
Scarcia, John J., M.Div., (Retired), P.O. Box 884, Eagle Lake, FL 33839
Sharrett, Victor F., M.A., (Retired), 101 Victoria Gardens Dr., Kennett Square, 19348
Sheehan, Michael J., M.Div., M.B.A., (Retired), 239 Crittenden Dr., Newtown, 18940-1323
Shelley, John J., (Retired), C/O Rev. Msgr. Richard T. Bolger: 685 York Rd., Warminster, 18974
Sherlock, James C., (Retired), Villa Saint Joseph, 1436 Lansdowne Ave., Darby, 19023-1218
Sibel, John J., Ph.D., M.Div., (Retired), Sacred Heart Rectory, 838 Walnut St., P.O. Box 64, Royersford, 19468
Silcox, John D. Jr., J.D., M.Div., (Retired), Villa Saint Joseph, 1436 Lansdowne Ave., Darby, 19023-1218
Silveri, Donato P., M.A., (Retired), Saint Joseph Rectory, 3640 Schuylkill Rd., Spring City, 19475-1523
Small, William T., M.A., (Retired), Villa St. Joseph, 1436 Lansdowne Ave., Darby, 19023-1218
Speitel, Edmond J., (Retired), Villa St. Joseph, 1436 Lansdowne Ave., Darby, 19023-1218
Sullivan, Charles J., (Retired), Immaculate Conception Rectory, 604 West Ave., Jenkintown, 19046-2708
Tribuiani, Raymond F., M.Div., (Retired), Saint Mary Center for Rehabilitation and Healthcare, 701 Lansdale Ave., Lansdale, 19446-2900
Williams, Richard C., (Retired), Our Lady of Charity Rectory, 231 Upland Rd., Brookhaven, 19015-3124
Witalec, Dennis J., (Retired), St. Monica Rectory, 2422 S. 17th St., 19145.

Permanent Deacons:

Alexander, Michael J., Saint Madeline Church, Ridley Park
Alicea, Angel L.
Amen, Charles R.
Anderson, James Jr., Archdiocese of Atlanta, GA
Angiolillo, Ernest W., Presentation B.V.M. Church, Wynnewood
Antrim, Harry D., Diocese of Venice, FL
Arno, Michael R.
Baratta, Gaspero P.
Basilio, James A., Our Lady of Peace Church, Milmont Park
Baxter, William T., Saint Francis of Assisi Church, Springfield
Belanger, A. Kenneth
Bell, Michael J., Our Lady of Calvary Church
Bellitto, Anthony J. Jr., Saint Stanislaus Church Lansdale
Benner, Robert L., St. Agnes Church, Sellersville
Bernauer, Joseph W. Jr., Maternity B.V.M. Church
Betancourt, Jose M.
Betzal, John M., St. Joseph Church, Aston
Bianco, Salvatore R., Immaculate Heart of Mary Church
Bingnear, Daniel, St. John Fisher Church, Boothwyn
Bizal, Francis M.
Bogdan, James E., St. Joseph Church, Downingtown
Bonilla, Victor M.
Bowie, John R., Saint John Chrysostom Church, Wallingford
Bradley, William C., St. Raymond of Penafort Church
Brady, Robert F., Our Lady of Guadalupe Church, Doylestown
Browne, James E., Holy Family Church
Burghart, Peter H.
Burke, Francis B.
Burns, Robert C., St. Matthew Church
Calabrese, Peter J., Archdiocese of Baltimore, MD
Campbell, John J.
Carr, Joseph C., St. Matthew Church, Conshohocken
Carrillo, Andres A., Holy Innocents Church
Catanese, Ralph M.
Cavaliere, Francis M.
Cella, William A., Presentation B.V.M. Church, Cheltenham
Ceneviva, Vincent G., Our Lady of Sacred Heart Church, Hilltown
Chavac, Cristobal, St. Thomas Aquinas Church
Cibenko, Michael L., Saint Ignatius Church, Yardley
Cincotta, Anthony J., St. Thomas the Apostle Church, Glen Mills
Clancy, Kenneth P.
Clay, Alvin A., Immaculate Conception Church, Jenkintown
Colgan, Francis M.
Concitis, Thomas C., Diocese of Orange, CA
Connors, Francis J., Saint Dennis Church, Havertown
Conroy, Michael G., St. Genevieve Church, Flourtown
Corwell, George V., Our Lady of Mt. Carmel Church, Doylestown
Coyne, Richard C.
Crespo, Adolfo, St. Charles Borromeo Church, Bensalem
Croke, Thomas M., St. Luke the Evangelist Church, Glenside
Cruz, Felipe, St. William Church, Philadelphia
Cuff, Edward M., St. Anthony of Padua Church, Ambler
Currie, B. Stephen, Corpus Christi, Lansdale
Cushing, Michael J., Saint Jude Church, Chalfont
D'Angelo, Ernest, St. John the Baptist Church, Ottsville
Dalton, James E.
Dayoc, Michael J.
DeBow, James P., St. Ephrem Church, Bensalem
DeGrasse, Michael J., Assumption B.V.M. Church, West Grove
DeJesus, Epifanio, Cathedral Basilica of SS. Peter & Paul
DeLucca, Daniel N.
DeMasi, Leonard D., St. Monica Church
Derivan, Albert T.
DeRosa, Joseph R., Diocese of Trenton, NJ
Diamond, Patrick J., Saint Cecilia Church, Philadelphia
Diana, Leonard J.
DiCarlo, Donald P. Jr., St. Thomas of Villanova Church, Rosemont
DiFerdinand, James A., St. Mary Magdalen Church, Media
DiIenno, Anthony J., Saint Rose of Lima Church, Eddystone
Dillon, Mark H., Mother of Providence Church, King of Prussia
Donnelly, John P., Saint Dorothy Church, Drexel Hill
Drewicz, Vincent M., Visitation B.V.M. Church, Norristown
Druding, Frederick C.
DuBois, John J.
Duess, Edward E., Saint Andrew Church, Newton
Duffy, James J., St. Katherine of Siena
Dymek, Edward J. Jr., St. Ephrem Church, Bensalem
Eliason, William F.
Elliot, James J., St. Patrick Church, Kennett Square
Ellis, John J., Our Lady of Peace Church, Milmont Park
Evans, William W., Corpus Christi Church, Lansdale
Farrell, John H., Saint Charles Borromeo Church, Drexel Hill
Favinger, M. Eugene, Our Lady of Consolation Church, Parkesburg
Ferreira, Joao A., Resurrection of Our Lord Church
Finn, Michael J.
Fitzpatrick, Thomas P., St. Bernadette Church, Drexel Hill
Flynn, Robert G., St. Philip Neri Church, Lafayette Hill
Fowkes, James J., Our Lady of Mount Carmel Church, Doylestown
Frankenberger, Robert
Franks, Michael J. Sr., St. Philip Neri Church, Pennsburg
Friel, Dennis J., Resurrection of Our Lord Church, Philadelphia
Gallagher, John J., St. Thomas Aquinas Church, Croydon
Garritano, Dominic A., Our Lady of Grace Church, Penndel
Gellentien, Robert P.
Gentilcore, Kevin F., St. Anthony of Padua Church, Ambler
Giblin, Daniel T., St. Ann Church, Phoenixville
Gohde, Robert P., Saint Rose of Lima Church, North Wales
Golaszewski, John M., St. Vincent De Paul Church, Richboro
Gonzalez, Victor, Diocese of Petersburg, FL
Gousie, Joseph N. Sr.
Granese, Claude B., St. Titus Church, Norristown
Guckin, Stephen A., St. Martha Church
Guy, Gary W., Our Lady of Fatima Church, Secane
Gwynn, Raymond F. Sr.
Haddon, Richard S. Sr., Diocese of Allentown, PA
Hall, Robert H., St. Katherine of Siena Church
Hanley, Edward F., St. Timothy Church
Hanna, Jeffrey S., Saint Mary of the Assumption Church, Phoenixville
Hannan, Thomas J., Assumption B.V.M. Church, West Grove
Harmansky, George S., Saint Aloysius Church, Pottstown
Harrington, Michael K., Holy Cross Church, Springfield
Harrison, A. Gerald
Hartmann, James E.
Hartmann, Karl J.
Hasson, John A., Saint Eleanor Church, Collegeville
Henriquez, Francisco E., Diocese of St. Petersburg, FL
Hernandez, Felipe, Our Lady of Hope Church
Hernandez, Jose
Hess, Jonathan P., St. John the Evangelist Church, Morrisville
Hickey, William L., Saint Maximilian Kolbe Church, West Chester
Hinson, Edward T., St. Eleanor Church, Collegeville
Hoelzle, Louis F., Saint Teresa of Calcutta Church, Schwenksville
Hopkins, Stephen
Horan, Thomas J.
Houser, Joseph F.
Hrobak, Matthew J., St. Paul Church, East Norriton
Hunter, John K., St. Hilary of Poitiers Church, Rydal
Hunter, Richard F., Diocese of St. Petersburg, FL
Huynh, Trac Mai
Hynes, John
Iacobellis, William F.
Iannucci, Joseph E.
Jacobucci, Raymond, Queen of Peace Church, Ardsley
Johnson, Dwight, St. Agnes Church, West Chester
Jones, David E.
Jones, Edward S.
Kane, James D. Sr.
Kelley, Ronald F., Our Lady of Perpetual Help Church, Morton
Kelly, Patrick J., St. Joseph Church, Collingdale
Kennedy, Patrick J., Office for Life and Family; St. Philip Neri, Pennsburg
Kern, Paul R.
Kerr, Frederick H., Our Lady of the Rosary Church, Coatesville
Knesis, John J., Resurrection of Our Lady Church, Philadelphia
Kolakowski, Michael J., Diocese of Camden, NJ
Kolesky, David J.
Kreczkevich, John J., St. Barnabas Church
Kubczak, David M., Saint Teresa of Calcutta Church, Schwenksville
Kubiak, Michael J., St. Matthias Church, Bala Cynwyd
Kuhn, Mark J., St. Joseph Church, Ambler
Kussamaul, William G. III, Nativity B.V.M. Church, Media
Lally, Francis C., Saint Teresa of Avila Church, Norristown
Lance, Walter C.
Langsdorf, Francis E., Corpus Christi Church, Lansdale
Leonard, Warren C., Holy Trinity, Morrisville
Lewis, Charles G., St. Stanislaus Church, Lansdale
Lewis, Ronald L., Assumption B.V.M. Church, West Grove
Libbi, Louis, St. Patrick Church, Malvern
Lindsay, Charles R., Maternity B.V.M. Church
Logan, Paul A., Mary Mother of the Redeemer Church, North Wales
Lonergan, Joseph W., Diocese of Camden, NJ
Lozada, Jose Luis, St. Veronica Church, Philadelphia
Lozano, John P., St. Norbert Church, Paoli
Lynch, Timothy P., St. Jude Church, Chalfont
Lyon, James E.
Madonna, James K., St. Patrick Church, Kennett Square
Mahar, James, St. Francis of Assisi Church, Norristown
Mahoney, James L., St. Athanasius Church, Philadelphia
Makoid, Eric T., Diocese of St. Petersburg, FL
Malamut, Richard S., St. Mark Church, Bristol
Maldonado, Rafael
Malfara, Louis S.
Mandracchia, Patrick J., Visitation B.V.M. Church, Norristown
Manzano, Edwin R.
Mars, Christopher J., Saint David Church, Willow Grove
Martino, Stephen J., St. Norbert Church, Paoli
Masapollo, William M.
Maskarinec, Gregory J., Mother of the Divine Providence Church, King of Prussia
Matour, David J., St. Teresa of Avila Church, Norristown
Mauriello, Alfred J., St. Maximilian Kolbe, West Chester
Mayes, William C., St. Charles Borromeo Church
Mazurek, Daniel E., Saint Isaac Jogues Church, Wayne
Mazzoni, Mace M., St. Frances Cabrini Church, Fairless Hills
McAndrews, Michael J., Our Lady of Peace Church, Milmont Park
McAvoy, James T., Saint Elizabeth Parish Office, Chester Springs
McBlain, Paul J.
McElwee, Robert V., Annunciation B.V.M. Church, Havertown
McGonigal, Joseph P., St. Dorothy Church, Drexel Hill
McGovern, Clement J.
McNally, Eugene J. III, St. Christopher Church
McPhillips, Gerard J., St. Bartholomew Church
Mead, Kevin T., St. Elizabeth Church, Chester Springs
Meinzer, Mark J.
Mendez, Jose M.
Mennilli, Olindo, Epiphany of Our Lord Church
Midwood, Barry R., St. Elizabeth Church, Chester Springs
Mirabelli, Mario G., St. Catherine of Siena Church, Horsham
Mischler, John J., St. Alphonsus Church, Maple Glen
Mitchell, David C., Saint Isidore Church, Quakertown
Morris, Edward J., Saint Albert the Great Church, Huntingdon Valley
Morris, George E. Jr., St. Robert Bellarmine Church, Warrington
Morris, Harry J., St. Cornelius Church, Chadds Ford
Moser, William J., St. William Church
Moskowitz, Myron A.
Murphy, Albert J., St. Gabriel Church, Norwood
Murphy, Francis X.
Murray, John K., Queen of the Universe Church, Levittown
Napoli, Richard G., Saint Vincent De Paul Church, Richboro

Nguyen, Phoung T., St. Maria Goretti Church, Hatfield
Niche, Peter L., St. Maria Goretti Church, Hatfield
Nichols, Donald O., St. Mary Church, Schwenksville
Nightingale, Richard G., St. Cyprian Church
Niland, Joseph W.
Nines, Joseph L., Our Mother of Consolation Church
Nucero, John J., Our Lady Help of Christians Church, Abington
Nungesser, Michael P., St. Isidore Church, Quakertown
O'Donnell, Patrick J., Saint Isidore Church, Quakertown
O'Neil, James, St. Christopher Church
Ortiz, Samuel, St. Laurence Church, Upper Darby
Owen, Joseph T., St. Cyril of Jerusalem Church, Jamison
Owens, James T., SS. Simon and Jude Church, West Chester
Panganiban, Homer A., Our Lady of Hope Church
Pascarella, Michael Jr., M.A., M.S., Office for Clergy; Epiphany Church, Norristown
Pfeifer, John J., St. Andrew Church, Newtown
Phillips, Francis X., Saint Pius X Church, Broomall
Phillips, Thomas G., St. Teresa of Calcutta Church, Schwenksville
Pierce, Robert F., SS. Peter & Paul Church, West Chester
Pileggi, John J., Saint Katherine Drexel Church, Chester
Poellnitz, Fredrick E.
Polley, Charles W. Jr., SS. Philip and James Church, Exton
Pomales, Victor M., St. Helena Church
Potter, Kevin J., Saint Luke the Evangelist Church, Glenside
Purnell, Edward M., Holy Cross Church
Quaglia, Louis, St. Charles Borromeo Church, Bensalem
Quinn, Paul A., St. Francis De Sales Church, Lenni
Quinn, Thomas P.
Raczkowski, Thaddeus C., Saint Anastasia Church, Newton Square
Ramos, Juan F., St. Peter the Apostle Church
Reyes, Jose A., St. Veronica Church
Riordan, John T., St. Jude Church, Chalfont
Roberts, Christopher C., Holy Martyrs Church, Oreland
Rodgers, John J., St. Colman Church, Ardmore
Rooney, Joseph T., Our Lady Help of Christians Church, Abington
Rosario, Israel
Rose, John P., Our Lady of the Assumption Church, Strafford
Rouse, Daniel J.
Ruggiero, Joseph A., SS. Simon and Jude Church, West Chester
Ryan, Frederick M.
Salvatore, Mark A., St. Dominic Church
Schaffer, David B., M.A., M.S., Saint John Neumann Church, Bryn Mawr
Schiappa, Edward R., St. Joseph Church, Downingtown
Schlegel, John F.
Schnepp, Lawrence P., St. Rose of Lima Church, Eddystone
Scipioni, Raymond N., St. Charles Borromeo Church, Bensalem
Seda, Victor I., St. Helena Church
Sexton, Joseph F.
Shearer, C. William, SS. Simon and Jude Church, West Chester
Shirley, Ralph J., Mother of Divine Grace Church, Philadelphia
Shurer, Thomas E., St. Agnes Church, West Chester
Simpson, Harry J.
Skawinski, Robert J.
Smith, H. W. Todd, St. Peter Church, West Brandywine
Stam, Bernardus C., Diocese of Wilmington, DE
Stewart, James J., St. Monica Church
Stewart, Robert J.
Stokely, Patrick M., SS. Peter and Paul Church, West Chester
Suplee, John J., Sacred Heart Church, Havertown
Szewczak, Mark R., St. Ann Church, Phoenixville
Taylor, Thomas L., St. Joseph Church, Collingdale
Teson, John P., Our Lady of Calvary Church
Thompson, Vincent J., St. Francis Xavier- The Oratory Church, Philadelphia
Thuel, Raymond H., St. Agnes Church, Sellersville
Tobin, Charles A.
Todor, John J., St. Cornelius Church, Chadds Ford
Tormey, James M., Diocese of Wilmington, DE
Toth, James, St. Alphonsus Church, Maple Glen
Tran, Huan C., Saint Helena Church, Philadelphia
Travaline, John M., Mary, Mother of the Redeemer Church, North Wales
Tucker, Henry E., St. Agnes Church, Sellersville
Umile, Eric M., Assumption B.V.M. Church, Feasterville
Urbanski, Timothy E.
Vadino, Raymond M., St. John Chrysostom Church, Wallingford
Valentin, Juan E., Saint Stanislaus Church, Lansdale
Vera, Jorge L., Diocese of Harrisburg, PA
Vondercrone, C. Stephens
Wallace, Mark M., St. Laurence Church, Upper Darby
Walsh, James V., St. Eugene Church, Primos
Warner, Dennis P., St. Anselm Church
Watkins, Justin J., Sacred Heart Church, Oxford
Wernert, Emil J., Epiphany of Our Lord, Plymouth Meeting
Whartenby, Gerald J., St. Anselm Church
Williams, William V., Sacred Heart Church, Havertown
Willoughby, Anthony O., St. Cyprian Church
Windish, Joseph F., St. Cyril of Jerusalem Church, Jamison
Wirth, Richard D.
Zaleski, Stanley M.
Ziff, Joel M.
Zurbach, E. Peter, St. Mary Magdalen Church, Media.

INSTITUTIONS LOCATED IN DIOCESE

[A] SEMINARIES, ARCHDIOCESAN

PHILADELPHIA. *Redemptoris Mater Archdiocesan Missionary Seminary* (2013) 821 W. Cobbs Creek Pkwy., Yeadon, 19050. Tel: 610-713-5697; Email: secretary@rmphiladelphia.org; Web: rmphiladelphia.org. Revs. Carlos A. Benitez, Rector; Mariano DellaGiovanna, Vice Rector. Priests 2; Students 15; Clergy / Religious Teachers 2.

WYNNEWOOD. *Theological Seminary of St. Charles Borromeo*, Administration: 100 E. Wynnewood Rd., Wynnewood, 19096. Tel: 610-667-3394;
Fax: 610-667-7635; Web: www.scs.edu. Most Rev. Timothy C. Senior, M.B.A., M.S.W., M.A., M.Div., Rector; Stephen P. Dolan Jr., M.B.A., CFO/COO; Barbara Coady, Dir. Finance; Revs. Augustine M. Esposito, O.S.A., M.Div., M.A., Ph.D., Dir. Apostolic Formation; Robert A. Pesarchick, M.A., S.T.L., S.T.D., Vice Pres. Academic Affairs, St. Charles Borromeo Seminary, Overbrook, 100 E. Wynnewood Rd., Wynnewood, 19096; Christopher R. Cooke, M.A., M.Div., Dir. Spirituality Year; Jared Haselbarth, M.A., Dir., School of Theological Studies; Revs. George J. Szparagowski, M.Div., Dean of Men, College Seminary, St. Charles Borromeo Seminary, Overbrook, 100 E. Wynnewood Rd., Wynnewood, 19096; Bernard Edward Shlesinger III, S.T.B., Dir. Spiritual Formation, Theological Seminary; Herbert J. Sperger, M.Div., Dir. Spiritual Formation, College Seminary; Patrick J. Brady, M.Div., S.S.L., S.T.D., Dean, School of Diaconal Formation; Cait Kokolus, M.S.L.S., M.A., M.S., Vice Pres. Info Svcs. & Assessment; James Humble, M.S.L.S., Dir. Ryan Memorial Library; Shura Sullivan, Registar; Nicholas Mancini, Dir. Safety & Security; Revs. Joseph T. Shenosky, S.T.D., M.A., M.Div., Vice Rector, College Seminary; Brian P. Kane, S.T.B., M.Div., M.A., Dean of Men, Theological Seminary; John J. Ames, S.T.D., M.A., M.Div., Dean, School of Theological Studies, St. Charles Seminary, 100 E. Wynnewood Rd., Wynnewood, 19096; Rudolph A. Lucente, Dir. Sacred Music; Catherine Peacock, Dir. External Affairs & Alumni Rels. Lay Staff 15; Priests 18; Sisters 1; School of Theological Studies 250; Seminarians from Other Dioceses 81; Seminarians from Archdiocese of Philadelphia 66; Spiritual Year 10; Pre-Theology Seminarians 19; Theology Seminarians 60; Seminarians from Religious Communities 8; School of Diaconal Formation: Aspirants 8; Candidates 58; College Seminarians 66.
Full Time Instructional Faculty: Kelly Anderson, M.A., S.T.L., S.T.D.; Luca D'Anselmi, B.A., M.A.; Rev. Keith J. Chylinski, M.A., M.Div.; James M. Despres, M.A., Dir., Philosophical Studies Program; Rev. Frank A. Giuffre, M.Div., M.A., S.S.L.; Janet Haggerty, M.A., Ph.D.; Rev. Msgr. Michael K. Magee, M.Div., M.A., S.S.L., S.T.L., S.T.D.; Eric Manchester, M.A., Ph.D.; Sr. Mary JoAnna Ruthland, R.S.M., S.T.L.; Michael Rombeiro, M.A., Ph.D.; Revs. Bernard J. Taglianetti, M.A., M.Div., S.T.L.; John P. Collins, M.Div., M.A., (Retired); Rev. Msgr. Gregory J. Fairbanks, H.Ed., M.A.
Adjunct Faculty: Rev. Mark C. Aita, S.J., M.D.; Robert Crewalk, B.A.; Nicole Patrice Dul, M.F.A.; Rabbi Alan Iser, M.A.; Rev. Mark J. Hunt, S.T.L., S.T.D.; Marie Joseph, M.A.; Atherton C. Lowry, M.A., Ph.D.; Sr. Matthew Anita MacDonald, S.S.J., M.A., Ph.D.; Revs. Daniel E. Mackle, M.Div., M.A.; Charles J. McElroy, M.S., (Retired); James P. Olson, M.Div., M.A., S.T.L.; Augustus C. Puleo, M.Div., M.A., M.S., Ph.D.; Daniel M. Ruff, S.J., M.Div., S.T.M., Ph.D.; Sisters Mary JoAnna Ruthland, R.S.M., S.T.L.; Kathleen Schipani, I.H.M., M.Ed., M.A.; Rev. Msgr. Gerard C. Mesure, J.D., J.C.D., M.A.; Rev. Sean P. Bransfield, J.C.L., M.A., M.Div.; Kristi Bushner, M.A., J.D.
Spirituality Year, 51 E. Third Ave., Conshohocken, 19428.

[B] SEMINARIES, RELIGIOUS OR SCHOLASTICATES

PHILADELPHIA. *Brothers of the Christian Schools*, Jeremy House, 6633 Ardleigh St., 19119-3824. Tel: 215-843-1884; Email: richfsc2003@gmail.com. Bro. Richard Buccina, F.S.C., Dir. Postulants. Students 3; Professed Brothers 3.
DePaul Novitiate, 5710 Magnolia St., 19144. Tel: 215-843-1581; Fax: 215-844-9634; Email: jacktimlimcm@gmail.com. Revs. Elmer Bauer III, C.M., In Res.; John P. Timlin, C.M., In Res. Novitiate for the Congregation of the Mission (Vincentians). Priests 2; Clergy / Religious Teachers 1.
St. Vincent's Seminary, 500 E. Chelten Ave., 19144-1296. Tel: 215-713-2400; Fax: 215-844-2085; Web: www.cmeast.org. Very Revs. Stephen M. Grozio, C.M., Prov.; Michael J. Carroll, C.M., Dir.; Thomas F. McKenna, C.M., Asst. Prov.; Revs. Gregory P. Cozzubbo, C.M., Supr.; Elmer Bauer III, C.M., Prov. Treas.; John W. Carven, C.M., Prov. Archivist; John B. Freund, C.M., Exec. Dir., FamVin; Mr. Allen Andrews, Exec. Dir. Finance. Central House of the Eastern Province of the Congregation of the Mission, (Vincentians). Residence for retired priests & brothers. Clergy / Religious Teachers 3.
Vincentian Theologate-DeAndreis House, 124 Cotton St., 19127. Tel: 267-437-2537. Revs. Gregory J. Semeniuk, C.M., Dir.; Charles P. Strollo, C.M., In Res. Vincentian Theologate House for Men studying at St. Charles Borromeo Seminary. Students 4; Clergy / Religious Teachers 3.

PAOLI. *Daylesford Abbey*, 220 S. Valley Rd., Paoli, 19301-1900. Tel: 610-647-2530; Fax: 610-651-0219; Email: nobertines@daylesford.org; Web: www.daylesford.org. Rt. Revs. Ronald J. Rossi, O.-Praem., Abbot Emeritus; Richard J. Antonucci, O.-Praem., Abbot; Very Rev. John Joseph Novielli, O.Praem., Prior & Dir.; Rev. Joseph A. Serano, O.-Praem., Treas.
Norbertine Fathers, Inc. Brothers 2; Priests 26; Seminarians 1.

[C] COLLEGES AND UNIVERSITIES

PHILADELPHIA. *Chestnut Hill College*, 9601 Germantown Ave., 19118-2693. Tel: 215-248-7000; Fax: 215-248-7155; Email: kmiller@chc.edu; Web: www.chc.edu. Sisters Carol Jean Vale, S.S.J., Ph. D., Pres.; Mary Josephine Larkin, S.S.J., Dean Library & Info. Resources. Lay Teachers 299; Priests 1; Sisters 17; Students 1,778.
Holy Family University (1954) 9801 Frankford Ave., 19114. Tel: 215-637-7700; Fax: 215-637-3787; Email: fonley@holyfamily.edu; Web: www.holyfamily.edu. Sr. Maureen McGarrity, C.S.F.N., Ph.D., Pres.; Revs. James MacNew, Chap. & Campus Ministry; Mark J. Hunt, S.T.L., S.T.D., Dept. of Rel. Studies; Shannon Brown, Dir. Library Svcs. Congregation of the Sisters of the Holy Family of Nazareth. Sisters 2; Undergraduate Students 1,819; Graduate Students 527; Doctoral Students 33; Lay Faculty 73; Accelerated Students 333.
**St. Joseph's University* Regis Hall Regis Hall, 5600 City Ave., 19131. Tel: 610-660-1000;
Fax: 610-660-1201; Web: www.sju.edu. Marc C. Reed, Pres. Under the direction of the Jesuit Fathers. Incorporated January 29, 1851. Lay Teachers 656; Priests 17; Sisters 1; Students 8,950.
Jesuit Fathers, Tel: 610-660-1400;
Fax: 610-664-6640. Revs. Mark C. Aita, S.J., M.D.; Anthony J. Berret, S.J.; John M. Braverman, S.J.; Thomas J. Brennan, S.J.; William J. Byron, S.J.; Peter A. Clark, S.J.; Joseph J. Feeney, S.J.; Vincent J. Genovesi, S.J.; Joseph J. Godfrey, S.J.; Daniel R.J. Joyce, S.J.; Brendan G. Lally, S.J.; Joseph L. Lombardi, S.J.; John Martin, S.J.; Dennis E. McNally, S.J.; Nicholas J. Rashford, S.J.; Damien Ruff, S.J.; Patrick H. Samway, S.J.; Christopher Grodecki, S.J.; Sr. Elizabeth Ann Linehan, R.S.M.; Anne Krakow, Librarian.
LaSalle University, 1900 W. Olney Ave., 19141. Tel: 215-951-1000; Fax: 215-951-1488. Colleen M. Hanycz, Ph.D., Pres.; Brian A. Goldstein, Ph.D., Provost & Vice Pres. Academic Affairs; Stephanie Pricken, Vice Pres. Fin. & Admin; Cathleen Par-

sons-Nikolie, Vice Pres. Univ. Advancement; Thomas Delahunt, Vice Pres. Enrollment Svcs.; Dawn Meza Soufleris, Ph.D., Vice Pres. Student Affairs & Dean, Students; Lynne A. Texter, Ph.D., Interim Dean; Gary A. Giamartino, Ph.D., Dean, School of Business Admin.; Kathleen Czekanski, Ph.D., R.N., C.N.E., Dean, School of Nursing & Health Sciences; James C. Plunkett, Exec. Dir., Admissions; Bro. Robert J. Kinzler, F.S.C., Dir. University Ministry & Svc.; John S. Baky, Dir. Connelly Library. (Incorporated under the auspices of the Brothers of the Christian Schools) Brothers 18; Lay Teachers 530; Students 7,820; Clergy 4.

ASTON. *Neumann University*, One Neumann Dr., Aston, 19014-1298. Tel: 610-558-5501;
Fax: 610-558-5643; Email: neumann@neumann.edu; Web: www.neumann.edu. Sponsored by the Sisters of St. Francis of Philadelphia.Opened September 1965. Administrators 133; Priests 1; Sisters 25; Students 2,901; Faculty and Staff 290; Adjuncts 232.

GWYNEDD VALLEY. *Gwynedd Mercy University*, 1325 Sumneytown Pike, P.O. Box 901, Gwynedd Valley, 19437. Tel: 215-646-7300; Fax: 215-641-5509; Email: mchale.b@gmercyu.edu; Web: www.gmercyu.edu. Brothers 1; Lay Teachers 78; Sisters of Mercy 2; Students 2,478.

IMMACULATA. *Immaculata University* (1920) 1145 King Rd., Immaculata, 19345. Tel: 610-647-4400;
Fax: 610-647-7635; Web: www.immaculata.edu. Barbara Lettiere, Pres.; Patricia Canterino, Vice Pres. Student Engagement & UG Admissions; Bruce Friedman, Vice Pres. Finance & Admin.; Sr. Mary Henrich, I.H.M., Vice Pres. Mission & Ministry; Angela Tekely, Ed.D., Vice Pres. Academic Affairs; Dr. Thomas O'Brien, Dean College of Graduate Studies; Jean Shingle, Ph.D., Dean College of UG Studies; Jeffrey Rollison, Exec. Dir. Library; Robert Forest, Dir. Financial Aid; Cecelia Oswald, Asst. Dir. Institutional Research & Effectiveness; Collette Delaney, Registrar; Susan Arnold, Institutional Advancement. Conducted by Sisters, Servants of the Immaculate Heart of Mary. Sisters 16; Total Staff 99; Enrollment 2,462.

RADNOR. *Cabrini University* (1957) 610 King of Prussia Rd., Radnor, 19087-3698. Tel: 610-902-8100;
Tel: 610-902-8200; Fax: 610-902-8204; Web: www.cabrini.edu. Donald Taylor, Pres.; Rev. Carl F. Janicki, Dir. Campus Min.
Legal Title: Missionary Sisters of the Sacred Heart of Jesus Lay Teachers 219; Priests 1; Students 2,285; Clergy / Religious Teachers 2.

ROSEMONT. *Rosemont College of the Holy Child Jesus*, 1400 Montgomery Ave., Rosemont, 19010-1699.
Tel: 610-527-0200; Fax: 610-527-0341; Email: shirsh@rosemont.edu; Web: www.rosemont.edu. Sharon Latchaw Hirsh, Ph.D., Pres.; Jeanne Marie Hatch, S.H.C.J., Vice Pres., Mission; Jay Verzosa, Dir. Campus Ministry; Catherine M. Fennell, Exec. Dir. Library Svcs.; Jennifer Hawkes, Dir. Institutional Research & Registar. Lay Teachers 150; Sisters of the Holy Child Jesus 2; Students 1,086.

VILLANOVA. *Villanova University*, 800 Lancaster Ave., Villanova, 19085. Tel: 610-519-7499;
Fax: 610-519-5333; Email: jleon.washington@villanova.edu; Web: www.villanova.edu. Rev. Peter M. Donohue, O.S.A., Pres. & Bd. Trustee; Very Rev. Michael F. DiGregorio, O.S.A., Bd. Trustee; Revs. Francis J. Doyle, O.S.A., Bd. Trustee; Peter G. Gori, O.S.A., Bd. Trustee; James R. Halstead, O.S.A., Bd. Trustee; Francis J. Horn, O.S.A.; Joseph L. Narog, O.S.A., Bd. Trustee; Very Rev. Bernard C. Scianna, O.S.A., Bd. Trustee; Richard P. Brennan, Bd. Trustee; Ms. Carolyn N. Everson, Board, Trustees; D. Douglas Gaston IV, Esq., Board, Trustees; Nance K. Dicciani, Ph.D., Bd. Trustee; Daniel DiLella, Bd. Trustee; Peter L. Fong, Bd. Trustee; Daryl J. Ford, Ph.D., Bd. Trustee; Justin G. Gmelich, Bd. Trustee; Helen M. Horstmann, M.D., Bd. Trustee; Sheila F. Klehm, Bd. Trustee; Tom Klein, Bd. Trustee; Patrick G. Lapore, Bd. Trustee; Nnenna J. Lynch, Bd. Trustee; Elizabeth T. Mazzeo, Bd. Trustee; Robert J. McCarthy, Bd. Trustee; Patrick McMahon, Bd. Trustee; Richard J. Kreider, Board, Trustee; Rev. Kevin C. Mullins, O.S.A., Bd. Trustee; Thomas Mulroy, Bd. Trustee; Mary D. Naylor, Ph.D., Bd. Trustee; James V. O'Donnell, Bd. Trustee; Thomas M. Quindlen, Bd. Trustee; Joseph V. Topper Jr., Bd. Trustee; Paul A. Tufano Esq., Bd. Trustee; Thomas A. Wagner III, Bd. Trustee; Edward J. Welsh, Bd. Trustee. Founded 1842 by the Augustinians, Province of St. Thomas of Villanova. Colleges of Liberal Arts and Sciences, Engineering, Nursing; The School of Law, the School of Business. Part-time and Continuing Education, Graduate Studies. Lay Teachers 673; Priests 24; Students 10,887; Clerical Faculty: Total Staff 13; Full-time Enrollment 6,494; Part-time Enrollment 484.
Administration: Patrick Maggitti, Ph.D., Provost; Ann Diebold, Vice Pres. Univ. Communications; Revs. Kail C. Ellis, O.S.A., Special Asst. to the Pres.; John P. Stack, O.S.A., Vice Pres. Student Life; Mr. Michael J. O'Neill, Senior Vice Pres. Advancement & Alumni Rels.; Barbara E. Wall, Vice Pres. Mission & Min.; Ms. Debra Fickler, Vice Pres. & Gen. Counsel; Mr. Kenneth G. Valosky, Exec. Vice Pres.; Mr. Stephen Fugale, Vice Pres. & CIO Information Tech. Svcs.; Mark C. Alexander, J.D., Dean, Law School; Mr. J. Leon Washington, Dean Enrollment Mgmt.; Joyce E. Russell, Ph.D., Dean, Villanova School of Business; Adele Lindenmeyr, Ph.D., Dean of Liberal Arts & Sciences; Dr. Gary Gabriele, Dean of Engineering; Mr. Paul Pugh, Dean of Students; Dr. M. Louise Fitzpatrick, Dean College of Nursing; Sr. Beth Hassel, P.B.V.M., Dir. Ctr. for Faith & Learning; Mr. Vincent Nicastro, Assoc. Dir. J. Moorad Ctr., Study of Sports Law; Mr. Mark Jackson, Dir. Athletics; Revs. Robert P. Hagan, O.S.A., Asst. Athletic Dir.; Joseph D. Calderone, O.S.A., Campus Min.; Thomas Murnane, O.S.A., Office of Univ. Admission; Francis Chambers, O.S.A., Assoc. Dir. of Univ. Admission; Dennis J. Gallagher, O.S.A., Archivist; Joseph S. Mostardi, O.S.A., Campus Min.; Bro. Michael Duffy, O.S.A., Campus Min.
Clerical Faculty: Revs. Stephen J. Baker, O.S.A., Education & Counseling Dept.; Richard G. Cannuli, O.S.A., Dir. Art Gallery, Curator Univ. & Art Collection; Francis J. Caponi, O.S.A., Theology & Religious Studies; David A. Cregan, O.S.A., Chm., Theatre Dept.; Allan Fitzgerald, O.S.A., Dir. Augustinian Institute; Richard Jacobs, O.S.A., Public Admin. Dept.; Martin Laird, O.S.A., Theology & Rel. Studies; Joseph Loya, O.S.A., Theology & Rel. Studies; Lee J. Makowski, O.S.A., Augustine & Culture Seminar Prog.; James J. McCartney, O.S.A., Faculty, Philosophy Dept.; Robert J. Murray, O.S.A., Education & Counseling Dept.; Arthur P. Purcaro, O.S.A., Campus Ministry; Joseph Ryan, O.S.A., History Dept.; Joseph A. Murray, O.S.A., Campus Ministry; Millicent Gaskell, Villanova University Librarian & Dir. Falvey Memorial Library.

[D] HIGH SCHOOLS, ARCHDIOCESAN

PHILADELPHIA. *Archbishop Ryan High School* Opened September 7, 1966. 11201 Academy Rd., 19154-3397. Tel: 215-637-1800; Fax: 215-637-8833; Email: information@archbishopryan.com; Web: www.archbishopryan.org. Rev. Jonathan J. Dalin, School Min.; Denise LaPera, Pres.; Joseph McFadden, Prin.; Mary Lorenzo Brelsford, Librarian. Lay Teachers 71; Priests 2; Sisters 3; Students 1,222; Total Staff 46.

Father Judge High School for Boys Opened September 1954. 3301 Solly Ave., 19136-2396.
Tel: 215-338-9494; Fax: 215-338-0250; Email: jdalton@fatherjudge.com; Web: fatherjudge.com. Mr. Brian P. King, Pres.; Revs. James E. Dalton, O.S.F.S., Prin.; Jack Kolodziej, O.S.F.S., Asst. Prin.; Mr. Kevin Williams, School Min. Oblates of St. Francis de Sales. Brothers 1; Lay Teachers 46; Priests 2; Sisters 2; Students 840.

St. Hubert's Catholic High School for Girls Opened September 1941. 7320 Torresdale Ave., 19136.
Tel: 215-624-6840; Fax: 215-624-5940; Email: contactus@huberts.org; Web: www.huberts.org. Lizanne Pando, Pres.; Courtney McHale, School Min. Lay Teachers 35; Priests 1; Sisters 11; Students 626.

SS. John Neumann and Maria Goretti Catholic High School (Formerly Southeast Catholic High School, St. John Neumann High School for Boys, St. Maria Goretti High School for Girls) (Boys and Girls 2004) 1736 S. Tenth St., 19148-1694.
Tel: 215-465-8437; Fax: 215-462-2410; Web: www.neumanngorettihs.org. Bruce Robinson, Pres.; Hugh Quigley, Prin. Lay Teachers 26; Priests 2; Students 450.

John W. Hallahan Catholic Girls' High School Opened September 18, 1901. 311 N. 19th St., 19103-1198. Tel: 215-563-8930; Fax: 215-563-3809; Email: dkassekert@jwhallahan.com; Web: www.jwhallahan.com. Denise Kassekert, Pres.; Michele B. Beachy, Prin.; Rev. Christopher D. Lucas, School Min. Lay Teachers 27; Priests 1; Sisters 5; Students 452.

Little Flower Catholic High School for Girls Opened September 1, 1939. 1000 W. Lycoming St., 19140.
Tel: 215-455-6900; Fax: 215-329-0478; Web: www.LittleFlowerHighSchool.org. Sisters Kathleen Klarich, R.S.M., Prin.; Donna Shallo, I.H.M., Pres.; Rev. Joseph C. McCaffrey, M.B.A., M.Div., School Min.; Brooke Hauer, Librarian. Lay Teachers 30; Sisters 3; Students 700.

Roman Catholic High School for Boys Opened September 8, 1890. 301 N. Broad St., 19107.
Tel: 215-627-1270; Tel: 215-627-1570;
Fax: 215-627-4979; Email: psticco@romancatholichs.com; Web: www.romancatholichs.com. Rev. Joseph W. Bongard, M.A., M.Div., Pres.; Mrs. Patricia C. Sticco, Prin.; Sandra Kolander, Librarian. Lay Teachers 48; Priests 2; Sisters 2; Students 920.

West Catholic Preparatory High School West Catholic High School for Boys opened in 1916. West Catholic High School for Girls opened in 1926. Consolidated September, 1989. 4501 Chestnut St., 19139. Tel: 215-386-2244;
Fax: 215-222-1651; Email: westcatholic@hotmail.org; Web: www.westcatholic.org. Andrew Brady, Dir. Advancement; Mr. James Gallagher, Prin.; Michael J. Field Jr., School Min. Brothers 2; Lay Teachers 20; Sisters 4; Students 404.

DOWNINGTOWN. *Bishop Shanahan High School*, 220 Woodbine Rd., Downingtown, 19335.
Tel: 610-518-1300; Fax: 610-343-6220; Email: rplunkett@shanahan.org; Web: www.shanahan.org. Sr. Regina Plunkett, I.H.M., Pres.; Mr. Michael J. McArdle, Prin.; Rev. John E. Donia, School Min. (Coed) Formerly St. Agnes High School opened in 1909; became diocesan high school September 1957, moved from West Chester to Downingtown in 1998. Lay Teachers 55; Priests 1; Sisters, Servants of the Immaculate Heart of Mary 9; Students 1,125.

DREXEL HILL. *Archbishop Prendergast High School* Opened September 1956. Restructured 2006. See Monsignor Bonner and Archbishop Prendergast Catholic High School.

Monsignor Bonner and Archbishop Prendergast Catholic High School, 403 N. Lansdowne Ave., Drexel Hill, 19026-1196. Tel: 610-259-0280;
Fax: 610-259-1630; Web: www.bonnerprendie.com. Dr. John E. Cooke, Pres.; Rev. Edward C. Kelly, Faculty; Mr. David Barr, Dir. School Min.; James Strandberg, Interim Prin. (Boys) Opened September 1953 as Archbishop Prendergast High School for Boys. New name adopted September 1956. Bonner and Prendergast merged under a co-institutional model of governance in September 2006. In September 2012, the school merged into a co-educational model. Faculty 42; Students 850.

FAIRLESS HILLS. *Conwell-Egan Catholic High School*, 611 Wistar Rd., Fairless Hills, 19030.
Tel: 215-945-6200; Fax: 215-945-6206; Web: conwell-egan.org. Michael Culnan, Prin.; Nicole Salvatore, Guidance Dir.; Eric Kindler, School Min. Formerly Bishop Egan High School, Fairless Hills, and Bishop Conwell High School, Levittown. Faculty 27; Students 545.

LANSDALE. *Lansdale Catholic High School*, 700 Lansdale Ave., Lansdale, 19446-2995.
Tel: 215-362-6160;
Tel: 215-242-6160 (Philadelphia);
Fax: 215-362-5746; Email: jcasey@lansdalecatholic.com; Web: www.lansdalecatholic.com. James W. Casey, Pres.; Rita McGovern, Prin.; Rev. John J. Nordeman, M.A., M.Div. Opened 1949. 1983 joined the System of Secondary Schools in Philadelphia. Lay Teachers 36; Priests 1; Students 715.

RADNOR. *Archbishop John Carroll High School* Opened September 1967. 211 Matson Ford Rd., Radnor, 19087. Tel: 610-688-7610;
Fax: 610-688-8326 (Prin.);
Fax: 610-971-0827 (Pres.); Web: www.jcarroll.org. Mr. Francis E. Fox, B.S., Pres.; Dr. Anchen Schulz, Prin.; Deacon Thomas G. Phillips Jr., Dir. Campus Min.; Charmaine Gates, Librarian. Lay Teachers 50; Priests 1; Sisters 2; Students 1,078.

ROYERSFORD. *Pope John Paul II High School* (2010) 181 Rittenhouse Rd., Royersford, 19468.
Tel: 484-975-6500; Web: www.pjphs.org. Jason Bozzone, Pres.; Rev. Brian M. Kean, Prin. Lay Teachers 41; Students 850.

SPRINGFIELD. *Cardinal O'Hara High School* (Coed) Opened September, 1963. 1701 S. Sproul Rd., Springfield, 19064. Tel: 610-544-3800;
Fax: 610-544-1189; Web: cohs.com. Eileen Vice, Prin.; Rev. John P. Masson, School Min. Lay Teachers 49; Priests 1; Sisters 1; Students 980.

WARMINSTER. *Archbishop Wood Catholic High School* Opened September 1964. 655 York Rd., Warminster, 18974. Tel: 215-672-5050;
Fax: 215-672-9572 (Academic Office);
Fax: 212-672-5451 (Business Office); Web: www.archwood.org. Gary V. Zimmaro, Pres.; Mrs. Mary Harkins, M.A., Prin.; Rev. Paul J. O'Donnell, M.Div., School Min. Faculty 65; Students 975.

WYNCOTE. *Bishop McDevitt High School*, 125 Royal Ave., Wyncote, 19095-1198. Tel: 215-887-5575;
Fax: 215-887-1371; Email: sfinley@mcdevitths.org; Web: www.mcdevitths.org. Opened September 1958. Lay Teachers 25; Priests 1; Sisters 2; Students 435.

[E] VOCATIONAL HIGH SCHOOLS

PHILADELPHIA. *Mercy Career & Technical High School*, 2900 W. Hunting Park Ave., 19129-1803. Tel: 215-226-1225; Fax: 215-228-6337; Email: generalinfo@mercycte.org; Web: www.mercycte.org. Sisters Rosemary Herron, R.S.M., Pres.; Susan Walsh, R.S.M., Prin.; Christian Aument, Vice Prin.; Catherine Glatts, Vice Prin.; Teena Weisler, School Min. Lay Teachers 36; Sisters of Mercy 9; Students 331.

[F] HIGH SCHOOLS, PRIVATE

PHILADELPHIA. **Cristo Rey Philadelphia High School*, 5218 N. Broad St., 19141. Tel: 215-219-3943; Fax: 215-525-9692; Web: www.cristoreyphiladelphia.org. John McConnell, Pres.; Michael Gomez, Prin.

St. Joseph's Preparatory School, Office of the President, 1733 W. Girard Ave., 19130. Tel: 215-978-1950; Fax: 215-765-1710; Web: www.sjprep.org. Rev. John W. Swope, S.J., Pres.; Albert Greene, Dean of Students; Mr. Richard Scanlan, CFO; Mrs. Rose Marie Kettinger, Registrar/Asst. Prin. for Academic Programs & Records; Dr. L. Stewart Barbera, Dir. of Ignatian Identity; Ms. Besty Courtney, Chief Devel. Officer; Mrs. Sonia Nelson, Librarian. Brothers 1; Lay Teachers 74; Priests 2; Sisters 1; Students 905.

Nazareth Academy High School, 4001 Grant Ave., 19114-2999. Tel: 215-637-7676; Fax: 215-637-8523; Email: sfanning@nazarethacademyhs.org; Web: www.nazarethacademyhs.org. Sr. Rita Fanning, C.S.F.N., Prin. Girls 356; Lay Teachers 37; Sisters 9.

AUDUBON. **Regina Luminis Academy*, (Grades K-12), 601 First Ave., Berwyn, 19312. Tel: 610-269-3905; Fax: 610-269-6235; Email: drattore@reginaluminis.org; Web: www.reginaluminis.org. Mark Anthony, Pres.; Dr. Denise D'Attore, Headmistress; Mrs. Miranda McClain, Librarian. Total Enrollment 53; Part-time Faculty 6; Full-time Faculty 6.

BENSALEM. *Holy Ghost Preparatory School*, 2429 Bristol Pike, Bensalem, 19020. Tel: 215-639-2102; Fax: 215-639-4225; Email: ggeruson@holyghostprep.org; Web: www.holyghostprep.org. Gregory J. Geruson, Pres., Tel: 215-639-2102; Revs. Christopher H. McDermott, C.S.Sp., Chap.; Philip Agber, C.S.Sp.; Mr. Jeffrey Danilak, Prin. Spiritan Fathers 2; Lay Teachers 43; Males 485.

BRYN MAWR. *Country Day School of the Sacred Heart*, 480 Bryn Mawr Ave., Bryn Mawr, 19010. Tel: 610-527-3915; Fax: 610-527-0942; Email: smacdonald@cdssh.org; Web: www.cdssh.org. Deirdre Cryor, Head, School; Rev. Thomas P. Gillin, M.S., Chap.; Catherine Scholl, Librarian. Lay Teachers 45; Sisters 2; Students 325.

DEVON. *Devon Preparatory School*, 363 N. Valley Forge Rd., Devon, 19333. Tel: 610-688-7337; Fax: 610-688-2409; Email: devoninfo@devonprep.com; Web: www.devonprep.com. Revs. Francisco Aisa, Sch.P., Prin.; James J. Shea, Sch.P., Rector; Javier Renteria, Sch.P., Chap. Piarist Fathers. Lay Teachers 46; Priests 3; Students 267. In Res. Rev. Geza Pazmany, Sch.P., (Retired).

FLOURTOWN. *Mt. St. Joseph Academy*, 120 W. Wissahickon Ave., Flourtown, 19031-1899. Tel: 215-233-3177; Fax: 215-233-4734; Email: kbrabson@msjacad.org; Web: www.msjacad.org. Sr. Kathleen Brabson, S.S.J., Pres.; Dr. Judith Caviston, Prin. Lay Teachers 56; Sisters of St. Joseph 5; Students 503.

GWYNEDD VALLEY. *Gwynedd Mercy Academy High School*, 1345 Sumneytown Pike, P.O. Box 902, Gwynedd Valley, 19437-0902. Tel: 215-646-8815; Fax: 215-646-4361; Web: www.gmahs.org. Denise Marbach, Pres.; Mary E. Kirby, Prin. Girls 375; Lay Teachers 42; Sisters 5.

HOLLAND. *Villa Joseph Marie High School*, 1180 Holland Rd., Holland, 18966. Tel: 215-357-8810; Fax: 215-357-2477; Email: lcarr@vjmhs.org; Web: www.vjmhs.org. Thomas Kardish, Pres.; Lauren Carr, Prin.; Marjene Hoffman, Librarian. Lay Teachers 46; Students 390.

MALVERN. *Malvern Preparatory School for Boys*, 418 S. Warren Ave., Malvern, 19355-2707. Tel: 484-595-1100; Email: cdrennen@malvernprep.org; Web: www.malvernprep.org. Rev. Donald F. Reilly, O.S.A., Headmaster; James Cassidy, Dir. Campus Min.; Revs. Christopher J. Drennen, O.S.A., Dir. Mission & Ministry; Harry J. Erdlen, O.S.A., Campus Min.; James R. Flynn, O.S.A., Faculty. Lay Teachers 77; Priests 5; Students 645; Clergy / Religious Teachers 5; Clergy / Religious Teachers 5.

Villa Maria Academy High School, 370 Central Ave., Malvern, 19355. Tel: 610-644-2551; Fax: 610-644-2866; Web: www.vmahs.org. Sr. Regina Ryan, I.H.M., Ed.D., Prin.; Melissa Norman, Librarian; Sr. Marie Claire Matsinger, I.H.M., School Min. Girls 440; Lay Teachers 56; Sisters, Servants of the Immaculate Heart of Mary 7.

MERION STATION. *Merion Mercy Academy*, 511 Montgomery Ave., Merion Station, 19066. Tel: 610-664-6655; Fax: 610-664-6322; Email: mma@merion-mercy.com; Web: www.merion-mercy.com. Sr. Barbara Buckley, R.S.M., Head of School. Day School for Girls. Lay Teachers 45; Sisters of Mercy 12; Students 460.

ORELAND. *Martin Saints Classical High School*, 120 Allison Rd., Oreland, 19075. Tel: 267-495-4865; Email: adickerson@martinsaintsclassical.org; Web: www.martinsaintsclassical.org. Deacon Christopher C. Roberts, Pres.; Mr. Adam A. Dickerson, J.C.L., M.A., Headmaster. Provides a Catholic, classical education for grades 9-12. Lay Teachers 15; Students 25; Clergy / Religious Teachers 1.

VILLANOVA. *Academy of Notre Dame de Namur*, 560 Sproul Rd., Villanova, 19085. Tel: 610-687-0650; Fax: 610-687-1912; Web: www.ndapa.org. Judith A. Dwyer, Pres.; Mrs. Jacqueline Coccia, Prin.; Mrs. Kim Eife, Academic Dean; Mrs. Jennifer Nobles, Dean, Students. Lay Teachers 63.

WYNDMOOR. *LaSalle College High School*, 8605 Cheltenham Ave., Wyndmoor, 19038. Tel: 215-233-2911; Fax: 215-233-1418; Email: admissions@lschs.org; Web: www.lschs.org. Bro. James Butler, F.S.C., Pres.; Mr. Daniel McGowan, Vice Pres. Inst. Advancement; Mr. Peter Sigmund, Chief Information Officer; Mr. Michael O'Toole, Prin.; Bro. Raymond T. Murphy, F.S.C., Dir.; Owen Schogsta, Librarian; Mr. Kevin Dougherty, Dean Admissions & Fin. Aid; Mr. Mark Gibbons, Bus. Mgr.; Mr. Christopher Carabello, Dir. Mktg., Communications & Public Rels.; Lewis Clark, Dir. Lasallian Mission & Min.; Mrs. Jill D'Angelo, Dir. Constituent Rels. Brothers of the Christian Schools 4; Lay Teachers 98; Students 1,085; Staff 60.

[G] REGIONAL PARISH SCHOOLS

PHILADELPHIA. *St. Anthony of Padua Regional Catholic School*, 913 Pierce St., 19148-1619. Tel: 215-468-0353; Fax: 215-334-4255; Email: srmaryesther@comcast.net; Web: teacherweb.com/pa/saintanthonyofpaduaregionalcatholicschool/schoolhomepage. Sisters Mary Esther Carsele, M.P.F., Prin.; Carmela Falcone, M.P.F., Vice Prin.; Dolores Duffy, O.S.F., Librarian. Faculty 17; Total Enrollment 230.

Blessed Trinity Regional Catholic School, 3033 Levick St., 19149. Tel: 215-338-9797; Fax: 215-331-6457. Linda Milewski, Prin.; James Zaccario, Dir. Advancement; Michael Skudar, Librarian. Faculty 31; Total Enrollment 576.

Holy Innocents Area Catholic School, 1312 E. Bristol St., 19124. Tel: 215-743-5909; Fax: 215-743-0199. Sr. Regina Mullen, I.H.M., Prin.; Mrs. Carol Hockensmith, Librarian. Lay Teachers 15; Sisters, Servants of the Immaculate Heart of Mary 4; Students 300.

St. Mary Interparochial School, (Grades K-8), 5th & Locust Sts., 19106. Tel: 215-923-7522; Fax: 215-923-8502; Email: schooloffice@saintmarys.us; Web: www.saintmarys.us. Mrs. Jayda Pugliese, Prin.; Millie Cammisa, Librarian; Christina Haciski, Dir. Lay Teachers 10; Students 255.

Our Lady of Hope Regional Catholic School, 1248 Jackson St., 19148. Tel: 215-467-5385; Fax: 215-336-5103; Email: pab0223@comcast.net; Web: www.ourladyofhopephilly.com. Patricia Cody, Prin.; Theresa T. Ford, Librarian. Faculty 19; Total Enrollment 315.

Our Lady of Port Richmond Regional School, 3233 Thompson St., 19134. Tel: 215-739-1920; Fax: 215-739-0519. Sisters Mary Ripp, S.C.C., Prin.; Angela Abbruzzese, S.C.C., Librarian. Regional School for St. Adalbert, Nativity of the Blessed Virgin Mary and Our Lady Help of Christians. Lay Teachers 26; Sisters 3.

St. Pio Regional Catholic School, (Grades PreSchool-8), 1826 Pollock St., 19145. Tel: 215-467-5430; Fax: 215-467-2391; Email: eileensharpwilson@gmail.com; Web: www.stpiocatholic.org. Eileen Wilson, Prin.; Maria Dunn, Admin. Asst. Lay Teachers 20; Total Enrollment 232.

Resurrection Regional Catholic School, (Grades PreK-8), 2020 Shelmire Ave., 19152-4209. Tel: 215-742-1127; Fax: 215-742-0947; Email: jbellantoni@resurrectschool.org; Web: www.resurrectschool.org. Jack Bellantoni, Prin. Lay Teachers 27; Students 485; Total Enrollment 485; Religious Teachers 1.

ARDSLEY. *Good Shepherd Catholic Regional School*, 835 N. Hills Ave, Ardsley, 19038. Tel: 215-886-4782; Fax: 215-517-6708; Email: spatriciahealey@gscregional.org; Web: www.gscregional.org. Sr. Patricia Healey, I.H.M., Prin. Lay Teachers 15; Sisters, Servants of the Immaculate Heart of Mary 3; Students 215.

ASTON. *Holy Family Regional Catholic School*, 3265 Concord Rd., Aston, 19014. Tel: 610-494-0147; Fax: 610-494-4615; Email: jdolores@holyfamilyaston.org; Web: www.holyfamilyaston.org. Jennifer Dolores, Prin. Faculty 19; Total Enrollment 252.

BRYN MAWR. *SS. Colman-John Neumann School*, 372 Highland Ln., Bryn Mawr, 19010. Tel: 610-525-3266; Fax: 610-525-6103; Web: www.scjnschool.org. Cathleen Lamberto, Prin.; Maryann Ratigan, Librarian. Regional school for St. Colman Parish and St. John Neumann Parish. Lay Teachers 21; Students 276.

COLLEGEVILLE. *Holy Cross Regional Catholic School*, 701 Locust St., Collegeville, 19426. Tel: 610-489-9434; Fax: 610-489-6137; Email: thealy@holycrossregionalschool.org; Web: holycrossregionalschool.org. Theresa A. Healy, Prin. Faculty 35; Total Enrollment 600.

HAVERTOWN. *Cardinal John Foley Regional Catholic School*, 300 E. Eagle Rd., Havertown, 19083. Tel: 610-446-4608; Fax: 610-446-5705; Email: principal@cardinalfoley.org. Mary Ann DeAngelo, Prin. Faculty 32; Total Enrollment 462.

HOLLAND. *St. Katharine Drexel Regional Catholic School*, 1053 Holland Rd., Holland, 18966. Tel: 215-357-4720; Fax: 215-355-9526; Email: mslauraclark@skdschool.org; Web: www.skdschool.org. Laura Clark, Prin. Total Enrollment 380.

KING OF PRUSSIA. *Mother Teresa Regional Catholic School*, 405 Allendale Rd., King of Prussia, 19406. Tel: 610-265-2323; Fax: 610-265-1816; Web: www.mtcschool.org. Christine Pagan, Prin.; Miranda Miller, Librarian. Faculty 22; Total Enrollment 310.

LANSDALE. *Mater Dei Catholic School*, 493 E. Main St., Lansdale, 19446. Tel: 215-368-0995; Fax: 215-393-4869; Email: info@materdeicatholic.com; Web: www.materdeicatholic.com. Diane E. McCaughan, Prin. Faculty 32; Total Enrollment 551.

LEVITTOWN. *Holy Family Regional Catholic School*, 2477 Trenton Rd., Levittown, 19056. Tel: 215-269-9600; Fax: 215-269-9609; Web: www.hfrcs.org. Linda Robinson, Prin. Lay Teachers 27; Sisters, Servants of the Immaculate Heart of Mary 2; Students 456.

MAPLE GLEN. *Our Lady of Mercy Regional Catholic School*, 29 Conwell Dr., Maple Glen, 19002. Tel: 215-646-0150; Fax: 215-646-7150; Email: olmcatholicschool@gmail.com; Web: www.olmcatholicschool.com. John C. McGrath, M.Ed., Prin.; Rosa Costanzo, Librarian. Faculty 29; Total Enrollment 430.

MORTON. *Our Lady of Angels Regional Catholic School*, (Grades PreK-8), 2130 Franklin Ave., Morton, 19070. Tel: 610-543-8350; Fax: 610-544-3203; Email: slowe@olaschool2.com; Web: www.ourladyofangelsmorton.org. Susan Lowe, Prin. Lay Teachers 30; Students 330; Total Enrollment 330; Clergy / Religious Teachers 2.

PHOENIXVILLE. *Holy Family School*, 221 Third Ave., Phoenixville, 19460. Tel: 610-933-7562; Fax: 610-933-8823; Email: abraca@myholyfamily.org; Web: www.myholyfamilyschool.org. Mrs. Ann Marie Braca, Prin.; Mrs. Susan Vickrey, Librarian. Regional school for St. Ann Parish; St. Mary of the Assumption Parish; St. Joseph, Spring City; St. Basil the Great, Kimberton. Lay Teachers 28; Students 368.

PLYMOUTH MEETING. *Holy Rosary Regional Catholic School*, 3040 Walton Rd., Plymouth Meeting, 19462-2361. Tel: 610-825-0160; Fax: 610-825-0460; Email: lhoban@holyrosaryregional.com. Mrs. Lisa Hoban, Prin. Total Enrollment 317.

RIDLEY PARK. *St. James Regional Catholic School*, 500 Tome St., Ridley Park, 19078. Tel: 610-583-3662; Fax: 610-583-3683; Email: principal@stjamesregional.com; Web: www.stjamesregional.com. Barbara Burke, Prin. Regional school for St. Madeline Parish, St. Rose of Lima Parish, and St. Gabriel Parish. Lay Teachers 21; Students 418.

WALLINGFORD. *Mother of Providence Regional Catholic School*, (Grades PreK-8), 607 S. Providence Rd., Wallingford, 19086. Tel: 610-876-7110; Fax: 610-876-5923; Email: twaters@mpregional.org; Web: www.mpregional.org. Therese Waters, Prin.; Linda Rooney, Advancement Dir. Faculty 24; Total Enrollment 270.

WARRINGTON. *St. Joseph-St. Robert School*, 850 Euclid Ave., Warrington, 18976. Tel: 215-343-5100; Fax: 215-343-7434; Web: stjstr.org. Mrs. Deborah R. Jaster, Prin.; Patricia Pfeil, Librarian. Regional school for St. Joseph Parish and St. Robert Bellarmine Parish. Lay Teachers 17; Students 250.

WEST BRANDYWINE. *Pope John Paul II Regional Catholic Elementary School*, (Grades PreK-8), 2875 Manor Rd., West Brandywine, 19320. Tel: 610-384-5961; Fax: 610-384-5730; Email:

skerins@popejohnpaul2sch.org; Web: www.popejohnpaul2sch.org. Sarah Kerins, Prin. Area school for St. Joseph, Our Lady of the Rosary, Coatesville; St. Peter Parish, West Brandywine; Our Lady of Consolation, Parkesburg. Lay Teachers 38; Students 623.

WILLOW GROVE. *Queen of Angels Regional Catholic School*, 401 N. Easton Rd., Willow Grove, 19090. Tel: 215-659-6393; Fax: 215-659-6377; Email: qoaschool@qoaschool.org; Web: www.qoaschool.org. Sr. Margaret Rose Adams, I.H.M., Prin. Faculty 22; Total Enrollment 280.

[H] INDEPENDENCE MISSION SCHOOLS

PHILADELPHIA. **Independence Mission Schools*, 640 Freedom Bus. Center Dr., Ste. 115, King of Prussia, 19406. Tel: 610-200-5100; Fax: 610-465-9887; Email: info@independencemissionschools.org; Web: www.independencemissionschools.org. Richard Auletta, Pres.; Brian McElwee, Bd. Dir.

DePaul Catholic School, (Grades PreK-8), 44 W. Logan St., 19144. Tel: 215-842-1266; Fax: 215-842-1400; Email: secretary@thedepaulcatholicschool.org; Web: depaulphila.org. Katie Wardlow, Prin. Lay Teachers 23; Students 424.

Holy Cross, (Grades K-8), 144 E. Mount Airy Ave., 19119. Tel: 215-242-0414; Email: holycrossoffice@holycrossphila.org; Web: holycrossphila.org. Emily Diefendorf, Prin. Lay Teachers 15; Students 242.

Our Mother of Sorrows/St. Ignatius of Loyola, (Grades PreK-8), 617 N. 43rd St., 19104. Tel: 215-222-3626; Email: info@omssiphila.org; Web: ommsiphila.org. Sr. Owen Patricia Bonner, S.S.J., Prin. Lay Teachers 14; Students 248; Religious Teachers 1.

St. Barnabas Catholic School, (Grades PreK-8), 6334 Buist Ave., 19142. Tel: 215-729-3603; Fax: 215-729-2315; Email: info@independencemissionschools.org; Web: stbarnabasphila.org. Sr. Catherine Clark, I.H.M., Prin. Lay Teachers 20; Sisters 4; Students 326; Religious Teachers 4.

St. Cyril of Alexandria, (Grades PreK-8), 716 Emerson Ave., East Lansdowne, 19050. Tel: 610-623-1113; Fax: 610-646-7294; Email: bmontague@stcyrilphila.org; Web: stcyrilphila.independencemissionschools.org. Sr. Barbara Montague, I.H.M., Prin.; Theresa Power, Admin. Lay Teachers 15; Students 241; Religious Teachers 1.

St. Frances Cabrini Regional Catholic School, (Grades PreK-8), 405 N. 65th St., 19151. Tel: 215-748-2994; Fax: 215-748-0288; Email: info@independencemissionschools.org; Web: stfrancescabriniphila.org. William Cascarina, Prin. Lay Teachers 17; Students 326; Total Enrollment 326.

St. Gabriel, (Grades PreK-8), 2917 Dickinson St., 19146. Tel: 215-468-7230; Fax: 215-468-2554; Email: info@independencemissionschools.org; Web: stgabrielphila.org. Sr. Noreen James Friel, I.H.M., Prin. Lay Teachers 16; Sisters 1; Students 184; Religious Teachers 1.

St. Helena - Incarnation Regional Catholic School, 6101 N. 5th St., 19120. Tel: 215-549-2947; Email: info@independencemissionschools.org; Web: www.sthelenaphila.org. Nick Huck, Prin. Faculty 29; Lay Teachers 29; Students 585; Total Enrollment 585.

St. Malachy, (Grades PreK-8), 1012 W. Thompson St., 19122. Tel: 215-232-0696; Fax: 215-236-1434; Email: info@independencemissionschools.org; Web: stmalachyphila.org. Stephen Janczewski, Prin. Lay Teachers 13; Sisters 1; Students 285; Religious Teachers 1.

**St. Martin de Porres School*, (Grades PreK-8), 2300 W. Lehigh Ave., 19132. Tel: 215-223-6872; Email: info@independencemissionschools.org; Web: stmartindeporresphila.org. Sr. Meaghan V. Patterson, S.S.J., Prin. Lay Teachers 25; Sisters 5; Students 505; Religious Teachers 5.

St. Martin of Tours, (Grades PreK-8), 5701 Loretto Ave., 19124. Tel: 215-744-0444; Email: info@stmartinoftoursphila.org; Web: www.stmartinoftoursphila.org. Sr. Ellen Giardino, I.H.M., Prin. Lay Teachers 31; Students 537; Religious Teachers 6.

St. Raymond of Penafort, (Grades PreK-8), 7940 Williams Ave., 19150. Tel: 215-548-1919; Fax: 215-548-1925; Email: info@independencemissionschools.org; Web: straymondphila.org. Patricia Wright, Prin. Lay Teachers 14; Students 283.

St. Rose of Lima, (Grades PreK-8), 1522 N. Wanamaker St., 19131. Tel: 215-473-6030; Fax: 215-473-2338; Email: info@independencemissionschools.org; Web: stroseoflimaphila.org. Sr. Rita James Murphy, I.H.M., Prin. Lay Teachers 13; Students 225; Religious Teachers 1.

St. Thomas Aquinas, (Grades PreK-8), 1631 S. 18th St., 19145. Tel: 215-334-0878; Email: info@stthomasphila.org; Web: stthomasphila.org. Nicole Unegbu, Prin. Lay Teachers 19; Students 267.

St. Veronica, (Grades PreK-8), 3521 N. 6th St., 19140. Tel: 215-225-1575; Email: info@independencemissionschools.org; Web: stveronicasphila.org. Sr. Eileen Buchanan, I.H.M., Prin. Lay Teachers 15; Students 213.

[I] ELEMENTARY SCHOOLS, PRIVATE

PHILADELPHIA. *The Gesu School*, (Grades PreK-8), 1700 W. Thompson Sts., 19121. Tel: 215-763-3660; Tel: 215-763-9077 (Development); Fax: 215-763-9844; Web: www.gesuschool.org. Bryan Carter, Pres.; Rev. Raymond J. Donaldson, S.J., Chap.; Sr. Ellen Convey, I.H.M., Prin.; Alana Lee, Vice Prin.; Rev. Neil L. Ver'Schneider, S.J., Vice Prin.; Sr. Mary E. Bur, I.H.M., Librarian. Clergy 2; Lay Teachers 28; Priests, Society of Jesus 2; Sisters, Servants of the Immaculate Heart of Mary 2; Students 450.

**La Salle Academy*, (Grades 3-8), 1434 N. 2nd St., 19122. Tel: 215-739-5804; Fax: 215-739-1664; Email: jmcgowan@lasalleacademy.net; Web: www.lasalleacademy.net. Sr. Jeanne McGowan, S.S.J., Pres.; Teresa Diamond, Prin. Brothers 4; Lay Teachers 14; Sisters 2; Students 90.

Nazareth Academy Grade School, 4701 Grant Ave., 19114. Tel: 215-637-7777; Fax: 215-637-5696; Email: nazarethacademygradeschool@yahoo.com; Web: www.nazarethacademy.net. Sisters Linda Joseph, C.S.F.N., Prin.; M. Yvette Ortiz, C.S.F.N., Finance Dir.; Mrs. Patricia McGarvey, Devel. Dir. Lay Teachers 18; Sisters of the Holy Family of Nazareth 3; Students 210.

Norwood-Fontbonne Academy, (Grades PreK-8), 8891 Germantown Ave., 19118. Tel: 215-247-3811; Email: rkilleen@norfon.org; Email: pingram@norfon.org; Web: www.norfon.org. Dr. Ryan Killeen, Pres.; Mrs. Nancy Nadler, Dir. Business Opers.; Mrs. Marianne Finnegan, Prin.; Mrs. Nancy Peluso, Prin.; Daniel O'Sullivan, Dir. Campus Min.; Erin Wallin, Dir. Admissions; Theresa Hutsell, Dir. Devel.; David Rodgers, Dir.; Pamela Ingram, Sec. Lay Teachers 39; Sisters of St. Joseph 4; Students 419; Religious Teachers 16; Clergy / Religious Teachers 2.

ABINGTON. *Regina Coeli Academy*, (Grades PreK-8), 1525 Marian Rd., Abington, 19001. Tel: 215-277-1386; Fax: 215-277-1489; Email: info@reginacoeliacademy.com; Web: www.reginacoeliacademy.com. Mr. Tim Murnane, Chm. Bd.; Christopher Keefe, Headmaster. A private independent school PreK-8. Classical curriculum and formation in the Catholic faith. Lay Teachers 16; Students 104.

BERWYN. **Regina Luminis Academy*, (Grades K-8), 601 First Ave., Berwyn, 19312. Tel: 610-269-3905; Email: drattore@reginaluminis.org; Web: www.reginaluminisacademy.com. Mark Anthony, Pres.; Dr. Denise D'Attore, Headmaster; Mrs. Miranda McClain, Librarian. Total Enrollment 52; Part-time Faculty 9; Full-time Faculty 6.

BRYN MAWR. *St. Aloysius Academy*, (Grades PreK-8), 401 S. Bryn Mawr Ave., Bryn Mawr, 19010. Tel: 610-525-1670; Fax: 610-525-5140; Email: mainoffice@staloysiusacademy.org; Web: www.staloysiusacademy.org. Sr. Stephen Anne Roderiguez, I.H.M., Ed.D., Prin. Lay Teachers 35; Sisters, Servants of the Immaculate Heart of Mary 10; Students 260.

CHESTER. *Drexel Neumann Academy*, (Grades PreK-8), 1901 Potter St., Chester, 19013-5497. Tel: 610-872-7358; Fax: 610-872-7833; Email: mgannonosf@comcast.net. Sisters Margaret Gannon, O.S.F., Pres.; Catherine McGowan, S.S.J., Prin. (Full-time, paid) 4; Lay Teachers 17; Sisters 2; Students 200.

DREXEL HILL. *Holy Child Academy*, (Grades N-8), 475 Shadeland Ave., Drexel Hill, 19026. Tel: 610-259-2712; Email: mfoxtully@holychildacademy.com; Web: holychildacademy.com. Mrs. Margaret Fox-Tully, Head, School; Anne M. Wood, Prin.; Amy Coleman, Dir. External Communications; Judy Clay, Librarian. Lay Teachers 19; Students 155.

IMMACULATA. *Villa Maria Academy*, (Grades PreK-8), 1140 King Rd., Immaculata, 19345-0600. Tel: 610-644-4864; Fax: 610-647-6403; Email: office@villamaria.org; Web: www.villamaria.org. Sr. Susan Joseph, I.H.M., Prin.; Dolores Lentz, Librarian. Girls 285; Lay Teachers 37; Sisters, Servants of the Immaculate Heart of Mary 3; Students 285.

MERION. *Waldron Mercy Academy*, 513 Montgomery Ave., Merion Station, 19066. Tel: 610-664-9847; Fax: 610-664-6364; Email: wma@waldronmercy.org; Web: www.waldronmercy.org. Mrs. Nell Stetser, Prin.; Sr. Joellen McDonnell, R.S.M., Admissions Dir. Private, co-educational elementary school with child care, preschool & Montessori programs. Lay Teachers 44; Sisters of Mercy 6; Students 495.

RADNOR. *Armenian Sisters Academy*, (Grades PreK-8), Montessori for ages 3-6. Elementary for ages 7-14. Toddler learning center 13 months to 2 1/2 years. 440 Upper Gulph Rd., Radnor, 19087. Tel: 610-687-4100; Fax: 610-687-2430; Email: sisteremma@asaphila.org; Web: www.asaphila.org. Sr. Emma Moussayan, Prin.; Lara Odabashian Croy, Librarian. Lay Teachers 27; Sisters 3; Students 137.

ROSEMONT. *Holy Child School at Rosemont*, 1344 Montgomery Ave., Rosemont, 19010. Tel: 610-992-1000; Fax: 610-922-1030; Email: info@holychildrosemont.org; Web: www.holychildrosemont.org. Mr. Thomas Lengel, Head of School; Deb Borden, Prin.; Catherine Stuart, Librarian. Lay Teachers 36; Students 295.

SPRING HOUSE. *Gwynedd-Mercy Academy Elementary School*, (Grades K-8), Elementary School, 816 Norristown Rd., P.O. Box 241, Spring House, 19477. Tel: 215-646-4916; Tel: 215-646-2406 (Business Office); Fax: 215-646-7250; Email: aslike@gmaelem.org; Web: www.gmaelem.org. Sr. Anne W. Knapke, R.S.M., Prin.; Mrs. Lindsey Rauch, Curriculum Coord.; Mary Johnson, Librarian. Lay Teachers 46; Sisters of Mercy 1; Students 410; Total Staff 64.

WYNCOTE. *Ancillae-Assumpta Academy*, (Grades PreK-8), (Coed) 2025 Church Rd., Wyncote, 19095. Tel: 215-885-1636; Fax: 215-885-2740; Email: alintner@ancillae.org; Email: mgillespie@ancillae.org; Web: www.ancillae.org. Amelia Lintner, Dir.; Sr. Maureen Gillespie, A.C.J., Prin.; Patricia Handel, Librarian; Maureen Rilling, D.R.E. Lay Teachers 63; Handmaids of the Sacred Heart of Jesus 4; Students 577.

YARDLEY. *Grey Nun Academy*, (Grades PreK-8), (Coed Day School) 1750 Quarry Rd., Yardley, 19067. Tel: 215-968-4151; Fax: 215-860-7418; Email: dkost@gnaedu.org; Web: www.greynunacademy.org. Deborah Kost, Head of School; Michelle Stewart, Dir.; Lisa Grabowski, Dir. Enrollment; Susy Kim, Dir. Advancement; Deborah Koehler, Multimedia Specialist. Lay Teachers 23; Grey Nuns of the Sacred Heart 1; Students 145.

[J] SPECIAL EDUCATION

PHILADELPHIA. *St. Lucy Day School for Children with Visual Impairments and Archbishop Ryan Academy for the Deaf*, 4251 L St., 19124. Tel: 215-289-4220; Fax: 215-289-4229; Email: principalarardslds@gmail.com; Web: stl.ocephila.org. Sr. Lisa Ann Lettiere, I.H.M., Prin. Lay Teachers 7; Sisters, Servants of the Immaculate Heart of Mary 4; Students 40.

Our Lady of Confidence Day School, Willow Grove. Tel: 215-657-9311; Fax: 215-657-9312; Email: jmoeller@ourladyofconfidence.org; Web: www.ourladyofconfidence.org. Intellectual Disability. Lay Teachers 8; Sisters Servants of the Immaculate Heart of Mary 3.

Main School and Office-St. David Site, 314 N. Easton Rd., Willow Grove, 19090-2506. Tel: 215-657-9311; Fax: 215-657-9312; Email: jmoeller@ourladyofconfidence.org.

Our Lady of Confidence Day School at Bishop McDevitt High School, 125 Royal Ave., Wyncote, 19095-1198. Tel: 215-887-5575, Ext. 251; Fax: 215-657-9312. Sr. Judith Moeller, I.H.M., Prin.

WYNNEWOOD. *St. Katherine Day School*, 930 Bowman Ave., Wynnewood, 19096. Tel: 610-667-3958; Fax: 610-667-3625; Email: principal@stkds.org. Mrs. Kathleen A. Gould, Prin. Children with Developmental Delay and/or Multiple Impairments. Lay Teachers 11; Students 99.

[K] CATHOLIC SOCIAL SERVICES OF THE ARCHDIOCESE OF PHILADELPHIA

PHILADELPHIA. *Catholic Social Services of the Archdiocese of Philadelphia*, 222 N. 17th St., 19103-1202. Tel: 267-331-2490; Fax: 215-587-2479; Email: cssphiladelphia@chs-adphila.org; Web: www.cssphiladelphia.org. James Amato, L.S.W., Sec. Catholic Human Svcs., Deputy Sec., Dir. Housing & Homeless Svcs.; Gary Miller, Divisional Controller; Amy Stoner, L.S.W., A.C.S.W., Dir. Community-Based Svcs. Division & Dir. Housing & Homeless Svcs. All addresses unless otherwise indicated.

St. Gabriel's System, 227 N. 18th St., 19103. Tel: 215-665-8777; Fax: 215-665-8821; Web: www.stgabes.org. Joseph Lavoritano, M.A., M.Ed., N.C.S.P., Dir. - Youth Svcs.

Developmental Programs Division Office, 20 E. Cleveland Ave., Norwood, 19074.

Tel: 484-472-5066; Fax: 610-543-5397; Web: www.developmentalprogramsphilly.org. Francis E. Swiacki Jr., M.S.W., Dir. Devel. Programs Div.

Adoption Services, Tel: 267-331-2443; Fax: 215-457-5418; Web: www.adoption-phl.org. Robert Montoro, M.S.W., Admin.

Foster Care, Tel: 267-331-2488; Fax: 215-457-5418. Robert Montoro, M.S.W., Admin.

Philadelphia County Community-Based Services Amy Stoner, L.S.W., A.C.S.W., Dir.

Casa del Carmen Family Services, 4440 N. Reese St., 19140. Tel: 267-331-2500; Fax: 215-329-6722. Christopher Gale, M.P.A., Admin.

Northeast Philadelphia Family Service Center, 7340 Jackson St., 19136. Tel: 215-624-5920; Fax: 215-624-9197. Yvonne Branch, Admin.

Southwest Philadelphia Family Service Center, 6214 Grays Ave., 19142. Tel: 215-724-8550; Fax: 215-724-8521. Lola DeCarlo Coles, Admin.

Catholic Community Services, 10125 Verree Rd., #200, 19116. Teresa Thompson, L.S.W., Dir.

Catholic Housing and Community Services, 222 N. 17th St., 19103. Tel: 215-587-3663. John M. Wagner, Contact Person. Provides support and services to older adults, including community-based multi-service centers for seniors, in-home support, parish-based support programs, housing social service coordination and the creation of affordable senior housing communities.

Suburban Counties

Bucks County Family Service Centers, 100 Levittown Pkwy., Levittown, 19054. Tel: 215-945-2550; Fax: 215-945-3595. Teri Mitchell, Admin.

Chester County Operating Base Cecilia, 605 E. Lincoln Hwy., Coatesville, 19320. Tel: 610-384-8387; Fax: 610-384-7873. Rick Pytlewski, M.S.W., Admin.

Delaware County Family Service Center 130 E. 7th St., Chester, 19013. Tel: 610-876-7101; Fax: 610-876-9183. Rick Pytlewski, M.S.W., Admin.

Montgomery County Family Service Center, 353 E. Johnson Hwy., Norristown, 19401. Tel: 610-279-7372; Fax: 610-270-0626. Susan Stier, Admin.

Specialized Services, 227 N. 18th St., 19103. The offices are all located at the Holy Family Center unless otherwise noted.

Immigration and Refugee Services, Tel: 215-854-7019; Fax: 215-854-7020. Catherine Baggiano Esq.

Senior Adult Services, Tel: 215-854-7087. Karen Becker, L.S.W., Dir.

Senior Centers and Clubs, 222 N. 17th St., 19103. Tel: 215-854-7087; Fax: 215-965-5712.

Miscellaneous Corporations

St. Joseph House for Boys, 222 N. 17th St., 19103.

St. Joseph Catholic Home for Children, 222 N. 17th St., 19103.

St. Vincent's Services, 222 N. 17th St., 19103.

St. Vincent's Home, Tacony, 222 N. 17th St., 19103.

[L] RESIDENTIAL SERVICES FOR CHILDREN

BENSALEM. *St. Francis - St. Joseph - St. Vincent Homes For Children*, 3400 Bristol Pike, Bensalem, 19020. Tel: 215-638-9310; Fax: 215-638-2498. James Logan, M.S.W., Admin. Operates the following programs for court adjudicated dependent females ages 12-21 who suffer from abuse and neglect. All facilities are staffed 24/7. Capacity 115; Total Staff 146.

St. Joseph's Hall Group Home (12 females ages 12-21) 477 E. Locust Ave., 19144. Tel: 215-849-1316; Fax: 215-438-2879.

Guardian Angel Group Home (16 females ages 12-21) 157 W. Carpenter Ln., 19111. Tel: 267-574-1100; Fax: 215-992-5189.

St. Francis - St. Joseph Homes for Children, 3400 Bristol Pike, Bensalem, 19020. Tel: 215-638-9310; Fax: 215-638-2498; Email: cssphiladelphia@chs-adphila.org; Web: www.sfsj.org. James Logan, M.S.W., Admin. Provides residential treatment at 8 sites for male youth, ages 12 to 20; also Supervised Living for male youth 17 & older. Out-patient clinic and on-grounds education. Capacity 106; Total Staff 141; Total Assisted 196.

[M] RESIDENTIAL SERVICES FOR MENTALLY CHALLENGED CHILDREN AND ADULTS

SPRINGFIELD. *Cardinal Krol Homes-Communities of Don Guanella*, 1799 S. Sproul Rd., Springfield, 19064. Tel: 484-475-2467; Fax: 610-237-7473; Web: communitiesofdonguanella.org. Rev. Dennis M. Weber, S.D.C., Dir. Ministry & Mission. A residential facility for 30 male adults with developmental/intellectual disabilities which provides an environment that contributes to the individuals own growth and development by fulfilling their potential in the physical, mental, emotional, social, psychological, and spiritual areas of their lives. Priests 1; Tot Asst. Annually 30; Total Staff 50; Residential Capacity 30.

1745 S. Sproul Rd., Springfield, 19064. Tel: 484-472-8074. 1755 S. Sproul Rd., Springfield, 19064. 1765 S. Sproul Rd., Springfield, 19064.

Communities of Don Guanella and Divine Providence, 686 Old Marple Rd., Springfield, 19064. Tel: 484-908-6501; Fax: 610-544-1710; Web: communitiesofdonguanella.org. Jean Calvarese-Donovan, L.S.W., Admin.; Rev. Dennis M. Weber, S.D.C., Chap. Residential care & specialized training for adult females and males with intellectual/developmental disabilities. Capacity 96.

NORWOOD. *Don Guanella Village Corporation*, 20 E. Cleveland Ave., Norwood, 19074. Tel: 484-472-5067; Fax: 610-237-7473; Email: fr.dweber@chs-adphila.org; Web: communitiesofdonguanella.org. Rev. Dennis M. Weber, S.D.C., Dir. Ministry & Mission. Also operates Cardinal Krol Homes-Communities of Don Guanella.; Community-based residential settings for 98 adult males with developmental/intellectual disabilities which provides an environment that contributes to the individuals' own growth and development by fulfilling their potential in the physical, mental, emotional, social, psychological and spiritual areas of their lives. Priests 1; Tot Asst. Annually 98; Total Staff 220; Residential Capacity 98.

Don Guanella Home at Bethel, 4317 Bethel Rd., Boothwyn, 19061. Tel: 610-494-4976.

Don Guanella Home at Broadview, 1302 Broadview E., Downingtown, 19335. Tel: 610-873-1536.

Don Guanella Home at Fairhill, 2 Fairhill Rd., Morton, 19070. Tel: 610-544-3987.

Don Guanella Home at Fairview, 990 Fairview Rd., Swarthmore, 19081. Tel: 610-544-3987.

Don Guanella Home at Frankford, 8538 Frankford Ave., 19136. Tel: 215-331-3615.

Don Guanella Home at Grant, 500-502 Grant Ave., Downingtown, 19335. Tel: 610-873-1917.

Don Guanella Home at Meetinghouse, 1834 Meetinghouse Rd., Boothwyn, 19061. Tel: 610-859-7962.

Don Guanella Home at Rolling Road, 813 W. Rolling Rd., Springfield, 19064. Tel: 610-543-2659.

Don Guanella Home at Sickles, 1545 Sickles Dr., Aston, 19014. Tel: 484-840-0358.

Don Guanella Home at Upland, 225 Upland Ave., Brookhaven, 19015. Tel: 610-872-1329.

Don Guanella Home at Whiteland, 125 Whiteland Ave., Downingtown, 19335. Tel: 610-873-1726.

Gula House, 1745 S. Sproul Rd., Springfield, 19064. Tel: 484-472-8074.

Servants of Charity House, 1755 S. Sproul Rd., Springfield, 19064. Tel: 484-479-3936.

Sisters Servants of the Immaculate Heart of Mary House, 1765 S. Sproul Rd., Springfield, 19064. Tel: 484-479-3806.

[N] RESIDENTIAL HOMES FOR PHYSICALLY HANDICAPPED CHILDREN

ROSEMONT. *St. Edmond's Home for Children*, 320 S. Roberts Rd., Rosemont, 19010. Tel: 610-525-8800; Fax: 610-525-2693; Web: cssmrserv.org. Denise Clofine, M.Ed., Admin.; Rev. Dennis M. Weber, S.D.C., Chap. Licensed I.C.F./M.R. Home for children ages birth to 21 with severe/profound intellectual and physical disabilities. Capacity 44; Total Staff 160.

[O] PROTECTIVE INSTITUTIONS

AUDUBON. *St. Gabriel's Hall*, 1350 Pawlings Rd., Box 7280, Audubon, 19407-7280. Tel: 215-247-2776 (Philadelphia); Tel: 610-666-7970 (Audubon); Fax: 610-666-1479; Email: jlavoritano@chs_adphila.org. Joseph Lavoritano, M.A., M.Ed., N.C.S.P., Exec. Dir.; Ralph Stinson, M.S.W., A.F.S.C., Dir. Offers residential treatment for court-committed delinquent boys, ages 10-18.

St. Gabriel's System, St. Gabriel's Hall, 1350 Pawlings Rd., Box 7280, Audubon, 19407-7280. Tel: 215-665-8777; Fax: 215-665-8821; Email: jlavoritano@chs-adphila.org; Web: www.st-gabes.org. Joseph Lavoritano, M.A., M.Ed., N.C.S.P., Exec. Dir. Administrative and Intake services for residential treatment; Day Treatment for Court-committed delinquent boys, ages 12-17. (See St. Gabriel's Hall, De LaSalle Vocational and St. Gabriel's System Reintegration Services). Total Staff 322; Total Assisted 1,581.

[P] DAY TREATMENT CENTERS

BENSALEM. *De La Salle Vocational Day Treatment Center*, 1265 Street Rd., Bensalem, 19020. Tel: 215-464-0344; Fax: 215-638-3767; Email: cgaus@chs-adphila.org. Charles E. Gaus Jr., M.Ed., Dir. A community based day treatment program for court-committed delinquent boys, ages 15-18. Capacity 120; Total Staff 35.

[Q] SENIOR COMMUNITY CENTERS

PHILADELPHIA. *St. Anne's Senior Community Center*, 2607 E. Cumberland St., 19125. Tel: 215-423-2772; Fax: 215-423-2423. Karen Rouse, Senior Center Mgr. Total Staff 6; Total Assisted 534.

St. Charles Senior Community Center, 1941 Christian St., 19146. Tel: 215-790-9530; Fax: 215-790-9765. Kathy Boles, Center Mgr. Total Staff 7; Total Assisted 1,409.

Norris Square Senior Community Center, 2121 N. Howard St., 19133. Tel: 215-423-7241; Fax: 215-634-7751. Bethzaida Butler Lopez, Center Mgr. Total Staff 8; Total Assisted 3,056.

Star Harbor Senior Community Center, 4700 Springfield Ave., 19143. Tel: 215-724-4414; Fax: 215-726-7496. Ernestine Patterson, Center Mgr. Total Staff 6; Total Assisted 974.

[R] OUTREACH CENTERS

PHILADELPHIA. *Casa del Carmen*, 4400 N. Reese St., 19140. Tel: 267-331-2500; Fax: 215-329-6722. Christopher Gale, M.P.A., Admin. Offers emergency crisis social services to the Spanish speaking community in Philadelphia and surrounding areas.

Drueding Center, 413 W. Master St., 19122. Tel: 215-769-1830; Fax: 215-787-0999; Email: acollins@holyredeemer.com; Web: www.druedingcenter.org. Anne Marie Collins, Exec. Dir. Sponsor: Sisters of the Holy Redeemer, C.S.R.Subsidiary of Holy Redeemer Health System; Provides transitional housing and support services for homeless women with children; daycare is provided for the children. Bed Capacity 58; Families Assisted Annually in All Programs 729; Families in Transitional Housing Only 56.

Marketing/Public Affairs Department, c/o 1602 Huntingdon Pike, Meadowbrook, 19046. Tel: 215-938-3226; Fax: 215-938-3232.

St. Francis Inn, 2441 Kensington Ave., 19125. Tel: 215-423-5845; Fax: 215-423-2289; Email: stfrancisinn@aol.com; Web: www.stfrancisinn.org. Rev. Michael A. Duffy, O.F.M., Contact Person. Meals for the needy every day and free clothing distribution three times a week. Brothers 2; (Full-time, paid) 2; Priests 2; Sisters 2; Tot Asst. Annually 145,000; Total Staff 8.

Thea Bowman's Women's Center, 2858 Kensington Ave., 19134. Tel: 215-739-1137. Kathryn Horan, Dir. & Contact Person. Women's day activity center.

St. John's Hospice, 1221 Race St., 19107. Tel: 215-563-7763; Fax: 215-563-0108; Web: www.saintjohnshospice.org. David Stier, Program Dir. Staffed by Catholic Social Services Archdiocese of Philadelphia. Total Staff 33; Total Assisted 50,000.

The Good Shepherd Program of St. John's Hospice, 1225 Race St., 19107. Tel: 215-569-1101; Fax: 215-569-1759. Barry Martin, Prog. Mgr.

McAuley House, 1800 Morris St., 19145. Tel: 215-271-5166; Fax: 215-271-1601. Marcia Cedeno, Prog. Supvr. Bed Capacity 6; Tot Asst. Annually 14; Total Staff 7.

Mercy Hospice, 334 S. 13th St., 19107. Tel: 215-545-5153; Fax: 215-545-1872. Kate Baumgardner, Dir. Provides residential case management and referral services to homeless women, women in recovery who are single or are with their children. Mercy Hospice also provides lunch Monday thru Friday from 12:00 - 12:45 p.m. to homeless women and children. Showers, clothing and the use of a telephone are available on a limited basis. Bed Capacity 35; Tot Asst. Annually 1,862; Total Staff 22; Lunch Program 1,540.

Visitation Homes, 2638 Kensington Ave., 19125. Tel: 215-425-2080; Fax: 215-425-1412. Sara Frisby-Simms, Prog. Dir. Residential service program for families making the transition from homelessness to permanent housing. The program offers 18 furnished one to three bedroom apartments and on site case management and life skill services. Referrals come through the City's Office of Emergency Shelter and Services. For a period of up to 18 months, residents are helped to achieve economic self sufficiency and address the other issues which led to their homelessness. Total Staff 10; Total Assisted 124.

Women of Hope Lombard, 1210 Lombard St., 19147. Tel: 215-732-1341; Fax: 215-732-0659. Rosemary Chetalo, L.S.W., Prog. Dir. Residential Facility for chronically mentally ill homeless women. Capacity 24; Tot Asst. Annually 25; Total Staff 20.

Women of Hope-Vine, 251 N. Lawrence St., 19106. Tel: 215-592-9116; Fax: 215-592-0650. Sr. Maureen Crissy, R.S.M., Prog. Dir. Residential facility for chronically mentally ill homeless women. Capacity 22; Total Staff 21; Total Assisted 26.

CHESTER. *The Bernardine Center (Bernardine Franciscans, Delaware County)*, 2625 W. Ninth St., Chester, 19013. Tel: 610-497-3225; Fax: 610-497-3659; Email: director@bernardinecenter.org; Web: www.

bernardinecenter.org. Sr. Sandra Lyons, O.S.F., Dir. West Side Brunch, Emergency Food Cupboard, Advocacy, Computer Classes, Parenting Classes, Anger Management Classes, Baby Cupboard, ESL (English as a Second Language). Sisters 1; Tot Asst. Annually 13,550; Total Staff 3; Volunteers 25.

Sisters of St. Francis of Philadelphia, Anna's Place, 226 Norris St., Chester, 19013. Tel: 484-361-5900; Fax: 484-361-5901; Email: jrupertus@osfphila.org; Web: annasplace.org. Sr. Jean Rupertus, Dir.

[S] DAY CARE CENTERS

PHILADELPHIA. *Casa del Carmen Day Care Center*, 4400 N. 5th St., 19140. Tel: 215-457-4325; Fax: 215-457-4339. Mailing Address: 4400 N. Reese St., 19140. Shari Gold, Dir.

St. Monica Early Learning Center, 1720 W. Ritner St., 19145. Tel: 215-334-6001; Fax: 215-467-4599; Email: rpeterson44@yahoo.com; Web: stmonicaparish.net. Sr. Rosemary Peterson, I.H.M., Dir. Sister, Servants of the Immaculate Heart of Mary. (Full-time, paid) 7; Sisters 2; Students 90; Religious Teachers 2.

[T] GENERAL HOSPITALS

PHILADELPHIA. *Mercy Catholic Medical Center* dba Mercy Philadelphia Hospital, 501 S. 54th St., 19143. Tel: 215-748-9300; Fax: 215-748-9709; Web: www.mercyhealth.org. Susan Croushore, Pres. & CEO, Mercy Health System; Kathryn Connelly-Conallen, M.S., B.S.N., Senior Vice Pres. & CEO, Mercy Acute Care Svcs.; Sr. Suzanne Gallagher, R.S.M., Ph.D., Vice Pres., Mission Integration. Opened July 2, 1918. Incorporated May 1, 1969. A member of Mercy Health System and Trinity Health. Bed Capacity 157; Patients Asst Anual. 88,027; Total Staff 763.

**Nazareth Hospital*, 2601 Holme Ave., 19152. Tel: 215-335-6039; Fax: 215-335-6598; Web: www.mercyhealth.org. Susan Croushore, Pres. & CEO, Mercy Health System; Kathryn Connelly-Conallen, M.S., B.S.N., Senior Vice Pres. & CEO, Mercy Acute Care Svcs.; Mary Ann Carter, Vice Pres. Mission Integration. A member of Mercy Health System and Trinity Health. Bed Capacity 231; Patients Asst Anual. 148,099; Total Staff 863.

DARBY. *Mercy Catholic Medical Center* dba Mercy Fitzgerald Hospital, 1500 Lansdowne Ave., Darby, 19023-1291. Tel: 610-237-4030; Fax: 610-237-4202; Web: www.mercyhealth.org. Susan Croushore, Pres. & CEO Mercy Health Systems; Kathryn Connelly-Conallen, M.S., B.S.N., Senior Vice Pres. & CEO, Mercy Acute Care Svcs.; Sr. Donna M. Watto, R.S.M., Vice Pres. Mission Integration. Opened July 1, 1933. Incorporated May 1, 1969.; A member of Mercy Health System and Trinity Health. Bed Capacity 204; Tot Asst. Annually 159,868; Total Staff 874.

HUNTINGDON VALLEY. *Holy Redeemer Ministries*, 667 Welsh Rd., Huntingdon Valley, 19006. Tel: 215-938-4650; Fax: 215-938-4671; Web: www.holyredeemer.com. Parent Corporation of Holy Redeemer Health System; Sponsor: Sisters of the Holy Redeemer, C.S.R. Total Staff 3,918; Total Assisted 111,708.

Marketing & Public Affairs Department, 521 Moredon Rd., Huntingdon Valley, 19006. Tel: 215-938-3226; Fax: 215-938-3232.

HRH Management Corporation, 667 Welsh Rd., Huntingdon Valley, 19006. Tel: 215-938-4650; Fax: 215-938-4671; Web: www.holyredeemer.com. Affiliate of Holy Redeemer Health System. Sponsor: Sisters of the Holy Redeemer, C.S.R.

MEADOWBROOK. *Holy Redeemer Hospital*, 1648 Huntingdon Pike, Meadowbrook, 19046. Tel: 215-947-3000; Fax: 215-938-2023; Email: cegan@holyredeemer.com; Web: www.holyredeemer.com. Catherine Egan, Exec. Vice Pres. & Chief Admin. Officer. Sponsor: Sisters of the Holy Redeemer, C.S.R.Subsidiary of Holy Redeemer Health System; Acute care community hospital, providing a broad spectrum of services, including preventive, rehabilitative, emergency and obstetrical care plus pastoral counseling. Bed Capacity 229; Total Staff 1,373; Total Assisted 63,078.

[U] SPECIALIZED HOSPITALS

PHILADELPHIA. *Mount Nazareth*, 2755 Holme Ave., 19152. Tel: 215-543-0124; Fax: 215-338-8752. Sr. Jeanette Lawlor, C.S.F.N., Local Supr. Sisters of the Holy Family of Nazareth.Home for retired and infirm sisters. Tot Asst. Annually 27; Total Staff 25; Resident Sisters 51.

ASTON. *Assisi House*, 600 Red Hill Rd., Aston, 19014. Tel: 610-459-8990; Fax: 610-558-5344; Email: megan@osphila.org; Web: www.osfphila.org. Sr. Peggy Egan, O.S.F., Admin.; Rev. Francis Sariego, O.F.M.Cap. Home for retired Sisters of St. Francis of Philadelphia. Capacity 130; Tot Asst. Annually 100; Total Staff 168.

DARBY. *Villa Saint Joseph*, 1436 Lansdowne Ave., Darby, 19023-1298. Tel: 610-586-8535; Fax: 610-586-2810. Rev. Msgr. William A. Dombrow, M.Div., Rector; Helen McConnell, R.N., M.S., Admin. Home for aged, infirm and convalescent priests of the Archdiocese of Philadelphia. Residents 62; Tot Asst. Annually 64; Total Staff 70.

DOWNINGTOWN. *St. John Vianney Center*, 151 Woodbine Rd., Downingtown, 19335. Tel: 610-269-2600; Tel: 888-993-8885; Email: info@sjvcenter.org; Web: www.sjvcenter.org. David Shellenberger, R.N., B.S.N., Pres. Private hospital treating behavioral health issues, addictions, and compulsive behaviors. Serving Catholic Clergy, Consecrated Men and Women Religious, and clergy of other Christian denominations worldwide. Holistic, inter-disciplinary, evidence-based, and individualized programs to get and stay healthy in mind, body, and spirit. Facility is open 24/7 for admissions, information, and resources. SJVC also provides consultations, interventions, mediations, and educational programs at your site. Bed Capacity 50; Tot Asst. Annually 125; Total Staff 120.

IMMACULATA. *Camilla Hall Nursing Home*, Camilla Dr., P.O. Box 100, Immaculata, 19345-0100. Tel: 610-386-2000; Fax: 610-695-0691; Email: ch@camillahall.org. Sisters Anne Veronica Burrows, I.H.M., Admin.; Dolores Joseph Bozzelli, I.H.M., Supr.; Rev. William E. Dean, M.Div., Chap.; Rev. Msgr. Joseph L. Logrip, M.A., M.Div., Chap. Sisters, Servants of the Immaculate Heart of Mary. Bed Capacity 239; Residents 210; Total Staff 207; Skilled Care 89.

MERION STATION. *McAuley Convent*, 517 Montgomery Ave., Merion Station, 19066. Tel: 610-667-2775; Fax: 610-667-9650. Sisters Maureen Murray, R.S.M., Life Coord.; Maryanne Werner, R.S.M., Dir., Nursing. Infirmary for Religious Sisters of Mercy. Total Staff 63; Total Assisted 34.

WARMINSTER. *Regina Coeli Residence for Priests*, 685 York Rd., Warminster, 18974. Tel: 215-441-4642. Rev. Msgr. J. Michael Flood, M.Div., Admin., (Retired); Helen McConnell, R.N., M.S., Admin. Home for retired priests of the Archdiocese of Philadelphia. Tot Asst. Annually 8; Total in Residence 11; Total Staff 4.

[V] AFFILIATED SERVICES

PHILADELPHIA. *Holy Redeemer Home Health and Hospice Services* Holy Redeemer Support Services 12265 Townsend Rd., Ste. 400, 19154. Tel: 215-671-9200; Fax: 215-671-1950; Web: www.holyredeemer.com. Patricia O'Brien, Senior Vice Pres. & Chief Admin. Officer. Affiliate of Holy Redeemer Health System. Sponsor: Sisters of the Holy Redeemer; Medicare certified home health agency serving patients in their own homes; Medicare certified hospice program serving terminally ill patients and their families.

Marketing & Public Affairs Department, 521 Moredon Rd., Huntingdon Valley, 19006. Tel: 215-938-3226; Fax: 215-938-3232.

PHOENIXVILLE. *St. Mary's Franciscan Shelter*, 209 Emmett St., Phoenixville, 19460. Tel: 610-933-3097; Fax: 610-917-9845; Email: stmarysfs@verizon.net; Web: stmarysfs.org. Total Staff 6; Families Assisted 28.

Staff: Sr. Bernadette Dougherty, S.S.J., Exec. Dir.; Kate Garges.

[W] NURSING AND CONVALESCENT HOMES

PHILADELPHIA. *St. Ignatius Nursing Home*, 4401 Haverford Ave., 19104. Tel: 215-349-8800; Fax: 215-222-3078; Email: jmeacham@stinrc.org; Web: www.stinrc.org. Susan McCrary, Admin. Attended from St. Ignatius Church. Bed Capacity 176; Felician Sisters 5; Total in Residence 176; Total Staff 235; Total Assisted 407.

FLOURTOWN. *Saint Joseph Villa*, 110 W. Wissahickon Ave., Flourtown, 19031-1898. Tel: 215-836-4179; Fax: 215-248-7802; Email: apprichd@stjosephvilla.org; Web: www.stjosephvilla.org. Sr. Dorothy Apprich, S.S.J., Exec. Dir. Bed Capacity 324; Total Staff 400; Licensed Beds 106; Convent Beds 216.

[X] LONG TERM RESIDENCES FOR THE ELDERLY

PHILADELPHIA. *Holy Family Home*, 5300 Chester Ave., 19143-4993. Tel: 215-729-5153; Fax: 215-727-5332. Sr. Catherine, L.S.P., Pres.; Rev. James F. Sullivan, M.Div., Chap. Little Sisters of the Poor. Residents 97; Tot Asst. Annually 123; Total Staff 118.

St. John Neumann Place, 2600 Moore St., 19145. Tel: 215-463-1101 (Main Number); Fax: 215-463-1119; Web: www.stjohnneumannplace.org. Caroline Morgan, M.S.S., L.S.W., Social Svcs. Coord.

St. Joseph Housing Corporation, Mount St. Joseph Convent, 9701 Germantown Ave., 19118-2694. Tel: 215-248-7200; Fax: 215-248-7277; Email: msjc@ssjphila.net; Web: www.ssjphila.org. Sr. Anne Myers, S.S.J., Supr. Staffed by the Sisters of St. Joseph. Total in Residence 100; Total Staff 4.

**Nativity BVM Place*, 3255 Belgrade St., 19134. Tel: 215-426-9422. Kimiko Doherty, Project Developer.

DARBY. *Little Flower Manor* All Skilled Nursing Care. 1201 Springfield Rd., Darby, 19023. Tel: 610-534-6000; Fax: 610-534-6039. Rosemary Port, Admin. Staffed by Sisters of the Divine Redeemer. Bed Capacity 127; Patients Asst Anual. 283; Total Staff 165.

ELVERSON. *St. Mary of Providence Center*, 227 Isabella Rd., Elverson, 19520. Tel: 610-942-4166; Fax: 610-942-4259; Email: stmaryofprov@comcast.net; Web: stmaryofprov-pa.org. Sr. Margaret Ann Hubler, D.S.M.P., Supr. Residence for Senior Citizens. Center of Spirituality, Retreats and Days of Recollection. Capacity 39; Sisters 3; Total in Residence 43; Total Staff 15; Overnight & Day Retreats 110.

FLOURTOWN. *Bethlehem Retirement Village*, 100 W. Wissahickon Ave., Flourtown, 19031. Tel: 215-233-0998; Fax: 215-233-9052. Sr. Judith Oliver, S.S.J., Mgr. Staffed by the Sisters of St. Joseph. Total in Residence 102; Total Staff 4; Apartments 100.

HUNTINGDON VALLEY. *Redeemer Village*, 1551 Huntingdon Pike, Huntingdon Valley, 19006. Tel: 215-947-8168; Web: www.holyredeemer.com. Marketing/Public Affairs Department, Holy Redeemer Health System, c/o 521 Moredon Rd., Huntingdon Valley, 19006. Tel: 215-938-3226; Fax: 215-938-3232. Joseph Munizza, Assoc. Vice Pres. Residential Svcs. Sisters of the Holy Redeemer, C.S.R.Subsidiary of Holy Redeemer Health System. Low income housing for the elderly or handicapped, subsidized by HUD. Apartments 151.

Redeemer Village II, 1551 Huntingdon Pike, Huntingdon Valley, 19006. Tel: 215-947-8168. Sisters of the Holy Redeemer, C.S.R.Subsidiary of Holy Redeemer Health System, Inc. Low income housing for the elderly or handicapped, subsidized by HUD. Apartments 49.

[Y] RESIDENCES FOR WOMEN

PHILADELPHIA. *St. Mary's Residence*, 247 S. 5th St., 19106. Tel: 215-922-4228; Fax: 215-922-0192. Kathleen Nelson, Prog. Dir. Catholic Social Services. Residents 38; Total Staff 5.

[Z] MONASTERIES AND RESIDENCES OF PRIESTS AND BROTHERS

PHILADELPHIA. *Augustinian Community (O.S.A.)*, 910 Watkins St., 19148. Tel: 215-463-1326; Fax: 215-463-0888; Email: stnicks910@verizon.net; Web: www.stnicksphila.com. Revs. Nicholas Martorano, O.S.A.; Dennis G. Wilde, O.S.A.; Howard McGraw, O.S.A.; Jorge Cleto, O.S.A.; Robert Terranova. Priests 5; Total Staff 5. In Res. Revs. Howard McGraw, O.S.A.; Denis G. Wilde, O.S.A.

The Brothers of the Christian Schools / Jeremy House Postulancy, 6633 Ardleigh St., 19119-3824. Tel: 215-843-1884. Bro. Richard Buccina, F.S.C., Dir. Postulants 4; Professed Brothers 3.

The Brothers of the Christian Schools, Roncalli Community, 6519 N. 12th St., 19126. Tel: 215-880-1180. Bro. Gerard Molyneaux, F.S.C., Dir.

Congregation of the Mission, St. Vincent's Seminary, 500 E. Chelten Ave., 19144-1203. Tel: 215-713-2400; Fax: 215-844-2085; Email: secretary@vincentiansusaeast.org; Web: www.cmeast.org. Revs. Gregory P. Cozzubbo, C.M., Supr.; Timothy V. Lyons, C.M., Supr.; Very Revs. Stephen M. Grozio, C.M., Prov.; Thomas F. McKenna, C.M., Asst. Prov.; Rev. Elmer Bauer III, C.M., Treas.; Bro. Peter A. Campbell, C.M., Treas.; Mr. Allen Andrews, Exec.; Revs. Stephen F. Cantwell, C.M.; Dennis H. Holtschneider, C.M.; John A. Kettelberger, C.M.; Joseph V. Agostino, C.M., In Res.; William J. Bamber, C.M., In Res.; Stephen Bicsko, In Res.; Henry Bradbury, In Res.; Michael Callaghan, C.M., In Res.; Michael J. Carroll, C.M., In Res.; John W. Carven, C.M., In Res.; Joseph V. Daly, C.M., In Res.; Joseph A. Elzi, C.M., In Res.; John B. Freund, C.M., In Res.; John E. Kane, C.M., In Res.; Richard J. Kehoe, C.M., In Res.; Michael J. Kennedy, C.M., In Res.; Thomas R. Kennedy, C.M., In Res.; Daniel J. Kramer, C.M., In Res.; Charles Krieg, In Res.; Robert P. Maloney, C.M., In Res.; William J. O'Brien, C.M., In Res.; Abel Osorio, C.M., In Res.; Alfred R. Pehrsson, C.M., In Res.; Flavio Pereira, C.M., In Res.; Carl L. Pieber, C.M., In Res.; Francis W. Sacks, C.M., In Res.; Thomas A. Sendlein, C.M., In Res.; Michael J. Shea, C.M., In Res.; William W. Sheldon, C.M., In Res.; Harold G. Skidmore, C.M., In Res.; Robert J. Stone, C.M.,

In Res.; Louis P. Trotta, C.M, In Res.; Stephen Trzecieski, In Res.; Bro. Joseph Zurowski, C.M., In Res. Central House of the Congregation of the Mission (Vincentian Community), Eastern Province. Novitiate, Central Shrine of the Miraculous Medal in the United States, The Central Association of the Miraculous Medal and St. Catherine's Infirmary, Assisted Living Facility, The Brother Bertrand Ducournau Archives of the Eastern Province of the Congregation of the Mission. Total in Residence 36.

Father Louis Brisson Residence, 3301 Solly Ave., 19136-2340. Tel: 215-624-1604; Fax: 215-332-3478. Revs. Leon V. Bonikowski, O.S.F.S., Oblate Mission of Appeals; Joseph G. Campellone, O.S.F.S., Pres.; James E. Dalton, O.S.F.S., Prin.; John J. Dolan, O.S.F.S., Spec. Ed. Teacher; Dominick F. Finn, O.S.F.S., (Retired); Joseph P. Jocco, O.S.F.S, Sophomore Counselor; Cornelius F. Kilty, O.S.F.S., Pastoral Min./Teaching; Jack Kolodziej, O.S.F.S., Vice Prin., Student Affairs; William Nessel, O.S.F.S., (Retired); John P. Spellman, O.S.F.S., Pastoral Min./Teacher; Bro. James F. Williams, O.S.F.S., Rel. Supvr. & Spec. Ed. Teacher. Total in Residence 11; Total Staff 5.

Gesu School Jesuit Community and Outreach Center (S.J.), 1700 W. Thompson St., 19121.
Tel: 215-763-3660, Ext. 108; Fax: 215-763-9844; Email: neil@gesuschool.org. Rev. Neil L. Ver'Schneider, S.J., Contact Person. Total Staff 1; Volunteers 1; Total Assisted 204.

Jesuit Community, Arrupe House, 1226 N. 18th St., 19121. Tel: 215-765-1875; Fax: 215-978-1920; Email: rmccouch@mdsj.org. Revs. Charles Frederico, S.J., Supr.; John W. Swope, S.J.; Raymond J. Donaldson, S.J.; Neil L. Ver'Schneider, S.J.; Chijioke A. Azuawusiefe, S.J. Residence of Jesuit Fathers and Brothers.

Monastery of Our Lady of Mercy, 6398 Drexel Rd., 19151-2596. Tel: 215-879-0594; Fax: 215-877-7625; Email: vocations@orderofmercy.org; Web: www.orderofmercy.org. Revs. Anthony M. Fortunato, O.de.M., Local Supr.; Eugene A. Costa, O.de.M.; Scottston F. Brentwood, O.de.M., Vocations & Master, Postulants; Bros. Gerard D. Snell, O.de.M.; Dominic (Matthew) Whetzel, O.de.M., Teacher, Neumann-Goretti High School. Order of the B.V.M. of Mercy (Mercedarian Friars).Pre-Novitiate House of Studies for the Order. Total in Residence 5.

Order of Friars Minor of the Province of the Most Holy Name aka Holy Name Province, The Franciscans, 1802 E. Hagert St., 19125.
Tel: 646-473-0265; Email: hnp@hnp.org. 129 West 31st St., 2nd Fl., New York, NY 10001. Rev. Kevin Mullen, Pres.

The Philadelphia Congregation of The Oratory of St. Philip Neri, 2321 Green St., 19130-3196.
Tel: 215-765-4568; Fax: 215-765-4049. Very Rev. Georges G. Thiers, C.O., Provost; Revs. Paul C. Convery, C.O., Vicar; James N. Dean, C.O.; Brian R. Gaffney, C.O.

ARDMORE. *Bellesini Friary*, 111 Argyle Rd., Ardmore, 19003. Tel: 610-642-1420; Email: fjdosa@gmail.com. Revs. Kevin M. DePrinzio, O.S.A., Prof.; Francis J. Doyle, O.S.A., Prior; Very Rev. Joseph L. Farrell, O.S.A.; Rev. Joseph L. Narog, O.S.A., Dir. In Res. Rev. Kevin De Prinzio, O.S.A.

AUDUBON. *Christian Brothers (F.S.C.)*, St. Gabriel Hall Community, 1350 Pawlings Rd., P.O. Box 7280, Audubon, 19407-7280. Tel: 215-247-2776;
Tel: 610-666-7970; Fax: 610-666-0743.

BENSALEM. *Congregation of the Holy Spirit*, Spiritan Hall, 2401 Bristol Pike, Bensalem, 19020.
Tel: 215-638-0845; Fax: 215-639-5438; Email: jmcmloskey@holyghostprep.org; Web: www.spiritans.org. Revs. James P. McCloskey, C.S.Sp., Supr.; Philip Agber, C.S.Sp.; Christopher H. McDermott, C.S.Sp., Bursar; Bro. Joseph T. Cannon. Faculty Residence for Priests Teaching at Holy Ghost Preparatory School.

Missionaries of the Blessed Sacrament (M.S.S.) aka Missionary Priests of the Blessed Sacrament, 2290 Galloway Rd., B7, Bensalem, 19020.
Tel: 215-244-9211; Fax: 215-244-9211; Email: apea@webtv.net; Web: www.perpetualadoration.org. Rev. Victor P. Warkulwiz, M.S.S., Supr.

BRYN MAWR. *Augustinians Friars (O.S.A.)*, Our Mother of Good Counsel Community, 31 Pennswood Rd., Bryn Mawr, 19010-3475. Tel: 610-525-0147;
Fax: 610-525-0157. Rev. James D. McBurney, O.S.A.; Bro. William C. Harkin, O.S.A. In Res. Bro. Richard Ekmann, O.S.A.

DEVON. *Piarist Fathers (Order of the Pious Schools)*, 363 N. Valley Forge Rd., Devon, 19333.
Tel: 610-688-7337; Fax: 610-688-2409; Email: HeadmasterEmeritus@DevonPrep.com. Revs. Francisco Aisa, Sch.P., Headmaster; James J. Shea, Sch.P., Rector; Javier Renteria, Sch.P., Chap.; Geza Pazmany, Sch.P., In Res., (Retired). Total in Residence 4; Total Staff 1.

DOYLESTOWN. *The Order of Saint Paul, First Hermit - The Pauline Fathers* aka Pauline Fathers Monastery, 654 Ferry Rd., P.O. Box 2049, Doylestown, 18901. Tel: 215-345-0607;
Fax: 215-348-2148; Email: reception@czestochowa.us; Web: www.czestochowa.us. Revs. Tadeusz Lizinczyk, Prov.; Krzysztof Drybka, O.S.P.P.E., Prior; Edward Volz, O.S.P.P.E., Dir.; Jan Michalak, O.S.P.P.E., Subprior; Mikolaj Socha, O.S.P.P.E., Admin.; Jan Kolmaga, O.S.P.P.E.; Jerzy Maj, O.S.P.P.E.; Bartlomiej Marciniak, O.S.P.P.E.; Tymoteusz Tarnacki, O.S.P.P.E.; Lucius Tyrasinski, O.S.P.P.E.; Bros. Tomasz Fabiszewsk, O.S.S.P.E.; Piotr Lisiecki, O.S.P.P.E.; Aniol Sokalski, O.S.P.P.E.; Kazimierz Kania, O.S.P.P.E.; Rev. Maciej Karpinski, O.S.P.P.E.; Bro. Bernard Kluczkowski, O.S.P.P.E.; Rev. Tadeusz Olzacki, O.S.P.P.E. Residents 17. Office:Tel: 215-345-0600;
Tel: 215-345-0601; Fax: 215-348-2148. Revs. Mikolaj Socha, O.S.P.P.E., Prov. Supr.; Tadeusz Lizinczyk, Prov.; Krzysztof Drybka, O.S.P.P.E., Prior; Jan Kolmaga, O.S.P.P.E.; Edward Volz, O.S.P.P.E., Shrine Dir.; Jerzy Maj, O.S.P.P.E.; Jan Michalak, O.S.P.P.E., Subprior; Bartlomiej Marciniak, O.S.P.P.E.; Tymoteusz Tarnacki, O.S.P.P.E.; Lucius Tyrasinski, O.S.P.P.E.; Bros. Tomasz Fabiszewsk, O.S.S.P.E.; Piotr Lisiecki, O.S.P.P.E.; Aniol Sokalski, O.S.P.P.E.; Rafal Kandora, Prov. Sec.; Bro. Kazimierz Kania, O.S.P.P.E.; Marek Kreis, O.S.P.P.E.; Rev. Dominik Libiszewski, O.S.P.P.E.

LAVEROCK. *Brothers of Charity (F.C.)*, Triest Hall, 7720 Doe Ln., Laverock, 19038. Tel: 215-887-6361;
Fax: 215-877-6372; Email: jfitzfc@aol.com; Web: www.brothersofcharity.org. Bro. John Fitzgerald, F.C., Regl. Supr. Total in Residence 14; Total Staff 9.

MALVERN. *Augustinian Friars (O.S.A.)*, Malvern Prep School, St. Augustine Friary at Albers Hall, 418 S. Warren Ave., Malvern, 19355-2707.
Tel: 484-595-1194; Web: www.augustinians.org. James Cassidy, Prof.; Revs. Christopher J. Drennen, O.S.A., Prior; Harry J. Erdlen, O.S.A., Campus Min.; James R. Flynn, O.S.A., Special Asst. to the Head of School; Thomas J. Meehan, O.S.A.; Donald F. Reilly, O.S.A., Headmaster. Students 650; Total in Residence 5.

MERION STATION. *Jesuit Community at St. Joseph's University*, 261 City Ave., Merion Station, 19066.
Tel: 610-660-1400; Fax: 610-660-1433; Email: blally@sju.edu; Web: www.sju.edu/jesuits. Revs. Vincent de P. Alagia, (Retired); David G. Allen, S.J., (Retired); George M. Anderson, S.J., (Retired); George Aschenbrenner, (Retired); Anthony J. Berret, S.J., Pastor Emeritus; John M. Braverman, S.J., Prof.; Thomas J. Brennan, Prof.; William J. Byron, S.J., University Prof. Emeritus; Peter A. Clark, S.J., Prof.; Robert S. Curry, S.J., (Retired); Richard Dimler, (Retired); James J. Ditillo, S.J., Chap.; Joseph J. Feeney, S.J., Prof. Emeritus; Vincent J. Genovesi, S.J., Prof.; Joseph J. Godfrey, S.J., Prof. Emeritus; Richard Gross, S.J., Chap.; Harry Hock, (Retired); Michael A. Hricko, S.J., (Retired); Manuel Hurtado, Prof.; Daniel R.J. Joyce, S.J., Admin.; John J. Kelly, Pastoral Asst.; Brendan G. Lally, S.J., Rector; John Lange, (Retired); Joseph L. Lombardi, S.J., Prof. Emeritus; Dominic W. Maruca, S.J., (Retired); James F. McAndrews, S.J., (Retired); John W. McDaniel, S.J., (Retired); Neil McLaughlin, (Retired); Dennis E. McNally, S.J., Prof.; Francis X. Moan, S.J., (Retired); James W. Moore, S.J., (Retired); Janez Percic, Prof.; Thomas A. Pesci, S.J., Admin.; Nicholas J. Rashford, S.J., Prof.; William C. Rickle, S.J., Chap.; Daniel M. Ruff, S.J., M.Div., S.T.M., Ph.D., Chap.; Patrick H. Samway, S.J., Prof. Emeritus; Edwin G. Sanders, S.J., (Retired); William J. Sneck, S.J., (Retired); Martin R. Tripole, S.J., Prof. Emeritus; Thomas Wheeler, S.J., (Retired); Kevin Wildes, University Prof. Priests 36. *Loyola Center* Revs. Brendan G. Lally, S.J., Rector; Thomas A. Pesci, S.J., Min.; Anthony J. Berret, S.J.; John M. Braverman, S.J.; Thomas J. Brennan, S.J.; William J. Byron, S.J.; Peter A. Clark, S.J.; James J. Ditillo, S.J.; Joseph J. Feeney, S.J.; Vincent J. Genovesi, S.J.; Joseph J. Godfrey, S.J.; Michael A. Hricko, S.J., (Retired); Daniel R.J. Joyce, S.J.; John J. Kelly, S.J.; Joseph L. Lombardi, S.J.; Gregory A. Lynch, S.J.; John W. McDaniel, S.J., (Retired); Dennis E. McNally, S.J.; Nicholas J. Rashford, S.J.; William C. Rickle, S.J.; Daniel M. Ruff, S.J., M.Div., S.T.M., Ph.D.; Patrick H. Samway, S.J.; Martin R. Tripole, S.J.

Manresa Hall Revs. David G. Allen, S.J., (Retired); George M. Anderson, S.J., (Retired); Robert S. Curry, S.J., (Retired); G. Richard Dimler, S.J.; G. Harry Hock, S.J.; Dominic W. Maruca, S.J., (Retired); Francis G. McManamin, S.J.; Francis X. Moan, S.J., (Retired); James W. Moore, S.J., (Retired); Edwin G. Sanders, S.J., (Retired); Joseph P. Sanders, S.J.; William J. Sneck, S.J., (Retired); Thomas F.X. Wheeler, S.J.

PAOLI. *Daylesford Abbey*, 220 S. Valley Rd., Paoli, 19301-1900. Tel: 610-647-2530; Fax: 610-651-0219; Email: norbertines@daylesford.org; Web: www.daylesford.org. Rt. Revs. Ronald J. Rossi, O.Praem., Abbot Emeritus; Richard J. Antonucci, O.Praem., Abbot; Very Rev. John Joseph Novielli, O.Praem., Dir. Devel. & Vocation, Prior; Revs. Steven J. Albero, O.Praem.; Joseph A. Serano, O.Praem., Treas.; Theodore J. Antry, O.Praem.; Maurice C. Avicolli, O.Praem.; Carl Braschoss, O.Praem.; Andrew D. Ciferni, O.Praem.; Francis X. Cortese, O.Praem.; Francis Danielski, O.Praem.; Paul J. DeAntoniis, O.Praem.; David Driesch, O.Praem.; Blaise R. Krautsack, O.Praem.; Joseph C. Laenen, O.Praem.; David T. Lawlor, O.Praem.; Michael J. Lee, O.Praem.; Joseph P. McLaughlin, O.Praem.; James C. Rodia, O.Praem.; Domenic A. Rossi, O.Praem.; Thomas J. Rossi, O.Praem.; Nicholas R. Terico, O.Praem.; William A. Trader, O.Praem., M.Div.; John C. Zagarella, O.Praem.; Rev. Frater James Garvey, O.Praem.; Bros. John B. Ginder, O.Praem.; Jeffrey Himes; Rev. A. Gerard Jordan, O.Praem.; Bro. Joseph P. Mulholland, O.Praem.

Daylesford Abbey, Inc. Brothers 3; Priests 26; Seminarians 1.

ROSEMONT. *Saxony Hall*, 110 Montrose Ave., Rosemont, 19010-1509. Tel: 610-520-4510;
Fax: 610-520-4510. Revs. Robert P. Hagan, O.S.A., Prior; Stephen J. Baker, O.S.A., Treas.; Martin S. Laird, O.S.A.; James J. McCartney, O.S.A.; Joseph Loya, O.S.A.; John J. McKenzie, O.S.A. Total in Residence 6.

SPRINGFIELD. *Servants of Charity (SdC)*, Divine Providence Village, 686 Old Marple Rd., Springfield, 19064. Tel: 484-472-5067;
Fax: 610-237-7473; Email: fr.dweber@chs-adphila.org. Rev. Dennis M. Weber, S.D.C. Total in Residence 1.

VILLANOVA. *St. Augustine Friary*, 214 Ashwood Rd., Villanova, 19085. Tel: 610-527-0325; Email: secretary@augustinian.org. Revs. Edward Dixey, O.S.A.; Arthur P. Purcaro, O.S.A. Priests 7.

Fray de Leon Community, Burns Hall - West Campus, Villanova University, 800 E. Lancaster Ave., Villanova, 19085. Tel: 610-519-5020. Revs. David A. Cregan, O.S.A., Prior; Peter M. Donohue, O.S.A.; Paul W. Galetto, O.S.A.; Bro. Michael Duffy, O.S.A. Augustinians. Total in Residence 4. P.O. Box 340, Villanova, 19085.
Tel: 610-527-3330, Ext. 279; Fax: 610-527-0618.

St. John Stone Friary, 37 Aldwyn Ln., Villanova, 19085. Tel: 610-519-0634. Revs. John E. Deegan, O.S.A., Supr.; Kail C. Ellis, O.S.A., Vice Pres. Academics, Villanova University.

Provincial Offices of the Order of St. Augustine, Province of St. Thomas of Villanova, 214 Ashwood Rd., P.O. Box 340, Villanova, 19085-0340.
Tel: 610-527-3330; Fax: 610-520-0618; Email: secretary@augustinian.org; Web: www.augustinian.org. Revs. John J. Sheridan, O.S.A., Prov. Archivist, Tel: 610-527-3330, Ext. 247; John E. Deegan, O.S.A., Dir. Justice & Peace; Joseph L. Narog, O.S.A., Dir.; Very Rev. Michael F. DiGregorio, O.S.A., Prior Prov.; Rev. Francis J. Horn, O.S.A., Treas. & Sec.; Paul Ashton, Psy.D., D.Min., Abuse Prevention & Educ. Coord.; Joanna Bowen, Dir. Augustinian Volunteers; Madonna Sutter, Dir.; Cher Rago, Dir.

St. Thomas Monastery, 800 E. Lancaster Ave., Villanova, 19085. Tel: 610-519-7500;
Fax: 610-519-5040; Email: lynn.walsh@villanova.edu. Revs. Stephen J. Baker, O.S.A., Treas. St. Thomas Monastery; John P. Betoni, O.S.A.; Robert M. Burke, O.S.A.; John J. Byrnes, O.S.A.; Francis J. Caponi, O.S.A., Friar; Thomas J. Casey, O.S.A.; Francis Cerullo, O.S.A.; Francis Chambers, O.S.A.; William M. Cleary, O.S.A.; Michael F. DiGregorio, O.S.A., Prior Prov., Province of St. Thomas of Villanova; Edward C. Doherty, O.S.A.; Thomas P. Dwyer, O.S.A.; Bro. Richard Ekmann, O.S.A.; Revs. Alfred J. Ellis, O.S.A.; Augustine M. Esposito, O.S.A., M.Div., M.A., Ph.D.; Francis A. Farsaci, O.S.A., Sub-Prior; John J. Ferrence, O.S.A.; Richard L. Foley, O.S.A.; Dennis J. Gallagher, O.S.A.; Very Rev. Anthony M. Genovese, O.S.A.; Revs. Joseph J. Getz, O.S.A.; Adrian Gilligan, O.S.A.; James G. Glennon, O.S.A.; John J. Hagen, O.S.A., Friar; Bro. William C. Harkin, O.S.A.; Revs. Francis J. Horn, O.S.A., Treas. Province of St. Thomas Villanova; Richard Jacobs, O.S.A.; Martin Laird, O.S.A.; George P. Magee, O.S.A.; Lee J. Makowski, O.S.A.; Gordon E. Marcellus, O.S.A.; James E. Martinez, O.S.A.; Thomas R. McCarthy, O.S.A., Friar; James J. McCartney, O.S.A.; Gary N. McCloskey, O.S.A.; Dennis M. McGowan, O.S.A., Prior; Thomas M. Murnane, O.S.A.; Joseph A. Murray, O.S.A.; Walter J. Quinn, O.S.A.; George F. Riley, O.S.A.; Joseph G. Ryan, O.S.A.; Michael J.

Scanlon, O.S.A.; Michael Scuderi, O.S.A.; John J. Sheridan, O.S.A.; Francis A. Sirolli, O.S.A.; Martin L. Smith, O.S.A.; John P. Stack, O.S.A.; Michael P. Sullivan, O.S.A.; James V. Vitali, O.S.A. Total in Residence 50; Total Staff 51.

St. Thomas of Villanova Friary, 109 Willowburn Rd., Villanova, 19085-1313. Tel: 610-527-0856; Email: joseph.calderone@villanova.edu. Revs. Joseph D. Calderone, O.S.A., Treas.; Richard G. Cannuli, O.S.A.; Russell Ortega, O.S.A.; Bro. Robert Thornton, O.S.A., Prior.

WYNDMOOR. *Christian Brothers (F.S.C.)*, LaSalle High School Community, 8605 Cheltenham Ave., Wyndmoor, 19038. Tel: 215-233-3030; Fax: 215-233-1418; Web: www.lschs.org. Bro. Raymond T. Murphy, F.S.C., Community Dir. Total in Residence 8.

Villa de Sales Oblate Residence, 8501 Flourtown Ave., Wyndmoor, 19038. Tel: 215-836-1472; Fax: 215-836-7213. Rev. Joseph F. Chorpenning, O.S.F.S., S.T.L., Ph.D.; Very Rev. Edward T. Fitzpatrick, O.S.F.S.; Revs. Thomas P. Gallagher, O.S.F.S.; William A. Guerin, O.S.F.S.; Charles J. Norman, O.S.F.S., M.A., Ph.D., M.Div.; Very Rev. Richard T. Reece, O.S.F.S., M.S., M.A., Ph.D., M.Div.; Revs. Robert G. Reece, O.S.F.S., M.S., M.A., M.Div.; Albert J. Smith, O.S.F.S., M.S., M.Div. Total in Residence 8.

[AA] CONVENTS AND RESIDENCES OF SISTERS

PHILADELPHIA. *St. Anna's Convent* St. Anna's Convent 1815 S. Alder St., 19148. Tel: 267-761-9573; Fax: 267-761-9572; Email: annassaint09@gmail.com. Elaine Swan Sr., Bus. Mgr.

Assumption Hall, Sisters of St. Joseph, 8900 Norwood Ave., 19118-2711. Tel: 215-247-3665; Tel: 215-248-2564. Sr. Marjorie Lawless, S.S.J., Contact. Residence for Norwood-Fontbonne Academy Faculty. Total Staff 15.

Assumption House, 1001 S. 47th St., 19143. Tel: 215-386-5016; Fax: 215-386-1780. Sr. Clare Teresa, R.A.

Blessed Trinity Mother Missionary Cenacle, 3501 Solly Ave., 19136. Tel: 215-335-7550; Fax: 215-335-7559; Email: msbtphl@msbt.org; Web: msbt.org. Sisters Joan Marie Keller, M.S.B.T., Gen. Custodian; Ellen Kieran, M.S.B.T., Gen. Sec. Generalate, Novitiate and Candidacy of the Missionary Servants of the Most Blessed Trinity. Mother Boniface Center. Sisters 58; Total in Residence 58; Total Staff 18.

Carmelite Monastery, 66th Ave. and Old York Rd., 19126. Tel: 215-424-6143; Fax: 215-424-6143. Mother Barbara of the Holy Ghost, O.C.D., Prioress.

Clare House, 2421 Jasper St., 19125. Tel: 215-739-6441. Franciscan Sisters of Allegany and Sisters of St. Francis of Philadelphia.

Congregation of the Sisters of St. Felix, St. Ignatius Convent, 4401 Haverford Ave., 19104. Tel: 215-222-2296; Fax: 215-222-3078; Email: smchristopher@feliciansisters.org; Web: www.feliciansistersna.org. Sr. Veronica Marie Lucero, C.S.S.F., Local Min. Sisters 2.

Daughters of Charity, 1020 E. Price St., 19138-1899. Tel: 267-336-7752; Web: www.daughtersofcharity.org. Sr. Jean Maher, D.C., Supr. Total in Residence 9.

Emmaus Convent, 5358 Cedar Ave., 19143. Tel: 215-471-7260; Email: rsmemmaus@aol.com. Sisters of Mercy (R.S.M.). Total in Residence 2.

St. Francis Convent, 1727 S. 11th St., 19148. Tel: 215-463-7343; Email: gpfrancia@verizon.net. Residence of Sisters of St. Francis of Philadelphia employed at John W. Hallahan High School, St. Nicholas Elementary School, St. Thomas Aquinas Elementary School, Children's Aid Society, University of Pennsylvania, Assisi House (Retirement), and Neumann University.

Grey Nuns of the Sacred Heart, Generalate, 14500 Bustelton Ave., 19116-1188. Tel: 215-968-4236; Fax: 267-538-3442; Email: jlanigan@greynun.org; Web: www.greynun.org. Sr. Julia C. Lanigan, G.N.S.H., Pres.
The Grey Nuns of the Sacred Heart, Inc. Sisters 90.

Handmaids of the Sacred Heart of Jesus, 1242 S. Broad St., 19146-3119. Tel: 215-468-6368; Web: acjusa.org. Sr. Asunta Than, Supr. Total in Residence 4.

Immaculate Heart Convent, 7310 Torresdale Ave., 19136. Tel: 215-332-8299; Fax: 215-624-5940; Email: ihc@comcast.net. Sr. M. Margaret Fleming, I.H.M., Supr. Faculty Residence for Sisters, Servants of the Immaculate Heart of Mary, teaching at St. Hubert High School. Sisters 11; Total in Residence 11.

Immaculate Heart Convent, 4904 Chestnut St., 19139. Tel: 215-474-8971. Sr. Sarah Lamb, I.H.M., Supr. Faculty Residence for Sisters, Servants of the Immaculate Heart of Mary, who teach at West Philadelphia Catholic High School and various Diocesan Apostolates. Total in Residence 9; Total Staff 4.

St. Joseph Convent, 7300 Torresdale Ave., 19136. Tel: 215-338-4884; Email: ssjtorr@netcarrier.com. Faculty Residence for Sisters of St. Joseph, who teach at Connell-Egan Catholic High School, St. Hubert High School and St. Francis-St Vincent Homes.

Little Sisters of the Poor, Holy Family Home, 5300 Chester Ave., 19143. Tel: 215-729-5153; Fax: 215-729-5158. Sr. Catherine Frain, L.S.P., Supr. Sisters 11.

Little Workers of the Sacred Hearts, Sacred Hearts Convent, 160 Carpenter Ln., 19119-2563. Tel: 215-843-2266. Sr. Leena Joseph, P.O.S.C., Supr.

Mary Immaculate Convent, 1731 S. 11th St., 19148. Tel: 215-336-2940; Tel: 215-468-9133; Fax: 215-336-7463; Email: maryim1731@yahoo.com. Sr. Margaret P. Reinking, I.H.M., Supr. Faculty Residence for Sisters, Servants of the Immaculate Heart of Mary, who teach at SS. John Neumann and Maria Goretti Catholic High School and John W. Hallahan High School. Total in Residence 10; Total Staff 12.

Medical Mission Sisters, North American Sector, 8400 Pine Rd., 19111. Tel: 215-742-6100; Fax: 215-342-3948; Email: mmsorg@medicalmissionsisters.org; Web: www.medicalmissionsisters.org. Sisters Patricia Lowery, M.M.S., NA Coord.; Maria Hornung, M.M.S., NA Coord.; Helen Lembeck, M.M.S., NA Coord. Sisters 82; Total in Residence 82.

St. Michael Hall, 9001 Germantown Ave., 19118. Tel: 215-247-3698. Faculty Residence for Sisters of St. Joseph who staff Chestnut Hill College. Total in Residence 11.

Monastery of the Visitation Nuns, 5820 City Ave., 19131-1295. Tel: 215-473-5888; Fax: 215-473-7512; Email: viznunphil@aol.com; Web: visitationuns.org. Mother Antoinette Marie Walker, V.H.M., Supr. Jesuit priests from St. Joseph's University, Chaplains. Sisters 8; Total in Residence 6.

Mt. St. Joseph Convent, 9701 Germantown Ave., 19118-2694. Tel: 215-248-7200; Fax: 215-248-7277; Email: msjc@ssjphila.org; Web: ssjphila.org. Sr. Anne Patricia Myers, S.S.J., Congregational Pres. Motherhouse of the Sisters of St. Joseph of Chestnut Hill, Philadelphia. Sisters 690.

Nazareth Convent, Religious Sisters of Mercy, 6369 Woodbine Ave., 19151. Tel: 215-477-3022. Sr. Kathleen Lyons, R.S.M., Contact Person & Treas.

Peace Hermitage, 8400 Pine Rd., 19111. Tel: 312-659-3655; Tel: 215-742-6100, Ext. 149; Fax: 215-342-3948. Society of Catholic Medical Missionaries (Medical Mission Sisters). Total in Residence 2.

School Sisters of Notre Dame, 3978 Constance Rd., 19114. Tel: 215-824-0754; Email: sisterbernie@yahoo.com; Web: www.ssnd.org. Sr. Bernadette Marie Ravenstahl, S.S.N.D., Contact.

Sister Servants of the Holy Spirit of Perpetual Adoration (S.Sp.S.A.P.), Convent of Divine Love, 2212 Green St., 19130. Tel: 215-567-0123; Fax: 215-569-8314; Email: conventofdivinelove@verizon.net; Web: www.adorationsisters.org. Sr. Mary Caritas, S.Sp. S.A.P., Supr.

Sisters of Life, St. Malachy's Convent, 1413 N. 11th St., 19122.

Sisters of St. Francis of Philadelphia, Santa Chiara, 2238 S. 12th St., 19148. Tel: 215-465-2227. Sisters Residence for those who work at Assisi House, Aston, and Epiphany Church.

Sisters of St. Francis of Philadelphia, Canticle House, 1624 Mifflin St., 19145. Tel: 215-551-2586; Web: www.osfphila.org.

Sisters of St. Joseph, Neumann House, 58 E. Northwestern Ave., 19118. Tel: 215-248-7200; Fax: 215-248-7277; Email: msjc@ssjphila.org; Web: ssjphila.org. Total in Residence 4.

Sisters of St. Joseph of Philadelphia, Cecilian Convent, 6818 Cresheim Rd., 19119. Tel: 215-438-7515. Total in Residence 8.

Sisters of St. Joseph of Philadelphia, Elizabeth House, 138 W. Carpenter Ln., 19119-2563. Tel: 215-849-3362. Sr. Kathryn Miller, S.S.J., Contact Person.

Sisters of St. Joseph of Philadelphia, Fournier Community, Administration, 9701 Germantown Ave., 19118-2694. Tel: 215-248-7200; Fax: 215-248-7277; Email: msjc@ssjphila.org; Web: ssjphila.org. Sr. Marie O'Brien, S.S.J., Contact Person. Sisters 5.

Sisters of the Holy Child, 2362 E. York St., 19125-3029. Tel: 215-423-9514; Email: americanprovince@shcj.org. Sr. Carroll Juliano, Prov.

Sisters of the Holy Family of Nazareth, 2755 Holme Ave., 19152. Tel: 215-543-0124; Fax: 215-338-8752; Email: bjwojnicki@yahoo.com; Web: nazarethcsfn.org. Sr. Barbara Jean Wojnicki, C.S.F.N., Prov. Supr.

Sisters of the Holy Family of Nazareth, Delaney Hall, 4800 Stevenson Ln., 19114. Tel: 267-341-3735; Fax: 267-341-3702; Email: bobrien42@gmail.com. Sr. Brendan O'Brien, Supr. Sisters 15.

Sisters of the Holy Family of Nazareth, Jesus of Nazareth Convent (aka Mount Nazareth), 2755 Holme Ave., 19152. Tel: 215-543-0124; Fax: 215-338-8752. Sr. Jeanette Lawlor, C.S.F.N., Local Supr. Total in Residence 51; Staff 25.

ARDMORE. *Missionary Sisters of the Holy Rosary (M.S.H.R.)*, 205 Cricket Ave., Ardmore, 19003. Tel: 610-896-1786; Web: holyrosarymissionarysisters.org. Total in Residence 3.

ASTON. *Anna Bachmann House*, 606 S. Convent Rd., Aston, 19014-1207. Tel: 610-558-3240; Web: www.osfphila.org. Sr. Patricia Smith, O.S.F., Contact Person.

Convent of Our Lady of Angels, 609 S. Convent Rd., Aston, 19014. Tel: 610-459-4125; Fax: 610-459-0195; Email: smonteleone@osfphila.org; Web: www.osfphila.org. Sr. Mary Kathryn Dougherty, O.S.F., Congregational Min. Motherhouse of the Sisters of St. Francis of Philadelphia.

Mt. Alvernia Convent, 602A S. Convent Rd., Aston, 19014. Tel: 610-459-5989. Sr. Kathleen M. Winkelman, O.S.F., Contact Person. Sisters of St. Francis of Philadelphia. Total in Residence 3.

Sisters of St. Francis, 607 S. Convent Rd., Aston, 19014. Tel: 610-358-5417; Email: cwright@osfphila.org; Web: www.osfphila.org. Sr. Marie Colette Gerry, O.S.F., Congregational Sec.

Sisters of St. Francis of Philadelphia, 6 Red Hill Rd., Aston, 19014. Tel: 610-459-1113.

Sisters of St. Francis of Philadelphia, Visitation Convent 609 S. Convent Rd., Aston, 19014. Tel: 610-558-7731; Web: www.osfphila.org. Sr. Marie Colette Gerry, O.S.F., Congregational Sec. Total in Residence 4.

Sisters of St. Francis of Philadelphia, Assisi House, 600 Red Hill Rd., Aston, 19014. Tel: 610-459-8990; Fax: 610-558-5344; Web: www.osfphila.org. Total in Residence 83; Total Staff 168.

Sisters of St. Francis of Philadelphia, Portiuncula Convent, 610 Red Hill Rd., Aston, 19014. Tel: 610-558-5350; Fax: 610-558-5344. Sisters 8.

Sisters of St. Francis of Philadelphia (Assumption Convent), Assumption Convent, 609 S. Convent Rd., Aston, 19014. Tel: 610-558-7672; Web: www.osfphila.org. Sr. Marie Colette Gerry, O.S.F., Congregational Sec. Total in Residence 4.

Sisters of St. Francis of Philadelphia, TAU Convent, 4000 Concord Rd., Aston, 19014. Tel: 610-494-7322 . Total in Residence 5.

AVONDALE. *Blessed Marie Catherine Formation Program*, 100 S. Williamson Rd., Avondale, 19311. Tel: 610-268-1373. Sr. Mary of Ephesus, S.S.V.M., Supr.

BENSALEM. *Sisters of the Blessed Sacrament* Administrative Offices 1663 Bristol Pike, Bensalem, 19020-5702. Tel: 215-244-7790; Fax: 215-244-8174; Email: schmidtsl@aol.com; Web: www.katharinedrexel.org. Sr. Donna Breslin, S.B.S., Pres.
Sisters of the Blessed Sacrament for Indians and Colored People Sisters 91; Total Staff 8.

BROOKHAVEN. *Dominican Sisters of Peace*, 245 Upland Rd., Brookhaven, 19015.

Sisters of St. Francis of Philadelphia, Claddagh House, 160 Meadowbrook Ln., Brookhaven, 19015. Tel: 610-490-5367; Fax: 610-490-5367; Email: mirmurray@comcast.net; Web: www.osfphila.org. Total in Residence 3.

BRYN MAWR. *Missionary Sisters of the Holy Rosary*, 741 Polo Rd., Bryn Mawr, 19010. Tel: 610-520-1974; Fax: 610-520-2002; Email: mcneillhelena@yahoo.com; Web: www.holyrosarymissionarysisters.com. Total in Residence 3.

Society of the Holy Child Jesus, 700 Old Lancaster Rd., Bryn Mawr, 19010. Tel: 610-527-5076; Fax: 610-527-4671; Email: emoughan@shcj.org. Residence for Sisters of the Holy Child Jesus. Total in Residence 5.

CHELTENHAM. *Sisters of the Good Shepherd (Contemplative)*, 7633 Waters Rd., Cheltenham, 19012. Tel: 215-782-8627; Fax: 215-782-8741; Email: judeelleng@aol.com. Sr. Martha Cardenas, Supr. Sisters 6; Total in Residence 6.

CHESTER. *Missionaries of Charity, Gift of Mary*, 2714 W. 9th St., Chester, 19013. Tel: 610-494-7424. Sr. Wini Marie, M.C., Supr. Total Staff 4; Total Assisted 704.

ELVERSON. *Daughters of St. Mary of Providence (D.S.M.P.)*, 227 Isabella Rd., Elverson, 19520. Tel: 610-942-4166; Fax: 610-942-4259; Email: stmaryofprov@comcast.net; Web: stmaryofprov-pa.

org. Sr. Gertrude La Barbera, D.S.M.P., Supr. Total in Residence 3; Total Staff 17.

ERDENHEIM. *Sisters of St. Joseph of Philadelphia*, Divine Shepherd Convent, 927 Bethlehem Pike, Erdenheim, 19038. Tel: 215-836-2082. Total in Residence 6.

Sisters of St. Joseph of Philadelphia, Nazareth House, 931 Bethlehem Pike, Erdenheim, 19038. Tel: 215-836-2613. Total in Residence 5.

FLOURTOWN. *Sisters of St. Joseph of Philadelphia, Mt. St. Joseph Academy*, Convent, 120 W. Wissahickon Ave., Flourtown, 19031-1899. Tel: 215-233-4368; Email: ssjmountcon@verizon.net. Total in Residence 14.

Sisters of St. Joseph of Philadelphia, St. Joseph Villa Staff Visitation Community, 110 W. Wissahickon Ave., Flourtown, 19031-1898. Tel: 215-836-4179; Fax: 215-248-7802; Email: visitationcommunity@msn.com. Total in Community 11.

FOX CHASE MANOR. *Sisters of St. Basil the Great (O.S.B.M.)* Motherhouse of the Sisters of St. Basil. 710 Fox Chase Rd., Fox Chase Manor, 19046-4198. Tel: 215-663-9153; Fax: 215-379-3999; Email: province@stbasils.com; Web: www.stbasils.com. Sr. Dorothy Ann Busowski, O.S.B.M., Prov. Supr.

Basilian Spirituality Center, 710 Fox Chase Rd., Jenkintown, 19046-4198. Tel: 215-780-1227; Fax: 215-379-4843.

GWYNEDD VALLEY. *Religious Sisters of Mercy - St. Joseph Convent*, 1349 Sumneytown Pike, P.O. Box 902, Gwynedd Valley, 19437-0902. Tel: 215-646-5259.

Religious Sisters of Mercy - Transfiguration Convent, 1325 Sumneytown Pike, P.O. Box 901, Gwynedd Valley, 19437-0901. Tel: 215-641-5512; Fax: 215-641-5509; Email: mcmahon.c@gmc.edu; Web: www.gmc.edu.

HAVERFORD. *Handmaids of the Sacred Heart of Jesus*, 616 Coopertown Rd., Haverford, 19041. Tel: 610-642-5715; Email: acjbelenes@gmail.com; Web: www.acjusa.org. Sr. Belen Escauriaza, A.C.J., Local Coord. Sisters 6.

Handmaids of the Sacred Heart of Jesus Provincialate, 616 Coopertown Rd., Haverford, 19041. Tel: 610-642-5715; Email: acjbelen@gmail.com; Web: www.acjusa.org. Sr. Belen Escauriaza, A.C.J., Prov. Supr. & Local Supr. Sisters 29; Total in Residence 6.

HUNTINGDON VALLEY. *Sisters of the Redeemer*, 521 Moredon Rd., Huntingdon Valley, 19006. Tel: 215-914-4101; Fax: 215-914-4111; Email: kkaufmann@holyredeemer.com; Email: amhaas@holyredeemer.com; Web: redeemersisters.org. 1600 Huntingdon Pike, Attn: Kathy Kaufmann, Meadowbrook, 19046. Sr. Anne Marie Haas, C.S.R., Prov. Leader. Sisters 4.

Sisters of the Redeemer, Visitation Community, 521 Moredon Rd., Huntingdon Valley, 19006. Tel: 215-914-4101; Fax: 215-914-4171; Email: kkaufmann@holyredeemer.com; Email: amhaas@holyredeemer.com; Web: redeemersisters.org. 1600 Huntingdon Pike, Attn: Kathy Kaufmann, Meadowbrook, 19046. Sr. Anne Marie Haas, C.S.R., Province Leader.

Sisters of the Redeemer-St. Teresa of Avila Convent, Sisters of the Redeemer-St. Teresa of Avila Convent, 619 Moredon Rd., Huntingdon Valley, 19006. Tel: 215-947-0135; Fax: 215-914-4171; Email: kkaufmann@holyredeemer.com; Email: amhaas@holyredeemer.com; Web: redeemersisters.org. 1600 Huntingdon Pike, Attn: Kathy Kaufmann, Meadowbrook, 19046. Sr. Anne Marie Haas, C.S.R., Province Leader. Sisters 4.

IMMACULATA. *Sisters, Servants of the Immaculate Heart of Mary (I.H.M.)*, Pacis Hall, 1145 King Rd., Immaculata, 19345-0700. Tel: 610-889-1668; Fax: 610-889-1667 (Camilla Hall); Email: pacishall@gmail.com. Sr. M. Patricia Micklos, I.H.M., Supr. Sisters 38; Total in Residence 39.

Sisters, Servants of the Immaculate Heart of Mary (I.H.M.), 100 Camilla Dr., P.O. Box 100, Immaculata, 19345. Tel: 610-386-2000; Fax: 610-695-0691; Email: ch@camillahall.org. Sr. Anne Veronica Burrows, I.H.M., Admin. Sisters 210.

Sisters, Servants of the Immaculate Heart of Mary (I.H.M.), 1145 King Rd., P.O. Box 400, Immaculata, 19345-0400. Tel: 610-647-4400, Ext. 3660; Fax: 610-640-5890; Email: gillet@immaculata.edu; Web: www.ihmimmaculata.org. Total in Residence 44.

Villa Maria House of Studies, 1140 King Rd., Immaculata, 19345-0200. Tel: 610-647-2160; Fax: 610-889-4874; Email: s.rita.lenihan@ihmimm.org.

Villa Maria House of Studies, Motherhouse of the Sisters, Servants of the Immaculate Heart of Mary Tot in Congregation 716.

JENKINTOWN. *Sisters of the Redeemer*, Sisters of the Redeemer-St. Elizabeth Convent, 615 Fox Chase Rd., Jenkintown, 19046. Tel: 215-379-0112; Tel: 215-914-4101; Fax: 215-914-4171; Email: amhaas@holyredeemer.com; Email: kkaufmann@holyredeemer.com; Web: redeemersisters.org. 1600 Huntingdon Pike, Meadowbrook, 19046. Sr. Anne Marie Haas, C.S.R., Prov.

LANGHORNE. *Monastery of St. Clare, Poor Clares*, 1271 Langhorne-Newtown Rd., Langhorne, 19047-1297. Tel: 215-968-5775; Fax: 215-968-6254; Email: stclare@poorclarepa.org; Web: www.poorclarepa.org. Cloistered Contemplative Nuns.Prayer and Altar Bread Ministry.

San Damiano Convent, 104 Alberts Way, Langhorne, 19047. Tel: 215-860-7185.

Sisters of St. Francis of Philadelphia Total in Residence 2.

Sisters of St. Francis of Philadelphia, St. Mary Medical Center Convent, 1207 Langhorne-Newton Rd., Langhorne, 19047-1233. Tel: 215-757-9494. Total in Residence 5.

Sisters of St. Francis of Philadelphia, Franciscan Residence, 113 Alberts Way, Langhorne, 19047. Tel: 215-860-1059. Sisters serving at St. Mary Medical Center.

LANSDALE. *Religious of the Assumption*, Assumption Convent, 506 Crestview Rd., Lansdale, 19446. Tel: 215-368-4427 (Main House); Tel: 215-362-6296 ; Email: raworcester@hotmail.com. Nuala Cotter, Prov.

Religious of the Assumption, North American Province, Inc. Sisters 22.

MALVERN. *Villa Maria Academy Convent*, 370 Old Lincoln Hwy., Malvern, 19355. Tel: 610-647-4878; Fax: 610-644-2866; Email: info@vmahs.org; Web: www.vmahs.org. Sisters, Servants of the Immaculate Heart of Mary (I.H.M.). Total in Residence 13.

MEADOWBROOK. *Sisters of the Redeemer Province Center*, 1600 Huntingdon Pike, Meadowbrook, 19046. Tel: 215-914-4101; Fax: 215-914-4171; Email: amhaas@holyredeemer.com; Email: kkaufmann@holyredeemer.com; Web: redeemersisters.org. Sisters Anne Marie Haas, C.S.R., Prov. Leader; Barbara Deitrich, C.S.R., Vicar Prov.; Ellen M. Marvel, C.S.R., Prov. Councilor; Revs. Timothy M. Judge, M.Div., Chap.; Dennis J.W. O'Donnell, Ph.D., Dir. Integrated Health Svcs.; Laurence J. Gleason, M.A., M.Div., Chap. Holy Redeemer Health System. Total in Residence 9.

MERION. *Sisters of Mercy of the Americas, Mid-Atlantic Community*, Sisters of Mercy Convent, Sisters of Mercy, 515 Montgomery Ave., Merion Station, 19066. Tel: 610-664-6650; Fax: 610-664-3429; Web: www.mercymidatlantic.org. Sisters Patricia Vetrano, R.S.M., Pres.; Sr. Mary Ann Clarahan, R.S.M., Local Coord. Sisters 77.

Sisters of Mercy of the Americas, Mid-Atlantic Community, Inc., 515 Montgomery Ave., Merion Station, 19066. Tel: 610-664-6650; Fax: 610-664-3429; Web: www.mercymidatlantic.org. Sisters Patricia Vetrano, R.S.M., Pres.; Sisters Kathleen Keenan, R.S.M., Leadership Team; Alicia Zapata, R.S.M., Leadership Team; Patricia Lapczynski, R.S.M., Leadership Team; Patricia Smith, R.S.M., Leadership Team. As of January 1, 2007 the Sisters of Mercy of the Americas, Regional Communities of Brooklyn, Dallas, Hartsdale, Merion and Watchung merged to create the Sisters of Mercy of the Americas, Mid-Atlantic Community, Inc. Sisters 887.

MORTON. *Sisters of St. Francis of Philadelphia (O.S.F.)*, 2130 Franklin Ave., Ct. No. 3, Morton, 19070-1217. Tel: 610-543-0186; Email: aboos@osfphila.org. Total in Residence 5; Total Staff 5.

NORRISTOWN. *Missionaries of Charity*, 630 DeKalb St., Norristown, 19401-3944. Tel: 610-277-5962. Sr. M. Lia Ann, M.C., Supr. Services include Food Distribution and Emergency Night Shelter and Soup Kitchen. Sisters 5.

RADNOR. *Armenian Sisters of the Immaculate Conception*, 440 Upper Gulph Rd., Radnor, 19087. Tel: 610-688-9360; Fax: 610-687-2430; Email: sisteremma@asaphila.org; Web: www.asaphila.org. Sr. Emma Moussayan, Supr. Sisters 3; Total in Residence 3.

Missionary Sisters of the Sacred Heart of Jesus (Cabrini Sisters), Cabrini College Convent Gatehouse, 610 King of Prussia Rd., Radnor, 19087-3698. Tel: 610-995-1210; Email: baltas40@aol.com; Web: www.mothercabrini.org.

ROSEMONT. *American Province Archives, Society of the Holy Child Jesus*, 1308 Wendover Rd., Rosemont, 19010. Tel: 610-525-8951; Fax: 610-525-8952; Email: rmcdougall@shcj.org; Web: www.shcj.org/american/contact/contact-us/. Sr. Roseanne McDougall, S.H.C.J., Dir. Archives; Emily Siegel, Archives Asst.

Holy Child Center, 1341 Montgomery Ave., Rosemont, 19010. Tel: 610-525-9900; Fax: 610-525-0662; Web: www.shcj.org. Total in Residence 30; Total Staff 58.

Society of the Holy Child, 105 County Line Rd., Rosemont, 19010. Tel: 610-520-2416; Email: emoughan@shcj.org. Residence for Sisters of the Holy Child Jesus. Total in Residence 4.

Society of the Holy Child Jesus, Provincial Office, 1341 Montgomery Ave., Rosemont, 19010-1628. Tel: 610-626-1400; Fax: 610-525-2919; Email: americanprovince@shcj.org; Web: www.shcj.org. Sr. Carroll Juliano, Prov.

Society of the Holy Child Jesus American Province, Inc.

SPRINGFIELD. *St. Anthony Convent*, 1715 S. Sproul Rd., Springfield, 19064. Tel: 610-544-4066. Residence for Sisters of St. Francis of Philadelphia who serve in various ministries of the Archdiocese. Total in Residence 7; Total Staff 7.

Immaculate Heart of Mary Convent, 1725 S. Sproul Rd., Springfield, 19064. Tel: 610-544-0275; Email: ihspringfield@hotmail.com. Sr. M. Rose Lawrence Harlan, I.H.M., Supr. Faculty Residence for Sisters, Servants of the Immaculate Heart of Mary.

St. Joseph Convent, 1705 S. Sproul Rd., Springfield, 19064. Tel: 610-544-4230. Sr. Mary Beth Kratzinger, S.S.J. Sisters of St. Joseph Faculty House, Cardinal O'Hara High School. Total in Residence 7.

Our Lady of Mercy Convent, 1735 S. Sproul Rd., Springfield, 19064. Tel: 610-544-0238. Faculty Residence for Sisters of Mercy who teach in Cardinal O'Hara and Mercy Vocational High Schools and who serve in other various ministries.

STRAFFORD. *Our Lady of the Assumption Convent*, 139 Fairfield Ln., Strafford, 19087. Tel: 610-688-7889; Email: olaihm@yahoo.com. Sr. Judith Ann Trumbore, I.H.M., Supr. Sisters, Servants of the Immaculate Heart of Mary. Total in Residence 6.

WARMINSTER. *Sisters of St. Joseph of Philadelphia*, Nativity of Our Lord Convent, 605 W. Street Rd., Warminster, 18974. Tel: 215-672-0147; Fax: 215-674-3787. Residence of Sisters St. Joseph.

WYNCOTE. *Handmaids of the Sacred Heart of Jesus*, 2025 Church Rd., Wyncote, 19095. Tel: 215-576-6250; Email: mgillespie@ancillae.org. Sr. Maureen Gillespie, A.C.J., Supr. Sisters 6.

WYNNEWOOD. *Sisters of the Holy Child Jesus (S.H.C.J.)*, Connell House, 105 Old Forest Rd., Wynnewood, 19096. Tel: 610-649-8462; Web: www.shcj.org. Total in Residence 3.

[BB] RETREAT HOUSES

PHILADELPHIA. *The Marianist Center for Lay Formation* dba NACMS, 1341 N. Delaware Ave., Ste. 301, 19125-4300. Tel: 215-634-4116; Email: marianistcenter@gmail.com; Web: www.marianist.com. Bro. Jack Ventura, S.M., Dir. The Marianist Center is committed to the spirit of Mary. This spirit mission fosters spiritual growth and formation, the building of lay faith/action communities and social justice according to the unique gifts of the Marianist tradition. Programs offered in Spirituality, Mary Community Building, for groups, staff, faculty, and parishes, as well as special programs specially designed for families. Total Staff 7; Total Assisted 600.

Mother Boniface Center, 3501 Solly Ave., 19136. Tel: 215-335-7541; Fax: 215-335-7541; Email: mbcretreat@msbt.org. Sponsored by Missionary Servants of the Most Blessed Trinity. Mid-week and weekend programs; retreats, days of recollection, scripture study, meetings, workshops and hosting programs. Capacity 67; Total Staff 8.

ASTON. *Clare House*, 608 B. Legion Rd., Aston, 19014. Tel: 610-558-6152; Fax: 610-558-5377; Email: fsc@osfphila.org; Web: www.fscaston.org. Sr. Christa Thompson, O.S.F. Directed and Private Retreats. 5 Hermitages on property also. Staffed by Sisters of St. Francis of Philadelphia. Capacity 6; Total Guests at Hermitages 937; Total Staff 2; Total Guests 694.

Franciscan Spiritual Center, 609 S. Convent Rd., Aston, 19014. Tel: 610-558-6152; Fax: 610-558-5377; Email: fsc@osfphila.org; Web: www.fscaston.org. Sr. Christa Marie Thompson, O.S.F., Dir. Private, directed and group retreats. Spiritual, human development and holistic programs. Staffed by the Sisters of St. Francis Philadelphia.

DOYLESTOWN. *National Shrine of Our Lady of Czestochowa*, 654 Ferry Rd., P.O. Box 2049, Doylestown, 18901. Tel: 215-345-0600; Tel: 215-345-0601; Fax: 215-348-2148; Email: info@czestochowa.us; Web: czestochowa.us. Rev. Krzysztof Drybka, O.S.P.P.E., Prior

Legal Title: The Order of Saint Paul, First Hermit the Pauline Fathers.

HAVERFORD. *Saint Raphaela Center*, 616 Coopertown Rd., Haverford, 19041. Tel: 610-642-5715; Email: straphaelacenter@gmail.com; Web: straphaelacenter.org. Sr. Lyan Tri, Dir.

MALVERN. *St. Joseph's-in-the-Hills* (The Malvern Retreat House) 315 S. Warren Ave., P.O. Box 315, Malvern, 19355-0315. Tel: 610-644-0400; Fax: 610-644-4363; Email: mail@malvernretreat.com; Web: malvernretreat.com. Rev. Msgr. Joseph T. Marino, M.Div., M.A., Rector, Tel: 610-644-0400, Ext. 28; Mark J. Poletunow, Pres.; Joseph Nardi, Chm. Owned and Operated by Catholic Laity since 1912, we serve the spiritual needs of lay men and women of all ages, clergy and religious of many denominations and provide a place of peaceful hospitality. Annual Retreatants over 20,000; Private Rooms 350.

[CC] NEWMAN APOSTOLATE

PHILADELPHIA. *Newman Apostolate for Archdiocese of Philadelphia*, 222 N. 17th St., 19103. Tel: 215-587-4544; Fax: 215-964-1749; Email: amena@archphila.org; Web: www.archdiocese-phl.org/offices/na.htm. Ann M. Menna, Deputy Sec.

Full Time Chaplaincies:.

Drexel University, Newman Catholic Center, 3720 Chestnut St., 19104-6189. Tel: 215-901-3602; Fax: 215-587-8634; Email: mjg395@drexel.edu; Email: amg556@drexel.edu; Web: saintsaj.org/drexel. Michael Gokie, Dir.

Temple University, Newman Center, 2129 N. Broad St., 19122-1193. Tel: 215-232-3779; Fax: 215-235-7302; Email: smahoney@temple.edu; Web: www.templenewmancenter.org. Rev. Shaun L. Mahoney, S.T.D., M.Div., Chap.; Patricia Lester, Asst. to Chap.

Tri-College Newman Cluster-Bryn Mawr, Haverford and Swarthmore Colleges, St. Anastasia, 3301 West Chester Pike, Newtown Square, 19073. Tel: 610-328-8578; Email: rev.johnames@gmail.com.

University of Pennsylvania, Newman Hall, 3720 Chestnut St., 19104-6189. Tel: 267-757-5000; Fax: 215-386-5899; Email: cshields@newman.upenn.edu; Email: ptraver7@newman.upenn.edu; Web: www.newman.upenn.edu. Adam Ureneck, Dir.; Carolyn Shields; Patrick Travers.

West Chester University, Newman Center, 409 Trinity Dr., West Chester, 19382-5362. Tel: 610-436-0891; Fax: 610-436-6247; Email: fathergardner@gmail.com; Web: www.wcunewman.org. Rev. Thomas J. Gardner, M.Div., Chap.; Daniel Pin, Asst. Dir.

Part-time Chaplaincies:.

Tenet Hahnemann (Center City Campus), Cathedral Basisilica SS Peter and Paul, 1723 Race St., 19103. Tel: 215-561-1313. Chaplaincy Vacant.

Arcadia University, St. Luke the Evangelist Church, 2316 Fairhill Ave., Glenside, 19038-4107. Tel: 215-572-0128. Rev. Joseph D. Brandt, Chap.

Bucks County Community College, St. Andrew Church, 81 Swamp Rd., Newtown, 18940. Tel: 215-968-2262. Rev. Msgr. Michael C. Picard, M.A.

Cheney University, Tel: 610-399-2353. Chaplaincy Vacant.

Community College of Philadelphia, 19130. Chaplaincy Vacant.

Delaware County Community College, St. Anastasia Church, 3301 W. Chester Pk., St. Anastasia, Newtown Square, 19073. Tel: 610-356-3303; Tel: 610-359-5206. Chaplaincy Vacant.

Delaware County Community College, Math Science Dept., Media, 19063. Tel: 610-359-5206.

St. Anastasia, 3301 West Chester Pike, Newtown Square, 19073. Tel: 610-356-1613; Tel: 610-356-3303; Fax: 610-356-8332.

Delaware Valley College of Science and Agriculture, St. Jude Church, 321 W. Butler Ave., Chalfont, 18914-2329. Tel: 215-822-0179; Fax: 215-822-0638 . Rev. Jeffrey M. Rott, M.Div.

Harcum College, Our Mother of Good Counsel, 31 Pennswood Rd., Bryn Mawr, 19010. Tel: 610-526-6050.

Lincoln University, Sacred Heart Church, 101 Church Rd., Oxford, 19363. Tel: 610-932-5040.

Montgomery County Community College, St. Helena Church, P.O. Box 5085, Center Square, 19422. Tel: 610-275-7711. Rev. Msgr. Joseph J. Nicolo, M.Div., Chap.

Pennsylvania State University-Abington, Our Lady Help of Christians, Brian Polk, 1600 Woodland Rd., Abington, 19001. Tel: 215-881-7548; Email: bep@psu.edu.

Pennsylvania State University - Delaware County Campus, St. Francis de Sales Church, 33 New Rd., Box 97, Lenni, 19062. Tel: 610-459-2203.

Pennsylvania State University-Great Valley Campus, 19104. Chaplaincy Vacant.

Philadelphia College of Pharmacy and Science, St. Agatha-St. James, 3728 Chestnut St., 19104. Tel: 215-898-7575. Adam Ureneck.

Philadelphia University, St. Bridget Church, 3667 Midvale Ave., 19129-1712. Tel: 215-844-4126. Rev. Robert T. Feeney, M.Div., Chap.

Roxborough Memorial School of Nursing, St. John the Baptist, 146 Rector St., 19107. Tel: 215-482-4600. Rev. Msgr. Kevin C. Lawrence, M.Div., Chap.

Temple University, Ambler Campus, St. Alphonsus Church, 33 Conwell Dr., Maple Glen, 19002. Tel: 215-646-4600; Fax: 215-646-0180; Web: www.libertynet.org/~tunewman.

Thomas Jefferson University, 111 S. 11th St., 19107.

University of the Arts, Assoc. Dean's Office, Broad and Pine Sts., 19102. Tel: 215-875-2236. Chaplaincy Vacant.

University of the Sciences in Philadelphia, 600 S. 43rd St., 19104. Tel: 215-596-8800. Rev. Louis C. Bier, St. Francis de Sales.

Ursinus College, St. Eleanor Church, 647 Locust St., Collegeville, 19426-2541. Tel: 610-489-1647; Fax: 610-489-7469. Rev. Msgr. Michael T. McCulken, M.Div., Chap.

Widener University, St. Katharine Drexel Church, 20th and Providence Ave., 1920 Providence Ave., Chester, 19013-5695. Tel: 610-872-0545; Email: fatherwhittingham@gmail.com. Rev. Thomas P. Whittingham, M.A., M.Div., Chap. St. Katharine Drexel.

[DD] MISCELLANEOUS LISTINGS

PHILADELPHIA. **American Academy of the Sacred Arts*, 1629 Porter St., 19145. Tel: 215-339-5041. Purpose is to glorify God in the cultural disciplines through the creation of original art, educational outreach and ecumenical dialogue.

**American Catholic Historical Society*, 263 S. 4th St., 19106. Tel: 215-925-5752; Email: info@amchs.org; Web: www.amchs.org. Michael H. Finnegan, Pres. ACHS promotes the documentation & interpretation of the history of the Catholic Church in the United States. It accomplishes its ongoing mission by publishing an award-winning academic journal, American Catholic Studies; sponsoring Society functions; & through the preservation of its historical collections, located at the Society's headquarters & at the Philadelphia Archdiocesan Historical Research Center.

**Augustinian Defenders of the Rights of the Poor*, 2130 S. 21st St., 2nd Fl., 19145. Tel: 215-925-3566; Email: info@rightsofthepoor.org; Web: www.rightsofthepoor.org. Joseph Micucci, Exec. Dir. ADROP is about collaborating with the poor and powerless in our society by matching identified needs with known resources across political, economic and religious spectra.

Catholic Clinical Consultants, 2433 S. 15th St., 19145. Tel: 855-518-2223. Most Rev. John J. McIntyre, D.D., Pres.; Rick Willgruber, Admin. Provides outsourced management, clinical and behavioral health consulting and other out-patient behavioral health services in Philadelphia and surrounding counties, including to skilled nursing facilities, assisted living facilities, adult day programs and other community-based elder care programs.

Catholic Kolping Society, 9130 Academy Rd., 19114. Tel: 267-255-2527; Email: phillykolpingnews@gmail.com; Web: www.kolpingphilly.com. Frank Staub, Pres.; Anna Nordin, Treas.

Catholic League For Persons With Disabilities, 911 Loney St., 19111. Tel: 215-725-9746. Rev. William E. Dean, M.Div., Chap.; Barbara M. Walter, Sec.

Catholics United for the Faith (St. John Neumann Philadelphia Area Chapter) 183 Hillcrest Ave., 19118. Tel: 215-247-2585; Email: annemwilson@yahoo.com. Mrs. Anne M. Wilson, Chm.

The Central Association of the Miraculous Medal, 475 E. Chelten Ave., 19144-5785. Tel: 215-848-1010; Tel: 800-523-3674; Fax: 215-848-1014; Email: bracine@cammonline.org; Web: www.miraculousmedal.org. Rev. William J. O'Brien, C.M., Dir.

Change for Change aka Change for Global Change, 9701 Germantown Ave., 19118-2694. Tel: 215-248-7220; Fax: 215-248-7277; Email: changeforglobalchange@earthlink.net. Sr. Anne Myers, S.S.J., Supr. Change for Global Change exists to address the global problem of sustainability through education, donations and grants to not-for-profit organizations for projects to aid those who have little or no means to provide a sustainable life for themselves.

The Collegium Institute An independent scholarly foundation devoted to fostering the Catholic intellectual tradition, and the liberal tradition of humane studies more broadly, within the University of Pennsylvania community. Leadership Hall, University of Pennsylvania, 3814 Walnut St., 19104-6197. Tel: 773-813-9011; Tel: 610-368-7288. Daniel Cheely, Pres.; Matthew O'Brien, Bd. Member.

Concerts at the Cathedral, 1723 Race St., 19103. Tel: 215-561-1313; Email: bm01003@aop222.org. Rev. Gerald Dennis Gill, M.Div., S.L.L., Rector & Pastor.

CORA Services, 8540 Verree Rd., 19111. Tel: 215-342-7660; Email: info@coraservices.org; Web: www.coraservices.org. AnnMarie Schultz, Pres. & CEO. Services provided for children and their families. Programs available: Intervention Services; Mental Health Treatment; Alcohol and Other Drug Treatment; After School Programming; Public, Charter and Nonpublic Schools Related/Remedial Services (Speech, Occupational/Physical Therapy, Counseling, Academic Remediation, Psyco-Educational Evaluations); Early Intervention Services; Early Years Programming.

CORA Services, Inc., Philadelphia, Pennsylvania Total Staff 300; Total Assisted 19,774.

CSFN Mission & Ministry, Inc., Sisters of the Holy Family of Nazareth, Holy Family Prov., 2755 Holme Ave., 19152. Tel: 215-335-4802; Email: ltfelici@aol.com. Sr. Loretta Felici, C.S.F.N., Pres.

**Depaul, USA*, 5725 Sprague St., 19138-1721. Tel: 215-438-1955; Fax: 215-438-1944; Email: charles.levesque@depaulusa.org; Web: www.depaulusa.org. Depaul USA offers homeless and disadvantaged people the opportunity to fulfill their potential and move towards an independent and positive future. Depaul USA is part of Depaul International and works in the spirit of St. Vincent de Paul and St. Louise De Marillac, believing that everyone should have a place to call home and a stake in their community.

Fournier Retirement Fund Corporation, Mount St. Joseph Convent, 9701 Germantown Ave., 19118-2694. Tel: 215-248-7205; Fax: 215-248-7277; Email: msjc@ssjphila.org; Web: www.ssjphila.org. Sr. Kathryn Shelly, Sec.

Franciscan Volunteer Ministry, Inc., P.O. Box 29276, 19125. Tel: 215-427-3070; Fax: 215-427-3059; Email: fvmadir@gmail.com; Email: fvmpd@aol.com; Web: www.franciscanvolunteerministry.org. Katie Sullivan, Exec. Dir.; Lizzy Heurich, Assoc. Dir. Purpose: To create and run a Franciscan lay volunteer program in the United States.

**Gianna Center of Philadelphia*, 7500 Central Ave., Ste. 203, 19111.

Good Shepherd Mediation Program, Chew Ave.: 2000 Hamilton St. Ste. 301, Rodin Place, 19130-3814. Tel: 215-843-5413; Fax: 267-534-2122; Email: gsmediation@phillymediators.org; Web: www.phillymediators.org. Cheryl Cutrona, Exec. Dir.

Good Shepherd Corporation, Philadelphia, Pennsylvania.

IHM Center for Literacy, 7341 Cottage St., 19136. Tel: 215-338-3120; Fax: 215-338-1003; Email: ihmcenter4literacy@yahoo.com; Web: www.ihmcenterforliteracy.com. Sisters Margaret Paul Longshore, I.H.M., Dir.; Sarah Lamb, I.H.M., Site Coord. Full-time program with courses in English for Speakers of Other Languages (ESOL)

2nd Sight, 929 S. Farragut St., 19143-3695. Tel: 215-382-0292; Fax: 215-382-4662; Email: ihmesldesales@verizon.net.

**International Institute for Culture*, Ivy Hall, 6331 Lancaster Ave., 19151. Tel: 215-877-9910; Fax: 215-877-9911; Web: www.iiculture.org. John M. Haas, Ph.D., S.T.L., M.Div., Pres. Purpose: for the evangelization of culture through international conferences, language and cultural programs, etc., which reflect the rich cultural heritage of the Catholic Church which serves to bring people to the Person of Jesus Christ.

Katherine Kiernan Chateau, Inc., c/o Catholic Social Services, 222 N. 17th St., Ste. 300, 19103. Tel: 215-587-3903; Fax: 215-587-2479; Email: CHSweb@chs-adphila.org.

Marianist Lay Community of North America (MLC-NA), 1341 N. Delaware Ave., #301, 19125-4300. Tel: 215-634-4116; Email: info@mlnna.org; Web: www.mlnna.org.

The Medaille Corporation, 9701 Germantown Ave., 19118.

Medical Mission Sisters Supplemental Subsidy Fund, Inc., 8400 Pine Rd., 19111. Tel: 215-742-6100; Fax: 215-742-2602; Email: camillia@medicalmissionsisters.org; Web: www.medicalmissionsisters.org. Sr. Frances Vaughan, M.M.S., Pres.

Society of Catholic Medical Missionaries, INC.

Missionary Cenacle Apostolate, 3501 Solly Ave, 19136. Tel: 410-772-5799. Pat Regan, Treas. & Gen. Custodian. The MCA is a branch of the Missionary Cenacle Family. Lay people called to be missionaries in the Church in the providence of everyday life. MCA members live and work in the United States, Mexico, Puerto Rico, Colombia, and Costa Rica.

National Catholic Bioethics Center, 6399 Drexel Rd., 19151. Tel: 215-877-2660; Fax: 215-877-2682; Email: info@ncbcenter.org; Web: www.ncbcenter.

org. John M. Haas, M.Div., S.T.L., Ph.D., Pres.; Donald J. Powers, Vice Pres. Fin., Tel: 401-289-0680; George E. Gunning IV, Exec. Vice Pres., Tel: 215-871-2009; Rev. Tadeusz Pacholczyk, Dir. Educ.; Edward J. Furton, M.A., Ph.D., Dir. Publications; Marie T. Hilliard, J.C.L., Ph.D., R.N., D.M., Dir. Bioethics & Pub. Policy; John F. Brehany, S.T.L., Ph.D., Dir. Institutional Rels.; John A. DiCamillo, Staff Ethicist.

National Shrine of Saint Rita of Cascia, 1166 S. Broad St., 19146. Tel: 215-546-8333; Fax: 215-732-3510; Tel: 215-546-8335; Email: ritashrine@aol.com; Web: www.saintritashrine.org. Chesley Turner, Dir. Center of Devotion to Saint Rita in the United States. Priests 4; Staff 7. In Res. Revs. Eugene DelConte, O.S.A.; Daniel McLaughlin, O.S.A.; William Recchuti, O.S.A.; James T. Spenard, O.S.A.

Natural Family Planning Center of Washington, DC, Inc., 8400 Pine Rd., 19111-1345. Tel: 301-897-9323; Email: hannaklaus@gmail.com; Web: www.teenstarprogram.org. Sr. Hanna Klaus, M.M.S., M.D., Exec. Dir. Teen STAR & Holistic Sexuality Programs. Total in Residence 1; Total Staff 5.

**New Jerusalem Now*, 2011 W. Norris St., 19121-2120. Tel: 215-763-8806. Sr. Margaret McKenna, M.M.S., Dir. Residential program that seeks to integrate all dimensions of recovery from drugs in the members' daily lives. Serves North Philadelphia.

Philadelphia Senatus of the Legion of Mary, 5109 N. Broad St., 19141. Tel: 215-457-6343; Email: info@philadelphiasenatus.org; Web: www.philadelphiasenatus.org. Rev. Addisalem T. Mekonnen, Spiritual Dir. The Legion of Mary is an international association of lay Catholics finding Jesus through prayer, works of mercy and evangelization rooted in Marian spirituality and commitment to the Holy Spirit.

Redemptorist Office for Mission Advancement, 1019 N. 5th St., 19123. Tel: 410-990-1680; Fax: 410-990-1683; Email: kwhaley@redemptorists.net; Web: redemptorists.net. PO Box 29308, 19125. Raymond Collins, Rector.

St. Raymond Nonnatus Foundation for Freedom, Family and Faith, 6398 Drexel Rd., 19151. Tel: 215-870-9913; Email: spirmod.srnf@gmail.com; Email: director.srnf@gmail.com. Rev. Matthew H. Phelan, O.de.M, Spiritual Moderator. Founded to give concrete application to the redemptive charism of the Order of the B.V.M. of Mercy by providing support and accompaniment to Catholic families in crisis situations, initially strengthening the Catholic faith and life of those wounded by divorce.

The Saint Thomas More Society of Philadelphia, P.O. Box 58060, 19102. Tel: 215-564-8106; Email: stmsphila@gmail.com; Web: www.saintthomasmoresociety.org. Purpose: The Society is an association of Catholic lawyers organized to strengthen the religious and charitable commitment of its members and to promote high ethical standards in the legal profession, as exemplified by the life of Saint Thomas More.

Sisters of Saint Joseph Welcome Center, 728 E. Allegheny Ave., 19134-2428. Tel: 215-634-1696; Fax: 215-634-0760; Email: kmcshane15@gmail.com; Web: www.ssjwelcomecenter.org. Sisters Kathleen McShane, Dir.; Connie Trainor, S.S.J., Dir. Sisters 4.

Society of Catholic Medical Missionaries Generalate, Inc. (Effective 1991) 8400 Pine Rd., 19111. Tel: 215-742-6100; Fax: 215-342-3948; Email: generalate@medicalmissionsisters.org.uk; Web: www.medicalmissionsisters.org.uk. Sisters Francine Poondikulam, General Treas.; Irene Fernandez, M.M.S., Society Coord. Corporation collects funds for charitable and missionary work, for Medical Mission Sisters; Assists in operation of hospitals, clinics and primary health care programs; Assists in care of poor, sick and infirm, in U.S. and overseas; Assists in training and educating men and women in medicine and nursing, and other health professions; Trains candidates for the Community; Provides assisted living care to sick and elder Medical Mission Sisters.

The Society of Catholic Scientists, 222 N. 17th St., 12th Fl., 19103. Tel: 302-831-6883; Fax: 302-831-1637; Email: smbarr@udel.edu; Web: www.catholicscientists.org. Stephen Barr, Pres. The Society of Catholic Scientists exists for fellowship and discussion among Catholic scientists.

Society of St. Vincent de Paul of Philadelphia, 3004 Keenwood Rd., East Norriton, 19403. Tel: 484-704-7153; Fax: 484-704-7262; Email: careygroberts@comcast.net. Larry Huber, Pres.; Ronald Mandel, Vice Pres. Catholic Lay Organization serving those in need with spiritual, moral, material and financial support regardless of race, creed, etc.

Vincentian Family Office, 500 E. Chelten Ave., 19144. Tel: 215-715-3984; Fax: 215-713-2404; Email: vfo@famvin.org; Web: www.famvin.org. Rev. Joseph V. Agostino, C.M. The Vincentian Family Office serves the international Vincentian Family by providing formation to its members and by enhancing the coordination & communication of the Vincentian Family in their service to persons living in poverty.

ASTON. *Association of Franciscan Colleges and Universities, Inc.*, Neumann University, 1 Neumann Dr., Aston, 19014. Tel: 601-358-4539; Email: haugd@neumann.edu. Debi Haug, Exec. Dir., Mission.

**Catholic Family Fun Club*, One Neumann Dr., RAB #326, Aston. Tel: 610-358-4224; Email: catholicfamilyfun@gmail.com; Web: www.meetup.com/Catholic-Family-Fun-Club. Mary Beth Yount, Exec. Dir. The CFFC provides a digital platform for Catholic families to attend - and create - local Catholic catechetical and social activities together and is run by families, for families to grow in the Catholic faith.

Legal Name: Educational Initiatives of PA.

Sisters of St. Francis Foundation, 609 S. Convent Rd., Aston, 19014. Tel: 610-558-7713; Fax: 610-558-5357; Email: dkrist@osfphila.org; Web: www.osfphila.org. Sr. Deborah Krist, O.S.F., Exec. Dir. Purpose: Raises funds to fulfill the needs of the Ministries and Retired Sisters of the Sisters of St. Francis of Philadelphia.

Sisters of St. Francis of Philadelphia, Charitable Trust II, Our Lady of Angels Convent, 609 S. Covent Rd., Aston, 19014. Tel: 610-558-7733; Fax: 610-459-0195; Email: mdougher@osfphila.org; Web: www.osfphila.org. Sr. Mary Kathryn Dougherty, O.S.F., Congregational Min.

BALA CYNWYD. *The Papal Foundation*, 150 Monument Rd., Ste. 609, Bala Cynwyd, 19004. Tel: 610-535-6340; Tel: 610-535-6341; Fax: 610-535-6343; Email: jschnatz@thepapalfoundation.com; Web: www.thepapalfoundation.com. Mr. James V. Coffey, M.A., Vice Pres. Advancement.

BERWYN. *AbbeyFest Ministries, Inc.*, 1200 Sugartown Rd., Berwyn, 19312. Tel: 215-569-5438; Email: megan@theabbeyfest.com; Web: www.theabbeyfest.com. Michael P. Broadhurst, Bd. Chair; Megan Schrieber, Pres.

COATESVILLE. *Franciscans of Mary*, 404 Charles St., Coatesville, 19320. Tel: 610-384-0360; Email: information@frmaria.org; Web: www.franciscansofmary.org. Rev. Santiago Martin Rodriguez, F.M., Pres. The mission of the Franciscans of Mary is to live and spread the spirituality of gratitude, helping everyone to understand that this is the heart of the Gospel, what God expects, and has the right to find in the heart of the Christian.

CONSHOHOCKEN. *Mercy Health System of Southeastern PA*, 1 West Elm St., Ste. 100, Conshohocken, 19428. Tel: 610-567-6107; Fax: 610-567-6150; Email: cweaver@mercyhealth.org; Web: www.mercyhealth.org. Susan Croushore, Pres. & CEO; Sr. Mary Christine McCann, R.S.M., Bd. Chm.; Catherine Weaver, Vice Pres. Mission & Integration. Mercy Health System is a regional health ministry of Trinity Health.

The health care services operated by Mercy Health System include:.

Mercy Catholic Medical Center dba Mercy Philadelphia Hospital, Tel: 215-748-9300; Fax: 215-748-9709.

Mercy Catholic Medical Center dba Mercy Fitzgerald Hospital, Tel: 610-237-4030; Fax: 610-237-4202.

Mercy Suburban Hospital, Tel: 610-278-2002; Fax: 610-272-4642.

St. Agnes Continuing Care Center, Tel: 610-567-6120; Fax: 610-567-6820.

**Nazareth Hospital*, Tel: 215-335-6039; Fax: 215-335-6598.

**Nazareth Health Care Foundation*, Tel: 215-335-6159; Fax: 215-335-6265.

**Nazareth Physician Services*, Tel: 610-567-6120; Fax: 610-567-6820.

**N.E. Physician Services, Inc.*, Tel: 610-567-6120; Fax: 610-567-6820.

**Mercy Family Support*, Tel: 610-690-2500; Fax: 610-690-4644.

**Mercy Health Plan*, Tel: 610-567-6120; Fax: 610-567-6820.

**Mercy Management Services of Southeastern PA*, Tel: 610-567-6120; Fax: 610-567-6820.

**Mercy Health Foundation*, Tel: 610-567-6120; Fax: 610-567-6820.

**Mercy Home Health*, Tel: 610-690-2500; Fax: 610-690-4644.

**Mercy Home Health Services*, Tel: 610-690-2500; Fax: 610-690-4644.

**East Norriton Physician Services*, Tel: 610-567-6120; Fax: 610-567-6820.

DOWNINGTOWN. **Theology of the Body Institute*, 400 Boot Rd., Ste. B1, Downingtown, 19335. Tel: 215-302-8200; Fax: 215-302-8200; Web: tobinstitute.org. Jennifer Settle, Managing Dir. Purpose: To educate and train men and women to understand, live and promote the Theology of the Body and to ensure that the teachings of John Paul II are promoted faithfully and effectively.

FLOURTOWN. *Saint Joseph Guild*, 110 W. Wissahickon Ave., P.O. Box 36, Flourtown, 19031-0036. Tel: 215-248-7838; Fax: 215-248-7802; Email: sjguild19@aol.com; Web: www.ssjphila.org. Sr. Frances DeLisle, S.S.J., Coord.

HUNTINGDON VALLEY. *Holy Redeemer Health System*, 667 Welsh Rd., Huntingdon Valley, 19006. Tel: 215-938-4650; Fax: 215-938-4671; Web: www.holyredeemer.com. Michael B. Laign, Pres. & CEO. Sponsor: Sisters of the Holy Redeemer, C.S.R.Parent organization which maintains, manages, and operates the health care system composed of the various corporations sponsored and established by the Sisters of the Holy Redeemer, C.S.R. as follows: Holy Redeemer Health System; Holy Redeemer Hospital; Holy Redeemer St. Joseph Manor; Holy Redeemer Lafayette; Holy Redeemer Home Health & Hospice Services; Holy Redeemer Multi-Care, Inc.; Holy Redeemer Transitional Care Unit; Redeemer Village; Redeemer Village II; Drueding Center; HRH Management Corporation; Convents Epiphany Community, St. Teresa of Avila Community, Visitation Community, Annunciation-Formation Community and Redeemer Community.

Holy Redeemer Hospital, Tel: 215-947-3000; Web: www.holyredeemer.com.

Holy Redeemer St. Joseph Manor, Tel: 215-938-4000; Web: www.holyredeemer.com. Benjamin Pieczynski, N.H.A., Vice Pres. & Admin.

Holy Redeemer Lafayette, Tel: 215-214-2800. Robin Frankwich, Group Vice Pres., Long Term Care & Residential Svcs.

Holy Redeemer Home Health and Hospice Services, Tel: 800-678-8678; Web: www.holyredeemer.com.

Holy Redeemer Transitional Care Unit, Tel: 215-947-3000.

Holy Redeemer Multi-Care, Inc.

IMMACULATA. *Enserv Inc.*, 1145 King Rd., Immaculata, 19345. Tel: 610-647-4400, Ext. 3147; Fax: 610-251-1668.

KING OF PRUSSIA. **The Living Scripture Institute*, 743 Roy Rd., King of Prussia, 19406. Tel: 610-888-9049; Email: ktdann@live.com. Katie Dannunzio, Vice Pres. The Marianist Center is committed to the spirit of Mary. This spirit mission fosters spiritual growth and formation, the building of lay faith/action communities and social justice according to the unique gifts of the Marianist tradition. Programs offered.

Rachel's Vineyard Ministries (International Headquarters), 808 N. Henderson Rd., King of Prussia, 19406. Tel: 610-354-0555 Toll Free: 877-HOPE-4-ME (877-4673-3463); Fax: 610-354-0311; Email: t.burke@rachelsvineyard.org; Web: www.rachelsvineyard.org. Theresa Burke, Ph.D., L.P.C., N.C.P., Founder & Exec. Dir.; Kevin Burke, M.S.S., L.S.W. Purpose: to provide retreats offering emotional and spiritual healing after abortion; and continuing education for professionals, clergy and lay persons.

MERION STATION. *The Mercy Foundation*, 515 Montgomery Ave., Merion Station, 19066-1297. Tel: 610-664-6650; Fax: 610-664-3429. Sr. Patricia Vetrano, R.S.M., Pres., Email: pvetrano@mercymidatlantic.org.

Sisters of Mercy of the Americas Mid-Atlantic Community, Inc., 515 Montgomery Ave., Merion Station, 19066. Tel: 610-664-6650; Fax: 610-664-3429; Web: www.mercymidatlantic.org. Sr. Patricia Vetrano, R.S.M., Pres.

NEWTOWN SQUARE. *Global Health Ministry*, 3805 West Chester Pike, Ste. 100, Newtown Square, 19073-2304. Tel: 610-355-2003; Fax: 610-271-9141; Email: mmcginley@trinity-health.org; Web: www.globalhealthvolunteers.net. Sr. Mary Jo McGinley, R.S.M., Pres. & Exec. Dir.

Trinity Health Life Pennsylvania, Inc. dba Mercy LIFE – West Philadelphia, 4508 Chestnut St., 19139. Tel: 267-787-8282; Email: kelly.hopkins@trinity-health.org; Web: www.trinity-health.org. Kelly Hopkins, Pres. Trinity Health PACE.

ORELAND. **Pro-Life Union of Greater Philadelphia*, 88 Pennsylvania Ave., Oreland, 19075. Edel Finnegan, Exec. Dir. Affirms the sanctity of life through our work in alternatives, education, outreach & public affairs.

ROSEMONT. *Holy Child Network of Schools*, 1341 Montgomery Ave., Rosemont, 19010. Tel: 610-626-1400; Fax: 610-525-2910; Email:

emcdevitt@shcj.org; Web: www.holychildschools.org. Sr. Eileen McDevitt, S.H.C.J., Dir. The Holy Child Network of Schools is a national network of ten elementary and secondary schools in the US and part of a larger body of schools in England, Ireland, France, Nigeria & Ghana. The Network office is organized/structured by a board of trustees.

VILLANOVA. *Augustinian Volunteers*, Business Office: 214 Ashwood Rd., Villanova, 19085. Tel: 610-527-3330, Ext. 291; Fax: 610-520-0618; Email: osavol@gmail.com; Web: www.osavol.org. Joanna Bowen, Dir.; Hannah Kunberger, Assoc. Dir.; Taylor Gostomski, Asst. Dir. A faith-based lay volunteer program serving the poor alongside the Augustinian Friars in the Archdioceses of Chicago, Boston, Philadelphia, and Los Angeles and the Diocese of San Diego. Also in Chulucanas, Pèru.

WAYNE. **Catholic Leadership Institute*, 440 E. Swedesford Rd., Ste. 3040, Wayne, 19087. Tel: 610-363-1315; Fax: 610-363-3731; Email: info@CatholicLeaders.org; Web: www.CatholicLeaders.org. Most Rev. Gregory M. Aymond, D.D., M.Div., Episcopal Mod.; Timothy C. Flanagan, Founder; Daniel Cellucci, CEO; Virgium Koehler, Vice Pres. Finance & Opers.; Lucille Smith, Client & Episcopal Svcs. Lay organization whose purpose is to provide bishops, priests, deacons, religious and lay persons in the Roman Catholic Church with world-class, pastoral leadership formation and consulting services that strengthen their confidence and competence in ministry, enabling them to articulate a vision for their local church, to call forth the gifts of those they lead and to create more vibrant faith communities rooted in Jesus Christ.

WEST CHESTER. *FIERCE Athlete, Inc.*, 227 N. Walnut St., Apt. 2, West Chester, 19380. Tel: 860-392-9225 ; Email: sam@fierceathlete.org; Web: www.fierceathlete.org. Samantha Kelley, Pres. FIERCE Athlete promotes true and authentic femininity within female athletics through the teachings of the Catholic Church.

WYNNEWOOD. **The Culture Project International*, P.O. Box 86, Wynnewood, 19096. Tel: 800-315-8684; Email: mail@restoreculture.com; Web: www.restoreculture.com. Cristina Barba, Pres.; Stephanie Deutsch, Asst. Dir.; Dee Simone, Devel. Asst. The Culture Project is an initiative of young people set out to restore culture through the experience of virtue. We proclaim the dignity of the human person and the richness of living sexual integrity, inviting our culture to become fully alive.

YARDLEY. **Legacy of Life Foundation*, 25 S. Main St., #217, Yardley, 19067. Tel: 215-788-4051; Fax: 215-826-9269; Email: marie@legacyoflifefoundation.org; Web: www.legacyoflifefoundation.org.

RELIGIOUS INSTITUTES OF MEN REPRESENTED IN THE ARCHDIOCESE

For further details refer to the corresponding bracketed number in the Religious Institutes of Men or Women section.

[0140]—*Augustinians* (Prov. of St. Thomas Villanova)—O.S.A.
[0290]—*Brothers of Charity*—F.C.
[0330]—*Brothers of the Christian Schools* (Baltimore Prov.)—F.S.C.
[0900]—*Canons Regular of Premontre*—O.Praem.
[0470]—*Capuchin Friars*—O.F.M.Cap.
[0650]—*Congregation of the Holy Spirit* (Eastern Prov.)—C.S.Sp.
[1330]—*Congregation of the Mission* (Eastern Prov.)—C.M.
[0685]—*Institute of the Incarnate Word*—I.V.E.
[0730]—*Legionaries of Christ*—L.C.
[0850]—*Missionaries of Africa*—M.Afr.
[0825]—*Missionaries of the Blessed Sacrament*—M.S.S.
[1110]—*Missionaries of the Sacred Heart* (American Prov.)—M.S.C.
[0910]—*Oblate Missionaries of Mary Immaculate*—O.M.I.
[0920]—*Oblates of St. Francis de Sales*—O.S.F.S.
[0520]—*Order of Friars Minor* (Assumption B.V.M. & Holy Name Provs.)—O.F.M.
[0970]—*Order of Our Lady of Mercy*—O.deM.
[0430]—*Order of Preachers*—O.P.
[1010]—*Pauline Fathers*—O.S.P.P.E.
[0950]—*The Philadelphia Congregation of the Oratory of Saint Philip Neri*—C.O.
[1040]—*Piarist Fathers*—Sch.P.
[1065]—*Priestly Fraternity of St. Peter*—F.S.S.P.
[1070]—*Redemptorist Fathers* (Baltimore Prov.)—C.SS.R.
[1220]—*Servants of Charity*—S.D.C.
[0690]—*Society of Jesus (Jesuits)* (Maryland Prov.)—S.J.
[0760]—*Society of Mary (Marianists)*—S.M.

RELIGIOUS INSTITUTES OF WOMEN REPRESENTED IN THE ARCHDIOCESE

[]—*All Saints Sisters of the Poor*—A.S.S.P.
[2120]—*Armenian Sisters of the Immaculate Conception*—A.S.I.C.
[1810]—*Bernardine Sisters of the Third Order of St. Francis*—O.S.F.
[0760]—*Daughters of Charity of St. Vincent de Paul*—D.C.
[0940]—*Daughters of St. Mary of Providence*—D.S.M.P.
[0420]—*Discalced Carmelite Nuns*—O.C.D.
[1115]—*Dominican Sisters of Peace*—O.P.
[1170]—*Felician Sisters*—C.S.S.F.
[1180]—*Franciscan Sisters of Allegany, New York*—O.S.F.
[1840]—*Grey Nuns of the Sacred Heart*—G.N.S.H.
[1870]—*Handmaids of the Sacred Heart of Jesus*—A.C.J.
[]—*Holy Spirit Sisters of Tanzania*—A.L.C.S.
[2340]—*Little Sisters of the Poor*—L.S.P.
[2345]—*Little Workers of the Sacred Hearts*—P.O.S.C.
[2490]—*Medical Mission Sisters*—M.M.S.
[2710]—*Missionaries of Charity*—M.C.
[2790]—*Missionary Servants of the Most Blessed Trinity*—M.S.B.T.
[2730]—*Missionary Sisters of the Holy Rosary*—M.S.H.R.
[2800]—*Missionary Sisters of the Most Sacred Heart of Jesus of Hill Twp.*—M.S.C.
[2860]—*Missionary Sisters of the Sacred Heart* (Eastern Prov.)—M.S.C.
[3730]—*Order of St. Basil the Great*—O.S.B.M.
[3760]—*Order of St. Clare*—O.S.C.
[3160]—*Parish Visitors of Mary Immaculate*—P.V.M.I.
[3390]—*Religious of the Assumption*—R.A.
[2519]—*Religious Sisters of Mercy of Alma*—R.S.M.
[3430]—*Religious Teachers Filippini*—M.P.F.
[2970]—*School Sisters of Notre Dame*—S.S.N.D.
[]—*Servants of the Lord and of the Virgin of Matara*—S.S.V.M.
[3540]—*Sister Servants of the Holy Spirit of Perpetual Adoration*—S.Sp.S.deA.P.
[0500]—*Sisters of Charity of Nazareth*—S.C.N.
[0660]—*Sisters of Christian Charity*—S.C.C.
[]—*Sisters of Life*—S.V.
[2575]—*Sisters of Mercy of the Americas, Merion*—R.S.M.
[3000]—*Sisters of Notre Dame de Namur*—S.N.D.deN.
[1650]—*Sisters of St. Francis of Philadelphia*—O.S.F.
[]—*Sisters of St. Joseph of Mombasa*—S.S.J.
[3893]—*Sisters of St. Joseph of Philadelphia*—S.S.J.
[0260]—*Sisters of the Blessed Sacrament for Indians and Colored People*—S.B.S.
[0970]—*Sisters of the Divine Compassion*—R.D.C.
[1830]—*Sisters of the Good Shepherd*—R.G.S.
[1970]—*Sisters of the Holy Family of Nazareth*—C.S.F.N.
[2000]—*Sisters of the Redeemer*—C.S.R.
[2160]—*Sisters Servants of the Immaculate Heart of Mary* (Scranton)—I.H.M.
[4060]—*Society of the Holy Child Jesus*—S.H.C.J.
[4120]—*Ursuline Sisters of the Immaculate Conception*—O.S.U.
[4190]—*Visitation Nuns*—V.H.M.

ARCHDIOCESAN CEMETERIES

PHILADELPHIA. *Cathedral*, 1032 N. 48th St., 19131. Tel: 215-302-9341
Holy Sepulchre, Cheltenham Ave. & Ivy Hill Rd., 19150. Tel: 215-302-9356
New Cathedral, 2nd & Butler Sts., 19140. Tel: 215-302-9364

BENSALEM. *Resurrection*, 5201 Hulmeville Rd., Bensalem, 19020. Tel: 215-302-9379

CHALFONT. *St. John Neumann*, 3797 County Line Rd., Chalfont, 18914. Tel: 215-302-9390

COATESVILLE. *All Souls*, 3215 Manor Rd., Coatesville, 19320. Tel: 484-200-8320

NEWTOWN. *All Saints*, 291 W. Durham Rd., Newtown, 18940. Tel: 215-302-9340

PENN TOWNSHIP. *Holy Saviour*

SPRINGFIELD. *SS. Peter and Paul*, 1600 S. Sproul Rd., Springfield, 19064. Tel: 484-200-8321

WEST CONSHOHOCKEN. *Calvary*, Gulph & Matsonford Rd., West Conshohocken, 19428. Tel: 610-232-7180

YEADON. *Holy Cross*, 626 Bailey Rd., Yeadon, 19050. Tel: 610-232-7182

NECROLOGY

† DeSimone, Louis A., Auxiliary Bishop Emeritus of Philadelphia, Died Oct. 5, 2018
† Close, John A., (Retired), Died Mar. 6, 2018
† Giliberti, Francis A., (Retired), Died Apr. 16, 2018
† Shields, James J., (Retired), Died Aug. 14, 2018
† Breen, Robert H., (Retired), Died Aug. 2, 2018
† Cavanaugh, Daniel J., (Retired), Died Sep. 19, 2018
† Gallagher, Joseph J., (Retired), Died Jun. 5, 2018
† Henry, James T., (Retired), Died Mar. 1, 2018
† Melle, James J., (Retired), Died Oct. 24, 2018
† Muir, Gavin W., Riegelsville, St. Lawrence, Died May. 15, 2018
† Murphy, Joseph T., (Retired), Died Nov. 19, 2018
† Nevins, John J., (Retired), Died Jun. 23, 2018
† Stec, Joseph C., (Retired), Died Sep. 17, 2018
† Whelan, James J., (Retired), Died Jun. 26, 2018
† Zeuner, Karl A., (Retired), Died Apr. 14, 2018

An asterisk (*) denotes an organization that has established tax-exempt status directly with the IRS and is not covered by the USCCB Group Ruling.

Diocese of Phoenix

(Dioecesis Phoenicensis)

Most Reverend

THOMAS J. OLMSTED, J.C.D.

Bishop of Phoenix; ordained July 2, 1973; appointed Coadjutor Bishop of Wichita February 16, 1999; Episcopal ordination April 20, 1999; appointed Bishop of Wichita October 4, 2001; appointed Bishop of Phoenix November 25, 2003; installed December 20, 2003. *Office: 400 E. Monroe St., Phoenix, AZ 85004-2336.*

Most Reverend

EDUARDO A. NEVARES

Auxiliary Bishop of Phoenix; ordained July 18, 1981; appointed Titular Bishop of Natchesium and Auxiliary Bishop of Phoenix May 11, 2010; episcopal ordination July 19, 2010. *Office: 400 E. Monroe St., Phoenix, AZ 85004-2336.*

Diocesan Pastoral Center: 400 E. Monroe St., Phoenix, AZ 85004-2336. Tel: 602-257-0030; Tel: 602-354-2000; Fax: 602-354-2427.

Web: www.dphx.org

Email: contact-us@dphx.org

ESTABLISHED DECEMBER 2, 1969.

Square Miles 43,967.

Comprises the Counties of Maricopa; Mohave; Yavapai & Coconino not to include the territorial boundaries of the Navajo Indian Reservation; Pinal–that portion of land known as the Gila River Indian Reservation in the State of Arizona.

Patroness of Diocese: Our Lady of Guadalupe.

For legal titles of parishes and diocesan institutions, consult the Chancery Office.

STATISTICAL OVERVIEW

Personnel	
Bishop	1
Auxiliary Bishops	1
Priests: Diocesan Active in Diocese	100
Priests: Retired, Sick or Absent	36
Number of Diocesan Priests	136
Religious Priests in Diocese	93
Total Priests in Diocese	229
Extern Priests in Diocese	78
Ordinations:	
Diocesan Priests	3
Religious Priests	1
Transitional Deacons	2
Permanent Deacons	6
Permanent Deacons in Diocese	222
Total Brothers	7
Total Sisters	134
Parishes	
Parishes	94
With Resident Pastor:	
Resident Diocesan Priests	53
Resident Religious Priests	16
Without Resident Pastor:	
Administered by Priests	25
Missions	23
Pastoral Centers	3
New Parishes Created	1
Professional Ministry Personnel:	
Sisters	14
Lay Ministers	28
Welfare	
Catholic Hospitals	1
Total Assisted	105,782
Health Care Centers	5
Total Assisted	17,177
Homes for the Aged	18
Total Assisted	849
Day Care Centers	20
Total Assisted	116
Specialized Homes	5
Total Assisted	1,639
Special Centers for Social Services	24
Total Assisted	10,250,757
Residential Care of Disabled	1
Total Assisted	15
Other Institutions	1
Total Assisted	1,817
Educational	
Diocesan Students in Other Seminaries	40
Total Seminarians	40
Colleges and Universities	2
Total Students	520
High Schools, Diocesan and Parish	6
Total Students	3,654
High Schools, Private	1
Total Students	1,336
Elementary Schools, Diocesan and Parish	28
Total Students	9,858
Elementary Schools, Private	1
Total Students	157
Catechesis/Religious Education:	
High School Students	2,330
Elementary Students	16,920
Total Students under Catholic Instruction	34,815
Teachers in the Diocese:	
Priests	9
Sisters	30
Lay Teachers	1,043
Vital Statistics	
Receptions into the Church:	
Infant Baptism Totals	4,895
Minor Baptism Totals	755
Adult Baptism Totals	287
Received into Full Communion	1,476
First Communions	6,757
Confirmations	7,745
Marriages:	
Catholic	740
Interfaith	120
Total Marriages	860
Deaths	2,905
Total Catholic Population	1,225,677
Total Population	4,883,177

Former Bishops—Most Revs. EDWARD A. MCCARTHY, D.D., installed Bishop of the Diocese of Phoenix, Dec. 2, 1969; transferred to Coadjutor Archbishop of Miami, July 7, 1976; installed Sept. 17, 1976; died June 7, 2005; JAMES S. RAUSCH, D.D., Ph.D., installed March 22, 1977; died May 18, 1981; THOMAS J. O'BRIEN, D.D., ord. May 7, 1961; cons. Jan. 6, 1982; installed Bishop of the Diocese of Phoenix Jan. 18, 1982; retired June 18, 2003; died Aug. 26, 2018.

Vicars General—Most Rev. EDUARDO A. NEVARES, V.G., Tel: 602-354-2488; Rev. FREDRICK J. ADAMSON, V.G., Tel: 602-354-2476.

Moderator of the Curia—Rev. FREDRICK J. ADAMSON, V.G., Diocesan Pastoral Center, 400 E. Monroe, Phoenix, 85004. Tel: 602-354-2180; Fax: 602-354-2427.

Diocesan Office—400 E. Monroe St., Phoenix, 85004-2336. Tel: 602-257-0030; Tel: 602-354-2000; Fax: 602-354-2427.

Chancellor—MARIA R. CHAVIRA, Ph.D., 400 E. Monroe St., Phoenix, 85004-2336. Tel: 602-354-2470; Fax: 602-354-2427.

College of Consultors—Revs. THOMAS BENNETT, V.F.; ROMEO DIONISIO; CHARLES GORAIEB, Chm.; STEVEN KUNKEL, V.F.; MATTHEW LOWRY; PEDRO VELEZ PRENSA; MICHAEL STRALEY.

Deans—Revs. EMILE C. "BUD" PELLETIER JR., V.F., Northwest Deanery; THOMAS BENNETT, V.F., East Deanery; STEVEN KUNKEL, V.F., Central Deanery; OSCAR GUTIERREZ, V.F., Southwest Deanery; JOHN BONAVITACOLA, V.F., South Deanery; DAVID KELASH, V.F., North Deanery; DONALD J. KLINE, V.F., Northeast Deanery.

Presbyteral Council—Revs. FREDRICK J. ADAMSON, V.G.; BRIAN BELL; THOMAS BENNETT, V.F., Chm.; DALE CRAIG, S.O.L.T.; ROMEO DIONISIO; JOHN PARKS, V.F.; CHRISTOPHER J. FRASER, J.C.L.; CHARLES GORAIEB; DANIEL MCBRIDE, V.F.; WILLIAM "BILLY" J. KOSCO; STEVEN KUNKEL, V.F., Sec.; MATTHEW LOWRY; JOHN MUIR, Vice Chm.; Most Revs. EDUARDO A. NEVARES, V.G.; THOMAS J. OLMSTED, J.C.D.; Revs. JESUS "JESS" G. TY; PEDRO VELEZ PRENSA; DAVID SANFILIPPO; GREGORY J. SCHLARB; MICHAEL STRALEY; PAUL SULLIVAN.

Diocesan Tribunal—Office: 400 E. Monroe St., Phoenix, 85004-2336. Tel: 602-354-2275; Fax: 602-354-2424.

Judicial Vicar—Rev. CHRISTOPHER J. FRASER, J.C.L.

Adjutant Judicial Vicar—Rev. ERNESTO REYNOSO, J.C.L.

Director—NICOLE M. DELANEY, J.C.L.

Diocesan Judges—Revs. F. NELSON LIBERA, J.C.D.; CHARLES G. KIEFFER, V.F.; JILSON PANAKAL, J.C.L.; AWTE WELDU, O.Cist., J.C.L.; Deacons WILLIAM FINNEGAN, J.C.L.; EDUARDO HUERTA.

Promoter of Justice—Rev. F. NELSON LIBERA, J.C.D.

Defenders of the Bond—Rev. PETER P. DOBROWSKI, (Retired); ROBERT FLUMMERFELT, J.D., J.C.L.; DANIELA KNEPPER, J.C.L.; Sr. ELLEN SINCLAIR, S.D.S.

Advocates—WILLIAM AHEARN; SANDI BEATTIE; CAMILLE O'MELIA; JAMES O'MELIA; DONNA WICKER; ASENCION MURGA; DEBORAH MALATIN; JOHN LOWERY; LEANA LOWERY; ISAURA

VALENZUELA; CLIFF MCGRAW; Sr. BRIDGET CHAPMAN, M.M., M.M.; Deacons JAMES BEATTIE; RUDY CAMPAS; WILLIAM JENKINS; DOMINICK BONAIUTO; PATRICK TOILOLO; Revs. H. FRED LECLAIRE, C.M.F.; MICAH MUHLEN, O.F.M.; MAUREEN SCHAAF; DENNIS SULLIVAN.

Auditor—JUSTINA SANCHEZ.

Notaries—NANCY PINA; LIANNA MARTINEZ; LEANA LOWERY; ASENCION MURGA; CATHERINE DUBE; VILMA HOGREVE.

Appellate Case Coordinator/Notary—HEIDI STOLL.

Diocesan Offices

Archives—400 E. Monroe St., Phoenix, 85004-2336. Tel: 602-354-2475; Fax: 602-354-2486. KATHERINE HERRICK, Archivist.

Arizona Catholic Conference—MR. RONALD JOHNSON, Exec. Dir., 400 E. Monroe St., Phoenix, 85004-2336. Tel: 602-354-2390; Fax: 602-354-2466; Fax: 602-354-2394.

Black Catholic Ministry—Diocesan Center, 400 E. Monroe St., Phoenix, 85004. Tel: 602-354-2025. DR. ROBERT WATSON, Dir.

Buildings & Properties—JOHN MINIERI, Dir. Real Property & Facilities, Diocesan Center, 400 E. Monroe St., Phoenix, 85004-2336. Tel: 602-354-2161; Fax: 602-354-2440.

Catholic Campaign for Human Development/Catholic Relief Services—Diocesan Center: 400 E. Monroe St., Phoenix, 85004-2336. Tel: 602-354-2125. Sr. MARY ANGELA ALEXANDER, R.S.M., Dir.

Catholic Cemeteries—St. Francis, Holy Redeemer, Holy Cross, Queen of Heaven, Calvary, All Souls Rev. MICHAEL L. DISKIN, Spiritual Advisor; MR. JOSEPH W. LANGE, Pres. & CEO, Calvary Cemetery, 201 W. University, Flagstaff, 86001. Tel: 928-220-2317; Fax: 928-774-1105 (Call First). Administrative Offices, 2033 N. 48th St., Phoenix, 85008. Tel: 602-267-1329; Fax: 602-267-7942. St. Francis Cemetery, 2033 N. 48th St., Phoenix, 85008. Holy Redeemer Cemetery, 23015 N. Cave Creek Rd., Phoenix, 85040. Tel: 480-513-3243; Fax: 480-513-3293. Queen of Heaven Cemetery, 1500 E. Baseline Rd., Mesa, 85204. Tel: 480-892-3729; Fax: 480-813-2826. All Souls Cemetery, 700 N. Bill Gray Rd., Cottonwood, 86326. Tel: 928-220-2317; Fax: 928-634-3326. Mortuary: Queen of Heaven Mortuary, 1562 E. Baseline Rd., Mesa, 85204. Tel: 480-892-3729; Fax: 480-813-2826. Holy Cross Cemetery, 9925 W. Thomas Rd., Avondale, 85323. Tel: 623-936-1710; Fax: 623-936-8089. Mortuary: Holy Cross Mortuary, 9925 W. Thomas Rd., Avondale, 85323.

Censor Librorum—Rev. Msgr. PETER DAI BUI; Rev. KEVIN C. GRIMDITCH.

The Catholic Sun—(Diocesan Newspaper) MR. ROB DEFRANCESCO, Assoc. Publisher; TONY GUTIERREZ, Editor, 400 E. Monroe St., Phoenix, 85004-2336. Tel: 602-354-2139; Fax: 602-354-2429; Email: info@catholicsun.org; Web: www.catholicsun.org.

Child and Youth Protection and Safe Environment Training—ANNE VARGAS-LEVERIZA, Ph.D., Dir., 400 E. Monroe, Phoenix, 85004. Tel: 602-354-2396; Fax: 602-354-2496.

Communications Office—MR. ROB DEFRANCESCO, Dir., 400 E. Monroe, Phoenix, 85004-2336. Tel: 602-354-2130; Fax: 602-354-2429.

Parish Finance and Corporate Services—DOUG PRITCHARD, Dir., Parish Admin. Svcs. Office: 400 E. Monroe St., Phoenix, 85004-2336. Tel: 602-354-2491.

Diaconate Office—Deacons JAMES TRANT, Dir., 400 E. Monroe, Phoenix, 85004. Tel: 602-354-2011; Fax: 602-354-2437; DOUGLAS BOGART, Assoc. Dir., Tel: 602-354-2012.

Ecumenical and Interreligious Affairs—400 E. Monroe, Phoenix, 85004. Tel: 602-354-2471. Rev. DAVID LOEFFLER, Dir., Tel: 602-943-4000, Ext. 157; Tel: 602-354-2220; Email: frloeffler@dphx.org.

Education and Evangelization, Division—Vicar of Evangelization: Rev. JOHN PARKS, 400 E. Monroe St., Phoenix, 85004. Tel: 602-354-2334; Fax: 602-354-2436.

Superintendent of Schools—HARRY PLUMMER, Tel: 602-354-2341; Fax: 602-354-2436.

Ethnic Ministries, Division of—Most Rev. EDUARDO A. NEVARES, V.G., Dir., Tel: 602-354-2477; IGNACIO RODRIGUEZ, Assoc. Dir., 400 E. Monroe, Phoenix, 85004. Tel: 602-354-2042; Fax: 602-354-2459.

Family Catechesis/Parish Leadership Support—400 E. Monroe St., Phoenix, 85004. ANGELA GAETANO, Dir. Parish Leadership Support, Tel: 602-354-2321; CARMEN PORTELA, Ph.D., Dir. Parish Hispanic Leadership Support, Tel: 602-354-2031.

Finance Office—JOSEPH ANDERSON, CFO; ANTHONY RABAGO, Controller, 400 E. Monroe St., Phoenix, 85004. Tel: 602-354-2186; Fax: 602-354-2448.

Hispanic Mission, Office of—CRISTOFER P. PEREYRA, Dir., 400 E. Monroe St., Phoenix, 85004. Tel: 602-354-2041.

Holy Childhood Association—MARGO GONZALEZ, Dir., 400 E. Monroe, Phoenix, 85004. Tel: 602-354-2005; Fax: 602-354-2442.

Human Resources—Parish Admin. Svcs. Office: 400 E. Monroe, Phoenix, 85004. Tel: 602-354-2201; Fax: 602-296-4385. MARIAN A. ENRIQUEZ, Dir.

John Paul II Resource Center—KATRINA ZENO, Coord., 400 E. Monroe St., Phoenix, 85004-2336. Tel: 602-354-2179.

Kino Catechetical Institute—400 E. Monroe St., Phoenix, 85004-2336. Tel: 602-354-2320; Fax: 602-354-2251. STEVE GREENE, Dir.

Kino Library—400 E. Monroe St., Phoenix, 85004-2336. Tel: 602-354-2251. Sr. DARCY PELETICH, O.S.F., M.A., M.L.S., Librarian.

Employee Benefits—MONIKA DALEY, Parish Admin. Svcs. Office: 400 E. Monroe St., Phoenix, 85004-2336. Tel: 602-354-2189.

Legal/General Counsel—DENNIS NAUGHTON, Gen. Counsel, Parish Admin. Svcs. Office: 400 E. Monroe, Phoenix, 85004. Tel: 602-354-2474; Fax: 602-354-2427.

Marriage and Respect Life, Office of—MIKE PHELAN, Dir., 400 E. Monroe, Phoenix, 85004. Tel: 602-354-2355; Fax: 602-354-2431.

Medical Ethics Board—St. Kateri Tekakwitha Friary, 5447 W. Pecos Rd., Laveen, 85339. Rev. IGNATIUS MAZANOWSKI, F.H.S., Chm. & Dir.

Native American Ministry, Office of—400 E. Monroe St., Phoenix, 85004. Tel: 602-354-2050. Rev. ANTONY TINKER, F.H.S., Dir.

Natural Family Planning, Office of—CINDY LEONARD, Coord., 400 E. Monroe St., Phoenix, 85004. Tel: 602-354-2123; Fax: 602-354-2124.

Priests' Assurance Association—Diocesan Pastoral Center: 400 E. Monroe St., Phoenix, 85004. Tel: 602-354-2478. Rev. MICHAEL DISKIN, Pres.; Rev. Msgr. RICHARD MOYER, Vice Pres.; Revs. JOHN SLOBIG, V.F., Treas., (Retired); EMILE C. "BUD" PELLETIER JR., V.F.; ROBERT CARUSO; DAN VANYO; JAMES TURNER; DANIEL MCBRIDE, V.F.; JOHN EBBESMIER; SCOTT M. SPERRY.

Priests, Vicar for—Rev. DAVID SANFILIPPO.

Priest Personnel—Rev. DAVID SANFILIPPO, Vicar for Priests, 400 E. Monroe, Phoenix, 85004. Tel: 602-354-2480; Fax: 602-354-2427.

Priestly Life and Ministry Board—Revs. JOSEPH BUI; KIERAN KLECZEWSKI, V.F.; EMILE C. "BUD" PELLETIER JR., V.F.; FAUSTO PENAFIEL; DAVID SANFILIPPO, Chm.; Rev. Msgr. ANTONIO SOTELO, (Retired).

Priests' Placement Board—Rev. DAVID SANFILIPPO, 400 E. Monroe, Phoenix, 85004. Tel: 602-354-2480. Members: Revs. CHARLES GORAIEB; DONALD J. KLINE; THADDEUS MCGUIRE, Chm.; ERNESTO REYNOSO, J.C.L.; DAVID SANFILIPPO; NIKKI WESTBY; Rev. CHAUNCEY WINKLER.

Prisons, Catholic Ministries to—400 E. Monroe St., Phoenix, 85004. MR. KEVIN STARRS, Dir., Tel: 602-354-2485.

Propagation of the FaithMARGO GONZALEZ, Dir., 400 E. Monroe, Phoenix, 85004. Tel: 602-354-2005; Fax: 602-354-2442.

Office of Consecrated Life—Sr. ANTHONY MARY DIAGO, R.S.M., Dir., 400 E. Monroe, Phoenix, 85004. Tel: 602-354-2472 (Direct); Fax: 602-354-2442.

Renewal Ministries, Catholic—Most Rev. EDUARDO A. NEVARES, V.G., Spiritual Dir.; MARGE CHAVEZ, Coord., Mailing Address: P.O. Box 13102, Chandler, 85248. Tel: 480-201-6691.

Schools, Catholic—HARRY PLUMMER, Supt. Schools, Tel: 602-354-2341; COLLEEN MCCOY-CEJKA, M.A., Asst. Supt., Tel: 602-354-2111; MR. DOMONIC SALCE, M.Ed., Asst. Supt., Tel: 602-354-2342.

Scouting, Catholic Committee on—St. Mary Magdalene Parish, 2654 E. Williams Field Rd., Gilbert, 85295. Tel: 480-279-6737. Rev. R. CHRISTOPHER AXLINE, Liaison.

Office of Mission Advancement—400 E. Monroe St., Phoenix, 85004. MR. CANDELARIO DELEON, Exec. Dir., Tel: 602-354-2216; Rev. GREGORY J. SCHLARB, Vicar Stewardship, Tel: 602-354-2215; Fax: 602-354-2215.

Vocations Office—Revs. PAUL SULLIVAN, Dir., 400 E. Monroe, Phoenix, 85004. Tel: 602-354-2004; Fax: 602-354-2442; Email: frsullivan@dphx.org; MATTHEW LOWRY, Assoc. Dir., 520 W. Riordan Rd., Flagstaff, 86001. Tel: 928-779-2903; Fax: 928-779-0698.

Worship and Liturgy, Office of—400 E. Monroe St., Phoenix, 85004. Revs. KIERAN KLECZEWSKI, V.F., Dir., Tel: 602-354-2113; JOHN MUIR, Asst. Dir., Tel: 602-354-2110; Deacon WILLIAM A. CHAVIRA, M.D.

CLERGY, PARISHES, MISSIONS AND PAROCHIAL SCHOOLS

CITY OF PHOENIX

(MARICOPA COUNTY)

1—SS. SIMON AND JUDE ROMAN CATHOLIC CATHEDRAL (1953)
6351 N. 27th Ave., 85017. Tel: 602-242-1300; Fax: 602-249-3768; Email: Contactus@simonjude.org; Web: www.simonjude.org. Very Rev. John Lankeit, Rector; Revs. Theilo Ramirez; John Nahrgang; Deacons Roy Drapeau; Anthony Smith; Doug Bogart. In Res., Most Rev. Thomas J. Olmsted, J.C.D.; Rev. David Loeffler.
School—SS. Simon and Jude Roman Catholic Cathedral School, (Grades PreK-8).
Catechesis Religious Program—Students 609.
Convent—Sisters of Loreto (I.B.V.M.), Tel: 602-242-2544; Fax: 602-633-7608. Sisters 8.

2—ST. AGNES ROMAN CATHOLIC PARISH (1940)
1954 N. 24th St., 85008. Tel: 602-244-0349; Fax: 602-244-0054; Email: info@stagnesphx.org; Web: www.stagnesphx.org. Revs. Bradley L. Peterson, O.Carm., Email: blpeterson@stagnesphx.org; Glenn Snow, O.Carm., Parochial Vicar; Deacon Jesse Sanchez.
School—St. Agnes Roman Catholic Parish School, (Grades PreK-8), 2311 E. Palm Ln., 85006. Tel: 602-244-1451. Christine Tax, Prin.; Mrs. Terry Kucera, Librarian.

3—ST. ANTHONY ROMAN CATHOLIC PARISH (1943)
909 S. First Ave., 85003. Tel: 602-252-1771; Email: anovoa@diocesephoenix.org; Web: www.stanthonyphoenix.com. Revs. Fabio Schilereff, I.V.E.; Alex Perez, I.V.E., Parochial Vicar; Rafael Umana.
Convent—Sister Servants of the Lord and the Virgin of Matura, S.S.V.M., Tel: 602-324-3579. Sisters 3.
Center-St. Pius X—Closed 2004. Currently used for Unity Mass for Black Catholic Ministry, the Croatian Community and the Sudanese Community.

4—ST. AUGUSTINE ROMAN CATHOLIC PARISH (1970)
3630 N. 71st Ave., 85033. Tel: 623-849-3131; Fax: 623-849-5689. Revs. Carlos Gomez-Rivera; Jose Ballesteros, Parochial Vicar; Octavio Delgado, Parochial Vicar; Deacons Lorenzo McKnight; Ernesto Ramirez.
Catechesis Religious Program—Martha Morales, D.R.E.

5—ST. BENEDICT ROMAN CATHOLIC PARISH (1985)
16223 S. 48th St., 85048. Tel: 480-961-1610; Email: stbenedict@stbenedict.org; Web: stbenedict.org. Revs. James Aboyi, V.C.; Wilfred Yinah, Parochial Vicar; Deacon Edwin Winkelbauer.
School—St. John Bosco Catholic School, (Grades PreSchool-8), 16035 S. 48th St., 85048. Tel: 480-219-4848; Fax: 480-219-5767; Email: info@sjbosco.org; Web: www.sjbosco.org. Anita Petitti, Prin.; Theresa Harvey, Librarian. Lay Teachers 28; Students 427.

6—ST. CATHERINE OF SIENA ROMAN CATHOLIC PARISH (1947)
6401 S. Central Ave., 85042. Tel: 602-276-5581; Email: st_catherine@diocesephoenix.org. Rev. Alonso Saenz; Deacon Carlos Terrazas. In Res., Rev. Raul Lopez Marzetti.
Schools—St. Catherine of Siena Roman Catholic Parish School—(Grades K-8), 6413 S. Central Ave., 85040. Tel: 602-276-2241, Ext. 251; Fax: 602-268-7886. Mr. Robert Rogers, Prin. & Preschool Dir. Lay Teachers 15; Students 208.
Preschool.

7—CORPUS CHRISTI ROMAN CATHOLIC PARISH (1985)
3550 E. Knox, 85044. Tel: 480-893-8770; Fax: 480-893-3291; Email: steve.mandarino@corpuschristiphx.org; Web: www.corpuschristiphx.org. Revs. Chad King; Reynaldo Clutario, Parochial Vicar; Deacons Alexander Gaudio, (Retired); Philip Simeone, (Retired); Dennis Lambert; Christopher Kellogg; Philip Amantia.
Catechesis Religious Program—Denise Halloran, D.R.E.

8—ST. EDWARD CONFESSOR ROMAN CATHOLIC PARISH (1976)
c/o 6802 S. 24th St., 85042. 4410 E. Southern Ave., 85042. Revs. Oscar Gutierrez, V.F., Parochial Admin.; Martin Munoz, M.D.M.

9—ST. FRANCIS XAVIER ROMAN CATHOLIC PARISH (1928)
4715 N. Central Ave., 85012-1796. Tel: 602-279-9547 ; Email: pastor@sfxphx.org; Email: stfrancisxavier@sfxphx.org; Web: www.sfxphx.org.

Revs. George Wanser, S.J.; Anthony P. Sauer, S.J.; Deacon Thomas Klein.
School—St. Francis Xavier Roman Catholic Parish School, (Grades PreK-8).

10—ST. GREGORY ROMAN CATHOLIC PARISH (1947)
3424 N. 18th Ave., 85015. Tel: 602-264-4488; Fax: 602-266-5210; Email: parishoffice@stgphx.org. Rev. Andres Arango, Parochial Admin.; Deacon Jose Torres. In Res., Revs. Paul Sullivan; F. Nelson Libera, J.C.D.
School—St. Gregory Roman Catholic Parish School, (Grades PreK-8), 3440 N. 18th Ave., 85015. Tel: 602-266-9527; Fax: 602-266-4055; Web: www.stgphx.com. Ms. Tanya Bartlett, Prin. Lay Teachers 26; Students 426.
Catechesis Religious Program—Rev. Guadalupe Ornelas, D.R.E.

11—HOLY FAMILY ROMAN CATHOLIC PARISH (1968)
6802 S. 24th St., 85042. Teletype: 602-268-2632. Revs. Oscar Gutierrez, V.F.; Martin Munoz, M.D.M., Parochial Vicar.

12—IMMACULATE HEART OF MARY ROMAN CATHOLIC PARISH aka Parroquia Inmaculado Corazón de María (1924)
909 E. Washington St., 85034. Tel: 602-253-6129; Fax: 602-253-4210; Email: iheart@diocesephoenix.org; Web: ihmphx.org. Revs. Fabio Schilereff, I.V.E.; Alex Perez, I.V.E., Parochial Vicar; Rafael Umana, Parochial Vicar; Deacon Jesus Morales.

13—ST. JEROME ROMAN CATHOLIC PARISH (1962)
10815 N. 35th Ave., 85029. Tel: 602-942-5555; Email: dvalencia@saintjerome.org; Web: www.saintjerome.org. Rev. Gary R. Regula; Deacons Schubert Wenzel; Dick Rein.
School—St. Jerome Roman Catholic Parish School, (Grades PreSchool-8), Tel: 602-942-5644; Email: akolden@saintjerome.org.

14—ST. JOAN OF ARC ROMAN CATHOLIC PARISH (1979)
3801 E. Greenway Rd., 85032-4698. Tel: 602-867-9171; Fax: 602-482-7930; Email: office@stjoanofarc.com. Revs. Donald J. Kline; Daniel Cruz, Parochial Vicar; Deacons Mark Salvato; Peter Auriemma. In Res., Rev. John Parks, V.F.
School—Preschool.

15—ST. JOSEPH ROMAN CATHOLIC PARISH (1969)
11001 N. 40th St., 85028. Tel: 602-966-5120; Fax: 602-996-4011; Email: finance@stjoephx.org. Rev. Regidor Carreon.
Rectory—11050 N. 38th St., 85028.

16—ST. LUKE ROMAN CATHOLIC PARISH (1985)
19644 N. 7th Ave., 85027. Tel: 623-582-0561; Fax: 623-434-3182; Email: parishoffice@saintlukecatholic.org. Rev. Pawel Stawarczyk.

17—ST. MARK ROMAN CATHOLIC PARISH (1946)
400 N. 30th St., 85008. Tel: 602-267-0503; Fax: 602-275-7261; Email: st_mark@dphx.org. Revs. Charles G. Kieffer, V.F., Canonical Pastor; Fausto Penafiel, Parochial Administrator.

18—ST. MARTIN DE PORRES ROMAN CATHOLIC PARISH (1973)
c/o 6802 S. 24th St., 85042. Tel: 602-268-2632; Fax: 602-268-8909; Email: men_sa_jero82@hotmail.com. 3851 W. Wier Ave., 85041. Revs. Oscar Gutierrez, V.F.; Martin Munoz, M.D.M.

19—ST. MARY'S ROMAN CATHOLIC BASILICA (1881)
231 N. Third St., 85004. Tel: 602-354-2100; Email: FrontDesk@smbphx.org; Web: www.smbphx.org. Very Rev. Michael Weldon, O.F.M., Rector; Revs. Micah Muhlen, O.F.M., Parochial Vicar; Edward Sarrazin, O.F.M., Parochial Vicar. In Res., Rev. Luis Baldonado, O.F.M., (Retired).
Catechesis Religious Program—Students 63.

20—MATER MISERICORDIAE MISSION
1537 W. Monroe St., 85007. Tel: 602-253-6090; Web: www.phoenixlatinmass.org; Email: office@phoenixlatinmass.org. Revs. Michael Passo, F.S.S.P.; Michael Malain, Parochial Vicar.
Catechesis Religious Program—Students 25.

21—ST. MATTHEW ROMAN CATHOLIC PARISH (1939)
320 N. 20th Dr., 85009. Tel: 602-258-1789; Email: respericueta@stmatthewaz.org. Revs. Nelson Libera, J.C.D., Parochial Admin.; Manoj John, Sch.P., Parochial Vicar; Deacon Anthony Beltran.
School—St. Matthew Roman Catholic Parish School, (Grades K-8), 2038 W. Van Buren, 85009. Tel: 602-254-0611. Gena McGowan, Prin. Lay Teachers 14; Students 221.

22—MOST HOLY TRINITY ROMAN CATHOLIC PARISH (1951)
8620 N. Seventh St., 85020. Tel: 602-944-3375; Email: pgalaviz@mht.org; Web: www.mht.org. Revs. Dale Craig, S.O.L.T.; Alphonsus Zaldy Abainza, S.O.L.T., Parochial Vicar; Deacons John Raphael Dalisay, D.S.; Lowell O'Grady. In Res., Rev. Edwardo Montemayor, S.O.L.T.; Bro. Ryan Avery.
School—Most Holy Trinity Roman Catholic Parish School, (Grades PreK-8), 535 E. Alice Ave., 85020. Tel: 602-943-9058. Margaret MacCleary, Prin. & Dir. (Preschool). Lay Teachers 18; Sisters 1; Students 234.
Catechesis Religious Program—Nayeli Ramirez, D.R.E.
Convent—Sisters of the Society of Our Lady of the Most Holy Trinity, Tel: 602-568-0601. Sr. Mary Claire Strasser, S.O.L.T., Supr.

23—OUR LADY OF CZESTOCHOWA ROMAN CATHOLIC PARISH (2008)
2828 W. Country Gables Dr., 85053. Tel: 602-212-1172; Fax: 602-212-1173; Web: www.polskaparafiaphoenix.com. Rev. Jacek Wesolowski, S.Ch.
Convent—Missionary Sisters of Christ the King for Polonia, Tel: 602-680-7646. Sr. Bozena Blad, M.Ch.R., Supr.

24—OUR LADY OF FATIMA MISSION
1418 S. 17th Ave., 85007. Tel: 602-254-4944; Email: olfparishmissionphx@gmail.com. Rev. Michael Accinni Reinhardt, Parochial Admin.
Convent—Missionaries of Charity, Gift of Mary Convent, 1414 S. 17th Ave., 85007. Gift of Maria Shelter and Home for the Needy, est. by Mother Teresa.

25—OUR LADY OF THE VALLEY ROMAN CATHOLIC PARISH (1973)
3220 W. Greenway Rd., 85053. Tel: 602-993-1213; Email: olv@olvstr.net. Rev. Edward J. Kaminski, C.S.C., Admin.; Deacons William Vivio; Eduardo Mirasol; Robert Manthie; Robert Meidl.
Catechesis Religious Program—Amelia Sury, Dir. Faith Formation; Leah Johnson, D.R.E. Students 32.

26—ST. PAUL ROMAN CATHOLIC PARISH (1976)
330 W. Coral Gables Dr., 85023. Tel: 602-942-2608; Email: admin@stpaulsphoenix.org; Web: www.stpaulsphoenix.org. Revs. Dindo C. Cuario, D.S.; Victor Yakubu, (Nigeria) Parochial Vicar; Deacon Gary Chatel; Craig Cullity, Pastoral Assoc.
Catechesis Religious Program—Email: ccullity@stpaulsphoenix.org. Craig Cullity, Pastoral Assoc, D.R.E. Students 269.

27—ST. PHILIP THE DEACON MISSION, A QUASI-PARISH
615 N. 20th St., Maricopa Co. 85006. Tel: 602-253-1076; Email: st_philip_the_deacon@dphx.org. Rev. Fausto Penafiel, Parochial Admin.

28—SACRED HEART ROMAN CATHOLIC PARISH (1962)
1421 S. 12th St., 85034. Tel: 602-258-2089; Fax: 602-258-2089; Email: sacred_heart@dphx.org. Rev. Paul Sullivan; Deacon Matias Valle.

29—ST. THERESA ROMAN CATHOLIC PARISH (1955) [CEM]
5045 E. Thomas Rd., 85018. Tel: 602-840-0850; Email: info@stphx.org; Web: www.stphx.org. Revs. Charles G. Kieffer, V.F.; Joachim Adeyemi, (Nigeria) Parochial Vicar; J.C. Ortiz, Parochial Vicar; Deacons Colin Campbell; Mark Kriese; Ralph Ulibarri. St. Theresa Parish and School
School—St. Theresa Catholic School, (Grades PreK-8), 5001 E. Thomas Rd., 85018. Tel: 602-840-0010; Email: info@stcs.us; Web: stcs.us. Dr. Thomas D. Dertinger, Prin. Lay Teachers 30; Students 397.

30—ST. THOMAS THE APOSTLE ROMAN CATHOLIC PARISH (1950)
2312 E. Campbell Ave., 85016-5597. Tel: 602-954-9089; Email: smadrid@staphx.org; Web: staphx.org. Revs. Steven A. Kunkel; Musie Tesfayohannes, O. Cist., Parochial Vicar; Deacon William A. Chavira, M.D. In Res., Revs. Robert Bolding; Awte Weldu, O.Cist., J.C.L.
School—St. Thomas the Apostle Roman Catholic Parish School, (Grades K-8), 4510 N. 24th St., 85016. Tel: 602-954-9088. Mary Coffman, Prin.; Meg Bushard, Librarian. Lay Teachers 36; Sisters 3; Students 516.
Catechesis Religious Program—Eric J. Westby, Dir. Parish & School Catechesis; Tom Parks, D.R.E. (Jr. High & High School).
Convent—4550 N. 24th St., 85016. Tel: 602-368-5238. Sr. Martin Therese, O.P., Supr. Dominican Srs. of Mary, Mother of the Eucharist.

31—VIETNAMESE MARTYRS PARISH ROMAN CATHOLIC PARISH (2004)
2915 W. Northern Ave., 85051. Tel: 602-395-0421; Email: dmnguyenop@yahoo.com. Revs. Duc Minh Nguyen, O.P.; Dominic Nguyen, O.P.
Catechesis Religious Program—Students 163.

32—ST. VINCENT DE PAUL ROMAN CATHOLIC PARISH (1957)
3140 N. 51st Ave., 85031. Tel: 623-247-6871; Email: stvincent@svdpphx.org. Revs. Jesus Lopez; Guillermo Rodriguez, M.D.M., Parochial Vicar; Thomas Tomson, Parochial Vicar; Deacons Sergio Estupinan; Lorenzo Salazar, (Retired); Rev. Jilson Panakkal, In Res.
School—St. Vincent de Paul Roman Catholic Parish School, (Grades PreSchool-8), 3130 N. 51st Ave., 85031. Tel: 623-247-8595; Fax: 623-245-0132. Sr. Julie Kubasak, D.C., Prin. Lay Teachers 25; Sisters 3; Students 611.
Convent—Daughters of Charity, Sisters Julie Kubasak, D.C., Supr.; Cabrini Thomas, D.C., Dir.

OUTSIDE THE CITY OF PHOENIX

ANTHEM, MARICOPA CO., ST. ROSE PHILIPPINE DUCHESNE ROMAN CATHOLIC PARISH (2004)
2825 W. Rose Canyon Cir., Anthem, 85086. Tel: 623-465-9740; Fax: 623-742-7031. Revs. Francisco Colasito, (Philippines) Parochial Admin.; Noel Ancheta.

ASHFORK, YAVAPAI CO., ST. ANNE ROMAN CATHOLIC MISSION, A QUASI-PARISH (1905)
47047 7th St., Ashfork, 86320. Teletype: 928-635-0177. P.O. Box 525, Ash Fork, 86320. Rev. John D. Ehrich, S.T.L., Parochial Vicar.

AVONDALE, MARICOPA CO., ST. THOMAS AQUINAS ROMAN CATHOLIC PARISH
13720 W. Thomas Rd., Avondale, 85392. Tel: 623-935-2151; Email: stawebmaster@stacc.net; Web: www.stacc.net. Revs. John Muir; Anwar Zomaya, Parochial Vicar; Venantius Yikore; Deacons Jason Robinson; Edgar Carnecer; Kenneth Porter; Chuck Shaw.
School—St. Thomas Aquinas Roman Catholic Parish School, (Grades PreK-8).

BAGDAD, YAVAPAI CO., ST. FRANCIS OF ASSISI ROMAN CATHOLIC PARISH (1959)
Mailing Address: P.O. Box 768, Bagdad, 86321. Rev. Camilo De Villa, Parochial Admin.; Jennie Martinez, D.R.E.
Church & Rectory: 220 Cook St., Bagdad, 86321. Tel: 928-633-2389.

BAPCHULE, PINAL CO., ST. PETER (1950)
Mailing Address: 400 E. Monroe St., 85004. Tel: 520-560-3716. Rev. Antony Tinker, F.H.S., Pastoral Admin.; Deacon Peter Fejes.
Church: 1500 N. St. Peter Rd., Bapchule, 85151.
School—St. Peter School, (Grades K-8), Tel: 520-315-3835; Fax: 520-315-3645. Sr. Martha Mary Carpenter, O.S.F., Prin.; Rev. Msgr. Ed Meulemans, Chap. Lay Teachers 1; Sisters 7; Students 231.
Convent—Consolata Missionary Sisters, P.O. Box 10840, Bapchule, 85151.
Missions—Holy Family—Blackwater Rd., Blackwater, Pinal Co.. Tel: 520-354-2050.
Our Lady of Victory, Sacaton Flats, Pinal Co.. Tel: 520-562-3716.
St. Anne, Santan, Pinal Co.. Tel: 520-562-3716.
St. Anthony, S. Church St., P.O. Box 783, Sacaton, Pinal Co. 85147.
Field House at St. Anthony—
St. Francis of Assisi - AK Chin, 16657 N. Church St., Maricopa, Pinal Co. 85139. Tel: 520-610-2937.

BLACK CANYON CITY, YAVAPAI CO., ST. PHILIP BENIZI ROMAN CATHOLIC MISSION
34621 Black Canyon Hwy., P.O. Box 138, Black Canyon City, 85324. Tel: 623-374-5392; Fax: 623-374-9768; Email: lstokes20@cox.net. Rev. Francisco Colasito, (Philippines) Parochial Admin.; Deacon Leslie Stokes, Mission Mgr.
Legal Name: St. Philip Benizi Roman Catholic Mission, A Quasi-Parish
Catechesis Religious Program—Students 5.

BUCKEYE, MARICOPA CO., SAINT HENRY ROMAN CATHOLIC PARISH (1956)
24750 W. Lower Buckeye Rd., Buckeye, 85326. Tel: 623-386-0175; Email: st_henry@dphx.org. Rev. William "Billy" J. Kosco; Deacons Mark Gribowski; Victor Leon; Dominick Bonaiuto.
Catechesis Religious Program—

BULLHEAD CITY, MOHAVE CO., ST. MARGARET MARY ROMAN CATHOLIC PARISH (1947)
1691 N. Oatman Rd., Bullhead City, 86442. Tel: 928-758-7117; Fax: 928-758-2345; Email: st_margaret_mary@dphx.org; Web: www.stmargaretmarybhc.com. Revs. Keith Edwin Kenney, Parochial Admin.; Jose Luis Gonzalez Aguayo, Parochial Vicar; Deacons John Del Quadro; Anthony Picciano, (Retired).
Catechesis Religious Program—Henry Castaneda, D.R.E. Students 126.

CAMP VERDE, YAVAPAI CO., ST. FRANCES CABRINI ROMAN CATHOLIC PARISH (1962)
S. 781 Cliff Parkway, Camp Verde, 86322. Tel: 928-567-3543; Fax: 928-567-7058; Email: st_frances_cabrini@dphx.org. Revs. Alphonsus Bakyil, S.O.L.T.; Alvin Cayetano, S.O.L.T.

CAREFREE, MARICOPA CO., OUR LADY OF JOY ROMAN CATHOLIC PARISH (1972)
Mailing Address: P.O. Box 1359, Carefree, 85377. Revs. Jesus "Jess" G. Ty; Clement Attah, Parochial Vicar; Deacons James Sejba; James Gall; Dennis Fleming.
Church: 36811 N. Pima Rd., Carefree, 85377. Tel: 480-488-2229 (Church); Fax: 480-437-1093.
School—Our Lady of Joy Roman Catholic Parish School.
Catechesis Religious Program—Carlos Gonzales, D.R.E.

CASHION, MARICOPA CO., ST. WILLIAM ROMAN CATHOLIC PARISH (1973)
Mailing Address: P.O. Box 329, Cashion, 85329. Rev. Mario Garcia-Icedo, Parochial Admin.; Deacon James Cascio.

Church: 11003 W. Third St., Cashion, 85329.
Tel: 623-936-6115; Fax: 623-936-8308; Email: st_william@dphx.org.
Chapel—Our Lady of Guadalupe, Santa Maria.

CAVE CREEK, MARICOPA CO., ST. GABRIEL ROMAN CATHOLIC PARISH (2002)
32648 N. Cave Creek Rd., Cave Creek, 85331.
Tel: 480-595-0883; Fax: 480-595-0886; Email: receptionist@stgacc.org; Web: www.stgacc.org. Revs. John Slobig, V.F., Parochial Admin. Pro Tem, (Retired); David Kulandaisamy, Parochial Vicar; Deacon William Clower.
School—Annunciation Catholic School, (Grades K-8).
Catechesis Religious Program—Roxanne Clower, D.R.E. Students 250.

CHANDLER, MARICOPA CO.
1—ST. ANDREW THE APOSTLE ROMAN CATHOLIC PARISH (1985)
3450 W. Ray Rd., Chandler, 85226.
Tel: 480-899-1990; Email: church@standrewchandler.com. Revs. Robert Aliunzi, A.J., V.F.; Teilo Lawande, A,J., Parochial Vicar; Edward Urassa, Parochial Vicar; Deacons Ernest Garcia; Donald Crawford; Paul Hursh; Mark Lishko.
Catechesis Religious Program—Suzie Malloy, C.R.E. (Elementary).
2—ST. MARY ROMAN CATHOLIC PARISH CHANDLER (1937)
230 W. Galveston, Chandler, 85225.
Tel: 480-963-3207; Email: parish@stmarychandler.org; Web: www.stmarychandler.org. Revs. Daniel McBride, V.F.; Sheunesu Bowora, Parochial Vicar; Rev Edgardo Iriarte; Deacons Bruce Bennett, Ed.D.; Manuel Olivas; Douglas Davaz; Joseph Ryan; Oliver Babbits; Marvin Silva; Antonio Alvarez; Rev. John Taylor, M.H.M., In Res., (Retired).
Juan Diego Roman Catholic Church, 3200 S. Cooper Rd., Chandler, 85286. Tel: 480-734-2187.
School—St. Mary-Basha Catholic Elementary, (Grades PreK-8), 200 W. Galveston, Chandler, 85225. Tel: 480-963-4951; Fax: 480-963-8959; Email: tseybert@stmarybashacatholic.org; Web: www.stmarybashacatholic.org. Tiffany Seybert, Prin.; Lisa Ballesteros, Librarian. Religious Teachers 2; Lay Teachers 23; Students 418.
Catechesis Religious Program—Debbie Sheahan, D.R.E. Students 865.

CHINO VALLEY, YAVAPAI CO., ST. CATHERINE LABOURE ROMAN CATHOLIC PARISH (1980)
Mailing Address: P.O. Box 152, Chino Valley, 86323-0152. Tel: 928-636-4071; Fax: 928-636-1945; Email: stcathlab@cableone.net; Web: stcatherinecv.org. 2062 N. Hwy. 89, Chino Valley, 86323. Rev. H. Fred LeClaire, C.M.F.; Deacons Michael Holmes; Michael Johnsen.
Catechesis Religious Program—Students 47.

CONGRESS, YAVAPAI CO., GOOD SHEPHERD OF THE DESERT MISSION (1952) Quasi-Parish.
26750 S. Congress Way, P.O. Box 1134, Congress, Yavapai Co. 85332. Tel: 928-685-4712; Email: goodshepherdotd@gmail.com. Rev. Jose R. Lobaton, O.F.M.

COTTONWOOD, YAVAPAI CO., IMMACULATE CONCEPTION ROMAN CATHOLIC PARISH (1966)
700 N. Bill Gray Rd., Cottonwood, 86326.
Tel: 928-634-2933; Email: immaculate_conception@diocesephoenix.org; Web: ic-cc.org. Revs. David Kelash, V.F.; Jose D. Cornelia, D.S.; Deacons David Kaminsky; Onofre Duran, (Retired); James Brown, (Retired); Peter Murphy.
School—Immaculate Conception Catholic School, (Grades PreK-8), 750 N. Bill Gray Rd., Cottonwood, 86326. Tel: 928-649-0624; Fax: 928-649-1191; Email: info@iccs-k8.org. Mrs. Jacqueline Kirkham, Prin. Religious Teachers 1; Lay Teachers 11; Students 188.
Missions—St. Cecilia—Clarkdale, Yavapai Co.. Currently site for Tridentine Mass. Closed 2002, for sacramental records contact Immaculate Conception, Cottonwood.
Holy Family, (Closed 2004) Jerome, Yavapai Co.

DOLAN SPRINGS, MOHAVE CO., OUR LADY OF THE DESERT MISSION, A QUASI-PARISH
15385 N. Pierce Ferry Rd., Dolan Springs, 86441.
Tel: 928-767-3397; Fax: 928-855-7172; Email: ourladyofthedesert@yahoo.com. Rev. Barnabas T. Duniya, Parochial Vicar.
Catechesis Religious Program—Rosemarie Poskarbiewicz, D.R.E.

EL MIRAGE, MARICOPA CO., SANTA TERESITA ROMAN CATHOLIC PARISH (1968)
14016 N. Verbena St., El Mirage, 85335. Email: santa_teresita@dphx.org; Web: www.stcaz.com. Rev. Stephen Schack.

FLAGSTAFF, COCONINO CO.
1—HOLY TRINITY NEWMAN CENTER, A QUASI-PARISH 1966
520 W. Riordan Rd., Flagstaff, 86001.
Tel: 928-779-2903; Fax: 928-779-0698; Email: info@catholicjacks.org; Web: www.catholicjacks.org. Revs. Matthew Lowry, Dir. and Chap.; Dan Connealy, Assoc. Dir, Parochial Vicar.
2—SAN FRANCISCO DE ASIS ROMAN CATHOLIC PARISH (1997) [CEM]
Mailing Address: 1600 E. Route 66, Flagstaff, 86001.
Tel: 928-779-1341; Fax: 928-779-5124; Email: church@sfdaparish.org; Web: sfdaparish.org. Rev. William Schmid; Deacons James Bret; Ronald Johnson; Robert Olberding; Dennis Revering, (Retired); Douglas Rade, (Retired); Jeffrey Hartin; Mark Veazie; Jim Myers.
School—San Francisco de Asis, (Grades PreSchool-8), Tel: 928-779-1337; Fax: 928-774-1943; Email: school@sfdaparish.org; Web: sfdaparish.org. Bill Carroll, Prin. Lay Teachers 13; Students 179.
Chapels—Nativity of B.V.M.—16 W. Cherry Ave., Flagstaff, 86001.
Our Lady of Guadalupe, 224 S. Kendrick, Flagstaff, 86001.

FOUNTAIN HILLS, MARICOPA CO., ASCENSION ROMAN CATHOLIC PARISH (1976)
12615 Fountain Hills Blvd., Fountain Hills, 85268.
Tel: 480-837-1066; Fax: 480-837-9093; Email: ascension@dphx.org; Web: www.ascensionfh.org. Rev. John T. McDonough; Deacons Richard Smith; Phillip LoCascio.
Mission—St. Dominic, 25603 N. Danny Ln., Ste. 2, Rio Verde, Maricopa Co. 85263.

GILA BEND, MARICOPA CO., ST. MICHAEL ROMAN CATHOLIC PARISH (1963)
Mailing Address: P.O. Box F, Gila Bend, 85337. 314 Dobson St., Gila Bend, 85337. Tel: 928-683-9997; Email: stmichaelgb@gmail.com. Rev. Leonardo J. Vargas, D.S., Parochial Admin.

GILBERT, MARICOPA CO.
1—ST. ANNE ROMAN CATHOLIC PARISH (1943)
440 E. Elliot Rd., Gilbert, 85299-0228.
Tel: 480-507-4400; Fax: 480-507-4800; Email: admin@stanneaz.org; Web: stanneaz.org. Revs. Sergio Munoz Fita, Pastor; Joal Bernales, Parochial Vicar; Job Kundoni, Parochial Vicar; Deacons Joe Spadafino; Keith Boswell; Robert Carey; Richard Nevins; John Berger.
Catechesis Religious Program—Donna Kano, D.R.E. Students 952.
Convent—Carmelite Sisters, M.C.S.T.N.J., 206 E. Palo Verde St., Gilbert, 85296.
2—ST. MARY MAGDALENE ROMAN CATHOLIC PARISH (2002)
Mailing Address: 2654 E. Williams Field Rd., Gilbert, 85295. Tel: 480-279-6737; Email: pastor@smarymag.org. Revs. R. Christopher Axline, Parochial Admin.; Ishaya S. Samaila, Parochial Vicar; Deacons Craig Hintze; Gerald O'Toole; Kevin Knapp.

GLENDALE, MARICOPA CO.
1—ST. HELEN ROMAN CATHOLIC PARISH (1974)
5510 W. Cholla, Glendale, 85304-3322.
Tel: 623-979-4202; Email: bfavot@sthelenglendale.org. Revs. John R. Ssegawa, A.J., (Uganda); Mark Nyeko, A.J., (Sudan) Parochial Vicar; Deacons Joseph Shinske, (Retired); Robert Campas, Email: dcncampas@sthelenglendale.org; William Jenkins; John Mickel.
Catechesis Religious Program—Sharon Nevels, Admin.
2—ST. JAMES ROMAN CATHOLIC PARISH (1982)
19640 N. 35th Ave., Glendale, 85308.
Tel: 623-581-0707; Email: admin@stjames-greater.com; Web: www.stjames-greater.com/. Rev. Benedict Onegiu, A.J.; Deacons Frank Devine; Ronald TenBarge; Marvin Hernandez; Rev. Felix Kauta, A.J., Parochial Vicar. In Res., Rev. William Okot, A.J.
Res.: 3118 W. Rose Garden Ln., 85027.
Catechesis Religious Program—
3—ST. LOUIS THE KING ROMAN CATHOLIC PARISH (1962)
Mailing Address: 4331 W. Maryland Ave., Glendale, 85301. Tel: 623-930-1127; Fax: 623-930-1129; Email: Office@slkparish.com. Revs. Joseph Bui; Charles Goraieb; Deacons Joseph Stickney; Gustavo Arteaga.
School—St. Louis the King Roman Catholic Parish School, (Grades PreK-8).
Catechesis Religious Program—Sr. Mary Ann Mahoney, I.H.M., D.R.E.
4—OUR LADY OF PERPETUAL HELP ROMAN CATHOLIC PARISH (1947)
5614 W. Orangewood Ave., Glendale, 85301.
Tel: 623-939-9758; Fax: 623-934-8854; Email: olph_glendale@dphx.org. Revs. Michael Straley; Mario Cortes; Miguel Noyola, S.O.L.T.; Deacons Albert Gonzalez; Anthony (Tony) Lopez; Christopher Georges; Dennis Raczkowski; Martin Gallo; Lani Bogart, Dir. Marriage & Family Life.
School—Our Lady of Perpetual Help Roman Catholic Parish School, (Grades PreSchool-8), 7521 N. 57th Ave., Glendale, 85301. Tel: 623-931-7288. Mrs. Catherine Lucero, Prin.; Brenda Castro, Librarian. Lay Teachers 30; Sisters 2; Students 329.
Catechesis Religious Program—
Chapel—Our Lady of Guadalupe, 6733 N. 55th Ave., Glendale, 85301.
5—ST. RAPHAEL ROMAN CATHOLIC PARISH (1974)
5525 W. Acoma, Glendale, 85306.
Teletype: 602-938-4227; Email: straphael@olvstr.net. Rev. Edward J. Kaminski, C.S.C., Canonical Pastor; Deacons Robert Manthie; Eduardo Mirasol; Richard Meidl, (Retired).
Catechesis Religious Program—Amelia Sury, D.R.E. Students 100.
6—ST. THOMAS MORE ROMAN CATHOLIC PARISH (1997)
6180 W. Utopia Rd., Glendale, 85308-7111.
Tel: 623-566-8222; Fax: 623-825-1468; Email: st_thomas_more@stmglendale. Rev. James Turner; Deacons Richard Kijewski; Salvatore Lema.
Catechesis Religious Program—Maria Buhrman, D.R.E.

GOODYEAR, MARICOPA CO., SAINT JOHN VIANNEY ROMAN CATHOLIC PARISH (1956)
539 La Pasada Blvd., Goodyear, 85338.
Tel: 623-932-3313; Fax: 623-932-1896; Email: st_john_vianney_az@dphx.org; Web: www.sjvaz.net. Revs. Thomas Eckert, C.S.C.; Eric Schimmel, C.S.C., Parochial Vicar.
School—Saint John Vianney Roman Catholic Parish School, (Grades PreSchool-8).
Catechesis Religious Program—David Portugal, D.R.E.
Convent—15 W. Loma Linda Blvd., Avondale, 85323. Tel: 623-932-2652; Fax: 623-932-1243.

GRAND CANYON, COCONINO CO., EL CRISTO REY ROMAN CATHOLIC PARISH (1960)
Mailing Address: P.O. Box 505, Grand Canyon, 86023. Tel: 928-638-2390; Email: elcristorey@msn.com. Rev. Rafael Bercasio.
Church: 44 Albright Ave., Grand Canyon, 86023.

GUADALUPE, MARICOPA CO., OUR LADY OF GUADALUPE ROMAN CATHOLIC PARISH (1970)
5445 San Angelo St., Guadalupe, 85283.
Tel: 480-839-2860; Email: olo_guad_guad@dphx.org. Revs. Alberto Villafan, O.F.M., Parochial Admin.; Louis Khoury, O.F.M., Parochial Vicar; Deacon Santino Bernasconi.
Res.: 9004 Calle Maravilla, Guadalupe, 85283.
Tel: 480-839-2376.

KINGMAN, MOHAVE CO., ST. MARY ROMAN CATHOLIC PARISH (1906)
302 E. Spring St., Kingman, 86401.
Tel: 928-753-3359; Fax: 928-263-6837; Email: stmarychurch@yahoo.com. Rev. Matthew Krempel, Parochial Admin.
Catechesis Religious Program—

LAKE HAVASU CITY, MOHAVE CO., OUR LADY OF THE LAKE ROMAN CATHOLIC PARISH (1969)
1975 Daytona Dr., Lake Havasu City, 86403.
Tel: 928-855-2685; Email: ourlady@ourladylhc.org; Web: www.ourladyofthelakeromancatholic.org/. Revs. Chauncey Winkler; Julius Kundi; Deacons Jeffrey Arner; Gilbert Lopez; John Navaretta; Patrick Toilolo; Andrew Kresha; John Woiwode.
School—(Grades PreK-1), Tel: 928-855-0154; Email: fmu@ourladylhc.org.
Catechesis Religious Program—
Mission—Our Lady of the Desert, 15385 N. Pierce Ferry Rd., Dolan Springs, 86441. Tel: 928-767-3397; Email: barry_duniya@yahoo.com. P.O. Box 337, Dolan Springs, 86441.

LAVEEN, MARICOPA CO., ST. JOHN THE BAPTIST (1950)
Mailing Address: P.O. Box 693, Laveen, 85339.
Tel: 520-550-2034; Email: stjohns@gilanet.net. 5427 W. Pecos Rd., Laveen, 85339. Revs. Antony Tinker, F.H.S., Parochial Admin.; Benedict Mary Lieb, F.H.S., Parochial Vicar; Alcuin Hurl, F.H.S., Parochial Vicar; Deacons James Trant, Parish Life Coord.; Ron Poulin, Assoc. Parish Admin. In Res., Revs. Antony Tinker, F.H.S.; Benedict Mary Lieb, F.H.S.; Alcuin Hurl, F.H.S.; Ignatius Mazanowski, F.H.S.; Joseph Francis LePage, F.H.S.
Missions—St. Catherine—3986 S. Santa Cruz Rd., Laveen, 85339. Tel: 602-292-4466.
St. Francis of Assisi, Pima-Maricopa Indian Community, Salt River. 3090 N. Longmore, Scottsdale, 85256.
San Lucy, 1120C St., Gila Bend, Pinal Co. 85337. Tel: 602-354-2050.
Blessed Kateri Tekakwitha Spirituality Center/St. John's Convent—
Chapel—St. Paschal Baylon, 850 E. Oak, Mesa, 85203.

MAYER, YAVAPAI CO., ST. JOSEPH ROMAN CATHOLIC MISSION, A QUASI-PARISH
Mailing Address: P.O. Box 171, Mayer, 86333-0171.
Tel: 928-632-4018. 10901 S. Hwy. 69, Mayer, 86333. Revs. Alphonsus Bakyil, S.O.L.T.; Alvin Cayetano, S.O.L.T.

MESA, MARICOPA CO.
1—ALL SAINTS ROMAN CATHOLIC PARISH (1972)
1534 N. Recker Rd., Mesa, 85205. Tel: 480-985-7655; Email: pjohnson@asccm.org; Web: www.asccm.org. Revs. Robert J. Caruso; Joevensie Balang, Parochial

Vicar; Deacons Gordon Aird, (Retired); Bernard Filzen; Michael Carr; Robert Bonura; Ronald Wilson.

2—ST. BRIDGET ROMAN CATHOLIC PARISH (1985)
2850 E. Lockwood St., Mesa, 85213.
Tel: 480-924-9111; Fax: 480-924-5255; Email: admin@stbridget.org. Rev. W. Scott Brubaker.
Church: 2213 N. Lindsay Rd., Mesa, 85213.
Tel: 480-924-9111; Fax: 480-924-3103.

3—CHRIST THE KING ROMAN CATHOLIC PARISH (1959)
1551 E. Dana Ave., Mesa, 85204. Tel: 480-964-1719; Fax: 480-844-4498; Email: christ_the_king@ctk-catholic.org; Web: www.ctk-catholic.org. Revs. Rolyn B. Francisco, Parochial Admin.; Benjamin Rivera, Parochial Vicar; Deacons Ronald Ruiz; Tom Bishop; Neil Tift.
School—Christ the King Catholic School, (Grades PreK-8), Tel: 480-844-4480; Email: ctk@ctk-catholicschool.org; Web: www.ctk-catholicschool.org. Shelley Conner, Prin. Lay Teachers 16; Students 240.
Convent—School Sisters of Notre Dame, 1534 E. Dana Ave., Mesa, 85204. Sr. Patricia Gehling, S.S.N.D., Admin. Sisters 2.

4—ST. COLUMBA KIM ROMAN CATHOLIC MISSION
1375 N. McClintock Dr., Chandler, 85226.
Tel: 480-446-7121. Rev. Kang Young Lee
Legal Name: St. Columba Kim Roman Catholic Mission, A Quasi Parish.

5—HOLY CROSS ROMAN CATHOLIC PARISH (1978)
1244 S. Power Rd., Mesa, 85206. Tel: 480-981-2021; Fax: 480-981-6844; Email: kknapp@holycrossmesa.org. Revs. Lawrence Merta; Simon Osuchukwu, Parochial Vicar; Jaya Rao Maddu, M.C.L., Parochial Vicar; Deacons Thomas Ferreira; James Gersitz; Joe Scaccia, (Retired); William Finnegan; Richard Conn; Clarence Vetter; Narciso Macia; Ted Childs.
Catechesis Religious Program—Cynthia M. Benzing, C.R.E.

6—QUEEN OF PEACE ROMAN CATHOLIC PARISH (1934)
30 W. 1st St., Mesa, 85201. Tel: 480-969-9166; Email: vchavez@qop.org. Revs. Thomas Bennett, V.F.; Frankie Cicero, Parochial Vicar; Timothy Seavey, Parochial Vicar; Deacons Richard Areyzaga; Santiago Rodriguez, (Retired); Jamie Whitford; Thomas Phelan, (Retired); Gene Messer.
School—Queen of Peace Roman Catholic Parish School, (Grades PreK-8), 141 N. Macdonald St., Mesa, 85201. Tel: 480-969-0226; Email: rbaeza@qop.org. Mrs. Renee Baeza, Prin. Religious Teachers 2; Lay Teachers 15; Sisters 1; Students 250.

7—ST. TIMOTHY ROMAN CATHOLIC PARISH (1978)
1730 W. Guadalupe, Mesa, 85202. Tel: 480-775-5200; Email: dmesa@sttimothymesa.org. Revs. Dan Vanyo; John Greb, Parochial Vicar; Deacons Richard Petersen, (Retired); Kevin Bassett; Abram Calderon; James Beattie.
Schools—St. Timothy Preschool—
St. Timothy Catholic School, (Grades K-8), 2520 S. Alma School Rd., Mesa, 85210. Tel: 480-775-2650; Fax: 480-775-2651; Web: www.sttimothymesa.org/school. Maureen Vick, Prin. Lay Teachers 16; Students 194.
Catechesis Religious Program—Bridgate Barcelo, D.R.E. (K-5th Grade); Ms. Meagan Martinez, D.R.E. (6th-12th Grade); Joe Cady, Dir. Adult Formation. Students 420.

NEW RIVER, MANICOPA CO., GOOD SHEPHERD MISSION, A QUASI-PARISH (1993)
45033 N. 12th St., New River, 85087.
Tel: 623-465-9740; Fax: 623-742-7031; Email: st.rose@dphx.org. Rev. Francisco Colasito, (Philippines) Parochial Admin.; Deacon Robert Head.

PEORIA, MARICOPA CO., ST. CHARLES BORROMEO ROMAN CATHOLIC PARISH (1968)
8615 W. Peoria Ave., Peoria, 85345-0819.
Tel: 623-979-3418; Email: frontoffice@scbpeoria.org; Web: www.scbpeoria.org. Rev. Arthur Nave; Deacons Joseph Badame; Catarino Portillo.
Res.: 8617 W. Peoria Ave., Peoria, 85345.
Tel: 623-979-3418; Fax: 623-412-2397.

PRESCOTT, YAVAPAI CO., SACRED HEART ROMAN CATHOLIC PARISH (1877)
150 Fleury Ave., Prescott, 86301. Tel: 928-445-3141; Fax: 928-717-1074; Email: parish@sacredheartprescott.com; Web: www.sacredheartprescott.com. Revs. Irudayaraj John Britto, C.M.F.; Vincente Montiel Romero; Ralph Berg, C.M.F., Pastoral Assoc.; Deacons Thomas Kayser, (Retired); Charles Tony Humphrey, (Retired); Peter Balland; Thomas Gregory, (Retired); Joseph Bueti; Ernie Gonzales; Rev. Gerald Caffrey, C.M.F., In Res.
School—Sacred Heart Roman Catholic Parish School, (Grades PreK-8), 131 N. Summit Ave., Prescott, 86301. Tel: 928-445-2621; Fax: 928-445-0966; Web: www.sacredhearteducation.com. Pamela Dickerson, Prin. Religious Teachers 1; Lay Teachers 16; Sisters 1; Students 174.
Convent—Institute of the Blessed Virgin Mary, 229 N. Summit St., Prescott, 86301. Sisters 2.

PRESCOTT VALLEY, YAVAPAI CO., ST. GERMAINE ROMAN CATHOLIC PARISH (1984)
7997 E. Dana Dr., Prescott Valley, 86314.
Tel: 928-772-6350; Fax: 928-772-4413; Email: stg-admin@cableone.net; Web: stgermaineinpv.com. Rev. Daniel Vollmer; Deacons Wayland Moncrief; Dennis Egan, Baptism Training; Dale Avery; James Fogle.

QUEEN CREEK, MARICOPA CO., OUR LADY OF GUADALUPE ROMAN CATHOLIC PARISH
20615 E. Ocotillo Rd., Queen Creek, 85142-0856.
Tel: 480-987-0315; Fax: 480-888-1159; Email: johns@ologparish.org. Revs. Craig Friedley; Clement Gyil, Parochial Vicar; John Simon, Admin.; Deacons David Barraza; Narciso Macia.

SCENIC, MOHAVE CO., LA SANTISIMA TRINIDAD MISSION, A QUASI-PARISH (2004)
3735 Scenic Blvd., Scenic, Mohave Co. 86432.
Tel: 602-242-7191; Email: alfredovaldez10@yahoo.com. Mailing Address: P.O. Box 1236, Mesquite, NV 89024. Rev. Alfredo Valdez Molina.

SCOTTSDALE, MARICOPA CO.

1—ST. BERNADETTE ROMAN CATHOLIC PARISH (1995)
16245 N. 60th St., Scottsdale, 85254.
Tel: 480-905-0221; Email: stbenedict@stbenedict.org. Revs. Donald J. Kline, Parochial Admin. Pro Tem; Edward Gilbert; Deacons Alfred Homiski; Frank Nevarez; Robert Torrigan.
School—Saint John XXIII Catholic School Community, (Grades K-8), 16235 N. 60th St., Scottsdale, 85254. Tel: 480-905-0939; Fax: 480-905-0955; Email: popejohnXXIII@diocesephoenix.org. Preston Colao, Prin.; Susan Houck, Librarian. Lay Teachers 29; Students 600.

2—ST. BERNARD OF CLAIRVAUX ROMAN CATHOLIC PARISH (1994)
10755 N. 124th St., Scottsdale, 85259.
Tel: 480-661-9843; Fax: 480-614-8092; Email: church@stboc.org. Rev. Brian Bell; Deacon Alan Hungate.
Catechesis Religious Program—Kathie Stine, D.R.E.

3—BLESSED SACRAMENT ROMAN CATHOLIC PARISH (1974)
11300 N. 64th St., Scottsdale, 85254.
Tel: 480-948-8370; Email: parish@bscaz.org; Web: www.bscaz.org. Revs. Greg Menegay; Quyen Nguyen, C.M.F., Parochial Vicar; Deacons Robert Evans; James Nazzal; Jeffrey Strom. In Res., Rev. Msgr. George Schroeder.
School—Preschool, (Grades PreSchool-K).

4—ST. DANIEL THE PROPHET ROMAN CATHOLIC PARISH (1961)
1030 N. Hayden Rd., Scottsdale, 85257.
Tel: 480-945-8437; Email: email@sdtp.net; Web: www.sdtp.net. Revs. Thaddeus McGuire; Vinshon Nguyen; Deacon Martin Dippre, (Retired).
Catechesis Religious Program—Students 151.
Convent—Carmelite Missionaries of St. Therese of the Child Jesus.

5—ST. MARIA GORETTI ROMAN CATHOLIC PARISH (1967)
6261 N. Granite Reef Rd., Scottsdale, 85250.
Tel: 480-948-8380; Email: smgoretti@smgaz.org; Web: www.smgaz.org. Rev. Gregory P. Rice, M.H.M., Interim Parochial Admin.; Deacons Gary Scott; Carmene Carbone.
School—Preschool, (Grades PreSchool-K), Email: preschool@smgaz.org; Web: www.smgazpreschool.org. Lay Teachers 6; Students 65.

6—OUR LADY OF PERPETUAL HELP ROMAN CATHOLIC PARISH (1949)
7655 E. Main St., Scottsdale, 85251.
Tel: 480-947-4331; Fax: 480-874-3798; Email: parish@olphaz.org. Revs. Gregory J. Schlarb; Anthony O. Okolo, C.S.Sp., Parochial Vicar. In Res., Rev. Michael J. Boyle, C.M.
School—Our Lady of Perpetual Help Roman Catholic Parish School, (Grades K-8), 3801 N. Miller Rd., Scottsdale, 85251. Tel: 480-874-3720; Fax: 480-874-3767; Email: school@olphaz.org; Web: olphaz.org/school. Ms. Donna Lauro, Prin. Lay Teachers 24; Students 380.
Convent—Sisters of Charity, 7634 E. Second St., Scottsdale, 85251. Sisters 2.

7—OUR LADY OF THE ANGELS CONVENTUAL CHURCH (2006) at the Franciscan Renewal Center.
5802 E. Lincoln Dr., Scottsdale, 85253.
Tel: 480-948-7460; Fax: 480-948-2325; Email: casa@thecasa.org; Web: www.thecasa.org. Revs. Peter Kirwin, O.F.M., Rector; William K. Bried, O.F.M., Parochial Vicar; Bro. Vincent Nguyen, O.F.M.; Deacon Herve Lemire; Revs. Page Polk, In Res.; Joseph Schwab, O.F.M., In Res.
Catechesis Religious Program—Email: dcm@thecasa.org. Patty Tafolla, D.R.E. Students 193.

8—ST. PATRICK ROMAN CATHOLIC PARISH (1980)
10815 N. 84th St., Scottsdale, 85260.
Tel: 480-998-3843; Email: generalmail@stpatcc.org. Rev. Eric Tellez; Deacons Louis Cornille III; John Meyer; James Hostutler; Richard Fettig.

SEDONA, YAVAPAI CO.

1—CHAPEL OF THE HOLY CROSS (1955)
780 Chapel Rd., Sedona, 86336. Tel: 928-282-7545; Fax: 928-282-3701. Rev. Kieran Kleczewski, V.F.; Dr. Charles E. Reaume, Admin.

2—ST. JOHN VIANNEY ROMAN CATHOLIC PARISH (1965)
180 St. John Vianney Ln., Sedona, 86336.
Tel: 928-282-7545; Email: stjohnvianney@sjvsedona.org; Web: www.sjvsedona.org. Rev. Kieran Kleczewski, V.F.; Deacons Ronald Martinez; Donald Henkiel; Dennis Sullivan.

SELIGMAN, YAVAPAI CO., ST. FRANCIS ROMAN CATHOLIC PARISH (1940)
P.O. Box 309, Seligman, 86337. Tel: 928-422-3354; Fax: 928-635-0177; Email: frehrich@dphx.org. 22440 Schoeney, Seligman, 86337. Rev. John D. Ehrich, S.T.L., Admin.
Church: 104 Schoeny, Seligman, 86337.

SUN CITY WEST, MARICOPA CO., OUR LADY OF LOURDES ROMAN CATHOLIC PARISH (1979) Revs. David M. Ostler; Michael Ashibuogwu, Parochial Vicar; Augustine Ogumere, C.S.Sp., Parochial Vicar.
Church: 19002 N. 128th Ave., Sun City West, 85375.
Tel: 623-214-5180; Fax: 623-214-1246; Email: info@oll-pp.com; Web: www.oll-pp.com.
Church: Prince of Peace, 14818 W. Deer Valley Dr., Sun City West, 85375. Fax: 623-584-2073.

SUN CITY, MARICOPA CO.

1—ST. CLEMENT OF ROME ROMAN CATHOLIC PARISH (1970)
15800 Del Webb Blvd., Sun City, 85351.
Tel: 623-974-5867; Email: dpo@stclementaz.org. Revs. Emile C. "Bud" Pelletier Jr., V.F.; Julius Kayiwa; Shia Reh Marino; Deacons Lee Beatrice; Kenneth Wedge.

2—ST. ELIZABETH SETON ROMAN CATHOLIC PARISH (1976)
9728 W. Palmeras Dr., Sun City, 85373.
Tel: 623-972-2129; Fax: 623-974-0654; Email: office@sescc.org. Revs. Kilian McCaffrey; Sylvester Modebei, (Nigeria) Parochial Vicar; Deacons Paul Csuy, (Retired); Larry Grey; Mike Napolitano; George Koch; Martin Pogioli.
Catechesis Religious Program—Mary Fogelson, D.R.E.

3—ST. JOACHIM & ST. ANNE (1961)
Mailing Address: P.O. Box 748, Youngtown, 85363.
Tel: 623-972-1179; Email: admin@sjasuncity.org. 11625 N. 111th Ave., Sun City, 85351-3746. Revs. John Ebbesmier; Nicholas A. Floridi, Parochial Vicar; Deacons Stephen Weiss; Dennis Luft
Legal Name: Church of St. Joachim & St. Anne Roman Catholic Parish.

SUN LAKES, MARICOPA CO., ST. STEVEN ROMAN CATHOLIC PARISH (1988)
Mailing Address: 24827 S. Dobson Rd., Sun Lakes, 85248. Tel: 480-895-9266; Fax: 480-895-9304; Email: freric@ststevensaz.org; Web: www.saintstevensparish.org. Revs. Eric Houseknecht; Enoch Okpa, Parochial Vicar; Deacons Richard Corwin; David Runyan; John Benware.
Catechesis Religious Program—Yadi De La Torre, D.R.E.

SURPRISE, MARICOPA CO., ST. CLARE OF ASSISI ROMAN CATHOLIC PARISH (2000)
Mailing Address: 17111 W. Bell Rd., Surprise, 85374.
Tel: 623-546-3444; Fax: 623-975-5615; Email: church@stcpaz.org; Web: www.saintcofa.com/. Revs. Hans P. Ruygt; Nicholas Erias Koro, A.J., Parochial Vicar; Deacons Donnan Lukaszewski; Michael Pirylis; David Opsahl; Joseph Lukaszewski, Pastoral Min.; Bernadette Wagner, Music Min.
Catechesis Religious Program—Brian Guillot, D.R.E.; Christopher Platt, Youth Evangelization.

TEMPE, MARICOPA CO.

1—ALL SAINTS ROMAN CATHOLIC NEWMAN CENTER
230 E. University Dr., Tempe, 85281-3700.
Tel: 480-967-7823; Email: mkilker@asucatholic.org; Web: www.asucatholic.org. Revs. Robert Clements; Bruce Downs, Parochial Vicar.

2—CHURCH OF THE RESURRECTION ROMAN CATHOLIC PARISH (1970)
3201 S. Evergreen Rd., Tempe, 85282.
Tel: 480-838-0207; Email: parishinfo@resurrectionaz.org. Revs. Romeo Dionisio, Parochial Admin.; Thomas R. Kagumisa, Parochial Vicar; Deacons Sione Hola, Ministry of Care; William Malatin.
Catechesis Religious Program—Web: www.resurrectionaz.org. Dee Dee Tamminen, C.R.E.; Rob Kubasko, C.R.E. Sisters 1; Students 158; Lay Ministers 4.

3—HOLY SPIRIT ROMAN CATHOLIC PARISH (1973)
1800 E. Libra Dr., Tempe, 85283. Tel: 480-838-7474; Email: parish@holyspirit-tempe-az.org; Web: www.holyspirit-tempe-az.org. Rev. Msgr. Peter Dai Bui; Rev. Cletus Kulah, S.O.L.T.; Deacons Stephen Beard; Gary Johnson; James Danovich.
Rectory—1871 E. Libra Dr., Tempe, 85283.
Catechesis Religious Program—Yvette Mayer, C.R.E. (Elementary & Jr. High); Bill Price, C.R.E. (Sr. High). Students 157.

4—ST. MARGARET ROMAN CATHOLIC PARISH (1972)

2435 E. McArthur Dr., Tempe, 85281.
Tel: 480-967-0379; Email: stmargaretcatholic@gmail.com; Web: www.stmargarettempe.org. Rev. Jesus Alfredo Quezada, Parish Admin.; Deacon Joseph "Tom" Swisher.
Catechesis Religious Program—Students 167.

5—OUR LADY OF MT. CARMEL ROMAN CATHOLIC PARISH (1932)
2121 S. Rural Rd., Tempe, 85282. Tel: 480-967-8791; Email: parish@olmctempe.com; Email: frjohn@olmctempe.com; Web: www.olmctempe.com. Revs. John Bonavitacola, V.F.; Jerome Cayetano; Deacons James Carbajal; James Brett; Thomas Glenn.
Schools—Our Lady of Mt. Carmel Roman Catholic Parish School—(Grades K-8), 2117 S. Rural Rd., Tempe, 85282. Tel: 480-967-5567; Fax: 480-967-6030 ; Email: info@olmcschool.info; Web: www.olmcschool.info/. Kelly Shewbridge, Prin.
Little Lambs Preschool, 3-5yrs. Tel: 480-966-1753; Email: monica@olmctempe.com. Monica Ferrance, Dir.
Catechesis Religious Program—Email: spdmariacristina@olmctempe.com. Sr. Maria Cristina, S.P.D., D.R.E.

TOLLESON, MARICOPA CO., BLESSED SACRAMENT ROMAN CATHOLIC PARISH (1953)
312 N. 93rd Ave., Tolleson, 85353. Tel: 623-936-7107; Email: welcome@blessedaz.org. Revs. Pedro Velez Prensa, Parochial Vicar; Paul Passant; Deacon Jose Garza.
Catechesis Religious Program—

WICKENBURG, MARICOPA CO., ST. ANTHONY OF PADUA ROMAN CATHOLIC PARISH (1941)
232 N. Tegner St., Wickenburg, 85390.
Tel: 928-684-2096; Fax: 928-684-3539; Email: stanthony@qwestoffice.net; Web: mystanthonyofpadua.com. Rev. Jose R. Lobaton, O.F.M.
Catechesis Religious Program—Rosemary Peterson, D.R.E.
Mission—Our Lady of Guadalupe, 50627 Eagle Eye Rd., P.O. Box 96, Aguila, Maricopa Co. 85320.

WILLIAMS, COCONINO CO., ST. JOSEPH ROMAN CATHOLIC PARISH (1928)
900 W. Grant, Williams, 86046. Tel: 928-635-2430; Email: frehrich@diocesephoenix.org; Web: ssjaf.weconnect.com/. Rev. John D. Ehrich, S.T.L., Admin.

YARNELL, YAVAPAI CO., ST. MARY MEDIATRIX MISSION, A QUASI PARISH, Closed. Supressed. Sacramental records are housed at Good Shepherd Quasi Parish, Congress, AZ.

Chaplains of Public Institutions

PHOENIX. *Arizona State Hospital*, 2500 E. Van Buren St., 85008. Tel: 602-244-1331;
Tel: 602-222-6193 Direct Line. Deacon James Cascio, Chap., Tel: 602-399-0315.
Banner University Medical Center, 1111 E. McDowell Rd., 85006. Tel: 602-239-2000;
Tel: 602-839-2000. Rev. William Okot, A.J., Chap.
John C. Lincoln Hospital - N. Mountain. Responsibility of Most Holy Trinity Parish, Phoenix; 602-944-3375. 2500 E. Dunlap, 85020.
Tel: 602-943-2381.
St. Joseph's Hospital, P.O. Box 2071, 85001.
Tel: 602-406-3275. Bonnie McCulley, Dir.
St. Luke's Medical Center. Responsibility of St. Mark, Phoenix; 602-267-0503. 1800 E. Van Buren St., 85006. Tel: 602-251-8100.
Maricopa Medical Center, 2601 E. Roosevelt St., 85008. Tel: 602-344-5437 (Chap. Svcs.);
Tel: 602-344-5011 (Main Hospital). Rev. George Ettuparayal, Chap., Dr. Gail M. Torres, D.C.E., P.C.C., Chap. Mgr.
Phoenix Indian Medical Center, 4212 N. 16th St., 85016. Tel: 602-263-1576. Responsibility of St. Francis Xavier, Phoenix; 602-279-9547.
Sky Harbor Interfaith Chaplaincy, Sky Harbor International Airport, Terminal 4, Level 3.
Tel: 602-244-1346. Deacon John Barelli, Chap. (Near security checkpoint B - Int'l arrivals gate).
United States Veterans Affairs Carl T. Hayden VA Medical Center, 650 E. Indian School Rd., 85012.
Tel: 602-222-6422. Rev. John T. Hannigan Jr., Chap.

CHANDLER. *Chandler Regional Medical Center*, 1955 W. Frye Rd., Chandler, 85224.
Tel: 480-728-5663 (Chap. Tel.). Rev. Fidelis Igwenwanne, Chap.Responsibility of St. Mary Parish, 230 W. Galveston St., Chandler, AZ, 85225, Tel: 480-963-3207.

GILBERT. *Mercy Gilbert Medical Center*, 3555 S. Val Vista Dr., Gilbert, 85296. Tel: 480-728-8000. Rev. Fidelis Igwenwanne, Chap.Responsibility of St. Mary Magdalene, 2654 E. Williams Field Rd., Gilbert, AZ 85295, Tel: 480-279-6737.

FLAGSTAFF. *Flagstaff Medical Center*, 1200 N. Beaver St., Flagstaff, 86001. Tel: 928-779-3366. Rev. William Schmid, San Francisco de Asis Parish, 1600 E. Rte. 66, Flagstaff, 86001. Tel: 928-779-1341 (Responsibility of San Francisco de Asis Parish, Flagstaff).

LUKE AIR FORCE BASE. *Luke Catholic Community*, 58 FW/HC, 13968 W. Shooting Star St., Bldg. #799, Luke Air Force Base, 85309-1932.
Tel: 623-856-6211; Fax: 623-856-6968. Rev. Msgr. Ronald Metha, Chap.To request a record of Sacraments received in a Military Chapel please contact, The Archdiocese of Military Services, U.S.A., P.O. Box 4469, Washington, D.C., 20017, Tel: 202-719-3600, Fax: 202-269-9022.

MESA. *Banner Desert Medical Center*, 1400 S. Dobson Rd., Mesa, 85202. Tel: 480-412-3198. Responsibility of Resurrection Parish, 3201 S. Evergreen Rd., Tempe, AZ, 85282, Tel: 480-838-0207.

PRESCOTT. *United States Veterans Hospital (Prescott)*, 500 Hwy. 89 N., Bldg #152, Prescott, 86313.
Tel: 928-445-4860, Ext. 6478. Rev. Gerald Caffrey, C.M.F., Chap.

SCOTTSDALE. *Honor Health Scottsdale Osborn Medical Center*, 7400 E. Osborn Rd., Scottsdale, 85251.
Tel: 480-882-4000 (Main Hospital);
Tel: 480-882-4028 (Chap. Svcs.). Rev. Greg Menegay(Responsibility of Blessed Sacrament Parish, 11300 N. 64th St., Scottsdale, AZ 85254-5047. Tel: 480-948-8370).

SUN CITY. *Banner Boswell Medical Center*, 10401 W. Thunderbird Blvd., Sun City, 85351.
Tel: 623-832-4000;
Tel: 623-832-3203 Spiritual Care.

Special Assignment:
Rev. Msgr.—
Sotelo, Antonio, Prison Chap., (Retired), 1421 S. 12th St., #154, 85034-4602. Tel: 602-258-2089
Revs.—
Accinni-Reinhardt, Michael D., Canonical Pastor, Our Lady of Fatima Mission, A Quasi-Parish, 1418 S. 17th Ave., 85007. Tel: 602-252-1771. Chap., Americare Hospice & Palliative Care, 1212 N. Spencer #2, Mesa, 85203. Tel: 480-726-7773
Igwenwanne, Fidelis, Chap., Mercy Gilbert Medical Center, 3555 S. Val Vista Dr., Gilbert, 85297. Tel: 480-728-8377.

On Leave:
Revs.—
Henry, Matthew J.
Mowrer, Patrick, V.F.

Retired:
Rev. Msgrs.—
Hever, Thomas, (Retired), 7828 E. Highland Ave., Scottsdale, 85251
Highberger, George, 8615 W. Peoria Ave., Peoria, 85345
Malone, Alan, (Retired), Eyrecourt, Ballinasloe, Co. Galway Ireland
Moyer, Richard W., (Retired), 3302 N. 7th St., #133, 85014
O'Grady, Michael, (Retired), 6301 N. 34th Ln., 85017
Sotelo, Antonio, (Retired), 700 W. University Dr., #154, Tempe, 85281
Revs.—
Bartel, Franklin L., (Retired), 10351 W. Burnett Rd., Peoria, 85382
Baumann, Lawrence L., (Retired), 4040 E. Comanche Dr., Cottonwood, 86326
Bormann, Charles P., (Retired), 13825 N. Cave Creek Rd., 85022
Brogan, Leo, (Retired), 3990 Centre St., Unit 401, San Diego, CA 92103
Canez, Jorge, (Retired), 9329 W. Georgia Ave., Glendale, 85305
Coleman, John R., (Retired), 1100 N. 115th St., Apt. 177, Scottsdale, 85259
Cunningham, John F., (Retired), 16709 E. Frye Rd., Gilbert, 85297
Diskin, Michael L., 170 E. Coronado Rd. #65, 85004-4522
Dobrowski, Peter P., (Retired), 3274 Shonto Trail, Flagstaff, 86005
Feit, Matthias, (Retired), Mount Claret, 4633 N. 54th St., 85018
Felt, Richard R., V.F., (Retired), 520 W. Clarendon, Apt. B-1, 85013
Fernandez, Frank, (Retired), 4112 E. Paradise Dr., 85028
Gauthier, John C., (Retired), 8931 Ferry Rd., New Roads, LA 70760-2078
Harrington, Mark, 12222 N. Paradise Village Pkwy S. #104, 85032
Healy, William, (Retired), 10815 N. 84th St., Scottsdale, 85260
Hennessy, Joseph I., (Retired), 24418 S. Starcrest, Sun Lakes, 85248
Hissey, L. Pierre, 1913 E. Buena Vista Dr., Chandler, 85249
Hoorman, Albert F.H., (Retired), 9439 Calle Bella Vista, Guadalupe, 85283
Kotnis, Gregory M., (Retired), 15735 W. Arrowhead Dr., Surprise, 85374
Lorig, Douglas E., 1403 E. Los Arboles Dr., Tempe, 85284-2460
Parker, Charles, (Retired), 725 S. Power Rd., #105, Mesa, 85206
Plathottam, Mathew, (Retired), Vianney Home, Dwaraka, Nalloornadu, P.O. Mananthavady 670645, Kerala, India
Riccitelli, Dennis, (Retired), 7145 E. Juanita Ave., Mesa, 85208
Robinson, Patrick, 5450 E. Deer Valley Dr. #2199, 85054
Ryan, Richard, (Retired), 18615 N. 125th Ave., Sun City West, 85375
Skagen, Robert, (Retired), 3422 W. Del Monico Ln., 85051
Slobig, John, V.F., (Retired), 540 North May, Apt. 2106, Mesa, 85201
Smith, Patrick, (Retired), 2620 N. 68th St., Scottsdale, 85257
Voss, Robert J., (Retired), 10742 N. 140th Pl., Scottsdale, 85259
Wasielewski, Henry R., (Retired), P.O. Box 939, Tempe, 85280-0939. 19920 N. 23rd Ave., Apt 1075, 85027
Wiedner, Larry W., (Retired), 13013 N. 100th Ave., Sun City, 85351.

Permanent Deacons:
Aird, Gordon, (Retired), All Saints, Mesa
Alvarez, Antonio, St. Mary Parish, Chandler
Amantia, Philip, Corpus Christi Parish, Phoenix (Extern)
Areyzaga, Richard, (Retired), Queen of Peace, Mesa
Arner, Jeffrey, Our Lady of the Lake, Lake Havasu City
Arteaga, Gustavo, St. Louis the King, Glendale
Auriemma, Peter, St. Joan of Arc Parish, Phoenix
Avery, Dale, St. Germaine Parish, Prescott Valley (Extern)
Babbits, Oliver, (Retired), St. Mary Parish, Chandler (Inactive)
Badame, Joseph, St. Charles Borromeo, Peoria
Balland, Peter, Sacred Heart, Prescott
Barelli, John, St. Daniel the Prophet, Scottsdale
Barraza, David, Our Lady of Guadalupe, Queen Creek
Bassett, Kevin, St. Timothy, Mesa
Beard, Stephen, Holy Spirit, Tempe
Beatrice, Lee, (Retired), St. Clement of Rome, Sun City
Beattie, James, St. Timothy Parish, Mesa
Beltran, Anthony, (Retired), St. Matthew, Phoenix
Bennett, Bruce, Ed.D., St. Mary, Chandler
Benware, John, (Retired), St. Steven Parish, Sun Lakes
Berger, John, (Retired), St. Anne Parish, Gilbert (Inactive)
Bernasconi, Santino, Our Lady of Guadalupe, Guadalupe
Bishop, Thomas, Christ the King, Mesa
Bogart, Douglas, SS. Simon and Jude Cathedral, Phoenix
Bonaiuto, Dominick, St. Henry Parish, Buckeye (Extern)
Bonura, Robert, All Saints Parish, Mesa
Boswell, Keith, St. Anne, Gilbert
Bret, James, San Francisco de Asis, Flagstaff (Extern)
Brett, James, Our Lady of Mount Carmel, Tempe
Brown, James, (Retired), Immaculate Conception, Cottonwood
Bueti, Joseph, Sacred Heart, Prescott
Calderon, Abram, St. Timothy, Mesa
Campas, Robert (Rudy), St. Helen, Glendale
Campbell, Colin, St. Theresa Parish, Phoenix
Carabajal, James, Our Lady of Mount Carmel Parish, Tempe (Extern)
Carbone, Carmene, St. Maria Goretti, Scottsdale
Carey, Robert, (Retired), St. Anne Parish, Gilbert

Carnecer, Edgar, (Retired), St. Thomas Aquinas Parish, Avondale (Extern)
Carr, Michael, All Saints, Mesa
Cascio, James, St. William, Cashion
Chatel, Gary, St. Paul Parish, Phoenix
Chavira, William A., M.D., St. Thomas the Apostle Parish, Phoenix
Childs, Ted, Holy Cross, Mesa
Clower, William, St. Gabriel Parish, Cave Creek
Conn, Richard, (Retired), Holy Cross Parish, Mesa
Cornille, Louis III, (Retired), St. Patrick, Scottsdale
Corwin, Richard, (Retired), St. Steven, Sun Lakes
Crawford, Donald, St. Andrew the Apostle, Chandler
Csuy, Paul, (Retired), St. Elizabeth Seton, Sun City
Dalisay, John Raphael, D.S., Most Holy Trinity, Phoenix (Extern)
Davaz, Douglas, St. Mary, Chandler
Del Quadro, John, St. Margaret Mary, Bullhead City
DeMarco, William, St. Francis Mission/Ak-Chin, Phoenix
Dennis, Irving, (Retired), St. Clement of Rome, Sun City
Devine, Frank, St. James, Glendale
Dippre, Martin, (Retired), St. Daniel the Prophet, Scottsdale
Drapeau, Roy, SS Simon & Jude Cathedral, Phoenix
Duran, Onofre, (Retired), Immaculate Conception, Cottonwood (Inactive)
Eckert, Richard, (Retired), (Inactive)
Egan, Dennis, (Retired), St. Germaine Parish, Prescott Valley
Ehrlich, Jacob, (Retired), (Inactive)
Estupinan, Sergio, St. Vincent de Paul Parish, Phoenix
Evans, Robert, (Retired), Blessed Sacrament Parish, Scottsdale
Fejes, Peter, St. Peter, Sacaton
Ferreira, Thomas, (Retired), Holy Cross, Mesa
Fettig, Richard, (Retired), St. Patrick Parish, Scottsdale
Filzen, Bernard, (Retired), All Saints, Mesa
Finnegan, William, J.C.L., (Retired), Holy Cross, Mesa
Fleming, Dennis, Our Lady of Joy Parish, Carefree (Seasonal)
Fogle, James, (Retired), St. Germaine Parish, Prescott Valley
Galarza, Frank, (Retired), Christ the King Parish, Mesa
Gall, James, Our Lady of Joy, Carefree
Gallo, Martin, Our Lady of Perpetual Help, Glendale
Garcia, Ernest, St. Andrew the Apostle, Chandler
Garza, Jose, Blessed Sacrament, Tolleson
Gaudio, Alexander, (Retired), Corpus Christi, Phoenix
Georges, Christopher, Our Lady of Perpetual Help, Glendale
Gersitz, James, (Retired), Holy Cross, Mesa
Giannola, Christopher, St. Joseph Parish, Williams
Giesner, Fred, (Retired), Blessed Sacrament, Scottsdale
Gilliland, Andrew, St. Anne, Gilbert
Giza, Stanley, (Retired)
Glenn, Thomas, Our Lady of Mount Carmel, Tempe
Gonzales, Ernie, Sacred Heart Catholic Church, Prescott (Extern)
Gonzalez, Albert, (Retired), Our Lady of Perpetual Help, Glendale
Gonzalez, Ricardo, (Inactive)
Goubeaux, Guy, (Inactive)
Gregory, Thomas, (Retired), Sacred Heart, Prescott (Inactive)
Grey, Larry, (Retired), St. Elizabeth Seton, Sun City
Gribowski, Mark, St. Henry, Buckeye (Extern)
Guzman, Angel
Guzman, Juan, (Retired), SS. Simon & Jude, Phoenix
Hamilton, James, (Retired)
Hartin, Jeffrey, San Francisco de Asis, Flagstaff
Head, Robert, (Retired), Good Shepherd Mission, New River
Henkiel, Donald, (Retired), St. John Vianney Catholic, Sedona
Hernandez, Marvin, St. James, Glendale
Hintze, Craig, St. Mary Magdalene, Gilbert
Hola, Sione, Resurrection Parish, Tempe
Holmes, Michael, St. Catherine Laboure, Chino Valley
Homiski, Alfred, St. Bernadette, Scottsdale
Hostutler, James, St. Patrick, Scottsdale (Extern)
Humphrey, Charles Tony, (Retired), Sacred Heart, Prescott
Hungate, Alan, St. Bernard of Clairvaux, Scottsdale
Hursh, Paul, St. Andrew the Apostle Parish, Chandler
Jenkins, William, St. Helen Parish, Glendale
Johnsen, Michael, St. Catherine Laboure Parish, Chino Valley
Johnson, Gary, Holy Spirit, Tempe
Johnson, Ronald, San Francisco de Asis, Flagstaff
Jolliffe, Garry, (Retired), St. Mary Parish, Chandler (Inactive)
Kaminsky, David, Immaculate Conception, Cottonwood
Kayser, Thomas, (Retired), Sacred Heart, Prescott
Kellogg, Christopher, Corpus Christi Parish, Phoenix
Kijewski, Richard, St. Thomas More, Glendale
Klein, Thomas, St. Francis Xavier, Phoenix
Kloft, Lee, (Retired), St. Clement of Rome, Sun City
Knapp, Kevin, St. Mary Magdalene Parish, Gilbert
Koch, George, (Retired), St. Elizabeth Seton Parish, Sun City
Kresha, Andrew, Our Lady of the Lake Parish, Lake Havasu City
Kriese, Mark, St. Theresa Parish, Phoenix
Kulinowski, Kenneth, (Retired), St. Andrew the Apostle Parish, Chandler
Lambert, Dennis, Corpus Christi Parish, Phoenix
Lema, Salvatore, St. Thomas More Parish, Glendale (Extern)
Lemire, Herve, Our Lady of the Angels, Scottsdale
Leon, Victor, St. Henry, Buckeye (Extern)
Lessard, Joseph, (Retired), (Inactive)
Lishko, Mark, St. Andrew the Apostle Parish, Chandler
LoCascio, Phillip, Ascension Parish, Fountain Hills (Extern)
Lopez, Anthony (Tony), (Retired), Our Lady of Perpetual Help, Glendale
Lopez, Gilbert, (Retired), Our Lady of the Lake, Lake Havasu City
Luft, Dennis, St. Joachim & St. Anne, Sun City (Seasonal)
Lukaszewski, Donnan, (Retired), St. Clare of Assisi, Surprise
Macia, Narciso, Our Lady of Guadalupe, Queen Creek
Malatin, William, Resurrection, Tempe
Manthie, Robert, St. Raphael, Glendale
Martin, Sidney, St. Anthony Mission, Sacaton
Martinez, Ronald, St. John Vianney, Sedona
McKnight, Lorenzo, St. Pius X, Phoenix
Meidl, Richard, (Retired), St. Raphael, Glendale
Mesa, Pedro, (Retired), St. Margaret, Tempe (Inactive)
Messer, Gene, Queen of Peace Parish, Mesa
Meyer, John, (Retired), St. Patrick, Scottsdale
Micek, Theodore, (Retired), (Inactive)
Mickel, John, St. Helen Parish, Glendale
Mirasol, Eduardo, St. Raphael Parish, Glendale
Moncrief, Wayland, St. Germaine, Prescott Valley (Extern)
Morales, Jesus, Immaculate Heart of Mary, Phoenix
Morton, Dwight, (Retired), (Inactive)
Mullaney, Roger, (Retired), Blessed Sacrament Parish, Scottsdale
Murphy, Peter, (Retired), Immaculate Conception Parish, Cottonwood
Myers, Jim, San Francisco de Asis, Flagstaff
Napolitano, Michael, (Retired), St. Elizabeth Seton Parish, Sun City
Navaretta, John, Our Lady of the Lake, Lake Havasu City
Nazzal, James, (Retired), Blessed Sacrament, Scottsdale
Nevarez, Frank, St. Bernadette, Scottsdale
Nevins, Richard, St. Anne Parish, Gilbert
O'Grady, Lowell, Most Holy Trinity, Phoenix
O'Toole, Gerald, (Retired), St. Mary Magdalene, Gilbert
Olberding, Robert, San Francisco de Asis, Flagstaff
Olivas, Manuel, St. Mary, Chandler
Opsahl, David, St. Clare of Assisi, Surprise (Extern)
Orozco, Jose, (Inactive)
Petersen, Richard, (Retired), St. Timothy, Mesa
Phelan, Michael, (Retired), St. Clement of Rome, Sun City
Phelan, Thomas J. III, (Retired), Queen of Peace, Mesa
Picciano, Anthony, (Retired), St. Margaret Mary, Bullhead City
Pirylis, Michael, (Retired), St. Clare of Assisi, Surprise
Pogioli, Martin, St. Elizabeth Seton Parish, Sun City (Extern)
Porter, Kenneth, St. Thomas Aquinas Parish, Avondale
Portillo, Catarino, St. Charles Borromeo Parish, Peoria
Poulin, Ronald, St. John the Baptist, Laveen
Raczkowski, Dennis, Our Lady of Perpetual Help, Glendale
Rade, Douglas, (Retired), San Francisco de Asis, Flagstaff (Inactive)
Ramirez, Ernesto, St. Augustine Parish, Phoenix
Rein, Richard, (Retired), St. Jerome, Phoenix
Revering, Dennis, (Retired), San Francisco de Asis, Flagstaff
Robinson, Jason, St. Thomas Aquinas, Avondale
Rodriguez, Santiago, (Retired), Queen of Peace, Mesa
Ruiz, Ronald, Christ the King, Mesa
Runyan, David, St. Steven Parish, Sun Lakes
Ryan, Joseph, St. Mary Parish, Chandler
Salazar, Lorenzo, (Retired), St. Vincent de Paul, Phoenix (Inactive)
Salvato, Mark, St. Joan of Arc Parish, Phoenix (Seasonal)
Sanchez, Jesse, (Retired), St. Agnes, Phoenix
Scaccia, Joseph, (Retired), Holy Cross, Mesa
Schmidt, Stephen, Holy Spirit Parish, Tempe
Scott, Gary, St. Maria Goretti Parish, Scottsdale
Sejba, James, (Retired), Our Lady of Joy, Carefree
Shaw, Chuck, (Retired), St. Thomas Aquinas Parish, Avondale
Shinske, Joseph, (Retired), St. Helen, Glendale
Silva, Marvin, St. Mary Parish, Chandler
Simeone, Philip, (Retired), Corpus Christi, Phoenix
Smith, Anthony, S.S. Simon & Jude Cathedral, Phoenix
Smith, Barry, (Retired), (Inactive)
Smith, Richard, (Retired), Ascension, Fountain Hills
Spadafino, Joseph, St. Anne, Gilbert
St. Onge, Lawrence, (Retired), St. Mary Magdalene Parish, Gilbert
Stickney, Joseph, St. Louis the King, Glendale
Stokes, Leslie, St. Philip Benizi, Black Canyon City
Strom, Jeffrey, Blessed Sacrament Parish, Scottsdale
Sullivan, Dennis, St. John Vianney Catholic Church, Sedona (Extern)
Swisher, Joseph "Tom", (Retired), St. Margaret, Tempe
TenBarge, Ronald, (Retired), St. James Parish, Glendale
Terrazas, Carlos, St. Catherine of Siena, Phoenix
Tift, John, Christ the King Parish, Mesa (Extern)
Toilolo, Patrick, Our Lady of the Lake, Lake Havasu City
Torigian, Robert, St. Bernadette Parish, Scottsdale
Torres, Jose, St. Gregory Parish, Phoenix
Torres, Vincent, (Retired), St. Helen Parish, Glendale
Trant, James, Dir. Office of Diaconate, St. Francis of Assisi Mission, Scottsdale
Ulibarri, Ralph, St. Theresa, Phoenix (Extern)
Valle, Matias, Sacred Heart, Phoenix
Veazie, Mark, San Francisco de Asis, Flagstaff
Vetter, Clarence, Holy Cross Parish, Mesa (Seasonal)
Vivio, William, (Retired), Our Lady of the Valley, Phoenix
Wedge, Kenneth, St. Clement of Rome, Sun City (Extern)
Weiss, Stephen, St. Joachim & St. Anne, Sun City
Wenzel, Schubert, St. Jerome, Phoenix
Whitford, Jaime, Queen of Peace Parish, Mesa
Wilson, Ronald, All Saints, Mesa
Winkelbauer, Edwin, St. Benedict Parish, Phoenix
Woiwode, John, Our Lady of the Lake Parish, Lake Havasu City (Extern).

INSTITUTIONS LOCATED IN DIOCESE

[A] HIGH SCHOOLS, DIOCESAN

PHOENIX. *Bourgade Catholic High School*, 4602 N. 31st Ave., 85017. Tel: 602-973-4000; Fax: 602-973-5854; Email: jbravo@bourgadecatholic.org; Web: www.bourgadecatholic.org. Mr. Javier Bravo, Prin.; Mr. Ryan Watson, Admin., Email: rwatson@bourgade.org; Rev. David Loeffler, Chap.; Miara Cash, Campus Min. Lay Teachers 28; Priests 1; Students 363; Chaplains 1.

St. Mary's Roman Catholic High School, 2525 N. Third St., 85004. Tel: 602-251-2500; Fax: 602-251-2595; Email: kmuir@smknights.org; Email: curias@smknights.org; Web: www.smknights.org. Rev. Robert Bolding, Pres.; Kevin Muir, Prin. Religious Teachers 5; Lay Teachers 34; Priests 2; Sisters 3; Students 502.

Xavier College Preparatory Roman Catholic High School, 4710 N. 5th St., 85012. Tel: 602-277-3772; Fax: 602-279-1346; Email: jnu@xcp.org; Web: www.xcp.org. Sisters M. Joan Fitzgerald, B.V.M., Pres.; Joan Nuckols, B.V.M., Prin.; Lynn Winsor, B.V.M., Vice Prin.; Rev. Kevin C. Grimditch, Chap.; Remi Fitzgerald, Dir. Library Technology. Religious Teachers 6; Lay Teachers 82; Priests 1; Sisters 5; Students 1,150.

St. John Paul II High School, 3120 N. 137th Ave., Avondale, 85392. Tel: 623-233-2777; Email:

smjhoover@jp2catholic.org; Web: www.jp2catholic.org. Sr. Mary Jordan Hoover, O.P., Prin.; Mr. Arthur Walker, Dean; Rev. Fernando Camou, Chap.

CHANDLER. *Seton Catholic Preparatory High School*, 1150 N. Dobson Rd., Chandler, 85224. Tel: 480-963-1900; Fax: 480-963-1974; Email: vserna@setoncatholic.org; Web: www.setoncatholic.org. Victor Serna, Prin.; David Sorkin, Asst. Prin.; Julie Grindey, Dean of Students; Rev. Timothy Seavey, Chap. Religious Teachers 1; Lay Teachers 47; Students 599.

SCOTTSDALE. *Notre Dame Preparatory Roman Catholic High School*, 9701 E. Bell Rd., Scottsdale, 85260. Tel: 480-634-8200; Fax: 480-634-8299; Email: info@ndpsaints.org. Jill Platt, Prin.; Rev. Kurt Perera, Chap. Religious Teachers 1; Deacons 1; Lay Teachers 81; Priests 2; Sisters 1; Students 886.

[B] HIGH SCHOOLS, PRIVATE

PHOENIX. *Brophy College Preparatory*, 4701 N. Central Ave., 85012. Tel: 602-264-5291; Fax: 602-234-1669; Email: awolf@brophyprep.org; Email: bryan@brophyprep.org; Web: www.brophyprep.org. Adria Renke, Pres.; Bob Ryan, Prin.; Patrick Higgins, Dean of Students; Kendra Krause, Admin.; Mica Mulloy, Admin.; Seamus Walsh, Admin.; Paul Fisko, Campus Min.; Tony Oldani, Dir. of Scheduling & Student Activities; Mike Ward, Dir., Admissions; Bill Woods, Athletic Dir.; Jonathan Londono, Advocacy & Outreach Coord. Jesuit Fathers.Boys Day School. Religious Teachers 2; Lay Teachers 98; Priests 1; Jesuit 1; Students 1,405.

[C] COLLEGES AND UNIVERSITIES

MESA. *Benedictine University* (Branch Campus at Mesa, AZ) Gillet Hall, 225 E. Main St., Mesa, 85201. Tel: 602-888-5500; Email: mesa@ben.edu; Web: www.ben.edu/mesa. Charles Gregory, CEO; Rev. James Aboyi, V.C., Chap.

[D] GENERAL HOSPITALS

GILBERT. *Mercy Gilbert Medical Center*, 3555 S. Val Vista Dr., Gilbert, 85297. Tel: 480-728-8000; Fax: 480-728-9640; Email: Robert.Sahagian@DignityHealth.org; Web: www.mercygilbert.org. Martin G. Breeden, Vice. Pres.; Rev. Fidelis Igwenwanne, Chap. Sponsored by Sisters of Mercy of the Americas-West Midwest Community. Bed Capacity 198; Tot Asst. Annually 105,782; Total Staff 1,348.

[E] HOMES FOR THE AGED & HANDICAPPED

PHOENIX. *Roeser Senior Village Apartments*, 1201 E. Thomas Rd., 85014. Tel: 602-268-5100; Fax: 602-268-5425; Email: Info@fsl.org. Units 80; Total Assisted 91.

Sweetwater Gardens Apartments (Handicapped) Tel: 602-867-4549; Fax: 602-867-4414; Email: Info@fsl.org. Units 24; Total Assisted 26.

AVONDALE. *Vianney Villas Apartments* (Retirement)-HUD Rent Subsidized 1201 E. Thomas Rd., 85014. Tel: 623-932-2036; Fax: 623-932-1134; Email: Info@fsl.org. Units 50; Total Assisted 57.

KINGMAN. *Amy Neal Retirement Center*, 1201 E. Thomas Rd., 85014. Tel: 928-757-7016; Fax: 928-757-2230; Email: Info@fsl.org. HUD rent subsidized. Units 24; Total Assisted 32.

Kingman Heights Apartments, 1201 E. Thomas Rd., 85014. Tel: 928-753-2425; Fax: 928-753-2590; Email: Info@fsl.org. (Retirement) - HUD rent subsidized. Units 33; Total Assisted 40.

LAKE HAVASU CITY. *Becket House Apartments* (Retirement) 1201 E. Thomas Rd., 85014. Tel: 928-855-7178; Fax: 928-855-1208; Email: Info@fsl.org. Units 50; Total Assisted 58.

Havasu Hills, Tel: 928-855-4743; Fax: 928-855-4760 . Total Staff 2; Units 50; Total Assisted 58.

PAYSON. *Pineview Manor Apartments*, 1201 E. Thomas Rd., 85014. Tel: 928-474-1317; Fax: 928-474-1321; Email: Info@fsl.org. Tot Asst. Annually 50; Total Staff 1; Units 49.

WICKENBURG. *Padua Hills Apartments* (Retirement)-HUD Rent Subsidized 460 S. West Rd., Wickenburg, 85390. Tel: 928-684-7034; Fax: 928-684-7253; Email: ainiguez@fsl.org; Web: www.fsl.org. Mr. Steve Hastings, Dir. Tot Asst. Annually 30; Total Staff 2; Units 25.

WILLIAMS. *St. Agnes Apartments* (Retirement) 1201 E. Thomas Rd., 85014. Tel: 928-635-2913; Fax: 928-635-2913; Email: Info@fsl.org. Tot Asst. Annually 30; Units 25.

[F] CONVENTS AND RESIDENCES OF SISTERS

PHOENIX. *Institute of Blessed Virgin Mary (I.B.V.M.)* (Regional House) 2521 W. Maryland Ave., 85017. Tel: 602-433-0658; Email: maryward@q.com; Web: ibvm.org. Sisters Kay Foley, I.B.V.M., Provincial; Dympna Doran, I.B.V.M., Supr. Sisters 2.

Institute of the Blessed Virgin Mary - Loreto, 7887 N. 16th St., #101, 85020. Tel: 602-331-9135. Sisters 3.

Missionaries of Charity, 1414 S. 17th Ave., 85007. Tel: 602-258-5504. Sr. Danette, M.C., Local Supr. Sisters 4.

Our Lady of Guadalupe Monastery Sisters of St. Benedict 8502 W. Pinchot Ave., 85037. Tel: 623-848-9608; Email: sisterlinda@olgmonastery.com; Web: www.olgmonastery.com. Sr. Linda Campbell, O.S.B., Prioress. Sisters 2; Oblates 95.

Sisters of Charity of the Blessed Virgin Mary (Xavier Convent) 311 E. Highland Ave., 85012. Tel: 602-264-0445; Email: jnu@xcp.org. Sr. Joan Nuckols, B.V.M., Community Representative. Sisters 7.

Sisters of Divine Savior, 323 E. Elm St., 85012-1703. Tel: 602-274-0228; Email: srgeorgene@yahoo.com; Web: www.sistersofthedivinesavior.org. Sr. Georgene Faust, S.D.S., Cluster Coord. for Region. Sisters 2.

Sisters of Notre Dame de Namur, 6635 S. 14th Way, 85042-4459. Tel: 602-243-9929. Sisters 2.

MESA. *Sisters of Notre Dame de Namur*, 548 W. Third St., Sister Nancy Wellmeier, SNDdeN, Mesa, 85201. Tel: 480-964-3685; Email: wellmier@aol.com. Sisters 2.

SCOTTSDALE. *Carmelite Missionaries of St. Therese of the Child Jesus*, 1030 N. Hayden Rd., Scottsdale, 85257. Tel: 480-633-3729. Sisters 3.

TONOPAH. *The Poor Clares of Perpetual Adoration, Our Lady of Solitude Monastery*, P.O. Box 639, Tonopah, 85354. Tel: 480-245-9614; Email: desertnuns@msn.com. Sisters 5.

[G] MONASTERIES AND RESIDENCES OF PRIESTS AND BROTHERS

PHOENIX. *Carmelite Community*, 1717 W. Flower, 85015. Tel: 602-274-0442; Fax: 602-274-3189. Revs. Silvan Boyle, O.Carm., (Retired); Tiernan O'Callaghan, O.Carm., (Retired). Priests 2.

Conventual Priory of the Holy Cross (Canons Regular of the Order of the Holy Cross), 717 E. Southern Ave., 85040-3142. P.O. Box 90428, 85066-0428. Tel: 602-443-7100; Email: crosier@crosier.org; Web: www.crosier.org. Rev. Thomas A. Enneking, O.S.C., Prior Prov.

Crosier Fathers and Brothers Province, Inc. Priests 1; Total Staff 3. In Residence Revs. Michael Cotone, O.S.C.; James Hentges, O.S.C.; Philip Suehr, O.S.C., (Retired).

Crosier Community of Phoenix (Canons Regular of the Order of the Holy Cross) aka Conventual Priory of the Holy Cross, 717 E. Southern Ave., 85040-3142. P.O. Box 90428, 85066-0428. Tel: 602-224-0434; Email: phoenix@crosier.org; Web: www.crosier.org. Very Rev. Thomas A. Enneking, O.S.C., Prior; Revs. Jude Verley, O.S.C., Community Coord.; Alex Juguilon, O.S.C.; Stephan Bauer, O.S.C.; John Christ, O.S.C.; Robert J. Rossi, O.S.C.; Bros. James Lewandowski, O.S.C.; Gus Schloesser, O.S.C.; Gabriel Guerrero, O.S.C., (Retired), (Retired); Gregory Madigan, O.S.C., (Retired), (Retired); Revs. Hubert Kavusa, O.S.C.; Ferdy Susilo, O.S.C. Brothers 4; Priests 8.

Crosier Village of Phoenix, 717 E. Southern Ave., 85040-3142. Tel: 602-443-7100; Email: village@crosier.org. Priests 1.

Disciples of Hope, 9241 N. 36th Dr., 85051. Tel: 602-841-7824; Web: www.disciplesofhopeds.org. Rev. Romuald P. Zantua, D.S.; Deacon Agerico Dalisjay, D.S. Brothers 1; Priests 1.

Holy Cross Congregation/Casa Santa Cruz, 7126 N. Seventh Ave., 85021. Tel: 602-944-6000; Fax: 602-944-1221. Revs. Duane Balcerski, C.S.C., Asst. Supr./Steward; Gerardo R. Barmasse, C.S.C.; James R. Blantz, C.S.C.; William W. Faiella, C.S.C.; Joseph F. O'Donnell, C.S.C., (Retired); John H. Pearson, C.S.C.; Stephen J. Sedlock; James W. Thornton, C.S.C., (Retired). Priests 7.

Society of Jesus, 120 E. Mariposa St., 85012. Tel: 602-264-5291; Email: gvwanser@gmail.com. Revs. Kevin Dilworth, S.J., Chap., Creighton Univ. Medical School; Daniel J. Sullivan, S.J., St. Francis Xavier Parish; Anastacio S. Rivera, S.J., St. Francis Xavier Parish, Email: arivera@jesuits.org; Anthony P. Sauer, S.J., St. Francis Xavier Parish; Peter J. Togni, S.J., St. Francis Xavier Parish, Email: ptogni@jesuits.org; Juan Pablo Marrufo del Torro, S.J., Brophy Prep.; Philip S. Postell, S.J.

St. Therese Priory, 75 E. Mariposa St., Apt. 1, 85012-1631. Tel: 602-604-2365. Revs. Kevin Lafey, O.-Carm.; James Mueller, O.Carm.

[H] RETREAT HOUSES

PHOENIX. *Mount Claret Roman Catholic Retreat Center*, 4633 N. 54th St., 85018. Tel: 602-840-5066; Email: info@mtclaret.org. Thomas McGuire, Dir.; Rev. Msgr. Gilbert J. Rutz, (Retired); Rev. Matthias Feit, (Retired). Priests 3. In Res. Rev. Msgr. Gilbert J. Rutz, (Retired); Revs. Matthias Feit, (Retired); Emile C. "Bud" Pelletier Jr., V.F.

Our Lady of Guadalupe Retreat/Conference Center, 8502 W. Pinchot, 85037. Tel: 623-848-9608; Email: sisterlydia@olgmonastery.com; Web: olgmonastery.com. Sisters Linda Campbell, O.S.B.; Lydia Armenta, O.S.B. Sisters 2; Conference Center Overnight Capacity 27; Conference Center Daytime Capacity 70; Scholastica House Daytime Capacity 30; Scholastica House Overnight Capacity 2; Hildegard House Overnight Capacity 2.

BLACK CANYON CITY. *Merciful Heart Hermitage: A House of Prayer for Priests*, 19950 E. St. Joseph Rd., Black Canyon City, 85324. P.O. Box 159, Black Canyon City, 85324. Tel: 623-374-9204; Email: mercifulheart@dphx.org. Rev. Eugene Florea, Dir.

SCOTTSDALE. *Franciscan Renewal Center, Inc. (Casa de Paz Y Bien)*, 5802 E. Lincoln Dr., Scottsdale, 85253. Tel: 480-948-7460; Fax: 480-948-2325; Email: casa@thecasa.org; Web: www.thecasa.org. Revs. Joseph Schwab, O.F.M., Exec. Dir.; Peter Kirwin, O.F.M., Rector. In Res. Rev. William K. Bried, O.F.M.

[I] NEWMAN CENTERS

PHOENIX. *Arizona State University*, All Saints Catholic Newman Center, 230 E. University Dr., Tempe, 85281. Tel: 480-967-7823; Email: mkilker@asucatholic.org; Web: www.asucatholic.org. Revs. Robert Clements, Dir.; Bruce Downs. (Tempe).

FLAGSTAFF. *Holy Trinity Newman Center, A Quasi-Parish*, 520 W. Riordan Rd., Flagstaff, 86001. Tel: 928-779-2903; Fax: 928-779-0698; Email: info@catholicjacks.org; Web: www.catholicjacks.org. Rev. Matthew Lowry, Chap. & Assoc. Vocations Dir.

[J] ACADEMIES OF RELIGIOUS TEACHING

PHOENIX. *Kino Catechetical Institute*, 400 E. Monroe, 85004. Tel: 602-354-2300; Fax: 602-354-2251; Web: www.kinoinstitute.org. Steve Greene, Dir. Kino Catechetical Institute; Luz Lobato, Registrar & Office Coord.; Sr. Darcy Peletich, O.S.F., M.A., M.L.S., Librarian. Program for Catechetical Studies & Adult Leadership Formation.

[K] MISCELLANEOUS LISTINGS

PHOENIX. *Andre House of Arizona*, 213 S. 11th Ave., 85007-3132. Tel: 602-255-0580; Fax: 602-257-4415; Email: director@andrehouse.org; Web: www.andrehouse.org. Rev. Tom Doyle, C.S.C., Dir. Hospitality House, U.S. Province of the Congregation of Holy Cross.

Caritas In Veritate International - USA, 3443 N. Central Ave., Ste. 1002, 85012. Tel: 602-795-9810; Email: henry@caritasinveritate.com. Henry Capello, Pres. & CEO.

**Catholic Charities Community Services*, 4747 N. 7th Ave., 85013. Tel: 602-285-1999; Fax: 602-285-0311; Email: info@cc-az.org; Web: www.catholiccharitiesaz.org. Paul S. Mulligan, M.T.S., Pres. & CEO; Jim LaBrie, Chm.

Catholic Charities Regional Service Centers:.

Catholic Charities Community Services, Phoenix, 1825 W. Northern Ave., 85021. Tel: 602-997-6105; Fax: 602-943-0377. Carrie Mascaro, Site Dir.

Catholic Charities Community Services, Flagstaff, 460 N. Switzer Canyon Dr., Ste. 400, Flagstaff, 86001. Tel: 928-774-9125; Fax: 928-774-0697. Brigid Wagner, Programs Dir.; Jean Littlehale, Sr. Program Dir.

Catholic Charities Community Services, Yavapai, 434 W. Gurley St., Prescott, 86301. Tel: 928-778-2531; Fax: 928-771-9531.

Catholic Charities Community Services, West Valley, 7400 W. Olive Ave., Ste. 10, Peoria, 85345. Tel: 623-486-9868; Fax: 623-486-9988. Larry Campbell, Dir., Head Start. 51 Head Start Classrooms.

Catholic Charities Parish & Community Engagement, 4747 N. 7th Ave., 85013. Tel: 602-285-1999; Fax: 602-285-0311. Tamara Bohannan.

Catholic Charities Residential Facilities:.

Dignity House, Tel: 602-361-0578. Group living for homeless women leaving prostitution.

Catholic Community Foundation for the Diocese of Phoenix, 400 E. Monroe St., 85004-2336. Tel: 602-354-2400; Fax: 602-354-2423; Email: info@ccfphx.org. Deacon James Carabajal, CEO.

Catholic Education Arizona, 2025 N. Third St., #165, 85004-1425. Tel: 602-218-6542; Fax: 602-218-6623; Web: www.catholiceducationarizona.org. Lewis Fellin, CFO; Deb Preach, Dir. Advancement & Donor Relations/Catholic Schools.

The Catholic Retreat for Young Singles, Inc., P.O. Box 16064, 85011. Tel: 480-540-4760; Email: atheis@gmail.com; Email: csc@cscarizona.org;

Email: jazzeline.perez@gmail.com; Web: www.cscarizona.org. 633 N. 54th St., 85018. Ms. Jazzeline Perez, Pres.; Andrew Theis.

Christ Child Society, 4633 N. 54th St., 85018-1904. Tel: 602-840-5066. Johanna Warner, Pres.; Sharon Casey, Treas.

Cursillo Movement, 4633 N. 54th St., 85018. Tel: 602-840-5066, Ext. 42; Email: info@phoenixcursillo.com; Web: www.phoenixcursillo.com. Dr. Dave Zeman, Dir.; Rev. Msgr. Michael O'Grady, Spiritual Dir., (Retired); Deacons Bob Carey, Assoc. Spiritual Dir.; Marvin Hernandez, Assoc. Spiritual Dir.

**Diocesan Council for the Society of St. Vincent De Paul*, P.O. Box 13600, 85002. Tel: 602-254-3338; Tel: 602-266-4673; Fax: 602-261-6829; Web: www.stvincentdepaul.net. Stephen J. Zabilski, Exec. Dir.

Foundation for Senior Living aka FSL, 1201 E. Thomas Rd., 85014. Tel: 602-285-1800; Email: info@fsl.org. Tom Egan, Pres.

Affordable Services for Seniors, Inc., 1201 E. Thomas Rd., 85014. Tel: 602-285-1800; Email: shastings@fsl.org. Tom Egan, Pres.

Foundation for Senior Adult Living, Inc., Tel: 602-285-1800; Fax: 602-285-1838; Email: info@fsl.org. Sweetwater Gardens (Apartments for the Handicapped), Phoenix; Kingman Heights Apartments, Kingman.

FSL Management, Tel: 602-285-1800; Fax: 602-285-1838; Email: info@fsl.org.

FSL Programs, Tel: 602-285-1800; Fax: 602-285-1838; Email: ainiguez@fsl.org; Email: info@fsl.org. Adult Day Health Care Centers; In-Home Care Services; Home Safety & Repair Program; Community Action Programs/ Senior Centers; Adult Foster Care; Oasis (Older Adult Service & Information System); Pathways Program (Resources and Referral-Care Management).

FSL Real Estate Services, Tel: 602-285-1800; Fax: 602-285-1838; Email: shastings@fsl.org. Mr. Steve Hastings.

FSL Rural Development, Tel: 602-285-1800; Fax: 602-285-1838; Email: jgreene@fsl.org. Becket House Apartments, Lake Havasu City; Vianney Villas Apartments, Avondale; Padua Hills Apartments, Wickenburg; St. Agnes Apartments, Williams, Amy Neal Retirement Center, Kingman.

FSL Home Improvements, 1201 E. Thomas Rd., 85014. Tel: 602-285-1800; Fax: 602-285-1838; Email: kmartin@fsl.org. Katie Martin, Dir.

FSL Pathways, 1201 E. Thomas Rd., 85014. Tel: 602-285-1800; Fax: 602-285-1838; Email: info@fsl.org. Carrie Smith, Contact Person. Assisted Group Living Program (11 Houses), Phoenix.

St. Clair Senior Living, 1201 E. Thomas Rd., 85014. Tel: 602-285-1800; Email: shastings@fsl.org.

FSL Christopher Properties, 1201 E. Thomas Rd., 85014. Tel: 602-285-0505, Ext. 181; Email: ainiguez@fsl.org. Mr. Steve Hastings, Dir.

St. Joseph the Worker (Job Service) 1125 W. Jackson St., 85007. Tel: 602-417-9854; Fax: 602-258-4940; Email: info@sjwjobs.org; Web: www.sjwjobs.org. P.O. Box 13503, 85002. Lieryn Jacobs, Board Chm.; Brent Downs, Exec. Dir.; Karl Johnson, Treas.; Joe McGovern, Brd. Sec. To assist homeless, low-income, and other disadvantaged individuals in their efforts to become self-sufficient through quality employment.

Saint Mary's Scholarship & Benefit Fund, 2525 N. Third St., 85004. Tel: 602-251-2506; Fax: 602-251-2595; Email: pmadigan@smknights.org; Web: www.smknights.org. Amy Lawrence, Dir. Development & Finance; Kevin Muir, Prin.

CHANDLER. *The Catholic Singles Ministry, Inc.*, 4589 W. Ivanhoe St., Chandler, 85226. Tel: 480-298-5158; Email: kmp.email@att.net; Web: www.catholicsinglesministry.org. Karina Penaranda, Contact Person.

GOODYEAR. *St. John Vianney School Development Fund*, 539 La Pasada Blvd., Goodyear, 85338. Tel: 623-932-3313; Fax: 623-932-1896; Email: eesquivel@sjvaz.net; Email: business@sjvaz.net; Web: www.sjvaz.net. Rev. Thomas J. Eckert, C.S.C., Pres.

MESA. **Life Teen, Inc.*, 2222 S. Dobson Rd., Ste. 601, Mesa, 85202. Tel: 480-820-7001; Fax: 480-820-8653; Email: jraus@lifeteen.com; Web: www.catholicyouthministry.com. Randy Raus, Pres. & CEO.

SCOTTSDALE. **Franciscan Friars of Arizona at the Franciscan Renewal Center*, 5802 E. Lincoln Dr., Scottsdale, 85253. Tel: 480-948-7460; Fax: 480-948-2325; Email: casa@thecasa.org. Charles Brown, Gen. Mgr.

SUN CITY. *Magnificat Phoenix Chapter*, 7203 W. Paradise Ln., Peoria, 85386. Tel: 623-979-9780; Email: aa-ok@cox.net; Email: azmtbriwal@gmail.com; Web: aa-ok0.wixsite.com/magnificat-arizona. 13611 N. 98th Ave. "G", Sun City, 85351. Laurie Walsh, Coord.; Mrs. Maureen Kight, Co-Coord.

TEMPE. **City of the Lord*, 711 W. University Dr., Tempe, 85281-3411. Tel: 480-968-5990; Fax: 480-921-9175; Email: phoenixbranch@cityofthelord.org; Web: www.cityofthelord.org. Peter Poppleton, Overall Coord.

**NPH USA*, 8925 E. Pima Center Pkwy., Ste. 145, Scottsdale, 85258-4407. Belinda Roda, Southwest Develop. Mgr. Total Staff 3; Total Assisted 3,471.

RELIGIOUS INSTITUTES OF MEN REPRESENTED IN THE DIOCESE

For further details refer to the corresponding bracketed number in the Religious Institutes of Men or Women section.

[]—*Apostles of Jesus* (Nairobi, Kenya, Africa)—A.J.
[0200]—*Benedictine Monks*—O.S.B.
[0600]—*Brothers of the Congregation of Holy Cross*—C.S.C.
[0400]—*Canons Regular of the Order of the Holy Cross*—O.S.C.
[0270]—*Carmelite Fathers and Brothers* (Prov. of Most Pure Heart of Mary)—O.Carm.
[0340]—*Cistercian Abbey*—O.Cist.
[0360]—*Claretian Missionaries*—C.M.F.
[0650]—*Congregation of the Holy Spirit*—C.S.Sp.
[1330]—*Congregation of the Mission Western Province*—C.M.
[]—*Disciples of Hope*—D.S.
[0520]—*Franciscan Friars* (Prov. of Santa Barbara; USA, Mexico, Venezuela)—O.F.M.
[]—*Franciscan Friars of the Holy Spirit.*
[0685]—*Institute of the Incarnate Word*—I.V.E.
[0690]—*Jesuit Fathers and Brothers* (California Prov.)—S.J.
[0800]—*Mary Knoll Missionaries*—M.M.
[]—*Miles Jesu*—M.J.
[0830]—*Mill Hill Missionaries*—M.H.M.
[0910]—*Oblates of Mary Immaculate*—O.M.I.
[0430]—*Order of Preachers (Dominicans)* (Canada)—O.P.
[1040]—*Piarist Fathers*—Sch.P.
[1065]—*Priestly Fraternity of St. Peter*—F.S.S.P.
[0610]—*Priests of the Congregation of Holy Cross*—C.S.C.
[1260]—*Society of Christ*—S.Ch.
[1200]—*Society of the Divine Savior* (North American Prov.)—S.D.S.
[0420]—*Society of the Divine Word*—S.V.D.
[0975]—*Society of Our Lady of the Most Holy Trinity*—S.O.L.T.
[1060]—*Society of the Precious Blood*—C.PP.S.
[]—*Via Christi* (Nigeria)—V.C.

RELIGIOUS INSTITUTES OF WOMEN REPRESENTED IN THE DIOCESE

[]—*Carmelite Sisters of St. Teresa*—C.S.S.T.
[2715]—*The Congregation of Missionary Sisters of Christ the King for Polish Immigrants* (Poznan, Poland; Chicago, IL)—M.Chr.
[3710]—*Congregation of the Sisters of St. Agnes* (Fond du Lac, WI)—C.S.A.
[1710]—*Congregation of the Third Order of St. Francis of Mary Immaculate* (Joliet, IL)—O.S.F.
[0720]—*Consolata Missionary Sisters* (Belmont, MI)—M.C.
[0760]—*Daughters of Charity* (Los Altos Hills, CA)—D.C.
[1070-13]—*Dominican Sisters* (Adrian, MI)—O.P.
[]—*Dominican Sisters of Mary Mother of the Eucharist* (Ann Arbor, MI)—O.P.
[1070-07]—*Dominican Sisters of St. Cecilia* (Nashville, TN)—O.P.
[1230]—*Franciscan Sisters of Christian Charity* (Manitowoc, WI)—O.S.F.
[2370]—*Institute of the Blessed Virgin Mary (Loretto Sisters)* (Prov. Wheaton, IL)—I.B.V.M.
[]—*La Siervas del Plan de Dios*—S.P.D.
[]—*Lovers of the Cross of Saigon*—L.H.C.
[2740]—*Maryknoll Sisters of St. Dominic* (Maryknoll, NY)—M.M.
[]—*Missionarias Carmelitas de Santa Teresa del Nino Jesus* (Puebla, Mexico)—M.C.S.T.N.J.
[2710]—*Missionaries of Charity* (Calcutta, India; Pacifica, CA)—M.C.
[3160]—*Parish Visitors of Mary Immaculate* (Monroe, NY)—P.V.M.I.
[3210]—*Poor Clares of Perpetual Adoration* (Tonopah, AZ)—P.C.P.A.
[]—*Sisters of the Sacred Heart*—S.H.S.
[2970]—*School Sisters of Notre Dame* (Central Pacific Province)—S.S.N.D.
[1680]—*School Sisters of St. Francis* (Milwaukee, WI)—S.S.S.F.
[3590]—*Servants of Mary Servite Sisters* (Lady Smith, WI)—O.S.M.
[]—*Servants of the Lord and the Virgin of Matura* (New York, NY)—S.S.V.M.
[0570]—*Sisters of Charity of Seton Hill* (Greensburg, PA)—S.C.
[0430]—*Sisters of Charity of the B.V.M.* (Dubuque, IA)—B.V.M.
[2519]—*Sisters of Mercy of Alma Michigan* (Alma, MI)—R.S.M.
[2575]—*Sisters of Mercy of the Americas* (Omaha, NE)—R.S.M.
[3000]—*Sisters of Notre Dame de Namur* (Cincinnati, OH)—S.N.D.deN.
[1540]—*Sisters of St. Francis* (Clinton, IA)—O.S.F.
[1570]—*Sisters of St. Francis of the Holy Family* (Dubuque, IA)—O.S.F.
[3830-15]—*Sisters of St. Joseph* (Concordia, KS)—C.S.J.
[1030]—*Sisters of the Divine Savior* (Milwaukee, WI)—S.D.S.
[]—*Sisters of the Sacred Heart* (Phoenix, AZ)—S.H.S.
[3105]—*Sisters of the Society of Our Lady of the Most Holy Trinity* (Bosque, NM)—S.O.L.T.

NECROLOGY

† O'Brien, Thomas J., Bishop Emeritus of Phoenix, Died Aug. 26, 2018
† Krynen, Joseph G., (Retired), Died Dec. 17, 2018
† O'Carroll, Eugene, (Retired), Died Sep. 1, 2018

An asterisk (*) denotes an organization that has established tax-exempt status directly with the IRS and is not covered by the USCCB Group Ruling.

Diocese of Pittsburgh

(Dioecesis Pittsburgensis)

Most Reverend

DAVID A. ZUBIK

Bishop of Pittsburgh; ordained May 3, 1975; appointed Auxiliary Bishop of Pittsburgh and Titular Bishop of Jamestown February 18, 1997; consecrated April 6, 1997; appointed Bishop of Green Bay October 10, 2003; installed December 12, 2003; appointed Bishop of Pittsburgh July 18, 2007; installed September 28, 2007. *Office: 111 Blvd. of the Allies, Pittsburgh, PA 15222-1618.*

Most Reverend

WILLIAM JOHN WALTERSHEID, V.G.

Auxiliary Bishop of Pittsburgh; ordained July 11, 1992; appointed Auxiliary Bishop of Pittsburgh and Titular Bishop of California February 25, 2011; consecrated April 25, 2011. *Office: 111 Blvd. of the Allies, Pittsburgh, PA 15222-1618.*

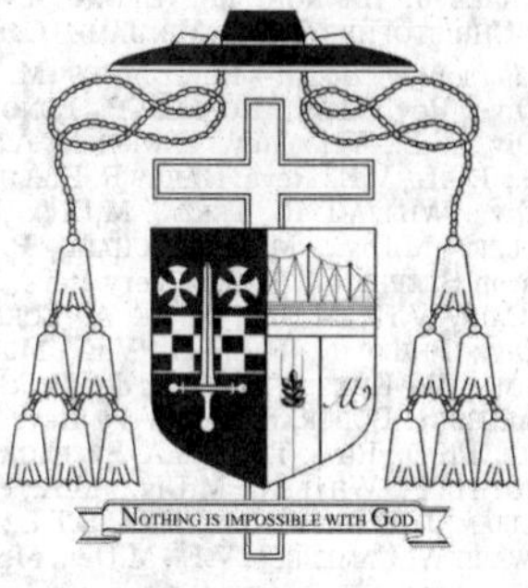

Pastoral Center: 111 Blvd. of the Allies, Pittsburgh, PA 15222-1618. Tel: 412-456-3000

Web: www.diopitt.org

Email: communications@diopitt.org

Most Reverend

WILLIAM J. WINTER, S.T.D.

Retired Auxiliary Bishop of Pittsburgh; ordained December 17, 1955; appointed Auxiliary Bishop of Pittsburgh and Titular Bishop of Uthina December 27, 1988; consecrated February 13, 1989; retired May 20, 2005. *Res.: St. John Vianney Manor, 2600 Morange Rd., Pittsburgh, PA 15205.*

ESTABLISHED AUGUST 11, 1843.

Square Miles 3,754.

Comprises the Counties of Allegheny, Beaver, Lawrence, Washington, Greene, and Butler in the State of Pennsylvania.

Legal Title: The Diocese of Pittsburgh and each parish in the diocese are organized as separate Pennsylvania Charitable Trusts.

STATISTICAL OVERVIEW

Personnel	
Bishop	1
Auxiliary Bishops	1
Retired Bishops	1
Priests: Diocesan Active in Diocese	201
Priests: Diocesan Active Outside Diocese	5
Priests: Retired, Sick or Absent	113
Number of Diocesan Priests	319
Religious Priests in Diocese	98
Total Priests in Diocese	417
Extern Priests in Diocese	23
Ordinations:	
Religious Priests	1
Transitional Deacons	4
Total Brothers	16
Total Sisters	746
Parishes	
Parishes	188
With Resident Pastor:	
Resident Diocesan Priests	177
Resident Religious Priests	11
Professional Ministry Personnel:	
Brothers	2
Sisters	60
Lay Ministers	410
Welfare	
Catholic Hospitals	1
Health Care Centers	1
Homes for the Aged	8
Specialized Homes	8
Special Centers for Social Services	29
Residential Care of Disabled	1
Educational	
Seminaries, Diocesan	1
Students from This Diocese	14
Diocesan Students in Other Seminaries	18
Total Seminarians	32
Colleges and Universities	3
Total Students	13,039
High Schools, Diocesan and Parish	8
Total Students	3,149
High Schools, Private	4
Total Students	783
Elementary Schools, Diocesan and Parish	64
Total Students	11,985
Elementary Schools, Private	3
Total Students	758
Non-residential Schools for the Disabled	2
Total Students	153
Catechesis/Religious Education:	
High School Students	3,932
Elementary Students	26,000
Total Students under Catholic Instruction	59,831
Teachers in the Diocese:	
Brothers	7
Sisters	17
Lay Teachers	1,397
Vital Statistics	
Receptions into the Church:	
Infant Baptism Totals	3,911
Minor Baptism Totals	223
Adult Baptism Totals	245
Received into Full Communion	320
First Communions	4,270
Confirmations	5,028
Marriages:	
Catholic	1,153
Interfaith	347
Total Marriages	1,500
Deaths	6,266
Total Catholic Population	630,033
Total Population	1,907,433

Former Bishops—Rt. Revs. MICHAEL J. O'CONNOR, S.J., D.D., ord. June 1, 1833; cons. Aug. 15, 1843; transferred to Erie and then to Pittsburgh Dec. 20, 1853; resigned May 23, 1860; entered the Society of Jesus Dec. 22, 1860; died at Woodstock College, MD, Oct. 18, 1872; MICHAEL DOMENEC, C.M., D.D., ord. June 30, 1839; cons. Dec. 9, 1860; transferred to Allegheny, Jan. 11, 1876; resigned July 29, 1877; died at Tarragona, Spain, Jan. 5, 1878; JOHN TUIGG, D.D., ord. May 14, 1850; cons. March 19, 1876; transferred to as Apostolic Administrator of Allegheny 1877; died at Altoona Dec. 7, 1889; RICHARD PHELAN, D.D., ord. May 4, 1854; cons. Aug. 2, 1885; Titular Bishop of Cibyra and Coadjutor to the Rt. Rev. John Tuigg; succeeded to Bishop Tuigg, Dec. 7, 1889; died at Idlewood Dec. 20, 1904; Most Revs. J. F. REGIS CANEVIN, D.D., ord. June 4, 1879; cons. Titular Bishop of Sabrata and Coadjutor, Feb. 24, 1903; succeeded to the See of Pittsburgh, Dec. 20, 1904; resigned Nov. 26, 1920; Titular Archbishop of Pelusium; appt. Jan. 9, 1921; died at Pittsburgh March 22, 1927; HUGH C. BOYLE, D.D., ord. July 2, 1898; succeeded to the See of Pittsburgh, June 16, 1921; cons. June 29, 1921; died at Pittsburgh Dec. 22, 1950; His Eminence JOHN CARDINAL DEARDEN, D.D., S.T.D., ord. Dec. 8, 1932; Titular Bishop of Sarepta and Coadjutor Bishop of Pittsburgh; appt. March 13, 1948; cons. May 18, 1948; succeeded to the See, Dec. 22, 1950; assistant at the Pontifical Throne, Oct. 15, 1957; installed at the Archdiocese of Detroit, Dec. 18, 1958; created Cardinal, April 28, 1969; died at Southfield, MI Aug. 1, 1988; JOHN CARDINAL WRIGHT, D.D., S.T.D., ord. Dec. 8, 1935; appt. May 10, 1947; cons. June 30, 1947; transferred to Bishop of Worcester, Jan. 28, 1950; transferred to Pittsburgh, Jan. 23, 1959; to the Roman Curia as Prefect of the Sacred Congregation for the Clergy; appt. April 23, 1969; created Cardinal, April 28, 1969; died at Cambridge, MA, Aug. 10, 1979; Most Rev. VINCENT M. LEONARD, D.D., ord. June 16, 1935; appt. Titular Bishop of Arsacal and Auxiliary, Feb. 28, 1964; cons. April 21, 1964; succeeded to the See, June 1, 1969; resigned June 30, 1983; died at Pittsburgh Aug. 28, 1994; His Eminence ANTHONY CARDINAL BEVILACQUA, D.D., J.C.D., J.D., ord. June 11, 1949; appt. Oct. 4, 1980; cons. Nov. 24, 1980; Bishop of Pittsburgh; appt. Oct. 10, 1983; installed Dec. 12, 1983; appt. Archbishop of Philadelphia, Feb. 11, 1988; created Cardinal, June 29, 1991; resigned Oct. 7, 2003; DONALD CARDINAL WUERL, ord. Dec. 17, 1966; appt. Titular Bishop of Rosemarkie and Auxiliary Bishop of Seattle Dec. 3, 1985; cons. Jan. 6, 1986; appt. and canonically installed Bishop of Pittsburgh Feb. 12, 1988; liturgically installed March 25, 1988; appt. Archbishop of Washington May 16, 2006; installed June 22, 2006; created Cardinal Nov. 20, 2010.

Pastoral Center—111 Blvd. of the Allies, Pittsburgh, 15222-1618. Tel: 412-456-3000. All official correspondence should be directed to this office. Prenuptial files and requests for marriage permissions should be sent to the Office for Matrimonial Concerns, 2900 Noblestown Rd., Pittsburgh, PA 15205.

Vicars General—Most Rev. WILLIAM J. WALTERSHEID, V.G., S.T.L.; Very Rev. LAWRENCE A. DINARDO, V.G., J.C.L., V.E.

Episcopal Vicars—Very Revs. FREDERICK L. CAIN, V.E., M.Div.; PHILIP N. FARRELL, V.E., M.A., M.Div.; HOWARD W. CAMPBELL, V.E., M.Div., M.A.; Most Rev. WILLIAM J. WALTERSHEID, V.G., S.T.L.

Vicar for Clergy Personnel—Very Rev. MARK A. ECKMAN, V.E., M.Div.

Vicar for Canonical Services—Very Rev. THOMAS W. KUNZ, V.E., V.J., J.C.D., S.T.L.

Vicar for Clergy & Consecrated Life—Very Rev. BRIAN J. WELDING, V.E., J.C.D., S.T.L.

Vicar for Leadership Development & Evangelization—Very Rev. JOSEPH M. MELE, Ph. D.

Vicar for Church Relations—Rev. Msgr. RONALD P. LENGWIN, V.G., M.Div., V.E.

Regional Vicars—

Vicariate 1—Most Rev. WILLIAM J. WALTERSHEID, V.G., S.T.L., Sisters of the Holy Spirit Motherhouse, 5246 Clarwin Ave., Pittsburgh, 15229. Tel: 412-456-5644.

Vicariate 2—Very Rev. FREDERICK L. CAIN, V.E., M.Div., Sisters of Saint Francis of the Providence of God, 1401 Hamilton Rd., Pittsburgh, 15234. Tel: 412-456-5645.

Vicariate 3—Very Rev. HOWARD W. CAMPBELL, V.E., M.Div., M.A., 373 Linmore Ave., Baden, 15005. Tel: 412-456-5648.

Vicariate 4—Very Rev. PHILIP N. FARRELL, V.E., M.A., M.Div., 125 Franklin St., Butler, 16001. Tel: 412-456-5649.

Chancellor—Tel: 412-456-3129. MRS. ELLEN M. MADY.

Vice Chancellor—Very Rev. THOMAS W. KUNZ, V.E., V.J., J.C.D., S.T.L.

Bishop's Office—Most Rev. DAVID A. ZUBIK, D.D.; MRS. JUDITH A. STYPERK, Exec. Asst.; Sr. MARIELLA BRADLEY, R.S.M., Administrative Asst.

General Secretary—Very Rev. LAWRENCE A. DINARDO, V.G., J.C.L., V.E., Tel: 412-456-3131; Fax: 412-456-3197.

Associate General Secretary—Very Rev. THOMAS W. KUNZ, V.E., V.J., J.C.D., S.T.L.

Vicar for Canonical Services—Very Rev. THOMAS W. KUNZ, V.E., V.J., J.C.D., S.T.L., Address all correspondence to: 111 Blvd. of the Allies, Pittsburgh, 15222-1698. Tel: 412-456-3135; Fax: 412-456-3183.

Matrimonial Concerns, Office for—Prenuptial files and requests for marriage permissions should be sent to the Office for Matrimonial Concerns, 2900 Noblestown Rd., Pittsburgh, PA 15205. Tel.: 412-456-3033.Canonical Consultants: Revs. LOUIS L. DENINNO, J.C.L., M.Div.; WILLIAM E. DORNER.

Tribunal Office—Address all correspondence to: 2900 Noblestown Rd., Pittsburgh, 15205-4227. Tel: 412-456-3033; Fax: 412-456-3118.

Judicial Vicar—Very Rev. BENEDETTO P. VAGHETTO, J.C.L.

Moderator of the Tribunal—MR. JAY CONZEMIUS, J.C.L.

Adjutant Judicial Vicar—VACANT.

Judges—Revs. ROBERT J. AHLIN, J.C.L.; LOUIS L. DENINNO, J.C.L., M.Div.; MR. JAY CONZEMIUS, J.C.L.; MRS. RITA F. JOYCE, J.D., J.C.L.; Rev. JAMES E. KUNKEL, S.T.M., (Retired); Most Rev. WILLIAM J. WINTER, V.G., S.T.D., (Retired); Revs. JAMES P. MCDONOUGH, S.T.L., J.C.L.; JOSEPH C. SCHEIB, J.C.L., M.Div., M.A.; Very Revs. BRIAN J. WELDING, V.E., J.C.D., S.T.L.; DENNIS P. YUROCHKO, J.C.L., S.T.L.

Promoter of Justice—Very Rev. LAWRENCE A. DINARDO, V.G., J.C.L., V.E.

Defender of the Bond—Rev. LOUIS L. DENINNO, J.C.L., M.Div.

Notaries—MS. MARTHA J. BRAUN; MS. SYLVIA VEHEC; MISS DIANE KASS.

Secretariat for Clergy and Consecrated Life—111 Blvd. of the Allies, Pittsburgh, 15222-1618. Tel: 412-456-3060; Fax: 412-456-3188; Tel: 888-808-1235 (Toll Free Victim's Assistance Hotline). Very Rev. BRIAN J. WELDING, V.E., J.C.D., S.T.L., Vicar for Clergy & Sec. Head; MRS. RITA E. FLAHERTY, M.S.W., Diocesan Assistance Coord.; Very Rev. MARK A. ECKMAN, V.E., M.Div., Vicar for Clergy Personnel.

Secretariat for External Affairs—111 Blvd. of the Allies, Pittsburgh, 15222-1618. Tel: 412-456-3166; Fax: 412-456-3183. MRS. ANNA TORRANCE, J.D., Sec. External Affairs.

Office of the Delegate for Consecrated Life—Sr. GERALDINE MARIE WODARCZYK, C.S.F.N., Delegate for Rel., 111 Blvd. of the Allies, Pittsburgh, 15222. Tel: 412-456-3067.

Priest Council—Most Rev. DAVID A. ZUBIK, D.D.; Very Revs. THOMAS W. KUNZ, V.E., V.J., J.C.D., S.T.L.; FREDERICK L. CAIN, V.E., M.Div.; Rev. JOSEPH V. KURUTZ, S.T.L., M.Ed., (Retired); Very Revs. LAWRENCE A. DINARDO, V.G., J.C.L., V.E.; MARK A. ECKMAN, V.E., M.Div.; PHILIP N. FARRELL, V.E., M.A., M.Div.; Revs. ALBERT J. SEMLER, (Retired); JOHN P. GALLAGHER, S.T.L.; JOHN P. SWEENEY, M.Div.; ALBIN C. MCGINNIS, V.F.; KENNETH W. MARLOVITS; ROBERT J. MILLER, M.Div., M.A.; Rev. Msgr. RONALD P. LENGWIN, V.G., M.Div., V.E.; Rev. MICHAEL A. CARIDI, S.T.L.; Very Rev. BRIAN J. WELDING, V.E., J.C.D., S.T.L.; Revs. KEVIN C. FAZIO; TERRENCE P. O'CONNOR, M.Div., J.D.; Most Rev. WILLIAM J. WALTERSHEID, V.G., S.T.L.; Rev. RICHARD J. ZELIK, O.F.M.Cap.; Very Rev. HOWARD W. CAMPBELL, V.E., M.Div., M.A.; Revs. PAUL J. ZYWAN, M.Div.; JOHN D. HARVEY, O.F.M.Cap.

College of Consultors—Most Rev. DAVID A. ZUBIK, D.D.; Very Revs. FREDERICK L. CAIN, V.E., M.Div.; PHILIP N. FARRELL, V.E., M.A., M.Div.; LAWRENCE A. DINARDO, V.G., J.C.L., V.E.; Revs. MICHAEL A. CARIDI, S.T.L.; JOHN P. GALLAGHER, S.T.L.; ALBIN C. MCGINNIS, V.F.; ROBERT J. MILLER, M.Div., M.A.; ALBERT J. SEMLER; JOHN P. SWEENEY, M.Div.; Most Rev. WILLIAM J. WALTERSHEID, V.G., S.T.L.; Very Rev. HOWARD W. CAMPBELL, V.E., M.Div., M.A.; Rev. KEVIN C. FAZIO.

Diocesan Development Board—PATRICK M. JOYCE, Ed. D., Chm.

Diocesan Finance Council—Most Rev. DAVID A. ZUBIK, D.D.; Very Rev. LAWRENCE A. DINARDO, V.G., J.C.L., V.E.; MRS. KATHLEEN W. BUECHEL; MS. KATHLEEN GEIS; MR. HOWARD HANNA III; MR. MICHAEL J. HANNON; MR. BRUNO A. BONACCHI; MR. CHRISTOPHER SOBEL; MR. JAMES C. STALDER.

Clergy Personnel Board—Rev. JAMES M. BACHNER, M.Div.; Rev. Msgr. RONALD P. LENGWIN, V.G., M.Div., V.E.; Very Rev. LAWRENCE A. DINARDO, V.G., J.C.L., V.E.; Revs. HARRY R. BIELEWICZ, V.E., M.Div.; WILLIAM R. TERZA, M.Div.; ROBERT J. MILLER, M.Div., M.A.; MICHAEL P. CONWAY; Deacon STEPHEN J. BYERS; Very Revs. FREDERICK L. CAIN, V.E., M.Div.; MARK A. ECKMAN, V.E., M.Div.; PHILIP N. FARRELL, V.E., M.A., M.Div.; THOMAS W. KUNZ, V.E., V.J., J.C.D., S.T.L.; Rev. CHARLES S. BOBER, S.T.D.; Very Rev. JOSEPH M. MELE, Ph.D.; Revs. THOMAS A. SPARACINO, M.Div.; TIMOTHY F. WHALEN, M.Div., M.A.; Most Rev. WILLIAM J. WALTERSHEID, V.G., S.T.L.; Very Rev. HOWARD W. CAMPBELL, V.E., M.Div., M.A.

Diocesan Administration

Administrative Procedures, Office for—Tel: 412-456-3126.

Archives and Record Center—MR. DENNIS WODZINSKI, Dir., 1050 Logue St., Pittsburgh, 15220. Tel: 412-456-3158.

Diocesan Assistance Coordinator—MRS. RITA E. FLAHERTY, M.S.W., Tel: 412-456-3060; Email: rflaherty@diopitt.org.

Auditors/Analysts, Office for the—MR. JAMES E. STIERHEIM, Supvr., Tel: 412-456-3029.

Catholic School Administrator - Finances—MR. ROY CARTIER, M.B.A., M.R.P., Dir. & Asst. Supt. Finance, Tel: 412-456-3108.

Building Commission—PAUL IURLANO, J.D.; MR. MICHAEL J. ARNOLD, Chm.; MR. JAMES J. ZIELINSKI, Exec. Sec., Tel: 412-456-3034.

Facilities Management & Maintenance, Dept. for—Tel: 412-456-3034; Fax: 412-456-3040. PAUL IURLANO, J.D., Chief Facilities Officer; MR. JAMES J. ZIELINSKI, Dir.; MR. JOSEPH KUBIAK, Plant Mgr.; DAVID J. SCHMIDT, Asbestos/Facilities Mgmt. Coord.; ANNETTE WRIGHT. Facilities Services Staff: MICHAEL DUNCAN; ANTHONY HARMS; JOHN HUDSON; MATT HUDSON; JONATHAN SCHMIDT; STEVE WALSH; WILLIAM WERME; THEODORE SZALLA JR.

Business Services, Dept. for—MR. BRUNO A. BONACCHI, CFO & Sec. Temporal Affairs, Tel: 412-456-3137.

Civil Law Services, Dept. for Secretariat for External Affairs—MR. CHRISTOPHER G. PONTICELLO, J.D., Gen. Counsel.

Canonical Services, Office for—Very Rev. THOMAS W. KUNZ, V.E., V.J., J.C.D., S.T.L.

Catechetical Ministries and Catechesis, Office for—Refer to Institute for Pastoral Leadership.

Catholic Charities—MS. SUSAN L. RAUSCHER, Exec. Dir., 212 9th St., Pittsburgh, 15222. Tel: 412-456-6999. Allegheny County, 212 9th St., Pittsburgh, 15222. Beaver County, 276 E. End Ave., Beaver, 15009. Tel: 724-775-0758. Butler County, 120 W. New Castle St., Butler, 16001. Tel: 724-287-4011. Greene County, 72 E. High St., Waynesburg, 15370. Tel: 724-627-6410. Lawrence County, 119 E. North St., New Castle, 16101. Tel: 724-658-5526. Washington County, 331 S. Main St., Washington, 15301. Tel: 724-228-7722. St. Joseph's House of Hospitality, 1635 Bedford Ave., Pittsburgh, 15219. Tel: 412-471-0666.

Catholic Charities Health Care Center, Inc.—212 Ninth St., Pittsburgh, 15222. Tel: 412-456-6911. AMY KIM, M.D.; AMY SUE LILLIE, Nurse Mgr.

Challenges: Options in Aging—Shenley Square, 2706 Mercer Rd., New Castle, 16105-1422. Tel: 724-658-3729.

Catholic Cemeteries Assoc., The—MR. MICHAEL SINNOTT, Exec. Dir., 718 Hazelwood Ave., Pittsburgh, 15217-2807. Tel: 412-521-9133.

Catholic Parish Cemeteries Assoc., The—100 Logue St., Pittsburgh, 15220. Tel: 412-680-0495. MS. MARIANNE LINN, Exec. Dir.

Catholic School Administration, Dept. for - Secretariat for External Affairs—MICHAEL A. LATUSEK, Ed.D., Supt. Catholic Schools; LILLIAN NACCARATI, Ed.D., Asst. Supt. Administration; Sr. PATRICIA LAFFEY, S.C., M.A., Asst. Supt. Curriculum Instruction & Assessment; MR. ROY CARTIER, M.B.A., M.R.P., Asst. Supt. Finance; Deacon JOHN C. MILLER, Public Policy & Devel.

Educational Consultants, Elementary—111 Blvd. of the Allies, Pittsburgh, 15222. Tel: 412-456-3070. CECILIA GRANDILLO, M.A.; Sr. CATHERINE ANN KOLLER, C.D.P., M.A.

Secretariat for Leadership, Development & Evangelization, Catholic School Mission & Identity—2900 Noblestown Rd., Pittsburgh, 15205. Tel: 412-456-3156. MR. CHRISTOPHER J. CHAPMAN; PATRICIA WASKOWIAK, Administrative Asst.

Family, Youth & Catholic School Ministries, Dept. for—St. Paul Seminary, 2900 Noblestown Rd., Pittsburgh, 15205-4227. Tel: 412-456-3112.

Family Ministry and Faith Formation—MS. JUDENE INDOVINA; CHRISTINE RADCLIFFE, Administrative Asst.

Youth Ministry—MR. GARY RONEY, Dir.; Deacon ANDREW J. WHITE SR., CYM Sports; PATRICIA WASKOWIAK, Administrative Asst.

Young Adult Ministry—JACOB WILLIAMSON.

Institutional Ministries, Office for—111 Blvd. of the Allies, Pittsburgh, 15222. ADAM BLAI, Dir., Tel: 412-456-3244.

Charismatic Prayer Groups—Rev. JOHN P. SWEENEY, M.Div., Moderator, St. Bonaventure Parish, 2001 Mount Royal Blvd., Glenshaw, 15116-2099. Tel: 412-486-2606.

Chief Facilities Officer, Secretariat for Temporal Affairs—PAUL IURLANO, J.D., Tel: 412-456-3093.

Chief Financial Officer & Secretary for Temporal Affairs—MR. BRUNO A. BONACCHI, Tel: 412-456-3137.

Vicar for Church Relations—Rev. Msgr. RONALD P. LENGWIN, V.G., M.Div., V.E., Tel: 412-456-3164.

Communications, Office for—Tel: 412-456-3020. Rev. NICHOLAS S. VASKOV, S.T.L., Exec. Dir.; MRS. ANN RODGERS, Dir.; MR. NICK SCIARAPPA, Diocesan Digital Media Strategist; MR. NATHAN SUDIE, Administrative Asst.

Clergy and Parish Leadership Development—Very Rev. JOSEPH M. MELE, Ph.D., Dir. & Secretariat Leadership, Devel. & Evangelization, St. Paul Seminary, 2900 Noblestown Rd., Pittsburgh, 15205-4227. Tel: 412-456-3048; Deacon STEPHEN J. BYERS, Dir., Deacon Ongoing Formation. Secretariat for Leadership Development & Evangelization.

Institute for Pastoral Leadership—DR. MICHEL THERRIEN, S.T.L., S.T.D., Pres. & Dir. Theological/Intellectual Formation; Very Rev. JOSEPH M. MELE, Ph.D., Dir. Pastoral Formation; MIMIKA GARESCHE, Dir. Spiritual Formation; MRS. SHARON TYBOROWSKI HACHMAN, Dean & Dir. Human Formation, Tel: 412-456-3110.

Cultural Diversity, Commission—MRS. BESS BIAMONTE, Chm., Tel: 412-456-3170; MRS. MARGRETTA STOKES TUCKER, Ph.D., Diocesan Liaison.

Deafness—See Evangelization and Missionary Outreach.

Permanent Diaconate—Deacon STEPHEN J. BYERS, Dir., Tel: 412-456-3124.

Diocesan National Black Catholic Congress Leadership Team—GWENDOLYN YOUNG, Team Leader, Tel: 412-456-3170; MRS. MARGRETTA STOKES TUCKER, Ph.D., Diocesan Liaison.

Disabilities, Persons with—See Evangelization and Missionary Outreach. Deacon TIMOTHY KILLMEYER, Ministry of Svc. to Persons with Disabilities, Tel: 412-456-3170 (Voice); Tel: 412-456-3122 (TTY).

Ecumenical and Interfaith Commission—Rev. Msgr. RONALD P. LENGWIN, V.G., M.Div., V.E., Dir., Tel: 412-456-3131.

Communications, Media and Technology, Office for - Secretariat for External Affairs—Rev. NICHOLAS S. VASKOV, S.T.L.; MR. NICK SCIARAPPA.

Ethnic Ministries—Tel: 412-456-3170. Chaplain to Korean Catholic Community: Rev. SHANG-HEE CHOI. Chaplain to Latino Catholic Community: VACANT. Chaplain to Vietnamese Catholic Community: Rev. DAM D. NGUYEN, M.Div. Coordinator of Latino Ministry: JORGE VELAS.

Financial Services, Office for—MR. WAYNE C. BOETTCHER, Dir., Tel: 412-456-3025.

Central Accounting Services—Tel: 412-456-3030.

Parish Accounting Services—Tel: 412-456-3025.

Foundation, Catholic Diocese of Pittsburgh—PATRICK M. JOYCE, Ed.D., Dir., Tel: 412-456-3085.

Health Care Liaison, Office of the - Secretariat for

External Affairs.—Very Rev. LAWRENCE A. DINARDO, V.G., J.C.L., V.E., Tel: 412-456-3131.

Information Technology & Personnel—Services provided by Vital Solutions International MR. EDWARD HANEY, Dir., Tel: 412-456-3152; Deacon KEVIN L. LANDER, Dir.

Insurance/Employee Benefits & Payroll, Office for—MR. DAVID S. STEWART, A.R.M., Dir., Tel: 412-456-3045.

Human Relations, Office for—Deacon JEFFREY A. HIRST, Dir., Tel: 412-456-3016.

Secretariat for Leadership, Development, & Evangelization—2900 Noblestown Rd., Pittsburgh, 15205. Tel: 412-456-3052. Very Rev. JOSEPH M. MELE, Ph.D., Sec.

Evangelization and Missionary Outreach, Dept. for—Saint Paul Seminary, 2900 Noblestown Rd., Pittsburgh, 15205-4227. Tel: 412-456-3156. DR. MICHEL THERRIEN, S.T.L., S.T.D., Dir.; Rev. ALEXANDER WROBLICKY, S.T.B., M.A., Assoc. Dir.; Deacon TIM M. KILLMEYER; SARAH JIMENEZ, Administrative Asst.; CHRISTINE RADCLIFFE, Administrative Asst.

Learning Media Center—(see Media and Technology, Office for) MICHAEL ANANIA; ANTHONY ACCETTULLA.

Legal Services, Office for—MR. CHRISTOPHER G. PONTICELLO, J.D., Gen. Counsel; KRISTIN BOOSE REPIN, J.D., Assoc. Gen. Counsel; PAUL IURLANO, J.D., Legal Counsel.

Matrimonial Concerns, Office for—Revs. WILLIAM E. DORNER, Canonical Consultant; LOUIS L. DENINNO, J.C.L., M.Div., Canonical Consultant, 2900 Noblestown Rd., Pittsburgh, 15205-4227. Tel: 412-456-3076.

Diocesan Review Board—Very Rev. THOMAS W. KUNZ, V.E., V.J., J.C.D., S.T.L., Exec. Sec., Tel: 412-456-3129.

Media and Technology, Office for - Department for Communication—Rev. NICHOLAS S. VASKOV, S.T.L., Dir.

Mission Office—Rev. Msgr. RONALD P. LENGWIN, V.G., M.Div., V.E., Dir., Tel: 412-456-3065.

Music, Office for—See Liturgy and Worship. Rev. JAMES J. CHEPPONIS, M.Div., M.A., Dir.; MR. DONALD FELLOWS, Assoc. Dir., St. Paul Seminary, 2900 Noblestown Rd., Pittsburgh, 15205-4227. Tel: 412-456-3042.

Natural Family Planning Advisory Committee—Deacon STEPHEN J. BYERS, Chm., Tel: 412-456-3124.

Newspaper—Pittsburgh Catholic MRS. ANN RODGERS, Gen. Mgr.; MR. WILLIAM CONE, Editor, 135 First Ave., #200, Pittsburgh, 15222-1506. Tel: 412-471-1252.

Department for Communications - Secretariat for External Affairs—Rev. NICHOLAS S. VASKOV, S.T.L., Dir.

Secretariat for Parish Services—2900 Noblestown Rd., Pittsburgh, 15205. DR. LINDA LEE RITZER, D.Min., Sec.

On Mission for the Church Alive Planning Initiative—2900 Noblestown Rd., Pittsburgh, 15205. Staff: EDWARD G. SCHEID, Ph.D.; MRS. MARGRETTA STOKES TUCKER, Ph.D.; MRS. MARY ANN MASON; MRS. ELLEN M. MADY, Tel: 412-456-3157; MRS. MARY ANN MOSER, Administrative Asst.

Payroll, Office for—MR. JOHN G. CVETIC, Dir., Tel: 412-456-3006.

Pilgrimage Office—Rev. Msgr. RONALD P. LENGWIN, V.G., M.Div., V.E., Dir., Tel: 412-456-3065.

Pornography, Commission to Counter—MRS. NORMA NORRIS, Chm.

Priest Ongoing Formation, Department for - Secretariat for Leadership & Evangelization—Very Rev. JOSEPH M. MELE, Ph.D., Dir., St. Paul Seminary, 2900 Noblestown Rd., Pittsburgh, 15205-4227. Tel: 412-456-3048.

Pre-Ordination Formation, Department for—St. Paul Seminary, 2900 Noblestown Rd., Pittsburgh, 15205-4227. Tel: 412-456-3048. Rev. THOMAS A. SPARACINO, M.Div.

Priestly Vocations, Office for—Tel: 412-456-3123. Rev. MICHAEL R. ACKERMAN, Dir.

Facilities Management & Maintenance—MR. JAMES J. ZIELINSKI, Dir., 135 First Ave., Pittsburgh, 15222. Tel: 412-456-3034; PAUL IURLANO, J.D., Chief Facilities Officer, Tel: 866-755-2373 (Disaster Hotline); MR. JOSEPH KUBIAK, Plant Mgr., St. Paul Seminary, 2900 Noblestown Rd., Pittsburgh, 15205.

Protection of Children and Young People, Office for the - Secretariat for External Affairs—PHYLLIS HANEY, Dir., St. Paul Seminary, 2900 Noblestown Rd., Pittsburgh, 15205. Tel: 412-456-5633.

Public and Community Affairs, Office for—Rev. Msgr. RONALD P. LENGWIN, V.G., M.Div., V.E., Dir., Tel: 412-456-3131.

Family, Youth, & Catholic School Ministries - Catholic School Mission/Identity—Tel: 412-456-3112. VACANT.

Retired Priests, Office for—Rev. LEROY A. DIPIETRO, Delegate, Tel: 412-931-4624.

St. Paul Cathedral—Very Rev. KRIS D. STUBNA, S.T.D., Rector & Pastor, 108 N. Dithridge St., Pittsburgh, 15213-2694. Tel: 412-621-4951.

St. Paul Seminary—2900 Noblestown Rd., Pittsburgh, 15205. Revs. THOMAS A. SPARACINO, M.Div., Rector, Tel: 412-456-3048; BRIAN W. NOEL, S.T.L., Spiritual Dir., Tel: 412-456-3048; Sr. CINDY ANN KIBLER, S.H.S., Apostolic Works Coord., Tel: 412-456-3053.

Society for the Propagation of the Faith
Tel: 412-456-3065. Deacon RICHARD M. TUCEK.

Stewardship, Office for—Tel: 412-456-3085. PATRICK M. JOYCE, Ed.D., Dir.; MRS. DOLORES C. NYPAVER, Asst. Dir.; MR. MICHAEL FRECKER, Dir. Planned Giving; Deacon JOHN C. MILLER, Dir. Public Policy & Devel., Catholic Schools Office.

Theological Commission—Very Rev. KRIS D. STUBNA, S.T.D., Tel: 412-621-4951.

Worship Commission—Tel: 412-456-3041. Rev. NICHOLAS S. VASKOV, S.T.L.

Liturgy & Worship, Dept. for—St. Paul Seminary, 2900 Noblestown Rd., Pittsburgh, 15205-4227.
Tel: 412-456-3041. Revs. NICHOLAS S. VASKOV, S.T.L., Worship & Liturgical Ministry; JAMES J. CHEPPONIS, M.Div., M.A., Dir. Office for Music.

Young Adult Outreach—Tel: 412-456-3156. Deacon FRANK J. SZEMANSKI.

CLERGY, PARISHES, MISSIONS AND PAROCHIAL SCHOOLS

CITY OF PITTSBURGH, PROPER

(ALLEGHENY COUNTY)

1—ST. PAUL CATHEDRAL (1834)
108 N. Dithridge St., 15213. Tel: 412-621-4951; Fax: 412-621-1079; Email: info@saintpaulcathedral.org; Web: stpaulpgh.org. Very Rev. Kris D. Stubna, S.T.D., Admin.; Revs. Adam C. Potter, Parochial Vicar; Daniel L. Walsh, C.S.Sp., Parochial Vicar; Mark L. Thomas, S.T.L., In Res.; Deacon Thomas J. Berna.
Catechesis Religious Program—Students 87.

2—ST. AGNES, Closed. For sacramental records contact St. Paul Cathedral.

3—ST. ANN, (Hungarian), Closed. See St. Stephen.

4—ST. AUGUSTINE, (German), Closed. See Our Lady of the Angels.

5—ST. BENEDICT THE MOOR (1889) (African American)
91 Crawford St., 15219. Tel: 412-281-3141; Email: sbtmoffice@verizon.net. Rev. Christopher D. Donley, Admin.
School—St. Benedict the Moor School, (Grades PreK-8), 631 Watt St., 15219. Tel: 412-682-3755; Fax: 412-682-4058; Email: stben@sbtmschool.org; Web: www.sbtmschool.org. Lay Teachers 20; Students 210.
Catechesis Religious Program—Students 20.
Convent—Tel: 412-621-0519. Revs. Stephen A. Kresak, M.Div.; Michael S. Sedor, S.T.L., Parochial Vicar; Deacons Michael J. Babcock; Tim Zenchak; James R. Grab.

6—ST. CATHERINE OF SIENA (Beechview) (1902)
1810 Belasco Ave., 15216. Tel: 412-531-2135; Fax: 412-531-8543. Revs. James M. Bachner, M.Div.; Fernando Torres, L.C., Parochial Vicar; Gary W. Oehmler, Parochial Vicar; Deacons Thomas O'Neill; Mark S. Bibro; Richard A. Longo.
Catechesis Religious Program—Marina Osthoff, D.R.E. (Spanish); Nancy Spinneweber, D.R.E. (English). Students 145.

7—CATHOLIC COMMUNITY OF THE EAST END OF PITTSBURGH (1922)
509 S. Dallas Ave., 15208. Tel: 412-661-7222; Fax: 412-661-9337; Email: mainoffice@stbedepgh.org. Rev. Thomas J. Burke, M.Div.
School—St. Bede School, 6920 Edgerton Ave., 15208. Tel: 412-661-9425; Fax: 412-661-0447; Email: 06941@diopitt.org. Rebecca Page, Prin. Lay Teachers 23; Students 278.
Catechesis Religious Program—Students 78.

8—ST. CHARLES LWANGA PARISH (1992) Rev. David H. Taylor, M.Div. Consolidated from the following churches: Corpus Christi, Holy Rosary, Mother of Good Counsel, Our Lady Help of Christians, Our Lady of the Most Blessed Sacrament, SS. Peter & Paul, and St. Walburga.
Res.: 7114 Kelly St., 15208. Tel: 412-731-3020; Fax: 412-731-1615; Email: frdht@aol.com.
See Sister Thea Bowman Catholic Academy, Pittsburgh under Consolidated Schools located in the Institution section.
Catechesis Religious Program—Email: mary15224@comcast.net. Students 15.

9—CORPUS CHRISTI, Closed. See St. Charles Lwanga.

10—ST. ELIZABETH OF HUNGARY, (Slovak), Closed. See St. Patrick-St. Stanislaus Kostka.

11—EPIPHANY (1902) (Irish)
Administrative Center, 164 Washington Pl., 15219. Tel: 412-471-0257; Email: churchoffice@epiphanychurch.net; Web: www.epiphanychurch.net. Rev. Christopher D. Donley, Admin.; Sr. Marlene Luffy, C.D.P., Pastoral Assoc.

12—HOLY APOSTLES PARISH
3198 Schieck St., 15227. Tel: 412-884-7744; Email: holyapostles@holyapostlesparish.org; Web: www.holyapostlesparish.org. Revs. Stephen A. Kresak, M.Div.; Levi D. Hartle, Parochial Vicar.

13—HOLY FAMILY, (Polish), Closed. See Our Lady of the Angels.

14—HOLY ROSARY, Closed. See St. Charles Lwanga.

15—ST. HYACINTH, (Polish), Closed. See St. Regis.

16—IMMACULATE CONCEPTION (1905) (Italian), Merged with St. Joseph, Pittsburgh to form St. Maria Goretti.

17—IMMACULATE HEART OF MARY (1897) (Polish)
3058 Brereton St., 15219. Tel: 412-621-5170; Fax: 412-621-7445. Revs. John D. Harvey, O.F.M.-Cap., Admin.; Dam D. Nguyen, M.Div., Parochial Vicar; Richard J. Zelik, O.F.M.Cap., Parochial Vicar; Deacon Richard T. Fitzpatrick.
Catechesis Religious Program—Tel: 412-682-2886; Fax: 412-682-6889. Twinned with Our Lady of Angels. Students 30.

18—ST. JOACHIM, Closed. See St. Rosalia.

19—ST. JOHN THE BAPTIST, Closed. See Our Lady of the Angels.

20—SAINT JOHN XXIII, A QUASI-PARISH FOR THE EXTRAORDINARY FORM OF MASS
1025 Haslage Ave., 15212. Tel: 412-434-1651; Email: office@stjohnxxiiiparish.org; Web: www.stjohnxxiiiparish.org. Revs. William Avis, Admin.; John O'Connor, Parochial Vicar.

21—ST. JOSEPH (1872) (German), Merged with Immaculate Conception, Pittsburgh to form St. Maria Goretti.

22—ST. KIERAN, Closed. See St. Matthew.

23—ST. LAWRENCE O'TOOLE (East End) (1897) Closed. For inquiries for parish records contact the chancery.

24—ST. MARIA GORETTI PARISH (2012) (German)
4712 Liberty Ave., 15224. Tel: 412-682-2354; Email: parish.secretary.smg@gmail.com. Revs. John D. Harvey, O.F.M.Cap., Admin.; Dam D. Nguyen, M.Div., Parochial Vicar; Richard J. Zelik, O.F.M.Cap., Parochial Vicar; Nicholas J. Argentieri, In Res.; Douglas A. Boyd, In Res.; Pierre G. Sodini, S.T.L., In Res.; Deacon Richard T. Fitzpatrick.
School—St. Maria Goretti School, 321 Edmond St., 15224. Tel: 412-621-5199; Fax: 412-621-5601; Email: parish.secretary.smg@gmail.com. Sr. Mary John Cook, Prin. Lay Teachers 15; Students 210.
Catechesis Religious Program—Students 49.

25—ST. MARTIN (West End) Closed. See Guardian Angels.

26—ST. MARY ASSUMPTION (Lawrenceville) Closed. See St. Matthew.

27—ST. MARY OF MERCY (1870)
202 Stanwix St., 15222. Tel: 412-261-0110; Email: office@stmaryofmercy.org. Revs. Christopher D. Donley, Admin.; Edward M. Bryce, V.F., S.T.L., In Res. (Retired); Rev. Msgr. Ronald P. Lengwin, V.G., M.Div., V.E., In Res.; Rev. Nicholas S. Vaskov, S.T.L., In Res.; Deacon Samuel Toney.

28—ST. MARY'S (Lawrenceville) Closed. See Our Lady of the Angels.

29—ST. MATTHEW (1993) Merged into St. Raphael Parish.

30—MOTHER OF GOOD COUNSEL, (Italian), Closed. See St. Charles Lwanga.

31—OUR LADY HELP OF CHRISTIANS, (Italian), Closed. See St. Charles Lwanga.

32—OUR LADY OF THE ANGELS (1993) [CEM]
Consolidated from St. Augustine, Holy Family, St. John the Baptist and St. Mary. Rev. John D. Harvey, O.F.M.Cap.; Deacon Richard T. Fitzpatrick. In Res., Revs. Reginald Russo, O.F.M.Cap.; Richard J. Zelik, O.F.M.Cap.; Reginald Lyimo, O.F.M.Cap.; Deacons Albert Carver, O.F.M.Cap.; Jonathan Ulrich.
Res.: 225 37th St., 15201. Tel: 412-682-0929; Fax: 412-682-6889; Email: parish@oloa.org; Web: www.oloa.org.
Catechesis Religious Program—Paula Calabrese, Catechetical Admin. Students 36.

33—OUR LADY OF THE MOST BLESSED SACRAMENT, Closed. See St. Charles Lwanga.

34—ST. PATRICK (Strip District) Closed. See St. Patrick-St. Stanislaus Kostka.

35—ST. PATRICK-ST. STANISLAUS KOSTKA (1993)

(Polish)
57 21st St., 15222. Tel: 412-471-4767;
Fax: 412-471-1209; Email: saintsinthestrip@comcast.net. Rev. Christopher D. Donley. Formerly St. Stanislaus, St. Patrick and St. Elizabeth of Hungary.
Catechesis Religious Program—Students 8.
36—SS. PETER AND PAUL (East Liberty) Closed. See St. Charles Lwanga.
37—ST. PHILOMENA (Squirrel Hill) Closed. See St. Bede.
38—ST. RAPHAEL (1911) Rev. Christopher D. Donley; Very Rev. Joseph M. Mele, Ph.D., In Res.; Deacon William O. Hahn.
Res.: 1118 Chislett St., 15206. Tel: 412-661-3100;
Fax: 412-661-0428; Email: parishcenter@straphaelpgh.org; Web: straphaelpgh.org.
School—St. Raphael School, (Grades PreSchool-8), 1154 Chislett St., 15206. Tel: 412-661-0288;
Fax: 412-661-0428; Email: school@straphaelpgh.org; Web: www.straphaelpgh.org/school/. Lay Teachers 12; Students 167.
Catechesis Religious Program—Nathan Wigfield, D.R.E. Students 167.
39—ST. REGIS (1993)
3235 Parkview Ave., 15213. Tel: 412-681-9365;
Fax: 412-681-1175; Email: 51101@diopitt.org. Very Rev. Kris D. Stubna, S.T.D., Admin.; Revs. Adam C. Potter, Parochial Vicar; Daniel L. Walsh, C.S.Sp., Parochial Vicar; Deacon Thomas J. Berna.
Res.: St. Paul Cathedral Rectory, 108 N. Dithridge St., 15213. Tel: 412-621-4951.
Catechesis Religious Program—Students 55.
40—ST. ROSALIA (1993)
411 Greenfield Ave., 15207. Tel: 412-421-5766;
Fax: 412-421-4529; Email: strosaliaparish@gmail.com; Web: www.strosaliaparish.org. Very Rev. Kris D. Stubna, S.T.D., Admin.; Revs. Adam C. Potter, Parochial Vicar; Daniel L. Walsh, C.S.Sp., Parochial Vicar; Deacon Thomas J. Berna.
41—SACRED HEART (1872)
310 Shady Ave., 15206. Tel: 412-661-0187;
Fax: 412-661-7932; Email: sacredheartshadyside@comcast.net. Revs. Thomas R. Miller, M.Div., M.A., Admin.; John P. Sweeney, M.Div., Parochial Vicar; Stephen M. Palsa, Chap.; Edward S. Litavec, In Res., (Retired); Deacons William O. Hahn; John A. Vaskov.
School—Sacred Heart School, (Grades K-8), 325 Emerson St., 15206. Fax: 412-441-2798; Email: slynn@sacredheartpgh.org; Web: www.sacredheartpgh.org. Sr. Lynn Rettinger, S.C., Prin. Lay Teachers 23; Sisters 4; Students 440; Religious Teachers 4.
Catechesis Religious Program—
Tel: 412-661-0187, Ext. 118; Email: faithformation@sacredheartpgh.org. Sharon Smoller, C.R.E. Merged with St. Raphael. Students 378.
42—ST. STANISLAUS (Strip District) (Polish), Closed. See St. Patrick-St. Stanislaus Kostka.
43—ST. STEPHEN (1993)
Mailing Address: 5115 Second Ave., 15207.
Tel: 412-421-9210; Fax: 412-421-6421; Email: saintstephen@verizon.net. Very Rev. Kris D. Stubna, S.T.D., Admin.; Revs. Adam C. Potter, Parochial Vicar; Daniel L. Walsh, C.S.Sp., Parochial Vicar; Deacon Thomas J. Berna.
Catechesis Religious Program—131 E. Elizabeth St., 15207. Tel: 412-421-4748; Fax: 412-421-4748. Students 50.

SOUTH SIDE
1—ST. ADALBERT, (Polish), Closed. See Prince of Peace.
2—ST. BASIL (1907) Merged to form Holy Apostles Parish.
3—ST. CANICE (Knoxville) Closed. See St. John Vianney.
4—ST. CASIMIR, (Lithuanian), Closed. See Prince of Peace.
5—ST. GEORGE (Allentown) Closed. See St. John Vianney.
6—GUARDIAN ANGELS (West End) (1994) [CEM] Closed. Merged with St. James and St. Martin.
7—ST. HENRY, Closed. See St. John Vianney.
8—HOLY ANGELS (1903)
408 Baldwin Rd., 15207. Tel: 412-461-6906;
Fax: 412-461-0961; Email: skresak@holyapostlesparish.org; Web: www.holyangelshays.com. Revs. Stephen A. Kresak, M.Div., Admin.; Robert J. Ahlin, J.C.L., Parochial Vicar; Levi D. Hartle, Parochial Vicar; Deacon Daniel E. Nizan.
Catechesis Religious Program—
Tel: 412-461-6906, Ext. 112; Email: elaine@holyangelshays.org. Students 180.
9—HOLY INNOCENTS (1900) Closed. All Sacramental Records have been taken to the Diocesan Archives Dept.
10—ST. JAMES (West End) Closed. See Guardian Angels.
11—ST. JOHN THE EVANGELIST, Closed. See Prince of Peace.
12—ST. JOHN VIANNEY (Hilltop) (1994) [CEM] Closed. Consolidation of the following churches: St. Canice, St. George, St. Henry and St. Joseph.
13—ST. JOSAPHAT, (Polish), Closed. See Prince of Peace.
14—ST. JUSTIN (Mt. Washington) (1917) Closed. For inquiries for parish records contact the chancery.
15—ST. MARY OF THE MOUNT (Mt. Washington) (1873)
407 Grandview Ave., 15211. Tel: 412-381-0212;
Fax: 412-381-9921; Email: smom@smomp.org; Web: www.smomp.org. Mailing Address: 403 Grandview Ave., 15211. Revs. Michael J. Stumpf; Daniel T. Straughn, S.T.L., Parochial Vicar; Peter C. Mawanda, In Res.
Catechesis Religious Program—Students 110.
16—ST. MATTHEW, (Slovak), Closed. See Prince of Peace.
17—ST. MICHAEL, (German), Closed. See Prince of Peace.
18—OUR LADY OF LORETO (1959)
1810 Belasco Ave., 15216. Tel: 412-531-2135; Email: ollpari1@verizon.net; Web: www.bbcatholic.com. Revs. James M. Bachner, M.Div.; Fernando Torres, L.C., Parochial Vicar; Gary W. Oehmler, Parochial Vicar; Deacons Thomas O'Neill; Mark S. Bibro; Richard A. Longo.
Res.: 1905 Pioneer Ave., 15226. Tel: 412-341-6161;
Fax: 412-341-3399; Email: ollpari@aol.com.
Catechesis Religious Program—
3040 Pioneer Ave.. Tel: 412-341-6163; Email: ololccd@aol.com. Patricia Schwerin, D.R.E. Students 57.
Convent—
1901 Pioneer Ave., 15226. Tel: 412-343-1377.
19—ST. PAMPHILUS (1960)
1000 Tropical Ave., 15216. Tel: 412-341-1000;
Tel: 412-531-8449; Fax: 412-341-6956; Email: 45801@diopitt.org. Rev. Alexis Anania, O.F.M.; Friar John-Michael Pinto, O.F.M., In Res.
Res.: 948 Tropical Ave., 15216.
Catechesis Religious Program—
Tel: 412-561-0330. Students 26.
20—ST. PETER, Closed. See Prince of Peace.
21—ST. PIUS X (1954)
3040 Pioneer Ave., 15226. Tel: 412-563-5423;
Fax: 412-561-3868. Revs. James M. Bachner, M.Div.; Gary W. Oehmler, Parochial Vicar; Fernando Torres, L.C., Parochial Vicar; Deacons Mark S. Bibro; Thomas O'Neill; Richard A. Longo.
See St. John Bosco Academy, Pittsburgh under Consolidated Schools located in the Institution section.
Catechesis Religious Program—
Tel: 412-563-1588. Patricia Schwerin, D.R.E. Students 85.
22—PRINCE OF PEACE (1992) [CEM 6]
Mailing Address: 81 S. 13th St., 15203-1897. Revs. Michael J. Stumpf, Admin.; Daniel T. Straughn, S.T.L., Parochial Vicar; Deacons Richard A. Longo; Frank J. Szemanski.
Res.: 162 S. 15th St., 15203-1897. Tel: 412-481-8380;
Fax: 412-431-0209; Email: princeofpeaceparish@verizon.net; Web: www.princeofpeacepittsburgh.org.
Catechesis Religious Program—
Tel: 412-381-5458. Students 31.
23—RESURRECTION (Brookline) (1909)
1100 Creedmoor Ave., 15226. Tel: 412-563-4400;
Fax: 412-563-4403; Email: resurrectionparishbrookline@gmail.com; Web: www.eressi.com. Revs. James M. Bachner, M.Div., Admin.; Gary W. Oehmler, Parochial Vicar; Fernando Torres, L.C., Parochial Vicar; Deacons Richard A. Longo; Thomas O'Neill; Mark S. Bibro.
Catechesis Religious Program—
Tel: 412-343-9551. Juanita Knouff, D.R.E. Students 138.
24—ST. VINCENT (Esplen) Closed. See St. John of God, McKees Rocks.
25—ST. WENDELIN (Carrick) (1873) Merged to form Holy Apostles Parish.

NORTH SIDE
1—ST. AMBROSE, Merged with St. Boniface to form Holy Wisdom.
2—ANNUNCIATION, Closed. See Incarnation of the Lord.
3—ST. BONIFACE, Merged with St. Ambrose to form Holy Wisdom.
4—ST. CYRIL OF ALEXANDRIA (1924)
3854 Brighton Rd., 15212-1696. Tel: 412-761-1552; Email: saintcyrilchurch@yahoo.com. Rev. Lawrence R. Smith, In Res., (Retired).
Catechesis Religious Program—
Tel: 412-734-0505; Email: stcyrilreled@yahoo.com. Jean D. Donato, D.R.E. Students 89.
5—ST. FRANCIS XAVIER, Closed. See Risen Lord.
6—ST. GABRIEL ARCHANGEL, (Slovak), Closed. See Risen Lord.
7—HOLY WISDOM (1994) [CEM 3]
1025 Haslage Ave., 15212-3429. Tel: 412-231-1116;
Fax: 412-231-1072; Email: office@holywisdomparish.org. Very Rev. Lawrence A. DiNardo, V.G., J.C.L., V.E., Mod.; Rev. Louis L. DeNinno, J.C.L., M.Div., In Res.
Catechesis Religious Program—
Tel: 412-321-3186; Fax: 412-321-7807. Twinned with St. Peter, North Side. Students 165.
8—INCARNATION OF THE LORD (1993) Consolidated from Annunciation and Nativity of Our Lord.
Mailing Address: 4071 Franklin Rd., 15214.
Tel: 412-931-2911; Fax: 412-931-2832; Email: businessmanagerincarnation@comcast.net. Revs. John R. Rushofsky, M.Ed., Admin.; Michael J. Maranowski, Snr. Parochial Vicar; Michael A. Zavage, Parochial Vicar; James W. Dolan, Chap.; Leroy A. DiPietro, In Res.; Innocent Onuh, In Res.; Deacons Richard R. Cessar; Robert E. Koslosky; William R. Palamara Jr.; David R. Witter Sr.; Marilyn Ruffner, Safe Environment Coord.; Ms. Naomi Wells, Office Mgr.; Mr. David Volcheck, Music Min.; Mr. John Dey, Maintenance; Mrs. Geraldine Seidl, Sec.
9—ST. JOSEPH, Closed. See St. Peter.
10—ST. LEO, Closed. See Risen Lord.
11—MOST HOLY NAME OF JESUS (Troy Hill) (1868) [CEM] (German)
Claim & Harpster Sts., 15212. Tel: 412-231-2994;
Fax: 412-231-7180; Email: mostholyname@hotmail.com. Mailing Address: 1700 Harpster St., 15212-4393. Very Rev. Lawrence A. DiNardo, V.G., J.C.L., V.E., Mod.; Deacon G. Gregory Jelinek.
See Northside Catholic School, Pittsburgh under Consolidated Schools located in the Institution section.
Catechesis Religious Program—
Tel: 412-231-3002; Tel: 412-759-9835. Students 74.
Chapel—St. Anthony's Chapel (1880) Carole Brueckner, Asst. Dir.
12—NATIVITY OF OUR LORD, Closed. See Incarnation of the Lord.
13—OUR LADY QUEEN OF PEACE, Closed. See St. Peter.
14—SAINT PETER PARISH (1993) [CEM] (Polish) Consolidated from St. Cyprian, St. Mary's, Mary Immaculate & Our Lady, Queen of Peace, St. Joseph, St. Peter and St. Wenceslaus. Rev. Vincent E. Zidek, O.S.B.
Res.: 720 Arch St., 15212. Tel: 412-321-0711;
Fax: 412-321-7807; Email: stpeter@winbeam.com; Web: www.stpeterparish.org.
See Northside Catholic School, Pittsburgh under Consolidated Schools located in the Institution section.
Catechesis Religious Program—
907 Middle St., 15212. Tel: 412-321-3186; Email: patkammersell@comcast.net. Patricia Kammersell, Faith Formation Prog. Mgr. Students 45.
15—REGINA COELI, (Italian), Closed. For sacramental records contact St. Cyril of Alexandria.
16—RISEN LORD (1993) Formerly the following churches: St. Francis Xavier, St. Gabriel Archangel, St. Leo and Our Lady of Perpetual Help.
Mailing Address: 3250 California Ave., 15212.
Tel: 412-761-1507; Fax: 412-761-6454; Email: risenlord@risenlordparish.org; Web: www.incandrl.org. Very Rev. Lawrence A. DiNardo, V.G., J.C.L., V.E., Mod.; Revs. Louis L. DeNinno, J.C.L., M.Div.; Anthony Gargotta, M.Div., M.A.; James R. Orr, M.Div., M.A.; Charles W. Speicher, Ph.D., S.T.M.; Clement Kanu, In Res.; Raymond Luther, In Res.; Lawrence R. Smith, In Res., (Retired); Deacons G. Gregory Jelinek; Gery G. Pielin; Mr. John Dey, Maintenance; Mrs. Mary Kay Ferrance, Music Min.; Marilyn Ruffner, Safe Environment Coord.; Ms. Naomi Wells, Office/Business Mgr.
17—ST. WENCESLAUS, Closed. See St. Peter.

OUTSIDE THE CITY OF PITTSBURGH

ALEPPO TOWNSHIP, ALLEGHENY CO., ST. MARY (1852) [CEM]
Mailing Address: 444 Glenfield Rd., Sewickley, 15143. Tel: 412-741-6460; Fax: 412-749-9271; Email: bcox@saintmaryaleppo.org; Web: www.saintmaryaleppo.org. Rev. David J. Jastrab.
Catechesis Religious Program—Tel: 412-741-3959; Email: b_venturella@saintmaryaleppo.org. Students 100.

ALIQUIPPA, BEAVER CO., ST. TITUS (1994) [CEM 2] [JC2]
952 Franklin Ave., Aliquippa, 15001.
Tel: 724-378-8561; Fax: 724-378-4851; Email: sttituschurch@comcast.net; Web: www.sttituschurch.org. Revs. Martin R. Bartel, O.S.B., Admin.; Joachim Morgan, Parochial Vicar; Thomas More Sikora, Parochial Vicar; Deacons Joseph N. Basko; Robert J. Bittner.
Catechesis Religious Program—Tel: 724-375-7940. Gloria Weaver, D.R.E. Students 28.

ALLISON PARK, ALLEGHENY CO., ST. URSULA (1908)
3937 Kirk Ave., Allison Park, 15101.
Tel: 412-486-6700; Fax: 412-486-2562; Email: ursula@stursula.com. Revs. Timothy F. Whalen,

M.Div., M.A., Admin.; Ernest Strelinski, P.A.; Joseph G. Luisi, In Res.
Catechesis Religious Program—
Tel: 412-486-6700, Ext. 7; Email: prep@stursula.com. Edith Bishop, D.R.E. Students 73.
AMBRIDGE, BEAVER CO.
1—CHURCH OF CHRIST THE KING, Closed. See Good Samaritan.
2—DIVINE REDEEMER, Closed. See Good Samaritan.
3—GOOD SAMARITAN (1994) [CEM] Consolidated from the following churches: St. Veronica, Divine Redeemer, St. Stanislaus, Christ the King and Holy Trinity.
Mailing Address: Administrative Center, 725 Glenwood Ave., Ambridge, 15003. Web: www.goodsam1.org. Rev. Joseph A. Carr.
Res.: 923 Melrose Ave., Ambridge, 15003.
Tel: 724-385-0356 (Res.); Tel: 724-266-6565 (Office); Fax: 724-266-5570.
Catechesis Religious Program— Combined with St. John the Baptist, Baden. Tel: 724-266-6565, Ext. 12; Email: ccd@goodsam1.org. Students 125.
4—HOLY TRINITY, (Croatian), Closed. See Good Samaritan.
5—ST. STANISLAUS, Closed. See Good Samaritan.
6—ST. VERONICA, Closed. See Good Samaritan.
ASPINWALL, ALLEGHENY CO., ST. SCHOLASTICA (1907)
309 Brilliant Ave., Aspinwall, 15215.
Tel: 412-781-0186; Fax: 412-781-4316; Email: parish@saintscholastica.com. Revs. Dale E. DeNinno; Michael W. Decewicz, V.F., M.Div., Parochial Vicar; Paul W. Merkovsky, Parochial Vicar.
See Christ the Divine Teacher Catholic Academy, Pittsburgh under Consolidated Schools located in the Institution section.
Catechesis Religious Program—
Tel: 412-781-0186, Ext. 21. Delia Barr, D.R.E. Students 175.
AVELLA, WASHINGTON CO., ST. MICHAEL (1917) [CEM]
97 Highland Ave., Avella, 15312. Tel: 724-587-3570; Email: stmike@hky.com. Revs. Harry R. Bielewicz, V.E., M.Div., Admin.; Zachary A. Galiyas, Parochial Vicar; Very Rev. Benedetto P. Vaghetto, J.C.L., In Res.
Catechesis Religious Program—Students 32.
BADEN, BEAVER CO., ST. JOHN THE BAPTIST (1866) [CEM]
Administrative Center, 375 Linmore Ave., P.O. Box 171, Baden, 15005. Tel: 724-869-2280;
Fax: 724-869-0305; Email: stjohnsbadenpa@gmail.com. Rev. Joseph A. Carr.
Res.: 923 Melrose Ave., Ambridge, 15003.
Tel: 724-385-0356.
Catechesis Religious Program—
Tel: 724-266-6565, Ext. 12; Email: ccd@goodsam1.org. This information is combined with Good Samaritan, Ambridge. Students 50.
BAIRDFORD, ALLEGHENY CO., ST. VICTOR (1919)
531 Bairdford Rd., P.O. Box 149, Bairdford, 15006.
Tel: 724-265-2070; Fax: 724-265-6316; Email: stvictors@consolidated.net. Rev. Charles W. Speicher, Ph.D., S.T.M.
Res.: 527 Bairdford Rd., Bairdford, 15006.
Catechesis Religious Program—535 Bairdford Rd., Bairdford, 15006. Tel: 724-265-4040;
Fax: 724-265-6313. Students 287.
BALDWIN BORO, ALLEGHENY CO., ST. ALBERT THE GREAT (1956) Merged to form Holy Apostles Parish.
BEAVER FALLS, BEAVER CO.
1—DIVINE MERCY (1994) [CEM] (Polish), Merged with Christ the Divine Teacher, Beaver Falls; St. Philomena, Beaver Falls & St. Rose of Lima, Darlington to form St. Monica, Beaver Falls.
2—HOLY TRINITY, (Polish), Closed. See Divine Mercy.
3—ST. MONICA (2013)
116 Thorndale Dr., Beaver Falls, 15010-1730.
Tel: 724-846-7540; Fax: 724-846-3819; Email: office@saintmonica.us. Rev. Kim J. Schreck, S.T.L.
Catechesis Religious Program—Heather Mineard, C.R.E. Students 555.
4—ST. PHILOMENA (1948) Merged with Christ the Divine Teacher, Beaver Falls; Divine Mercy, Beaver Falls & St. Rose of Lima, Darlington to form St. Monica, Beaver Falls.
BEAVER, BEAVER CO., SS. PETER AND PAUL (1830) [CEM]
200 Third St., Beaver, 15009. Tel: 724-775-4111;
Fax: 724-775-1117; Email: office@ssppbeaver.org. Rev. Robert J. Miller, M.Div., M.A.
School—SS. Peter and Paul School, 370 E. End Ave., Beaver, 15009. Tel: 724-774-4450; Fax: 724-774-5192; Email: school@ssppbeaver.org. Lay Teachers 15; Students 194.
Catechesis Religious Program—Students 200.
BELLEVUE, ALLEGHENY CO., ASSUMPTION OF THE BLESSED VIRGIN MARY ON THE BEAUTIFUL RIVER (1903)
45 N. Sprague Ave., Bellevue, 15202.
Tel: 412-766-6660; Fax: 412-766-4836; Email: parish@assumptionchurch.org; Web: www.assumptionchurch.org. Very Rev. John M. Bachkay, V.F., M.Div., M.Ed., Admin.; Revs. David Green, Parochial Vicar; John L. McKenna, In Res.
Catechesis Religious Program—35 N. Jackson Ave., Bellevue. Tel: 412-766-4046; Email: maryvictaylor@gmail.com. Mary Vic Taylor, C.R.E. Students 167.
BENTLEYVILLE, WASHINGTON CO.
1—AVE MARIA (1994) [CEM 2] Merged with St. Katherine Drexel Parish.
2—ST. KATHARINE DREXEL PARISH 2017
126 Church St., Bentleyville, 15314.
Tel: 724-209-1370, Ext. 404; Web: www.katharinedrexelpgh.org. Revs. Edward L. Yuhas, M.Div., Admin.; Donald Chortos, Parochial Vicar, (Retired).
3—ST. LUKE, Closed. See St. Katherine Drexel, Bentleyville.
BESSEMER, LAWRENCE CO., ST. ANTHONY (1909) Merged with St. Lawrence, Hillsville to form Christ the King, Hillsville.
BETHEL PARK, ALLEGHENY CO.
1—ST. GERMAINE (1957)
7003 Baptist Rd., Bethel Park, 15102.
Tel: 412-833-0661; Fax: 412-833-4036; Email: church_stgermaine@comcast.net. Rev. John J. Baver; Mary Beth Green, Pastoral Assoc.
Catechesis Religious Program—Tel: 412-833-6662. Students 11.
2—ST. THOMAS MORE (1953)
126 Fort Couch Rd., 15241. Tel: 412-833-0031;
Fax: 412-833-5995; Email: parishoffice@stmpgh.org; Web: www.stmpgh.org. Revs. W. Peter Horton, M.A., M.Div., Admin.; James J. Chepponis, M.Div., M.A., Parochial Vicar; James R. Bedillion, J.C.L., Chap.; Deacon William G. Batz.
School—St. Thomas More School, (Grades PreK-8), 134 Fort Couch Rd., 15241. Tel: 412-833-1412;
Fax: 412-833-5597; Email: info@stmcs.org; Web: www.stmcs.org. Joseph Rosi, Prin. Associated with St. Thomas More Parish, OCD ID 141003 Lay Teachers 26; Students 393.
Catechesis Religious Program—Tel: 412-835-6996;
Fax: 412-283-0256; Email: lynchl@stmpgh.org. Lynne Lynch, C.R.E. Students 340.
3—ST. VALENTINE (1931)
2710 Ohio St., Bethel Park, 15102. Tel: 412-835-4415; Fax: 412-835-4417; Email: svoffice@comcast.net; Web: www.stvals.org. Rev. Victor J. Molka Jr.
Catechesis Religious Program—2709 Mesta St., Bethel Park, 15102. Tel: 412-835-3780. Cary Dabny, Dir. Faith Formation. Students 423.
BLAWNOX, ALLEGHENY CO.
1—ST. EDWARD (1938) Merged to form St. Pio of Pietrelcina Parish, Pittsburgh.
2—ST. PIO OF PIETRELCINA PARISH (2011)
450 Walnut St., 15238. Tel: 412-828-4066; Email: sted-fran@verizon.net. Revs. Dale E. DeNinno; Michael W. Decewicz, V.F., M.Div., Parochial Vicar; Paul W. Merkovsky, Parochial Vicar; Dozie Romanus Egbe, (Nigeria) In Res.; Deacon Robert F. Wertz Jr.
Catechesis Religious Program—Tel: 412-781-0186. Students 40.
BOBTOWN, GREENE CO., ST. IGNATIUS OF ANTIOCH (1924)
305 Grant Ave., P.O. Box 63, Bobtown, 15315.
Tel: 724-839-7122; Fax: 724-839-7315; Email: gcatholiccommunities@gmail.com. Revs. Albin C. McGinnis, V.F., Admin.; J. Francis Frazer, Parochial Vicar; Deacons Elbert A. Kuhns; James M. Sheil.
Catechesis Religious Program—Jennifer Dickerson. Students 31.
BRADDOCK HILLS, ALLEGHENY CO., SACRED HEART (1897) (Polish), Merged with Good Shepherd, Braddock.
BRADDOCK, ALLEGHENY CO., GOOD SHEPHERD (1985) Merged with Sacred Heart, Braddock Hills & Holy Cross, East Pittsburgh.
1024 Maple Way, Braddock, 15104.
Tel: 412-271-1515; Fax: 412-271-1222; Email: gshepoffice@comcast.net; Web: www.goodshepherdbraddock.org. Revs. Lawrence D. Adams, Admin.; Jeremy J. Mohler, Parochial Vicar; Vincent F. Kolo, Chap.; Deacons Joseph M. Dougherty; Keith G. Kondrich.
Res.: 1600 Brinton Rd., 15221.
BRENTWOOD, ALLEGHENY CO., ST. SYLVESTER (1924)
3754 Brownsville Rd., 15227. Tel: 412-882-8593;
Fax: 412-882-0153; Email: office@saintsylvesterparish.org; Web: www.saintsylvesterparish.org. Very Rev. John M. Bachkay, V.F., M.Div., M.Ed.
School—St. Sylvester School, 30 W. Willock Rd., 15227. Tel: 412-882-9900; Fax: 412-882-0153; Email: 54841@diopitt.org. Lay Teachers 11; Students 135.
Catechesis Religious Program—Tel: 412-881-4142;
Tel: 412-882-8593, Ext. 219. Carolyn Eisenbarth, D.R.E. Students 20.
BRIDGEVILLE, ALLEGHENY CO.
1—ST. AGATHA (1894) Closed. See Holy Child.
2—ST. ANTHONY (1915) (Lithuanian), Closed. See Holy Child.
3—ST. BARBARA (1894) [CEM]
45 Prestley Rd., Bridgeville, 15017-1971.
Tel: 412-221-5152; Email: stbarb@comcast.net. Very Rev. Dennis P. Yurochko, J.C.L., S.T.L.; Rev. David G. Rombold. Bridgeville-Cecil Grouping - St. Barbara, St. Mary & Holy Child.
Catechesis Religious Program—Students 267.
4—HOLY CHILD Holy Child (1994) [CEM]
212 Station St., Bridgeville, 15017.
Tel: 412-221-5213; Fax: 412-257-2461; Email: holychildparish@verizon.net; Web: holychildrcparish.org. Very Rev. Dennis P. Yurochko, J.C.L., S.T.L.; Revs. David G. Rombold, Parochial Vicar; Stan M. Gregorek, Chap.; Deacons Lee Miles; Brian M. Podobnik; Leonard M. Thomas Jr. Bridgeville-Cecil Grouping - St. Barbara, St. Mary & Holy Child.
Catechesis Religious Program—Tel: 412-221-6514; Email: holychildccd@comcast.net. Mary Elizabeth Hand, D.R.E. Students 380.
BULGER, WASHINGTON CO., ST. ANN (1917)
965 Grant St., Bulger, 15019. Tel: 724-796-3791;
Tel: 724-796-9151; Fax: 724-796-5173; Email: stannrectory@gmail.com. Mailing Address: 967 Grant St., P.O. Box 488, Bulger, 15019-0488. Revs. Harry R. Bielewicz, V.E., M.Div., Admin.; Zachary A. Galiyas, Parochial Vicar.
Catechesis Religious Program—Colleen Jastrzebski, D.R.E. Students 42.
BURGETTSTOWN, WASHINGTON CO., OUR LADY OF LOURDES (1916) [CEM]
1109 Main St., Burgettstown, 15021.
Tel: 724-947-3363; Fax: 724-947-9348; Email: olol@verizon.net. Rev. Harry R. Bielewicz, V.E., M.Div., Admin.
Catechesis Religious Program—Tel: 724-947-5076; Email: ololccd@verizon.net. Mary Lou Dowler, C.R.E. Students 65.
BUTLER, BUTLER CO.
1—ST. FIDELIS OF SIGMARINGEN (1995)
125 Buttercup Rd., Butler, 16001. Tel: 724-482-2690;
Fax: 724-482-2315. Revs. Kevin C. Fazio, Admin.; John J. Baver, Parochial Vicar; Daniel Waruszewski, Parochial Vicar; William D. Wuenschel, Chap.; Deacon Mitchell M. Natali.
Catechesis Religious Program—Tel: 724-482-2362. Amanda Kramer, C.R.E.; Celine Mitchell, C.R.E. Students 206.
2—ST. MARY OF THE ASSUMPTION (1842) [CEM]
821 Herman Rd., Butler, 16002. Tel: 724-285-3285;
Fax: 724-285-4715; Email: saintmaryinherman@zoominternet.net; Web: www.stsjjmcatholic.org. Revs. Ward Stakem, O.F.M.Cap.; James Kurtz, O.F.M.Cap., Parochial Vicar; Albert Alexandrunas, O.F.M.Cap., In Res.; Victor Kriley, O.F.M.Cap., In Res.; Gary Stakem, O.F.M.Cap., In Res.
Catechesis Religious Program—Barbara Moran, D.R.E. Students 25.
3—ST. MICHAEL THE ARCHANGEL (1909) [CEM] (Italian—French)
432 Center Ave., Butler, 16001. Tel: 724-282-4107;
Fax: 724-282-3156; Email: stmikearch1@zoominternet.net. Revs. Kevin C. Fazio, Admin.; John J. Baver, Parochial Vicar; Daniel Waruszewski, Parochial Vicar; William D. Wuenschel, Chap.; Deacon Mitchell M. Natali.
See Butler Catholic School, Butler under Consolidated Schools located in the Institution section.
Catechesis Religious Program—Sr. Teresa Baldi, S.H.S., D.R.E. Students 40.
4—ST. PAUL (1867) [CEM]
128 N. McKean St., Butler, 16001. Tel: 724-287-1759; Email: stpaulchurch@zoominternet.net; Web: butlercitycatholicparishes.org. Revs. Kevin C. Fazio, Admin.; John J. Baver, Parochial Vicar; Daniel Waruszewski, Parochial Vicar; William D. Wuenschel, Chap.; Deacon Mitchell M. Natali.
Res.: 432 Center Ave., Butler, 16001.
See Butler Catholic School, Butler under Consolidated Schools located in the Institution section.
Catechesis Religious Program—Sr. Teresa Baldi, S.H.S., D.R.E. Students 200.
5—ST. PETER (1821) [CEM] (German)
127 Franklin St., Butler, 16001. Tel: 724-287-2743; Email: stpeterbutler@zoominternet.net; Web: butlercitycatholicparishes.org. Revs. Kevin C. Fazio, Admin.; John J. Baver, Parochial Vicar; Daniel Waruszewski, Parochial Vicar; William D. Wuenschel, Chap.; Deacon Mitchell M. Natali.
Res.: 432 Center Ave., Butler, 16001.
See Butler Catholic School, Butler under Consolidated Schools located in the Institution section.
Catechesis Religious Program—128 N. McKean St., Butler, 16001. Tel: 724-287-1759; Email: stpauloffice@zoominternet.net. Sr. Teresa Baldi, S.H.S., D.R.E. Students 59.
6—ST. WENDELIN (1863) [CEM]

210 Saint Wendelin Rd., Butler, 16002-1065.
Tel: 724-287-0820; Fax: 724-287-6253; Email: parish@stwendelinbutler.org; Web: www.stwendelinbutler.com. Revs. Matthew R. McClain, Admin.; Louis F. Pascazi, Parochial Vicar.
Child Care—Preschool, Tel: 724-285-4986. Students 22.
School—St. Wendelin School, (Grades 1-8), 211 Saint Wendelin Rd., Butler, 16002. Tel: 724-285-4986; Email: Stwend@zoominternet.net. Jolynn Clouse, Prin. Lay Teachers 12; Students 132.
Catechesis Religious Program—Gina Beaver, D.R.E. Students 126.

CABOT, BUTLER CO., ST. JOSEPH (1904)
315 Stoney Hollow Rd., Cabot, 16023.
Tel: 724-352-2149; Email: parishofficesj@yahoo.com; Email: stjosephcabot@zoominternet.net; Web: stsjjmcatholic.org. Revs. Ward Stakem, O.F.M.Cap.; James Kurtz, O.F.M.Cap.
St. Mary Friary, Res.: 821 Herman Rd., Butler, 16002.
Catechesis Religious Program—Tel: 724-352-3030; Fax: 724-352-3443; Email: sjreled@zoominternet.net. Debi Gross, Coord. Faith Formation. Includes Good Shepherd through Grade 8. Students 197; Youth Group 8.

CALIFORNIA, WASHINGTON CO., ST. THOMAS AQUINAS (1888) [CEM] Merged to form St. Katharine Drexel Parish.

CANONSBURG, WASHINGTON CO.
1—ST. GENEVIEVE, (Polish), Closed. See St. Patrick.
2—ST. PATRICK (1892) [CEM] Consolidated with St. Genevieve in 2009. Revs. John J. Batykefer; Camillus Okechukwu Njoku, Parochial Vicar; Deacons Joseph Cerenzia; Philip D. Martorano.
Res.: 317 W. Pike St., Canonsburg, 15317.
Tel: 724-745-6560; Fax: 724-746-1112; Email: stpatparish@verizon.net.
School—St. Patrick School, 200 Murdock St., Canonsburg, 15317. Tel: 724-745-7977;
Fax: 724-746-9778; Email: drmstpats@gmail.com; Web: www.stpatschool.org. Lay Teachers 15; Priests 2; Students 174.
Catechesis Religious Program—Tel: 724-745-3787. Students 479.

CARMICHAELS, GREENE CO., ST. HUGH (1951) (Polish)
408 Rt. 88, Carmichaels, 15320. Tel: 724-966-7270; Fax: 724-966-9118; Email: sthugholcpc@windstream.net. Revs. Albin C. McGinnis, V.F., Admin.; J. Francis Frazer, Parochial Vicar; Deacons Elbert A. Kuhns; James M. Sheil.
Catechesis Religious Program—Students 130.

CARNEGIE, ALLEGHENY CO.
1—ST. ELIZABETH ANN SETON (1992) [CEM] [JC4] (Italian—German)
Mailing Address: 330 3rd Ave., Carnegie, 15106-2519. Tel: 412-276-1011; Email: SEAS@SEAScarnegie.org; Web: www.SEAScarnegie.org. Revs. Robert J. Grecco, M.Div., Admin.; Aleksandr Schrenk, Parochial Vicar; Robin Evanish, Chap.
Catechesis Religious Program—Mary Kay Smith, C.R.E. Students 218.
2—HOLY SOULS, Closed. See St. Elizabeth Ann Seton.
3—ST. IGNATIUS DE LOYOLA, (Polish), Closed. See St. Elizabeth Ann Seton.
4—IMMACULATE CONCEPTION, (Polish), Closed. See St. Elizabeth Ann Seton.
5—ST. JOSEPH, (German), Closed. See St. Elizabeth Ann Seton.
6—ST. LUKE, Closed. See St. Elizabeth Ann Seton.

CASTLE SHANNON, ALLEGHENY CO., ST. ANNE (1889) [CEM]
400 Hoodridge Dr., 15234. Tel: 412-531-5964;
Fax: 412-531-6901; Web: www.stanneparish.com. Revs. Michael A. Caridi, S.T.L.; Richard A. Infante, M.F.A., M.L.S., M.Div., M.A., Parochial Vicar.
School—St. Anne School, 4040 Willow Ave., 15234.
Tel: 412-561-7720; Fax: 412-561-7927; Email: hstewart@saintanneschool.org. Lay Teachers 13; Students 165.
Catechesis Religious Program—Tel: 412-561-0101. Elise Wilson, D.R.E. Students 377.

CECIL, WASHINGTON CO., ST. MARY (1909) [CEM]
10 St. Mary's Ln., Cecil, 15321. Tel: 412-221-1560; Fax: 412-221-9544; Email: stmarysch@comcast.net. Very Rev. Dennis P. Yurochko, J.C.L., S.T.L., Admin.; Revs. David G. Rombold, Parochial Vicar; Stan Gregorkek, Chap.; Deacons Leon F. Miles; Brian M. Podobnik; Leonard M. Thomas Jr. Bridgeville-Cecil Grouping - St. Barbara, St. Mary & Holy Child.
Catechesis Religious Program—19 Cecil Elementary Dr., Cecil, 15321. Tel: 412-221-0595. Students 213.

CENTER TOWNSHIP, BEAVER CO., ST. FRANCES CABRINI (1961)
115 Trinity Dr. Center Twp., Aliquippa, 15001.
Tel: 724-775-6363; Fax: 724-775-3848; Email: info@sfcabrini.us; Web: www.sfcabrini.us. Revs. Martin R. Bartel, O.S.B.; Joachim Morgan, Parochial Vicar; Thomas More Sikora, Parochial Vicar; Deacons Joseph N. Basko; Robert J. Bittner.
Catechesis Religious Program—Tel: 724-774-4888. Deanna Stacho, C.R.E. Students 355.

CENTER TOWNSHIP, BUTLER CO., ST. ANDREW (1964)
1660 N. Main St. Ext., Butler, 16001.
Tel: 724-287-7781; Fax: 724-287-7346; Email: standrewbutler@zoominternet.net. Revs. Kevin C. Fazio, Admin.; John J. Baver, Parochial Vicar; Daniel Waruszewski, Parochial Vicar; William D. Wuenschel, Chap.; Deacon Mitchell M. Natali.
Catechesis Religious Program—Students 90.

CHARLEROI, WASHINGTON CO.
1—SS. CYRIL AND METHODIUS, (Slovak), Closed. See Mary Mother of the Church.
2—ST. JEROME, Closed. See Mary Mother of the Church.
3—MARY MOTHER OF THE CHURCH (1992) [CEM]
624 Washington Ave., Charleroi, 15022-1932.
Tel: 724-483-5533; Fax: 724-483-0122. Rev. Gerald S. Mikonis, (Retired).
Catechesis Religious Program—Students 161.
4—MOTHER OF SORROWS, (Italian), Closed. See Mary Mother of the Church.

CHICORA, BUTLER CO., MATER DOLOROSA (1875)
409 N. Main St., Chicora, 16025. Tel: 724-445-2275; Fax: 724-445-7507; Email: materdol@zoominternet.net. Mailing Address: P.O. Box 243, Chicora, 16025. Revs. Matthew R. McClain; Louis F. Pascazi, Parochial Vicar.
Catechesis Religious Program—Vanessa Birch, D.R.E. Combined with St. Joseph, North Oakland. Students 31.

CHIPPEWA TOWNSHIP, BEAVER CO., CHRIST THE DIVINE TEACHER (1969) Merged with Divine Mercy, Beaver Falls; St. Rose of Lima, Darlington & St. Philomena, Beaver Falls to form St. Monica, Beaver Falls.

CHURCHILL BOROUGH, ALLEGHENY CO., ST. JOHN FISHER (1960)
33 Lewin Ln., 15235. Tel: 412-241-4722;
Fax: 412-241-4653; Email: st_john_fisher@comcast.net. Revs. Frank D. Almade, Ph.D., Admin.; Martin F. Barkin, M.Div., Parochial Vicar; Deacon Herbert E. Riley Jr.
Catechesis Religious Program—Tel: 412-241-4653. Students 210.

CLAIRTON, ALLEGHENY CO.
1—ST. CLARE OF ASSISI (1994) [CEM] Consolidated from the following churches: St. Joseph, St. Paulinus and St. Clare.
Mailing Address: 460 Reed St., Clairton, 15025.
Tel: 412-233-7870; Fax: 412-233-0742; Email: stclareparish2@comcast.net; Web: www.stclareofassisiparish.com. Rev. Charles J. Baptiste.
Catechesis Religious Program— Combined with Holy Spirit Parish, West Mifflin.
2—ST. JOSEPH, Closed. See St. Clare of Assisi.
3—ST. PAULINUS, Closed. See St. Clare of Assisi.

CLARKSVILLE, WASHINGTON CO., ST. THOMAS (1992) (Polish—Italian)
30 Main St., Clarksville, 15322. Tel: 724-377-2588;
Fax: 724-377-0707; Email: stthomastheapostle@atlanticbbn.net. Revs. Albin C. McGinnis, V.F., Admin.; J. Francis Frazer, Parochial Vicar; Deacons Elbert A. Kuhns; James M. Sheil.
Catechesis Religious Program—Students 46.

CONWAY, BEAVER CO., OUR LADY OF PEACE (1941)
Mailing Address: 1000 Third Ave., Conway, 15027.
Tel: 724-869-3024; Fax: 724-869-3025; Web: olopconway.com. Rev. John F. Donahue II, Admin.
Res.: 372 E. End Ave., Beaver, 15009.
Catechesis Religious Program—Tel: 724-869-4723; Email: olopdre@verizon.net. Students 125.

CORAOPOLIS, ALLEGHENY CO., ST. JOSEPH (1891) [CEM]
1304 Fourth Ave., Coraopolis, 15108.
Tel: 412-264-6162; Fax: 412-264-5370; Email: secretary13-4@gmail.com. Revs. Frank M. Kurimsky, Admin.; Sean M. Francis, Parochial Vicar; Michael L. Yaksick, Chap.; Deacon Robert A. Jancart; Kathleen A. Cosnotti, Sec.; Eileen Fratangelo, Sec.
Catechesis Religious Program—1313 Fifth Ave., Coraopolis, 15108. Email: ccdsaintjoseph@gmail.com. Kathleen Petley, Contact Person. Students 93.

COYLESVILLE, BUTLER CO., ST. JOHN THE EVANGELIST (1853) [CEM]
668 Clearfield Rd., Fenelton, 16034.
Tel: 724-287-7590; Fax: 724-287-3550; Email: stjohnchurch@zoominternet.net; Web: stsjjmcatholic.org. Revs. Ward G. Stakem, O.F.M.Cap.; James Kurtz, O.F.M.Cap., Parochial Vicar.
Catechesis Religious Program—Tel: 724-287-0426; Email: stjohnccd@zoominternet.net. Laura Eakman, C.R.E. Students 55.

CRAFTON, ALLEGHENY CO., ST. PHILIP (1839) [CEM] (Irish)
50 W. Crafton Ave., 15205. Tel: 412-922-6300;
Fax: 412-920-7310; Email: parishoffice@saintphilipchurch.org; Web: www.saintphilipchurch.org. Administrative Offices: 114 Berry St., 15205. Revs. John B. Gizler III; Francis J. Murhammer, Parochial Vicar.
Ascension Worship Site, 114 Berry St., 15205.
School—St. Philip School, 52 W. Crafton Ave., 15205. Tel: 412-928-2742; Web: www.spsangelway.org. Lay Teachers 21; Sisters of Charity 1; Students 355.
Catechesis Religious Program—
Tel: 412-922-6300, Ext. 8. Maryann Garfold, D.R.E. Students 150.

CRANBERRY TOWNSHIP, BUTLER CO.
1—ST. FERDINAND (1961)
2535 Rochester Rd., Cranberry Township, 16066-6496. Tel: 724-776-2888; Fax: 724-776-2378; Email: parish@stferd.org. Rev. John P. Gallagher, S.T.L.
Catechesis Religious Program—Tel: 724-776-9177; Fax: 724-776-6640; Email: sue@stferd.org. Students 736.
Saint Ferdinand Parish Charitable Trust - A Pennsylvania Charitable Trust.
2—ST. KILIAN (1917) Revs. Charles S. Bober, S.T.D.; Robert Guay, In Res., (Retired); Deacons Ralph W. Bachner Jr., Pastoral Assoc. & Dir. Evangelization; Robert M. Marshall, Youth Ministry/SKY Ministry (High School); William Carver, Pastoral Care & Institutional Ministry.
Res.: 7076 Franklin Rd., Cranberry Township, 16066-5302. Tel: 724-625-1665; Fax: 724-625-1922; Email: parish@saintkilian.org; Web: www.saintkilian.org.
School—St. Kilian School, (Grades PreK-8),
Tel: 724-625-1665; Fax: 724-625-1922; Email: school@stkilian.org. Lay Teachers 35; Students 627.
Catechesis Religious Program—Mary French, Dir. Faith Formation. Students 878.

CREIGHTON, ALLEGHENY CO., HOLY FAMILY (East Deer Twp.) (1949)
787 Freeport Rd., Creighton, 15030.
Tel: 724-224-1626; Fax: 724-224-0609; Email: holyfamilyparishpa@gmail.com; Web: upperavrcc.org. Revs. John B. Lendvai; Andrew C. Fischer, V.F., M.Div., Parochial Vicar; Aaron J. Kriss, Parochial Vicar; John D. Brennan, Chap.; Deacon Patrick Wood.
Catechesis Religious Program—Jean Tatananni, D.R.E. Students 25.

CRESENT, ALLEGHENY CO., ST. CATHERINE OF SIENA (1959)
199 McGovern Blvd., Crescent, 15046.
Tel: 724-457-7026. Revs. Louis F. Vallone, M.Div., M.A., J.C.B., (Retired); Robert J. Zajdel, M.A.; Deacon Leonard M. Thomas Jr.
Catechesis Religious Program—Students 70.

DARLINGTON, BEAVER CO., ST. ROSE OF LIMA (1854) [CEM] Merged with Christ the Divine Teacher, Beaver Falls; Divine Mercy, Beaver Falls & St. Philomena, Beaver Falls to form St. Monica, Beaver Falls.

DONORA, WASHINGTON CO.
1—ST. CHARLES, Closed. See Our Lady of the Valley.
2—ST. DOMINIC, (Slovak), Closed. See Our Lady of the Valley.
3—HOLY NAME OF THE BLESSED VIRGIN MARY, Closed. See Our Lady of the Valley.
4—OUR LADY OF THE VALLEY (1992) [CEM] Consolidated from the following churches: St. Charles Borromeo, St. Dominic, Holy Name of the Blessed Virgin Mary and St. Philip Neri. Rev. Pierre M. Falkenhan, V.F.
Res.: 1 Park Manor Rd., Donora, 15033.
Tel: 724-379-4777; Fax: 724-379-6242; Email: olv@verizon.net.
Catechesis Religious Program—Mary, Mother of the Church Parish, 624 Washington Rd., Charleroi, 15022-1932. Students 19.
5—ST. PHILIP NERI, (Italian), Closed. See Our Lady of the Valley.

DUQUESNE, ALLEGHENY CO.
1—CHRIST THE LIGHT OF THE WORLD (1994) [CEM 2] Consolidated from St. Hedwig and Holy Name. Rev. Thomas J. Lewandowski.
Res.: 32 S. First St., Duquesne, 15110.
Tel: 412-469-0196; Fax: 412-466-6845; Email: 09901@diopitt.org.
Catechesis Religious Program—Students 130.
2—HOLY NAME, Closed. See Christ the Light of the World.
3—ST. JOSEPH (1897) [CEM] (German)
32 S. First St., Duquesne, 15110. Tel: 412-469-0196; Fax: 412-466-6845; Email: 27101@diopitt.org. Rev. Thomas J. Lewandowski; Deacon Barry A. Krofcheck.
Catechesis Religious Program—Twinned with Christ the Light of the World. Students 18.

EAST MCKEESPORT, ALLEGHENY CO., ST. ROBERT BELLARMINE (1951)
1313 Fifth Ave., East McKeesport, 15035.
Tel: 412-824-2644; Fax: 412-824-4786; Email: strobertbellarmine@comcast.net; Web: saintrobertbellarmine.org. Revs. Terrence P. O'Connor, M.Div., J.D., Admin.; Jack Demnyan, Parochial Vicar; Joseph C. Beck, Chap.; Deacons Dale J. DiSanto; Reynold Wilmer.

Catechesis Religious Program—1301 Fifth Ave., East McKeesport, 15035. Tel: 412-824-3688; Email: srbcf@comcast.net. Students 112.

EAST PITTSBURGH, ALLEGHENY CO.

1—ST. HELEN, (Slovak), Closed. See Holy Cross.

2—HOLY CROSS (1994) Closed. Merged with Good Shepherd, Braddock.

3—ST. WILLIAM, Closed. See Holy Cross.

ELIZABETH, ALLEGHENY CO., ST. MICHAEL (1851) [CEM] 101 McLay Dr., Elizabeth, 15037. Tel: 412-751-0663; Fax: 412-751-2161; Email: 40101@diopitt.org. Rev. Thomas A. Wagner.

Catechesis Religious Program—Students 260.

ELLWOOD CITY, LAWRENCE CO.

1—ST. AGATHA (1895) (Territorial), Merged with Purification of the Blessed Virgin Mary, Ellwood City to form Holy Redeemer, Ellwood City.

2—HOLY REDEEMER PARISH (2000) [CEM] 415 4th St., Ellwood City, 16117. Tel: 724-758-4411; Fax: 724-752-1466; Web: www.holyredeemerparishpgh.com. Revs. John P. Gallagher, S.T.L., Admin.; Mark L. Thomas, S.T.L., Parochial Vicar; James R. Torquato, Parochial Vicar; James G. Young, M.Div., Chap., (Retired); Deacon Donald C. Pepe.

Catechesis Religious Program—603 Bridge St., Ellwood City, 16117. Fax: 724-752-1271; Email: hrreledu@zoominternet.net; Web: www.holyredeemerpgh.com. Students 260.

Convent—300 Crescent Ave., Ellwood City, 16117. Tel: 724-758-3741.

3—PURIFICATION OF THE BLESSED VIRGIN MARY (1914) Merged with St. Agatha, Ellwood City to form Holy Redeemer, Ellwood City.

ELRAMA, ALLEGHENY CO., ST. ISAAC JOGUES (1950) Mailing Address: 3609 Washington Ave., Finleyville, 15332. Tel: 412-384-4406; Fax: 412-384-5740; Email: stisaac@comcast.net. Revs. Richard J. Tusky, Parochial Vicar, (Retired); Robert Miller.

Church: 1216 Collins Ave., Jefferson Hills, 15025.

Catechesis Religious Program—Students 45.

EMSWORTH, ALLEGHENY CO., SACRED HEART (1891) 154 Orchard Ave., Emsworth, 15202. Tel: 412-761-6651; Fax: 412-766-8298; Email: sacredheartemsworth@gmail.com; Web: www.sacredheartavonworth.org. Very Rev. John M. Bachkay, V.F., M.Div., M.Ed., Admin.; Revs. David Green, Parochial Vicar; Kenneth R. Keene, M.Div., Parochial Vicar.

Catechesis Religious Program—Students 120.

Mission—Sacred Heart.

ETNA, ALLEGHENY CO., ALL SAINTS (1902) 19 Wilson St., 15223-1798. Tel: 412-781-0530; Fax: 412-784-8769; Email: 01701@diopitt.org. Revs. James R. Gretz, D.Min., MTS, Admin.; James K. Mazurek, M.Div., Parochial Vicar; Miroslaw Stelmaszczyk, Parochial Vicar; Gerald J. Lutz, In Res., (Retired); Deacons Stephen J. Byers; Stephen J. Kisak; Charles H. Rhoads.

Catechesis Religious Program—Tel: 412-781-5183; Fax: 412-781-5273; Email: allsaintsreled@comcast.net. Students 100.

SOCIAL SERVICE, Tel: 412-781-0530.

EVANS CITY, BUTLER CO., ST. MATTHIAS (1939) Merged into St. Gregory Parish.

FINLEYVILLE, WASHINGTON CO., ST. FRANCIS OF ASSISI (1893) [CEM] 3609 Washington Ave., Finleyville, 15332. Tel: 724-348-7145; Fax: 724-348-7522; Email: stfran1893@comcast.net. Revs. Robert Miller, Admin.; Pierre M. Falkenhan, V.F.; Robert L. Seeman; Deacon Victor P. Satter. Grouping With St. Benedict the Abbot, St. Isaac Jogues.

Catechesis Religious Program—Tel: 724-348-6190. Carol Cicci, D.R.E. Students 130.

FOREST HILLS, ALLEGHENY CO., ST. MAURICE (1949) 2001 Ardmore Blvd., 15221. Tel: 412-271-0809; Fax: 412-271-2415; Email: jkosar@saintmauriceparish.org. Revs. Larry Adams, Admin.; Jeremy J. Mohler, Parochial Vicar; Vincent F. Kolo, Chap.; Daniel A. Adjei, In Res.

School—East Catholic School, Tel: 412-351-5403; Fax: 412-273-9114; Email: principal@eastcatholicschool.org; Web: www.eastcatholicschool.org. Sr. Judith Stojhovic, Prin. Lay Teachers 17; Students 250; Clergy 1.

Catechesis Religious Program—Tel: 412-351-6710. Students 120.

FRANKLIN PARK BOROUGH, ALLEGHENY CO.

1—ST. JOHN NEUMANN (1979) Mailing Address: 2230 Rochester Rd., 15237. Tel: 412-366-2020; Fax: 412-366-2866; Email: jkiliany@stjohnneumannpgh.org. Rev. Albin C. McGinnis, V.F.

Res.: 1543 Old Orchard Rd., 15237.

Catechesis Religious Program—2230 Rochester Rd., 15237. Tel: 412-366-5885. Students 740.

2—SAINTS JOHN AND PAUL (1994) 2586 Wexford-Bayne Rd., Sewickley, 15143. Tel: 724-935-2104; Fax: 724-935-8320; Email: info@sts-jp.org. Revs. John F. Donahue II, Admin.; John J. Batykefer, Parochial Vicar; Michael J. Roche, Parochial Vicar; Joseph A. Carr, Chap.

Catechesis Religious Program—Students 1,235.

FREDERICKTOWN, WASHINGTON CO.

1—ST. MICHAEL THE ARCHANGEL, Closed. See St. Oliver Plunkett, Marianna.

2—ST. OLIVER PLUNKETT (1994) [CEM] Merged Consolidated from Saints Mary & Ann, Marianna, and St. Michael Archangel, Fredericktown before parish closed to become part of St. Katharine Drexel.

FREEDOM, BEAVER CO., ST. FELIX (1906) [CEM] 450 13th St., Freedom, 15042. Tel: 724-775-1476; Email: secretary@stfelix.comcasbiz.net. Revs. Paul Kuppe, O.F.M.Cap.; Mark Carter, O.F.M.Cap., Parochial Vicar.

Catechesis Religious Program—Danielle Tabin, D.R.E. Students 23.

GLADE MILLS, BUTLER CO., HOLY SEPULCHER (1955) 1304 E. Cruikshank Rd., Butler, 16002. Tel: 724-586-7610; Fax: 724-586-7247; Web: www.holysepulcher.org. Rev. Charles S. Bober, S.T.D.; Deacon David S. Miller.

School—Holy Sepulcher School, (Grades PreK-8), 6515 Old Rte. 8, Butler, 16002. Tel: 724-586-5022; Fax: 724-586-5073; Email: 19041@diopitt.org. Sr. Anna Marie Gaglia, C.S.J., Prin. Lay Teachers 12; Students 134; Religious Teachers 1.

Catechesis Religious Program—Tel: 724-586-7276. Sr. Benita DeMatteis, O.S.B., Dir. Faith Formation. Students 309.

GLASSPORT, ALLEGHENY CO.

1—ST. CECILIA, Closed. See Queen of the Rosary.

2—QUEEN OF THE ROSARY (1994) [JC] Consolidated from Holy Cross and St. Cecilia. Rev. Miroslaus A. Wojcicki, Admin.

Res.: 530 Michigan Ave., Glassport, 15045. Tel: 412-672-7209; Fax: 412-672-6390; Email: qorglasspt@comcast.net.

Catechesis Religious Program—Students 42.

GLENSHAW, ALLEGHENY CO.

1—ST. BONAVENTURE (1957) 2001 Mt. Royal Blvd., Glenshaw, 15116. Tel: 412-486-2606; Fax: 412-492-9329; Email: parish@stbonaventureparish.org. Revs. James R. Gretz, D.Min., MTS, Admin.; James K. Mazurek, M.Div., Parochial Vicar; Miroslaw Stelmaszczyk, Parochial Vicar; Deacons Stephen J. Byers; Stephen J. Kisak; Charles H. Rhoads.

Catechesis Religious Program—
Tel: 412-486-2606, Ext. 200. Faith Mosher, C.R.E. Students 400.

2—ST. MARY OF THE ASSUMPTION (1834) [CEM] Merged with St. Ursula.

2510 Middle Rd., Glenshaw, 15116. Tel: 412-486-4100; Fax: 412-486-4150; Email: rectory@stmaryglenshaw.org; Web: www.stmaryglenshaw.org. Rev. Timothy F. Whalen, M.Div., M.A.; Deacon Francis J. Dadowski Jr.

Catechesis Religious Program—Tel: 412-486-5521; Fax: 412-486-5177. Rose Stegman, Dir. Faith Formation. Students 405.

GREEN TREE, ALLEGHENY CO., ST. MARGARET (1938) 310 Mansfield Ave., 15220. Tel: 412-921-0745; Fax: 412-921-0707; Email: parish@stmargparish.org; Web: stmargparish.org. Revs. Robert J. Grecco, M.Div., Admin.; Aleksandr Schrenk, Parochial Vicar.

School—St. Margaret School, (Grades PreK-8), 915 Alice St., 15220. Tel: 412-922-4765; Fax: 412-922-4647; Email: rmunz@stmargschool.com; Web: www.stmargschool.com. Robert Munz, Prin. Lay Teachers 13; Students 154.

Catechesis Religious Program—Tel: 412-921-1613; Fax: 412-921-0707. Nancy Spinneweber, C.R.E. Students 110.

HARMAR, ALLEGHENY CO., ST. FRANCIS OF ASSISI (1940) Merged to form St. Pio of Pietrelcina Parish, Pittsburgh.

HARWICK, ALLEGHENY CO., OUR LADY OF VICTORY (1944) 1319 Low Grade Rd., Harwick, 15049. Tel: 724-274-8575; Fax: 724-274-0529; Email: olov1@verizon.net; Web: upperavrcc.org. Revs. John B. Lendvai, Admin.; Andrew C. Fischer, V.F., M.Div., Parochial Vicar; Aaron J. Kriss, Parochial Vicar; John D. Brennan, Chap.; Deacon Patrick G. Wood.

Catechesis Religious Program—Email: olovreligioused@outlook.com. Students 26.

HILLSVILLE, LAWRENCE CO.

1—CHRIST THE KING (2000) [CEM 2] Mailing Address: P.O. Box 23, Hillsville, 16132. 175 Martin Kelly Spear Rd., Hillsville, 16132. Tel: 724-667-7721; Fax: 724-667-0827; Email: 09301@diopitt.org. Revs. Joseph R. McCaffrey, Admin.; Anthony R. Sciarappa; William P. Siple; Victor J. Molka Jr., Chap.; Deacon John J. Carran, Deacon Admin.

Catechesis Religious Program—Students 83.

2—ST. LAWRENCE (1904) (Italian), Merged with St. Anthony, Bessemer to form Christ the King, Hillsville.

HOLIDAY PARK, ALLEGHENY CO., OUR LADY OF JOY (1968) Rev. Albert L. Zapf; Gregory Callaghan, Pastoral Assoc.

Res.: 2000 O'Block Rd., 15239. Tel: 412-795-3388; Fax: 412-793-5308; Email: p@ourladyofjoy.org.

Catechesis Religious Program—Tel: 412-795-4389. Jane Siatkosky, C.R.E. Students 370.

HOMESTEAD, ALLEGHENY CO.

1—ST. ANNE, Closed. See St. Maximilian Kolbe, Homestead.

2—ST. ANTHONY, Closed. See St. Maximilian Kolbe, Homestead.

3—ST. MARY MAGDALENE, Closed. See St. Maximilian Kolbe, Homestead.

4—ST. MAXIMILIAN KOLBE (1992) [CEM 3] Consolidated from the following churches: St. Anne, Homestead; St. Anthony, Homestead; St. Margaret, Homestead; St. Mary Magdalene, Homestead; St. Michael, Homestead; SS. Peter & Paul, Homestead. Rev. E. Daniel Sweeney. In Res., Revs. Mark W. Glasgow, Tel: 412-462-1807; Martin Ene.

Parish Center: 363 W. 11th Ave. Ext., Homestead, 15120. Tel: 412-461-1054; Fax: 412-462-1744; Email: stmaximiliankolbe@comcast.net.

Catechesis Religious Program—Students 74.

5—SS. PETER AND PAUL, (Lithuanian), Closed. See St. Maximilian Kolbe, Homestead.

HOPEWELL TOWNSHIP, BEAVER CO., OUR LADY OF FATIMA (1954) 2270 Brodhead Rd., Aliquippa, 15001. Tel: 724-375-7626; Fax: 724-375-0219; Email: olofo1@yahoo.com; Web: www.olof.us. Revs. Martin R. Bartel, O.S.B., Admin.; Joachim Morgan, Parochial Vicar; Thomas More Sikora, Parochial Vicar; Deacons Joseph N. Basko; Robert J. Bittner.

School—Our Lady of Fatima School, (Grades PreK-8), Tel: 724-375-7565; Email: olofschool@yahoo.com. Mrs. Cindy Baldrige, Prin.; Rev. Martin R. Bartel, O.S.B., Admin. Students 177.

Catechesis Religious Program—Tel: 724-378-8020. Students 200.

IMPERIAL, ALLEGHENY CO., ST. COLUMBKILLE (1908) [CEM] 103 Church Rd., Imperial, 15126. Tel: 724-695-7325; Fax: 724-695-9202; Email: stcolumbkilleparish@comcast.net. Revs. Harry R. Bielewicz, V.E., M.Div., Admin.; Zachary A. Galiyas, Parochial Vicar.

Catechesis Religious Program—101 Church Rd., Imperial, 15126. Tel: 724-695-2146. Students 493.

INDUSTRY, BEAVER CO., ST. CHRISTINE, Closed. See St. Blaise, Midland.

INGRAM, ALLEGHENY CO., ASCENSION (1967) Merged into St. Philip.

JEFFERSON HILLS, ALLEGHENY CO., ST. THOMAS A'BECKET (1957) 139 Gill Hall Rd., Jefferson Hills, 15025. Tel: 412-655-2885; Fax: 412-655-0615; Email: becketst@comcast.net; Web: www.saintthomasabecket.com. Rev. Robert J. Cedolia, M.Div., M.A., Admin.

Catechesis Religious Program—Tel: 412-653-4322; Fax: 412-653-9979. Sr. Dolores Ann Therasse, S.C.N., D.R.E. Students 502.

Convent—Tel: 412-655-4122.

KENNEDY TOWNSHIP, ALLEGHENY CO., ST. MALACHY (1953) 343 Forest Grove Rd., Coraopolis, 15108. Tel: 412-771-5483; Fax: 412-331-7312; Email: parish@stmalachypgh.org. Revs. David G. Poecking, S.T.L., Admin.; Alan E. Morris, Parochial Vicar; Robert J. Zajdel, M.A., Parochial Vicar; Michael R. Ruffalo, Chap.

School—St. Malachy School, (Grades PreSchool-8), Tel: 412-771-4545; Email: schooloffice@stmalachyschool.net. Lay Teachers 11; Students 196.

Catechesis Religious Program—Tel: 412-771-7480. Students 282.

KOPPEL, BEAVER CO.

1—QUEEN OF HEAVEN (1992) Closed. For inquiries for parish records contact the chancery. Consolidated from St. Monica, Wampum and St. Teresa, Koppel.

2—ST. TERESA, Closed. See Queen of Heaven.

LAWRENCE, WASHINGTON CO., ST. ELIZABETH, Closed. See St. Mary, Cecil.

LIBERTY BORO, ALLEGHENY CO., ST. EUGENE, Closed. See St. Mark, Port Vue.

LYNDORA, BUTLER CO.

1—ST. JOHN (1904) (Slovak), Closed. See St. Fidelis of Sigmaringen, Butler.

2—ST. STANISLAUS KOSTKA (1919) (Polish), Merged with St. Conrad, Meridian and St. John, Lyndora, to form St. Fidelis, Butler.

MCDONALD, WASHINGTON CO., ST. ALPHONSUS (1892) 219 W. Lincoln Ave., McDonald, 15057. Tel: 724-926-2984; Fax: 724-926-9251; Email: st.alphonsus@verizon.net. Rev. Harry R. Bielewicz, V.E., M.Div.

Catechesis Religious Program—Tel: 724-926-2160; Email: st.alphonsusccd@gmail.com. Brenda Ford. Students 83.

MCKEES ROCKS, ALLEGHENY CO.
1—SS. CYRIL AND METHODIUS, (Polish), Closed. See St. John of God.
2—ST. FRANCIS DE SALES, Closed. See St. John of God.
3—ST. JOHN OF GOD (1993) [CEM 2]
1011 Church Ave., McKees Rocks, 15136.
Tel: 412-771-5646; Fax: 412-331-0678; Email: parish@sjogparish.com; Web: www.sjogparish.com. Revs. David G. Poecking, S.T.L., Admin.; Alan E. Morris, Parochial Vicar; Robert J. Zajdel, M.A., Parochial Vicar; Michael R. Ruffalo, Chap.; Regis J. Ryan, In Res., (Retired); Deacons Leonard M. Thomas Jr.; Tim M. Killmeyer; Elna Johnson, Music Min.
4—ST. MARIA GORETTI CHAPEL, Closed. See St. John of God.
5—ST. MARK, (Slovak), Closed. See St. John of God.
6—ST. MARY HELP OF CHRISTIANS, (German), Closed. See St. John of God.
7—MOTHER OF SORROWS, (Italian), Closed. See St. John of God.
MCKEESPORT, ALLEGHENY CO.
1—CORPUS CHRISTI PARISH
2515 Versailles Ave., McKeesport, 15132.
Tel: 412-672-0765; Email: corpuschristi3@comcast.net; Web: corpuschristimckeesport.com. Rev. Terrence P. O'Connor, M.Div., J.D.
2—HOLY TRINITY, Closed. See St. Martin de Porres.
3—ST. MARTIN DE PORRES (1993) [CEM 3] Closed. For inquiries for parish records contact the chancery.
4—ST. MARY, (German), Closed. For inquiries for parish records contact the chancery.
5—ST. MARY CZESTOCHOWA (1893) [CEM] (Polish), Closed. For inquiries for parish records contact the chancery.
6—ST. PATRICK (1993) [CEM] Merged with St. Denis, Versailles and St. Perpetua, McKeesport.
310 32nd St., McKeesport, 15132. Tel: 412-673-4110; Fax: 412-678-7259; Email: stpatmck@comcast.net; Web: www.stpatrickmckeesport.com. Rev. Terrence P. O'Connor, M.Div., J.D., Admin.
Catechesis Religious Program—305 32nd St., McKeesport, 15132. Students 43.
7—ST. PERPETUA, Closed. See St. Patrick, Versailles.
8—ST. PETER, Closed. For inquiries for parish records contact the chancery.
9—ST. PIUS V (1903) [CEM] Closed. For inquiries for parish records contact the chancery.
10—SACRED HEART, (Croatian), Closed. For inquiries for parish records contact the chancery.
11—ST. STEPHEN (1899) (Hungarian), Closed. See St. Pius V.
MEADOW LANDS, WASHINGTON CO., OUR LADY OF THE MIRACULOUS MEDAL (1949) [JC] Combined with St. Patrick, Canonsburg & Holy Rosary, Muse
300 Pike St., P.O. Box 366, Meadow Lands, 15347.
Tel: 724-222-1911; Tel: 724-206-9677 (Spanish);
Fax: 724-222-5688; Email: olmm@comcast.net. Rev. Carmen A. D'Amico, V.F., M.Div.
Catechesis Religious Program—Tel: 724-228-9088; Tel: 724-228-8575 (CCD Activities Center);
Fax: 724-228-1488; Email: rgeckehs@comcast.net. Students 144.
MERIDIAN, BUTLER CO., ST. CONRAD, Merged with St. John and St. Stanislaus Kostka, Lyndora to form St. Fidelis, Butler.
MIDLAND, BEAVER CO., ST. BLAISE (1994)
772 Ohio Ave., Midland, 15059. Tel: 724-643-4050;
Fax: 724-643-6533; Email: office@stblaiseparish.com. Rev. Kim J. Schreck, S.T.L.
Catechesis Religious Program—Tel: 724-643-4663. Students 137.
MILLVALE, ALLEGHENY CO.
1—ST. ANN, Closed. See Holy Spirit.
2—ST. ANTHONY, (German), Closed. See Holy Spirit.
3—HOLY SPIRIT (1994) Formerly St. Anthony and St. Ann.
Mailing Address: 608 Farragut St., 15209.
Tel: 412-821-4424; Fax: 412-253-4732; Email: pastor@holyspiritmillvale.org. Rev. James R. Gretz, D.Min., MTS; Deacon Stephen J. Kisak.
Catechesis Religious Program—Tel: 412-821-2099. Students 127.
4—ST. NICHOLAS, (Croatian), Closed. See the new St. Nicholas.
5—ST. NICHOLAS (1894) [JC2] (Croatian)
24 Maryland Ave., 15209-2738. Tel: 412-821-3438;
Fax: 412-821-8726; Email: office@holyspiritmillvale.org. Revs. James R. Gretz, D.Min., MTS, Admin.; James K. Mazurek, M.Div., Parochial Vicar; Miroslaw Stelmaszczyk, Parochial Vicar; Deacons Stephen J. Byers; Stephen J. Kisak; Charles H. Rhoads.
Catechesis Religious Program—Clustered with Holy Spirit Parish, Millvale. Students 10.
MONACA, BEAVER CO., ST. JOHN THE BAPTIST (1888) [CEM]
1501 Virginia Ave., Monaca, 15061.
Tel: 724-775-3940; Fax: 724-775-6886; Email: officesjbp@gmail.com; Web: www.stjbparish.org. Revs. Martin R. Bartel, O.S.B., Admin.; Joachim Morgan, Parochial Vicar; Thomas More Sikora, Parochial Vicar; Deacons Joseph N. Basko; Robert J. Bittner.
Res.: 1409 Pennsylvania Ave., Monaca, 15061. Email: pastoralassociate@stjbparish.org.
Catechesis Religious Program—Tel: 724-775-2389. Students 148.
MONONGAHELA, WASHINGTON CO.
1—ST. ANTHONY (1904) [CEM] (Italian—Slovak), Merged with Transfiguration, Monongahela to become St. Damien of Molokai Parish, Monongahela.
2—ST. DAMIEN OF MOLOKAI PARISH (2011) [CEM 2]
722 W. Main St., Monongahela, 15063.
Tel: 724-258-7742; Fax: 724-258-8733. Rev. William R. Terza.
Catechesis Religious Program—Students 169.
3—TRANSFIGURATION (1865) [CEM 2] Merged with St. Anthony, Monongahela to become St. Damien of Molokai Parish, Monongahela.
MONROEVILLE, ALLEGHENY CO.
1—ST. BERNADETTE (1955)
245 Azalea Dr., Monroeville, 15146.
Tel: 412-373-0050; Fax: 412-374-8113; Email: 07201@diopitt.org. Rev. Anthony Gargotta, M.Div., M.A.; Deacon Michael W. Kelly.
School—St. Bernadette School, (Grades PreK-8),
Tel: 412-372-7255; Fax: 412-372-7649; Email: schooloffice@stbrnadet.org. Lay Teachers 23; Students 275; Religious Teachers 1.
Catechesis Religious Program—Tel: 412-373-1797; Email: mvkopper@stbrnadet.org. Marlene Kopper, D.R.E. Students 325.
2—NORTH AMERICAN MARTYRS (2010)
2526 Haymaker Rd., Monroeville, 15146.
Tel: 412-373-0330; Fax: 412-380-1306; Email: office@namcatholicchurch.org. Rev. Richard J. Thompson, In Res.
Catechesis Religious Program—Tel: 412-349-0942. Students 180.
MOON TOWNSHIP, ALLEGHENY CO., ST. MARGARET MARY (1956) Revs. Frank M. Kurimsky; Michael L. Yaksick, Chap.; Sean M. Francis, In Res.; Deacon Robert A. Jancart; Sherri Kappas, Business Mgr.
Res.: One Parish Place, Moon Township, 15108-2697.
Tel: 412-264-2573; Fax: 412-264-4327; Email: contactus@stmargaretmary-moon.org.
Catechesis Religious Program—Tel: 412-264-9368; Email: reoffice@stmargaretmary-moon.org. Kathleen Petley, C.R.E. Students 435.
MT. LEBANON, ALLEGHENY CO.
1—ST. BERNARD (1919) Merged with Our Lady of Grace, Scott Twp.
311 Washington Rd., 15216. Tel: 412-561-3300;
Fax: 412-563-0211; Email: dbonnar@stbpgh.org; Web: stbernardchurchpgh.org. Revs. David J. Bonnar, V.E., S.T.B., Admin.; Benjamin Barr, Parochial Vicar; Thomas Gramc, Parochial Vicar; Robin S. Evanish, Chap.; Gilbert Z. Puznakoski, Chap.; Very Rev. Mark A. Eckman, V.E., M.Div., In Res.; Deacons Frederick N. Eckhardt; Lawrence R. Sutton, Ph.D.
School—St. Bernard School, (Grades PreK-8), 401 Washington Rd., 15216. Tel: 412-341-5444;
Fax: 412-341-2044; Email: 07341@diopitt.org; Web: www.stbschool.net. Regina Glitz, Librarian. Lay Teachers 22; Students 265.
Catechesis Religious Program—Tel: 412-561-0199;
Fax: 412-561-1005; Web: stbernardchurch.com/ccd. Students 778.
2—ST. WINIFRED (Pittsburgh) (1960)
550 Sleepy Hollow Rd., 15228. Tel: 412-344-5010;
Fax: 412-563-7279; Email: winoffice@comcast.net. Revs. Michael A. Caridi, S.T.L., Admin.; Richard A. Infante, M.F.A., M.L.S., M.Div., M.A., Parochial Vicar; Deacon Joseph J. Kosko Jr.
Catechesis Religious Program—Tel: 412-563-1414. Colette Speca, Dir. Faith Formation; Dana Mahr, Dir. Faith Formation (7-12). Students 157.
MUNHALL, ALLEGHENY CO.
1—ST. MARGARET, Closed. See St. Maximilian Kolbe, Homestead.
2—ST. MICHAEL, (Slovak), Closed. See St. Maximilian Kolbe, Homestead.
3—ST. RITA (1936) Merged with Resurrection, West Mifflin.
219 W. Schwab Ave., Munhall, 15120.
Tel: 412-461-8087; Fax: 412-461-0142; Email: resurrection15122@gmail.com; Web: resurrection-strita.org. 1 Majka Dr., West Mifflin, 15122. Revs. E. Daniel Sweeney, Admin.; Nicholas Mastrangelo, Parochial Vicar.
Catechesis Religious Program—St. Rita, Combined with Resurrection, West Mifflin. Tel: 412-461-5787. Students 15.
4—ST. THERESE OF LISIEUX (1925)
1 St. Therese Ct., Munhall, 15120-3701.
Tel: 412-462-8161; Fax: 412-462-4817; Email: cpicciafoco@st-therese.net. Revs. Terrence P. O'Connor, M.Div., J.D.; Nicholas Mastrangelo, Parochial Vicar; Emmanuel Abbey-Quaye, In Res.; Ms. Lori Ellis, Pastoral Assoc.
School—St. Therese of Lisieux School, 3 St. Therese Ct., Munhall, 15120. Tel: 412-462-8163;
Fax: 412-462-5865; Email: sttherese@sttheresesschoolmunhall.org; Web: www.sttheresesschoolmunhall.org. Jonathan Cuniak, Prin. Lay Teachers 20; Students 305.
Catechesis Religious Program—Students 165.
MUSE, WASHINGTON CO., HOLY ROSARY (1963)
One Orchard St., P.O. Box 447, Muse, 15350-0447.
Tel: 724-745-3531; Fax: 724-745-0669; Email: administrator@holyrosarymuse.org; Web: www.holyrosarymuse.org. Revs. Carmen A. D'Amico, V.F., M.Div., Admin.; George T. DeVille, Parochial Vicar; Thomas L. Gillespie, Parochial Vicar; Thomas J. Galvin, Chap.; Robert M. Staszewski, In Res., (Retired); Deacons Joseph Cerenzia; Philip D. Martorano; Anton V. Mobley.
Catechesis Religious Program—Clyde House, D.R.E. Students 240.
NATRONA HEIGHTS, ALLEGHENY CO.
1—BLESSED SACRAMENT, Closed. See Our Lady of the Most Blessed Sacrament.
2—OUR LADY OF PERPETUAL HELP, Closed. See Our Lady of the Most Blessed Sacrament.
3—OUR LADY OF THE MOST BLESSED SACRAMENT (1992) (Slovak)
1526 Union Ave., Natrona Heights, 15065-2008.
Tel: 724-226-4900; Fax: 724-224-3559; Email: churchoffice@olmbs.org. Revs. John B. Lendvai, Admin.; Andrew C. Fischer, Parochial Vicar; Aaron J. Kriss, Parochial Vicar; John D. Brennan, Chap.; Deacon Patrick Wood.
School—Our Lady of the Most Blessed Sacrament School, 800 Montana Ave., Natrona Heights, 15065.
Tel: 724-226-2345; Fax: 724-226-4934; Email: leadadmin@olmbs.org; Web: www.olmbss.org. Rev. John Lendvai, Admin. Lay Teachers 12; Students 168; Religious Teachers 2.
Catechesis Religious Program—Tel: 724-224-3339;
Fax: 724-226-8655; Email: olmbsccd@verizon.net. Students 150.
NATRONA, ALLEGHENY CO.
1—ST. JOSEPH (1992) [CEM] [JC]
Mailing Address: 1526 Union Ave., Natrona Heights, 15065. Tel: 724-224-1336; Fax: 724-224-3559; Email: stjosephnatrona@hotmail.com. Revs. John B. Lendvai, Admin.; Andrew C. Fischer, V.F., M.Div., Parochial Vicar; Aaron J. Kriss, Parochial Vicar; John D. Brennan, Chap.; Deacon Patrick G. Wood.
Res.: 1283 Carolina & 10th Sts., Natrona Heights, 15065. Tel: 724-226-4903.
High School—St. Joseph High School, 800 Montana Ave., Natrona Heights, 15065. Tel: 724-224-5552;
Fax: 724-224-0235; Email: bkaniecki@saintjosephhs.com. Students 200.
Catechesis Religious Program—Tel: 724-224-3339; Email: ccd@olmbs.org. Clustered with Our Lady of the Most Blessed Sacrament, Natrona Heights. Students 150.
2—ST. LADISLAUS, (Polish), Closed. See St. Joseph.
3—ST. MATHIAS, Closed. See St. Joseph.
NEMACOLIN, GREENE CO., OUR LADY OF CONSOLATION (1923) [CEM] (Polish)
837 Wood St. Extension, Nemacolin, 15351.
Tel: 724-966-7270; Email: sthugholcpc@windstream.net. 408 Rte. 88, Carmichaels, 15320. Revs. Albin C. McGinnis, V.F., Admin.; J. Francis Frazer, Parochial Vicar; Deacons Elbert A. Kuhns; James M. Sheil.
Catechesis Religious Program— CCD & Youth Group combined with St. Hugh Parish. All clases held at Ft. Hugh church. Linette Kerr, D.R.E.
Missions—Sacred Heart—Rices Landing, Greene Co.
St. Mary, Crucible, Greene Co.
NESHANNOCK, LAWRENCE CO., ST. CAMILLUS DE LELLIS (1959)
314 W. Englewood Ave., New Castle, 16105-1806.
Tel: 724-652-9471; Fax: 724-654-1430; Email: rectory@stcamillusparish.org. Revs. Joseph R. McCaffrey, Admin.; Anthony R. Sciarappa, Parochial Vicar; William P. Siple, Parochial Vicar; Victor J. Molka Jr., Chap.; Sisters Annie Bremmer, Pastoral Assoc.; Barbara Ann Johnston, C.S.J., Pastoral Assoc.; Deacons John J. Carran; S. Daniel Kielar.
Catechesis Religious Program—Students 236.
NEW BRIGHTON, BEAVER CO.
1—SS. CYRIL AND METHODIUS, (Slovak), Closed. See Holy Family.
2—HOLY FAMILY (1994) [CEM]
521 7th Ave., New Brighton, 15066.
Tel: 724-847-3538; Email: hfp18001@verizon.net; Web: holyfamilynb.com. 1851 3rd Ave., New Brighton, 15066. Rev. Robert J. Miller, M.Div., M.A., Admin.; Larry Tavlarides, Music Min.
Catechesis Religious Program—Tel: 724-846-9622. Suzan Bauer, D.R.E. Students 130.
3—ST. JOSEPH, Closed. See Holy Family.
NEW CASTLE, LAWRENCE CO.
1—ST. JOSEPH THE WORKER (1888) [JC]
Mailing Address: 910 S. Mercer St., New Castle, 16101. 1111 S. Cascade St., New Castle, 16101.
Tel: 724-658-1683; Fax: 724-652-2322; Email: cascade1111@comcast.net; Web: www.catholicnewcastle.org. Revs. Joseph R. McCaffrey,

Admin.; Anthony R. Sciarappa; William P. Siple; Victor J. Molka Jr., Chap.; Deacons John J. Carran, Admin.; S. Daniel Kielar.
Res.: 124 N. Beaver St., New Castle, 16101.
Tel: 724-658-2564; Fax: 724-658-9024.
Catechesis Religious Program—Tel: 724-698-7136; Fax: 724-654-7076; Email: ladyjoe04@aol.com. Louis Bosco, CCD-Jr. High; Sheryl Skowronski, CCD. Students 111.
2—St. Lucy, (Italian), Closed. See St. Vincent de Paul.
3—Madonna of Czestochowa, Closed. See Mary, Mother of Hope.
4—St. Margaret, Closed. See St. Vincent de Paul.
5—St. Mary, Closed. See Mary, Mother of Hope.
6—Mary, Mother of Hope (1993) [CEM] [JC] (Irish—Polish)
910 S. Mercer St., New Castle, 16101. Revs. Joseph R. McCaffrey, Admin.; Anthony R. Sciarappa, Parochial Vicar; William P. Siple, Parochial Vicar; Victor J. Molka Jr., Chap.; Deacons John J. Carran, Admin.; S. Daniel Kielar.
Res.: 124 N. Beaver St., New Castle, 16101.
Tel: 724-658-2564; Fax: 724-652-2322; Email: jbookmmoh@comcast.net; Web: www.catholicnewcastle.org.
Catechesis Religious Program—
Tel: 724-658-2564, Ext. 21; Fax: 724-654-7076. Louis Bosco, CCD-Jr. High; Sheryl Skowronski, CCD. Students 208.
7—St. Michael, (Slovak), Closed. See St. Vincent de Paul.
8—SS. Philip and James, (Polish), Closed. See St. Vincent de Paul.
9—St. Vincent de Paul (1993) [CEM 2]
Mailing Address: 910 S. Mercer St., New Castle, 16102. 1 Lucymont Dr., New Castle, 16102.
Tel: 724-652-5829; Fax: 724-652-2322; Email: svdpbulletin@verizion.net; Web: www.catholicnewcastle.org. Revs. Joseph R. McCaffrey, Admin.; Anthony R. Sciarappa, Parochial Vicar; William P. Siple, Parochial Vicar; Victor J. Molka Jr., Chap.; Deacons John J. Carran, Admin.; S. Daniel Kielar.
Res.: Mary Mother of Hope, 124 N. Beaver St., New Castle, 16101. Tel: 724-658-2564.
Catechesis Religious Program—Louis Bosco, CCD-Jr. High; Sheryl Skowronski, CCD. Students 22.
10—St. Vitus (1901) [JC] (Italian)
910 S. Mercer St., New Castle, 16101.
Tel: 724-652-3422; Email: stvitusec@verizon.net; Web: www.catholicnewcastle.org. Revs. Joseph R. McCaffrey, Admin.; Anthony R. Sciarappa, Parochial Vicar; William P. Siple, Parochial Vicar; Victor J. Molka Jr., Chap.; Nicholas A. Spirko, In Res., (Retired); Deacons John J. Carran, Admin.; S. Daniel Kielar.
Res.: 124 N. Beaver St., New Castle, 16101.
Tel: 724-658-2564; Fax: 724-652-2322.
School—St. Vitus School, (Grades 1-8), 915 S. Jefferson St., New Castle, 16101. Tel: 724-654-9297; Fax: 724-654-9364; Email: cryan@stvituscatholicschool.com. Lay Teachers 10; Students 110.
Catechesis Religious Program—Tel: 724-654-9371. Students 366.
North Oakland, Butler Co., St. Joseph (1845) [CEM]
864 Chicora Rd., Chicora, 16025. Tel: 724-445-2275; Fax: 724-445-7507; Email: mbirch@zoominternet.net. Mailing Address: P.O. Box 243, Chicora, 16025. Revs. Matthew R. McClain; Louis F. Pascazi, Parochial Vicar.
Catechesis Religious Program— Combined with Mater Dolorosa. Vanessa Birch, D.R.E. Students 16.
North Rochester, Beaver Co., St. Pudentiana, Closed. See St. Cecilia, Rochester.
O'Hara Township, Allegheny County, St. Joseph (1845)
Mailing Address: 342 Dorseyville Rd., 15215.
Tel: 412-963-8885, Ext. 305; Fax: 412-963-1945; Email: parishoffice@stjosephohara.com; Web: www.stjosephohara.com. Rev. Dale E. DeNinno, Admin.; Ms. Lori McKinniss, Business Mgr.
Res.: 330 Dorseyville Rd., 15215.
Tel: 412-963-8885, Ext. 304.
Catechesis Religious Program—342 Dorseyville Rd., 15215. Tel: 412-963-8885, Ext. 301; Email: ccd@stjosephohara.com. Delia Barr, D.R.E. Students 280.
Oakdale, Allegheny Co., St. Patrick (1866) [CEM]
7322 Noblestown Rd., Oakdale, 15071-1919.
Tel: 724-693-9260; Fax: 724-693-9247; Email: 46201@diopitt.org. Revs. Harry R. Bielewicz, V.E., M.Div., Admin.; Zachary A. Galiyas, Parochial Vicar; Very Rev. Benedetto P. Vaghetto, J.C.L., In Res.
Catechesis Religious Program—Tel: 724-693-8447; Email: saintpatyouth@yahoo.com. Students 108.
Oakmont, Allegheny Co., St. Irenaeus (1907)
387 Maryland Ave., Oakmont, 15139.
Tel: 412-828-3065; Fax: 412-828-8749; Email: office@opvcatholic.org; Web: www.opvcatholic.org. Rev. Kevin G. Poecking, Admin.
School—St. Irenaeus School, 637 Fourth St., Oakmont, 15139. Tel: 412-828-8444;
Fax: 412-828-8749; Email: 21641@diopitt.org. Jill Hubert, Preschool Dir. Preschool Only Lay Teachers 3; Students 32.
Catechesis Religious Program—Tel: 412-828-9450. Michael Shipe, Dir. Faith Formation. Students 160.
Overbrook, Allegheny Co., St. Norbert (1914) Merged with St. Basil, St. Albert the Great and St. Wendlin to form Holy Apostle Parish.
Penn Hills, Allegheny Co.
1—St. Bartholomew (1950)
111 Erhardt Dr., 15235. Tel: 412-242-3374;
Fax: 412-242-1488; Email: melissa@stbartsparish.com. Rev. Albert L. Zapf, Admin.
Catechesis Religious Program—Tel: 412-242-7207; Email: cford@stbartsparish.com. Students 30.
2—St. Gerard Majella (1964)
121 Dawn Dr., Verona, 15147. Tel: 412-793-3333;
Fax: 412-793-4726; Email: saintgerardmajella@comcast.net; Email: stgerardbulletin@gmail.com. Revs. Albert L. Zapf, Admin.; Edwin J. Wichman, Senior Parochial Vicar; Kenneth A. Sparks, Parochial Vicar; Richard J. Thompson, Chap.; Faustine Furaha, In Res.; Deacons Michael W. Kelly; Richard M. Tucek.
Catechesis Religious Program—200 Stotler Rd., 15235. Tel: 412-798-3591; Email: stsusannae@gmail.com. Students 44.
3—St. Susanna (1960)
200 Stotler Rd., Penn Hills, 15235-3554.
Tel: 412-798-5596; Fax: 412-798-0479; Email: 54601@diopitt.org. Rev. Martin F. Barkin, M.Div.
Catechesis Religious Program—Tel: 412-798-3591; Email: stsusannare@verizon.net. Students 27.
Perrysville, Allegheny Co., St. Teresa of Avila (1867) [CEM]
1000 Avila Ct., 15237. Tel: 412-367-9001;
Fax: 412-366-8415; Email: 55201@diopitt.org. Revs. John R. Rushofsky, M.Ed., Admin.; Michael J. Maranowski, Parochial Vicar; Michael A. Zavage, Parochial Vicar; James W. Dolan, Chap.; Deacons Richard R. Cessar; Gary L. Comer; Robert E. Koslosky; William R. Palamara Jr.; David R. Witter Sr.
Catechesis Religious Program—
Tel: 412-367-9001, Ext. 549. Kate Giuffre, D.R.E. Students 220.
Convent—900 Avila Ct., 15237.
Tel: 412-367-9001, Ext. 544.
Peters Township, Washington Co., St. Benedict the Abbot (1962)
120 Abington Dr., McMurray, 15317.
Tel: 724-941-9406; Fax: 724-941-9517; Email: staff@sbapeters.org. Revs. Robert M. Miller, S.T.L.; Pierre M. Falkenhan, V.F., Parochial Vicar; Robert L. Seeman, Parochial Vicar; Deacon Victor P. Satter; Dennis Gehlrlein, Pastoral Assoc.
Catechesis Religious Program—Tel: 724-941-9587. Elizabeth Jesserer, Dir. Faith Formation; Janet Roberto, Young Adult Min. Students 1,099.
Pitcairn, Allegheny Co., St. Michael (2010) Closed. For inquiries for parish records contact the chancery.
Pleasant Hills, Allegheny Co., Saint Elizabeth of Hungary (1942)
One Grove Pl., 15236. Tel: 412-882-8744;
Fax: 412-882-8320; Email: stelizabethchurch@st-elizabeth.org. Rev. Robert J. Cedolia, M.Div., M.A.
School—Saint Elizabeth of Hungary School, (Grades PreK-8), Tel: 412-881-2958; Email: 13441@diopitt.org. Linda M. Bechtol, Prin. Lay Teachers 13; Students 160.
Catechesis Religious Program—Tel: 412-882-5023; Fax: 412-207-1647; Email: kcentinaro@st-elizabeth.org. Kristina Centinaro, Dir. Faith Formation. Students 245.
Plum, Allegheny Co.
1—St. Januarius (1946)
1450 Renton Rd., Plum, 15239. Tel: 412-793-4439;
Fax: 412-793-7135; Email: stjanplum@comcast.net; Web: opvcatholic.org. Rev. Kevin G. Poecking, Admin.
Catechesis Religious Program—Diana Bullick, D.R.E. Students 67.
2—St. John the Baptist (1915) [CEM]
444 St. John St., 15239. Tel: 412-793-4511;
Tel: 412-793-4580; Fax: 412-793-4311; Email: parishoffice@stjohnplum.org; Email: manager@stjohnplum.org. Rev. Kevin G. Poecking; Deacons Joseph R. Vannucci; Timothy F. Noca.
School—St. John the Baptist School, (Grades PreSchool-8), 418 Unity Center Rd., 15239.
Tel: 412-793-0555; Fax: 412-793-4001; Email: quattronesjbs@gmail.com; Web: www.stjohnthebaptistschool.org. Lay Teachers 19; Preschool 80; Students 100; Preschool Teachers 6.
Catechesis Religious Program—Tel: 412-795-6536; Email: reled@stjohnthebaptist.org; Web: www.stjohnreled.org. Stephanie Williams, Dir. Faith Formation. Students 333.
Port Vue, Allegheny Co.
1—St. Joseph, Closed. See St. Mark.
2—Saint Mark Parish (1993)
1125 Romine Ave., Port Vue, 15133.
Tel: 412-678-6275; Fax: 412-673-1393; Email: saintmarkparishdiopitt@gmail.com. Rev. Thomas A. Wagner, Admin.
Port Vue Worship Site—
Res. & Liberty Worship Site—3210 Liberty Way, Liberty Borough, 15133. Tel: 412-678-6275.
Catechesis Religious Program—Students 113.
Prospect, Butler Co., St. Christopher at the Lake (1974)
229 N. Franklin St., Prospect, 16052.
Tel: 724-865-2430; Fax: 724-865-1120; Email: stchristopher@zoominternet.net. Revs. Adam M. Verona, S.T.L., Admin.; Steven V. Neff, Parochial Vicar.
Catechesis Religious Program—Tel: 724-865-9840. Students 55.
Pulaski, Lawrence Co., St. James the Apostle aka Lawrence County Grouping (1844) [CEM]
4019 US 422, Pulaski, 16143. Tel: 724-964-8276;
Fax: 724-964-1108; Email: 22601@diopitt.org; Web: www.stjamestheapostle.org. Revs. Joseph R. McCaffrey, Admin.; William P. Siple, Senior Parochial Vicar; Anthony R. Sciarappa, Parochial Vicar; Victor J. Molka Jr., Chap.; Deacons John J. Carran, Deacon Admin.; S. Daniel Kielar. In process of implementing the On Mission procedure for the Lawrence County Grouping.
Catechesis Religious Program—Students 36.
Rankin, Allegheny Co., Visitation of the Blessed Virgin Mary, (Croatian), Closed. See Word of God, Swissvale.
Reserve Township, Allegheny Co., St. Aloysius (1892)
3616 Mt. Troy Rd., 15212. Tel: 412-821-2351; Web: www.saintaloysiuspittsburgh.org. Mailing Address: 1700 Harpster St., 15212. Very Rev. Lawrence A. DiNardo, V.G., J.C.L., V.E., Mod.
Richeyville, Washington Co., St. Agnes (1994) Merged into St. Katherine Drexel Parish.
Richland Township, Allegheny Co., Saint Richard (1992)
3841 Dickey Rd., Gibsonia, 15044. Tel: 724-444-1971;
Fax: 724-444-6001; Email: officeadm@saintrich.org; Web: www.saintrichardparish.org. Revs. Robert J. Vular; Christopher J. Mannerino, Parochial Vicar; Deacons Clifford M. Homer Sr.; Gary Molitor.
Res.: 5717 Wesleyann Dr., Gibsonia, 15044.
Catechesis Religious Program—Students 575.
Robinson Township, Allegheny Co., Holy Trinity (Moon Run) (1944)
5718 Steubenville Pike, McKees Rocks, 15136-1311.
Tel: 412-787-2140; Fax: 412-787-3799; Email: info@holytrinityrobinson.org; Email: 19801@diopitt.org; Web: holytrinityrobinson.org. Revs. David G. Poecking, S.T.L., Admin.; Alan E. Morris, Parochial Vicar; Robert J. Zajdel, M.A., Parochial Vicar; Michael R. Ruffalo, Chap.; Robert W. Herrmann, In Res., (Retired); Russell J. Maurer, In Res., (Retired); Regis J. Ryan, In Res., (Retired); Louis F. Vallone, M.Div., M.A., J.C.B., In Res., (Retired); Deacon Timothy Killmeyer.
School—Holy Trinity School, (Grades PreK-8), 5720 Steubenville Pike, Mc Kees Rocks, 15136-1311.
Tel: 412-787-2656; Fax: 412-787-9487; Email: schooloffice@holytrinityrobinson.org; Web: www.holytrinityelementary.org. Mrs. Kimberly Stevenson, Prin. Lay Teachers 24; Students 441.
Catechesis Religious Program—
Tel: 412-787-2656, Ext. 156. D. Carl Stuvek, Young Adult Min. Students 357.
Rochester, Beaver Co., St. Cecilia (1856) [CEM] (German—Italian)
628 Virginia Ave., Rochester, 15074.
Tel: 724-775-0801; Email: secretary@stcecilia.comcastbiz.net; Web: www.steciliaroch.org. Revs. Paul Kuppe, O.F.M.Cap.; Mark Carter, O.F.M.Cap.
Tel: 724-312-2058.
Church: 632 Virginia Ave., Rochester, 15074.
Catechesis Religious Program—633 California Ave., Rochester, 15074. Tel: 724-775-2761. Students 168.
See St. Fidelis Friary under Monasteries & Residences of Priests & Brothers in the Institution section.
Roscoe, Washington Co., St. Joseph (1904) Merged to form St. Katharine Drexel Parish.
Ross Township, Allegheny Co., St. Sebastian (North Hills) (1952)
311 Siebert Rd., 15237. Tel: 412-364-8999;
Fax: 412-364-6330; Email: info@saintsebastianparish.org; Web: www.ssebastianparish.org. Revs. John R. Rushofsky, M.Ed.; Michael A. Zavage, Parochial Vicar; William E. Dorner, In Res.; Deacon Richard R. Cessar, Pastoral Assoc.
Catechesis Religious Program—Students 444.

RUSSELLTON, ALLEGHENY CO., TRANSFIGURATION (1916) [CEM]
94 McKrell Rd., Russellton, 15076. Tel: 724-265-1030 ; Fax: 724-265-1032; Email: rctransroman@gmail.com; Web: www.trcparish.org. Rev. James P. Holland.
Church: 100 McKrell Rd., Russellton, 15076-1305.
Catechesis Religious Program—Tel: 724-265-3284; Email: rctransroman@gmail.com. Mary Etta Filotei, Catechetical Admin. Students 40.

SCOTT TOWNSHIP, ALLEGHENY CO.
1—OUR LADY OF GRACE (1947)
310 Kane Blvd., 15243. Tel: 412-279-7070; Fax: 412-279-2385; Email: rectory@olgscott.org; Web: www.olgscott.org. Revs. David J. Bonnar, V.E., S.T.B.; Benjamin Barr, Parochial Vicar; Thomas Gramc, Parochial Vicar; Robin S. Evanish, Chap.; Gilbert Z. Puznakoski, Chap.; Deacons Frederick N. Eckhardt; Lawrence R. Sutton, Ph.D.; Kristian Sherman, Seminarian.
School—Our Lady of Grace School, (Grades PreK-8), 1734 Bower Hill Rd., 15243. Tel: 412-279-6611; Fax: 412-279-6755; Email: sbrown@olgscott.net. Lay Teachers 12; Students 180.
Catechesis Religious Program—1730 Bower Hill Rd., 15243. Tel: 412-276-0277. Geoff Schnieder, Dir. Adult Catechesis & Evangelization; Don Fontana, D.R.E.; Isaac Summers, Dir. Youth Ministry. Students 256.
2—SS. SIMON AND JUDE (1955)
1607 Greentree Rd., 15220. Tel: 412-563-3189; Fax: 412-563-8524; Email: parish@ssjpittsburgh.org; Web: www.ssjpittsburgh.org. Revs. Robert J. Grecco, M.Div., Admin.; Aleksandr Schrenk, Parochial Vicar; Jerome Etenduk, (Africa) In Res.; Deacon James S. Mackin; Christine Manion, Business Mgr.; Laura O'Keeffe.
Child Care—Saints Simon & Jude Early Childhood Program, 1625 Greentree Rd., 15220.
Tel: 412-563-1199; Email: preschool@ssjpittsburgh.org. Maureen Torcasi, Dir.
Catechesis Religious Program—
Tel: 412-563-3189, Ext. 209. Bethann Petrovich, Faith Formation Program Mgr. & RCIA; Rory Mitrik, Coord. Evangelization & Youth, Tel: 412-563-3189, Ext. 205; Rich Moser, Dir. Music Ministry, Tel: 412-563-3189, Ext. 210; Kathryn Blythe, Dir. Young Adult Ministry. Students 151.

SEWICKLEY, ALLEGHENY CO., ST. JAMES (1863) [CEM]
200 Walnut St., Sewickley, 15143. Tel: 412-741-6650; Fax: 412-741-4782; Email: saintjamesparish@comcast.net. Rev. James B. Farnan, Admin.
School—St. James School, (Grades PreSchool-8), 201 Broad St., Sewickley, 15143. Tel: 412-741-5540; Fax: 412-741-9038; Email: chill@saintjames-sewickley.org; Web: www.stjamesschool.us. Cindy Meurer, Librarian. Part of North Hills Regional Catholic Schools Lay Teachers 18; Preschool 22; Students 187.
Catechesis Religious Program—
Tel: 412-741-6650, Ext. 503; Email: stjamesreled@comcast.net. Students 377.

SHARPSBURG, ALLEGHENY CO.
1—ST. JOHN CANTIUS (1906) (Polish), Closed. See Saint Juan Diego Parish.
2—MADONNA OF JERUSALEM (1904) (Italian), Closed. See Saint Juan Diego Parish.
3—ST. MARY (1994) [CEM] Closed. See Saint Juan Diego Parish.
4—SAINT JUAN DIEGO PARISH (2009) [CEM]
201 9th St., Sharpsburg, 15215-2304.
Tel: 412-784-8700; Fax: 412-781-1101; Email: saintjuandiegopgh@comcast.net; Web: www.saintjuandiegopgh.org. Rev. Michael W. Decewicz, V.F., M.Div.
Catechesis Religious Program—Students 38.

SLIPPERY ROCK, BUTLER CO., ST. PETER (1938) [CEM]
342 Normal Ave., Slippery Rock, 16057.
Tel: 724-794-2880; Fax: 724-794-1255. Rev. Robert L. Seeman.
Church: 670 S. Main St., Slippery Rock, 16057.
Catechesis Religious Program—Katrina Boosel, D.R.E. Students 25.
Mission—St. Anthony Church, 232 Boyers Rd., Forestville, Butler Co. 16035.

SOUTH PARK, ALLEGHENY CO.
1—ST. JOAN OF ARC (1923) Merged with St. Louise DeMarillac.
6414 Montour St., South Park, 15129.
Tel: 412-833-2400; Fax: 412-835-1764; Web: www.mystjoan.org. Revs. Joseph E. Sioli, Admin.; Jon J. Brzek, Parochial Vicar; Daniel J. Maurer, S.T.L., Parochial Vicar.
Catechesis Religious Program—Tel: 412-835-3724. Students 262.
2—NATIVITY (1905) Merged with St. Gabriel, St. Germaine & St. Valentine.
5811 Curry Rd., 15236. Tel: 412-655-3000; Email: nativitychurch@comcast.net. Revs. John W. Skirtich, Admin.; Michael S. Suslowicz, Parochial Vicar; John E. Hissrich, Chap.
Catechesis Religious Program—Students 110.

SPRINGDALE, ALLEGHENY CO., ST. ALPHONSUS (1901)
750 Pittsburgh St., Springdale, 15144-1699.
Tel: 724-274-5084; Fax: 724-274-7035; Email: office@StAlphonsus.comcastbiz.net. Rev. Kenneth E. Kezmarsky.
Catechesis Religious Program—Tel: 724-274-2547. Students 25.

SWISSVALE, ALLEGHENY CO.
1—ST. ANSELM, Closed. See Word of God.
2—SAINT BARNABAS, (Slovak), Closed. See Word of God.
3—MADONNA DEL CASTELLO (1920) (Italian)
2021 S. Braddock Ave., 15218. Tel: 412-271-5666; Fax: 412-271-2335; Email: madonnadelcastello1920@gmail.com. Revs. Larry Adams, Admin.; Jeremy J. Mohler, Parochial Vicar; Vincent F. Kolo, Chap.
Catechesis Religious Program—Students 18.
4—WORD OF GOD (1994) Consolidated from the following churches: St. Anselm, St. Barnabas and Visitation of the Blessed Virgin Mary, Rankin.
2021 S. Braddock Ave., 15218. Tel: 412-241-1372; Fax: 412-271-2335; Email: wordofgod1994@gmail.com. 7446 McClure Ave., 15218. Revs. Larry Adams; Jeremy J. Mohler, Parochial Vicar; Deacons Ronald D. Demblowski, Pastoral Assoc.; Joseph M. Dougherty; Keith G. Kondrich.
Catechesis Religious Program—Students 21.

TARENTUM, ALLEGHENY CO.
1—ST. CLEMENT, Closed. See Holy Martyrs.
2—HOLY MARTYRS (1992) [CEM] [JC2] Consolidated from St. Clement and Sacred Heart, St. Peter. Rev. Thomas L. Gillespie.
Res.: 353 W. Ninth Ave., Tarentum, 15084.
Tel: 724-224-0770; Fax: 724-224-7070; Email: holymartyrsparish@comcast.net.
Catechesis Religious Program—344 W. 9th Ave., Tarentum, 15084. Tel: 724-224-1234; Email: michelestruhar@gmail.com. Michele Struhar, D.R.E. Students 40.
3—SACRED HEART - ST. PETER, Closed. See Holy Martyrs.

TURTLE CREEK, ALLEGHENY CO., ST. COLMAN (1882)
100 Tri-Boro Ave., Turtle Creek, 15145.
Tel: 412-823-2564; Fax: 412-823-6350; Email: stcolman@verizon.net. Revs. Frank D. Almade, Ph. D., Admin.; Martin F. Barkin, M.Div., Parochial Vicar; Deacon Herbert E. Riley Jr.
Catechesis Religious Program—Students 88.

UPPER ST. CLAIR, ALLEGHENY CO.
1—ST. JOHN CAPISTRAN (1968)
1610 McMillan Rd., 15241. Tel: 412-221-6275; Fax: 412-257-3789; Web: www.sjcusc.org. Revs. W. Peter Horton, M.A., M.Div.; James J. Chepponis, M.Div., M.A., Parochial Vicar; James R. Bedillion, J.C.L., Chap.; Deacon William G. Batz.
Catechesis Religious Program—Tel: 412-221-5445; Email: sjcreled@comcast.net. Denise DeCapria, D.R.E. Students 240.
2—ST. LOUISE DE MARILLAC (1961)
Mailing Address: 320 McMurray Rd., 15241.
Tel: 412-833-1010; Fax: 412-833-6624; Email: stl@stlouisedemarillac.org; Web: stlouisedemarillac.org. Revs. Joseph E. Sioli; Daniel J. Maurer, S.T.L., Parochial Vicar; Deacon William F. Strathmann Jr.; Sr. M. Faith Balawejder, C.S.S.F., Pastoral Assoc.; Greg Fincham, Music Min.
School—St. Louise de Marillac School, (Grades K-8), 310 McMurray Rd., 15241. Tel: 412-835-0600; Fax: 412-835-2898; Email: kklase@stlouisedemarillac.org; Web: www.stlouiseschoolpa.org. Ken Klase, Prin. Lay Teachers 27; Students 449.
Catechesis Religious Program—Tel: 412-835-1155; Fax: 412-833-3952. Loretta Uhlmann, D.R.E.; Jason Zych, Youth Min. Students 646.

VERONA, ALLEGHENY CO., ST. JOSEPH (1866) [CEM]
825 Second Ave., Verona, 15147-1498.
Tel: 412-795-5114; Email: joevchurch@verizon.net. Revs. Kevin G. Poecking, Admin.; George R. Dalton, Parochial Vicar; David D. DeWitt, Parochial Vicar.
School—St. Joseph School, Tel: 412-828-7213; Email: stjosephelementary@comcast.net. Lay Teachers 13; Students 125; Religious Teachers 1.

VERSAILLES, ALLEGHENY CO., ST. DENIS, Closed. See St. Patrick, McKeesport.

WAMPUM, LAWRENCE CO., ST. MONICA, Closed. See Queen of Heaven, Koppel.

WASHINGTON, WASHINGTON CO.
1—ST. HILARY (1919)
320 Henderson Ave., Washington, 15301.
Tel: 724-222-4087; Fax: 724-222-2130; Email: sthilarychurch@comcast.net; Web: sthilaryparish.org. Revs. Michael John Lynam; Michael P. Conway, Parochial Vicar; Michael R. Peck, Parochial Vicar; Camillus Okechukwu Njoku, Chap.
Catechesis Religious Program—340 Henderson Ave., Washington, 15301. Tel: 724-222-1381. Students 90.
2—IMMACULATE CONCEPTION (1855) [CEM 3]
119 W. Chestnut St., Washington, 15301.
Tel: 724-225-1425; Fax: 724-229-7946; Email: office@icwashpa.net; Web: icwashpa.net. Revs. Michael John Lynam; Michael P. Conway, Parochial Vicar; Michael R. Peck, Parochial Vicar; Camillus Okechukwu Njoku, Chap.; George F. Chortos, In Res., (Retired); Deacon Jeffrey A. Hirst; Sr. Margaretta Nussbaumer, C.D.P., Pastoral Assoc.
Worship Site: Sacred Heart, Claysville, PA.
Res.: 119 W. Chestnut St., Washington, 15301-4422.
Tel: 724-225-1425; Fax: 724-229-7946; Email: office@icwashpa.net; Web: www.icwashpa.org.
School—John F. Kennedy Catholic, 111 W. Spruce St., Washington, 15301-4356. Tel: 724-225-1680; Fax: 724-225-4651. Lay Teachers 20; Preschool 61; Students 225.
Catechesis Religious Program—119 W. Chestnut St., Washington, 15301. Tel: 724-225-0382; Fax: 724-229-7942. Sheryl Giovanelli, C.R.E. Students 227.

WAYNESBURG, GREENE CO., ST. ANN (1839) [CEM]
232 E. High St., Waynesburg, 15370.
Tel: 724-627-7568; Fax: 724-627-3735; Email: saintannchurch@comcast.net. Revs. Albin C. McGinnis, V.F., Admin.; J. Francis Frazer, Parochial Vicar; Deacons Elbert A. Kuhns; James M. Sheil.
Catechesis Religious Program—Students 63.

WEST ALIQUIPPA, BEAVER CO., ST. JOSEPH, Closed. See St. Titus, Aliquippa.

WEST MIFFLIN, ALLEGHENY CO.
1—ST. AGNES (1867) [CEM]
622 St. Agnes Ln., West Mifflin, 15122.
Tel: 412-466-6545. Rev. Thomas J. Lewandowski, Admin.
School—St. Agnes School, (Grades PreSchool-8), 653 St. Agnes Ln., West Mifflin, 15122.
Tel: 412-466-6238; Fax: 412-466-2013. Lay Teachers 8; Sisters of the Holy Spirit 2; Students 120; Religious Teachers 2.
Catechesis Religious Program—
Convent— Sisters of the Holy Spirit 635 St. Agnes Ln., West Mifflin, 15122. Tel: 412-466-3554; Email: stagnes11@verizon.net.
2—HOLY SPIRIT (1963)
2603 Old Elizabeth Rd., West Mifflin, 15122-2598.
Tel: 412-346-0477; Fax: 412-466-4983; Email: hsrectory2603@comcast.net. Revs. Robert J. Cedolia, M.Div., M.A.; Kenneth E. Kezmarsky, Parochial Vicar; William R. Terza, Parochial Vicar.
Catechesis Religious Program—Tel: 412-346-0475; Tel: 412-346-0476 (Music Office); Fax: 412-466-3444; Email: hsccd@comcast.net. Students 203.
3—HOLY TRINITY (1901) [CEM] (Slovak)
529 Grant Ave. Ext., West Mifflin, 15122.
Tel: 412-466-6545; Fax: 412-466-6968; Email: h.trinity@verizon.net. Rev. Thomas J. Lewandowski, Admin.
4—RESURRECTION (1936) Merged with St. Rita, Munhall.
1 Majka Dr., West Mifflin, 15122. Tel: 412-461-8087; Fax: 412-461-0142; Email: resurrection15122@gmail.com; Web: resurrection-strita.org. Rev. Nicholas Mastrangelo, Parochial Vicar.
Catechesis Religious Program— Combined with St. Rita. Catherine Ratay, D.R.E. Students 30.

WEST PITTSBURG, LAWRENCE CO., HOLY CROSS, Closed. See St. Vincent de Paul, New Castle.

WEST SUNBURY, BUTLER CO.
1—ST. ALPHONSUS, [CEM] [JC3] (Est. 1993)
202 W. State St., P.O. Box 246, West Sunbury, 16061. Tel: 724-476-1476; Fax: 724-476-1477; Email: stalphparish@zoominternet.net. Rev. James R. Bedillion, J.C.L.; connie malinski, Sec.; Suzanne Colon, Music Min.
Catechesis Religious Program—Amy J. Baptiste, D.R.E. Students 62.
2—ST. LOUIS, Closed. See St. Alphonsus, Boyers.

WEST VIEW, ALLEGHENY CO., ST. ATHANASIUS (1905)
7 Chalfonte Ave., 15229. Tel: 412-931-4624; Fax: 412-939-3516; Email: mcooper@stathanasiuswv.org. Revs. John R. Rushofsky, M.Ed.; Leroy A. DiPietro, In Res.; Innocent Ohuh, In Res.
Catechesis Religious Program—
Tel: 412-931-4624, Ext. 213. Victor Boerio, Dir. Faith Formation. Students 316.

WEXFORD, ALLEGHENY CO.
1—ST. ALEXIS (1961)
10090 Old Perry Hwy., Wexford, 15090.
Tel: 724-935-4343; Fax: 724-935-1270; Email: parish@stalexis.org; Web: stalexis.org. Revs. Paul J. Zywan, M.Div., Admin.; Joseph M. Freedy, Parochial Vicar.
Catechesis Religious Program—Tel: 724-935-0877. Paula Green, D.R.E. Students 245.
2—ST. ALPHONSUS (1840) [CEM]
201 Church Rd., Wexford, 15090. Tel: 724-935-1151; Fax: 724-934-3788; Email: bookkeeper@saintalphonsuswexford.org; Web: www.

saintalphonsuswexford.org. Revs. Paul J. Zywan, M.Div.; Joseph M. Freedy, Parochial Vicar.
Catechesis Religious Program—Tel: 724-935-1160. Louis Bosco, D.R.E. Students 222.

WHITE OAK BORO, ALLEGHENY CO., ST. ANGELA (1958) 1640 Fawcett Ave., White Oak, 15131.
Tel: 412-672-9641; Fax: 412-672-1576; Email: 03401@diopitt.org; Web: www.stangelamericiparish.org. Rev. Terrence P. O'Connor, M.Div., J.D.
Res.: 1732 Fawcett Ave., White Oak, 15131.
School—Mary of Nazareth Catholic School, (Grades PreK-8), 1640 Fawcett Ave., White Oak, 15131.
Tel: 412-672-2360; Fax: 412-672-0880; Email: 66241@diopitt.org. Lynda McFarland, Prin. Consolidated Elementary School serving Saint Angela Merici, Corpus Christi, Saint Jude the Apostle, Saint Mark, Saint Michael, Saint Patrick, Queen of the Rosary, St. Robert Bellarmine Parishes Lay Teachers 20; Students 266.
Catechesis Religious Program—Tel: 412-672-0913; Fax: 412-672-1576. Students 90.

WHITEHALL, ALLEGHENY CO., ST. GABRIEL OF THE SORROWFUL VIRGIN (1944)
5200 Greenridge Dr., 15236. Tel: 412-881-8115;
Tel: 412-881-8117; Fax: 412-440-0160. Revs. John W. Skirtich, Admin.; Michael S. Suslowicz, Parochial Vicar; John R. Haney, M.Div., In Res., (Retired).
School—St. Gabriel of the Sorrowful Virgin School, Tel: 412-882-3353; Fax: 412-882-2125; Email: militzer@stgabrielpgh.org. Lay Teachers 22; Students 440.
Catechesis Religious Program—5300 Greenridge Dr., 15236. Tel: 412-881-7950. Students 240.

WILDWOOD, ALLEGHENY CO., ST. CATHERINE OF SWEDEN (1943)
2554 Wildwood Rd., Allison Park, 15101.
Tel: 412-486-6001; Fax: 412-486-6004; Email: info@scospgh.org; Web: stcatherineofsweden.org. Revs. Robert J. Vular, Admin.; Christopher J. Mannerino, Parochial Vicar; Deacon Clifford M. Homer Sr.
Res.: 4701 Sylvan Dr., Allison Park, 15101.
Catechesis Religious Program—Email: ccd@stcatherineofsweden.org. Students 549.

WILKINSBURG, ALLEGHENY CO., ST. JAMES (1869)
718 Franklin Ave., 15221. Tel: 412-241-1392;
Fax: 412-241-6625. 7114 Kelly St., 15208. Rev. David H. Taylor, M.Div.
Catechesis Religious Program—Fax: 412-241-6625. Students 25.

WILMERDING, ALLEGHENY CO.
1—ST. JUDE THE APOSTLE (1994) [CEM] Consolidated from St. Aloysius and St. Leocadia. Rev. John D. Brennan.
Res.: 405 Westinghouse Ave., Wilmerding, 15148.
Tel: 412-823-8390; Fax: 412-823-8399; Email: jbrennan@diopitt.org.
2—ST. LEOCADIA, (Polish), Closed. See St. Jude the Apostle.

ZELIENOPLE, BUTLER CO., ST. GREGORY (1906) [CEM]
2 W. Beaver St., Zelienople, 16063.
Tel: 724-452-7245; Fax: 724-452-4064; Email: parishoffice@stgregzelie.org; Web: stgregparish.org. Revs. John P. Gallagher, S.T.L., Admin.; Mark L. Thomas, S.T.L., Parochial Vicar; James R. Torquato, Parochial Vicar; James G. Young, M.Div., Chap., (Retired); Deacon Donald C. Pepe.
School—St. Gregory School, 115 Pine St., Zelienople, 16063. Tel: 724-452-9731; Fax: 724-452-4064; Email: schooloffice@stgregzelie.org. Lay Teachers 16; Students 230.
Catechesis Religious Program—Students 250.

Chaplains of Public Institutions

BEAVER COUNTY. *McGuire Memorial Home*, 2119 Mercer Rd., New Brighton, 15066.
Tel: 724-843-3400, Ext. 1127; Email: jlewisandrews@mecguirememorial.org. Rev. Michael P. Greb, O.F.M.Cap., Dir. Pastoral Care, Tel: 724-774-1242 Home; Tel: 724-843-3400, Ext. 1127 Work(Vacant).

Hospitals

ALLEGHENY COUNTY. *Children's Hospital*, Allegheny County. Tel: 412-692-5325. Rev. Nicholas J. ArgentieriUPMC Chaplains, Tel: 412-692-7253.
St. Clair Memorial Hospital, Tel: 412-561-4900. Revs. Robin Evanish, Gilbert Z. Puznakoski.
Heritage Valley Sewickley, Tel: 412-741-6600. Attended by Catholic Parishes in the Area.
Jefferson Regional Medical Center, Allegheny County. Tel: 412-469-5000. Rev. Jason Charron.
Life Care Hospital of Pittsburgh, Allegheny County. Tel: 412-247-2585. Attended by St. James Parish, Wilkinsburg. Tel:412-241-1392.
Magee-Women's Hospital, Allegheny County. Tel: 412-647-1000. Rev. Douglas A. Boyd, Kathleen Klocek, Pastoral Min.
McKeesport UPMC, Allegheny County. Tel: 412-664-2000. Rev. Joseph C. BeckAttended by Corpus Christi Parish 412-672-0765.
Mercy Health System of Pittsburgh-Pittsburgh Mercy Hospital, Allegheny County. Tel: 412-232-8111. Revs. Richard S. Jones, M.Div., M.A., Christopher Mbogu, John G. Oesterle, Albert Schempp, M.I., Tel: 412-232-8198.
Ohio Valley General Hospital, Allegheny County. Tel: 412-777-6161. Rev. Michael RuffaloAttended by St. Malachy Parish. Tel: 412-771-5483 and St. John of God Parish. Tel: 412-771-5646.
UPMC East, Tel: 412-357-3587. Rev. Richard J. ThompsonAttended by Saint Bernadette Parish. Tel: 412-373-0050.
UPMC Passavant Hospital, Allegheny County. Tel: 412-367-6700. Rev. Joseph G. Luisi.
UPMC Shadyside Hospital, Allegheny County. Tel: 412-623-2121. Rev. Pierre G. Sodini, S.T.L., Tel: 412-623-1691.
UPMC St. Margaret Hospital, Allegheny County. Tel: 412-767-4672. Attended by: St. Scholastica Parish: Tel: 412-784-8700; Pastoral Care, Tel: 412-784-4749 & St. Juan Diego Parish: Tel: 412-784-8700.
UPMC University of Pittsburgh Medical Center, Allegheny County. Tel: 412-647-7560. Revs. Dozie Romanus Egbe, (Nigeria) Tel: 412-647-7560, Francis Oranefo, (Nigeria)Patient and Family Support, Tel: 412-647-7615.
West Penn Allegheny Health System-Alle-Kiski Medical Center, Allegheny County. Tel: 724-224-5100. Rev. John D. Brennan, Tel: 724-226-4900.
West Penn Allegheny Health System-Allegheny General, Allegheny County. Tel: 412-359-3131.
West Penn Allegheny Health System-Forbes Regional, Tel: 412-858-2960. Rev. Richard J. Thompson, Tel: 412-456-5645.
Western Pennsylvania Hospital, Allegheny County. Tel: 412-578-5000. Rev. Reginald Lyimo, O.F.M.-Cap.

BEAVER COUNTY. *Heritage Valley Beaver*, Beaver County. Tel: 724-728-7000. Attended by St. Frances Cabrini Parish Grouping. Tel: 724-775-4111.

BUTLER COUNTY. *Butler Memorial Hospital*, Butler County. Tel: 724-283-6666. Rev. William Wuenchel, Tel: 724-287-7781.
UMPC Passavant Health Center. Rev. James G. YoungButler County, PA 724-452-5400.

GREENE COUNTY. *Greene County Memorial*, Greene County. Tel: 724-627-3101. Attended by St. Ann Parish, Waynesburg. Tel:724-627-7568.

LAWRENCE COUNTY. *Ellwood City Hospital*, Lawrence County. Tel: 724-752-0081. Rev. Victor J. Molka Jr., Tel: 724-758-4441.
Jameson Hospital North Campus. Rev. Victor J. Molka Jr.Attended by Vicariate 4 District 1, Tel. 412-456-5649.
Jameson Hospital South Campus. Rev. Victor J. Molka Jr.Lawrence County, PA 724-658-9001.

WASHINGTON COUNTY. *Mon Valley Hospital*, Washington County. Tel: 724-258-2000. Rev. Gerald S. Mikonis, (Retired), Tel: 724-258-7742.
Washington Hospital, Washington County. Tel: 724-225-7000. Rev. Camillus Okechukwu Njoku.
West Penn Allegheny Health System-Canonsburg Hospital, Washington County. Tel: 724-745-6100. Rev. Thomas J. Galvin.

Veterans Administration Hospitals

ALLEGHENY COUNTY. *VA Hospital Pittsburgh*, Allegheny County. Tel: 412-688-6000. Tel: 1-866-482-7488 (24-Hour)
University Drive. Rev. Msgr. Joseph R. Lamonde, Revs. Robert Craig, O.F.M.Cap., Tel: 412-954-4001 (Pastoral Care), Charles Soto, O.F.M.
H.J. Heinz III (Aspinwall). Rev. Robert Craig, O.F.M.Cap., Tel: 412-954-4001 (Pastoral Care).
VA Pittsburgh Health Care System. Rev. Msgr. Joseph R. Lamonde, Revs. Robert Craig, O.F.M.Cap., Mark W. Glasgow, Pastoral Care, Tel: 412-954-4001, Charles Soto, O.F.M.University Drive DivisionHJ Heinz Progressive Care Center. Pastoral Care 412-954-4001.

BUTLER COUNTY. *VA Medical Center Butler*, Tel: 800-362-8262. Rev. James F. Murphy, (Retired).

Rehabilitation, Nursing and Geriatric Care Facilities

ALLEGHENY COUNTY. *Arden Courts*, Tel: 412-795-3388.
Arden Courts North Hills, Tel: 412-369-7887. Attended by Our Lady of the Assumption Parish Grouping Bellvue. 412-367-9001; Tel: 412-369-7887.
Asbury Heights, Allegheny County. Tel: 412-341-1030. Revs. Robin Evanish, Gilbert Z. Puznakoski.
Baldwin Health Care, Allegheny County. Tel: 412-885-8400. Rev. Jason Charron.
Baptist Home. Attended by St. Winifred Parish 412-344-5010 Allegheny County, PA 412-563-6550.
Beverly Healthcare Mt. Lebanon, Allegheny County. Tel: 412-257-4444.
Beverly Manor Nursing Home, Allegheny County. Tel: 412-856-7570.
Canterbury Place, Allegheny County. Tel: 412-622-9000. Attended by Our Lady of the Angels Parish, Pittsburgh. Tel: 412-682-0929.
Cedars of Monroeville, Tel: 412-373-3900. Rev. Richard J. Thompson.
Children's Institute, Allegheny County. Tel: 412-661-7222; Fax: 412-420-2400. Attended by St. Bede Parish, Tel: 412-661-7222.
Collins Nursing Center. Attended by St. Bede Parish. Tel: 412-661-7222 Allegheny County. Tel: 412-661-1740.
Concordia at Rebecca. Attended by St. Victor Parish 724-265-2070 Allegheny County, PA 724-444-0600.
Concordia of Fox Chapel. Attended by St. Pio of Pietrelcina Parish 412-828-4066 Allegheny County, PA 412-767-5808.
Concordia of South Hills. Revs. Robin Evanish, Gilbert Z. Puznakoski.
Consulate Health Care. Attended by St. Victor Parish 724-265-2070 Allegheny County, PA 412-767-4998.
Country Meadows. Allegheny County, PA 412-257-2474 Rev. Stan M. Gregorek.
DT Watson Rehab Hospital, Allegheny County. Tel: 412-741-9000. Attended by St. James Parish, Sewickley. Tel: 412-741-6650.
Forbes Hospice. Allegheny County, PA 412-578-7208.
Forbes Road Nursing Center, Allegheny County. Tel: 412-665-3232. Rev. Stephen M. Palsa.
Golden Living Center Monroeville. Allegheny County, PA 412-856-7570 Rev. Frederick W. Gruber.
Golden Living Center Oakmont. Rev. Frederick W. Gruber.
Hamilton Hills Personal Care. Rev. Stephen M. Palsa, Tel: 412-795-3388.
Health South Hospital of Pittsburgh, Allegheny County. Tel: 412-856-2400. Rev. Joseph C. Beck.
Healthsouth Harmarville Hospital, Allegheny County. Tel: 412-826-4929. Rev. John D. Brennan.
Heartland Health Care Center, Allegheny County. Tel: 412-665-2400. Attended by St. Bede Parish. Tel: 412-661-7222.
Heritage Shadyside, Allegheny County. Tel: 412-422-5100. Rev. Stephen M. Palsa.
Independence Court of Mt. Lebanon, Allegheny County. Tel: 412-341-4400.
Independent Court of Monroeville, Allegheny County. Tel: 412-373-3030. Rev. Frederick W. Gruber.
Kane Regional Center - Glen Hazel, Allegheny County. Tel: 412-422-6800. Rev. Stephen M. Palsa.
Kane Regional Center - McKeesport, Allegheny County. Tel: 412-675-8600. Rev. Joseph C. Beck, Tel: 412-675-8640.
Kane Regional Center - Ross, Allegheny County. Tel: 412-369-2000. Rev. James W. Dolan.
Kane Regional Center - Scott, Allegheny County. Tel: 412-429-3000. Rev. Gilbert Z. Puznakoski, Chap., Tel: 412-279-7070.
Kindred Hospital Pittsburgh. Rev. Michael L. Yaksick.
Kindred Hospital Pittsburgh North Shore. Attended by St. Peter Parish 412-321-0711 Allegheny County, PA 412-323-5800.
Ladies of the Grand Army Republic (LGAR), Allegheny County. Tel: 412-825-9000. Rev. David Green.
Little Sisters of the Poor, 1028 Benton Ave., E Pittsburgh, 15212-1694. Tel: 412-307-1100; Email: mspittsburgh@littlesistersofthepoor.org. Rev. William P. Feeney, M.Div., (Retired).
Longwood at Oakmont, Allegheny County. Tel: 412-826-5917. Rev. Frederick W. Gruber.
Manorcare Health Services, Highland Dr., Allegheny, 15212. Tel: 412-831-6050. Rev. James R. Bedillion, J.C.L.
Manorcare Health Services Green Tree, Greentree Rd., Allegheny, 15212. Tel: 412-344-7744. Rev. Robin Evanish.
Manorcare Health Services McMurray. Attended by St. Benedict the Abbot Parish. Tel: 724-941-9406. McMurray Rd., Allegheny, 15212. Tel: 412-941-3080.
Manorcare Health Services Monroeville, Allegheny County. Rev. Frederick W. GruberTel: 412-856-7071.
Manorcare Health Services North Hills, Allegheny County. Tel: 412-369-9955. Rev. James W. Dolan.
Marian Manor, Inc., Allegheny County. Tel: 412-563-6866.
Oakmont Nursing Center, Allegheny County. Tel: 412-828-7300. Rev. Frederick W. Gruber.
Presbyterian Seniorcare Westminister Place,

Allegheny County. Tel: 412-826-6136. Rev. Frederick W. Gruber.
Providence Point Nursing Home. Revs. Robin Evanish, Gilbert Z. Puznakoski.
Ridgepoint, Allegheny County. Tel: 412-653-6870. Rev. John E. Hissrich.
Riverview Center for Jewish Seniors, Allegheny County. Tel: 412-521-5900. Rev. Stephen M. Palsa.
Seneca Manor Assisted Living. Rev. Frederick W. Gruber.
Seneca Place. Rev. Frederick W. Gruber.
Shadyside Nursing and Rehabilitation Center. Attended by St. Bede Parish. Tel: 412-661-7222. Allegheny County. Tel: 412-362-3500.
Southwestern Nursing and Rehabilitation Center, Allegheny County. Tel: 412-466-0600, Ext. 5989. Rev. Jason Churran.
Sunrise Assisted Living. Rev. Frederick W. Gruber.
UPMC Rehabilitation Hospital, Allegheny County. Tel: 412-420-2400. Attended by St. Bede Parish, Pittsburgh. Tel: 412-661-7222.
Vincentian Collaborative System, Tel: 412-630-9980. Sr. Laverne Sihelnik, V.S.C.
Vincentian de Marillac Home. Attended by St. Raphael Tel: 412-661-3100; Tel: 412-361-2833. Rev. Stephen M. Palsa.
Vincentian Home, Allegheny County. Tel: 412-366-5600; Email: info@vcs.org. Sisters Karen Kellerski, Chap., Tel: 412-366-5600, Ext. 569, Linda Soltis, SCN, Chap., Tel: 412-366-5600, Ext. 567.
Vincentian Regency Home, Allegheny County. Tel: 412-366-8540. Sr. Denise Hibel, Chap.Tel: 412-366-8540.
Woodhaven Convalescent Center, Allegheny County. Tel: 412-856-4770. Rev. Stephen M. Palsa.

BEAVER COUNTY. *Beaver Elder Care Rehab*. Attended by St. Titus Parish 724-378-8561 Beaver County, PA 724-375-0345.
Blair Personal Care Home. Rev. James G. Young.
Friendship Ridge Skilled Nursing, Beaver County. Tel: 724-775-7100. Rev. William J. Schwartz, (Retired), Tel: 724-775-7100.
Hunter's Personal Care. Beaver County, PA 724-378-1205Attended by St. Titus Parish 724-378-8561.
Maplewood Personal Care. Rev. Joseph A. CarrBeaver County, PA 724-266-4485.
Providence Care Center. Rev. Ladis CizikBeaver County, PA 724-846-8504.
Villa St. Joseph, 1030 State St., Baden, 15005. Tel: 724-869-6300; Email: pphillips@stjosephvilla.org. Rev. Frank Mitolo, Chap.

BUTLER COUNTY. *Autumn Grove Care Center*. Rev. William WuenchelButler County, PA 724-735-4224.
Concordia Lutheran Ministries. Deacon Toby GainesButler County, PA 724-352-1571.
Creek Meadows. Butler County, PA 724-452-7378.
Evergreen Nursing Center. Rev. James G. YoungButler County, PA 724-452-6970.
St. John Specialty Care Center. Attended by St. Kilian Parish, Tel: 724-625-1665 or Tel: 724-625-1571.
Sunnyview Home, Butler County. Tel: 724-282-1800. Rev. William Wuenchel.
Sunrise of Cranberry. Attended by St. Kilian Parish, Tel: 724-625-1665 or Tel: 724-779-4300.
UPMC/Passavant Cranberry and UPMC Cranberry Place. Attended by St. Killian Parish, Tel: 724-625-1665, 724-775-5350, or Tel: 724-772-5350.
Valencia Woods at St. Barnabas. Attended by St. Kilian Parish, Tel: 724-625-1665 or Tel: 724-625-4000.
Worthington of Adams. Attended by St. Kilian Parish, Tel: 724-625-1665 or Tel: 724-779-5020.

GREENE COUNTY. *Beverly Health Care*, Greene County. Tel: 724-852-2020. Attended by St. Ann Parish, Waynesburg. Tel: 724-627-7568.
Rolling Meadows, Greene County. Tel: 724-627-3153. Attended by St. Ann Parish, Waynesburg. Tel: 724-627-7568.

LAWRENCE COUNTY. *Almira Home*, Lawrence County. Tel: 724-652-4131. Rev. Victor J. Molka Jr.
Belvedere Residence, Inc., Lawrence County. Tel: 724-924-2191. Rev. Victor J. Molka Jr. Attended by Vicariate 4, District 1 Parishes, Tel: 412-456-5649.
Castle Manor, Lawrence County. Tel: 724-654-4377. Rev. Victor J. Molka Jr.Attended by Vicariate 4, District 1 Parishes, Tel: 412-456-5649.
Cedar Manor, Lawrence County. Tel: 724-654-8050. Rev. Victor J. Molka Jr.Attended by Vicariate 4, District 1 Parishes, Tel: 412-456-5649.
Edison Manor Nursing & Rehab. Lawrence County, PA 724-652-6340 Rev. Victor J. Molka Jr.Attended by Vicariate 4, District 1 Parishes, Tel: 412-456-5649.
Golden Hill Nursing, Inc., Lawrence County. Tel: 724-654-7791. Attended by Vicariate 4 Parishes.
Haven Convalescent Home, Lawrence County. Tel: 724-654-8833. Rev. Victor J. Molka Jr. Attended by Vicariate 4 Parishes, Tel. 412-456-5649.
Highland Hall Care Center, Lawrence County. Tel: 724-658-4781. Rev. Victor J. Molka Jr. Attended by Vicariate 4 Parishes, Tel: 412-456-5649.
Hillview Manor, Lawrence County. Tel: 724-658-1521. Rev. Victor J. Molka Jr. Attended by Vicariate 4 Parishes, Tel: 412-456-5649.
Jameson Care Center. Rev. Victor J. Molka Jr. Lawrence County, PA 724-596-3411Attended by St. Camillus Parish 724-652-9471.
Majors Manor, Lawrence County. Tel: 724-924-9568. Rev. Victor J. Molka Jr.Attended by Vicariate 4, District 1 Parishes, Tel: 412-465-5649.
Overlook Nursing Home. Attended by St. Camillus Parish 724-652-9471 Lawrence County. Tel: 724-946-3511. Rev. Victor J. Molka Jr.
Shenango United Presbyterian Home. Attended by: St. Camillus Parish 724-652-9471 Lawrence County. Tel: 724-946-3516. Rev. Victor J. Molka Jr.
Silver Oak Nursing. Attended by Mary Mother of Hope Parish 724-658-2564 Lawrence County. Tel: 724-652-3863. Rev. Victor J. Molka Jr.
Southpoint at Jameson PCH. Rev. Victor J. Molka Jr.Lawrence County, PA 724-658-1100Attended by Mary Mother of Hope Parish 724-658-2564.

WASHINGTON COUNTY. *Beverly South Hills*, Washington County. Tel: 724-746-1300. Rev. Thomas J. Galvin.
Canon House, Washington County. Tel: 724-745-7771. Revs. Thomas J. Galvin, John D. Nanz, D.Div., (Retired)Attended by St. Patrick Parish, Canonsburg. Tel. 724-745-6560, Tel: 724-745-7771.
Charles House Home for the Aged, Washington County. Tel: 724-745-6355. Revs. Thomas J. Galvin, John D. Nanz, D.Div., Chap., (Retired)Tel: 724-745-0950, Tel: 724-745-6355Attended by St. Patrick Parish, Canonsburg.
Greenery Nursing Home, Washington County. Tel: 724-745-8000. Revs. Thomas J. Galvin, John D. Nanz, D.Div., Chap., (Retired)Tel: 724-745-6560, Tel: 724-745-8000Attended by St. Patrick Parish, Canonsburg.
Havencrest. Washington County, PA 724-258-3000Attended by St. Damien of Molokai Parish 724-258-7742.
Horizon Senior Care, Washington County. Tel: 724-746-5040. Revs. Thomas J. Galvin, John D. Nanz, D.Div., (Retired)Tel: 724-745-6560, Tel: 724-746-5040Attended by St. Patrick Parish, Canonsburg.
Humbert Lane Health Care. Rev. Camillus Okechukwu Njoku.
Kade's Nursing Home, Washington County. Tel: 724-222-2148. Rev. Camillus Okechukwu NjokuAttended by St. Hilary Parish 724-222-4087.
Mon Valley Care Center. Washington County, PA 724-310-1111Attended by St. Damien of Molokai Parish 724-258-7742.
Presbyterian Senior Care, Washington County. Tel: 724-222-4300. Rev. Camillus Okechukwu Njoku.
Rest Haven Personal Care Home, Washington County. Tel: 724-745-3333. Revs. Thomas J. Galvin, John D. Nanz, D.Div., Chap., (Retired) Attended by: St. Patrick Parish, Canonsburg, Tel: 724-745-6560.
Washington County Health Center. Attended by Immaculate Conception Parish, Washington 724-225-1425 Washington County. Tel: 724-228-5010. Rev. Camillus Okechukwu Njoku.

Mental Health Facilities

ALLEGHENY COUNTY. *Western Psychiatric Institute & Clinic*, Allegheny County. Tel: 412-647-3060. Attended by UPMC Chaplains. Tel: 412-647-7615.

Correctional Institutions

ALLEGHENY COUNTY. *Allegheny County Jail*, Allegheny County. Tel: 412-350-2000. Rev. Peter C. Mawanda, Deacon Thomas J. Berna.
Shuman Center, Allegheny County. Tel: 412-661-6806. Social Services. Tel: 412-665-4135.

BEAVER COUNTY. *Beaver County Jail*. Deacon Joseph N. Basko.

BUTLER COUNTY. *Butler County Jail*. Rev. William Wuenchel.

GREENE COUNTY. *State Correctional Institute at Greene*, Greene County. Tel: 724-852-2902. Rev. Malcolm McDonald.
Waynesburg County Jail, Greene County. Tel: 724-627-7780. Attended by St. Ann Parish (724-627-7780).

On Duty Outside the Diocese:
Rev. Msgr.—
Kozar, John E., 1011 First Ave., New York, NY 10022-4195
Very Rev.—
Wehner, James A., S.T.D., 2901 S. Carrollton Ave., New Orleans, LA 70118-4391
Revs.—
Schluep, Thomas G. Jr.
Sedor, Michael S., S.T.L.

Absent on Sick Leave:
Rev. Msgr.—
Ogrodowski, William M., S.T.L.
Very Rev.—
Esposito, Samuel J., V.E., M.Div.
Revs.—
Cillo, David M.
Fix, Donald P.
McKnight, Kevin F.
Moneck, George J.
Patriquin, Garry D.
Walsh, John F.
Yagesh, Richard C.

Retired:
Revs.—
Alberth, Regis, (Retired), 115 Trinity Drive, Aliquippa, 15001
Ayoob, John, (Retired), 2349 Railroad St., #1502, 15222
Baily, Harold, (Retired), 12 Maple Ave., Carnegie, 15106
Bischof, Donald R., (Retired), 2600 Morange Rd., 15205
Bleichner, Howard P., S.S., S.T.D., (Retired), 1050 McNeilly Rd., 15226
Boyle, Robert, (Retired), 2600 Morange Rd., 15205
Breier, Donald P., (Retired), 511 Payne Hill Rd., V-239, Jefferson Hills, 15025
Bryce, Edward M., V.F., S.T.L., (Retired), 202 Stanwix St., 15222
Buchleitner, Donald N., (Retired), 202 Carpenter Ln., 15212
Buranosky, Dennis M., (Retired), 7076 Franklin Rd., Cranberry Township, 106066
Campbell, Norbert J., (Retired)
Chortos, Donald, (Retired), 119 W. Chestnut St., Washington, 15301
Chortos, George F., (Retired), 119 W. Chestnut St., Washington, 15301
Cirilli, Matthew R., (Retired), 708 Sturbridge Ln., Export, 15632
Conley, Roy H., (Retired), 2600 Morange Rd., 15205
Connolly, Robert P., (Retired), 633 Cannelton Rd., Darlington, 16115
Costello, Bernard B., (Retired), 2600 Morange Rd., 15205
Czapinski, Richard J., (Retired), 702 Dehaven Ct., Glenshaw, 15116
Dansak, Thomas E., (Retired)
Dascenzo, Joseph J., (Retired), Villa St. Joseph, 1030 W. State St., Baden, 15005
Dixon, David C., (Retired), 2600 Morange Rd., 15205
Dixon, Jerome A., J.C.L., (Retired), 1020 Benton Ave., 15212
Dorsey, Garrett D., (Retired), Canongate Apartments, 200 White Hampton Ln., #618, 15236-1550
Downs, James A., (Retired), 12076 Sagwaw Ave., Conneaut Lake, 16316
Duch, Robert G., Ph.D., (Retired), 411 Hickory Ct., 15238
Dworak, Walter W., (Retired), P.O. Box 502, Aubrey, TX 76227
Elanjileth, J. Matthew, (Retired), 1500 Fifth Ave. Kelly Bldg., McKeesport, 15132
Fay, William J., (Retired), 124 Rana Ln., Gibsonia, 15044
Feeney, William P., M.Div., (Retired), 1028 Benton Ave., 15212
Fitzgerald, John P., C.A.C., (Retired), 2600 Morange Rd., 15205
Garvey, James W., (Retired), 1700 Harpster St., 15212
Geinzer, John A., S.T.L., M.Ed, (Retired), 2600 Morange Rd., 15205
Gentile, Carl J., V.F., (Retired), 337 W. 12th Ave. Extension, Homestead, 15120
George, Robert J., (Retired), 4720 5th Ave., 15213
Grosko, Joseph R., M.Div., (Retired), 2695 Winchester Dr., 15220
Gualtieri, Raymond A., (Retired), c/o Barbara Arnone, 4940 Brightwood Rd., Apt. A406, Bethel Park, 15102
Guay, Robert, (Retired), St. Kilian Parish, 7076 Franklin Rd, Cranberry Twp., 16066

Gudewicz, John L., (Retired), 346 Finley Ave., Carnegie, 15106
Gutierrez, Alvin P., (Retired), 3401 Rigel St., 15212
Haney, John R., M.Div., (Retired)
Harcarik, Bernard M., (Retired), 81 South 13th St., 15203
Harvey, John A., (Retired), Arrowood #359, 512 N. Lewis Run Rd., West Mifflin, 15122
Herrmann, Robert W., (Retired), Holy Trinity Parish, 5718 Steubenville Pike, McKees Rocks, 15136-1311
Holpp, Lawrence V., (Retired), 500 E. Bruceton Rd., #316, 15236
Householder, Paul C., (Retired), 207 Patton Dr., Aliquippa, 15001-9167
Jordan, John M., (Retired)
Keenan, Joseph F., M.Div., (Retired), 2413 Mission St., 15203
Kirby, Thomas M., (Retired), 999 Rock Run Rd., Elizabeth, 15037
Kleppner, Joseph J., S.T.L., Ph.D., (Retired), 1136 Timberwood Dr., Beaver Falls, 15010
Kohler, William F., (Retired), 2270 Brodhead Rd., Aliquippa, 15001
Koser, Albert C., (Retired), 2600 Morange Rd., 15205
Kredel, Thomas E., (Retired), 2600 Morange Rd., 15205
Kunco, Edward J., (Retired), P.O. Box 4248, Hidden Valley, 15502
Kunkel, James E., S.T.M., (Retired), 2600 Morange Rd., 15205
Kurutz, Joseph V., S.T.L., M.Ed., (Retired), 1317 Berryman Ave., Bethel Park, 15102
Lang, Hugh J., M.Ed., (Retired), 400 Hoodridge Dr., 15234
Litavec, Edward S., (Retired)
Lutz, Gerald J., (Retired), 19 Wilson St., 15223
Maida, Thaddeus S., (Retired), 44045 Five Mile Rd., Plymouth, MI 48170
Manion, Thomas F., (Retired), 2600 Morange Rd., 15205
Marcucci, John A., (Retired), 458 Amherst Ave., Coraopolis, 15108
Maurer, Russell J., (Retired), 343 Forest Grove Rd., Coraopolis, 15108-3797
McDermott, Michael A., (Retired), 2600 Morange Rd., 15205
Meyer, Robert J., (Retired)
Mikonis, Gerald S., (Retired), 1163 Country Club Rd., Rte. 88, Monongahela, 15063
Mitolo, Frank A., (Retired), 807 Pine St., Ambridge, 15003-1734
Mueller, Richard J., (Retired), 889 Charlemagne Blvd., Naples, FL 34112
Murphy, James F., (Retired), 16 Blueberry Ln., Wexford, 16090
Murphy, Peter P., (Retired), 2600 Morange Rd., 15205
Nanz, John D., D.Div., (Retired)
Nichols, Harry E., (Retired), 2600 Morange Rd., 15205
Norton, Robert A., 9817 Three Degree Rd., Allison Park, 15101
O'Brien, Patrick J., S.T.D., M.S.Ed., (Retired), 5703 Holden St., 15205
O'Donnell, Thomas M., M.Div., (Retired), 1321 Apaloosa Ln. Apt. 317, Fort Myers, FL 33912
O'Malley, John J., (Retired), 1103 N. Highland Ave., 15206
O'Neil, Thomas D., M.Div., (Retired), 207 Chambers Dr., Washington, 15301
O'Shea, Jeremiah T., (Retired), 417 LeCove Rd., Greensburg, 15601
Oldenski, Kenneth E., (Retired), 6698 41st St. Cir. E., Sarasota, FL 34243
Palick, George J., (Retired), Vincentian Home, 111 Perrymont Rd., 15237-5239
Palko, John A., (Retired), 1028 Benton Ave., 15212
Petrarulo, John D., (Retired), 2600 Morange Rd., 15205
Pribonic, Phillip, (Retired), 173 Bluestone Dr., Bethel Park, 15102
Pudichery, Joseph P., (Retired), 1 Lucymont Dr., New Castle, 16102
Ritzert, William J., (Retired), 954 Gameland Rd., Chicora, 16025
Rutkowski, Theodore A., S.T.L., (Retired), 2848 Darlington Rd., Beaver Falls, 15010
Ryan, Regis J., (Retired), 1011 Church Ave., Mc Kees Rocks, 15136
Rydzon, Walter G., (Retired), 20 Deerskin Ave., Ormond Beach, FL 32174
Schleicher, Edward R., (Retired), 2600 Morange Rd., 15205
Schwartz, William J., (Retired), 200 3rd St., Beaver, 15009
Semler, Albert J., (Retired), 1304 E. Cruikshank Rd., Butler, 16002
Smith, Lawrence R., (Retired), St. Cyril of Alexandria Parish, 3854 Brighton Rd., 15212-1602
Smoley, Rudolph F., (Retired), 1160 Bower Hill Rd., Apt. 501-B, 15243
Sobon, Walter A., V.F., M.Ed., (Retired), 402 Red Deer Ln., Coraopolis, 15108
Spirko, Nicholas A., (Retired), St. Vitus Parish, 910 South Mercer St., New Castle, 16101-4670
Staszewski, Robert M., (Retired), 317 W. Pike St., Canonsburg, 15317
Suhoza, John E., (Retired), c/o Rev. Frank Mitolo, 807 Pine St., Ambridge, 15003-1734
Swiderski, Gregory C., (Retired), 2600 Morange Rd., 15205
Terdine, Richard G., (Retired), 2600 Morange Rd., 15205
Tosello, Matthew, Ph.D., (Retired), 211 Osborne Ln., Sewickley, 15143
Trance, F. Raymond, M.Div., M.R.E., M.B.A., (Retired), 3309 McRoberts Rd., 15234
Trzeciakowski, Edward J., (Retired), 2600 Morange Rd., 15205
Tusky, Richard J., (Retired), 2710 Ohio St., Bethel Park, 15102
Utz, Raymond M., (Retired), 2600 Morange Rd., 15205
Vallone, Louis F., M.Div., M.A., J.C.B., (Retired), 1011 Church Ave., McKees Rocks, 15136
Ward, Richard E., S.T.D., (Retired), 108 N. Dithridge St., 15213
Wesoloski, Richard J., (Retired), 2600 Morange Rd., 15205
White, Kenneth R., (Retired), 115 Green Commons Dr., 15243
Wilt, George A., (Retired), 2600 Morange Rd., 15205
Young, James G., M.Div., (Retired).

Permanent Deacons:
Babcock, Michael J., Holy Apostles, Baldwin/ Carrick/Overbrook; Holy Angels, Hays; St. Sylvester, Brentwood
Bachner, Ralph W. Jr., St. Kilian, Adams/Cranberry Townships; Holy Sepulcher, Glade Mills
Barth, Robert V., (Retired)
Basko, Joseph N., St. Frances Cabrini, Center Twp.; St. John the Baptist, Monaca; Our Lady of Fatima, Hopewell Township; St. Titus, Aliquippa
Batz, William G., St. Thomas More, Bethel Park; St. John Capistran, Upper St. Clair
Berna, Thomas J., St. Stephen, Hazelwood; St. Paul Cathedral, St. Regis, Oakland; St. Rosalia, Greenfield
Bibro, Mark S., St. Pius X, Brookline; Our Lady of Loreto, Brookline; St. Catherine of Siena, Beechview; Resurrection, Brookline
Bittner, Robert J., Our Lady of Fatima, Hopewell Twp.; St. Titus, Aliquippa, St. Francis Cabrini, Center Township; St. John the Baptist, Monaca
Byers, Stephen J., St. Bonaventure, Glenshaw; All Saints, Etna; Holy Spirit, Millvale; St. Nicholas, Millvale
Carran, John J., Christ the King, Bessemer/ Hillsville; St. James the Apostle, Pulaski; St. Camillus, Neshannock Twp.; St. Joseph the Worker, Mary Mother of the Church, St. Vincent de Paul, St. Vitus, New Castle
Caruso, Richard J., St. John Neumann, Franklin Park; Assumption of the Most Blessed Virgin Mary, Bellvue; Sacred Heart, Emsworth
Carver, William H., St. Kilian, Adams/Cranberry Twps.; Holy Sepulcher, Glade Mills
Cerenzia, Joseph A., St. Patrick, Canonsburg; Holy Rosary, Muse; Our Lady of the Miraculous Medal, Meadow Lands
Cessar, Richard R., St. Sebastian, Ross Twp.; St, Athanasius, West View; Incarnation, N. Side; St. Teresa of Avila, Perrysville
Christmann, Edwin P., St. Peter, Slippery Rock; St. Alphonsus, Boyers; St. Christopher, Prospect
Comer, Gary L., St. Athanasius, West View; Incarnation, N. Side; St. Sebastian, Ross Township; St. Teresa of Avila, Perrysville
Como, Gerard A., St. Thomas a Becket, Jefferson Hills; St. Clare of Assisi, Clairton; St. Elizabeth of Hungary, Pleasant Hills, Holy Spirit, West Mifflin
Compomizzi, Joseph, (Outside the Diocese)
Dadowski, Francis J. Jr., St. Mary of the Assumption, Glenshaw; St. Ursula, Allison Park
DeFazio, Victor P., St. Anne, Castle Shannon; St. Winifred, Mt. Lebanon
Demblowski, Ronald D., St. Maximilian Kolbe, Homestead; Resurrection, West Mifflin; St. Rita, Munhall; St. Therese of Lisieux, Munhall
DeNome, Harry J., St. Monica, Beaver Falls/ Chippewa Twp./Darlington; St. Blaise, Midland
Deskevich, Stephen M., St. James, Sewickley; St. Mary, Aleppo
DiSanto, Dale J., St. Angela Merici, White Oak; Corpus Christi, St. Patrick, McKeesport; St. Robert Bellarmine, East McKeesport
Dougherty, Joseph M., Good Shepherd, Braddock; Madonna del Castello, Swissvale; St. Maurice, Forest Hills; Word of God, Rankin
Eckhardt, Frederick N., St. Bernard, Mount Lebanon; Our Lady of Grace, Scott Township
Ernst, Richard D., St. Ursula, Allison Park; St. Mary of the Assumption, Glenshaw
Fitzpatrick, Richard T., Our Lady of the Angels, Lawrenceville; Immaculate Heart of Mary, Polish Hill; St. Maria Goretti, Bloomfield
Gaines, George W., Concordia at Cabot Nursing Home
Giordano, Anthony J., St. John the Baptist, Monaca; Good Samaritan, Baridge; Sts. John and Paul, Franklin Park; Our Lady of Peace, Conway
Grab, James R., Ministry for Retired Clergy; Holy Apostles, South Pittsburgh; Holy Angels, Hays; St. Sylvester, Brentwood
Gruseck, David J., (Outside the Diocese)
Hahn, William O., St. Raphael, Morningside / Stanton Heights / Upper Lawrenceville; Sacred Heart, Shadyside
Heiles, Albert E. Jr., St. Alphonsus, St. Alexis, Wexford
Hirst, Jeffrey A., Immaculate Conception, St. Hilary, Washington
Homer, Clifford M. Sr., St. Catherine of Sweden, Hampton Twp.; St. Richard, Richland Township
Jancart, Robert A., St. Margaret Mary, Moon Twp.; St. Catherine of Siena, Crescent; St. Joseph, Coraopolis
Jelinek, G. Gregory, Most Holy Name of Jesus, Troy Hill; St. Aloysius, Reserve Township; St. Cyril of Alexandria, Brighton heights; Holy Wisdom, St. Peter, N. Side; Risen Lord, Marshall
Kelly, Michael W., St. Bernadette, North American Martyrs, Monroeville; St. Bartholomew, St. Gerard Majella, St. Susanna, Penn Hills
Kenny, James A., St. Germaine, Bethel Park; Nativity, South Park
Kielar, S. Daniel, St. Camillus, Neshannock Township; Christ the King, Bessemer; st. james the Apostle, Pulaski; St. Joseph the Worker, Mary Mother of the Church, St. Vincent de Paul, St. Vitus, New Castle
Killmeyer, Tim M., Holy Trinity, Robinson Township; St. John of God, McKees Rocks; St. Malachy, Kennedy Township
Kisak, Stephen J., Holy Spirit, Millvale: St. Nicholas, Millvale/N. Side; All Saints, Etna; St. Bonaventure, Glenshaw
Kondrich, Keith G., Word of God, Rankin/Swissvale; Madonna del Costello, Swissvale; Good Shepherd, Braddock; St. Maurice, Forest Hills
Kosko, Joseph J. Jr., St. Winifred, Mt. Lebanon; St. Anne, Castle Shannon
Koslosky, Robert E., Incarnation of the Lord, Observatory Hill/Perry North; St. Athanasius, West View; St. Sebastian, Ross Township; St. Teresa of Avila, Perrysville
Krofcheck, Barry A., St. Agnes, West Mifflin; Christ the Light of the World, St. Joseph, Duquesne; Holy Trinity, West Mifflin
Krulikowski, Thomas E., Primary Episcopal Master of Ceremonies
Kuhns, Elbert A., St. Thomas, Clarksville; Our Lady of Consolation, Nemacolin; St. Ignatius of Antioch, Bobtown; St. Hugh, Carmichaels; St. Ann, Waynesburg
Lander, Kevin L., St. Margaret, Green Tree; St. Elizabeth Ann Seton, Carnegie; Sts. Simon and Jude, Scott Township
Longo, Richard A., St. Mary of the Mount, Mt. Washington; Prince of Peace, South Side
Lopus, Thomas A., St. James, Sewickley; St. Mary, Aleppo
Ludwikowski, Jeffrey J., St. Alexis, St. Alphonsus, Wexford
Mackin, James S., Ss. Simon and Jude, Scott Twp.; St. Elizabeth Ann Seton, Carnegie; St. Margaret of Scotland, Greentree
Marshall, Robert M., St. Kilian, Adams/Cranberry Twps.; Holy Sepulcher, Glade Mills
Martorano, Philip D., St. Patrick, Canonsburg; Holy Rosary, Muse; Our Lady of the Miraculous Medal, Meadow Lands
Meyer, Joseph C. Jr., (Retired)
Miles, Leon F., St. Barbara and Holy Child, Bridgeville; St. Mary, Cecil
Miller, David S., Holy Sepulcher, Glade Mills; St. Kilian, Cranberry Township
Miller, John C., St. Teresa of Avila, Perrysville
Mills, Thomas B., St. Valentine, St. Germaine, Bethel Park; St. Gabriel of the Sorrowful Virgin, Whitehall; Nativity, South Park
Mobley, Anton V., Our Lady of the Miraculous Medal, Meadow Lands; Holy Rosary, Muse; St. Patrick, Canonsburg
Molitor, Gary, St. Richard, Richland Twp.; St. Catherine of Sweden, Hampton
Natali, Mitchell M., St. Paul, St. Michael the

Archangel, St. Peter, Butler; St. Andrew, Center Township; St. Fidelis of Sigmaringen, Lyndora
Nizan, Daniel E., Holy Angels, Hays; Holy Apostles, South Pittsburgh; St. Sylvester, Brentwood
Noca, Timothy F., St. John the Baptist, St. Januarius, Plum; St. Irenaeus, Oakmont; St. Joseph, Verona; Our Lady of Peace, Conway
O'Keefe, Charles L., (Retired)
O'Neill, Thomas J., St. Catherine of Sienna, Beechview; Our Lady of Loreto, Brookline; St. Pius X, Brookline; Resurrection, Brookline; St. Pamphilus, Beechview
Olson, James R., Good Samaritan, Ambridge; St. John the Baptist, Baden; Sts. John & Paul, Franklin Park; Our Lady of Peace, Conway
Palamara, William R. Jr., St. Athanasius, West View; Incarnation, N. Side; St. Sebastian, Ross Township; St. Teresa of Avila, Perrysville
Pepe, Donald C., St. Gregory, Zelienople; St. Ferdinand, Cranberry Township; holy Redeemer, Ellwood City
Pielin, Gery G., St. Aloysius, Reserve Twp.; St. Cyril of Alexandria, Brighton Heights; Holy Wisdom, St. Peter, N. Side; Most Holy Name of Jesus, Troy Hill; Risen Lord, Marshall
Pikula, Stephen C., St. Mark, Liberty Borough; St. Michael, Elizabeth; Queen of Rosary, Glassport
Podobnik, Brian M., Holy Child, St. Barbara, Bridgeville; St. Mary, Cecil
Poroda, Alexander J. II, St. Damien of Molokai, Monongahela; Mary Mother of the Church, Charleroi; Our Lady of the Valley, Donora
Ragan, John E., St. Michael, Elizabeth; St. Mark, Libery Borough; Queen of Rosary, Glassport
Raymond, Thomas W., St. Katharine Drexel, Southeast Washington County
Rhoads, Charles H., All Saints, Etna; St. Bonaventure, Glenshaw; Holy Spirit, St. Nicholas, Millvale
Riley, Herbert E. Jr., St. Colman, Turtle Creek; St. John Fisher, Churchill; St. Jude the Apostle, Wilmerding
Rubio, Silverio, (Outside the Diocese)
Satter, Victor P., St. Benedict the Abbot, McMurray; St. Francis of Assis, Finleyville; St. Isacc Jogues, Jefferson Hills
Sheil, James M., St. Ann, Waynesburg; St. Hugh, Carmichael; St. Ignatius of Antioch, Bobtown; Our Lady of Consolation, Nemacolin; St. Thomas, Clarksville
Stein, Robert J., St. Germaine, St. Valentine, Bethel Park; Nativity, South Park; St. Gabriel of the Sorrowful Virgin, Whitehall
Strathmann, William F. Jr., St. Louise de Marillac, Upper Saint Clair; St. Joan of Arc, South Park
Sutton, Lawrence R., Ph.D., Our Lady of Grace, Scott Township; St. Bernard, Mt. Lebanon
Szemanski, Frank J., Prince of Peace, South Side; St. Mary of the Mount, Mt. Washington
Thomas, Leonard M. Jr., St. Mary, Cecil; St. Barbara, Holy Child; Bridgeville
Toney, Samuel, St. Mary of Mercy, The Point / Gateway Center; St. Benedict the Moor, Hill District; Epiphany, Uptown; St. Patrick-St. Stanislaus Kostka, Strip District
Tucek, Richard M., St. Bartholomew, St. Gerard Majella, St. Susanna, Penn Hills; St. Bernadette, North American Martyrs, Monroeville
Vannucci, Joseph R., St. John the Baptist, St. Januarius, Plum; St. Irenaeus, Oakmont; St. Joseph, Verona; Our Lady of Joy, Holiday Park
Vaskov, John A., Sacred Heart, Shadyside; St. Raphael, Morningside/Stanton Heights/Upper Lawrenceville
Vukotich, Charles J. Jr., Asbury Heights
Weiland, James T., (Outside the Diocese)
Wertz, Robert F. Jr., St. Juan Diego, Sharpsburg; St. Joseph, O'Hara Twp., St. Pio of Pietrelcina, Blawnox; St. Scholastica, Aspinwall
White, Andrew J. Sr., St. Sylvester, Brentwood; Holy Apostles, South Pittsburgh; Holy Angels, Hays
Wilmer, Reynold, St. Robert Bellarmine, East McKeesport; St. Angela Merici, White Oak; Corpus Christi, St. Patrick, McKeesport
Witter, David R. Sr., St. Teresa of Avila, Perrysville; St. Athanasius, West View; Incarnation, North Side; St. Sebastian, Ross Township
Wood, Patrick G., Our Lady of the Most Blessed Sacrament, Natrona Heights; St. Joseph, Natrona; Our Lady of Victory, Harwick; St. Alphonsus, Springdale; Holy Family, Creighton; Holy Martyrs, Tarentum
Zenchak, Timothy B., Holy Apostles, South Pittsburgh; Holy Angels, Hays; St. Sylvester, Brentwood.

INSTITUTIONS LOCATED IN DIOCESE

[A] SEMINARIES, RELIGIOUS OR SCHOLASTICATES

PITTSBURGH. *Saint Paul Seminary* (1965) College & Pre-Theology, 2900 Noblestown Rd., 15205-4227. Tel: 412-456-3048; Fax: 412-456-3187; Email: seminaryprog@diopitt.org; Web: www.diopitt.org. Rev. Brian W. Noel, S.T.L., Spiritual Dir. & Dir. of Pastoral Formation; Sr. Cindy Ann Kibler, S.H.S., Apostolic Works Coord.; Rev. Thomas A. Sparacino, M.Div., Rector. Priests 2; Sisters 1; Students 13; Students (attending Duquesne University) 13; Religious Teachers 3.

[B] COLLEGES AND UNIVERSITIES

PITTSBURGH. *Carlow University* (1929) 3333 Fifth Ave., 15213. Tel: 412-578-6059; Fax: 412-578-6668; Email: admission@carlow.edu; Web: www.carlow.edu. Suzanne K. Mellon, Pres.; Deanne H. D'Emilio, J.D., Vice Pres. of Academic Affairs & Provost; Andrea Leyko, Interim Librarian. Sisters of Mercy. Lay Teachers 95; Sisters 2; Total Enrollment 2,272; Total Staff 289.

Duquesne University of the Holy Spirit (1878) 600 Forbes Ave., 15282. Tel: 412-396-6000;
Fax: 412-396-4334; Email: walshd@duq.edu; Web: www.duq.edu. Ken Gormley, Pres.; Revs. John Fogarty, Supr. Gen., Spiritan Congregation; Sean M. Hogan, C.S.Sp., Pres., Duquesne University Scholarship Assoc.; Sean Kealy, C.S.Sp., (Retired); Raymond D. French, C.S.Sp., Vice Pres. Mission & Identity; Naos McCool, C.S.Sp., Asst. Dean Student Formation School of Educ., (Retired); Peter I. Osuji, Campus Min. & Asst. Prof.; Very Rev. Jeffrey T. Duaime, C.S.Sp., Prov. Supr., Spiritan U.S. Province & Chm. Duquesne Univ. Corp.; Revs. John A. Sawicki, C.S.Sp., Sec./Treas. Duquesne Univ. Corp.; Jocelyn Gregoire, C.S.Sp.; Daniel L. Walsh, C.S.Sp., Campus Min. & Dir., Spiritan Campus Ministry; Brian Cronin, C.S.Sp., Visiting Prof., Philosophy; James C. Okoye, Dir., Spiritan Studies & Vice Chm. Duquesne Univ. Corp.; Eugene Uzukwu, C.S.Sp., Assoc. Prof., Theology; William H. Christy, C.S.Sp., Asst. Dir., Spiritan Campus Ministry; George J. Spangenberg, C.S.Sp., Visiting Instructor Intl. Educ.; Gregory Olikenyi, C.S.Sp., Asst. Prof., Theology; Jean-Michael Gelmetti, C.S.Sp., Spiritan Fellow; William Cleary, Scholar in Residence; James P. McCloskey, C.S. Sp., Senior Adviser to the Pres. The Spiritans. Faculty 514; Priests 16; Students 9,403; Total Staff 1,578.

The University is coeducational and comprises the following Colleges, Schools and Institutes:

College of Liberal Arts, Tel: 412-396-6389;
Fax: 412-396-4859. Dr. James Swindal, Dean, College & Graduate School of Liberal Arts.

School of Business Administration,
Tel: 412-396-6238; Fax: 412-396-4764. Dr. Dean B. McFarlin, Dean.

School of Music, Tel: 412-396-6080;
Fax: 412-396-5479. Seth Beckman, Dean.

School of Law, Tel: 412-396-6300;
Fax: 412-396-5219. The Honorable Maureen Lally-Green, Interim Dean.

School of Education, Tel: 412-396-6093;
Fax: 412-396-5585. Dr. Cindy M. Walker, Dean.

School of Nursing, Tel: 412-396-6550;
Fax: 412-396-6346. Dr. Mary Ellen Smith Glasgow, Dean.

School of Pharmacy, Tel: 412-396-6380;
Fax: 412-396-1810. Dr. J. Douglas Bricker, Dean, Mylan School of Pharmacy.

School of Health Sciences, Tel: 412-396-6652;
Fax: 412-396-5554. Dr. Paula Sammahone Turocy, Interim Dean; Dr. Philip Reeder, Dean Bayer School of Natural & Environmental Sciences, Tel: 412-396-4900; Dr. Timothy R. Austin, Provost & Academic Vice Pres.; Matthew Frist, Vice Pres. Mgmt. & Business; Dr. Douglas K. Frizzel, Vice Pres. Student Life; Madelyn A. Reilly Esq., Gen. Counsel & Univ. Sec.; Dr. Sara Baron, Librarian.

La Roche College (1963) 9000 Babcock Blvd., 15237-5898. Tel: 412-367-9300; Fax: 412-536-1199; Email: admissions@laroche.edu; Web: www.laroche.edu. Sr. Candace Introcaso, C.D.P., Ph.D., Pres.; Michael Andreola, Vice Pres. Inst. Advancement; Colleen Ruefle, Vice Pres. for Student Life & Dean of Students; Rev. Thomas G. Schaefer, Assoc. Vice Pres., Academic Affairs; Dr. Howard Ishiyama, Vice Pres. for Academic Affairs & Academic Dean; Dr. Rosemary McCarthy, Ph.D., Assoc. Vice Pres., Academic Affairs & Dean, Grad. Student & Adult Ed.; Robert Vogel, Vice Pres. Business & Finance; CFO; Sr. Michele Bisbey, C.D.P., Senior Advisor to Pres.; James Weisgerber, Ph.D., Vice Pres. for Enrollment Mgmt. Sisters of Divine Providence. Religious Teachers 1; Lay Teachers 220; Priests 3; Sisters 15; Students 1,555; Total Staff 190.

[C] HIGH SCHOOLS, DIOCESAN

PITTSBURGH. *Bishop Canevin High School, Inc.* (1957) 2700 Morange Rd., 15205. Tel: 412-922-7400;
Fax: 412-922-7403; Email: mainoffice@bishopcanevin.org; Web: www.bishopcanevin.org. Mr. Kenneth M. Sinagra, Prin.; Rev. Brian W. Noel, S.T.L., Chap.; Mrs. Karen M. Walker, Asst. Prin.; Mrs. Susan Rakaczky, Librarian. Lay Teachers 27; Priests 1; Students 300.

Central Catholic High School, Inc. (1927) 4720 Fifth Ave., 15213. Tel: 412-208-3400 Main;
Tel: 412-208-3421; Fax: 412-208-0555; Email: abaginski@centralcatholichs.com; Web: www.centralcatholichs.com. Bro. Anthony Baginski, F.S.C., Pres. & Prin.; Vincent Ciaramella, Admin. The school is a Diocesan institution under the care of the Brothers of the Christian Schools (F.S.C.). Brothers 7; Lay Teachers 65; Priests 2; Students 845; Total Staff 100.

Oakland Catholic High School, Inc. (1989) 144 N. Craig St., 15213. Tel: 412-682-6633;
Fax: 412-682-2496; Email: webmaster@oaklandcath.org; Web: www.oaklandcatholic.org. Nicole Modarelli, Asst. Prin.; Sharyn Zalno, Asst. Prin.; Marisa Greco, Asst. Prin.; Mary Claire Kasunic, Pres. Lay Teachers 46; Priests 1; Students 556; Total Staff 20.

BADEN. *Quigley Catholic High School, Inc.* (1967) 200 Quigley Dr., Baden, 15005. Tel: 724-869-2188;
Fax: 724-869-3091; Email: office@qchs.org; Web: www.qchs.org. Mrs. Rita McCormick, Prin. Religious Teachers 1; Lay Teachers 14; Sisters 1; Students 112; Total Staff 17.

CRANBERRY TOWNSHIP. *North Catholic High School* (1939) 1617 Rte. 228, Cranberry Twp, 16066.
Tel: 412-321-4823; Fax: 724-776-2287; Email: school@cwnchs.org; Web: www.cwnchs.org. Mr. Luke Crawford, Prin.; Rev. Charles Bober, Chap. Lay Teachers 39; Students 442; Total Staff 49.

MCKEESPORT. *Serra Catholic High School, Inc.* (1961) 200 Hershey Dr., McKeesport, 15132.
Tel: 412-751-2020; Fax: 412-751-3488; Email: 73781@diopitt.org; Web: www.serrahs.com. Timothy Chirdon, Prin.; Mrs. Wendy Seibert, Librarian. Lay Teachers 25; Students 350.

MT. LEBANON. *Seton-LaSalle Catholic High School, Inc.* (1979) 1000 McNeilly Rd., 15226.
Tel: 412-561-3583; Fax: 412-561-9097; Email: slshs@slshs.org; Web: www.slshs.org. Lisa Osterhaus, Pres.; Lauren Martin, Prin.; Stephanie Schmidt, Librarian; Rev. Jack Demnyan, Chap. Religious Teachers 1; Lay Teachers 34; Students 406.

NATRONA HEIGHTS. *Saint Joseph High School, Inc.*, 800 Montana Ave., Natrona Heights, 15065.
Tel: 724-224-5552; Fax: 724-224-3205; Email: cjagodrinski@saintjosephhs.com; Email: bkaniecki@saintjosephhs.com; Web: www.saintjosephhs.com. Beverly K. Kaniecki, Prin. Religious Teachers 1; Lay Teachers 20; Sisters 1; Students 180.

[D] HIGH SCHOOLS, PRIVATE

PITTSBURGH. **Holy Family Academy*, 8235 Ohio River Blvd., 15202. Tel: 412-307-0230;
Fax: 412-307-0249; Email: abel-palmieri.lisa@hfa-pgh.org; Web: www.hfa-pgh.org. Lisa Abel-Palmieri, Ph.D., Head of School & Chief Learning Office; Joseph Oliphant, Prin. Holy Family Academy is an independent Catholic high school that provides an affordable, innovative education focused on college and career readiness. The Academy partners with families and uses evidence-based practices to equip each student for success. Through a rigorous yet personalized college preparatory program and unique internship program, Academy students build skills that will transform their lives. Lay Teachers 20; Students 171; Chaplains 1; CSFN 1.

Vincentian Academy (1932) 8100 McKnight Rd., 15237. Tel: 412-364-1616; Fax: 412-367-5722; Email: paul.zavolta@vincentianacademy.org; Web: www.vincentianacademy.org. Mrs. Rita B. Canton, Prin. Lay Teachers 24; Sisters of Charity of Nazareth 1; Students 251; Total Staff 35.

CORAOPOLIS. *Our Lady of the Sacred Heart High School* (1932) 1504 Woodcrest Ave., Coraopolis, 15108. Tel: 412-264-5140; Fax: 412-264-4143; Email: info@olsh.org; Web: www.olsh.org. Tim Plocinik, Prin.; Bethany Cvitkovic, Librarian. Felician Sisters, C.S.S.F.State approved day high school. Lay Teachers 32; Sisters 1; Students 356; Total Staff 49.

[E] CONSOLIDATED SCHOOLS

PITTSBURGH. *Christ the Divine Teacher Catholic Academy*, (Grades PreK-8), 205 Brilliant Ave., 15215. Tel: 412-781-7927; Fax: 412-781-0891; Email: office@cdtca.org. Mark Grgurich, Prin.; Kathy Goreczny, Librarian. (Aspinwall); Serving 24 parishes (Regional).; Part of North Hills Regional Catholic Elementary Schools, Inc Lay Teachers 14; Students 160; Total Staff 15.

St. John Bosco Academy, Inc., (Grades PreK-8), 2690 Waddington Ave., 15226. Tel: 412-563-0858; Fax: 412-341-5610; Email: stjbapgh@gmail.com; Web: www.sjbpgh.com. Janet Salley Rakoczy, Prin. (Brookline); Serving the parishes of Our Lady of Loreto, St. Pius X, Resurrection, St. Catherine of Siena, St. Pamphilus, Prince of Peace & St. Mary of the Mount Lay Teachers 10; Students 90; Total Staff 20.

North Hills Regional Catholic Elementary Schools, Inc., 800 Avila Ct., 15237.

Blessed Francis Seelos Academy, 201 Church Rd., Wexford, 15090.

Blessed Francis Seelos Academy Early Childhood Center, 10090 Old Perry Hwy., Wexford, 15090.

Blessed Trinity Academy, 2510 Middle Rd., Glenshaw, 15116. Tel: 412-486-7611.

Blessed Trinity Academy Early Childhood Center, 2001 Mt. Royal Blvd, Glenshaw, 15116.

Holy Cross Academy, 307 Siebert Rd., 15237.

Holy Cross Academy Early Childhood Center, 800 Avila Ct., 15237.

Northside Catholic, 3854 Brighton Rd., 15212. Tel: 412-761-5043; Fax: 412-761-0840; Email: nscprincipal1@gmail.com. Mrs. Rosanne Kwiatkowski, Prin. Aides 1; Lay Teachers 10.

Sister Thea Bowman Catholic Academy, (Grades PreK-8), Previously St. James School. Merged with Holy Rosary School in 2010. 721 Rebecca Ave., 15221. Tel: 412-242-3515; Fax: 412-241-3199; Email: vmorris@stbca.net; Email: info@stbca.net; Web: www.sistertheabowman.org. Nicholas Tisak, Prin. Lay Teachers 13; Priests 2; Students 133.

BUTLER. *Butler Catholic School* (1969) (Grades K-8), 515 E. Locust St., Butler, 16001. Tel: 724-285-4276 ; Fax: 724-285-4896; Email: bcsoffice@butlercatholic.org; Web: www.butlercatholic.org. Sr. John Ann Mulhern, C.D.P., Prin., Prin. Serving the parishes of St. Paul, St. Michael, St. Fidelis, St. Andrew and St. Peter's, Butler. Lay Teachers 23; Preschool 42; Students 235; Full-time Faculty 18; Part-time Faculty 4; Religious Teachers 1.

MONONGAHELA. *Madonna Catholic Regional School* (1998) (Grades PreSchool-8), 731 Chess St., Monongahela, 15063. Tel: 724-258-3199; Fax: 724-258-6764; Email: info@madonnacatholic.com; Web: www.madonnacatholic.com. Mrs. Kathryn Miller, Admin. Serving the parishes of Mary, Mother of the Church, Our Lady of the Valley, and St. Damien of Molokai. Lay Teachers 13; Students 132; Total Staff 18.

[F] ELEMENTARY SCHOOLS, PRIVATE

PITTSBURGH. *The Campus School of Carlow University* (1963) (Grades PreSchool-8), 3333 5th Ave., 15213. Tel: 412-578-6158; Fax: 412-578-6676; Email: mapeduto@carlow.edu; Web: www.campusschool.carlow.edu. Michelle Peduto, Prin.; Julie Marcoux, Librarian. Sisters of Mercy. Lay Teachers 30; Students 272; Total Staff 12.

ALLISON PARK. *Providence Heights Alpha School*, (Grades K-8), 9000 Babcock Blvd., Allison Park, 15101. Tel: 412-366-4455; Fax: 412-635-6317; Email: 87041@diopitt.org; Web: www.alphaschool.org. Ms. Margaret Ruefle, Prin.; Heather Parker, Sec. Sisters of Divine Providence. Religious Teachers 1; Lay Teachers 20; Sisters 3; Students 153.

[G] DEPARTMENT OF SPECIAL EDUCATION

PITTSBURGH. *DePaul School for Hearing and Speech* (1908) 6202 Alder St., 15206. Tel: 412-924-1012; Fax: 412-924-1036; Email: mjmac@depaulinst.com; Web: www.speakmiracles.org. Dr. Ruth Auld, Exec. Dir.; Mary Jo Maynard, Prin. A listening and spoken language day school for children who are deaf or hard of hearing. Lay Teachers 16; Sisters 1; Students 53; Total Staff 40.

NEW BRIGHTON. *McGuire Memorial* (1963) 2119 Mercer Rd., New Brighton, 15066-3437. Tel: 724-843-3400; Fax: 724-847-2004; Email: mcgm@mcguirememorial.org; Web: www.mcguirememorial.org. Residential Facility- Intermediate Care for Intellectually Disabled, The School at McGuire Memorial, Life Enrichment Adult Program, Community Homes, Employment Option Center. Bed Capacity 141; Lay Staff 500; Lay Teachers 25; Priests 1; Sisters 3; Tot Asst. Annually 468; ICF Residents 53; Additional Services: Adult Training 213; Community Living Residents 88; Private Academic School 71.

WEXFORD. **St. Anthony School Programs*, 2000 Corporate Dr., Ste. 580, Wexford, 15090. Tel: 724-940-9020; Fax: 724-940-9064; Email: lgeorge@stanthonyschoolprograms.com. Lisa George, Program Dir. Resource rooms for students with special needs in 4 elementary schools, 3 high schools and 1 Post-Secondary Program. Lay Teachers 12; Students 112; Total Staff 45.

[H] CHILD CARE INSTITUTIONS

PITTSBURGH. *Franciscan Child Day Care Center*, 1401 Hamilton Rd., 15234-2399. Tel: 412-882-5085; Fax: 412-885-7247; Email: fcdcc@osfprov.org; Web: www.osfprov.org/fcdcc.htm. Mrs. Sandra Merlo, Dir.; Sr. Barbara Zilch, O.S.F., Pres. Students 119; Total Staff 21; Religious Teachers 1; Total Assisted 119.

Holy Family Institute (1900) 8235 Ohio River Blvd., 15202. Tel: 412-766-4030; Fax: 412-766-5434; Email: kearns.megan@hfi-pgh.org; Web: www.hfi-pgh.org. Sr. Linda Yankoski, C.S.F.N., Ed.D., Pres. & CEO. Sisters of the Holy Family of Nazareth. Holy Family Institute is committed to helping children, preserving families and strengthening communities by providing an integrated network of social services and programs. These programs and services include in-home family counseling services, a youth workforce development program, SNAP (Stop Now and Plan) program, (early intervention for at-risk youth), Strong Families Collaborative (financial stabilization), substance abuse and addiction counseling, mental health counseling, energy assistance programs and specialized schools for grades K through 12. C.S.F.N. 2; Total Staff 225; Total Assisted 40,264.

Mt. Alvernia Day Care & Learning Center, 146 Hawthorne Rd., 15209. Tel: 412-821-4302; Fax: 412-821-3318; Web: www.sosf.org; Email: mtalverniadaycare@sosf.org. Sr. Karen Krebs, Dir. Sisters of St. Francis of the Neumann Communities.Provides infant, toddler, and preschool care as well as before- and after-school care for school age children, school age care on non-school days and summer. Total Staff 47; Total Assisted 280.

Providence Connections, Inc. (1994) Corporate Office, 3113 Brighton Rd., 15212-2456. Tel: 412-766-3860; Fax: 412-766-6775; Email: sellwood@providenceconnections.org; Web: www.providenceconnections.org. Samantha Ellwood, M.S., Exec. Dir. Students 125; Staff 39.

Providence Family Support Center (1994) 3113 Brighton Rd., 15212-2456. Tel: 412-766-3860; Fax: 412-766-6775; Email: sellwood@providenceconnections.org; Web: www.providenceconnections.org. Samantha Ellwood, M.S., Dir. Children 303; Families 342; (Full-time, paid) 38; Total Assisted 500.

Vincentian Child Development Center, 8150 McKnight Rd., 15237. Tel: 412-366-8588; Fax: 412-366-7315; Email: jparagi@vcs.org. Jill Paragi, Dir. Lay Teachers 22; Sisters 1.

[I] GENERAL HOSPITALS

PITTSBURGH. *UPMC Mercy* (An affiliate of the University of Pittsburgh Medical Center) 1400 Locust St., 15219. Tel: 412-232-8111; Fax: 412-232-7380; Email: eisemanp@upmc.edu; Web: www.upmcmercy.com. Michael Grace, Pres. Bed Capacity 487; Patients Asst Anual. 221,990; Total Staff 2,604.

[J] HOMES FOR THE AGED

PITTSBURGH. *Little Sisters of the Poor Home for the Aged* (1839) 1028 Benton Ave., 15212. Tel: 412-307-1100; Fax: 412-307-1104; Email: mspittsburgh@littlesistersofthepoor.org; Web: www.littlesistersofthepoorpittsburgh.org. Sr. Mary Vincent Mannion, M.S., Supr.; Rev. William P. Feeney, M.Div., Chap., (Retired). Bed Capacity 93; Sisters 12; Tot Asst. Annually 120; Total Staff 115.

Marian Manor Corp. (1956) 2695 Winchester Dr., 15220. Tel: 412-440-4365 (Admin.); Tel: 412-440-4343 (Nursing); Fax: 412-440-4426; Email: slewandowski@vcs.org; Web: www.vcs.org/marianmanor. Rev. John F. Walsh. Marian Manor is a ministry of Vincentian Collaborative System Residents 184; Sisters of the Holy Spirit 3; Tot Asst. Annually 540; Total Staff 275; Child Day Care 73.

[K] REHABILITATION, NURSING AND GERIATRIC CARE FACILITIES

PITTSBURGH. *Marian Hall Home, Inc.* (1970) 934 Forest Ave., 15202-1118. Tel: 412-761-1999; Fax: 412-761-2556; Email: msgriccia@marianhall.org; Web: www.marianhall.org. Sr. Marian Sgriccia, O.S.F., Admin. Purpose: to provide programs, facilities, and services, including, but not limited to, residential personal care, and long-term care homes for the elderly, ill, or disabled, including supportive services. Bed Capacity 81; Tot Asst. Annually 93; Total in Residence 55; Total Staff 58.

The Community at Holy Family Manor, Inc., 301 Nazareth Way, 15229-5105. Tel: 412-931-6996; Fax: 412-931-7255; Email: DPawlus@chfmanor.org; Web: chfmanor.org. Programs operating under The Community at Holy Family Manor: Mt. Nazareth Learning Center; Nazareth Housing Services; Holy Family Manor Personal Care Home. Bed Capacity 59; Tot Asst. Annually 1,550; Total Staff 88.

Vincentian de Marillac (1943) 5300 Stanton Ave., 15206. Tel: 412-361-2833; Fax: 412-361-1237; Email: jpruett@vcs.org. Linda Schoyer, Pastoral Care; Jennifer Pruett, Admin. Catholic, skilled nursing home. Bed Capacity 50; Tot Asst. Annually 150; Total Staff 80.

Vincentian Home (1924) 111 Perrymont Rd., 15237. Tel: 412-366-5600; Fax: 412-366-1408; Email: info@vcs.org; Web: www.vcs.org. Maureen M. Coyne, B.S., M.S.W., M.P.M., L.N.H.A., Admin. Sisters of Charity of Nazareth. Bed Capacity 180; Sisters 5; Tot Asst. Annually 1,025; Total Staff 245; Assisted Living: Total Assisted 60.

BADEN. **Villa St. Joseph of Baden, Inc.*, 1030 State St., Baden, 15005. Tel: 724-869-6300; Fax: 724-869-6399; Email: mmurray@villastjoseph.org; Web: www.villastjoseph.org. Mr. Gary Chace, Pres.; Ms. Mary M. Murray, N.H.A., M.P.H., Exec. Dir. Purpose: To provide a home-like environment for 120 residents in need of skilled nursing, rehabilitation and long-term intermediate care. Villa St. Joseph is a place of healing committed to "excellence in compassionate care" serving the health needs of older adults, as well as those in the wider community in need of our expanding services. Our staff focuses on building relationships, while providing therapy, clinical nursing, activities, spiritual, and other support in a holistic manner. Specialty services include short-term rehabilitation for orthopedic surgeries and other diagnoses, dementia care, and home-like long term living. Villa St. Joseph's Center for outpatient rehabilitation provides therapy services for persons in the local community. Bed Capacity 120; Tot Asst. Annually 500; Total Staff 229; Beds for Patients with Dementia or Alzheimer's 30.

[L] PERSONAL PRELATURES

PITTSBURGH. *Prelature of the Holy Cross and Opus Dei* (1928) Warwick House, 5090 Warwick Ter., 15213. Tel: 412-683-8448; Fax: 412-687-3806; Email: info@warwickhouse.org; Web: www.opusdei.org. Revs. Rene J. Schatteman; Martin J. Miller.

[M] MONASTERIES AND RESIDENCES OF PRIESTS AND BROTHERS

PITTSBURGH. *St. Augustine Friary*, 221 36th St., 15201. Tel: 412-682-6430; Fax: 412-682-6148; Email: brgregb@juno.com; Web: www.capuchin.com. Revs. Thomas Betz, O.F.M.Cap., Prov.; Gregory J. Brown, O.F.M.Cap., Guardian; Vernon Busch, O.F.M.Cap.; Robert Craig, O.F.M.Cap., Vicar; Gervase Degenhardt, O.F.M.Cap., Confessor; Francis Fugini, O.F.M.Cap., Archivist; William Henn, O.F.M.Cap., Prof. Pontifical Gregorian Univ.; Robert E. McCreary, O.F.M.Cap.; John Pfannenstiel, O.F.M.-Cap., Dir. Seraphic Mass Assn.; Joseph Tuscan, O.F.M.Cap., Preaching Ministry; Emilio Biosca, O.F.M.Cap., Pastoral work; Moises Villalta, O.F.M.Cap.; Dennis Klemash, O.F.M.Cap., Pastoral work. Brothers 1; Priests 18. In Res. Revs. Jerome Dunn, O.F.M.Cap.; Dismas Young, O.F.M.Cap.; Michael P. Masich, O.F.M.Cap.; Leon Leitem, O.F.M.Cap.; Robert E. McCreary, O.F.M.Cap., Tel: 724-774-1242; Senan Glass, O.F.M.Cap.; Thomas Betz, O.F.M.Cap., Prov. Min.; Bro. James Gavin, O.F.M.-Cap.

The Capuchin Franciscan Friars Province of Saint Augustine, 220 37th St., 15201. Tel: 412-682-6011; Fax: 412-682-0506; Email: joekusnir@capuchin.com. Revs. Michael Joyce, O.F.M.Cap., Vicar Prov.; Thomas Betz, O.F.M.Cap., Prov. Min.; Francis X. Yacobi, O.F.M.Cap., Exec. Secy.; Rafael Anguiano-Rodriguez, O.F.M.Cap., Dir. Vocations; R. Joseph Kusnir, CFO; Revs. Stephen Fernandes, O.F.M.-Cap., Definitor; Robert Marva, O.F.M.Cap., Definitor; Bro. James Mungovan, O.F.M.Cap., Definitor.

Congregation of the Oratory of St. Philip Neri, The Pittsburgh Oratory, 4450 Bayard St., 15213. Tel: 412-681-3181; Fax: 412-681-2922; Email: info@pittsburghoratory.org; Web: www.thepittsburghoratory.org. Very Revs. Drew P. Morgan, C.O., Chap.; David S. Abernethy, C.O., Provost; Revs. Michael J. Darcy, C.O., Vice Provost & Campus Min.; Joshua Kibler, C.O., Sec. & Campus Min.; Stephen Lowery, C.O., Dir. of Campus Min.; Paul M. Werley, C.O., Chap. to the Secular Oratory; Peter J. Gruber, C.O., Campus Min.; Bros. Reed Frey, C.O., Seminarian; Thomas Skamai, C.O., Seminarian. Total Staff 9.

St. Conrad Friary (1983) 9448 Babcock Blvd., Allison Park, 15101. Tel: 412-364-8240; Fax: 412-366-8331

; Email: joekusnir@capuchin.com; Web: www.capuchin.com. Rev. Francis X. Yacobi, O.F.M.Cap., Exec. Sec./Guardian; Bro. Richard Lubomski, O.F.M.Cap., Vicar; Revs. John Getsy, O.F.M.Cap.; Scott Seethaler, O.F.M.Cap., Preaching Ministry; Urbano Vazquez, O.F.M.Cap. Total in Residence 5.

Franciscan Friars, T.O.R., Queen of Peace Friary, 5324 Carnegie St., 15201. Tel: 412-449-1020; Fax: 412-449-1035; Email: martinzatsick@gmail.com; Email: bfttor@aol.com. Rev. Bernard Tickerhoof, T.O.R., Vicar; Bro. Martin, TOR, Supr. In Res. Revs. David Pivonka, T.O.R.; Jude Ventiquattro, T.O.R.

St. John Vianney Manor, 2600 Morange Rd., 15205. Tel: 412-928-0825; Tel: 412-928-0908; Fax: 412-928-1947; Email: pprzybyla@diopitt.org. Retired priests' residence. Total in Residence 23; Total Staff 7. In Res. Most Rev. William J. Winter, V.G., S.T.D., (Retired); Revs. Norbert J. Campbell, (Retired), St. John Vianney Manor, 2600 Morange Rd., 15205; Roy H. Conley, (Retired); Bernard B. Costello, (Retired); David C. Dixon, (Retired), 2600 Morange Rd., 15205; John M. Jordan, (Retired), St. John Vianney Manor, 2600 Morange Rd., 15205; Albert C. Koser, (Retired); Thomas F. Manion, (Retired); Michael A. McDermott, (Retired); Malcolm McDonald; Robert J. Meyer, (Retired), St. John Vianney Manor, 2600 Morange Rd., 15205; John D. Petrarulo, (Retired); Philip J. Przybyla; David E. Scharf; Edward R. Schleicher, (Retired); Miroslaw Stelmaszczyk; Richard G. Terdine, (Retired); Edward J. Trzeciakowski, (Retired); Raymond M. Utz, (Retired); George A. Wilt, (Retired); Rev. Msgr. William M. Ogrodowski, S.T.L., (Health Leave); Rev. Donald R. Bischof, (Health Leave), (Retired).

Our Lady of the Angels Friary, 225-37th St., 15201. Tel: 412-682-6888; Fax: 412-682-6889; Email: joekusnir@capuchin.com. Revs. John D. Harvey, O.F.M.Cap., Admin., Our Lady of the Angels; Reginald Russo, O.F.M.Cap., Vicar; Reginald Lyimo, O.F.M.Cap., Chap.; Bro. David Cira, O.F.M.Cap., Chap.; Rev. Richard J. Zelik, O.F.M.Cap., Parochial Vicar. Brothers 1; Priests 4. In Res. Revs. Reginald Russo, O.F.M.Cap., Replacement Ministry; Richard J. Zelik, O.F.M.Cap.; Bro. David Cira, O.F.M.Cap., UPMC Mercy Hospital Chap.

St. Paul of the Cross Monastery Monastery & Retreat Center. 148 Monastery Ave., 15203. Tel: 412-381-1188 (Monastery); Tel: 412-381-7676 (Retreat Center); Fax: 412-481-5049 (Monastery); Fax: 412-431-3044 (Retreat Center); Email: stpaulsmonastery@cpprov.org; Web: http://stpaulofthecrossmonastery.com/. Revs. Justin Kerber, C.P., Rector; Gerald Laba, C.P., Retreat Dir.; Patrick Geinzer, C.P., Vicar; Donald Ware, C.P.; Timothy Fitzgerald, C.P.; John F. McMillan, C.P.; Edwin Moran, C.P.; Michael Salvagna, C.P.; Joseph Sedley, C.P.; Jerome Vereb, C.P., De Familia; Junesh Xavier, C.P., Retreat Team; Bro. Leo DiFiore, C.P., De Familia; Rev. Richard A. Nalepa, C.P. Brothers 1; Priests 13.

Society of The Divine Word, 207 Lytton, 15213. Tel: 412-683-4030; Fax: 412-683-5033; Email: luhal@dwci.edu. Revs. Walter Ostrowski, S.V.D., Mission Dir., Tel: 412-683-0640; Raymond Hober, S.V.D.; Bros. John DeBold, S.V.D.; Gerard Raker, S.V.D., Supr. Total in Residence 4.

AVALON. *Holy Family Friary* (Friars Minor), The Franciscans. 232 S. Home Ave., 15202-2899. Tel: 412-761-2550; Tel: 412-721-7092; Email: DMoczulskiOFM@gmail.com; Fax: 412-202-2559. Revs. David Moczulski, O.F.M., M.Div., Guardian, Chaplain: Allegheny General Hsp. Sisters of the Holy Family of Nazareth, Sisters of Charity of Nazareth & School Sisters of St. Francis.; Leonard Cornelius, O.F.M., Vicar; John Joseph Gonchar, O.F.M. Friars 3.

BEAVER. *St. Fidelis Friary*, 372 East End Ave., Beaver, 15009. Fax: 724-774-3056; Email: stcecilia@verizon.net; Web: www.stceciliaroch.org. Church: St. Cecilia, 632 Virginia Ave., Rochester, 15074. Tel: 725-775-0801. Revs. Mark Carter, O.F.M.Cap., Parachial Vicar; Michael P. Greb, O.F.M.Cap., Dir. Pastoral Care, McGuire Memorial; Paul Kuppe, O.F.M.Cap. Capuchin Friars. Total in Residence 3.

BETHEL PARK. *Congregation of the Holy Spirit Province of the United States*, 6230 Brush Run Rd., Bethel Park, 15102. Tel: 412-831-0302; Email: usprovince@spiritans.org. Very Rev. Jeffrey T. Duaime, C.S.Sp., Prov. Supr.

Holy Spirit Fathers and Brothers Provincialate, 6230 Brush Run Rd., Bethel Park, 15102. Tel: 412-831-0302; Fax: 412-831-0970; Email: usprovince@spiritans.org; Web: www.spiritans.org. Very Rev. Jeffrey T. Duaime, C.S.Sp., Prov. Supr.; Bro. Michael Suazo, C.S.Sp., Vocation Dir. Residents 2; Total Staff 5.

BUTLER. *St. Mary's Friary*, 821 Herman Rd., Butler, 16002. Tel: 724-282-1485; Fax: 724-285-4715. Revs. James Kurtz, O.F.M.Cap., Parochial Vicar; Gary Stakem, O.F.M.Cap., Replacement Ministry; Ward Stakem, O.F.M.Cap., Pastor & Guardian; Bro. Joseph Day, O.F.M.Cap., Pastoral Assoc.; Rev. Albert Alexandrunas, O.F.M.Cap., Replacement Ministry. Capuchin Franciscan FriarsProvince of St. Augustine Brothers 1; Priests 4.

[N] CONVENTS AND RESIDENCES FOR SISTERS

PITTSBURGH. *Mount Assisi Convent*, Motherhouse of the School Sisters of the Third Order Regular of St. Francis United States Province, 934 Forest Ave., 15202. Tel: 412-761-6004; Fax: 412-761-0290; Email: administrationusa@schoolsistersosf.org; Web: schoolsistersosf.org. Sr. Frances Marie Duncan, O.S.F., Prov.

Civil Law Entity: The School Sisters of the Third Order Regular of St. Francis, a Pennsylvania corporation. Residents 27; Sisters 69; Total Staff 5. In Res. Rev. David Moczulski, O.F.M., M.Div., Chap.

Our Lady of Sorrows Monastery of the Passionist Nuns (1910) 2715 Churchview Ave., 15227. Tel: 412-881-1155; Fax: 412-881-1091. Mother Mary Ann, C.P., Supr. Motherhouse and Novitiate of the Religious of the Passion. (Passionist Nuns). Professed Sisters 8.

Sisters of Charity of Nazareth, Sisters of Charity of Nazareth Pittsburgh Campus, 8200 McKnight Rd., 15237. Tel: 412-364-3000; Fax: 412-364-9055. Rev. David Moczulski, O.F.M., M.Div. (formerly VSCs).

Sisters of Mercy of the Americas - New York, Pennsylvania, Pacific West Community, Convent of Mercy, 3333 Fifth Ave., 15213. Tel: 412-578-6225; Fax: 412-578-6180; Email: gloncki@mercynyppaw.org. Rev. Robert J. George, Chap., (Retired). Convent of Mercy Total Professed Sisters 107; Associates 28.

Sisters of Our Lady of Charity of the Good Shepherd Central South US Province (1872) 4100 Vinceton St., P.O. Box 340, 15214. Tel: 412-931-2299; Fax: 412-931-6044; Email: cs.provincial@gssweb.org. Sr. Sheila Rooney, Local Supr. Sisters of Our Lady of Charity of the Good Shepherd-Central South U.S. Province, Inc. Sisters 1.

Sisters of St. Francis of the Providence of God, 3757 Library Rd., 15234-2267. Tel: 412-882-9911; Fax: 412-885-7247; Email: usa@osfprov.org; Web: www.osfprov.org. Sr. Joanne Brazinski, O.S.F., Gen. Min.; Very Rev. Frederick L. Cain, V.E., M.Div., Chap. Sisters 26.

Sisters of the Holy Family of Nazareth, 201 Nazareth Way, 15229. Tel: 412-415-0988, Ext. 303; Fax: 412-415-0390; Email: info@nazarethcsfn.org; Web: www.nazarethcsfn.org.

Sisters of the Holy Family of Nazareth, Holy Family Province USA Inc.

Sisters of the Holy Spirit (S.H.S.) (Ross Township) 5246 Clarwin Ave., 15229-2208. Tel: 412-931-1917; Email: SRSHS@verizon.net; Web: www.sistersoftheholyspirit.com. Most Rev. William J. Waltersheid, V.G., S.T.L., Chap.; Sr. Grace Fabich, S.H.S., Gen. Supr. Professed Sisters 26.

ALLISON PARK. *Congregation of the Sisters of Divine Providence of Allegheny County* (1881) Providence Heights Motherhouse, 9000 Babcock Blvd., Allison Park, 15101-2793. Tel: 412-931-5241; Fax: 412-635-5416; Email: mbisbey@cdpsisters.org; Web: www.cdpsisters.org. Sr. Michele Bisbey, C.D.P., Prov. Motherhouse of the Sisters of Divine Providence in the Diocese (Pittsburgh); Novitiate of the Sisters of Divine Providence (Allison Park, PA). Sisters 180; In Motherhouse 60; In Province (including Puerto Rico) 120.

BADEN. *Ladies of Bethany* (1919) 1018 W. State St., Baden, 15001. Tel: 729-869-6083; Email: mimovodi@msn.com. Sr. Monique Dietz, L.B., Pres.; Eleanor Doidge, Sec.; Sr. Geraldine Marie Wodarczyk, C.S.F.N., Delegate for Rel., Dio. of Pittsburgh. Sisters 2.

Sisters of St. Joseph (1869) St. Joseph Convent Motherhouse 1020 State St., Baden, 15005. Tel: 724-869-2151; Tel: 412-761-3700; Fax: 724-869-3336; Email: kzaffuto@stjoseph-baden.org; Web: www.stjoseph-baden.org. Rev. Frank Mitolo, Chap.; Sr. Mary Pellegrino, C.S.J., B.A., M.S., M.A., Congregational Moderator. Residents 24; Sisters 156; Total in Community 156.

BAKERSTOWN. *St. Benedict Monastery* (1870) Benedictine Sisters of Pontifical Jurisdiction, 3526 Bakerstown Rd., Bakerstown, 15007-9705. Tel: 724-502-2600; Fax: 724-502-2601; Email: osbpgh@osbpgh.org; Web: www.osbpgh.org. Sr. Karen R. Brink, O.S.B., Prioress. Motherhouse and Novitiate of the Benedictine Sisters in the Diocese. Sisters 41.

BEAVER FALLS. *Felician Sisters of North America, Inc. Congregation of the Sisters of St. Felix of Cantalice, Our Lady of Hope Province*, 871 Mercer Rd., Beaver Falls, 15010-6815. Tel: 724-384-5300; Fax: 724-384-5301; Email: smchristopher@feliciansiters.org. Sr. Mary Christopher Moore, C.S.S.F., Provincial Min. Sisters 511.

BETHEL PARK. *Sisters of Charity of Seton Hill Generalate*, Seton House International, 7005 Baptist Rd., Bethel Park, 15102.

CORAOPOLIS. *Our Lady of the Sacred Heart Convent* (1932) 1500 Woodcrest Ave., Coraopolis, 15108. Tel: 412-264-2890; Fax: 412-264-7047; Email: sconniet@feliciansisters.org; Web: www.feliciansistersna.org. Sr. Mary Christopher Moore, C.S.S.F., Prov. Min. Home of the Felician Sisters of Pennsylvania C.S.S.F. Sisters 39.

ELIZABETH. *Divine Redeemer Motherhouse* (1912) 999 Rock Run Rd., Elizabeth, 15037-2613. Tel: 412-751-8600; Fax: 412-751-0355; Email: sdrarusa@gmail.com; Web: www.divine-redeemer-sisters.org. Sr. M. Alojziana Spisakova, S.D.R., Regl. Supr.; Rev. Thomas M. Kirby, Chap., (Retired). Motherhouse and Novitiate of the Sisters of the Divine Redeemer. Sisters 15.

GIBSONIA. *Disciples of the Lord Jesus Christ*, 10745 Babcock Blvd., Gibsonia, 15044.

MILLVALE. *Sisters of St. Francis of the Neumann Communities, Western Pennsylvania Region*, Sisters of St. Francis of the Neumann Communities, 146 Hawthorne Rd., 15209. Tel: 412-821-2200; Fax: 412-821-3318; Email: bschaad@sosf.org. Rev. Gervase Degenhardt, O.F.M.Cap., Chap. Attended by Capuchin Fathers from St. Augustine, Pittsburgh. Associates 41; In the Region 91.

VILLA MARIA. *Sisters of the Humility of Mary, Inc.* (1854) 288 Villa Dr., P.O. Box 914, Villa Maria, 16155. Tel: 724-964-8861; Fax: 724-964-8082; Email: scunningham@humilityofmary.org; Email: cbender@humilityofmary.org; Web: www.humilityofmary.org. Sisters Jean Tobin Lardie, H.M., Major Supr.; Joanne Gardner, H.M., Archivist. Founded in France in 1854.; First foundation in the United States in 1864 at Villa Maria, Lawrence County, Pennsylvania, 16155

Sisters of the Humility of Mary (Motherhouse), Villa Maria PA; Sisters of the Humility of Mary Charitable Trust, Villa Maria PA; Magnificat High School, Rocky River OH; Villa Maria Education and Spirituality Center, Villa Maria PA; Humility of Mary Housing, Inc., Akron OH; HM Life Opportunity Services, Akron OH; Villa Maria Residential Services, Villa Maria PA Sisters 125.

[O] RETREAT HOUSES

PITTSBURGH. *Martina Spiritual Renewal Center, Inc.* (1986) 5244 Clarwin Ave., 15229-2208. Tel: 412-931-9766; Fax: 412-931-1823; Email: info@martinacenter.com; Web: martinacenter.com. Sisters Grace Fabich, S.H.S., Pres.; Donna Smith, S.H.S., Admin. To provide a facility to individuals and groups for retreats and spiritual programs. Ministry of the Sisters of the Holy Spirit.

St. Paul of the Cross Retreat Center, 148 Monastery Ave., 15203. Tel: 412-381-7676; Tel: 412-381-7677; Fax: 412-431-3044; Email: stpaulrcpa@cpprov.org; Web: stpaulsretreatcenter-pittsburgh.org. Revs. Patrick Geinzer, C.P., Aux. Retreat Team; Gerald Laba, C.P., Retreat Dir.; John Colaizzi, Bus. Admin.; Revs. Michael Salvagna, C.P., Aux. Retreat Team; Timothy Fitzgerald, C.P., Aux. Retreat Team; Donald Ware, C.P., Aux Retreat Team. Total in Residence 1; Total Staff 25.

ALLISON PARK. *Kearns Spirituality Center* (1983) 9000 Babcock Blvd., Allison Park, 15101-2713. Tel: 412-366-1124; Fax: 412-635-6318; Email: kearns@cdpsisters.org; Web: www.cdpsisters.org. Sisters of Divine Providence.Conference room for 250; overnight accommodations for 60; dining facilities for 70. Call for more information on programs offered. Total Staff 4.

BETHEL PARK. *The Spiritan Center*, 6230 Brush Run Rd., Bethel Park, 15102. Tel: 412-835-3510; Fax: 412-835-3541; Email: thespiritancenter@gmail.com. Revs. Thomas J. Byrne, C.S.Sp.; Huy Q. Dinh, C.S.Sp.; Girard J. Kohler, C.S.Sp., (Retired); Louis G. Perreault, C.S.Sp.; Ralph J. Poirier, C.S.Sp.; Joseph A. Seiter, C.S.Sp.; Bro. Michael Suazo, C.S.Sp.; Rev. Adrien Hebert, CSSp. Total in Residence 9; Total Staff 22.

[P] OFFICES FOR CAMPUS MINISTRY

PITTSBURGH. *Office for Institutional Ministries*, 111 Blvd. of the Allies, 15222. Tel: 412-456-3060; Fax: 412-456-3188; Email: ablai@diopitt.org.

CRAFTON. *Office for Campus Ministry*, Saint Paul Seminary, 2900 Noblestown Rd., Crafton, 15205. Tel: 412-456-3140; Fax: 412-456-3141; Email: groney@diopitt.org. Mr. Gary Roney, Dir. Campus Min.

Art Institute of Pittsburgh, St. Mary of Mercy, Stanwix St., 15212-5296. Tel: 412-321-0711. Rev. Nicholas S. Vaskov, S.T.L.

La Roche College (1963) 9000 Babcock Blvd., 15237.

Tel: 412-536-1050; Fax: 412-536-1048. Sr. M. Elena Almendarez, C.D.P., M.A.

Carlow University, 3333 5th Ave., 15213. Tel: 412-578-6069. Mrs. Siobhan DeWitt.

Carnegie-Mellon University, Ryan Catholic Newman Center, 4450 Bayard St., 15213. Tel: 412-681-3181; Fax: 412-681-2922; Email: info@pittsburghoratory.org. Revs. Joshua Kibler, C.O., Dir., Campus Min.; Stephen Lowery, C.O., Dir.; Michael J. Darcy, C.O., Campus Min.; Deacon Peter Gruber, C.O., Campus Min.

Chatham College, Ryan Catholic Newman Center, 4450 Bayard St., 15213. Tel: 412-681-3181; Fax: 412-681-2922; Email: info@pittsburghoratory.org. Revs. Joshua Kibler, C.O., Dir. Campus Ministry; Stephen Lowery, C.O., Dir.; Michael J. Darcy, C.O., Campus Min.; Peter Gruber, Campus Min.

Duquesne University, Campus Ministry, 15282. Tel: 412-396-6020; Email: walshd@duq.edu. Rev. Daniel L. Walsh, C.S.Sp.; Linda Donovan, Campus Min.; Katherine Lecci, Campus Min.; Debbie Kostosky, Campus Min.

Geneva College, Campus Ministry, 289 Ridge Rd., New Brighton, 15066. Tel: 724-846-5978. Rev. Kim J. Schreck, S.T.L., Dir.

Pennsylvania State University, Beaver Campus, Office of Student Life, 6001 University Blvd., Moon Township, 15108. Tel: 724-773-3839; Email: gslifkey@diopitt.org. Mr. Gary M. Slifkey, M.A., M.S., Dir.

Point Park College, St. Mary of Mercy Church, 202 Stanwix St., 15222. Tel: 412-261-0110; Fax: 412-261-0113; Email: nvaskov@diopitt.org. Rev. Nicholas S. Vaskov, S.T.L.

Robert Morris College, Moon Township Campus Mr. Gary M. Slifkey, M.A., M.S.

University of Pittsburgh, Ryan Catholic Newman Center, 4450 Bayard St., 15213. Tel: 412-681-3181 ; Fax: 412-681-2922; Email: info@pittsburghoratory.org. Revs. Joshua Kibler, C.O., Dir., Campus Min.; Stephen Lowery, C.O., Dir.; Michael J. Darcy, C.O., Campus Min.; Peter Gruber, Campus Min.

California University (California), 250 University Ave., California, 15419. Tel: 724-938-3204; Fax: 724-938-0434. Rev. Michael A. Zavage, Dir.

Westminster College, Westminster College Catholic Campus Ministry, 314 W. Englewood Ave., New Castle, 16105. Tel: 724-652-9471; Fax: 724-654-1430; Email: frmrp@stcamillusparish.org. Rev. Michael R. Peck.

Slippery Rock University, Newman Center (Slippery Rock), 342 Normal Ave., Slippery Rock, 16057. Tel: 724-794-8459; Fax: 724-794-1150; Email: campusministry@rockcatholic.org. Rev. Robert L. Seeman, Dir.; Ms. Diane Magliocca, Campus Min.

Washington and Jefferson College (Washington), St. John Paul the Great Regional Campus Ministry, 213 Fourth St., California, 15419. Tel: 724-938-3204; Email: mzavage@diopitt.org. Rev. Michael A. Zavage.

Waynesburg College (Waynesburg), St. John Paul the Great Regional Campus Ministry, 213 Fourth St., California, 15419. Tel: 724-938-3204; Email: mzavage@diopitt.org. Rev. Michael A. Zavage.

[Q] MISCELLANEOUS LISTINGS

PITTSBURGH. *The Capuchin Franciscan Volunteer Corps, Inc.*, 220 37th St., 15201. Tel: 412-682-6011; Fax: 412-682-0506; Email: capcorpseast@gmail.com; Web: www.capuchin.com. Rev. Francis X. Yacobi, O.F.M.Cap., Dir. Province of St. Augustine of the Capuchin Order.Purpose: To promote, train, supervise and support Catholic lay missions and missionaries throughout the world, especially in conjunction with the ministries and fraternities of the Capuchin Order.

Cardinal Wuerl North Catholic Endowment Fund, 111 Blvd. of the Allies, 15222. Web: www.diopitt.org.

Catholic Benefits Trust, 111 Blvd. of the Allies, 15222. Tel: 412-456-3149; Fax: 412-456-3050; Email: dstewart@catholicbenefitstrust.org. Mr. David S. Stewart, A.R.M., CEO.

Catholic Diocese of Pittsburgh Foundation dba Sharing In Faith (Tm) Our Catholic Legacy Foundation, 111 Blvd. of the Allies, 15222. Tel: 412-456-3085; Fax: 412-456-3169; Email: stewardship@diopitt.org; Web: www.diopitt.org.

The Catholic Historical Society of Western Pennsylvania, 2900 Noblestown Rd., 15205-4227. Tel: 412-921-4421; Email: joyecho@aol.com; Web: www.catholichistorywpa.org. Blanche McGuire, Pres. Purpose: To promote the teaching of the Catholic Church in the United States, especially the Church in Western Pennsylvania; to recognize the growth, development and contribution of the Catholic Church by the preservation of artifacts, records and documents related to that history; to make available the results of research and study.

The Catholic Institute of Pittsburgh, PA, 111 Blvd. of the Allies, 15222. Tel: 412-456-3137; Fax: 412-456-3139; Email: bbonacchi@diopitt.org. Mr. Bruno A. Bonacchi, CFO.

Catholic Parish Cemeteries Association, 1000 Logue St., 15220. Tel: 412-680-0495; Email: linn@cpca-pgh.org.

Catholic Sisters Leadership Council (Western PA), 111 Boulevard of the Allies, 15222-1618. Tel: 412-477-2333; Email: sjgardner@osfprov.org. Sisters Janet Gardner, O.S.F., Co-Chair; Maria Kruszewski, Co-Chair; Constance M. Tomyl, C.S.S.F., Sec.

Chimbote Foundation, 111 Blvd. of the Allies, 15222-1618. Tel: 412-456-3085; Fax: 412-456-3169; Email: rlengwin@diopitt.org; Web: www.diopitt.org.

Christ Child Society of Pittsburgh (1992) P.O. Box 11324, 15238-1324. Tel: 412-682-4102. Rev. Jeremy J. Mohler, Spiritual Advisor/Care Svcs.; Dottie Talerico, Pres. Purpose: To foster a personal love of Christ expressed in service for needy children and youths. Volunteers 59; Total Assisted 900.

Cursillo Movement-Diocese of Pittsburgh, 1138 Windmill Ln., 15237. Tel: 412-837-9450; Email: pghcursillo@gmail.com; Web: www.pghcursillo.org. Rev. Thomas J. Galvin, Spiritual Advisor/Care Svcs.; Dan Kubisiak, Dir.

Elizabeth Seton Center Inc. (1985) 1900 Pioneer Ave., 15226. Tel: 412-561-8400; Fax: 412-561-8488; Email: srbarb@setoncenter.com; Web: www.setoncenter.com. Sr. Barbara Ann Boss, S.C., CEO. Care Programs for Children and Adults; Senior Citizens Center; School of Art. Sisters of Charity 9; Total Staff 75; Total Assisted 2,500.

Epiphany Association, 820 Crane Ave., 15216-3050. Tel: 412-341-7494; Fax: 412-341-7495; Email: samuto.epiphanyassociation@gmail.com; Web: www.epiphanyacademyofformativespirituality.org. Dr. Susan Muto, Dean. Purpose: Under the auspices of the Epiphany Association, the Epiphany Academy of Formative Spirituality strives with God's help to meet the needs of parents, pastors, teachers, counselors, chaplains and directors in pursuit of a deeper understanding of the spiritual life in accordance with the wisdom of their faith and formation traditions. Total Staff 7.

Holy Family Foundation (1992) 8235 Ohio River Blvd., 15202. Tel: 412-766-4030; Fax: 412-766-5434; Web: www.hfi-pgh.org. Sr. Linda Yankoski, C.S.F.N., Ed.D., Pres. & CEO; Michael Sexauer, M.B.A., Exec. Dir. The mission of Holy Family Foundation is to promote & support the public charitable works & educational purposes of Holy Family Institute and any other exempt activities affiliated with Holy Family Institute.

Institutional Common Fund Trust, 111 Blvd. of the Allies, 15222. Tel: 412-456-3137; Email: klander@diopitt.org. Mr. Wayne C. Boettcher, Dir.

Institutional Deposit and Loan Fund Trust, 111 Blvd. of the Allies, 15222. Tel: 412-456-3137; Email: klander@diopitt.org. Mr. Wayne C. Boettcher, Dir.

Knights of Columbus Bishop of Pittsburgh Diocese Project, P.O. Box 9691, 15226-0691. Tel: 724-422-7136 (Seals Chairman); Web: www.bishopsprojectkofc.org. Project for benefit of St. Anthony School Programs and McGuire Memorial.

Mount Assisi Academy Preschool (1980) 934 Forest Ave., 15202. Tel: 412-761-0381; Fax: 412-761-0290; Email: kduncan@maapreschool.com. Sr. Frances Marie Duncan, O.S.F., Prov. Min.; Kathy Duncan, Dir. Lay Teachers 5; Sisters 2; Students 84.

National Institute for Newman Studies, 211 N. Dithridge St., 15213. Tel: 412-681-4375; Fax: 412-681-4376; Email: admin@ninsdu.org; Web: www.newmanstudies.org. Kenneth L. Parker, Ph.D., Exec. Dir.; Catharine Ryan, M.A., Pres., Bd. of Dirs.

Nazareth Family Foundation (1996) 201 Nazareth Way, 15229. Tel: 814-660-2559; Fax: 814-695-2606; Email: mcollins.nff@gmail.com. Sr. Thea Krause, C.S.F.N., Pres. Purpose: To promote family life through financial support of facilities, programs, and services which enhance individual and family well-being. Total Assisted 3,200.

Nazareth Global Missions, Inc., 201 Nazareth Way, 15229. Tel: 814-660-2559; Fax: 814-695-2606; Email: mcollins.csfn@gmail.com. Sr. Michele Collins, C.S.F.N., Dir.

Our Campaign for the Church Alive!, Inc., 111 Blvd. of the Allies, 15222. Tel: 412-456-3085; Fax: 412-456-3169; Email: stewardship@diopitt.org.

Parish Common Fund Trust, 111 Blvd. of the Allies, 15222. Tel: 412-456-3025; Email: wboettcher@diopitt.org. Mr. Wayne C. Boettcher, Dir.

Parish Deposit and Loan Fund Trust, 111 Blvd. of the Allies, 15222. Tel: 412-456-3025; Email: klander@diopitt.org. Mr. Wayne C. Boettcher, Dir.

Pension Plan for the Diocese of Pittsburgh (Lay Pension Plan) 111 Blvd. of the Allies, 15222. Tel: 412-456-3137; Fax: 412-456-3139; Email: benefits@diopitt.org. Mr. Bruno A. Bonacchi, Dir.

Pittsburgh Catholic Publishing Associates, Inc. (1954) Purpose: To promote for Catholics and other readers an understanding of the mission and teachings of the Church and its role in the community. 111 Blvd. of the Allies, Ste. 200, 15222-1618. Tel: 412-471-1252; Tel: 800-392-4670; Fax: 412-471-4228; Email: info@pittsburghcatholic.org; Web: www.pittsburghcatholic.org. Mrs. Ann Rodgers, Gen. Mgr.; Ms. Carmella A. Weismantle, Opers. Mgr./Dir. Advertising; Mr. William Cone, Editor. Total Staff 12.

Pittsburgh Mercy Health System, Inc., McAuley Hall, 3333 Fifth Ave., 15213. Tel: 412-578-6675; Fax: 412-697-0266; Web: www.pittsburghmercy.org. Sr. Susan Welsh, R.S.M., Pres. & CEO. Part of Trinity Health, serving in the tradition of the Sisters of Mercy

Parent company of the following subsidiaries:.

Mercy Life Center Corporation, 1200 Reedsdale St., 15233. Tel: 412-323-8026; Fax: 412-323-4507; Web: www.pittsburghmercy.org.

McAuley Ministries, McAuley Hall, 3333 Fifth Ave., 15213. Tel: 412-578-6223; Fax: 412-697-0266; Web: www.mcauleyministries.org; Email: MRCooprt@mcauleymninistries.org. Michele Rone Cooper, Exec. Dir.

Portiuncula Foundation of the Sisters of St. Francis of the Neumann Communities, 146 Hawthorne Rd., 15209. Tel: 412-821-2200, Ext. 430; Fax: 412-821-3318; Email: portiuncula@sosf.org. Natalie Kasievich, Dir. Sisters of St. Francis of the Neumann Communities.

Priests' Benefit Plan of the Diocese of Pittsburgh (1955) 111 Blvd. of the Allies, 15222. Tel: 412-456-3060; Fax: 412-456-3139; Email: centralaccounting@diopitt.org. Rev. Charles S. Bober, S.T.D., Chm. Purpose: To provide certain retirement and health-related benefits to eligible priests.

Procurator Assurance, Inc., c/o 111 Blvd. of the Allies, 15222. Tel: 412-456-3137; Fax: 412-456-3139; Email: insurance@diopitt.org. Mr. David S. Stewart, A.R.M., Vice. Pres.; Mr. Bruno A. Bonacchi, Dir.

Scholastic Opportunity Scholarship Program, 111 Blvd. of the Allies, 15222. Tel: 412-456-3100; Fax: 412-456-3101; Email: rbowes@diopitt.org; Web: www.diopitt.org.

**Society of Saint Vincent de Paul*, Council of Pittsburgh, 1243 N. Franklin St., 15233. Tel: 412-321-1071, Ext. 206; Fax: 412-321-9131; Email: council@svdppitt.org; Web: www.svdppitt.org. Al Bannon, Pres., Email: bannon1313@aol.com; Deacon Keith G. Kondrich, B.A., Exec. Dir. Total Staff 135; Total Assisted 110,660.

Saint Thomas More Society (1960) 400 County Office Bldg., 542 Forces Ave., 15219. Tel: 412-350-2547; Email: rita.murillo@alleghenycounty.us. Sr. Rita C. Murillo Esq., C.S.J., Pres.

Totus Tuus, 4205 Bigelow Blvd., 15213. Tel: 603-630-2637; Tel: 412-996-7980; Email: mimikag3@gmail.com; Email: rmdonahue10@gmail.com; Email: totustuus.pittsburgh@gmail.com. Rhodora M. Donahue, Pres.; Marie Garesche, Treas.

Vincentian Collaborative System, 8250 Babcock Blvd., 15237. Tel: 412-630-9980; Fax: 412-348-0186; Email: vcsinfo@vcs.org; Web: www.vcs.org. Mark Alexander, Pres. Purpose: To provide coordination and supervision of facilities and services operating under the auspices of the Sisters of Charity of Nazareth.

Vincentian Collaborative System Charitable Foundation, 8250 Babcock Blvd., 15237. Tel: 412-548-4055; Fax: 412-348-0186; Email: info@vcs.org.

Vincentian Collaborative System Rehabilitation Services (2000) 111 Perrymont Rd, 15237. Tel: 412-348-1593; Fax: 412-348-1597; Email: lparkinson@vcs.org. Linda Parkinson, Dir., Vincentian Collaborative System Rehabilitation Svcs.

ALLISON PARK. *Sisters of Divine Providence Charitable Trust* (1985) 9000 Babcock Blvd., Allison Park, 15101-2793. Tel: 412-635-5414; Fax: 412-635-5416; Email: mbisbey@cdpsisters.org; Web: www.cdpsisters.org. Sr. Mary Jane Beatty, C.D.P., Chm.

BADEN. *Bethany Community*, 1018 W. State St., Baden, 15001. Tel: 729-869-6083; Email: mimovodi@msn.com. Timothy Giltinan, Admin.

The City of God Foundation, 1020 State St., Baden, 15005. Tel: 724-869-6594; Email: dicauley@yahoo.com. Sr. Diane Cauley, C.S.J., Coord.

BEAVER FALLS. *Felician Sisters of North America*

Endowment Trust, 871 Mercer Rd., Beaver Falls, 15010-6815. Tel: 724-384-5300; Fax: 724-384-5301; Email: smchristopher@feliciansisters.org. Sr. Mary Christopher Moore, C.S.S.F., Trustee.

Felician Sisters of North America Marian Corporation, 871 Mercer Rd., Beaver Falls, 15010-6815. Tel: 724-384-5300; Fax: 724-384-5301; Email: smchristopher@feliciansisters.org. Sr. Mary Christopher Moore, C.S.S.F., Pres.

Felician Sisters of North America Real Estate Holding Corporation, 871 Mercer Rd., Beaver Falls, 15010-6815. Tel: 724-384-5300; Fax: 724-384-5301; Email: smchristopher@feliciansisters.org. Sr. Mary Christopher Moore, C.S.S.F., Pres.

Felician Sisters of North America Real Estate Trust, 871 Mercer Rd., Beaver Falls, 15010. Tel: 724-384-5300; Fax: 724-384-5301; Email: sconniet@feliciansisters.org. Sr. Constance M. Tomyl, C.S.S.F., Trustee.

Felician Sisters of North America Retirement and Continuing Care Trust, 871 Mercer Rd., Beaver Falls, 15010. Tel: 724-384-5300; Fax: 724-384-5301 ; Email: smchristopher@feliciansisters.org. Sr. Mary Christopher Moore, C.S.S.F., Trustee.

BETHEL PARK. *Spiritan Support Trust*, 6320 Brush Run Rd., Bethel Park, 15102. Tel: 412-831-0302; Fax: 412-831-0970; Email: usprovince@spiritans.org; Web: www.spiritans.org. Very Rev. Jeffrey T. Duaime, C.S.Sp., Prov. Supr.

CLAIRTON. *Sisters Place, Inc.* (1993) 418 Mitchell Ave., Clairton, 15025. Tel: 412-233-3903; Fax: 412-233-3904; Email: info@sistersplace.org; Web: www.sistersplace.org. Robert Barth Jr., Pres.; Sr. Mary Parks, C.S.J., Exec. Dir. Purpose: To provide housing and supportive services to single parents and children who are homeless. Total Staff 11; Families 32.

CORAOPOLIS. **Girls Hope of Pittsburgh, Inc.*, 1005 Beaver Grade Rd., Ste. 103, Coraopolis, 15108. Tel: 412-329-7172; Fax: 412-474-3796; Email: twiese@bhgh.org. Mr. Tom Wiese, Exec. Dir. Purpose: To provide a supportive home environment and a quality education through college for girls who have potential for leadership but who because of poverty, abuse, neglect or abandonment cannot remain in their own homes. Total Staff 12; Total Assisted 24.

CRANBERRY TOWNSHIP. *Magnificat Pittsburgh*, 114 Bayberry Ln., Cranberry Township, 16066. Tel: 724-452-1150; Email: msamsa@zoominternet.net. Kay Burkot, Contact Person.

ELIZABETH. *Divine Redeemer Health Care Ministries Corp.* (1990) 999 Rock Run Rd., Elizabeth, 15037-2613. Tel: 412-751-8600; Fax: 412-751-0355; Email: sdrarusa@gmail.com; Web: www.divine-redeemer-sisters.org.

Sisters of Divine Redeemer Charitable Trust (1990) 999 Rock Run Rd., Elizabeth, 15037-2613. Tel: 412-751-8600; Fax: 412-751-0355; Email: info@divine-redeemer-sisters.org; Web: www.divine-redeemer-sisters.org.

MCKEESPORT. *Auberle*, 1101 Hartman St., McKeesport, 15132-1500. Tel: 412-673-5800, Ext. 1310; Fax: 412-673-8587; Email: johnly@auberle.org; Web: www.auberle.org. John Patrick Lydon, CEO; Darla Poole, COO. Helping build strong individuals, families and communities. Total Staff 260; Total Served 4,000.

Pauline Auberle Foundation (1952) 1101 Hartman St., McKeesport, 15132-1500. Tel: 412-673-5800; Fax: 412-673-8587; Email: johnly@auberle.org; Web: www.auberle.org. John Patrick Lydon, CEO; Nichole Williams, Contact Person. Helping build strong individuals, families, and communities Total Staff 6.

VILLA MARIA. *Sisters of the Humility of Mary Charitable Trust*, 288 Villa Dr., P.O. Box 313, Villa Maria, 16155. Tel: 724-964-8861; Fax: 724-964-8082; Email: scunningham@humilityofmary.org; Email: cbender@humilityofmary.org; Web: www.humilityofmary.org. Sr. Carol Anne Smith, H.M., Treas.

Villa Maria Education & Spirituality Center (1989) P.O. Box 424, Villa Maria, 16155. Tel: 724-964-8886; Fax: 724-964-8815; Email: jmkudlacz@humilityofmary.org; Web: www.vmesc.org. Jane Marie Kudlacz, H.M., Pres. & CEO; Matt Abramowski, Progam Dir. VMESC provides and promotes educational and spiritual experiences in a unique setting for people of all ages, faiths and economic status. Total Staff 12; Total Assisted 10,000.

Villa Maria Residential Services, 380 Villa Dr., P.O. Box 230, Villa Maria, 16155. Tel: 724-964-8920, Ext. 3340; Fax: 724-964-1321; Email: jbird@humilityofmary.org; Web: www.villaapartments.org. Sr. Jean Tobin Lardie, H.M., Rel. Order Leader. The Villa Maria Apartments provide housing for low and moderate income adults age 55 and over. (Number of apartments) 40.

WEXFORD. **St. Anthony Charitable Foundation*, 2000 Corporate Dr., Ste. 580, Wexford, 15090. Tel: 724-940-9020; Fax: 724-940-9064; Email: jgaughan@stanthonykids.org; Web: stanthonykids.org. Jerome Gaughan, CEO.

**St. Anthony Programs*, 2000 Corporate Dr., Ste. 580, Wexford, 15090. Tel: 724-940-9020; Fax: 724-940-9064; Email: msieg@stanthonyschoolprograms.com.

RELIGIOUS INSTITUTES OF MEN REPRESENTED IN THE DIOCESE

For further details refer to the corresponding bracketed number in the Religious Institutes of Men or Women section.

[0200]—*Benedictine Monks* (St. Vincent Archabbey)—O.S.B.
[0330]—*Brothers of the Christian Schools* (Prov. of Baltimore)—F.S.C.
[0470]—*The Capuchin Friars* (Prov. of St. Augustine)—O.F.M.Cap.
[0650]—*Congregation of the Holy Spirit* (Eastern Prov.)—C.S.Sp.
[1000]—*Congregation of the Passion* (Eastern Prov.)—C.P.
[0520]—*Franciscan Friars* (Immaculate Conception & St. John the Baptist)—O.F.M.
[0950]—*Oratorians*—C.O.
[0560]—*Third Order Regular of Saint Francis* (Prov. of Sacred Heart of Jesus)—T.O.R.

RELIGIOUS INSTITUTES OF WOMEN REPRESENTED IN THE DIOCESE

[0230]—*Benedictine Sisters of Pontifical Jurisdiction*—O.S.B.
[3730]—*Byzantine Sisters of Saint Basil the Great*—O.S.B.M.
[0885]—*Daughters of Mary Mother of Mercy.*
[]—*Disciples of Our Lord Jesus Christ.*
[1070-02]—*Dominican Sisters of Our Lady of the Springs of Bridgeport*—O.P.
[1115]—*Dominican Sisters of Peace*—O.P.
[1170]—*Felician Sisters*—C.S.S.F.
[2575]—*Institute of the Sisters of Mercy of the Americas* (Pittsburgh, PA)—R.S.M.
[]—*Ladies of Bethany*—L.B.
[2340]—*Little Sisters of the Poor*—L.S.P.
[2720]—*Mission Helpers of the Sacred Heart*—M.H.S.H.
[3071]—*North American Union Sisters of Our Lady of Charity*—O.L.C.
[3170]—*Religious of the Passion of Jesus Christ*—C.P.
[3430]—*Religious Teachers Filippini* (St. Lucy Filippini Prov.)—M.P.F.
[2970]—*School Sisters of Notre Dame*—S.S.N.D.
[1690]—*School Sisters of St. Francis*—O.S.F.
[0500]—*Sisters of Charity of Nazareth*—S.C.N.
[0570]—*Sisters of Charity of Seton Hill, Greensburg, Pennsylvania*—S.C.
[0990]—*Sisters of Divine Providence*—C.D.P.
[1805]—*Sisters of St. Francis of the Neumann Communities*—O.S.F.
[1660]—*Sisters of Saint Francis of the Providence of God*—O.S.F.
[3830-13]—*Sisters of Saint Joseph*—C.S.J.
[1620]—*Sisters of St. Francis*—O.S.F.
[1020]—*Sisters of the Divine Redeemer*—S.D.R.
[1970]—*Sisters of the Holy Family of Nazareth*—C.S.F.N.
[2040]—*Sisters of the Holy Spirit*—S.H.S.
[2110]—*Sisters of the Humility of Mary*—H.M.
[]—*Sisters of the Merciful Jesus.*
[2160]—*Sisters, Servants of the Immaculate Heart of Mary*—I.H.M.

DIOCESAN CEMETERIES

PITTSBURGH. *The Catholic Cemeteries Association of the Diocese of Pittsburgh* (1952) Central Office, 718 Hazelwood Ave., 15217-2807. Tel: 412-521-9133; Fax: 412-521-7019; Email: cca@ccapgh.org; Web: www.ccapgh.org.

All Saints Catholic Cemetery & Mausoleum (Braddock Catholic), 1560 Brinton Rd., 15221-4899. Tel: 412-271-5950; Fax: 412-271-8219

Calvary Catholic Cemetery & Mausoleum, 718 Hazelwood Ave., 15217-2807. Tel: 412-521-9133; Fax: 412-521-7019

Christ Our Redeemer Catholic Cemetery & Mausoleum (North Side Catholic), 204 Cemetery Ln., 15237-2722. Tel: 412-931-2206; Fax: 412-931-2229. formerly North Side Catholic Cemetery and Mausoleum

St. Mary Catholic Cemetery, c/o Calvary Cemetery, 718 Hazelwood Ave., 15217-2807. Tel: 412-421-9959; Fax: 412-621-6439

St. Stanislaus Catholic Cemetery & Mausoleum & St. Anthony Catholic Cemetery, 700 Soose Rd., 15209-1544. Tel: 412-821-4324; Fax: 412-821-4718 . Mr. Michael Sinnott, Dir.

Queen of Heaven Catholic Cemetery & Mausoleum, 2900 Washington Rd., McMurray, 15317-3278. Tel: 724-941-7601; Fax: 724-942-2550

Resurrection Catholic Cemetery & Mausoleum, 100 Resurrection Rd., Moon Township, 15108-7759. Tel: 724-695-2999; Fax: 724-695-3032

Sacred Heart Catholic Cemetery and Mausoleum, 97 Sacred Heart Rd., Monongahela, 15063-9605. Tel: 724-258-2885; Fax: 724-258-2275

Good Shepherd Catholic Cemetery & Mausoleum, 733 Patton St., Monroeville, 15146-4530. Tel: 412-824-0355; Fax: 412-823-9083; Email: cca@ccapgh.org

Saint Joseph Catholic Cemetery & Mausoleum, 1443 Lincoln Hwy., North Versailles, 15137-2448. Tel: 412-823-9111; Fax: 412-823-6655

Holy Souls Catholic Cemetery, c/o Resurrection Cemetery, 100 Resurrection Rd., Moon Twp, 15108-7759. Tel: 724-695-2999; Fax: 412-249-8970 . Mr. Michael Sinnott, Dir.

Our Lady of Hope Catholic Cemetery & Mausoleum, 1898 Bakerstown Rd., Tarentum, 15084-3213. Tel: 724-224-2785; Fax: 724-224-0211

Holy Savior Catholic Cemetery, 4629 Bakerstown Rd., Gibsonia, 15044-8993. Tel: 724-625-3822; Fax: 724-625-3880

Mount Carmel Catholic Cemetery & Mausoleum, 7601 Mt. Carmel Rd., Verona, 15147-1518. Tel: 412-241-1260; Fax: 412-241-5041

NECROLOGY

† Bergman, Charles B., (Retired), Died Feb. 27, 2018
† Connolly, Brian W., (Retired), Died May. 16, 2018
† Czemerda, Edward M., M.A., M.Div., Duquesne, St. Joseph, Died Nov. 17, 2018
† Graff, Francis C., (Retired), Died Oct. 12, 2018
† Lauer, Eugene F., (Retired), Died May. 20, 2018
† Salberg, James G., (Retired), Died Mar. 24, 2018
† Vecchio, Michael J., (Retired), Died Oct. 2, 2018

An asterisk (*) denotes an organization that has established tax-exempt status directly with the IRS and is not covered by the USCCB Group Ruling.

Diocese of Portland (In Maine)

(Dioecesis Portlandensis)

Most Reverend

ROBERT P. DEELEY

Bishop of Portland; ordained July 14, 1973; appointed Titular Bishop of Kearney and Auxiliary Bishop of Boston November 9, 2012; ordained Bishop January 4, 2013; appointed Bishop of Portland December 18, 2013; installed February 14, 2014. *Office: 510 Ocean Ave., Portland, ME 04103-4936.*

Most Reverend

JOSEPH JOHN GERRY, O.S.B.

Retired Bishop of Portland; ordained priest June 12, 1954; ordained Titular Bishop of Praecausa and Auxiliary Bishop of Manchester April 21, 1986; appointed Bishop of Portland December 21, 1988; installed February 21, 1989; retired February 10, 2004. *Mailing Address: St. Anselm Abbey, 100 St. Anselm Dr., Manchester, NH 03102-1310.*

Chancery: 510 Ocean Ave., Portland, ME 04103-4936. Tel: 207-773-6471; Fax: 207-773-0182.

ESTABLISHED JULY 29, 1853.

Square Miles 35,385.

Comprises the State of Maine.

Corporate Title: Roman Catholic Bishop of Portland, a Corporation Sole. This Corporation is comprised of the Diocesan parishes, missions, churches, rectories, cemeteries, schools, departments and other Diocesan activities. Those listings do not connote separate civil status (legal, tax, or otherwise) for any such listed activities, departments, entities or personnel that are comprised within the Roman Catholic Bishop of Portland, a Corporation Sole.

The list below also includes organizations which are separate from the Roman Catholic Bishop of Portland, a Corporation Sole.

For the legal titles of other diocesan-related institutions that are not part of the Roman Catholic Diocese of Portland, please consult Chancery.

STATISTICAL OVERVIEW

Personnel	
Bishop	1
Retired Bishops	1
Priests: Diocesan Active in Diocese	44
Priests: Diocesan Active Outside Diocese	1
Priests: Retired, Sick or Absent	71
Number of Diocesan Priests	116
Religious Priests in Diocese	31
Total Priests in Diocese	147
Extern Priests in Diocese	12
Ordinations:	
Diocesan Priests	1
Permanent Deacons in Diocese	45
Total Brothers	12
Total Sisters	181
Parishes	
Parishes	55
With Resident Pastor:	
Resident Diocesan Priests	32
Resident Religious Priests	1
Without Resident Pastor:	
Administered by Priests	22
Professional Ministry Personnel:	
Sisters	6
Lay Ministers	71
Welfare	
Catholic Hospitals	2
Total Assisted	423,171
Homes for the Aged	3
Total Assisted	1,344
Day Care Centers	2
Total Assisted	190
Specialized Homes	3
Total Assisted	651
Special Centers for Social Services	1
Total Assisted	220
Other Institutions	6
Total Assisted	593
Educational	
Diocesan Students in Other Seminaries	7
Total Seminarians	7
Colleges and Universities	1
Total Students	2,167
High Schools, Diocesan and Parish	1
Total Students	161
High Schools, Private	1
Total Students	431
Elementary Schools, Diocesan and Parish	9
Total Students	1,565
Elementary Schools, Private	1
Total Students	222
Catechesis/Religious Education:	
High School Students	601
Elementary Students	3,381
Total Students under Catholic Instruction	8,535
Teachers in the Diocese:	
Priests	1
Scholastics	1
Sisters	2
Lay Teachers	442
Vital Statistics	
Receptions into the Church:	
Infant Baptism Totals	816
Minor Baptism Totals	56
Adult Baptism Totals	88
Received into Full Communion	76
First Communions	950
Confirmations	1,007
Marriages:	
Catholic	255
Interfaith	102
Total Marriages	357
Deaths	2,372
Total Catholic Population	279,159
Total Population	1,338,404

Former Bishops—Very Rev. J. COSKERY, V.G., of Baltimore, The first Bishop-Elect, declined the nomination; Rt. Revs. DAVID W. BACON, D.D., ord. Dec. 13, 1838 in Baltimore, MD; cons. Bishop of Portland April 22, 1855; died Nov. 5, 1874; JAMES AUGUSTINE HEALY, D.D., ord. June 10, 1854 in Paris, France; cons. Bishop of Portland June 2, 1875; died Aug. 5, 1900; His Eminence WILLIAM CARDINAL O'CONNELL, ord. June 8, 1884; cons. Bishop of Portland, May 19, 1901; named Coadjutor Archbishop of Boston, Feb. 8, 1906; succeeded to the See of Boston, Aug. 30, 1907; created Cardinal, Nov. 27, 1911; died April 22, 1944; Rt. Revs. LOUIS S. WALSH, D.D., ord. Dec. 23, 1882 in Rome, Italy; cons. Bishop of Portland Oct. 18, 1906; died May 12, 1924.; JOHN GREGORY MURRAY, D.D., ord. April 14, 1900 in Louvain, France; appt. Titular Bishop of Flavias & Auxiliary Bishop of Hartford Nov. 15, 1919; cons. Bishop April 28, 1920; appt. Bishop of Portland, Maine May 29, 1925; installed Oct. 12, 1925; appt. Archbishop of Saint Paul Oct. 29, 1931; installed Jan. 27, 1932; died Oct. 11, 1956.; Most Revs. JOSEPH EDWARD MCCARTHY, D.D., ord. July 4, 1903; cons. Bishop of Portland Aug. 24, 1932; died Sept. 8, 1955; DANIEL JOSEPH FEENEY, D.D., LL.D., ord. May 21, 1921; appt. Titular Bishop of Sita and Auxiliary of Portland, June 22, 1946; cons. Sept. 12, 1946; Apostolic Administrator of the Diocese; appt. July 27, 1948; Coadjutor "cum jure successionis"; appt. March 4, 1952; succeeded to See, Sept. 8, 1955; died Sept. 15, 1969; PETER LEO GERETY, D.D., ord. June 29, 1939; appt. Titular Bishop of Crepedula and Coadjutor Bishop of Portland March 4, 1966; cons. June 1, 1966; appt. Apostolic Administrator, Feb. 18, 1967; succeeded to See, Sept. 15, 1969; transferred to Archdiocese of Newark, April 2, 1974; EDWARD C. O'LEARY, D.D., ord. June 15, 1946; Titular Bishop of Moglaena and Auxiliary Bishop of Portland; appt. Nov. 17, 1970; cons. Jan. 25, 1971; Apostolic Administrator; appt. June 29, 1974; ninth Bishop of Portland, Dec. 4, 1974; installed Dec. 18, 1974; retired Sept. 27, 1988; died April 2, 2002; JOSEPH J. GERRY, O.S.B., D.D., (Retired), ord. June 12, 1954; cons. Titular Bishop of Praecausa and Auxiliary Bishop of Manchester April 21, 1986; appt. Bishop of Portland Dec. 21, 1988; installed Feb. 21, 1989; retired Feb. 10, 2004; RICHARD J. MALONE, ord. priest May 20, 1972; appt. Auxiliary Bishop of Boston and Titular Bishop of Aptuca Jan. 27, 2000; ord. March 1, 2000; appt. Bishop of Portland Feb. 10, 2004; installed March 31, 2004; appt. Bishop of Buffalo May 29, 2012; appt. Apostolic Admin. of Portland Aug. 10, 2012.

Vicars General—Very Rev. Msgr. ANDREW DUBOIS, S.T.L., V.G.; Very Rev. DANIEL P. GREENLEAF, V.G., S.T.L.

Chancery—510 Ocean Ave., Portland, 04103-4936. Tel: 207-773-6471; Fax: 207-773-0182. Office Hours: Mon.-Fri. 9-4:30 Labor Day to Memorial Day; Mon.-Thurs. 8-5, Fri. closed, Memorial Day to Labor Day. Closed Holidays. This is the address for all offices unless otherwise listed.

Moderator of the Curia—Very Rev. Msgr. ANDREW DUBOIS, S.T.L., V.G., Email: andrew.dubois@portlanddiocese.org.

Chancellor—Sr. RITA-MAE BISSONNETTE, R.S.R., J.C.L., Email: ritamae.bissonnette@portlanddiocese.org.

Vicar for Priests—Rev. Msgr. PAUL F. STEFANKO, J.C.L., Email: paul.stefanko@portlanddiocese.org.

Vicars Forane—Very Revs. JEAN-PAUL LABRIE, V.F.; JOHN R. SKEHAN, V.F.; FRANK J. MURRAY, V.F.; ROBERT D. LARIVIERE, V.F.; LOUIS J. PHILLIPS, V.F.; PHILIP A. TRACY, V.F.

Diocesan Consultors—Very Rev. Msgr. ANDREW DUBOIS, S.T.L., V.G.; Very Rev. DANIEL P. GREENLEAF, V.G., S.T.L.; Revs. TIMOTHY J. NADEAU; GREGORY P. DUBE; Very Rev. LOUIS J. PHILLIPS, V.F.; Rev. Msgr. PAUL F. STEFANKO, J.C.L.

Diocesan Review Board—MR. MICHAEL MCGOVERN,

Chm.; Sr. MAUREEN WALLACE, R.S.M.; MRS. EDNA CHACE; MR. DANIEL COTE; MR. TODD DIFEDE; MS. KATHERINE COSTER; MS. PATRICIA PALMER; IRA SHAPIRO; Deacon JOHN MURPHY. Staff: Very Rev. Msgr. ANDREW DUBOIS, S.T.L., V.G.; MRS. YVONNE BORELLI-CHACE; MR. MICHAEL MAGALSKI.

Diocesan Offices and Directors

Department of Pastoral and Educational Services—

Diocesan Office of Lifelong Faith Formation—DR. LORI DALHLOFF, Ed.D., Dir., Email: lori.dalhloff@portlanddiocese.org.

Coordinator of Youth Ministry—SHAWN GREGORY.

Children and Adult Ministry—46 St. Agatha Ave., Frenchville, 04745-6038. Tel: 207-321-7884. MRS. JUDY MICHAUD, Coord., Email: judy.michaud@portlanddiocese.org; HANNAH GONNEVILLE, Asst. Coord.

Catholic Schools Superintendent—MR. JAMES KING, Email: jim.king@portlanddiocese.org.

Office for Missions—MRS. YVONNE BORELLI-CHACE, Email: yvonne.chace@portlanddiocese.org.

Director of Chaplaincies—Very Rev. Msgr. ANDREW DUBOIS, S.T.L., V.G.

Latin Mass—Rev. ROBERT A. PARENT, Coord., 1313 Riverside Dr., Auburn, 04210-9662. Tel: 207-212-3218.

Hospital Chaplaincy—Deacon PETER J. BERNIER.

Hispanic Ministry—Sr. PATRICIA PORA, R.S.M., Dir., Email: patricia.pora@portlanddiocese.org.

Prison Ministry—Deacon ROBERT CURTIS, Email: robert.curtis@portlanddiocese.org.

Ecumenical & Interreligious Services—Deacon DANIEL P. SHERIDAN, Ph.D., Coord., Email: daniel.sheridan@portlanddiocese.org.

Charismatic Renewal—Rev. RICHARD P. RICE, (Retired), 66 Ward Circle, Brunswick, 04011-9342.

Campus Ministry—Rev. WILFRED P. LABBE, Email: bill.labbe@portlanddiocese.org.

Catholic Scouting—(refer to the Office of Lifelong Faith Formation).

Department of Financial Services—MR. DAVID P. TWOMEY JR., CPA, CFO, Email: david.twomey@portlanddiocese.org.

Parish Financial Services—MR. NICHOLAS PAQUETTE, CPA, Dir., Email: nick.paquette@portlanddiocese.org.

Controller—MRS. LAURIE J. DOWNEY, CPA, Email: laurie.downey@portlanddiocese.org.

Human Resources—MS. ELIZABETH ALLEN, S.P.H.R., Dir., Email: elizabeth.allen@portlanddiocese.org.

Property Management—MR. JAMES SOMMA, Dir., Email: james.somma@portlanddiocese.org.

Risk Management—MR. JOHN CAVALLARO, Dir., Email: john.cavallaro@portlanddiocese.org.

DICON - Diocesan Construction—MR. ALAN HINCKLEY, Supt., Email: alan.hinckley@portlanddiocese.org.

Safe Environment—MR. GERALD COUTU, Coord., Email: gerry.coutu@portlanddiocese.org.

Information Technology—MR. MICHAEL MOORE, Dir., Email: michael.moore@portlanddiocese.org.

Department of Canonical Services—Very Rev. JOHN D. DICKINSON, J.C.L., J.V.

Tribunal—

Officialis—Very Rev. JOHN D. DICKINSON, J.C.L., J.V., Email: jack.dickinson@portlanddiocese.org.

Promoter of Justice—VACANT.

Defenders of the Bond—MRS. SHANNON FOSSETT, Email: shannon.fossett@portlanddiocese.org; Rev. MARK P. NOLETTE, J.C.L., Email: mark.nolette@portlanddiocese.org; Sr. RITA-MAE BISSONNETTE, R.S.R., J.C.L.

Advocates—MRS. SHANNON FOSSETT; Sr. RITA-MAE BISSONNETTE, R.S.R., J.C.L.; MR. CHRISTOPHER SIUZDAK, J.C.L.

Notary—Rev. CLAUDE R. GENDREAU, Email: claude.gendreau@portlanddiocese.org.

Associate Judges—Sr. RITA-MAE BISSONNETTE, R.S.R., J.C.L.; Rev. Msgr. PAUL F. STEFANKO, J.C.L.

Guardian—Very Rev. Msgr. ANDREW DUBOIS, S.T.L., V.G.

Office Coordinator—Very Rev. JOHN D. DICKINSON, J.C.L., J.V.

Due Process—(examination of violation of rights within the church) MRS. SHANNON FOSSETT, Dir.

Department of Administrative & Ministerial Services— Very Rev. Msgr. ANDREW DUBOIS, S.T.L., V.G.

Diocesan Office of Communications—MR. DAVID W. GUTHRO, Dir., Email: dave.guthro@portlanddiocese.org.

Harvest Magazine—MS. LOIS CZENIAK, Editor, Email: lois.czeniak@portlanddiocese.org.

Public Policy—MRS. SUZANNE LAFRENIERE, Dir., Email: suzanne.lafreniere@portlanddiocese.org.

Professional Responsibility—MR. MICHAEL MAGALSKI, Dir., Tel: 207-321-7836; Email: michael.magalski@portlanddiocese.org.

Diaconate—Deacon PETER J. BERNIER, Dir., Email: peter.bernier@portlanddiocese.org.

Ministry to Priests—Deacon PETER J. BERNIER, Dir.

Vocations—Rev. SEAMUS P. GRIESBACH, Email: seamus.griesbach@portlanddiocese.org.

Seminarians—Very Rev. DANIEL P. GREENLEAF, V.G., S.T.L., Email: daniel.greenleaf@portlanddiocese.org.

Delegate for Religious—Sr. RITA-MAE BISSONNETTE, R.S.R., J.C.L., Email: ritamae.bissonnette@portlanddiocese.org.

Support and Assistance Ministry—(Victims Assistance) MRS. YVONNE BORELLI-CHACE, Email: yvonne.chace@portlanddiocese.org; MS. CAROLYN BLOOM, Independent Clinician, Tel: 207-782-1051; Email: cbloomlcsw@gmail.com.

Department of Development and Annual Appeal—MR. DAVID DINAPOLI, Dir., Email: dave.dinapoli@portlanddiocese.org.

Catholic Foundation of Maine—MRS. ELIZABETH BADGER, Exec. Dir., Email: elizabeth.badger@portlanddiocese.org.

Campaign for Human Development—MRS. SUZANNE LAFRENIERE, Email: suzanne.lafreniere@portlanddiocese.org.

Catholic Relief Services—MRS. YVONNE BORELLI-CHACE.

Diocesan Priests' Benefit Plan - Members—Most Rev. ROBERT P. DEELEY, J.C.D., Pres.; Very Rev. Msgr. ANDREW DUBOIS, S.T.L., V.G.; Very Rev. PHILIP A. TRACY, V.F.; Rev. EDWARD R. CLIFFORD; Rev. Msgr. PAUL F. STEFANKO, J.C.L., Vicar for Priests; MR. DAVID P. TWOMEY JR., CPA, CFO; MR. NICHOLAS PAQUETTE, CPA, Dir. Parish Fin. Svcs.; MS. ELIZABETH ALLEN, S.P.H.R., Dir. Human Resources; MRS. NANCY LOMBARDI, Benefits Coord.; Sr. RITA-MAE BISSONNETTE, R.S.R., J.C.L., Sec.

Diocesan Archivist—Sr. RITA-MAE BISSONNETTE, R.S.R., J.C.L. Contact Chancellor's Office:.

Diocesan Board of Education—MR. JAMES KING, Exec. Sec. Members: MS. DENISE GOULET; MRS. DONNA JACQUES; MR. GREGORY DESJARDINS; MR. MICHAEL KOMICH; Rev. SEAMUS P. GRIESBACH; MR. ROBERT PHELAN; MR. JOSEPH GALLANT; MR. ROBERT E. DANIELSON; MR. MARK ANTOINE SR.

Diocesan Bureau of Housing—Most Rev. ROBERT P. DEELEY, J.C.D., Bishop of Portland & Pres.; MR. DAVID P. TWOMEY JR., CPA, Treas.; THOMAS KELLY ESQ., Clerk.

Diocesan Finance Council—Most Rev. ROBERT P. DEELEY, J.C.D.; Very Rev. Msgr. ANDREW DUBOIS, S.T.L., V.G.; MR. GREGG H. GINN, Chm.; MR. MARK FERNANDEZ; MS. PAULA MOSES; MR. GENE MILIARD; MR. MICHAEL COSTER; MR. ROBERT BLAISDELL; MS. CYNTHIA O'ROURKE; MR. JAMES GEARY; MR. GENE ARDITO; MR. NORMAN BELANGER; MR. ERIC WYCOFF; MR. JAMES HANLEY. Ex Officio Members: Sr. RITA-MAE BISSONNETTE, R.S.R., J.C.L.; MR. DAVID P. TWOMEY JR., CPA, CFO. Staff: MRS. LAURIE J. DOWNEY, CPA; MR. NICHOLAS PAQUETTE, CPA.

Diocesan Pastoral Council—MS. CHERYL DEMERCHANT; MR. DAVID GRANT; MR. JOSEPH LASQUADRO; MS. JULIA SOCKBESON; MR. JOHN BOBROWIECKI JR.; MR. JAMES HEBERT; MS. SANDRA THOMPSON; MR. CHRISTOPHER CRAWFORD; MR. KENNETH RUSINEK; MR. KENNETH GREENLEAF; MS. MARY COLOMBO, Chair; MRS. ELIZABETH GALLAGHER. Ex Officio: Most Rev. ROBERT P. DEELEY, J.C.D.; Very Rev. Msgr. ANDREW DUBOIS, S.T.L., V.G.; Sr. RITA-MAE BISSONNETTE, R.S.R., J.C.L.

General Counsel—MR. THOMAS R. KELLY, Robinson Kriger & McCallum, 12 Portland Pier, Portland, 04101-4713. Tel: 207-772-6565.

Maine Diocesan Council of Catholic Women—Most Rev. ROBERT P. DEELEY, J.C.D., Episcopal Chm.; Sr. ALINE PLANTE, P.M.; RUTH WARREN, Pres.

Newman Apostolate—Rev. WILFRED P. LABBE, Dir.

Personnel Board—Revs. GREGORY P. DUBE; CLAUDE R. GENDREAU; Very Rev. FRANK J. MURRAY, V.F.; Rev. JAMES S. PLOURDE. Ex Officio Members: Most Rev. ROBERT P. DEELEY, J.C.D., Pres.; Very Rev. Msgr. ANDREW DUBOIS, S.T.L., V.G., Moderator of the Curia; Very Rev. DANIEL P. GREENLEAF, V.G., S.T.L., Dir., Seminarians; Rev. Msgr. PAUL F. STEFANKO, J.C.L., Vicar for Priests.

Pontifical Association of Missionary Childhood—MRS. YVONNE BORELLI-CHACE.

Pontifical Society for the Propagation of the FaithMRS. YVONNE BORELLI-CHACE.

Presbyteral Council—Most Rev. ROBERT P. DEELEY, J.C.D., Pres. Ex Officio: Rev. Msgr. PAUL F. STEFANKO, J.C.L., Vicar for Priests; Very Rev. DANIEL P. GREENLEAF, V.G., S.T.L.; Very Rev. Msgr. ANDREW DUBOIS, S.T.L., V.G., Moderator of the Curia; Very Rev. JOHN D. DICKINSON, J.C.L., J.V., Judicial Vicar. Members: Rev. Msgrs. RENE T. MATHIEU, S.T.L.; J. JOSEPH FORD, (Retired); Revs. DAVID R. RAYMOND; TIMOTHY J. NADEAU; Very Rev. FRANK J. MURRAY, V.F.; Rev. GREGORY P. DUBE; Very Rev. LOUIS J. PHILLIPS, V.F.; Revs. AARON L. DAMBOISE; DOMINIC SAVIO, H.G.N.

CLERGY, PARISHES, MISSIONS AND PAROCHIAL SCHOOLS

CITY OF PORTLAND

(CUMBERLAND COUNTY)

1—CATHEDRAL OF THE IMMACULATE CONCEPTION (1853) 307 Congress St., 04101-3695. Tel: 207-773-7746; Email: portlandpeninsula@portlanddiocese.org; Web: www.portlandcatholic.org. Revs. Gregory P. Dube, Rector; Kyle L. Doustou, Parochial Vicar; Kevin Upham, Parochial Vicar; Deacon Michael Augustino; Denis Lafreniere, Business Mgr.

Catechesis Religious Program—Email: melissa.maurais@portlanddiocese.org. Melissa Maurais, P.C.L. Students 61.

2—ST. CHRISTOPHER'S (Peaks Island) (1923)
Mailing Address: 307 Congress St., 04101-3695. Tel: 207-773-7446; Email: portlandpeninsula@portlanddiocese.org; Web: www.portlandcatholic.org. Revs. Gregory P. Dube; Kyle L. Doustou, Parochial Vicar; Kevin Upham, Parochial Vicar.

Church: 15 Central Ave., Peaks Island, 04108.

Catechesis Religious Program—Email: melissa.maurais@portlanddiocese.org. Melissa Maurais, D.R.E.

Mission—Our Lady Star of the Sea, 8 Beach Ave., Long Island, 04050. Tel: 207-773-7746.

3—ST. DOMINIC'S (1830) Merged See Sacred Heart/St. Dominic's, Portland.

4—ST. JOSEPH'S (1909) Merged See Our Lady of Hope Parish, Portland.

5—ST. LOUIS (1915) (Polish)
279 Danforth St., 04102. Tel: 207-773-7746; Email: portlandpeninsula@portlandcatholic.org; Web: www.portlandcatholic.org. Mailing Address: 307 Congress St., 04101-3695. Revs. Gregory P. Dube; Kyle L. Doustou, Parochial Vicar; Kevin Upham, Parochial Vicar; Denis Lafreniere, Business Mgr.; Revs. Anthanasius S. Wirsiy, In Res.; Antonydass Pichaimuthu, H.G.N., In Res.; Amandus B. Sway, A.J., In Res.

Catechesis Religious Program—Email: melissa.maurais@portlanddiocese.org. Melissa Maurais, D.R.E. Students 1.

6—OUR LADY OF HOPE PARISH (2011)
673 Stevens Ave., 04103-2640. Tel: 207-797-7026; Email: Linda.Mccormack@portlanddiocese.org; Web: www.ladyofhopemaine.org. Revs. Paul Sullivan, S.J.; John R. d'Anjou, S.J., Parochial Vicar; Vincent Curtin, Parochial Vicar; Mary Cafazzo, Business Mgr.

Res.: 492 Ocean Ave., 04103.

Worship Sites:—

St. Joseph Church—673 Stevens Ave., 04103-2640.

St. Pius X Church, 492 Ocean Ave., 04103.

School—St. Brigid School, (Grades PreK-8), 695 Stevens Ave., 04103-2682. Tel: 207-797-7073; Fax: 207-797-7078; Email: william.burke@portlanddiocese.org. Mr. William Burke, Prin. Full time 19; Students 277.

Catechesis Religious Program—Email: sandra.litcher@portlanddiocese.org. Sandra Litcher, D.R.E. Students 40.

7—ST. PATRICK'S (1922) Closed. See Our Lady of Hope Parish, Portland.

8—ST. PETER'S (1911) (Italian)
Mailing Address: 307 Congress St., 04101. Revs. Gregory P. Dube; Kyle L. Doustou, Parochial Vicar; Kevin Upham, Parochial Vicar; Denis Lafreniere, Business Mgr. In Res., Rev. Claude R. Gendreau; Very Rev. Msgr. Andrew Dubois, S.T.L., V.G.

Church: 72 Federal St., 04101-3695. Tel: 207-773-7746; Email: portlandpeninsula@portlanddiocese.org; Web: www.portlandcatholic.org.

Catechesis Religious Program—Email: melissa.maurais@portlanddiocese.org. Melissa Maurais, P.C.L. Students 12.

9—ST. PIUS X (1962) Merged See Our Lady of Hope Parish, Portland.

10—SACRED HEART/ST. DOMINIC (1997)
65 Mellen St., 04101-3695. Tel: 207-773-7746; Email: portlandpeninsula@portlanddiocese.org; Web: www.portlandcatholic.org. Mailing Address: 307 Congress

St., 04101. Revs. Gregory P. Dube; Kyle L. Doustou, Parochial Vicar; Kevin Upham, Parochial Vicar.
Church: 80 Sherman St., 04101-2290.
Tel: 207-772-6182.
Catechesis Religious Program—Email: melissa.maurais@portlanddiocese.org. Melissa Maurais, D.R.E. Students 35.

OUTSIDE THE CITY OF PORTLAND

ASHLAND, AROOSTOOK CO., ST. MARK'S (1902) Merged See Parish of the Precious Blood, Caribou.

AUBURN, ANDROSCOGGIN CO.

1—IMMACULATE HEART OF MARY PARISH (2008)
24 Sacred Heart Pl., Auburn, 04210-4938.
Tel: 207-782-8096; Email: ihmadmin@portlanddiocese.org; Web: ihm-auburn.org. Very Rev. Robert D. Lariviere, V.F.; Deacon Denis Mailhot; Sr. Elizabeth A. Platt, C.O.C., Pastoral Coord.; Gladys Garlarneau, Communications Admin.
Churches—
Sacred Heart Church—8 Sacred Heart Pl., Auburn, 04210.
St. Philip's Church, 2365 Turner Rd., Auburn, 04210.
Catechesis Religious Program—Email: donald.smith@portlanddiocese.org. Donald Smith, Faith Formation Dir. Students 45.

2—ST. LOUIS (1902) Closed. See Immaculate Heart of Mary Parish, Auburn.

3—ST. PHILIP'S (1968) Merged See Immaculate Heart of Mary Parish, Auburn.

4—SACRED HEART (1923) Merged See Immaculate Heart of Mary Parish, Auburn.

AUGUSTA, KENNEBEC CO.

1—ST. ANDREW'S (1968) Closed. See St. Michael Parish, Augusta.

2—ST. AUGUSTINE'S (1888) Merged See St. Michael Parish, Augusta.

3—ST. MARY OF THE ASSUMPTION (1834) Merged See St. Michael Parish, Augusta.

4—ST. MICHAEL PARISH (2007) [CEM 4]
24 Washington St., Augusta, 04330-4239.
Tel: 207-623-8823; Email: noreen.hare@portlanddiocese.org; Email: st.michael@portlanddiocese.org; Web: stmichaelmaine.org. Very Rev. John R. Skehan, V.F.; Revs. Michael J. Seavey, Parochial Vicar; Arockiasmy Santhiyagu, H.G.N., Parochial Vicar; Gail Gould, Pastoral Min./Coord.; Noreen Hare, Business Mgr.
Res.: 41 Western Ave., Augusta, 04330-6324.
Churches—
St. Augustine Church—1 Kendall St., Augusta, 04330.
St. Mary of the Assumption Church, 41 Western Ave., Augusta, 04330.
St. Joseph Church, 1 Lincoln St., Gardiner, 04345.
St. Denis Church, 298 Grand Army Rd., Whitefield, 04353.
St. Francis Xavier Church, 130 Rte. 133, Winthrop, 04364.
Sacred Heart Church, 12 Summer St., Hallowell, 04347.
School—St. Michael Parish School, (Grades PreK-8), 56 Sewall St., Augusta, 04330-7327.
Tel: 207-623-3491; Fax: 207-623-2971; Email: kevin.cullen@portlanddiocese.org. Kevin Cullen, Prin. Lay Teachers 15; Students 185.
Catechesis Religious Program—Sarah Wick, D.R.E. Students 200.

BAILEYVILLE, WASHINGTON CO., ST. JAMES THE GREATER (1905) Merged See Saint Kateri Tekakwitha Parish, Calais.

BANGOR, PENOBSCOT CO.

1—ST. JOHN'S (1856) Merged See Saint Paul the Apostle Parish, Bangor.

2—ST. MARY (1872) Merged See Saint Paul the Apostle Parish, Bangor.

3—SAINT PAUL THE APOSTLE PARISH (2009) [CEM]
217 York St., Bangor, 04401-5442. Tel: 207-217-6740; Email: cheryl.whalen@portlanddiocese.org; Web: www.stpaulbangor.me. 207 York St., Bangor, 04401-5442. Very Rev. Frank J. Murray, V.F.; Deacons Timothy R. Dougherty; Michael E. Whalen; Mr. Thomas Pendergast, Dir. Pastoral Admin.; Mrs. Cheryl Whalen, Business Mgr. In Res., Revs. Apolinary Kavishe, A.J., Chap.; Robert Tumwekwase, A.J., Chap.
Res. for Chaplains: 531 N. Main St., Brewer, 04412-1219.
Churches—
St. John Church—207 York St., Bangor, 04401-5442.
St. Mary Church, 768 Ohio St., Bangor, 04401-3106.
St. Joseph Church, 531 N. Main St., Brewer, 04412-1219.
St. Theresa Church, 425 S. Main St., Brewer, 04412-2327.
St. Matthew Church, 70 Western Ave., Hampden, 04444-1427.
St. Gabriel Church, 435 S. Main St., Winterport, 04496.
Schools—All Saints Catholic School—(Grades PreK-8), 768 Ohio St., P.O. Box 1749, Bangor, 04402-1749.
Tel: 207-947-7063; Tel: 207-942-0955; Email: joseph.gallant@portlanddiocese.org; Web: allsaintsmaine.org. Mr. Joseph Gallant, Prin. St. Mary's and St. John's Campuses. Lay Teachers 14; Students 193.
St. Mary's Campus, (Grades PreK-3), 768 Ohio St., Bangor, 04401-3165. Email: joseph.gallant@portlanddiocese.org. Mr. Joseph Gallant, Prin. Lay Teachers 14; Students 193.
St. John's Campus, (Grades 4-8), 166 State St., P.O. Box 1749, Bangor, 04402-1749. Tel: 207-947-0955; Email: joseph.gallant@portlanddiocese.org. Mr. Joseph Gallant, Prin. Lay Teachers 14; Students 193.
Catechesis Religious Program—Tel: 207-217-6740; Email: tracy.guerrette@portlanddiocese.org. Tracy Guerrette, Faith Formation. Students 275.

BAR HARBOR, HANCOCK CO.

1—HOLY REDEEMER (1907) Merged See Parish of the Transfiguration, Bar Harbor.

2—PARISH OF THE TRANSFIGURATION (2011) [CEM]
56 Mount Desert St., Bar Harbor, 04609-1324. 231 Main St., Ellsworth, 04605-1613. Tel: 207-667-2342; Tel: 207-288-3526; Email: holyredeemer@roadrunner.com; Web: www.mdicatholics.com/. Very Rev. John R. Skehan, V.F.; Revs. Joseph W. Cahill, Parochial Vicar; Stan Ukwe, O.P., Parochial Vicar.
Res.: 21 Ledgelawn Ave., Bar Harbor, 04609-1303.
Worship Sites:—
Holy Redeemer Church—
St. Ignatius Church, 8 Lookout Way, Northeast Harbor, 04679.
Our Lady Star of the Sea Chapel, Little Cranberry Island Islesford, ME (only summers).
St. Peter's Church, 5 Ocean House Hill Rd., Manset, 04656.
Catechesis Religious Program—Tel: 207-667-2342; Email: edith.forst@portlanddiocese.org. Edith Forst, D.R.E. Students 6.

BATH, SAGADAHOC CO., ST. MARY (1849) Merged See All Saints Parish, Brunswick.

BELFAST, WALDO CO., ST. FRANCIS OF ASSISI (1891) Merged See Saint Brendan the Navigator Parish, Camden.

BENEDICTA, AROOSTOOK CO., ST. BENEDICT'S (1834) [CEM]
Mailing Address: P.O. Box 27, Benedicta, 04733-0027. Tel: 207-365-4294; Email: stbens@fairpoint.net. 1063 Benedicta Rd., Benedicta, 04733. Rev. Bruce Siket.
Catechesis Religious Program—Tel: 207-365-4269. Anna Robinson, D.R.E. Students 9.

BERWICK, YORK CO.

1—OUR LADY OF PEACE (1927) Closed. See Parish of the Ascension of the Lord, Kittery.

2—OUR LADY OF THE ANGELS (2006) Closed. See Parish of the Ascension of the Lord, Kittery.

BIDDEFORD, YORK CO.

1—ST. ANDRE'S (1899) [JC] Closed. See Good Shepherd Parish, Saco.

2—ST. JOSEPH'S (1870) Merged See Good Shepherd Parish, Saco.

3—ST. MARY'S (1855) Closed. See Good Shepherd Parish, Saco.

BINGHAM, SOMERSET CO., ST. PETER'S (1920) Merged See Christ the King Parish, Skowhegan.

BOOTHBAY HARBOR, LINCOLN CO., OUR LADY QUEEN OF PEACE (1928) Merged See All Saints Parish, Brunswick.

BRADLEY, PENOBSCOT CO., ST. ANN (1934) [JC] Merged See Parish of the Resurrection of the Lord, Old Town.

BREWER, PENOBSCOT CO.

1—ST. JOSEPH'S (1926) [JC] Merged See Saint Paul the Apostle Parish, Bangor.

2—ST. TERESA'S (1894) Merged See Saint Paul the Apostle Parish, Bangor.

BRIDGTON, CUMBERLAND CO., ST. JOSEPH (1971) Revs. Edward R. Clifford; Peter Shaba, S.M.A., Parochial Vicar.
Rectory—174 S. High St., Bridgton, 04009.
Church & Mailing Address: 225 S. High St., Bridgton, 04009-4104. Tel: 207-647-2334; Email: StJosephBridgton@portlanddiocese.org; Web: www.cluster30.org.
Catechesis Religious Program—Email: joanne.fortier@portlanddiocese.org. Joanne Fortier, D.R.E. Students 19.
Mission—St. Elizabeth Ann Seton, 857 Main St., Fryeburg, 04037-1521. Tel: 207-743-2606.

BRUNSWICK, CUMBERLAND CO.

1—ALL SAINTS PARISH (2009) [CEM 2]
132 McKeen St., Brunswick, 04011-2980.
Tel: 207-725-2624; Email: allsaints@portlanddiocese.org; Web: www.allsaintsmaine.com. Very Rev. Thomas M. Murphy, V.F.; Revs. Dominic Azaghbor, O.P., Parochial Vicar; Patrick Agbodi, Parochial Vicar; Deacons John Murphy; Robert Curtis; Martha Corkery, Parish Life Coord.
Churches—
St. Mary Church—144 Lincoln St., Bath, 04530-2198.
St. Charles Church, 132 McKeen St., Brunswick, 04011-2980.
St. John the Baptist Church, 39 Pleasant St., Brunswick, 04011-2279.
Our Lady Queen of Peace Church, 82 Atlantic Ave., Boothbay Harbor, 04538-2129.
St. Patrick Church, 380 Academy Hill Rd., Newcastle, 04553-3473.
St. Ambrose Church, 27 Kimball St., Richmond, 04357-1106.
St. Katharine Drexel Church, 419 Mountain Rd., Harpswell, 04079.
School—St. John's Catholic School, (Grades PreK-8), 37 Pleasant St., Brunswick, 04011-2279.
Tel: 207-725-5507; Fax: 207-782-5508. Shelly Wheeler, Prin. Lay Teachers 13; Students 90.
Catechesis Religious Program—Email: amy.ford@portlanddiocese.org; Email: merissa.newton@portlanddiocese.org; Email: marcy.brenner@portlanddiocese.org. Ms. Amy Ford, P.C.L.; Ms. Merissa Newton, D.R.E.; Marcy Brenner, RCIA Coord. Students 160.

2—ST. CHARLES (1930) Merged See All Saints Parish, Brunswick.

3—ST. JOHN THE BAPTIST (1877) Merged See All Saints Parish, Brunswick.

BUCKSPORT, HANCOCK CO.

1—STELLA MARIS PARISH (2008) [CEM 2]
Mailing Address: 60 Federal St., P.O. Box S, Bucksport, 04416-1219. Tel: 207-469-3322; Email: stellamaris@portlanddiocese.org. Very Rev. John R. Skehan, V.F.; Revs. Joseph W. Cahill, Parochial Vicar; Stan Ukwe, O.P., Parochial Vicar.
Office: 231 Main St., Ellsworth, 04605-1613.
Worship Sites:—
Our Lady of Hope Church—137 Perkins St., Castine, 04421.
St. Mary Star of the Sea, 8 Granite St., Stonington, 04681.
St. Vincent de Paul, 64 Franklin St., Bucksport, 04416.
Catechesis Religious Program—Students 15.

2—ST. VINCENT DE PAUL (1892) Merged See Stella Maris Parish, Bucksport.

CALAIS, WASHINGTON CO.

1—IMMACULATE CONCEPTION (1859) Merged See Blessed Saint Tekakwitha Parish, Calais.

2—SAINT KATERI TEKAKWITHA PARISH (2008) [CEM]
Mailing Address: P.O. Box 898, Calais, 04619-0898.
Tel: 207-454-0680; Email: kevin.martin@portlanddiocese.org. 31 Calais Ave., Calais, 04619-0898. Rev. Kevin J. Martin.
Churches—
Immaculate Conception Church—31 Calais Ave., Calais, 04619.
St. Ann Church, Peter Dana Point Rd., Indian Twp, 04668.
St. Ann Church, 126 Bayview Dr., Perry, 04667.
St. James the Greater Church, 15 Hillside St., Baileyville, 04694.
St. John the Evangelist Church, 39 Hersey Ln., Pembroke, 04666.
St. Joseph Church, 51 Washington St., Eastport, 04631.
Catechesis Religious Program—Sr. Aline Roy, D.R.E. Students 47.

CAMDEN, KNOX CO.

1—SAINT BRENDAN THE NAVIGATOR PARISH (2009) [CEM 2]
7 Union St., Camden, 04843-2015. Tel: 207-236-4785; Email: stbrendan@portlanddiocese.org. Revs. Robert C. Vaillancourt; Hyacinth Fornkwa, Parochial Vicar; Deacon Robert Cleveland; Christine Cammelieri, Parish Life Coord.; Karol Skoby, Business Mgr.
Churches—
St. Francis of Assisi Church—81 Court St., Belfast, 04915-6134.
St. Mary of the Isles, Pendleton Point Rd., Islesboro, 04848.
Our Lady of Good Hope Church, 7 Union St., Camden, 04843.
St. Bernard Church, 150 Broadway, Rockland, 04841-2698.
St. James Church, Main St., Thomaston, 0486.
Catechesis Religious Program—Kathleen Luppens, D.R.E. Students 122.

2—OUR LADY OF GOOD HOPE (1967) Merged See Saint Brendan the Navigator Parish, Camden.

CAPE ELIZABETH, CUMBERLAND CO., ST. BARTHOLOMEW (1968)
8 Two Lights Rd., Cape Elizabeth, 04107.
Tel: 207-883-0334; Email: katie.benedict@portlanddiocese.org; Web: www.saintbarts.com. 150 Black Point Rd., Scarborough, 04074. Rev. Msgr. Paul F. Stefanko, J.C.L.; Rev. Innocent Okozi, S.M.A., Parochial Vicar; Kathleen Benedict, Business Mgr.; Kristina Benson, Parish Life Coord.
Catechesis Religious Program—Students 101.

CARIBOU, AROOSTOOK CO.

1—HOLY ROSARY (1896) Merged See Parish of the Precious Blood, Caribou.

2—PARISH OF THE PRECIOUS BLOOD (2009) [CEM 10]
Mailing Address: P.O. Box 625, Caribou, 04736-0625. Tel: 207-498-2536; Email: janet.beckwith@portlanddiocese.org; Web: www.theppb.org. 31 Thomas Ave., Caribou, 04736-1721. Revs. David R. Raymond; Nehru Stephen Savarayia, H.G.N., Parochial Vicar; Agustin Sebasthiyan; Janet Beckwith, Parish Life Coord.; Martha Frank, Business Mgr.
St. Mary Rectory, 6 Roberts St., Presque Isle, 04769-8813.
Churches—
St. Mark's Church—113 Allen Farm Rd., Ashland, 04732.
Our Lady of the Lakes, 2111 Portage Rd. US #11, Portage, 04768.
St. Catherine, 24 McManus St., Washburn, 04786.
Holy Rosary Church, 34 Vaughn St., Caribou, 04736-1721.
Sacred Heart Church, 1141 Van Buren Rd., Caribou, 04736-3527.
St. Joseph Church, 17 Main St., Mars Hill, 04758-0000.
St. Denis Church, 147 Main St., Fort Fairfield, 04742-1223.
St. Louis Church, 106 Main St., Limestone, 04750-1116.
St. Therese Church, 239 Main St., Stockholm, 04783-0000.
Nativity of the Blessed Virgin Mary Church, 333 Main St., Presque Isle, 04769-0813.
Catechesis Religious Program—Tel: 207-768-3671; Email: stella.carlstrom@portlanddiocese.org. Stella Carlstrom, D.R.E. Students 180.

3—SACRED HEART (1881) Merged See Parish of the Precious Blood, Caribou.

DAIGLE, AROOSTOOK CO., HOLY FAMILY (1906) Closed. For inquiries for parish records please contact St. John Vianney Parish, Fort Kent.

DEXTER, PENOBSCOT CO.

1—ST. ANNE (1893) Merged See Our Lady of the Snows Parish, Dexter.

2—OUR LADY OF THE SNOWS PARISH (2007)
Mailing Address: P.O Box 193, Dexter, 04930-0193. Tel: 207-924-7104; Email: olofthesnows@portlanddiocese.org. 60 Free St., Dexter, 04930-1507. Rev. Robert L. Lupo; Deacon David Denbow.
Res.: 45 High St., Dover Foxcroft, 04426.
Tel: 207-564-2612.
Churches—
St. Anne Church—64 Free St., Dexter, 04930.
St. Thomas Aquinas Church, 43 High St., Dover Foxcroft, 04426.
Sts. Francis & Paul the Apostle Church, 128 Riverside St., Milo, 04463.
Catechesis Religious Program—

DOVER-FOXCROFT, PISCATAGUIS CO., ST. THOMAS AQUINAS (1898) Merged See Our Lady of the Snows Parish, Dexter.

EAGLE LAKE, AROOSTOOK CO., ST. MARY'S (1892) Merged See St. John Vianney Parish, Fort Kent.

EAST MILLINOCKET, PENOBSCOT CO.

1—CHRIST THE DIVINE MERCY PARISH (2007)
Mailing Address: P.O Box 400, East Millinocket, 04430-0400. 58 Cedar St., East Millinocket, 04430-1031. Rev. Bruce Siket; Charleen Rossignol, Business Mgr.
Churches—
St. Peter's Church—58 Cedar St., East Millinocket, 04430.
St. Martin of Tours Church, 19 Colby St., Millinocket, 04462.
Catechesis Religious Program—Tel: 207-723-6395; Email: tina.mcleod@portlanddiocese.org. Tina McLeod, D.R.E. Students 41.

2—ST. PETER'S (1907) Merged See Christ the Divine Mercy Parish, East Millinocket.

EASTPORT, WASHINGTON CO., ST. JOSEPH (1828) [JC] Merged See Saint Kateri Tekakwitha Parish, Calais.

ELLSWORTH, HANCOCK CO., ST. JOSEPH (1862) [CEM]
Mailing Address: 231 Main St., Ellsworth, 04605-1613. Tel: 207-667-2342; Fax: 207-667-2043; Email: stjoseph.church@roadrunner.com. Revs. Emile H. Dube; Benedict Olusegun Faneye, O.P., Parochial Vicar; Joseph W. Cahill, Parochial Vicar; Laurence Fernald, Business Mgr.
Res.: 4 Park St., Ellsworth, 04605-1628.
Catechesis Religious Program—Students 51.
Missions—Our Lady of the Lake—(summers only) Dedham, 04429.
St. Margaret, (summers only) Winter Harbor.

FAIRFIELD, SOMERSET CO., IMMACULATE HEART OF MARY (1871) Closed. See Corpus Christi Parish, Waterville.

FALMOUTH, CUMBERLAND CO.

1—HOLY MARTYRS (1968) Merged See Parish of the Holy Eucharist, Falmouth.

2—PARISH OF THE HOLY EUCHARIST
266 Foreside Rd., Falmouth, 04105-1405.
Tel: 207-847-6890; Email: pothe@portlanddiocese.org; Web: pothe.org/. Revs. Daniel P. Greenleaf, V.F.; Peter Kaseta, O.F.M.Cap., Parochial Vicar; Deacon Dennis J. Popadak; Rev. Paul R. Marquis, In Res.
Holy Martyrs of North America Church—266 Foreside Rd., Falmouth, 04105.
Sacred Heart Church, 326 Main St., Yarmouth, 04096.
St. Gregory Church, 24 N. Raymond Rd., Gray, 04039.
St. Jude Church, 134 Main St., Freeport, 04034.
Catechesis Religious Program—Georgette Dionne, D.R.E.; Sr. Kate Walsh, Asst. Faith Formation; Joy Segovia, Coord. Youth Ministry. Students 99.

FARMINGTON, FRANKLIN CO., ST. JOSEPH'S (1885)
Mailing Address: 133 Middle St., Farmington, 04938-1598. Tel: 207-778-2778; Email: stjfarmington@portlanddiocese.org. Rev. Paul H. Dumais.
Catechesis Religious Program—Students 19.

FORT FAIRFIELD, AROOSTOOK CO., ST. DENIS (1894) Merged See Parish of the Precious Blood, Caribou.

FORT KENT, AROOSTOOK CO.

1—ST. JOHN VIANNEY PARISH (2007) [CEM 11]
26 E. Main St., Fort Kent, 04743-1395.
Tel: 207-834-5656; Email: stjohnvianneyparish@portlanddiocese.org. Very Rev. Jean-Paul Labrie, V.F.; Rev. Selvaraj Kasi, Parochial Vicar; Deacon Luis Sanclemente; Mrs. Gale Rioux, Office Mgr. & Bookkeeper.
Churches—
St. Mary Church—3443 Aroostock Rd., Eagle Lake, 04739.
St. Louis Church, 26 E. Main St., Fort Kent, 04743.
St. Charles Church, 912 Main St., St. Francis, 04774.
St. Joseph Church, 7 Church St., Wallagrass, 04781.
Catechesis Religious Program—Ms. Barbara Pelletier, P.C.L.; Lisa Charette, D.R.E. K-6; Meliss Babin, D.R.E. (7-8); Ms. Lynette Sirois, Youth Min. 9-12. Students 352.

2—ST. LOUIS (1870) Merged See St. John Vianney Parish, Fort Kent.

FRENCHVILLE, AROOSTOOK CO., ST. LUCE (1843) Merged See Our Lady of the Valley, St. Agatha.

GARDINER, KENNEBEC CO., ST. JOSEPH'S (1863) Merged See St. Michael Parish, Augusta.

GORHAM, CUMBERLAND CO., ST. ANNE (1967)
299 Main St., Gorham, 04038-1330.
Tel: 207-839-4857; Fax: 207-839-3082; Email: stannegorham@portlanddiocese.org; Web: www.stannegorham.com. Mailing Address: P.O. Box 69, Westbrook, 04098-0069. Revs. Louis J. Phillips, V.F.; Steven G. Cartwright.
Office: Pastoral Center, 268 Brown St., Westbrook, 04098.
Catechesis Religious Program—Tel: 207-839-3082; Email: jackie.moreau@portlanddiocese.org. Sr. Jackie Moreau, R.S.M., D.R.E. Students 87.
Mission—Our Lady of Sebago, Rte. 114, East Sebago.

GRAND ISLE, AROOSTOOK CO., ST. GERARD-MT. CARMEL (1930) Merged See Notre Dame du Mont Carmel Parish, Madawaska.

GRAY, CUMBERLAND CO., ST. GREGORY (1967) Merged See Parish of the Holy Eucharist, Falmouth.

GREENVILLE, PISCATAQUIS CO., HOLY FAMILY (1916) [CEM]
P.O. Box 457, Greenville, 04441-0457.
Tel: 207-695-2262; Email: bette.diangelo@portlanddiocese.org; Web: portlanddiocese.org/holy-family. 145 Pritham Ave., Greenville, 04441. Rev. Aaron L. Damboise.
Catechesis Religious Program—Students 7.
Mission—St. Joseph's, Rockwood Rd., Rockwood.

HALLOWELL, KENNEBEC CO., SACRED HEART (1878) Merged See St. Michael Parish, Augusta.

HAMLIN, AROOSTOOK CO., ST. JOSEPH (1920) Merged See Saint Peter Chanel Parish, Van Buren.

HAMPDEN, PENOBSCOT CO., ST. MATTHEW (1968) Merged See Saint Paul the Apostle Parish, Bangor.

HOULTON, AROOSTOOK CO., ST. MARY OF THE VISITATION (1839) [CEM]
112 Military St., Houlton, 04730-2507.
Tel: 207-532-2871; Fax: 207-532-4401; Email: maryagnespaul@portlanddiocese.org; Web: maryagnespaul.org. Rev. Kent R. Ouellette; Deacons Albert Burleigh; Ronald Ouellette.
Catechesis Religious Program—Email: clare.desrosiers@portlanddiocese.org. Clare Desrosiers, D.R.E. Students 60.

HOWLAND, PENOBSCOT CO., ST. LEO THE GREAT (1945) [CEM]
Mailing Address: P.O. Box 22, Howland, 04448-0022. Tel: 207-732-3495; Email: stleohowland@gmail.com. 18 River Rd., Howland, 04448-0000. Very Rev. Richard C. Malo, V.F.
Catechesis Religious Program—Ms. Karen Carson, D.R.E. Students 12.

INDIAN TOWNSHIP, WASHINGTON CO., ST. ANN (1929) (Native American), Merged See Saint Kateri Tekakwitha Parish, Calais.

ISLAND FALLS, AROOSTOOK CO., ST. AGNES (1920) [CEM]
76 Sewall St., Island Falls, 04747. Rev. Kent R. Ouellette; Deacons Albert Burleigh; Ronald Ouellette.
Office & Mailing Address: 112 Military St., Houlton, 04730. Tel: 207-532-2871; Fax: 207-532-4401; Email: maryagnespaul@portlanddiocese.org; Web: maryagnespaul.org.
Catechesis Religious Program—Clare Desrosiers, D.R.E. Students 11.
Mission—St. Paul, 34 Katahdin St., Patten, 04765.

JACKMAN, SOMERSET CO., ST. ANTHONY (1892) [CEM]
Mailing Address: P.O. Box 457, Greenville, 04441-0457. Tel: 207-668-2881; Email: aaron.damboise@portlanddiocese.org. Rev. Aaron L. Damboise; Lorraine Auclair, Business Mgr.
Res.: 145 Pritham Ave., Greenville, 04441.
Church: St. Faustina Church, 370 Main St., Jackman, 04945.
Catechesis Religious Program—Students 14.

JAY, FRANKLIN CO., ST. ROSE OF LIMA (1894) [CEM]
One Church St., Jay, 04239-1801. Tel: 207-897-2173; Fax: 207-897-2478; Email: strose@portlanddiocese.org; Web: strosejayme.com. Rev. Paul H. Dumais.
Catechesis Religious Program—Students 52.

KENNEBUNK, YORK CO., ST. MARTHA'S (1909) Merged See Holy Spirit Parish, Wells.

KITTERY, YORK CO.

1—PARISH OF THE ASCENSION OF THE LORD (2011)
6 Whipple Rd., Kittery, 03904-1739.
Tel: 207-439-0442; Email: bill.green@portlanddiocese.org; Web: pal-me.org. Revs. Scott M. Mower; Antonydass Piachaimuthu.
Rectory—8 Whipple Rd., Kittery, 03904-1758.
Worship Sites:—
Our Lady of the Angels Church—160 Agamenticus Rd., South Berwick, 03908.
St. Christopher-by-the-Sea Church, 4 Barrell Ln., York, 03909-1020.
St. Raphael's Church, 6 Whipple Rd., Kittery, 03904-1739.
Star of the Sea Church, 13 Church St., York Beach, 03910. (Seasonal).
Catechesis Religious Program—Julie Webber, D.R.E. Students 110.

2—ST. RAPHAEL'S (1916) Merged See Parish of the Ascension of the Lord, Kittery.

LEWISTON, ANDROSCOGGIN CO.

1—HOLY CROSS (1923) [JC] Merged See Prince of Peace Parish, Lewiston.

2—HOLY FAMILY (1923) Merged See Prince of Peace Parish, Lewiston.

3—ST. JOSEPH (1857) [JC] Closed. See Prince of Peace Parish, Lewiston.

4—ST. MARY (1907) Closed. For inquiries for parish records contact Prince of Peace Parish, Lewiston.

5—ST. PATRICK (1887) [CEM] Closed. See Prince of Peace Parish, Lewiston.

6—SS. PETER AND PAUL BASILICA (1870) Merged See Prince of Peace Parish, Lewiston.

7—PRINCE OF PEACE PARISH (2009) [CEM] Revs. Timothy J. Nadeau; Matthew J. Gregory, H.G.N., Admin.; Antony Chinnaiyah, H.G.N., Parochial Vicar; Deacon Irenee Richard, O.P. In Res., Rev. Dominic Savio, H.G.N., Hospital Chap.
Catholic Center—16 Ste. Croix St., P.O. Box 1540, Lewiston, 04241-1540. Tel: 207-777-1200; Email: sue.tuttle@portlanddiocese.org.
Res.: 607 Sabattus St., Lewiston, 04240-4193.
Churches—
Basilica of Ss. Peter & Paul—27 Bartlett St., Lewiston, 04240.
Holy Cross Church, 1080 Lisbon St., Lewiston, 04240.
Holy Family Church, 607 Sabattus St., Lewiston, 04240.
Catechesis Religious Program—Lisa Daigle, D.R.E. Students 143.

LIMERICK, YORK CO., ST. MATTHEW (1921)
19 Dora Ln., Limerick, 04048-3527.
Tel: 207-793-2244; Email: heather.silva@portlanddiocese.org; Web: www.stmatthewlimerick.org. Very Revs. Philip A. Tracy, V.F.; John D. Dickinson, J.C.L., J.V., Parochial Vicar; Deacon Paul Lissandrello.
Catechesis Religious Program—Students 95.

LIMESTONE, AROOSTOOK CO., ST. LOUIS (1919) Merged See Parish of the Precious Blood, Caribou.

LINCOLN, PENOBSCOT CO., ST. MARY (1902) Very Rev. Richard C. Malo, V.F.
Church: 164 Main St., P.O. Box 310, Lincoln, 04457-0310. Tel: 207-794-6333; Fax: 207-794-8044; Email: saintmarys3@myfairpoint.net.
Catechesis Religious Program—Students 32.
Missions—Sacred Heart—Winn.
St. Ann, Danforth.

LISBON FALLS, ANDROSCOGGIN CO.

1—SS. CYRIL AND METHODIUS (1925) (Slovak), Closed. See Holy Trinity, Lisbon Falls.

2—HOLY TRINITY (1995) [CEM 3] Revs. Timothy J.

Nadeau; Matthew J. Gregory, H.G.N., Admin.; Antony Chinnaiyah, H.G.N., Parochial Vicar.
Res.: 7 Highland Ave., Lisbon Falls, 04252-1105.
Church, Office & Mailing: 67 Frost Hill Ave., Lisbon Falls, 04252-1126. Tel: 207-353-2792 (Office); Fax: 207-353-6192; Email: holytrinity@portlanddiocese.org.
Catechesis Religious Program—Cammy Reny, D.R.E. Students 67.

LISBON, ANDROSCOGGIN CO., ST. ANNE'S (1885) Closed. See Holy Trinity, Lisbon Falls.

LUBEC, WASHINGTON CO., SACRED HEART (1913) Merged See Saint Peter the Fisherman Parish, Machias.

LYMAN, YORK CO., ST. PHILIP (1981) [JC] Merged See Good Shepherd Parish, Saco.

MACHIAS, WASHINGTON CO.
1—HOLY NAME OF JESUS (1828) Merged See Saint Peter the Fisherman Parish, Machias.
2—SAINT PETER THE FISHERMAN PARISH (2008)
Mailing Address: P.O. Box 898, Machias, 04654-0248. Tel: 207-255-3731; Email: stpeterthefisherman@portlanddiocese.org; Web: www.stpeterthefisherman.me. 8 Free St., Machias, 04654-0248. Rev. Philip Clement, Admin.; Deacon James J. Gillen, Business Mgr.; Kathy Lawrence, Business Mgr.
Holy Name of Jesus Church—8 Free St., Machias, 04654.
Sacred Heart Church, 14 Hamilton St., Lubec, 04652.
St. Michael Church, 51 Elm St., Cherryfield, 04622.

MADAWASKA, AROOSTOOK CO.
1—ST. DAVID'S (1872) Merged See Notre Dame du Mont Carmel Parish, Madawaska.
2—NOTRE DAME DU MONT CARMEL PARISH (2007) [CEM 4]
309 St. Thomas St., Ste. 103, Madawaska, 04756-1278. Tel: 207-728-7531; Email: Judy.Lavoie@portlanddiocese.org. Revs. James S. Plourde; Alex Anthony Maria Doss, H.G.N.; Selvaraj Kasi; Deacon Donald R. Clavette; Mr. Gregory Cyr, Business Mgr.
Res.: 774 Main St., Madawaska, 04756.
Churches—
St. Gerard-Mt. Carmel Church—361 Main St., Grand Isle, 04746.
St. Thomas Aquinas Church, 321 St. Thomas St., Madawaska, 04756.
St. David Church, 774 Main St., Madawaska, 04756.
Catechesis Religious Program—Tel: 207-728-7135; Email: annmarie.clavette@portlanddiocese.org. Ann Marie Clavette, D.R.E. Students 102.
3—ST. THOMAS AQUINAS (1929) Merged See Notre Dame du Mont Carmel Parish, Madawaska.

MADISON, SOMERSET CO., ST. SEBASTIAN (1907) Merged See Christ the King Parish, Skowhegan.

MARS HILL, AROOSTOOK CO., ST. JOSEPH (1927) Merged See Parish of Precious Blood, Caribou.

MECHANIC FALLS, ANDROSCOGGIN CO., OUR LADY OF RANSOM (1931) Merged See Blessed Teresa of Calcutta Parish, Norway.

MEXICO, OXFORD CO., ST. THERESA (1926) [JC] Closed. See Parish of the Holy Savior, Rumford.

MILLINOCKET, PENOBSCOT CO., ST. MARTIN OF TOURS (1899) Merged See Christ the Divine Mercy Parish, East Millinocket.

MILO, PISCATAQUIS CO., ST. FRANCIS XAVIER (1929) Merged See Our Lady of the Snows Parish, Dexter.

NEWCASTLE, LINCOLN CO., ST. PATRICK (1796) Merged See All Saints Parish, Brunswick.

NORTH VASSALBORO, KENNEBEC CO., ST. BRIDGET'S (1911) Merged See Corpus Christi Parish, Waterville.

NORTHEAST HARBOR, HANCOCK CO., ST. IGNATIUS (1929) Merged See Parish of the Transfiguration, Bar Harbor.

NORWAY, OXFORD CO.
1—SAINT TERESA OF CALCUTTA PARISH (2008)
32 Paris St., Norway, 04268-5633. Tel: 207-743-2606; Email: btcadmin@portlanddiocese.org; Web: www.cluster30.org. Revs. Edward R. Clifford; Peter Shaba, S.M.A., Parochial Vicar.
Churches—
Our Lady of Ransom Church—117 Elm St., Mechanic Falls, 04256.
St. Catherine of Sienna Church, 32 Paris St., Norway, 04268.
St. Mary Church, 276 King St., Oxford, 04270.
Catechesis Religious Program—Email: joanne.fortier@portlanddiocese.org. Joanne Fortier, D.R.E. Students 28.
2—ST. CATHERINE OF SIENNA (1914) Merged See Blessed Teresa of Calcutta Parish, Norway.

OAKLAND, KENNEBEC CO., ST. THERESA (1963) Merged See Corpus Christi Parish, Waterville.

OLD ORCHARD BEACH, YORK CO., ST. MARGARET'S (1926) Merged See Good Shepherd Parish, Saco.

OLD TOWN, PENOBSCOT CO.
1—ST. ANN CHURCH, INDIAN ISLAND (1688) (Native American), Merged See Parish of the Resurrection of the Lord, Old Town.
2—HOLY FAMILY (1992) [JC] Merged See Parish of the Resurrection of the Lord, Old Town.
3—ST. JOSEPH'S (1862) Closed. All records at Parish of the Resurrection of the Lord, Old Town.
4—ST. MARY'S (1928) Closed. All records at Parish of the Resurrection of the Lord, Old Town.
5—PARISH OF THE RESURRECTION OF THE LORD (2009)
429 Main St., Old Town, 04468-1718.
Tel: 207-827-4000; Email: resurrectionparish@portlanddiocese.org; Web: resurrectionofthelord.org/. Rev. Wilfred P. Labbe; Deacon Michael Boggs; Linda Lawrence, Business Mgr.; Jessica Moore, Music Min. & D.R.E.; Audrey Aylmer, RCIA Coord.
Churches—
St. Ann Church—84 Main St., Bradley, 04411.
St. Ann Church, 6 Down St., Indian Island, 04468.
Holy Family Church.
Our Lady of Wisdom Newman Center Chapel, 83 College Ave., Orono, 04473. Tel: 207-866-2155; Fax: 207-866-4543.
Catechesis Religious Program—Email: jessica.moore@portlanddiocese.org. Students 78.

OQUOSSOC, FRANKLIN CO., OUR LADY OF THE LAKES (1927)
Mailing Address: 43 Rangeley Ave., P.O. Box 333, Oquossoc, 04964-0333. Tel: 207-864-3796; Email: paul.murray@portlanddiocese.org. Rev. Paul G. Murray, Admin.
Catechesis Religious Program—Students 3.
Missions—St. Luke—9 Lake St., Rangeley, 04964.
St. John, Main St., Stratton, 04964.
Richard H. Bell Memorial Chapel, Sugarloaf Ski Area, Sugarloaf U.S.A., 04964.

ORONO, PENOBSCOT CO.
1—ST. MARY'S (1888) [JC] Closed. See Parish of the Resurrection of the Lord, Old Town.
2—OUR LADY OF WISDOM PERSONAL CAMPUS PARISH (1946) Merged See Parish of the Resurrection of the Lord, Old Town.

PERRY, WASHINGTON CO., ST. ANN (Pleasant Point) (1907) (Native American), Merged See Saint Kateri Tekakwitha Parish, Calais.

PITTSFIELD, SOMERSET CO., ST. AGNES (1909)
238 Detroit St., Pittsfield, 04967-3522.
Tel: 207-924-7104; Email: olofthesnows@portlanddiocese.org. P.O. Box 193, Dexter, 04930-0193. Rev. Robert L. Lupo; Deacon David Denbow. In Res., Rev. Mark P. Nolette, J.C.L.
Res.: 113 Leonard St., Pittsfield, 04967.
Tel: 207-924-7104; Email: olofthesnows@portlanddiocese.org; Web: www.ourladyofthesnowsme.org.
Office: 60 Free St., P.O. Box 193, Dexter, 04930.
Catechesis Religious Program—Students 21.

PRESQUE ISLE, AROOSTOOK CO., NATIVITY OF B.V.M. (1895) Merged See Parish of the Precious Blood, Caribou.

RICHMOND, SAGADAHOC CO., ST. AMBROSE (1866) Merged See All Saints Parish, Brunswick.

ROCKLAND, KNOX CO., ST. BERNARD'S (1857) Merged See Saint Brendan the Navigator Parish, Camden.

RUMFORD, OXFORD CO.
1—ST. ATHANASIUS-ST. JOHN (1906) [JC] Merged See Parish of the Holy Savior, Rumford.
2—PARISH OF THE HOLY SAVIOR (2008) [CEM]
7 Brown St., Mexico, 04257. Tel: 207-364-4556; Email: holysaviorparish@portlanddiocese.org; Web: www.parishoftheholysavior.com. Rev. Nathan D. March; Cheryl Cox, Business Mgr.
St. Athanasius & St. John Church—126 Maine Ave., Rumford, 04276.
Our Lady of the Snows Church, 265 Walkers Mills Rd., Bethel, 04217.
Catechesis Religious Program—Email: laura.koch@portlanddiocese.org. Laura A. Koch, P.C.L. Students 19.

ST. AGATHA, AROOSTOOK CO.
1—ST. AGATHA'S (1889) Merged See Our Lady of the Valley, St. Agatha.
2—OUR LADY OF THE VALLEY (2006) [CEM 3]
379 Main St., St. Agatha, 04772. Tel: 207-543-7447; Email: Judy.Lavoie@portlanddiocese.org. Mailing Address: 309 St. Thomas St., Ste. 103, Madawaska, 04756-1278. Revs. James S. Plourde; Alex Anthony Maria Doss, H.G.N.; Selvaraj Kasi; Mr. Gregory Cyr, Business Mgr.
Churches—
St. Luce Church—437 U.S. Route 1, Frenchville, 04745.
St. Agatha Church, 379 Main St., St. Agatha, 04772.
St. Joseph Church, 413 Shore Rd., Sinclair, 04779.
St. Michael Church, 31 Chapel Rd., St. David, 04773.
Catechesis Religious Program—Tel: 207-543-6119; Fax: 207-543-6019. Janice Young, D.R.E. Students 95.

ST. FRANCIS, AROOSTOOK CO., ST. CHARLES (1891) Merged See St. John Vianney Parish, Fort Kent.

ST. JOHN, AROOSTOOK CO., ST. JOHN (1930) Merged See St. John Vianney Parish, Fort Kent.

SABATTUS, ANDROSCOGGIN CO., OUR LADY OF THE ROSARY (1975)
131 High St., Sabattus, 04280-4250.
Tel: 207-375-6951; Email: ourladyoftherosary@portlanddiocese.org. Revs. Timothy J. Nadeau; Matthew J. Gregory, H.G.N., Admin.; Antony Chinnaiyah, H.G.N., Parochial Vicar; Seamus P. Griesbach, In Res.
Catechesis Religious Program—Cammy Reny, D.R.E. Students 14.
Mission—St. Francis, Rte. 202, Greene, 04236.

SACO, YORK CO.
1—GOOD SHEPHERD PARISH (2008) [CEM 2] Rev. Msgr. Rene T. Mathieu, S.T.L.; Revs. Dominic Tumusii, H.G.N., A.J., Parochial Vicar; Brad Morin, Parochial Vicar; Deacons Kevin N. Jacques; Robert M. Parenteau; Richard Huot; Elizabeth Williams, Pastoral Life Coord.; Mr. David Gadbois, Business Mgr.
Office & Res.: 271 Main St., Saco, 04072-1510.
Tel: 207-282-3321; Email: goodshepherd@portlanddiocese.org; Web: www.goodshepherdparish.us.
Churches—
St. Brendan Church—40 Lester B. Orcutt Blvd., Biddeford Pool, 04006. (Summers Only).
St. Joseph Church, 178 Elm St., Biddeford, 04005.
Most Holy Trinity Church, 271 Main St., Saco, 04072.
St. Margaret Church, 6 Saco Ave., Old Orchard Beach, 04064.
St. Philip Church, 404 Goodwins Mills Rd., Lyman, 04002.
School—St. James School, (Grades PreK-8), 25 Graham St., Biddeford, 04005-3297.
Tel: 207-282-4084; Fax: 207-286-3693; Email: nancy.naimey@portlanddiocese.org; Email: helen.fournier@portlanddiocese.org. Ms. Nancy Naimey, Prin.; Helen Fournier, Sec. Administrators 1; Lay Teachers 15; Total Students 153.
Catechesis Religious Program—Students 200.
2—MOST HOLY TRINITY (1916) Merged See Good Shepherd Parish, Saco.
3—NOTRE DAME DE LOURDES (1929) [JC] Closed. See Good Shepherd Parish, Saco.

SANFORD, YORK CO.
1—HOLY FAMILY (1923) [JC] Merged See Saint Therese of Lisieux Parish, Sanford.
2—ST. IGNATIUS MARTYR (1892) Closed. See Saint Therese of Lisieux Parish, Sanford.
3—SAINT THERESE OF LISIEUX PARISH (2007) [CEM 2]
66 North Ave., Sanford, 04073-2997.
Tel: 207-324-2420; Fax: 207-324-6630; Email: philip.tracy@portlanddiocese.org; Email: laura.alexandre@portlanddiocese.org; Web: www.stthereseparishmaine.org. Very Revs. Philip A. Tracy, V.F.; John D. Dickinson, J.C.L., J.V., Parochial Vicar.
Res.: 10 Payne St., Springvale, 04083-1312.
Churches—
Holy Family Church.
Notre Dame Church—10 Payne St., Springvale, 04083.
School—St. Thomas Consolidated School, (Grades PreK-8), 69 North Ave., Sanford, 04073-2542.
Tel: 207-324-5832; Fax: 207-324-2549; Email: donna.jacques@portlanddiocese.org; Web: www.saintthomassanford.org. Mrs. Donna Jacques, Prin. Lay Teachers 11; Students 176.
Catechesis Religious Program—Email: shelly.carpenter@portlanddiocese.org. Shelly Carpenter, D.R.E. Students 95.

SCARBOROUGH, CUMBERLAND CO., ST. MAXIMILIAN KOLBE (1988)
150 Black Point Rd., Scarborough, 04074-9349.
Tel: 207-883-0334; Email: katie.benedict@portlanddiocese.org; Web: www.saintmax.com. Rev. Msgr. Paul F. Stefanko, J.C.L.; Rev. Innocent Okozi, S.M.A., Parochial Vicar; Katie Benedict, Business Mgr.; Kristina Benson, Parish Life Coord.
Catechesis Religious Program—Tel: 207-883-1742; Email: stmaxre@maine.rr.com. Students 163.

SINCLAIR, AROOSTOOK CO., ST. JOSEPH (1936) Merged See Our Lady of the Valley, St. Agatha.

SKOWHEGAN, SOMERSET CO.
1—CHRIST THE KING PARISH (2007) [CEM 2]
273 Water St., Skowhegan, 04976-0369.
Tel: 207-474-2039; Email: christthekingparish@portlanddiocese.org; Email: nddlourdes@myfairpoint.net. P.O. Box 369, Skowhegan, 04976-0369. Rev. James L. Nadeau, S.T.L.
Churches—
St. Peter Church—26 Owens St., Bingham, 04920.
St. Sebastian Church, 161 Main St., Madison, 04950. Tel: 207-696-3203.
Notre Dame de Lourdes Church, 273 Water St., Skowhegan, 04976.
Catechesis Religious Program—Email: alicia.

benson@portlanddiocese.org. Alicia Benson, D.R.E. Students 41.
2—NOTRE DAME DE LOURDES (1881) Merged See Christ the King Parish, Skowhegan.
SOUTH BERWICK, YORK CO., ST. MICHAEL (1886) Closed. See Parish of the Ascension of the Lord, Kittery.
SOUTH PORTLAND, CUMBERLAND CO.
1—CHURCH OF THE HOLY CROSS (1913) Merged See St. John and Holy Cross Parish, South Portland.
2—ST. JOHN AND HOLY CROSS PARISH
Mailing Address: 150 Black Point Rd., Scarborough, 04074-9349. Rev. Msgr. Paul F. Stefanko, J.C.L.; Rev. Innocent Okozi, S.M.A., Parochial Vicar; Kathleen Benedict, Business Mgr.; Kristina Benson, Parish Life Coord.
Church of the Holy Cross, 124 Cottage Rd., South Portland, 04116.
School—Holy Cross School, (Grades PreK-8), 436 Broadway, South Portland, 04106-2996.
Tel: 207-799-6661; Fax: 207-799-8345; Email: chris.labbe@portlanddiocese.org; Email: william.ridge@portlanddiocese.org; Web: www.holycrossmaine.com. Mrs. Christine L'Abbe, Prin. Religious Teachers 1; Lay Teachers 12; Students 116.
Catechesis Religious Program—Students 69.
3—ST. JOHN THE EVANGELIST (1940) Closed. See St. John and Holy Cross Parish, South Portland.
SPRINGVALE, YORK CO., NOTRE DAME (1887) Merged See Saint Therese of Lisieux Parish, Sanford.
STOCKHOLM, AROOSTOOK CO., ST. THERESE (1926) Merged See Parish of the Precious Blood, Caribou.
STONINGTON, HANCOCK CO., ST. MARY STAR OF THE SEA (1931) Merged See Stella Maris Parish, Bucksport.
VAN BUREN, AROOSTOOK CO.
1—ST. BRUNO - ST. REMI (1991) Merged See Saint Peter Chanel Parish, Van Buren.
2—SAINT PETER CHANEL PARISH (2007) [CEM 2]
174 Main St., Van Buren, 04785-1237.
Tel: 207-868-2718; Email: Judy.Lavoie@portlanddiocese.org. Revs. James S. Plourde; Alex Anthony Maria Doss, H.G.N.; Selvaraj Kasi; Mr. Gregory Cyr, Business Mgr.
Churches—
St. Joseph Church—1779 Hamlin Rd., Hamlin, 04785.
St. Bruno-St. Remi Church, 174 Main St., Van Buren, 04785.
Catechesis Religious Program—Ann Marie Clavette, D.R.E. Students 57.
3—ST. REMI (1923) Closed. See listing for Saint Peter Chanel Parish, Van Buren.
WALLAGRASS, AROOSTOOK CO., ST. JOSEPH'S (1890) Closed. See St. John Vianney Parish, Fort Kent.
WATERVILLE, KENNEBEC CO.
1—CORPUS CHRISTI PARISH (2007) [CEM]
70 Pleasant St., Waterville, 04901-5405.
Tel: 207-872-2281; Email: ccmoffice@gwi.net; Web: www.corpuschristimaine.org. Revs. Daniel J. Baillargeon; Patrick Finn; Ms. Kimberly Suttie, Parish Life Coord.; Deborah Hebert, Business Mgr.
Res.: 26 Monument St., Winslow, 04901.
Churches—
Notre Dame Church, 116 Silver St., Waterville, 04901.
Sacred Heart Church—72 Pleasant St., Waterville, 04901.
St. John Church—
St. Helena Church, Belgrade Lakes, 04918. (Summers only).
School—St. John Regional Catholic School, (Grades PreK-7), 15 S. Garand St., Winslow, 04901.
Tel: 207-872-7115; Fax: 207-872-2500; Email: sjcs@portlanddiocese.org; Web: www.stjohnschoolwinslow.org. Mrs. Valerie Wheeler, Prin. Lay Teachers 5; Students 68.
Catechesis Religious Program—Tel: 209-660-9027; Email: elaine.gordon@portlanddiocese.org. Mrs. Elaine Gordon, D.R.E. Students 118.
2—NOTRE DAME (1910) Merged See Corpus Christi Parish, Waterville.
3—PARISH OF THE HOLY SPIRIT (1996) [JC] Merged See Corpus Christi Parish, Waterville.
4—SACRED HEART (1906) Merged See Corpus Christi Parish, Waterville.
WELLS, YORK CO.
1—HOLY SPIRIT PARISH (2008)
236 Eldridge Rd., Wells, 04090-4050.
Tel: 207-646-5605; Email: stmarywells@myfairpoint.net; Web: www.holyspiritme.org. Rev. Fredrick H. Morse; Deacon Darrell Blackwell.
Churches—
St. Martha Church—30 Portland Rd., Kennebunk, 04043-6631.
St. Mary Church.
All Saints Church, 45 School St., Ogunquit, 03907. (Summers only).
Catechesis Religious Program—Tel: 207-985-6252; Email: churchlady5605@gmail.com; Email: rosanne.smith@portlanddiocese.org. Carolyn Houston, Catechetical Leader; Mrs. Rosanne Smith, Adult Faith Formation. Students 147.
2—ST. MARY (1970) Merged See Holy Spirit Parish, Wells.
WESTBROOK, CUMBERLAND CO.
1—ST. ANTHONY OF PADUA PARISH (2005) [CEM]
Mailing Address: P.O. Box 69, Westbrook, 04098-0069. Tel: 207-854-0490; Email: stanthonyparish@verizon.net; Web: www.ac.net/portland/stanthony. 268 Brown St., Westbrook, 04098. Very Rev. Louis J. Phillips, V.F.; Rev. Michael J. Seavey, Parochial Vicar; Deacon Lawrence Guertin, Parish Life Coord. In Res., Rev. Reginald R. Brissette, (Retired).
St. Hyacinth.
Res.: 63 Dana Ct., Westbrook, 04092-2912.
Catechesis Religious Program—Students 87.
2—ST. EDMUND (Prides Corner) (1975) Closed. See St. Anthony of Padua, Westbrook.
3—ST. HYACINTH (1892) Merged See St. Anthony of Padua, Westbrook.
4—ST. MARY'S (1920) [JC] Closed. See St. Anthony of Padua, Westbrook.
WHITEFIELD, LINCOLN CO., ST. DENIS (1818) Merged See St. Michael Parish, Augusta.
WILTON, FRANKLIN CO., ST. MARY (1928) Closed. All records at St. Joseph, Farmington.
WINDHAM, CUMBERLAND CO., OUR LADY OF PERPETUAL HELP (1974)
919 Roosevelt Tr., Windham, 04062-5641. Email: Donnamarie.Inman@portlanddiocese.org. Mailing Address: P.O. Box 69, Westbrook, 04098-0069.
Tel: 207-892-8288. Very Rev. Louis J. Phillips, V.F.; Rev. Steven G. Cartwright; Deacons Lawrence Guertin, Parish Life Coord.; Frank Chambers; Peter J. Bernier; Dean Lachance.
Office: Pastoral Center, 268 Brown St., Westbrook, 04098.
Catechesis Religious Program—Email: jill.russell-morey@portlanddiocese.org. Jill Russell-Morey, D.R.E. Students 65.
WINSLOW, KENNEBEC CO., ST. JOHN THE BAPTIST (1926) [JC] Merged See Corpus Christi Parish, Waterville.
WINTERPORT, WALDO CO., ST. GABRIEL (1850) Merged See Saint Paul the Apostle Parish, Bangor.
WINTHROP, KENNEBEC CO., ST. FRANCIS XAVIER (1910) [JC] Merged See St. Michael Parish, Augusta.
YARMOUTH, CUMBERLAND CO., SACRED HEART (1876) Merged See Parish of the Holy Eucharist, Falmouth.
YORK HARBOR, YORK CO., ST. CHRISTOPHER-BY-THE-SEA (1947) Merged See Parish of the Ascension of the Lord, Kittery.

Chaplains of Public Institutions

PORTLAND. *Maine Medical Center*, Tel: 207-871-0111. Revs. Amandus B. Sway, A.J., Anthanasius S. Wirsiy, Chaplain Mr. Michael Vaughn.
Mercy Hospital, 144 State St., 04101-3776.
Tel: 207-879-3000; Web: mercyhospital.org. Sr. Patricia Mooney, R.S.M., Chap., Pastoral Care.
AUGUSTA. *Augusta Mental Health Institute*, Riverview Psychiatric Center, 250 Arsenal St, Augusta, 04330. Tel: 207-623-8823; Email: st.michael@portlanddiocese.org. 24 Washington St., Augusta, 04330-4239. Tel: 207-624-4600. Served by the staff of St. Michael Parish, Augusta.
Maine General Medical Center. Alfond Center for Health Care, Riverview Psychiatric Center Augusta. Tel: 207-626-1000. Rev. Arockiasamy Santhiyagu, H.G.N.
Togus VA Medical Center, Togus.
Tel: 207-623-8411, Ext. 5176. Rev. Jacob C. George.
BANGOR. *Eastern Maine Medical Center*, Bangor.
Tel: 207-943-7000. Rev. Apolinary Kavishe, A.J. Taylor Hospital, Bangor Convalescent Center,.
St. Joseph Healthcare Foundation, 360 Broadway, Bangor, 04401-3979. Tel: 207-907-1000;
Fax: 207-907-1922; Email: maryprybylo@sjhhealth.com; Web: www.stjoehealing.org. Mary Prybylo, Pres.
BIDDEFORD. *Southern Maine Medical Center*, Biddeford. Tel: 207-283-3663. Served by Good Shepherd Parish, Biddeford.
LEWISTON. *Central Maine Medical Center*, Lewiston.
Tel: 207-795-0111. Rev. Dominic Savio, H.G.N., Mr. Jonathan Hoffman, Pastoral Care.
St. Mary's Regional Medical Center. Rev. Dominic Savio, H.G.N., Anne-Marie Bourque, R.S.M., Charles Demm, Daniel Doyon
Campus Ave., P.O. Box 291, Lewiston, 04243-0291.
Tel: 207-777-8520.
SOUTH PORTLAND. *Maine Youth Center*. Vacant.
WARREN. *Super Maximum Facility & Minimum Facility*, 807 Cushing Rd., Warren, 04864-4603.
Tel: 207-273-5300; Email: robert.curtis@portlanddiocese.org. 510 Ocean Ave., 04103-4936. Deacon Robert Curtis, Chap.
WINDHAM. *Maine Correctional Center*, 17 Mallison Falls Rd., Windham, 04062-4101. Sr. Marian Zimmerman, R.S.M., Chap., Tel: 207-893-7063.

Special or Other Diocesan Assignment:
Very Rev. Msgr.—
Dubois, Andrew, S.T.L., V.G., 510 Ocean Ave., 04103-4936. Tel: 207-773-6471. Res.: St. Peter Rectory, 72 Federal St., 04101
Rev. Msgrs.—
Caron, Marc B., S.T.L., St. John Seminary, 127 Lake St., Brighton, MA 02135-3848
Henchal, Michael J., J.C.L., 510 Ocean Avenue, 04103-4936
Revs.—
Daniels, Joseph E., V.F., 510 Ocean Ave., 04103-4936
Gendreau, Claude R., Tribunal, 510 Ocean Ave., 04103-4936. St. Peter Rectory, 72 Federal St., 04101
Griesbach, Seamus P., Diocesan Vocation Dir., 510 Ocean Ave., 04103-4936
LaBree, Paul, 510 Ocean Ave., 04103-4936
Nolette, Mark P., J.C.L., 113 Leonard St., Pittsfield, 04967-3533
Reinhardt, Mark S., 510 Ocean Ave., 04103-4936. Tel: 207-773-6471.

Retired:
Rev. Msgrs.—
Begin, Raymond F., S.T.L., J.C.D., (Retired), Venetian Gardens, 1450 Venice E. Blvd., #110, Venice, FL 34292-4001. Tel: 941-493-6869
Ford, J. Joseph, (Retired), 12 Willow Grove Rd., Brunswick, 04011-2958
Goudreau, Joseph L., 2516 1st Rd. S., Arlington, VA 22204-1921. Tel: 703-521-0918. Died Oct. 15, 2018
Murphy, Charles M., S.T.D., (Retired), P.O. Box 378, Kennebunkport, 04046-0378. Tel: 207-967-3788
Revs.—
Affleck, David M., (Retired), 23 Rocky Hill Rd., York, 03909-5081
Albert, James R., (Retired), 290 St. Peter St., Cross Lake, 04779-0000. Tel: 207-834-2083
Amato, Antonio, (Retired), Mallview Terrace, 27A Marston St., Apt. 311, Lewiston, 04240-6171. Tel: 207-795-5095
Andrus, Albin A., (Retired), Park Danforth, Apt. 217, 777 Stevens Ave., 04103-2684. Tel: 207-879-0827
Auger, Raymond D., (Retired), 4675 Appletree Cir., Apt. A, Boynton Beach, FL 33436-1231. Tel: 752-561-0417
Boisvert, Ralph J., (Retired), P.O. Box 733, Augusta, 04332. Tel: 207-446-1013
Brewer, James P., (Retired), P.O. Box 582, Old Orchard Beach, 04064-0582
Brissette, Reginald R., (Retired), 63 Dana Ct., Westbrook, 04092-2912. Tel: 207-857-0490
Cameron, Hilary J., (Retired), St. Catherine's Hall, 242 Walton St., Apt. 103, 04103-3381. Tel: 207-899-3329
Chabot, Roger P., (Retired), Winter: 1000 Hillcrest Ct., #105, Hollywood, FL 33021-7822. Summer: 58 Larry Dr., Monmouth, 04259-6504. Tel: 207-513-6218
Chouinard, Lionel G., (Retired), 10 Seville Pl., Apt. 22, Lewiston, 04240-2420. Tel: 207-795-0707
Colpitts, Albert B., (Retired), 17 Orchard St., Biddeford, 04005-2911
Concannon, Stephen F., (Retired), Our Lady Miraculous Medal Rectory, 289 Lafayette Rd., Hampton, NH 03842-2109. Tel: 603-926-2206
Cote, David P., (Retired), P.O. Box 372, Limestone, 04750-0372. Tel: 207-325-4202
Coughlin, Paul E., (Retired), 4159 Mayo St., Brooksville, FL 34601-8357
Cyr, Joel R., (Retired), 25 Blockhouse Rd., Apt. 201, Fort Kent, 04743-1202. Tel: ; Tel: 207-944-3577
Cyr, L. Philip, (Retired), 25 Blockhouse Rd., Apt. 201, Fort Kent, 04743-1202. Tel: 207-316-3050
Davis, John P., (Retired), 68 Webster Ave., Lewiston, 04240-6463. Tel: 207-784-6235
Gaffey, Eugene F., (Retired), 596 County Rd., Lubec, 04652-3515
Irving, Alfred E., (Retired), 301 Buddington Rd., Lot 35, Groton, CT 06340-3254. Tel: 207-380-5620
Koury, Joseph J., J.C.D., (Retired), 148 Breakwater Dr., Unit 418, South Portland, 04106-1657. Tel: 207-505-5825
L'Heureux, Ernest L., (Retired), The Landing at Saco Bay #114, 392 Main St., Saco, 04072-1521

Labarre, Renald D., (Retired), 31 Esper Court, Fort Myers, FL 33912-2036. Tel: 207-615-1378
Lavoie, Rene G., (Retired), St. Mary's d'Youville Pavillion, 102 Campus Ave., Lewiston, 04240-6019
Lebel, Maurice T., (Retired), 64 Flintlock Village, #64, Wells, 04090-5326. Tel: 207-641-8790
Lee, Thomas M., (Retired), 257 Canco Rd. Apt. 327, 04103-4292
Lequin, Thomas, (Retired), 1018 New Sharon Rd., Starks, 04911-000. Tel: 207-735-8865
Leveille, Rudolph J., (Retired), 65 Juniper St., Bangor, 04401-4163. Tel: 207-942-9715
Levesque, Gerald A., (Retired), 31 Esper Ct., Fort Myers, FL 33912-2036. Tel: 207-409-5445
Levesque, Sylvio J., (Retired), 2 Tenney Way, Apt. 104, Hallowell, 04347-1740. Tel: 207-263-9231
MacDonough, Richard, S.S., (Retired), St. John's Seminary, 5012 Seminary Rd., Camarillo, CA 93012-2500
Manship, D. Joseph, (Retired), 19 Memorial Dr., Biddeford, 04005-2927. Tel: 207-494-8400
Martel, C. James, (Retired), 163 N. Parish Rd., Turner, 04282-0016. Tel: 207-225-3001
McKenna, Joseph R., (Retired), 100 State St., #321, 04101-3729. Tel: 207-775-1084
McLaughlin, Richard C., V.F., (Retired), 323 N. 13th St., Arkadelphia, AR 71923-4606. Tel: 207-955-5341
Modlin, William F., (Retired), 31 Monarch Dr., Augusta, 04330-3712. Tel: 207-446-5301
Morency, Raymond P., (Retired), 211 Randall Rd., Apt. 48, Lewiston, 04240-1741. Tel: 207-784-6822
Moreshead, Harold D., (Retired), 148 Breakwater Dr., Unit 713, South Portland, 04106-1658. Tel: 207-828-8638
Morin, Eddy, (Retired), P.O. Box 129, Saint David, 04773-0129
Mulkern, Stephen M., (Retired), Deering Pavilion, 880 Forest Ave., Apt. 10-20, 04103-4164. Tel: 207-797-3519
Nadeau, Roland P., (Retired), Winterberry Heights Assisted Living, 932 Ohio St., Bangor, 04401-1913. Tel: 207-922-2922
Neault, Armand R., (Retired), 54 Blacksmith Rd., #11, Wells, 04090-5748. Tel: 207-646-6417
Nguyen, Thanh, (Retired), 115 Birchwood Dr., Apt. H, Bristol, CT 06010-2876. Tel: 860-585-6663
O'Hara, John, (Retired), P.O. Box 141, Machias, 04654-0141. Tel: 207-735-8865
Paquet, Hubert J., (Retired), 46 Wentworth St., Biddeford, 04005-3153. Tel: 207-286-9674
Picard, Raymond, (Retired), 8 Lufkin Rd., North Yarmouth, 04097-6045. Tel: 207-809-1049
Piselli, Costanzo J., (Retired), Mount St. Joseph, Apt. 4, 7 Highwood St., Waterville, 04901-5739. Tel: 207-616-0570
Poussard, Bertrand R., (Retired), St. Joseph Rehab & Residence, 1133 Washington Ave., 04103-3629. Tel: 207-878-5488
Rice, Richard P., (Retired), 66 Ward Cir., Brunswick, 04011-9342
Richard, Normand P., (Retired), 13 Fawn Dr., Saco, 04072-9605. Tel: 207-494-8320
Roux, G. Albert, (Retired), 944 Sabattus St., Lewiston, 04240-3712. Tel: 207-783-3590
Senghas, Richard E., (Retired), 15 Piper Rd., Apt. J320, Scarborough, 04074-7555. Tel: 207-833-6394
Tracy, Philip Michael, (Retired), 148 Breakwater Dr., #404, South Portland, 04106-1656. Tel: 207-767-6501
Welch, Bernard J., (Retired), Coastal Landing, 142 Neptune Dr., Brunswick, 04011-2882. Tel: 207-504-5743.

INSTITUTIONS LOCATED IN DIOCESE

[A] COLLEGES AND UNIVERSITIES

STANDISH. *Saint Joseph's College*, (Grades Associate-Masters), Attn: President's Office, 278 Whites Bridge Rd., Standish, 04084-5263.
Tel: 207-893-7711; Fax: 207-893-7867; Email: lsullivan@sjcme.edu; Email: lschiraldi@sjcme.edu; Web: www.sjcme.edu. Dr. James Dlugos, Ph.D., Pres.; Rev. Gabriel Muteru, Chap. Religious Teachers 4; Deacons 1; Lay Teachers 215; Sisters 2; Students 2,167; Graduate Students 758; Undergraduate Students 968; Undergraduate Students in Distance Education 441.

Residential College Program, (Grades Associate-Masters), Attn: President's Office, 278 Whites Bridge Rd., Standish, 04084-5263.
Tel: 207-893-6641; Fax: 207-893-7861; Email: lsullivan@sjcmaine.edu. Richelle Davis, Dir. Library Svcs. Full-time Enrollment 998; Part-time Enrollment 49.

[B] HIGH SCHOOLS, REGIONAL

AUBURN. *Saint Dominic Academy* (1941) (Grades PreK-12), Grades 7-12: 121 Gracelawn Rd., Auburn, 04210-0452. Tel: 207-782-6911;
Fax: 207-795-6439; Email: Donald.Fournier@PortlandDiocese.org; Web: www.stdomsmaine.org. Mr. Donald Fournier, Pres.; Shelly Wheeler, Prin. (Gr. 7-12); Marianne Pellefier, Prin. (PreK-6); Rev. Seamus P. Griesbach, Chap. Lay Teachers 50; PreK - 8 306; 9-12 16.

[C] HIGH SCHOOLS, PRIVATE

PORTLAND. *Cheverus High School* (1917) 267 Ocean Ave., 04103-5707. Tel: 207-774-6238;
Fax: 207-828-0207; Email: moran@cheverus.org; Web: www.cheverus.org. Rev. Robert Pecoraro, Pres.; Dr. John Moran, Ph.D., Prin. Faculty resides at St. Ignatius Residence. See separate listing for details. Religious Teachers 1; Lay Teachers 47; Scholastics 1; Students 431.

[D] ELEMENTARY SCHOOLS, PRIVATE

WATERVILLE. *Mount Merici Academy* (1911) (Grades PreK-8), 18 Mount Merici Ave., Waterville, 04901-4645. Tel: 207-873-3773; Fax: 207-873-6377; Email: info@mountmerici.org; Web: www.mountmerici.org. Susan H. Cote, Prin.; Mary Ellen Fitzpatrick, Librarian. Lay Teachers 10; Students 222.

[E] CATHOLIC CHARITIES MAINE, INC.

PORTLAND. *Catholic Charities Maine*, 307 Congress St., P.O. Box 10660, 04101-6060. Tel: 207-781-8550;
Fax: 207-781-8560; Email: info@ccmaine.org; Web: www.ccmaine.org. Most Rev. Robert P. Deeley, J.C.D., Pres.; Mr. Stephen P. Letourneau, CEO; Ms. Constance Browning Jones, Human Resources Dir., Tel: 207-781-8550; Mr. Michael Smith, Assoc. Dir.; Very Rev. Msgr. Andrew Dubois, S.T.L., V.G., Chap. Tot Asst. Annually 50,655; Total Staff 570.

St. Elizabeth's Child Development Center, 87 High St., 04101-3811. Tel: 207-871-7444;
Fax: 207-871-1178; Email: info@ccmaine.org. Leslie Pierce, Program Dir. Lay Staff 13; Students 90.

St. Michael's Center, 1066 Kenduskeag Ave., Bangor, 04401-2914. Tel: 207-941-2855;
Fax: 207-941-2835; Email: info@ccmaine.org; Web: www.ccmaine.org. Bob Colby, Dir. (Functional Family Therapy and Case Management Services and Children Behavioral Health Home Services) Tot Asst. Annually 540; Full-Time Staff 12.

[F] SPECIAL RESIDENTIAL SERVICES

BIDDEFORD. *St. Andre Home, Inc.*, Admin. Office, 168 Prospect St., Biddeford, 04005-3841.
Tel: 207-282-3351; Fax: 207-282-8733; Email: stgauvin@saintandrehome.org; Web: www.SaintAndreHome.org. Sr. Theresa Gauvin, S.C.I.M., Dir. Pregnant and Parenting Young Women, Adoption Services,Clinical and Case Management Supportive Visitation, Services for Sex Trafficking Victims, Emergency Placement; Public Information-Education; Community Outreach Services; Residences in Biddeford, Bangor. Bed Capacity 6; Residents 5; Tot Asst. Annually 100; Total Staff 17.

LEWISTON. **St. Martin de Porres Residence, Inc.* aka St. Catherine of Siena Residence, 23 Bartlett St., Lewiston, 04240-6804. Tel: 207-786-4690;
Fax: 207-786-8866; Email: mdeporres@roadrunner.com. Mailing Address: P.O. Box 7227, Lewiston, 04243-7227. Deacon Irenee Richard, O.P., Exec. Dir. Bed Capacity 18; Tot Asst. Annually 220; Total Staff 7.

SACO. *Esther Residence*, 27 Thornton Ave., Saco, 04072-2720. Tel: 207-283-0323; Email: estherres@gwi.net; Email: joanne_roy@aol.com; Web: www.Esther Residence.org. Sr. Joanne Roy, S.C.I.M., Dir. Servants of the Immaculate Heart of MaryTransitional housing for women. Bed Capacity 7; Lay Staff 1; Nuns 3; Tot Asst. Annually 11; Total Staff 4; Volunteers 19.

[G] HOMES FOR THE AGED

PORTLAND. *DBH Management II, Inc.* (2014) 510 Ocean Ave., 04103. Tel: 207-773-6471, Ext. 7823; Email: david.twomey@portlanddiocese.org. Most Rev. Robert P. Deeley, J.C.D., Pres.; Mr. David Twomey, Treas.

DBH Management, Inc., 510 Ocean Ave., 04103-4936. Tel: 207-773-6471, Ext. 7823;
Fax: 207-321-7863; Email: david.twomey@portlanddiocese.org. Helen McGuinness, Exec. Dir.; Mr. David P. Twomey Jr., CPA, Treas. Sponsored by: Roman Catholic Diocese of Portland.

Deering Pavilion, 880 Forest Ave., 04103-4128.
Tel: 207-797-8777; Fax: 207-797-8963; Email: info@deeringpavilion.com; Web: www.deeringpavilion.com. Joanne Bean, Exec. Dir. Residents 213; Apartments 200.

AUGUSTA. *Roncalli Apartments, Inc.*, 144 State St., Augusta, 04330. Tel: 207-512-4248; Email: david.twomey@portlanddiocese.org; Fax: 207-512-4250. Mailing Address: 510 Ocean Ave., 04103-4936.
Tel: 207-773-6471, Ext. 7823; Fax: 207-773-0182. Mr. David P. Twomey Jr., CPA, Treas.; Michael Pease, Site Mgr. Sponsor: Roman Catholic Diocese of Portland.Purpose: to provide very low and extremely low cost housing for the elderly in the capital city of the state. Employees 3; Residents 31; Units 30.

BANGOR. *St. Xavier's Home*, 119 Somerset St., Bangor, 04401-5334. Tel: 207-942-2108; Email: David.twomey@portlanddiocese.org. 510 Ocean Ave., 04103-4936. Mr. David Twomey, Treas. & Contact Person, Tel: 207-773-6471; Fax: 207-773-0182; Bob Chandler, Site Mgr., C & L Realty. Sponsor: Roman Catholic Diocese of Portland.Purpose: to provide very low and extremely low cost housing for the elderly in the Bangor, Maine area. Residents 20; Units 19; Staff 3.

BIDDEFORD. *St. Andre Health Care & Facility*, 407 Pool St., Biddeford, 04005-9716. Tel: 207-282-5171;
Fax: 207-282-5372; Email: salaimo@standre.org; Email: psullivan@standre.org; Web: standre.org. Stephen Alaimo, CEO & Admin.; Sr. Patricia Sullivan, Spiritual Advisor/Care Svcs. Sponsored by Covenant Health, Inc., Tewksbury, MA. Bed Capacity 96; Tot Asst. Annually 325; Total Staff 150.

LEWISTON. **St. Mary's Regional Medical Center* dba St. Mary's d'Youville Pavilion, 102 Campus Ave., Lewiston, 04240-6019. Tel: 207-777-4200;
Fax: 207-777-4255; Email: ltame@covh.org; Web: www.stmarysmaine.com. Mr. Peter Holden, Pres.; Philip Hickey, Vice Pres.; Charles Demm, Dir. Chaplaincy; Rev. Dominic Savio, H.G.N., Chap.; Anne-Marie Bourque, R.S.M., Chap., Chap.; Sarah Gillespie, Chap.; David Deluca, Chap. St. Mary's Health System (a member of Covenant Health in Tewksbury, MA) Bed Capacity 210; Tot Asst. Annually 839; Total Staff 420.

St. Mary's Residences (Formerly: Maison Marcotte) 100 Campus Ave., Lewiston, 04240-6040.
Tel: 207-786-0062; Fax: 207-777-8570; Email: ltame@covh.org; Web: www.stmarysmaine.com. Mr. Peter Holden, Pres. Sponsored by St. Mary's Health System. Total in Residence 126; Staff 2.

WATERVILLE. *St. Francis Apartments, Inc.*, 52 Elm St., Waterville, 04901-6015. Tel: 207-773-7471; Email: david.twomey@portlanddiocese.org. Mailing Address: 510 Ocean Ave., 04103-4936. Mr. Harlan Cooper, Admin.; Michael Pease, Site Mgr., Tel: 207-660-9256; Fax: 207-660-9258; Mr. David Twomey, Treas. Residents 40; Personnel 3; Units 40.

Mt. St. Joseph Residence & Rehabilitation, 7 Highwood St., Waterville, 04901-5797.
Tel: 207-873-0705; Email: dsinclair@mtsj.org; Web: www.mtsj.org. Steven Kastner, Pres. (Part of Trinity Health-Trinity Senior Living Communities) Bed Capacity 138; Tot Asst. Annually 180; Total Staff 200; Assisted Living 27; Nursing Facility 111. In Res.

Seton Village Inc., 1 Carver St., Waterville, 04901-5739. Tel: 207-873-0178; Fax: 207-873-1233; Email: David.twomey@portlanddiocese.org. 510 Ocean Ave., 04103-4936. Most Rev. Robert P. Deeley, J.C.D., Pres.; Mr. David P. Twomey Jr., CPA, Treas., Tel: 207-773-6471, Ext. 7823; Fax: 207-773-0182; Mr. Harlan Cooper, Admin. Purpose: to provide very low and extremely low cost housing for the elderly in the Waterville, Maine area. Guests 163; Personnel 6; Units 140.

[H] GENERAL HOSPITALS

BANGOR. *St. Joseph Hospital*, 360 Broadway, Bangor, 04401-3974. Tel: 207-262-1000; Fax: 207-262-1922; Email: mary.prybylo@sjhhealth.com; Web: www.stjoeshealing.com. Revs. Augustine A. Nellary, Vice Pres.; Robert Tumwekwase, A.J., Chap. Sponsored by Covenant Health, Inc. Bed Capacity 112; Felician Sisters 2; Tot Asst. Annually 115,205; Total Staff 1,134; Lay Nurses 283.

Pastoral Care Dept., 360 Broadway, Bangor, 04401.
Tel: 207-262-1798; Fax: 207-262-1922; Email: Mary.Prybylo@sjhhealth.com; Web: stjoeshealing.com. Rev. Augustine A. Nellary, Vice Pres., Mission Integration; Andrew Files, Dir. Spiritual Care; Rev. Robert Tumwekwase, A.J., Chap.

**Alternative Health Services of St. Joseph, Inc.*, 360 Broadway, Bangor, 04401-3979. Tel: 207-907-1000 ; Fax: 207-907-1922; Email: maryprybylo@sjhhealth.com; Web: www.stjoehealing.org. Mary Prybylo, Pres. & CEO. Home Health and Hospice Services.

**St. Joseph Ambulatory Care, Inc.*, 360 Broadway,

Bangor, 04401-3979. Tel: 207-907-1100; Fax: 207-907-1922; Email: maryprybylo@sjhhealth.com; Web: www.stjoehealing.org. Mary Prybylo, Pres.& CEO. Corporate entity for all employed physicians and their related office practices for St. Joseph Hospital.

St. Joseph Healthcare Foundation, 360 Broadway, Bangor, 04401-3979. Tel: 207-907-1100; Fax: 207-907-1922; Email: maryprybylo@sjhhealth.com; Web: www.stjoehealing.org. Mary Prybylo, Pres. & CEO; Rev. Augustine A. Nellary, Vice Pres. Parent corporation of St. Joseph Hospital and affiliates.

LEWISTON. *St. Mary's Health System*, 93 Campus Ave., P.O. Box 7291, Lewiston, 04243-7291. Tel: 207-777-8802; Tel: 207-777-8546; Fax: 207-777-8803; Email: ltame@covh.org; Web: www.stmarysmaine.com. Mr. Peter Holden, Pres. St. Mary's Health System is a member of Covenant Health in Tewksbury, MA. Total Staff 155.

Services Include:.

St. Mary's WorkMed, Tel: 207-753-3080; Fax: 207-753-3088. Occupational Health Program.

St. Mary's Health Steps, Tel: 207-777-8898; Fax: 207-777-3499.

St. Mary's Development, Tel: 207-777-8863; Fax: 207-755-3380.

St. Mary's Maine Covenant, Tel: 207-777-8553; Fax: 207-777-8800.

St. Mary's Take Charge, Tel: 207-777-8898; Fax: 207-755-3499. Health screening programs. Total Staff 203.

St. Mary's Regional Medical Center (1880) 93 Campus Ave., P.O. Box 291, Lewiston, 04243-0291. Tel: 207-777-8802; Fax: 207-777-8803; Email: ltame@covh.org; Web: www.stmarysmaine.com. Mr. Peter Holden, Pres.; Charles Demm, Dir. & Chaplaincy Svcs.; Rev. Dominic Savio, H.G.N., Chap.; David Deluca, Chap.; Sarah Gillespie, Chap. Sponsored by St. Mary's Health System (a member of Covenant Health in Tewksbury, MA) Bed Capacity 170; Nurses 309; Sisters 2; Tot Asst. Annually 307,966; Total Staff 1,450; LPNs 3; CNAs 86.

St. Mary's Lifeline, Tel: 207-777-8827; Fax: 207-777-8839. Serving 466.

St. Mary's Nutrition Center of Maine, Tel: 207-513-3847. Nutrition services.

[I] MONASTERIES AND RESIDENCES OF PRIESTS AND BROTHERS

PORTLAND. *St. Ignatius Residence (The Jesuits of Maine)*, 492 Ocean Ave., 04103-4936. Tel: 207-775-3032; Fax: 207-775-1229; Email: rlevens@jesuits.org. Rev. Robert Levens, Supr. Jesuit Fathers (Northeast Prov.). Priests 6; Scholastics 1.

ALFRED. *LaMennais-North American Province: American Delegation* (House of Brothers of Christian Instruction) 132 Shaker Hill Rd., P.O. Box 159, Alfred, 04002-0159. Tel: 207-324-6612; Email: djcaron43@yahoo.com. Bro. Daniel Caron, F.I.C., F.I.C., Prov. Delegate, Supr., Tel: 207-324-6612; Fax: 207-324-9772; Jerome Lessand, F.I.C., Local Supr. Brothers 12.

KENNEBUNK. *St. Anthony's Friary*, 28 Beach Ave., Kennebunk, 04043-7628. Tel: 207-967-2011; Fax: 207-967-0423; Email: jonasbac@gmail.com; Web: www.framon.net. Mailing Address: P.O. Box 980, Kennebunkport, 04046-0980. Revs. John J. Bacevicius, O.F.M., Supr.; Andrew R. Bisson, O.F.M., Pastoral Ministry; Raimundas Bukauskas, O.F.M., Vicar & Treas.; Aurelijus Gricius, O.F.M., Vicar & Pastoral Ministry. Priests 5.

[J] CONVENTS AND RESIDENCES OF SISTERS

PORTLAND. *Frances Warde Convent*, 37 Capisic St., 04102-2203. Tel: 207-772-1140; Fax: 207-772-1873; Email: mmorey@mercyne.org. Sr. Edward Mary, R.S.M., Facilitator. Sisters 12.

Sisters of Charity, 41 Tamarlane, 04103-4257. Tel: 207-773-8607; Fax: 207-874-6086. Sr. Claire Pouliot, Contact Person. Sisters 1.

Sisters of Mercy of the Americas, 84 Plymouth St., 04103-2005. Tel: 207-797-6957; Email: mmorey@mercyne.org. Sr. Mary M. Morey, R.S.M., Contact Person. Sisters of Mercy of the Americas 1.

Sisters of Mercy of the Americas-Northeast Community, Life & Ministry Office: 966 Riverside St., 04103-1046. Tel: 207-797-7861; Fax: 207-797-0146; Email: mmorey@mercyne.org. Sr. Mary M. Morey, R.S.M., Local Coord. Sisters 42.

ACTON. *The Sisters of the Presentation of Mary of Maine, Inc. Presentation Villa*, 246 Rte. 109, Acton, 04001. Tel: 978-688-1920; Email: pmtreasurer209@gmail.com; Web: www.presentationofmary-usa.org. Sr. Annette Laliberte, P.M., Treas. Sisters 10.

AUBURN. *Companions of Christ*, 503 Park Ave., Auburn, 04210-8526. Tel: 207-784-5960; Email: elizabeth.platt@portlanddiocese.org. Sr. Elizabeth Platt, C.O.C., Contact Person. Sisters 2.

BANGOR. *St. Joseph Convent*, 754 Ohio St., Bangor, 04401-3165. Tel: 207-404-4717; Email: stjoseph@feliciansisters.org. Sr. Barbara Theresa Martis, C.S.S.F., Supr. Felician Sisters 2.

Missionary Sisters of the Immaculate Conception of the Mother of God, 121 Fern St., Bangor, 04401-4039. Tel: 207-262-3532; Email: bridie59@earthlink.net. Sr. Miriam Devlin, S.M.I.C., Supr. & Contact Person. Sisters 2.

BIDDEFORD. *St. Joseph Convent*, 409 Pool St., Biddeford, 04005. Tel: 207-283-9051; Fax: 207-284-8381; Email: anadeau409@maine.rr.com. Sr. Annette Nadeau, S.C.I.M., Supr. Servants of the Immaculate Heart of Mary (Good Shepherd) 27.

Marie Fitzbach Convent, 283 Elm St., Biddeford, 04005-3027. Tel: 207-283-9051; Email: clambert409@maine.rr.com. Sr. Claire Lambert, S.C.I.M., Contact Person. Sisters 5.

Marie Joseph Spiritual Center (Sisters of the Presentation of Mary) 10 Evans Rd., Biddeford, 04005-9290. Tel: 207-284-5671; Fax: 207-286-1371; Email: mariejosephcenter@yahoo.com; Web: www.mariejosephspiritual.org. Sr. Ruth Ouellette, P.M., Supr. Sisters 12.

Provincial Residence, 409 Pool St., Biddeford, 04005-9506. Tel: 207-283-9051; Fax: 207-282-7376; Email: scimprove@outlook.com. Sr. Theresa Gauvin, S.C.I.M., Prov. Supr. Servants of the Immaculate Heart of Mary. Sisters 1.

CASCO. *Community of the Resurrection A Lataste Community, Inc.*, P.O. Box 284, Casco, 04015-0284. Tel: 207-627-7184; Email: comres123@gmail.com. 205 Popular Ridge Rd., Ottisfield, 04270. Sr. Renata Camenzind, Supr. Sisters 4; Total in Residence 5.

LEWISTON. *Dominican Sisters of the Roman Congregation*, Provincial Residence, 123 Dumont Ave., Apt. 1, Lewiston, 04240-6107. Tel: 207-786-5058; Email: moniqueb@megalink.net; Web: www.crsdop.org. Sr. Monique Belanger, O.P., Prov. Sisters 14.

Holy Cross, 16 Saint Croix St., Apt. 2, Lewiston, 04240-5061. Tel: 207-782-0263; Email: ccmondor@yahoo.com; Email: pmtreasurer209@gmail.com. Sr. Cecile Mondor, P.M., Supr. Sisters of the Presentation of Mary 2.

OLD ORCHARD BEACH. *Sisters of Our Lady of the Holy Rosary*, Regional House, 25 Portland Ave., Old Orchard Beach, 04064-2211. Tel: 207-934-0592; Email: roy-jen@excite.com. Sr. Jeannette Roy, R.S.R., Regl. Coord. Sisters 8.

SABATTUS. *Dominican Sisters*, 61 Lisbon Rd., Sabattus, 04280-4209. Tel: 207-375-6583; Fax: 207-375-2694; Email: japro43@gmail.com. Sisters Monique Belanger, O.P., Prov.; Jacqueline Provencher, O.P., Prioress. Dominican Sisters of the Roman Congregation 7.

ST. AGATHA. *Our Lady of Wisdom Community*, Montfort Heights, 384 Main St., Apt. 221, St. Agatha, 04772-6169. Tel: 207-543-9395. Sr. Jacqueline Ayotte, D.W., Coord. Sisters 3.

WATERVILLE. *Blessed Sacrament Convent*, 101 Silver St., Waterville, 04901-5923. Tel: 207-872-7072; Fax: 207-873-2317; Email: jjroneysss@gmail.com; Web: www.blesacrament.org. Sr. Josephine Roney, S.S.S., Supr. Servants of the Blessed Sacrament. Sisters 12.

Sisters of St. Joseph of Lyon - Maine, 80 Garland Rd., Winslow, 04901-0600. Tel: 207-873-4512; Email: hrjafd@gmail.com; Web: www.csjwinslowmaine.org. Sr. Judith Donovan, Leader. Sisters 22.

Ursuline Sisters, 1 St. Angela Way, Waterville, 04901-4640. Tel: 207-873-3515; Fax: 207-873-4926; Email: marieposta@gmail.com. Sr. Rita Ann Bregenhorn, Prioress. Sisters 9.

WINTHROP. *Little Franciscans of Mary*, 130 Rte. 133, Winthrop, 04364-1356. Tel: 207-395-5338; Email: carol.martin@portlanddiocese.org. Sisters Carol Martin, P.F.M., Contact Person; Juanita Robichaud, P.F.M., (Retired). Little Franciscans of Mary 2.

[K] HERMITAGES

ELLSWORTH. *John of the Cross Monastery*, 19 Trinity Way, Ellsworth, 04605-2800. Tel: 207-664-0026; Email: gaudeamusjm@gmail.com. Sr. Margaret Dorgan, D.C.M. Carmelite Sisters 1.

ST. ALBANS. *Sky-Arch Hermitage*, 47 Bryant Rd., St. Albans, 04971-7327. Email: skyarchhermitage@gmail.com. Sr. B. Emmanuel Bryant. Hermit 1.

WINDSOR. *Transfiguration Hermitage*, 205 Windsor Neck Rd., Windsor, 04363-3202. Tel: 207-445-8031; Email: benedicite@fairpoint.net; Web: www.transfigurationhermitage.org. Sr. Elizabeth Wagner, Contact Person. Novices 1; Hermits 2.

[L] RETREAT HOUSES

BIDDEFORD. *Marie Joseph Spiritual Center*, 10 Evans Rd., Biddeford, 04005-9290. Tel: 207-284-5671; Fax: 207-286-1371; Email: mariejosephcenter@yahoo.com; Web: www.mariejosephspiritual.org. Sr. Sue Bourret, P.M., Admin. Sisters of the Presentation of Mary. Total Staff 24; Served 3,850.

FRENCHVILLE. *Christian Life Center*, 444 U.S. Rte. 1, Frenchville, 04745-0530. Tel: 207-728-7531; Email: Judy.Lavoie@portlanddiocese.org. 309 St. Thomas St., Madawaska, 04756. Rev. James S. Plourde, Admin. Retreatants 200.

[M] NEWMAN CENTERS

PORTLAND. *University of Southern Maine*, University of Southern Maine, 37 College Ave., Gorham, 04038-1032. St. Anne Parish - Campus Ministry, P.O. Box 69, Westbrook, 04098-0069. Revs. Louis J. Phillips, V.F., Pastor; Steven G. Cartwright, Parochial Vicar. Ministry Provided by St. Anne Parish, Gorham.

Gorham Campus Joy Segovia, Campus Min., Tel: 207-839-4857.

BIDDEFORD. *University of New England*, University of New England, 11 Hills Beach Rd, Biddeford, 04005-9526. Tel: 207-282-3321; Email: goodshepherd@portlanddiocese.org. Good Shepherd Parish - Campus Ministry, 271 Main St., Saco, 04072-1510. Rev. Msgr. Rene T. Mathieu, S.T.L., Pastor; Catherine Gallerizzo, Campus Min. Ministry Provided by Good Shepherd Parish, Saco.

BRUNSWICK. *Bowdoin College*, Bowdoin College, 255 Maine St,, Brunswick, 04011. Tel: 207-725-2624; Email: allsaints@portlanddiocese.org. All Saints Parish - Campus Ministry, 132 McKeen St, Brunswick, 04011-2980. Very Rev. Thomas M. Murphy, V.F., Campus Chap.; Joy Segovia, Campus Min. Ministry Provided by All Saints Parish, Brunswick.

CASTINE. *Maine Maritime Academy*, Stella Maris Parish - Campus Ministry, P.O. Box S, Bucksport, 04416-1219. Tel: 207-773-6471; Email: stellamaris@roadrunner.com. Maine Maritime Academy, 1 Pleasant St., Castine, 04420. Rev. Emile H. Dube, Chap. Ministry provided by Stella Maris Parish.

FARMINGTON. *University of Maine at Farmington*, University of Maine at Farmington, 224 Main St., Farmington, 04938-1953. St Joseph Parish - Campus Ministry, 133 Middle St., Farmington, 04938-1598. Rev. Paul H. Dumais, Campus Chap. Ministry provided by St. Joseph Parish staff.

FORT KENT. *University of Maine at Fort Kent*, University of Maine at Fort Kent, 23 University Dr., Fort Kent, 04743-1248. Tel: 207-834-5656; Fax: 207-834-7461; Email: stjohnvianneyparish@portlanddiocese.org. Very Rev. Jean-Paul Labrie, V.F., Pastor. Ministry provided by St. John Vianney Parish, Fort Kent Staff.

LEWISTON. *Bates College*, 163 Wood St., Lewiston, 04240-7687. Tel: 207-777-1200; Email: pop@portlanddiocese.org; Email: frank.daggett@portlanddiocese.org; Web: www.bates.edu/chaplaincy. Prince of Peace Parish - Campus Ministry, PO Box 1540, Lewiston, 04241-1540. Mr. Frank Daggett, Campus Min. Served by the personnel of Prince of Peace Parish, Lewiston, ME.

MACHIAS. *University of Maine at Machias*, University of Maine at Machias, 116 O'Brien Ave., Machias, 04654-1329. Mailing Address: St. Peter the Fisherman Parish - Campus Ministry, P.O. Box 248, Machias, 04654-0248. Rev. Philip Clement, Admin. Ministry Provide by St. Peter the Fisherman Parish, Machias Staff.

ORONO. *University of Maine*, University of Maine at Orono, 83 College Ave., Orono, 04473-4210. Tel: 207-866-2155; Email: resurrectionparish@portlanddiocese.org; Web: www.umaine.edu/newman. Rev. Wilfred P. Labbe; Audrey Aylmer, Campus Min.

PRESQUE ISLE. *University of Maine at Presque Isle*, University of Maine at Presque Isle, 181 Main St., Presque Isle, 04769-2844. Tel: 207-498-2536; Email: pbb@portlanddiocese.org. Precious Blood Campus Ministry, Caribou, 04736-0625. Rev. David R. Raymond, Pastor. Ministry provided by Parish of the Precious Blood, Caribou.

SCARBOROUGH. *Southern Maine Community College*, Southern Maine Community College, 2 Fort Rd., South Portland, 04106-1611. Tel: 207-883-0334; Fax: 207-883-4246; Email: paul.stefanko@portlanddiocese.org. St. John and Holy Cross Parish - Campus Ministry, 150 Black Point Rd., Scarborough, 04074-9349. Rev. Msgr. Paul F. Stefanko, J.C.L., Pastor. Ministry provided by staff of St. John and Holy Cross Parish, South Portland.

STANDISH. *Saint Joseph's College*, St. Joseph College - Campus Ministry Office, 278 Whites Bridge Rd., Standish, 04084-5263. Tel: 207-892-6766; Fax: 207-893-7867; Email: lsullivan@sjcme.edu;

Email: lschiraldi@sjcme.edu; Email: gmuteru@sjcme.edu. Dr. James Dlugos, Ph.D., Pres.; Rev. Gabriel Muteru, Chap. Campus Ministry Office.

WATERVILLE. *Colby College*, Colby College, 4000 Mayflower Hill Dr., Waterville, 04901-8840.
Tel: 207-859-4273; Email: ccmoffice@corpuschristimaine.org. Colby College - Lorimer Chapel, 4272 Mayflower Hill Dr., Waterville, 04901-8842. Rev. Patrick Finn, Chap.; Charles Demm, Campus Min. Ministry provided by Chancery Employee.

Thomas College, Thomas College, 180 W. River Rd., Waterville, 04901-5061. Tel: 207-872-2281; Email: ccmoffice@corpuschristimaine.org. Christi Parish - Campus Ministry, 70 Pleasant St., Waterville, 04901-5463. Rev. Patrick Finn, Chap.

[N] MISCELLANEOUS LISTINGS

PORTLAND. **Catholic Foundation of Maine*, 510 Ocean Ave., P.O. Box 799, 04104-0799. Tel: 207-321-7820; Tel: 207-321-7871; Fax: 207-773-0182; Email: elizabeth.badger@catholicfoundationmaine.org. Mrs. Elizabeth Badger, Exec. Dir.

The Presence Radio Network, Inc, P.O. Box 10660, 04104-6060. Tel: 207-689-9939; Email: cnickless@thepresenceradio.org; Web: www.thepresenceradio.org. 4 Washington St., Auburn, 04210-4859. Ms. Cynthia Nickless, Exec. Dir.

SOUTH PORTLAND. *Magnificat-Scarborough ME Chapter*, 143 Westbrook St., South Portland, 04106-5233. Email: cathykoenig88@gmail.com; Web: magnificat-ministry.net/chapters/chapter-states-l-m/me-scarborough/. 125 Ash Swamp Rd., Scarborough, 04074. Catherine Koenig, Treas.

RELIGIOUS INSTITUTES OF MEN REPRESENTED IN THE DIOCESE

For further details refer to the corresponding bracketed number in the Religious Institutes of Men or Women section.

[0320]—*Brothers of Christian Instruction*—F.I.C.
[0470]—*Capuchin Franciscan Friars*—O.F.M. Cap.
[0430]—*Dominican Province of St. Joseph the Worker*—O.P.
[0520]—*Franciscan Friars*—O.F.M.
[0585]—*Heralds of Good News*—H.G.N.
[0690]—*Jesuit Fathers and Brothers* (New England Prov.)—S.J.
[0780]—*Marist Fathers* (Boston Prov.)—S.M.
[0800]—*Maryknoll*—M.M.
[]—*Missionary Institute of Apostles of Jesus* (U.S.A. Zone)—A.J.
[0430]—*Order of Preachers (Dominicans)* (Canadian Prov.)—O.P.
[0610]—*Priests of the Congregation of Holy Cross*—C.S.C.
[0110]—*Society of African Missions*—S.M.A.
[0925]—*Society of Our Lady of the Most Holy Trinity*—S.O.L.T.

RELIGIOUS INSTITUTES OF WOMEN REPRESENTED IN THE DIOCESE

[]—*Community of the Resurrection.*
[]—*Companions of Christ*—C.O.C.
[3100]—*Congregation of Our Lady of the Holy Rosary*—R.S.R.
[0960]—*Daughters of Wisdom*—D.W.
[]—*Diocesan Carmelites of Maine*—D.C.M.
[2655]—*Diocesan Sisters of Mercy*—R.S.M.
[1120]—*Dominican Sisters of the Roman Congregation*—O.P.
[1170]—*Felician Sisters*—C.S.S.F.
[1430]—*Franciscan Sisters of Our Lady of Perpetual Help*—O.S.F.
[2575]—*Institute of the Sisters of Mercy of the Americas*—R.S.M.
[2280]—*Little Franciscans of Mary*—P.F.M.
[2760]—*Missionary Sisters of the Immaculate Conception of the Mother of God*—S.M.I.C.
[3500]—*Servants of the Blessed Sacrament*—S.S.S.
[3550]—*Servants of the Immaculate Heart of Mary*—S.C.I.M.
[0610]—*Sisters of Charity of St. Hyacinthe (Grey Nuns)*—S.C.S.H.
[3750]—*Sisters of St. Chretienne*—S.S.Ch.
[3870]—*Sisters of St. Joseph (Lyons, France)*—C.S.J.
[0150]—*Sisters of the Assumptions*—S.A.S.V.
[3310]—*Sisters of the Presentation of Mary*—P.M.
[4110]—*Ursuline Nuns (Roman Union)* (Northeastern Prov.)—O.S.U.

DIOCESAN CEMETERIES

BANGOR. *Mount Pleasant Catholic Cemetery*, 449 Ohio St., Bangor, 04401-3736. Tel: 207-947-4322; Email: gene.gagnon@portlanddiocese.org. 207 York St., Bangor, 04401-5442. Mr. Lawrence Gagnon, Supt.

BIDDEFORD. *St. Joseph Cemetery and St. Mary Cemetery*, 120 West St. (& 530 FLM St.), Biddeford, 04005. Tel: 207-282-0747;
Tel: 207-282-3321; Email: stjosephscemetery@portlanddiocese.org; Email: GoodShepherd@portlanddiocese.org; Email: john.fencik@portlanddiocese.org; Web: goodshepherdparish.us/cemeteries. Good Shepherd Parish Cemeteries, 271 Main St., Saco, 04072-1510. Rev. Msgr. Rene T. Mathieu, S.T.L., Admin.

LEWISTON. *St. Peter Cemetery*, 217 Switzerland Rd., Lewiston, 04240-5177. Tel: 207-782-8721;
Fax: 207-784-3432; Email: robert.leblanc@portlanddiocese.org. Robert E. LeBlanc, Exec. Dir.

SOUTH PORTLAND. *Calvary Cemetery*, 1461 Broadway, South Portland, 04106-2601. Tel: 207-773-5796;
Fax: 207-773-5796; Email: calvarycem@portlanddiocese.org; Web: www.portlanddiocese.net/calvary. Mr. John Fencik, Dir.

WATERVILLE. *St. Francis Catholic Cemetery*, 78 Grove St., P.O. Box 575, Waterville, 04901-0575.
Tel: 207-872-2770; Fax: 207-872-2770; Email: stfrancem@myfairpoint.net; Web: www.portlanddiocese.org/stfranciscemetery. Deborah Hebert, Dir.

NECROLOGY

† Goudreau, Joseph L., (Retired), Died Oct. 15, 2018
† Feeney, John J., (Retired), Died Feb. 21, 2018
† McAllister, Donald L., (Retired), Died Aug. 26, 2018

An asterisk (*) denotes an organization that has established tax-exempt status directly with the IRS and is not covered by the USCCB Group Ruling.

Archdiocese of Portland in Oregon

(Archidioecesis Portlandensis in Oregon)

Most Reverend

JOHN G. VLAZNY, D.D.

Archbishop Emeritus of Portland in Oregon; ordained December 20, 1961; appointed Auxiliary Bishop of Chicago and Titular Bishop of Stagno October 31, 1983; consecrated December 13, 1983; appointed Bishop of Winona May 19, 1987; installed July 29, 1987; appointed Archbishop of Portland in Oregon October 28, 1997; installed December 19, 1997; retired January 29, 2013.

Most Reverend

PETER LESLIE SMITH

Auxiliary Bishop of Portland in Oregon; ordained June 9, 2001; appointed Titular Bishop of Tubunae in Mauretania and Auxiliary Bishop of Portland in Oregon March 4, 2014; ordained April 29, 2014.

Most Reverend

ALEXANDER K. SAMPLE

Archbishop of Portland in Oregon; ordained June 1, 1990; appointed Bishop of Marquette December 13, 2005; installed January 25, 2006; appointed Archbishop of Portland in Oregon January 29, 2013; installed April 2, 2013.

VULTUM CHRISTI CONTEMPLARI

Archdiocesan Pastoral Center: 2838 E. Burnside St., Portland, OR 97214-1895. Tel: 503-234-5334; Fax: 503-234-2545.

Web: www.archdpdx.org

Email: commdir@archdpdx.org

Most Reverend

KENNETH D. STEINER, D.D.

Retired Auxiliary Bishop of Portland in Oregon; ordained May 19, 1962; appointed Titular Bishop of Avensa and Auxiliary Bishop of Portland in Oregon December 6, 1977; ordained March 2, 1978l; retired Nov. 25, 2011. *Office: 2838 E. Burnside St., Portland, OR 97214.*

Square Miles 29,717.

Erected as a Vicariate-Apostolic December 1, 1843

Created Archdiocese of Oregon City, July 24, 1846; Name changed by Papal Decree to "Archdiocese of Portland in Oregon," September 26, 1928

Comprises that part of the State of Oregon lying between the summit of the Cascades and the Pacific Ocean.

For legal titles of parishes and archdiocesan institutions, consult the Archdiocesan Pastoral Center

STATISTICAL OVERVIEW

Personnel	
Archbishops	1
Retired Archbishops	1
Auxiliary Bishops	1
Retired Bishops	1
Abbots	2
Retired Abbots	3
Priests: Diocesan Active in Diocese	103
Priests: Diocesan Active Outside Diocese	2
Priests: Retired, Sick or Absent	58
Number of Diocesan Priests	163
Religious Priests in Diocese	132
Total Priests in Diocese	295
Extern Priests in Diocese	18
Ordinations:	
Diocesan Priests	2
Transitional Deacons	2
Permanent Deacons in Diocese	82
Total Brothers	51
Total Sisters	322
Parishes	
Parishes	124
With Resident Pastor:	
Resident Diocesan Priests	88
Resident Religious Priests	22
Without Resident Pastor:	
Administered by Priests	14
Missions	23
Professional Ministry Personnel:	
Brothers	6
Sisters	39
Lay Ministers	247
Welfare	
Catholic Hospitals	10
Total Assisted	2,019,615
Health Care Centers	12
Total Assisted	36,537
Homes for the Aged	9
Total Assisted	3,987
Day Care Centers	3
Total Assisted	2,359
Specialized Homes	5
Total Assisted	1,881
Special Centers for Social Services	16
Total Assisted	922,008
Educational	
Diocesan Students in Other Seminaries	8
Seminaries, Religious	1
Students Religious	104
Total Seminarians	112
Colleges and Universities	1
Total Students	3,975
High Schools, Diocesan and Parish	3
Total Students	1,450
High Schools, Private	7
Total Students	4,164
Elementary Schools, Diocesan and Parish	37
Total Students	8,140
Elementary Schools, Private	4
Total Students	958
Catechesis/Religious Education:	
High School Students	3,839
Elementary Students	9,544
Total Students under Catholic Instruction	32,182
Teachers in the Diocese:	
Priests	9
Brothers	5
Sisters	9
Lay Teachers	1,149
Vital Statistics	
Receptions into the Church:	
Infant Baptism Totals	3,812
Minor Baptism Totals	383
Adult Baptism Totals	339
Received into Full Communion	319
First Communions	4,666
Confirmations	3,072
Marriages:	
Catholic	633
Interfaith	179
Total Marriages	812
Deaths	1,654
Total Catholic Population	467,610
Total Population	3,597,001

Former Bishops—Most Revs. FRANCIS NORBERT BLANCHET, D.D., First Vicar Apostolic of Oregon Territory; cons. July 25, 1845, Titular Bishop of Drasa; appt. Archbishop of Oregon City, July 24, 1846 when the Vicariate was erected into an ecclesiastical province; resigned 1880; died June 18, 1883; CHARLES JOHN SEGHERS, D.D., cons. June 29, 1873; Bishop of Vancouver Island, British Columbia; coadjutor to the Archbishop of Oregon City, Dec. 10, 1880; Archbishop, Dec. 20, 1880; resigned 1884; and transferred to Vancouver Island, British Columbia; died Nov. 28, 1886; WILLIAM H. GROSS, C.Ss.R., D.D., Archbishop of Oregon City; cons. Bishop of Savannah, GA April 27, 1873; promoted by His Holiness Leo XIII Feb. 1, 1885 from Savannah to the Archiepiscopal See of Oregon City; died Nov. 14, 1898; ALEXANDER CHRISTIE, D.D., Archbishop of Oregon City; consecrated June 29, 1898, Bishop of Vancouver Island, B.C.; promoted by His Holiness Leo XIII February 12, 1899 from Vancouver Island to the Archiepiscopal See of Oregon City; died April 6, 1925; EDWARD D. HOWARD, D.D., LL.D., Titular Archbishop of Albule; ord. June 12, 1906; cons. Titular Bishop of Isauria and Auxiliary Bishop of Davenport, April 6, 1924; appt. to the See of Oregon City, April 30, 1926; asst. at the Pontifical Throne, May 2, 1939; transferred to the Titular See of Albule and as Archbishop of Portland in Oregon, Dec. 9, 1966; died Jan. 2, 1983; ROBERT JOSEPH DWYER, D.D., Ph.D., ord. June 11, 1932; cons. Bishop of Reno, Aug. 5, 1952; appt. Archbishop of Portland in Oregon, Dec. 9, 1966; resigned Jan. 22, 1974; died March 24, 1976; CORNELIUS MICHAEL POWER, D.D., J.C.D., ord. June 3, 1939; appt. Bishop of Yakima, Feb. 5, 1969; cons. May 1, 1969; appt. Archbishop of Portland in Oregon, Jan. 22, 1974; retired July 3, 1986; died May 22, 1997; WILLIAM J. LEVADA, S.T.D., ord. Dec. 20, 1961; appt. Titular Bishop of Capri and Auxiliary Bishop of Los Angeles, March 29, 1983; appt. Archbishop of Portland in Oregon, July 1, 1986; installed Sept. 21, 1986; appt. Coadjutor Archbishop of San Francisco, Aug. 17, 1995; transferred to Oct. 24, 1995; FRANCIS E. GEORGE, O.M.I., Ph.D., S.T.D., ord. Dec. 21, 1963; appt. Bishop of Yakima July 10, 1990; installed Sept. 21, 1990; appt. Archbishop of Portland in Oregon, April 29, 1996; installed May 27, 1996; appt. Archbishop of Chicago April 8, 1997; installed May 7, 1997; created Cardinal Priest Feb. 21, 1998; died April 17, 2015.; JOHN G. VLAZNY, ord. Dec. 20, 1961; appt. Auxiliary Bishop of Chicago and Titular Bishop of Stagno Oct. 31, 1983; cons. Dec. 13, 1983; appt. Bishop of Winona May 19, 1987; installed July 29, 1987; appt. Archbishop of Portland in Oregon Oct. 28, 1997; installed Dec. 19, 1997; retired Jan. 29, 2013.

Office of the Archbishop

Archdiocesan Pastoral Center—2838 E. Burnside St., Portland, 97214-1895. Tel: 503-234-5334; Fax: 503-234-2545.

Archdiocesan Canonical Officials

Auxiliary Bishop, Vicar General and Moderator of the Curia—Most Rev. PETER L. SMITH, J.C.L., Pastoral Center, 2838 E. Burnside St., Portland, 97214. Tel: 503-233-8331; Fax: 503-234-2545.

Vicar for Clergy and Ministry Personnel—Rev. TODD MOLINARI.
Chancellor—Sr. VERONICA SCHUELER, F.S.E.
Finance Officer—JO WILLHITE.
Departments—
General Counsel—G. KEVIN KIELY.
Archdiocesan Administrative Department—JO WILLHITE, Chief Admin. Officer.
Office of the Vicar for Clergy and Ministry Personnel—Rev. TODD MOLINARI.
Department of Catholic Schools—Bro. WILLIAM DYGERT, C.S.C., Supt.
Office of the Chancellor and Public Affairs—Sr. VERONICA SCHUELER, F.S.E.
Department of Pastoral Ministries—Deacon KEVIN WELCH, Dir.
Oregon Catholic Conference (OCC) - Board of Directors—Most Revs. ALEXANDER K. SAMPLE, Archbishop of the Archdiocese of Portland in Oregon, Pres.; LIAM CARY, Bishop of Baker, Vice Pres.; PETER L. SMITH, J.C.L., Auxiliary Bishop of the Archdiocese of Portland in Oregon, Sec./Treas.; TODD COOPER, Reprensentative.
Tribunal—Rev. Msgr. PATRICK BRENNAN, Judicial Vicar.
Canonical Advisory Groups—
Finance Council—Most Revs. ALEXANDER K. SAMPLE; PETER L. SMITH, J.C.L.; JO WILLHITE, Ex Officio Chair; CARMEN GASTON, Ex Officio; DOUG WHITE; CAROLYN WINTER; RON BASILE.
College of Consultors—Most Rev. PETER L. SMITH, J.C.L.; Revs. MICHAEL WALKER; MARIANO ESCANO; Rev.s Msgr. JOSEPH BETSCHART; Revs. JOSE LUIS GONZALEZ; RONALD NELSON JR.; Rev. Msgr. RICHARD HUNEGER; Revs. JOHN W. KERNS; LUAN Q. TRAN.
Area Vicars—Revs. MARTIN L. KING, Downtown Portland; MATTHEW LIBRA, Northeast Portland; JOHN J. BOYLE, J.C.L., Southeast Portland; JOSE LUIS GONZALEZ, East Portland Suburban; MAXY D'COSTA, S.F.X., South Portland Suburban; JOHN HENDERSON, West Portland Suburban; CARY RENIVA, Beaverton Suburban; MIKE WALKER, Yamhill County; JEFFREY MEEUWSEN, Tualatin Valley; NICOLAUS MARANDU, A.L.C.P., Columbia County; AMAL IRUDAYARAJ, North Coast; JAMES J. COLEMAN, Marion County; GARY L. ZERR, Metropolitan Salem; DICK ROSSMAN, Santiam; FRANCISCO BRINGUELA, Albany-Corvallis; DAVID BROWN, Metropolitan Eugene; JAMES D. GRAHAM, South Coast; WILLIAM HOLTZINGER, Southern Oregon.
Clergy Personnel Board—Revs. TIMOTHY J. MOCKAITIS; CARY RENIVA; TIMOTHY FURLOW; Rev.s Msgr. JOSEPH BETSCHART; Most Rev. ALEXANDER K. SAMPLE, Archbishop & Ex Officio; Rev. TODD MOLINARI; Most Rev. PETER L. SMITH, J.C.L.; Rev. JEFFREY EIRVIN.

Tribunal

Judicial Vicar—Very Rev. Msgr. PATRICK S. BRENNAN, J.C.L.
Adjutant Judicial Vicars—Most Rev. PETER L. SMITH, J.C.L.; Rev. JOHN J. BOYLE, J.C.L.
Director of the Tribunal—MR. STEPHEN V GARBITELLI, J.C.L.
Judges—Revs. NAZARIO ATUKUNDA, J.C.L.; MICHAEL VUKY, J.C.L.; MR. STEPHEN V GARBITELLI, J.C.L.; Revs. JEFFREY MEEUWSEN; AMALRAJ RAYAPPAN, J.C.D.
Defender of the Bond—VACANT.
Auditor—RACHEL WELDON.
Notaries—SUSAN OUFFOUE; Rev. MICHAEL VUKY, J.C.L.; RACHEL WELDON.
Advocates—Clergy and others approved for this function.

Archdiocesan Offices and Agencies

Administrative—JO WILLHITE, Chief Administrative Officer.
Archives—JOSEPH SCHIWEK, Records Mgr., 2838 E. Burnside St., Portland, 97214-1895. Tel: 503-233-8334; Email: archives@archdpdx.org.
Building Commission—Most Rev. PETER L. SMITH, J.C.L., (Ex Officio); Revs. DON GUTMANN; PATRICK MCNAMEE, Chair, Chair, (Retired); GARY L. ZERR; JIM KILPATRICK; BRIAN SHEA; JIM EVANS; ROBERT BOILEAU; BILL PARRY; JOSEPH GEHLEN; DELIA WILSON; JO WILLHITE, (Ex Officio); SAMUEL RODRIGUEZ; TONY ROOS; MICHELLE BRAULICK; MARY FRANCES CASCIATO, Sec.
Campus Ministry—2838 E. Burnside St., Portland, 97214-1895. Tel: 503-233-8335. RICKY SHOOP, Contact.
Catholic Charities, Inc.—Deacon RICHARD BIRKEL, Ph. D., Exec. Dir., 2740 S.E. Powell Blvd., Portland, 97202. Tel: 503-231-4866; Fax: 503-231-4327; Email: rbirkel@catholiccharitiesoregon.org.
Catholic Deaf Ministry—JILENE MODLIN, Coord., 2838 E. Burnside St., Portland, 97214. Tel: 971-340-4769 (Videophone); Email: jmodlin@archdpdx.org.
Catholic Sentinel—(Official Newspaper of the Archdiocese), *2838 E. Burnside St., Portland, 97202.* Tel: 503-460-5353. *Mailing Address: P.O. Box 18030, Portland, 97218-0030.* Most Rev. ALEXANDER K. SAMPLE, Publisher-in-Chief; WADE WISLER, Publisher; ED LANGLOIS, Mng. Editor.
Catholic Youth Organization/Camp Howard—Sr. KRISTA VON BORSTEL, S.S.M.O., Exec. Dir., 825 N.E. 20th Ave., Oregon Plaza, Ste. 120, Portland, 97232. Tel: 503-231-9484, Ext. 104; Fax: 503-231-9531; Email: srkrista@cyocamphoward.org; Web: cyocamphoward.org.
Cemeteries—JO WILLHITE, Tel: 503-234-5334; TIM CORBETT, Dir., Mt. Calvary Cemetery, 333 S.W. Skyline Blvd., Portland, 97221. Tel: 503-292-6621. Gethsemani Funeral Home & Cemetery, 11666 S.E. Stevens Rd., Happy Valley, 97086. Tel: 503-659-1350. Mount Calvary Cemetery, Eugene, 300 Mary Lane, Eugene, 97405. Tel: 541-686-8722.
Child & Youth Protection—CATHY SHANNON, Dir., 2838 E. Burnside St., Portland, 97214-1895. Tel: 503-416-8810 Victim Assistance; Tel: 503-233-8302 Child Protection; Email: cshannon@archdpdx.org.
Clergy Personnel—Rev. TODD MOLINARI, Vicar for Clergy & Ministry Personnel, 2838 E. Burnside St., Portland, 97214-1895. Tel: 503-233-8366; Fax: 503-230-1477.
Communications—DAVID RENSHAW, Dir., 2838 E. Burnside St., Portland, 97214-1895. Tel: 503-233-8373; Fax: 503-234-0019.
Continuing Education for Clergy—Rev. MICHAEL VUKY, J.C.L., Dir., Tel: 503-233-8368. Board Members: Revs. TIMOTHY J. MOCKAITIS; TODD MOLINARI; CHARLES A. WOOD; JAMES HERRERA; THEODORE LANGE.
Diaconate Office—Deacons BRIAN DIEHM, Dir., Tel: 503-233-8337; Email: bdiehm@archdpdx.org; GEOFF SCHMITT, Assoc., 2838 E. Burnside St., Portland, 97214-1895. Tel: 503-233-8344; Email: gschmitt@archdpdx.org.
Ecumenical and Interreligious Affairs—2838 E. Burnside St., Portland, 97214. TODD COOPER, Dir.
Episcopal Delegate for Religious—2838 E. Burnside St., Portland, 97214. Tel: 503-233-8322. Sr. VERONICA SCHUELER, F.S.E., Email: vschueler@archdpdx.org.
Department of Pastoral Ministries—2838 E. Burnside St., Portland, 97214-1895. Tel: 503-233-8335. Deacon KEVIN WELCH.
Hispanic Ministries—2838 E. Burnside St., Portland, 97214. Tel: 541-646-0032. Rev. JAMES COLEMAN, Vicar for Hispanic Ministry; Deacon FELIX GARCIA, Coord.
Historical Commission—MARY BETH HERKERT, Pres., 2838 E. Burnside St., Portland, 97214-1895. Tel: 503-234-5334.
Holy Childhood, Pontifical Association of—2838 E. Burnside St., Portland, 97214-1895. VACANT.
Human Resources—ALANA WILSON, Dir., 2838 E. Burnside St., Portland, 97214-1895. Tel: 503-233-8327; Email: awilson@archdpdx.org.
General Counsel—2838 E. Burnside St., Portland, 97214. Tel: 508-233-8356. G. KEVIN KIELY, Email: gkkiely@archdpdx.org; ELISE FERGUSON, Legal Asst., Email: eferguson@archdpdx.org.
Life, Justice & Peace—MATT CATO, Dir., 2838 E. Burnside St., Portland, 97214-1895. Tel: 503-233-8361; Email: justiceandpeace@archdpdx.org; Rev. MATTHEW LIBRA, Assoc. Dir. Respect for Life Activities.
Marriage & Family Life—JASON KIDD, 2838 E. Burnside St., Portland, 97214-1895. Tel: 503-233-8304; Email: jkidd@archdpdx.org.
Ministry Formation—2838 E. Burnside St., Portland, 97214-1895. Tel: 503-233-8315. ROLANDO MORENO, Dir., Email: rmoreno@archdpdx.org.
Mission Office—2838 E. Burnside St., Portland, 97214-1895. Sr. VERONICA SCHUELER, F.S.E.
Oregon Catholic Conference—Most Revs. ALEXANDER K. SAMPLE, Pres.; LIAM CARY, Vice Pres.; PETER L. SMITH, J.C.L., Sec. & Treas., 2838 E. Burnside St., Portland, 97214-1895. Tel: 503-234-5334.
Oregon Catholic Press—5536 N.E. Hassalo St., Portland, 97213-3638. Mailing Address: P.O. Box 18030, Portland, 97218-0030. Tel: 503-281-1191. Most Rev. ALEXANDER K. SAMPLE, Publisher-in-Chief; WADE WISLER, Publisher.
Pastoral Ministries—2838 E. Burnside St., Portland, 97214-1895. Tel: 503-233-8335. Deacon KEVIN WELCH, Dir.
People with Disabilities—2838 E. Burnside St., Portland, 97214-1895.
Teletype: 503-233-8399 (V/TTY). KELSEY BELL, Coord., Email: kbell@archdpdx.org.
Pro-Life Activities—(See Life, Justice and Peace).
Project Rachel—2740 S.E. Powell Blvd., #7, Portland, 97202. Tel: 800-249-8074.
Propagation of the Faith, Pontifical Society for the2838 E. Burnside St., Portland, 97214-1895.
Tel: 503-234-5334; Email: VSchueler@archdpdx.org. Sr. VERONICA SCHUELER, F.S.E., Dir.
Catechesis & Faith Formation—ROLANDO MORENO, Dir., Tel: 503-234-5334.
Refugee Resettlement—2740 S.E. Powell Blvd., Portland, 97202. Tel: 971-222-1883;
Fax: 971-222-1887. KELSEY KESWANI, Interim Dir.
Religious Education—ROLANDO MORENO, Dir.
Stewardship & Development—CARMEN GASTON, Dir. Stewardship & Devel.; CHRISTY UHRICH, ACA/Capital Campaign Contact, 2838 E. Burnside St., Portland, 97214-1895. Tel: 503-233-8336; Fax: 503-235-6675; Email: cuhrich@archdpdx.org.
St. Mary's Home for Boys—FRANCIS MAHER, Exec. Dir., 16535 S.W. Tualatin Valley Hwy., Beaverton, 97006. Tel: 503-649-5651.
School Office—Bro. WILLIAM DYGERT, C.S.C., Supt. Catholic Schools, Tel: 503-233-8300; Fax: 503-236-3683. Associate Superintendents: GARY BECKLEY; JEANNIE RAY-TIMONEY.
Vocations—Rev. JEFFREY EIRVIN, Dir., 2838 E. Burnside St., Portland, 97214-1895. Tel: 503-233-8368; Email: jeirvin@archdpdx.org.
Divine Worship—2838 E. Burnside St., Portland, 97214-1895. Tel: 503-233-8321. Rev. Msgr. GERARD O'CONNOR, Dir., Email: goconnor@archdpdx.org.
Youth and Young Adult Ministry—Tel: 503-233-8310; Email: rshoop@archdpdx.org. RICKY SHOOP, Coord.

CLERGY, PARISHES, MISSIONS AND PAROCHIAL SCHOOLS

CITY OF PORTLAND

(MULTNOMAH COUNTY)
PORTLAND

1—CATHEDRAL OF THE IMMACULATE CONCEPTION (1851) 1716 N.W. Davis St., 97209.
Tel: 503-228-4397; Email: hello@maryscathedralpdx.org. Rev. Msgr. Patrick Brennan; Ms. Elizabeth Stephenson, Admin. Asst.; Ms. Jennifer Overbay, Business Mgr.
School—Cathedral of the Immaculate Conception School, (Grades PreK-8),
110 N.W. 17th Ave., 97209. Tel: 503-275-9370;
Fax: 503-275-9378; Email: info@cathedral-or.org; Web: www.cathedral-or.org. Mrs. Amy Biggs, Prin. Lay Teachers 16; Students 247.
Catechesis Religious Program—Students 11.

2—ST. AGATHA aka St. Agatha School (1911) 1430 S.E. Nehalem St., 97202. Tel: 503-236-4747. Rev. Luan Quach Tran.
School—St. Agatha School, (Grades PreK-8),
7960 S.E. 15th Ave., 97202. Tel: 503-234-5500;
Fax: 503-232-7240; Web: www.stagathaschoolpdx.us. Christopher Harris, Prin.; Stacey Dunn, Librarian. Lay Teachers 16; Students 204.

3—ALL SAINTS (1917) 3847 N.E. Glisan, 97232.
Tel: 503-232-4305; Web: www.allsaintsportland.org. Rev. Paul Jeyamani.
School—All Saints School, (Grades PreK-8),
601 N.E. Cesar E Chavez Blvd., 97232.
Tel: 503-236-6205; Fax: 503-236-0781; Email: office@allsaintsportland.com; Web: www.allsaintsportland.com. Mary Wallulis, Librarian. Lay Teachers 40; Students 500; Clergy / Religious Teachers 1.
Catechesis Religious Program—Students 106.

4—ST. ANDRE BESSETTE CHURCH (1919) (Downtown Chapel), 601 W. Burnside St., 97209.
Tel: 503-228-0746; Fax: 503-972-1063; Email: frtom@saintandrechurch.org; Email: andrew@saintandrechurch.org; Email: tgornick@archdpdx.org; Email: brjoe@saintandrechurch.org; Web: saintandrechurch.org. Rev. Tom Gaughan; Bro. Joseph DeAgostino, Pastoral Asst.; Mr. Andrew Rakestraw, Parish Office Mgr.; Mr. Tom Gornick, Fin. and Facilities Mgr.

5—ST. ANDREW (1907) 806 N.E. Alberta St., 97211.
Tel: 503-281-4429; Fax: 503-281-4411; Email: OurOffice@standrewchurch.com; Email: dzegar@archdpdx.org; Web: standrewchurch.com.

Rev. David E. Zegar; Mr. Edward Prindle, Pastoral Council; Mr. John Kelly, Administrative Council.
Catechesis Religious Program—
Email: asandoval@archdpdx.org. April Sandoval, D.R.E. Students 107.
6—ST. ANTHONY (1917) 3720 S.E. 79th Ave., 97206. Tel: 503-771-6039; Email: pdonoghue@archdpdx.org; Email: alewis@archdpdx.org; Email: StAnthonyPortland@archdpdx.org; Web: stanthonypdx.com. Rev. Patrick Donoghue; Ms. Anna Lewis, Admin. Asst.; Ms. Jeanne McPherson, Bookkeeper.
Catechesis Religious Program—
Email: grymsza@archdpdx.org. Glenn Rymsza, D.R.E. Students 61.
7—ASCENSION (1892) 743 S.E. 76th Ave., 97215. Tel: 503-256-3897; Fax: 503-257-4681; Email: vaguilar@ascensionpdx.org; Web: ascensionpdx.org. Rev. David Leo Jaspers.
Catechesis Religious Program—
Tel: 503-256-3897, Ext. 21; Email: sgrigar@ascensionpdx.org. Sharon Grigar, Pastoral Assoc.; Maria Solis, Dir. Hispanic Ministry. Students 206.
8—ASSUMPTION (1909) Closed. For inquiries for parish records contact the chancery. (Holy Cross).
9—ST. BIRGITTA (1954) 11820 N.W. St. Helens Rd., 97231-2319. Tel: 503-286-3929; Email: secretarystb@gmail.com; Web: www.stbirgittapdx.com. Revs. Joshua Clifton; Luan Q. Tran.
Chapel—Portland, Chapel of Our Lady of Sinj.
Catechesis Religious Program—Students 9.
10—BLESSED SACRAMENT (1913) Closed. For inquiries for parish records please contact Holy Cross, Portland.
11—ST. CHARLES (1914) 5310 N.E. 42nd, 97218. Tel: 503-281-6461; Fax: 503-281-6828; Email: stchas@stcharlespdx.org; Web: www.stcharlespdx.org. Rev. Elwin Schwab, Admin.; Leif Kehrwald, Pastoral Assoc.; Gabriel Triplett, Pastoral Assoc./Youth Coord.
Catechesis Religious Program—
Email: jhommes@stcharlespdx.org. Mayra Torres, D.R.E. Students 40.
12—CHURCH OF ST. JOSEPH THE WORKER (1885) 2310 S.E. 148th Ave., 97233. Tel: 503-761-8710; Web: www.stjosephtheworkerpdx.org. Rev. Ted Prentice; Deacons Mike Caldwell; Larry Loumena.
Catechesis Religious Program—Students 75.
13—CHURCH OF ST. MICHAEL THE ARCHANGEL (1894) (Italian) 424 S.W. Mill St., 97201. Tel: 503-228-8629. Revs. Ignacio Llorente, S.S.J.; Juan Pablo Segura, Parochial Vicar; Deacon Chuck Amsberry, Pastoral Assoc.
Catechesis Religious Program—Students 6.
14—ST. CLARE (1913) 8535 S.W. 19th Ave., 97219. Tel: 503-244-1037; Email: office@saintclarechurch.org; Web: www.saintclarechurch.org. Rev. Donald Gutmann; Deacon Bill McNamara.
School—St. Clare School, (Grades K-8),
1807 S.W. Freeman St., 97219. Tel: 503-244-7600; Fax: 503-293-2076; Email: info@stclarepdx.org; Web: www.stclarepdx.org. Debbi Monahan, Prin.; Lynn Napoli, Librarian. Lay Teachers 14; Students 200.
Catechesis Religious Program—
Tel: 503-244-1037, Ext. 104; Email: dcnbill@saintclarechurch.org. Students 86.
15—ST. ELIZABETH OF HUNGARY (1953) 4112 S.W. Sixth Ave. Dr., 97239. Tel: 503-222-2168; Email: office@stelizabethportland.net; Web: www.stelizabethportland.net. Rev. James M. Kolb, C.S.P.
Catechesis Religious Program—Ms. Elizabeth Duncan, Parish Asst. Students 35.
16—ST. FRANCIS OF ASSISI (1876) 1131 S.E. Oak St., 97214. Tel: 503-232-5880; Email: office@stfrancispdx.org; Web: stfrancispdx.org. Rev. George Kuforiji, Admin.
Res.: 330 SE 11th Ave, 97214.
17—HOLY CROSS CATHOLIC CHURCH (1901) 5227 N. Bowdoin St., 97203. Tel: 503-289-2834; Email: holycrossoffice@archdpdx.org. Rev. Mark Bachmeier; Ana Carmina Perez-Flores, Hispanic Ministry; Deb Volker, Business Mgr.; Susan Unger, Spiritual Advisor/Care Svcs.
School—Holy Cross Catholic Church School, (Grades PreK-8),
5202 N. Bowdoin St., 97203. Tel: 503-289-3010; Fax: 503-286-5006; Email: jjohnson@archdpdx.org; Web: www.holycrosspdx.org/school. Julie Johnson, Prin.; Amanda Louie, Librarian. Lay Teachers 20; Sisters 1; Students 245; Clergy / Religious Teachers 1.
Catechesis Religious Program—Andrea Swanson, D.R.E. Students 70.
Chapel—Christ The Teacher, University of Portland
5000 N. Willamette Blvd., 97203.
18—HOLY FAMILY (1931) Business Office: 3732 S.E. Knapp, 97202. Tel: 503-774-1428; Email: churchlady@holyfamilyportland.com; Web: www.holyfamilyportland.org. Rev. Rodel de Mesa; Deacon Timothy Dooley.
Res.: 3708 S.E. Flavel.
Church: 7525 S.E. Cesar E. Chavez Blvd., 97202.
School—Holy Family Catholic School, (Grades PreSchool-8),
7425 Cesar E. Chavez Blvd., 97202.
Tel: 503-774-8871; Fax: 503-774-8872; Email: school@holyfamilyportland.org. Loretta Wiltgen, Prin.; Tamara Beecroft, Librarian. Lay Teachers 18; Students 220.
Catechesis Religious Program—
Tel: 503-774-1428, Ext. 123 (D.R.E.);
Tel: 503-774-1428, Ext. 107 (Youth Min.);
Fax: 503-774-1854. Students 63.
19—HOLY REDEEMER (1906) 25 N. Rosa Parks Way, 97217. Tel: 503-285-4539; Email: holyredeemerchurch@comcast.net. Revs. Pat Neary, C.S.C.; Chris Brennan, Parochial Vicar; Deacons Robert Lukosh; John Rilatt.
School—Holy Redeemer School, (Grades PreSchool-8),
127 N. Rosa Parks Way, 97217. Tel: 503-283-5197; Fax: 503-283-9479; Email: araineri@holyredeemerpdx.org; Web: www.holyredeemerpdx.org. Anna Raineri, Prin. Lay Teachers 17; Students 305; Clergy / Religious Teachers 3.
Catechesis Religious Program—
Email: kbattilega@holyredeemerpdx.org. Ms. Kathy Battilega, Business Mgr. Students 97.
20—HOLY ROSARY PARISH & DOMINICAN PRIORY (1894) 375 N.E. Clackamas St., 97232.
Tel: 503-235-3163; Email: holyrosarypdx@parishmail.com; Web: holyrosarypdx.org. Rev. Joseph Sergott, O.P., Dir.; Very Rev. Vincent Kelber, O.P.; Revs. Corwin Low, O.P., Parochial Vicar; Gabriel T. Mosher, O.P., Parochial Vicar; Paul A. Duffner, O.P., In Res., (Retired); Brian T.B. Mullady, O.P., In Res.; Paschal Donald Salisbury, O.P., In Res., (Retired).
Catechesis Religious Program—Janine Applegate, D.R.E. Students 147.
21—ST. IGNATIUS (1907) [JC] 3400 S.E. 43rd Ave., 97206. Tel: 503-777-1491; Email: office@sipdx.org; Web: www.sipdx.org. Revs. Craig Boly, S.J.; Daniel Sullivan, S.J.
Legal Titles: St Ignatius Catholic Church, Portland Oregon.
School—St. Ignatius School, (Grades PreSchool-8),
3330 S.E. 43rd St., 97206. Tel: 503-774-5533; Fax: 503-788-1134; Email: school@sipdx.org; Web: www.sispdx.org. Kelli Clark, Prin. Lay Teachers 18; Students 214.
Catechesis Religious Program—
Email: jingman@sipdx.org. Grace Byrd, D.R.E. Students 235.
22—IMMACULATE HEART OF MARY (1885) 2926 N. Williams Ave., 97227-1628. Tel: 503-287-3724; Email: immaculateheart_portland@archdpdx.org. Rev. Paulinus Mangesho, A.L.C.P.; Deacons Harold Burke-Sivers; Paul Pham.
Catechesis Religious Program—Students 4.
23—ST. JOHN FISHER (1959) 4567 S.W. Nevada St., 97219. Tel: 503-244-4945; Email: office@johnfisher.org. Rev. Richard B. Thompson; Mrs. Kim Cox, Business Mgr.
School—St. John Fisher School, (Grades K-8),
4581 S.W. Nevada St., 97219. Tel: 503-246-3234; Fax: 503-246-4117; Email: mwasman@sjfschool.org. Sundi Pierce, Librarian. Administrators 1; Lay Teachers 15; Students 220; Clergy / Religious Teachers 1.
Catechesis Religious Program—
Email: mtimoneydeville@johnfisher.org. Students 12.
24—ST. JUAN DIEGO CATHOLIC CHURCH (2002) 5995 N.W. 178th Ave., 97229. Tel: 503-644-1617; Email: office@stjuandiego.org. Rev. Terry O'Connell; Deacon Dennis Desmarais; Peggy Brice, Business Mgr.
Catechesis Religious Program—
Email: jdelaney@stjuandiego.org. Jean Delaney, Pastoral Assoc./Faith Formation. Students 178.
25—KOREAN MARTYRS CATHOLIC CHURCH (1990) [JC] (Korean) 10840 S.E. Powell Blvd., 97266.
Tel: 503-762-6880; Email: chrkor@yahoo.com; Web: kmccp.org. Rev. Jaebum (Raphael) Park.
Catechesis Religious Program—
Tel: 503-997-2538. Paul Park, D.R.E. Students 68.
26—ST. MARY MAGDALENE (1911) (The Madeleine) 3123 N.E. 24th Ave., 97212. Tel: 503-281-5777; Email: fathermike@themadeleine.edu; Email: jreilly@themadeleine.edu; Web: www.themadeleine.edu. Rev. Michael Biewend.
School—St. Mary Magdalene School, (Grades K-8),
3240 N.E. 23rd Ave., 97212. Tel: 503-288-9197; Fax: 503-280-1196; Email: ssteele@themadeleine.edu; Email: aanderson@themadeleine.edu. Susan J. Steele, Prin.; Alison Anderson, Librarian. Lay Teachers 21; Students 258.
Catechesis Religious Program—
Email: jonderko@themadeleine.edu. Julie Onderko, D.R.E. Students 90.
27—OUR LADY OF LAVANG (1999) (Vietnamese) 5404 N.E. Alameda Dr., 97213. Tel: 503-249-5892; Fax: 503-249-1776; Email: APham@archdpdx.org. Revs. Angsar Pham, S.D.D.; Francis X. Nguyen, S.D.D.; Joseph Mink Van Nguyen, S.D.D.; Thanh Vo; Deacon Tien Nguyen.
Catechesis Religious Program—Students 924.
Mission—St. Andrew Dung-Lac
7390 S.W. Grabhorn Rd., Aloha, Washington Co. 97007.
28—OUR LADY OF SORROWS (1917) 5239 S.E. Woodstock Blvd., 97206-6822. Tel: 503-775-6731; Email: ebrush@olspdx.org; Email: ourladyofsorrowspdx@gmail.com; Web: www.olspdx.org. Revs. Ronald C. Millican; Joseph Heuberger, In Res.; Deacon An Thanh Vu; Evelyn Brush, OFS, Pastoral Min./Coord.
Res.: 5313 S.E. Knight St., 97206.
Catechesis Religious Program—Evelyn Brush, OFS, D.R.E. Students 34.
29—ST. PATRICK (1885) 1623 N.W. 19th Ave., 97209. Tel: 503-222-4086; Email: office@stpatrickpdx.org; Email: tfurlow@archdpdx.org; Web: stpatrickpdx.org. P.O. Box 10146, 97296. Rev. Timothy Furlow, Admin.
Catechesis Religious Program—Students 32.
30—ST. PETER (1911) Mailing Address: 8623 S.E. Woodstock Blvd., 97266. Tel: 503-777-3321; Fax: 503-777-3351; Email: stpeterportland@archdpdx.org. Rev. Raul O. Marquez.
Res.: 5736 S.E. 86th St., 97266.
Catechesis Religious Program—
Email: mscott@archdpdx.org. Ms. Marcy Scott, D.R.E. Students 57.
31—ST. PHILIP NERI (1912) Mailing Address: 2408 S.E. 16th Ave., 97214. Tel: 503-231-4955; Fax: 503-736-1383; Email: info@stphilipneripdx.org; Email: debbieg@stphilipneripdx.org; Web: www.stphilipneripdx.org. Rev. Msgr. J. Richard Paperini; Rev. Nazario Atukunda, J.C.L.
Res.: 2411 S.E. Tamarack Ave., 97214.
Catechesis Religious Program—
Email: barbarah@stphilipneripdx.org. ms. Barbara Harrison, D.R.E.; Ms. Debbie Guthrie, Admin. Asst. Students 10.
32—ST. PIUS X (Cedar Mill) (1953) 1280 N.W. Saltzman Rd., 97229. Tel: 503-644-5264; Email: frontdesk@stpius.org; Web: www.stpius.org. Revs. Sean M. Weeks; Julio Cesar Torres Montejo; Deacon Robert Little.
School—St. Pius X School, (Grades K-8),
1260 N.W. Saltzman Rd., 97229. Tel: 503-644-3244; Fax: 503-646-6568; Email: mthompson@stpius.org. Margaret Burd, Librarian. Lay Teachers 31; Students 487.
Catechesis Religious Program—
Email: nsoares@stpius.org; Email: jhoekstra@stpius.org; Email: kmombert@stpius.org. Kristen Mombert, Dir. Faith Form. & Youth Min.; Ms. Noreen Soares, Faith Form. Preschool-Grade 5; Ms. Janell Hoekstra, Middle School Min. Students 200.
33—QUEEN OF PEACE, Closed. For inquiries for parish records contact the chancery. (Holy Cross).
34—ST. RITA (1923) 10029 N.E. Prescott St., 97220. Tel: 503-252-3403; Fax: 503-256-9682; Email: stritapdx@qwestoffice.net; Web: stritapdx.org. Rev. Todd Molinari, Priest Mod.; Lisa Porter, Pastoral Admin.
Catechesis Religious Program—Ms. Barbara Stanton, D.R.E. Students 31.
35—ST. ROSE OF LIMA (1911) 2727 N.E. 54th Ave., 97213. Tel: 503-281-5318; Email: dcooper@strosepdx.org; Web: strosepdxparish.org. Rev. Matthew Libra; Ms. Dianna Cooper, Office Mgr.
School—St. Rose School, (Grades PreSchool-8),
5309 N.E. Alameda St., 97213. Tel: 503-281-1912; Fax: 503-281-0554; Email: kasbury@strosepdx.org; Web: www.strosepdx.org. Karen Asbury, Prin.; Heather Mott, Business Mgr.; Daniel Woytek, Librarian. Lay Teachers 14; Students 250.
Catechesis Religious Program—Students 45.
36—SACRED HEART (1893) 3910 S.E. 11th Ave., 97202. Tel: 503-231-9636; Email: sacredheart@sacredheartportland.org; Web: www.sacredheartportland.org. Rev. Robert L. Barricks.
37—ST. STANISLAUS (1907) (Polish) 3916 N. Interstate Ave., 97227-1063. Tel: 503-281-7532; Email: parish@ststanislausparish.com. Rev. Piotr Dzikowski, S.Ch.
Catechesis Religious Program—Christ Our Life, Students 32.
38—ST. STEPHEN (1907) 1112 S.E. 41st Ave., 97214. Tel: 503-234-5019; Email: saintstephenpdx@gmail.com. Revs. Eric Andersen; John J. Boyle, J.C.L., In Res.
Catechesis Religious Program—Mr. Joseph Salazar, Rel. Education Coord. Students 38.
39—ST. THERESE OF THE CHILD JESUS (1955) 1260 N.E. 132nd AVE., 97230. Tel: 503-256-5850; Email: amy@sttheresor.org. Rev. Stephen Geer.

Res.: 1224 N.E. 131st Pl., 97230. Email: frsteve@sttheresesor.org.
School—St. Therese of the Child Jesus School, (Grades PreSchool-8),
Tel: 503-256-5850; Fax: 503-253-3560; Email: huntj@stthereseschool.org. Joy Hunt, Prin. Lay Teachers 17; Students 191.
Catechesis Religious Program—Ms. Johnee Bennett, Recptionist. Students 27.
40—ST. THOMAS MORE (1936) 3525 S.W. Patton Rd., 97221. Tel: 503-222-2055; Email: stmparish@stmpdx.org. Rev. Martin L. King.
School—St. Thomas More School, (Grades K-8), 3521 S.W. Patton Rd., 97221. Tel: 503-222-6105; Fax: 503-227-5661; Email: stmschool@stmpdx.org; Web: www.stmpdxschool.org. Lauren Morgan, (a) Librarian. Lay Teachers 20; Students 220; Clergy / Religious Teachers 1.
Catechesis Religious Program—
Tel: 503-222-2055, Ext. 14; Email: mschuster@stmpdx.org. Mrs. Margaret Schuster, D.R.E. Students 12.

OUTSIDE THE CITY OF PORTLAND

ALBANY, LINN CO., OUR LADY OF PERPETUAL HELP (ST. MARY) (1885)
706 Ellsworth St., S.W., Albany, 97321.
Tel: 541-926-1449; Email: stmarysbusiness@comcast.net; Web: www.stmarysalbany.com. Revs. Edwin Sanchez Romero, Admin.; Leonard Omolo, ACLP, Parochial Vicar.
Catechesis Religious Program—Students 208.
ALOHA, WASHINGTON CO., ST. ELIZABETH ANN SETON (1982)
3145 SW 192nd Ave, Aloha, 97006.
Tel: 503-649-9044; Fax: 503-848-2915; Email: fjmeeuwsen@seas-aloha.org; Email: re@seas-aloha.org. Rev. Jeffrey Meeuwsen; Deacon Jesus Espinoza, Pastoral Assoc., Hispanic Ministry; Pati Izquierdo, Rel. Ed. Admin.
Catechesis Religious Program—Email: re@seas-aloha.org. Sandi Campos, Pastoral Assoc. Students 232.
ASHLAND, JACKSON CO., OUR LADY OF THE MOUNTAIN (1887)
987 Hillview Dr., Ashland, 97520. Tel: 541-482-1146; Email: sperry@mind.net; Email: olmop@mind.net. Rev. Mariano Escano; Deacon Ricardo Cervantes, Pastoral Assoc.
Catechesis Religious Program—Email: etlibrary@yahoo.com. Evelyn Tucker, D.R.E. Students 73.
ASTORIA, CLATSOP CO., ST. MARY, STAR OF THE SEA (1874) [JC]
1465 Grand Ave., Astoria, 97103. Tel: 503-325-3671; Web: www.stmaryastoria.com. Rev. William Oruko, Admin.
Rectory—1860 S.E. 3rd St., Astoria, 97103.
Mission—St. Francis de Sales, 867 5th Ave., Hammond, Clatsop Co. 97121.
Catechesis Religious Program—Email: amyr@stmaryastoria.com. Rose Marie Doyle, D.R.E.; Ms. Tatiana Pitstick, D.R.E. Students 88.
BANDON, COOS CO., HOLY TRINITY (1883) [CEM]
355 Oregon Ave. SE, Bandon, 97411.
Tel: 541-329-0697; Tel: 541-347-2309; Email: holytrinitybandon@yahoo.com; Web: www.holytrinitybandon.org. Rev. Anthony Ahamefule, Admin.
Mission—St. John the Baptist, 15th and Hwy 101, Port Orford, Curry Co. 97465. Tel: 541-332-0139; Email: gmdietel@icloud.com.
Catechesis Religious Program—Tel: 541-297-5555; Email: hennicksr@hotmail.com. Sharon Hennick, D.R.E. Students 10.
BEAVERTON, WASHINGTON CO.
1—ST. CECILIA (1876)
5105 S.W. Franklin Ave., Beaverton, 97005.
Tel: 503-644-2619; Email: jcassinelli@stceciliachurch.org; Email: cmotal@stceciliachurch.org. Revs. Cary Reniva; Brent Crowe.
School—St. Cecilia School, (Grades PreSchool-8), 12250 S.W. 5th, Beaverton, 97005.
Tel: 503-644-2619, Ext. 3; Fax: 503-646-4217; Email: creniva@archdpdx.org; Web: www.stceciliaschool.us. Wendy Casale, Librarian. Lay Teachers 17; Students 295.
Catechesis Religious Program—Mr. Jim Cassinelli, Business Mgr. Students 305.
2—HOLY TRINITY (1962) [CEM]
13715 S.W. Walker Rd., Beaverton, 97005.
Tel: 503-643-9528; Email: Parish@h-t.org; Email: Ingrid@h-t.org. Rev. David Gutmann.
School—Holy Trinity School, (Grades PreK-8), 13755 S.W. Walker Rd., Beaverton, 97005.
Tel: 503-644-5748; Fax: 503-643-4475; Email: holytrinity@pvt.k12.or.us; Web: htsch.org. Lay Teachers 19; Students 310; Clergy / Religious Teachers 1.
Catechesis Religious Program—Email: cstorm@htsch.org. Chris Storm, D.R.E. Students 340.
BROOKINGS, CURRY CO., STAR OF THE SEA CATHOLIC CHURCH (1923)
Mailing Address: 820 Old County Rd., Brookings, 97415. Tel: 541-469-2313; Fax: 541-469-9644; Email: pastor@sosstc.org; Email: parishoffice@sosstc.org; Email: starofthesea@frontier.com; Web: staroftheseastcharles.org. Rev. Justus Alaeto; Deacons Leo H. Appel II; Roger Hogan.
Mission—St. Charles Borromeo, 94323 Gauntlet, P.O. Box 529, Gold Beach, Curry Co. 97444.
Catechesis Religious Program—Valarie Cowan, D.R.E.; Ms. Carol Richardson, Admin. Asst. Students 26.
CANBY, CLACKAMAS CO., ST. PATRICK (1882) [CEM]
498 N.W. Ninth, P.O. Box 730, Canby, 97013.
Tel: 503-266-9411; Tel: 503-263-1286; Email: dnewbury@canby.com; Email: stpatricks@canby.com; Web: stpatcanby.org. Rev. Arturo Romero.
Catechesis Religious Program—488 N.W. 9th, Canby, 97013. Tel: 503-263-1287; Email: jpatershall@canby.com. Jody Patershall, D.R.E.; Ms. Debbie Newbury, Admin. Asst. Students 173.
CENTRAL POINT, JACKSON CO., SHEPHERD OF THE VALLEY (1978)
600 Beebe Rd., Central Point, 97502.
Tel: 541-664-1050; Web: shepherdcatholic.com. Rev. Fredy Bonilla Moreno, Admin.
Catechesis Religious Program—Students 107.
COOS BAY, COOS CO., ST. MONICA (1888)
357 S. 6th St., Coos Bay, 97420. Tel: 541-267-7421; Email: carole@saintmonicacoosbay.org; Web: saintmonicacoosbay.org. Rev. Robert Wolf
Legal Title: St. Monica Catholic Church, Coos Bay, Oregon.
Catechesis Religious Program—Pam Romanko, C.R.E. Students 81.
COQUILLE, COOS CO., HOLY NAME (1915)
50 S. Dean St., P.O. Box 368, Coquille, 97423.
Tel: 541-396-3849; Email: lorigunther@cvcatholic.com. Revs. James D. Graham; Henry Rufo, Parochial Vicar.
Res.: 2250 16th St., North Bend, 97459.
Mission—Sts. Ann and Michael, 209 Second St., P.O. Box 368, Myrtle Point, Coos Co. 97458.
CORNELIUS, WASHINGTON CO., ST. ALEXANDER (1881) (Hispanic)
170 N. 10th Ave., P.O. Box 644, Cornelius, 97113.
Tel: 503-359-0304; Fax: 503-992-8634; Email: jvillarreal@archdpdx.org; Email: nkale@archdpdx.org; Email: dschiferl.sac@comcast.net; Email: esoto@archdpdx.org; Email: ealvarado@archdpdx.org; Web: www.stalexandercornelius.org. Rev. David E. Schiferl; Sr. Juanita Villarrea, Pastoral Assoc.; Ms. Kim Folsom, Dir.; Ms. Ermelinda Soto-Avalos, Office Mgr.; Ms. Eva Alvarado, Business Office.
Res.: 268 N. 17th Ave., Cornelius, 97113.
Catechesis Religious Program—Students 402.
CORVALLIS, BENTON CO., ST. MARY (1861) [CEM]
501 N.W. 25th St., Corvallis, 97330.
Tel: 541-757-1988; Web: www.stmarycorvallis.org. Matias Perez Constanzo; Deacons Michael Cihak; Chris Anderson; Lynette Martin, Admin. Asst.
Catechesis Religious Program—Email: gmerritt@stmarycorvallis.org. Gabrielle Merritt, D.R.E.; Ms. Catherine Myers, Business Mgr. Students 188.
COTTAGE GROVE, LANE CO., OUR LADY OF PERPETUAL HELP (1897)
1025 N. 19th St., Cottage Grove, 97424.
Tel: 541-942-3420; Email: office@olphcg.net; Web: Olphcg.net. Rev. John J. Boyle, J.C.L., Parochial Vicar.
Mission—St. Philip Benizi, 552 Holbrook, Creswell, Lane Co. 97426.
Catechesis Religious Program—
Tel: 541-942-3420, Ext. 103; Email: passoc@olphcg.net. Mrs. Loralyn Eckstine, Pastoral Assoc. Students 35.
DALLAS, POLK CO., ST. PHILIP (1920) [JC]
825 S.W. Mill St., Dallas, 97338. Tel: 503-623-2440; Web: stphilipdallas.org. Rev. Michael Johnston.
Catechesis Religious Program—Students 109.
ESTACADA, CLACKAMAS CO., ST. ALOYSIUS (1924) [JC]
192 NW 3rd Ave, P.O. Box 1199, Estacada, 97023.
Tel: 503-630-2416; Email: tpagano@staloysiusestacada.org; Web: mjaparishescluster.org/contact-st-aloysius. 18090 SE Langensand Rd., Sandy, 97055. Rev. Gregg Bronsema.
Catechesis Religious Program—Tel: 503-630-2416;
Tel: 503-668-4446, Ext. 101; Email: tpagano@stmichaelsandy.org.
EUGENE, LANE CO.
1—ST. JUDE (1969)
4330 Willamette, Eugene, 97405. Tel: 541-344-1191; Email: parishstjude@comcast.net. Rev. Thomas D. Yurchak; Ms. Christina VanderPlaat, Pastoral Assoc.
Catechesis Religious Program—Students 40.
2—ST. MARK (1961)
1760 Echo Hollow Rd., Eugene, 97402.
Tel: 541-689-0725; Email: saintmark1760@hotmail.com; Web: www.saintmarkeugene.org. Revs. Michael Jeeva Antony; Peter Nhat Hoang, Parochial Vicar; Deacon Darrell Meter.
Catechesis Religious Program—Email: sparkministrieseugene@gmail.com. Mariah Harris, D.R.E.; Ms. Darralynn Nemechek, D.R.E. Asst. Students 101.
3—ST. MARY (1887) [CEM]
1062 Charnelton St., Eugene, 97401.
Tel: 541-342-1139; Email: info@stmaryeugene.com; Web: www.stmaryeugene.com. Revs. Ronald Nelson; Henry Guillen-Vega, Parochial Vicar; Edgar Eloy Rivera Torres, Parochial Vicar.
Catechesis Religious Program—Students 211.
4—ST. PAUL CATHOLIC CHURCH (1955)
1201 Satre St., Eugene, 97401. Tel: 541-686-2345; Email: stpaulcommunity@archpdx.org; Email: pvdmehden@archdpdx.org. Rev. David Brown; Deacon Greg Wilhelm; Ms. Pat Von der Mehden, Pastoral Assoc.
School—St. Paul Catholic Church School, (Grades PreK-8), Tel: 541-344-1401; Email: kbraud@saintpaul-school.org; Web: saintpaul-school.org. Kelli Braud, Prin. Lay Teachers 22; Students 289.
Catechesis Religious Program—Students 59.
5—ST. PETER (1955) [JC]
1150 Maxwell Rd., P.O. Box 40518, Eugene, 97404.
Tel: 541-688-1051; Email: stpetercc@stpetereugene.org; Web: www.stpetereugene.org. Revs. Michael Jeeva Antony; Peter Nhat Hoang, Parochial Vicar; Deacon David Sorensen.
Catechesis Religious Program—Tel: 541-689-0725; Email: sparkministrieseugene@gmail.com; Email: telliott@stpetereugene.org. Mariah Harris, Coord. Family & Spark Ministries; Ms. Darralynn Nemechek, D.R.E. Asst. Students 26.
6—ST. THOMAS MORE CHURCH (1915) (Catholic Campus Ministry)
1850 Emerald St., Eugene, 97403. Tel: 541-343-7021; Fax: 541-686-8028; Email: secretary@uonewman.org; Email: Pastor@uonewman.org; Email: bookkeeper@uonewman.org; Web: www.uonewman.org. Revs. Peter Do, O.P.; Vincent Benoit, O.P.; Garry Cappleman, O.P.
Res.: 1386 E. 18th, Eugene, 97403.
Catechesis Religious Program—Corinne M. Lopez, S.T.M., D.R.E. Students 7.
St. Thomas More Community—Canonical Religious House of the Western Dominican Province.
FLORENCE, LANE CO., ST. MARY, OUR LADY OF THE DUNES (1951)
85060 U.S. Hwy. 101 S., P.O. Box 2640, Florence, 97439. Tel: 541-997-2312; Email: rcassidy@archdpdx.org. Rev. Panneer Selvam; Ms. Nancy Ervin, Office Asst.
Res./Rectory: 1369 Zebra Wood St., Florence, 97439.
Catechesis Religious Program—Ms. Renee LaCosse, Youth Min. Coord. Students 48.
FOREST GROVE, WASHINGTON CO., ST. ANTHONY OF PADUA (1908) [JC]
1660 Elm St., Forest Grove, 97116.
Tel: 503-357-2989; Fax: 503-357-2217; Email: office@safg.org; Email: diana@safg.org; Web: www.safg.org. Rev. Benjamin Tapia; Ms. Diana Wuertz, Business Mgr.
Catechesis Religious Program—Tel: 503-359-0660. Rafael Manríquez, D.R.E. Students 137.
GERVAIS, MARION CO., SACRED HEART-ST. LOUIS (1847) [CEM]
605 7th St., P.O. Box 236, Gervais, 97026.
Tel: 503-792-4231; Email: secretary@shstl.org. Rev. James Herrera.
School—Sacred Heart-St. Louis School, (Grades PreK-8), 515 7th St., Gervais, 97026.
Tel: 503-792-4541; Fax: 503-792-3826; Email: lucy.shawn@shstl.org; Web: www.shstl.org. Lucy Shindler Shawn, Prin.; Marion Zellner, Librarian. Clergy 1; Lay Teachers 5; Students 57.
Catechesis Religious Program—Students 65.
GRAND RONDE, YAMHILL CO., ST. MICHAEL (1860)
48520 Hebo Rd., Grand Ronde, 97347.
Tel: 503-472-5232; Email: churchoffice@stjamesmac.com; Web: stjamesmac.com. 1145 NE 1st St., McMinnville, 97128-6064. Rev. Mike Walker.
GRANTS PASS, JOSEPHINE CO., ST. ANNE (1896) Revs. William Holtzinger; Tetzel Umingli; Deacon Robert Chapin, Rogue River Catholic Community: P.O. Box 1596, Rogue River, Jackson Co. 97537. Tel: 541-582-1373.
Res.: 1131 N.E. 10th St., Grants Pass, 97526.
Tel: 541-476-2240; Tel: 541-479-4848;
Tel: 541-479-1582; Tel: 541-787-4711; Email: office@stannegp.com; Web: www.stannegp.com.
Parish Center—Tel: 541-479-4848.
School—St. Anne School, (Grades PreK-5), 1131 N.E. 10th St., Grants Pass, 97526. Tel: 541-479-1582;

Email: stanneschool@stannegp.com; Web: www.stanneschoolgp.com. Lay Teachers 6; Students 58.
Child Care—Kelly Youth Center, Tel: 541-476-5802. Randi Lauby, Youth Min.
Catechesis Religious Program—Students 90.
Missions—St. Patrick of the Forest—407 W. River St., Cave Junction, Josephine Co. 97523.
Our Lady of the River Mission, 3625 N. River Rd., Gold Hill, Jackson Co. 97525.

GRESHAM, MULTNOMAH CO.
1—ST. ANNE (1957)
1015 S.E. 182nd Ave., Gresham, 97233-5099.
Tel: 503-665-4935; Email: stannecatholicchurch@gmail.com; Web: www.stannechurchingresham.org. Revs. Jose Luis Gonzalez; Miguel Figueroa Farias; Deacon Jose Gonzalez.
Catechesis Religious Program—Ms. Becci Stanton, Bookkeeper. Students 328.
2—ST. HENRY (1913)
346 N.W. First St., Gresham, 97030.
Tel: 503-665-9129; Email: sthenry_gresham@archdpdx.org; Email: theitzman@archdpdx.org; Web: sthenrygresham.org. Rev. Charles E. Zach.
Catechesis Religious Program—Email: jchambers@archdpdx.org. Jeanne Chambers, D.R.E.; Ms. Terri Heitzman, Admin. Asst. Students 316.

HILLSBORO, WASHINGTON CO., ST. MATTHEW CATHOLIC CHURCH (1902) [CEM]
475 S.E. 3rd Ave., Hillsboro, 97123-4499.
Tel: 503-648-1998; Fax: 503-648-4489; Email: parishoffice@stmattewhillsboro.com; Email: ewaters@stmatthewhillsboro.org; Web: www.stmatthewhillsboro.org. Revs. Hugo O. Maese, M.Sp.S.; Rito Guzman, M.Sp.S., Parochial Vicar; Agustin Rodriguez, M.Sp.S., Parochial Vicar; Jose Ortega, M.Sp.S., (In Res.); Guillermo Flores, M.Sp.S, (In Res.).
School—St. Matthew School, (Grades PreK-8), 221 S.E. Walnut St., Hillsboro, 97123. Tel: 503-648-2512; Fax: 503-648-4518; Email: pdunn@stmatthewschoolhillsboro.org; Web: www.stmatthewschoolhillsboro.org. Ms. Becky Smith, Business Mgr,. Lay Teachers 13; Students 231; Clergy / Religious Teachers 1.
Catechesis Religious Program—
Tel: 503-648-1998, Ext. 230; Email: mteeter@stmatthewhillsboro.org; Email: BSmith@stmatthewhillsboro.org. Molly Teeter, D.R.E. Students 264.

INDEPENDENCE, POLK CO., ST. PATRICK CHURCH (1908)
1275 E St., Independence, 97351. Tel: 503-838-1242; Email: deaconrobpage@gmail.com. Rev. Francisco Bringuela.
Res.: 1258 E St., Independence, 97351.
Catechesis Religious Program—Ms. Diana Lindskog, Sec. Students 164.

JORDAN, LINN CO., OUR LADY OF LOURDES (1885) [CEM] [JC2]
39043 Jordan Rd., Scio, 97374. Tel: 503-394-2437; Email: jmsh@nettigers.com. Rev. Luan D. Nguyen.
Catechesis Religious Program—Tel: 503-769-2050; Email: jmsh@nettigers.com. Bob Bjornstedt, D.R.E.; Ms. Jeanne Howe, Office Admin. Students 5.
Mission—St. Patrick, 362 7th St., Lyons, Linn Co. 97358.

JUNCTION CITY, LANE CO., ST. HELEN (1959) [CEM]
1350 W. 6th Ave., Junction City, 97448.
Tel: 541-998-8053; Fax: 541-998-9474; Email: parishesofsthelenandstrose@gmail.com; Web: strosesthelen.org. Revs. Edgar Rivera Torres, Admin.; John Arcidiacono, Admin.
Catechesis Religious Program—Students 50.

KEIZER, MARION CO., ST. EDWARD (1967)
5303 River Rd. N., Keizer, 97303. Tel: 503-393-5323; Email: grace@sainteds.com. Rev. Gary L. Zerr.
Catechesis Religious Program—Fax: 503-463-5439; Email: cyndie.harris@sainteds.com. Ms. Cyndie Harris, Office Mgr. Students 495.

LAKE OSWEGO, CLACKAMAS CO., OUR LADY OF THE LAKE (1890) [CEM]
650 A Ave., Lake Oswego, 97034-2943.
Tel: 503-636-7687; Fax: 503-636-9415; Email: office@ollparish.com; Web: www.ollparish.com. Revs. John W. Kerns; Gregg Bronsema; Deacon Kevin Welch; Mr. Boras Georgeann, Pastoral/Admin. Asst.
School—Our Lady of the Lake Catholic School, (Grades K-8), Tel: 503-636-2121; Email: office@ollschool-lakeoswego.org. Corrine Buich, Prin. Administrators 2; Lay Teachers 16; Students 227.
Catechesis Religious Program—Email: laurap@ollparish.com; Email: georgeannb@ollparish.com. Laura Patton, D.R.E.; Mr. Georgeann Boras, Pastoral/Admin. Asst. Students 305.

LEBANON, LINN CO., ST. EDWARD (1903)
Office: 100 Main St., Lebanon, 97355.
Tel: 541-258-5333; Fax: 541-258-2511; Email: stedwardslebanon@comcast.net. Rev. Peter O'Brien; Deacon Richard E. Triska.
Res.: 67 Oakway Pl., Lebanon, 97355.
Catechesis Religious Program—Tel: 541-258-2224. Students 109.

LINCOLN CITY, LINCOLN CO., ST. AUGUSTINE (1925) [CEM]
1139 N.W. Hwy. 101, Lincoln City, 97367.
Tel: 541-994-2216; Fax: 541-994-6554; Email: staugustinechurch@lincolncitycoast.com; Web: www.staugustinelincolncity.com. 1151 N.W. Inlet Ave., Lincoln City, 97367. Rev. Joseph Sebasty.
Catechesis Religious Program—Students 27.

MCMINNVILLE, YAMHILL CO., ST. JAMES (1876) [CEM]
1145 N.E. First St., McMinnville, 97128.
Tel: 503-472-5232; Fax: 503-472-4414; Email: churchoffice@stjamesmac.com; Web: stjamesmac.com. Revs. Mike Walker; Zani Pacanza; Deacon Raul Rodriguez, Pastoral Assoc.
School—St. James School, (Grades PreK-5), 206 N.E. Kirby St., McMinnville, 97128. Tel: 503-472-2661; Fax: 503-472-5201; Email: schooloffice@stjamesmac.com. Sally Breidwell, Librarian. Lay Teachers 10; Students 82; Clergy / Religious Teachers 3.
Catechesis Religious Program—Email: earellano@stjamesmac.com. Engracia Arellano, D.R.E. Students 271.

MEDFORD, JACKSON CO., SACRED HEART OF JESUS (1928) [JC]
517 W. Tenth St., Medford, 97501. Tel: 541-779-4661. Revs. Kenneth Sampson; Moises Kumulmac; Deacons Ron Filardi; Dennis Macey.
School—Sacred Heart School, (Grades PreSchool-8), 431 S. Ivy, Medford, 97501. Tel: 541-772-4105; Fax: 541-732-0633; Email: ljones@shcs.org; Web: www.shcs.org. Leslie Jones, Prin.; Terry Fry, Bus. Mgr. Lay Teachers 16; Students 192.
Mission—St. Joseph, 280 N. 4th, Jacksonville, Jackson Co. 97530.
Catechesis Religious Program—Ms. Brenda Woodburn, Dir. of Admin. Students 300.

MILWAUKIE, CLACKAMAS CO.
1—CHRIST THE KING (1961)
7414 S.E. Michael Dr., Milwaukie, 97222.
Tel: 503-659-1475; Web: www.ctk.cc. Rev. John Cihak.
School—Christ the King School, (Grades K-8), 7414 S.E. Michael Dr., Milwaukie, 97222.
Tel: 503-785-2411; Email: office@ctk.pvt.k12.or.us; Web: www.ctkweb.org. Dr. Patrick Jefferies, Prin.; Mrs. Christina Baker, Librarian. Lay Teachers 15; Students 244.
Catechesis Religious Program—Tel: 503-785-2413; Email: re@ctk.cc. Stacey Pinder, D.R.E. Students 92.
2—ST. JOHN THE BAPTIST (1912)
10955 S.E. 25th, Milwaukie, 97222.
Tel: 503-654-5449; Email: parishoffice@sjbcatholicchurch.org; Email: frjorge@sjbcatholicchurch.org; Web: sjbcatholicchurch.org. Revs. Jorge Hernandez, O.F.M.; Richard Juzix, O.F.M., Parochial Vicar; Ms. Mary Jenck, Sec.; Ms. Kim Zea, Pastoral Assoc.
School—St. John the Baptist School, (Grades PreSchool-8), 10956 S.E. 25th, Milwaukie, 97222.
Tel: 503-654-0200; Fax: 503-654-8419; Email: lsilva@sjbcatholicschool.org; Web: www.sjbcatholicschool.org. Dr. Angie Gomez, Prin.; Cheryl Biehl, Librarian. Lay Teachers 15; Students 172; Clergy / Religious Teachers 1.
Catechesis Religious Program—Tel: 503-659-2760; Email: jcrenshaw@sjbcatholicchurch.org. Jessica Crenshaw, D.R.E. Students 115.

MOLALLA, CLACKAMAS CO., ST. JAMES (1938)
301 Frances St., Molalla, 97038. Tel: 503-829-2080; Fax: 503-829-2806; Email: st_james@molalla.net; Email: mserrano@archdpdx.org; Email: mgardner@archdpdx.org; Web: www.stjamesmolalla.org. Rev. Aniceto Guiriba; Mr. Miguel Serrano, Pastoral Asst.; Charles Gardner, Admin. Asst.
Catechesis Religious Program—Email: stjamesmolalla957@gmail.com. Students 159.

MONROE, BENTON CO., ST. ROSE OF LIMA (1883) [CEM]
470 S. 5th St., Monroe, 97456. Tel: 541-998-8053; Fax: 541-998-9474; Email: parishesofsthelenandstrose@gmail.com; Web: strosesthelen.org. Mailing Address & Office: 1350 W. 6th Ave., Junction City, 97448. Revs. Edgar Rivera Torres, Admin.; John Arcidiacono, Admin.
Catechesis Religious Program—Students 10.

MOUNT ANGEL, MARION CO., ST. MARY (1881) [CEM 2] (German)
575 E. College St., Mount Angel, 97362.
Tel: 503-845-2296; Web: www.stmarymtangel.org. Rev. Philip Waibel, O.S.B.
Catechesis Religious Program—Tel: 503-845-4282; Email: bwagner@archdpdx.org. Bernadette Wagner, D.R.E. Students 325.
Mission—Holy Rosary, [CEM] Scotts Mills, Marion Co.

MYRTLE CREEK, DOUGLAS CO., ALL SOULS CATHOLIC CHURCH (1952) [JC]
1242 N.E. Spruce St., P.O. Box 810, Myrtle Creek, 97457. Tel: 541-863-3271; Email: allsoulsparish@gmail.com; Email: kschray@gmail.com. Rev. Karl Schray, Admin., (Retired).
Catechesis Religious Program—Students 36.
Mission—Holy Family, 243 Marshall Ave., P.O. Box 136, Glendale, Douglas Co. 97442.

NEWBERG, YAMHILL CO., ST. PETER (1907)
2315 N. Main, Newberg, 97132-6081.
Tel: 503-538-4312; Fax: 503-538-5693; Email: stpeter.office@frontier.com; Web: stpeternewbergor.org. Rev. Martin Tavares, Admin.; Deacon Jose Montoya, Hispanic Coord.; Ms. Nancy Gooden, Business Mgr.
Catechesis Religious Program—Email: shellydidway@gmail.com. Shelly Didway, D.R.E. Students 143.

NEWPORT, LINCOLN CO., SACRED HEART PARISH (1889) [JC]
927 N. Coast Hwy., P.O. Box 843, Newport, 97365.
Tel: 541-265-5101; Email: office@sacredheartnewport.com. Rev. William E. Palmer.
Rectory—140 N.W. 10th St., Newport, 97365.
Mission—Our Lady of Guadalupe, 231 E. Logsden Rd., Siletz, Lincoln Co. 97380. Tel: 541-444-1164.
Catechesis Religious Program—Email: scramer@archdpdx.org. Sandy Cramer, D.R.E.; Ms. Rose English, Admin. Asst. Students 128.

NORTH BEND, COOS CO., HOLY REDEEMER (1906) [JC]
2250 16th St., North Bend, 97459. Tel: 541-756-0633; Email: businessoffice@holyredeemernb.org; Email: Parishoffice@holyredeemernb.org; Web: holyredeemerbn.org. Revs. James D. Graham; Henry Rufo, Parochial Vicar; Ms. Susan Uehara, Business Mgr.
Catechesis Religious Program—Tel: 541-756-0161; Email: religious.ed@holyredeemernb.org. James DeLong, D.R.E. Students 63.

NORTH PLAINS, WASHINGTON CO., ST. EDWARD (1913) [CEM]
10990 N.W. 313th Ave., P.O. Box 507, North Plains, 97133. Tel: 503-647-2131; Email: mail@stedwardnp.org; Email: mvuky@yahoo.com; Web: www.stedwardnp.org. Rev. Michael Vuky, J.C.L., Admin.
Catechesis Religious Program—Students 20.

OAKRIDGE, LANE CO., ST. MICHAEL CATHOLIC CHURCH (1941)
76387 Crestview St. #422, Oakridge, 97463.
Tel: 541-782-3262; Email: ecoleman@archdpdx.org. Rev. Ed Coleman.
Mission—St. Henry, [JC] 38925 Dexter Rd., P.O. Box 65, Dexter, Lane Co. 97431.
Catechesis Religious Program—

OREGON CITY, CLACKAMAS CO., ST. JOHN THE APOSTLE (1842) [CEM]
417 Washington St., Oregon City, 97045.
Tel: 503-742-8200; Email: office@sja-catholicchurch.com; Web: www.sja-catholicchurch.com. Rev. Maxy D'Costa, S.F.X.
School—St. John the Apostle School, (Grades PreSchool-8), Tel: 503-742-8230; Email: office@sja-eagles.com; Web: sja_eagles.com. Lay Teachers 14; Students 190; Clergy / Religious Teachers 8.
Catechesis Religious Program—Tel: 503-742-8228; Email: religious-ed@sja-catholicchurch.com. Elizabeth Link, D.R.E.; Ms. Felix Barba, Admin. Asst. Students 135.

OREGON CITY-REDLAND, CLACKAMAS CO., ST. PHILIP BENIZI (1966)
18211 S. Henrici Rd., Oregon City, 97045.
Tel: 503-631-2882; Fax: 503-631-7443; Email: stphilipbenizi_redland@archpdx.org; Email: mpattyn@archdpdx.org; Web: www.philipbenizi.com. Rev. Paschal Ezurike, Admin.; Deacon Jim Pittman; Ms. Sherrie Havens, Sec.
Catechesis Religious Program—Tel: 503-631-7124. Ms. Mary Pattyn, Business Mgr,. Students 47.

RAINIER, COLUMBIA CO., NATIVITY B.V.M. (1910)
204 E. C St., P.O. Box 340, Rainier, 97048.
Tel: 503-556-5641; Email: mgikenyi@archdpdx.org. Rev. Mark O. Gikenyi; Deacon Paul Cramer; Linda Bailey, Business Mgr.
Catechesis Religious Program—Students 11.
Mission—St. John the Baptist (1917) 100 High St., Clatskanie, Columbia Co. 97016.

REEDSPORT, DOUGLAS CO., ST. JOHN THE APOSTLE (1924)
12 St. John's Way, P.O. Box 207, Reedsport, 97467.
Tel: 541-271-5621; Tel: 541-997-2312; Email: pansel@ourladyofthedunes.org; Email: nervin@archdpdx.org; Email: pansel@questoffice.net; Web: ourladyofthedunes.org. Rev. Panneer Selvam; Mrs. Patricia Horning, Business Mgr.; Mrs. Nancy Lane, Sec.
Catechesis Religious Program—Students 3.

ROCKAWAY, TILLAMOOK CO., ST. MARY BY THE SEA (1927) [JC]
275 S. Pacific St, P.O. Box 390, Rockaway, 97136.
Tel: 503-355-2661; Email: stmarys1927@gmail.com. Rev. Laurence L. Gooley, S.J.

ROSEBURG, DOUGLAS CO., ST. JOSEPH (1867) [CEM]
800 W. Stanton St., Roseburg, 97471.

Tel: 541-673-5157; Email: jcampos@archdpdx.org; Email: pschulze@archdpdx.org; Web: sjfx-church.org. Revs. Jose Campos-Garcia; Cletus Osuji, Mercy Medical Center Chap.; Ms. Pauline Schulze, Business/ Parish Admin.
Rectory—2425 W. Military Rd., Roseburg, 97471.
Catechesis Religious Program—Email: pschulze@qwestoffice.net. Lourdes Clyde, D.R.E. Students 167.

ROY, WASHINGTON CO., ST. FRANCIS OF ASSISI (1908) [CEM]
39135 N.W. Harrington Rd., Banks, 97106.
Tel: 503-324-2231; Fax: 503-324-7032. Rev. Michael Vuky, J.C.L.
School—St. Francis of Assisi School, (Grades K-8), 39085 N.W. Harrington Rd., Banks, 97106.
Tel: 503-324-2182; Fax: 503-324-7032; Email: sfa.royschool@gmail.com. Lay Teachers 5; Students 86; Clergy / Religious Teachers 1.
Catechesis Religious Program—Students 6.

ST. HELENS, COLUMBIA CO., ST. FREDERIC (1910)
175 S. 13th St., St. Helens, 97051. Tel: 503-397-0148; Fax: 503-366-3870; Email: stfred@comcast.net; Web: stfredericchurch.org. Rev. Nicolaus Marandu, A.L.C.P.

ST. LOUIS, MARION CO., ST. LOUIS, Closed. For sacramental records contact Sacred Heart-St. Louis, Gervias.

ST. PAUL, MARION CO., ST. PAUL (1839) [CEM 2]
20217 Christie St., N.E., P.O. Box 454, St. Paul, 97137. Tel: 503-633-4611; Email: stpaulparish@stpaultel.com. Rev. Msgr. Gregory Moys.
School—St. Paul School, (Grades PreK-8), 20327 Christie St., N.E., P.O. Box 188, St. Paul, 97137.
Tel: 503-633-4622; Fax: 503-633-4624; Email: office@saintpaulparochial.org; Web: www.saintpaulparochial.org. Amanda Davidson, Prin. Lay Teachers 6; Students 85.
Catechesis Religious Program—Students 21.

SALEM, MARION CO.
1—ST. JOSEPH (1864) [JC]
721 Chemeketa St., N.E., Salem, 97301.
Tel: 503-581-1623; Fax: 503-581-7271; Email: jennifer@stjosephchurch.com; Email: frontdesk@stjosephchurch.com; Web: www.stjosephchurch.com. Rev. Msgr. Richard Huneger; Revs. Paolo Dayto, Parochial Vicar; Jonah Lynch, Parochial Vicar.
School—St. Joseph School, (Grades PreK-8), 373 Winter St., N.E., Salem, 97301. Tel: 503-581-2147; Fax: 503-399-7045; Email: school@stjosephchurch.com; Web: www.stjoseph.com/school. Michelle Bartholomew, Admin.; Mrs. Deb Dewar, Prin. Lay Teachers 10; Students 178; Clergy / Religious Teachers 1.
Catechesis Religious Program—Tel: 503-585-5095; Email: re@stjosephchurch.com. Isabelle Rico. Students 422.
Mission—Sunday Spanish Off-Campus Mass, East Salem Community Center, 1850 45th Ave., N.E., Salem, 97305.

2—QUEEN OF PEACE (1963)
4227 Lone Oak Rd. SE, Salem, 97302.
Tel: 503-364-7202; Email: church@qpsalem.org; Web: qpsalem.org. Rev. Timothy J. Mockaitis; Debbie Davis, Pastoral Asst.; Michelle Unger, Children's Min.
School—Queen of Peace School, (Grades PreSchool-5), 4227 Lone Oak Rd., S.E., P.O. Box 3696, Salem, 97302. Tel: 503-362-3443; Fax: 503-589-9411; Email: school@qpsalem.org; Web: qpschool.org. Carl Mucken, Prin.; Mr. Karon Willburn, Admin. Asst. Lay Teachers 12; Students 127.
Catechesis Religious Program—Michelle Unger, D.R.E.; Cheri Posedel, Youth Ministry Coord., D.R.E. (Grades 6-12); Eddie Caudel, Coord. Faith Formation. Students 245.

3—ST. VINCENT DE PAUL (1925) [JC]
1010 Columbia St. N.E., Salem, 97301.
Tel: 503-363-4589; Email: stvdp@questoffice.net; Email: office@svdpchurchsalem.org. P.O. Box 7548, Salem, 97303-0155. Revs. Joseph Heuberger; Fredy Bonilla-Moreno, Parochial Vicar; Deacon Jose Roman Mendez; Sr. Maria Guadalupe Carrillo, Pastoral Assoc.
School—St. Vincent de Paul School, (Grades PreK-6), 1015 Columbia St., N.E., Salem, 97301.
Tel: 503-363-8457; Fax: 503-363-1516; Web: www.stvincentsalem.org. David Spink, Librarian. Lay Teachers 4; Students 90.
Catechesis Religious Program—1010 Columbia St. N.E., Salem, 97301-7207. Sheila Machado, D.R.E.; Lisa Mangers, Youth Min., (Young Adults). Students 483.

SANDY, CLACKAMAS CO., ST. MICHAEL THE ARCHANGEL (1898)
18090 S.E. Langensand Rd., Sandy, 97055-9427.
Tel: 503-668-4446; Email: gbronsema@stmichaelsandy.org; Web: www.stmichaelsandy.org. Rev. Gregg Bronsema; Ms. Tammy Pagano, Pastoral Assoc.
Catechesis Religious Program—Tel: 503-228-8629; Email: pastoralassociate@stmichaelportland.org. Deacon Chuck Amsberry, D.R.E. Students 75.
Mission—St. John the Evangelist, Email: tpagano@stmichaelsandy.org.

SCAPPOOSE, COLUMBIA CO., ST. WENCESLAUS (1911) [CEM]
51555 Old Portland Rd., Scappoose, 97056.
Tel: 503-543-2110, Ext. 201; Email: office@stwenceslaus-scappoose.com. Rev. Charles A. Wood; Ms. Janell Greisen, Office Mgr.
Catechesis Religious Program—Tel: 503-543-7425; Fax: 503-543-5159. Students 95.

SCIO, LINN CO., ST. BERNARD (1912)
Mailing Address: P.O. Box 45, Scio, 97374.
Tel: 503-394-2625; Email: pobrien@archdpdx.org. 38810 Cherry St., Scio, 97374. Rev. Peter O'Brien.
Catechesis Religious Program—Tel: 503-394-2848. James Brown, D.R.E. at St. Bernard.
Mission—St. Thomas, 647 Third St., P.O. Box 928, Jefferson, Marion Co. 97352.

SEASIDE, CLATSOP CO., OUR LADY OF VICTORY (1900)
120 Oceanway St., P.O. Box 29, Seaside, 97138.
Tel: 503-738-6616; Cell: 503-717-2952; Email: olvoffice@archdpdx.org; Web: www.ourladyofvictoryseaside.org. Rev. Joseph Barita, A.L.C.P./O.S.S.
Mission—St. Peter the Fisherman, 79441 Hwy. 101 S., Arch Cape, 97102. Tel: 503-436-2876.
Catechesis Religious Program—Mr. Joseph Salazar, Family Rel. Educ. Coord. Students 92.

SHADY COVE, JACKSON CO., OUR LADY OF FATIMA (1955)
56 Williams Ln., P.O. Box 116, Shady Cove, 97539.
Tel: 541-878-2479; Email: cholden@archdpdx.org; Web: www.fatimacatholic.org. Rev. Charles E. Holden.
Office: 37 Church Ln., Shady Cove, 97539.
Catechesis Religious Program—Ms. Connie Snider, D.R.E. Students 6.

SHAW, MARION CO., ST. MARY - SHAW (1906) [CEM]
9168 Silver Falls Hwy., P.O. Box 338, Aumsville, 97325-0338. Tel: 503-362-6159; Tel: 503-769-2656; Fax: 503-371-6435; Email: bonipast@wvi.com; Email: kmcnulty@qwestoffice.net. Revs. Paul Materu, A.L.C.P.; Richard Rossman, In Res., (Retired); Ms. Kathy McNulty, Admin. Asst.
Catechesis Religious Program—Students 10.

SHERIDAN, YAMHILL CO., GOOD SHEPHERD (1908)
127 N.E. Hill St., Sheridan, 97378. Tel: 503-472-5232 ; Email: churchoffice@stjamesmac.com; Web: stjamesmac.com/goodshepherd. 1145 N.E. 1st St., McMinnville, 97128-6064. Rev. Mike Walker; Deacon David J. Briedwell, Pastoral Admin.
Catechesis Religious Program—Marie Scett, D.R.E. Students 20.

SHERWOOD, WASHINGTON CO., ST. FRANCIS (1921)
15651 S.W. Oregon St., Sherwood, 97140.
Tel: 503-625-6185; Email: church@stfrancissherwood.org; Email: bill@stfrancissherwood.org; Web: www.stfrancissherwood.org. Rev. James Herrera; Deacon Bill Bloudek.
Res.: 22942 S.W. Pine St., Sherwood, 97140.
School—St. Francis School, (Grades K-8), 15643 S.W. Oregon St., Sherwood, 97140.
Tel: 503-625-0497; Email: gretchen.brown@stfrancissherwoodschool.org; Web: stfrancissherwoodschool.org. Gretchen Brown, Sec. Lay Teachers 13; Students 135.
Catechesis Religious Program—Tel: 503-625-6187. Students 143.

SILVERTON, MARION CO., ST. PAUL (1914) [CEM]
1410 Pine St., Silverton, 97381. Tel: 503-873-3114; Email: jaker@stpaulsilverton.com; Email: office@stpaulsilverton.com; Web: stpaulsilverton.com. Rev. Basil Lawrence, O.S.B.
Catechesis Religious Program—Ms. Jennifer Aker, Sec./Admin. Asst. Students 144.

SPRINGFIELD, LANE CO., ST. ALICE (1947)
1520 E St., Springfield, 97477-4161.
Tel: 541-747-7041, Ext. 210; Email: pries@archdpdx.org; Web: stalice.org. Rev. Mark A. Bentz.
Catechesis Religious Program—Mr. Fernando Rivas, D.R.E. Students 89.

STAYTON, MARION CO., IMMACULATE CONCEPTION (1903) [CEM]
1077 N. Sixth Ave., Stayton, 97383.
Tel: 503-769-2656; Email: pastor@immacstayton.org. Rev. Luan D. Nguyen.
Res.: 1035 N. Sixth Ave., Stayton, 97383. Email: sec@immacstayton.org.
Catechesis Religious Program—Email: gschmitt@archdpdx.org. Students 83.
Mission—St. Catherine of Siena, 716 S First Ave., Mill City, 97360.

SUBLIMITY, MARION CO., ST. BONIFACE (1879) [CEM]
375 S.E. Church St., Sublimity, 97385.
Tel: 503-769-5664; Fax: 503-769-4292; Email: bonipast@wvi.com; Email: boniface@wvi.com. Rev. Paul Materu, A.L.C.P.
Catechesis Religious Program—Email: bonirel@wvi.com. Bernadette Kintz, D.R.E. Students 67.

SUTHERLIN, DOUGLAS CO., ST. FRANCIS XAVIER (1957)
323 N. Comstock Ave., Sutherlin, 97479.
Tel: 541-673-5157; Fax: 541-672-5022; Email: pschulze@archdpdx.org; Email: jcampos@archdpdx.org; Web: sjfx-church.org. Revs. Jose Manuel Campos-Garcia; Cletus Osuji, Mercy Medical Center Chap.

SWEET HOME, LINN CO., ST. HELEN CATHOLIC CHURCH (1953) [JC]
600 Sixth Ave., Sweet Home, 97386.
Tel: 541-367-2530; Email: sthelenholytrinitysho@centurtel.net. Mailing Address: 815 5th Ave., Sweet Home, 97386. Rev. Fred Jeffrey Anthony; Deacon Robert Malone.
Catechesis Religious Program—Ms. Nancy Ellis, Pastoral Assoc. Students 27.
Mission—Holy Trinity, 104 Blakely Ave., P.O. Box 145, Brownsville, Linn Co. 97327.

TIGARD, WASHINGTON CO., ST. ANTHONY (1878) [CEM]
Mailing Address: 9905 S.W. McKenzie St., Tigard, 97223. Tel: 503-639-4179, Ext. 112; Email: jhenderson@satigard.org. Revs. John Henderson; Scott Baier, Parochial Vicar; Deacons Marco Espinoza, Dir. of Hispanic Min.; Dave Hammes.
Res.: 8391 SW Arthur Ct., Tigard, 97223.
Tel: 503-639-4179, Ext. 112; Email: jhenderson@satigard.org; Web: www.satigard.org.
School—St. Anthony School, (Grades PreK-8), 12645 S.W. Pacific Hwy., Tigard, 97223. Tel: 503-639-4179; Fax: 503-620-5117; Email: school@satigard.org. Andrew Nichols, Prin.; Julie Stump, Librarian. Lay Teachers 25; Students 333.
Catechesis Religious Program—Students 476.
Mission—Mission of the Atonement, 7400 S.W. Scholls Ferry Rd., Beaverton, Washington Co. 97008.

TILLAMOOK, TILLAMOOK CO., SACRED HEART (1890) [CEM]
2410 Fifth St., Tillamook, 97141. Tel: 503-842-6647; Fax: 503-842-3897; Email: sacredheart2405@gmail.com; Web: www.tillamooksacredheart.org. Rev. Amal Irudayaraj.
Catechesis Religious Program—2411 Fifth St., Tillamook, 97141. Tel: 503-842-6647, Ext. 23. Patrick Matthews, D.R.E.; Ms. Anna Orta, Sec. Students 77.
Mission—St. Joseph, 34560 Parkway Dr., Cloverdale, Tillamook Co. 97112.

TUALATIN, CLACKAMAS CO., RESURRECTION CATHOLIC CHURCH (1981)
21060 S.W. Stafford Rd., Tualatin, 97062.
Tel: 503-638-1579; Fax: 503-638-8754; Email: office@rcparish.org; Web: www.rcparish.org. Rev. William C. Moisant; Anna Arnesen Mosey, Pastoral Assoc.; Ms. Maya Bashoury, Business Mgr.
Catechesis Religious Program—Email: mbashoury@rcparish.org. Students 200.

VENETA, LANE CO., ST. CATHERINE OF SIENA (1954)
25181 E. Broadway Ave., P.O. Box 277, Veneta, 97487-0277. Tel: 541-935-3933; Tel: 541-505-2190; Email: StCofSienaVeneta@aol.com; Email: tlange@archdpdx.org; Web: www.StCVeneta.com. Rev. Theodore Lange; Ms. Deanna Valenzuela, Pastoral Assoc.
Catechesis Religious Program—Students 25.

VERBOORT, WASHINGTON CO., VISITATION B.V.M. (1875) [CEM] (Dutch)
4285 N.W. Visitation Rd., Forest Grove, 97116.
Tel: 503-357-6990; Tel: 503-575-5608; Email: bookkeeper@vcsknights.org; Email: churchsecretary@vcsknights.org; Web: verboort.org. Rev. Michael Vuky, J.C.L.; Ms. Laura Nevis, Parish/ Pastoral Admin. Asst.
School—Visitation B.V.M. School, (Grades PreK-8), 4189 N.W. Visitation Rd., Forest Grove, 97116.
Tel: 503-357-6990; Email: churchsecretary@vcsknights.org. Carol Funk, Prin.; Lisa McMullen, Sec. Lay Teachers 10; Students 194.
Catechesis Religious Program—Students 79.

VERNONIA, COLUMBIA CO., ST. MARY OF IMMACULATE CONCEPTION (1923)
960 Missouri Ave., P.O. Box 312, Vernonia, 97064.
Tel: 503-429-8841; Email: maryscatholicchurch@frontier.com. Rev. Joshua Clifton, Admin.
Catechesis Religious Program—Tel: 503-429-8092. Students 21.

WALDPORT, LINCOLN CO., ST. ANTHONY (1949)
685 N. Broadway, P.O. Box 770, Waldport, 97394.
Tel: 541-563-3246; Fax: 541-563-3734; Email: stanthony@peak.org; Web: www.stanthonywaldport.org. Rev. Joseph Hoang.
Catechesis Religious Program—Students 4.

WILSONVILLE, CLACKAMAS CO., ST. CYRIL (1926)
9205 S.W. Fifth St., Wilsonville, 97070.
Tel: 503-682-2332; Fax: 503-685-9294; Web: www.stcyrilparish.org. Rev. Brian V. Allbright.
Catechesis Religious Program—Students 51.

WOODBURN, MARION CO., ST. LUKE (1899) [CEM]

417 Harrison St., Woodburn, 97071.
Tel: 503-981-5011; Email: STLUKECH@WBCABLE.NET; Email: sbaier@archdpdx.org; Web: www.stlukewoodburn.org. Rev. James J. Coleman.
School—St. Luke School, (Grades PreK-8), 529 Harrison St., Woodburn, 97071. Tel: 503-981-7441; Fax: 503-982-4697; Email: office@stlukeschoolwoodburn.org; Web: www.stlukeschoolwoodburn.org. Lay Teachers 10; Students 164.
Catechesis Religious Program—Students 360.
Mission—St. Agnes, 3052 D St., Hubbard, Marion Co. 97032.

YAMHILL, YAMHILL CO., ST. JOHN THE EVANGELIST (1911)
445 N. Maple St., P.O. Box 580, Yamhill, 97148.
Tel: 503-662-4291; Fax: 503-662-0047; Email: st.johnyamhill@gmail.com; Email: mleal@archdpdx.org; Email: bluengas@archdpdx.org; Web: stjohnyamhill.org. Rev. Moises Leal Gonzalez, Admin.
Catechesis Religious Program—Brisa Luengas, D.R.E. Students 20.

SOUTHEAST ASIAN VICARIATE

PORTLAND, MULTNOMAH CO., SOUTHEAST ASIAN VICARIATE (1982) Please refer to Our Lady of Lavang Church, Portland, OR.
Our Lady of LaVang: 5404 N.E. Alameda Dr., 97213.
Tel: 503-249-5892; Email: apham@archdpdx.org; Web: www.gxlavangoregon.com. Rev. Ansgar Pham.
Catechesis Religious Program—Students 924.

Chaplains of Public Institutions

PORTLAND. *Department of Veterans' Affairs Medical Center*, 3710 S.W. U.S. Veterans' Hospital Rd., Box 1034, 97207. Tel: 503-220-8262, Ext. 57027;
Tel: 503-220-8262, Ext. 57201; Fax: 503-721-7819.
Oregon Health Sciences University, 3181 S.W. Sam Jackson Park Rd., 97239. Tel: 503-222-2168. Rev. James M. Kolb, C.S.P., Tel: 503-222-2168.

EUGENE. *Lane County Adult Corrections*, 101 W. Fifth Ave., Eugene, 97401. Tel: 541-682-2174;
Fax: 541-682-2278.

NORTH BEND. *Shutter Creek Correctional Institution*, 95200 Shutters Landing Ln., North Bend, 97459-0303. Tel: 541-756-6666; Fax: 541-756-6888.

ROSEBURG. *U.S. Veterans' Administration Hospital*, 913 N.W. Garden Valley Blvd., Roseburg, 97470-6513. Tel: 541-440-1000.

SALEM. *Mill Creek Correctional Facility*, 5465 Turner Rd. S.E., Salem, 97317. Tel: 503-378-2601. Rev. Msgr. Richard Huneger.
Oregon State Correctional Institution, 3405 Deer Park Dr., S.E., Salem, 97310. Tel: 503-373-0100. Rev. Msgr. Richard Huneger.
Oregon State Penitentiary, 2605 State St., Salem, 97310. Tel: 503-373-1673. Rev. Msgr. Richard Huneger.
Santiam Correctional Institution, 4005 Aumsville Hwy., S.E., Salem, 97301-9112. Tel: 503-378-2144. Rev. Msgr. Richard Huneger.

SHERIDAN. *Federal Correctional Institution*, 27072 Ballston Rd., Sheridan, 97378-9601.
Tel: 503-843-6357. Revs. Moises Leal, Zani Pacanza, Martin Tavares, Michael WalkerServed by volunteers from local parishes; St. James Parish, McMinnville.

WHITE CITY. *U.S. Veterans Affairs Domiciliary*, 8495 Crater Lake Hwy., White City, 97503.
Tel: 541-826-2111, Ext. 3321; Tel: 800-809-8725; Email: felix.vistal@va.gov. Rev. Felix Vistal, Chap.

WILSONVILLE. *Coffee Creek Correctional Facility*, 24499 S.W. Grahams Ferry Rd., Wilsonville, 97070.
Tel: 503-570-6604; Fax: 503-570-6617. Served by St. Cyril Parish, Wilsonville.

WOODBURN. *MacLaren Youth Correctional Facility*, 2630 N. Pacific Hwy., Woodburn, 97071.
Tel: 503-981-9531, Ext. 315; Fax: 503-982-4414. Served by St. Luke Parish, Woodburn.

Special Assignment:
Revs.—
Carey, Raymond, P.O. Box 3019, Salem, 97302
Kueber, Michael I., 215 8th St., Minneapolis, MN 55402.

Absent on Leave:
Revs.—
Hoang, Petrus Binh
Patrick, Michael, J.C.L.
Stobie, Stephen A.
Te, Angelo
Thomas, Andrew R.

Retired:
Rev. Msgrs.—
Buxman, Donald, (Retired)
Dernbach, Arthur, (Retired), Maryville Nursing Home, 14645 S.W, Farmington Rd., Beaverton, 97007
O'Donovan, Dennis, (Retired)
Pham, James Ninh Van, (Retired), 12510 N.E. Beech St., 97230
Revs.—
Betts, John C., (Retired), P.O. Box 3177, Albany, 97321
Bliven, Edmond, (Retired), 9347 SW 35th, 97219
Brouillard, John, (Retired), 17704 Shady Fir Loop, Beaverton, 97006-8204
Chun, Francis, (Retired), 4525-B S.W. St. John Vianney Way, Beaverton, 97078
Cullings, David Ronald, (Retired), 638 Wimbleton Ct., Eugene, 97401
Cunniff, Vincent, (Retired), 4525-D S.W. St. John Vianney Way, Beaverton, 97078
Dieringer, James J., (Retired), P.O. Box 683, Pacific City, 97135
Dowd, James, (Retired), 1875 N. Country Club Dr., Canby, 97013-2349
Durand, Donald, (Retired), 62 N.W. Ava Ave., Gresham, 97030
Fister, Stephen J., (Retired), P.O. Box 310, Gold Hill, 97525
Frison, Theodore, (Retired), 4843 S.E. 30th Ave., #38, 97202
Galluzzo, James, (Retired), 1314 N.W. Irving, #512, 97209
Hume, Kenneth, (Retired), 19453 Stillmeadow Dr., Oregon City, 97045
Jacobson, Gary, (Retired), 1400 N.E. 2nd Ave., Apt. 1118, 97232
Janes, David, (Retired), 90971 Hwy. 101, #74, Warrenton, 97146
Knusel, Frank, (Retired), 34799 N. Honeyman Rd., Scappoose, 97056
Krueger, Robert, (Retired), 3825 SE 8th Ave., Apt. 120, 97206-2378
Lau, Michael, (Retired), 2838 E Burnside St., 97214-1895
Layton, Thomas Michael, (Retired), 516 Kenosia Ave. S, #A-207, Kent, WA 98030-5909
Mayo, James, (Retired), 4655-D SW St. John Vianney Way, Beaverton, 97078
McGrann, John, (Retired), 336 S.E. 50th Ave., #1, 97215
McGuire, John F., (Retired), 7145 Park Valley Ct., Reno, NV 89523-7710
McMahon, Joseph S., (Retired), 3040 N. Hunt St., 97217
McNamee, Patrick, (Retired), 4630 SW St. John Vianney Way, APt. A, Beaverton, 97078-7743
McProud, Bryce, (Retired), 360 Loretta Way, Eugene, 97404
Moore, Neil, (Retired), 1619 N.W. Bridgeway Ln., Beaverton, 97006
Mosbrucker, Jacob A., (Retired), 3828 N.E. 79th St., 97213
Nguyen, Joseph Hau Duc, (Retired), 5404 N.E. Alameda Dr., 97213
Olsen, Kenneth, (Retired), 1480 Walnut Rd., Springfield, 97477
Peri, Paul, (Retired), 5124 N. 31st Pl. #518, Phoenix, AZ 85016
Quintal, Gerald, (Retired), P.O. Box 9, Cloverdale, 97112
Remington, Leo, (Retired), 8012 N. Interstate Ave., 97217
Rodrigues, Amancio J., (Retired), 53 S.E. 171st Ave., 97233
Rossman, Richard, (Retired), P.O. Box 338, Aumsville, 97325
Sassano, Rock, (Retired), 4655-C SW St. John Vianney Way, Beaverton, 97078
Sieg, Leslie, (Retired), 7454 S.W. Cascara Dr., Gaston, 97119
Sirianni, Richard, (Retired), S.W. St. John Vianney Dr., 4525-A, Beaverton, 97078
Sprauer, Michael, (Retired), 4598 Beth St., NE, Salem, 97301
Urbanski, Louis, (Retired), 10904 NW 195th St., Hillsboro, 97214
Waddill, Dale T., (Retired), 208 Madison St., Oregon City, 97045-2535
Waldron, John, (Retired), P.O. Box 972, Canby, 97013
Weber, Theodore, (Retired), 9709 SE Causey Way, Happy Valley, 97086
Wheatley, Herbert, (Retired), 1936 S.W. Sunset Blvd., 97239.

Permanent Deacons:
Altenhofen, Tom, (Retired)
Amsberry, Chuck, St. Michael the Archangel, Portland
Anderson, Chris, St. Mary, Corvallis
Appel, Leo, Star of the Sea, Brookings
Bartos, James
Birkel, Rick, (Unassigned)
Bloudek, Bill, St. Francis, Sherwood
Boone, Ken E., (On Leave)
Briedwell, David, Good Shepherd, Sheridan; St. Michael, Grand Ronde
Brinker, Ken, (On Leave)
Broussard, Pete, Holy Redeemer, North Bend
Burke-Sivers, Harold, Immaculate Heart, Portland
Caldwell, Mike, St. Joseph the Worker, Portland
Cervantes, Ricardo, Our Lady of the Mountain, Ashland
Chapin, Bob, St. Anne, Grants Pass
Ciffone, Don, (Retired)
Cihak, Michael, St. Mary, Corvallis
Corey, Charles, (Retired)
Cramer, Paul, Nativity of the Blessed Virgin Mary, Rainier
Cummings, Owen
De Sitter, Lou, St. Henry, Gresham
DeSart, Del, (On Leave)
Desmarais, Dennis, St. Juan Diego, Portland
Diehm, Brian, St. Rose of Lima, Portland
Dooley, Timothy, Holy Family, Portland
Edmonson, Brett, Holy Trinity, Beaverton
Espinoza, Jesus, St. Elizabeth Ann Seton, Aloha
Espinoza, Marco, St. Anthony, Tigard
Filardi, Ron, Sacred Heart, Medford
Fillo, Kevin, (On Leave)
Garcia, Felix
Giger, Jerry, St. Patrick, Canby
Gonzalez, Jose, St. Anne, Gresham
Gornick, Tom, (Retired)
Gutierrez, Jose, St. John the Apostle, Oregon City
Hammes, Dave, St. Anthony, Tigard
Hayward, Tom, Ascension Parish, Portland
Hix, Jim, St. John the Baptist, Milwaukie
Hogan, Roger, Star of the Sea, Brookings
Jacob, Ramon, St. Andrew, Portland
Jimenez, Romeo, St. Andrew, Portland
Kolbet, Scott, St. Mary Cathedral, Portland
Krebsbach, John, St. Anthony Church, Forest Grove
Little, Bob, St. Pius X, Portland
Loumena, Larry, St. Joseph the Worker, Portland
Lukosh, Robert, Holy Redeemer, Portland
Macey, Dennis, Sacred Heart, Medford
Malone, Robert, St. Helen, Sweet Home
McNamara, Bill, St. Clare, Portland
McVeigh, Jim G., (Retired)
Mendez, Jose, (Retired)
Meter, Darrell, St. Mark, Eugene
Montoya, Jose, St. Peter, Newberg
Murdy, Don, St. Mary, Mount Angel
Myers, Jim, (Retired)
Nguyen, Tien, Our Lady of Lavang, Portland
O'Mahoney, Mike, St. Mary Magdalene Parish (The Madeleine), Portland
Page, Bob, St. Patrick, Independence
Pham, Chau, Our Lady of Lavang, Portland; St. Andrew Dung-Lac Mission, Aloha
Pham, Paul, Immaculate Heart, Portland
Pittman, Jim, (Retired)
Potts, Francis, (On Leave)
Rasca, Leo, St. Joseph, Salem
Richardson, Bill, St. Cecilia, Beaverton
Riherd, John, (Retired)
Rilatt, John, Holy Redeemer, Portland
Rodriguez, Raul, St. James, McMinnville; St. Martin de Porres Mission, Dayton
Schmitt, Geoff, Immaculate Conception, Stayton; Our Lady of Lourdes Parish, Jordan; St. Catherine of Siena Mission, Mill City; St. Patrick Mission, Lyons
Soper, Leonard, (Retired)
Sorensen, David, (Retired)
Tabor, Steve, St. Boniface, Sublimity; St. Mary, Shaw
Triska, Richard, St. Edward, Lebanon; St. Bernard, Scio; St. Thomas, Jefferson
Vandecoevering, Allen, St. Joseph, Salem
Vu, An Thanh, (Retired)
Welch, Kevin, Our Lady of the Lake, Lake Oswego
Wilhelm, Greg, St. Paul, Eugene.

INSTITUTIONS LOCATED IN DIOCESE

[A] SEMINARIES AND SCHOLASTICATES

MOUNT ANGEL. *Felix Rougier House of Studies*, 585 E. College St., Mount Angel, 97362. Tel: 503-845-1181; Email: mspsmahos@gmail.com. P.O. Box 499, St. Benedict, 97373. Revs. Juan Pablo Patino, M.Sp.S, Supr.; Alex Rubio, M.Sp.S., Spiritual Dir., Mt. Angel Seminary; Pedro Arteaga, M.Sp.S., Formation Dir. in Mt. Angel Seminary. Priests 4; Students 2.

ST. BENEDICT. *Mount Angel Seminary*, Office of the Rector, 1 Abbey Dr., St. Benedict, 97373.
Tel: 503-845-3951; Fax: 503-845-3128; Email: seminaryinfo@mtangel.edu; Web: www.mountangelabbey.org/seminary/. Rev. Msgr. Joseph V. Betschart, Pres.-Rector; Revs. Terrence P. Tompkins, Vice Rector; Stephen Clovis, Vice Pres. for Administration & Dir. Human Formation; Ralph Recker, O.S.B., Dir., Student Svcs.; Marina Keys, Registrar; Revs. William Dillard, Dir. of Spiritual Formation; Teresio Caldwell, O.S.B., Dir., Admissions; Dr. Shawn Keough, Vice Pres of Academics & Academic Dean. Brothers 2; Deacons 1; Lay Teachers 20; Priests 15; Sisters 1; Students 170; Permanent Staff 6.
Formation Directors: Rt. Rev. Peter Eberle, O.S.B., (Retired); Revs. Peter Arteaga, M.Sp.S., Dir. Pastoral Formation; Ralph Recker, O.S.B.; Terrence P. Tompkins; Teresio Caldwell, O.S.B.; Ms. Victoria Ertelt, Librarian.

[B] COLLEGES AND UNIVERSITIES

PORTLAND. **University of Portland*, (Grades Bachelors-Masters), 5408 N. Strong St., 97203.
Tel: 503-943-7101; Tel: 503-943-8000; Email: admissions@up.edu; Email: president@up.edu; Web: www.up.edu. Rev. Mark Poorman, C.S.C., Pres. Endowed by the Congregation of Holy Cross; established 1901. Brothers 2; Religious Teachers 17; Lay Teachers 254; Priests 16; Sisters 3; Students 4,000; Adjunct Faculty 250.
Executive Officers of the University: Dr. Thomas G. Greene, Provost; Rev. Mark Poorman, C.S.C., Pres.; Laurie Kelley, Vice Pres. Univ. Rels.; Alan P. Timmins, Vice Pres. Fin. Affairs; James Ravelli, Vice Pres., Univ. Opers.; Kaley McCauley, Admin. Asst., CSC Office.
Faculty Staff: Revs. Jeffrey Allison, C.S.C.; Robert Antonelli, C.S.C., (Retired); Jeffrey Cooper, C.S.C.; John Donato, C.S.C., Assoc. Vice Pres. Student Life; Jim Gallagher, C.S.C.; Mark Ghyselinck, C.S.C.; Charles Gordon, C.S.C.; Patrick Hannon, C.S.C.; Thomas Hosinski, C.S.C.; Charles McCoy, C.S.C.; Edwin Obermiller, C.S.C.; Gerry Olinger, C.S.C.; Dan Parrish, C.S.C.; Claude Pomerleau, C.S.C., (Retired); Mark Poorman, C.S.C.; Richard Rutherford, C.S.C., (Retired); Jeffrey Schneibel, C.S.C.; Ronald Wasowski, C.S.C.; Arthur F. Wheeler, C.S.C.; Bro. Thomas Giumenta, C.S.C. In Res. Revs. Richard Berg, C.S.C., (Retired); George C. Bernard, C.S.C., (Retired); William Hund, C.S.C., (Retired); James Rigert, C.S.C., (Retired); Charles D. Sherrer, C.S.C., (Retired); William E. Wickham, C.S.C., (Retired); John Wironen, C.S.C., (Retired); Bro. Ken Allen, C.S.C., (Retired).
Following is the Academic Structure of the University: Dr. Thomas G. Greene, Provost.
College of Arts and Sciences, (Grades Bachelors-Masters), 5000 N. Willamette Blvd., 97203.
Tel: 503-943-7760; Fax: 503-943-7804; Email: egger@up.edu. Religious Teachers 6; Lay Teachers 50; Students 1,400.
School of Nursing, (Grades Bachelors-Masters), School of Nursing Buckley Center 301, 5000 N. Willamette Blvd., 97203. Tel: 503-943-7509;
Tel: 503-943-7211; Fax: 503-943-7729; Email: nursing@up.edu. Dr. Joane T. Moceri, Dean. Students 913.
Pamplin School of Business, (Grades Bachelors-Masters), 5000 N. Willamette Blvd., 97203.
Tel: 503-943-7224; Email: anderson@up.edu; Web: https://business.up.edu/index.html. Dr. Robin D. Anderson, Dean. Religious Teachers 1; Students 750.
School of Engineering, (Grades Bachelors-Masters), Shiley Hall, 5000 N. Willamette Blvd., 97203. Tel: 503-943-7314; Tel: 503-943-7292;
Fax: 503-943-7316; Email: engineering@up.edu; Web: https://engineering.up.edu. Dr. Sharon A. Jones, Dean; Jason S. McDonald, Dean, Admissions, Tel: 503-943-7751; Email: mcdonaja@up.edu. Students 655.
School of Education, (Grades Bachelors-Masters), 5000 N. Willamette Blvd. MSC 149, 97203.
Tel: 503-943-7135; Fax: 503-943-8042; Email: watzke@up.edu; Email: soed@up.edu; Web: https://education.up.edu. John Watzke, Dean. Students 411.
Graduate School, (Grades Bachelors-Masters), 5000 N. Willamette Blvd., 97203.
Tel: 503-943-7107; Email: gradschl@up.edu. Dr. Thomas G. Greene, Dean; Drew Harrington, Dean, Library, Tel: 503-943-7111; Fax: 503-943-7491. Religious Teachers 17; Students 493.

[C] HIGH SCHOOLS, ARCHDIOCESAN

PORTLAND. *Central Catholic High School* (1939) (Coed) 2401 S.E. Stark St., 97214. Tel: 503-235-3138;
Fax: 503-233-0073; Email: info@centralcatholichigh.org; Web: www.centralcatholichigh.org. Colin McGinty, Pres.; Rev. Timothy Murphy, Pres. Emeritus; John Garrow, Prin.; Sara Bruins, Asst. Prin.; Nic Netzel, Librarian; Sherril Acton, Contact Person. Religious Teachers 2; Lay Teachers 70; Priests 2; Sisters 1; Students 880.

EUGENE. *Marist Catholic High School* (Coed) 1900 Kingsley Rd., Eugene, 97401. Tel: 541-686-2234; Email: sbaker@marists.org; Web: www.marists.org. Stacey Baker, Prin. & Contact; Rev. Ed Coleman. Religious Teachers 1; Lay Teachers 37; Priests 1; Students 496.

STAYTON. *Regis St. Mary Catholic School* (1963) (Grades PreK-12), (Coed) 550 W. Regis St., Stayton, 97383. Tel: 503-769-2159;
Fax: 503-769-1706; Email: principal@regisstmary.org; Web: www.regisstmary.org. Richard Schindler, Prin.; Selena Schumacher, Guidance Counselor. Religious Teachers 9; Lay Teachers 25; Students 300.
Regis High School Foundation dba Regis - St. Mary Foundation, 550 W. Regis St., Stayton, 97383.
Tel: 503-769-2159; Fax: 503-769-1706; Email: rhsprincipal@regishighschool.net; Email: office@regishighschool.net; Web: www.regishighschool.net. John Meldrum, Pres.

[D] HIGH SCHOOLS, PRIVATE

PORTLAND. *De La Salle North Catholic High School (Coed)*, 7528 N. Fenwick Ave., 97217.
Tel: 503-285-9385; Fax: 503-285-9546; Email: info@dlsnc.org; Web: www.delasallenorth.org. Oscar Leong, Pres.; Tim Joy, Prin.; Dr. Zulema Naegele, Vice Prin., Academics; James Broadhous, Dean of Students. Lay Teachers 22; Students 270.
Jesuit High School (1956) (Coed) 9000 S.W. Beaverton-Hillsdale Hwy., 97225-2491.
Tel: 503-292-2663; Fax: 503-292-0134; Email: tarndorfer@jesuitportland.org; Email: dgolik@jesuitportland.org; Web: www.jesuitportland.org. Thomas D. Arndorfer, Pres.; Mr. Paul Hogan, Prin.; Dr. Chris Smart, Academic Vice Prin.; Mrs. Diane Salzman, Vice Pres. Development; Mr. Khalid Maxie, Vice Pres. Student Life; Emily Hagelgans, Vice Pres. Student Life; Mrs. Erin DeKlotz, Admissions Dir.; Mr. Donald Clarke, Campus Min.; Mr. Gregory Lum, Librarian; Erika Tuenge, Vice Pres Communications & Public Affairs; Alyssa Tormala, Vice Prin. Prof. Dev. & Innovation. The Society of Jesus. Religious Teachers 2; Lay Teachers 76; Priests 2; Scholastics 2; Students 1,260.
Faculty: Mr. Patrick Couture, S.J., Supr.; Rev. Christopher Calderon, S.J., Prof. In Res. Revs. Kevin T. Clarke, S.J.; Lawrence F. Robinson, S.J.
St. Mary's Academy (1859) (Girls) 1615 S.W. Fifth Ave., 97201. Tel: 503-228-8306; Fax: 503-223-0995; Tel: 971-256-9972; Email: jennifer.masi@smapdx.org; Web: www.smapdx.org. Christina Friedhoff, Pres.; Nicole Foran, Prin.; Emily Niedermeyer Becker, Vice Pres. Development; Jennifer Masi, Dir. Marketing & Comm.; Alena Kelly, Asst. Prin. Academics; Liane Rae, Asst. Prin. Curriculum Design & Instruction; Michele Taylor, Dean, Student Leadership & Activities; Patty Gorman, Dean of Students. Religious Teachers 1; Lay Teachers 62; Sisters 1; Students 710.

BEAVERTON. *Valley Catholic Middle High Schools*, (Grades 6-12), (Coed) 4275 S.W. 148th Ave., Beaverton, 97078. Tel: 503-644-3745;
Fax: 503-646-4054; Email: tdow@valleycatholic.org; Web: www.valleycatholic.org. Jennifer Gfroerer, Prin.; Doug Ierardi, Prin. Sisters of St. Mary of Oregon Lay Teachers 70; Students 640.

MEDFORD. *St. Mary's School*, (Grades 6-12), (Middle School & High School) (Coed) 816 Black Oak Dr., Medford, 97504. Tel: 541-773-7877;
Fax: 541-772-8973; Email: fphillips@smschool.us; Web: www.smschool.us. Frank Phillips, Pres.; Jim Meyer, Prin. Lay Teachers 55; Students 497.

MILWAUKIE. *La Salle Catholic College Preparatory* (1966) La Salle Catholic College Preparatory (Coed) 11999 S.E. Fuller Rd., Milwaukie, 97222.
Tel: 503-659-4155; Fax: 503-659-2535; Email: akuffner@lsprep.org; Web: www.lsprep.org. Andrew Kuffner, Pres. & Prin.; Ann Poteet, Librarian. Lay Teachers 49; Students 718.

SALEM. **Archbishop Francis Norbert Blanchet School* dba Blanchet Catholic School (1995) (Grades 6-12), 4373 Market St., N.E., Salem, 97301.
Tel: 503-391-2639; Fax: 503-399-1259; Email: info@blanchetcatholicschoolcom; Web: www.blanchetcatholicschool.com. Bob Weber, Pres. Lay Teachers 29; Students 320.

[E] ELEMENTARY SCHOOLS, AREA

EUGENE. *O'Hara Area Elementary Catholic School* (1889) (Grades PreSchool-8), 715 W. 18th, Eugene, 97402. Tel: 541-485-5291; Fax: 541-484-9138; Email: tconway@oharaschool.org; Web: www.oharaschool.org. Mrs. Tammy Conway, Prin.; Leslie Jones, Religious Coord.; Lynn Gori, Librarian; Ellen Booth, Librarian. Comprised of students from the following parishes in Eugene: St. Jude, St. Mark, St. Mary, St. Paul, St. Peter, St. Alice, the Newman Center, Our Lady of Perpetual Help, St. Catherine, St. Helen, St. Henry, Nativity Ukrainian Catholic Church, St. Philip Benizi Catholic Church, St. Rose of Lima Catholic Church Lay Teachers 27; Students 507.

[F] ELEMENTARY SCHOOLS, PRIVATE

PORTLAND. **St. Andrew Nativity School* (2000) (Grades 6-8), 4925 N.E. 9th Ave., P.O. Box 11127, 97211-4513. Tel: 503-335-9600; Fax: 503-335-9494; Email: info@nativityportland.org; Web: www.nativityportland.org. Mike Chambers, Prin.; Carolyn Becic, Pres.; Mr. Justin Scalzo, Bus. Mgr. Religious Teachers 1; Lay Teachers 8; Students 83.
Franciscan Montessori Earth School/St. Francis Academy, 14750 S.E. Clinton St., 97236.
Tel: 503-760-8220; Fax: 503-760-8333; Email: sistertheresegutting@fmes.org; Web: www.fmes.org. Sr. Therese Gutting, F.S.E., Head of School. Staffed by Franciscan Sisters of the Eucharist. Religious Teachers 5; Lay Teachers 28; Sisters 5; Students 312.

BEAVERTON. *Valley Catholic Elementary School*, (Grades PreK-5), 4420 S.W. St. Mary's Dr., Beaverton, 97078. Tel: 503-718-6500;
Fax: 503-718-6520; Email: kjacobson@valleycatholic.org; Web: www.valleycatholic.org. John Matcovich, Pres.; Krista Jacobson, Prin.; Shauna Jasperson, Librarian. Sisters of St. Mary of Oregon Lay Teachers 22; Sisters 1; Students 328.

[G] SOCIAL AND MINISTERIAL SERVICES

PORTLAND. *Catholic Charities Oregon*, 2740 S.E. Powell Blvd., #5, 97202. Tel: 503-608-2502;
Fax: 503-231-4327; Email: info@catholiccharitiesoregon.org; Web: www.catholiccharitiesoregon.org. Deacon Richard Birkel, Ph.D., Exec. Dir. Programs include: pregnancy and parenting support, mental health and trauma services, peer support, case management, migration services including refugee resettlement and immigration legal services, affordable housing, resident services and homeless services, Project Rachel, financial empowerment services, financial coaching, individual development (matched) savings accounts. Tot Asst. Annually 56,376; Total Staff 239.
Catholic Youth Organization/Camp Howard, 825 N.E. 20th, Ste. 120, 97232-2295. Tel: 503-231-9484
; Fax: 503-231-9531; Email: srkrista@cyocamphoward.org; Web: www.cyocamphoward.org. Sr. Krista Von Borstel, S.S.M.O., Exec. Dir. Programs include: Youth recreation & camping. Tot Asst. Annually 15,000; Total Staff 14.
Catholic Community Services of Lane County, 1025 G. St., Springfield, 97477. Email: info@ccslc.org;
Tel: 541-345-3628; Fax: 541-744-2272; Web: www.ccslc.org. Thomas Mulhern, Exec. Dir. Basic needs svcs. (help for today) include: emergency food distribution; utility bill payment assistance; free distribution of donated clothing, hygiene and household items; help paying for prescription medications, bus passes and identification documents; and referral to other sources of help. Self-sufficiency programs (hope for tomorrow) include: transitional housing; family support and connections; and fathers parenting prg., day svcs. for homeless families, refugee resettlement.
**Caritas Community Housing Corporation*, 2740 S.E. Powell Blvd. #5, 97202. Tel: 503-231-4866; Email: info@ccoregon.org. Trell Anderson, Exec. Tot Asst. Annually 1,510; Total Staff 4.
**El Programa Hispano Catolico*, 333 S.E. 223rd Ave., Ste. 100, Gresham, 97030. Tel: 503-669-8350 ; Email: rdiaz@elprograma.org. Patricia Rojas, Exec. Tot Asst. Annually 7,998; Total Staff 108.
Refugee Resettlement Servivces.

[H] CHILD DEVELOPMENT CENTERS

PORTLAND. *Providence Health & Services-Oregon* dba *Providence Child Center, 830 N.E. 47th Ave., 97213. Tel: 503-215-2400; Fax: 503-215-0660; Email: joann.vance@providence.org. Joann Vance, Exec.; Kelly Schmidt, Dir. Patients Asst Anual. 1,922; Total Staff 202.
Providence Health & Services-Oregon dba Center for Medically Fragile Children, 830 N.E. 47th Ave., 97213. Tel: 503-215-2400; Email: jvance@providence.org. Joann Vance, Dir. The Center for Medically Fragile Children at Providence Child Center is the only nursing facility in the Northwest providing skilled nursing care for children with complex medical needs in a residential setting. Fifty-eight beds are dedicated to children needing long-term chronic care, short-term assessment and/or respite care, and end-of-life

care. Bed Capacity 133; Patients Asst Anual. 90; Total Staff 58.

Providence Health & Services-Oregon dba Providence Wee Care, Tel: 503-215-6832; Fax: 503-215-0333. Child development program for children of Providence Health System employees and the community, ages 6 weeks to 6 years. Developmental and age-appropriate activities support child's growth and development. Students 107; Staff 29.

Providence Health & Services-Oregon dba Providence Neurodevelopmental Center for Children, Tel: 503-215-2233; Fax: 503-215-2478. Providence Neurodevelopmental Center for Children (PNCC) provides diagnostic and therapy services for children with complex developmental medical needs as well as children with developmental delays. Staff 33; Total Assisted 1,725.

[I] RESIDENTIAL SCHOOLS FOR YOUTHS WITH EMOTIONAL-SOCIAL PROBLEMS

BEAVERTON. *St. Mary's Home for Boys, Inc.*, 16535 S.W. Tualatin Valley Hwy., Beaverton, 97003. Tel: 503-649-5651; Fax: 503-649-7405; Email: smiller@stmaryshomeforboys.org; Web: www.stmaryshomeforboys.org. Francis Maher, Exec. Dir. & Contact Person. Residential & day treatment center for behaviorally & emotionally disturbed children. Out patient mental health services. Students 102; Staff 114.

[J] GENERAL HOSPITALS

PORTLAND. *Providence Health & Services-Oregon* dba Providence Portland Medical Center (1941) 4805 N.E. Glisan St., 97213. Tel: 503-215-1111; Fax: 503-215-6858; Email: bruce.cwiekowski@providence.org; Web: www.providence.org. 4400 N.E. Halsey St., Bldg. 2, Ste. 595, 97213. Krista Farnham, CEO; Revs. Kevin T. Clarke, S.J., Chap.; Bruce Cwiekowski, Dir. Pastoral Care & Contact, Tel: 503-215-6833; Fax: 203-215-5619; Augustine Manyama, A.J., Chap.; Vernetta Ollison, Chap.; Gordon MacDonald, Catholic Chap.; Jean McQuiggin, Catholic Chap.; Sandra J. Walker, E.L.C.A., Clinical Pastoral Educ. Supvr.; Rev. Jon Andres, Clinical Chap.; Thomas Ayepa; Julie Dreyer, Chap.; Rev. Michael L. Harvey, O.F.M., Chap.; Carl Jensen, Chap.; Revs. Dominic Mtenga, A.J., (Tanzania) Chap.; Frederick Nkwasibwe, A.J., Chap.; Thomas Payne, Chap.

Providence Health & Services-Oregon Bed Capacity 483; Priests 6; Tot Asst. Annually 410,787; Total Staff 4,700.

Providence Health & Services-Oregon dba Providence St. Vincent Medical Center, 9205 S.W. Barnes Rd., 97225. Tel: 503-216-1234; Fax: 503-216-2468; Email: sisterlynda.thompsonsnjm@providence.org; Web: www.providence.org. 4400 N.E. Halsey St., Bldg. 2, Ste. 595, 97213. Janice Burger, Chief Exec., Providence St. Vincent Medical Center; Revs. Godfred Ocun, A.J., Spiritual Care Dir.; Cornelius Ssekitto, A.J., Chap.; Melinda Smith, Chap.; Connie Knyoth-Smith, Chap.; Stephen Kelson, Chap.; Simon Ho, Chap.; Sr. Lynda Thompson, S.N.J.M., Mission Integration Dir.; Veniamin Bilan, Chap.; Christopher Fabre, Chap.; Sr. Patricia Marie Landin, S.S.M.O., Chap.; Letha McCleod, Chap.; Rev. Francis Njau, A.J., Chap.; Aimee Niles, Chap.; Denise Denniston, Chap.; Jesse Pickott, Chap.; Ashton Roberts, Chap.

Providence Health & Services-Oregon. Bed Capacity 523; Patients Asst Anual. 462,529; Priests 4; Total Staff 3,320.

COTTAGE GROVE. *Peace Health - Cottage Grove Community Medical Center*, 1515 Village Dr., Cottage Grove, 97424. Tel: 360-729-1000; Email: sbrewer@peacehealth.org; Web: www.peacehealth.org. Mailing Address: 1115 S.E. 164th Ave., Ste. 314, Vancouver, WA 98686. Tel: 541-767-5500. Liz Dunne, Pres.; Dianna Kielian, Exec. Bed Capacity 14; Tot Asst. Annually 12,476; Total Staff 174.

EUGENE/SPRINGFIELD. **Sacred Heart Medical Center*, 3333 River Bend Dr., Springfield, 97477. Tel: 360-729-1000; Tel: 541-222-7300; Email: sbrewer@peacehealth.org; Web: www.peacehealth.org. 1115 S.E. 164th Ave., Vancouver, WA 98683. Liz Dunne, Pres.& CEO; Dianna Kielian, Exec. Sisters of St. Joseph of Peace.Div. of PeaceHealth. Bed Capacity 451; Tot Asst. Annually 123,517; Total Staff 4,341.

FLORENCE. *Peace Health - Peace Harbor Medical Center*, 400 Ninth St., Florence, 97439. Tel: 360-729-1000; Email: sbrewer@peacehealth.org; Web: www.peacehealth.org. Mailing Address: 1115 S.E. 164th Ave., Dept. 314, Vancouver, WA 98683. Liz Dunne, Pres. & CEO; Dianna Kielian, Exec. Critical access hospital owned and operated by Peace Health, Vancouver, WA. Bed Capacity 21; Tot Asst. Annually 11,197; Total Staff 248.

MEDFORD. *Providence Health & Services-Oregon* dba Providence Medford Medical Center, 1111 Crater Lake Ave., Medford, 97504-6225. Tel: 541-732-5000; Fax: 541-732-5872; Email: tim.serban@providence.org. 4400 N.E. Halsey St., Bldg. 2, Ste. 595, 97213. Lee Casey, Dir.; Rev. James Clifford, O.S.A., Chap.; Josue Delgado, Chap.; John Dungey, On Call Chap.; Joel Maiorano, Chap.; Constance Wilkerson, Chap.; Valerie Garrick, Chap.

Providence Health & Services-Oregon Bed Capacity 134; Patients Asst Anual. 138,662; Priests 1; Total Staff 1,600.

**Providence Community Health Foundation, Medford*, 940 Royal Ave., Ste. 410, Medford, 97504. Tel: 541-732-6766; Fax: 541-772-2861; Email: kelly.buechler@providence.org; Web: www.providence.org/medford/foundation. Kelly Buechler, Exec.

MILWAUKIE. *Providence Health & Services-Oregon* dba *Providence Milwaukie Hospital (1968) 10150 S.E. 32nd Ave., Milwaukie, 97222. Tel: 503-513-8300; Fax: 503-513-8191; Email: julie.dirmunoz@providence.org; Web: www.providence.org/milwaukie. 4400 N.E. Halsey St., Bldg. 2, Ste. 595, 97213. Julie Dir-Munoz, Dir., Mission Integration and Spiritual Care; Patty Douglass, Chap.; Sherri Kulink, Exec.; Ben Rrustemaj, Chap.

Providence Health & Services-Oregon. Bed Capacity 77; Tot Asst. Annually 142,110; Total Staff 536.

NEWBERG. *Providence Health & Services-Oregon* dba Providence Newberg Medical Center, 1001 Providence Dr., Newberg, 97132-1887. Tel: 503-537-1555; Fax: 503-537-5611; Email: bonnie.mcculley@providence.org. 4400 N.E. Halsey St., Bldg. 2, Ste. 595, 97213. Lori Bergen, Exec.; Bonnie McCulley, Dir. Mission and Spiritual Care; John Mahaffy, Chap.; Jonathan Brewer, Chap.; Mark Campbell, Chap.; David Jacob, Chap.; Shelley Campbell, Chap.; David Jones, Chap.; Ken Vanden Hoek, Chap. Bed Capacity 40; Tot Asst. Annually 129,896; Total Staff 540.

OREGON CITY. *Providence Health & Services-Oregon* dba Providence Willamette Falls Medical Center, 1500 Division St., Oregon City, 97045. Tel: 503-656-1631; Fax: 503-650-6807; Web: www.providence.org; Email: russell.reinhard@providence.org. 4400 N.E. Halsey St., 97213. Russ Reinhard, Chief Exec., Willamette Faus Medical Center; Julie Dir-Munoz, Dir. Mission Integration and Spiritual Care; Mary Follen, Chap.; Thomas Struck, Chap. Bed Capacity 143; Tot Asst. Annually 96,146; Total Staff 697.

Providence Willamette Falls Medical Foundation, 1500 Division St., Oregon City, 97045. Tel: 503-656-1631; Fax: 503-650-6807; Email: laurie.kelley@providence.org. 4400 N.E. Halsey St., Bldg. 2, Ste. 595, 97213. Laurie Kelley, Exec.

ROSEBURG. *Mercy Medical Center, Inc.*, 2700 Stewart Pkwy., Roseburg, 97471. Tel: 541-673-0611; Email: kellymorgan@chiwest.com; Email: davidprice@chiwest.com; Email: cletusosuji@chiwest.com; Web: www.chimercyhealth.com. Kelly C. Morgan, Pres. & CEO; David Price, Ph.D., Dir., Mission Integration; Rev. Cletus Osuji, Catholic Chap. Bed Capacity 174; Tot Asst. Annually 417,576; Total Staff 1,150.

Mercy Foundation, Inc., 2700 N.W. Stewart Pkwy., Roseburg, 97471. Tel: 541-677-4818; Fax: 541-677-4891. 1600 N.W. Garden Valley Blvd., Ste 110, Roseburg, 97471. David Price, Ph. D., Dir.; Rev. Cletus Osuji, Chap.

SEASIDE. *Providence Health & Services-Oregon* dba Providence Seaside Hospital, 725 S. Wahanna Rd., Seaside, 97138-7735. Tel: 503-717-7000; Fax: 503-717-7505; Email: cherilyn.frei@providence.org; Web: www.providence.org/northcoast. 4400 N.E. Halsey St., Bldg. 2, Ste. 595, 97213. Kendall Sawa, Chief Exec., Providence Seaside Hospital; Cherilyn Frei, Mission & Spiritual Care Dir.

Sisters of Providence in Oregon. Bed Capacity 25; Patients Asst Anual. 87,195; Total Staff 350.

[K] RETIREMENT AND ASSISTED LIVING

PORTLAND. **St. Anthony Village (activity of St. Anthony Village Enterprise)*, 3560 S.E. 79th Ave., 97206. Tel: 503-775-4414; Fax: 503-771-9189; Email: mmaslowsky@villageenterprises.org; Email: jmittelstaedt@villageenterprises.org; Web: www.villageenterprises.org. Rev. Michael Maslowsky, Pres.; Janice Mittelstaedt, Admin. & Contact Person; Tracy Koslicki, Leasing Coord. Assisted living facility centered around Catholic Parish. Independent, assisted living and memory care unit. Bed Capacity 127; Tot Asst. Annually 100; Staff 70.

**Assumption Village (activity of St. Anthony Village Enterprise)* (2002) 9121 N. Burr Ave., 97203. Tel: 503-283-5644; Fax: 503-283-5692; Email: smunsell@villageenterprises.org; Web: www.villageenterprises.org. Rev. Michael Maslowsky, Pres.; Stacey Munsell, Admin. Retirement Village, Senior independent and assisted living, chapel with daily Mass multiple activities, gardens, intergenerational interaction with neighborhood and local social service agencies. Bed Capacity 109; Tot Asst. Annually 85; Total Staff 40.

Providence Health & Services-Oregon dba Providence ElderPlace, 4531 S.E. Belmont, Ste. 100, 97215. Tel: 503-215-6556; Fax: 503-215-0685; Email: luann.trutwin@providence.org. Ellen Garcia, Exec. Dir.; Luann Trutwin, Dir. Mission Integration & Spiritual Care. Bed Capacity 230; Patients Asst Anual. 1,578; Total Staff 465.

BEAVERTON. *Maryville Nursing Home*, 14645 S.W. Farmington Rd., Beaverton, 97007. Tel: 503-643-8626; Fax: 503-520-1435; Email: cfo@ssmoministries.org. Kathleen Parry, Exec.; Mylene Cepedia, Dir. Nurses. Bed Capacity 165; Total Staff 245; RCF Beds 16; Hospice Care 40; Total Assisted 746.

MOUNT ANGEL. *Providence Health & Services-Oregon* dba Providence Benedictine Nursing Center, 540 S. Main St., Mount Angel, 97362-9532. Tel: 503-845-6841; Fax: 503-845-9229; Email: luann.trutwin@providence.org; Web: www.providence.org/benedictine. 4400 N.E. Halsey St., Bldg. 2, Ste. 595, 97213. Emily Dazey, Exec. Dir.; Luann Trutwin, Dir. Mission Integration & Spiritual Care; David Horn, Chap.; Jennifer Gringerich, Chap.; Barbara Harrend, Chap. Providence Health & Services. Patients Asst Anual. 684; Total Staff 152; Beds 98.

Providence Benedictine Orchard House, Tel: 503-845-2544; Fax: 503-845-2560. Personalized Living Center (ALF). Bed Capacity 50; Total Staff 25; Total Assisted 74.

Providence Benedictine Home Health, Tel: 503-845-9226; Fax: 503-845-9880. Patients Asst Anual. 2,490; Total Staff 236.

ROSEBURG. *Linus Oakes, Inc.*, 2665 Van Pelt Blvd., Roseburg, 97471. Tel: 541-677-4800; Fax: 541-677-2106; Email: miryan@chilivingcomm.org. Mike Ryan, Admin. Part of CHI Living Communities, a subsidiary of Catholic Health Initiatives.

[L] MONASTERIES AND RESIDENCES OF PRIESTS

PORTLAND. *Colombiere Jesuit Community*, 3220 S.E. 43rd Ave., 97206-3104. Tel: 503-595-1930; Fax: 503-595-1929; Email: asholander@jesuits.org; Web: www.jesuitswest.org. Very Rev. Scott R. Santarosa, S.J., Prov.; Revs. Robert Niehoff, S.J., Prov. Asst.; Michael Weiler, S.J., Asst. Tertian Dir.; Kevin T. Clarke, S.J., Chap.; Daniel Sullivan, S.J.; Michael S. Bayard, S.J.; Craig Boly, S.J.; Richard H. Ganz, S.J.; Michael C. Gilson, S.J.; Thomas McCarthy, S.J.; Christopher S. Weekly, S.J.; Charles Moutenot, S.J.; Roger De La Rosa, S.J.; Gary N. Smith, S.J.; Dat T. Tran, S.J.; Anthony Sholander, S.J.; Steven Dillard, S.J.; Dan Mai, S.J.; E. O'Keefe, S.J. Priests 19.

The Grotto, The National Sanctuary of Our Sorrowful Mother (1924) 85th and N.E. Sandy Blvd., 8840 N.E. Skidmore St., P.O. Box 20008, 97294-0008. Tel: 503-254-7371; Fax: 503-254-7948; Email: office@thegrotto.org; Web: www.thegrotto.org. Christopher Blanchard, Exec.; Rev. Richard R. Boyle, O.S.M., Spiritual Advisor/Care Svcs. Priests 6; Sisters 4. In Res. Revs. Eugene S. Smith, O.S.M., Prior; Donald Siple, O.S.M, Rector; Marciano Doloroso, Spiritual Advison/Care Svcs.; Ignatius M. Kissel, O.S.M., Spiritual Advisor/Care Svcs.

Holy Rosary Priory, 375 N.E. Clackamas St., 97232-1103. Tel: 503-235-3163; Email: holyrosarypdx@parishmail.com; Web: holyrosarypdx.org. Revs. Joseph Sergott, O.P., Prior; Corwin Low, O.P., Subprior; Gabriel Mosher, O.P., Treas.; Very Rev. Vincent Kelber, O.P., Pastor; Revs. Paul A. Duffner, O.P., (Retired); Brian T.B. Mullady, O.P.; Paschal Donald Salisbury, O.P., (Retired).

Society of Jesus, Oregon Province, 3215 S.E. 45th Ave., 97206. Tel: 503-226-6977; Fax: 503-228-6741; Email: uweprovince@jesuits.org; Web: www.jesuitswest.org. P.O. Box 86010, 97286-0010. Very Rev. Scott R. Santarosa, S.J., Prov.; Revs. John Martin, S.J., Treas.; Michael S. Bayard, S.J., Socius.

Priests of Holy Cross in Oregon, Inc., 5000 N. Willamette Blvd., 97203. Tel: 503-943-8024; Fax: 503-943-7313; Email: ssimmonds@holycrossusa.org. Revs. Charles McCoy, C.S.C., Vice Pres.; Robert Antonelli, C.S.C., (Retired); Richard Berg, C.S.C., (Retired); George C. Bernard, C.S.C., (Retired); John Donato, C.S.C.; Jim Gallagher, C.S.C.; Mark Ghyselinck, C.S.C.; Charles Gordon, C.S.C.; Patrick Hannon, C.S.C.; Thomas Hosinski, C.S.C.; William Hund, C.S.C., (Retired); Edwin Obermiller, C.S.C.; Dan Parrish, C.S.C.; Claude Pomerleau, C.S.C., (Retired); Mark Poorman, C.S.C.; James Rigert, C.S.C., (Retired); Richard Rutherford, C.S.C.,

(Retired); Jeffrey Schneibel, C.S.C.; Arthur F. Wheeler, C.S.C.; William E. Wickham, C.S.C., (Retired); Bros. Ken Allen, C.S.C., (Retired); William Dygert, C.S.C.; Thomas Giumenta, C.S.C.; Revs. Pat Neary, C.S.C.; Timothy Weed, C.S.C.

AMITY. *Brigittine Priory of Our Lady of Consolation - The Order of the Most Holy Savior* (1976) 23300 Walker Ln., Amity, 97101. Tel: 503-835-8080; Fax: 503-835-9662; Email: monks@brigittine.org; Web: www.brigittine.org. Bro. Bernard Ner Suguitan, O.Ss.S., Prior & Contact. Brothers 9; Novices 2; Professed 7.

BANKS. *Missionaries of the Holy Spirit, M.Sp.S.*, Provincial House (Christ the Priest Province), 39085 N.W. Harrington Rd., P.O. Box 130, Banks, 97106. Email: jgmsps@me.com; Web: www.mspsusa.org. Revs. Roberto Saldivar-Ureno, M.Sp.S., Prov. Supr.; Mario Rodriguez, M.Sp.S, Prov. Asst.; Juan Jose Gonzalez, M.Sp.S., Treas.

CARLTON. *The Cistercian (Trappist) Abbey of Our Lady of Guadalupe* (1948) 9200 N.E. Abbey Rd., Carlton, 97111-9504. Tel: 503-852-7174; Fax: 503-852-0193; Email: community@trappistabbey.org; Web: www.trappistabbey.org. Rt. Rev. Peter McCarthy, O.C.S.O., Abbot; Revs. M. Dominique-Savio Nelson, O.C.S.O., Prior; Richard Layton, O.C.S.O., Business Mgr.; Martin Cawley, O.C.S.O.; Timothy Clark, O.C.S.O.; Howard Curtis, O.C.S.O.; Francis King, O.C.S.O.; Timothy Michell, O.C.S.O.; Peter Plakut, O.C.S.O.; Mark Weidner, O.C.S.O. Order of Cistercians of the Strict Observance. Priests 10; Solemnly Professed 22; Total in Community 23.

CORVALLIS. *Saint John Society*, 501 N.W. 25th St., Corvallis, 97330. Tel: 541-753-1392; Fax: 541-753-1392; Email: stjohnsociety@socsj.org; Web: www.socsj.org. Revs. Lucas Laborde, S.S.J.; Ignacio Llorente, S.S.J.; Juan Pablo Segura; Maximo Stock, S.S.J. Brothers 2; Priests 4.

HILLSBORO. *Missionaries of the Holy Spirit, M.Sp.S.*, 642 S.E. 20th Ct., Hillsboro, 97123. Tel: 503-648-1998; Fax: 503-648-4489; Email: jgmsps@me.com. Revs. Lucio Villalobos, M.Sp.S., Pastor; Rito Guzman, M.Sp.S.; Agustin Rodriguez, M.Sp.S.

MILWAUKIE. *St. John the Baptist Friary* (Province of St. Barbara, Franciscan Friars of Oregon, Franciscan Friars of California) 10955 S.E. 25th Ave., Milwaukie, 97222. Tel: 503-954-2180; Email: frjorge@sjbcatholicchurch.org. Revs. Jorge Hernandez, O.F.M.; Richard Juzix, O.F.M., Guardian.

MOUNT ANGEL. *Discalced Carmelite Friars (O.C.D.)*, Carmelite House of Studies, 300 Humpert Ln., Mount Angel, 97362. Tel: 503-845-2240; Email: davidguzman@live.com. Revs. Thomas Koller, O.C.D., Rector; John Melka, O.C.D.; David Guzman, O.C.D.; Bros. John Cannon, O.C.D.; Joseph Mary, O.C.D. Brothers 2; Priests 3.

Missionaries of the Holy Spirit, M.Sp.S., 585 E. College St., Mount Angel, 97362. Tel: 503-845-1181 ; Email: jpmsps@gmail.com. P.O. Box 499, St. Benedict, 97373. Revs. Pedro Arteaga, M.Sp.S., Formation Dir., Mt. Angel Seminary; Gerardo Cisneros, Formation Dir., Mt. Angel Seminary; Alex Rubio, M.Sp.S., Spiritual Dir., Mt. Angel Seminary; Bros. Ren Alvarez, Rel. in Formation; Jesus Romo, Rel. in Formation. Serving the Felix Rougier House of Studies.

MYRTLE CREEK. *Augustinian Community*, P.O. Box 810, Myrtle Creek, 97457-0116. Tel: 541-863-3271; Fax: 541-863-6759; Email: jamesclifford@charter.net. 318 N. Seventh St., Medford, 97502. Rev. James Clifford, O.S.A., Regl. Supr.

ST. BENEDICT. *Mt. Angel Abbey*, One Abbey Dr., St. Benedict, 97373. Tel: 503-845-3030; Fax: 503-845-3594; Email: info@mtangel.edu; Web: www.mountangelabbey.org. Revs. Jeremy Driscoll, O.S.B., Abbot, (Retired); Gregory Duerr, O.S.B., (Retired); Very Rev. Vincent Trujillo, O.S.B., Prior; Revs. William Hammelman, O.S.B., Subprior; Odo Recker, O.S.B., Vocation Dir.; Rt. Revs. Nathan Zodrow, O.S.B., (Retired); Peter Eberle, O.S.B., (Retired); Revs. Benedict Suing, O.S.B.; Augustine DeNoble, O.S.B.; Edmund Smith, O.S.B.; Paul Thomas, O.S.B.; Philip Waibel, O.S.B.; John Paul Le, O.S.B.; Aelred Yockey, O.S.B.; Pius X Harding, O.S.B.; Vincent Liem Nguyen, O.S.B.; Ralph Recker, O.S.B.; Martin Grassel, O.S.B.; Joseph Nguyen, O.S.B.; Jacob Stronach, O.S.B.; Andrew Schwenke, O.S.B.; Teresio Caldwell, O.S.B.; Basil Lawrence, O.S.B. Brothers 25; Priests 25; Monks in Perpetual Vows 48.

[M] CONVENTS AND RESIDENCES FOR SISTERS

PORTLAND. *Convent of Sisters of Reparation of the Sacred Wounds of Jesus*, Novitiate, 2120 S.E. 24th Ave., 97214-5504. Tel: 503-236-4207; Fax: 503-236-3400; Email: repsrs@comcast.net; Web: www.reparationsisters.org. Mother Mary of the Angels, S.R., Supr. Gen. Sisters 2; Donne Members 164.

Holy Spirit Sisters (1950) 2736 N.E. 54th Ave., 97213. Tel: 503-239-0328; Fax: 503-239-0328; Cell: 503-830-2809; Email: hssportland@gmail.com. Sisters Euphemia M. Mkenda, Contact Person; M. Winifrida Anthony Okutu, CNA. Sisters 6.

Rose Hall Reparation and Prayer Center, 2120 S.E. 24th Ave., 97214-5504. Tel: 503-236-4207; Fax: 503-236-3400; Email: mmangels@comcast.net; Web: www.reparationsisters.org. Mother Mary of the Angels, S.R., Dir. Sisters 2.

Sister Adorers of the Holy Cross Convent (1670) 7408 S.E. Alder, 97215. Tel: 503-254-3284; Fax: 503-255-3097; Email: mtgdlhn@yahoo.com; Email: kimchibuimtg@gmail.com. Sr. Mary Kim Chi Bui, M.T.G., Supr. First foundation in the United States in 1976, founded by Bishop Pierre Lambert de la Motte. Represented in the Archdiocese of Portland in Oregon, the Diocese of Arlington, VA and the Diocese of Sacramento, CA. *Adorers of the Holy Cross Sisters* Sisters 31.

ALOHA. *Lovers of the Holy Cross of Thu Thiem*, 6955 SW 201st, Aloha, 97078. Tel: 503-330-5411; Email: nph.jun4@gmail.com. Sr. Mary Therese Nguyen, Contact Person. Sisters 8.

BEAVERTON. *Convent, Franciscan Missionary Sisters of Our Lady of Sorrows* (1939) 3600 S.W. 170th Ave., Beaverton, 97003-4467. Tel: 503-649-7127; Fax: 503-259-9507; Email: franmisisters39@gmail.com; Web: www.olpretreat.org. Sr. Anne Marie Warren, O.S.F., Supr. Gen., Contact Person. Sisters 13.

Sisters of St. Mary of Oregon (1886) 4440 S.W. 148th Ave., Beaverton, 97078. Tel: 503-644-9181; Fax: 503-646-1102; Email: srcharleneh@ssmo.org; Email: cfo@ssmoministries.org; Web: www.ssmo.org. Sisters Charlene Herinckx, S.S.M.O., Supr. Gen.; Julie Doan, S.S.M.O., Admin.; Rev. Godfred Ocun, A.J., Chap. Motherhouse of the Sisters of St. Mary of Oregon. Sisters 59; Professed Sisters 57.

BRIDAL VEIL. *Franciscan Sisters of the Eucharist Convent* (1973) Administrative Center, 48100 E. Historic Columbia R. Hwy., P. O. Box 23, Bridal Veil, 97010-0023. Tel: 503-695-2375; Fax: 503-695-2368; Web: www.fsecommunity.org. Sr. Mary Margaret Delaski, F.S.E., Supr. Sisters 10.

EUGENE. *Carmel of Maria Regina* (1957) (Contemplative Order) 87609 Green Hill Rd., Eugene, 97402. Tel: 541-345-8649; Fax: 541-345-4857; Email: carmeleugene@gmail.com; Web: http://carmelitesinoregon.org/. Mother Elizabeth Mary, O.C.D., Prioress. Novices 1; Professed Sisters 5.

MARYLHURST. *Convent of the Holy Names*, P.O. Box 398, Marylhurst, 97036. Tel: 503-675-7100; Fax: 503-675-7138; Email: alindsay@snjmuson.org; Web: www.snjmusontario.org. 17410 Holy Names Dr., Lake Oswego, 97034. Anita Lindsay, Sisters Svcs. Coord. Provincial House of the Sisters of the Holy Names of Jesus & Mary, S.N.J.M. Sisters 130.

MOUNT ANGEL. *Queen of Angels Monastery* (1882) 840 S. Main St., Mount Angel, 97362-9527. Tel: 503-845-6141; Fax: 503-845-6585; Email: info@benedictine-srs.org; Web: www.benedictine-srs.org. Sr. Jane Hibbard, S.N.J.M., Prioress. Monastery of the Benedictine Sisters of Mt. Angel.; See separate listing for Shalom Prayer Center (retreat center). Sisters 28.

[N] RETREAT HOUSES

BEAVERTON. *Our Lady of Peace Retreat* (1953) 3600 S.W. 170th Ave., Beaverton, 97003-4467. Tel: 503-649-7127; Fax: 503-259-9507; Email: sisters@olpretreat.org; Web: www.olpretreat.org. Sr. Anne Marie Warren, O.S.F., Supr. Gen. & Contact Person. Employees 11; Franciscan Missionary Sisters of Our Lady of Sorrows 13.

GOLD HILL. *St. Rita's Retreat Center*, P.O. Box 310, Gold Hill, 97525. Tel: 541-855-1333; Email: paterretreat@gmail.com; Web: stritaretreat.org. Rev. Stephen J. Fister, Dir. & Contact Person, (Retired). Bed Capacity 30; Retreatants 30; Volunteers 3.

MCKENZIE BRIDGE. *St. Benedict Lodge Dominican Retreat & Conference Center* (1955) 56630 N. Bank Rd., McKenzie Bridge, 97413-9614. Tel: 541-822-3572 (Office & Dominican Res.); Email: sblodge@opwest.org; Web: sblodge.opwest.org. Revs. Kieren Healy, Dir. & Chap.; David Willis Geib, O.P., Chap. & Asst. Dir.; Deacon Tom Hayward.

55433 McKenzie Hwy., Mc Kenzie Bridge, 97413. Tel: 541-822-6087; Email: dcnlgjms@earthlink.net.

MILWAUKIE. *Franciscan Spiritual Center* (2002) 2512 S.E. Monroe St., Milwaukie, 97222. Tel: 503-794-8542; Fax: 503-794-8556; Email: info@francisspctr.com; Web: francisspctr.com. Sisters Mary Jo Chaves, O.S.F., Spiritual Dir.; Celeste Clavel, O.S.F., Business Mgr.; Emma Holdener, O.S.F., Office Mgr. & Body-work; Michelle Kroll, Admin. Asst.; Larry Peacock, Dir.; Eileen Parfrey, Spiritual Dir.; Paula Gamble-Grant, Dir.; Mark Lesniewski, Dir.; Thomas Welch, Dir. Sisters of St. Francis of Philadelphia.Spiritual direction; day retreats; workshops and body-work. Sisters 3; Staff 5.

MOUNT ANGEL. *Benedictine Sisters Shalom Prayer Center*, 840 S. Main St., Mount Angel, 97362-9527. Tel: 503-845-6773; Fax: 503-845-6585; Email: shalom@mtangel.net; Web: www.benedictine-srs.org/shalom. Sr. Dorothy Jean Beyer, O.S.B., Dir. Sisters 1.

ST. BENEDICT. *Mount Angel Abbey Guest House & Retreat Center*, 1 Abbey Dr., St. Benedict, 97373. Tel: 503-845-3025; Email: retreat@mtangel.edu; Web: www.mountangelabbey.org. Rev. Pius X Harding, O.S.B., Guest Master/ Retreat Cntr. Dir.

[O] SOCIETY OF ST. VINCENT DE PAUL

PORTLAND. *Society of St. Vincent de Paul Portland Council* (1869) Portland Council 8101 S.E. Cornwell St., P.O. Box 42157, 97242-0157. Tel: 503-234-5287; Fax: 503-233-5581; Email: brian.f@svdpportland.org; Web: svdppdx.org. Brian Ferschweiler, Exec. Dir. Tot Asst. Annually 79,692; Staff 10.

EUGENE. *St. Vincent de Paul Society of Lane County, Inc.* Lane County District Council 2890 Chad Dr., P.O. Box 24608, Eugene, 97402. Tel: 541-687-5820; Fax: 541-683-9423; Email: askme@svdp.us; Web: www.svdp.us. Charlie Burnham, Pres.; Terrence R. McDonald, Exec. Dir. & Contact Person. Employees 625.

MEDFORD. *Society of St. Vincent de Paul* (1982) Rogue Valley District Council 2424 N. Pacific Hwy., P.O. Box 1663, Medford, 97501. Tel: 541-772-3828; Fax: 541-772-6886; Email: vincent@mind.net; Web: www.stvincentdepaulmedford.info. Kathleen Begley, Pres. Tot Asst. Annually 136,120; Volunteers 300.

MYRTLE CREEK. *Conference of St. Vincent de Paul of Myrtle Creek* (1997) 116 N. Main St., P.O. Box 1258, Myrtle Creek, 97457. Tel: 541-839-2109; Fax: 541-863-5489; Email: tamistax@frontier.com. Tamara E. Whiteley, Treas. Total Assisted 8,156.

SALEM. *St. Vincent de Paul Society of Mid-Williamette Valley* (1957) 3745 Portland Rd., N.E., Salem, 97303. Tel: 503-364-3210; Fax: 503-361-7475; Email: shari@svdpsalem.org. Carolyn Criteser, District Council Pres.; Shari Crawford, Exec. Dir. Tot Asst. Annually 87,701.

[P] NEWMAN CENTERS

PORTLAND. *Lewis & Clark College*, 0615 S.W. Palatine Hill Rd., P.O. Box 171, 97219. Tel: 503-768-7085; Tel: 574-229-6513; Tel: 503-780-2886; Fax: 503-768-7084; Email: dhaug@lclark.edu; Email: amlechevallier@lclark.edu. Debi Haug, Catholic Student Life Coord.

PDX Newman Center, 926 S.W. Clifton St., 97201. Tel: 503-241-4281; Email: campusminister@stmichaelportland.org; Web: www.pdxcatholic.org. Sr. Teresa Harrell, Campus Min.

University of Portland, Campus Ministry, 5000 N. Willamette Blvd., 97203. Tel: 503-943-7131; Fax: 503-943-8567; Email: ministry@up.edu; Web: www.up.edu. Revs. Jim Gallagher, C.S.C., Dir., Campus Ministry; Timothy Weed, C.S.C., Liturgy Dir.; Maureen Briare, Assoc. Dir. Liturgical Music; Beth Barsotti, Asst. Dir., Faith Formation; Annie Boyle, Asst. Dir. Retreat & Student Devel.; Anthony Paz, Asst. Dir. Liturgy & Catechesis; Theresa McCreary, Office Mgr.

ASHLAND. *Southern Oregon University (Ashland)* Walsh Memorial Newman Center c/o Our Lady of the Mountain Church, 987 Hillview Dr., Ashland, 97520. Tel: 541-482-0825; Fax: 541-488-5174; Email: sperry@mind.net; Web: www.newmansou.com. Rev. Mariano Escano, Chap.

CORVALLIS. *Newman Center at Oregon State University (Corvallis)*, Newman Center, 2127 N.W. Monroe St., Corvallis, 97330. Tel: 541-752-6818; Email: info@osunewman.org; Web: www.osunewman.org. Rev. Maximo Stock, S.S.J., Dir.; Connor York, Asst. Dir.

EUGENE. *Lane Community College*, 1850 Emerald St., Eugene, 97403. Tel: 541-343-7021; Fax: 541-686-8028; Email: secretary@uonewman.org; Web: UOnewman.org. Revs. Vincent Benoit, O.P., In Residence; Peter Do, O.P.; Garry Cappleman, O.P.

St. Thomas More Catholic Church, Eugene, Newman Center.

University of Oregon (Eugene), Newman Center, St. Thomas More Catholic Church, 1850 Emerald St., Eugene, 97403. Tel: 541-343-7021; Fax: 541-686-8028; Email: secretary@uonewman.org; Web: www.uonewman.org. Revs. Peter Do, O.P.; Garry Cappleman, O.P.; Corinne M. Lopez, S.T.M., Dir. Faith Formation.

MARYLHURST. *Marylhurst University*, 17600 Pacific Hwy., Marylhurst, 97036. Tel: 800-634-9982; Tel: 503-636-8141; Email: president@marylhurst.edu; Email: jsaalfeld@marylhurst.edu; Web: www.marylhurst.edu. Sr. Joan Saalfeld, S.N.J.M., Vice Pres., Mission Integration.

MCMINNVILLE. *Linfield College (McMinnville)*, St. James Church, 1145 N.E. First St., McMinnville, 97128. Tel: 503-472-5232; Fax: 503-472-4414; Email: mdouglass@stjamesmac.com. Michael Douglass, Campus Min.

MONMOUTH. *Western Oregon University (Monmouth)*, 315 N. Knox, Monmouth, 97361. Tel: 503-838-1242 ; Tel: 503-606-0113 (Campus House); Email: catholic_campus_ministry@hotmail.com. Rev. Francisco Bringuela, Admin.; Lisa Silbernagel, Campus Min., Tel: 503-606-0113. Students 5,300.

SALEM. *Willamette University (Salem)*, St. Joseph Church, 721 Chemeketa St., N.E., Salem, 97301. Tel: 503-581-1623; Email: chrelibar3@gmail.com. Rev. Msgr. Richard Huneger; Christina Barth, Youth & Young Adult Min.

[Q] MISCELLANEOUS

PORTLAND. *Blanchet House of Hospitality* (1952) 310 N.W. Glisan St., 97209. Tel: 503-241-4340; Fax: 503-222-4071; Email: gbaker@blanchethouse.org; Web: www.blanchethouse.org. Gregory Baker, Exec. Dir., Tel: 503-807-4330. Served 354,598.

Brotherhood of the People of Praise, 7709 N. Denver Ave., 97217. Tel: 503-230-9999; Cell: 612-720-3067; Email: joelkibler@gmail.com. Most Rev. Peter L. Smith, J.C.L., Contact Person. Total in Community 10.

Catholic Broadcasting Northwest, Inc., Mater Dei Radio, KBVM-FM 88.3, KMME-FM 94.9 & 100.5 (1989) P.O. Box 5888, 97228-5888. Tel: 503-285-5200; Fax: 503-285-3322; Email: info@materdeiradio.com; Web: www.materdeiradio.com. Patrick Ryan, Dir. Total Staff 7.

**The Gamelin-Oregon Association-Emilie House* dba Emilie House Apartments (1986) 5520 N.E. Glisan, 97213-3170. Tel: 503-236-9779; Fax: 503-239-1867; Email: shannan.stickler@providence.org; Web: www.providencesupportivehousing.org. Shannan Stickler, Dir. & Contact. Providence Health and Services.Apartments for the elderly and mobility impaired subsidized by the Department of Housing and Urban Development. Total Apartments 40.

**Jesuit Volunteer Corps Northwest* (1956) 2780 S.E. Harrison St., Ste 201, P.O. Box 22125, 97269-2125. Tel: 503-335-8202; Fax: 503-249-1118; Email: info@jvcnorthwest.org; Web: www.jvcnorthwest.org. Jeanne Haster, Exec. Dir. & Contact Person. Jesuit Volunteers Encorps 6,500; Jesuit Volunteer Program 6,600.

St. Joseph the Worker Corporate Work Study Program, Inc., 7528 N. Fenwick, 97217. Tel: 503-285-9385, Ext. 125; Fax: 503-285-9546; Email: thennessy@dlsnc.org; Web: www.dlsnc.org. Aiyana Ashley, Dir., Corp. Internship Prog.

**The Northwest Catholic Counseling Center*, 8383 N.E. Sandy, Ste. 205, 97220. Tel: 503-253-0964; Fax: 503-253-7659; Email: info@nwcounseling.org; Web: nwcounseling.org. Erin Peters, CEO; Sisters Barbara Kennedy, O.S.M., Co-founder; Sarah Deeby, O.S.M., Co-founder. Patients Asst Anual. 1,200.

Oregon Catholic Conference (1979) 2838 E. Burnside St., 97214. Tel: 503-233-8386; Fax: 503-234-2545; Email: tcooper@archdpdx.org. Most Revs. Alexander K. Sample, Pres.; Liam Cary, Vice Pres.; Peter L. Smith, J.C.L., Sec. & Treas.

Parish Funds Trust, 2838 E. Burnside St., 97214-1895. Tel: 503-234-5334; Fax: 503-234-2545; Email: JWillhite@archdpdx.org. Joanne K. Willhite, Admin. Trustee.

Providence Health & Services-Oregon dba Providence Home & Community Services, 6410 N.E. Halsey St., Ste. 100, 97213-4778. Tel: 503-215-4321; Fax: 503-215-4778; Email: luann.trutwin@providence.org. James Arp, Exec.; Luann Trutwin, Dir. Mission Integration & Spiritual Care.

Providence Health & Services-Oregon dba Providence Hospice, Tel: 503-215-2273. Providence Hospice provides expert, compassionate care for individuals as they face the end of life. We understand that each family is special. That's why we tailor our team approach to the specific needs of each patient and family. Hospice services are provided in the patient's home, no matter where that home is. It may be a private residence, an assisted living community, an adult care home, or a residential or intermediate care community. We know you have a choice for hospice care. As hospice professionals, we are honored to be invited into your home at such a sacred time. Total Staff 237; Total Assisted 3,580.

Providence Health & Services-Oregon dba Providence Home Health, Tel: 503-215-4646. Home is often the best place for healing. Surrounded by familiar settings, family and friends, you can relax and allow the healing process to begin. To aid in your recovery, your doctor may recommend medical care provided in your home. Whether you are returning home from the hospital or a skilled rehabilitation center, and whether your require skilled nursing care or rehab therapies, Providence Home Health provides a continuum of services and support at any stage of illness or recovery. Total Staff 432; Total Assisted 12,601.

Providence Health & Services-Oregon dba Providence Home Medical Equipment, Tel: 503-215-5435. Providence Home Medical Equipment provides a wide variety of products and services patients may need at home, or out enjoying activities. Whether patients choose to visit a service center for pick-up, or have a home delivery, we are here to help. Our credentialed respiratory therapists and dietitians work to ensure that our patients receive the appropriate care and products. Home delivery and patient education are an essential part of our program. We also have an experienced team of insurance specialists who obtain authorizations and bill insurance companies directly for services provided. Total Staff 132; Total Assisted 58,118.

Providence Health & Services-Oregon dba Providence Specialty Pharmacy, Tel: 503-215-4633 . Providence Specialty Pharmacy Services offers a full line of pharmacy services at home, in our infusion suites or in long-term care facilities. Total Staff 100; Total Assisted 6,241.

The Rosary Center (The Rosary Confraternity, Inc.), Western Dominican Province 1331 N.E. Third Ave., 97232. Tel: 503-236-8393; Email: rosary@rosary-center.org; Web: www.rosary-center.org. P.O. Box 3617, 97208-3617. Rev. Joseph Sergott, O.P., Dir.

Sharing Our Faith, Shaping Our Future, Capital Campaign, 2838 E. Burnside St., 97214-1895. Tel: 503-234-5334; Fax: 503-234-2545; Email: MSilvagnia@archdpdx.org. Joanne K. Willhite, Board Ex-Officio & Contact Person.

BANKS. *Felix Rougier Religious Care Trust*, 39085 N.W. Harrington Rd., P.O. Box 130, Banks, 97106. Tel: 503-324-2492; Fax: 503-324-2493; Email: jgmsps@me.com. Revs. Jose Gerardo Alberto, M.Sp.S., Trustee; Juan Jose Gonzalez, M.Sp.S., Trustee; Alex Rubio, M.Sp.S., Trustee.

BEAVERTON. *Our Lady of Peace Institute in Catholic Teaching*, 3600 S.W. 170th Ave., Beaverton, 97003-4467. Tel: 503-649-7127; Fax: 503-259-9507; Email: sisters@olpretreat.org; Web: www.olpretreat.org. Sr. Anne Marie, O.S.F., Coord. & Contact Person. Students 30; Staff 5.

Sisters of St. Mary of Oregon Campus Schools Corporation, 4440 S.W. 148th Ave., Beaverton, 97078. Tel: 503-644-9181; Fax: 503-646-1102; Email: jmatcovich@valleycatholic.org; Web: www.valleycatholic.org. John Matcovich, Pres. Lay Teachers 89; Sisters 1; Students 978.

Valley Catholic Middle & High Schools, (Grades 7-12), (Coed) 4275 S.W. 148th Ave., Beaverton, 97078. Tel: 503-644-3745; Email: dierardi@valleycatholic.org.

Valley Catholic Elementary School, (Grades K-5), 4420 S.W. St. Mary's Dr., Beaverton, 97078. Tel: 503-718-6500; Email: kjacobson@valleycatholic.org; Web: www.valleycatholic.org. Krista Jacobson, Prin. Religious Teachers 1; Lay Teachers 12; Students 336.

Sisters of St. Mary of Oregon Little Flower Development Center, 4450 S.W. St. Mary's Dr., Beaverton, 97078. Tel: 503-520-0214; Fax: 503-626-6220; Email: mdoxtator@valleycatholic.org. Melissa Doxtator, Prin. Lay Teachers 22; Students 201.

Sisters of St. Mary of Oregon Ministries Corporation, 4440 S.W. 148th Ave., Beaverton, 97078. Tel: 503-644-9181; Fax: 503-646-1102; Email: info@ssmoministries.org; Web: www.ssmoministries.org. Sr. Adele Marie Altenhofen, S.S.M.O., Pres.

LAKE OSWEGO. **Friends of Our Lady Queen of Africa*, P.O. Box 1061, Lake Oswego, 97034. Tel: 503-968-2211; Email: bverheggen@comcast.net. Deacon Kevin Welch, Chm.; Bill Verheggen, Treas.; Jean Verheggen, Sec.; Greg Heinrich, Dir.; Susan Welch, Dir.; Kathleen Wendland, Dir. Girls 500; Patients Asst Anual. 4,000; Professed Sisters 450.

Holy Names Heritage Center Inc., 17425 Holy Names Dr., Lake Oswego, 97034. Tel: 503-607-0595; Fax: 503-607-0609; Email: scantor@snjmuson.org; Web: www.holynamesheritagecenter.org. Sarah Cantor, Dir. Heritage Center.

**Mary's Woods at Marylhurst, Inc.*, 17400 Holy Names Dr., Lake Oswego, 97034. Tel: 503-675-2004; Fax: 503-675-2015; Email: ssharma@marywoods.org; Web: www.maryswoods.org. Jacki Gallo, Chm.; Diane Hood, COO & CFO; Sr. Roswitha Frawley, S.N.J.M., Mission Dir.; Kimberly Scott, Dir.; Lynn Szender, Dir. Marie Rose Health Center. Current Residency 499.

MARYLHURST. *Holy Names Sisters Foundation* (1859) c/o Development Office, P.O. Box 398, Marylhurst, 97036. Tel: 503-697-6435; Fax: 503-697-6436; Email: acarr@snjmuson.org. 17590 Gleason Dr., Lake Oswego, 97034. Vicki Cummings, CFO; Adrianna Carr, Devel. Dir.

Sisters of the Holy Names of Jesus and Mary, Community Support Charitable Trust, P.O. Box 398, Marylhurst, 97036. Tel: 503-675-7123; Fax: 503-675-7138; Email: snjmkirk@yahoo.com. 17590 Gleason Dr., Lake Oswego, 97034. Marguerite Kirk, Contact Person.

Sisters of the Holy Names of Jesus and Mary U.S.-Ontario Province Corporation, P.O. Box 398, Marylhurst, 97036. Tel: 503-675-7123; Fax: 503-675-7138; Email: vcummings@snjmuson.org; Web: www.snjmusontario.org. 17590 Gleason Dr., Lake Oswego, 97034. Sisters Maureen Delaney, S.N.J.M., Prov.; Mary Breiling, S.N.J.M., Vice Pres.; Margaret Kennedy, S.N.J.M., Sec.; Mary Rita Rohde, S.N.J.M., Treas.; Guadalupe Guajardo, S.N.J.M., Leadership Team.

MILWAUKIE. *La Salle Catholic College Preparatory Educational Foundation*, 11999 S.E. Fuller Rd., Milwaukie, 97222. Tel: 503-353-1417; Fax: 503-496-1754; Email: mwinningham@lsprep.org; Email: savery@lsprep.org; Web: www.lsprep.org. Mr. Matthew Winningham, Treas. & Contact Person; Stephanie Avery, Exec. Asst. to the Pres.

MOUNT ANGEL. *Benedictine Foundation of Oregon* (1980) 840 Main St., Mount Angel, 97362. Tel: 503-845-2556; Fax: 503-845-6585; Email: benedictinefoundation@gmail.com; Web: www.benedictine-srs.org. Sr. Dorothy Jean Beyer, O.S.B., Devel. Coord.

**Fr. Bernard Youth Center, Inc.* Lay Ministry Youth and Young Adult Retreat Center 980 S. Main St., P.O. Box 790, Mount Angel, 97362-0790. Tel: 503-845-4097; Fax: 503-845-2208; Email: adminoffice@fbyc.info; Email: mark@fbyc.info; Email: michelle@fbyc.info; Web: www.fbyc.info. Mark Dol, Exec.; Michelle Wodtli, Exec. Retreatants 3,000.

St. Joseph Shelter (1988) 925 S. Main, Mount Angel, 97362-9527. Tel: 503-845-6147; Fax: 503-845-2815; Email: sjshelter@mtangel.net; Web: stjosephshelter.org. Mike Norman, Operations Dir.; Contact Person. Special center for social services and assistance. Total Staff 7; Total People Served 105; Total Shelter Nights 20,931; Total Meals Served 15,532.

SALEM. *Salem Catholic Schools Foundation*, 1850 45th Avenue N.E., Salem, 97305. Tel: 503-371-9068; Email: dana@salemcatholicschools.org; Web: www.SalemCatholicSchools.org. Dana North, Contact Person.

ST. BENEDICT. *The Abbey Foundation of Oregon* (2002) 1 Abbey Dr., P.O. Box 497, St. Benedict, 97373-0497. Tel: 503-845-3030; Email: info@mtangel.edu; Web: www.mountangelabbey.org. Rev. Martin Grassel, O.S.B., Treas. & Procurator.

RELIGIOUS INSTITUTES OF MEN REPRESENTED IN THE ARCHDIOCESE

For further details refer to the corresponding bracketed number in the Religious Institutes of Men or Women section.

[]—*Apostles of Jesus*—A.J.
[]—*Apostolic Life Community Of Priests (Holy Spirit Fathers)*—A.L.C.P.
[0140]—*Augustinian Community*—O.S.A.
[0200]—*Benedictine Monks* (Mt. Angel, OR)—O.S.B.
[]—*Brotherhood of the People of Praise.*
[0350]—*The Cistercians (Trappists)*—O.C.S.O.
[]—*Discalced Carmelite Friars*—O.C.D.
[]—*Domus Dei Clerical Society of Apostolic Life*—S.D.D.
[0520]—*Franciscan Friars*—O.F.M.
[0690]—*Jesuit Fathers and Brothers* (Oregon Prov. Office)—S.J.
[]—*Maronite Monks of Jesus, Mary and Joseph*—M.M.J.M.J.
[0660]—*Missionaries Of The Holy Spirit*—M.Sp.S.
[0430]—*Order of Preachers (Dominicans)* (Western Prov.)—O.P.
[0895]—*Order of the Most Holy Savior (Brigittine Monks)*—O.Ss.S.
[1030]—*Paulist Fathers*—C.S.P.
[0610]—*Priests of the Congregation of Holy Cross*—C.S.C.
[]—*St. John Society*—S.S.J.
[1240]—*Servite Friars (The Grotto)* (Western Prov.)—O.S.M.
[1260]—*Society of Christ*—S.Ch.
[]—*Society of the Missionaries of St. Francis Xavier*—S.F.X.

RELIGIOUS INSTITUTES OF WOMEN REPRESENTED IN THE ARCHDIOCESE

[]—*Adrian Dominican Sisters*—O.P.
[0230]—*Benedictine Sisters of Pontifical Jurisdiction* (Mount Angel, OR)—O.S.B.
[0420]—*Discalced Carmelite Sisters*—O.C.D.
[]—*Dominican Sisters* (Blauvelt, NY)—O.P.
[]—*Dominican Sisters of Caldwell, NJ*—O.P.
[1390]—*Franciscan Missionary Sisters of Our Lady of Sorrows*—O.S.F.
[]—*Holy Spirit Sisters*—A.L.C.S.
[1250]—*The Institute of the Franciscan Sisters of the Eucharist*—F.S.E.
[]—*The Lovers of The Holy Cross Sisters*—T.H.C.S.
[]—*Maryknoll Sisters of St. Dominic*—M.M.
[]—*Missionaries of the Rosary of Fatima*—M.R.F.
[]—*Oblates of Saint Martha*—O.S.M.
[3590]—*Servants of Mary (Servite Sisters)*—O.S.M.
[]—*Sisters for Christian Community*—S.F.C.C.
[0430]—*Sisters of Charity of the Blessed Virgin Mary*—B.V.M.
[]—*Sisters of Jesus the Saviour*—S.J.S.
[]—*Sisters of Mary of Kakamega*—S.M.K.
[2575]—*Sisters of Mercy of the Americas* (Omaha, NE)—R.S.M.
[3350]—*Sisters of Providence* (Mother Joseph Province)—S.P.
[3475]—*Sisters of Reparation of the Sacred Wounds of Jesus*—S.R.
[]—*Sisters of St. Francis* (Clinton, Iowa)—O.S.F.
[1650]—*The Sisters of St. Francis of Philadelphia*—O.S.F.
[3890]—*Sisters of St. Joseph of Peace* (Our Lady Prov.)—C.S.J.P.
[3960]—*Sisters of St. Mary of Oregon*—S.S.M.O.
[1830]—*The Sisters of the Good Shepherd*—R.G.S.
[1990]—*Sisters of the Holy Names of Jesus and Mary*—S.N.J.M.
[]—*Society of Mary.*
[4060]—*Society of the Holy Child Jesus* (American Prov.)—S.H.C.J.
[4155]—*Vietnamese Adorers of the Holy Cross*—M.T.G.

ARCHDIOCESAN CEMETERIES

PORTLAND. *Gethsemani*, 11666 S.E. Stevens Rd., Happy Valley, 97086. Tel: 503-659-1350; Email: TCorbett@ccpdxor.com; Web: www.ccpdxor.com. Tim Corbett, Dir.

EUGENE. *Mount Calvary*, 333 S.W. Skyline Blvd., 97221. Tel: 503-292-6621; Fax: 503-292-6622; Email: tcorbett@ccpdxor.com; Web: www.ccpdxor.com. Tim Corbett, Pres.

SALEM. *St. Barbara*, Liberty Rd S & Missouri Ave S, Salem, 97302. Tel: 503-581-1623; Email: irico@stjosephchurch.com. Isabelle Rico, Sec. Run by St. Joseph's. Salem.

An asterisk (*) denotes an organization that has established tax-exempt status directly with the IRS and is not covered by the USCCB Group Ruling.

Diocese of Providence

(Dioecesis Providentiensis)

Most Reverend

THOMAS J. TOBIN

Bishop of Providence; ordained July 21, 1973; appointed Titular Bishop of Novica and Auxiliary Bishop of Pittsburgh, November 3, 1992; consecrated December 27, 1992; appointed Fourth Bishop of Youngstown installed February 2, 1996; appointed eighth Bishop of Providence March 31, 2005; installed May 31, 2005. *Office: One Cathedral Square, Providence, RI 02903-3695.*

Most Reverend

ROBERT C. EVANS

Auxiliary Bishop of Providence; ordained July 2, 1973; appointed Titular Bishop of Aquae Regiae and Auxiliary Bishop of Providence October 15, 2009; consecrated December 15, 2009. *Office: One Cathedral Square, Providence, RI 02903-3695.*

Bishop's Office & Chancery Office: One Cathedral Square, Providence, RI 02903-3695. Tel: 401-278-4500

Web: www.dioceseofprovidence.org

Most Reverend

LOUIS E. GELINEAU

Bishop Emeritus of Providence; ordained June 5, 1954; appointed Bishop of Providence December 6, 1971; consecrated January 26, 1972; retired June 11, 1997. *Res.: 400 Mendon Rd., North Smithfield, RI 02896.*

ESTABLISHED APRIL 16, 1872.

Square Miles 1,085.

Corporate Title: Roman Catholic Bishop of Providence, a corporation sole

Comprises the State of Rhode Island.

STATISTICAL OVERVIEW

Personnel	
Bishop	1
Auxiliary Bishops	1
Retired Bishops	2
Abbots	1
Priests: Diocesan Active in Diocese	127
Priests: Diocesan Active Outside Diocese	7
Priests: Retired, Sick or Absent	106
Number of Diocesan Priests	240
Religious Priests in Diocese	75
Total Priests in Diocese	315
Extern Priests in Diocese	10
Ordinations:	
Diocesan Priests	1
Transitional Deacons	2
Permanent Deacons in Diocese	102
Total Brothers	60
Total Sisters	352
Parishes	
Parishes	133
With Resident Pastor:	
Resident Diocesan Priests	109
Resident Religious Priests	5
Without Resident Pastor:	
Administered by Priests	17
Administered by Deacons	2
Missions	8
Pastoral Centers	15
New Parishes Created	1
Closed Parishes	7
Professional Ministry Personnel:	
Brothers	1
Sisters	20
Lay Ministers	96
Welfare	
Homes for the Aged	7
Total Assisted	44,500
Day Care Centers	2
Total Assisted	115
Specialized Homes	2
Total Assisted	150
Special Centers for Social Services	8
Total Assisted	103,315
Other Institutions	4
Total Assisted	41,780
Educational	
Seminaries, Diocesan	1
Students from This Diocese	5
Students from Other Diocese	11
Diocesan Students in Other Seminaries	8
Total Seminarians	13
Colleges and Universities	2
Total Students	7,521
High Schools, Diocesan and Parish	4
Total Students	1,889
High Schools, Private	3
Total Students	2,567
Elementary Schools, Diocesan and Parish	27
Total Students	5,033
Elementary Schools, Private	4
Total Students	878
Catechesis/Religious Education:	
High School Students	2,632
Elementary Students	10,353
Total Students under Catholic Instruction	30,886
Teachers in the Diocese:	
Priests	11
Brothers	5
Sisters	24
Lay Teachers	1,053
Vital Statistics	
Receptions into the Church:	
Infant Baptism Totals	1,876
Minor Baptism Totals	148
Adult Baptism Totals	76
Received into Full Communion	46
First Communions	2,105
Confirmations	2,365
Marriages:	
Catholic	546
Interfaith	93
Total Marriages	639
Deaths	3,706
Total Catholic Population	623,815
Total Population	1,057,315

Former Bishops—Rt. Revs. THOMAS F. HENDRICKEN, D.D., cons. first Bishop of Providence, April 28, 1872; died June 11, 1886; MATTHEW HARKINS, D.D., cons. second Bishop of Providence, April 14, 1887; died May 25, 1921; Most Revs. WILLIAM A. HICKEY, D.D., ord. Dec. 22, 1893; appt. Coadjutor Bishop of Providence, Cum jure successionis, March 10, 1919; cons. Titular Bishop of Claudiopolis, April 10, 1919; succeeded to the See of Providence, May 25, 1921; died Oct. 4, 1933; FRANCIS P. KEOUGH, D.D., cons. fourth Bishop of Providence, May 22, 1934; appt. Archbishop of Baltimore, Nov. 29, 1947; died Dec. 8, 1961; RUSSELL J. MCVINNEY, D.D., appt. May 29, 1948; cons. July 14, 1948 fifth Bishop of Providence; died Aug. 10, 1971; LOUIS E. GELINEAU, D.D., S.T.L., J.C.L., (Retired), appt. Dec. 6, 1971; cons. sixth Bishop of Providence, Jan. 26, 1972; retired June 11, 1997; ROBERT E. MULVEE, ord. June 30, 1957; appt. Auxiliary Bishop of Manchester and Titular Bishop of Summa Feb. 15, 1977; cons. April 14, 1977; appt. Bishop of Wilmington Feb. 19, 1985; installed April 11, 1985; appt. Coadjutor Bishop of Providence Feb. 9, 1995; succeeded to See June 11, 1997; retired March 31, 2005; died Dec. 28, 2018.

Vicars General—Most Rev. ROBERT C. EVANS, D.D., J.C.L.; Rev. Msgr. ALBERT A. KENNEY, S.T.L.

Episcopal Vicars and Secretaries—

Vicar for Judicial Matters—Rev. Msgr. RONALD P. SIMEONE, M.Div., J.C.L.

Secretary for Diocesan Administration—Rev. Msgr. ALBERT A. KENNEY, S.T.L.

Secretary for Ministerial Services—Most Rev. ROBERT C. EVANS, D.D., J.C.L.

Secretary for Planning & Financial Services—Rev. Msgr. RAYMOND B. BASTIA.

Secretary for Catholic Charities and Social Ministry—MR. JOHN J. BARRY III.

Deans—

Deanery I—Rev. Msgr. JOHN J. DARCY, M.A., J.C.L.

Deanery II—Very Rev. FRANCIS A. O'LOUGHLIN.

Deanery III—VACANT.

Deanery IV—VACANT.

Deanery V—Very Rev. EDWARD S. CARDENTE.

Deanery VI—Very Rev. WILLIAM J. LEDOUX.

Deanery VII—Very Rev. BERNARD A. HEALEY.

Deanery VIII—VACANT.

Bishop's Office—One Cathedral Sq., Providence, 02903-3695. Tel: 401-278-4546; Fax: 401-278-4654. Rev. JEREMY J. RODRIGUES, Administrative Sec. to the Bishop. Office Hours: Mon.-Fri. 8:30-4:30.

Vicars General—Most Rev. ROBERT C. EVANS, D.D., J.C.L., Tel: 401-278-4518; Fax: 401-278-4623; Rev. Msgr. ALBERT A. KENNEY, S.T.L., Tel: 401-278-4519; Fax: 401-278-4623.

Moderator of the Curia—Rev. Msgr. ALBERT A. KENNEY, S.T.L., Tel: 401-278-4519; Fax: 401-278-4623.

Chancellor—Rev. TIMOTHY D. REILLY, S.T.B., J.C.L., Tel: 401-278-4663; Fax: 401-278-4623.

Assistant Chancellor—Tel: 401-278-4664; Fax: 401-278-4623. Rev. NATHAN J. RICCI.

Diocesan Tribunal—

Judicial Vicar—Rev. Msgr. RONALD P. SIMEONE, M.Div., J.C.L., Tel: 401-278-4666; Fax: 401-278-4622.

Judges—Rev. Msgrs. RONALD P. SIMEONE, M.Div.,

J.C.L.; PAUL D. THEROUX, S.T.B., J.C.L.; Rev. DEAN P. PERRI, J.C.L., S.T.L.
Assessor and Auditor—Deacon JOHN P. PRYOR.
Defenders of the Bond—Revs. DAVID W. MASELLO, J.C.L., (part-time); ALBERT P. MARCELLO III.
Advocate—Rev. TIMOTHY D. REILLY, S.T.B., J.C.L.
Assessor and Counselor—MRS. NANCY GOULD.
Notaries—MRS. PATRICIA COSTA; MRS. LINDA L. NASTARI.
Notary & Secretary—MRS. PATRICIA COSTA.

Council of Priests—One Cathedral Sq., Providence, 02903-3695. Tel: 401-278-4567; Fax: 401-278-4623.
Officers—Most Rev. THOMAS J. TOBIN, Pres.; Very Rev. WILLIAM J. LEDOUX, Moderator; Rev. Msgr. ALBERT A. KENNEY, S.T.L., Sec.
Ex Officio—Most Rev. ROBERT C. EVANS, D.D., J.C.L.; Rev. Msgrs. RAYMOND B. BASTIA; ALBERT A. KENNEY, S.T.L.; Rev. TIMOTHY D. REILLY, S.T.B., J.C.L.
Elected Members—Constituency I: Rev. JOSEPH R. UPTON. Constituency II: Rev. BRIAN M. SISTARE. Constituency III: Rev. JAMES T. RUGGIERI. Constituency IV: Very Rev. WILLIAM J. LEDOUX. Constituency V: Rev. STEPHEN P. AMARAL. Constituency VI: Rev. ROGER C. GAGNE. Constituency VII: Rev. EUGENE J. MCKENNA, (Retired). Constituency VIII: Rev. ALBERT DUGGAN, O.P.
Appointed Members—Revs. JOSHUA A. BARROW; FRANCESCO FRANCESE; MICHAEL A. KELLEY; RICHARD A. NARCISO; ALBERT D. RANALLO JR.; JOHN P. SOARES.
College of Consultors—Most Rev. ROBERT C. EVANS, D.D., J.C.L.; Rev. Msgrs. RAYMOND B. BASTIA; ALBERT A. KENNEY, S.T.L.; Revs. JOHN C. CODEGA; JAIME A. GARCIA; OTONIEL J. GOMEZ; EUGENE J. MCKENNA, (Retired); MICHAEL J. NAJIM, M.Div.; RICHARD A. NARCISO; TIMOTHY D. REILLY, S.T.B., J.C.L.

Finance Council—Most Revs. THOMAS J. TOBIN, Pres.; ROBERT C. EVANS, D.D., J.C.L.; Rev. Msgrs. RAYMOND B. BASTIA, Sec.; ALBERT A. KENNEY, S.T.L.; PAUL D. THEROUX, S.T.B., J.C.L.; Revs. ROGER C. GAGNE; JARED J. COSTANZA; Sr. DOROTHY SCHWARZ, S.S.D.; MS. KATHLEEN A. RYAN, Esq.; MR. ALMON C. HALL; MR. WILLIAM K. WRAY; MR. GLENN M. CREAMER; Deacon JOHN P. PRYOR; MRS. DEBORAH A. IMONDI; MRS. PATRICIA SMOLLEY. Staff: MR. MICHAEL F. SABATINO, CPA.
Chief Financial Officer—MR. MICHAEL F. SABATINO, CPA.

Diocesan Offices and Directors

Diocesan Administration—
Secretariat for Diocesan Administration—One Cathedral Sq., Providence, 02903-3695. Tel: 401-278-4519; Fax: 401-278-4623. Rev. Msgr. ALBERT A. KENNEY, S.T.L.
Archives—MRS. LISA A. VESPIA, Archives Clerk, One Cathedral Sq., Providence, 02903-3695. Tel: 401-278-4522.
Censor of Books—Rev. TIMOTHY D. REILLY, S.T.B., J.C.L.
Communications—(Legal Title: Diocesan Catholic Telecommunications Network of Rhode Island); (News Media, TV, Public Relations) MS. CAROLYN CRONIN, Dir. Communications; Ms. KAREN DAVIS, Public Affairs Mgr., One Cathedral Sq., Providence, 02903-3695. Tel: 401-278-4600.
Telecommunications—(Produces Catholic Programming, Liaison with State Interconnect and CATV Companies, ETWN Liaison) MISS SUSAN MCCARTHY, Tel: 401-278-4609.
Website Coordinator—MRS. LAURA H. TESTA, Tel: 401-278-4602; Fax: 401-278-4659.
Education and Compliance—MR. KEVIN O'BRIEN, Dir., 80 St. Mary's Dr., Cranston, 02920. Tel: 401-941-0760; Fax: 401-941-1195.
RI Catholic Conference—Very Rev. BERNARD A. HEALEY, Dir., One Cathedral Sq., Providence, 02903. Tel: 401-278-4525; Tel: 401-333-1568; Fax: 401-333-8941; Email: ricc@dioceseofprovidence.org; Web: www.faithfulcitizenri.org.
Human Resources Office—MR. JOHN BITTNER, Dir., One Cathedral Square, Providence, 02903-3695. Tel: 401-278-4584; Fax: 401-278-4659; KATE HANCOCK, Human Resources Mgr., Tel: 401-278-4586.
Newspaper—"Rhode Island Catholic", Diocesan weekly. *One Cathedral Sq., Providence, 02903.* Tel: 401-272-1010; Fax: 401-421-8418. RICK SNIZEK, Editor; Rev. NATHAN J. RICCI, Theological Advisor.
Propagation of the Faith—(Legal Title: Society for the Propagation of the Faith, Diocese of Providence) Rev. ROBERT P. PERRON, Dir., Tel: 401-278-4520; MS. PAULA MOLLO, Sec., One Cathedral Sq., Providence, 02903-3695. Tel: 401-278-4519; Email: pmollo@dioceseofprovidence.org.
Catholic Relief Services—Rev. ROBERT P. PERRON, Dir., Tel: 401-278-4520.

Ministerial Services—
Secretariat for Ministerial Services—Most Rev. ROBERT C. EVANS, D.D., J.C.L., Sec., One Cathedral Sq., Providence, 02903-3695. Tel: 401-278-4518; Fax: 401-278-4623.
Post-Ordination Formation—Rev. CARL B. FISETTE, 485 Mt. Pleasant Ave., Providence, 02908. Tel: 401-331-1316; Fax: 401-521-4192.
Pre-Ordination Formation—Rev. DAVID F. GAFFNEY, M.Div., Coord., 485 Mt. Pleasant Ave., Providence, 02908. Tel: 401-331-1316; Fax: 401-521-4192.
Priests' Personnel Committee—Most Rev. ROBERT C. EVANS, D.D., J.C.L., Chm., One Cathedral Sq., Providence, 02903-3695. Tel: 401-278-4518; Fax: 401-278-4623. Members: Rev. Msgr. PAUL D. THEROUX, S.T.B., J.C.L.; Very Rev. WILLIAM J. LEDOUX; Revs. CARL B. FISETTE; FRANCIS C. SANTILLI; DAVID F. GAFFNEY, M.Div.
Ecumenical Officer—Rev. JOHN A. KILEY, (Retired), 247 Highland St., Woonsocket, 02895. Tel: 401-787-4093; Email: highlandstreet@verizon.net.
Clergy Benefit Fund—(Legal Title: Our Lady, Queen of the Clergy) Most Rev. ROBERT C. EVANS, D.D., J.C.L., Dir.
Permanent Diaconate—One Cathedral Sq., Providence, 02903-3695. Tel: 401-278-4604. Deacon NOEL EDSALL, Dir.
Religious—Sr. ELIZABETH CASTRO, H.M.S.P., Dir., 34 Fenner St., Providence, 02903. Tel: 401-278-4633.
Council of Religious—Sr. ELIZABETH CASTRO, H.M.S.P., Coord.
Seminary of Our Lady of Providence—House of Formation for college students and pre-theologians) *485 Mt. Pleasant Ave., Providence, 02908.* Tel: 401-331-1316; Fax: 401-521-4192. Revs. DAVID F. GAFFNEY, M.Div., Rector; THOMAS J. WOODHOUSE, Dir. Spiritual Formation; TIMOTHY D. REILLY, S.T.B., J.C.L., Asst. Spiritual Dir.; CHRISTOPHER J. MURPHY; DR. MICHAEL HANSEN, Ph.D., Human Formation, Email: mhansen@dioceseofprovidence.org.
Vocations—Rev. CHRISTOPHER J. MURPHY, Dir., 485 Mt. Pleasant Ave., Providence, 02908. Tel: 401-831-8011; Fax: 401-521-4192; Sr. ELIZABETH CASTRO, H.M.S.P., Assoc. Dir. Rel. Vocations, 34 Fenner St., Providence, 02903. Tel: 401-278-4633.

Catholic Schools—MR. DANIEL FERRIS, Supt., One Cathedral Sq., Providence, 02903. Tel: 401-278-4550; Fax: 401-278-4596; Email: cso@dioceseofprovidence.org; Web: www.catholicschools.org.

Handicapped Persons Apostolate—Rev. RICHARD A. NARCISO, Chap.

SPRED (Special Religious Education)—MRS. IRMA I. RODRIQUEZ, Coord., 34 Fenner St., Providence, 02903-3603. Tel: 401-278-4578; Email: irodriguez@dioceseofprovidence.org.

Office of Faith Formation—MR. EDWARD TRENDOWSKI, Dir., Email: etrendowski@dioceseofprovidence.org; MRS. MICHELLE DONOVAN, M.A., Asst. Dir., 34 Fenner St., Providence, 02903-3603. Tel: 401-278-4646; Email: mdonovan@dioceseofprovidence.org; Web: www.discovercatholicfaith.org.

Worship—Rev. JEREMY J. RODRIGUES, Dir., One Cathedral Sq., Providence, 02903. Tel: 401-278-4587; Fax: 401-278-4654; Email: jrodrigues@dioceseofprovidence.org.

Catholic Youth Ministry—MISS LOUISE DUSSAULT, Dir., One Cathedral Sq., Providence, 02903-3695. Tel: 401-278-4626; Fax: 401-278-4596; Email: ldussault@dioceseofprovidence.org; Web: www.catholicyouthri.org.
Catholic Scouting-Boy Scouts, Girl Scouts, Camp Fire—Rev. ADAM A. YOUNG, Chap., Tel: 401-278-4626; Sr. DIANE RUSSO, R.S.M., Pastoral Assoc.
Catholic Youth Organization—Tel: 401-278-4626.
Youth Summer Camp—Mother of Hope Camp, Box W, Chepachet, 02814. Tel: 401-568-3580. MICHELLE LOSARDO, Dir., Email: mlosardo@dioceseofprovidence.org; Web: www.motherofhopecamp.com.

Marriage Preparation and Enrichment—One Cathedral Sq., Providence, 02903. Tel: 401-278-4577; Tel: 401-278-4576; Email: marriage@dioceseofprovidence.org.

Social Ministry—
Secretariat for Catholic Charities and Social Ministry—MR. JOHN J. BARRY III, Sec., One Cathedral Sq., Providence, 02903-3695. Tel: 401-421-7833, Ext. 205; Fax: 401-274-5450; Email: jbarry@dioceseofprovidence.org.
Catholic Social Services of RI—One Cathedral Sq., Providence, 02903-3695. Tel: 401-421-7833, Ext. 206; Fax: 401-453-6135.
AIDS Ministry—MR. JAMES JAHNZ, One Cathedral Sq., Providence, 02903-3695. Tel: 401-421-7833, Ext. 222; Fax: 401-453-6135; Email: jjahnz@dioceseofprovidence.org.
Catholic Campaign for Human Development and Catholic Charities Advocacy Fund—MR. JOHN J. BARRY III, Tel: 401-421-7833, Ext. 204; Email: jmonteiro@dioceseofprovidence.org.
Chaplains of Public Institutions—Catholic Chaplaincy Team (All Correctional and Detention Institutions) Rev. LAZARUS ONUH, (Nigeria) Chap.; MRS. MARTHA PAONE, Chap. Coord., Tel: 401-421-7833, Ext. 204; Tel: 401-462-5215 (Prison); Email: martha.paone@doc.ri.gov.
Elder Care Services—Respite Care; Friendly Visitor Tel: 401-421-7833, Ext. 228. MR. HECTOR MUNOZ, Tel: 401-421-7833, Ext. 211; Email: hmunoz@dioceseofprovidence.org; JO ELLEN MISTARZ, Tel: 401-421-7833, Ext. 202.
Emmanual House—MR. JAMES JAHNZ, One Cathedral Sq., Providence, 02903-3695. Tel: 401-421-7833, Ext. 222; Fax: 401-453-6135; Email: jjahnz@dioceseofprovidence.org.
Health Care Ministries—One Cathedral Sq., Providence, 02903-3695. Tel: 401-421-7833, Ext. 204; Fax: 401-274-5450; Email: jmonteiro@dioceseofprovidence.org.
Immigration and Refugee Services— Tel: 401-421-7833, Ext. 229; Fax: 401-277-9027. NANCY GONZALEZ, Coord., Email: ngonzalez@dioceseofprovidence.org.
Keep the Heat On—MR. JAMES JAHNZ, One Cathedral Sq., Providence, 02903-3695. Tel: 401-421-7833, Ext. 222; Fax: 401-453-6135; Fax: 401-453-6135; Email: jjahnz@dioceseofprovidence.org.
Office for Multi-Cultural Ministry—Rev. NOLASCO TAMAYO, (Colombia) Dir., One Cathedral Sq., Providence, 02903-3695. Tel: 401-421-7833, Ext. 237; Email: ntamayo@dioceseofprovidence.org. Hispanic Ministry: MR. SILVIO CUELLAR, Coord., Tel: 401-421-7833, Ext. 220; Tel: 401-421-7833, Ext. 233; Email: scuellar@dioceseofprovidence.org. Black Catholic Ministry: MS. PATTY JANUARY, Coord., Tel: 401-421-7833, Ext. 4552; Email: pjanuary@dioceseofprovidence.org.
Peace and Justice—Tel: 401-421-7833, Ext. 206; Fax: 401-453-6135.
Catholic Social Services of RI - South County and Newport Satellite—114 High St., Wakefield, 02879. Tel: 401-783-3149; Fax: 401-783-3149. MS. EILEEN NOBLE, Email: enoble@dioceseofprovidence.org.
Catholic Social Services of RI - Kent County Satellite—145 Washington St., West Warwick, 02893. Tel: 401-823-6211; Fax: 401-615-1410. MS. DARLENE LEMOI, Tel: dlemoi@dioceseofprovidence.org.
Catholic Social Services of RI - Northern RI Satellite—323 Rathbun St., Woonsocket, 02895. Tel: 401-762-2849; Fax: 401-356-0271. MRS. ROSANNA LENUS, Email: rlenus@dioceseofprovidence.org.
Catholic Social Services of RI - Newport County Satellite—Tel: 401-619-4677.

Life and Family Ministry—(Legal Title: Retreat House of the Immaculate Heart of Mary) *One Cathedral Sq., Providence, 02903-3695.* Tel: 401-421-7833, Ext. 218; Fax: 401-453-6135.
Newport County Satellite, 1 Vernon St., Newport, 02840. Tel: 401-278-4508. MRS. CAROL OWENS, Dir., Email: cowens@dioceseofprovidence.org.
Adoption Searches—MR. PETER MAGNOTTA, M.S.W., L.I.C.S.W., C.C.D.P.-D., Tel: 401-421-7833, Ext. 217; Fax: 401-453-6135; Email: pmagnotta@dioceseofprovidence.org.
Evaluations for Maturity for Marriage—MR. PETER MAGNOTTA, M.S.W., L.I.C.S.W., C.C.D.P.-D., Tel: 401-421-7833, Ext. 217; MRS. CAROL OWENS, Elizabeth Ministry, Tel: 401-421-7833, Ext. 107; Tel: 401-421-7833, Ext. 218; Email: cowens@dioceseofprovidence.org.
Project Rachel—(Abortion Helpline 24/7) Tel: 1-888-456-HOPE.
Rachel's Vineyard's Retreats—MRS. CAROL OWENS, Liaison, Tel: 401-421-7833, Ext. 218.
Respect Life Activities—MRS. CAROL OWENS, Coord., Tel: 401-421-7833, Ext. 118; Tel: 401-421-7833, Ext. 218 (St. Gabriel's Call); Email: cowens@dioceseofprovidence.org.

Project Hope/Proyecto Esperanza—(Legal Title: Project Hope/Proyecto Esperanza) MR. JAMES JAHNZ, Prog. Supvr., One Cathedral Sq., Providence, 02903. Tel: 401-728-0515; Fax: 401-728-2330; Email: jjahnz@dioceseofprovidence.org.

St. Martin de Porres Multi-Service Center—(Legal Title: St. Martin de Porres Center) *160 Cranston St., Providence, 02907-2396.* Tel: 401-274-6783;

Fax: 401-274-5930. LINDA AVANT-DEISHINNI, Email: lavant-deishinni@dioceseofprovidence.org.

Planning and Financial Services—

Secretariat for Planning and Financial Services— Rev. Msgr. RAYMOND B. BASTIA, Vicar; MR. MICHAEL F. SABATINO, CPA, CFO, One Cathedral Sq., Providence, 02903-3695. Tel: 401-278-4540; Fax: 401-831-1786.

Diocesan Facilities Department—One Cathedral Sq., Providence, 02903-3695. Tel: 401-278-4636. MR. SEAN BRENNAN, Dir. Facilities.

*Cemeteries—*MR. ANTHONY J. CARPINELLO, Dir., 80 St. Mary's Drive, Cranston, 02920. Tel: 401-944-8383; Fax: 401-944-8394.

*Fiscal Office—*MS. CHERYL BRENNAN, Diocesan Controller, One Cathedral Sq., Providence, 02903-3695. Tel: 401-278-4616; Fax: 401-751-6808.

*Insurance Commission—*Rev. Msgr. RAYMOND B. BASTIA, Chm., One Cathedral Sq., Providence, 02903-3695. Tel: 401-278-4547.

*Catholic Mutual Group—*MR. JOSEPH WALSH, Claims & Risk Mgr., 80 St. Mary's Dr., Cranston, 02920-5200. Tel: 401-944-5375; Tel: 401-944-5379; Fax: 401-944-5380; Email: jwalsh@catholicmutual.org.

*Management Information Services—*MS. MARGARET RYAN, Dir., One Cathedral Sq., Providence, 02903-3695. Tel: 401-278-4611.

*Parish Financial Assistance—*MRS. CATHERINE MESSIER, Dir., One Cathedral Sq., Providence, 02903. Tel: 401-278-4644; Email: cmessier@dioceseofprovidence.org.

Stewardship and Development—(Annual Appeal, Stewardship, Planned Giving, Major Gifts, Anchor of Hope Fund) Tel: 401-277-2121. MR. ROBERT CORCORAN, Dir.

Catholic Charity Appeal—(Legal Title: Catholic Charity Fund) Tel: 401-277-2121.

Catholic Foundation of R.I.—(Legal Title: Catholic Foundation of Rhode Island) Tel: 401-277-2121 . ANDREA H. KRUPP, Esq., Dir.

*Victim Assistance—*Office of Outreach & Prevention DR. MICHAEL HANSEN, Ph.D., Dir., Tel: 401-946-0728; Fax: 401-946-1587; Email: mhansen@dioceseofprovidence.org.

CLERGY, PARISHES, MISSIONS AND PAROCHIAL SCHOOLS

CITY OF PROVIDENCE

(PROVIDENCE COUNTY)

1—CATHEDRAL OF SS. PETER AND PAUL (1837)
30 Fenner St., 02903. Tel: 401-331-2434; Email: aiello@providencecathedral.org; Web: providencecathedral.org. Rev. Msgr. Anthony Mancini, V.F., Rector
*SS. Peter and Paul's Church*In Res., Revs. Robert W. Hayman, M.A., Ph.D., (Retired); Jeremy J. Rodrigues; Rev. Msgr. Raymond B. Bastia.
*Catechesis Religious Program—*Email: religious_education@providencecathedral.org. Sr. Elizabeth Castro, H.M.S.P., D.R.E. Students 15.
Convent—Cathedral Convent.

2—ST. ADALBERT (1902) (Polish)
866 Atwells Ave., 02909-2596. Tel: 401-351-9306; Email: fathermarek@hotmail.com; Web: www.stadalberts.us. Rev. Marek S. Kupka; Sisters Mary Bernice Pikul, C.S.S.F., Pastoral Assoc. & C.R.E.; Janice M. Gaudette, C.S.S.F., Pastoral Assoc.
Saint Adalbert's Church
*Convent—*Tel: 401-831-3336. Felician Sisters of St. Francis 3.
*Catechesis Religious Program—*Students 31.

3—ST. AGNES (1904)
351 Branch Ave., 02904. Tel: 401-861-7265; Email: stagnesprov@verizon.net; Web: www.saintagnesprovidence.org. Rev. Frank S. Salmani; Ms. Cathy Cadden, Pastoral Assoc.
St. Agnes Church
*Catechesis Religious Program—*Tel: 401-487-1486. Students 50.

4—ST. ANN (1895) (Italian) Revs. Albert D. Ranallo Jr.; Antony Jeya Siluvai Rayan, (In Res.)
Saint Ann's Catholic Church of Providence, Rhode Island
Res.: 2 Russo St., 02940-9207. Tel: 401-861-5111; Email: stann1@cox.net.
*Catechesis Religious Program—*Students 19.

5—ASSUMPTION OF THE BLESSED VIRGIN MARY (1871)
791 Potters Ave., 02907. Tel: 401-941-1248; Email: assumptionsouthprovidence@yahoo.com. Rev. Gildardo Suarez, (Colombia); Deacon Rony Lopez; Sr. Angela Daniels, C.P., Pastoral Assoc.
The Church of the Assumption, Providence, Rhode Island
*Catechesis Religious Program—*Tel: 401-941-3768; Email: religiouseducation791@yahoo.com. Mrs. Luz Lopez, D.R.E. Students 195.
Mission—St. Anthony (Olneyville) (1900) 549 Plainfield St., 02909. Tel: 401-943-2300.
Saint Anthony's Church Corporation, Rhode Island.

6—ST. AUGUSTINE (1929) Revs. Robert H. Forcier; Joseph Brice
Saint Augustine's Church, Providence, Rhode Island
Res.: 20 Old Rd., 02908. Tel: 401-831-3503; Email: staugprov@verizon.net; Web: www.churchofsaintaugustineprov.com.
School—St. Augustine School, (Grades PreK-8), 635 Mt. Pleasant Ave., 02908. Tel: 401-831-1213;
Fax: 401-831-4256; Email: principal@staugustinesri.com. Janet Rufful, Prin. Lay Teachers 25; Sisters 1; Students 240.
*Catechesis Religious Program—*Sr. Dorothy Schwartz, D.R.E. Students 202.

7—ST. BARTHOLOMEW (1907) (Italian) Revs. Vilmar Orsolin; Joseph Pranzo, C.S.; Deacon Robert L. Gallo, Pastoral Assoc.
Saint Bartholomew's Church Corporation
Res.: 297 Laurel Hill Ave., 02909-3897.
Tel: 401-944-4466; Fax: 401-946-5866; Email: stbartholomewparish@hotmail.com; Web: www.rc.net/providence/stbartholomew.
*Catechesis Religious Program—*Students 140.

8—BLESSED SACRAMENT (1888)
239 Regent Ave., 02908. Tel: 401-751-7575; Email: blessacprov@gmail.com; Web: blessedsacramentpvd.org. Rev. Charles R. Grondin; Deacon Luis Garcia
The Church of the Blessed Sacrament in Providence, Rhode Island
School—Blessed Sacrament School, (Grades PreK-8), 240 Regent Ave., 02908. Tel: 401-831-3993; Email: dfioravanti@blessedschoolpvd.org; Web: blessedschoolpvd.com. Christopher Weber, Prin. Lay Teachers 20; Students 190; Religious Teachers 1.
*Catechesis Religious Program—*Students 90.

9—ST. CASIMIR (1919) [JC] (Lithuanian), Closed.
Saint Casimir's Church, Providence, Rhode Island.

10—ST. CHARLES BORROMEO (1874) (French) Rev. Jaime A. Garcia; Deacons Jose Rico, Pastoral Assoc.; Joseph Braga
Saint Charles Borromeo Roman Catholic Church, Providence, Rhode Island
Res.: 178 Dexter St., 02907. Tel: 401-421-6441;
Fax: 401-421-4009; Email: stcharlesprov@verizon.net.
*Catechesis Religious Program—*Students 316.

11—ST. EDWARD (1874)
10 Caxton St., 02904. Tel: 401-331-4035; Email: stanthonynp@cox.net. 997 Branch Ave., 02904. Very Rev. Edward S. Cardente; Rev. Nolasco Tamayo, (Colombia)
The Church of St. Joseph Geneva Rhode Island
*Catechesis Religious Program—*Tel: 401-353-5215. Students 29.

12—GENESIS COMMUNITY, Closed. For inquiries for parish records contact Cathedral of SS. Peter & Paul, Providence.

13—ST. HEDWIG, Closed. For inquiries for sacramental records contact St. Adalbert Parish, Providence.

14—HOLY CROSS (1949) (Italian) Mission of St. Thomas Parish, Providence. For sacramental records, contact St. Thomas Parish.
5 Fruit Hill Ave., 02909. Tel: 401-272-7118; Email: stthomaschurch@cox.net. Rev. John P. Soares, Admin.
Corporation of the Church of the Holy Cross
*Catechesis Religious Program—*Tel: 401-751-1144. Mrs. June Carnevale, D.R.E. Students 95.

15—HOLY GHOST (1889) (Italian)
472 Atwells Ave., 02909. Tel: 401-421-3551;
Fax: 401-421-2615; Email: holyghostchurchri@gmail.com; Web: www.holy-ghost-church.org. Revs. Francesco Francese; Saji Thengumkudiyil, In Res.
Corporation of the Church of the Holy Ghost, Rhode Island
*Catechesis Religious Program—*Students 14.

16—HOLY NAME OF JESUS (1882) (Cape Verdean)
99 Camp St., 02906-1799. Tel: 401-272-4515; Email: theholyname@cox.net; Web: www.holynameprovidence.org. Rev. Joseph D. Santos Jr., (Portugal)
*Church of the Holy Name of Jesus at Providence, Rhode Island*In Res., Revs. John Wydeven; Lazarus Onuh, (Nigeria).
*Catechesis Religious Program—*Students 78.

17—IMMACULATE CONCEPTION, Closed. For inquiries for sacramental records contact St. Patrick Parish, Providence.

18—ST. JOHN, Closed. Sacramental records are located at St. Mary Church, Providence.
St. John Church of Providence Rhode Island.

19—ST. JOSEPH (Foxpoint) (1851)
92 Hope St., 02906. Tel: 401-421-9137; Email: stjoe1851@cox.net; Web: stjosephprovidence.org. Revs. Edward A. Sousa Jr.; Stanley R. Azaro, O.P., (Retired); Maurice L. Brindamour, (Retired); Domingos M. da Cunha, (Retired); Sr. Mary Ellen Maytum, R.S.M., Pastoral Assoc.
St. Joseph's Church Providence Rhode Island
*Catechesis Religious Program—*Virginia DiMasi, D.R.E. Students 42.

20—ST. MARON, Rev. Timothy D. Reilly, S.T.B., J.C.L.
Church of St. Maron in Providence
Res.: One Cathedral Sq., 02903-3695.
Tel: 401-278-4500; Email: chancellor@dioceseofprovidence.org.

21—ST. MARY (Broadway) (1853)
538 Broadway, 02909-3329. Tel: 401-274-3434; Email: Secretary@stmaryonbroadway.org; Web: StMaryonBroadway.org. Rev. John Berg, F.S.S.P.
St. Mary's Church Providence Rhode Island
*Catechesis Religious Program—*Email: faithformation@stmaryonbroadway.org. Students 72.

22—ST. MICHAEL THE ARCHANGEL (South Providence) (1859) Rev. Robert P. Perron; Deacon Juan Andres Perez
St. Michael's Providence, Rhode Island
Res.: 239 Oxford St., 02905. Tel: 401-781-7210; Email: rpperron2@gmail.com.
*Catechesis Religious Program—*Students 76.

23—OUR LADY OF CHARITY, Rev. Timothy D. Reilly, S.T.B., J.C.L.
Church of Our Lady of Charity of Providence
Res.: One Cathedral Sq., 02903-3695.
Tel: 401-278-4500; Email: chancellor@dioceseofprovidence.org.

24—OUR LADY OF LOURDES (1904) (French)
901 Atwells Ave., 02909. Tel: 401-272-8127; Email: fathermarek@hotmail.com. Rev. Marek S. Kupka; Deacon Anthony J. Wendoloski Jr.
Church of Our Lady of Lourdes.

25—OUR LADY OF MT. CARMEL (1921) (Italian), Closed. For inquiries of sacramental records. contact Holy Ghost, Providence, One Cathedral Sq., Providence, RI 02903.
Church of Our Lady of Mount Carmel, Providence.

26—OUR LADY OF THE ROSARY (1886) (Portuguese)
463 Benefit St., 02903. Tel: 401-421-5621; Email: rosary463@aol.com; Web: www.rosary463.com. Rev. Joseph A. Escobar; Deacon Victorino Andrade
Church of Our Lady of the Rosary
*Catechesis Religious Program—*Tel: 401-273-1685; Email: olrccd463@aol.com. Elisa Guerra Thibeault, D.R.E. Students 302.

27—ST. PATRICK (1841)
244 Smith St., 02908. Tel: 401-421-7070; Email: stpatrickprov@outlook.com; Web: www.saintpatrickchurch.net. Rev. James T. Ruggieri; Deacons Charles Andrade; Robert MacLure; Eduardo Birbuet, Pastoral Assoc.
St. Patrick's Church, Providence, Rhode Island
School—St. Patrick Academy, (Grades 9-12),
Tel: 401-421-9300; Fax: 401-490-4511; Email: bdaigle@stpatrickacademyri.org; Web: www.stpatrickacademyri.org. Bruce Daigle, Prin.; Mrs. Jessica Hauk, Librarian. Lay Teachers 15; Students 77.
*Catechesis Religious Program—*c/o Blessed Sacrament Church, 239 Regent Ave., 02908.
Tel: 401-781-8403. Maria Batista, D.R.E. Students 119.

28—ST. PIUS V (1918)
55 Elmhurst Ave., 02908. Tel: 401-751-4871;
Fax: 401-273-1089; Email: esther@spvchurch.org; Web: spvchurch.org/. Revs. James Mary Sullivan, O.P.; Patrick Mary Briscoe, O.P.
*Saint Pius Church, Providence, Rhode Island*In Res., Very Rev. John P. Burchill, O.P.; Rev. Albert Duggan, O.P.
School—St. Pius V School, (Grades PreK-8), 49 Elmhurst Ave., 02908. Tel: 401-421-9750;
Fax: 401-455-3928; Email: principal@spvri.org. Maria Francesca Wiley, Prin. Religious Teachers 3; Lay Teachers 19; Religious 4; Students 226.
*Catechesis Religious Program—*Tel: 401-684-3063; Email: spvfaithformation@gmail.com. Charles A. da Silva, D.R.E. Students 226.
*Convent—*30 Elmhurst Ave., 02908.

29—ST. RAYMOND (1911)
2 Matilda St., 02904-1812. Rev. Edward L. Pieroni
Saint Raymond's Church Corporation
Church: 1240 N. Main St., 02904.
*Catechesis Religious Program—*Students 33.

30—ST. SEBASTIAN (1915)
67 Cole Ave., 02906. Tel: 401-751-0196;
Fax: 401-273-2753; Email: office@stsebastianri.org; Web: stsebastianri.org. Rev. Jordan Kelly
*Church of Saint Sebastian*In Res.
*Catechesis Religious Program—*Tel: 401-272-6062. Students 63.

31—ST. TERESA OF AVILA (Olneyville) (1883) Closed. For inquiries for sacramental records contact Blessed Sacrament, Providence.
Saint Teresa's Church Providence, Rhode Island.

32—ST. THOMAS (Fruit Hill) (1886) Rev. John P. Soares; Deacon Albert DePetrillo
St. Thomas' Church of Manton Rhode Island

Res.: 65 Fruit Hill Ave., 02909-5598.
Tel: 401-272-7118; Email: stthomaschurch@cox.net.
See St. Thomas Regional School, Providence under Regional Elementary Schools located in the Institution section.
Catechesis Religious Program—Tel: 401-272-1443; Fax: 401-272-8431. Students 169.

OUTSIDE THE CITY OF PROVIDENCE

BARRINGTON, BRISTOL CO.
1—HOLY ANGELS (1913) (Italian)
341 Maple Ave., Barrington, 02806.
Tel: 401-245-7743; Email: hangels@fullchannel.net. Rev. Raymond J. Ferrick
Holy Angel's Church Corporation
Catechesis Religious Program—Tel: 401-247-1764. Marie Mascena, D.R.E. Students 14.
2—ST. LUKE (West Barrington) (1942)
108 Washington Rd., Barrington, 02806-1133.
Tel: 401-246-1212; Email: revtj23@gmail.com. Very Rev. TJ Varghese; Rev. Brian Morris
Saint Luke's Church Corporation, Barrington
School—St. Luke School, (Grades PreK-8), 10 Waldron Ave., Barrington, 02806. Tel: 401-246-0990; Fax: 401-246-2120; Email: pbartel@stlukesri.org; Web: www.stlukesri.org. Mrs. Patricia Bartel, Prin.; Mr. Neil Kiely, Admissions Dir.; Karen Lico, Librarian. Lay Teachers 20; Students 218.
Catechesis Religious Program—110 Washington Rd., Barrington, 02806. Students 616.

BRISTOL, BRISTOL CO.
1—ST. ELIZABETH (1913) (Portuguese)
577 Wood St., Bristol, 02809-2395. Tel: 401-253-8366 ; Email: office@saintelizabethchurch.net; Web: www.saintelizabethchurch.net. Rev. Marinaldo A. Batista, C.S.P.
Saint Elizabeth's Church of Bristol
Catechesis Religious Program—Tel: 401-253-3501; Email: dccdbristol@gmail.com. Aurendina Veiga, D.R.E. Students 310.
2—ST. MARY (1869) [CEM]
330 Wood St., P.O. Box 120, Bristol, 02809.
Tel: 401-253-3300; Fax: 401-253-4057; Email: frbjg@aol.com; Web: www.stmarybristolri.org. Rev. Barry J. Gamache; Deacons Paul Bisbano; Bernard G. Theroux
Saint Mary's Church, Bristol, Rhode Island
Res.: 330 Wood St., Bristol, 02809.
Catechesis Religious Program—Tel: 401-253-2270. Students 203.
Mission—Our Lady of Prudence, Prudence Island, 02872.
3—OUR LADY OF MOUNT CARMEL (1917) [JC] (Italian)
141 State St., Bristol, 02809. Revs. Henry P. Zinno Jr.; Stephen Battey
Church of Our Lady of Mount Carmel, Bristol
School—Our Lady of Mount Carmel School, (Grades PreK-8), 127 State St., Bristol, 02809.
Tel: 401-253-8455; Fax: 401-254-8234; Email: jwalters@olmcri.org; Web: www.olmcri.org. Jessica Walters, Prin. Lay Teachers 11; Filippini Sisters 4; Students 158.
Catechesis Religious Program—131 State St., Bristol, 02809. Students 205.

BURRILLVILLE, PROVIDENCE CO.
1—ST. JOSEPH (Pascoag) (1884)
183 Sayles Ave., P.O. Box 188, Pascoag, 02859-0188.
Tel: 401-568-2411; Fax: 401-568-2586; Email: stjosephpascoag@cox.net; Web: www.stjosephri.org. Rev. Scott J. Carpentier
Saint Joseph's Roman Catholic Church of Pascoag
Catechesis Religious Program—Students 85.
2—OUR LADY OF GOOD HELP (Mapleville) (1905)
1063 Victory Hwy., Mapleville, 02839.
Tel: 401-568-8280; Email: ourladyofgoodhelp@gmail.com; Web: www.ourladyofgoodhelp.org. Rev. Michael J. McMahon; Deacon Richard J. Lapierre
Eglise de Notre Dame de Bonsecours
Catechesis Religious Program—Students 145.
3—ST. PATRICK (Harrisville) (1854) [CEM] [JC2] Rev. Scott J. Carpentier
St. Patrick's Church, Burrillville, Rhode Island
Res.: 45 Main St., Harrisville, 02830.
Tel: 401-568-5600; Fax: 401-568-7132; Email: stpatsri01@verizon.com; Web: www.stpatrickri.org.
Catechesis Religious Program—Students 46.
4—ST. THERESA OF THE CHILD JESUS (Nasonville) (1923) [CEM]
35 Dion Dr., Harrisville, 02830. Tel: 401-568-8280; Email: ourladyofgoodhelp@gmail.com. Rev. Michael J. McMahon; Deacon Richard J. Lapierre
Church of Saint Teresa of the Child Jesus, Nasonville
Catechesis Religious Program—Tel: 401-568-3057. Students 43.

CENTRAL FALLS, PROVIDENCE CO.
1—HOLY SPIRIT PARISH (2009) [CEM] Unification of Holy Trinity (Legal Title: Church of the Holy Trinity, Central Falls); Notre Dame (Legal Title: Notre Dame Church); and St. Matthew (Legal Title: Saint Matthew's Church of Central Falls)
1030 Dexter St., Central Falls, 02863-1717.
Tel: 401-726-2600; Email: the.holy.spirit.parish@gmail.com; Web: www.holyspiritcentralfalls.parishesonline.com. Rev. Otoniel J. Gomez
Holy Spirit Parish, Central Falls.
Catechesis Religious Program—901 Lonsdale Ave., Central Falls, 02863. Tel: 401-722-3717; Email: holy.spirit.religious.education@gmail.com. Pierre Larivee, D.R.E. Students 282.
2—HOLY TRINITY (1989) Merged See Holy Spirit Parish, Central Falls.
3—ST. JOSEPH (1906) (Polish) Rev. Dariusz J. Jonczyk
St. Joseph's Church of Central Falls
Res.: 391 High St., Central Falls, 02863-3109.
Tel: 401-723-5427; Fax: 401-726-5971; Email: st.joseph1@verizon.net.
Catechesis Religious Program—Students 57.
4—ST. MATTHEW'S (1906) (French), Merged See Holy Spirit Parish, Central Falls.
5—NOTRE DAME (1873) (French), Merged See Holy Spirit Parish, Central Falls.

CHARLESTOWN, WASHINGTON CO., ST. MARY (Carolina) (1946) Rev. Paul E. Desmarais; Deacons Paul A. Theroux; John S. Shea; Raphael Castaldi
Saint Mary's Church Corporation, Carolina, RI
Res.: 437 Carolina Back Rd., P.O. Box 475, Carolina, 02812. Tel: 401-364-7214; Fax: 401-213-6327; Email: stmjparish@aol.com; Web: www.stmjparish.org.
Catechesis Religious Program—Sally Lambert, D.R.E. Students 262.
Mission—St. James, 2079 Matunuck School House Rd., Charlestown, 02813.

COVENTRY, KENT CO.
1—SS. JOHN AND PAUL (1955)
341 S. Main St., Coventry, 02816. Tel: 401-821-5764; Email: father.woolley@verizon.net; Email: ssjp341@stjp.necoxmail.com; Web: stsjohnpaulri.com/. Very Rev. Michael J. Woolley; Rev. Nicholas T. Fleming; Deacon Robert Persson
*SS. John and Paul Parish Corporation, Coventry*In Res., Rev. John J. Duggan, (Ireland) (Retired).
Father John V. Doyle School—343 S. Main St., Coventry, 02816. Tel: 401-821-3756;
Fax: 401-828-5351; Email: jaesmith@fjvd.org; Web: www.ri.net/rinet/fr_doyle. Mrs. Jae T. Smith, Prin. Lay Teachers 18; Students 240.
Catechesis Religious Program—Tel: 401-821-4780. Ann Sartell, D.R.E.; Patricia Jarvis, D.R.E. Students 680.
2—OUR LADY OF CZENSTOCHOWA (Quidnick) (1905) (Polish)
Tel: 401-821-7991; Email: olczenstochowa@aol.com; Web: olcsvp.org. Rev. Jacek Ploch
Church of Our Lady of Czenstochowa
Catechesis Religious Program—Students 92.
3—ST. VINCENT DE PAUL (Anthony) (1937) (French)
6 St. Vincent de Paul St., Coventry, 02816.
Tel: 401-821-8719; Email: stvincentcoventry@gmail.com; Web: olcsvp.org. Rev. Jacek Ploch
Church of Saint Vincent de Paul, Anthony, Rhode Island
Catechesis Religious Program—2 St. Vincent de Paul St., Coventry, 02816. Students 72.

CRANSTON, PROVIDENCE CO.
1—ST. ANN (1858) Closed. Sacramental records kept at St. George Maronite Church, 1493 Cranston St., Cranston, RI 02920; Tel: 401-723-8444.
2—HOLY APOSTLES (1991)
800 Pippin Orchard Rd., Cranston, 02921.
Tel: 401-946-5586; Email: parishoffice@holyapostles.com; Web: www.holyapostles.com. Rev. Msgr. Paul D. Theroux, S.T.B., J.C.L.
*Holy Apostles Church, Cranston, Rhode Island*In Res., Rev. Msgr. Albert A. Kenney, S.T.L.
Catechesis Religious Program—Email: mms@holyapostles.com. Margaret Simms, D.R.E. Students 617.
3—IMMACULATE CONCEPTION (Oaklawn) (1958)
237 Garden Hills Dr., Cranston, 02920.
Tel: 401-942-1854; Email: iccriooffice@gmail.com; Web: www.iccatholicchurch.org. Rev. Edward J. Wilson Jr.; Deacons Thomas R. Raspallo, (Retired); Scott Brown
Immaculate Conception Church Corporation, Cranston
See Immaculate Conception Catholic Regional School, Cranston under Regional Elementary Schools in the Institution section.
Catechesis Religious Program—Email: iccrireligiousedu@gmail.com. Deanna Marinucci, D.R.E. Students 425.
4—ST. MARK (Garden City) (1950)
9 Garden Ct., Cranston, 02920-5701.
Tel: 401-942-1616; Fax: 401-942-1747; Email: welcome@stmarkri.org; Web: www.stmarkri.org. Rev. Anthony W. Verdelotti; Matthew Gebhart, Business Mgr.; Renee Brissette, D.R.E.
Saint Mark's Church Corporation of Cranston.
5—ST. MARY (Knightsville) (1925) (Italian) (Santa Maria della Civita)
1525 Cranston St., Cranston, 02920-5297.
Tel: 401-942-1492; Email: dditraglia@stmc.necoxmail.com; Web: www.saintmarycranston.org. Very Rev. William J. Ledoux; Deacons Armand R. Ragosta, (Retired); Peter A. Ceprano, (Retired)
*Saint Mary's Church, Cranston*In Res., Rev. James R. Collins, (Retired).
School—St. Mary School, (Grades PreK-8), 85 Chester Ave., Cranston, 02920-5297.
Tel: 401-944-4107; Fax: 401-944-2395; Email: llepore@stmaryschoolri.org; Web: www.stmaryschoolri.org. Miss Lisa Lepore, Prin. Students 176.
Catechesis Religious Program—85 Chester Ave., Cranston, 02920. Tel: 401-944-1323; Email: nnasser@stmaryschoolri.org. Mrs. Nancy Nasser, D.R.E. Students 188.
6—ST. MATTHEW (Auburn) (1909)
15 Frances Ave., Cranston, 02910. Tel: 401-461-7172 ; Email: stmatthewri@cox.net. Rev. Ronald J. Bengford
*St. Matthew's Church Corporation*In Res., Rev. Chinnaiah Yerrnini.
Church: Elmwood & Park Ave., Cranston, 02910.
Catechesis Religious Program—Sr. Mercian Hassett, R.S.M., D.R.E. Students 200.
7—ST. PAUL (Edgewood) (1907) Rev. Adam A. Young; Deacon Paul Shea
Saint Paul's Church of Edgewood
Res.: One St. Paul Pl., Cranston, 02905.
Tel: 401-461-5734; Fax: 401-785-3613; Email: stpauledgewood@gmail.com; Web: www.saintpaulcranston.org.
School—St. Paul School, (Grades PreK-8), 1789 Broad St., Cranston, 02905. Tel: 401-941-2030;
Fax: 401-941-0644; Email: johncorry@stpaulcranston.org; Web: www.saintpaulschoolcranston.com. Mr. John F. Corry, Prin. Lay Teachers 17; Students 194.
Catechesis Religious Program—Tel: 401-941-5576. Julie Bradley, D.R.E. Students 154.

CUMBERLAND, PROVIDENCE CO.
1—ST. AIDAN, Merged with St. Patrick, Cumberland to form St. Aidan-St. Patrick Parish, Cumberland.
2—ST. AIDAN-ST. PATRICK (1962)
P.O. Box 7058, Cumberland, 02864. 1460 Diamond Hill Rd., Cumberland, 02864. Tel: 401-333-5897;
Tel: 401-725-0344; Fax: 401-333-5078; Email: office@aidan-patrick.org; Web: saintaidanparish.weconnect.com/. Rev. Msgr. Jacques L. Plante; Deacon Robert L. Lafond, M.T.S.
St. Aidan Church Corporation, Cumberland DBA St. Aidan-St. Patrick Parish
Catechesis Religious Program—Tel: 401-333-9074; Email: faithformation@aidan-patrick.com. Darlyn Gomes Hidalgo, D.R.E. Students 81.
3—ST. JOAN OF ARC (Cumberland Hill) (1929)
3357 Mendon Rd., Cumberland, 02864-2195.
Tel: 401-658-2084; Email: stjoanschurch@gmail.com; Web: www.stjoanschurchri.org. Rev. Norman W. Bourdon
Saint Joan's Church, Cumberland, Rhode Island
Catechesis Religious Program—Tel: 401-658-0734. Mrs. Francine M. Salinger, D.R.E. Students 284.
4—ST. JOHN BAPTIST MARY VIANNEY (Diamond Hill) (1953)
3609 Diamond Hill Rd., Cumberland, 02864.
Tel: 401-333-6060; Fax: 401-334-4548; Email: sjvdenise@gmail.com; Web: www.sjvparish.org. 3655 Diamond Hill Rd., Cumberland, 02864. Rev. Joseph A. Pescatello; Deacon Paul H. Lambert
Saint John Baptist Mary Vianney Church Corporation, Diamond Hill
Catechesis Religious Program—Students 607.
5—ST. JOSEPH (Ashton) (1872) [CEM]
1303 Mendon Rd., P.O. Box 7005, Cumberland, 02864. Tel: 401-333-4013; Email: historicstjosephchurch@gmail.com. Rev. Charles H. Galligan; Deacon James Walsh
St. Joseph's Church, Ashton, Rhode Island
Catechesis Religious Program—Tel: 401-333-4014. Mrs. Kayne D'Amore, D.R.E. Students 167.
6—OUR LADY OF FATIMA (Valley Falls) (1953) (Portuguese)
1 Fatima Dr., Cumberland, 02864. Tel: 401-723-6719 ; Email: olf@olfchurch.com; Web: www.olfchurch.com. Rev. Fernando A. Cabral, (Portugal); Deacon Amandio Bartolo
Church of Our Lady of Fatima, Valley Falls
Catechesis Religious Program—7 Fatima Dr., Cumberland, 02864. Tel: 401-724-3454; Email: olffaithformation@gmail.com. Melissa DiFonzo, D.R.E. Students 261.
7—ST. PATRICK (Valley Falls) (1861) [CEM 2] Merged with St. Aidan, Cumberland to form St. Aidan-St. Patrick, Cumberland.
St. Patrick's Church Corporation, Valley Falls, Rhode Island.

EAST GREENWICH, KENT CO., OUR LADY OF MERCY (1853) [CEM]
65 Third St., East Greenwich, 02818.
Tel: 401-224-4968; Email: parish@olmparish.org; Web: www.olmparish.org. Very Rev. Bernard A. Healey; Rev. Joshua A. Barrow; Deacon John Dowd
Our Lady of Mercy, Greenwich, Rhode Island

Catechesis Religious Program—Tel: 401-884-1061; Email: reled@olmparish.org; Email: confirmation@olmparish.org. Mrs. Michele St. Jean, D.R.E., Grades 1-5; Mr. Douglas E. Green, D.R.E., Grades 6-8 & Confirmation. Students 450.

EAST PROVIDENCE, PROVIDENCE CO.

1—ST. BRENDAN (Riverside) (1909) Rev. John C. Codega
St. Brendan's Church
Res.: 60 Turner Ave., Riverside, 02915.
Tel: 401-433-2600; Email: stbrendan@cox.net; Web: www.stbren.com.
Catechesis Religious Program—55 Turner Ave., Riverside, 02915. Tel: 401-433-2680. Tamara Primmer, D.R.E. Students 450.

2—ST. FRANCIS XAVIER (1915) (Portuguese)
81 N. Carpenter St., East Providence, 02914.
Tel: 401-434-1878; Email: sfxsecretary@yahoo.com. Revs. Jorge V. Rocha; Nathan J. Ricci, Parochial Vicar
Saint Francis Xavier's Church
Catechesis Religious Program—Tel: 401-434-3153. Doris Wigginton, D.R.E. Students 350.

3—ST. MARGARET (Rumford) (1888)
1098 Pawtucket Ave., Rumford, 02916.
Tel: 401-438-3230; Email: office-stmargaretchurch@cox.net; Web: www.stmargaretchurch.org. Rev. Msgr. John J. Darcy, M.A., J.C.L.; Deacon John F. Needham; Mr. Charles Moreira, Pastoral Assoc. & D.R.E.
Saint Margaret's Church Corporation, East Providence Rhode Island
School—St. Margaret School, (Grades PreK-8), 42 Bishop Ave., Rumford, 02916. Tel: 401-434-2338; Fax: 401-431-0266; Email: lunes@stmargaretsch.org. Mrs. Lee Ann Nunes, Prin. Lay Teachers 16; Students 220.
Catechesis Religious Program—Tel: 401-438-3231; Email: cmoreira@cox.net. Students 129.

4—ST. MARTHA (1956)
2595 Pawtucket Ave., East Providence, 02914.
Tel: 401-434-4060; Tel: 401-434-4070;
Fax: 401-434-4849; Email: stmarthaschurch@cox.net; Web: stmarthaschurchepri.org. Rev. David E. Green; Deacon Dominic P. DiOrio
*St. Martha's Church Corporation, East Providence*In Res., Rev. Albert P. Marcello III.
Catechesis Religious Program—Matthew J. Burns, D.R.E. Students 197.

5—OUR LADY OF LORETO (1920) (Italian—Brazilian)
346 Waterman Ave., East Providence, 02914.
Tel: 401-434-3535; Fax: 401-434-8204; Email: loreto5@ymail.com. Rev. Dean P. Perri, J.C.L., S.T.L.
Church of Our Lady of Loreto, East Providence
Catechesis Religious Program—Mr. Douglas E. Green, D.R.E. Students 67.

6—SACRED HEART (1876)
118 Taunton Ave., East Providence, 02914.
Tel: 401-434-0326; Email: sdn249@hotmail.com. Revs. Silvio DeNard, S.d.C.; Peter S. DiTullio, S.d.C.
Church of the Sacred Heart
School—Sacred Heart School, (Grades K-8), 56 Purchase St., East Providence, 02914.
Tel: 401-434-1080; Fax: 401-434-1080; Email: jwoodmansee@sacredheartepri.com. Mr. James Woodmansee, Prin. Lay Teachers 13; Students 160.
Child Care—Nursery-Day Care, 101 Taunton Ave., East Providence, 02914. Tel: 401-434-2462. Children 75; Total Staff 7.
Catechesis Religious Program—Students 48.

EXETER, WASHINGTON CO., SAINT KATERI TEKAKWITHA CATHOLIC COMMUNITY (1981)
84 Exeter Rd., Exeter, 02822. Tel: 401-212-0855; Email: gsabourin@dioceseofprovidence.org; Web: www.kateritekakwitha.org/katerichurch. Rev. Msgr. Gerard O. Sabourin, Admin., (Retired); Deacon John A. Corey
Saint Kateri Tekakwitha Catholic Community
Catechesis Religious Program—Students 25.

FOSTER, PROVIDENCE CO., ST. PAUL THE APOSTLE (1972)
116A Danielson Pike, Foster, 02825-1468.
Tel: 401-647-3664; Email: church@stpaulsfoster.org; Web: www.stpaulsfoster.org. Rev. M.J. Bernard Dore; Deacon Fernando Botelho
St. Paul's Church Corporation, Foster
Catechesis Religious Program—Students 87.

GLOCESTER, PROVIDENCE CO., ST. EUGENE (Chepachet) (1956) Rev. Stephen J. Dandeneau
St. Eugene's Church Corporation, Chepachet
Res.: 1251 Putnam Pike, P.O. Box A, Chepachet, 02814. Tel: 401-568-5102; Fax: 401-567-7847; Email: steugenechurch@verizon.net; Web: www.sainteugeneschurch.com.
Catechesis Religious Program—Students 218.

HOPKINTON, WASHINGTON CO.

1—ST. JOSEPH (Hope Valley) (1939)
1105 Main St., P.O. Box 388, Hope Valley, 02832.
Tel: 401-539-8311; Email: stjosephhv@verizon.net; Web: www.stjosephhv.org. Rev. Michael J. Leckie, Admin.; Deacon Ronald Preuhs
Saint Joseph's Church, Hope Valley
Catechesis Religious Program—Tel: 401-539-8312; Email: reledstjosephhv@aol.com. Mrs. Shannon Reed, D.R.E. Students 47.

2—OUR LADY OF VICTORY (Ashaway) (1946) Rev. Michael A. Colello, Admin.; Deacon Costa Adamopoulos
*Church of Our Lady of Victory, Ashaway*In Res., Rev. Msgr. William J. McCaffrey, (Retired).
Res.: 169 Main St., Ashaway, 02804.
Tel: 401-377-8830; Email: olv_svp@cox.net.
Catechesis Religious Program—Email: ggolv@yahoo.com. Students 80.

JAMESTOWN, NEWPORT CO., ST. MARK (Jamestown) (1909) [CEM]
60 Narragansett Ave., Jamestown, 02835.
Tel: 401-423-1421; Web: stmarkchurchri@icloud.com. Rev. Stephen P. Amaral
Saint Mark Church of Jamestown
Catechesis Religious Program—Students 174.

JOHNSTON, PROVIDENCE CO.

1—ST. BRIGID (Thornton) (1915) Merged and now a mission of St. Rocco, Johnston.
Saint Brigid's Church of Johnston.

2—OUR LADY OF GRACE (1913) (Italian)
4 Lafayette St., Johnston, 02919. Tel: 401-231-2220; Email: ourladyofgraceri@aol.com; Web: www.ourladyofgraceri.org. Rev. Peter J. Gower
Church of Our Lady of Grace
Catechesis Religious Program—Tel: 401-231-8959. Students 140.

3—ST. ROBERT BELLARMINE (1963)
1804 Atwood Ave., Johnston, 02919-3215.
Tel: 401-232-5600; Email: srbp1804@aol.com; Web: www.strobertsparish.org. Rev. John G. LaPointe; Deacon Joseph Tumminelli
St. Robert Bellarmine Church Corporation, Johnston
Catechesis Religious Program—Tel: 401-232-9321. Students 197.

4—ST. ROCCO (1903) (Italian)
927 Atwood Ave., Johnston, 02919.
Tel: 401-942-5203; Email: churchofstrocco@gmail.com; Web: www.churchofstrocco.org. Rev. Angelo N. Carusi; Deacon Robert P. Troia
Saint Rocco Church of Johnston
School—St. Rocco School, (Grades PreK-8), 931 Atwood Ave., Johnston, 02919. Tel: 401-944-2993; Fax: 401-944-3019; Email: principal@stroccoschool.org; Web: www.stroccoschool.org. Lorraine Moschella, Prin. Lay Teachers 14; Sisters 3; Students 194; Religious Teachers 2.
Catechesis Religious Program—Tel: 401-944-6040. Sr. Mary Antoinette Cappelli, F.M.H., D.R.E.; Mrs. Robin Okolowitcz, C.R.E. Students 100.

LINCOLN, PROVIDENCE CO.

1—ST. AMBROSE (Albion) (1905) [CEM]
191 School St., P.O. Box 67, Albion, 02802.
Tel: 401-333-1568; Email: stambrosechurch@cox.net; Web: stambrosechurchri.org. Rev. Thomas J. Ferland
St. Ambrose Church, Albion, Rhode Island
Catechesis Religious Program—Tel: 401-333-1568. Students 160.

2—ST. JAMES (Manville) (1874) [CEM]
45 Division St., Manville, 02838. Tel: 401-766-1558; Email: office.stjames@verizon.net; Web: www.saintjamesmanville.org. P.O. Box 60, Manville, 02838. Rev. Thomas J. Ferland
Saint James Church of Manville, Rhode Island
Res.: 33 Division St., Manville, 02838.
Catechesis Religious Program—Email: fern.stjames@verizon.net. Fern Dery, D.R.E. Students 125.

3—ST. JUDE (Lincoln) (1946)
301 Front St., Lincoln, 02865. Tel: 401-725-8140; Email: officeatst.jude@verizon.net; Web: www.saintjude.us. Rev. Bernard C. Lavin; Deacon L.J. (Bud) Remillard
St. Jude's Church, Lincoln
Catechesis Religious Program—Tel: 401-725-8120; Email: stjudereled@gmail.com. Sr. Mary Higgins, R.S.M., D.R.E. Students 271.

LITTLE COMPTON, NEWPORT CO., ST. CATHERINE OF SIENA (1930) [CEM] Rev. Stephan A. Silipigni
St. Catherine's Church Corporation, Little Compton
Res.: 74 Simmons Rd., P.O. Box 208, Little Compton, 02837-0208. Tel: 401-635-4420; Fax: 401-635-2214; Email: scs7474@aol.com.
Catechesis Religious Program—Karen Lambert, D.R.E. Students 175.

MIDDLETOWN, NEWPORT CO., ST. LUCY (Middletown) (1952) Rev. John W. O'Brien; Deacon John E. Croy; Sr. Sheila Murphy, S.S.J., Pastoral Min./Coord.
Saint Lucy's Church Corp.
Res.: 909 W. Main Rd., Middletown, 02842-6351.
Tel: 401-847-6153; Fax: 401-846-1545; Email: stlucyoffice@gmail.com; Web: www.stlucy.org.
Catechesis Religious Program—Colette Savaria, Coord. Faith Formation; Jane Parillo, Adult Faith Formation; Colleen Earnshaw, Confirmation & Baptism Coord. Students 87.

NARRAGANSETT, WASHINGTON CO.

1—ST. MARY, STAR OF THE SEA (Point Judith) (1960)
864 Pt. Judith Rd., Narragansett, 02882. Email: stmarys@dioceseofprovidence.org; Web: www.stmarystarofthesearі.org. Rev. Francis P. Kayatta; Mrs. Darie Lavallee, Pastoral Assoc. & D.R.E.
St. Mary, Star of the Sea Church Corporation, Point Judith
Catechesis Religious Program—Tel: 401-789-7308. Students 118.

2—ST. THOMAS MORE (1917) Revs. Marcel L. Taillon; Vijay Kiran Anthony Raj; Deacon Paul J. Sullivan
St. Thomas More Church, Narragansett Pier, Rhode Island
Res.: 53 Rockland St., Narragansett, 02882.
Tel: 401-789-7682; Fax: 401-783-8646; Email: sthomasmore@cox.net; Web: www.stthomasmoreri.org.
Catechesis Religious Program—Tel: 401-783-2113. Connie DiOrio, D.R.E. Students 242.
Chapel—St. Veronica Chapel, 1035 Boston Neck Rd., Narragansett, 02882.

NEW SHOREHAM, WASHINGTON CO., ST. ANDREW (Block Island) (1917) [JC] Rev. Joseph Protano Jr.
Saint Andrew's Church Corporation, Block Island
Res.: Spring St., Box 279, Block Island, 02807.
Tel: 401-466-5519; Fax: 401-466-3118; Email: standrewblockisland@verizon.net; Web: www.standrewblockisland.com.
Catechesis Religious Program—Students 26.

NEWPORT, NEWPORT CO.

1—ST. AUGUSTIN (1911)
12 William St., P.O. Box 357, Newport, 02840. Rev. Kris M. von Maluski; Sr. Josephine St. Leger, S.J.C., Pastoral Assoc.
Saint Augustin's Church of Newport
Res.: 2 Eastnor Rd., Newport, 02840.
Tel: 401-847-0518; Fax: 401-845-9497; Email: staugustinnewp@verizon.net; Web: www.staugustinnewport.org.
Catechesis Religious Program—Deborah Circosta, D.R.E. Students 45.

2—JESUS SAVIOUR (1926) (Portuguese)
1 Vernon Ave., Newport, 02840. Tel: 401-847-1267;
Tel: 401-846-4095; Fax: 401-846-3375; Email: jsaviour@jesussaviour.necoxmail.com; Web: www.jsaviournewportri.org. Very Rev. Francis A. O'Loughlin
Church of Jesus-Saviour, Newport
Catechesis Religious Program—Email: prinfret@cox.net. Clotilde Rinfret, D.R.E. Students 80.

3—ST. JOSEPH (1885)
5 Mann Ave., Newport, 02840. Tel: 401-847-0065; Email: office@stjosephsnewport.org; Web: www.stjosephsnewport.org. Very Rev. Francis A. O'Loughlin
Saint Joseph's Church of Newport, Rhode Island
Catechesis Religious Program—Tel: 401-847-9248; Email: religioused@stjosephsnewport.org. Students 126.

4—ST. MARY (1826) [CEM] Rev. Kris M. von Maluski
St. Mary's, Newport, Rhode Island
Res.: 12 William St., P.O. Box 547, Newport, 02840.
Tel: 401-847-0475; Fax: 401-845-9497; Email: stmarynewport@aol.com; Web: www.stmarynewport.org.
Catechesis Religious Program—Tel: 401-846-6057. Students 142.

NORTH KINGSTOWN, WASHINGTON CO.

1—ST. BERNARD (Wickford) (1874) [CEM] Rev. John E. Unsworth; Angelo Giacchi, Pastoral Assoc.
St. Bernard's Roman Catholic Church of Wickford, Rhode Island
Office & Mailing Address: 275 Tower Hill Rd., Wickford, 02852. Tel: 401-295-0387; Email: sbc.bus@verizon.net; Web: www.stbernardnk.org.
Catechesis Religious Program—Email: sbc.gof@verizon.net. Dawn Masterson, D.R.E. Students 520.

2—ST. FRANCIS DE SALES (Davisville) (1960)
381 School St., North Kingstown, 02852.
Tel: 401-884-2105; Email: parishoffice@saintfds.org; Web: www.saintfds.org. Rev. David C. Procaccini; Deacon Ronald DePietro
St. Francis de Sales Church Corporation, North Kingstown
Catechesis Religious Program—Tel: 401-885-3639. Kathleen Kane, D.R.E.; Kristen Soucie, D.R.E. Students 320.

NORTH PROVIDENCE, PROVIDENCE CO.

1—ST. ANTHONY (1944) (Italian)
5 Gibbs St., North Providence, 02904.
Tel: 401-353-3120; Email: stanthonynp@cox.net. 1413 Mineral Spring Ave., North Providence, 02904. Very Rev. Edward S. Cardente
Saint Anthony's Church Corporation, North Providence
Catechesis Religious Program—Tel: 401-353-5215. Maryann Pallotta, D.R.E. Students 327.

2—ST. LAWRENCE (Centredale) (1907) Closed. For inquiries for parish records contact Mary Mother of Mankind Parish, North Providence.
Saint Lawrence Church of Centredale.

3—MARY, MOTHER OF MANKIND (1967)
25 Fourth St., North Providence, 02911.

Tel: 401-231-3542; Email: mmmchurch@hotmail.com; Web: www.marymotherofmankind.org. Rev. Dennis J. Kieton; Deacon Stephen M. Risi
Mary, Mother of Mankind Church Corporation, North Providence
Catechesis Religious Program—Tel: 401-231-3544. Students 128.

4—PRESENTATION OF THE BLESSED VIRGIN MARY (Marieville) (1912) (French—Italian)
1081 Mineral Spring Ave., North Providence, 02904.
Tel: 401-722-7140; Email: pbvm1081@cox.net. 5 Gibbs St., North Providence, 02904. Very Rev. Edward S. Cardente; Deacon Louis A. Vani
The Church of the Presentation of the Blessed Virgin Mary
Catechesis Religious Program—Fax: 401-353-5126. Maryann Dempsey, D.R.E. Students 11.

NORTH SMITHFIELD, PROVIDENCE CO., ST. JOHN THE EVANGELIST (Slatersville) (1872) [CEM]
63 Church St., Box 266, Slatersville, 02876.
Tel: 401-762-0946; Tel: 401-762-0966;
Fax: 401-762-0944; Email: stjohn02876@yahoo.com; Web: stjohntheevangelist.weconnect.com/. Rev. Gerard J. Caron
St. John's Church Society, Rhode Island
Catechesis Religious Program—Tel: 401-762-0966. Mrs. Celeste Baillargeon, D.R.E. Students 316.

PAWTUCKET, PROVIDENCE CO.

1—ST. ANTHONY (1926) (Portuguese)
32 Lawn Ave., Pawtucket, 02860. Tel: 401-723-9138; Email: stanthony32@pawtucket.necoxmail.com. Rev. Jose F. Rocha
Saint Anthony's Church Corporation, Pawtucket
Catechesis Religious Program—Students 117.

2—ST. CECILIA (1910) (French), Merged with St. Leo the Great, Pawtucket to form Saint John Paul II Pawtucket Rhode Island.
Saint Cecilia's Church Corporation.

3—ST. EDWARD (1904) Closed. Mission of St. Mary of the Immaculate Conception Parish, Pawtucket.
St. Edward's Church of Pawtucket.

4—HOLY FAMILY PARISH, PAWTUCKET (2009) Unification of the following parishes: St. Joseph, Pawtucket, est. 1873 (Legal title: St. Joseph's Church); Our Lady of Consolation, Pawtucket, est. 1895 (Legal title: Church of Our Lady of Consolation, Rhode Island); Sacred Heart of Jesus, Pawtucket, (Irish), est. 1872 (Legal title: The Church of the Sacred Heart of Jesus of Pawtucket, Rhode Island)
Mailing Address: 195 Walcott St., Pawtucket, 02860.
Tel: 401-724-9190; Fax: 401-724-9314; Email: holyfamily195@gmail.com; Web: www.holyfamilypawtucket.org. Rev. Joseph F. Craddock
Holy Family Parish, Pawtucket, Rhode Island
Catechesis Religious Program—Students 100.

5—IMMACULATE HEART OF MARY (1979) (Cape Verdean) (An operation of Church of St. Maron in Providence)
35 Clay St., Central Falls, 02863. Tel: 401-725-1126; Email: immheartofmarypawtucket@gmail.com. Rev. Joao Baptista Barros, C.S.Sp.
Church: 291 High St., Pawtucket, 02860.
Catechesis Religious Program—Students 30.

6—ST. JOHN PAUL II PARISH (2011)
697 Central Ave., Pawtucket, 02861-2191.
Tel: 401-722-1220; Tel: 401-722-1101;
Fax: 401-726-3392; Email: stjpii697@gmail.com; Web: www.saintjohnpaulri.com. Rev. Michael A. Sisco
Saint John Paul II Parish, Pawtucket, Rhode Island
School—St. Cecilia School, Pawtucket, (Grades PreK-8), 755 Central Ave., Pawtucket, 02861.
Tel: 401-723-9463; Fax: 401-722-1444; Email: mtetzner@scsri.org; Web: www.scsri.org. Mrs. Mary E. Tetzner, Prin. Lay Teachers 17; Students 198.
Catechesis Religious Program—Mrs. Debra Zagorski, D.R.E. Students 181.

7—ST. JOHN THE BAPTIST (1884) (French)
69 Quincy Ave., Pawtucket, 02860.
Tel: 401-722-9054; Email: st.johnthebaptist@verizon.net. Rev. Brian M. Sistare; Deacon Vicente Caban
The Church of St. John the Baptist of Pawtucket Rhode Island
Catechesis Religious Program—Email: carapialilian@gmail.com. Sr. Lilian Carapia, D.R.E. Students 0.

8—ST. JOSEPH (1873) Closed. See Holy Family Parish, Pawtucket
St. Joseph's Church.

9—ST. LEO THE GREAT (1916) (Irish), Merged with St. Cecilia, Pawtucket to form Saint John Paul II Pawtucket Rhode Island.
Church of Saint Leo the Great in Pawtucket.

10—ST. MARIA GORETTI (1953) Closed. For inquiries for sacramental records, contact Rev. Timothy D. Reilly, One Cathedral Square, Providence, RI 02903, 401-278-4516.
St. Maria Goretti Church Corporation, Pawtucket.

11—ST. MARY OF THE IMMACULATE CONCEPTION (1829) [JC]
103 Pine St., P.O. Box 518, Pawtucket, 02862.
Tel: 401-722-5425; Email: stmarypawt@cox.net; Web: www.saintmaryri.org. Rev. Mark A. Sauriol, Admin.; Deacon C. Patrick Sheehy
The Church of the Immaculate Conception of Pawtucket, Rhode Island
Catechesis Religious Program—Elizabeth Roach, D.R.E. Students 50.

12—OUR LADY OF CONSOLATION (1895) Closed. See Holy Family Parish, Pawtucket.
Church of Our Lady of Consolation Rhode Island.

13—SACRED HEART OF JESUS (1872) (Irish), Closed. See Holy Family Parish, Pawtucket.
The Church of the Sacred Heart of Jesus of Pawtucket, Rhode Island.

14—ST. TERESA OF THE CHILD JESUS (1929) Rev. David G. Thurber Jr.; Deacon N. David Bouley
Church of Saint Teresa of the Child Jesus, Pawtucket, Rhode Island
Res.: 358 Newport Ave., Pawtucket, 02861.
Tel: 401-722-4470; Fax: 401-722-2958; Email: mlombardi@stteresa.necoxmail.com; Web: www.stteresari.com.
School—St. Teresa of the Child Jesus School, (Grades PreK-8), 140 Woodhaven Rd., Pawtucket, 02861. Tel: 401-726-1414; Fax: 401-722-6998; Email: aamodie@stteresapawtucket.org; Web: www.stteresaschoolpawtucket.com. Mrs. Allison Amodie, Prin. Lay Teachers 19; Students 235.
Catechesis Religious Program—Tel: 401-722-8650. Mrs. Susan Levesque, D.R.E. Students 304.

PORTSMOUTH, NEWPORT CO.

1—ST. ANTHONY (1901)
2836 E. Main Rd., P.O. Box 570, Portsmouth, 02871.
Tel: 401-683-0089; Fax: 401-683-9680; Email: stanthonych@msn.com. Rev. Daniel J. Gray; Deacon Paul St. Laurent
Saint Anthony's Church of Portsmouth
Catechesis Religious Program—Tel: 401-683-3636. Students 30.

2—ST. BARNABAS (1963)
1697 E. Main Rd., Portsmouth, 02871-2427.
Tel: 401-683-1343; Email: sbchurch@stbarnabas.necoxmail.com; Web: www.stbarnabasportsmouth.weconnect.com. Rev. Peter J. Andrews; Deacon John Silvia
St. Barnabas Church Corporation, Portsmouth
Catechesis Religious Program—Tel: 401-683-3147; Email: faithformation@stbarnabas.necoxmail.com. Students 481.

SCITUATE, PROVIDENCE CO., ST. JOSEPH (North Scituate) (1940)
144 Danielson Pk., P.O. Box 236, North Scituate, 02857. Tel: 401-647-2255; Email: dmc948@verizon.net. Very Rev. Paul R. Grenon; Deacon Paul A. Ullucci
*Saint Joseph's Church Corporation, North Scituate*In Res., Rev. Eugene R. Lessard, (Retired).
Res.: 151 Danielson Pk., P.O. Box 236, North Scituate, 02857.
Catechesis Religious Program—
Tel: 401-647-2650 (D.R.E.); Fax: 401-647-2968. Mrs. Lisa Woodhead, D.R.E.; Andrea Olson, Youth Min.; Laurence Hall, Youth Min. Students 323.

SMITHFIELD, PROVIDENCE CO.

1—ST. MICHAEL (Georgiaville) (1875)
80 Farnum Pike, Smithfield, 02917.
Tel: 401-231-5119; Email: info@stmikegeo.necoxmail.com; Web: stmichaelsmithfield.org. Rev. Richard A. Valentine
St. Michael's Church, Georgiaville, Rhode Island
Catechesis Religious Program—Tel: 401-231-1340. Students 360.

2—ST. PHILIP (Greenville) (1852)
622 Putnam Pike, Greenville, 02828-1403.
Tel: 401-949-1500; Fax: 401-949-3504; Email: office@saintphilip.com; Web: www.saintphilip.com. Revs. Francis C. Santilli; Ryan J. Simas; Deacons Anthony E. Muscatelli; Carlo J. Sabetti
St. Philip's Church Greenville Rhode Island
School—St. Philip School, (Grades PreK-8), Parish School (St. Philip, Greenville) 618 Putnam Pike, Greenville, 02828. Tel: 401-949-1130. Mrs. Cynthia Senenko, Prin. Lay Teachers 14; Students 191; Religious Teachers 2.
Catechesis Religious Program—Tel: 401-949-0330; Email: reled@saintphilip.com. Mr. Dennis Sousa, D.R.E. Students 536.

SOUTH KINGSTOWN, WASHINGTON CO.

1—CHRIST THE KING (Kingston) (1950)
180 Old North Rd., Kingston, 02881.
Tel: 401-783-7459; Fax: 401-789-3671; Email: info@ctkri.org. Rev. Jared J. Costanza
Christ the King Church Corporation, Kingston
Catechesis Religious Program—Tel: 401-789-0417. Students 524.

2—ST. FRANCIS OF ASSISI (Wakefield) (1879) [CEM] Rev. Henry J. Bodah; Tony Romeo, Music Min.
Saint Francis's Church
Res.: 114 High St., Wakefield, 02879-3141.
Tel: 401-783-4411; Fax: 401-783-9667; Email: saintfrancis00@aol.com; Web: stfranciswakefield.com.
Catechesis Religious Program—Tel: 401-792-8684; Email: cullen_stfrancis@verizon.net; Email: castro_stfrancis@verizon.net. Barbette Cullen, D.R.E.; Mrs. Diane Castro, C.R.E. Students 281.
Chapel—St. Romuald Chapel, 61 Atlantic Ave., Wakefield, 02879.

TIVERTON, NEWPORT CO.

1—ST. CHRISTOPHER (1910)
Mailing Address: 265 Stafford Rd., Tiverton, 02878.
Tel: 401-624-6644. Rev. Przemyslaw Lepak; Deacon Dr. Timothy Flanigan, M.D.
Saint Christopher's Church of Tiverton
Res.: 1554 Main Rd., Tiverton, 02878.
Tel: 401-624-8746; Email: nancy@sstandctiverton.org; Web: www.sstandctiverton.org.
Church: 1584 Main Rd., Tiverton, 02878.
Catechesis Religious Program—Email: lynne@sstandctiverton.org. Lynne Swass, D.R.E. Students 0.

2—HOLY GHOST (North Tiverton) (1913)
316 Judson St., Tiverton, 02878. Email: FrFinelli@holyghostcc.org; Web: www.HolyGhostCC.org. 311 Hooper St., Tiverton, 02878.
Tel: 401-624-8131; Email: FRogers@HolyGhostCC.org. Rev. Jay A. Finelli
Church of the Holy Ghost, North Tiverton
Catechesis Religious Program—Tel: 401-624-3664. Students 56.

3—ST. MADELEINE SOPHIE (1948) (Portuguese) Rev. Stephan A. Silipigni
Saint Madeleine's Church Corporation of Tiverton
Res.: 35 Lake Rd., Tiverton, 02878.
Tel: 401-624-4226; Email: stmadeleinesophietiverton@gmail.com.
Catechesis Religious Program—Students 62.

4—ST. THERESA (1960)
265 Stafford Rd., Tiverton, 02878. Tel: 401-624-8746; Fax: 401-625-5384; Email: cindy@sstandctiverton.org; Web: www.sstandctiverton.org. Rev. Przemyslaw Lepak; Deacon Dr. Timothy Flanigan, M.D.
St. Theresa's Parish Corporation, Tiverton
Catechesis Religious Program—Email: lynne@sstandctiverton.org. Lynne Swass, D.R.E. Students 125.

WARREN, BRISTOL CO.

1—ST. ALEXANDER (1915) [CEM] (Italian)
221 Main St., Warren, 02885. Tel: 401-245-6369; Email: parishoffice@saintalexanders.com. Rev. David W. Masello, J.C.L., Admin.
Saint Alexander's Church Corporation, Warren
Catechesis Religious Program—Tel: 401-247-1764; Email: mhm7@verizon.net. Marie Mascena, D.R.E.; Martha Delekta, D.R.E. Students 9.

2—ST. CASIMIR (1908) [JC] (Polish), Closed. For Inquiries for parish records please see St. Mary of the Bay, Warren.
Saint Casimir's Church of Warren.

3—ST. MARY OF THE BAY (1851) [CEM]
645 Main St., Warren, 02885. Tel: 401-245-7000; Email: stmary02885@gmail.com; Web: stmaryofthebay.org. Rev. W. Douglas Grant; Deacon John P. Pryor
Church of Saint Mary of the Bay
Catechesis Religious Program—
Tel: 401-245-7000, Ext. 21. Students 192.

4—ST. THOMAS THE APOSTLE (1952) (Portuguese)
500 Metacom Ave., Warren, 02885-2808.
Tel: 401-245-4469; Email: stthomasap500@fullchannel.net. Rev. John E. Abreu
Saint Thomas the Apostle Church Corporation of Warren
Catechesis Religious Program—Tel: 401-245-4488. Anne Furtado, C.R.E. Students 36.

WARWICK, KENT CO.

1—ST. BENEDICT (Conimicut) (1914) Rev. Robert L. Marciano, Admin.
St. Benedict's Church, Conimicut
Res.: 135 Beach Ave., Warwick, 02889.
Tel: 401-737-9492; Email: stbenedicts@verizon.net.
Catechesis Religious Program—70 Transit St., Warwick, 02889. Students 61.

2—ST. CATHERINE (Apponaug) (1916)
3252 Post Rd., Warwick, 02886. Tel: 401-737-4455; Email: pastor@stcat.necoxmail.com. Rev. Pierre J. Plante; Deacon John F. Baker
Saint Catherine's Roman Catholic Church of Warwick, Rhode Island
Catechesis Religious Program—Fax: 401-736-0960. Kelly Francoeur, D.R.E. Students 43.

3—ST. CLEMENT'S (1961) Merged with St. Rose of Lima to form St. Rose of Lima/St. Clement, Warwick.

4—ST. FRANCIS OF ASSISI (Hillsgrove) (1943)
596 Jefferson Blvd., Warwick, 02886.
Tel: 401-737-5191; Email: stfrancis737@cox.net. Rev. Pierre J. Plante
Saint Francis Church Corporation, Hillsgrove
Catechesis Religious Program—Students 10.
Convent—249 Chestnut St., Warwick, 02888.

5—ST. GREGORY THE GREAT (Cowesett) (1961)
360 Cowesett Rd., Warwick, 02886.
Tel: 401-884-1666; Email: info@sgg.necoxmail.com; Web: www.stgregorychurchri.com. Rev. Alfred V. Ricci; Deacon Paul F. Kirk

*St. Gregory the Great Church Corporation, Warwick*In Res., Rev. David F. Ricard, (Retired).
Catechesis Religious Program—Email: achristianson@sgg.necoxmail.com. Angela Christianson, D.R.E. Students 333.
6—ST. KEVIN (1956) Rev. Robert L. Marciano; Deacon John Fulton
St. Kevin's Church Corporation, Warwick
Res.: 333 Sandy Ln., Warwick, 02889.
Tel: 401-737-2638; Email: secretary@saintkevinri.org.
School—St. Kevin School, (Grades PreK-8), 39 Cathedral Rd., Warwick, 02889. Tel: 401-737-7172; Fax: 401-738-2832; Email: dirving@saintkevinschool.org; Web: www.saintkevinschool.org. Mr. David Irving, Prin. Lay Teachers 26; Students 251.
Catechesis Religious Program—Tel: 401-739-6309. Michael Curran, C.R.E. (Grade 1-8); Christopher Tanguay, C.R.E. (Grade 9); Brian Callahan, C.R.E. (Grade 9). Students 200.
7—ST. PETER (Pawtuxet) (1933)
350 Fair St., Warwick, 02888. Tel: 401-467-4895; Email: info@stpeterswarwick.com. Rev. Roger C. Gagne; Deacon Robert M. Morisseau
*St. Peter's Church, Warwick, Rhode Island*In Res., Rev. Msgr. Nicholas J. Iacovacci, (Retired).
School—St. Peter School, (Grades PreK-8), 120 Mayfair Rd., Warwick, 02888. Tel: 401-781-9242; Fax: 401-467-5673; Email: stpeters5@cox.net. Mrs. Joan Sickinger, Prin. Lay Teachers 17; Students 221.
Catechesis Religious Program—Tel: 401-461-5691. Margaret Andreozzi, D.R.E.; Elaine Morisseau, D.R.E. Students 345.
8—ST. RITA (Oakland Beach) (1935)
722 Oakland Beach Ave., Warwick, 02889.
Tel: 401-738-1800; Email: saintrita02889@ahoo.com. Rev. Peter J. D'Ambrosia
Saint Rita's Church Corporation, Oakland Beach
Catechesis Religious Program—Cheryl Picard, D.R.E. Students 71.
9—STS. ROSE & CLEMENT (1998) Consolidation of St. Rose of Lima (Legal Title: St. Rose's Church Corporation, Warwick) and St. Clement (Legal Title: St. Clement's Church Corporation, Warwick).
111 Long St., Warwick, 02886. Rev. S. Matthew Glover; Deacon Noel Edsall.
Res.: 171 Inman Ave., Warwick, 02886-1700.
Tel: 401-739-1212; Email: office@ssrc4.necoxmail.com.
School—St. Rose of Lima, (Grades PreK-8), 200 Brentwood Ave., Warwick, 02886. Tel: 401-739-6937; Fax: 401-737-4632; Email: kizzi@saintroseschool.com; Web: www.saintroseschool.com. Ms. Kimberly Izzi, Prin. Lay Teachers 18; Students 241.
Catechesis Religious Program—Students 273.
10—ST. ROSE OF LIMA (Greenwood) (1950) Merged with St. Clement to form St. Rose of Lima/St. Clement, Warwick.
11—ST. TIMOTHY (Hoxie) (1950) Rev. D. Andrew Messina
Saint Timothy's Church Corporation, Warwick
Res.: 1799 Warwick Ave., Warwick, 02889.
Tel: 401-739-9552; Email: sttim1799@aol.com.
Catechesis Religious Program—Tel: 401-738-9079. Students 122.
12—ST. WILLIAM (Norwood) (1933) [CEM] Closed.
Saint William Church Corporation, Norwood.
WEST WARWICK, KENT CO.
1—ST. ANTHONY (Riverpoint) (1925) (Portuguese) Rev. Victor T. Silva; Deacon Carlos Botelho
Saint Anthony's Church Corporation, River Point
Res.: 10 Sunset Ave., West Warwick, 02893.
Tel: 401-821-8342; Email: stanthonyswwri@hotmail.com.
Catechesis Religious Program—Students 125.
2—CHRIST THE KING (Centreville) (1931) (French)
130 Legris Ave., West Warwick, 02893.
Tel: 401-821-9228; Email: ctkwwri@cox.net. Rev. Timothy J. Lemlin; Deacon William J. Schofield
Church of Christ the King, West Warwick
Res.: 120 Legris Ave., West Warwick, 02893.
Catechesis Religious Program—Students 86.
3—ST. JAMES (1908) Merged with St. John the Baptist, West Warwick to form SS. John and James Parish, West Warwick.
4—SS. JOHN AND JAMES PARISH (2003) [CEM]
20 Washington St., West Warwick, 02893-4919.
Tel: 401-821-7661; Email: ssjohnandjames@cox.net. Rev. Eddy E. Lopez-Bolanos, Admin.
Catechesis Religious Program—Mrs. Christine Daneault, D.R.E. Students 142.
5—ST. JOHN THE BAPTIST (Arctic) (1874) [CEM] (French), Merged with St. James, West Warwick to form SS. John and James Parish, West Warwick.
6—ST. JOSEPH (Natick) (1873)
854 Providence St., West Warwick, 02893-1140.
Tel: 401-821-4072; Email: stjoseph854@gmail.com. Rev. Gregory P. Stowe; Deacon Cyrille W.J. Cote
St. Joseph's Church, Natick RI
School—St. Joseph School, (Grades PreK-8), 850 Wakefield St., West Warwick, 02893.
Tel: 401-821-3450. Mr. Joseph Pasonelli, Prin. Lay Teachers 22; Students 208.
Catechesis Religious Program—Students 85.
7—ST. MARY (Crompton) (1844) [CEM]
70 Church St., West Warwick, 02893.
Tel: 401-821-5555; Email: stmaryschurch1@cox.net. Rev. Douglas J. Spina, Ph.D.
St. Mary's Church, Crompton Rhode Island
Catechesis Religious Program—Tel: 401-828-8756. Students 71.
8—OUR LADY OF GOOD COUNSEL (Phenix) (1897) [CEM] (French)
62 Pleasant St., West Warwick, 02893.
Tel: 401-821-6428; Email: olgc60@verizon.net. Rev. Paul R. Lemoi
Church of Our Lady of Good Counsel, Warwick RI
Catechesis Religious Program—Tel: 401-822-1869. Susan Cinieri, D.R.E. Students 54.
9—SS. PETER AND PAUL (Phenix) (1853) [CEM]
48 Highland St., West Warwick, 02893-5699.
Tel: 401-821-2198; Email: sspeterandpaulchurch@verizon.net. Rev. Robert J. Giardina
SS. Peter and Paul's Church, Phoenixville, Rhode Island
Catechesis Religious Program—Students 40.
10—SACRED HEART CHURCH (Natick) (1929) (Italian)
820 Providence St., West Warwick, 02893.
Tel: 401-821-4184; Email: sacredheartww@cox.net. Rev. Richard A. Bucci
Church of the Sacred Heart, Natick RI
Catechesis Religious Program—Students 26.
WESTERLY, WASHINGTON CO.
1—ST. CLARE (Misquamicut) (1946)
4 Saint Clare Way, Westerly, 02891.
Tel: 401-348-8765; Email: stclareri2@cox.net. Rev. Kenneth J. Suibielski; Deacons Stephen R. Cote; John D. McGregor; W. Carl LaFleur, (Retired)
Saint Clare's Church Corporation, Misquamicut
Catechesis Religious Program—Students 120.
2—IMMACULATE CONCEPTION (1885) [CEM] (Italian)
Mailing Address: 111 High St., Westerly, 02891-0556. Tel: 401-596-2130; Email: icc@immcon.org; Web: immcon.org. Rev. Giacomo D. Capoverdi Jr.
Church of the Immaculate Conception of Westerly, Rhode Island
Catechesis Religious Program—Tel: 401-596-0900. Mrs. Catherine Kimmel, C.R.E. (Grades 1-8). Students 208.
3—ST. PIUS X (1955)
44 Elm St., Westerly, 02891. Tel: 401-596-2535; Email: stpiusx@cox.net. Rev. Michael J. Najim, M.Div.; Deacon Francis J. Valliere; Rev. Raymond N. Suriani, In Res., (Retired), 44 Elm St., Westerly, 02891
St. Pius X Parish Corporation, Westerly
Catechesis Religious Program—Tel: 401-596-8530; Email: chrismagowan@cox.net. Christine Magowan, D.R.E. Students 90.
4—ST. VINCENT DE PAUL (Bradford) (1946)
Mailing Address: 169 Main St., Ashaway, 02804. Rev. Michael A. Colello, Admin.; Deacon Costa Adamopoulos
Saint Vincent's Church Corporation, Bradford
Church: 5 Church St., Bradford, 02808.
Catechesis Religious Program—Email: ggolv@yahoo.com. Students 79.
WOONSOCKET, PROVIDENCE CO.
1—ST. AGATHA (1953) Rev. Michael A. Kelley; Deacon Eugene Garceau
*Saint Agatha's Church Corporation, Woonsocket*In Res., Rev. Wilfrid G. Gregoire, (Retired).
Res.: 34 Joffre Ave., Woonsocket, 02895.
Tel: 401-767-2950; Email: stagathaschurch@cox.net.
Catechesis Religious Program—Students 126.
2—ALL SAINTS PARISH (2009) [JC] An alliance of the following three parishes: Our Lady of Victories, (French), est. 1909, (Legal title: Church of Notre Dame des Victoires); St. Aloysius, (French) est. 1902, (Legal title: Saint Aloysius Church of Woonsocket); and St. Ann, (French) est. 1890 (Legal title: St. Ann's Church Corporation of Woonsocket RI).
323 Rathbun St., Woonsocket, 02895.
Tel: 401-762-1100; Email: allsaintsrectory2@hotmail.com; Web: www.allsaintswoonsocket.org. Deacon Robert L. Gallo, Admin.
All Saints Parish, Woonsocket, Rhode Island
Catechesis Religious Program—Tel: 401-766-5771. Students 231.
3—ST. ALOYSIUS (1902) Merged See All Saints Parish, Woonsocket.
4—ST. ANN (1890) Merged See All Saints Parish, Woonsocket.
5—ST. ANTHONY (1924) [JC] (Italian) Rev. Msgr. Ronald P. Simeone, M.Div., J.C.L.
Saint Anthony's Church, Woonsocket, RI
Res.: 128 Greene St., Woonsocket, 02895.
Tel: 401-766-2640; Email: saintanthonywoonsocket@verizon.net.
Catechesis Religious Program—Students 17.
6—ST. CHARLES (1846) [CEM]
Mailing Address: 323 Rathbun St., Woonsocket, 02895. Tel: 401-766-0176; Email: rectory@stcharlesborromeo.com; Web: stcharlesborromeo.com. 8 Daniels St., Woonsocket, 02895. Deacon Robert L. Gallo, Admin.
St. Charles Borromeo's Church, Woonsocket, RI
Church: 190 N. Main St., Woonsocket, 02895-3140.
Catechesis Religious Program—Students 9.
7—HOLY FAMILY (1902) [JC] (French), Merged See Holy Trinity, Woonsocket.
Church of the Holy Family.
8—HOLY TRINITY PARISH WOONSOCKET (2018) Unification of Holy Family, (Legal Title: Church of the Holy Family); Our Lady, Queen of Martyrs (Legal Title: Our Lady, Queen of Martyrs Church Corporation); and Sacred Heart (Legal Title: Church of the Sacred Heart, Woonsocket, Rhode Island)
1409 Park Ave., Woonsocket, 02895.
Tel: 401-762-5117; Fax: 401-765-8875; Email: holy.trinity1409@gmail.com; Web: www.holytrinityri.com. Rev. Daniel J. Sweet, Admin.
9—ST. JOSEPH (East Woonsocket) (1929) (French-Canadian) Rev. Carl B. Fisette
Saint Joseph's Church, Woonsocket
Res.: 1200 Mendon Rd., Woonsocket, 02895-3999.
Tel: 401-766-0626; Email: father.woolley@verizon.net; Web: saintjosephwoonsocket.org.
Catechesis Religious Program—1210 Mendon Rd., Woonsocket, 02895. Students 121.
Stations—Woonsocket Health Center—Woonsocket.
Wyndemere Woods, Woonsocket.
10—OUR LADY OF VICTORIES (1909) Merged See All Saints Parish, Woonsocket.
11—OUR LADY, QUEEN OF MARTYRS (1953) Merged Sacramental records are maintained at Holy Trinity Parish, Woonsocket.
12—PRECIOUS BLOOD (1843) [CEM] (French)
94 Carrington Ave., Woonsocket, 02895.
Tel: 401-767-2950; Email: preciousblood@cox.net. 34 Joffre Ave., Woonsocket, 02895. Rev. Michael A. Kelley
The Church of the Precious Blood Corporation, Woonsocket, RI
Catechesis Religious Program—Students 35.
13—SACRED HEART (1895) Closed. Sacramental records are maintained at Holy Trinity Parish, Woonsocket.
14—ST. STANISLAUS (1905) [JC] (Polish) Rev. Dariusz J. Jonczyk, Admin.
Saint Stanislaus Kostka Church of Woonsocket
Res.: 174 Harris Ave., Woonsocket, 02895.
Tel: 401-762-0021; Email: st.joseph1@verizon.net.
Catechesis Religious Program—Students 25.

Chaplains of Public Institutions

PROVIDENCE. *Miriam Hospital*, 164 Summit Ave., 02906. Tel: 401-274-3700. Rev. Edward L. Pieroni
Res., 2 Matilda St., 02904-1812.
Rhode Island Hospital, 593 Eddy St., 02902.
Tel: 401-277-4000. Revs. Jose Q. dos Reis, Francesco Francese, Albert P. Marcello III, Albert A. Ranallo Jr., Dir. Catholic Chaplaincy, Antony Jeya Siluvai Rayan, Saji Thengumkudiyil, Chap.
Roger Williams Hospital, 825 Chalkstone Ave., 02908. Tel: 401-456-2000. Pastoral care provided by local parishes.
Veterans Administration Hospital, Davis Park, 02908. Tel: 401-273-7100. Rev. John L. Wydeven.
BURRILLVILLE. *Rhode Island-Zambarano State Hospital*, 1 Cathedral Sq., 02903. Pastoral care provided by Office of Health Ministries.
CRANSTON. *Department of Corrections*, 1 Cathedral Sq., 02903. Tel: 401-421-7833. Mrs. Martha Paone, Chap. Coord.
Eleanor Slater Hospital. Rev. Lazarus Onuh, (Nigeria).
NEWPORT. *Newport Hospital*. Very Rev. Francis A. O'Loughlin, 1 Vernon Ave., Newport, 02840. Teletype: 401-847-0065.
NORTH SMITHFIELD. *Saint Antoine Residence*. Rev. Roger A. Houle.
Landmark Medical Center, Fogarty Unit. Pastoral care provided by local parishes.
SOUTH KINGSTOWN. *South County Hospital*,
Tel: 401-782-8000. Rev. Henry J. Bodah, 114 High St., Wakefield, 02879-3141.
WARWICK. *Kent County Memorial Hospital*. Pastoral Care provided by local parishes.
WESTERLY. *The Westerly Hospital*, 25 Wells St., Westerly, 02891. Tel: 401-596-6000. Pastoral care provided by local parishes.
WOONSOCKET. *Landmark Medical Center, Woonsocket Unit*. Pastoral care provided by local parishes.

On Duty Outside the Diocese:
Revs.—
Berthelette, Ernest H., U.S. Air Force; Diocese of St. John's-Basseterre, Antigua & Barbuda, West Indies
Cardenas Bonilla, Jose C., Diocese of Charlotte

Connors, Ryan W., Rome, Italy
Rev—
Dufour, Phillip J., Rome, Italy
Revs.—
Mahar, Christopher M., S.T.L., Rome, Italy
Pontes, Scott J., Archdiocese of Newark
Prendiville, Edmond P., 2480 Presidential Way-Envoy 1202, West Palm Beach, FL 33401
Willenberg, Lukasz J., Archdiocese for the Military Services, U.S.A.

Absent on Leave:
Revs.—
Abruzzese, Joseph A.
Fisette, Kevin R.
Jimenez-Londono, Fredy A.
Manchester, Roman R.
Petrocelli, John N.
Puleo, Derek J.

Retired:
Most Revs.—
Boland, Ernest B., O.P., (Retired), 964 Main St., Pawtucket, 02860
Gelineau, Louis E., D.D., S.T.L., J.C.L., (Retired), 400 Mendon Rd., North Smithfield, 02896
Roque, Francis, (Retired), 964 Main St., Pawtucket, 02860
Rev. Msgrs.—
Connerton, Barry R.L., (Retired), P.O. Box 2553, Taunton, MA 02780
Frappier, George L., (Retired), 400 Mendon Rd., Apt. 232, North Smithfield, 02896
Halloran, John C., (Retired), 36 Coffey Ave., Narragansett, 02882
Iacovacci, Nicholas J., (Retired), 350 Fair St., Warwick, 02888
McCaffrey, William J., (Retired), 169 Main St., Ashaway, 02804
Montecalvo, Carlo F., (Retired)
Sabourin, Gerard O., (Retired), 84 Exeter Rd., Exeter, 02822
Sheahan, Richard D., (Retired), 19 Penguin Dr., Narragansett, 02882
Vieira, Victor M., (Retired), 2155 Chestnut St., North Dighton, MA 02764
Revs.—
Allard, George L., (Retired), 715 Putnam Pike, Apt. 312, Greenville, 02828
Beirne, Gerald E., (Retired), 75 Circuit Dr., Narragansett, 02882
Beirne, Robert M., (Retired), 493 Mt. Pleasant Ave., 02908
Blais, Robert L., (Retired), 10 Hall St., West Warwick, 02893
Bolton, Paul J., (Retired), 3700 N. 55th Ave., Hollywood, FL 33021
Brassard, Ronald E., (Retired), 21 Normandy Dr., Cranston, 02920
Brindamour, Maurice L., (Retired), 92 Hope St., 02906
Cabral, Clifford J., (Retired), 15 St. Elizabeth's Way, East Greenwich, 02818
Caul, Robert F., (Retired), 964 Main St., Pawtucket, 02860
Charland, Paul A., (Retired), c/o 1 Cathedral Sq., 02903
Chew, Randolph G., (Retired), P.O. Box 1361, Charlestown, 02813
Collins, James R., (Retired), 1525 Cranston St., Cranston, 02920
Collins, Raymond F., (Retired), P.O. Box 507, Saunderstown, 02874
Courtemanche, Normand L., (Retired), 10 Rhodes Ave., North Smithfield, 02896
Creedon, Joseph D., (Retired), 54 Woodbridge Rd., Narragansett, 02882
da Cunha, Domingos M., (Retired), 92 Hope St., 02906
Davenport, Christopher M., (Retired), 110 Booth Ave., Pawtucket, 02861
Depatie, Donald L., (Retired), 170 Centre St., Rumford, 02916
Desaulniers, Richard P., (Retired), 417 Maple St., Woonsocket, 02895
Dreher, John D., (Retired), 493 Mt. Pleasant Ave., Apt. 8, 02908
Duggan, John J., (Ireland) (Retired), 341 S. Main St., Coventry, 02816
Farley, James V., (Retired), P.O. Box 254, Dayville, CT 06249
Finerty, D. Bryan, (Retired), 15323 Lime Dr., Punta Gorda, FL 33955
Fitzgerald, Edmund H., (Retired), c/o One Cathedral Sq., 02903
Friedrichs, Richard M., (Retired), P.O. Box 876, Glendale, 02826
Gibowski, Boguslaw T., (Retired), Poland
Giudice, Francis J., (Retired), 400 Mendon Rd., Apt. 229, North Smithfield, 002896
Gorton, Timothy J., (Retired), 1 Cathedral Sq., 02903
Gray, John W., (Retired), 964 Main St., Apt. 402, Pawtucket, 02860
Greaves, John G., (Retired), 2730 Sailors Way, Naples, FL 34109-7643
Gregoire, Wilfrid G., (Retired), 34 Joffre Ave., Woonsocket, 02895
Harbour, Gerald G., (Retired), 1209 Ocean Rd., Narragansett, 02882
Hawkins, Robert F., (Retired), 467 North Ln., Bristol, 02809
Hayman, Robert W., M.A., Ph.D., (Retired), 30 Fenner St., 02903
Hazebrouck, Maurice L., (Retired), c/o One Cathedral Sq., 02903
Heaney, John F., (Retired), 10 Brightman Way, Westerly, 02891
Henry, Joseph P., (Retired), 225 Capstan St., Jamestown, 02835
Hunt, John W., (Retired), P.O. Box 796, Chepachet, 02814
Hussey, Gerald W., (Retired), 1401 Capella South, Newport, 02840
Iwuc, Anthony D., (Retired), 493 Mt. Pleasant Ave., Apt. 6, 02908
Johnson, Edward D., (Retired), 1417 Ronald Reagan Ln., Jefferson, GA 30549-7144
Kachel, Czeslaw L., (Retired), 493 Mt. Pleasant Ave., 02908
Kelley, Edward J., (Retired), C/O One Cathedral Sq., 02903
Kiley, John A., (Retired), 247 Highland St., Woonsocket, 02895
LaMontagne, Bernard L., (Retired), 2604 Garfield Ave., Terre Haute, IN 47804
Laporte, Paul J., (Retired), 218 Baxter St., Pawtucket, 02861
Lavin, John J., (Retired), 56 Boxwood Ave., Cranston, 02910
Lessard, Eugene R., (Retired), P.O. Box 236, North Scituate, 02857-0236
Lonardo, Alfred C., (Retired), P.O. Box 228, Jamestown, 02835
Luft, Raymond P., (Retired), 493 Mt. Pleasant Ave., 02908
Maher, Charles E., (Retired), 188 Col. John Gardner Rd., Narragansett, 02882
Malm, Raymond B., (Retired), 1180 Narragansett Blvd., Cranston, 02905
Maynard, Richard C., (Retired), 493 Mt. Pleasant Ave., Apt 10, 02908
McCarthy, George B., (Retired), 302 America, Goat Island, Newport, 02840
McElroy, John J., (Retired), 493 Mt. Pleasant Ave., 02908
McGovern, Edward J., (Retired), 493 Mt. Pleasant Ave., Apt. 1, 02908
McKenna, Eugene J., (Retired), 30 Blackberry Hill Dr., Wakefield, 02879
McLaughlin, Farrell E., (Retired), 493 Mt. Pleasant Ave., 02908
McNulty, John T., (Retired), P.O. Box 16176, Rumford, 02916
Micarelli, Edmond C., (Retired), c/o One Cathedral Sq., 02903-3695
Mongeon, Peter M., (Retired), 26 Fairview Ave., Cranston, 02905
Natalizia, Louis T., (Retired), 96 Dunedin St., Cranston, 02920
O'Hara, Francis W., (Retired), 36 Eden Crest Dr., Cranston, 02920
O'Neill, Thomas D., (Retired), 309 Spring St., Newport, 02840
O'Neill, William J., (Retired), 9 Spring St., Jamestown, 02835
O'Reilly, Bernard M., M.A., Ph.D., D.Min., (Retired), 111 Ballston Ave., Pawtucket, 02861
Paquette, Joseph, (Retired), 220 Hilltop Rd., Cumberland, 02864
Piacentini, David A., (Retired), C/O 16 Arbor Dr., 02908
Pincince, Gerald P., (Retired), 2280 S. Flagler Ave., Flagler Beach, FL 32136
Quinn, Charles P., (Retired), 685 Steere Farm Rd., Pascoag, 02859
Rainone, John J., (Retired), 493 Mt. Pleasant Ave., 02908
Randall, Robert J., (Retired), P.O. Box 5617, Wakefield, 02880
Reardon, Dennis A., (Retired), 124 Frigate St., Jamestown, 02835
Ricard, David F., (Retired), 41 Sandro Dr., Warwick, 02886
Rochon, Robert A., (Retired), 27 Andrews Dr., Uxbridge, MA 01569-3151
Simoneau, Roland L., (Retired), 35 Peabody Dr., Warwick, 02889
Slota, Frederick V., (Retired), 84 Kulas Rd., West Warwick, 02893
Smith, Nicholas P., (Retired), 493 Mt. Pleasant Ave., 02908
Stokes, David L., (Retired), 86 Frigate St., Jamestown, 02835
Strumski, Matthew J., (Retired), C/O 735 Willett Ave., #701, Riverside, 02915
Suriani, Raymond N., (Retired), 44 Elm St., Westerly, 02891
Tanguay, William H., (Retired), c/o One Cathedral Sq., 02903
Tetrault, Raymond L., (Retired), 66 Appleton St., 02909
Tetreault, Raymond A., (Retired), 13 Ledgebrook Dr., Blackstone, MA 01504
Theroux, Bertrand L., (Retired), 209 Legend Rock Rd., Wakefield, 02879
Theroux, Raymond C., (Retired), 309 Spring St., Apt. 320, Newport, 02840
Toole, Lawrence E., (Retired), 77 King Philip Rd., Pawtucket, 02861
Trainor, Daniel M., (Retired), 493 Mt. Pleasant Ave., Apt. 2, 02908
Turillo, B. Samuel, (Retired), One Cathedral Sq., 02903
Verdelotti, James J., (Retired), 493 Mt. Pleasant Ave., Apt. 3, 02908
Walsh, Richard A., (Retired), C/O P.O. Box 389, Newport, 02840
Watterson, John E., (Retired), 700 Shore Dr., Unit 1109, Fall River, MA 02721.

Permanent Deacons:
Adamopoulos, Costa, Our Lady of Victory, Ashaway; St. Vincent DePaul, Bradford
Albanese, Gregory, Holy Apostles, Cranston
Andrade, Charles, (Retired), St. Patrick, Providence
Andrade, Kenneth, St. Timothy, Warwick
Andrade, Victorino, Our Lady of the Rosary, Providence
Baker, John F., St. Catherine, Warwick
Barboza, Benjamin, (Retired), St. Thomas, Warren
Bartolo, Amandio, Our Lady of Fatima, Cumberland
Batalon, Raymond E., (L.O.A)
Birbuet, Eduardo, St. Patrick, Providence
Bisbano, Paul, St. Mary, Bristol
Botelho, Carlos, St. Anthony, West Warwick
Botelho, Fernando, St. Paul, Foster
Boutier, Thomas F., (Retired)
Braga, Joseph F., (Retired), St. Patrick, Providence
Brown, Scott, Immaculate Conception, Cranston; Veterans' Home, Bristol
Caban, Vicente, St. John the Baptist, Pawtucket
Castaldi, Raphael, St. Mary, Carolina
Ceprano, Peter A., (Retired), St. Mary, Cranston
Corey, John A., Saint Kateri Tekakwitha Catholic Community, Exeter
Cote, Cyrille W.J., St. Joseph, West Warwick; Chaplain, Kent County Hospital
Cote, Stephen R., St. Clare, Misquamicut
Croy, John E., (Retired), St. Lucy, Middletown
DePetrillo, Albert, St. Thomas, Providence
DePietro, Ronald H., St. Francis de Sales, North Kingstown
DiOrio, Dominic P., (Retired), St. Martha, East Providence
Dowd, John, Our Lady of Mercy, East Greenwich
Dunbar, James N., (Retired), Jesus Saviour, Newport
Edsall, Noel, Immaculate Conception, Cranston
Fajardo, Jose, (Retired), (Cursillo Movement)
Dr. Flanigan, Timothy, M.D., St. Christopher & St. Theresa, Tiverton
Foster, Walter, Sts. John & Paul, Coventry
Fulton, John, St. Kevin, Warwick
Gallo, Robert L., Pastoral Admin., All Saints & St. Charles Borromeo, Woonsocket
Garceau, Eugene, (Retired), St. Agatha, Woonsocket
Garcia, Luis, Blessed Sacrament, Providence
Geoffroy, Roland R., (Diocese of Charlotte)
Gomez, Oscar, (Leave of Absence)
Hanrahan, Charles L., (Diocese of Charlestown)
Hester, Stephan, St. Andrew, Block Island
Horton, Gregory R., (Diocese of West Palm Beach)
Kirk, Paul, D.D.S., St. Gregory the Great, Warwick
Konold, Paul C., (Diocese of Arlington)
LaFleur, W. Carl, (Retired), St. Clare, Westerly
Lafond, Robert L., M.T.S., St. Aidan-St. Patrick, Cumberland
Lambert, Paul H., St. John Vianney, Cumberland
Lapierre, Richard J., Our Lady of Good Help, Mapleville
Lopez, Rony, Assumption/St. Anthony, Providence
Lucian, Robert C., (Retired), (Diocese of Bridgeport)
MacLure, Robert, (Retired)
Martins, Jesse L., (Diocese of Fall River)
McCarthy, Charles F., St. Benedict, Warwick
McGregor, John D., St. Clare, Misquamicut
Morisseau, Robert M., St. Peter, Warwick

Muscatelli, Anthony E., St. Philip, Greenville
Natalizia, John J., Holy Cross, Providence
Needham, John F., St. Margaret, East Providence
Owen, Jimmie H., (Retired), Blessed Sacrament, Providence
Perez, Juan Andres, St. Michael, Providence
Persson, Robert, (Retired), SS. John & Paul, Coventry
Preuhs, Ronald, St. Joseph, Hope Valley
Pryor, John P., St. Mary of the Bay, Warren
Ragosta, Armand R., (Retired), St. Mary, Cranston
Raspallo, Thomas R., (Retired), Immaculate Conception, Cranston
Raymond, Stephen, Holy Ghost, Providence
Remillard, Lionel J., St. Jude, Lincoln
Riccio, Raymond L., (Retired), St. Rocco, Johnston
Rico, Jose, St. Charles Borromeo, Providence
Risi, Stephen M., Mary, Mother of Mankind, North Providence
Sabetti, Carlo J., St. Philip, Greenville
Schofield, William J., Christ the King, West Warwick
Shea, John S., (Retired), (St. Mary, Carolina)
Shea, Paul M., St. Paul, Cranston
Sheehy, C. Patrick, St. Mary, Pawtucket
Silvia, John, St. Barnabas, Portsmouth
St. Laurent, Paul, St. Anthony, Portsmouth
Sullivan, Paul J., St. Thomas More, Narragansett
Tanguay, Paul A., Chap., ACI, Cranston
Theroux, Bernard G., (Retired), Chap., R.I. Veteran's Home
Theroux, Paul A., (Retired), St. Mary, Carolina
Troia, Robert, St. Rocco's, Thornton
Tumminelli, Joseph, St. Robert Bellarmine, Johnston
Turbitt, Robert A. II, Diocese of Orlando
Turcios, Jose, All Saints, Woonsocket
Ullucci, Paul A., St. Joseph, Scituate
Valliere, Francis J., St. Pius X, Westerly
Vani, Louis A., Presentation of the Blessed Virgin Mary, North Providence
Walsh, James T., St. Joseph, Cumberland
Wendoloski, Anthony, (Retired), Our Lady of Lourdes, Providence
Yany, George, (Retired), St. Basil Melkite, Lincoln.

INSTITUTIONS LOCATED IN DIOCESE

[A] SEMINARIES, DIOCESAN

PROVIDENCE. *Seminary of Our Lady of Providence*, 485 Mt. Pleasant Ave., 02908. Tel: 401-331-1316; Fax: 401-521-4192; Email: cdeangelis@dioceseofprovidence.org. Revs. Christopher J. Murphy, Dir. Vocations; David F. Gaffney, M.Div., Rector; Timothy D. Reilly, S.T.B., J.C.L., Asst. Dir. Spiritual Form.; Thomas J. Woodhouse, Dir. Spiritual Formation; Dr. Michael Hansen, Ph. D., Dir. Human Formation/Staff Psychologist. House of Formation for College Students and Pre-Theologians.
Seminary of Our Lady of Providence Religious Teachers 4; Students 25; Total Staff 6.

[B] COLLEGES AND UNIVERSITIES

PROVIDENCE. *Providence College*, One Cunningham Sq., 02918. Tel: 401-865-1000; Fax: 401-865-2057; Email: pcadmiss@providence.edu; Web: www.providence.edu. Revs. Brian J. Shanley, O.P., Pres.; Kenneth Sicard, O.P., Exec. Vice Pres. & Treas.; Dr. Hugh V. Lena, Provost & Senior Vice Pres. Academic Affairs; John Sweeney, Senior Vice Pres. Finance & Business & CFO; Kristine Goodwin, Vice Pres. Student Affairs; Revs. J. Stuart McPhail, O.P., Assoc. Chap., Natl. Alumni Assoc.; Mark D. Nowel, O.P., Dean Undergraduate & Graduate Studies; Gregory T. Waldron, Senior Vice Pres. Inst. Advancement; Revs. Peter Martyr Joseph Yungwirth, O.P., Chap.; R. Gabriel Pivarnik, O.P., Vice Pres. Mission & Ministry; Marifrances McGinn, Vice Pres. & Gen. Counsel; Robert Driscoll, Assoc. Vice Pres. & Athletic Dir.; Kathleen M. Alvino, Assoc. Vice Pres. Human Resources. Conducted by the Dominican Friars.
Providence College Dominican Priests Teaching 24; Diocesan Priests Teaching 2; Franciscan Priests Teaching 1; Sisters Teaching 1; Lay Professors 318; Undergraduate Students 4,133; Graduate Students 547; School of Continuing Education 319.

NEWPORT. *Salve Regina University* (1934) 100 Ochre Point Ave., Newport, 02840-4192.
Tel: 401-847-6650; Fax: 401-847-0372; Email: sruadmis@salve.edu; Web: www.salve.edu. Sisters M. Therese Antone, R.S.M., Chancellor; Jane Gerety, R.S.M., Pres.; Dr. Anna Mae Mayer, Dir. Campus Min.; Ms. Amy Cady, Campus Min. Sisters of Mercy of the Americas.
Salve Regina University Religious Teachers 2; Lay Teachers 121; Sisters 6; Students 2,823.

[C] HIGH SCHOOLS, DIOCESAN

PAWTUCKET. *St. Raphael Academy*, 123 Walcott St., Pawtucket, 02860. Tel: 401-723-8100, Ext. 113; Fax: 401-723-8740; Web: www.saintrays.org; Email: drichard@saintrays.org. Rev. Carl B. Fisette, Chap.; Michelle Carrara, Admissions Dir.; Mr. Daniel J. Richard, Prin. Conducted by the Brothers of the Christian Schools.
Saint Raphael Academy Lay Teachers 30; Priests 1; Sisters 1; Students 518.

SOUTH KINGSTOWN. *The Prout School*, 4640 Tower Hill Rd., Wakefield, 02879. Tel: 401-789-9262; Fax: 401-782-2262; Email: sdeluca@theproutschool.org; Web: www.theproutschool.org. David Estes, Prin.; Rev. Joseph R. Upton, Chap.; Sharon DeLuca, Admissions Dir.
The Prout School Lay Teachers 35; Priests 1; Students 405.

WARWICK. *Bishop Hendricken High School* (1959) (Grades 8-12), 2615 Warwick Ave., Warwick, 02889. Tel: 401-739-3450; Fax: 401-732-8261; Email: hawks@hendricken.com; Web: www.hendricken.com. Rev. Robert L. Marciano, Pres.; Mark DeCiccio, Prin.; Rev. Christopher J. Murphy, Chap. Congregation of Christian Brothers.
Bishop Hendricken High School Boys 882; Lay Teachers 85; Priests 1; Sisters 1.

[D] HIGH SCHOOLS, PRIVATE

PROVIDENCE. *La Salle Academy*, (Grades 6-12), 612 Academy Ave., 02908. Tel: 401-351-7750; Fax: 401-444-1782; Email: dkavanagh@lasalle-academy.org; Email: pmeehan@lasalle-academy.org; Web: www.lasalle-academy.org. Bro. Thomas Gerrow, F.S.C., Pres.; Mr. Donald Kavanagh, Prin.; Rev. Thomas J. Woodhouse, Chap.; Thomas Glavin, Vice Pres. Institutional Advancement; Patrick Meehan, CFO. Conducted by the Brothers of the Christian Schools.
St. John Baptist de LaSalle Institute Brothers 2; Lay Teachers 115; Priests 1; Students 1,584; High School Students 1,391; Middle School Students 193.

EAST PROVIDENCE. *St. Mary Academy - Bay View*, St. Mary Academy-Bayview, 3070 Pawtucket Ave., Riverside, 02915. Tel: 401-434-0113, Ext. 156; Fax: 401-434-0335; Email: mberetta@bayviewacademy.org; Web: www.bayviewacademy.org. Sr. Marybeth Beretta, R.S.M., Pres.; Ms. Colleen Gribbin, Prin.; Laura Laurence, Librarian. Mercy Education System of the Americas (MESA) Religious Teachers 4; Girls 329; Lay Teachers 47; Sisters 4.

PORTSMOUTH. *Portsmouth Abbey School*, 285 Cory's Ln., Portsmouth, 02871. Tel: 401-683-2000; Fax: 401-682-7150; Email: mcd@portsmouthabbey.org; Email: hmassist@portsmouthabbey.org; Web: www.portsmouthabbey.org. Mr. Daniel McDonough, Headmaster
Order of St. Benedict in Portsmouth, Rhode Island dba Portsmouth Abbey School Brothers 2; Religious Teachers 4; Lay Teachers 44; Priests 8; Students 360.

WOONSOCKET. *Mount Saint Charles Academy* (1924) (Grades 6-12), 800 Logee St., Woonsocket, 02895-5599. Tel: 401-769-0310; Fax: 401-762-2327; Email: tenreiroa@mtstcharles.org; Web: mountsaintcharles.org. Mr. Alan Tenreiro, Pres.; Edwin F. Burke, Prin.; Mrs. Jessie Butash, Principal, Middle School. Brothers of the Sacred Heart.
Mount Saint Charles Academy, Inc. Brothers 3; Lay Teachers 53; Students 555.

[E] ELEMENTARY SCHOOLS, PRIVATE

PROVIDENCE. *San Miguel School* (1993) (Grades 5-8), 525 Branch Ave., 02904. Tel: 401-467-9777; Fax: 401-785-4976; Web: www.sanmiguelprov.org. Carol Soltys, Academic Dean; John Wolf, Exec.
San Miguel Education Center Lay Teachers 8; Students 64.

CUMBERLAND. *Mercymount Country Day School* (1948) (Grades PreK-8), 35 Wrentham Rd., Cumberland, 02864. Tel: 401-333-5919; Fax: 401-333-5150; Email: principal@mercymount.org; Web: www.mercymount.org. Dr. Gretchen Hawley, Ed.D., Prin.; Sr. Diane Russo, R.S.M., Librarian. Sisters of Mercy Northeast Community. Brothers 1; Lay Teachers 33; Sisters 4; Students 305.

EAST PROVIDENCE. *St. Mary Academy-Bay View*, (Grades PreK-8), St. Mary Academy-BayView, 3070 Pawtucket Ave., Riverside, 02915.
Tel: 401-434-0113, Ext. 156; Fax: 401-434-0335; Email: mcummings@bayviewacademy.org; Web: www.bayviewacademy.org. Sr. Marybeth Beretta, R.S.M., Pres.; Ms. Margaret Cummings, Prin. Mercy Education System of the Americas (MESA) Day Pupils. Religious Teachers 1; Lay Teachers 11; Sisters 1; Students 209.

PORTSMOUTH. *St. Philomena School* (1953) (Grades PreK-8), 324 Cory's Ln., Portsmouth, 02871.
Tel: 401-683-0268; Fax: 401-683-6554; Email: acoakley@saintphilomena.org; Email: bcordeiro@saintphilomena.org; Web: www.saintphilomena.org. Brian Cordeiro, Prin.; Jeffrey Moniz, Vice Prin. Sisters Faithful Companions of Jesus. Lay Teachers 33; Students 430.

[F] REGIONAL ELEMENTARY SCHOOLS

PROVIDENCE. *Bishop McVinney Regional School*, (Grades PreK-8), 155 Gordon Ave., 02905.
Tel: 401-781-2370; Fax: 401-785-2618; Email: lhebertbmv@gmail.com. Mr. Louis Hebert, Prin.
Catholic Association for Regional Education Lay Teachers 12; Students 205.
St. Thomas Regional School, (Grades PreK-8), 15 Edendale Ave., 02911. Tel: 401-351-0403; Fax: 401-351-0403 (call first); Email: mdimuccio@saintthomasregional.com. Mary DiMuccio, Prin. Lay Teachers 10; Students 112.

CRANSTON. *Immaculate Conception Catholic Regional School*, (Grades PreK-8), 235 Garden Hills Dr., Cranston, 02920. Tel: 401-942-7245; Fax: 401-943-5738; Email: aspaziante@iccatholicschool.org. Andrea Spaziante, Prin.; Kristine Mahone, Librarian. Lay Teachers 26; Students 313.

EAST GREENWICH. *Our Lady of Mercy Regional School* (1950) (Grades PreK-8), 55 Fourth Ave., East Greenwich, 02818. Tel: 401-884-1618; Fax: 401-885-3138; Email: principal@olmschool.org; Web: www.olmschool.org. Mr. Scott W. Fuller, Prin.; Camille Craybas, Librarian. Administrators 2; Lay Teachers 25; Sisters 2; Students 252.

GREENVILLE. *Overbrook Academy*, (Grades 6-9), (Boarding School) 60 Austin Ave., Greenville, 02828. Tel: 401-349-3444; Fax: 401-349-3375; Email: information@overbrookacademy.org; Web: www.overbrookacademy.com. Ms. Susan Mansfield, Prin.
Overbrook, Incorporated Religious Teachers 3; Lay Teachers 6; Sisters 7; Students 73.

MIDDLETOWN. *All Saints Academy* (1971) (Grades PreK-8), 915 W. Main Rd., Middletown, 02842.
Tel: 401-848-4300; Fax: 401-848-5587; Email: office@allsaintsacademy.org; Web: allsaintsacademy.org. Anita Brouse, Prin. Lay Teachers 13; Students 146.

PAWTUCKET. *Woodlawn Catholic Regional School* (1972) (Grades PreK-8), 61 Hope St., Pawtucket, 02860. Tel: 401-723-3759; Fax: 401-722-4090; Email: mrbennettwcrs@gmail.com; Web: www.woodlawncrs.com. Mary-Regina Bennett, Prin. Lay Teachers 12; Sisters 1; Students 121.

WAKEFIELD. *Monsignor Matthew F. Clarke Regional School* (1967) (Grades PreK-8), 5074 Tower Hill Rd., Wakefield, 02880. Tel: 401-789-0860; Fax: 401-789-3164; Email: alisi@monsignorclarkeschool.org; Web: www.monsignorclarkeschool.org. Dr. Arthur Lisi, Prin. Provides "Little Angels" daycare program, 18 to 36 months. Lay Teachers 23; Students 241.

[G] THE GREATER WOONSOCKET CATHOLIC REGIONAL SCHOOL SYSTEM

WOONSOCKET. *Greater Woonsocket Catholic Regional School System*, Office: 64 Hamlet St., Woonsocket, 02895. Tel: 401-762-1095; Fax: 401-767-5901; Email: phurteau@gwcrs.org; Web: www.gwcrs.org. Mrs. Paula Hurteau, Admin.
Greater Woonsocket Catholic Regional School System.

Member Schools

WOONSOCKET.
Good Shepherd Catholic Regional School, (Grades 3-8), 1210 Mendon Rd., Woonsocket, 02895.
Tel: 401-767-5906; Fax: 401-767-5905; Email: goodshepherdprincipal@gwcrs.org; Web: www.gwcrs.org. Mrs. Jennifer DeOliveira, Prin. Lay Teachers 10; Students 130.
Monsignor Gadoury Catholic Regional School, (Grades PreK-2), Three year old program-Grade 2 1371 Park Ave., Woonsocket, 02895.
Tel: 401-767-5902; Fax: 401-767-5923; Email: mgprincipal@cox.net; Web: www.gwcrs.org. Shawn A. Capron, Prin. Lay Teachers 7; Sisters 1; Students 100.

[H] CHILD CARING FACILITIES

PROVIDENCE. *Group Home for Adolescent Boys* (Whitmarsh House) 1055 N. Main St., 02904.
Tel: 401-351-7230; Fax: 401-421-0198; Email: whitmarsh@whitmarshhouse.org. Bro. John McHale, O.L.P., Dir. Students 40; Staff 50.

NARRAGANSETT. *Ocean Tides*, 635 Ocean Rd., Narragansett, 02882-1314. Tel: 401-789-1016; Fax: 401-788-0924; Email: martino@oceantides.org; Web: www.oceantides.org. Bro. James Martino, F.S.C., Pres.; Charlie Coutro, Prin.

Ocean Tides, Inc. Brothers 3; (Full-time, paid) 36; Lay Teachers 20; Students 107.

[I] HOMES FOR AGED

CUMBERLAND. *Mount St. Rita Health Centre* (1971) 15 Sumner Brown Rd., Cumberland, 02864.
Tel: 401-333-6352; Fax: 401-333-1012; Email: mail@mountstrita.org; Web: www.mountstrita.org. William P. Fleming, Admin. Sponsored by Covenant Health, Inc.Licensed Nursing Home.
Mount St. Rita Health Centre Inc. Residents 98; Total Staff 115.

NEWPORT. *St. Clare Home* (1909) 309 Spring St., Newport, 02840. Tel: 401-849-3204;
Fax: 401-849-5780; Email: mbdaigneault@stclarenewport.org; Web: stclarenewport.org. Mary Beth Daigneault, Admin.; Rev. Raymond C. Theroux, Chap., (Retired). Nursing Facility.
The Saint Clare Home Residents 73; Tot Asst. Annually 100; Total Staff 100; Lay Nurses 20; Lay Employees 80. In Res. Revs. Thomas D. O'Neill, Chap., (Retired); Richard A. Walsh, (Retired).

NORTH KINGSTOWN. *Scalabrini Villa* (1957) 860 N. Quidnessett Rd., North Kingstown, 02852.
Tel: 401-884-1802; Fax: 401-884-4727; Email: admin@scalabrinivilla.com; Web: www.scalabrinivilla.com. Rev. Peter Polo, C.S., Chap.; Sr. Nemesia Licayu, F.A.S., Supr. Full Skilled Nursing Facility.
Scalabrini Villa Inc. Residents 120; Franciscan Apostolic Sisters 3; Total Staff 138; Scalabrinian Missionaries 1; Total Assisted 43,800.

NORTH PROVIDENCE. *Our Lady, Queen of Peace, Assisted Living Community*, 399 Fruit Hill Ave., North Providence, 02911. Tel: 401-353-5800;
Fax: 401-354-8296; Email: lapfmm@aol.com. Sr. Lois Ann Pereira, F.M.M., Supr.; Ms. Stephanie Dyer, Admin.
Franciscan Missionaries of Mary Sisters 9.

NORTH SMITHFIELD. *Saint Antoine Residence* (1913) 10 Rhodes Ave., North Smithfield, 02896.
Tel: 401-767-3500; Fax: 401-769-5249; Email: jwoznicki@stantoine.net; Web: www.stantoine.net. Rev. Roger A. Houle, Chap.
Saint Antoine Residence Residents 260; Total Staff 415.
The Villa at Saint Antoine (2000) 400 Mendon Rd., North Smithfield, 02896-6999. Tel: 401-767-2574;
Fax: 401-767-2581; Email: tsummiel@stantoine.net; Web: www.stantoine.net. Tammy Summiel, Admin.
The Frassati Residence Total Staff 62; Total Assisted 90.
The Frassati Residence dba The Villa at Saint Antoine, 400 Mendon Rd., North Smithfield, 02896. Tel: 401-767-2574; Fax: 401-767-2581; Email: tsummiel@stantoine.net. Tammy Summiel, Admin.

PAWTUCKET. *Jeanne Jugan Apartments*, 310 Sayles Ave., Pawtucket, 02860. Tel: 401-723-4314;
Fax: 401-723-4316; Email: pwmothersuperior@littlesistersofthepoor.org. Sr. Mercy Stella Andrades, L.S.P., Supr. Residents 30; Total Staff 1; Apartments for Elderly 27.
Jeanne Jugan Residence, 964 Main St., Pawtucket, 02860. Tel: 401-723-4314; Fax: 401-723-4316; Email: pwmothersuperior@littlesistersofthepoor.org. Sr. Mercy Stella Andrades, L.S.P., Supr.
Jeanne Jugan Residence of the Little Sisters of the Poor Residents 70; Little Sisters of the Poor 11; Total Staff 84; Total Assisted 70. In Res. Most Rev. Ernest B. Boland, O.P., (Retired), (Retired); Rev. Robert F. Caul, (Retired), (Retired); Most Rev. Francis Roque, (Retired), (Retired); Rev. John W. Gray, (Retired).

[J] CAMPS AND COMMUNITY CENTERS

PROVIDENCE. *St. Martin de Porres Multi-Purpose Center*, 160 Cranston St., 02907. Tel: 401-274-6783; Fax: 401-274-5930; Email: priceesther4@gmail.com. Ms. Esther E. Price, Dir.
St. Martin de Porres Center Total Staff 13; Total Under Care 2,100; Total Assisted 2,500.
The McAuley Corporation dba McAuley Ministries, 622 Elmwood Ave., P.O. Box 73195, 02907.
Tel: 401-941-9013; Fax: 401-941-6862; Email: dwolfe@mcauleyri.org; Web: www.mcauleyri.org. Donald P. Wolfe, Exec. Dir. Sisters of Mercy of the Americas Northeast Community.
The McAuley Corporation, DBA McAuley Ministries.
McAuley Ministries - McAuley House (1975) 622 Elmwood Ave., P.O. Box 27009, 02907-3352.
Tel: 401-941-9013; Fax: 401-941-6862; Email: dwolfe@mcauleyri.org; Web: www.mcauleyri.org. Rev. Mary Margaret Earl, Admin. Meal site assisting 10,000 homeless annually. Total Staff 5.
McAuley Ministries - McAuley Village (1990) 325 Niagara St., 02907. Tel: 401-467-3630;
Fax: 401-467-2760; Email: dwolfe@mcauleyri.org; Web: www.mcauleyri.org. Rev. Michele L. Matott, Admin. Transitional Housing and Child Care assisting 23 families, 40 children in Daycare. Students 40; Total Staff 20.
McAuley Ministries - The Warde-robe (1997) 1286 Broad St., Central Falls, 02863. Tel: 401-729-0405; Email: dwolfe@mcauleyri.org; Web: www.mcauleyri.org. Donna Benetti, Admin. Clothing and housewares for the working poor. Tot Asst. Annually 10,000; Total Staff 4.

CRANSTON. *Rejoice in Hope Youth Center*, 804 Dyer Ave., Cranston, 02920. Tel: 401-942-6571; Email: pkane@dioceseofprovidence.org; Web: catholicyouthri.com/rejoice-in-hope-youth-center. Pat Kane, Dir.

GLOCESTER. *Mother of Hope Camp*, Mailing Address: 1 Cathedral Sq., 02903. Tel: 401-278-4626; Email: mlosardo@dioceseofprovidence.org; Web: www.motherofhopecamp.com. 1589 Putnam Pike, Chepachet, 02814. Tel: 401-568-3580. Michelle Losardo, Dir.
Mother of Hope Camp.

WARWICK. *OLP Center, Inc.*, 836 Warwick Neck Ave., Warwick, 02889. Tel: 401-739-6850;
Fax: 401-738-8058; Email: info@aldrichmansion.com; Web: aldrichmansion.com. Mr. John Gazerro, Dir.
OLP Center, Inc. Staff 10.

WOONSOCKET. *Fr. Marot CYO Center* (1970) 53 Federal St., P.O. Box 518, Woonsocket, 02895-0518.
Tel: 401-762-3252; Fax: 401-762-3255; Email: FrMarotCYO@gmail.com; Web: catholicyouthri.com/fr-marot-cyo-center. Leo Fontaine, Dir.
CYO of Northern Rhode Island, Inc.

[K] PERSONAL PRELATURES

PROVIDENCE. *Prelature of the Holy Cross and Opus Dei*, Mathewson House, 224 Bowen St., 02906.
Tel: 401-272-7834; Fax: 401-272-7854; Email: info@opusdei.org; Web: www.opusdei.org. Rev. George Crafts.

[L] MONASTERIES AND RESIDENCES OF PRIESTS AND BROTHERS

PROVIDENCE. *Brothers of Our Lady of Providence* (1959) 1055 N. Main St., 02904. Tel: 401-351-7230;
Fax: 401-421-0198; Email: Whitmarsh@whitmarshcorp.org. Bro. John McHale, O.L.P., Supr. Brothers 1.
St. John Vianney Residence (1978) 493 Mt. Pleasant Ave., 02908. Tel: 401-331-9870; Fax: 401-331-5092; Email: dgaffney@dioceseofprovidence.org. Rev. David F. Gaffney, M.Div., Dir. Residence for Senior Priests. Priests 15.
Residents: Revs. Robert M. Beirne, (Retired); Jose Q. dos Reis; Anthony D. Iwuc, (Retired); Czeslaw L. Kachel, (Retired); Raymond P. Luft, (Retired); John J. McElroy, (Retired); Edward J. McGovern, (Retired); John J. Rainone, (Retired); Nicholas P. Smith, (Retired); Daniel M. Trainor, (Retired); James J. Verdelotti, (Retired); Farrell E. McLaughlin, (Retired); Richard C. Maynard, (Retired); John D. Dreher, (Retired).
St. Pius V Priory, 55 Elmhurst Ave., 02908.
Tel: 401-751-4871; Fax: 401-273-1089; Email: info@spvchurch.org; Web: https://spvchurch.org/. Rev. Patrick Mary Briscoe, O.P.; Very Rev. John P. Burchill, O.P.; Revs. Albert Duggan, O.P.; Augustine Judd, O.P.
Dominican Fathers Priests 4.
St. Thomas Aquinas Priory at Providence College, 1 Cunningham Sq., 02918. Tel: 401-865-2101 (office); Fax: 401-865-2959; Email: dmaioran@providence.edu. Rev. Vincent Bagan, O.P.; Most Rev. Ernest B. Boland, O.P., (Retired); Revs. Justin Brophy, O.P.; Bonaventure Chapman, O.P.; Raymond Daley, O.P.; Thomas Davenport, O.P.; Thomas J. Ertle, O.P.; Humbert Kilanowski, O,P,; Richard A. McAlister, O.P.; Thomas P. McCreesh, O.P., Prior; Isaac Morales, O.P.; Damian Myett, O.P.; Alan Piper, O.P.; Philip Neri Reese, O.P.; Augustine Reisenauer, O.P.; Dominic M. Verner, O.P. Dominican Friars.
Priory of St. Thomas Aquinas
Assigned & Residing in the Priory: Most Rev. Ernest B. Boland, O.P., Bishop Emeritus of Multan, (Retired); Revs. Edward T. Myers, O.P., Prior; John E. Allard, O.P.; J. Iriarte Andujar, O.P.; Nicanor P.G. Austriaco, O.P.; Albino F. Barrera, O.P.; Peter Batts, O.P.; Ronald Leo Checkai, O.P.; Paul M. Conner, O.P.; G. Adrian Dabash, O.P.; Thomas J. Ertle, O.P.; William David Folsey, O.P.; Joseph J. Guido, O.P.; G. Nicholas Ingham, O.P.; Terence Keegan, O.P.; Bernard F. Langton, O.P.; Ambrose Little, O.P.; Richard A. McAlister, O.P.; Thomas P. McCreesh, O.P.; J. Stuart McPhail, O.P.; Robert D. Myett, O.P.; Mark D. Nowel, O.P.; Michael D. O'Connor, O.P., (Resides in Rome); David T. Orique, O.P.; John S. Peterson, O.P.; R. Gabriel Pivarnik, O.P.; Matthew D. Powell, O.P.; Philip Neri Reese, O.P.; Kevin D. Robb, O.P.; Paul E. Seaver, O.P.; Brian J. Shanley, O.P.; Kenneth Sicard, O.P.; Joseph Torchia, O.P.; John C. Vidmar, O.P.; Walter Urban Voll, O.P.; Dominic M. Verner, O.P.; Peter Martyr Joseph Yungwirth, O.P.

BRISTOL. *St. Columban's Retirement House*, 65 Ferry Rd., Box 65, Bristol, 02809. Tel: 401-253-6909;
Fax: 401-253-7099; Email: jburger@columban.org. Revs. William Brunner, S.S.C.; John Buckley, S.S.C.; John E. Burger, S.S.C., Vicar/Bursar; Salvatore S. Caputo, S.S.C., (Retired); Francis P. Carroll, S.S.C., Supr., (Retired); Michael J. Donnelly, S.S.C., (Retired); James Dwyer, S.S.C., (Retired); Victor Gaboury, S.S.C., (Retired); Francis Grady, S.S.C., (Retired); Charles Lintz, S.S.C., Supr.; John Marley, S.S.C., (Retired); Daniel McGinn, S.S.C., (Retired); Joseph McSweeney, S.S.C., (Retired); John Moran, S.S.C., (Retired); Paul O'Malley, S.S.C., (Retired); Francis D. O'Mara, S.S.C.; Robert O'Rourke, S.S.C., (Retired); Richard L. Pankratz, S.S.C., (Retired); Francis J. Royer, S.S.C., (Retired); Alban Sueper, S.S.C., (Retired); William F. Sullivan, S.S.C., (Retired); William F. Sweeney, S.S.C.; Thomas Vaughan, S.S.C.; John Q. Wanaurny, S.S.C., (Retired); Gerard P. Wilmsen, S.S.C., (Retired); Vincent Youngkamp, S.S.C., (Retired)
St. Columban's Foreign Mission Society Priests 26.

BURRILLVILLE. *Brothers of the Sacred Heart Residence*, 685 Steere Farm Rd., Pascoag, 02859-4601.
Tel: 401-568-8686; Fax: 401-568-1450; Email: brothercarlsc@gmail.com; Web: brothersofthesacredheart.org. Bros. Carl Bouchereau, S.C., Dir.; Robert T. Gagne, S.C., Accounts Mgr.
The Brothers of the Sacred Heart of New England, Inc. Brothers 25.

NARRAGANSETT. *Christian Brothers' Center*, 635 Ocean Rd., Narragansett, 02882. Tel: 401-789-0244;
Fax: 401-783-5303; Email: cheryl@dlcb.org; Web: www.dlcb.org. Bro. Edmond Precourt, F.S.C., Exec. Dir.; Laura Wallace, Health Care Coord. Brothers of the Christian Schools.
Brothers of the Christian Schools, Long Island-New England Province Brothers 22.

PORTSMOUTH. *Order of St. Benedict in Portsmouth, Rhode Island* dba Portsmouth Abbey School, 285 Corys Ln., Portsmouth, 02871. Tel: (401) 683-2000; Email: abbot@portsmouthabbey.org; Web: www.portsmouthabbey.org. Very Rev. Gregory Mohrman, O.S.B., Prior.
Abbey of St. Gregory the Great (1918) 285 Cory's Lane, Portsmouth, 02871. Tel: 401-683-2000;
Fax: 401-643-1388; Email: abbott@portsmouthabbey.org; Web: www.portsmouthabbey.org. Bro. Joseph Byron, O.S.B., Prior; Rev. Michael Brunner, O.S.B., Admin.; Bro. Francis Crowley, O.S.B.; Revs. Christopher Davis, O.S.B.; Gregory Havill, O.S.B.; Rt. Rev. Caedmon Holmes, O.S.B., (Retired); Revs. Paschal Scotti, O.S.B.; Geoffrey Chase, O.S.B.; Rt. Rev. Matthew Stark, O.S.B., (Retired); Rev. Julian Stead, O.S.B. Benedictines of the English Congregation.
Order of St. Benedict in Portsmouth, Rhode Island Brothers 2; Priests 6; Abbots 2.

WOONSOCKET. *Brothers of the Sacred Heart* (1821) 800 Logee St., Woonsocket, 02895. Tel: 401-769-0313;
Fax: 401-769-0065; Email: unitedstatesprovince@gmail.com. Bro. Ronald Champagne, Dir. Brothers 4.
Brothers of the Sacred Heart, 159 Earle St., Woonsocket, 02895. Tel: 401-766-9677; Email: bxwerneth@catholichigh.org; Web: www.Brothersofthesacredheart.org. Bros. Xavier Werneth, S.C., Dir.; Donald Sukanek, S.C., Dir. Novices. Brothers 7.

[M] CONVENTS AND RESIDENCES FOR SISTERS

BARRINGTON. *Monastery of Discalced Carmelites* (1930) 25 Watson Ave., Barrington, 02806-4009.
Tel: 401-245-3421; Fax: 401-245-6872; Email: sllbarr@juno.com; Web: home.att.net/~barringtoncarmel. Sr. Susan L. Lumb, Prioress
Monastery of Discalced Carmelites at Nayatt, Barrington, RI Postulants 1; Professed Sisters 14.

BRISTOL. *Mt. St. Joseph Spiritual Life Center and Provincialate*, 13 Monkeywrench Ln., Bristol, 02809-2916. Tel: 401-253-5434; Email: nuninbristol@yahoo.com; Web: Sisters of St. Dorothy.org. Sisters Sharon A. McCarthy, S.S.D., Provincial Coord.; Dorothy Schwarz, S.S.D., Local Coord. Sisters of St. Dorothy. Sisters 5.

CUMBERLAND. *Sisters of Mercy of the Americas Northeast Community, Inc.* (1851) 15 Highland View Rd., Cumberland, 02864-1124.
Tel: 401-333-6333; Fax: 401-333-6450; Email: info@mercyne.org. Sr. Maureen Mitchell, R.S.M., Pres.; Jill Gemma, COO/CFO; Sisters Peg Sullivan, R.S.M., Vice Pres.; Ruth Kelly, R.S.M., Leadership Team; Patricia Moriarty, R.S.M., Leadership Team; Daniel Justynski, Dir. Northeast Real Estate Portfolio; Beth Watson, Dir. of Devel.; Lisa Driscoll, Dir. of Human Resources; Jennifer Giuf-

frida, Dir. of Long Term Care & Retirement Strategy; Brigitte Buxton, Dir.; Mary Lauzon, Dir.
Sisters of Mercy of the Americas Northeast Community, Inc. Sisters 493; Associates 425. *Sisters of Mercy of the Americas Northeast Community, Inc., Administrative Offices*, 15 Highland View Rd., Cumberland, 02864-1124. Tel: 401-333-6333; Fax: 401-333-6450; Email: info@mercyne.org. Sr. Maureen Mitchell, R.S.M., Pres. *Mercycrest Convent*, 125 Wrentham Rd., Cumberland, 02864. Tel: (401) 333-6333; Email: info@mercyne.org. 15 Highland Rd., Cumberland, 02864. Sr. Maureen Mitchell, R.S.M., Pres. *Mercymount Convent*, 75 Wrentham Rd., Cumberland, 02864. Tel: 401-333-6333; Email: info@mercyne.org; Web: sistersofmercy.org/northeast. 15 Highland View Rd., Cumberland, 02864. Sr. Maureen Mitchell, R.S.M., Pres. Sisters of Mercy 1.

EAST GREENWICH. *Franciscan Apostolic Sisters* (1953) 66 Fifth Ave., East Greenwich, 02818. Tel: 401-336-3145; Email: srnemfas@yahoo.com; Email: srloufas@yahoo.com; Web: www.geocities.com/franapsisters. Sisters Lourdes DeLeon, F.A.S., Local Animator/Regl. Treas./Regl. Sec.; Emma Salvador, F.A.S., Member. Sisters 5. *Franciscan Apostolic Sisters Regional House*, 860 N. Quidnessett Rd., North Kingstown, 02852. Tel: 401-884-4594; Email: srnemfas@yahoo.com; Web: www.geocities.com/franapsisters. Sisters Nemesia Licayu, F.A.S., Regl. Mgr./Local Animator; Jane Molitas, F.A.S.; Marizza Manicap, F.A.S. Sisters 3.

MIDDLETOWN. *Cluny Provincial House* (1807) 7 Restmere Ter., Middletown, 02842. Tel: 401-846-4757 (Prov.); Tel: 401-846-4826 (Office); Fax: 401-846-4826 (Office); Email: clunyprosecretary@hotmail.com. Sr. Luke Parker, S.J.C., Prov. St. Joseph of Cluny Sisters' School. Sisters 2,838; Sisters in Diocese 7.
Provincial House, Tel: 401-846-4826; Fax: 401-846-4826. Sr. Luke Parker, S.J.C., Prov. Supr. *St. Joseph of Cluny Convent*, Tel: 401-847-3637; Fax: 401-846-4826.

NEWPORT. *St. Clare Convent, Cutting Memorial*, 301 Spring St., Newport, 02840. Tel: 401-846-1025. *The Saint Clare Home* Daughters of the Holy Spirit 2.
Javouhey House (2002) 78 Carroll Ave., Newport, 02840. Tel: 401-849-5124; Email: ellenliston@yahoo.com. Sr. Anne-Marie Liston, S.J.C., Local Coord. Sisters of St. Joseph of Cluny 3.

NORTH KINGSTOWN. *Sisters of the Cross and Passion*, 1 Wright Ln., North Kingstown, 02852. Tel: 401-667-4813; Email: passcom12@gmail.com; Web: www.passionistsisters.org. Sr. Bernadette Hughes, C.P., Province Leader. Provincial Office of the Sisters of the Cross and Passion.
Sisters of the Holy Cross and Passion Sisters 3.

NORTH PROVIDENCE. *Daughters of Mary Mother of Mercy*, 2 Pope St., North Providence, 02904. Tel: 401-353-8654; Fax: 401-353-5126; Email: ponyeje@yahoo.com. Sr. Patricia Onyeje, D.M.M.M., Supr. Sisters 2.
Franciscan Missionaries of Mary (1903) 399 Fruit Hill Ave., North Providence, 02911. Tel: 401-353-5800; Fax: 401-353-2674; Email: lapfmm@aol.com; Web: www.fmmusa.org. Sr. Lois Ann Pereira, F.M.M., Supr.
Franciscan Missionaries of Mary Sisters 37.
Holy Family Community, 399 Fruit Hill Ave., North Providence, 02911. Tel: 401-353-5800; Fax: 401-353-2674; Email: lapfmm@aol.com. Sr. Mildred Morrissey, R.S.M., Supr. Sisters 11.
Trinity Community, Assisted Living Community, 399 Fruit Hill Ave., North Providence, 02911. Tel: 401-353-5800; Email: lapfmm@aol.com. Sr. Maria C. Zunzarren, F.M.M., Supr. Sisters 14.
Our Lady of the Lourdes Convent, 385 Fruit Hill Ave., North Providence, 02911. Tel: 401-353-6381; Email: lapfmm@aol.com. Sr. Yvette Hubert, F.M.M. Sisters 4.
De Chappotin Community, 399 Fruit Hill Ave., North Providence, 02911. Tel: 401-353-9412; Fax: 401-353-2674; Email: lapfmm@aol.com. Sr. Barbara Dopierala, R.S.M., Supr. Sisters 3.

NORTH SMITHFIELD. *Franciscan Missionaries of Mary*, Ein Karim Community, 318 Mendon Rd., North Smithfield, 02896. Tel: 401-766-8242; Fax: 401-766-6492; Email: karimfmm@aol.com. Sr. Emilie Duchaney, F.M.M. Sisters 2.

SOUTH KINGSTOWN. *Congregation of the Sisters of Divine Providence Generalate* (1851) 12 Christopher St., Wakefield, 02878. Sr. Maria Fest, C.D.P., Supr.
Mother of Providence Convent, 12 Christopher St., Wakefield, 02879. Tel: 401-782-1785; Fax: 401-782-6967. Sr. Maria Fest, C.D.P., Congregational Leader. Sisters 2.

WOONSOCKET. *Emmanuel House*, 67 Highland St., Woonsocket, 02895. Tel: 401-766-0525; Email: pmtreasurer209@gmail.com. Sr. Paulette Lefebvre, Supr. Sisters 1.

[N] RETREAT HOUSES

NORTH PROVIDENCE. *Bethany Renewal Center*, 397 Fruit Hill Ave., North Providence, 02911. Tel: 401-353-5860; Email: bethanyfmm@aol.com; Web: www.fmmusa.org. Sr. Yvette Hubert, F.M.M. Conducted by the Franciscan Missionaries of Mary.

[O] NEWMAN CENTERS

PROVIDENCE. *Brown University* aka Brown-RISD Catholic Community, Office of Chaplains & Religious Life, 69 Brown St., Ste. 410, Box 1931, 02912. Tel: 401-863-2344; Fax: 401-863-9359; Email: chaplain@brownrisdcatholic.org; Web: www.brownisdcatholic.org. Rev. Albert Duggan, O.P., Catholic Chap. Priests 1; Total Staff 2.
Johnson & Wales University The Newman Club Catholic Campus Ministry, CBCSI Bldg., 8 Abbott Park Pl., 02903. Tel: (401) 598-1830; Email: pvd@admissions.jwu.edu. Jessica Grady, Assoc. Dir. for Student Engagement.
Rhode Island College, Catholic Campus Ministry, Donovan Lower Level, 600 Mt. Pleasant Ave., 02908. Tel: 401-456-8346; Fax: 401-456-2849 (Call first); Email: RICInterfaithCenter@ric.edu; Web: http://www.ric.edu/interfaithcenter. Frank Sanchez, Pres. Interfaith Center.

BRISTOL. *Roger Williams University*, 1 Old Ferry Rd., Bristol, 02809. Tel: 401-254-3433; Email: nsoukup@rwu.edu. Donald Farrish, Pres.

SMITHFIELD. *Bryant University*, 1150 Douglas Pk., Box 33, Smithfield, 02917-1284. Tel: 401-232-6045; Fax: 401-232-6362; Email: rburgess2@bryant.edu.

SOUTH KINGSTOWN. *University of Rhode Island Catholic Center*, 90 Chapel Way, Kingston, 02881. Tel: 401-874-2324; Fax: 401-874-2095; Email: chaplain@rhodycatholic.com; Web: www.rhodycatholic.com. Rev. Joseph R. Upton, Chap.

[P] SECULAR INSTITUTES

GREENVILLE. *Regnum Christi*, 60 Austin Ave., Greenville, 02828. Tel: 401-349-3444; Fax: 401-349-3375; Email: fformolo@legionaries.org; Web: www.regnumchristi.org. Rev. Frank Formolo, Authorized Rep.

[Q] MISCELLANEOUS LISTINGS

PROVIDENCE. **The Haitian Project, Inc.*, 650 Ten Rod Rd., North Kingstown, 02852. Tel: 401-351-3624; Email: operations@haitianproject.org; Web: www.haitianproject.org. P.O. Box 6891, 02940. Deacon Patrick Moynihan, Pres.
**The Interfaith Community Dire Emergency Fund*, One Cathedral Sq., 02903. Tel: (401) 421-7833, Ext. 207; Fax: (401) 453-6135; Email: jjahnz@dioceseofprovidence.org. Mr. James Jahnz, Coord., Tel: 401-421-7833, Ext. 207; Fax: 401-453-6135.
**Mandamiento Nuevo Corporation*, One Cathedral Sq., 02903. Tel: 401-421-7833, Ext. 104; Fax: 401-274-5450; Email: jbarry@dioceseofprovidence.org. Mr. John J. Barry III, Sec.
Miscellaneous Listings for the Diocese of Providence Mailing address for all Providence listings Chancery Office: 1 Cathedral Sq., 02903. Tel: 401-278-4663; Fax: 401-278-4623; Email: treilly@dioceseofprovidence.org; Web: www.dioceseofprovidence.org. Rev. Timothy D. Reilly, S.T.B., J.C.L., Chancellor. For further information contact:
Catholic Charity Fund.
Catholic Foundation of Rhode Island.
Catholic Information Center of Newport.
Catholic Inner City Apostolate, Inc.
Catholic Investment Trust, Inc.
Catholic Social Services of RI, Email: treilly@dioceseofprovidence.org. Rev. Timothy D. Reilly, S.T.B., J.C.L., Contact Person.
Catholic Teachers' College of Providence.
Christ the Redeemer Academy.
Cluny School, (Grades PreK-8).
Corpus Christi Carmel.
The Church of the Immaculate Conception, North Providence.
De LaSalle Academy Corporation.
Deliverance Ministry.
DiMed Corp.
Diocesan Administration Corporation, Tel: 401-278-4616; Fax: 401-751-6808.
Diocesan Catholic Telecommunications Network of Rhode Island.
Diocesan Plant Fund.
Diocesan School Financial Services, Tel: 401-278-4500; Email: treilly@dioceseofprovidence.org. Rev. Timothy D. Reilly, S.T.B., J.C.L., Contact Person.
Diocesan Service Corporation, Tel: 401-278-4616; Fax: 401-751-6808.
F.A.C.E. of Rhode Island (Financial Aid for Children's Education of Rhode Island).
Father Barry CYO Center.
Father Holland Catholic Regional Elementary School.
Grateful for God's Providence, Inc.
Holy Name Society.
House of the Good Shepherd of Providence.
Homes for Hope Foundation.
Inter-Parish Loan Fund, Inc.
LaSalle Academy.
Little Sisters of the Assumption of Woonsocket.
Marian Association of Northern Rhode Island.
The Mercy Home and School.
Mother of Hope Novitiate.
Mount St. Francois of Woonsocket, RI.
Nazareth Home.
New England Conference of Diocesan Directors of Religious Education.
Our Lady of Fatima High School.
Our Lady of Peace Retreat House.
Our Lady of Providence Preparatory Seminary.
Our Lady, Queen of the Clergy.
Parish Investment Group.
Pius X Salvage Bureau.
Retreat House of the Immaculate Heart of Mary.
The Rhode Island Catholic Orphan Asylum (St. Aloysius Home).
Rhode Island Home for Working Boys.
Roman Catholic Bishop of Providence (A Corporation Sole).
St. Benedict's Hearth Corporation, East Providence.
St. Casimir.
Saint Casimir's Church of Warren.
St. Dominic Savio Youth Center.
St. Elizabeth Ann Seton Academy.
Saint Francis House.
Saint Hedwig's Church Corporation, Providence.
The Church of Saint Jean Baptiste of Warren, Rhode Island.
ST. JOHN'S CHURCH OF PROVIDENCE.
Saint Margaret's Home.
Saint Maria Society.
St. Martin de Porres Center.
St. Mary Academy of the Visitation.
Saint Raphael's Industrial Home and School.
St. Vincent de Paul Home, Woonsocket.
Saint Vincent de Paul Infant Asylum.
Saint William Church Corporation, Norwood.
Shepherds of Hope, Inc. Rev. Timothy D. Reilly, S.T.B., J.C.L., Contact Person.
Stella Maris Home for Convalescents.
Vision of Hope, Inc.

BURRILLVILLE. *Father Andre Coindre Charitable Trust*, 685 Steere Farm Rd., Pascoag, 02859-4601. Tel: 401-568-3361, Ext. 3202; Fax: 401-568-1450; Email: bileblancsc@gmail.com. Bro. Ivy LeBlanc, S.C., Treas.

COVENTRY. *Cursillo Movement*, 461 Shady Valley Rd., Coventry, 02816. Tel: 401-392-1252. Edward Overton, Lay Coord.

CUMBERLAND. *Northeast FIDES, Inc.*, 15 Highland View Rd., Cumberland, 02864-1124. Tel: 401-333-6333; Fax: 401-333-6450; Email: info@meryne.org. Sr. Patricia Moriarty, R.S.M., Pres.
Northeast FIDES, Inc.

GREENVILLE. *Overbrook, Incorporated*, 60 Austin Ave., Greenville, 02828. Tel: 770-828-4950; Email: Javier.valenzuela@oakinternational.org. Rev. Frank Formolo, Sec.

MAPLEVILLE. *Society of St. Vincent de Paul of Providence*, 525 Maureen Cir., Mapleville, 02839. Tel: 401-568-4709; Fax: 401-568-4709; Email: jmar10@cox.net; Web: www.svdpri.org. James Martufi, Pres., Diocesan Council of Providence.

MIDDLETOWN. *Charismatic Renewal*, 909 West Main Rd., Middletown, 02842-6351. Tel: 401-847-6153; Email: stlucyoffice@gmail.com. Rev. John W. O'Brien.

NARRAGANSETT. *Ocean Tides Christian Brothers Charitable Trust* (2016) 635 Ocean Rd., Narragansett, 02882. Tel: (401) 789-1016; Email: administrator@oceantides.org. Bro. James Martino, F.S.C., Pres.

NORTH PROVIDENCE. *Franciscan Missionaries of Mary* (1903) 399 Fruit Hill Ave., North Providence, 02911. Tel: 401-636-4470; Email: mmottefmm@gmail.com; Web: www.fmmusa.org. Sr. Mary Motte, R.S.M., Contact Person
Franciscan Missionaries of Mary
Mission Resource Center (1988) Tel: 401-353-4470; Email: mmottefmm@gmail.com. Sr. Mary Motte, R.S.M., Dir.

NORTH SMITHFIELD. *Hombre Nuevo (RI), Inc.* (1993) 275 Mechanic St., North Smithfield, 02896-7718. Tel: 770-828-4950; Email: fformolo@legionaries.org. Rev. Frank Formolo, Sec.
Ocean Pastoral Center, Inc., 275 Mechanic St., North Smithfield, 02896-7718. Tel: 770-828-4950; Email: fformolo@legionaries.org. Rev. Frank Formolo, Sec.

PAWTUCKET. *Bishop Francis P. Keough Regional High School* (1971) (Closed in 2015) 165 Power Rd., Pawtucket, 02860. Tel: 401-726-0335; Email: treilly@dioceseofprovidence.org. Rev. Timothy D. Reilly, S.T.B., J.C.L., Contact Person.

SMITHFIELD. *Conference of Regional Treasurers*, P.O. Box 17372, Smithfield, 02917. Tel: 401-349-4960; Fax: 401-349-4970; Email: vgladu@bmtconsults.com. Virginia Gladu, Contact Person.

LC Pastoral Services, Inc., 60 Austin Ave., Greenville, 02828. Tel: 401-949-3444; Fax: 401-949-3375; Email: fformolo@legionaries.org. Rev. Frank Formolo, Sec.

Mater Ecclesiae, Inc. (1993) 60 Austin Ave., Greenville, 02828. Tel: 401-949-3444; Fax: 401-949-3375; Email: sbaldwin@regnumchristi.net; Web: www.regnumchristi.org. Sonia Baldwin, Sec.

WARWICK. **Poverello Corporation*, 222 Jefferson Blvd., Ste. 200, Warwick, 02888. Tel: (646) 473-0265; Email: hnp@hnp.org. Mailing Address: c/o Holy Name Provincial Office, 129 W 31st St., 2nd Fl., New York, NY 10001-3403. Rev. Kevin Mullen, Pres.

WEST WARWICK. *Tides Family Services*, 215 Washington St., West Warwick, 02893. Tel: 401-822-1360; Fax: 401-823-4694; Email: mail@tidesfs.org; Web: www.tidesfs.org. Bro. Michael Reis, F.S.C., CEO. Total Staff 125; Total Assisted 6,000.

Branch Offices:

Youth Transition Center, 790 Broad St., 02907. Tel: 401-467-8888; Fax: 401-467-8899; Email: mail@tidesfs.org. Bro. Michael Reis, F.S.C., CEO.

Youth Transition Center, 242 Dexter St., Pawtucket, 02860. Tel: 401-724-8100; Fax: 401-724-8899; Email: mail@tidesfs.org. Bro. Michael Reis, F.S.C., CEO.

Preserving Families Network, 242 Dexter St., Pawtucket, 02860. Tel: 401-724-8201; Fax: 401-724-8899; Email: mail@tidesfs.org. Bro. Michael Reis, F.S.C., CEO.

Outreach and Tracking Program, 242 Dexter St., Pawtucket, 02860. Tel: 401-724-8380; Fax: 401-724-8899; Email: mail@tidesfs.org. Bro. Michael Reis, F.S.C., CEO.

Woonsocket Outreach Project, 55 Main St., Ste. 1, Woonsocket, 02895. Tel: 401-766-9320; Fax: 401-766-9324; Email: mail@tidesfs.org. Bro. Michael Reis, F.S.C., CEO.

Learning Centers:

242 Dexter St., Pawtucket, 02860. Tel: 401-724-8060 ; Fax: 401-724-8899.

790 Broad St., 02907. Tel: 401-467-8228; Fax: 401-467-8899.

222 Washington St., West Warwick, 02893. Tel: 401-823-0157; Fax: 401-823-4694.

Youth Diversion Projects:

215 Washington St., West Warwick, 02893. Tel: 401-822-1360; Fax: 401-823-4694.

242 Dexter St., Pawtucket, 02860. Tel: 401-724-8380 ; Fax: 401-724-8899.

Preserving Families Network

242 Dexter St., Pawtucket, 02860. Tel: 401-724-8380 ; Fax: 401-724-8899.

55 Main St., Ste. 1, Woonsocket, 02895. Tel: 401-766-9320; Fax: 401-766-9324.

790 Broad St., 02907. Tel: 401-467-8888; Fax: 401-467-8899.

215 Washington St., West Warwick, 02893. Tel: 401-822-1360; Fax: 401-823-4694.

RELIGIOUS INSTITUTES OF MEN REPRESENTED IN THE DIOCESE

For further details refer to the corresponding bracketed number in the Religious Institutes of Men or Women section.

[0200]—*Benedictine Monks*—O.S.B.
[]—*Brothers of Our Lady of Providence*—O.L.P.
[0330]—*Brothers of the Christian Schools* (New England-Long Island Prov.)—F.S.C.
[1100]—*Brothers of the Sacred Heart*—S.C.
[]—*Company of Saint Paul*—C.S.P.
[0650]—*Congregation of the Holy Spirit* (Portuguese Prov. & Irish Prov.)—C.S.SP.
[0730]—*Legionaries of Christ*—L.C.
[1210]—*Missionaries of St. Charles (Scalabrinians)*—C.S.
[0430]—*Order of Preachers (Dominicans)* (Prov. of St. Joseph)—O.P.
[1065]—*Priestly Fraternity of Saint Peter*—F.S.S.P.
[1220]—*Servants of Charity*—S.C.
[0370]—*Society of St. Columban*—S.S.C.

RELIGIOUS INSTITUTES OF WOMEN REPRESENTED IN THE DIOCESE

[0990]—*Congregation of Divine Providence*—C.D.P.
[0885]—*Daughters of Mary Mother of Mercy*—D.M.M.M.
[]—*Daughters of Our Lady of the Garden*—F.M.H.
[0940]—*Daughters of St. Mary of Providence*—D.S.M.P.
[0420]—*Discalced Carmelite Nuns*—O.C.D.
[1105]—*Dominican Sisters of Hope*—O.P.
[1115]—*Dominican Sisters of Peace*—O.P.
[1070-05]—*Dominicans* (Amityville)—O.P.
[1070-13]—*Dominicans* (Adrian)—O.P.
[1070-15]—*Dominicans* (Blauvelt)—O.P.
[1070-07]—*Dominicans* (St. Cecilia of Nashville, TN)—O.P.
[1170]—*Felician Sisters*—C.S.S.F.
[]—*Franciscan Apostolic Sisters*—F.A.S.
[1370]—*The Franciscan Missionaries of Mary*—F.M.M.
[3790]—*Institute of the Sisters of St. Dorothy*—S.S.D.
[2340]—*Little Sisters of the Poor*—L.S.P.
[1360]—*Missionary Franciscan Sisters of the Immaculate Conception*—M.F.I.C.
[]—*Missionary Sisters Servants of the Word*—H.M.S.P.
[3230]—*Poor Handmaids of Jesus Christ*—P.H.J.C.
[3450]—*Religious of Jesus and Mary*—R.J.M.
[2070]—*Religious of the Holy Union of the Sacred Hearts*—S.U.S.C.
[3430]—*Religious Teachers Filippini*—M.P.F.
[2575]—*Sisters of Mercy of the Americas*—R.S.M.
[3750]—*Sisters of St. Chretienne*—S.S.CH.
[3860]—*Sisters of St. Joseph of Cluny*—S.J.C.
[3830]—*Sisters of St. Joseph of Springfield*—S.S.J.
[]—*Sisters of the Adoration of the Blessed Sacrament*—S.A.B.S.
[0150]—*Sisters of the Assumption*—S.A.S.V.
[2980]—*Sisters of the Congregation of Notre Dame*—C.N.D.
[3180]—*Sisters of the Cross and Passion*—C.P.
[3310]—*Sisters of the Presentation of Mary*—P.M.
[3320]—*Sisters of the Presentation of the B.V.M.*—P.B.V.M.
[4040]—*Society of St. Ursula*—S.U.
[4048]—*Society of the Sisters, Faithful Companions of Jesus*—F.C.J.

DIOCESAN CEMETERIES

PROVIDENCE. *St. Patrick's*

BARRINGTON. *Maria Del Campo*

CRANSTON. *St. Ann's*

CUMBERLAND. *Resurrection*

EAST PROVIDENCE. *Gate of Heaven*, 555 Wampanoag Trl., East Providence, 02915. Tel: 401-434-2579; Email: cemetery@dioceseofprovidence.org. Mr. Anthony J. Carpinello, Dir.

MIDDLETOWN. *St. Columba*

PAWTUCKET. *St. Francis*

Mount St. Mary's

WEST GREENWICH. *St. Joseph*

NECROLOGY

† Mulvee, Robert E., Bishop Emeritus of Providence, Died Dec. 28, 2018
† Allard, John C., (Retired), Died Apr. 27, 2018
† Varsanyi, William I., (Retired), Died Jan. 7, 2019
† Bouressa, Donald J., (Retired), Died Oct. 15, 2018
† Brassil, Kevin J., (Retired), Died Jun. 5, 2018
† Demers, Normand J., (Retired), Died Jul. 21, 2018
† Paiva, Antonio M., (Retired), Died Apr. 9, 2018

An asterisk (*) denotes an organization that has established tax-exempt status directly with the IRS and is not covered by the USCCB Group Ruling.

Diocese of Pueblo

(Dioecesis Pueblensis)

Most Reverend

STEPHEN J. BERG

Bishop of Pueblo; ordained May 15, 1999; appointed Bishop of Pueblo January 15, 2014; ordained and installed February 27, 2014. *Pastoral Center, 101 N. Greenwood St., Pueblo, CO 81003-3164.*

Most Reverend

FERNANDO ISERN, D.D.

Bishop Emeritus of Pueblo; ordained April 16, 1993; appointed Bishop of Pueblo October 15, 2009; ordained and installed December 10, 2009; retired June 13, 2013. *Catholic Pastoral Center, 101 N. Greenwood St., Pueblo, CO 81003-3164.*

Catholic Pastoral Center: 101 N. Greenwood St., Pueblo, CO 81003. Tel: 719-544-9861; Fax: 719-544-5202.

Web: www.dioceseofpueblo.org

Email: officeofbishop@dioceseofpueblo.org

Square Miles 48,155.

Diocesan Patron: St. Therese of the Child Jesus. Secondary Patroness: Our Lady of Guadalupe.

Erected a Diocese November 15, 1941.

Comprises the 29 Counties of Alamosa, Archuleta, Baca, Bent, Conejos, Costilla, Crowley, Custer, Delta, Dolores, Fremont, Gunnison, Hinsdale, Huerfano, Kiowa, La Plata, Las Animas, Mesa, Mineral, Montezuma, Montrose, Otero, Ouray, Prowers, Pueblo, Rio Grande, Saguache, San Juan and San Miguel in the southern and western part of the State of Colorado.

For legal titles of parishes and diocesan institutions, consult the Finance Office.

STATISTICAL OVERVIEW

Personnel	
Bishop	1
Retired Bishops	1
Priests: Diocesan Active in Diocese	28
Priests: Diocesan Active Outside Diocese	1
Priests: Retired, Sick or Absent	11
Number of Diocesan Priests	40
Religious Priests in Diocese	15
Total Priests in Diocese	55
Extern Priests in Diocese	10
Permanent Deacons in Diocese	56
Total Sisters	34
Parishes	
Parishes	52
With Resident Pastor:	
Resident Diocesan Priests	21
Resident Religious Priests	9
Without Resident Pastor:	
Administered by Priests	22
Missions	38
Pastoral Centers	1
Professional Ministry Personnel:	
Sisters	4
Lay Ministers	30
Welfare	
Catholic Hospitals	4
Total Assisted	781,539
Health Care Centers	1
Total Assisted	195,367
Educational	
Diocesan Students in Other Seminaries	1
Total Seminarians	1
High Schools, Diocesan and Parish	1
Total Students	8
Elementary Schools, Diocesan and Parish	3
Total Students	863
Elementary Schools, Private	1
Total Students	130
Catechesis/Religious Education:	
High School Students	1,167
Elementary Students	3,353
Total Students under Catholic Instruction	5,522
Teachers in the Diocese:	
Lay Teachers	92
Vital Statistics	
Receptions into the Church:	
Infant Baptism Totals	410
Minor Baptism Totals	298
Adult Baptism Totals	113
Received into Full Communion	121
First Communions	885
Confirmations	613
Marriages:	
Catholic	120
Interfaith	37
Total Marriages	157
Deaths	818
Total Catholic Population	57,762
Total Population	792,670

Former Bishops—Most Revs. JOSEPH CLEMENT WILLGING, D.D., First Bishop of Pueblo; ord. June 20, 1908; appt. Dec. 6, 1941; cons. Feb. 24, 1942; Assistant at Pontifical Throne, Feb. 20, 1958; died March 3, 1959; CHARLES A. BUSWELL, ord. July 9, 1939; appt. Bishop of Pueblo Aug. 8, 1959; cons. Sept. 30, 1959; installed Oct. 6, 1959; retired Sept. 18, 1979; died June 14, 2008.; ARTHUR N. TAFOYA, D.D., ord. May 12, 1962; appt. Bishop of Pueblo July 1, 1980; ord. and installed Sept. 10, 1980; retired Oct. 15, 2009; died March 24, 2018.; FERNANDO ISERN, ord. April 16, 1993; appt. Bishop of Pueblo Oct. 15, 2009; ord. and installed Dec. 10, 2009; retired June 13, 2013.

Chancery—*101 N. Greenwood St., Pueblo, 81003-3164.* Tel: 719-544-9861; Fax: 719-544-5202. Office Hours: Mon.-Fri. 8-12 & 1-5.

Delegate—Tel: 719-544-9861. VACANT.

Vicar General—Rev. Msgr. EDWARD H. NUNEZ, V.G., Tel: 719-544-9861, Ext. 1121.

Moderator of the Curia—VACANT.

Chancellor—Rev. MATTHEW WERTIN, J.C.L., Tel: 719-544-9861, Ext. 1171.

Vicar for Clergy—Rev. Msgr. EDWARD H. NUNEZ, V.G., Tel: 719-544-9861, Ext. 1121.

Director of Pastoral Services—Deacon DANIEL T. LEETCH.

Director of Administrative Services—VACANT.

Diocesan Tribunal—Rev. Msgr. MARK A. PLEWKA, J.C.L., J.V., Tel: 719-544-9861, Ext. 1161.

Judicial Vicar—Rev. Msgr. MARK A. PLEWKA, J.C.L., J.V., Tel: 719-544-9861, Ext. 1161.

Secretarial to the Tribunal—MS. PAULA GUITERREZ, Tel: 719-544-9861, Ext. 1161.

Judge—Rev. Msgr. MARK A. PLEWKA, J.C.L., J.V., Tel: 719-544-9861, Ext. 1161.

Ecclesiastical Notaries—MRS. PAULA GUTIERREZ; Rev. MARK T. BETTINGER.

College of Consultors—Rev. Msgr. JAMES F. KOENIGSFELD, V.F., (Retired); Rev. MATTHEW WERTIN, J.C.L., Chancellor; Very Revs. STEVEN J. MURRAY; DERREK D. SCOTT; Rev. Msgr. EDWARD H. NUNEZ, V.G.; Revs. MICHAEL CHRISMAN; STEPHEN OLAMOLU; Very Rev. JOSEPH A. VIGIL.

Deans—Very Revs. DONALD P. MALIN, Alamosa Deanery; KEVIN F. NOVACK, Durango Deanery; STEVEN J. MURRAY, La Junta Deanery; JOSEPH A. VIGIL, Pueblo Deanery; Rev. CARLOS A. ALVAREZ, Grand Junction Deanery.

Diocesan Offices

Administrative Services—

Moderator of the Curia—VACANT.

Office of Missionary Discipleship—MR. SETH WRIGHT, Tel: 719-544-9861, Ext. 1140.

Communications—MS. MICHELLE HILL, Tel: 719-544-9861, Ext. 1193.

Finance—MR. JOHN DANELUK, CFO, Tel: 719-544-9861, Ext. 1141.

Finance Advisory Council—Tel: 719-544-9861, Ext. 1141. MR. JOHN DANELUK, Contact Person.

Foundation—MR. STEVEN S. CHARGIN, Tel: 719-544-9861, Ext. 1131.

Human Resources—Tel: 719-544-9861, Ext. 1110. MS. NANCY MARTINEZ.

Institutional Ministries—Deacon DANIEL T. LEETCH, Tel: 719-544-9861, Ext. 1117.

Superintendent of Catholic Schools—Deacon DANIEL T. LEETCH, Tel: 719-544-9861, Ext. 1117.

Tribunal—Rev. Msgr. MARK A. PLEWKA, J.C.L., J.V., Dir., Tel: 719-544-9861, Ext. 1161.

Vocations—Rev. CARL F. WERTIN, Tel: 719-544-9861, Ext. 1114.

Worship—Rev. MICHAEL CHRISMAN, Tel: 719-544-9861, Ext. 1115.

Catholic Charismatic Renewal—Liaison: Very Rev. DONALD P. MALIN, Coord., Tel: 719-852-2673.

Respect Life Office—Rev. MATTHEW WERTIN, J.C.L., Tel: 719-544-9861, Ext. 1171.

Diocesan Liturgical Commission—Rev. MICHAEL CHRISMAN, Contact Person, Tel: 719-544-9861, Ext. 1115.

Catholic Charities of the Diocese of Pueblo, Inc.—MR. JOE MAHONEY, Dir., Tel: 719-544-4233, Ext. 115.

Victim Assistance Coordinator—MR. JOE MAHONEY, Tel: 719-544-4233, Ext. 115.

The Bishop Charles A. Buswell Trust—

Tel: 719-544-9861, Ext. 1141. MR. JOHN DANELUK, CFO.

Boy Scouts of America—RIK BERGETHON, Catholic Committee Chm., Tel: 719-544-1255.

Clergy Benefit Society of the Diocese of Pueblo, Inc.—Rev. Msgr. JAMES E. KING, Contact Person, Tel: 719-561-3580.

Diocesan Council of Catholic Women—Tel: 719-846-3369. Very Rev. STEVEN J. MURRAY, Mod.

Diocesan Pastoral Committee—VACANT.

Father John Powers Memorial Basketball League, Inc.—JIM VIGIL, Contact Person, Tel: 719-564-3811.

Girl Scouts of America—MRS. VICTORIA KAMPA, Tel: 719-545-1768.

Catholic Campaign for Human Development—MR. JOE MAHONEY, Tel: 719-544-4233, Ext. 115.

Nocturnal Adoration Society—Sr. GORGONIA PARCERO, S.S.S., Tel: 719-545-7729.

Presbyteral Council—Rev. Msgr. EDWARD H. NUNEZ, V.G., Tel: 719-544-9861, Ext. 1121; Rev. MATTHEW WERTIN, J.C.L., Tel: 719-544-9861, Ext. 1171; Rev. Msgr. JAMES F. KOENIGSFELD, V.F., (Retired), Tel: 970-946-4143; Revs. ANDRES AYALA SANTIAGO, Tel: 970-641-0805; MICHAEL CHRISMAN, Tel: 719-544-9861, Ext. 1115; ALBEIRO HERRERA-CIRO, Tel: 970-874-3300; Very Revs. DONALD P. MALIN, Tel: 719-852-2673; STEVEN J. MURRAY, Tel: 719-846-3369; KEVIN F. NOVACK, Tel: 970-247-0044; Revs. STEPHEN OLAMOLU, Tel: 719-738-1204; JESSE L. PEREZ, (Retired), Tel: 719-275-7549; Very Revs. DERREK D. SCOTT, Tel: 719-544-5175; JOSEPH A. VIGIL, Tel: 719-544-1886; Rev. CARLOS A. ALVAREZ, Tel: 970-243-0209.

Clergy Personnel—Rev. Msgr. EDWARD H. NUNEZ, V.G., Tel: 719-544-9861, Ext. 1121.

Search of Pueblo—MS. SANDY HANSEN, Tel: 719-542-6513; Tel: 719-320-2707; Email: sandyrosehansen@gmail.com.

Legion of Mary—MS. MARINA ZAMORA, Tel: 719-821-4276.

CLERGY, PARISHES, MISSIONS AND PAROCHIAL SCHOOLS

CITY OF PUEBLO

(PUEBLO COUNTY)

1—CATHEDRAL OF THE SACRED HEART (1872)
414 W. 11th St., 81003-2888. Tel: 719-544-5175; Fax: 719-586-9922; Email: shcathedral@shcathedral.net; Web: shcathedral.net. Most Rev. Stephen J. Berg; Very Rev. Derrek D. Scott, Rector; Deacons Ben Davis; Daniel T. Leetch.
Catechesis Religious Program—Margaret Ursick Leetch, Faith Formation Coord. Students 18.

2—ST. ANNE (1956)
2701 E. 12th St., 81001-4708. Tel: 719-545-2644; Tel: 719-544-0959; Email: splsrus@hotmail.com. Rev. Msgr. Mark A. Plewka, J.C.L., J.V., Sacramental Min.; Deacon Steve Lumbert, Pastoral Life Admin.
Catechesis Religious Program—Students 26.

3—ST. ANTHONY OF PADUA, Closed. For inquiries for parish records contact the chancery.

4—CHRIST THE KING (1956)
1708 Horseshoe Dr., 81001. Tel: 719-542-9248; Fax: 719-542-3482; Email: mmeissner@ctkpueblo.org; Web: www.ctkpueblo.org. Rev. John Ozella; Deacons Corey Compton; Steve Escalera.
Catechesis Religious Program—Laura Escalera, D.R.E. Students 125.

5—ST. FRANCIS XAVIER (1903)
611 Logan Ave., 81004-3505. Tel: 719-564-1125; Fax: 719-564-1141; Email: stfrancisxavierpueblo@yahoo.com; Web: www.sfxavierpueblo.org. Rev. Selvakumar Xavier, Admin.; Deacon Paul Villegas.
Catechesis Religious Program—Students 84.
Mission—Our Lady of Lourdes, 8800 Maryknoll, Beulah, Pueblo Co. 81023.

6—HOLY FAMILY (1954)
2827 Lakeview Ave., 81005-2495. Tel: 719-564-2696; Fax: 719-564-4396. Revs. Tomas Carvajal-Basto, C.R.; Douglas Hunt, C.R.; Deacon Marco Vegas.
Catechesis Religious Program—Students 162.
Mission—St. Aloysius (1936) 8006 Hwy. 165 W., Rye, 81069. Tel: 719-489-3543; Email: homim73@yahoo.com. P.O. Box 186, Rye, Pueblo Co. 81069-0186. Rev. Gregory Ezeanya, Admin.

7—HOLY ROSARY (1954)
2400 W. 22nd St., 81003. 2217 W. 22nd St., 81003-3842. Rev. Msgr. James E. King.
Catechesis Religious Program—Students 11.

8—ST. JOSEPH (1960)
1145 S. Aspen Rd., 81006-9998. Very Rev. Joseph A. Vigil; Deacons Peter A. Massaro; Ben Davis.
Catechesis Religious Program—Students 296.

9—ST. LEANDER (1902)
1402 E. 7th St., 81001-3510. Rev. Charles A. Sena, V.F.; Deacon Edward Riccillo.
Catechesis Religious Program—Students 100.

10—ST. MARY HELP OF CHRISTIANS (1895)
307 E. Mesa Ave., 81006. Tel: 719-296-8778; Fax: 719-562-1195; Email: stmaryhev@hotmail.com. 217 E. Mesa Ave., 81006-1014. Rev. Prabhu Arockiasamy, Admin.
Catechesis Religious Program—Belinda Castro, C.R.E. Students 87.

11—OUR LADY OF GUADALUPE CHAPEL (1968) Closed. For inquiries for parish records please contact St. Leander, Pueblo.

12—OUR LADY OF MT. CARMEL (1901)
421 Clark St., 81003. Tel: 719-542-5952; Fax: 719-542-2310; Email: ourladyofmtcarmel@live.com. Rev. Martin Frias; Deacon Jake Arellano.
Catechesis Religious Program—Students 146.

13—OUR LADY OF THE ASSUMPTION (1949) Closed. For inquiries for parish records contact the chancery.

14—OUR LADY OF THE MEADOWS (1979)
23 Starling Dr., 81005-1878. Tel: 719-561-3580; Fax: 719-561-1271. Rev. Msgr. James E. King.
Catechesis Religious Program—Students 62.

15—ST. PATRICK (1882) Closed. For inquiries for parish records contact the chancery.

16—ST. PAUL THE APOSTLE (2009)
1132 W. Oro Grande Dr., Pueblo West, 81007. P.O. Box 7199, Pueblo West, 81007-0199. Rev. Edmundo Valera, Ph.D.; Deacon Philip Medina.
Catechesis Religious Program—Students 161.

17—ST. PIUS X (1955)
3130 Morris Ave., 81008-1338. Tel: 719-542-4264; Email: pmonte2@comcast.net. Rev. Matthew Wertin, J.C.L.; Deacon Roy Stringfellow.
Catechesis Religious Program—Students 55.

18—SHRINE OF ST. THERESE (1948)
300 Goodnight Ave., 81004-1097. Tel: 719-542-1788; Fax: 719-545-3161; Email: parish@sostpueblo.org. Rev. Michael Chrisman; Deacon Buddy P. Rodriguez; Mrs. Theresa R. Farley, Office Admin.
Catechesis Religious Program—Students 50.

OUTSIDE THE CITY OF PUEBLO

AGUILAR, LAS ANIMAS CO., ST. ANTHONY OF PADUA (1875) [CEM] [JC] (Spanish—Italian)
125 S. Fir St., Aguilar, 81020-0577.
Tel: 719-941-4124; Fax: 719-941-4124. Mailing Address: P.O. Box 577, Aguilar, 81020-0577. Rev. Stephen Olamolu.
Catechesis Religious Program—Students 9.

ALAMOSA, ALAMOSA CO., SACRED HEART (1887)
715 E. 4th St., P.O. Box 547, Alamosa, 81101-057. Tel: 719-589-5829; Tel: 719-589-9788; Fax: 719-589-5820; Email: admin@sacredheartalamosa.org; Email: pastor@sacredheartalamosa.org; Web: www.sacredheartalamosa.org. Rev. Uju Patrick Okeahialam, C.S.Sp.
Catechesis Religious Program—Students 272.

AVONDALE, PUEBLO CO., SACRED HEART (1960) (Spanish)
210 Hwy. 50 E., Avondale, 81022. Tel: 719-947-3092; Fax: 719-947-3005. P.O. Box 279, Avondale, 81022-0279. Very Rev. Joseph A. Vigil, Admin.; Deacon Michael LaConte.
Catechesis Religious Program—Students 34.
Mission—Avondale Sacred Heart Parish, 210 E. Hwy. 501, P.O. Box 279, Avondale, 81027. Email: shcparish@hotmail.com.

CANON CITY, FREMONT CO., ST. MICHAEL (1880)
10th St. & College Ave., Canon City, 81212.
Tel: 719-275-7549; Fax: 719-275-7540; Email: office@stmikescanoncity.org; Web: www.stmikescanoncity.org. 1029 College Ave., Canon City, 81212. Rev. Jesse L. Perez, (Retired); Deacon Merle E. Runck.
Catechesis Religious Program—Students 85.

CAPULIN, CONEJOS CO., ST. JOSEPH (1912) [CEM] (Hispanic)
19895 County Rd. 8, Capulin, 81124.
Tel: 719-274-5304; Fax: 719-274-4454; Email: saintjosephp@gmail.com. P.O. Box 40, Capulin, 81124-0040. Rev. Arturo Anonuevo, S.O.L.T.
Catechesis Religious Program—Students 125.
Missions—Our Lady of the Valley—19617 S. Hwy. 285, La Jara, Conejos Co. 81140. Tel: 719-274-5647.
St. Therese of the Child Jesus, 115 Main St., Manassa, Conejos Co. 81141.
St. Anthony, 18900 County Rd. 28, Los Sauces, Conejos Co. 81151.
Our Lady of the Immaculate Conception, 211 Blanca St., Romeo, Conejos Co. 81148.

CENTER, SAGUACHE CO., ST. FRANCIS JEROME (1951) [CEM] (San Juan Catholic Community)
781 Warden St., Center, 81125-9367.
Tel: 719-852-2673; Fax: 719-852-0623; Email: sanjuancatholiccommunity@gmail.com; Web: sjccommunity.org. P.O. Box 590, Monte Vista, 81144-0590. Very Rev. Derrek D. Scott; Rev. Albert Berkmans; Deacons Jerry LeBlanc, D.R.E.; Ray Torres.
Catechesis Religious Program—215 S. Worth St., Center, 81125. Students 51.
Mission—St. Agnes, 505 Gunnison St., Saguache, 81149.

CONEJOS, CONEJOS CO., OUR LADY OF GUADALUPE (1857) [CEM]
6633 County Rd. 13, Antonito, 81120.
Tel: 719-376-5985; Fax: 719-376-2530; Email: chiquilinmedallas@yahoo.com; Email: info@ologp.org. P.O. Box 305, Antonito, 81120-0305. Rev. Sergio Cardenas-Robles, C.R.
Catechesis Religious Program—Students 73.
Missions—St. Augustine—803 Pine St., Antonito, 81120.
Sagrada Familia, 17344 Co. Rd. G, Lobatos, Conejos Co. 81120.
San Juan Nepomuceno y San Cayetano, 684 Co. Rd. B, Ortiz, Conejos Co. 81120.
San Antonio de Padua, 13148 Co. Rd. C, San Antonio, Conejos Co. 81120.
San Pedro y San Rafael, 5308 Co. Rd. 10.75, San Rafael, Conejos Co. 81120.
San Isidro Labrador, Las Mesitas, Conejos Co.
San Miguel Church.
Shrine—El Santuario de Los Pobladores.

CORTEZ, MONTEZUMA CO., ST. MARGARET MARY (1945)
28 E. Montezuma Ave., Cortez, 81321-3299.
Tel: 970-565-7308 (Office); Fax: 970-565-0822; Email: SMM@fone.net; Web: www.montelorescatholic.org. Rev. Pat Valdez, C.R. Montelores Catholic Community
Catechesis Religious Program—Students 98.
Missions—Immaculate Heart of Mary—
St. Jude.

CRESTED BUTTE, GUNNISON CO., QUEEN OF ALL SAINTS (1880) Attended by St. Peter Parish, Gunnison.
400 W. Georgia Ave., Gunnison, 81230-3021. Rev. Andres Ayala-Santiago; Deacons Vincent Rogalski; John Stroop; Joseph W. Fitzpatrick.
Catechesis Religious Program—401 Sopris, Crested Butte, 81224. Students 24.

DEL NORTE, RIO GRANDE CO., HOLY NAME OF MARY (1879) [CEM 2] (San Juan Catholic Community)
645 Pine St., Del Norte, 81132-2246.
Tel: 719-852-2673; Fax: 719-852-0623; Email: sanjuancatholiccommunity@gmail.com; Web: sjccommunity.org. Mailing Address: P.O. Box 590, Monte Vista, 81144-0590. Very Rev. Donald P. Malin; Rev. Albert Berkmans; Deacons Jerry LeBlanc, D.R.E.; Ray Torres.
Catechesis Religious Program—Students 22.
Missions—St. Francis of Assisi—5615 W. CR 5 N., Monte Vista, Rio Grande Co. 81144.
San Jose, County Rd. 63, Agua Ramon, Rio Grande Co. 81154.
Holy Family, 0204 Church St., South Fork, Rio Grande Co. 81154.
Immaculate Conception, 104 W. 3rd St., Creede, Mineral Co. 81130.

DELTA, DELTA CO., ST. MICHAEL (1910)
628 Meeker St., Delta, 81416-1923.
Tel: 970-874-3300; Cell: 970-275-0069; Email: secretary@stmichaelsdelta.org; Web: www.stmichaelsdelta.org. Rev. Albeiro Herrera-Ciro; Deacon Price Hatcher, Business Mgr.
Catechesis Religious Program—Students 118.
Mission—St. Philip Benizi, P.O. Box 713, Cedaredge, Delta Co. 81413-0713. Tel: 970-856-6495.

DURANGO, LA PLATA CO.

1—ST. COLUMBA (1881)
1830 E. 2nd Ave., Durango, 81301-5019.
Tel: 970-247-0044; Fax: 970-385-5737; Email: parishoffice@stcolumbacatholic.org; Web: www.stcolumbacatholic.org. Very Rev. Kevin F. Novack; Deacon Stephen Johnson III.
School—St. Columba School, (Grades K-8), 1801 E 3rd Ave., Durango, 81301. Tel: 970-247-5527; Fax: 970-382-9355; Email: office@stcolumbaschooldurango.org. Kevin C. Chick, Prin. Lay Teachers 26; Preschool 71; Students 261.
Catechesis Religious Program—Students 70.

2—SACRED HEART (1906) (Hispanic)
254 E. 5th Ave., Durango, 81301-5649.
Tel: 970-247-3997; Fax: 970-375-2385. Rev. Douglas Hunt, C.R., Admin.; Deacons José Benito Martinez; Toby Romero.
Catechesis Religious Program—

FLORENCE, FREMONT CO., ST. BENEDICT (1895)
622 W. 2nd St., Florence, 81226-1015.
Tel: 719-784-4879; Fax: 719-784-2070; Email: stbenedict_81226@yahoo.com. Rev. Stephen Injoalu; Deacon Richard Madison.
Catechesis Religious Program—Email: joyce_stb@yahoo.com. Joyce Archuletta, D.R.E. Students 43.

FRUITA, MESA CO., SACRED HEART (1890)
1210 17 1/2 Rd., Fruita, 81521-9717.
Tel: 970-858-9605; Fax: 970-639-9343; Email: sacredheartfruita@yahoo.com; Web: sacredheartfruita.com. Rev. Samuel Auta, Admin.
Catechesis Religious Program—Students 130.

GARDNER, HUERFANO CO., SACRED HEART aka St. Mary Parish (1912)
121 E. 7th St., Walsenburg, 81089. Tel: 719-738-1204 ; Fax: 719-738-1206. P.O. Box 86, Walsenburg, 81089-0086. Rev. Stephen Olamolu; Deacon John Luginbill.
Catechesis Religious Program—
Mission—Sacred Heart, Tel: 719-746-2037.

GRAND JUNCTION, MESA CO.
1—IMMACULATE HEART OF MARY (1955)
790 26 1/2 Rd., Grand Junction, 81506-8350.
Tel: 970-242-6121; Fax: 970-256-0276; Email: wwilliams@ihmgjt.org; Web: www.ihmgjt.org. Revs. Chrysogomus Nwele; Isaac Kariuki, Parochial Vicar; Timothy Okeahialam, Parochial Vicar; Deacons Luke Konantz; Leo Truscott; Beverly Goodrich, Pastoral Assoc.
Catechesis Religious Program—Irene Fritzler, D.R.E. Students 133.
Mission—St. Ann, 535 W. 1st St., Palisade, Mesa Co. 81526-8786. Tel: 970-464-5024; Fax: 970-256-0276.
Stations—Debeque.
Collbran.
2—ST. JOSEPH (1884)
230 N. 3rd St., Grand Junction, 81501-2439.
Tel: 970-243-0209; Fax: 970-243-7493; Email: parish@stjosephgj.org; Email: belle@stjosephgj.org; Web: stjosephgj.org. Rev. Carlos A. Alvarez, Tel: 719-647-1500; Deacons Fred Bartels; Douglas Van Houten.
Catechesis Religious Program—Carol Schneider, D.R.E. Students 284.

GUNNISON, GUNNISON CO., ST. PETER (1881)
400 W. Georgia Ave., Gunnison, 81230-3021. Email: stpeters@montrose.net. Rev. Andres Ayala-Santiago; Deacons Vincent Rogalski; Lloyd Hawes.
Catechesis Religious Program—Students 74.
Mission—St. Rose of Lima.

HOLLY, PROWERS CO., ST. FRANCES OF ROME (1920)
131 S. Main St., Holly, 81047. P. O. Box 130, Holly, 81047-0130. Revs. Mariusz Wirkowski, (Poland) Admin.; Nicodemus Urassa, Parochial Vicar.
Catechesis Religious Program—Students 42.
Mission—St. Mary, 211 N. Labelle, Holly, Prowers Co. 81047. P.O. Box 130, Holly, 81047-0130.

IGNACIO, LA PLATA CO., ST. IGNATIUS PARISH (1898)
15449 Hwy. 172, Ignacio, 81137. Tel: 970-563-4241; Fax: 970-563-1032; Email: stignatius@frontier.net; Web: www.stignatiuschurch-ignacio.com. P.O. Box 1350, Ignacio, 81137-1350. Rev. Salvador Cisneros; Deacons John O'Hare; Larry Tucker.
Catechesis Religious Program—Students 55.
Missions—St. Bartholemew—1749 CR 526, Bayfield, 81122. Web: stbartsbayfield.com. P.O. Box 488, Bayfield, 81122-0488.
SS. Peter & Rose, 1917 CR 975, Ignacio, Archuleta Co. 81137.

LA JUNTA, OTERO CO., OUR LADY OF GUADALUPE / ST. PATRICK PARISH (1889)
202 Lincoln Ave., La Junta, 81050-1181.
Tel: 719-384-4342; Tel: 719-384-4372;
Fax: 719-384-7894; Email: ljcp@bresnan.net. Henry J. Wertin.

LAMAR, PROWERS CO., ST. FRANCIS DE SALES-OUR LADY OF GUADALUPE (1907)
600 E. Parmenter St., Lamar, 81052-3523.
Tel: 719-336-7759; Fax: 719-336-0291; Email: catholicchurchlamar@bresnan.net; Web: secolocatholics.org. Revs. Mariusz Wirkowski, (Poland); Nicodemus Urassa, Parochial Vicar; Deacon Allan J. Medina.
Catechesis Religious Program—Students 219.

LAS ANIMAS, BENT CO., ST. MARY (1910)
650 Elm Ave., Las Animas, 81054-1738.
Tel: 719-456-1104; Fax: 719-456-1104; Email: stmaryla@yahoo.com. 714 Elm Ave., Las Animas, 81054-1738. Rev. Henry James Wertin.
Catechesis Religious Program—Students 40.

MANCOS, MONTEZUMA CO., ST. RITA OF CASCIA (1914)
203 S. Main St., Mancos, 81238. Tel: 970-565-7308; Fax: 970-565-0822. Mailing Address: 28 E. Montezuma Ave., Cortez, 81321-3217. Rev. Pat Valdez, C.R.
Missions—Our Lady of Victory Church—101 N. 7th St., Dolores, 81323.
Immaculate Heart of Mary Chapel, Rico.

MONTE VISTA, RIO GRANDE CO., ST. JOSEPH (1920) (San Juan Catholic Community)
425 Batterson, Monte Vista, 81144.
Tel: 719-852-2673; Fax: 719-852-0623; Email: sanjuancatholiccommunity@gmail.com; Web: sjccommunity.org. P.O. Box 590, Monte Vista, 81144-0590. Very Rev. Donald P. Malin; Rev. Albert Berkmans, Pastoral Assoc.; Deacons Jerry LeBlanc, D.R.E.; Ray Torres.
Catechesis Religious Program—Students 133.
Stations—Monte Vista Estates—2277 East Dr., Monte Vista, 81144. Tel: 719-852-5138.
Colorado State Veterans Center, 3749 Sherman Ave., Monte Vista, 81144. Tel: 719-852-5118.
The Legacy Assisted Living Home, 100 Chico Camino, Monte Vista, 81144. Tel: 719-852-5179.

MONTROSE, MONTROSE CO., ST. MARY (1906)
1855 St. Mary Dr., Montrose, 81401-5011. Rev. Mark T. Bettinger; Deacons Dennis Putnam, (Retired); Michael Rovella; Scott McIntosh.
Catechesis Religious Program—Students 362.
Mission—Our Lady of Fatima, 211 Main St., Olathe, 81425.

OURAY, OURAY CO., ST. DANIEL THE PROPHET (1883)
614 5th St., Ouray, 81427. Tel: 970-325-4373; Email: sdouray@centurylink.net. P.O. Box 565, Ouray, 81427-0565. Rev. Nathanael Foshage, O.S.B.
Catechesis Religious Program—Students 14.
Mission—St. Patrick, 1005 Reece, Silverton, San Juan Co. 81433.

PAGOSA SPRINGS, ARCHULETA CO.
1—IMMACULATE HEART OF MARY (1923) [CEM] (Hispanic)
451 Lewis St., Pagosa Springs, 81147.
Tel: 970-731-5744; Fax: 970-731-2151. 353 S. Pagosa Blvd., Pagosa Springs, 81147-4300. Rev. Kenny Udumka.
Catechesis Religious Program—Students 81.
Missions—St. Francis—Frances, Archuleta Co.
St. John Baptist, Pagosa Junction, Archuleta Co.
St. James, Trujillo, Archuleta Co.
2—POPE JOHN PAUL II aka Immaculate Heart of Mary
353 S. Pagosa Blvd., Pagosa Springs, 81147-4300.
Tel: 970-731-5744; Fax: 970-731-2151. Rev. Kenny Udumka.
Catechesis Religious Program—Students 81.

PAONIA, DELTA CO., SACRED HEART (1923)
235 N. Fork Ave., Paonia, 81428. Tel: 970-527-3214; Email: sacredheart@tds.net; Web: www.facebook.com/sacredheartcatholicchurchpaonia/. P.O. Box 988, Paonia, 81428-0988. Rev. Wojciech Pelczarski.
Catechesis Religious Program—Students 39.
Mission—St. Margaret Mary, 289 Bridge & Piñon, Paonia, 81428. Tel: 970-872-2117.

ROCKY FORD, OTERO CO., ST. PETER THE APOSTLE (1910)
1209 Swink Ave., Rocky Ford, 81067-1835.
Tel: 719-254-3565; Fax: 719-254-3921; Email: sprockyford@centurytel.net. Rev. Paul Ekeh; Deacon Terry Marinelli.
Catechesis Religious Program—Students 51.
Missions—St. Peter Chapel—905 Main St., Ordway, Crowley Co. 81063. Tel: 719-267-4645. P.O. Box 218, Ordway, 81063-0218.
Mary Queen of Heaven, 602 7th St., Fowler, Otero Co. 81039. Tel: 719-263-4455. P.O. Box 214, Fowler, 81039-0384.

SAN LUIS, COSTILLA CO., SANGRE DE CRISTO (1881) [CEM] (Hispanic)
511 Church Pl., San Luis, 81152. P.O. Box 326, San Luis, 81152-0326. Damian de la Cruz Nuñez; Deacon Margarito Duarte.
Catechesis Religious Program—Students 37.
Missions—St. James—Blanca, Costilla Co.
Holy Family, Fort Garland, Costilla Co.
Immaculate Conception, Chama, Costilla Co.
San Acacio, San Acacio, Costilla Co.
SS. Peter and Paul, San Pedro, Costilla Co.
St. Isidro, San Isidro, Costilla Co.
St. Francis of Assisi, San Francisco, Costilla Co.
Sacred Heart of Jesus, Garcia, Costilla Co.

SILVERTON, SAN JUAN CO., ST. PATRICK (1883)
1005 Reese St., Silverton, 81433. Tel: 970-325-4373. Mailing Address: P.O. Box 565, Ouray, 81433-0565. Rev. Nathanael Foshage, O.S.B.
Catechesis Religious Program—Students 8.

SPRINGFIELD, BACA CO., OUR LADY OF THE ANNUNCIATION (1932)
140 Kansas St., P.O. Box 174, Springfield, 81073.
Tel: 719-336-7759; Tel: 719-523-6645. Revs. Mariusz Wirkowski, (Poland); Nicodemus Urassa, Parochial Vicar.
Catechesis Religious Program—Students 26.
Station—Springfield.

TELLURIDE, SAN MIGUEL CO., ST. PATRICK (1896)
301 N Spruce, Telluride, 81435. Tel: 970-728-3387; Email: stpatrickstelluride@yahoo.com. P.O. Box 398, Telluride, 81435-0398. Rev. Nathanael Foshage, O.S.B., Supvr.; Deacon Michael Doehrman, Parish Life Dir.
Catechesis Religious Program—Students 12.
Mission—Our Lady of Sorrows Nucla, 325 Fox St., Nucla, 81424. Email: stpatrickstelluride@yahoo.com. P.O. Box 451, Nucla, 81424-0451.

TRINIDAD, LAS ANIMAS CO.
1—ST. JOSEPH, TRINIDAD AREA CATHOLIC COMMUNITY, Closed. For inquiries for parish records contact Most Holy Trinity, 719-846-3369.
2—MOST HOLY TRINITY (1866)
235 N. Convent St., Trinidad, 81082-2692.
Tel: 719-846-3369; Fax: 719-846-4856; Email: tacc@trinidadcatholic.org; Web: www.trinidadcatholic.org. Very Rev. Steven J. Murray; Rev. Isaac Kariuki, Parochial Vicar; Deacon Phil Martin.
Catechesis Religious Program—Students 225.
Missions—San Isidro—Vigil, Las Animas Co.
St. Ignatius, Segundo, Las Animas Co.
3—OUR LADY OF MT. CARMEL, Closed. For inquiries for parish records contact Most Holy Trinity, 719-846-3369.

VINELAND, PUEBLO CO., ST. THERESE (1928)
1133 Ln. 35, 81006. Tel: 719-948-2410;
Tel: 719-544-1886; Fax: 719-544-5137. Mailing Address: 1145 S. Aspen Rd., 81006-1655. Very Rev. Joseph A. Vigil.
Catechesis Religious Program—Students 5.

WALSENBURG, HUERFANO CO., ST. MARY (1896) [CEM]
121 E. 7th St., Walsenburg, 81089. Tel: 719-738-1204 ; Fax: 719-738-1206. P.O. Box 86, Walsenburg, 81089-0086. Rev. Stephen Olamolu; Sr. Carol Tlach, S.N.D., Pastoral Assoc.; Deacon John Luginbill.
Catechesis Religious Program—Students 25.
Missions—Christ the King—505 S. Main St., La Veta.
Sacred Heart, Colorado State Hwy. 69, Gardner.

WESTCLIFFE, CUSTER CO., OUR LADY OF THE ASSUMPTION (1870)
109 S. 5th St., P.O. Box 359, Westcliffe, 81252.
Tel: 719-783-3507; Fax: 719-783-3510; Email: ola.westcliffe@gmail.com; Web: www.olawestcliffe.org. Rev. Stephen Injoalu, Admin.; Deacon Michael Patterson.
Catechesis Religious Program—Students 7.

Chaplains of Public Institutions

PUEBLO. *St. Mary Corwin Medical Center*, 1008 Minnequa Ave., 81004. Tel: 719-557-4000. Rev. Konaku Kuosegmeh, Deacon Marco Vegas.
Parkview Hospital, 400 W. 16th St., 81003.
Tel: 719-584-4000. Rev. Gregory Ezenya.

GRAND JUNCTION. *St. Mary Hospital & Medical Center*, 2635 N. 7th St., P.O. Box 1628, Grand Junction, 81501. Rev. Joachim Adione.

On Duty Outside the Diocese:
Rev.—
Haberman, C. Robert, Asst. Prof. & Dir. of Campus Min., 50 Acadia, San Rafael, CA 94901. Tel: 415-479-1249.

Retired:
Rev. Msgrs.—
Huber, Dan, (Retired)
Kapushion, Marvin, M.S.W., J.C.L., L.C.S.W., (Retired), Tel: 719-545-4599
Koenigsfeld, James F., V.F., (Retired)
Revs.—
Cerwonka, Clarence J., (Retired), Tel: 607-862-3216
Costanzo, John J., (Retired), Tel: 303-477-4853
Courtney, William Liam, (Retired), Tel: 011 353 43333 24421
DeSciose, Michael C., (Retired), Tel: 303-873-1051
Huber, J. William, Ph.D., (Retired), Tel: 719-586-9622
Kennedy, Gary L., (Retired), Tel: 719-561-8917
Marcantonio, Clement, (Retired)
Perez, Jesse L., (Retired)
Plough, James H., (Retired), Tel: 970-255-1228.

Permanent Deacons:
Anderson, Michael, St. Peter, Gunnison
Arellano, Jake, Our Lady of Mt. Carmel, Pueblo
Bartels, Fred, St. Joseph, Grand Junction
Brotherton, Robert E., (Retired)
Byrne, Patrick, St. Paul, Pueblo West
Compton, Cory, Christ the King, Pueblo
Davis, Ben, Sacred Heart Cathedral, Pueblo
Diaz, Mario, St. Mary, Montrose
Doehrman, Michael J., Parish Dir., St. Patrick, Telluride
Duarte, Margarito, Sangre de Cristo, San Luis
Escalera, Stephen, Christ the King, Pueblo
Fitzpatrick, Joseph W., Queen of All Saints, Crested Butte
Gundrum, Henry, (Retired)
Hatcher, E. Price, St. Michael, Delta; St. Philip, Cedaredge
Hawes, Lloyd, St. Peter, Gunnison
Johnson, Stephen III, St. Columba, Durango
Konantz, Luke, IHM, Grand Junction
LaConte, Michael, Sacred Heart, Avondale
Lamb, Donald, (Retired), St. Joseph, Monte Vista
LeBlanc, Jerry, St. Joseph, Monte Vista
Leetch, Daniel T., Dir., Inst. Ministries; Permanent Deacons, Sacred Heart Cathedral, Pueblo
Luginbill, John, St. Mary, Walsenburg

Lumbert, Steven, Pastoral Life Admin., St. Anne, Pueblo
Madison, Richard, St. Benedict, Florence
Manley, Douglas, Our Lady of Guadalupe, La Junta
Marinelli, Terry, St. Peter, Rocky Ford
Martin, Philip, Holy Trinity, Trinidad
Martinez, José Benito, (Retired)
Massaro, Peter A., St. Joseph, Pueblo
McIntosh, Scott, St. Mary, Montrose
McKenzie, Patrick, (Retired)
Medina, Allan J., St. Francis de Sales/Our Lady of Guadalupe, Lamar
Medina, Philip, St. Paul the Apostle, Pueblo West
O'Hare, John, St. Ignatius, Ignacio
Pacheco, Jose (Pepe), St. Mary, Montrose
Patterson, Michael, (Retired)
Putnam, Dennis, (Retired)
Riccillo, Edward, St. Leander, Pueblo
Rodriguez, Buddy P., Shrine of St. Therese, Pueblo
Rogalski, Vincent, Queen of All Saints, Crested Butte
Romero, Octaviano, Sacred Heart, Durango
Runck, Merle, St. Michael, Canon City
Sadler, E. Jerome, (Retired)
Sanchez, Michael, St. Paul the Apostle, Pueblo West
Sanchez, Robert, Holy Family, Pueblo
Shafer, Jacob, (Retired)
Stringfellow, Roy, St. Pius X, Pueblo
Stroop, John, (Retired)
Torres, Ray, St. Joseph, Monte Vista
Truscott, Leo, Immaculate Heart of Mary, Grand Junction
Tucker, Lawrence, St. Ignatius, Ignacio
Van Cleave, Milton, (Retired)
Van Houten, Douglas, St. Joseph, Grand Junction
Vegas, Marco, Holy Family, Pueblo; Chap., St. Mary Corwin Hospital, Pueblo
Villegas, Paul, St. Francis Xavier, Pueblo
Yatch, Lawrence, (Retired).

INSTITUTIONS LOCATED IN DIOCESE

[A] ELEMENTARY SCHOOLS, DIOCESAN

PUEBLO. *St. Therese Catholic School*, (Grades PreK-12), 320 Goodnight Ave., 81004. Tel: 719-561-1121; Fax: 719-561-2252; Email: mfuruto@sttheresepueblo.org. Nadine Montoya, Prin. Lay Teachers 18; Students 134; Total Enrollment 134.

DURANGO. *St. Columba*, (Grades PreK-8), 1801 E. 3rd Ave., Durango, 81301-5072. Tel: 970-247-5527; Fax: 970-382-9355; Email: office@stcolumbaschooldurango.org. Kevin C. Chick, Prin. Students 261; Teachers 26.

GRAND JUNCTION. *Holy Family Catholic School*, (Grades PreSchool-8), 786 26 1/2 Rd., Grand Junction, 81506. Tel: 970-242-6168; Fax: 970-242-4244; Email: jake.aubert@hfcs-gj.org; Email: coni.gibson@hfcs-gj.org; Email: kathy.menck@hfcs-gj.org; Web: holyfamily-gj.org. Jake T. Aubert, Prin. Lay Teachers 35; Students 477.

[B] ELEMENTARY SCHOOLS, PRIVATE

PUEBLO. *St. John Neumann Catholic Schools*, (Grades PreK-8), 2415 E. Orman Ave., 81004. Tel: 719-561-9419; Fax: 719-561-4718; Email: admissions@stjohneumannschool.org; Web: www.stjohneumannpueblo.com. Joyce Baca-Anderson, Prin. & Admin. Lay Teachers 16; Students 130.

[C] GENERAL HOSPITALS

PUEBLO. *Centura Health-St. Mary-Corwin Medical Center*, 1008 Minnequa Ave., 81004. Tel: 719-557-4000; Fax: 719-557-5950; Email: michaelcafasso@centura.org; Email: krisordelheide@centura.org; Web: www.stmarycorwin.org. 9100 E. Mineral Cir., Centennial, 80112. Michael Cafasso, Interim Admin.; Kris Ordelheide, Contact Person; Rev. Konaku Kuusegme, Chap. An operating unit of Catholic Health Initiatives Colorado (an affiliate of Catholic Health Initiatives). Bed Capacity 408; Patients Asst Anual. 224,537; Total Staff 693.

CANON CITY. *Centura Health-St. Thomas More Hospital*, 9100 E, Mineral Cir., Centennial, 80112. Tel: 719-285-2000; Web: www.stmhospital.org. Sheri Trahern, CEO; Kris Ordelheide, Contact Person & Gen. Counsel. An operating unit of Catholic Health Initiatives Colorado (an affiliate of Catholic Health Initiatives). Bed Capacity 25; Patients Asst Anual. 107,820; Staff 335.

DURANGO. *Mercy Regional Medical Center*, 1010 Three Springs Blvd., Durango, 81301. Tel: 970-247-4311; Fax: 970-764-3919; Email: krisordelheide@centura.org; Web: www.mercydurango.org. 9100 E. Mineral Cir., Centennial, 80112. Will McConnell, CEO; Kris Ordelheide, Contact Person. An operating unit of Catholic Health Initiatives Colorado (an affiliate of Catholic Health Initiatives). Bed Capacity 82; Patients Asst Anual. 311,658; Total Staff 1,321.

GRAND JUNCTION. *St. Mary Hospital and Medical Center*, 2635 N. 7th St., P.O. Box 1628, Grand Junction, 81501. Tel: 970-298-2273; Web: www.stmarygj.org. Dr. Brian Davidson, M.D., M.B.A., Pres.; Pat Montgomery, Exec. Asst., Email: pat.montgomery@sclhs.net. Bed Capacity 346; Tot Asst. Annually 40,575; Total Staff 2,050; Sisters of Charity of Leavenworth, Kansas 10.

[D] SPECIAL CARE FACILITIES

CANON CITY. *Centura Health-Progressive Care Center*, 1338 Phay Ave., Canon City, 81212. Tel: 719-285-2540; Fax: 719-285-2256; Email: krisordelheide@centura.org; Email: roschellelucero@centura.org; Email: karenburnett@centura.org. 9100 E. Mineral Cir., Centennial, 80112. Kris Ordelheide, Senior Vice Pres. & General Council; Roschelle Lucero, Dir. An operating unit of Catholic Health Initiatives Colorado (an affiliate of Catholic Health Initiatives). Bed Capacity 68; Tot Asst. Annually 102; Total Staff 64.

[E] MONASTERIES AND RESIDENCES OF PRIESTS AND BROTHERS

TRINIDAD. *Trinidad Area Catholic Community*, Pastoral Center, 235 N. Convent St., Trinidad, 81082. Tel: 719-846-3369; Fax: 719-846-4856; Email: tacc@trinidadcatholic.org. Very Rev. Steven J. Murray, Pastor; Rev. Carl F. Wertin, Parochial Vicar.

[F] CONVENTS AND RESIDENCES FOR SISTERS

PUEBLO. *Capuchin Poor Clares O.S.C.Cap.*, 806 E. B St., 81003. Tel: 719-295-2236; Email: osccappueblo@yahoo.com.

Servants of the Blessed Sacrament, 311 E. Mesa Ave., 81006. Tel: 719-545-7729; Tel: 719-544-4506; Fax: 719-544-2203; Email: ssspueblo@outlook.com; Web: www.blesacrament.org. Sisters Resillia Llanto, Supr.; Gorgonia Parcero, S.S.S., Treas. Sisters 3.

[G] NEWMAN CENTERS

PUEBLO. *Campus Ministry - Diocese of Pueblo*, 101 N. Greenwood St., 81003. Tel: 719-544-9861; Fax: 719-544-5202. Deacon Daniel T. Leetch.

Sacred Heart Parish, P.O. Box 547, Alamosa, 81101-0547. Tel: 719-589-5829; Fax: 719-589-5820 . Rev. Michael Chrisman, Pastor.

St. Columba Parish, 1830 E. 2nd St., Durango, 81301-5019. Tel: 970-247-0044; Fax: 970-385-5737 . Very Rev. Kevin F. Novack, Pastor.

Immaculate Heart of Mary Parish, 790 26 1/2 Rd., Grand Junction, 81506-8350. Tel: 970-242-6121; Fax: 970-243-7493. Very Rev. Donald P. Malin, Pastor.

St. Peter Parish, 400 W. Georgia Ave., Gunnison, 81230-3021. Rev. Andres Ayala Santiago, Pastor.

St. Joseph Parish, 1145 Aspen Dr., 81006-9998. Tel: 719-544-1886; Fax: 719-544-5137. Very Rev. Joseph A. Vigil, Dean.

[H] RETREAT WORK

CRESTONE. *Spiritual Life Institute of America, Inc.*, P.O. Box 219, Crestone, 81131. Tel: 719-256-4778; Email: nada@spirituallifeinstitute.org; Web: www.spirituallifeinstitute.org. Rev. Eric Haarer, Prior; Sr. Connie Bielecki, Contact; Susan Ryan, Contact. Priests 1; Sisters 1.

[I] MISCELLANEOUS

PUEBLO. *Catholic Charities of the Diocese of Pueblo Works Corp.*, 429 W. 10th St., 81003.

**Catholic Diocese of Pueblo Foundation*, 101 N. Greenwood St., 81003. Tel: 719-544-9861, Ext. 1131; Fax: 719-544-5202; Email: schargin@dioceseofpueblo.org; Web: www.catholicfoundationdop.org. Mr. Steven S. Chargin, Exec. Dir.

St. Charles Community, 18 Dartmouth, 81005. Tel: 719-566-1620. Mr. Ed Sajbel, Contact Person.

Deacon Candidate Formation Committee, 101 N. Greenwood St., 81003. Tel: 719-544-9861, Ext. 1110; Fax: 719-544-5202; Email: smspm2@aol.com; Web: www.dioceseofpueblo.org. Deacon Scott McIntosh, Deacon Formation Dir.

Pueblo Community Soup Kitchen, Inc., 422 W. Seventh, 81003. Tel: 719-545-6540. Eva L. Matola, Dir.; John Martinez, Coord.

Pueblo Step Up, 1925 E. Orman Ave., Ste. 640-A, 81004. Tel: 719-557-5886; Fax: 719-557-3770; Email: jeffreyporter@centura.org. Jeffrey Porter, Exec. Dir.; Kris Ordelheide, Contact Person. A division of Catholic Health Initiatives Colorado.; Purpose: A ministry to low-income, disadvantaged, and underserved persons, providing wellness clinics, fitness and education for empowerment and transformation. Enroll children into federal and state healthcare programs and provide community resource referrals to clients.

Search of Pueblo, 1402 E. 7th, 81001. Tel: 719-542-6513; Tel: 719-320-2707; Email: sandyrosehansen@gmail.com. 2 Bear Claw Ct., 81001. Ms. Sandy Hansen, Coord.

Serra Club of Pueblo, 101 N. Greenwood St., 81003. Tel: 719-846-3369; Email: cwertin@gmail.com. Rose Marie Stimpfl, Pres.; Rev. Carl F. Wertin.

Spe Salvi Institute, P.O. Box 1515, Westcliffe, 81252. Tel: 719-924-9303; Email: info@spesalviinstitute.org; Web: www.spesalviinstitute.org. Lisa Guarnere, Exec. Dir.

DURANGO. *Mercy Health Foundation*, 1010 Three Springs Blvd., Ste. 248, Durango, 81301. Tel: 970-764-2800; Fax: 970-764-2809; Email: karenmidkiff@centura.org; Web: www.mercydurango.org. Ms. Karen Midkiff, Exec. Dir. & Contact. Affiliate of Catholic Health Initiatives.

GRAND JUNCTION. *Grand Valley Catholic Outreach*, 245 S. 1st St., Grand Junction, 81501. Tel: 970-241-3658; Fax: 970-254-1262; Email: kabland@catholicoutreach.org; Web: www.catholicoutreach.org. Sr. Karen Bland, O.S.B., Exec. Dir. Bed Capacity 80; Tot Asst. Annually 1,642,000; Total Staff 14.

Grand Valley Peace and Justice, 740 Gunnison Ave., Grand Junction, 81501. Tel: 970-243-0136; Fax: 970-314-9692; Email: director@gvpeacejustice.org; Web: gvpeacejustice.org. Julie Mamo, Exec. Dir.; Ms. Sherry Cole, Project Coord.

St. Mary's Hospital Foundation, 2635 N. 7th St., P.O. Box 1628, Grand Junction, 81502-1628. Tel: 970-298-1954; Fax: 970-298-7605; Email: richelle.barton@sclhs.net; Web: www.stmarygj.org/aboutfoundation. Carmen Shipley, Dir.

St. Mary's Physical Medicine & Rehabilitation, 2686 Patterson Rd., Grand Junction, 81506. Tel: 970-298-6005. Valerie Hedgecock, Supvr.

PAGOSA SPRINGS. *Archuleta Housing Corporation*, 703 San Juan St., P.O. Box 355, Pagosa Springs, 81147-0355. Tel: 970-264-2195; Fax: 970-264-4229; Email: archie@centurytel.net.

RELIGIOUS INSTITUTES OF MEN REPRESENTED IN THE DIOCESE

For further details refer to the corresponding bracketed number in the Religious Institutes of Men or Women section.

[]—*Apostles of Jesus*—A.J.
[]—*Brothers for Christian Community*—B.F.C.C.
[]—*Congregation of the Holy Spirit*—C.S.Sp.
[0260]—*Discalced Carmelite Fathers*—O.C.D.
[0690]—*Jesuit Fathers and Brothers* (Missouri Prov.)—S.J.
[]—*Society of Our Lady of the Most Holy Trinity*—S.O.L.T.
[1300]—*Theatine Fathers* (Rome, Italy)—C.R.

RELIGIOUS INSTITUTES OF WOMEN REPRESENTED IN THE DIOCESE

[]—*Adrian Dominican Sisters*—O.P.
[0230]—*Benedictine Sisters of Pontifical Jurisdiction* (Chicago, IL; Covington, KY; Colorado Springs, CO; Yankton, SD)—O.S.B.
[3765]—*Capuchin Poor Clares*—O.S.C.Cap.
[0420]—*Discalced Carmelite Nuns*—O.C.D.
[1115]—*Dominican Sisters of Peace*—O.P.
[]—*Notre Dame Sisters*—N.D.
[]—*Servants of Mary*—O.S.M.
[3500]—*Servants of the Blessed Sacrament*—S.S.S.
[]—*Sisters for Christian Community*—S.F.C.C.
[0440]—*Sisters of Charity of Cincinnati, Ohio*—S.C.
[0480]—*Sisters of Charity of Leavenworth, Kansas*—S.C.L.
[]—*Sisters of Loretto at the Foot of the Cross*—S.L.
[2575]—*Sisters of Mercy of the Americas*—R.S.M.
[3830-15]—*Sisters of St. Joseph*—C.S.J.
[]—*Society of Our Lady of the Most Holy Trinity Sisters*—S.O.L.T.
[]—*Society of the Holy Child of Jesus*—S.H.C.J.
[1570]—*Third Order Regular of Rochester, MN*—O.S.F.

CEMETERIES, DIOCESAN AND PAROCHIAL

AGUILAR. *St. Anthony*
(St. Anthony Parish).
CAPULIN. *St. Joseph*
(St. Joseph Parish).
CONEJOS. *Conejos; Las Mesitas; Ortiz*
(Our Lady of Guadalupe Parish).
DEL NORTE. *St. Francis of Assisi*, Plaza de Los Valdeses, Monte Vista, 81144. Tel: 719-852-2673; Email: sanjuancatholiccommunity@gmail.com. Mailing Address: P.O. Box 590, 425 Batterson St., Monte Vista, 81144. (Holy Name of Mary Parish).

FRUITA. *Fruita Catholic*
(Sacred Heart Parish).
PAGOSA SPRINGS. *St. John the Baptist; St. Andrew Avelino; St. Francis; and St. James*
(Pope John Paul II & Immaculate Heart of Mary Parish).
RYE. *Mount Olivet*
(St. Aloysius Mission Parish)
The Rye Mount Olivet Cemetery.
SAN LUIS. *San Luis; San Pedro; San Acacio; San Francisco; and Chama*
(Sangre de Cristo Parish).
TRINIDAD. *Trinidad Catholic*
Legal Title: Trinidad Catholic Cemetery Assoc. (Cemetery Bd.).
WALSENBURG. *St. Mary*
Legal Title: St. Mary South Cemetery (St. Mary Parish).
WESTCLIFFE. *Silver Cliff Assumption Catholic*
(Our Lady of the Assumption Parish).

NECROLOGY

† Adrians, Thomas M., (Retired), Died Sep. 15, 2018
† Gleeson, William, (Retired), Died Feb. 7, 2018

An asterisk (*) denotes an organization that has established tax-exempt status directly with the IRS and is not covered by the USCCB Group Ruling.

Diocese of Raleigh

(Dioecesis Raleighiensis)

Most Reverend

LUIS RAFAEL ZARAMA, J.C.L.

Bishop of Raleigh; ordained November 27, 1993; appointed Auxiliary Bishop of Atlanta and Titular Bishop of Bararus July 27, 2009; consecrated September 29, 2009; appointed Sixth Bishop of Raleigh July 5, 2017; installed August 29, 2017.

DEUS CARITAS EST

Catholic Center: 7200 Stonehenge Dr., Raleigh, NC 27613-1620. Tel: 919-821-9700; Fax: 919-821-9705.

Web: www.dioceseofraleigh.org

Square Miles 31,875.

Established as Vicariate-Apostolic of North Carolina by Pope Pius IX, March 3, 1868.

Established as Diocese of Raleigh by Pope Pius XI, December 12, 1924.

Comprises the following Counties in the State of North Carolina: Alamance, Beaufort, Bertie, Bladen, Brunswick, Camden, Carteret, Caswell, Chatham, Chowan, Columbus, Craven, Cumberland, Currituck, Dare, Duplin, Durham, Edgecombe, Franklin, Gates, Granville, Greene, Halifax, Harnett, Hertford, Hoke, Hyde, Johnston, Jones, Lee, Lenoir, Martin, Moore, Nash, New Hanover, Northampton, Onslow, Orange, Pamlico, Pasquotank, Pender, Perquimans, Person, Pitt, Robeson, Sampson, Scotland, Tyrrell, Vance, Wake, Warren, Washington, Wayne and Wilson.

For legal titles of parishes and diocesan institutions, consult the Chancery.

STATISTICAL OVERVIEW

Personnel	
Bishop	1
Priests: Diocesan Active in Diocese	67
Priests: Diocesan Active Outside Diocese	1
Priests: Retired, Sick or Absent	30
Number of Diocesan Priests	98
Religious Priests in Diocese	49
Total Priests in Diocese	147
Extern Priests in Diocese	24
Ordinations:	
Diocesan Priests	3
Transitional Deacons	2
Permanent Deacons in Diocese	73
Total Brothers	4
Total Sisters	32
Parishes	
Parishes	79
With Resident Pastor:	
Resident Diocesan Priests	47
Resident Religious Priests	24
Without Resident Pastor:	
Administered by Priests	8
Missions	18
Pastoral Centers	4
Professional Ministry Personnel:	
Brothers	4
Sisters	9
Welfare	
Special Centers for Social Services	12
Total Assisted	62,500
Educational	
Diocesan Students in Other Seminaries	26
Total Seminarians	26
High Schools, Diocesan and Parish	2
Total Students	1,612
High Schools, Private	1
Total Students	194
Elementary Schools, Diocesan and Parish	27
Total Students	7,447
Catechesis/Religious Education:	
High School Students	5,216
Elementary Students	15,745
Total Students under Catholic Instruction	30,240
Teachers in the Diocese:	
Priests	4
Sisters	5
Lay Teachers	621
Vital Statistics	
Receptions into the Church:	
Infant Baptism Totals	4,064
Minor Baptism Totals	1,139
Adult Baptism Totals	248
Received into Full Communion	273
First Communions	4,976
Confirmations	4,055
Marriages:	
Catholic	626
Interfaith	287
Total Marriages	913
Deaths	1,345
Total Catholic Population	237,281
Total Population	5,032,241

Former Bishops of Diocese—Most Revs. WILLIAM J. HAFEY, D.D., cons. June 24, 1925; transferred to the See of Scranton, PA, Oct. 2, 1937; installed Nov. 15, 1937; died May 12, 1954; EUGENE J. MCGUINNESS, D.D., cons. Dec. 21, 1937; transferred to the See of Oklahoma City and Tulsa, OK, Dec. 8, 1944; installed Jan. 10, 1945; died Dec. 27, 1957; VINCENT S. WATERS, D.D., cons. May 15, 1945; installed June 6, 1945; died Dec. 3, 1974; F. JOSEPH GOSSMAN, D.D., J.C.D., (Retired), ord. Dec. 17, 1955; appt. Titular Bishop of Aguntum and Auxiliary Bishop of Baltimore July 15, 1968; ord. Sept. 11, 1968; appt. Fourth Bishop of Raleigh April 8, 1975; installed May 19, 1975; retired June 8, 2006; died Aug. 12, 2013.; MICHAEL F. BURBIDGE, Ed.D., D.D., ord. May 19, 1984; appt. Auxiliary Bishop of Philadelphia and Titular Bishop of Cluain Iraird June 21, 2002; cons. Sept. 5, 2002; appt. Fifth Bishop of Raleigh June 8, 2006; installed Aug. 4, 2006; appt. fourth Bishop of Arlington Oct. 4, 2016; installed Dec. 6, 2016.

Former Bishops of Vicariate-Apostolic—His Eminence JAMES CARDINAL GIBBONS, D.D., consecrated Aug. 16, 1868, Titular Bishop of Adramyttum, first Vicar-Apostolic; transferred to Richmond, VA, July 30, 1872; promoted to the See of Baltimore, Oct. 3, 1877; created Cardinal-Priest of S. Maria in Trastevere, June 7, 1886; died March 24, 1921; Most Rev. JOHN J. KEANE, consecrated Bishop of Richmond and Vicar-Apostolic of North Carolina, Aug. 25, 1878; transferred to the Titular See of Jasso, Aug. 12, 1888; elevated to the Archepiscopal Dignity with the title of Archbishop of Damascus, Jan. 9, 1897; transferred to the See of Dubuque, July 24, 1900; resigned April 3, 1911; appt. Titular Archbishop of Cios, April 28, 1911; died June 23, 1918; Rt. Revs. H. P. NORTHROP, consecrated Titular Bishop of Rosalia and Vicar-Apostolic of North Carolina, Jan. 8, 1882; transferred to Charleston, Jan. 27, 1883; died June 7, 1916; LEO HAID, O.S.B., Vicar Apostolic of North Carolina and Abbot-Ordinary of Belmont Abbey; consecrated Titular Bishop of Messene, July 1, 1888; died July 24, 1924.

Office of the Bishop—7200 Stonehenge Dr., Raleigh, 27613-1620. Tel: 919-821-9731; Fax: 919-821-9779. Most Rev. LUIS RAFAEL ZARAMA, J.C.L.

Vicar General—7200 Stonehenge Dr., Raleigh, 27613-1620. Tel: 919-821-9708. Rev. Msgr. DAVID D. BROCKMAN, S.T.L., J.C.L.

Vicar Judicial & Chancellor—Rev. Msgr. GIRARD M. SHERBA, V.J., J.C.D., Ph.D., 7200 Stonehenge Dr., Raleigh, 27613-1620. Tel: 919-821-9756.

Chancery—7200 Stonehenge Dr., Raleigh, 27613-1620. Tel: 919-821-8145; Fax: 866-955-8449.

Chief Financial Officer / Chief Administrative Officer—MR. RUSSELL C. ELMAYAN, M.B.A., M.P.S., 7200 Stonehenge Dr., Raleigh, 27613-1620. Tel: 919-821-9704.

Deans—Very Revs. CARLOS N. ARCE, V.F., Albemarle; SCOTT E. MCCUE, V.F., Piedmont; JOHN E. MCGEE, O.S.F.S., V.F., Cape Fear; STEPHEN E. SHOTT, O.S.F.S., V.F., Fayetteville; THOMAS R. DAVIS, V.F., New Bern; KEVIN J. MOLEY, C.Ss.R., V.F., Newton Grove Deanery; Rev. Msgr. JEFFREY A. INGHAM, V.F., Raleigh; Very Rev. JEFFREY A. BOWKER, V.F., Tar River.

Diocesan Attorney—7200 Stonehenge Dr., Raleigh, 27613. Tel: 919-821-9728. MR. FRANK TORTORA III.

Diocesan Consultors—Rev. Msgr. DAVID D. BROCKMAN, S.T.L., J.C.L., V.G.; Rev. JAMES F. GARNEAU, Ph. D.; Rev. Msgr. JEFFREY A. INGHAM, V.F.; Very Rev. CARLOS N. ARCE, V.F.; Rev. SAMUEL JAMES BUCHHOLZ; Rev. Msgr. GIRARD M. SHERBA, V.J., J.C.D., Ph.D.

Diocesan Tribunal—7200 Stonehenge Dr., Raleigh, 27613-1620. Tel: 919-821-9759. All rogatorial commissions should be directed to the Tribunal.

Vicar Judicial—Rev. Msgr. GIRARD M. SHERBA, V.J., J.C.D., Ph.D.

Adjutant Vicar Judicial—VACANT.

Defenders of the Bond—MICHAEL DOIRON, J.C.D., Ph. D.; Revs. ARTHUR J. ESPELAGE, O.F.M., J.C.D.; THOMAS S. DUGGAN, J.C.L.; RAFAEL A. LEON-VALENCIA, J.C.L.

Promoter of Justice—VACANT.

Diocesan Judges—Rev. Msgr. DAVID D. BROCKMAN, S.T.L., J.C.L., V.G.; Rev. JAVIER CASTREJON, J.C.L., Ph.D., M.A., S.T.D.; Rev. Msgr. JOHN A. RENKEN, Ph.D., M.A., S.T.D., J.C.D.; Rev. JOSEPH G. MULRONEY, J.C.L.

Director of the Tribunal—MRS. VIKKI NEWELL.

Notaries—MRS. VIKKI NEWELL; MS. VERONICA ALVARADO TREJO; MRS. SUSAN STANTON; MRS. ANNE WOLFF; MRS. PAULA ZANKER.

Council of Priests—Revs. JAMES F. GARNEAU, Ph.D.; THOMAS S. TULLY; STEVEN R. PATTI, O.F.M.; Very Revs. STEPHEN E. SHOTT, O.S.F.S., V.F.; SCOTT E. MCCUE, V.F.; Rev. Msgr. JEFFREY A. INGHAM, V.F.; Revs. SAMUEL JAMES BUCHHOLZ; PHILIP R. HURLEY, S.J.; Very Revs. JOHN MCGEE, O.S.F.S., V.F.; CARLOS N. ARCE, V.F.; THOMAS R. DAVIS, V.F.; Rev. DONALD F. STAIB; Rev. Msgrs. GERALD LEWIS, (Retired); MICHAEL SHUGRUE; Very Revs. KEVIN J. MOLEY, C.Ss.R., V.F.; JEFFREY A. BOWKER, V.F. Ex Officio: Rev. Msgrs. DAVID D. BROCKMAN, S.T.L., J.C.L., V.G.; GIRARD M. SHERBA, V.J., J.C.D., Ph.D.; JOHN WILLIAMS, V.E.

Council of Women Religious—Sr. MARY JEAN KOREJWO, S.N.D.; Rev. Msgr. GIRARD M. SHERBA, V.J., J.C.D., Ph.D., Ex Officio; Sisters MARY ANN CZAJA, C.S.A.; CONSTANCE GILDER; CAROL MAROZZI, S.S.J.; MAXINE TANCRAITOR, C.D.P.; THERESINE GILDA, C.D.P.; JANET SCHEMMEL, S.N.D.; MARY JOSEPHINE ELY, I.H.M.; ROSEMARY G. MCNAMARA, S.U.

Vicar for Priests—Rev. Msgr. JOHN WILLIAMS, V.E.

Bishop's Delegate for Religious—Rev. Msgr. GIRARD M. SHERBA, V.J., J.C.D., Ph.D.

Diocesan Offices and Departments

All addresses are 7200 Stonehenge Dr., Raleigh, NC 27613-1620 unless noted otherwise.

Archives—Rev. Msgr. GERALD L. LEWIS, (Retired), Tel: 919-821-9709.

Information Technology—MR. STEPHEN WOLFE, Tel: 919-821-9766.

Stewardship and Advancement—Tel: 919-821-9721. VACANT, Exec. Dir. Devel.

Property and Construction—MR. ARTHUR WESCHE, Tel: 919-821-9726.

Catholic Charities of the Diocese of Raleigh, Inc.—Tel: 919-821-9752. MS. LISA E. PERKINS, M.S.W., L.C.S.W., Exec. Dir.

Catholic Formation and Education—DR. MICHAEL J. FEDEWA, Ed.D., Supt., Tel: 919-821-9748.

Campus Ministry—DR. MICHAEL J. FEDEWA, Ed.D., Dir., Office of Catholic Formation and Education, 7200 Stonehenge Dr., Raleigh, 27613-1620.

Evangelization and Discipleship—Tel: 919-821-9724. MRS. AMY DANIELS, D.Min., Exec. Dir.

Associate Director of Faith Formation—Tel: 919-821-9702. MR. PATRICK GINTY.

Associate Director of Marriage and Family Life—Tel: 919-821-9770. MR. GABRIEL HERNANDEZ.

Communications—Tel: 919-821-9732. MR. JOHN DORNAN, Dir.

NC Catholics Magazine—Tel: 919-821-9738. MRS. KATE TURGEON WATSON, Editor.

Web Administrator—MRS. MICHELLE KING, Tel: 919-821-9737.

Ecumenical Commission—Tel: 919-417-3264. Deacon BERTRAND PAUL L'HOMME.

Human Resources—MR. GARY ROSIA, Dir., Tel: 919-821-9711.

Office of African Ancestry Ministry and Evangelization—Tel: 919-821-9762. Rev. Msgr. JOSEPH K. NTUWA, Delegate.

Office for Child & Youth Protection—DR. JOHN A. PENDERGRASS, Dir., Tel: 866-535-7233; Tel: 866-535-7233.

Office of Hispanic Ministry—Rev. BILL JOHN ACOSTA-ESCOBAR, Delegate, Tel: 919-821-9738.

Office of Permanent Diaconate—Rev. JAMES F. GARNEAU, Ph.D., Dir., Tel: 919-658-4023.

Office for Vocations and Seminarian Formation—Rev. PHILIP M. TIGHE, Dir., 7200 Stonehenge Dr., Raleigh, 27613-1620. Tel: 919-832-6279.

Office of Divine Worship—7200 Stonehenge Dr., Raleigh, 27613-1620. Tel: 919-832-6281. Rev. JAMES SABAK, O.F.M.

Miscellaneous Offices—

Apostleship of the Sea—Rev. Msgr. FRANCIS R. MOESLEIN, (Retired), 2106 Joslyn Dr., Morehead City, 28557-9200. Tel: 252-726-3579.

Censor Librorum—VACANT.

Holy Childhood Pontifical Association—

Home Mission Society of the Diocese of Raleigh—7200 Stonehenge Dr., Raleigh, 27613. Tel: 919-658-4023. Rev. JAMES F. GARNEAU, Ph. D., Dir.

Pontifical Mission Societies in the United States—Rev. Msgr. DAVID D. BROCKMAN, S.T.L., J.C.L., V.G., Tel: 919-821-9708.

Victim Assistance Coordinator—MS. LOUISE DILLON, M.S.W., L.C.S.W., Tel: 919-790-8533.

CLERGY, PARISHES, MISSIONS AND PAROCHIAL SCHOOLS

CITY OF RALEIGH

(WAKE COUNTY)

1—HOLY NAME OF JESUS CATHEDRAL (1834)
219 W. Edenton St., 27603-1724. Tel: 919-832-6030; Email: info@hnojnc.org; Web: raleighcathedral.org. 715 Nazareth St., 27606. Rev. Msgr. David D. Brockman, S.T.L., J.C.L., Rector; Revs. John A. Kane, Parochial Vicar; Pedro Manuel Munoz Munoz, O.F.M.Cap., Parochial Vicar; Deacons Michael Boyd Alig; Juan Banda.
Sacred Heart Church, 200 Hillsborough St, 27603.
School—Cathedral School, (Grades PreK-8), 204 Hillsborough St., 27603. Tel: 919-832-4711; Fax: 919-832-8329; Email: cathedralschool@cathedral-school.net; Web: www.cathedral-school.net. Dr. Janice Jett, Prin. Lay Teachers 16; Students 245.
Catechesis Religious Program—Mrs. Andrea Blanco, Dir.; Mrs. Stacie Miller, Dir. Students 227.

2—CATHOLIC STUDENT CENTER (1974)
1720 Hillsborough St. LL One, 27605.
Tel: 919-301-8812; Email: Fr.Philip.Tighe@raldioc.org. Rev. Philip M. Tighe
Legal Name: Catholic Student Center, North Carolina State University
Doggett Center at Aquinas House—Tel: 919-833-9668.
Catechesis Religious Program—Students 2.

3—ST. FRANCIS OF ASSISI (1982) [CEM]
11401 Leesville Rd., 27613. Tel: 919-847-8205; Email: tresa.pickup@stfrancisraleigh.org; Web: www.stfrancisraleigh.org. Revs. Steven R. Patti, O.F.M.; Stephen E. Kluge, Parochial Vicar; James Sabak, O.F.M., Parochial Vicar.
Child Care—Pre-School, Tel: 919-847-8205, Ext. 240; Web: www.preschoolatstfrancis.com. Ms. Dawn Eagan, Prin. Lay Teachers 26; Students 220.
School—The Franciscan School, 10000 St. Francis Dr., 27613. Tel: 919-534-4837; Email: terri.layer@stfrancisraleigh.org; Web: www.franciscanschool.org. Michael Watson, Prin. Lay Teachers 47; Students 668.
Catechesis Religious Program—Jennifer Fiduccia, Dir., Formation & Evangelization. Students 3,888.

4—ST. JOSEPH (1968)
2817 Poole Rd., 27610. Tel: 919-231-6364; Email: P.st.joseph.raleigh@raldioc.org. Rev. Msgr. Jeffrey A. Ingham, V.F.; Rev. Lourduraj Alapaty, (India) In Res.; Deacon Stephen Lewandowski.
Res.: 2809 Poole Rd., 27610.
Catechesis Religious Program—Students 343.

5—ST. LUKE THE EVANGELIST (1985)
12333 Bayleaf Church Rd., 27614-9165.
Tel: 919-848-1533; Web: stlukesraleigh.org. Rev. Robert P. Staley, D.Min.; Deacon Michael Sanchez.
Catechesis Religious Program—Students 324.

6—OUR LADY OF LA VANG PARISH
11701 Leesville Rd., 27613. Tel: 919-307-4023; Email: queenmaria_2000@yahoo.com; Web: www.ducmelavangraleigh.org. Rev. Martin Tran Van Ban.

7—OUR LADY OF LOURDES (1954) [CEM]
2718 Overbrook Dr., 27608. Tel: 919-861-4600; Email: mhouse@ourladyoflourdescc.org; Web: ourladyoflourdescc.org. Very Rev. Dr. James F. Garneau, Ph.D., V.F.; Rev. Michael G. Schuetz, Parochial Vicar; Deacons Myles J. Charlesworth; D. Thomas Mack.
Res.: 2912 Anderson Dr., 27608.
Catechesis Religious Program—Students 202.

8—ST. RAPHAEL THE ARCHANGEL (1966) [CEM]
5801 Falls of Neuse Rd., 27609. Tel: 919-865-5700. Revs. Philip R. Hurley, S.J.; Bruce Bavinger, S.J., Parochial Vicar; Peter J. Murray, S.J., Parochial Vicar; Christopher Ryan, Parochial Vicar; Deacons Hector Velazco; Louis Philip Clark; John Robert Wetsch.
School—St. Raphael, (Grades K-8), 5815 Fall of Neuse Rd., 27609. Tel: 919-865-5750; Fax: 919-865-5751; Email: srcs@saintraphael.org; Web: saintraphaelschool.org. John Mihalyo, Prin. Lay Teachers 27; Students 384.
Child Care—St. Raphael Catholic Early Childhood Center, Carrie Griffith, Dir. Students 166.
Catechesis Religious Program—Students 917.

OUTSIDE THE CITY OF RALEIGH

AHOSKIE, HERTFORD CO., ST. CHARLES BORROMEO (1944)
122 NC 561 W, Ahoskie, 27910. Tel: 252-332-2939; Email: Fr.Michael.Burbeck@raldioc.org; Web: saintcharlescatholic.org. P.O. Box 605, Ahoskie, 27910. Rev. Michael J. Burbeck.
Catechesis Religious Program—Students 56.
Mission—St. Anne, 1715 Main St., Scotland Neck, Halifax Co. 27874. Tel: 252-332-2939; Email: Fr.Michael.Burbeck@raldioc.org. P.O. Box 605, Ahoskie, 27910.

APEX, WAKE CO.

1—ST. ANDREW THE APOSTLE (1983) [CEM]
3008 Old Raleigh Rd., Apex, 27502.
Tel: 919-362-0414; Web: www.saintandrew.org. Revs. John G. Durbin; Robert T. Schriber, Parochial Vicar; Deacon Richard Mickle.
Res.: 536 Metro Sta., Apex, 27502.
Catechesis Religious Program—Students 810.

2—ST. MARY MAGDALENE (1997)
625 Magdala Pl., Apex, 27502.
Tel: 919-657-4800, Ext. 7281; Fax: 919-657-4805; Email: info@stmm.net; Web: www.stmm.net. Rev. Donald F. Staib.
Catechesis Religious Program—Mrs. Suzanne Will, D.R.E.; Mrs. Elizabeth Sams, Youth Min.; Janine McGann, Youth Min. Students 1,221.

BURGAW, PENDER CO., ST. JOSEPH (1908) [CEM]
1303 Hwy. 117 S., Burgaw, 28425. Tel: 910-259-2601; Web: stjosephcatholicnc.org. Rev. Roger Malonda Nyimi, (Democratic Republic of Congo) Admin.
Catechesis Religious Program—Students 35.

BUTNER, GRANVILLE CO., ST. BERNADETTE (1957)
Parish House & Mailing Address: 311 Eleventh St., Butner, 27509. Tel: 919-575-4537; Email: st_bernadette@frontier.com; Web: myplace.frontier.com/~st_bernadette/index.html. 804 W. D St., Butner, 27509. Very Rev. Marcos Leon-Angulo, V.F., V.E., Admin.
Catechesis Religious Program—Students 127.

BUXTON, DARE CO., OUR LADY OF THE SEAS (1935) Mission; Parish Erected (2002)
Mailing Address: 48478 Hwy. 12, P.O. Box 399, Buxton, 27920. Tel: 252-995-6613; Fax: 252-995-6398; Email: olssecretary@aol.com; Web: www.ourladyoftheseas.org. Rev. Alfred J. Smuda, O.S.F.S.
Catechesis Religious Program—Students 18.

CARY, WAKE CO., ST. MICHAEL THE ARCHANGEL (1962)
804 High House Rd, Cary, 27513. Tel: 919-468-6100; Email: office@stmichaelcary.org; Web: www.stmichaelcary.org. Revs. Douglas Reed; James Labosky, Parochial Vicar; Joseph Kalu Oji, C.S.Sp., Parochial Vicar; Edisson Urrego Restrepo, Parochial Vicar; Rev. Msgr. John A. Wall, Pastor Emeritus, (Retired); Deacons Patrick Daniel Pelkey; Terry Mancuso; Brian John Phillips.
Res.: 1610 Castalia Dr., Cary, 27513.
Catechesis Religious Program—Students 1,347.
Mission—Blessed Teresa of Calcutta Mission, 10030 Green Level Church Rd., Ste. 802 #1092, Cary, 27513. Email: MtccFinAssist@gmail.com; Web: www.mtccary.org. Rev. Daniel B. Oschwald, Admin.

CASTLE HAYNE, NEW HANOVER CO., ST. STANISLAUS (1914) [CEM] (Polish)
4849 Castle Hayne Rd., Castle Hayne, 28429-4849.
Tel: 910-675-2336; Email: ststans4@ec.rr.com; Web: ststanislauscatholic.org. Rev. Roger Malonda Nyimi, (Democratic Republic of Congo) Admin.; Deacon Edwin Jeffress Jolly.
Catechesis Religious Program—Students 56.

CHAPEL HILL, ORANGE CO.

1—NEWMAN CATHOLIC STUDENT CENTER (1968)
218 Pittsboro St., Chapel Hill, 27516-2738.
Tel: 919-929-3730; Email: info@uncnewman.org; Web: uncnewman.org. Revs. Justin Ross, O.F.M.-Conv.; William J. Robinson, O.F.M.Conv., Parochial Vicar
Legal Name: Newman Catholic Student Center, University of North Carolina
Catechesis Religious Program—Students 92.

2—ST. THOMAS MORE (1940)
940 Carmichael St., Chapel Hill, 27514-4203.
Tel: 919-942-1040; Email: parishofficestaff@stmchapelhill.org; Web: stmchapelhill.org. Very Rev. Scott E. McCue, V.F.; Rev. Christopher Koehn, Parochial Vicar; Deacons Luis Royo; Stephen Yates; Robert Edward Troy Jr.; Mary Ellen McGuire, Pastoral Assoc.
Res. (Parochial Vicar): 211 McCauley St., Chapel Hill, 27516.
Rectory—301 Rossburn Way, Chapel Hill, 27516.
Catechesis Religious Program—Students 925.

CLAYTON, JOHNSTON CO., ST. ANN (1935)
4057 U.S. 70 Bus. Hwy. W., Clayton, 27520.
Tel: 919-934-2084; Email: st.ann.frontdesk@gmail.com; Web: www.st-annschurch.org. Revs. Peter A. Grace, C.P.; Philip G. Johnson, Parochial Vicar.
Catechesis Religious Program—Students 820.

CLINTON, SAMPSON CO., IMMACULATE CONCEPTION (1910)
104 E. John St., Clinton, 28328. Tel: 910-592-1384; Email: inri@icclintonnc.org; Web: www.icclintonnc.org. Revs. Joseph Dionne, C.Ss.R.; Mark B. Wise, C.Ss.R., Parochial Vicar.
Catechesis Religious Program—Students 116.
Mission—San Juan, 1710 Old U.S. Hwy. 701, Ingold, Sampson Co. 28446.

DUNN, HARNETT CO., SACRED HEART (1916)
106 S McKay Ave., Dunn, 28334. Tel: 910-891-1972; Web: www.shdunn.org. Mailing Address: P.O. Box 535, Dunn, 28335. Rev. Joseph G. Mulroney, J.C.L.
Res.: 311 S. Orange Ave., Dunn, 28334.
Catechesis Religious Program—Students 89.

DURHAM, DURHAM CO.

1—HOLY CROSS (1939) (African American)
2438 S. Alston Ave., Durham, 27713.
Tel: 919-957-2900; Email: office@holycrossdurham.org. Rev. Bart Karwacki; Deacon Phil Rzewnicki.
Res.: 510 Massey Ave., Durham, 27701.
Catechesis Religious Program—Students 72.

2—HOLY INFANT (1970) [CEM]
5000 Southpark Dr., Durham, 27713-9470.
Tel: 919-544-7135; Fax: 919-973-0071; Email: info@holyinfantchurch.org; Web: holyinfantchurch.org. Rev. Robert M. Rutledge, O.S.F.S.
Catechesis Religious Program—Tel: 919-973-0018. Ms. Lynn Sale, Pastoral Assoc. Students 150.

3—IMMACULATE CONCEPTION (1906)
Mailing Address: 901A W. Chapel Hill St., Durham, 27701. Tel: 919-682-3449; Email: info@icdurham.org; Web: www.icdurham.org. Revs. Christopher C. Van Haight, O.F.M.; Hugh Macsherry, Parochial Vicar;

Deacons Mario Gomez, O.F.M.Cap., Parochial Vicar; Laurence DeCarolis; Gerardo Chavez.
Res.: 720 Vickers Ave., Durham, 27701.
School—Immaculata Catholic School, (Grades PreK-8), 721 Burch Ave., Durham, 27701.
Tel: 919-682-5847; Fax: 919-956-7073; Email: corcorand@icdurham.org. Dana Corcoran, Prin. Lay Teachers 32; Students 460.
Catechesis Religious Program—Students 821.
4—ST. MATTHEW (1990) [CEM]
1001 Mason Rd., Durham, 27712. Tel: 919-479-1001; Email: saintmatthew@frontier.com; Web: www.stmatthewcc.org. Rev. Thanh N. Nguyen.
Rectory—7 Timbercreek Ct., Durham, 27712.
Catechesis Religious Program—Students 157.
EDENTON, CHOWAN CO., ST. ANNE (1858) [CEM]
207 N. Broad St., Edenton, 27932. Tel: 252-482-2617; Email: churchoffice@stanne-edenton.org; Web: edentoncatholic.weebly.com. Mailing Address: P.O. Box 422, Edenton, 27932. Very Rev. Carlos N. Arce, V.F.; Deacon Frank T. Jones III.
Catechesis Religious Program—Students 34.
Mission—All Souls, 917 Main St., Columbia, 27925.
ELIZABETH CITY, PASQUOTANK CO., HOLY FAMILY (1915)
1453 N. Road St., Elizabeth City, 27909.
Tel: 252-338-2521; Email: hfoffice@holyfamilyec.org. Revs. Nicholas Cottrill; Alberto Ortega, Parochial Vicar.
Catechesis Religious Program—Students 246.
Mission—St. Katharine Drexel, 154 Maple Rd., P.O. Box 64, Maple, Currituck Co. 27956.
Tel: 252-453-6035.
FARMVILLE, PITT CO., ST. ELIZABETH OF HUNGARY (1931)
Mailing Address: 3447 S. Contentnea St., Farmville, 27828-1686. Tel: 252-753-4367; Fax: 252-753-4400; Email: stelizabethoffarmville@gmail.com; Web: stelizabethoffarmville.org. 3455 S. Contentnea St., Farmville, 27828. Rev. Marco Antonio Gonzalez-Hernandez.
Catechesis Religious Program—Students 79.
FAYETTEVILLE, CUMBERLAND CO.
1—ST. ANDREW KIM (2000) (Korean)
1401 Valencia Dr., Fayetteville, 28303.
Tel: 910-630-2316; Fax: 910-487-8737; Email: Fr. Sanghyun.Lee@raldioc.org. Rev. Sanghyun Lee.
2—ST. ANN (1939) (African American)
361 N. Cool Spring St., Fayetteville, 28301.
Tel: 910-483-3216; Email: info@stanncatholicchurch.org; Web: www.stanncatholicchurch.org. Mailing Address: 357 N. Cool Spring St., Fayetteville, 28301. Very Rev. Stephen E. Shott, O.S.F.S., V.F.; Deacon Gary Stemple.
Res.: 228 Temple Ave., Fayetteville, 28301.
Catechesis Religious Program—365 N. Cool Spring St., Fayetteville, 28301. Tel: 910-483-3902; Email: principal@stanncatholicchurch.org; Web: www.stanncatholicschool.net. N. Rene Corders, Prin. Lay Teachers 14; Students 71.
3—ST. ELIZABETH ANN SETON (1981)
1000 Andrews Rd., Fayetteville, 28311.
Tel: 910-488-1797; Fax: 910-488-7116; Email: cjohnson@seaschurch.net; Web: www.seaschurch.net. Rev. John J. Kelly, O.S.F.S.
Catechesis Religious Program—Students 231.
4—ST. PATRICK (1824)
2840 Village Dr., Fayetteville, 28304.
Tel: 910-323-2410; Fax: 910-323-3006; Email: churchoffice@stpatnc.org; Web: stpatnc.org. Mailing Address: 2844 Village Dr., Fayetteville, 28304-3813. Very Rev. Gregory Lowchy, V.F.; Rev. Marlon Mendieta Rodas, Parochial Vicar; Deacon Vincent Joseph Mescall.
Res.: 433 Holly Ln., Fayetteville, 28305.
Catechesis Religious Program—Students 328.
FUQUAY-VARINA, WAKE CO., ST. BERNADETTE (1987) [CEM]
Mailing Address: 1005 Wilbon Rd., Fuquay-Varina, 27526-9702. Tel: 919-552-8758; Fax: 919-552-1846; Email: office@stbnc.net; Web: www.stbnc.net. Revs. Fernando Torres; Michael Coveyou, Parochial Vicar; Deacon Charles Edward Zlamal.
Catechesis Religious Program—Students 680.
Social Outreach Office—
GARNER, WAKE CO., ST. MARY, MOTHER OF THE CHURCH (1966)
1008 Vandora Springs Rd., Garner, 27529.
Tel: 919-772-5524; Email: smgoffice@stmarygarner.org; Web: www.stmarygarner.org. Revs. David M. Chiantella; Amaro Vasquez Ortiz, Parochial Vicar; Deacon Ronald Soriano.
Res.: 1408 Cane Creek Dr., Garner, 27529.
Catechesis Religious Program—Students 349.
GOLDSBORO, WAYNE CO., ST. MARY (1889)
1603 Edgerton St., Goldsboro, 27530-3141.
Tel: 919-734-5033; Email: office@saintmarygoldsboro.org; Web: www.saintmarygoldsboro.org. Rev. Roch T. Drozdzik, (Poland).
Catechesis Religious Program—Students 194.
GRAHAM, ALAMANCE CO., BLESSED SACRAMENT (1929)
Mailing Address: P.O. Box 619, Burlington, 27216.
Tel: 336-226-8796; Fax: 336-227-2896; Email: joe@blessedsacramentnc.org; Web: www.blessedsacramentnc.org. 1620 Hanford Rd., Graham, 27235. Revs. Paul D. Lininger, O.F.M.Conv.; Vincent P. Rubino, O.F.M.Conv.; Briant Cullinane, O.F.M.-Conv., Pastor Emeritus; Peter C. Tremblay, O.F.M.-Conv., In Res.; Deacon Leo Tapler.
Res.: 514 Parkview Dr., Burlington, 27215.
School—(Grades PreK-8), 515 Hillcrest Ave., Burlington, 27215. Tel: 336-570-0019; Fax: 336-570-9623; Email: office@bssknights.org; Web: www.bssknights.org. Mrs. Maria Gomez, Prin. Lay Teachers 20; Students 230.
Catechesis Religious Program—710 Koury Dr., Burlington, 27215. Tel: 336-226-8796, Ext. 308. Ann Imrick, D.R.E. Students 918.
GREENVILLE, PITT CO.
1—ST. GABRIEL (1936)
3250 Dickinson Ave., Greenville, 27834.
Tel: 252-758-1504; Email: secretarystgabriel@gmail.com; Web: www.stgabrielgreenville.org. Rev. Romen A. Acero.
Res.: 402 Trey Dr., Greenville, 27834.
Catechesis Religious Program—Students 169.
2—ST. PETER'S (1884)
2700 E. Fourth St., Greenville, 27858.
Tel: 252-757-3259; Email: parishoffice@spccnc.org; Web: www.saintpetercatholicchurch.org. Revs. Samuel James Buchholz; Ian C. Van Heusen, Parochial Vicar; Deacon Arthur Charles Schneider.
School—St. Peter's School, (Grades PreK-8), Tel: 252-752-3529; Email: djones@spcsnc.net; Web: www.stpeterscatholicschool.com. Douglas Jones, Prin. Lay Teachers 45; Students 432.
Catechesis Religious Program—Students 250.
HAMPSTEAD, PENDER CO., ALL SAINTS CATHOLIC CHURCH (1992)
18737 U.S. Hwy. 17 N., Hampstead, 28443.
Tel: 910-270-1477; Fax: 888-368-9203; Email: admin@allsaintsccnc.org; Web: www.allsaintsccnc.org. Rev. Msgr. Joseph K. Ntuwa. St. Jude the Apostle Catholic Church (Hampstead) and St. Mary Gate of Heaven Catholic Church (Surf City) merged.
Res.: 557 Osprey Dr., Hampstead, 28443.
Catechesis Religious Program—Students 190.
Mission—All Saints Catholic Church, 18737 U.S. Hwy. 17 N, Hampstead, Pender Co. 28443. Email: Msgr.Joseph.Ntuwa@raldioc.org. 420 N. Topsail Dr., Surf City, 28445.
HAVELOCK, CRAVEN CO., ANNUNCIATION (1953) [CEM]
Mailing Address: 246 E. Main St., Havelock, 28532-0720. Tel: 252-447-2112; Fax: 252-447-2113; Email: pastor@annunciationparish.org; Web: annunciationparish.org. Rev. William J. Upah, V.F.; Deacons Walter Calabrese; James Richard Strange.
Catechesis Religious Program—Students 150.
HENDERSON, VANCE CO., ST. JAMES (1995) [CEM] [JC]
Consolidated St. Paul and St. Catherine of Siena, Oxford merged to form St. James.
3275 Hwy. 158 Bypass, Henderson, 27536.
Tel: 252-438-3124; Email: stjamescath@embarqmail.com; Web: stjamescatholichenderson.org. Rev. Rafael A. Leon-Valencia, J.C.L.
Mission—St. Joseph the Worker, 842 U.S. Hwy. 158 W. Business, P.O. Box 934, Warrenton, Warren Co. 27589. Tel: 252-257-5605; Email: info@st-joseph-church.com; Web: www.st-joseph-church.com.
HILLSBOROUGH, ORANGE CO., HOLY FAMILY (1989)
Mailing Address: 216 Governor Burke Rd., Hillsborough, 27278. Tel: 919-732-1030; Email: office@hfch.org; Web: www.hfcch.org. Rev. Ryan W. Elder, Admin.
Rectory—700 Miller Rd., Hillsborough, 27278.
Catechesis Religious Program—Students 255.
HOPE MILLS, CUMBERLAND CO., GOOD SHEPHERD (1981)
5050 Oak St., Hope Mills, 28348. Tel: 910-425-1590; Email: gdshprd81@gmail.com. Rev. Thomas J. Gaul, Pastor Emeritus & Admin., (Retired).
Catechesis Religious Program—Patricia Martin-Kamionka, D.R.E. Students 122.
Mission—St. Isidore, 4733 Macedonia Church Rd., Fayetteville, Cumberland Co. 28312.
Tel: 910-424-2698. Deacon Juan Nay Henriquez, Pastoral Min./Coord.
JACKSONVILLE, ONSLOW CO., INFANT OF PRAGUE, CHURCH OF THE HOLY SPIRIT (1941)
210 Marine Blvd., Jacksonville, 28540.
Tel: 910-347-4196; Fax: 910-347-9338; Email: psecretary.iop@gmail.com; Web: iopnc.org. Mailing Address: 205 Chaney Ave., Jacksonville, 28540. Very Rev. Gregory D. Spencer, V.F.; Rev. Thomas S. Duggan, J.C.L., Parochial Vicar; Deacon James Anthony Marapoti.
Res.: 330 Mildred Ave., Jacksonville, 28540.
School—Infant of Prague, Church of the Holy Spirit School, (Grades PreK-8), 501 Bordeaux St., Jacksonville, 28540. Tel: 910-353-1300; Email: ioprincipal@gmail.com; Web: www.iopschool.net. Ms. Jennifer Cupsta, Prin. Lay Teachers 15; Students 155; Clergy / Religious Teachers 1.
Catechesis Religious Program—Students 427.
KINSTON, LENOIR CO., HOLY SPIRIT CATHOLIC CHURCH (1921) (Formerly Holy Trinity-Our Lady of the Atonement)
400 Academy Heights Rd., Kinston, 28504.
Tel: 252-523-8898; Fax: 252-527-9495; Email: hscatholicchurch@embarqmail.com; Web: www.hscatholicchurchkinston.com. P.O. Box 1455, Kinston, 28503. Rev. M. Arturo Cabra.
Res.: 137 Rae Rd., Kinston, 28504.
Catechesis Religious Program—Students 186.
KITTY HAWK, DARE CO., HOLY REDEEMER BY THE SEA (1937)
301 W. Kitty Hawk Rd., Kitty Hawk, 27949.
Tel: 252-261-4700; Fax: 252-261-1405; Email: info@obxcatholicparish.org; Web: obxcatholicparish.org. P.O. Box 510, Kitty Hawk, 27949. Revs. Dr. William F. Walsh, O.S.F.S.; John A. Hanley, O.S.F.S.
Res.: 109 Sunrise View, Kitty Hawk, 27949.
Res.: 101 E. Gulfstream Way, Nags Head, 27959.
Catechesis Religious Program—Students 145.
Station—Holy Trinity by the Sea Catholic Mission, 7335 Virginia Dare Tr., Nags Head, 27959. Email: contact@obxcatholicparish.org.
LAURINBURG, SCOTLAND CO., ST. MARY (1946) [JC]
Mailing Address: P.O. Box 1148, Laurinburg, 28353-1148. Tel: 910-276-4468; Fax: 910-276-9519; Email: st-mary-lbg@att.net; Web: www.stmary-laurinburg-nc.org. 800 S Main St, Laurinburg, 28352. Rev. John Alex Gonzalez; Deacon Alexander Vicent.
Catechesis Religious Program—Students 40.
LOUISBURG, FRANKLIN CO., OUR LADY OF THE ROSARY (1999) Mission of Saint Eugene Church, Wendell
2227 Hwy 39 N, PO Box 593, Louisburg, 27549.
Tel: 919-340-0556; Email: olrcatholic@gmail.com; Web: catholicolr.org. Rev. Marlee Abao, C.I.C.M., Admin.; Deacon Patrick Gerald McIlmoyle.
Catechesis Religious Program—Students 83.
LUMBERTON, ROBESON CO., ST. FRANCIS DE SALES (1938)
2000 E. Elizabethtown Rd., P.O. Box 2249, Lumberton, 28358. Tel: 910-739-4723; Fax: 910-739-5443; Email: office@stfrancisdesalescatholic.org; Web: www.stfrancisdesalescatholic.org. Rev. Zacharie Lukielo Tati.
Catechesis Religious Program—Students 106.
MOREHEAD CITY, CARTERET CO., ST. EGBERT (1929)
Arendal at 17th St., Morehead City, 28557.
Tel: 252-726-3559; Email: camedy@stegbert.org; Web: www.crystalcoastcatholic.org. 1706 Evans St., Morehead City, 28557. Very Rev. Thomas R. Davis, V.F.; Rev. Msgr. Francis R. Moeslein, Pastor Emeritus, (Retired); Joseph McKenzie, Pastoral Assoc.
Res.: 1612 Evans St., Morehead City, 28557.
Catechesis Religious Program—Students 200.
MOUNT OLIVE, DUPLIN CO., MARIA, REINA DE LAS AMERICAS, (Mary, Queen of the Americas)
Mailing Address: P.O. Box 978, Beulaville, 28518.
Tel: 910-298-4300; Email: mreinacatholic@gmail.com; Web: mariareinacatholic.org. 636 Whitfield Rd., Mount Olive, 28365. Revs. Bernard Kayimbw Mbay, C.I.C.M.; Eric Imbao, Parochial Vicar.
Res.: 208 Cavenaugh St., Beulaville, 28518.
Mission—St. Teresa del Nino Jesus, 206 Cavenaugh St., Beulaville, Duplin Co. 28518. Email: fr.bernard.mbay@raldioc.org; Web: santateresacatholic.org.
Catechesis Religious Program—Veronica Rivera, D.R.E.
MOUNT OLIVE, WAYNE CO., ST. MARY OF THE ANGELS (1916) [CEM] [JC]
3262 N. US Hwy 117 BYP, P.O. Box 1145, Mount Olive, 28365. Tel: 919-658-4023; Fax: 919-658-4023; Email: Amy.Breindel@raldioc.org; Web: stmarysmtolive.org. Rev. John J. Granados, Admin.; Deacon David William Kierski.
Catechesis Religious Program—Students 200.
NEW BERN, CRAVEN CO., ST. PAUL (1821) [CEM]
3005 Country Club Rd., New Bern, 28562.
Tel: 252-638-1984; Email: dconway@spccnb.org; Web: stpccnb.org. Revs. Thomas S. Tully; Robert L. Schmid Jr., Parochial Vicar; Deacons Frederick Melvin Fisher Jr.; Michael A. Mahoney; Sr. Monique Dissen, I.H.M., Pastoral Assoc.
School—St. Paul Catholic School, (Grades PreK-8), 3007 Country Club Rd., New Bern, 28562.
Tel: 252-633-0100; Fax: 252-633-4457; Email: info@stpaulcs.org; Web: stpaulcs.org. Deacon David William Kierski, Prin.; Kathleen Fisher, Librarian. Lay Teachers 13; Students 120; Clergy / Religious Teachers 2.
Catechesis Religious Program—Students 263.
Mission—St. Peter the Fisherman, 1149 White Farm Rd., Oriental, 28571. Tel: 252-249-3687.
NEW HILL, WAKE CO., ST. HA-SANG PAUL JUNG (1988)
3031 Holland Rd., Apex, 27502. Tel: 919-414-9256; Email: hellospjcc@gmail.com; Web: www.spjcc.org/xe/home. Rev. Jae Kim.
Catechesis Religious Program—Students 35.
NEWTON GROVE, SAMPSON CO., OUR LADY OF GUADALUPE (1871) [CEM]

211 Irwin Dr., P.O. Box 100, Newton Grove, 28366. Tel: 910-594-0287; Email: ologoffice@aol.com; Web: ourladyofguadalupenewtongrove.org. Very Rev. Kevin J. Moley, C.Ss.R., V.F.; Rev. Mark B. Wise, C.Ss.R., Parochial Vicar; Deacon Louise Vincent Parente.
Catechesis Religious Program—Students 314.
ORIENTAL, PAMLICO CO., SAINT PETER THE FISHERMAN (2000) [CEM] Mission of St. Paul, New Bern.
1149 White Farm Rd., Oriental, 28571.
Tel: 252-249-3687; Email: stpeteronc@embarqmail.com; Web: stpeteronc.org. Rev. Thomas S. Tully.
Catechesis Religious Program—Students 20.
PINEHURST, MOORE CO., SACRED HEART (1919)
300 Dundee Rd., Pinehurst, 28374.
Tel: 910-295-6550; Fax: 910-255-0299; Email: shrcc@sacredheartpinehurst.org; Email: Jeanne.ryan@sacredheartpinehurst.org; Web: sacredheartpinehurst.org. Very Rev. John F. Forbes, V.F.; Rev. Javier Castrejon, J.C.L., Ph.D., M.A., S.T.D., Parochial Vicar, Email: fr.javier.castrejon@raldioc.org; Deacon Guy Berry.
Child Care—Early Childhood Center,
Tel: 910-295-3514; Email: stephanie.hinds@sacredheartpinehurst.org. Stephanie Hinds, Dir. Students 30.
Catechesis Religious Program—Paul Abbe, D.R.E. Students 321.
Mission—Saint Juan Diego, 6963 Hwy. 705 S., Robbins, Moore Co. 27325.
PLYMOUTH, WASHINGTON CO., ST. JOAN OF ARC (1959)
506 E. Main St., P.O. Box 822, Plymouth, 27962.
Tel: 252-741-9335; Fax: 252-793-5315; Email: stjoanplymouth@gmail.com; Web: stjoanplymouth.org. Rev. Aaron Wessman; Julian Crespo, Pastoral Min./Coord.
Catechesis Religious Program—Students 43.
RAEFORD, HOKE CO., ST. ELIZABETH OF HUNGARY (1959)
6199 Fayetteville Rd., Raeford, 28376-0665.
Tel: 910-875-8803; Fax: 910-875-8802; Web: www.stelizabethofhungaryraeford-nc.org. P.O. Box 665, Raeford, 28376. Rev. JaVan Saxon.
Res.: 210 W. Elwood Ave., Raeford, 28376.
Catechesis Religious Program—Students 168.
RED SPRINGS, ROBESON CO., ST. ANDREW
301 Mercer Ave., P.O. Box 649, Red Springs, 28377.
Tel: 910-359-8022; Fax: 910-359-8077; Web: standrewredsprings.org. Rev. Giovanni de Jesus Romero Bermudez, Admin.
Res.: 518 S. Main St., Red Springs, 28377.
Station—Our Lady of Mount Carmel, Saint Pauls, 28384.
RIEGELWOOD, COLUMBUS CO., CHRIST THE KING (1964) (Hispanic)
Mailing Address: 1011 Eastwood Rd., Wilmington, 28403. Tel: 910-392-0720; Fax: 910-392-6777; Email: staffassistant@stmarkcatholicchurch.com; Web: www.stmarkcatholicchurch.com. 100 Burns Rd., Riegelwood, 28456. Rev. Patrick A. Keane.
Catechesis Religious Program—Students 10.
Mission—Christ the King, 100 Burns Rd., Riegelwood, 28456.
ROANOKE RAPIDS, HALIFAX CO., ST. JOHN THE BAPTIST (1931) [CEM]
900 Hamilton St., P.O. Box 116, Roanoke Rapids, 27870. Tel: 252-537-4667; Fax: 252-535-2076; Email: stjohnbaptist@hotmail.com; Web: saintjohnthebaptistcc.wordpress.com. Rev. Pius S. Wekesa, Admin.
Res.: 71 Dalton Ct., Roanoke Rapids, 27870.
Catechesis Religious Program—Students 66.
Station—Immaculate Conception, King St., Halifax, 27839.
ROCKY MOUNT, NASH & EDGECOMBE COS., OUR LADY OF PERPETUAL HELP (1892)
Mailing Address: 328 Hammond St., Rocky Mount, 27804. Tel: 252-972-0452; Fax: 252-972-4780; Email: church@olphrm.com; Web: www.olphrm.com. 331 Hammond St., Rocky Mount, 27804. Rev. Clyde Timberlake Meares.
Res.: 501 Hammond St., Rocky Mount, 27804.
Catechesis Religious Program—Students 155.
Mission—Immaculate Conception, 721 Virginia Ave., Rocky Mount, Nash & Edgecombe Cos. 27804.
ROXBORO, PERSON CO., STS. MARY AND EDWARD (1935)
611 N. Main St., Roxboro, 27573-5040.
Tel: 336-599-4122; Web: stmaryandedward.org. Rev. William H. Rodriguez.
Catechesis Religious Program—Students 43.
SANFORD, LEE CO., ST. STEPHEN THE FIRST MARTYR (1932) [CEM]
901 N. Franklin Dr., Sanford, 27330.
Tel: 919-766-1532; Email: secretaryststephen@earthlink.net; Web: www.ststephensanford.org. Revs. Robert F. Ippolito, M.S.; Hector LaChapelle, M.S., In Res.; Deacons Gustavo Castro-Reynoso; Mark Alan Westrick; Robert Lawrence Bridwell.
Res.: 2402 Wicker St., Sanford, 27330.
Catechesis Religious Program—Students 436.
SHALLOTTE, BRUNSWICK CO., ST. BRENDAN THE NAVIGATOR (1983) [JC]
5101 Ocean Hwy. W., Shallotte, 28470.
Tel: 910-754-8544; Fax: 910-755-6046; Email: brenavigator@atmc.net; Web: saintbrendan-shallotte.org. Mailing Address: P.O. Box 2984, Shallotte, 28459. Rev. Mark J. Betti; Deacons Andrew Robert McGahran; Thomas Kronyak.
Catechesis Religious Program—Students 79.
SILER CITY, CHATHAM CO., ST. JULIA (1961)
Mailing Address: 210 Harold Hart Rd., Siler City, 27344. Tel: 919-742-5584; Fax: 919-742-4917; Email: info@saintjulianc.org; Web: www.stjulianc.org. Rev. Julio Martinez.
Catechesis Religious Program—Students 250.
SMITHFIELD, JOHNSTON CO., ST. ANN (1935) See separate listing. See new location under Clayton, NC.
SOUTHERN PINES, MOORE CO., ST. ANTHONY OF PADUA (1895) [CEM]
Mailing Address: 175 E. Connecticut Ave., Southern Pines, 28387. Tel: 910-692-6613; Fax: 910-692-4964; Email: dwake@stanthonyparish.net; Web: www.stanthonyparish.net. 160 E. Vermont Ave, Southern Pines, 28387. Rev. M. Andrew McNair; Deacon Joseph Pius Piyasiri Gabriel.
Rectory—2952 Camp Easter Rd., Southern Pines, 28387.
School—St. John Paul II School, (Grades PreK-8), 2922 Camp Easter Rd., Southern Pines, 28387-0029. Tel: 910-692-6241; Fax: 910-692-2286; Email: kstepnoski@jp2catholicschool.org; Web: www.jp2catholicschool.org. Mr. John J. Donohue III, Prin. Lay Teachers 16; Students 155.
Catechesis Religious Program—Diana Wake, D.R.E. Students 175.
SOUTHPORT, BRUNSWICK CO., SACRED HEART (1941)
Mailing Address: 5269 Dosher Cutoff, S.E., Southport, 28461. Tel: 910-457-6173;
Fax: 910-457-6421; Email: sacheart@earthlink.net. Very Rev. John Victor Gournas, V.F.; Patricia Ciemnicki, Dir. Pastoral Svcs.
Res.: 213 Yaupon Dr., Southport, 28461.
Catechesis Religious Program—Students 65.
SWANSBORO, ONSLOW CO., ST. MILDRED (1947) [CEM]
653 Old Hammock Rd, Swansboro, 28584.
Tel: 910-326-5589; Email: stmildred@embarqmail.com; Web: www.stmildred.info. Mailing Address: 616 Sabiston Dr., Swansboro, 28584-9674. Rev. Donald G. Baribeau, M.S.
Catechesis Religious Program—Students 285.
TARBORO, EDGECOMBE CO., ST. CATHERINE OF SIENA (1897)
1004 St. David St., Tarboro, 27886.
Tel: 252-563-6096; Email: fr.raffo@raldioc.org; Web: stcatherinetarboro.org. Rev. Frank M. Raffo, Admin.
Catechesis Religious Program—Students 52.
WAKE FOREST, WAKE CO., ST. CATHERINE OF SIENA (1940)
520 W. Holding Ave., Wake Forest, 27587.
Tel: 919-570-0070; Web: www.scswf.org. Revs. Bill John Acosta Escobar; James Magee, Parochial Vicar; Deacon Bradley Evans Watkins.
Child Care—Early Childhood Center,
Tel: 919-556-4104.
WALLACE, DUPLIN CO., TRANSFIGURATION OF JESUS
506 E. Main St., P.O. Box 1601, Wallace, 28466.
Tel: 910-665-1530; Email: transfigurationofjesus.wallace@gmail.com; Web: www.transfigurationofjesusparish.org. Rev. Fernando Melendez Castaneda, Admin.; Deacon Michael Dean Vandiver.
Catechesis Religious Program—Students 51.
WASHINGTON, BEAUFORT CO., MOTHER OF MERCY (1963)
112 W. 9th St., Washington, 27889.
Tel: 252-946-2941; Email: momchurchnc@gmail.com. Rev. Brendan J. Buckler.
Res.: 412 Crown Dr., Washington, 27889.
Church: 111 W. Ninth St., Washington, 27889.
Catechesis Religious Program—Students 129.
WENDELL, WAKE CO., ST. EUGENE (1948)
608 Lions Club Rd., P.O. Box 188, Wendell, 27591.
Tel: 919-365-7114; Fax: 919-365-9431; Email: steugeneoffice@gmail.com; Web: www.catholicste.org. Rev. Archie Tacay; Bro. Emmanuel Mandona, Intern; Deacon Willie Foggie, (Retired).
Catechesis Religious Program—
Tel: 919-365-7114, Ext. 202; Email: steeducation@gmail.com. Sue Mahon, D.R.E. Students 367.
Mission—Our Lady of the Rosary, 2227 U.S. 401, Louisburg, 27549. Tel: 919-340-0556;
Fax: 919-340-0556; Email: olrcatholic@gmail.com.
WHITEVILLE, COLUMBUS CO., SACRED HEART (1938)
302 N Lee St., Whiteville, 28472. Tel: 910-642-3895; Email: P.SacredHeart.Whiteville@raldioc.org; Web: www.sacredheartwhiteville.org/. Rev. Joseph J. Yaeger.
Res.: 119 W. College St., Whiteville, 28472.
Catechesis Religious Program—Students 48.
Mission—Our Lady of the Snows, 701 W. Broad St., P.O. Box 1766, Elizabethtown, Bladen Co. 28337-1766. Tel: 910-862-4998; Fax: 910-862-7298. Ms. Joan Marion, Pastoral Min./Coord.
WILLIAMSTON, MARTIN CO., HOLY TRINITY (1951)
P.O. Box 894, Williamston, 27892. Tel: 252-332-2939; Fax: 252-792-4091; Web: www.williamstoncatholic.org. 830 E Boulevard (Hwy17/13), Williamston, 27892. Rev. John Brown.
Catechesis Religious Program—Students 20.
WILMINGTON, NEW HANOVER CO.
1—BASILICA SHRINE OF SAINT MARY (1912)
220 S. 5th Ave., Wilmington, 28401.
Tel: 910-762-5491; Email: secretary@thestmaryparish.org; Web: www.thestmaryparish.org. Mailing Address: 412 Ann St., Wilmington, 28401. Revs. Ryszard Kolodziej; Francisco Javier Garcia Gonzalez, Parochial Vicar.
Catechesis Religious Program—Students 388.
2—IMMACULATE CONCEPTION (1925)
6650 Carolina Beach Rd., Wilmington, 28412.
Tel: 910-791-1003; Fax: 910-791-0081; Email: Info@iccwilm.org; Web: www.iccwilm.org. Very Rev. John E. McGee, O.S.F.S., V.F.
Catechesis Religious Program—Email: Lfetzer@iccwilm.org. Mrs. Loraine Fetzer, D.R.E. Students 129.
3—ST. MARK (1978)
1011 Eastwood Rd., Wilmington, 28403.
Tel: 910-392-0720; Email: staffassistant@stmarkcatholicchurch.com; Web: stmarkcatholicchurch.com. Revs. Patrick A. Keane; Cesar Torres Martinez, Parochial Vicar.
Catechesis Religious Program—Students 261.
Mission—Christ the King, 100 Burns Rd., Riegelwood, Columbus Co. 28456-0155.
WILSON , WILSON CO.
1—ST. ALPHONSUS DE LIGUORI, Closed. For sacramental records contact St. Therese, Wilson.
2—CHURCH OF ST. THERESE (1923)
700 Nash St., N.E., Wilson, 27893-3047.
Tel: 252-237-3019; Email: st.therese.wilson@gmail.com. Very Rev. Jeffrey A. Bowker, V.F.; Rev. Paul W. Brant, S.J.; Deacon Michel du Sablon.
Res. & Rectory: 3311 Berkshire Dr., Wilson, 27896.
Catechesis Religious Program—Students 440.
WINDSOR, BERTIE CO., HOLY SPIRIT CATHOLIC CHURCH (2004)
Mailing Address: 403 Belmont St., P.O. Box 1394, Windsor, 27983. Tel: 252-794-5086; Email: aaronwessman@hotmail.com; Web: holyspiritwindsor.org. Rev. Aaron Wessman.
Catechesis Religious Program—Students 5.
WRIGHTSVILLE BEACH, NEW HANOVER CO., ST. THERESE (1939)
209 S. Lumina Ave., Wrightsville Beach, 28480.
Tel: 910-256-2471; Email: office@catholicwb.org; Web: www.catholicwb.org. Rev. Trent L. Watts.
Catechesis Religious Program—Email: formation@catholicwb.org. Students 60.

Special Assignment:
Rev. Msgr.—
Clay, Michael G., D.Min., Faculty School of Theology & Religious Studies at The Catholic University of America, Washington, DC 20069.

Absent on Leave:
Revs.—
DeCandia, Anthony
Fitzgerald, R. Martin, Chap. Lt. Col.
Ospina-Briceno, Walter.

Retired:
Rev. Msgrs.—
Leach, Phillip, (Retired), 202-1835 Barclay St., Vancouver, BC Canada V6G 1K7
Lewis, Gerald L., (Retired), 7200 Stonehenge Dr., 27613. Tel: 919-376-3911
Moeslein, Francis R., (Retired), 2106 Joslyn Dr., Morehead City, 26557-9200. Tel: 252-726-3579
Shugrue, Michael P., (Retired), 2651 Mellow Field Dr., 27604
Wall, John A., (Retired), 1418 Castalia Dr., Cary, 27513
Williams, John J., (Retired), P.O. Box 1, Paint Bank, VA 24131
Very Revs.—
Carlson, Steven V., V.F., (Retired), 465 Lands End, East Fayetteville, 28314
Kus, Robert J., (Retired), Honduras
Ruede, Ernest, V.F., (Retired), 210 Hayden Pl., Jacksonville, 28540
Revs.—
Burch, Edward, (Retired), 538 Rockwood Dr., Graham, 27253
Collins, Terrence, (Retired), P.O. Box 729, Hampstead, 28443
Diegelman, Robert W., (Retired), 2673 Hitchcock Dr., Durham, 27705

Gaul, Thomas J., (Retired), 5407 Gales St., Hope Mills, 28348. Tel: 910-426-3728
Ghisalberti, Giacomo G., (Retired), P.O. Box 70338, Myrtle Beach, SC 29572
Gillespie, John, (Retired), 300 Waters Dr., Apt. B-205, Southern Pines, 28387
Grabowski, Eugene M., (Retired), 116 Sutton Dr., Cape Carteret, 28584. Tel: 252-762-3330
Kelly, John R., (Retired), 779 Galloway Dr., Fayetteville, 28303. Tel: 910-867-2803
Lawson, Douglas J., (Retired), 1449 South Shore Dr., Southport, 28461. Tel: 910-845-2353
Maloney, Francis G., (Retired), 590 Central Ave., Villa F.3, Southern Pines, 28387. Tel: 910-246-2123
Parker, Kenneth, (Retired), 704 McIntosh Rd., Carthage, 28327. Tel: 910-245-4640
Perry, Francis, (Retired), P.O. Box 506, La Grange, 28551
Pitts, William L., V.F., (Retired), P.O. Box 3645, Pinehurst, 27374
Richardson, John L., (Retired), 592 Central Dr., Villa F., Southern Pines, 28387. Tel: 910-579-8270
Smiley, Douglas J., (Retired), 109 Grayton Ln., Enterprise, AL 36330
Turner, Richard W., (Retired), P.O. Box 1039, Spring Hope, 27882. Tel: 252-475-3360
Woodhall, Jonathan A., (Retired), 200 Waters Dr., Apt. A-218, Southern Pines, 28387. Tel: 919-412-3388.

Permanent Deacons:
Alig, Michael Boyd, Holy Name of Jesus Cathedral
Andrews, Stephen William, Saint Francis of Assisi, Raleigh
Baffa, John Thomas, St. Brendan the Navigator, Shallotte
Banda, Jose Juan, Holy Name of Jesus Cathedral, Raleigh
Bandiera, Albert, St. Ann, Clayton
Berry, Guy, Sacred Heart, Pinehurst
Bridwell, Robert Lawrence, St. Stephen, the First Martyr, Sanford
Calabrese, Walter, Annunciation, Havelock
Campos, Juan Carlos, Saint Elizabeth of Hungary, Raeford
Castro-Reynoso, Gustavo, Saint Stephen, the First Martyr, Sanford
Champagne, Byron M., Our Lady of Lourdes, Raleigh
Charlesworth, Myles, Our Lady of Lourdes, Raleigh
Chavez, Gerardo, Immaculate Conception, Durham
Clark, Louis Philip, St. Raphael the Archangel, Raleigh
DeCarolis, Laurence, Immaculate Conception, Durham
du Sablon, Michel, St. Therese, Wilson
Evans, Forest
Fatica, Gerald, St. Mildred, Swansboro
Ferrer, Ramon de los Reyes, Saint Patrick, Fayetteville
Fisher, Frederick Melvin Jr., St. Paul, New Bern
Foggie, Willie, St. Eugene, Wendell
Gabriel, Joseph Pius Piyasiri, St. Anthony of Padua, Southern Pines
Hackett, James, St. Paul, New Bern
Henriquez, Juan Nay, St. Isidore Mission, Stedman
Hoffert, Daniel, St. Andrew, Mars Hills
James, Webster A.
Jolly, Edwin Jeffress, St. Stanislaus, Castle Hayne
Jones, Frank T. III, St. Anne, Edenton
Kierski, David William, St. Mary of the Angels, Mount Olive
Kronyak, Thomas, Saint Brendan the Navigator, Shallotte
L'Homme, Bertrand Paul, Holy Family, Hillsborough
Lacina, Dick, (Retired)
LaPierre, Joseph, St. Mary Magdalene, Apex
Lewandowski, Stephen, St. Joseph, Raleigh
Mack, Tom, Our Lady of Lourdes, Raleigh
Mahoney, Michael A., St. Paul, New Bern
Mancuso, Terry, St. Michael the Archangel, Cary
Marapoti, James Anthony, Infant of Prague, Jacksonville
McGahran, Andrew Robert, St. Brendan, Shallotte
McIlmoyle, Patrick Gerald, Our Lady of the Rosary, Louisburg
Meier, Anthony
Mejia, Emilio, St. Stephen the First Martyr, Sanford
Mescall, Vincent Joseph, St. Patrick, Fayetteville
Mickle, Richard, St. Andrew the Apostle, Apex
Nguyen, Anthony Hoang, Our Lady of LaVang, Raleigh
Oguledo, Valentine, St. Mary, Laurinburg
Parente, Louise Vincent, Our Lady of Guadalupe, Newton Grove
Pelkey, Patrick Daniel, St. Michael the Archangel, Cary
Phillips, Brian John, St. Michael the Archangel, Cary
Porter, Thomas, St. Anthony of Padua, Southern Pines
Price, Robert, Transfiguration of Jesus, Wallace
Royo-Camacho, Luis Alfonso, Saint Thomas More, Chapel Hill
Rzewnicki, Phil, Holy Cross, Durham
Saez, Felix Jr., Our Lady of Lourdes, Raleigh
Sanchez, Michael, St. Luke the Evangelist, Raleigh
Schneider, Arthur Charles, St. Peter, Greenville
Schoebel, James, (Retired)
Snyder, Patrick, Good Shepherd, Hope Mills
Soriano, Ronald, St. Mary, Mother of the Church, Garner
Stemple, Gary, St. Ann, Fayetteville
Stonikinis, George, Holy Family, Elizabeth City
Strange, James Richard, Annunciation, Havelock
Tapler, Leopold, Blessed Sacrament
Troy, Robert Edward Jr., St. Thomas More, Chapel Hill
Vandiver, Michael Dean, Transfiguration of Jesus, Wallace
Velazco Bonilla, Hector, St. Raphael the Archangel, Raleigh
Vicent Martinez, Juan Alexander, St. Mary, Laurinburg
Vikor, Desider, St. Matthew, Durham
Walsh, Michael, Mission of St. Teresa of Calcutta, Cary
Watford, Scott, New Hanover Detention Facility
Watkins, Bradley Evans, St. Catherine of Siena, Wake Forest
Welch, James, (Retired)
Westrick, Mark Alan, St. Stephen the First Martyr, Sanford
Wetsch, John Robert, St. Raphael the Archangel, Raleigh
Yates, Stephen, St. Thomas More, Chapel Hill
Zlamal, Charles Edward, St. Bernadette, Fuquay-Varina.

INSTITUTIONS LOCATED IN DIOCESE

[A] HIGH SCHOOLS

RALEIGH. *Cardinal Gibbons High School* (1909) 1401 Edwards Mill Rd., 27607. Tel: 919-834-1625; Fax: 919-834-9771; Email: jcurtis@cghsnc.org; Web: www.cghsnc.org. Mr. Jason D. Curtis, Prin.; Tripp Reade, Librarian & Media Specialist. Lay Teachers 95; Priests 1; Sisters 2; Students 1,520; Total Staff 149; Clergy/Religious Teachers 1.

GREENVILLE. *St. John Paul II Catholic High School*, 2725 E. 14th St., Greenville, 27858. Tel: 252-215-1224; Email: cconticchio@jp2highschool.com; Web: www.jp2highschool.com. 3250A Dickinson Ave., Greenville, 27834. Craig Conticchio, Prin. Lay Teachers 14; Spiritual Director 1; Students 60.

[B] HIGH SCHOOLS-PRIVATE

RALEIGH. *St. Thomas More Academy*, 3109 Spring Forest Rd., 27616. Tel: 919-878-7640; Fax: 919-878-7641; Email: admissions@stmacademy.org; Web: www.stmacademy.org. Deacon Bradley Evans Watkins, Headmaster. Deacons 1; Lay Teachers 4; Students 180; Clergy/Religious Teachers 1.

[C] CHILD CARE CENTERS

RALEIGH. *St. Raphael Preschool*, 5801 Falls of the Neuse Rd., 27609. Tel: 919-865-5717; Fax: 919-865-5701; Email: bjcady@saintraphael.org; Web: straphaelpreschool.org. Molly DeAngelo, Dir. Lay Teachers 14; Students 163.

APEX. *Saint Andrew Early Childhood Center*, 3008 Old Raleigh Rd., Apex, 27502. Tel: 919-387-8656; Fax: 919-362-5778; Email: ecc@saintandrew.org; Web: www.saintandrew.org. Nancy Wujek, Prin. Students 108; Total Staff 19.

CARY. *St. Michael Early Childhood Center* (1983) 804 High House Rd., Cary, 27513. Tel: 919-468-6110; Fax: 919-468-6130; Email: preschool@stmcary.org; Web: www.stmichaelcary.org. Mrs. Lisa Ciesla, Prin. Students 160; Total Staff 21.

[D] GENERAL HOSPITALS

SOUTHERN PINES. *St. Joseph of the Pines*, 100 Gossman Dr., Ste. B, Southern Pines, 28387. Tel: 910-246-3100; Email: lportfleet@sjp.org; Web: www.sjp.org. Lori Portfleet, Pres.
St. Joseph of the Pines, Inc.

[E] CATHOLIC SOCIAL SERVICES

RALEIGH. *Catholic Charities of the Diocese of Raleigh, Inc.*, 7200 Stonehenge Dr., 27613-1620. Tel: 919-821-9750; Fax: 919-821-9712; Email: lisa.perkins@raldioc.org; Web: catholiccharitiesraleigh.org. Ms. Lisa E. Perkins, M.S.W., L.C.S.W., Dir. Tot Asst. Annually 63,000; Total Staff 55.
Raleigh Office, 3000 Highwoods Blvd., Ste. 128, 27604. Tel: 919-790-8533; Fax: 919-790-8836; Email: donna.walker@raldioc.org. Rick Miller-Haraway, L.C.S.W., Dir. Total Staff 17.
Cape Fear Office, 20 N. 4th St. Ste. 300, Harrelson Center, Wilmington, 28401. Tel: 910-251-8130; Fax: 910-251-8491; Email: Emilie.Hart@raldioc.org. Emilie Hart, M.S.W., L.C.S.W.A., Dir. Total Staff 4.
Piedmont Office, 3711 Univ. Dr., Ste. B, Durham, 27707. Tel: 919-286-1964; Fax: 919-286-4001; Email: barbara.mazza@raldioc.org. Jeremy Ireland, M.A., Dir. Total Staff 3.
Fayetteville Office, 726 Ramsey St., Ste. 10 & 11, Fayetteville, 28301. Tel: 910-424-2020; Fax: 910-424-8435; Email: wanda.collaza@raldioc.org. Wanda I. Collazo, M.A., L.P.C., Dir. Total Staff 7.
New Bern Office, 502 Middle St., New Bern, 28560. P.O. Box 826, New Bern, 28563. Tel: 252-638-2188 ; Fax: 252-638-2417; Email: agnes.barber@raldioc.org. Agnes Barber, Dir. Total Staff 3.
Tar River Office, 2780 B Dickinson Ave., Greenville, 27834. Tel: 252-355-5111; Fax: 252-355-1088; Email: maria.bick@raldioc.org. Ethel Higgins, Dir. Total Staff 5.
Albemarle Office, 113 Market St., Hertford, 27944. Tel: 252-426-7717; Fax: 252-426-8189; Email: Maria.Rogers@raldioc.org. Daniel Altenau, Dir. Total Staff 2.
Newton Grove Office, 4057 US-70 BUS, Clayton, 27520. Tel: 919-821-9750; Email: gabby.amos@raldioc.org. Ms. Lisa E. Perkins, M.S.W., L.C.S.W., Dir.

[F] MONASTERIES AND RESIDENCE OF PRIESTS AND BROTHERS

RALEIGH. *Jesuit Community* (1996) 5801 Falls of the Neuse Rd., 27609. Tel: 919-865-5700; Fax: 919-865-5701; Email: pastorsoffice@saintraphael.org; Web: www.saintraphael.org. Priests 6.
Jesuits in Eastern North Carolina: Revs. Bruce Bavinger, S.J.; Paul W. Brant, S.J.; Philip R. Hurley, S.J.; Matthew S. Monnig, S.J.

BURLINGTON. *Conventual Franciscans*, Blessed Sacrament Church, 1236 Westbrook Ave., Elon, 27244. Tel: 336-446-6753; Fax: 336-227-2896; Email: catholic@netpath.net; Web: www.blessedsacramentnc.org. Revs. Briant Cullinane, O.F.M.Conv.; Paul D. Lininger, O.F.M.Conv.; Vincent P. Rubino, O.F.M.Conv. Total in Residence 4.

PITTSBORO. *Our Lady of Guadalupe Friary*, 1983 Thompson Street, Pittsboro, 27312. Tel: 919-545-5600; Fax: 919-545-5650; Email: aljumar11@yahoo.com; Web: www.franciscanseast.org. P.O. Box 1638, Pittsboro, 27312. Rev. Julio Martinez, Contact Person; Bro. Raymond Sobocinski, Supr.

[G] CONVENTS AND RESIDENCES FOR SISTERS

RALEIGH. *Congregation of the Sisters of the Holy Cross*, 2017 Quail Forest Dr., 27609. Tel: 919-878-0741; Email: sbrennan@cscsisters.org. Sr. Suzanne Brennan, Treas. A Place for Women to Gather
Sisters of the Holy Cross, Inc. Sisters 2.
A Place for Women to Gather, 8380 Six Forks Rd. #201, 27615. Tel: 919-846-3601; Email: sbrennan@cscsisters.org. Sr. Suzanne Brennan, Treas.
Sisters of the Holy Cross, Inc.
Sisters, Servants of the Immaculate Heart of Mary, 1012 Tyrrell Rd., 27609. Tel: 919-803-3363. Sisters 5.

CHAPEL HILL. *Sisters, Servants of the Immaculate Heart of Mary*, 1194 Great Ridge Pkwy., Chapel Hill, 27516. Tel: 919-240-5612 (Home); Tel: 919-490-5253 (Office); Email: cgellings@aol.com; Web: ihmsisters.org. Sisters 2.

DURHAM. *Sisters of St. Francis of Philadelphia* (1855) 724 Mason Rd., Durham, 27712. Tel: 919-451-3429 ; Email: damian711@nc.rr.com. Sisters 1.

JACKSONVILLE. *Sisters of St. Ursula* (1606) 518 East Ct., Jacksonville, 28546. Tel: 910-389-1742; Email: bmcady@aol.com. Mailing Address: 205 Chaney Ave., Jacksonville, 28540. Sisters 1.

NEW BERN. *St. Paul Convent*, 210 Tobiano Dr., New Bern, 28562. Tel: 252-675-0333; Email: IMHERE4U@suddenlink.net. Sisters 1; Total in Residence 1.

TARBORO. *Congregation of St. Agnes* (1858) 4934 Howard Ave. Ext., Tarboro, 27886.
Tel: 252-823-0540; Email: tcoutreach@tarboronc.com; Web: csasisters.org. Sisters 1.

[H] RETREAT HOUSES

DURHAM. *Avila Retreat Center* (1980) 711 Mason Rd., Durham, 27712-9229. Tel: 919-985-3015; Email: avila@raldioc.org; Web: www.avila-retreat-center.com. Max Martin, Dir. Total in Residence 1; Total Staff 7.

[I] COLLEGE CAMPUS MINISTRY CENTERS

RALEIGH. *Doggett Center for Catholic Campus Ministry at Aquinas House*, North Carolina State University, 1720 Hillborough St., 27605.
Tel: 919-301-8812; Email: doggett.priest@gmail.com; Web: www.ccmraleigh.org. Rev. Philip M. Tighe, Chap. Parish Population 330.

CHAPEL HILL. *Newman Catholic Student Center*, 218 Pittsboro St., Chapel Hill, 27516.
Tel: 919-929-3730; Email: info@uncnewman.org; Web: www.uncnewman.org. Revs. Justin Ross, O.F.M.Conv.; William J. Robinson, O.F.M.Conv.

DURHAM. *Duke Catholic Center*, Box 90976, Durham, 27708. Tel: 919-684-3354; Email: catholic@duke.edu; Web: catholic.duke.edu. 404 Chapel Dr., Page Bldg., Ste. 309, Durham, 27708. Revs. Michael T. Martin, O.F.M.Conv., Dir.; Brad Heckathorne, O.F.M.Conv., Assoc. Dir.; Sisters Marcia Ternes, D.R.E.; Mary Agnes Ryan, I.H.M., Dir.; Catherine Preston, Campus Min., Faith Formation; Ruth Anne Kennedy, Business Mgr.; Michelle Sutton, Devel. Dir.; Andrew Witchger, Music Dir.; Emma Miller, Communication Dir.; Evan Wescott, Peer Ministry Coord.; Michelle Naehring, Devel. Asst.

ELON. *Elon University* (1889) Catholic Campus Ministry, Campus Box 2960, Elon, 27244-2010.
Tel: 336-278-7355; Fax: 336-278-7439; Email: ptremblay@elon.edu; Web: org.elon.edu/ccm. Mr. Trung Huynh-Duc, Dir.; Rev. Peter C. Tremblay, O.F.M.Conv., Campus Min. & Assoc. Chap., Catholic Life.

GREENVILLE. *Newman Catholic Student Center at East Carolina University* (1948) 953 E. 10th St., Greenville, 27858. Tel: 252-757-1991;
Fax: 252-757-1991; Email: chaplin@ecunewman.org; Email: assistant@ecunewman.org; Web: www.ecunewman.org. Rev. Ian C. Van Heusen, Dir.

WILMINGTON. *Newman Catholic Student Center* (1986) 4802 College Acres Dr., Wilmington, 28402.
Tel: 910-792-0507; Fax: 910-792-0507; Email: mcnamarar@uncw.edu; Web: www.newman-uncw.org. University of North Carolina at Wilmington, UNC-W Station, P.O. Box 20044, Wilmington, 28407. Sr. Rosemary G. McNamara, S.U., Dir. & Campus Min.

[J] MISCELLANEOUS

RALEIGH. *Catholic Housing Corporation*, 7200 Stonehenge Dr., 27613-1620. Tel: 919-821-9704; Fax: 919-821-9705; Email: elmayan@raldioc.org.

Catholic Parish Outreach, 2013 N. Raleigh Blvd., 27604. Tel: 919-873-0245; Fax: 919-873-0260; Email: cpo@raldioc.org; Web: www.cporaleigh.org. Rick Miller-Haraway, L.C.S.W., Dir. Catholic Parish Outreach is a program of Catholic Charities of the Diocese of Raleigh Tot Asst. Annually 100,000; Total Staff 4; Average Assisted Per Month 8,700.

The Clergy Retirement Plan of Diocese of Raleigh, 7200 Stonehenge Dr., 27613-1620.
Tel: 919-821-9711; Fax: 919-821-9712; Email: gary.rosia@raldioc.org; Web: www.dioceseofraleigh.org.

The Foundation of the Roman Catholic Diocese of Raleigh, Inc., 7200 Stonehenge Dr., 27613.
Tel: 919-821-9707; Email: shane.nolan@raldioc.org. Mr. Shane Nolan, B.A., Dir.

Vocations Office, 7200 Stonehenge Dr., 27613-1620.
Tel: 919-832-6280; Fax: 919-832-9723; Email: Fiorella.simonidecannon@raldioc.org; Email: fr.philip.tighe@raldioc.org; Web: raleighvocations.org. Rev. Philip M. Tighe, Dir.

FAYETTEVILLE. *LIFE St. Joseph of the Pines, Inc.*, 4900 Raeford Rd., Fayetteville, 28304.
Tel: 910-483-4911; Email: lifefay@sjp.org; Web: www.trinityhealthseniorcommunities.org/pace. Lori Portfleet, Pres.

SOUTHERN PINES. *St. Joseph of the Pines Retirement Villa*, 100 Gossman Dr., Ste. B, Southern Pines, 28387. Tel: 910-246-1000; Email: info@sjp.org; Web: www.sjp.org. Lori Portfleet, Pres.

St. Joseph of the Pines, Inc., 100 Gossman Dr., Ste. B, Southern Pines, 28387. Tel: 910-246-1000; Email: lportfleet@sjp.org; Web: www.sjp.org. Lori Portfleet, Pres.
St. Joseph of the Pines, Inc.

RELIGIOUS INSTITUTES OF MEN REPRESENTED IN THE DIOCESE

For further details refer to the corresponding bracketed number in the Religious Institutes of Men or Women section.

[0650]—*Congregation of the Holy Spirit*—C.S.Sp.
[]—*Congregation of the Mother of the Redeemer* (US Assumption Prov.)—C.R.M.
[1000]—*Congregation of the Passion*—C.P.
[0480]—*Conventual Franciscans*—O.F.M.Conv.
[0520]—*Franciscan Friars*—O.F.M.
[0570]—*Glenmary Home Missioners*—G.H.M.
[0690]—*Jesuit Fathers and Brothers* (Maryland & New York Provs.)—S.J.
[0720]—*The Missionaries of Our Lady of La Salette*—M.S.
[0860]—*Missionhurst Congregation of the Immaculate Heart of Mary*—C.I.C.M.
[0920]—*Oblates of St. Francis De Sales* (American Prov.)—O.S.F.S.
[]—*Redemptorists*—C.Ss.R.

RELIGIOUS INSTITUTES OF WOMEN REPRESENTED IN THE DIOCESE

[3710]—*Congregation of the Sisters of Saint Agnes*—C.S.A.
[1920]—*Congregation of the Sisters of the Holy Cross*—C.S.C.
[]—*Daughters of St. Mary of Guadalupe*—D.S.M.G.
[0960]—*Daughters of Wisdom*—D.W.
[1250]—*Franciscan Sisters of the Eucharist, Inc.*—F.S.E.
[]—*Sister of the Blessed Sacrament of Nigeria*.
[0590]—*Sisters of Charity of Saint Elizabeth N.J.*—S.C.
[0990]—*Sisters of Divine Providence*—C.D.P.
[2520]—*Sisters of Mercy*—R.S.M.
[2990]—*Sisters of Notre Dame* (Chardon, OH)—S.N.D.
[1650]—*Sisters of St. Francis of Philadelphia*—O.S.F.
[2150]—*Sisters, Servants of the Immaculate Heart of Mary*—I.H.M.
[2160]—*Sisters, Servants of the Immaculate Heart of Mary*—I.H.M.
[2170]—*Sisters, Servants of the Immaculate Heart of Mary*—I.H.M.
[4040]—*Society of St. Ursula*—S.U.
[3830]—*Sisters of St. Joseph*—S.S.J.

NECROLOGY

† Keenan, Desmond R., (Retired), Died Jan. 25, 2018
† Vetter, Joseph G., (Retired), Died May. 7, 2018

An asterisk (*) denotes an organization that has established tax-exempt status directly with the IRS and is not covered by the USCCB Group Ruling.

Diocese of Rapid City

(Dioecesis Rapidopolitana)

Most Reverend

ROBERT D. GRUSS

Bishop of Rapid City; ordained July 2, 1994; appointed Bishop of Rapid City May 26, 2011; installed July 28, 2011.

Chancery Office: 606 Cathedral Dr., Rapid City, SD 57701. Tel: 605-343-3541; Fax: 605-348-7985.

Email: chancery@diorc.org

Square Miles 43,000.

Formerly the Diocese of Lead.

Erected August 4, 1902; See transferred to Rapid City, August 1, 1930.

Comprises the Counties of Bennett, Butte, Corson, Custer, Dewey, Fall River, Gregory, Haakon, Harding, Jackson, Jones, Lawrence, Lyman, Meade, Mellette, Pennington, Perkins, Stanley, Oglala Lakota, Todd, Tripp and Ziebach in the State of South Dakota.

For legal titles of parishes and diocesan institutions, consult the Chancery Office.

STATISTICAL OVERVIEW

Personnel	
Bishop	1
Priests: Diocesan Active in Diocese	25
Priests: Diocesan Active Outside Diocese	2
Priests: Retired, Sick or Absent	7
Number of Diocesan Priests	34
Religious Priests in Diocese	12
Total Priests in Diocese	46
Extern Priests in Diocese	1
Ordinations:	
Transitional Deacons	1
Permanent Deacons in Diocese	29
Total Brothers	3
Total Sisters	23
Parishes	
Parishes	78
With Resident Pastor:	
Resident Diocesan Priests	22
Resident Religious Priests	5
Without Resident Pastor:	
Administered by Priests	51
Missions	18
Pastoral Centers	4
Closed Parishes	1
Professional Ministry Personnel:	
Brothers	3
Sisters	7
Lay Ministers	21
Welfare	
Catholic Hospitals	1
Total Assisted	29,351
Specialized Homes	1
Total Assisted	12,405
Special Centers for Social Services	5
Total Assisted	11,676
Educational	
Diocesan Students in Other Seminaries	7
Total Seminarians	7
High Schools, Diocesan and Parish	1
Total Students	255
High Schools, Private	1
Total Students	214
Elementary Schools, Diocesan and Parish	3
Total Students	604
Elementary Schools, Private	3
Total Students	408
Catechesis/Religious Education:	
High School Students	528
Elementary Students	2,103
Total Students under Catholic Instruction	4,119
Teachers in the Diocese:	
Scholastics	2
Brothers	2
Sisters	3
Lay Teachers	167
Vital Statistics	
Receptions into the Church:	
Infant Baptism Totals	410
Minor Baptism Totals	44
Adult Baptism Totals	26
Received into Full Communion	64
First Communions	399
Confirmations	384
Marriages:	
Catholic	56
Interfaith	48
Total Marriages	104
Deaths	487
Total Catholic Population	23,934
Total Population	227,211

Former Bishops—Most Revs. JOHN STARIHA, D.D., cons. Oct. 28, 1902; retired March 29, 1909 and named Titular Bishop of Antipatride; died in Laibach, Austria, Nov. 28, 1915; JOSEPH F. BUSCH, D.D., cons. May 19, 1910; transferred to Saint Cloud, MN, Feb. 21, 1915; died May 31, 1953; JOHN J. LAWLER, S.T.D., cons. Titular Bishop of Greater Hermopolis and Auxiliary Bishop of St. Paul, Minnesota, May 19, 1910; transferred to the See of Lead, Jan. 29, 1916; died March 11, 1948; LEO F. DWORSCHAK, D.D., cons. Titular Bishop of Tium and Coadjutor Bishop of Rapid City "cum jure successionis," Aug. 22, 1946; transferred to Fargo, ND, April 10, 1947; WILLIAM T. MCCARTY, C.Ss.R., D.D., appt. Titular Bishop of Anaea and Delegate to the Military Vicar, Jan. 2, 1943; appt. Coadjutor Bishop of Rapid City "cum jure successionis," April 10, 1947; succeeded to March 11, 1948; retired Sept. 17, 1969; appt. Titular Bishop of Rotdon; died Sept. 14, 1972; HAROLD J. DIMMERLING, D.D., appt. Bishop of Rapid City, Sept. 17, 1969; ord. May 2, 1940; cons. Oct. 30, 1969; died Dec. 13, 1987; CHARLES J. CHAPUT, D.D., appt. Bishop of Rapid City, April 11, 1988; appt. Archbishop of Denver, Feb. 18, 1997; BLASE J. CUPICH, ord. Aug. 16, 1975; appt. Bishop of Rapid City July 7, 1998; ord. and installed Sept. 21, 1998; appt. Bishop of Spokane June 30, 2010.

Vicar General—Very Rev. MICHEL MULLOY.

Chancery Office—606 Cathedral Dr., P.O. Box 678, Rapid City, 57709. Tel: 605-343-3541; Fax: 605-348-7985; Email: chancery@diorc.org. Office Hours: Mon.-Fri. 8-5Address all official business to this office.

Chancellor—MARGARET SIMONSON.

Diocesan Tribunal—2101 City Springs Rd., Ste. 200, Rapid City, 57702-9616. Tel: 605-716-5214; Fax: 605-348-7985.

Officialis—Rev. TIMOTHY S. HOAG, J.C.L.

Diocesan Consultors—Rev. BRYAN SORENSEN, Eagle Butte; Very Rev. MICHEL MULLOY, Rapid City; Revs. DANIEL JUELFS, J.C.L., Wall; KERRY PRENDIVILLE, Rapid City; ED WITT, S.J., Rapid City; LEO HAUSMANN, J.C.L., Lead.

Deaneries—Very Rev. MICHEL MULLOY, Rapid City; Rev. Msgr. MICHAEL WOSTER, J.C.L., Spearfish; Revs. RONALD S. SEMINARA, S.J., Pine Ridge; TONY GROSSENBURG, Lemmon; RON GARRY, Fort Pierre.

Presbyteral Council—Very Rev. MICHEL MULLOY.

Vicar for Clergy—Very Rev. MICHEL MULLOY.

Permanent Diaconate Program—606 Cathedral Dr., Rapid City, 57701. Tel: 605-343-3541. Very Rev. BRIAN PATRICK CHRISTENSEN, Dir.; Deacon GREGORY SASS, Asst. Dir.

Stewardship Director—SHAWNA HANSON.

Development Program—TODD TOBIN, Dir.

Continuing Education of Clergy—Very Rev. MICHEL MULLOY.

Vocation Program—Rev. MARK MCCORMICK, Dir., 2101 City Springs Rd., Ste. 200, Rapid City, 57702-9616. Tel: 605-716-5214.

Chief Financial Officer/Administrator of Temporal Affairs—MR. RICHARD SOULEK.

Diocesan Finance Council—DAN DUFFY; TIMOTHY FROST; Rev. BRIAN LANE; S. ROY DISHMAN; LES LINDSKOV; BOB WENTZ; LEISA NASH; BRUCE BYRUM; Very Rev. MICHEL MULLOY; MARGARET SIMONSON; JEFF BERZINA; DON STUKEL; PAT BURCHILL; STEPHANIE HURD.

Missionary Childhood Pontifical Association—TERESA SPIESS.

Propagation of the FaithDeacon MARLON J. LENEAUGH.

National Collections—TERESA SPIESS.

Mission Co-op—Deacon MARLON LENEAUGH.

Catholic Relief Service—TERESA SPIESS, 606 Cathedral Dr., Rapid City, 57701-5498.

Native Ministry Office—2101 City Springs Rd., Ste. 200, Rapid City, 57702-9616. Tel: 605-716-5214; Fax: 605-348-7985. Deacon MARLON LENEAUGH.

Director of Committee of Ongoing Priest Formation—

Superintendent of Schools—MS. BARBARA HONEYCUTT.

Director of Rural Life—Rev. TYLER DENNIS.

Office of Family Life—AMY JULIAN, Dir., 2101 City Springs Rd., Ste. 200, Rapid City, 57702-9616. Tel: 605-716-5214; Fax: 605-348-7985.

Family Life Sponsored Ministries—

Marriage Preparation—Heart to Heart weekend Retreat for the Engaged.

Social Justice Commission—2101 City Spring Rd., Ste. 200, Rapid City, 57701. Deacon GREG PALMER, Chair.

Retreat Ministry—2101 City Springs Rd., Ste. 200, Rapid City, 57702-9616. Tel: 605-716-5214.

Separated and Divorced Support Group—

Bereavement Ministry—2101 City Springs Rd., Ste. 200, Rapid City, 57702-9616. Tel: 605-716-5214.

Natural Family Planning Ministry—2101 City Springs Rd., Ste. 200, Rapid City, 57702-9616. Tel: 605-716-5214.

Rachel's Vineyard—2101 City Springs Rd., Ste. 200, Rapid City, 57702-9616. Tel: 605-716-5214

Courage and Encourage—

Returning Catholics Ministry—

Independent Ministries—

Retrouvaille—2101 City Springs Rd., Ste. 200, Rapid City, 57702-9616. Tel: 605-716-5214.

Rapid City Right to Life—Tel: 605-718-5215 (local contact).

Birthright—Tel: 605-343-1732.

Cursillo—

Worldwide Marriage Encounter—2101 City Springs Rd., Ste. 200, Rapid City, 57702-9616. Tel: 605-716-5214.

Sacred Heart Guild of the Catholic Medical Association—

Pastoral Ministries Director—SUSAN SAFFORD, Dir.

Diocesan Office of Faith Formation—SUSAN SAFFORD, Dir., 2101 City Springs Rd., Ste. 200, Rapid City, 57702-9616. Tel: 605-716-5214.

Diocesan Office of Ministry to Youth and Young Adults—2101 City Springs Rd., Ste. 200, Rapid City, 57702-9616. Tel: 605-716-5214. VACANT, Dir.

Campaign for Human Development—2101 City Springs Rd., Ste. 200, Rapid City, 57702-9616. Tel: 605-716-5214. Deacon MARLON LENEAUGH.

Victim Assistance Coordinator—BARBARA SCHERR, Tel: 605-209-3418.

Director of Communications—MARGARET SIMONSON, 606 Cathedral Dr., Rapid City, 57701. Tel: 605-343-3541.

West River Catholic Newspaper—LAURIE HALLSTROM, Editor, 606 Cathedral Dr., Rapid City, 57701.

Catholic Youth Commission—2101 City Springs Rd., Ste. 200, Rapid City, 57702-9616. Tel: 605-716-5214. CRAIG DYKE, Dir.

Archives—KATHY CORDES.

CLERGY, PARISHES, MISSIONS AND PAROCHIAL SCHOOLS

CITY OF RAPID CITY

(PENNINGTON COUNTY)

1—CATHEDRAL OF OUR LADY OF PERPETUAL HELP (1890) Affiliated with St Michael in Hermosa, Rapid City Newman Center.
520 Cathedral Dr., 57701-5499. Tel: 605-342-0507; Fax: 605-721-5986; Web: www.cathedralolph.org. Very Rev. Brian Patrick Christensen; Rev. Matthew Fallgren; Deacons George Gladfelter, (Retired); Raul Daniel; James Scherr.
See St. Elizabeth Elementary, St. Thomas More Middle School, and St. Thomas More High School, Rapid City under Diocesan Catholic School System located in the Institution section.
Catechesis Religious Program—Amy Dyke, D.R.E. Students 213.
Chapel—Rapid City Catholic Newman Center, St. John de la Salle Newman Center, 316 E. Kansas City St., 57701. Tel: 605-716-4130; Web: www.rcnewmancenter.com. Rev. Mark McCormick, Chap.; Mr. Jacques Daniel, Dir.

2—BLESSED SACRAMENT (1947)
4500 Jackson Blvd., 57702-4999. Tel: 605-342-3336; Email: bsc@blessedsacramentchurch.org; Web: www.blessedsacramentchurch.org. Revs. Timothy S. Hoag, J.C.L.; Adam Hofer, Parochial Vicar; Deacons Larry Kopriva; Greg Palmer; James VanLoan.
Catechesis Religious Program—Mary Farrell, D.R.E., Email: mfarrell@diorc.org. Students 427.

3—IMMACULATE CONCEPTION CHURCH OF RAPID CITY
922 Fifth St., 57701. Tel: 605-341-1578; Fax: 605-341-8751. 522 Columbus St., 57701. Rev. Christopher Hathaway, F.S.S.P. Personal parish.
Catechesis Religious Program—Mr. Matt Bruch, D.R.E. Students 44.

4—ST. ISAAC JOGUES (1949) (Native American)
211 Knollwood Dr., P.O. Box 1304, 57709-1304. Tel: 605-343-2165; Fax: 605-343-3257; Email: stisaac@rushmore.com. Rev. Ed Witt, S.J.; Deacons Luis Usera Sr., D.R.E.; Marlon J. Leneaugh.
Catechesis Religious Program—Students 70.
Mother Butler Center—231 Knollwood Dr., 57701. Catechetical and Social Center for Indians.

5—ST. THERESE THE LITTLE FLOWER (1941) [JC] Formerly known as The Church of St. John the Evangelist.
532 Adams St., 57701. Tel: 605-342-1556; Fax: 605-348-6272; Email: sttherese@diorc.org; Web: sainttheresechurch.org. Rev. Kerry Prendiville; Deacon Charles Rausch.
Catechesis Religious Program—Bobby Myers, Youth Formation Coord. Students 94.

OUTSIDE THE CITY OF RAPID CITY

BELLE FOURCHE, BUTTE CO., ST. PAUL (1905) [JC]
855 Fifth Ave., Belle Fourche, 57717-1701. Tel: 605-723-3226; Email: stpaulbellefourche@outlook.com. Rev. Msgr. Michael Woster, J.C.L.; Rev. John Paul Trask; Deacon Ray Klein.
Catechesis Religious Program—Tina Barrie, D.R.E. Students 80.

BISON, PERKINS CO., BLESSED SACRAMENT (1918) [JC] Served from Buffalo.
P.O. Box 382, Bison, 57620. 202 Rogers St., Bison, 57620. Tel: 605-244-5547; Email: evanorny@diorc.org. Rev. Ed Vanorny, Admin., (Retired).
Catechesis Religious Program—Angela Thompson, D.R.E., Email: athompson@diorc.org. Students 37.

BONESTEEL, GREGORY CO., IMMACULATE CONCEPTION (1906) [CEM] Served from St. Joseph, Gregory.
607 Mallette St., Bonesteel, 57317. Tel: 605-654-2204; Tel: 605-605-6542; Email: imconsta@gwtc.net; Web: www.gregorycountycatholic.org. P.O. Box 376, Bonesteel, 57317-0376. Rev. Jonathan Dillon, Admin.
Catechesis Religious Program— Combined with St. Anthony, Fairfax. Ms. Roberta Witt, D.R.E. Students 42.

BUFFALO, HARDING CO., ST. ANTHONY (1917) [CEM 2] [JC] Affiliated with Blessed Sacrament, Bison as well as the mission at St. Isidore in Ralph.
410 Allison St., Buffalo, 57720-0085. Tel: 605-375-3438. P.O. Box 85, Buffalo, 57720. Rev. Ed Vanorny, Admin., (Retired).
Catechesis Religious Program—Marisa Hett, D.R.E. Students 69.
Mission—St. Isidore, Ralph, General Delivery, Ralph, Harding Co. 57650.

BURKE, GREGORY CO., SACRED HEART (1905) [CEM 2] [JC] Served from St. Joseph, Gregory.
Mailing Address: P.O. Box 354, Burke, 57523. Tel: 605-775-2532. 934 Lincoln Ave., Burke, 57523. Rev. Jonathan Dillon, Admin.
Catechesis Religious Program—Ms. Annie York, D.R.E. Students 49.

CLEARFIELD, TRIPP CO., ST. BONIFACE, Closed. For inquiries for parish records contact the chancery.

COLOME, TRIPP CO., ST. ISIDORE (1909) [JC] Served from Immaculate Conception, Winner.
301 Carr St., Colome, 57528. Tel: 605-842-3520; Email: parishsec@gwtc.net. P.O. Box 765, Winner, 57580-0765. Rev. Kevin Lee Achbach.
Catechesis Religious Program—Email: dreic@gwtc.net. Students 20.

CUSTER, CUSTER CO., ST. JOHN THE BAPTIST (1911) [JC] Served from St. Anthony, Hot Springs.
449 Harney St., Custer, 57730-0632. Tel: 605-673-4426; Email: stjohns@gwtc.net. P.O. Box 632, Custer, 57730. Rev. Grant Gerlach.
Catechesis Religious Program—Ms. Belinda Wickham, D.R.E. Students 63.

DEADWOOD, LAWRENCE CO., ST. AMBROSE (1877) [CEM]
760 Main St., Deadwood, 57732. Tel: 605-584-2002. Mailing Address: 141 Siever St., Lead, 57754. Rev. Leo Hausmann, J.C.L.
Catechesis Religious Program— Twinned with St. Patrick's, Lead. Ms. Mary DeMarcus, D.R.E. Students 8.

EAGLE BUTTE , DEWEY CO., ALL SAINTS (1911) [JC] (Native American) Cheyenne River Reservation Parishes.
325 S. Spruce St., Eagle Butte, 57625-0110. Tel: 605-964-3391; Fax: 605-964-3300. P.O. Box 110, Eagle Butte, 57625. Rev. Bryan Sorensen.
Catechesis Religious Program—138 Spruce St., Eagle Butte, 57625-0110. Students 32.
Missions—Immaculate Conception, Bridger—Unnamed Rd., Bridger, Ziebach Co. 57748.
St. Joseph, Cherry Creek, Main Rd., Cherry Creek, Ziebach Co. 57553.
Catechesis Religious Program—
Sacred Heart, 410 1st St., Dupree, Ziebach Co. 57623. Tel: 605-365-5273. P.O. Box 110, Eagle Butte, 57625.
Catechesis Religious Program—Students 18.
St. Catherine, Promise, Promise Rd., Promise, Dewey Co. 57601.
Sacred Heart, Red Scaffold, BIA Hwy. 6, Red Scaffold, Ziebach Co. 57626.
Catechesis Religious Program—
St. Joseph, Ridgeview, 220 6th St. W., Ridgeview, Dewey Co. 57652.
St. Therese, Whitehorse Rd., White Horse, Dewey Co. 57661.

FAIRFAX, GREGORY CO., ST. ANTHONY'S (1904) [CEM] Served from St. Joseph's, Gregory.
2nd St., Fairfax, 57335-0186. Tel: 605-654-2204; Tel: 605-835-9290; Email: stjoseph@gwtc.net. Mailing Address: P.O. Box 186, Fairfax, 57335-0186. Rev. Jonathan Dillon, Admin.
Catechesis Religious Program—Students 7.

FAITH, MEADE CO., ST. JOSEPH (1917) [CEM]
413 W. 4th Ave., Faith, 57626. Tel: 605-967-2201; Email: stjoseph@faithsd.com. P.O. Box 307, Faith, 57626-0307. Rev. James Hoerter; Deacon Larry Brown.
Catechesis Religious Program—Students 26.
Missions—St. Anthony in Red Owl—Red Owl Rd., 9 miles North of Hwy. 34, Faith, Meade Co. 57626.
Catechesis Religious Program—Students 10.
St. Joseph, Mud Butte, 16601 Old 212, Mud Butte, Meade Co. 57758.
Catechesis Religious Program—Students 2.

FORT PIERRE, STANLEY CO., ST. JOHN (1905) [JC]
206 W. Main Ave., Fort Pierre, 57532. Tel: 605-223-2176; Web: stjohnsfortpierre.org. Rev. Ron Garry.
Catechesis Religious Program—Josie Tardiff, D.R.E. Students 117.

GREGORY, GREGORY CO., ST. JOSEPH (1905) [CEM 3]
414 Church Ave., Gregory, 57533. Tel: 605-835-9290; Email: stjoseph@gwtc.net. Rev. Jonathan Dillon.
Catechesis Religious Program—Mary Vale Hall, 411 Church St., Gregory, 57533. Ms. Sandy Stukel, D.R.E. Students 50.

HERMOSA, CUSTER CO., ST. MICHAEL'S, Attended by Cathedral of Our Lady of Perpetual Help, Rapid City.
13480 Hwy. 40, Hermosa, 57744. Very Rev. Brian Patrick Christensen; Rev. Matthew Fallgren.
Catechesis Religious Program—Students 13.

HILL CITY, PENNINGTON CO., ST. ROSE OF LIMA (1898) [JC]
250 Park St., Hill City, 57745. Tel: 605-574-2479. P.O. Box 236, Hill City, 57745-0236. Rev. Mark E. Horn, Admin.; Deacon Frederick G. Tully.
Catechesis Religious Program—100 Park St., Hill City, 57745. Students 59.
Mission—Our Lady of Mt. Carmel, 1014 Madill St., Keystone, Pennington Co. 57751. Students 5.

HOT SPRINGS, FALL RIVER CO., ST. ANTHONY OF PADUA (1890) [JC] Affiliated with St. John in Custer and St. James in Edgemont.
538 University Ave., Hot Springs, 57747. Tel: 605-745-3393; Tel: 605-745-3278; Email: sohillscatholic@gwtc.net; Web: StAnthonyHotSprings.org. P.O. Box 969, Hot Springs, 57747-0969. Rev. Grant Gerlach; Deacons Earl F. Witte, (Retired); James Hayes; Thomas Adams; Craig Pearson.
Catechesis Religious Program—Students 54.
Mission—St. James the Apostle, 310 3rd Ave., P.O. Box 568, Edgemont, Fall River Co. 57735. Tel: 605-662-7801; Email: stjames@goldenwest.net.
Catechesis Religious Program—Ms. Linda Tidball, D.R.E. Students 22.

KADOKA, JACKSON CO., OUR LADY OF VICTORY (1908) [JC] Served from Our Lady of the Sacred Heart, Martin.
600 Maple St., P.O. Box 159, Kadoka, 57543. Tel: 605-837-2219. Rev. Tyler Dennis.
Catechesis Religious Program—Students 17.

KENEL, CORSON CO., ASSUMPTION OF THE BLESSED VIRGIN MARY (1879) (Native American), Attended by St. Bernard, McLaughlin.
Kenel Rd., Kenel, 57642. Tel: 605-823-4401; Email: jhoerter@diorc.org. P.O. Box 539, McLaughlin, 57642-0539. Rev. James Hoerter, Email: jhoerter@diorc.org.
Catechesis Religious Program— Twinned with St. Bernard, McLaughlin. Sr. Jacqueline Schroeder, O.S.F., D.R.E.

KENNEBEC, LYMAN CO., ST. MICHAEL'S (1906) [CEM] Served from St. Mary, Lower Brule.
300 Hotchkiss St., Kennebec, 57544. Tel: 605-473-5335; Fax: 605-473-5453; Email: pastteam@gwtc.net. c/o St. Mary Church, P.O. Box 185, Lower Brule, 57548-0185. Rev. Mark Mastin, S.C.J.
Catechesis Religious Program—Students 11.

KYLE, OGLALA SIOUX CO., OUR LADY OF SORROWS (1910) [CEM 2] (Native American) Reservation Chapel. Served from Holy Rosary Mission, Pine Ridge.
1 Church Rd., Kyle, 57770. Tel: 605-455-2888; Tel: 605-455-1521; Fax: 605-455-2899; Email: ronaldseminara@redcloudschool.org. P.O. Box 567, Kyle, 57752-0567. Rev. Ronald S. Seminara, S.J.
Catechesis Religious Program—Students 2.
Mission—St. John of the Cross, Reservation Chapel in Allen, SD. Rural, Allen, Bennett Co. 57714. Tel: 605-454-6261.

LEAD, LAWRENCE CO., ST. PATRICK'S (1878) [CEM] [JC]
141 Siever St., Lead, 57754. Tel: 605-584-2002. Rev. Leo Hausmann, J.C.L.
Catechesis Religious Program— Twinned with St. Ambrose, Deadwood. Ms. Mary DeMarcus, D.R.E. Students 26.

LEMMON, PERKINS CO., ST. MARY'S (1908) [JC] Affiliated with Sacred Heart in Morristown, St. Bonaventure in McIntosh, St. Michael in Watauga.
410 3rd Ave. W., Lemmon, 57638. Tel: 605-374-3767; Tel: 605-374-3768; Email: stmarys@sdplains.com. P.O. Box 210, Lemmon, 57638-0210. Rev. Tony Grossenburg; Deacon Bill Dustman.
Catechesis Religious Program—Ms. Jenny Dirk, D.R.E. Students 66.

LOWER BRULE, LYMAN CO., ST. MARY'S (1923) [CEM] (Native American) Affiliated with St. Michael in Kennebec and St. Mary in Reliance.

508 Gall St., Lower Brule, 57548. Tel: 605-473-5335; Fax: 605-473-5453; Email: pastteam@gwtc.net. P.O. Box 185, Lower Brule, 57548-185. Rev. Mark Mastin, S.C.J.; Deacon Steve McLaughlin; Sr. Charles Palm, D.R.E.

Catechesis Religious Program—Students 17.

MANDERSON, OGLALA SIOUX CO., ST. AGNES (1901) [CEM] (Native American)

101 Main St., Manderson, 57756. Tel: 605-867-2267. P.O. Box 88, Manderson, 57756-0088. Rev. Edmund Yainao, S.J. Served by Holy Rosary Mission, Pine Ridge.

Catechesis Religious Program—Students 4.

MARTIN, BENNETT CO., OUR LADY OF THE SACRED HEART (1918) [CEM] [JC] Affiliated with Our Lady of Victory, Kadoka.

802 1st Ave., Martin, 57551. Tel: 605-685-6232; Email: olshofmartin@gmail.com. P.O. Box 567, Martin, 57551-0567. Rev. Tyler Dennis, Admin.; Deacon Calvin Clifford.

Catechesis Religious Program—Tel: 605-685-6274. Students 33.

MCINTOSH, CORSON CO., ST. BONAVENTURE'S (1913) [CEM] Served from St. Mary, Lemmon.

140 1st Ave. W., McIntosh, 57641. Tel: 605-374-3767; Tel: 605-273-4334; Email: lcarda@diorc.org. P.O. Box 210, Lemmon, 57638. Rev. Tony Grossenburg.

Catechesis Religious Program—Ms. Mandy Mollman, D.R.E. Students 35.

MCLAUGHLIN, CORSON CO., ST. BERNARD (1918) [CEM]

410 1st Ave., E., P.O. Box 539, McLaughlin, 57642. Tel: 605-823-4401; Tel: 605-823-2484; Email: jhoerter@diorc.org. Rev. James Hoerter; Sr. Jacqueline Schroeder, O.S.F., D.R.E.

Catechesis Religious Program— Twinned with Assumption of the Blessed Virgin Mary, Kenel. Sr. Jacqueline Schroeder, O.S.F., Faith Formation. Students 30.

Mission—St Aloysius, Bullhead, Mission parish, no resident priest. 401 Tatanka St., Bullhead, Corson Co. 57642.

Catechesis Religious Program— Twinned with St. Bernard's McLaughlin. Students 1.

MIDLAND, HAAKON CO., ST. WILLIAM (1911) Served from Sacred Heart, Philip.

307 Elm St., Midland, 57552. Tel: 605-859-2664; Tel: 605-843-2544. c/o Sacred Heart Church, P.O. Box 309, Philip, 57567. Rev. Gary Oreshoski.

Catechesis Religious Program—203rd St., Midland, 57552. Students 8.

MISSION, TODD CO., ST. THOMAS THE APOSTLE (1933) [CEM] (Native American) Served from St. Francis Mission.

150 Jefferson St., P.O. Box 151, Mission, 57555. Tel: 605-856-4018; Tel: 605-856-4618. Rev. Jacob Boddicker, Parochial Vicar.

Catechesis Religious Program—Tel: 605-856-2273. Gladys Bordeaux, D.R.E. Students 3.

Mission—Our Lady of Good Counsel - Wood, Served from St. Francis Mission. Rural, Wood, 57585.

MORRISTOWN, CORSON CO., SACRED HEART (1912) [JC] Attended by Served from St. Mary, Lemmon.

308 2nd Ave. E., Morristown, 57645. Tel: 605-374-3767; Tel: 605-524-3486; Fax: 605-374-3768; Email: stmarys@sdplains.com. P.O. Box 210, Lemmon, 57638-0210. Rev. Tony Grossenburg.

Catechesis Religious Program—

MURDO, JONES CO., ST. MARTIN (1906) [CEM] Served from Christ the King, Presho.

502 E. 2nd St., Murdo, 57559. Tel: 605-895-2534. Mailing Address: P.O. Box 399, Presho, 57568. Rev. John Heying.

Catechesis Religious Program—Tel: 605-895-2534. Students 20.

NEW UNDERWOOD, PENNINGTON CO., ST. JOHN THE EVANGELIST (1921) [JC] Served from St. Therese, Rapid City.

106 S. A St., New Underwood, 57761. Tel: 605-342-1556. P.O. Box 305, New Underwood, 57761-0305. Rev. Kerry Prendiville.

Catechesis Religious Program—Email: sttherese@rushmore.com. Ms. Stacey Nelson, D.R.E.; Ms. Georgine Wolf, D.R.E. Students 23.

NEWELL, BUTTE CO., ST. MARY STAR OF THE SEA (1910) Served from St. Francis of Assisi, Sturgis.

306 6th St., Newell, 57760. Tel: 605-720-3579; Email: stfrancis@rushmore.com. Mailing Address: P.O. Box 72, Newell, 57760-0072. Rev. Timothy William Castor.

Catechesis Religious Program—Students 28.

OGLALA SIOUX, OGLALA SIOUX CO., OUR LADY OF THE SIOUX (1916) [CEM] (Native American) Served by Holy Rosary Mission, Pine Ridge.

100 Church Hill Rd., Oglala, 57764. Tel: 605-867-1518; Email: sioux@gwtc.net. P.O. Box 140, Oglala, 57764-0140. Rev. Joseph Daoust, S.J.; Sr. Barbara Ann Bogenschutz, O.P., Parish Life Coord.

Catechesis Religious Program—Students 11.

Missions—St. Bernard, Red Shirt Table—Served from Holy Rosary Mission, Pine Ridge. Rural, Red Shirt Table, 57738.

Our Lady of Good Counsel, No Water (Drywood), Served by Holy Rosary Mission, Pine Ridge. Rural, Oglala, 57764.

PHILIP, HAAKON CO., SACRED HEART (1907) [JC] Affiliated with St. William, Midland and St. Mary, Milesville.

307 W. Elm, P.O. Box 309, Philip, 57567. Tel: 605-859-2664; Email: sacred@gwtc.net. Rev. Gary Oreshoski.

Catechesis Religious Program—Students 48.

Mission—St. Mary, Milesville, 203rd St., Milesville, Haakon Co. 57553.

Catechesis Religious Program—Students 7.

PIEDMONT-BLACK HAWK, MEADE CO., OUR LADY OF THE BLACK HILLS (1916) [JC]

12365 Sturgis Rd., Piedmont, 57769-2007. Tel: 605-787-5168; Email: olbh@olbh.org; Web: olbh.org. Rev. Andrzej Wyrostek; Deacons Walt Wilson; John Osnes; Gregory Sass.

Catechesis Religious Program—Ms. Rhonda Gehlsen, D.R.E.; Ms. Joni Osnes, D.R.E. Students 141.

PINE RIDGE, OGLALA SIOUX CO., SACRED HEART (1890) [JC] (Lakota) Attended from Holy Rosary Mission.

40 E. Hwy. 18, P.O. Box 359, Pine Ridge, 57770. Tel: 605-867-5551; Tel: 605-867-6287. Rev. Edmund Yainao, S.J.

See Red Cloud Indian School under Holy Rosary, Pine Ridge.

Catechesis Religious Program—Mrs. Carol LaDeaux, D.R.E. Students 50.

PORCUPINE, OGLALA SIOUX CO., CHURCH OF CHRIST THE KING (1901) [CEM] (Native American) Served by Holy Rosary Mission, Pine Ridge.

500 Our Lady of Lourdes Ln., Porcupine, 57772. Tel: 605-867-1614. P.O. Box 367, Porcupine, 57772-0367. Rev. Edmund Yainao, S.J., Email: eyainao@diorc.org.

See Red Cloud Indian School under Holy Rosary, Pine Ridge.

Catechesis Religious Program—Students 2.

PRESHO, LYMAN CO., CHRIST THE KING (1906) [CEM] Affiliated with St. Martin, Murdo and St. Anthony, Draper.

401 S. Fir Ave., Presho, 57568. Tel: 605-895-2534. P.O. Box 399, Presho, 57568-0399. Rev. John Heying.

Catechesis Religious Program—Students 13.

Mission—St. Anthony of Padua, Draper, Elm & 1st St., Draper, 57531. Students 1.

RELIANCE, LYMAN CO., ST. MARY'S (1911) [CEM] Served from St. Mary's, Lower Brule.

32984 SD Hwy. 47, Reliance, 57569. Tel: 605-473-5335; Fax: 605-473-5453; Email: pastteam@gwtc.net. P.O. Box 185, Lower Brule, 57548-0185. Rev. Mark Mastin, S.C.J.

Catechesis Religious Program—Students 13.

ROSEBUD, TODD CO., ST. BRIDGET, (Native American)

130 Rosebud St., Rosebud, 57570. Tel: 605-747-2361; Web: sfmission.org. P.O. Box 340, Rosebud, 57570-0340. Revs. James Kubicki; James Lafontaine, S.J. Served by St. Francis Mission.

Catechesis Religious Program—

ST. FRANCIS, TODD CO., ST. CHARLES BORROMEO (1886) [CEM] (Native American) Served from St. Francis Mission.

350 Oak St., P.O. Box 499, St. Francis, 57572. Tel: 605-747-2361; Web: sfmission.org. Revs. James Kubicki; James Lafontaine, S.J.

Catechesis Religious Program—Tel: 605-747-2436. Mrs. Jenny Black Bear, D.R.E. Students 225.

Mission—St. Agnes, Served from St. Francis Mission. 1 W. Service Rd., Parmelee, Todd Co. 57566.

SPEARFISH, LAWRENCE CO., ST. JOSEPH (1907) [JC] Affiliated with St. Paul, Belle Fourche.

844 5th St., Spearfish, 57783-2005. Tel: 605-642-2306; Email: diane@stjosephspearfish.com; Web: www.stjosephspearfish.com. Rev. Msgr. Michael Woster, J.C.L.; Rev. John Paul Trask, Parochial Vicar.

Catechesis Religious Program—Ms. Patsy Custis, D.R.E. Students 303.

STURGIS, MEADE CO., ST. FRANCIS OF ASSISI (1840) [CEM] Affiliated with St. Mary Star of the Sea, Newell.

1049 Howard St., Sturgis, 57785-1999. Tel: 605-720-3579; Email: stfrancis@rushmore.com. Rev. Timothy William Castor.

Catechesis Religious Program—Tel: 605-720-3996; Email: stfrancisccd@rushmore.com. Machell Sauer, D.R.E. Students 102.

TIMBER LAKE, DEWEY CO., HOLY CROSS (1910) Affiliated with Holy Rosary, Trail City and St. Mary, Isabel.

511 E. St., Timber Lake, 57656. Tel: 605-865-3653; Email: holycrosschurch57656@gmail.com; Web: www.HolyCrossTimberLake.com. P.O. Box 70, Timber Lake, 57656-0070. Rev. Brian Lane.

Catechesis Religious Program—Sarah Schweitzer, Faith Formation; LuAnn Lindskov, Faith Formation. Students 86.

Missions—St. Mary, Isabel—220 E. Idaho, Isabel, Dewey Co. 57633. Students 17.

Queen of the Holy Rosary, 200 1st Ave. W., Trail City, Corson Co. 57657. Students 4.

WALL, PENNINGTON CO., ST. PATRICK'S (1917) [JC] Affiliated with St. Margaret, Lakeside.

701 Norris St., Wall, 57790-0405. Tel: 605-279-2542; Email: stpatrickwall@gwtc.net. P.O. Box 405, Wall, 57790-0405. Rev. Daniel Juelfs, Admin.

Catechesis Religious Program—Students 51.

Mission—St. Margaret, 22100 Wicksville Rd., Owanka, Meade Co. 57767.

WANBLEE, JACKSON CO., SAINT IGNATIUS LOYOLA (1920) [CEM 3] [JC5] (Native American) Chapel in Wanblee, served from Holy Rosary Mission, Pine Ridge. Affiliated with Our Lady of Sorrows in Kyle.

100 Washington Ave., Wanblee, 57577. Tel: 605-455-2888. P.O. Box 567, Kyle, 57752. Rev. Ronald S. Seminara, S.J.

Catechesis Religious Program—

WATAUGA, CORSON CO., ST. MICHAEL (1912) [CEM] Served from St. Mary, Lemmon.

1st Ave. E. & Cemetery St., Watauga, 57660. Tel: 605-374-3767; Fax: 605-374-3768. Mailing Address: P.O. Box 210, Lemmon, 57638. Rev. Tony Grossenburg.

Catechesis Religious Program—

WHITE RIVER, MELLETTE CO.

1—ST. IGNATIUS (1899) [CEM] [JC] (Native American), Merged with Sacred Heart.

2—SACRED HEART (1919) [JC] Served from St. Francis Mission.

100 S. McKinley St., P.O. Box 185, White River, 57579-0185. Tel: 605-856-4018; Tel: 605-856-4618; Email: jboddicker@jesuits.org. Rev. Jacob Boddicker, Parochial Vicar.

Catechesis Religious Program—Students 3.

WINNER, TRIPP CO., IMMACULATE CONCEPTION (1910) [JC] Affiliated with St. Isidore, Colome.

302 W. 4th St., P.O. Box 765, Winner, 57580. Rev. Kevin Lee Achbach.

Catechesis Religious Program—Email: dreic@gwtc.net. Students 105.

INDIAN MISSIONS

EAGLE BUTTE, DEWEY CO., CHEYENNE RIVER RESERVATION (1911) [CEM 8] [JC2] (Native American)

All Saints, 138 N. Spruce St., Eagle Butte, 57625. Tel: 605-964-3391; Fax: 605-964-3300; Email: bsorensen@diorc.org. Mailing Address: P.O. Box 110, Eagle Butte, 57625-0100. Rev. Bryan Sorensen. Cheyenne River Indian Reservation Ministry Team. Serves All Saints Parish, Eagle Butte and its mission parishes.

LOWER BRULE, LYMAN CO., LOWER BRULE RESERVATION (1895) [CEM] (Native American) Lower Brule Reservation Ministry. Serves parishes in Lower Brule, Kennebec, Reliance.

508 Gall St., Lower Brule, 57548. Mailing Address: P.O. Box 185, Lower Brule, 57548-0185. Tel: 605-473-5487; Tel: 605-473-5335; Email: mmastin@diorc.org. Rev. Mark Mastin, S.C.J.

PINE RIDGE, OGLALA SIOUX CO., HOLY ROSARY/RED CLOUD INDIAN SCHOOL INC. (Pine Ridge Reservation) (1888) [CEM] (Native American) Ministry on the Pine Ridge Indian Reservation. Serving parishes in Pine Ridge, Porcupine, Manderson, Oglala, Drywood, Red Shirt Table, Kyle and Wanblee.

Mailing Address: 100 Mission Dr., Pine Ridge, 57770-2100. Tel: 605-867-5491; Tel: 605-867-9600; Tel: 605-867-2330; Email: gwinzenburg@redcloudschool.org; Web: www.redcloudschool.org. Revs. Edmund Yainao, S.J.; Ronald S. Seminara, S.J.; George E. Winzenburg, S.J., Pres.; Peter J. Klink, S.J., Dir. Mission/Identity; Joseph Daoust, S.J., Supr.

Schools—Our Lady of Lourdes Elementary—(Grades K-8), 500 Lourdes Ln., Porcupine, 57772. Mailing Address: P.O. Box 7, Porcupine, 57772-0007. Tel: 605-967-2801; Fax: 605-867-5874; Email: tlessert@redcloudschool.org. Theresa Lessert, Prin. Lay Teachers 28; Students 132; Staff 4.

Red Cloud Elementary School, (Grades K-8), Tel: 605-867-5889; Email: annmarieamiotte@redcloudschool.org; Web: www.redcloudschool.org. Ms. Ann-Marie Amiotte, Prin. Lay Teachers 31; Students 226; Clergy/Religious Teachers 2.

Red Cloud High School, (Grades 9-12), Tel: 605-867-1289; Email: clarehuerter@redcloudschool.org; Web: www.redcloudschool.org. Clare Huerter, Prin. Lay Teachers 33; Students 214; Clergy/Religious Teachers 2.

The Heritage Center—(Museum) 100 Mission Dr., Pine Ridge, 57770-2100. Tel: 605-867-8267; Fax: 605-867-1291; Email: marymaxon@redcloudschool.org; Web: www.redcloudschool.org/museum. Mary Maxon, Dir.

ST. FRANCIS, TODD CO., ST. FRANCIS MISSION (1886) [CEM] (Native American) Serving the Rosebud

Indian Reservation. Parishes in St. Francis, Rosebud, Parmelee, Mission, White River and Wood. 350 Oak St., St. Francis, 57572. Tel: 605-747-2361; Tel: 605-747-2362; Fax: 605-747-5057; Email: frjkubickisj@gmail.com; Web: sfmission.org. St. Francis Mission Foundation, P.O. Box 499, St. Francis, 57572-0499. Revs. James Lafontaine, S.J., Supr.; James Kubicki; Jacob Boddicker; Deacon Ben Black Bear Jr.

STANDING ROCK, CORSON CO., STANDING ROCK RESERVATION (1918)
410 1st Ave. E., McLaughlin, 57642.
Tel: 605-823-4401; Tel: 605-823-2484; Email: jhoerter@diorc.org. Mailing Address: P.O. Box 539, McLaughlin, 57642. Revs. James Hoerter; Tony Grossenburg.
Missions—St. Bernard Church-McLaughlin—410 1st Ave. E., McLaughlin, 57642. Tel: 605-823-4401. P.O. Box 539, McLaughlin, 57642. Rev. James Hoerter.
Missions—St. Aloysius - Bullhead—
Assumption - Kenel.
St. Mary - Lemmon, 410 2nd Ave. W., Lemmon, 57638. Tel: 605-374-3767; Fax: 605-374-3768; Email: stmarys@sdplains.com. P.O. Box 210, Lemmon, 57638-0210. Rev. Tony Grossenburg.
Missions—St. Bonaventure - McIntosh—
St. Michael - Watauga.
Sacred Heart - Morristown.

Chaplains of Public Institutions

ELLSWORTH. *Ellsworth AFB*. Rev. Msgr. Gerald D. McManus, M.Div.

On Duty Outside the Diocese:
Revs.—
Novotny, Richard
Sparks, Nathan.

Retired:
Revs.—
Hight, Michael, (Retired), 416 6th Ave., #3, Wall, 57790
Kari, Arnold, (Retired), 532 Adams St., 57701
Pennati, Riccardo, (Retired)
Vanorny, Ed, Temporary Admin., (Retired), P.O. Box 85, Buffalo, 57720-0085
Zandri, William A., (Retired), (Hospital Ministry), 4001 Derby Ln., Apt. 202, 57701.

Permanent Deacons:
Black Bear, Ben Jr., St. Francis Mission, St. Francis
Brown, Larry, Faith
Bush, Gerald, (Retired), Wanblee
Clark, Andrew, Gregory
Clifford, Calvin, Martin
Condon, Harold, Howes
Coy, Patrick, Hill City
Curtin, Michael, (Retired), El Paso, TX
Daniel, Raul, Rapid City
Dustman, Bill, (Retired), Lemmon
Freece, Tom, Gull Lake, MN
Frein, Lloyd, Philip
Garnett, James W., (Retired), Hot Springs
Gladfelter, George, (Retired), Rapid City
Keller, Paul, Mobridge
Klein, Ray, Belle Fourche
Kopriva, Larry, Rapid City
Leneaugh, Marlon, Rapid City
Osnes, John, Piedmont
Palmer, Greg, Rapid City
Rausch, Charles, Rapid City
Sass, Gregory, Piedmont
Scherr, James, Rapid City
Tully, Frederick G., Hill City
Usera, Luis Sr., Rapid City
VanLoan, James, Rapid City
Wilson, Walt, (Retired), Piedmont
Witte, Earl Joseph, (Retired), Piedmont.

INSTITUTIONS LOCATED IN DIOCESE

[A] DIOCESAN CATHOLIC SCHOOL SYSTEM

RAPID CITY. *St. Thomas More High School* (Rapid City Catholic School System) 300 Fairmont Blvd., 57701. Tel: 605-343-8484; Fax: 605-343-1315; Email: wsully@rccss.org; Web: www.rccss.org. Wayne Sullivan, Prin.; Ms. Barbara Honeycutt, Supt.; Rev. Mark McCormick, Chap. Lay Teachers 24; Priests 1; Students 255.

St. Elizabeth Elementary School, (Grades PreSchool-5), 2101 City Springs Rd., Ste. 100, 57702. Tel: 605-716-5213; Fax: 605-716-5216; Email: clecy@rccss.org; Web: www.rccss.org. Colleen Lecy, Prin., PreK - 5th. Lay Teachers 30; Students 391.

St. Thomas More Middle School, (Grades 6-8), 424 Fairmont Blvd., 57701. Tel: 605-348-1477; Fax: 605-342-4367; Email: mholsen@rccss.org; Web: www.rccss.org. Mary Helen Olsen, Prin. Lay Teachers 21; Students 185.

[B] GENERAL HOSPITALS

GREGORY. *Avera McKennan* dba Avera Gregory Hospital, 400 Park Ave., Gregory, 57533-0400. Tel: 605-835-8394; Fax: 605-835-9422. Mailing Address: P.O. Box 408, Gregory, 57639-0408. Mr. Anthony Timanus, CEO. Sponsored by Presentation of the B.V.M. of Aberdeen, SD & Benedictine Sisters of Sacred Heart Monastery, Yankton, SD. Bed Capacity 25; Total Staff 172; Total Assisted 29,351.

[C] MONASTERIES AND RESIDENCES OF PRIESTS & BROTHERS

HOWES. *Kino Jesuit Community*, 350 Oak St., Saint Francis, 57572. Mailing Address: P.O. Box 499, St. Francis, 57572-0499. Tel: 605-747-2361; Email: jlafontainesj@diorc.org. Revs. James Lafontaine, S.J., Supr.; James Kubicki; Jacob Boddicker, Assoc. Pastor. Priests 3.

LOWER BRULE. *SCJ Community House*, P.O. Box 185, Lower Brule, 57548-0185. Tel: 605-473-5335; Tel: 605-473-5487; Email: mmastin@diorc.org. 508 Gall St., Lower Brule, 57548-0185. Revs. Christianus Hendrick, S.C.J.; Mark Mastin, S.C.J., Parochial Vicar; Deacon Steve McLaughlin. Priests also serve the Sioux Falls Diocese. Priests 2; Total in Residence 2; Total Staff 1.

PIEDMONT. *Casa Maria Residence for Retired Priests*, 12541 Sturgis Rd., Piedmont, 57769. Cell: 605-850-1468; Email: mmulloy@diorc.org. Mailing Address: P.O. Box 678, 57709-0678. Ronald Johnsen, Mgr.; Very Rev. Michel Mulloy, Chm.; Mr. Richard Soulek, CFO. Total in Residence 1.

PINE RIDGE. *Holy Rosary Mission Jesuit Community*, 100 Mission Dr., Pine Ridge, 57770-2100. Tel: 605-867-5491; Fax: 605-867-1291; Email: josephdaoust@jesuits.org; Web: www.redcloudschool.org. Revs. Joseph Daoust, S.J., Supr.; George E. Winzenburg, S.J., Pres.; Peter J. Klink, S.J.; Edmund Yainao, S.J.; Bros. Michael Baranek, S.J.; Michael Zimmerman, S.J.; Joseph Fleischman, S.J. Brothers 3; Priests 5; Scholastics 2; Total in Residence 10.

[D] CONVENTS AND RESIDENCES FOR SISTERS

RAPID CITY. **Benedictine Convent of St. Martin* (1889) 1851 City Springs Rd., 57702-9613. Tel: 605-343-8011; Fax: 605-399-2723; Email: srmarywegher@yahoo.com; Web: www.blackhillsbenedictine.com. Sr. Mary Wegher, Prioress. Motherhouse and Novitiate of the Sisters of St. Benedict. Sisters 17.

PORCUPINE. *Our Lady of Lourdes School Convent*, 500 Lourdes Ln., Porcupine, 57772. Mailing Address: P.O. Box 7, Porcupine, 57772-0007. Tel: 605-867-1056; Email: sistersusan@yahoo.com. Sr. Susan Biegert, Rel. Teacher. School Sisters of Notre Dame. Sisters 1.

[E] MISCELLANEOUS

RAPID CITY. *Catholic Parish Association Contingency Fund, Inc.*, 606 Cathedral Dr., 57701. Tel: 605-343-3541; Fax: 605-348-7985; Email: rsoulek@diorc.org. Mailing Address: P.O. Box 678, 57709-0678. Brett Hanson, Pres.

Catholic Social Services, 529 Kansas City St., Ste. 100, 57701. Tel: 605-348-6086; Fax: 605-348-1050; Email: css@cssrapidcity.com; Web: www.catholicsocialservicesrapidcity.com. James Kinyon, Exec. Dir. Number Served 11,676; Total Staff 20.

Priest Retirement and Aid Association/Pension Plan Board, 606 Cathedral Dr., 57701. Mailing Address: P.O. Box 678, 57709-0678. Tel: 605-343-3541; Email: rsoulek@diorc.org. Rev. Msgr. Michael Woster, J.C.L., Exec. Sec., Email: mwoster@diorc.org; Rev. Ron Garry, Pres.; Mr. Richard Soulek, Business Mgr.

Western South Dakota Catholic Foundation, Inc., 10 E. Mall Dr., Ste. B, 57701. Tel: 605-721-6843; Email: thenderson@wsdcf.org; Web: wsdcf.org. Timothy Henderson, Exec. Dir.

EAGLE BUTTE. *Sacred Heart Center* (Social Service Agency) 121 Landmark St., Eagle Butte, 57625. Tel: 605-964-6062; Fax: 605-964-6060; Email: info@shconline.org; Web: www.shconline.org. Mailing Address: P.O. Box 2000, Eagle Butte, 57625-2000. Gregory Fisher, Exec. Dir.; Mr. Kirk Beyer, Dir. Programs/Oper.; Mr. John Lemke, Business Mgr. Total Staff 32; Total Assisted (Including Informational & Educational Outreach) 12,405.

HOWES. *The Diocese of Rapid City Mahpiya na Maka Okoigna* Sioux Spiritual Center 20100 Center Rd., Howes, 57748-7703. Tel: 605-985-5906; Fax: 605-985-5908; Email: ssc@gwtc.net; Web: www.siouxspiritualcenter.org. Carole Brown, Dir. Total in Residence 1; Total Staff 5.

RELIGIOUS INSTITUTES OF MEN REPRESENTED IN THE DIOCESE

For further details refer to the corresponding bracketed number in the Religious Institutes of Men or Women section.

[1130]—*Congregation of the Priests and Brothers of the Sacred Heart*—S.C.J.
[]—*Holy Spirit Fathers*—A.L.C.P. / O.S.S.
[0690]—*Jesuit Fathers and Brothers*—S.J.
[1065]—*Priestly Fraternity of St. Peter*—F.S.S.P.

RELIGIOUS INSTITUTES OF WOMEN REPRESENTED IN THE DIOCESE

[0230]—*Benedictine Sisters of Pontifical Jurisdiction* (Rapid City, SD)—O.S.B.
[1076]—*Dominican Sisters of Springfield Illinois*—O.P.
[]—*North East Province of Ursuline Franciscan Congregation* (Dimapur, Nagaland, India).
[2970]—*School Sisters of Notre Dame*—S.S.N.D.
[]—*Sisters of St. Francis of Assisi of Tshumbe* (Democratic Republic of Congo)—S.S.F.A.T.
[]—*Sisters of St. Francis of the Immaculate Conception* (Peoria, IL)—O.S.F.

NECROLOGY

† Baden, Robert D., (Retired), Died Sep. 12, 2018

An asterisk (*) denotes an organization that has established tax-exempt status directly with the IRS and is not covered by the USCCB Group Ruling.

Diocese of Reno

(Dioecesis Renensis)

Most Reverend

RANDOLPH R. CALVO, D.D., J.C.D.

Bishop of Reno; ordained May 21, 1977; appointed Bishop of Reno December 23, 2005; ordained and installed February 17, 2006. *Office: 290 S. Arlington Ave., Reno, NV 89501-1713.*

Pastoral Center: 290 S. Arlington Ave., Reno, NV 89501-1713. Tel: 775-329-9274; Fax: 775-348-8619.

Web: www.renodiocese.org

Email: donnak@catholicreno.org

Most Reverend

PHILLIP F. STRALING, D.D.

Bishop Emeritus of Reno; ordained March 19, 1959; appointed Bishop of San Bernardino July 18, 1978; installed November 6, 1978; appointed Bishop of Reno March 21, 1995; installed June 29, 1995; retired June 21, 2005. *Office: 290 S. Arlington Ave., Reno, NV 89501-1713.*

Square Miles 70,852.

Erected as the Diocese of Reno by His Holiness Pope Pius XI March 27, 1931. Canonical Erection of the Diocese August 19, 1931; Redesignated Diocese of Reno-Las Vegas by Pope Paul VI, October 13, 1976; Reformed Diocese of Reno by His Holiness Pope John Paul II March 21, 1995.

Comprises the Counties of Carson City, Churchill, Douglas, Elko, Eureka, Humboldt, Lander, Lyon, Mineral, Pershing, Storey, and Washoe.

Patrons of the Diocese: Our Lady of the Snows (August 5); The Holy Family (Sunday in the Octave of Christmas); Established through an Apostolic brief dated August 24, 1933.

Legal Title: "The Roman Catholic Bishop of Reno and His Successors, a Corporation Sole".
For legal titles of parishes and diocesan institutions, consult the Pastoral Center.

STATISTICAL OVERVIEW

Personnel	
Bishop	1
Retired Bishops	1
Priests: Diocesan Active in Diocese	26
Priests: Diocesan Active Outside Diocese	1
Priests: Retired, Sick or Absent	11
Number of Diocesan Priests	38
Religious Priests in Diocese	2
Total Priests in Diocese	40
Extern Priests in Diocese	9
Ordinations:	
Diocesan Priests	2
Permanent Deacons in Diocese	29
Total Brothers	3
Total Sisters	15
Parishes	
Parishes	28
With Resident Pastor:	
Resident Diocesan Priests	24
Resident Religious Priests	1
Without Resident Pastor:	
Administered by Priests	2
Missions	6
Professional Ministry Personnel:	
Sisters	2
Lay Ministers	11
Welfare	
Day Care Centers	4
Total Assisted	280
Specialized Homes	1
Total Assisted	115
Special Centers for Social Services	1
Total Assisted	218,000
Educational	
Diocesan Students in Other Seminaries	4
Total Seminarians	4
High Schools, Diocesan and Parish	1
Total Students	621
Elementary Schools, Diocesan and Parish	4
Total Students	846
Catechesis/Religious Education:	
High School Students	907
Elementary Students	2,898
Total Students under Catholic Instruction	5,276
Teachers in the Diocese:	
Lay Teachers	109
Vital Statistics	
Receptions into the Church:	
Infant Baptism Totals	1,501
Minor Baptism Totals	126
Adult Baptism Totals	78
Received into Full Communion	128
First Communions	1,556
Confirmations	713
Marriages:	
Catholic	213
Interfaith	37
Total Marriages	250
Deaths	397
Total Catholic Population	89,838
Total Population	734,093

Former Bishops—Most Revs. THOMAS K. GORMAN, D.D., D.Sc.Hist., ord. June 23, 1917; appt. Bishop, April 24, 1931; cons. July 22, 1931; appt. Coadjutor Bishop of Dallas "cum jure successionis," Feb. 8, 1952; succeeded to the See, Aug. 19, 1954; resigned Aug. 27, 1969; died Aug. 16, 1980; ROBERT J. DWYER, D.D., Ph.D., ord. June 11, 1932; appt. May 20, 1952; cons. Aug. 5, 1952; elevated to Archiepiscopal Dignity and promoted to Portland in Oregon, Dec. 14, 1966; resigned Jan. 22, 1974; died March 24, 1976; JOSEPH GREEN, D.D., ord. July 14, 1946; appt. Titular Bishop of Trisipa and Auxiliary of Lansing, June 22, 1962; cons. Aug. 28, 1962; appt. Bishop of Reno, March 10, 1967; installed May 25, 1967; resigned Dec. 6, 1974; died Aug. 30, 1982; NORMAN F. MCFARLAND, D.D., J.C.D., ord. June 15, 1946; appt. Titular Bishop of Bida and Auxiliary of San Francisco, June 5, 1970; ord. Bishop, Sept. 8, 1970; appt. Apostolic Admin. of Reno, Dec. 6, 1974; appt. Bishop of Reno, Feb. 10, 1976; installed March 31, 1976; appt. Bishop of Orange, Dec. 29, 1986; installed Feb. 24, 1987; retired June 30, 1998; died April 16, 2010.; DANIEL F. WALSH, D.D., ord. March 30, 1963; appt. Titular Bishop of Tigia and Auxiliary of San Francisco June 30, 1981; ord. Bishop, Sept. 24, 1981; appt. Bishop of Reno-Las Vegas, June 9, 1987; installed Aug. 6, 1987; appt. first Bishop of the newly established Diocese of Las Vegas, March 21, 1995; installed June 28, 1995; appt. Bishop of Santa Rosa April 11, 2000; installed May 22, 2000; retired June 30, 2011.; PHILLIP F. STRALING, D.D., ord. March 19, 1959; appt. Bishop of San Bernardino July 18, 1978; installed Nov. 6, 1978; appt. Bishop of Reno March 21, 1995; installed June 29, 1995; retired June 21, 2005.

Bishop's Office—Most Rev. RANDOLPH R. CALVO, D.D., J.C.D.

Bishop Emeritus—Most Rev. PHILLIP F. STRALING, D.D.

Secretary—MRS. DONNA KENNEDY, Tel: 775-326-9428.

Vicar General—Very Rev. CHARLES DURANTE, V.G.

Moderator of the Curia/Chancellor—Rev. ROBERT W. CHOREY, Tel: 775-326-9429.

Secretary—MS. MARIAN HULL, Tel: 775-326-9410.

Tribunal—

Judicial Vicar/Officialis—Rev. JOSEPH ABRAHAM, J.C.L.

Adjutant Judicial Vicar—Rev. THOMAS FRANSISCUS, C.Ss.R., J.C.L.

Vicar for Clergy—Rev. JOSEPH ABRAHAM, J.C.L.

Secretary/Notary—PIEDAD GONZALEZ, Sec., Tel: 775-326-9411.

Promoter of Justice—Revs. GARY M. LUIZ, C.P.P.S., J.C.L.; ROBERT E. HAYES, J.C.L.

Defenders of the Bond—Revs. GARY M. LUIZ, C.P.P.S., J.C.L.; ROBERT E. HAYES, J.C.L.

Judges—Revs. JOSEPH ABRAHAM, J.C.L.; THOMAS FRANSISCUS, C.Ss.R., J.C.L.

Advocates—Rev. PHILIP GEORGE, M.O.C.L.; Bro. MATTHEW CUNNINGHAM, F.S.R.

Department of Education—

Superintendent of Catholic Schools—MRS. KAREN L. BARRERAS, Tel: 775-326-9430.

Diocesan School Board—Most Rev. RANDOLPH R. CALVO, D.D., J.C.D.; Rev. JORGE HERRERA; MRS. KAREN L. BARRERAS; DR. JOHN ANXO, Past Pres.; DR. RANDY PANE, Vice Pres.; MR. MICHAEL DICUS; MS. JOANN BARD; MS. CATHERINE FRENCH; MS. AMY FANTER; MR. JIM CAVILIA, Pres.; MS. LAURA SEDAR, Sec.; MS. MARY CROW; MS. JESSE DANNEN; MR. ANDREW STEWART; MR. MATTHEW SCHAMBARI; MRS. STEPHANIE HIX, Prin. Representative.

Pastoral Ministry Offices—

Office of Faith Formation—MS. MONIQUE JACOBS, Dir., Tel: 775-326-9439.

Conference Associate—MS. BREANNA BALMUT, Tel: 775-326-9440.

Office of Lay Ministry Formation—DR. LAURI-ANNE REINHART, Dir., Tel: 775-326-9431.

Office of Youth and Young Adult Ministry—MRS. CHRISTINA DAVIS, Dir., Tel: 775-372-6456.

Office of Ethnic Ministries—Tel: 775-326-9423. MRS. MARIPAZ RAMOS, Dir.

Office of Permanent Diaconate Formation, Family Life and Spirituality Director—Tel: 775-326-9786. Deacon JOSEPH BELL.

Office of Safe Environment—Tel: 775-326-9430. MRS. KAREN L. BARRERAS, Dir.; MS. ELDA JUAREZ, Coord. Secretaries: MS. BREANNA BALMUT, Tel: 775-326-9434; MS. JUDIT CARBAJAL, Tel: 775-326-9415; MS. PAT GIANNOTTI, Tel: 775-326-9441; MRS. CARLA MISCHEL, Tel: 775-326-9413.

Archives—Rev. ROBERT W. CHOREY, Tel: 775-326-9429; MS. MARIAN HULL, Tel: 775-326-9410.

Curia—Most Rev. RANDOLPH R. CALVO, D.D., J.C.D.; Very Rev. CHARLES DURANTE, V.G., Vicar Gen.; MRS. KAREN L. BARRERAS; MS. MONIQUE JACOBS; MR. MIKE QUILICI; MRS. MARIPAZ RAMOS; MR. FRED WEBER; DR. LAURI-ANNE REINHART; Rev. JOSEPH ABRAHAM, J.C.L.; MRS. CHRISTINA DAVIS; Deacon JOSEPH BELL; MRS. MARIE BAXTER.

Department of Stewardship and Development—MR. MICHAEL QUILICI, Chief Devel. Officer, Tel: 775-326-9432. Secretaries: CARMEN GODOY, Tel: 775-326-9433; BRIZEIDA GONZALEZ, Tel: 775-326-9444.

Diocesan Communications—Rev. ROBERT W. CHOREY, Moderator of the Curia/Chancellor.

Diocesan Board of Consultors—Most Rev. RANDOLPH R. CALVO, D.D., J.C.D.; Very Rev. CHARLES DURANTE, V.G.; Revs. MARK HANIFAN; JORGE HERRERA; MICHAEL Q. MAHONE; ROBERT W. CHOREY, Moderator of the Curia/Chancellor; NATHAN MAMO; JESUS BALLESTEROS; THOMAS BABU; PHILIP GEORGE, M.O.C.L.; JOSEPH ABRAHAM, J.C.L.; JOSEPH INFANTE.

Lists of Deans—Revs. TOMY MAMPARAMPIL JOSEPH; MARK HANIFAN; JAMES SETELIK; MICHAEL Q. MAHONE.

Finance Office—

Finance Council—Most Rev. RANDOLPH R. CALVO, D.D., J.C.D.; Very Rev. CHARLES DURANTE, V.G.; Rev. ROBERT W. CHOREY; MR. FRED WEBER; MRS. DEBBIE GRIFFIN; MR. MIKE QUILICI; MR. JOHN MURPHY; MR. TIM RUFFIN; MR. JOE HAGGERTY; MR. JIM PILZNER; MR. JOHN DESMOND.

Chief Financial Officer—MR. FRED WEBER, Tel: 775-326-9420.

Payroll and Employee Benefits Coordinator—JUDIE DAY, Tel: 775-326-9424.

Human Resources—Tel: 775-326-9425. MS. MARY JEAN SNOW.

Parish Audit Support—RICHARD TODD, Tel: 775-326-9417.

Accountant and Bookkeeper—RITA SAN PAOLO-OUEILHE, Tel: 775-326-9435.

Parish Accounting Support—DIANE LACEBAL, Tel: 775-326-9422.

Frontier of the Faith—Mailing Address: P.O. Box 10930, Reno, 89510. Tel: 775-326-9433.

Director—Rev. ROBERT W. CHOREY.

Missionary Co-Op—Rev. ROBERT W. CHOREY.

High Desert Catholic Magazine—MS. LISA LAUGHLIN, Editor-in-Chief, 290 S. Arlington, Ste. 200, Reno, 89501-1713. Tel: 775-329-9274; Fax: 775-348-8619; Email: hdc@catholicreno.org.

Ongoing Formation for Permanent Deacons—Rev. JOSEPH ABRAHAM, J.C.L., Vicar for Clergy.

Our Mother of Sorrows Cemetery—2700 N. Virginia St., Reno, 89503. Tel: 775-323-0133. *Mailing Address: P.O. Box 8505, Reno, 89507.* Fax: 775-323-1229; Email: omos@catholicreno.org. MS. CHRISTINE LUNA, Oper. Mgr.

Presbyteral Council—Most Rev. RANDOLPH R. CALVO, D.D., J.C.D.; Very Rev. CHARLES DURANTE, V.G.; Revs. THOMAS BABU; JORGE HERRERA; MICHAEL Q. MAHONE; MARK HANIFAN; PHILIP GEORGE, M.O.C.L.; ROBERT W. CHOREY; NATHAN MAMO; JOSEPH ABRAHAM, J.C.L.; JOSEPH INFANTE.

Priest Personnel Board—Most Rev. RANDOLPH R. CALVO, D.D., J.C.D.; Very Rev. CHARLES DURANTE, V.G.; Revs. JOSEPH INFANTE; MARK HANIFAN; ROBERT W. CHOREY; MICHAEL Q. MAHONE.

Detention Ministry—Carson City Area: Deacon MICHAEL JOHNSON.

Reno Area—Deacon JOSE CASTRO, Tel: 775-322-2255.

Lovelock Prison—Tel: 775-273-2189. Rev. MARK HANIFAN.

Property Management—MR. FRED WEBER.

Respect Life Commission—Rev. MARK HANIFAN, Priest Moderator, Priest Moderator; MS. JULIANNA JERVIS; MS. WENDY AVANSINO; MS. LINDA UGALDE, Exec. Sec.; MS. TONI BERRY; MS. SUE BARNES; DR. STEVE BROWN; MS. MELISSA CLEMENT; MS. LORI COURTNEY; ED HORODKO; MRS. KAREN MOWRY; ROSEANN GRACZA; MIKE GRACZA; CHRIS WATTERS.

Project Rachel—MRS. KAREN MOWRY, Dir.

Seminary Board—Most Rev. RANDOLPH R. CALVO, D.D., J.C.D.; Very Rev. CHARLES DURANTE, V.G.; Revs. MICHAEL MAHONE; ROBERT W. CHOREY; MARGARET GRAHAM; Rev. JESUS BALLESTEROS; Sr. MARIA AHEARN, O.C.D.; MRS. KITTY BERGIN.

Victims' Advocate—MARILYN JANKA, Tel: 775-753-9543; DAVID CALOIARO, Tel: 775-450-3618.

Vocations Team—Revs. MICHAEL MAHONE; ROBERT W. CHOREY; Sr. MARIA AHEARN, O.C.D.

Secretary—MS. PAT GIANNOTTI, Tel: 775-326-9426.

Life, Peace & Justice Commission—Very Rev. CHARLES DURANTE, V.G.; MIDGE BREEDEN; JEFF HARDCASTLE; DONNA CARAVELLI; BETTY BISHOP; BOB MCGINTY; CELIA MCGINTY; FRAN MCMILLAN, Co-Chair; SHERRY LAGIER; RITA SLOAN, Coord.; JIM KELLEHER; CHRISTINE SEXTON.

Liturgy Commission—Revs. ROBERT W. CHOREY, Chm.; THOMAS NELSON; MS. CAROL SARA; MS. MARIA LEMAN; MS. SANDY MCGOWEN, Liturgical Coord.; MRS. DONNA KENNEDY; MS. TERI IACONIS; MR. JEFF LOFY; MS. TINA ACKERLEY; MR. VICTOR GONZALES; MS. THERESA BOULDIN; MR. TONY PINEDA; MR. DANIEL LANG.

CLERGY, PARISHES, MISSIONS AND PAROCHIAL SCHOOLS

CITY OF RENO

(WASHOE COUNTY)

1—ST. THOMAS AQUINAS CATHEDRAL aka St. Thomas Aquinas Cathedral Catholic Corporation (1907)
310 W. Second St., 89503-5398. Tel: 775-329-2571; Email: office@stacathedral.com; Web: www.stacathedral.com. Very Rev. Charles Durante, V.G., Rector; Deacons Robert Dangle; Joseph Bell; Revs. Paul Fazio, O.F.M.Conv.; Lucio Zuñiga Rocha, Parochial Vicar.
Catechesis Religious Program—Tel: 775-544-3737; Email: aquinasccd@stacathedral.com. Tammie Sheely, D.R.E. Students 87.

2—ST. ALBERT THE GREAT (1948)
1250 Wyoming Ave., 89503. Tel: 775-747-0722; Email: StAlbert@stalbertreno.org; Web: www.stalbertreno.org. 1259 St. Albert Dr., 89503. Revs. Honesto Agustin; Thomas Nelson, Parochial Vicar; Deacons Richard Ramm; Charles Lanham.
Res.: 3100 Coronado Dr., 89503.
School—St. Albert the Great School, (Grades K-8), 1255 St. Albert Dr., 89503. Tel: 775-747-3392; Fax: 775-747-6296; Email: lkane@stalbertreno.org; Web: www.stalbertreno.org. Mrs. Stephanie Hix, Prin.; Laurie Vasquez, Librarian. Lay Teachers 13; Students 289.
Child Care—St. Albert's Child Development Center, Kristen Mareno, Dir. Students 90; Teachers 15.
Catechesis Religious Program—Beth Lujan, D.R.E.; David Willems, Youth Min. Students 191.

3—OUR LADY OF THE SNOWS aka Our Lady of the Snows Parish Corp (1939)
1138 Wright St., 89509. Tel: 775-323-6894; Email: parishadministrator@olsparish.com; Web: www.olsparish.com. Revs. Robert W. Chorey; Michael Mahone, Parochial Vicar; Deacons David Norman; Brian Callister.
School—Our Lady of the Snows School, (Grades K-8), 1125 Lander St., 89509. Tel: 775-322-2773; Fax: 775-322-0827; Email: tfuetsch@ourladyofthesnowsschool.org; Web: www.snowsnv.org. Tim Fuetsch, Prin.; Christine Vikre, Librarian. Full-time Lay Teachers 15; Students 331; Part-time Lay Teachers 7.
Catechesis Religious Program—Tel: 775-329-6147; Email: dre@olsparish.org. Dr. Lauri-Anne Reinhart, D.R.E. Students 290.

4—OUR LADY OF WISDOM (1965)
1101 N. Virginia St., 89503. Tel: 775-322-4336; Email: church@olwnreno.com; Web: www.olwnreno.com. Rev. Nathan Mamo; Therese Gaikowski, Pastoral Assoc.
Our Lady of Wisdom Catholic Parish Corporation
Children's Liturgy of the Word—(Attend on Sunday morning).

5—ST. ROSE OF LIMA (1996)
100 Bishop Manogue Dr., 89511. Tel: 775-851-1874; Fax: 775-851-1727; Email: srl@strosereno.com; Web: www.strosereno.com. Revs. Joseph Abraham, J.C.L.; Bobin Babu; Deacon Auguste Lemaire; Jane Lucero, Pastoral Assoc.
Catechesis Religious Program—Tel: 775-850-2535; Tel: 775-850-2544; Email: DRE@strosereno.com; Email: Youth@strosereno.com. Lydia Aberasturi, D.R.E.; Linda Walsh, Youth Min. Students 162.
Mission—Holy Spirit, 1025 N. U.S. Hwy. 395, Washoe Valley, Washoe Co. 89704.

6—ST. THERESE OF THE LITTLE FLOWER CATHOLIC CHURCH (1947)
875 E. Plumb Ln., 89502. Tel: 775-322-2255; Fax: 775-322-0196; Email: yocelin@littleflowerchurchreno.org; Web: www.littleflowerchurchreno.org. Revs. Jorge Herrera; Justin Lazar, Parochial Vicar; Deacons Robert Ruggiero; Rigoberto Ruano.
Res.: 339 Urban Rd., 89509.
School—St. Therese Church of the Little Flower School, (Grades K-8), 1300 Casazza Dr., 89502. Tel: 775-323-2931; Fax: 775-323-2997; Email: colts@littleflowerschoolnv.org; Web: www.littleflowerschoolnv.org. Vicki Rossolo, Prin. Clergy 2; Lay Teachers 22; Students 298.
Catechesis Religious Program—
Tel: 775-322-2255, Ext. 114; Email: deacon@littleflowerchurchreno.org. Students 298.

OUTSIDE THE CITY OF RENO

BATTLE MOUNTAIN, LANDER CO., ST. JOHN BOSCO (1940)
392 S. Reese St., Battle Mountain, 89820.
Tel: 775-635-2576; Email: stjboscosm@hotmail.com. Mailing Address: 384 S. Reese St., Battle Mountain, 89820. Rev. Tomy Mamparampil Joseph; Deacon Dennis Cahill.
Catechesis Religious Program—Tel: 775-635-2576. Yolanda Rodriguez, D.R.E. Students 69.

CARLIN, ELKO CO., SACRED HEART (1910)
562 4th St., P.O. Box 235, Carlin, 89822.
Tel: 775-754-6425; Email: carlincatholic@yahoo.com.
Catechesis Religious Program—Tel: 775-754-6415; Email: thaub@frontiernet.net. Laurie Haub, D.R.E. Students 9.

CARSON CITY, CARSON CITY CO.

1—CORPUS CHRISTI (1949)
3597 N. Sunridge Dr., Carson City, 89705.
Tel: 775-267-3200; Email: generaloffice@ccchurchcc.org; Web: www.ccchurchcc.org. Rev. James Setelik.
Catechesis Religious Program—Email: karens@ccchurchcc.org. Karen Smeath, D.R.E. Students 59.

2—ST. TERESA OF AVILA (1858)
3000 N. Lompa Ln., Carson City, 89706.
Tel: 775-882-1968; Email: stteresa@stteresaofavila.net; Web: www.stteresaofavila.net. Revs. Thomas Babu; Hermes Binlayo, Parochial Vicar; Deacons Gilbert Coleman; Michael Johnson; Craig LaGier; Dennis Schreiner; Sr. Marie McGloin, S.A., Pastoral Assoc.
St. Teresa of Avila Parish Corporation
School—St. Teresa of Avila School, (Grades K-8), 567 S. Richmond Ave., Carson City, 89703.
Tel: 775-882-2079; Fax: 775-882-6135; Email: pburger@stts.org; Web: www.stts.org. Peggy Burger, Prin.; Teya Cantwell, Librarian. Lay Teachers 13; Students 199.
Child Care—St. Teresa Child Development Center, 561 Richmond Ave., Carson City, 89703.
Tel: 775-283-0261; Email: csupko@stts.org. Cindi Supko, Dir. Students 33; Teachers 6.
Catechesis Religious Program—Tel: 775-882-2130; Email: kanderson@stteresaofavila.net; Email: grace@stteresaofavila.net. Kari Anderson, D.R.E.; Grace Kengle, Youth Min. Students 364.
St. Teresa of Avila Columbarium & Memorial Gardens—

DAYTON, LYON CO., ST. ANN (1937)
Mailing Address: 3 Melanie Dr., P.O. Box 309, Dayton, 89403. Tel: 775-246-7578;
Fax: 775-246-7560; Email: admin@stannsdayton.org. Rev. Thomas Fransiscus, C.Ss.R., J.C.L.
Catechesis Religious Program—Marna Zachry, D.R.E. Students 72.

ELKO, ELKO CO., ST. JOSEPH'S (1917)
1035 C St., Elko, 89801. Tel: 775-738-6432; Email: stjoech@frontier.com; Web: stjoech.org. Revs. Varghese Malancheruvil; Kuriakose Mambrakatt; Deacons Joseph Walsh; Franklin Martinez.
Catechesis Religious Program—Tel: 775-738-8770; Email: sjcc@frontiernet.net. Catherine Higginbotham, D.R.E.; Catherine Valdez, Youth Min. Students 398.
Mission—Our Lady of Guadalupe, P.O. Box 200, Jackpot, Elko Co. 89825.

EUREKA, EUREKA CO., ST. BRENDAN'S (1872)
70 N. O'Neill Ave., P.O. Box 305, Eureka, 89316.
Tel: 775-754-6425; Email: catholiceurekanv@yahoo.com. Rev. Varghese Malancheruvil.

FALLON, CHURCHILL CO., ST. PATRICK (1920)
850 W. Fourth St., Fallon, 89406. Tel: 775-423-2846; Email: st.patricksfallon@yahoo.com; Web: stpatricksparish.org. Rev. Antonio Quijano Jr., M.S.; Deacons Kurt Carlson; Ronald Cherry; Wayne Crooks.
Catechesis Religious Program—Tel: 775-427-3916. Judy Northrup, D.R.E.; Paul Loop, Youth Min. Students 121.

FERNLEY, LYON CO., ST. ROBERT BELLARMINE (1957)
625 Desert Shadows Ln., Fernley, 89408.
Tel: 775-575-4011; Fax: 775-575-9167; Email: books@strobertbellarmine.org; Web: www.strobertbellarmine.org. Rev. Joseph Infante; Deacon Ruben Cervantes.
Catechesis Religious Program—Linda Harrison, C.R.E. Students 121.
Mission—St. Joseph the Worker, Empire, Washoe Co. 89412.

GARDNERVILLE, DOUGLAS CO., ST. GALL (1917) Rev. Paul McCollum; Deacon Emilio Gonzales.
Office & Mailing Address—1343 Centerville Rd.,

Gardnerville, 89410. Tel: 775-782-2852; Email: church@saintgall.org; Web: www.saintgall.org.
Catechesis Religious Program—Tel: 775-782-3784; Email: dimelli@saintgall.org; Email: mhedwall@saintgall.org. DeAnna Imelli, D.R.E.; Marina Hedwall, Youth Min. Students 256.

HAWTHORNE, MINERAL CO., OUR LADY OF PERPETUAL HELP (1938)
804 A St., P.O. Box 850, Hawthorne, 89415.
Tel: 775-463-2882; Fax: 775-945-2020. Rev. Jesus Ballesteros.
Office: 838 A St., Hawthorne, 89415.
Res.: 794 A St., Hawthorne, 89415.
Catechesis Religious Program—Ms. Suzanne Welch, D.R.E. Students 8.

INCLINE VILLAGE, WASHOE CO., ST. FRANCIS OF ASSISI (1965)
701 Mount Rose Hwy., Incline Village, 89451.
Tel: 775-831-0490; Fax: 775-831-2045; Email: Katiec@sftahoe.org; Web: www.sftahoe.org. Rev. William Nadeau.
Catechesis Religious Program—Email: beckym@sftahoe.org. Rebecca Massingill, D.R.E.; Ms. Sarah Morris, Youth Min. Students 82.

LOVELOCK, PERSHING CO., ST. JOHN THE BAPTIST (1875)
1045 Franklin Ave., P.O. Box 177, Lovelock, 89419-0177. Tel: 775-273-2189; Email: stjohns_lovelock@yahoo.com; Web: www.stjohnthebaptist.today. Rev. Mark Hanifan.
Church: 1085 Franklin Ave., Lovelock, 89419-0177.
Catechesis Religious Program—Tel: 775-273-7903; Tel: 775-422-3240; Email: twmaita@hotmail.com; Email: bekirosas@yahoo.com. Tera Maita, Co-D.R.E.; Beki Rosas, Co-D.R.E. Students 57.

SPARKS, WASHOE CO.
1—HOLY CROSS CATHOLIC COMMUNITY (1967)
5650 Vista Blvd., Sparks, 89436. Tel: 775-358-2544; Email: hccchurch@sbcglobal.net; Web: www.holycrosssparks.com. Rev. Jose Issac; Deacon Antonio Baptista.
Catechesis Religious Program—Rosa Martinez, C.R.E., Grades K-8. Students 418.
2—IMMACULATE CONCEPTION (1904)
2900 N. McCarran Blvd., Sparks, 89431.
Tel: 775-358-5977; Email: office@icsparks.org; Web: www.icsparks.org. Revs. Philip George, M.O.C.L.; Arlon Vergara.
Catechesis Religious Program—Diedre Cenac, D.R.E.; Mrs. Dorothy Gonzalez, D.R.E.; Mrs. Gabriela Woodward, D.R.E. Students 406.

STEAD, WASHOE CO., ST. MICHAEL'S (1967)
14075 Mt. Vida St., 89506. Tel: 775-972-7462; Email: stmreno@stmichaelreno.org; Web: www.stmichaelreno.org. Rev. Elberto Melendez.
Catechesis Religious Program—Tel: 775-737-9337; Email: martha@stmichaelreno.org. Ms. Martha Ibarra, D.R.E. Students 197.

SUN VALLEY, WASHOE CO., ST. PETER CANISIUS (1976)
225 E. Fifth Ave., Sun Valley, 89433.
Tel: 775-673-6800; Fax: 775-673-2028; Email: st.petercanisius@hotmail.com. Rev. Edgar Villanueva; Deacon Russ Bergin.
Catechesis Religious Program—Tel: 775-762-0738. Ms. Imelda Lopez, D.R.E. Students 248.

VIRGINIA CITY, STOREY CO., ST. MARY'S IN THE MOUNTAINS (1862)
111 S. E St., Virginia City, 89440. Tel: 775-847-9099; Fax: 775-847-9098; Email: info.stmarysvc@gmail.com; Web: dioceseofreno.org/mary-mountains.aspx.
Mailing Address: P.O. Box 510, Virginia City, 89440.
Revs. Joseph Abraham, J.C.L.; Bobin Babu.

WELLS, ELKO CO., ST. THOMAS AQUINAS
619 Sixth St., P.O. Box 369, Wells, Elko Co. 89835-0369. Tel: 775-752-3400; Email: taaquinaschurch@hotmail.com. Rev. Varghese Malancheruvil.
Catechesis Religious Program—Ann Battenfield, D.R.E. Students 18.

WINNEMUCCA, HUMBOLDT CO., ST. PAUL (1883)
350 Melarkey St., Winnemucca, 89445.
Tel: 775-626-2928; Fax: 775-623-2816; Email: stpaulswimmsec@gmail.com. Rev. Jose Sobarzo Guerra.
Catechesis Religious Program—Tel: 775-623-2928; Email: stpaulswmcaccd@gmail.com. Ms. Catherine Whitman, Diocesan D.R.E. Students 288.
Missions—St. Alphonsus—Main St., Paradise Valley, Humboldt Co. 89426.
Sacred Heart, Olivarria St., McDermitt, Humboldt Co. 89421.

YERINGTON, LYON CO., HOLY FAMILY (1901)
103 N. West St., Yerington, 89447. Tel: 775-463-2882 ; Fax: 775-463-2162; Email: holyfamily104@yahoo.com; Web: www.holyfamilyyerington.parishesonline.com. Rev. Jesus Ballesteros.
Catechesis Religious Program—Tel: 775-721-1829; Email: ccdcomdu@yahoo.com. Cindy Hitchcock, D.R.E. Students 100.
Mission—St. John the Baptist, Wellington.

ZEPHYR COVE, DOUGLAS CO., OUR LADY OF TAHOE (1966)
One Elks Point Rd., P.O. Box 115, Zephyr Cove, 89448. Tel: 775-588-2080; Email: office@ourladyoftahoe.org; Web: www.ourladyoftahoe.org. Rev. Larry Morrison.
Catechesis Religious Program—P.O. Box 115, Zephyr Cove, 89448. Ms. Patty Smith, D.R.E. Students 22.

Chaplains of Public Institutions

RENO. *St. Mary's Regional Medical Center*, 235 W. 6th St., 89503. Rev. Conrado Lomibao, Chap.

Retired:
Revs.—
Apassa, Cyril, (Retired), 9700 McCann Rd., #145, Longview, TX 75605
Arias, Ariel, (Retired), 5561 Crestlock Dr., Las Vegas, 89113
Bain, John, (Retired), 2875 Idlewild Dr., 89509
Corona, John, (Retired), 1740 Lavender Ct., Minden, 89423
Curran, Oliver, (Retired), 1772 Bella Casa Dr., Minden, 89423
Hanley, Gerald T., (Retired), 5339 Dogwood Dr., White Lake, MI 48383
King, Norman, (Retired), 855 Emerson Way, Sparks, 89434
Simpson, Robert, (Retired), 2870 Halo Dr., Sparks, 89436
Sommer, Anton, (Retired), P.O. Box 27, Virginia City, 89440
Torrente, Lorenzo, (Retired)
Vercellone, Anthony, (Retired), 9620 Renner Way, 89521
Wolf, George C., (Retired), P.O. Box 50097, Sparks, 89435.

Permanent Deacons:
Baptista, Antonio, 6717 Magical Dr., Sparks, 89436. Tel: 775-626-2196. Diocese of Oakland, CA
Bell, Joseph, 9330 Tomahawk Way, 89506. Tel: 775-972-1596
Bergin, Russ, 125 Guildwood Dr., Sun Valley, 89433. Tel: 775-673-5286
Cahill, Dennis, 435 W. Antelope, Battle Mountain, 89820. Tel: 775-635-0355
Callister, Brian, 3689 Cashill Blvd., 89509
Carasco, Anthony, 3782 Westwood Dr., Sparks, 89509. Diocese of Sacramento
Carlson, Kurt, 1888 Ryan Way, Fallon, 89406. Tel: 775-428-2055
Castro, Jose, 1586 Oxford Ave., Sparks, 89434. Tel: 775-358-8518
Cervantes, Ruben, 670 Sage Dr., Fernley, 89408. Tel: 775-575-2134
Cherry, Ronald, 428 N. Taylor St., Fallon, 89406. Tel: 775-423-7537
Coleman, Gilbert, 40 Pine View Ct., 89511. Tel: 775-852-1989
Crooks, Wayne, 5100 Workman Rd., Fallon, 89406. Tel: 775-463-2882
Dangle, Robert, 1529 Foster Dr., 89509. Diocese of Bismark, ND
Evans, Robert, 887 Thompson St., Carson City, 89703. Tel: 775-883-2341
Garcia, Joseph, (Retired), 1715 Teal Dr., Carson City, 89706. Tel: 775-885-2546
Gonzales, Emilio, 1185 Sage Ocean Dr., Gardnerville, 89460. Tel: 775-783-8880. Archdiocese of Galveston-Houston, TX
Henderson, William, 1343 Centerville Ln., Gardnerville, 89410. Diocese of Oakland
Johnson, Michael, 399 Pasture Dr., Carson City, 89701. Tel: 775-885-9782
Klonicke, Ron, 490 Golden Vista, 89506. Tel: 775-971-3258. Archdiocese of Chicago, IL
Korson, Donald, 9345 Oakley St., 89521. Tel: 775-852-3650
LaGier, Craig, (Retired), 4771 Lango Dr., Carson City, 89706. Tel: 775-720-2218
Lanham, Charles, 4742 Cougar Creek Tr., 89519
Lemaire, Auguste, P.O. Box 8512, 89507. Tel: 775-786-4657
Martinez, Franklin, 891 Blue Jay Dr., Spring Creek, 89815. Tel: 775-777-1648
Norman, David, 3785 Gibraltar Dr., 89509. Tel: 775-826-1314
Ramm, Richard, 3440 Kalispell Ct., 89523. Tel: 775-787-8839
Ruano, Rigoberto, 312 Smithridge Park, 89502. Diocese of San Bernardino
Ruggiero, Robert L., 1280 Davidson Way, 89509. Tel: 775-337-0735. Archdiocese of Los Angeles, CA
Schreiner, Dennis, (Retired), 3365 Lyon Ln., Carson City, 89704. Tel: 775-849-0910.

INSTITUTIONS LOCATED IN DIOCESE

[A] HIGH SCHOOLS, DIOCESAN

RENO. *Bishop Manogue Catholic High School, a Nevada non-profit corporation*, 110 Bishop Manogue Dr., 89511. Tel: 775-336-6000;
Fax: 775-336-6015; Email: karenb@catholicreno.org; Web: www.bishopmanogue.org. Mr. Matthew Schambari, Pres.; Mrs. Brianne Thoreson, Prin.; Lauren McBride, Ph.D., Vice Prin.; Frank Lazarek, Vice Prin.; Rev. Richard Kayizzi, Chap. Lay Teachers 47; Priests 1; Students 665.

[B] MONASTERIES AND RESIDENCES FOR PRIESTS AND BROTHERS

RENO. *Brothers of Our Lady of the Holy Rosary Monastery*, 232 Sunnyside Dr., 89503-3510.
Tel: 775-747-4441; Email: bros-reno@charter.net. Bros. Philip Napolitano, F.S.R.; Matthew Cunningham, F.S.R., Supr.; Edward Zuber, F.S.R. Brothers 3.

[C] CONVENTS AND RESIDENCES FOR SISTERS

RENO. *Sisters of Our Lady of Mount Carmel (OCD)*, 1950 La Fond Dr., 89509-3099. Tel: 775-323-3236;
Fax: 775-322-1532; Email: renocarmel@carmelofreno.net; Web: www.carmelofreno.com. Sr. Susan Weber, O.C.D., Prioress. Discalced Carmelite Nuns 13.
Sisters of the Holy Family, S.H.F., 5599 Quail Manor Ct., #48, 89511. Tel: 775-827-5370; Email: carolb@holyfamilysisters.org. Sr. Carol Bettancourt, Supr. Holy Family Sisters. Sisters 2.

[D] CAMPUS MINISTRY

RENO. *University of Nevada, Newman Community*, 1101 N. Virginia St., 89503. Tel: 775-322-4336;
Fax: 775-322-3616; Email: olwnewmancenter@gbis.com; Web: ladyofwisdomnewman.org. Rev. Nathan Mamo, Pastor. Served by Our Lady of Wisdom.

[E] CATHOLIC CHARITIES OF NORTHERN NEVADA

RENO. *Catholic Charities of Northern Nevada*, 500 E. 4th St., 89512. Tel: 775-322-7073;
Fax: 775-322-8197; Email: mbaxter@ccsnn.org; Web: www.ccsnn.org. P.O. Box 5099, 89513. Mrs. Marie Baxter, CEO. Tot Asst. Annually 327,444; Total Staff 180.
Adoption (Program temporarily suspended).
Tel: 775-322-7073, Ext. 231.
St. Vincent's Helping Hands, Email: ymyers@ccsnn.org; Web: ccsnn.org/pages/resource-network. Yvette Myers, Exec. Dir. Tot Asst. Annually 10,000.
St. Vincent's Food Pantry, Email: CCarrillo@ccsnn.org. Carlos Carrillo, Dir., Tel: 775-322-7073, Ext. 440. Tot Asst. Annually 180,000.
St. Vincent's Thrift Shop, Email: jfisher@ccsnn.org. John Fisher, Dir., Tel: 775-322-7073, Ext. 545.
Immigration Assistance, Tel: 775-322-7073, Ext. 740. Annie Allen, Dir. Tot Asst. Annually 300.
Holy Child Early Learning Center, 440 Reno Ave., 89509. Tel: 775-329-2979; Fax: 775-329-8537; Email: holychild@ccsnn.org. Yvette Myers, Exec.; Nicole Koehler-White, Dir. Religious Teachers 35; Students 100.
St. Vincent's Residence/Crossroads Program, 395 Gould St., 89502. Tel: 775-322-7073; Email: ymyers@ccsnn.org; Web: ccsnn.org/pages/crossroads-housing-program. Mailing Address: P.O. Box 5099, 89512. Yvette Myers, Exec. Bed Capacity 160.
St. Vincent's Dining Room, 325 Valley Rd., 89512.
Tel: 775-323-7073, Ext. 455; Email: eenglund@ccsnn.org; Web: ccsnn.org/pages/dining-room. P.O. Box 5099, 89513-5099. Eric Englund, Dir. Tot Asst. Annually 156,000.

[F] MISCELLANEOUS

RENO. *The Catholic Community Foundation of the Diocese of Reno*, 290 S. Arlington, Ste. 200, 89501-1713. Tel: 775-326-9420; Fax: 775-348-8619; Email: fredw@catholicreno.org. Mr. Fred Weber, CFO.
**Fertility Care Center of Reno, Inc.*, 1281 Terminal Way #114, 89502. Tel: 775-827-5111;
Fax: 775-851-2114; Email: juliannajervis@att.net. Ms. Julianna Jervis, Pres. Offer Creighton Model FertilityCare System and NaProTechnology.
Nevada Catholic Conference, 290 S. Arlington Ave.,

Ste. 200, 89501-1713. Fax: 775-348-8619; Email: nevadacatholicconference@gmail.com. Mike Dyer, Contact Person.

RELIGIOUS INSTITUTES OF MEN REPRESENTED IN THE DIOCESE

For further details refer to the corresponding bracketed number in the Religious Institutes of Men or Women section.

[0142]—*Augustinians*—O.S.A.

[0960]—*Brothers of the Congregation of Our Lady of the Holy Rosary*—F.S.R.

[1070]—*Redemptorist Father* (Denver Prov.)—C.SS.R.

RELIGIOUS INSTITUTES OF WOMEN REPRESENTED IN THE DIOCESE

[0420]—*Discalced Carmelite Nuns*—O.C.D.

[1190]—*Franciscan Sisters of the Atonement*—S.A.

[]—*Holy Family Sisters of the Needy*—H.F.S.N.

[1960]—*Sisters of the Holy Family*—S.H.F.

DIOCESAN CEMETERIES

RENO. *Our Mother of Sorrows Cemetery & Mausoleum*, 2700 N. Virginia St., 89503. Tel: 775-323-0133; Fax: 775-323-1229; Email: omos@catholiccemetery.org; Web: www.CatholicCemeteryReno.org. P.O. Box 8505, 89507. Ms. Christine Luna, Mgr.

NECROLOGY

† Donnelly, Thomas Fabian, (Retired), Died Aug. 31, 2018

An asterisk (*) denotes an organization that has established tax-exempt status directly with the IRS and is not covered by the USCCB Group Ruling.

Diocese of Richmond

(Dioecesis Richmondiensis)

Most Reverend

BARRY C. KNESTOUT

Bishop of Richmond; ordained June 24, 1989; appointed Auxiliary Bishop of Washington and Titular Bishop of Leavenworth November 18, 2008; Episcopal ordination December 29, 2008; appointed Bishop of Richmond December 5, 2017; installed January 12, 2018. *Pastoral Center: 7800 Carousel Lane, Richmond, VA 23294.*

Catholic Diocese of Richmond Pastoral Center: 7800 Carousel Lane, Richmond, VA 23294. Tel: 804-359-5661; Fax: 804-358-9159.

Web: www.richmonddiocese.org

Email: Bishop@richmonddiocese.org

ESTABLISHED IN 1820.

Square Miles 36,711.

Comprises the State of Virginia, with the exception of the Counties of Arlington, Clarke, Culpeper, Fairfax, Fauquier, Frederick, King George, Lancaster, Loudoun, Madison, Northumberland, Orange, Page, Prince William, Rappahannock, Richmond, Shenandoah, Spotsylvania, Stafford, Warren and Westmoreland.

For legal titles of parishes and diocesan institutions, consult the Chancery Office.

STATISTICAL OVERVIEW

Personnel	
Bishop	1
Retired Abbots	1
Priests: Diocesan Active in Diocese	86
Priests: Diocesan Active Outside Diocese	4
Priests: Retired, Sick or Absent	40
Number of Diocesan Priests	130
Religious Priests in Diocese	18
Total Priests in Diocese	148
Extern Priests in Diocese	52
Ordinations:	
Diocesan Priests	3
Transitional Deacons	5
Permanent Deacons	19
Permanent Deacons in Diocese	165
Total Brothers	7
Total Sisters	180
Parishes	
Parishes	138
With Resident Pastor:	
Resident Diocesan Priests	98
Resident Religious Priests	6
Without Resident Pastor:	
Administered by Priests	34
Missions	6
Closed Parishes	1
Professional Ministry Personnel:	
Brothers	5
Sisters	180
Lay Ministers	150
Welfare	
Catholic Hospitals	8
Total Assisted	1,024,697
Homes for the Aged	7
Total Assisted	1,453
Day Care Centers	2
Total Assisted	310
Special Centers for Social Services	6
Total Assisted	32,507
Residential Care of Disabled	3
Total Assisted	582
Educational	
Diocesan Students in Other Seminaries	30
Total Seminarians	30
High Schools, Diocesan and Parish	5
Total Students	1,004
High Schools, Private	3
Total Students	600
Elementary Schools, Diocesan and Parish	24
Total Students	7,356
Elementary Schools, Private	4
Total Students	1,317
Catechesis/Religious Education:	
High School Students	3,059
Elementary Students	8,532
Total Students under Catholic Instruction	21,898
Teachers in the Diocese:	
Priests	2
Brothers	1
Sisters	9
Lay Teachers	926
Vital Statistics	
Receptions into the Church:	
Infant Baptism Totals	2,521
Minor Baptism Totals	118
Adult Baptism Totals	59
First Communions	2,576
Confirmations	1,774
Marriages:	
Catholic	340
Interfaith	239
Total Marriages	579
Deaths	1,355
Total Catholic Population	248,822
Total Population	5,220,225

Former Bishops—Rt. Revs. PATRICK KELLY, D.D., ord. July 18, 1802; first Bishop; cons. Aug. 24, 1820; transferred to Waterford and Lismore in 1822; died Oct. 8, 1829; RICHARD V. WHELAN, D.D., ord. May 1, 1831; second Bishop; cons. March 21, 1841; transferred to Wheeling, July 23, 1850; died July 7, 1874; JOHN MCGILL, D.D., ord. June 13, 1835; cons. Nov. 10, 1850; died Jan. 14, 1872; His Eminence JAMES CARDINAL GIBBONS, D.D., ord. June 30, 1861; cons. Aug. 16, 1868; Bishop of Adramyttum, and Vicar-Apostolic of North Carolina; transferred to the See of Richmond, July 30, 1872; transferred to the See of Baltimore, Oct. 3, 1877; created Cardinal Priest of S. Maria in Trastevere, June 7, 1886; died March 24, 1921; Rt. Revs. JOHN J. KEANE, D.D., ord. July 2, 1866; cons. Aug. 25, 1878; resigned August, 1888; rector of the Catholic University, Washington, DC; transferred to Archbishopric of Dubuque, July 24, 1900; died June 27, 1918; AUGUSTINE VAN DE VYVER, D.D., ord. July 21, 1870; cons. Oct. 20, 1889; died Oct. 16, 1911; DENIS JOSEPH O'CONNELL, D.D., ord. May 26, 1877; cons. May 3, 1908; Titular Bishop of Sebaste and Auxiliary Bishop of San Francisco; appt. Bishop of Richmond, Jan. 19, 1912; resigned Jan. 15, 1926 and appt. Titular Archbishop of Marianne; died Jan. 1, 1927; Most Revs. ANDREW J. BRENNAN, D.D., ord. December 17, 1904; cons. Titular Bishop of Thapsus and Auxiliary Bishop of Scranton, April 25, 1923; appt. Bishop of Richmond, May 28, 1926; resigned April 14, 1945; appt. Titular Bishop of Telmissus; died May 23, 1956; PETER L. IRETON, D.D., ord. June 20, 1906; appt. Titular Bishop of Cime Coadjutor Bishop and Apostolic Administrator of Richmond, Aug. 3, 1935; cons. Oct. 23, 1935; named Bishop of Richmond, April 14, 1945; named Assistant at the Pontifical Throne, May 21, 1956; died April 27, 1958; JOHN J. RUSSELL, D.D., ord. July 8, 1923; appt. Bishop of Charleston, Jan. 28, 1950; cons. March 14, 1950; appt. Bishop of Richmond, July 3, 1958; retired April 3, 1973; died March 17, 1993; WALTER F. SULLIVAN, D.D., ord. May 9, 1953; appt. Titular Bishop of Selsey and Auxiliary Bishop of Richmond Oct. 20, 1970; cons. Dec. 1, 1970; appt. Apostolic Administrator of Richmond April 30, 1973; succeeded to the See, June 6, 1974; resigned Sept. 16, 2003; died Dec. 11, 2012.; FRANCIS X. DILORENZO, ord. May 18, 1968; appt. Titular Bishop of Tigia and Auxiliary Bishop of1 Scranton Jan. 26, 1988; cons. March 8, 1988; appt. Apostolic Admin. of Honolulu Oct. 12, 1993; succeeded to See Nov. 29, 1994; appt. Bishop of Richmond March 31, 2004; installed May 24, 2004; ret. April 15, 2017; died Aug. 17, 2017.

Central Administrative Offices

Unless otherwise indicated all Diocesan Offices are located at: *7800 Carousel Ln., Richmond, 23294.* Tel: 804-359-5661; Fax: 804-358-9159.

Vicar General and Moderator of the Curia—Very Rev. MICHAEL G. BOEHLING. Regional Vicars: Very Rev. Msgrs. WALTER C. BARRETT JR., Eastern Vicariate, Tel: 757-851-8800; R. FRANCIS MUENCH, J.C.L., Central Vicariate, Tel: 804-355-9155; Very Rev. KEVIN L. SEGERBLOM, Western Vicariate, Tel: 276-669-8200, Ext. 30

Deanery - Eastern Vicariate—Very Rev. Msgr. WALTER C. BARRETT JR., (Episcopal Vicar).

Deanery 1—Very Rev. WILLIAM DANIEL BEEMAN, V.F.

Deanery 2—Very Rev. DANIEL J. MALINGUMU, V.F.

Deanery 3—Very Rev. ROMEO D. JAZMIN, V.F.

Deanery 4—Very Rev. JOHN DAVID RAMSEY, V.F.

Deanery 5—Very Rev. GERALD S. KAGGWA, V.F.

Central Vicariate—Very Rev. Msgr. R. FRANCIS MUENCH, J.C.L., (Episcopal Vicar).

Deanery 6—Very Rev. Msgr. PATRICK D. GOLDEN, V.F.

Deanery 7—Very Rev. JAMES J. BEGLEY JR., V.F.

Deanery 8—Very Rev. JOHN C. KAZIBWE, (Uganda) V.F.

Deanery 9—Very Rev. DANIEL ANDREW COGUT, V.F.

Deanery 10—Very Rev. JOSEPH MARY LUKYAMUZI, V.F.

Western Viciariate—Very Rev. KEVIN L. SEGERBLOM, (Episcopal Vicar).

Deanery 11—Very Rev. SILVIO KABERIA, V.F.

Deanery 12—Very Rev. KENNETH J. SHUPING, V.F.

Deanery 13—Very Rev. ANTHONY O. SENYAH, V.F.

Deanery 14—Very Rev. FRANCIS XAVIER MUSOLOOZA, V.F.

Deanery 15—Very Rev. SALVADOR ANONUEVO, V.F.

Other Vicar—Very Rev. WILLIAM DANIEL BEEMAN, V.F., Catholic Schools' Mission & Identity.

Assistant to the Bishop—MRS. ANNE C. EDWARDS.

Chancellor—Very Rev. Msgr. R. FRANCIS MUENCH, J.C.L., Tel: 804-355-9155; Fax: 804-359-2810.

Vice Chancellor—MS. EDITH MCNEIL JETER, Tel: 804-359-5661, Ext. 218.

Diocesan Tribunal—Tel: 804-355-9155; Fax: 804-359-2810.

Judicial Vicar—Very Rev. Msgr. R. FRANCIS MUENCH, J.C.L.
Adjutant Judicial Vicar—Very Rev. MICHAEL M. DUFFY, J.C.L.

Judges—Rev. Msgr. J. KENNETH RUSH JR., D.Min.; Revs. WAYNE L BALL, J.C.L.; KEVIN J. O'BRIEN, Ph. D.; MR. JEFFREY M. STAAB, J.C.D.; H. ROBERTA SMALL, J.C.L.; JUDITH A. DOUGLAS, J.C.D.; SUSAN L. VANNICE, J.C.L.; Deacon J. MICHAEL FITZGERALD, J.C.L.

Defenders of the Bond—CHRISTINA HIP-FLORES, J.C.D.; AMY JILL STRICKLAND, J.C.L.; ELISA E. UGARTE, J.C.L.; E. MAGDALEN ROSS, J.C.L.

Ecclesiastical Notaries—MRS. CHERYL GAMBARDELLA; MRS. KATHLEEN M. MCINTOSH; MRS. LISA MURILLO.

Propagation of the Faith—Deacon ROBERT H. GRIFFIN.

Vicar for Clergy—Very Revs. TIMOTHY M. KUHNEMAN; JOHN C. KAZIBWE, (Uganda) V.F., Asst. to Vicar for Clergy for African Priests; SALVADOR ANONUEVO, V.F., Asst. to Vicar for Clergy for Filipino Priests.

Registrar & Coordinator Permanent Diaconate—MRS. GERALDINE MANCUSO.

Ethnic and Special Liturgies—Filipino, Hispanic, Korean, Vietnamese; Tridentine Latin Mass, Deaf/Hearing Impaired. Please refer to the diocesan website for location and schedule.

Vicar for Ecumenism & Ecumenical Affairs—Rev. Msgr. JOSEPH P. LEHMAN, Tel: 540-774-0066; Email: pastor@OLN-parish.org.

Vicar for Vocations—Very Rev. MICHAEL G. BOEHLING; Rev. BRIAN W. CAPUANO, Assoc. Dir. & Promoter of Vocations.

Director of Archives and Museum—MS. EDITH MCNEIL JETER.

Office of Human Resources—MRS. DOROTHY MAHANES, Human Resource Officer; MRS. MARYJANE M. FULLER, Dir. Safe Environment & Dir. Human Resources; MRS. CATHERINE M. CARNEY, Benefits Mgr.; MRS. TINA B. TUPPER, Onboarding Specialist; MS. JENNIFER SLOAN, Victim Assistance/Safe Environment Coord.; Ms. MS. SARA BOARD, HR Coord./Recruiter; MRS. SARAH FOLGER, HRMS & Payroll Mgr.; MS. ANGELA ZALESWKI, Payroll Specialist.

Catholic Community Foundation—MRS. MARGARET KEIGHTLEY, Exec. Dir.; MR. ALEX PREVITERA, CFRE, Dir.; MS. JOYCE A. SCHREIBER, Dir. McMahon Parater Scholarship Foundation; MRS. MARIA GABRIELA GONZALEZ, Dir. Parish Devel. Svcs.; MS. MARYAGNES F. KEENAN, Dir. Planned Giving; MR. DONALD S. ROSS, Major Gifts Officer.

Office of Information Technology—MR. ERIC SUND, Dir.; MR. IAN REYES, Systems Admin.; MS. LYNN MOONEY, Web Svcs. & Database Devel.; MR. DANIEL DEHART, Desktop Support Technician; MRS. PAULA DULLAS, Technology Support Specialist.

Office of Communications—MS. DEBORAH M. COX, Dir.

Office of Printing—MR. JOEL CLIBORNE, Dir.

Office of Finance—MR. MICHAEL J. MCGEE, CFO; MRS. SARAH W. RABIN, Dir. Finance; Deacon PAUL MAHEFKY, Dir. Real Estate; MRS. AIMEE W. CHAPPELL, Asst. Dir. Finance.
Diocesan Housing Corporation—MR. WILLIAM B. MURPHY, Exec. Dir.

Facilities Management—MR. JOHN W. MURPHY JR., Dir.

Office of Risk Management—MR. KURT HICKMAN, Dir.

Office of Christian Formation—MRS. EMILY FILIPPI, Dir.; MS. SHERI KEMP, Assoc. Dir.; MRS. BERNADETTE E. HARRIS, Assoc. Dir., Dir. Lay Ecclesial Ministry Inst.; MRS. MELANIE CODDINGTON, Regl. Min. Christian Formation.

Office of Catholic Schools—MR. RAYMOND E. HONEYCUTT, Supt.; MRS. KELLY LAZZARA, Assoc. Supt. Opers.; DR. ANGELA M. ALLEN, Assoc. Supt. Curriculum & Instruction; MS. PAMELA WRAY, Enrollment Mgmt. Coord.

Office of Evangelization—MR. MICHAEL F. SCHOOL, Dir.; MS. CARRIE POSTON, Prog. Coord.

Center for Marriage, Family & Life—Tel: 804-622-5109 ; Fax: 804-358-9159; Email: cmfl@richmonddiocese.org; Email: marriageprep@richmonddiocese.org. MR. MICHAEL F. SCHOOL, Exec. Dir.; MS. CARRIE POSTON, Prog. Coord.

Youth & Young Adult—MS. KATIE YANKOSKI, Assoc. Dir.

Campus Ministry—MR. ANDREW WARING, Assoc. Dir.

Office of Worship—Rev. SEAN M. PRINCE, Dir.

Office for the Hispanic Apostolate—Sr. INMA CUESTA-VENTURA, C.M.S., Dir.

Office for Black Catholics & Asian Ministry—Deacon CHARLES WILLIAMS JR., Interim Dir.

Office of Social Ministries—MR. MICHAEL F. SCHOOL, Dir.; MS. RACHAEL LAUSTRUP, Assoc. Dir.; MS. CARRIE POSTON, Prog. Coord.; Rev. RICHARD T. MOONEY, Prison Ministry.

Diocesan Councils and Organizations

Catholic Relief Services—(See Office of Social Ministry).

Catholic Daughters of America—State Regent: EILEEN DUMANSKY, 7306 Parkline Dr., Richmond, 23226. Tel: 804-662-5663.

Catholic Virginian (Diocesan Newspaper)—MR. BRIAN OLSZEWSKI, Editor, Tel: 804-359-5654; Fax: 804-359-5689.

Council of Catholic Women—Contact: MRS. LOUISE HARTZ, Tel: 804-741-2487.

Cemeteries—Deacon ED HANDEL, Dir., Tel: 804-359-5661.

Council of Priests—See Presbyteral Council.

Catholic Charities—
Commonwealth Catholic Charities—1601 Rolling Hills Dr., Richmond, 23229. Tel: 804-285-5900. MS. JOANNE D. NATTRASS, M.B.A., B.S.N., R.N., Exec. Dir.
Catholic Charities of Eastern Virginia, Inc.—5361-A Virginia Beach Blvd., Virginia Beach, 23462. Tel: 757-467-7707. MR. CHRISTOPHER R. TAN, Exec. Dir.

Commission for Ecumenical & Interreligious Affairs—Rev. Msgr. JOSEPH P. LEHMAN, Tel: 540-774-0066; Email: Pastor@OLN-Parish.com.

Finance Council—Contact: MR. MICHAEL J. MCGEE, CFO.

Haitian Ministry Commission—Office of Social Ministries. Tel: 804-622-5222.

Knights of Columbus—State Deputy: MR. EDWARD R. POLICH, Email: statedeputy@vakofc.org.

Diocesan Pastoral Council—VACANT.

Diocesan School Board—3650 Hermitage Rd., Richmond, 23227. Tel: 804-822-3947. MS. JANE JOHNSON, Chm.

Presbyteral Council—Very Rev. WILLIAM DANIEL BEEMAN, V.F., Chm.

Propagation of the FaithDeacon ROBERT H. GRIFFIN.

Respect Life—MR. MICHAEL F. SCHOOL, Exec. Dir.

Secular Carmelite Communities—
Community of the Holy Spirit—SUNNI COWLING, O.C.D.S., Pres., 1211 Mt. Erin Dr., Richmond, 23231.
Community of Our Lady of the Annunciation—TIRA KNIPSEL, O.C.D.S., Pres., 1288 Alanton Dr., Virginia Beach, 23454.

Third Order of the Dominicans—
Lay Fraternity of St. Dominic—St. Thomas Aquinas Chapter *401 Alderman Rd., Charlottesville, 22903*. Very Rev. JOSEPH BARRANGER, O.P., Supvr.
Lay Fraternity of St. Dominic—Church of the Vietnamese Martyrs Rev. PAUL TRAN NGUYEN, O.P., 12500 Patterson Ave., Richmond, 23238.

Victim Assistance Coordinator—MS. JENNIFER SLOAN, Tel: 804-622-5175.

Youth Ministry Council—MR. MICHAEL F. SCHOOL.

Liturgical Commission—Rev. SEAN M. PRINCE.

Commission for Black Catholic—2609 Mountain Berry Ct., Glen Allen, 23060. Tel: 804-314-8556. MS. CANDRA PARKER, Chm.

Building and Renovation Committee—Rev. ROBERT J. COLE, 800 Los Conaes Way, Virginia Beach, 23456. Tel: 757-426-2180.

Campus & Young Adult Ministry—MR. MICHAEL F. SCHOOL.

Christian Formation Commission—Our Lady of Perpetual Help, 314 Turner Rd., Salem, 24153. Tel: 540-387-0491. MS. BARBARA HAIRFIELD.

CLERGY, PARISHES, MISSIONS AND PAROCHIAL SCHOOLS

CITY OF RICHMOND

1—CATHEDRAL OF THE SACRED HEART (1906) [JC] Very Rev. Msgr. Patrick D. Golden, V.F., Rector; Deacons Christopher M. Malone; Marshall D. Banks; Mark C. Matte; Charles Williams Jr.; Michael David DeNoia; Mary Rebecca Pugsley, Interim Campus Min.
Bishop's Office—
7800 Carousel Ln., 23294.
Cathedral Office—
800 S. Cathedral Pl., 23220-1569. Tel: 804-359-5651; Fax: 804-358-8043; Email: info@richmondcathedral.org; Web: www.richmondcathedral.org.
Church: 18 N. Laurel, 23220.
Catechesis Religious Program—Students 117.

2—ST. AUGUSTINE (Chesterfield Co.) (1973) Rev. Marlon Portillo Munoz, Admin.; Deacons Eric Christopher Broughton; Christopher Corrigan; Albert Hallat.
Res.: 9608 Verlinda Ct., 23237.
Church: 4400 Beulah Rd., 23237-1850.
Tel: 804-275-7962; Fax: 804-271-4604; Email: sta@staugustineparish.net; Web: www.staugustineparish.net.
Catechesis Religious Program—Students 356.

3—SAINT BENEDICT (1911) [JC]
Email: ioleary@saintbenedictparish.org. Rev. Anthony E. Marques.
Res.: 2900 Garrett St., 23221.
Church: 300 N. Sheppard St., 23221-2407.
Tel: 804-254-8810; Fax: 804-355-5112; Email: ioleary@saintbenedictparish.org; Web: www.saintbenedictparish.org.
School—Saint Benedict School
3100 Grove Ave., 23221. Tel: 804-254-8850;
Fax: 804-254-9163; Email: scress@saintbenedictschool.org; Web: www.saintbenedictschool.org. Mr. Sean M. Cruess, Prin. Lay Teachers 16; Students 182.
Catechesis Religious Program—
Email: rhamrick@saintbenedictparish.org. Robert Hamrick, D.R.E. Students 215.

4—ST. BRIDGET (Richmond, VA) (1949) Rev. Msgr. William H. Carr; Rev. John Christian, Parochial Vicar; Deacons Patrick Joseph White; Robert B. Giovenco; Victor Petillo. In Res., Very Rev. Msgr. R. Francis Muench, J.C.L.
Church: 6006 Three Chopt Rd., 23226-2730. Email: parishmail@saintbridgetchurch.org; Web: www.saintbridgetchurch.org.
School—Saint Bridget Catholic School
6011 York Rd., 23226. Tel: 804-288-1994;
Fax: 804-288-5730; Email: information@saintbridget.org; Web: www.saintbridget.org. Mr. George Sadler, Prin. Lay Teachers 35; Students 456.
Catechesis Religious Program—Students 271.

5—CHURCH OF THE EPIPHANY (Chesterfield Co.) (1979)
Mailing Address: 11000 Smoketree Dr., 23236-3144.
Tel: 804-794-0222; Fax: 804-378-2013; Email: epiphany@epiphanychurch.org; Web: www.epiphanychurch.org. Very Rev. John C. Kazibwe, (Uganda) V.F.; Deacons Stephen Haut; Belardino Lupini; Arthur Mendez.
See Regional School St. Edward - Epiphany, Richmond under St. Edward, Richmond for details.
Catechesis Religious Program—Students 465.

6—CHURCH OF THE VIETNAMESE MARTYRS (1983) (Vietnamese)
Mailing Address: 12486 Patterson Ave., 23238.
Tel: 804-784-5450; Email: cvmrectory@gmail.com. Rev. Paul Tuan Nguyen, O.P.; John Baptist Khoi Nguyen, Parochial Vicar.
Catechesis Religious Program—Students 257.

7—ST. EDWARD THE CONFESSOR (1959)
Mailing Address: 2700 Dolfield Dr., North Chesterfield, 23235. Tel: 804-272-2948;
Fax: 804-560-3565; Email: stedward@stedwardch.org; Web: www.stedchurch.com. Rev. Donald H. Lemay; Deacons James D. Greer; Thomas B. Elliott; Kevin Hogan; Robert D. Ewan.
Res. & Church: 10908 Ashburn Rd., North Chesterfield, 23237-2618.
School—Regional School St. Edward-Epiphany
10701 Huguenot Rd., 23235. Tel: 804-272-2881;
Fax: 804-272-2904. Mrs. Emily Elliott, Prin. Lay Teachers 50; Students 491.
Catechesis Religious Program—Students 667.

8—ST. ELIZABETH (1923) [JC] (African American)
Mailing Address: 1301 Victor St., 23222-3935. Revs. Daniel O. Brady; James M. Arsenault, Parochial Vicar.
Church: 2712 2nd Ave., 23222-3935.
Tel: 804-329-4599; Fax: 804-321-0741; Email: stelizcc@verizon.net; Web: www.stelizcc.org.
School—All Saints
3418 Noble Ave., 23222. Tel: 804-329-7524;
Fax: 804-329-4201. Mr. Kenneth Soistman, Prin.
Catechesis Religious Program—Students 7.

9—HOLY ROSARY (1953) (African American) Rev. David J. Stanfill; Deacons Francis Nelson Jr.; Melvin D. Dowdy.
Parish Office & Mailing Address: 3300 "R" St., 23223-0416. Tel: 804-222-1105; Fax: 804-226-2204; Email: office@hrccrichmond.org; Web: hrccrichmond.org.
Res.: 901 Hunters Run Dr., 23223.
Catechesis Religious Program—Students 48.

10—ST. JOSEPH (1991)
828 Buford Rd., 23235. Tel: 804-320-4932;
Fax: 804-451-1009; Email: office@stjosephrichmond.org; Web: www.stjosephrichmond.org. Revs. Robert

Novokowsky, F.S.S.P.; Terrence Gordon, F.S.S.P., Parochial Vicar.
Catechesis Religious Program—Students 103.
11—ST. KIM TAEGON (1986) (Korean)
Mailing Address: 3103 Maury St., 23224-3559.
Tel: 804-232-0993; Fax: 804-232-0992. Rev. Myoung-sang Lee.
Church: 3100 Logandale Ave., 23224.
Catechesis Religious Program—Students 49.
12—ST. MARY (1962)
Mailing Address: 9505 Gayton Rd., 23229-5319.
Tel: 804-740-4044; Fax: 804-740-2197; Email: parish@stmarysrichmond.org; Web: www.stmarysrichmond.org. Rev. Michael A. Renninger; Deacons Joseph Thomas Morlino; Frank Ronald Baskind, Ph.D.; Sr. Pat McCarthy, S.F.C.C., Pastoral Assoc.; Laura Stapleton, Youth Min.; Rebecca Oxenreider, Human Concerns; Joe Lenich, Music Min.; Mark Yeager, Dir. Parish Admin.; Gregg Kamper, Business Mgr.; Sharon Vrtis, Liturgy Dir.; Teresa Lee, Dir. Evangelism. In Res., Rev. James M. Arsenault.
School—St. Mary School
9501 Gayton Rd., 23229. Tel: 804-740-1048;
Fax: 804-740-1310. Dr. Thomas D. Dertinger, Prin. Lay Teachers 34; Students 450.
Catechesis Religious Program—John Sweet, D.R.E.; Christopher Jenkins, Youth Min. Students 454.
13—ST. MICHAEL (Glen Allen) (1992) [CEM]
Mailing Address: 4491 Springfield Rd., Glen Allen, 23060. Tel: 804-527-1037; Fax: 804-527-1039; Email: admin@saint-mikes.org; Web: www.saint-mikes.org. Revs. Daniel O. Brady; James M. Arsenault, Parochial Vicar; Deacons Andrew M. Ferguson, Business Mgr.; David S. Nemetz, Pastoral Assoc.; Robert H. Griffin.
Catechesis Religious Program—
Tel: 804-527-1037, Ext. 13; Email: pmundy@saint-mikes.org. Students 876.
14—OUR LADY OF LOURDES (Henrico Co.) (1944) [JC] Very Rev. James J. Begley Jr., V.F.; Rev. Valencia Zepeda, Parochial Vicar; Deacon James Van Wyk.
Church: 8200 Woodman Rd., 23228-3237.
Tel: 804-262-7315; Fax: 804-262-7337; Email: lourdes@ollrichva.org; Web: www.ollrichva.org.
School—Our Lady of Lourdes School
8250 Woodman Rd., 23228. Tel: 804-262-1770;
Fax: 804-200-6295; Email: admissions@lourdesrva.org; Email: frontoffice@lourdesrva.org; Web: www.lourdesrva.org. Mrs. Kelly Taylor, Prin. Lay Teachers 19; Students 375.
Catechesis Religious Program—
Email: mcottam@ollrichva.org. Students 150.
15—ST. PATRICK (1859)
Mailing Address: 213 N. 25th St., 23223-7115.
Tel: 804-737-8028; Fax: 804-328-4683; Email: office@saintpatrickchurchhill.org; Web: www.saintpatrickchurchhill.org. Revs. Gino P. Rossi; Frank Wiggins; Ernest Livasia Bulinda.
Catechesis Religious Program—Paulita Matheny, D.R.E. Students 12.
16—ST. PAUL (1921) [CEM]
Mailing Address: 909 Rennie Ave., 23227.
Tel: 804-329-0473; Fax: 804-321-6454; Email: churchoffice@saintpaulscc.com. Rev. James C. Griffin; Deacons John Tucker III; R. Wayne Snellings, Music Min., Dir. Worship, Business Mgr. & Administrative Asst. In Res., Rev. Wayne L Ball, J.C.L.
School—All Saints
3418 Noble Ave., 23222. Tel: 804-329-7524;
Fax: 804-321-1538. Wanda Wallin, Prin. Lay Teachers 10; Students 161.
Catechesis Religious Program—Students 40.
17—ST. PETER (1834)
Mailing Address: 800 E. Grace St., P.O. Box 933, 23219-0933. Email: stpeterchurch2@aol.com. Revs. Gino P. Rossi; Frank Wiggins; Ernest Livasia Bulinda.
Res.: 213 N. 25th St., 23223.
Church: 800 E. Grace St., 23219.
Catechesis Religious Program—Students 4.
18—SACRED HEART (1901) [JC]
Mailing Address: 1400 Perry St., 23224-2057.
Tel: 804-232-8964; Email: office@sacredheartrva.org. Rev. Shay W. Auerbach, S.J. In Res., Rev. John Podsiadlo, S.J., Email: jjpodsiadlo@gmail.com.
Res.: 1409 Perry St., 23224.
Church: 1401 Perry St., 23224.
Catechesis Religious Program—Students 174.

OUTSIDE THE CITY OF RICHMOND

ABINGDON, WASHINGTON CO., CHRIST THE KING (1983)
Mailing Address: P.O. Box 1201, Abingdon, 24212-1201. Very Rev. Francis Xavier Musolooza, V.F.
Res.: 168 Roger St., Abingdon, 24210.
Church: 820 E. Main St., Abingdon, 24210.
Tel: 276-628-2941; Email: office@ctk-abingdon.org; Web: www.ctk-abingdon.org.
Catechesis Religious Program—Students 52.
AMELIA, WASHINGTON CO., GOOD SAMARITAN (1980)
13441 Patrick Henry Hwy., Amelia, 23002.
Tel: 804-639-6712; Fax: 804-639-6591; Email: stgabrielmail@saintgabriel.org. Mailing Address: 8901 Winterpock Rd., Chesterfield, 23832. Rev. Dr. Felix Rex Amofa; Deacons Armando DeLeon, Pastoral Min./Coord.; Gerald Wyngaard, Pastoral Min./ Coord.
Catechesis Religious Program—Students 12.
AMHERST, AMHERST CO., ST. FRANCIS OF ASSISI (1995)
Mailing Address: 332 S. Main St., P.O. Box 663, Amherst, 24521. Tel: 434-946-2053; Email: parish@stfrancisamherst.comcastbiz.net; Web: stfrancisamherst.org. Rev. Carlos H. Lerma.
Catechesis Religious Program—Students 8.
APPOMATTOX, APPOMATTOX CO., OUR LADY OF PEACE (1982)
Mailing Address: 2938 Oakleigh Ave., P.O. Box 668, Appomattox, 24522-0668. Tel: 434-352-0104; Email: jimg301@juno.com. Rev. James E. Gallagher Jr.
Catechesis Religious Program—Students 22.
ASHLAND, HANOVER CO., ST. ANN (1892) Rev. Christian J. Haydinger, L.C.S.W.; Deacon Eugene P. Kamper; Lise Mikkelson, Pastoral Assoc.; Wanda Clarke, Admin. Asst.; Elizabeth Whitehead, Bookkeeper.
Res.: 105 S. Snead St., Ashland, 23005-1811.
Tel: 804-798-5039; Email: office@stannscc.org; Web: www.stannsashland.org.
Catechesis Religious Program—Students 275.
BEDFORD, BEDFORD CO., HOLY NAME OF MARY (1874)
Tel: 540-586-8988; Fax: 540-587-9080; Email: rbailey.hnm@gmail.com; Web: HolyNameofMary.net. Very Rev. Salvador Anonuevo, V.F.; Deacon William Edward Craig.
Res.: 1531 Newton Cir., Bedford, 24523.
Church: 1307 Oakwood St., Bedford, 24523.
Tel: 540-586-8988; Fax: 540-587-9080; Email: rbailey.hnm@gmail.com; Web: holynameofmary.net.
Catechesis Religious Program—Email: rporterfield.hnm@gmail.com. Rebecca Porterfield, D.R.E. Students 151.
BIG STONE GAP, WISE CO., SACRED HEART (1902) Rev. Jose Arnel Ayo. In Res., Rev. Leslie Schmidt, G.H.M.
Rectory—1821 Holton Ave. E., Big Stone Gap, 24219-2611. Tel: 276-523-1588; Fax: 276-523-1588; Email: stanthony3@verizon.net.
Catechesis Religious Program—Students 7.
BLACKSBURG, MONTGOMERY CO., ST. MARY (1938)
Mailing Address: 1205 Old Mill Rd., Blacksburg, 24060-3618. Tel: 540-552-1091; Fax: 540-953-2962; Email: officestaff@stmarysblacksburg.org; Email: businessmanager@stmarysblacksburg.org; Web: www.stmarysblacksburg.org. Revs. John Asare; David M. Sharland, Y.A., Campus Min., VA Tech.; Deacons Mike Ellerbrock; Richard Lee Furman.
NEWMAN COMMUNITY, 203 Otey St., Blacksburg, 24060. Tel: 540-951-0032.
Catechesis Religious Program—Email: formation@stmarysblacksburg.org. Susan Ellerbrock, D.R.E.
BLACKSTONE, NOTTOWAY CO., IMMACULATE HEART OF MARY (1947)
Mailing Address: 903 S. Main St., P.O. Box 266, Blackstone, 23824-0266. Tel: 434-292-5535;
Fax: 434-392-6677; Email: centralvacluster@gmail.com. Revs. Stefan Migac, (Slovakia); Paul Kkonde; Deacons Dr. Emmett R. McLane III, Pastoral Assoc.; Peter J. Menting.
Catechesis Religious Program—Students 28.
BRISTOL, BRISTOL CO., ST. ANNE (1903) [CEM]
Mailing Address: 350 Euclid Ave., Bristol, 24201-4014. Tel: 276-669-8200; Fax: 276-669-7825; Email: stannes@stannes-bristol.org; Web: www.stannes-bristol.org. Rev. Nicholas Mammi; Deacon Juan Ibarra, (Retired).
Res.: 922 Chester St., Bristol, 24201.
School—St. Anne School, (Grades PreK-8), 300 Euclid Ave., Bristol, 24201. Tel: 276-669-0048;
Fax: 276-669-3523; Email: schooloffice@stanneschoolbristol.org. Ms. Billie Schneider, Prin.; Mrs. Angie Bush, Librarian. Lay Teachers 21; Students 155.
Catechesis Religious Program—Students 97.
BROOKNEAL, CAMPBELL CO., ST. ELIZABETH OF HUNGARY (1957) Closed. For inquiries for parish records contact the chancery.
BUCKINGHAM, BUCKINGHAM, CO., CHURCH OF THE NATIVITY (1981) [CEM] Closed. For inquiries for parish records contact St. Theresa, Farmville.
BUMPASS, LOUISA CO., IMMACULATE CONCEPTION (1876) [CEM] See separate listing. See St. Jude, Mineral.
CAPE CHARLES, NORTHAMPTON CO., ST. CHARLES BORROMEO (1886) [CEM]
Mailing Address: 545 Randolph Ave., Cape Charles, 23310-3305. Tel: 757-331-1724 (Rectory);
Tel: 757-331-2040 (Office); Email: saintcharles545@gmail.com; Web: www.stcharlescatholicchurch.org. Rev. J. Michael Breslin.
Catechesis Religious Program—Students 42.
CAROLINE COUNTY, CAROLINE CO., ST. MARY OF THE ANNUNCIATION (1914) [CEM 2]
Mailing Address: P.O. Box 396, Ladysmith, 22501. Rev. Alexander Muddu; Deacons David J. Geary; Francis Leaming Jr.
Office & Church: 10306 Ladysmith Rd., Ruther Glen, 22546. Tel: 804-448-9064; Email: office.saintmarycc@gmail.com.
Catechesis Religious Program—Students 110.
CHARLOTTESVILLE, ALBEMARLE CO.
1—HOLY COMFORTER CATHOLIC CHURCH (1880) Very Rev. Joseph Mary Lukyamuzi, V.F.
Res.: 133 Old Fifth Cir., Charlottesville, 22903.
Crozet Catholic Community, 208 E. Jefferson St., Charlottesville, 22902-5105. Tel: 804-295-7185;
Fax: 434-220-1464; Email: office@holycomforterparish.org; Email: jlukyajm@holycomforterparish.org; Web: www.holycomforterparish.org.
Catechesis Religious Program—Tel: 434-295-6559; Email: cre@holycomforterparish.org. Ms. Susan Dougherty, C.R.E. Students 90.
2—CHURCH OF THE INCARNATION (1976)
1465 Incarnation Dr., Charlottesville, 22901-1716.
Tel: 434-973-4381; Email: office@incarnationparish.org; Web: www.incarnationparish.org. Revs. Gregory R. Kandt; Jaime Guardado, Parochial Vicar; Deacons Christopher G. Morash, Dir. Worship & Music; Thomas Healey.
Res.: 838 Belvedere Blvd., Charlottesville, 22901-3201.
School—Charlottesville Catholic School, 1205 Pen Park Rd., Charlottesville, 22901. Tel: 434-964-0400;
Fax: 434-964-1373; Email: info@cvillecatholic.org; Web: www.cvillecatholic.org. Mr. Michael J. Riley, Prin. Lay Teachers 26; Students 309.
Catechesis Religious Program—1465 Incarnation Drive, Charlottesville, 22901. Tel: 434-973-4381. Mrs. Maria Nootbaar, D.R.E. Total Students 324; Elementary School Students 243; High School Students 81.
3—ST. THOMAS AQUINAS (1963) [JC]
Tel: 434-293-8081; Email: admin@stauva.org; Web: www.stauva.org. Very Rev. Joseph Barranger, O.P.; Revs. Mario Aquinas Calabrese, O.P., Parochial Vicar; Anthony Di Tolve; David Mott, Parochial Vicar; Joseph-Anthony Kress, Campus Min.; William Garrott, O.P., Chap.; Deacon Joseph Michael Fitzgerald Jr. In Res.
Res.: St. Thomas Aquinas Priory, 98 Midmont. Ln., Charlottesville, 22903. Tel: 434-977-5658; Email: frdavid@stauva.org.
Church & Mailing Address: 401 Alderman Rd., Charlottesville, 22903. Tel: 434-293-8083;
Tel: 434-293-8081; Email: admin@stauva.org; Web: www.stauva.org.
Catechesis Religious Program—Tel: 434-293-8081; Email: dre@stauva.org; Email: edge@stauva.org; Email: youth@stauva.org. Eleanor Nicholson, D.R.E.; Ms. Mariah Naegele, Admin.; Karl Meier, Youth Min. (High School). Students 327.
CHESAPEAKE, CHESAPEAKE CO.
1—ST. BENEDICT (1992) Revs. Neal Nichols; Anthony Forte, Parochial Vicar.
Office & Res.: 521 McCosh Dr., Chesapeake, 23320-6111. Tel: 757-543-0561; Fax: 757-543-3510; Email: frdamian521@hrcoxmail.com; Web: www.stbenedictsparish.org.
Catechesis Religious Program—Students 81.
2—CHURCH OF ST. THERESE OF LISIEUX (1954) Rev. Kevin J. O'Brien, Ph.D.; Deacon Frederick Clarence Allen III.
Res.: 321 Saunders Dr., Portsmouth, 23701.
Church: 4137 Portsmouth Blvd., Chesapeake, 23321-2127. Tel: 757-488-2553; Fax: 757-465-4086; Email: info@sttheresechesva.org; Web: www.sttheresechesva.org.
Catechesis Religious Program—Students 235.
3—ST. MARY (1915)
Mailing Address: 3501 Cedar Ln., Portsmouth, 23703. Revs. Anthony William Morris; Paul Kkonde.
Church: 536 Homestead Rd., Chesapeake, 23321.
Tel: 757-484-7335; Fax: 757-484-5857; Email: saintmary@clusterparishes.com.
Catechesis Religious Program—Students 10.
4—PRINCE OF PEACE (1975)
Mailing Address: 621 Cedar Rd., Chesapeake, 23322.
Tel: 757-547-0356; Fax: 757-436-6477; Email: pop.office@popparish.org; Web: www.popparish.org. Very Rev. Romeo D. Jazmin, V.F.; Deacon Adrian A. Marchi, Ph.D.
Res.: 303 Elberon Ct., Chesapeake, 23322.
Catechesis Religious Program—Students 371.
5—ST. STEPHEN, MARTYR (1997)
Mailing Address: 1544 S. Battlefield Blvd., Chesapeake, 23322-2041. Tel: 757-421-7416;
Fax: 757-421-7488; Email: ssm@ssmrcc.org; Web: ssmrcc.org. Rev. Brian M. Rafferty; Deacons Keith A. Fournier; Kevin F. Trail.
Res.: 1560 S. Battlefield Blvd., Chesapeake, 23322.
Catechesis Religious Program—Students 671.
CHESTERFIELD, CHESTERFIELD CO., ST. GABRIEL (1997) Rev. Dr. Felix Rex Amofa; Deacons Roy Smith; Gerald Wyngaard.

Office & Mailing Address: 8901 Winterpock Rd., Chesterfield, 23832. Tel: 804-639-6712;
Fax: 804-639-6591; Email: stgabrielemail@stgabriel.org; Web: www.saintgabriel.org.
Catechesis Religious Program—Email: lisa.gorton@saintgabriel.org. Lisa Gorton, D.R.E. Students 276.

CHINCOTEAGUE ISLAND, ACCOMACK CO., ST. ANDREW THE APOSTLE (1965) Rev. Michael Montalban Imperial, Admin.
Res. & Mailing Address: 6319 Mumford St., Chincoteague Island, 23336. Tel: 757-336-5432;
Fax: 757-336-3515; Email: saintandrewcatholicchurch@gmail.com.
Church: 6288 Church St., Chincoteague Island, 23336.
Catechesis Religious Program—Students 18.

CHRISTIANSBURG, MONTGOMERY CO., HOLY SPIRIT CATHOLIC CHURCH (1995) Very Rev. Anthony O. Senyah, V.F.
Church: 355 Independence Blvd., Christiansburg, 24073. Tel: 540-381-0299; Email: officemanager@holyspiritcatholic.net.
Catechesis Religious Program—Students 75.

CLARKSVILLE, MECKLENBURG CO., ST. CATHERINE OF SIENA (1947) [CEM]
Mailing Address: 805 Virginia Ave., P.O. Box 1537, Clarksville, 23927. Tel: 434-374-8408;
Fax: 434-374-9442; Email: saintcatherines@usa.net. Revs. Rogelio A. S. Largoza; Eric Baffour Asamoah, Parochial Vicar; Deacon John E. Sadowski.
Res.: 810 Market St., Clarksville, 23927.
Catechesis Religious Program—Camille Borowski, D.R.E. Students 24.

CLIFTON FORGE, ALLEGHANY CO., ST. JOSEPH (1889) [CEM]
Mailing Address: 620 Jefferson Ave., Clifton Forge, 24422-1715. Tel: 540-863-5371. Revs. Stephen McNally; Thomas R. Collins, Parochial Vicar, (Retired). In Res., Rev. Daniel L. Kelly.
Catechesis Religious Program—

CLINTWOOD, DICKENSON CO., ST. JOSEPH (1979)
Mailing Address: P.O. Box 1250, Clintwood, 24228-1250. Tel: 276-926-5451; Web: www.clintwoodva.catholicweb.com. Rev. Jose Arnel Ayo.
Church: 478 Clintwood Main St., Clintwood, 24228.
Catechesis Religious Program—Students 1.

COLONIAL HEIGHTS, COLONIAL HEIGHTS CO., ST. ANN (1925) [CEM]
Mailing Address: 17111 Jefferson Davis Hwy., Colonial Heights, 23834-5396. Tel: 804-526-2548;
Email: saintann@stanncc.com; Web: www.stanncc.com. Very Rev. Daniel Andrew Cogut, V.F.
Res.: 16024 Searchlight Ct., Chester, 23831.

COLUMBIA, FLUVANNA CO., ST. JOSEPH'S/SHRINE OF ST. KATHARINE DREXEL (1884)
Mailing Address & Parish House: 28 Cameron St., P.O. Box 808, Columbia, 23038-0808.
Tel: 434-842-3970. Rev. Gerald F. Musuubire; Deacon Robert Allen.
Res.: 15 Dogleg Rd., Palmyra, 22963.
Catechesis Religious Program—5125 Rosewood Tr., Columbia, 23038. Students 22.

COVINGTON, ALLEGHANY CO., SACRED HEART (1924) Revs. Stephen McNally; Thomas R. Collins, Parochial Vicar, (Retired).
Office: 214 W. Locust St., Covington, 24426-1537.
Tel: 540-962-6541; Email: sacredheart24426@yahoo.com.
Res.: 220 W. Locust St., Covington, 24426-1537.
Catechesis Religious Program—Students 1.

CREWE, NOTTOWAY CO., ST. JOHN THE BAPTIST (1939) [CEM] Closed. For inquiries for parish records contact the chancery.

DANVILLE, PITTSYLVANIA CO., SACRED HEART (1878)
Mailing Address: 538 Central Blvd., Danville, 24541.
Tel: 434-792-9456; Fax: 434-792-9463; Email: shc_adm@comcast.net; Web: www.sheartchurch.org. Rev. Jonathan Goertz.
Res.: 154 College Ave., Danville, 24541.
School—Sacred Heart School, 540 Central Blvd., Danville, 24541. Tel: 434-793-2656;
Fax: 434-793-2658; Email: kskania@sheartschool.com; Web: www.sheartschool.com. Kira S. Kania, Prin. Lay Teachers 17; Students 163.
Catechesis Religious Program—Students 184.

DINWIDDIE, DINWIDDIE CO., ST. JOHN (1907) [CEM]
Mailing Address: 7215 Squirrel Level Rd., Petersburg, 23805-7035. Tel: 804-861-0123;
Fax: 804-861-0123; Email: info@stjohndinwiddie.org; Web: www.stjohndinwiddie.org. Revs. Christopher Martin Hess; Ernest Livasia Bulinda; Julio Ciraco Barrameda Buena; Deacon Matthew C. MacLaughlin.
Church: 7310 Squirrel Level Rd., Petersburg, 23805.
Catechesis Religious Program—

ELKTON, ROCKINGHAM CO., HOLY INFANT (1951)
Mailing Address & Church: 101 W. Marshall Ave., P.O. Box 301, Elkton, 22827. Tel: 540-298-1341;
Email: holy_infant@verizon.net; Web: www.holyinfant-elkton.org. Rev. Michael Mugomba.
Catechesis Religious Program—Mrs. Connie Youngman, D.R.E. Students 26.

EMPORIA, GREENSVILLE CO., ST. RICHARD (1940)
117 Laurel St., Emporia, 23847.
Tel: 434-634-3524 (Church Office); Email: sptamail@buggs.net. Rev. Joker R. Bayta.
Catechesis Religious Program—Ann Thomas, D.R.E.

FARMVILLE, PRINCE EDWARD CO.

1—SACRED HEART (1913) Rev. Paul Kkonde, Parochial Vicar; Deacons Dr. Emmett R. McLane III, Pastoral Assoc.; Peter J. Menting.
Church: 2597 Bruceville Rd., Meherrin, 23954.
Tel: 434-736-9390; Fax: 434-392-6677; Email: centralvacluster@gmail.com.

2—ST. THERESA (1939)
Mailing Address: 709 Buffalo St., Farmville, 23901-1109. Tel: 434-315-0311; Fax: 434-392-6677 (Office);
Email: sttheresa@embarqmail.com. Rev. Paul Kkonde, Parochial Vicar; Deacons Dr. Emmett R. McLane III; Peter J. Menting.
Res.: 816 Buffalo St., Farmville, 23901.
Catechesis Religious Program—Email: sttheresa2@embarqmail.com. Karel Bailey, D.R.E. Students 87.
LONGWOOD UNIVERSITY.
HAMPDEN-SYDNEY COLLEGE.

FINCASTLE, BOTETOURT CO., CHURCH OF THE TRANSFIGURATION (1989)
Tel: 540-473-2646. Rev. Stephen McNally.
Church & Mailing Address: 7624 Roanoke Rd., Fincastle, 24090. Tel: 540-473-2656; Email: transfigure@ntelos.net; Web: www.churchofthetransfiguration.com.
Catechesis Religious Program—Students 50.
Mission—St. John the Evangelist (2000) 99 Second St., New Castle, 24127.

FORT MONROE, HAMPTON CO., ST. MARY STAR OF THE SEA (1860)
Mailing Address: 7 Frank Ln., Fort Monroe, 23651-1010. Tel: 757-722-9855; Tel: 757-722-3138;
Fax: 757-726-0083; Email: stmary@starofthesea.hrcoxmail.com; Web: www.smsschurch.com. Very Rev. Msgr. Walter C. Barrett Jr.; Rev. Gerard Leoval C. Guadalupe; Deacon Michael Swisher; Kimberly A. Primo, Admin.
School—St. Mary Star of the Sea, 14 N. Willard Ave., Hampton, 23663. Tel: 757-723-6358;
Fax: 757-723-6544. Sr. Mary John, O.P., Prin. Lay Teachers 13; Sisters 4; Students 167.
Catechesis Religious Program—Students 10.

FRANKLIN, SOUTHAMPTON CO., ST. JUDE (1948)
Mailing Address: 1014 Clay St., Franklin, 23851-1309. Tel: 757-569-9600;
Fax: 757-569-9600 (Call First); Email: st_jude1@stjudefranklin.org. Rev. Charles A. Saglio Jr.
Catechesis Religious Program—Students 36.
Mission—Infant of Prague, Rte. 460, Wakefield, 23888.

GATE CITY, SCOTT CO., ST. BERNARD (1956)
Mailing Address: 139 Linda St., Gate City, 24251.
Tel: 276-386-9665; Email: frkevin@stannes-bristol.org. Rev. Nicholas Mammi. In Res., Rev. Timothy A. Drake.
Catechesis Religious Program—
Mission—St. Patrick (1946) Dungannon.

GLOUCESTER, GLOUCESTER CO., ST. THERESE, THE LITTLE FLOWER (1939) Rev. James Cowles.
Church & Mailing Address: 6262 Main St., Gloucester, 23061. Tel: 804-693-5939 (Office);
Fax: 804-693-4766; Email: office.1@stthersglo.org; Web: www.sainttheresechurch.info.
Catechesis Religious Program—Students 75.

HAMPTON, HAMPTON CO.

1—CATHOLIC COMMUNITY OF THE KOREAN MARTYRS (1989) (Korean), Merged with St. Rose of Lima, Hampton to form St. Rose of Lima and the Korean Martyrs Catholic Parish, Hampton.

2—IMMACULATE CONCEPTION (1968)
Tel: 757-826-0393; Email: parish@icchampton.org; Web: www.icchampton.org. Rev. John A. Grace.
Res.: 40 Pine Cone Dr., Hampton, 23669.
Church: 2150 Cunningham Dr., Hampton, 23666.
Tel: 757-826-0393; Email: churchoffice@icchampton.org; Web: www.icchampton.org.
Catechesis Religious Program—Students 96.

3—ST. JOSEPH (1955)
Mailing Address: 512 Buckroe Ave., Hampton, 23664. Tel: 757-851-8800; Fax: 757-851-1875; Web: stjosephscatholicchurch.net. Very Rev. Msgr. Walter C. Barrett Jr.; Rev. Gerard Leoval C. Guadalupe, Parochial Vicar; Deacons Jose M. Gonzalez; Guillermo Gonzalez. In Res:, Rev. John Bosco Walugembe.
Res.: 410 Buckroe Ave., Hampton, 23664-0126.
Church: 414 Buckroe Ave., Hampton, 23664-0126.
Catechesis Religious Program—Students 75.

4—OUR LADY OF VIETNAM CHAPEL (1994) (Vietnamese)
Mailing Address: 1806 Ashland Ave., Norfolk, 23509.
Tel: 757-531-7214; Tel: 757-232-1424. Rev. Joseph Phien Nguyen.
Chapel—1307 LaSalle Ave., Hampton, 23669.
Catechesis Religious Program—John Baptist Khoi Nguyen, D.R.E. Students 70.

5—ST. ROSE OF LIMA (1948) Merged with Catholic Community of the Korean Martyrs, Hampton to form St. Rose of Lima and the Korean Martyrs Catholic Parish, Hampton.

6—ST. ROSE OF LIMA AND THE KOREAN MARTYRS (2012)
2114 Bay Ave., Hampton, 23661. Tel: 757-245-5513;
Fax: 757-245-1277; Email: roselimakm@gmail.com; Web: www.strosekmcp.org. Rev. Simon Hyo Sung Ahn
Legal Name: St. Rose of Lima and the Korean Martyrs Catholic Parish
Res.: 2108 Bay Ave., Hampton, 23661.
Catechesis Religious Program—Students 35.

HARRISONBURG, ROCKINGHAM CO., BLESSED SACRAMENT (1906)
Tel: 540-434-4341; Email: office@bsccva.com; Web: blessedsacramentva.org. Very Rev. Silvio Kaberia, V.F.; Rev. Jose Melendez II, Parochial Vicar.
Mailing Address & Church: 154 N. Main St., Harrisonburg, 22802. Tel: 540-434-4341;
Fax: 540-434-5549; Email: mmoyers@bsccva.com; Web: www.bsccva.com.
Res.: 1682 Sherry Ln., Harrisonburg, 22801.
Catechesis Religious Program—Students 450.

HIGHLAND SPRINGS, HENRICO CO., ST. JOHN THE EVANGELIST (1929) Revs. Gino P. Rossi; Frank Wiggins, Parochial Vicar; Ernest Livasia Bulinda, Parochial Vicar.
Res.: 213 N. 25th St., 23223.
Church: 813 W. Nine Mile Rd., Highland Springs, 23075. Tel: 804-737-8028; Fax: 804-328-4683; Email: office@stjohnscatholicchurch.org; Web: www.stjohnscatholicchurch.org.
Catechesis Religious Program—Email: pmatheny@stjohnscatholicchurch.org. Paulita Matheny, D.R.E. Students 175.

HOPEWELL, HAMPTON CO., ST. JAMES CHURCH (1918)
Mailing Address: 510 W. Poythress St., Hopewell, 23860-2508. Tel: 804-458-9223; Email: office@stjameshopewell.comcastbiz.net. Revs. Christopher Martin Hess; Julio Ciraco Barrameda Buena, Parochial Vicar.
Res.: 102 N. Fifth Ave., Hopewell, 23860.
Church: 500 W. Poythress St., Hopewell, 23860.
Catechesis Religious Program—Students 40.

HOT SPRINGS, BATH CO., THE SHRINE OF THE SACRED HEART (1922)
Mailing Address: 1499 Shady Ln., Hot Springs, 24445-0047. Tel: 540-839-2603. Rev. John McGinnity, (Retired).
Catechesis Religious Program—Email: shrine@tds.net.

HURT, PITTSYLVANIA CO., ST. VICTORIA (1962)
Mailing Address: P.O. Box 640, Hurt, 24563-0640.
Tel: 434-324-4824; Email: stviccach@fairpoint.net. Rev. James E. Gallagher Jr.; Deacon Christopher Barrett.
Res.: 305 Victoria Dr., Hurt, 24563.
Catechesis Religious Program—Mrs. Kassaundra Carey, D.R.E. Students 11.

JONESVILLE, LEE CO., CHURCH OF THE HOLY SPIRIT (1956)
Mailing Address: P.O. Box 923, Jonesville, 24263.
Tel: 276-346-0269; Email: stanthonys3@verizon.net. Rev. Jose Arnel Ayo.
Church: 384 Eagle Ridge Dr., Jonesville, 24263.
Catechesis Religious Program—Students 6.

LAKE GASTON, MECKLENBERG CO., ST. PETER THE APOSTLE (1995) Rev. Joker R. Bayta.
Church: 31 Ebony Rd., Ebony, 23845.
Tel: 434-636-7782; Fax: 434-636-6277; Email: sptamail@buggs.net; Web: www.st-peter-the-apostle.org.
Catechesis Religious Program—

LEBANON, RUSSELL CO., GOOD SHEPHERD (1959)
Mailing Address: 890 W. Main St., Lebanon, 24266-0730. Tel: 276-889-1690; Email: smstgscatholicchurch@gmail.com; Web: www.spiritofthemountain.org. P.O. Box 730, Lebanon, 24266-0730. Rev. Zaverio Banasula, (Uganda) Admin.
Catechesis Religious Program—Students 13.

LEXINGTON, ROCKBRIDGE CO., ST. PATRICK (1873)
P.O. Box 725, Lexington, 24450. Rev. Joseph A. D'Aurora.
Office & Mailing: 221 W. Nelson St., P.O. Box 725, Lexington, 24450-0725. Tel: 540-463-3533;
Fax: 540-464-3790; Email: officestpats@embarqmail.com; Web: stpatrickslexington.com.
Res.: 225 Denny Ln., Lexington, 24450-1700.
Church: 219 W. Nelson St., Lexington, 24450.
Catechesis Religious Program—Email: restpats@embarqmail.com. Kathleen Nowacki-Correia, D.R.E. Students 25.
Missions—Virginia Military Institute—
Washington and Lee University.
Southern Virginia University.

LOVINGSTON, NELSON CO., ST. MARY CATHOLIC CHURCH (1979)

Mailing Address: 9900 Thomas Nelson Hwy., Lovingston, 22949-0735. Tel: 434-263-8509; Email: stmarystfrancischurch@verizon.net; Web: www.stmarycatholicchurch.org. Rev. Carlos H. Lerma; Deacon Richard J. Nees.
Catechesis Religious Program—Tel: 434-263-6923. Students 50.

LYNCHBURG, CAMPBELL CO.

1—HOLY CROSS (1859) [CEM] Rev. Msgr. J. Kenneth Rush Jr., D.Min. In Res., Rev. James E. Gallagher Jr.
Church & Office Address: 710 Clay St., Lynchburg, 24504-2530. Tel: 434-846-5245; Fax: 434-846-7022; Web: www.holycrosslynchburg.org.
Res.: 2000 Burnt Bridge Rd., Lynchburg, 24503.
School—Holy Cross Regional Catholic School, (Grades PreK-12), 2125 Langhorne Rd., Lynchburg, 24501. Tel: 434-847-5436; Fax: 434-847-4156. Mrs. Mary Sherry, Prin.; Holly Main, Librarian. Lay Teachers 35; Students 190.
Catechesis Religious Program—Students 200.

2—ST. THOMAS MORE (1978)
3015 Roundelay Rd., Lynchburg, 24502-2036.
Tel: 434-237-5911; Fax: 434-237-8854; Email: info@stmva.com; Web: www.stmva.com. Rev. Msgr. Michael D. McCarron; Deacon Frederick Scarletto.
Catechesis Religious Program—Tel: 434-237-8852; Email: faithformation@stmva.com. Students 105.

MARION, SMYTH CO., ST. JOHN THE EVANGELIST CHURCH (1974) Very Rev. Francis Xavier Musolooza, V.F.; Deacon Juan Ibarra, Hispanic Ministry.
Church: 124 Park Blvd., Marion, 24354.
Tel: 276-783-7282; Fax: 276-783-7282.
Catechesis Religious Program—Students 17.

MARTINSVILLE, HENRY CO., ST. JOSEPH (1949) (Hispanic)
Mailing Address: 2481 Spruce St., Martinsville, 24112. Tel: 276-638-4779; Tel: 276-638-1192; Fax: 276-638-2218; Email: office.stjoe24221@comcastbiz.net; Web: www.stjoechurch.net. Rev. Mark White.
Res.: 1810 Spruce St., #117, Martinsville, 24112.
Catechesis Religious Program—Students 80.

MATHEWS, MATHEWS CO., CHURCH OF FRANCIS DE SALES (1983) [JC] Very Rev. Gerald S. Kaggwa, V.F.
Church: 176 Lover's Ln., Mathews, 23109.
Tel: 804-725-2776; Fax: 804-725-0528; Email: fdschurch@gmail.com; Web: www.churchoffrancisdesales.org.
Catechesis Religious Program—Students 37.

MECHANICSVILLE, HANOVER CO., CHURCH OF THE REDEEMER (1976) Rev. John J. Wagner III; Deacons Christopher Stephen Colville; Ronald A. Reger.
Church & Mailing Address: 8275 Meadowbridge Rd., Mechanicsville, 23116. Tel: 804-746-4911; Fax: 804-746-8657; Email: sphillips@churchredeemer.org; Web: www.churchredeemer.org.
Res.: 8222 N. Mayfield Ln., Mechanicsville, 23111.
Catechesis Religious Program—Mrs. Terry Colville, D.R.E.; Mr. LeRoy Orie Jr., Youth Min.; Mrs. Loraine Tracy, Coord. (Adult). Students 408.

MINERAL, LOUISA CO., ST. JUDE (1974) [CEM]
Mailing Address: 1937 Davis Hwy., P.O. Box 40, Mineral, 23117-0040. Tel: 540-894-4266; Fax: 540-894-4993; Email: office@louisacatholics.org; Web: www.louisacatholics.org. Very Rev. Michael M. Duffy, J.C.L.; Deacon Alfonso Benet.
Rectory—Email: louisacatholics@verizon.net.
Church: 1883 Davis Hwy., P.O. Box 541, Louisa, 23093-0541. Tel: 540-894-8209.
Catechesis Religious Program—Tel: 540-223-1563; Email: dre.louisacatholics@gmail.com. Jess Johnson, D.R.E. Students 100.
Mission—Immaculate Conception (1876) [CEM] 1107 Fredericks Hall Rd., P.O. Box 128, Bumpass, 23024-0128.
Catechesis Religious Program—Students 23.

MONETA, BEDFORD CO., RESURRECTION (1984) [CEM]
Mailing Address: 15353 Moneta Rd., Moneta, 24121-9804. Tel: 540-297-5530; Fax: 540-297-6316; Email: info@resurrectioncatholic.org; Web: www.resurrectioncatholic.org. Very Rev. Salvador Anonuevo, V.F.; Deacon Barry Dwayne Welch, Pastoral Assoc.; Joe Day, Business Admin.
Catechesis Religious Program—Students 67.

NEW CASTLE, CRAIG CO., SAINT JOHN THE EVANGELIST MISSION (1997)
99 Second St., New Castle, 24127. Tel: 540-864-8686; Email: stjohnnewcastle@tds.net. Rev. Stephen McNally.
Catechesis Religious Program—Students 7.

NEWPORT NEWS, NEWPORT CO.

1—ST. JEROME (1966)
Mailing Address: 116 Denbigh Blvd., Newport News, 23608-3333. Tel: 757-877-5021; Fax: 757-898-1437; Email: stjerome@stjeromennva.org; Web: www.stjeromennva.org. Rev. Patrick Baffour-Akoto; Deacon Peter Eric Palm.
Catechesis Religious Program—Tel: 757-877-3771; Email: margie@stjeromennva.org. Students 323.

2—OUR LADY OF MOUNT CARMEL (1953)
100 Harpersville Rd., Newport News, 23601-2324.
Tel: 757-595-0385; Fax: 757-599-9285; Email: frjdramsey@olmc.org; Web: www.olmc.org. Very Rev. John David Ramsey, V.F.; Revs. Peter Tran, (Retired); Nicholas Redmond, Parochial Vicar; Deacons Antonio Siochi; Edwin Anleu Sandoval; Daniel F. Johnson.
School—Our Lady of Mount Carmel School, Tel: 757-596-2754; Email: principal@olmc-school.com; Web: www.olmc-school.com. Students 275.
Catechesis Religious Program—
Tel: 757-595-0385, Ext. 107. Students 249.

3—ST. VINCENT DE PAUL (1881) Rev. John Bosco Walugembe.
Church & Mailing Address: 230 33rd St., P.O. Box 258, Newport News, 23607-0258. Tel: 757-245-4234; Fax: 757-245-0039; Email: stvdpcc@verizon.net; Web: www.stvincentsnn.org.
Catechesis Religious Program—Students 16.

NORFOLK, NORFOLK CITY CO.

1—BASILICA OF ST. MARY OF THE IMMACULATE CONCEPTION (1791) [JC] (African American)
Tel: 757-622-4487. Rev. James P. Curran, Rector; Deacons Calvin J. Bailey; Harold L. Sampson.
Office & Rectory: 1000 Holt St., Norfolk, 23504-4201. Tel: 757-622-4487; Fax: 757-625-7969; Email: admin@stmary.hrcoxmail.com; Web: www.basilicaofsaintmary.org.
Church: 232 Chapel St., Norfolk, 23504.
Catechesis Religious Program—Students 104.

2—BLESSED SACRAMENT (1921) [CEM]
Mailing Address: 6400 Newport Ave., Norfolk, 23505-4557. Tel: 757-423-8305; Fax: 757-451-3335; Email: office@blessed-sacrament.com; Web: www.blessed-sacrament.com. Rev. Joseph H. Metzger III.
Res.: 110 W. Severn Rd., Norfolk, 23505.
Catechesis Religious Program—Email: cmccrary@blessed-sacrament.com; Email: hkallenbach@blessed-sacrament.com. Claire McCrary, D.R.E.; Hannah Kallenbach, Youth Min. Students 356.

3—CHRIST THE KING (1949) Rev. Matthias Lusembo.
Office & Mailing Address—1803 Columbia Ave., Norfolk, 23509-1200. Tel: 757-622-1120; Tel: 757-622-9196; Fax: 757-627-8808; Email: office@christtheking.hrcoxmail.com; Web: www.ctkparish-norfolk.org.
Res.: 1804 Ashland Ave., Norfolk, 23509.
School—Christ the King School, 3401 Tidewater Dr., Norfolk, 23509. Tel: 757-625-4951; Fax: 757-623-5212; Email: info@ctkparish.org; Web: www.ctkparish.org. Dr. Francine Gagne, Ed.D., Prin. Lay Teachers 26; Students 278.
Catechesis Religious Program—
Tel: 757-622-1120, Ext. 4. Students 100.

4—HOLY TRINITY (1921) [JC]
Mailing Address: 154 W. Government Ave., Norfolk, 23503-2905. Tel: 757-480-3433; Fax: 757-480-8749; Email: parish.office@trinitynorfolk.org; Web: www.trinitynorfolk.org. Very Rev. William Daniel Beeman, V.F.
Catechesis Religious Program—Students 240.

5—OUR LADY OF LAVANG (1991) [JC]
1806 Ashland Ave., Norfolk, 23509-1236.
Tel: 757-232-1424; Tel: 757-531-7214. Rev. Joseph Phien Nguyen.
Church: 409 Compostella Rd., Norfolk, 23523.
Catechesis Religious Program—Joseph Trinh Tu, D.R.E. Students 50.

6—ST. PIUS X (1955)
7800 Halprin Dr., Norfolk, 23518-4408.
Tel: 757-583-0291; Fax: 757-583-0293; Email: church@piusxparish.org; Web: www.piusxparish.org. Rev. Nixon Negparanon; Deacon Robert S. Wash.
Res.: 1615 Longdale Dr., Norfolk, 23518.
School—St. Pius X School, Tel: 757-588-6171; Fax: 757-587-6580; Email: school@piusxparish.org; Web: stpiusxschoolva.org. Sr. Linda Taber, I.H.M., Pres. Lay Teachers 18; Sisters Servants of the Immaculate Heart of Mary 3; Students 247.
Catechesis Religious Program—Email: religioused@piusxparish.org; Email: youth@piusxparish.org. Yaylin Aponte, Youth Min. Students 72.

7—SACRED HEART (1894) [CEM] Rev. Paul Muyimbwa.
Office: 520 Graydon Ave., Norfolk, 23507-1711.
Tel: 757-625-6763; Fax: 757-627-1965; Email: office@sacredheartnorfolk.org; Web: www.sacredheartnorfolk.org.
Catechesis Religious Program—Students 88.

NORGE, JAMES CITY CO., ST. OLAF, PATRON OF NORWAY (1992)
Mailing Address: 104 Norge Ln., Williamsburg, 23188-7229. Tel: 757-564-3819; Fax: 757-565-1099; Email: office@stolaf.cc; Web: www.stolaf.cc. Rev. Thomas E. Mattingly; Deacons Robert R. Thompson; Neil Zachary; James Conklin.
Catechesis Religious Program—Students 179.

NORTON, WISE CO., ST. ANTHONY (1938) Rev. Jose Arnel Ayo.
Mailing Address & Church: 1009 Virginia Ave., N.W., Norton, 24273-1897. Tel: 276-679-2336; Email: tdrake@richmonddiocese.org; Web: www.stanthonycatholic.org.
Catechesis Religious Program—Students 32.
Station—University of Virginia at Wise, Wise.

ONLEY, ACCOMACK CO., ST. PETER THE APOSTLE CATHOLIC CHURCH (1942) Rev. Rogelio L. Abadano, Admin.
Church & Mailing Address: 25236 Coastal Blvd., P.O. Box 860, Onley, 23418-0860. Tel: 757-787-4592; Fax: 757-787-2899; Email: stpeterapostle@verizon.net.
Catechesis Religious Program—Students 62.

PALMYRA, FLUVANNA CO., SS. PETER & PAUL (1986)
Mailing Address: 4309 Thomas Jefferson Pkwy., Palmyra, 22963-9506. Tel: 434-589-5201; Fax: 434-589-4463; Email: office@saintspeterpaul.org; Web: www.saintspeterpaul.org. Rev. Gerald F. Musuubire.
Catechesis Religious Program—Students 105.

PEARISBURG, GILES CO., HOLY FAMILY (1965)
Mailing Address: 516 Mason Court Dr., Pearisburg, 24134-1832. Tel: 540-921-3547; Email: holyfamilyva@lycos.com. Very Rev. Anthony O. Senyah, V.F.
Catechesis Religious Program—

PETERSBURG, PRINCE GEORGE CO., ST. JOSEPH (1842) [CEM] Rev. Brian W. Capuano; Deacons Robert (Bob) Young; Donatus Theukwumere Amaram.
Church, Office & Mailing Address: 151 W. Washington St., P.O. Box 2006, Petersburg, 23804-1306. Tel: 804-733-3115; Fax: 804-862-9931; Email: st_joseph_church@sjcpetersburg.com; Web: www.sjcpetersburg.com.
Res.: 19 Centre Hill Ct., Petersburg, 23803.
School—St. Joseph School, 123 Franklin St., Petersburg, 23803. Tel: 804-732-3931; Fax: 804-732-6479. Joseph Whitmore, Prin. Lay Teachers 18; Students 156.
Catechesis Religious Program—
Tel: 804-733-3115, Ext. 15. Students 55.

POCAHONTAS, TAZEWELL CO., ST. ELIZABETH (1896) Merged with St. Mary, Richlands, St. Theresa, Tazewell & St. Joseph, Grundy to form Holy Family Parish, Tazewell.

PORTSMOUTH, PORTSMOUTH CO.

1—CHURCH OF THE HOLY ANGELS (1917) [JC]
34 Afton Pkwy., Portsmouth, 23702.
Tel: 757-484-7335; Fax: 757-484-5857; Email: holyangels@clusterparishes.com; Web: www.clusterparishes.com. Mailing Address: 3501 Cedar Ln., Portsmouth, 23703. Revs. Anthony W. Morris; Paul Kkonde, Parochial Vicar.
Catechesis Religious Program—Email: christianformation@clusterparishes.com. Kristi Harriman, D.R.E.

2—CHURCH OF THE RESURRECTION (1971)
Mailing Address: 3501 Cedar Ln., Portsmouth, 23703. Tel: 757-484-7335; Fax: 757-484-5857; Email: resurrection@clusterparishes.com; Web: www.clusterparishes.com. Revs. Anthony W. Morris; Paul Kkonde, Parochial Vicar.
Catechesis Religious Program—Email: christianformation@clusterparishes.com. Kristi Harriman, D.R.E.

3—ST. PAUL (1804) [CEM] [JC] Revs. Anthony W. Morris; Paul Kkonde, Parochial Vicar.
Office: 3501 Cedar Ln., Portsmouth, 23703-3803.
Tel: 757-484-7335; Fax: 757-484-5857; Email: saintpaul@clusterparishes.com; Web: www.clusterparishes.com.
Church: 522 High St., Portsmouth, 23704-3516.
Catechesis Religious Program—Email: christianformation@clusterparishes.com. Kristi Harriman, D.R.E.

POWHATAN, CAMPBELL CO., ST. JOHN NEUMANN (1948) [CEM] Rev. Walter G. Lewis; Deacons Edward P. Schmidt; James O. Tubbs; Mr. Gary Fitzgerald, Music Min.; Mrs. Lee Mecca, Business Mgr.
Church: 2480 Batterson Rd., Powhatan, 23139-7513.
Tel: 804-598-3754; Email: sjn_general@yahoo.com; Web: www.sjnpowhatan.org.
Catechesis Religious Program—Students 215.

QUINQUE, GREENE COUNTY, SHEPHERD OF THE HILLS (1980)
Mailing Address: P.O. Box 83, Quinque, 22965-0083.
Tel: 434-985-3929; Email: holy_infant@verizon.net. Rev. Michael Mugomba.
Church: Rte. 633, 6562 Amicus Rd., Quinque, 22965-0083.
Catechesis Religious Program—Jane Lilly, D.R.E. Students 28.

QUINTON, NEW KENT CO., ST. ELIZABETH ANN SETON (1986)
Mailing Address: P.O. Box 648, Quinton, 23141-0648. Rev. J. Scott Duarte, J.C.D.
Church: 2631 Pocahontas Tr., Quinton, 23141-0245.
Tel: 804-932-4125; Email: seascatholic@verizon.net; Web: www.seascatholicchurch.org.
Catechesis Religious Program—Tel: 804-932-3388;

Email: seas.dthomson@verizon.net. Donna Thomson, D.R.E. Students 52.

RADFORD, MONTGOMERY CO., ST. JUDE (1967)
Mailing Address: 1740 Tyler Rd., Christiansburg, 24073-6154. Tel: 540-639-5341; Email: stjuderadfordva@gmail.com; Web: stjuderadfordva.org. Rev. Charles Ssebalamu; Deacon Michael J. Ellerbrock.
Res.: 1800 Tyler Rd., Christiansburg, 24073.
Catechesis Religious Program—Email: stjudechurch@gmail.com. Susan Ellerbrock, D.R.E. Students 16.

RICHLANDS, TAZEWELL CO., ST. MARY (1962) Merged with St. Theresa, Tazewell, St. Elizabeth, Pocahontas & mission church of St. Joseph, Grundy to form Holy Family, Tazewell.

ROANOKE, ROANOKE CO.

1—ST. ANDREW (1890) Very Rev. Kevin L. Segerblom; Rev. Matthew Allen Kiehl, Parochial Vicar.
Res. & Mailing Address: 631 N. Jefferson St., Roanoke, 24016-1401.
Catechesis Religious Program—Students 265.

2—ST. GERARD (1946)
809 Orange Ave., N.W., Roanoke, 24016-1117.
Tel: 540-343-7744; Fax: 540-343-3599; Email: mail@stgerard.roacoxmail.com; Web: stgerardroanokeva.org. Very Rev. Kenneth J. Shuping, V.F.; Rev. Jose Alberto Moran Arce, Parochial Vicar.
Catechesis Religious Program—Tel: 540-343-3599. Maria Morales, D.R.E. Students 132.

3—OUR LADY OF NAZARETH (1914)
Mailing Address: 2505 Electric Rd., S.W., Roanoke, 24018-3599. Tel: 540-774-0066; Tel: 540-774-0857; Fax: 540-774-2148; Email: secretary@oln-parish.com; Web: www.oln-parish.org. Rev. Msgr. Joseph P. Lehman; Rev. James P. O'Reilly; Deacon Richard Surrusco, M.D.
Catechesis Religious Program—Tel: 540-774-0773; Email: cf@oln-parish.org. Students 185.

ROCKY MOUNT, FRANKLIN CO., ST. FRANCIS OF ASSISI (1984)
Mailing Address: 15 Glennwood Dr., Rocky Mount, 24151-2111. Tel: 540-483-9591; Email: churchsecretary556@gmail.com; Web: www.francis-of-assisi.org. Rev. Mark White; Mrs. Kayla Acosta, Sec.; Mrs. Pat Prillaman, Bookkeeper.
Catechesis Religious Program—Email: crefoa@gmail.com. Linda Siler, D.R.E. Students 118.

ST. PAUL, WISE CO., ST. THERESE (1954)
Mailing Address: 16661 Wise St., P.O. Box 56, St. Paul, 24283-0056. Tel: 276-889-1690; Email: smstgscatholicchurch@gmail.com; Web: www.spiritofthemountain.org. Rev. Zaverio Banasula, (Uganda) Admin.
Catechesis Religious Program—Students 1.

SALEM, PAGE CO., OUR LADY OF PERPETUAL HELP (1947)
Mailing Address: 314 Turner Rd., Salem, 24153-2399. Tel: 540-387-0491; Fax: 540-389-8237; Email: office@olphsalem.org; Web: www.olphsalem.org. Very Rev. Kenneth J. Shuping, V.F.; Deacons Eric M. Surat; John Eric Beach.
Catechesis Religious Program—Ms. Barbara Hairfield, D.R.E. Students 101.

SCOTTSVILLE, ALBEMARLE CO., ST. GEORGE (1975) [CEM]
Mailing Address: 7240 Scottsville Rd., P.O. Box 9, Scottsville, 24590-0009. Tel: 434-286-3724; Email: stgeorge604@juno.com. Very Rev. Joseph Barranger, O.P.; Deacon Michael Stinson.
Catechesis Religious Program—Anglea Scolfora, D.R.E. Students 42.

SMITHFIELD, ISLE OF WIGHT CO., CHURCH OF THE GOOD SHEPHERD (1984) Rev. Pio Antonio Yllana.
Church: 300 Smithfield Blvd., Smithfield, 23430.
Tel: 757-365-0579; Email: admin@cgsparish.org.
Catechesis Religious Program—Email: formation@cgsparish.org. Mary Langhill, D.R.E. Students 42.

SOUTH BOSTON, HALIFAX CO., ST. PASCHAL BAYLON (1953) [JC] Revs. Rogelio A. S. Largoza; Eric Baffour Asamoah, Parochial Vicar; Deacons Paul Buckman, Ph.D.; Richard Bolgiano.
Church: 800 John Randolph Blvd., South Boston, 24592-2943. Tel: 434-572-2285; Fax: 434-572-1725; Email: stpaschalchurch@embarqmail.com.
Catechesis Religious Program—Students 14.

SOUTH HILL, MECKLENBURG CO., GOOD SHEPHERD (1922)
1664 N. Mecklenburg Ave., South Hill, 23970-0621.
Tel: 434-447-3622; Fax: 434-447-4729; Email: goodsh23970@embarqmail.com. P.O. Box 621, South Hill, 23970-0621. Revs. Rogelio A. S. Largoza; Eric Baffour Asamoah, Parochial Vicar.
Catechesis Religious Program—Students 70.

SOUTH PRINCE GEORGE, PRINCE GEORGE CO., CHURCH OF THE SACRED HEART (1906) [CEM]
Mailing Address: 9300 Community Ln., South Prince George, 23805. Tel: 804-732-6385; Fax: 804-732-6385 ; Email: church@churchsacredheart.com; Web: www.churchsacredheart.com. Rev. Christopher Martin Hess; Deacons Edward G. Hanzlik; Edward Christ; Esaud Feliciano; Robert Straub.
Catechesis Religious Program—Students 148.

STAUNTON, AUGUSTA CO., ST. FRANCIS OF ASSISI (1844)
118 N. New St., Staunton, 24401-3636.
Tel: 540-886-9121; Fax: 540-885-5743; Email: office@stfrancisparish.org; Web: www.stfrancisparish.org. Rev. Joseph Wamala; Deacon James Kledzik.
Res.: 126 N. New St., Staunton, 24401.
Catechesis Religious Program—Students 151.

SUFFOLK, SUFFOLK CO., ST. MARY OF THE PRESENTATION (1927) Rev. Emmanuel Tobi Mensah.
Office: 202 S. Broad St., Suffolk, 23434-5715.
Tel: 757-539-5732; Fax: 757-538-0103; Email: office@stmarysuffolk.org; Web: www.stmarysuffolk.org.
Church: 200 S. Broad St., Suffolk, 23434.
Catechesis Religious Program—Students 77.

TABB, YORK CO., SAINT KATERI TEKAKWITHA (1986)
Tel: 757-766-3800; Fax: 757-766-1125; Email: lyankoski@stkateri.cc; Web: www.stkateri.cc. Rev. Robert M. Spencer; Mrs. Lori Yankoski, Admin.
Church & Office: 3800 Big Bethel Rd., Tabb, 23693-3814. Tel: 757-766-3800; Email: lyankoski@stkateri.cc; Web: www.stkateri.cc.
Catechesis Religious Program—Email: dgausmann@stkateri.cc. Mrs. Debra Gausmann, D.R.E. Students 178.

TAPPAHANNOCK, ESSEX CO., ST. TIMOTHY (1972)
Mailing Address: 413 St. Timothy Ln., Tappahannock, 22560-0129. Email: sttimothychurch@va.metrocast.net; Web: www.sttimothysparish.org. Rev. Herman Katongole.
Church: 708 N. Church Ln., Tappahannock, 22560.
Catechesis Religious Program—Students 35.

TAZEWELL, TAZEWELL CO.

1—HOLY FAMILY PARISH (1875)
312 Tazewell Ave., Tazewell, 24651.
Tel: 276-988-4626; Email: theword1875@verizon.net; Web: www.holyfamilyva.com. Rev. Jugene Uyola Espeleta.
Catechesis Religious Program—Students 7.

2—ST. THERESA (1980) Merged with St. Mary, Richlands, St. Elizabeth, Pochontas & mission church of St. Joseph, Grundy to form Holy Family, Tazewell.

TOPPING, MIDDLESEX CO., CHURCH OF THE VISITATION (1983) [JC]
Mailing Address: P.O. Box 38, Topping, 23169-0038.
Tel: 804-758-5160; Fax: 804-758-0676; Email: churchofthevisitation@va.metrocast.net; Web: www.church-of-the-visitation.org. Very Rev. Gerald S. Kaggwa, V.F.
Res.: 119 Club Dr., Hartfield, 23071.
Church: 8462 Puller Hwy., Topping, 23169.
Catechesis Religious Program—Students 6.

VIRGINIA BEACH, VIRGINIA BEACH CO., CHURCH OF THE ASCENSION (1972) Very Rev. Daniel J. Malingumu, V.F.; Rev. John R. Baab; Deacons Thomas E. McFeely; Gary R. Harmeyer; Lisa Liedl, Business Mgr.; Diane Nestor, Music Min.
Office: 4853 Princess Anne Rd., Virginia Beach, 23462-4446. Tel: 757-495-1886, Ext. 410; Fax: 757-495-1516; Email: secretary@ascensionvb.org.
Catechesis Religious Program—
Tel: 757-495-1886, Ext. 423. Janet Jones, D.R.E.; Travis Hayes, Youth Min. Students 222.

VIRGINIA BEACH, VIRGINIA CO.

1—CATHOLIC CHURCH OF ST. MARK (1978) [CEM]
Mailing Address: 1505 Kempsville Rd., Virginia Beach, 23464-7210. Tel: 757-479-1010;
Tel: 757-479-9897; Fax: 757-479-9453; Email: secretary@stmark-parish.org; Email: franthony@stmark-parish.org; Web: www.stmark-parish.org. Rev. Anthony Mpungu; Deacons Michael Johnson, Pastoral Assoc.; John J. Kren.
Res.: 4901 Whitewood Ln., Virginia Beach, 23464.
Catechesis Religious Program—Email: sharon@stmark-parish.org. Sharon Katzman, D.R.E. Students 390.

2—CHURCH OF THE HOLY APOSTLES (1977) (Anglican-Roman Catholic Congregation of Hampton Roads) Deacon Gary R. Harmeyer, Senior Pastoral Assoc.
Church: 1593 Lynnhaven Pkwy., Virginia Beach, 23453-2008. Tel: 757-427-0963; Fax: 757-427-9434; Email: admin@holyapostlesvb.org; Web: www.holyapostlesvb.org.
Catechesis Religious Program—Students 32.

3—ST. GREGORY THE GREAT (1957) Revs. Eric Vogt; Lee R. Yoakam, O.S.B., Parochial Vicar; Cristiano Aparecido Brito, O.S.B., Parochial Vicar; John J. Peck, O.S.B., Parochial Vicar; Deacons Robert Beardsworth, Sacramental Prep.; Paul Minner, Hispanic Min.; Darrell G. Wentworth; Bro. Tobias Yott, O.S.B., Liturgy Coord.; Toni Redifer, Business Mgr.; Diana Cuffley, Fin. Mgr.; Janice Figueroa-Lopez, Hispanic Min. Coord.; Laura Sage, Pastoral Assoc.
Office: 5345 Virginia Beach Blvd., Virginia Beach, 23462. Tel: 757-497-8330; Email: stgregoryg@aol.com; Web: stgregoryvabeach.org.
Child Care—St. Gregory the Great Daycare Center.
School—St. Gregory the Great School, 5343 Virginia Beach Blvd., Virginia Beach, 23462-1896.
Tel: 757-497-1811; Fax: 757-497-7005; Email: office@sggsvb.org. Gina Coss, Prin. Clergy 8; Lay Teachers 43; Religious 1; Students 660.
Catechesis Religious Program—Email: cwhisman@stgregorysva.org. Dr. Cathryn Whisman, D.R.E.; Sr. Brenda Query, I.H.M., Adult Faith Formation/RCIA; Thomas Gallagher, Youth Min. Students 1,051.

4—HOLY FAMILY (1977) Rev. Gaudencio G. Pugat; Deacon Robert May.
Parish Center—1279 N. Great Neck Rd., Virginia Beach, 23454-2117. Tel: 757-481-5702;
Tel: 757-481-0799; Fax: 757-481-3989; Email: businessmanager@holyfamilyvb.org; Web: www.holyfamilyvb.org.
Catechesis Religious Program—Students 318.

5—HOLY SPIRIT (1975) [CEM] Rev. Merlito M. Abiog; Deacon Robert J. Durel, Ph.D.
Office: 1396 Lynnhaven Pkwy., Virginia Beach, 23453-2710. Tel: 757-468-3600; Tel: 757-468-3601; Fax: 757-468-3342; Email: office@holyspiritvb.org; Web: www.holyspiritvb.org.
Res.: 3345 Clubhouse Rd., Virginia Beach, 23452.
Catechesis Religious Program—Students 413.

6—ST. JOHN THE APOSTLE CHURCH (1989)
1968 Sandbridge Rd., Virginia Beach, 23456.
Tel: 757-426-2180; Email: parish@sjavb.org; Web: www.sjavb.org. Rev. Robert J. Cole; Deacons Joseph F. Grillo; Vernon Krajeski, (Retired); Chris James Finocchio Jr.
School—St. John the Apostle Church School, 1968B Sandbridge Rd., Virginia Beach, 23456.
Tel: 757-821-1100; Fax: 757-821-1047. Ms. Miriam Cotton, M.Ed., Prin. Students 333; Staff 45.
Catechesis Religious Program—Email: jdomingo@sjavb.org. Mr. John Domingo, D.R.E. Students 367.

7—ST. LUKE (1986)
Mailing Address: 2304 Salem Rd., Virginia Beach, 23456-1215. Tel: 757-427-5776; Fax: 757-427-2260; Email: stlukecc@aol.com; Web: www.stlukevabeach.org. Rev. Msgr. Raphael A. Owusu Peprah, Admin.; Deacons Lawrence P. Illy; Anacleto Magsombol.
Catechesis Religious Program—Students 163.

8—ST. MATTHEW (1924) Revs. John Adam Abe; Stephen Opoku-Boaheng, Parochial Vicar; Deacons Cris Romero; William J. Blatnik; Daniel Sorady.
Office: 3314 Sandra Ln., Virginia Beach, 23464-1736.
Tel: 757-420-6310; Tel: 757-420-6311;
Fax: 757-420-7734; Email: office@saintmatts.net; Web: www.saintmatts.net.
Res.: 1020 Josephine Crescent, Virginia Beach, 23464.
School—St. Matthew School, 3316 Sandra Ln., Virginia Beach, 23464. Tel: 757-420-2455;
Fax: 757-420-4880; Email: office@smsvb.net; Web: www.smsvb.net. Mr. Louis Goldberg, Prin. Lay Teachers 44; Students 550.
Catechesis Religious Program—Students 164.

9—ST. NICHOLAS (1963) Rev. Venancio R. Balarote Jr.; Mrs. Lora Di Nardo, Pastoral Assoc.
Office & Church: 712 Little Neck Rd., Virginia Beach, 23452. Tel: 757-340-7231; Tel: 757-340-4551; Email: stnicholas@stnicholasvb.com; Email: thostutler@verizon.net; Web: www.stnicholasvb.com.
Res.: 3340 Old Kirkwood Dr., Virginia Beach, 23452-5807. Email: frvb@stnicholasb.com.
Catechesis Religious Program—Email: awhitehouse@stnicholasvb.com. Mrs. Angela Whitehouse, D.R.E. Students 271.

10—STAR OF THE SEA (1915) Rev. Esteban DeLeon.
Office: 1404 Pacific Ave., Virginia Beach, 23451-3439. Tel: 757-428-8547; Fax: 757-428-0788; Email: parishoffice@staroftheseaparish.com; Web: www.staroftheseaparish.com.
School—Star of the Sea School, 309 15th St., Virginia Beach, 23451. Tel: 757-428-8400;
Fax: 757-428-2794; Email: carey.averill@sosschool.org; Email: information@sosschool.org; Web: www.sosschool.org. Carey Averill, Prin. Lay Teachers 35; Students 182.
Catechesis Religious Program—Students 150.

WAYNESBORO, AUGUSTA CO., ST. JOHN THE EVANGELIST (1946)
Mailing Address: 344 Maple Ave., Waynesboro, 22980-4706. Email: jdunford@stjohnevan.com; Web: www.stjohnevan.com. Rev. Rolo B. Castillo.
Church: 300 Maple Ave., Waynesboro, 22980.
Catechesis Religious Program—Students 500.

WEST POINT, KING WILLIAM CO., OUR LADY OF THE BLESSED SACRAMENT (1918) [CEM 2]
Mailing Address: 207 W. Euclid Blvd., West Point, 23181-9378. Tel: 804-843-3125; Fax: 804-843-9158; Email: olbs@olbs.hrcoxmail.com; Email: pam.

watkins@olbs.hrcoxmail.com; Web: www.olbs-catholic.org. Rev. Oscar Paraiso.
Church: 3570 King William Ave., West Point, 23181.
Catechesis Religious Program—3510 King William Ave., Van den Boogaard Hall, West Point, 23181. Email: lrkryalls@cox.net. Mrs. Lorraine Ryalls, D.R.E. Students 47.

WILLIAMSBURG, JAMES CITY CO., ST. BEDE (1932)
Tel: 757-229-3631; Email: stboffice@bedeva.org. Rev. Msgr. Timothy E. Keeney; Revs. James M. Glass, O.S.B., William & Mary Chap.; Francis Boateng; Peter B. Naah; Deacons Gregory Ballentine; Francis Roettinger; William Westerman.
Res.: 4524 The Foxes, Williamsburg, 23188-2424.
Church & Mailing Address: 3686 Ironbound Rd., Williamsburg, 23188-5207. Tel: 757-229-3631; Fax: 757-229-7845; Email: stboffice@bedeva.org; Web: www.bedeva.org.
Catechesis Religious Program—Students 560.

WOODLAWN, CARROLL CO., ST. JOSEPH'S (1981)
Mailing Address: 3579 Carrollton Pike, Woodlawn, 24381-3651. Tel: 276-236-7814; Fax: 276-236-4897; Email: sjoffice@embarqmail.com. Revs. Pio Antonio Yllana; David Martin Ssentamu, Admin.
Catechesis Religious Program—Students 119.
Mission—Church of the Risen Lord, 59 Mountainview Loop, Stuart, 24171.
Catechesis Religious Program—Students 4.
Mission—Church of All Saints, 598 Needmore Rd., N.E., Floyd, 24091.
Catechesis Religious Program—Students 9.

WYTHEVILLE, WYTHE CO., ST. MARY THE MOTHER OF GOD St. Mary's Catholic Church (1845) [CEM]
Mailing Address: 370 E. Main St., Wytheville, 24382-0007. Tel: 276-228-3104; Fax: 276-228-3322; Email: stmarys10@embarqmail.com; Web: www.stmaryswytheville.com. P.O. Box 7, Wytheville, 24382. Rev. Bernie A. Ramirez; Deacon Charles William May.
Catechesis Religious Program—Students 12.
Mission—St. Edward, P.O. Box 1670, Pulaski, 24301.
Catechesis Religious Program—Students 23.

YORKTOWN, YORK CO., ST. JOAN OF ARC (1954) Rev. Michael Joly; Deacons James L. Satterwhite; Mark Mueller; Phillip Wilkinson.
Office & Res.: 315 Harris Grove Ln., Yorktown, 23692-4014. Tel: 757-898-5570; Fax: 757-898-0737; Email: cmacababbad@stjoanofarcva.org; Web: www.stjoanofarcva.org.
Catechesis Religious Program—Tel: 757-898-7190. Students 139.

Chaplains of Public Institutions

RICHMOND. *International Airport*. Rev. Gino P. Rossi, Chap., Tel: 804-737-8028.
McGuire VA Medical Center. Rev. Sean Labat, Chap., Tel: 804-675-5000, Ext. 5125.
St. Francis Hospital, 13710 St. Francis Blvd., Midlothian, 23114. Tel: 804-594-7300. Rev. Msgr. Thomas F. Shreve, PA., J.C.L., (Retired).

BLACKSBURG. *Virginia Polytechnic Institute & University*. Rev. David M. Sharland, Y.A., Email: fatherdavid.vtccm@gmail.com.

HAMPTON. *VA Medical Center*, Chaplain Service, Bldg. 69, Hampton, 23667. Tel: 757-722-9961, Ext. 3600. Rev. Donald J. Cavey.

HARRISONBURG. *James Madison University*. Rev. Peter Nassetta, Y.A., Chap., Tel: 540-434-7360.

SALEM. *Salem VA Medical Center*, Salem.
Tel: 540-982-2463. Rev. Evan Spencer, Tel: 540-982-2463.

VIRGINIA BEACH. *Holy Apostles Community*, 1593 Lynnhaven Pkwy., Virginia Beach, 23453.
Tel: 757-427-0963. Rev. Rene R. Castillo, Chap.

Military Chaplains:
Revs.—
Albano, Alwyn
Barakeh, Imad N.
Bruno, Robert
Butler, Timothy
Connolly, James M.T.
Creed, Peter M., (Retired)
Ianucci, Thomas
Kirk, David
Labat, Sean
McGuire, David V.
Milewski, John
Szamreta, John.

Unassigned:
Revs.—
Asher, Steven
Bostwick, John
Fosnot, James, (Retired)
Murphy, Dennis
Rule, Steven R.
Smith, Russell E., S.T.D.

Retired:
Rev. Msgrs.—
Barton, Raymond A., (Retired), 717 Runnymeade Cir., Virginia Beach, 23452
Perkins, Robert M., (Retired), 7501 River Rd., #9-D, Newport News, 23607. Tel: 757-244-0258
Schmied, Michael S., (Retired), 1538 Heritage Hill Dr., 23238
Shreve, Thomas F., PA., J.C.L., (Retired), 1001 Clayborne Ln., Midlothian, 23114. Tel: 804-339-7731
Revs.—
Apuzzo, Pasquale, (Retired), 200 N. Grove Ave., Highland Springs, 23075
Bain, Daniel, (Retired), 141 Green Turtle Ln., Apt. 8, Charlottesville, 22901. Tel: 434-974-7730
Benoit, Louis, (Retired), 3106 H Honeywood Ln., Roanoke, 24018. Tel: 540-958-0422
Bond, B. Daniel, (Retired), 8280 Woodman Rd., 23228. Tel: 804-684-5293
Brickner, Charles W., (Retired), 3991 Floyd Pike, Hillsville, 24343. Tel: 276-237-2339
Caiazzo, Gregory G., (Retired), 210 Glenwood Dr., Conway, SC 29526
Carr, James V., (Retired), 217 Beach 99th St., Rockaway Park, NY 11694
Clark, Joseph L., (Retired), 1016 Donation Dr., Virginia Beach, 23455. Tel: 757-464-1816
Collins, Thomas R., (Retired), St. Joseph, 620 Jefferson Ave., Clifton Forge, 24422
Creed, Peter M., (Retired), Tel: 757-250-3205
Cummins, Robert L. Jr., (Retired), 725 Brunswick Rd., Portsmouth, 23701
Dinga, William, (Retired)
Dorson, James E., (Retired), 133 Routier Hill, Hot Springs, 24445
Facura, Joseph C., J.C.L., S.L.D., (Retired), Blk. 3, St. Gabriel Sub.Div., Koronadal City, South Cotabato Philippines 9506
Feusahrens, Frederick J., (Retired), 909 Rennie Ave., 23227-4808
Funk, Virgil C., (Retired), 12960 S.W. Park Way, Portland, OR 97225. Tel: 503-643-3734
Goodman, Julian, (Retired), 11800 Paddock Dr., Midlothian, 23113
Guarnieri, Leo J., (Retired), P.O. Box 193, Sarita, TX 78385. Tel: 361-294-5301
Hai-Nguyen, Joseph, Ph.D., (Retired), 2027 Richland Ct., Sugar Land, TX 77478
Hickman, J. Stephen, (Retired), 197 Big Sky S.W., Los Lunas, NM 87031
Huan, Joseph Van Tran, (Retired)
Ilano, Jovencio, Ph.B., M.Div., (Retired), P.O. Box 4902, Virginia Beach, 23454
Klem, Daniel N., (Retired), 520 Graydon Ave., Norfolk, 23507. 520 Graydon Ave., Norfolk, 23507
Maier, Paul, (Retired), 650 N. Jefferson St., Rm. 305, P.O. Box 11586, Roanoke, 24016
Majewski, Joseph B., (Retired), 1991 Beaverdam Rd., Spring Grove, 23881
Malabad, Antonio R., (Retired), 400 Waters Dr. #D-104, Southern Pines, NC 28387
Moran, Edward, (Retired), 2001 Jefferson Davis Hwy, Suite 511, Arlington, 22202
Natale, Samuel, (Retired), 236 E. Market St., Long Beach, NY 11561. Email: sammymn@aol.com
Ngo, Anthony, (Retired), 12500 Patterson Ave., 23233-6411. Tel: 804-784-5450
Przywara, Gerald A., (Retired), 5500 Holly Fork Rd., Barhamsville, 23011
Ruoff, Lou W., (Retired), 3702 W. Steeple Chase Way, Apt. A, Williamsburg
Slattery, Joseph A., (Retired), P.O. Box 12898, South Africa Centrahil 6006
Slowik, Joseph S., (Retired), 1257 Marywood Ln. #127, 23229
Teslovic, Eugene, (Retired), 107 Maryland Ave., Portsmouth, 23707
Torretto, Joseph, (Retired), 1635 SE Pomeroy St., Unit 4-7, Stuart, FL 34997
Tran, Peter, (Retired), 100 Harpersville Rd., Newport News, 23601-7722. Tel: 757-597-7722.

Permanent Deacons:
Brown, Michael, Christ the King, Norfolk
Ahearn, James, Church of the Ascension, Virginia Beach
Allen, Frederick Clarence III, Church of St. Therese, Chesapeake
Allen, Robert, (Retired)
Allison, Mark D., St. Andrew, Roanoke
Amaram, Donatus Theukwumere, (Retired), St. Joseph, Petersburg
Anleu Sandoval, Edwin, Our Lady of Mt. Carmel, Newport News
Arkesteyn, John Aster, (Retired)
Bailey, Calvin J., Basilica of Saint Mary of the Immaculate Conception, Norfolk
Baker, Robert Dennis, (Retired)
Ballentine, Gregory, St. Bede, Williamsburg
Barrett, Christopher, St. Elizabeth, Richmond
Baskind, Frank Ronald, Ph.D., St. Mary, Richmond
Beach, John Eric, Our Lady of Perpetual Help, Salem
Beardsworth, Robert, St. Gregory the Great, Virginia Beach
Benet, Alfonso, St. Jude, Mineral
Blatnik, William J., (Retired)
Bolgiano, Richard, St. Paschal Baylon, South Boston
Broughton, Eric Christopher, Saint Augustine, Richmond
Buckman, Paul, Ph.D., St. Paschal Baylon, South Boston
Burgess, Lou, Our Lady of Peace, Appomattox
Cartwright, Gordon Kenneth, (Retired)
Christ, Edward, Church of the Sacred Heart, Petersburg
Coleman, Peter, Sts. Peter and Paul, Palmyra
Colville, Christopher Stephen, Church of the Redeemer, Mechanicsville
Conklin, James, (Unassigned)
Corrigan, Christopher, St. Augustine, Richmond
Craig, William Edward, Holy Name of Mary, Bedford
de Leon, Armando J., Good Samaritan, Amelia
DeNoia, Michael David, Cathedral of the Sacred Heart, Richmond
di Stefano, Thomas, Raleigh
DiTolve, Anthony, St. Thomas Aquinas, Charlottesville
Donovan, Donald, (Retired)
Dowdy, Melvin D., Holy Rosary, Richmond; Cathedral of the Sacred Heart, Richmond
Durel, Robert J., Ph.D., (Retired)
Dwyer, Bruce K., (Retired)
Ellerbrock, Michael J., St. Mary, Blacksburg
Elliott, Thomas B., (Retired)
Esposito, Robert M., (Retired)
Ewan, Robert D., St. Edward the Confessor, Richmond; St. Edward, Richmond
Feliciano, Esaud, Church of the Sacred Heart, Prince George County
Ferguson, Andrew M., Saint Michael, Richmond
Fernando-Lopez, Arturo, Holy Cross, Lynchburg
Finocchio, Chris James Jr., St. John the Apostle, VA Beach
Fitzgerald, Joseph Jr., J.D., J.C.L., (Retired), St. Thomas Aquinas, Charlottesville, Tribunal
Fournier, Keith A., St. Stephen Martyr, Chesapeake
Fox, Donald, Mission Outside Diocese
Funk, Charles, St Joseph, Petersburg
Furman, Richard Lee, St. Mary, Blacksburg
Geary, David J., (Retired), St. Mary of the Annunciation, Caroline County
Giovannetti, Charles, St. Bridget, Richmond
Giovenco, Robert B., Saint Bridget, Richmond
Gonzalez, Guillermo, St. Joseph, Hampton
Gonzalez, Jose Miguel, (Retired)
Gorman, Kevin, St. Gregory the Great, Virginia Beach
Greer, James D., (Retired), Saint Edward the Confessor, Richmond
Greer, Timothy, St. Theresa, Farmville; Sacred Heart, Farmville; Immaculate Heart of Mary, Blackstone; Church of the Nativity, Burke
Griffin, Robert H., (Retired), St. Michael's, Glen Allen
Grillo, Joseph F., St. John the Apostle, Virginia Beach; Saint Paul, Portsmouth
Hallat, Albert, St. Augustine, Richmond
Handel, Ed, St. Olaf, Norge
Hanzlik, Edward G., (Retired)
Harmeyer, Gary R., Church of the Ascension, Virginia Beach; Sr. Pastoral Assoc., Holy Apostles, VA Beach
Harriman, Mark, Portsmouth Cluster: Church of the Holy Angels, Church of the Resurrection, St. Paul
Haut, Stephen, Church of the Epiphany, Richmond
Healey, Thomas, Incarnation, Charlottesville
Hogan, Kevin, St. Edward the Confessor, Richmond
Holly, Chester, (Retired)
Hoppe, Daniel, Mission Outside Diocese
Hornstra, Curtis L., (Unassigned)
Ibarra, Juan, (Retired)
Illy, Lawrence P., (Retired)
Johnson, Daniel F., Our Lady of Mt. Carmel, Newport News
Johnson, Michael, St. Mark, Virginia Beach; Saint Mark, Virginia Beach
Kamper, Eugene P., (Retired)
Kapral, Vincent, Mission Outside Diocese
King, Walker P., (Retired)
Kledzik, James, (Retired)
Kohut, David, St. John the Evangelist, Waynesboro
Krajeski, Vernon, (Retired), St. John the Apostle, Virginia Beach
Kren, John J., Saint Mark, Virginia Beach
Kudrav, Paul, Holy Infant, Elkton
LaSpina, Fred C., Unassigned

Lupini, Belardino, (Retired)
MacLaughlin, Matthew C., Saint John, Petersburg
Magsombol, Anacleto, St. Luke, Virginia Beach
Mahefky, Paul, Diocesan Dir. of Real Estate
Malone, Christopher M., Cathedral of the Sacred Heart, Richmond
Marchi, Adrian A., Ph.D., Prince of Peace, Chesapeake
Matte, Mark C., Cathedral of the Sacred Heart, Richmond
Mattson, Martin, (Unassigned)
Maurelli, Louis A., (Retired)
May, Charles William, St. Edward Mission, Pulaski; St. Mary the Mother of God, Wytheville
May, Robert, Church of the Holy Family, Virginia Beach
McClelland, Gary, St. John the Apostle, Virginia Beach
McCourt, Peter, St. Mary, Richmond
McFeely, Thomas E., (Retired), Church of the Ascension, Virginia Beach
Dr. McLane, Emmett R. III, St. Theresa; Immaculate Heart of Mary; Church of the Nativity; Sacred Heart, Farmville
Melendez, Jose Miguel, Holy Family, Pearisburg; Holy Spirit Catholic Community, Jonesville
Mendez, Arthur, Church of the Epiphany, Richmond
Menting, Peter J., (Retired), (Retired)
Minner, Paul, St. Gregory the Great, Virginia Beach
Moczygemba, Gregory, St. Michael, Glen Allen
Morash, Christopher G., Incarnation, Charlottesville
Morgan, James, Archdiocese of Atlanta
Morlino, Joseph Thomas, St. Mary, Richmond
Moro, Michael, (Retired)
Morrison, Kevin Robert, Church of the Holy Angels, St. Paul; Church of the Resurrection, St. Mary, Chesapeake
Mueller, Mark, St. Joan of Arc, Yorktown
Mugnolo, Charles Louis, Holy Cross, Lynchburg
Mullen, Thomas, U of R Campus Ministry, Richmond
Murphy, Christopher, Holy Cross, Lynchburg
Nees, Richard J., (Retired)
Nelson, Francis Jr., Holy Rosary, Richmond
Nemetz, David S., St. Michael, Richmond
Nguyen, Hung, Church of the Epiphany, Richmond
O'Connell, Stephen, (Retired)
O'Donnell, Fulton Patrick, (Retired)
Ovalle, Francisco, Sacred Heart, Richmond
Owen, Edward, St. Benedict, Richmond
Palm, Peter Eric, St. Jerome, Newport News
Petillo, Victor, St. Bridget, Richmond
Reaves, David, St. Joan of Arc, Yorktown
Reger, Ronald A., Church of the Redeemer, Mechanicsville
Riss, Joseph N., (Unassigned)
Rivera, Robies Ramon, St. John, Highland Springs
Roettinger, Francis, St. Bede, Williamsburg
Romero, Crisanto D., (Retired)
Sadowski, John E., (Retired)
Satterwhite, James L., St. Joan of Arc, Yorktown
Schmidt, Edward P., St. John Neumann, Powhatan
Siochi, Antonio, Our Lady of Mt. Carmel, Newport News
Smith, Roy, (Retired)
Smithberger, Robert, Church of the Holy Spirit, Virginia Beach
Snellings, Rodney, Our Lady of Lourdes, Richmond
Sorady, Daniel, St. Matthew, Virginia Beach
Stefanowicz, Stanley J., (Retired)
Stinson, Charles, St. George, Scottsville
Straub, Robert, Church of the Sacred Heart, Prince George
Surat, Eric M., Our Lady of Perpetual Help, Salem
Surrusco, Richard, M.D., (Retired)
Swisher, Michael, St. Mary of the Star, Fort Monroe
Taylor, Bernard F., (Unassigned)
Taylor, Bernard H., (Retired)
Thomas, John H., J.D., (Retired)
Thompson, Robert R., St. Olaf, Norge
Trail, Kevin F., St. Stephen Martyr, Chesapeake
Tran, Thoai, Church of the Vietnamese Martyrs, Richmond
Tubbs, James O., St. John Neumann, Powhatan
Tucker, John III, St. Paul, Richmond
Turrietta, James Derek, Blessed Sacrament, Norfolk
Valle, Victor, Church of the Epiphany, Richmond
Van Wyk, James, Our Lady of Lourdes, Richmond
Wash, Robert S., St. Pius X, Norfolk
Welch, Barry Dwayne, Resurrection, Moneta
Wentworth, Darrell G., St. Gregory the Great, VA Beach; New Creation Charismatic
Westerman, William, St. Bede, Williamsburg
White, Patrick Joseph, St. Bridget, Richmond
Wilkinson, Phillip, St. Joan of Arc, Yorktown
Williams, Charles Jr., Cathedral of the Sacred Heart
Wyngaard, Gerald, St. Gabriel, Richmond; Good Samaritan, Amelia
Young, Robert (Bob), St. Joseph, Petersburg
Zachary, Neil, St. Olaf, Norge.

INSTITUTIONS LOCATED IN DIOCESE

[A] HIGH SCHOOLS, DIOCESAN

LYNCHBURG. *Holy Cross Regional School* (1879) (Grades PreK-12), 2125 Langhorne Rd., Lynchburg, 24501. Tel: 434-847-5436; Tel: 434-847-5464; Fax: 434-847-4156; Email: office@hcfaculty.com; Web: www.hcrs-va.org. Mrs. Mary Sherry, Prin.; Holly Main, Library Aide. Lay Teachers 26; Students 189.

NEWPORT NEWS. *Peninsula Catholic High School*, (Grades 8-12), 600 Harpersville Rd., Newport News, 23601. Tel: 757-596-7247; Fax: 757-952-1038; Web: www.peninsulacatholic.com. Janine C. Franklin, Prin.; Cheryl Loughran, Librarian. Lay Teachers 29; Students 260; Total Staff 15.

ROANOKE. *Roanoke Catholic School*, (Grades PreK-12), 621 N. Jefferson St., Roanoke, 24016-1401. Tel: 540-982-3532; Fax: 540-345-0785; Email: ppatterson@roanokecatholic.com; Web: www.roanokecatholic.com. Patrick Patterson, Prin., Head School; Julie Frost, Asst. Prin.; Kurt Axt, Librarian. Lay Teachers 40; Students 452.

VIRGINIA BEACH. *Bishop Sullivan Catholic High School*, 4552 Princess Anne Rd., Virginia Beach, 23462. Tel: 757-467-2881; Fax: 757-467-0284; Web: www.chsvb.org. Daniel J. Miani, Asst. Prin.; Dana St. John, Librarian. Lay Teachers 44; Students 460; Administrative Staff 3.

[B] HIGH SCHOOLS, PRIVATE

RICHMOND. *Benedictine College Preparatory* (1911) 12829 River Rd., 23238. Tel: 804-708-9500; Fax: 804-784-5410; Email: bcpinfo@benedictinecollegeprep.org; Web: www.benedictinecollegeprep.org. Jesse Grapes, Headmaster; Rt. Rev. Placid Solari, O.S.B. A Catholic Military High School operated by the Benedictine Monks. Lay Teachers 32; Priests 1; Students 251.

**Cristo Rey Richmond High School*, 304 N. Sheppard St., 23221.

Saint Gertrude High School (1922) 3215 Stuart Ave., 23221. Tel: 804-358-9114; Fax: 804-355-5682; Email: sghs@saintgertrude.org; Web: www.saintgertrude.org. Mrs. Renata Rafferty, Head of School; Mrs. Peggy Boon, Dean of Faculty and Academics. Lay Teachers 26; Students 238; Staff 25.

WILLIAMSBURG. *Walsingham Academy*, (Grades PreK-12), 1100 Jamestown Rd., Williamsburg, 23185. Tel: 757-229-6026; Fax: 757-259-1401; Email: mjo@walsingham.org; Web: www.walsingham.org. Sr. Mary Jeanne Oesterle, R.S.M., Pres.; Angie Baker, Dir. of Academic Affairs; Mary Johnston, Lower School Dir. Private Day School for Boys and Girls. Administrators 7; Lay Teachers 72; Students 512.

[C] ELEMENTARY SCHOOLS, DIOCESAN

RICHMOND. *All Saints Catholic School*, (Grades PreK-8), 3418 Noble Ave., 23222. Tel: 804-329-7524; Fax: 804-329-4201; Email: wwallin@allsaintsric.org; Web: www.allsaintsric.org. Mr. Kenneth W. Soistman, Pres.; Wanda Wallin, Prin. Lay Teachers 19; Total Enrollment 191; Total Staff 35.

St. Benedict School (1919) (Grades PreK-8), 3100 Grove Ave., 23221. Tel: 804-254-8850; Fax: 804-254-9163; Email: scruess@saintbenedictschool.org; Web: www.saintbenedictschool.org. Mr. Sean M. Cruess, Prin.; Leda Ansbro, Librarian. Students 213; Teachers 17; Total Enrollment 213; Total Staff 9.

St. Bridget School, (Grades K-8), 6011 York Rd., 23226. Tel: 804-288-1994; Fax: 804-288-5730; Email: aallen@saintbridget.org; Web: www.saintbridget.org. Mr. George Sadler, Prin.; Elizabeth Kerr, Librarian. Lay Teachers 37; Priests 2; Total Enrollment 447; Total Staff 62.

St. Edward/Epiphany Catholic School (1961) (Grades PreK-8), 10701 W. Huguenot Rd., 23235. Tel: 804-272-2881; Fax: 804-327-0788; Email: office@seeschool.com; Web: www.seeschool.com. Mr. Michael Kelleher III, Prin.; Mrs. Allison Zabel, Librarian; Mr. Justin Andrew, Vice Pres.; Mrs. Mindy Gerloff, Business Mgr. Lay Teachers 30; Students 491; Total Enrollment 491.

St. Mary's Catholic School (1965) (Grades PreK-8), 9501 Gayton Rd., 23229. Tel: 804-740-1048; Fax: 804-740-1310; Email: albisese@saintmary.org; Web: www.saintmary.org. Jenni Ellis, Prin. Lay Teachers 39; Students 426.

Our Lady of Lourdes School, (Grades PreK-8), 8250 Woodman Rd., 23228. Tel: 804-262-1770; Fax: 804-200-6295; Web: www.lourdesrva.org. Mrs. Kelly Taylor, Prin.; Amy Gouldman, Librarian. Lay Teachers 26; Total Enrollment 349.

BRISTOL. *St. Anne Catholic School*, (Grades PreK-8), 300 Euclid Ave., Bristol, 24201. Tel: 276-669-0048; Fax: 276-669-3523; Email: schooloffice@stanneschoolbristol.org; Web: www.stanneschoolbristol.org. Ms. Billie Schneider, Prin.; Mrs. Patricia Johnson, Asst. Prin.; Angelina Bush, Librarian. Lay Teachers 12; Total Enrollment 146; Total Staff 32.

CHARLOTTESVILLE. *Charlottesville Catholic Elementary School*, (Grades PreK-8), 1205 Pen Park Rd., Charlottesville, 22901. Tel: 434-964-0400; Fax: 434-964-1373; Email: info@cvillecatholic.org; Web: www.cvillecatholic.org. Mr. Michael J. Riley, Prin. Aides 4; Lay Teachers 30; Students 338.

DANVILLE. *Sacred Heart Elementary School* (1953) 540 Central Blvd., Danville, 24541. Tel: 434-793-2656; Fax: 434-793-2658; Email: kskania@sheartschool.com; Web: www.sheartschool.com. Kira S. Kania, Prin.; Jayne Church, Librarian. Lay Teachers 20; Total Enrollment 184; Total Staff 29.

HAMPTON. *St. Mary Star of the Sea*, (Grades PreK-8), 14 N. Willard Ave., Hampton, 23663. Tel: 757-723-6358; Fax: 757-723-6544; Email: admin@saintmarystarofthesea.com; Web: www.saintmarystarofthesea.com. Sr. Mary John Slonkosky, O.P., Prin.; Jamie Green, Librarian. Lay Teachers 12; Sisters 4; Total Enrollment 170; Total Staff 8.

NEWPORT NEWS. *Our Lady of Mt Carmel* (1954) (Grades PreK-8), 52 Harpersville Rd., Newport News, 23601. Tel: 757-596-2754; Fax: 757-596-1570; Web: www.olmc-school.com. Sr. Anna Joseph, Prin. Clergy 4; Lay Teachers 26; Sisters 4; Students 275; Total Enrollment 275; Total Staff 45.

NORFOLK. *Christ the King Catholic School*, (Grades PreK-8), 3401 Tidewater Dr., Norfolk, 23509. Tel: 757-625-4951; Fax: 757-623-5212; Email: fgagne@ctkparish.org; Web: www.ctkparish.org. Dr. Francine Gagne, Ed.D., Prin., Email: fgagne@ctkparish.org; Mrs. Jan Mislan, Asst. Prin.; Ms. Dawn Lindey, Librarian. Lay Teachers 25; Total Enrollment 255.

St. Pius X School, (Grades PreK-8), 7800 Halprin Dr., Norfolk, 23518. Tel: 757-588-6171; Fax: 757-587-6580; Email: school@piusxparish.org; Web: www.stpiusxschoolva.org. Mr. Mark Zafra, Prin. Lay Teachers 17; Sisters 1; Students 218; Total Enrollment 218; Total Staff 33.

PETERSBURG. *St. Joseph School*, (Grades PreK-8), 123 Franklin St., Petersburg, 23803. Tel: 804-732-3931 ; Fax: 804-732-6479; Email: school@saintjosephschool.com; Web: www.saintjosephschool.com. Joseph Whitmore, Prin.; Teresa Fisher, Librarian. Lay Teachers 16; Total Enrollment 114; Total Staff 21.

PORTSMOUTH. *Portsmouth Catholic Regional*, 2301 Oregon Ave., Portsmouth, 23701. Tel: 757-488-6744; Fax: 757-465-8833; Email: philcampbell@portsmouthcatholic.net; Email: maryellenpaul@portsmouthcatholic.net; Web: www.portsmouthcatholic.com. Mary Ellen Paul, Prin.; Mr. Franklin Baker, Librarian. Lay Teachers 18; Total Enrollment 172; Total Staff 34.

POWHATAN. *Blessed Sacrament Huguenot High School* (1998) (Grades PreSchool-12), 2501 Academy Rd., Powhatan, 23139. Tel: 804-598-4211; Fax: 804-598-1053; Email: pledbetter@bshknights.org; Web: www.BlessedSacramentHuguenot.com. Mrs. Paula Ledbetter, Head of School; Mr. Brian Kieran, Asst. Prin.; Mimi Ziletti, Librarian. Lay Teachers 39; Students 295.

VIRGINIA BEACH. *St. Gregory the Great School* (1964) (Grades PreK-8), 5343 Virginia Beach Blvd., Virginia Beach, 23462. Tel: 757-497-1811; Fax: 757-497-7005; Email: office@sggsvb.org; Web: www.sggsvb.org. Gina Coss, Prin.; Eric Landon, Asst. Prin. Clergy 23; Lay Teachers 41; Priests 4; Sisters 1; Students 663; Total Enrollment 663; Total Staff 106.

St. John the Apostle Catholic School (2002) (Grades PreK-8), 1968-B Sandbridge Rd., Virginia Beach, 23456. Tel: 757-821-1100; Fax: 757-821-1047; Email: sja@sjavb.org; Web: www.sjavb.org. Ms. Miriam Cotton, M.Ed., Prin.; Melissa Foster, M.Ed., Librarian. Lay Teachers 26; Total Enrollment 364; Total Staff 17.

St. Matthew School St. Matthew's Catholic School, (Grades PreK-8), 3316 Sandra Ln., Virginia Beach, 23464. Tel: 757-420-2455; Fax: 757-420-4880; Email: office@smsvb.net; Web: www.smsvb.net. Mr. Louis Goldberg, Prin.; Mrs. Ziegenfuss, Librarian. Clergy 3; Lay Teachers 42; Students 520; Total Enrollment 520; Total Staff 87.

Star of the Sea School (1958) (Grades PreK-8), 309

15th St., Virginia Beach, 23451. Tel: 757-428-8400; Fax: 757-428-2794; Email: information@sosschool.org; Web: www.sosschool.org. Mrs. Kelly Lazzara, Prin. Lay Teachers 23; Total Enrollment 188; Total Staff 5.

[D] ELEMENTARY SCHOOLS, PRIVATE

BLACKSBURG. **St. John Neumann Academy*, 3600 Yellow Sulphur Road, Blacksburg, 24060. Tel: 540-552-7562; Fax: 540-302-8020; Email: julia.wharton@sjnacademy.org. Julia Wharton, Dir. Lay Teachers 10; Students 120.

NORFOLK. **Barry Robinson Schools of Norfolk* (2001) P.O. Box 1180, Norfolk, 23501. Tel: 757-440-5500. Charles V. McPhillips, Pres.

St. Patrick Catholic School, (Grades PreK-8), 1000 Bolling Ave., Norfolk, 23508. Tel: 757-440-5500; Fax: 757-440-5200; Email: info@stpcs.org; Web: www.stpcs.org. Mr. Stephen Hammond, Prin.; Mrs. Betsy Cox, Librarian, Email: bcox@stpcs.org. Teachers & TA 49; Total Enrollment 415; Support 27; Aftercare 14.

[E] GENERAL HOSPITALS

RICHMOND. *Bon Secours Richmond Health System*, 5875 Bremo Rd., Ste 710, 23226. Tel: 804-281-8330 ; Fax: 804-282-1243; Email: gennette_cameron-reid@bshsi.org; Web: www.bonsecours.com. Peter Bernard, CEO. Sisters of Bon Secours. Bed Capacity 850; Sisters 2; Total Staff 7,513; Inpatients 47,371; Outpatients 427,203.

Bon Secours-Richmond Health Care Foundation, 7229 Forest Ave., Ste. 200, 23226. Tel: 804-287-7700; Fax: 804-287-7316. Cynthia Reynolds, CEO.

Bon Secours-Richmond Community Hospital, 1500 N. 28th St., 23233. Tel: 804-225-1701; Fax: 804-225-1725. Michael D. Robinson, CEO. Bed Capacity 104; Total Staff 260; Inpatients 2,854; Outpatients 46,158.

St. Mary's Hospital Toni R. Ardabell, CEO. Bed Capacity 391; Sisters 2; Total Staff 2,440; Inpatients 21,084; Outpatients 147,505.

Bon Secours Memorial Regional Medical Center, 8260 Atlee Rd., Mechanicsville, 23116. Tel: 804-764-6000; Fax: 804-764-6420. Michael D. Robinson, CEO. Bed Capacity 225; Total Staff 1,738; Inpatients 14,374; Outpatients 140,398.

MIDLOTHIAN. *St. Francis Medical Center (Bon Secours Richmond Health System)*, 13700 St. Francis Blvd., Ste. 100, Midlothian, 23114. Tel: 804-594-7400; Fax: 804-594-7410. Mark M. Gordon, CEO; Peter J. McCourt, Mission Leader. Bed Capacity 130; Sisters 1; Tot Asst. Annually 9,054; Total Staff 1,203.

NEWPORT NEWS. *Mary Immaculate Hospital* (1952) 2 Bernardine Dr., Newport News, 23602-4499. Tel: 757-886-6000; Fax: 757-886-6751; Web: www.bonsecourshamptonroads.com. Darlene Stephenson, CEO, Tel: 757-886-6768; Fax: 757-886-6751; Email: darlene_stephenson@bshsi.org; Sr. Bernard Marie Magill, O.S.F., M.S., N.A.C.C., M.A., Dir. Mission. Bed Capacity 123; The Bernardine Sisters of the Third Order of St. Francis 5; Total Staff, Bon Secours Mary Immaculate 853; Outpatients 75,578; Inpatients 7,841.

Bernardine Franciscan Sisters Foundation, Inc., 2 Bernardine Dr., Newport News, 23602. Tel: 757-886-6025; Fax: 757-886-6881; Email: david_niski@bshsi.org. Sr. David Ann Niski, Dir.

NORFOLK. *Bon Secours De Paul Medical Center, Inc.*, 150 Kingsley Ln., Norfolk, 23505. Tel: 757-889-5000; Fax: 757-889-5837; Web: bonsecourshamptonroads.com. John Barrett, CEO. Bon Secours Ministries
Bon Secours DePaul Medical Center
Bon Secours DePaul Health Foundation
Bon Secours Bayley Properties Bed Capacity 204; Outpatients 83,842; Inpatients 7,315; Staff 787.

PORTSMOUTH. *Bon Secours Hampton Roads Health Systems, Inc.*, 3636 High St., Portsmouth, 23707-3236. Tel: 757-398-2122. Joseph M. Oddis, CEO. Bed Capacity 346; Total Staff 1,913.

Bon Secours Maryview Medical Center, 3636 High St., Portsmouth, 23707. Tel: 757-398-2200; Fax: 757-398-2359; Web: www.bonsecourshamptonroads.com. Joseph M. Oddis, CEO; Richard Chasse, Dir. Pastoral Care; Rita Hickey; Rev. Pantaleon O. Manalo, Chap. Sisters of Bon Secours.
Maryview Hospital Bed Capacity 346; Total Staff 1,569; Outpatients 187,915; Inpatients 1,400.

Maryview Behavioral Medicine Center, 3636 High St., Portsmouth, 23707. Tel: 757-398-2589; Fax: 757-398-2396; Web: www.BonSecoursHamptonRoads.com. Lucy Kooiman, Admin. Bed Capacity 54; Patients Asst Anual. 2,352; Total Staff 70.

[F] CHILD LEARNING CENTERS

RICHMOND. *Sacred Heart Center, Inc.*, 1400 Perry St., 23224. Tel: 804-230-4399; Fax: 804-231-7247; Email: tanya-gonzalez@shcrichmond.org. Tanya Gonzalez, Exec. Dir.; Rev. John Podsiadlo, S.J., Dir. Leadership & Volunteer Prog. Adult Education, Social Services, Latino Outreach.

BLACKSBURG. *St. Mary's Little Angels Preschool* (1988) 1205 Old Mill Rd., Blacksburg, 24060-3618. Tel: 540-951-0916; Fax: 540-953-2962; Email: littleangels@stmarysblacksburg.org; Web: www.stmarysblacksburg.org/smla. Kimberly Keesee, Preschool Coord. Preschool: ages 3-5 year olds; Parent Morning Out: 18-36 months Lay Teachers 12; Students 63.

VIRGINIA BEACH. *Holy Family Day School*, 1279 N. Great Neck Rd., Virginia Beach, 23454-2117. Tel: 757-481-1180; Fax: 757-481-3989; Email: dayschoolprincipal@holyfamilyvb.org; Web: www.holyfamilyvb.org. Cynthia Girard, Prin.; Colleen Oates, Bookkeeper. Lay Teachers 5.

[G] HOMES FOR THE AGED

RICHMOND. *St. Francis Home, Inc.*, 65 W. Clopton St., 23225. Tel: 804-231-1043; Fax: 804-231-1065; Email: bslough@saintfrancishome.com. Bruce M. Slough, Exec. Dir. Bed Capacity 135; Tot Asst. Annually 170; Total Staff 52.

St. Joseph's Home for the Aged/Jeanne Jugan Pavilion (1874) 1503 Michaels Rd., Henrico, 23229. Tel: 804-288-6245; Fax: 804-288-8906; Email: msrichmond@littlesistersofthepoor.org. Sr. Marie Edward Quinn, Supr. & Admin. Attended by Rev. Kenneth Wood (Chap.) Bed Capacity 96; Guests 98; Little Sisters of the Poor 10; Tot Asst. Annually 96; Total Staff 130; Direct Care 125.

St. Mary's Woods (1986) 1257 Marywood Ln., 23229. Tel: 804-741-8624; Fax: 804-740-7912; Email: randy.scott@stmaryswoods.com; Web: stmaryswoods.com. Randy Scott, Admin. Total Staff 75; Independent Units 34; Total Assisted Living 86; Units 120.

Our Lady of Hope Health Center, Inc., 13700 N. Gayton Rd., 23233. Tel: 804-360-1960; Fax: 804-364-0737; Email: mfarmer@ourladyofhope.com; Web: www.ourladyofhope.com. Julia Fretwell, L.N.H.A., Admin. Total Staff 203; Nursing Home Residents 60; Assisted Living 77.

CHARLOTTESVILLE. *Our Lady of Peace*, 751 Hillsdale Dr., Charlottesville, 22901. Tel: 434-973-1155; Fax: 434-973-3397; Web: www.our-lady-of-peace.com. Sara Warden, L.N.H.A., Exec. Dir. Total Staff 124; Nursing Bed Capacity 30; Independent Units 32; Assisted Units 94.

NEWPORT NEWS. *St. Francis Nursing Center*, 4 Ridgewood Pkwy., Newport News, 23602. Tel: 757-886-6500; Fax: 757-886-6539; Web: www.bshsihr.com. Robin Smith, Admin. Bed Capacity 115; Tot Asst. Annually 102; Total Staff 110; Total Assisted 1,582.

ROANOKE. *Our Lady of the Valley Retirement Community*, 650 N. Jefferson St., Roanoke, 24016. Tel: 540-345-5111; Fax: 540-985-6561; Web: www.OurLadyoftheValley.com. Mary Lynn Yengst, L.N.H.A., Admin. Assisted Living Beds 98; Skilled Nursing Facility Beds 70; Staff 136.

SUFFOLK. *Bon Secours-Maryview Nursing Care*, 4775 Bridge Rd., Suffolk, 23435. Tel: 757-686-0488; Fax: 757-686-8211. Diana L. Jarrett, Admin. Bed Capacity 120.
Martha W. Davis Cancer Center.
Maryview Employee Assistance Program.
Maryview MedCare Centers (Urgent Care).
Maryview Wellspring Home Health Agency.
Maryview Hospice Program.

VIRGINIA BEACH. *Marian Manor* (1988) 5345 Marian Ln., Virginia Beach, 23462. Tel: 757-456-5018; Fax: 757-497-7561; Email: karen@marian-manor.com; Web: www.marian-manor.com. Karen Land, Exec. Dir. Tot Asst. Annually 186; Total Staff 100; IAL Beds 18; Assisted Living Beds 109.

Our Lady of Perpetual Help Health Center, Inc., 4560 Princess Anne Rd., Virginia Beach, 23462-7905. Tel: 757-495-4211; Fax: 757-495-7366; Email: tanderson@ourladyperpetualhelp.com; Web: www.OurLadyPerpetualHelp.com. Theresa Anderson, L.N.H.A., Admin. Bed Capacity 123; Tot Asst. Annually 123; Total Staff 160.

[H] SPECIALIZED SERVICES

RICHMOND. *Commonwealth Catholic Charities* (1923) 1601 Rolling Hills Dr., 23229-5011. Tel: 804-285-5900; Fax: 804-285-9130; Email: agency@cccofva.org; Web: www.cccofva.org. Ms. Joanne D. Nattrass, M.B.A., B.S.N., R.N., Exec. Dir. Total Staff 152; Total Assisted 66,630.
Satellite Offices:
918 Harris St., Ste. 1G, Charlottesville, 22903. Tel: 434-974-6880; Fax: 434-296-6002.
541 Luck Ave. S.W., Ste. 118, Roanoke, 24016-5055. Tel: 540-342-0411; Fax: 540-342-3307.
507 Park Ave., S.W., Norton, 24273. Tel: 276-679-1195; Fax: 276-679-2719.
820 Campbell Ave., S.W., Roanoke, 24016-3536. Tel: 540-342-7561; Fax: 540-344-7513.
836 Camnpbell Ave., S.W., Roanoke, 24016-3536. Tel: 540-342-7561; Fax: 540-344-7513.
St. Francis House, 820 Campbell Ave., S.W., Roanoke, 24016-3536. Tel: 540-342-7561, Ext. 319; Fax: 540-344-7513.
12284 Warwick Blvd., Ste. 1-A, Newport News, 23606-3855. Tel: 757-247-3600; Fax: 757-247-1070.
827 Commerce St., Petersburg, 23803. Tel: 804-733-6207; Fax: 804-733-0099.
511 W. Grace St., 23220-4911. Tel: 804-648-4177; Fax: 804-648-4931.

VIRGINIA BEACH. *Catholic Charities of Eastern Virginia, Inc.*, 5361-A Virginia Beach Blvd., Virginia Beach, 23462. Tel: 757-456-2366; Fax: 757-456-2367; Email: help@cceva.org; Web: www.cceva.org. Mr. Christopher R. Tan, CEO.
Branch Offices:
4855 Princess Anne Rd., Virginia Beach, 23462. Tel: 757-467-7707; Fax: 757-495-3206.
1301 Colonial Ave., Norfolk, 23517. Tel: 757-533-5217; Fax: 757-533-9562.
3804 Poplar Hill Rd., Ste. A, Chesapeake, 23321. Tel: 757-484-0703; Fax: 757-484-1096.
12829 Jefferson Ave., Ste. 101, Newport News, 23608. Tel: 757-875-0060; Fax: 757-877-7883.
Other Offices:
Catholic Charities Outreach Center, 5361-A Virginia Beach Blvd., Virginia Beach, 23462. Tel: 757-490-4931; Fax: 757-456-2367.

[I] MONASTERIES AND RESIDENCES OF PRIESTS AND BROTHERS

RICHMOND. *Mary Mother of the Church Abbey*, 12829 River Rd., 23238-7206. Tel: 804-784-3508; Fax: 804-784-2214; Email: abbeyinfo@richmondmonks.org; Web: www.richmondmonks.org. Rt. Revs. Placid Solari, O.S.B., Admin.; Benedict R. McDermott, O.S.B., (Retired); Bro. Ambrose Okema, O.S.B.; Revs. Gregory Gresko, O.S.B.; Adrian W. Harmening, O.S.B.; Bros. David Owen, O.S.B.; Jeffery Williams, O.S.B.; Robert Nguyen, O.S.B.; Rev. John Mary Lugemwa, O.S.B., Prior; Bro. Vincent McDermott, O.S.B. Benedictine Monks. Brothers 5; Priests 4.

[J] CONVENTS AND RESIDENCES FOR SISTERS

RICHMOND. *Benedictine Sisters of Virginia, Saint Gertrude Convent*, 6826 Monument Avenue, 23226. Tel: 804-814-2793; Email: srkatpers@gmail.com; Web: osbva.org. Sr. Kathleen L. Persson, O.S.B., L.C.S.W. Sisters 2.

Comboni Missionary Sisters, Delegation House, 1307 Lakeside Ave., 23228-4710. Tel: 804-262-8827; Web: www.combonimissionarysistersusa.org. Sr. Olga Sanchez Caro, Supr. Sisters 14.

BARHAMSVILLE. *Bethlehem Monastery of the Poor Clare Nuns*, 5500 Holly Fork Rd., Barhamsville, 23011. Tel: 757-566-1684; Fax: 757-566-1697; Email: mtstfrancis@gmail.com; Web: www.poor-clares.org. Mother Mary Therese, P.C.C., Abbess. Observing the Primitive Rule of St. Clare, Constitutions of the Poor Clare Federation of Mary Immaculate (strictly cloistered, solemn vows). Novices 3; Sisters 25; Solemnly Professed 16; Junior Professed 2.

CROZET. *Our Lady of the Angels Monastery* (1987) Cistercian Nuns of the Strict Observance in Virginia, Inc., 3365 Monastery Dr., Crozet, 22932. Tel: 434-823-1452; Fax: 434-823-6379; Email: sisters@olamonastery.org; Web: www.olamonastery.org. Mother Kathy Ullrich, O.C.S.O., Prioress. Professed 13; Sisters 12.

NEWPORT NEWS. *Bernardine Sisters of the Third Order of St. Francis*, 6A Ridgewood Pkwy., Newport News, 23602-4484. Tel: 757-886-6391; Fax: 757-886-6751; Web: www.bfranciscan.org. Sr. Bernard Marie Magill, O.S.F., M.S., N.A.C.C., M.A., Team Leader, Bernardine Franciscans in Newport News, VA. Sisters 5.

NORFOLK. *Sisters Servants of the Immaculate Heart of Mary* (1845) Tel: 757-769-7009; Tel: 757-588-6171; Fax: 757-587-6580; Email: piusihmva@aol.com; Web: www.ihmimmaculata.org.

St. Pius X Convent, 7813 Halprin Dr., Norfolk, 23518. Tel: 757-769-7009 (Home); Tel: 757-588-6171 (School); Fax: 757-587-6580; Email: piusihmva@aol.com (Home). Sr. Linda Taber, I.H.M., Supr. Sisters 5.

PORTSMOUTH. *Sisters of Bon Secours* (1824) 412 West Rd., Portsmouth, 23707. Tel: 757-397-3869; Email: rita_thomas@bshsi.com. Sr. Rita Thomas, M.S.N., Pres.

ROCKVILLE. *Monastery of the Visitation Monte Maria*, 12221 Bienvenue Rd., Rockville, 23146-1620. Tel: 804-749-4885; Email: info@visitmontemaria.com; Web: www.visitmontemaria.com. Mother Mary Paula Zemienieuski, V.H.M., Supr. Novices 2; Visitation Sisters 9.

VIRGINIA BEACH. *Franciscan Sisters of St. Joseph*, 6112 Level Green Ct., Virginia Beach, 23464-4511. Tel: 757-420-1431; Email: mbogaever@yahoo.com.

Sisters Servants of I.H.M., St. Gregory the Great, 5349 Virginia Beach Blvd., Virginia Beach, 23462. Tel: 757-497-7517; Fax: 757-497-7005; Email: smaryihm@stgregory.pvt.k12.va.us; Email: stgregsihms@aol.com Convent. Sr. Mary Catherine Chapman, I.H.M., Ed.D., Supr./Prin.

WILLIAMSBURG. *Sisters of Mercy*, Walsingham Academy, 1100 Jamestown Rd., P.O. Box 8702, Williamsburg, 23187-8702. Tel: 757-229-2642 (Lower School); Tel: 757-229-6026 (Upper School); Tel: 757-220-8735 (Convent); Fax: 757-259-1401; Web: www.walsingham.org. Sisters Mary Jeanne Oesterle, R.S.M., Pres.; Rose Morris, R.S.M, Volunteer. Sisters 2.

[K] RETREAT HOUSES

ABINGDON. *Jubilee House Retreat Center*, 822 E. Main St., Abingdon, 24210-4415. Tel: 276-619-0919; Fax: 276-619-0919; Email: info@jubileeretreat.org; Web: www.jubileeretreat.org.

MONTPELIER. *Shalom House*, P.O. Box 196, Montpelier, 23192. Tel: 804-883-6149; Fax: 804-883-5298. Mary E. Alexander, Dir.

ROANOKE. *Madonna House*, 828 Campbell Ave., S.W., Roanoke, 24016. Tel: 540-343-8464; Email: mhrke79@gmail.com; Web: www.madonnahouse.org. Ms. Marie McLaughlin, Dir.

[L] CAMPUS MINISTRY

RICHMOND. *Catholic Campus Ministry, Virginia Commonwealth University*, 800 Cathedral Pl., 23220.

ASHLAND. *Catholic Campus Ministry, Randolph Macon College*, 105 S. Snead St., Ashland, 23005.

BLACKSBURG. *Virginia Tech, Newman Community*, 203 Otey St., Blacksburg, 24060. Tel: 540-951-0032.

CHARLOTTESVILLE. *Catholic Campus Ministry, University of Virginia*, 401 Alderman Rd., Charlottesville, 22903.

FARMVILLE. *Catholic Campus Ministry, Hampden-Sydney & Longwood Univ.*, 114 Midtown Ave., Farmville, 23901.

HARRISONBURG. *Catholic Campus Ministry, James Madison University*, 1052 S. Main St., Harrisonburg, 22801.

LEXINGTON. *Catholic Campus Ministry, Washington & Lee Univ. & VMI*, P.O. Box 725, Lexington, 24450.

LYNCHBURG. *Catholic Campus Ministry, Lynchburg College*, 710 Clay St., Lynchburg, 24504.

NEWPORT NEWS. *Catholic Campus Ministry, Christopher Newport University*, 100 Harpersville Rd., Newport News, 23601.

NORFOLK. *Catholic Campus Ministry, Norfolk State University*, 1000 Holt St., Norfolk, 23504.

Catholic Campus Ministry, Old Dominion University, 1306 W. 49th St., Norfolk, 23508. Mrs. Marissa O'Neil, Dir.; Rev. George Prado, Chap.

NORTON. *Catholic Campus Ministry, University of Virginia at Wise*, 1009 Virginia Ave., N.W., Norton, 24273.

RADFORD. *Catholic Campus Ministry, Radford University*, 1024A Clement St., Radford, 24141.

SALEM. *Catholic Campus Ministry, Roanoke College*, 221 College Ln., Salem, 24153.

WILLIAMSBURG. *Catholic Campus Ministry, College of William & Mary*, 10 Harrison Ave., Williamsburg, 23185.

[M] MISCELLANEOUS

RICHMOND. *The Catholic Community Foundation of the Diocese of Richmond*, 7800 Carousel Ln., 23294. Tel: 804-359-5661; Email: mkeightley@richmonddiocese.org; Web: www.richmondcatholicfoundation.org. Mrs. Margaret Keightley, Exec.

St. Francis Home of Richmond Foundation, Ltd., 65 W. Clopten St., 23225. Tel: 804-231-1043; Fax: 804-231-1065. Bruce M. Slough, Exec. Dir. Provides grants to subsidize cost of care for aged, infirm and disabled residents of limited means.

Shroud of Turin Center, 12829 River Rd., 23238. Tel: 804-977-4820; Email: bryan1106@comcast.net; Email: Shroud_Center@comcast.net. Bryan Walsh, Dir. Provides educational services and conducts historical research into the Shroud of Turin.

CHARLOTTESVILLE. *Saint Anselm Institute for Catholic Thought* (2001) P.O. Box 6432, Charlottesville, 22906-6432. Tel: 434-924-6993; Fax: 434-924-3389; Email: info@stanselminstitute.org; Web: www.stanselminstitute.org. Charles A. Kromkowski.

ROANOKE. *Catholic Historical Museum of the Roanoke Valley* (Museum & Religious Goods) 501A Marshall Ave., S.W., Roanoke, 24016-3627. Tel: 540-556-7240; Tel: 540-397-4028; Email: chmrv1@gmail.com. Karl Kleinhenz, Pres.; Cheri Hughes, Exec. Dir.

VIRGINIA BEACH. *Catholic Charities of Eastern Virginia Foundation*, 5361-A Virginia Beach Blvd., Virginia Beach, 23462. Tel: 757-456-2366; Fax: 757-456-2367; Web: www.cceva.org. Christopher Tan, CEO.

**Missioners of Christ*, 5880 Oak Terrace Dr., Virginia Beach, 23464.

San Lorenzo Spiritual Center, P.O. Box 64458, Virginia Beach, 23467-4458. Tel: 757-471-8949; Fax: 757-471-3114.

RELIGIOUS INSTITUTES OF MEN REPRESENTED IN THE DIOCESE

For further details refer to the corresponding bracketed number in the Religious Institutes of Men or Women section.

[0200]—*Benedictine Monks* (Latrobe, PA)—O.S.B.
[]—*Benedictine Monks* (Richmond, VA)—O.S.B.
[1350]—*Brothers of St. Francis Xavier*—C.F.X.
[0690]—*Jesuits Fathers and Brothers*—S.J.
[0430]—*Order of Preachers (Dominicans)* (Province of St. Joseph)—O.P.

RELIGIOUS INSTITUTES OF WOMEN REPRESENTED IN THE DIOCESE

[0230]—*Benedictine Sisters of Pontifical Jurisdiction*—O.S.B.
[1810]—*Bernardine Sisters of the Third Order of St. Francis*—O.S.F.
[0670]—*Cistercian Nuns of the Strict Observance*—O.C.S.O.
[0690]—*Comboni Missionary Sisters*—C.M.S.
[0270]—*Congregation of Bon Secours*—C.B.S.
[1070-09]—*Congregation of St. Catherine of Siena, Racine*—O.P.
[1070-07]—*Congregation of St. Cecelia, Nashville*—O.P.
[1070-13]—*Congregation of the Most Holy Rosary, Adrian*—O.P.
[0760]—*Daughters of Charity of St. Vincent de Paul*—D.C.
[0820]—*Daughters of the Holy Spirit*—D.H.S.
[0960]—*Daughters of Wisdom*—D.W.
[1180]—*The Franciscan Sisters*—O.S.F.
[1840]—*Grey Nuns of the Sacred Heart*—G.N.S.H.
[2575]—*Institute of the Sisters of Mercy of the Americas*—R.S.M.
[2340]—*Little Sisters of the Poor*—L.S.P.
[2490]—*Medical Mission Sisters*—S.C.M.M.
[2490]—*Medical Mission Sisters*—M.M.S.
[2480]—*Medical Missionaries of Mary*—M.M.M.
[3760]—*Order of St. Clare*—P.C.C.
[3640]—*Poor Servants of the Mother of God*—S.M.G.
[3465]—*Religious of the Sacred Heart of Mary* (Eastern American Prov.)—R.S.H.M.
[2970]—*School Sisters of Notre Dame*—S.S.N.D.
[1070-03]—*Sinsinawa Dominican Congregation of the Most Holy Rosary*—O.P.
[]—*Sisters for Christian Community*—S.F.C.C.
[0500]—*Sisters of Charity of Nazareth*—S.C.N.
[0990]—*Sisters of Divine Providence* (Our Lady of Divine Providence Prov.)—C.D.P.
[2990]—*Sisters of Notre Dame*—S.N.D.
[1530]—*Sisters of St. Francis of the Congregation of Our Lady of Lourdes, Sylvania, Ohio*—O.S.F.
[2980]—*Sisters of the Congregation of Notre Dame*—C.N.D.
[1990]—*Sisters of the Holy Names of Jesus and Mary*—S.N.J.M.
[2170]—*Sisters, Servants of the Immaculate Heart of Mary* (Immaculata, PA)—I.H.M.
[4130]—*Ursuline Sisters of the Congregation of Tildonk, Belgium*—O.S.U.
[4190]—*Visitation Nuns*—V.H.M.

DIOCESAN CEMETERIES

RICHMOND. *Holy Cross Cemetery*, 1628 Matthews St., 23222. Tel: 804-321-5936

Mount Calvary, 1400 S. Randolph St., 23220. Tel: 804-355-5271; Fax: 804-355-5277; Email: jim.glass@mcalvary.com. Mr. Jim Glass, Business Mgr.

LYNCHBURG. *Holy Cross*, 710 Clay St., Lynchburg, 24504. Tel: 434-846-5245; Fax: 434-846-7022

NORFOLK. *St. Mary's Catholic Cemetery*, 3000 Church St., Norfolk, 23504. Tel: 757-627-2874; Fax: 757-627-0369

PORTSMOUTH. *All Saints Catholic Cemetery (formerly St. Paul's Cemetery)*, P.O. Box 155, Portsmouth, 23705. Tel: 757-483-6201

ROANOKE. *St. Andrew's Diocesan Cemetery*, 3601 Salem Tpke., N.W., Roanoke, 24017. Tel: 540-595-7173; Fax: 540-342-9180; Email: standrewscemetery@gmail.com

SOUTH PRINCE GEORGE. *Sacred Heart Cemetery Corporation*, 9300 Community Ln., South Prince George, 23805. Tel: 804-732-6385; Email: dhanzlik87@gmail.com. Rev. Joseph F. Goldsmith, Pres.; Mr. David Hanzlik, Dir.; Mr. Michael Hanzlik, Dir.; Mr. Lewis Hanzlik, Dir.; Mr. Thomas McCormick, Dir.

NECROLOGY

† Dorgan, John J., (Retired), Died Oct. 24, 2018
† Kanicki, Philip A., (Retired), Died Apr. 3, 2018

An asterisk (*) denotes an organization that has established tax-exempt status directly with the IRS and is not covered by the USCCB Group Ruling.

Diocese of Rochester

(Dioecesis Roffensis)

Most Reverend

SALVATORE R. MATANO, D.D., S.T.L., J.C.D.

Bishop of Rochester; ordained December 17, 1971; appointed Coadjutor Bishop of Burlington March 3, 2005; ordained April 19, 2005; succeeded November 9, 2005; appointed Bishop of Rochester November 6, 2013; installed as Ninth Bishop of Rochester January 3, 2014. *Office: 1150 Buffalo Rd., Rochester, NY 14624.*

Most Reverend

MATTHEW H. CLARK, D.D.

Retired Bishop of Rochester; ordained December 19, 1962; appointed Bishop of Rochester April 23, 1979; consecrated May 27, 1979; installed June 26, 1979; retired September 21, 2012. *Res.: 1150 Buffalo Rd., Rochester, NY 14624.*

Pastoral Center: 1150 Buffalo Rd., Rochester, NY 14624-1890. Tel: 585-328-3210; Tel: 800-388-7177; Fax: 585-328-3149.

Web: www.dor.org

ESTABLISHED MARCH 3, 1868.

Square Miles 7,107.

Comprises the Counties of Cayuga, Chemung, Livingston, Monroe, Ontario, Schuyler, Seneca, Steuben, Tioga, Tompkins, Wayne and Yates in the State of New York.

Legal Title of Diocese: The Diocese of Rochester.
For legal titles of parishes and diocesan institutions, consult the Pastoral Center.

STATISTICAL OVERVIEW

Personnel	
Bishop	1
Retired Bishops	1
Abbots	1
Retired Abbots	2
Priests: Diocesan Active in Diocese	93
Priests: Diocesan Active Outside Diocese	3
Priests: Retired, Sick or Absent	60
Number of Diocesan Priests	156
Religious Priests in Diocese	35
Total Priests in Diocese	191
Extern Priests in Diocese	14
Ordinations:	
Diocesan Priests	1
Transitional Deacons	2
Permanent Deacons	3
Permanent Deacons in Diocese	96
Total Brothers	26
Total Sisters	526
Parishes	
Parishes	86
With Resident Pastor:	
Resident Diocesan Priests	65
Resident Religious Priests	2
Without Resident Pastor:	
Administered by Priests	16
Administered by Deacons	1
Administered by Religious Women	1
Missions	2
New Parishes Created	1
Closed Parishes	2
Welfare	
Health Care Centers	2
Total Assisted	1,600
Homes for the Aged	4
Total Assisted	1,700
Day Care Centers	1
Total Assisted	132
Specialized Homes	7
Total Assisted	820
Special Centers for Social Services	73
Total Assisted	230,000
Residential Care of Disabled	11
Total Assisted	83
Educational	
Diocesan Students in Other Seminaries	11
Total Seminarians	11
Colleges and Universities	1
Total Students	108
High Schools, Private	6
Total Students	2,970
Elementary Schools, Diocesan and Parish	18
Total Students	3,020
Elementary Schools, Private	2
Total Students	212
Catechesis/Religious Education:	
High School Students	4,578
Elementary Students	5,896
Total Students under Catholic Instruction	16,795
Teachers in the Diocese:	
Priests	1
Sisters	10
Lay Teachers	554
Vital Statistics	
Receptions into the Church:	
Infant Baptism Totals	1,578
Minor Baptism Totals	376
Adult Baptism Totals	127
Received into Full Communion	233
First Communions	1,738
Confirmations	1,470
Marriages:	
Catholic	429
Interfaith	159
Total Marriages	588
Deaths	3,076
Total Catholic Population	296,178
Total Population	1,438,485

Former Bishops—Rt. Rev. BERNARD J. MCQUAID, D.D., ord. Jan. 16, 1848; appt. March 31, 1868; cons. July 12, 1868; died Jan. 18, 1909; Most Revs. THOMAS F. HICKEY, D.D., ord. March 25, 1884; cons. May 24, 1905; succeeded to the See, Jan. 18, 1909; appt. assistant at the Pontifical Throne, May 4, 1925; made Archbishop of the Titular See of Viminacium, Oct. 30, 1928; died Dec. 10, 1940; JOHN FRANCIS O'HERN, D.D., ord. Feb. 17, 1901; appt. Bishop of Rochester, Jan. 4, 1929; cons. March 19, 1929; died May 22, 1933; His Eminence EDWARD CARDINAL MOONEY, D.D., appt. Papal Delegate to India Jan. 1, 1926; cons. Jan. 31, 1926; appt. Apostolic Delegate to Japan Jan. 1, 1931; appt. Bishop of Rochester Jan. 1, 1933; installed Bishop of Rochester Oct. 12, 1933; transferred to Detroit, May 26, 1937; installed Archbishop of Detroit, Aug. 3, 1937; created Cardinal, Feb. 18, 1946; died Oct. 25, 1958; Most Revs. JAMES E. KEARNEY, D.D., ord. Sept. 19, 1908; appt. Bishop of Salt Lake, Utah, July 1, 1932; cons. Oct. 28, 1932; transferred to Rochester, July 31, 1937; installed Nov. 11, 1937; retired Oct. 26, 1966; died Jan. 12, 1977; FULTON J. SHEEN, D.D., ord. Sept. 30, 1919; appt. Titular Bishop of Cesariana and Auxiliary of New York, May 28, 1951; cons. June 11, 1951; appt. to Rochester, Oct. 26, 1966; installed Dec. 15, 1966; resigned Oct. 15, 1969; appt. Titular Archbishop of Newport; died Dec. 9, 1979; JOSEPH L. HOGAN, S.T.D., D.D., ord. June 6, 1942; appt. to Rochester, Oct. 15, 1969; cons. and installed Nov. 28, 1969; retired Nov. 28, 1978; died Aug. 27, 2000; MATTHEW H. CLARK, ord. Dec. 19, 1962; appt. Bishop of Rochester April 23, 1979; cons. May 27, 1979; installed June 26, 1979; retired Sept. 21, 2012.

Pastoral Center Administration

Pastoral Center—1150 Buffalo Rd., Rochester, 14624-1890. Tel: 585-328-3210;
Tel: 800-388-7177 (Toll Free within Diocese);
Fax: 585-328-3149; Web: www.dor.org.

Vicar General—Very Rev. PAUL J. TOMASSO, V.G.

Moderator of the Curia—Very Rev. PAUL J. TOMASSO, V.G.

Priest Secretary to Bishop Matano—Rev. DANIEL E. WHITE.

Chancellor—Rev. DANIEL J. CONDON, J.C.L.

Judicial Vicar—Rev. LOUIS A. SIRIANNI, J.C.L.

Executive Assistant to the Bishop, Moderator of the Curia, Vicar General—MRS. KATHLEEN MCMAHON.

Secretary to Bishop Emeritus Matthew H. Clark—Sr. MARY ANN BINSACK, R.S.M., Fax: 585-328-3149.

Office of the Chancellor and Department of Legal Services

Chancellor and Director of the Department of Legal Services—Rev. DANIEL J. CONDON, J.C.L.

Judicial Vicar—Rev. LOUIS A. SIRIANNI, J.C.L.

Legal Assistant to the Chancellor—MRS. KATE CZARNECKI.

Diocesan Archives—Sr. CONNIE DERBY, R.S.M., Dir. Archival Svcs., Email: archives@dor.org.

Censores Librorum—Rev. JOSEPH A. HART, S.T.D.; Very Rev. WILLIAM F. LAIRD, J.C.L.; Revs. WILLIAM E. GRAF, D.Min., (Retired); JOSEPH W. MARCOUX, S.T.L.

Tribunal—

Director—VACANT.

Judges—Rev. LOUIS A. SIRIANNI, J.C.L., Judicial Vicar; MS. RENEE LISS-SIRACO, J.C.L.; Very Rev. KEVIN E. MCKENNA, J.C.D.; Rev. T. PIUS PATHMARAJAH, J.C.L.; Very Rev. WILLIAM F. LAIRD, J.C.L., Adjutant Judicial Vicar.

Defender of the Bond—Rev. Msgr. GERARD C. KRIEG, J.C.L., (Retired).

Staff—Rev. WILLIAM E. GRAF, D.Min., Expert, (Retired); Deacon JAMES STEIGER, Ecclesiastical Notary; Rev. R. RICHARD BRICKLER, Assesor, (Retired); MR. JOSE RIVERA, Judicial Asst.

Consultative Bodies

Bishop's Stewardship Council—MR. ROBERT NAPIER, Chairperson.

College of Consultors—Rev. DANIEL J. CONDON, J.C.L., Contact.

Priest Consultors—Very Rev. WILLIAM G. COFFAS; Revs. PAUL GITAU; GEORGE P. HEYMAN; DANIEL J. CONDON, J.C.L.; WILLIAM B. LEONE; Very Revs. FRANK E. LIOI; PAUL J. TOMASSO, V.G.; Revs. THOMAS P. MULL; DANIEL E. WHITE.

Priests' Council—Most Rev. SALVATORE R. MATANO, Pres.; Very Revs. TIMOTHY E. HORAN, Monroe East Deanery (Region); JAMES P. JAEGER, West Deanery (Region); Rev. PATRICK L. CONNOR, South Deanery (Region); Very Revs. JUSTIN D. MILLER, East Deanery (Region); EDISON TAYAG, Central Deanery (Region); WILLIAM G. COFFAS, Monroe Central Deanery (Region); LEE P. CHASE, S.T.L., Monroe West Deanery (Region); Revs. MICHAEL W. TWARDZIK, Secular Priests not Incarnated in the Diocese; PAUL ENGLISH, C.S.B., Religious Order; PETER B. BAYER, (Retired); PAUL GITAU. Ex Officio: Rev. DANIEL J. CONDON, J.C.L., (Chancellor); Very Rev. PAUL J. TOMASSO, V.G., (Vicar Gen.); Rev. GEORGE P. HEYMAN, Chair, Convocation Committee.

Deans—Very Revs. LEE P. CHASE, S.T.L., Monroe West Deanery; JAMES P. JAEGER, West Deanery; EDISON TAYAG, Central Deanery; JUSTIN D. MILLER, East Deanery; PATRICK CONNOR, South Deanery; WILLIAM G. COFFAS, Monroe Central Deanery; TIMOTHY E. HORAN, Monroe East Deanery.

Catholic Charities—

Catholic Charities of the Diocese of Rochester—1150 Buffalo Rd., Rochester, 14624. Tel: 585-328-3210. JACK BALINSKY, Diocesan Dir.; MICHAEL GABRIELLI, Chm. Bd. Directors. (refer to Catholic Charities section under Institutions located in the Diocese for further listings).

Rochester Catholic Press Association "Catholic Courier"—El Mensajero Catolico Tel: 585-529-9530 ; Tel: 800-600-3628. KAREN FRANZ, Gen. Mgr. & Editor.

Board of Directors—Very Rev. PAUL J. TOMASSO, V.G., Vice Pres.; Rev. DANIEL J. CONDON, J.C.L., Sec.; WILLIAM H. KEDLEY, Treas.; MARK HARE; ANDREA COLARUOTOLO-O'NEILL; Very Rev. KEVIN E. MCKENNA, J.C.D.; Rev. PETER MOTTOLA; KEVIN FOY; LEONORE RIVERA; JAMES SCHNELL; JANE SUTTER; DAVID PEROTTO; COLLEEN TREVISANI; LAURETTA BEALE; VICTORIA RIPPEL; Sr. SHEILA STEVENSON, R.S.M.; DEREK DALTON; MEGAN HENRY; Deacon FRANK PETTRONE; Rev. DANIEL E. WHITE. Honorary Members: CAROLINE RIBY; RICHARD HARE; HELEN MCDERMOTT; TIMOTHY FITZGERALD.

Faith Development Ministry—

Department of Catholic Schools—DR. ANTHONY COOK III, Ed.D., Supt. Schools; MR. JAMES TAUZEL, Assoc. Supt.; MS. SHARON HOCKWATER, Administrative Asst.; MS. ANN FRANK, Coord. Assessment & Professional Growth; MS. REBECCA WILLIAMS, Business Mgr.

Department of Evangelization and Catechesis—MS. LINDA MEHLENBACHER, Dir.

AV Resource Librarian—Sr. CONNIE DERBY, R.S.M.

Coordinator of Sports—MR. ROBERT NALEPA JR.

Coordinator of Diocesan Youth & Young Adult Ministry—MS. LESLIE BARKIN.

Coordinator for Evangelization and Sacramental Catechesis—MR. DONALD SMITH.

Project Coordinators—MS. KATEY BOURNE; MR. MARK CAPELLAZZI.

Office of Stewardship and Communications—MR. DOUG MANDELARO, Dir.

Associate Director—MS. COLLEEN BRADE.

Administrative Assistant—MS. COLLEEN TALARICO.

Department of Financial Services—

Chief Financial Officer—MS. LISA M. PASSERO.

Administrative Assistant—MS. JANA THOMPSON.

Director of Financial Services—MS. MARY ZIARNIAK.

Information Technology—MR. THOMAS VEEDER, Dir.; MR. DAVID KILPATRICK, Network Systems Admin. Computer Coordinators: MR. MARK DARLING, IT Mgr.; MS. BRENDA CHEVALIER, Accounting Applications Analyst; MR. CHRIS MCDONALD, System Analyst; MR. BRENDAN PARKER, Web Developer; MR. JADON CRAWFORD, Network Technician; MR. RYAN HART, Network Technician; MR. SHAWN MLECZYNSKI, Systems Analyst; MR. CODY HALTERMAN, Technician; MS. SHAYNA MACLARTY, Technician; MR. ROB HENNING, Technician; MR. MIKE MELI, Technician; MR. TOM SMALLWOOD, Help Desk & Field Technician.

Buildings and Properties—MR. SEAN MORAN, Mgr.

Controller—MR. SCOTT MOSMAN.

Human Resources—MS. TAMMY SYLVESTER, Dir.; MS. RENATA PARKS, IT Implementation Mgr.

Benefits Administration—MS. KATE GRAY, HRIS/ Pension Analyst.

Department of Priest Personnel—Very Rev. PAUL J. TOMASSO, V.G., Dir.

Department of Human Resources for Catholic Schools—MS. TAMMY SYLVESTER, Dir.

Ministry to Priests—Rev. WILLIAM E. GRAF, D.Min., Coord., (Retired), 681 High St., Victor, 14564. Email: graf@dor.org.

Newly Ordained Priests—Very Rev. PAUL J. TOMASSO, V.G.

Pension Committee (Lay and Priests)—Very Rev. PAUL J. TOMASSO, V.G.; Rev. DANIEL J. CONDON, J.C.L.; Very Rev. ROBERT J. SCHRADER; MS. TAMMY SYLVESTER; MS. MAUREEN DEMPSEY-FRAZER; MS. LISA M. PASSERO; MS. SUSAN MILLER; MR. STEPHEN OBERST; MR. BRIAN KOPP; MS. FRAN PULLANO.

Priests' Personnel Board—Very Rev. PAUL J. TOMASSO, V.G., Dir.

Priests' Sabbatical Committee—Rev. GEORGE P. HEYMAN, Pres. St. Bernard's School of Theology & Ministry.

Office of Vocations—Revs. WILLIAM J. COFFAS, Dir., Our Mothers of Sorrows, 500 Mount Read Blvd., Rochester, 14612. Tel: 585-663-5432; Email: fcoffas@dor.org; PETER VANLIESHOUT; MATTHEW F. JONES.

Vicar for Religious—Rev. DANIEL J. CONDON, J.C.L.

Pastoral Services—Tel: 585-328-3228, Ext. 1337.

Director—MR. BERNARD GRIZARD.

Associate Director—DR. SHANNON LOUGHLIN.

Administrative Assistant—MRS. LAURIE MCMAHON.

Project Managers—MS. CARMEN ROLLINSON; MR. NICHOLAS FREGA.

Liturgical Commission—Rev. DANIEL E. WHITE.

Leadership Formation for Parishes—MS. KAREN RINEFIERD.

Office of Migrant Ministry—Rev. JESUS FLORES.

Urban Hispanic Ministry—MR. JORGE SALGADO, N.W. Monroe & Livingston Counties; MS. LUCI ROMERO-PONCE, Wayne County; Sr. KAY E. SCHWENZER, R.S.M., Ontario & Yates Counties.

Intercultural Program Specialist—VACANT.

Director of Cultural Diversity—MS. LYNETTE SAENZ, Dir.

The Society for the Propagation of the Faith—Rev. ROBERT C. BRADLER, Dir., (Retired); MS. JOSEPHINE CONLON, Sec. & Bookkeeper.

Clergy Services—

Priest & Seminarian Services Associate Director—MRS. DARLENE SERBICKI.

Administrative Assistant—MRS. LAURIE MCMAHON.

Deacon Personnel & Formation—Deacon EDWARD GIBLIN, Dir. Deacon Personnel.

Ministry Offices—Rev. JESUS FLORES.

Office of Seminarians—Very Rev. PAUL J. TOMASSO, V.G.

Specialized Ministries—

Bishop Sheen Ecumenical Housing Foundation—935 East Ave., Ste. 300, Rochester, 14607. Tel: 585-461-4263; Fax: 585-461-5177; Email: sheen@rochester.rr.com; Web: sheenhousing.org. MS. ALLYNN SMITH, Exec. Dir.; MS. ROSEANNE HENNESSEY, Pres. Bd. Directors, Subsidiary: Bloomfield Meadows, Inc.

Clergy Relief Society—130 Exchange St., Geneva, 14456. Tel: 315-789-0930. Rev. THOMAS P. MULL.

Diocesan Building Commission—MR. SEAN MORAN, Contact.

Diocesan Women's Commission—DR. SHANNON LOUGHLIN, Diocesan Liaison.

Holy Sepulchre Cemetery—MS. LYNN SULLIVAN, CEO, 2461 Lake Ave., Rochester, 14612. Tel: 585-458-4110.

Victim Assistance Coordinator—MRS. DEBORAH HOUSEL, Tel: 585-328-3228, Ext. 1555; Email: victimassistance@dor.org.

Safe Environment Education & Compliance—MS. KAREN RINEFIERD, Tel: 585-328-3228, Ext. 1255; Email: karen.rinefierd@dor.org.

CLERGY, PARISHES, MISSIONS AND PAROCHIAL SCHOOLS

METROPOLITAN ROCHESTER

(MONROE COUNTY)

1—SACRED HEART CATHEDRAL (1910) Very Rev. Kevin E. McKenna, J.C.D.; Deacons Lynn W. Kershner, (Retired); Bruno Petrauskas. In Res., Most Rev. Salvatore R. Matano; Rev. Daniel E. White.
The Cathedral Community—(Holy Rosary, Most Precious Blood, Sacred Heart Cathedral) 296 Flower City Pk., 14615. Tel: 585-254-3221;
Fax: 585-254-8970.

2—ST. AMBROSE (1921) Merged with St. James, Rochester & St. John the Evangelist, Rochester to form Peace of Christ Roman Catholic Parish of Rochester, NY.

3—ST. ANDREW (1914) Closed. Inquiries for Parish records should contact St. Francis Xavier Cabrini Parish.

4—ST. ANNE (1930) [CEM] Rev. Gary L. Tyman, Sacramental Min.; Deacons John McDermott; David Hudzinski. In Res., Revs. Frederick Asuming; Dennis Bonsignore; James F. Lawlor, (Retired).
Res.: 1600 Mt. Hope Ave., 14620-4598.
Tel: 585-271-3260; Fax: 585-271-7160.

5—ST. ANTHONY OF PADUA (1906) (Italian—Vietnamese), Closed. For inquiries for parish records, contact Holy Apostles Church, Rochester, NY.

6—ST. AUGUSTINE (1898) Closed. For inquiries for parish records contact St. Monica, Rochester.

7—BLESSED SACRAMENT (1902) Revs. John Loncle; Felicjan Sierotowicz, Parochial Vicar; Deacon David Palma.
Parish—534 Oxford St., 14607.
Res. & Mailing Address: 259 Rutgers St., 14607.
Tel: 585-271-7240.
Convent—247 Rutgers St., 14607. Tel: 585-271-7736.

8—ST. BONIFACE (1860) [CEM] (German) Revs. John Loncle; Matthew F. Jones; Deacon David Palma.
Res.: 330 Gregory St., 14620. Tel: 585-473-4271;
Fax: 585-256-0868.

9—ST. BRIDGET (1854) Merged with Immaculate Conception, Rochester to form the parish of Immaculate Conception/St. Bridget, Rochester. For inquiries on records contact Immaculate Conception Parish.

10—ST. CECILIA (1949) [CEM] Merged with Christ the King, St. Margaret Mary, St. Salome & St. Thomas the Apostle, Rochester to form the Parish of Saint Kateri Tekakwitha, Rochester.

11—ST. CHARLES BORROMEO (1925) Revs. John A. Firpo; T. Pius Pathmarajah, J.C.L.; Deacons Daniel Callan; Richard J. Lombard, (Retired). In Res., Rev. Thomas R. Statt, (Retired).
Res.: 3003 Dewey Ave., 14616. Tel: 585-663-3230;
Fax: 585-663-8055.

12—CHRIST THE KING (1955) Merged with St. Cecilia, St. Margaret Mary, St. Salome & St. Thomas the Apostle, Rochester to form the Parish of Saint Kateri Tekakwitha, Rochester.

13—CHURCH OF THE ANNUNCIATION (1917) (Italian), Merged with Our Lady of the Americas, St. Michael's and Our Lady of Perpetual Help to form St. Frances Xavier Cabrini.

14—EMMANUEL CHURCH OF THE DEAF (1981) Rev. Raymond H. Fleming; Deacon Patrick A. Graybill, (Retired)
Legal Name: Emmanuel Church of the Deaf of the Diocese of Rochester
Res.: 34 St. Monica St., 14619. Tel: 585-235-3244;
Tel: 585-235-1812.

15—ST. FRANCES XAVIER CABRINI, Revs. William McGrath, Co-Pastor; Robert Thomas Werth, Co-Pastor; Deacons Jose Berrios; Jorge Malave; Robert Meyer; Carlos Vargas; Agenol Rodriguez
Legal Name: Roman Catholic Parish of St. Frances Xavier Cabrini
Office: 124 Evergreen St., 14605. Tel: 585-325-4041;
Fax: 585-287-5160.

16—ST. FRANCIS ASSISI (1929) Closed. For inquiries for parish records, please contact: Holy Apostles, 7 Austin St., Rochester, NY 14606; Tel: 585-254-7171; Fax: 585-254-5813; Email: rholyapo@dor.org.

17—ST. FRANCIS XAVIER, Closed. All inquiries should be directed to St. Frances Xavier Cabrini Parish.

18—ST. GEORGE (1907) (Lithuanian)
Mailing Address: 150 Varinna Dr., 14618.
Tel: 585-319-5689. Rev. Gary L. Tyman.

19—GUARDIAN ANGELS (1960) Merged with Church of the Good Shepherd, Henrietta & St. Joseph's, Rush. For inquiries on records Marianne Cope Roman Catholic Parish, Monroe County.
Res.: 2061 E. Henrietta Rd., 14623-3999.
Tel: 585-334-1412; Fax: 585-334-7145.

20—ST. HELEN (1940) Merged with Holy Ghost & St. Jude. For records contact The Parish of the Holy Family, Gates, NY.

21—HOLY APOSTLES (1884) Very Rev. Anthony P. Mugavero; Deacons Salvador Otero; Nemesio Vellon Martinez.

Parish: 530 Lyell Ave., 14606.
Res.: 7 Austin St., 14606. Tel: 585-254-7170; Fax: 585-254-5813.

22—HOLY CROSS (1873) Revs. John F. Gagnier; John Reif, Parochial Vicar, (Retired); Deacon Joseph Placious.
Res.: 4492 Lake Ave., 14612. Tel: 585-663-2244; Fax: 585-865-5379.
School—Holy Cross School, (Grades PreK-6), 4488 Lake Ave., 14612. Tel: 585-663-6533; Email: hcdcs@dor.org. Mary Martell, Prin. Lay Teachers 26; Students 334.
Convent—4490 Lake Ave., 14612. Tel: 716-663-5351.

23—HOLY GHOST (1875) [CEM] Merged with St. Helen & St. Jude. For parish records contact The Parish of the Holy Family, Gates, NY.

24—HOLY FAMILY (1864) (German), Merged with Holy Apostles, Rochester. For inquiries for parish records contact Holy Apostles, Rochester.

25—HOLY NAME OF JESUS (1964) Closed. For inquiries for parish records contact St. Charles Borromeo, Rochester.

26—HOLY REDEEMER-ST. FRANCIS XAVIER (1867-1888) Merged with Our Lady of the Americas, Our Lady of Mount Carmel, Light of Christ, Our Lady of the Angels & Our Lady of Perpetual Help, Rochester. For inquiries for the records contact the Parish of St. Francis Xavier Cabrini, Rochester.

27—HOLY ROSARY (1889) Merged with Most Precious Blood & Sacred Heart Cathedral, Rochester. For inquiries for parish records contact The Cathedral Community.

28—IMMACULATE CONCEPTION (1849) Merged with St. Bridget, Rochester to form the parish of Immaculate Conception/St. Bridget, Rochester.

29—IMMACULATE CONCEPTION/ST. BRIDGET, Revs. Raymond H. Fleming; Robert C. Bradler, (Retired); Deacon Richard Rall.
Office: 445 Frederick Douglass St., 14608.

30—ST. JAMES (1949) Merged with St. Ambrose, Rochester & St. John the Evangelist, Rochester. For inquiries for records, Peace of Christ Roman Catholic Parish of Rochester, NY.

31—ST. JOHN THE EVANGELIST (1914) Merged with St. Ambrose, Rochester & St. James, Rochester. For inquiries for records, Peace of Christ Roman Catholic Parish of Rochester, NY.

32—ST. JOHN THE EVANGELIST (1865) Rev. Peter Enyan-Boadu; Deacons Robert Burke; Ed Knauf.
Res.: 2400 Ridge Rd., W., 14626. Tel: 585-225-8980; Fax: 585-723-9825.

33—ST. JOSEPH (1836) Closed. For inquiries for parish records contact Our Lady of Victory.

34—KATERI TEKAKWITHA ROMAN CATHOLIC PARISH, Revs. Paul English, C.S.B.; Michael Buentello, C.S.B., Parochial Vicar; Evan Simington, Parochial Vicar. In Res., Revs. Walter Cushing, (Retired); Joseph A. Trovato, C.S.B., (Retired).
Office: 445 Kings Hwy. S., 14617. Tel: 585-266-1288.
School—Saint Kateri School, (Grades PreK-6), Tel: 585-467-8730; Fax: 585-467-5392; Email: sksdcs@dor.org. Sr. Kathleen Lurz, S.S.J., Prin. Lay Teachers 16; Students 200; Religious Teachers 2.

35—ST. LAWRENCE (1959) Very Rev. Lee P. Chase, S.T.L.; Rev. Scott Caton; Deacons Emmanuel Asis; Thomas Beck; David Squilla.
Res.: 1000 N. Greece Rd., 14626. Tel: 585-723-1350; Fax: 585-723-1361.
School—St. Lawrence School, (Grades PreK-5), Tel: 585-225-3870; Email: slawrdcs@dor.org. Frank Arvizzigno, Prin. Lay Teachers 28; Students 170.
Catechesis Religious Program—Tel: 585-225-7320.

36—LIGHT OF CHRIST ROMAN CATHOLIC PARISH, Merged with Our Lady of the Americas, Our Lady of the Angels & Our Lady of Perpetual Help, Rochester. For inquiries for parish records contact Roman Catholic Parish of St. Francis Xavier Cabrini, Rochester.

37—ST. LUCY (1912) Closed. For inquiries for parish records contact Immaculate Conception Church.

38—ST. MARGARET MARY (1929) Merged with St. Cecilia, Christ the King, St. Salome & St. Thomas the Apostle, Rochester. For inquiries for parish records contact Parish of Saint Kateri Tekakwitha, Rochester.

39—ST. MARK (1964) Rev. Louis A. Sirianni, J.C.L.; Deacons Frank Pettrone; David Cadregari.
Res.: 54 Kuhn Rd., 14612. Tel: 585-225-3710; Fax: 585-227-6824.

40—ST. MARY (1834) Revs. John Loncle; Matthew F. Jones, Parochial Vicar; Deacon David Palma, Pastoral Assoc.
Res.: 15 St. Mary's Pl., 14607. Tel: 585-232-7142; Fax: 585-232-6289.

41—ST. MICHAEL (1872) Merged with Our Lady of the Americas, Our Lady of the Angels & Our Lady of Perpetual Help, Rochester. For inquiries for parish records contact the Roman Catholic Parish of St. Frances Xavier Cabrini, Rochester.

42—ST. MONICA (1898) Rev. Raymond H. Fleming; Deacons Matthew Dudek; Brian J. McNulty.
Office: 34 Monica St., 14611. Tel: 585-235-3340; Fax: 585-235-8315.

43—MOST PRECIOUS BLOOD (1930) Closed. For inquiries for parish records contact the Cathedral Community, Rochester.

44—OUR LADY OF GOOD COUNSEL (1928) Closed. For inquiries for parish records contact St. Monica, Rochester.

45—OUR LADY OF LOURDES (1928) Revs. Gary L. Tyman; James F. Lawler, (Retired); Deacons John McDermott; William Rabjohn.
Res.: 150 Varinna Dr., 14618. Tel: 585-473-9656; Fax: 585-271-6472.
School—Seton Catholic School, (Grades PreK-6), 165 Rhinecliff Dr., 14618-1525. Tel: 585-473-6604; Email: csoffice@rochester.rr.com. Mrs. Patty Selig, Prin. Lay Teachers 19; Students 260.

46—OUR LADY OF MERCY (1957) Closed. For inquiries for parish records please see Our Mother of Sorrows, Rochester.

47—OUR LADY OF MOUNT CARMEL (1909) Merged with Our Lady of the Americas, Light of Christ, Our Lady of the Angels, Our Lady of Perpetual Help, Holy Redeemer, St. Francis Xavier & Corpus Christi, Rochester. For inquiries for parish records contact the Parish of St. Frances Xavier Cabrini, Rochester.

48—OUR LADY OF PERPETUAL HELP (1905) Merged with Our Lady of the Americas, Our Lady of the Angels & Light of Christ, Rochester. For inquiries for parish records contact the Roman Catholic Parish of St. Francis Xavier Cabrini, Rochester.

49—OUR LADY OF THE AMERICAS OF ROCHESTER, NY (1888) Merged with Light of Christ, Our Lady of the Angels & Our Lady of Perpetual Help, Rochester to form the Roman Catholic Parish of St. Francis Xavier Cabrini, Rochester.

50—OUR LADY OF VICTORY-ST. JOSEPH (1848) Rev. Ronald A. Antinarelli, K.C.H.S.
Res.: 210 Pleasant St., 14604. Tel: 585-454-2244; Fax: 585-454-2246.

51—OUR LADY QUEEN OF PEACE (1960) Rev. Joseph A. Hart, S.T.D.; Deacon Arthur Cuestas; Margaret Ostromecki, Pastoral Assoc. In Res., Most Rev. Matthew Harvey Clark, D.D.
Parish—601 Edgewood Ave., 14618-4329.
Res.: 18 Viennawood Dr., 14618.
Tel: 585-244-3010 (Office);
Fax: 585-242-7733 (Office).

52—OUR MOTHER OF SORROWS (1829) [CEM] (Irish) Revs. William J. Coffas; Anthony Nketiah, Parochial Vicar; Deacon Donald Eggleston. In Res., Rev. Winfried Kellner, (Retired).
Res.: 5000 Mt. Read Blvd., 14612. Tel: 585-663-5432; Fax: 585-663-7683.

53—THE PARISH OF THE HOLY FAMILY, MONROE COUNTY, NY
4100 Lyell Ave., 14606. Revs. Michael J. Schramel; Thomas Akowuah, Parochial Vicar; Deacon Patrick M. Shanley.

54—ST. PATRICK (1832) Closed. (Old Cathedral). For inquiries for records contact Holy Apostles, 7 Austin St., Rochester, NY 14608. Tel: 585-254-5813.

55—PEACE OF CHRIST
Mailing Address: 25 Empire Blvd., 14609.
Tel: 585-288-5000; Fax: 585-654-7658; Email: rpeace@dor.org; Web: www.peaceofchristparish.org. Very Rev. Robert J. Schrader; Revs. Timothy Brown; Carlos Sanchez-Betancur
Legal Name: Peace of Christ Roman Catholic Parish of Rochester, NY
Res.: 549 Humboldt St., 14610.
School—St. Ambrose Academy, (Grades PreK-5), 31 Empire Blvd., 14609-4335. Tel: 585-255-0580; Email: sjndcs@dor.org. Jacqueline Senecal, Prin. Lay Teachers 13; Students 119.
Catechesis Religious Program—

56—SS. PETER AND PAUL (1843) Closed. For inquiries for parish records contact St. Monica, Rochester.

57—ST. PHILIP NERI (1929) Closed. For inquiries for parish records, contact St. Francis Xavier Cabrini Parish.

58—ST. PIUS TENTH (1954) [CEM]
Mailing Address: 3010 Chili Ave., 14624. Rev. Paul Bonacci; Deacons Elmer Smith; James Briars.
Res.: 3032 Chili Ave., 14624.
Tel: 585-247-2566 (Office); Fax: 585-247-8848.
School—St. Pius X School, (Grades PreK-6), 3000 Chili Ave., 14624-4598. Tel: 585-247-5650; Email: spxdcs@dor.org. Daniel Pitnell, Prin. Lay Teachers 16; Students 173.

59—ST. SALOME (1925) Merged with St. Cecilia, St. Margaret Mary, Christ the King & St. Thomas the Apostle, Rochester to form the Parish of Blessed Kateri Tekakwitha, Rochester.

60—ST. STANISLAUS (1890) (Polish) Rev. Roman Caly.
Res. & Mailing: 34 St. Stanislaus St., 14621.
Tel: 585-467-3068; Fax: 585-467-3072.
Church: 1124 Hudson Ave., 14621.

61—ST. THEODORE (1924) Revs. Stephen Kraus; Frederick Asuming, Admin.; Deacons Craig Stratton; Dennis Lohouse; Angelo Coccia, (Retired); Laurence Feasel, (Retired).
Res.: 168 Spencerport Rd., 14606. Tel: 585-429-6811; Fax: 585-429-7726.

62—ST. THERESA (1927) (Polish), Closed. For inquiries for parish records contact St. Stanislaus, Rochester.

63—ST. THOMAS MORE (1953) Rev. Joseph A. Hart, S.T.D.; Deacon Arthur Cuestas; Margaret Ostromecki, Pastoral Assoc.
Res.: 2617 East Ave., 14610. Tel: 585-381-4200; Fax: 585-381-6327.

64—ST. THOMAS THE APOSTLE (1922) Merged with St. Cecilia, St. Margaret Mary, St. Salome & Christ the King, Rochester. For inquiries for records contact the Parish of Blessed Kateri Tekakwitha, Rochester.

OUTSIDE METROPOLITAN ROCHESTER

ADDISON, STEUBEN CO.

1—ST. CATHERINE OF SIENA (1854) [CEM] Merged with St. Joseph, Campbell & St. Stanislaus, Bradford. For inquiries for parish records contact the Catholic Parish of Saints Isidore and Maria Torribia, Addison.

2—SAINTS ISIDORE AND MARIA TORRIBIA, Revs. Patrick L. Connor; Francis J. Erb, (Retired); Deacon Douglas Farwell
Legal Name: The Catholic Parish of Saints Isidore and Maria Torribia
Office: 51 Maple St., Addison, 14801.
Tel: 607-359-2115; Fax: 607-359-2121.

APALACHIN, TIOGA CO., ST. MARGARET MARY (1955) Merged with St. Francis, Catatonk; St. John the Evangelist, Newark Valley; St. Pius the Tenth, Van Etten; and St. James, Waverly. For inquiries for parish records contact Blessed Trinity, Owego.

AUBURN, CAYUGA CO.

1—ST. ALOYSIUS, Closed. For inquiries for parish records please see Holy Family, Auburn.

2—ST. ALPHONSUS (1853) [JC] (German) Very Rev. Timothy L. Niven; Deacon Gregg Lawson, (Retired).
Parish—85 E. Genesee St., Auburn, 13021.
Mailing & Res.: 10 S. Lewis St., Auburn, 13021.
Tel: 315-252-7261; Fax: 315-252-7262.
See St. Joseph's School (Auburn), Auburn under Schools Outside Monroe County located in the Institution section.
Catechesis Religious Program—

3—ST. FRANCIS OF ASSISI (1907) [JC] (Italian) Merged with St. Hyacinth, Auburn. For inquiries for parish records contact Saints Mary and Martha Roman Catholic Parish, Cayuga County, NY.

4—HOLY FAMILY (1834) Rev. John Gathenya. In Res., Rev. Ronald E. Gaesser, (Retired).
Parish—85 North St., Auburn, 13021.
Tel: 315-252-9576; Fax: 315-255-1506.
School—St. Joseph's School, Tel: 315-253-8327; Fax: 315-253-2401. Michael Carney, Prin.
Catechesis Religious Program—

5—ST. HYACINTH (1905) [JC] (Polish), Merged with St. Francis of Assisi, Auburn. For inquiries for parish records contact Saints Mary and Martha Roman Catholic Parish, Cayuga County, NY.
In Res—Rev. Michael F. Conboy, (Retired).
Church & Res.: 61 Pulaski St., Auburn, 13021.
Tel: 315-252-7297; Fax: 315-252-2447.
Church Office: 299 Clark St., Auburn, 13021.
School—St. Joseph School, Tel: 315-253-8327. Mr. Michael W. Carney, Prin. A consolidation of the following parishes: Holy Family; Sacred Heart; St. Alphonsus; and St. Hyacinth.

6—ST. MARY (1868) (Irish) Very Rev. Frank E. Lioi; Deacon Dennis Donahue.
Res.: 15 Clark St., Auburn, 13021. Tel: 315-252-9545 ; Fax: 315-252-9546.
School—St. Joseph's School, Tel: 315-253-8357. Michael Carney, Prin. Also serving the parishes of Auburn.

7—SAINTS MARY AND MARTHA, Very Rev. Frank E. Lioi
Legal Name: Saints Mary and Martha Roman Catholic Parish Cayuga County, NY
Res.: 299 Clark St., Auburn, 13021.
Tel: 315-252-7593; Fax: 315-252-2447.
Catechesis Religious Program—

8—SACRED HEART (1955) [JC] Rev. Michael R. Brown; Deacon Nicholas Valvo.
Res.: 90 Melrose Rd., Auburn, 13021.
Tel: 315-252-7271; Fax: 315-255-0716.
School—St. Joseph School, 89 E. Genesee St., Auburn, 13021. Tel: 315-253-8327;
Fax: 315-253-2401. Mr. James Tauzel, Prin. A consolidation of the following parishes: Holy Family; Sacred Heart; and St. Alphonsus. Lay Teachers 14; Students 152.
Mission—St. Ann (1912) Main St., Owasco, Cayuga Co. 13021.

AURORA, CAYUGA CO.

1—GOOD SHEPHERD CATHOLIC COMMUNITY, [CEM]
Mailing Address: P.O. Box 296, Aurora, 13026-0296.
Tel: 315-364-7197; Fax: 315-364-7197. Rev. William A. Moorby; Deacon Dennis Donahue.

2—ST. PATRICK (1858) Closed. For inquiries for parish

records contact Good Shepherd Catholic Community, Aurora.

AVON, LIVINGSTON CO., ST. AGNES (1866) [CEM] Rev. Michael G. Fowler, Admin.; Deacons Peter Dohr; Gregory Emerton; Eugene Edwards, (Retired).
Res.: 108 Prospect St., Avon, 14414.
Tel: 585-226-2100; Fax: 585-226-6436.
School—St. Agnes School, (Grades PreK-6), For detailed school information please see Category Schools outside Monroe located in the Institution section.

BATH, STEUBEN CO.
1—ST. JOHN VIANNEY, Very Rev. James P. Jaeger; Deacons David LaFortune, Admin.; Robert Colomaio
Legal Name: St. John Vianney Roman Catholic Parish, Steuben County, NY
Res.: 32 E. Morris St., Bath, 14810.
Tel: 607-776-3327; Fax: 607-776-3409.
2—ST. MARY (1860) [CEM] Merged with St. Gabriel, Hammondsport. For inquiries for parish records contact St. John Vianney Roman Catholic Parish, Steuben County, NY.

BRADFORD, STEUBEN CO., ST. STANISLAUS (1922) (Polish), Merged with St. Joseph, Campbell & St. Catherine, Addison. For inquiries for parish records contact the Catholic Parish of Saints Isidore and Maria Torribia, Addison.

BROCKPORT, MONROE CO., NATIVITY OF THE BLESSED VIRGIN MARY (1848) [CEM] Rev. Joseph P. McCaffrey; Deacons Paul Virgilio; Thomas Schrage.
Res.: 152 Main St., Brockport, 14420-1972.
Tel: 585-637-4500; Fax: 585-637-4232.

CALEDONIA, LIVINGSTON CO.
1—ST. COLUMBA (1885) Merged with St. Vincent de Paul's Catholic Church Society, Churchville and St. Mary's Catholic Church, Scottsville. For inquiries for parish records contact The Parish of St. Martin de Porres, Livingston County.
2—THE PARISH OF SAINT MARTIN DE PORRES, LIVINGSTON COUNTY, NY (2017)
198 North Rd., Caledonia, 14423. Tel: 585-538-2126. Revs. John H. Hayes; Theodore J. Auble; Deacon Matthew Dudek.

CANANDAIGUA, ONTARIO CO.
1—ST. BENEDICT
95 N. Main St., Canandaigua, 14424. Revs. Michael Costik, Admin.; Clifford Dorkenoo, Parochial Vicar; Kevin P. Murphy, (Retired); Deacon Claude Lester
Legal Name: St. Benedict Roman Catholic Parish Ontario County, NY.
2—ST. MARY (1844) [CEM] Merged with St. Bridget, East Bloomfield to form St. Benedict Roman Catholic Parish Ontario County, NY.
Res.: 95 N. Main St., Canadaigua, 14424.
Tel: 585-394-1220; Fax: 585-396-3230.
See St. Mary (Canandaigua), Canandaigua under Finger Lakes & Southern Tier Schools located in the Institution section.

CANISTEO, STEUBEN CO., ST. JOACHIM (1880) Closed. For inquiries for parish records contact Our Lady of the Valley, Hornell.

CATO, CAYUGA CO., ST. PATRICK (1875) Merged with St. Joseph, Weedsport and St. John, Port Byron. For inquiries for the parish records contact Our Lady of the Snow, Weedsport.

CAYUGA, CAYUGA CO., ST. JOSEPH (1870) Closed. For inquiries for parish records contact Good Shepherd Catholic Community, Aurora.

CHURCHVILLE, MONROE CO., ST. VINCENT DE PAUL (1869) [CEM] Merged with St. Columba's Church, Caledonia and St. Mary's Catholic Church of Scottsville. For inquiries for parish records contact The Parish of Saint Martin de Porres, Livingston County.

CLIFTON SPRINGS, ONTARIO CO.
1—ST. FELIX (1856) Clustered with St. Francis, Phelps to form St. Felix/St. Francis Parish Cluster, Clifton Springs.
2—ST. FELIX/ST. FRANCIS PARISH CLUSTER (1992) [CEM 2] Merged with St. Dominic, Shortsville. For inquiries for parish records contact St. Peter's Roman Catholic Parish, Ontario County.
Office: 12 Hibbard Ave., Clifton Springs, 14432.
Tel: 315-548-5331 (St. Francis);
Tel: 315-462-2961 (St. Felix); Fax: 315-462-3608.
3—ST. PETER'S ROMAN CATHOLIC PARISH, ONTARIO COUNTY
12 Hibbard Ave., Clifton Springs, 14432. Rev. Peter VanLieshout, Admin.; Deacons Robert Cyrana; Edward A. Smith.

CLYDE, WAYNE CO.
1—ST. JOHN THE EVANGELIST (1852) [CEM] (Italian) Merged with St. Michael, Lyons. For inquiries for parish records contact St. Joseph the Worker Roman Catholic Parish, Wayne County.
2—ST. JOSEPH THE WORKER
43 Dezeng St., Clyde, 14433. Rev. David Tedesche; Deacon Gregory Kiley
Legal Name: St. Joseph the Worker Roman Catholic Parish, Wayne County
Res.: 114 Sodus St., Clyde, 14433. Tel: 315-923-3941; Fax: 315-923-3941.
Mission—St. Patrick (1875) Grand Ave., Savannah, Wayne Co. 13146. Tel: 315-365-3244.

COHOCTON, STEUBEN CO., ST. PIUS V (1861) (German), Closed. For inquiries for parish records contact the chancery. see Holy Family Catholic Community, Wayland.

CORNING, STEUBEN CO.
1—ALL SAINTS
Mailing Address: 222 Dodge Ave., Corning, 14830.
Tel: 607-936-4689; Fax: 607-936-0222. Rev. Matthew F. Jones, Admin.; Deacons Raymond Defendorf; James D. Hankey.
Rectory—15 E. High St., Painted Post, 14870.
Tel: 607-962-0422.
School—All Saints School, Mr. James Tauzel, Prin. For detailed school information please see All Saints Academy.
2—ST. MARY (1848) Closed. with St. Vincent de Paul, Corning and Immaculate Heart of Mary, Painted Post. For inquiries for parish records contact All Saints, Corning.
3—ST. PATRICK (1903) Closed. For inquiries for parish records contact All Saints, Corning.
4—ST. VINCENT DE PAUL (1913) Closed. with St. Mary Corning and Immaculate Heart of Mary, Painted Post. For inquiries for parish records contact All Saints, Corning.

DANSVILLE, LIVINGSTON CO., ST. MARY (1845) Closed. For inquiries for parish records contact the chancery. see Holy Family Catholic Community, Wayland.

DRYDEN, TOMPKINS CO., HOLY CROSS (1962) Rev. Daniel Ruiz-Sierra, Admin.; Deacon George Kozak. In Res., Rev. Gerard R. McKeon, S.J.
Parish—375 S. George Rd., Freeville, 13068.
Tel: 607-844-8314; Fax: 607-844-8358.

EAST BAY, WAYNE CO., ST. JOHN FISHER (1935) Closed. All inquiries for mission records can be made at Blessed Trinity, Wolcott.

EAST BLOOMFIELD, ONTARIO CO., ST. BRIDGET (1850) [CEM] Merged with St. Mary, Canandaigua to form St. Benedict Roman Catholic Parish, Ontario County.

EAST ROCHESTER, MONROE CO., ST. JEROME (1905) Rev. William B. Leone; Sr. Clare Brown, S.S.J., Pastoral Assoc.; Deacons Thomas R. Ecker, (Retired); Dermot M. Loughran. In Res., Rev. William Endres, (Retired).
Res.: 207 S. Garfield St., East Rochester, 14445.
Tel: 585-586-3231; Fax: 585-586-0537.

ELMIRA HEIGHTS, CHEMUNG CO., ST. CHARLES BORROMEO (1904) Merged with Our Lady of Lourdes, Elmira, and St. Casamir, Elmira. For inquiries for parish records contact Christ the Redeemer, Elmira.

ELMIRA, CHEMUNG CO.
1—ST. ANTHONY (1908) (Italian), Merged with St. Patrick, Elmira & Sts. Peter & Paul Catholic Parish, Elmira. For inquiries for parish records contact Blessed Sacrament Roman Catholic Church of Elmira, NY.
2—BLESSED SACRAMENT, Merged with Christ the Redeemer, Elmira and St. Mary, Elmira to form The Parish of the Most Holy Name of Jesus Chemung County NY.
Legal Name: Blessed Sacrament Roman Catholic Church of Elmira, NY.
3—ST. CASIMIR (1890) (Polish), Merged with Our Lady of Lourdes, Elmira & St. Charles Borromeo, Elmira Heights. For inquiries for parish records contact Christ the Redeemer, Elmira.
4—ST. CECILIA OF EASTSIDE CATHOLIC PARISH (1904) Closed. For inquiries for parish records contact Blessed Sacrament, Elmira.
5—CHRIST THE REDEEMER, Merged with Blessed Sacrament, Elmira and St. Mary, Elmira to form The Parish of the Most Holy Name of Jesus Chemung County NY.
6—ST. JOHN THE BAPTIST OF EASTSIDE CATHOLIC PARISH (1866) (German), Closed. For inquiries for parish records contact Blessed Sacrament, Elmira.
7—ST. MARY (1873) [CEM] (Irish) Revs. Scott Kubinski; Richard T. Farrell, Parochial Vicar; Deacon Paul Sartori.
Res.: 224 Franklin St., Elmira, 14904.
Tel: 607-734-6254; Fax: 607-733-8890.
See Holy Family Primary, Elmira under Schools Outside Monroe County located in the Institution section.
8—OUR LADY OF LOURDES (1940) Merged with St. Charles Borromeo, Elmira Heights & St. Casimir, Elmira. For inquiries for parish records contact Christ the Redeemer, Elmira.
9—THE PARISH OF THE MOST HOLY NAME OF JESUS, CHEMUNG COUNTY, NY (2018)
1010 Davis St., Elmira, 14901.
10—ST. PATRICK (1871) (Irish), Merged with St. Anthony, Elmira & Sts. Peter & Paul Catholic Parish, Elmira. For inquiries for parish records contact Blessed Sacrament Roman Catholic Church of Elmira, NY.
11—STS. PETER AND PAUL CATHOLIC PARISH (1848) Merged with St. Anthony, Elmira & St. Patrick, Elmira. For inquiries for parish records contact Blessed Sacrament Roman Catholic Church of Elmira, NY.

FAIRPORT, MONROE CO.
1—CHURCH OF THE ASSUMPTION (1866) [CEM] Rev. George P. Heyman; Deacons Robert Corsaro; John Pattison; Marcelo G. De Risio.
Res.: 20 East Ave., Fairport, 14450.
Tel: 585-388-0040; Fax: 585-388-0248.
2—CHURCH OF THE RESURRECTION (1973) Rev. George P. Heyman; Deacon Marcelo G. De Risio.
Res.: 52 Mason Rd., Fairport, 14450.
Tel: 585-223-6686; Fax: 585-223-6958.
Church: 63 Mason Rd., Fairport, 14450.
Tel: 585-223-5500.
3—ST. JOHN OF ROCHESTER OF PERINTON, NEW YORK (1962) Rev. Peter C. Clifford; Deacon Thomas J. Cleary, (Retired)
*Legal Name: Church of St. John of Rochester of Perinton, New York*In Res., Revs. James E. Boyle, (Retired); Alexander H. Bradshaw, (Retired).
Ministry Bldg.—8 Wickford Way, Fairport, 14450.
Tel: 585-248-5993; Fax: 585-387-0517.
Rectory—18 Wickford Way, Fairport, 14450.

FLEMING, CAYUGA CO., ST. ISAAC JOGUES (1946) Closed. For sacramental records contact Good Shepherd Catholic Community, Aurora, NY.

GENESEO, LIVINGSTON CO.
1—ST. LUKE THE EVANGELIST (1854) [CEM] Revs. Bernard Dan, Admin.; Edward J. Dillon, (Retired); Deacon Paul Clement
Legal Name: St. Luke the Evangelist Roman Catholic Church Society of Livingston County
Office: 13 North St., Geneseo, 14454.
Tel: 585-243-1100; Fax: 585-243-0240.

2—ST. MARY, Merged with Holy Angels, Nunda, St. Patrick, Mt. Morris & St. Thomas Aquinas, Leicester & St. Mary, Retsof. For inquiries for parish records contact St. Luke the Evangelist Roman Catholic Church Society of Livingston County.

GENEVA, ONTARIO CO.
1—ST. FRANCIS DE SALES (1835) [CEM] [JC2] Merged with St. Stephen, Geneva. For inquiries for parish records contact Our Lady of Peace Roman Catholic Church of Geneva, NY.
2—OUR LADY OF PEACE
Mailing Address: 130 Exchange St., Geneva, 14456.
Tel: 315-789-0930; Fax: 315-781-1985; Email: gourladyofpeace@dor.org; Web: www.genevarc.org. Rev. Thomas P. Mull; Deacon Kevin Carges
Legal Name: Our Lady of Peace Roman Catholic Church of Geneva, NY
School—St. Francis DeSales/St. Stephen School, (Grades K-8), 17 Elmwood Ave., Geneva, 14456.
Tel: 315-789-1828; Fax: 315-789-9179; Email: sfssdcs@dor.org. Mary C. Mantelli, Prin.
3—ST. STEPHEN (1904) [JC] Merged with St. Francis de Sales, Geneva, NY. For inquiries for parish records contact Our Lady of Peace Roman Catholic Church of Geneva, NY.

GROTON, TOMPKINS CO., ST. ANTHONY (1873) [CEM] Rev. Daniel Ruiz-Sierra, Admin.; Deacon George Kozak.
Res.: 312 Locke Rd., R.D. 2, Groton, 13073.
Tel: 607-898-5135; Fax: 607-898-7608.

HAMLIN, MONROE CO., ST. ELIZABETH ANN SETON (1982)
Mailing Address: P.O. Box 149, Hamlin, 14464. Rev. William V. Spilly; Deacon Christopher Fisher Jr.
Res.: 1634 Lake Rd., P.O. Box 149, Hamlin, 14464.
Tel: 585-964-8560; Fax: 585-964-3352.

HAMMONDSPORT, STEUBEN CO., ST. GABRIEL (1845) [JC] Merged with St. Mary, Bath. For inquiries for parish records contact St. John Vianney Roman Catholic Parish Steuben County.
Res.: 78 Shethar St., Hammondsport, 14840.
Tel: 607-569-3501; Fax: 607-569-3226.

HENRIETTA, MONROE CO.
1—CHURCH OF THE GOOD SHEPHERD (1911) [CEM] Merged with Guardian Angels, Rochester & St. Joseph, Rush. For inquiries for parish records contact Marianne Cope Roman Catholic Parish, Monroe County.
2—MARIANNE COPE, Sr. Sheila Stevenson, R.S.M., Admin.; Rev. Eloo Malachy Nwosu; Deacons Herbert Bietry; Robert Lyons
Legal Name: Marianne Cope Roman Catholic Parish, Monroe County NY
Res.: 3318 E. Henrietta Rd., Henrietta, 14467.
Tel: 585-334-3518; Fax: 585-334-6015.

HILTON, MONROE CO., ST. LEO (1884) Rev. Joseph R. Catanise; Deacons Lon Smith; James Steiger, (Retired).
Res.: 167 Lake Ave., Hilton, 14468.
Tel: 585-392-2710, Ext. 2; Fax: 585-392-9254.

HONEOYE FALLS, MONROE CO., ST. PAUL OF THE CROSS (1870) [CEM] Rev. Michael G. Fowler, Admin.; Deacons Peter Dohr; Gregory Emerton.
Res.: 37 Monroe St., Honeoye Falls, 14472.
Tel: 585-624-1443; Fax: 585-624-5169.

HONEOYE, ONTARIO CO., ST. MARY, OUR LADY OF THE

HILLS (1868) [CEM] Rev. Hoan Q. Dinh; Deacon John Hoffman.
Parish—8961 Main St., P.O. Box 725, Honeoye, 14471.
Res.: Rte. 20A, Box 725, Honeoye, 14471.
Tel: 585-229-5007.

HORNELL, STEUBEN CO.
1—ST. ANN (1849) [CEM] [JC2] Merged with St. Mary's, Rexville. For inquiries for parish records contact Our Lady of the Valley, Hornell.
2—ST. IGNATIUS LOYOLA (1931) Closed. For inquiries for parish records contact Our Lady of the Valley, Hornell.
3—OUR LADY OF THE VALLEY (2004) Merger of St. Ann's, Hornell; St. Joachim, Canisteo; St. Ignatius Loyola, Hornell; St. Mary's, Rexville.
Mailing Address: 27 Erie Ave., Hornell, 14843.
Tel: 607-324-5811; Fax: 607-324-0116; Email: ourladyofthevalley@dor.org. Rev. Stanley Kacprzak; Deacons Mark Clark; Robert W. McCormick.

HORSEHEADS, CHEMUNG CO., ST. MARY OUR MOTHER (1866) [CEM] Rev. Christopher E. Linsler. In Res., Rev. Joseph Francis Shetui.
Res.: 816 W. Broad St., Horseheads, 14845.
Tel: 607-739-3817; Fax: 607-739-5628.
School-See St. Mary Our Mother (Horseheads), Horseheads under Schools Outside Monroe County located in the Institution section.

INTERLAKEN, SENECA CO., ST. FRANCIS SOLANUS (1875) Merged with Holy Cross, Ovid and St. James, Trumansburg. For inquiries for parish records contact Mary, Mother of Grace, Seneca County.

ITHACA, TOMPKINS CO.
1—ST. CATHERINE OF SIENA (1960) Rev. Joseph W. Marcoux, S.T.L.
Res. & Church: 309 Siena Dr., Ithaca, 14850.
Tel: 607-257-2493; Fax: 607-257-5901.
Catechesis Religious Program—
2—IMMACULATE CONCEPTION (1848) [CEM 2] Rev. Augustine Chumo; Deacon Daniel R. Hurley.
Res.: 113 N. Geneva St., Ithaca, 14850.
Tel: 607-273-6121; Fax: 607-273-0185.
See Immaculate Conception, Ithaca under Schools Outside Monroe County located in the Institution section.

KING FERRY, CAYUGA CO., OUR LADY OF THE LAKE, KING FERRY (1868) Closed. For inquiries for parish records contact Good Shepherd Catholic Community, Aurora.

LANSING, TOMPKINS CO., ALL SAINTS (1913) Deacon George Kozak; Rev. Daniel Ruiz-Sierra, Admin.
Res.: 347 Ridge Rd., Lansing, 14882.
Tel: 607-533-7344.
Catechesis Religious Program—

LEICESTER, LIVINGSTON CO., ST. THOMAS AQUINAS (1897) Merged with Holy Angels, Nunda, St. Lucy, Retsof, St. Mary, Geneseo & St. Patrick, Mt. Morris. For inquiries for parish records contact St. Luke the Evangelist Roman Catholic Church Society of Livingston County, Geneseo.

LIMA, LIVINGSTON CO., ST. ROSE (1848) [CEM]
Mailing Address: P.O. Box 8A, Lima, 14485. Rev. Michael G. Fowler, Admin.; Deacons Gregory Emerton; Peter Dohr; Eugene Edwards, (Retired).
Church: 1985 Lake Ave., Lima, 14485.

LIVONIA CENTER, LIVINGSTON CO., ST. MICHAEL (1848) Closed. For inquiries for parish records contact St. Mary's, Honeoye.

LIVONIA, LIVINGSTON CO.
1—ST. JOSEPH (1911) Closed. For inquiries for parish records contact St. Matthew Catholic Church Society, Livonia.
2—ST. MATTHEW CATHOLIC CHURCH SOCIETY, [CEM] Merged with St. William, Conesus and St. Joseph, Livonia.
Mailing Address: P.O. Box 77, Livonia, 14487.
Tel: 585-346-3815; Fax: 585-346-9445. Rev. Hoan Q. Dinh; Deacon John Hoffman.

LYONS, WAYNE CO., ST. MICHAEL (1852) (Italian) Merged with St. John the Evangelist, Clyde & Mission St. Patrick, Savannah. For inquiries for parish records contact St. Joseph the Worker Roman Catholic Parish, Wayne County.

MACEDON, WAYNE CO., ST. PATRICK (1883) [CEM] Merged with St. Gregory, Marion & St. Anne, Palmyra. For inquiries for parish records contact Parish of St. Katharine Drexel, Palmyra.

MARION, WAYNE CO., ST. GREGORY (1914) Merged with St. Anne, Palmyra & St. Patrick, Macedon. For inquiries for parish records contact the Parish of St. Katherine Drexel, Palmyra.

MENDON, MONROE CO., ST. CATHERINE OF SIENA (1902) Rev. Robert Scott Bourcy; Deacon James Carra.
Res.: 26 Mendon-Ionia Rd., Mendon, 14506.
Tel: 585-624-4990; Fax: 585-624-4996.
Convent—15 Mendon-Ionia Rd., Mendon, 14506.
Tel: 716-624-1538.

MONTEZUMA, CAYUGA CO., ST. MICHAEL (1865) Closed. For inquiries for parish records contact Our Lady of the Snows, Weedsport.

MORAVIA, CAYUGA CO., ST. PATRICK (1872) Closed. For inquiries for parish records contact Good Shepherd Catholic Community, Aurora.

MOUNT MORRIS, LIVINGSTON CO., ST. PATRICK (1869) [CEM] Merged with Holy Angels, Nunda, St. Mary, Geneseo, St. Thomas Aquinas, Leicester & St. Mary, Retsof. For inquiries for parish records contact St. Luke the Evangelist Roman Catholic Church Society of Livingston County, Geneseo.

NEWARK VALLEY, TIOGA CO., ST. JOHN THE EVANGELIST (1880) Merged with St. Francis of Assisi, Catatonk; St. Margaret Mary, Apalachin; St. Pius the Tenth, Van Etten and St. James, Waverly. For inquiries for parish records contact Blessed Trinity, Owego.

NEWARK, WAYNE CO., ST. MICHAEL (1863) Rev. Jeffrey Tunnicliff.
Res.: 401 Main St., Newark, 14513.
Tel: 315-331-6753; Fax: 315-331-2925.

NORTH CHILI, MONROE CO., ST. CHRISTOPHER (1968) Deacon David Kepler.
Res.: 3350 Union St., P.O. Box 399, North Chili, 14514. Tel: 585-594-1400.

NUNDA, LIVINGSTON CO., HOLY ANGELS (1854) Merged with St. Patrick, Mt. Morris, St. Mary, Geneseo, St. Thomas Aquinas, Leicester & St. Lucy, Retsof. For inquiries for parish records contact St. Luke the Evangelist Roman Catholic Church Society of Livingston County, Geneseo.

ODESSA, SCHUYLER CO., ST. BENEDICT (1965)
Mailing Address: c/o St. Mary's of the Lake, P.O. Box 289, Watkins Glen, 14891. Rev. Steven W. Lape; Deacon Daniel Pavlina.
Res.: 1101 1/2 Tenth St., Watkins Glen, 14891.
Tel: 607-535-2786; Fax: 607-535-2990.
Church: 304 Speedway, Odessa, 14869.
Tel: 607-594-2226.

ONTARIO, WAYNE CO.
1—ST. MARY OF THE LAKE (1869) [CEM] Merged with Epiphany, Sodus. For inquiries for parish records contact St. Maximilian Kolbe, Ontario.
2—ST. MAXIMILIAN KOLBE, Rev. Symon Peter Ntaiyia; Deacon Edward Kohlmeier.
Res.: 5823 Walworth Rd., P.O. Box 499, Ontario, 14519. Tel: 315-524-2611; Fax: 607-524-8353.
Catechesis Religious Program—

OVID, SENECA CO.
1—HOLY CROSS (1849) [CEM] Merged with St. Francis Solanus, Interlaken and St. James, Tumansburg. For inquiries for parish records contact Mary, Mother of Mercy, Seneca County.
2—THE PARISH OF MARY, MOTHER OF MERCY, SENECA COUNTY, NY
P.O. Box 403, Interlaken, 14847. 3660 Orchard St., Interlaken, 14847. Rev. Bernard Maloney, O.F.M.-Cap.

OWEGO, TIOGA CO.
1—BLESSED TRINITY (2003)
Mailing Address: Blessed Trinity and St. Patrick Parishes, 300 Main St., Owego, 13827.
Tel: 607-687-1068; Tel: 607-625-3192 (Rectory); Fax: 607-687-8122; Email: blessedtrinity@dor.org. Rev. Anthony Amato, Parochial Vicar; Deacons Michael Donovan; Richard DeMars.
Res.: 1110 Pennsylvania Ave., Apalachin, 13732.
2—ST. PATRICK (1842) [CEM]
Mailing Address: 300 Main St., Owego, 13827.
Tel: 607-687-1068; Fax: 607-687-8122. Rev. Anthony Amato, Parochial Vicar; Deacons Michael Donovan; Richard DeMars.
Res.: 1110 Pennsylvania Ave., Apalachin, 13732.
Tel: 607-625-3192.

PAINTED POST, STEUBEN CO., IMMACULATE HEART OF MARY (1952) Closed. Merged with St. Mary, Corning and St. Vincent de Paul, Corning. For inquiries for parish records contact All Saints, Corning.

PALMYRA, WAYNE CO.
1—ST. ANNE (1850) [CEM] Merged with St. Gregory, Marion & St. Patrick, Macedon. For inquiries for parish records contact the Parish of St. Katharine Drexel, Palmyra.
2—THE PARISH OF ST. KATHARINE DREXEL, Very Rev. William F. Laird, J.C.L.
Office: 52 Main St., Macedon, 14502.
Tel: 315-597-4571; Fax: 315-597-5252.

PENFIELD, MONROE CO.
1—HOLY SPIRIT (1965) Revs. James A. Schwartz; Jeff Chichester, Parochial Vicar; Deacon Raymond Garbach.
Parish Address—1355 Hatch Rd., Webster, 14580.
Tel: 585-671-5520; Fax: 585-671-7262.
2—ST. JOSEPH (1860) [CEM] Rev. James A. Schwartz; Very Rev. Justin D. Miller; Rev. Jeff Chichester; Deacons Don Germano; Duncan Harris; William Coffey, (Retired). In Res., Revs. Robert G. Kreckel, (Retired); William Amann, (Retired).
Parish—43 Gebhardt Rd., Penfield, 14526.
Res.: 35 Gebhardt Rd., Penfield, 14526.
Tel: 585-586-8089; Fax: 585-586-0674.
School—St. Joseph School, (Grades PreK-6), 39 Gebhardt Rd., Penfield, 14526-1398.
Tel: 585-586-6968; Email: sjpendcs@dor.org. Amy Johnson, Prin. Lay Teachers 23; Students 285.

PENN YAN, YATES CO.
1—ST. MICHAEL (1850) [CEM 2] Merged with St. Januarius, Naples; St. Patrick's, Prattsburg; St. Theresa's Stanley, St. Andrew, Dundee & St. Mary, Rushville. For inquiries for parish records contact Our Lady of the Lakes Catholic Community.
2—OUR LADY OF THE LAKES CATHOLIC COMMUNITY, Formed by merge of St. Januarius & Our Lady of the Grapes Shrine, Naples, St. Patrick's, Prattsburg, St. Theresa's Stanley and St. Michael's Penn Yan. Revs. Leo J. Reinhardt; Felicjan Sierotowicz; John L. O'Connor, (Retired); Deacon Timothy Hebding.
Rectory & Mailing Address: 210 Keuka St., Penn Yan, 14527. Tel: 585-374-2414; Fax: 585-374-2415.
See St. Michael, Penn Yan under Schools Outside Monroe County located in the Institution section.

PERKINSVILLE, STEUBEN CO., SACRED HEART OF JESUS, Merged with St. Joseph's, Wayland; St. Mary's, Dansville; and St. Pius V, Cohocton. For inquiries for parish records contact Holy Catholic Community, Cohocton.

PHELPS, ONTARIO CO., ST. FRANCIS (1869) Merged with St. Felix, Clifton Springs & St. Dominic, Shortsville. For inquiries for parish records contact St. Peter's Roman Catholic Parish, Ontario County.

PITTSFORD, MONROE CO.
1—CHURCH OF THE TRANSFIGURATION (1983)
50 W. Bloomfield Rd., Pittsford, 14534.
Tel: 585-248-2427; Fax: 585-385-9870. Rev. Michael Bausch; Deacons Eric Bessette; Patrick DiLaura.
Catechesis Religious Program—
2—ST. LOUIS (1911)
64 S. Main St., Pittsford, 14534. Very Rev. Robert P. Ring; Rev. Juan Benitez, Parochial Vicar; Deacon David Snyder. In Res., Rev. Msgr. Gerard C. Krieg, J.C.L., (Retired).
Res.: 60 S. Main St., Pittsford, 14534.
Tel: 585-586-5675; Fax: 585-387-9888.
Saint's Place—46 S. Main St., Pittsford, 14534.
Tel: 585-385-6860; Email: saintlady@stlouischurch.org; Web: www.saintsplace.org. Isabel Miller, Dir.
School—St. Louis School, (Grades PreK-5), 11 Rand Pl., Pittsford, 14534-2084. Tel: 585-586-5200; Email: sisdcs@dor.org. Fran Barr, Prin.; Susan Conlogue, Librarian. Lay Teachers 26; Students 302.

RED CREEK, WAYNE CO., ST. THOMAS THE APOSTLE (1882) [CEM] Merged with St. Mary Magdalen, Wolcott & St. Jude Chapel, Fair Haven to form Catholic Community of the Blessed Trinity. For inquiries for parish records contact Blessed Trinity, Wolcott.

REXVILLE, STEUBEN CO., ST. MARY (1845) [CEM 4] (Irish) Merged with St. Ann, Hornell. For inquiries for parish records contact Our Lady of the Valley, Hornell.

RUSH, MONROE CO., ST. JOSEPH (1863) Merged with Guardian Angels, Rochester & Church of the Good Shepherd, Henrietta. For inquiries for parish records contact Marianne Cope Roman Catholic Parish, Monroe County.

SCIPIO CENTER, CAYUGA CO., ST. BERNARD (1867) Closed. For inquiries for parish records contact Good Shepherd Catholic Community, Aurora.

SCOTTSVILLE, MONROE CO., ST. MARY OF THE ASSUMPTION (1853) [CEM] Merged with St. Columba's Church, Caledonia and St. Vincent de Paul's Catholic Church Society, Churchville. For inquiries for parish records contact The Parish of Saint Martin de Porres, Livingston County.

SENECA FALLS, SENECA CO., ST. PATRICK (1831) [CEM] Merged with St. Mary's, Waterloo. For inquires for parish records contact St. Francis and St. Clare Roman Catholic Parish, Seneca County, NY.

SHORTSVILLE, ONTARIO CO., ST. DOMINIC (1885) [CEM] Merged with St. Felix, Clifton Springs & St. Francis, Phelps. For inquiries for parish records contact St. Peter's Roman Catholic Parish, Ontario County.
Church, Church: 6 Canandaigua St., Shortsville, 14548.

SODUS, WAYNE CO., EPIPHANY (1922) Merged with St. Mary of the Lake, Ontario. For inquiries for parish records contact St. Maximilian Kolbe, Ontario.

SPENCERPORT, MONROE CO., ST. JOHN THE EVANGELIST (1867) [CEM] Rev. Peter Mottola, Admin.; Deacon Thomas Uschold. In Res., Rev. Daniel F. Holland, (Retired).
Parish—55 Martha St., Spencerport, 14559.
Res.: 60 Martha St., Spencerport, 14559.
Tel: 585-352-5481; Fax: 585-352-3759.

STANLEY, ONTARIO CO., ST. THERESA (1875) [CEM] Merged with St. Januarius, Naples; St. Patrick's, Prattsburgh; St. Michaels, Penn Yan; St. Andrews, Dondee & St. Mary's Rushville to form Our Lady of the Lakes Catholic Community.

TRUMANSBURG, TOMPKINS CO., ST. JAMES THE APOSTLE (1857) [CEM] Merged Merged with St. Francis Solanus, Interlaken and Holy Cross, Ovid. For inquiries for parish records contact Mary, Mother of Mercy, Seneca County.

UNION SPRINGS, CAYUGA CO., ST. MICHAEL'S (1851)

Closed. For inquiries for parish records contact Good Shepherd Catholic Community, Aurora.

VAN ETTEN, CHEMUNG CO., ST. PIUS THE TENTH (1954) Merged with St. Francis, Catatonk, St. Margaret Mary, Apalachin, St. John the Evangelist, Newark Valley and St. James, Waverly. For inquiries for parish records contact Blessed Trinity, Owego.

VICTOR, ONTARIO CO., ST. PATRICK (1856) [CEM] (Irish) Very Rev. Edison Tayag; Deacon John Payne.
Res.: 115 Maple Ave., Victor, 14564.
Tel: 585-924-7111; Fax: 585-742-3296.
Catechesis Religious Program—

WATERLOO, SENECA CO.
1—ST. FRANCIS & ST. CLARE
25 Center St., Waterloo, 13165. Revs. James Fennessy; Michael Merritt, Parochial Vicar
Legal Name: St. Francis & St. Clare Roman Catholic Parish, Seneca County, NY
Res.: 35 Center St., Waterloo, 13165.
Tel: 315-539-2944; Fax: 315-539-8841.
2—ST. MARY (1868) [CEM] Merged with St. Patrick's, Seneca Falls. For inquires for parish records contact St. Francis and St. Clare Roman Catholic Parish, Seneca County, NY.

WATKINS GLEN, SCHUYLER CO., ST. MARY OF THE LAKE (1846) [CEM 2] (Irish—Italian) Rev. Steven W. Lape; Deacons Daniel Pavlina; George Roy.
*Parish—*905 N. Decatur St., P.O. Box 289, Watkins Glen, 14891.
Res.: 110 1/2 Tenth St., Watkins Glen, 14891.
Tel: 607-535-2786; Fax: 607-535-2990.
*Parish Center—*10th St., Watkins Glen, 14891.

WAVERLY, TIOGA CO., ST. JAMES (1881) [CEM] Merged with St. Francis of Assisi, Catatonk; St. Margaret Mary, Apalachin; St. John the Evangelist, Newark Valley and St. Pius the Tenth, Van Etten. For inquiries for parish records contact Blessed Trinity, Owego.

WAYLAND, STEUBEN CO.
1—HOLY FAMILY CATHOLIC COMMUNITY
Mailing Address: 206 Fremont St., Wayland, 14572-1298. Tel: 585-728-2228; Fax: 585-728-2232. Very Rev. Stephen Karani; Rev. Michael W. Twardzik.
Rectory—St. Mary's, 40 Elizabeth St., Dansville, 14437. Tel: 585-335-2700.
2—ST. JOSEPH'S (1881) (German), Merged with St. Pius V, Cohocton; St. Mary's, Dansville; and Sacred Heart of Jesus, Perkinsville Holy Family Catholic Community, Cohocton.

WEBSTER, MONROE CO.
1—HOLY TRINITY (1861) [CEM] Very Rev. Timothy E. Horan. In Res., Rev. John M. Mulligan, (Retired).
Res.: 1460 Ridge Rd., Webster, 14580.
Tel: 585-265-0391; Fax: 585-265-1627.
2—ST. PAUL (1967) Rev. Paul Gitau; Deacon Mark Robbins.
Res.: 783 Hard Rd., Webster, 14580.
Tel: 585-671-2112; Fax: 585-787-8907.
3—ST. RITA (1950) Rev. Lance Gonyo; Deacons Richard Rall; James J. Fien.
Res.: 1008 Maple Dr., Webster, 14580.
Tel: 585-671-1100; Fax: 585-671-5446.
School—St. Rita School, Webster, (Grades PreK-6), 1008 Maple Dr., Webster, 14580. Tel: 585-671-3132; Email: sritadcs@dor.org. Mary Ellen Wagner, Prin. Lay Teachers 14; Students 150.

WEEDSPORT, CAYUGA CO.
1—ST. JOHN (1865) Merged with St. Joseph, Weedsport and St. Patrick, Cato. For inquiries for parish records contact Our Lady of the Snow, Weedsport.
2—ST. JOSEPH (1854) [CEM] Merged with St. John, Port Byron and St. Patrick, Cato. For inquiries contact Our Lady of the Snow, Weedsport.
3—OUR LADY OF THE SNOW (2005)
Mailing Address: 2667 Hamilton St., Weedsport, 13166. Tel: 315-834-6266; Fax: 315-834-6278; Email: wstjosep@dor.org. Rev. William G. Darling.

WOLCOTT, WAYNE CO.
1—CATHOLIC COMMUNITY OF THE BLESSED TRINITY (2006) Merged
11956 Washington St., Wolcott, 14590-1133.
Tel: 315-594-9430; Fax: 315-594-9430. Rev. Michael Upson; Deacon Robert Lee. with St. Thomas the Apostle, Red Creek; St. Mary Magdalene, Wolcott and St. Jude Chapel, Fair Haven.
Legal Name: Catholic Community of the Blessed Trinity of Wolcott, NY.
2—ST. MARY MAGDALENE (1940) Merged with St. Thomas the Apostle, Red Creek & St. Jude Chapel, Fair Haven. For inquiries for parish records contact Catholic Community of the Blessed Trinity of Wolcott, NY.

Chaplains of Public Institutions.

Health Care Facilities

ROCHESTER. *St. Ann's Home/Heritage*, 1500 Portland Ave., 14621. Tel: 585-697-6446. Sheila Kinsky, Pastoral Care Coord., Sisters Mary Louise Mitchell, S.S.J., Dir. Spiritual Care, Livia Ruocco, Pastoral Care Coord.
Highland Hospital, 1000 South Ave., 14620.
Tel: 585-341-6890. Revs. Dennis Bonsignore, Chap., Carlos Sanchez, Chap.
Monroe Community Hospital, 435 E. Henrietta Rd., 14620. Tel: 585-760-6164. Rev. Dennis Bonsignore, Sr. Marie Susanne Hoffman, S.S.J., Pastoral Care.
Rochester General Hospital/Via Health, 1425 Portland Ave., 14621. Tel: 585-922-5121. Deacon Dermot M. Loughran, Sr. Margaret Kunder, S.S.J., Chap.
Strong Health System, 601 Elmwood Ave., 14642.
Tel: 585-275-2187. Revs. Dennis Bonsignore, Carlos Sanchez, Deacon Mark Bovenzi, Sr. Virginia Schmitz.
Unity Health System, Park Ridge Hospital, 1555 Long Pond Rd., 14626. Tel: 585-723-7969. Rev. Thomas Akowuah, Chap., Marianne Katz, Chap., Tel: 585-723-7969.
Unity Health System, St. Mary's Campus, 89 Genesee St., 14611. Tel: 585-328-3268. Rev. Thomas Akowuah.

BATH. *Soldiers' Home and Veterans' Hospital*, Bath.
Tel: 607-664-4402, Ext. 1382. Vacant.

CANANDAIGUA. *Veteran's Hospital*, Canandaigua.
Tel: 585-394-2000, Ext. 3052. Very Rev. James P. Jaeger, Rev. William B. Leone.

HORNELL. *St. James Mercy Hospital*, 411 Canisteo St., Hornell, Steuben Co. 14843. Tel: 607-324-8153. Deacon Robert W. McCormick.

State Facilities

ROCHESTER. *Finger Lakes DDSO - Rochester Site*, 620 Westfall Rd., 14620. Tel: 585-461-8676. Vacant.
Rochester Psychiatric Center, 1111 Elmwood Ave., 14620. Tel: 585-241-1200; Email: elaine.hollis@omh.ny.gov. Sr. Elaine Hollis, S.S.J., Chap.

AUBURN. *Auburn Correctional Facility*, 135 State St., P.O. Box 618, Auburn, 13021.
Tel: 315-253-8401, Ext. 4321. Rev. Michael R. Brown, Chap., Deacon John Tomandl.

ELMIRA. *Elmira Correctional Facility, Center and Camp Monterey*, P.O. Box 500, Elmira, 14902.
Tel: 607-734-3901. Rev. Richard T. Farrell, Deacon Douglas Farwell.
Elmira Psychiatric Center, 100 Washington St., Elmira, 14901. Tel: 607-737-4991. Vacant.

GENESEO. *Finger Lakes DDSO - Geneseo Site*, 3 Park St., Geneseo, 14454-1217. Tel: 585-243-6405. Vacant.

INDUSTRY. *State Agricultural & Industrial School, Div. of Youth*, Industry, 14474. Tel: 585-533-2600. Deacon Peter Dohr.

MORAVIA. *Cayuga Correctional*, P.O. Box 1150, Moravia, 13118. Tel: 315-497-1110, Ext. 4000. Vacant.

NEWARK. *Finger Lakes DDSO - Newark Site*, 703 E. Maple Ave., Newark, 14513. Tel: 315-331-1700. Vacant.

PINE CITY. *Southport Correctional Facility*, P.O. Box 2000, Pine City, 14871-2000. Tel: 607-737-0850. Rev. Richard T. Farrell, Chap., Deacon Alberto Pacete, Chap.

ROMULUS. *Five Points Correctional Facility*, State Rte. 96, Romulus, 14541. Tel: 607-869-5111. Maureen Collins.

SONYEA. *Groveland Correctional Facility*, 7000 Sonyea Rd., P.O. Box 50, Sonyea, 14556.
Tel: 585-658-2871, Ext. 4807. Rev. Michael R. Brown, Deacon Paul Clement, Barbara Clement.
Livingston Correctional Facility and Seneca Correctional Facility, Rt. 36, P.O. Box 49, Sonyea, 14556. Tel: 585-658-3710. Rev. Michael R. Brown, Deacon Nemesio Vellon Martinez.

WILLARD. *Drug Treatment Center*, 7116 County Rd. 132, P.O. Box 303, Willard, 14588-0303.
Tel: 607-869-5500, Ext. 4800; Email: tom.ruda@dor.org. Deacon Thomas Ruda, Chap.

County Jail Chaplains

ROCHESTER. *Livingston County Jail*, 4 Court St., Geneseo, 14454. Tel: 585-243-1100. Vacant.
Monroe County Jail. Deacon Michael Zuber.
Tompkins County Jail. Vacant.
Yates County Jail. Vacant.

Retired:
Rev. Msgr.—
Krieg, Gerard C., J.C.L., (Retired), 64 S. Main St., Pittsford, 14534
Revs.—
Amann, William, (Retired), 35 Gebhardt Rd., Penfield, 14526
Barrett, William, (Retired), 15 Washington St., Mayville, 14757
Bartolotta, Victor W. Jr., (Retired), 16147 Vanderbilt Dr., Odessa, FL 33556
Bayer, Peter T., (Retired), 844 Cottage Cove Ln., Webster, 14580
Beligotti, Richard J., (Retired), 320 Clearbrook Cir. U201, Venice, FL 34292
Beligotti, Robert L., (Retired), 320 Clearbrook Cir. U201, Venice, FL 34292
Billotte, Philip J., (Retired), 777 Germania Rd., P.O. Box 135, Frenchville, PA 16836
Boyle, James E., (Retired), 8 Wickford Way, Fairport, 14450
Bradler, Robert C., (Retired), 269 Garford Rd., 14622
Bradshaw, Alexander H., (Retired), 8 Wickford Way, Fairport, 14450
Brennan, Paul P., (Retired), 345 Waters Edge, Auburn, 13021
Brickler, R. Richard, (Retired), 1961 #1 Traditions Pl., Henrietta, 14467
Brown, Lewis, (Retired), 6 Eagle Dr., Painted Post, 14870
Burke, James C., (Retired), 2123 S.E. 5th Ter., Cape Coral, FL 33990
Conboy, Michael F., (Retired), 3113 W. Lake Rd., Skaneateles, 13152
Cosgrove, William, (Retired), Sisters of St. Joseph Motherhouse, 150 French Rd., 14618
Cushing, Walter F., (Retired), 2732 Culver Rd., 14622
Deckman, Peter, (Retired), Sisters of St. Joseph Motherhouse, 150 French Rd., 14618
Delmonte, Albert L., (Retired), 1550 Portland Ave. Apt. 1315, 14621
Dillon, Edward J., (Retired), 13 North St., Geneseo, 14454
Dollen, Bernard, (Retired), 4477 Buffalo Rd., North Chili, 14514
Donnelly, William, (Retired), #1216 1500 Portland Ave., 14621
Eisemann, Frederick F., (Retired), 1500 Portland Ave., 14612
Endres, William, (Retired), St. Jerome's, 220 West Ave., East Rochester, 14445
Erb, Francis J., (Retired), P.O. Box 96, Painted Post, 14870
Erdle, Thomas M., (Retired), 100 McAuley Dr., Apt. 275, 14610
Falletta, Frank J., (Retired), 70 Heberton Rd., 14621
Fleming, Terence, (Retired), 1385 River Oaks Ct., Oldsmar, FL 34677
Forni, John V., (Retired), 152 Main St., Brockport, 14420
Fratts, Ralph J., (Retired), 113 Genesee St., New Hartford, 13413
Gaesser, Ronald E., (Retired), 85 North St., Auburn, 13021
Golden, Edward, (Retired), Sisters of St. Joseph, 150 French Rd., 14618
Graf, William E., D.Min., (Retired), 681 High St., Victor, 14564
Helfrich, P. Frederick, (Retired), 300 Cranberry Landing, 14609
Holland, Daniel F., (Retired), 1550 Portland Ave., 14621
Kellner, Winfried, (Retired), Sisters of St. Joseph Motherhouse, 150 French Rd., 14618
Kennedy, Robert J., (Retired), 66 Meadowbrook Rd., 14620
Kiggins, Roy, (Retired), 97 W. Bayard St., Seneca Falls, 13148
Kreckel, Robert G., (Retired), 35 Gebhardt Rd., 14626
Latus, Charles J., (Retired), 833 Cottage Cove Ln., Webster, 14580
Lawlor, James F., (Retired), 1600 Mount Hope Ave., 14620
Mans, Leo J., (Retired), 2990 Carlisle Pike, PC Rm. 3913, New Oxford, PA 17350
Michatek, William C., (Retired), 8286 W. Port Bay Rd., Wolcott, 14590-9447
Miller, Mark, (Retired), St. Theodores, 168 Spencerport Rd., 14606
Mulligan, John M., (Retired), 1460 Ridge Rd., Webster, 14580
Murphy, Kevin P., (Retired), Sisters of St. Joseph Motherhouse, 150 French Rd., 14618
Nellis, Thomas F., (Retired), 22 Greenwood Ave., Statesboro, GA 30458
O'Connor, John L., (Retired), 3351 James Rd., Keuka Park, 14478
Palumbos, Edward L., (Retired), 259 Rutgers St., 14607
Reif, John, (Retired), 4492 Lake Ave., 14612
Sasso, Joseph M., (Retired), 8112 Oatka Tr., LeRoy, 14482

Statt, Thomas R., (Retired), P.O. Box 752, Honeoye, 14471
Tormey, Daniel, (Retired), Sisters of St. Joseph Motherhouse, 150 French Rd., 14618
Wainwright, Walter L., (Retired), 1502 Maple Ave., Elmira, 14904
Weis, Eugene R., (Retired), Sisters of St. Joseph Motherhouse, 150 French Rd., 14168.

Permanent Deacons:
Abballe, Dominick, (Retired)
Almeter, Robert C., Diocese of Burlington
Aman, Leo, (Retired)
Antenucci, John, (Retired), Diocese of Venice
Asis, Emmanuel, St. Lawrence, Greece
Baker, William, (Leave of Absence)
Behe, Thomas, (Inactive)
Berrios, Jose, St. Francis Xavier Cabrini
Bessette, Eric, Church of the Transfiguration, Pittsford
Bietry, Herbert, Holy Family, Gates
Birx, Charles, (Inactive, Out of State)
Bovenzi, Mark, URMC
Bowers, Owen F., (Retired)
Brasley, John, (Unassigned)
Briars, James, St. Pius X, Chili
Burke, Robert, St. John the Evangelist, Greece
Cadregari, David, St. Mark, Greece
Callan, Daniel, St. Charles Borromeo, Greece
Carges, Kevin, Our Lady of Peace Parish, Geneva; Catholic Charities, CRS
Carra, James, St. Catherine of Siena, Mendon
Caruso, Anthony, (Retired)
Casey, Lawrence B., Diocese of Atlanta
Cass, K. Thomas, Diocese of Burlington
Chatterton, James, (Retired)
Clark, Mark, Our Lady of the Valley, Hornell
Cleary, Thomas J., (Retired)
Clement, Paul F., Groveland Correctional Facility, Sonyea; St. Luke the Evangelist, Geneseo
Coccia, Angelo, (Retired), St. Theodore
Coffey, William, (Retired)
Colomaio, Robert, St. John Vianney, Bath
Condon, Dean, (Unassigned)
Corsaro, Robert, Church of the Assumption, Fairport
Crego, John, (Retired)
Cuestas, Arthur, Our Lady Queen of Peace, St. Thomas More, Brighton, NY
Cunningham, John, Diocese of Palm Beach
Curtin, Claude, (Retired)
Cyrana, Robert, St. Peter's, Clifton Springs
Dardess, George, (Retired)
Datz, Ramon, (Retired)
De Risio, Marcelo G., Church of the Assumption & Church of the Resurrection, Fairport
Defendorf, Raymond, (Unassigned)
Dejesus, Benny, St. Francis Xavier Cabrini
DiLallo, Gary R., Diocese of Syracuse
DiLaura, Patrick, Church of the Transfiguration, Pittsford
Dohr, Peter, St. Agnes; St. Paul of the Cross; St. Rose
Donahue, Dennis, St. Mary Church, Auburn
Donovan, Michael, Blessed Trinity/St. Patrick, Owego
Dougherty, William P., (Retired)
Douglas, Stanley, (Retired)
Dudek, Matthew, St. Columba; St. Mary of the Assumption; St. Vincent DePaul, St. Monica
Edwards, Eugene L. Jr., (Retired)
Eggleston, Donald
Emerton, Gregory, St. Paul of the Cross, Honeoye Falls; St. Rose, Lima; St. Agnes, Avon
Erb, John, (Retired)
Erway, Joseph, Blessed Sacrament, Elmira
Farwell, Douglas, Ss. Isidore & Maria Torribia, Addison; NYSDOCCS, Elmira
Feasel, Laurence, (Retired)
Federowicz, Joseph F., (Retired)
Fien, James J., St. Rita, Webster
Fisher, Christopher Jr., St. Elizabeth Ann Seton, Hamlin
Fitch, James E., (Retired)
Garbach, Raymond, Holy Spirit, Webster
Germano, Donald, St. Joseph, Penfield
Giblin, Edward, Dir., Office of Permanent Diaconate, Clergy Svcs.
Giugno, John M., The Cathedral Community, Rochester
Graybill, Patrick A., (Retired)
Haber, Francis, Diocese of Richmond
Hankey, James D., Care First Corning, All Saints Parish, Corning
Harris, Duncan, St. Joseph, Penfield
Hebding, Timothy, Our Lady of the Lakes, Penn Yan
Henry, Murray, (Inactive)
Hoerner, Gerard A., Diocese of Birmingham
Hoffman, John, St. Matthew/Livonia; St. Mary Honeoye
Hudzinski, David, RIT Newman
Hurley, Daniel R., Immaculate Conception, Ithaca; NYSDOCCS Midstate
Jack, Thomas, St. John Vianney, Bath; Liasion to Prison Chap.
Jewell, Thomas, Our Mother of Sorrows, Greece
Johnson, H. Wilson, Diocese of Knoxville
Kepler, David, St. Christopher, North Chili
Kershner, Lynn W., (Retired)
Kiley, Gregory, St. Joseph the Worker; Clyde
Kinsky, Daniel M., (Retired)
Kluchko, Thomas J., (Retired)
Knauf, Ed, St. John the Evangelist, Greece
Kohlmeier, Edward, St. Maximilian Kolbe, Ontario
Kozak, George, Holy Cross, Freeville; St. Anthony, Groton; All Saints, Lansing
Kristan, Michael, The Cathedral Community, Rochester
LaFortune, David, St. John Vianney, Bath
Lawson, Gregg K., (Retired)
Lebron, Juan, Diocese of St. Petersburg
Lee, Robert, Blessed Trinity, Wolcott
Lenhart, William, (Retired)
Lester, Claude E., St. Benedict, Canandaigua
Lohouse, Dennis, St. Theodore, Gates
Lombard, Richard J., (Retired)
Loomis, Roger, (Inactive)
Loughran, Dermot M., St. Jerome, East Rochester; Rochester General Hospital
Lyons, Robert, St. Marianne Cope, Henrietta
Mack, Joseph, (Retired)
Mahany, Richard E., (Retired)
Mahoney, Brian, (Leave of Absence)
Malave, Jorge, St. Frances Xavier Cabrini Parish, Rochester
Mangione, Michael, Cornell Catholic Community & Ithaca College Newman Center
Martinez, Nemesio, Holy Apostles, Rochester; Livingston Correctional Facility
Mathis, Edward, (Retired)
Maune, William D., (Retired), Archdiocese of Chicago
McCormick, Robert W., Our Lady of the Valley, Hornell
McDermott, John, St. Anne & Our Lady of Lourdes, Rochester
McGuire, Michael R., St. Benedict, Canandaigua
McNulty, Brian J., St. Monica, Rochester; Diocesan Medical Health Ministry
Mercadel, Anthony J., (Retired)
Mercado, Conrado, Diocese of Mayaguez
Meyer, Robert, St. Frances Xavier Cabrini, Rochester
Mielcarek, Raymond, (Retired)
Nail, James B., (Retired), St. Maximilian, Kolbe, Ontario
Nelson, John, Diocese of Rockford
Nguyen, Bin-Yen, Holy Family, Gates; Vietnamese Catholic Community
Niche, Peter, Archdiocese of Philadelphia
Otero, Salvador, Holy Apostles Church, Rochester
Pacete, Alberto, Southport Correctional Facility; Christ the Redeemer, Elmira; NYSDOCCS
Palma, David, St. Boniface, Blessed Sacrament, St. Mary, Rochester; Southeast Rochester Catholic Community
Paluskiewicz, David L., Edna Tina Wilson Living Center
Pattison, John, Church of the Assumption, Fairport
Pavlina, Daniel, Schuyler Catholic Community, Watkins Glen
Payne, John F. X., St. Patrick, Victor
Pegoni, James, St. John of Rochester, Fairport
Petrauskas, Bruno, St. Stanislaus, Rochester
Pettrone, Frank, St. Mark, Greece
Piehler, Michael J., (Retired)
Placious, Joseph, Holy Cross, Charlotte
Rabjohn, William, St Anne, Rochester; Our Lady of Lourdes, Rochester
Rall, Richard, St. Rita, Webster; Immaculate Conception/St. Bridget, Rochester
Robbins, Mark, St. Paul, Webster
Rodriguez, Agenol, St. Francis Xavier Cabrini, Rochester
Roy, George, Schuyler Catholic Community, Watkins Glen
Ruda, Thomas, Willard Drug Treatment; Schuyler Catholic Community
Rutan, Warren, Diocese of Orlando
Sartori, Paul, St. Mary, Elmira
Schmitz, William F., (Retired)
Schrader, Robert, (Retired)
Schrage, Thomas, Nativity of the Blessed Virgin Mary, Brockport; Coordinating Chap., Orleans Men's Correctional Facility
Sciolino, Anthony, Unassigned
Serbicki, Jeffrey P., Jewish Home of Rochester
Shanley, Patrick M., The Parish of the Holy Family, Gates
Skerrett, Jerry, (Retired)
Slattery, Daniel P., (Retired)
Smith, Edward A., St. Peter's, Clifton Springs
Smith, Elmer, St. Pius Tenth, Chili
Smith, Lon, St. Kateri Tekakwith, Irondequoit
Snyder, David, St. Louis, Pittsford, NY; Project Rachel Coord.
Spezzano, George, (Retired)
Squilla, David, St. Lawrence, Greece
Steiger, James P., (Retired), Diocese of Rochester Tribunal
Stowell, Robert, (Retired)
Stratton, W. Craig, (Retired)
Tocci, Ronald J., (Retired)
Tomandl, John D., Auburn Correctional, Auburn Hospital
Toot, Walter, Unassigned
Uschold, Thomas, St. John the Evangelist, Spencerport
Valvo, Nicholas, Sacred Heart, Auburn
Van Etten, Laurence A., Unassigned
Vargas, Carlos H., St. Frances Xavier Cabrini Parish, Rochester
Virgilio, Paul, Nativity of the Blessed Virgin Mary, Brockport
Welch, George J., Blessed Sacrament, Elmira
Williams, Daniel, (Leave of Absence)
Yawman, Philip, (Retired)
Zuber, Michael, Monroe County Jail; Monroe County Correctional Facility.

INSTITUTIONS LOCATED IN DIOCESE

[A] GRADUATE SCHOOL OF THEOLOGY

ROCHESTER. *St. Bernard's School of Theology & Ministry*, 120 French Rd., 14618. Tel: 585-271-3657; Fax: 585-271-2045; Email: registrar@stbernards.edu; Web: www.stbernards.edu. Dr. Stephen Loughlin, Pres.; Deacon Frank Berning, Dir., Albany Site; Mark Capellazzi, Dir.; Corinne DerCola, Business Mgr.; Deacon Edward Giblin, Dir.; Sr. Nancy Hawkins, Prof.; Dr. Roslyn Karaban, Prof.; Dr. Matthew Kuhner, Dean; Mr. Marko Pranic, Registrar; Matthew Brown, Dir.; Ms. Lynette Saenz, Dir., Hispanic Pastoral Institute; Revs. Peter VanLieshout, Prof.; Jack Healy, O.Carm., Prof.; David Tedesche, Prof.; Patrick Sweeney, Dir. Lay Teachers 3; Priests 1; Sisters 1; Total Enrollment 102; Total Staff 12; Religious Teachers 2.

[B] HIGH SCHOOLS

ROCHESTER. *The Aquinas Institute* (1902) 1127 Dewey Ave., 14613-9989. Tel: 585-254-2020; Fax: 585-254-7401; Email: jknapp@aquinasinstitute.com; Web: www.aquinasinstitute.com. Michael Daley, Pres.; Ted Mancini, Prin.; Ms. Michelleq Beechey, Librarian. Lay Teachers 66; Religious 2; Students 744.

Bishop Kearney High School (Coed) 125 Kings Hwy. S., 14617-5596. Tel: 585-342-4000; Fax: 585-342-4694; Email: jsimoni@bkhs.org; Web: www.bkhs.org. Mr. Steve Salluzzo, Pres.; Mr. Jason Simoni, Prin.; Fred Tillinghast, Dir. Admissions; Mary Slifer, Librarian. Sponsored by the Congregation of Christian Brothers in association with the School Sisters of Notre Dame, Wilton Province. Clergy 1; Lay Teachers 36; Sisters 1; Students 314.

McQuaid Jesuit High School (1954) 1800 S. Clinton Ave., 14618. Tel: 585-473-1130; Fax: 585-256-6171; Web: www.mcquaid.org. Revs. Edward F. Salmon, S.J.; Robert E. Reiser, S.J., Pres.; Mr. Adam R. Baber, Prin. Northeast Province of the Society of Jesus (The Jesuits) Lay Teachers 84; Students 868.

Our Lady of Mercy School for Young Women, (Grades 6-12), 1437 Blossom Rd., 14610. Tel: 585-288-7120; Fax: 585-288-7966; Web: www.mercyhs.com. Mr. Terry Quinn, Prin.; Mary Szlosek, Prin.; Kimberly Rouleau, Librarian. Lay Teachers 69; Sisters of Mercy 3; Students 807.

ELMIRA. *Notre Dame High School* (1955) 1400 Maple Ave., Elmira, 14904. Tel: 607-734-2267; Fax: 607-737-8903; Email: kellyn@notredamehighschool.com; Web: www.notredamehighschool.com. Sisters Mary Walter Hickey, R.S.M., Pres.; Nancy Kelly, R.S.M., Exec. Asst., Pres.; Mrs. Deborah Franklin, Prin.; Mrs.

Susan Tanner, Librarian. Lay Teachers 41; Sisters of Mercy 2; Students 325.

[C] ELEMENTARY SCHOOLS

ROCHESTER. *Nazareth Elementary School* (1871) (Grades PreSchool-6), 311 Flower City Park, 14615-3614. Tel: 585-458-3786; Fax: 585-647-8717; Web: nazarethschools.org. Sr. Margaret Mancuso, S.S.J., Prin. Aides 3; Lay Teachers 15; Sisters of St. Joseph 5; Students 178.

[D] MONROE COUNTY CATHOLIC SCHOOLS

ROCHESTER. *Diocese of Rochester Department of Catholic Schools*, 1150 Buffalo Rd., 14624.
Tel: 585-328-3210; Fax: 585-328-3149; Web: www.dor.org. Dr. Anthony Cook III, Ed.D., Supr.; Ms. Ann Frank, Coord. Assessment & Professional Growth; Ms. Sharon Hockwater, Admin. Asst.; Ms. Rebecca Williams, Bus. Mgr. Lay Teachers 382; Sisters 4; Students 3,963.
Junior High Schools:.
Siena Catholic Academy, (Grades 6-8), 2617 East Ave., 14610-3111. Tel: 585-381-1220;
Fax: 585-381-1223; Email: scadcs@dor.org. Martin Kilbridge, Prin. Lay Teachers 19; Students 211.

[E] FINGER LAKES AND SOUTHERN TIER SCHOOLS

AUBURN. *St. Joseph School (Auburn)*, (Grades PreK-8), 89 E. Genesee St., Auburn, 13021-4161.
Tel: 315-253-8327; Fax: 315-253-2401; Web: schools.dor.org/stjoauburn. Mr. Michael W. Carney, Prin. Lay Teachers 17; Preschool 38; Students 200.

AVON. *St. Agnes School*, (Grades PreK-6), 60 Park Pl., Avon, 14414-1053. Tel: 585-226-8500;
Fax: 585-226-8500; Email: sagnesdcs@dor.org. Elizabeth Jensen, Prin. Lay Teachers 13; Preschool 30; Students 70.

CANANDAIGUA. *St. Mary School (Canandaigua)*, (Grades PreK-8), 16 E. Gibson St., Canandaigua, 14424-1310. Tel: 585-394-4300; Fax: 585-394-3954; Email: smcdcs@dor.org; Web: www.stmaryscanandaigua.org. Ms. Ann Marie Deutsch, Prin.; Christine Pohorence, Librarian. Lay Teachers 18; Students 159.

CORNING. *All Saints Academy*, (Grades PreK-8), 158 State St., Corning, 14830-2594. Tel: 607-936-9234; Fax: 607-936-1797; Email: asadcs@dor.org; Web: schools.dor.org/allsaints. TJ Verzillo, Prin. Aides 1; Lay Teachers 15; Students 115.

ELMIRA. *Holy Family Elementary*, (Grades PreK-6), 421 Fulton St., Elmira, 14904-1709.
Tel: 607-732-3588; Fax: 607-732-1850; Email: hfpdcs@dor.org; Web: www.schools.dor.org/holyfamilypri. Lori Brink, Prin.; Mark Schoonover, Info. Tech. Coord. Lay Teachers 17; Preschool 22; Students 163.

GENEVA. *St. Francis de Sales - St. Stephen School*, (Grades PreK-8), 17 Elmwood Ave., Geneva, 14456-2299. Tel: 315-789-1828; Fax: 315-789-9179; Email: sfssdcs@dor.org; Web: www.stfrancisststephen.org. Mary C. Mantelli, Prin. Lay Teachers 15; Preschool 6; Students 111.

HORSEHEADS. *St. Mary Our Mother (Horseheads)* (1959) (Grades PreK-6), 811 Westlake St., Horseheads, 14845-2099. Tel: 607-739-9157;
Fax: 607-739-2532; Email: smomdcs@dor.org. Jean Yorio, Prin.; Karen Solometo, Librarian. Lay Teachers 20; Preschool 31; Students 105.

PENN YAN. *St. Michael (Penn Yan)* (1884) (Grades PreSchool-5), 214 Keuka St., Penn Yan, 14527-1143. Tel: 315-536-6112; Fax: 315-536-6112; Email: smpydcs@dor.org; Web: stmichaelschoolpy.com. Tom Flood, Prin.; Liz Castner, Librarian. Lay Teachers 11; Preschool 28; Students 63.

[F] HOMES FOR AGED

ROCHESTER. *St. Ann's Home for the Aged*, 1500 Portland Ave., 14621. Tel: 585-697-6000;
Fax: 585-342-9585; Email: info@stannscommunity.com; Web: www.stannscommunity.com. Michael E. McRae, Pres. & CEO; Sr. Mary Louise Mitchell, S.S.J., Dir., Pastoral Care. Residents 388.
St. Ann's Nursing Home Co., Inc. (The Heritage) 1450 Portland Ave., 14621. Tel: 585-697-6000;
Fax: 585-342-9585; Email: info@stannscommunity.com; Web: www.stannscommunity.com. Michael E. McRae, Pres. & CEO; Sr. Livia Ann Ruocco, R.S.M., Pastoral Care Coord.; Sheila Kinsky, Pastoral Care Coord. Residents 203.
Chapel Oaks:, 1550 Portland Ave., 14621.
Tel: 585-342-3052; Fax: 585-338-3453; Email: info@stannscommunity.com; Web: www.stannscommunity.org. Michael E. McRae, Pres. & CEO; Deacon Daniel M. Kinsky, Chap.; Sr. Livia Ann Ruocco, R.S.M., Pastoral Care Coord.; Sheila Kinsky, Pastoral Care Coord.; Sr. Gertrude Erb, R.S.M., Pastoral Care Coord. - Cherry Ridge.

[G] SPECIALTY HOUSING

ROCHESTER. *Providence Housing Development Corporation*, 1150 Buffalo Rd., 14624.
Tel: 585-529-9555, Ext. 1393; Fax: 585-529-9525; Email: mark.greisberger@dor.org; Web: www.providencehousing.org. Mark Greisberger, Exec. Dir.; Jack Balinsky, Pres. Bd. of Directors; Helen Bianchi, Vice Pres., Property Mgmt.; Daniel Sturgis, Dir., Finance. Mission Statement: To strengthen families & communities by creating & providing access to quality affordable housing enriched by the availability of supportive services. Providence, a not-for-profit corporation affiliated with Catholic Charities of the Diocese of Rochester, develops, finances, & manages housing for individuals & families in the 12 counties of the Diocese of Rochester.
Clark Park Apartments Housing Development Fund Company, Inc., 1150 Buffalo Rd., 14624.
Tel: 585-529-9555; Tel: 585-529-9525; Email: mgreisberger@dor.org; Web: www.providencehousing.org. Mark Greisberger, Vice Pres.
Providence Atwood Park Housing Development Fund Company, Inc., 1150 Buffalo Rd., 14624.
Tel: 585-529-9555; Tel: 585-529-9525; Email: mark.greisberger@dor.org; Web: www.providencehousing.org. Mark Greisberger, Vice Pres.
Providence Clemens Housing Corporation, 1150 Buffalo Rd., 14624.
Providence LaFrance Housing Corporation, 1150 Buffalo Rd., 14624.
Providence Lyons Housing Development Fund Company, Inc., 1150 Buffalo Rd., 14624.
Tel: 585-328-3228, Ext. 1434; Fax: 585-529-9525; Email: mark.greisberger@dor.org; Web: www.providencehousing.org. Lori VanAuken, Pres.; Kathy Termine, Sec.
Providence Northstar Housing Development Fund Company, Inc., 1150 Buffalo Rd., 14624.
Tel: 585-328-3228, Ext. 1434; Fax: 585-529-9525; Email: mgreisberger@dor.org; Web: www.providencehousing.org. Mark Greisberger, Vice Pres.
Providence Rivendell Court Apartments, Inc., 1150 Buffalo Rd., 14624. Tel: 585-328-3228, Ext. 1434; Fax: 585-529-9525. Mark Greisberger, Vice Pres.
Providence Yates Housing Development Fund Company, Inc., 1150 Buffalo Rd., 14624.
Tel: 585-529-9555, Ext. 1434; Fax: 585-529-9525; Email: mark.greisberger@dor.org; Web: www.providencehousing.org. Lori VanAuken, Pres.; Kathy Termine, Sec.
Son House Housing Development Fund Company, Inc., 1150 Buffalo Rd., 14624. Tel: 585-529-9555; Fax: 585-529-9525; Email: mark.greisberger@dor.org; Web: www.providencehousing.org. Mark Greisberger, Vice Pres.
Union Meadows Housing Development Fund Company, Inc. (1997) 1150 Buffalo Rd., 14624.
Tel: 585-529-9555; Email: mark.greisberger@dor.org; Web: www.providencehousing.org.
West Town Village Housing Development Fund Company, Inc. (1999) 1150 Buffalo Rd., 14624.
Tel: 585-529-9555; Email: mark.greisberger@dor.org.

[H] CAMPS

LIVONIA. *Camp Stella Maris*, 4395 E. Lake Rd., Livonia, 14487. Tel: 585-346-2243;
Fax: 585-346-6921; Email: info@campstellamaris.org; Web: campstellamaris.org. John Quinlivan, CEO. Purpose: Residential camp (ages 7-15) and day camp (ages 5-12) under Catholic auspices, for boys & girls of all faiths. Encampment period: Nine weeks during summer (June/July/August). ACA Accredited. Rental of facility available September-June for family/youth development retreats as well as Adventure Based Learning Experience (ABLE) high and low challenge ropes course ideal for building trust, confidence, cooperation, teamwork, self-esteem, communication, and leadership skills. Students 5,000; Total Staff 9; Summer/Seasonal 140.

[I] GENERAL HOSPITALS

ELMIRA. *St. Joseph's Hospital* (1908) Skilled Nursing Facility. A Member of the Arnot Health System 555 St. Josephs Blvd., Elmira, 14901.
Tel: 607-733-6541, Ext. 2264; Fax: 607-737-7837; Email: vkastenhuber@arnothealth.org; Web: www.arnothealth.org. H. Fred Farley, Pres. & COO; Deacon George Welch. Bed Capacity 224; Total Staff 772; Skilled Nursing Facility 85.
St. Joseph's Hospital Foundation, Inc., 555 E. St. Josephs Blvd., Elmira, 14901. Tel: 607-737-7004;
Fax: 607-271-3418. Anthony J. Cooper, Interim Pres. & CEO.

[J] CATHOLIC CHARITIES

ROCHESTER. *Catholic Charities of the Diocese of Rochester*, 1150 Buffalo Rd., 14624.
Tel: 585-328-3210; Fax: 585-546-6396; Email: jack.balinsky@dor.org; Web: www.dor.org/charities/index.htm. Michael Gabrielli, Chm.; Jack Balinsky, Diocesan Dir.; Suzanne Stack, Life Issues Coord.; Barbara Poling, H.R. Dir. Total Staff 6.
Regional Diocesan Administration,
Tel: 607-734-9748; Fax: 607-734-3764. Anthony T. Barbaro, Assoc. Diocesan Dir., Tel: 607-734-9784; Fax: 607-734-3764; Lee Randall, Dir. Fin. Svcs., Tel: 607-734-9784; Fax: 607-733-3614; Donna L. Rieker, H.R. Dir., Tel: 607-734-9784, Ext. 165; Fax: 607-734-3764.
Regional Offices:.
Catholic Charities Community Services, 1099 Jay St., Bldg. J, 14611. Tel: 585-339-9800;
Fax: 585-339-9377; Email: cccs@dor.org; Web: www.cccsrochester.org. Lori VanAuken, Exec. Dir.; Tim Mason, Chm.; Kathleen Termine, Dir. Devel. Disabilities; Joan Brandenburg, Dir. Devel.; James Kennedy, Dir. Clinical & Medicaid Initiatives; Penny Coon, Dir. Quality Mgmt.; Tracy McNett, Dir. Care Coordination. Tot Asst. Annually 3,000; Total Staff 350.
Catholic Family Center, 87 N. Clinton Ave., 14604.
Tel: 585-546-7220; Fax: 585-546-6396; Email: CFC@cfcrochester.org. Marlene Bessette, Pres. & CEO; Roger W. Brandt Jr., Chm.; Kristie Elias, Vice Pres., Behavioral Health; Lindsay Gozzi-Theobald, Chief Quality & Compliance Officer; Kathy Grant, Dir., Mktg. & Communications; Kathleen Johnson, Chief Fin. Officer; Lisa Lewis, Vice Pres., Crisis Stabilization/Res. Svcs.; Marvin Mich, Dir., Advocacy & Parish Social Min.; James Morris, Vice Pres., Family Svcs.; Sarah F. Partner, Vice Pres., Mission Advancement; John Paul Perez, Vice Pres., Strategic Initiatives; Cathy Saresky, Vice Pres., Clinical Innovation. Tot Asst. Annually 23,134; Total Staff 461.
Departments of Catholic Family Center:.
Mission Advancement, Tel: 585-262-7115;
Fax: 585-325-3867. Sally Partner, Vice Pres.
Crisis & Intervention / Housing Services,
Tel: 585-546-7220; Fax: 585-262-7006. Lisa Lewis, Vice Pres.; Kathleen Johnson, CFO.
Family Services James Morris, Assoc. Vice Pres.
Mental Health Kristie Elias, Dir.
Compliance Lindsay Gozzi-Theobald, Vice Pres.
Office of Advocacy & Parish Social Ministry,
Tel: 585-546-7220; Fax: 585-325-3867. Marvin Mich, Dir.
Restart Services, Tel: 585-546-7220;
Fax: 585-546-3062. Cathy Saresky, Pres.
Fund Development & Marketing, Tel: 585-546-7220; Fax: 585-262-7166. Kathy Grant, Dir., Mktg. & Communications.
Catholic Charities Finance Office, 94 Exchange St., Geneva, 14456-2235. Tel: 315-789-1377;
Fax: 315-789-4339; Email: tony.barbaro@dor.org. Anthony T. Barbaro, Dir.; Lee Randall, Dir., Finance; Donna L. Rieker, Dir. Total Staff 15.
Catholic Charities of Chemung / Schuyler, 215 E. Church St., Elmira, 14901. Tel: 607-734-9784;
Fax: 607-734-6588; Email: test@test.com; Web: www.cs-cc.org. Greg Stewart, Chm. Bd.; Chuck Nocera, Exec. Dir.; Kathy Dubel, Justice & Peace Coord., Tel: 607-734-9784, Ext. 135; Tel: 607-734-9784, Ext. 135; Ellen Topping, Assoc. Dir.; Lindsay Winters, Devel.; Marty McInerny, Property Dept.; Suzianna Fritz, Emergency Svcs.; Teri Gursky, Quality Assurance; Jane Sokolowski, Housing Counseling Svcs.; Debra MacDonald, Schuyler Svcs. Dir.; Mary Canali, Bus. Mgr. Tot Asst. Annually 7,000; Total Staff 77.
Homeless Intervention Program Samaritan Center.
Catholic Charities of the Finger Lakes, 94 Exchange St., Geneva, 14456. Tel: 315-789-2686. Ellen Wayne, Exec. Dir.; Mary Luckern, Chm. Bd.; William Lamb, Dir., Svcs.; Rhonda Zettlemoyer, Dir., Administrative Svcs.; Deacon Gregory Kiley, Justice & Peace Coord. (Serving Yates, Ontario, Seneca, and Cayuga Counties).
Catholic Charities of Livingston County, 34 E. State St., Mt. Morris, 14510. Tel: 585-658-4466; Email: tabitha.brewster@dor.org; Web: www.aboutcclc.org. Tabitha Brewster, Exec. Dir.; Jessica Pierce, Transportation Svcs. & Emergency Payment Svcs.; Michelle Dourie, Individual & Family Therapist & Parenting Educator, Community of Caring; Nicole Ricker, Employment Svcs. Caseworker; Carrie Lyons, Parenting Educator & Emergency Payment Svcs.; Amy Patterson, Lead Employment Svcs. & Community Based Svcs. Case Mgr.; Brandy Swain, Transitional Jail Counselor, Youth Mentoring Social Worker; Heather Wagner, Disability Social Worker & Children's Health Homes Care Mgr.; Elijah Truth, Housing Svcs. & Soc. Sec. Disability Advocate; Deborah Farberman, Chm.; Kelsey Speicher, Youth Mentoring Social Work Asst. Tot Asst. Annually 9,000; Total Staff 10; Volunteers 185.

Catholic Charities of Steuben County, 23 Liberty St., Bath, 14810. Tel: 607-776-8085; Email: ckinship@dor.org; Web: www.catholiccharitiessteuben.org. Laura Opelt, Exec. Dir.; Paula Smith, Dir., Fundraising & Communications; Jamie Fuller, Admin. Specialist; Sue Bozman, Dir., Grant Devel. & Data Mgmt.; Jim Bassage, Dir., Substance Free Living Prevention; Melissa Nichols Mahany, S.H.A.P.E., Therapeutic Foster Care; Theresa McKinley, Dir., Turning Point; Heather Meehan, Dir., Residential Svcs.; Gary Pease, Chm.; Gina Reagan, Asst. Dir.; Jill Smith, Prog. Mgr. Healthy Families. Tot Asst. Annually 27,428; Total Staff 100.

Substance Free Living Prevention Jim Bassage, Dir.

S.H.A.P.E. & Bath Community Child Day Care Svcs. M. Duff, Dir.

Kinship Family & Youth Svcs., Healthy Families Lisa Galatio, Dir.

Residential Kim Robards-Smith, Dir.

Catholic Charities of Tompkins/Tioga, 324 W. Buffalo St., Ithaca, 14850. Tel: 607-272-5062. Renee Spear, Exec. Dir.; Joseph D'Abbracci, Bd. Chm.; Laurie Konwinski, Deputy Dir. & Justice & Peace Coord., Tompkins; Tommy Miller, Dir. Family & Empowerment; Susan Chaffe, Dir. Immigrant Svcs.; Laurie Ellis, Dir. Community Svcs.; Virginia Ubari, Dir. Samaritan Center; Annie Benjamin, Outreach & Educational Specialist; Sondra Siegfried, Coord., YES.

Justice and Peace, Tompkins Laurie Konwinski, Deputy Dir.

Justice and Peace, Tioga K. Dubel, Contact Person.

Family Empowerment Services Tommy Miller, Dir., Family Empowerment.

Development Susan Chaffe, Coord.

Immigrant Support Services Laurie Ellis, Community Svcs. Coord.

Samaritan Center Virginia Ubari, Samaritan Center Dir.

Catholic Charities of Wayne County, 180 E. Union St., Newark, 14513. Tel: 315-331-4867; Email: Peter.Dohr@dor.org. Emily Howard, Chm. Bd.; Deacon Peter Dohr, Exec. Dir.; Inga Rojas, Dir. Clinical Svcs.; Sharon VanLiew, Supvr., PINS & DAS; Jill Lee, Volunteer Mgr., Community Clothing Center; Alicia Diehl, Supvr., CCIP; Scott Cameron, Supvr., PARC; Allison Huff, Mgr., College Bound; Cathy Thiell-Kamp, Admin. & Community Connections; Sandy Thomas, Admin. & Community Resources; Peter Mares; Deacon Gregory Kiley, Justice & Peace Coord.

Early Intervention Inga Rojas, Contact Person.

Justice & Peace/Parish Social Ministry Peter Mares, Contact Person.

General Counseling/College Bound/PARC Inga Rojas, Clinical Svcs.

LaCasa/Community Outreach Peter Mares.

PINS & DAS Sharon VanLiew.

Wolcott Clothing Center Jill Lee.

Food Bank of the Southern Tier, 945 County Rt. 64, Elmira, 14903. Tel: 607-796-6061. Dave Patterson, Dir. Warehouse Opers.; Jennifer Edger, Dir. Community Progs.; Natasha Thompson, Exec. Dir.; Stephen Fowler, Bd. Chm.; Timothy Currie, COO; Michelle Benedict-Jones, Vice Pres., Devel. & Community Engagement; Matt Griffin, Dir., Agency Svcs. & Nutrition; Janet Wells, Dir., Business Svcs.

[K] MONASTERIES AND RESIDENCES OF PRIESTS AND BROTHERS

ROCHESTER. *Basilian Fathers*, Christ the King Church, 445 Kings Hwy., S., 14617. Tel: 585-266-1288. Very Rev. George T. Smith, Supr.; Revs. Albert W. Cylwicki, C.S.B.; Thomas P. Dugan; Paul English, C.S.B.; Kevin Mannara, C.S.B.; Joseph A. Trovato, C.S.B., (Retired).

Basilian Residence, 3497 East Ave., 14618. Tel: 585-586-4600; Fax: 585-385-6383. Revs. T. Paul Broadhurst, C.S.B.; Albert W. Cylwicki, C.S.B.; Leo A. Hetzler, C.S.B., Rector; Donald J. Lococo, C.S.B.; Thomas P. Dugan.

Priests of the Region Serving Elsewhere: Revs. George Kosicki, C.S.B., c/o Companions of Christ the Lamb, P.O. Box 12, Paradise, MI 49768. Tel: 906-492-3647; Paul F. O'Connor, C.S.B.

Missionaries of the Precious Blood (1815) 1261 Highland Ave., 14620-1873. Tel: 585-244-2692; Email: jcolacino@sjfc.edu. Rev. John A. Colacino, C.PP.S.

Whitefriars Priory, 625 Colebrook Dr., 14617. Tel: 585-266-2560. Revs. Joseph DeMaio, O.Carm.; Jack Healy, O.Carm., Prior & Treas.; Matthew Temple, O.Carm. Total in Residence 3.

INTERLAKEN. *St. Fidelis Friary* (1951) 7790 County Rd. 153, Interlaken, 14847. Tel: 607-532-4423; Fax: 607-532-9271. Bro. Antonine Lizama, O.F.M.-Cap.; Revs. Bernard Maloney, O.F.M.Cap., Guardian; Eugene O'Hara, O.F.M.Cap., Vicar. Province of St. Mary (Order of Friars Minor Capuchin) NY-NE Brothers 1; Priests 3.

PIFFARD. *Abbey of the Genesee* (1951) 3258 River Rd., Piffard, 14533. Tel: 585-243-0660; Fax: 585-243-4816; Email: community@geneseeabbey.org; Web: www.geneseeabbey.org. Rev. John Eudes Bamberger, O.C.S.O., Retired Abbot, (Retired); Bro Louis Petruska, O.C.S.O.; Revs. Justin R. Sheehan, O.C.S.O.; Aelred W. Wentz, O.C.S.O.; Rt. Rev. Gerard D'Souza, O.C.S.O., Abbot; Revs. Michael M. Hayden, O.C.S.O.; Stephen Muller, O.C.S.O.; Eugene Chung, O.C.S.O.; Isaac Slater, O.C.S.O.; Bros. James Almeter, O.C.S.O.; David Baumbach, O.C.S.O.; Revs. John Vianney Hamill, O.C.S.O.; Jerome J. Machar, O.C.S.O.; Bros. Gregory Chan, O.C.S.O.; Benedict Drgan, O.C.S.O.; Alberic Gardner, O.C.S.O.; Augustine Jackson, O.C.S.O.; Lawrence Jenny, O.C.S.O.; Brian Kerns, O.C.S.O.; Paul Richards, O.C.S.O.; Walter Thomann, O.C.S.O.; Christian Walsh, O.C.S.O.; Anthony Weber, O.C.S.O.; David Wilson, O.C.S.O.; Rev. Sanjay Lopes, O.C.S.O. The Order of Cistercians of the Strict Observance (Trappists). Priests 11; Professed Monks 28; Total in Community (Piffard) 31.

PINE CITY. *Mount Saviour Monastery* (1950) 231 Monastery Rd., Pine City, 14871-9787. Tel: 607-734-1688; Fax: 607-734-1689; Email: info@msaviour.org; Web: www.msaviour.org. Bros. John Thompson, O.S.B, Prior; Antonio Bravo Lara, O.S.B.; Rev. James Cronen, O.S.B.; Bros. Gabriel Duffee, O.S.B.; Bruno Lane, O.S.B.; Michael O'Connor, O.S.B.; Pierre Pratte, O.S.B., Subprior; Luke Zimnicky, O.S.B. Novices 1; Professed Monks 11.

[L] CONVENTS AND RESIDENCES FOR SISTERS

ROCHESTER. *Sisters of Mercy of the Americas - New York, Pennsylvania, Pacific West Community*, 1437 Blossom Rd., 14610. Tel: 585-288-2710; Fax: 585-288-2756; Email: nhoff@mercynyppaw.org; Web: www.sistersofmercy.org. Sr. Nancy Hoff, R.S.M, Rel. Order Leader. Associates 197; Professed Sisters & Perpetual Vows 117.

Sisters St. Joseph of Rochester (1854) 150 French Rd., 14618-3822. Tel: 585-641-8100; Fax: 585-641-8524; Email: cong@ssjrochester.org; Web: www.ssjrochester.org. Sr. Sharon Bailey, S.S.J., Congregational Pres.; Rev. George P. Heyman, Assisting Priest. Sisters of St. Joseph of Rochester, Inc. Priests 12; Professed Sisters in Community 189.

PITTSFORD. *Monastery of Our Lady and St. Joseph Carmelite Monastery*, 1931 W. Jefferson Rd., Pittsford, 14534-1041. Tel: 585-427-7094; Web: carmelitesofrochester.org. Mother Therese Marie of Jesus Crucified, O.C.D., Prioress. Discalced Carmelite Nuns. Professed Nuns with Solemn Vows 13.

[M] RETREAT HOUSES

ROCHESTER. *Mercy Spirituality Center* (1978) 65 Highland Ave., 14620. Tel: 585-473-6893; Fax: 585-473-6414; Email: info@mercyspiritualitycenter.org; Web: www.mercyspiritualitycenter.org. Ms. Karen Kosciolek, Admin. Sponsored by Sisters of Mercy, New York, Pennsylvania, Pacific West Community. Total Staff 5.

CANANDAIGUA. *Notre Dame Retreat House* (1967) 5151 Foster Rd., Box 342, Canandaigua, 14424. Tel: 585-394-5700; Fax: 585-394-9215; Web: ndretreat.org. Rev. Francis Jones, CSsR, Rector.

[N] CAMPUS MINISTRY

ROCHESTER. *Campus Ministry*, Pastoral Center, 1150 Buffalo Rd., 14624. Tel: 585-328-3210; Fax: 585-328-3149; Email: Shannon.Loughlin@dor.org. Dr. Shannon Loughlin, Dir., Campus Min.

The Catholic Community of Ithaca College, 1001 Muller Chapel, Ithaca College, 953 Danby Rd., Ithaca, 14850. Tel: 607-274-3103; Fax: 607-274-1909; Email: Fr.Carsten.Martensen@dor.org.

Catholic Newman Community at the University of Rochester, Interfaith Chapel, 320 Wilson Blvd., 14627. Tel: 585-275-8515; Email: catholicnewmancommunity@rochester.edu. Rev. Brian Cool, Dir. of Campus Ministry; Sr. Leandra Kosmoski, Campus Min.

The Cornell Catholic Community, Inc. (Ithaca), Cornell University, G-22 Anabel Taylor Hall, Ithaca, 14853. Tel: 607-255-4228; Fax: 607-255-7793; Email: catholic@cornell.edu.

Eastman School of Music Catholic Students Organization, Interfaith Chapel, 320 Wilson Blvd., 14627. Tel: 585-275-8515; Email: catholicnewmancommunity@rochester.edu. Rev. Brian Cool, Contact Person.

Elmira College, c/o Blessed Sacrament, Christ the Redeemer, St. Mary's, 1010 Davis St., Elmira, 14901. Tel: 607-733-3484; Email: Fr.Scott.Kubinski@dor.org. One Park Pl., Elmira, 14901. Very Rev. Scott M. Kubinski, Contact Person.

Hobart and William Smith College, c/o Our Lady of Peace, 130 Exchange St., Geneva, 14456. Tel: 315-789-0930; Email: Fr.Thomas.Mull@dor.org. Rev. Thomas P. Mull, Tel: 315-789-0930. Roman Catholic Community.

St. John Fisher College, 3690 East Ave., 14618. Tel: 585-385-8368; Fax: 585-385-8129; Email: campusministry@sjfc.edu; Web: www.sjfc.edu/student-life/campus-ministry/. Mrs. Sarah Mancini-Goebert, Music Min.; Rev. Kevin Mannara, C.S.B., Dir.; Jonathan Schott, Pastoral Min./Coord.

Keuka College c/o Our Lady of the Lakes, 210 Keuka St., Penn Yan, 14527. Tel: 315-536-7459; Fax: 315-536-6964; Email: Fr.Leo.Reinhardt@dor.org. Rev. Leo J. Reinhardt, Our Lady of the Lakes.

Monroe Community College c/o Our Lady of Lourdes / St. Anne, 1600 Mount Hope Ave., 14620. Tel: 585-271-3260; Email: Fr.Gary.Tyman@dor.org. Rev. Gary L. Tyman.

Nazareth College of Rochester, 4245 East Ave., 14618. Tel: 585-389-2303; Email: jfazio1@naz.edu. Jamie Fazio, Campus Min.

Newman (Catholic Campus) Parish, RIT/NTID, Interfaith Center, 40 Lomb Memorial Dr., 14623. Tel: 585-475-5172; Fax: 585-475-5485; Email: bcool@admin.rochester.edu; Web: www.rit.edu/~newman/. Rev. Brian Cool, Dir. of Campus Ministry.

New York Chiropractic College, c/o St. Francis & St. Clare, 25 Center St., Waterloo, 13165. Tel: 315-252-7297 (Rectory); Email: Fr.James.Fennessy@dor.org. Rev. James Fennessy. Priests 11; Total Staff 23; Total Assisted 120,721.

Roberts Wesleyan College c/o St. Christopher Church, 3350 Union St., North Chili, 14514. Tel: 585-595-1400; Email: Fr.Robert.Gaudio@dor.org.

State University College at Brockport, the Newman Oratory of Brockport, 101 Kenyon St., Brockport, 14420. Tel: 585-637-4500; Email: Fr.Joe.McCaffrey@dor.org. Rev. Joseph P. McCaffrey, Chap.

State University College at Geneseo (Geneseo), Newman Catholic Community at the Interfaith Center, 11 Franklin St., Geneseo, 14454. Tel: 585-243-1460; Email: Mike.Sauter@dor.org. Michael Sauter, Dir.; Revs. Edward J. Dillon, Sacramental Min., (Retired); Bernard Dan.

Wells College, c/o Good Shepherd Catholic Community, 299 Main St, Aurora, 13026. Tel: 315-364-7197; Email: Fr.William.Moorby@dor.org. Rev. William A. Moorby, Chap.

[O] MISCELLANEOUS LISTINGS

ROCHESTER. *Apostleship of Prayer*, Diocesan Pastoral Center, 1150 Buffalo Rd., 14624. Tel: 585-328-3210. Rev. Thomas P. Mull.

Archivist (Diocese of Rochester Archives), 1150 Buffalo Rd., 14624. Tel: 585-328-3210, Ext. 1204; Fax: 585-328-3149; Email: department.archive@dor.org. Sr. Connie Derby, R.S.M., Dir. of Archives and Records.

Catholic Committee on Scouting, 1150 Buffalo Rd., 14624. Tel: 585-328-3210; Fax: 585-328-3149; Email: linda.mehlenbacher@dor.org; Web: www.dor.org. Rev. William McGrath; Ms. Alison Lechase, Diocesan Scouting Liaison.

Catholic Gay & Lesbian Family Ministry, 66 Meadowbrook Rd., 14620. Tel: 585-303-8605. Ms. Karen Rinefierd, Diocesan Liaison.

Communis Fund of the Diocese of Rochester, Inc., 1150 Buffalo Rd., 14624. Tel: 585-328-3228, Ext. 1269.

DOR Holding, Inc., 1150 Buffalo Rd., 14624. Tel: 585-328-3228, Ext. 1269; Fax: 585-328-4142.

Dunn Tower Apartments, Inc. (1976) 100 Dunn Tower Dr., 14606. Tel: 585-429-6820; Fax: 585-429-9720; Email: dt1@dunntower.com; Web: www.dunntower.com. Housing for Seniors; Under 62 with Physical or Mobility; Disabled Vets Total in Residence 192; Total Staff 6.

Family Rosary For Peace, Inc. (1950) 51 Hazelhurst Dr., Apt. C, 14606. Tel: 585-436-8179. Very Rev. Paul J. Tomasso, V.G., Dir.; Dolores Mary Brien, Sec.

Finger Lakes Guild, P.O. Box 25223, 14625.

St. Joseph's House of Hospitality, 402 South Ave., 14620. Tel: 585-232-3262; Email: stjoes@frontier.net. Mailing Address: P.O. Box 31049, 14603. Tel: 585-232-3262. Services provide soup kitchen, personal assistance to the needy, emergency men's housing and social justice advocacy. Total Staff 5; Total Assisted 120.

St. Joseph's Neighborhood Center, Inc., 417 South Ave., 14620. Tel: 585-325-5260.

Magnificat - Rochester, P.O. Box 24787, 14624.

Tel: 585-233-8674. Louise Carson, Coord. & Contact.

Marriage Encounter Apostolate (Worldwide) 132 Clay Ave., 14613. Tel: 585-719-9848; Email: jbrasley@dor.org; Web: www.wwme.org. Deacon John Brasley, Spiritual Dir.; Belinda Brasley, Spiritual Dir. Total Staff 12.

Mercy Community Services, Inc. (1980) 142 Webster Ave., 14609. Tel: 585-288-2634; Fax: 585-288-0252; Email: info@mercycommunityservices.org; Web: www.mercycommunityservices.org. Nikisha Johnson, Pres. & CEO. Supportive Housing for Single Mothers and their Children and primary healthcare for the uninsured. Total Staff 15; Families Assisted 90; Total Assisted 600.

Missionary Childhood Association, 1150 Buffalo Rd., 14624. Tel: 585-436-9200; Fax: 585-529-9501; Email: jconlon@dor.org; Web: www.dor.org/missions. Rev. Robert C. Bradler, Dir., (Retired).

Nativity Preparatory Academy of Rochester, 15 Whalin St., 14620. Tel: 585-271-1630; Fax: 585-271-1633; Email: nativityrochester@frontiernet.net; Web: www.nativityrochester.org. Maria Cahill, Prin.

Notre Dame Learning Center, Inc., P.O. Box 77175, 14617. Tel: 585-254-5110; Fax: 585-254-2378; Email: ndlc@frontiernet.net; Web: www.ndlcenter.org. 71 Pkwy., 14608. Sr. Mary Lennon, Treas. Ministry for children and adults by providing educational opportunities in literacy, reading & math to enable them to reach the fullness of their potential & become successful & productive citizens.

Providence St. Andrew's Housing Development Fund Company, Inc., 1150 Buffalo Rd., 14624.

Rochester Catholic Worker Bethany House (1978) 1111 Joseph Ave., 14621. Tel: 585-454-4197; Fax: 585-730-8042; Email: rbethan1@rochester.rr.com. Donna Ecker, Contact Person. Total Staff 4.

Sisters of Saint Joseph of Rochester Charitable Trust, c/o Presiding Trustee, 150 French Rd., 14618. Tel: 585-641-8166; Fax: 585-641-8524. Alicia Pender, Contact Person.

Sisters of Saint Joseph of Rochester Ministry Foundation, Inc. (2004) 150 French Rd., 14618-3822. Tel: 585-641-8120; Fax: 585-641-8524; Email: mpray@ssjrochester.org; Web: www.ssjrochester.org. Mr. Stephen Uebbing, Contact Person.

The Diocese of Rochester Lay Employees' Retirement Accumulation Plan, 1150 Buffalo Rd., 14624.

The Diocese of Rochester Priests' Retirement Plan, 1150 Buffalo Rd., 14624.

St. Theodore's Apartment Housing Development Fund Co., Inc. (Dunn Tower II Apts.) (1980) 200 Dunn Tower Dr., 14606. Tel: 585-429-6840; Fax: 585-247-3723; Email: dt2@dunntower.com; Web: www.dunntower.com.

CORNING. *Anawim Community Center*, 122 E. First St., Corning, 14830. Tel: 607-936-4965; Fax: 607-936-0207; Email: shirleyfernandes@anawim.com; Web: www.anawim.com. Revs. Daniel Healy, Dir.; Richard M. Rusk, Missions & Vocations Dir. Priests 2; Total in Residence 5; Total Staff 11.

OWEGO. *Owego -Tioga County Rural Ministry* (1978) 143 North Ave., Owego, 13827. Tel: 607-687-3021; Fax: 607-687-3033; Email: mobriencsj@stny.rr.com. Sr. Mary O'Brien, C.S.J., Exec. Dir. This ministry serves as a food pantry and an emergency outreach to the poor and elderly of the county. Total Staff 4; Total Assisted 2,496.

SENECA FALLS. *Patrician Fund Trust*, 25 Center St., Waterloo, 13165. Tel: 315-651-4349; Fax: 315-539-8841; Email: sstpatri@dor.org; Web: www.senecafallsonline.com/stpats/. Rev. James Fennessy.

SPENCERPORT. *Rochester Comitium*, 71 Thorntree Cir., Penfield, 14526. Jim Alessi, Pres.

WEBSTER. *Catholic Charismatic Renewal*, 929 Gravel Rd., Webster, 14580. Tel: 585-671-5275; Email: bomba_14580@yahoo.com. Deacon Robert Meyer, Diocesan Liaison.

RELIGIOUS INSTITUTES OF MEN REPRESENTED IN THE DIOCESE

For further details refer to the corresponding bracketed number in the Religious Institutes of Men or Women section.

[0170]—*Basilian Fathers*—C.S.B.
[0200]—*Benedictine Monks*—O.S.B.
[0470]—*The Capuchin Friars* (Province of St. Mary)—O.F.M.Cap.
[0270]—*Carmelite Fathers and Brothers*—O.Carm.
[0350]—*Cistercians Order of the Strict Observance (Trappists)*—O.C.S.O.
[0690]—*Jesuit Fathers and Brothers* (New York Province)—S.J.
[]—*Maryknoll Fathers and Brothers*—M.M.
[1070]—*Redemptorist Fathers* (Baltimore Province)—C.SS.R.
[1060]—*Society of the Precious Blood*—C.PP.S.

RELIGIOUS INSTITUTES OF WOMEN REPRESENTED IN THE DIOCESE

[3110]—*Congregation of Our Lady of the Retreat in the Cenacle*—R.C.
[0760]—*Daughters of Charity of St. Vincent de Paul*—D.C.
[0420]—*Discalced Carmelite Nuns*—O.C.D.
[2575]—*Institute of the Sisters of Mercy of the Americas* (Rochester, NY)—R.S.M.
[2970]—*School Sisters of Notre Dame*—S.S.N.D.
[3840]—*Sisters of St. Joseph of Carondolet*—C.S.J.
[3830-14]—*Sisters of St. Joseph (Rochester)*—S.S.J.
[3730]—*Sisters of the Order of St. Basil the Great*—O.S.B.M.
[1490]—*Sisters of the Third Franciscan Order*—O.S.F.

DIOCESAN CEMETERIES

ROCHESTER. *Holy Sepulchre Cemetery*, 2461 Lake Ave., 14612. Tel: 585-458-4110; Fax: 585-458-3059; Web: www.holysepulchre.org; Email: lynn@holysepulchre.org. Ms. Lynn Sullivan, CEO

REGIONAL CEMETERIES

AUBURN. *St. Joseph's*
CORNING. *St. Mary*
ELMIRA. *SS. Peter and Paul's*
GENEVA. *St. Mary's and St. Patrick's*

NECROLOGY

† MacNamara, Robert C., (Retired), Died Feb. 9, 2019
† Metzger, Edwin, (Retired), Died Jul. 2, 2018
† Plominski, Walter J., (Retired), Died Oct. 4, 2018
† Tracy, Laurence C., (Retired), Died Aug. 16, 2018

An asterisk (*) denotes an organization that has established tax-exempt status directly with the IRS and is not covered by the USCCB Group Ruling.

Diocese of Rockford

(Dioecesis Rockfordiensis)

Most Reverend

DAVID J. MALLOY

Bishop of Rockford; ordained July 1, 1983; appointed Bishop of Rockford March 20, 2012. *Office: 555 Colman Center Dr., Rockford, IL 61125.*

Diocesan Chancery: 555 Colman Center Dr., P.O. Box 7044, Rockford, IL 61125. Tel: 815-399-4300; Fax: 815-399-5266.

Web: www.rockforddiocese.org

Email: info@rockforddiocese.org

ESTABLISHED SEPTEMBER 23, 1908.

Square Miles 6,457.

Comprises Jo Daviess, Stephenson, Winnebago, Boone, McHenry, Carroll, Ogle, DeKalb, Kane, Whiteside and Lee Counties in the State of Illinois.

For legal titles of parishes and diocesan institutions, consult the Chancery Office.

STATISTICAL OVERVIEW

Personnel	
Bishop	1
Abbots	1
Retired Abbots	1
Priests: Diocesan Active in Diocese	115
Priests: Diocesan Active Outside Diocese	3
Priests: Retired, Sick or Absent	65
Number of Diocesan Priests	183
Religious Priests in Diocese	36
Total Priests in Diocese	219
Extern Priests in Diocese	16
Ordinations:	
Diocesan Priests	1
Transitional Deacons	3
Permanent Deacons	14
Permanent Deacons in Diocese	186
Total Brothers	7
Total Sisters	73
Parishes	
Parishes	104
With Resident Pastor:	
Resident Diocesan Priests	75
Resident Religious Priests	9
Without Resident Pastor:	
Administered by Priests	20
Pastoral Centers	1
Professional Ministry Personnel:	
Brothers	7
Sisters	17
Lay Ministers	193
Welfare	
Catholic Hospitals	3
Total Assisted	980,000
Health Care Centers	19
Total Assisted	150,000
Homes for the Aged	8
Total Assisted	800
Day Care Centers	1
Total Assisted	26
Special Centers for Social Services	7
Total Assisted	84,090
Educational	
Diocesan Students in Other Seminaries	21
Total Seminarians	21
Colleges and Universities	1
Total Students	301
High Schools, Diocesan and Parish	6
Total Students	2,622
High Schools, Private	2
Total Students	850
Elementary Schools, Diocesan and Parish	35
Total Students	7,621
Catechesis/Religious Education:	
High School Students	6,259
Elementary Students	19,993
Total Students under Catholic Instruction	37,667
Teachers in the Diocese:	
Priests	9
Brothers	2
Sisters	6
Lay Teachers	734
Vital Statistics	
Receptions into the Church:	
Infant Baptism Totals	4,218
Minor Baptism Totals	124
Adult Baptism Totals	111
Received into Full Communion	199
First Communions	5,407
Confirmations	5,086
Marriages:	
Catholic	682
Interfaith	165
Total Marriages	847
Deaths	2,021
Total Catholic Population	411,217
Total Population	1,509,566

Former Bishops—Most Revs. PETER J. MULDOON, D.D., ord. Dec. 18, 1886; cons. Titular Bishop of Tamassus and Auxiliary Bishop of Chicago, July 25, 1901; appt. Bishop of Rockford, Sept. 28, 1908; made Assistant to the Pontifical Throne, June 8, 1921; died Oct. 8, 1927; EDWARD F. HOBAN, S.T.D., ord. July 11, 1903; cons. Titular Bishop of Colonia and Auxiliary Bishop of Chicago, Dec. 21, 1921; appt. Bishop of Rockford, Feb. 10, 1928; appt. Assistant at the Pontifical Throne, Nov. 25, 1937; appt. Titular Bishop of Listra and Coadjutor Bishop of Cleveland, Nov. 16, 1942; succeeded to the See of Cleveland, Nov. 2, 1945; died Sept. 22, 1966; JOHN J. BOYLAN, D.D., Ph.D., ord. July 28, 1915; appt. Nov. 21, 1942; cons. Feb. 17, 1943; died July 19, 1953; RAYMOND P. HILLINGER, D.D., ord. April 2, 1932; appt. Nov. 3, 1953; cons. Dec. 29, 1953; appt. Titular Bishop of Derbe and Auxiliary Bishop of Chicago, June 27, 1956; died Nov. 13, 1971; Rt. Rev. DONALD M. CARROLL, D.D., ord. April 7, 1934; appt. June 27, 1956; resigned Sept. 25, 1956; died Jan. 3, 2002; Most Revs. LORAS T. LANE, D.D., ord. March 19, 1937; appt. Titular Bishop of Bencenna and Auxiliary of Dubuque, May 29, 1951; cons. Aug. 20, 1951; appt. to Rockford, Oct. 11, 1956; died July 22, 1968; ARTHUR J. O'NEILL, D.D., V.G., ord. March 27, 1943; appt. Bishop of Rockford Aug. 19, 1968; cons. and installed Oct. 11, 1968; retired April 19, 1994; died April 27, 2013.; THOMAS G. DORAN, D.D., J.C.D., ord. Dec. 20, 1961; appt. Bishop of Rockford April 19, 1994; cons. and installed June 24, 1994; retired March 20, 2012; died Sept. 1, 2016.

Diocesan Chancery—555 Colman Center Dr., P.O. Box 7044, Rockford, 61125. Tel: 815-399-4300; Fax: 815-399-5266. Address all official business to this office. Office Hours: Mon.-Fri. 8:30-12, 1-4:30.

Vicar General—Mailing Address: P.O. Box 7044, Rockford, 61125. Tel: 815-399-4300; Fax: 815-399-5266. Rev. Msgr. GLENN L. NELSON, V.G., J.C.L.

Moderator of the Curia—Rev. Msgr. GLENN L. NELSON, V.G., J.C.L.

Vicar for Clergy and Religious—Rev. Msgr. DANIEL J. DEUTSCH.

Parish Services and Directors—MR. PATRICK WINN, Dir. Social Svcs., 555 Colman Center Dr., P.O. Box 7044, Rockford, 61125; MS. JENNIFER COLLINS, Dir. Pastoral Svcs., P.O. Box 7044, Rockford, 61125; MR. JOHN MCGRATH, Dir. Educational Svcs., Catholic Education Office, 555 Colman Center Dr., P.O. Box 7044, Rockford, 61125; MR. MICHAEL KAGAN, Asst. Dir. Educational Svcs., Catholic Education Office, 555 Colman Center Dr., P.O. Box 7044, Rockford, 61125; MR. VITO DEFRISCO, Asst. Supt. of Schools, Catholic Education Office, 555 Colman Center Dr., P.O. Box 7044, Rockford, 61125; MRS. ELIZABETH HEITKAMP, Asst. Supt. of Schools, Catholic Education Office, 555 Colman Center Dr., P.O. Box 7044, Rockford, 61125; MRS. JODI RIPPON, CPA, Dir. Fin. & Admin. Svcs., 555 Colman Center Dr., P.O. Box 7044, Rockford, 61125; MRS. LORI GRABER, CPA, Asst. Dir. Fin. & Admin. Svcs., 555 Colman Center Dr., P.O. Box 7044, Rockford, 61125.

Chancellor—ELLEN B. LYNCH.

Vice Chancellor—Very Rev. MATTHEW M. BERGSCHNEIDER, J.C.L.

Secretary to the Bishop—Deacon THOMAS MCKENNA.

Bishop's Secretary for Retired Priests—Rev. Msgr. DANIEL J. DEUTSCH.

Diocesan Master of Ceremonies—1891 Kanesville Rd., Geneva, 60134. Tel: 630-232-0124. Rev. JONATHAN P. BAKKELUND, S.T.L.

Diocesan Tribunal—555 Colman Center Dr., P.O. Box 7044, Rockford, 61125. Tel: 815-399-4300; Fax: 815-399-4861. Address all official business to this office.

Judicial Vicar—Very Rev. MATTHEW M. BERGSCHNEIDER, J.C.L.

Adjunct Judicial Vicars—Rev. Msgr. ARQUIMEDES VALLEJO, J.C.D., V.F.; Rev. JOSEPH F. JASKIERNY, J.C.L.

Promoter of Justice—Rev. Msgr. ARQUIMEDES VALLEJO, J.C.D., V.F.

Defenders of the Bond—Rev. Msgrs. ARQUIMEDES VALLEJO, J.C.D., V.F.; MICHAEL A. HACK, J.C.D.; Rev. JOSEPH F. JASKIERNY, J.C.L.

Advocates—Rev. JOSEPH F. JASKIERNY, J.C.L.; Deacon JAMES EASTON.

Expert—MR. KERRY BURD.

Notaries—MRS. DENISE GEORGE; MRS. DONNA HAYES.

Diocesan Consultors—Rev. GODWIN N. ASUQUO; Rev. Msgr. P. WILLIAM MCDONNELL, S.T.L.; Rev. F. WILLIAM ETHEREDGE; Rev. Msgr. DANIEL J. DEUTSCH; Revs. PATRICK S. GILLMEYER, O.S.B.; MICHAEL G. LAVAN; Rev. Msgr. STEPHEN J. KNOX, S.T.L., V.F.; Rev. TIMOTHY J. SIEGEL; Rev. Msgrs.

ARQUIMEDES VALLEJO, J.C.D.; GLENN L. NELSON, V.G., J.C.L.

Deans—Rev. Msgr. ARQUIMEDES VALLEJO, J.C.D., V.F., Aurora Deanery; Very Rev. MATTHEW J. MCMORROW, S.T.L., V.F., DeKalb Deanery; Rev. Msgr. STEPHEN J. KNOX, S.T.L., V.F., Elgin Deanery; Very Revs. KENNETH J. ANDERSON, V.F., Freeport Deanery; BRIAN D. GRADY, V.F., McHenry Deanery; J. STEPHEN ST. JULES, V.F., Rockford Deanery; JAMES R. KEENAN, V.F., Sterling Deanery.

Diocesan Offices and Directors

Accounting and Data Processing Office—DAN O'MALLEY, Dir. Accounting; ROBERT WHITE, Dir. Information Technology; LORI GLENN, Office Mgr., Mailing Address: P.O. Box 7044, Rockford, 61125. Tel: 815-399-4300; Fax: 815-399-5657.

Catholic Campaign for Human Development—555 Colman Center Dr., P.O. Box 7044, Rockford, 61125. Tel: 815-399-4300; Fax: 815-399-6303.

Catholic Charismatic Renewal Services—1910 Bracknel Blvd., Rockford, 61103. Tel: 815-654-4111. MR. RON BERGMAN, Diocesan Liaison; Revs. CHRISTOPHER J. KUHN, Spiritual Dir.; ANDRES SALINAS, Hispanic Spiritual Dir.

Catholic Office of the Deaf—Rev. Msgr. GLENN L. NELSON, V.G., J.C.L., Dir., P.O. Box 7044, Rockford, 61125. Tel: 815-399-4300 (Voice); Tel: 815-217-2234 (Video Phone); Fax: 815-399-5266; Email: rockfordhi@aol.com; Web: rockforddiocese.org/deafapostolate.

Catholic Relief Services—Deacon THOMAS MCKENNA, 555 Colman Center Dr., P.O. Box 7044, Rockford, 61125. Tel: 815-399-4300; Fax: 815-399-6303.

Catholic Social Services and Catholic Charities—Mailing Address: P.O. Box 7044, Rockford, 61125. Tel: 815-399-4300; Fax: 815-399-6303. MR. PATRICK WINN, Dir. Offices: *314 Lake St., Ste. 1-A, Aurora, 60506. 521 State St., Ste. 2, Belvidere, 61008. 33 N. Geneva St., Elgin, 60120. 5141 W. Bull Valley Rd., McHenry, 60050. 431 Phelps Ave., Ste. 608, Rockford, 61108. Refugee Svcs., 6116 Mulford Village Dr., Ste. 8, Rockford, 61107.*

Cemeteries—MRS. JODI RIPPON, CPA, Admin.; CAROL GIAMBALVO, Dir., 8616 W. State St., Winnebago, 61088. Tel: 815-965-1450; Fax: 815-965-9632.

Censores Librorum—Revs. RYAN B. BROWNING, S.T.L.; JARED TWENTY, S.T.L.

Clergy Relief Society, Priests' Retirement Committee—Rev. Msgr. DANIEL J. DEUTSCH, Exec. Sec., P.O. Box 7044, Rockford, 61125. Tel: 815-399-4300; Fax: 815-399-5266.

Communications—MRS. PENNY WIEGERT, Dir., 555 Colman Center Dr., P.O. Box 7044, Rockford, 61125. Tel: 815-399-4300; Fax: 815-399-6225.

General Counsel—ELLEN B. LYNCH, 555 Colman Center Dr., P.O. Box 7044, Rockford, 61125. Tel: 815-399-4300; Fax: 815-399-6168.

Council of Catholic Women, Diocesan—Rev. Msgr. THOMAS L. DZIELAK, S.T.L., Moderator, (Retired), P.O. Box 70, Maple Park, 60151. Tel: 815-827-3218; CATHY VENDEMIA, Pres., 107 Wenatchee Way, Poplar Grove, 61065. Tel: 815-566-1843.

Cursillo Movement—VACANT, Spiritual Dir.; Rev. MANUEL G. GOMEZ, Spanish Spiritual Dir., Tel: 630-892-5918; KEN MEEKER, Lay Dir., Tel: 630-430-9879; MARISELA RODRIGUEZ, Spanish Lay Dir., Tel: 630-853-9202.

Charitable Giving Office—555 Colman Center Dr., P.O. 7044, Rockford, 61125. Tel: 815-399-4300; Fax: 815-399-5657. DENISE DOBROWOLSKI, Dir.

Courage—Rev. PHILLIP A. KAIM, S.T.L., Chap., Web: www.couragerc.org.

Divine Worship, Office for—(and RCIA Resources)–*1891 Kanesville Rd., Geneva, 60134.* Tel: 630-232-0124. Rev. JONATHAN P. BAKKELUND, S.T.L., Dir.

Ecumenism, Office of—Rev. ALEJANDRO DEL TORO, S.T.L., 2505 School St., Rockford, 61101. Tel: 815-965-9539.

Education—MR. MICHAEL KAGAN, Supt. Schools & DRE; MR. JOHN MCGRATH, Dir. Educ. & Ministry Formation, 555 Colman Center Dr., P.O. Box 7044, Rockford, 61125. Tel: 815-399-4300; Fax: 815-399-6278; MS. JENNIFER COLLINS, Dir. Youth & Young Adult Ministry, Mailing Address: P.O. Box 7044, Rockford, 61125.

Ethicist for Health Care Issues, Diocesan—Rev. KENNETH WASILEWSKI, S.T.L., P.O. Box 7044, Rockford, 61125. Tel: 815-399-4300; Fax: 815-399-6303.

EnCourage—Rev. RYAN B. BROWNING, S.T.L., Chap., Web: www.couragerc.org.

Office of Life and Family Evangelization—MS. JENNIFER COLLINS, Dir., Mailing Address: P.O. Box 7044, Rockford, 61125. Tel: 815-399-4300; Fax: 815-399-6303.

Finance and Administration—555 Colman Center Dr., P.O. Box 7044, Rockford, 61125. Tel: 815-399-4300; Fax: 815-399-5591. MRS. JODI RIPPON, CPA, Dir. Fin. & Admin. Svcs.; MRS. LORI GRABER, CPA, Asst. Dir. Fin. & Admin. Svcs.

Hispanic Ministry Offices—Office for Aurora Deanery: Hispanic Ministry Center, St. Nicholas Parish, 308 High St., Aurora, 60505. Tel: 630-851-1890. *DeKalb Deanery: Hispanic Ministry Center, St. Mary Parish, 308 Fisk Ave., DeKalb, 60115.* Tel: 815-758-1377. Office for Aurora Deanery: *Hispanic Ministry Center, St. Nicholas Parish, 308 High St., Aurora, 60505.* Tel: 630-851-1890. DeKalb Deanery: *Hispanic Ministry Center, St. Mary Parish, 308 Fisk Ave., DeKalb, 60115.* Tel: 815-758-1377. Freeport Deanery: *St. Mary Parish, 229 W. Washington Pl., Freeport, 61032.* Rev. DIEGO F. OSPINA. Episcopal Vicar and Rockford Deanery: Rev. Msgr. ARQUIMEDES VALLEJO, J.C.D., V.F., 555 Colman Center Dr., P.O. Box 7044, Rockford, 61125. Tel: 815-399-4300; Fax: 815-399-4861.

Immigration Services—IOSDEL TRUJILLO, Dir., Mulford Village Mall, 6116 Mulford Village Dr., Ste. 8, Rockford, 61107. Tel: 815-399-1709; Fax: 815-399-1731.

Investment and Loan—555 Colman Center Dr., P.O. Box 7044, Rockford, 61125. Tel: 815-399-4300; Fax: 815-399-5591. MRS. JODI RIPPON, CPA.

Liturgical Commission, Diocesan—1891 Kanesville Rd., Geneva, 60134. Tel: 630-232-0124. Rev. JONATHAN P. BAKKELUND, S.T.L., Chm.

Ministry Formation, Office of—MR. JOHN MCGRATH, Dir., 555 Colman Center Dr., P.O. Box 7044, Rockford, 61125. Tel: 815-399-4300; Fax: 815-399-6278.

Ministry to Priests Program—Rev. Msgr. DANIEL J. DEUTSCH, Vicar, Clergy Sabbaticals and Diocesan Priests' Retreats, 555 Colman Center Dr., P.O. Box 7044, Rockford, 61125. Tel: 815-399-4300; Fax: 815-399-5962.

Newman-Campus Ministry—Very Rev. MATTHEW J. MCMORROW, S.T.L., V.F., 512 Normal Rd., DeKalb, 60115. Tel: 815-787-7770; Fax: 815-758-2053.

Newspaper—The Observer MRS. PENNY WIEGERT, Mng. Editor, 555 Colman Center Dr., P.O. Box 7044, Rockford, 61125. Tel: 815-399-4300; Fax: 815-399-6225.

Permanent Diaconate Program Diocesan—Rev. KENNETH WASILEWSKI, S.T.L., Dir., 555 Colman Center, P.O. Box 7044, Rockford, 61125. Tel: 815-399-4300; Fax: 815-399-6303.

Priest Personnel—Rev. Msgr. DANIEL J. DEUTSCH, Vicar, Clergy and Religious, 555 Colman Center Dr., P.O. Box 7044, Rockford, 61125. Tel: 815-399-4300; Fax: 815-399-5962.

Propagation of the Faith555 Colman Center Dr., P.O. Box 7044, Rockford, 61125. Tel: 815-399-4300; Fax: 815-399-4861. Rev. Msgr. GLENN L. NELSON, V.G., J.C.L., Dir.

Property Management Office—Mailing Address: P.O. Box 7044, Rockford, 61125. Tel: 815-399-4300; Fax: 815-399-5657. MR. BRIAN HEINKEL, Dir.

Research and Planning—555 Colman Center Dr.`, P.O. Box 7044, Rockford, 61125. Tel: 815-399-4300; Fax: 815-399-6306. MR. KEVIN FUSS, Dir.

Rural Life Conference—Deacon THOMAS MCKENNA, Dir., 555 Colman Center Dr., P.O. Box 7044, Rockford, 61125. Tel: 815-399-4300; Fax: 815-399-6303.

Scouts—St. Elizabeth Ann Seton Parish, 1023 McHenry Ave., Crystal Lake, 60014. Tel: 815-459-3033. Rev. COLIN EASTON.

Diocesan Administration Offices—555 Colman Dr., P.O. Box 7044, Rockford, 61125. Tel: 815-399-4300; Fax: 815-399-6303. MR. BRIAN HEINKEL, Bldg. Mgr.; JAKI PARSONS, Asst. Bldg. Mgr.

Unemployment Insurance Office—LORI GLENN, Mgr., Mailing Address: P.O. Box 7044, Rockford, 61125. Tel: 815-399-4300; Fax: 815-399-5657.

Victim Assistance Coordinator—DR. VIRGINIA DESJARLAIS, Tel: 815-293-7540; Email: vdesjarlais@rockforddiocese.org.

Vocations—555 Colman Center Dr., P.O. Box 7044, Rockford, 61125. Tel: 815-399-4300; Fax: 815-399-6085. Rev. KYLE A. MANNO, Dir.

CLERGY, PARISHES, MISSIONS AND PAROCHIAL SCHOOLS

CITY OF ROCKFORD

(WINNEBAGO COUNTY)

1—ST. PETER CATHEDRAL aka Cathedral of St. Peter (1922)
1243 N. Church St., 61103. Tel: 815-965-2765; Email: StPeterCathedral-Rockford@RockfordDiocese.org. Very Rev. Stephen St. Jules, Rector; Deacons Robert Mitchison; James Easton.
School—St. Peter Cathedral School, (Grades K-8), 1231 N. Court St., 61103. Tel: 815-963-3620; Fax: 815-963-0551; Email: stpetercathedralschool-rockford@rockforddiocese.org; Web: cathedralofstpeter.org/school. Mr. James Burns, Prin. Lay Teachers 15; Students 131.
Catechesis Religious Program—Students 52.

2—ST. ANTHONY OF PADUA (1909) (Italian)
1010 Ferguson St., 61102. Tel: 815-965-2761; Email: stanthony-rockford@rockforddiocese.org; Web: Stanthonyrockford.org. Revs. James M. Ciaramitaro, O.F.M.Conv.; Lucjan Szymanski, Parochial Vicar; Deacon Peter J. Addotta; Bro. James D. Dufresne, O.F.M.Conv., Spiritual Advisor/Care Svcs.
Catechesis Religious Program—Mrs. Heather Dunaway, D.R.E. Students 58.

3—ST. BERNADETTE (1957)
2400 Bell Ave., 61103. Tel: 815-968-0904; Email: mGroeninger@RockfordDiocese.org; Web: stbernadetterockford.com. Revs. Kenneth J. Stachyra, V.F.; Ricardo F. Hernandez, Parochial Vicar; Deacons Richard Gerdeman; Ronald Meadors; Gregg Cox; Mary Groeninger, Business Mgr.; Dr. Joan Wagner, Ph.D., Liturgy & Music Dir.
Church: Rockton Ave. & Bell Ave., 61103.
Catechesis Religious Program—2300 Bell Ave., 61103. Email: stbernadetterockford@rockforddiocese.org. Mr. Kevin Rilott, D.R.E. Students 25.

4—ST. EDWARD (1929)
3004 11th St., 61109. Tel: 815-229-0282; Fax: 815-229-8912; Email: stedward-rockford@rockforddiocese.org; Web: www.stedwardrockford.org. Revs. Johnson Lopez, Parochial Admin.; William E. Vallejo.
Res.: 3026 11th St., 61109.
School—St. Edward School, 3020 S. 11th St., 61109. Tel: 815-398-2631; Fax: 815-398-3134; Email: stedwardschool-rockford@rockforddiocese.org. Mrs. Patricia Wackenhut, Prin. Lay Teachers 14; Students 134.
Catechesis Religious Program—Tel: 815-229-8914. Nancy Perez-Renteria, D.R.E. Students 198.

5—HOLY FAMILY (1963)
4401 Highcrest Rd., 61107. Tel: 815-398-4280; Fax: 815-398-4287; Email: HolyFamily-Rockford@rockforddiocese.org; Web: www.holyfamilyrockford.org. Revs. Phillip A. Kaim, S.T.L.; Charles P. Fitzpatrick, Parochial Vicar; Kenneth Wasilewski, S.T.L., (In Res.); Deacons Frank Zammuto; Jason Stewart.
School—Holy Family School, 4407 Highcrest Rd., 61107. Tel: 815-398-5331; Fax: 815-398-5902; Email: holyfamilyschool-rockford@rockforddiocese.org. Mrs. Corine Gendron, Prin. Lay Teachers 31; Students 364.
Catechesis Religious Program—Email: bbeckett@holyfamilyrockford.org. Barbara Beckett, C.R.E. Students 153.

6—ST. JAMES (1853) [JC]
428 N. Second St., 61107. Tel: 815-962-1214; Email: StJames-Rockford@RockfordDiocese.org; Web: www.stjamesrockford.com. Rev. Leonard Jacobs; Deacon William Dean; Kim Carlson, Business Mgr.
School—St. James School, (Grades K-8), 409 N. First St., 61107. Tel: 815-962-8515; Email: stjamesschool-rockford@rockforddiocese.org. Renee Payne, Prin. Lay Teachers 14; Students 137.
Catechesis Religious Program—Tel: 815-962-5588. Kathy Wilson, C.R.E. Students 37.

7—ST. MARY ORATORY (1997)
126 S. Winnebago St., 61102. Tel: 815-965-5971; Email: StMary-Rockford@RockfordDiocese.org; Web: www.institute-Christ-king.org/rockford/. Mailing Address: 517 Elm St., 61102. Rev. Canon Benjamin L. Coggeshall, Rector; Bro. Matthew O'Hora, Clerical Oblate.

8—ST. PATRICK (1919) [JC]
2505 School St., 61101. Tel: 815-965-9539; Email: stpatrick-rockford@rockforddiocese.org; Web: stpatrickrockford.org. Rev. Jhakson Garcia, Parochial Admin.
Catechesis Religious Program—Maria Magana, C.R.E. Students 210.

9—SS. PETER AND PAUL (1911) (Hispanic)
617 Lincoln Ave., 61102. Tel: 815-962-7171; Email: SSPeterandPaul-Rockford@RockfordDiocese.org.
Rev. Zbigniew Zajchowski, O.F.M.Conv., (Poland).
Catechesis Religious Program—Sylvia Escamilla, D.R.E.

10—ST. RITA (1914)
6254 Valley Knoll Dr., 61109-1898.
Tel: 815-398-0853; Fax: 815-397-7499; Email:

StRita-Rockford@RockfordDiocese.org; Web: www.stritarockford.org. Rev. Ervin Pio M. Caliente, Admin.; Deacons John Huntley; Joseph Achino.

School—St. Rita School, (Grades PreK-8), 6284 Valley Knoll Dr., 61109-1898. Tel: 815-398-3466; Fax: 815-398-6104; Email: stritaschool-rockford@rockforddiocese.org. Patrick Flanagan, Prin. Lay Teachers 13; Students 261.

Catechesis Religious Program—Tel: 815-398-6483; Email: DColloton@RockfordDiocese.org. Doug Colloton, C.R.E. Students 100.

11—ST. STANISLAUS KOSTKA (1912) (Polish)
201 Buckbee, 61104. Tel: 815-965-3913; Fax: 815-965-3915; Email: ststanislaus-rockford@rockforddiocese.org; Web: www.st-stanislaus.org. Rev. Mieczyslaw Wit, O.F.M.Conv.; Mrs. Margaret Borowski, Business Mgr.; Mrs. Mary Strand, Music Min.

Catechesis Religious Program—Email: church@st-stanislaus.org. Randee Hansen, D.R.E. Students 0.

OUTSIDE THE CITY OF ROCKFORD

ALBANY, WHITESIDE CO., ST. PATRICK (1948)
1201 N. Bluff St., Albany, 61230. Tel: 815-589-3542; Fax: 815-589-4915; Email: stpatrick-albany@rockforddiocese.org; Web: www.icspchurches.org. Mailing Address: 703 12th Ave., Fulton, 61252. Revs. Slawomir Zimodro, Parochial Admin.; Matthew J. Camaioni, Parochial Vicar.

Catechesis Religious Program—Mrs. Marie Currie, C.R.E. Combined with Immaculate Conception, Fulton Students 3.

ALGONQUIN, MCHENRY CO., ST. MARGARET MARY (1954) (Polish)
111 S. Hubbard St., Algonquin, 60102. Tel: 847-658-7625; Email: StMargaretMary-Algonquin@RockfordDiocese.org; Web: www.saintmargaretmary.org. Revs. Piotr Sarnicki, O.F.-M.Conv.; Witold Adamczyk, O.F.M.Conv., Parochial Vicar; Daniel P. Zdebik, O.F.M.Conv., Parochial Vicar; Deacons Howard Fischer; Donald Miller; Michael LeRoy; James McDonough; Robert Christopher Armstrong.

School—St. Margaret Mary School, (Grades PreK-8), 119 S. Hubbard St., Algonquin, 60102. Tel: 847-658-5313; Fax: 847-854-0501; Email: stmargaretmaryschool-algonquin@rockforddiocese.org. Brenna O'Hearn, Prin. Lay Teachers 26; Students 312.

Catechesis Religious Program—113 S. Hubbard St., Algonquin, 60102. Tel: 847-658-9339; Tel: 847-658-7881; Email: enelson@saintmargaretmary.org; Email: tchiappone@saintmargaretmary.org. 119 S. Hubbard St., Algonquin, 60102. Mrs. Ellie Nelson, D.R.E.; Mrs. Teresa Chiappone, Youth Min. Students 503.

AMBOY, LEE CO., ST. PATRICK (1857) [CEM]
32 N. Jones Ave., Amboy, 61310. Tel: 815-857-2315; Email: StPatrick-Amboy@RockfordDiocese.org; Web: www.stpatrickamboy.org. Rev. Timothy J. Draper; Deacon Kevin Prunty.

Catechesis Religious Program—Susan McCoy, C.R.E. Students 116.

APPLE RIVER, JO DAVIESS CO., ST. JOSEPH (1868) [CEM]
105 W. Webster St., Apple River, 61001. Tel: 815-745-2312; Fax: 815-745-2326; Email: stjoseph-appleriver@rockforddiocese.org. Mailing Address: P.O. Box 665, Warren, 61087. Rev. Andrew T. Skrobutt.
Res./Rectory: 608 E. Railroad St., Warren, 61087.

Catechesis Religious Program—Jan Bussan, D.R.E. Twinned with St. Ann, Warren. Students 0.

AURORA, KANE CO.

1—ANNUNCIATION OF THE BLESSED VIRGIN MARY (1875) [CEM]
1820 Church Rd., Aurora, 60505. Tel: 630-851-1436, Ext. 204; Email: AnnunciationBVM-Aurora@RockfordDiocese.org. Rev. Patrick S. Gillmeyer, O.S.B.; Deacons Michael Giblin; Kenneth Gay; Domenic Petitti.

School—Annunciation of the Blessed Virgin Mary School, (Grades K-8), 1840 Church Rd., Aurora, 60505. Tel: 630-851-4300; Fax: 630-851-4316; Email: annunciationschool-aurora@rockforddiocese.org. Jennifer Wardynski, Prin.; Michelle Sojka, Librarian; Barbara Tews, Librarian. Lay Teachers 10; Students 187.

Catechesis Religious Program—Email: mfletcher@rockforddiocese.org. Mr. Mark Fletcher, D.R.E. Students 195.

2—HOLY ANGELS (1892)
180 S. Russell Ave., Aurora, 60506. Tel: 630-897-1194; Fax: 630-897-1370; Email: holyangels-aurora@rockforddiocese.org; Web: www.holy-angels.org. Revs. Michael G. Lavan; Selvaraj Lucas, M.S.C., Parochial Vicar; Deacons Tim White; Tom Hawksworth; Jim Hall.
Res.: 720 Hardin Ave., Aurora, 60506-4997.

School—Holy Angels School, 720 Kensington Pl., Aurora, 60506. Tel: 630-897-3613; Fax: 630-897-8233; Email: holyangelsschool-aurora@rockforddiocese.org; Web: www.holyangelsschool.net. Mrs. Tonya Forbes, Prin. Clergy 3; Lay Teachers 33; Students 451.

Catechesis Religious Program—Tel: 630-897-1194, Ext. 156; Email: releducation@holy-angels.org. Rose Gatze, D.R.E.; Mimi Steinwart, D.R.E. Students 145.

3—ST. JOSEPH (1899) [CEM]
722 High St., P.O. Box 4395, Aurora, 60507. Tel: 630-844-3780; Fax: 630-844-1338; Email: stjoseph-aurora@rockforddiocese.org; Web: www.stjosephaurora.weconnect.com. Rev. Jerome L. Leake; Rev. Msgr. Robert J. Willhite, In Res., (Retired).
Res.: 405 St. Joseph Ave., Aurora, 60505.

School—St. Joseph School, 706 High St., Aurora, 60505. Tel: 630-844-3781; Fax: 630-844-3656; Email: stjosephschool-aurora@rockforddiocese.org. Ms. Nancy Coughlin, Prin. Lay Teachers 12; Students 144.

Catechesis Religious Program—Tel: 630-844-3782. Students 77.

4—ST. MARY (1851) [CEM] (Irish)
430 E. Downer Pl., Aurora, 60505-3475. Tel: 630-892-0480; Email: StMary-Aurora@rockforddiocese.org. 432 E. Downer Pl., Aurora, 60505-3475. Rev. Timothy Piasecki; Deacon Jose Falcon.

Catechesis Religious Program—Mrs. Mary Ann Bennett, D.R.E. Students 161.

5—ST. NICHOLAS (1862) [CEM] (Hispanic)
308 High St., Aurora, 60505. Tel: 630-898-8707; Email: stnicholas-aurora@rockforddiocese.org; Web: www.stnicholasaurora.org. Rev. Andres Salinas; Deacon Bruce Watermann.

Catechesis Religious Program—Sr. Irma Luna, D.R.E.

6—OUR LADY OF GOOD COUNSEL (1909)
620 S. Fifth St., Aurora, 60505. Tel: 630-851-1100; Email: olgc-aurora@rockforddiocese.org; Web: ourladyofgoodcounsel.net. Rev. Timothy P. Mulcahey, L.C.; Deacons Carlos Navarro; Ray Weaver.

Rectory—620 S. Fifth St., Aurora, 60505.

Catechesis Religious Program—Email: sr.maria.olgc@gmail.com. Sr. Maria Romero, D.R.E. Students 417.

7—ST. PETER (1929)
925 Sard Ave., Aurora, 60506. Tel: 630-896-6816; Email: stpeter-aurora@rockforddiocese.org; Web: www.stpeteraurorail.org. 915 Sard Ave., Aurora, 60506. Rev. Joachim B. Tyrtania; Deacon Carlos Navarro.

Catechesis Religious Program—Students 110.

8—ST. RITA OF CASCIA (1927)
750 Old Indian Trail Rd., Aurora, 60506. Tel: 630-892-5918; Email: strita-aurora@rockforddiocese.org; Web: www.saintritaofcascia.org. Revs. Oscar Cortes; Adalberto Sanchez; Deacons Ignacio Felix; Richard Martin; Luis Patino.

School—St. Rita of Cascia School, 770 Old Indian Trail Rd., Aurora, 60506. Tel: 630-892-0200; Fax: 630-892-4236; Email: stritaofcasciaschool-aurora@rockforddiocese.org. Ms. Elizabeth Faxon, Prin. Lay Teachers 18; Students 195.

Catechesis Religious Program—Tel: 630-892-9507; Fax: 630-264-7104. Rae Eigenhauser, D.R.E. Students 591.

9—SACRED HEART (1861) [CEM] (Hispanic)
125 N. State St., Aurora, 60505. Tel: 630-898-4165; Email: SacredHeart-Aurora@RockfordDiocese.org. Rev. Msgr. Arquimedes Vallejo, J.C.D., V.F.; Jocelyn Quiles, Bookkeeper.
Res.: 771 Fulton St., Aurora, 60505.

Catechesis Religious Program—755 Fulton St., Aurora, 60505. Students 600.

10—ST. THERESE OF JESUS (1925)
271 N. Farnsworth Ave., Aurora, 60505. Tel: 630-898-5422; Email: StTherese-Aurora@RockfordDiocese.org; Web: www.stojcc.org. Rev. Ernesto Odilio Caicedo, M.S.C.; Deacons Bruce M. Watermann, D.R.E.; Julio Rosado.

School—St. Therese of Jesus School, Now part of St. John Paul II Catholic Academy, South Campus, Aurora. 255 N. Farnsworth Ave., Aurora, 60505. Tel: 630-898-0620; Fax: 630-898-3087; Email: stthereseofjesusschool-aurora@rockforddiocese.org. Mr. Michael G. Neis, Prin. Lay Teachers 10; Students 135.

Catechesis Religious Program—Students 296.

BATAVIA, KANE CO., HOLY CROSS (1871) [JC]
2300 Main St., Batavia, 60510-7625. Tel: 630-879-4750; Email: holycross-batavia@rockforddiocese.org; Web: www.holycross-batavia.org. Revs. James W. Parker; Rico Paril; Romeo Pavino; Deacons Gregory Norris; Raymond J. Martin; Larry J. Motyka; Kenneth Ramsey.

Rectory—260 S. Deerpath Rd., Batavia, 60510-7625.

School—Holy Cross School, (Grades PreK-8), Tel: 630-593-5290; Email: holycrossschool-batavia@rockforddiocese.org; Web: www.holycrosscatholicschool.org. Mr. Michael Puttin, Prin. Clergy 1; Lay Teachers 20; Students 423.

Catechesis Religious Program— (2008)
Tel: 630-879-4751. Karen A. McQuillan, D.R.E.; Mr. Steve Johnson, Youth Min.; Patricia A. Roatch, Children's Min.; Tim Glemkowski, H.S. Youth Min. Students 862.

BELVIDERE, BOONE CO., ST. JAMES (1886) [CEM]
Mailing Address: 402 Church St., Belvidere, 61008. Tel: 815-547-6397; Fax: 815-547-0607; Email: stjames-belvidere@rockforddiocese.org; Web: www.stjamesbelvidere.org. Rev. Brian A. Geary; Deacons Steven Johnson; James D. Olson.
Res.: 554 S. Main St., Belvidere, 61008.

School—St. James School, (Grades K-8), 320 Logan Ave., Belvidere, 61008. Tel: 815-547-7633; Fax: 815-544-2294; Email: stjamesschool-belvidere@rockforddiocese.org. Dr. Kathleen Miller, Prin. Lay Teachers 10; Students 123.

Catechesis Religious Program—320 Logan Ave., Belvidere, 61008. Tel: 815-544-3698; Email: b.graybiel@stjamesbelvidere.org. Barbara Graybiel, D.R.E. Students 471.

BYRON, OGLE CO., ST. MARY (1895) [CEM]
226 E. 2nd St., P.O. Box 1070, Byron, 61010. Tel: 815-234-7431; Fax: 815-234-2133; Email: stmary-byron@rockforddiocese.org; Web: www.saintmaryinbyron.org. Rev. Howard C. Barch; Deacon Thomas Petit.
Res.: 3954 E. Mockingbird Ln., Byron, 61010.

Catechesis Religious Program—Email: beth@saintmaryinbyron.org. Joetta Hass, C.R.E.; Beth Hildreth, C.R.E. Students 200.

CARPENTERSVILLE, KANE CO., ST. MONICA (1957) (Hispanic)
90 N. Kennedy Dr., Carpentersville, 60110-1695. Tel: 847-428-2646; Fax: 847-428-1021; Email: stmonica-carpentersville@rockforddiocese.org. Revs. Josue Lara, Parochial Admin.; Manuel G. Gomez-Reza, Parochial Vicar; Deacon Dennis Garber.

Catechesis Religious Program—Tel: 847-428-7562. Velveth Garcia, D.R.E. Students 699.

CARY, MCHENRY CO., SS. PETER & PAUL (1904)
410 N. First St., Cary, 60013. Tel: 847-516-2636; Fax: 847-639-3474; Email: sspeterandpaul-cary@rockforddiocese.org; Web: www.peterpaulchurchcary.org. Revs. Jeremy A. Trowbridge, S.T.L.; Juan Arciniegas, Parochial Vicar; Timothy J. Seigel, Parochial Vicar; Deacons Howard Ganschow II; Michael Boyce; Michael O'Connor; Donald Siciliano; Kenneth Wasko.

School—SS. Peter & Paul School, 416 N. First St., Cary, 60013. Tel: 847-639-3041; Fax: 847-639-5329; Email: sspeterandpaulschool-cary@rockforddiocese.org. Ms. Carolyn Strong, Prin. Clergy 4; Lay Teachers 23; Students 325.

Catechesis Religious Program—Tel: 847-639-0414. Diana Gallagher, C.R.E.; Jennifer Lombrowski, Dir. Youth Ministry. Students 450.

CRYSTAL LAKE, MCHENRY CO.

1—ST. ELIZABETH ANN SETON (1978)
1023 McHenry Ave., Crystal Lake, 60014. Tel: 815-459-3033; Fax: 815-459-3040; Email: StElizabethAnnSeton-CrystalLake@RockfordDiocese.org. Very Rev. Brian D. Grady, V.F.; Rev. Colin Easton, Parochial Vicar; Deacons Kenneth Giacone; Richard Marcantonio.
Res.: 991 McHenry Ave., Crystal Lake, 60014.

Catechesis Religious Program—Tel: 815-459-3096. Vicky Serio, D.R.E.; Denise Ramis, Youth Min. Students 411.

2—ST. THOMAS THE APOSTLE (1881)
451 W. Terra Cotta Ave., Crystal Lake, 60014. Tel: 815-455-5400; Fax: 815-455-2733; Email: stthomas-crystallake@rockforddiocese.org; Web: www.stthomascl.church. Mailing Address: 272 King St., Crystal Lake, 60014. Revs. John R. Evans; Akan S. Simon, Parochial Vicar; William Tunarosa, Parochial Vicar; Jerome P. Koutnik, Parochial Vicar; Deacons David Deitz; Allen Bondi; Edward Morrison.
Res.: 200 Washington St., Crystal Lake, 60014.

School—St. Thomas the Apostle School, (Grades PreK-8), 265 King St., Crystal Lake, 60014. Tel: 815-459-0496; Fax: 815-459-0591; Web: www.stthomascl.org. Mrs. Gina Houston, Prin. Lay Teachers 26; Students 325.

Catechesis Religious Program—Tel: 815-455-9787; Email: ckolodzik@saintthomascatholicchurch.org. Charlotte Kolodzik, D.R.E. Students 734.

DEKALB, DEKALB CO.

1—CHRIST THE TEACHER (1963)
512 Normal Rd., DeKalb, 60115. Tel: 815-787-7770. Very Rev. Matthew J. McMorrow, S.T.L., V.F.; Rev. Kyle A. Manno, Parochial Vicar; Deacon James Dombek

Legal Name: Christ the Teacher, University Parish of Northern Illinois University

Catechesis Religious Program—Email: newmanniudre@gmail.com. Mrs. Cheryl Lehman, D.R.E. Students 301.

2—ST. MARY (1861) [CEM]
329 Pine St., DeKalb, 60115.
Tel: 815-758-5432, Ext. 100; Email: StMary-DeKalb@RockfordDiocese.org; Web: www.stmarydekalb.org. Mailing Address: 302 Fisk Ave., DeKalb, 60115. Revs. Dean E. Russell; Darwin Flores, In Res.; Anthony Vu Khac Long, In Res.
Res.: 321 Pine St., DeKalb, 60115.
School—St. Mary School, 210 Gurler Rd., DeKalb, 60115. Tel: 815-756-7905; Fax: 815-758-1459; Email: stmaryschool-dekalb@rockforddiocese.org. Roseann Feldman, Prin. Lay Teachers 11; Students 204.
Catechesis Religious Program—Annalisa McMaster, C.R.E. Students 100.

DIXON, LEE CO.
1—ST. ANNE (1928)
1104 N. Brinton Ave., Dixon, 61021.
Tel: 815-288-3131; Email: stanne-dixon@rockforddiocese.org; Web: www.stanneparishdixon.org. Rev. Thomas J. Doyle; Deacon Joseph Achino; Ms. Karen Didier, Business Mgr.; Virginia Sollars, Sec.
School—St. Anne School, (Grades PreK-8), 1112 N. Brinton Ave., Dixon, 61021. Tel: 815-288-5619; Fax: 815-288-5820; Email: stanneschool-dixon@rockforddiocese.org; Web: www.stanneschooldixon.org. Kathleen Howard, Prin. Lay Teachers 15; Students 109.
Catechesis Religious Program—(Grades K-8), Tel: 815-288-3131, Ext. 105; Email: evangelizestanne@gmail.com. Piper Grazulis, D.R.E. Students 35.
2—ST. PATRICK (1854)
612 Highland Ave., Dixon, 61021. Tel: 815-284-7719; Fax: 815-284-4758; Email: stpatrick-dixon@rockforddiocese.org; Web: www.stpatrickdixon.org. Rev. Keith D. Romke; Deacons Sam Berard; Terry Wagner; Rhonda Jahn, Business Mgr.; Rita VanWassenhove, Liturgy Dir.; Kara Grot, Sec.
School—St. Mary Elementary & Junior High, (Grades PreK-8), 704 S. Peoria Ave., Dixon, 61021. Tel: 815-284-6986; Fax: 815-284-6905; Email: stmaryschool-dixon@rockforddiocese.org; Web: www.stmarysdixon.org. Mrs. Jean Spohn, Prin.; Caroline Toppert, Business Mgr.; Rev. Colin Easton, Parochial Vicar; Michele Blair, Sec. Lay Teachers 14; Students 192.
Catechesis Religious Program—Sarah Campbell, C.R.E. Students 63; Catechists 9.

DUNDEE, KANE CO., ST. CATHERINE OF SIENA (1912)
845 W. Main St., West Dundee, 60118.
Tel: 847-426-2217; Email: StCatherine-Dundee@RockfordDiocese.org. Revs. Matthew M. DeBlock; John Gow, Parochial Vicar; Deacons William Whitehead Jr.; Steven Fox; Hank Schmalen.
School—St. Catherine of Siena School, (Grades PreK-8), c/o St. Catherine of Siena Parish, 845 W. Main St., West Dundee, 60118. Tel: 847-426-4808; Email: stcatherineofsienaschool-dundee@rockforddiocese.org; Web: www.st-cath.net. Colleen Cannon, Prin. Lay Teachers 15; Students 204.
Catechesis Religious Program—Email: dschmalen@RockfordDiocese.org. Jessica Cranston, Youth Min. Students 460.
Mission—St. Mary, [CEM] 10 Matteson Rd., Gilberts, 60136.

DURAND, WINNEBAGO CO., ST. MARY (1862) [CEM 2] (Irish)
606 W. Main St., Durand, 61024. Tel: 815-248-2490; Fax: 815-248-9100; Email: stmary-durand@rockforddiocese.org; Web: www.stmarystpatrick.org. Very Rev. Matthew M. Bergschneider, J.C.L.; Deacons Richard Mulcahey; Steven Pulkrabek.
Catechesis Religious Program—Terry Cravens, C.R.E. Students 128.
Mission—St. Patrick, [CEM] 5333 N. Irish Grove Rd., Davis, 61019.

EAST DUBUQUE, JO DAVIESS CO., ST. MARY (1868) [JC]
170 Montgomery Ave., East Dubuque, 61025.
Tel: 815-747-3221; Email: StMary-EastDubuque@RockfordDiocese.org. Rev. Dean M. Smith; Deacons Douglas Kremer; Anthony Keppler.
School—St. Mary School, 701 Rte. 35 N., East Dubuque, 61025. Tel: 815-747-3010; Fax: 815-747-6188; Email: stmaryschool-eastdubuque@rockforddiocese.org; Web: www.stmary-ed.org. Angela Jones, Prin. Lay Teachers 5; Students 55.
Catechesis Religious Program—Kelly Puls, C.R.E. Students 93.

ELBURN, KANE CO., ST. GALL (1870) [CEM] (Irish)
43W885 Hughes Rd., Elburn, 60119.
Tel: 630-365-6030; Email: StGall-Elburn@RockfordDiocese.org. Rev. Christopher P. Di Tomo. St. Gall built and moved to a new location in 2017.
Catechesis Religious Program—Donna Doherty, D.R.E. Students 176.

ELGIN, KANE CO.
1—ST. JOSEPH (1887) (German—Spanish)
272 Division St., Elgin, 60120. Tel: 847-931-2800; Fax: 847-931-2810; Email: stjoseph-elgin@RockfordDiocese.org; Web: www.stjosephelgin.org. Mailing Address: 33 N. Geneva St., Elgin, 60120. Revs. Jesus Dominguez; Yovanny Dorado, Parochial Vicar; Eliserio Palencia, Parochial Vicar; Deacon Francisco Fausto; Sr. Herlinda Rodriguez, M.R.F., Youth Min.
School—St. Joseph School, 274 Division St., Elgin, 60120. Tel: 847-931-2804; Fax: 847-931-2811; Email: stjosephschool-elgin@rockforddiocese.org. Dr. Peter Trumblay, Prin. Lay Teachers 10; Students 180.
Catechesis Religious Program—Tel: 847-931-2808. Students 1,108.
2—ST. LAURENCE (1929)
225 Jewett St., Elgin, 60123. Tel: 847-468-6900; Email: StLaurence-Elgin@RockfordDiocese.org. Mailing Address: 565 Standish St., Elgin, 60123. Revs. Robert J. Camacho, In Res., (Retired); Andrew T. Mulcahey; Deacons Robert Plazewski; Joe Bermea.
Res.: 226 Orchard St., Elgin, 60123.
School—St. Laurence School, (Grades PreK-8), 572 Standish St., Elgin, 60123. Tel: 847-468-6100; Fax: 847-468-6104; Email: stlaurenceschool-elgin@rockforddiocese.org. Mrs. Wendy Kelly, Prin. Clergy 1; Lay Teachers 11; Students 114.
Catechesis Religious Program—Email: office@stlaurencechurchelgin.com. Agnes Mozdzen, Bookkeeper; Belinda Bermea, Sec. Students 105.
3—ST. MARY (1851)
397 Fulton St., Elgin, 60120. Tel: 847-888-2828; Email: StMary-Elgin@RockfordDiocese.org; Web: www.stmaryelgin.org. Revs. Christopher J. Kuhn; Jorge H. Loaiza, Parochial Vicar; Deacons Henry Orlik; Loc Nguyen; David Mattoon.
Res.: 390 Fulton St., Elgin, 60120. Email: CKuhn@RockfordDiocese.org.
School—St. Mary School, (Grades PreK-8), 103 S. Gifford St., Elgin, 60120. Tel: 847-695-6609; Fax: 847-695-6623; Email: stmaryschool-elgin@rockforddiocese.org. Mr. Michael G. Neis, Prin. Lay Teachers 12; Students 188.
Catechesis Religious Program—Tel: 847-888-2718. Students 329.
4—ST. THOMAS MORE (1959) [JC]
215 Thomas More Dr., Elgin, 60123.
Tel: 847-888-1682; Fax: 847-888-3198; Email: stthomasmore-elgin@RockfordDiocese.org; Web: www.stthomasmorechurch.org. Rev. Richard A. Rosinski; Deacons Jack Roder; Gregory Stevens.
School—St. Thomas More School, (Grades PreK-8), 1625 W. Highland Ave., Elgin, 60123.
Tel: 847-742-3959; Fax: 847-931-1066; Email: stthomasmoreschool-elgin@rockforddiocese.org; Web: www.stmcentral.org. Denise Ostrem, Librarian; Sonja Keane, Prin. Lay Teachers 16; Students 177.
Catechesis Religious Program—Tel: 847-888-4887; Email: mtack@rockforddiocese.org. Mrs. Michelle Tack, D.R.E. Students 508.

ELIZABETH, JO DAVIESS CO., ST. MARY (1886) [CEM]
112 E. Washington St., P.O. Box 246, Elizabeth, 61028. Tel: 815-858-3422; Email: stmary-elizabeth@rockforddiocese.org; Web: www.stmaryelizabethil.org. Revs. Dennis M. Morrissy; Stanislaw Kos, In Res., (Retired); Ms. Norma Schwirtz, D.R.E.; Ms. Marilyn Gollmer, Sec.

ERIE, WHITESIDE CO., ST. AMBROSE (1936)
5th & Main St., P.O. Box 746, Erie, 61250.
Tel: 309-659-2781; Fax: 815-537-2077; Email: stambrose-erie@rockforddiocese.org. Rev. Antoni Kretowicz, (Poland).
Catechesis Religious Program—Cindy Weaver, D.R.E. Students 12.

FREEPORT, STEPHENSON CO.
1—ST. CATHERINE, Closed. For inquiries for parish records contact the chancery.
2—ST. JOSEPH (1862) [CEM] (German)
229 W. Washington Pl., Freeport, 61032.
Tel: 815-232-8271; Email: stjoseph-freeport@rockforddiocese.org. Rev. Timothy J. Barr.
School—Aquin Catholic Elementary School, 202 W. Pleasant St., Freeport, 61032. Tel: 815-232-6416; Email: aquinelementaryschool-freeport@rockforddiocese.org. Rosemarie Brubaker, Supt.; Jeremy Keesee, Prin. Lay Teachers 25; Students 84.
3—ST. MARY (1846) [CEM]
704 S. State Ave., Freeport, 61032. Tel: 815-232-8271; Email: stmary-freeport@rockforddiocese.org. Mailing Address: 229 Washington Place, Freeport, 61032. Revs. Timothy J. Barr; Diego F. Ospina, (In Res.); Deacon Paul Ranney.
4—ST. THOMAS AQUINAS (1921)
1400 Kiwanis Dr., Freeport, 61032.
Tel: 815-232-3225; Email: StThomasAquinas-Freeport@RockfordDiocese.org; Web: www.stthomasfreeport.org. Very Rev. Kenneth J. Anderson, V.F.; Deacons H. Donald Brunette; Richard Dinneen; Vincent Drees; Stephen Pospischil; Kim Hemesath.
Catechesis Religious Program—Marie Dinneen, C.R.E.; Julie Dorsey, C.R.E. Students 48.

FULTON, WHITESIDE CO., IMMACULATE CONCEPTION (1863)
703 12th Ave., Fulton, 61252. Tel: 815-589-3542; Fax: 815-589-4915; Email: ImmaculateConception-Fulton@RockfordDiocese.org; Web: www.icspchurches.org. Revs. Slawomir Zimodro, Admin.; Matthew J. Camaioni, Parochial Vicar.
Catechesis Religious Program—Mrs. Marie Currie, D.R.E. Students 34.

GALENA, JO DAVIESS CO.
1—ST. MARY (1850) [CEM] (German)
406 Franklin St., Galena, 61036. Tel: 815-777-2053; Email: stmary-galena@rockforddiocese.org; Web: www.catholicgalena.com. 231 S. Bench St., Galena, 61036. Rev. David J. Reese; Deacon Joseph Achino.
Catechesis Religious Program—Email: re@catholicgalena.com. Heidi O'Shea, C.R.E./D.R.E. Students 0.
2—ST. MICHAEL (1832) [CEM] (Irish)
227 S. Bench St., Galena, 61036. Tel: 815-777-2053; Email: stmichael-galena@rockforddiocese.org; Web: www.catholicgalena.com. 231 S. Bench St., Galena, 61036. Rev. David J. Reese; Deacon Joseph Achino.
Res.: 227 S. Bench St., Galena, 61036.
Catechesis Religious Program—c/o St. Mary's, 406 Franklin St., Galena, 61036. Heidi O'Shea, D.R.E./C.R.E. Students 0.

GENEVA, KANE CO., ST. PETER (1911) [JC]
1891 Kaneville Rd., Geneva, 60134.
Tel: 630-232-0124; Email: StPeter-Geneva@RockfordDiocese.org; Web: www.stpeterchurch.com. Revs. Jonathan P. Bakkelund, S.T.L.; Adrian Ladines; Deacons Gregory D'Anna; Dennis White.
Res.: 1771 Kaneville Rd., Geneva, 60134.
Tel: 630-232-0124.
School—St. Peter School, (Grades PreK-8), 1881 Kaneville Rd., Geneva, 60134. Tel: 630-232-0476; Fax: 630-262-0308; Email: stpeterschool-geneva@rockforddiocese.org; Web: www.stpeterrockets.org. Becky Ward, Prin. Lay Teachers 18; Students 200; Staff 2.
Catechesis Religious Program—(Grades PreSchool-8), Email: re.director@stpetergeneva.org. Miss Nicole Billapando, D.R.E. Students 683.

GENOA, DEKALB CO., ST. CATHERINE OF GENOA (1912) [CEM]
340 S. Stott St., Genoa, 60135. Tel: 815-784-2355; Email: stcatherine-genoa@rockforddiocese.org. Rev. Zdzislaw F. Wawryszuk; Deacon William A. Stankevitz.
Catechesis Religious Program—Email: ReligiousEd@st-catherine-genoa.org. Alaisa Emmens, D.R.E./DYM. Students 0.

GILBERTS, KANE CO., ST. MARY'S OF GILBERTS, [CEM]
10 Matteson Rd., Gilberts, 60136. Tel: 847-426-2217; Fax: 847-426-1130; Email: stmary-gilberts@rockforddiocese.org. Mailing Address: 845 W. Main St., 60118. Revs. Matthew M. DeBlock; John Gow, Parochial Vicar; Deacons William Whitehead Jr.; Steven Fox; Hank Schmalen.

HAMPSHIRE, KANE CO., ST. CHARLES BORROMEO (1878) [CEM]
Mailing Address: 297 E. Jefferson Ave., Hampshire, 60140-7646. Tel: 847-683-2391; Fax: 847-683-2396; Email: stcharlesborromeo-hampshire@rockforddiocese.org; Web: www.scbparish.org. Rev. Sylvester A. Nnaso; Deacons John Nelson; Jerome Ryndak; James Ward.
Res.: 309 Jake Ln., Hampshire, 60140.
School—St. Charles Borromeo School, (Grades PreK-8), 288 E. Jefferson Ave., Hampshire, 60140.
Tel: 847-683-3450; Fax: 847-683-3209; Email: stcharlesborromeoschool-hampshire@rockforddiocese.org. Maureen Jackson, Prin. Lay Teachers 15; Students 150.
Catechesis Religious Program—Tel: 847-683-1536; Email: JOlson@RockfordDiocese.org. Jane Olson, D.R.E. Students 135.

HANOVER, JO DAVIESS CO., ST. JOHN THE EVANGELIST (1925)
103 Savanna Rd., Hanover, 61041. Tel: 815-591-2258; Fax: 815-591-2259; Email: stjohntheevangelist-hanover@rockforddiocese.org. Rev. Dennis M. Morrissy; Mrs. Karen Harkness, Sec.; Laura Kuzniar, C.R.E.

HARMON, LEE CO., ST. FLANNEN (1898) [CEM] (Irish)
213 S. Second St., Harmon, 61042. Tel: 815-857-2670; Email: StFlannen-Harmon@RockfordDiocese.org. Mailing Address: 32 N. Jones Ave., Amboy, 61310. Rev. Timothy J. Draper.
Catechesis Religious Program—Susan McCoy, C.R.E. Twinned with St. Patrick, Amboy.

HARTLAND, MCHENRY CO., ST. PATRICK (1837) [CEM]
15012 St. Patrick Rd., Hartland, 60098.
Tel: 815-338-7883; Email: StPatrick-

Hartland@RockfordDiocese.org. Rev. Burt H. Absalon; Deacon Joseph Kayser.
Catechesis Religious Program—Students 27.
HARVARD, MCHENRY CO., ST. JOSEPH (1866) [CEM]
206 E. Front St., Harvard, 60033. Tel: 815-943-6406; Email: StJoseph-Harvard@RockfordDiocese.org; Web: stjosephharvard.org. 101 Church St., Harvard, 60033. Revs. Steven P. Clarke; Carlos A. Monsalve; Deacons Anthony Koss; Michael Keane.
Catechesis Religious Program—Tel: 815-943-1644. Mrs. Kelly Sergent, D.R.E. Students 283.
HUNTLEY, MCHENRY CO., ST. MARY (1873) [CEM]
10307 Dundee Rd., Huntley, 60142.
Tel: 847-669-3137; Fax: 847-669-3138; Email: StMary-Huntley@RockfordDiocese.org; Web: www.stmaryhuntley.org. Revs. Max J. Striedl; Ervin Pio M. Caliente, Parochial Vicar; Sean Grismer, Parochial Vicar; Deacons Policarpo Jimenez; Anthony Schubert; John A. McPhee; Louis Farinella; George Coltman; Christopher Lincoln; Frank Englert; James Conrey.
Catechesis Religious Program—Tel: 847-669-5953. Roberta Christian, D.R.E. Students 1,382.
JOHNSBURG, MCHENRY CO., ST. JOHN THE BAPTIST (1841) [CEM]
2302 W. Church St., Johnsburg, 60051.
Tel: 815-385-1477; Email: StJohntheBaptist-Johnsburg@RockfordDiocese.org; Web: www.stjohnsjohnsburg.org. Rev. Jacek Junak, C.R.; Deacons Jerry Giessinger; David Gillespie.
School—St. John the Baptist School, (Grades PreK-5), 2304 W. Church St., Johnsburg, 60051.
Tel: 815-385-3959; Fax: 815-363-3337; Email: stjohnthebaptistschool-johnsburg@rockforddiocese.org. Brenda Baldassano, Prin. Lay Teachers 6; Students 58.
Catechesis Religious Program—Ellie Nusser, D.R.E. Students 163.
LEE, LEE CO., ST. JAMES (1878) [CEM 2]
221 W. Kirke Gate, P.O. Box 100, Lee, 60530.
Tel: 815-824-2053; Fax: 815-824-2043; Email: stjames-lee@rockforddiocese.org; Web: www.saintjamesinlee.org. Rev. Bonaventure Okoro, (Nigeria); Jean Henning, Business Mgr.
Res.: 321 S. Viking Vie, Lee, 60530.
Tel: 815-824-2004.
Catechesis Religious Program—Melissa Muetze, C.R.E. Students 37.
LENA, STEPHENSON CO., ST. JOSEPH (1870) [CEM]
Mailing Address: 410 W. Lena St., Lena, 61048.
Tel: 815-369-2810; Fax: 815-369-9137; Email: stjoseph-lena@rockforddiocese.org. Rev. Andrew T. Skrobutt.
Res.: 416 W. Lena St., Lena, 61048.
Catechesis Religious Program—Teresa Brown, C.R.E. Students 52.
LOVES PARK, WINNEBAGO CO., ST. BRIDGET (1946)
600 Clifford Ave., Loves Park, 61111.
Tel: 815-633-6311; Fax: 815-633-6314; Email: parish@stbridgetlovespark.org. Rev. Msgr. Daniel J. Deutsch; Revs. Ryan B. Browning, S.T.L., Parochial Vicar; John P. McNamara, Parochial Vicar; Deacons Philip Abel; William Riseley; Jovie Reyes; Richard Broderick; John Gibson.
School—St. Bridget School, (Grades PreK-8), 604 Clifford Ave., Loves Park, 61111. Tel: 815-633-8255; Fax: 815-633-5847; Email: stbridgetschool-lovespark@rockforddiocese.org; Web: www.stbridgetlovespark.org. Mrs. Mary Toldo, Prin.; Mrs. Linda Lynch, Librarian. Clergy 1; Lay Teachers 24; Religious 1; Students 374.
Catechesis Religious Program—Mr. Nick Frank, Youth Min. Students 290.
MAPLE PARK, DEKALB CO., ST. MARY (1850) [CEM 2]
123 S. County Line Rd., P.O. Box 70, Maple Park, 60151-0070. Tel: 815-827-3205; Email: StMary-MaplePark@RockfordDiocese.org; Web: www.stmarymaplepark.org. Rev. Ariel A. Valencia, Parochial Admin.; Rev. Msgr. Thomas L. Dzielak, S.T.L., In Res., (Retired); Deacon Gregory Urban.
Novak Center—211 S. County Line Rd., P.O. Box 70, Maple Park, 60151-0070.
Catechesis Religious Program—Sarah Poynton, C.R.E. Students 72.
MARENGO, MCHENRY CO., SACRED HEART (1902) [CEM]
323 N. Taylor St., Marengo, 60152.
Tel: 815-568-7878; Fax: 815-568-7929; Email: sacredheart-marengo@RockfordDiocese.org; Web: www.sacredheartmarengo.org. Rev. William R. Antillon; Deacon Robert Anchor.
Catechesis Religious Program—Tel: 815-568-6230; Email: DSakowski@RockfordDiocese.org. Mrs. Debbie Sakowski, D.R.E. Students 179.
MAYTOWN, LEE CO., ST. PATRICK (1840) [CEM] [JC2]
1336 Maytown Rd., Amboy, 61310. Tel: 815-849-5412 ; Fax: 815-849-5412; Email: stpatrick-maytown@rockforddiocese.org. Mailing Address: P.O. Box 80, Sublette, 61367. Rev. Randy J. Fronek.
Catechesis Religious Program—Teresa Machen, C.R.E. Held at our Lady of Perpetual Help, Sublette. Students 8.
MCHENRY, MCHENRY CO.
1—CHURCH OF HOLY APOSTLES (1989) [CEM]
5211 W. Bull Valley Rd., McHenry, 60050.
Tel: 815-385-5673; Fax: 815-385-6045; Email: holyapostles-mchenry@RockfordDiocese.org; Web: www.thechurchofholyapostles.org. Revs. Paul C. White; Johnson Lopez, Parochial Vicar; Deacons Joseph Phelan; Curtis Fiedler; Daniel Krey; Craig Robinson; Daniel Torres Paredes; Mark Kinnare.
Catechesis Religious Program—John Jelinek, D.R.E. Students 470.
2—ST. MARY (1894) [CEM] (German)
1401 N. Richmond Rd., McHenry, 60050.
Tel: 815-385-0024; Email: StMary-McHenry@RockfordDiocese.org; Web: www.stmarymchenryil.org. 1407 N. Richmond Rd., McHenry, 60050. Rev. David M. Austin; Barbara Russell, Business Mgr.; Celeste Mann, Liturgy Dir.; Mary Schneider, Sec.
School—Montini-Middle Grades, 1405 N. Richmond Rd., McHenry, 60050. Tel: 815-385-1022;
Fax: 815-363-7536; Email: montinimiddleschool-mchenry@rockforddiocese.org. Mr. Michael J. Shukis, Prin. Consolidated with St. Patrick and Church of Holy Apostles. Lay Teachers 10; Students 98.
Catechesis Religious Program—Tel: 815-385-7809; Email: tmiller@rockforddiocese.org. Students 29.
3—ST. PATRICK CHURCH (1840) [CEM 2] (Irish)
Mailing Address: 3500 W. Washington St., McHenry, 60050. Tel: 815-385-0025; Fax: 815-385-0861; Email: stpatrick-mchenry@rockforddiocese.org; Web: www.stpatrickmchenry.org. Rev. Godwin Nsikan-Ubom Asuquo; Deacon Dennis Holian.
Res.: 3425 W. Washington St., McHenry, 60050.
School—Montini Catholic School, (Grades PreK-3), c/o St. Patrick Church, 3504 W. Washington St., McHenry, 60050. Tel: 815-385-5380; Email: montinischool-mchenry@rockforddiocese.org; Web: www.montinischool.com. Lay Teachers 6; Students 132.
Catechesis Religious Program—Email: bcurry@stpatrickmchenry.org. Bonnie Curry, D.R.E. Students 112.
MENOMINEE, JO DAVIESS CO., NATIVITY OF THE BLESSED VIRGIN MARY (1864) [CEM] (German)
15406 W. Creek Valley Rd., East Dubuque, 61025.
Tel: 815-747-3670; Fax: 815-747-2050; Email: NativityBVM-Menominee@RockfordDiocese.org; Web: www.stmaryedbq.org. Rev. Dean M. Smith; Deacons Douglas Kremer; Anthony Keppler.
Res.: 170 Montgomery Ave., East Dubuque, 61025.
Tel: 815-986-9608.
Catechesis Religious Program—Kelly Puls, D.R.E. (at St. Marys, East Debuque).
MORRISON, WHITESIDE CO., ST. MARY (1904)
13320 Garden Plain Rd., Morrison, 61270.
Tel: 815-772-4890; Email: StMary-Morrison@RockfordDiocese.org; Web: www.stmarymorrison.org. Rev. Slawomir Zimodro.
Res.: 611 Greenwood Dr., Morrison, 61270.
Catechesis Religious Program—Shayne Prange, C.R.E. Students 21.
MOUNT CARROLL, CARROLL CO., SS. JOHN AND CATHERINE (1923) Attended by Savanna.
314 S. Main St., P.O. Box 193, Mount Carroll, 61053.
Tel: 815-244-1835; Email: stjccatholic@gmail.com. Rev. Moises A. Apostol, Parochial Admin.
Catechesis Religious Program—Marlene Muscha-Taylor, C.R.E. Students 10.
NORTH AURORA, KANE CO., BLESSED SACRAMENT CATHOLIC CHURCH (1970)
801 Oak St., North Aurora, 60542-1063.
Tel: 630-897-1029; Fax: 630-897-1062; Email: blessedsacrament-northaurora@rockforddiocese.org; Web: blessedsacrament-na.org. Rev. Max Lasrado.
Catechesis Religious Program—Email: re@blessedsacrament-na.org. Melissa Heinen, C.R.E. Students 129.
OREGON, OGLE CO., ST. MARY (1885) [CEM]
301 N. 4th St., Oregon, 61061. Tel: 815-732-7383;
Fax: 815-732-4742; Email: stmary-oregon@rockforddiocese.org. Mailing Address: 881 Mongan Dr., Oregon, 61061. Rev. Joseph P. Naill, M.A.; Deacons John Ley; Ronald Abramowicz.
Catechesis Religious Program—Students 66.
PECATONICA, WINNEBAGO CO., ST. MARY (1872) [CEM] (Irish—German)
126 W. Fifth St., P.O. Box 656, Pecatonica, 61063-0656. Tel: 815-239-1271. Rev. Joseph F. Jaskierny, J.C.L.; Deacon Warren LaMont.
Catechesis Religious Program—Students 93.
POLO, OGLE CO., ST. MARY CHURCH (1854) [CEM] [JC]
211 N. Franklin Ave., Polo, 61064. Tel: 815-946-2535 ; Email: stmary-polo@rockforddiocese.org; Web: www.stmaryop.org. Rev. Joseph P. Naill, M.A.; Deacons Ronald Abramowicz; John Ley.
Catechesis Religious Program—Students 15.
PROPHETSTOWN, WHITESIDE CO., ST. CATHERINE (1917)
308 E. Third St., Prophetstown, 61277.
Tel: 815-537-2077; Email: StCatherine-Prophetstown@RockfordDiocese.org. Rev. Antoni Kretowicz, (Poland).
Catechesis Religious Program—Tel: 815-499-8887. Lori Border, C.R.E. (Attended at St. Ambrose).
RICHMOND, MCHENRY CO., ST. JOSEPH (1899) [CEM] (German)
10519 Main St., Richmond, 60071. Tel: 815-678-7421 ; Fax: 815-678-6961; Email: stjoseph-richmond@rockforddiocese.org; Web: stjosephrichmondil.weconnect.com. Rev. Msgr. Martin G. Heinz; Deacons Albert Dietz; Norman Kocol.
Catechesis Religious Program—Tel: 815-678-4720. Lisa Sachs, C.R.E. Students 48.
ROCHELLE, OGLE CO., ST. PATRICK (1868) [CEM]
244 Kelley Dr., P.O. Box 329, Rochelle, 61068.
Tel: 815-562-2370; Fax: 815-562-5250; Email: stpatrick-rochelle@rockforddiocese.org; Web: www.stpatricksrochelle.com. Rev. Ruben Herrera; Deacons George Schramm; Fermin Garcia.
Res.: 250 Kelley Dr., Rochelle, 61068.
Catechesis Religious Program—903 Caron Rd., Rochelle, 61068. Tel: 815-561-0079. Kalah Williams, D.R.E. Students 262.
ROCK FALLS, WHITESIDE CO., ST. ANDREW (1950) [JC]
708 10th Ave., Rock Falls, 61071. Tel: 815-625-4508; Email: standrew-rockfalls@rockforddiocese.org. Rev. Richard M. Russo.
School—St. Andrew School, (Grades PreK-8), 701 11th Ave., Rock Falls, 61071. Tel: 815-625-1456;
Fax: 815-625-1724; Email: standewschool-rockfalls@rockforddiocese.org. Deacon Mr. William Lemmer, Prin. Lay Teachers 10; Students 125.
Catechesis Religious Program—701 11th Ave., Rock Falls, 61071. Tel: 815-716-8134; Email: bzdonsm@gmail.com. Sr. Marcianne Bzdon, S.S.N.D., D.R.E. Students 0.
ROSCOE, WINNEBAGO CO., CHURCH OF THE HOLY SPIRIT (1980)
5637 Broad St., P.O. Box 478, Roscoe, 61073.
Tel: 815-623-6930; Fax: 815-623-1890; Email: holyspirit-roscoe@rockforddiocese.org. Rev. Steven M. Sabo.
Catechesis Religious Program—Kate Elliot, D.R.E. Students 30.
SAINT CHARLES, KANE CO.
1—ST. JOHN NEUMANN (1977)
2900 E. Main St., St. Charles, 60174.
Tel: 630-377-2797; Email: StJohnNeumann-StCharles@RockfordDiocese.org. Revs. David A. Peck; Ma Carlos Datu Saligumba, S.O.L.T., Parochial Vicar; Deacons Tom Elms; Paul Iwanski; Ronald Williams; Michael Monteleone; Ray Mills.
Catechesis Religious Program—Tel: 630-377-2803; Email: tstahl@RockfordDiocese.org. Therese Stahl, D.R.E.; Eric Groth, H.S. Youth Min.; Becky Groth, H.S. Youth Min. Students 555.
2—ST. PATRICK (1851)
6N491 Crane Rd., St. Charles, 60175.
Tel: 630-338-8000; Fax: 630-338-8008; Email: StPatrick-StCharles@RockfordDiocese.org; Web: www.stpatrickparish.org. Mailing Address: 6N487 Crane Rd., St. Charles, 60175. Rev. Msgr. Stephen J. Knox, S.T.L., V.F.; Revs. Jorge H. Loaiza, Parochial Vicar; Jhonatan Sarmiento, Parochial Vicar; Robert Gonnella, Parochial Vicar; Deacons James Mellin; Michael Smith; David Stowell.
Church (downtown): 400 Cedar St., St. Charles, 60174.
Schools—Preschool—(Grades PreK-PreK), (Extended Day Care) 118 N. Fifth St., St. Charles, 60174. Tel: 630-338-8200; Fax: 630-338-8208; Email: vday@stpatrickparish.org. Veronica Day, Dir. Lay Teachers 8; Students 192.
St. Patrick School, 787 Crane Rd, St. Charles, 60175.
Tel: 630-338-8100; Fax: 630-338-8108; Email: stpatrickschool-stcharles@rockforddiocese.org. Lisa Brown, Prin. Lay Teachers 28; Students 500.
Catechesis Religious Program—Tel: 630-338-8164;
Tel: 630-338-8165; Email: jryndak@rockforddiocese.org; Email: apoziombka@stpatrickparish.org. Alyce Poziombka, D.R.E.; Deacon Jerome Ryndak, D.R.E. Students 1,238.
SANDWICH, DEKALB CO., ST. PAUL THE APOSTLE (1910) [CEM]
340 W. Arnold Rd., Sandwich, 60548.
Tel: 815-786-9266; Email: stpaul-sandwich@rockforddiocese.org; Web: Saintpaulscc.net. Rev. Bernard J. Sehr.
Rectory—505 W. Lisbon St., Sandwich, 60548.
Catechesis Religious Program—Tel: 815-786-2004. Students 68.
SAVANNA, CARROLL CO., ST. JOHN THE BAPTIST (1884) [CEM]
318 Chicago Ave., Savanna, 61074.
Tel: 815-273-3961; Email: StJohntheBaptist-Savanna@RockfordDiocese.org. Rev. Moises A. Apostol, Parochial Admin.
Catechesis Religious Program—Mimi Rucobo, C.R.E. Students 32.
SCALES MOUND, JO DAVIESS CO., HOLY TRINITY (1863) [CEM 2]

231 S. Bench St., Galena, 61036. Rev. David J. Reese; Deacon Joseph Achino.
Catechesis Religious Program—Tel: 815-275-3907. Carol Bilgri, C.R.E. Students 0.

SHANNON, CARROLL CO., ST. WENDELIN (1870) [CEM]
18 S. Linn St., P.O. Box 23, Shannon, 61078.
Tel: 815-864-2548; Fax: 815-864-2729; Email: stwendelin-shannon@rockforddiocese.org; Web: www.saintwen.org. Rev. Michael J. Bolger.
Catechesis Religious Program—Students 35.

SOMONAUK, DEKALB CO., ST. JOHN THE BAPTIST (1865) [CEM]
320 S. Depot St., Somonauk, 60552-0276.
Tel: 815-498-2010; Fax: 815-498-2770; Email: stjohnthebaptist-somonauk@rockforddiocese.org; Web: www.stjbsom.org. P.O. Box 276, Somonauk, 60552. Rev. Kevin M. Butler; Deacon Armando Regalado, D.R.E.
Catechesis Religious Program—Tel: 815-498-2627. Carol Shelton, D.R.E. Students 91.

SOUTH BELOIT, WINNEBAGO CO., ST. PETER (1909)
620 Blackhawk Blvd., South Beloit, 61080.
Tel: 815-525-3400; Fax: 815-525-3409; Email: stpeter-sbeloit@rockforddiocese.org; Web: st-peter-church.com. 325 Oak Grove Ave., South Beloit, 61080. Revs. Steven Sabo; Robert J. McClellan, Parochial Vicar; Deacon Ignacio Badillo.
School—St. Peter School, 320 Elmwood Ave., South Beloit, 61080. Tel: 815-525-3400; Fax: 779-475-0562; Email: stpeterschool-southbeloit@rockforddiocese.org; Web: st-peter-school.com. Erica Schwartz, Prin. Lay Teachers 12; Students 100.
Catechesis Religious Program—Clara Fragozo, C.R.E. Students 188.

SPRING GROVE, MCHENRY CO., ST. PETER (1900) [CEM] (German)
2118 Main St., P.O. Box 129, Spring Grove, 60081.
Tel: 815-675-2288; Email: StPeter-SpringGrove@RockfordDiocese.org; Web: stpetercatholicchurch.org. Rev. Msgr. Joseph F. Jarmoluk; Deacon Gregory Duffey.
Catechesis Religious Program—Tel: 815-675-2576. Aimee Thomas, C.R.E. Students 176.

STERLING, WHITESIDE CO.
1—ST. MARY (1898) [CEM]
509 Ave. B, Sterling, 61081. Tel: 815-625-0640; Fax: 815-625-1684; Email: stmary-sterling@rockforddiocese.org; Web: www.stmarysterling.com. Mailing Address: 600 Ave. B, Sterling, 61081. Very Rev. James R. Keenan, V.F.; Rev. Jorge Bravo, Parochial Vicar; Jane Olson, Pastoral Assoc.
Res.: 507 Ave. B, Sterling, 61081.
School—St. Mary School, 6 W. Sixth St., Sterling, 61081. Tel: 815-625-2253; Fax: 815-625-8942; Email: stmaryschool-sterling@rockforddiocese.org; Web: www.smsterling.webs.com. Mrs. Rebecca Schmitt, Prin. Lay Teachers 14; Students 167.
Catechesis Religious Program—6 W. 6th St., Sterling, 61081. Tel: 815-625-6688. Lisa Bales, D.R.E. Students 139.
2—SACRED HEART (1870) [CEM] (German)
2224 Ave. J, Sterling, 61081. Tel: 815-625-1134; Fax: 815-625-1138; Email: sacredheart-sterling@RockfordDiocese.org; Web: www.sacredheartparish.net. Rev. Bruce J. Ludeke; Deacon Kenneth Funk.
Catechesis Religious Program—Melinda Hutchison, D.R.E. Students 56.

STOCKTON, JO DAVIESS CO., HOLY CROSS (1893) [CEM] (German)
223 E. Front Ave., Stockton, 61085.
Tel: 815-947-2545; Fax: 815-947-3705; Email: holycross-stockton@rockforddiocese.org; Web: www.holycross.weconnect.com. Rev. Michael E. Morrissey, Parochial Admin.; Deacon Charles Loehr.
Res.: 216 E. Benton Ave., Stockton, 61085.
Catechesis Religious Program—Julie Baysinger, D.R.E. Students 59.

SUBLETTE, LEE CO., OUR LADY OF PERPETUAL HELP (1860) [CEM]
201 S. Locust St., P.O. Box 80, Sublette, 61367.
Tel: 815-849-5412; Fax: 815-849-5412; Email: ourladyof perpetualhelp-sublette@rockforddiocese.org. Rev. Randy J. Fronek.
Catechesis Religious Program—Students 20.

SUGAR GROVE, KANE CO., ST. KATHARINE DREXEL PARISH (2008)
8S055 Dugan Rd., P.O. Box 1189, Sugar Grove, 60554. Tel: 630-466-0303; Fax: 630-466-0333; Email: stkatharinedrexel-sugargrove@rockforddiocese.org; Web: www.stkatharinedrexel.org. Rev. Robert W. Jones; Deacon Michael Lane.
Catechesis Religious Program—
Tel: 630-466-0303, Ext. 109. Mrs. Patricia Weis, D.R.E. Students 424.

SYCAMORE, DE KALB CO., ST. MARY (1885) [CEM]
244 Waterman St., Sycamore, 60178.
Tel: 815-895-3275; Fax: 815-991-5340; Email: stmary-sycamore@RockfordDiocese.org; Web: www.stmarysycamore.com. 322 Waterman St., Sycamore, 60178. Rev. Carl Edward Beekman; Deacon Michael Zibrun.
Res.: 305 Waterman St., Sycamore, 60178.
School—St. Mary School, (Grades PreK-8), 222 Waterman St., Sycamore, 60178. Tel: 815-895-5215; Fax: 815-895-5295; Email: stmaryschool-sycamore@rockforddiocese.org. Guy Herrmann, Prin. Lay Teachers 15; Students 149.
Catechesis Religious Program—
Tel: 815-895-3726, Ext. 1; Email: lrivers@stmarysycamore.com. Leila Rivers, D.R.E. Students 143.

TAMPICO, WHITESIDE CO., ST. MARY (1875) [CEM]
105 N. Benton St., P.O. Box 159, Tampico, 61283.
Tel: 815-438-5425; Email: stmary-tampico@rockforddiocese.org. Rev. Richard M. Russo; Deacon Mr. William Lemmer.
Catechesis Religious Program—Joan Cooney, Business Mgr. Students 4.

VIRGIL, KANE CO., SS. PETER AND PAUL (1909) [CEM]
5 N. 939 Meredith Rd., Virgil, 60151.
Tel: 630-365-6618; Email: SSPeterandPaul-Virgil@RockfordDiocese.org; Web: ssppvirgil.org. Rev. Ariel A. Valencia; Rev. Msgr. Thomas L. Dzielak, S.T.L., In Res., (Retired); Deacon Jim Newhouse.
Catechesis Religious Program—Email: tdzielak@rockforddiocese.org. Students 0.

WALTON, LEE CO., ST. MARY (1913) [JC]
912 Walton Rd., Walton, 61021. Tel: 815-857-2670; Email: StMary-Walton@RockfordDiocese.org; Web: www.stpatrickamboy.org. Mailing Address: 32 N. Jones Ave., Amboy, 61310. Rev. Timothy J. Draper.
Catechesis Religious Program—Susan McCoy, C.R.E. Twinned with St. Patrick, Amboy.

WARREN, JO DAVIESS CO., ST. ANN (1914) [CEM]
608 E. Railroad St., P.O. Box 665, Warren, 61087.
Tel: 815-745-2312; Fax: 815-745-2326; Email: stann-warren@rockforddiocese.org. Rev. Andrew T. Skrobutt.
Catechesis Religious Program—Email: parishes.wa@gmail.com. Jan Bussan, D.R.E. Students 30.

WEST BROOKLYN, LEE CO., ST. MARY (1889) [CEM]
2520 Johnson St., West Brooklyn, 61378.
Tel: 815-849-5412; Fax: 815-849-5412; Email: stmary-westbrooklyn@rockforddiocese.org. Mailing Address: P.O. Box 80, Sublette, 61367. Rev. Randy J. Fronek.
Catechesis Religious Program—Teresa Machen, C.R.E. Held at Our lady of Perpetual Help, Sublette. Students 4.

WONDER LAKE, MCHENRY CO., CHRIST THE KING (1949) [CEM]
5006 E. Wonder Lake Rd., Wonder Lake, 60097.
Tel: 815-653-2561; Fax: 815-653-9401; Email: christtheking-wonderlake@rockforddiocese.org; Web: Christthekingchurch.org. Rev. Joel N. Lopez, Parochial Admin.; Deacon Mark Raz.
Catechesis Religious Program—Tel: 815-653-2581. Odette Conroy, D.R.E. Students 69.

WOODSTOCK, MCHENRY CO.
1—ST. MARY (1853) [CEM]
312 Lincoln Ave., Woodstock, 60098.
Tel: 815-338-3377; Email: StMary-Woodstock@RockfordDiocese.org; Web: www.stmary-woodstock.org. Rev. Burt H. Absalon; Deacons Hans Rokus; Jim Devona; William Johnson.
School—St. Mary School, 320 Lincoln Ave., Woodstock, 60098. Tel: 815-338-3598; Fax: 815-338-3408; Email: stmaryschool-woodstock@rockforddiocese.org; Web: stmary-woodstock.org/school. Vincent Sossong, Prin. Clergy 3; Lay Teachers 19; Students 227.
Catechesis Religious Program—Tel: 815-338-3413; Email: dodonnell@stmary-woodstock.org. Mrs. Diane O'Donnell, D.R.E. Students 349.
2—RESURRECTION (1978)
2918 S. Country Club Rd., Woodstock, 60098.
Tel: 815-338-7330; Fax: 815-338-7365; Email: resurrection-woodstock@RockfordDiocese.org; Web: www.resurrectionwoodstock.church. Rev. Stephen Glab, C.R.; Deacons Paul Oswald; Mark Priniski.
Catechesis Religious Program—Nancy Neumeister, D.R.E. Students 103.

Chaplains of Public Institutions

ELGIN. *Elgin State Hospital*, 750 S. State St., Elgin, 60123. Vacant.

MOOSEHEART. *School of the Loyal Order of Moose*, 240 W James J Davis Dr, Mooseheart, 60539.
Tel: 630-859-2000; Email: gurwiler@mooseheart.org; Web: www.mooseheart.org.

SAINT CHARLES. *Illinois State Youth Center*, IL Youth Center, Chapel of the Immaculate Conception, 3825 Campton Hills Rd., St. Charles, 60175.
Tel: 630-584-0506; Email: hbarch@rockforddiocese.org. Rev. Howard C. Barch, Dir. of Prison MinistryRecords kept at St. Patrick, St. Charles.

Special Assignment:
Rev. Msgrs.—
Deutsch, Daniel J., Episcopal Vicar for Clergy & Religious, 555 Colman Center Dr., P.O. Box 7044, 61125. Tel: 815-399-4300
Nelson, Glenn L., V.G., J.C.L., Vicar Gen., Mod. of the Curia, Propagation of the Faith & Dir. Deaf Apostolate, 555 Colman Center Dr., P.O. Box 7044, 61125. Tel: 815-399-4300
Vallejo, Arquimedes, J.C.D., V.F., Episcopal Vicar for Hispanic Ministry and Tribunal, 555 Colman Center Dr., P.O. Box 7044, 61125. Tel: 815-399-4300
Very Rev.—
Bergschneider, Matthew M., J.C.L., Judicial Vicar & Vice Chancellor, 61125
Revs.—
Bakkelund, Jonathan P., S.T.L., Master of Ceremonies & Office Divine Worship, 61125
Barch, Howard C., Diocesan Prison Ministry
Birungyi, George, Chap., St. Joseph Hospital, Elgin
Bolger, Michael J., Asst. Principal, Aquin Central Catholic High School, Freeport, Freeport, IL
Browning, Ryan B., S.T.L., Censor Librorum and Encourage Chaplain
Dietz, Andrew J., Spiritual Dir., St. Edward Central Catholic High School
Dorado, E. Yovanny, Spiritual Dir. for the Hispanic Catholic Emaus
Easton, Colin, Chap., Boy Scouts
Etheredge, F. William, Supt., Aurora CC High School, Aurora
Federspiel, Nicholas, Chap., Prison Ministry & Poor Clares Monastery, Rockford, IL
Finn, David C., Asst. Prin. & Spiritual Dir., Boylan Central Catholic High School, Rockford, IL
Flores, Darwin, Hispanic Ministry, DeKalb Deanery
Gomez, Manuel G., Asst. Vocation Dir.
Gonnella, Robert, Asst. Vocation Dir.
Grismer, Sean, Asst. Vocation Dir.
Jaskierny, Joseph F., J.C.L., Adjutant Judicial Vicar
Kaim, Phillip A., S.T.L., Chap., Courage
Lange, Steven J., Asst. Chap., OSF St. Anthony Hospital, Rockford, IL
Long, Anthony Vu Khac, Vietnamese Catholic Ministry, 321 Pine St., DeKalb, 60115
Ludeke, Bruce J., Asst. Prin. Newman Central Catholic High School, Sterling, IL
Manno, Kyle A., Vocation Dir.
Ospina, Diego F., Hispanic Ministry, Freeport Deanery
Polycarpe, Pierre G., Chap., St. Anthony Hospital, Rockford
Salinas, Andres, Spiritual Dir., Hispanic Cursillo
Trowbridge, Jeremy A., S.T.L., Spiritual Dir. of Diocesan Life & Family Evangelization Office
Twenty, Jared, S.T.L., Censor Librorum & Spiritual Dir., Marian Central Catholic High School, Woodstock
Vasquez, Perfecto L., Filipino Ministry, Sts. Peter & Paul, (Retired), 5N939 Meredith Rd., Virgil, 60151
Wasilewski, Kenneth, S.T.L., Diocesan Dir. Permanent Deacons & Diocesan Ethicist.

Active Outside the Diocese:
Revs.—
Emeh, Martins C., J.C.L., Archdiocese of Galveston-Houston
Fuller, Michael J.K., S.T.D., USCCB, Washington, DC
Garrity, Robert M., Ave Maria Univ., Naples, FL.

Retired:
Rev. Msgrs.—
Barr, Eric R., S.T.L., (Retired), 1061 Anee Dr., 61108
Brady, Thomas C., P.A., V.G., Ph.D., (Retired), 16 Country Club Beach, 61103
Dempsey, Thomas J., (Retired), 13750 White Oak Rd., Huntley, 60142
Dzielak, Thomas L., S.T.L., (Retired), P.O. Box 70, Maple Park, 60151
Hermes, Daniel J., (Retired), 1962 Hidden Shores Dr., Dixon, 61021
Kobbeman, Gerald P., S.T.L., (Retired), 12795 Edgewater Pointe, Winnebago, 61088
Linster, Joseph B., (Retired), 244 S. Randall PMB 102, Elgin, 60123
McDonnell, William, S.T.L., (Retired), 4444 Brendenwood Rd. #313, 61107
McLoughlin, James W., (Retired), 11335 Bellflower Ln., Huntley, 60142
Monahan, Thomas J., Ph.D., (Retired), 4141 N. Rockton Ave., 61103
Schwartz, William H., S.T.L., P.A., (Retired), P.O. Box 1283, Williams Bay, WI 53191
Sweeney, Robert J., S.T.B., (Retired), 2542 W. 117th Pl., Chicago, 60655
Tierney, Michael J., (Retired), 15 Delbourne Dr., Davis, 61019

Willhite, Robert J., (Retired), 405 St. Joseph Ave., Aurora, 60505
Revs.—
Ahles, Donald M., (Retired), 1271 Anee Dr., 61108
Barry, Michael T., (Retired), 7431 E. State St., #233, 61107
Beauvais, David E., (Retired), P.O. Box 94, Rock City, 61070
Burr, Thomas E., (Retired), St. Joseph Village, 1201 E. Sandy Lake Rd., Coppell, TX 75019
Camacho, Robert J., (Retired), 565 Standish St., Elgin, 60123
Donahugh, Donald E., (Retired), 6755 Ridgmar Blvd., Apt. 238, Fort Worth, TX 76116
Engbarth, David R., (Retired), 980 7th St., N.W. Lot 32, Largo, FL 33770
Falcone, Emilio, (Retired), P.O. Box 7044, 61125
Ganss, Karl P., (Retired), 15 Delburne Dr., Davis, 61019
Gillespie, Edward F., (Retired), Gail Quinn, 126 Central Ave., Naperville, 60506
Guagliardo, Salvatore J., (Retired), 4444 Brendenwood Rd., 61107
Heraty, John T., S.T.L., (Retired), 11936 Tuliptree Ln., Huntley, 60142
Jones, Ronald A., (Retired), P.O. Box 7044, 61125
Kos, Stanislaw, (Retired), P.O. Box 246, Elizabeth, 61028
Kraemer, John A., (Retired), 1571 W. Ogden Ave., Apt. 1204, La Grange Park, 60526
Kramer, Richard R., (Retired), 209 W. Shellhammer Rd., P.O Box 130, Harmon, 61042
Kulak, Joseph F., (Retired), 1213 Oakdale, Elgin, 60123
Lewandowski, Theodore V., (Retired), N1829 William Dr., Waupaca, WI 54981
Lipinski, Paul M., (Retired), 2731 Cobblestone Dr., Prairie Grove, 60012
Lutz, Joseph L., (Retired), 378 Brittany Ct., Apt. A, Geneva, 60134
Maldonado, Leonardo, (Retired), 1915 Clinton Ave., Berwyn, 60402
Mallari, Arturo O., (Retired), 17201 Birchleaf Ter., Bowie, MD 20716
McDonnell, Francis E., S.T.L., (Retired), 3330 Maria Linden Dr., 61114
McKitrick, James V., (Retired), N.1555 Shadow Ln., Fontana, WI 53125
Mullane, Bernard J., (Retired), P.O. Box 1403, Williams Bay, WI 53191
Neumann, Aloysius J., (Retired), 837 Carillon Dr., Bartlett, 60103
Peters, Daniel E., (Retired), 1934 Schomer Ct., Aurora, 60505
Schuessler, William R., S.T.D., (Retired), 402 Church St., Belvidere, 61008
Sherry, Robert N., (Retired), 5081 Olympic Blvd., Erlanger, KY 41018
Slampak, John A., (Retired), Rev. William Etheredge, 1255 N. Edgelawn Dr., Aurora, 60506
Stringini, John L., (Retired), 241 Yacht Club Dr., Niceville, FL 32578
Tosto, Louis F., (Retired), 312 W. Lincoln Ave., Woodstock, 60098
Urbaniak, Lawrence M., (Retired), 13640- N. 107th Ln., Sun City, AZ 85351
Vasquez, Perfecto L., (Retired), 796 Portsmouth St., Pingree Grove, 60140
Vlasz, Melvyn J., (Retired), 3330 Maria Linden Dr., 61114
Wentink, William R., (Retired), P.O. Box 8786, 61126
Wirth, Geoffrey D., (Retired), 12450 Russet Lake, Huntley, 60142.

Permanent Deacons:
Abel, Philip, St. Bridget, Loves Park
Abramowicz, Ronald, St. Mary, Oregon
Achino, Joseph, St. Anne, Dixon
Addotta, Peter J., St. Anthony, Rockford
Anchor, Robert, Sacred Heart, Marengo
Armstrong, Robert Christopher, St. Margaret Mary, Algonquin
Badillo, Ignacio, St. Peter, South Beloit
Barone, Frank, (Retired)
Barone, Louis, (Retired)
Berard, Samuel, St. Patrick, Dixon
Bermea, Jose, St. Laurence, Elgin
Bondi, Allen, (Retired)
Boyce, Michael, SS. Peter & Paul, Cary
Brandenburg, Robert, (Retired)
Broderick, Richard, St. Bridget, Loves Park
Bronzi, William, (Retired)
Brunette, Donald J., St. Thomas Aquinas, Freeport
Chaplin, Mark, St. Gall, Elburn
Ciochon, Thaddeus, (Retired)
Coltman, George, St. Mary, Huntley
Conrey, James, St. Mary, Huntley
Cooper, Charles, St. Peter, St. Helena, NC
Cox, Gregg, St. Bernadette, Rockford
Dr. Cristoforo, Michael, (Retired)
Czerniewski, Martin, (Retired)
D'Anna, Gregory, St. Peter, Geneva
Dall, William, (Leave of Absence)
Dean, William, St. James, Rockford
Deatherage, Lee, (Leave of Absence)
Deitz, David, St. Thomas the Apostle, Crystal Lake
DeLeon, Luis, St. Mary, Elgin
Devona, James, St. Mary, Woodstock
Dietz, Albert, St. Joseph, Richmond
Dinneen, Richard, St. Thomas Aquinas, Freeport
Dombek, James, Christ the Teacher, DeKalb
Drees, Vincent, St. Thomas Aquinas, Freeport
Duffey, Gregory, St. Peter, Spring Grove
Easton, James, St. Peter Cathedral, Rockford
Elms, Thomas, St. John Neumann, St. Charles
Emmert, Phillip, (Leave of Absence)
Englert, Frank, St. Mary, Huntley
Falcón, Jose, St. Mary, Aurora
Farinella, Louis, St. Mary, Huntley
Fausto, Francisco, St. Joseph, Elgin
Felix, Ignacio, St. Rita of Cascia, Aurora
Fiedler, Curtis, Church of Holy Apostles, McHenry
Fischer, Howard, St. Margaret Mary, Algonquin; St. Mary, Gilberts
Fox, Kenneth, (Retired)
Fox, Steven, St. Catherine of Siena, Dundee
Frazier, J. Michael, (Retired)
Freund, Walter, (Retired)
Funk, Kenneth, Sacred Heart, Sterling
Gagnon, Charles, (Retired)
Ganshow, Howard, SS. Peter & Paul, Cary
Garber, Dennis, St. Monica, Carpentersville
Garcia, Fermin, St. Patrick, Rochelle
Gartland, William, St. Patrick, St. Charles
Gay, Kenneth, Annunciation BVM, Aurora
Geinosky, Larry, (Retired)
Gerdeman, Richard, St. Bernadette, Rockford
Giacone, Kenneth, St. Elizabeth Ann Seton, Crystal Lake, IL
Giambalvo, Michael, (Retired)
Giblin, Michael, Annunciation B.V.M., Aurora
Gibson, John, St. Bridget, Loves Park
Giessinger, Jerry, St. John the Baptist, Johnsburg
Gillespie, David, St. John the Baptist, Johnsburg
Goetz, Daniel A., (Retired)
Graw, Ronald, (Retired)
Grossmayer, Simon, (Retired)
Hall, James, Holy Angels, Aurora
Hawksworth, Thomas, Holy Angels, Aurora
Hemesath, Kim, St. Thomas Aquinas, Freeport
Hetzel, Martin, (Retired)
Holian, Dennis, St. Patrick, McHenry
Holt, Arthur, (Retired)
Hunter, Kevin, St. Rita, Rockford
Huntley, John, St. Rita, Rockford
Iwanski, Paul, St. John Neumann, St. Charles
Jimenez, Policarpo, St. Mary, Huntley
Johnson, Steven, St. James, Belvidere
Johnson, William, St. Patrick, St. Charles
Johnston, William, St. Mary, Woodstock
Jones, Michael, (Leave of Absence)
Kayser, Joseph, St. Patrick, Hartland
Keane, Michael, St. Joseph, Harvard
Kellen, John, St. Mary, Sterling
Keppler, Anthony, St. Mary, East Dubuque
Kinnare, Mark, Holy Apostles, McHenry
Kocol, Norman, St. Joseph, Richmond
Koss, Anthony, St. Joseph, Harvard
Kremer, Douglas, St. Mary, East Dubuque
Krey, Daniel, Church of the Holy Apostles, McHenry
LaMont, Warren R., St. Mary, Pecatonica
Lane, Michael, St. Katharine Drexel, Sugar Grove
Lemmer, William, St. Mary, Tampico
LeRoy, Michael, St. Margaret Mary, Algonquin
Ley, John, St. Mary, Oregon; St. Mary, Polo
Lincoln, Christopher, St. Mary, Huntley
Loehr, Charles, Holy Cross, Stockton
Lopez, James, (Retired)
Luna, Juan, Sts. Peter and Paul, Cary
Maher, Patrick, St. Margaret Mary, Algonquin
Marcantonio, Richard, St. Elizabeth Ann Seton, Crystal Lake
Marcheschi, David, St. Mary, Huntley
Martin, Raymond J., Holy Cross, Batavia
Martin, Richard, St. Rita of Cascia, Aurora
Martinez, Armando, (Retired)
Mattoon, David, St. Mary, Elgin
McDonough, James, St. Margaret Mary, Algonquin
McKenna, Thomas, Diocese Rockford Chancery
McNealy, Ken, (Retired)
McPhee, John, St. Mary, Huntley
Meadors, Ronald, St. Bernadette, Rockford
Mellin, James, St. Patrick, St. Charles
Miller, Donald, St. Margaret Mary, Algonquin
Mills, Ray, St. John Neuman, St. Charles
Mitchison, Robert, Cathedral of St. Peter, Rockford
Monteleone, Michael, St. John Neumann, St. Charles
Morrison, Edward, St. Thomas the Apostle, Crystal Lake
Motyka, Larry J., Holy Cross, Batavia
Moynihan, Patrick, The Haitian Project
Mulcahey, Richard, (Retired)
Murray, Thomas III, St. Mary, Woodstock
Navarro, Carlos, St. Peter, Aurora; Our Lady of Good Counsel, Aurora
Nelson, John, St. Charles Borromeo, Hampshire
Newhouse, James, SS. Peter & Paul, Virgil
Newton, Robert, St. Thomas Moore, Elgin
Nguyen, Loc, St. Mary, Elgin
Norris, Gregory, Holy Cross, Batavia
O'Connor, Michael, SS. Peter & Paul, Cary
O'Leary, Jack, Sacred Heart, Marengo
Olson, James D., (Retired)
Orlik, Henry, St. Mary, Elgin
Oswald, Paul, Resurrection, Woodstock
Patino, Luis, St. Rita, Aurora
Petit, Thomas, St. Mary, Byron
Petitti, Domenic, Annunciation BVM, Aurora
Phelan, Joseph, Church of Holy Apostles, McHenry
Pipitone, Michael, St. Patrick, Hartland
Plazewski, Robert, St. Laurence, Elgin
Pospischil, Steven, St. Thomas Aquinas, Freeport
Priniski, Mark, Resurrection, Woodstock
Prunty, Kevin, St. Patrick, Amboy
Pulkrabek, Steven, St. Mary, Durand; St. Patrick, Irish Grove
Puscas, Stephen, St. Mary, DeKalb
Ramsey, Kenneth, Holy Cross, Batavia
Ranney, Paul, St. Mary, Freeport
Raz, Mark, Christ the King, Wonder Lake
Real, Robert, (Retired)
Regalado, Armando, St. Mary, DeKalb
Reyes, Reynaldo, St. Bridget, Loves Park
Riseley, William, St. Bridget, Loves Park
Roberts, Timothy, SS. Peter and Paul, Cary
Robinson, Craig, Church of Holy Apostles, McHenry
Roder, John, St. Thomas More, Elgin
Rokus, Hans, St. Mary, Woodstock
Rosado, Julio, St. Therese of Jesus, Aurora
Ryan, Michael, (Retired)
Ryndak, Jerry, St. Charles Borromeo, Hampshire
Schmalen, Hank, St. Catherine of Siena, Dundee; St. Mary, Gilbert
Schramm, George, St. Patrick, Rochelle
Siciliano, Donald, SS. Peter & Paul, Cary
Sims, Fred, (Retired)
Skrade, Fred, (Retired)
Smith, Daniel, (Leave of Absence)
Smith, Michael, St. Patrick, St. Charles
Stankevitz, William A., St. Catherine, Genoa
Statter, Ralph, (Retired)
Stevens, Greg, St. Thomas More, Elgin
Stewart, Jason, Holy Family, Rockford
Stowell, David, Church of Holy Apostles, McHenry
Sullivan, Michael, (Retired)
Sweeney, Robert, (Retired)
Szudarski, Norbert, (Retired)
Timmerman, Mike, OSF, Mendota, IL
Torres Paredes, Daniel, Church of Holy Apostle, McHenry
Urban, Gregory, St. Mary, Maple Park
Wagner, Terrence, St. Patrick, Dixon
Ward, James, St. Charles Borromeo, Hampshire
Wasko, Kenneth, Sts. Peter & Paul, Cary
Watermann, Bruce, St. Therese, Aurora; St. Nicholas, Aurora
Weaver, Raymond, Our Lady of Good Counsel, Aurora
White, Dennis, St. Peter, Geneva
White, Thomas, Holy Angels, Aurora
Whitehead, William Jr., St. Catherine of Siena, Dundee; St. Mary, Gilbert
Wilbricht, David, (Retired)
Williams, Ronald, St. John Neumann, St. Charles
Woeste, James, (Retired)
Zammuto, Frank, Holy Family, Rockford
Zarembski, David, Deaf Apostolate
Zibrun, Michael, St. Mary, Sycamore
Zitkus, Lawrence, (Retired).

INSTITUTIONS LOCATED IN DIOCESE

[A] HIGH SCHOOLS, DIOCESAN

ROCKFORD. *Boylan Central Catholic High School*, 4000 St. Francis Dr., 61103. Tel: 815-877-0531; Fax: 815-877-2544; Email: boylan@boylan.org; Web: www.boylan.org. Mr. Christopher Lindstedt, Dean of Students; Mrs. Amy Ott, Pres.; Mr. Christopher Rozanski, Prin.; Rev. David Finn, Asst. Prin. & Spiritual Dir.; Mrs. Penny Yurkew, Asst. Prin., Academic Affairs; Mrs. Angela Long, Librarian. Religious Teachers 1; Lay Teachers 64; Priests 2; Students 798.

AURORA. *Aurora Central Catholic High School*, 1255 N. Edgelawn Dr., Aurora, 60506. Tel: 630-907-0095; Fax: 630-907-1076; Email: auroracentralhighschool@rockforddiocese.org; Web: www.auroracentral.com. Rev. F. William Etheredge, Prin. & Supt.; Mr. Paul Mayer, Asst. Prin.; Sr. Mary Catherine Martini, Librarian. Religious Teachers 3; Lay Teachers 52; Priests 1; School Sisters of St. Francis 2; Students 615.

ELGIN. *St. Edward Central Catholic High School*, 335 Locust St., Elgin, 60123. Tel: 847-741-7535; Fax: 847-695-4682; Email: stedwardhighschool@rockforddiocese.org; Web: www.stedhs.org. Mrs. Barbara Villont, Supt.; Rev. Andrew Deitz, Dir. Lay Teachers 30; Students 382.

FREEPORT. *Aquin Central Catholic High School*, 1419 S. Galena Ave., Freeport, 61032. Tel: 815-235-3154 ; Fax: 815-235-3185; Email: aquinhighschool-freeport@rockforddiocese.org; Web: www.aquinschools.org. Rosemarie Brubaker, Supt.; Rev. Michael J. Bolger, Asst. Prin. & Chm. Rel. Studies Dept.; Mrs. Connie Gogel, Librarian. Lay Teachers 17; Priests 2; Students 148.

STERLING. *Newman Central Catholic High School* (1915) 1101 W. 23rd St., Sterling, 61081-9002. Tel: 815-625-0500; Fax: 815-625-8444; Email: newmanhighschool-sterling@rockforddiocese.org; Web: www.newmancchs.org. Kathleen Howard, Prin.; Rev. Bruce J. Ludeke, Asst. Prin.; Timothy Nelson, Admin.; Shelley McCarty, LIbrarian. Lay Teachers 25; Priests 1; Students 225.

WOODSTOCK. *Marian Central Catholic High School* (1959) 1001 McHenry Ave., Woodstock, 60098. Tel: 815-338-4220; Fax: 815-338-4253; Email: marianhighschool-woodstock@rockforddiocese.org; Email: dnovy@rockforddiocese.org; Web: www.marian.com. Mr. Vito DeFrisco, Supt.; Debra Novy, Prin.; Cheryl Loy, Asst. Prin. Religious Teachers 1; Lay Teachers 38; Students 592.

[B] HIGH SCHOOLS, PRIVATE

AURORA. *Marmion Academy*, 1000 Butterfield Rd., Aurora, 60502. Tel: 630-897-6936; Fax: 630-897-7086; Email: atinerella@marmion.org; Web: www.marmion.org. Rev. Michael Burrows, O.S.B., Chap.; Rt. Rev. John Brahill, O.S.B., Pres., 850 Butterfield Rd., Aurora, 60504. Tel: 630-897-1881; Fax: 630-897-0393; Email: jbrahill@marmion.org; Web: www.marmion.org; Mr. Anthony Tinerella, Prin. Day School for Boys. Religious Teachers 5; Lay Teachers 51; Students 548; Benedictines 3.

Rosary High School (1962) 901 N. Edgelawn Ave., Aurora, 60506. Tel: 630-896-0831; Fax: 630-896-8372; Email: rosaryhighschool-aurora@rockforddiocese.org; Web: www.rosaryhs.com. Dr. Thomas Choice, Pres.; Sisters Mary Megan Farrelly, O.P., Prin.; Katrina Lamkin, O.P., Admin.; Mrs. Jennifer Stasinopoulos, Librarian. Girls 303; Lay Teachers 25; Sisters 5.

[C] ELEMENTARY SCHOOLS

ROCKFORD. *All Saints Catholic Academy*, (Grades PreK-8), 409 N. First St., 61104. Email: jparsons@RockfordDiocese.org.

[D] GENERAL HOSPITALS

ROCKFORD. *Saint Anthony College of Nursing* (1915) Health Sciences Center, 3301 N Mulford Rd, 61108. Tel: 815-282-7900; Fax: 815-282-7901; Email: sandiesoldwisch@sacn.edu; Web: www.sacn.edu. Sandie Soldwisch, Ph.D., A.P.N., A.N.P.-B.C., Pres., College. Faculty 42; Students 303; Staff 13.

Saint Anthony Medical Center, 5666 E. State St., 61108. Tel: 815-226-2000; Fax: 815-395-5449; Email: robert.brandfass@osfhealthcare.org; Web: www.osfhealthcare.org. Ms. Paula Carynski, Pres.; Rev. Pierre G. Polycarpe, Chap. Bed Capacity 254; Tot Asst. Annually 345,828; Total Staff 2,052.

AURORA. *Presence Mercy Medical Center*, 1325 N. Highland Ave., Aurora, 60506. Tel: 630-859-2222; Fax: 630-906-2939; Email: Judy.MacPhersonSchumacher@presencehealth.org; Web: www.presencehealth.org. Michael L. Brown, Regl. Pres. & CEO; Edward J. Hunter, Regl. Vice Pres. Mission Svcs.; Mrs. Dorothy Van Dyke, Spiritual Care Mgr.

Presence Central and Suburban Hospitals Network dba Presence Mercy Medical Center. Licensed Beds 293; Tot Asst. Annually 161,470; Total Staff 944.

Center for Diabetic Wellness, 1325 N. Highland Ave., Aurora, 60506. Tel: 630-897-4000; Fax: 630-897-9032; Email: Judy.MacPhersonSchumacher@presencehealth.org. Edward J. Hunter, Regl. Mission Officer.

Health Institute, 1975 Melissa Ln., Aurora, 60505. Tel: 630-907-1129; Fax: 630-907-1354; Email: Judy.MacPhersonSchumacher@presencehealth.org. Edward J. Hunter, Regl. Mission Officer.

ELGIN. *Presence Saint Joseph Hospital-Elgin* (1902) 77 N. Airlite St., Elgin, 60123. Tel: 847-695-3200; Fax: 847-931-5550; Email: Judy.MacPhersonSchumacher@presencehealth.org; Web: www.presencehealth.org. Michael L. Brown, Regl. Pres. & CEO; Edward J. Hunter, Regl Mission Officer; Rev. George Birungyi, Spiritual Care Mgr.

Presence Central and Suburban Hospitals Network dba Presence Saint Joseph Hospital-Elgin. Bed Capacity 184; Priests 1; Tot Asst. Annually 73,469; Total Staff 751.

Presence Family Care, Carpentersville, 2201 Randall Rd., Carpentersville, 60110. Tel: 847-844-7800; Fax: 847-783-0628; Email: Judy.MacPhersonSchumacher@presencehealth.org. Edward J. Hunter, Regl. Mission Officer.

Presence Family Care, Hampshire, 895 S. State St., Ste. 201, Hampshire, 60140. Tel: 847-683-7099; Fax: 847-683-7104; Email: Judy.MacPhersonSchumacher@presencehealth.org. Edward J. Hunter, Regl. Mission Officer.

[E] SCHOOLS FOR EXCEPTIONAL ADOLESCENTS AND ADULTS

FREEPORT. *Presence Saint Vincent Community Living Facility and Supported Living Arrangement*, 659 E. Jefferson St., Freeport, 61032. Tel: 815-232-6181; Fax: 815-232-6143; Email: michelle.lindeman@presencehealth.org; Web: presencehealth.org. Ms. Michelle Lindeman, Admin.

Presence Life Connections dba Presence Saint Vincent Community Living Facility; Presence Life Connections dba Presence Saint Vincent Supported Living Arrangement. Bed Capacity 20; Tot Asst. Annually 35; Total Staff 11.

[F] HOMES FOR AGED AND ADULT DAY CARE CENTERS

ROCKFORD. *Presence Cor Mariae Center*, 3330 Maria Linden Dr., 61114. Tel: 815-877-7416; Email: sherry.gillihan@presencehealth.org; Web: www.presencehealth.org/cormariae. Sherry Gillihan, Admin.

Presence Life Connections dba Presence Cor Mariae Center. Bed Capacity 162; Tot Asst. Annually 364; Total Staff 102.

Presence Saint Anne Center, 4405 Highcrest Rd., 61107. Tel: 815-229-1999; Fax: 815-229-1560; Email: Amy.Swanson@presencehealth.org; Web: www.presencehealth.org. Sr. Marie Ange Marcotte, Spiritual Care Dir.

Presence Life Connections dba Presence Saint Anne Center. Bed Capacity 179; Tot Asst. Annually 900; Total Staff 160.

AURORA. *Presence Fox Knoll*, 421 N. Lake St., Aurora, 60506. Tel: 630-844-0380; Fax: 630-844-0702; Email: james.brady@presencehealth.org; Web: www.presencehealth.org/foxknoll. Deacon Jack Roder, Spiritual Care Dir.; James F. Brady, Admin.

Presence Life Connections dba Presence Fox Knoll. Bed Capacity 163; Tot Asst. Annually 154; Total Staff 41.

Presence McAuley Manor (1985) 400 W. Sullivan Rd., Aurora, 60506. Tel: 630-859-3700; Fax: 630-264-1862; Email: Judy.MacPhersonSchumacher@presencehealth.org; Web: www.presencehealth.org/mcauley. James F. Brady, Admin.; Helena Mathews, Admin.

Presence Life Connections dba Presence McAuley Manor. Bed Capacity 87; Tot Asst. Annually 470; Total Staff 82.

BATAVIA. *Assisi Homes-Batavia Apartments, Inc.* (1993) 1259 E. Wilson St., Batavia, 60510. Tel: 630-879-3117; Tel: 303-830-3300; Fax: 630-879-0665; Email: mrankin@mercyhousing.org; Web: www.mercyhousing.org. Melissa Clayton, Contact Person. Housing Units 290; Staff 10.

ELGIN. *Presence Home Care*, 799 S. McLean Blvd, Elgin, 60123. Tel: 847-931-5553; Fax: 847-622-2055; Email: Judy.MacPhersonSchumacher@presencehealth.org. Jan Cotter, Admin.; Michael Gordon, Pres.

FREEPORT. *Presence Saint Joseph Adult Day Center*, 659 E. Jefferson St., Freeport, 61032. Tel: 815-266-8067; Fax: 815-266-8001; Email: michelle.lindeman@presencehealth.org. Ms. Michelle Lindeman, Admin.; Ms. Sharon Batten, Dir.

Presence Life Connections dba Presence Saint Joseph Adult Day Center. Bed Capacity 55; Tot Asst. Annually 48; Total Staff 6.

Presence Saint Joseph Center, 659 E. Jefferson St., Freeport, 61032. Tel: 815-232-6181; Fax: 815-232-6143; Email: michelle.lindeman@presencehealth.org. Ms. Michelle Lindeman, Admin.

Presence Life Connections dba Presence Saint Joseph Center Bed Capacity 124; Tot Asst. Annually 358; Total Staff 120.

SAINT CHARLES. *Presence Pine View Care Center*, 611 Allen Ln., St. Charles, 60174. Tel: 630-377-2211; Fax: 630-377-4352; Email: Judy.MacPhersonSchumacher@presencehealth.org; Web: presencehealth.org. Susan Puchalla, B.A., M.A., Ed.D., Chap. Spiritual Care Dir.; Amrit Jacob, Admin.

Presence Life Connections dba Presence Pine View Care Center. Bed Capacity 120; Tot Asst. Annually 250; Total Staff 115.

[G] MONASTERIES AND RESIDENCES OF PRIESTS AND BROTHERS

AURORA. *Marmion Abbey* (1933) 850 Butterfield Rd., Aurora, 60502. Tel: 630-897-7215; Email: jbrahill@marmion.org; Web: www.marmion.org. Rt. Revs. John Brahill, O.S.B., Abbot; Vincent Bataille, O.S.B., Abbot Emeritus; Revs. Thomas Bailey, O.S.B.; Michael Burrows, O.S.B.; Rene Otzoy Colaj, O.S.B.; Patrick S. Gillmeyer, O.S.B., Pastor; Orlando Perez Gomez, O.S.B.; Juan Francisco Peren Mux, O.S.B.; Frederick Peterson, O.S.B.; Cristobal Coche Quic, O.S.B.; Charles Reichenbacher, O.S.B.; Joel Rippinger, O.S.B.; Marcos Rivas, O.S.B.; Nathanael Roberts, O.S.B.; Bernard Schaefer, O.S.B.; Kenneth Theisen, O.S.B.; Bros. Andre Charron, O.S.B.; Theodore Haggerty, O.S.B.; Antony Minardi, O.S.B.; Armando Menchu, O.S.B.; Benedict Robert, O.S.B.; Rev. Paul Weberg, O.S.B., Prior; Bro. Francis Knott, O.S.B.; Rt. Rev. Leo M. Ryska, O.S.B.

Marmion. Brothers 4; Priests 20.

Missionaries of the Sacred Heart Community (1854) 305 S. Lake St., P.O. Box 270, Aurora, 60507. Tel: 630-892-2371; Fax: 630-892-1678; Email: rwkpng03@mscparish.com; Web: www.misacor-usa.org. Very Rev. Richard Kennedy, M.S.C., Prov.; Revs. Steve Boland, M.S.C.; Hilary Fischer, M.S.C.; Frank John Timar, M.S.C.; Very Revs. Joseph Jablonski, M.S.C., Retreat Dir.; Luis Alfonso Segura, M.S.C., Pastor; Rev. Selvaraj Lucas, M.S.C., Parochial Vicar. Provincial Administrative Office of the Missionaries of the Sacred Heart.

Missionaries of the Sacred Heart of Jesus Priests 7.

Priests and Brothers of the Aurora Community Serving Elsewhere:

In Chicago, IL Revs. Hugo Leon Londono, M.S.C.; Andrew Torma, M.S.C., Admin.

In Milwaukee, WI Rev. Abraham Yoo, M.S.C., Admin.

MCHENRY. *Villa Desiderata Retreat House*, 3015 N. Bayview Ln., McHenry, 60051-9641. Tel: 815-385-2264; Email: villaretreats@att.net; Web: www.villadesiderata.com. Bro. Patrick T. Drohan, C.S.V., Facilities Mgr.

[H] CONVENTS AND RESIDENCES FOR SISTERS

ROCKFORD. *The Poor Clares of Rockford* (1916) Corpus Christi Monastery, 2111 S. Main St., 61102-3591. Tel: 815-963-7343; Fax: 815-963-7369; Email: vicarforclergy@rockforddiocese.org; Web: www.poorclares.org/rockford/. Mother Mary Dominica Stein, P.C.C., Abbess. Poor Clare Colettines. Postulants 1; Sisters 21; Cloistered Sisters 20; Extern Sisters 1; Junior Sr. 1.

FREEPORT. *Congregation of the Sisters of the Immaculate Heart of Mary, Mother of Christ-Nigeria* (1937) 1209A S. Walnut Ave., Freeport, 61032. Tel: 815-297-8287; Fax: 815-297-1786; Email: guadaluperegion@gmail.com; Web: www.ihmguadaluperegion.org. Mother Mary Clause Oguh, Supr. Gen.; Sr. Mary Theonilla Chukwu, Regl. Supr. Sisters 8; Total in U.S. 46.

[I] COMMUNITY SERVICES

ROCKFORD. *St. Elizabeth Catholic Community Center* (1911) 1536 S. Main St., 61102. Tel: 815-969-6526; Fax: 815-969-0541; Email: thill@rockforddiocese.org; Web: catholiccharities.rockforddiocese.org. Terri Hill, Dir. Tot Asst. Annually 86,579; Total Staff 15.

AURORA. *Public Action to Deliver Shelter, Inc. (PADS)*, 659 S. River St., Aurora, 60506. Tel: 630-897-2165; Fax: 630-801-9759; Email: info@hesedhouse.org; Web: www.hesedhouse.org. Ryan J. Dowd, M.P.A., J.D., Exec. Dir. Ecumenical advocacy, overnight and transitional shelters, daytime drop-in center for homeless persons, and comprehensive resource center. Total Assisted 76,890.

[J] RETREAT HOUSES

ROCKFORD. *Bishop Lane Retreat Center* (1966) 7708 E. McGregor Rd., 61102. Tel: 815-965-5011; Fax: 815-965-5811; Email: bishoplane@rockforddiocese.org; Web: www.bishoplane.org. Kristen Sapoznik, Dir.

BATAVIA. *Holy Heart of Mary Novitiate*, 717 N. Batavia Ave., Batavia, 60510. Tel: 630-879-1296;

Fax: 630-879-7831; Email: evelynbv@sbcglobal.net; Web: www.sscm-usa.org. Sr. Evelyn Varboncoeur, S.S.C.M., Supr. Servants of the Holy Heart of Mary. Professed Sisters 4.

Nazareth Spirituality Center, 717 N. Batavia Ave., Batavia, 60510. Tel: 630-879-1296;
Fax: 630-879-7831; Email: sscm.vocations@gmail.com; Web: www.sscm-usa.org. Linda Isleib, Dir.

[K] FOUNDATIONS

ROCKFORD. *Boylan Educational Foundation, Inc.* (1980) 4000 St. Francis Dr., 61103.
Tel: 815-877-0531; Fax: 815-877-2544; Email: aott@rockforddiocese.org; Web: www.boylan.org. Mr. Christopher Lindstedt, Dean; Mrs. Amy Ott, Pres.; Mr. Christopher Rozanski, Prin.; Rev. David Finn, Admin.; Lynn McConville, Admin.; Mrs. Penny Yurkew, Admin.; Jeffrey Marrs, Admin.; Jeffrey Hohn, Admin.

The Catholic Foundation for the People of the Diocese of Rockford, 555 Colman Center Dr., P.O. Box 7044, 61125-7044. Tel: 815-399-4300;
Fax: 815-399-5657; Email: domalley@rockforddiocese.org; Web: www.foundationrockford.org. Dan O'Malley, Exec. Dir.

AURORA. *Aurora Catholic Education Foundation* (1973) 1141 Trask St., Aurora, 60505. Tel: 630-898-2998; Email: bigal7ll@comcast.net. P.O. Box 234, Aurora, 60507. Alan Schuler, Treas.

DEKALB. *Newman Center of Northern Illinois University Educational Program*, 512 Normal Rd., DeKalb, 60115. Tel: 815-787-7770;
Fax: 815-758-2053; Email: bwelsh@rockforddiocese.org; Web: www.newmanniu.org. Very Rev. Matthew J. McMorrow, S.T.L., V.F., Dir.

Newman Center of Northern Illinois University Educational Program and Development Fund, Inc. Total Staff 9.

ELGIN. *St. Edward Central Catholic High School Education Foundation*, 335 Locust St., Elgin, 60123. Tel: 847-741-7535; Fax: 847-695-4682; Email: stedwardhighschool@rockforddiocese.org; Web: www.stedhs.org. Mrs. Barbara Villont, Chm.

FREEPORT. *Education Through the 90's Foundation*, 1419 S. Galena Ave., Freeport, 61032.
Tel: 815-235-3154; Fax: 815-235-3185; Email: rosemarie.brubaker@aquinschools.org; Web: www.aquinschools.org. Rosemarie Brubaker, Admin. The foundation provides financial support for the Aquin Catholic School System.

Freeport Catholic Education Foundation, 1419 S. Galena Ave., Freeport, 61032. Tel: 815-235-3154;
Fax: 815-235-3185; Email: rosemarie.brubaker@aquinschools.org; Web: www.aquinschools.org. Rosemarie Brubaker, Admin. The foundation provides financial support for the Aquin Catholic School System.

[L] NEWMAN CENTERS

DEKALB. *Newman Foundation for Catholic Students of Northern Illinois University*, 512 Normal Rd., DeKalb, 60115. Tel: 815-787-7770;
Fax: 815-758-2053; Email: bwelsh@rockforddiocese.org; Web: www.newmanniu.org. Very Rev. Matthew J. McMorrow, S.T.L., V.F., Dir. Campus Ministries & Pastor; Rev. Kyle A. Manno, Parochial Vicar; Denise Sanders, Campus Min.

[M] MISCELLANEOUS

ROCKFORD. *Catholic Office of the Deaf*, 555 Colman Center Dr., P.O. Box 7044, 61125.
Tel: 815-399-4300 (Voice); Tel: 815-217-2234 (V.P.); Fax: 815-399-5266; Email: RockfordHI@aol.com; Web: www.rockforddiocese.org/deafapostolate. Rev. Msgr. Glenn L. Nelson, V.G., J.C.L., Dir.

AURORA. **Dominican Literacy Center, Aurora* (1993) 260 Vermont Ave., Aurora, 60505-3100.
Tel: 630-898-4636; Fax: 630-898-4636; Email: domlitctr@sbcglobal.net; Web: www.dominicanliteracycenter.org. Sr. Kathleen Ryan, O.P., Dir.

HARVARD. *Magnificat, A Ministry to Catholic Women*, 2101 Coolidge Avenue, McHenry, 60051.
Tel: 815-236-6027; Email: rooney@sbcglobal.net. Gina Rooney, Contact Person.

SAINT CHARLES. *Cultivation Ministries* (1990) 818 Gray Strret, P.O. Box 662, St. Charles, 60174.
Tel: 630-513-8222; Fax: 630-549-3031; Email: frank@cultivationministries.com; Web: www.cultivationministries.com. Frank Mercadante, Dir. To cultivate team-based, intergenerational and disciple-making Catholic youth ministries by training, resourcing and supporting adult and student leaders.

Queen of Americas Guild, 311 Kautz Rd., St. Charles, 60174. Tel: 630-584-1822;
Fax: 630-587-2200; Email: staff@queenoftheamericasguild.org; Web: www.queenoftheamericasguild.org. His Eminence Raymond Cardinal Burke, D.D., J.C.D., Dir.; Most Rev. Arturo Cepeda, S.T.L., S.T.D., Episcopal Moderator; Mr. Stephen Banaszak, Vice Pres.; Mr. Leif Arvidson, Dir.; Christopher Smoczynski, Pres.; Rebecca Nichols, Sec.; Matthew Smoczynski, Dir.

SAVANNA. *Mercy Homecare/Hospice*, 9317A IL Route 84, Savanna, 61074. Tel: 815-273-2628; Email: Lisa.Mason-Hagen@mercyhealth.com; Email: Timothy.Shinbori@Trinity-health.org; Web: www.mercyclinton.com. 638 S Bluff Blvd, Clinton, IA 52732. Timothy T. Shinbori, Exec. Dir. Sponsor: CHE Trinity Health of Livonia, Michigan, Catholic Health Ministries. Tot Asst. Annually 200; Total Staff 50.

STERLING. *St. Vincent DePaul Society*, 7 W. 6th St., Sterling, 61081. Tel: 815-625-0311;
Fax: 815-625-1684; Email: svdsaukvalley@gmail.com; Email: StMary-Sterling@RockfordDiocese.org; Web: www.stmarysterling.com. Ed Mulvaney, Pres. Total Staff 26; Total Assisted 7,200.

St. Mary's Conference, 600 Ave. B, Sterling, 61081.
Tel: 815-625-0640; Fax: 815-625-1684; Email: stmary-sterling@rockforddiocese.org. Very Rev. James R. Keenan, V.F., Pastor.

STOCKTON. *Christ in the Wilderness* (1980) 7500 S. Randecker Rd., Stockton, 61085-8922.
Tel: 815-947-2476; Fax: 815-947-2476; Email: citw@citwretreat.com; Web: www.citwretreat.com. Sr. Julia Marie Bathon, O.S.F., Exec. Dir. Christ in the Wilderness.

SYCAMORE. **5 Stones Group, NFP* 5 Stones Group. NFP, 1915 Aster Rd., Sycamore, 60178.
Tel: 630-517-4839; Fax: 815-895-0333; Email: veronica.cammuca@lighthousecatholicmedia.org; Web: weare5stones.com. Mr. Michael Pacer, Pres. Employees 42.

RELIGIOUS INSTITUTES OF MEN REPRESENTED IN THE DIOCESE

For further details refer to the corresponding bracketed number in the Religious Institutes of Men or Women section.

[0200]—*Benedictine Monks* (Marmion Abbey, Aurora)—O.S.B.
[1320]—*Clerics of St. Viator*—C.S.V.
[]—*Congregation of the Blessed Sacrament* (Province of the Assumption)—S.S.S.
[1080]—*Congregation of the Resurrection* (Chicago Prov.)—C.R.
[0480]—*Conventual Franciscans* (St. Bonaventure Province)—O.F.M.Conv.
[]—*Conventual Franciscans of St. Anthony, Poland*—O.F.M.Conv.
[]—*Institute of Christ the King Sovereign Priest* (Provincial House, Italy).
[1110]—*Missionaries of the Sacred Heart* (U.S. Province)—M.S.C.
[]—*Order of Discalced Carmelites*—O.C.D.
[]—*Scalabrinian Missionaries*—C.S.
[]—*Society of Our Lady of the Most Holy Trinity*—S.O.L.T.

RELIGIOUS INSTITUTES OF WOMEN REPRESENTED IN THE DIOCESE

[2100]—*Congregation of the Humility of Mary*—C.H.M.
[1070-03]—*Dominican Sisters*—O.P.
[1070-10]—*Dominican Sisters*—O.P.
[1070-13]—*Dominican Sisters*—O.P.
[1430]—*Franciscan Sisters of Our Lady of Perpetual Help*—O.S.F.
[1450]—*Franciscan Sisters of the Sacred Heart*—O.S.F.
[]—*Josephine Sisters*—H.J.
[]—*Missionaries of the Rosary of Fatima*—M.R.F.
[]—*Passionist Sisters*—C.F.P.
[3760]—*Poor Clare Colettines*—P.C.C.
[2970]—*School Sisters of Notre Dame*—S.S.N.D.
[1680]—*School Sisters of St. Francis*—O.S.F.
[3520]—*Servants of the Holy Heart of Mary*—S.S.C.M.
[0430]—*Sisters of Charity of the Blessed Virgin Mary*—B.V.M.
[2360]—*Sisters of Loretto at the Foot of the Cross*—S.L.
[2575]—*Sisters of Mercy of the Americas* (Chicago, IL)—R.S.M.
[]—*Sisters of Providence*—S.P.
[]—*Sisters of St. Francis* (Clinton, IA)—O.S.F.
[]—*Sisters of St. Joseph of Concordia*—C.S.J.
[3930]—*Sisters of St. Joseph of the Third Order of St. Francis*—S.S.J.-T.O.S.F.
[2183]—*Sisters of the Immaculate Heart of Mary Mother of Christ, Nigeria*—I. H. M.
[1770]—*Sisters of the Third Order of St. Francis* (Peoria, Illinois)—O.S.F.
[]—*Workers of the Holy Trinity*—Op.S.F.

DIOCESAN CEMETERIES

ROCKFORD. *Calvary-St. Mary's/St. James*, 8616 W. State St., Winnebago, 61088. Tel: 815-965-1450;
Fax: 815-965-9632; Email: CGiambalvo@RockfordDiocese.org. 917 Auburn St., 61103. Ken Giambalvo, Contact Person

AURORA. *Mount Olivet*, 278 Ashland Ave., Aurora, 60505. Tel: 630-897-9250; Fax: 630-897-9261; Email: CGiambalvo@RockfordDiocese.org. Beverly Hampton, Contact Person

BATAVIA. *Geneva-St. Charles Resurrection*, 37W210 Fabyan Pkwy, Geneva, 60134. Tel: 331-248-0289; Email: CGiambalvo@RockfordDiocese.org. Carol Schwendner, Contact Person

ELGIN. *Mount Hope*, 1001 Villa St., Elgin, 60120.
Tel: 847-468-6910; Fax: 847-468-6909; Email: CGiambalvo@RockfordDiocese.org. Ken Giambalvo, Contact Person

WINNEBAGO. *Calvary*, 8616 W. State St., Winnebago, 61088. Tel: 815-965-1450; Fax: 815-965-9632; Email: CGiambalvo@RockfordDiocese.org. Ken Giambalvo, Contact Person

NECROLOGY

† Bales, Thomas E., (Retired), Died Apr. 21, 2018
† Kurz, Michael A., (Retired), Died Jan. 8, 2019
† O'Neil, Philip E., S.T.L., (Retired), Died Jan. 19, 2018
† Balog, Robert A., (Retired), Died Apr. 5, 2018
† Bartolomeo, Thomas, (Retired), Died Sep. 18, 2018
† Budden, William A., (Retired), Died Dec. 20, 2018
† Clapsaddle, Harlan, (Retired), Died Dec. 17, 2018
† DeSalvo, Donald D., (Retired), Died Feb. 28, 2018
† Holdren, John C., (Retired), Died Apr. 16, 2018
† Knott, William P., (Retired), Died Sep. 26, 2018

An asterisk (*) denotes an organization that has established tax-exempt status directly with the IRS and is not covered by the USCCB Group Ruling.

Diocese of Rockville Centre

(Dioecesis Petropolitana In Insula Longa)

Most Reverend

WILLIAM FRANCIS MURPHY, S.T.D., L.H.D.

Bishop Emeritus of Rockville Centre; ordained December 16, 1964; appointed Auxiliary Bishop to the Archbishop of Boston and Titular Bishop of Saia Maggiore, November 21, 1995; consecrated December 27, 1995; appointed Fourth Bishop of Rockville Centre, June 26, 2001; installed September 5, 2001; retired December 9, 2016. *Mailing Address: Diocesan Pastoral Center, P.O. Box 9023, Rockville Centre, NY 11571-9023.* Email: bishopsoffice@drvc.org.

Most Reverend

EMIL A. WCELA

Retired Auxiliary Bishop of Rockville Centre; ordained June 2, 1956; appointed Titular Bishop of Filaca and Auxiliary Bishop of Rockville Centre October 21, 1988; ordained December 13, 1988; retired April 3, 2007. *Church of St. John the Evangelist, 546 St. John's Pl., Riverhead, NY 11901.* Tel: 631-727-2030.

Most Reverend

JOHN C. DUNNE, D.D.

Retired Auxiliary Bishop of Rockville Centre; ordained June 1, 1963; appointed Titular Bishop of Abercorn and Auxiliary Bishop of Rockville Centre October 21, 1988; ordained December 13, 1988; retired June 22, 2013. *Church of Saint Kilian, 485 Conklin St., Farmingdale, NY 11735.*

Most Reverend

JOHN O. BARRES, S.T.D., J.C.L., D.D.

Bishop of Rockville Centre; ordained October 21, 1989; appointed Bishop of Allentown May 27, 2009; installed July 30, 2009; appointed Bishop of Rockville Centre December 9, 2016; installed January 31, 2017. *Pastoral Center, P.O. Box 9023, Rockville Center, NY 11571-9023.*

Pastoral Center: P.O. Box 9023, Rockville Centre, NY 11571-9023. Tel: 516-678-5800; Fax: 516-764-3316.

Web: drvc.org

Most Reverend

ANDRZEJ JERZY ZGLEJSZEWSKI

Auxiliary Bishop of Rockville Centre; ordained May 26, 1990; appointed Titular Bishop of Nicives and Auxiliary Bishop of Rockville Centre February 11, 2014; ordained March 25, 2014. *Mailing Address: 42 Bermingham Pl., Williston Park, NY 11596.*

Most Reverend

ROBERT J. COYLE

Auxiliary Bishop of Rockville Centre; ordained May 25, 1991; appointed Titular Bishop of Zabi and Auxiliary Bishop of the Archdiocese for the Military Services February 11, 2013; ordained April 25, 2013; appointed Auxiliary Bishop of Rockville Centre February 20, 2018.

Most Reverend

RICHARD G. HENNING

Auxiliary Bishop of Rockville Centre; ordained May 30, 1992; appointed Titular Bishop of Tabla and Auxiliary Bishop of Rockville Centre June 8, 2018; installed July 24, 2018. *Mailing Address: P.O. Box 9023, Rockville Centre, NY 11571-9023.*

ESTABLISHED APRIL 6, 1957.

Square Miles 1,198.

The Roman Catholic Diocese of Rockville Centre, New York.

Comprises the Counties of Nassau and Suffolk (excepting Fishers Island) in the State of New York.

For legal titles of parishes and diocesan institutions, consult the Chancery Office.

STATISTICAL OVERVIEW

Personnel	
Bishop	1
Auxiliary Bishops	3
Retired Bishops	3
Priests: Diocesan Active in Diocese	218
Priests: Diocesan Active Outside Diocese	5
Priests: Retired, Sick or Absent	114
Number of Diocesan Priests	337
Religious Priests in Diocese	62
Total Priests in Diocese	399
Extern Priests in Diocese	107
Ordinations:	
Diocesan Priests	1
Religious Priests	1
Transitional Deacons	6
Permanent Deacons	5
Permanent Deacons in Diocese	285
Total Brothers	34
Total Sisters	801
Parishes	
Parishes	133
With Resident Pastor:	
Resident Diocesan Priests	123
Resident Religious Priests	10
Missions	1
Professional Ministry Personnel:	
Brothers	6
Sisters	27
Lay Ministers	336
Welfare	
Catholic Hospitals	6
Total Assisted	1,024,573
Health Care Centers	3
Total Assisted	34,684
Homes for the Aged	3
Total Assisted	3,190
Specialized Homes	9
Total Assisted	4,774
Special Centers for Social Services	44
Total Assisted	55,667
Residential Care of Disabled	55
Total Assisted	449
Other Institutions	16
Total Assisted	1,530
Educational	
Diocesan Students in Other Seminaries	25
Students Religious	4
Total Seminarians	29
Colleges and Universities	1
Total Students	4,980
High Schools, Diocesan and Parish	4
Total Students	3,022
High Schools, Private	5
Total Students	7,490
Elementary Schools, Diocesan and Parish	41
Total Students	12,422
Elementary Schools, Private	4
Total Students	1,300
Non-residential Schools for the Disabled	1
Total Students	70
Catechesis/Religious Education:	
High School Students	2,442
Elementary Students	73,285
Total Students under Catholic Instruction	105,040
Teachers in the Diocese:	
Priests	8
Brothers	27
Sisters	14
Lay Teachers	1,647
Vital Statistics	
Receptions into the Church:	
Infant Baptism Totals	13,219
Minor Baptism Totals	1,085
Adult Baptism Totals	938
Received into Full Communion	204
First Communions	13,638
Confirmations	14,714
Marriages:	
Catholic	2,569
Interfaith	487
Total Marriages	3,056
Deaths	9,955
Total Catholic Population	1,428,296
Total Population	3,004,366

Former Bishops—Most Revs. WALTER P. KELLENBERG, D.D., first Bishop of Rockville Centre; ord. June 2, 1928; appt. Titular Bishop of Joannina and Auxiliary Bishop of New York, Aug. 25, 1953; cons. Oct. 5, 1953; appt. Bishop of Ogdensburg, Jan. 19, 1954; appt. first Bishop of Rockville Centre, April 16, 1957; installed May 27, 1957; retired May 3, 1976; died Jan. 11, 1986; JOHN R. MCGANN, D.D., second Bishop of Rockville Centre; ord. June 3, 1950; appt. Titular Bishop of Morosbisdus and Auxiliary to the Bishop of Rockville Centre, Nov. 12, 1970; cons. Jan. 7, 1971; appt. second Bishop of Rockville Centre, May 3, 1976; installed June 24, 1976; retired Jan. 4, 2000; died Jan. 29, 2002; JAMES T. MCHUGH, S.T.D., third Bishop of Rockville Centre; ord. May 25, 1957; appt. Titular Bishop of Morosbisdo and Auxiliary Bishop of Newark, Nov. 20, 1987; cons. Jan. 25, 1988; appt. Bishop of Camden, May 13, 1989; installed June 20, 1989; appt. Coadjutor Bishop of Rockville Centre, Dec. 7, 1998; installed Feb. 22, 1999; succeeded to the See, Jan. 4, 2000; died Dec. 10, 2000; WILLIAM FRANCIS MURPHY, S.T.D., L.H.D., ord. Dec. 16, 1964; appt. Auxiliary Bishop to the Archbishop of Boston and Titular Bishop of Saia Maggiore, Nov. 21, 1995; cons. Dec. 27, 1995; appt. Fourth Bishop of Rockville Centre, June 26, 2001; installed Sept. 5, 2001; retired Dec. 9, 2016.

Diocesan Bishop—Most Reverend JOHN O. BARRES, S.T.D., J.C.L., D.D.

Auxiliary Bishops—Most Revs. EMIL A. WCELA, D.D., (Retired); JOHN C. DUNNE, D.D., (Retired); ROBERT J. BRENNAN, D.D.; ANDRZEJ JERZY ZGLEJSZEWSKI, D.D.; ROBERT J. COYLE, D.D., M.Div.

Secretary to the Bishop—Rev. ERIC R. FASANO, M.Div., J.C.L., Tel: 516-678-5800, Ext. 402; Email: efasano@drvc.org.

Vicar General and Moderator of the Curia—Most Rev. ROBERT J. BRENNAN, V.G., P.O. Box 9023, Rockville Centre, 11571-9023. Tel: 516-678-5800, Ext. 622; Fax: 516-678-3138; Email: rbrennan@drvc.org.

Episcopal Vicars—Western Vicariate: Most Rev. ANDRZEJ JERZY ZGLEJSZEWSKI, D.D., 42 Bermingham Ave., Williston Park, 11596. Tel: 516-744-6850. Central Vicariate: Most Rev. RICHARD G. HENNING, S.T.D., 125 Half Hollow Rd., Deer Park, 11729. Tel: 631-446-2977. Eastern Vicariate: Most Rev. ROBERT J. COYLE, D.D., M.Div., Mailing Address: Church of Good Shepherd, 1370 Grundy Ave., Holbrook, 11741. Tel: 631-588-7689; Fax: 631-588-7603; Email: rcoyle@drvc.org.

Chancery Office—

Co Chancellors—Sr. MARYANNE FITZGERALD, S.C.;

Rev. ERIC R. FASANO, M.Div., J.C.L., Tel: 516-678-5800, Ext. 583; Email: chancellor@drvc.org.
Secretary to the Bishop—Rev. ERIC R. FASANO, M.Div., J.C.L.

Cabinet—
Secretary for Diocesan Administration—MR. KEVIN T. MURPHY, Tel: 516-678-5800, Ext. 543; Email: ktmurphy@drvc.org; Email: ktmurphy@drvc.org.
Secretary for Communications—MR. SEAN P. DOLAN, Tel: 516-678-5800, Ext. 625; Email: rvcinfo@drvc.org.
Office of Education—DR. KATHLEEN WALSH, Ed.D., Supt. Schools, Diocese of Rockville Centre, 128 Cherry Ln., Hicksville, 11801. Tel: 516-280-2479; Fax: 516-280-2963; Email: kwalsh@drvc.org.
Secretary for Faith Formation—Sr. MARY ALICE PIIL, C.S.J., Ph.D., Tel: 516-678-5800, Ext. 512; Email: mapiil@drvc.org.
Secretary for Ministerial Personnel—
Tel: 516-678-5800, Ext. 585. Rev. EDWARD M. SHERIDAN, Email: esheridan@drvc.org.
Secretary for New Evangelization—Deacon FRANCISCO CALES, Tel: 516-678-5800, Ext. 618.
Secretary for Social Services—LAURA CASSELL, Tel: 516-733-7013; Email: cassell.laura@catholiccharities.cc.
Secretary for Institutional Advancement—BARBARA KILARJIAN, Tel: 516-678-5800, Ext. 235; Email: bkilarjian@drvc.org.
Secretary for Operations and General Counsel—MR. THOMAS RENKER, Tel: 516-678-5800, Ext. 241; Email: trenker@drvc.org.
Secretary to the Bishop—Rev. ERIC R. FASANO, M.Div., J.C.L., Tel: 516-678-5800, Ext. 402.
Co Chancellors—Sr. MARYANNE FITZGERALD, S.C., Tel: 516-678-5800, Ext. 583; Email: chancellor@drvc.org; Rev. ERIC R. FASANO, M.Div., J.C.L., Tel: 516-678-5800, Ext. 583; Email: .

Censors of Books—Rev. Msgr. JOHN A. ALESANDRO, P.A., J.C.D.; Rev. CHARLES CACCAVALE, S.T.L., S.T.D.; Rev. Msgrs. JOSEPH DE GROCCO; ROBERT O. MORRISSEY, M.Div., J.C.D.; FRANCIS J. SCHNEIDER, M.Div., J.C.D.; Rev. ROBERT J. SMITH, S.T.L.; Rev. Msgr. PETER I. VACCARI, S.T.L.

Diocesan Tribunal—P.O. Box 9023, Rockville Centre, 11571-9023. Tel: 516-678-5800; Fax: 516-594-1548.

Judicial Vicar—Rev. Msgr. ROBERT O. MORRISSEY, M.Div., J.C.D., Tel: 516-678-5800, Ext. 565; Email: jpereda@drvc.org.

Adjutant Judicial Vicars—Revs. THOMAS V. ARNAO, M.Div., J.C.D., Tel: 516-678-5800, Ext. 558; LEE R. DESCOTEAUX, M.Div., J.C.L.

Diocesan Judge/Defender of the Bond—Deacon THOMAS B. RICH, J.C.L., D.Min., Tel: 516-678-5800, Ext. 559.

Promoter of Justice/Defender of the Bond—Rev. IRINEL RACOS, J.U.D., Tel: 516-678-5800, Ext. 564.

Notaries—MRS. CAROL GATZ; CAROL MCCARTHY; LUCILLE VETRANO.

Medical Experts—THOMAS P. DEMARIA, Ph.D.; Sr. THOMAS MORE FAHEY, R.G.S., Psy.D.

Coordinator of Post-Annulment Counseling Program—KATHRYN SPENCER, Tel: 516-526-7205.

Procurator & Advocates—MRS. LORRAINE ANISANSEL; Deacon RICHARD BECKER; MRS. TERRI BLAKENEY; MRS. MARIAN BOPP; Rev. Msgr. WILLIAM G. BRESLAWSKI; Deacon FRANCISCO CALES; Rev. Msgr. THOMAS C. COSTA; Rev. LAWRENCE T. DUNCKLEE; MR. WILLIAM DWYER; Deacon THOMAS J. EVRARD; Rev. THOMAS J. HAGGERTY; DR. JOANNE HEANY-HUNTER; MR. RICHARD KUMINSKI; Rev. WALTER F. KEDJIERSKI; ROBERT M. MANGIONE; Rev. JAMES P. MANNION JR.; Deacon JAMES MCQUADE; MS. ANN MESSINA; Rev. Msgr. JOSEPH A. MIRRO; Deacons CHARLES MUSCARNERA; MONTFORD D. NAYLOR; Rev. CHRISTOPHER NOWAK; Deacons JOHN O'CONNOR; THOMAS O'CONNOR; MS. EILEEN PHILLIPS; MR. JOHN P. REALI; Deacon GEORGE REICH; MRS. LINDA REICH; Rev. ROBERT A. ROMEO; CARMEN RONCAL; Deacons NEIL SQUITIERI; JOHN F. SULLIVAN; Sr. PATRICIA TURLEY, C.S.J.; MS. JULIE VAN NOSTRAND; Revs. MICHAEL A. VETRANO, Ph. D.; KENNETH M. ZACH; Sr. ELLEN ZAK, C.S.F.N.

Presbyteral Council—Most Revs. ANDRZEJ JERZY ZGLEJSZEWSKI, D.D., Ex Officio; ROBERT J. BRENNAN, V.G., Ex Officio; RICHARD G. HENNING, S.T.D.; ROBERT J. COYLE, D.D., M.Div.; Revs. ERIC R. FASANO, M.Div., J.C.L.; JOSEPH BAIDOO; Rev. Msgrs. FRANK J. CALDWELL, C.S.W.; STEVEN CAMP; Revs. CHRISTOPHER M. COSTIGAN; LAWRENCE T. DUNCKLEE; NASIR GULFAM; Rev. Msgr. THOMAS J. HAROLD; Revs. MICHAEL F. HOLZMANN; ANTHONY IACONIS; THOMAS MORIARTY; GONZALO OAJACA-LOPEZ; FRANCIS PIZZARELLI, S.M.M.; HENRY W. REID; PIOTR ROZEK; JOSEPH SCOLARO; FRANK ZERO; KEVIN SMITH.

College of Consultors—Most Revs. ANDRZEJ JERZY ZGLEJSZEWSKI, D.D.; ROBERT J. BRENNAN, V.G.; RICHARD G. HENNING, S.T.D.; ROBERT J. COYLE, D.D., M.Div.; Revs. ERIC R. FASANO, M.Div., J.C.L.; GONZALO OAJACA-LOPEZ; Rev. Msgr. THOMAS J. HAROLD.

Deans—Rockville Centre Deanery: Rev. Msgr. JAMES P. SWIADER, M.Div. North Hempstead Deanery: Rev. ROBERT A. ROMEO. Oyster Bay Deanery: Rev. MICHAEL T. MAFFEO. Belmont Deanery: Rev. THOMAS M. FUSCO. Five Towns Deanery: Rev. BRIAN P. BARR. Seaford Deanery: Rev. Msgr. ROBERT L. HAYDEN. Hicksville Deanery: Rev. JOHN M. DERASMO. Huntington Deanery: Rev. ROBERT J. SMITH, S.T.L. Babylon Deanery: VACANT. Islip Deanery: Rev. ANTHONY IACONIS. Smithaven Deanery: Rev. MICHAEL F. HOLZMANN. North Brookhaven Deanery: Rev. PATRICK M. RIEGGER. South Brookhaven Deanery: Rev. Msgr. CHARLES R. FINK, M.Div. Peconic Deanery: Rev. MICHAEL J. BARTHOLOMEW.

Diocesan Offices

Pastoral Center—P.O. Box 9023, Rockville Centre, 11571-9023. Tel: 516-678-5800; Fax: 516-764-3316.

Director of Diocesan Administration—MR. KEVIN T. MURPHY, Tel: 516-678-5800, Ext. 543; Email: ktmurphy@drvc.org.

Archives—Seminary of the Immaculate Conception, 440 W. Neck Rd., Huntington, 11743.
Tel: 631-423-0483; Fax: 631-423-7922; Email: archives@drvc.org. KRISTA H. AMMIRATI.

Healthcare Apostolate—Catholic Health Services of Long Island, 992 N. Village Ave., Rockville Centre, 11570. Tel: 516-705-3700; Fax: 516-705-3730. DR. ALAN D. GUERCI, M.D., Pres. & CEO, Tel: 631-465-6000.

Institutional Advancement—BARBARA KILARJIAN, Tel: 516-678-5800, Ext. 235; Email: bkilarjian@drvc.org.

Catholic Ministries Appeal—Mailing Address: P.O. Box 4000, Rockville Centre, 11571.
Tel: 516-678-5800, Ext. 296; Fax: 516-379-5043; Email: catholicministries@drvc.org. BARBARA KILARJIAN.

Parish Stewardship—Tel: 516-678-5800, Ext. 297; Fax: 516-379-3234; Email: stewardship@drvc.org; Web: www.stewardshipli.org.

Religious & Priest Retirement Fund—
Tel: 516-678-5800, Ext. 257; Fax: 516-379-5043; Email: catholicministries@drvc.org. BARBARA KILARJIAN.

Catholic Charities—LAURA A. CASSELL, Exec. Dir., 90 Cherry Ln., Hicksville, 11801. Tel: 516-733-7013. See separate listing below.

Cemeteries—MR. PETER RYAN, Dir., Mailing Address: Catholic Cemeteries, Diocese of Rockville Centre, P.O. Box 182, Westbury, 11590. Tel: 516-334-7990; Fax: 516-334-4383; Email: director@ccdrvcinc.org; Web: www.holyroodcemetery.org. Holy Rood Cemetery, 111 Old Country Rd., Westbury, 11590. Tel: 516-334-7990; Fax: 516-333-2837. Holy Sepulchre Cemetery, 3442 Rte. 112, Coram, 11727. Tel: 631-732-3460; Fax: 631-732-3476. Queen of All Saints Cemetery, 115 Wheeler Rd., Central Islip, 11722. Tel: 631-234-8297; Fax: 631-234-8632. Queen of Peace Cemetery, Old Westbury. Tel: 516-334-7990; Fax: 516-333-2837.

Parish Cemeteries—Parish of St. Patrick, Old Brookville. Parish of St. Boniface, Elmont.
Tel: 516-334-7990. *Parish of The Sacred Heart, Cutchogue. Parish of St. Frances de Sales, Patchogue. Parish of St. John the Evangelist, Riverhead*. Tel: 631-732-3460. *Parish of St. John of God, Central Islip*. Tel: 631-234-8297.

Chaplains (Uniformed)—
Chaplain of the Nassau County Firemen's Association—Nassau County Fire Marshal's Office Rev. KEVIN M. SMITH, St. Dominic, Oyster Bay.; Rev. Msgr. STEVEN CAMP; Rev. CHRISTOPHER M. COSTIGAN.
Chaplains of the Nassau County Police Department—Revs. JOSEPH D'ANGELO, (Retired), Sacred Heart, North Merrick.; GERARD GORDON, St. Martin of Tours, Amityville.
Chaplain of the Suffolk County Police Department—Rev. BRUCE J. POWERS, St. Kilian's, Farmingdale.
Chaplain of the Emerald Society—Rev. SEAN J. GANN, St. Joseph, Kings Park.

Fe Fuerza Vida Newspaper—50 N. Park Ave., Rockville Center, 11571. Tel: 516-678-5800, Ext. 221. MARTHA MOSCOSCO, Editor.

Deacons—Mailing Address: Office of Deacons, P.O. Box 9023, Rockville Center, 11571.
Tel: 631-678-5800, Ext. 632. Deacon LAWRENCE FAULKENBERRY, Dir. Deacon Personnel, Email: lfaulkenberry@drvc.org.

Diaconate Formation—Rev. WALTER F. KEDJIERSKI.

Education—Mailing Address: 128 Cherry Ln., Hicksville, 11801. Tel: 516-280-2479. DR. KATHLEEN WALSH, Ed.D., Supt. Schools, Tel: 516-678-5800, Ext. 845; Email: kwalsh@drvc.org; MS. MARIAN HERNANDEZ, M.S., Asst. Supt. Admin., Tel: 516-678-5800, Ext. 8; Email: mhernandez@drvc.org; MR. ANTHONY BISCIONE, M.S., Asst. Supt. Curriculum, Instruction & Assessment, Email: abiscione@drvc.org; MRS. NORA AUFIERO, B.A., Advocate for Hispanic Initiative, Email: naufiero@drvc.org; MRS. MAUREEN HANNAN, B.S., M.B.A., Coord. Finances, Tel: 516-678-5800, Ext. 825; Email: mhannan@drvc.org; MR. BIAGIO M. ARPINO, M.S., P.D., Asst. Supt. Personnel, Tel: 516-678-5800, Ext. 853; Email: barpino@drvc.org; MRS. KATHLEEN RAZZETTI, M.S., C.A.S., Asst. Supt. for Govt. Progs. & Student Svcs., Tel: 516-678-5800, Ext. 850; Email: krazzetti@drvcschools.org; MRS. EMILY GUARNIERI, M.S., Dir. Educational Technology, Tel: 516-678-5800, Ext. 804; Email: eguarnieri@drvc.org; MR. GARY LAYTON, B.S., Dir. Mktg. & Enrollment, Tel: 516-678-5800, Ext. 817; Email: glayton@drvc.org.

Office of Faith Formation—50 N. Park Ave., P.O. Box 9023, Rockville Centre, 11571. Tel: 516-678-5800; Fax: 516-536-3473. Sr. MARY ALICE PIIL, C.S.J., Ph.D., Dir. Faith Formation, Tel: 516-678-5800, Ext. 512; Email: mapiil@drvc.org.

Temporal Affairs—
Director of Diocesan Administration—MR. KEVIN T. MURPHY, Tel: 516-678-5800, Ext. 543; Fax: 516-536-6554; Email: ktmurphy@drvc.org.
Chief Financial Officer—MR. THOMAS DOODIAN, Tel: 516-678-5800, Ext. 522; Email: tdoodian@drvc.org.
Chief Operations Officer and General Counsel—MR. THOMAS RENKER, Tel: 516-678-5800, Ext. 241; Email: trenker@drvc.org.
Facilities and Risk Management—MR. WILLIAM G. CHAPIN, Dir., Tel: 516-678-5800, Ext. 261; Fax: 516-763-2606; Email: wgchapin@drvc.org.

Health Care Apostolate—Catholic Health Services of Long Island, 992 N. Village Ave., Rockville Centre, 11570. Tel: 516-705-3701; Fax: 516-705-3705; Fax: 516-705-3728. DR. ALAN D. GUERCI, M.D., Pres. & CEO, Tel: 516-705-3708; MR. SALVATORE SODANO, Exec. Chm. Catholic Health Svcs., Tel: 516-705-3708; JAMES SPENCER, Senior Vice Pres. Mission & Ministry, CHS, 992 N. Village Ave., Rockville Center, 11570. Tel: 516-705-7189. For individual hospitals and other healthcare institutions see separate listings below.

Hispanic Apostolate of the South Fork—16 Hill St., Southampton, 11968. Tel: 631-287-9647.

Human Resources—MS. PATRICIA KERNER, Dir., Tel: 516-678-5800, Ext. 282; ARTHUR A. CANDIDO, Tel: 516-678-5800, Ext. 520; Fax: 516-678-9566.

Office of Public Information—MR. SEAN P. DOLAN, Dir., Tel: 516-678-5800, Ext. 625; Fax: 516-594-0984; Email: sdolan@drvc.org.

Immigrant Services—MS. CARMEN MAQUILON, Dir. Immigrant Svcs. Catholic Charities, 143 Schleigel Blvd., Amityville, 11701. Tel: 631-789-5210; Fax: 631-789-5245.

Information Technology—EDWARD COSTELLO, Co Dir.; JACK WEBER, Co Dir., Tel: 516-678-5800, Ext. 405; Email: helpdesk@drvc.org.

Office of Liturgy and Worship—Rev. NICHOLAS A. ZIENTARSKI, S.T.L., Dir., Tel: 516-678-5800, Ext. 504.

The Long Island Catholic Magazine—MR. SEAN P. DOLAN, Assoc. Publisher & Editor, 50 N. Park Ave., Rockville Center, 11571. Tel: 516-678-5800, Ext. 221; Fax: 516-594-1092; Email: sdolan@drvc.org.

Ministry to Senior Priests—Rev. Msgr. THOMAS C. COSTA, St. Pius X Residence, 565 Albany Ave., Amityville, 11701. Tel: 631-608-2622.

Office of New Evangelization—Deacon FRANCISCO CALES, Dir., Tel: 516-678-5800, Ext. 618; Email: fcales@drvc.org.
Office of Multicultural Diversity—DARCEL WHITTEN-WILAMOWSKI, Coord., Tel: 516-678-5800, Ext. 239; Email: dwhitten@drvc.org.
Campus Ministry—Rev. JOSEPH FITZGERALD, M.Div., Coord., Tel: 516-678-5800, Ext. 214; Email: jfitzgerald@drvc.org.
Catholic Scouting—MR. AUSTIN CANNON JR., Coord., Tel: 516-678-5800, Ext. 245; Email: acannon@drvc.org.
Office of Hispanic Ministry—Deacon ROBERTO POLANCO, Tel: 516-678-5800, Ext. 606; Email: rpolanco@drvc.org.
Mission and Propagation of the Faith—Society for the Propagation of the Faith, Holy Childhood Association, Catholic Relief Services, Diocesan Mission in the Dominican Republic, American Home Missions, Secretariat for Latin America.

Deacon FRANCISCO CALES, Dir., Tel: 516-678-5800, Ext. 618.

Renewal Apostolate—MR. PHILIP MANDATO, Tel: 516-678-5800, Ext. 638; Email: pmandato@drvc.org.

Youth Ministry Director—NOLAN REYNOLDS, Tel: 516-678-5800, Ext. 615; Email: nreynolds@drvc.org.

Young Adult Ministry Director—MARY MAILLOUX, Tel: 516-678-5800, Ext. 277; Email: mmailloux@drvc.org.

Clergy Personnel—Rev. EDWARD M. SHERIDAN, Tel: 515-678-5800, Ext. 585; Fax: 516-764-3467; Email: esheridan@drvc.org.

Priestly Life and Ministry—Rev. Msgr. JAMES P. SWIADER, M.Div., Church of Saint Joseph, 130 Fifth St., Garden City, 11530. Tel: 516-747-3535.

Priests' Personnel Assignment Board—Most Revs. JOHN O. BARRES; ANDRZEJ JERZY ZGLEJSZEWSKI, D.D.; ROBERT J. BRENNAN, V.G.; Rev. EDWARD M. SHERIDAN, Ex Officio; Most Revs. RICHARD G. HENNING, S.T.D.; ROBERT J. COYLE, D.D., M.Div.; Rev. THOMAS M. FUSCO; Rev. Msgrs. RICHARD C. BAUHOFF, J.C.D., Ph.D.; ROBERT L. HAYDEN; Revs. ROBERT J. SMITH, S.T.L.; STEPHEN J. PIETROWSKI; IRINEL RACOS, J.U.D.; JAMES T. STACHACZ; ROBERT A. HOLZ.

Priests' Personnel Policy Board—Revs. EDWARD M. SHERIDAN; ANTONY ASIR; Rev. Msgr. JAMES P. SWIADER, M.Div.; Rev. DAVID ATANASIO; Rev. Msgr. THOMAS M. COOGAN; Revs. MICHAEL F. DUFFY; PATRICK M. RIEGGER; FRANK ZERO.

Priests' Retirement Board—Rev. EDWARD M. SHERIDAN, Ex Officio; Rev. Msgrs. THOMAS C. COSTA; RICHARD M. FIGLIOZZI; ROMUALDO SOSING; Revs. JOSEPH V. DAVANZO; ANTONY ASIR; ROBERT A. HOLZ; Most Rev. JOHN C. DUNNE, D.D., (Retired); Rev. Msgr. CHRISTOPHER J. HELLER.

SDR Board Executive Committee Members—(Sick, Disabled, Retired) Revs. EDWARD M. SHERIDAN; ROBERT H. OLZ; Rev. Msgrs. THOMAS C. COSTA; RICHARD M. FIGLIOZZI; MR. KEVIN T. MURPHY; MR. MIKE CONNORS; MS. PATRICIA KERNER; MR. THOMAS DOODIAN.

Prison Ministry and Criminal Justice Affairs—1727 N. Ocean Ave., Medford, 11763. Tel: 631-758-1969. Deacon JAMES MCLAUGHLIN, Dir.; LAURA CASSELL, CEO, Catholic Charities; VICKI MARTINEZ.

Nassau County Correctional Center—100 Carman Ave., East Meadow, 11554-1146. Tel: 516-572-3622. Chaplains: Deacons JOHN H. MCGONIGLE; MANUEL J. RAMOS; S. SUSAN SMOLINSKY, S.C.

Suffolk County Correctional Facility—100 Center Dr., Riverhead, 11901. Tel: 631-852-2294. Chaplains: Sr. MICHELLE BREMER, C.S.F.N.; Deacon JOSE B. VALDEZ.

Suffolk County Minimum Security Facility—Mailing Address: 200 Suffolk Ave., Yaphank, 11980. Tel: 631-852-7296. Prison Chaplains: Sr. MICHELLE BREMER, C.S.F.N.; Deacons JOSE B. VALDEZ; MIGUEL ROMERO; ROGER MOTT. Religious: Vicar for Religious: Sr. PATRICIA MORAN, C.I.J., Tel: 516-678-5800, Ext. 589; Email: pmoran@drvc.org.

Respect Life—ALLISON O'BRIEN, Dir., Tel: 516-678-5800, Ext. 381; Email: aobrien@drvc.org.

The Catholic Faith Network (TV 29)—1200 Glenn Curtiss Blvd., Uniondale, 11553. Tel: 516-538-8700; Fax: 516-489-9701; Email: info@cfntv.org. Rev. Msgr. JAMES C. VLAUN, Tel: 516-538-8704, Ext. 148.

Victim Assistance Coordinator—MARY MCMAHON, Tel: 516-678-5800, Ext. 573; Email: mmcmahon@drvc.org.

Vocations—Fax: 516-255-3796. Rev. JOSEPH FITZGERALD, M.Div., Dir., Mailing Address: Diocese of Rockville Centre, Vocation Office, P.O. Box 9023, Rockville Centre, 11571-9023. Tel: 516-678-5800, Ext. 409; Email: vocations@drvc.org; Web: www.drvc.org/vocations.

Worship—Rev. NICHOLAS A. ZIENTARSKI, S.T.L., Dir., Tel: 516-678-5800, Ext. 503.

Diocesan Organizations

Catholic Accountants' Guild—MISS MARY R. GOELLER, Contact Person, 155 Garfield Ave., Mineola, 11501. Tel: 516-746-1223.

Catholic Lawyer's Guild—Rev. Msgr. JAMES F. PEREDA, M.Div., M.A., J.C.D., Diocesan Chap., Tel: 516-678-5800, Ext. 565; Email: jpereda@drvc.org; Most Rev. ROBERT J. BRENNAN, V.G., Nassau County Chap.

Catholic Youth Organization of Nassau and Suffolk—MR. PAUL EUCHAUSSE, Exec. Dir., Tel: 516-433-1145; MS. MARGARET JOHNSON, Prog. Dir., Tel: 516-433-1145, Ext. 13; Rev. JOSEPH V. DAVANZO, Priest Moderator, 20 E. Cherry St., Hicksville, 11801.

Society of St. Vincent de Paul—THOMAS J. ABBATE, Exec. Dir., 249 Broadway, Bethpage, 11714. Tel: 516-822-3132; Fax: 516-822-2728.

CLERGY, PARISHES, MISSIONS AND PAROCHIAL SCHOOLS

VILLAGE OF ROCKVILLE CENTRE

(NASSAU COUNTY)

1—ST. AGNES CATHEDRAL (1894)

29 Quealy Pl., 11570. Tel: 516-766-0205; Email: parishoffice@stagnescathedral.org; Web: www.stagnescathedral.org. Rev. Msgrs. James C. Vlaun, Pres. and C.E.O. of Telecare; William E. Koenig, Rector; Revs. German Villabon, O.S.A.; Seth N. Awo Doku; James H. Hansen; Rev. Msgr. Robert O. Morrissey, M.Div., J.C.D., In Res.; Most Rev. William Francis Murphy, S.T.D., L.H.D., Former Bishop; Rt. Rev. Msgr. James P. Kelly, Rector Emeritus, (Retired); Deacon Thomas McDaid.

School—St. Agnes Cathedral School, (Grades K-8), 70 Clinton Ave., 11570. Tel: 516-678-5550; Fax: 516-678-0437; Email: cstjohn5546@stagnes-school.org; Web: stagnes-school.org. Mrs. Cecilia St. John. Lay Teachers 45; Students 627.

Catechesis Religious Program—Tel: 516-678-2306; Email: jlong@stagnescathedral.org. Joseph R. Long, D.R.E. Students 1,550.

2—CAMPUS PARISH OF LONG ISLAND (1972)

P.O. Box 9023, 11571. Tel: 516-678-5800; Fax: 516-763-1078. Most Rev. Robert J. Brennan, V.G., Admin.; Marianne Sheridan, Dir. Youth, Campus, Young Adults.

Catechesis Religious Program—Ellen Zafonte, Dir. Faith Formation.

For details, please refer to Campus Ministries and Newman Centers under the Institution section.

OUTSIDE VILLAGE OF ROCKVILLE CENTRE

AMITYVILLE, SUFFOLK CO., ST. MARTIN OF TOURS (1897) Revs. Gerard Gordon; Joseph Madsen; Deacons Michael Aprile; Richard Ferri; Larry McPartland.

Res.: 37 Union Ave., Amityville, 11701.

Tel: 631-264-0124; Tel: 631-264-0166; Fax: 631-264-0139; Email: martours@optonline.net; Web: www.stmartinschurch.net.

School—St. Martin of Tours School, 30 Union Ave., Amityville, 11701. Tel: 631-264-7166; Fax: 631-264-0136; Email: mmartinez5606@smtschool.org; Web: smtschool.org. Maria Martinez, Prin. Lay Teachers 24; Students 359.

Catechesis Religious Program—Tel: 631-691-1617; Email: stmartinreo@gmail.com. Jennifer Kennedy, D.R.E. Students 25.

BABYLON, SUFFOLK CO., ST. JOSEPH (1877) [CEM] Rev. Msgr. Christopher J. Heller; Revs. Joseph V. Arevalo; Francis A. Samuel, O.C.I.; Ethel Anarado, (Nigeria); Deacons Michael J. Leyden; John F. Sullivan; Barry P. Croce.

Res.: 39 N. Carll Ave., Babylon, 11702-2701.

Tel: 631-669-0068; Fax: 631-669-9175; Email: parishoffice@stjosephsbabylon.org; Web: www.stjosephsbabylon.org.

Catechesis Religious Program—Tel: 631-587-4717. Claire Moule, D.R.E. Students 1,207.

Mission—West Gilgo Beach, Suffolk Co. 11702. (Summer).

BALDWIN, NASSAU CO., ST. CHRISTOPHER (1915) Revs. Nicholas A. Zientarski, S.T.L.; Brandon O'Brien; Deacons Anthony Banno; James Carroll; Ralph J. Muscente. In Res., Rev. Sylvester Ileka.

Res.: 11 Gale Ave., Baldwin, 11510-3202.

Tel: 516-223-0723; Email: info@stchrisbaldwin.org; Web: www.stchris.com.

School—St. Christopher School, 15 Pershing Blvd., Baldwin, 11510. Tel: 516-223-4404; Fax: 516-223-1409. Anne Lederer, Prin. Lay Teachers 23; Sisters of St. Joseph, Brentwood 1; Students 295.

Catechesis Religious Program—Tel: 516-223-5813; Fax: 516-223-5609. Sr. Joan Klimski, O.P., D.R.E. (Adult & Faith Formation); James Montalbano, Music & Liturgy Dir. Students 525.

BAY SHORE, SUFFOLK CO., ST. PATRICK'S (1883) [CEM] Rev. Msgr. Thomas M. Coogan; Revs. David Atanasio; Cyril Obi Bayim; Deacons Joseph Peralta; Frank Keach; Tom Quinn; Gregory Nardone.

Res.: 9 N. Clinton Ave., Bay Shore, 11706.

Tel: 631-665-4911; Fax: 631-665-8388.

School—St. Patrick's School, Tel: 631-665-0569; Fax: 631-968-6007; Web: www.spsbayshore.org. Mrs. Roseann Petruccio, Prin. Lay Teachers 30; Students 490.

Catechesis Religious Program—Tel: 631-665-4914; Fax: 631-665-9009. Students 1,263.

BAYVILLE, NASSAU CO., ST. GERTRUDE'S (1959) Rev. Stephen J. Brigandi.

Res.: 28 School St., Bayville, 11709.

Tel: 516-628-1113; Fax: 516-628-9032.

School—Pre School, Tel: 516-628-3710. Students 40.

Catechesis Religious Program—Tel: 516-628-2432; Fax: 516-628-0224. Students 420.

BELLMORE, NASSAU CO., ST. BARNABAS THE APOSTLE (1912) Revs. Adrian McHugh, (Ireland); Charles Omotu, (Nigeria); Francis Agyeman, (Ghana); Deacons Bernard Sherlock; Richard Iandoli.

Res.: 2320 Bedford Ave., Bellmore, 11710.

Tel: 516-785-0054; Fax: 516-221-7789; Web: www.stbarnabasny.org.

See St. Elizabeth Ann Seton Regional School, Bellmore under Regional Schools located in the Institution section.

Catechesis Religious Program—Tel: 516-785-0130; Fax: 516-221-0391; Email: stbarnabasocf@yahoo.com. Students 1,450.

BELLPORT, SUFFOLK CO., MARY IMMACULATE (1905) Rev. Msgr. William A. Hanson.

Res.: 16 Brown's Ln., Bellport, 11713.

Tel: 631-286-0154; Fax: 631-286-2937; Email: frbill@miparish.net; Web: miparish.net.

See Holy Angels Regional School, Patchogue under Regional Schools located in the Institution section.

Catechesis Religious Program—Tel: 631-286-3504. Students 465.

BETHPAGE, NASSAU CO., ST. MARTIN OF TOURS (1923) Revs. Patrick Wood, C.Ss.R.; James McCabe, C.Ss.R., Pastoral Assoc.; Ciya Thomas, C.Ss.R., Pastoral Assoc.; Deacon Thomas Hennessy.

Res.: 40 Seaman Ave., Bethpage, 11714.

Tel: 516-931-0818; Fax: 516-931-0559.

See St. John Baptist de LaSalle Regional School, Farmingdale under Regional Schools located in the Institution section.

Catechesis Religious Program—220 Central Ave., Bethpage, 11714. Patricia Ryan, C.R.E.; Laura Leigh Agnese, C.R.E. Students 1,151.

BLUE POINT, SUFFOLK CO., OUR LADY OF THE SNOW (1917) Rev. Msgr. Charles R. Fink, M.Div.; Deacons Robert Gronenthal, (Retired); Frank Hartmann; Edward Karan.

Res.: 175 Blue Point Ave., Blue Point, 11715.

Tel: 631-363-6385, Ext. 111; Email: ourladyofthesnowbp@gmail.com; Web: www.ourladyofthesnowbluepoint.com.

Catechesis Religious Program—Tel: 631-363-6394. Students 1,056.

BOHEMIA, SUFFOLK CO., ST. JOHN NEPOMUCENE (1919) [CEM] Revs. Joseph M. Schlafer; Lawrence A. Chadwick; Deacons James Bohuslaw; George Reich; Roger Mott.

Res.: 1140 Locust Ave., Bohemia, 11716.

Tel: 631-589-0540; Fax: 631-244-8086; Email: stjohnep@optonline.net; Web: mychurchandtown.com.

Catechesis Religious Program—1150 Locust Ave., Bohemia, 11716. Tel: 631-567-1765. Mrs. Kathy Russell-Sica, D.R.E. Students 1,216.

BRENTWOOD, SUFFOLK CO.

1—ST. ANNE'S (1895)

88 Second Ave., Brentwood, 11717.

Tel: 631-273-8113; Email: stannesbrentwood@gmail.com. Revs. Stanislaw Wadowski, (Poland); Victor Evangelista; Charlince Vendredy; Deacons Jay Alvarado; John E. Walters; Andres Colpa; Mrs. Marge Baum, Pastoral Assoc.; Mrs. Sue Lindsay, Dir. Music; Mrs. Janet Lambert, Parish Life Coord.; Mr. Anthony (Tony) Bellizzi, Youth Min.

See Our Lady of Providence Regional School, Central Islip under Regional Schools located in the Institution section.

Catechesis Religious Program—Tel: 631-231-7344. Students 565.

2—ST. LUKE (1965) [JC]

266 Wicks Rd., Brentwood, 11717. Tel: 631-273-1110; Email: info@sanlukes.org; Web: sanlukes.org. Revs. Cristobal Martin, M. Id, Ph.D.; Biju Choothamparambil; Camillo Lugo, (Colombia) (In Res.); Bro. Carlos Lindao, M. Id, Youth Min.; Deacons Richard A. Luken; Orlando Mancilla; Jose Arevalo; Debby Cristaldo, Office Mgr.

See Our Lady of Providence Regional School, Central Islip under Regional Schools located in the Institution section.

Catechesis Religious Program—Sr. Elaine Schenk, M.Id., D.R.E. Students 256.

BRIDGEHAMPTON, SUFFOLK CO., QUEEN OF THE MOST HOLY ROSARY (1922)

P.O. Box 3035, Bridgehampton, 11932.

Tel: 631-537-0156; Fax: 631-537-7116; Email: qmhrnybh@aol.com. Rev. Peter Devaraj, S.A.C.

Catechesis Religious Program—Sr. Maryann McCarthy, C.S.J., D.R.E. Students 8.

BROOKVILLE, NASSAU CO., ST. PAUL THE APOSTLE

(1962) Rev. Msgr. James F. Pereda, M.Div., M.A., J.C.D.; Deacon Raymond P. D'Alessio.
Res.: 2534 Cedar Swamp Rd., Rte. 107, Brookville, 11545. Tel: 516-935-1880; Email: info@stpaulsbrookville.org.
Catechesis Religious Program—Tel: 516-938-4530; Fax: 516-938-4531. Mrs. Louise Shannon, Faith Formation Admin.; Bro. Joseph Bellizzi, S.M., D.R.E. Students 323.

CARLE PLACE, NASSAU CO., CHURCH OF OUR LADY OF HOPE (1987) Rev. Thomas V. Arnao, M.Div., J.C.D.; Deacons Thomas B. Rich, J.C.L., D.Min.; Raymond J. Tirelli; Patrick J. Dunphy; Raymond J. Henderson, Music Min.
Church: 534 Broadway, Carle Place, 11514-1712.
Tel: 516-334-6288; Web: www.olhope.org.
School—St. Brigid / Our Lady of Hope Regional School, 101 Maple Ave., Westbury, 11590.
Tel: 516-333-0580; Fax: 516-333-0590.
Catechesis Religious Program—Tel: 516-334-4781. Students 480.

CEDARHURST, NASSAU CO., ST. JOACHIM (1894) Rev. Thomas Moriarty Jr., Admin.; Rev. Msgr. Paul F. Rahilly, Pastor Emeritus, (Retired); Deacons Frank J. Bono; Charles R. Goldburg.
Res.: 614 Central Ave., Cedarhurst, 11516.
Tel: 516-569-1845; Fax: 516-569-0117; Email: joachimrcc@yahoo.com.

CENTER MORICHES, SUFFOLK CO., ST. JOHN THE EVANGELIST (1898) Revs. Walter F. Kedjierski; John Sureau; Felix Akpabio; Dennis Suglia; Deacon John C. Pettorino.
Res.: 25 Ocean Ave., Center Moriches, 11934.
Tel: 631-878-0009; Fax: 631-874-2466; Email: rectory@sjecm.org.
See Our Lady, Queen of the Apostles Regional School, Center Moriches under Regional Schools located in the Institution section.
Catechesis Religious Program—Tel: 631-878-4141. Students 1,825.

CENTEREACH, SUFFOLK CO., ASSUMPTION OF THE BLESSED VIRGIN MARY (1955)
20 Chestnut St., Centereach, 11720.
Tel: 631-585-8760; Email: rectory@abvmcentereach.com. Revs. Christopher J. Aridas; Joseph Alenchery, (India); Deacon Michael Montelione.
Catechesis Religious Program—Tel: 631-588-6408; Email: lrobustelli@abvmcentereach.com. Lisette Robustelli, Coord. Evangelization & Faith Formation. Students 533.

CENTERPORT, SUFFOLK CO., OUR LADY QUEEN OF MARTYRS (1966) Rev. Stephen J. Pietrowski; Bro. Etienne Jaeckel, Pastoral Assoc.; Deacon John Rieger.
Res.: 53 Prospect Rd., Centerport, 11721.
Tel: 631-757-8184; Email: rectory@olqmparish.org; Web: www.olqmparish.org.
See Trinity Regional School, East Northport under Regional Schools located in the Institution section.
Catechesis Religious Program—Email: neuler@OLQMparish.org. Ninette Euler, D.R.E. Students 0.

CENTRAL ISLIP, SUFFOLK CO., ST. JOHN OF GOD (1904) [CEM]
84 Carleton Ave., Central Islip, 11722.
Tel: 631-234-6535; Email: sjogno1@aol.com; Web: www.stjohnofgodparish.org. Revs. Christopher Nowak; Fidel Cruz Vicencio; Sr. Valerie Scholl, C.S.J., Pastoral Assoc. Admin.; John Lafferty, Pastoral Assoc., Fundraising; Deacon Jose B. Valdez; Carmen Roncal, Pastoral Assoc.; Ana Sullivan, Pastoral Assoc.; Mr. Giovanni Mayo, Pastoral Assoc.; Mr. Guillermo Felix, Music Min.
See Our Lady of Providence Regional School, Central Islip under Regional Schools located in the Institution section.
Catechesis Religious Program—Tel: 631-234-4040; Email: sjogre@verizon.net. Margaret Martin, D.R.E. Students 557.
PARISH OUTREACH, Tel: 631-234-1884. Ana Sullivan, Dir.
Convent—Sisters of St. Joseph, 330 St. John St., Central Islip, 11722.

COMMACK, SUFFOLK CO., CHRIST THE KING (1959)
2 Indian Head Rd., Commack, 11725.
Tel: 631-864-1623; Fax: 631-864-8891; Email: parishoffice@ctkrcc.org. Revs. Joseph V. Davanzo; Robert C. Scheckenback; Brian J. Brinker, In Res.; Deacons Joseph Marfoglio; Louis Anetrella.
See Holy Family Regional School, Commack under Regional Schools located in the Institution section.
Catechesis Religious Program—Email: cff@ctkrcc.org. Students 1,653.

COPIAGUE, SUFFOLK CO., OUR LADY OF THE ASSUMPTION (1928)
1 Molloy St., Copiague, 11726. Tel: 631-842-5211;
Tel: 631-626-4174 (Emergency Number); Email: assumptioncopia@optonline.net; Web: www.olacopiague.org. Revs. Dariusz Koszyk; Jose Gustavo Perez Alzate; Deacons Michael Appel; Philip A. Mills Jr.
Catechesis Religious Program—Tel: 631-842-3545. Mr. Biagio M. Arpino, M.S., P.D., D.R.E. Students 729.

CORAM, SUFFOLK CO., ST. FRANCES CABRINI (1953) Revs. Donald M. Baier; James Akpan, (Nigeria); Deacons Carmen L. Pagnotta; Monte Naylor Jr., (Retired); Peter Acquaro.
Res.: 134 Middle Country Rd., Coram, 11727.
Tel: 631-732-8445; Fax: 631-732-8978; Email: coramcab@aol.com; Web: sfccoram.org.
See Holy Angels Regional School, Patchogue under Regional Schools located in the Institution section.
Catechesis Religious Program—Tel: 631-698-3149. Students 560.

CUTCHOGUE, SUFFOLK CO.
1—OUR LADY OF OSTRABRAMA (1909) [JC] (Polish) Rev. Msgr. Joseph W. Staudt, Admin.
Res.: 3000 Depot Ln., Box 997, Cutchogue, 11935.
Tel: 631-734-6446; Fax: 631-734-4117.
School—North Fork Regional Catholic School, Cutchogue, Tel: 631-734-5166. See Regional Schools under Institutions Located in the Diocese.
Catechesis Religious Program—Students 72.
2—SACRED HEART (1901) [CEM] Rev. Msgr. Joseph W. Staudt; Deacon Jeffrey Sykes.
Res.: 27905 Main Rd., P.O. Box 926, Cutchogue, 11935-0926. Tel: 631-734-6722; Fax: 631-734-7906.
See Our Lady of Mercy Regional School, Cutchogue under Regional Schools located in the Institution section.
Catechesis Religious Program—Tel: 631-734-2568. Mrs. Suzanne Sykes, D.R.E. Students 330.
Mission—Our Lady of Good Counsel, Main Rd., Mattituck, Suffolk Co. 11952.

DAVIS PARK, FIRE ISLAND SUFFOLK CO., MOST PRECIOUS BLOOD (1962) (Summer Mission) Rev. Francis Pizzarelli, S.M.M.
Res.: 10 Spindrift Walk, Fire Island, Davis Park, 11728.

DEER PARK, SUFFOLK CO., SS. CYRIL AND METHODIUS (1956) Rev. Msgr. Robert J. Clerkin; Revs. Patrick Grace; Francis D. Sang, (Vietnam) (Retired); Moise Aime, (Haiti); Deacons John F. Fitzpatrick; Charles F. Huber, (Retired); James A. Murano, Music Dir.; Philip A. Mills Jr., Pastoral Assoc. Admin./Business Mgr.; William Sperl.
Res.: 125 Half Hollow Rd., Deer Park, 11729-4288.
Tel: 631-667-4044; Email: saintcm@optonline.net.
School—SS. Cyril and Methodius School, Fax: 631-667-0093. Sr. Susan Snyder, C.S.J., Prin. Lay Teachers 21; Preschool 48; Students 162.
Catechesis Religious Program—Email: amora.laucella@gmail.com. Amora Laucella, D.R.E. Students 1,000.

DIX HILLS, SUFFOLK CO., ST. MATTHEW (1965) Revs. Robert S. Hewes; Allan Sikorski; Deacons James M. McQuade; Carmine DeStefano; Luis Roberto Polanco; Dolores Tiernan, Business Mgr.
Res.: 35 N. Service Rd., Dix Hills, 11746.
Tel: 631-499-8520; Fax: 631-499-1530; Email: pastor@smrcc.org; Web: www.smrcc.org. In Res., Rev. Lawrence B. Rafferty, (Retired).
See Holy Family Regional School, Commack under Regional Schools located in the Institution section.
Catechesis Religious Program—Tel: 631-864-3321. Mary Donaldson, D.R.E. Students 1,426.

EAST HAMPTON, SUFFOLK CO., MOST HOLY TRINITY (1894) [CEM]
Mailing Address: 57 Buell Ln., East Hampton, 11937. Tel: 631-324-0134, Ext. 712. Rev. Ryan Creamer; Deacon Lawrence Faulkenberry.
Res.: 53 Buell Ln., East Hampton, 11937.
Business: 79 Buell Ln., East Hampton, 11937. Email: pastor@mht-eh.org.
Catechesis Religious Program—44 Meadow Way, East Hampton, 11937. Students 267.
Mission—St. Peter the Apostle, 286 Main St., Amagansett, Suffolk Co. 11930.

EAST ISLIP, SUFFOLK CO., CHURCH OF ST. MARY (1898)
20 Harrison Ave., East Islip, 11730.
Tel: 631-581-4266; Fax: 631-581-0112; Email: tvanburen@parishofstmary.org; Web: www.parishofstmary.org. Rev. Donald E. Babinski, M.Div.; Rev. Msgr. Michael P. Flynn; Revs. Jaime Calderon-Hernandez; Robert W. Ketcham, In Res.; Sr. Patricia Tippen, I.H.M., Pastoral Assoc.; Deacon Stephen Behar.
School—Church of St. Mary School, 16 Harrison Ave., East Islip, 11730. Tel: 631-581-4266, Ext. 5; Fax: 631-581-7509. Mr. Biagio M. Arpino, M.S., P.D., Prin. Lay Teachers 23; Students 497.
Catechesis Religious Program—Linda Crowley, D.R.E. Students 1,387.

EAST MEADOW, NASSAU CO., ST. RAPHAEL (1941)
600 Newbridge Rd., East Meadow, 11554.
Tel: 516-785-0236; Fax: 516-783-9578; Email: vincenzarectory@optonline.net; Web: www.straphaelparish.org. Revs. Robert A. Holz; Tomasz Jarzynka; Anthony Saliba; Deacons Victor R. Costa; Angelo D'Aversa; Dennis Schlosser; Sr. Judy Fay, C.S.J., Dir. Parish Social Ministry; Diane Lawlor, Business Mgr.
See St. Elizabeth Ann Seton Regional School, Bellmore under Regional Schools located in the Institution section.
Catechesis Religious Program—Tel: 516-221-9096; Fax: 516-221-9084; Email: raphaelreo@hotmail.com. Sr. Karen Lademann, O.P., Dir. Faith Formation. Students 1,382.

EAST NORTHPORT, SUFFOLK CO., ST. ANTHONY OF PADUA (1951) Rev. Msgr. Joseph A. Mirro; Revs. Innocent Amasiorah; Vian Ntegerejlmana; Deacon Robert Braun. In Res., Rev. Msgr. Thomas E. Molloy, (Retired).
Res.: 20 Cheshire Pl., East Northport, 11731-2591.
Tel: 631-261-1077; Fax: 631-757-0572; Email: pastor@saintanthonyofpadua.org; Web: www.saintanthonyofpadua.org.
See Trinity Regional School, East Northport under Regional Schools located in the Institution section.
Catechesis Religious Program—Tel: 631-261-1306. Mrs. Patricia Seibert, D.R.E. Students 500.

EAST PATCHOGUE, SUFFOLK CO., ST. JOSEPH THE WORKER (1955)
510 Narragansett Ave., East Patchogue, 11772.
Tel: 631-286-9133; Fax: 631-286-9145; Email: sjw510@gmail.com; Web: www.stjosephtheworker.weconnect.com. Rev. Martin Curtin, O.F.M.Cap.
See Holy Angels Regional School, Patchogue under Regional Schools located in the Institution section.
Catechesis Religious Program—Tel: 631-286-2550. Judy Hansen, D.R.E. Students 510.

EAST ROCKAWAY, NASSAU CO., ST. RAYMOND'S (1909) Revs. Charles Romano; Francis X. Eisele; Deacons Richard W. LaRossa, Pastoral Assoc.; Robert C. Campbell; Thomas W. Connolly; Guy Donza, Pastoral Assoc.; Thomas Malone.
Res.: 263 Atlantic Ave., East Rockaway, 11518.
Tel: 516-593-5000; Fax: 516-887-0554; Email: strayrcc@optonline.net; Web: www.saintraymonds.org.
School—St. Raymond's School, Tel: 516-593-9010; Fax: 516-593-0986. Sr. Ruthanne Gypalo, I.H.M., Prin. Lay Teachers 23; Sisters, Servants of the Immaculate Heart of Mary 3; Students 300.
Catechesis Religious Program—Tel: 516-593-9075; Email: econtaldisrre@optonline.net. Mrs. Evelyn Contaldi, D.R.E. Students 850.

ELMONT, NASSAU CO.
1—ST. BONIFACE (1852) [CEM] Rev. Msgr. William J. Gomes, Email: stbonfac@aol.com; Revs. Charlince Vendredy; Cerino Bunao; Sr. Evelyn Lamoureux, D.W., Human Svcs.; Deacons Salvatore Marino; Dominique Silien. In Res., Rev. George Punti, (Retired).
Res.: 631 Elmont Rd., Elmont, 11003.
Tel: 516-354-0715; Fax: 516-354-0446.
Catechesis Religious Program—Tel: 516-437-7112. Nancy Cosgrove, D.R.E. Students 475.
2—ST. VINCENT DE PAUL (1951)
1510 De Paul St., Elmont, 11003. Tel: 516-352-2127; Fax: 516-352-2358; Email: parishoffice@stvincentdepaulparish.org; Web: stvincentdepaulparish.org. Rev. Msgr. Richard M. Figliozzi, Admin.
Res.: 33 New Hyde Park Rd., Franklin Square, 11010.
Catechesis Religious Program—St. Catherine School, 990 Holzheimer St., Franklin Square, 11010. Students 85.

FARMINGDALE, NASSAU CO., ST. KILIAN (1896) Revs. Bruce J. Powers; Michael F. Duffy; Jose Luis Tenas Calidonio Medrano; Deacons Frank D. Barone; Lucio Cotone, (Retired); Francis P. Marino; George Owen, (Retired); Mark Wetzel; William Weiss Jr.; Edward Fronckwicz, Business Mgr. In Res., Most Rev. John C. Dunne, D.D., (Retired); Rev. Augustine Fernado, (India) (Retired).
Res.: 485 Conklin St., Farmingdale, 11735.
Tel: 516-249-0127; Fax: 516-249-7131; Email: info@stkilian.com; Web: www.stkilian.com.
Catechesis Religious Program—50 Cherry St., Farmingdale, 11735. Tel: 516-694-0633; Fax: 516-454-8612. Claire Stiglic, Assoc. D.R.E.; Kathleen Singleton, Assoc. D.R.E.; Mr. Paul C. Phinney, Music Dir. Students 1,301.
PARISH SOCIAL MINISTRY/OUTREACH, 140 Elizabeth St., Farmingdale, 11735. Tel: 516-756-9656; Fax: 516-293-2667. Mrs. Nina Petersen, Dir. Social Ministry.

FARMINGVILLE, SUFFOLK CO., CHURCH OF THE RESURRECTION (1988) Rev. Gonzalo Oajaca-Lopez; Deacons James DiGiovanna; Juan Diaz; Vincent Barreca Jr.
Church: 50 Granny Rd., Farmingville, 11738.
Tel: 631-696-0232; Fax: 631-696-0271; Email: info@resurrectionrcchurch.org; Web: resurrectionrcchurch.org.
Catechesis Religious Program—
Tel: 631-696-0270, Ext. 25; Email:

religioused@resurrectionrcchurch.org. Laurie Thorp, D.R.E. Students 2.

FLORAL PARK, NASSAU CO.

1—ST. HEDWIG'S (1902) (Polish)
One Depan Ave., Floral Park, 11001.
Tel: 516-354-0042; Email: contact@sthedwig.church; Web: www.sthedwig.church. Rev. Piotr Rozek, Admin.
Catechesis Religious Program—Tel: 631-875-8413; Email: contact@sthedwigfloralpark.org. Krzysztof Gospodarzec, D.R.E. Students 58.

2—OUR LADY OF VICTORY (1921)
2 Floral Pkwy., Floral Park, 11001-3198.
Tel: 516-354-0482; Email: tfusco@olvfpny.org; Web: www.olvfpny.org. Revs. Thomas M. Fusco; Christopher Sullivan; John V. O'Farrell, Pastor Emeritus, (Retired); Deacon Lawrence P. Mulligan.
School—Our Lady of Victory School, 2 Bellmore St., Floral Park, 11001. Tel: 516-352-4466;
Tel: 516-354-2150; Fax: 516-352-2998; Email: paugello5628@olvfp.org; Web: olvfp.org. Margaret M. Augello, Prin. Lay Teachers 26; Students 368.
Catechesis Religious Program—Tel: 516-352-0510. Christine Fuchs, D.R.E. Students 984.

FRANKLIN SQUARE, NASSAU CO., ST. CATHERINE OF SIENNA (1913)
33 New Hyde Park Rd., Franklin Square, 11010.
Tel: 516-352-0146; Email: parishoffice@stcatherineofsienna.org; Web: stcatherineofsienna.org. Rev. Msgr. Richard M. Figliozzi; Revs. Jerzy Bres; Allan Arnaud; Deacons Joseph Benincasa; Frank Gonzalez.
Catechesis Religious Program—Email: dhurley@stcatherineofsienna.org. Debbie Hurley, Faith Formation Coord. Students 1,183.

FREEPORT, NASSAU CO., OUR HOLY REDEEMER (1903)
Revs. Douglas R. Arcoleo; Carlos Urrego Arenas, Parochial VIcar; Alessandro da Luz; Deacons Francisco Cales; Bruce A. Burnham; Cristobal Sanchez, Pastoral Assoc.; Alfonso Martinez, Dir. Parish Human Svcs. In Res., Rev. Msgr. Donald T. Bennett, (Retired).
Res.: 37 S. Ocean Ave., Freeport, 11520.
Tel: 516-378-0665; Email: ohr37@aol.com; Web: ohrfreeport.org.
Catechesis Religious Program—87 Pine St., Freeport, 11520. Tel: 516-546-1057; Email: ohrreled@optimum.net. Mrs. Deneen Vukelic, D.R.E. Students 490.

GARDEN CITY, NASSAU CO.

1—ST. ANNE (1929)
35 Dartmouth St., Garden City, 11530.
Tel: 516-352-5904; Email: parishoffice@stannesgc.org; Web: www.stannesgc.org. Rev. Msgrs. Thomas J. Harold; Timothy Valentine; Deacons George Browne; James J. O'Brien; Basil Bliss; Robert McCarthy.
School—St. Anne School, 25 Dartmouth St., Garden City, 11530. Tel: 516-352-1205; Fax: 516-352-5969. Mr. Gene Fennell, Prin. Lay Teachers 30; Students 530.
Catechesis Religious Program—Tel: 516-488-1032; Email: vflood@stannesgc.org. Vivian Flood, Faith Formation Program Admin. Students 900.

2—ST. JOSEPH'S (1901) Rev. Msgr. James P. Swiader, M.Div.; Revs. Joseph Scolaro; Prasanna Costa; Deacons John J. McKenna; Andrew Ciccaroni; Jack McKenna, Dir. Stewardship & Family Ministry; Joseph Cangialosi, Dir. Music & Liturgy.
Res.: 130 Fifth St., Garden City, 11530.
Tel: 516-747-3535; Email: msgrjswiader@stjosephsgc.com; Web: www.stjosephchurchgc.org.
School—St. Joseph's School, 450 Franklin Ave., Garden City, 11530. Tel: 516-747-2730;
Fax: 516-747-2854. Mr. Brian Colomban, Prin.; Regina A. Cioffi, Asst. Prin.; Anna Maria Sirianni, L.C.S.W., Dir. Human Svcs. Lay Teachers 27; Students 356.
Catechesis Religious Program—Tel: 516-741-7787; Fax: 516-741-5049. Mrs. Lisa Spohr, D.R.E.; Sr. Kathleen Corr, O.P., Dir. Adult Faith Formation. Students 1,400.

GLEN COVE, NASSAU CO.

1—ST. PATRICK'S (1856) [CEM] Very Revs. Dom Daniel Stephen Nash, Can.Reg.; Dom Gabriel Rach, Can. Reg., Parochial Vicar; Dom Ambros Boyd, Can.Reg., Parochial Vicar; Mr. Cantalicio Gamarra, Spanish Min.; Deacons Frank Borchardt; Juan Guilfu; Frances Howlett, Music Min. In Res., Very Rev. Dom Elias Carr, Can.Reg.
Res.: 235 Glen St., Glen Cove, 11542.
Tel: 516-676-0276; Fax: 516-674-9137; Email: stpatshill@aol.com.
FOR HISPANIC MINISTRY, Tel: 516-759-6039.
See All Saints Regional Catholic School, Glen Cove under Regional Schools located in the Institution section.
Catechesis Religious Program—Tel: 516-671-7223. Bernadette Heym, D.R.E. Students 445.

2—ST. ROCCO (1937) (Italian) Very Rev. Dom Elias Carr, Can.Reg.
Res.: 18 Third St., Glen Cove, 11542.
Tel: 516-676-2482; Fax: 516-676-2117; Email: saintroccochurch@gmail.com; Web: www.stroccoglencove.com.
See All Saints Regional Catholic School, Glen Cove under Regional Schools located in the Institution section.
Catechesis Religious Program—Students 352.

GLEN HEAD, NASSAU CO., ST. HYACINTH (1909) (Polish) Revs. Marian Bicz; Jerzy Bres.
Res.: 319 Cedar Swamp Rd., Glen Head, 11545.
Tel: 516-676-0361; Fax: 516-674-4728; Email: sthyacinth@optonline.net.
See All Saints Regional Catholic School, Glen Cove under Regional Schools located in the Institution section.
Catechesis Religious Program—
Tel: 516-676-0361, Ext. 123. Miss Eileen Meserole, D.R.E. Students 106.

GREAT NECK, NASSAU CO., ST. ALOYSIUS (1876) (Hispanic—Korean)
592 Middle Neck Rd., Great Neck, 11023. Revs. Rene O. Tapel, (Philippines); Seung Yi, Korean Ministry, Tel: 516-466-8700 (Office); Fax: 516-466-6006.
Catechesis Religious Program—Tel: 516-482-5660; Fax: 516-829-4054. Students 256.

GREENLAWN, SUFFOLK CO., ST. FRANCIS OF ASSISI (1966) Rev. Peter Kaczmarek; Rev. Msgr. Patrick Armshaw, Pastor Emeritus, (Retired); Deacons Allan Longo; David Campbell; Jean Cantave; James Byrne.
Res.: 29 Northgate Dr., Greenlawn, 11740.
Tel: 631-757-7435; Fax: 631-757-0469; Web: www.stfrancisgreenlawn.org.
See Trinity Regional School, East Northport under Regional Schools located in the Institution section.
Catechesis Religious Program—Tel: 631-754-6436. Students 440.

GREENPORT, SUFFOLK CO., ST. AGNES (1886) [CEM] (Hispanic)
523 Front St., Greenport, 11944. Tel: 631-477-0048; Email: rectory@optonline.net; Web: www.saintagnesgreenport.org. Rev. Richard P. Hoerning.
See Our Lady of Mercy Regional School, Cutchogue under Regional Schools located in the Institution section.
See McGann-Mercy High School, Riverton under High Schools Diocesan located in the Institution section.
Catechesis Religious Program—Tel: 631-477-1422. Students 140.

HAMPTON BAYS, SUFFOLK CO., ST. ROSALIE'S (1901)
31 E. Montauk Hwy., Hampton Bays, 11946.
Tel: 631-728-9461; Email: StRosalies@optonline.net; Web: www.saintrosalie.com. Revs. Steve Maddaloni, Admin.; John Wachowicz; Deacons Christopher Ervin, Pastoral Assoc.; James E. Leopard.
See Our Lady of the Hamptons Regional School, Southampton under Regional Schools located in the Institution section.
Catechesis Religious Program—Email: rfeileen@optonline.net. Eileen McPhelin, D.R.E. Students 433.
Mission—Montauk Hwy. & Walnut Ave., East Quogue, Suffolk Co. 11946.

HAUPPAUGE, SUFFOLK CO., ST. THOMAS MORE (1967)
115 Kings Hwy., Hauppauge, 11788-4221.
Tel: 631-234-5551; Fax: 631-234-6412; Email: rectory@stmli.org; Web: www.stmli.org. Rev. Antony Asir; Deacons Robert Weisz; Edward R. Vigneaux; Matt Surico.
See Holy Family Regional School, Commack under Regional Schools located in the Institution section.
Catechesis Religious Program—119 Kings Hwy., Hauppauge, 11788. Tel: 631-234-0397; Email: stmreled@yahoo.com. Mrs. Mary Ellen Carroll, D.R.E.; Mrs. Patricia Chapin, D.R.E. Students 688.

HEMPSTEAD, NASSAU CO.

1—ST. JOHN CHRYSOSTOM MALANKARA MISSION (1999)
115 Greenwich St., Hempstead, 11550.
Tel: 516-775-1779; Fax: 516-216-5350. Rev. Joseph Nedumankuzhiyil, (India) Admin.

2—ST. LADISLAUS (1915) (Polish) Rev. Piotr Wasek, Admin.
Res.: 18 Richardson Pl., Hempstead, 11550.
Tel: 516-489-0368; Fax: 516-489-0368.
See St. Martin de Porres Regional School, Uniondale under Regional Schools located in the Institution section.

3—OUR LADY OF LORETTO (1870) Revs. Luis M. Romero, M.Id; Felipe R. Vazquez; Deacon Juan Perez.
Res.: 104 Greenwich St., Hempstead, 11550.
Tel: 516-489-3675; Fax: 516-485-8371; Email: OLLoretto1@hotmail.com; Email: lromerofernandez@drvc.org; Web: www.ourladyoflorettohempstead.org.
See St. Martin de Porres Regional School, Uniondale under Regional Schools located in the Institution section.
Catechesis Religious Program—Tel: 516-483-3643. Cecilia Bradley, D.R.E. Students 340.

HEWLETT, NASSAU CO., ST. JOSEPH'S (1872) Revs. Thomas Moriarty Jr.; James F. Drew; Deacons Thomas Costello; Daniel Otton.
Res.: 1346 Broadway, Hewlett, 11557.
Tel: 516-374-0290; Fax: 516-374-2598; Email: joehewlett@aol.com; Web: saintjoseph-hewlett.org.
Catechesis Religious Program—1355 Noel Ave., Hewlett, 11557. Tel: 516-569-6080;
Fax: 516-374-3664. Julianne Markey, D.R.E. Students 320.

HICKSVILLE, NASSAU CO.

1—HOLY FAMILY (1951) (Irish—Italian)
17 Fordham Ave., Hicksville, 11801.
Tel: 516-938-3846; Email: response@holyfamilyparishny.org; Web: www.holyfamilyparishny.org. Revs. Gerard J. Gentleman, M.A., M.Div.; Daniel Opoku-Mensah; Liam McDonald; R. Michael Reid, In Res.; Deacons John H. McGonigle; David J. White; Sr. Carol Radosti, Pastoral Min.; Mr. Steven Benner, Youth Min.; Ronald Land, Music Dir.
Res.: 5 Fordham Ave., Hicksville, 11801.
School—Holy Family School, 25 Fordham Ave., Hicksville, 11801. Fax: 516-938-5041; Email: ccalabro@hfsli.org; Web: hfsli.org. Mrs. MaryAlice Doherty, Prin. Lay Teachers 26; Students 303.
Catechesis Religious Program—
Tel: 516-938-3846, Ext. 320; Email: cweiss@holyfamilyparishny.org. Mrs. Cathy Weiss, D.R.E. Students 500.
Outreach—15 Fordham Avenue, Hicksville, 11801.
Tel: 516-938-3846, Ext. 331; Email: outreach@holyfamilyparishny.org. Sr. Carol Radosti, Coord. Tot Asst. Annually 4,100.

2—ST. IGNATIUS LOYOLA (1859)
129 Broadway, Hicksville, 11801. Tel: 516-931-0056; Fax: 516-939-0852; Email: stignatius1859@aol.com; Web: st-ignatius-parish.org. Revs. James T. Stachacz; Andres A. Fernandez Lopez-Pelaz; Deacon George A. Mais Jr.; Ms. Jennifer Toohey, Music Min. In Res., Revs. Benjamin Uzuegbunam; Emmanuel Debrah.
Catechesis Religious Program—Tel: 516-935-6873. Colleen Tuzzolo, C.R.E. Students 367.

3—OUR LADY OF MERCY (1953) Rev. Stephen J. Pietrowski; Rev. Msgr. Thomas C. Costa; Revs. Patrick Grace; Martin L. Klein, (Retired); Nasir Giulfam.
Res.: 500 S. Oyster Bay Rd., Hicksville, 11801.
Tel: 516-931-4351; Fax: 516-433-8702; Email: therectory@olmrcc.com; Web: www.ourladyofmercy.org.
School—Our Lady of Mercy School, 520 S. Oysterbay Rd., Hicksville, 11801. Tel: 516-433-7040;
Fax: 516-433-8286; Email: jharrigan@olmshicks.org. Mrs. Jane Harrigan, Prin. Lay Teachers 19; Sisters of Mercy 2; Students 223; Religious Teachers 2.
Catechesis Religious Program—Tel: 516-681-1228; Fax: 516-681-1527; Email: religioused@olmrcc.com. Kevin Kwasnik, Youth Min. Students 576.

HOLBROOK, SUFFOLK CO., GOOD SHEPHERD (1970)
1370 Grundy Ave., Holbrook, 11741.
Tel: 631-588-7689; Email: goodshepherdstaf@aol.com; Web: www.goodshepherdRCchurch.org. Most Rev. Robert J. Coyle, D.D., M.Div.; Revs. Gennaro J. DiSpigno; Rudy Pesongco; Rev. Msgrs. Gerard A. Ringenback, M.S.Ed., M.A., Pastor Emeritus; Thomas L. Spadaro, Pastor Emeritus, (Retired); Rev. Lachlan T. Cameron, In Res.; Deacons John Newhall; Thomas O'Connor; Edward Tappin; Mrs. Christine Fitzgerald, Youth Min.; Annmarie Camporeale, Business Mgr.
See Prince of Peace Regional School, Sayville under Regional Schools located in the Institution section.
Catechesis Religious Program—Tel: 631-981-3889; Email: gsspiritualformation@gmail.com. Sr. Ellen Zak, C.S.F.N., D.R.E. Students 1,044.

HUNTINGTON STATION, SUFFOLK CO., ST. HUGH OF LINCOLN (1913) Rev. Robert J. Smith, S.T.L.; Very Rev. Daniel Rivera, M.Sp.S.; Deacons Edward W. Billia; Vito B. Taranto; Luis Giraldo; Richard Bilella. In Res., Rev. Khoa T. Le.
Res.: 21 E. Ninth St., Huntington Station, 11746.
Tel: 631-427-0638; Email: rectory@sthugh.org.
Parish Center—1450 New York Ave., Huntington Station, 11746.
See Trinity Regional School, East Northport under Regional Schools located in the Institution section.
Catechesis Religious Program—Tel: 631-271-6081. Mrs. Helen Schramm, D.R.E. Students 725.

HUNTINGTON, SUFFOLK CO., ST. PATRICK'S (1849) [CEM] Rev. Msgr. Steven Camp; Revs. Michael Bissex; Scott Daniels; Deacons William Casey; Dale Bonocore; Louis Consentino. In Res., Revs. Thomas Edamattan, (India); Daniel Neyoh, Chap. Huntington Hospital.
Res.: 400 Main St., Huntington, 11743-3208.

Tel: 631-385-3311; Fax: 631-673-4102; Web: www.stpatrickchurchhunt.org.
School—St. Patrick's School, 360 Main St., Huntington, 11743-3298. Tel: 631-673-5325; Fax: 631-673-4609. Sr. Maureen McDade, Prin.; Mrs. Jean Grasso, Asst. Prin. Lay Teachers 34; Sisters 1; Students 633.
Catechesis Religious Program—Mrs. Jill Rowbo, D.R.E. Students 1,220.

INWOOD, NASSAU CO., OUR LADY OF GOOD COUNSEL (1910) Revs. Thomas Moriarty Jr.; James F. Drew. In Res., Rev. Eric R. Fasano, M.Div., J.C.L.
Res.: 68 Wanser Ave., Inwood, 11096.
Tel: 516-239-0953; Fax: 516-239-0386.
Catechesis Religious Program—90 Henry St., Inwood, 11096. Tel: 516-239-0662. Mrs. Maureen O'Louglin, D.R.E. Students 167.

ISLAND PARK, NASSAU CO., SACRED HEART (1938) Rev. Msgr. John J. Tutone, M.Div., J.C.D.
Res.: 282 Long Beach Rd., Island Park, 11558.
Tel: 516-432-0655; Email: ship282@verizon.net.
Catechesis Religious Program—Tel: 516-431-7877. Mrs. Carmel Caracciolo, D.R.E. Students 211.

ISLIP TERRACE, SUFFOLK CO., ST. PETER THE APOSTLE (1962)
94 Valley Stream St., Islip Terrace, 11752.
Tel: 631-277-9448; Email: stpeters11752@gmail.com; Web: stpetersnyit.org. Rev. Anthony Iaconis; Deacon Everett Lackenbauer.
See Our Lady of Providence Regional School, Central Islip under Regional Schools located in the Institution section.

KINGS PARK, SUFFOLK CO., ST. JOSEPH'S (1888)
59 Church St., Kings Park, 11754. Tel: 631-269-6635; Email: stjosephkp@optonline.net; Web: www.stjosephskp.org. Revs. Sean J. Gann; Francis P. Vattakudiyil, (Retired); Thomas W. Tassone; Deacon John E. Trodden.
See Holy Family Regional School, Commack under Regional Schools located in the Institution section.
Catechesis Religious Program—Tel: 631-269-4383. Students 1,100.

LAKE RONKONKOMA, SUFFOLK CO., ST. ELIZABETH ANN SETON (1988)
800 Portion Rd., Lake Ronkonkoma, 11779.
Tel: 631-737-4388; Email: steas@optonline.net. Rev. Kevin Thompson; Deacons Joseph Maffeo; John Grebe; David Vallone; Pat Mystkowski, Pastoral Assoc.; Lori Marando, Business Mgr.
Res.: 59 Frances Blvd., Holtsville, 11742.
Catechesis Religious Program—Tel: 631-737-8915; Email: mhahnstliz@optonline.net. Mrs. Michele Hahn, D.R.E. Students 700.

LEVITTOWN, NASSAU CO., ST. BERNARD (1948) Rev. Msgr. Ralph Sommer; Rev. Joseph E. Nohs; Deacons John Blakeney; James W. Flannery. In Res., Rev. Patrick Abem, Chap.
Res.: 3100 Hempstead Tpke., Levittown, 11756.
Tel: 516-731-4220; Email: parish@stbernardchurch.org; Web: www.stbernardchurch.org.
Catechesis Religious Program—Email: reled@stbernardchurch.org. Mrs. Susan Martin, D.R.E. Students 980.

LINDENHURST, SUFFOLK CO., OUR LADY OF PERPETUAL HELP (1871)
210 S. Wellwood Ave., Lindenhurst, 11757-4989.
Tel: 631-226-7725; Email: jdwyer@oloph.org; Web: www.olphlindenhurst.com. Rev. Msgr. Joseph DeGrocco, D.Min.; Revs. Frank Zero; Fidelis Ezeani, (Nigeria); Deacons Robert A. Becker; Douglas Smith; William Crosby.
Catechesis Religious Program—Email: akleinlaut@oloph.org. April Kleinlaut, Dir. Faith Formation. Students 1,100.

LONG BEACH, NASSAU CO.
1—ST. IGNATIUS MARTYR (1926) Rev. Msgr. Donald M. Beckmann; Rev. Anthony Osuagwu, (Nigeria).
Res.: 721 W. Broadway, Long Beach, 11561.
Tel: 516-432-0045; Fax: 516-432-6848; Email: saintignatiusmar@yahoo.com; Web: home.catholicweb.com/stignatiusmartyr/index.cfm.
See Long Beach Regional Catholic School, Long Beach under Regional Schools located in the Institution section.
Catechesis Religious Program—722 W. Penn St., Long Beach, 11561. Tel: 516-432-6788. Mrs. Gail Milne, D.R.E. Students 598.
Parish Social Ministry/Outreach—
Tel: 516-432-4899. Sr. Diane Morgan, O.P., Pastoral Assoc.; Deacon Phillip J. Newton.
2—ST. MARY OF THE ISLE (1915) Rev. Brian P. Barr; Vicki Ayala-Solis, Business Mgr., Tel: 516-432-0157, Ext. 16.
Res.: 315 E. Walnut St., Long Beach, 11561.
Tel: 516-432-0157; Fax: 516-897-0566; Email: stmarylb@gmail.com.
See Long Beach Regional Catholic School, Long Beach under Regional Schools located in the Institution section.
Catechesis Religious Program—Tel: 516-432-1320. Andrew Santos, C.R.E. Students 279.

LYNBROOK, NASSAU CO., OUR LADY OF PEACE (1940) Rev. Richard T. Stelter; Deacons Thomas J. Evrard; Kevin McCormack.
Res.: 25 Fowler Ave., Lynbrook, 11563.
Tel: 516-599-6414; Email: olprcc@olplynbrook.com; Web: www.olplynbrook.com.
School—Our Lady of Peace School, 21 Flower Ave., Lynbrook, 11563. Tel: 516-593-4884; Fax: 516-593-9861; Email: olpschool@optonline.net. Lay Teachers 19; Sisters of Mercy 1; Students 283.
Catechesis Religious Program—Tel: 516-593-5150; Email: srgracem@olplynbrook.com. Students 436.

MALVERNE, NASSAU CO., OUR LADY OF LOURDES (1926) Revs. Michael F. Duffy; Cosmas Ozoagu; Deacon Richard H. Portuese. In Res., Rev. Richard R. Donovan, (Retired).
Res.: 65 Wright Ave., Malverne, 11565.
Tel: 516-599-1269; Email: ollmalvchurch@aol.com; Web: www.ollchurchmalverne.org.
School—Our Lady of Lourdes School, 76 Park Blvd., Malverne, 11565. Tel: 516-599-7328; Fax: 516-599-3813. Mary Carmel Murphy, Prin. Lay Teachers 19; Students 262.
Catechesis Religious Program—Tel: 516-599-7222; Email: ollreld@gmail.com. Miss Mary Lasar, D.R.E. Students 350.

MANHASSET, NASSAU CO., ST. MARY'S (1853)
1300 Northern Blvd., Manhasset, 11030.
Tel: 516-627-0385; Email: information@stmary.ws. Revs. Robert A. Romeo; Jiha Lim, Parochial Vicar; Jude Dioka, Parochial Vicar.
School—St. Mary's Elementary School, 1340 Northern Blvd., Manhasset, 11030.
Tel: 516-627-0184; Fax: 516-627-3795; Web: www.stmary11030.org. (Elementary) Lay Teachers 25; Students 306.
High School—St. Mary's High School, (Coed) 51 Clapham Ave., Manhasset, 11030. Tel: 516-627-2711 ; Fax: 516-627-3209; Web: www.stmary.ws/highschool. Marist Brothers 2; Lay Teachers 35; Students 585.
Catechesis Religious Program—Tel: 516-627-4028; Fax: 516-627-5543. Students 1,065.

MANORHAVEN, NASSAU CO., OUR LADY OF FATIMA (1948) Rev. Steven J. Peterson; Deacon Arthur Candido; Sr. Kathy Somerville, O.P., Parish Social Ministry; Barbara Minerva, Business Mgr.
Res.: 6 Cottonwood Rd., Port Washington, 11050.
Tel: 516-767-0781; Fax: 516-767-2981.
Catechesis Religious Program—Tel: 516-944-8322. Sr. Gerri O'Neil, O.P., D.R.E. Students 120.

MANORVILLE, SUFFOLK CO., STS. PETER & PAUL (1995) Rev. Jose Jacob, S.M.M.
Res.: 781 Wading River Rd., Manorville, 11949.
Tel: 631-369-1273; Fax: 631-369-7141; Email: pmc207@optonline.net.
Catechesis Religious Program—Tel: 631-208-1978. Students 379.

MASSAPEQUA PARK, NASSAU CO., OUR LADY OF LOURDES (1955) Rev. Msgr. James P. Lisante; Revs. Gregory Heinlein, (Retired); Edward M. Seagriff; Deacons Domenick Valdaro; Frank Gariboldi; Ferdinando Ferrara; John Brosnan, Business Mgr.; J.C. Laws, Music Dir. In Res., Rev. Cletus Nwaogwugwu.
Res.: 855 Carmans Rd., Massapequa Park, 11762.
Tel: 516-541-3270; Fax: 516-797-9851; Email: ollmpk@aol.com; Web: www.ollmp.org.
Catechesis Religious Program—379 Linden St., Massapequa Park, 11762. Bernadette Schaefer, D.R.E. Students 458.

MASSAPEQUA, NASSAU CO., ST. ROSE OF LIMA (1952)
2 Bayview Ave., Massapequa, 11758-7299.
Tel: 516-798-4992; Email: michelez@srolchurch.org; Web: www.srolchurch.org. Revs. Kenneth M. Zach; Collins Adutwum; Leo Song; Joseph Fitzgerald, M.Div., In Res.; Deacons Frank J. Flood; Michael Gambardella; Francis B. McGuinness.
School—St. Rose of Lima School, 4704 Merrick Rd., Massapequa, 11758. Tel: 516-541-1546; Fax: 516-797-0351; Email: kgallina@stroseschool.net; Web: www.stroseschool.net. Sr. Kathleen Gallina, O.P., Prin. Lay Teachers 26; Sisters of St. Dominic 1; Students 365.
Catechesis Religious Program—Tel: 516-541-1712; Email: religioused@stroseoflimaparish.org. Students 2,439.

MASTIC BEACH, SUFFOLK CO., ST. JUDE (1949)
89 Overlook Dr., Mastic Beach, 11951.
Tel: 631-281-5743, Ext. 12; Email: rectory@stjudemb.org; Web: www.stjudemb.org. Rev. John David Ryan; Deacons Joseph Simeone; John Gagliardi. In Res., Rev. Msgr. John T. Heinlein, (Retired).
See Our Lady, Queen of the Apostles Regional School, Center Moriches under Regional Schools located in the Institution section.
Catechesis Religious Program—Tel: 631-281-2835; Email: faithformation@stjudemb.org. Mrs. Eileen C. Will, D.R.E. Students 550.
Parish Human Services Center—Tel: 631-281-5634; Email: outreach@stjudemb.org.

MEDFORD, SUFFOLK CO., ST. SYLVESTER (1948) [CEM]
68 Ohio Ave., Medford, 11763. Tel: 631-475-4506; Fax: 631-475-1057; Email: parishoffice@stsylvesterli.org; Web: www.stsylvesterli.org. Rev. Thomas W. Coby; Deacons George J. Riegger, (Retired); Frank Rivera; Joseph Mystkowski; Justin McMahon, Dir. Parish Social Ministry/Outreach; Mrs. Lori Zito, Dir.
See Holy Angels Regional School, Patchogue under Regional Schools located in the Institution section.
Catechesis Religious Program—Email: fmcmahon@stsylvesterli.org. Frances McMahon, Dir. Faith Formation. Students 716.

MELVILLE, SUFFOLK CO., ST. ELIZABETH OF HUNGARY (1962) Rev. Irinel Racos; Deacons Joseph Mercolino, (Retired); John Failla; Maryann Giannettino, Dir. Parish Social Ministry; Virgil Barkauskas, Dir. Music; Harry Perepeluk, Business/Facilities Mgr.; Mary Calabrese, Sacramental & Adult Formation.
Res.: 181 Wolf Hill Rd., Melville, 11747.
Tel: 631-271-4455; Fax: 631-271-1415.
Church: 175 Wolf Hill Rd., Melville, 11747. Email: center@stelizabeth.org; Web: www.stelizabeth.org.
See Trinity Regional School, East Northport under Regional Schools located in the Institution section.
Catechesis Religious Program—Lois Szypot, D.R.E.; Elizabeth Teixerira, Dir. Youth Ministry. Students 951.

MERRICK, NASSAU CO., CURÉ OF ARS (1926) Rev. Msgr. Francis J. Caldwell, C.S.W.; Revs. Henry Leuthardt; Zachary Callahan, (In Res.), (Retired); Joseph Fitzgerald, M.Div., (In Res.); Deacons Joseph Zubrovich; Ronald Federici; Lisa Hudson, Parish Social Ministry & Stewardship; Sr. Patricia A. Ryan, C.S.J., Music Min.; Louis Cicalese, Youth Min.; William Geasor, Business Mgr.
Res.: 2323 Merrick Ave., Merrick, 11566.
Tel: 516-623-1400; Email: rectory@cureofarschurch.org; Web: www.cureofarschurch.org.
See St. Elizabeth Ann Seton Regional School, Bellmore under Regional Schools located in the Institution section.
Catechesis Religious Program—
Tel: 516-623-1400, Ext. 101; Fax: 516-223-7401. Lee Hlavacek, D.R.E. Students 772.

MINEOLA, NASSAU CO., CORPUS CHRISTI (1901) (Spanish—Portuguese)
155 Garfield Ave., Mineola, 11501. Tel: 516-746-1223 ; Email: Rectory@corpuschristi-mineola.net; Web: www.corpuschristi-mineola.net. Revs. Malcolm J. Burns; Richard F. Kammerer; John Victor, O.M.I.; Deacon Brian J. Mannix. In Res., Most Rev. Andrzej Jerzy Zglejszewski, D.D.; Rev. Patrick J. Callan, (Retired).
Catechesis Religious Program—120 Searing Ave., Mineola, 11501. Tel: 516-294-0631; Fax: 516-294-0352. Mrs. Susan Anaischik, D.R.E. Students 349.

MONTAUK, SUFFOLK CO., ST. THERESE OF LISIEUX (1950)
67 S. Essex St., Montauk, 11954. Mailing Address: P.O. Box 5027, Montauk, 11954. Tel: 631-668-2200; Fax: 631-668-2384; Email: sttheresedesk@optimum.net. Rev. Thomas P. Murray; Mr. Christopher Murray, Business Mgr.
Child Care—Day Care/Nursery School,
Tel: 631-668-5353. (2 & 3 years old) Children 25.
Catechesis Religious Program—Tel: 631-668-2460. Louise Carman, D.R.E. Students 150.

NESCONSET, SUFFOLK CO., CHURCH OF THE HOLY CROSS (1988)
95 Old Nichols Rd., Nesconset, 11767. Rev. Michael F. Holzmann; Deacon Ralph Rivera, Pastoral Min.; Mrs. Judith Pickel, Pastoral Assoc.
Res.: 85 Old Nichols Rd., Nesconset, 11767.
Tel: 631-265-2200; Email: pothc@optonline.net.
Catechesis Religious Program—
Tel: 631-265-2200, Ext. 12; Email: hcreled@optonline.net. Ms. Ellen Fox, D.R.E. Students 1,339.

NEW HYDE PARK, NASSAU CO.
1—HOLY SPIRIT (1893) Rev. Frank M. Grieco; Deacons Lachlan J. Cameron; Douglas Ferreiro.
Rectory—Holy Spirit Parish Rectory, 16 S. Sixth St., New Hyde Park, 11040. Tel: 516-354-0359; Fax: 516-354-2611 (Rectory); Email: holyspchurch@aol.com; Web: www.holyspiritchurch.com.
Catechesis Religious Program—13 S. 6th St., New Hyde Park, 11040. Tel: 516-354-2363. Students 350.
2—NOTRE DAME (1941) Revs. William T. Slater; Aloysius Melly. In Res., Rev. John Denniston.
Res.: 45 Mayfair Rd., New Hyde Park, 11040.
Tel: 516-352-7203; Fax: 516-326-7988.
School—Notre Dame School, 25 Mayfair Rd., New Hyde Park, 11040. Tel: 516-354-5618; Fax: 516-354-5373. Mrs. Caryn Durkin Flores, Prin. Lay Teachers 34; Sisters of St. Dominic (Amityville) 1.
Catechesis Religious Program—Tel: 516-437-5604. Sr. Mary Jane Coleman, R.S.M., D.R.E.

NORTH MERRICK, NASSAU CO., SACRED HEART (1952)

Mailing Address: 720 Merrick Ave., North Merrick, 11566. Tel: 516-379-1356; Fax: 516-379-1610; Email: frontdesk@sacredheartnm.org; Web: www.sacredheartnm.org. Revs. Joseph J. Nixon, M.A., M.Div.; Kevin Thompson.

Catechesis Religious Program—Tel: 516-868-9406. Mrs. Maryann Specht, D.R.E. Students 657.

NORTHPORT, SUFFOLK CO., ST. PHILIP NERI (1894) [CEM] Rev. Msgr. Peter C. Dooley; Deacon Richard Becker.

Office: 15 Prospect Ave., Northport, 11768.

Res.: 344 Main St., Northport, 11768. Email: frpeter@stphilipnerinpt.org.

See Trinity Regional School, East Northport under Regional Schools located in the Institution section.

Catechesis Religious Program—

Tel: 631-261-2485, Ext. 108. Linda Oristano, D.R.E.; Patricia Merenda, D.R.E. Students 754.

OCEAN BEACH, (FIRE ISLAND) SUFFOLK CO., OUR LADY OF THE MAGNIFICAT (1921)

36 Bungalow Walk, P.O. Box 445, Ocean Beach, 11770. Tel: 631-860-8962;

Tel: 631-423-0483, Ext. 114; Email: oceanbeachmagnificat@yahoo.com; Email: rhenning@icseminary.edu. Rev. Richard G. Henning, M.A., M.Div., Admin. Summer Mission ParishParish operates weekends-only in the spring & fall, and full time in the summer months.

Catechesis Religious Program—

OCEANSIDE, NASSAU CO., ST. ANTHONY (1927) Revs. Donald C. Gannon, S.J., Admin.; James Donovan; Daniel A. O'Brien, S.J.; Vincent J. Ritchie, S.J., M.B.A., M.Div., S.T.M.; Deacons Michael Monahan; James O'Neill; John O'Connor, Business Mgr.; Richard Nichols, Contact Person; Daniel Gibbons, Dir. Music.

Res.: 110 Anchor Ave., Oceanside, 11572.

Tel: 516-764-0048, Ext. 2513; Email: saoffice3@aol.com.

Catechesis Religious Program—Tel: 516-282-2520. Mrs. Rose Dillon, D.R.E.

OYSTER BAY, NASSAU CO., ST. DOMINIC'S (1894) Revs. Kevin M. Smith; John Ekwoanya, (Nigeria). In Res., Rev. Msgr. Robert J. Batule, S.T.L.

Res.: 93 Anstice St., Oyster Bay, 11771.

Tel: 516-922-4488, Ext. 1197; Email: lnalick@stdoms.org.

School—Elementary School, 35 School St., Oyster Bay, 11771. Tel: 516-922-4233; Fax: 516-624-7613; Email: esorge7485@stdomsob.org. Lay Teachers 27; Sisters of the Immaculate Heart of Mary 1; Students 261.

High School—High School, 110 Anstice St., Oyster Bay, 11771. Tel: 516-922-4888; Fax: 516-922-5794; Email: mchirichella@stdoms.org. Lay Teachers 36; Students 440.

Catechesis Religious Program—Email: coneil@stdoms.org; Email: cmangiarotti@stdoms.org. Cathy O'Neil, D.R.E.; Carolyn Mangiarotti, D.R.E. Students 714.

PATCHOGUE, SUFFOLK CO.

1—ST. FRANCIS DE SALES (1888) [CEM] Rev. Steven J. Hannafin; Deacons Martin McIndoe; Francisco Diaz-Granados; Robert Mongillo; Lizbeth Carrillo, Outreach Coord.

Res.: 7 Amity St., Patchogue, 11772.

Tel: 631-475-0161; Email: sanfraninpatch@hotmail.com; Web: www.stfrancispatchogue.com.

See Holy Angels Regional School, Patchogue under Regional Schools located in the Institution section.

Catechesis Religious Program—Tel: 631-289-4339; Email: sanfraninpatch@hotmail.com. Elaine Heschl, D.R.E. Students 600.

2—OUR LADY OF MT. CARMEL (1925) (Italian) Rev. Henry W. Reid; Deacon Anthony Graviano.

Res.: 495 New North Ocean Ave., Patchogue, 11772.

Tel: 631-475-4739; Email: info@olmcpatchogue.org; Web: www.olmcpatchogue.org.

See Holy Angels Regional School, Patchogue under Regional Schools located in the Institution section.

Catechesis Religious Program—Tel: 631-289-7327. Students 276.

PLAINVIEW, NASSAU CO., ST. PIUS X (1955)

1 St. Pius X Ct., Plainview, 11803. Tel: 516-938-3956 ; Fax: 516-433-6138; Email: admstpx@gmail.com; Web: www.stpiusxrc.com. Revs. Valentine D. Rebello, (India); Chux Okochi, In Res.; Deacon John F. Burkart; Miss Rosann Kelly, Parish Admin.; Mr. Salvatore Spano, Pastoral Assoc.; Mrs. Anne Bantleon, Pastoral Assoc.; Mrs. Maryanne Rietschlin, Ph.D., Pastoral Assoc.; Mrs. Marion Celenza, Pastoral Assoc.; Mrs. Teresa Arrigo, Dir. Music; Mr. Steve Rhoads, Youth Min.

Catechesis Religious Program—Tel: 516-822-8348. Miss Michelle Mascolo, Faith Formation Coord.; Mr. Steve Rhoads, Youth Min.; Mr. Steve Rhoads, Youth Min. Students 255.

POINT LOOKOUT, NASSAU CO., OUR LADY OF THE MIRACULOUS MEDAL (1937) (Irish)

75 Parkside Dr., P.O. Box 20, Point Lookout, 11569. Tel: 516-431-2772; Email: rectory@olmmc.com; Web: www.olmmc.com. Rev. Joseph J. Nixon, M.A., M.Div., Admin.

See Long Beach Regional Catholic School, Long Beach under Regional Schools located in the Institution section.

Catechesis Religious Program—Tel: 516-432-8074; Email: relegiousED@olmmc.com. Mrs. Georgette Levesque, D.R.E. Students 14.

PORT JEFFERSON STATION, SUFFOLK CO.

1—ST. GERARD MAJELLA (1968)

Mailing Address: 300 Terryville Rd., Port Jefferson Station, 11776. Rev. Gennaro J. DiSpigno; Deacons Vincent Beckles; John Panzica.

Res.: 65 Nadine Ln., Port Jefferson Station, 11776.

Tel: 631-473-2900; Fax: 631-473-0015; Web: www.stgmajella.org.

See Our Lady of Wisdom Regional School, Port Jefferson under Regional Schools located in the Institution section.

Catechesis Religious Program—Tel: 631-928-2550. John Aleksak, D.R.E. Students 825.

2—INFANT JESUS (1903)

110 Myrtle Ave., Port Jefferson, 11777.

Tel: 631-473-0165; Tel: 631-928-0447;

Tel: 631-331-6045; Email: Rectory@InfantJesus.org; Web: www.infantjesus.org. Revs. Patrick M. Riegger; Francis Lasrado; Rolando Ticllasuca, (Peru); Martin Bancroft, In Res.; Henry Vas, O.F.M.Cap., In Res.; Deacons William J. Powers; Richard E. Waldmann; Robert A. Kruse; Kenneth Clifford; Carlito Roman; Michael Byrne.

See Our Lady of the Wisdom Regional School, Port Jefferson under Regional Schools located in the Institution section.

Catechesis Religious Program—110 Hawkins St., Port Jefferson, 11777. Email: religiouseducation@infantjesus.org. Corrine Addiss, Faith Formation Coord. Students 1,200.

PORT WASHINGTON, NASSAU CO., ST. PETER OF ALCANTARA (1901) Rev. Patrick J. Whitney; Deacon Joseph Bianco.

Res.: 1327 Port Washington Blvd., Port Washington, 11050. Tel: 516-883-6675; Email: stpetesecretary@gmail.com; Web: stpeterofalcantara.org.

School—St. Peter of Alcantara School,

Tel: 516-944-3772; Fax: 516-767-8075. Marianne Carberry, Prin. Lay Teachers 25; Students 275.

Catechesis Religious Program—Tel: 516-883-5584; Fax: 516-767-6194. Mary Christine Thomsen, D.R.E. Students 735.

Convent—IHM Spirituality Center, 1317 Port Washington Blvd., Port Washington, 11050.

RIVERHEAD, SUFFOLK CO.

1—ST. ISIDORE (1903) [CEM] (Polish)

622 Pulaski St., Riverhead, 11901. Tel: 631-727-2114 ; Email: sisidore@optonline.net; Web: saintisidoreriverhead.org. Revs. Robert Kuznik; Piotr Narkiewicz; Deacon Michael A. Bonocore.

Catechesis Religious Program—Tel: 631-727-1650; Email: mfitzgerald@sisriverhead.com. Kathy Tysz, D.R.E.; Marypat Fitzgerald, D.R.E. Students 198.

2—ST. JOHN THE EVANGELIST (1861) [CEM] Rev. Lawrence Duncklee; Deacons Peter F. Schultz; Dan Waloski; William Austin. In Res., Most Rev. Emil A. Wcela, D.D., (Retired).

Res.: 546 St. John's Pl., Riverhead, 11901.

Tel: 631-727-2030; Fax: 631-369-5228; Email: stjohnriverhead@aol.com; Web: www.saintjohnriverhead.org.

Catechesis Religious Program—Tel: 631-727-6774; Email: stjohnrelformation@gmail.com. Students 410.

ROCKY POINT, SUFFOLK CO., ST. ANTHONY OF PADUA (1948) Rev. Msgr. William G. Breslawski; Sr. Mary Schoberg, I.H.M., Pastoral Assoc.

Res.: 614 Rte. 25A, Rocky Point, 11778.

Tel: 631-744-2609; Email: stasrp@optonline.net.

Catechesis Religious Program—Tel: 631-821-0872. Sr. Phylis O'Dowd, O.P., D.R.E. Students 1,245.

RONKONKOMA, SUFFOLK CO., ST. JOSEPH (1910) Revs. Michael J. Rieder; Gilbert D. Lap; Belevendiram S. Rathinam, (India); Deacons Edward S. Grieb, Business Mgr.; James Altonji, (Retired); Michael J. DeBellis; Joseph Dougherty, (Retired); Joseph Califano, (Retired); Michael Devenney; William Dobbins; Frank Dell'Aglio.

Res.: 45 Church St., Ronkonkoma, 11779-3300.

Tel: 631-588-8456; Email: info@stjoronk.org; Web: stjosephronkonkoma.org.

School—St. Joseph School, 25 Church St., Ronkonkoma, 11779. Tel: 631-588-4760;

Fax: 631-588-0543; Email: school@stjoronk.org. Richard F. Kuntzler Jr., Prin. Lay Teachers 22; Students 208.

Catechesis Religious Program—Tel: 631-981-1805; Email: mtrezza@stjoronk.org. Ms. Maryanne Trezza, D.R.E. Students 1,100.

ROOSEVELT, NASSAU CO., QUEEN OF THE MOST HOLY ROSARY (1919) Revs. Joseph Baidoo; Miguel Angel Rivera-Franco, (El Salvador); Deacons Clinton Lewis; Thomas Jackson; Elena A. Powers, Music Dir. In Res., Most Rev. Andrzej Jerzy Zglejszewski, D.D.

Res.: 196 W. Centennial Ave., Roosevelt, 11575.

Tel: 516-378-1315; Fax: 516-378-5754; Email: qmhr@optonline.net.

Catechesis Religious Program—Tel: 516-623-1391; Email: cherylwhite@optonline.net. Cheryl White, D.R.E. Students 180.

ROSLYN, NASSAU CO., ST. MARY'S (1871) Rev. John J. McCartney.

Res.: 110 Bryant Ave., Roslyn, 11576.

Tel: 516-621-2222; Fax: 516-621-7892.

See All Saints Regional Catholic School, Glen Cove under Regional Schools located in the Institution section.

Catechesis Religious Program—Tel: 516-621-6798. Nora Toal, Rel. Educ. Admin. Students 276.

SAINT JAMES, SUFFOLK CO., SS. PHILIP AND JAMES (1907) Revs. Thomas J. Haggerty; Patrick Osei-Poku; Deacons Kenneth Maher; Robert Heschl, (Retired); John Keenan; Gerard Reda; Ronald Blasius.

Res.: 1 Carow Pl., St. James, 11780.

Tel: 631-584-5454; Fax: 631-862-9675; Email: info@sspj.org; Web: www.sspj.org.

School—SS. Philip and James School, (Grades PreK-8), Tel: 631-584-7896; Fax: 631-584-3258; Web: sspjschool.net. Mrs. Ruth Testa, Prin.; Mrs. Ledna Gallagher, Librarian. Lay Teachers 18; Students 259.

Catechesis Religious Program—Tel: 631-584-3204. Students 1,254.

SAG HARBOR, SUFFOLK CO., ST. ANDREW'S (1859) [CEM] Rev. Peter Devaraj, S.A.C. In Res., Rev. Andrew P. Blake, Pastor Emeritus, (Retired).

Res.: 122 Division St, Sag Harbor, 11963-3154.

Tel: 631-725-0123; Email: cbkvm@yahoo.com.

Catechesis Religious Program—Students 142.

SALTAIRE, SUFFOLK CO., OUR LADY STAR OF THE SEA, MISSION CHAPEL, (Summer Mission)

210 Pilot Walk, Saltaire, 11706. Rev. Richard R. Viladesau, S.T.D., Admin.

Res.: 2000 Jackson Ave., Seaford, 11783.

Tel: 516-785-1266, Ext. 15.

Church: 310 Pilot Walk, Saltaire, 11706.

Tel: 631-583-7613.

SAYVILLE, SUFFOLK CO., ST. LAWRENCE THE MARTYR (1895) [CEM]

27 Handsome Ave., Sayville, 11782.

Tel: 631-589-0042; Email: office@stlawrencesayville.org; Web: www.stlawrencesayville.org. Revs. Brian Ingram; Thomas J. Pers; Deacon Patrick LaBella; Jeanmarie Smith, Pastoral Assoc.; Lorraine Magyar, Pastoral Min./Coord.; Christopher Koch, Business Mgr.; Joseph Mankowski, Music Min.

Catechesis Religious Program—Email: mdavidson@stlawrencesayville.org. Mrs. Maria Davidson, D.R.E. Students 1,188.

SEA CLIFF, NASSAU CO., ST. BONIFACE MARTYR (1898) Rev. Kevin J. Dillon; Deacon Tom Fox; Eileen Krieb, Business Mgr.; Jeff Schneider, Music Dir.

Rectory, Office & Parish Center: 145 Glen Ave., Sea Cliff, 11579. Tel: 516-676-0676; Fax: 516-674-6742; Email: stbonchurch@gmail.com; Web: saintboniface.org.

Res.: 220 Carpenter Ave., Sea Cliff, 11579.

See All Saints Regional Catholic School, Glen Cove under Regional Schools located in the Institution section.

Catechesis Religious Program—Tel: 516-671-0418; Email: stbonccd@gmail.com. Karen Croce, D.R.E.; Chris Mandato, Youth Min. Students 536.

SEAFORD, NASSAU CO.

1—ST. JAMES (1951) Revs. John Derasmo; Innocent Mbaegbu; Aaron T. Vellaramparampil; Deacons James G. Beirne; Richard Brunner; Chris Daniello; Alfred Allongo, Music Min.

Res.: 80 Hicksville Rd., Seaford, 11783.

Tel: 516-731-3710; Email: parishoffice@stjamesrcchurch.org; Web: www.stjamesrcchurch.org.

See St. John Baptist de LaSalle Regional School, Farmingdale under Regional Schools located in the Institution section.

Catechesis Religious Program—Tel: 516-796-2979; Email: mmirkow@stjamesrcchurch.org; Email: gdrost@stjamesrcchurch.org. Gina Drost, Dir. of Faith Formation; Marianne Mirkow, Coord. Faith Formation. Students 1,500.

2—MARIA REGINA (1954)

3945 Jerusalem Ave., Seaford, 11783.

Tel: 516-798-2415; Email: rderose@mariaregina.com; Web: www.mariaregina.com. Revs. Frank M. Nelson; Ignatius Okwuonu; Rev. Msgr. Peter J. Pflomm, In Res.; Rev. Thomas Edamattam, In Res., (Retired); Deacons Gerald F. Whitfield; Joseph Oliva; Paul Neuhedel.

School—Maria Regina School, 4045 Jerusalem Ave., Seaford, 11783. Tel: 516-541-1229;

Fax: 516-541-1235. Mrs. Leona Arpino, Prin. Lay Teachers 27; Students 400.

Catechesis Religious Program—Tel: 516-541-0921; Fax: 516-795-2510. Alice Moran, D.R.E. (Grades 1-5); Tina Rine, D.R.E. (Grades 6-8). Students 1,466.

3—ST. WILLIAM THE ABBOT (1928)
2000 Jackson Ave., Seaford, 11783.
Tel: 516-785-1266; Email: information@stwilliam.org; Web: www.stwilliam.org. Rev. Msgr. Robert L. Hayden; Revs. Edmund Ani; Joseph Augustine Kadungamparambil, (India); Richard R. Viladesau, S.T.D., In Res.; Deacons Anthony M. Cedrone; John Lynch; Michael C. Metzdorff; Joseph Tumbarello; Sr. Jo Ann Bonauro, S.C., Pastoral Assoc.
School—St. William the Abbot School, 2001 Jackson Ave., Seaford, 11783. Tel: 516-785-6784; Fax: 516-785-2752; Email: ebricker5651@stwilliamtheabbot.net; Web: www.stwilliamtheabbot.net. Mrs. Elizabeth Bricker, Prin. Lay Teachers 30; Students 454.
Catechesis Religious Program—Tel: 516-679-9558; Fax: 516-679-1649; Email: reled@stwilliam.org. Mrs. Laura Walsh, D.R.E. Students 1,362.

SELDEN, SUFFOLK CO., ST. MARGARET OF SCOTLAND (1948)
81 College Rd., Selden, 11784. Tel: 631-732-3131; Fax: 631-732-8827; Email: jburtoff@saintmargaret.com; Web: www.saintmargaret.com. Revs. James L. Wood; Paul F. Butler; Deacon Edward Hayes; Lisa Boyd, Business Mgr.
See Holy Angels Regional School, Patchogue under Regional Schools located in the Institution section.
Catechesis Religious Program—Email: FF@saintmargaret.com. Jackie Mirenda, D.R.E. Students 518.

SETAUKET, SUFFOLK CO., ST. JAMES (1949) [CEM]
429 Rte. 25-A, Setauket, 11733. Tel: 631-941-4141; Email: parish@stjamessetauket.org. Revs. James P. Mannion Jr.; Gerald Cestare; John J. Fitzgerald, In Res., (Retired).
See Our Lady of the Wisdom Regional School, Port Jefferson under Regional Schools located in the Institution section.
Catechesis Religious Program—Mrs. Louise DiCarlo, D.R.E.; Mr. Richard Foley, Liturgy Dir.; Mrs. Cristinia O'Keefe, RCIA Coord.; Mrs. Miriam Salerno, Liturgy Dir.; Mrs. Kathy Vaeth, Dir. Students 1,500.

SHELTER ISLAND, SUFFOLK CO., OUR LADY OF THE ISLE (1911) [CEM]
7 Prospect Ave., P.O. Box 3027, Shelter Island Heights, 11965. Tel: 631-749-0001; Fax: 631-749-4218; Email: ourladyoftheisle@gmail.com; Web: www.ourladyoftheisle.org. Rev. Peter DeSanctis; Ms. Amber Brach-Williams, C.P.A., Business Mgr.; Suzanne Wilutis, C.P.A., Trustee; Frank Vecchio, Trustee; JoAnn Kirkland-Hundgen, Sec.
See Regional School, Our Lady of the Hamptons, Southampton under Regional Schools located in the Institution section.
Catechesis Religious Program—Sr. Kathryn Schlueter, C.S.J., D.R.E.; Ginny Gibbs, M.S., D.R.E. Students 48.

SHOREHAM, SUFFOLK CO., ST. MARK (1973) Rev. Msgr. Jeffrey J. Madley; Revs. Theodore J. Howard, Pastor Emeritus, (Retired); Thomas Tuite; Deacons Patrick Gerace; Igino Aceto.
Res.: 105 Randall Rd., Shoreham, 11786.
Tel: 631-744-2800; Fax: 631-821-1628; Email: stmarksrcc@aol.com; Web: stmarksrcc-shoreham.org.
Catechesis Religious Program—Tel: 631-821-0550; Email: relform@verizon.net. Mrs. Lynn Fein, D.R.E. Students 775.

SMITHTOWN, SUFFOLK CO., ST. PATRICK (1952) [CEM] (Irish—Italian)
280 E. Main St., Smithtown, 11787.
Tel: 631-265-2271; Email: rectory@stpatricksmithtown.org; Email: stpatrickssmithtown@gmail.com; Web: www.stpatricksmithtown.org. Rev. Msgr. Ellsworth R. Walden; Revs. Sean T. Magaldi; Abraham Thannickal; Deacon Jerry Reda. In Res., Revs. Frederick Hill; Corneille Boyeye, (Democratic Republic of Congo).
School—St. Patrick School, 284 E. Main St., Smithtown, 11787. Tel: 631-724-0285; Fax: 631-265-4841; Web: www.spssmith.org. Linda Pymm, Prin. Lay Teachers 32; Students 429.
Catechesis Religious Program—Tel: 631-724-7454; Email: stpatsrfc@optonline.net. Mrs. Elaina Kedjierski, D.R.E. Students 1,327.

SOUND BEACH, SUFFOLK CO., ST. LOUIS DE MONTFORT (1971)
75 New York Ave., Sound Beach, 11789-2506.
Tel: 631-744-8566; Fax: 631-744-8611; Email: tkretz@sldmrc.org; Web: www.stlouisdm.org. Rev. Msgr. Christopher J. Heller; Rev. Lennard Sabio, (Philippines); Rev. Msgr. Donald Hanson, (In Res.); Deacons Joseph T. Bartolotto; Gary F. Swane; Robert Mullane.
See Our Lady of the Wisdom Regional School, Port Jefferson under Regional Schools located in the Institution section.
Catechesis Religious Program—Tel: 631-744-9515; Email: jmcnamara@sldmrc.org; Email: ksweeney@sldmrc.org; Email: elizabethteixeira717@gmail.com. Mr. John McNamara, D.R.E.; Kathleen Sweeney, D.R.E.; Elizabeth Teixeira, Youth Min. Students 1,892.

SOUTHAMPTON, SUFFOLK CO.

1—BASILICA CHURCH OF SACRED HEARTS OF JESUS AND MARY (1896) [CEM]
168 Hill St., Southampton, 11968. Tel: 631-283-0097; Email: parishoffice@shjmbasilica.org; Email: mvetrano@drvc.org. Rev. Michael A. Vetrano, Ph.D. In Res., Rev. Msgr. William J. Gill, (Retired).
See Our Lady of the Hamptons Regional School, Southampton under Regional Schools located in the Institution section.
Catechesis Religious Program—Tel: 631-283-0508. Students 360.

2—OUR LADY OF POLAND (1918) (Polish)
35 Maple St., Southampton, 11968.
Tel: 631-283-0667; Fax: 631-287-4146; Email: olpchurch@optonline.net; Web: olpchurch.org. Rev. Janusz Lipski; Deacon James Ashe.
See Our Lady of the Hamptons Regional School, Southampton under Regional Schools located in the Institution section.
Catechesis Religious Program—168 Hill St., Southampton, 11968. Students 20.

SOUTHOLD, SUFFOLK CO., ST. PATRICK'S (1865) [CEM]
Rev. John J. Barrett.
Res.: 52125 Main Rd., P.O. Box 1117, Southold, 11971-1401. Tel: 631-765-3442; Fax: 631-765-9631; Email: saintpat@optonline.net.
See Our Lady of Mercy Regional School, Cutchogue under Regional Schools located in the Institution section.
Catechesis Religious Program—Tel: 631-765-2338. Students 215.

SYOSSET, NASSAU CO., ST. EDWARD CONFESSOR (1952)
205 Jackson Ave., Syosset, 11791-4218.
Tel: 516-921-8030, Ext. 150; Email: MMaffeo@St-Edwards.Org; Web: www.st-edwards.org. Revs. Michael T. Maffeo; Hyacinth Jemigbola, (Nigeria); Deacons James Murphy, Pastoral Min./Coord.; Barry Croce, Pastoral Min./Coord.
School—St. Edward Confessor School, 2 Teibrook Ave., Syosset, 11791. Tel: 516-921-7767; Fax: 516-496-0001. Mr. Vincent Albrecht, Prin. Lay Teachers 25; Students 286.
Catechesis Religious Program—Tel: 516-921-8543; Email: RPetti@St-Edwards.Org. Mrs. Rosemary Pettei, D.R.E. Students 150.

UNIONDALE, NASSAU CO., ST. MARTHA (1949)
546 Greengrove Ave., Uniondale, 11553.
Tel: 516-481-2550; Email: info@stmartha.org; Web: saintmarta.org. Revs. Christopher M. Costigan; Cesar Bejarano, Parochial Vicar; Eden Jean Baptiste, Parochial Vicar; Deacon Trevor S. Mathurin, D.R.E.
See St. Martin de Porres Marianist School, Uniondale under Elementary Schools, Private located in the Institution section.
Catechesis Religious Program—
Tel: 516-481-2550, Ext. 311. Mrs. Marlene Jean-Baptiste, Dir. Parish Social Ministry; Ms. Barbara Powell, Co-Dir. Parish Social Ministry. Students 360.

VALLEY STREAM, NASSAU CO.

1—BLESSED SACRAMENT (1950) Revs. Peter Dugandzic, S.T.D.; Romulo Cesar Gomez; Charlince Vendredy. In Res., Rev. Sathyan Naduviledath, O.I.C.
Res.: 201 N. Central Ave., Valley Stream, 11580.
Tel: 516-568-1027; Fax: 516-872-1499.
Catechesis Religious Program—Randell Hochenberger, M.Div., Dir. Faith Formation. Students 263.

2—HOLY NAME OF MARY (1902)
55 E. Jamaica Ave., Valley Stream, 11580.
Tel: 516-825-1450; Fax: 516-568-1906; Email: holynamemary@aol.com; Web: www.hnom.org. Rev. Msgr. Romualdo Sosing; Rev. Henry W. Reid; Deacons James O'Hara; Clyde Ruggieri; Richard F. Raad; Scott Baker.
School—Holy Name of Mary School, 90 S. Grove St., Valley Stream, 11580. Tel: 516-825-4009; Fax: 516-825-2710. Pamela Sanders, Prin. Lay Teachers 16; Students 280.
Catechesis Religious Program—Religious Education, Tel: 516-825-1810; Fax: 516-256-0724. Matthew Zinser, D.R.E.; Sr. Margie Kelly, C.S.J., Parish Outreach Dir.; Kevin Faughey, Music Min. Students 576.

WADING RIVER, SUFFOLK CO., ST. JOHN BAPTIST (1922)
Rev. Msgr. Francis J. Schneider, M.Div., J.C.D.; Deacons Frederick Finter; Vincent Pozzolano.
Res.: 1488 North Country Rd., Wading River, 11792.
Tel: 631-929-4339; Email: office@stjohnthebaptistchurch.org.
Catechesis Religious Program—Students 600.

WANTAGH, NASSAU CO., ST. FRANCES DE CHANTAL (1952) Revs. Gregory J. Cappuccino; Aloysius Pakianather, (Sri Lanka); Vincent Schifano; Sr. Jocelyn Panzetta, C.I.J.; Deacons Robert O'Donovan; Joseph Torres; Thomas Anderson; Anthony M. Cedrone.
Res.: 1309 Wantagh Ave., Wantagh, 11793.
Tel: 516-785-2333; Fax: 516-826-7645; Web: www.saintjanefrances.org.
See St. Elizabeth Ann Seton Regional School, Bellmore under Regional Schools located in the Institution section.
Catechesis Religious Program—
Tel: 516-785-2333, Ext. 205. Lucy Creed, D.R.E.; Donna Mugno, Admin. Students 1,501.

WEST BABYLON, SUFFOLK CO., OUR LADY OF GRACE (1962)
666 Albin Ave., West Babylon, 11704.
Tel: 631-587-5185; Email: parish@ourladyofgrace.net. Rev. Msgr. Vincent Rush; Revs. Gabriel Miah, Parochial Vicar; Francisco Gius Garcia, (Philippines); Deacons Irwin Saffran; Brian Miller.
Catechesis Religious Program—Tel: 631-661-9354; Email: faithformation@ourladyofgrace.net. Margaret Harnisch, Dir. Ministries for Children & Families A.R.E. Students 1,260.

WEST HEMPSTEAD, NASSAU CO., ST. THOMAS, THE APOSTLE (1931)
24 Westminster Rd., West Hempstead, 11552.
Tel: 516-489-8585; Fax: 516-292-2651; Email: stthomasap@optonline.net; Web: stthomasapostle.org. Rev. Msgrs. Francis J. Maniscalco; Michael Barimah-Apau; Rev. Anthony Cardone; Deacons John E. Ford; Edward Cunningham; Jacques Philippeaux. In Res., Rev. Msgr. John A. Alesandro, P.A., J.C.D.; Rev. Damian Umeokeke.
School—St. Thomas, the Apostle School, 12 Westminster Rd., West Hempstead, 11552.
Tel: 516-481-9310; Fax: 516-481-8769. Mrs. Valerie Gigante, Prin. Lay Teachers 22; Sisters 2; Students 292.
Catechesis Religious Program—Tel: 516-538-7460. Mrs. Mary Ann Pellegrino, D.R.E. Students 549.
Mission—Chapel, 875 Hempstead Ave., West Hempstead, Nassau Co. 11552.

WEST ISLIP, SUFFOLK CO., OUR LADY OF LOURDES (1956)
455 Hunter Ave., West Islip, 11795.
Tel: 631-661-3224; Email: parishoffice@ollchurch.org; Web: www.ollchurch.org. Rev. Msgr. Brian J. McNamara; Revs. Gregory Breen; Sylvester Chukwumalume, Chap.; Freddy Lozano, (Colombia) In Res.; Deacons John Teufel; John DeGuardi; Jack Meehan; Thomas Lucie; Richard P. Maher.
Catechesis Religious Program—Tel: 631-661-5440; Fax: 631-661-3606. Sisters Diane Liona, D.R.E.; Nancy Campkin, D.R.E. Students 1,829.

WESTBURY, NASSAU CO., ST. BRIGID (1850) Revs. Anthony M. Stanganelli; Jason Grisafi; Romulo Cesar Gomez; Nesly Jean-Jaques; Deacons Manuel J. Ramos, (Retired); Darrell Buono; James Morris, (Retired); Frank Pesce. In Res., Rev. Msgr. John P. Martin, (Retired).
Res.: 50 Post Ave., Westbury, 11590.
Tel: 516-334-0021; Fax: 516-334-0082; Email: parish@saintbrigid.net; Web: www.saintbrigid.net.
School—St. Brigid / Our Lady of Hope Regional School, 101 Maple Ave., Westbury, 11590.
Tel: 516-333-0580; Fax: 516-333-0590. Paul P. Clagnaz, Prin. Lay Teachers 21; School Sisters of Notre Dame 1; Students 339.
Catechesis Religious Program—101 Maple Ave., Westbury, 11590. Sr. Ann Horn, O.P., Pastoral Assoc., Faith Formation; Socorro Moreno, D.R.E.; Meg Westfall, Part-Time D.R.E. Students 950.

WESTHAMPTON BEACH, SUFFOLK CO., IMMACULATE CONCEPTION (1891)
580 Main St., P.O. Box 1227, Westhampton Beach, 11978. Tel: 631-288-1423; Email: parishoffice@iccwhb.org; Web: www.iccwhb.org. Rev. Michael J. Bartholomew; Deacons Joseph Byrne; Mark Herrmann.
See Our Lady, Queen of the Apostles Regional School, Center Moriches under Regional Schools located in the Institution section.
Catechesis Religious Program—18 Ocame Ave., Westhampton Beach, 11978. Starr Alleyne, Dir. Faith Formation. Students 525.

WILLISTON PARK, NASSAU CO., ST. AIDAN'S CHURCH (1928) Revs. Jerry Matthew; Jeff Yildirmaz; Deacons Francis J. Love; Salvatore Villani, (Retired); Rudy Martin.
Res.: 505 Willis Ave., Williston Park, 11596.
Tel: 516-746-6585; Fax: 516-746-6055.
School—St. Aidan's Church School, (Grades N-3), 525 Willis Ave., Williston Park, 11596.
Tel: 516-746-6585, Ext. 9202; Fax: 516-746-8817. Eileen Oliver, Prin.; Mrs. Julie O'Connell, Asst. Prin.; Mrs. Patti Serrano, Librarian. Lay Teachers 31; Students 459.
Catechesis Religious Program—508 Willis Ave.,

Williston Park, 11596. Tel: 516-746-6585, Ext. 9404. Mrs. Elaine Smith. Students 1,000.

WOODBURY, NASSAU CO., HOLY NAME OF JESUS (1962) 690 Woodbury Rd., Woodbury, 11797-2504.
Tel: 516-921-2334; Fax: 516-682-8161; Email: rsullivan@hnjchurch.net; Web: www.hnjchurch.net. Rev. Msgr. Richard C. Bauhoff, J.C.D., Ph.D.; Revs. Damien Lee; John Melapuram.
Catechesis Religious Program—Students 75.

WYANDANCH, SUFFOLK CO., OUR LADY OF THE MIRACULOUS MEDAL (1932) Rev. William F. Brisotti; Deacons Alfredo Mora; Irwin Saffran.
Res.: 1434 Straight Path, Wyandanch, 11798.
Tel: 631-643-7568; Fax: 631-643-5935.
GERALD RYAN OUTREACH CENTER, INC.,
Tel: 631-643-7591. Noelle Campbell, Dir.; Naycha Florival, Religious Education & Youth Ministry.
Catechesis Religious Program—Tel: 631-643-3364. Students 240.

Chaplains of Public Institutions

ROCKVILLE CENTRE. *Catholic Health Services of Long Island*, 992 N. Village Ave., 11570.
Tel: 516-705-3700.
Mercy Medical Center, 1000 N. Village Ave., 11570. Tel: 516-705-2525. Revs. Michael Aggrey, Chap., Emilce Erato, Chap., Emery Kibal, C.P., Chap., Deacon Jacques Philippeaux, Chap., Sr. Norma Jean Lokcinski, C.I.J., Chap., Eileen Vassallo, Chap.
Good Shepherd Hospice (Nassau), 245 Old Country Rd., Melville, 11747. Tel: 631-465-6300. Rev. Robert Dawley, Chap., Deacon Richard Becker, Chap., Sr. Alice Benedict, Chap., Pauline T. Lavelle, Chap., Sisters Joyce Osgood, O.P., Chap., Patricia Pelletier, Chap.

AMITYVILLE. *The Long Island Home Specialty Healthcare System*. South Oaks Psychiatric Hospital/Broadlawn Manor Nursing and Rehabilitation Center 400 Sunrise Hwy., Amityville, 11701. Tel: 631-264-4000. Rev. Emmanuel Otiaba, Chap.

BAY SHORE. *NSLIJ Southside Hospital*.

BETHPAGE. *St. Joseph Hospital*, New Island Hospital, 4295 Hempstead Tpke., Bethpage, 11714.
Tel: 631-520-0222. Rev. Emmanuel Otiaba.

EAST MEADOW. *Nassau County Police Department*. Revs. Joseph D'Angelo, (Retired), Gerard Gordon.
Nassau County, Fire Chiefs, Council of. Rev. Kevin M. Smith.
Nassau University Medical Center, 2201 Hempstead Tpke., East Meadow, 11554. Tel: 516-572-3195; Tel: 516-572-6069. Sr. Maureen Chase, Dir. Pastoral Care.

FRANKLIN. *NSLIJ Franklin*. Rev. Casmir Obi, Chap.

GLEN COVE. *NSLIJ Glen Cove*. Rev. Azubuike Igwegbe, Chap.

LONG BEACH. *Beach Terrace Care Center*. Rev. Anthony Osuagwu, (Nigeria) Chap.
Grandell Rehab. Rev. Anthony Osuagwu, (Nigeria) Chap.
Komanoff Center, 455 E. Bay Dr., Long Beach, 11561. Rev. Anthony Osuagwu, (Nigeria) Chap.
Park Avenue Extended Care Facility. Rev. Anthony Osuagwu, (Nigeria) Chap.
South Point Plaza Nursing and Rehab Center. Rev. Anthony Osuagwu, (Nigeria) Chap.

MANHASSET. *NSLIJ Manhasset*. Rev. Gilbert Omolo, Chap.

MELVILLE. *Long Island Developmental Center*, Box 788, Melville, 11747. Tel: 516-385-2700. Rev. Malachy Flaherty, O.F.M.Cap.

MINEOLA. *Winthrop Hospital*, First St., Mineola, 11501. Tel: 516-663-0333. Revs. Evans Fwamba, C.P., Chap., Charles Ugwu, Chap.
Corpus Christi, 155 Garfield Ave., Mineola, 11501-2583. Tel: 516-746-1223.

NESCONSET. *Nesconset Nursing Home*, Nesconset, 11767. Tel: 516-361-8800. Vacant.

NORTHPORT. *Veteran's Administration Hospital*, Northport, 1176. Tel: 631-261-4400, Ext. 7194. Revs. John Malone, David Lazar Mani.

OCEANSIDE. *South Nassau Communities Hospital*, Oceanside. Tel: 516-763-2030.

PATCHOGUE. *Brookhaven Hospice*, Patchogue.
Tel: 631-687-2960. Deacon Bob Gronenthal.
Brookhaven Memorial Hospital, 100 Hospital Rd., Patchogue, 11772. Tel: 631-654-7100.

PLAINVIEW. *North Shore Hospital at Plainview*, 888 Old Country Rd., Plainview, 11083.
Tel: 516-681-8900. Rev. Benjamin Uzuegbunam, Chap.
St. Pius X: 1 St. Pius Ct., Plainview, 11803-4023.
Tel: 516-938-3959.
NSLIJ Plainview. Rev. Benjamin Uzuegbunam, Chap.

PORT JEFFERSON. *St. Charles Hospital, Port Jefferson, New York*, Port Jefferson, 11777.
Tel: 631-474-6411. Rev. Henry Vas, O.F.M.Cap., Chap., Sr. Edith Menegus, O.S.U., Chap., Dir. Pastoral Care.
Maryhaven Center of Hope, 51 Terryville Rd., Port Jefferson, 11777. Tel: 631-474-3400; Email: john.connolly@chsli.org; Web: www.maryhaven.chsli.org. Sisters Cathy Smith, O.P., Maryaline Zierle, O.P.
Mather Memorial Hospital, Port Jefferson, 11777.
Tel: 631-473-1320, Ext. 4007. Vacant.

ROSLYN. *St. Francis Hospital*, Roslyn, 11576. Rev. Emmanuel Bae, Chap., Mary Ellen Beneivenga, Sisters Minda Castrillo, F.M.M., Elisa Fernando, F.M.M., Pauline Gilmore, F.M.M., Dir., Pastoral Care, Claire MacDonald, O.P., Stella Slonski, C.J.S., Chap., Patricia Tarpinian, Ms. Mary Toole.

SAYVILLE. *Good Samaritan Nursing Home.*, Sayville, 11782. Tel: 631-244-2400. Jeanette Zerella.

SMITHTOWN. *St. Catherine of Siena Hospital*, Smithtown, 11787. Tel: 631-360-2000. Revs. Cornelius Dery, (Ghana) Chap., Xavier Lakra, (India) Chap.
280 E. Main St., Smithtown, 11787.
Tel: 631-862-3000; Tel: 631-979-1292.

STONY BROOK. *L.I. State Veterans' Home*, Stony Brook.
Tel: 631-444-8737. Vacant.
Stony Brook University Hospital, SUNY at Stony Brook, Stony Brook, 11790. Tel: 631-444-8157. Revs. Thomas Aidoo, Chap., Vitus Arinze Ezeiruaku, Chap., (M T W on-call).

UNIONDALE. *Holly Patterson Geriatric Center*, 875 Jerusalem Ave., Uniondale, 11553.
Tel: 516-572-1500. Rev. R. Michael Reid, (Retired)
Res.: Holy Family, Hicksville, 11801.
Tel: 516-938-3846.

VALLEY STREAM. *Franklin Medical Center Hospital*, Valley Stream, 11580. Tel: 516-256-6000. Rev. Patrick Onuegbu
Our Lady of Peace, 25 Fowler Ave., Lynbrook, 11563.
Tel: 516-399-6414.

WEST BRENTWOOD. *Pilgrim Psychiatric Center*, P.O. Box A, West Brentwood, 11717. Tel: 631-761-2828. Rev. Franklin Ezeora.

WEST ISLIP. *Consolation Nursing Home*, West Islip, 11795. Tel: 631-587-1600. Rev. Martin Bancroft, Chap., Mrs. Peggy Nixdorf, Dir., Pastoral Care.
Good Samaritan Hospital Medical Center, West Islip, 11795. Tel: 631-376-3000. Deacon Richard Becker, Sisters Mona Garrett, D.W., Chap., Jean Agnes Geraghty, O.P., Chap., Rosemary Jermusryk, O.P., Chap., Ellen Moore, O.P., Chap., Ann Marie Pierce, O.P., Chap., Carmen Springer, Chap.
Catholic Home Care, 15 Park Ave., Hauppauge, 11749. Tel: 631-929-8200. Samuel Blair, Chap., Alex Daszewski, Chap.

Serving Outside the Diocese:
Rev. Msgrs.—
Batule, Robert J., S.T.L., Dunwoodie.
Calledo, James
Rowan, Mark P.
Revs.—
Denniston, John
Mocarski, Janusz.

Medical Leave:
Revs.—
Johnston, Jeffrey, (Retired)
Lubrano, Robert, (Retired).

Retired:
Most Revs.—
Wcela, Emil, (Retired), Church of St. John the Evangelist, 546 St. John's Pl., Riverhead, 11901-4691
Dunne, John C., D.D., (Retired), St. Kilian, 485 Conklin St., Farmingdale, 11735
Rev. Msgrs.—
Armshaw, Patrick, (Retired), St. Francis of Assisi, 29 Northgate Dr., Greenlawn, 11740
Bennett, Donald T., (Retired), Church of the Holy Redeemer, 37 S. Ocean Ave., Freeport, 11520
Boccafola, Kenneth, (Retired), 50 Sutton Pl., Islandia, 11749
Candreva, Thomas D., S.T.L., J.C.D., (Retired), St. Pius X Residence, 565 Albany Ave., Amityville, 11701
Curley, Joseph K., (Retired), Assumption of BVM, 20 Chestnut St., Centereach, 11720
Gaeta, Francis X., (Retired), St. Pius X Residence, 565 Albany Ave., Amityville, 11701
Gallagher, Thomas G., (Retired), 1345 Martin Ct. #928, Bethlehem, PA 18018
Gill, William J., (Retired), Sacred Hearts of Jesus & Mary, 168 Hill St., Southampton, 11968
Graziadio, Domenick T., M.A., (Retired), Diocese of Rockville Center, P.O. Box 9023, 11571-9023
Hamilton, Daniel S., (Retired), St. Pius X Residence, 565 Albany Ave., Amityville, 11701
Heinlein, John T., (Retired), St. Jude, 89 Overlook Dr., Mastic Beach, 11951
Kane, Thomas S., (Retired), 2850 75th St., West #2, Bradenton, FL 34209
Kopinski, Richard P., (Retired), St. Joseph's Guest Home, Greenlawn, 11740
Martin, John P., (Retired), St. Brigid, 75 Post Ave., Westbury, 11590
Molloy, Thomas E., (Retired), St. Pius X Residence, 565 Albany Ave., Amityville, 11701
Nosser, John C., M.S., M.Div., (Retired), St. Patrick, 9 N. Clinton Ave., Bay Shore, 11706
Placa, Alan J., (Retired), 200 Eagleton Estates Blvd., Palm Beach Gardens, FL 33414
Rahilly, Paul F., (Retired), 83 Acapulco St., Atlantic Beach, 11509
Regan, Dennis M., (Retired), 52 Rocky Point Rd., Middle Island, 11953
Richardson, Ronald A., (Retired), 59 Eric Dr., Middle Island, 11953
Riordan, Brendan P., (Retired), 1714 Consulate Pl., Unit 101, West Palm Beach, FL 33401
Rowan, John J., (Retired), 78 Sprucewood Blvd., Central Islip, 11722
Ryan, T. Peter, (Retired), St. Pius X Residence, 565 Albany Ave., Amityville, 11701
Saccacio, Robert J., (Retired), 2163 Lima Loop-130-173, Laredo, TX 78045
Spadaro, Thomas L., (Retired), 53 Virginia Ave., Ronkonkoma, 11779
Wawerski, Edward, (Retired), Church of St. Hedwig, 1 Depan Ave., Floral Park, 11001-2294
Revs.—
Alarcon, Felix, (Retired), Calle de San Bernardo 112, Madrid, Spain 28015
Allen, Peter, (Retired), 151 Union Ave, Lynbrook, 11563
Blake, Andrew P., (Retired), St. Andrew, 122 Division St., Sag Harbor, 11963-3154
Bogert, James, (Retired), 1507 NM State Rd., 76, Santa Cruz, NM 87567
Bowman, James C., (Retired), 6780 Sinsonte Ct., Fort Pierce, FL 34951
Buckley, Harold P., (Retired), 100 Discover Way, Palm Beach Gardens, FL 33418
Callahan, Zachary, (Retired), Church of Cure of Ars, 2323 Merrick Ave., Merrick, 11566
Callan, Patrick J., (Retired), Corpus Christi, 155 Garfield Ave., Mineola, 11501
Connolly, Andrew P., (Retired), 309 Brookside Ct., Copiague, 11726-4001
Coschignano, Joseph C., (Retired), 600 Pine Hollow Rd., #14-4A, East Norwich, 11732
D'Angelo, Joseph, (Retired), 490 Lupton Point Rd., Mattituck, 11952
D'Souza, Claude J., (Retired), 4525 N.W. 2nd St., Apt. B, Delray Beach, FL 33445
Dahm, Paul J., (Retired), St. Pius X Residence, 565 Albany Ave., Amityville, 11701
De Vita, James C., (Retired), 4760-A Greentree Way, Boynton Beach, FL 33436
Ditta, Angelo J., (Retired), 109 Harbor South, Amityville, 11701
Dolan, Paul, (Retired), P.O. Box 9023, 11571-9023
Donovan, Richard R., (Retired), Our Lady of Lourdes, 65 Wright Ave., Malverne, 11565
Driscoll, Paul G., (Retired), 16 Croyden Rd., Mineola, 11501
Edamattam, Thomas, (Retired), Maria Regina, 3945 Jerusalem Ave., Seaford, 11783
Fernando, Simon, (Retired), Suwinda Dummalademoya, Wennappuwa, Sri Lanka
Figliola, Nicholas J., (Retired), 50 Myson St., West Islip, 11795
Fitzgerald, John J., (Retired), Church of St. James, 429 Route 25A, East Setauket, 11733
Gallagher, William G., (Retired), Our Lady of Consolation, 111 Beach Dr., West Islip, 11795
Gomide, Tomaz, (Retired), 559 Rockland St., Westbury, 11590
Heinlein, Gregory, (Retired), Our Lady of Lourdes, 855 Carmans Rd., Massapequa Park, 11762
Howard, Theodore J., (Retired), ATRIA, 4089 Nesconset Hwy., South Setauket, 11720
Johnston, Jeffrey, (Retired), 751 E. Red House Branch Rd., St. Augustine, FL 32084
Kealey, Edward J., (Retired), St. Pius X Residence, 565 Albany Ave., Amityville, 11701
Klein, Martin L., (Retired), St. Pius X Residence, 565 Albany Ave., Amityville, 11701
Kline, Robert J., (Retired), 40 Moriches Ave., East Moriches, 11940
Kohli, Charles F., (Retired), St. Joseph Guest House, 350 Cuba Hill Rd., Huntington, 11743
Liu, Peter T., (Retired), St. Pius X Residence, 565 Albany Ave., Amityville, 11701
McCabe, John H., (Retired), St. Pius X Residence, 565 Albany Ave., Amityville, 11701

McCarthy, William E., M.M., (Retired), St. Teresa's Residence, P.O. Box 321, Maryknoll, 10545-0305
McComiskey, Joseph C., (Retired), P.O. Box 1268, Smithtown, 11787
McGratty, John J., (Retired), 2203 Cedar Path, Riverhead, 11901
McMullen, Francis R., (Retired), 20550 Falcons Landing Cir., #5203, Potomac Falls, VA 20165
Michell, George J., (Retired), St. Pius X Residence, 565 Albany Ave., Amityville, 11701
Minturn, Joseph, (Retired), 58 Oyster Cove Ln., Blue Point, 11715
Moore, John R., (Retired), 1101 Cabot Ct. N., Saint James, 11780
Niewczas, Taddeus, (Retired), 84 Berry St., Apt. 1L, Brooklyn, 11211
Palliparambil, Jose Simon, (Retired), St. Pius X Residence, 565 Albany Ave., Amityville, 11701
Pedzik, Vitalis B., (Retired), 6615 Wetherole St., D9, Rego Park, 11374
Punti, George, (Retired), St. Pius X Residence, 565 Albany Ave., Amityville, 11701
Quesada, Manuel, (Retired), Ave. Huayna Capac, 1-396, Cyenca, Ecuador
Rafferty, Lawrence B., (Retired), St. Pius X Residence, 565 Albany Ave., Amityville, 11701
Reid, R. Michael, (Retired), Church of the Holy Family, 17 Fordham Ave., Hicksville, 11801
Saloy, Thomas, (Retired), Diocese of Rockville Centre, P.O. Box 9023, 11570-9023
Sang-Nguyen, Francis, (Retired), S.S. Cyril & Methodius, 125 Half Hollow Rd., Deer Park, 11729
Soriano, Mamerto, (Retired), Our Lady of Gate, Daranga, Albay, Philippines 4501
Swiatocha, Bruno, (Retired), c/o Veronica Czebotar, 4210 Rose Petal Ct., Ellicott City, MD 21043
Torpey, Michael J., (Retired), 2606 Timber Cove, Annapolis, MD 21401
Vattakudiyil, Francis P., (Retired), St. Joseph, 59 Church St., Kings Park, 11754
Walas, Joseph, (Poland) (Retired), Diocese of Rockville Centre, P.O. Box 9023, 11571-9023
Weerasinghe, Felix M., (Sri Lanka) (Retired), 52 Alles Rd., Negombo, Sri Lanka
Whelan, Dennis J., (Retired), St. Pius X Residence, 565 Albany Ave., Amityville, 11701
Whelan, John F., (Retired), 640 W. Broadway, Long Beach, 11561
Worthley, John, (Retired), 30 Town Path, Glen Cove, 11542.

Permanent Deacons:
Acquaro, Peter, St. Frances Cabrini, Coram
Altonji, James F., (Retired), St. Joseph, Ronkonkoma
Alvarado, Jesus, (Retired), St. Anne, Brentwood
Alvarado, Rene, St. Joseph, Ronkonkoma
Anderson, Thomas, St. Frances de Chantal, Wantagh
Anetrella, Louis, Christ the King, Commack
Appel, Michael, Our Lady of the Assumption, Copiague
Aprile, Michael, (Retired), St. Martin of Tours, Amityville
Arevalo, Jose, St. Luke, Brentwood
Ashe, James C., (Retired), Our Lady of Poland, Southampton (Inactive)
Austin, William, St. John the Evangelist, Riverhead
Baker, Scott, Holy Name of Mary, Valley Stream
Banno, Anthony, St. Christopher, Baldwin
Barone, Frank D., St. Kilian, Farmingdale
Barreca, Vincent Jr., Resurrection, Farmingville
Bartolotto, Joseph T., (Retired), St. Louis De Montfort, Sound Beach (Inactive)
Bast, Thomas, (Retired), (Out of Diocese, NV)
Becker, Richard, (Retired), St. Philip Neri, Northport
Becker, Robert A., Our Lady of Perpetual Help, Lindenhurst
Beckles, Vincent, St. Gerard Majella (Out of Diocese, Diocese of Orlando)
Bedell, Paul, (Retired), Campus Ministry, Adelphi University
Behar, Stephen, St. Mary, East Islip
Bellevue, Hernst, St. Martha, Uniondale
Benincasa, Joseph, (Retired), St. Catherine of Sienna, Franklin Square
Bianco, Joseph, St. Peter of Alcantara, Port Washington
Bice, Frank, (Out of Diocese, CT)
Bilella, Richard, St. Hugh of Lincoln, Huntington Station
Billia, Edward W., (Retired), St. Hugh of Lincoln, Huntington Station
Blakeney, John, St. Bernard, Levittown
Blasius, Ronald, (Retired), Ss. Philip & James, St. James
Bliss, Basil, St. Anne, Garden City
Bohuslaw, James, St. John Nepomucene, Bohemia
Bono, Frank J., (Retired), St. Joachim, Cedarhurst
Bonocore, Dale, St. Patrick, Huntington
Bonocore, Michael A., St. Isidore, Riverhead
Borchardt, Frank, (Retired), St. Patrick, Glen Cove
Bowe, Martin J., (Retired)
Braun, Robert G., (Retired), St. Anthony of Padua, East Northport
Browne, George J., (Retired), St. Anne, Garden City (Inactive)
Brunner, Richard, St. James, Seaford
Bueno, Jose M., St. Martha, Uniondale
Buono, Darrell, St. Brigid, Westbury
Burkart, John F., (Retired), St. Pious X, Plainview
Burnham, Bruce A., Our Holy Redeemer, Freeport
Byrne, James, St. Francis of Assisi, Greenlawn
Byrne, Joseph, (Retired), Immaculate Conception, Westhampton Beach
Byrne, Michael, Infant Jesus, Port Jefferson
Cales, Francisco, Our Holy Redeemer, Freeport
Califano, Joseph, (Retired), St. Joseph, Ronkonkoma (Inactive)
Cameron, Lachlan J., Holy Spirit, New Hyde Park
Campbell, Robert, (Retired), St. Raymond, East Rockaway (Inactive)
Candido, Arthur, Our Lady of Fatima, Manorhaven
Cantave, Jean, St. Francis of Assisi, Greenlawn
Carroll, James P., St. Christopher, Baldwin
Case, Edward M., (Out of Diocese, SC)
Casey, William, St. Patrick, Huntington
Cedrone, Anthony M., Our Lady of Peace, Lynbrook
Cepeda, Jose A., Our Lady of the Assumption, Copiague
Chamberlain, Anthony J., (Retired), St. Anthony, Rocky Point (Inactive)
Choi, Stephen Gil Soo, St. Aloysius, Great Neck
Ciccaroni, Andrew, St. Joseph, Garden City
Clifford, Kenneth, Infant Jesus, Port Jefferson
Coleman, Thomas, St. Barnabas the Apostle, Bellmore
Colon, Ralph E., Our Lady of Mercy, Hicksville
Colpa, Andres, St. Anne, Brentwood
Connolly, Thomas, St. Raymond, East Rockaway
Contreras, Jose A., St. Ignatious Loyola, Hicksville
Cosentino, Louis, St. Patrick, Huntington
Costa, Victor R., St. Raphael, East Meadow
Costello, Thomas P., (Retired), St. Joseph, Hewlett
Cotone, Louis, (Retired), St. Kilian, Farmingdale
Cove, Francis K., (Inactive)
Croce, Barry, St. Edward the Confessor, Syosset
Crosby, William, O.L.P.H., Lindenhurst
Cunningham, Edward F., St. Thomas the Apostle, West Hempstead
D'Alessio, Raymond P., St. Paul, Brookville
D'Angelo, Frank G., (Suspended), St. Peter of Alcantara, Port Washington
D'Aversa, Angelo D., (Retired), St. Raphael, East Meadow
Daniello, Chris, St. James, Seaford
Daza, Heriberto, (Retired), St. Mary of the Isle, Long Beach
DeBellis, Michael J., (Retired), St. Joseph, Ronkonkoma
DeGuardi, John P., (Retired), Our Lady of Lourdes, West Islip
Dejewski, Robert, (Retired), (Inactive)
Dell'Aglio, Frank, St. Gerard Majella, Port Jefferson Station
DeStefano, Carmine E., St. Matthew, Dix Hills
Devenney, Michael L., (Retired), St. Joseph, Ronkonkoma
Diaz, Juan, (Retired), Resurrection, Farmingville
Diaz-Granados, Francisco, St. Francis de Sales, Patchogue
DiGiovanna, James R., Resurrection, Farmingville
DiGiuseppe, Peter A., (Retired), (Out of Diocese, TX)
Dobbins, William, St. Joseph, Ronkonkoma
Donza, Gaetano, (Retired), St. Raymond, East Rockaway
Dunphy, Patrick J., Our Lady of Hope, Carle Place
Ervin, Christopher, Sacred Heart, Cutchogue
Evrard, Thomas J., Our Lady of Peace, Lynbrook
Failla, John, (Retired), St. Elizabeth, Melville
Farley, Owen, St. Anthony, Rocky Point
Faulkenberry, Lawrence, Church of the Most Holy Trinity, East Hampton
Federici, Ronald, Cure of Ars, Merrick
Ferrara, Fernando, Our Lady of Lourdes, Massapequa Park
Ferreiro, Douglas, Holy Spirit, New Hyde Park
Ferri, Richard, St. Martin of Tours, Amityville
Fielding, John, St. Rocco, Glen Cove
Finter, Frederick E., St. John the Baptist, Wading River
Fitzpatrick, John F., Ss. Cyril and Methodius, Deer Park
Flannery, James W., St. Bernard, Levittown
Flood, Frank J., (Retired), St. Rose of Lima, Massapequa
Forbes, Thomas J., (Retired), St. Rose of Lima, Massapequa
Ford, John E., (Retired), St. Thomas the Apostle, West Hempstead
Fox, Thomas, St. Boniface Martyr, Sea Cliff
Gagliardi, John, St. Jude, Mastic Beach
Gagnon, Jules O. A., (Retired), Our Lady of the Miraculous Medal, Wyandanch (Inactive)
Gambardela, Michael, St. Rose of Lima, Massapequa
Gargiulo, Andrew T., (Retired), Maria Regina, Seaford
Gariboldi, Frank, (Retired), Our Lady of Lourdes, Massapequa Park
Gerace, Patrick C., St. Mark, Shoreham
Gillette, Ronald J., (Retired), St. John of God, Central Islip
Giraldo, Luis D., (Retired), St. Hugh of Lincoln, Huntington Station
Goldburg, Charles R., (Retired), St. Joachim, Cedarhurst
Gomes, Mario R., St. Ignatious Loyola, Hicksville
Gomes, Michael, (Out of Diocese, VA)
Gonzalez, Frank, St. Catherine of Sienna, Franklin Square
Graff, Charles, (Retired), (Inactive) Our Lady of Grace, Babylon
Graviano, Anthony, (Retired), Our Lady of Mount Carmel, Patchogue
Grebe, John, St. Elizabeth Ann Seton, Lake Ronkonkoma
Grieb, Edward S., St. Joseph, Ronkonkoma
Gronenthal, Robert W., (Retired), Our Lady of Snow, Blue Point
Guilfu, Juan, St. Patrick, Glen Cove
Hartmann, Frank C., (Retired), Our Lady of the Snow, Blue Point (Inactive)
Hayes, Edward, St. Margaret of Scotland, Selden
Hennessy, Thomas R., (Retired), St. Martin of Tours, Bethpage
Herrmann, Mark, Immaculate Conception, Westhampton Beach
Hogan, John J., Holy Spirit, New Hyde Park
Horn, John D., St. James, Seaford
Huber, Charles F., (Retired), SS. Cyril & Methodius, Deer Park (Out of Diocese, GA)
Iandoli, Richard, (Leave of Absence)
Jennings, Paul, Good Samaritan Hospital (Returned to CT)
Kammerer, Charles, Sacred Heart, North Merrick
Karan, Edward, Our Lady of the Snow, Blue Point
Keach, Frank, St. Patrick, Bay Shore
Keenan, John, Sts. Philip & James, St. James
Kogler, William E., (Retired), St. Margaret of Scotland, Selden
Kolakowski, Theodore, (Retired), St. Gertrude, Bayville
Kruse, Robert A., Infant Jesus, Port Jefferson
Kurre, Frank, Notre Dame, New Hyde Park
LaBella, Patrick, St. Lawrence the Martyr, Sayville
Lackenbauer, Everett, St. Peter the Apostle, Islip Terrace
LaRossa, Richard W., St. Raymond, East Rockaway
Lemme, Thomas, Notre Dame, New Hyde Park
Leopard, James E., St. Rosalie, Hampton Bays
Lewis, Clinton, (Retired), Queen of the Most Holy Rosary, Roosevelt
Leyden, Michael J., (Retired), St. Joseph, Babylon
Logan, George, (Retired), Most Holy Trinity, East Hampton
Longo, Allan D., St. Francis of Assisi, Greenlawn
Lucie, Thomas, Our Lady of Lourdes, West Islip
Luken, Richard A., St. Luke, Brentwood
Lynch, John, St. William the Abbot, Seaford
Lyon, Robert, (Retired), Mary Immaculate, Bellport
Maffeo, Joseph R., St. Elizabeth Ann Seton, Lake Ronkonkoma
Maggipinto, V. Anthony, SS. Philip and James, St. James (Leave of Absence)
Maher, Kenneth, SS. Philip & James, St. James
Maher, Richard P., Our Lady of Lourdes, West Islip
Mais, George A. Jr., St. Ignatius Loyola, Hicksville
Malone, Thomas, St. Raymond's, East Rockaway
Mancilla, Orlando, St. Luke, Brentwood
Mannix, Brian, Corpus Christi, Mineola
Marfoglio, Joseph, (Retired), Christ the King, Commack
Marino, Francis, St. Kilian, Farmingdale
Marino, Salvatore, St. Boniface, Elmont
Martin, Rodolfo, St. Aidan, Williston Park
Mathurin, Trevor S., St. Martha, Uniondale
McCarthy, Robert, St. Anne, Garden City
McCormack, Kevin, Our Lady of Peace, Lynbrook
McDaid, Thomas P., (Retired), St. Agnes, Rockville Centre
McGauvran, John W., (Retired), (Inactive)
McGonigle, John H., (Retired), Holy Family, Hicksville
McGowan, John, (Retired), Notre Dame, New Hyde Park
McGuinness, Francis B., St. Rose of Lima, Massapequa
McIndoe, Martin B., St. Francis de Sales, Patchogue

McKenna, John J., K.H.S., St. Joseph, Garden City
McKenna, Michael A., (Retired), St. Joseph, Ronkonkoma
McLaughlin, James, St. Anthony of Padua, Rocky Point
McPartland, Lawrence E., St. Martin of Tours, Amityville
McQuade, James J., (Retired), St. Matthew, Dix Hills
Meehan, John J., Our Lady of Lourdes, West Islip
Mercolino, Joseph T., (Retired), St. Elizabeth, Melville (Inactive)
Metzdorff, Michael C., St. William the Abbot, Seaford
Mildeberger, William, (Retired), St. Boniface, Elmont (Inactive)
Miller, Brian, Our Lady of Grace, West Babylon
Mills, Philip A. Jr., Our Lady of the Assumption, Copiague
Monahan, Michael, St. Anthony, Oceanside
Mongillo, Robert, St. Francis de Sales, Patchogue
Montelione, Michael, St. Raphael, East Meadow; Assumption of BVM, Centereach
Mora, Alfredo, OL Miraculous Medal, Wyndanch
Moran, John, (Suspended), (Inactive)
Morris, James, (Retired), St. Brigid, Westbury (Inactive)
Mott, Roger P., (Retired), St. John Nepomucene, Bohemia
Mullane, Robert, St. Louis de Montfort, Sound Beach
Mulligan, Lawrence, Our Lady of Victory, Floral Park
Murano, James A., SS. Cyril and Methodius, Deer Park; Ss. Cyril & Methodius, Deer Park
Muratore, Biagio V., (Retired), St. Margaret of Scotland, Selden
Murillo, Julio, St. Joseph, Babylon
Murphy, James, St. Edward the Confessor, Syosset
Muscarnera, Charles, (Retired), St. Christopher, Baldwin
Muscente, Ralph J., St. Christopher, Baldwin
Mystkowski, Joseph J., St. Sylvester, Medford
Nardone, Gregory, St. Patrick, Bay Shore
Naylor, Montford D., (Retired), St. Frances Cabrini, Coram
Neuhedel, Paul W., Maria Regina, Seaford
Newhall, John, Good Shepherd, Holbrook
Newton, Philip, (Returned to Home Diocese)
Nuzzi, John, (Retired), Maria Regina, Seaford
O'Brien, James J., St. Anne, Garden City
O'Connor, John, St. Anthony, Oceanside
O'Connor, Thomas F., Good Shepherd, Holbrook
O'Donovan, Robert S., St. Frances de Chantal, Wantagh
O'Hara, James, Holy Name of Mary, Valley Stream
O'Neill, James, (Retired), St. Anthony, Oceanside
Odin, Francis, (Retired), Our Lady of Perpetual Help, Lindenhurst
Oliva, Joseph, Maria Regina, Seaford
Otton, Daniel, St. Joseph, Hewlett
Owen, George, (Retired), St. Kilian, Farmingdale
Padula, Wayne, (Retired), St. James, Setauket
Pagnotta, Carmen, St. Frances Cabrini, Coram
Panzica, John, (Out of Diocese, NC)
Peralta, Joseph F., St. Patrick, Bay Shore
Perez, Juan, Our Lady of Loretto, Hempstead
Pesce, Frank V., St. Brigid, Westbury
Pettorino, John C., (Retired), St. John the Evangelist, Center Moriches
Philppeaux, Jacques, St. Thomas the Apostle, West Hempstead
Pickford, Albert, St. Joseph the Worker, East Patchogue
Polanco, Luis Roberto, St. Matthew, Dix Hills
Portuese, Richard, Our Lady of Lourdes, Malverne
Pozzolano, Vincent, St. John the Baptist, Wading River
Quinn, Tom, St. Patrick, Bayshore
Raad, Richard, Holy Name of Mary, Valley Stream
Ramos, Manuel, (Retired), St. Brigid, Westbury
Rapacki, John, St. Thomas More, Hauppauge (Out of Diocese, Archdiocese of Galveston-Houston)
Reda, Gerard, St. Patrick, Smithtown
Reed, Robert R., St. Ignatious Martyr, Long Beach
Reich, George F., (Retired), St. John Nepomucene, Bohemia
Reilly, Thomas Jr., (Suspended), St. Edward the Confessor, Syosset (Leave of Absence)
Rich, Thomas B., J.C.L., D.Min., Our Lady of Hope, Carle Place
Rieger, John, Our Lady Queen of Martyrs, Centerport
Riegger, George J., (Retired), St. Sylvester, Medford
Rivera, Franklin, St. Sylvester, Medford
Rivera, Ralph, Holy Cross, Nesconset
Rivera, Wenceslao, (Retired), (Inactive)
Roman, Carlito, Infant Jesus, Port Jefferson
Romero, Miguel A., (Retired), St. Martha, Uniondale
Rorke, Gerard J., St. Patrick, Huntington
Ruggieri, Clyde, Holy Name of Mary, Valley Stream
Saffran, Irwin, Our Lady of Grace, West Babylon
Saint-Louis, Evenou, St. Martha, Uniondale
Samson, Thomas R., (Retired), St. Anne, Brentwood
Sanchez, Cristobal, (Retired), Our Holy Redeemer, Freeport
Sandberg, Louis C., (Retired), Queen of the Most Holy Rosary, Roosevelt (Inactive)
Savarese, Philip E., St. Anthony, Oceanside
Schlosser, Dennis, St. Raphael, East Meadow
Schultz, Peter F., (Retired), St. John the Evangelist, Riverhead
Sherlock, Bernard F., (Retired), St. Barnabas Apostle, Bellmore
Silien, Dominique, (Retired), St. Boniface, Elmont
Simeone, Joseph, St. Jude, Mastic Beach
Sisinni, Christopher, Holy Name of Jesus, Woodbury
Smith, Douglas, Our Lady of Perpetual Help, Lindenhurst
Sorico, Matthew, St. Thomas More, Happauge
Sperl, William, Ss. Cyril & Methodius, Deer Park
Squiteri, Aniello, (Retired), Our Lady of Peace, Lynbrook
Stamm, Donald, (Retired, Inactive), (Inactive)
Sullivan, John F., (Retired), St. Joseph, Babylon
Swane, Gary, St. Louis de Montfort, Sound Beach
Sykes, Jeffrey, (Retired), (Inactive)
Tappin, Edward, (Retired), Church of the Good Shepherd, Holbrook
Taranto, Vito, (Retired), St. Hugh of Lincoln, Huntington Station
Taylor, Timm, St. Bernard, Levittown & Archdiocese of Miami
Teufel, John G., (Retired), Our Lady of Lourdes, West Islip (Inactive)
Tirelli, Raymond J., (Retired), Our Lady of Hope, Carle Place
Torres, Joseph, (Out of Diocese) FL
Trodden, John E., St. Joseph, Kings Park
Tumbarello, Joseph, St. William the Abbot, Seaford
Valdaro, Domenick, (Retired), Our Lady Lourdes, Massapequa Park
Valdes, Jesus, St. Dominic, Oyster Bay
Valdez, Jose B., St. John of God, Central Islip
Vallone, David, St. Elizabeth Ann Seton, Lake Ronkonkoma
Vigliotta, Albert C., (Retired), (Inactive)
Vigliotta, Crescenzo T., (Out of Diocese, CT)
Vigneaux, Edward, St. Thomas More, Hauppauge
Villani, Salvatore B., (Retired), St. Aidan, Williston Park
Waldmann, Richard E., Infant Jesus, Port Jefferson
Walters, John, St. Anne, Brentwood
Weiss, William Jr., St. Kilian, Farmingdale
Weisz, Robert D., St. Thomas More, Hauppauge
Wetzel, Mark, St. Kilian, Farmingdale
White, David J., Holy Family, Hicksville
Whitecomb, MIchael T., St. Patrick, Huntington
Whitfield, Gerald F., Maria Regina, Seaford
Yosko, Stephen E., St. Joseph, Babylon
Zubrovich, Joseph, Cure of Ars, Merrick.

INSTITUTIONS LOCATED IN DIOCESE

[A] SEMINARIES, DIOCESAN

HUNTINGTON. *Diocesan Seminary of the Immaculate Conception*, 440 West Neck Rd., Huntington, 11743. Tel: 631-423-0483; Fax: 631-423-2346; Email: info@icseminary.edu. Most Revs. William Murphy, S.T.D., L.H.D., D.D., Chm., Bd. of Governors; Richard G. Henning, S.T.D., Rector & Prof. of Scripture; Rev. Walter F. Kedjierski, Vice Rector; Elyse B. Hayes, M.L.S., Dir. Library & Information Technologies; Deacon Dennis J. Schlosser, M.A.P.S., Dir. Fin. & Opers. Priests 2; Support Lay Staff 16.

[B] COLLEGES AND UNIVERSITIES

ROCKVILLE CENTRE. *Molloy College* (1955) 1000 Hempstead Ave., P.O. Box 5002, 11571-5002. Tel: 516-323-3000; Tel: 516-323-4710; Email: cmuscente@molloy.edu; Email: dfornieri@molloy.edu; Web: www.molloy.edu. Drew Bogner, Ph.D., Pres.; Susan Williams, Vice Pres. Finance & Treas.; Janine Payton, Vice Pres. Student Affairs; Catherine Muscente, Vice Pres. Mission & Ministry; Linda Albanese, Vice Pres. for Enrollment Mgmt.; Ann Branchini, Vice Pres. Academic Affairs & Dean Faculty; Edward J. Thompson, Vice Pres. for Advancement; Michael Torres, Vice Pres. Technology & Institutional Effectiveness; Diane Fornieri, Chief of Staff & Secy, to Brd. of Trustees. Lay Teachers 715; Sisters of St. Dominic (Amityville Community) 6; Students 4,728.

[C] HIGH SCHOOLS, DIOCESAN

NASSAU COUNTY

HICKSVILLE.
Holy Trinity Diocesan High School (1966) 98 Cherry Ln., Hicksville, 11801. Tel: 516-433-2900; Fax: 516-433-2827; Email: hths98@holytrinityhs.echalk.com; Web: www.holytrinityhs.org. Kathleen Moran, Prin.; Rev. John D. McCarthy, Chap. Lay Teachers 59; Sisters 2; Students 1,001.

SUFFOLK COUNTY

RIVERHEAD.
Bishop McGann - Mercy Diocesan High School, 1225 Ostrander Ave., Riverhead, 11901. Tel: 631-727-5900; Fax: 631-369-7328; Email: principal@mcgann-mercy.org; Web: www.mcgann-mercydhs.org. Dr, Carl A. Semmler, Prin.; Mrs. Lisa Navarra, Asst. Prin.; Mr. Charles Bender, Dean of Students; Ms. Jill Weiler, Librarian. Directed by the Diocese of Rockville Centre/Sisters of Mercy.(Coed) Lay Teachers 44; Priests 1; Students 405.

WEST ISLIP.
St. John the Baptist Diocesan High School, 1170 Montauk Hwy., West Islip, 11795. Tel: 631-587-8000; Fax: 631-587-8996; Web: www.stjohnthebaptistdhs.net. Nan Doherty, Prin.; Rev. Robert W. Ketcham, Chap.; Cheryl Westerfeld, Librarian. Lay Teachers 110; Priests 1; Sisters 3; Students 1,500.

[D] HIGH SCHOOLS, PRIVATE

HEMPSTEAD. *Sacred Heart Academy* College preparatory-girls 47 Cathedral Ave., Hempstead, 11550. Tel: 516-483-7383; Fax: 516-483-1016; Email: sha@sacredheartacademyhempstead.org; Web: www.sacredheartacademyhempstead.org. Kristin Lynch Graham, Pres.; Sr. Joanne Forker, C.S.J., Prin.; Regina Foge, Librarian. Lay Teachers 67; Sisters 3; Students 795.

MINEOLA. *Chaminade High School (Boys)* (1930) Directed by the Society of Mary (Marianists) 340 Jackson Ave., Mineola, 11501. Tel: 516-742-5555; Fax: 516-742-1989; Email: flyers@chaminade-hs.org; Web: www.chaminade-hs.org. Bros. Thomas J. Cleary, S.M., Pres.; Joseph D. Bellizzi, S.M., Prin.; Mr. Daniel Petruccio, Asst. Prin. Guidance; Mr. John Callinan, Asst. Prin. Athletics & Campus Activities; Mr. Robert Paul, Prin.; Rev. Garrett J. Long, S.M., Chap.; Mr. Gregory Kay, Asst. Prin. Curriculum & Technology; Mr. Michael Foley, Dir. Campus Ministry; Mr. Thomas Dillon, Dir. Student Activities; Mr. Patrick Kemp, Asst. Dean Students. Brothers 16; Religious Teachers 19; Lay Teachers 95; Priests 2; Students 1,700.

SOUTH HUNTINGTON. *St. Anthony's High School* (1933) College Prep. 275 Wolf Hill Rd., South Huntington, 11747-1394. Tel: 631-271-2020; Fax: 631-547-6820; Email: officeoftheprincipal@stanthonyshs.org; Web: www.stanthonyshs.org. Bro. Gary Cregan, O.S.F., Prin. Directed by the Franciscan Brothers of Brooklyn. Brothers 8; Lay Teachers 126; Priests 1; Students 2,350; Intercommunity Sisters 2.

SYOSSET. *Our Lady of Mercy Academy* College prep for young women. 815 Convent Rd., Syosset, 11791-3895. Tel: 516-921-1047; Fax: 516-921-3634; Web: www.olma.org. Ms. Margaret Myhan, Pres.; Ms. Lisa Harrison, Prin.; Mrs. Sheila Wilson, Librarian. Sisters of Mercy/Mid-Atlantic Community. Lay Teachers 47; Sisters of Mercy 3; Students 464; Sisters of St. Ursula 1.

UNIONDALE. *Kellenberg Memorial High School* (1987) 1400 Glenn Curtiss Blvd., Uniondale, 11553. Tel: 516-292-0200; Fax: 516-292-0877; Email: brokenneth@kellenberg.org; Web: www.kellenberg.org. Bro. Kenneth M. Hoagland, S.M., Prin.; Mr. John Benintendi, Asst. Prin. Admissions; Mr. Kenneth Conrade, Asst. Prin. Academics; Rev. Albert Bertoni, S.M., Asst. Prin. Guidance; Miss Maria Korzekwinski, Asst. Prin. Latin School; Bro. Roger Poletti, S.M., Asst. Prin. Activities; Rev. Thomas A. Cardone, S.M., Chap.; Ms. Jennifer Mulligan, Dean of Women; Mr. John McCutcheon, Dean of Students; Mr. Bryan Finn, Dir. Apostolic Activities; Bro. Donald Nussbaum, S.M., Suprv. New Construction, Vehicles; Mrs. Marietta Tartamella, Financial Supvr.; Bro. David Bruner, S.M., Librarian; Christopher Cartier, Admin.; Rev. Daniel Griffin, S.M., Chap.; Ruth Marconi, Admin.; Robert York, Admin. Directed by the Society of Mary. Brothers 9; Religious Teachers 23; Lay Teachers 123; Priests 3; Students 2,583.

[E] REGIONAL SCHOOLS

BELLMORE. *St. Elizabeth Ann Seton Regional School*, (Grades N-8), 2341 Washington Ave., Bellmore, 11710. Tel: 516-785-5709; Fax: 516-785-4468; Email: lgraziose@steas.com. Leeann Graziose, Prin. Supported by the following parishes: St. Barnabas, Bellmore; St. Raphael, East Meadow; Cure of Ars, Merrick; St. Frances de Chantal, Wantagh. Lay Teachers 25; Students 325.

CENTER MORICHES. *Our Lady, Queen of Apostles Regional School*, 2 St. Johns Pl., Center Moriches, 11934. Tel: 631-878-1033; Fax: 631-878-1059; Email: derlanger@olqany.org. David Erlanger, Prin. Supported by the following parishes: St. John Evangelist, Center Moriches; St. Jude, Mastic Beach; Immaculate Conception, Westhampton Beach; Ss. Peter & Paul, Manorville. Lay Teachers 25; Students 200.

CENTRAL ISLIP. *Our Lady of Providence Regional School* (1992) 82 Carleton Ave., Central Islip, 11722. Tel: 631-234-6324; Fax: 631-234-6360; Email: lfitzpatrick@olprov.org; Web: www.olprov.org. Sharon Swift Imperati, Prin.; Lorena Fitzpatrick, School Sec. Supported by the following parishes: St. Anne, Brentwood; St. Luke, Brentwood; St. John of God, Central Islip; St. Peter the Apostle, Islip Terrace. Lay Teachers 19; Sisters 1; Students 287.

COMMACK. *Holy Family Regional School*, Indian Head Rd., P.O. Box 729, Commack, 11725.
Tel: 631-543-0202; Fax: 631-543-2818; Email: hfrs@aol.com. Mr. Anthony Giordano, Prin.; Wendy Sokol, Librarian. Supported by the following parishes: Christ the King, Commack; St. Matthew, Dix Hills; St. Thomas More, Hauppauge; St. Joseph, Kings Park. Lay Teachers 20; Students 260.

CUTCHOGUE. *Our Lady of Mercy Regional School*, 27685 Main Rd., P.O. Box 970, Cutchogue, 11935.
Tel: 631-734-5166; Fax: 631-734-4266; Email: olm@olmregional.org; Web: www.olmregional.org. Alexandra Conlan, Prin. Supported by the following parishes: Sacred Heart, Cutchogue; Our Lady of Ostrabrama, Cutchogue; St. Agnes, Greenport; St. Patrick, Southold; St. John the Evangelist, Riverhead. Lay Teachers 13; Students 90.

EAST NORTHPORT. *Trinity Regional School*, 1025 Fifth Ave., East Northport, 11731. Tel: 631-261-5130; Email: tregion@optonline.net. Miss Jeanne Morcone, Prin. Supported by the following parishes: Our Lady Queen of Martyrs, Centerport; St. Anthony of Padua, East Northport; St. Francis of Assisi, Greenlawn; St. Hugh of Lincoln, Huntington Station; St. Elizabeth, Melville; St. Philip Neri, Northport. Administrators 2; Employees 11; Faculty 26; Elementary School Students 355.

GLEN COVE. *All Saints Regional Catholic School*, (Grades N-8), 12 Pearsall Ave., Glen Cove, 11542-3052. Tel: 516-676-0762; Fax: 516-676-0660; Web: www.asrcatholic.com. Very Rev. Dom Elias Carr, Can.Reg., Headmaster; Mrs. Joanne Fitzgerald, Academic Dean. Supported by the following parishes: St. Boniface, Sea Cliff; St. Hyacinth, Glen Head; St. Mary, Roslyn; St. Patrick, Glen Cove; St. Rocco, Glen Cove. Lay Teachers 17; Students 180.

LONG BEACH. *Long Beach Catholic Regional School*, (Grades PreK-8), 735 W. Broadway, Long Beach, 11561. Tel: 516-432-8900; Fax: 516-432-3841; Email: kkahn@lbcrs.org; Web: lbcrs.org. Mrs. Kerry Kahn, Prin.; Marianne Carberry, Asst. Prin.; Patricia Esposito, Librarian. Supported by the following parishes: St. Ignatius, Long Beach; St. Mary of the Isle, Long Beach, and Our Lady of the Miraculous Medal, Point Lookout. Lay Teachers 25; Sisters 2; Students 440.

PATCHOGUE. *Holy Angels Regional School* (1923) (Grades PreK-8), 1 Division St., Patchogue, 11772. Tel: 631-475-0422; Fax: 631-475-2036; Email: mconnell@holyangelsregional.org; Web: www.holyangelsregional.org. Michael Connell, Prin.; Karen Weibke, Business Mgr.; Katie Mitchell, Librarian & Technology Coord. Supported by the following parishes: Mary Immaculate, Bellport; St. Frances Cabrini, Coram; St. Joseph the Worker, E. Patchogue; St. Sylvester, Medford; Our Lady of Mount Carmel, Patchogue; St. Frances de Sales, Patchogue, and St. Margaret of Scotland, Selden. Lay Teachers 18; Students 262.

PORT JEFFERSON. *Our Lady of Wisdom Regional Catholic School*, 114-116 Myrtle Ave., Port Jefferson, 11777. Tel: 631-473-1211;
Fax: 631-473-1064; Email: jpiropato@ourladyofwisdomschool.com; Web: www.ourladyofwisdomschool.com. John W. Piropato, Prin. Supported by the following parishes: Infant Jesus, Port Jefferson; St. Louis de Montfort, Sound Beach; St. James, Setauket; St. Gerard Majella, Port Jefferson Station. Lay Teachers 15; Students 117; Total Staff 21.

RIVERHEAD. *Saint John Paul II Regional School*, 515 Marcy Ave., Riverhead, 11901. Tel: 631-727-1650;
Fax: 631-727-3945; Email: aswiatkowski@sjp2regional.org; Web: www.sjp2regional.org. Abbey Swiatkowski, Prin.

SOUTHAMPTON. *Our Lady of the Hamptons Regional School*, (Grades PreK-8), 160 N. Main St., Southampton, 11968. Tel: 631-283-9140;
Fax: 631-287-3958; Email: sks@hamptons.com; Web: www.olh.org. Sr. Kathryn Schlueter, C.S.J., Prin.; Melissa Meyer, Librarian. Nursery and PreK.; Supported by the following parishes: St. Rosalie, Hampton Bays; Our Lady of Poland, Southampton; Sacred Hearts Jesus Mary, Southampton; Queen of the Most Holy Rosary; St. Andrew; Most Holy Trinity; St. Therese of Lisieux; Our Lady of the Isle. Lay Teachers 26; Sisters 1; Students 340.
31 Montauk Hwy., Hampton Bays, 11946.
Tel: 631-723-3740; Fax: 631-728-2559. Sr. Kathryn Schlueter, C.S.J., Prin. Lay Teachers 26; Sisters 1; Students 344.

[F] ELEMENTARY SCHOOLS, PRIVATE

FREEPORT. *The De La Salle School* (2001) (Grades 5-8), 87 Pine St., Freeport, 11520-3615.
Tel: 516-379-8660; Fax: 516-379-8806; Email: Learn@delassalleschool.org; Web: www.delasalleschool.org. Kathleen Boniello; Mrs. Jeanmarie Becker, Dir.; Jeanne Mulry, Dir., Development; William L. Gault, Exec. Dir. Brothers 1; Lay Teachers 8.

MANHASSET. *Our Lady of Grace Montessori School and Center*, (Grades N-3), 29 Shelter Rock Rd., Manhasset, 11030. Tel: 516-365-9832 (School);
Tel: 516-627-9255 (Center); Fax: 516-365-9329. Sisters Ann Barbara DeSiano, I.H.M., Admin.; Kelly Quinn, I.H.M., Prin. Lay Teachers 17; Sisters, Servants of the Immaculate Heart of Mary 2; Students 165.

OLD WESTBURY. *Holy Child Academy*, (Grades Toddler-8), 25 Store Hill Rd., Old Westbury, 11568.
Tel: 516-626-9300; Fax: 516-626-7914; Email: cbowen@holychildacademy.org; Web: www.holychildacademy.org. Mr. Michael O'Donoghue, Head of School; Palma Gartland, Campus Min. & Div. Head 3 & 4; Tara Presti, Asst. Prin. Grades 5-8; Marie O'Donoghue, ECC Dir. & Div. Head 1 & 2. Lay Teachers 50; Students 225.

UNIONDALE. *St. Martin de Porres Marianist School* (2004) (Grades PreK-8), 530 Hempstead Blvd., Uniondale, 11553. Tel: 516-481-3303;
Fax: 516-483-4138; Email: jholian@stmartinmarianist.org; Web: www.stmartinmarianist.org. Bro. Kenneth M. Hoagland, S.M., Prin.; Mr. John Holian, Headmaster; Bro. James W. Conway, S.M., Dir. Student Svcs. Brothers 2; Religious Teachers 2; Lay Teachers 30; Students 377.

[G] SPECIALIZED CHILD CARE AGENCIES

NESCONSET. *Cleary Deaf Child Center, Inc.* (1925) 301 Smithtown Blvd., Nesconset, 11767.
Tel: 631-588-0530 (Voice and TTY);
Fax: 631-588-0016; Email: jsimms@clearyschool.org; Web: www.clearyschool.org. Jaqueline Simms, Exec. Dir. Directed by Catholic Charities.Day School (Infants thru 21 years). Students 85.

SYOSSET. *MercyFirst* (1894) 525 Convent Rd., Syosset, 11791-3864. Tel: 516-921-0808; Fax: 516-921-4542; Email: gmccaffery@mercyfirst.org; Web: www.mercyfirst.org. Gerard McCaffery, Pres. & CEO. Under the sponsorship of the Sisters of Mercy.Residential services provided in campus and group home settings, including diagnostic, non secure detention, hard to place (JD and clinically intensive), abuse treatment and prevention, mother/child, OMH programs, Immigrant Youth Program and Care Management Services; Family Foster Care/Adoption, Youth Development Services and Prevention Services programs provide services in Queens and Brooklyn. Serving youth and families in Nassau, Suffolk, Queens and Brooklyn. Bed Capacity 585; Tot Asst. Annually 3,000; Total Staff 540.

WADING RIVER. **Little Flower Children & Family Services of New York* (1929) 2450 N. Wading River Rd., Wading River, 11792-1402. Tel: 631-929-6200; Fax: 631-929-6121; Web: www.LittleFlowerNY.org. Sr. Rita Wasilewski, C.S.F.N., Supr.; Corinne Hammons, Exec. Dir.; Kevin Kundmueller, CFO. Sisters of the Holy Family of Nazareth.Affiliated with the Diocese of Brooklyn. Foster care, adoption & Post-Adoption Services for Developmentally Disabled Adults; Residential Treatment Center; Bricfs to Health; Medicaid service provider services. Therapeutic foster boarding homes. Eldercare Solutions: Counseling for employees of client organizations. Bed Capacity 95; Total Staff 547; Total Assisted 1,072.

[H] CATHOLIC CHARITIES

HICKSVILLE. *Catholic Charities*, 90 Cherry Ln., Hicksville, 11801-6299. Tel: 516-733-7000;
Fax: 516-733-7099; Email: info@catholiccharities.cc; Web: www.catholiccharities.cc. Laura A. Cassell, CEO, Tel: 516-733-7013; Paul F. Engelhart, COO, Tel: 516-733-7012; Fax: 516-733-7099; Richard Balcom, CFO; Gerard Bragg, Facilities & Maintenance Admin.; James Contessa, Purchasing Admin.; Jennifer Regan Haight, Contact Person. Tot Asst. Annually 62,400; Total Staff 744.

Catholic Charities Health Systems Corp. of the Diocese of Rockville Centre, Inc., 90 Cherry Ln., Hicksville, 11801-6299. Tel: 516-733-7000. Richard Balcom, Exec.

Catholic Charities Support Corp., 90 Cherry Ln., Hicksville, 11801-6299. Tel: 516-733-7032. Richard Balcom, Exec.

Chemical Dependency Services, 155 Indian Head Rd., Commack, 11725. Tel: 631-543-6200;
Fax: 631-543-6203. Kathleen Brown, Dir. Chemical Dependence Svcs. Tot Asst. Annually 5,124; Total Staff 72.

Outpatient Clinics and Wraparound Services, 155 Indian Head Rd., Commack, 11725.
Tel: 631-543-6200. Kathleen Brown, Dir. Chemical Dependence Svcs. Tot Asst. Annually 775; Total Staff 31.

Talbot House - Crisis Center, 30-C Carlough Rd., Bohemia, 11716. Tel: 631-589-4144;
Fax: 631-589-3281. Kathleen Brown, Dir. Chemical Dependence Svcs. Bed Capacity 35; Tot Asst. Annually 4,349; Total Staff 41.

Development and Communications, 90 Cherry Ln., Hicksville, 11801. Tel: 516-733-7000;
Fax: 516-733-7098. Jennifer Regan Haight, Dir. Devel. & Communications. Total Staff 6.

Finance, 90 Cherry Ln., Hicksville, 11801-6299.
Tel: 516-733-7015; Fax: 516-733-7099. Richard Balcom, CFO; Erin Shirvell, Dir. Finance. Total Staff 15.

Food and Nutrition Services, 90 Cherry Ln., Hicksville, 11801-6299. Tel: 516-733-7000; Email: agiato.amy@catholiccharities.cc. Amy Agiato, Dir. Nutrition and Maternity Svcs. Tot Asst. Annually 17,087; Total Staff 32.

Commodity Supplemental Food Program, 38 St. John's Pl., Freeport, 11520. Amy Agiato, Dir. Nutrition & Maternity Svcs. Tot Asst. Annually 5,427; Total Staff 12.

Housing Services (1980) 90 Cherry Ln., Hicksville, 11801-6299. Tel: 516-733-7076; Fax: 516-733-7098 . Jay Korth, Dir. Housing & Legal Affairs. Tot Asst. Annually 4,042; Total Staff 8.

Human Resources, 90 Cherry Lane, Hicksville, 11801-6299. Tel: 516-733-7000; Fax: 516-733-7038 . Kristy D'Errico, Dir. Human Resources, Tel: 516-733-7005; Fax: 516-733-7038. Total Staff 8.

Immigrant Services, 143 Schleigel Blvd., Amityville, 11701. Tel: 631-789-5210; Fax: 631-789-5245. Carmen Maquilon, Dir. Immigrant Svcs., Tel: 631-789-5225. Tot Asst. Annually 27,895; Total Staff 16.

Mental Health Programs, 333 N. Main St., Freeport, 11520. Tel: 516-634-0012, Ext. 126;
Fax: 516-634-0017. Howard G. Duff, Dir. Mental Health Svcs. Tot Asst. Annually 2,036; Total Staff 108.

Mental Health Residential Services, 333 N. Main St., Freeport, 11520. Howard G. Duff, Dir. Mental Health Svcs. Tot Asst. Annually 145; Total Staff 69.

Parish Social Ministry, 90 Cherry Ln., Hicksville, 11801. Tel: 516-733-7061; Fax: 516-733-7098. Paula Malloy, Dir. Parish Social Min. Tot Asst. Annually 1,617; Total Staff 5.

Central Intake & Referral Developers, 90 Cherry Ln., Hicksville, 11801. Tel: 516-733-7045; Email: info@catholiccharities.cc. Paula Malloy, Dir. Parish Social Ministry. Tot Asst. Annually 1,617; Total Staff 1.

Regina Maternity Services Corporation, 90 Cherry Ln., Hicksville, 11801. Tel: 516-223-7888;
Fax: 516-223-2752. Amy Agiato, Dir. Nutrition & Maternity Svcs. Tot Asst. Annually 176; Total Staff 25.

Regina Maternity Services/Mentoring, 90 Cherry Ln., Hicksville, 11801. Tel: 516-223-7888. Amy Agiato, Dir. Nutrition & Maternity Svcs. Tot Asst. Annually 6.

Residential Services - Developmental Disabilities, 147 Schleigel Blvd., Amityville, 11701.
Tel: 631-665-3434; Tel: 631-532-2150. Diane Ammirati, Dir. Disability Svcs. Tot Asst. Annually 271; Total Staff 187.

Senior Services, 90 Cherry Ln., Hicksville, 11801. Kim Parbst, Dir. Senior Svcs. Tot Asst. Annually 3,995; Total Staff 81.

Senior Services Case Management, 333 N. Main St., Freeport, 11520. Paulette Jones, Prog. Coord. Senior Case Mgmt. Tot Asst. Annually 1,720.

[I] HOSPITALS

BETHPAGE. **WSNCHS North Inc.* dba St. Joseph Hospital, 4295 Hempstead Tpke., Bethpage, 11714. Tel: 516-579-6000; Fax: 516-579-0417. Dr. Alan D. Guerci, M.D., Pres. & CEO; Mr. Peter Scaminaci, Exec. Vice Pres. & Chief Admin. Officer.

[J] CATHOLIC HEALTHCARE APOSTOLATE

ROCKVILLE CENTRE. *Catholic Health System of Long Island, Inc.* dba Catholic Health Services of Long Island, 992 N. Village Ave., 11570.
Tel: 516-705-3700; Fax: 516-705-3730; Web: www.chsli.org. Mr. Salvatore Sodano, Chm.; Mr. Brian McGuire, Vice Chm.; Mr. Christopher Pasucci, Treas.; Dr. Alan D. Guerci, M.D., CEO; Mr. Dennis Verzi, COO; Daniel DeBarba, CFO; Dr. Patrick M. O'Shaughnessy, Exec. Vice Pres. & Chief Medical Officer; Mr. David DeCerbo, Exec. Vice Pres. & Gen. Counsel.

Catholic Healthcare Network of Long Island, 992 N. Village Ave., 11570. Tel: 516-705-3700; Fax: 516-705-3730; Web: www.chsli.org. Dr. Alan D. Guerci, M.D., CEO.

Hospitals:

Good Samaritan Hospital Medical Center, 1000 Montauk Hwy., West Islip, 11795.
Tel: 631-376-4001; Fax: 631-376-4208. Dr. Alan D. Guerci, M.D., Pres.; Ruth Hennessey, Exec. Bed Capacity 437; Tot Asst. Annually 106,021; Total Staff 3,657.

Mercy Medical Center, 1000 N. Village Ave., 11571.
Tel: 516-705-2525; Fax: 516-705-1406. Dr. Alan D. Guerci, M.D., Pres.; Mr. Peter Scaminaci, Exec. Vice Pres. & Chief Admin. Officer. Bed Capacity 513; Tot Asst. Annually 44,812; Total Staff 1,606.

St. Catherine of Siena Medical Center, 50 Rte. 25A, Smithtown, 11787. Tel: 631-862-3000;
Fax: 631-862-3105. Dr. Alan D. Guerci, M.D., Pres.; James O'Connor, Exec. Bed Capacity 306; Tot Asst. Annually 33,156; Total Staff 1,690.

St. Charles Hospital and Rehabilitation Center, 200 Belle Terre Rd., Port Jefferson, 11777.
Tel: 631-474-6600; Fax: 631-474-6884. Dr. Alan D. Guerci, M.D., Pres.; James O'Connor, Exec. Bed Capacity 243; Tot Asst. Annually 33,156; Total Staff 1,859.

St. Francis Hospital, 100 Port Washington Blvd., Roslyn, 11576. Tel: 516-562-6000;
Fax: 516-629-2448. Dr. Alan D. Guerci, M.D., CEO; Mr. Charles Lucore, Pres. Bed Capacity 364; Tot Asst. Annually 65,566; Total Staff 3,896.

Long Term Care Facilities:

Good Samaritan Nursing Home, 101 Elm St., Sayville, 11782. Tel: 631-244-2400;
Fax: 631-244-2405. Frank Misiano, Chief Admin. Officer. Operating under the license of Good Samaritan Hospital Medical Center.

Our Lady of Consolation Nursing and Rehabilitative Care Center, 111 Beach Dr., West Islip, 11795.
Tel: 631-587-1600; Fax: 631-587-5960. Mr. James Ryan, Chief Admin. Officer.

St. Catherine of Siena Nursing and Rehabilitation Care Center, 52 Rte. 25A, Smithtown, 11787.
Tel: 631-862-3900; Fax: 631-862-3983. Mr. John Chowske, Chief Admin. Officer. Operating under the license of St. Catherine of Siena Medical Center.

Hospice and Palliative Care Services:

Good Shepherd Hospice, 110 Bi-County Blvd., Farmingdale, 11735. Tel: 631-465-6300;
Fax: 631-828-7493. Mary Ellen Polit, Chief Admin. Officer.

Nursing Sisters Home Care, Inc. dba Catholic Home Care, 110 Bi-County Blvd., Farmingdale, 11735.
Tel: 631-828-7400; Fax: 631-828-7475. Mary Ellen Polit, Chief Admin. Officer.

Behavioral/Developmentally Disabled Programs:

Maryhaven Center of Hope, Inc., 51 Terryville Rd., Port Jefferson Station, 11776. Tel: 631-474-4120;
Fax: 631-474-4110. Mr. Lewis Grossman, CEO.

Adult Day Services (over age 18):

Vocational Training/Supported Work/Sheltered Center, Tel: 631-924-5900; Fax: 631-924-2464. Participants develop skills necessary to obtain employment within an array of community-based options, or within the agency's work center; receive assistance with learning skills necessary for independent living, intensive therapeutic services and increased community integration.

Day Habilitation, Tel: 631-474-4100;
Fax: 631-474-4156.

Adult Residential Services:

Adult Residences, Tel: 631-474-4100;
Fax: 631-474-9014. The agency operates a variety of housing alternatives within community-based settings. Individuals still living at home receive assistance in accessing needed support services.

Mental Health Services:

Personalized Recovery Oriented Services for People with Psychiatric Disabilities (PROS East & West), Tel: 631-727-4044; Fax: 631-727-6531. These day programs work to develop individual skills to improve a person's living, working, learning, and social situations. Staff offer individuals assistance with accessing supports and services, advocacy and individual follow-up.

Children Services (Ages 5-21):

Maryhaven School, 51 Terryville Rd., Port Jefferson Station, 11776. Tel: 631-474-4120;
Fax: 631-474-4110. Mr. Lewis Grossman, CEO, Email: lou.grossman@chsli.org. Progressive educational programming for children with developmental disabilities providing 24-hour programming for students requiring greater support than can be provided at home. The school is committed to the IEP diploma recipient and has a specialization in autism.

Children's Residences, Tel: 631-474-3400;
Fax: 631-474-4181.

**Maryhaven Transportation Services, Inc.*, 51 Terryville Rd., Port Jefferson Station, 11776.
Tel: 631-474-4100; Fax: 631-474-4110. Mr. Lewis Grossman, CEO.

Miscellaneous Entities:

Center of Hope Foundation, 51 Terryville Rd., Port Jefferson Station, 11776. Tel: 631-474-4120;
Fax: 631-474-4110. Mr. Lewis Grossman, CEO.

CHS Home Support Services, Inc., 15 Power Dr., Hauppauge, 11788. Tel: 631-694-3435;
Fax: 631-940-3405.

CHS Services, Inc., 992 N. Village Ave., 11570.
Tel: 516-705-3700; Fax: 516-705-3730. Dr. Alan D. Guerci, M.D., CEO.

**Good Samaritan Hospital Self Insurance Against Malpractice Trust*, 1000 Montauk Hwy., West Islip, 11795. Tel: 631-376-3000. Thomas Ockers, Exec. Vice Pres. & Chief Admin. Officer.

Good Shepherd Hospice Foundation, Inc., 110 Bi-County Blvd., Farmingdale, 11735.
Tel: 631-465-6300; Fax: 631-465-6534.

St. Francis-Mercy Corporation, 100 Port Washington Blvd., Roslyn, 11576.
Tel: 516-562-6000; Fax: 516-629-2448. Dr. Alan D. Guerci, M.D., CEO.

Siena Retirement Community Realty, LLC, 50 Rte. 25A, Smithtown, 11787. Tel: 631-862-3100;
Fax: 631-862-3105. James O'Connor, Exec.

Siena Village, Inc., 2000 Bishop's Rd., Smithtown, 11787. Tel: 631-360-3000; Fax: 631-360-6006. Kim Parbst, Admin. A low income housing program.

Suffolk Hearing & Speech Center, Inc., 369 E. Main St., East Islip, 11730. Tel: 631-376-4001;
Fax: 631-376-4208. Thomas Ockers, Exec. A diagnostics & treatment center.

The Good Samaritan Hospital Foundation, 1000 Montauk Hwy., West Islip, 11795.
Tel: 631-376-4001; Fax: 631-376-4208.

The Mercy Medical Center Foundation, 1000 N. Village Ave., 11570. Tel: 516-705-2525;
Fax: 516-705-1406. Mr. Peter Scaminaci, Exec.

The Our Lady of Consolation Foundation, 111 Beach Dr., West Islip, 11795. Tel: 631-587-1600;
Fax: 631-587-5960. Mr. James Ryan, Pres.

The St. Catherine of Siena Medical Center Foundation, 48 Rte. 25A, Med. Office Bldg, Suite 205, Smithtown, 11787. Tel: 631-862-3000;
Fax: 631-862-3805.

The St. Charles Corporation, 200 Belle Terre Rd., Port Jefferson, 11777. Tel: 631-474-6600;
Fax: 631-474-6884. James O'Connor, Pres.

The St. Charles Hospital Foundation, 200 Belle Terre Rd., Port Jefferson, 11777.
Tel: 631-474-6000; Fax: 631-474-6884. James O'Connor, Pres.

**The St. Francis Hospital Foundation, Inc.*, 100 Port Washington Blvd., Roslyn, 11576.
Tel: 516-562-6000; Fax: 516-629-2448. Dr. Alan D. Guerci, M.D., CEO.

The St. Francis Research and Educational Corporation, 100 Port Washington Blvd., Roslyn, 11576. Tel: 516-562-6000; Fax: 516-629-2448. Ruth Hennessey, Pres.

The Samaritan Corporation, 992 N. Village Ave., 11570. Tel: 516-705-3700; Fax: 516-705-3730. Thomas Ockers, Exec.

**Wisdom Gardens Housing Development Fund Company, Inc.*, c/o Maryhaven Center of Hope, 51 Terryville Rd., Port Jefferson Station, 11776.
Tel: 631-474-4100; Fax: 631-474-4110. Mr. Lewis Grossman, CEO.

[K] RESIDENCES FOR AGED

AMITYVILLE. *Dominican Village, Inc.*, 565 Albany Ave., Amityville, 11701. Tel: 631-842-6091;
Fax: 631-842-6131; Email: info@dominicanvillage.org. Kenneth Ruthinoski, Pres. & CEO; Sr. Maureen Muir, Vice Pres. Opers. Total Staff 130; Housing Units 266; Total Assisted 66.

HUNTINGTON. *Missionary Sisters of St. Benedict Home for the Aged, Inc.*, 350 Cuba Hill Rd., Huntington, 11743. Tel: 631-368-9528; Fax: 631-266-1015; Email: sjgh350@yahoo.com; Email: admin@stjosephsosb.org; Web: www.stjosephs-home.org. Sr. Agnieszka Owsiejko, O.S.B., Admin. Missionary Sisters of St. Benedict. Bed Capacity 44; Tot Asst. Annually 48; Total Staff 26.

[L] SOCIETY OF ST. VINCENT DE PAUL

BETHPAGE. **Society of St. Vincent de Paul-Central Council* (1833) 249 Broadway, Bethpage, 11714.
Tel: 516-822-3132; Fax: 516-822-2728; Email: tabbate@svdpli.org; Web: svdpli.org. Rev. Msgr. Gerard A. Ringenback, M.S.Ed., M.A., Spiritual Dir.; Robert Meekins, Pres.; Thomas J. Abbate, Exec. Dir. & CEO. Total Staff 82; Volunteers 1,420; Total Assisted 203,985.

[M] HOME HEALTH SERVICES

HAMPTON BAYS. *Dominican Sisters Family Health Service*, 103-6 W. Montauk Hwy., Hampton Bays, 11946. Tel: 631-728-0181; Fax: 631-723-0866; Email: pjablow@dsfhs.org; Web: www.dsfhs.org. Patricia Jablow, B.S.N., Admin. Suffolk Offices.
3237 Rte. 112, Bldg. #6, Medford, 11763.
Tel: 631-736-1527; Fax: 631-736-1747; Web: www.dsfhs.org.

DSFHS Special Programs, P.O. Box 1028, Hampton Bays, 11946. Tel: 631-728-0937;
Fax: 631-728-7162; Web: www.dsfhs.org.

[N] MONASTERIES AND RESIDENCES OF PRIESTS AND BROTHERS

AMITYVILLE. *St. Pius X Residence*, Dominican Village: Province Building, 595 Albany Ave., Amityville, 11701. Tel: 631-608-2622; Fax: 631-608-2624; Email: tcosta@drvc.org. Rev. Msgr. Thomas C. Costa, Vicar for Senior Priests; Deacon Jay Valdes, Pastoral Assoc. for Senior Priests. Total in Residence 19. In Res. Rev. Msgrs. Francis X. Gaeta, (Retired); Thomas E. Molloy, (Retired); Thomas D. Candreva, S.T.L., J.C.D., (Retired); Daniel S. Hamilton, (Retired); T. Peter Ryan, (Retired); Rt. Rev. Msgr. James P. Kelly, (Retired); Revs. John H. McCabe, (Retired); Jose Simon Palliparambil, (Retired); Martin L. Klein, (Retired); Andrew P. Blake, (Retired); Paul J. Dahm, (Retired); Edward J. Kealey, (Retired); Peter T. Liu, (Retired); Robert Lubrano, (Retired); George J. Michell, (Retired); George Punti, (Retired); Lawrence B. Rafferty, (Retired); Dennis J. Whelan, (Retired). Total in Residence 19.

BAY SHORE. *Montfort Missionaries*, 26 S. Saxon Ave., Bay Shore, 11706. Tel: 631-666-7500;
Fax: 631-665-4349; Email: montfort.secretariat@gmail.com. Revs. Francis Pizzarelli, S.M.M., Admin.; James Manning, S.M.M., (Retired); Thomas Poth, S.M.M., Supr.; James Brady, S.M.M., Trustee; Gerald Fitzsimmons, S.M.M., Preacher; Bernard Brault, S.M.M., (Retired); John Breslin, S.M.M., (Retired); John McCann, S.M.M., (Retired). Montfort Spiritual Center and Headquarters of "Montfort Publications"

The Missionaries of the Company of Mary; Montfort Missionaries; Montfort Publications; Montfort Spiritual Association Priests 8. *Montfort Missionaries - Spiritual Center* (1928) 26 S. Saxon Ave., Bay Shore, 11706. Tel: 631-666-7500; Fax: 631-666-4349; Email: montfort.secretariat@gmail.com. Rev. Thomas Poth, S.M.M., Dir.

GLEN COVE. *St. Josaphat's Monastery, Novitiate and Retreat House*, East Beach Dr., Glen Cove, 11542.
Tel: 516-671-0545; Fax: 516-676-7465; Email: stjosaphatnvtt@gmail.com. Revs. Theodosius (Roman) Ilnicki, O.S.B.M., Provincial Sec.; Eugene (Andriy) Khdmyn, O.S.B.M., Asst. Master of Novices, Vicar. Basilian Fathers.

MANORVILLE. *Shrine of Our Lady of the Island*, 258 Eastport Manor Rd., Manorville, 11949.
Tel: 631-325-0661; Fax: 631-325-5592; Email: montfort.secretariat@gmail.com; Web: ourladyoftheisland.org. Revs. Roy Tvrdik, S.M.M., Dir.; Peter D'Abele, S.M.M.; Hugh Gillespie, S.M.M.

Our Lady of the Island Shrine Gift Shop Priests 3.

MINEOLA. *Provincial Residence and Novitiate*, 240 Emory Rd., Mineola, 11501. Tel: 516-742-5555;
Fax: 516-742-1989; Email: tdriscoll@chaminade-hs.org. Bro. Thomas J. Cleary, S.M., Councilor; Revs. Garrett J. Long, S.M., Councilor & Novice Master; Thomas A. Cardone, S.M., Asst. Prov. & Asst. Rel. Life; Bros. James W. Conway, S.M., Asst. Temporalities; Timothy S. Driscoll, S.M., Prov. & Asst. Educ. Society of Mary (Marianists).

[O] CONVENTS AND RESIDENCES FOR SISTERS

ROCKVILLE CENTRE. *Congregation of the Infant Jesus* (1905) 984 N. Village Ave., 11570.
Tel: 516-823-3808; Fax: 516-594-0412; Email: marylou.kelly@nursingsisterscij.org; Web: www.cijnssp.org. Congregation of the Infant Jesus (Nursing Sisters of the Sick Poor). Professed Sisters 36.

AMITYVILLE. *Queen of the Rosary, Motherhouse* (1853) 555 Albany Ave., Amityville, 11701-1197.
Tel: 631-842-6000; Fax: 631-842-0240; Email: prioress@amityop.org; Web: www.amityvilleop.org. Sr. Mary Patricia Neylon, O.P., Prioress; Jennifer E. Friedman, Exec. Dir. Sisters of St. Dominic.
Sisters of the Order of St. Dominic

Amityville Dominican Sisters, Inc. Total in Residence 123.

BAY SHORE. *New Jerusalem*, 106 N. Penataquit Ave., Bay Shore, 11706-6939. Tel: 631-968-8859. Sisters 4.

BLUE POINT. *St. Ursula Center*, 186 Middle Rd., Blue Point, 11715. Tel: 631-363-2422; Fax: 631-363-0319; Email: shoran@tildonkursuline.org; Web: www.tildonkursuline.org. Sandy Horan, Admin. Ursuline Sisters, Congregation of Tildonk.

BRENTWOOD. *Saint Joseph Convent* (1856) Motherhouse, 1725 Brentwood Rd., Brentwood, 11717. Tel: 631-273-4531; Fax: 631-273-1451; Email: rooney@csjbrentwood.org; Web: www.brentwoodcsj.org. Sisters Helen M. Kearney, C.S.J., Pres.; Helen Rooney, C.S.J., Gen. Sec.; Eileen M. Kelly, C.S.J., Gen. Treas.; Virginia Dowd, Community Archivist. Sisters of Saint Joseph Generalate. Sisters 480.

Saint Joseph Novitiate, 1725 Brentwood Rd., Brentwood, 11717. Tel: 631-273-1187; Fax: 631-273-1451; Web: www.brentwoodcsj.org. Sr. Mary Walsh, C.S.J., Dir. Formation.

Maria Regina Residence, Inc. Sisters of St. Joseph 1725 Brentwood Rd., Bldg. 1, Brentwood, 11717-5589. Tel: 631-299-3000; Fax: 631-952-2378; Email: ebartoldus@mariareginaresidence.org; Web: www.mariareginaresidence.org.

HAMPTON BAYS. *St. Joseph's Villa Retreat and Renewal Center*, 81 Lynn Ave., Hampton Bays, 11946. Tel: 631-728-6074; Fax: 631-273-1451; Email: stjosephvilla@optonline.net; Web: www.csjbrentwoodny.org. Sisters of St. Joseph 2.

HUNTINGTON. *Missionary Sisters of St. Benedict*, 350 Cuba Hill Rd., Huntington, 11743. Tel: 631-368-9528; Fax: 631-266-1015; Email: mssb350@yahoo.com; Web: www.osbhuntington.org. Sr. Lyudmyla Varhatyuk, O.S.B., Supr. Sisters 24.

ISLIP. *Daughters of Wisdom (Administration)*, 385 Ocean Ave., Islip, 11751. Tel: 631-277-2660; Fax: 631-277-3274; Email: eeckhardt@daughtersofwisdom.org; Web: www.daughtersofwisdom.org. Sr. Catherine Sheehan, D.W., Prov. Administration Offices. Sisters 5.

OCEANSIDE. *St. Anthony's Parish House*, 111 Anchor Ave., Oceanside, 11572. Tel: 516-536-3308; Email: oceansideop@verizon.net. Sr. Margaret Sammon, O.P., Contact Person. Sisters of St. Dominic 3.

POINT LOOKOUT. *St. Clare Convent-Franciscan Sisters of Allegany*, 104 Ocean Blvd., P.O. Box 823, Point Lookout, 11569. Tel: 516-665-3389; Tel: 347-963-4552; Email: smcm1082@aol.com. Sr. Catherine Moran, O.S.F., Contact Person. Sisters 10.

St. Elizabeth Convent-Franciscan Sisters of Allegany, 29 Ocean Blvd., Point Lookout, 11569. Email: congsecretary@fsallegany.org; Tel: 718-665-3063; Tel: 347-963-4552. Sr. Catherine Moran, O.S.F., Contact Person. Sisters 10.

RONKONKOMA. *Congregation of Our Lady of the Retreat in the Cenacle, (R.C.)* aka Ronkonkoma Cenacle, Inc., 310 Cenacle Rd., Ronkonkoma, 11779-0430. Tel: 631-588-8366; Fax: 631-737-3375; Email: kathrynmadden@hotmail.com; Web: www.cenaclesisters.org.

Cenacle Convent, 310 Cenacle Rd., Ronkonkoma, 11779. Tel: 631-588-8366; Fax: 631-471-0031. Sr. Kathryn Madden, R.C., Local Leader.

Therese's Well Community, 312 Cenacle Rd., Ronkonkoma, 11779-2203. Tel: 631-285-3999. Sr. Monica Kaufer, R.C., Contact Person.

Ronkonkoma Cenacle Retreat Center, 310 Cenacle Rd., Ronkonkoma, 11779. Tel: 631-588-8366; Fax: 631-738-9511. Sr. Margaret Rohde, R.C., Ministry Coord.

ROOSEVELT. *Oblate Sisters of the Most Holy Redeemer*, Mother of Good Counsel Home, 290 Babylon Tpke., P.O. Box 329, Roosevelt, 11575-0329. Tel: 516-223-1013; Fax: 516-223-4254; Email: ossr290@earthlink.net. Sr. Matilde Murillo, O.SS.R., Dir. Mother of Good Counsel Home is a group home for pregnant and parenting teenage mothers and their infants.

SOUND BEACH. *Our Lady of Perpetual Help Convent*, 49 Convent Dr., Sound Beach, 11789. Tel: 631-744-2477; Fax: 631-744-2515; Email: convsb@optimum.net. Gayle Walkowiak, Facility Coord. Daughters of Wisdom 23.

[P] RETREAT HOUSES

CENTERPORT. *St. Francis Center, Inc.* (1961) 105 Prospect Rd., P.O. Box 301, Centerport, 11721. Tel: 631-261-5730; Fax: 631-754-4204; Email: alverniacenterportny@gmail.com; Web: www.alvernia.org. Directed by Franciscan Bros. of Brooklyn.

PATCHOGUE. *St. Joseph's Prayer Center*, 312 Maple Ave., Patchogue, 11772. Tel: 631-730-6210; Fax: 631-730-6210; Email: stjoepc@optonline.net. Louise Kramer, Dir.; Rev. James J. Wheeler, S.J., Apostolic Dir. Priests 1; Total Staff 15; Total Assisted 500.

RONKONKOMA. *Cenacle Retreat Center*, 310 Cenacle Rd., P.O. Box 4005, Ronkonkoma, 11779-0430. Tel: 631-588-8366; Fax: 631-738-9511; Email: retreat@cenaclesisters.org; Web: www.cenaclesisters.org. Sr. Margaret Rohde, R.C., Dir. Ministry. Religious of the Cenacle. Ministry Staff 9.

SAG HARBOR. *Cormaria Retreat Center, Inc.* (1949) 77 Bay St., P.O. Box 1993, Sag Harbor, 11963. Tel: 631-725-4206; Fax: 631-725-1837; Email: cormaria@aol.com; Web: www.cormaria.org. Sr. Ann Thaddeus Marino, R.S.H.M., Retreat Dir. Directed by the Religious of the Sacred Heart of Mary. Sisters 5; Total Staff 17.

[Q] MISCELLANEOUS

ROCKVILLE CENTRE. **Ecclesia Assurance Company*, P.O. Box 9023, 11571.

Magnificat Rockville Centre, 219 Hempstead Ave., 11570.

Mission Assistance Corporation, P.O. Box 9023, 11571. Tel: 516-678-5800. Joseph Young, Sec. & Treas.

**Tomorrow's Hope Foundation, Inc.*, P.O. Box 9023, 11571. Tel: 516-678-5800. Joseph Young, Treas.

Unitas Investment Fund Inc., P.O. Box 9023, 11571-9023. Tel: 516-678-5800. Mr. Thomas Doodian, Pres.

Welfare Benefit Trust of the Diocese of Rockville Centre and Other (2016) c/o The RC Diocese of Rockville Centre, 50 N. Park Ave., Rockville Center.

AMITYVILLE. *Dominican Sisters Of Amityville-Finance Dept.*, 555 Albany Ave., Amityville, 11701. Tel: 631-842-6000; Fax: 631-842-0240; Email: prioress@amityop.org; Web: www.amityvilleop.org. Sisters Mary Patricia Neylon, O.P., Pres.; Patricia Hanvey, O.P., Vice Pres.; Patricia Koehler, O.P., Sec. & Treas.

**Dominican Youth Movement USA*, 555 Albany Ave., Amityville, 11701.

Queen of the Rosary Motherhouse, Dominican Sisters of Amityville, 555 Albany Ave., Amityville, 11701. Tel: 631-842-6000, Ext. 212; Fax: 631-842-0240; Web: www.amityvilleop.org.

BAY SHORE. *Missionaries of the Company of Mary General House Charitable Trust*, 28 S. Saxon Ave., Bay Shore, 11706. Tel: 631-627-1836; Email: jpbsmm@gmail.com.

Montfort Missionaries Charitable Trust, 26 S. Saxon Ave., Bay Shore, 11706.

Pronto of Long Island, Inc., 128 Pine Aire Dr., Bay Shore, 11706. Tel: 631-231-8290; Fax: 631-231-8390; Email: kbennett@prontolongisland.org; Web: www.prontoli.org. Vivian Hart, Sec., BOD.

BETHPAGE. **Partnership for Global Justice*, 4108 Hicksville Rd., Bethpage, 11714. Tel: 212-682-6481 ; Email: partnershipforglobaljustice@gmail.com; Web: www.partnershipforglobaljustice.com. Sr. JoAnn Mark, A.S.C., Exec. Dir.

BRENTWOOD. *Congregation of the Sisters of St. Joseph* (1856) 1725 Brentwood Rd., Brentwood, 11717-5587. Tel: 631-273-1187; Fax: 631-273-1345; Web: www.brentwoodcsj.org. Sr. Eileen M. Kelly, C.S.J., Treas.

The CSJ Learning Connection for Adult Education, Inc., 1725 Brentwood Rd., Brentwood, 11717. Tel: 631-951-4783; Fax: 631-951-0642; Email: CSJTLC@optonline.net. Sr. Kathleen Carberry, C.S.J., Dir.

Sisters of Saint Joseph Lay Employee Pension Plan Charitable Trust, 1725 Brentwood Rd., Brentwood, 11717. Tel: 631-273-1187; Fax: 631-273-1451; Web: www.brentwoodcsj.org. Sr. Eileen M. Kelly, C.S.J., Trustee.

CENTERPORT. *Mt. Alvernia, Inc.* (1888) 105 Prospect Rd., P.O. Box 301, Centerport, 11721. Tel: 631-261-5730; Fax: 631-754-4204; Email: alverniacenterportny@gmail.com; Email: natalie@campalvernia.org. Bro. Lawrence Makofske, O.S.F., Dir. Directed by the Franciscan Brothers. Bed Capacity 70.

Camp Alvernia, Tel: 631-261-5730; Fax: 631-754-4204; Email: info@campalvernia.org. Directed by the Franciscan Brothers.

Mt. Alvernia Center for Retreats, Tel: 631-261-5730; Fax: 631-754-4204; Email: alverniacenterportny@gmail.com. Directed by the Franciscan Brothers.

EASTPORT. *Magnificat - Suffolk County NY Chapter*, 200 Bach Ct., Eastport, 11941. Tel: 631-325-1923; Email: corndang@optonline.net.

GREENPORT. *North Fork Parish Outreach, Inc.*, 69465 Main Rd., P.O. Box 584, Greenport, 11944.

HAMPTON BAYS. *Centro Corazon de Maria, Inc.*, 31 Montauk Hwy. E., Hampton Bays, 11946. Tel: 631-728-5558; Fax: 631-728-5559.

HICKSVILLE. **Department of Education, Diocese of Rockville Centre*, 128 Cherry Ln., Hicksville, 11801. Tel: 516-280-2479; Email: kwalsh@drvc.org; Web: drvcschools.org. Dr. Kathleen Walsh, Ed.D., Supt.; Mr. Biagio M. Arpino, M.S., P.D., Asst. Supt. for Personnel; Mrs. Kathleen Razzetti, M.S., C.A.S., Asst. Supt. for Govt. Prog. & Student Svcs.; Mr. Anthony Biscione, M.S., Asst. Supt. for Curriculum, Instruction & Assessment; Ms. Marian Hernandez, M.S., Asst. Supt. for Admin.; Mrs. Emily Guarnieri, M.S., Dir. of Educ. Technology; Mrs. Nora Aufiero, B.A., Advocate for Hispanic Initiative; Mrs. Maureen Hannan, B.S., M.B.A., Coord. of Finance; Mr. Gary Layton, B.S., Dir. Mktg. & Enrollment.

HUNTINGTON. *Sacred Heart Institute*, 440 W. Neck Rd., Huntington, 11743. Tel: 631-423-0483, Ext. 185; Fax: 631-423-2357; Email: kgarcia@cor-jesu.org; Web: www.cor-jesu.org. Most Rev. Richard G. Henning, S.T.D., Dir.

ISLIP. *Wisdom Charitable Trust*, 385 Ocean Ave., Islip, 11751. Tel: 631-277-2660; Fax: 631-277-3274; Email: bswiss@daughtersofwisdom.org. Sr. Catherine Sheehan, D.W., Trustee.

NESCONSET. **Cleary Foundation for the Deaf, Inc.*, 301 Smithtown Blvd., Nesconset, 11767-2007. Tel: 631-588-0530; Fax: 631-588-0016.

NEW HYDE PARK. *Sisters of the Imitation of Christ United States Mission, Inc.*, 1653 Highland Ave., New Hyde Park, 11040. Tel: 516-358-4597.

OAKDALE. *Saint John Baptist De La Salle of New York, Inc.*, P.O. Box 538, Oakdale, 11769. Tel: 401-789-0244; Fax: 401-783-5303; Email: eprecourt@cbc.necoxmail.com. Bro. Edmond Precourt, F.S.C., Provincial.

RIVERHEAD. *Sisters of the Holy Family of Nazareth, Holy Family Province*, 3560 Sound Ave., Riverhead, 11901. Tel: 631-727-5122; Fax: 631-369-5685; Email: rwlodarczyk@csfn.org. Sr. Mary Ronald Wlodarczyk, C.S.F.N., Admin.

ROOSEVELT. *Friends of Mother of Good Counsel Home, Inc.*, 290 Babylon Tpke., Roosevelt, 11575. Tel: 516-223-1013; Fax: 516-223-4254; Email: ossr290@earthlink.net. Sr. Matilde Murillo, O.SS.R., Dir. Bed Capacity 7; Tot Asst. Annually 12; Total Staff 3.

SOUTH HUNTINGTON. *St. Anthony's High School, South Huntington*, 275 Wolf Hill Rd., South Huntington, 11747. Bro. Gary Cregan, O.S.F., Prin.

St. Anthony's Threshold of Hope Inc., 275 Wolf Hill Rd., South Huntington, 11747.

Seraphic Properties, Inc., 275 Wolf Hill Rd., South Huntington, 11747. Bro. Gary Cregan, O.S.F., Admin.

SYOSSET. **Emmaus House Foundation, Inc.* dba Harvest Houses, 235 Cold Spring Rd., Syosset, 11791. Tel: 516-496-9796; Fax: 516-496-9796; Email: jabharvest@yahoo.com; Web: www.harvesthouse.org. Sr. Jeanne A. Brendel, O.P., Exec. Dir.

UNIONDALE. *TELECARE of the Diocese of Rockville Centre*, 1200 Glenn Curtiss Blvd., Uniondale, 11553. Tel: 516-538-8704; Fax: 516-489-9701; Email: info@telecaretv.org; Web: www.telecaretv.org. Rev. Msgr. James C. Vlaun, Pres. & CEO; Joseph Perrone, Gen. Mgr.

WESTBURY. *Sisters, Lovers of the Holy Cross, Inc.* (1993) 43 Crown Ln, Westbury, 11590. Tel: 516-333-9464; Fax: 516-333-9464; Email: sr.theresanguyen@yahoo.com.

St. Theresa Convent, 43 Crown Ln., Westbury, 11590. Tel: 516-333-9464; Fax: 516-333-9464; Email: srteresanguyen@yahoo.com. Sr. Theresa Nguyen, L.H.C., Pres.

WYANDANCH. *Gerald J. Ryan Outreach Center, Inc.*, 1434 Straight Path, Wyandanch, 11798. Tel: 631-643-7591; Fax: 631-643-1871; Email: ryanouthreach@optonline.net. Myrna Salmeron, Hispanic Ministry Coord./Asst. to Dir.; Ivonne Taveras, Support Svcs. Total Staff 4; Volunteers 35; Total Assisted 20,150.

The Opening Word Program, Inc. (1991) 1434 Straight Path, Wyandanch, 11798. Tel: 631-643-0541; Fax: 631-643-5935; Email: opword@optonline.net. Sisters Margaret A. Krajci, O.P., Treas.; Lenore Toscano, O.P., Exec. Dir.; Mary Patricia Neylon, O.P., Chairperson. Directed by the Sisters of St. Dominic.

RELIGIOUS INSTITUTES OF MEN REPRESENTED IN THE DIOCESE

For further details refer to the corresponding bracketed number in the Religious Institutes of Men or Women section.

[0330]—*Brothers of the Christian Schools*—F.S.C.

[]—*Canons Regular of St. Augustine*—Can.Reg.

[0470]—*The Capuchin Friars* (St. Mary Prov.)—O.F.M.Cap.

[]—*Cong. Missionaros de la Reconciliacion.*

[1330]—*Congregation of the Mission-Vincentians* (Eastern Prov.)—C.M.

[1000]—*Congregation of the Passion* (Prov. of St. Paul of the Cross)—C.P.
[0490]—*Franciscan Brothers of Brooklyn*—O.S.F.
[]—*Franciscan Misioneros of Hope*—F.M.H.
[]—*Idente Missionaries.*
[0690]—*Jesuit Fathers and Brothers* (NY Prov.)—S.J.
[0770]—*The Marist Brothers*—F.M.S.
[]—*Missionaries of the Sacred Heart*—M.S.C.
[0870]—*Montfort Missionaries*—S.M.M.
[0430]—*Order of Preachers-Dominicans*—O.P.
[]—*Order of St. Augustine*—O.S.A.
[]—*Order of the Imitation of Christ*—O.I.C.
[0990]—*Pallotines*—S.A.C.
[1070]—*Redemptorist Fathers*—C.SS.R.
[0760]—*Society of Mary* (Provs. of NY; Meribah)—S.M.

RELIGIOUS INSTITUTES OF WOMEN REPRESENTED IN THE DIOCESE

[]—*Adorers of the Blood of Christ*—A.S.C.
[3110]—*Congregation of Our Lady of the Retreat in the Cenacle*—R.C.
[2240]—*Congregation of the Infant Jesus*—C.I.J.
[]—*Daughters of Mary* (Haiti)—F.de M.
[0960]—*Daughters of Wisdom*—D.W.
[1070-05]—*Dominican Sisters* (Amityville)—O.P.
[1070-11]—*Dominican Sisters* (Sparkill)—O.P.
[1370]—*Franciscan Missionaries of Mary*—F.M.M.
[2070]—*Holy Union Sisters*—S.U.S.C.
[]—*Idente Missionaries.*
[2575]—*Institute of the Sisters of Mercy of the Americas* (Mid-Atlantic Community)—R.S.M.
[0210]—*Missionary Benedictine Sisters*—O.S.B.
[3030]—*Oblate Sisters of M.H. Redeemer*—O.SS.R.
[3465]—*Religious of the Sacred Heart of Mary*—R.S.H.M.
[2970]—*School Sisters of Notre Dame*—S.S.N.D.
[0640]—*Sisters of Charity of St. Vincent de Paul* (Halifax)—S.C.
[2990]—*Sisters of Notre Dame de Namur*—S.N.D.
[3000]—*Sisters of Notre Dame de Namur* (Baltimore & Base Communities Provinces)—S.N.D.deN.
[3830-05]—*Sisters of St. Joseph* (Brentwood, NY)—C.S.J.
[3180]—*Sisters of the Cross and the Passion*—C.P.
[1830]—*Sisters of the Good Shepherd*—R.G.S.
[1970]—*Sisters of the Holy Family of Nazareth*—C.S.F.N.
[]—*Sisters of the Imitation of Christ*—S.I.C.
[2392]—*Sisters, Lovers of the Holy Cross* (Brookville, N.Y.)—L.H.C.
[2160]—*Sisters, Servants of the Immaculate Heart of Mary*—I.H.M.
[4130]—*Ursuline Sisters of the Congregation of Tildonk, Belgium*—O.S.U.

DIOCESAN CEMETERIES

CENTRAL ISLIP. *Queen of All Saints Cemetery*, 115 Wheeler Rd., Central Islip, 11722. Tel: 631-234-8297; Fax: 631-234-8632

CORAM. *Holy Sepulchre Cemetery*, 3442 Rte. 112, Coram, 11727. Tel: 631-732-3460; Fax: 631-732-3476

WESTBURY. *Cemetery of the Holy Rood*, 111 Old Country Rd., Box 182, Westbury, 11590-0182. Tel: 516-334-7990; Fax: 516-334-4383

NECROLOGY

† Brassil, James A., (Retired), Died Jan. 21, 2018
† Colgan, Thomas J., (Retired), Died Feb. 2, 2018
† Jablonski, William W., (Retired), Died Nov. 11, 2018
† McDonald, James M., (Retired), Died Nov. 16, 2018
† Blyman, Robert Y., (Retired), Died Jan. 5, 2019
† Carmody, James P., (Retired), Died Aug. 1, 2018
† Costa, Caetano F., (India) (Retired), Died Mar. 23, 2018
† Dineros, Santiago A., (Retired), Died Nov. 7, 2018
† Hall, Martin J., (Retired), Died Feb. 20, 2018
† Hien, John, (Retired), Died May. 20, 2018
† Noviello, Harold J., Died Aug. 11, 2018

An asterisk (*) denotes an organization that has established tax-exempt status directly with the IRS and is not covered by the USCCB Group Ruling.

Diocese of Sacramento

(Dioecesis Sacramentensis)

Most Reverend

JAIME SOTO, D.D., M.S.W.

Bishop of Sacramento; ordained June 12, 1982; appointed Auxiliary Bishop of Orange and named Titular Bishop of Segia March 23, 2000; installed May 31, 2000; appointed Coadjutor Bishop of Sacramento October 11, 2007; installed November 18, 2007; Succeeded to the See November 30, 2008. *Diocesan Pastoral Center: Office of the Bishop, 2110 Broadway, Sacramento, CA 95818-2541.* Tel: 916-733-0200; Fax: 916-733-0215.

Most Reverend

WILLIAM K. WEIGAND, D.D.

Retired Bishop of Sacramento; ordained May 25, 1963; appointed Bishop of Salt Lake City September 3, 1980; ordained and installed November 17, 1980; appointed Bishop of Sacramento November 30, 1993; installed January 27, 1994; retired November 30, 2008. *Diocesan Pastoral Center, Office of the Bishop, 2110 Broadway, Sacramento, CA 95818-2541.* Tel: 916-733-0200; Fax: 916-733-0215.

Diocesan Pastoral Center: 2110 Broadway, Sacramento, CA 95818-2541. Tel: 916-733-0100; Fax: 916-733-0195.

Web: www.scd.org

Square Miles 42,597.

Erected by His Holiness, Leo XIII, May 28, 1886.

Comprises the Counties of Amador, Butte, Colusa, El Dorado, Glenn, Lassen, Modoc, Nevada, Placer, Plumas, Sacramento, Shasta, Sierra, Siskiyou, Solano, Sutter, Tehama, Trinity, Yolo and Yuba in the State of California.

Co-Patrons of Diocese: St. Patrick; Our Lady of Guadalupe.

Legal Title: "Roman Catholic Bishop of Sacramento, A Corporation Sole."
For legal titles of parishes and diocesan institutions, consult the Diocesan Pastoral Center.

STATISTICAL OVERVIEW

Personnel	
Bishop	1
Retired Bishops	1
Abbots	1
Priests: Diocesan Active in Diocese	92
Priests: Diocesan Active Outside Diocese	3
Priests: Retired, Sick or Absent	63
Number of Diocesan Priests	158
Religious Priests in Diocese	69
Total Priests in Diocese	227
Extern Priests in Diocese	29
Ordinations:	
Diocesan Priests	3
Religious Priests	1
Transitional Deacons	3
Permanent Deacons in Diocese	178
Total Brothers	6
Total Sisters	120
Parishes	
Parishes	102
With Resident Pastor:	
Resident Diocesan Priests	93
Resident Religious Priests	9
Without Resident Pastor:	
Administered by Priests	2
Missions	42
Pastoral Centers	1
Professional Ministry Personnel:	
Sisters	15
Lay Ministers	237
Welfare	
Catholic Hospitals	6
Total Assisted	631,453
Special Centers for Social Services	15
Total Assisted	216,000
Educational	
Diocesan Students in Other Seminaries	12
Total Seminarians	12
High Schools, Diocesan and Parish	3
Total Students	1,650
High Schools, Private	3
Total Students	2,599
Elementary Schools, Diocesan and Parish	35
Total Students	8,799
Catechesis/Religious Education:	
High School Students	872
Elementary Students	23,758
Total Students under Catholic Instruction	37,690
Teachers in the Diocese:	
Sisters	8
Lay Teachers	522
Vital Statistics	
Receptions into the Church:	
Infant Baptism Totals	6,268
Minor Baptism Totals	585
Adult Baptism Totals	386
Received into Full Communion	701
First Communions	7,575
Confirmations	6,365
Marriages:	
Catholic	993
Interfaith	178
Total Marriages	1,171
Deaths	2,514
Total Catholic Population	1,038,026
Total Population	3,720,284

Former Bishops—Rt. Revs. EUGENE O'CONNELL, D.D., ord. May 21, 1842; cons. Titular Bishop of Flaviopolis and appt. Vicar Apostolic of Marysville, Feb. 3, 1861; appt. First Bishop of Grass Valley, March 22, 1868; resigned March 17, 1884 and appt. Titular Bishop of Joppa; died Dec. 4, 1891; PATRICK MANOGUE, D.D., ord. Dec. 21, 1861; cons. Titular Bishop of Ceremos, Coadjutor to Bishop O'Connell of Grass Valley, Jan. 16, 1881; succeeded to the See of Grass Valley on Bishop O'Connell's resignation, March 17, 1884; became the first Bishop of Sacramento, May 1886; died Feb. 27, 1895; THOMAS GRACE, D.D., cons. June 16, 1896; died Dec. 27, 1921; PATRICK J. KEANE, D.D., ord. June 20, 1895; cons. Bishop of Samaria, Dec. 14, 1920; appt. to See of Sacramento, March 17, 1922; died Sept. 1, 1928; Most Revs. ROBERT J. ARMSTRONG, D.D., Litt.D., ord. Dec. 10, 1910; cons. March 12, 1929; died Jan. 14, 1957; JOSEPH T. MCGUCKEN, D.D., S.T.D., LL.D., ord. Jan. 16, 1928; cons. Titular Bishop of Sanavo and Auxiliary Bishop of Los Angeles, March 19, 1941; Coadjutor Bishop of Sacramento, Oct. 26, 1955; succeeded to Jan. 14, 1957, as Bishop of Sacramento; promoted to the See of San Francisco, Feb. 21, 1962; died Oct. 6, 1983; ALDEN J. BELL, D.D., M.S.S.W., ord. May 14, 1932; appt. Titular Bishop of Rhodopolis and Auxiliary Bishop of Los Angeles, April 18, 1956; cons. June 4, 1956; appt. Bishop of Sacramento, March 30, 1962; retired March 15, 1979; died Aug. 28, 1982; JOHN S. CUMMINS, D.D., ord. Jan. 24, 1953; appt. Titular Bishop of Lambesi and Auxiliary Bishop of Sacramento, Feb. 26, 1974; cons. May 26, 1974; appt. Bishop of Oakland, May 3, 1977; FRANCIS A. QUINN, D.D., Ed.D., ord. June 15, 1946; appt. Titular Bishop of Numana and Auxiliary Bishop of San Francisco, April 28, 1978; Episcopal Ordination, June 29, 1978; appt. Bishop of Sacramento, Dec. 18, 1979; retired Nov. 30, 1993; died March 21, 2019.; ALPHONSE GALLEGOS, O.A.R., D.D., ord. May 24, 1958; appt. Titular Bishop of Sassabe and Auxiliary Bishop of Sacramento, Sept. 1, 1981; cons. Nov. 4, 1981; died Oct. 6, 1991; WILLIAM K. WEIGAND, D.D., ord. May 25, 1963; appt. Bishop of Salt Lake City Sept. 3, 1980; ord. and installed Nov. 17, 1980; appt. Bishop of Sacramento Nov. 30, 1993; installed Jan. 27, 1994; retired Nov. 30, 2008.

Moderator of the Curia—Tel: 916-733-0200; Fax: 916-733-0215. Very Rev. MICHAEL D. VAUGHAN.

Vicar General—Tel: 916-733-0200; Fax: 916-733-0215. Very Rev. MICHAEL D. VAUGHAN.

Director of Finance—MR. THOMAS J. MCNAMARA, Tel: 916-733-0277; Fax: 916-733-0295.

Director of Pastoral Services—Tel: 916-733-0200; Fax: 916-733-0215. DR. LOIS T. LOCEY.

Episcopal Vicar for Clergy—Very Rev. GLENN GIOVANNI JARON, M.S.P., (Philippines) Tel: 916-733-0200; Fax: 916-733-0215.

Director of Hispanic Institute—Tel: 916-733-0123; Fax: 916-733-0195. TERESA DONAN.

Director of Permanent Diaconate—ULI SCHMITT, Tel: 916-733-0244; Fax: 916-733-0215.

Director of Catholic Charities & Social Concerns—JOHN WATKINS, Dir., Tel: 916-733-0253; Fax: 916-733-0224.

Chancellor—Tel: 916-733-0200; Fax: 916-733-0215. DR. LOIS T. LOCEY.

Delegate for Religious—Sr. SUSAN MCCARTHY, R.S.M., Tel: 916-733-0246; Fax: 916-733-0215.

Coordinator for Retired Priests—Very Rev. GLENN GIOVANNI JARON, M.S.P., (Philippines) Tel: 916-733-0200; Fax: 916-733-0215.

Clergy Care Manager—LOUELLA GARCIA, Tel: 916-733-0200.

Delegate for Deacons—Deacon LUIGI DEL GAUDIO, 2110 Broadway, Sacramento, 95818-2541. Tel: 916-733-0256; Fax: 916-733-0224.

Vicars Forane—Revs. FREDHELITO E. GUCOR, (Shasta); SYLVESTER KWIATKOWSKI, (Colombia) (Gold

Country); CHRISTOPHER R. FRAZER, (Mother Lode); RONALD V. TORRES, (Siskiyou); BRIAN J. SOLIVEN, (Ridge); AVRAM E. BROWN, (Sutter Buttes); PHILIP V. MASSETTI, O.S.J., (West Placer); JACOBO A. CACERES, (Yolo); VICENTE C. TENEZA, (Solano); ALEXANDER A. ESTRELLA, (Southern Suburbs); DARIUSZ T. MALCZUK, (Poland) (American River); MIECZYSLAW MITCH MALESZYK, (City).

Diocesan Tribunal—Please direct all requests to the Tribunal. *2110 Broadway, Sacramento, 95818-2541.* Tel: 916-733-0225; Fax: 916-733-0224.

Moderator of the Tribunal Chancery—CHERYL M. THOLCKE.

Judicial Vicar—Very Rev. MARK R. RICHARDS, J.C.L.

Judges—Revs. JOSEPH HUYEN NGUYEN, J.C.L.; CESAR R. AGEAS, J.C.L.; SANTIAGO E. RAUDES, J.C.L.

Promoter of Justice—Rev. DAVID L. DEIBEL, J.D., J.C.L.

Defenders of the Bond—Rev. Msgr. RAYMOND GOEHRING, J.C.L.; Sr. KARLA FELIX-RIVERA, V.D.M.F., J.C.L.; CHRISTINA HIP-FLORES, J.C.D.

Auditors—CHERYL M. THOLCKE; MARIA GARCIA; MEGHAN RANGEL; Rev. BRIAN J. ATIENZA; CARLO PEREZ.

Notaries—CHERYL M. THOLCKE; MEGHAN RANGEL; MARIA GARCIA; Rev. BRIAN J. ATIENZA; CARLO PEREZ.

College of Consultors—Revs. ALDRIN G. BASARTE; OSCAR GOMEZ-MEDINA; Rev. Msgrs. ALBERT G. O'CONNOR, (Retired); JAMES T. MURPHY, (Retired); Very Rev. MARK R. RICHARDS, J.C.L.; Rev. JOHN P. SULLIVAN, (Retired); Very Rev. MICHAEL D. VAUGHAN.

Diocesan Offices and Directors

AIDS, Ministry to—JOHN WATKINS, Tel: 916-733-0253.

Alcoholism Advisory Board—Rev. PHILIP J. WELLS, Tel: 530-365-8573.

Archives—2110 Broadway, Sacramento, 95818-2541. Tel: 916-733-0299. PHILIP DELEON, Archivist.

Bereavement Ministry—Office: 2110 Broadway, Sacramento, 95818. Tel: 916-733-0133. STEVE PATTON.

Catholic Committee on Scouting—JENNIFER CAMPBELL, Tel: 530-389-2780; Email: scouting@scd.org; Rev. CHRISTOPHER R. FRAZER, Chap.

Black Catholic Ministry—Office: 2110 Broadway, Sacramento, 95818-2541. Tel: 916-733-0123; Tel: 415-622-7466; Fax: 916-733-0195. Rev. BART LANDRY, C.S.P.

Building Committee—Direct inquiries to: MR. THOMAS J. MCNAMARA, Staff, Diocesan Pastoral Center, 2110 Broadway, Sacramento, 95818-2541. Tel: 916-733-0277; Fax: 916-733-0295.

Office of Youth and Young Adult Ministries—Deacon KEVIN STASZKOW, Dir.; ALEX BARRAZA, Regl. Coord. Youth & Young Adult Ministry, Pastoral Juvenil; RICHARD CHERVENEY, Youth & Young Adult, North State; LINDSEY WEST, Regl. Coord. Youth & Young Adult Ministry, Sacramento; JENNIFER CAMPBELL, Dir. Trinity Pines Catholic Center, Colfax; WESTON RUIZ, Newman Catholic Center, Chico; EDRICK BONDOC, B.A., Dir., Newman Catholic Center, Davis; CECILIA FLORES, M.A., Dir., Newman Catholic Center, Sacramento; ANDREA FLOREZ, Campus Min., Chico; AARON SANTOS, Campus Min., Sacramento; Rev. BART LANDRY, C.S.P., Coord., Black Catholic Min.

Office of Family and Faith Formation—CHRIS OWENS, Dir.; STEVE PATTON, Assoc. Dir., Family & Respect Life Ministries; TERESA DONAN, Coord. Lay Ministry Formation & Support; MARTHA HAIG, Coord., Lay Ministry Formation & Support; LAURALYN SOLANO, B.A., Coord., Lay Ministry Formation & Support; HECTOR VELASCO, North State Revival Coord.; PAULA SEGNO, Project Rachel Coord.; JO KRISTINE CLARK, Deaf Ministry Contact.

Department of Catholic Charities & Social Concerns—JOHN WATKINS, Dir., 2110 Broadway, Sacramento, 95818. Tel: 916-733-0253; Fax: 916-733-0224.

Catholic Charities of Sacramento, Inc.—JOHN WATKINS, Dir., 2110 Broadway, Sacramento, 95818. Tel: 916-733-0253; Fax: 916-733-0224.

Communications—2110 Broadway, Sacramento, 95818. Tel: 916-733-0154. BEEJAE VISITACION.

Presbyteral Council—Direct all correspondence to: 2110 Broadway, Sacramento, 95818-2541. Most Rev. JAIME SOTO, M.S.W.; Revs. MARTIN J. RAMAT; LAWRENCE J. BECK; ANTONIO B. RACELA III; JONATHAN B. MOLINA; MICHAEL D. RITTER; MICHAEL J. HEBDA; ERIC FLORES; BLAISE R. BERG; VINCENT P. O'REILLY, (Retired); ANDRES EMMANUELLI; STANLEY T. POLTORAK; ENRIQUE ALVAREZ; RONALD V. TORRES; ERIC D. LOFGREN; RODOLFO D. LLAMAS; BRIAN J. ATIENZA; RAJ R. DERIVERA. Ex Officio: Very Revs. GLENN GIOVANNI JARON, M.S.P., (Philippines); MICHAEL D. VAUGHAN. Staff: DR. LOIS T. LOCEY.

The Catholic Foundation of the Diocese of Sacramento—2110 Broadway, Sacramento, 95818-2541. Tel: 916-733-0266; Fax: 916-733-0195. MR. THOMAS J. MCNAMARA, Dir.

Diocesan Pastoral Council—Please direct all inquiries to: DR. LOIS T. LOCEY, Chancellor, Tel: 916-733-0200.

Diocese of Sacramento Priests' Pension Trust—Most Rev. JAIME SOTO, M.S.W., Plan Sponsor. Please direct all inquiries to: JULIANNA AGUILERA, Tel: 916-733-0282.

Divorced and Separated Ministry—STEVE PATTON, Assoc. Dir., Family & Respect Life Ministries, Direct Inquiries to: Office of Family & Faith Formation, 2110 Broadway, Sacramento, 95818-2541. Tel: 916-733-0133; Fax: 916-733-0195.

Eastern Catholic Churches—2110 Broadway, Sacramento, 95818. Tel: 916-733-0200. Very Rev. MICHAEL D. VAUGHAN, Liaison Officer.

Ecclesia Dei Community (Latin Mass)—Rev. JOHN LYONS, F.S.S.P., Mailing Address: 5461 44th St., Sacramento, 95820. Tel: 916-455-5114; Fax: 916-455-1018.

Ecumenical & Interreligious Affairs—2110 Broadway, Sacramento, 95818-2541. Tel: 916-733-0200; Fax: 916-733-0215. Very Rev. MICHAEL D. VAUGHAN.

Finance Council—Members: JOHN HASBROOK; MR. MICHAEL PROFUMO, CPA; CHRISTINE SANFILIPPO; Very Rev. MARK R. RICHARDS, J.C.L.; SUSAN GOODWIN; MR. LON BURFORD; MR. JOHN MATZOLL; MR. JAMES PONS; BERNARD BOWLER. Ex Officio: Very Rev. MICHAEL D. VAUGHAN. Staff: MR. THOMAS J. MCNAMARA, Chancery Office, 2110 Broadway, Sacramento, 95818-2541. Tel: 916-733-0277.

Finance Office—MR. THOMAS J. MCNAMARA, Dir., 2110 Broadway, Sacramento, 95818-2541. Tel: 916-733-0277; Fax: 916-733-0295.

Lay Personnel—ANNA SCHIELE, Mgr., 2110 Broadway, Sacramento, 95818-2541. Tel: 916-733-0240; Fax: 916-733-0238.

Magazine—Catholic Herald MS. JULIE SLY, Editor, 2110 Broadway, Sacramento, 95818. Tel: 916-733-0175.

Office of Clergy—2110 Broadway, Sacramento, 95818. Tel: 916-733-0200; Fax: 916-733-0215. Very Rev. GLENN GIOVANNI JARON, M.S.P., (Philippines) Episcopal Vicar for Clergy.

Office of Clergy Formation—ULI SCHMITT, Dir., 2110 Broadway, Sacramento, 95818. Tel: 916-733-0244; Fax: 916-733-0215. Delegate for Deacons: Deacon LUIGI DEL GAUDIO, Office, 2110 Broadway, Sacramento, 95818-2541. Tel: 916-733-0244.

Priests' Personnel Board, Diocesan—Please direct all inquiries to: Priest Personnel, Office of the Bishop, 2110 Broadway, Sacramento, 95818. Tel: 916-733-0200. Most Rev. JAIME SOTO, M.S.W.; Very Rev. GLENN GIOVANNI JARON, M.S.P., (Philippines); Rev. HUMBERTO GOMEZ, Chm.; Rev. Msgr. JAMES C. KIDDER, (Retired); Revs. AVRAM E. BROWN; GEORGE T. SNYDER JR.; LEON JUCHNIEWICZ; Very Rev. MICHAEL D. VAUGHAN; Rev. FREDHELITO E. GUCOR.

Propagation of the FaithJOHN WATKINS, Dir., 2110 Broadway, Sacramento, 95818-2541. Tel: 916-733-0253; Fax: 916-733-0224.

Properties Committee—Please direct all inquiries to: MR. THOMAS J. MCNAMARA, Staff, 2110 Broadway, Sacramento, 95818-2541. Tel: 916-733-0277.

Radio—2110 Broadway, Sacramento, 95818-2541. Tel: 916-733-0168; Fax: 916-733-0195. BOB DUNNING.

Schools—MR. LINCOLN SNYDER, Dir. Catholic Schools, 2110 Broadway, Sacramento, 95818-2541. Tel: 916-733-0110; Fax: 916-733-0120.

Pastoral Care Coordinator—LOREE LIPPSMEYER, Tel: 916-733-0142.

Safe Environment Coordinator—KATITA SCHLOEMANN, Tel: 916-733-0227.

Vocations—Rev. JOVITO D. RATA; Sr. MARIA CAMPOS, R.S.M., Tel: 916-733-0258.

Worship, Office of—JAMES P. CAVANAGH, Dir., 2110 Broadway, Sacramento, 95818. Tel: 916-733-0221; Fax: 916-733-0224.

Lay Organizations—

Catholic Alumni Club—P.O. Box 1777, Carmichael, 95609-1777. Email: sactocac@yahoo.com. CYNTHIA SPEED.

Catholic Daughters of the Americas—

Court Sacramento #172—St. Paul Parish, Florin Rev. JOYLE T. MARTINEZ, Chap.; NELLIE BASQUEZ, Regent, 5430 Emerson Rd., Sacramento, 95820. Tel: 916-381-1365; Email: nell44@comcast.net.

Court Our Lady of the Visitation #1890—St. Philomene Parish, Sacramento ELSIE GENTRY, Regent, 2691 Bell St., Sacramento, 95821. Tel: 916-927-8943.

Court St. Felicitas #1939—St. Lawrence Parish, North Highlands DOROTHY KNAGGS, Regent, 1640 San Antonio Ln., Roseville, 95747. Tel: 916-774-9365.

Court Our Lady of Wisdom #2392—St. John Vianney Parish, Rancho Cordova JOAN DUBOIS, Regent, 8313 Pillares Dr., Sacramento, 95827. Tel: 916-363-2847.

Catholic Ladies Relief Society—ALICE VICTORINO, Pres., 8126 Hemlock Ln., Oregon House, 95962. Tel: 530-273-2171.

Charismatic Renewal—CARLOS ORINO, Assoc. Diocesan Liaison, 1210 Bitten Way, Suisun City, 94585. Tel: 707-426-1401.

Cursillo Movement—

Cursillo in Christianity Movement—285 Devonshire Ct., Vallejo, 94591. Tel: 707-853-0206. HELEN DRIS, Lay Dir., Email: helen285@comcast.net.

Movimiento de Cursillos de Cristiandad—MARIA DEL REFUGIO RUIZ, Lay Dir., Tel: 530-844-4174.

Daughters of Isabella—Tel: 209-200-1897. LINDA DULANEY, Regent.

Diocesan Council of Catholic Women—Rev. JOHN CANTWELL, (Retired); SHEILA TAVANA, Pres. (2017-2019), 476 Canal St., Placerville, 95667.

Italian Catholic Federation—TIM ANATONOPOLOS, District Pres., 6204 Fairfax Way, North Highlands, 95660. Tel: 916-949-8894.

Knights of Peter Claver and Ladies Auxiliary—CHARLES GLOVER, Grand Knight, Council #175, 166 Fairbanks Ave., Sacramento, 95838. Tel: 916-927-3925; BARBARA MONTGOMERY, Grand Lady Court 175, 6761 Narrowgate Way, Sacramento, 95823. Tel: 916-689-0215.

Knights of Columbus—JIM JORDAN, Chapter Pres., Tel: 916-663-1946; Email: jimj@sbcglobal.net.

Legion of Mary—CHARLES MCGLOUGHLIN, Pres., 8654 Bluefield Way, Sacramento, 95823. Tel: 916-832-0654; Email: charlesmcg@gmail.com.

Marriage Encounter Worldwide—Tel: 916-489-3464; Web: www.sacramentowwme.org. TERRY DOANE; JANET DOANE. Hispanic Coordinators: Tel: 530-312-1071; Tel: 530-681-2547; Web: www.emm17.org. HECTOR VILLEGAS; MONICA VILLEGAS.

Scouting, Diocesan Catholic Committee on—2110 Broadway, Sacramento, 95818. Rev. CHRISTOPHER R. FRAZER, Chap., Tel: 916-733-0225; Deacon KEVIN STASZKOW, Contact, Tel: 916-733-0152; Fax: 916-733-0195; JENNIFER CAMPBELL, Tel: 530-389-2780.

Secular Franciscan Order—

Little Portion Fraternity—KATHLEEN MOLARO, SFO Regl. Min., Tel: 530-272-1416.

Sacramento-St. Francis of Assisi Parish—Fraternidad De San Juan (Spanish) GENARO GONZALEZ, Min., Tel: 916-969-2567; Tel: 916-967-4233. St. Francis of Assisi Fraternity (English).

Secular Order of Discalced Carmelites—LILLIAN KELLY, St. Mary, 1333 58th St., Sacramento, 95819. Web: www.ocdssacramento.org.

Serra Club of Sacramento—ROBERT LEACH, Pres., Tel: 916-797-0830.

Society of St. Vincent de Paul—JUDY DIETLIAN, Pres., Tel: 707-315-3368; Email: jdietlein@svdp-sacramento.org; Web: www.svdp-sacramento.org.

Young Ladies Institute—MARILYN WALTER, Mailing Address: 2605 Zinfandel Dr., Rancho Cordova, 95670. Tel: 916-638-7905.

St. Thomas More Society—MICHAEL A. TERHORST, Pres., Tel: 916-444-3400; Web: www.sacstms.org.

CLERGY, PARISHES, MISSIONS AND PAROCHIAL SCHOOLS

CITY OF SACRAMENTO

(SACRAMENTO COUNTY)

1—CATHEDRAL OF THE BLESSED SACRAMENT (1889)
1017 Eleventh St., 95814. Tel: 916-444-3071; Email: blessed@cathedralsacramento.org; Web: www.cathedralsacramento.org. Most Rev. Jaime Soto, M.S.W., Ordinary; Very Rev. Michael O'Reilly, Rector; Deacons Don De Haven; John Gisla; Rex Rallanka, Music Dir.; Deacons Edgar Hilbert; Omar Bardales. Catechetical Center Cathedral Parish Hall conducted by parish CCD and Daughters of Charity of Canossa.

Legal Name: Pastor of Cathedral of the Blessed Sacrament Parish, Sacramento, a corporation sole
Catechesis Religious Program—Email: blessed@cathedralsacramento.org. Sr. Jenny Aldeghi, D.R.E. Students 589.

2—ALL HALLOWS (1942) Merged with St. Peter, Sacramento to form St. Peter & All Hallows Parish, Sacramento.

3—ST. ANNE (1961)
7724 24th St., 95832. Tel: 916-422-8380; Email: joehuong@yahoo.com. Rev. Joseph Huong Xuan Nguyen; Deacon Pedro Manriquez, (Retired)
Legal Name: Pastor of St. Anne Parish, Sacramento, a corporation sole
Catechesis Religious Program—Vera Teresa, D.R.E. Students 195.

4—ST. ANTHONY (1974)
660 Florin Rd., 95831. Tel: 916-428-5678; Email: office@stasac.org; Web: www.stasac.org. Rev. Mieczyslaw Mitch Maleszyk, Parochial Admin.; Rev. Msgr. T. Brendan O'Sullivan, Pastor Emeritus, (Retired); Deacons Richard Koppes; David Cabrera
Legal Name: Pastor of St. Anthony Parish, Sacramento, a corporation sole
Catechesis Religious Program—Tel: 916-392-6362; Email: linda@stasac.org. Linda DiNinni, D.R.E. Students 176.

5—ST. CHARLES BORROMEO (1960) (Spanish)
7584 Center Pkwy., 95823. Tel: 916-421-5177; Email: scbchurch@sbcglobal.net; Web: www.scbchurchsac.org. Revs. Oscar Gomez-Medina; Alexander A. Estrella, Parochial Vicar
Legal Name: Pastor of St. Charles Borromeo Parish, Sacramento, a corporation sole
School—St. Charles Borromeo School, 7580 Center Pkwy., 95823. Tel: 916-421-6189; Fax: 916-421-3954; Email: scboffice@scbsac.net. Mrs. Antoinette Perez, Prin. Lay Teachers 11; Students 163.
Catechesis Religious Program—Tel: 916-421-7174; Tel: 916-421-1063. Sisters Josie Tanudtanud, D.R.E.; Patricia Ortega, D.R.E. (Spanish). Students 745.

6—DIVINE MERCY (2005)
2231 Club Center Dr., 95835. Tel: 916-256-3134; Email: parish@divinemercynatomas.com; Web: www.divinemercynatomas.com. Rev. Soane T. Kaniseli
Legal Name: Pastor of Divine Mercy Parish, Sacramento, a corporation sole
Catechesis Religious Program—Email: divinemercy.parish@sbcglobal.net. Luz Manrique, D.R.E. Students 377.

7—ST. ELIZABETH (1909) (Portuguese)
1817 12th St., 95811. Tel: 916-442-2333; Email: stelizportugal@gmail.com; Web: www.stelizabethsac.org. Revs. Mark Richards, J.C.L.; Eduino T. Silveira, Chap. to the Portuguese Community
Legal Name: Pastor of St. Elizabeth Parish, Sacramento, a corporation sole
Catechesis Religious Program—Students 12.

8—ST. FRANCIS OF ASSISI (1894)
1066 26th St., 95816. Tel: 916-443-8084; Fax: 916-443-7356; Email: info@stfrancisparish.com; Web: www.stfrancisparish.com. Rev. Desmond T. O'Reilly; J.D. Warrik, Admin.; Elizabeth White, Liturgy Dir. & D.R.E.; Richard Hernandez, Dir. Outreach; John Iosega, Music Min.
*Legal Name: Pastor of St. Francis of Assisi Parish, Sacramento, a corporation sole*In Res., Bros. John Summers, O.F.M.; Mark Schroeder, O.F.M.; Rev. Raymond Bucher, O.F.M.
School—St. Francis of Assisi School, 2500 K St., 95816. Tel: 916-442-5494; Fax: 916-442-1390; Email: mainoffice@stfranciselem.org; Web: www.stfranciselem.org. Ivan Hrga, Prin. Lay Teachers 20; Students 321.
Catechesis Religious Program—Email: dff@stfrancisparish.com. Students 120.

9—HOLY SPIRIT (1940)
3159 Land Park Dr., 95818. Tel: 916-443-5442; Email: office@hs-sacramento.org; Web: www.hs-sacramento.org. Rev. Michael J. Hebda
Legal Name: Pastor of Holy Spirit Parish, Sacramento, a corporation sole
School—Holy Spirit School, (Grades 4-8), 3920 W. Land Park Dr., 95822. Tel: 916-448-5663; Fax: 916-448-1465; Email: mreel@hs-ps.com; Email: afaires@hs-ps.com. Ann Marie Faires, Prin. Lay Teachers 15; Students 287.
Catechesis Religious Program—Email: patricia@hs-sacramento.org. Patricia Scott, D.R.E. Students 400.

10—ST. IGNATIUS LOYOLA (1954)
3235 Arden Way, 95825-2014.
Tel: 916-482-9666, Ext. 200; Email: lvchacon@stignatiussac.org; Web: www.stignatiussac.org. Revs. Michael E. Moynahan, S.J.; Arthur J. Wehr, S.J., Parochial Vicar; David J. Ayotte, S.J., Dir. of Advancement, Associate Pastor; Charles Tilley, S.J., Business Mgr.; Deacons Jackson Gualco; Sergio Diaz
Legal Name: Pastor of St. Ignatius Loyola Parish, Sacramento, a corporation sole
Res.: 1200 Jacob Ln., Carmichael, 95608.
School—St. Ignatius Loyola School, 3245 Arden Way, 95825. Tel: 916-488-3907, Ext. 103; Fax: 916-488-0569; Email: PKochis@stignatiussacschool.org. Patricia Kochis, Prin. Lay Teachers 20; Preschool 50; Students 351.
Catechesis Religious Program—
Tel: 916-482-9666, Ext. 238; Email: fohlsen@stignatiussac.org. Fatima Avila-Ohlsen, D.R.E. Students 191.
Ignatian Institute for Family Life—
Tel: 916-482-9666, Ext. 205.

11—IMMACULATE CONCEPTION (1909)
Parish Office: 3263 First Ave., 95817.
Tel: 916-452-6866; Email: info@immaculateconceptionsacramento.org; Web: www.immaculateconceptionsacramento.org. Rev. Rodolfo D. Llamas, Parochial Admin.; Deacon Gerald Pauly
Legal Name: Pastor of Immaculate Conception Parish, Sacramento, a corporation sole
Catechesis Religious Program—Email: religiousedimmaculateconceptionsacramento.org. Mrs. Laura Rios, D.R.E. Students 240.

12—ST. JEONG-HAE ELIZABETH (1993) [CEM] (Korean)
9354 Kiefer Blvd., 95826. Tel: 916-368-9204; Email: Khm8517@hannail.net. Rev. Han Mo Kim
Legal Name: Pastor of St. Jeong-Hae Elizabeth Parish, Sacramento, a corporation sole
Catechesis Religious Program—Andrew Kim, D.R.E. Students 60.

13—ST. JOSEPH (1924)
1717 El Monte Ave., 95815. Tel: 916-925-3584; Fax: 916-925-1045; Email: stjoseph1924@gmail.com. Revs. Luis F. Urrego, (Colombia); Joseph Nguyen, Parochial Vicar; Deacons Antonio Ponce; Antonio Latu
Legal Name: Pastor of St. Joseph Parish, Sacramento, a corporation sole
Catechesis Religious Program—
Tel: 916-925-3485, Ext. 124; Email: latu_cffsjc@yahoo.com. Sr. Soledad Castillo, H.R.F., D.R.E. (Spanish); Atonio Latu, C.R.E.; Vera Garay, RCIA Coord. Students 520.

14—ST. MARY (1906)
1333 58th St., 95819. Tel: 916-452-0296; Email: traci@stmarysacto.org; Web: www.stmarysacto.org. Revs. James Narithookil, C.M.I.; Sijo Chirayath, C.M.I., Parochial Vicar; Deacons George Kriske; Luigi Del Gaudio
Legal Name: Pastor of St. Mary Parish, Sacramento, a corporation sole
School—St. Mary School, (Grades PreK-8), 1351 58th St., 95819. Tel: 916-452-1100; Fax: 916-453-2750; Email: lallen@saintmaryschool.com; Web: www.saintmaryschool.com. Laura Allen, Prin., Tel: 916-452-1100, Ext. 110. Religious Teachers 2; Lay Teachers 21; Students 308.
Catechesis Religious Program—
Tel: 916-452-0296, Ext. 12; Email: cff@stmarysacto.org; Email: rcia@stmarysacto.org. Cindy Blecha, D.R.E.; Michelle Mills, RCIA Coord. Students 72.

15—OUR LADY OF GUADALUPE (1958) (Hispanic)
711 T St., 95811. Tel: 916-442-3211; Fax: 916-442-3679; Email: office@shrinegpe.org; Web: www.guadalupe-sacramento.org. Mailing Address: 1909 7th St., 95811. Revs. Francisco J. Hernandez-Gomez; Jose Edgardo Rodriquez, Parochial Vicar
Legal Name: Pastor of Our Lady of Guadalupe Parish, Sacramento, a corporation sole
Catechesis Religious Program—Tel: 916-446-3500; Email: catechesis@shrinegpe.org. Sr. Violeta Morales, D.R.E. Students 400.

16—OUR LADY OF LOURDES (1957)
1951 North Ave., 95838. Tel: 916-925-5313; Email: OurLadyofLourdes@comcast.net; Web: ollsacramento.org. Revs. Dariusz T. Malcuck, Parochial Admin.; Anthony Traynor, Pastor Emeritus, (Retired)
Legal Name: Pastor of Our Lady of Lourdes Parish, Sacramento, a corporation sole
Catechesis Religious Program—Sr. Linda Carandang, D.R.E. Students 215.
Convent—Daughters of Charity of Canossa, 1949 North Ave., 95838.

17—ST. PAUL (1958)
8720 Florin Rd., 95828. Tel: 916-381-5200; Email: saintpaulcatholic@comcast.net; Web: www.stpaulflorin.org. P.O. Box 292280, 95829. Revs. Joyle T. Martinez; Felipe H. Paraguya, (Philippines); Deacon Antonio Ramirez; Shirley Brown, Business Mgr.
*Legal Name: Pastor of St. Paul Parish, Sacramento, a corporation sole*In Res.
Res.: 7200 Gardner Ave., 95828.
Catechesis Religious Program—Email: saintpauldre@comcast.net. Sr. Elizabeth Siguenza, D.R.E. & Youth Min.

18—ST. PETER (1955) Merged with All Hallows Parish, Sacramento to form St. Peter & All Hallows Parish, Sacramento.

19—ST. PETER AND ALL HALLOWS (2012)
5500 13th Ave., 95820. Revs. Jovito D. Rata; Julian Medina, (In Res.), (Retired); Deacons Tou Moua; Orin Rovito, Email: orinrovito471@gmail.com; Manuel Ocon
Legal Name: Pastor of St. Peter and All Hallows Parish, Sacramento, a corporation sole
Worship Sites—
All Hallows, 5501 14th Ave., 95820.
Catechesis Religious Program—Sherryll Mayo, D.R.E.; Lupita Perez, D.R.E. (Spanish); Ray Moreno, RCIA Coord. Students 485.

20—ST. PHILOMENE (1948)
2428 Bell St., 95825. Tel: 916-481-6757; Email: stphilomene@stphilomene.com; Web: www.stphilomene.com. Revs. Martin J. Ramat; Gerald J. Ryle, Pastor Emeritus, (Retired); Deacons Charles Cheever; Alfredo Anguiano
Legal Name: Pastor of St. Philomene Parish, Sacramento, a corporation sole
School—St. Philomene School, 2320 El Camino Ave., 95821. Tel: 916-489-1506; Fax: 916-489-2642; Email: office@stphilomene.org; Web: www.stphilomene.org. Ann Marie Faires, Prin.; Kerri Bray-Smith, Prin. Lay Teachers 10; Students 123.
Catechesis Religious Program—Students 482.

21—PRESENTATION OF THE BLESSED VIRGIN MARY (1961)
Mailing Address: 4123 Robertson Ave., 95821-0208.
Tel: 916-481-7441; Email: communications@presentationparish.org; Web: www.presentationparish.org. Rev. Stanley T. Poltorak; Deacons Lawrence Klimecki; David Leatherby
Legal Name: Pastor of Presentation of the Blessed Virgin Mary Parish, Sacramento, a corporation sole
School—Presentation of the Blessed Virgin Mary School, 3100 Norris Ave., 95821. Tel: 916-482-0351; Fax: 916-482-0377; Email: pdhamrait@presentationschool.net; Email: wpavelchik@presentationschool.net; Email: cdonahue@presentationschool.net; Web: www.presentationschool.net. Carrie Donohue, Prin. Religious Teachers 5; Lay Teachers 10; Students 281.
Convent—Dominican Sisters of Mary, Mother of the Eucharist, 3110 Norris Ave., 95821.
Catechesis Religious Program—Tel: 916-482-8883; Email: sid@presentationparish.org. Sidney Curry, D.R.E. Students 0.

22—ST. ROBERT (1955)
2243 Irvin Way, 95822. Tel: 916-451-1475, Ext. 10; Email: churchst.robert@comcast.net; Web: www.saintrobertsac.org. Rev. Arnold P. Parungao, Admin.; Deacon Preciliano Ramirez
Legal Name: Pastor of St. Robert Parish, Sacramento, A Corporation sole
School—St. Robert School, 2251 Irvin Way, 95822.
Tel: 916-452-2111; Fax: 916-452-5765; Email: office@strobertschool.org; Web: www.strobertschool.org. Samara Palko, Prin. Lay Teachers 15; Students 229.
Catechesis Religious Program—Tel: 916-451-1475; Email: cpulliam48@gmail.com; Email: deacon_preciliano@yahoo.com. Candy Pulliam, D.R.E. (English). Students 0.

23—ST. ROSE (1942)
Mailing Address: 5961 Franklin Blvd., P.O. Box 246070, 95824. Tel: 916-421-1414; Fax: 916-421-0460; Email: strosesac@att.net; Web: www.stroseinsacramento.com. Revs. Guillermo Hernandez; Francisco Velazquez; Cirilo Cervantes, Parochial Vicar; Deacon Gilberto Coss
Legal Name: Pastor of St. Rose Parish, Sacramento, a corporation sole
School—St. Patrick Academy, 5945 Franklin Blvd., 95824. Tel: 916-421-4963; Fax: 916-421-1379; Email: info@saintpatricksacademy.net. Leslie Lastra, Prin. Lay Teachers 19; Students 270.
Catechesis Religious Program—Tel: 510-287-1241; Tel: 916-421-1777 (Spanish); Email: religedstrose@gmail.com; Email: chiocjc@hotmail.com; Email: mary.maucieri.sr@gmail.com; Email: ayaladianaa@gmail.com. Sr. Rocio De Todos Los Santos, D.R.E. (Spanish); Mr. Markton Ross, D.R.E. (English); Mrs. Mary Maucieri, RCIA Coord.; Ms. Diana Ayala, Youth Min. Students 670.

24—SACRED HEART (1926)
1040 39th St., 95816. Tel: 916-452-4136, Ext. 2; Email: shchurchoffice@gmail.com; Web: sacheart.org. Rev. Msgr. Robert P. Walton; Deacons Gilbert Parra, (Retired); William Riehl, (Retired)
*Legal Name: Pastor of Sacred Heart Parish, Sacramento, a corporation sole*In Res., Very Rev. Glenn Giovanni Jaron, M.S.P., (Philippines).
School—Sacred Heart, 856 39th St., 95816.
Tel: 916-456-1576; Fax: 916-456-4773; Email: tsparks@sacredheartschool.net; Web: www.sacredheartschool.net. Theresa Sparks, Prin., Email: tsparks@sacredheartschool.net. Lay Teachers 14; Students 292.
Catechesis Religious Program—Tel: 916-947-2683; Tel: 916-452-4830; Email: tilamadrigal@gmail.com; Email: ritaspillane@gmail.com. Tila Madrigal, C.R.E.; Rita Spillane, RCIA Coord. & Adult Faith Formation; Paul Sunderman, Youth Min. Students 106.

25—St. Stephen the First Martyr (2002) (Tridentine Latin Mass)
5461 44th St., 95820. Tel: 916-455-5114; Email: stephenproto@yahoo.com; Web: www.sacfssp.com. Revs. Joshua Curtis; Dominic Savoie, Parochial Vicar; Graham Latimer, F.S.S.P.
Legal Name: Pastor of St. Stephen the First Martyr Parish, Sacramento, a corporation sole
Catechesis Religious Program—Religion classes provided at St. Stephen Students 0.
26—Vietnamese Martyrs Parish aka Giao Xu Cac Thanh Dao Viet Name (1976) (Vietnamese)
8181 Florin Rd., 95828-9714. Tel: 916-383-4276; Email: thoanmen@gmail.com; Web: cttd.org. Revs. Louis Nhien Vu, C.R.M.; Thomas Luu Vu, C.R.M.; Deacon An Binh Nguyen
Legal Name: Pastor of Vietnamese Catholic Martyrs Parish, Sacramento, a corporation sole
Res.: 8195 Florin Rd., 95828-9714.
Catechesis Religious Program—Mrs. Lynn Nguyen, D.R.E. Students 662.
Mission—St. Dominic, 475 E. I St., Benicia, 94510-0756.

OUTSIDE THE CITY OF SACRAMENTO

Alturas, Modoc Co., Sacred Heart (1883)
507 E. Fourth St., Alturas, 96101-3406.
Tel: 530-233-2119; Email: shpalturas@gmail.com; Web: webservant@sacredheart-alturas.org. Rev. Lawrence M. Kithiniji
Legal Name: Pastor of Sacred Heart Parish, Alturas, a corporation sole
Catechesis Religious Program—Students 18.
Mission—St. James, Bonner St. & Garfield St., Cedarville, 96104.
Anderson, Shasta Co., Sacred Heart (1949)
3141 St. Stephen's Dr., Anderson, 96007.
Tel: 530-365-8573; Fax: 530-365-9544; Email: sacredheartanderson@outlook.com; Web: sacredheartparish.com. Rev. Eric Flores; Deacons Michael Evans; Anthony Short, (Retired); Rich Valles; Jesus Madrigal
Legal Name: Pastor of Sacred Heart Parish, Anderson, a corporation sole
Catechesis Religious Program—Renae Magana, D.R.E. Students 51.
Mission—St. Anne, 3415 Main St., Cottonwood, 96022.
Auburn, Placer Co.
1—St. Joseph (1861) [CEM]
1162 Lincoln Way, Auburn, 95603. Tel: 530-885-2956 ; Email: frcesarcdo@yahoo.com; Web: www.stjoseph.auburncatholic.com. Rev. Cesar R. Ageas, J.C.L.; Deacon Mark Ruiz
Legal Name: Pastor of St. Joseph Parish, Auburn, a corporation sole
School—St. Joseph School, 11610 Atwood Rd., Auburn, 95603. Tel: 530-885-4490;
Fax: 530-885-0182; Email: info@saintjosephauburn.org. Mrs. Jenny Oliver, Prin. Lay Teachers 13; Students 153.
Catechesis Religious Program—Tel: 530-320-8810; Email: katie_prust@auburncatholic.com. Katie Prust, C.R.E.; Tracy Steele, D.R.E. Students 132.
Mission—St. Joseph of Foresthill (1994) 22200 Foresthill Rd., Foresthill, 95631.
Station—
2—St. Teresa of Avila (1994)
11600 Atwood Rd., Auburn, 95603.
Tel: 530-889-2254; Email: info@stteresaauburn.com; Web: stteresaauburn.com. Rev. Innocent Subiza; Jo Ann Drummond, Business Mgr.; Jean Sawyer, Music Dir.
Legal Name: Pastor of St. Teresa of Avila Parish, Auburn, a corporation sole
Catechesis Religious Program—Judy Jones, C.R.E. Students 114.
Benicia, Solano Co., St. Dominic (1854) [CEM]
475 E. I St., Benicia, 94510-0756. Tel: 707-747-7220; Email: tstone@stdombenicia.org; Web: www.stdombenicia.org. Revs. Jerome Cudden, O.P., Pastor & Dominican Superior; Bradley Elliot, O.P.; Deacons Errol Kissinger; Shawn Carter. In Res., Revs. Vincent Serpa, O.P., (Retired); David Farrugia, O.P.
Res. & Church: 436 E. I St., Benicia, 94510-3427. Email: vaserpa@yahoo.com.
School—St. Dominic School, 935 E. 5th St., Benicia, 94510-3427. Tel: 707-745-1266; Fax: 707-745-1841; Email: admissions@sdbenicia.org. Katie Perata, Prin. Lay Teachers 16; Students 325.
Catechesis Religious Program—433 E. I St., Benicia, 94510-3427. Tel: 707-747-7240; Email: ekissinger@stdombenicia.org. Students 288.
Burney, Shasta Co., St. Francis of Assisi (1948)
Mailing Address: 37464 Juniper Ave., P.O. Drawer 160, Burney, 96013. Tel: 530-335-2372; Email: pastor@stfrancisburney.org; Web: www.stfrancisburney.org. Rev. Hector Montoya
Legal Name: Pastor of St. Francis of Assisi Parish, Burney, a corporation sole
Res. & Church: 37464 Juniper Ave., Burney, 96013.
Missions—St. Stephen's—43118 State Hwy. 299 E., Bieber, 96009.
Our Lady of the Valley, 43434 Main St., Fall River Mills, 96028.
Carmichael, Sacramento Co.
1—St. John the Evangelist (1960)
5751 Locust Ave., Carmichael, 95608.
Tel: 916-483-8454; Email: office@sjecarmichael.org; Web: www.sjecarmichael,org. Revs. Bernardin Mugabo; Thomas A. Bland, Pastor Emeritus, (Retired); Deacons Lawrence Niekamp; Keith Johnson; Jack Wilson
*Legal Name: Pastor of St. John the Evangelist Parish, Carmichael, a corporation sole*In Res., Rev. Alban Uba, S.M.M.M., (Nigeria).
School—St. John the Evangelist School, 5701 Locust Ave., Carmichael, 95608. Tel: 916-481-8845; Fax: 916-481-1319; Email: principal@stjohnev.com; Web: www.stjohnev.com. Christine Horton, Prin. Lay Teachers 22; Students 221.
Catechesis Religious Program—Tel: 916-483-4628. Sr. Hannah O'Donoghue, D.R.E. Students 90.
2—Our Lady of the Assumption (1952)
5057 Cottage Way, Carmichael, 95608.
Tel: 916-481-5115; Email: parish@olaparish.net; Web: www.olaparish.net. Revs. Eduino T. Silveira; Michael F. Kiernan, Pastor Emeritus, (Retired); Brendan McKeefry, Pastor Emeritus, (Retired); Deacon Michael Tateishi
Legal Name: Pastor of Our Lady of the Assumption Parish, Carmichael, a corporation sole
School—Our Lady of the Assumption School, 2141 Walnut Ave., Carmichael, 95608. Tel: 916-489-8958; Fax: 916-489-3237; Email: albers@olaparish.net; Email: ministrycoordinator@olaparish.net; Web: school.olaparish.net. Nicole Grant, Prin. Lay Teachers 18; Students 331.
Catechesis Religious Program—Tel: 916-488-4626; Email: faithformation@olaparish.net. Joan Cotton, C.R.E. Students 100.
Chico, Butte Co.
1—St. John the Baptist (1878)
435 Chestnut St., Chico, 95928. Tel: 530-343-8741; Email: stjohn33@sbcglobal.net; Web: www.stjohnthebaptistchico.org. 416 Chestnut St., Chico, 95928. Rev. Michael D. Ritter, Parochial Vicar; Deacons Jesus Padilla Campos; Stephen Schwartz; F. Paul Sajben; William Bruening
Legal Name: Pastor of St. John the Baptist Parish, Chico, a corporation sole
School—Notre Dame Elementary School, (Grades K-8), 435 Hazel St., Chico, 95928. Tel: 530-342-2502; Fax: 530-342-6292; Email: tschwabauer@ndschico.org; Web: www.ndschico.org. Mrs. Teresa Schwabauer, Prin. Lay Teachers 14; Students 243.
Catechesis Religious Program—Linda Givens, D.R.E. (English); Raquel Ruiz, D.R.E. (Spanish). Students 350.
Mission—St. James, [JC] Corner of Holland & Faber, Durham, 95938.
2—Our Divine Savior (1967)
566 E. Lassen Ave., Chico, 95973. Tel: 530-343-4248; Email: ourdivines@yahoo.com; Web: ourdivinesavior.org. Rev. R. Francis Stevenson
Legal Name: Pastor of Our Divine Savior Parish, Chico, a corporation sole
Catechesis Religious Program—Students 187.
Citrus Heights, Sacramento Co., Holy Family (1949)
7817 Old Auburn Rd., Citrus Heights, 95610.
Tel: 916-723-2494; Email: holyfamilychurch@surewest.net; Web: holyfamilycitrusheights.org. Rev. Enrique Alvarez; Deacons Mark Holt; Mark Hronicek
Legal Name: Pastor of Holy Family Parish, Citrus Heights, a corporation sole
School—Holy Family School, Tel: 916-722-7788; Email: mgustason@holyfamilyca.org. Jude Mikal, Prin. Lay Teachers 12; Students 189.
Child Care—Preschool, Tel: 916-722-4620;
Fax: 916-722-4509. Lucy Eberhardt, Preschool Dir. Lay Teachers 14; Students 64.
Catechesis Religious Program—Tel: 916-726-7217; Email: bjohnson4310@yahoo.com. Bonnie Johnson, D.R.E. (English). Students 413.
Clarksburg, Yolo Co., St. Joseph (1893)
32890 S. River Rd., Clarksburg, 95612.
Tel: 916-665-1132; Email: office@stjosephsclarksburg.org; Web: stjosephsclarksburg.org. Revs. Santiago E. Raudes, J.C.L.; Daniel Madigan, Pastor Emeritus, (Retired)
Legal Name: Pastor of St. Joseph Parish, Clarksburg, a corporation sole
Catechesis Religious Program—Students 88.
Colfax, Placer Co., St. Dominic (1929) [CEM]
Mailing Address: 58 E. Oak St., P.O. Box 752, Colfax, 95713. Tel: 530-346-2286; Fax: 530-346-8122; Email: st.dominicpastor@gmail.com; Email: st.dominicsecretary@gmail.com. Rev. Walter M. (Waldystaw) Borkowski
Legal Name: Pastor of St. Dominic Parish, Colfax, a corporation sole
Catechesis Religious Program—Tel: 530-346-2314. Students 10.
Colusa, Colusa Co., Our Lady of Lourdes (1870)
345 Oak St., Colusa, 95932. Tel: 530-458-4170; Email: ollcolusa@yahoo.com; Web: www.ourladyoflourdescolusa.com. 745 Ware Ave., Colusa, 95932. Rev. Matthew J. Blank, Parochial Admin.; Deacons Ruben Fuentes; Julian Delgado
Legal Name: Pastor of Our Lady of Lourdes Parish, Colusa, a corporation sole
School—Our Lady of Lourdes School, (Grades PreK-8), 741 Ware Ave., Colusa, 95932. Tel: 530-458-8208; Fax: 530-458-8657; Email: kstocksoll@frontier.com; Web: www.theollschool.com. Mrs. Barbara Genera, Prin. Religious Teachers 1; Lay Teachers 9; Students 100.
Catechesis Religious Program—Tel: 530-458-4170; Email: dianneluoma@frontier.com. Dianne Luoma, D.R.E. Students 180.
Mission—St. Joseph, 1st St. & Center St., Princeton, 95970.
Station—Our Lady of Sorrows, [CEM] [JC] Grimes, 95950.
Corning, Tehama Co., Immaculate Conception (1946) [JC]
814 Solano St., Corning, 96021. Tel: 530-824-5879; Email: iccorning@att.net. 818 Solano St., Corning, 96021. Rev. Orlando R. Gomez
Legal Name: Pastor of Immaculate Conception Parish, Corning, a corporation sole
Catechesis Religious Program—Mary Caputo, D.R.E. Students 298.
Mission—St. Stanislaus, 4th St. & D St., Tehama, 96090.
Davis, Yolo Co., St. James (1875) [JC]
1275 B St., Davis, 95616. Tel: 530-756-3636;
Fax: 530-756-5342; Email: pkelleher@stjamesdavis.net; Web: stjamesdavis.org. Revs. Rey B. Bersabal; Richard Sia; Deacons Sam Colenzo; Moises Guadarrama; Joseph O'Donnell
Legal Name: Pastor of St. James Parish, Davis, a corporation sole
School—St. James School, 1215 B St., Davis, 95616. Tel: 530-756-3946; Fax: 530-753-9765; Email: info@sjsdavis.com; Web: www.sjsdavis.com. Heather Church, Prin. Lay Teachers 18; Students 287.
Catechesis Religious Program—
Tel: 530-756-3636, Ext. 210; Email: jmislang@stjamesdavis.net. Josephine Mislang, D.R.E. Students 250.
Newman Center, 514 C St., Davis, 95616.
Tel: 530-753-7393; Fax: 530-753-2794.
Dixon, Solano Co., St. Peter (1877)
105 S. 2nd St., Dixon, 95620. Tel: 707-678-9424;
Fax: 707-678-9432; Email: stpeterschurchdixon@gmail.com; Web: stpeterschurchdixon.com. Rev. Jose J. Beltran, Admin.; Deacons Robert H. Ikelman, (Retired); Daniel Blanton; John King; Felix Lupercio, (Spanish); John Fio
*Legal Name: Pastor of St. Peter Parish, Dixon, a corporation sole*In Res., Rev. Pius Amah.
Res.: 1510 Folsom Downs Cr., Dixon, 95620.
Catechesis Religious Program—Students 170.
Downieville, Sierra Co., Immaculate Conception (1853) [CEM] [JC]
Mailing Address: 110 Sunnyside Dr., P.O. Box 302, Downieville, 95936. Tel: 530-289-3644;
Tel: 530-289-3102; Email: icp110@att.net; Email: foekej@gmail.com. Revs. Christopher R. Frazer; Robert E. Brooks, Parochial Vicar
Legal Name: Pastor of Immaculate Conception Parish, Downieville, a corporation sole
Catechesis Religious Program—
Mission—St. Thomas, 109 Butte Ave., Sierra City, 96125.
Dunsmuir, Siskiyou Co., St. John the Evangelist (1899) [JC]
c/o St. Anthony Catholic Church, 507 Pine St., Mount Shasta, 96067. Tel: 530-926-4477; Email: holyfamilyweed@gmail.com. Mailing Address: c/o Holy Family Parish, 1051 N. Davis Ave., Weed, 96094. Rev. Michael T. Canny, (Retired)
Legal Name: Pastor of St. John the Evangelist Parish, Dunsmuir, a corporation sole
Church: 5603 Shasta Ave., Dunsmuir, 96025.
Catechesis Religious Program—Tel: 530-235-4705; Fax: 530-235-4759. Eileen Congi, D.R.E. Twinned with St. Anthony, Mt. Shasta. Students 3.
El Dorado Hills, El Dorado Co., Holy Trinity (1992)
3111 Tierra de Dios Dr., El Dorado Hills, 95762-8008. Tel: 530-677-3234; Email: holytrinity@holytrinityparish.org; Web: www.holytrinityparish.org. Revs. Lawrence J. Beck; Jesus Hernandez, Parochial Vicar; Deacons James Hopp; Robert T. Shauger; Daniel Haverty; Rob Sabino, Music Min.
Legal Name: Pastor of Holy Trinity Parish, El Dorado Hills, a corporation sole
School—Holy Trinity School, 3115 Tierra de Dios Dr., El Dorado Hills, 95762-8008. Tel: 530-677-3591;

Fax: 530-350-3032; Email: hts@holytrinityparish.org; Web: www.holytrinityparish.org/school. Mr. Christopher Nelson, Prin. Lay Teachers 25; Students 248.
Catechesis Religious Program—
Tel: 530-677-3234, Ext. 133; Email: holytrinity@holytrinityparish.org. Hannah Terbrack, Youth Min.; Mrs. Susie Hahn, D.R.E. Students 638.

ELK GROVE, SACRAMENTO CO.

1—GOOD SHEPHERD (1993)
9539 Racquet Ct., Elk Grove, 95758.
Tel: 916-684-5722; Email: goodshepherdchurch@frontiernet.net; Web: gscceg.org. Revs. Leon Juchniewicz; Edgardo Garcia-Velazquez
Legal Name: Pastor of Good Shepherd Parish, Elk Grove, a corporation sole
Res.: 6808 Kilconnell Dr., Elk Grove, 95758.
School—St. Elizabeth Ann Seton Elementary School, (Grades PreSchool-8), Tel: 916-684-7903; Email: mswain@stelizabetheg.org. Marci Greene, Prin. Lay Teachers 17; Students 408.
Catechesis Religious Program—
Tel: 916-683-2963, Ext. 30. Sr. Sibele Moreira, V.D.M.F., D.R.E. Students 992.

2—ST. JOSEPH (1962)
9961 Elk Grove-Florin Rd., Elk Grove, 95624.
Tel: 916-685-3681; Email: aurora.aguirre@stjoseph-elkgrove.net; Web: www.stjoseph-elkgrove.net. Rev. Julito R. Orpilla
Legal Name: Pastor of St. Joseph Parish, Elk Grove, a corporation sole
Catechesis Religious Program—Email: sjp.dre@stjoseph-elkgrove.net. Sr. Imelda Grace Danas, Coord. Faith Formation. Students 432.
Mission— Mission Church of Saint Vincent De Paul 14673 Cantova Way, Rancho Murieta, 95683.

3—ST. MARIA GORETTI (2007)
8700 Bradshaw Rd., Elk Grove, 95624.
Tel: 916-647-4538, Ext. 204; Email: business@smgcc.net; Email: admin@smgcc.net; Web: www.smgcc.net. Rev. Joshy Matthew, C.M.I.; Deacon Al Llenos, Business Mgr.
Legal Name: Pastor of St. Maria Goretti Parish, Elk Grove, a corporation sole
Catechesis Religious Program—Students 232.

FAIR OAKS, SACRAMENTO CO., ST. MEL (1948)
4745 Pennsylvania Ave., P.O. Box 1180, Fair Oaks, 95628. Tel: 916-967-1229; Email: stmeloffice@yahoo.com; Web: www.stmelchurch.org. Rev. Aldrin G. Basarte; Deacons David Lehman; Anthony Pescetti; Jack Roland
Legal Name: Pastor of St. Mel Parish, Fair Oaks, a corporation sole
School—St. Mel School, Tel: 916-967-2814; Email: jnagel@stmelschool.org; Web: www.stmelschool.org. Janet Nagel, Prin. Lay Teachers 9; Students 217.
Catechesis Religious Program—Tel: 916-966-4314. Sara Donnelly, D.R.E. Students 82.

FAIRFIELD, SOLANO CO.

1—HOLY SPIRIT (1950)
Mailing Address: 1050 N. Texas St., P.O. Box X, Fairfield, 94533. Revs. Joel S. Genabia; Michael D. Downey, Pastor Emeritus, (Retired); Juan Francisco Bracamontes
Legal Name: Pastor of Holy Spirit Parish, Fairfield, a corporation sole
Res. & Church: 1050 N. Texas St., Fairfield, 94533.
Tel: 707-425-3138; Email: lfaivre@holyspiritfairfield.org; Email: bsouza@holyspiritfairfield.org; Web: www.holyspiritfairfield.org.
School—Holy Spirit School, (Grades K-8),
Tel: 707-422-5016; Email: mregello@hsschool.org; Email: jthompson@hsschool.org; Web: www.hsschool.org. Mrs. Julie Thompson, Prin. Students 295.
Catechesis Religious Program—Tel: 707-425-9042; Email: shernandez@holyspiritfairfield.org. Suselia Hernandez, D.R.E. Students 1,106.

2—OUR LADY OF MOUNT CARMEL (1979) (Carmelite Fathers)
2700 Dover Ave., Fairfield, 94533. Tel: 707-422-7767; Email: olmc.geo@gmail.com; Email: olmc.val@gmail.com. Revs. David A. Fontaine, O.Carm.; Patrick Gavin, O.Carm, Parochial Vicar; Deacon Raymond Elias
Legal Name: Pastor of Our Lady of Mount Carmel Parish, Fairfield, a corporation sole
Catechesis Religious Program—Tel: 707-422-2814; Email: elainebruno@comcast.net. Elaine Bruno, D.R.E. Students 305.

FOLSOM, SACRAMENTO CO., ST. JOHN THE BAPTIST (1857) [CEM]
307 Montrose Dr., Folsom, 95630. Tel: 916-985-2065; Fax: 916-985-7579; Email: parishoffice@stjohnsfolsom.org; Web: folsomcatholic.org. Revs. Sylvester Kwiatkowski; F. Ignatius Haran, Pastor Emeritus, (Retired); Jossy G. Vattothu, C.M.I., Parochial Vicar
Legal Name: Pastor of St. John the Baptist Parish, Folsom, a corporation sole
Res.: 107 Joseph Way, Folsom, 95630.
School—St. John's-Notre Dame, Tel: 916-985-4129; Email: michelle.zalles@sjnds.org. Keith Martin, Prin. Lay Teachers 19; Students 333.
Catechesis Religious Program—309 Montrose Dr., Folsom, 95630. Tel: 916-985-7338; Email: lmueller@folsomcatholic.org. Lissa Mueller, D.R.E.; Danielle Leyva, D.R.E. Students 545.
Stations—Folsom State Prison—P.O. Box W, Represa, 95671. Tel: 916-985-2561;
Fax: 916-351-3070. Deacons William Goeke, Chap.; James McFadden, Tel: 916-989-1731.
California State Prison, P.O. Box 29, 95671.
Tel: 916-985-8610; Fax: 916-985-6425.

FORT JONES, SISKIYOU CO., SACRED HEART (1921) [CEM]
101 Carlock St., P.O. Box 126, Fort Jones, 96032-0126. Tel: 530-842-4874; Email: stjoseph310@nctv.com. 314 Fourth St., Yreka, 96097. Rev. Ronald V. Torres, Parochial Admin.
Legal Name: Pastor of Sacred Heart Parish, Fort Jones, a corporation sole
Catechesis Religious Program—Students 60.
Missions—St. Mary's—Etna.
All Saints, 1321 Indian Creek Rd., Happy Camp, 96093.
St. Joseph.

GALT, SACRAMENTO CO., ST. CHRISTOPHER (1885)
Mailing Address: 950 S. Lincoln Way, P.O. Box 276, Galt, 95632. Tel: 209-745-1389; Email: mariapolanco@saint-christophers.com; Web: www.st-christopherchurch.com. Rev. Miguel J. Silva
Legal Name: Pastor of St. Christopher Parish, Galt, a corporation sole
Res.: P.O. Box 276, Galt, 95632.
Catechesis Religious Program—
Tel: 209-745-1389, Ext. 304. Manuel Ramirez, D.R.E. Students 423.

GRANITE BAY, PLACER CO., ST. JOSEPH MARELLO (2004)
7200 Auburn Folsom Rd., Granite Bay, 95746. Rev. Philip V. Massetti, O.S.J.; Deacons Dennis Gorsuch; Jeffery McClure
Legal Name: Pastor of St. Joseph Marello Parish, Granite Bay, a corporation sole
Catechesis Religious Program—Tel: 916-786-5001;
Tel: 916-474-6459; Email: marellok5@gmail.com; Email: marelloedge@gmail.com; Email: marellolifeteen@gmail.com. Karen Chappelear, D.R.E. (Grades K-5); Lisa Nollette, Youth Min. (Grades 6-8) & Lifeteen (Grades 9-12). Students 241.

GRASS VALLEY, NEVADA CO., ST. PATRICK (1855) [CEM]
235 Chapel St., Grass Valley, 95945.
Tel: 530-273-2347; Email: stpatchurch@sbcglobal.net; Web: www.stpatrickgrassvalley.org. Revs. Christopher R. Frazer; Robert E. Brooks, Parochial Vicar; Deacons James Chatigny, (Retired); Brian Moore, (Retired); Richard Soria
Legal Name: Pastor of St. Patrick Parish, Grass Valley, a corporation sole
School—Mt. St. Mary's Academy, 400 S. Church St., Grass Valley, 95945. Tel: 530-273-4694;
Fax: 530-273-1724; Email: info@mtstmarys.org. Edee Wood, Prin. Lay Teachers 15; Religious 1; Students 129.
Catechesis Religious Program—425 Dalton St., Grass Valley, 95945. Tel: 530-273-2336; Email: stpatsdcnrick@gmail.com. Students 45.

GRIDLEY, BUTTE CO., SACRED HEART (1926)
Mailing Address: 1560 Hazel St., Gridley, 95948.
Tel: 530-846-2140; Email: sacredheartgridley@gmail.com; Web: sacredheartgridley.wixsite.com/sac-diocese. Rev. Roland B. Ramirez
Legal Name: Pastor of Sacred Heart Parish, Gridley, a corporation sole
Catechesis Religious Program—P.O. Box 205, Gridley, 95948. Email: joannhamman@sbcglobal.net. Joann Hamman, D.R.E. Students 340.
Mission—Our Lady of Guadalupe, 9660 Broadway, Live Oak, 95953.

IONE, AMADOR CO., SACRED HEART OF JESUS (1932) [JC] Merged with Immaculate Conception, Sutter Creek & St. Patrick's, Jackson to form St. Katharine Drexel, Martell.

ISLETON, SACRAMENTO CO., ST. THERESE (1953)
100 4th St., P.O. Box 697, Isleton, 95641.
Tel: 916-776-1330; Email: fralvaro@churchofsaintanthony.org. Rev. Alvaro Perez
Legal Name: Pastor of St. Therese Parish, Isleton, a corporation sole
Church: 4th St. & Jackson Blvd., Isleton, 95641.
Catechesis Religious Program—Mrs. Andrea Diaz, D.R.E. Students 48.

JACKSON, AMADOR CO., ST. PATRICK'S (1864) [CEM 2] Merged with Immaculate Conception, Sutter Creek & Sacred Heart of Jesus, Ione to form St. Katharine Drexel, Martell.

KNIGHTS LANDING, YOLO CO., ST. PAUL (1949) [CEM]
222 Sycamore Way, P.O. Box 176, Knights Landing, 95645. Tel: 530-735-6478; Email: eugeniolopez74@gmail.com. Rev. Eugenio Lopez-Restrepo, Parochial Admin.; Deacons Antonio Gonzalez; Hermennegildo Valera
Legal Name: Pastor of St. Paul Parish, Knights Landing, a corporation sole
Catechetical Center—6th St. & Locust St., Knights Landing, 95645.
Catechesis Religious Program—Students 80.
Mission—St. Agnes, 9865 Main St., Zamora, 95645.

LAKE ALMANOR, PLUMAS CO., OUR LADY OF THE SNOWS (1929)
220 Clifford Dr., P.O. Box 1970, Lake Almanor, 96137. Tel: 530-259-3932; Email: tmylfrd@yahoo.com; Web: www.ourladyofsnows.org. Mailing Address: P.O. Box 1970, Chester, 96020. Rev. Alfredo L. Tamayo
Legal Name: Pastor of Our Lady of the Snows Parish, Lake Almanor, a corporation sole
Catechesis Religious Program—

LINCOLN, PLACER CO., ST. JOSEPH (1892) [CEM] [JC]
280 Oak Tree Ln., Lincoln, 95648. Tel: 916-645-2102; Email: stjosephlincoln@gmail.com; Web: www.stjosephlincoln.com. Rev. Eric D. Lofgren; Deacons Jesus Rodriguez, (Retired); Roberto Ruiz; Stan S. Rudger; Juvencio Vela; Emmett Pogue
Legal Name: Pastor of St. Joseph Parish, Lincoln, a corporation sole
Catechesis Religious Program—Tel: 916-645-2684; Email: stjoelincolndre@gmail.com. Rosalinda Guadarrama, D.R.E. Students 530.
Missions—St. Boniface—1028 Marcum Rd., Nicolaus, 95659.
St. Daniel, 214 Main St., Wheatland, 95692.
Shrine—Our Lady of Guadalupe, 3rd St. & K St., Lincoln, 95648.

MARTELL, AMADOR CO., ST. KATHARINE DREXEL (2011) [JC8]
11361 Prospect Dr., Jackson, 95642.
Tel: 209-223-2970; Email: office@stkatharinedrexel.com; Web: www.stkatharinedrexel.com. Revs. Colin C. Wen, Parochial Admin.; Thomas Relihan, Pastor Emeritus, (Retired); Deacons Ed Pogue, (Retired); Jaime Garcia
Legal Name: Pastor of St. Katharine Drexel Parish, Martell, a corporation sole
Missions—Immaculate Conception—125 Amelia St., Sutter Creek, 95685.
Our Lady of the Pines, 26750 Tiger Creek Rd., Pioneer, 95666.
Sacred Heart of Jesus, 20 Relihan Dr., Ione, 95640.
St. Bernard, 16285 Immigrant St., Volcano, 95689.
St. Patrick, 115 Church St., Jackson, 95642.
St. Mary of the Mountains, 18765 Church St., Plymouth, 95669.
Stations—Mule Creek State Prison—4001 Hwy. 104, P.O. Box 409099, Ione, Amador Co. 95640.
Tel: 209-274-4911.
Plasse's Resort, 30001 Plasse Rd., Pioneer, 95666.

MARYSVILLE, YUBA CO., ST. JOSEPH (1852) [CEM]
Mailing: 223 Eighth St., Marysville, 95901.
Tel: 530-742-6461; Fax: 530-742-0346; Email: stjosephmarysville@gmail.com; Web: stjoseph-marysville.org. 702 C St., Marysville, 95901. Rev. Avram E. Brown, Admin.; Deacons David Perez; Barry Johnson; Rafael Moreno
Legal Name: Pastor of St. Joseph Parish, Marysville, a corporation sole
Res.: 319 Seventh St., Marysville, 95901.
Catechesis Religious Program—715 C St., Marysville, 95901. Students 711.
Mission—Sacred Heart Church, P.O. Box 208, Dobbins, 95953.

MAXWELL, COLUSA CO., SACRED HEART (1881)
P.O. Box 1327, Williams, 95987. Tel: 530-473-2432; Email: sh_maxwell@frontiernet.net; Web: www.sacredheart-maxwell.org. 627 8th St., Williams, 95987. Revs. Michael Olszewski, (Poland) Parochial Admin.; John J. Myles, Pastor Emeritus, (Retired); Maria Lozano, D.R.E.
Legal Name: Pastor of Sacred Heart Parish, Maxwell, a corporation sole
Church: 45 Elm St., Maxwell, 95955.
Missions—Holy Cross—412 Laurel St., Arbuckle, 95912.
Church of the Annunciation, 617 8th St., Williams, 95987.

MCCLOUD, SISKIYOU CO., ST. JOSEPH (1933) [JC]
507 Pine St., Mount Shasta, 96067.
Tel: 530-926-4477; Email: sta@nctv.com. Rev. Lester T. Menor
Legal Name: Pastor of St. Joseph Parish, McCloud, a corporation sole
Church: 213 Colombero Dr., Mccloud, 96057.
Catechesis Religious Program—(In Mt. Shasta).

MOUNT SHASTA, SISKIYOU CO., ST. ANTHONY (1954)
507 Pine St., Mount Shasta, 96067.
Tel: 530-926-4477; Email: sta@nctv.com. Rev. Lester T. Menor
Legal Name: Pastor of St. Anthony Parish, Mount Shasta, a corporation sole
Catechesis Religious Program—Students 15.

NEVADA CITY, NEVADA CO., ST. CANICE (1851) [CEM]
Tel: 530-265-2049; Email: stcanice@sbcglobal.net. Revs. Christopher R. Frazer; Robert E. Brooks, Parochial Vicar

Legal Name: Pastor of St. Canice Parish, Nevada City, a corporation sole
Church: 316 Washington St., Nevada City, 95959.
Catechesis Religious Program—236 Reward St., Nevada City, 95959. Tel: 530-265-2712. Kim Mello, D.R.E. Students 30.

NORTH HIGHLANDS, SACRAMENTO CO., ST. LAWRENCE (1955)
4325 Don Julio Blvd., North Highlands, 95660.
Tel: 916-332-4777; Email: gnydozer@gmail.com; Web: saintlawrencechurch.org. Rev. Isnardo Serrano, C.O.; Deacons Donald Galli; Kevin Staszkow
Legal Name: Pastor of St. Lawrence Parish, North Highlands, a corporation sole
Catechesis Religious Program—Email: mtd.tov@gmail.com. Margarita Toledo, D.R.E. Students 352.

ORANGEVALE, SACRAMENTO CO., DIVINE SAVIOR (1987)
Mailing Address: 9079 Greenback Ln., Orangevale, 95662-4703. Tel: 916-989-7400; Fax: 916-989-7410; Email: kathleen@divinesavior.com; Web: www.divinesavior.com. Revs. Roman C. Mueller, S.D.S.; Marcel Emeh, S.D.S., Parochial Vicar
Legal Name: Pastor of Divine Savior Parish, Orangevale, a corporation sole
Res.: 8680 Hickory Leaf Pl., Orangevale, 95662-3444.
Catechesis Religious Program—Email: denise@divinesavior.com. Denise Hackett, D.R.E. Students 281.

ORLAND, GLENN CO., ST. DOMINIC (1884)
Mailing Address: 830 A St., Orland, 95963.
Tel: 530-865-4550; Email: stdominicorland@gmail.com. Rev. Antonio B. Racela III
Legal Name: Pastor of St. Dominic Parish, Orland, A corporation sole
Catechesis Religious Program—Martha Rico, D.R.E. Students 323.
Mission—St. Mary, 400 Los Robles Ave., Hamilton City, 95951.

OROVILLE, BUTTE CO., ST. THOMAS THE APOSTLE (1857)
1330 Bird St., Oroville, 95965. Tel: 530-533-0262; Fax: 530-533-1148; Email: st.thomas.oroville@gmail.com; Web: www.orovillecatholic.org. Rev. Gerome D. Hernandez, M.S.P.; Deacons Jesus Venegas; Tom O'Connell
Legal Name: Pastor of St. Thomas the Apostle Parish, Oroville, a corporation sole
Rectory—1355 First Ave., Oroville, 95965.
School—St. Thomas the Apostle School, 1380 Bird St., Oroville, 95965. Tel: 530-534-6969; Fax: 530-534-9374; Email: kheinert@stschool.net; Web: www.stschool.net. Kasia Heinert, Prin. Lay Teachers 5; Students 88.
Catechesis Religious Program—Tel: 530-693-7438; Email: mainoffice@orovillecatholic.org. Lucia Navarro-Imsdahl, D.R.E. Students 62.
Mission—St. Anthony of Padula, 10184 La Porte Rd., Challenge, 95925.

PARADISE, BUTTE CO., ST. THOMAS MORE (1949)
767 Elliott Rd., Paradise, 95969. Tel: 530-877-4501; Email: office@stmparadise.org; Web: www.stmparadise.org. Rev. Godwin Xavier; Deacons Gary Zellmer; Ray Helgeson, M.A.
Legal Name: Pastor of St. Thomas More Parish, Paradise, a corporation sole
Catechesis Religious Program—Deon Nagan, D.R.E. Students 39.

PLACERVILLE, EL DORADO CO., ST. PATRICK (1852)
3109 Sacramento St., Placerville, 95667.
Tel: 530-622-0373; Email: parishoffice@stpatpv.org; Web: stpatpv.org. Revs. Hernando Gomez-Amaya, (Colombia); John Cantwell, Pastor Emeritus, (Retired); Lupita Gonzalez, Business Mgr.
Legal Name: Pastor of St. Patrick Parish, Placerville, a corporation sole
Catechesis Religious Program—3090 Benham St., Placerville, 95667. Tel: 530-622-7692; Email: faithformation@stpatpv.org. Kathleen Hill-Kasnic, D.R.E. Students 0.
Mission—St. James, 2831 Harkness St., Georgetown, 95634. Tel: 530-333-9432.
St. Patrick Ladies Society—
St. Patrick Aid Ministry (S.P.A.M.)—
St. James Society—Tel: 530-333-2946; Email: bearstate@hughes.net.

PORTOLA, PLUMAS CO., HOLY FAMILY (1929)
108 Taylor Ave., Portola, 96122. Rev. Brian J. Soliven, Parochial Admin.
Legal Name: Pastor of Holy Family Parish, Portola, a corporation sole
Catechesis Religious Program—Students 61.
Mission—Holy Rosary, 614 4th St., Loyalton, 96118.

QUINCY, PLUMAS CO., ST. JOHN (1947) [JC6]
Mailing Address: 170 Lawrence St., P.O. Box 510, Quincy, 95971. Tel: 530-283-0890; Email: salvadorbringas@yahoo.com. Rev. Stephen M. Borlang, (Retired)
Legal Name: Pastor of St. John Parish, Quincy, a corporation sole
Res. & Church: 170 Lawrence St., Quincy, 95971.
Catechesis Religious Program—
Mission—St. Anthony, 209 Jesse St., Greenville, 95947.

RANCHO CORDOVA, SACRAMENTO CO., ST. JOHN VIANNEY (1958)
10497 Coloma Rd., Rancho Cordova, 95670.
Tel: 916-362-1385; Email: frgiovanni79@yahoo.com; Web: www.sjvparish.com. Revs. Giovanni B. Gamas; Raj R. Derivera, Parochial Vicar; Deacons Walter Little; Daniel Rangel
Legal Name: Pastor of St. John Vianney Parish, Rancho Cordova, a corporation sole
School—St. John Vianney School, 10499 Coloma Rd., Rancho Cordova, 95670. Tel: 916-363-4610; Fax: 916-363-3243; Email: ahale@sjvschool.org. Amy Hale, Prin. Lay Teachers 15; Students 210.
Catechesis Religious Program—Email: josfinaperalta777@yahoo.com. Sr. Josefina Peralta, D.R.E. Students 122.

RED BLUFF, TEHAMA CO., SACRED HEART (1867) [JC]
Rev. Charles P. Kelly
Legal Name: Pastor of Sacred Heart Parish, Red Bluff, a corporation sole
Parish Hall—2355 Monroe Ave., Red Bluff, 96080.
Tel: 530-527-1351; Tel: 530-527-2229;
Fax: 530-529-2586; Email: bmudd@sacredheartrb.org; Email: kramirez@sacredheartrb.org; Web: www.sacredheartredbluff.com.
School—Sacred Heart School, 2255 Monroe Ave., Red Bluff, 96080. Tel: 530-527-6727;
Fax: 530-527-5026; Email: rcherveny@shsredbluff.org; Web: sacredheartredbluffschool.org. Paul Weber, Prin. Lay Teachers 7; Students 82.
Catechesis Religious Program—Email: awilson@sacredheartrb.org. Ann Wilson, D.R.E. Students 8.

REDDING, SHASTA CO.
1—ST. JOSEPH (1907) [CEM]
2040 Walnut Ave., Redding, 96001.
Tel: 530-243-3463; Email: stjoeparish@sbcglobal.net. Revs. Fredhelito E. Gucor; Hector Rene Jauregui; Deacons David Gasman; Michael Mangas
Legal Name: Pastor of St. Joseph Parish, Redding, a corporation sole
School—St. Joseph School, 2460 Gold St., Redding, 96001. Tel: 530-243-2302; Fax: 530-243-2747; Email: contact@sjsr.org. Bill Koppes, Prin. Lay Teachers 10; Students 165.
Catechesis Religious Program—Mrs. Susan Riffel, D.R.E. Students 70.
Mission—St. Michael, 3440 Shasta Dam Blvd., Shasta Lake City, 96019.
2—OUR LADY OF MERCY (1980)
2600 Shasta View Dr., Redding, 96002.
Tel: 530-222-3424; Email: jessica@olmredding.net. Rev. Jhay B. Galeon, Admin.; Deacons Ray Arnold; Raymond Hemenway
Legal Name: Pastor of Our Lady of Mercy Parish, Redding, a corporation sole
Catechesis Religious Program—
Tel: 530-222-3424, Ext. 130; Email: jesus@olmredding.net. Jesus Carillo, D.R.E.; Michelle Pineda, D.R.E. Students 157.
Mission—Mary Queen of Peace, 30725 Shingletown Ridge Rd., Shingletown, 96088.

RIO VISTA, SOLANO CO., ST. JOSEPH (1885) [CEM 2]
130 S. 4th St., Rio Vista, 94571. Tel: 707-374-2155;
Tel: 707-374-2607 (Parish Hall); Email: stjosephoffice@stjosephriovista.org; Web: www.stjosephriovista.org. Revs. Mervin P. Concepcion; William K. Walsh, Pastor Emeritus, (Retired); Deacon Bill Bolduc
Legal Name: Pastor of St. Joseph Parish, Rio Vista, a corporation sole
Catechesis Religious Program—Email: stjosephcatechism@comcast.net. Suzette Sutton, D.R.E. Students 75.

ROCKLIN, PLACER CO., SS. PETER AND PAUL (1981)
Mailing Address: 4450 Granite Dr., Rocklin, 95677.
Tel: 916-624-5827; Email: sarah.peterson@rocklincatholic.org; Web: www.rocklincatholic.org. Revs. Bony Arackal, Parochial Admin.; Michael J. Dillon, Pastor Emeritus, (Retired); Deacon David Haproff
Legal Name: Pastor of SS. Peter and Paul Parish, Rocklin, a corporation sole
Catechesis Religious Program—Kris Dahla, Faith Formation Coord. (Prek-6th Grade), Tel: 916-624-5827, Ext. 213; Jennifer Gordon, Faith Formation Coord. (Grades 7-8); Nancy Von Thaden, High School Youth Min. Coord.; Darcy Wharton, Adult Faith Formation Coord.; Michelle Pfister, RCIA Coord. & Liturgy Coord., Tel: 916-624-5827, Ext. 210; Melissa Stutts, Faith Formation Asst. Students 774.

ROSEVILLE, PLACER CO.
1—ST. CLARE (1992) [JC]
Mailing Address: 1950 Junction Blvd., Roseville, 95747. Tel: 916-772-4717; Fax: 916-772-4152; Email: paulas@stclareroseville.org; Web: stclareroseville.org. Revs. George T. Snyder Jr.; German Plaza Ramos, Parochial Vicar; Deacons Larry Bertrand; Ken Crawford; Carl Kube, (Retired); Ned Quigley, (Retired); Marinko Kraljevich; JoJo Lazaro, Coord. Liturgy; Paula Staszkow, Parish Dir.
Legal Name: Pastor of St. Clare Parish, Roseville, a corporation sole
Res.: 1900 Santa Ines Ave., Roseville, 95747.
Catechesis Religious Program—Email: agness@stclareroseville.org; Email: timr@stclareroseville.org. Agnes Soria, Coord. K-5th Grade Ministry; Tim Rumery, Coord. 6th-12th Grade Ministry. Students 750.
2—ST. ROSE OF LIMA (1907)
615 Vine Ave., Roseville, 95678. Tel: 916-783-5211; Email: office@strosechurch.org; Web: strosechurch.org. Revs. J. Michael B. Baricuatro, Admin.; Michael J. Cormack, Pastor Emeritus, (Retired); Michael J. Estaris, Parochial Vicar; Deacons Mark Van Hook; Michael Turner
Legal Name: Pastor of St. Rose of Lima Parish, Roseville, a corporation sole
School—St. Rose of Lima School, 633 Vine Ave., Roseville, 95678. Tel: 916-782-1161;
Fax: 916-782-7862; Email: rweinreich@strose.org. Suzanne Smolley, Prin. Lay Teachers 20; Students 231.
Catechesis Religious Program—Dona Gentile, D.R.E. & R.C.I.A.; Frida Callejas, Spanish Rel. Educ. Coord. Students 565.

SOUTH LAKE TAHOE, EL DORADO CO., ST. THERESA (1951)
1041 Lyons Ave., South Lake Tahoe, 96150.
Tel: 530-544-3533; Email: sttheresa@tahoecatholic.com; Web: www.tahoecatholic.com. Rev. Mauricio Hurtado, Parochial Admin.; Rev. Msgr. Murrough C. Wallace, Pastor Emeritus, (Retired); Rev. John J. Grace, Pastor Emeritus, (Retired)
Legal Name: Pastor of St. Theresa Parish, South Lake Tahoe, a Corporation Sole
Catechesis Religious Program—Tel: 530-544-4788. Danette Winslow, D.R.E. Students 246.
Mission—Our Lady of the Sierra, Camp Sacramento.

SUSANVILLE, LASSEN CO., SACRED HEART (1894)
Mailing Address: 120 N. Union St., P.O. Box 430, Susanville, 96130. Tel: 530-257-3230; Email: secretaryshpsusanville@gmail.com; Web: sacredheartsusanville.org. Rev. Arbel S. Cabasagan
Legal Name: Pastor of Sacred Heart Parish, Susanville, a corporation sole
Catechesis Religious Program—Msgr. Moran Hall, 140 N. Weatherlow St., Susanville, 96130-3935. Students 74.
Station—170 DS Hall St., Herlong, 96113.

SUTTER CREEK, AMADOR CO., IMMACULATE CONCEPTION (1864) [CEM 4] Merged with St. Patrick's, Jackson & Sacred Heart of Jesus, Ione to form St. Katharine Drexel, Martell.

TAHOE CITY, PLACER CO., CORPUS CHRISTI (1961)
Mailing Address: 905 W. Lake Blvd., P.O. Box 1878, Tahoe City, 96145. Tel: 530-583-4409; Email: secretary@corpuschristi-tahoe.org; Web: www.corpuschristi-tahoe.org. Rev. Benedict S. DeLeon, (Retired); Deacon Michael Holley
Legal Name: Pastor of Corpus Christi Parish, Tahoe City, a corporation sole
Church & Res.: 905 W. Lake Blvd., Hwy. 89, Tahoe City, 96145.
Catechesis Religious Program—Teresa Mills, D.R.E. Students 24.
Mission—Queen of the Snows, 1550 Squaw Valley Rd., Olympic Valley, 96146.
Station—Marie Sluchak Community Park, Pine & Wilson Sts., Tahoma, 96142. (July & August only).

TRUCKEE, NEVADA CO., ASSUMPTION OF THE BLESSED VIRGIN MARY (1869)
Mailing Address: 10930 Alder Dr., Truckee, 96161.
Tel: 530-587-3595; Fax: 530-582-8648; Email: info@assumptiontruckee.com; Web: assumptiontruckee.com. Rev. Vincent R. Juan, J.C.L.; Deacon Ray Craig
Legal Name: Pastor of Assumption of the Blessed Virgin Mary Parish, Truckee, a corporation sole
Catechesis Religious Program—Email: dreassumtiontruckee@outlook.com. Carol Fowler, D.R.E. Students 196.
Mission—Our Lady of the Lake, 8263 Steelhead, Kings Beach, 96143.

TULELAKE, SISKIYOU CO., HOLY CROSS (1949)
Mailing Address: 765 First St., P.O. Box 266, Tulelake, 96134. Tel: 530-667-2727; Email: holycrossandolgc@gmail.com. Rev. Guillermo Ramirez, Parochial Admin.
Legal Name: Pastor of Holy Cross Parish, Tulelake, a corporation sole
Catechesis Religious Program—Tel: 530-640-2613; Email: cmarquez.cm10@gmail.com. Christian Marquez, D.R.E. Students 85.
Mission—Our Lady of Good Counsel, W. 3rd St., Dorris, 96023.

VACAVILLE, SOLANO CO.
1—ST. JOSEPH (1992) [JC]
1791 Marshall Rd., Vacaville, 95687.
Tel: 707-447-2354; Fax: 707-447-9322; Email: melissav@stjoseph-vacaville.org. Revs. Renier C.

Siva; Vincent P. O'Reilly, Pastor Emeritus, (Retired); Juan Carlos Villavicencio, P.E.S., Parochial Vicar. (Spanish Mass Sundays 5:00 PM)
Legal Name: Pastor of St. Joseph Parish, Vacaville, a corporation sole
School—Notre Dame, 1781 Marshall Rd., Vacaville, 95687. Tel: 707-447-1460; Fax: 707-447-1498; Email: office@notredamevacaville.org. Susan Kealy, Prin. Lay Teachers 19; Students 332.
Catechesis Religious Program—Email: jeromeb@stjoseph-vacaville.org. Jerome Baybayan, D.R.E. Students 200.

2—ST. MARY (1947)
350 Stinson Ave., Vacaville, 95688.
Tel: 707-448-2390; Fax: 707-448-2818; Email: office@stmarysvacaville.com; Web: stmarysvacaville.com. Revs. Blaise R. Berg; Michael McFadden, Pastor Emeritus, (Retired); Carlo Paul G. Tejano, Parochial Vicar; Deacons Gilberto Miranda; Robert Vandergraaf
Legal Name: Pastor of St. Mary Parish, Vacaville, a corporation sole
Catechesis Religious Program—Tel: 707-446-1881; Tel: 707-446-7067. Martha Batres-Martin, D.R.E.; Carmen Espinal, D.R.E. (Spanish); Guillermina Rodriguez, D.R.E.; Andreya Arvelao, Youth Min. Students 480.

VALLEJO, SOLANO CO.
1—ST. BASIL (1941)
1200 Tuolumne St., Vallejo, 94590.
Tel: 707-644-5251; Email: fatheramby@gmail.com; Web: stbasilvallejo.org. Mailing: 1225 Tuolumne St., Vallejo, 94590. Revs. Ambrose O. Ugwuegbu, (Nigeria) Parochial Admin.; Lawrence M. Kithinji, (Kenya) Parochial Vicar; Deacon Mike Urick
Legal Name: Pastor of St. Basil Parish, Vallejo, a corporation sole
School—St. Basil School, 1230 Nebraska St., Vallejo, 94590. Tel: 707-642-7629; Fax: 707-642-8635; Email: kwidenmann@stbasilschool.org. Mrs. Julia Boen, Prin. Lay Teachers 28; Preschool 55; Students 283.
Catechesis Religious Program—Tel: 707-644-8309; Email: stbasilvallejore@gmail.com. Julie Kissinger, Dir. of Rel. Ed. & Youth Coord. Students 246.

2—ST. CATHERINE OF SIENA (1964) [CEM]
3450 Tennessee St., Vallejo, 94591.
Tel: 707-553-1355; Email: stcatherine@stcsv.org; Web: stcatherinevallejo.org. Revs. Restituto O. Galang, M.S.P., Parochial Admin.; Percy Singco; Deacons Pedro Lobo; Rudy David; Renato Peregrino; Dennis Purificacion; Juan Moreno; Alejandro Madero
Legal Name: Pastor of St. Catherine of Siena Parish, Vallejo, a corporation sole
School—St. Catherine of Siena School, (Grades PreK-8), 3460 Tennessee St., Vallejo, 94591.
Tel: 707-643-6691; Fax: 707-647-4441; Email: cwalsh@scstars.net. Christine Walsh, Prin. Lay Teachers 24; Students 282.
Catechesis Religious Program—Tel: 707-647-4445. Janet Brandon, D.R.E. Students 311.

3—ST. VINCENT FERRER (1855) [CEM]
420 Florida St., Vallejo, 94590. Tel: 707-644-8396;
Tel: 707-644-8795; Fax: 707-644-1330; Email: alobo@stvincentferrer.org; Web: www.stvincentferrer.org. 816 Santa Clara St., Vallejo, 94590. Revs. Vicente C. Teneza; Andres Emmanuelli, Parochial Vicar
Legal Name: Pastor of St. Vincent Ferrer Parish of Vallejo, a Corporation Sole
School—St. Vincent Ferrer School, 411 Kentucky St., Vallejo, 94590. Tel: 707-642-4311; Fax: 707-642-1329; Email: jessica.dare@svfsvallejo.org; Web: svfsvallejo.org. Jessica Dare, Prin. Lay Teachers 12; Students 250.
Catechesis Religious Program—Tel: 707-643-0188; Email: stvincentferrercff@gmail.com. Sr. Fe Bigwas, R.V.M., D.R.E. Students 259.
Chapel—St. Louis Bertrand Chapel, 651 Sonoma Blvd., Vallejo, 94590.

WALNUT GROVE, SACRAMENTO CO., ST. ANTHONY (1881)
Mailing Address: 14012 Walnut Ave., Walnut Grove, 95690. Tel: 916-776-1330; Email: fralvaro@churchofsaintanthony.org. Rev. Andrzej A. Koziczuk
Legal Name: Pastor of St. Anthony Parish, Walnut Grove, a corporation sole
Catechesis Religious Program—Mrs. Cathy Baranek, D.R.E. Students 89.

WEAVERVILLE, TRINITY CO., ST. PATRICK (1853) [CEM]
P.O. Box 1219, Weaverville, 96093-1219.
Tel: 530-623-4383; Email: padpatgit@yahoo.com; Web: wwwstpatricksparish.net. 102 Church St., Weaverville, 96093. Revs. Patrick Gitonga Nyaga; Keith E. Canterbury, Pastor Emeritus, (Retired)
Legal Name: Pastor of St. Patrick Parish, Weaverville, a corporation sole
Catechesis Religious Program—Cathy Black, D.R.E. Students 17.
Missions—Holy Trinity—Hayfork.
St. Gilbert, Lewiston.
Trinity Center, Trinity Center, 96091.

WEED, SISKIYOU CO., HOLY FAMILY (1933)
1051 N. Davis Ave., Weed, 96094. Tel: 530-938-4334; Email: holyfamilyweed@gmail.com. Rev. Valmorida Mario
Legal Name: Pastor of Holy Family Parish, Weed, a corporation sole
Catechesis Religious Program—256 Broadway, Weed, 96094. Tel: 530-261-1013; Email: tapia75@sbcglobal.net. Chela Tapia, D.R.E. Students 13.

WEST SACRAMENTO, YOLO CO.
1—HOLY CROSS (1913)
1321 Anna St., West Sacramento, 95605.
Tel: 916-371-1211; Email: holycrossws@gmail.com. Rev. Jacobo A. Caceres; Maria del Refugio Martinez, Pastoral Assoc.
Legal Name: Pastor of Holy Cross Parish, West Sacramento, a corporation sole
Res.: 1321 Anna St., West Sacramento, 95605.
Tel: 916-371-1211; Email: holycrossws@gmail.com.
Catechesis Religious Program—Students 339.

2—OUR LADY OF GRACE (1949)
911 Park Blvd., West Sacramento, 95691.
Tel: 916-371-4814; Fax: 916-371-4816; Email: westsacolg@gmail.com; Email: olgoffice@wavecable.com; Web: www.westsacolg.com. Rev. Mathew Rappu; Deacon David Campbell
Legal Name: Pastor of Our Lady of Grace Parish, West Sacramento, a corporation sole
School—Our Lady of Grace School, (Grades PreK-8), 1990 Linden Rd., West Sacramento, 95691.
Tel: 916-371-9416; Email: lmacdonald@olgwestsac.com; Web: olgwestsac.com. Laura MacDonald, Prin. Aides 9; Lay Teachers 11; Students 327.
Catechesis Religious Program—Email: olgwestsaccff@gmail.com; Email: thomcarson52@gmail.com; Email: rampalm@sbcglobal.net. Carmela Torres, D.R.E.; Thom Carson, RCIA Coord.; Maggie Carson, RCIA Coord.; Ana Ramirez-Palmer, Youth Min.; Bro. Steve Ramirez-Palmer, Youth Min.; Jeremy Arcinas, Youth Min.; Helen Kanosky, D.R.E.; Cyndi Thompson, D.R.E. Students 105.

WILLOWS, GLENN CO., ST. MONICA PARISH (1877) [CEM]
1129 W. Wood St., Willows, 95988. Tel: 530-934-3314; Email: stmonicawillows@outlook.com; Web: stmonicawillows.com. Rev. Cormac R. Lacre
Legal Name: Pastor of St. Monica Parish, Willows, a corporation sole
Catechesis Religious Program—Tel: 530-774-7150. Maribel Palomino, D.R.E. Students 226.
Mission—St. Mary of the Mountain Church, 2nd St. & Geary St., Stonyford, 95979.

WINTERS, YOLO CO., ST. ANTHONY PARISH, WINTERS, A CORPORATION SOLE (1913) [JC]
511 Main St., Winters, 95694. Tel: 530-795-2230; Email: stanthonystmartin@gmail.com; Web: www.stanthonystmartin.org. Rev. Perlito G. De la Cruz; Deacon Jorge Villalobos.
Res.: 507 Main St., Winters, 95694.
Catechesis Religious Program—Email: stanthonystmartin@gmail.com. Katie Long, D.R.E. Students 177.
Mission—St. Martin, 25633 Grafton Rd., Esparto, 95627.

WOODLAND, YOLO CO., HOLY ROSARY (1870) [CEM]
Mailing Address: 503 California St., Woodland, 95695. Rev. Jonathan B. Molina; Deacons Gonzalo Chavez; Jose Luis Collazo
Legal Name: Pastor of Holy Rosary Parish, Woodland, a corporation sole
(Corner of Walnut & Court Sts.) Church: 301 Walnut St., Woodland, 95695.
School—Holy Rosary School, 505 California St., Woodland, 95695. Tel: 530-662-3494;
Fax: 530-668-2442; Email: office@hrsaints.com; Web: www.hrsaints.com. Natalie McCullough, Prin. Lay Teachers 9; Students 95.
Catechesis Religious Program—575 California St., Woodland, 95695. Students 670.

YREKA, SISKIYOU CO., ST. JOSEPH (1855)
314 Fourth St., Yreka, 96097. Tel: 530-842-4874; Email: stjoseph310@nctv.com. Rev. Ronald V. Torres, Parochial Admin.
Legal Name: Pastor of St. Joseph Parish, Yreka, a corporation sole
Catechetical Center—310 Fourth St., Yreka, 96097.
Catechesis Religious Program—Students 40.
Mission—Immaculate Conception, Hawkinsville.

YUBA CITY, SUTTER CO., ST. ISIDORE (1952)
222 S. Clark Ave., Yuba City, 95991.
Tel: 530-673-1573; Email: pastor@stisidore-yubacity.org; Web: stisidore-yubacity.org. Revs. Avram E. Brown; J. Fernando Meza, Parochial Vicar; Helen Gomez, Business Mgr.; Rodolfo Quijano, Bookkeeper
Legal Name: Pastor of St. Isidore Parish, Yuba City, a corporation sole
School—St. Isidore School, 200 Clark Ave., Yuba City, 95991. Tel: 530-673-2217; Fax: 530-673-3673; Email: tblankenship@stisidoreschool.org. Mrs. Barbara Genera, Prin. Lay Teachers 13; Students 235.
Catechesis Religious Program—
Tel: 530-673-1573, Ext. 17; Email: rramos@stisidore-yubacity.org. Rita Ramos, D.R.E.; Daniel Quiroz, Youth Min. Students 804.

Chaplains of Public Institutions

SACRAMENTO. *Beale AFB*, P.O. Box 5495, 95817. Rev. Michael F. Kiernan.
Mercy General Hospital, 832 41st St., 95819. Rev. Brent Hall.
Sacramento International Airport. Rev. Soane T. Kaniseli.
Sutter General Hospital, 2801 L St., 95816. Rev. Paul McNamee.
Sutter Memorial Hospital, 52nd & F Sts., 95819. Tel: 916-454-3333. Vacant.
University of California, Davis Medical Center, 2315 Stockton Blvd., 95817. Tel: 916-453-2011. Rev. Joseph Huyen Van Nguyen.

CARMICHAEL. *Mercy San Juan Hospital*, 6501 Coyle Ave., Carmichael, 95608. Rev. Alban Uba, S.M.M.M., (Nigeria).

FAIRFIELD. *Travis Air Force Base*, 60 AMW/HC 200 Hackett St., Travis AFB, 94535. Rev. Jeffrey F. Henry.

FOLSOM. *California State Prison*, Folsom.
Tel: 916-985-8610, Ext. 6025. Deacon William Goeke.
Folsom State Prison, P.O. Box 71, Represa, 95671. Tel: 916-985-2561, Ext. 4206. Rev. Humberto Gomez.

IONE. *Mule Creek State Prison*, P.O. Box 409099, Ione, 95640. Tel: 209-274-4911. Rev. Diogo Baptista.

REDDING. *Mercy Medical Center*, 2175 Rosaline Ave., Redding, 96001. Vacant.

SUSANVILLE. *California Correctional Center*, P.O. Box 790, Susanville, 96130.
Tel: 530-257-2181, Ext. 1180.
High Desert State Prison, P.O. Box 750, Susanville, 96130. Tel: 916-251-5100, Ext. 6722. Joseph McLachlan.

VACAVILLE. *California State Prison, Solano*, P.O. Box 4000, Vacaville, 95696.
Tel: 707-451-0182, Ext. 5474. Vacant.

VANDENBERG AFB. *Vandenberg AFB*, 747 Nebraska Ave., Vandenberg AFB, 93437. Rev. Arthur Nejera.

Special or Other Diocesan Assignment:
Rev.—
Ternullo, Joseph P., Chap. to Sacramento Law Enforcement, (Retired), 2610 F St., 95816. Tel: 916-448-5690.

On Duty Outside the Diocese:
Revs.—
Colaste, Sherwin S.
Najera, Arthur Jr.

Excardinated:
Rev.—
Bosque, Peter J.

Graduate Studies:
Rev.—
Rojas, Loreto Bong B.

Retired and in Senior Ministry:
Rev. Msgrs.—
Kidder, James C., (Retired)
Murphy, James T., (Retired)
O'Connor, Albert G., (Retired), 6600 Van Maren Ln., Unit 2A, Citrus Heights, 95621
O'Sullivan, T. Brendan, (Retired), 3865 J St., 95816
Terra, Russell G., (Retired), 2040 Walnut Ave., Redding, 96001
Wallace, Murrough C., (Retired), P.O. Box 612043, South Lake Tahoe, 96150
Revs.—
Bland, Thomas A., (Retired)
Boll, John E., (Retired), 6600 Van Maren Ln., Unit 7B, Citrus Heights, 95621
Borlang, Stephen M., (Retired)
Brady, Charles, (Retired)
Canny, Michael T., (Retired)
Canterbury, Keith E., (Retired), P.O. Box 2663, Weaverville, 96093
Cantwell, John, (Retired)
Carroll, Michael A., (Retired)
Copsey, Robert A., (Retired)
Cormack, Michael J., (Retired), 6600 Van Maren Ln., #2B, Citrus Heights, 95621
Dare, Glenn, (Retired)
DeLeon, Benedict S., (Retired)
Dillon, Michael J., (Retired), 3700 Argonaut Ave., Rocklin, 95677. Tel: 916-624-1947

Dinelli, William J., (Retired), P.O. Box 162021, 95816
Doner, Roy, (Retired)
Downey, Michael D., (Retired)
Grace, John J., (Retired), 3035 Berkeley Ave., South Lake Tahoe, 96150
Hall, Rodney L., (Retired), 3865 J St., #319, 95816
Haran, F. Ignatius, (Retired), 105 Joseph Way, Folsom, 95630
Healy, John J., (Retired), 6600 Van Maren Ln, 3B, Citrus Heights, 95621
Henry, Patrick J., (Retired)
Ho, Nicholas, (Retired)
Kiernan, Michael F., (Retired)
Kinane, William P., (Retired), 6600 Van Maren Ln., #4B, Citrus Heights, 95621
Koziczuk, Andrzej A., (Retired)
Lawrence, John M., (Retired)
Leslie, Patrick J., (Retired)
Looney, Daniel, (Retired), 6600 Van Maren Ln, 6A, Citrus Heights, 95621
MacCarthy, Liam J., (Retired), 6600 Van Maren Ln., Unit 6B, Citrus Heights, 95621
Madigan, Daniel, (Retired)
Maguire, Thomas J., (Retired)
McFadden, Michael, (Retired), 319 Buck Ave., Vacaville, 95688
McKeefry, Brendan, (Retired)
McKnight, James, (Retired)
McMahon, Kieran M., (Retired), 6600 Van Maren Ln., Unit 8B, Citrus Heights, 95621
McSweeney, Liam P., (Retired), P.O. Box 1180, Fair Oaks, 95628
Medina, Julian, (Retired), c/o St. Peter and All Hallows Parish
Moroney, Martin J., (Retired), 3544 Riojo Way, Rancho Cordova, 95670
Myles, John J., (Retired)
O'Brien, Maurice, (Retired), 6600 Van Maren Ln., Unit 11B, Citrus Heights, 95621
O'Connor, Patrick J., (Retired), 6600 Van Maren Ln., Unit 5A, Citrus Heights, 95621
O'Kelly, P. Colm, (Retired), 6600 Van Maren Ln., Unit 7A, Citrus Heights, 95621
O'Leary, Sean R., (Retired)
O'Rafferty, Patrick, (Retired), 6600 VanMaren Ln., #3A, Citrus Heights, 95621
O'Reilly, Aidan, (Retired), Virginia, Co. Cavan Ireland
O'Reilly, Vincent P., (Retired), 7012 Bucktown Ln., Vacaville, 95688
Pepka, Edward P., (Retired)
Perez, Juan, (Retired)
Relihan, Thomas, (Retired), P.O. Box 4, Ione, 95640
Ricks, Paul C., (Retired), 2208 Kendrick Ln., Waco, TX 76711
Ryle, Gerald J., (Retired)
Schloeder, Paul J., (Retired)
Seabridge, Thomas L., (Retired), 3401 Nesscliff Way, Carmichael, 95608
Serpa, Vincent, O.P., (Retired), c/o St. Dominic Parish, Benicia
Sheets, James P., (Retired)
Soria, Manuel B., (Retired)
Soriano, Jesus T., (Retired)
Sullivan, John P., (Retired)
Ternullo, Joseph P., (Retired), 2610 F St., 95816
Traynor, Anthony, (Retired)
Twomey, Simon D., (Retired)
Walsh, James B., (Retired)
Walsh, William K., (Retired)
Wells, Philip J., (Retired), P.O. Box 1082, Anderson, 96007.

Retired Religious & Externs Living in the Diocese:
Revs.—
Bucher, Raymond, O.F.M.
Coddaire, Louis C.
Ho, Nicholas, (Retired)
Klein, David F., S.J.
Lester, Thomas
Ndugbu, Polycarp E.
Paraguya, Felipe H., (Philippines).

Permanent Deacons:
Anguiano, Alfredo, St. Philomene, Sacramento
Arnold, Ray, Our Lady of Mercy, Redding
Bardales, Omar, Cathedral of the Blessed Sacrament, Sacramento
Bell, Brad, St. Isidore, Yuba City
Bertrand, Larry, St. Clare, Roseville
Blanton, Daniel, St. Peter, Dixon
Bockman, John, St. Vincent Ferrer, Vallejo
Bolduc, Bill, (Retired)
Bruening, William, St. John the Baptist, Chico
Brys, Gary, St. Maria Goretti, Elk Grove
Bullen, Jack, (Retired)
Burke, Keith, (Retired)
Burkett, James, Our Divine Savior Parish, Chico
Cabrera, David, St. Anthony, Sacramento
Cadenasso, Richard, (Retired)
Campbell, David, Our Lady of Grace, West Sacramento
Campos, Jesus Padilla, St. John the Baptist, Chico
Carter, Shawn, St. Dominic, Bernicia
Ceja, Jose, Our Lady of the Mercy Parish, Redding
Chatigny, James, (Retired)
Chavarria, Modesto, (Retired)
Chavez, Gonzalo, Holy Rosary, Woodland
Cheever, Charles, St. Philomene, Sacramento
Colenzo, Sam, (Retired-Active), St. James, Davis
Collazo, Jose Luis, Holy Rosary, Woodland
Coss, Gilberto, St. Rose, Sacramento
Crawford, Ken, St. Clare, Roseville
Declines, Rommel, Good Shepherd, Elk Grove
DeHaven, Donald, (Retired)
Del Gaudio, Luigi, St. Mary, Sacramento
Delgado, Julian, Our Lady of Lourdes, Colusa
Diaz, Roman, Holy Rosary, Woodland
Diaz, Sergio, St. Ignatius of Loyola, Sacramento
Driggs, Richard, (Retired)
Elias, Raymond, Our Lady of Mt. Carmel, Fairfield
Enos, Richard, (Retired)
Evans, Michael, (Retired)
Fernandes, Rudolph, St. Rose, Sacramento
Fernandez, Miguel, (Retired)
Fio, John, St. Peter, Dixon
Flanagan, John, (Retired-Active), St. Dominic, Benicia
Friedrich, Paul, Our Lady of Lourdes, Sacramento
Fuentes, Ruben, Our Lady of Lourdes, Colusa
Galli, Donald, St. Lawrence, North Highlands
Garcia, Henry, (Retired)
Garcia, Jaime, St. Katharine Drexel, Martell
Gasman, David H., (Retired-Active)
Gisla, John, Cathedral of the Blessed Sacrement, Sacramento
Goeke, William, St. John the Baptist, Folsom
Gonzalez, Antonio, St. Paul, Knights Landing
Gorsuch, Dennis, St. Joseph Marello, Granite Bay
Guadarrama, Moises, St. James, Davis
Gualco, Jack, St. Ignatius of Loyola, Sacramento
Guzman, Jose, Holy Cross, West Sacramento
Haproff, David, (Retired-Active), SS. Peter & Paul, Rocklin
Haverty, Daniel, Holy Trinity, El Dorado Hills
Healy, James, (Retired-Active), St. Anthony, Sacramento
Helgeson, Raymond, St. Thomas More, Paradise
Hemenway, Raymond, Our Lady of Mercy, Redding
Henning, Patrick, (Retired)
Hilbert, Edgar, Cathedral of the Blessed Sacrament, Sacremento
Hiner, Lawrence, St. Joseph, Elk Grove
Hintz, Eric, Holy Spirit, Sacramento
Holley, Michael, Corpus Christi, Tahoe City
Holt, Mark, Holy Family, Citrus Heights
Hopp, James, (Retired-Active), Holy Trinity, El Dorado Hills
Hronicek, Mark, Holy Family, Citrus Heights
Ikelman, Robert, (Retired)
Johnson, Barry, St. Joseph, Marysville
Johnson, Keith, St. John the Evangilist, Carmichael
Kim, Byung, St. Jeong-Hae Elizabeth (Korean Catholic Church), Sacramento
Kim, Sang Dominic, St. Jeong-Hae Elizabeth (Korean Catholic Church), Sacrmento
Kimball, Earle, (Retired-Active), St. Peter & Paul, Rocklin
King, John, St. Peter, Dixon
Kissinger, Errol, St. Dominic, Benicia
Klimecki, Lawrence, Presentation of the Blessed Virgin Mary, Sacramento
Kochany, Kenneth M., Our Lady of Peace, Bay City
Koppes, Richard, (Retired-Active), St. Anthony, Sacramento
Kraatz, David, Our Divine Savior, Chico
Kraljevich, Marinko, St. Clare, Roseville
Kriske, George, (Retired-Active), St. Mary, Sacramento
Kube, Carl, (Retired-Active), St. Clare, Roseville
Kull, Edward, (Retired)
Lara, Joaquin, St. Monica, Willows
Latu, Antonio, St. Joseph, Sacramento
Leatherby, David, Presentation of the Blessed Virgin Mary, Sacramento
Lehman, David, St. Mel, Fair Oaks
Leon, Raul, (Retired)
Link, Robert, (Retired)
Little, Walter, St. John Vianney, Rancho Cordova
Llenos, Antonio, Good Shepherd, Elk Grove
Lobo, Pedro, (Retired-Active), St. Catherine of Siena, Vallejo
Louis, Timothy, Holy Family, Weed
Lupercio, Felix, (Retired)
Madrigal, Jesus, (Retired-Active), Sacred Heart, Anderson
Mangas, Michael, St. Joseph, Redding
Manriquez, Pedro, (Retired)
Martin, Jose Gerardo, St. Joseph Parish, Elk Grove
McClure, Jeffery, St. Joseph Marello, Granite Bay
McFadden, James, St. John the Baptist, Folsom
Medero, Alejandro, St. Catherine of Siena, Vallejo
Merino, Dennis, (Retired)
Miranda, Gilberto, St. Mary, Vacaville
Montes, Ignacio, Sacred Heart, Red Bluff
Moore, Brian, (Retired)
Morales, Rick, Divine Mercy, Sacramento
Moreno, Juan, St. Catherine of Siena, Vallejo
Moreno, Rafael, St. Joseph, Marysville
Morgado, Edwin, Teresa of Avila, Auburn
Morrison, Charles, (Retired)
Moua, Tou, St. Peter and All Hallows, Sacramento
Nguyen, An Binh, Vietnamese Martyrs, Sacramento
Niekamp, Lawrence, (Retired-Active), St. John the Evangelist, Carmichael
O'Connell, Tom, St. Thomas the Apostle, Oroville
O'Donnell, Joseph, St. James, Davis
Ocon, Manuel, St. Peter/All Hallows, Sacramento
Ogbonna, James, Divine Mercy, Sacramento
Parra, Gilbert, (Retired-Active), Sacred Heart, Sacramento
Patterson, Daniel, Holy Spirit, Sacramento
Pauly, Gerald, (Retired-Active), Immaculate Conception, Sacramento
Pecis, Ed, St. Anthony, Mount Shasta
Peregrino, Renato, St. Catherine of Siena, Vallejo
Perez, David, (Retired)
Pescetti, Anthony, St. Mel, Fair Oaks
Pierre, Allen, (Retired)
Pogue, Edwin, (Retired-Active), St. Katharine Drexel, Martell
Pogue, Emmett, St. Joseph, Lincoln
Ponce, Antonio, St. Joseph, Sacramento
Purificacion, Dennis, St. Catherine of Siena, Vallejo
Quigley, Ned, (Retired)
Ramirez, Antonio, St. Paul, Sacramento
Ramirez, Jose, (Retired)
Ramirez, Preciliano, St. Robert, Sacramento
Randall, Paul, St. Dominic, Orland
Rangel, Daniel, St. John Vianney, Rancho Cordova
Revelo, Jose, (Retired)
Rey, Rafael, St. Vincent Ferrer, Vallejo
Reyna, Pedro, Sacred Heart, Maxwell
Rico, Benito, St. Dominic, Orland
Riehl, William, (Retired)
Rodriguez, Jesus, (Retired)
Rojo, Ruben, St. Isidore, Yuba City
Roland, Jack, St. Mel, Fair Oaks
Rovito, Orin, St. Peter and All Hallows, Sacramento
Rudger, Stanley, St. Joseph, Lincoln
Ruiz, Mark, St. Joseph, Auburn
Ruiz, Roberto, St. Joseph, Lincoln
Sajben, F. Paul, St. John the Baptist, Chico
Schwartz, Steve, (Retired)
Sexton, Scott, St. Joseph, Vacaville
Shauger, Robert T., (Retired-Active), Holy Trinity, El Dorado Hills
Sheehan, John, St. Teresa of Avila, Auburn
Short, Anthony, (Retired)
Smith, Edward, (Retired)
Soria, Richard, St. Patrick, Grass Valley
Sousa, William, (Retired-Active), Good Shepherd, Elk Grove
Staszkow, Kevin, a, St. Lawrence, North Highlands
Symkowick, Joseph, (Retired-Active), St. Ignatius of Loyola, Sacramento
Tateishi, Michael, Our Lady of the Assumption, Carmichael
Tokuno, Doug, (Retired)
Turner, Michael, St. Rose of Lima, Roseville
Urick, Michael, St. Basil, Vallejo
Valles, Rich, Sacred Heart, Anderson
Van Hook, Mark, St. Rose of Lima, Roseville
Vandergraaf, Robert, St. Mary, Vacaville
Varela, Hermengildo, St. Paul, Knights Landing
Vargas, Alberto, St. Dominic, Orland
Vela, Juvencio, St. Joseph, Lincoln
Venegas, Jesus, St. Thomas, Oroville
Verba, Pelagio L. (Phil) Jr., (Retired-Active), St. Mary, Vacaville
Vignery, Eldon, St. Isidore, Yuba City
Villalobos, Jorge, St. Anthony, Winters
Walker, Casey, St. Basil, Vallejo
Werner, Charles, Sacred Heart, Fort Jones
Wilson, Jack, St. John the Evangelist, Carmichael
Ya, Jacques, All Hallows, Sacramento
Zellmer, Gary, (Retired-Active), St. Thomas More, Paradise
McAvoy-Jensen, Greg, M.Div., St. Joseph, Elk Grove.

INSTITUTIONS LOCATED IN DIOCESE

[A] SEMINARY, RELIGIOUS

LOOMIS. *Mount St. Joseph Novitiate and Seminary* (1964) 6530 Wells Ave., P.O. Box 547, Loomis, 95650. Tel: 916-652-6336; Fax: 916-652-0620; Email: mspencer@osjusa.org; Web: www.osjusa.org. Revs. Sergio Perez, O.S.J., Dir., Youth Retreats; Philip V. Massetti, O.S.J., Pastor; Matthew Spencer, O.S.J., Rector; Bro. David Pohorsky, O.S.J., Treas. Novitiate of Oblates of St. Joseph. Brothers 1; Priests 3.

VINA. *Abbey of New Clairvaux, Trappist Seminary* (1955) 26240 7th St., P.O. Box 80, Vina, 96092.
Tel: 530-839-2161; Fax: 530-839-2332; Email: pmschwan@newclairvaux.org; Web: www.newclairvaux.org. Rt. Revs. Paul Mark Schwan, O.C.S.O., Abbot/Rector; Thomas X. Davis, O.C.S.O., J.C.L., Dean of Students, Librarian. Brothers 11; Priests 8. In Res. Revs. Paul Jerome Konkler, O.C.S.O.; Harold K. Meyer, O.C.S.O.; Placid Morris, O.C.S.O.

[B] HIGH SCHOOLS, DIOCESAN

SACRAMENTO. *St. Francis Catholic High School* (All Girls Catholic High School) 5900 Elvas Ave., 95819. Tel: 916-452-3461; Fax: 916-452-1591; Email: sfhsinfo@stfrancishs.org; Web: www.stfrancishs.org. Theresa Rodgers, Pres.; Elias Mendoza, Prin.; Judy Walker, Librarian; Rev. Arnold P. Parungao, Chap.
St. Francis Catholic High School of the Diocese of Sacramento, Inc. Religious Teachers 6; Deacons 1; Lay Teachers 76; Nuns 1; Priests 1; Students 1,081.

RED BLUFF. *Mercy Catholic High School*, 233 Riverside Way, Red Bluff, 96080. Tel: 530-527-8313;
Fax: 530-527-3058; Email: pweber@mercy-high.org; Web: www.mercy-high.org. John Davis, Prin. Lay Teachers 13; Students 82.

VALLEJO. *St. Patrick-St. Vincent High School*, 1500 Benicia Rd., Vallejo, 94591. Tel: 707-644-4425;
Fax: 707-644-3107; Email: c.martin@spsv.org; Web: www.spsv.org. Coleen Martin, Prin. Lay Teachers 43; Students 456.

[C] HIGH SCHOOLS, PRIVATE

SACRAMENTO. *Christian Brothers High School of Sacramento, Inc.* (1876) 4315 Martin Luther King, Jr. Blvd., 95820. Tel: 916-733-3600;
Tel: 916-733-3636; Email: jmcbride@cbhs-sacramento.org; Web: www.cbhs-sacramento.org. Lorcan P. Barnes, Pres.; Christopher Orr, Prin. Lay Teachers 70; Priests 1; Students 1,156.
Cristo Rey High School, 8475 Jackson Rd., 95826.
Tel: 916-733-2660; Fax: 916-739-1310; Email: aagos@crhss.org; Web: www.crhss.org. Andreas Agos, Prin. Lay Teachers 20; Priests 1; Students 365.

CARMICHAEL. *Jesuit High School* (1963) 1200 Jacob Ln., Carmichael, 95608-6024. Tel: 916-482-6060;
Fax: 916-482-2310; Web: www.jesuithighschool.org. Very Rev. John P. McGarry, S.J., Pres.; Michael Wood, Prin.; Revs. Thomas H. O'Neill, S.J., Supr.; Charles R. Olsen, S.J., Campus Min. Asst.; Aaron Engebretson, S.J.; James Schaukowitch, S.J.; Matthew Pyrc, S.J. (Boys) Lay Teachers 83; Jesuit Priests 4; Students 1,068.

[D] DAY NURSERY AND CHILD CARE HOMES

SACRAMENTO. *St. Patrick's Fund for Children, Inc.*, 2110 Broadway, 95818. Tel: 916-733-0200;
Fax: 916-733-0215; Email: Mvaughan@scd.org. Very Rev. Michael D. Vaughan, Exec.

[E] HOMES FOR SENIOR CITIZENS

SACRAMENTO. *Mercy McMahon Terrace*, 3865 J St., 95816. Tel: 916-733-6510; Fax: 916-733-6515; Email: Mary.Erickson@DignityHealth.org; Web: www.mercymcmahonterrace.org. Mary Erickson, CEO/Exec. Dir. Bed Capacity 118; Tot Asst. Annually 150; Total Staff 81.

[F] GENERAL HOSPITALS

SACRAMENTO. *Mercy General Hospital* (1897) 4001 J St., 95819. Tel: 916-453-4545; Fax: 916-453-4587; Email: Robert.Sahagian@DignityHealth.org; Web: www.mercygeneral.org. Edmundo Castaneda, Pres. Sponsored by Sisters of Mercy of the Americas West Midwest Community. Bed Capacity 419; Sisters of Mercy 6; Tot Asst. Annually 117,370; Total Staff 1,966.

CARMICHAEL. *Mercy San Juan Medical Center* (1967) 6501 Coyle Ave., Carmichael, 95608.
Tel: 916-537-5000; Fax: 916-537-5111; Email: Robert.Sahagian@DignityHealth.org; Web: www.mercysanjuan.org. Michael Korpiel, Pres. Sponsored by Sisters of Mercy of the Americas West Midwest Community. Bed Capacity 370; Sisters 4; Tot Asst. Annually 123,283; Total Staff 2,560.

FOLSOM. *Mercy Hospital of Folsom* (1962) 1650 Creekside Dr., Folsom, 95630. Tel: 916-983-7400;
Fax: 916-983-7406; Email: Robert.Sahagian@DignityHealth.org; Web: www.mercyfolsom.org. Randall Ross, Pres. Sponsored by Sisters of Mercy of the Americas West Midwest Community. Bed Capacity 106; Sisters of Mercy 1; Tot Asst. Annually 67,731; Total Staff 742.

MT. SHASTA. *Mercy Medical Center Mt. Shasta* (1938) 914 Pine St., Mount Shasta, 96067.
Tel: 530-926-6111; Fax: 530-926-0517; Email: Robert.Sahagian@DignityHealth.org; Web: www.mercy.org. Rodger Page, Pres. Sponsored by Sisters of Mercy of the Americas West Midwest Community. Bed Capacity 33; Sisters 1; Tot Asst. Annually 62,409; Total Staff 289.

RED BLUFF. *St. Elizabeth Community Hospital* (1906) 2550 Sr. Mary Columba Dr., Red Bluff, 96080-4397. Tel: 530-529-8000; Fax: 530-529-8009; Email: Robert.Sahagian@DignityHealth.org; Web: www.mercy.org. Jordan Wright, Pres. Sponsored by Sisters of Mercy of the Americas West Midwest Community. Bed Capacity 76; Sisters 1; Tot Asst. Annually 85,116; Total Staff 500.

REDDING. *Mercy Medical Center Redding* (1944) 2175 Rosaline Ave., Redding, 96001. Tel: 530-225-6000; Fax: 530-225-6125; Email: Robert.Sahagian@DignityHealth.org; Web: www.mercy.org. Todd Smith, Pres. Sponsored by Sisters of Mercy of the Americas West Midwest Community. Bed Capacity 267; Sisters of Mercy 1; Tot Asst. Annually 175,544; Total Staff 1,805.

[G] MONASTERIES AND RESIDENCES OF PRIESTS AND BROTHERS

CARMICHAEL. *Sacramento Jesuit Community* (1963) 1200 Jacob Ln., Carmichael, 95608.
Tel: 916-482-6060; Fax: 916-482-2310; Email: toneill@jesuits.org. Very Rev. John P. McGarry, S.J., Pres.; Revs. Edwin Harris, S.J., Chap.; Charles J. Tilley, S.J., Parochial Vicar; Aaron Engebretson, S.J.; Thomas H. O'Neill, S.J., Supr.; Michael E. Moynahan, S.J., Pastor, St. Ignatius Parish, Email: mmoynahan@jesuits.org; Thomas G. Piquado, S.J., Email: tpiquado@jesuits.org; Matthew Pyrc, S.J.; James Schaukowitch, S.J.; David J. Ayotte, S.J.; David F. Klein, S.J.; Mr. Edin Barrera, S.J., Scholastic (seminarian); Rev. Arthur J. Wehr, S.J., Email: awehr@jesuits.org; Matthew Yim, S.J., Spiritual Advisor/Care Svcs. (Jesuits West, Portland) Priests 11; Scholastics 2.

CITRUS HEIGHTS. *Christ the King Passionist Retreat Center, Inc.*, 6520 Van Maren Ln., Citrus Heights, 95621. Tel: 916-725-4720; Fax: 916-725-4812; Email: christtheking@passionist.org; Web: christthekingretreatcenter.org. Revs. Joseph Moons, C.P., Prov.; James G. Strommer, C.P., Supr.; Giltus Mathias, C.P., Exec., Exec.; Clemente Barron, C.P.; Blaise Czaja, C.P.; John Hilgert, C.P.; Bro. Carl Hund, C.P. The Passionists (Chicago, IL).A community residence for the Passionist priests and brothers who conduct missions and retreats. Brothers 1; Priests 6.

VINA. *Abbey of New Clairvaux, Trappist*, 26240 7th St., P.O. Box 80, Vina, 96092. Tel: 530-839-2161;
Fax: 530-839-2332; Email: monks@newclairvaux.org; Email: mikeprym@newclairvaux.org; Web: www.newclairvaux.org. Rt. Revs. Paul Mark Schwan, O.C.S.O., Abbot; Thomas X. Davis, O.C.S.O., J.C.L., Prior; Bro. Peter Damian, O.C.S.O., Sec. Cistercian Abbey, Cistercians of the Strict Observance. Priests 8; Professed Brothers 8.

WALNUT GROVE. *Our Lady of Sacramento Monastery*, 14080 Leary Rd., P.O. Box 96, Walnut Grove, 95690. Tel: 916-776-1356; Fax: 916-776-1921; Cell: 916-477-0595; Email: osm.ocist@gmail.com. Revs. Vincent Dinh Hau, O.Cist., Prior; Dominic Tran, O.Cist., Admin.; Nicolas Thanh Le; Leo Tien Nguyen; Bro. Anthony Hao Ngo; Rev. Francis de Sales Nam Vu
Our Lady Sacramento Monastery.

[H] CONVENTS AND RESIDENCES FOR SISTERS

SACRAMENTO. *Canossian Daughters of Charity* (1808) Our Lady of Lourdes Convent, 1949 North Ave., 95838. Tel: 916-925-4001; Fax: 267-629-8904; Email: jennyfdcc@yahoo.com; Web: www.canossiansacramento.wordpress.com. Sr. Jenny Aldeghi, Contact Person. Sisters 4.
Missionaries of Charity, Inc., 3971 39th Ave., 95824.
Tel: 916-454-3591; Email: smcCarthy@scd.org. Sr. Mary Lourdes, Supr.
Religious of the Institute of the Blessed Virgin Mary, 3606 Chadsworth Way, 95821. Tel: 916-485-6384;
Fax: 916-485-6385; Email: ibvmesther@comcast.net. Sr. Judy Illig, Contact Person. Sisters 3.
Religious of the Virgin Mary, 10816 Richert Ln., Elk Grove, 95624. Tel: 916-682-1203;
Fax: 916-682-1203. Sisters Maria Josielinda Tanudtanud, R.V.M., Local Supr., District Supr.; Maria Fe Bigwas, R.V.M., Local Supr. Sisters 4.
Sister Servants of the Blessed Sacrament (1904, Congregation); (1971, Community) 5929 61st St., 95824. Tel: 916-457-0182; Email: sacramentosjs@yahoo.com.mx. Sisters Marcela G. de la Pena, S.J.S., Supr.; Ana Marie Guzman, S.J.S., Campus Ministry at St. Patrick's Acad.; Maria Guadalupe Quezada, S.J.S., Teacher. Sisters 3.
Sisters Catechists of Jesus Crucified (1962) 5712 Muskingham Way, 95823. Tel: 916-395-1875; Email: hermanascjc@aol.com. Sisters Patricia Ortega Carranco; Maria Teresa Arellano Barrera; Maria del Rocio de los Santos Aquino; Maria Virginia Alcala Ruesga. Sisters 4.
Sisters of the Holy Rosary of Fatima (1952) 1708 U St., 95818. Tel: 916-442-8646; Email: vicentalemus@sbcglobal.net. Sr. Vicenta Lemus, Contact Person. Sisters 2.

AUBURN. *Sisters of Mercy of the Americas West Midwest Community, Inc.*, 535 Sacramento St., Auburn, 95603-5699. Tel: 530-887-2000; Fax: 530-887-0789; Email: sistersofmercy@mercywmw.org; Web: www.sistersofmercy.org/west-midwest/. Sisters Susan Sanders, R.S.M., Pres.; Ana Maria Pineda, R.S.M., Vice Pres.; Rebecca VandenBosch, CFO; Sisters Margaret Maloney, R.S.M., Leadership Team; Margaret Mary Hinz, R.S.M., Leadership Team; Maria Klosowski, R.S.M., Leadership Team. Sisters 531; Associates 605.

FAIRFIELD. *Sisters of the Holy Faith* (1867) 1881 Norwalk Ct., Fairfield, 94534. Tel: 707-759-5806; Email: verashiells@yahoo.com. Sisters Veronica M. Shiells; Dorothea Glennon. Sisters 2.

GEORGETOWN. *Discalced Carmelite Nuns* (1935) 6981 Teresian Way, P.O. Box 4210, Georgetown, 95634.
Tel: 530-333-1617; Fax: 530-333-1617; Email: georgetown2004@juno.com; Web: www.carmelitemonastery.org. Sr. Mary Beck-Meyer, Prioress. Carmel of the Holy Family and Saint Therese. Sisters 15.

[I] RETREAT HOUSES

SACRAMENTO. *Pendola Center*, 2110 Broadway, 95818-2541. Tel: 530-389-2780; Fax: 916-733-0195; Email: jcampbell@scd.org; Web: www.pendola.org. Jennifer Campbell, Dir.; Joe Rose, Asst. Dir. Center located in Sierra-Nevada foothills near Camptonville. Summer camp for boys and girls 6-18. Contact: Dir. of Pendola Center.

AUBURN. *Sisters of Mercy of the Americas West Midwest Community, Inc., Mercy Center Auburn*, 535 Sacramento St., Auburn, 95603-5699.
Tel: 530-887-2019; Fax: 530-887-1154; Email: info@mercycenter.org; Web: www.mercycenter.org. Colleen Gregg, Dir. A ministry of the Sisters of Mercy of the Americas West Midwest Community. Overnight Capacity 40; Daytime Capacity 250; Staff 9.

LOS GATOS. *Jesuit Retreat Center of the Sierra*, 1001 Boole Rd., Applegate, 95703. Tel: 530-878-2776; Email: jrc@uccr.org. Rev. Charles J. Tilley, S.J., Dir., Tel: 916-482-9666; Kris Holland, Res. Site Dir., Tel: 530-878-2776. Available for retreats and conferences from August 14 to May 15 & July.

[J] CAMPUS MINISTRIES AND NEWMAN CENTERS

SACRAMENTO. *Newman Catholic Center - Chico*, 346 Cherry St., Chico, 95928. Tel: 530-342-5180; Email: wruiz@scd.org; Web: www.chiconewman.org. Weston Ruiz, Dir.; Andrea Florez, Campus Min.
Newman Catholic Center - Davis, 514 C St., Davis, 95616. Tel: 530-753-7393; Email: Director@davisnewman.org; Web: www.davisnewman.org. Roberta Siebert, Campus Min.
Newman Catholic Center - Sacramento (1967) Mailing Address: 5900 Newman Ct., 95819-2610.
Tel: 916-454-4188; Fax: 916-454-4180; Email: campusministry@sacnewman.org; Web: www.sacnewman.org. Aaron Santos, Campus Min.

[K] CATHOLIC SOCIAL WELFARE ACTIVITIES

SACRAMENTO. *Catholic Charities of Sacramento, Inc.*, 2110 Broadway, 95818. Tel: 916-733-0254;
Fax: 916-733-0224; Email: jwatkins@scd.org; Web: catholiccharitiessacramento.org. John Watkins, Pres. Tot Asst. Annually 1,500,000; Total Staff 2.
Member Agencies of Catholic Charities of Sacramento, Inc.:.
Northern Valley Catholic Social Service, 2400 Washington Ave., Redding, 96001.
Tel: 530-241-0552; Fax: 530-247-3354; Email: cwyatt@nvcss.org; Web: www.nvcss.org. Dan Ghidinelli, Chm.; Cathy Wyatt, Dep. Dir. Tot Asst. Annually 24,629; Total Staff 210.
Catholic Charities of Solano, Inc. aka Catholic

Charities of Yolo Solano, 125 Corporate Pl., Ste. A, Vallejo, 94590. Tel: 707-644-8909; Fax: 707-644-6314; Email: miriam@ccyoso.org; Web: www.csssolano.org. Rich Fowler, Chm.; Miriam Sammartino, Dir. Tot Asst. Annually 3,200; Total Staff 15.

Subsidiaries of Catholic Charities of Sacramento:.

Sacramento Food Bank and Family Services, 3333 Third Ave., 95817. Tel: 916-456-1980; Fax: 916-451-5920; Email: jwatkins@scd.org; Web: www.sacramentofoodbank.org. Karen Woodruff, Chm.; Blake Young, CEO. Tot Asst. Annually 135,000; Total Staff 86.

Administrative Project of Catholic Charities of Sacramento:.

Mother Teresa Maternity Home, Inc., 3109 Sacramento St., Placerville, 95667. Tel: 530-295-8006; Email: jwatkins@scd.org. Jane Meuser, Chm. Bed Capacity 6; Tot Asst. Annually 18; Total Staff 12; Total Served 100.

Society of St. Vincent de Paul, Sacramento District Council, Thrift Store: 2275 Watt Ave., P.O. Box 162487, 95816. Tel: 916-972-1212; Fax: 916-972-1242; Email: jdietlein@svdp-sacramento.org; Web: svdp-sacramento.org. Judy Dietlian, Admin.

Society St. Vincent de Paul, Sacramento Diocesan Council, 680 University Ave., 95825. Tel: 916-649-2214; Fax: 916-649-9241; Email: jdietlein@svdp-sacramento.org; Web: www.svdp-sacramento.org. Judy Dietlian, Council Pres. Total Staff 20; Total Assisted 250,000.

COLUSA. *Grand Council, Catholic Ladies Relief Society of the Diocese of Sacramento*, c/o Alice Victorino, 8126 Hemlock Ln., Oregon House, 95962. Email: grandmavict@yahoo.com. Yvonne Moore, Pres.; Alice Victorino, Pres.

ROSEVILLE. *Society of St. Vincent DePaul* (1983) 503 Giuseppe Ct. #8, Roseville, 95678. Tel: 916-781-3303 (Office & Food Locker); Tel: 916-472-6629 (Thrift Store); Fax: 916-781-8105 (Office Fax); Email: jwatkins@scd.org. Karl Thompson, Pres. Emergency Services, Clothing Vouchers, Food Assistance, Baby Supplies, Hygiene, Dining Room, Thrift Store, Mail Service. Also free medical clinic on Wednesday mornings 9:00 a.m. to 11:00 a.m. Provide triage and urgent care; no longitudinal care. Tot Asst. Annually 43,922.

VALLEJO. *Society of St. Vincent de Paul*, 1225 Tuolumne St., Vallejo, 94590. Tel: 707-644-0376; Fax: 707-644-1423; Email: stbasilsvdpconf@gmail.com. Charmaine Ferrez, Pres. Tot Asst. Annually 4,590.

[L] YOUTH AND YOUNG ADULT MINISTRIES

SACRAMENTO. *Catholic Committee on Scouting*, 2110 Broadway, 95818. Tel: 916-733-0123; Fax: 916-733-0224; Email: jcampbell@scd.org; Web: www.scd.org/evangelization-and-catechesis/catholic-scouting. Jon Kantola, Chm.; Rev. Chris Frazier, Diocesan Chap.; Jennifer Campbell, DEC Staff Liason.

[M] MISCELLANEOUS

SACRAMENTO. *California Catholic Conference, Inc.* (1971) 1119 K St., 95814. Tel: 916-313-4000; Fax: 916-313-4066; Email: arivas@cacatholic.org; Web: www.cacatholic.org. Most Rev. Jaime Soto, M.S.W., Pres.; Robert McElroy, Vice Pres.; Most Rev. Kevin Vann, Treas.; Andy Rivas, Executive Dir.; Debbie McDermott, Exec. Asst./Assoc. Dir. Restorative Justice CA Catholic Conference; Mrs. Linda Wanner, Assoc. Dir. Governmental Rels.; Stephen J. Pehanich, Senior Dir. Advocacy & Educ. CA Catholic Conference; Mr. Raymond Burnell, Assoc. Dir. Governmental Rels.

California Conference of Catholic Bishops, 1119 K St., 95814. Tel: 916-313-4000; Fax: 916-313-4066; Web: www.cacatholic.org; Email: leginfo@cacatholic.org. Most Rev. Jaime Soto, M.S.W., Pres.; Robert McElroy, Vice Pres.; Andy Rivas, Exec. Dir.; Debbie McDermott, Exec. Asst./Assoc. Dir. Restorative Justice CA Catholic Conference; Mrs. Linda Wanner, Assoc. Dir. Govt. Rels.; Ms. Sandra Palacios, Assoc. Dir. Govt. Rels.; Barbara Caselli, Office Mgr.; Stephen J. Pehanich, Senior Dir. Advocacy & Ed.; Mr. Raymond Burnell, Assoc. Dir. Govt. Rels.

Camp ReCreation, 2110 Broadway, 95818.

Catholic Charities of California, Inc. (1987) 1107 9th St. Ste. 707, 95814. Tel: 916-313-4005; Email: smlahey@catholiccharitiesca.org; Web: www.catholiccharitiesca.org. Shannon M. Lahey, Exec. Dir.; Ken Sawa, Pres.; Rev. Msgr. Gregory Cox, Sec. & Treas. Tot Asst. Annually 1,000,000; Total Staff 8.

The Catholic Foundation of the Diocese of Sacramento, Inc., 2110 Broadway, 95818. Tel: 916-733-0266; Fax: 916-733-0195; Email: foundation@scd.org. Thomas L. McNamara, Exec. Dir.

Catholic Schools of Solano, Inc., 2110 Broadway, 95818. Tel: 916-733-0110; Email: csd@scd.org. Mr. Lincoln Snyder, Supt.

Catholic Schools of the Northern Sacramento Valley, Inc., 2110 Broadway, 95818. Mr. Lincoln Snyder, Supt.

One Campaign of the Diocese of Sacramento, Inc., 2110 Broadway, 95818. Tel: 916-733-0266; Fax: 916-733-0195; Email: info@onerevival.org. Thomas L. McNamara, Exec.

The Parochial Fund, Inc., 2110 Broadway, P.O. Box 189666, 95818. Tel: 916-733-0277; Fax: 916-733-0295; Email: tmcnamara@scd.org. Rev. Msgr. Albert G. O'Connor, Pres., (Retired).

PAX Ministerio Foundation Trust Fund, 2110 Broadway, 95818. Tel: 916-733-0245; Email: uschmitt@scd.org; Web: www.scd.org. Uli Schmitt, Dir., Clergy Formation.

The Preserving Our Past, Building Our Future Foundation of Northern California, Inc., 2110 Broadway, 95818. Tel: 916-733-0266; Fax: 916-733-0295; Email: foundation@scd.org. Thomas L. McNamara, Exec.

Radio Santisimo Sacramento, Inc., 1909 7th St., 95811. Tel: 916-442-7389; Email: lorenaa@radiosantisimosacramento.com. Lorena Albarran, Pres. & Gen. Mgr.

Sacramento Catholic Forum (2002) P.O. Box 254848, 95865-4848. Tel: 916-572-3171; Email: ncardin@relevantradio.com; Web: www.saccatholicforum.org. Nicole Cardin, Contact Person.

**Stanford Settlement* (1936) 450 W. El Camino Ave., 95833-2299. Tel: 916-927-1303; Fax: 916-922-1694; Email: sisterjeanne@stanfordsettlement.org; Web: www.stanfordsettlement.org. Sr. Jeanne Felion, S.S.S., Exec. Dir. Tot Asst. Annually 8,000.

COLFAX. *Trinity Pines Catholic Center*, 28000 Rollins Lake Rd., Colfax, 95713. Tel: 530-389-2780; Email: jcampbell@scd.org; Web: www.trinitypinescatholic.org. Jennifer Campbell, Dir.; Charles Huckins, Contact Person.

LOOMIS. *Dominican Sisters of Mary, Mother of the Eucharist - Loomis*, 5820 Rocklin Rd., Loomis, 95650. Tel: 734-994-7437; Email: sjdr@sistersofmary.org. Sr. John Dominic Rasmussen, Treas.

**IHR Educational Broadcasting* dba Immaculate Heart Radio, 3256 Penryn Rd., Ste. 100, Loomis, 95650. Tel: 888-887-7120; Fax: 916-535-0504; Email: amcfarland@relevantradio.com. Andrew McFarland, Pres.

PLACERVILLE. *Upper Room Dining Hall, Inc.*, 1868 Broadway, P.O. Box 484, Placerville, 95667. Tel: 530-621-7730; Cell: 530-919-1036; Email: plsaindon293@gmail.com; Email: director@upperroomdininghall.org true. Paul Saindon, Chm.; Charles McDonald, Dir.

PLEASANTON. *Catholic Funeral and Cemetery Services of the Diocese of Sacramento, Inc.*, 2110 Broadway, 95818. Tel: 916-733-0252; Email: jdelcore@scd.org. Jerry Del Core, CEO.

RANCHO CORDOVA. *Holy Trinity Community North America (HTCNA)*, 4216 Silver Water Way, Rancho Cordova, 95742. Tel: 916-213-9281. Erick Yo, Pres.; Yanliwaty S. Guerzon, Sec.

Mercy Foundation (1954) 3400 Data Dr., Rancho Cordova, 95670. Tel: 916-851-2700; Fax: 916-851-2724; Email: mercyfoundationsac@dignityhealth.org; Web: www.supportmercyfoundation.org. Trigna Panna, Business Mgr.

VACAVILLE. *Pro Ecclesia Sancta of California*, 3945 Joslin Ln., Vacaville, 95688. Tel: 707-685-0370; Email: frcarlos.pes@gmail.com. Rev. Carlos A. Farfan, P.E.S., Pres.

RELIGIOUS INSTITUTES OF MEN REPRESENTED IN THE DIOCESE

For further details refer to the corresponding bracketed number in the Religious Institutes of Men or Women section.

[0270]—*Carmelite Fathers & Brothers* (Darin, IL)—O.Carm.

[]—*Carmelite of Mary Immaculate* (India)—C.M.I.

[]—*Cistercians of the Common Observance* (Rome, Italy)—O.Cist.

[0350]—*Cistercians Order of the Strict Observance-Trappists* (Vina, CA)—O.C.S.O.

[]—*Congregation of the Mother of the Redeemer* (Carthage, MO)—C.M.C.

[1000]—*Congregation of the Passion* (Chicago, IL)—C.P.

[]—*Crusade of the Holy Spirit.*

[0520]—*Franciscan Friars* (Prov. of St. Barbara, Oakland, CA)—O.F.M.

[0690]—*Jesuit Fathers and Brothers* (California Prov., Los Gatos, CA)—S.J.

[0930]—*Oblates of St. Joseph* (Santa Cruz, CA)—O.S.J.

[0950]—*Oratorians* (Columbia)—C.O.

[0430]—*Order of Preachers-Dominicans* (Oakland, CA)—O.P.

[1065]—*Priestly Fraternity of St. Peter*—F.S.S.P.

[]—*Pro Ecclesia Santa* (Lima, Peru)—P.E.S.

[1200]—*Society of the Divine Savior* (Milwaukee, WI)—S.D.S.

RELIGIOUS INSTITUTES OF WOMEN REPRESENTED IN THE DIOCESE

[]—*Adorers of the Holy Cross* (Portland, OR)—M.T.G.

[]—*Cistercian Nuns* (Vietnam)—O.Cist.

[0730]—*Daughters of Charity of Canossa* (Albuquerque, NM)—Fd.CC.

[0820]—*Daughters of the Holy Spirit* (Putnam, CT)—D.H.S.

[0420]—*Discalced Carmelite Nuns* (Georgetown, CA)—O.C.D.

[]—*Dominican Sisters of Mary, Mother of the Eucharist - Sacramento* (Ann Arbor, MI).

[2370]—*Institute of the Blessed Virgin Mary (Loretto Sisters)* (Wheaton, IL)—I.B.V.M.

[2575]—*Institute of the Sisters of Mercy of the Americas* (WMW, Omaha, NE)—R.S.M.

[]—*Missionaries of Charity* (Pacifica, CA)—M.C.

[]—*Religious of the Virgin Mary* (Quezon City, Philippines)—R.V.M.

[]—*Sisters Catechists of Jesus Crucified* (Mexico)—S.J.C.

[]—*Sisters of Mercy* (Redlands, CA, U.S. Province)—R.S.M.

[]—*Sisters of Notre Dame de Namur* (Belmont, CA)—S.N.D.

[4080]—*Sisters of Social Service of Los Angeles, Inc.* (Encino, CA)—S.S.S.

[1630]—*Sisters of St. Francis of Penance and Christian Charity* (Redwood City, CA)—O.S.F.

[]—*Sisters of the Holy Rosary of Fatima* (Salvatierra, Mexico)—H.R.F.

[]—*Verbum Dei Missionary Confraternity, San Francisco.*

DIOCESAN CEMETERIES

SACRAMENTO. *Catholic Funeral and Cemetery Services of the Diocese of Sacramento, Inc. (CFCS)* dba Calvary Catholic Cemetery & Mausoleum, 7101 Verner Ave., 95841. Tel: 707-644-5209; Email: tdinh@scd.org. 2110 Broadway, 95818. Jerry Del Core, CEO

Catholic Funeral and Cemetery Services of the Diocese of Sacramento, Inc. (CFCS) dba St. Joseph Catholic Cemetery, 2615 21st St., 95818. Tel: 916-452-4831; Fax: 916-452-1364; Email: tdinh@scd.org. 2110 Broadway, 95818. Jerry Del Core, CEO

Catholic Funeral and Cemetery Services of the Diocese of Sacramento, Inc. (CFCS) dba St. Mary's Catholic Cemetery & Mausoleum, 6509 Fruitridge Rd., 95820-5981. Tel: 916-452-4831; Fax: 916-452-1364; Email: tdinh@scd.org. 2110 Broadway, 95818. Jerry Del Core, CEO

COLUSA. *Catholic Funeral and Cemetery Services of the Diocese of Sacramento, Inc. (CFCS)* dba Holy Cross Catholic Cemetery, 1741 Westscott, Colusa, 95932. Tel: 916-726-1232; Fax: 916-726-4821. 2110 Broadway, 95818. Email: tdinh@scd.org. Jerry Del Core, CEO

FAIRFIELD. *Catholic Funeral and Cemetery Services of the Diocese of Sacramento, Inc. (CFCS)* dba St. Alphonsus Catholic Cemetery, 1801 Union Ave., Fairfield, 94533. Tel: 707-644-5209; Fax: 707-554-4091; Email: tdinh@scd.org. 2110 Broadway, 95818. Jerry Del Core, CEO

GRASS VALLEY. *St. Patrick's Cemetery*, 18044 Rough & Ready Hwy., Grass Valley, 95945. Tel: 916-733-0252; Email: jdelcore@scd.org. Jerry Del Core, CEO

RANCHO MURIETA. *Catholic Funeral and Cemetery Services of the Diocese of Sacramento, Inc. (CFCS)* dba St. Vincent DePaul Catholic Cemetery, Jackson Hwy., Rancho Murieta, 95683. Tel: 916-452-4831; Fax: 916-452-1364; Email: tdinh@scd.org. 2110 Broadway, 95818. Jerry Del Core, CEO

RIO VISTA. *Catholic Funeral and Cemetery Services of the Diocese of Sacramento, Inc. (CFCS)* dba St. Joseph Catholic Cemetery, Hwy. 12, Rio Vista, 94571. Tel: 916-452-4831; Fax: 916-452-1364; Email: jdelcore@scd.org. 2110 Broadway, 95818. Jerry Del Core, CEO

VALLEJO. *Catholic Funeral and Cemetery Services of the Diocese of Sacramento, Inc. (CFCS)* dba All Souls Catholic Cemetery & Mausoleum, 550 Glen Cove Rd., Vallejo, 94591. Tel: 707-644-5209; Fax: 707-554-4091; Email: tdinh@scd.org. 2110 Broadway, 95818. Jerry Del Core, CEO

Catholic Funeral and Cemetery Services of the Diocese of Sacramento, Inc. (CFCS) dba St. Vincent Cemetery, 550 Glen Cove Rd., Vallejo, 94591. Tel: 707-644-5209; Fax: 707-554-4091; Email: tdinh@scd.org. 2110 Broadway, 95818. Jerry Del Core, CEO

WOODLAND. *Catholic Funeral and Cemetery Services of*

the Diocese of Sacramento, Inc. (CFCS) dba St. Joseph Catholic Cemetery & Mausoleum, 503 California St., Woodland, 95695. Tel: 530-662-8645 ; Fax: 530-662-0796; Email: tdinh@scd.org. 2110 Broadway, 95818. Jerry Del Core, CEO

NECROLOGY

† Quinn, Francis A., Bishop Emeritus of Sacramento., Died Mar. 21, 2019
† Kavanagh, Edward J., (Retired), Died Mar. 17, 2018
† Brennan, Ronan P., (Retired), Died Oct. 26, 2018
† Duggan, Nicholas S., (Retired), Died Oct. 3, 2018
† Lawlor, Eugene Francis, (Retired), Died May. 17, 2018
† O'Hara, Edward, (Retired), Died Feb. 24, 2018

An asterisk (*) denotes an organization that has established tax-exempt status directly with the IRS and is not covered by the USCCB Group Ruling.

Diocese of Saginaw

(Dioecesis Saginavensis)

Most Reverend

WALTER A. HURLEY, J.C.L.

Apostolic Administrator of Saginaw and Retired Bishop of Grand Rapids; ordained June 5, 1965; appointed Titular Bishop of Chunavia and Auxiliary Bishop of Detroit July 7, 2003; consecrated August 12, 2003; appointed Bishop of Grand Rapids June 21, 2005; installed August 4, 2005; retired April 18, 2013; appointed Apostolic Administrator of Saginaw October 17, 2018.

(VACANT SEE)

Chancery: 5800 Weiss St., Saginaw, MI 48603-2762. Tel: 989-799-7910; Fax: 989-797-6670.

Web: www.saginaw.org

ESTABLISHED FEBRUARY 26, 1938.

Square Miles 6,955.

Comprises the following Counties in the State of Michigan: Arenac, Bay, Clare, Gladwin, Gratiot, Huron, Isabella, Midland, Saginaw, Sanilac and Tuscola.

For legal titles of parishes and diocesan institutions, consult the Chancery Office.

STATISTICAL OVERVIEW

Personnel	
Priests: Diocesan Active in Diocese	37
Priests: Diocesan Active Outside Diocese	7
Priests: Retired, Sick or Absent	36
Number of Diocesan Priests	80
Religious Priests in Diocese	5
Total Priests in Diocese	85
Extern Priests in Diocese	6
Ordinations:	
Diocesan Priests	1
Transitional Deacons	2
Permanent Deacons in Diocese	21
Total Sisters	60
Parishes	
Parishes	56
With Resident Pastor:	
Resident Diocesan Priests	37
Resident Religious Priests	4
Without Resident Pastor:	
Administered by Priests	4
Administered by Deacons	4
Administered by Religious Women	5
Administered by Lay People	2
Professional Ministry Personnel:	
Sisters	5
Lay Ministers	36
Welfare	
Catholic Hospitals	2
Total Assisted	131,467
Health Care Centers	1
Total Assisted	810
Homes for the Aged	1
Total Assisted	229
Residential Care of Children	2
Total Assisted	257
Specialized Homes	5
Total Assisted	809
Special Centers for Social Services	4
Total Assisted	1,060
Other Institutions	2
Total Assisted	23,000
Educational	
Diocesan Students in Other Seminaries	7
Total Seminarians	7
High Schools, Diocesan and Parish	3
Total Students	373
Elementary Schools, Diocesan and Parish	11
Total Students	1,711
Catechesis/Religious Education:	
High School Students	623
Elementary Students	2,906
Total Students under Catholic Instruction	5,620
Teachers in the Diocese:	
Lay Teachers	180
Vital Statistics	
Receptions into the Church:	
Infant Baptism Totals	650
Minor Baptism Totals	59
Adult Baptism Totals	75
Received into Full Communion	129
First Communions	697
Confirmations	783
Marriages:	
Catholic	167
Interfaith	109
Total Marriages	276
Deaths	1,399
Total Catholic Population	86,333
Total Population	688,110

Former Bishops—Most Revs. WILLIAM F. MURPHY, J.C.L., LL.D., S.T.D., ord. June 13, 1908; appt. first Bishop of Saginaw, March 17, 1938; cons. May 17, 1938; died Feb. 7, 1950; STEPHEN S. WOZNICKI, D.D., second Bishop; ord. Dec. 22, 1917; appt. Titular Bishop of Pelte and Auxiliary Bishop of Detroit, Dec. 13, 1937; cons. Jan. 25, 1938; transferred to Saginaw, March 28, 1950; Assistant at the Pontifical Throne, Dec. 22, 1967; resigned and transferred to the Titular See of Tiava, Oct. 30, 1968; died Dec. 10, 1968; FRANCIS F. REH, S.T.L., J.C.D., third Bishop; ord. Dec. 8, 1935; appt. Bishop of Charleston, June 4, 1962; cons. June 29, 1962; transferred to the Titular See of Macrinna in Maurentania; Rector Pontifical North American College in Rome, Sept. 5, 1964; transferred to Saginaw, Dec. 18, 1968; installed Feb. 26, 1969; retired April 29, 1980; died Nov. 14, 1994; KENNETH E. UNTENER, ord. June 1, 1963; ord. and installed as Bishop of Saginaw Nov. 24, 1980; died March 27, 2004.; ROBERT J. CARLSON, ord. May 22, 1970; appt. Titular Bishop of Aviocala and Auxiliary Bishop of Saint Paul and Minneapolis Nov. 22, 1983; cons. Jan. 11, 1984; appt. Coadjutor Bishop of Sioux Falls Jan. 13, 1994; Succeeded to the See March 21, 1995; appt. Bishop of Saginaw Dec. 29, 2004; installed Feb. 24, 2005; appt. Archbishop of St. Louis April 21, 2009.; JOSEPH R. CISTONE, ord. May 17, 1975; appt. Titular Bishop of Casae Medianae and Auxiliary Bishop of Philadelphia; ord. July 28, 2004; appt. Bishop of Saginaw May 20, 2009; installed July 28, 2009; died Oct. 16, 2018.

Vicar General—Very Rev. WILLIAM J. RUTKOWSKI.

Vicar for Priests—Rev. RONALD F. WAGNER, 5800 Weiss St., Saginaw, 48603. Tel: 989-797-6649.

Episcopal Vicars—

Territorial Vicars—Revs. RICHARD A. BOKINSKIE; ANDREW D. BOOMS; PETER J. GASPENY; ROBERT J. HOWE; PATRICK M. JANKOWIAK.

Hispanic Ministries Vicar—Rev. ALBERTO E. VARGAS, Tel: 989-797-6604.

Delegate for Religious—Sr. JANET FULGENZI, O.P., Ph. D., 5800 Weiss St., Saginaw, 48603-2799. Tel: 989-799-7910.

Chancery—5800 Weiss St., Saginaw, 48603-2799. Tel: 989-799-7910; Fax: 989-797-6670.

Chancellor—Sr. MARY JUDITH O'BRIEN, R.S.M., J.D., J.C.D., Tel: 989-797-6620.

Director of Human Resources—CONNIE HUISKENS WOJDA, Tel: 989-797-6687.

Financial and Business Operations—

Chief Financial Officer—DEBRA BIERLEIN, Tel: 989-797-6688.

Comptroller—MELISSA SEEGER, Tel: 989-797-6642.

Accounting Assistant—Tel: 989-797-6629. TAMMY SAMBORN.

Catholic Cemeteries—Tel: 989-797-6627. MRS. ALICE LEFEVRE.

Diocesan Finance Council—JOHN HUNT, Chm.

Diocesan Building Commission—RANDY BEYER, Chm., 5800 Weiss St., Saginaw, 48603-2799. Tel: 989-799-7910.

Diocesan Investment Committee—TIM DIJAK, Chm.

Inter-Parish Deposit & Loan—VACANT, Chm.

Catholic Services Appeal—LYNN BAERWOLF, 5800 Weiss St., Saginaw, 48603-2799. Tel: 989-797-6626.

Tribunal—5800 Weiss St., Saginaw, 48603-2799. Tel: 989-797-6623.

Judicial Vicar—Tel: 989-797-6622. Rev. RICHARD M. FILARY, J.C.L.

Auditor—Sr. JEAN T. BAUMANN, O.S.F., Tel: 989-797-6667.

Defenders of the Bond—Sr. VICTORIA VONDENBERGER, R.S.M., J.C.L.; Rev. THOMAS E. SUTTON, J.C.L.

Judges—Sr. MARY JUDITH O'BRIEN, R.S.M., J.D., J.C.D.; Revs. RICHARD M. FILARY, J.C.L.; EDWIN C. DWYER, J.C.L.

Promoter of Justice—

Notary—KIMBERLY VOELKER.

Diocesan Presbyteral Council—Rev. PETER J. GASPENY, Chm., 1035 N. River Rd., Saginaw, 48609. Tel: 989-781-2457.

Diocesan College of Consultors—Revs. ROBERT H. BYRNE, (Retired); PETER J. GASPENY; FREDERICK J. KAWKA, (Retired); Very Rev. WILLIAM J. RUTKOWSKI; Rev. RONALD F. WAGNER.

Clergy Personnel Board—Rev. WILLIAM R. TAYLOR, Chm., (Retired), 1525 S. Washington, Saginaw, 48601-2895. Tel: 989-755-8020.

Diocesan Council of Catholic Women—RITA FAITH MAHER, Pres., 3028 McGill St., Marlette, 48453.

Office of Communication—ERIN LOOBY CARLSON; TIM SPEAR; CHRISTOPHER PHAM, 5800 Weiss St., Saginaw, 48603-2799. Tel: 989-797-6630.

Mission Office—Tel: 989-797-6633.

Education/Formation—DR. DANIEL OSBORN, S.T.D., Dir. Center for Ministry, 5802 Weiss St., Saginaw, 48603. Tel: 989-797-6662; KELLIE DEMING, Coord. Lay Ministry, Tel: 989-797-6609; MARGARET MCEVOY, Coord. Faith Formation, Tel: 989-797-6608; MR. MARK GRAVELINE, Dir. Youth Ministry, Tel: 989-797-6639; PATRICIA D. PRESTON, Sec., Tel: 989-797-6654.

Catholic Schools—5800 Weiss St., Saginaw, 48603. Tel: 989-797-6651. CORMAC J. LYNN, Supt. Schools.

Bay Area Catholic Schools—607 E. South Union, Bay City, 48706. Tel: 989-894-8777. BRIAN CAMPBELL, Prin.

Saginaw Area Catholic Schools—MARK FROST, Pres. & Prin. Nouvel Catholic Central High School, 2555 Weineke Rd., Saginaw, 48603. Tel: 989-399-2221; Tel: 989-797-6632; Fax: 989-399-2257; MRS. IZABELLA LOPEZ, Prin., Nouvel Catholic Central Elementary, 21365 Berberovich St., Saginaw, 48603.

Ecumenism Ministry—Rev. JAMES R. CARLSON, (Retired), 5800 Weiss St., Saginaw, 48603. Tel: 989-790-5086.

Ministry to Charismatic Renewal—JUDY TROXELL, Dir., Charismatic Renewal Center, 1110 State St., Bay City, 48706. Tel: 989-684-4640.

Ministry to Priests—Rev. RONALD F. WAGNER, Vicar for Priests, Tel: 989-797-6649.

Office of Christian Service—TERRI GRIERSON, Dir., Tel: 989-797-6650; LORI BECKER, Respect Life Coord., Tel: 989-797-6652.

Coordinator of Marriage and Family Ministry—LINDA MILCO, Tel: 989-797-6660.

Office of Liturgy—Tel: 989-797-6664. Rev. JAMES W. BESSERT, Dir.; Sr. ESTHER MARY NICKEL; PAM BOURSCHEIDT, Assoc. Liturgical Music.

Organizations and Services—

Diocese of Saginaw Priests' Retirement Association—Rev. PETER J. GASPENY.

Holy Childhood Association—5800 Weiss St., Saginaw, 48603-2799. Tel: 989-797-6633.

Director of Development—Tel: 989-797-6624.

Office of Stewardship and Planned Giving—MS. GERI RUDOLF.

Victim Assistance Coordinator—Sr. JANET FULGENZI, O.P., Ph.D., Tel: 989-797-6682; Email: jfulgenzi@dioceseofsaginaw.org.

CLERGY, PARISHES, MISSIONS AND PAROCHIAL SCHOOLS

CITY OF SAGINAW

(SAGINAW COUNTY)

1—CATHEDRAL OF MARY OF THE ASSUMPTION (1853)
615 Hoyt Ave., 48607. Tel: 989-752-8119; Email: cathedral@cscluster.com. Most Reverend Walter A. Hurley, J.C.L., Apostolic Admin., (Retired); Rev. Richard E. Jozwiak, Sacramental Min.; Sr. Yvonne Mary Loucks, R.S.M., Pastoral Care Coord.
Convent—Our Lady of the Assumption Convent, Religious Sisters of Mercy Sisters 3.
Catechesis Religious Program—
Endowment—St. Mary Cathedral Parish Inter-Parish Endowment Fund.

2—ST. ANDREW, Merged with St. Helen, Saginaw to form Christ the Good Shepherd, Saginaw.

3—ST. ANTHONY OF PADUA, [JC] Merged with St. Casimir & St. George Church, Saginaw to form St. Francis of Assisi Parish, Saginaw.

4—SS. CASIMIR & ST. GEORGE, [JC] Merged with St. Anthony of Padua, Saginaw to form St. Francis of Assisi Parish, Saginaw.

5—CHRIST THE GOOD SHEPHERD PARISH
2445 N. Charles St., 48602. Tel: 989-793-0618; Email: ctgssaginaw@sbcglobal.net. Rev. Ronald F. Wagner.
St. Andrew Church, 612 N. Michigan Ave., 48602.

6—ST. DOMINIC PARISH
2711 Mackinaw St., 48602. Tel: 989-799-2334; Fax: 989-793-3611; Email: stdominic@stdominicsaginaw.org; Email: mary@stdominicsaginaw.org; Web: www.stdominicsaginaw.org. Rev. Steven M. Gavit.
Ss. Peter and Paul Church—4735 Washington Ave., 48638.
St. Stephen Church.
Catechesis Religious Program—Students 140.

7—ST. FRANCIS OF ASSISI
3680 S. Washington Rd., 48601. Tel: 989-752-1971; Email: stfrancissaginaw@gmail.com. Rev. Gerald Pehler. The parish office holds the sacramental records of St. George Church (closed), Saginaw.
St. Anthony of Padua—3680 S. Washington Rd., 48601-4966. Tel: 989-752-1971; Fax: 989-752-1441; Email: stfrancissaginaw@gmail.com.
St. Casimir Church, 2122 S. Jefferson Ave., 48601.
Catechesis Religious Program—Students 57.

8—ST. HELEN, [JC] Merged with St. Andrew, Saginaw to form Christ the Good Shepherd, Saginaw.

9—HOLY FAMILY, [CEM]
1525 S. Washington Ave., 48601. Tel: 989-755-8020; Email: office@holyfamilysaginaw.org; Web: www.holyfamilycatholicchurch-saginaw.org. Deacon Roger Pasionek, Pastoral Admin.

10—HOLY ROSARY, Closed. For inquiries for parish records contact St. Francis de Sales Parish, Bridgeport.

11—ST. JOHN VIANNEY
6400 McCarty Rd., 48603. Tel: 989-790-5086; Email: stjvianney6@aol.com; Web: www.sjvsaginaw.org. Sr. Janet Pewoski, C.S.J., Pastoral Admin.; Rev. William J. Rutkowski, Sacramental Min.; Deacon Richard A. Warner.
Catechesis Religious Program—Sr. Janet Pewoski, C.S.J., Faith Formation. Students 26.

12—ST. JOSEPH
936 N. Sixth Ave., 48601. Tel: 989-755-7561; Email: ddsasiela@stjosephsaginaw.org. Rev. Francis Voris, O.F.M.Cap.; Deacon Librado Gayton.
Catechesis Religious Program—Students 86.

13—OUR LADY HELP OF CHRISTIANS, Closed. For inquiries for parish records contact St. Francis de Sales Parish, Bridgeport.

14—OUR LADY OF MOUNT CARMEL, Closed. For inquiries for parish records contact St. Francis de Sales Parish, Bridgeport.

15—SS. PETER AND PAUL, Merged with St. Stephen Church, Saginaw to form St. Dominic Parish, Saginaw.

16—ST. RITA, Closed. For inquiries for parish records contact St. Francis de Sales Parish, Bridgeport.

17—SACRED HEART, Closed. For inquiries for parish records contact St. Francis de Sales Parish, Bridgeport.

18—SS. SIMON AND JUDE, Merged with St. Christopher, Bridgeport to form St. Francis de Sales, Bridgeport.

19—ST. STEPHEN, Merged with Ss. Peters and Paul Church, Saginaw to form St. Dominic Parish, Saginaw.

20—ST. THOMAS AQUINAS, [JC]
5376 State Rd., 48603. Tel: 989-799-2460; Email: rickb@stasaginaw.org; Email: dawnd@stasaginaw.org; Web: www.stasaginaw.org. Rev. Richard A. Bokinskie; Sr. Ann de Guise, O.S.F., Pastoral Assoc.
School—Nouvel Catholic Elementary Bernardine Sisters of Third Order of St. Francis, (Grades PreSchool-8), 2136 Berberovich, 48603.
Tel: 989-792-2361; Email: jsprague@nouvelcatholic.org; Web: www.nouvelcatholic.org. Mrs. Izabella Lopez, Prin.; Sr. Ann de Guise, O.S.F., Prin. (Farmington, MI) Lay Teachers 27; Sisters 3; Students 476.
Catechesis Religious Program—Students 26.

OUTSIDE THE CITY OF SAGINAW

ALBEE, SAGINAW CO., ST. MARY, Merged with Immaculate Conception Church, Saint Charles to form Mary of the Immaculate Conception, Saint Charles.

ALMA, GRATIOT CO.

1—ST. MARY, Merged with Mount St. Joseph, Saint Louis to form Nativity of the Lord Parish, Alma.

2—NATIVITY OF THE LORD PARISH
Tel: 989-463-5370; Email: nschultz@nativityparish.net. Rev. Nathan E. Harburg.
St. Mary Church—510 Prospect Ave., Alma, 48801-1633. Tel: 989-463-5370; Email: secretary@nativityparish.net; Web: www.nativityparish.net.
Mt. St. Joseph Church, 605 S. Franklin St., Saint Louis, 48880.
School—St. Mary School, Tel: 989-463-4579; Email: lseeley@nativityparish.net. Lisa Seeley, Prin. Lay Teachers 10; Students 107.
Catechesis Religious Program—Email: secretary@nativityparish.net. Students 36.

ARGYLE, SANILAC CO., ST. JOSEPH, [CEM] Merged with St. John the Evangelist Church, Ubly, St. Ignatius Church, Freiburg & St. Columbkille Church, Sheridan Corners to form Good Shepherd Parish, Ubly.

AUGRES, ARENAC CO., ST. MARK
415 S. Court St., Au Gres, 48703. Tel: 989-876-7925; Fax: 989-876-7778; Email: stmark@centurytel.net. Revs. Gerald E. Balwinski, Sacramental Min., (Retired); Thomas M. Kowalczyk, Sacramental Min., (Retired); Colleen McCormick Snyder, Pastoral Min./Coord. Parish office has sacramental records of closed St. Edward Church, Omer.
Catechesis Religious Program—Yolanda Collier, Faith Formation. Students 17.

AUBURN, BAY CO., ST. GABRIEL PARISH, Rev. Thomas E. Sutton, J.C.L. Parish office has sacramental records of St. Anthony Church, Auburn (Fisherville).
St. Joseph Church—84 W. Midland Rd., Auburn, 48611.
St. Anthony Church, 1492 W. Midland Rd., Auburn, 48611.
Schools—Area School—(Grades PreSchool-5), Tel: 989-662-6431; Email: rmilne@auburnac.org. Mr. Robert Milne, Prin. Lay Teachers 8; Students 100.
Auburn Area Catholic, Early Childhood Center, (Grades PreSchool-5), 114 W. Midland Rd., Auburn, 48611. Tel: 989-662-6431; Fax: 989-662-3391.
Catechesis Religious Program—Students 67.

BAD AXE, HURON CO.

1—ST. HUBERT PARISH
Tel: 989-269-7729; Email: st.hubertparish@yahoo.com. Rev. Robert J. Howe.
Sacred Heart Church—311 Whitelam St., Bad Axe, 48413-1205.
St. Joseph Church, 3455 Rapson Rd., Rapson, 48413.
Catechesis Religious Program—Students 123.

2—SACRED HEART, [CEM] Merged with St. Joseph, Rapson and Most Holy Trinity, Smith Corners to form St. Hubert Parish, Bad Axe.

BANNISTER, GRATIOT CO., ST. CYRIL
517 E. Main St., PO Box 96, Bannister, 48807. Tel: 989-862-5207; Email: ckleinstcyrilchurch@gmail.com. Rev. William J. Gruden.
Catechesis Religious Program—Students 26.

BAY CITY, BAY CO.

1—ALL SAINTS PARISH
Tel: 989-893-4693; Email: allsaintsparishbaycity@gmail.com; Web: www.allsaintsparishbaycity.org. Revs. Jose Maria Cabrera; Stephen Fillion, In Res., (Retired); Thomas J. Fleming, In Res.
St. James Church—710 Columbus Ave., Bay City, 48708.
St. Boniface Church, 500 N. Lincoln St., Bay City, 48708.
Our Lady of Guadalupe Church, 1619 Broadway, Bay City, 48708.
School—All Saints, (Grades PreK-5),
Tel: 989-892-4371. Lisa Rhodus, Prin. Lay Teachers 10; Students 216.
Catechesis Religious Program—Students 82.
Convent—200 S. Farragut St., Bay City, 48708.

2—ST. BONIFACE, Merged with St. James, Bay City & Our Lady of Guadalupe, Bay City to form All Saints, Bay City.

3—ST. CATHERINE OF SIENA PARISH
Tel: 989-684-1203; Email: office@scsparish.com; Web: www.scsparish.com. Rev. John S. Sarge, Sacramental Min., (Retired); Jane Grzegorczyk, Pastoral Admin.
St. Vincent de Paul Church—2956 E. North Union Rd., Bay City, 48706. Tel: 989-684-1203; Email: office@scsparish.com.
St. Maria Goretti Church, 2872 N. Euclid Rd., Bay City, 48706.
Catechesis Religious Program—Students 72.

4—CORPUS CHRISTI PARISH
1008 S. Wenona St., Bay City, 48706.
Tel: 989-893-4073; Email: parish2014@corpus-christi-parish.com. Revs. Robert J. Kelm, Parochial Admin.; Kevin Kerbawy.
St. Hedwig Church, 1504 S. Kiesel St., Bay City, 48706.
Catechesis Religious Program—Students 129.

5—ST. HEDWIG, Merged with Holy Trinity, Bay City to form Corpus Christi Parish, Bay City.

6—HOLY TRINITY, Merged with St. Hedwig, Bay City to form Corpus Christi, Bay City.

7—ST. HYACINTH, [CEM] Merged with St. Stanislaus Kostka, Bay City to form Our Lady of Czestochowa, Bay City.

8—ST. JAMES (1983) [CEM] Merged with St. Boniface, Bay City and Our Lady of Guadalupe, Bay City to form All Saints, Bay City.

9—ST. JOSEPH, Merged with St. John the Evangelist, Essexville & St. Norbert, Munger to form St. Jude Thaddeus, Essexville.

10—ST. MARIA GORETTI, Merged with St. Vincent de Paul, Bay City to form St. Catherine of Siena, Bay City.

11—ST. MARY OF THE ASSUMPTION, Merged with Our Lady of the Visitation, Bay City to form Our Lady of Peace, Bay City.

12—OUR LADY OF CZESTOCHOWA PARISH
Tel: 989-893-6421; Email: parisholc@baycityolc.com; Web: www.baycityolc.com. Rev. Richard M. Filary, J.C.L.; Deacon Stanley Kuczynski.
St. Stanislaus Kostka Church—1503 Kosciuszko Ave., Bay City, 48708.
St. Hyacinth Church, 1515 Cass Ave., Bay City, 48708.
Catechesis Religious Program—Email: eileena@baycityolc.com. Students 76.

13—OUR LADY OF GUADALUPE, Merged with St. James, Bay City and St. Boniface, Bay City to form All Saints, Bay City.

14—OUR LADY OF PEACE PARISH
607 E. S. Union St., Bay City, 48706.
Tel: 989-892-6031; Email: office@baycityourladyofpeace.com. Rev. Edwin C. Dwyer, J.C.L., Admin.; Deacon Kenneth M. Kochany. Parish has records of Our Lady of Visitation Parish, Bay City.
Catechesis Religious Program—Students 33.

15—ST. STANISLAUS KOSTKA, Merged with St.

Hyacinth, Bay City to form Our Lady of Czestochowa, Bay City.
16—ST. VINCENT DE PAUL, Merged with St. Maria Goretti, Bay City to form St. Catherine, Bay City.
BEAL CITY, ISABELLA CO., ST. JOSEPH THE WORKER, [CEM]
2163 N. Winn Rd., Mount Pleasant, 48858.
Tel: 989-644-2041; Email: stjosephtheworkerbcparish@gmail.com. Rev. Thomas R. Held, Parochial Admin.
School—St. Joseph the Worker School, (Grades PreK-6), Tel: 989-644-3970; Email: mhauck325@gmail.com. Mrs. Mary Hauck, Prin. Lay Teachers 9; Students 89.
Catechesis Religious Program—Students 49.
BEAVER, BAY CO., ST. VALENTINE, [CEM] Merged with St. Anne, Linwood & Sacred Heart, Kawkawlin to form Prince of Peace, Linwood.
BIRCH RUN, SAGINAW CO.
1—SS. FRANCIS & CLARE PARISH
12157 Church St., Birch Run, 48415.
Tel: 989-624-9098; Email: ssfandcparishoffice@gmail.com. Revs. Randy J. Kelly, Sacramental Min., (Retired); Thomas J. McNamara, Sacramental Min., (Retired); Sr. Kathy Onderbeke, Admin. Parish office has sacramental records of Assumption of the Blessed Virgin Mary Church, Bridgeport (closed).
Catechesis Religious Program—Students 102.
2—SACRED HEART, Merged with Assumption of the Blessed Virgin Mary Church, Bridgeport to form Ss. Francis and Clare Parish, Birch Run.
BRIDGEPORT, SAGINAW CO.
1—ST. CHRISTOPHER, Merged with SS. Simon & Jude, Saginaw to form St. Francis de Sales, Bridgeport.
2—ST. FRANCIS DE SALES PARISH
3945 Williamson Rd., 48601. Tel: 989-777-2091; Email: sfdssaginaw@yahoo.com. Rev. John Mancini, O.S.F.S. Parish offices have the sacramental records of the following closed Saginaw churches: St. Simon & Jude; Holy Rosary; Our Lady Help of Christians; St. Rita; and Sacred Heart.
St. Christopher Church.
Catechesis Religious Program—Students 13.
CARO, TUSCOLA CO.
1—ST. CHRISTOPHER PARISH
910 W. Frank St., Caro, 48723. Tel: 989-673-2346; Email: scp@cmstchristopher.org. Rev. Jerzy Dobosz, Admin.
Sacred Heart Church—140 Atwood St., Caro, 48723.
St. Joseph Church, 315 W. Ohmer Rd., Mayville, 48744.
Catechesis Religious Program—Students 100.
2—SACRED HEART, [CEM] Merged with St. Joseph, Mayville to form St. Christopher, Caro.
CARROLLTON, SAGINAW CO.
1—SAINT JOHN PAUL II PARISH
3431 Jefferson, Carrollton, 48724. Tel: 989-755-0828; Email: office@stjohnpauliicc.org. Rev. James W. Bessert, Sacramental Min.; Sr. Christine Gretka, C.S.J., Pastoral Admin. Parish office has sacramental records of St. John the Baptist Church, Carrollton (closed).
St. Josaphat Church—469 Shattuck Rd., 48604.
St. Matthew Church, 511 W. Cornell St., 48604.
Catechesis Religious Program—Students 26.
2—ST. JOSAPHAT, Merged with St. John the Baptist, Carrollton & St. Matthew, Zilwaukee to form St. John Paul II, Carrollton.
CASEVILLE, HURON CO.
1—OUR LADY OF PERPETUAL HELP PARISH
Tel: 989-856-4933; Email: OLPH6.27@gmail.com. Rev. Robert Pare.
St. Roch Church—6253 Main St., P.O. Box 1238, Caseville, 48725-1238.
St. Francis Borgia Church, 25 Moeller St., Pigeon, 48755.
St. Felix of Valois Church, 3515 Limerick Rd., Pigeon, 48755.
Catechesis Religious Program—Students 14.
2—ST. ROCH, Merged with St. Francis Borgia Church, Pigeon and St. Felix of Valois Church, Pinnebog to form Our Lady of Perpetual Help Parish, Caseville.
CASS CITY, TUSCOLA CO.
1—OUR LADY CONSOLATA PARISH
4618 South St, P.O. Box 139, Gagetown, 48735-0139. Rev. Adam Maher, Parochial Admin. Parish church has records of former St. Jude Church in Fairgrove.
St. Pancratius Church—4292 S. Seeger St., Cass City, 48726.
Holy Family Church, 8370 Unionville Rd., Sebewaing, 48759.
St. Agatha Church, 4618 South St., Box 139, Gagetown, 48735.
St. Michael Church, 1951 Kingston Rd., Deford, 48729.
Catechesis Religious Program—Email: parishoffice@stpancc.com. Students 59.
2—ST. PANCRATIUS, Merged with Holy Family, Sebewaing, St. Agatha, Gagetown & St. Michael, Wilmot to form Our Lady Consolata, Cass City.
CHESANING, SAGINAW CO.
1—OUR LADY OF PERPETUAL HELP, [CEM] Merged with St. Michael Church, Oakley to form St. Peter Parish, Chesaning.
2—ST. PETER PARISH
404 S. Wood St., P.O. Box 454, Chesaning, 48616.
Tel: 989-845-1794; Email: kapullman@gmail.com; Web: www.stpeterchesaning.org. Rev. William J. Gruden.
Our Lady of Perpetual Help Church—
St. Michael Church, 509 Parshall St., Oakley, 48649.
Catechesis Religious Program—Students 94.
CLARE, CLARE CO.
1—ST. CECILIA, [CEM] Merged with St. Henry-St. Charles, Rosebush to form Our Lady of Hope, Clare.
2—OUR LADY OF HOPE PARISH
Tel: 989-386-9862; Fax: 989-386-3550; Email: parish@olhclare.org. Rev. Peter Nwokoye, Parochial Admin. Parish offices has the sacramental records of St. Charles, Leaton,
St. Cecilia Church—106 E. Wheaton Ave., Clare, 48617.
St. Henry Church, 4079 E. Vernon Rd., Rosebush, 48878.
Catechesis Religious Program—Students 53.
COLEMAN, MIDLAND CO., ST. PHILIP NERI, Merged with St. Anne Church, Edenville & St. Agnes Church, Sanford to form Our Lady of Grace Parish, Sanford.
ESSEXVILLE, BAY CO.
1—ST. JOHN THE EVANGELIST, Merged with St. Norbert, Munger & St. Joseph, Bay City to form St. Jude Thaddeus, Essexville.
2—ST. JUDE THADDEUS PARISH
Tel: 989-894-2701, Ext. 111; Email: stjudebkkpr@gmail.com; Web: www.stjudethaddeus.org. Rev. Dale A. Orlik; Deacon Timothy S. Hartwig. The parish office has sacramental records of St. Joseph Church, Bay City (closed) and St. Norbert Church, Munger (closed).
St. John the Evangelist Church—614 Pine St., Essexville, 48732.
St. Joseph Church, 1005 Third St., Bay City, 48708.
Catechesis Religious Program—Students 168.
FRANKENMUTH, SAGINAW CO., BLESSED TRINITY
958 E. Tuscola St., Frankenmuth, 48734.
Tel: 989-652-3259; Email: lsnyder@blessedtrinityfrankenmuth.org; Web: www.blessedtrinityfrankenmuth.org. Deacon Lawrence Deford.
Catechesis Religious Program—Students 161.
FREELAND, SAGINAW CO., ST. AGNES
300 Johnson St., Freeland, 48623. Tel: 989-695-5652; Email: StAgnesParish@aol.com. Sheila Bugbee, Pastoral Admin Pro Tem.
Catechesis Religious Program—Students 232.
GAGETOWN, TUSCOLA CO., ST. AGATHA, Merged with St. Pancratius, Cass City, Holy Family, Sebewaing & St. Michael, Wilmot to form Our Lady Consolata, Cass City.
GLADWIN, GLADWIN CO., SACRED HEART
330 N. Silverleaf St., Gladwin, 48624.
Tel: 989-426-7154; Email: sacredheartgladwin@gmail.com; Web: gladwinharrisoncatholic.com. Rev. Joseph Marcel Portelli.
Catechesis Religious Program—Students 40.
HARBOR BEACH , HURON CO.
1—HOLY NAME OF MARY PARISH
Tel: 989-479-3393; Email: hnomp@holynameofmaryparish.org; Web: www.holynameofmaryparish.org. Rev. George Amos, Parochial Admin.
Our Lady of Lake Huron Church—413 S. 1st St., Harbor Beach, 48441-1324.
St. Anthony of Padua Church, 8239 Helena Rd., Harbor Beach, 48441.
School—Our Lady of Lake Huron School, (Grades PreK-8), Tel: 989-479-3427; Email: cgoulet@ollhschool.org. Mrs. Cathryne Goulet, Prin. Lay Teachers 7; Students 132.
Catechesis Religious Program—Students 88.
2—OUR LADY OF LAKE HURON, [CEM] Merged with St. Anthony of Padua Church, Helena to form Holy Name of Mary Parish, Harbor Beach.
HARRISON, CLARE CO., ST. ATHANASIUS
310 S. Broad St., Harrison, 48625. Tel: 989-539-6232 ; Email: stathanasiusparish@gmail.com. Rev. Joseph Marcel Portelli, Parochial Admin.
Catechesis Religious Program—Students 6.
HELENA, HURON CO., ST. ANTHONY, [CEM] Merged with Our Lady of Lake Huron Church, Harbor Beach to form Holy Name of Mary Parish, Harbor Beach.
HEMLOCK, SAGINAW CO.
1—ST. JOHN XXIII PARISH
Tel: 989-642-5606; Email: secretary@stjohn23.net. Rev. Dennis H. Kucharczyk.
St. Mary Church—151 St. Mary's Dr., Hemlock, 48626.
Sacred Heart Church, 419 S. Midland St., Merrill, 48637.
St. Patrick Church, 4708 S. Meridian Rd., Merrill, 48637.
Catechesis Religious Program—Students 47.
2—ST. MARY, [CEM] Merged with Sacred Heart, Merrill & St. Patrick, Ryan to form St. John XXIII, Hemlock.
IRISHTOWN, ISABELLA CO., ST. PATRICK CHURCH, Merged Please see listing under St. Vincent de Paul, Shepherd.
ITHACA, GRATIOT CO., ST. PAUL THE APOSTLE PARISH
121 N. Union St., Ithaca, 48847. Tel: 989-875-2852; Email: stpaultheapostle@yahoo.com. Rev. Andrzej Boroch.
Catechesis Religious Program—Students 29.
St. Martin De Porres Church, 4010 W. Cleveland Rd., Perrinton, Gratiot Co. 48871.
KAWKAWLIN, BAY CO., SACRED HEART, Merged with St. Anne, Linwood & St. Valentine, Beaver to form Prince of Peace, Linwood.
KINDE, HURON CO., ST. MARY-ST. EDWARD, Merged with St. Michael Church, Port Austin to form Annunciation of the Lord Parish, Port Austin.
LEXINGTON, SANILAC CO.
1—AVE MARIA PARISH
Tel: 810-359-5400; Email: avemariaparish@gmail.com; Web: www.avemariaparishmi.org. Rev. Donald J. Eppenbrock, Sacramental Min., (Retired); Sr. Maria Inviolata Honma, S.M.D.G., Parochial Admin.
St. Mary, Our Lady of Sorrows Church, 7066 Main St., Port Sanilac, 48469.
Catechesis Religious Program—Students 72.
2—ST. DENIS, [CEM] Merged with St. Mary, Our Lady of Sorrows Church, Port Sanilac and St. Patrick Church, Croswell to form Ave Maria Parish, Lexington.
LINWOOD, BAY CO.
1—ST. ANNE, Merged with Sacred Heart, Kawkawlin & St. Valentine, Beaver to form Prince of Peace, Linwood.
2—PRINCE OF PEACE PARISH
Tel: 989-697-4443, Ext. 221; Email: office@princeofpeaceparish.net; Web: www.princeofpeaceparish.net. Rev. Nicholas F. Coffaro; Deacons Michael Arnold; Lee Stillwell, (Retired).
St. Anne Church—315 W. Center St., Linwood, 48634. Tel: 989-697-4443; Email: office@princeofpeace.net; Web: www.princeofpeaceparish.net.
Sacred Heart Church, 2510 Fraser Rd., Kawkawlin, 48631.
St. Valentine Church, 999 S. 9 Mile Rd., Kawkawlin, 48631.
Catechesis Religious Program—Students 82.
MAPLE GROVE, SAGINAW CO., ST. MICHAEL, [CEM]
17994 Lincoln Rd., New Lothrop, 48460.
Tel: 989-845-7010; Fax: 989-845-4729; Email: stmichaelchurchmg@hotmail.com; Web: stmichaelsmaplegrove.org. Rev. John F. Cotter.
Catechesis Religious Program—Students 235.
MARLETTE, SANILAC CO., ST. ELIZABETH, Merged with St. Joseph Church, Sandusky & St. John the Evangelist Church, Peck to form Holy Family Parish, Sandusky.
MAYVILLE, TUSCOLA CO., ST. JOSEPH, Merged with Sacred Heart, Caro to form St. Christopher, Caro.
MERRILL, SAGINAW CO., SACRED HEART, [CEM] Merged with St. Mary, Hemlock & St. Patrick, Ryan to form St. John XXIII, Hemlock.
MIDLAND, MIDLAND CO.
1—ASSUMPTION OF THE BLESSED VIRGIN MARY
3516 E. Monroe Rd., Midland, 48642.
Tel: 989-631-4447; Email: assumption@assumptionmidland.org. Rev. Joseph M. Griffin.
2—BLESSED SACRAMENT
3109 Swede Ave., Midland, 48642. Tel: 989-835-6777 ; Email: admin@blessed-midland.org. Rev. Kevin M. Maksym.
School—Blessed Sacrament School, (Grades PreSchool-5), Mr. Patrick Bevier, Prin. Lay Teachers 7; Students 100.
Catechesis Religious Program—Students 434.
3—ST. BRIGID
207 Ashman St., Midland, 48640. Tel: 989-835-7121; Email: stbrigid@stbrigid-midland.org. Rev. Andrew D. Booms; Deacons Daniel J. Corbat, Chap.; Francis W. Hudson; Aloysius J. Oliver.
School—St. Brigid School, (Grades K-8), 130 W. Larkin St., Midland, 48640-6579. Tel: 989-835-9481; Fax: 989-835-9141; Email: school@stbrigid-midland.org. Ms. Laura Wilkowski, Prin. Lay Teachers 14; Students 128.
Catechesis Religious Program—Anne Marie Graham, D.R.E. Students 94.
MOUNT PLEASANT, ISABELLA CO.
1—ST. MARY UNIVERSITY PARISH
1405 S. Washington St., Mount Pleasant, 48858.
Tel: 989-773-3931; Email: office@stmarycmu.org. Rev. Patrick M. Jankowiak.
Endowment—St. Mary University Parish Inter-Parish Endowment Fund.

2—MOST SACRED HEART OF JESUS, [CEM]
302 S. Kinney Ave., Mount Pleasant, 48858.
Tel: 989-772-1385; Email: brau@sha.net; Web: www.sha.net. Revs. Loren M. Kalinowski; Donald Henkes, Sacramental Min., (Retired); Deacons James Damitio; Larry Fussman.
High School—Sacred Heart Academy, (Grades 7-12), 316 E. Michigan Ave., Mount Pleasant, 48858.
Tel: 989-772-1457; Email: myonker@sha.net. Mary Kay Yonker, Prin. Lay Teachers 16; Priests 1; Students 224.
Catechesis Religious Program—Students 73.
MUNGER, BAY CO., ST. NORBERT, Merged with St. John the Evangelist, Essexville & St. Joseph, Bay City to form St. Jude Thaddeus, Bay City.
OAKLEY, SAGINAW CO., ST. MICHAEL, [CEM] Merged with Our Lady of Perpetual Help, Chesaning to form St. Peter Parish, Chesaning.
PALMS, SANILAC CO., ST. PATRICK, Merged with St. Mary Church, Parisville to form St. Isidore Parish, Parisville.
PARISVILLE, HURON CO.
1—ST. ISIDORE PARISH
Tel: 989-864-3523; Email: stisadoreparish@yahoo.com. Rev. Todd Arnberg.
St. Mary Church—4190 Parisville Rd., Parisville, 48470-0022.
St. Patrick Church, 1801 Palms Rd., Palms, 48465-9604.
Catechesis Religious Program—Tel: 989-864-3164; Email: stisadoreparish@yahoo.com. Students 33.
2—ST. MARY CHURCH, Merged with St. Patrick Church, Palms to form St. Isidore Parish, Parisville.
PIGEON, HURON CO., ST. FRANCIS BORGIA, [CEM] Merged with St. Roch Church, Caseville and St. Felix of Valois Church, Pinnebog to form Our Lady of Perpetual Help Parish, Caseville.
PINCONNING, BAY CO.
1—HOLY TRINITY PARISH
Tel: 989-879-2141; Email: denise@holytrinitypinconning.org. Rev. James R. Carlson, Sacramental Min., (Retired); Deacon Gary Patelski, Pastoral Admin. Records of St. Agnes Church maintained by Holy Trinity Parish Office.
St. Mary Church—739 W. Cody-Etsey Rd., Pinconning, 48650.
St. Michael Church, 225 S. Jenning St., Pinconning, 48650. Tel: 989-879-2141; Fax: 989-879-6633; Email: dlp3364@hotmail.com.
School—St. Michael School, (Grades PreK-8), Tel: 989-879-3063; Email: ayers.ashley@gmail.com. Ashley Kanuszewski, Prin.; Mrs. Norma Vallad, Admin. Lay Teachers 8; Students 109.
Endowment—St. Michael Catholic School Foundation Endowment Fund, St. Michael Catholic School Foundation Endowment Fund.
Catechesis Religious Program—Ashley Kanuszewski, Prin. Students 100.
2—ST. MARY, [CEM] Merged with St. Michael Parish, Pinconning to form Holy Trinity Parish, Pinconning.
3—ST. MICHAEL, Merged with St. Mary Parish, Pinconning to form Holy Trinity Parish, Pinconning.
PINNEBOG, HURON CO., ST. FELIX, [CEM] Merged with St. Francis Borgia Church, Pigeon and St. Roch Church, Caseville to form Our Lady of Perpetual Help Parish, Caseville.
PORT AUSTIN, HURON CO.
1—ANNUNCIATION OF THE LORD PARISH
8661 Independence St., P.O. Box 355, Port Austin, 48467-0355. Tel: 989-738-7521; Email: annunciationparish@centurytel.net; Web: www.annunciationofthelordparish.weebly.com. Rev. Craig Carolan, Parochial Admin.
St. Edward Church—5083 Park St., Kinde, 48445.
St. Mary Church, 1709 Moeller Rd., Kinde, 48445.
Catechesis Religious Program—8650 Independence St., Port Austin, 48467. Students 28.
2—ST. MICHAEL, [CEM] Merged with St. Mary-St. Edward, Kinde to form Annunciation of the Lord Parish, Port Austin.
PORT SANILAC, SANILAC CO., ST. MARY, [CEM] Merged with St. Denis Church, Lexington and St. Patrick Church, Croswell to form Ave Maria Parish, Lexington.
RAPSON, HURON CO., ST. JOSEPH, [CEM] Merged with Sacred Heart Church, Bad Axe and Most Holy Trinity, Smith Corners to form St. Hubert Parish, Bad Axe.
REESE, TUSCOLA CO., ST. ELIZABETH, [CEM]
12835 E. Washington Rd., P.O. Box 392, Reese, 48757. Tel: 989-868-4081; Email: stelizabethreese@gmail.com. Rev. Christian F. Tabares.
School—(Grades PreSchool-8), Tel: 989-868-4108. M. Gabriela Marguery Costoya, Prin. Lay Teachers 7; Students 81.
Catechesis Religious Program—Students 65.
ROSEBUSH, ISABELLA CO., ST. HENRY-ST. CHARLES, [CEM] Merged with St. Cecilia Church, Clare & St. Charles Church, Beal City to form Our Lady of Hope Parish, Clare.
RUTH, HURON CO.
1—HOLY APOSTLES PARISH
7121 E. Atwater Rd., Ruth, 48470-8507.
Tel: 989-864-3649; Email: holyapostlesruth@gmail.com. 7135 E. Atwater Rd., P.O. Box 55, Ruth, 48470-0055. Rev. Christopher M. Coman, Parochial Admin.
SS. Peter and Paul Church—
St. John Chrysostom Church, 7939 3rd St., Forestville, 48434.
Catechesis Religious Program—Students 51.
2—SS. PETER AND PAUL, [CEM] Merged with St. John Chrysostom Church, Pt. Sanilac to form Holy Apostles Parish, Ruth.
RYAN, MIDLAND CO., ST. PATRICK, [CEM] Merged with St. Mary, Hemlock & Sacred Heart, Merrill to form St. John XXIII, Hemlock.
ST. CHARLES, SAGINAW CO.
1—IMMACULATE CONCEPTION, [CEM] Merged with St. Mary Church, Albee to form Mary of the Immaculate Conception, Saint Charles.
2—MARY OF THE IMMACULATE CONCEPTION PARISH
708 Sanderson St., PO Box 39, St. Charles, 48655.
Tel: 989-865-9460; Fax: 989-865-6699; Email: maryoftheimmaculatec@yahoo.com. Rev. John F. Cotter.
St. Mary Church, 5661 Fergus Rd., Saint Charles, 48655-9694.
Catechesis Religious Program—Students 48.
ST. LOUIS, GRATIOT CO., MOUNT ST. JOSEPH, Merged with St. Mary, Alma to form Nativity of the Lord Parish, Alma.
SANDUSKY, SANILAC CO.
1—HOLY FAMILY PARISH
Tel: 810-648-2968; Email: holyfamilyparish1@gmail.com; Web: www.holyfamilyparishsanilaccounty.com. Rev. Robert Schikora.
St. Joseph Church—59 N. Moore St., Sandusky, 48471-0249.
St. Elizabeth Church, 6785 Marlette St., Marlette, 48453.
St. John the Evangelist Church, 5335 Sandusky Rd., Peck, 48466.
Catechesis Religious Program—Students 76.
2—ST. JOSEPH, Merged with St. Elizabeth Church, Marlette & St. John the Evangelist Church, Peck to form Holy Family Parish, Sandusky.
SANFORD, MIDLAND CO.
1—ST. AGNES, Merged with St. Anne Church, Edenville & St. Philip Neri Church, Coleman to form Our Lady of Grace Parish, Sanford.
2—OUR LADY OF GRACE PARISH
Tel: 989-687-5657; Email: father.dan@ourladyofgracemi.org. Rev. Daniel Fox, O.F.M.-Cap.
St. Agnes Church—2500 N. West River Rd., Sanford, 48657-9418.
St. Anne Church, 5738 M-30, Edenville, 48620.
St. Philip Neri Church, 5199 Shaffer Rd., Coleman, 48618. Records of St. Philip Neri Church are at St. Agnes Church, Sanford.
Catechesis Religious Program—Students 116.
SEBEWAING, HURON CO., HOLY FAMILY, [CEM] Merged with St. Pancratius, Cass City, St. Agatha, Gagetown & St. Michael, Wilmot to form Our Lady Consolata, Cass City.
SHEPHERD, ISABELLA CO., ST. VINCENT DE PAUL, [CEM]
168 Wright Ave., Shepherd, 48883.
Tel: 989-828-5720; Email: office@stvincentdp.com; Web: stvincentdp.com. Rev. Frederick J. Kawka, Sacramental Min., (Retired); Deacon Todd S. Lovas. Parish office has sacramental records of St. Leo the Great Parish, Winn (closed).
St. Patrick Church, 7631 N. County Line, Irishtown, Gratiot Co. 48883.
Catechesis Religious Program—Students 52.
SHIELDS, SAGINAW CO., HOLY SPIRIT
1035 N. River Rd., 48609. Tel: 989-781-2457; Email: angela@saginawhsp.org; Web: www.saginawhsp.org. Rev. Peter J. Gaspeny; Deacon Steven George; Kathleen Myles, Pastoral Min./Coord.
Catechesis Religious Program—Students 141.
STANDISH, ARENAC CO., RESURRECTION OF THE LORD, [CEM]
423 W. Cedar St., P.O. Box 306, Standish, 48658.
Tel: 989-846-9565; Email: resurrectionchurchstandish@yahoo.com. Rev. David L. Parsch.
St. Joseph Church, 7842 Newberry St., Alger, Arenac Co. 48610.
Catechesis Religious Program—Students 45.
UBLY, HURON CO.
1—ST. COLUMBKILLE, [CEM] Merged with St. John the Evangelist Church, Ubly, St. Ignatius Church, Freiburg & St. Joseph Church, Argyle to form Good Shepherd Parish, Ubly.
3031 McAlpin Rd., Sheridan Corners, 48475.
2—GOOD SHEPHERD PARISH
Tel: 989-658-8824; Email: goodshepherd48475@yahoo.com. Rev. Charles A. Hammond.
St. John the Evangelist Church—4470 N. Washington St., Ubly, 48475. Tel: 989-658-8824; Email: goodshepherd48475@yahoo.com.
St. Columbkille Church, 3031 McAlpin Rd., Sheridan Corners, 48475.
St. Ignatius Church, 1826 Cumber Rd., Freiburg, 48410.
St. Joseph Church, 4960 Ubly Rd., Argyle, 48410.
Catechesis Religious Program—Students 109.
3—ST. JOHN THE EVANGELIST, [CEM] Merged with St. Columbkille Church, Sheridan Corners, St. Ignatius Church, Freiburg & St. Joseph Church, Argyle to form Good Shepherd Parish, Ubly.
VASSAR, TUSCOLA CO., ST. FRANCES XAVIER CABRINI, Records of St. Bernard, Millington are kept at the parish office.
334 Division St., Vassar, 48768. Tel: 989-823-2911; Email: office@stfrancescabrini.co. Rev. Christian F. Tabares.
Catechesis Religious Program—Students 6.
WILMOT, TUSCOLA CO., ST. MICHAEL, [CEM] Merged with St. Pancratius, Cass City, Holy Family, Sebewaing & St. Agatha, Gagetown to form Our Lady Consolata, Cass City.
ZILWAUKEE, SAGINAW CO., ST. MATTHEW, Merged with St. Josaphat, Carrollton & St. John the Baptist, Carrollton to form St. John Paul II, Carrollton.

Chaplains of Public Institutions

BAY CITY. *Bay Medical Center and Bay Osteopathic Hospital*, 1201 S. Erie, Bay City, 48706. Sr. Jean Woloszak, O.P.

Outside the Diocese:
Revs.—
Falsey, James E., (Retired), 1237 Bradway Rd., North Pole, AK
Fitzpatrick, James M., (Retired), 2906 Connon St., Alpena, 49707
Friske, Joseph P., (Retired), Burgermeister-Keller Strasse, Munich, Germany 81829
Jenuwine, David, Diocese of Santa Rosa, 985 Airway Ct., Santa Rosa, CA 95403
Loos, Frederick C., (Retired), Sierra San Pedro #1, Col/Benita Juarez, Naucalpan, Mexico 53790. Apdo. 77-02 Lomas de Sotelo, Mexico City, D.F. Mexico C.P. 11201
Mullet, John, 1200 Seventh Ave., Saint Petersburg, FL 33705
Roa, Daniel, St. Eugene Cathedral, 2323 Montgomery Dr., Santa Rosa, CA 95405
Spencer, William W., (Retired), 2348 Nixon Rd., Ann Arbor, 48105-1419
Tipton, Prentice Jr., Our Lady of Good Counsel Parish, Plymouth
Varner, Rick M., Epiphany Cathedral Parish, 350 Tampa Ave. W., Venice, FL 34285-1739.

Retired:
Revs.—
Balwinski, Gerald E., (Retired)
Byrne, Robert H., (Retired)
Carlson, James R., (Retired)
Dombrowski, Ronald J., (Retired)
Ederer, John A., (Retired)
Eppenbrock, Donald, (Retired)
Falsey, James E., (Retired)
Fillion, Stephen, (Retired)
Fitzpatrick, James M., (Retired)
Friske, Joseph P., (Retired)
Gohm, Robert S., (Retired)
Heller, James, (Retired)
Henkes, Donald, (Retired)
Johnson, John R., (Retired)
Jozwiak, Richard, (Retired)
Kawka, Frederick J., (Retired)
Kelly, Randy J., (Retired)
Konieczka, Edward J., (Retired)
Kowalczyk, Thomas M., (Retired)
LeFleur, R. Keith, (Retired)
Loos, Frederick C., (Retired)
Maher, Michael L., (Retired)
McNamara, Thomas J., (Retired)
Meissner, Robert J., (Retired)
Miller, Joseph K., (Retired)
Moeggenberg, Raymond, (Retired)
O'Connor, Patrick C., (Retired)
Sarge, John S., (Retired)
Schabel, Joseph A., (Retired)
Serour, George J., (Retired)
Sikorski, Harold R., (Retired)
Skornia, Bernard L., (Retired)
Spencer, William W., (Retired)
Surman, Stanley, (Retired)
Taylor, William R., (Retired)
Yaroch, Kenneth E., (Retired).

Permanent Deacons:
Arnold, Michael, Prince of Peace, Linwood

Corbat, Daniel J., St. Brigid of Kildare, Midland
Cremin, John J., (Retired), St. Mary, Alma
Damitio, James, Mt. Pleasant, Sacred Heart
Deford, Larry, Cathedral of Mary of the Assumption, Saginaw
Fussman, Lawrence, Sacred Heart Church, Mount Pleasant
Gayton, Librado, St. Joseph, Saginaw
George, Steven, Holy Spirit, Shields
Hartwig, Timothy S., St. Jude Thaddeus, Essexville
Hudson, Francis W., St. Brigid, Midland
Keller, George, (Retired)
Kuczyunski, Stanislaw, Bay City, Our Lady of Czestochowa
Lovas, Todd S., Nativity of the Lord, Alma
Oliver, Aloysius J., St. Brigid, Midland
Pasionek, Roger, Holy Family, Saginaw
Patelski, Gary, Pinconning, St. Michael
Smith, Michael, (Retired)
Stilwell, Lee, Prince of Peace, Linwood
Warner, Richard A., St. John Vianney, Saginaw.

INSTITUTIONS LOCATED IN DIOCESE

[A] HIGH SCHOOLS, INTER-PAROCHIAL

SAGINAW. *Nouvel Catholic Central High School* (1984) 2555 Wieneke Rd., 48603. Tel: 989-791-4330; Fax: 989-797-6603; Email: mfrost@nouvelcatholic.org; Web: www.sacschools.org. Mark Frost, Prin. Lay Teachers 24; Students 250.

Nouvel Catholic Central Educational Foundation Endowment Fund.

BAY CITY. *All Saints Central Catholic Middle and High School*, (Grades 6-12), 217 S. Monroe St., Bay City, 48708. Tel: 989-892-2533; Fax: 989-892-7188; Email: brian.campbell@ascbaycity.org; Web: www.ascbaycity.org. Brian Campbell, Prin.; Laura Tacey, Librarian. Lay Teachers 32; Students 247.

[B] ELEMENTARY SCHOOLS

AUBURN. *Auburn Area Catholic Schools*, (Grades PreK-5), East Campus: W. 114 Midland Rd., Auburn, 48611. Tel: 989-662-6431; Fax: 989-662-3391; Email: rmilne@auburnac.org; Web: www.auburnac.org. Mr. Robert Milne, Prin. Lay Teachers 8; Students 103.

[C] CHILDREN'S HOMES

SAGINAW. *Holy Cross Services-Mid-Michigan CB*, 625 Yale St., 48602. Tel: 989-799-2503; Tel: 989-596-3557; Email: cdevaux@hccsnet.org; Web: www.HolyCrossServices.org. 1013 N. River Rd., 48609. Sharon Berkobien, L.M.S.W., CEO. (Part of HCS, Diocese of Lansing); Provides Specialized Foster Care and Independent Living Services for boys and girls. Students 127; Religious Teachers 3.

Holy Cross Services-Mid-Michigan CB, 614 E. Holland, 48601. Tel: 989-799-2503; Tel: 989-596-3557; Email: mmadaj@hccsnet.org; Web: www.HolyCrossServices.org. 1013 N. River Rd., 48609. Sharon Berkobien, L.M.S.W., CEO. (Part of HCS, Diocese of Lansing); Provides Independent Living Services. Total Assisted 19.

Holy Cross Services - Queen of Angels, 3400 S. Washington, 48601. Tel: 989-755-1072; Fax: 989-755-1401; Tel: 989-596-3557; Email: cdevaux@hccsnet.org; Web: www.HolyCrossServices.org. Mailing Address: 1013 N. River Rd., 48609. Sharon Berkobien, L.M.S.W., CEO. Residential and out-patient substance abuse treatment programs for boys, girls, women and their children with facilities located throughout the state of Michigan under the auspices of the Brothers of the Holy Cross, Notre Dame, Indiana. Bed Capacity 112; Tot Asst. Annually 364; Total Staff 66.

Boysville of Michigan, Inc. dba Holy Cross Services, 925 N. River Rd., 48609. Tel: 989-781-2780; Tel: 989-596-3557; Fax: 989-781-5422; Email: cdevaux@hccsnet.org; Web: HolyCrossServices.org. Sharon Berkobien, L.M.S.W., CEO. Residential treatment programs for troubled youth and families with facilities located throughout the state of Michigan, under the auspices of the Brothers of the Holy Cross at Notre Dame. Includes Residential Treatment and Assessment Center. Students 64; Religious Teachers 3; Youths 120.

[D] GENERAL HOSPITALS

SAGINAW. *Ascension St. Mary's Hospital*, 800 S. Washington Ave., 48601-2524. Tel: 898-907-8000; Email: paula.caruso@ascension.org. Dr. Stephanie Duggan, CEO; Joanne Sparks, Spiritual Advisor/Care Svcs. Daughters of Charity of St. Vincent de Paul, East Central Province, Evansville, IN. Bed Capacity 293; Tot Asst. Annually 131,103; Total Staff 2,061.

Field Neurosciences Institute, 800 S. Washington Ave., 48601-2524. Tel: 989-907-8000; Email: betsy.aderholdt@ascension.org. Joanne Sparks, Spiritual Advisor/Care Svcs.

St. Mary's-St. Joseph Health System, 800 S. Washington Ave., 48601. Tel: 989-907-8000; Email: paula.caruso@ascension.org. Dr. Stephanie Duggan, Pres.; Joanne Sparks, Spiritual Advisor/Care Svcs.

[E] HOMES FOR AGED

SAGINAW. *St. Francis Home of Saginaw* (1953) 915 N. River Rd., 48609. Tel: 989-781-3150; Fax: 989-781-3791; Email: tiffanyp@stfrhome.org; Web: stfrhome.org. Rev. Thai Hung Nguyen, Chap.; Ms. Tiffany Patrick, Admin. Residents 80; Total Staff 150.

[F] FAMILY SERVICE

SAGINAW. *Catholic Family Service of the Diocese of Saginaw*, 710 N. Michigan Ave., 48602-4372. Tel: 989-763-8446; Fax: 989-797-7436; Email: rkoterba@dioceseofsaginaw.org; Web: www.cfssite.org. Sr. Mary Rebecca Koterba, R.S.M., M.D., Exec. Dir.

Counseling Centers:

SAGINAW.

710 N. Michigan Ave., 48602-4372.
Tel: 989-753-8336; Fax: 989-753-2582.

MT. PLEASANT.

210 Court St., Mount Pleasant, 48858.
Tel: 989-773-9328; Fax: 989-773-9803.

Adoption Center:

BAY CITY.

915 Columbus Ave., Bay City, 48708-6690.
Tel: 989-892-2504; Fax: 989-892-1923.

[G] CONVENTS AND RESIDENCES FOR SISTERS

SAGINAW. *Franciscan Poor Clare Nuns, O.S.C.* (1991) 4875 Shattuck Rd., 48603-2962. Tel: 989-797-0593; Email: sisters@srsclare.org; Web: www.srsclare.com. Sr. Dianne Doughty, O.S.C., Abbess. Sisters 3; Solemnly Professed 3.

Motherhouse and Novitiate of the Mission Sisters of the Holy Spirit (1932) 1030 N. River Rd., 48609. Tel: 989-781-0934; Email: marylou.owczarzak@gmail.com. Sr. Mary Lou Owczarzak, M.S.Sp., Pres. Sisters 4.

ALMA. *Motherhouse and Novitiate of the Religious Sisters of Mercy* (1973) 1965 Michigan Ave., Alma, 48801. Tel: 989-463-6035; Fax: 989-463-5811; Email: religious.sisters.of.mercy@gmail.com; Web: www.rsmofalma.org. Mother Mary McGreevy, R.S.M., Supr. Gen.; Sr. Mary Judith O'Brien, R.S.M., J.D., J.C.D., Vicar. Sisters 25.

[H] MISCELLANEOUS LISTINGS

SAGINAW. **Catholic Community Foundation of Mid-Michigan*, P.O. Box 6883, 48608-6883. Tel: 989-797-6627; Tel: 989-797-6684; Email: CCFMM@dioceseofsaginaw.org; Web: ccfmm.com. Jerome Blaxton, Pres.; Colleen Rabine, Dir.

Holy Spirit Sisters Charitable Trust (1988) 1030 N. River Rd., 48609. Tel: 989-781-0934; Email: marylou.owczarzak@gmail.com. Sr. Mary Lou Owczarzak, M.S.Sp., Pres.

**Little Books of the Diocese of Saginaw, Inc.*, 5802 Weiss St., P.O. Box 6009, 48608-6009. Tel: 989-797-6653; Fax: 989-797-6606; Email: ljones@dioceseofsaginaw.org. Leona Jones, Admin.; Catherine Haven, Editor.

**Partnership Center*, 723 Emerson St., 48607. Tel: 989-907-5610; Fax: 989-907-7702; Email: reynoldspatty@yahoo.com. Patricia L. Reynolds, Prog. Coord.

**St. Robert Bellarmine Trust*, 5800 Weiss St., 48603. Tel: 989-797-6620; Tel: 989-797-6614; Email: mcurtiss@dioceseofsaginaw.org. Mrs. Mary Elizabeth Curtiss, Admin.

Roman Catholic Diocese of Saginaw Inter-Parish Endowment Fund, 5800 Weiss St., 48603-2799. Tel: 989-797-6683; Email: grudolf@dioceseofsaginaw.org. Ms. Geri Rudolf, Contact Person.

ALMA. *Saint Joseph Corporation*, 1965 Michigan Ave., Alma, 48801. Tel: 989-463-6035; Fax: 989-463-5811; Email: olgrecords@gmail.com. Mother Mary McGreevy, R.S.M., Pres.

**Sacred Heart Mercy Health Care Center* (1981) 2025 W. Cheesman Rd., Alma, 48801. Tel: 989-463-3451 ; Fax: 989-463-4956; Email: business@sacredheartmercy.com; Web: www.sacredheartmercy.org. Sr. Mary Juanita Gonsalves, Admin.

BAY CITY. *Society of St. Vincent de Paul, Bay County Council*, 523 Michigan Ave., Bay City, 48708. Tel: 989-893-5772; Email: bcsvdp@mail.speednetllc.com. Mr. Thomas LeFevre, Pres. Member Conferences: Bay City, Our Lady of Peace, St. Catherine of Siena, Our Lady of Czestochowa, All Saints, Corpus Christi; Essexville-St. Jude Thaddeus.

PORT SANILAC. *Sisters of Our Mother of Divine Grace*, St. Mary-Our Lady of Sorrow Church, 7066 W. Main St., Port Sanilac, 48469. Tel: 810-622-9904, Ext. 3; Fax: 810-622-7953; Email: smphilomena@gmail.com. Sr. Mary Philomena Fuire, Supr. Sisters 4.

RELIGIOUS INSTITUTES OF MEN REPRESENTED IN THE DIOCESE

For further details refer to the corresponding bracketed number in the Religious Institutes of Men or Women section.

[0470]—*The Capuchin Friars* (St. Joseph Prov.)—O.F.M.Cap.
[0920]—*Oblates of St. Francis De Sales*—O.S.F.S.
[0690]—*Society of Jesus*—S.J.

RELIGIOUS INSTITUTES OF WOMEN REPRESENTED IN THE DIOCESE

[1810]—*Bernadine Sisters of Third Order of St. Francis*—O.S.F.
[1150]—*Congregation of St. Joseph*—C.S.J.
[]—*Congregation of the Holy Cross* (Amityville)—O.P.
[1070-13]—*Dominican Sisters* (Adrian, MI)—O.P.
[1070-14]—*Dominican Sisters* (Grand Rapids)—O.P.
[2740]—*Mission Sisters of the Holy Spirit*—M.S.Sp.
[2790]—*Missionary Servants of the Most Blessed Trinity*—M.S.B.T.
[3760]—*Order of St. Clare*—O.S.C.
[2519]—*Religious Sisters of Mercy of Alma, Michigan*—R.S.M.
[3560]—*Servants of Jesus*—S.J.
[0440]—*Sisters of Charity of Cincinnati, Ohio*—S.C.
[2575]—*Sisters of Mercy of the Americas* (Detroit, MI)—R.S.M.
[3260]—*Sisters of the Precious Blood (Dayton, Ohio)*—C.PP.S.
[2150]—*Sisters, Servants of the Immaculate Heart of Mary* (Monroe)—I.H.M.

DIOCESAN CEMETERIES

SAGINAW. *St. Andrew's, Mt. Olivet & Calvary*, 381 St. Andrews Rd, 48638. Tel: 989-797-6672; Email: alefevre@dioceseofsaginaw.org. 3440 S. Washington, 48638. Mrs. Alice Lefevre, Dir.

BAY CITY. *St. Patrick's, Calvary & St. Stanislaus*, 2000 Columbus Ave., Bay City, 48708. Tel: 989-797-6672; Email: alefevre@dioceseofsaginaw.org; Web: saginaw.org/cemeteries. 2977 Old Kawkawlin Rd., Kawkawlin. Mrs. Alice Lefevre, Dir.

LINWOOD. *St. Anne*, 1673 E. Linwood Rd., Linwood, 48634. Tel: 989-797-6672; Email: alefevre@dioceseofsaginaw.org; Web: saginaw.org/catholic-cemeteries/st-anne-cemetery. Mailing Address: c/o Diocese of Saginaw Catholic Cemeteries, 5800 Weiss St., 48603. Mrs. Alice Lefevre

MIDLAND. *Calvary*, 2743 E. Bombay Rd., Midland, 48642. Tel: 989-689-3739; Email: alefevre@dioceseofsaginaw.org; Web: saginaw.org/cemeteries. Mrs. Alice Lefevre, Dir.

NECROLOGY

† Cistone, Joseph R., Bishop of Saginaw, Died Oct. 16, 2018
† Boucher, Edward F., (Retired), Died Nov. 22, 2018
† Marceau, Emmett L., (Retired), Died Feb. 16, 2018

An asterisk (*) denotes an organization that has established tax-exempt status directly with the IRS and is not covered by the USCCB Group Ruling.

Diocese of St. Augustine

(Dioecesis Sancti Augustini)

Most Reverend

FELIPE DE JESUS ESTEVEZ, S.T.D.

Bishop of St. Augustine; ordained May 30, 1970; appointed Titular Bishop of Kearney and Auxiliary Bishop of Miami November 21, 2003; consecrated January 7, 2004; appointed Bishop of St. Augustine April 27, 2011; installed June 2, 2011. *Office: 11625 Old St. Augustine Rd., Jacksonville, FL 32258.*

Catholic Center: 11625 Old St. Augustine Rd., Jacksonville, FL 32258. Tel: 904-262-3200

Web: www.dosafl.com

Most Reverend

VICTOR BENITO GALEONE, S.T.L.

Bishop Emeritus of St. Augustine; ordained December 18, 1960; appointed Bishop of St. Augustine June 26, 2001; consecrated and installed August 21, 2001; retired April 27, 2011.

Most Reverend

JOHN J. SNYDER, D.D.

Bishop Emeritus of St. Augustine; ordained June 9, 1951; appointed Titular Bishop of Forlimpopuli December 19, 1972; consecrated February 2, 1973; appointed Bishop of St. Augustine October 2, 1979; installed December 5, 1979; retired December 12, 2000.

Square Miles 11,032.

Florida, east of the Apalachicola River, was erected by Pope Pius IX into a Vicariate-Apostolic in the year 1857, and in 1870 into the Diocese of St. Augustine.

Comprises all of the northeastern Counties of the State of Florida including Alachua, Baker, Bradford, Clay, Columbia, Dixie, Duval, Flagler, Gilchrist, Hamilton, Lafayette, Levy, Nassau, Putnam, St. Johns, Suwannee and Union Counties.

For legal titles of parishes and diocesan institutions, consult the Catholic Center.

STATISTICAL OVERVIEW

Personnel	
Bishop	1
Retired Bishops	2
Priests: Diocesan Active in Diocese	49
Priests: Diocesan Active Outside Diocese	4
Priests: Retired, Sick or Absent	52
Number of Diocesan Priests	105
Religious Priests in Diocese	28
Total Priests in Diocese	133
Extern Priests in Diocese	37
Ordinations:	
Diocesan Priests	2
Transitional Deacons	4
Permanent Deacons in Diocese	76
Total Brothers	2
Total Sisters	108
Parishes	
Parishes	52
With Resident Pastor:	
Resident Diocesan Priests	46
Resident Religious Priests	6
Missions	14
Pastoral Centers	2
Welfare	
Catholic Hospitals	3
Total Assisted	1,291,440
Homes for the Aged	1
Total Assisted	1,224
Day Care Centers	7
Total Assisted	810
Special Centers for Social Services	9
Total Assisted	87,756
Residential Care of Disabled	1
Total Assisted	30
Other Institutions	5
Total Assisted	653
Educational	
Diocesan Students in Other Seminaries	26
Total Seminarians	26
High Schools, Diocesan and Parish	5
Total Students	2,192
Elementary Schools, Diocesan and Parish	25
Total Students	8,721
Non-residential Schools for the Disabled	1
Total Students	135
Catechesis/Religious Education:	
High School Students	512
Elementary Students	8,939
Total Students under Catholic Instruction	20,525
Teachers in the Diocese:	
Sisters	7
Lay Teachers	587
Vital Statistics	
Receptions into the Church:	
Infant Baptism Totals	1,488
Minor Baptism Totals	144
Adult Baptism Totals	148
Received into Full Communion	421
First Communions	1,907
Confirmations	1,913
Marriages:	
Catholic	377
Interfaith	117
Total Marriages	494
Deaths	1,081
Total Catholic Population	142,440
Total Population	2,163,676

Former Bishops—Most Revs. AUGUSTIN VEROT, S.S., D.D., ord. Sept. 20, 1828; cons. April 25, 1858; Vicar-Apostolic of Florida; translated to the See of Savannah in July, 1861; appt. Bishop of St. Augustine March, 1870; died June 10, 1876; JOHN MOORE, D.D., ord. 1860; cons. May 13, 1877; died July 30, 1901; WILLIAM JOHN KENNY, D.D., ord. Jan. 15, 1879; cons. May 18, 1902; died Oct. 23, 1913; M. J. CURLEY, D.D., ord. 1903; cons. June 30, 1914; promoted to See of Baltimore Aug. 10, 1921; died May 16, 1947; PATRICK BARRY, D.D., ord. June 9, 1895; appt. Feb. 22, 1922; cons. May 3, 1922; died Aug. 13, 1940; JOSEPH P. HURLEY, D.D., ord. May 25, 1919; appt. Aug. 16, 1940; cons. Oct. 6, 1940; Received Personal title of Archbishop Aug. 18, 1950; died Oct. 30, 1967; PAUL F. TANNER, D.D., ord. May 30, 1931; appt. Titular Bishop of Lamasba, Oct. 20, 1965; cons. Dec. 21, 1965;; appt. Bishop of St. Augustine, Feb. 21, 1968; retired April 21, 1979; Remained as Administrator to Dec. 4, 1979; died July 29, 1994; JOHN J. SNYDER, D.D., (Retired), ord. June 9, 1951; appt. Titular Bishop of Forlimpopuli Dec. 19, 1972; cons. Feb. 2, 1973; appt. Bishop of St. Augustine Oct. 2, 1979; installed Dec. 5, 1979; retired Dec. 12, 2000; remained as Administrator to Aug. 21, 2001; VICTOR B. GALEONE, S.T.L., ord. Dec. 18, 1960; appt. Bishop of St. Augustine June 26, 2001; cons. and installed Aug. 21, 2001; retired April 27, 2011.

Vicar General—Rev. Msgr. KEITH R. BRENNAN, J.C.D., V.G.

Chancellor—Deacon DAVID A. WILLIAMS, M.A.

Secretary to the Bishop—JERRY WILAMOWSKI.

Secretary to the Vicar General/Chancellor—JUDY T. PINSON.

Episcopal Vicar for Development and Finance—Rev. MICHAEL HOULE, M.Ed., E.V.

Fiscal Office—STEPHEN R. BELL, CPA, CGMA.

Diocesan Tribunal—5110 Lourcey Rd., Jacksonville, 32257. Tel: 904-800-2393; Tel: 904-800-2613; Fax: 904-800-2647.

Judicial Vicar—Rev. PETER AKIN-OTIKO, J.C.L., Ph. D., J.V.

Moderator of the Tribunal—Sr. ANN KUHN, S.S.J.

Judges—Rev. Msgr. DANIEL B. LOGAN, (Retired); Rev. PETER AKIN-OTIKO, J.C.L., Ph.D., J.V.; KAREN KIGHT, J.D., J.C.L.; Rev. JOHN R. REYNOLDS, J.C.L.

Defender of the Bond—Rev. Msgr. KEITH R. BRENNAN, J.C.D., V.G.

Promoter of Justice—Rev. Msgr. KEITH R. BRENNAN, J.C.D., V.G.

Diocesan Consultors—Rev. Msgr. KEITH R. BRENNAN, J.C.D., V.G.; Rev. MICHAEL HOULE, M.Ed., E.V.; Rev. Msgr. MICHAEL P. MORGAN, J.D., J.C.L.; Revs. WILLIAM A. KELLY, (Retired); PETER AKIN-OTIKO, J.C.L., Ph.D., J.V.; JOHN M. PHILLIPS, V.F.; JHON GUARNIZO, V.F.; JAMES R. BODDIE JR.

Diocesan Pastoral Council—ERIN MCGEEVER, M.A., M.Ed., Sec., Diocese of St. Augustine Catholic Center, 11625 Old St. Augustine Rd., Jacksonville, 32258. Tel: 904-262-3200.

Presbyteral Council—Most Rev. FELIPE J. ESTEVEZ, S.T.D., Pres.; Rev. Msgr. KEITH R. BRENNAN, J.C.D., V.G.; Revs. MICHAEL HOULE, M.Ed., E.V., Sec. & Treas.; WILLIAM A. KELLY, (Retired); GUY NOONAN, M.B.A., S.T.D.; TERRY MORGAN; Rev. Msgr. VINCENT J. HAUT, M.S.W., (Retired); Revs. PETER AKIN-OTIKO, J.C.L., Ph.D., J.V.; JOHN GILLESPIE; ROBERT TRUJILLO; GREGORY J. FAY; CHRISTOPHER LIGUORI; JOSE PANTHAPLAMTHOTTIYIL, C.M.I.; ALEXANDER CARANDANG, O.S.J.; JOHN SOLLEE.

Deans—Revs. TIMOTHY M. LINDENFELSER, V.F., St. Augustine Deanery; JOHN M. PHILLIPS, V.F., Gainesville Deanery; JOSE J. KULATHINAL, C.M.I., V.F., North Jacksonville Deanery; AMARNATH NAGOTHU, M.S.F.S., V.F., South Jacksonville Deanery; JOHN H. TETLOW, V.F., St. Johns River Deanery.

Building Commission—Most Rev. FELIPE J. ESTEVEZ, S.T.D., Chm.; Rev. GUY NOONAN, M.B.A., S.T.D.; RONALD SCALISI; TOM BRENNAN; Deacon DAVID A. WILLIAMS, M.A., Chancellor; DR. DAVID CRATEM; MICHAEL COFFEY; CHARLES DAVID, Dir. Construction & Business Opers.

Catholic Foundation of Diocese of St. Augustine—CLIFF EVANS, O.F.S., M.A., Planned Giving Officer;

MICHAEL MCNAMARA, Chm.; Most Rev. FELIPE J. ESTEVEZ, S.T.D., Pres.; JOHN MCLAUGHLIN, Vice Chm.; Rev. MICHAEL HOULE, M.Ed., E.V., Treas.

Finance Council—BROOKES BURKHARDT, Chm.

Insurance Committee, Diocesan—GREG C. REED, PHR, SHRM-CP, Chm.

Diocesan Offices and Directors

Apostleship of the Sea—11625 Old St. Augustine Rd., Jacksonville, 32258. Tel: 904-613-3489. Deacon MILTON VEGA, Dir.

Archives of Diocese—Sr. CATHERINE BITZER, S.S.J., Archivist, P.O. Box 3506, St. Augustine, 32085. Tel: 904-823-8707.

Multicultural Ministry—134 E. Church St., Jacksonville, 32202. Tel: 904-353-3243. MS. ALBA M. OROZCO, Dir., Tel: 904-854-0669; Rev. JAMES R. BODDIE JR., Black Catholic Commission Coord.

Catholic Campaign for Human Development—8523 Normandy Blvd., Jacksonville, 32202. Tel: 904-786-1192. Rev. TIMOTHY R. LOZIER, Dir.

Christian Formation—ERIN MCGEEVER, M.A., M.Ed., Dir., 11625 Old St. Augustine Rd., Jacksonville, 32258. Tel: 904-262-3200.

Catholic Burse Endowment Fund, Inc.—(Education of Priests), *11625 Old St. Augustine Rd., Jacksonville, 32258.* Tel: 904-262-3200.

Catholic Charities Bureau, Inc.—134 E. Church St., Jacksonville, 32202. Tel: 904-224-0080. ANITA HASSELL, Diocesan Dir., See separate listing for more details.

Catholic Relief Services—134 E. Church St., Jacksonville, 32202. Tel: 904-224-0080. ANITA HASSELL, Diocesan Dir.

Catholic Women, Council of—Rev. JAMES R. BODDIE JR., Christ the King, 742 Arlington Rd., Jacksonville, 32211. Tel: 904-724-0080.

Charismatic Renewal—KATHERINE A. PERNINI, Sec., P.O. Box 13888, Gainesville, 32604. Tel: 352-371-2185.

Hispanic Charismatic Renewal—Rev. RODOLFO GODINEZ, Spiritual Dir., San Jose Parish, 3619 Toledo Rd., Jacksonville, 32217. Tel: 904-733-1630; MARIO MENDIETA, Coord., 2079 Forest Gate Dr. W., Jacksonville, 32246. Tel: 904-314-9211.

Civil Institutions—St. Mary Parish, P.O. Box 1120, Macclenny, 32063. Tel: 904-259-6414. Rev. RICHARD RASCH, O.de.M.

Communications—KATHLEEN BAGG, Dir., 11624 Old St. Augustine Rd., Jacksonville, 32258. Tel: 904-262-3200.

Continuing Education for Clergy—Deacon ROBERT DELUCA, Dir., 12366 Brady Place Blvd., Jacksonville, 32223. Tel: 904-880-2692.

Cursillos de Cristiandad—Revs. AMARNATH NAGOTHU, M.S.F.S., V.F., Diocesan Spiritual Advisor, Holy Spirit, 11665 Fort Caroline Rd., Jacksonville, 32225; HERIBERTO VERGARA, Diocesan Spiritual Advisor (Spanish), St. John the Baptist Parish, 2725 Hwy. 17S, Crescent City, 32112. Tel: 386-698-2055; CARL LUDWIG, Lay Dir., Tel: 904-241-0919.

Development & Stewardship Office—5110 Lourcey Rd., Jacksonville, 32257. Tel: 904-262-3200. CHARLIE SLOAN, Dir.; PATRICIA DISANDRO, Assoc. Dir.

Planned Giving Officer for the Catholic Foundation—CLIFF EVANS, O.F.S., M.A.

Disabilities, Ministry of Persons with—REBECCA ALEMAN, Dir., 235 Marywood Dr., St. Johns, 32259. Tel: 904-230-7447.

Ecumenism and Interfaith—Deacon DAVID A. WILLIAMS, M.A., Chancellor, 11625 Old St. Augustine Rd., Jacksonville, 32258. Tel: 904-262-3200. Associate Diocesan Ecumenical Officer: Rev. ALBERTO ESPOSITO, Queen of Peace Parish, 10900 S.W. 24th Ave., Gainesville, 32607.

Educational Services—Deacon SCOTT J. CONWAY, M.Ed., Supt. Catholic Schools; RHONDA ROSE, Asst. Supt. Schools.

Family Life, Diocesan Center—MICHAEL DAY, Dir.

Farmworker Services Program—OLGA LARA-MOSER, Coord., 234 S. Summit St., Crescent City, 32112. Tel: 386-698-4234.

Florida Catholic Conference—MICHAEL B. SHEEDY, Exec. Dir., 201 W. Park Ave., Tallahassee, 32301-7715. Tel: 850-222-3803.

Holy Childhood Association—Deacon BRYAN OTT, Dir., 107A 15th St., St. Augustine, 32080. Tel: 904-461-5762.

Justice and Peace—134 E. Church St., Jacksonville, 32202. Tel: 904-899-5500. ANITA HASSELL.

Legalization—Providence Center, 134 E. Church St., Rm D-21, Jacksonville, 32202. Tel: 904-354-5904. IRAIDA MARTINEZ, Dir.

Legion of Mary—6175 Datil Pepper Rd., St. Augustine, 32086. Tel: 904-797-4842. Rev. EDWARD W. MURPHY, Diocesan Chap.

Office of Liturgy—Revs. THOMAS S. WILLIS, Dir., 35 Treasury St., St. Augustine, 32084. Tel: 904-824-2806; JOHN M. PHILLIPS, V.F., Chm., Liturgical Commission, 747 N.W. 43rd St., Gainesville, 32607.

Priests' Spirituality Committee—Rev. DAVID RUCHINSKI, Chm., St. Augustine Parish, 1738 W. University Ave., Gainesville, 32603. Tel: 352-372-3533.

Propagation of the FaithDeacon BRYAN OTT, Dir., 107A 15th St., St. Augustine, 32080. Tel: 904-461-5762.

Refugee Resettlement—MICHELLE KAROLAK, Dir., Providence Center, 134 E. Church St., Jacksonville, 32202-3130. Tel: 904-354-4846.

Human Life & Dignity—MAY OLIVER, Dir., 11625 Old St. Augustine Rd., Jacksonville, 32258. Tel: 904-262-3200.

Scouts—ROBIN SHIPLEY, Dir. Youth & Young Adult, 11625 Old St. Augustine Rd., Jacksonville, 32258; Revs. JAMES R. BODDIE JR., Chap.; EDWARD W. MURPHY, Asst. Chap., Mailing Address: 121 E. Duval St., Jacksonville, 32202. Tel: 904-359-0331.

Seminarians—11625 Old St. Augustine Rd., Jacksonville, 32258. Tel: 904-262-3200. Rev. DAVID KEEGAN, Dir.

Senior Priest Care—Tel: 904-703-7910. LAUREN AUSTIN, Coord., Assistance for Senior Priests; Rev. WILLIAM A. KELLY, Vicar for Senior Priests, (Retired).

Vicar for Priests—Rev. MICHAEL PENDERGRAFT, V.F., 7190 Hwy. 17 S., Fleming Island, 32003. Tel: 904-284-3811.

Vicar for Deacons—1718 State Rd. 13, St. Johns, 32259. Tel: 904-287-0519. Rev. JOHN H. TETLOW, V.F.

Delegate for Religious—Sr. VICTORA WILL, S.N.D., 746 W. 41st St., Jacksonville, 32206. Tel: 904-477-0549.

Vicar for Senior Priests—Rev. WILLIAM A. KELLY, (Retired), 5201 Atlantic Blvd., #228, Jacksonville, 32207. Tel: 904-348-3983.

Victim Assistant Coordinator—JUDY PINSON, Diocese of St. Augustine, 11625 Old St. Augustine Rd., Jacksonville, 32258. Tel: 904-262-3200.

Vocations—11625 Old St. Augustine Rd., Jacksonville, 32258. Tel: 904-262-3200. Revs. DAVID KEEGAN, Diocesan Dir.; STEVEN ZEHLER, Assoc. Dir.; DAVID RUCHINSKI, Assoc. Dir.

Youth and Young Adult Ministry—11625 Old St. Augustine Rd., Jacksonville, 32258. Tel: 904-262-3200. ROBIN SHIPLEY, Dir.

CLERGY, PARISHES, MISSIONS AND PAROCHIAL SCHOOLS

CITY OF ST. AUGUSTINE

(ST. JOHN'S COUNTY)

1—CATHEDRAL - BASILICA OF ST. AUGUSTINE (1565) [CEM]
38 Cathedral Pl., St. Augustine, 32084.
Tel: 904-824-2806; Email: cathparish@gmail.com; Web: thefirstparish.org. 35 Treasury St., St. Augustine, 32086. Revs. Thomas S. Willis; D. Terrence Morgan, Parochial Vicar; Joseph Kuhlman, Parochial Vicar; Livinus "Martin" Ibeh, Parochial Vicar; Deacon Charles Kanaszka.
School—Cathedral Parish School, (Grades K-8), 259 St. George St., St. Augustine, 32084.
Tel: 904-824-2861; Fax: 904-829-2059; Email: kboice@cpsschool.org; Web: www.thecathedralparishschool.org. Kathy Boice, Prin. Clergy 7; Lay Teachers 23; Students 267.
Catechesis Religious Program—Email: cathedralcfp@gmail.com. Andrew Tierney, D.R.E. Students 98.
Mission—St. Benedict the Moor (1911) .

2—ST. ANASTASIA (1985)
Mailing Address: 5205 A1A S., St. Augustine, 32080-8006. Tel: 904-471-5364; Email: sec@saccfl.org; Web: www.saccfl.org. Rev. Timothy M. Lindenfelser; Deacon Bryan Ott.
Catechesis Religious Program—
Tel: 904-471-5364, Ext. 112; Email: dre@saccfl.org. Denise Pressley, D.R.E. Students 190.

3—MISSION NOMBRE DE DIOS AND SHRINE OF OUR LADY OF LA LECHE (1565) [JC]
27 Ocean Ave., St. Augustine, 32084.
Tel: 904-824-2809; Email: fathercarrilloparis@missionandshrine.org; Email: jstark@missionandshrine.org. Revs. Ivan Carillo Paris, I.C.C., Shrine Rector; Carlos Manuel Sosa, I.C.C., Asst. to Rector; Joanna R. Stark.
Rectory—34 Ocean Ave., St. Augustine, 32084.
Mission Nombre de Dios Museum—
Shrine—Shrine Church of Our Lady of La Leche, 101 San Marco, St. Augustine, 32084.

4—OUR LADY OF GOOD COUNSEL (2008) [CEM]
5950 State Rd. 16, St. Augustine, 32092-0626.
Tel: 904-824-8688; Email: mknightolgc@gmail.com; Web: www.olgc-church.org. Rev. Guy Noonan, M.B.A., S.T.D.; Deacon Mark Sciullo.
Catechesis Religious Program—Email: olgc.amy@gmail.com. Amy Kirk, D.R.E. Students 130.

5—SAN SEBASTIAN (1968)
1112 State Rd. 16, St. Augustine, 32084.
Tel: 904-824-6625; Email: tyra@sansebastiancatholicchurch.com; Web: www.sansebastiancatholicchurch.com. Rev. John D. Gillespie; Deacons Santiago Rosado; James Swanson.
Catechesis Religious Program—Email: susan@sansebastiancatholicchurch.com. Susan Boehm-Donlon, D.R.E. Students 255.

OUTSIDE THE CITY OF ST. AUGUSTINE

CALLAHAN, NASSAU CO., OUR LADY OF CONSOLATION (1974)
541668 U.S. Hwy. One, P.O. Box 692, Callahan, 32011. Tel: 904-879-3662; Email: olccatholicchurch@comcast.net. Rev. Dung Quang Bui.
Catechesis Religious Program—Email: olcdre@comcast.net. Joseph Smith, D.R.E. Students 31.

CHIEFLAND, LEVY CO., ST. JOHN THE EVANGELIST (1981) (Hispanic)
4050 N.W. US Hwy. 27 Alt., P.O. Box 863, Chiefland, 32644. Tel: 352-493-9723; Email: stjhc@bellsouth.net; Web: stjhc.org. Rev. Cesar Torres-Pinzon, Admin.
Catechesis Religious Program—St. Andrew Mission, 12513 S.R 24, Cedar Key, 32625. Students 53.
Missions—Holy Cross— (1971) 2090 S.W. Highway 19, Cross City, Levy Co. 32628.
Christ the Good Shepherd, 9679 US Hwy. 129, Trenton, 32693.

CRESCENT CITY, PUTNAM CO., ST. JOHN THE BAPTIST (1906) [CEM] [JC]
2725 S Hwy 17, P.O. Box 908, Crescent City, 32112.
Tel: 386-698-2055; Email: church@sjbcc.com. Rev. Heriberto Vergara, Admin.
Catechesis Religious Program—Students 172.

ELKTON, ST. JOHN CO., ST. AMBROSE (1875) [CEM] (Minorcan)
6070 Church Rd., Elkton, 32033. Tel: 904-692-1366; Fax: 904-692-1136; Email: choffice1@windstream.net; Web: www.saintambrose-church.org. Rev. Steven Zehler.
Catechesis Religious Program—Tel: 904-540-2419; Email: stamreled@windstream.net. Christine Humphries, D.R.E. Students 10.

FERNANDINA BEACH, AMELIA ISLAND NASSAU CO., ST. MICHAEL'S (1872) [JC]
505 Broome St., Fernandina Beach, 32034.
Tel: 904-261-3472; Email: wedwards@stmichaelscatholic.com; Web: www.stmichaelscatholic.com. Revs. Jose Kallukalam, (India); Briggs Hurley, Parochial Vicar; Sisters Rose Madassery, Admin.; Nayva Thekkumthala, Pastoral Assoc.; Deacon Art Treadwell; Mr. Walt Edwards, Business Mgr.
School—St. Michael's Academy, (Grades PreK-8), 228 N. 4th St., Fernandina Beach, 32034.
Tel: 904-321-2102; Fax: 904-321-2330. Dr. Christopher Hampton, Prin.; Colleen Hodge, Librarian. Students 219.
Catechesis Religious Program—Students 130.

FLAGLER BEACH, FLAGLER CO., SANTA MARIA DEL MAR (1970)
Mailing Address: 915 N. Central Ave., Flagler Beach, 32136. Tel: 386-439-2791; Fax: 386-439-1362; Email: nick@smdmcc.org; Web: www.smdmcc.org. Rev. Kazimierz Ligeza.
Catechesis Religious Program—Students 206.

FLEMING ISLAND, CLAY CO., SACRED HEART (1954) [CEM]
7190 Hwy. 17 S., Fleming Island, 32003.
Tel: 904-284-3811; Fax: 904-529-8845; Email: shbulletin3811@bellsouth.net; Web: www.sacredheartcatholicchurch.org. Revs. Michael Pendergraft, V.F.; Alexis Diaz, C.M.F., Hispanic Min. Asst.
Res.: 1065 Live Oak Ln., Fleming Island, 32003.
Catechesis Religious Program—Tel: 904-284-9983. Kristin Michler-Belleza, C.R.E. (Elementary); Sandra Curtis, C.R.E. (High School). Students 382.

GAINESVILLE, ALACHUA CO.

1—ST. AUGUSTINE CHURCH AND CATHOLIC STUDENT CENTER (1923) (Student Center)
1738 W. University Ave., Gainesville, 32603.

Tel: 352-372-3533; Fax: 352-378-9010; Email: info@catholicgators.org; Web: www.catholicgators.org. Revs. David Ruchinski; Wilson Colmenares, Parochial Vicar; Philip Timlin, Parochial Vicar.

2—HOLY FAITH (1973)
747 N.W. 43rd St., Gainesville, 32607.
Tel: 352-376-5405; Email: holyfaithoffice@holyfaithchurch.org; Web: www.holyfaithcatholicchurch.org. Revs. John M. Phillips, V.F.; Emmanuel J. Pazhayapurackal, C.M.I., (India); Deacon Michael J. Demers.
Catechesis Religious Program—Holy Faith Children's Christian Formation, Email: sr.adell@holyfaithchurch.org. Sr. Adell Lininger, D.R.E. Students 281.

3—ST. PATRICK CHURCH (1887)
500 N.E. 16th Ave., Gainesville, 32601.
Tel: 352-372-4641, Ext. 100; Email: stpatsjoy@saintpatricksparish.org; Email: frlawrence@saintpatricksparish.org; Web: www.saintpatricksparishgnv.org. Rev. Lawrence Peck, Admin.

4—QUEEN OF PEACE (1987) [JC]
10900 S.W. 24th Ave., Gainesville, 32607.
Tel: 352-332-6279; Email: office@qopparish.org; Web: qopparish.org. Revs. Alberto Esposito; Marialal Joseph.
School—Queen of Peace Academy, Tel: 352-332-8808; Email: office@qopacademy.org; Web: www.qopacademy.org. Tammie Vassou, Prin. Lay Teachers 33; Students 463.
Catechesis Religious Program—Tel: 352-448-4542; Email: bcaulson@qopparish.org. Sr. Beatrice Caulson, I.H.M., D.R.E. Students 420.

HIGH SPRINGS, ALACHUA CO., ST. MADELEINE SOPHIE PARISH AND SANTA FE SHRINE OF OUR LADY OF LA LECHE (1925) [CEM]
17155 N.W. US Hwy. 441, High Springs, 32643.
Tel: 386-454-2358; Fax: 386-454-4985; Email: stmadeleinecc@windstream.net; Web: www.stmadeleinecatholicchurch.com. Rev. Mark Dzien; Deacons Henry Zmuda; Angel Cuesta, D.P.M.; Paul Pettie.
Catechesis Religious Program—Students 53.
Mission—San Juan, Mailing Address: 304 S.E. Plant Ave., Branford, Alachua Co. 32008.
Tel: 386-935-2632; Fax: 386-935-4050; Email: sanjuancruz@live.com; Web: sanjuanmission.org.

INTERLACHEN, PUTNAM CO., ST. JOHN THE EVANGELIST (1968) [JC]
P.O. Box 207, Interlachen, 32148. Tel: 386-684-2528; Email: sjcc1200@aol.com. Revs. Amarnath Nagothu, M.S.F.S., V.F.; Pablo Fuentes, Parochial Vicar.

JACKSONVILLE BEACH, DUVAL CO., ST. PAUL'S (1930)
224 N. Fifth St., Jacksonville Beach, 32250.
Tel: 904-249-2600; Email: office@stpaulsjaxbeach.org; Web: www.stpaulsjaxbeach.org. Revs. Michael Houle, M.Ed., E.V.; Bartlomiej Gadaj, Parochial Vicar; Valanarasu Irudayanathan, Parochial Vicar; Deacon Michael J. O'Brien.
School—St. Paul's School, 428 2nd Ave. N., Jacksonville Beach, 32250. Tel: 904-249-5934; Fax: 904-241-2911. Krissy Thompson, Prin. Lay Teachers 32; Students 690.
Catechesis Religious Program—578 1st Ave N, Jacksonville Beach, 32250. Tel: 904-249-2660; Tel: 904-222-0608; Email: mimistpaulre@gmail.com; Email: mjstpaulre@gmail.com. Mary Coleman, D.R.E.; Mary Jo Antone, D.R.E. Students 510.
Mission—St. Peter's Mission (2008) 960 Girvin Rd., Duval Co. 32225. Tel: 904-619-2860; Email: other@stpaulsjaxbeach.org. Maggie Bilas, Contact Person.

JACKSONVILLE, DUVAL CO.

1—ASSUMPTION (South Jacksonville) (1913)
2403 Atlantic Blvd., 32207. Tel: 904-398-1963; Email: assumption@assumptioncatholicchurch.org; Web: www.assumptioncatholicchurch.org. Revs. Frederick R. Parke; Jose Panthaplamthottiyil, C.M.I., Parochial Vicar; Martin Orokia Raj, O.S.B., Parochial Vicar; Donald Lum, In Res.
School—Assumption School, 2431 Atlantic Blvd., 32207. Tel: 904-398-1774; Fax: 904-398-6712; Email: mjimenez@assumptionjax.org; Web: assumptionjax.org. Maryann Jimenez, Prin. Lay Teachers 41; Students 526.
Catechesis Religious Program—Email: assumptionrciadm@gmail.com. Sr. Kathryn Shea, S.H.M., D.R.E.; Daniel Mull, D.R.E. Students 60.

2—BASILICA OF THE IMMACULATE CONCEPTION (1854) [CEM] [JC]
121 E. Duval St., 32202. Tel: 904-359-0331; Fax: 904-356-8133; Email: pmoore@icjax.org; Web: icjax.org. Rev. Blair Gaynes, Admin.; Deacon Lawrence Geinosky.

3—BLESSED TRINITY (1957)
10472 Beach Blvd., 32246. Tel: 904-641-1414; Fax: 904-641-8171; Email: btccjax10472@gmail.com; Web: btccjax.org. Revs. Jhon Guarnizo, V.F.; Rafael Lavilla Jr., O.S.J.; Deacons Brian Hughes; Angel Sanchez.
School—Blessed Trinity School, (Grades PreK-8), Tel: 904-641-6458; Email: btschool@comcast.net. Marie Davis, Prin. Clergy 4; Lay Teachers 19; Students 236.
Catechesis Religious Program—Tel: 904-646-4320; Email: dre@btccjax.org. Linda Miranda, D.R.E. Students 217.

4—CHRIST THE KING (1954)
742 Arlington Rd. N., 32211. Tel: 904-724-0080; Email: rectory@ctkcatholic.com; Web: ctkcatholic.com. Revs. James R. Boddie Jr.; Lam Nguyen, Parochial Vicar; Deacon George Barletta.
School—Christ the King School, 6822 Larkin Rd., 32211. Tel: 904-724-2954; Fax: 904-721-8004; Email: ctk@ctkschooljax.com. Stephanie Engelhardt, Prin. Lay Teachers 21; Students 256.
Catechesis Religious Program—
Tel: 904-724-0080, Ext. 308. Sandy Hill, D.R.E. Students 42.

5—CHURCH OF THE CRUCIFIXION (1974) (African American)
3183 W. Edgewood Ave., 32209-2209.
Tel: 904-765-5284; Email: crucifixion@comcast.net; Web: www.crucifixionjax.org. Rev. Bernardine Eikhuemelo.
Catechesis Religious Program—

6—ST. EPHREM SYRIAC ANTIOCHIAN CATHOLIC CHURCH (1986)
4650 Kernan Blvd. S., 32224. Tel: 904-998-7800; Fax: 904-998-7801. Revs. Muntaser Hadden, Admin.; Caesar Russo, M.A., J.C.L., S.T.L., Admin., (Retired).

7—ST. FRANCIS CHOE CHAPEL (1997) (Korean)
8051 Rampart Rd., 32244. Tel: 904-573-1833; Fax: 904-573-1833. Rev. Stephano Young Su Kim.
Catechesis Religious Program—Students 15.

8—HOLY FAMILY (1974)
9800 Baymeadows Rd., 32256. Tel: 904-641-5838; Email: plombardo@holyfamilyjax.com; Web: www.holyfamilyjax.com. Revs. David Keegan; Matthew Ibok; Rev. Msgrs. Mortimer Danaher, In Res., (Retired); Daniel B. Logan, In Res., (Retired); Deacon Doug Nullet, Pastoral Assoc.; Matthew Daniel, Music Min.; Stael Dantes, Youth Min.; Mrs. Patricia Lombardo, Contact Person.
School—Holy Family School, 9800-3 Baymeadows Rd., 32256. Tel: 904-645-9875; Fax: 904-899-6060; Email: tcusick@holyfamilyjax.com; Web: hfcatholicschool.com/. Matt Moloney, Prin. Lay Teachers 32; Students 389.
Catechesis Religious Program—Email: mpetrotta@holyfamilyjax.com. Maria Petrotta, D.R.E. Students 162.

9—HOLY ROSARY (1921)
4731 Norwood Ave., 32206. Tel: 904-764-3241; Fax: 904-765-4995; Email: holyrosaryjax@comcast.net; Web: holyrosaryjax.org. Rev. Bernardine Eikhuemelo.
Catechesis Religious Program—Students 7.

10—HOLY SPIRIT (1966)
Mailing Address: 11665 Fort Caroline Rd., 32225. Rev. Amarnath Nagothu, M.S.F.S., V.F.; Deacons Patrick J. Goin; Edward Prisby.
Res.: 11324 Oak Landings Dr., 32225.
Tel: 904-641-7244; Email: amarmsfs@gmail.com; Email: vslade@holyspiritchurchjax.org; Web: holyspiritchurchjax.org.
School—Holy Spirit School, (Grades PreK-8), Tel: 904-642-9165; Fax: 904-642-1047; Web: www.hscatholicschool.com. John Luciano, Prin. Lay Teachers 17; Students 249.
Catechesis Religious Program—Email: sraines@holyspiritchurchjax.org. Stefanie Raines, D.R.E. Students 139.

11—ST. JOHN THE BAPTIST (1967)
P.O. Drawer 330005, 32233. Tel; 904-246-6014; Fax: 904-246-1219; Email: SAMatthews.StJohn@outlook.com; Web: www.saintjohnsatlanticbeach.org. 2400 Mayport Rd., 32233. Rev. Mark S. Waters.
Catechesis Religious Program—Email: Samatthews.stjohn@outlook.com. Samantha Matthews, D.R.E. Students 108.

12—ST. JOSEPH (1883) [CEM]
11730 Old St. Augustine Rd., 32258-2002.
Tel: 904-268-5422; Email: pkinnare@stjosephsjax.org. Revs. Sebastian K. George, C.M.I.; John Sollee, Parochial Vicar; Bernie Ahern, In Res.; Deacons Kevin Boudreaux; Bob Gardner; Lowell Hecht; Robert Repke.
School—St. Joseph School, 11600 Old St. Augustine Rd., 32258. Tel: 904-268-6688; Fax: 904-268-8989; Email: schoolbilling@stjosephcs.org; Web: www.stjosephcs.org. Mrs. Robin Fecitt, Prin. Lay Teachers 33; Students 501.
Catechesis Religious Program—Tel: 904-880-6404; Email: religious-ed@stjosephsjax.org. Mrs. Katie Weikert, Diocesan D.R.E. Students 471.

13—MARY, QUEEN OF HEAVEN (1988)
Mailing Address: 9401 Staples Mill Dr., 32244.
Tel: 904-777-3168; Web: www.maryqueenofheaven.org. Rev. Denis O'Shaughnessy; Deacons David A. Williams, M.A.; Paul Testa.
Res.: 8804 Bandera Cir. S., 32244. Tel: 904-777-3168; Email: mqoh@att.net; Web: maryqueenofheaven.org.
Catechesis Religious Program—Students 160.

14—ST. MATTHEW (Lake Shore) (1949)
1773 Blanding Blvd., 32210. Tel: 904-388-8698; Email: stmatthews@stmatthewsjax.com; Web: www.stmatthewsjax.com. Rev. Jose J. Kulathinal, C.M.I., V.F.; Deacons George Good; David Yazdiya.
School—St. Matthew School, Tel: 904-387-4401; Fax: 904-388-4404; Email: stmatthewsoffice@comcast.net; Web: www.stmatthewscs.org. Mrs. Kathy Tuerk, Prin. Lay Teachers 14; Students 236.
Catechesis Religious Program—Tel: 904-388-1207; Email: donna@stmatthewsjax.com. Donna Burney, D.R.E. Students 135.

15—MOST HOLY REDEEMER (1962)
8523 Normandy Blvd., 32221-6701.
Tel: 904-786-1192; Email: mhr@mhrjax.org. Rev. Timothy R. Lozier; Deacons John Baker, M.D.; Milton Vega.
Catechesis Religious Program—Email: jkollasch@mhrjax.org. Jennifer Kollasch, D.R.E. Students 88.

16—OUR LADY OF THE ANGELS (1917) [CEM] Closed. Records moved to St. Paul's Parish, 2609 Park St., Jacksonville, FL 32204, Tel: 904-387-2554.

17—ST. PATRICK (1959)
601 Airport Center Dr. E., 32218. Tel: 904-768-2593; Email: fatherliguori@hotmail.com; Web: stpatrickjacksonville.org. Rev. Christopher Liguori; Deacon David Belanger.
Res.: 505 Tidal Wave Ln., 32218.
School—St. Patrick School, (Grades PreK-8), Tel: 904-768-6323; Fax: 904-768-2144. Mrs. Mary Margaret Martin, Prin. Lay Teachers 32; Students 322.
Catechesis Religious Program—Email: cataylor@addressplus.net. Students 80.

18—ST. PAUL'S (1923)
2609 Park St., 32204. Tel: 904-387-2554; Email: parishoffice@spsjax.org. Rev. George Vaniyapurackal; Deacon James Scott, D.R.E.
School—St. Paul's School, Tel: 904-387-2841; Fax: 904-388-1781. Lay Teachers 17; Students 200.
Catechesis Religious Program—Tel: 904-534-2506. Sr. Florence Bryan, D.R.E. Students 24.

19—ST. PIUS V (1919) (African American)
2110 Blue Ave., 32209. Tel: 904-354-1501; Email: spvbm@outlook.com; Web: www.stpiusjax.org. Rev. Bernardine Eikhuemelo.
Catechesis Religious Program—Students 31.

20—PRINCE OF PEACE (1970)
6320 Bennett Rd., 32216. Tel: 904-733-6860;
Tel: 904-733-6011; Fax: 904-367-0215; Email: popofficemanager@yahoo.com. Revs. Callistus, O. C. Onwere, (Nigeria); Calonge Lemaine, Vicar; Deacon Michael Federico.
Catechesis Religious Program—Tel: 904-733-6011; Fax: 904-367-0215; Web: www.princeofpeacecatholicchurch.net. Students 10.

21—RESURRECTION (1959)
3383 University Blvd. N., 32277-2483.
Tel: 904-744-0833; Email: secretary@respar.net; Web: www.respar.net. Revs. Peter Akin-Otiko, J.C.L., Ph.D., J.V.; Richard Pagano, Parochial Vicar.
School—Resurrection School, (Grades PreK-8), 5710 Jack Rd., 32277. Tel: 904-744-1266; Fax: 904-744-5800; Email: principal@resurrectioncatholic.com; Web: www.resurrectionschooljax.com. Timothy Connor, Prin. Lay Teachers 18; Students 185.
Catechesis Religious Program—Students 35.

22—SACRED HEART (1959)
5752 Blanding Blvd., 32244. Tel: 904-771-2152; Email: sacredheartbm@gmail.com; Web: www.sacredheartjax.com. Revs. James Kaniparampil, C.M.I.; Slawomir S. Podsiedlik, O.C.D., In Res.; Deacon Jeffrey P. Burgess Sr.
School—Sacred Heart School,
Tel: 904-771-5800, Ext. 15; Email: sr.rosario@sacredheartjax.com; Web: sacredheartcatholicjax.org. Sr. M. Rosario Vega-R., HMSS, Prin. Lay Teachers 25; Students 376; Clergy / Religious Teachers 2.
Catechesis Religious Program—
Tel: 904-771-5800, Ext. 23. Santa Cochran, C.R.E. Students 140.

23—SAN JOSE (1959)
3619 Toledo Rd., 32217. Tel: 904-733-1630; Email: admin@sjcatholic.org; Web: www.sjcatholic.org. Revs. Gregory J. Fay; Rodolfo Godinez, Parochial Vicar; Deacon Christopher Supple.
School—San Jose School, Tel: 904-733-2313; Email: courtney@sanjoseschool.com. Brian Wheeler, Prin. Lay Teachers 36; Students 407.
Catechesis Religious Program—
Tel: 904-733-1630, Ext. 18; Fax: 904-731-4335;

Email: dre@sjcatholic.org. Anita Michaels, D.R.E. Students 193.

KEYSTONE HEIGHTS, CLAY CO., ST. WILLIAM (1948) [JC]
210 S.W. Peach St., Keystone Heights, 32656.
Tel: 352-473-4136; Email: stwilliamcatholi@bellsouth.net. Rev. Andrzej Mitera.
Catechesis Religious Program—Tel: 352-473-4223. Janie Phillips, D.R.E.; Peyton Phillips, D.R.E. Students 44.

KORONA, FLAGLER CO., ST. MARY (1914) [CEM]
89 St. Mary's Pl., Bunnell, 32110-1537.
Tel: 386-437-5098; Email: Karen@stmaryccfl.net; Web: www.stmaryccfl.net. Mailing Address: 230 S. Old Dixie Hwy, Bunnell, 32110-1537. Rev. Slawomir Bielasiewicz.
Catechesis Religious Program—Mary Araya, D.R.E. Students 4.

LAKE CITY, COLUMBIA CO., EPIPHANY (1965)
1905 S.W. Epiphany Ct., Lake City, 32025.
Tel: 386-752-4470; Email: office@epiphanycatholiclc.com; Web: www.epiphanycatholiclc.com. Revs. Robert Trujillo; Wilson Colmenares, Parochial Vicar.
School—Epiphany School, Epiphany Catholic School, 1937 S.W. Epiphany Ct., Lake City, 32025.
Tel: 386-752-2320; Fax: 386-752-2364; Email: epiphanyeagles@ecslc.org. Ms. Rita Klenk, Prin. Lay Teachers 17; Students 138; Clergy / Religious Teachers 1.
Catechesis Religious Program—Tel: 386-269-1646; Email: dre@epiphanycatholiclc.com. Susi Pittman, D.R.E. Students 27.

LIVE OAK, SUWANNEE CO., ST. FRANCIS XAVIER (1979)
928 E. Howard St., Live Oak, 32064.
Tel: 386-364-1108; Fax: 386-364-1836; Email: stfxoff@comcast.net. Rev. Anthony Basso, Contact Person.
Catechesis Religious Program—Sherri Ortega, D.R.E. Students 93.
Missions—Our Lady of Guadalupe— (2004) 137 E. Main St., Mayo, Lafayette Co. 32066. Email: lili@claretiansisters.org. Mailing Address: P.O. Box 506, Mayo, 32066. Tel: 386-294-2126. Sr. Martha Lili Tututi, Contact Person.
St. Therese of the Child Jesus (1975) 5430 N.W. Hwy. 41, Jasper, Hamilton Co. 32052.

MACCLENNY, BAKER CO., ST. MARY, MOTHER OF MERCY (1960) [JC]
1143 W. Macclenny Ave., P.O. Box 1120, Macclenny, 32063. Tel: 904-570-7765; Email: stmarychurchmacclenny@gmail.com; Web: www.stmarymacclenny.com. Deacon Kenneth L. Cochran Sr.
Res.: 894 Jacqueline Cir., Macclenny, 32063.
Catechesis Religious Program—Tel: 904-710-6246. Julie Johnson, D.R.E. Students 41.
Chaplaincy—Northeast Florida State Hospital, Macclenny; Union Correctional Institute, Raiford; and Florida State Prison, Starke.

MIDDLEBURG, CLAY CO., ST. LUKE (1982)
1606 Blanding Blvd., Middleburg, 32068.
Tel: 904-282-0439; Email: office@stlukesparish.org; Web: www.stlukesparish.org. Revs. Andy Blaszkowski, Admin.; Jaisemon Xaviour, Parochial Vicar; Deacons Robert DeLuca; Stephen Arnold.
Res.: 4113 Old Jennings Rd., Middleburg, 32068.
Catechesis Religious Program—Students 330.

ORANGE PARK, CLAY CO., ST. CATHERINE OF SIENA (1877)
1649 Kingsley Ave., Orange Park, 32073.
Tel: 904-264-0577; Fax: 904-264-7999; Email: parish@stcatherineop.com; Email: busmgr@stcatherineop.com; Web: www.stcatherineop.com. Revs. Ignatius J. Plathanam, C.M.I., (India); Adam Izbicki, Parochial Vicar; William Villa.
Catechesis Religious Program—Email: formation@stcatherineop.com. Vincent Reilly, Dir. Faith Formation. Students 250.

PALATKA, PUTNAM CO., ST. MONICA (1858) [CEM]
114 S. 4th St., Palatka, 32177. Tel: 386-325-9777; Email: stmonicacatholic@bellsouth.net. Rev. Ronald A. Camarda.
Catechesis Religious Program—Catherine Webb, CCF Coord. Students 31.

PALM COAST, FLAGER CO., ST. ELIZABETH ANN SETON (1978) [CEM]
4600 Belle Terre Pkwy., Palm Coast, 32164.
Tel: 386-445-2246; Email: info@seaspcfl.org; Web: www.seaspcfl.org. Revs. Jason Trull; Arulanantham Yagappan, M.S.F.S., Parochial Vicar; Alexander Carandang, O.S.J., Parochial Vicar; Deacons Perlito (Tom) Alayu; Bob Devereaux; Jose Homem.
Catechesis Religious Program—Email: kallio@seaspcfl.org. Katherine Allio, D.R.E. Students 420.

PONTE VEDRA BEACH, ST. JOHN CO., OUR LADY STAR OF THE SEA (1972)
545 Hwy. A1A N., Ponte Vedra Beach, 32082.
Tel: 904-285-2698; Fax: 904-285-2502; Email: office@olsspvb.org; Web: www.olsspvb.org. Rev. Msgr. Keith R. Brennan, J.C.D., V.G.; Rev. Bastian Mathew, Parochial Vicar; Sr. Lucille Clynes, D.W, Pastoral Assoc.; Deacons Donald DeLorenzo; Anthony Marini, (Retired); Daniel Scrone.
Child Care—Preschool, Tel: 904-567-1970; Fax: 904-273-9740. Chris Saliba, Dir. Lay Teachers 9; Students 134.
School—Palmer Catholic Academy, 4889 Palm Valley Rd., Ponte Vedra Beach, 32082.
Tel: 904-543-8515; Fax: 904-543-8750; Web: www.pcapvb.org. Mrs. Linda Earp, Prin. Lay Teachers 36; Students 439; Clergy / Religious Teachers 1.
Catechesis Religious Program—Email: dvoutour@olsspvb.org. Dina Voutour, D.R.E. Students 285.
Mission—St. John Paul II Catholic Church, 127 Stonemason Way, Ponte Vedra, 32081.
Tel: 904-330-0153; Email: dre@stjp2.net. Rev. Edward Shaner, O.S.P.P.E.; Dodi Flora, Contact Person.

ST. AUGUSTINE SHORES, ST. JOHN CO., CORPUS CHRISTI (1975) [CEM]
6175 Datil Pepper Rd., St. Augustine, 32086.
Tel: 904-797-4842; Fax: 904-797-2746; Email: office@ccstaug.com; Web: www.corpuschristicatholicchurch.org. Rev. Edward W. Murphy.
Catechesis Religious Program—Students 70.

ST. JOHN, ST. JOHN CO., SAN JUAN DEL RIO (1977)
1718 State Rd., No. 13, St. John, 32259.
Tel: 904-287-0519; Email: padre@sjdrparish.org. Revs. John H. Tetlow, V.F.; Dilip Pally; Deacons Peter Dang; Stan Boschert; Michael Edison.
School—San Juan Del Rio School, 1714 State Rd. 13, 32259. Tel: 904-287-8081; Fax: 904-287-4574; Email: saints@sjdrschool.org; Web: www.sjdrsaints.org. Mr. Michael Masi, Prin. Lay Teachers 31; Students 391; Clergy / Religious Teachers 1.
Catechesis Religious Program—Tel: 904-287-2801. Students 609.

STARKE, BRADFORD CO., ST. EDWARD (1941)
441 N. Temple Ave., Starke, 32091-3207.
Tel: 904-964-6155; Email: stedward441@gmail.com. Rev. Jan A. Ligeza.
Catechesis Religious Program—Web: www.stedstarke.com. Students 8.

WILLISTON, LEVY CO., HOLY FAMILY (1970)
17353 N.E. Hwy. 27 Alt., Williston, 32696.
Tel: 352-528-2893; Fax: 352-528-6002; Email: holyfamilywilliston@gmail.com; Web: www.holyfamilychurch.org. Rev. Manny Lopez.
Catechesis Religious Program—Students 81.
Mission—St. Anthony the Abbot (1974) 6090 S.E. 193rd Pl., Inglis, Levy Co. 34449. Tel: 352-447-4573. P.O. Box 1070, Inglis, 34449. Fax: 352-528-6004. Heather Barly, Coord.

YULEE, NASSAU CO., ST. FRANCIS OF ASSISI CATHOLIC CHURCH
86000 St. Francis Way, Yulee, 32097.
Tel: 904-849-1256; Fax: 904-849-7622; Email: secretary@stfrancisyulee.org; Web: www.stfrancisyulee.org. Rev. Rafal Mazurowski, (Poland).

Special Assignment:
Revs.—
Augustun Nwagbara, 590 NE 16th Ave., Gainesville, 32601
Bower, Alan, 1806 N.W. 21st St., Gainesville, 32605
Nguyen, Lam, 6320 Bennett Rd., 32216
Young, Dennis M., 1601 S.W. Archer Rd., Gainesville, 32608-1197.

On Duty Outside the Diocese:
Rev. Msgr.—
Morgan, Michael P., J.D., J.C.L., Apostolic Nunciature to the United States, Washington, DC
Rev.—
Blaszkowski, Remiguiusz, J.C.D., Seminary.

On Graduate Studies:
Revs.—
Cusick, Timothy S., Post Graduate Studies
Hurley, Briggs, Rome, Italy.

Retired:
Rev. Msgrs.—
Conesa, Diego, (Retired)
Danaher, Mortimer, (Retired)
Haut, Vincent J., M.S.W., (Retired)
Heslin, James J., (Retired)
Ignacio, Simon Peter G., (Retired)
Kohls, Eugene C., P.A., J.C.D., (Retired)
Logan, Daniel B., (Retired)
Revs.—
Ahern, Bernard, (Retired)
Booth, Edward, (Retired)
Carroll, Patrick, C.S.Sp., (Retired)
Cody, Daniel, (Retired)
Cody, Thomas, (Retired)
Colasurdo, Peter, (Retired)
Cowart, Conrad, (Retired)
DePascale, Daniel, (Retired)
DiFazio, Silverio, (Retired)
Ducci, Alex, (Retired)
Dux, John H., (Retired)
Eburn, Brian, (Retired)
Florez, Luis, (Retired)
Frazer, Joseph, (Retired)
Gagan, Phillip R., (Retired)
Johnston, Jefferey, (Retired)
Julien, Roland M., V.F., (Retired)
Keene, Warren, (Retired)
Kelly, William A., (Retired)
Larkin, Michael J., (Retired)
Maniangat, Joseph, (Retired)
Maniyangat, Jose, (India)
May, James, (Retired)
McDermott, Robert, (Retired)
McDonnell, Joseph, (Retired)
McElroy, John, (Retired)
McGowan, Jeffrey A., (Retired)
McLoughlin, Luke, (Retired)
Mooney, William, (Retired)
Moore, Frederick Thomas, (Retired)
Nelson, Dennis (Dan), (Retired)
O'Flynn, Seamus, (Retired)
O'Neal, James E., (Retired)
Palazzolo, Anthony P., (Retired)
Perko, Richard, (Retired)
Raczynski, Paul, (Retired)
Revilla, Francisco, (Retired)
Rooney, Edward K., (Retired)
Russo, Caesar, M.A., J.C.L., S.T.L., (Retired)
Sankoorikal, George, (Retired)
Sebra, Anthony G., V.F., (Retired)
Sullivan, Donal, (Retired)
Sullivan, Thomas K., (Retired)
Walsh, Thomas P., (Retired)
Williams, Michael S., (Retired).

Permanent Deacons:
Deacons—
Abrahams, Vincent
Alayu, Perlito
Arnold, Stephen
Arsenault, Richard
Bajraktari, Gjet
Baker, John, M.D.
Barletta, George
Belanger, David
Boschert, Stan
Boudreaux, Kevin
Bretz, John
Brown, Frederic H., D.M.D.
Burgess, Jeffrey P. Sr.
Campbell, Brian
Casapulla, James
Cochran, Kenneth L. Sr.
Colichio, Tony
Consbruck, Paul
Conway, Scott J., M.Ed.
Cuesta, Angel, D.P.M.
Dang, Peter
DeLorenzo, Donald
DeLuca, Robert
Demers, Michael J.
Devereux, Robert
Dugan, Richard
Elison, Michael
Federico, Michael
Gagne, Ron
Gardner, Robert
Geinosky, Lawrence
Goin, Patrick J.
Good, George
Grenn, Stanley
Hart, Larry
Hecht, Corky
Holmes, Michael
Homem, Jose
Hughes, Brian
Kanaszka, Charles
Kidwell, Earl
Leahy, Michael
Lucian, Bob
Marini, Anthony
Martinez, Ralph
Moniz, John
Moody, Michael
Murati, George
Nullet, Doug
O'Brien, Michael J.
Ott, Bryan
Patterson, Chuck
Pelletier, John
Pettie, Paul
Prisby, Edward
Raymond, Jack
Repke, Robert
Richards, Thomas
Rosado-Rodriguez, Santiago, M.D.
Rounds, Jack

Sanchez, Angel
Sciullo, Mark
Scott, James
Scrone, Daniel
Shami, Elias
Silvernale, Jeffrey
Supple, Christopher
Swanson, James
Tatum, Dale
Testa, Paul
Treadwell, Art
Turkowski, Gerald
Vega, Milton
Williams, David A., M.A.
Wolff, Ed
Yazdiya, David
Zmuda, Henry.

INSTITUTIONS LOCATED IN DIOCESE

[A] DIOCESAN SCHOOLS

ST. AUGUSTINE. *Cathedral Parish Early Education Center*, 10 Sebastian Ave., St. Augustine, 32084. Tel: 904-829-2933; Email: valleycpeec@aol.com. Jill Valley, Dir.; Kathy Boice, Prin. (Preschool with Before and After School Care) Lay Teachers 8; Students 93.

St. Joseph's Academy, Inc., 155 State Rd. 207, St. Augustine, 32084. Tel: 904-824-0431; Fax: 904-826-4477; Email: todd.declemente@sjaweb.org; Web: www.sjaweb.org. Todd DeClemente, Prin. Day School. Religious Teachers 2; Lay Teachers 26; Students 314.

GAINESVILLE. *St. Anne Early Learning Center*, 4300 Newberry Rd., Gainesville, 32607. Tel: 352-448-9395; Email: sconway@dosafl.com. Deacon Scott J. Conway, M.Ed., Supt.

St. Francis Catholic High School, Inc., 4100 N.W. 115 Ter., Gainesville, 32606. Tel: 352-376-6545; Fax: 352-248-0418; Email: info@sfcawolves.org; Web: www.sfcawolves.org. Jason Acosta, Prin. Religious Teachers 1; Lay Teachers 21; Students 205.

JACKSONVILLE. *Bishop John Snyder High School, Inc.*, 5001 Samaritan Way, 32221. Tel: 904-771-1029; Fax: 904-908-8988; Email: davidyazdiya@bishopsnyder.org; Web: www.bishopsnyder.org. Deacon David Yazdiya, Prin. Religious Teachers 1; Lay Teachers 35; Students 459.

Bishop Kenny High School, Inc. (1952) 1055 Kingman Ave., 32207. Tel: 904-398-7545; Fax: 904-398-5728; Email: torlando@bishopkenny.org. Mr. Todd Orlando, M.Ed., Prin. Religious Teachers 1; Lay Teachers 82; Students 1,214.

Christ the King Early Learning Center, 720 Arlington Rd., 32211.

Guardian Catholic Schools, Inc., 4920 Brentwood Ave., 32206. Tel: 904-765-1920; Fax: 904-765-8155; Email: guardian@guardiancatholicschools.org. Sr. Dianne Rumschlag, S.N.D., Headmaster. This alliance includes the following schools: Religious Teachers 3; Lay Teachers 34; Students 409.

Holy Rosary Catholic School, (Grades PreK-8), 4920 Brentwood Ave., 32206. Tel: 904-765-6522; Fax: 904-765-9486; Email: sr.dianne.rumschlag@holyrosaryschooljax.org. Sr. Dianne Rumschlag, S.N.D., Prin.; April Rice, Librarian/Media Specialist. Lay Teachers 15; Sisters 5; Students 190.

St. Pius V Catholic School, (Grades PreK-8), 1470 W. 13th St., 32209. Tel: 904-354-2613; Fax: 904-356-4522; Email: principal@stpiusjax.com; Web: www.stpiusjax.com. Mrs. Lauren May, Prin. Lay Teachers 14; Sisters 3; Students 215.

MIDDLEBURG. *St. Luke Early Learning Center*, 1608 Blanding Blvd., Middleburg, 32068.

PONTE VEDRA. *St. John Paul II Early Learning Center*, 127 Stonemason Way, Bldg. 100, Ponte Vedra, 32081. Tel: 904-800-2445; Email: director@stjp2elc.net. Ms. Kathy Blanchard, Dir. Lay Teachers 10; Students 25.

ST. JOHNS. *St. Therese Early Learning Center*, 2468 County Rd. 210 W., St. Johns, 32259. Tel: 904-429-7637; Email: tlittle@sttheresee lc.org. Theresa Little, Dir. Lay Teachers 18; Students 142.

[B] ELEMENTARY SCHOOLS, INTERPAROCHIAL

GAINESVILLE. *St. Patrick School*, 550 N.E. 16th Ave., Gainesville, 32601. Tel: 352-376-9878; Fax: 352-371-6177; Email: info@stpatrickschoolgnv.org; Web: www.stpatrickschoolgnv.org. Frank Mackritis, Prin. Interparish school composed of students from St. Patrick, Holy Faith & St. Augustine, Gainesville. Lay Teachers 27; Students 383.

MIDDLEBURG. *Annunciation School* (1993) (Grades PreK-8), 1610 Blanding Blvd., Middleburg, 32068. Tel: 904-282-0504; Email: principal@annunciationcatholic.org; Web: www.annunciationcatholic.org. Victoria Farrington, Prin. Interparish school composed of students from Sacred Heart, Green Cove Springs; St. Catherine's, Orange Park; and St. Luke, Middleburg. Lay Teachers 19; Students 378.

[C] CATHOLIC CHARITIES

JACKSONVILLE. *Catholic Charities Bureau, Inc.*, 134 E. Church St., 32202. Tel: 904-354-4846; Fax: 904-899-5510; Email: ahassell@ccbdosa.org; Web: www.ccbdosa.org. Anita Hassell, CEO. Tot Asst. Annually 87,746; Total Staff 96.

Catholic Charities Bureau, Gainesville, 1701 N.E. 9th St., Gainesville, 32609. Tel: 352-372-0294; Fax: 352-371-3157; Email: jbarli@ccgnv.org; Web: www.catholiccharitiesgainesville.org. John C. Barli, Dir. (Emergency services, pregnancy counseling, adoptions, adult finance education, and weekend hunger backpack program.).

Catholic Charities Bureau, Jacksonville (1945) 134 E. Church St., 32202. Tel: 904-354-4718; Fax: 904-224-0092, Ext. 228; Email: lhopkins@ccbjax.org; Email: hjarvis@ccbjax.org; Web: www.ccbjax.org. Lauren Weedon Hopkins, Dir. Emergency financial assistance for housing/utilities, food pantry, immigration legal assistance, workforce development and refugee resettlement. Tot Asst. Annually 15,000; Total Staff 57.

Catholic Charities Bureau, Lake City, 553 N.W. Railroad St., Lake City, 32055. Tel: 386-754-9180; Fax: 386-754-5325; Email: cclc@bellsouth.net; Web: www.catholiccharitieslakecity.org. Suzanne M. Edwards, COO.

Catholic Charities Bureau, St. Augustine, 3940 Lewis Speedway, Ste. 2103, St. Augustine, 32084. Tel: 904-829-6300; Fax: 904-829-0494; Email: info@ccbstaug.org; Web: ccbstaug.org. Jill Leslie, Dir. Tot Asst. Annually 9,621; Total Staff 8.

[D] SPECIAL APOSTOLATES

ST. AUGUSTINE. *Religious Education for Catholic Deaf and Blind*, 1112-1120 State Rd. 16, St. Augustine, 32084. Tel: 904-824-6625; Fax: 904-829-0459; Email: susan@sansebastiancatholicchurch.com.

JACKSONVILLE. *L'Arche Jacksonville, Inc.* (1985) 700 Arlington Rd. N., 32211. Tel: 904-721-5992; Fax: 904-721-7143; Email: hello@larchejacksonville.org; Web: larchejacksonville.org. Melanie Saxon, Exec. Dir. & Community Leader. A residential community for adults with intellectual disabilities and those who choose to share life with them (assistants). We also have an adult day program called the Rainbow Workshop. Founded on the gospel teachings. Bed Capacity 20; Tot Asst. Annually 30; Total Staff 39.

Morning Star School (1956) 725 Mickler Rd., 32211. Tel: 904-721-2144; Fax: 904-721-1040; Email: principal@morningstar-jax.org; Web: www.morningstar-jax.org. Jean Barnes, Prin. A school for exceptional children. Lay Teachers 5; Students 42.

[E] GENERAL HOSPITALS

JACKSONVILLE. *St. Vincent's Medical Center, Inc.*, 1 Shircliff Way, P.O. Box 2982, 32204. Tel: 904-308-7300; Fax: 904-308-7326; Email: Hugh.Middlebrooks@ascension.org; Web: www.jaxhealth.com. Thomas VanOsdol, CEO; Tracie Loftis, Chief Mission Officer. Ascension Health MinistriesMember St. Vincent's Health System, Inc. Bed Capacity 528; Total Assisted Annually (inc. sub-orgs.) 503,482; Total Staff (inc. sub-orgs.) 3,639.

St. Luke's - St. Vincent's HealthCare, Inc. dba St. Vincent's Medical Center Southside Member: St. Vincent's Health System, Inc. 4201 Belfort Rd., 32216. Tel: 904-296-3700; Fax: 904-296-3760; Email: Hugh.Middlebrooks@ascension.org; Web: www.jaxhealth.com. J. Hugh Middlebrooks, Chief Legal Officer. Ascension Health Ministries Bassinets 17; Bed Capacity 309; Nurses 383; Tot Asst. Annually 55,940; Total Staff 931.

St. Vincent's Medical Center-Clay County, Inc., 1 Shircliff Way, 32204. Tel: 904-602-1000; Email: hugh.middlebrooks@ascension.org. 1670 St. Vincent's Way, Middleburg, 32068. J. Hugh Middlebrooks, Chief Legal Officer. Bassinets 12; Bed Capacity 106; Nurses 219; Tot Asst. Annually 55,526; Total Staff 567.

St. Vincent's Foundation, Inc., 1 Shircliff Way, 32204. Tel: 904-308-7306; Fax: 904-308-7573; Email: Hugh.Middlebrooks@ascension.org. Jane Lanier, Pres.; Thomas VanOsdol, Dir.

St. Vincent's Ambulatory Care, Inc., 1 Shircliff Way, 32204. Tel: 904-308-1290; Fax: 904-308-4085. J. Hugh Middlebrooks, Chief Legal Officer.

St. Vincent's Health System, Inc., 1 Shircliff Way, 32204. Tel: 904-308-7300; Fax: 904-308-2947; Email: Hugh.Middlebrooks@ascension.org. Thomas VanOsdol, Pres.; J. Hugh Middlebrooks, Chief Legal Officer.

[F] HOMES FOR AGING

JACKSONVILLE. *Casa San Pedro*, 365 Marywood Dr., St. Johns, 32259. Tel: 904-230-2562; Fax: 904-230-2563; Email: csanpedr@bellsouth.net; Web: www.marywoodcenter.org. Matt Achorn, Dir.

St. Catherine Laboure Manor aka St. Catherine Laboure Place, 1750 Stockton St., 32204. Tel: 904-308-4700; Fax: 904-308-2987; Email: neil.ramski@ascension.org; Web: www.ascensionliving.org. Neil Ramski, Admin. Long term health care skilled nursing facility. Bed Capacity 240; Sisters 3; Tot Asst. Annually 1,224; Total Staff 265.

[G] CATHOLIC CHARITIES OFFICE OF HOUSING

JACKSONVILLE. *Jacksonville, Family Housing Management Co.* (1986) 134 E. Church St., 32202. Tel: 904-632-1255; Fax: 904-632-2135; Email: aballard@ccbjax.org. Norberto Cruz, Pres.; Alma C. Ballard, Exec. Dir. Tot Asst. Annually 326; Total Staff 4.

Jacksonville, Office of Housing Development, 134 E. Church St., 32202. Tel: 904-632-1255; Fax: 904-632-2135; Email: aballard@ccbjax.org. Alma C. Ballard, Exec. Dir.

Hurley Apartments (1984) 3333-35 University Blvd. N., 32277. Tel: 904-744-6022; Fax: 904-744-6037; Email: fpgimenez@hurleyapts.org. Donald Zehnder, Pres.; Franceli Gimenez, Mgr. Parent Co., Catholic Charities Housing Association of Jacksonville, Inc. Tot Asst. Annually 152; Total Staff 10.

Barry Apartments (1984) 1000 Husson Ave., Palatka, 32177. Tel: 386-328-5137; Fax: 386-328-5138; Email: office@barryapts.org. Wilhelmina Clay, Pres. Parent Co., Palatka Retirement Villas, Inc. Tot Asst. Annually 75; Total Staff 7.

Providence Center, 134 E. Church St., 32202. Tel: 904-632-1255; Fax: 904-632-2135; Email: aballard@ccbjax.org. Alma C. Ballard, Contact Person. Total Staff 2.

San Jose I Apartments (1991) 3630 Galicia Rd., 32217. Tel: 904-739-0555; Fax: 904-739-0559; Email: sja@sanjoseapts.comcastbiz.net. Betty Trad, Pres.; Jacqueta Nash, Mgr. (Parent Company: Housing Association of the Diocese of St. Augustine.) Tot Asst. Annually 50; Total Staff 3.

San Jose II Apartments (2000) 3622 Galicia Rd., 32217. Tel: 904-739-0555; Fax: 904-739-0559; Email: sja@sanjoseapts.comcastbiz.net. Joe DeSalvo, Pres.; Jacqueta Nash, Mgr. (Parent Company: San Jose Catholic Housing Assoc., Inc.) Tot Asst. Annually 50; Total Staff 3.

[H] MONASTERIES AND RESIDENCES OF PRIESTS AND BROTHERS

BUNNELL. *Discalced Carmelite Fathers of Florida*, 141 Carmelite Dr., Bunnell, 32110. Tel: 386-437-2910; Email: carmelitefathers@aol.com. Revs. Joseph F. Zawada, O.C.D.; Artur Chojda, O.C.D., Prior; Slawomir S. Podsiedlik, O.C.D.; Bro. Patrick Gemmato, O.C.D. Total Staff 4.

[I] CONVENTS AND RESIDENCES FOR SISTERS

ST. AUGUSTINE. *Motherhouse of the Sisters of St. Joseph of St. Augustine, Florida*, 241 St. George St., P.O. Box 3506, St. Augustine, 32085. Tel: 904-824-1752; Fax: 904-826-0949; Web: ssjfl.org. Sr. Jane Stoecker, S.S.J., Gen. Supr. Professed Sisters 60.

The Sisters of St. Joseph Continuing Community Support Trust Fund., St. Augustine. Tel: 904-824-1752; Fax: 904-826-0949.

St. Joseph Ministries, P.O. Box 3506, Saint Augustine, 32085.

[J] RETREAT HOUSES

JACKSONVILLE. *Marywood Center for Spirituality and Ministry*, 235 Marywood Dr., St. Johns, 32259. Tel: 904-287-2525; Fax: 904-287-9738; Email: info@marywoodcenter.org; Web: www.marywoodcenter.org. Charles David, Admin., Email: charlesjdavid@yahoo.com; Ginger Eddy, Dir. Total Staff 15.

[K] NEWMAN CENTERS

ST. AUGUSTINE. *Flagler College Catholic Fellowship*, c/o Cathedral Basilica of St. Augustine, 35 Treasury St., St. Augustine, 32084. Tel: 904-824-2806; Fax: 904-824-0761; Email: frtomstaug@gmail.com. Rev. Thomas S. Willis.

JACKSONVILLE. *U.N.F. Catholic Student Center*, 11277 Alumni Way, 32246. Cell: 904-687-8883; Tel: 904-516-8140; Email: awilson@dosafl.com; Email: bsamuelson@dosafl.com; Email: staugustineccm@gmail.com. Rev. Blair Gaynes, Dir.; Sr. Brittany Samuelson, S.C.T.J.M., Campus Min.; Alex Wilson, Campus Min.

[L] MISCELLANEOUS

ST. AUGUSTINE. *St. Augustine House of Prayer & Evangelization Center*, 30 Ocean Ave., St. Augustine, 32084. Tel: 904-824-4831.

Sisters of St. Joseph's Architectural Stained Glass, 2745 Industry Center Rd., #6, St. Augustine, 32084. Tel: 904-669-5388; Email: liteart@aol.com; Web: www.ssjstainedglass.com. Sr. Diane Couture, S.S.J., Dir.

GAINESVILLE. *Spirit Radio of North Florida, Inc.*, 500 N.E. 16th Ave., Gainesville, 32601. Tel: 352-372-2191; Fax: 352-376-0575; Email: rolandjulien@hotmail.com; Web: www.spirit-radio.org. Rev. Roland M. Julien, V.F., (Retired).

JACKSONVILLE. **Association of St. Lawrence Comunita Cenacolo America Inc.*, 1050 Talleyrand Ave., 32206. Tel: 904-353-5353; Fax: 904-353-4707; Email: cenacolo@bellsouth.net; Web: www.hopereborn.org. Albino Aragno, Exec. Dir.

DSA Land, Inc., 11625 Old St. Augustine Rd., 32258. Tel: 904-262-3200, Ext. 190; Email: mnedrich@dosafl.com. Deacon David A. Williams, M.A., Chancellor.

RELIGIOUS INSTITUTES OF MEN REPRESENTED IN THE DIOCESE

For further details refer to the corresponding bracketed number in the Religious Institutes of Men or Women section.

[]—*Apostles of Jesus*—A.J.
[0275]—*Carmelites of Mary Immaculate*—C.M.I.
[]—*Community of the Immaculate Conception*—I.C.C.
[]—*Congregation of the Most Holy Redeemer*—C.Ss.R.
[]—*Congregation of the Sacred Stigmata*—C.S.S.
[0260]—*Discalced Carmelite Friars*—O.C.D.
[0650]—*Holy Ghost Fathers*—C.S.Sp.
[1160]—*Marist Brothers*—F.M.S.
[0920]—*Missionaries of St. Francis de Sales*—M.S.F.S.
[]—*Missionary Congregation of the Blessed Sacrament*—M.C.B.S.
[]—*Missionary Society of St. Thomas the Apostle*—M.S.T.
[1161]—*Missionary Sons of the Immaculate Heart of Mary, Claretians*—C.M.F.
[1163]—*Oblates of St. Joseph*—O.S.J.
[]—*Order of St. Benedict, Benedictines*—O.S.B.
[1164]—*Order of St. Paul the First Hermit*—O.S.P.P.E.
[]—*Order of the BVM of Mercy*—O.deM.

RELIGIOUS INSTITUTES OF WOMEN REPRESENTED IN THE DIOCESE

[]—*Carmelite Sisters*—O.Carm.
[0685]—*Claretian Missionary Sisters*—R.M.I.
[]—*Daughters of Wisdom*—D.W.
[1070-13]—*Dominican Sisters*—O.P.
[]—*Mercedarian Sisters of the Blessed Sacrament*—H.M.S.S.
[]—*Missionary Sisters of the Holy Family*—M.S.F.
[]—*Sacred Heart Congregation*—S.H.
[]—*Servant Sisters of the Home of the Mother*—S.S.H.M.
[2170]—*Servants of the Immaculate Heart of Mary*—I.H.M.
[]—*Servants of the Pierced Hearts of Jesus & Mary*—S.C.T.J.M.
[]—*Sisters for Christian Community*—S.F.C.C.
[]—*Sisters of Mercy of Ireland*—R.S.M.
[2990]—*Sisters of Notre Dame* (Toledo Prov.)—S.N.D.
[]—*Sisters of St. Francis Xavier*—S.F.X.
[3900]—*Sisters of St. Joseph of St. Augustine, FL*—S.S.J.
[]—*Trinitarian Handmaids of the Divine Word*—T.H.D.W.

DIOCESAN CEMETERIES

ST. AUGUSTINE. *St. Augustine Diocesan Cemeteries* Operates San Lorenzo Cemetery in St. Augustine and St. Mary Cemetery in Bunnell. 1635 U.S. 1 S., St. Augustine, 32084. Tel: 904-824-6680; Fax: 904-824-3845; Email: krezendes@dosafl.com. Keith Rezendes, Dir.

An asterisk (*) denotes an organization that has established tax-exempt status directly with the IRS and is not covered by the USCCB Group Ruling.

Diocese of St. Cloud

(Dioecesis S. Clodoaldi)

Most Reverend

DONALD J. KETTLER, J.C.L.

Bishop of St. Cloud; ordained May 29, 1970; appointed Bishop of Fairbanks June 7, 2002; ordained and installed August 22, 2002; appointed Bishop of St. Cloud September 20, 2013; installed November 7, 2013. *Office: 214 Third Ave. S., P.O. Box 1248, Saint Cloud, MN 56302-1248.* Tel: 320-251-2340.

Chancery: 214 Third Ave. S., P.O. Box 1248, St. Cloud, MN 56302-1248. Tel: 320-251-2340; Fax: 320-251-0470.

Web: www.stcdio.org

Square Miles 12,251.

Corporate Title: "The Diocese of St. Cloud."

Erected as the Vicariate of Northern Minnesota, February 12, 1875.

Created as the Diocese of St. Cloud, September 22, 1889.

Comprises the Counties of Stearns, Sherburne, Benton, Morrison, Mille Lacs, Kanabec, Isanti, Pope, Stevens, Traverse, Grant, Douglas, Wilkin, Otter Tail, Todd and Wadena in the State of Minnesota.

For legal titles of parishes and diocesan institutions, consult the Chancery Office.

STATISTICAL OVERVIEW

Personnel	
Bishop	1
Retired Bishops	1
Abbots	1
Priests: Diocesan Active in Diocese	55
Priests: Diocesan Active Outside Diocese	1
Priests: Retired, Sick or Absent	32
Number of Diocesan Priests	88
Religious Priests in Diocese	98
Total Priests in Diocese	186
Ordinations:	
Religious Priests	2
Transitional Deacons	3
Permanent Deacons	2
Permanent Deacons in Diocese	57
Total Brothers	56
Total Sisters	305
Parishes	
Parishes	131
With Resident Pastor:	
Resident Diocesan Priests	55
Resident Religious Priests	11
Without Resident Pastor:	
Administered by Priests	61
Administered by Deacons	2
Welfare	
Catholic Hospitals	3
Homes for the Aged	11
Special Centers for Social Services	1
Total Assisted	73,821
Residential Care of Disabled	7
Educational	
Seminaries, Diocesan	1
Diocesan Students in Other Seminaries	13
Total Seminarians	13
Colleges and Universities	2
Total Students	3,621
High Schools, Diocesan and Parish	1
Total Students	670
High Schools, Private	1
Total Students	275
Elementary Schools, Diocesan and Parish	27
Total Students	5,028
Catechesis/Religious Education:	
High School Students	3,754
Elementary Students	9,825
Total Students under Catholic Instruction	23,186
Teachers in the Diocese:	
Priests	3
Sisters	3
Lay Teachers	728
Vital Statistics	
Receptions into the Church:	
Infant Baptism Totals	1,861
Adult Baptism Totals	16
Received into Full Communion	113
First Communions	1,503
Confirmations	1,258
Marriages:	
Catholic	320
Interfaith	120
Total Marriages	440
Deaths	1,318
Total Catholic Population	124,974
Total Population	576,936

Former Bishops—Rt. Revs. RUPERT SEIDENBUSCH, O.S.B., D.D., ord. June 22, 1853; cons. Bishop of Halia, Vicar-Apostolic of Northern Minnesota, May 30, 1875; resigned Nov. 15, 1888; died June 2, 1895; OTTO ZARDETTI, D.D., ord. Aug. 21, 1870; cons. Oct. 20, 1889; transferred to Bucharest, Romania, and raised to the Archiepiscopal Dignity, Feb. 23, 1894; died May 9, 1902; MARTIN MARTY, O.S.B., D.D., ord. Sept. 14, 1856; cons. Bishop of Tiberias, Feb. 1, 1880; Bishop of Sioux Falls, 1889; transferred to St. Cloud, Jan. 21, 1895; died Sept. 19, 1896; JAMES TROBEC, D.D., ord. Sept. 8, 1865; cons. Bishop of St. Cloud, Sept. 21, 1897; resigned April 15, 1914; appt. Titular Bishop of Lycopolis; died Dec. 14, 1921; Most Revs. JOSEPH F. BUSCH, D.D., ord. July 28, 1889; appt. Bishop of Lead, S. D., April 9, 1910; cons. May 19, 1910; transferred to See of St. Cloud, Jan. 19, 1915; died May 31, 1953; PETER W. BARTHOLOME, D.D., ord. June 12, 1917; appt. Titular Bishop of Lete and Coadjutor Bishop of St. Cloud "cum jure successionis", Dec. 6, 1941; cons. March 3, 1942; succeeded to See May 31, 1953; appt. Assistant at the Pontifical Throne July 23, 1954; resigned Jan. 31, 1968; died June 17, 1982; GEORGE H. SPELTZ, D.D., Ph.D., ord. June 2, 1940; appt. Auxiliary Bishop of Winona and Titular Bishop of Claneus February 13, 1963; cons. March 25, 1963; appt. Coadjutor of St. Cloud April 4, 1966; succeeded Jan. 31, 1968; resigned Jan. 13, 1987; died Feb. 1, 2004; JEROME HANUS, O.S.B., D.D., ord. July 30, 1966; appt. Bishop of St. Cloud, July 6, 1987; ord. and installed Aug. 24, 1987; appt. Coadjutor Archbishop of Dubuque, IA, Aug. 23, 1994; JOHN F. KINNEY, D.D., J.C.D., ord. Feb. 2, 1963; appt. Titular Bishop of Caorle and Auxiliary Bishop of St. Paul and Minneapolis Nov. 16, 1976; cons. Jan. 25, 1977; appt. Bishop of Bismarck June 28, 1982; installed Aug. 23, 1982; appt. Bishop of St. Cloud May 9, 1995; installed July 6, 1995; resigned Nov. 7, 2013.

Chancery—214 Third Ave. S., P.O. Box 1248, St. Cloud, 56302. Tel: 320-251-2340; Tel: 320-259-5227 (after hours); Fax: 320-251-0470. Office Hours: Mon.-Fri. 8:30-12 & 1-4:30.

Vicar General—Very Rev. ROBERT ROLFES, J.C.L.

Chancellor—JANE MARRIN, Email: jmarrin@gw.stcdio.org.

Diocesan Tribunal—305 Seventh Ave. N., St. Cloud, 56303. All marriage cases are to be directed to: The Tribunal, Box 576, St. Cloud, 56302. Tel: 320-251-6557.

Judicial Vicar—Rev. VIRGIL A. HELMIN, J.C.L.

Adjutant Judicial Vicar—Rev. MARVIN ENNEKING, J.C.L.

Promoter Justitiae—Rev. ROBERT C. HARREN, J.C.L., (Retired).

Defensor Vinculi—Revs. GREGORY LIESER, (Retired); JONATHAN LICARI, O.S.B.; THOMAS OLSON, (Retired); NICHOLAS LANDSBERGER, (Retired).

Judges—Rev. MARVIN ENNEKING, J.C.L.; Very Rev. ROBERT ROLFES, J.C.L.; Rev. VIRGIL HELMIN, J.C.L.; THERESA A. WYBURN, J.C.L.

Notaries—Rev. VIRGIL A. HELMIN, J.C.L.; Very Rev. ROBERT ROLFES, J.C.L.; KARRIE MOLLNER.

Advocates—Revs. JOSEPH KORF; MARK INNOCENTI; MRS. DOLORES SALCHERT.

Marriage Counseling—Caritas Family Services, 911 18th St. N., St. Cloud, 56303. Tel: 320-650-1660.

Diocesan Consultors—Very Rev. ROBERT ROLFES, J.C.L.; Revs. ROBERT HARREN, J.C.L., (Retired); JOSEPH HERZING; BENJAMIN KOCIEMBA; MATTHEW LUFT, O.S.B; EDWARD VEBELUN, O.S.B.

Deans—Revs. STEVEN BINSFELD, Alexandria/Morris; GLENN A. KRYSTOSEK, Cold Spring; ARLIE SOWADA, Fergus Falls/Wadena; DONALD WAGNER, Cambridge; VACANT, Foley/Princeton; Revs. DAVID MACIEJ, Little Falls; MARVIN ENNEKING, J.C.L., Melrose/Sauk Centre; ROBERT HARREN, J.C.L., St. Cloud, (Retired).

Diocesan Corporate Board—Most Rev. DONALD J. KETTLER, J.C.L.; Very Rev. ROBERT ROLFES, J.C.L., Vice Pres.; Revs. JOSEPH KORF; DONALD WAGNER; JANE MARRIN.

Diocesan Finance Council—Most Rev. DONALD J. KETTLER, J.C.L.; JOSEPH SPANIOL, Finance Officer; Very Rev. ROBERT ROLFES, J.C.L.; Rev. RONALD WEYRENS; Sr. ARDELLA KVAMME, O.S.B.; JEAN HART; GREGORY SIMONES; GARY MEYER; PAUL PFANNENSTEIN; NIKOLI SAEHR; TIM DIMBERIO; KRIS LEVANDOWSKI.

Conciliation / Arbitration Process—JANE MARRIN, Dir.

Liturgical Commission—Rev. KEVIN ANDERSON; KRISTI BIVENS; AARON CARPENTER.

Presbyteral Council—Most Rev. DONALD J. KETTLER, J.C.L.; Revs. ROBERT E. ROLFES, J.C.L., V.G., Vicar Gen.; MATTHEW KUHN; PETER VANDERWEYST; OMAR GUANCHEZ; VIRGIL HELMIN, J.C.L.; ROBERT HARREN, J.C.L., (Retired); EDWARD VEBELUN, O.S.B.; MATTHEW LUFT, O.S.B.

Pastoral Council—Most Rev. DONALD J. KETTLER, J.C.L.; PATRICIA LOXTERCAMP, Exec. Sec.; JASON STOCK; DARRELL WELLE; ABIGAIL LONDE; CAROL BRUNN; RUSS VANDENHEUVEL; Deacon GERALD THEIS; JIM SCHWARTZ; DARLENE FELLING; Sr. BETTY LARSON, O.S.B.; JOSEPH TOWALKI; KRISTI ANDERSON; EMILY PRIMUS; CHERYL WELLE; Rev. GREGORY MILLER, O.S.B.

Diocesan Offices and Programs

Archives—VACANT.

Boy Scouts—Rev. BENJAMIN KOCIEMBA, Chap., 1125 11th Ave. N., Saint Cloud, 56303.

Catholic Campaign for Human Development—911 18th St. N., P.O. Box 2390, St. Cloud, 56302. Tel: 320-229-6020. KATERI MANCINI.

Campus Ministry—Newman Center, 396 First Ave. S., St. Cloud, 56301. Rev. JOSEPH HERZING.

Catholic Charities—911 18th St., N., P.O. Box 2390, St.

Cloud, 56302. Tel: 320-650-1550; Fax: 320-650-1528. Deacon STEPHEN PAREJA, Exec. Dir. Community Services (Senior Dining, Central Minnesota Foster Grandparent Program, Support and Advocacy for Independent Living, Supportive Housing for Youth, Youth Transitional Housing; In Home Program for Persons with Disabilities, Community Alternative for Handicapped Individuals, Mother Teresa Home, St. Anne's Home, St. Francis Home, St. Luke's Home, Bethany Home); Caritas Family Services (Caritas Mental Health Clinic; Emergency Services: Food, Clothing, Financial; Financial and Housing Counseling; Hope Community Support Program; St. Elizabeth's Home; St. Margaret's Home & St. Michael's Home); Housing Services (Housing Management and Transitional Housing including Domus Transitional Housing, Emily's Place & V.A. Home); Day Services (St. Cloud Children's Home, Intensive Treatment Unit, Young Learners & Day Treatment); Social Concerns (Immigrant & Refugee Community Organizing & Rural Life Leadership Development Initiative).

Catholic Foundation of the Diocese of St. Cloud—MR. DAVID EICKHOFF, Exec. Dir., 305 7th Ave. N., St. Cloud, 56303. Tel: 320-258-0390.

Catholic Relief Services—Rev. WILLIAM VOS, Dir., (Retired), 11 Eighth Ave. S., St. Cloud, 56301. Tel: 320-251-1100; Fax: 320-251-2061.

Catholic Women, Council of—308 Third St. S., Sauk Rapids, 56379. Tel: 320-281-3775. Rev. LAURN VIRNIG, Spiritual Advisor, (Retired).

Cemeteries Assumption-Calvary—2341 Roosevelt Rd., St. Cloud, 56301. Tel: 320-251-5511.

Censores Librorum—Rev. ROBERT C. HARREN, J.C.L., (Retired); Sr. RENEE DOMEIER, O.S.B.

Clerical Aid Association—Address Mail To: The Chancery, P.O. Box 1248, St. Cloud, 56302. Most Rev. DONALD J. KETTLER, J.C.L.; Very Rev. ROBERT ROLFES, J.C.L., Sec.; JANE MARRIN; Revs. JOSEPH KORF; LAUREN GERMANN. Directors: Revs. GLENN A. KRYSTOSEK; DONALD WAGNER; ARLIE SOWADA, (Retired); DAVID MACIEJ; BENJAMIN KOCIEMBA; RONALD WEYRENS; ROBERT KIEFFER, (Retired).

Communications Office—(Radio, Television, Public Information), MR. JOSEPH TOWALSKI, 305 N. 7th Ave., Saint Cloud, 56303. Tel: 320-251-3022.

Continuing Formation of Priests—305 7th Ave. N., St. Cloud, 56303. Tel: 320-251-8335. Rev. JOSEPH HERZING.

Development Office—305 7th Ave. N., Ste. 105, St. Cloud, 56303. Tel: 320-258-0390. MR. JOSEPH TOWALSKI, Dir., Stewardship & Devel.

Diocesan Education Council—LINDA KAISER, Dir.; JOAN KRAUSE; BRENDA KRESKY; KENT SCHMITZ; MAYULI BALES; TIMOTHY WELCH; CHRISTINE CODDEN; JOAN HAIDER; CHRISTINE FRIEDERICHS; KATY LENZ; SHIRLEY SCAPANSKI; KRISTI BIVENS; Rev. BENJAMIN KOCIEMBA.

Office of Catholic Education Ministries—Address all correspondence to: Catholic Education Ministries, Pastoral Center, Diocese of St. Cloud, 305 Seventh Ave., N., St. Cloud, 56303. Tel: 320-251-0111. LINDA KAISER, Dir.; TIMOTHY WELCH, Consultant, Educational Technology; KENT SCHMITZ, Consultant for Youth Ministry & Rel. Educ.; KRISTI BIVENS, Assoc. Dir., Lay Leadership Formation; LAURA GORDER, Receptionist/Sec.

Diocesan Commission on Ecumenical and Interreligious Affairs—Sr. HELEN ROLFSON, O.S.F., 3402 22nd St. S., Saint Cloud, 56301.

Diocesan Planning Council—Most Rev. DONALD J. KETTLER, J.C.L.; Rev. TIMOTHY BALTES; Very Rev. ROBERT ROLFES, J.C.L.; Deacon CRAIG KORVER; Revs. EUGENE DOYLE; AARON J. KUHN; MATTHEW LUFT, O.S.B; DR. WILLIAM CAHOY; DR. BARBARA SUTTON; MS. RITA CLASEMANN, Chm.; EDITH HERNANDEZ-FUSSY; Sr. JULIE SCHLEPER, O.S.B.; HANNAH VOSS; CAROL BRUNN; BERNIE CULLEN; AL PEKAREK; ANDY KLINNERT; KAREN PUNDSCK; MARY KAY BODEEN; Deacon DAVID HERNANDEZ; ADELA HERNANDEZ; JANE MARRIN; Deacon STEPHEN PAREJA; BAILEY ZIEGLER; BRENDA KRESKY, Dir., Pastoral Planning; JAYNE BRUEMMER, Administrative Asst.

Diocesan Priests Pension Plan Trustees—Most Rev. DONALD J. KETTLER, J.C.L.; Very Rev. ROBERT ROLFES, J.C.L.; Revs. RONALD WEYRENS; TIMOTHY WENZEL, (Retired); DANIEL WALZ; KEVIN ANDERSON; GLENN A. KRYSTOSEK; RICHARD LEISEN, (Retired); JANE MARRIN, Chancellor.

Vicar for Retired Priests—Very Rev. ROBERT ROLFES, J.C.L.

Health Ministry—Rev. THOMAS KNOBLACH, Ph.D., Consultant for Healthcare Ethics.

Holy Childhood Association—ELIZABETH NEVILLE, Dir., 11 8th Ave., S., St. Cloud, 56301.

Koinonia Program of Central Minnesota—Rev. DAVID MACIEJ, Mailing Address: P.O. Box 38, Lastrup, 56344.

Legion of Decency—Very Rev. ROBERT ROLFES, J.C.L., Mailing Address: P.O. Box 1248, St. Cloud, 56302.

Legion of Mary—Rev. RICHARD LEISEN, (Retired), 308 3rd St. S., Sauk Rapids, 56379.

Multicultural Ministry—MAYULI BALES, Dir., 305 N. 7th Ave., Saint Cloud, 56303. Tel: 320-529-4614.

Office of Marriage and Family—CHRISTINE CODDEN, Dir., 305 N. 7th Ave., Ste. 100, St. Cloud, 56303. Tel: 320-252-4721; Tel: 320-252-4721; Fax: 320-258-7658.

Newspaper "The Visitor"—Pastoral Center, Diocese of St. Cloud, 305 N. Seventh Ave., Box 1068, St. Cloud, 56302. Tel: 320-251-3022. MR. JOSEPH TOWALSKI, Editor.

Office of Diaconate—VACANT, Dir., 214 Third Ave. S., Saint Cloud, 56303. Tel: 320-251-2340; Fax: 320-251-0470; Deacon ERNEST KOCIEMBA, Consultant for Diaconate; Rev. RALPH G. ZIMMERMAN, Vicar for Permanent Deacons; Deacon FRANK RINGSMUTH, Pres. Diaconal Community, 851 5th Ave., S., Waite Park, 56387. Tel: 320-253-6032.

Personnel Committee—Most Rev. DONALD J. KETTLER, J.C.L.; Very Rev. ROBERT ROLFES, J.C.L., Dir.; Revs. TIMOTHY BALTES, Chair, Mailing Address: P.O. Box 150, Sartell, 56377-0150; LEROY SCHEIERL; SCOTT POGATCHNIK; STEPHEN BEAUCLAIR, O.S.B.; Deacon ERNEST KOCIEMBA.

Propagation of the FaithELIZABETH NEVILLE, Dir., 11 8th Ave. S., Saint Cloud, 56301. Tel: 320-251-2061.

Rural Life Program—911 18th St. N., P.O. Box 2390, St. Cloud, 56302. Tel: 320-229-6020. KATERI MANCINI.

TEC (Central Minnesota TEC) (Together Encountering Christ)—MICHAEL LENTZ, Coord., Mailing Address: P.O. Box 500, Onamia, 56359. Tel: 320-532-3103.

Assistance Coordinator—ROXANNE STORMS, Tel: 320-248-1563.

Vocations—214 Third Ave. S., St. Cloud, 56301. Tel: 320-251-5001; Fax: 320-251-0470. Revs. SCOTT POGATCHNIK, Dir.; BENJAMIN KOCIEMBA, Asst. Dir.

Worship, Office of—Pastoral Center, Diocese of St. Cloud, 305 N. Seventh Ave., St. Cloud, 56303. Tel: 320-255-9068. AARON CARPENTER, Dir.

CLERGY, PARISHES, MISSIONS AND PAROCHIAL SCHOOLS

CITY OF ST. CLOUD

(BENTON, STEARNS, SHERBURNE COUNTIES)

1—ST. MARY'S CATHEDRAL OF ST. CLOUD, [JC]
25 Eighth Ave. S., 56301-4279. Tel: 320-251-1840; Email: office@stmarysstcloud.org. Revs. Scott Pogatchnik, Rector; Douglas Liebsch; Robert E. Rolfes, J.C.L., V.G., In Res.; Deacons Richard Scheierl; John Wocken.
School-See St. Katherine Drexel School, St. Cloud under Inter-Parochial Schools located in the Institution section.
Catechesis Religious Program—Nikki Walz, D.R.E. Students 54.

2—ST. ANTHONY OF PADUA (1920)
2405 1st St. N., 56303. Tel: 320-251-5966; Email: saps@spiritandsaints.org. Revs. Thomas Knoblach, Ph.D.; Douglas Wiechmann, Parochial Vicar.
School-See St. Elizabeth Ann Seton School, St. Cloud under Inter-Parochial Schools located in the Institution section.
Catechesis Religious Program—2410 1st. St. N., 56303. Virginia Duschner, D.R.E. Students 91.

3—ST. AUGUSTINE (1919)
442 Second St., S.E., 56304. Tel: 320-251-8335; Email: info@staugs.com. Revs. Scott Pogatchnik; Douglas Liebsch; Deacons Richard Scheierl; John Wocken.
Res.: 25 8th Ave. S., 56301.
School-See St. Katharine Drexel School under Inter-Parochial Schools located in the Institution section.
Catechesis Religious Program—Tel: 320-252-6042; Fax: 320-529-3236. Nikki Walz, D.R.E. Students 73.

4—CHRIST CHURCH (1964) (Newman Center)
396 First Ave. S., 56301. Tel: 320-251-3260; Email: newmancenter@scsucatholic.org. Rev. Joseph Herzing.
Catechesis Religious Program—Students 91.

5—HOLY ANGELS, Closed. For inquiries for parish records contact St. Mary's Cathedral, St. Cloud.

6—HOLY SPIRIT (1952) [JC]
2405 Walden Way, 56301. Tel: 320-251-3764; Email: hspirit@spiritandsaints.org. Revs. Thomas Knoblach, Ph.D.; Douglas Wiechmann, Parochial Vicar; Deacon Vernon Schmitz; Roxanne Storms, Pastoral Assoc.
School-See St. Elizabeth Ann Seton School, St. Cloud under Inter-Parochial Schools located in the Institution section.
Catechesis Religious Program—2405 N. First St., 56303. Tel: 320-252-0535; Email: faith.formation.ginny@hotmail.com. Ginny Duschner, D.R.E. Students 159.

7—ST. JOHN CANTIUS (1901)
1515 Third St. N., 56303. Tel: 320-251-4455; Email: stjohncantius@charter.net; Web: www.stjohncantius.org. Revs. Thomas Knoblach, Ph.D.; Derek Wiechmann; Deacon Frank Ringsmuth.
Catechesis Religious Program—2405 First St. N., 56303-4307. Tel: 320-252-0535, Ext. 101; Email: faith.formation.ginny@hotmail.com. Ginny Duschner, D.R.E. Students 18.

8—ST. MICHAEL (1970) [CEM]
1036 Co. Rd. 4, 56303. Tel: 320-251-6923; Email: churchofstmichael@churchofstmichael.net. Rev. Timothy Gapinski; Deacons Jim Trout; Todd Warren.
School-See All Saints Academy, St. Cloud under Inter-Parochial Schools located in the Institutions section.
Catechesis Religious Program—Students 120.

9—ST. PAUL (1946) [JC]
1125 11th Ave. N., 56303. Tel: 320-251-4831; Email: jrudnitski@stpetestpaul.org. Rev. LeRoy Scheierl; Deacons David Lindmeier; Chris Goenner.
School-See All Saints Academy, St. Cloud under Inter-Parochial Schools located in the Institutions section.
Catechesis Religious Program—Geralyn Nathe Evans, D.R.E. Students 322.

10—ST. PETER (1947) [JC]
Office: 1125 11th Ave., N., 56303. Tel: 320-252-2113; Email: lscheierl@stpetestpaul.org. Rev. LeRoy Scheierl; Deacon Chris Goenner.
Res.: 930 31st Ave., N., 56303.
Tel: 320-251-4831, Ext. 201; Email: mainoffice@stpetestpaul.org.
School-See All Saints Academy, St. Cloud under Inter-Parochial Schools located in the Institutions section.
Catechesis Religious Program— (Combined with St. Paul.) Geralyn Nathe Evans, D.R.E.

OUTSIDE THE CITY OF ST. CLOUD

ALBANY, STEARNS CO., SEVEN DOLORS (1868) [CEM]
24328 Trobec St., P.O. Box 277, Albany, 56307. Tel: 320-845-2705; Email: 7dolors@albanytel.com. Rev. Edward Vebelun, O.S.B.
School—Holy Family School, (Grades K-6), Tel: 320-845-2011; Fax: 320-845-7380; Email: hfamily@albanytel.com. Bonnie Massmann, Prin.; Donna Huckenpoehler, Librarian.
Catechesis Religious Program—Tel: 320-845-4335. Antionette (Toni) Hudock, D.R.E. Students 328.

ALEXANDRIA, DOUGLAS CO., ST. MARY'S (1882) [CEM]
420 Irving St., Alexandria, 56308. Tel: 320-763-5781; Email: stmary@stmaryalexandria.org. Rev. Steven Binsfeld.
School—St. Mary's School, (Grades K-6), Tel: 320-763-5861; Fax: 320-763-7992; Email: stmaryss@stmaryalexandria.org. Troy Sladek, Prin.; Aaron Korynta, Librarian.
Catechesis Religious Program—Tel: 320-763-9202; Email: stmreled@stmaryalexandria.org. Students 424.

AVON, STEARNS CO., ST. BENEDICT'S (1868) [CEM]
P.O. Box 98, Avon, 56310. Tel: 320-250-5618; Email: stbenedicts7121@benedictavon.org. Revs. Gregory Miller, O.S.B.; Ian Dommer, O.S.B., Pastoral Min./Coord.; Cyril Gorman, O.S.B., Parochial Vicar.
Catechesis Religious Program—Timothy Stanoch, Dir. Faith Formation. Students 235.

BATTLE LAKE, OTTER TAIL CO., OUR LADY OF THE LAKE (1953) [CEM]
407 Lake Ave. N., P.O. Box 671, Battle Lake, 56515. Tel: 218-864-5747; Email: church@olldj.org. Rev. LeRoy Schik.
Catechesis Religious Program—Students 73.

BECKER, SHERBUNE CO., IMMACULATE CONCEPTION (1918) [CEM] Merged with Our Lady of the Lake, Big Lake to form The Church of Mary of the Visitation, Becker/Big Lake.

BELGRADE, STEARNS CO., ST. FRANCIS DE SALES (1890) [CEM]
541 Martin Ave., P.O. Box 69, Belgrade, 56312. Rev. David Grundman.
Catechesis Religious Program—Annette Fischer, D.R.E. Students 59.

BELLE PRAIRIE, MORRISON CO., HOLY FAMILY (1852) [CEM]
18777 Riverwood Dr., Little Falls, 56345.

Tel: 320-632-5720; Email: holyfam@fallsnet.com. Revs. Benjamin Kociemba; Matthew Langager.
Catechesis Religious Program—Tel: 320-632-5754. Cindy Loidolt, D.R.E. Students 103.

BELLE RIVER, DOUGLAS CO., ST. NICHOLAS (1871) [CEM]
P.O. Box F, Osakis, 56360. Tel: 320-852-7041; Email: st.nick@arvig.net. Rev. David Jeffrey Petron; Deacon Stanley Hennen.
Church: 9473 County Rd. 3, N.E., Carlos, 56319.
Catechesis Religious Program—Tonya Beulke, D.R.E. Students 71.

BERTHA, TODD CO., ST. JOSEPH (1914) [CEM]
P.O. Box 83, Browerville, 56438. Tel: 218-756-2205; Email: stjoseph_bertha@yahoo.com. Rev. Mitchell Bechtold.
Catechesis Religious Program—Elizabeth Schwartz, D.R.E. Students 66.

BIG LAKE, SHERBURNE CO.
1—THE CHURCH OF MARY OF THE VISITATION OF BECKER/BIG LAKE (2012) [CEM 2]
440 Lake St., N., P.O. Box 100, Big Lake, 55309. Tel: 763-447-3339; Email: parish@maryofthevisitation.org. Rev. Michael Kellogg.
Catechesis Religious Program—Katy Hager, C.R.E.; Barb Olson, C.R.E. Students 623.
Worship Site: The Church of Mary of the Visitation, Becker Site: 12100 Sherburne Ave; Big Lake Site: 440 Lake St.
2—OUR LADY OF THE LAKE (1958) [CEM] Merged with Immaculate Conception, Becker to form Mary of the Visitation, Becker/ Big Lake.

BLUEGRASS, WADENA CO., ST. HUBERT (1908) [CEM]
22008 County Rd. 23, Sebeka, 56477. Tel: 218-445-5204; Email: vbmcatholic@wcta.net. P.O. Box C, Verndale, 56481. Rev. Lauren Germann. Res.: 20 Brown St. N., P.O. Box C, Verndale, 56481. Tel: 218-445-5786.
Catechesis Religious Program—Tel: 218-631-1771; Email: sthubert171@hotmail.com. Shirley Malone, D.R.E. Students 48.

BLUFFTON, OTTER TAIL CO., ST. JOHN THE BAPTIST (1902) [CEM]
310 Main St., P.O. Box 36, Bluffton, 56518. Tel: 218-385-2608; Email: sjc428@eot.com. Rev. Aaron J. Kuhn.
Catechesis Religious Program—Students 101.

BOWLUS, MORRISON CO., ST. STANISLAUS KOSTKA, [CEM]
Mailing Address: P.O. Box 249, Upsala, 56384. Tel: 320-573-2132; Fax: 320-573-9133; Email: 238catholic@surfsota.com. Rev. Gregory Mastey. Res.: P.O. Box 8, Bowlus, 56314. Tel: 320-746-2231.
Catechesis Religious Program—Cindy Fussy, D.R.E. Students 72.

BRAHAM, ISANTI CO., ST. PETER & PAUL (1986) [CEM]
1050 Southview Ave., P.O. Box 483, Braham, 55006. Tel: 320-396-3105; Email: stspeter_paulchurch@yahoo.com. Rev. Donald Wagner; Deacon Eugene Kramer.
Catechesis Religious Program—Students 100.

BRANDON, DOUGLAS CO., CHURCH OF ST. ANN (1867) [CEM]
402 Nelson St., P.O. Box 256, Brandon, 56315. Tel: 320-643-5173; Email: stanns@gctel.com. Rev. Peter VanderWeyst; Deacon Joseph Wood.
Catechesis Religious Program—Sheri Streasick, D.R.E. Students 75.

BRECKENRIDGE, WILKIN CO., ST. MARY OF THE PRESENTATION (1898) [CEM 2]
221 Fourth St. N., Breckenridge, 56520-1496. Tel: 218-643-5173; Email: marypresentation@hotmail.com; Web: kentbreckcatholics.org. Rev. Joseph Backowski; Ms. Theodosia Orlando, Pastoral Assoc.
School—St. Mary of the Presentation School, (Grades PreK-8), Tel: 218-643-5443. Linda Johnson, Prin.; Sandra Olson, Librarian.
Catechesis Religious Program—Students 84.

BRENNYVILLE, BENTON CO., ST. ELIZABETH OF HUNGARY (1927) [CEM]
16426 125th Ave., N.E., Foley, 56329. Tel: 320-387-2255; Email: sesjppchurch@jetup.net. Mailing Address: P.O. Box 86, Gilman, 56333. Rev. Leo Moenkedick.
Catechesis Religious Program—Tel: 320-387-3332. Students 48.

BROOTEN, STEARNS CO., ST. DONATUS (1911) [CEM]
301 Eastern Ave. S., P.O. Box 159, Brooten, 56316. Tel: 320-346-2431; Email: stdonatus@tds.net. Rev. David Grundman.
Catechesis Religious Program—Annette Fischer, D.R.E. Students 41.

BROWERVILLE, TODD CO., CHRIST THE KING (1978) [CEM]
201 Cherry St., Bertha, 56437. Tel: 320-594-2291. Rev. Mitchell Bechtold.
School—Christ the King School, (Grades PreK-6), Tel: 320-594-6114; Fax: 320-594-6313. Sarah Becker, Dean, Students.
Catechesis Religious Program—Beverly Geraets, D.R.E. Students 66.

BROWNS VALLEY, TRAVERSE CO., ST. ANTHONY'S (1896) [CEM]
122 2nd St. S., P.O. Box 359, Browns Valley, 56219. Tel: 320-695-2622; Email: wheatoncatholiccommunity@hotmail.com. Rev. Gregory Frankman.
Catechesis Religious Program—Students 28.

BUCKMAN, MORRISON CO., ST. MICHAEL'S, [CEM]
P.O. Box 428, Pierz, 56364. Tel: 320-468-2316; Email: stmichaelbuckman@yahoo.com. Rev. Kenneth Popp.
Catechesis Religious Program—Tel: 320-468-2640. Students 125.

BUTLER, OTTER TAIL CO., HOLY CROSS (1910) [CEM]
234 2nd Ave. S.W., Perham, 56573. Tel: 164944; Email: fayeadell@yahoo.com. Rev. Matthew Kuhn.
Catechesis Religious Program—Mary Peeters, D.R.E.; Glenda Hofland, D.R.E. Students 40.

CAMBRIDGE, ISANTI CO., CHRIST THE KING, [CEM]
230 Fern St. N., Cambridge, 55008-1094. Tel: 763-689-1221; Email: crkgcbmn@aol.com. Rev. Donald Wagner; Deacon Eugene Kramer.
Catechesis Religious Program—Tel: 763-689-3728. Students 92.

CHOKIO, STEVENS CO., ST. MARY'S (1897) [CEM]
P.O. Box 187, Chokio, 56221. Tel: 320-563-4421; Email: stmarych@fedtel.net. Rev. John Paul Knopik.
Catechesis Religious Program—Students 28.

CLARISSA, TODD CO., ST. JOSEPH (1896) [CEM]
105 John St. S., P.O. Box 5, Clarissa, 56440. Tel: 218-756-2205; Email: stjoschu@hcctel.net. Rev. Mitchell Bechtold.
Res.: Box 83, Browerville, 56438. Tel: 320-594-2291; Fax: 320-594-6313.
Catechesis Religious Program—Tel: 218-756-3614. Bev Desotell, D.R.E., Tel: 320-594-6383; Eileen Uhlenkamp, D.R.E. Students 48.

CLEAR LAKE, SHERBURNE CO., ST. MARCUS (1888) [CEM]
8701 Main Ave., P.O. Box 237, Clear Lake, 55319-0237. Tel: 320-743-2481; Email: stmarcus@frontiernet.net. Rev. Virgil A. Helmin, J.C.L.
Catechesis Religious Program—Tel: 320-743-3346; Email: stmarcusff@frontiernet.net. Peggy Berger, D.R.E. Students 162.

COLD SPRING, STEARNS CO., CHURCH OF SAINT BONIFACE (1878) [CEM]
501 Main St., Cold Spring, 56320. Tel: 320-685-3280; Email: rschwartz@stboniface.com. Revs. Matthew Luft, O.S.B; Cletus Connors, O.S.B., Parochial Vicar; Deacon Lawrence Sell.
School—Church of Saint Boniface School, (Grades PreSchool-6), Tel: 320-685-3541. Sr. Sharon Waldoch, S.S.N.D., Prin.; Shelly Giswold, Librarian. Students 274; Parish or Independent 1.
Catechesis Religious Program—
Tel: 320-685-8222, Ext. 103. Ashley Barker, Pastoral Leader Youth Ministries. Students 270.

COLLEGEVILLE, STEARNS CO., ST. JOHN THE BAPTIST (1875) [JC]
14241 Fruit Farm Rd., St. Joseph, 56374. Tel: 320-363-2569; Email: jortloff@csbsju.edu. Revs. Gregory Miller, O.S.B.; Gorman Cyril, Parochial Vicar; Ian Dommer, O.S.B., Pastoral Min./Coord.
Catechesis Religious Program—Julie Warner, D.R.E. Students 68.

DENT, OTTER TAIL CO., SACRED HEART (1921) [CEM]
36963 State Hwy. 108, Dent, 56528. Tel: 218-758-2700; Email: sacredheart@ect.com. Rev. George Michael, V.C.; Deacon Mark Stenger.
Catechesis Religious Program—Joe Sazama, D.R.E.; Diane Sazama, D.R.E. Students 61.

DONNELLY, STEVENS CO., ST. THERESIA, Closed. For inquiries for parish records contact St. Charles, Herman.

DUELM, BENTON CO., ST. LAWRENCE'S (1863) [CEM]
10915 Duelm Rd., N.E., Foley, 56329. Tel: 320-968-7502; Fax: 320-743-2481; Email: st_lawrence@victorcc.net. Rev. Virgil Helmin, J.C.L. Res.: P.O. Box 237, Clear Lake, 55319.
Catechesis Religious Program—Tel: 320-968-6595. Betty Pundsack, D.R.E. Students 201.

DUMONT, TRAVERSE CO., ST. PETER'S, Closed. For inquiries for Parish Records contact: Ave Maria, Wheaton. Mailing address: 201 9th St. S., Wheaton, MN 56296.

EDEN VALLEY, STEARNS CO., THE CHURCH OF THE ASSUMPTION (1892) [CEM 2]
464 State St. N., P.O. Box 9, Eden Valley, 55329. Tel: 320-453-2788; Email: assumptionev@meltel.net; Web: www.churchoftheassumptionedenvalley.org. Rev. Aaron Nett.
Catechesis Religious Program—Tel: 320-453-7388. Sherry Braegelmen, D.R.E.; Sherri Lego, D.R.E. Students 62.

ELBOW LAKE, GRANT CO., ST. OLAF, [CEM]
Mailing Address: 518 Division St., Elbow Lake, 56531. Tel: 218-685-5372; Email: stolaf@runestine.net. Rev. Jeremy Ploof.
Res.: 110 Minnesota Ave., Tintah, 56583. Tel: 218-369-2188.
Catechesis Religious Program—Students 68.

ELIZABETH, OTTER TAIL CO., ST. ELIZABETH (1875) [CEM]
706 Pleasant Ave., Elizabeth, 56533. Tel: 218-736-5230; Email: frjdethen@yahoo.com. Rev. Jeffrey D. Ethen; Deacon Peter Bellavance.
Catechesis Religious Program—Tel: 218-739-1140. Jan Dumas, D.R.E. Students 60.

ELK RIVER, SHERBURNE CO., THE CHURCH OF ST. ANDREW (1890) [CEM]
566 Fourth St., Elk River, 55330. Tel: 763-441-1483; Email: minnocenti@saint-andrew.net. Rev. Mark Innocenti.
School—The Church of St. Andrew School, (Grades PreK-5), 428 Irving Ave., Elk River, 55330. Tel: 763-441-2216; Fax: 763-441-1146. Susan Scipioni, Prin.; Aaron Johnson, Librarian. Lay Teachers 12; Sisters 1; Students 178.
Catechesis Religious Program—Tel: 763-441-3202. Students 781.

ELMDALE, MORRISON CO., ST. EDWARD'S, [CEM]
P.O. Box 249, Upsala, 56384. Tel: 320-573-2132; Email: 238catholic@surfsota.com. Rev. Jeremy Theis. Res.: 8550 State Hwy. 238, Bowlus, 56314. Tel: 320-573-2975.
Catechesis Religious Program—308 S. Main St., Upsala, 56384. Tel: 320-573-2132. Students 49.

ELROSA, STEARNS CO., SS. PETER AND PAUL (1891) [CEM]
302 State St., P.O. Box 95, Elrosa, 56325. Tel: 320-697-5541; Email: francisdesales@willmarnet.com. Rev. David Grundman.
Catechesis Religious Program—Tel: 320-254-8218. Jo Braegelman, D.R.E. Students 54.

FARMING, STEARNS CO., ST. CATHERINE'S (1879) [CEM] Closed. For inquiries for parish records please see St. Martin, MN.

FERGUS FALLS, OTTER TAIL CO., OUR LADY OF VICTORY (1881) [CEM]
207 N. Vine St., Fergus Falls, 56537. Tel: 218-736-2429; Email: olv@prtel.com. Rev. Alan Wielinski; Deacons Charles Kampa; Dean Pawlowski.
School—Our Lady of Victory School, (Grades PreSchool-6), 426 W. Cavour Ave., Fergus Falls, 56537. Tel: 208-736-6661; Fax: 218-736-6931. Sandy Carpenter, Prin.; Sue Herder, Librarian. Lay Teachers 9; Students 100.
Catechesis Religious Program—Tel: 218-736-6837. Jennifer Dummer, Faith Formation Coord.; Mayme Hofland, Faith Formation Dir. Students 122.

FLENSBURG, MORRISON CO., SACRED HEART, [CEM 2]
9406 Church Cir., Little Falls, 56345. Tel: 320-632-6930; Fax: 320-632-5644; Email: ststan@littlefalls.net. Rev. Jimmy Joseph, V.C.
Catechesis Religious Program—Sheila Gardner, D.R.E. Students 12.

FOLEY, BENTON CO., CHURCH OF ST. JOHN, [CEM]
Mailing Address: 621 Dewey St., P.O. Box 337, Foley, 56329. Tel: 320-968-7913; Email: hyperdulia@arvig.net. Rev. Michael Wolfbauer.
School—St. John's Area School, (Grades PreSchool-6), Tel: 320-968-7972; Fax: 320-968-9956; Email: principal@saintjohnsschool.net; Web: www.saintjohnsschool.net. Christine Friederichs, Prin. Lay Teachers 8; Students 101.
Catechesis Religious Program—Fax: 320-968-4424. Sheila Matteson, D.R.E. Students 180.

FORESTON, MILLE LACS CO., ST. LOUIS BERTRAND, [CEM]
187 First St. S., P.O. Box 128, Foreston, 56330. Tel: 320-294-5460; Email: stlouis@ecenet.com. Rev. James H. Remmerswaal, O.S.C., Canonical Pastor; Deacon Kenneth Rosha.
Catechesis Religious Program—Students 111.

FOXHOME, WILKIN CO., ST. JOSEPH, Closed. For inquiries for parish records contact St. Mary of the Presentation, Breckenridge.

FREEPORT, STEARNS CO., SACRED HEART (1881) [CEM]
106 3rd Ave., N.E., P.O. Box 155, Freeport, 56331-0155. Tel: 320-836-2143; Email: triparish@albanytel.com. Rev. Daniel Walz; Deacon Richard Scherping.
School—Sacred Heart School, (Grades PreK-6), 303 2nd St. N.E., P.O. Box 39, Freeport, 56331. Tel: 320-836-2591; Fax: 320-836-2514; Email: shs@albanytel.com. Kristie Harren, Prin. Lay Teachers 6; Students 144.
Catechesis Religious Program—Amy Hoeschen, Tri-Parish D.R.E. Students 50.

GILMAN, BENTON CO., SS. PETER AND PAUL (1872) [CEM]
Mailing Address: P.O. Box 86, Gilman, 56333. Tel: 320-387-2255; Tel: sesjppchurches@jetup.net. Rev. Leo Moenkedick.
See St. John's School, Foley under Inter-Parochial Schools located in the Institution section.

Catechesis Religious Program—Tel: 320-387-3332. Students 112.

GLENWOOD, POPE CO., SACRED HEART (1903) [CEM 2]
122 N.W. 1st St., Glenwood, 56334.
Tel: 320-634-3813; Email: sheartchurch@gmail.com. Rev. Joseph Vanderberg.
Res.: 105 Franklin St. N., Glenwood, 56334.
Catechesis Religious Program—Tel: 320-634-4828. Paula Johnson, D.R.E.; Mike Sopcyk, D.R.E. Students 142.

GREENWALD, STEARNS CO., ST. ANDREW'S (1924) [CEM]
Mailing Address: 211 2nd Ave. N., P.O. Box 136, Greenwald, 56335. Tel: 320-987-3205; Email: stjohn1@meltel.net. Revs. Marvin Enneking, J.C.L.; Oswaldo Roche, Parochial Vicar.
School—St. Andrew's School, (Grades K-2), Tel: 320-987-3133. Sr. Suzanne Slominski, O.S.B., Prin.
Catechesis Religious Program—Tel: 320-256-3498. Ruth Klaphake, D.R.E. Students 29.

GREY EAGLE, TODD CO., ST. JOSEPH'S, [CEM 2]
118 Minnesota St., P.O. Box 366, Grey Eagle, 56336.
Tel: 320-285-2545; Email: stjoseph@meltel.net. Rev. Ronald Dockendorf.
Catechesis Religious Program—Students 80.

HARDING, MORRISON CO., HOLY CROSS (1904) [CEM]
28520 Church St., P.O. Box 38, Lastrup, 56344.
Tel: 320-468-2111; Email: holycrossstjohn@centurytel.net. Rev. David Maciej.
Catechesis Religious Program—Students 63.

HENNING, OTTER TAIL CO., CHURCH OF ST. EDWARD OF HENNING (1945) [CEM]
201 Douglas Ave., Henning, 56551.
Tel: 218-583-2490; Email: stedward@arvig.net. Rev. LeRoy Schik.
Catechesis Religious Program—Lyn Andrews, D.R.E. Students 89.

HERMAN, GRANT CO., ST. CHARLES (1913) [CEM]
Mailing Address: 61 Berlin Ave., S., Herman, 56248.
Tel: 320-677-2433; Email: stcharles@frontier.com. Rev. Jeremy Ploof.
Res.: 110 Minnesota Ave., Tintah, 56583.
Catechesis Religious Program—Katy Blume, D.R.E. Students 23.

HILLMAN, MORRISON CO., CHURCH OF ST. RITA OF HILLMAN (1920) [CEM]
Mailing Address: 16691 371st Ave., Hillman, 56338.
Tel: 320-277-3807; Email: strita@brainerd.net. Revs. Jerome Schik, O.S.C.; Gregory Poser, O.S.C., Parochial Vicar.
Catechesis Religious Program—Students 48.

HOLDINGFORD, STEARNS CO.

1—CHURCH OF ALL SAINTS
311 River St., P.O. Box 308, Holdingford, 56340.
Tel: 320-228-0105; Email: secretary@tworiverscatholic.com; Web: tworiverscatholic.com. Rev. Gregory Mastey.
Catechesis Religious Program—Tel: 320-292-1575; Email: allsaintsff@tworiverscatholic.com. Katrina Kolles, D.R.E.

2—ST. HEDWIG'S, [CEM] Closed. For inquiries for parish records please see Church of All Saints, Holdingford, MN.

3—ST. MARY'S (1883) [CEM] Closed. For inquiries for parish records please see Church of All Saints, Holdingford, MN.

ISANTI, ISANTI CO., ST. ELIZABETH ANN SETON (1976)
Mailing Address: 207 County Rd. 23, N.W., Isanti, 55040. Tel: 763-444-4035; Fax: 763-444-6019; Email: annseton76@yahoo.com. Revs. Donald Wagner; Derek Weichmann, Parochial Vicar.
Res.: 230 Fern St. N., Cambridge, 55008.
Tel: 763-645-1189.
Catechesis Religious Program—Michelle Fedewa, D.R.E. Students 93.

JACOB'S PRAIRIE WAKEFIELD TOWNSHIP, STEARNS CO., ST. JAMES, [CEM]
25042 County Rd. 2, Cold Spring, 56320.
Tel: 320-685-3479; Email: stjamesjp@clearwire.net. Revs. Matthew Luft, O.S.B; Efrain Rosado, O.S.B., Parochial Vicar.
Catechesis Religious Program—Students 24.

KENSINGTON, GRANT CO., OUR LADY OF THE RUNESTONE, [CEM]
25890 110th St., Lowry, 56349-4580.
Tel: 320-965-2596; Email: snepomuk@runestone.net. Rev. Peter K. Kirchner.
Catechesis Religious Program—Students 29.

KENT, WILKIN CO., ST. THOMAS (1891) [CEM]
115 Harris St., P.O. Box 23, Kent, 56553.
Tel: 218-557-8312; Email: sharonl@702com.net; Web: www.kentbreckcatholics.org. Rev. Joseph Backowski; Ms. Theodosia Orlando, Pastoral Assoc.
Catechesis Religious Program—Combined with St. Mary of the Presentation, Breckenridge, MN. Students 20.

KIMBALL, STEARNS CO., CHURCH OF SAINT ANNE (1919) [CEM]
441 Hazel Ave. E., P.O. Box 99, Kimball, 55353.
Tel: 320-398-2211; Email: sannekim@meltel.net. Rev. James Statz.
Catechesis Religious Program—Students 102.

LAKE HENRY, STEARNS CO., ST. MARGARET'S, [CEM]
505 Burr St., Paynesville, 56362. Tel: 320-243-4413; Email: frglenn@saintalm.org. Rev. Glenn A. Krystosek.
Catechesis Religious Program—Hannah Voss, D.R.E. Students 29.

LAKE RENO, POPE CO., ST. JOHN NEPOMUK, [CEM]
25890 110th St., Lowry, 56349-4580.
Tel: 320-283-5273; Email: snepomuk@runestone.net. Rev. Peter K. Kirchner.
Catechesis Religious Program—Students 31.

LASTRUP, MORRISON CO., ST. JOHN NEPOMUK (1900) [CEM]
28520 Church St., P.O. Box 38, Lastrup, 56344.
Tel: 320-468-2111; Email: holycrossstjohn@centurytel.net. Rev. David Maciej.
Catechesis Religious Program—Students 66.

LITTLE FALLS, MORRISON CO.

1—ST. MARY, [CEM 3]
305 Fourth St., S.E., Little Falls, 56345.
Tel: 320-632-5640; Email: office@stmaryslf.org. Revs. Benjamin Kociemba; Matthew Langager, Parochial Vicar; Deacon Bruce Geyer.
See Mary of Lourdes Elementary and Middle School, Little Falls under Inter-Parochial Schools located in the Institution section.
Catechesis Religious Program—Tel: 320-632-3911. Brenda Przybilla, D.R.E. Students 154.

2—OUR LADY OF LOURDES (1917) [CEM]
208 W. Broadway, Little Falls, 56345.
Tel: 320-632-8243; Email: ololoffice@yahoo.com. Revs. Benjamin Kociemba; Matthew Langager; Deacon Craig Korver.
See Mary of Lourdes Elementary and Middle School, Little Falls under Inter-Parochial Schools located in the Institution section.
Catechesis Religious Program—Tel: 320-616-9689. Linda Pilarski, D.R.E. Students 290.

LONG PRAIRIE, TODD CO., ST. MARY OF MT. CARMEL (1868) [CEM] [JC]
409 Central Ave., Long Prairie, 56347.
Tel: 320-732-2635; Email: stmarysrectory@stmaryslp.org. Rev. Omar Guanchez; Deacon James Schulzetenberg.
School—St. Mary of Mt. Carmel School, (Grades PreK-6), Tel: 320-357-0813; Email: bgugglberger@stmaryslp.org. Brenda Gugglberger, Prin.
Catechesis Religious Program—Fax: 320-323-4394; Email: vpeterson@stmaryslp.org. V. Bucher, D.R.E. Students 146.

LUXEMBURG, STEARNS CO., ST. WENDELIN'S (1859) [CEM]
22714 State Hwy. 15, 56301. Tel: 320-251-6944; Email: stwencc@live.com. Rev. Ronald Weyrens.
School—St. Wendelin's School, (Grades PreK-6), Tel: 320-251-9175; Fax: 320-654-9030; Email: stwend@citescape.com. Lynn Rasmussen, Prin.
Catechesis Religious Program—Students 28.

MAINE, OTTER TAIL CO., CHURCH OF SAINT JAMES AT MAINE, [CEM]
32009 County Hwy. 74, Underwood, 56586.
Tel: 218-864-5619; Email: church@ollsj.org. Rev. LeRoy Schik.
Catechesis Religious Program—Students 22.

MAYHEW LAKE, BENTON CO., ANNUNCIATION (1896) [CEM]
9965 Mayhew Lake Rd., N.E., Sauk Rapids, 56379.
Tel: 320-252-1729; Email: annunciation@cloudnet.com. Rev. Thomas Becker.
Catechesis Religious Program—Tel: 320-259-4941. Shirley Scapanski, D.R.E. Students 85.

MEIRE GROVE, STEARNS CO., ST. JOHN'S (1858) [CEM]
211 5th Ave., S.E., Melrose, 56352.
Tel: 320-256-4207; Email: stmarys@stmarysofmelrose.com. Revs. Marvin Enneking, J.C.L.; Oswaldo Roche, Parochial Vicar.
Church: 105 County Rd., E., Melrose, 56352.
School—St. John's - St. Andrew's Catholic School, (Grades 3-6), Tel: 320-987-3491; Tel: 320-987-3133; Email: stjohnstandrew@gmail.com; Web: sjsaschool.org. Mrs. Mary Miller, Prin.; Brenda Nathe, Bookkeeper; Kristen Pattinson, Sec. Lay Teachers 4; Students 52.
Catechesis Religious Program—Tel: 320-256-3498. Ruth Klaphake, D.R.E. Students 15.

MELROSE, STEARNS CO., ST. MARY'S (1958) [CEM 2]
402 2nd St., S.E., Melrose, 56352-1427.
Tel: 320-256-4207; Email: stmarys@stmarysofmelrose.com. Revs. Marvin Enneking, J.C.L.; Oswaldo Roche, Parochial Vicar; Deacon Ernest Kociemba.
School—St. Mary's School, (Grades PreSchool-6), 320 5th S.E., Melrose, 56352. Tel: 320-256-4257; Email: sms@meltel.net. Robert Doyle, Prin.; Autumn Nelson, Librarian & Media Specialist. Lay Teachers 8; Students 120.
Catechesis Religious Program—Tel: 320-256-4258. Dawn Carrillo, D.R.E. Students 277.

MENAHGA, WADENA CO., ASSUMPTION OF OUR LADY OF MENAHGA (1953) [CEM 4]
Mailing Address: P.O. Box C, Verndale, 56481.
Tel: 218-445-5786; Fax: 218-445-5087; Email: vbmcatholic@wcta.net. Rev. Lauren Germann
Legal Name: The Church of the Assumption of Our Lady of Menahga
Church: 113 Aspen Ave. N.W., Menahga, 56464.
Catechesis Religious Program—Students 9.

MILACA, MILLE LACS CO., ST. MARY'S (1954) [CEM]
625 3rd Ave., S.E., Milaca, 56353. Tel: 320-983-3255; Email: stmary.milaca@frontiernet.net. Rev. James H. Remmerswaal, O.S.C., Canonical Pastor; Deacon Kenneth Rosha, Parish Life Coord.
Catechesis Religious Program—Students 105.

MILLERVILLE, DOUGLAS CO., SEVEN DOLORS (1870) [CEM]
16921 County Rd. 7, N.W., Brandon, 56315.
Tel: 320-876-2240; Email: sevendolors@gctel.net. Rev. Peter VanderWeyst; Deacon Joseph Wood.
Catechesis Religious Program—Students 85.

MORA, KANABEC CO., ST. MARY'S (1895) [CEM]
201 Forest Ave. E., Mora, 55051. Tel: 320-679-1593; Email: ritac@stmarysmora.org. Rev. Michael Kellogg, Canonical Pastor; Ms. Rita Clasemann, Parish Life Coord.
Catechesis Religious Program—Sue Grabowski, D.R.E. Students 135.

MORAN, TODD CO., ST. ISIDORE, [CEM] Closed. For inquiries for parish records contact Christ the King, Browerville.

MORRILL, MORRISON CO., ST. JOSEPH'S (1914) [CEM]
33009 Nature Rd., Foley, 56329. Tel: 320-355-2454; Email: sesjppchurches@jetup.net. Mailing Address: P.O. Box 86, Gilman, 56333. Rev. Leo Moenkedick.
Catechesis Religious Program—Students 36.

MORRIS, STEVENS CO., ASSUMPTION OF THE BLESSED VIRGIN MARY, [CEM]
207 E. Third, P.O. Box 287, Morris, 56267.
Tel: 320-589-3003; Email: assump@info-link.net. Rev. Todd Schneider.
Res.: 301 E. Third, Morris, 56267.
School—Assumption of the Blessed Virgin Mary School, (Grades K-6), 411 Colorado Ave., Morris, 56267. Tel: 320-589-1704; Fax: 320-589-1703. Joseph Ferriero, Prin. Lay Teachers 7; Students 83.
Catechesis Religious Program—Nicole Berlinger, C.R.E. Youth. Students 114.

MOTLEY, MORRISON CO., ST. MICHAEL (1888)
Mailing Address: P.O. Box 177, Staples, 56479.
Tel: 218-894-2291; Email: sheart@arvig.net. Rev. Gabriel Walz; Deacons John Wolak; Robert Shaffer.
Catechesis Religious Program—Tel: 218-352-6782. Students 41.

NEW MUNICH, STEARNS CO., IMMACULATE CONCEPTION (1857) [CEM]
Mailing Address: P.O. Box 155, New Munich, 56356.
Tel: 320-836-2143; Email: triparish@albanytel.com. Rev. Daniel Walz; Deacon Richard Scherping.
Church: 650 Main St., New Munich, 56356-9028.
Catechesis Religious Program—Kristen Herdering, Tri-Parish D.R.E. Students 56.

NORTH PRAIRIE, MORRISON CO.

OGILVIE, KANABEC CO., ST. KATHRYN'S (1947) [CEM]
201 Forest Ave. E., Mora, 55051. Tel: 320-679-1593; Email: ritac@stmarysmora.org. Revs. Michael Kellogg, Canonical Pastor; Eugene D. Plaisted, O.S.C., Sacramental Min.; Ms. Rita Clasemann, Parish Life Coord.
Catechesis Religious Program—Students 36.

ONAMIA, MILLE LACS CO., THE CHURCH OF THE HOLY CROSS OF ONAMIA (1910) [CEM]
Crosier Priory of the Holy Cross, 102 Crosier Dr. N., P.O. Box 500, Onamia, 56359. Tel: 320-532-3122; Fax: 320-532-5222; Email: hconamia@gmail.com. Revs. Jerome Schik, O.S.C.; Gregory Poser, O.S.C., Parochial Vicar.
Catechesis Religious Program—Students 20.

OPOLE, STEARNS CO., OUR LADY OF MT. CARMEL (1887) [CEM]
St. Mary's Rectory, 42942 125th Ave., Holdingford, 56340. Tel: 320-746-2449; Email: parishes@greatrivercatholic.org; Web: greatrivercatholic.org. Rev. Eugene Doyle; Deacon Jeffrey Fromm.
Catechesis Religious Program—Tel: 320-309-3280; Email: opolefaith@gmail.com. Melyssa Sakry, D.R.E. Students 110.

OSAKIS, DOUGLAS CO., IMMACULATE CONCEPTION (1899) [CEM]
306 W. Oak St., P.O. Box F, Osakis, 56360.
Tel: 320-859-2390; Email: iccosakis@arvig.net. Rev. David Jeffrey Petron.
School—St. Agnes, (Grades PreSchool-6), 307 4th Ave. W., P.O. Box O, Osakis, 56360.
Tel: 320-859-2130; Fax: 320-859-5850. Pat Pospisil, Prin.; Rosalie Kreemer, Librarian. Lay Teachers 6; Students 46.
Catechesis Religious Program—Jennifer Wolbeck, D.R.E.; Greta Petrich, D.R.E. Students 119.

PADUA, STEARNS CO., CHURCH OF ST. ANTHONY OF

PADUA, Closed. For inquiries for parish records contact St. Donatus Church, Brooten.
PARKERS PRAIRIE, OTTER TAIL CO., CHURCH OF ST. WILLIAM (1951) [CEM]
209 W. Soo St., P.O. Box 339, Parkers Prairie, 56361. Tel: 218-338-2761; Email: stwm@midwestinfo.net. Rev. Peter VanderWeyst; Deacon Joseph Wood.
Catechesis Religious Program—Students 38.
PAYNESVILLE, STEARNS CO., ST. LOUIS (1899) [CEM]
505 Burr St., Paynesville, 56362. Tel: 320-243-4413; Email: frglenn@saintalm.org. Rev. Glenn A. Krystosek.
Catechesis Religious Program—Hannah Voss, D.R.E. Students 246.
PEARL LAKE, STEARNS CO., HOLY CROSS (1897) [CEM]
10651 County Rd. 8, Kimball, 55353.
Tel: 320-398-3900; Email: church@holycrossmn.org. Rev. Ronald Weyrens.
School—Holy Cross School, (Grades PreK-6), Tel: 320-398-7885; Fax: 320-398-7873. Lorraine Gregory, Librarian.
Catechesis Religious Program— Twinned with Rockville & Luxemburg. Students 21.
PELICAN RAPIDS, OTTER TAIL CO., ST. LEONARD'S (1951) [CEM]
36 1st Ave. N.E., P.O. Box 378, Pelican Rapids, 56572. Tel: 218-863-4240; Email: stleonard@loretel.net. Rev. Jeffrey D. Ethen; Deacons Joseph Hilber; Peter Bellavance.
Catechesis Religious Program—Ann Bergquist, D.R.E. Students 85.
PERHAM, OTTER TAIL CO.
1—ST. HENRY'S (1875) [CEM]
234 2nd Ave. S.W., Perham, 56573.
Tel: 218-346-4240; Email: sthenry@arvig.net. Rev. Matthew Kuhn; Deacon Randy Alstadt.
School—St. Henry Area School, (Grades K-6), 253 2nd St. S.W., Perham, 56573. Tel: 218-346-6190; Fax: 218-346-6190; Email: sthenryschool@arvig.net. Jason Smith, Prin.; Lisa Silbernagel, Librarian. Lay Teachers 8; Students 87.
Catechesis Religious Program—Tel: 218-346-7030. Students 142.
2—ST. STANISLAUS (1895) [CEM] Closed. For inquiries for parish records contact St. Henry, Perham.
PIERZ, MORRISON CO., ST. JOSEPH'S, [CEM]
68 Main St., P.O. Box 428, Pierz, 56364.
Tel: 320-468-6033; Email: stjoes@midco.net. Rev. Kenneth Popp.
See Holy Trinity School, Pierz under Inter-Parochial Schools located in the Institution section.
Catechesis Religious Program—P.O. Box 205, Pierz, 56364. Tel: 320-468-2640. Students 198.
PRINCETON, MILLE LACS CO.
1—THE CHURCH OF CHRIST OUR LIGHT (2010) [CEM]
804 7th Ave. S., Princeton, 55371. Tel: 763-389-2115; Email: jamiea@christourlightmn.org. Rev. Kevin Anderson; Deacon Mark Barder.
Catechesis Religious Program—Molly Weyrens, D.R.E. Students 358.
2—ST. EDWARD'S (1898) [CEM] Merged With St. Pius X, Zimmerman to form The Church of Christ Our Light Princeton/Zimmerman.
RANDALL, MORRISON CO., ST. JAMES, [CEM]
Mailing Address: P.O. Box 225, Randall, 56475.
Tel: 320-632-6930; Email: ststans@littlefalls.net. Rev. Jimmy Joseph, V.C., Canonical Admin.
Catechesis Religious Program—Students 101.
RICE, BENTON CO., IMMACULATE CONCEPTION (1885) [CEM]
130 First Ave., N.E., P.O. Box 189, Rice, 56367.
Tel: 320-393-2725; Email: iccrice@jetup.net. Rev. Thomas G. Becker.
Catechesis Religious Program—Tel: 320-393-2826. Jean Skroch, C.R.E. Students 210.
RICHMOND, STEARNS CO., SS. PETER AND PAUL (1856) [CEM]
110 Central Ave. N., P.O. Box 69, Richmond, 56368.
Tel: 320-597-2575; Email: parish@ssppr.com. Revs. Matthew Luft, O.S.B; Efrain Rosado, O.S.B., Parochial Vicar.
Res.: 56 - 1st St. N.E., P.O. Box 69, Richmond, 56368.
School—SS. Peter and Paul School, (Grades K-5), 111 Central Ave. N., Richmond, 56368.
Tel: 320-597-2565; Fax: 320-597-4385; Email: jwalz@ssppr.com. Jacqueline Walz, Prin. & Librarian. Lay Teachers 6; Students 44.
Catechesis Religious Program—Teri Krowka-Ansberry, D.R.E. Students 130.
ROCKVILLE, STEARNS CO., MARY OF THE IMMACULATE CONCEPTION (1911) [CEM]
113 Broadway, P.O. Box 7, Rockville, 56369.
Tel: 320-251-7801; Email: micrparish@gmail.com; Email: micchurch@mywdo.com. Rev. Ronald Weyrens.
Catechesis Religious Program—Students 128.
ROSCOE, STEARNS CO., ST. AGNES, [CEM]
505 Burr St., Paynesville, 56362. Tel: 320-243-4413; Email: frglenn@saintalm.org. Rev. Glenn A. Krystosek.
Catechesis Religious Program—Students 15.
ROYALTON, MORRISON CO.
1—HOLY CROSS (1876) [CEM]
14891 Gable Rd., Royalton, 56314. Tel: 320-584-5484 ; Email: htrinityhcross@gmail.com; Web: holytrinitychurchroyalton.yolasite.com. Rev. Roger Klassen, O.S.B.
Catechesis Religious Program—Students 28.
2—HOLY TRINITY (1897) [CEM]
216 N. 2nd St., P.O. Box 258, Royalton, 56373.
Tel: 320-584-5484; Email: htriniy@fallsnet.com. Rev. Roger Klassen, O.S.B.
Catechesis Religious Program—Students 278.
RUSH LAKE, OTTER TAIL CO., ST. LAWRENCE aka St. Lawrence Catholic Church of Rush Lake (1886) [CEM]
46404 County Hwy. 14, Perham, 56573.
Tel: 218-346-7729; Email: stlawrence@arvig.net; Web: sacredheartstlawrencecatholicchurches.com. Rev. George Michael, V.C., Canonical Admin.; Deacon Mark Stenger; Jeannie Guck, Contact Person.
Res.: 36963 State Hwy. 108, Dent, 56528.
Tel: 218-758-2888; Fax: 218-346-5946.
Catechesis Religious Program—Students 68.
ST. ANNA, STEARNS CO., IMMACULATE CONCEPTION, [CEM]
St. Mary's Rectory, P.O. Box 308, Holdingford, 56340. Tel: 320-746-2449; Email: fivepoffice@yahoo.com. Rev. Gregory Mastey; Deacon Jeffrey Fromm.
Catechesis Religious Program—Students 86.
ST. ANTHONY, STEARNS CO., ST. ANTHONY'S (1874) [CEM]
24326 Trobec St., Albany, 56307. Tel: 320-845-2416; Email: stanthony@albanytel.com. Rev. Edward Vebelun, O.S.B.
Catechesis Religious Program—Joyce Ostendorf, D.R.E. Students 76.
ST. AUGUSTA, STEARNS CO., ST. MARY HELP OF CHRISTIANS (1856) [CEM]
24588 County Rd. 7, 56301. Tel: 320-252-1799; Email: nancym@smhoc.org. Rev. Jose Edayadiyil, V.C.
School—St. Mary Help of Christians School, (Grades K-6), Tel: 320-251-3937; Fax: 320-251-3937. Kelly Kirks, Prin.
Catechesis Religious Program—Jan Minke, D.R.E. Students 191.
ST. FRANCIS, STEARNS CO., ST. FRANCIS OF ASSISI, [CEM]
44055 State Hwy. 238, Freeport, 56331.
Tel: 320-573-2132; Email: 238catholic@surfsota.com. Rev. Jeremy Theis.
Res.: 8550 State Hwy. 238, Bowlus, 56314.
Tel: 320-573-2975.
Catechesis Religious Program—Mr. John Young, D.R.E. Students 63.
ST. JOSEPH, STEARNS CO., ST. JOSEPH'S (1856) [CEM]
12 W. Minnesota St., St. Joseph, 56374.
Tel: 320-363-7505; Email: parish@churchstjoseph.org. Rev. Jerome Tupa, O.S.B.; Deacon Bertrum Bliss.
School-See All Saints Academy, St. Cloud under Inter-Parochial Schools located in the Institutions section.
Catechesis Religious Program—Students 217.
ST. MARTIN, STEARNS CO., ST. MARTIN (1858) [CEM]
119 Maine St., P.O. Box 290, St. Martin, 56376.
Tel: 320-548-3550; Email: parishofstmartin@arvig.com. Rev. Edward Vebelun, O.S.B.
Catechesis Religious Program—Tel: 320-548-3209. Deb Goebel, D.R.E. Students 110.
ST. NICHOLAS, STEARNS CO., ST. NICHOLAS (1857) [CEM]
15862 County Rd. 165, Watkins, 55389.
Tel: 320-764-7345; Email: stnicholas@meltel.net. Rev. James Statz.
Catechesis Religious Program—Students 47.
ST. ROSA, STEARNS CO., ST. ROSE OF LIMA (1898) [CEM]
Mailing Address: P.O. Box 155, Freeport, 56331.
Tel: 320-836-2143; Fax: 320-836-2142; Email: triparish@albanytel.com. Rev. Daniel Walz; Deacon Richard Scherping.
Church: 28905 County Rd. 17, Freeport, 56331.
Catechesis Religious Program—Amy Hoeschen, Tri-Parish D.R.E. Students 44.
ST. STEPHEN, STEARNS CO., ST. STEPHEN'S (1871) [CEM]
42942 125th Ave., Holdingford, 56340.
Tel: 320-251-1520; Email: ststephen@churchofststephen.org. Rev. Eugene Doyle; Deacon Jeffrey Fromm.
Res.: 103 Central Ave. S., St. Stephen, 56375.
Tel: 320-746-2449; Email: parishes@greatrivercatholic.org; Web: greatrivercatholic.org.
Catechesis Religious Program—Tel: 320-251-5066; Email: ststephenfaith@outlook.com. Danna Gasperlin, D.R.E. Students 181.
ST. WENDEL, STEARNS CO., ST. COLUMBKILLE'S, [CEM]
12536 County Rd. 4, Avon, 56310. Tel: 320-746-2449; Email: parishes@greatrivercatholic.org; Web: greatrivercatholic.org. Mailing Address: 42942 125th Ave., Holdingford, 56340. Rev. Eugene Doyle; Deacon Jeffrey Fromm.
Catechesis Religious Program—Tel: 320-249-9939; Email: stwendelfaith@gmail.com. Jen Revermann, D.R.E. Students 68.
SARTELL, STEARNS CO., ST. FRANCIS XAVIER (1948) [CEM]
219 2nd St. N., P.O. Box 150, Sartell, 56377.
Tel: 320-252-1363; Email: bdingmann@stfrancissartell.org. Rev. Timothy Baltes; Deacons Stephen Pareja; Stephen Yanish.
School—St. Francis Xavier School, (Grades PreSchool-6), Tel: 320-252-9940; Email: kkockler@stfrancissartell.org. Kathryn Kockler, Prin.
Catechesis Religious Program—Tel: 320-252-8761; Email: svaske@stfrancissartell.org; Email: larnold@stfrancissartell.org; Email: sfxyouthmin@stfrancissartell.org. Shelby Vaske, D.R.E.; Linda Arnold, D.R.E.; Melissa Fox, Youth Min. Students 640.
SAUK CENTRE, STEARNS CO.
1—OUR LADY OF THE ANGELS, [CEM]
207 S. 7th St., Sauk Centre, 56378-1505.
Tel: 320-352-3502; Email: angels@mainstreetcom.com; Web: www.catholic-sc.org. Mailing Address: 304 Sinclair Lewis Ave., Sauk Centre, 56378. Revs. Gregory Paffel; James Maderak, Parochial Vicar.
Catechesis Religious Program—Tel: 320-352-5580. Students 178.
2—ST. PAUL'S (1870) [CEM]
304 Sinclair Lewis Ave., Sauk Centre, 56378.
Tel: 320-352-2196; Email: stpaulschurch@mainstreetcom.com. Revs. Gregory Paffel; James Maderak, Parochial Vicar; Deacon Thomas McFadden.
See Holy Family School, Sauk Centre under Inter-Parochial Schools located in the Institution section.
Catechesis Religious Program—220 S. Birch, Sauk Centre, 56378. Tel: 320-352-5580. Students 200.
SAUK RAPIDS, BENTON CO.
1—CHURCH OF SACRED HEART (1919) [CEM]
2875 10th Ave. N.E., Sauk Rapids, 56379.
Tel: 320-251-8115; Fax: 320-252-0710; Email: parish@sacredheartsaukrapids.org. Rev. Ralph G. Zimmerman; Deacon Joseph Kresky.
See St. Katharine Drexel under Inter-Parochial Schools, St. Cloud for details.
Catechesis Religious Program—Joan Krause, D.R.E. Students 230.
2—ST. PATRICK, [CEM]
7286 Duelm Rd., N.E., Sauk Rapids, 56379.
Tel: 320-252-2069; Email: stpatsmn@earthlink.net. Rev. Michael Wolfbauer.
Res.: P.O. Box 337, Foley, 56329. Tel: 320-968-7913.
Catechesis Religious Program—Toni Hammond, D.R.E. Students 43.
SEDAN, POPE CO., IMMACULATE CONCEPTION, Closed. For inquiries for parish records contact Sacred Heart, Glenwood.
SOBIESKI, MORRISON CO., ST. STANISLAUS (1884) [CEM]
9406 Church Cir., Little Falls, 56345-9803.
Tel: 320-632-6930; Email: ststans@littlefalls.net. Rev. Jimmy Joseph, V.C.
Catechesis Religious Program—Students 29.
SPRING HILL, STEARNS CO., ST. MICHAEL'S (1857) [CEM]
211 5th Ave. S.E., Melrose, 56352. Tel: 320-256-4702 ; Email: stmarys@stmarysofmelrose.com. Revs. Marvin Enneking, J.C.L.; Oswaldo Roche, Parochial Vicar.
Church: P.O. Box 136, Greenwald, 56335.
Catechesis Religious Program—Tel: 320-987-3672. Diane Welle, D.R.E. Students 35.
STAPLES, TODD CO., SACRED HEART
310 Fourth St., N.E., P.O. Box 177, Staples, 56479.
Tel: 218-894-2296; Email: sheart@arvig.net. Rev. Gabriel Walz; Deacons Robert Shaffer; John Wolak.
School—Sacred Heart Area School, (Grades PreSchool-6), 324 - 4th St. N.E., Staples, 56479.
Tel: 218-894-2077. James Opelia, Prin. Lay Teachers 7; Students 80.
Catechesis Religious Program—Tel: 218-894-1095. Students 96.
SWANVILLE, MORRISON CO., ST. JOHN THE BAPTIST, [CEM]
P.O. Box 68, Swanville, 56382. Tel: 320-547-2920; Email: stjohns@gctel.net. Rev. Ronald Dockendorf.
Catechesis Religious Program—Students 105.
TINTAH, TRAVERSE CO., ST. GALL (1881) [CEM]
110 Minnesota Ave., Tintah, 56583.
Tel: 218-369-2188; Email: stgall@runestone.net. Rev. Jeremy Ploof.
Catechesis Religious Program—Students 7.
UPSALA, MORRISON CO., ST. MARY, [CEM]
P.O. Box 249, Upsala, 56384. Tel: 320-573-2132; Email: 238catholic@surfsota.com. Revs. Gregory Mastey; Jeremy Theis.
Res.: 8550 State Hwy. 238, Bowlus, 56314.
Tel: 320-584-5313; Tel: 320-573-2975.
Catechesis Religious Program—Students 87.

URBANK, OTTER TAIL CO., SACRED HEART (1902) [CEM]
60 Central Ave. N., Parkers Prairie, 56361.
Tel: 218-894-2296; Email: gloriajb@midwestinfo.net. Rev. Peter VanderWeyst; Deacon Joseph Wood.
Catechesis Religious Program—Students 41.

VERNDALE, WADENA CO., ST. FREDERICK (1910) [CEM]
20 Brown St. N., P.O. Box C, Verndale, 56481.
Tel: 218-445-5204; Email: vbmcatholic@wcta.net. Rev. Lauren Germann.
Catechesis Religious Program—20 Mason Ave. N.W., Verndale, 56481. Shirley Malone, D.R.E. Students 46.

VILLARD, POPE CO., ST. BARTHOLOMEW'S (1883) [CEM]
105 N. Franklin, Glenwood, 56334.
Tel: 320-634-3813; Fax: 320-634-0590; Email: vbmcatholic@wcta.net. Rev. Joseph Vanderberg.
Catechesis Religious Program—Paula Johnson, D.R.E.; Micki Morrissey, D.R.E. Students 11.

VINELAND, MILLE LACS CO., ST. THERESE, [CEM] [JC]
Mailing Address: P.O. Box 26, Onamia, 56359.
Tel: 320-532-3601; Fax: 320-532-5222; Email: sacredheart56386@yahoo.com. Revs. Jerome Schik, O.S.C.; Gregory Poser, O.S.C., Parochial Vicar.
Catechesis Religious Program—Students 5.

WADENA, WADENA CO., ST. ANN'S (1895) [CEM]
514 First St., S.E., Wadena, 56482.
Tel: 218-631-1593; Email: bbutter@saintanns.net. Rev. Aaron J. Kuhn; Deacon Gerald Snyder.
Catechesis Religious Program—Students 108.

WAHKON, MILLE LACS CO., SACRED HEART, [CEM]
P.O. Box 68, Wahkon, 56386. Tel: 320-495-3324; Email: sacredheart56386@yahoo.com. Revs. Jerome Schik, O.S.C.; Gregory Poser, O.S.C., Parochial Vicar.
Catechesis Religious Program—Tel: 320-495-3324. Jessica Faust, D.R.E. Students 41.

WAITE PARK, STEARNS CO., ST. JOSEPH'S (1916) [CEM]
106 7th Ave. N., Waite Park, 56387.
Tel: 320-251-5231; Email: churchofstjosephwp@waitepark.org. Rev. Timothy Gapinski; Deacons Jim Trout; Lucio Hernandez.
School-See All Saints Academy, St. Cloud under Inter-Parochial Schools located in the Institutions section.
Catechesis Religious Program—Students 42.

WARD SPRINGS, TODD CO., ST. BERNARD'S, Closed. For inquiries for parish records contact St. Joseph, Grey Eagle.

WEST UNION, TODD CO., ST. ALEXIUS, [CEM]
11 Oak St., P.O. Box 104, West Union, 56378.
Tel: 320-352-2563; Email: stralexius@wisper-wireless.com. Revs. Gregory Paffel; James Maderak, Parochial Vicar.
Res.: 211 S. 7th St., Sauk Centre, 56378.
Catechesis Religious Program—Box 4A, West Union, 56389. Students 22.

WHEATON, TRAVERSE CO., AVE MARIA (1899) [JC]
201 Ninth St. S., Wheaton, 56296. Tel: 320-563-4421; Email: stmarych@fedtel.net. Rev. John Paul Knopik.
Catechesis Religious Program—Barb Tauber, D.R.E. Students 77.

ZIMMERMAN, SHERBURNE CO., ST. PIUS X, [CEM] Merged With St. Edward's, Princeton to form The Church of Christ Our Light, Princeton.

Chaplains of Public Institutions

ST. CLOUD. *Minnesota State Reformatory for Men*. Vacant.
U.S. Veteran's Hospital, 56301.

CAMBRIDGE. *Cambridge State School and Hospital*, Cambridge, 55008. Vacant.

FERGUS FALLS. *State Hospital Chapel*, Fergus Falls, 56537. Vacant.

Special Assignment:
Revs.—
Belland, David
Marfori, Antonio
Nordick, Jerome.

Retired:
Revs.—
Dalseth, Gerald, (Retired), 308 3rd St. S., #105, Sauk Rapids, 56379
Folsom, Paul, (Retired), 39880 Crane Lake Dr., Battle Lake, 56515
Harren, Robert C., J.C.L., (Retired), 1515 No. 3rd St., 56303
Holmes, Albert, (Retired), 302 Balmoral Ave., Henning, 56551
Hoppe, Arthur, (Retired), 125 5th Ave., N.W., #117, Melrose, 56352
Kieffer, Robert, (Retired), 509 12th Ave. E., P.O. Box 11, Alexandria, 56308
Kleinschmidt, Sylvester, (Retired), 606 Main St. N., Apt. 207, Sauk Centre, 56378
Kraemer, Edwin, (Retired), 828 Village Ave., Sartell, 56377
Kroll, Anthony, (Retired), 308-3rd St. S., #203, Sauk Rapids, 56379
Landsberger, Nicholas, (Retired), 308 3rd St. S., #101, Sauk Rapids, 56379
Leisen, Richard, (Retired), 308-3rd St. S., #107, Sauk Rapids, 56379
Lieser, Gregory, (Retired), 308-3rd St. S., #103, Sauk Rapids, 56379
Lieser, Vincent, (Retired), 30582 440th St., Melrose, 56352
Marthaler, Andrew, (Retired), 750 Railroad Ave., Apt. 132, Sauk Centre, 56378
Maus, Le Roy, (Retired), 11367 Phoenix Dr., #75, Yuma, AZ 85367
Mischke, Gerald, (Retired), 25-8th Ave. S., Saint Cloud, 56301
Olson, Thomas, (Retired), 6221 19th St. N., 56303
Pavelis, Harold, (Retired), Box 88, Concord, CA 94522
Riedemann, Kenneth, (Retired), 21398 Alcott Ln., Sauk Centre, 56378
Schefers, Eberhard, (Retired), 702-2nd Ave., N.E., Saint Joseph, 56374
Schmitt, Silverius, (Retired), 5290-175th St., N.W., Box 353, Royalton, 56373
Sowada, Arlie, (Retired), 117 6th St., Bluffton, 56518
Thielman, Kenneth, (Retired), 125 N. Fifth Ave. W., Apt. 121, Melrose, 56352
Thoennes, James, (Retired), P.O. Box 1248, Saint Cloud, 56302
Tomasiewicz, Frank, (Retired), 308 3rd St. S., #201, Sauk Rapids, 56379
Vogel, Arthur, (Retired), 617 Pinecone Rd., Apt. 308, Sartell, 56377
Vos, William, (Retired), 1664 Payton Ct., N.E., Sauk Rapids, 56379
Wenzel, Timothy, (Retired), 21949 100th Ave., Randall, 56475
Wieser, Stanley, (Retired), 909 1st Ave. S., Wheaton, 56296
Zimmer, Nicholas, (Retired), 400 3rd St., S.W., Apt. 211, Braham, 55006.

Permanent Deacons:
Altstadt, Randall, St. Henry, Perham
Anderberg, George, (Retired)
Arnold, Stephen
Barder, Mark, Christ Our Light, Princeton/Zimmerman
Beck, Guy, (Retired)
Benda, Michael
Bliss, Bertrum
Bobertz, Charles A.
Clack, James
Curry, Dirck, Epiphany, Normal, IL
Dullinger, Dan
Dupay, Steven C.
Fromm, Jeffrey, Holdingford; Our Lady of Mt. Carmel, Opole; St. Wendel, St. Columbkille; Church of St. Stephen, St. Stephen
Froslee, Hans
Geyer, Bruce, St. Mary, Little Falls; Holy Family, Belle Prairie; Our Lady of Lourdes, Little Falls
Goenner, Chris
Hennen, Stanley, (Retired)
Hernandez, David
Hilber, Joseph, St. Leonard's, Pelican Rapids; St. Elizabeth, Elizabeth
Kaas, Lawrence, Our Lady of the Angels, Sauk Centre; St. Paul, Sauk Centre; St. Alexius, West Union
Kampa, Charles, Our Lady of Victory, Fergus Falls
Keable, Michael, (Retired)
Kociemba, Ernest, St. Mary, Melrose
Korver, Craig, Our Lady of Lourdes, Little Falls
Kosiba, Leo, (Retired)
Kramer, Eugene, Christ the King, Cambridge; St, Mary's, Milaca; St. Louis, Foreston
Krebs, Brian
Kresky, Joseph, Sacred Heart, Sauk Rapids
Kunkel, Andrew, (Retired)
Lindmeier, David, St. Paul, St. Cloud
Maltzen, Bruce H.
McFadden, Thomas
Murray, Thomas A., (Retired), St. Joseph, St. Joseph.
Nord, Carl, Immaculate Conception, Rice
Pareja, Stephen, St. Francis, Sartell
Pinataro, Thomas
Quistorff, Richard
Ringsmuth, Frank, St. John Cantius, St. Cloud
Ritchie, William, St. Peter, St. Cloud
Rosha, Kenneth
Roth, Jerome, (Retired)
Salchert, John J., (Retired)
Scheierl, Richard, St. Augustine, St. Cloud; St. Mary, St. Cloud
Scherping, Richard, Sacred Heart, Freeport; Immaculate Conception, New Munich; St. Rose, St. Rosa
Schmainda, Frank, (Retired)
Schmitz, Vernon, Holy Spirit, St. Cloud
Schulzetenberg, James, St. Mary of Mt. Carmel, Long Prairie
Schwarzbauer, Jerome, (Retired)
Sell, Lawrence, St. Boniface, Cold Spring
Shaffer, Robert, St. Michael, Motley; Sacred Heart, Staples
Snyder, Gerald, St. Ann, Wadena; St. John, Bluffton
St. Jean, Fred, (Retired), St. Andrew, Elk River
Steele, Gregory J.
Stenger, Mark, Sacred Heart, Dent; St. Lawrence, Rush Lake
Theis, Gerald, St. Martin, St. Martin; Ss. Peter & Paul, Richmond
Trout, James, St. Michael, St. Cloud
Tzinski, Donald, J.C.L., (Diocesan Tribunal)
Warren, Todd, St. Michael, St. Cloud
Wocken, John, St. Mary, St. Cloud; St. Augustine, St. Cloud
Wolak, John, Sacred Heart, Staples; St. Michael, Motley
Wood, Joseph, St. Olaf, Elbow Lake; St. Gall, Tintah
Yanish, Stephen, St. Francis, Sartell.

INSTITUTIONS LOCATED IN DIOCESE

[A] SEMINARIES, RELIGIOUS OR SCHOLASTICATES

COLLEGEVILLE. *St. John's School of Theology and Seminary*, P.O. Box 7288, Collegeville, 56321.
Tel: 320-363-2100; Fax: 320-363-3145; Email: sot@csbsju.edu; Web: www.csbsju.edu/sot. Revs. Michael Patella, O.S.B., Rector; Dale Launderville, O.S.B., Dean; David Wuolu, Librarian
Legal Title: St. John's School of Theology and Seminary Religious Teachers 1; Lay Teachers 15; Priests 5; Students 112.

[B] COLLEGES AND UNIVERSITIES

COLLEGEVILLE. *Saint John's University* (1857) (Men) 2850 Abbey Plaza, Box 2222, Collegeville, 56321.
Tel: 320-363-3161; Fax: 320-363-3519; Email: kosborne@csbsju.edu; Web: www.csbsju.edu. Dr. Michael Hemesath, Pres.; Richard Adamson, Treas.; Patti Epsky, Sec. An undergraduate college of liberal arts and sciences that educates 1,650 men in the Catholic Benedictine tradition. SJU has a partnership with College of Saint Benedict, a liberal arts college for women. The partnership expands the resources of both institutions. Other sponsored programs include the graduate School of Theology (co-ed) and Seminary (men), the Hill Museum and Manuscript Library, The Saint John's Bible, and Artist in Residence Program. Religious Teachers 12; Students 1,777; Monks 29; Lay Faculty 151; Staff 367.

SAINT JOSEPH. *College of Saint Benedict* (1913) (Women) 37 College Ave. S., St. Joseph, 56374.
Tel: 320-363-5011; Fax: 320-363-5136; Email: csbcampusministry@csbsju.edu; Web: www.csbsju.edu. Sr. Sharon Nohner, Dir. Sisters of the Order of Saint Benedict.A 1,977-student national liberal arts college for women educating students in the Catholic, Benedictine tradition. CSB has a partnership with Saint John's University, a liberal arts college for men. The partnership expands the resources of both institutions including more than 60 areas of study and 38 majors and 33 minor programs and 20 study-abroad programs. Clergy 2,019; Faculty 166; Sisters 8; Students 1,977; Staff 497.
Officers Group: Mary Geller, Vice Pres. Student Devel.; Mary Dana Hinton, Pres.; Kathy Hansen, Vice Pres., Inst. Advancement - Interim; Susan Palmer, Vice Pres. of Finance & Admin.; Dr. Richard Ice, Ph.D., Interim Provost.
Administrative Group: Jon McGee, Vice Pres. Planning & Public Affairs; Tammy Moore, Dir. CSB Media Rels.

[C] HIGH SCHOOLS, DIOCESAN

ST. CLOUD. *The Cathedral High School*, (Grades 7-12), 312 7th Ave. N., 56303. Tel: 320-251-3421;
Fax: 320-253-5576; Email: mmullin@chsj23.org. Mr. Michael Mullin, Prin. Emeritus; Ms. Lynn Grewing, Prin.; Rev. Benjamin Kociemba, Chap.; Julie Notsch, Librarian. Religious Teachers 1; Lay Teachers 46; Priests 1; Students 655.
Cathedral High School Education Foundation, P.O.

Box 1579, 56302. Tel: 320-251-3421; Fax: 320-253-5576.

[D] HIGH SCHOOLS, PRIVATE

COLLEGEVILLE. *Saint John's Preparatory School*, (Grades 6-12), College Preparatory. 2280 Water Tower Rd., P.O. Box 4000, Collegeville, 56321. Tel: 320-363-3315; Fax: 320-363-3322; Email: admissions@sjprep.net; Web: www.sjprep.net. Rev. Jonathan Licari, O.S.B., Headmaster; Katie Bergstrom, Prin.; Stephanie Johnson, Technology & Library. Brothers 2; Religious Teachers 2; Lay Teachers 28; Priests 1; Sisters 1; Students 284.

[E] INTER-PAROCHIAL SCHOOLS

ST. CLOUD. *All Saints Academy*, (Grades PreK-6), 1215 11th Ave. N., 56303. Fax: 320-251-7014; Email: paula.leiter@allsaintsmn.org; Web: www.allsaintsacademymn.org. Paula Leiter, Prin.; Karl Terhaar, Admin. Consolidation of the following parishes: St. Joseph, Waite Park, St. Joseph, St. Joseph and Sts. Peter, Paul & Michael, St. Cloud. Faculty 28; Students 385.

St. Elizabeth Ann Seton School, (Grades PreK-6), 1615 Eleventh Ave. S., 56301. Tel: 320-251-1988; Fax: 320-229-2149; Email: kvangsness@seasmn.org. Kelly Vangsness, Prin.; Alyssa Sauerer, Librarian. Consolidation of schools of the following parishes: Holy Spirit and St. Anthony, St. Cloud. Lay Teachers 12; Students 131.

St. Katharine Drexel School, (Grades PreK-6), 428 2nd St., S.E., 56304. Tel: 320-251-2376; Fax: 320-529-3222; Email: ehatlestad@ourcatholicschool.org; Web: www.ourcatholicschool.org. Erin Hatlestad, Prin.; Sr. Karen Niedzielski, O.S.F., Librarian. Consolidation of schools of the following parishes: St. Mary's Cathedral and St. Augustine, St. Cloud, and Sacred Heart, Sauk Rapids

St. Augustine's/St. Mary's Cathedral School and Sacred Heart School Religious Teachers 3; Lay Teachers 20; Students 300.

FOLEY. *St. John's Area School*, (Grades PreK-6), Tel: 320-968-7972; Fax: 320-968-9956; Email: office@saintjohnsschool.net; Email: principal@saintjohnsschool.net; Web: www.saintjohnsschool.net. Christine Frederichs, Prin. Consolidation of the following parishes: St. John's, Foley; St. Lawrence, Duelm; St. Elizabeth, Brennyville; St. Joseph, Morrill; SS. Peter and Paul, Gilman; St. Louis, Foreston; St. Patrick of Minden Township Lay Teachers 8; Students 90.

LITTLE FALLS. *Mary of Lourdes School (Elementary Campus)*, (Grades PreK-4), 307 Fourth St., S.E., Little Falls, 56345. Tel: 320-632-5408; Fax: 320-632-5409; Email: mhbecker@molschool.org; Web: www.molschool.org. Maria Heymans-Becker, Prin.; Mary Sowado, Asst. Prin. Consolidation of following parishes: St. Mary and Our Lady of Lourdes, Little Falls Lay Teachers 13; Students 145.

Mary of Lourdes School (Middle School Campus), (Grades 5-8), 205 N.W. Third St., Little Falls, 56345. Tel: 320-632-6742; Fax: 320-632-3556; Email: molmsoffice@molschool.org; Web: www.molschool.org. Maria Heymans-Becker, Prin.; Mary Sowada, Asst. Prin. Clergy 1; Students 102; Teachers 10.

PIERZ. *Holy Trinity Catholic School*, (Grades PreK-6), 80 Edward St. S., P.O. Box 427, Pierz, 56364. Tel: 320-468-6446; Fax: 320-468-6446; Email: dmm@holytrinitypierz.org; Web: holytrinitypierz.org. Debra Meyer-Myrum, Prin.; Kristi Schmidtbauer, Librarian. Consolidation of the following parishes: St. Michael's, Buckman; Holy Cross, Harding; St. John Nepomuk, Lastrup; St. Joseph, Pierz. Lay Teachers 14; Students 177.

SAUK CENTRE. *Holy Family School*, (Grades K-6), 231 Sinclair Lewis Ave., Sauk Centre, 56378. Tel: 320-352-6535; Fax: 320-352-6537; Email: lynn_peterson@isd743.k12.mn.us; Web: www.holyfamilysc.stclouddiocese.org. Lynn Peterson, Prin.; Patty Dirkes, Librarian. Consolidation of the following parishes: St. Paul's and Our Lady of the Angels, Sauk Centre. Religious Teachers 1; Lay Teachers 16; Students 199.

[F] HOMES FOR EMOTIONALLY DISTURBED AND HANDICAPPED

ST. CLOUD. *Bethany Home*, 13 8th Ave. S., Cold Spring, 56320. Tel: 320-685-7899; Fax: 320-685-9808; Email: betsy.holan@ccstcloud.org. Deacon Stephen Pareja, Exec. Dir.; Betsy Holan, Dir. Bed Capacity 4; Residents 4; Tot Asst. Annually 4; Total Staff 4.

St. Cloud Children's Home of the Diocese of St. Cloud, 1726 Seventh Ave. S., 56301. Tel: 320-251-2340; Email: RRolfes@gw.stcdio.org. Very Rev. Robert Rolfes, J.C.L., Vicar. Bed Capacity 60.

St. Elizabeth Home, 306 15th Ave. N., 56303. Tel: 320-650-1550; Email: betsy.holan@ccstcloud.org. Deacon Stephen Pareja, Exec. Dir.; Betsy Holan, Dir. Board and Lodging Home for Functionally Impaired Adults. Bed Capacity 18; Tot Asst. Annually 27; Total Staff 2.

St. Francis Home, 1727 Roosevelt Rd., 56301. Tel: 320-650-1550; Email: betsy.holan@ccstcloud.org. Deacon Stephen Pareja, Exec. Dir. Supervised Living Situation for Persons with Developmental Disabilities. Bed Capacity 4; Tot Asst. Annually 4; Total Staff 4.

LaPaz Community Inc., Catholic Charities Housing Services, 530 S. 16th St., 56301. Tel: 320-229-4580; Email: sheri.brown@ccstcloud.org. Deacon Stephen Pareja, Exec. Dir.; Sheri Brown, Dir. Bed Capacity 36; Tot Asst. Annually 146; Total Staff 1; Units 36.

COLD SPRING. *St. Anne's Home* Contact Catholic Charities 103 10th Ave. N., Cold Spring, 56320. Tel: 320-650-1550; Email: betsy.holan@ccstcloud.org. Deacon Stephen Pareja, Exec. Dir.; Betsy Holan, Dir. Supervised Living Situation for Persons with Developmental Disabilities. Bed Capacity 4; Tot Asst. Annually 4; Total Staff 4.

St. Luke's Home Contact Catholic Charities 411 8th Ave. N., Cold Spring, 56320. Tel: 320-650-1550. Deacon Stephen Pareja, Exec. Dir.; Ruth Hunstiger, Dir. Community Svc. Adults with mild to moderate developmental disabilities. Bed Capacity 4; Tot Asst. Annually 4; Total Staff 4.

Mother Teresa Home, 101 Tenth Ave., Cold Spring, 56320. Tel: 320-685-8626; Fax: 320-685-8626; Email: Betsy.Holan@ccstcloud.org. Deacon Stephen Pareja, Exec. Dir.; Betsy Holan, Dir. Supervised Living Situation for Persons with Developmental Disabilities. Bed Capacity 4; Residents 4; Tot Asst. Annually 4; Total Staff 4.

LITTLE FALLS. *St. Camillus Place*, 1100 S.E. Fourth St., Little Falls, 56345. Tel: 320-631-5020; Fax: 320-631-5025. Lisa Thielman, Dir.; Barbara A. Miller, Admin.; Bea Britz, Chap. Bed Capacity 14.

PAYNESVILLE. *Adult Foster Care for Handicapped Individuals*, 1790 W. Mill St., Paynesville, 56362. Tel: 320-243-3750; Fax: 320-243-3718; Email: Betsy.Holan@ccstcloud.org. P.O. Box 2390, 56302. Deacon Stephen Pareja, Exec. Dir.; Betsy Holan, Dir. Bed Capacity 4; Tot Asst. Annually 4; Total Staff 5.

[G] GENERAL HOSPITALS

ST. CLOUD. *St. Cloud Hospital*, 1406 Sixth Ave. N., 56303. Tel: 320-251-2700; Fax: 320-255-5711; Email: administrator@centracare.com; Web: www.stcloudhospital.com. Craig Broman, Pres.; Bret Reuter, Dir. Mission and Spiritual Care; Revs. Roger Botz, O.S.B., Chap.; Mark Stang, Chap. Bassinets 43; Bed Capacity 489; Tot Asst. Annually 309,304; Total Staff 6,108; Sisters of St. Benedict 1.

BRECKENRIDGE. *St. Francis Medical Center* (1899) 2400 St. Francis Dr., Breckenridge, 56520. Tel: 218-643-3000; Fax: 218-643-0850; Email: davidnelson@catholichealth.net; Web: www.sfcare.org. David Nelson, Pres.; Ann Trebsch, Vice Pres. Mission; Rev. Joseph Backowski, Chap. Bassinets 8; Bed Capacity 25; Tot Asst. Annually 26,000; Total Staff 175.

LITTLE FALLS. *St. Gabriel's Hospital*, 815 S.E. Second St., Little Falls, 56345. Tel: 320-632-5680; Fax: 320-631-5480; Email: luanntrutwin@catholichealth.net. Joseph Messmer, Pres.; LuAnn Trutwin, Chap. Bassinets 10; Bed Capacity 178; Total Staff 307; Total Assisted 120,000.

[H] HOMES FOR AGED

ST. CLOUD. *St. Benedict's Senior Community* (1978) 1810 Minnesota Blvd., S.E., 56304. Tel: 320-252-0010; Fax: 320-654-2351; Email: doerrl@centracare.com. Linda Doerr, Exec. Dir.; Rebecca Calderone, Dir. of Pastoral Care & Lay Ecclesial Health Care Min.; Rev. Stephen Beauclair, O.S.B., Chap.; Sr. Janelle Sietsema, O.S.B., Lay Ecclesial Minister. Corporate Division of the St. Cloud Hospital. Operated under the auspices of the local Catholic Church of St. Cloud.; Care Center managed by St. Benedict's Senior Community. A division of the St. Cloud Hospital. Operated under the auspices of the local Catholic Church of St. Cloud. Residents 146; Short Stay Units/Beds 76.

Benedict Village, Benedict Village: 2000 15th Ave., S.E., 56304. Tel: 320-252-4380; Fax: 320-654-2351. Linda Kappel, Vice Pres.; Robin Theis, Admin., Housing and Community Svcs. Managed by St. Benedict's Senior Community. A Division of the St. Cloud Hospital. Operated under the auspices of the local Catholic Church of St. Cloud. Residents 115.

Benedict Homes (4), 1342 Minnesota Blvd., S.E., 56304. Tel: 320-252-0010. Residential Homes for residents with memory loss diseases. All Benedict Homes are managed by St. Benedict's Senior Community. A division of the St. Cloud Hospital. Operated under the auspices of the local Catholic Church of St. Cloud. Residents 24.

Benedict Court, 1980 15th Ave., S.E., 56304. Tel: 320-252-0010; Fax: 320-654-2351. Linda Kappel, Vice Pres.; Robin Theis, Admin., Housing and Community Svcs. 39 assisted living apartments; Managed by St. Benedict's Senior Community. A Division of the St. Cloud Hospital. Operated under the auspices of the local Catholic Church of St. Cloud. Residents 40.

Benet Place North, 1420 Minnesota Blvd., S.E., 56304. Tel: 320-252-2557; Fax: 320-654-2351. Subsidized apartments with supportive services for older adults only. Managed by St. Benedict's Senior Community. Tenants 40.

Benet Place South, 1975 15th Ave., S.E., 56304. Tel: 320-529-8700; Fax: 320-654-2351. Tenants 36.

ALBANY. *Mother of Mercy Senior Living*, 230 Church Ave., Box 676, Albany, 56307. Tel: 320-845-2195; Fax: 320-845-7092; Email: dmcdevitt@momcampus.org; Web: www.motherofmercymn.org. Dean McDevitt, Admin. & CEO. Bed Capacity 142; Patients Asst Anual. 205.

BRECKENRIDGE. *Appletree Court* (1998) 601 Oak St., Breckenridge, 56520. Tel: 218-643-0407; Fax: 218-643-0850; Email: jolynDohman@catholichealth.net; Web: sfcare.org. David Nelson, CEO. Residents 18.

St. Francis Home, 2400 St. Francis Dr., Breckenridge, 56520. Tel: 218-643-3000; Fax: 218-643-0850; Web: www.sfcare.org. David Nelson, CEO; Rev. Joseph Backowski, Chap. Bed Capacity 80; Patients Asst Anual. 143.

COLD SPRING. *Assumption Home* (1963) 715 First St. N., Cold Spring, 56320. Tel: 320-685-3693; Fax: 320-685-7044; Email: lindseys@assumptionhome.com; Web: assumptionhome.org. Rev. Thomas Andert, O.S.B., Chap.; Lindsey Sand, Admin. Residents 82.

Assumption Home, Inc., 715 First St. N., Cold Spring, 56320. Tel: 320-685-3693; Fax: 320-685-7044; Email: lindseys@assumptionhome.com; Web: www.assumptionhome.org. Rev. Thomas Andert, O.S.B., Chap.; Lindsey Sand, Admin. Assumption Home, Inc. is made up of Assumption Home and Assumption Court, a nursing home and a housing with services apartment complex. Skilled Nursing Beds 82; Total Apartments 59; Total Staff 180.

John Paul Apartments, 200 Eighth Ave. N., Cold Spring, 56320. Tel: 320-685-4429; Fax: 320-685-7044; Email: lindseys@assumptionhome.com. Rev. Thomas Andert, O.S.B., Chap.; Lindsey Sand, Admin. Apartments 61.

LITTLE FALLS. *Alverna Apartments*, 300 Eighth Ave., S.E., Little Falls, 56345. Tel: 320-631-5030; Fax: 320-631-5035. Bea Britz, Chap.; Allysa Barnes, Mgr. (An Affiliate of Catholic Health Initiatives) Units 60.

MORA. *Benedictine Living Community of Mora*, 110 N. 7th St., Mora, 55051. Tel: 320-679-1411; Fax: 320-679-8350. Jack L'Heureux, CEO. Skilled care and assisted living facility.

MORRIS. *West Wind Village*, 1001 Scotts Ave., Morris, 56267. Tel: 320-589-1133; Fax: 320-589-7955; Email: msyltie@sfhs.org. Paula Viker, Admin. Beds 88; Patients Asst Anual. 115.

PARKERS PRAIRIE. *St. William's Living Center* (1963) P.O. Box 30, Parkers Prairie, 56361. Tel: 218-338-4671; Fax: 218-338-5917; Email: administrator@stwilliamslivingcenter.com. Tim Kelly, Admin. Bed Capacity 58; Tot Asst. Annually 110.

[I] MONASTERIES AND RESIDENCES OF PRIESTS AND BROTHERS

COLLEGEVILLE. *Holy Cross Trust*, 2900 Abbey Plaza, P.O. Box 2400, Collegeville, 56321. Tel: 320-363-2547; Email: bjenniges@csbsju.edu. Very Rev. Bradley Jenniges, O.S.B., Trustee.

St. John's Abbey, of the Order of St. Benedict and St. John's University, School of Theology, Seminary, Preparatory School and Novitiate. 2900 Abbey Plaza, P.O. Box 2015, Collegeville, 56321-2015. Tel: 320-363-2011; Email: sjainfo@csbsju.edu; Web: saintjohnsabbey.org. Rt. Rev. John Klassen, O.S.B., Ph.D., Abbot; Very Rev. Bradley Jenniges, O.S.B., Prior; Ven. Bro. David Paul Lange, O.S.B.; Revs. Thomas Andert, O.S.B.; Knute Anderson, O.S.B.; Timothy Backous, O.S.B.; Stephen Beauclair, O.S.B.; Nickolas Becker, O.S.B.; Luigi Bertocchi, O.S.B.; Michael Bik, O.S.B.; Roger Botz, O.S.B.; Allan Bouley, O.S.B.; Jerome Coller, O.S.B.; Corwin Collins, O.S.B.; Cletus Connors, O.S.B.; Alberic Culhane, O.S.B.; Meinrad Dindorf, O.S.B.; Ian Dommer, O.S.B.; John Patrick Earls, O.S.B.; Geoffrey Fecht, O.S.B.; Joseph Feders, O.S.B.; Jonathan Fischer, O.S.B.; Thomas Gillespie, O.S.B.; Michael Leonard Hahn, O.S.B.; Nathanael Hauser, O.S.B.; Eric Hollas, O.S.B.; Roger Kasprick, O.S.B.; Chrysostom Kim, O.S.B.; Roger Klassen, O.S.B.; Nickolas Kleespie, O.S.B., Univ. Chap.; Robert Koopmann, O.S.B.; Lewis Grobe, O.S.B.; Luke Mancuso, O.S.B.; Michael Kwatera, O.S.B.; Bernadine Ness, O.S.B.; Michael Peterson, O.S.B.; Very Rev. Thomas Wahl, O.S.B.; Revs. Dale Launderville, O.S.B.; Donald LeMay, O.S.B.; Jonathan Licari, O.S.B.; Matthew Luft, O.S.B; Brennan Maiers, O.S.B.; Kilian McDonnell, O.S.B.; Rene McGraw, O.S.B.; John Meoska, O.S.B.; Gregory Miller, O.S.B.; Dunstan Moorse, O.S.B.; Douglas Mullin, O.S.B.; Michael Naughton, O.S.B.; Kieran Nolan, O.S.B.; Michael Patella, O.S.B.; James Reichert, O.S.B.; Anthony Ruff, O.S.B.; Dominic Ruiz, O.S.B.; William Schipper, O.S.B., (On leave); Francisco Schulte, O.S.B.; William Skudlarek, O.S.B.; Columba Stewart, O.S.B., HMML Dir.; Don Talafous, O.S.B.; Donald Tauscher, O.S.B.; Gordon Tavis, O.S.B.; Mel Taylor, O.S.B.; Wilfred Theisen, O.S.B.; Hilary Thimmesh, O.S.B.; Jerome Tupa, O.S.B.; Blane Wasnie, O.S.B.; Isaiah Frederick, O.S.B.; Efrain Rosado, O.S.B., Sacramental Min.; Simeon Thole, O.S.B. Brothers 37; Priests Within Diocese 72; Priests Elsewhere 3; Permanent Deacons 1.

On Special Assignments: Revs. Joel Kelly, O.S.B.; Daniel Ward, O.S.B., 2613 Woodedge Rd., Silver Spring, MD 20906. Tel: 301-933-0447; Fax: 301-589-2897; Cyprian Weaver, O.S.B.; Blane Wasnie, O.S.B.

Priests of the Abbey Serving Abroad: Revs. Anthony Gorman, O.S.B.; Roman Paur, O.S.B., Prior, Holy Trinity Benedictine Monastery, 3110 Fujimi-Fujimi Machi, Nagano Ken, Japan 399-0211. Tel: 011-81-266-62-8770; Fax: 011-81-266-8765.

ONAMIA. *Crosier Priory* (1922) Crosier Priory of the Holy Cross, 104 Crosier Dr. N., P.O. Box 500, Onamia, 56359. Tel: 320-532-3103;
Fax: 320-532-5222; Email: onamia@crosier.org; Web: www.crosier.org. Revs. Kermit Holl, O.S.C., Prior; Thomas Carkhuff, O.S.C.; Neil Emon, O.S.C., (On restriction/charter); John J. Fleischhacker, O.S.C.; Clement N. Gustin, O.S.C.; John Hawkins, O.S.C.; Bro. Daniel Hernandez, O.S.C.; Rev. Ernest Martello, O.S.C.; Bros. Javier Garcia Nunez, O.S.C.; Timothy Tomczak, O.S.C.; Rev. James Moeglein, O.S.C., (On restriction/charter); Bro. Emil Hartman, O.S.C.; Rev. Virgil Petermeier, O.S.C.; Bros. Leo Schoenberg, O.S.C.; Daniel Stang, O.S.C.; Rev. Eugene D. Plaisted, O.S.C.; Bro. Ralph Dahl, O.S.C.; Rev. Gregory Poser, O.S.C., (Suspended); Bros. Robert Mandernach, O.S.C.; Albert Becker, O.S.C.; Jeffrey Mario Breer, O.S.C.; Revs. James H. Remmerswaal, O.S.C.; Jerome Schik, O.S.C.; Raymond Steffes, O.S.C.; Dale Ettel, (In Res.); John Phillip Suehr, O.S.C., (In Long Term Care); Steven Henrich, O.S.C.; Bro. James Scher, O.S.C.; Rev. Zawadi Jean-Marie Kambale Sambya, O.S.C. The National Shrine of St. Odilia is sponsored and maintained by the Crosier Fathers of Onamia
Crosier Fathers of Onamia Priests in Residence 17; Priests Elsewhere 5; Brothers in Residence 10.

[J] CONVENTS AND RESIDENCES FOR SISTERS

LITTLE FALLS. *St. Francis Convent* (1891) 116 Eighth Ave., S.E., Little Falls, 56345. Tel: 320-632-2981; Fax: 320-632-6313; Email: akruchten@fslf.org; Web: www.fslf.org. Sr. Beatrice Eichten, O.S.F., Community Min. Motherhouse of Franciscan Sisters of Little Falls, MN. On Mother House Campus 52; Total in Community 117.

Franciscan Life Center Rick Dietz, Contact Person.

SAINT JOSEPH. *St. Benedict's Monastery* (1857) 104 Chapel Ln., St. Joseph, 56374. Tel: 320-363-7100; Fax: 320-363-7130; Email: dmanuel@csbsju.edu; Web: www.sbm.osb.org. Sisters Susan Rudolph, O.S.B., Prioress; Elaine Schroeder, O.S.B., Coord. Eucharistic Presiders. Motherhouse and Formation House for Sisters of the Order of Saint Benedict. Sisters 145; Total in Community 204.

SAUK RAPIDS. *St. Clare's Monastery* (1923) Major Papal Cloister 421 4th St. S., Sauk Rapids, 56379.
Tel: 320-251-3556; Fax: 320-203-7052. Sr. Marie Immaculata, O.S.C., Abbess; Rev. Jerome Nordick, Chap. Franciscan Poor Clare Nuns. Sisters 20; Cloistered Nuns: Solemn Professed 20; Extern Sisters: Perpetual Professed 1.

[K] RETREAT HOUSES

ISANTI. *Pacem in Terris Center for Spirituality*, Mailing Address: Hermitage Retreats, 26399 MN 47, N.W., Isanti, 55040. Tel: 763-444-6408;
Fax: 763-444-9649; Email: staff@paceminterris.org; Email: tim.drake@paceminterris.org; Web: www.paceminterris.org. P.O. Box 418, St. Francis, 56374. Timothy Drake, Dir,.

[L] NEWMAN CENTERS

ST. CLOUD. *Newman Center, Inc.*, 396 First Ave. S., 56301. Tel: 320-251-3260; Fax: 320-252-3930; Email: newmancenter@scsucatholic.org; Web: scsucatholic.org. Rev. Anthony Oelrich, S.T.L., Admin.

MORRIS. *Newman Catholic Student Center*, 306 E. Fourth St., Morris, 56267. Tel: 320-589-1947; Email: newman@hometownsolutions.net; Web: www.mrs.umn.edu/~catholic. Scott Crumb, Dir. Campus Ministry.

[M] MISCELLANEOUS

ST. CLOUD. *Affordable Community Housing, Inc.*, P.O. Box 2390, 56303. Tel: 320-650-1530; Email: steve.pareja@ccstcloud.org. Deacon Stephen Pareja, Exec. Dir.

Central Minnesota Residents Encountering Christ (1998) 6667 County Rd. 91, S.E., 56304.
Tel: 320-251-0098; Email: ccarolt@yahoo.com. Carol Tembreull, Prog. Coord.

Domus Transitional Housing, 17 S. 19 1/2 Ave., 56301. Tel: 320-229-4576; Fax: 320-253-7464; Email: sheri.brown@ccstcloud.org. Deacon Stephen Pareja, Exec. Dir.; Sheri Brown, Dir. Tot Asst. Annually 35; Total Staff 2.

BROWNS VALLEY. **Browns Valley Health Center*, 114 Jefferson St. S., Browns Valley, 56219.
Tel: 320-695-2165; Fax: 320-695-2166; Email: cward@bvhc.sfhs.org. Claudia Ward, Admin. Capacity 41.

CAMBRIDGE. *Benedictine Care Centers* (Includes: St. Crispin Living Community, Red Wing, MN; Benedictine Health Center at Innsbruck, New Brighton, MN) 1995 E. Rum River Dr. S., Cambridge, 55008. Tel: 763-689-1162;
Fax: 763-689-1197; Email: jerry.carley@bhshealth.org. Jerry Carley, CEO.

Benedictine Health Dimensions, Inc., 1995 E. Rum River Dr., S., Cambridge, 55008. Tel: 763-689-1162 ; Fax: 763-689-1197; Email: webmaster@bhshealth.org; Web: www.bhshealth.org. Jerry Carley, CEO.

COLLEGEVILLE. *Dialogue Interreligieux Monastique (Monastic Interreligious Dialogue) (DIMMID)*, Saint John's Abbey, 2900 Abbey Plaza, Collegeville, 56321-2015. Tel: 320-363-3921; Email: wskudlarek@csbsju.edu. Rev. William Skudlarek, O.S.B., Contact Person.

MELROSE. *Rose Mill Apartments, LLC*, 407 E. 5th St. N., Melrose, 56352. Tel: 320-229-4580; Email: sheri.brown@ccstcloud.org. Mailing Address: P.O. Box 2390, 56302. Deacon Stephen Pareja, Exec. Dir.; Sheri Brown, Dir.

MORRIS. *St. Francis Health Services of Morris, Inc.* (1984) 801 Nevada Ave., Morris, 56267.
Tel: 320-589-2004; Fax: 320-589-1270; Email: jmichaelson@sfhs.org; Email: craw@sfhs.org; Web: www.sfhs.org. Carol Raw, CEO.

West Wind Village (1987) 1001 Scotts Ave., Morris, 56267. Tel: 320-589-1133; Fax: 320-589-7955; Web: www.pcs.sfhs.org.

ONAMIA. *Crosier Continuing Care and Support Trust*, 104 Crosier Dr., Onamia, 56359. Tel: 320-532-3103 ; Email: kholl@crosier.org. P.O. Box 500, Onamia, 56359-0500. Rev. Kermit Holl, O.S.C.

Crosier International Trust for Religious Life and Service, 104 Crosier Dr. N., P.O. Box 500, Onamia, 56359-0500. Rev. David Donnay, O.S.C., Trustee.

National Shrine of St. Odilia, Tel: 320-532-3103;
Fax: 320-532-5222; Email: info@crosier.org; Web: www.crosier.org. Bro. Albert Becker, O.S.C., Contact Person & Dir. Devel. Sponsored and maintained by Crosier Fathers of Onamia.

RICHMOND. *Maple Apartments of Richmond, Inc.*, 488 1st St., N.E., Richmond, 56368. Tel: 320-229-4580;
Fax: 320-253-7464; Email: sheri.brown@ccstcloud.org. P.O. Box 2390, 56302. Sheri Brown, Dir.; Deacon Stephen Pareja, Exec. Dir.

SAINT JOSEPH. *St. Joseph Apartment, Inc.*, 410 W. Minnesota St., St. Joseph, 56374.
Tel: 320-229-4580; Email: sheri.brown@ccstcloud.org. P.O. Box 2390, 56302. Deacon Stephen Pareja, Exec,; Sheri Brown, Dir.

Monastic Interreligious Dialogue, St. Benedict's Monastery, 104 Chapel Ln., St. Joseph, 56374.
Tel: 320-363-7070; Fax: 320-363-7173; Email: hmercier@csbsju.edu; Web: www.monasticdialog.org. Sr. Helene Mercier, O.S.B., Contact Person.

SAUK CENTRE. *Sauk Centre Apts.*, 217 Railroad Ave. Ct., Sauk Centre, 56378. Tel: 320-229-4580; Email: sheri.brown@ccstcloud.org. Mailing Address: P.O. Box 2390, 56302. Deacon Stephen Pareja, Exec.; Sheri Brown, Dir.

RELIGIOUS INSTITUTES OF MEN REPRESENTED IN THE DIOCESE

For further details refer to the corresponding bracketed number in the Religious Institutes of Men or Women section.

[0200]—*Benedictine Monks* (Collegeville, MN)—O.S.B.

[0400]—*Canons Regular of the Order of the Holy Cross* (Province of St. Odilia)—O.S.C.

[]—*Vincentian Congregation* (St. Joseph Prov.)—V.C.

RELIGIOUS INSTITUTES OF WOMEN REPRESENTED IN THE DIOCESE

[0230]—*Benedictine Sisters of Pontifical Jurisdiction*—O.S.B.

[1920]—*Congregation of the Sisters of the Holy Cross*—C.S.C.

[1310]—*Franciscan Sisters of Little Falls, Minnesota*—O.S.F.

[3760]—*Order of St. Clare*—O.S.C.

[2970]—*School Sisters of Notre Dame* (Northwestern Prov.)—S.S.N.D.

[1710]—*Sisters of St. Francis of Mary Immaculate*—O.S.F.

NECROLOGY

† Kahlhamer, Bernard, (Retired), Died Oct. 17, 2018
† Landsberger, Robert, (Retired), Died Feb. 6, 2018
† Ludwig, Alexander, (Retired), Died Apr. 26, 2018

An asterisk (*) denotes an organization that has established tax-exempt status directly with the IRS and is not covered by the USCCB Group Ruling.

Archdiocese of St. Louis

(Archidioecesis S. Ludovici)

Most Reverend

ROBERT JAMES CARLSON

Archbishop of St. Louis; ordained May 22, 1970; appointed Titular Bishop of Aviocala and Auxiliary Bishop of Saint Paul and Minneapolis November 22, 1983; consecrated January 11, 1984; appointed Coadjutor Bishop of Sioux Falls January 13, 1994; Succeeded to the See March 21, 1995; appointed Bishop of Saginaw December 29, 2004; installed February 24, 2005; appointed Archbishop of St. Louis April 21, 2009; installed June 10, 2009. *Office: 20 Archbishop May Dr., St. Louis, MO 63119-5738.*

Most Reverend

ROBERT J. HERMANN, D.D.

Retired Auxiliary Bishop of St. Louis; ordained March 30, 1963; appointed Auxiliary Bishop of St. Louis October 16, 2002; ordained December 12, 2002; retired December 1, 2010. *Office: 20 Archbishop May Dr., St. Louis, MO 63119.*

Office: 20 Archbishop May Dr., St. Louis, MO 63119-5738. Tel: 314-792-7005

Web: www.archstl.org

Email: communications@archstl.org

Most Reverend

MARK S. RIVITUSO

Auxiliary Bishop of St. Louis; ordained January 16, 1988; appointed Titular Bishop of Turuzi and Auxiliary Bishop of St. Louis March 7, 2017; installed May 2, 2017. *Office: 20 Archbishop May Dr., St. Louis, MO 63119-5738.*

Square Miles 5,968.

Diocese July 18, 1826; Archdiocese July 20, 1847.

Comprises that portion of the State of Missouri bounded on the north by the northern line of the County of Lincoln; on the west by the western lines of the Counties of Lincoln, Warren, Franklin and Washington; on the south by the southern lines of the Counties of Washington, St. Francois and Perry; on the east by the Mississippi River.

Heavenly Patrons–Saint Louis, King, Saint Vincent de Paul and Saint Rose Philippine Duchesne.

For legal titles of parishes and archdiocesan institutions, consult the Catholic Center.

STATISTICAL OVERVIEW

Personnel	
Archbishops	1
Auxiliary Bishops	1
Retired Bishops	1
Abbots	1
Retired Abbots	1
Priests: Diocesan Active in Diocese	206
Priests: Diocesan Active Outside Diocese	14
Priests: Diocesan in Foreign Missions	3
Priests: Retired, Sick or Absent	95
Number of Diocesan Priests	318
Religious Priests in Diocese	260
Total Priests in Diocese	578
Extern Priests in Diocese	12
Ordinations:	
Diocesan Priests	2
Religious Priests	4
Transitional Deacons	7
Permanent Deacons	25
Permanent Deacons in Diocese	280
Total Brothers	96
Total Sisters	1,131
Parishes	
Parishes	179
With Resident Pastor:	
Resident Diocesan Priests	144
Resident Religious Priests	13
Without Resident Pastor:	
Administered by Priests	15
Administered by Deacons	5
Administered by Religious Women	1
Administered by Lay People	1
Missions	6
Closed Parishes	2
Welfare	
Catholic Hospitals	12
Total Assisted	3,193,152
Homes for the Aged	12
Total Assisted	2,962
Residential Care of Children	2
Total Assisted	700
Day Care Centers	6
Total Assisted	26,410
Specialized Homes	12
Total Assisted	10,709
Special Centers for Social Services	39
Total Assisted	59,524
Educational	
Seminaries, Diocesan	2
Students from This Diocese	42
Students from Other Diocese	88
Diocesan Students in Other Seminaries	4
Seminaries, Religious	1
Students Religious	25
Total Seminarians	71
Colleges and Universities	2
Total Students	14,448
High Schools, Diocesan and Parish	11
Total Students	3,805
High Schools, Private	15
Total Students	7,138
Elementary Schools, Diocesan and Parish	94
Total Students	23,989
Elementary Schools, Private	8
Total Students	1,369
Non-residential Schools for the Disabled	3
Total Students	71
Catechesis/Religious Education:	
High School Students	86
Elementary Students	14,580
Total Students under Catholic Instruction	65,557
Teachers in the Diocese:	
Priests	24
Scholastics	3
Brothers	1
Sisters	28
Lay Teachers	2,695
Vital Statistics	
Receptions into the Church:	
Infant Baptism Totals	4,596
Minor Baptism Totals	307
Adult Baptism Totals	206
Received into Full Communion	337
First Communions	5,132
Confirmations	5,296
Marriages:	
Catholic	1,052
Interfaith	423
Total Marriages	1,475
Deaths	3,786
Total Catholic Population	509,280
Total Population	2,250,000

Former Bishops—Most Revs. LOUIS WILLIAM VALENTINE DUBOURG, Archbishop of the Cardinalatial See of Besancon; ord. 1788; cons. in Rome, Sept. 24, 1815, Bishop of Louisiana, Upper and Lower, took his first residential seat in St. Louis, Jan. 6, 1818. On July 18, 1826, the Diocese of Louisiana was divided and the Sees of St. Louis and New Orleans erected. Bishop DuBourg having resigned the See of Louisiana, was transferred to the Diocese of Montauban in France, Aug. 13, 1826, and made Archbishop of the Cardinalatial See of Besancon, Feb. 15, 1833, where he died Dec. 12 of the same year; JOSEPH ROSATI, C.M., Bishop of St. Louis; born Jan. 12, 1789 in Lazio, Italy; ord. Feb. 10, 1811; cons. Bishop of the Titular See of Tenagra and constituted Coadjutor of Bishop DuBourg of Louisiana at Donaldsville, LA, March 25, 1824. When the See of Louisiana was divided Bishop Rosati was made Bishop of St. Louis and Administrator of New Orleans. He died while on business in Rome on Sept. 25, 1843; PETER RICHARD KENRICK, D.D., Archbishop of St. Louis; born Aug. 17, 1806 in Dublin, Ireland; ord. March 6, 1832; cons. Nov. 30, 1841, Bishop of Drasa and Coadjutor to Bishop of St. Louis; Succeeded as Bishop Sept. 25, 1843; appt. Archbishop of St. Louis July 12, 1847; retired May 21, 1895; died March 4, 1896; JOHN JOSEPH KAIN, D.D., Archbishop of St. Louis; born May 31, 1841 in Martinsburg, Virginia; ord. July 2, 1866; cons. Bishop of Wheeling, WV on May 23, 1875; Titular Archbishop of Oxyrynchia and Coadjutor "cum jure successionis" of Archbishop of St. Louis, 1893; Administrator of Archdiocese of St. Louis, Dec. 14, 1893; created Archbishop of St. Louis on May 21, 1895; died Oct. 13, 1903; His Eminence JOHN CARDINAL GLENNON, D.D., Archbishop of St. Louis; born June 14, 1862; ord. Dec. 20, 1884; appt. Titular Bishop of Pinara and Coadjutor to the Bishop of Kansas City, March 14, 1896; cons. June 29, 1896; transferred to St. Louis, April 27, 1903, as Coadjutor to the Archbishop of St. Louis "cum jure successionis"; Archbishop of St. Louis, Oct. 13, 1903; Pallium received May 14, 1905; Assistant at the Pontifical Throne, June 21, 1921; created Cardinal Priest, Feb. 18, 1946; died March 9, 1946; JOSEPH CARDINAL RITTER, D.D., Archbishop of St. Louis; born July 20, 1892; ord. May 30, 1917; appt.

Titular Bishop of Hippo, Feb. 3, 1933 and Auxiliary Bishop of Indianapolis; cons. March 28, 1933; appt. Archbishop of Indianapolis, Nov. 11, 1944; appt. Archbishop of St. Louis, July 20, 1946 assistant at the Pontifical Throne, Oct. 5, 1956; created Cardinal, Priest Jan. 16, 1961; died June 10, 1967; JOHN JOSEPH CARDINAL CARBERRY, D.D., S.T.D., J.C.D., Ph.D., Archbishop of St. Louis; born July 31, 1904 in Brooklyn, New York; ord. July 28, 1929; appt. Titular Bishop of Elis and Coadjutor of Lafayette in Indiana, May 3, 1956; cons. July 25, 1956; Succeeded to See, Nov. 20, 1957; transferred to Columbus, Jan. 16, 1965; appt. Archbishop of St. Louis, Feb. 17, 1968; installed March 25, 1968; created Cardinal, April 28, 1969; retired July 31, 1979; died June 17, 1998; Most Rev. JOHN L. MAY, D.D., Archbishop of St. Louis; born March 31, 1922 in Evanston, Illinois; ord. May 3, 1947; appt. Auxiliary Bishop of Chicago, June 21, 1967; cons. Aug. 24, 1967; transferred to Mobile, Oct. 8, 1969; installed as Bishop of Mobile, Dec. 10, 1969; appt. Archbishop of St. Louis, Jan. 29, 1980; installed March 25, 1980; resigned Dec. 9, 1992; died March 24, 1994; His Eminence JUSTIN CARDINAL RIGALI, J.C.D., Archbishop of St. Louis; born April 19, 1935; ord. April 25, 1961; appt. Titular Archbishop of Bolsena, June 8, 1985; cons. Sept. 14, 1985; appointed Archbishop of St. Louis, Jan. 25, 1994; installed March 15, 1994; Pallium received June 29, 1994; transferred to Archdiocese of Philadelphia, July 15, 2003; created Cardinal, Sept. 28, 2003; installed as Archbishop of Philadelphia, Oct. 7, 2003; retired July 19, 2011; RAYMOND CARDINAL BURKE, D.D., J.C.D., born June 30, 1948 in Richland Center, Wisconsin; ord. June 29, 1975; appt. to the Residential See of La Crosse Dec. 10, 1994; cons. Jan. 6, 1995; installed as Eighth Bishop of La Crosse Feb. 22, 1995; appt. Archbishop of St. Louis Dec. 2, 2003; installed Jan. 26, 2004; appt. Prefect of the Apostolic Signatura June 27, 2008; created Cardinal Nov. 20, 2010; Patron of the Sovereign Order of the Knights of Malta, Nov. 8, 2014.

Vicars General—Most Rev. MARK S. RIVITUSO, J.C.L., M.C.L., M.A., M.Div., V.G.; Rev. Msgr. DENNIS R. STEHLY, V.G.; Rev. MICHAEL P. BOEHM, V.G.

Moderator of the Curia—Rev. Msgr. DENNIS R. STEHLY, V.G.

Chancellor—MS. NANCY J. WERNER, 20 Archbishop May Dr., St. Louis, 63119. Tel: 314-792-7836; Fax: 314-792-7842.

Chancellor for Canonical Affairs—Rev. Msgr. JEROME D. BILLING, S.T.L., J.C.L., 20 Archbishop May Dr., St. Louis, 63119. Tel: 314-792-7408; Fax: 314-792-7401.

Vice Chancellor for Special Projects—20 Archbishop May Dr., St. Louis, 63119. Tel: 314-792-7812. MRS. JENNIFER STANARD.

Metropolitan Tribunal—20 Archbishop May Dr., St. Louis, 63119. Tel: 314-792-7400; Fax: 314-792-7401.

Judicial Vicar—Rev. NICHOLAS E. KASTENHOLZ, J.C.L.

Adjutant Judicial Vicars—Revs. PHILIP J. BENE, J.C.D.; AARON P. NORD, J.C.D.

Defender of the Bond—Rev. DENNIS M. DOYLE, J.C.L.

Judges—Revs. NICHOLAS E. KASTENHOLZ, J.C.L.; PHILIP J. BENE, J.C.D.; AARON P. NORD, J.C.D.; Sr. ROBIN NORDYKE, C.D.P., J.C.L.

Promoter of Justice—Rev. Msgr. JEROME D. BILLING, S.T.L., J.C.L.

Notaries—MRS. PATRICIA LANASA; MRS. RENA HILL.

Missouri Appellate Tribunal—20 Archbishop May Dr., St. Louis, 63119. Tel: 314-792-7166; Fax: 314-792-7401.

Appellate Tribunal Officer—Rev. Msgr. JOHN B. SHAMLEFFER, J.C.L., M.C.L., M.A., M.Div.

Defender of the Bond—Rev. Msgr. JEROME D. BILLING, S.T.L., J.C.L.

Archdiocesan Consultors—Most Revs. ROBERT J. HERMANN, D.D., (Retired); MARK S. RIVITUSO, J.C.L., M.C.L., M.A., M.Div., V.G.; Rev. Msgrs. JOHN B. SHAMLEFFER, J.C.L., M.C.L., M.A., M.Div.; JOHN J. LEYKAM; VERNON E. GARDIN, Ph. D.; JOHN J. BRENNELL; MICHAEL E. DIECKMANN; Rev. JOHN M. SEPER; Rev. Msgr. DENNIS R. STEHLY, V.G.; Very Rev. MICHAEL P. BOEHM, V.G.

Deaneries/Deans—Very Revs. TIMOTHY R. COOK, V.F., North City Deanery; CARL J. SCHEBLE, V.F., South City Deanery; Very Rev. Msgr. MARK C. ULLRICH, M.Div., M.S.W., V.F., North County Deanery; Very Revs. THOMAS M. MOLINI, M.A., V.F., West County Deanery; CHARLES W. BARTHEL, V.F., South County Deanery; MICHAEL J. ESSWEIN, V.F., Mid-County Deanery; CHRISTOPHER F. HOLTMANN, V.F., Festus Deanery; BRIAN R. FISCHER, V.F., St. Charles Deanery; RICKEY J. VALLEROY, V.F., Ste. Genevieve Deanery; EUGENE G. ROBERTSON, V.F., Washington Deanery.

Archdiocesan Council of Priests—c/o 20 Archbishop May Dr., St. Louis, 63119.

Vicar for Priests—Very Rev. MICHAEL P. BOEHM, V.G., 20 Archbishop May Dr., St. Louis, 63119. Tel: 314-792-7550; Fax: 314-792-7554.

Archbishop's Liaison to Senior Priests—Rev. PHILIP G. KRAHMAN, 20 Archbishop May Dr., St. Louis, 63119. Tel: 314-963-0706.

Chief Financial Officer—MR. ROBERT BOUCHE.

Archdiocesan Offices and Directors

Archdiocesan Archives—MR. ERIC B. FAIR, Dir., 20 Archbishop May Dr., St. Louis, 63119. Tel: 314-792-7020; Fax: 314-792-7029.

Saint Louis Counseling—MR. THOMAS DUFF, L.C.S.W., Exec. Dir., 9200 Watson Rd., G101, Saint Louis, 63126. Tel: 314-544-3800; Fax: 314-843-0552. See MISCELLANEOUS section for more information.

Annual Catholic Appeal—MR. BRIAN NIEBRUGGE, Exec. Dir., 20 Archbishop May Dr., St. Louis, 63119. Tel: 314-792-7680; Fax: 314-792-7699. See MISCELLANEOUS section for more information.

Catholic Relief Services—MRS. JENNIFER STANARD, 20 Archbishop May Dr., St. Louis, 63119. Tel: 314-792-7812.

Catholic Cemeteries of St. Louis—Rev. Msgr. DENNIS M. DELANEY, Dir., 6901 Mackenzie, St. Louis, 63123. Tel: 314-792-7737; Fax: 314-351-1782. See CEMETERIES section for more information.

Central Purchasing—MR. MARK WEAVER, Dir., 20 Archbishop May Dr., St. Louis, 63119. Tel: 314-792-7065; Fax: 314-792-7019.

Catholic Renewal Center—Most Rev. ROBERT J. HERMANN, D.D., Liaison, (Retired); MS. JANE GUENTHER, Dir., 1406 S. Sappington, Crestwood, 63126. Tel: 314-801-8688; Fax: 314-792-7364.

Finance Office—20 Archbishop May Dr., St. Louis, 63119-5738. Tel: 314-792-7281; Fax: 314-792-7148. MS. MARILISSA HEIDERSCHEID, Controller.

Parish Services—20 Archbishop May Dr., St. Louis, 63119. Tel: 314-792-7716; Fax: 314-792-7149. MR. SCOTT WELZ, Dir.

Internal Audit—20 Archbishop May Dr., St. Louis, 63119. Tel: 314-792-7241; Fax: 314-792-7145. MS. KATIE FEISE.

Catholic Charities—MRS. THERESA E. RUZICKA, Pres., 4445 Lindell Blvd., St. Louis, 63108. Tel: 314-367-5500; Fax: 314-289-8037; Web: www.ccstl.org. See MISCELLANEOUS section for more information.

Cardinal Ritter Senior Services—7601 Watson Rd., St. Louis, 63119. Tel: 314-961-8000; Fax: 314-961-1934. MR. CHRISTOPHER BAECHLE, CEO, Email: cbaechle@crsstl.org. See SERVICES FOR THE ELDERLY section for more information.

Office of Child and Youth Protection—20 Archbishop May Dr., St. Louis Air Mail Center, 63119. Tel: 314-792-7704; Fax: 314-792-7714. MRS. SANDRA PRICE, Exec. Dir.

Office of Information Technology—MR. PAUL GILJUM, Dir., 20 Archbishop May Dr., St. Louis, 63119. Tel: 314-792-7570; Fax: 314-792-7579.

Office for Ecumenical & Interreligious Affairs—DR. F. JAVIER OROZCO, Dir., 20 Archbishop May Dr., St. Louis, 63119. Tel: 314-792-7162; Fax: 314-792-7164.

Office of Consecrated Life—Sr. MARYSIA WEBER, R.S.M., Dir., 20 Archbishop May Dr., St. Louis, 63119. Tel: 314-792-7250; Fax: 314-792-7259.

Office of General Counsel—20 Archbishop May Dr., St. Louis, 63119. Tel: 314-792-7075; Fax: 314-792-7079.

Archdiocesan Office of Worship—Rev. NICHOLAS W. SMITH, Dir., 20 Archbishop May Dr., St. Louis, 63119. Tel: 314-792-7231; Fax: 314-792-7239.

Council of Catholic Youth—MR. BRIAN MILLER, Exec. Dir., 20 Archbishop May Dr., St. Louis, 63119. Tel: 314-792-7600; Fax: 314-792-7619.

Missionary Childhood Association—20 Archbishop May Dr., St. Louis, 63119. Tel: 314-792-7655; Fax: 314-792-7669. Rev. TIMOTHY J. NOELKER, Dir.

Human Resources—20 Archbishop May Dr., St. Louis, 63119. Tel: 314-792-7540; Fax: 314-792-7549. MS. CHERYL FLAHERTY, Exec. Dir.

Latin America Apostolate, Archdiocese of St. Louis—20 Archbishop May Dr., St. Louis, 63119. Tel: 314-792-7655; Fax: 314-792-7669. Rev. TIMOTHY J. NOELKER, Dir.

Pan y Amor—20 Archbishop May Dr., St. Louis, 63119. Tel: 314-792-7655; Fax: 314-792-7669. Rev. TIMOTHY J. NOELKER, Dir.

Archdiocesan Newspaper "St. Louis Review"—MR. TEAK PHILLIPS, Editor, 20 Archbishop May Dr., St. Louis, 63119. Tel: 314-792-7500; Fax: 314-792-7534.

Pastoral Planning, Office of—MR. JOHN SCHWOB, Tel: 314-792-7237; Fax: 314-792-7312.

Archdiocesan Office of Stewardship & Development—MR. BRIAN NIEBRUGGE, Exec. Dir., 20 Archbishop May Dr., St. Louis, 63119-5004. Tel: 314-792-7680; Fax: 314-792-7229.

Archdiocesan Planned Giving and Endowment Council—See MISCELLANEOUS section for more information.

Risk Management—20 Archbishop May Dr., St. Louis, 63119. Tel: 314-792-7203; Fax: 314-792-7079. MR. BRANDON S. ROTHKOPF, Dir.

Priests' Mutual Benefit Society—MRS. KATHY EGGERING, Mgr., 20 Archbishop May Dr., St. Louis, 63119. Tel: 314-792-7034; Fax: 314-792-7548.

Priests' Purgatorial Society—20 Archbishop May Dr., St. Louis, 63119. Tel: 314-792-7408. Rev. Msgr. JEROME D. BILLING, S.T.L., J.C.L., Pres.

Respect Life Apostolate—MS. KAREN NOLKEMPER, Dir., 20 Archbishop May Dr., St. Louis, 63119. Tel: 314-792-7555; Fax: 314-792-7569.

Project Rachel—20 Archbishop May Dr., St. Louis, 63119. Tel: 314-792-7565; Email: projectrachel@archstl.org.

Regina Cleri—10 Archbishop May Dr., St. Louis, 63119. Tel: 314-968-2240; Fax: 314-968-1049. MR. MICHAEL MILLER, Admin.

The Society for the Propagation of the Faith, Archdiocese of St. Louis20 Archbishop May Dr., St. Louis, 63119. Tel: 314-792-7655; Fax: 314-792-7669. Rev. TIMOTHY J. NOELKER, Dir.

Building and Real Estate—MR. RANDY RATHERT, Dir., 20 Archbishop May Dr., Saint Louis, 63119. Tel: 314-792-7087; Fax: 314-961-6234.

Today and Tomorrow Educational Foundation—MS. SHARON GERKEN, Exec. Dir., 20 Archbishop May Dr., St. Louis, 63119. Tel: 314-792-7735; Fax: 314-792-7629.

Office of Communications and Planning—20 Archbishop May Dr., St. Louis, 63119. Tel: 314-792-7500; Fax: 314-792-7639. MR. TEAK PHILLIPS, Dir. Publications, Tel: 314-792-7504; MS. ELIZABETH WESTHOFF, Dir. Communications, Tel: 314-792-7635; MR. JOHN SCHWOB, Dir. Pastoral Planning, Tel: 314-792-7237.

Office of Catholic Education and Formation—20 Archbishop May Dr., St. Louis, 63119. Tel: 314-792-7300; Fax: 314-792-7399. Sr. NATHALIE MEYER, O.P., Interim Dir. See SCHOOLS section for more information.

St. Louis Roman Catholic Theological Seminary—20 Archbishop May Dr., St. Louis, 63119. Tel: 314-792-6100; Fax: 314-792-6500. Rev. JAMES MASON, Rector.

Kenrick School of Theology—(St. Louis Roman Catholic Theological Seminary-Kenrick School of Theology) *5200 Glennon Dr., St. Louis, 63119*. Tel: 314-792-6100; Fax: 314-792-6500. Rev. JAMES MASON, Pres. & Rector.

Cardinal Glennon College—Rev. JAMES MASON, Pres. & Rector, 5200 Glennon Dr., St. Louis, 63119. Tel: 314-792-6100; Fax: 314-792-6500. See SEMINARIES section for more information.

Office of Vocations—5200 Glennon Dr., St. Louis, 63119. Tel: 314-792-6460; Fax: 314-792-6502. Rev. BRIAN S. FALLON, Dir.

Continuing Education & Formation of Priests—20 Archbishop May Dr., St. Louis, 63119. Tel: 314-792-6100. Rev. LAWRENCE C. BRENNAN, S.T.D., Dir.

Priests' Wellness Program—MRS. SUSAN K. ROCKAMANN, Coord., 20 Archbishop May Dr., St. Louis, 63119. Tel: 314-792-7648.

Safe Environment Program Office—MRS. SANDRA PRICE, Dir., 20 Archbishop May Dr., St. Louis, 63119. Tel: 314-792-7271; Fax: 314-792-7279.

Archdiocesan Office of the Permanent Diaconate—Deacons CHRISTOPHER M. AST, Dir.; DALE J. FOLLEN, Assoc. Dir. Formation; MS. SUE CURRAN, Sec., 20 Archbishop May Dr., St. Louis, 63119. Tel: 314-792-7431; Fax: 314-792-7439.

Office of Laity and Family Life—MRS. JULIE BOSTICK, Dir., 20 Archbishop May Dr., St. Louis, 63119-5738. Tel: 314-792-7180; Fax: 314-792-7199.

Cardinal Rigali Center—MR. STEPHEN LUDWIG, Bldg. Admin., 20 Archbishop May Dr., St. Louis, 63119. Tel: 314-792-7000; Fax: 314-792-7710.

Office of Youth Ministry—MR. BRIAN MILLER, Exec. Dir.

Victim Assistance Coordinator—MRS. CAROL BRESCIA.

CLERGY, PARISHES, MISSIONS AND PAROCHIAL SCHOOLS

CITY OF ST. LOUIS

ST. LOUIS COUNTY

1—CATHEDRAL BASILICA OF SAINT LOUIS CATHOLIC CHURCH (1896)
4431 Lindell Blvd., 63108. Tel: 314-373-8202; Email: parish@cathedralstl.org; Email: laurav@cathedralstl.org; Web: www.cathedralstl.org. Rev. Msgr. Joseph M. Simon, Rector; Revs. Nicholas W. Smith; Joseph Xiu Hui Jiang; Deacons John A. Curtin; John J. Stoverink; H. Matthew Witte.
See St. Louis the King School at the Cathedral under Archdiocesan-Based Elementary Schools located in the Institution section (G).

2—ST. AGATHA CATHOLIC CHURCH (1871) (Polish)
Mailing Address: 3239 S. Ninth St., 63118.
Tel: 314-772-1603; Fax: 314-772-3979; Email: parishoffice@polishchurchstlouis.org; Web: www.polishchurchstlouis.org. Rev. Hubert Zasada, S.Ch.R., Admin.

3—ST. ALBAN ROE CATHOLIC CHURCH (1980)
2001 Shepard Rd., Wildwood, 63038.
Tel: 636-458-2977; Email: rstoltz@stalbanroe.org; Web: www.stalbanroe.org. Revs. Richard L. Stoltz; Fredrick Devaraj, C.Ss.R.; Richard Wosman, S.M.; Deacons Keith G. Mallon; Timothy G. Michaelree.
School—St. Alban Roe Catholic Church School, 2005 Shepard Rd., Wildwood, 63038. Tel: 636-458-6084. Tara Smith, Prin. Lay Teachers 27; Religious 3; Students 305.
Catechesis Religious Program—Email: emccormack@stalbanroe.org. Dr. Ellen McCormack, C.R.E. Students 468.

4—ALL SAINTS CATHOLIC CHURCH, UNIVERSITY CITY (1901) Rev. Michael J. Witt; Deacon Stephen L. Murray.
Res.: 6403 Clemens Ave., University City, 63130.
Tel: 314-721-6403; Fax: 314-659-9799; Email: all_saintschurch@sbcglobal.net.
Catechesis Religious Program—Students 11.

5—ALL SOULS CATHOLIC CHURCH (1906)
9550 Tennyson Ave., Overland, 63114.
Tel: 314-427-0442; Fax: 314-427-3872; Email: secretaryallsouls@charter.net; Email: allsouls@charter.net; Web: allsoulsparish.com. Rev. James C. Gray; Deacon Samuel Lee.
Catechesis Religious Program—Students 32.
Convent—9600 Tennyson Ave., Overland, 63114. Tel: 314-427-3413.

6—ST. ALOYSIUS (SPANISH LAKE) (1871) Closed. For inquiries regarding sacramental records, contact the Archdiocesan Archives, 20 Archbishop May Dr., Saint Louis, MO 63119.

7—ST. ALOYSIUS GONZAGA (1892) Closed. For inquiries regarding sacramental records, contact the Archdiocesan Archives, 20 Archbishop May Dr., Saint Louis, MO 63119.

8—ST. ALPHONSUS LIGUORI CATHOLIC CHURCH (1867) Very Rev. Richard M. Potts, C.Ss.R., V.F.; Rev. Stephen Joseph Benden, C.Ss.R. In Res., Rev. David Polek, C.Ss.R.; Deacon Richard W. Fischer, C.Ss.R.
Res.: 1118 N. Grand Blvd., 63106. Tel: 314-533-0304; Email: parish130@archstl.org.
Catechesis Religious Program—Ms. Donna Lane, D.R.E.

9—ST. AMBROSE CATHOLIC CHURCH (1903)
5130 Wilson Ave., 63110. Tel: 314-771-1228; Email: secretary@stambroseonthehill.com; Web: stambroseonthehill.com. Rev. Msgr. Vincent R. Bommarito; Deacon Joseph A. Fragale.
School—St. Ambrose Catholic Church School, (Grades K-8), 5110 Wilson Ave., 63110.
Tel: 314-772-1437. Ms. Barbara Zipoli. Lay Teachers 22; Students 265; Sisters (Apostles of the Sacred Heart of Jesus) 1.
Catechesis Religious Program—Students 332.

10—ST. ANDREW CATHOLIC CHURCH (1905) Very Rev. Charles W. Barthel, V.F.; Deacon C. Allen Boedeker, Pastoral Admin.
Res.: 309 Hoffmeister Ave., 63125-1609.
Tel: 314-631-0691; Email: saintandrew@sbcglobal.net.
Catechesis Religious Program—Tel: 314-631-5135; Fax: 314-631-5633. Mrs. Mary Boedeker, D.R.E. Students 50.

11—ST. ANDREW KIM CATHOLIC CHURCH (2001) (Korean) Rev. Sanghyun Kim, Admin.
Church: 8665 Olive Blvd., University City, 63132.
Tel: 314-993-1277; Fax: 314-993-2031.

12—ST. ANGELA MERICI CATHOLIC CHURCH (1962)
3860 N. Hwy. 67, Florissant, 63034.
Tel: 314-838-6565; Fax: 314-838-6566; Email: brindley@stangelam.org; Web: www.saintangelamerici.org. Rev. Msgr. Matthew M. Mitas; Deacon Joseph C. Kroutil.
School—St. Angela Merici Catholic Church School, (Grades K-8), 3860 N. Hwy. 67, Florissant, 63034.
Tel: 314-831-8012. Lay Teachers 13; Students 188.

13—ST. ANN CATHOLIC CHURCH, NORMANDY (1856) [CEM]
7530 Natural Bridge Rd., Normandy, 63121.
Tel: 314-385-5090; Fax: 314-385-6527; Email: secretary@sacs-stl.org; Email: pastor@sacs-stl.org; Web: stannchurch-stl.org. Rev. Nicklaus E. Winker.
School—St. Ann Catholic Church, Normandy School, (Grades K-8), 7532 Natural Bridge, Normandy, 63121. Tel: 314-381-0113; Fax: 314-381-1367; Email: principal@sacs-stl.org. Jacob Reft, Prin. Religious Teachers 1; Lay Teachers 13; Students 143.
Catechesis Religious Program—

14—ST. ANN, MOTHER B.V.M., Closed. For inquiries regarding sacramental records, contact the Archdiocesan Archives, 20 Archbishop May Dr., Saint Louis, MO 63119.

15—ANNUNCIATION CATHOLIC CHURCH (1950)
12 W. Glendale Rd., Webster Groves, 63119. Tel: ; Email: parishsecretary@goannunciation.com; Web: www.goannunciation.com. Very Rev. Michael J. Esswein, V.F. In Res., Most Rev. Mark S. Rivituso, J.C.L., M.C.L., M.A., M.Div., V.G.
See Holy Cross Academy, St. Louis under Inter-Parochial, Consolidated Elementary Schools in the Institution section (H).
Catechesis Religious Program—Email: psr@goannunciation.com. Students 78.

16—ST. ANSELM CATHOLIC CHURCH (1966)
530 S. Mason Rd., 63141-8522. Tel: 314-878-2120; Email: parishoffice299@att.net; Web: www.stanselmstl.org. Revs. Aidan McDermott, O.S.B.; R. Benedict Allin, O.S.B.; Finbarr Dowling, O.S.B., In Res.; Very Rev. Gerard Garrigan, O.S.B., Pastor Emeritus; Deacons Charles Durban, Pastoral Assoc.; James Sigillito, Pastoral Assoc. & Liturgy Dir.
Catechesis Religious Program—Email: mmeiners@stanselmstl.org. Marge Meiners, D.R.E. Students 155.

17—ST. ANTHONY OF PADUA CATHOLIC CHURCH (1863)
3140 Meramec St., 63118. Tel: 314-353-7470; Email: mjfofm@aol.com; Web: www.stanthonyofpaduastl.com. Revs. Michael Fowler, O.F.M.; Andrew Lewandowski, O.F.M.; Sr. Dolores Sanchez, O.F.M., Pastoral Assoc.
Catechesis Religious Program—Tel: 314-655-0550. Students 41.

18—ASCENSION CATHOLIC CHURCH, CHESTERFIELD (1923)
230 Santa Maria Dr., Chesterfield, 63005.
Tel: 636-532-3304; Email: parishoffice@ascensionchesterfield.org; Web: asc.church. Very Rev. Thomas M. Molini, M.A., V.F.; Revs. Michael Lampe; Richard J. Bockskopf; Deacons C. Frank Chauvin; Robert Keeney; John Marino.
Child Care—Preschool, Ascension Early Childhood Center, 238 Santa Maria Dr., Chesterfield, 63005.
Tel: 636-532-3375; Email: littleschool@acsls.org; Web: ascensionchesterfield.org/LS-home. Erica Argue, Dir. Students 97.
School—Ascension Catholic Church, Chesterfield School, (Grades K-8), 238 Santa Maria Dr., Chesterfield, 63005. Tel: 636-532-1151;
Fax: 636-532-6502; Email: principal207@archstl.org; Web: www.ascensioncatholicschool.org. Joseph Kilmade, Prin. Lay Teachers 26; Students 284.
Catechesis Religious Program—Tel: 636-532-1136; Email: rseiler@ascensionchesterfield.org. Robin Seller, D.R.E. Students 486.

19—ASCENSION-ST. PAUL (1995) Closed. For inquiries for sacramental records contact the Archdiocesan Archives, 20 Archbishop May Dr., St. Louis, MO 63119.

20—ASSUMPTION CATHOLIC CHURCH, MATTESE (1839) [CEM]
4725 Mattis Rd., 63128. Tel: 314-487-7970; Email: riekd@assumptionstl.org; Web: www.assumptionstl.org. Revs. Thomas G. Keller; Ryan M. Weber; Deacons Charles T. Ryder; William G. Meister; David M. Schaefer.
School—Assumption Catholic Church, Mattese School, (Grades PreK-8), 4709 Mattis Rd., 63128.
Tel: 314-487-6520; Fax: 314-487-3598; Email: sykorai@assumptionstl.org. Ms. Maria Billhartz, Librarian. Lay Teachers 20; Students 207.
Catechesis Religious Program—
Tel: 314-487-6520, Ext. 2219. Laura Benson, Dir. Faith Formation (Adult); Donna Koppy, Dir. Faith Formation (Children). Students 160.

21—ST. AUGUSTINE CATHOLIC CHURCH (1992) [JC]
1371 Hamilton Ave., 63112. Tel: 314-385-1934;
Fax: 314-385-2949; Email: st.augustine.cc@sbcglobal.net; Web: st-augustine-stl.org. Rev. Msgr. Robert J. Gettinger; Deacon Edward R. Grotpeter. In Res., Rev. Christopher Adinuba.
Catechesis Religious Program—Students 214.

22—ST. BARBARA, Closed. For inquiries regarding sacramental records, contact the Archdiocesan Archives, 20 Archbishop May Dr., Saint Louis, MO 63119.

23—ST. BARTHOLOMEW (HAZELWOOD) (1959) Closed. For inquiries regarding sacramental records, contact the Archdiocesan Archives, 20 Archbishop May Dr., Saint Louis, MO 63119.

24—BASILICA OF ST. LOUIS, KING OF FRANCE CATHOLIC CHURCH (1770)
209 Walnut St., 63102. Tel: 314-231-3250; Email: oldcathedral@att.net. Rev. Msgr. Jerome D. Billing, S.T.L., J.C.L.; Rev. Richard J. Quirk, Ph.D.

25—ST. BERNADETTE CATHOLIC CHURCH (1947)
68 Sherman Rd., Lemay, 63125. Rev. Robert J. Reiker; Deacons Michael Buckley; Phillip Warren.

26—ST. BLAISE (MARYLAND HEIGHTS) (1961) Closed. For inquiries regarding sacramental records, contact the Archdiocesan Archives, 20 Archbishop May Dr., Saint Louis, MO 63119.

27—BLESSED TERESA OF CALCUTTA CATHOLIC CHURCH (2005)
Mailing Address: 120 N. Elizabeth, Ferguson, 63135.
Tel: 314-524-0500; Fax: 314-524-0744; Email: parishoffice@btcparish.org; Web: btcparish.org. Rev. Thomas J. Haley; Deacon Allen F. Love. In Res.
School—Blessed Teresa of Calcutta Catholic Church School, 150 N. Elizabeth, Ferguson, 63135.
Tel: 314-522-3888; Fax: 314-521-3173. Addie Govero, Prin.
Catechesis Religious Program—Debbie Davisson, P.S.R. Dir. Students 35.

28—ST. BONIFACE (1859) Closed. For inquiries regarding sacramental records, contact the Archdiocesan Archives, 20 Archbishop May Dr., Saint Louis, MO 63119.

29—ST. BRIDGET OF ERIN (1853) Closed. For inquiries regarding sacramental records, contact the Archdiocesan Archives, 20 Archbishop May Dr., Saint Louis, MO 63119.

30—ST. CASIMIR (HATHAWAY MANOR), Closed. For inquiries regarding sacramental records, contact the Archdiocesan Archives, 20 Archbishop May Dr., Saint Louis, MO 63119.

31—ST. CATHERINE LABOURE CATHOLIC CHURCH (1953) Rev. Charles E. Prost, C.M.; Deacon Timothy J. Woods.
Res.: 9740 Sappington Rd., 63128. Tel: 314-843-3245; Fax: 314-843-3196; Web: www.sclparish.org.
School—St. Catherine Laboure Catholic Church School, (Grades K-8), 9750 Sappington Rd., 63128.
Tel: 314-843-2819; Fax: 314-843-7687. Mrs. Laurie Jost, Prin. Lay Teachers 36; Students 445.
Catechesis Religious Program—
Tel: 314-843-3245, Ext. 223. Peggy Brinkmann, D.R.E. Students 218.

32—ST. CATHERINE OF ALEXANDRIA CATHOLIC CHURCH, COFFMAN (1921) Closed. For inquiries regarding sacramental records, contact the Archdiocesan Archives, 20 Archbishop May Dr., Saint Louis, MO 63119.

33—ST. CATHERINE OF SIENA (PAGEDALE) (1909) Closed. For inquiries regarding sacramental records, contact the Archdiocesan Archives, 20 Archbishop May Dr., Saint Louis, MO 63119.

34—ST. CECILIA CATHOLIC CHURCH (1906) (Hispanic)
5418 Louisiana Ave., 63111. Tel: 314-351-1318; Email: parish140@archstl.org; Web: www.stceciliaparishstl.org. Rev. Anthony B. Ochoa.
Church: Eiler & Alaska Ave., 63111.
See St. Cecilia School and Academy under Archdiocesan-Based Elementary Schools located in the Institution section (G).
Catechesis Religious Program—Students 83.

35—CHRIST, PRINCE OF PEACE CATHOLIC CHURCH (1971)
415 Weidman Rd., Manchester, 63011.
Tel: 636-391-1307; Email: cdunlap@cpopschool.com; Web: www.christprinceofpeace.com. Rev. Christopher J. Dunlap; Deacon Patrick J. Belding. In Res., Rev. Dennis J. Doyle, (Retired).
School—Christ, Prince of Peace Catholic Church School, (Grades K-8), 417 Weidman Rd., Manchester, 63011. Tel: 636-394-6840; Fax: 636-394-3860; Web: www.cpopschool.com. Dr. Marlise Albert, Prin.; Joan Bowe, Librarian; Karen Costa, Librarian. Lay Teachers 20; Students 220.
Catechesis Religious Program—Tel: 636-391-1560; Email: lthornbrugh@christprinceofpeace.com. Students 124.

36—CHRIST THE KING CATHOLIC CHURCH (1927) Rev. Msgr. Michael E. Turek, V.F.; Deacons E. Ray Kiely; David P. Dille.
Res.: 7316 Balson Ave., University City, 63130.
Tel: 314-721-8737; Fax: rectory@ctkstl.com.
School—(Grades PreK-8), 7324 Balson Ave., University City, 63130. Tel: 314-725-5855;
Fax: 314-725-5981. Mrs. Susan E. Hooker, Prin. Lay Teachers 22; Students 230.

37—ST. CHRISTOPHER (FLORISSANT) (1967) Closed. For inquiries regarding sacramental records, contact the Archdiocesan Archives, 20 Archbishop May Dr., Saint Louis, MO 63119.

38—CHURCH OF THE ANNUNZIATA CATHOLIC CHURCH

(1929) Rev. Msgr. John J. Leykam; Deacon Thomas J. Gottlieb.
Res.: 9305 Clayton Rd., Ladue, 63124.
Tel: 314-993-4422; Fax: 314-994-7877.
Catechesis Religious Program—Students 176.

39—ST. CLARE OF ASSISI CATHOLIC CHURCH (1963)
15642 Clayton Rd., Ellisville, 63011.
Tel: 636-394-7307; Email: stclare@saintclareofassisi.org; Web: www.saintclareofassisi.org. Revs. Christopher M. Martin; Brian E. Hecktor.
School—St. Clare of Assisi Catholic Church School, (Grades PreK-8), 15668 Clayton Rd., Ellisville, 63011. Tel: 636-227-8654; Fax: 636-394-0359. Mrs. Marie Sinnett, Prin.; Susan Gier, Librarian. Lay Teachers 26; Students 328.
Catechesis Religious Program—Tel: 636-394-4368; Fax: 636-591-0024. Students 277.

40—ST. CLEMENT OF ROME CATHOLIC CHURCH (1952)
1510 Bopp Rd., 63131. Tel: 314-965-0709;
Fax: 314-965-1486; Email: saintclementoffice@yahoo.com; Web: www.stclementcatholicchurch.org. Rev. Msgrs. Michael T. Butler; Timothy P. Cronin; Deacon Richard Vehige.
School—St. Clement of Rome Catholic Church School, (Grades PreK-8), 1508 Bopp Rd., 63131.
Tel: 314-822-1903; Fax: 314-822-8371; Web: www.stclementschool.com. Susan Cunningham, Prin. Lay Teachers 34; Students 317.
Catechesis Religious Program—Jesse Egbert, D.R.E.; Barb Yoffie, C.R.E. Students 120.

41—CORPUS CHRISTI (JENNINGS) (1915) Closed. For inquiries regarding sacramental records, contact the Archdiocesan Archives, 20 Archbishop May Dr., Saint Louis, MO 63119.

42—ST. CRONAN CATHOLIC CHURCH (1878)
1202 S. Boyle Ave., 63110. Tel: 314-289-9384; Email: parish143@archstl.org; Web: www.stcronan.org. Rev. Msgr. A. John Schuler, V.F.; Sisters Chabanel Mathison, O.S.U., Admin.; Lynne Schmidt, S.S.N.D., Pastoral Assoc.; Samantha Chumley, Sec.
Catechesis Religious Program—Tel: 314-256-9350. Students 65.

43—CURE' OF ARS CATHOLIC CHURCH (1966)
670 S. Laclede Station Rd., 63119-4910.
Tel: 314-962-5883; Email: cureofarsparishoffice@gmail.com; Web: cureofarsparish.org. Rev. James J. Byrnes; Deacon Patrick G. Monahan.

44—ST. DISMAS (FLORISSANT) (1956) Closed. For inquiries regarding sacramental records, contact the Archdiocesan Archives, 20 Archbishop May Dr., Saint Louis, MO 63119.

45—ST. DOMINIC SAVIO CATHOLIC CHURCH (1956) Rev. Paul J. Rothschild; Deacon John W. Beckmann, Pastoral Assoc. In Res., Rev. Michael J. Lydon.
Res.: 6120 Pebble Hill Dr., Affton, 63123.
Tel: 314-353-7629; Email: frprothschild@stdominicsavio.org; Email: rlukasek@stdominicsavio.org; Web: www.stdominicsavio.org.
Church: 7748 MacKenzie Rd., Affton, 63123.
School—St. Dominic Savio Catholic Church School, (Grades PreK-8), Tel: 314-832-4161;
Fax: 314-352-6331. Chris Cheak, Prin. Lay Teachers 23; Students 290.
Catechesis Religious Program—Students 82.

46—ST. EDWARD (1893) Closed. For inquiries regarding sacramental records, contact the Archdiocesan Archives, 20 Archbishop May Dr., Saint Louis, MO 63119.

47—ST. ELIZABETH OF HUNGARY CATHOLIC CHURCH (1956) Deacon Robert Snyder.
Res.: 1420 S. Sappington Rd., Crestwood, 63126.
Tel: 314-968-0760; Email: steeliz@sbcglobal.net.
Catechesis Religious Program—Tel: 314-963-8868. Students 54.
Convent—1406 S. Sappington Rd., Crestwood, 63126. Tel: 314-961-2630.

48—ST. ELIZABETH, MOTHER OF JOHN THE BAPTIST CATHOLIC CHURCH (1891) (African American) Rev. Stephen P. Giljum. In Res., Rev. J. Edward Vogler, (Retired).
Res.: 4330 Shreve Ave., 63115. Tel: 314-381-4145;
Fax: 314-381-2212.
See St. Louis Catholic Academy under Inter-Parochial, Consolidated Elementary Schools located in the Institution section (H).

49—EPIPHANY OF OUR LORD CATHOLIC CHURCH (1911)
6596 Smiley Ave., 63139. Tel: 314-781-1199; Email: parish104@archstl.org; Web: www.epiphanystl.org. Rev. Michael Rennier.
Catechesis Religious Program—Students 60.

50—ST. FERDINAND CATHOLIC CHURCH (1788)
1765 Charbonier Rd., Florissant, 63031.
Tel: 314-837-3165; Fax: 314-837-5799; Email: stferdinandchurch@stferdinandstl.org; Web: www.stferdinandstl.org. Revs. Michael G. Murphy; David E. Rauch.
Catechesis Religious Program—Tel: 314-831-8988; Email: dharpring@stferdinandstl.org. Students 244.

51—ST. FRANCES XAVIER CABRINI (JENNINGS) (1965) Closed. For inquiries regarding sacramental records, contact the Archdiocesan Archives, 20 Archbishop May Dr., Saint Louis, MO 63119.

52—ST. FRANCIS OF ASSISI CATHOLIC CHURCH, OAKVILLE (1927)
4556 Telegraph Rd., 63129. Tel: 314-487-5736; Email: parishoffice@sfastl.org; Web: sfastl.org. Revs. Anthony R. Yates; Kent M. Pollman.
School—(Grades K-8), 4550 Telegraph Rd., 63129. Fax: 314-416-7118. Mr. D. Gregory Sturgill, Ph.D., Prin. Lay Teachers 19; Students 231.
Catechesis Religious Program—
Tel: 314-487-5736, Ext. 125. Students 157.

53—ST. FRANCIS XAVIER CATHOLIC CHURCH (1841) (College)
3628 Lindell Blvd., 63108. Tel: 314-977-7300;
Fax: 314-977-7315; Email: church@slu.edu; Web: sfxstl.org. Revs. Daniel P. White, S.J.; Thomas G. Cwik, S.J.
Catechesis Religious Program—Tel: 314-977-7302. Katie Jansen-Larson, Admin. Students 150.

54—ST. GABRIEL THE ARCHANGEL CATHOLIC CHURCH (1934)
6303 Nottingham Ave., 63109. Tel: 314-353-6303; Email: millerj@stgabrielstl.org. Rev. Msgr. John B. Shamleffer, J.C.L., M.C.L., M.A., M.Div.; Rev. Steve Kuhlmann, O.P., Parochial Vicar; Deacons James P. Hoefl; David J. Willis.
School—4711 Tamm Ave., 63109. Tel: 314-353-1229; Fax: 314-353-6737. Lay Teachers 39; Students 477.
Catechesis Religious Program—Students 490.

55—ST. GEORGE CATHOLIC CHURCH (1915) Rev. Paul J. Rothschild.
Res.: 4980 Heege Rd., 63123. Tel: 314-352-3544; Email: rlukasek@stdominicsavio.org; Email: frprothschild@stdominicsavio.org; Email: mrusch@stdominicsavio.org; Web: www.saintgeorgeaffton.com.

56—ST. GERARD MAJELLA CATHOLIC CHURCH (1955)
1969 Dougherty Ferry Rd., Kirkwood, 63122.
Tel: 314-965-3985; Fax: 314-965-7650; Email: office@sgmparish.org; Web: www.sgmparish.org. Revs. David P. Skillman; Larry T. Huber; Deacons Timothy Dolan; Donald Denham.
School—St. Gerard Majella School, (Grades K-8), 2005 Dougherty Ferry Rd., Kirkwood, 63122.
Tel: 314-822-8844; Fax: 314-822-8588; Email: principal@sgmschool.org. Ms. Chrisell Guthrie, Prin. Lay Teachers 32; Students 384.
Catechesis Religious Program—Students 225.

57—GOOD SHEPHERD (FERGUSON) (1958) Closed. For inquiries regarding sacramental records, contact the Archdiocesan Archives, 20 Archbishop May Dr., Saint Louis, MO 63119.

58—ST. GREGORY (ST. ANN) (1942) Closed. For inquiries regarding sacramental records, contact the Archdiocesan Archives, 20 Archbishop May Dr., Saint Louis, MO 63119.

59—ST. HEDWIG (1904) Closed. For inquiries regarding sacramental records, contact the Archdiocesan Archives, 20 Archbishop May Dr., Saint Louis, MO 63119.

60—HOLY ANGELS (KINLOCH) (1931) (African American), Closed. For inquiries regarding sacramental records, contact the Archdiocesan Archives, 20 Archbishop May Dr., Saint Louis, MO 63119.

61—HOLY FAMILY (1898) Closed. For inquiries regarding sacramental records, contact the Archdiocesan Archives, 20 Archbishop May Dr., Saint Louis, MO 63119.

62—HOLY GHOST (BERKELEY) (1923) Closed. For inquiries regarding sacramental records, contact the Archdiocesan Archives, 20 Archbishop May Dr., Saint Louis, MO 63119.

63—HOLY GUARDIAN ANGELS (1866) Closed. For inquiries regarding sacramental records, contact the Archdiocesan Archives, 20 Archbishop May Dr., Saint Louis, MO 63119.

64—HOLY INFANT CATHOLIC CHURCH (1954)
627 Dennison Dr., Ballwin, 63021. Tel: 636-227-7440 ; Email: rectoryoffice@holyinfantballwin.org; Web: www.holyinfantballwin.org. Revs. Edward J. Stanger; Andrew V. Burkemper; Rev. Msgr. Michael E. Dieckmann.
School—Holy Infant Catholic Church School, (Grades PreK-8), 248 New Ballwin Rd., Ballwin, 63021. Tel: 636-227-0802; Fax: 636-227-9184; Email: schooloffice@holyinfantballwin.org; Web: www.holyinfantschool.org. Rebecca R. McQuaide, Prin.; Carolanne Ryle, Librarian. Lay Teachers 37; Students 460.
Catechesis Religious Program—
Tel: 636-227-0802, Ext. 3; Email: psroffice@holyinfantballwin.org. Patricia Foley, D.R.E. Students 450.

65—HOLY INNOCENTS (1893) Closed. For inquiries regarding sacramental records, contact the Archdiocesan Archives, 20 Archbishop May Dr., Saint Louis, MO 63119.

66—HOLY NAME OF JESUS CATHOLIC CHURCH (2005)
Mailing Address: 10235 Ashbrook Dr., 63137.
Tel: 314-868-2310; Fax: 314-868-3919; Email: parishoffice10235@sbcglobal.net; Web: www.holynamestlouis.org. Rev. Michael L. Henning; Deacons George Watson; Matthew E. Duban. In Res., Rev. Raymond Iwuji.
School—Christ Light of the Nations, 1650 Redman Rd., 63138. Tel: 314-741-0400; Fax: 314-653-2531; Email: st_mary@christlightofthenations.com; Web: www.christlightofthenations.com. Sr. Mary Lawrence, S.S.N.D., Prin. Lay Teachers 15; Students 157.
Catechesis Religious Program—1650 Redman Rd., 63138. Students 175.

67—HOLY REDEEMER CATHOLIC CHURCH (1886) Rev. Kenneth A. Brown, V.F.; Deacon Stephen L. Murray.
Res.: 17 Joy Ave., Webster Groves, 63119.
Tel: 314-962-0038; Fax: 314-962-2084; Web: www.holyr.org.
School—Holy Redeemer Catholic School, (Grades PreK-8), Tel: 314-962-0038; Tel: 314-962-8989; Email: principal@holyr.org; Web: www.holyr.org. Wayne Schiefelbein, Prin. Lay Teachers 21; Students 234.
Catechesis Religious Program—Tel: 314-962-2043; Email: cre@holyr.org. Patricia Maloney, C.R.E. Students 170.

68—HOLY SPIRIT CATHOLIC CHURCH (2004) Formerly St. Blaise and St. Lawrence.
3130 Parkwood Ln., Maryland Heights, 63043.
Tel: 314-739-0230; Email: parish@holyspiritstl.org; Web: www.holyspiritstl.org. Revs. Robert T. Evans; Gerald A. Meier, V.F., (Retired); Deacons James T. DeNatale; Scott C. Kaufman.
School—Holy Spirit Catholic Church School, (Grades K-8), Tel: 314-739-1934; Fax: 314-739-7703. Lay Teachers 12; Students 127.
Catechesis Religious Program—Sharon Kaufman, C.R.E. Students 134.

69—HOLY TRINITY CATHOLIC CHURCH (2002)
3500 St. Luke Ln., St. Ann, 63074. Tel: 314-733-1463 ; Email: jlivengood720@gmail.com. 3400 St. Gregory Ln., St. Ann, 63074. Revs. Eric F. Olsen, Parochial Admin.; Gerson Parra-Meza; Deacon William F. Priesmeyer.
School—Holy Trinity Catholic Church School, (Grades K-8), 10901 St. Henry Ln., St. Ann, 63074.
Tel: 314-426-8966; Fax: 314-428-7084. Margaret Ahle, Prin. Students 150.
Catechesis Religious Program—Students 200.

70—IMMACOLATA CATHOLIC CHURCH (1945)
8900 Clayton Rd., Richmond Heights, 63117.
Tel: 314-991-5700; Email: choffmeyer@immacolata.org. Rev. Denny M. Schaab; Rev. Msgr. Vernon E. Gardin, Ph.D.; Deacon Joseph LaMartina, (Retired).
School—Immacolata Catholic Church School, (Grades K-8), 8910 Clayton Rd., Richmond Heights, 63117. Tel: 314-991-5700, Ext. 302;
Fax: 314-991-9354; Web: www.immacolata.org. Dr. Jennifer Stutsman, Prin. Lay Teachers 22; Students 271.
Catechesis Religious Program—
Tel: 314-991-5700, Ext. 303. Students 96.

71—IMMACULATE CONCEPTION CATHOLIC CHURCH, MAPLEWOOD (1904) [JC] Rev. Peter M. Blake, Sacramental Min.; Deacon John P. Flanigan Jr., Parish Life Coord.
Res.: 2934 Marshall Ave., Maplewood, 63143.
Tel: 314-645-3307; Email: icmaplewood@gmail.com; Web: icmaplewood.com.
Catechesis Religious Program—7240 Anna Ave., Maplewood, 63143. Tel: 314-644-6787. Students 62.

72—IMMACULATE CONCEPTION-ST. HENRY (1865) Closed. For inquiries regarding sacramental records, contact the Archdiocesan Archives, 20 Archbishop May Dr., Saint Louis, MO 63119.

73—IMMACULATE HEART OF MARY CATHOLIC CHURCH, ST. LOUIS (1951) Rev. Kristian C. Teater; Deacon James W. Murphey Jr.
Res.: 4092 Blow St., 63116. Tel: 314-481-7543; Email: adonohue@ihm-stl.org; Web: www.ihm-stl.org.

74—INCARNATE WORD CATHOLIC CHURCH (1965)
13416 Olive Blvd., Chesterfield, 63017.
Tel: 314-576-5366; Email: generalmailbox@incarnate-word.org; Web: www.incarnate-word.org. Revs. Kevin M. Schroeder; James M. Sullivan, Senior Assoc., (Retired); David J. Hogan; Deacons Ronald Lee Reuther; Donald J. Funke Jr.
School—Incarnate Word Catholic Church School, (Grades K-8), Tel: 314-576-5366, Ext. 11. C. Michael Welling, Prin. Lay Teachers 23; Students 356.
Catechesis Religious Program—
Tel: 314-576-5366, Ext. 26; Email: lflanagan@incarnate-word.org; Email: abrockmann@incarnate-word.org. Laura Flanagan, D.R.E. Students 175.

75—ST. JAMES THE GREATER CATHOLIC CHURCH (1860) (Irish)
6401 Wade Ave., 63139. Tel: 314-481-7543; Email:

adonohue@ihm-stl.org; Web: www.stjamesthegreater.org. Rev. Rajpaul Sundararaj, C.Ss.R., (India); Deacon Michael A. Nicolai. In Res., Rev. Augustine Kizhakkedam, O.C.D.

School—St. James the Greater Catholic Church School, (Grades K-8), 1360 Tamm Ave., 63139. Tel: 314-647-5244; Fax: 314-647-8237; Email: stjames152@yahoo.com. Lay Teachers 19; Students 168.

Catechesis Religious Program—Students 151.

76—ST. JEROME (BISSELL HILLS) (1952) Closed. For inquiries regarding sacramental records, contact the Archdiocesan Archives, 20 Archbishop May Dr., Saint Louis, MO 63119.

77—ST. JOAN OF ARC CATHOLIC CHURCH (1941) 5800 Oleatha St., 63139. Tel: 314-832-2838; Email: mcooper@stjoanofarcstl.com. Rev. Craig T. Holway; Rev. Msgr. Thomas J. Dempsey, (Retired); Deacon Daniel H. Henroid.

School—South City Catholic Academy, 5821 Pernod, Saint Louis, 63139.

78—STS. JOHN AND JAMES (FERGUSON) (1882) Closed. For inquiries regarding sacramental records, contact the Archdiocesan Archives, 20 Archbishop May Dr., Saint Louis, MO 63119.

79—ST. JOHN BOSCO CATHOLIC CHURCH (1972) 12934 Marine Ave., Maryland Heights, 63146. Tel: 314-434-1312; Fax: 314-514-0478; Email: sjb@stjohnboscostl.com; Web: sjjohnboscostl.com. Rev. Gerard R. Welsch; Deacons Paul D. Craska; John J. O'Hara.

Catechesis Religious Program—Tel: 314-878-6492; Email: cindy.meirink@stjohnboscostl.com. Cindy Meirink. Students 106.

80—ST. JOHN NEPOMUK CATHOLIC CHURCH (1854) Deacon Joseph Iovanna, Dir.

Res.: 1625 S. 11th St., 63104. Tel: 314-231-0141; Email: smredfearn@swbell.net.

81—ST. JOHN THE APOSTLE AND EVANGELIST CATHOLIC CHURCH (1847) 15 Plaza Sq., 63103. Tel: 314-421-3467; Email: stjohnsae@netzero.net. Rev. Msgr. Dennis M. Delaney.

Catechesis Religious Program—

82—ST. JOHN THE BAPTIST CATHOLIC CHURCH, ST. LOUIS (1914) 4200 Delor St., 63116. Tel: 314-353-1255; Fax: 314-752-3154; Email: sjb4200@sjbstl.org; Email: rectory@sjbstl.org. Very Rev. Carl J. Scheble, V.F.; Deacon John Robert Wolffer. In Res., Rev. John L. Mayer, (Retired).

Catechesis Religious Program—South City Deanery at St. John the Baptist Parish, 4170 Delor St., 63116. Tel: 314-773-3070; Fax: 314-773-3070. Nancy Haselhorst, C.R.E. Students 120.

83—ST. JOSEPH CATHOLIC CHURCH, CLAYTON (1842) 106 N. Meramec Ave., Clayton, 63105. Tel: 314-726-1221; Email: pat_stj@hotmail.com; Web: www.stjosephclayton.org. Revs. Nicholas E. Kastenholz, J.C.L.; Philip J. Bene, J.C.D.; Deacon Delfin S. Leonardo.

Catechesis Religious Program—Tel: 314-727-9059; Fax: 314-727-2271. Mrs. Terri Venneman, C.R.E. Students 206.

84—ST. JOSEPH CATHOLIC CHURCH, MANCHESTER (1865) [CEM] 567 St. Joseph Ln., Manchester, 63021. Tel: 636-227-5247; Email: info@stjoemanchester.org; Web: www.stjoemanchester.org. Revs. Thomas M. Pastorius; Ricardo Escobar; Timothy J. Noelker; Deacons George Miller; Daniel R. Donnelly; Jimmy D. Broyles.

School—St. Joseph Catholic School, (Grades PreK-8), 555 St. Joseph Ln., Manchester, 63021. Tel: 636-391-1253; Fax: 636-391-1462. Mr. D. Gregory Sturgill, Ph.D., Prin. Lay Teachers 19; Students 185.

Catechesis Religious Program—Tel: 636-391-1404; Email: mfoster@stjoemanchester.org. Michelle Foster, D.R.E. Students 372.

85—ST. JOSEPH CROATIAN CATHOLIC CHURCH (1904) (Croatian) Rev. Stjepan Pandzic, O.F.M.

Res.: 2112 S. 12th St., 63104. Tel: 314-771-0958; Fax: 314-772-2675.

Catechesis Religious Program—Students 39.

86—ST. JUDE CATHOLIC CHURCH (1953) Rev. James C. Gray.

Res.: 2218 N. Warson Rd., Overland, 63114. Tel: 314-428-2262.

87—ST. JUSTIN MARTYR CATHOLIC CHURCH (1964) 11910 Eddie & Park Rd., Sunset Hills, 63126. Rev. William Kempf; Deacon Mark J. Jaeger. In Res., Rev. John J. Johnson, (Retired).

School—St. Justin Martyr Catholic Church School, (Grades PreK-8), 11914 Eddie and Park Rd., 63126. Tel: 314-843-6447; Fax: 314-843-9257. Amy Schroff, Prin. Lay Teachers 24; Students 288.

Catechesis Religious Program—Tel: 314-635-2499; Email: maurer@stjustinmartyr.org. Donna Maurer, C.R.E. Students 109.

88—ST. KEVIN (ST. ANN) (1953) (Irish), Closed. For inquiries regarding sacramental records, contact the Archdiocesan Archives, 20 Archbishop May Dr., Saint Louis, MO 63119.

89—ST. LAWRENCE THE MARTYR (BRIDGETON) (1960) Closed. For inquiries regarding sacramental records, contact the Archdiocesan Archives, 20 Archbishop May Dr., Saint Louis, MO 63119.

90—ST. LIBORIUS (1856) Closed. For inquiries regarding sacramental records, contact the Archdiocesan Archives, 20 Archbishop May Dr., Saint Louis, MO 63119.

91—LITTLE FLOWER CATHOLIC CHURCH (1925) 1264 Arch Ter., Richmond Heights, 63117. Email: littleflower@little-flower-parish.org; Web: www.little-flower-parish.org. Rev. Lawrence A. Herzog.

School—Little Flower Catholic Church School, (Grades PreK-8), 1275 Boland Pl., Richmond Heights, 63117. Tel: 314-781-4995; Fax: 314-781-9177. Robert Baird, Prin. Lay Teachers 15; Students 176.

92—ST. LOUISE DE MARILLAC (JENNINGS) (1935) Closed. For inquiries regarding sacramental records, contact the Archdiocesan Archives, 20 Archbishop May Dr., Saint Louis, MO 63119.

93—ST. LUCY (JENNINGS) (1957) Closed. For inquiries regarding sacramental records, contact the Archdiocesan Archives, 20 Archbishop May Dr., Saint Louis, MO. 63119.

94—ST. LUKE THE EVANGELIST CATHOLIC CHURCH (1914) Rev. Peter M. Blake; Deacon David Osmack.

Res.: 7230 Dale Ave., 63117. Tel: 314-644-2144; Fax: 314-644-4624; Email: office@stukestl.org; Web: www.stlukestl.org.

95—ST. MARGARET MARY ALACOQUE CATHOLIC CHURCH (1962) 4900 Ringer Rd., 63129. Tel: 314-487-2522, Ext. 201; Fax: 314-487-4475; Email: sbrandt@smmaparish.org; Web: www.smmaparish.org. Rev. Msgr. Norbert A. Ernst; Rev. Scott L. Scheiderer; Rev. Msgr. William J. Leach, (Retired); Deacons Andrew Daus; Robert Orr.

Res.: 5056 Faust Ct., 63129. Tel: 314-487-2522.

School—St. Margaret Mary Alacoque Catholic Church School, (Grades K-8), Tel: 314-487-1666. Lay Teachers 40; Students 491.

Catechesis Religious Program—Students 235.

96—ST. MARGARET OF SCOTLAND CATHOLIC CHURCH (1899) 3854 Flad Ave., 63110. Tel: 314-776-0363; Email: parishoffice@stmargaretstl.org. Rev. Matthew L. O'Toole.

School—St. Margaret of Scotland Catholic Church School, (Grades PreK-8), 3964 Castleman, 63110. Tel: 314-776-7837; Fax: 314-776-7955; Web: smos-school.org. Lay Teachers 27; Students 384.

97—ST. MARK CATHOLIC CHURCH, AFFTON (2003) 4200 Ripa Ave., 63125. Tel: 314-743-8600; Fax: 314-743-8618; Web: www.stmarkstl.com. Rev. Msgr. Patrick K. Hambrough.

Rectory—4230 Ripa Ave., 63125. Tel: 314-743-8620.

School—St. Mark Catholic School, 4220 Ripa Ave., 63125. Tel: 314-743-8640; Fax: 314-743-8690; Email: malthage@stmarkstl.com; Email: dianelittle@archstl.org; Web: www.stmarkstl.com. Lay Teachers 10; Religious 1; Students 220.

Catechesis Religious Program—Students 76.

98—ST. MARK, EVANGELIST (PAGE & ACADEMY) (1893) Closed. For inquiries regarding sacramental records, contact the Archdiocesan Archives, 20 Archbishop May Dr., Saint Louis, MO 63119.

99—ST. MARTIN DE PORRES CATHOLIC CHURCH (1962) 615 Dunn Rd., Hazelwood, 63042-1799. Tel: 314-895-1100; Email: mdpparishmo@gmail.com. Rev. Lijo Stephen Kallarackal, O.S.B.Silv., Admin.; Deacons David Pacino; Edward Bierne.

Child Care—Knobbe House, 627 Undercliff, Hazelwood, 63042.

Catechesis Religious Program—Marilyn Saunders, Sacramental Coord. C.R.E. Students 71.

100—ST. MARTIN OF TOURS CATHOLIC CHURCH (1939) Rev. Noah A. Waldman; Deacons Edward Fronick; Phillip Warren.

Res.: 610 W. Ripa Ave., Lemay, 63125. Tel: 314-544-5664; Fax: 314-631-3118.

Catechesis Religious Program—Students 25.

101—ST. MARY (BRIDGETON) (1852) Closed. For inquiries regarding sacramental records, contact the Archdiocesan Archives, 20 Archbishop May Dr., Saint Louis, MO 63119.

102—STS. MARY AND JOSEPH CATHOLIC CHURCH (1821) Rev. Ronald J. Hopmeir, Chap.

Res.: 6304 Minnesota Ave., 63111. Tel: 314-481-6304 ; Fax: 314-481-6337.

Catechesis Religious Program—Students 2.

103—ST. MARY MAGDALEN CATHOLIC CHURCH, BRENTWOOD (1912) Rev. John S. Siefert; Deacon William A. Preiss. In Res., Rev. Msgr. James J. Ramacciotti, J.C.L.

Res.: 2618 Brentwood Blvd., Brentwood, 63144. Tel: 314-961-8400; Fax: 314-961-7019; Email: info@stmmchurch.com.

School—St. Mary Magdalen Catholic School, 8750 Magdalen Ave., Brentwood, 63144. Tel: 314-961-0149; Fax: 314-961-7208; Email: office@stmmschool.com; Web: stmmlab.com. Mrs. Kathy Wiseman, Prin. Lay Teachers 16; Students 157.

Catechesis Religious Program—Students 100.

104—ST. MARY MAGDALEN CATHOLIC CHURCH, ST. LOUIS (1919) Rev. Msgr. John J. Borcic; Deacon William G. Weiss. In Res.

Res.: 4924 Bancroft Ave., 63109. Tel: 314-352-2111; Fax: smmadmin@sbcglobal.net.

Catechesis Religious Program—Southside Regional Parish School of Religion, 4170 Delor, 63116. Tel: 314-773-3070. Students 70.

105—ST. MARY OF VICTORIES CATHOLIC CHURCH (1843) St. Stephen of Hungary Chapel

744 S. 3rd St., 63102. Tel: 314-231-8101; Email: materdei82@hotmail.com; Web: www.smov.info. Rev. Brian W. Harrison, O.S., Chap. In Res., Rev. Msgr. John F. McCarthy, P.A., Chap. & D.R.E., (Retired).

106—MARY, MOTHER OF THE CHURCH CATHOLIC CHURCH (1971) 5901 Kerth Rd., 63128. Tel: 314-894-1373; Fax: 314-894-3801; Email: parish228@archstl.org; Email: agaravaglia@marymother.org; Web: www.marymother.org. Very Rev. Charles W. Barthel, V.F.; Deacons Richard Coffman; Robert S. Smerek; Randy C. Howe.

Catechesis Religious Program—Email: edlew@marymother.org. Ed Lewandowski, D.R.E. Students 288.

107—MARY, QUEEN OF PEACE CATHOLIC CHURCH (1922) 676 W. Lockwood Ave., Webster Groves, 63119. Tel: 314-962-2311; Email: afiordelisi@mqpwg.org; Email: mqpparishoffice@mqpwg.org. Revs. John Rogers Vien; Aaron P. Nord, J.C.D., Part-time Assoc. Pastor; Deacons Thomas O. Mulvihill; Joseph M. Wientge. In Res., Rev. Msgr. Robert P. Jovanovic, M.Ed.

School—Mary, Queen of Peace Catholic School, (Grades PreSchool-8), 680 W. Lockwood Ave., Webster Groves, 63119. Tel: 314-961-2891; Fax: 314-961-7469; Email: afinke@mqpwg.org; Web: www.mqpwg.org/school. Mr. Michael Nieman, Prin. Lay Teachers 35; Students 395.

Catechesis Religious Program—Leslie Walrath, D.R.E. Students 166.

108—MARY, QUEEN OF THE UNIVERSE (1955) Closed. For inquiries regarding sacramental records, contact the Archdiocesan Archives, 20 Archbishop May Dr., Saint Louis, MO 63119.

109—ST. MATTHEW, APOSTLE CATHOLIC CHURCH (1893) [CEM] (African American) Rev. Patrick T. Quinn, S.J. In Res., Rev. Kevin L. Cullen, S.J.

Res.: 2715 N. Sarah St., 63113. Tel: 314-531-6443; Fax: 314-533-7318; Email: stmatthews@sbcglobal.net; Web: stmatthewtheapostlecatholicchurch.org.

Catechesis Religious Program—Students 45.

110—ST. MATTHIAS CATHOLIC CHURCH (1959) Rev. Dennis R. Port; Deacon Charles R. Bacher.

Res.: 796 Buckley Rd., 63125. Tel: 314-892-5109; Fax: 314-892-0629; Email: st.matthiasoffice@sbcglobal.net.

Catechesis Religious Program—Students 84.

111—ST. MICHAEL CATHOLIC CHURCH (1895) Rev. Michael J. Grosch.

Res.: 7622 Sutherland Ave., Shrewsbury, 63119. Tel: 314-647-5611; Email: msteingruby@stmike.org; Email: rectory@stmike.org; Web: stmike.org.

See Holy Cross Academy, St. Louis under Inter-Parochial, Consolidated Elementary Schools in the Institution section (H).

Catechesis Religious Program—Students 60.

112—ST. MONICA CATHOLIC CHURCH (1872) [CEM] Revs. Joseph A. Weber; Michael L. Donald, Senior Assoc.; Deacons Carl J. Sommer; James P. Martin.

Res.: 12136 Olive Blvd., Creve Coeur, 63141-6629. Tel: 314-434-4211; Fax: 314-434-5978.

School—St. Monica Catholic School, (Grades PreK-8), 12132 Olive Blvd., Creve Coeur, 63141-6698. Tel: 314-434-2173; Fax: 314-434-7689. Genevieve Callier, Prin. Lay Teachers 13; Students 154.

Catechesis Religious Program—Tel: 314-205-9276; Email: jcombs@stmonicastl.org. James Combs, D.R.E. Students 78.

113—MOST BLESSED SACRAMENT (1907) Closed. For inquiries regarding sacramental records, contact the Archdiocesan Archives, 20 Archbishop May Dr., Saint Louis, MO 63119.

114—MOST HOLY NAME OF JESUS (EAST GRAND) (1875) Closed. For inquiries regarding sacramental records, contact the Archdiocesan Archives, 20 Archbishop May Dr., Saint Louis, MO 63119.

115—MOST HOLY ROSARY (1891) Closed. For inquiries regarding sacramental records, contact the Archdiocesan Archives, 20 Archbishop May Dr., Saint Louis, MO 63119.

116—MOST HOLY TRINITY CATHOLIC CHURCH (1848)

Rev. Aidan McDermott, O.S.B., Sacramental Min.; Sr. Janice Munier, S.S.N.D., Parish Life Coord.
Res.: 3519 N. Fourteenth St., 63107-3796.
Tel: 314-241-9165; Fax: 314-436-9291.
See Most Holy Trinity School, St. Louis under Archdiocesan-Based Elementary Schools located in the Institution section (G).
Catechesis Religious Program—Students 80.

117—MOST PRECIOUS BLOOD (LEMAY) (1961) Closed. For inquiries regarding sacramental records, contact the Archdiocesan Archives, 20 Archbishop May Dr., Saint Louis, MO 63119.

118—MOST SACRED HEART CATHOLIC CHURCH, EUREKA (1889)
350 E. Fourth St., Eureka, 63025. Tel: 636-938-5048; Email: parishsecretary@sacredhearteureka.org; Email: bizmgr@sacredhearteureka.org; Web: www.sacredhearteureka.org. Revs. Joseph G. Kempf; Leo J. Spezia; Deacons Thomas L. Eultgen; Leo S. Fehner; Alan W. Whitson.
School—Most Sacred Heart School, (Grades K-8), Tel: 636-938-4602; Fax: 636-938-5802. Monica Wilson, Prin.; Kelly Schumacher. Lay Teachers 13; Students 206.
Catechesis Religious Program—Tel: 636-938-9507. Students 235.

119—ST. NICHOLAS CATHOLIC CHURCH (1865) Rev. Arthur J. Cavitt. In Res., Rev. McDonald Nah.
Res.: 701 N. 18th St., 63103. Tel: 314-231-2860; Fax: 314-241-9823; Email: stnickscatholicchurch@gmail.com; Web: snrcc.org.
See St. Louis the King School at the Cathedral under Archdiocesan-Based Elementary Schools located in the Institution section (G).
Catechesis Religious Program—Students 10.

120—ST. NORBERT CATHOLIC CHURCH (1965) Very Rev. James M. Mitulski, V.F.; Deacons David A. Felber; William H. Twellman, Pastoral Assoc.; Donald J. Funke Jr.
Res.: 16455 New Halls Ferry Rd., Florissant, 63031.
Tel: 314-831-3874; Email: frjim@saintnorbert.com; Web: www.saintnorbert.com.
School—St. Norbert Catholic Church School, (Grades PreK-8), 16475 New Halls Ferry Rd., Florissant, 63031. Tel: 314-839-0948; Fax: 314-839-3053; Email: school@saintnorbert.com. Mr. David Watkins, Prin. Lay Teachers 24; Students 309.
Catechesis Religious Program—Email: deaconbill@saintnorbert.com. Students 200.

121—NORTH AMERICAN MARTYRS (FLORISSANT) (1955) Closed. For inquiries regarding sacramental records, contact the Archdiocesan Archives, 20 Archbishop May Dr., Saint Louis, MO 63119.

122—NOTRE DAME DE LOURDES (WELLSTON) (1902) Closed. For inquiries regarding sacramental records, contact the Archdiocesan Archives, 20 Archbishop May Dr., Saint Louis, MO 63119.

123—ORATORY OF SAINT GREGORY AND SAINT AUGUSTINE (2007)
6403 Clemens Ave., Saint Louis, 63130. Rev. Michael J. Witt.
Catechesis Religious Program—Marilyn Lonigro, D.R.E. Students 36.

124—ORATORY OF ST. FRANCIS DE SALES (2005)
2653 Ohio Ave., 63118. Tel: 314-771-3100; Email: sfds@institute-christ-king.org; Web: www.institute-christ-king.org. Rev. Canon Michael K. Wiener, Rector; Revs. Pierre Dumain, Vicar; Luke Zignego. Extraordinary Form of the Roman Rite Administered by the Institute of Christ the King Sovereign Priest.

125—OUR LADY OF FATIMA (FLORISSANT) (1950) Closed. For inquiries regarding sacramental records, contact the Archdiocesan Archives, 20 Archbishop May Dr., Saint Louis, MO 63119.

126—OUR LADY OF GOOD COUNSEL (BELLEFONTAINE NEIGHBORS) (1951) Closed. For inquiries regarding sacramental records, contact the Archdiocesan Archives, 20 Archbishop May Dr., Saint Louis, MO 63119.

127—OUR LADY OF GUADALUPE CATHOLIC CHURCH (1954) (Hispanic)
1115 S. Florissant Rd., 63121. Tel: 314-522-9264; Fax: 314-522-8461. Rev. John J. O'Brien; Sr. Cathy Doherty, S.S.N.D., Pastoral Assoc.
School—Our Lady of Guadalupe Catholic Church School, (Grades PreK-8), Tel: 314-524-1948. Peggy O'Brien, Prin. Lay Teachers 10; Students 177.
Catechesis Religious Program—Students 96.

128—OUR LADY OF LORETTO (SPANISH LAKE) (1959) Closed. For inquiries regarding sacramental records, contact the Archdiocesan Archives, 20 Archbishop May Dr., Saint Louis, MO 63119.

129—OUR LADY OF LOURDES CATHOLIC CHURCH, UNIVERSITY CITY (1916)
7148 Forsyth Blvd., University City, 63105.
Tel: 314-726-6200; Email: rectory@ucitylourdes.org. Rev. Msgr. Richard E. Hanneke; Deacon Patrick G. Waldschmidt.
School—Our Lady of Lourdes Catholic School, (Grades K-8), 7157 Northmoor Dr., University City, 63105. Tel: 314-726-3352; Fax: 314-726-0503; Email: jeanne.gearon@ucitylourdes.org. Lay Teachers 24; Religious 1; Students 222.

130—OUR LADY OF MERCY (HAZELWOOD) (1964) Closed. For inquiries regarding sacramental records, contact the Archdiocesan Archives, 20 Archbishop May Dr., Saint Louis, MO 63119.

131—OUR LADY OF MOUNT CARMEL (1872) Closed. For inquiries regarding sacramental records, contact the Archdiocesan Archives, 20 Archbishop May Dr., Saint Louis, MO 63119.

132—OUR LADY OF PERPETUAL HELP (1873) Closed. For inquiries regarding sacramental records, contact the Archdiocesan Archives, 20 Archbishop May Dr., Saint Louis, MO 63119.

133—OUR LADY OF PROVIDENCE CATHOLIC CHURCH (1954) Rev. Richard J. Schilli; Deacon David Amelotti.
Res.: 8866 Pardee Rd., 63123. Tel: 314-843-3570; Fax: 314-843-8033; Email: ladyprov@charter.net; Web: www.olpstl.com.
See Holy Cross Academy, St. Louis under Inter-Parochial, Consolidated Elementary Schools in the Institution section (H).
Catechesis Religious Program—Students 60.

134—OUR LADY OF SORROWS CATHOLIC CHURCH (1907)
5020 Rhodes Ave., 63109. Tel: 314-351-1600; Fax: 314-351-1602; Email: rectory@olsorrows.org; Web: olsorrows.org. Rev. Sebastian Mundackal, O.S.B.; Deacon Daniel Skillman. In Res., Rev. Andrew J. Sigmund, (Retired).

135—OUR LADY OF THE HOLY CROSS CATHOLIC CHURCH (1864)
8115 Church Rd., 63147. Tel: 314-381-0323; Email: olhc2@msn.com; Web: www.ourladyoftheholycross.com. Rev. Vincent R. Nyman.

136—OUR LADY OF THE PILLAR CATHOLIC CHURCH (1938)
401 S. Lindbergh Blvd., 63131. Revs. Thomas French, S.M.; George Cerniglia, S.M.; Deacon Frederick S. Tustanowsky.
School—Our Lady of the Pillar Catholic School, (Grades PreK-8), 403 S. Lindbergh Blvd., 63131.
Tel: 314-993-3353; Fax: 314-993-2172; Email: hfanning@olpillar.com. Lay Teachers 19; Students 150.
Catechesis Religious Program—
Tel: 314-993-2280, Ext. 208; Email: ftustanowsky@olpillar.com. Students 130.

137—OUR LADY OF THE PRESENTATION CATHOLIC CHURCH (1915) Rev. Mark A. Dolan.
Res.: 8860 Tudor Ave., Overland, 63114.
Tel: 314-427-0486; Email: olpresentation@hotmail.com; Web: olpchurch.weconnect.com.

138—OUR LADY OF THE ROSARY CATHOLIC CHURCH (2005) Closed. For inquires regarding sacramental records contact Archdiocesan Archives, 20 Archbishop May Dr., Saint Louis, MO 63119.

139—ST. PATRICK (1981) Closed. For inquiries for parish records contact the chancery.

140—ST. PATRICK (UNIVERSITY CITY) (1940) Closed. For inquiries regarding sacramental records, contact the Archdiocesan Archives, 20 Archbishop May Dr., Saint Louis, MO 63119.

141—ST. PAUL CATHOLIC CHURCH, FENTON (1878) [CEM] Rev. Msgr. Michael E. Dieckmann; Revs. Michael J. Benz; Philip J. Bene, J.C.D., In Res.; Deacons John Weatherholt, (Retired); Paul Crafts.
Res.: 15 Forest Knoll, Fenton, 63026-3105.
Tel: 636-343-1234, Ext. 130; Fax: 636-343-4809; Email: stpo@swbell.net; Web: www.stpaulfenton.org.
School—St. Paul Catholic Church, Fenton School, (Grades PreK-8), 465 New Smizer Mill Rd., Fenton, 63026. Tel: 636-343-4333; Fax: 636-343-1769; Web: www.stpaulfenton.org/school. Lay Teachers 26; Students 293.
Catechesis Religious Program—Email: stpaulpsr@swbell.net. Students 146.

142—ST. PAUL THE APOSTLE, Merged to form Ascension-St. Paul, Normandy.

143—STS. PETER AND PAUL CATHOLIC CHURCH (1849)
1919 S. 7th St., 63104. Tel: 314-231-9923; Email: pssspeterpaul@charter.net; Web: stspeterandpaulstl.org. Rev. Bruce H. Forman; Deacons Thomas Gorski; Dennis K. Stovall.

144—ST. PETER CATHOLIC CHURCH, KIRKWOOD (1832) [CEM]
243 W. Argonne Dr., Kirkwood, 63122.
Tel: 314-966-8600; Fax: 314-966-5721; Email: info@stpeterkirkwood.org; Web: www.stpeterkirkwood.org/. Rev. Msgr. John M. Costello; Rev. Paul J. Hamilton; Deacons John W. Komotos; Richard L. Renard; Kevin Stillman, Dir. In Res., Rev. Msgr. Gregory L. Schmidt, (Retired).
School—St. Peter Catholic Church, Kirkwood School, (Grades PreK-8), 215 N. Clay St., Kirkwood, 63122.
Tel: 314-821-0460; Fax: 314-821-0833. Lay Teachers 45; Students 468.
Catechesis Religious Program—
Tel: 314-821-0460, Ext. 4208; Email: abonsanti@stpeterkirkwood.org. Andrea Bonsati, C.R.E. Students 517.

145—ST. PIUS V CATHOLIC CHURCH (1905) Rev. Paul J. Niemann, V.F.
Res.: 3310 S. Grand Blvd., 63118. Tel: 314-772-1525; Fax: 314-772-5615; Web: www.stpiusv.org.
See St. Frances Cabrini Academy, St. Louis under St. Wenceslaus, St. Louis for details.

146—ST. PIUS X (GLASGOW VILLAGE) (1954) Closed. For inquiries regarding sacramental records, contact the Archdiocesan Archives, 20 Archbishop May Dr., Saint Louis, MO 63119.

147—QUEEN OF ALL SAINTS CATHOLIC CHURCH (1972) Rev. Msgr. Henry J. Breier, V.F.; Rev. Peter J. Fonseca; Deacons Richard Schellhase; Joseph Wingbermuehle.
Res.: 6603 Christopher Dr., 63129. Tel: 314-846-8207; Email: queenparish@qasstl.org.
School—Queen of All Saints Catholic Church School, (Grades K-8), 6611 Christopher Dr., 63129.
Tel: 314-846-0506; Fax: 314-846-4939. Mrs. Shannon Sanchez, Prin. Students 297.
Catechesis Religious Program—Tel: 314-846-8126. Mrs. Ann Bender, C.R.E. Students 292.

148—ST. RAPHAEL THE ARCHANGEL CATHOLIC CHURCH (1950) Rev. Robert J. Reiker; Deacons Gerald Geiser; Ronald A. Holmes, Pastoral Assoc.
Res.: 6047 Bishops Pl., 63109. Tel: 314-352-8100; Email: parish@straphaelarchangel.org; Web: www.straphaelarchangel.org.
School—St. Raphael the Archangel Catholic Church School, (Grades K-8), 6000 Jamieson, 63109.
Tel: 314-352-9474; Fax: 314-352-7285. Mrs. Kim Vangel, Prin. Lay Teachers 14; Students 194.
Catechesis Religious Program—Students 175.

149—RESURRECTION OF OUR LORD CATHOLIC CHURCH (1930) (Vietnamese)
3900 Meramec St., 63116. Tel: 314-832-7023; Fax: 314-832-7024; Email: thuynguyenmtg@gmail.com. Revs. Khien Mai (John) Luu, S.V.D.; Chinh Quang Tran, S.V.D.; Bro. Larry Camilleri, S.V.D., In Res.
Catechesis Religious Program—Students 131.

150—ST. RICHARD CATHOLIC CHURCH (1963)
11223 Schuetz Rd., 63146. Tel: 314-432-6224; Email: vtonsor@strichardstl.org; Web: www.strichardstl.org. Rev. Philip D. Krill; Deacon John A. Bischof.

151—ST. RITA CATHOLIC CHURCH (1919)
8240 Washington St., 63114. Tel: 314-428-4845; Email: Parish249@archstl.org; Web: www.stritacatholicchurch.org. Rev. Msgr. Michael E. Turek, V.F.; Deacon David I. Harpring, Parish Life Coord.
Catechesis Religious Program—Students 2.

152—ST. ROCH CATHOLIC CHURCH (1911)
6052 Waterman Blvd., 63112. Tel: 314-721-6340; Email: linda@strochparish.org; Web: strochparish.com. Rev. Msgr. Salvatore E. Polizzi.
School—St. Roch Catholic School, (Grades PreK-8), 6040 Waterman Blvd., 63112. Tel: 314-721-2595; Fax: 314-721-0868; Email: markg@strochschool.org. Mark Gilligan, Prin. Lay Teachers 17; Students 223.

153—ST. ROSE OF LIMA (1884) Closed. For inquiries regarding sacramental records, contact the Archdiocesan Archives, 20 Archbishop May Dr., Saint Louis, MO 63119.

154—ST. ROSE PHILIPPINE DUCHESNE CATHOLIC CHURCH
Mailing Address: 1210 Paddock Dr., Florissant, 63033. Tel: 314-837-3410; Fax: 314-837-6628; Email: secretary@strpdparish.org; Web: www.strpdparish.org. Revs. Thomas W. Wyrsch; John C. Nickolai; Deacons William P. Johnson; Dennis J. Barbero.
School—All Saints Academy, St. Rose Campus, 3500 St. Catherine, Florissant, 63033. Tel: 314-921-3023; Fax: 314-921-3025. Religious Teachers 2; Lay Teachers 18; Students 270.
Catechesis Religious Program—Students 50.

155—ST. SABINA CATHOLIC CHURCH (1960)
1365 Harkee Dr., Florissant, 63031.
Tel: 314-837-1365; Fax: 314-837-7680; Email: jhofmann@stsabina.com. 1625 Swallow Ln., Florissant, 63031. Rev. Joseph W. Banden; Deacons Harold A. Strauss, (Retired); Gerard M. Lauterwasser; John G. Hofmann. In Res., Rev. Eugene P. Brennan, (Retired).
Catechesis Religious Program—Tel: 314-837-0146. Students 50.

156—SACRED HEART CATHOLIC CHURCH, FLORISSANT (1866)
751 N. Jefferson St., Florissant, 63031.
Tel: 314-837-3757; Email: cdunard@sh-flo.org; Web: www.sacredheartflorissant.org. Very Rev. Msgr. Mark C. Ullrich, M.Div., M.S.W., V.F.; Rev. Peter J. Fonseca; Deacons Bruce A. Burkhard; J. John Heithaus.
School—Sacred Heart Catholic Church, Florissant School, (Grades K-8), 501 St. Louis St., Florissant, 63031. Tel: 314-831-3372; Fax: 314-831-2844. Lois Vollmer, Prin. Lay Teachers 22; Students 317.
Catechesis Religious Program—
Tel: 314-837-3757, Ext. 222. Students 56.

157—SACRED HEART CATHOLIC CHURCH, VALLEY PARK

(1903) [CEM] Revs. Thomas J. Haley; Patrick J. Christopher; Scott Jones, S.D.S.; Deacons Gary Peterson; Charles R. Snyder.
Res.: 8 Fernridge, Valley Park, 63088.
Tel: 636-225-5268; Fax: 636-225-6969.
School—Sacred Heart Catholic School, (Grades PreK-8), 12 Ann Ave., Valley Park, 63088.
Tel: 636-225-3824; Fax: 636-225-8941. Lay Teachers 24; Students 390.
Catechesis Religious Program—Students 585.

158—ST. SEBASTIAN (GLEN OWEN), Closed. For inquiries regarding sacramental records, contact the Archdiocesan Archives, 20 Archbishop May Dr., Saint Louis, MO 63119.

159—SEVEN HOLY FOUNDERS CATHOLIC CHURCH (1927) Rev. Msgr. John J. Brennell; Deacons Thomas A. Schiller; Charles Lombardo; Thomas E. Forster.
Office: 6820 Aliceton Ave., Affton, 63123.
Tel: 314-638-3938; Email: gailshf@aol.com; Web: www.foundersaffton.org.
Church: 6741 Rock Hill Rd., 63123.
Tel: 314-631-3938.
See Holy Cross Academy, St. Louis under Inter-Parochial, Consolidated Elementary Schools in the Institution section (H).
Catechesis Religious Program—Bro. Arnaldo M. Sanchez, O.S.M., Dir. Faith Formation. Students 120.

160—SHRINE OF ST. JOSEPH (1844)
1220 N. 11th St., 63106-4614. Tel: 314-231-9407; Fax: 314-231-0802; Email: kdfinazzo@yahoo.com; Email: allen4651@yahoo.com; Web: www.shrineofstjoseph.org. Rev. Dale P. Wunderlich, Rector.

161—ST. SIMON OF CYRENE (1993) Closed. For inquiries regarding sacramental records, contact the Archdiocesan Archives, 20 Archbishop May Dr., Saint Louis, MO 63119.

162—ST. SIMON THE APOSTLE CATHOLIC CHURCH (1959) Revs. Bradley E. Modde; Thomas J. Santen, Sr. Assoc.; Deacons David Camden; Paul F. Stackle.
Res.: 11011 Mueller Rd., 63123.
Tel: 314-842-3848, Ext. 1; Fax: 314-842-9829; Email: stsimon@sbcglobal.net; Web: www.stsimonchurch.org.
Child Care—Preschool, 11015 Mueller Rd., 63123.
Tel: 314-842-3848, Ext. 3; Fax: 314-842-4935; Email: simonsays@stsimonchurch.org; Web: www.simonsaysecc.com.
School—St. Simon the Apostle Catholic Church School, (Grades K-8), 11019 Mueller Rd., 63123.
Tel: 314-842-3848, Ext. 2; Fax: 314-849-6355; Email: principal@stsimonschool.org. Lay Teachers 21; Students 333.
Catechesis Religious Program—Students 134.

163—STE. GENEVIEVE DU BOIS CATHOLIC CHURCH, WARSON WOODS (1956) Rev. Daniel E. Mosley; Rev. Msgr. John M. Unger, (Retired); Deacon H. Matthew Witte.
Res.: 1575 N. Woodlawn Ave., Warson Woods, 63122.
Tel: 314-966-3780; Fax: 314-966-4687; Email: stegen@sbcglobal.net; Web: www.stegenevievedubois.org.
School—Ste. Genevieve Du Bois School, (Grades PreK-8), Tel: 314-821-4245; Fax: 314-822-4881. Mr. Anthony Van Gessel, Prin. Lay Teachers 15; Students 120.
Catechesis Religious Program—Students 77.

164—ST. STEPHEN PROTOMARTYR CATHOLIC CHURCH (1926)
3949 Wilmington Ave., 63116. Tel: 314-481-1133; Email: junetessinssp@gmail.com. Rev. Ronald J. Hopmeir.
School—St. Stephen Protomartyr Catholic Church School, (Grades K-8), 3923 Wilmington Ave., 63116.
Tel: 314-752-4700; Fax: 314-752-5165. Michel Wendell, Prin. Lay Teachers 15; Students 194.
Catechesis Religious Program—Students 7.

165—STS. TERESA AND BRIDGET CATHOLIC CHURCH (2003)
3636 N. Market, 63113. Tel: 314-371-1190;
Fax: 314-531-1047; Email: pastor@ststb.org; Email: drt@cicbservice.com; Web: www.ststb.org. Very Rev. Timothy R. Cook, V.F.; Deacon Charles M. Allen.

166—ST. TERESA OF AVILA (1865) Closed. For inquiries regarding sacramental records, contact Sts. Teresa & Bridget Church, 3636 N. Market St., Saint Louis, MO 63113.

167—ST. THOMAS MORE (BEL-RIDGE) (1955) Closed. For inquiries regarding sacramental records, contact the Archdiocesan Archives, 20 Archbishop May Dr., Saint Louis, MO 63119.

168—ST. THOMAS OF AQUIN (1882) Closed. For inquiries regarding sacramental records, contact the Archdiocesan Archives, 20 Archbishop May Dr., Saint Louis, MO 63119.

169—ST. THOMAS THE APOSTLE (FLORISSANT) (1960) Closed. For inquiries regarding sacramental records, contact the Archdiocesan Archives, 20 Archbishop May Dr., Saint Louis, MO 63119.

170—ST. TIMOTHY (1958) Closed. For inquiries regarding sacramental records, contact the Archdiocesan Archives, 20 Archbishop May Dr., Saint Louis, MO 63119.

171—TRANSFIGURATION (FLORISSANT) (1965) Closed. For inquiries regarding sacramental records, contact the Archdiocesan Archives, 20 Archbishop May Dr., Saint Louis, MO 63119.

172—ST. VINCENT DE PAUL CATHOLIC CHURCH, ST. LOUIS (1841)
1408 S. Tenth St., 63104. Tel: 314-420-8450; Email: efmurphy@stvstl.org; Web: www.stvstl.org. Revs. Edward F. Murphy, C.M.; James T. Beighlie, C.M.
Catechesis Religious Program—Email: lmertz@stvstl.org. Linda Mertz, D.R.E. Students 30.

173—VISITATION-ST. ANN SHRINE CATHOLIC CHURCH (1881) Closed. For inquiries regarding sacramental records contact Archdiocesan Archives, 20 Archbishop May Dr., Saint Louis, MO 63119.

174—ST. WENCESLAUS CATHOLIC CHURCH (1895) Rev. James Wasser, M.S.F.; Deacon George W. Miller.
Res.: 3014 Oregon Ave., 63118. Tel: 314-865-1020; Email: stwencebulletin@sbcglobal.net.
Catechesis Religious Program—St. Frances Cabrini Academy, 3022 Oregon Ave., 63118.
Tel: 314-776-0883; Fax: 314-776-4912. Students 175.

175—ST. WILLIAM (WOODSON TERRACE) (1953) Closed. For inquiries regarding sacramental records, contact the Archdiocesan Archives, 20 Archbishop May Dr., Saint Louis, MO 63119.

CHURCHES OUTSIDE ST. LOUIS CITY AND ST. LOUIS COUNTY

APPLE CREEK, PERRY CO., ST. JOSEPH CATHOLIC CHURCH, APPLE CREEK (1828) [CEM] [JC2]
138 St. Joseph Ln., Apple Creek, 63775.
Tel: 573-788-2330; Email: stjoeapc@gmail.com. Rev. James R. French.
Catechesis Religious Program—10198 Hwy. B, Perryville, 63775. Tel: 573-768-0338; Email: ashlyr82@gmail.com. Ashly Richardet, D.R.E. Students 71.

ARNOLD, JEFFERSON CO.

1—ST. DAVID CATHOLIC CHURCH (1963)
2334 Tenbrook Rd., Arnold, 63010. Tel: 636-296-5485; Fax: 636-296-8717; Email: stdavid@swbell.net; Web: www.stdavidarnold.org. Rev. Charles F. Ferrara; Deacons Thomas G. Politte; Scott D. Schardan.
See Arnold, Holy Child School under Inter-Parochial, Consolidated Elementary Schools located in the Institution section (H).
Catechesis Religious Program—Tel: 636-287-1551; Email: garycathy@sbcglobal.net. Cathy Whitlock, D.R.E. Students 99.

2—IMMACULATE CONCEPTION CATHOLIC CHURCH, ARNOLD (1840) [CEM] Revs. Larry T. Huber; Timothy M. Foley, (Retired); Deacons Steven M. Schisler; Donald J. Walker.
Res.: 2300 Church Rd., Arnold, 63010.
Tel: 636-321-0002; Fax: 636-321-0004; Email: parishsecretary@icarnold.com; Web: icarnold.com.
See Arnold, Holy Child School under Inter-Parochial, Consolidated Elementary Schools located in the Institution section (H).
Catechesis Religious Program—
Tel: 636-321-0004, Ext. 74. Mary Winkelmann, D.R.E. Students 300.

AUGUSTA, ST. CHARLES CO., IMMACULATE CONCEPTION CATHOLIC CHURCH, AUGUSTA (1851) [CEM] Very Rev. Eugene G. Robertson, V.F.
Res.: 5912 S. Hwy. 94, Augusta, 63332.
Tel: 636-482-4455; Fax: 636-228-4529; Email: icaugustamo@yahoo.com; Web: www.svdutzow.org.
Catechesis Religious Program—Students 22.

BELGIQUE, PERRY CO., NATIVITY OF THE BLESSED VIRGIN MARY, Closed. For inquiries regarding sacramental records, contact the Archdiocesan Archives, 20 Archbishop May Dr., Saint Louis, MO 63119.

BERGER, FRANKLIN CO., ST. PAUL CATHOLIC CHURCH, BERGER (1853) [CEM] (German) Rev. John C. Deken; Deacon H. Wayne Groner.
Res.: 603 Miller St., New Haven, 63068.
Tel: 573-237-3372; Fax: 573-237-3372.
Catechesis Religious Program—Students 7.

BIEHLE, PERRY CO., ST. MAURUS CATHOLIC CHURCH (1870) [CEM] [JC]
10198 Hwy. B, Perryville, 63775. Tel: 573-547-5246; Email: stjoeapc@gmail.com. Rev. James R. French.
Catechesis Religious Program—Tel: 573-768-0338; Email: ashlyr82@gmail.com. Ashly Richardet, D.R.E. Students 42.

BLOOMSDALE, STE. GENEVIEVE CO., ST. AGNES CATHOLIC CHURCH (1835) [CEM]
40 St. Agnes Dr., P.O. Box 124, Bloomsdale, 63627.
Tel: 573-483-2555; Email: office@stagnesandstlawrence.org. Very Rev. Rickey J. Valleroy, V.F.; Deacon James Basler.
School—St. Agnes Catholic Church School, (Grades PreK-8), 30 St. Agnes Dr., Bloomsdale, 63627.
Tel: 573-483-2506; Email: principal@stagneselementary.org. Erin O'Driscoll, Prin. Lay Teachers 9; Students 96.
Catechesis Religious Program—Students 23.

BONNE TERRE, ST. FRANCOIS CO., ST. JOSEPH CATHOLIC CHURCH, BONNE TERRE (1872) [CEM]
15 St. Joseph St., Bonne Terre, 63628.
Tel: 573-358-2112; Email: bernieburle@yahoo.com. Rev. Stephen F. Bauer.
Catechesis Religious Program—Students 24.
Mission—St. Anne, 5425 Brickey Rd., French Village, St. Francois Co. 63036. Tel: 573-358-2112.

BREWER, PERRY CO., CHRIST THE SAVIOR CATHOLIC CHURCH (1907) [CEM]
Mailing Address: 1010 Rosati Ct., Perryville, 63775.
Tel: 573-547-4300; Email: svdepaul@svdepaul.org. 55 Shady Ln., Perryville, 63775. Revs. Joseph C. Geders, C.M.; Richard L. Wehrmeyer, C.M.

CATAWISSA, FRANKLIN CO., ST. JAMES CATHOLIC CHURCH, CATAWISSA (1913) [CEM]
1587 Hwy. AM, Villa Ridge, 63089.
Tel: 636-451-4685; Email: frmarkbozada@gmail.com; Web: www.stmarys-moselle.com. 1107 Summit Dr., Catawissa, 63015. Rev. Mark S. Bozada.
Mission—St. Patrick, [CEM] Hwy. NN & Rock Church Rd., Armagh, Franklin Co. 63015.
Tel: 636-257-2227.

CLOVER BOTTOM, FRANKLIN CO., ST. ANN CATHOLIC CHURCH, CLOVER BOTTOM (1883) [CEM] Rev. Philip D. Krill; Deacon Stephen J. Young.
Res.: 7851 Hwy. YY, Washington, 63090-4050.
Tel: 636-239-3222; Email: stann.mills@yhti.net; Web: www.stannchurchcloverbottom.org.
Catechesis Religious Program—Students 46.

COFFMAN, STE. GENEVIEVE CO., ST. CATHERINE OF ALEXANDRIA (1929) [CEM] [JC]
Mailing Address: 10 N. Long St., Farmington, 63640.
Tel: 573-756-4250; Email: secretary@stjosephfarmington.com. 23496 State Rte. WW, Ste. Genevieve, 63670. Rev. William C. Thess.
Catechesis Religious Program—Students 2.

CONCORD HILL, WARREN CO., ST. IGNATIUS LOYOLA CATHOLIC CHURCH (1857) [CEM 3] Deacon Paul J. Hecktor.
Res.: 19127 Mill Rd., Marthasville, 63357-1439.
Tel: 636-932-4445; Email: info@saintig.com.
School—St. Ignatius Loyola Catholic School, (Grades K-8), Tel: 636-932-4444; Fax: 636-932-4479; Web: www.saintig.com. Dr. Arlesa Leopold, Prin. Clergy 6; Lay Teachers 6; Students 43.

COTTLEVILLE, ST. CHARLES CO., ST. JOSEPH CATHOLIC CHURCH, COTTLEVILLE (1873) [CEM]
1355 Motherhead Rd., St. Charles, 63304.
Tel: 636-441-0055; Fax: 636-926-7341; Email: parish@stjoecot.org; Web: www.stjoecot.org. Rev. Msgr. James P. Callahan, V.F.; Revs. Mark A. Chrismer; John Schneier; Jane Brown, Pastoral Assoc.; Deacons Michael Piva; Eugene Schaeffer III; Thomas A. Burke III.
School—St. Joseph Catholic School, (Grades PreK-8), 1351 Motherhead Rd., St. Charles, 63304.
Tel: 636-441-0055, Ext. 200; Fax: 636-441-9932; Email: info@stjoecot.org; Web: www.stjoecot.org/school. Sr. Mary Shelia Maksim, O.P., Prin.; Brad Benne, Vice Prin.; Tricia Bauche, Vice Prin. Religious Teachers 4; Lay Teachers 53; Students 991.
Catechesis Religious Program—1351 Motherhead Road, Cottleville, 63304. Email: mdoerr@stjoecot.org. Mary Doerr, D.R.E. Students 500.
Convent—1353 Motherhead Rd., St. Charles, 63304.
Tel: 636-244-2257. Sisters 4.

CRYSTAL CITY, JEFFERSON CO., SACRED HEART CATHOLIC CHURCH, CRYSTAL CITY (1881) [CEM]
555 Bailey Rd., Crystal City, 63019-1798.
Tel: 636-937-4662; Fax: 636-931-5507; Email: sh324cc@sbcglobal.net. Rev. Clark B. Maes; Deacon Gerard G. Stoverink.
Catechesis Religious Program—Students 152.

DARDENNE PRAIRIE, ST. CHARLES CO., IMMACULATE CONCEPTION CATHOLIC CHURCH, DARDENNE (1880) [CEM] Rev. Msgr. Ted L. Wojcicki, Ed.D., V.F.; Revs. Alexander M. Nord; Henry K. Purcell; Christopher Rubie; Deacons Lonnie G. Weishaar; Paul Bast; Brett C. LePage.
Res.: 7701 Hwy. N., Dardenne Prairie, 63368.
Tel: 636-561-6611; Email: parishoffice@icdparish.org; Web: www.icdparish.org.
School—Immaculate Conception Catholic School, (Grades PreK-8), 2089 Hanley Rd., Dardenne Prairie, 63368. Tel: 636-561-4450; Fax: 636-625-9020; Email: dan.mullenschlader@icdschool.org; Web: www.icdschool.org. Mr. Daniel Mullenschlader, Prin. Lay Teachers 51; Students 928.
Catechesis Religious Program—Tel: 636-561-1974; Email: psr@icdparish.org. Students 914.

DE SOTO, JEFFERSON CO., ST. ROSE OF LIMA CATHOLIC CHURCH, DESOTO (1866) [CEM] Rev. Alexander R. Anderson; Deacon Edward J. Boyer.
Res.: 504 S. Third St., De Soto, 63020.
Tel: 636-337-2212; Fax: 636-337-2394.
School—St. Rose of Lima Catholic School, (Grades PreSchool-8), Email: limaatstrose@sbcglobal.net;

Web: www.stroseparish.info. Lay Teachers 11; Students 102.
Catechesis Religious Program—Students 120.

DUTZOW, WARREN CO., ST. VINCENT CATHOLIC CHURCH, DUTZOW (1856) [CEM]
13497 S. State Hwy. 94, Marthasville, 63357.
Tel: 636-433-2678; Email: svchurch@centurytel.net; Web: svdutzow.org. Very Rev. Eugene G. Robertson, V.F.
School—St. Vincent Catholic Church, Dutzow School, 13495 S. State Hwy. 94, Marthasville, 63357. Tel: 636-433-2466. Lay Teachers 9; Sisters 1; Students 75.
Catechesis Religious Program—Students 6.

ELSBERRY, LINCOLN CO., SACRED HEART CATHOLIC CHURCH, ELSBERRY (1905)
714 Lincoln St., Elsberry, 63343. Tel: 573-898-2202; Email: parish@sacredheartelsberry.org. Rev. Charles P. Tichacek.
Catechesis Religious Program—Tel: 636-662-2407. Rachele Presley, D.R.E. Students 42.

FARMINGTON, ST. FRANCOIS CO., ST. JOSEPH CATHOLIC CHURCH, FARMINGTON (1890) [JC2]
10 N. Long St., Farmington, 63640. Rev. William C. Thess; Deacon Mark A. Byington.
School—St. Joseph Catholic Church, Farmington School, (Grades K-8), 501 Ste. Genevieve Ave., Farmington, 63640. Tel: 573-756-6312;
Fax: 573-756-0738. Students 158.
Catechesis Religious Program—Students 75.

FESTUS, JEFFERSON CO., OUR LADY CATHOLIC CHURCH (1956)
1550 St. Mary Ln., Festus, 63028-1543.
Tel: 636-937-5513; Email: gklump@olparish.org; Web: olparish@org. Rev. Gregory S. Klump; Deacon Timothy L. Dunn.
School—Our Lady Catholic School, (Grades K-8), 1599 St. Mary Ln., Festus, 63028-1557.
Tel: 636-937-5008; Email: tkempfer@olparish.org. Lay Teachers 16; Students 206.
Catechesis Religious Program—Students 105.

FLINT HILL, ST. CHARLES CO., ST. THEODORE CATHOLIC CHURCH (1883) [CEM]
5051 Hwy. P, Wentzville, 63385-2118.
Tel: 636-332-9269, Ext. 226;
Fax: 636-332-9269, Ext. 225; Email: bulletin@sainttheodore.org; Email: info@sainttheodore.org; Web: www.sainttheodore.org/. 5085 Hwy. P, Wentzville, 63385-2118. Rev. Anthony J. Gerber; Deacons Patrick Rankin; Robert J. Mayo II.
School—St. Theodore Catholic Church School, 5059 Hwy. P, Wentzville, 63385. Tel: 636-332-9269, Ext. 4; Fax: 636-327-5115; Email: sttheodore.school@centurytel.net. Lay Teachers 13; Students 204.
Catechesis Religious Program—
Tel: 636-332-9269, Ext. 283; Email: psr@sainttheodore.org. Students 20.

GILDEHAUS, FRANKLIN CO., ST. JOHN THE BAPTIST CATHOLIC CHURCH, GILDEHAUS (1839) [CEM] Deacon Randall G. Smith.
Res.: 5567 Gildehaus Rd., Villa Ridge, 63089.
Tel: 636-583-2488; Fax: 636-583-6114; Email: stjohnsgild@yhti.net.
School—St. John the Baptist Catholic School, (Grades PreSchool-8), 5579 Gildehaus Rd., Villa Ridge, 63089. Tel: 636-583-2392. Mr. Gary Menke, Prin. Lay Teachers 13; Students 114.
Catechesis Religious Program—Students 50.

HAWK POINT, LINCOLN CO., ST. MARY CATHOLIC CHURCH, HAWK POINT (1919) [CEM 2]
458 Main St., P.O. Box 205, Hawk Point, 63349. Email: marysrectory@centurytel.net;
Tel: 636-338-4331. Rev. John A. Keenoy.
Catechesis Religious Program—Fax: 636-338-4331. Students 38.

HERCULANEUM, JEFFERSON CO., CHURCH OF THE ASSUMPTION OF B.V.M. CATHOLIC CHURCH (1916) [CEM] Closed. For inquiries regarding sacramental records contact Archdiocesan Archives, 20 Archbishop May Dr., Saint Louis, MO 63119.

HIGH RIDGE, JEFFERSON CO., ST. ANTHONY CATHOLIC CHURCH, HIGH RIDGE (1944)
3009 High Ridge Blvd., High Ridge, 63049.
Tel: 636-677-4868; Email: rusalynesahr@att.net. Rev. John Reiker; Deacons Richard L. Stevens; James R. G'Sell.
Catechesis Religious Program—Email: mrskathyjoslin@yahoo.com. Mrs. Kathy Joslin, D.R.E. Students 193.

HILLSBORO, JEFFERSON CO., CHURCH OF THE GOOD SHEPHERD CATHOLIC CHURCH, HILLSBORO (1934) [CEM] Very Rev. Christopher F. Holtmann, V.F.; Deacons Paul A. Martin; Daniel A. Raidt.
Res.: 703 Third St., Hillsboro, 63050-4342.
Tel: 636-789-3356; Fax: 636-789-9986; Email: parishsecretary@mygoodshepherd.com; Web: mygoodshepherd.com.
School—Church of the Good Shepherd Catholic Church, Hillsboro School, (Grades PreK-8), 701 Third St., Hillsboro, 63050. Tel: 636-797-2300;
Fax: 636-797-2300. Mrs. Mariann Jones, Prin. Lay Teachers 10; Students 82.
Catechesis Religious Program—Students 150.

HOUSE SPRINGS, JEFFERSON CO., OUR LADY, QUEEN OF PEACE CATHOLIC CHURCH (1961) [CEM 2] Revs. Dennis C. Schmidt; James T. Beighlie, C.M.; Deacons Thomas Gerling; Paul Turek.
Res.: 4696 Notre Dame Ln., House Springs, 63051.
Tel: 636-671-3062; Fax: 636-671-0003; Email: parishoffice@olqpparish.org; Email: parishbookkeeping@olqpparish.org.
School—Our Lady, Queen of Peace Catholic Church School, (Grades K-8), 4675 Notre Dame Ln., House Springs, 63051. Tel: 636-671-0247;
Fax: 636-671-0418. Mr. John Boyd, Prin.; Tiffany Leicht, Librarian. Lay Teachers 12; Students 106.
Catechesis Religious Program—Students 130.

IMPERIAL, JEFFERSON CO.
1—ST. JOHN, THE BELOVED DISCIPLE CATHOLIC CHURCH (1869) [CEM] Rev. Richard V. Coerver, V.F.; Deacons Norbert Gawedzinski; Lawrence Nava.
Res.: 4614 Blue Springs Dr., Imperial, 63052.
Tel: 636-296-8061, Ext. 4; Email: office@stjohnimperial.org.
Catechesis Religious Program—Students 60.
2—ST. JOSEPH CATHOLIC CHURCH, IMPERIAL (1905) [CEM]
6020 Old Antonia Rd., Imperial, 63052-0968.
Tel: 636-464-1013; Email: agriffard@sjiparish.org; Web: stjosephimperial.org. Revs. Daniel G. Shaughnessy; Thomas A. Vordtriede; Gary L. Vollmer; Deacons Brian T. Selsor; Donald Kintz.
School—St. Joseph Catholic Church, Imperial School, (Grades K-8), 6024 Old Antonia Rd., Imperial, 63052. Tel: 636-464-9027;
Fax: 636-464-3574. Sr. Carol Sansone, A.S.C.J. Students 260.
Catechesis Religious Program—Students 367.

JOSEPHVILLE, ST. CHARLES CO., ST. JOSEPH CATHOLIC CHURCH, JOSEPHVILLE (1852) [CEM]
1390 Josephville Rd., Wentzville, 63385.
Tel: 636-332-6676; Email: trish.seaman@stjojo.net; Web: www.stjojo.net. Rev. Robert J. Samson; Deacon David L. Billing.
School—St. Joseph Catholic Church, Josephville School, (Grades PreK-8), 1410 Josephville Rd., Wentzville, 63385. Tel: 636-332-5672. Jill Nance, Prin. Lay Teachers 10; Students 107.
Catechesis Religious Program—Larry Bean, D.R.E. Students 23.

KRAKOW, FRANKLIN CO., ST. GERTRUDE CATHOLIC CHURCH (1845) [CEM] Rev. Philip D. Krill; Deacon Charles Gildehaus. In Res., Rev. Bernard J. Wilkins, (Retired).
Res.: 6535 Hwy. YY, Washington, 63090.
Tel: 636-239-4216; Email: stger@charter.net.
School—St. Gertrude Catholic Church School, (Grades K-8), 6520 Hwy. YY, Washington, 63090.
Tel: 636-239-2347; Fax: 636-239-3550; Email: stgertrude@primary.net. Dr. Steve Young, Prin. Lay Teachers 19; Students 228.
Catechesis Religious Program—Rosie Heidmann, D.R.E. Students 48.

LAWRENCETON, STE. GENEVIEVE CO., ST. LAWRENCE CATHOLIC CHURCH (1872) [CEM] Attended by St. Agnes Rectory.
8055 State Rt. Y, P.O. Box 124, Bloomsdale, 63627.
Tel: 573-483-2555; Fax: 573-483-9497; Email: office@stagnesandstlawrence.org. Very Rev. Rickey J. Valleroy, V.F.
Catechesis Religious Program—Students 3.

LUEBBERING, FRANKLIN CO., ST. FRANCIS OF ASSISI CATHOLIC CHURCH (1874) [CEM]
1000 Luebbering Rd., Luebbering, 63061-3100.
Tel: 636-629-1717; Email: parish338@archstl.org. Rev. Robert D. Knight.
Catechesis Religious Program—Alison Byerley, D.R.E. Students 19.

MILLWOOD, LINCOLN CO., ST. ALPHONSUS CATHOLIC CHURCH, MILLWOOD (1850) [CEM] Rev. Charles P. Tichacek, Admin.
Res.: 29 St. Alphonsus Rd., Silex, 63377.
Tel: 573-384-6223; Fax: 573-384-5981.
School—St. Alphonsus School, Tel: 573-384-5305; Fax: 573-384-6190. Lay Teachers 5; Students 42.
Catechesis Religious Program—Students 30.

NEIER, FRANKLIN CO., ST. JOSEPH CATHOLIC CHURCH, NEIER (1881) [CEM] Rev. Donald E. Henke, D.Th.M.
Res.: 2401 Neier Rd., Union, 63084.
Tel: 636-583-2806; Fax: 636-583-0627.
Catechesis Religious Program—Students 72.

NEW HAVEN, FRANKLIN CO., ASSUMPTION CATHOLIC CHURCH, NEW HAVEN (1892) [CEM] Rev. John C. Deken; Deacon H. Wayne Groner.
Res.: 603 Miller St., New Haven, 63068.
Tel: 573-237-3372; Fax: 573-237-3372.
Catechesis Religious Program—Students 107.

NEW MELLE, ST. CHARLES CO., IMMACULATE HEART OF MARY CATHOLIC CHURCH, NEW MELLE (1945) [CEM]
Box 100, New Melle, 63365-0100. Tel: 636-398-5270; Email: secretary@ihm-newmelle.org; Web: www.ihm-newmelle.org. 8 W. Hwy. D, New Melle, 63365. Rev. Thomas C. Miller; Deacons Christopher M. Ast; Anthony Falbo; Laura Orf, Business Mgr.; Mr. Shawn Mueller, D.R.E.; Marilyn O'Neill, Music Min.
Chapel—Immaculate Heart of Mary.

O'FALLON, ST. CHARLES CO.
1—ASSUMPTION CATHOLIC CHURCH, O'FALLON (1871) [CEM] Rev. Mitchell S. Doyen; Rev. Msgr. William W. McCumber, M.A.L.; Deacon Gerald R. Hurlbert.
Res.: 403 N. Main St., O'Fallon, 63366.
Tel: 636-240-3721; Email: peggy.assumption@yahoo.com; Web: assumptionbvm.org.
School—Assumption Catholic Church, O'Fallon School, (Grades PreK-8), 203 W. Third St., O'Fallon, 63366. Tel: 636-240-4474; Fax: 636-240-5795. Lay Teachers 23; Students 445.
Catechesis Religious Program—Tel: 636-240-1020. Students 497.
2—ST. BARNABAS CATHOLIC CHURCH (1961) Rev. Raymond D. Hager.
Res.: 1400 N. Main St., O'Fallon, 63366.
Tel: 636-240-4556; Email: parish@stbarnabasofallon.org; Web: www.stbarnabasofallon.org.
Catechesis Religious Program—Email: mvomund@cpps-ofallon.org. Sr. Michaleen Vomund, D.R.E. Students 48.

OLD MINES, WASHINGTON CO., ST. JOACHIM CATHOLIC CHURCH, OLD MINES (1723) [CEM 3] Rev. Anthony A. Dattilo.
Res.: 10120 Crest Rd., Cadet, 63630.
Tel: 573-438-6181; Fax: 573-438-3685; Email: stjoachimparish@hotmail.com; Web: stjoachimchurch.com.
School—St. Joachim School, Tel: 573-438-3973; Fax: 573-438-3161; Email: stjoachimschool_63630@yahoo.com; Web: stjoachimschool.com. Carmen Litton, Prin. Lay Teachers 6; Students 61.
Catechesis Religious Program—Students 60.

OLD MONROE, LINCOLN CO., IMMACULATE CONCEPTION CATHOLIC CHURCH, OLD MONROE (1867) [CEM]
110 Maryknoll Rd., Old Monroe, 63369.
Tel: 636-661-5002; Email: parish@icomparish.org; Web: www.icomparish.org. Rev. Richard J. Rath; Deacon Neal R. Westhoff.
School—Immaculate Conception Catholic School, (Grades PreK-8), 120 Maryknoll Rd., Old Monroe, 63369. Tel: 636-661-5156; Fax: 636-661-5307; Email: jpalmer@icomparish.org; Web: icomparish.org/school. Janice Palmer, Prin. Lay Teachers 13; Students 204.
Catechesis Religious Program—Students 30.

OZORA, STE. GENEVIEVE CO., SACRED HEART CATHOLIC CHURCH, OZORO (1898) [CEM] Rev. James W. Schaefer, V.F.
Res.: 17742 State Rte. N., St. Mary, 63673.
Tel: 573-543-2209; Fax: 573-543-5576.
Catechesis Religious Program—Students 18.
Convent—17740 State Rte. N, St. Mary, 63673.
Tel: 573-543-2997.

PACIFIC, FRANKLIN CO., ST. BRIDGET OF KIDARE CATHOLIC CHURCH (1841) [CEM 2] Rev. James A. Holbrook; Deacon Michael E. Suden, D.D.S.
Res.: 111 W. Union St., Pacific, 63069.
Tel: 636-271-3993; Fax: 636-257-6265.
School—St. Bridget of Kidare Catholic Church School, Tel: 636-257-4533; Fax: 636-257-2504. Lay Teachers 9; Students 110.
Catechesis Religious Program—Students 68.

PARK HILLS, ST. FRANCOIS CO., IMMACULATE CONCEPTION CATHOLIC CHURCH, PARK HILLS (1903) [CEM] [JC]
Box 66, Park Hills, 63601-0066. Tel: 573-431-2427; Fax: 573-431-4060; Email: icsja@icsja.net; Email: icsjapastor@icsja.net; Web: www.icsja.org. 1020 W. Main St., Park Hills, 63601. Rev. Mark S. Ebert; Deacon Michael D. Burch.
Catechesis Religious Program—Students 43.
Mission—St. John (1879) [CEM] [JC] Maple St. & Walnut St., Bismarck, St. Francois Co. 63624.

PERRYVILLE, PERRY CO., ST. VINCENT DE PAUL CATHOLIC CHURCH, PERRYVILLE (1817) [CEM 4]
1010 Rosati Court, Perryville, 63775.
Tel: 573-547-4300; Email: svdepaul@svdepaul.org. 1000 Rosati Ct., Perryville, 63775. Revs. Joseph C. Geders, C.M.; Richard L. Wehrmeyer, C.M.
School—St. Vincent De Paul Catholic Church, Perryville School, (Grades K-6), 1007 W. St. Joseph St., Perryville, 63775. Dr. Ben Johnson, Elem. Prin. Lay Teachers 21; Students 292.
High School—St. Vincent De Paul Catholic Church, Perryville High School, 210 S. Water St., Perryville, 63775. Dr. Patricia Hensley, Prin. Lay Teachers 22; Students 225.
Catechesis Religious Program—Parish School of Religion, Email: ldauster@svdepaul.org. Students 275.
Missions—St. Joseph—Highland, Perry Co.
St. James, Crosstown, Perry Co.

PORT HUDSON, FRANKLIN CO., HOLY FAMILY CATHOLIC

CHURCH, PORT HUDSON (1872) [CEM]
124 Holy Family Church Rd., New Haven, 63068.
Tel: 573-459-6441; Email: parish352@archstl.or. Rev. James J. Foster.
Catechesis Religious Program—Tel: 573-459-6594; Tel: 573-764-3292. Students 30.
Mission—St. Gerald, 404 E. Fitzgerald, Gerald, 63037.

PORTAGE DES SIOUX, ST. CHARLES CO., ST. FRANCIS OF ASSISI CATHOLIC CHURCH, PORTAGE DES SIOUX (1799) [CEM 2] (French—German) Rev. Robert L. Banken, (Retired).
Res.: 1355 Farnham St., P.O. Box 129, Portage Des Sioux, 63373. Tel: 636-899-0906.
Mission—Immaculate Conception, 14060 Hwy. 94 N., P.O. Box 129, West Alton, 63386.

POTOSI, WASHINGTON CO., ST. JAMES CATHOLIC CHURCH, POTOSI (1829) [CEM 2] Rev. Rodger P. Fleming.
Res.: 201 N. Missouri Ave., Potosi, 63664.
Tel: 573-438-4686; Email: stjameschurch@centurylink.net; Web: www.stjamespotosi.org.
Catechesis Religious Program—Students 104.

RICHWOODS, WASHINGTON CO., ST. STEPHEN CATHOLIC CHURCH (1841) [CEM] Rev. Robert D. Knight.
Res.: 11514 Hwy. A, P.O. Box 233, Richwoods, 63071-0233. Tel: 573-678-2207; Email: parish354@archstl.org; Web: www.ststephenrichwoodsmo.com.

RIVER AUX VASES, STE. GENEVIEVE CO., STS. PHILIP AND JAMES CATHOLIC CHURCH (1840) [CEM] Rev. Gregory S. Klump.
Res.: 18411 RAV Church Rd., Ste. Genevieve, 63670.
Tel: 573-883-2923; Fax: 573-883-9605.
Catechesis Religious Program—Students 32.

ST. CHARLES, ST. CHARLES CO.

1—ST. CHARLES BORROMEO CATHOLIC CHURCH (1792) Revs. William F. Dotson; Ricardo Escobar; Deacons Donald L. McElroy; Jorge A. Perez. In Res., Rev. Msgr. Donald C. Schramm, (Retired).
Res.: 601 N. 4th St., St. Charles, 63301.
Tel: 636-946-1893; Email: marydubois@borromeoparish.com; Web: www.borromeoparish.com.
School—St. Charles Borromeo Catholic Church School, (Grades K-8), 431 Decatur, St. Charles, 63301. Tel: 636-946-2713; Fax: 636-946-3096; Web: borromeoschool.com. Lay Teachers 20; Sisters of Notre Dame 1; Students 259.
Catechesis Religious Program—Tel: 636-946-2916. Students 215.

2—ST. CLETUS (1965) Revs. James J. Benz; Mark Whitman; Deacons Frank Olmsted; Mark McCarthy.
Res.: 2705 Zumbehl Rd., St. Charles, 63301.
Tel: 636-946-6327; Fax: 636-946-6466.
School—St. Cletus School, 2721 Zumbehl Rd., St. Charles, 63301. Tel: 636-946-7756;
Fax: 636-946-6526. Lay Teachers 20; Students 214.
Catechesis Religious Program—Tel: 636-255-1717. Students 135.

3—ST. ELIZABETH ANN SETON CATHOLIC CHURCH (1975) Revs. Robert W. Burkemper; Frank A. D'Amico; Deacons Daniel K. Graham; Robert Brunton; David W. Ewing.
Res.: 2 Seton Ct., St. Charles, 63303.
Tel: 636-946-6717; Email: info@setonscene.org; Web: setonscene.org.
School—Seton Regional Catholic School, 1 Seton Ct., St. Charles, 63303. Tel: 636-946-6716;
Fax: 636-946-2670. Lay Teachers 17; Students 189.
Catechesis Religious Program—Tel: 636-669-6706; Email: lrathz@setonscene.org. Linda Rathz, D.R.E. Students 165.

4—STS. JOACHIM AND ANN CATHOLIC CHURCH, ST. CHARLES (1981)
Mailing Address: 4112 McClay Rd., St. Charles, 63304. Tel: 636-441-7503; Email: frbrockland@stsja.org; Web: www.stsja.org. Revs. John A. Brockland, V.F., J.C.L., M.A., M.Div.; James L. Gahan, (Retired); Deacons Timothy Schultz; A. John Lipin; Joseph A. Hartz; William L. Scarry.
School—Sts. Joachim and Ann Catholic School, (Grades PreK-8), 4110 McClay Rd., St. Charles, 63304-7915. Tel: 636-441-4835; Fax: 636-441-9534; Email: martinezj@stsja.org; Web: www.stsja.org. Jason Martinez, Prin. Lay Teachers 16; Students 212.
Catechesis Religious Program—Tel: 314-926-0021. Students 267.

5—ST. PETER CATHOLIC CHURCH, ST. CHARLES (1850) [CEM] Rev. John Paul Hopping; Deacons Fred M. Haehnel; Lawrence R. Boldt; Timothy H. Dallas. In Res., Rev. Frederick A. Meyer, (Retired).
Office: 221 First Capitol Dr., St. Charles, 63301.
Tel: 636-946-6641; Email: stpeterparish@stpstc.org.
Catechesis Religious Program—Students 134.

6—ST. ROBERT BELLARMINE CATHOLIC CHURCH (1964)
1424 First Capitol Dr. S., St. Charles, 63303.
Tel: 636-946-6799; Email: deaconjohn@strbellarmine.com; Web: www.strbellarmine.com. Rev. Mark Whitman; Deacons John Schiffer, Parish Life Coord.; Joseph C. Meiergerd; Phillip King. In Res., Rev. Msgr. Raymond A. Hampe, (Retired).
School—St. Elizabeth / St. Robert Regional School.
Catechesis Religious Program—Tel: 636-946-6461; Email: pamolimpio@strbellarmine.com. Pamela Olimpio, D.R.E. Students 86.

ST. CLAIR, FRANKLIN CO., ST. CLARE CATHOLIC CHURCH, ST. CLAIR (1916) [CEM]
165 E. Springfield St., St. Clair, 63077.
Tel: 636-629-0315; Email: parish358@archstl.org. Rev. Eric J. Kunz; Deacons Harvey Dubbs; Trevor J. Wild Sr.
Catechesis Religious Program—Students 23.

ST. MARY, STE. GENEVIEVE CO., IMMACULATE CONCEPTION CATHOLIC CHURCH, ST. MARY (1869) [CEM] Rev. Richard C. Kasznel, (Retired).
Res.: 481 Pine St., P.O. Box 27, St. Mary, 63673.
Tel: 573-543-2536; Fax: 573-543-2536.

ST. PAUL, ST. CHARLES CO., ST. PAUL CATHOLIC CHURCH, ST. PAUL (1850) [CEM]
1223 Church Rd., St. Paul, 63366. Tel: 636-978-1900; Email: parishcenter@st-paulchurch.org; Web: www.st-paulchurch.org. Rev. Gerald J. Blessing; Deacon Robert J. Marischen.
School—St. Paul Catholic Church, St. Paul School, (Grades PreK-8), 1235 Church Rd., St. Paul, 63366.
Tel: 636-978-1900, Ext. 231; Email: principal@stpaulknights.org. Kelly Kaimann, Prin. Religious Teachers 1; Lay Teachers 14; Students 196.
Catechesis Religious Program—Tel: 314-574-4483; Email: bmarishchen@st-paulchurch.org. Students 56.

ST. PETERS, ST. CHARLES CO., ALL SAINTS CATHOLIC CHURCH, ST. PETERS (1815) [CEM]
7 McMenamy Rd., St. Peters, 63376.
Tel: 636-397-1440; Email: asparish@allsaints-stpeters.org; Web: www.allsaints-stpeters.org. Revs. Donald R. Wester; Robert J. Suit; Peter Faimega; Deacons Gerald Knobbe; Gary Meyerkord.
School—All Saints Catholic School, (Grades K-8), 5 McMenamy Rd., Saint Peters, 63376.
Tel: 636-397-1477; Fax: 636-970-3735. Rae Ann Kielty, Prin. Lay Teachers 23; Students 291; Religious Teachers 1.
Catechesis Religious Program—Tel: 636-397-6995. Ms. Marya Pohlmeier, D.R.E. Students 294.

SERENO, PERRY CO., OUR LADY OF VICTORY CATHOLIC CHURCH (1908) [JC]
172 PCR 920, Perryville, 63775. Mailing Address: 1010 Rosati Ct., Perryville, 63775. Tel: 573-547-4300; Email: svdepaul@svdepaul.org. Revs. Joseph C. Geders, C.M.; Richard L. Wehrmeyer, C.M.

SILVER LAKE, PERRY CO., ST. ROSE OF LIMA CATHOLIC CHURCH, SILVER LAKE (1885) [CEM]
10138 Hwy. T, Perryville, 63775. Tel: 573-547-4300; Email: svdepaul@svdepaul.org; Web: www.svdepaul.org. Mailing Address: 1010 Rosati Ct., Perryville, 63775. Revs. Joseph C. Geders, C.M.; Richard L. Wehrmeyer, C.M.

STE. GENEVIEVE, STE. GENEVIEVE CO., STE. GENEVIEVE CATHOLIC CHURCH, STE. GENEVIEVE (1759) [CEM]
Mailing Address: 20 N. 4th St., Ste. Genevieve, 63670. Tel: 573-883-2731; Email: nemethe@stegenevieveparish.com. Revs. Edward G. Nemeth; David M. Miloscia; Deacons John F. Meere; James M. Robert.
Res.: 49 Du Bourg Pl., Ste. Genevieve, 63670.
School—Ste. Genevieve Catholic Church, Ste. Genevieve School, 40 N. Fourth St., Ste. Genevieve, 63670. Tel: 573-883-2403; Fax: 573-883-7413. Lay Teachers 20; Students 235.
High School—Valle High School, Tel: 573-883-7496; Fax: 573-883-9142. Religious Teachers 1; Lay Teachers 15; Students 133.
Catechesis Religious Program—Tel: 573-883-6110; Email: tinamarie6110@gmail.com. Tina Ringwald, D.R.E. Students 53.

SULLIVAN, FRANKLIN CO.

1—ST. ANTHONY CATHOLIC CHURCH, SULLIVAN (1891) [CEM]
201 W. Springfield Ave., Sullivan, 63080.
Tel: 573-468-6101; Email: sachurch@fidmail.com. Rev. Paul E. Telken; Deacon Kevin R. Miller.
School—St. Anthony Catholic School, (Grades K-8), 119 W. Springfield Ave., Sullivan, 63080.
Tel: 573-468-4423; Email: principal365@archstl.org. Mary Wooley, Prin. Lay Teachers 5; Students 69.
Catechesis Religious Program—Students 39.

2—CHURCH OF THE HOLY MARTYRS OF JAPAN CATHOLIC CHURCH (1879) [CEM 2]
8244 Hwy. AE, Sullivan, 63080-3229.
Tel: 573-627-3378; Email: parish333@archstl.org. Rev. Timothy J. Henderson, Admin.
Catechesis Religious Program—Students 40.

TIFF, WASHINGTON CO., ST. JOSEPH CATHOLIC CHURCH, TIFF (1905) [CEM] Rev. Anthony A. Dattilo.
Res.: 10120 Crest Rd., Cadet, 63630.
Tel: 573-438-6181; Fax: 573-438-3685.

TROY, LINCOLN CO., SACRED HEART CATHOLIC CHURCH, TROY (1891) [CEM] Rev. Thomas Wissler.
Res.: 100 Thompson Dr., Troy, 63379.
Tel: 636-528-8219; Fax: 636-528-3983; Email: tlwsheart@lincoln.mo.us; Web: sacredhearttroy.org.
School—Sacred Heart Catholic Church, Troy School, 110 Thompson Dr., Troy, 63379. Tel: 636-528-6684; Fax: 636-528-3923. Mrs. Ann Hoffman, Prin. Lay Teachers 13; Students 298.
Catechesis Religious Program—Students 290.

UNION, FRANKLIN CO., IMMACULATE CONCEPTION CATHOLIC CHURCH, UNION (1866) [CEM]
100 N. Washington Ave., Union, 63084.
Tel: 636-583-5144; Email: icunionoffice@gmail.com. Rev. Joseph S. Post; Deacon Gerald H. Becker.
School—Immaculate Conception Catholic Church, Union School, 6 W. State St., Union, 63084.
Tel: 636-583-2641; Fax: 636-583-3073. Lay Teachers 23; Students 330.
Catechesis Religious Program—Students 60.
Convent—111 N. Washington Ave., Union, 63084.
Tel: 636-583-2188.

VILLA RIDGE, FRANKLIN CO., ST. MARY OF PERPETUAL HELP CATHOLIC CHURCH, MOSELLE (1905) [CEM] Rev. Mark S. Bozada.

WARRENTON, WARREN CO., HOLY ROSARY CATHOLIC CHURCH (1868) [CEM]
724 E. Booneslick Rd., Warrenton, 63383.
Tel: 636-456-3698; Email: brownd@holyrosarywm.com; Web: holyrosarywm.com. Rev. Msgr. Francis X. Blood; Deacons Ray Burle; Mark L. Schmierbach.
School—Holy Rosary Catholic School, (Grades PreK-8), 716 Booneslick Rd., Warrenton, 63383.
Tel: 636-456-3698, Ext. 2; Fax: 636-456-6181; Email: racinel@holyrosarywm.com; Web: www.school.holyrosarywm.com. Lori Racine, Prin. Lay Teachers 13; Students 148.
Catechesis Religious Program—Students 75.

WASHINGTON, FRANKLIN CO.

1—ST. FRANCIS BORGIA CATHOLIC CHURCH (1834) [CEM]
115 Cedar St., Washington, 63090. Tel: 636-239-6701; Email: parish@borgiaparish.org; Email: jhill@borgiaparish.org; Web: www.borgiaparish.org. 310 W. Main St., Washington, 63090. Revs. Joseph E. Wormek, V.F.; Raymond D. Buehler; Kevin V. Schmittgens; Deacon Leon Noelker.
Res.: 311 W. 2nd St., Washington, 63090.
School—225 Cedar St., Washington, 63090.
Tel: 636-239-2590; Fax: 636-239-3501. Lay Teachers 24; Students 223.
Catechesis Religious Program—Tel: 636-239-2530; Email: kgulledge@borgiaparish.org. Kyra Gulledge, D.R.E. Students 62.

2—OUR LADY OF LOURDES CATHOLIC CHURCH, WASHINGTON (1958)
1014 Madison Ave., Washington, 63090-4806.
Tel: 636-239-3520; Email: rectory@ollwashmo.org; Web: www.ollwashmo.org. Rev. James D. Theby; Deacon Donald A. Elbert. In Res., Rev. Donald A. Glastetter, (Retired).
School—Our Lady of Lourdes Catholic School, 950 Madison Ave., Washington, 63090. Tel: 636-239-5292; Fax: 636-390-9050. Lay Teachers 13; Students 222.

WEINGARTEN, STE. GENEVIEVE CO., OUR LADY, HELP OF CHRISTIANS CATHOLIC CHURCH (1872) [CEM]
13370 Hwy. 32, Ste. Genevieve, 63670-9402.
Tel: 573-883-3796; Email: helpofchristians@hughes.net. Rev. Francis F. Koeninger.

WENTZVILLE, ST. CHARLES CO.

1—ST. GIANNA CATHOLIC CHURCH (2006)
450 E. Hwy. N., Wentzville, 63385.
Tel: 636-327-3639; Email: rschulte@stgiannaparish.org; Web: www.stgiannaparish.org. Rev. Timothy P. Elliott.
Res.: 460 E. Highway N., Lake Saint Louis, 63367.
Catechesis Religious Program—Students 120.

2—ST. PATRICK CATHOLIC CHURCH (1905) [CEM] [JC] Very Rev. Brian R. Fischer, V.F.; Rev. Daniel J. Kavanagh; Deacons Bernard A. Buckman; James P. Davies.
Res.: 405 S. Church St., Wentzville, 63385.
Tel: 636-332-9225; Fax: 636-332-6998.
School—St. Patrick Catholic School, (Grades PreSchool-8), 701 Church St., Wentzville, 63385.
Tel: 636-332-9913; Fax: 636-332-4877; Email: principal@stpatsch.org; Web: www.stpatrickwentzville.org. Mrs. Denise Brickler, Prin. Lay Teachers 28; Students 476.
Catechesis Religious Program—Tel: 636-332-9036. Students 360.

ZELL, STE. GENEVIEVE CO., ST. JOSEPH CATHOLIC CHURCH, ZELL (1845) [CEM] Rev. Msgr. Jeffrey N. Knight, V.F.
Res.: 11824 Zell Rd., Ste. Genevieve, 63670.
Tel: 573-883-3481; Email: stjozell@aptitudeinternet.com.
School—St. Joseph School, Tel: 573-883-5097. Lay Teachers 4; Students 21.
Catechesis Religious Program—Students 102.

Chaplains of Public Institutions

ST. LOUIS. *St. Anthony's Medical Center*, Tel: 314-525-1000. Rev. William Cardy, Chap.

Barnes - Jewish Hospital. Rev. Augustine Kizhakkedam, O.C.D., Chap., Tel: 314-747-3000.

Christian Hospital Northeast-Northwest, 11133 Dunn Rd., 63136. Tel: 314-653-5000 (Northeast); Tel: 314-953-6000 (Northwest). Rev. Raymund Iwuji, Chap.

Lambert - St. Louis International Airport.

Mercy Hospital St. Louis, Tel: 314-569-6000. Deacon Ken Potzman.

SSM Health DePaul Hospital. Rev. Lawrence F. Asma, C.M.

SSM Health St. Mary's Hospital, Tel: 314-768-8000. Vacant.

ST. CHARLES. *SSM Health St. Joseph Hospital - St. Charles*, St. Charles. Tel: 636-946-6641. Rev. Msgr. Raymond A. Hampe, (Retired), Tel: 636-947-5000.

WASHINGTON. *Mercy Hospital Washington*, Washington. Tel: 636-239-8000.

Special Assignment:

Revs.—

Aten, Robert L., 20542 Echo Valley Rd., Rocky Mount, 65072. Tel: 573-648-2467

Braun, Gary G., Catholic Student Center, Washington University, St. Louis

Doyle, Dennis M., J.C.L., Chap., 10341 Manchester Rd., Kirkwood, 63122

Heil, John P., S.S.D., 620 Michigan Ave. N.E., Washington, DC 20069

Krahman, Philip G., 10 Archbishop May Dr., 63119

Muenks, Nicholas J., Catholic University of America

O'Brien, John J., Faculty, St. John Seminary, Archdiocese of Los Angeles

O'Connor, Andrew, Chap., 2 Nazareth Ln., Saint Louis, 63129

Sullivan, Conor M., Catholic Student Center, University of Maryland, College Park, MD.

On Duty Outside the Archdiocese:

Rev. Msgr.—

Mesa, Luis, Colombia, South America

Revs.—

Driscoll, Patrick J., Archdiocese of San Francisco

Hayden, Patrick T., La Paz, Bolivia

Kirsch, Gregory G., Irvine, CA

Kopfensteiner, Thomas R., Englewood, CO

Means, David A., Chamois, MO

Michler, James R., La Paz, Bolivia

Seiler, Christopher M., Rome.

Military Chaplains:

Revs.—

Breig, Gary R.

Kirchhoefer, Thomas A.

Ramatowski, Edward F.

On Medical Leave:

Rev.—

Vowels, G. Timothy.

On Leave of Absence:

Rev.—

Houser, Michael J.

Retired:

Rev. Msgrs.—

Baker, Joseph W., (Retired), 3200 Southern Aire Pl., 63125

Buchheit, Jerome J., (Retired), 10 Archbishop May Dr., Shrewsbury, 63119

Dempsey, Thomas J., (Retired), 5800 Oleatha Ave., Saint Louis, 63139

Griesedieck, Edmund O., (Retired), 5200 Glennon Dr., 63119

Hampe, Raymond A., (Retired), 1424 S. First Capitol Dr., Saint Charles, 63301

Hanson, James E., (Retired), 10021 Grouse Rd., Cadet, 63630

Hickel, John J., (Retired), 10341 Manchester Rd., Saint Louis, 63122

Jovanovic, Robert P., (Retired), Mary, Queen of Peace, 676 W. Lockwood, Webster Groves, 63119

Leach, William J., (Retired), 4900 Ringer Rd., Saint Louis, 63129

McCarthy, Robert, (Retired), 6825 Natural Bridge Rd., Saint Louis, 63121

O'Laughlin, Patrick J., (Retired), 1046 Silo Bend Dr., Wentzville, 63385

Pieper, James E., (Retired), 51 Muirfield, Saint Louis, 63141

Schmidt, Gregory L., (Retired), 243 W. Argonne Dr., Saint Louis, 63122

Schneider, Nicholas A., (Retired), 6333 S. Rosebury Ave. 2W, Clayton, 63105

Schramm, Donald C., (Retired), 601 N. Fourth St., Saint Charles, 63301

Sudekum, Edward J., (Retired), 63119

Telthorst, James T., V.F., (Retired), 7601 Watson Rd., Saint Louis, 63119

Unger, John M., (Retired), 1575 N. Woodlawn Ave., Warson Woods, 63122

Whited, Walter M., (Retired), 10 Archbishop May Dr., 63119

Revs.—

Argent, Robert W., (Retired), 10 Archbishop May Dr., 63119

Baier, William J., (Retired), 10 Archbishop May Dr., Saint Louis, 63119

Banken, Robert L., (Retired), 10 Archbishop May Dr., Saint Louis, 63119

Bendel, Eugene F., (Retired), 10 Archbishop May Dr., 63119

Brennan, Eugene P., (Retired), 1365 Harkee Dr., Florissant, 63031

Brennan, George P., (Retired), 300 N. Fourth St., #901, 63102

Bryon, Thomas C., (Retired), 1 Hawthorne Estates S., 63131

Buhr, Donald L., (Retired), 10 Archbishop May Dr., Saint Louis, 63119

Burgoon, Charles E., (Retired), Regina Cleri, 6825 Natural Bridge Rd., 63121

Chochol, Ronald C., (Retired), P.O. Box 210911, Saint Louis, 63121

Creason, Richard H., (Retired)

Deister, Charles C., (Retired), 10341 Manchester Rd., 63122

Doyle, Dennis J., (Retired), 415 Weidman Rd., Manchester, 63011

Dyer, James W., (Retired), 5145 B Nova Ln., Perryville, 63775

Edwards, James T., (Retired), 10 Archbishop May Dr., 63119

Everding, Richard F., (Retired), 10341 Manchester Rd., 63122

Foley, Timothy M., (Retired), 2300 Church Rd., Arnold, 63010

Gahan, James L., (Retired), 4112 McClay Rd., Saint Louis, 63304

Gebelein, Gary M., V.F., (Retired), 9814 Huntingdon Ln., Saint Louis, 63123

Heim, Edward L., (Retired), 655 Loyola Dr., Florissant, 63031

Heimos, Robert L., (Retired), P.O. Box 85, Gray Summit, 63039

Heman, Richard J., (Retired), 450 E. Lockwood, Apt. 104, Webster Groves, 63119

Hughes, John Jay, (Retired), 10341 Manchester Rd., 63122

Johnson, John J., (Retired), 11910 Eddie & Park Rd., 63126

Kasznel, Richard C., (Retired), Regina Cleri, 10 Archbishop May Dr., Saint Louis, 63119

Kester, William J., (Retired), Regina Cleri, 10 Archbishop May Dr., 63119

Kleba, Gerald J., (Retired), 3914 Botanical Ave., Saint Louis, 63110

Knoll, Urban H., (Retired), 723 1st Capito Dr., St. Charles, 63301

Kovalcin, John, (Retired), 27 Glenwood Dr., Saint Louis, 63026

Lampert, Robert E., (Retired), 9321 Kathi Creek Dr., Colorado Springs, CO 80924

Lane, Robert C., (Retired), 100 Timber Creek Dr., O'Fallon, 63368

Leibrecht, Robert G., (Retired), 10 Archbishop May Dr., 63119

Lewis, Leo T., (Retired), 73 Kings Rd., Evergreen, CO 80439

Liss, Robert C., (Retired), 10 Archbishop May Dr., 63119

Mahoney, Kevin J., (Retired)

Mannion, Martin K., (Retired), 3225 N. Florissant, Saint Louis, 63107

Mattler, Albert A., (Retired), 10 Archbishop May Dr., 63119

Mayer, John L., (Retired), 4200 Delor St., Lake St. Louis, 63116

Meier, Gerald A., V.F., (Retired), 3130 Parkwood Ln., Maryland Heights, 63043

Menner, Robert J., (Retired), 10 Archbishop Dr., Saint Louis, 63119

Meyer, Frederick A., (Retired), 324 S. 3rd St., Saint Charles, 63301

Molitor, Donald F., (Retired), 10341 Manchester Rd., 63122

Mulvihill, Martin J., (Retired), 6825 Natural Bridge Rd., Saint Louis, 63121

Novak, David A., (Retired), 10 Archbishop May Dr., 63119

Parisi, Joseph L., J.C.L., (Retired)

Robertson, Thomas M., (Retired), 10 Archbishop May Dr., Saint Louis, 63119

Rosebrough, Robert T., (Retired), 146 Geneva Cove, Saint Louis, 63390

Rubbelke, Ronald J., (Retired), 10 Archbishop May Dr., 63119

Ryan, Patrick, (Retired), 1293 Poseidon Court, St. Peters, 63376

Sandweg, Michael J., Ph.D., (Retired), 1364 Haute Loire Dr., Manchester, 63011

Schloemer, Bernard J., (Retired), 10 Archbishop May Dr., 63119

Schneider, John H., (Retired), 434 Rue Bergerac, Bonne Terre, 63628

Selzer, Eugene P., (Retired), 10341 Manchester Rd., 63122

Sigmund, Andrew J., (Retired), 5020 Rhodes Ave., Saint Louis, 63109

Spielman, Paul J., (Retired), 6315 Weber Rd., Saint Louis, 63123

Sullivan, James M., (Retired), 13416 Olive Blvd., Saint Louis, 63017

Tillman, Richard J., (Retired), Bell Fountain Rd., P.O. Box 187, Cadet, 63630

Toohey, Timothy J., (Retired), Rodgersville, MO.

Utrup, Eugene E., (Retired), 22 Heather Dr., Saint Louis, 63123

Voelker, Harold H., (Retired), 10 Archbishop May Dr., 63119

Vogler, J. Edward, (Retired), 4330 Shreve Ave., Saint Louis, 63115

Wichlan, David L., (Retired), 10 Archbishop May Dr., Saint Louis, 63119

Wigand, William J., (Retired), 10 Archbishop May Dr., 63119

Wilkins, Bernard J., (Retired), 6535 Hwy. YY, Washington, 63090

Winzerling, James L., (Retired), 12685 Dorsett Rd., #228, Maryland Heights, 63043

Zinzer, Walter W., (Retired), 3310 McHenry, San Antonio, TX 78239.

Permanent Deacons:

Allen, Charles M., Sts. Teresa & Bridget, St. Louis

Amelotti, David, Our Lady of Providence, Crestwood; St. Mary's Health Center

Arthur, Paul J., St. Gerard Majella, Kirkwood

Ast, Christopher M., Immaculate Heart of Mary, New Melle; Permanent Diaconate Office

Bacher, Charles R., St. Matthias, St. Louis

Bansbach, Paul, (Retired)

Barbero, Dennis J., St. Rose Philippine Duchesne, Florissant; Elder Care Service, Northeast Deanery

Basler, James H., St. Agnes, Bloomsdale

Bast, Paul, Immaculate Conception, Dardenne Prairie

Becker, Gerald H., Immaculate Conception, Union

Beckmann, John W., St. John Paul II, Affton

Beirne, Edward R., St. Martin De Porres, Hazelwood

Belding, Patrick J., Christ, Prince of Peace, Manchester

Billing, David L., St. Joseph, Josephville

Birkenmaier, Robert G., (Retired)

Bischof, John A., St. Richard, Creve Coeur

Boedeker, C. Allen, St. Andrew, Lemay

Boland, Richard J., (Retired)

Boldt, Lawrence R., St. Peter, St. Charles, MO

Boyer, Edward J., (Retired)

Brancato, Michael G., St. John Paul II, Affton

Brindley, Joseph R., St. Vincent de Paul, Perryville

Broom, James E., St. Clare of Assisi, Ellisville

Broyles, Jimmy D., St. Joseph, Manchester

Brunton, Robert, St. Elizabeth Ann Seton, St. Charles

Buchek, Bradford M., (Retired)

Buckley, James Mike, (Retired)

Buckley, Michael L., St. Bernadette, Lemay

Buckman, Bernard A., St. Patrick, Wentzville

Burch, Michael D., Immaculate Conception, Park Hills

Burkard, Bruce A., Sacred Heart, Florissant; Magdala Foundation

Burke, Thomas A. III, St. Joseph, Cottleville

Burkemper, Thomas B., (Retired)

Burle, Raymond J. Jr., Holy Rosary, Warrenton

Butler, James R., (Retired)

Byington, Mark A., St. Joseph, Farmington

Camden, David M., St. Simon the Apostle, Green Park

Carroll, Kevin, (Serving Outside the Archdiocese)

Carter, James K., (Leave of Absence)

Casseau, William U., (Retired)

Chauvin, C. Frank, Ascension, Chesterfield

Chitwood, Dennis M., (Retired)

Clark, Lawrence L., (Serving Outside the Archdiocese)

Clemens, Kenneth C. Jr., (Retired)

Coffman, Richard W., (Retired)

Collins, Terrence C., St. Vincent de Paul, St. Louis

Conley, Allen M., (Retired)

Coppage, Michael J. Jr., (Retired)

Crafts, R. Paul, St. Paul, Fenton

Craska, Paul D., (Retired)
Curtin, John A., Cathedral Basilica of St. Louis
Dallas, Timothy H., St. Peter, St. Charles
Damato, Larry, (Retired)
Darin, John, St. Vincent de Paul, Perryville
Daugherty, G. Joseph, (Retired)
Daus, Andrew C., St. Margaret Mary Alacoque, Oakville; CJM - Potosi Correctional Center
Davanzo, Charles R., (Retired)
Davies, James P., St. Patrick, Wentzville
Dehler, Thomas F., (Retired)
DeNatale, James T., Holy Spirit, Maryland Heights
Denham, Donald C., St. Gerard Majella, Kirkwood
Dille, David P., Christ the King, University City
Dodson, Fred, (Retired)
Dolan, Timothy C., St. Gerard Majella, Kirkwood; SSM St. Clare Health Center
Donnelly, Daniel R., St. Joseph, Manchester
Driscoll, Donald L., (Retired)
Duban, Matthew E., Holy Name of Jesus, Bissell Hills
Dubbs, Harvey, (Retired)
DuFaux, John C., St. Francis of Assisi, Oakville
Dunn, Timothy L., Our Lady, Festus
Durban, Charles, St. Anselm, Creve Coeur
Ecker, Alan E., (Retired)
Elbert, Donald A., Our Lady of Lourdes, Washington
Eultgen, Thomas L., Most Sacred Heart, Eureka
Ewing, David G., St. Ann, Clover Bottom; St. Gertrude, Krakow
Ewing, David W., St. Elizabeth Ann Seton, St. Charles
Falbo, Anthony, Immaculate Heart of Mary, New Melle
Fehner, Leo S., Most Sacred Heart, Eureka
Felber, David A., St. Norbert, Florissant
Fink, George Russ, (Retired)
Flanigan, John P. Jr., Parish Life Coord., Immaculate Conception, Maplewood
Follen, Dale J., St. Michael the Archangel, Shrewsbury; Permanent Diaconate Office
Forster, Thomas E., (Retired)
Fragale, Joseph A., St. Ambrose, Saint Louis
Fronick, Edward C., St. Martin of Tours, Lemay
Funke, Donald J. Jr., Incarnate Word, Chesterfield
G'Sell, James R., St. Anthony of Padua, High Ridge
Gawedzinkski, Norbert L., (Retired)
Gearon, William A., (Retired)
Geiser, Gerald J., (Retired)
Gerling, Thomas J., Our Lady, Queen of Peace, House Springs
Germain, Carl J., St. Mary of Perpetual Help, Moselle; St. James, Catawissa
Gettemeier, Herbert B., (Retired)
Gildehaus, Charles R., St. Gertrude, Krakow
Gorski, Thomas, Sts. Peter and Paul, St. Louis
Gottlieb, Thomas J., Church of the Annunziata, Ladue
Gounis, Peter E., (Retired)
Graham, Daniel K., St. Elizabeth Ann Seton, St. Charles; Elder Care Service, St. Charles Deanery
Griffard, James M., St. Francis Xavier, Saint Louis
Groner, H. Wayne, Assumption, New Haven; St. Paul, Berger
Grotpeter, Edward R., St. Augustine, St. Louis, MO
Guilford, Mark A., (Leave of Absence)
Gunsaullus, Roland J., (Retired)
Haehnel, Fred M., St. Peter, St. Charles
Harpring, David I., Parish Life Coord., St. Rita, Vinita Park
Harrison, R. Fielding, (Retired)
Hartz, Joseph A., Sts. Joachim and Ann, St. Charles; St. Joseph Hospital, St. Charles
Hayes, Ralph, (Retired)
Hecktor, Paul J., St. Ignatius Loyola, Concord Hill
Heithaus, J. John, Sacred Heart, Florissant
Hengen, Philip R., Washington University, Newman Center
Henke, Daniel L., Holy Infant, Ballwin
Henning, Kenneth A., (Retired)
Henroid, Daniel H., St. Joan of Arc, St. Louis
Hivner, John W., (Retired)
Hoefl, James P., St. Gabriel the Archangel, St. Louis
Hofmann, John G., St. Sabina, Florissant
Holmes, Charles E., (Retired)
Holmes, Ronald A., (Leave of Absence)
Holtmeyer, Gilbert C., (Retired)
Howe, Randy C., Mary, Mother of the Church, Mattese
Hurlbert, Gerald R., (Retired)
Iovanna, Joseph, Dir., St. John Nepomuk Chapel, Saint Louis
Jaeger, Mark J., St. Justin Martyr, Sunset Hills
Johnson, Leslie A., (Retired)
Johnson, William P., St. Rose Philippine Duchesne, Florissant
Jurek, Thomas F., (Serving Outside the Archdiocese)
Kaiser, Roland G., (Retired)
Kaufman, Scott C., Holy Spirit, Maryland Heights
Keeney, Robert J., Ascension, Chesterfield
Kiefer, William A., (Serving Outside the Archdiocese)
Kiely, Edward Ray, Christ the King, University City
King, Philip, St. Robert Bellarmine, St. Charles
Kintz, Donald, St. Joseph, Imperial
Knight, Brian K., St. Mary of Perpetual Help, Moselle; St. James, Catawissa
Knobbe, Gerald E., All Saints, St. Peters
Komotos, John W., St. Peter, Kirkwood
Kroutil, Joseph C., St. Angela Merici, Florissant
La Martina, Joseph A., (Retired)
LaBozzetta, Walter F., St. Cletus, St. Charles
Lackas, Kirk A., St. Patrick, Wentzville
Lauterwasser, Gerard M., St. Sabina, Florissant
Le Fors, Ronald S., (Serving Outside the Archdiocese)
Lee, Samuel, All Souls, Overland; St. Jude, Overland
Lemoine, David E., (Retired)
Leonardo, Delfin S., St. Joseph, Clayton; Mercy Hospital
LePage, Brett C., Immaculate Conception, Dardenne Prairie
Lipin, A. John, Sts. Joachim & Ann, St. Charles
Litteken, James J., (Retired)
Loeffler, Kurt S., Queen of All Saints, Oakville
Lombardo, Charles W., (Retired)
Love, Allen F., Blessed Teresa of Calcutta, Ferguson
Mallon, Keith G., St. Alban Roe, Wildwood
Maranan, Diosdado L., (Retired)
Marino, John, Ascension, Chesterfield
Marischen, Robert J., St. Paul, St. Paul
Martin, James P., St. Monica, Creve Coeur; Airport Chaplaincy
Martin, Leroy A. Jr., (Retired)
Martin, Paul A., Church of the Good Shepherd, Hillsboro
Maune, Randall W., St. John the Baptist, Gildehaus
Maxwell, Perez E., (Leave of Absence)
Mayo, Robert J. II, (Leave of Absence)
McCarthy, Mark J., St. Cletus, St. Charles
McCruden, Patrick, St. Pius V, Saint Louis
McElroy, Donald L., St. Charles Borromeo, St. Charles
McEntire, Clyde W., (Retired)
McGuire, Jerry N., (Retired)
McKee, Paul R., Ph.D., (Retired)
Meere, John F., (Retired)
Meiergerd, Joseph C., St. Robert Bellarmine, St. Charles
Meinert, Dennis M., St. Francis Borgia, Washington
Meister, William G., Assumption, Mattese
Menard, Louis A., (Retired)
Meyerkord, Gary A., All Saints, St. Peters
Michaelree, Timothy G., St. Alban Roe, Wildwood
Miller, George A., St. Joseph, Manchester
Miller, George W., (Retired)
Miller, Kevin R., St. Anthony, Sullivan
Miller, Millard Ray, (Retired)
Minicky, John S., St. Gianna, Wentzville
Moeller, Steven G., St. Charles Borromeo, St. Charles
Monahan, Patrick G., Cure of Ars, Shrewsbury
Moore, Richard R., (Retired)
Mulvihill, Thomas O., Mary, Queen of Peace, Webster Groves
Murphey, James W. Jr., Immaculate Heart of Mary, St. Louis
Murphy, James L., (Retired)
Murray, Stephen L., Holy Redeemer, Webster Groves
Naumann, Eugene J., (Retired), Holy Spirit, Maryland Heights
Nava, Lawrence, St. John the Beloved Disciple, Imperial
Nesbitt, Frank E., (Retired)
Nicolai, Michael A., St. James the Greater, St. Louis
Noelker, Leon R., St. Francis Borgia, Washington
Nuelle, Norman C., (Retired)
O'Hara, John J., St. John Bosco, Creve Coeur
O'Neail, Matthew M., St. Rose of Lima, DeSoto
Olmsted, Francis J., St. Cletus, St. Charles; DeSmet Jesuit High School
Orr, Robert J., St. Margaret Mary Alacoque, Oakville
Osmack, David, St. Luke the Evangelist, Richmond Heights
Pacino, David, St. Martin De Porres, Hazelwood
Penberthy, Robert S., (Retired)
Perez, Jorge A., St. Charles Borromeo, St. Charles
Peterson, Gary, Sacred Heart, Valley Park
Peterson, Stanley M. Jr., (Retired)
Pimmel, Terrance, (Leave of Absence)
Piva, Michael J., St. Joseph, Cottleville
Politte, Glennon P. Sr., (Retired)
Politte, Stephen A., (Retired)
Politte, Thomas J., St. David, Arnold
Potzman, Kenneth M., Mercy Hospital
Powers, James R., Ph.D., Holy Infant, Ballwin
Preiss, William A., St. Mary Magdalen, Brentwood
Prideaux, Frank W., (Retired)
Priesmeyer, William F. Jr., Holy Trinity, St. Ann
Quinn, J. Gerard, Senior Deacon, (Serving Outside the Archdiocese)
Quistorff, Richard, (Serving Outside the Archdiocese)
Raidt, Daniel A., Church of the Good Shepard, Hillsboro
Rankin, Patrick J., St. Theodore, Flint Hill
Renard, Richard L., St. Peter, Kirkwood
Reuther, Ronald Lee, Incarnate Word, Chesterfield
Rivera, Manolo D., St. Robert Bellarimine, St. Charles
Roberson, Robert L., (Retired)
Robert, James M., Ste. Genevieve, Ste. Genevieve
Rodis, Theodore J., (Retired)
Rohaly, Ernest G., (Retired)
Rosenkoetter, Richard H., St. Mark, Saint Louis
Rothermich, Thomas N., (Serving Outside the Archdiocese)
Russell, James W., (Leave of Absence)
Ryder, Charles T., Assumption, Mattese
Scarry, William L., Sts. Joachim and Ann, St. Charles
Schaefer, David M., Assumption, Mattese
Schaeffer, Eugene W. III, St. Joseph, Cottleville
Schardan, Scott D., St. David, Arnold
Schellhase, Richard H., Queen of All Saints, Oakville
Schiffer, John, St. Robert Bellarmine, St. Charles
Schiller, Thomas A., Seven Holy Founders, Affton
Schisler, Steven M., Immaculate Conception, Arnold
Schmierbach, Mark L., Holy Rosary, Warrenton
Schmitt, Daniel F., Immaculate Conception, Dardenne Prairie
Schmitt, Donald J., (Retired)
Schultheis, Glennon J., (Retired)
Schultz, Timothy, Sts. Joachim and Ann, St. Charles; Cardinal Ritter Institute
Selsor, Brian T., St. Joseph, Imperial
Seveska, Richard A., (Retired)
Shannon, John R., (Retired)
Sigillito, James, St. Anselm, Creve Coeur
Sinak, William S., (Retired)
Sisul, Leonard A., St. John Paul II, Affton; St. Mary's Heath Center
Skillman, Daniel, Our Lady of Sorrows, St. Louis
Smerek, Robert S., Mary Mother of the Church, Mattese
Smith, George J., St. Clare of Assisi, Ellisville; Queen of Peace Center
Smith, Randall G., St. John the Baptist, Gildehaus
Snyder, Charles R., Sacred Heart, Valley Park
Snyder, Robert J., (Retired)
Sommer, Carl J., St. Monica, Creve Coeur
Stackle, Paul F., St. Simon the Apostle, Green Park
Stallings, Larry J., (Retired)
Stevens, Richard L., St. Anthony of Padua, High Ridge
Stigall, Donald R., (Retired)
Stovall, Dennis K., Sts. Peter & Paul, Saint Louis; Disabled Ministry, Mission Work
Stoverink, Gerard G., Sacred Heart, Crystal City
Stoverink, John J., Cathedral Basilica, St. Louis
Strauss, Harold A., (Retired)
Streckfuss, Joseph C., (Retired)
Suden, Michael E., D.D.S., St. Bridget of Kildare, Pacific
Sulze, Joseph W., (Retired)
Tadlock, Richard, Assumption, O'Fallon
Tetreault, James E., (Retired)
Towey, Martin G., Ph.D., (Retired)
Trani, Lee W., St. Clare of Assisi, Ellisville
Turek, Paul J. Sr., Our Lady, Queen of Peace, House Springs
Tustanowsky, Frederick S., Our Lady of the Pillar, St. Louis
Twellman, William H., St. Norbert, Florissant; Parish Lif Coord., St. Francis of Assisi, Portage des Souix; Immaculate Conception, West Alton.
Vehige, Richard J., St. Clement of Rome, Des Peres
Volansky, Fred N., Assumption, O'Fallon
Volansky, James M., (Retired)
Vonesh, Frank, (Serving Outside the Archdiocese)
Walbridge, William F., (Retired)
Waldschmidt, Patrick G., Our Lady of Lourdes, University City; Elder Care in SW Deanery
Walker, Donald J., Immaculate Conception, Arnold
Warren, Phillip C., St. Bernadette, Lemay
Watson, George H., Holy Name of Jesus, Bissel Hills
Weatherholt, H. John, (Retired)
Weishaar, Lonnie G., Immaculate Conception, Dardenne Prairie
Weiss, William G., St. Mary Magdalen, St. Louis
Westhoff, Neal R., Immaculate Conception, Old Monroe
Wheadon, Patrick M., Our Lady of Providence, Crestwood
Whitson, Alan W., Most Sacred Heart, Eureka

Wientge, Joseph M., Mary, Queen of Peace, Webster Groves
Wild, Trevor J. Sr., St. Clare, St. Clair
Willbrand, Thomas J., (Retired)
Williams, Albert C., (Retired)
Willis, David J., St. Gabriel the Archangel, St. Louis
Wingbermuehle, Joseph, Queen of All Saints, Oakville
Winkelmann, Christian H., (Retired)
Witte, H. Matthew, Ste. Genevieve du Bois, Warson Woods; Cathedral Basilica of St. Louis
Wolffer, John Robert, St. Joseph, Imperial
Wood, Robert A., (Serving Outside the Archdiocese)
Woods, Timothy J., St. Catherine Laboure, Sappington
Young, Stephen J., (Serving ouside the Archdiocese).

INSTITUTIONS LOCATED IN DIOCESE

[A] SEMINARIES, ARCHDIOCESAN

ST. LOUIS. *Kenrick-Glennon Seminary* (1818) (St. Louis Roman Catholic Theological Seminary) 5200 Glennon Dr., 63119. Tel: 314-792-6100; Fax: 314-792-6500; Email: marshafeingold@kenrick.edu; Web: www.kenrick.edu. Marsha Feingold, Archivist.

Kenrick School of Theology, 5200 Glennon Dr., 63119. Tel: 314-792-6100; Fax: 314-792-6500; Email: marshafeingold@kenrick.edu; Web: www.kenrick.edu. Rev. James Mason, Rector & Pres.; Rev. Msgr. Gregory R. Mikesch, Vice-Rector for Formation; Rev. Jason J. Schumer, Vice Rector; Rev. Msgrs. Edmund O. Griesedieck, Assoc. Spiritual Dir., (Retired); James J. Ramacciotti, J.C.L., Canon Law; Revs. Michael J. Witt, Assoc. Prof. Church History; Kristian C. Teater, Asst. Prof. Spiritual Theology; Donald T. Anstoetter, Dir. Worship; Paul Hoesing, Dean Seminarians; Mark Kramer, S.J., Dir. Spiritual Formation; Very Rev. Thomas M. Molini, M.A., V.F., Dir.; Dr. Susanne M. Harvath, Ph.D., Dir.; Dr. Lawrence Feingold, Assoc. Prof. Theology & Philosophy; Dr. Lawrence J. Welch, Ph.D., Prof. Systematic Theology; Mr. Jeffrey Wisniewski, Dir. Sacred Music; Revs. Edward Ahn, A.V.I., Spiritual Dir.; Donald E. Henke, D.Th.M., Assoc. Prof.; Mirco Sosio, A.V.I., Spiritual Dir.; Dr. Andrew Chronister, Assoc. Prof.; Dr. Shawn Welch, Prof.; Rev. Fadi Thomas M. Auro, Asst. Prof.; Dr. Randall Colton, Prof.; Dr. John Finley, Prof.; Most Rev. Robert J. Hermann, D.D., Spiritual Dir., (Retired); Revs. Scott Jones, S.D.S., Spiritual Advisor; Charles K. Samson, Prof.; Dr. Edward Hogan, Dean; Ms. Mary Ann Aubin, Librarian. Lay Staff 9; Priests 15; Sisters 1; Students 89; St. Louis Students 26.

Cardinal Glennon College, 5200 Glennon Dr., 63119. Tel: 314-792-6100; Fax: 314-792-6500. Rev. Christopher M. Martin, Vice Rector, Cardinal Glennon College & Assoc. Prof.; Dr. Randall Colton, Asst. Prof. Philosophy/Assoc. Academic Dean; Dr. John Finley, Assoc. Prof. Philosophy; Ms. Mary Ann Aubin, Library Dir. & Asst. Prof. Lay Teachers 5; Students 33; St. Louis Students 20; Permanent Staff: Priests 10.

[B] SEMINARIES, RELIGIOUS, OR SCHOLASTICATES

ST. LOUIS. *Aquinas Institute of Theology*, 23 S. Spring Ave., 63108. Tel: 314-256-8800; Fax: 314-256-8888; Email: info@ai.edu; Web: www.ai.edu. Revs. Seán Martin, Pres.; Gregory J. Heille, O.P., Vice Pres. & Academic Dean; Thomas Barbarak, Business Mgr.; David Werthmann, Dir. Admissions; Erin Hammond, Registrar; Very Rev. Jay M. Harrington, O.P., Regent, Studies & Assoc. Dean, Academic. Priests 7; Sisters 3; Lay Faculty & Administrative Staff 19.

Faculty: Michael Anthony Abril; Revs. Leobardo Almazan, O.P.; Harry M. Byrne, O.P., Emeritus; George R. Boudreau, O.P.; Donald Goergen, O.P., Ph.D., S.T.M.; Kevin Stevens, O.P.; Sisters Jean deBlois, C.S.J., Emeritus; Colleen Mary Mallon, O.P.; Honora Werner, O.P.; Juliet Mousseau, R.S.C.J.; Carla Mae Streeter, O.P., Emeritus; Thomas Bushlack, Ph.D.; Hsin-Hsin Huang; Kathleen Tehan, Librarian; Marian Love; Carolyn Wright; Stacey Krieg, Dir. Institutional Advancement; Jan Lingua, Dir. Communications; Dan Moore, Dir. IT; Kevin Sweeney, Dir. Student Svcs.

[C] COLLEGES AND UNIVERSITIES

ST. LOUIS. *Fontbonne University* (1923) 6800 Wydown Blvd., 63105. Tel: 314-862-3456; Fax: 314-889-1451; Email: smccaslin@fontbonne.edu; Web: www.fontbonne.edu. J. Michael Pressimone, Ed.D., Pres.; Sharon McCaslin, Ph.D., Librarian. Lay Teachers 80; Sisters 1; Students 1,534.

Saint Louis University (1818) Corporate Title: Saint Louis University, One North Grand Blvd., St. Louis, MO 63103 One North Grand Blvd., DuBourg Hall, Rm. 100, 63103. Tel: 800-758-3678; Fax: 314-977-7136; Email: admission@slu.edu; Web: www.slu.edu. 3634 Lindell Blvd., Verhaegen Hall, Rm. 315, 63108. Tel: 314-977-2223; Fax: 314-977-3079. Joseph Conran, Chm. Bd. of Trustees; Fred P. Pestello, Ph.D., Pres.; Nancy Brickhouse, Ph.D., Provost; Philip O. Alderson, M.D., Vice Pres. Medical Affairs. Brothers 1; Lay Teachers 2,069; Priests 22; Total Enrollment 12,914; Total Staff 2,917.

Vice Presidents: David Heimburger, Vice Pres. & CFO; Jeff L. Fowler, Vice Pres. Mktg. & Communications; William R. Kauffman, J.D., Vice Pres. & Gen. Counsel; Michael J. Luna, J.D., Vice Pres. Human Resources; Kent Porterfield, Ed.D., Vice Pres. Student Devel.; David Hakanson, M.B.A., Vice Pres., Chief Information Officer; Sheila M. Manion, Vice Pres. Devel.; Kenneth A. Olliff, Vice Pres. Research; Jay W. Goff, M.A., Vice Pres., Enrollment & Retention Mgmt.; Michael Lucido, Assoc. Vice Pres. Facilities Svcs.; Robert Wood, Ph.D., Assoc. Provost, Academic Affairs.

Deans:
Doisy College of Health Sciences, Tel: 314-977-8501; Fax: 314-977-8503. Mardell A. Wilson, Ed.D., R.D., L.D.N., Dean.
Arts and Sciences, College of, Tel: 314-977-2710; Fax: 314-977-3649. Christopher Duncan, Ph.D., Dean; Rev. Theodore Vitali, O.P.
John Cook School of Business, Tel: 314-977-3800; Fax: 314-977-1412. Mark M. Higgins, Ph.D., C.P.A., Dean.
School of Law, 100 N. Tucker Ave., Scott Hall, 63101. Tel: 314-977-2800; Fax: 314-977-1464. Michael A. Wolff, J.D., Dean.
School of Medicine, Tel: 314-977-9870; Fax: 314-977-9899. Philip O. Alderson, M.D., Dean.
School of Nursing, Tel: 314-977-8900; Fax: 314-977-8950. Teri A. Murray, Ph.D., R.N., A.P.H.N.-B.C., F.A.A.N., Dean.
Parks College of Engineering, Aviation and Technology, Tel: 314-977-8283; Fax: 314-977-8403. Michelle B. Sabick, Ph.D., Dean.
College of Philosophy and Letters, Tel: 314-977-3827 ; Fax: 314-977-3696. Bro. William R. Rehg, S.J., Dean.
School for Professional Studies, Tel: 800-734-6736; Tel: 314-977-2330; Fax: 314-977-2333. Jennifer Giancola, Ph.D., Interim Dean.
College for Public Health & Social Justice, Tel: 314-977-8100; Fax: 314-977-6310. Collin O. Airhihenbuwa, M.P.H., Dean.
School of Education, Tel: 314-977-3292; Fax: 314-977-3290. Ann Rule, Ph.D., Interim Dean.
Retention and Academic Success, Tel: 314-977-3484 Frost Campus; Tel: 314-977-8992 Medical Campus; Fax: 314-977-3486 Frost Campus; Fax: 314-977-8757 Medical Campus. Lisa B. Israel, Dir. Student Success Center.
Pius XII Memorial Library, Tel: 314-977-3095; Fax: 314-977-3587. David Cassens, M.A., T.M.L.S., Dean Univ. Libraries.
Madrid Spain Campus, Tel: 314-977-3445; Fax: 314-977-3412; Tel: 1+34-915 54 58 58, Ext. 207 (Intl. Phone); Fax: +1+34-915 54 62 02 (Intl. Fax). Paul A. Vita, Ph.D., Dean & Dir.
Center for Advanced Dental Education, Tel: 314-977-8363; Fax: 314-977-8617. John F. Hatton, D.M.D., Exec. Dir.
Albert Gnaegi Center for Health Care Ethics, Tel: 314-977-1060; Fax: 314-977-5150. Jeffrey P. Bishop, M.D., Ph.D., Dir.
Center for Outcomes Research, Tel: 314-977-9300; Fax: 314-977-1101. Thomas Burroughs, Ph.D., Exec. Dir.
Center for Sustainability, Tel: 314-977-3608; Fax: 314-977-5155. Jason Knouft, Ph.D., Interim Dean.

Other Jesuits Associated with the University: Revs. John A. Apel, S.J.; Michael D. Barber, S.J.; Richard Buhler, S.J.; James J. Burshek, S.J.; Christopher S. Collins, S.J.; David J. Corrigan, S.J.; Kevin L. Cullen, S.J.; Anthony C. Daly, S.J.; J. Daniel Daly, S.J.; Terrence E. Dempsey, S.J.; Donald Highberger, S.J.; Michael K. May, S.J.; David V. Meconi, S.J.; Robert E. Murphy, S.J.; Mr. Ronald R. O'Dwyer, S.J.; Revs. James M. O'Leary, S.J.; Albert C. Rotola, S.J.; Francis X. Ryan, S.J.; Steven A. Schoenig, S.J.; James A. Sebesta, S.J.; Daniel P. White, S.J.; Bro. William R. Rehg, S.J.

Pastoral Care Dept. of SSM Health Saint Louis University Hospital: M. Cristina Stevens, B.C.C., B.C.C., Dir. Pastoral Care & Educ.; Sr. Joyce Williams, O.P., B.C.C., Staff Chap; Rev. Rob Hartmann, B.C.C., Mgr., Pastoral Care Svcs.; Jennifer Tummond, Admin. Asst.; Susan Burke Kellett, B.C.C., Staff Chap; Thomas Sanger, B.C.C., Staff Chap.; Bob Crecelius, Staff Chap.; John Cline, Staff Chap.; Rev. K'Lynne McKinley, D.Min., Supervisory Educ. Res.; Brian Mason, Chap. Res.; Mary Brutcher, Office Asst.; Teresa Sullivan, B.C.C., Staff Chap.

[D] RELIGIOUS EDUCATION

ST. LOUIS. *Paul VI Institute of Catechetical and Pastoral Studies*, 20 Archbishop May Dr., 63119. Tel: 314-792-7450; Fax: 314-792-7459; Email: paul6@archstl.org; Web: www.archstl.org/paul6. Dr. Barbara Blackburn, Interim Dir.; Mary L. Beier, Registrar - Business Mgr.; Patrick Iver, Technology Coord. Lay Teachers 20; Priests 2; Sisters 2; Total Enrollment 689.

[E] HIGH SCHOOLS, ARCHDIOCESAN

ST. LOUIS. *Bishop DuBourg High School* (1950) 5850 Eichelberger St., 63109. Tel: 314-832-3030; Fax: 314-832-0529; Email: dschnable@bishopdubourg.org; Web: www.bishopdubourg.org. Rev. Michael J. Lydon, Pres.; Dr. Bridget Timoney, Prin. A Co-Educational School Staffed by Diocesan Priests, Religious and Lay Teachers. Deacons 1; Lay Teachers 30; Priests 1; Students 325.

Cardinal Ritter College Prep, 701 N. Spring, 63108. Tel: 314-446-5501; Fax: 314-446-5570; Email: chall@archstl.org; Web: info.csd.org/ritter.htm. Leon Henderson, Pres.; Michael R. Blackshear, Prin.; Christine Turland, Librarian. Co-Educational High School Staffed by Religious and Laity. Lay Teachers 25; Priests 1; Sisters 1; Students 315.

Saint Mary's High School (1931) 4701 S. Grand Blvd., 63111. Tel: 314-481-8400; Fax: 314-481-3670; Email: mainoffice@stmaryshs.com; Web: www.stmaryshs.com. Mr. Michael F. England, Pres.; Mr. Kevin Hacker, B.A., M.Ed., Prin.; Matt Purcell, Librarian. For boys. Lay Teachers 30; Total Enrollment 342.

Rosati-Kain High School (1911) 4389 Lindell Blvd., 63108-2701. Tel: 314-533-8513; Fax: 314-533-1618; Email: rkoffice@rosati-kain.org; Web: www.rosati-kain.org. Sr. Joan Andert, S.S.N.D., Pres.; Elizabeth Ann Goodwin, Pres.; Terence McNamee, Prin. Conducted for Girls by the Archdiocese of St. Louis, the Sisters of St. Joseph and the School Sisters of Notre Dame. Girls 290; Lay Teachers 30; Sisters 1.

Trinity Catholic High School (2002) 1720 Redman Rd., 63138. Tel: 314-741-1333; Fax: 314-741-1335; Email: office@trinitycatholichigh.org; Web: www.trinitycatholichighschool.org. Mrs. Kristen Shipp, Prin. Lay Teachers 33; Sisters 1; Students 338.

FESTUS. *St. Pius X High School*, 1030 St. Pius Dr., Festus, 63028. Tel: 636-937-3695; Tel: 636-931-7488; Fax: 636-931-7487; Email: lancer@stpius.com; Web: stpius.com. Mrs. Karen DeCosty, Prin. A Co-Educational High School Conducted by Diocesan Priests and Lay Faculty. Lay Teachers 23; Priests 2; Students 278.

O'FALLON. *St. Dominic High School* (1962) 31 St. Dominic Dr., O'Fallon, 63366. Tel: 636-240-8303; Fax: 636-240-9884; Email: mainoffice@stdominichs.org; Web: www.stdominichs.org. Sr. Mary H. Bender, S.S.N.D., Pres.; Cathy Fetter, Prin.; Mary Fridley, Librarian. A co-educational high school conducted by diocesan priests, laymen and laywomen. Lay Teachers 54; Priests 1; Sisters 1; Students 707.

ST. CHARLES. *Duchesne High School*, 2550 Elm St., St. Charles, 63301-1494. Tel: 636-946-6767; Fax: 636-946-6267; Email: cnolan@duchesne-hs.org; Web: www.duchesne-hs.org. Charles L. Nolan Jr., Pres.; Frederick Long, Prin.; Kristina Radley, Campus Min. A Co-Educational College Prep High School Conducted by Archdiocesan Priests and Catholic Lay Staff. Under the Auspices of the Catholic Education Office and the Archdiocese of St. Louis. Lay Teachers 30; Priests 1; Students 307.

WASHINGTON. *St. Francis Borgia Regional High School* (1982) 1000 Borgia Dr., Washington, 63090. Tel: 636-239-7871; Fax: 636-239-1198; Email: mtraffas@borgia.com; Web: www.borgia.com. Marilyn Traffas, Admin.; Mr. George Wingbermuehle, Prin.; Rebecca Price, Librarian. A Co-Educational High School Staffed by Diocesan Priests and dedicated lay faculty. Lay Teachers 41; Priests 1; Sisters 1; Students 545.

[F] HIGH SCHOOLS, PRIVATE

ST. LOUIS. *Christian Brothers College High School (C.B.C.)* (1850) 1850 De La Salle Dr., 63141. Tel: 314-985-6100; Fax: 314-985-6115; Email: admin@cbchs.org; Web: www.cbchs.org. Mr. Michael Jordan, Pres.; Mr. Tim Seymour, Prin. Brothers 2; Lay Teachers 83; Students 875.

Cor Jesu Academy (1956) 10230 Gravois Rd., 63123. Tel: 314-842-1546; Fax: 314-842-6061; Email: principal@corjesu.org; Web: www.corjesu.org. Sisters Barbara Thomas, A.S.C.J., Pres.; Veronica Beato, A.S.C.J., Prin.; Mrs. Kathleen Koboldt, Librarian. Apostles of the Sacred Heart of Jesus. Lay Teachers 60; Sisters 6; Students 597.

Incarnate Word Academy (1932) 2788 Normandy Dr., 63121. Tel: 314-725-5850; Fax: 314-725-2308; Email: hmonahan@iwacademy.org; Web: www.iwacademy.org. Sr. Helena Monahan, C.C.V.I., Ph. D., Pres.; Molly Grumich, Ph.D., Prin.; Julie Schmidt, Librarian; Sr. Eileen O'Keeffe, C.C.V.I., Mission Integration. Sisters of Charity of Incarnate Word of San Antonio. Lay Teachers 32; Students 350.

St. Joseph's Academy (1840) 2307 S. Lindbergh Blvd., 63131. Tel: 314-965-7205; Fax: 314-965-9114; Email: pdunphy@stjosephacademy.org; Web: www.stjosephacademy.org. Anita Reznicek, Pres.; Diane Cooper, Prin.; Jennifer Millikan, Librarian. Girls 548; Lay Teachers 51; Sisters of St. Joseph of Carondelet 5.

St. Louis University High School, George H. Backer Memorial, 4970 Oakland Ave., 63110. Tel: 314-531-0330; Fax: 314-534-3441; Web: www.sluh.org. Revs. Carl J. Heumann, S.J., Supr.; Michael A. Marchlewski, S.J.; Ralph D. Houlihan, S.J.; John Moran, Ed.D., Prin.; Cortney Schraut, M.S., Librarian. Lay Teachers 95; Priests 6; Students 1,038; Jesuit Scholastics 1.

Notre Dame High School (1934) 320 E. Ripa Ave., 63125. Tel: 314-544-1015; Fax: 314-544-8003; Email: emmem@ndhs.net; Web: www.ndhs.net. Meghan Bohac, Prin.; Amy Bush, Head, Academics. Girls 220; Lay Teachers 40; Sisters 3.

CREVE COEUR. *Chaminade College Preparatory School Inc.*, 425 S. Lindbergh Blvd., Creve Coeur, 63131-2799. Tel: 314-993-4400; Fax: 314-993-4403; Email: archstl851@impresso.com; Web: www.chaminademo.com. Rev. Ralph A. Siefert, S.M., Pres.; Mr. Philip Rone, Prin.; James Zolnowski, Librarian. Society of Mary.Residents and Day Students. Brothers 1; Lay Teachers 66; Priests 2; Students 562.

De Smet Jesuit High School, 233 N. New Ballas Rd., Creve Coeur, 63141. Tel: 314-567-3500; Fax: 314-567-1519; Web: www.desmet.org. Trevor Bonat, Prin.; Rev. Walter T. Sidney, S.J., Pres.; Mrs. Lynn G. Maitz, Librarian. Brothers 1; Lay Teachers 75; Priests 3; Scholastics 2; Sisters 1; Students 773.

St. Louis Priory School, 500 S. Mason Rd., Creve Coeur, 63141-8500. Tel: 314-434-3690; Fax: 314-576-7088; Email: frcuthbert@priory.org; Web: www.priory.org. Revs. Cuthbert Elliott, O.S.B., Headmaster; J. Gregory Mohrman, O.S.B., Abbot; Susanne M. Kress, Librarian; Revs. Ambrose Bennett, O.S.B.; Michael Brunner, O.S.B.; Linus Dolce, O.S.B.; Francis Hein, O.S.B.; Cassian Koenemann, O.S.B.; John McCusker, O.S.B.; Aidan McDermott, O.S.B.; Augustine Wetta, O.S.B.; D. Ralph Wright, O.S.B.; Maximilian Toczylowski, O.S.B. Brothers 6; Religious Teachers 12; Lay Teachers 46; Priests 13; Students 407; Students (9-12) 280; Students (7-8) 127.

FRONTENAC. *Villa Duchesne and Oak Hill School* (1929) 801 S. Spoede Rd., Frontenac, 63131. Tel: 314-432-2021; Fax: 314-432-0199; Email: vdoh@vdoh.org; Web: www.vdoh.org. Sr. Donna Collins, R.S.C.J., Prin.; Ms. Katie Komos, Prin. Elementary School; Mr. Michael F. Baber, Head, School. Religious of the Sacred Heart.(Girls: PreK-12; Boys: PreK-6) Lay Teachers 67; Sisters 4; Elementary School Students 158; Middle & High School Students 293.

KIRKWOOD. *St. John Vianney High School* (1960) 1311 S. Kirkwood Rd., Kirkwood, 63122. Tel: 314-965-4853; Fax: 314-965-1950; Email: lkeller@vianney.com; Web: www.vianney.com. Mr. Michael Loyet, Pres.; Mr. Lawrence D. Keller, Prin.; Mr. Gerard Stevison, Librarian. Conducted for Boys by the Society of Mary (Marianists). Brothers 3; Lay Teachers 45; Priests 1; Students 625.

Ursuline Academy (1848) 341 S. Sappington Rd., Kirkwood, 63122. Tel: 314-984-2800; Fax: 314-966-3396; Email: pslater@ursulinestl.org; Web: www.ursulinestl.org. Peggy Slater, Pres.; Dr. Mark Michalski, Prin.; Mrs. Lisa Vance, Business Mgr. Ursuline Sisters of the Roman Union. Religious Teachers 2; Lay Teachers 35; Sisters 3; Students 375.

TOWN AND COUNTRY. *Visitation Academy* (1833) 3020 N. Ballas Rd., Town and Country, 63131. Tel: 314-625-9100; Fax: 314-432-5355; Email: swilliams@visitationacademy.org; Web: www.visitationacademy.org. Mr. David Colon, Head of School; Barbara McMullen, Upper School Prin.; Mrs. Jane Eschmann, Middle School Prin.; Dr. Marlise Albert, Lower School Prin. Lay Teachers 71; Sisters in the Monastery 7; Upper & Middle School (6-12) Enrollment 419; Lower School Enrollment 113.

WEBSTER GROVES. *Nerinx Hall* (1924) 530 E. Lockwood, Webster Groves, 63119. Tel: 314-968-1505; Fax: 314-968-0604; Email: broche@nerinxhs.org; Web: www.nerinxhs.org. Mr. John E. Gabriel, Pres.; Mrs. Jane W. Kosash, Prin.; Mrs. Patricia Crenshaw, Interim Assoc. Prin.; Alison Rollins, Librarian. Lay Teachers 61; Religious 2; Sisters of Loretto at the Foot of the Cross 2; Students 598.

[G] ARCHDIOCESAN-BASED ELEMENTARY SCHOOLS

ST. LOUIS. *St. Cecilia School and Academy*, 906 Eichelberger Ave., 63111. Tel: 314-351-3372; Fax: 314-353-2114; Web: http://stc-stl.org. Mary Loux, Prin.

Most Holy Trinity School, 1435 Mallinckrodt St., 63107. Tel: 314-231-9014; Fax: 314-435-9291; Web: www.mht-stl.org. Jessica Kilmade, Prin.

FLORISSANT. *All Saints Academy - St. Ferdinand Campus*, (Grades K-8), 1735 Charbonier Rd., Florissant, 63031. Tel: 314-921-2201; Fax: 314-921-2253. Lay Teachers 18; Students 222.

[H] INTER-PAROCHIAL, CONSOLIDATED ELEMENTARY SCHOOLS

ST. LOUIS. *All Saints Academy*, 20 Archbishop May Dr., 63119. Tel: 314-792-7300; Email: jphelps@archstl.org; Web: www.archstl.org/education. All Saints Academy is the parent organization for a partnership model with schools located on three campuses: All Saints Academy-St. Ferdinand Campus; All Saints Academy-St. Norbert Campus; All Saints Academy-St. Rose Philippine Duchesne Campus.

Christ, Light of the Nations, 1650 Redman Ave., 63138.

St. Frances Cabrini Academy, (Grades K-8), 3022 Oregon Ave., 63118. Tel: 314-776-0883; Fax: 314-776-4912. Mr. Peter Schroeder, Prin.

St. Francis of Assisi, (Grades PreK-8), Tel: 314-487-5736; Fax: 314-416-7118; Email: schooloffice@sfastl.org. Mrs. Elizabeth Bartolotta, Prin. Lay Teachers 23; Students 289.

Holy Cross Academy, (Grades PreK-8), 8874 Pardee Rd., 63123. Tel: 314-475-3436; Email: holycross@hca-stl.org; Web: www.holycross-stl.org. Dr. Gregory A. Densberger, Ph.D., Pres.

Legal Title: Holy Cross Academy - St. Louis Lay Teachers 72; Students 700.

Holy Cross Academy at the Annunciation Campus, (Grades 6-8), 16 W. Glendale Rd., Webster Groves, 63119.

Holy Cross Academy at Our Lady of Providence Campus, (Grades K-5), 8874 Pardee Rd., 63123. Tel: 314-475-3436.

Holy Cross Academy - St. John Paul II Campus, 7748 Mackenzie Rd., 63123. Tel: 314-832-4161.

Holy Cross Academy at St. Michael the Archangel Campus, (Grades K-5), 7630 Sutherland Ave., Shrewsbury, 63119. Tel: 314-647-7159.

St. Justin Martyr, 11914 Eddie & Park Rd., 63126. Tel: 314-843-6447; Fax: 314-843-9257. Mrs. Elizabeth Bartolotta, Prin.; Karim Reich, Librarian.

St. Louis Catholic Academy, 4720 Carter, 63112. Tel: 314-389-0401; Fax: 314-389-7042; Web: http://www.slca-stl.org. Sandra Morton, Prin.

South City Catholic Academy, 5821 Pernod, 63139. Tel: 314-752-4171; Fax: 314-351-8562; Web: southcitycatholicacademy.org. Laura Hirschman, Prin.

ARNOLD. *Holy Child School*, 2316 Church Rd., Arnold, 63010.

Immaculate Conception, (Grades PreK-8), 2300 Church Rd., Arnold, 63010. Tel: 636-321-0002; Email: delmore@holychildarnold.org; Web: icarnold.com. Mailing Address: 2316 Church Rd., Arnold, 63010. Fax: 636-296-5639. Lay Teachers 18; Students 277.

St. David, 2334 Tenbrook Rd., Arnold, 63010.

FESTUS. *Our Lady*, (Grades K-8), 1599 St. Mary Ln., Festus, 63028. Tel: 636-937-5008; Email: ourladyschool@sbcglobal.net; Web: www.ourladycatholicschool.org. Lay Teachers 20; Students 223.

FLORISSANT. *St. Norbert*, 16475 New Halls Ferry Rd., Florissant, 63031. Tel: 314-839-0948.

O'FALLON. *Assumption*, 203 W. Third St., O'Fallon, 63366. Tel: 636-240-4474. Genevieve Callier, Prin.

ST. CHARLES. *St. Elizabeth/St. Robert School*, (Grades K-8), 1 Seton Ct., St. Charles, 63303. Tel: 636-946-6716; Fax: 636-946-2670. Ms. Joanna Collins, Prin.

UNION. *Immaculate Conception*, 6 W. State St., Union, 63084. Tel: 636-583-2641; Fax: 636-583-3073. Mr. Dennis Lottmann, Prin.

UNIVERSITY CITY. *Christ the King*, 7324 Balson Ave., University City, 63130. Tel: 314-725-5855; Fax: 314-725-5981. Mrs. Susan E. Hooker, Prin. Lay Teachers 21; Students 245.

WASHINGTON. *St. Francis Borgia*, (Grades PreK-8), 225 Cedar St., Washington, 63090. Fax: 636-316-9384; Email: lpahl@borgiagradeschool.org. Linda Pahl, Prin. Lay Teachers 24; Students 228.

[I] ELEMENTARY SCHOOLS, PRIVATE

ST. LOUIS. *Loyola Academy of St. Louis* (1994) 3851 Washington Blvd., 63108. Tel: 314-531-9091; Fax: 314-531-3603; Email: eclark@loyolaacademy.org; Web: www.loyolaacademy.org. Dr. H. Eric Clark, Pres.; Mr. Paul Bozdech, Prin. Lay Teachers 7; Religious 1; Students 60.

Marian Middle School (1999) 4130 Wyoming, 63116. Tel: 314-771-7674; Fax: 314-771-7679; Email: sheger@mms-stl.org; Web: www.mms-stl.org. S. Sarah Heger, Prin. Lay Teachers 7; Students 75.

CREVE COEUR. *Chaminade College Preparatory*, (Grades 6-12), 425 S. Lindbergh Blvd., Creve Coeur, 63131. Tel: 314-993-4400; Fax: 314-993-4403; Email: archstl851@impresso.com; Web: www.chaminademo.com. Rev. Ralph A. Siefert, S.M., Pres.; Mr. Todd Guidry, Prin.; James Zolnowski, Librarian. Society of Mary.(Middle School), Residents and Day Students (Boys) Brothers 1; Lay Teachers 28; Priests 2; Students 265.

FESTUS. *Ursuline Learning Center*, 201 Brierton Ln., Festus, 63028. Tel: 636-937-3344. Carolyn Meinhardt, Dir.

FRONTENAC. *Villa Duchesne and Oak Hill School* (1929) (Grades Toddler-12), 801 S. Spoede Rd., 63131-2699. Tel: 314-432-2021; Fax: 314-432-0199; Email: admissions@vdoh.org; Email: news@vdoh.org; Web: www.vdoh.org. Mr. Michael F. Baber, Head, School. Lay Teachers 76; Sisters 1; Students 470.

ST. CHARLES. *Academy of the Sacred Heart* (1818) (Coed) 619 N. 2nd St., St. Charles, 63301. Tel: 636-946-6127; Fax: 636-949-6659; Email: mglavin@ash1818.org; Web: www.ash1818.org. Sr. Maureen Glavin, Head of School; Mrs. Marcia Renken, Prin.; Elizabeth Metcalf, Librarian. Lay Teachers 45; Students 348.

TOWN AND COUNTRY. *Visitation Academy* (1833) (Grades PreK-12), 3020 N. Ballas Rd., Town and Country, 63131. Tel: 314-625-9100; Fax: 314-432-5355; Email: swilliams@visitationacademy.org; Web: www.visitationacademy.org. Mr. David Colon, Head of School; Dr. Marlise Albert, Prin. Lower School; Barbara McMullen, Prin. Upper School; Mrs. Jane Eschmann, Prin. Middle School. Lower School (Preschool-5th Grade) Lay Teachers 71; Visitation Sisters 7; Students 532; Lower School 113; Upper & Middle School 419.

[J] DEPARTMENT OF SPECIAL EDUCATION

ST. LOUIS. *Department of Special Education* (1950) 20 Archbishop May Dr., 63119. Tel: 314-792-7320; Fax: 314-792-7325; Email: cathyjohns@archstl.org. Dr. Catherine Johns, Ph.D., Dir. Curriculum, Instruction, Assessment & Dept. Spl. Educ. Special education programs at five sites for children in grades PreK-8 who have one or more diagnosed learning disorders or disability who would benefit from a more restrictive setting than general education. The settings range from a special education setting for core curriculum classes to full time special education services to a customized program with intensive speech-language therapy and sensory integration therapy. Tot Asst. Annually 80; Total Staff 30.

St. Joseph Institute for the Deaf, 1314 Strassner Ave., 63144. Tel: 636-532-3211 (Voice/TTY); Fax: 636-532-4560; Web: www.sjid.org. Cheryl Broekelmann, STL Dir. Opers., Tel: 314-918-1369; Fax: 314-918-1609. School for the Deaf; Listening and spoken language facility for children who are deaf or hard of hearing. Offering Early Intervention, Pediatric Audiology and Tele-intervention via the internet. Proud to offer solutions for nearly 200 families seeking spoken language services for their children who are deaf. Lay Teachers 4; Students 141; Personnel 10; Therapists 1.

St. Mary's Special Services for Exceptional Children (1952) Administrative Office: 20 Archbishop May Dr., 63119. Tel: 314-792-7320; Fax: 314-792-7325; Email: cathyjohns@archstl.org. Rev. Msgr. Vernon E. Gardin, Ph.D., Exec. Dir.; Catherine Johns, Asst. Supt. Early Intervention services at ten parish elementary sites for children in preschool and/or primary grades who have a diagnosed learning need and/or considered at-risk for educational success and would benefit from services in the areas of speech/language and social/emotional development.

St. Mary's Special School for Exceptional Children Tot Asst. Annually 100; Total Staff 3.

[K] SERVICES FOR THE ELDERLY

ST. LOUIS. *Cardinal Carberry Senior Living Center*, 7601 Watson Rd., 63119. Tel: 314-961-8000; Fax: 314-961-1934; Email: swesley@crssstl.org; Web: www.cardinalritterseniorservices.org. Karen Ledbetter, Interim CEO.

Cardinal Ritter Senior Services, 7601 Watson Rd., 63119. Tel: 314-961-8000; Fax: 314-961-1934; Email: cbaechle@crssstl.org; Web: www.cardinalritterseniorservices.org. Mr. Christopher Baechle, CEO. Catholic Charities network of agencies provides compassionate care through a continuum of high quality residential, healthcare and supportive social services. Tot Asst. Annually 3,609; Total Staff 521.

Cardinal Ritter Senior Services - Adult Day Program, 7663 Watson Rd., 63119. Tel: 314-962-7501; Fax: 314-962-7140; Email: Cbaechle@crssstl.org; Web: www.cardinalritterseniorservices.org. Mr. Christopher Baechle, CEO.

Cardinal Ritter General Partner Corporation, 7601 Watson Rd., 63119.

Cardinal Ritter Institute Residential Services Corporation, 7601 Watson Rd., 63119. Tel: 314-961-8000; Fax: 314-961-4850; Email: cbaechle@crssstl.org; Web: www.cardinalritterseniorservices.org. Mr. Christopher Baechle, CEO. Provides housing management, housing & assisted living facilities for the elderly.

St. John Neumann Apartments, Inc., 8424 Lucas and Hunt Rd., 63136. Tel: 314-385-0707; Fax: 314-385-5299; Email: cbaechle@crssstl.org; Web: www.cardinalritterseniorservices.org. Mr. Christopher Baechle, CEO.

St. Joseph Apartments, Inc., 7677 Watson Rd., 63119. Tel: 314-962-0969; Fax: 314-962-1393; Web: www.cardinalritterseniorservices.org.

Holy Infant Apartments, Inc., 7663 Watson Rd., 63119. Tel: 314-962-7878; Fax: 314-962-1393; Web: www.cardinalritterseniorservices.org.

St. Agnes Apartments, Inc., 2840 Wisconsin, 63118. Tel: 314-664-1255; Fax: 314-664-1192; Web: www.cardinalritterseniorservices.org.

Pope John Paul II Apartments, Inc., 6325 Waterways Dr., 63033. Tel: 314-653-0400, Ext. 294; Fax: 314-653-2840; Web: www.cardinalritterseniorservices.org.

St. Elizabeth Hall, 325 N. Newstead, 63108. Tel: 314-652-9525; Fax: 314-652-8879; Email: cbaechle@crssstl.org; Web: www.cardinalritterseniorservices.org.

DuBourg House, 5890 Eichelberger, 63109. Tel: 314-752-1901; Fax: 314-752-0572; Web: www.cardinalritterseniorservices.org.

Cardinal Carberry Senior Living Center, 7601 Watson, St Louis, 63119. Tel: 314-961-8000; Fax: 314-961-1934; Email: cbaeche@crssstl.org. Mr. Christopher Baechle, CEO.

Our Lady of Life Apartments, Inc., 7655 Watson Rd., 63119. Tel: 314-968-9447; Fax: 314-968-1758; Web: www.cardinalritterseniorservices.org.

Mother of Perpetual Help Residence, Inc., Mother of Perpetual Help Residence, Inc., 7609 Watson Rd., 63119. Tel: 314-918-2260; Fax: 314-961-3061; Email: cbaechle@crssstl.org; Web: www.cardinalritterseniorservices.org. Mr. Christopher Baechle, CEO; Karen Ledbetter, Admin. Total Assisted 90.

Mary, Queen and Mother Center, 7601 Watson Rd., 63119. Tel: 314-961-8000; Fax: 314-961-3580; Email: skruep@crssstl.org; Web: www.cardinalritterseniorservices.org. Sharrill Kruep, Admin.

Holy Angels Apartments I, Inc., 3455 DePaul Ln., Bridgeton, 63044. Tel: 314-298-9505; Fax: 314-298-2414; Web: www.cardinalritterseniorservices.org.

Holy Angels Apartments II, Inc., 3499 DePaul Ln., Bridgeton, 63044. Tel: 314-291-1345; Fax: 314-291-2851; Web: www.cardinalritterseniorservices.org.

St. Clare of Assisi Senior Village, Inc., 409 Warrenton Village Dr., Warrenton, 63383. Tel: 636-695-4200; Fax: 636-695-4208; Web: www.cardinalritterseniorservices.org.

St. William Apartments I, Inc., 1979 Hanley Rd., Dardenne Prairie, 63368. Tel: 636-695-4200; Fax: 636-695-4208.

St. William Apartments II, Inc., 1983 Hanley Rd., Dardenne Prairie, 63368. Tel: 636-695-4205; Fax: 636-695-4216.

St. Elizabeth's Adult Day Care Center, Inc. (1981) 3683 Cook St., 63113. Tel: 314-772-5107; Fax: 314-772-3674; Email: sjamiller@seadcc.org; Web: www.seadcc.org. Sr. John Antonio Miller, C.PP.S., Admin. Conducted by the Sisters of the Most Precious Blood to Provide Day Care for the Elderly and Handicapped.

St. Elizabeth Adult Day Care Center of Florissant (1994) 1831 N. New Florissant Rd., Florissant, 63033. Tel: 314-838-5005; Fax: 314-838-5005.

St. Elizabeth Adult Day Care Center of Overland (1997) 2543 Hood, Overland, 63114. Tel: 314-890-0005; Fax: 314-890-0005; Web: www.seadcc.org.

St. Elizabeth Arnold Adult Day Care Center, 308 Plaza Way, Arnold, 63010. Tel: 636-282-0345; Fax: 636-282-0345; Web: www.seadcc.org.

St. Elizabeth Adult Day Care Center - Olivette, 9723 Grandview, Olivette, 63132. Tel: 314-994-9165; Fax: 314-994-9165; Web: www.seadcc.org.

St. Elizabeth Adult Day Care Center - Lemay, 317 Hoffmeister, Lemay, 63125. Tel: 314-638-8850; Fax: 314-638-8850; Web: www.seadcc.org.

St. Elizabeth Adult Day Care Center - St. Charles, 1424 First Capitol Dr., S., St. Charles, 63303. Tel: 636-724-2110; Fax: 636-724-2110; Web: www.seadcc.org.

St. Elizabeth Adult Day Care Center - Ste. Genevieve, 765 Market St., Sainte Genevieve, 63670. Tel: 573-883-7603; Fax: 573-883-7603; Web: www.seadcc.org.

San Luis Apartments, Inc., 20 Archbishop May Dr., 63119. Tel: 314-792-7408; Email: Billing@archstl.org. Rev. Msgr. Jerome D. Billing, S.T.L., J.C.L., Chancellor.

[L] GENERAL HOSPITALS

ST. LOUIS. *St. Anthony's Medical Center* (1900) 10010 Kennerly Rd., 63128. Tel: 314-525-1000; Email: Thomas.Edelstein@Mercy.net; Web: www.stanthonysmedcenter.com. Rev. William Cardy, O.F.M., Chap. Bed Capacity 562; Total Staff 3,827.

SSM Health St. Mary's Hospital (1924) 6420 Clayton Rd., 63117. Tel: 314-768-8000; Fax: 314-768-8011; Email: travis.capers@ssmhealth.com; Web: www.stmarys-stlouis.com. Travis Capers, Pres. Member of SSM Health Care Bed Capacity 492; Patients Asst Anual. 230,699; Total Staff 1,989.

BRIDGETON. *SSM Health De Paul Hospital - St. Louis* (1828) 12303 De Paul Dr., Bridgeton, 63044. Tel: 314-344-6000; Fax: 314-344-6840; Email: ellis.hawkins@ssmhealth.com; Web: www.ssmdepaul.com. Ellis D. Hawkins, Pres.; Revs. David Boyle, Chap.; Glenn Reitz, Chap.; Michael Southcombe, Chap.; Daniel DeVilder, Chap.; John Morton, Chap.; Chacko Issac, Chap.; Kevin Cook, Chap.; John Sharp, Chap. Member of SSM Health Care. Bed Capacity 529; Tot Asst. Annually 238,877; Total Staff 2,139.

*SSM Health De Paul Hospital - St. Louis*Bed Capacity 477; Patients Asst Anual. 257,424; Sisters 1; Volunteers 11; Staff 2,252.

St. Vincent Division, 12303 De Paul Dr., Bridgeton, 63044. Tel: 314-344-7955; Email: vicki.holtmann@ssmhealth.com. Michelle Schafer, Admin. Pre-Adolescent, Adolescent, Adult & Gero Psychiatric Care and Outpatient Chemical Dependency.

CREVE COEUR. *Mercy Hospital St. Louis*, 615 S. New Ballas Rd., Creve Coeur, 63141. Tel: 314-251-6000; Fax: 314-251-4168; Web: www.mercy.net. 14528 S. Outer 40 Rd., Ste. 100, Chesterfield, 63017. Susan Hannasch. Conducted by the Sisters of Mercy of the Americas South Central Community, Inc. merged 7/1/2008.(See Branch Unit under Mercy Hospital East Community).

FENTON. *SSM St. Clare Health Center* (1954) 1015 Bowles Ave., Fenton, 63026. Tel: 636-496-2000; Fax: 636-496-4901; Email: tina.garrison@ssmhealth.com; Web: www.ssmhealth.com. Tina Garrison, Pres. Member of SSM Health Care. Bed Capacity 180; Tot Asst. Annually 126,902; Total Staff 994; Total Nurses 451.

LAKE ST. LOUIS. *SSM St. Joseph Hospital West*, 100 Medical Plaza, Lake Saint Louis, 63367. Tel: 314-625-5200; Fax: 636-755-3876; Email: SSMHealthCareOfficialCatholicDirectoryNotices@ssmhealth.com; Web: www.ssmstjoseph.com. Lisle Wescott, Pres.; Sisters Donna Olson, Pastoral Care; Charlotte Lehman, Pastoral Care. Member of SSM Health Care.

Legal Title: SSM Health St. Joseph Hospital - Lake Saint Louis Bed Capacity 215; Tot Asst. Annually 156,156; Total Staff 1,043.

ST. CHARLES. *SSM Health St. Joseph Hospital - St. Charles*, 300 First Capitol Dr., St. Charles, 63301. Tel: 314-947-5000; Fax: 314-947-5392; Email: ssmhealthcareofficialcatholidirectorynotices@ssmhealth.com; Web: www.ssmstjoseph.com. Lisle Wescott, Pres.; Gail Holstein, Chap.; Rev. Charles Dey, Team Leader & Chap.; Rev. Msgr. Raymond A. Hampe, (Retired). Member of SSM Health. Bed Capacity 410; Tot Asst. Annually 183,242; Total Staff 1,259.

TROY. *Mercy Hospital Lincoln*, 1000 E. Cherry St., Troy, 63379. Tel: 314-628-3608; Email: Marynell.Ploch@Mercy.Net. Susan Hannasch, Regl. Gen. Counsel.

WASHINGTON. *Mercy Hospital Washington* (1926) 901 E. 5th St., Washington, 63090. Tel: 636-239-8000; Fax: 636-569-6733; Email: Marynell.Ploch@Mercy.Net. Eric Eoloff, Pres.; Mark Covington, Vice Pres., Mission; Mary Salois, Mgr. Pastoral Svcs.; Rev. Catherine Gamblin, Chap. (Protestant); Sr. Michaelanne Estoup, R.S.M., (Retired); Rev. James Austin, Chap. (Protestant). (See Listing Under Creve Coeur, MO). Bed Capacity 166; Tot Asst. Annually 311,988; Total Staff 734.

WENTZVILLE. *SSM St. Joseph Health Center-Wentzville*, 500 Medical Dr., Wentzville, 63385. Tel: 636-327-1000; Fax: 636-327-1110; Email: SSMHealthCareOfficialCatholicDirectoryNotices@ssmhealth.com; Web: www.ssmstjoseph.com. Lisle Wescott, Pres.; Gail Holstein, Team Leader, Pastoral Care. Bed Capacity 77; Tot Asst. Annually 14,132; Total Staff 248.

[M] SPECIAL HOSPITALS

ST. LOUIS. *SSM Health - Cardinal Glennon Children's Hospital* (1956) 1465 S. Grand Blvd., 63104. Tel: 314-577-5613; Fax: 314-268-6440; Email: steven.burghart@ssmhealth.com; Web: www.cardinalglennon.com. Mr. Steven Burghart, Pres. Member of SSM Health Care. Sisters 5; Tot Asst. Annually 245,022; Total Staff 1,945.

CREVE COEUR. *SSM Rehab*, 10101 Woodfield Ln., Creve Coeur, 63132. Tel: 314-768-5300; Fax: 314-768-5355; Email: SSMHealthCareOfficialCatholicDirectoryNotices@ssmhealth.com; Web: www.ssmrehab.com. Robert Pritts, CEO. Member of SSM Health Care; For rehabilitation of pediatrics, adolescents and adults. Bed Capacity: SSM St. Mary's Health Center, St. Louis 80; SSM St. Joseph Health Center, St. Charles 20; Outpatient Locations 24.

[N] PROTECTIVE INSTITUTIONS

Day Care Centers

ST. LOUIS.

Guardian Angel Settlement Association, 1127 N. Vandeventer Ave., 63113. Tel: 314-231-3188; Fax: 314-231-8126; Email: info@gasastl.org; Web: www.gasastl.org. Jessica Brandon, Pres. & CEO. Founded by the Daughters of Charity of St. Vincent de Paul.Child Care Services and Social Services. Tot Asst. Annually 4,000; Total Staff 55.

Guardian Angel Settlement Association, 1127 N. Vandeventer Ave, 63113. Tel: 314-231-3188; Fax: 314-231-8126. Child Care Center.

Guardian Angel Settlement Association, 2700 Cherokee St., 63118. Tel: 314-773-9027; Fax: 314-773-6140.

Peace for Kids, 4415 Maryland, 63108. Tel: 314-531-0511, Ext. 104; Fax: 314-531-2954; Email: sspruell@ccstl.org. Sharon Spruell, CEO. A child development center providing high quality child development education and care to children 6 weeks to 6 years. Licensed by the State of Missouri and accredited by Counsel on Accreditation (COA) and Missouri Accreditation of Programs for Children and Youth (MOA). Students 36.

Sacred Heart Villa (1940) 2108 Macklind Ave., 63110. Tel: 314-771-2224; Fax: 314-771-1262; Web: sacredheartvilla.org. Sr. Jude Ruggeri, A.S.C.J., Exec. Dir.; Kristine Doder, Dir. Conducted by the Apostles of the Sacred Heart of Jesus.Full-time care from 6:30 a.m. to 6:00 p.m. for children 2-6 years old. Clergy 6; Students 151; Total Staff 51; Total Assisted 151.

IMPERIAL.

Queen of Apostles Center (1989) 800 Montebello Camp Rd., Imperial, 63052. Tel: 636-464-0163; Email: cantinora@ascjus.org. Sr. Catherine Antinora, A.S.C.J., Dir. Days of Recollection, conferences for adults; spiritual direction. Total Staff 2; Apostles of the Sacred Heart of Jesus 5.

KIRKWOOD.

Carmelite Child Development Center, 1111 N. Woodlawn Ave., Kirkwood, 63122. Tel: 314-822-0058; Fax: 314-822-3573; Email: vocations@carmelitedcj.org; Web: www.carmelitedcj.org. Ann Cunningham, Dir. Operated by the Carmelite Sisters of the Divine Heart of Jesus. Provides child development, child care and services. Total Staff 15; Full Day 106.

[O] HOMES FOR CHILDREN

ST. LOUIS. *Boys Hope Girls Hope of St. Louis, Inc.*, 755 S. New Ballas Rd., Ste. 120, 63141. Tel: 314-692-7477; Fax: 314-692-7810; Email: hopestlouis@bhgh.org; Web: www.boyshopegirlshopestl.org. Brian Hipp, Exec. Dir., Email: bhipp@bhgh.org. Residential Care for Adolescent Boys and Girls, Troubled by Family Disruptions, who are Capable of College Preparatory High School Work. Ages 10-18. Tot Asst. Annually 84; Total Staff 20.

FLORISSANT. *Child Center - Marygrove* aka Marygrove (1849) 2705 Mullanphy Ln., Florissant, 63031. Tel: 314-837-1702; Fax: 314-830-6263; Email: info@mgstl.org; Web: www.marygrovechildren.org. Joseph Bestgen, CEO. Owned and operated under the auspices of Catholic Charities. Residential treatment for males and females (ages 6-21). Special education, therapy, medical services, crisis care for males and females (birth-21), transitional/independent living programs for males and females (16-21), therapeutic Foster Homes, in-home counseling and respite care. Bed Capacity 225; Total Staff 235; Total Assisted 1,300.

NORMANDY. *St. Vincent Home for Children* (1850) 7401 Florissant Rd., Normandy, 63121. Tel: 314-261-6011; Fax: 314-385-1467; Email: info@saintvincenthome.org; Web: www.saintvincenthome.org. Carla Monroe-Posey, Ph.D., L.C.S.W., M.S.H.A., Exec. Dir.; A'eesha Bell, Dir.; Deborah Jackson, Dir.; Courtney Graves, Dir. Chapel of the Sacred Heart.

The German St. Vincent Orphan Association Bed Capacity 40; Tot Asst. Annually 500; Total Staff 73.

[P] HOMES FOR AGED

ST. LOUIS. *Alexian Brothers Lansdowne Village* aka Ascension Living Lansdowne Place (1988) 4624 Lansdowne, 63116. Tel: 314-351-6888; Fax: 314-351-5825; Email: brian.cooper@ascension.org; Web: ascensionliving.org. Brian D. Cooper, Exec. Dir. Bed Capacity 145; Tot Asst. Annually 547; Total Staff 115.

Alexian Brothers Sherbrooke Village (1991) 4005 Ripa Ave., 63125. Tel: 314-544-1111; Fax: 314-544-5134; Email: mroth@alexianbrothers.net; Web: ascensionliving.org. C. Michael Roth, Pres. Tot Asst. Annually 825; Total Staff 167; Total in Residence (Assisted Living) 88; Total Assisted (Nursing Care) 167.

Alexian Court Apartments, 2636 Chippewa St., 63118. Tel: 314-771-5604; Fax: 314-771-7629; Email: 0931@nationalchurchresidences.org; Web: www.alexianbrothers.net. Sponsored by Alexian Brothers Senior Ministries. Managed by National Church Residence.

Alexian Brothers Services, Inc. Total Apartments 109.

Little Sisters of the Poor, Home for the Aged (1869) 3225 N. Florissant Ave., 63107. Tel: 314-421-6022; Fax: 314-436-9069. Sr. Gonzague Castro, L.S.P., Supr.; Rev. James Beegan, M.S.F., Chap. Residents 116; Sisters 8; Total Staff 125; Total Assisted 125.

Mary, Queen and Mother Center, 7601 Watson Rd., 63119. Tel: 314-961-8000; Fax: 314-961-3580; Email: mbarth@ccstl.org; Web: www.ccstl.org/crss. Shari Kruep, Admin. Skilled Nursing Facility.; A part of Cardinal Carberry Living Center Bed Capacity 230; Tot Asst. Annually 630; Total Staff 255.

Mother of Good Counsel Home (1932) 6825 Natural Bridge Rd., (St. Louis Co.), 63121. Tel: 314-383-4765; Fax: 314-383-7256; Email: smchristine@mogch.org; Web: mogch.org. Sr. M. Christine Crowder, F.S.G.M., Admin. Conducted by Sisters of St. Francis of the Martyr St. George. Skilled Nursing Facility for Men and Women. Residents 70; Sisters 12; Total Staff 120.

Mother of Perpetual Help Residence, 7609 Watson Rd., 63119. Tel: 314-918-2260; Fax: 314-961-3061; Web: www.cardinalritterseniorservices.org. Sr. Suzanne Wesley, C.S.J., CEO; Kimberly Brown, Admin. A part of Cardinal Ritter Senior Services Bed Capacity 160; Total Staff 65; Total Assisted 80.

Nazareth Living Center, 2 Nazareth Ln., 63129. Tel: 314-487-3950; Fax: 314-487-8001; Email: ron.mantia@bhshealth.org; Web: www.nazarethlivingcenter.com. Rev. Andrew O'Connor, Chap.; Ronald Mantia, CEO & Admin.; Ronda Griffin, Asst. Admin.; Betty Fuller, Dir. Mission & Pastoral Care. Sisters of St. Joseph of Carondelet & Benedictine Health System (Ministry Partners). Skilled Nursing Care Facility, Assisted Living & Independent Living. Total Staff 310; Total Assisted Skilled 140; Total Assisted Living 150; Total Independent Living 50.

Our Lady of Life Apartments, Inc., 7655 Watson Rd., 63119. Tel: 314-968-9447; Fax: 314-968-1758; Web: www.cardinalritterseniorservices.org. A part of Cardinal Ritter Senior Services. Total Staff 41; Total Independent Living Apartments 206.

Regina Cleri Residence (1959) 10 Archbishop May Dr., 63119. Tel: 314-968-2240; Fax: 314-968-1049; Email: reginacleri@earthlink.net. Ms. Nancy Bryant, Admin. A Residence for Retired Diocesan Priests of the Archdiocese of St. Louis. Conducted by the Archdiocese of St. Louis. Priests 37; Sisters of the Most Precious Blood (O'Fallon, MO) 2; Franciscan Sisters of Our Lady of Perpetual Help 2; Tot Asst. Annually 45; Total Staff 26.

EUREKA. *St. Andrew's at Francis Place*, 300 Forby Rd., Eureka, 63025. Tel: 636-938-5151; Fax: 636-938-5266. Mary Alice Ryan, CEO; Sr. Rita A. Bregenhorn, O.S.U., Vice Chairperson. Sponsored by the Ursuline Sisters and managed by St. Andrew's Management Services, Inc. Residents 95; Total Staff 55; Total Assisted 44.

KIRKWOOD. *St. Agnes Home for the Elderly*, 10341 Manchester Rd., Kirkwood, 63122. Tel: 314-965-7616; Fax: 314-965-3179; Web: www.stagneshome.com. Ruth Dotson, Admin.; Rev. Dennis M. Doyle, J.C.L., Chap.

Carmelite Sisters of the Divine Heart of Jesus of Missouri Bed Capacity 150; Sisters 16; Tot Asst. Annually 124; Total Staff 130.

[Q] MONASTERIES AND RESIDENCES OF PRIESTS AND BROTHERS

ST. LOUIS. *The Abbey of St. Mary and St. Louis* (1955) 500 S. Mason Rd., 63141-8522. Tel: 314-434-3690; Fax: 314-434-0795; Email: frdominic@priory.org; Web: www.stlouisabbey.org. Revs. J. Gregory Mohrman, O.S.B., Abbot; Cassian Koenemann, O.S.B., Prior; Ambrose Bennett, O.S.B., Subprior; Cuthbert Elliott, O.S.B., Headmaster; D. Ralph Wright, O.S.B., Vocations Dir.; Very Rev. Gerard Garrigan, O.S.B.; Rev. Francis Hein, O.S.B.; Very Rev. M. Paul Kidner, O.S.B.; Revs. J. Laurence Kriegshauser, O.S.B.; Dominic Lenk, O.S.B.; Edward Mazuski, O.S.B.; John McCusker, O.S.B.; Aidan McDermott, O.S.B.; Andrew Senay, O.S.B.; Maximilian Toczylowski, O.S.B.; Augustine Wetta, O.S.B.; R. Benedict Allin, O.S.B.; Rt. Rev. Thomas Frerking, O.S.B., Abbot Emeritus; Revs. Michael Brunner, O.S.B.; Linus Dolce, O.S.B.; Finbarr Dowling, O.S.B. Benedictines of the English Congregation. Priests 21; Total Staff 28; Brother Monks 7.

Bellarmine House of Studies, 3737 Westminster Pl., 63108-3407. Tel: 314-652-8862; Fax: 314-535-4597; Email: bellarminehouse@gmail.com. Revs. Steven A. Schoenig, S.J., Rector; John J. Vowells, S.J., Min. & Treas.; James K. Coughlin, S.J., Pastoral Coord.; Robert F. O'Toole, S.J.; Daniel P. White, S.J. Jesuit Residence for Students in the College of Philosophy and Letters of St. Louis University. Priests 5; Students 23; Total Staff 3.

Congregation of the Mission Vincentian Fathers Lazarist Residence, 13245 Tesson Ferry Rd., 63128-3888. Tel: 314-843-0108; Fax: 314-849-1267; Email: pgrivett@vincentian.org. 13663 Rider Trl. N., Earth City, 63045. Revs. Raymond Van Dorpe, C.M., Rel. Order Leader; Lawrence F. Asma, C.M.; Andrew E. Bellisario, C.M.; Bro. David Berning, C.M.; Revs. Robert J. Brockland, C.M.; Guillermo Campozano, C.M., Rep. to United Nations; James B. Cormack, C.M.; John F. Clark, C.M., M.A.; Philip J. Coury, C.M.; William Hartenbach, C.M.; Ronald Hoye, C.M.; Stephen Gallegos, C.M.; Daniel P. Kearns, C.M.; Richard L. Lause, C.M.; Kevin P. McCracken, C.M.; Paul O. Schneebeck, C.M.; Daniel Schulte, C.M.; Daniel R. Thiess, C.M.; Bernard Quinn, C.M.; Joseph S. Williams, C.M.; Henry W. Grodecki, C.M.; Prosper Molengi, C.M.; Donald Ours, C.M.; Charles E. Prost, C.M.; James G. Ward, C.M.; Clayton Kilburn, C.M.; Patrick Mullin, C.M. Brothers 1; Priests 27.

Congregation of the Resurrection, Resurrection Seminary, 4252 W. Pine Blvd., 63108. Tel: 314-652-8814; Email: gary9756@yahoo.com; Web: www.resurrectionseminary.com. Rev. Gary Hogan, C.R., Dir. Formation.

De Smet Jesuit High School Community, 330 Emerson Rd., 63141. Tel: 314-567-3500; Fax: 314-567-1519; Email: jcraig@desmet.org. Revs. John V. Craig, S.J., Supr.; John J. Bergin, S.J.; Robert E. Bosken, S.J., (Retired); Michael H. Durso, S.J.; Walter T. Sidney, S.J.; Bro. Donald E. Lee, S.J.; Mr. Vincent A. Giacabazi, S.J.; Mr. Ronald R. O'Dwyer, S.J. Brothers 1; Priests 5; Scholastics 2; Jesuits 8.

St. Dominic Priory, 3407 Lafayette Ave., 63104. Tel: 314-678-9427; Fax: 314-256-8888; Web: www.domcentral.org/locations/st-dominic-priory. Rev. Leobardo Almazan, O.P., Prior; Very Rev. Jay M. Harrington, O.P.; Revs. Vincent W. Bryce, O.P.; David L. Delich, O.P., Syndic; Donald Goergen, O.P., Ph.D., S.T.M.; Steve Kuhlmann, O.P.; Victor Laroche, O.P., Student Master; DePorres Dorham, O.P.; Kevin Stephens, O.P. Priests 9; Total in Residence 31; Student Brothers 22.

Dominican Community of St. Louis (1982) St. Louis Bertrand House - Province of St. Albert the Great. 97 Waterman Pl., 63112-1820. Tel: 314-361-4445; Fax: 314-256-8888; Email: byrne@ai.edu. Revs. Harry M. Byrne, O.P., Supr.; Gregory J. Heille, O.P., Business Mgr.; Charles E. Bouchard, O.P.; James Dominic A.C. Rooney, O.P. Priests 4.

Dominican Studentate (2010) 3407 Lafayette Ave., 63104. Tel: 314-678-9427; Fax: 314-678-9526. Very Rev. James V. Marchionda, O.P., Prior Prov.

Franciscan Friary of St. Anthony of Padua Headquarters for the Franciscan (O.F.M.) Province of the Sacred Heart. 3140 Meramec St., 63118-4339. Tel: 314-353-7470; Fax: 314-353-0935; Email: provsec@thefriars.org; Web: www.thefriars.org. Very Rev. Thomas Nairn, O.F.M., Prov.; Revs. James Lause, O.F.M., Prov. Sec.; Michael Hill, O.F.M., Treas.; Andrew Lewandowski, O.F.M.; Edmund Mundwiller, O.F.M., Contemplative & Visual Ministry, Tel: 314-353-7470; John Abts, O.F.M., Prov. Health Care Office; Ralph Parthie, O.F.M., Vicar/Dir. Office of Friar Life and Sec. Formation & Studies; Glenn Phillips, O.F.M., Chap.; Raymond Rickels, O.F.M., Counselor; Eulogio Roselada, O.F.M.; Bros. Patrick Darnell, O.F.M., Fraternal Svc.; Robert Gross, O.F.M., Computer Technician; Patrick Hanrahan, O.F.M.; James Lammers, O.F.M., Fraternal Svc.; Damian Pfeifer, O.F.M., Fraternal Svc.; Rev. Damien Dougherty, O.F.M.; Bros. Charles Reid, O.F.M.; Joseph Rogenski, O.F.M., Dir. Franciscan Missionary Union; Revs. Michael Fowler, O.F.M.; William Cardy, O.F.M.; Frank Folino, O.F.M.; David Rodriguez, O.F.M.; Bro. Joseph Manning, O.F.M.; Rev. Dat Hoang, O.F.M.

The Franciscan Friars of the State of Missouri Brothers 9; Priests 18.

Friars of Sacred Heart Province Serving Abroad: Revs. Jesus Aguirre-Garza, O.F.M., Fgn. Missionary, South Africa; Joseph Tan Doan Nguyen, O.F.M., Fgn. Missionary, Vietnam; Bro. Jeffery Haller, O.F.M., Fgn. Missionary, Thailand.

Ignatius House (1990) 4517 W. Pine Blvd., 63108-2191. Tel: 314-361-6145; Email: jarnold@jesuits-mis.org; Web: www.jesuits-mis.org. Revs. John D. Arnold, S.J., Supr.; Kevin L. Cullen, S.J., Province Treas.; Daniel C. O'Connell, S.J., Writer; Paul C. Pilgram, S.J., Aide in Province Offices. Total in Residence 4.

Saint Jean de Brebeuf Jesuit Community, 4948 Wise Ave., 63110. Tel: 314-255-4851; Email: jburshek@jesuits.org. Revs. James J. Burshek, S.J., Supr.; Ralph D. Houlihan, S.J.; Ian R. Gibbons, S.J.; Michael A. Marchlewski, S.J.; Kevin L. Cullen, S.J.; Joseph M. Hill, S.J.; Christopher Schroeder, S.J. Priests 7.

Jesuit Community Corporation at Saint Louis University - Jesuit Hall, 3601 Lindell Blvd., 63108-3393. Tel: 314-633-4400; Fax: 314-633-4404; Email: rbuhler@jesuits.org. Revs. John A. Apel, S.J.; James H. Baker, S.J.; Peter W. Bayhi, S.J.; Luke J. Byrne, S.J.; Robert E. Bosken, S.J., (Retired); Francis C. Brennan, S.J.; Richard O. Buhler, S.J., Rector, Email: rbuhler@jesuits-mis.org; Christopher S. Collins, S.J., Asst. to St. Louis Univ. Pres. for Mission & Identity; J. David Corrigan, S.J.; James J. Costello, S.J.; Thomas W. Cummings, S.J.; Donald M. Cunningham, S.J.; Anthony C. Daly, S.J.; Justin Daffron, S.J.; Terrence E. Dempsey, S.J.; Michael H. Durso, S.J., Teacher, DeSmet Jesuit High; John B. Foley, S.J.; John N. Folzenlogen, S.J., (Retired); Michael D. French, S.J., Dir. of Pavillion; Garth L. Hallett, S.J.; Steven Hawkes-Teeples, S.J., Loyola Academy; Donald E. Highberger, S.J.; John M. Hunthausen, S.J.; William J. Hutchison, S.J.; Thomas E. J. Kelly, S.J., (Retired); James G. Knapp, S.J.; David L. Koesterer, S.J.; Philip D. Kraus, S.J.; Edward L. Maginnis, S.J.; L. Gene Martens, S.J.; Michael K. May, S.J.; John L. McCarthy, S.J.; Frederick G. McLeod, S.J.; David V. Meconi, S.J., Prof.; Thomas J. Melancon, S.J.; Glenn R. Mueller, S.J.; John J. Mueller, S.J.; Earl C. Muller, S.J., Counsellor, Kenrick Seminary; Daniel C. O'Connell, S.J.; James M. O'Leary, S.J.; John W. Padberg, S.J.; Christopher Pinné, S.J., Teacher, St. Louis Univ. High School; Eugene C. Renard, S.J.; Albert C. Rotola, S.J.; Francis X. Ryan, S.J., Pastoral Care, St. Louis Univ. Hospital; Edward Salazar, S.J.; James A. Sebesta, S.J.; Gary G. Seibert, S.J.; Anthony J. Short, S.J.; James M. Short, S.J.; James H. Swetnam, S.J., (Retired); John G. Valenta; Curtis E. Van Del, S.J., (Retired); Richard J. Vogt, S.J.; Martin J. Whealen, S.J., (Retired); William T. Miller, S.J.; Mr. Ronald R. O'Dwyer, S.J.; Revs. Louis J. Oldani, S.J.; Frank J. Schmitt, S.J.; Paul G. Sheridan, S.J.; Timothy Thompson, S.J.; Bros. Robert L. Aug, S.J.; Albert Dorsey, S.J.; Rev. Michael V. Tueth, S.J.; Bros. John C. Fava, S.J.; Donald E. Lee, S.J., Loyola Academy; Robert C. Snyder, S.J.; Harold A. Teel, S.J., (Retired); Gerrard A. Schroeder, S.J.; Henry E. Welch, S.J. Brothers 8; Priests 70.

Leo Brown Jesuit Community, 3550 Russell Blvd., 63104. Tel: 314-771-5884; Fax: 314-771-6953; Email: jarmstrong@jesuits.org. Revs. Michael D. Dooley, S.J., Supr.; John F. Armstrong, S.J.; Jason Brauninger, S.J.; Richard E. Hadel, S.J.; Mark D.

McKenzie, S.J.; Ronald A. Mercier, S.J.; Jaroslaw Mikuczewski, S.J.; Robert E. Murphy, S.J. Priests 8; Total in Residence 8.

Marianist Community, P.O. Box 718, Eureka, 63025. Tel: 636-938-5470; Fax: 636-938-3493; Email: mcmrcc@aol.com. Rev. Jose Ramirez, S.M.; Bros. James Droste, S.M., Dir.; Joseph Markel, S.M.; Leo Slay, S.M.; Irwin Wachtel, S.M. Brothers 4; Priests 1.

Marianist Province of the United States (Society of Mary), 4425 W. Pine, 63108-2301. Tel: 314-533-1207; Fax: 314-533-0778; Email: msolma@sm-usa.org; Web: www.marianist.com. Revs. Martin A. Solma, S.M., Prov.; William J. Meyer, S.M., Asst. Rel. Life; Bros. Thomas Giardino, S.M., Asst. Educ.; Joseph Kamis, S.M., Asst. Prov.; Ronald Overman, S.M., Asst. Temporalities. Total Staff 23.

Priests of the Province on Special Assignment: Revs. James Schimelpfening, S.M.; Patrick Philbin, S.M., 7734 Santiago Canyon Rd., Orange, CA 92869-1829. Tel: 714-633-2698; Bros. Robert Donovan, S.M., 1516 Elm St., #10, Cincinnati, OH 45202; Frank Gomes, S.M.; Robert Juenemann, S.M.; Robert Metzger, S.M.; Robert Moriarty, S.M.; Edward Violett, S.M., 253 W. Ligustrum Dr., San Antonio, TX 78228-4020. Tel: 210-433-9114.

Priests of the Province Serving Outside the USA: Revs. David L. Fleming, S.J.; Michael R. Reaume, S.M., St. Columba's, Church Ave., Ballybrack, Dublin Ireland. Tel: 011-353-1285-8301; Fax: 011-353-1235-2789; Bros. James Contadino, S.M., St. Columba's, Church Ave., Ballybrack, Dublin Ireland. Tel: 011-353-1285-8301; Fax: 011-353-1235-2789; Lester Kaehler, S.M.; Gerard McAuley, S.M., Dir., St. Columba's, Church Ave., Ballybrack, Dublin Ireland. Tel: 011-353-1285-8301; Fax: 011-353-1235-2789; Fred Rech, S.M., St. Columba's, Church Ave., Ballybrack, Dublin Ireland. Tel: 011-353-1285-8301; Fax: 011-353-1235-2789; Revs. Quentin Hakenwerth, S.M.; John Thompson, S.M.; Bro. Delmar Jorn, S.M.

Priests of the Province Serving in the Missions: Rev. Gerald R. Hammel, S.M., Zambia; Bros. William Farrell, S.M., Guatemala; Steven Grazulis, S.M., Zambia; David Herbold, S.M., (Japan) Japan; Lawrence McBride, S.M., Patna, India. *Chaminade Community*, 401 S. Lindbergh Blvd., Creve Coeur, 63131. Tel: 314-993-1254; Fax: 314-993-6462. Revs. Thomas French, S.M., Pastor; Ralph A. Siefert, S.M.; Joseph Uvietta, S.M.; Oscar Vasquez, S.M., Dir.; Bro. James Eppy. Brothers 1; Priests 5. *Marycliff Marianist Community*, 4000 Hwy. 109, Box 718, Eureka, 63025-0178. Tel: 636-938-5470; Fax: 636-938-3493. Bros. James Droste, S.M.; Joseph Markel, S.M., Dir.; Irwin Wachtel, S.M.; Rev. Jose Ramirez, S.M. Brothers 3; Priests 1. *Maryland Avenue Marianist Community*, 4528 Maryland Ave., 63108. Tel: 314-367-0390. Bros. William Campbell, S.M., Dir.; Francis Heyer; Thomas Giardino, S.M.; James Maus, S.M.; Robert Resing, S.M.; Kenneth Straubinger, S.M.; Revs. Martin A. Solma, S.M.; Alvin McMenamy, S.M. Brothers 6; Priests 2. *Salve Marianist Community*, 4108 W. Pine Blvd., 63108. Tel: 314-289-9499. Rev. William J. Meyer, S.M., Dir.; Bros. Joseph Kamis, S.M.; Ronald Overman, S.M. Brothers 2; Priests 1. *Vianney Marianist Community*, 6029 Terri Lynn Dr., Saint Louis, 63123. Rev. Timothy Kenney, S.M.; Bro. Roy McLoughlin, S.M. Brothers 1; Priests 1.

St. Matthew Jesuit Community, 2715 N. Sarah St., 63113-2940. Tel: 314-531-6443; Fax: 314-533-7318; Email: stmatthews@sbcglobal.net; Web: www.stmatthewtheapostle.org. Revs. Patrick T. Quinn, S.J., Pastor; Kevin L. Cullen, S.J. Priests 2.

Missionaries of LaSalette, Province of Mary, Mother of the Americas, 4650 S. Broadway, 63111-1398. Tel: 314-353-5000; Email: lasalette.STL@gmail.com; Web: www.lasalette.org. Revs. John Nuelle, M.S., Supr., (Retired); Richard Lavoie, M.S.; Dennis J. Meyer, M.S., Treas.; Thomas Vellappallil, M.S.; James Winiarski, M.S.; Bro. Luke D. Bauer *Missionaries of La Salette Corp. of MissouriLaSalette Spirituality Center*, Tel: 314-353-5000. *La Salette Novitiate*, 4650 S. Broadway, 63111-1398. Tel: 314-353-5000. Rev. Dennis J. Meyer, M.S. *North American La Salette Mission Center*, 4650 S. Broadway, 63111. Tel: 314-352-0064; Fax: 314-352-3737; Email: lsmc2@charter.net; Web: www.lsmc.org. Rev. Thomas Vellappallil, M.S., Exec. Dir.; Connie Evans, Sec. *North American La Salette Mission Center*.

Redemptorist Fathers (1867) 1118 N. Grand Blvd., 63106. Tel: 314-533-0304; Fax: 314-533-4260; Email: the-rock@saintly.com; Web: www.stalphonsusrock.org. Total Staff 6. In Res. Revs. David Polek, C.Ss.R.; Kyle Fisher, C.Ss.R.; Very Rev. Richard M. Potts, C.Ss.R., V.F.; Bro. Terrence Burke, C.Ss.R.

Sacred Heart Jesuit Community, 3900 Westminster Pl., 63108-3902. Tel: 314-531-5400; Email: jddalysj@gmail.com. Revs. Michael D. Barber, S.J.; J. Daniel Daly, S.J., Supr.; Michael G. Harter, S.J.; Mark Kramer, S.J.; Robert L. Poirier, S.J.; Bro. William R. Rehg, S.J.; Mr. William A. McCormick, S.J.

U.S. Central & Southern Province, Society of Jesus, 4511 W. Pine Blvd., 63108-2191. Tel: 314-361-7765 ; Fax: 314-758-7164; Email: ucsprov@jesuits.org; Web: www.jesuitscentralsouthern.org. Very Rev. Ronald A. Mercier, S.J., Prov.; Revs. Francis Huete, S.J., Prov. Asst.; John F. Armstrong, S.J., Socius; Michael G. Harter, S.J., Asst. Formation; Michael D. Dooley, S.J., Vocation Dir.; Thomas P. Greene, S.J., Asst. Intl. Ministries; Geoffrey Miller, Asst. Secondary & Pre-secondary Educ.; Thomas Reynolds, Asst. Higher Educ.; Mary Baudouin, Asst. for Social Ministries; Ana Casey, Asst. for Health Care; Mr. John Fitzpatrick, Dir. Advancement; Therese Meyerhoff, Dir. Communications; David P. Miros, Ph.D., Archivist, Jesuit Archives, Central US. Brothers 21; Novices 18; Priests 294; Students in Major Seminary 40.

White House Retreat Jesuit Community (1922) 7410 Christopher Dr., 63129-5701. Tel: 314-846-2575; Fax: 314-293-0931; Email: whretreat@whretreat.org; Web: www.whretreat.org. Rev. Ralph G. Huse, S.J. *Office* (1922) 7400 Christopher Dr., 63129-5701. Tel: 314-416-6400; Tel: 800-643-1003; Fax: 314-416-6464; Email: reservations@whretreat.org; Web: www.whretreat.org. Revs. James A. Blumeyer, S.J., Assoc. Dir.; Edward Arroyo, S.J., Assoc. Dir.; Anthony J. Wieck, S.J., Spiritual Advisor.

DARDENNE PRAIRIE. *Franciscan Brothers of the Holy Cross St. Charles Friary*, 12 Dardenne Woods Ct., Dardenne Prairie, 63368. Tel: 636-561-0589; Email: bdavids61@gmail.com; Web: www.franciscanbrothers.net. Bros. David Sarnecki, F.F.S.C., Supr.; Raphael Kreikemeier, F.F.S.C.

DITTMER. *Franciscan Friars Province of the Sacred Heart*, St. Germain Friary, 7992 St. Francis Ln., Eime Rd., P.O. Box 278, Dittmer, 63023-0278. Tel: 636-285-7362 (Friary); Tel: 636-274-0554 (Il Ritiro). Revs. Bertin Miller, O.F.M., Guardian & Exec. Dir. RECON - Wounded Brothers Program; Pio Jackson, O.F.M., Chap.; Luis Runde, O.F.M., Food for the Poor. Priests 6.

Servants of the Paraclete (1947) St. Michael's Community, 6476 Eime Rd., Dittmer, 63023. Tel: 636-274-5226; Fax: 636-274-1430; Email: liamhsp@yahoo.com; Web: www.theservants.org. Rev. Benedict Livingston, s.P.; Very Rev. Liam Hoare, s.P.; Rev. Edward Rolph, s.P. *Vianney Renewal Center* (1989) 6476 Eime Rd., Dittmer, 63023. Tel: 636-274-5226; Fax: 636-274-1430.

EARTH CITY. *Congregation of the Mission Western Province (Vincentians)*, 13663 Rider Trail N., Earth City, 63045-1512. Tel: 314-344-1184; Fax: 314-344-2989; Email: provinceoffice@vincentian.org; Web: www.vincentian.org. Very Rev. Raymond Van Dorpe, C.M., Prov.; Revs. Joseph S. Williams, C.M., Asst. Prov.; Kevin P. McCracken, C.M., Prov. Treas.

EUREKA. *Franciscan Brothers House of Studies*, 300 Forby Rd., P.O. Box 129, Eureka, 63025. Tel: 636-938-5539; Email: shrine1olc@aol.com. Bro. John A. Spila, O.S.F., Dir. House of Studies of Franciscan Missionary Brothers of the Sacred Heart of Jesus. Total in Residence 2; Total Staff 1.

HIGH RIDGE. *Society of Our Mother of Peace* (1966) Sons of Our Mother of Peace, Mary the Font Solitude, 6150 Antire Rd., High Ridge, 63049-2135. Tel; 636-677-3235; Fax: 636-677-5284; Email: marythefont@gmail.com; Web: marythefont.org. Rev. Placid Guste, S.M.P., Supr. Gen. Brothers 1; Priests 3; Total in Residence 4; Total Staff 3.

LIGUORI. *Alphonsian Foundation*, One Liguori Dr., Liguori, 63057-9998. Tel: 636-223-1455; Fax: 636-223-1394; Email: foundation@alfonsiana.org; Web: www.alphonsianfoundation.org. Rev. Andrzej Wodka, C.Ss.R., Pres. Alphonsian Academy. Purpose: to provide public relations and financial support for the Alphonsian Academy of Moral Theology in Rome.

St. Clement Health Care Center (1988) 300 Liguori Dr., Liguori, 63057. Tel: 636-464-3656; Fax: 636-464-1361; Email: stclementliguori@gmail.com. Very Rev. John Schmidt, C.Ss.R., Rector; Revs. Vincent H. Aggeler, C.Ss.R., (Retired); Albert C. Babin, C.Ss.R.; Vincent Minh Cao, C.Ss.R., Consultor; Albert J. Castellino, C.Ss.R.; Warren Drinkwater, C.Ss.R.; Wilfred E. Lowery, C.Ss.R., (Retired); Raymond Maiser, C.Ss.R., (Retired); Byron J. Miller, C.Ss.R., Vicar; Edward T. Morgan, C.Ss.R., (Retired); Michael P. Quinn, C.Ss.R.; Carl Schindler, C.Ss.R., (Retired); Joseph H. Stenger, C.SS.R., (Retired); John F. Willett, C.Ss.R., (Retired); William Wright, C.Ss.R., (Retired); Bros. James Burke, C.Ss.R., (Retired); Marvin Hamman, C.Ss.R., (Retired), (Retired); Robert T. Ruffing, C.Ss.R., (Retired); Deacon Richard W. Fischer, C.Ss.R., Consultor; Revs. Lamar Partin, C.Ss.R.; Victor Karls, C.Ss.R.; Richard Boever, C.Ss.R.; Peter Schavitz, C.Ss.R.; Joseph M. Curalli, C.Ss.R.; Bros. Paul Yasenak, C.Ss.R.; Stephen Fruge, C.Ss.R.; Revs. Rudy Papes, C.Ss.R.; Martin Stillmock, C.Ss.R.; Bro. Daniel Korn, C.Ss.R.; Revs. John Cody, C.Ss.R.; Richard Quinn, C.Ss.R. Total in Residence 32; Total Staff 4.

Liguori Mission House/Redemptorists, Ten Liguori Dr., Liguori, 63057. Tel: 636-464-6999; Fax: 636-464-6765; Email: gmaycssr@aol.com. Revs. Gregory May, C.Ss.R., Rector; Lamar Partin, C.Ss.R., Vicar; Richard Boever, C.Ss.R.; John Cody, C.Ss.R.; Joseph M. Curalli, C.Ss.R.; Victor Karls, C.Ss.R.; Rudy Papes, C.Ss.R.; Peter Schavitz, C.Ss.R.; Martin Stillmoch, C.Ss.R.; Bros. Stephen Fruge, C.Ss.R.; Daniel Korn, C.Ss.R.; Paul Yasenak, C.Ss.R. Brothers 3; Priests 9.

Order of the Most Holy Redeemer, Monastery of the Most Holy Redeemer, Thailand, The Redemptoristine Nuns, 200 Liguori Dr., Liguori, 63057. Tel: 636-464-1093; Email: rednuns@gmail.com. Sr. Joan E. Calver, O.SS.R., Prioress.

PACIFIC. *Franciscan Missionary Brothers of the Sacred Heart of Jesus*, 265 St. Joseph's Hill Rd., Pacific, 63069. Tel: 636-938-5361; Email: shrine1olc@aol.com; Web: www.franciscancaring.org. Bro. John Spila, O.S.F., Dir. Gen. Generalate of Franciscan Missionary Brothers of the Sacred Heart of Jesus. Professed Brothers 4.

Black Madonna Shrine, 100 St. Joseph Hill Rd., Pacific, 63069. Tel: 636-938-5361; Email: shrine1olc@aol.com. Bro. John A. Spila, O.S.F., Dir. Staff 2.

PERRYVILLE. *Congregation of the Mission* aka St. Mary's of the Barrens, 1701 W. St. Joseph St., Perryville, 63775-1599. Tel: 573-547-6533; Fax: 573-547-2204; Email: mjoyce@vincentian.org. Rev. Michael P. Joyce, C.M., Supr.; Bro. Timothy Opferman, C.M., Treas.; Revs. Thomas A. Grace, C.M.; John F. Gagnepain, C.M.; Edward J. Tomasiewicz, C.M.; Charles F. Shelby, C.M.; Robert Wood, C.M.; Thomas R. Hinni, C.M.; Walter Housey, C.M.; Edward Gallagher, C.M.; Binh Nguyen, C.M.; Walter J. Reisinger, C.M., (Dixon, MO); Ronald W. Ramson, C.M.; William Rhinehart, C.M.; George Weber, C.M.; Richard L. Wehrmeyer, C.M.; J. Godden Menard, C.M.; Bros. Harvey Goertz, C.M.; Richard A. Hermann, C.M.; Thomas Juneman, C.M.; John Mangogna, C.M.; Francis Keigher, C.M.; Richard Zoellner, C.M.; Revs. Francis H. Agnew, C.M.; Thomas Croak, C.M.; Joseph C. Geders, C.M.; Bro. David P. Goodman, C.M.; Revs. Stafford Poole, C.M.; John Richardson, C.M.; John Shine, C.M.; Deacon Arnold Hernandez, C.M. U.S. Motherhouse of the Congregation of the Mission (Vincentian Fathers, Western Prov.). Priests 22; Professed Brothers 8.

ROCKY MOUNT. *Contemplative Heart of Mary Hermitage*, 20542 Echo Valley Rd., Rocky Mount, 65072. Tel: 573-557-2119. Rev. Robert L. Aten.

[R] PERSONAL PRELATURES

KIRKWOOD. *Prelature of the Holy Cross and Opus Dei*, Wespine Study Center, 100 E. Essex Ave., Kirkwood, 63122. Tel: 314-821-1608; Fax: 314-821-4722; Email: info@wespine.org; Web: www.opusdei.org. Revs. Michael E. Giesler; Gregory Coyne.

[S] CONVENTS AND RESIDENCES FOR SISTERS

ST. LOUIS. *Adorers of the Blood of Christ, United States Region*, 4233 Sulphur Ave., 63109. Tel: 314-351-6294; Fax: 314-351-6789; Email: adminassistant@adorers.org; Web: www.adorers.org. Sr. Vicki Bergkamp, A.S.C., Rel. Order Leader. Sisters 183.

Carmel of St. Joseph (1863) 9150 Clayton Rd., 63124-1898. Tel: 314-993-4394; Fax: 314-993-4346; Email: prioress@stlouiscarmel.org. Mother Marya Williams, O.C.D., Prioress. Discalced Carmelites. Chapel of the Precious Blood. Novices 2; Professed 14; Extern Sisters 1.

Carmelite Religious of Trivandrum, 5200 Glennon Dr., 63119. Sr. Vivienne Gemma Mendonca, C.C.R., Contact Person.

Clelian House Convent, 5324 Wilson Ave., 63110. Tel: 314-803-2600; Email: jruggeri@ascjus.org. Sr. Jude Ruggeri, A.S.C.J., Supr. Sisters 6.

Congregation of Mary, Queen, 3815 Westminster Pl., 63108. Tel: 314-371-1294; Email: vocation@trinhvuong.org; Web: www.trinhvuong.org. Sr. Pauline Nguyen, C.M.R., Supr.

Congregational Office of the Sisters of St. Joseph of Carondelet, 10777 Sunset Office Dr., Ste. 10, 63127. Tel: 314-394-1985; Fax: 314-735-4476; Email: congctroffice@csjcarondelet.org; Web: www.csjcarondelet.org. Sisters Danielle Bonetti, C.S.J., Congregational Leadership Team; Barbara Dreher, C.S.J., Congregational Leadership Team; Mary

Ann Leininger, C.S.J., Congregational Leadership Team; Mary McKay, C.S.J., Congregational Leadership Team; Miriam D. Ukeritis, C.S.J., Congregational Leadership Team; Pam Harding, C.S.J., Exec. Asst.; Eleanor Ortega, C.S.J., Asst. Mission Coord. (Los Angeles Office); Barbara Siderewicz, O.S.F., Receptionist/Sec.; Carol Marie Wildt, S.S.N.D., Archivist; Mr. Tom Ratz, Fin. Office; Mrs. Kim Westerman, Congregational Communications Coord. Sisters 10.

Contemplative Sisters of the Good Shepherd (1859) 7660 Natural Bridge Rd., 63121. Tel: 314-837-1719 ; Fax: 314-837-5925; Email: cgsflo@mindspring.com; Web: www.archstl.org. Sr. Sharon Rose Authorson, C.G.S., Supr. Sisters 10.

Cor Jesu Academy Convent, 10230 Gravois Rd., 63123. Tel: 314-843-8272; Email: bthomas@ascjus.org. Sr. Barbara Thomas, A.S.C.J., Supr. Sisters 7.

Daughters of Charity of St. Vincent de Paul, Province of St. Louise (1910) 4328 Westminster, 63108-2624. Tel: 314-533-3004; Email: tom.beck@doc.org; Web: www.daughtersofcharity.org. Sr. Catherine Mary Norris, Prov. Provincial House for Daughters of Charity of St. Vincent de Paul, Province of St. Louise. Sisters 415. *Provincial Offices*, 4330 Olive St., 63108-2622. Tel: 314-533-4770;
Fax: 314-561-4676; Email: tom.beck@doc.org; Web: www.daughtersofcharity.org. Sr. Catherine Mary Norris, Prov. Sisters 430.

Daughters of St. Paul Convent, 9804 Watson Rd., 63126. Tel: 314-965-6935; Fax: 314-984-8431; Email: stlouis@pauline.org; Web: www.pauline.org. Postulants 3; Sisters 5.

Eucharistic Missionaries of St. Theresa, 12934 Marine Ave., 63146. Tel: 314-434-1312.

The Federation of the Congregations of Sisters of Saint Joseph of the United States of America, 6400 Minnesota Ave., 63111-2807. Tel: 314-925-7662; Email: info@cssjfed.org; Web: cssjfed.org. Sr. Patricia Johnson, C.S.J., Exec. Dir. Sisters 4,203.

Franciscan Sisters of Mary Administration (1872) 3221 McKelvey Rd. - Ste 107, Bridgeton, 63044.
Tel: 314-768-1824; Fax: 314-768-1880; Email: sscholl@fsmonline.org; Email: rhutchins@fsmonline.org; Web: www.fsmonline.org. Sr. Susan Scholl, F.S.M., Pres. Offices of the Franciscan Sisters of Mary. Professed Sisters Elsewhere 4.

Franciscan Sisters of Mary Novitiate (1872) 3221 McKelvey Rd. - Ste. 107, Bridgeton, 63044.
Tel: 314-768-1828; Fax: 314-768-1880; Email: fhaarmann@fsmonline.org; Web: www.fsmonline.org.

Franciscan Sisters of Our Lady of Perpetual Help (1901) 335 S. Kirkwood Rd., 63122.
Tel: 314-965-3700; Fax: 314-965-3710; Email: srrenita@fsolph.org; Web: www.franciscansisters-olph.org. Sr. Renita Brummer, O.S.F., Min. Gen. Motherhouse and Novitiate of Franciscan Sisters of Our Lady of Perpetual Help. Sisters 81; Total Staff 6; Total in Community 81.

Heart of Mary Center, 6220 Westway Pl., 63109-3417. Web: www.dhmna.org. Daughters of the Heart of Mary 4.

St. Joseph's Provincial House (1836) 6400 Minnesota Ave., 63111-2899. Tel: 314-481-8800;
Fax: 314-481-2366; Email: mjohnson@csjsl.org; Web: www.csjsl.org. Sisters Mary Margaret Lazio, C.S.J., Province Leadership Team; Marilyn Lott, C.S.J., Province Leadership Team; Mary F. Johnson, C.S.J., Province Treas.; Rita Marie Schmitz, C.S.J., Province Leadership Team; Deacon Joseph Wingbermuehle, Admin. Prov. House of the Sisters of St. Joseph of Carondelet. Sisters 269; In Archdiocese 202.

Loretto Center, c/o Loretto St. Louis Staff Office, Millennium Centre, 9201 Watson Rd., Ste. 220, 63126. Tel: 314-962-8112; Fax: 314-962-0400; Email: dday@lorettocommunity.org; Web: www.lorettocommunity.org. Sr. Donna Day, Admin. Sisters 1; Total Staff 3.

Missionaries of Charity, 3629 Cottage Ave., 63113-3539. Tel: 314-533-2777. Sisters M. Jonathan, M.C., Regl. Supr.; M. Marilyn, M.C., Supr. Missionaries of Charity also in: Peoria, IL; Chicago, IL; Detroit, MI; Memphis, TN; Dallas, TX; Little Rock, AR; Baton Rouge, LA; Lafayette, LA; Lexington, KY; Atlanta, GA; Charlotte, NC; Gary, IN; Indianapolis, IN., Houston, TX; Minneapolis, MN. Sisters 7.

Monastery of St. Clare of the Immaculate Conception, 200 Marycrest Dr., 63129-4813. Tel: 314-846-2618. Mother Mary Elizabeth, O.S.C., Abbess. Poor Clare Nuns. Cloistered Nuns 10.

Mount Grace Convent and Chapel of Perpetual Adoration, 1438 E. Warne Ave., 63107.
Tel: 314-381-2654; Fax: 314-381-6756; Email: holyspiritadoration@gmail.com; Web: www.mountgraceconvent.org. P.O. Box 16459, 63125. Sr. Mary Catherine, S.Sp.S.deAP., Supr. Sister Servants of the Holy Spirit of Perpetual Adoration (Generalate, Bad Driburg, Germany). Attended by Divine Word Fathers. Professed 18; Sisters 18.

Religious Sisters of Mercy, 5047 Washington Pl., 63108. Tel: 314-932-7326; Fax: 314-932-7327. Sr. Mary Charles Mayer, R.S.M., Local Supr.

Sacred Heart Villa Convent, 2108 Macklind Ave., 63110. Tel: 314-771-2224; Email: jruggeri@ascjus.org. Sr. Jude Ruggeri, A.S.C.J., Supr. Sisters 6.

Salesian Missionaries of Mary Immaculate, 798 Buckley Rd., 63125. Tel: 314-416-1778; Email: smmi.us@gmail.com. Sr. Jolly Joseph, S.M.M.I., Supr. Sisters 3.

School Sisters of Notre Dame aka SSND (1895) Sancta Maria in Ripa, 320 E. Ripa Ave., 63125-2897. Tel: 314-544-0455; Fax: 314-544-6754; Email: mhummert@ssndcp.org; Web: www.ssnd.org. Sr. Mary Anne Owens, S.S.N.D., Rel. Order Leader
School Sisters of Notre Dame, Central Pacific Province. Sisters 919.

Liturgical Fabric Arts (1983) Sancta Maria in Ripa, 320 E. Ripa Ave., 63125-2897. Tel: 314-544-0455;
Tel: 314-633-7030; Fax: 314-544-6754; Email: josephinessnd@yahoo.com; Web: www.liturgicalfabricarts.com.

Maria Center (1980) 336 E. Ripa Ave., 63125.
Tel: 314-544-6757; Tel: 314-633-7050;
Fax: 314-633-7052; Email: mariacenter@ssndcp.org. 325 E. Ripa Ave., St Louis, 63125.

Resource Development (1991) Sancta Maria in Ripa, 320 E. Ripa Ave., St Louis, 63125-2897.
Tel: 314-631-3530; Fax: 314-633-7056; Email: missionadv@ssndcp.org; Web: www.ssndcp.org.

School Sisters of Notre Dame Central Pacific Province, Inc., 320 E. Ripa, 63125.
Tel: 314-544-0455; Fax: 314-544-6754; Email: mhummert@ssndcp.org; Web: www.ssnd.org. Sr. Mary Anne Owens, S.S.N.D., Prov. Supr. Sisters 919.

School Sisters of Notre Dame Worldwide, Inc., 320 E. Ripa Ave., 63125. Tel: 262-787-1499; Email: joanfrey@ssnd.org. Sr. Joan Frey, S.S.N.D., Office Mgr. Sisters 2,423.

Sisters of Good Shepherd Province of Mid North America (1999) 7654 Natural Bridge Rd., 63121.
Tel: 314-381-3400; Fax: 314-381-7102; Email: mmunday@gspmna.org; Web: goodshepherdsisters.org. Sr. Madeleine Munday, R.G.S., Prov. Leader. Sisters 125.

Sisters of St. Francis of the Martyr St. George, 6825 Natural Bridge Rd., 63121. Tel: 314-383-4765;
Fax: 314-383-7256; Email: smchristine@mogch.org; Web: mogch.org. Sr. M. Christine Crowder, F.S.G.M., Supr. Sisters 11.

Mother of Good Counsel Home, 6825 Natural Bridge Rd., 63121. Tel: 314-383-4765; Fax: 314-383-7256; Email: smbeata@mogch.org. Sr. M. Christine Crowder, F.S.G.M., Admin. Sisters 12.

Sisters of the Good Shepherd (1835) 7654 Natural Bridge Rd., 63121. Tel: 314-381-3400;
Fax: 314-382-5294; Email: ceballos@gspmna.org; Web: www.goodshepherdsisters.org. Sr. Marta Ceballos, R.G.S., Local Leader. Sisters 12; Total Staff 16.

Society of Helpers (Paris 1856) (St. Louis 1903) 2800 Olive St., Apt 12K, 63103. Tel: 314-535-2622; Email: hottinger12k@att.net; Web: www.helpers.org. Sr. Patricia A. Hottinger, S.H., Contact. Spiritual Direction, Parish Weeks & Months of Guided Prayer, Visiting homebound and frail elders.
Society of the Helpers of the Holy Souls.

Society of the Sacred Heart, United States-Canada Province, Provincial House, 4120 Forest Park Ave., 63108. Tel: 314-652-1500; Fax: 314-534-6800; Email: provincialhouse@rscj.org; Web: www.rscj.org. Sr. Barbara Dawson, R.S.C.J., Prov. Province Corporations: California Province of the Society of the Sacred Heart, Inc.; Ladies of the Sacred Heart of St. Louis, Missouri; Society of the Sacred Heart, Chicago Province, Inc.; Religious of the Sacred Heart, Washington Province, Inc.; Religious of the Sacred Heart, New York Province, Inc.; Religious of the Sacred Heart in Massachusetts, Inc. Sisters in Archdiocese 30.

BRIDGETON. *Incarnate Word Sisters* (1869) 3393 McKelvey Rd., Apt. 326, Bridgeton, 63044.
Tel: 314-387-3326; Email: mseeker314@aol.com; Web: www.ccrtsantonio.org. Sisters Bette Bluhm, C.C.V.I., Prov. Coord.; Mary Ann Seeker, C.C.V.I., Contact (Retired). Sisters 24.

Sisters of Divine Providence, 3415 Bridgeland Dr., Bridgeton, 63044. Tel: 314-397-3382;
Fax: 314-209-9207; Email: mbisbey@cdpsisters.org; Web: www.cdpsisters.org. Sisters Michele Bisbey, C.D.P., Prov.; Mary Michael McCulla, C.D.P., Area Asst. Room at the Inn.
Sisters of Divine Providence of Missouri
Sisters of Divine Providence of Missouri Charitable Trust Sisters 22.

CHESTERFIELD. *Missionary Sisters of St. Peter Claver* (1894) 667 Woods Mill Rd. S., P.O. Box 6067, Chesterfield, 63006-6067. Tel: 314-469-4932;
Fax: 314-469-0869; Email: stl1928@charter.net. Sr. Genevieve Kudlik, Delegate. Sisters 4.

ELLISVILLE. *Passionist Nuns Monastery* (1948) 15700 Clayton Rd., Ellisville, 63011-2300.
Tel: 636-527-6867; Fax: 636-527-6867; Web: passionistnunsofstlouis.org. Mother Mary Veronica, C.P., Supr. Cloistered Contemplatives. Novices 1; Sisters 5; Professed Religious 4.

FLORISSANT. *Pallottine Missionary Sisters-Queen of Apostles Province* (Rome 1838) (U.S. 1912) 15270 Old Halls Ferry Rd., Florissant, 63034-1611.
Tel: 314-837-7100; Fax: 314-837-1041; Email: srgailb@gmail.com; Web: www.pallottinesac.org. Sr. Gail Borgmeyer, S.A.C., Prov. Sisters of the Catholic Apostolate. Sisters at Provincial House 1.

FRONTENAC. *Religious of the Sacred Heart Convent* (1929) Villa Duchesne, #1 Jaccard Ln., Frontenac, 63131. Tel: 314-872-8597; Fax: 314-432-7713; Email: nghio@rscj.org. Sisters 3.

HIGH RIDGE. *Society of Our Mother of Peace, Daughters of Our Mother of Peace* (1966) Mary the Font Solitude, 6150 Antire Rd., High Ridge, 63049-2135.
Tel: 636-677-3235; Fax: 636-677-5284; Email: marythefont@gmail.com; Web: marythefont.org. Sisters Therese Marie Labicane, S.M.P., Local Supr.; Anne Marie DeFord, S.M.P., Treas. & Sec. Total in Residence 9.

IMPERIAL. *Our Lady Queen of Apostles Convent*, 800 Montebello Camp Rd., Imperial, 63052.
Tel: 636-464-0163; Email: csansone@ascjus.org. Sr. Carol Sansone, A.S.C.J., Supr.

KIRKWOOD. *Carmelite Sisters of the Divine Heart of Jesus Provincial House and Novitiate* (1891) 10341 Manchester Rd., Kirkwood, 63122.
Tel: 314-965-7616; Fax: 314-822-3154; Email: vocations@carmelitedcj.org; Web: carmelitedcj.org. Sr. M. Angela Therese Kim, Prov. Supr. The Sisters own and operate two nursing homes and one day care center in their Province. Novices 1; Postulants 3; Sisters 15; Temporary Vows 3; Final Professed 8.

Ursuline Provincialate, 353 S. Sappington Rd., Kirkwood, 63122. Tel: 314-821-6884;
Fax: 314-821-6888; Email: ursulines@osucentral.org; Web: www.osucentral.org. Sr. Rita A. Bregenhorn, O.S.U., Prov. Prioress. Central Province of the Ursuline Nuns of the Roman Union. Sisters: In Province 98; In the Archdiocese 31.
Other Locations:*Ursuline Sisters*, 500 Clemens Dr., Florissant, 63033. Tel: 314-839-2803; Email: osumjb@sbcglobal.net. Sr. Marilyn Burkemper. Sisters 2.

Ursuline Sisters, 105 N. Holmes Ave., 63122.
Tel: 314-698-2506. Sisters 3.

Ursuline Sisters, 5821 Sutherland, 63109.
Tel: 314-353-5745; Email: madooling@ursulinestl.org. Sr. Mary Ann Dooling, O.S.U. Sisters 5.

Ursuline Sisters, 801 Fairdale Ave., Rock Hill, 63119. Tel: 314-942-9861; Email: rita@osucentral.org. Sr. Rita A. Bregenhorn, O.S.U. Sisters 5.

Ursuline Sisters, 921 H Carriage Circle Ln., Kirkwood, 63122. Tel: 314-394-0931; Email: adele@osucentral.org. Sr. Maria Teresa de Llano, Rel. Order Leader. Sisters 3.

Ursuline Sisters, 244 W. Adams Ave., 63122.
Tel: 314-858-1120. Sisters 2.

LIGUORI. *Monastery of St. Alphonsus* (1960) 200 Liguori Dr., Liguori, 63057-9999.
Tel: 636-464-1093; Fax: 636-464-1073; Email: rednun@redemptoristinenuns.org; Email: prayerrequest@redemptoristinenuns.org; Web: www.redemptoristinenuns.org. Sr. Margaret Wilkinson, O.Ss.R., Prioress. Order of the Most Holy Redeemer (Redemptoristine Nuns). Professed 12.

NORMANDY. *Convent of the Immaculate Heart*, 7626 Natural Bridge Rd., Normandy, 63121.
Tel: 314-383-0300; Fax: 314-383-0337; Email: srmpbrgs@aol.com; Web: www.goodshepherdsisters.org. A residence for aged & infirm. Good Shepherd Sisters of the Mid-North America Prov. Total in Residence 25; Total Staff 35.

O'FALLON. *St. Mary's Institute of O'Fallon*, 204 N. Main St., O'Fallon, 63366-2299. Tel: 636-240-6010; Fax: 636-272-5031; Email: jbader@cpps-ofallon.org; Web: www.cpps-ofallon.org. Sr. Janice Bader, C.PP.S., Supr. Gen. Motherhouse of the Sisters of the Most Precious Blood.Chapel of St. Joseph. Sisters in Archdiocese 96.

ST. CHARLES. *Religious of the Sacred Heart* (1800) 301 Decatur St., St. Charles, 63301-2089.
Tel: 636-946-7276; Fax: 636-949-6659; Email: mmmunch@rscj.org. Religious 3; Sisters 3.

ST. LOUIS COUNTY. *Religious of the Sacred Heart*, 541 S. Mason Rd., St. Louis County, 63141-8550.
Tel: 314-878-6705; Email: khughes@rscj.org; Web: www.rscj.org. Sisters 6.

TOWN AND COUNTRY. *Monastery of the Visitation, St. Louis*, 2039 N. Geyer Rd., Frontenac, 63131.
Tel: 314-625-9260; Email: srmtr@visitationmonastery.org; Web: www.

visitationmonastery.org/stlouis. Sr. Marie Therese Ruthmann, V.H.M., Supr. Residence of Visitation Nuns Living at the Monastery of the Visitation. Sisters 6.

Offices of Visitation Nuns at the Monastery of the Visitation, 3020 N. Ballas Rd., Town and Country, 63131. Tel: 314-625-9247; Tel: 314-625-9260; Email: srmtr@visitationmonastery.org. Sr. Marie Therese Ruthmann, V.H.M., Supr. Sisters 7.

Residence of Visitation Nuns, 2039 N. Geyer Rd., 63131. Tel: 314-625-9247; Email: srmtr@visitationmonastery.org. Sr. Marie Therese Ruthmann, V.H.M., Supr. Sisters 7.

[T] HOMES FOR MEN AND WOMEN

ST. LOUIS. *Cathedral Tower*, 325 N. Newstead Ave., 63108. Tel: 314-367-5500, Ext. 121; Fax: 314-361-5099; Web: www.ccstl.org. Building which houses several agencies of Catholic Charities: Queen of Peace Center; St. Elizabeth Hall; and Peace for Kids, Inc. Residents 150.

Father Dempsey's Hotel, Inc., 3427 Washington Ave., 63103. Tel: 314-535-7221; Fax: 314-535-7289; Email: maboussie@archstl.org. Martie Aboussie, Exec. Dir. Total in Residence 77; Total Staff 4.

Father Jim's Home, 3427 Washington Ave., 63103. Tel: 314-535-7221; Fax: 314-535-7289; Email: maboussie@archstl.org. Martie Aboussie, Exec. Dir. Total in Residence 77; Total Staff 4.

St. Martha's Hall, P.O. Box 4950, 63108. Tel: 314-533-1313; Fax: 314-533-2035; Email: stmarthashall@sbcglobal.net; Web: www.saintmarthas.org. Michelle Schiller-Baker, Exec. Dir. Provides Shelter, Advocacy and Support to Abused Women & their Children. Bed Capacity 24; Tot Asst. Annually 220; Total Staff 15.

St. Philippine Home (1996) 1015 Goodfellow Blvd., 63112. Tel: 314-454-1012; Fax: 314-367-7455; Email: lpennington@ccstl.org. Lara B. Pennington, Exec. Dir. Transitional housing for St. Louis homeless women with addiction and their children, accredited by COA Council on Accreditation. Bed Capacity 30; Tot Asst. Annually 100; Total Staff 12; Outpatients 20.

Queen of Peace Center (1985) 325 N. Newstead Ave., 63108. Tel: 314-531-0511; Fax: 314-652-2637; Email: sspruell@ccstl.org; Web: www.qopcstl.org. Sharon Spruell, CEO. Comprehensive residential and outpatient behavioral healthcare for women with substance abuse, their children and families. Specialty in pregnant women, trauma and co-occurring disorders. Permanent and transitional housing programs. Licensed by DMH. Bed Capacity 16; Tot Asst. Annually 2,900; Total Staff 100; Vouchers 600.

Rural Parish Clinic, 10120 Crest Rd., Cadet, 63630.

Rosati Center, 4220-24 N. Grand Ave., 63107. Tel: 314-534-6624; Fax: 314-535-4394. Permanent supportive housing for former homeless single adults. Managed by St. Patrick Center. Total Staff 8; Studio Apartments 26; Total Assisted 30.

Rosati Group Home, Inc., 4218 N. Grand Blvd., 63107. Tel: 314-534-6624; Fax: 314-535-4394; Email: nboland@stpatrickcenter.org; Web: stpatrickcenter.org. Greg Vogelweid, Admin. Group Home for homeless mentally ill adults. Managed by St. Patrick Center. Total Staff 10; Total Assisted 140.

[U] RETREAT HOUSES

ST. LOUIS. *Mercy Center*, 2039 N. Geyer Rd., 63131-3332. Tel: 314-966-4313; Fax: 314-909-4600; Email: dhartman@mercysc.org. Sr. Donella Hartman, R.S.M., Admin. Sisters of Mercy of the Americas, South Central Community, Inc.Conference and Renewal Ministry.

**Mercy Conference and Retreat Center*, 2039 N. Geyer Rd., 63131. Tel: 314-966-4686; Fax: 314-909-4600; Email: dstringfield@mercycenterstl.org; Web: www.mercycenterstl.org. Dawn Stringfield, Exec. Dir., Tel: 314-909-4656.

White House Retreat (1922) 7400 Christopher Dr., 63129. Tel: 314-416-6400; Fax: 314-416-6464; Tel: 800-643-1003; Email: whretreat@whretreat.org; Web: www.whretreat.org. Rev. Ralph G. Huse, S.J., Supr.

Retreat House (1922) 7400 Christopher Dr., 63129. Tel: 314-416-6400. William F. Schmidt, Dir.; Revs. Richard E. Hadel, S.J., Assoc. Dir.; Eugene C. Renard, S.J., Assoc. Dir.; Leonard E. Kraus, S.J., Assoc. Dir.; Bro. John C. Fava, S.J., Assoc. Dir.; Rev. Ralph G. Huse, S.J., Assoc. Dir. Total in Residence 6; Total Staff 6.

DITTMER. *Il Ritiro-The Little Retreat* dba Il Ritiro Franciscan Retreat Center (1981) 7935 St. Francis Ln., P.O. Box 38, Dittmer, 63023. Tel: 636-274-0554 (Toll Free from St. Louis); Email: il.ritiro@gmail.com; Web: www.il-ritiro.org. Sr. Ann Pierre Wilken, O.S.F., Dir.; Revs. Bertin Miller, O.F.M.; Pio Jackson, O.F.M. Operated by the Franciscan Friars. Priests 2; Total Staff 8.

Vianney Renewal Center (1988) 6476 Eime Rd., P.O. Box 130, Dittmer, 63023. Tel: 636-274-5226; Fax: 636-274-1430; Web: www.theservants.org. Very Rev. David Fitzgerald, s.P., Father Servant; Dr. Rob Furey, Ph.D., Clinical Dir. Operated by the Servants of the Paraclete. Total in Residence 33; Total Staff 12.

EUREKA. *Marianist Retreat & Conference Center* (1967) P.O. Box 718, Eureka, 63025-0718. Tel: 636-938-5390; Fax: 636-938-3493; Email: info@mretreat.org; Web: www.mretreat.org. Mr. Jim Ford, Dir.; Rev. Jose Ramirez, S.M. Conducted by the Marianist Province of the U.S.Center for Formation and Growth in the Christian Life. Total in Residence 5; Total Staff 20.

FLORISSANT. *Pallottine Renewal Center, Inc.* (1969) 15270 Old Halls Ferry Rd., Florissant, 63034-1611. Tel: 314-837-7100; Fax: 314-837-1041; Email: director@pallottinerenewal.org; Web: www.pallottinerenewal.org. Sr. Gail Borgmeyer, S.A.C., Prov. Supr.; Marilyn S. Webb, Dir. Pallottine Missionary Sisters, Queen of Apostles Province. Total Staff 7.

HIGH RIDGE. *Society of Our Mother of Peace at Mary the Font Solitude* (1966) 6150 Antire Rd., High Ridge, 63049-2135. Tel: 636-677-3235; Fax: 636-677-5284; Email: marythefont@gmail.com; Web: marythefont.org. Sisters Therese Marie Labicane, S.M.P., Local Supr.; Anne Marie DeFord, S.M.P., Treas.; Rev. Placid Guste, S.M.P.

PEVELY. *Vision of Peace Ministries* (1977) 1000 Abbey Ln., P.O. Box 69, Pevely, 63070. Tel: 636-475-3697; Fax: 636-475-3697; Email: visofpeace@juno.com. Ms. Jane Guenther, Treas. Total in Residence 2.

WILDWOOD. *La Salle Institute - Retreat and Conference Center* (1886) 2101 Rue De La Salle, Wildwood, 63038-2299. Tel: 636-938-5374; Fax: 636-587-9792; Email: Cblasalle@sbcglobal.net.

Christian Brothers (De La Salle) (1886) Tel: 636-938-6142; Fax: 636-587-9792. Bro. Bill Brynda, Community Dir.; Mr. Michael Sawicki, Pres.; Gerri Schroeder, Retreat Coord., Email: Cblasalle@sbcglobal.net. Total in Residence 4; Total Staff 11; Community 4.

[V] NEWMAN CENTERS

ST. LOUIS. *University of Missouri, St. Louis, Catholic Newman Center* (1965) 8200 Natural Bridge Rd., 63121. Tel: 314-385-3455; Fax: 314-385-1523; Email: cnc@cncumsl.org; Email: frnick@cncumsl.org; Web: www.cncumsl.org. Rev. Nicklaus E. Winker, Dir.

Washington University Newman Centers Catholic Student Center 6352 Forsyth Blvd., 63105-2269. Tel: 314-935-9191; Fax: 314-727-6053; Email: braun@washucsc.org; Email: hederman@washucsc.org; Web: www.washucsc.org. Rev. Gary G. Braun, Archdiocesan Dir. Campus Ministries. Total in Residence 1; Total Staff 15.

[W] ASSOCIATIONS OF THE FAITHFUL

ST. LOUIS. *Oblates of Wisdom Study Center*, P. O. Box 13230, 63157. Tel: 314-621-2055; Email: jfmccarthy1@sbcglobal.net. Rev. Msgr. John F. McCarthy, P.A., Dir. Gen., (Retired). In Res. Rev. Brian W. Harrison, O.S., Scholar.

[X] MISCELLANEOUS

ST. LOUIS. *Alexian Brothers Services, Inc.*, 12250 Weber Hill Rd., Ste. 200, 63127. Tel: 314-729-3500; Fax: 314-843-5227; Email: amy.flynn-jones@ascension.org. Rev. Michael Lampe, Admin.

Almost Home (1993) 3200 St. Vincent Ave., 63104-1336. Tel: 314-771-4663; Fax: 314-865-4692; Email: smukhtiar@almosthomestl.org; Web: www.almosthomestl.org. Sheroo Mukhtiar, Exec. Dir. Transitional living program for teenage mothers and their children who are homeless. Total Staff 20; Members and Children 40.

American Academy of FertilityCare Professionals, 11700 Studt Ave., Ste. C, 63141. Tel: 314-997-7576 ; Fax: 314-692-8097; Email: diane.daly@mercy.net; Web: aafcp.org. Mrs. Diane Daly.

Anna Foundation, c/o Sisters of St. Joseph of Carondelet, St. Louis Province, 6400 Minnesota Ave., 63111. Tel: 314-481-8800, Ext. 321; Fax: 314-481-2366; Email: mjohnson@csjsl.org. Sr. Mary Frances Johnson, C.S.J., Treas. & Contact Person.

Annual Catholic Appeal, 20 Archbishop May Dr., 63119. Tel: 314-792-7681; Fax: 314-792-7229; Email: niebruggeb@archstl.org; Web: www.archstl.org/aca. Mr. Brian Niebrugge, Exec. Dir., Stewardship & Annual Catholic Appeal. Staff 10.

Archdiocesan Elementary Schools of the Archdiocese of St. Louis, 20 Archbishop May Dr., 63119. Tel: 314-792-7300; Fax: 314-792-7399; Web: www.archstl.org/education.

The Archdiocese of St. Louis Real Estate Corporation, 20 Archbishop May Dr., 63119.

Archdiocesan Stewardship Education Committee, 20 Archbishop May Dr., 63119. Tel: 314-792-7215; Fax: 314-792-7229; Web: www.archstl.org/stewardship. Mr. David Baranowski, Dir. Stewardship Educ.; Ms. Silvina Baez; Mr. John Drabik; Rev. John Paul Hopping; Ms. Ann Love; Rev. Msgr. Gregory R. Mikesch; Mr. Jon Nienas; Ms. Diane Valentine; Rev. John Rogers Vien.

ASC Health, 4233 Sulphur Ave., 63109. Tel: 314-351-6294; Fax: 314-351-6789; Email: schumerf@adorers.org. Sr. Jan E. Renz, A.S.C., Chm.

ASC Investment Group Inc., 4233 Sulphur Ave., 63109. Tel: 314-351-6294; Email: renzj@adorners.org. Sisters Barbara Hudock, A.S.C., Pres.; Jan E. Renz, A.S.C., Treas.

Ascension Health aka Ascension Healthcare, 4600 Edmundson Rd., 63134. Tel: 314-733-8000; Fax: 314-733-8013; Email: atersigni@ascension.org; Web: www.ascension.org. Patricia Maryland, Dr.PH, Pres & CEO. Sponsored by Ascension Health Ministries, a public juridic person.

Legal Title: Ascension Health, Inc. Total Staff 100,000.

Ascension Health Alliance dba Ascension, 101 S. Hanley Rd., Ste. 450, 63105. Tel: 314-733-8000; Fax: 314-733-8013; Email: jimpicciche@ascension.org; Web: www.ascension.org. Joseph R. Impicciche, Gen. Counsel.

Ascension Health Global Mission dba Ascension Global Mission, Ascension Health Alliance, 101 S. Hanley Rd., Ste. 450, 63105. Tel: 314-733-8286; Fax: 314-733-8013; Email: jimpicciche@ascension.org; Web: www.ascension.org. Joseph R. Impicciche, Exec. Vice Pres. & Gen. Counsel; Susan Huber, Sr. Vice Pres.

Ascension Health Senior Care dba Ascension Living, 4600 Edmundson Rd., 63134. Tel: 314-733-8000; Fax: 314-733-8013; Email: Gayle.Trupiano@ascension.org. Gayle Trupiano, Pres.

Legal Title: Ascension Living / Ascension Senior Living.

Ascension Health-IS, Inc. aka Ascension Technologies, 101 S. Hanley Rd., Ste 450, 63105. Tel: 314-733-8000; Fax: 314-733-8013; Email: jimpicciche@ascension.org; Web: www.ascension.org. Joseph R. Impicciche, Exec. Vice Pres. & Gen. Counsel; Gerry X. Lewis, Pres. & CEO

Legal Title: Ascension Technologies / Ascension Information Services.

Ascension Ministry and Mission Fund dba Ascension Associate Assistance Fund, 101 S. Hanley Rd., Ste., 200, Clayton, 63105. Tel: 314-733-8000; Fax: 314-733-8474; Email: jimpicciche@ascension.org; Web: www.ascension.org. Joseph R. Impicciche, Exec. Vice Pres. & Gen. Counsel

Legal Title: Ascension Associate Assistance Fund.

Aware, Inc. (1973) St. Anthony's Medical Center, 10016 Kennerly Rd., 63128. Tel: 314-525-1622. Karen Molner, Pres.

Birthright, 2525 S. Brentwood Blvd., Ste. 102, 63144. Tel: 314-962-5300; Fax: 314-962-7606; Web: www.birthrightstlouis.org. Ruth A. Bradberry, Admin. Dir. Total Staff 25; Total Assisted 5,679.

Branch Offices:

6680 Chippewa, 63109. Tel: 314-962-3653; Fax: 314-351-4531.

3435-C Bridgeland, Bridgeton, 63044. Tel: 314-298-0945; Fax: 314-298-0813.

205 N. 5th St., St. Charles, 63301. Tel: 636-724-1200 ; Fax: 636-946-0447.

625 N. Euclid, 63108. Tel: 636-946-4900; Fax: 314-361-0129.

800 N. Tucker Blvd., 63101. Tel: 636-916-4300; Fax: 314-588-1179.

Cardinal Glennon Children's Foundation, 3800 Park Ave., 63110. Tel: 314-577-5605; Fax: 314-268-6416; Email: info@glennon.org; Web: www.glennon.org. Sandy Koller, Vice Pres. Member of SSM Health.

Catholic Charities Foundation, 4445 Lindell Blvd., 63108. Tel: 314-367-5500; Fax: 314-289-8037; Email: info@ccstl.org; Web: www.ccstl.org. Mrs. Theresa E. Ruzicka, Pres.; Brian Thouvenot, Chief Devel. Officer. A Charitable Fund Established to Support the Activities of Catholic Charities.

Language Access Multicultural People (LAMP), 8050 Watson, Ste. 340, 63119. Tel: 314-842-0062; Fax: 314-842-1303. Jelena Mujanovic, Dir.

St. Francis Community Services, 4445 Lindell Blvd., 63108-2497. Tel: 314-932-3300; Fax: 314-289-8037; Email: kwallensak@ccstl.org; Web: www.sfcsstl.org. Karen Wallensak, Dir. Provides legal aid for immigrants, veterans, victims of violence and others; bilingual immigrant services, including youth programs, case management, and counseling; and long-term case management for disaster survivors and impoverished families.

Catholic Legal Assistance Ministry, 100 N. Tucker Blvd., Ste. 726, 63101. Tel: 314-977-3993; Fax: 314-977-3334; Email: amy.diemer@slu.edu;

Web: www.sfcsstl.org. Amy Diemer, Dir. Providing legal advocacy and representation in civil matters and immigration for low-income clients.

St. Francis Community Services Southside Center (Vietnamese and Hispanic Programs), 4222 Delor, 63116. Tel: 314-773-6100; Fax: 314-664-6200. Meredith Rataj, Dir.

The Catholic Health Association of the United States, 4455 Woodson Rd., 63134-3797. Tel: 314-427-2500; Fax: 314-427-0029; Web: www.chausa.org. Sr. Carol Keehan, D.C., Pres. & CEO. Established June 24, 1915. Total Staff 72.

Office of Catholic Education and Formation, 20 Archbishop May Dr., 63119. Maureen DePriest, Supt., Elementary Schools.

Catholic High School Association, 20 Archbishop May Dr., 63119. Tel: 314-792-7300; Fax: 314-792-7399; Email: jphelps@archstl.org; Web: www.archstl.org/education/.

Catholic Kolping Society of America, 5410 Oakvilla Manor Dr., 63129. Tel: 314-894-2136.

Central Bureau of the C.C.V.A., 3835 Westminster Pl., 63108-3472. Tel: 314-371-1653; Fax: 314-371-0889; Email: centbur@sbcglobal.net; Web: www.socialjusticereview.org. Rev. Edward Krause, C.S.C., Dir. & Editor of the Social Justice Review.

Chaminade Foundation, 4425 W. Pine Blvd., 63108. Tel: 314-533-1207; Fax: 314-533-0778; Email: roverman@sm-usa.org. Bro. Ronald Overman, S.M., Dir.

St. Charles Lwanga Center (1978) 4746 Carter Ave., Ste. 100, 63115-2238. Tel: 314-367-7929; Fax: 314-367-4134; Email: info@lwangacenter.org; Web: www.archstl.org/lwangacenter/. Rev. Arthur J. Cavitt, Exec. Dir. A spiritual formation Center for leadership in the African American Catholic Community, in the Archdiocese of St. Louis. The Center collaborates with other Christians and provides leadership training for junior high and teenage youth and adult laity. In conjunction with our service to sponsoring parishes, we conduct workshops on the Sacrament of Confirmation, coping with grief and loss, marriage preparation, days of reflection, pastoral care and retreats. Bible study, evangelization/consultation services. Total Staff 2.

Collaborative Dominican Novitiate, 4928 Washington Blvd., 63108-1621. Tel: 314-956-7748; Email: mmcelroy@grdominicans.org. John Rich, Contact Person; Megan E. McElroy, O.P., Contact Person.

**Covenant House Missouri*, 2727 N. Kingshighway Blvd., 63113.

CSJ Ministries, 6400 Minnesota Ave., 63111. Tel: 314-481-8800; Fax: 314-481-2366; Email: mjohnson@csjsl.org. Sr. Mary Frances Johnson, C.S.J., Treas.

Congregation Sisters of St. Joseph Education Association, 2767 Ashrock Dr., 63129.

Daughters of Charity Foundation (1996) c/o Ascension Health, 4600 Edmundson Rd., 63134. Tel: 314-802-2060; Tel: 314-733-8000; Fax: 314-802-2051; Email: jimpicciche@ascension.org; Web: www.daughtersofcharityfdn.org. Joseph R. Impicciche, Exec. Vice Pres. & Gen. Counsel, Tel: 314-733-8286.

Daughters of Charity Foundation of St. Louis (1995) 4600 Edmundson Rd., 63134. Tel: 314-733-8000; Email: jimpicciche@ascension.org; Web: www.ascension.org. Joseph R. Impicciche, Exec.

Daughters of Charity Ministries, Inc., 4330 Olive St., 63108-2622. Tel: 314-533-4770; Fax: 314-561-4676; Email: tom.beck@doc.org; Web: www.daughtersofcharity.org. Sr. Catherine Mary Norris, Prov.

Daughters of Charity National Health System, Inc., 4600 Edmundson Rd., 63134. Tel: 314-733-8000; Fax: 314-733-8013; Email: jimpicciche@ascension.org; Web: www.ascension.org. Joseph R. Impicciche, Exec. Vice Pres.

Daughters of Charity, Inc., 4330 Olive St., 63108-2622. Tel: 314-533-4770; Fax: 314-533-3226; Email: tom.beck@doc.org; Web: www.daughtersofcharity.org. Sr. Catherine Mary Norris, Prov. Sisters 415.

Dismas House of St. Louis, 5025 Cote Brilliante Ave., 63113. Tel: 314-361-2802; Fax: 314-849-2430. John R. Flatley, Exec. Dir. Total in Residence 170; Total Staff 60.

Equestrian Order of the Holy Sepulchre of Jerusalem, 2870 S. Lindbergh Blvd., 63131. Tel: 314-984-5077; Fax: 314-984-9390; Email: nardance@aol.com. Nancy Ross, Sec.

St. Francis de Sales Association (Paris 1872) (St. Louis 1950) 9328 Pine Ave., 63144. Tel: 651-592-6645; Email: webteam@sfdsassociation.org; Web: www.sfdsassociation.org. 1772 Highland Pky., St Paul, MN 55116. Ann Wiedl, Contact Person. A call to the laity to live their individual vocation in the spirit of Jesus, using the writings of St. Francis de Sales as a means to see and do God's will and grow in holiness.; Private Universal Association of the Faithful.

The Franciscan Connection (1991) 2903 Cherokee St., 63118. Tel: 314-773-8485; Email: franciscanconnection@thefriars.org. Rev. Lawrence M. Nickels, O.F.M., Exec. Dir.

Franklin County Catholic Church Real Estate Corporation (1834) 20 Archbishop May Dr., 63119. Tel: 314-792-7408; Fax: 314-792-7401; Email: Billing@archstl.org. Rev. Msgr. Jerome D. Billing, S.T.L., J.C.L., Contact Person.

Friends of St. Francis de Sales Oratory, Inc., 2653 Ohio Ave., 63118. Tel: 314-771-3100; Fax: 314-771-3295; Email: sfds@institute-christking.org; Web: www.traditionfortomorrow.com.

Good Shepherd Children and Family Services, 1340 Partridge Ave., 63130. Tel: 314-854-5700; Fax: 314-854-5747; Email: goodshepinfo@ccstl.org; Web: www.goodshepherdstl.org. Michael P. Meehan, Ph.D., Exec. Dir. A Catholic Charities agency merging the services of Catholic Services for Children & Youth, Father Dunne's Newsboys' Home, Marian Hall Agencies, St. Joseph's Home and Family Support Services, and Villa Maria Center. Provides child welfare services including foster care, adoption, expectant parent counseling, advocacy, and shelter and transitional living services for teen mothers and their babies.

Good Shepherd Mission Development Corporation, 7654 Natural Bridge Rd., 63121. Tel: 314-381-3400 ; Email: cmcquaid@gspmna.org. Sr. Mary Carolyn McQuaid, R.G.S., Sec.

Good Shepherd Programs of St. Louis (1979) 7654 Natural Bridge Rd., 63121. Tel: 314-381-3400; Web: cmcquaid@gspmna.org. Sr. Mary Carolyn McQuaid, R.G.S., Pres.

Hispanic Ministry of the Archdiocese of St. Louis (1995) 20 Archbishop May Dr., 63119. Tel: 314-792-7645; Fax: 314-792-7710.

Incarnate Word Foundation, Missouri (1997) 5257 Shaw Ave., Ste. 309, 63110. Tel: 314-773-5100; Fax: 314-773-5102; Email: marty.glosemeyer@iwfdn.org; Web: www.iwfdn.org. Bridget M. Flood, Exec. Dir.

Institute for Theological Encounter with Science & Technology (ITEST), 20 Archbishop May Dr., 63119. Tel: 314-792-7221; Email: mariannepost@archstl.org; Web: www.itest-faithscience.org. Sr. Marianne Postiglione, R.S.M., Assoc. Dir.

Intercommunity Housing Association (1993) 1049 N. Clay, Ste. 300, Kirkwood, 63122. Tel: 314-965-4700 ; Email: donald.schneiber@sbcglobal.net; Web: www.intercommunityhousing.org. Provides safe, affordable housing & supportive svcs. for economically disadvantaged & working poor families in St. Louis; operates Pillar Place Apartments, Compton Place Apartments.

Jefferson County Catholic Church Real Estate Corporation, 20 Archbishop May Dr., 63119. Tel: 314-792-7408; Fax: 314-792-7401; Email: Billing@archstl.org. Rev. Msgr. Jerome D. Billing, S.T.L., J.C.L., Contact Person.

Ladies of Charity of St. Catherine Laboure, 12160 Leelaine Dr., 63126. Susan Tumminia, Pres. Affiliate with Ladies of Charity of the United States & the Assoc. of Intl. Charities of St. Vincent de Paul.

Ladies of Charity of St. Vincent-Guardian Angel, Tel: 314-231-9328; Fax: 314-621-2232; Email: stvstl@swbell.net. Affiliate with Ladies of Charity of the United States & the Assoc. of Intl. Charities of St. Vincent de Paul.

St. Vincent's Church: 1408 S. Tenth St., 63104. Tel: 314-231-9328; Fax: 314-621-2232.

Ladies of Charity Service Center, 7500 Natural Bridge Rd., 63121. Tel: 314-383-4207; Fax: 314-383-0605. Phyllis A. Makowski, Pres. Ladies of Charity Service Center; Thrift Store & Food Pantry.

Ladies of Charity Service Center Total Staff 25; Total Assisted 1,065.

Lincoln County Catholic Church Real Estate Corporation, 20 Archbishop May Dr., 63119. Tel: 314-792-7408; Fax: 314-792-7401; Email: Billing@archstl.org. Rev. Msgr. Jerome D. Billing, S.T.L., J.C.L., Contact Person.

The St. Louis Archdiocesan Fund, 20 Archbishop May Dr., Shrewsbury, 63119-5738. Tel: 314-792-7129; Fax: 314-792-7867. Michael J. Rizzo.

St. Louis Area Women Religious Collaborative Ministries (1998) 4330 Olive St., 63108. Tel: 314-265-3683; Email: info@englishtutoringproject.org. Sr. Carmen Schnyder, C.PP.S., Contact Person. Includes English Tutoring Project for Immigrant/Refugee Children and Intercommunity Environmental Council.

St. Louis Catholic Charismatic Renewal, 1406 S. Sappington, Crestwood, 63126. Tel: 314-792-7734; Email: janeguenther@archstl.org; Web: www.archstl.org/renewal. Most Rev. Robert Hermann, Liaison; Ms. Jane Guenther, Dir.

Abiding Bible Companion (2001) Tel: 314-725-6527.

Healing & Deliverance Ministry.

Magnificat, Tel: 314-792-7734.

Theotokos Ministry, 4311 S. Compton, 63111. Tel: 314-351-6061. Center with books & tapes, prayer time, ministry times, retreats for parishes, leaders training, small faith groups, conferences, special events & days of renewal.

Two Alike, Tel: 314-792-7734.

Saint Louis Counseling, Inc. (1992) 9200 Watson Rd., Ste. G-101, 63126. Tel: 314-544-3800; Fax: 314-843-0552; Email: tduff@ccstl.org; Web: www.saintlouiscounseling.org. Mr. Thomas Duff, L.C.S.W., Dir. Provides professional counseling services to children, adolescents, adults, and the elderly in various settings, including eight outpatient offices, schools, and places of employment, throughout the St. Louis area. Tot Asst. Annually 7,000; Staff 93.

Locations:.

Saint Louis Counseling - O'Fallon Office, 311 S. Main St.. Ste. 100, O'Fallon, 63366. Tel: 636-281-1990; Fax: 636-281-1995; Web: www.saintlouiscounseling.org. Provides professional counseling services to children, adolescents, adults, and the elderly in the O'Fallon, MO, area.

Saint Louis Counseling School Partnership Program, 9200 Watson Rd, G-101, 63126. Tel: 314-544-3800; Fax: 314-843-0552; Web: www.saintlouiscounseling.org.

Saint Louis Counseling - Troy Office, 140 Professional Pkwy., Troy, 63379. Tel: 636-528-5911; Fax: 636-528-5912; Web: www.saintlouiscounseling.org.

Saint Louis Counseling - West County Office, 498 Woods Mill Rd., Manchester, 63011-4144. Tel: 636-391-9966; Fax: 636-394-4678; Web: www.saintlouiscounseling.org. Provides professional counseling services to children, adolescents, adults, and the elderly in the West County area of St. Louis.

Saint Louis Counseling - Union Office, 102 E. Springfield, Ste. 202, Union, 63084. Tel: 636-583-1800; Fax: 636-583-0836; Web: www.saintlouiscounseling.org. Provides professional counseling services to children, adolescents, adults, and the elderly in the Union, MO area.

Saint Louis Counseling - Florissant Office, 1385 Harkee Rd., Florissant, 63031. Tel: 314-831-1533; Fax: 314-831-1391; Web: www.saintlouiscounseling.org. Provides professional counseling services to children, adolescents, adults, and the elderly in the Florissant, MO area.

St. Louis Consultation Center, 1750 S. Brentwood, Ste. 602, 63144. Tel: 314-909-4620; Email: director@stlconsult.org. Dr. Rob Furey, Ph.D., Dir. Tot Asst. Annually 125.

St. Louis County Catholic Church Real Estate Corporation, 20 Archbishop May Dr., 63119. Tel: 314-792-7408; Fax: 314-792-7401; Email: Billing@archstl.org. Rev. Msgr. Jerome D. Billing, S.T.L., J.C.L., Contact Person.

Lovers of the Holy Cross of St. Louis, 4211 Hydraulic Ave., 63116. Tel: 314-832-7321.

St. Luke Consultation Center, 1750 S. Brentwood Blvd., Ste. 602, 63144.

Maria Droste Foundation, 7654 Natural Bridge Rd., 63121. Tel: 314-381-3400; Email: cmcquaid@gspmna.org. Sr. Mary Carolyn McQuaid, R.G.S., Sec.

Mary and Joseph Trust, 3221 McKelvey Rd. Ste 107, Bridgeton, 63044. Tel: 314-768-1817; Fax: 314-768-1880; Email: joshaughnessy@fsmonline.org. Sr. Susan Scholl, F.S.M., Supr.

Mercy Health Foundation (2003) 14528 S. Outer Forty, Ste. 100, Chesterfield, 63017. Tel: 314-579-6100; Fax: 314-628-3732; Email: marynell.ploch@mercy.net. Shannon Sock.

Mercy Health Foundation Jefferson, 1400 Hwy. 61 S., P.O. Box 350, Crystal City, 63019. Tel: 314-628-3608; Email: Marynell.Ploch@Mercy.Net. Susan Hannasch, Counsel.

Mercy Health Foundation Lincoln, 1000 E. Cherry St., Troy, 63379. Tel: 314-628-3608; Email: Marynell.Ploch@Mercy.Net. Mailing Address: 14528 S. Outer 40 Rd., Ste. 100, Chesterfield, 63017. Philip Wheeler, Sr. Vice Pres. & Gen. Counsel.

Mercy Investment Services, Inc., 2039 N. Geyer Rd., 63131. Tel: 314-909-4609; Fax: 314-909-4694; Email: bbrockmeyer@mercyinvestments.org. Bryan Pini, Pres. & CIO.

Midwest Coalition for Responsible Investment, 6400 Minnesota Ave., 63111. Tel: 314-678-0471; Email: midwest.coalition@yahoo.com; Web: www.midwestcri.com. Sr. Barbara Jennings, C.S.J., Coord.

Missionaries of the Holy Family Retirement Trust

Fund, 3014 Oregon Ave., 63118. Tel: 314-577-6300; Fax: 314-577-6301; Email: msf@msf-america.org; Web: www.msf-america.org. Rev. Philip Sosa, M.S.F., Supr.

National Christian Life Community of the United States of America (CLC) (1540) 3601 Lindell Blvd., 63108-3393. Tel: 713-246-3785; Web: www.clc-usa.org. Edward Plocha, Pres. Founded c. 1540 & approved 1584, a public, intl. assn. of the Faithful of Pontifical Right which builds small Faith-Communities for mission & svc. to the church. It uses the Spiritual Exercises of Saint Ignatius of Loyola as its specific source & characteristic instrument for its spirituality. Membership equally open to primarily Catholic Christian men, women, youth & young adults, clergy, brothers & sisters.

Network of Sacred Heart Schools, Inc., 700 N. Third St., St. Charles, 63301. Tel: 636-724-7003; Fax: 636-724-4049; Email: nshoffice@sofie.org; Web: www.sofie.org. Madeleine Ortman, Dir.

Our Lady's Inn (1981) 8790 Manchester Rd., 63114. Tel: 314-351-4590; Fax: 314-351-2119; Email: pforrest@ourladysinn.org; Web: www.ourladysinn.org. 3607 Hwy. D., Defiance, 63341.
Tel: 636-398-5375; Fax: 636-398-5376. Peggy Forrest, Contact Person. Residential shelters for pregnant women who have no home, who are being abused, who have no one who cares, and/or who are being pressured to abort their baby. We provide living facilities, food, clothing, counseling, vocational guidance and follow up care. Total Staff 49; Total Assisted 700.
3607 Hwy. D, Defiance, 63341. Tel: 636-398-5375; Fax: 636-398-5376.

Pathways to Progress, 10235 Ashbrook Dr., 63137.

St. Patrick Center (1983) 800 N. Tucker, 63101. Tel: 314-802-0700; Fax: 314-802-1981; Email: lphillips@stpatrickcenter.org; Web: www.stpatrickcenter.org. Laurie Phillips, CEO. Located in downtown St. Louis, St. Patrick Center provides opportunities for self-sufficiency and dignity to persons who are homeless or at risk of becoming homeless. Individuals achieve permanent, positive changes in their lives through education, affordable housing, sound mental health, employment, and financial stability. Total Staff 140; Total Assisted 5,900.
St. Patrick Partnership Center, 800 N. Tucker, 63101. Tel: 314-802-0700; Email: lphillips@stpatrickcenter.org; Web: www.stpatrickcenter.org. Laurie Phillips, CEO.

Pauline Books and Media, 9804 Watson Rd., 63126. Tel: 314-965-3512; Tel: 314-965-5273; Fax: 314-821-8401; Email: stlouis@pauline.org; Web: www.pauline.org. Daughters of St. Paul.

Pelletier Trust, a Charitable Trust of the Sisters of the Good Shepherd (1990) 7654 Natural Bridge Rd., 63121. Tel: 314-381-3400; Email: cmcquaid@gspmna.org. Sr. Mary Carolyn McQuaid, R.G.S., Trustee.

Perpetual Help Retirement Corporation (2002) 335 S. Kirkwood Rd., 63122. Tel: 314-965-3700; Fax: 314-965-3710; Email: srmaryanne@fsolph.org; Web: www.fsolph.org. Sr. Renita Brummer, O.S.F., Vice Pres. Established by the Franciscan Sisters of Our Lady of Perpetual Help to Support the Religious and Charitable Purposes of the Franciscan Sisters of Our Lady of Perpetual Help.

Perry County Catholic Church Real Estate Corporation, 20 Archbishop May Dr., 63119. Tel: 314-792-7408; Fax: 314-792-7401; Email: Billing@archstl.org. Rev. Msgr. Jerome D. Billing, S.T.L., J.C.L., Contact Person.

Redemptorists of Mattese (1989) 1118 N. Grand Blvd., 63106. Tel: 314-533-0304; Fax: 314-533-4260. Bro. Terrence Burke, C.Ss.R.

Rosati Center, 4220 N. Grand Ave., 63107.

Sisters of the Good Shepherd Province of Mid-North America Foundation (2001) 7654 Natural Bridge Rd., 63121. Tel: 314-381-3400; Fax: 314-381-7102; Email: cmcquaid@gspmna.org; Web: goodshepherdsisters.org. Sr. Mary Carolyn McQuaid, R.G.S.

Society Devoted to the Sacred Heart, 9600 Tennyson Ave., 63114. Tel: 314-429-0526; Fax: 314-429-0794; Email: shsuperior@outlook.com; Web: www.sacredheartsisters.com.

**Society of St. Vincent de Paul, Council of St. Louis* (1845) 100 N. Jefferson Ave., 63103. Tel: 877-238-3228; Tel: 314-881-6000; Fax: 314-531-6712; Email: info@svdpstl.org; Web: www.svdpstl.org.
Christy Thrift Store, 4928 Christy, 63116. Tel: 314-881-6043.
Dellwood Thrift Store, 10052 W. Florissant Ave., 63136.
Lemay Ferry Thrift Store, 3924 Lemay Ferry Rd., 63125. Tel: 314-881-6046.
St. Charles Thrift Store, 1063 Regency Pkwy., St. Charles, 63303. Tel: 314-881-6047.
West County Thrift Store, 14660 Manchester Rd., Ballwin, 63011. Tel: 314-811-6034.

SSM Health Businesses, 10101 Woodfield Ln., 63132. Tel: 314-994-7800; Email: SSMHealthCareOfficialCatholicDirectoryNotices@ssmhealth.com. Laura Kaiser, Pres. Member of SSM Health.

SSM Health Care Corporation, 10101 Woodfield Ln., 63132. Tel: 314-994-7800; Email: SSMHealthCareOfficialCatholicDirectoryNotices@ssmhealth.com. Laura Kaiser, Pres. Member of SSM Health.

SSM Health Care Portfolio Management Company, 10101 Woodfield Ln., 63132. Tel: 314-994-7800; Email: SSMHealthCareOfficialCatholicDirectoryNotices@ssmhealth.com. Laura Kaiser, Pres. Member of SSM Health.

SSM Health Care St. Louis, 1173 Corporate Lake Dr., 63132. Tel: 314-989-2000; Fax: 314-989-2400; Email: SSMHealthCareOfficialCatholicDirectoryNotices@ssmhealth.com; Web: www.ssmhealth.com. Candace Jennings, Pres. Member of SSM Health Care.

SSM Hospice and Home Care Foundation aka SSM Health Hospice and Home Health Foundation, 12312 Olive Blvd., Ste. 400, 63141. Tel: 314-989-2775; Fax: 314-682-1388; Email: hospicefoundation@ssmhealth.com; Web: www.ssmhealthathomecom/foundation. Jeanne Hampson, Prog. Coord.; Heather Selsor, Foundation Coord.

SSM Health Foundation - St. Louis, 10101 Woodfield Ln., 63132. Tel: 314-523-8044; Fax: 314-523-8767; Email: amy.collard@ssmhealth.com; Web: www.ssmhealth.com/foundation. Mr. Paul Ross, Exec. Dir. Member of SSM Health.

SSM Regional Health Services, 10101 Woodfield Ln., 63132. Tel: 314-994-7800; Email: SSMHealthCareOfficialCatholicDirectoryNotices@ssmhealth.com. Laura Kaiser, Pres. Member of SSM Health.

SSM-SLUH, Inc., 10101 Woodfield Ln., 63132. Tel: 314-577-8000; Email: SSMHealthCareOfficialCatholicDirectoryNotices@ssmhealth.com; Web: www.ssmhealth.com/slu-hospital-academic-hospital. Kate Becker, Pres. Bed Capacity 352; Employees 1,689; Nurses 611.

SSND Central Pacific Retirement, Inc., 320 E. Ripa Ave., 63125. Tel: 314-544-0455; Fax: 314-544-6754; Email: finance-sl@ssndcp.org; Email: finance-ndeg@ssndcp.org. Sr. Marjorie Klein, S.S.N.D., Dir.

St. Charles County Catholic Church Real Estate Corporation, 20 Archbishop May Dr., 63119. Tel: 314-792-7408; Fax: 314-792-7401; Email: Billing@archstl.org. Rev. Msgr. Jerome D. Billing, S.T.L., J.C.L., Contact Person.

St. Francois County Catholic Church Real Estate Corporation, 20 Archbishop May Dr., 63119. Tel: 314-792-7408; Fax: 314-792-7401; Email: Billing@archstl.org. Rev. Msgr. Jerome D. Billing, S.T.L., J.C.L., Contact Person.

St. Louis City Catholic Church Real Estate Corporation, 20 Archbishop May Dr., 63119. Tel: 314-792-7408; Fax: 314-792-7401; Email: Billing@archstl.org. Rev. Msgr. Jerome D. Billing, S.T.L., J.C.L., Contact Person.

Stand Up for CBC, Inc., 1850 De La Salle Dr., Town and Country, 63131.

Ste. Genevieve County Catholic Church Real Estate Corporation, 20 Archbishop May Dr., 63119. Tel: 314-792-7408; Fax: 314-792-7401; Email: Billing@archstl.org. Rev. Msgr. Jerome D. Billing, S.T.L., J.C.L., Contact Person. Priests 1.

US Central & Southern Province, Society of Jesus, Office of Advancement, 4511 W. Pine Blvd., 63108-2191. Tel: 314-361-7765; Fax: 314-758-7163; Email: ucsadvancement@jesuits.org; Web: www.jesuitscentralsouthern.org. Mr. John Fitzpatrick, Dir.

US Central and Southern Province, Society of Jesus Aged/Infirm Fund, 4511 W. Pine Blvd., 63108.

US Central and Southern Province, Society of Jesus Formation Fund, 4511 W. Pine Blvd., 63108.

Visitation Association of the Christian Faithful, Inc., 3020 N. Ballas Rd., Saint Louis, 63131. Tel: 314-625-9247; Email: srmtr@visitationmonastery.org. Sr. Marie Therese Ruthmann, V.H.M., Supr.

Visitation Real Property Foundation, 3020 N. Ballas Rd., Saint Louis, 63131. Tel: 314-625-9247; Email: srmtr@visitationmonastery.org. Sr. Marie Therese Ruthmann, V.H.M., Supr.

Warren County Catholic Church Real Estate Corporation, 20 Archbishop May Dr., 63119. Tel: 314-792-7408; Fax: 314-792-7401; Email: Billing@archstl.org. Rev. Msgr. Jerome D. Billing, S.T.L., J.C.L., Contact Person.

Washington County Catholic Church Real Estate Corporation (1821) 20 Archbishop May Dr., 63119. Tel: 314-792-7408; Fax: 314-792-7401; Email: Billing@archstl.org. Rev. Msgr. Jerome D. Billing, S.T.L., J.C.L., Contact Person.

We & God Spirituality Center, 3601 Lindell Blvd., Ste. 617, 63108. Tel: 314-633-4630; Fax: 314-633-4404; Email: wgsc@weandgod.org; Web: www. weandgod.org.

**Women for Faith and Family* (1984) 6415 Sutherland, 63109. Web: www.wf-f.org. Susan J. Benofy, Treas.

Young Catholic Musicians, 1919 S. 7th St., 63104. Tel: 314-962-9260; Fax: 314-231-7464; Email: revycm@charter.net. Mary Smith, Contact Person.

BRIDGETON. *Boys Hope Girls Hope*, 12120 Bridgeton Square Dr., Bridgeton, 63044. Tel: 314-298-1250; Fax: 314-298-1251; Email: hope@bhgh.org; Web: www.boyshopegirlshope.org. Paul A. Minorini, Pres. & CEO. A College Preparatory Residential Child Care Agency Serving Abandoned, Abused and Neglected Children. Founded in 1977; With affiliated programs in: Baton Rouge; Chicago; Cincinnati; Denver; Detroit; New Orleans; New York; Northeast Ohio; Orange County, CA; Phoenix; Pittsburgh; St. Louis; San Francisco, Baltimore, Kansas City. Total Staff 225; Total Assisted 1,050.

Room at the Inn (1998) 3415 Bridgeland Dr., Bridgeton, 63044. Tel: 314-209-9198; Fax: 314-209-9207; Email: mbisbey@cdpsisters.org; Web: www.roomstl.org. Sr. Michele Bisbey, C.D.P., Prov.

The Sarah Community, 3221 McKelvey Rd. Ste 107, Bridgeton, 63044. Tel: 314-768-1817; Fax: 314-768-1880; Email: joshaughnessy@fsmonline.org. Purpose: provides a continuing care retirement community for members of religious congregations and laity. Operates the following: Anna House, a skilled nursing facility; Veronica House, an assisted living facility; Naomi House, a retirement living facility.

The Sarah Community Foundation, 3221 McKelvey Rd., Ste. 107, Bridgeton, 63044. Tel: 314-768-1817; Fax: 314-768-1880; Email: joshaughnessy@fsmonline.org. Mr. John O'Shaughnessy, Contact Person.

Sisters of Divine Providence, 3415 Bridgeland Dr., Bridgeton, 63044. Tel: 314-209-9181; Fax: 314-209-9207; Email: mbisbey@cdpsisters.org; Web: www.divineprovidenceweb.org. Sisters Michele Bisbey, C.D.P., Prov.; Mary Michael McCulla, C.D.P., Contact Person. Sisters 24.

CADET. *Rural Parish Workers of Christ the King* (1942) 15540 Cannon Mines Rd., Cadet, 63630. Tel: 636-586-5171; Fax: 636-586-5918; Email: villmer15540@wildblue.net; Web: rpwck.net. Miss Natalie Villmer, Gen. Dir. A Secular Institute of the Archdiocese of St. Louis. Total in Residence 3; Total Staff 6; Workers 4; Total Assisted 2,500.

CHESTERFIELD. *McAuley Portfolio Management Company*, Attn: Mercy Corp. Paralegal - Legal Dept, 14528 S. Outer 40, Ste. 100, Chesterfield, 63017. Tel: 314-579-6100; Fax: 314-628-3732; Email: Marynell.Ploch@Mercy.net. Mr. Philip Wheeler.

Mercy Health, 14528 S. Outer Forty, Ste. 100, Chesterfield, 63017. Tel: 314-579-6100; Fax: 314-628-3732; Email: marynell.ploch@mercy.net; Web: www.mercy.net. Philip Wheeler.

MHM Support Services, 14528 S. Outer Forty, Ste. 100, Chesterfield, 63017. Tel: 314-579-6100; Fax: 314-628-3732; Email: marynell.ploch@mercy.net. Mr. Philip Wheeler.

DARDENNE PRAIRIE. *Saint William Apartments, Inc.*, 1979 Hanley Rd., Dardenne Prairie, 63368. Tel: 636-695-4200; Fax: 636-695-4208.

St. William Apartments II, Inc., 1983 Hanley Rd., Dardenne Prairie, 63368. Tel: 636-695-4205; Fax: 636-695-4216.

DITTMER. *Our Lady of Victory Charitable Foundation*, 6476 Eime Rd., Dittmer, 63023. Tel: 636-274-5226; Fax: 636-274-1430. Marian Wolaver, Dir. Opers.

Servants of the Paraclete Missouri Generalate Corporation, 6476 Eime Rd., Dittmer, 63023. Tel: 636-274-5226; Fax: 636-274-1430. Very Revs. David Fitzgerald, s.P., Dir.; Liam Hoare, s.P., Sec.; Revs. Peter Lechner, s.P., Trustee; Benedict Livingstone, s.P., Trustee; Philip Taylor, s.P., Trustee.

EARTH CITY. *Congregation of the Mission International Fund*, 13663 Rider Tr. N., Earth City, 63045-1512. Tel: 314-344-1184; Fax: 314-344-2989; Email: provinceoffice@vincentian.org. Rev. Kevin P. McCracken, C.M., Treas.

Lazarist Trust Fund, 13663 Rider Tr. N., Earth City, 63045-1512. Tel: 314-344-1184; Fax: 314-344-2989; Email: provinceoffice@vincentian.org. Rev. Kevin P. McCracken, C.M., Treas.

Vincentian Marian Youth, U.S.A., 13663 Rider Trail N., Earth City, 63045. Tel: 573-768-7011; Tel: 314-344-1184; Fax: 314-344-2989; Email: provinceoffice@vincentian.org; Web: www.vmy.us. Mailing Address: National Office, P.O. Box 202, Perryville, 63775. Rev. Kevin P. McCracken, C.M., Treas.

Vincentian Solidarity Office, Congregation of the Mission Western Province, 13663 Rider Trail N., Earth City, 63045. Tel: 314-344-1184;

Fax: 314-344-2989; Email: provinceoffice@vincentian.org. Rev. Kevin P. McCracken, C.M., Treas.

FLORISSANT. *Child Center Foundation* (1947) 2705 Mullanphy Ln., Florissant, 63031.
Tel: 314-837-1702; Fax: 314-830-6263; Email: info@mgstl.org; Web: www.marygrovechildren.org. Joseph Bestgen, CEO. Child Center Foundation provides financial support to Child Center - Marygrove, a residential and day treatment facility serving severely emotionally disturbed children and their families.

KIRKWOOD. *Ursuline Provincialate Foundation, Central Province of the United States*, 353 S. Sappington Rd., Kirkwood, 63122.
Tel: 314-821-6884; Email: ellette@osucentral.org. Sr. Rita A. Bregenhorn, O.S.U., Prov.

Ursuline Sisters Trust Fund, 353 S. Sappington Rd., 63122. Tel: 314-821-6884; Fax: 314-821-6888; Email: ellette@osucentral.org; Web: www.osucentral.org. Ellette Gibson, Contact Person.

LIGUORI. *Redemptorist Fathers* dba Liguori Publications, One Liguori Dr., Liguori, 63057.
Tel: 636-464-2500; Fax: 636-223-1593; Email: dwillard@liguori.org; Web: www.liguori.org. Rev. Donald Willard, C.SS.R., Pres.

MARYLAND HEIGHTS. **Society of St. Vincent de Paul, National Administration Services, Inc.*, 58 Progress Pkwy., Maryland Heights, 63043-3706.
Tel: 314-576-3993; Fax: 314-576-6755; Email: usacouncil@svdpusa.org; Web: www.svdpusa.org. Mr. David Barringer, CEO; Mr. Frank Karpowicz, NAS Chair.

**Society of St. Vincent DePaul, National Council of the United States* (1845) 58 Progress Pkwy., Maryland Heights, 63043-3706. Tel: 314-576-3993; Fax: 314-576-6755; Email: usacouncil@svdpusa.org; Web: www.svdpusa.org. Rev. Donald J. Hying, Natl. Episcopal Advisor; Mr. David Barringer, CEO; Ralph Middlecamp, Pres.

O'FALLON. *Centers for Professional and Pastoral Services*, 204 N. Main St., O'Fallon, 63366-2299.
Tel: 636-240-6010; Fax: 636-272-5031; Email: jbader@cpps-ofallon.org. Sisters Joni Belford, C.PP.S., Admin.; Janice Bader, C.PP.S., Supr. Gen. Sponsored by Sisters of the Most Precious Blood of O'Fallon, MO. Total Staff 6; Centers 1; Total Assisted 371.

Charitable Trust, Sisters of the Most Precious Blood of O'Fallon, MO, 204 N. Main St., O'Fallon, 63366-2299. Tel: 636-240-6010; Fax: 636-272-5031; Email: cschnyder@cpps-ofallon.org; Web: www.cpps-ofallon.org. Sr. Carmen Schnyder, C.PP.S., Treas. Trust fund for support of retired Sisters of the Most Precious Blood.

St. Dominic Endowment Fund, St. Dominic High School, 31 St. Dominic Dr., O'Fallon, 63366.
Tel: 314-240-8303; Fax: 314-240-9884; Email: mainoffice@stdominichs.org; Web: www.stdominichs.org. Sr. Mary H. Bender, S.S.N.D., Treas.

PACIFIC. *Franciscan Missionary Brothers Foundation*, 265 St. Joseph's Hill Rd., Pacific, 63069.
Tel: 636-938-5361; Email: shrine1olc@aol.com. Bro. John Spila, O.S.F., Dir.

Providence Trust, Our Lady of the Angels Monastery, 265 St. Joseph Rd., Pacific, 63069.
Tel: 636-938-5361; Email: shrine1olc@aol.com; Web: www.franciscancaring.org. Bro. John A. Spila, O.S.F., Dir. Purpose: To support the religious and charitable purposes of the Franciscan Missionary Brothers of the Sacred Heart.

PERRYVILLE. *Association of the Miraculous Medal* (1918) 1811 W. Saint Joseph St., Perryville, 63775.
Tel: 573-547-8343; Fax: 573-547-1389; Email: ammfather@amm.org; Web: www.amm.org. Don Fulford, CEO; Rev. Kevin P. McCracken, C.M., Interim Spiritual Dir.

Catholic Home Study, P.O. Box 363, Perryville, 63775. Tel: 573-547-4084; Email: catholichomestudy@gmail.com; Web: www.catholichomestudy.org. Rev. Ronald Hoye, C.M., Dir. Offers free correspondence courses on the Catholic Faith. Priests 1; Total Staff 3; Total Assisted 12,000.

Ladies of Charity of St. Vincent de Paul Parish, 1010 Rosati Ct., Perryville, 63775. Tel: 573-846-1100;
Fax: 573-547-4145; Email: svdepaul@svdepaul.org. Claire E. Schemel, Pres. Affiliate with Ladies of Charity of the United States & the Assoc. of Intl. Charities of St. Vincent de Paul. Total Assisted 8,084.

St. Vincent De Paul Educational Foundation, 1010 A Rosati Ct., Perryville, 63775. Tel: 573-547-4591;
Fax: 573-547-4145; Email: svdepaul@svdepaul.org; Web: www.svdepaul.org. Rev. Milton F. Ryan, C.M., Moderator. Develops, Promotes and Sustains Catholic Education in Perry County.

ST. CHARLES. *Academy of the Sacred Heart of St. Charles, Missouri Endowment Trust Fund* (1818) 619 N. 2nd St., St. Charles, 63301.
Tel: 636-946-6127; Fax: 636-949-6659; Email: mglavin@ash1818.org; Web: www.ash1818.org.

St. Clare of Assisi Senior Village, Inc., 409 Warrenton Village Dr., Warrenton, 63383.
Tel: 636-695-4205; Fax: 636-695-4216.

Duchesne High School Endowment Fund Inc., 2550 Elm St., St. Charles, 63301. Tel: 636-946-6767;
Fax: 636-946-6267; Email: cnolan@duchesne-hs.org; Web: www.duchesne-hs.org. Charles L. Nolan Jr., Pres. Receives Bequests and Gifts from Various Donors for the Express Purpose of Aiding and Benefitting Duchesne High School, St. Charles, and by Investment and Use of Such Bequests and Gifts and Income there from Aids and Benefits the High School in Fulfilling its Educational Purposes.

Sts. Joachim and Ann Care Service, 4116 McClay Rd., St. Charles, 63304. Tel: 636-441-1302;
Fax: 636-229-4684; Email: jlipin@jacares.org; Web: jacares.org. Deacon Jack Lipin, Exec. Dir.

STE. GENEVIEVE. *Vincentian Marian Youth Southeast Missouri*, 751 Center Dr., Ste. Genevieve, 63670.
Tel: 573-517-2212; Email: vincentianmarianyouth@gmail.com. Mr. Curt Buerck, Pres. Total Staff 7.

RELIGIOUS INSTITUTES OF MEN REPRESENTED IN THE ARCHDIOCESE

For further details refer to the corresponding bracketed number in the Religious Institutes of Men or Women section.

[0120]—*Alexian Brothers* (Immaculate Conception Prov.)—C.F.A.
[]—*Apostles of Jesus Missionaries* (Kenya; Regional: Northampton, PA)—A.J.
[0200]—*Benedictine Monks* (English Benedictine Congregation [St. Louis Abbey])—O.S.B.
[0330]—*Brothers of the Christian Schools* (Midwest Prov.)—F.S.C.
[]—*Congregation Messengers of Fatima*—C.M.F.
[1330]—*Congregation of the Mission* (Western Prov.)—C.M.
[0630]—*Congregation of the Missionaries of the Holy Family* (North American Prov.)—M.S.F.
[1000]—*Congregation of the Passion* (St. Paul of the Cross Prov.)—C.P.
[1080]—*Congregation of the Resurrection of Our Lord Jesus Christ* (USA Prov.)—C.R.
[0510]—*Franciscan Brothers of the Holy Cross*—F.F.S.C.
[0520]—*Franciscan Friars. (Croatian Franciscan Commissariat, Sacred Heart Prov.)*—O.F.M.
[0540]—*Franciscan Missionary Brothers of the Sacred Heart of Jesus* (Eureka, MO)—O.S.F.
[]—*Institute of Christ The King Sovereign Priest.*
[0690]—*Jesuit Fathers and Brothers* (U.S. Central and Southern Province, Society of Jesus)—S.J.
[0720]—*The Missionaries of Our Lady of La Salette*—M.S.
[0870]—*Monfort Missionaries*—S.M.M.
[0430]—*Order of Preachers* (Prov. in Columbia, South America)—O.P.
[0430]—*Order of Preachers* (Prov. of St. Albert the Great/Central Dominican Prov.)—O.P.
[1070]—*Redemptorist Fathers* (Denver Prov.)—C.Ss.R.
[1070]—*Redemptorist Fathers* (Prov. in India)—C.Ss.R.
[1230]—*Servants of the Paraclete*—s.P.
[1260]—*Society of Christ*—S.Ch.
[0760]—*Society of Mary* (United States Prov.)—S.M.
[0420]—*Society of the Divine Word* (Chicago Prov.)—S.V.D.
[]—*Sons of Our Mother of Peace*—S.M.P.

RELIGIOUS INSTITUTES OF WOMEN REPRESENTED IN THE ARCHDIOCESE

[0100]—*Adorers of the Blood of Christ* (U.S. Prov.)—A.S.C.
[0130]—*Apostles of the Sacred Heart of Jesus* (U.S. Prov.)—A.S.C.J.
[0360]—*Carmelite Sisters of the Divine Heart of Jesus* (Central Prov.)—Carmel D.C.J.
[1010]—*Congregation of Divine Providence, San Antonio, TX*—C.D.P.
[0397]—*Congregation of Mary, Queen* (American Region)—C.M.R.
[1070-09]—*Congregation of St. Catherine of Siena*—O.P.
[1070-07]—*Congregation of St. Cecilia* (Nashville, TN)—O.P.
[]—*Congregation of the Carmelite Religious* (St. Louis Centre)—C.C.R.
[]—*Congregation of the Most Holy Rosary.*
[0470]—*Congregation of the Sisters of Charity of the Incarnate Word, Houston, TX*—CCVI.
[0460]—*Congregation of the Sisters of Charity of the Incarnate Word, San Antonio, TX*—C.C.V.I.
[1730]—*Congregation of the Sisters of the Third Order of St. Francis* (Oldenburg, IN)—O.S.F.
[1830]—*Contemplatives of the Good Shepherd* (Mid-North) American Prov.)—R.G.S.
[0760]—*Daughters of Charity of St. Vincent de Paul*—D.C.
[]—*Daughters of Our Mother of Peace*—S.M.P.
[0810]—*Daughters of the Heart of Mary*—D.H.M.
[0420]—*Discalced Carmelite Nuns*—O.C.D.
[1115]—*Dominican Sisters of Peace* (Columbus, OH)—O.P.
[]—*Eucharist Missionaries of St. Theresa*—M.E.S.T.
[]—*Franciscan Sisters of Christian Charity*—FSSC.
[1415]—*Franciscan Sisters of Mary*—F.S.M.
[1430]—*Franciscan Sisters of Our Lady of Perpetual Help*—O.S.F.
[]—*Hospital Sisters of St. Francis*—O.S.F.
[]—*Institute of Salesian Missionaries of Mary Immaculate*—S.M.M.I.
[]—*Lovers of the Holy Cross of Hanoi, Vietnam*—L.H.C.
[]—*Lovers of the Holy Cross of St. Louis*—L.H.C.
[2710]—*Missionaries of Charity*—M.C.
[3990]—*Missionary Sisters of St. Peter Claver*—S.S.P.C.
[3760]—*Order of St. Clare*—O.S.C.
[2010]—*Order of the Most Holy Redeemer*—O.Ss.R.
[]—*Pallotine Missionary Sisters* (Queen of Apostles Prov.)—S.A.C.
[0950]—*Pious Society Daughters of St. Paul*—F.S.P.
[3170]—*Religious of the Passion of Jesus Christ*—C.P.
[]—*Religious Sisters of Mercy of Alma, Michigan*—R.S.M.
[2970]—*School Sisters of Notre Dame* (Central Pacific Prov.)—S.S.N.D.
[]—*Sinsinawa Dominican Congregation of the Most Holy Rosary*—O.P.
[0430]—*Sisters of Charity of the Blessed Virgin Mary*—B.V.M.
[0990]—*Sisters of Divine Providence* (Marie de la Roche Prov.)—C.D.P.
[2360]—*Sisters of Loretto at the Foot of the Cross*—S.L.
[2575]—*Sisters of Mercy of the Americas*—R.S.M.
[2575]—*Sisters of Mercy of the Americas* (Northeast)—R.S.M.
[2575]—*Sisters of Mercy of the Americas* (South Central)—R.S.M.
[2575]—*Sisters of Mercy of the Americas* (West Midwest)—R.S.M.
[1600]—*Sisters of St. Francis of the Martyr St. George*—F.S.G.M.
[3840]—*Sisters of St. Joseph of Carondelet*—C.S.J.
[1830]—*Sisters of the Good Shepherd* (Mid-North American Prov.)—R.G.S.
[3270]—*Sisters of the Most Precious Blood* (O'Fallon, MO)—C.PP.S.
[3540]—*Sisters Servants of the Holy Spirit of Perpetual Adoration*—S.Sp.S.deA.
[4070]—*Society of the Sacred Heart*—R.S.C.J.
[4110]—*Ursuline Nuns*—O.S.U.
[]—*US Federation of Sisters of St. Joseph.*
[4190]—*Visitation Nuns*—V.H.M.

ARCHDIOCESAN CEMETERIES

ST. LOUIS. *Calvary*, Business Office: 5239 W. Florissant Ave., 63115. Tel: 314-792-7738;
Fax: 314-381-3218.
Location:
Calvary Cemetery, 5239 W. Florissant Ave., 63115. Tel: 314-792-7738; Fax: 314-381-3218
Sacred Heart Cemetery, Graham Rd., Florissant, 63033. Tel: 314-792-7738; Fax: 314-381-3218
Saint Ferdinand Cemetery, Graham Rd., Hazelwood, 63042. Tel: 314-792-7738;
Fax: 314-381-3218
Saint Mary Cemetery, 5200 Fee Fee Rd., Hazelwood, 63042. Tel: 314-792-7738; Fax: 314-381-3218
Saint Peter Cemetery, Geyer at W. Monroe Ave., Kirkwood, 63122. Tel: 314-792-7738;
Fax: 314-381-3218
Cemetery of Our Lady, Lake St. Louis Blvd. & Orf Rd., Lake St. Louis, 63366. Tel: 314-792-7738;
Fax: 314-381-3218
Saint Charles Borromeo Cemetery, Randolph St., St. Charles, 63301. Tel: 314-792-7738;
Fax: 314-381-3218
Ste. Philippine Cemetiere, 4057 Towers Rd., St. Charles, 63304. Tel: 314-792-7738;
Fax: 314-381-3218
Holy Cross Cemetery, 16200 Manchester Rd., Ellisville, 63011. Tel: 314-792-7738;
Fax: 314-381-3218

Resurrection, Business Office: 6901 Mackenzie Rd., 63123. Tel: 314-792-7737; Fax: 314-351-1782.
Location:
Resurrection Cemetery, 6901 Mackenzie Rd., 63123. Tel: 314-792-7737; Fax: 314-351-1782
Saints Peter and Paul Cemetery, 7030 Gravois Ave., 63116. Tel: 314-792-7737; Fax: 314-351-1782
Saint Vincent Cemetery, 1488 Romaine Creek Rd., Fenton, 63026. Tel: 314-792-7737;
Fax: 314-351-1782
Mount Olive Cemetery, 3906 Mt. Olive Rd., Lemay, 63125. Tel: 314-792-7737; Fax: 314-351-1782
Ascension Cemetery, 5563 Country Club Rd., Washington, 63090. Tel: 314-792-7737;
Fax: 314-351-1782

NECROLOGY

† Lubeley, Richard J., (Retired), Died May. 2, 2018
† Borgerding, Terry J., Died Aug. 16, 2018
† Ditenhafer, John A., (Retired), Ladue, MO, Annunziata Parish, Died Jun. 9, 2018
† Fitzgibbon, Edmond J., (Retired), Died Sep. 18, 2018
† Fleiter, Robert V., (Retired), Died May. 7, 2018
† Kerber, John V., (Retired), Died Feb. 28, 2018
† Koch, Donald J., (Retired), Died Oct. 24, 2018
† Marshall, Robert A., (Retired), Died Sep. 28, 2018
† Wesloh, Ferdinand J., (Retired), Died Oct. 22, 2018

An asterisk (*) denotes an organization that has established tax-exempt status directly with the IRS and is not covered by the USCCB Group Ruling.

Archdiocese of St. Paul and Minneapolis

(Archidioecesis Paulopolitana et Minneapolitana)

Most Reverend

JOHN C. NIENSTEDT, S.T.D., D.D.

Archbishop Emeritus of Saint Paul and Minneapolis; ordained July 27, 1974; appointed Auxiliary Bishop of Detroit June 12, 1996; episcopal ordination July 9, 1996; appointed Bishop of New Ulm June 12, 2001; installed August 6, 2001; appointed Coadjutor Archbishop of Saint Paul and Minneapolis April 24, 2007; succeeded to the See May 2, 2008; resigned June 15, 2015. *Office: 777 Forest St., St. Paul, MN 55106-3857.* Tel: 651-291-4511; Fax: 651-291-4549.

Most Reverend

HARRY J. FLYNN, D.D.

Archbishop Emeritus of Saint Paul and Minneapolis; ordained May 28, 1960; appointed Coadjutor of Lafayette April 19, 1986; episcopal ordination June 24, 1986; appointed Bishop of Lafayette May 13, 1989; appointed Coadjutor Archbishop of Saint Paul and Minneapolis February 22, 1994; succeeded to the See September 8, 1995; retired May 2, 2008. *Office: 777 Forest St., St. Paul, MN 55106-3857.* Tel: 651-291-4420; Fax: 651-291-4549.

Most Reverend

BERNARD A. HEBDA

Archbishop of Saint Paul and Minneapolis; ordained July 1, 1989; appointed Bishop of Gaylord October 7, 2009; Episcopal Ordination December 1, 2009; appointed Coadjutor Archbishop of Newark September 24, 2013; ordained November 5, 2013; appointed Apostolic Administrator of St. Paul and Minneapolis June 15, 2015; appointed Archbishop of St. Paul and Minneapolis March 24, 2016; installed May 13, 2016. *Office: 777 Forest St., St. Paul, MN 55106-3857.* Tel: 651-291-4511; Fax: 651-291-4545; Email: archbishop@archspm.org.

Archdiocesan Catholic Center: 777 Forest St., St. Paul, MN 55106-3857. Tel: 651-291-4400; Fax: 651-290-1629.

Web: www.archspm.org

Email: catholiccenter@archspm.org

Most Reverend

ANDREW H. COZZENS

Auxiliary Bishop of Saint Paul and Minneapolis; ordained May 31, 1997; appointed Auxiliary Bishop of Saint Paul and Minneapolis and Titular Bishop of Bisica October 11, 2013; episcopal ordination December 9, 2013. *Office: 777 Forest St., St. Paul, MN 55106-3857.* Tel: 651-291-4521; Fax: 651-290-1637; Email: bishopcozzens@archspm.org.

Most Reverend

LEE ANTHONY PICHÉ

Former Auxiliary Bishop of Saint Paul and Minneapolis; ordained May 26, 1984; appointed Auxiliary Bishop of Saint Paul and Minneapolis and Titular Bishop of Tamata May 27, 2009; episcopal ordination June 29, 2009; resigned June 15, 2015. *Office: 777 Forest St., St. Paul, MN 55106-3857.* Tel: 651-291-4521; Fax: 651-290-1637; Email: bishoppiche@archspm.org.

Square Miles 6,187.

Diocese Established, July 19, 1850. Archdiocese Established, May 4, 1888.

Comprises the following twelve Counties of the State of Minnesota: Ramsey, Hennepin, Anoka, Carver, Chisago, Dakota, Goodhue, Le Sueur, Rice, Scott, Washington and Wright.

Corporate Title: The Archdiocese of Saint Paul and Minneapolis.

For legal titles of parishes and archdiocesan institutions, consult the Catholic Center.

STATISTICAL OVERVIEW

Personnel	
Archbishops	1
Retired Archbishops	2
Auxiliary Bishops	1
Retired Bishops	1
Priests: Diocesan Active in Diocese	198
Priests: Diocesan Active Outside Diocese	5
Priests: Diocesan in Foreign Missions	1
Priests: Retired, Sick or Absent	171
Number of Diocesan Priests	375
Religious Priests in Diocese	81
Total Priests in Diocese	456
Extern Priests in Diocese	45
Ordinations:	
Diocesan Priests	4
Religious Priests	1
Transitional Deacons	5
Permanent Deacons in Diocese	210
Total Brothers	45
Total Sisters	456
Parishes	
Parishes	187
With Resident Pastor:	
Resident Diocesan Priests	142
Resident Religious Priests	15
Without Resident Pastor:	
Administered by Priests	30
Missions	2
Professional Ministry Personnel:	
Brothers	9
Sisters	24
Lay Ministers	414
Welfare	
Catholic Hospitals	4
Total Assisted	214,228
Health Care Centers	1
Total Assisted	1,500
Homes for the Aged	22
Total Assisted	60,490
Day Care Centers	1
Total Assisted	70
Specialized Homes	3
Total Assisted	94
Special Centers for Social Services	18
Total Assisted	20,000
Residential Care of Disabled	2
Total Assisted	12
Educational	
Seminaries, Diocesan	2
Students from This Diocese	49
Students from Other Diocese	131
Diocesan Students in Other Seminaries	5
Seminaries, Religious	1
Students Religious	16
Total Seminarians	70
Colleges and Universities	3
Total Students	14,894
High Schools, Diocesan and Parish	2
Total Students	923
High Schools, Private	12
Total Students	7,132
Elementary Schools, Diocesan and Parish	78
Total Students	20,636
Elementary Schools, Private	1
Total Students	499
Catechesis/Religious Education:	
High School Students	5,410
Elementary Students	21,039
Total Students under Catholic Instruction	70,603
Teachers in the Diocese:	
Priests	36
Brothers	5
Sisters	18
Lay Teachers	2,643
Vital Statistics	
Receptions into the Church:	
Infant Baptism Totals	5,121
Minor Baptism Totals	1,306
Adult Baptism Totals	208
Received into Full Communion	922
First Communions	6,637
Confirmations	6,836
Marriages:	
Catholic	1,002
Interfaith	445
Total Marriages	1,447
Deaths	3,792
Total Catholic Population	825,000
Total Population	3,405,652

Former Bishops—Rt. Rev. JOSEPH CRETIN, D.D., cons. Jan. 26, 1851; died Feb. 22, 1857; Most Revs. THOMAS L. GRACE, O.P., D.D., cons. July 24, 1859; resigned July 31, 1884; named Titular Bishop of Menith, and later, Titular Archbishop of Siunia; died Feb. 22, 1897; JOHN IRELAND, D.D., cons. Dec. 21, 1861; Bishop of Maronea, and Coadjutor to; died Sept. 25, 1918; THOMAS L. GRACE, O.P., D.D., succeeded to the See of St. Paul, July 31, 1884; appt. Archbishop, May 15, 1888; died Sept. 25, 1918; AUSTIN DOWLING, D.D., Archbishop of St. Paul; ord. June 24, 1891; appt. Bishop of Des Moines, Iowa, Jan. 31, 1912; cons. April 25, 1912; Nominated Archbishop of St. Paul, Feb. 1, 1919; died Nov. 29, 1930; JOHN GREGORY MURRAY, S.T.D., ord. April 14, 1900; appt. Titular Bishop of Flavias, Auxiliary to the Bishop of Hartford, Nov. 15, 1919; cons. April 28, 1920; transferred to the Diocese of Portland, May 29, 1925; appt. Archbishop of St. Paul, Oct. 29, 1931; died Oct. 11, 1956; WILLIAM O. BRADY, D.D., Archbishop of St. Paul; ord. Dec. 21, 1923; appt. Bishop of Sioux Falls, June 10, 1939; cons. Aug. 24, 1939; appt. Titular Archbishop of Selymbria and Coadjutor "cum jure successionis" of St. Paul, June 16, 1956; succeeded to See, Oct. 11, 1956; died Oct. 1, 1961; LEO C. BYRNE, D.D., Coadjutor Archbishop "cum jure successionis" of Saint Paul and Minneapolis; ord. June 10, 1933; appt. titular Bishop of Sabidia and Auxiliary of St. Louis, May 21, 1954; cons. June 29, 1954; transferred to Wichita, "cum jure successionis" 1961; appt. Apostolic Administrator of Wichita, Feb. 25, 1963; promoted to St. Paul and Minneapolis, Aug. 2, 1967; died Oct. 21, 1974; LEO BINZ, D.D., ord. March 15, 1924; appt. Titular Bishop of Pinara and Coadjutor Bishop of Winona, Nov. 21, 1942; cons. Dec. 21, 1942; Titular Archbishop of Silyum and Coadjutor to the Archbishop of Dubuque "cum jure successionis," Oct. 15, 1949; Archbishop of Dubuque, Dec. 2, 1954; appt. Archbishop of Saint Paul, Dec. 16, 1961; resigned May 21, 1975; died Oct. 9, 1979; JOHN R. ROACH, D.D., Archbishop of St. Paul and Minneapolis; ord. June 8, 1946; appt. Titular Bishop of Cenae and Auxiliary Bishop of St. Paul and Minneapolis, July 12, 1971; cons. Sept. 8, 1971; appt. Archbishop of St. Paul and Minneapolis, May 21, 1975; resigned Sept. 8, 1995;

died July 11, 2003; HARRY J. FLYNN, D.D., ord. May 28, 1960; appt. Coadjutor of Lafayette April 19, 1986; cons. June 24, 1986; appt. Bishop of Lafayette May 13, 1989; appt. Coadjutor Archbishop of Saint Paul and Minneapolis Feb. 22, 1994; appt. Archbishop of Saint Paul and Minneapolis Sept. 8, 1995; retired May 2, 2008.; JOHN C. NIENSTEDT, ord. July 27, 1974; appt. Auxiliary Bishop of Detroit June 12, 1996; episcopal ord. July 9, 1996; appt. Bishop of New Ulm June 12, 2001; installed Aug. 6, 2001; appt. Coadjutor Archbishop of Saint Paul and Minneapolis April 24, 2007; succeeded to the See May 2, 2008; resigned June 15, 2015.

Archdiocesean Catholic Center—777 Forest St., St. Paul, 55106-3857. Tel: 651-291-4400; Fax: 651-290-1629.

Office of the Archbishop—Most Rev. BERNARD HEBDA, Archbishop; PATRICE ZANGS, Exec. Asst. to the Archbishop, Tel: 651-291-4511; Fax: 651-291-4549; Email: archbishop@archspm.org.

Office of the Auxiliary Bishop—Tel: 651-291-4510; Email: bishopcozzens@archspm.org. Most Rev. ANDREW H. COZZENS, S.T.D.; ALISON KAARDAL, Exec. Asst. to Bishop Cozzens.

Vicar General and Moderator of the Curia—Email: vicargeneral@archspm.org. Very Rev. CHARLES V. LACHOWITZER; MS. LAURIE WOHLERS, Administrative Asst.

Presbyteral Council—

Executive Director—Rev. MICHAEL VAN SLOUN.
Deanery 1—Rev. JOSEPH JEROME BAMBENEK.
Deanery 2—Rev. PATRICK J. HIPWELL.
Deanery 3—Rev. JOHN L. UBEL.
Deanery 4—Rev. JOHN PAUL ERICKSON.
Deanery 5—Rev. ANDREW R. BRINKMAN.
Deanery 6—Rev. RANDAL J. KASEL.
Deanery 7—Rev. BRANDON MICHAEL THEISEN.
Deanery 8—Rev. DOUGLAS ALLEN EBERT.
Deanery 9—Rev. LUKE C. MARQUARD.
Deanery 10—Rev. WILLIAM DEZIEL.
Deanery 11—Rev. ANTHONY G. VANDERLOOP.
Deanery 12—Rev. THOMAS W. DUFNER.
Deanery 13—Rev. DAVID HASCHKA, S.J.
Deanery 14—Rev. JOSEPH P. GILLESPIE, O.P.
Deanery 15—Rev. RICHARD KALEY, O.F.M.Conv.
Deanery 16—(Academic) VACANT.
Deanery 17—(Specialized) Very Rev. MICHAEL C. JOHNSON, J.C.L.
Deanery 18—(Retired) Revs. KENNETH J. PIERRE, (Retired); JOHN M. MALONE, (Retired).
Appointees—Revs. DAVID R. HENNEN; JAMES J. STILES; THOMAS (T.J.) MCKENZIE.
Ex Officio—Most Revs. BERNARD HEBDA; ANDREW H. COZZENS, S.T.D.; Very Rev. CHARLES V. LACHOWITZER.

Archdiocesan Finance Council (AFC)—Rev. JOHN L. UBEL; Deacon ROBERT SCOTT DURHAM; MR. STEWART W. LAIRD; MR. MARK MISUKANIS; MS. JACKIE DAYLOR; MR. THOMAS ABOOD, Chm.; MR. RICHARD J. PEARSON; Sr. CATHERINE MARY ROSENGREN, C.S.J.; MR. DANIEL STATSICK; Very Rev. CHARLES V. LACHOWITZER, Vicar Gen. & Moderator of the Curia.

Office for the Mission of Catholic Education—MR. JASON SLATTERY, Dir. Catholic Education.

College of Consultors—Very Rev. JOHN BAUER; Revs. DAVID BLUME; STAN P. MADER; NATHANIEL MEYERS; CHRISTOPHER L. SHOFNER; MICHAEL VAN SLOUN; ROLF R. TOLLEFSON; JOHN L. UBEL; Very Rev. CHARLES V. LACHOWITZER; Most Rev. ANDREW H. COZZENS, S.T.D.

Archdiocesan Curia

Members of the Corporation—Most Revs. BERNARD HEBDA, Archbishop; ANDREW H. COZZENS, S.T.D., Auxiliary Bishop; MR. THOMAS MERTENS, CFO; Very Rev. CHARLES V. LACHOWITZER, Vicar Gen.; MR. JOSEPH KUEPPERS, Chancellor.

Board of Directors—Very Rev. CHARLES V. LACHOWITZER, Vicar Gen.; MR. JOSEPH KUEPPERS, Chancellor; MR. JOHN F. BIERBAUM; PETER DALY, M.D.; MR. THOMAS MERTENS, CFO; KAREN RAUENHORST; Most Rev. ANDREW H. COZZENS, S.T.D.; MR. BRIAN SHORT; Rev. STEPHEN D. ULRICK; Most Rev. BERNARD HEBDA, Archbishop.

Chancellor for Civil Affairs—MR. JOSEPH KUEPPERS, Email: kueppersj@archspm.org.

Chancellor for Canonical Affairs—MS. SUSAN MULHERON, Email: mulherons@archspm.org.

Legal Assistant to the Chancellors—MS. THERESA KLEINFEHN, Email: kleinfehnt@archspm.org.

Vice Chancellor—MR. SEAN MCDONOUGH, Email: mcdonoughs@archspm.org.

Director of Ministerial Standards and Safe Environment—Judge TIMOTHY O'MALLEY, Tel: 651-290-1618; Email: omalleyt@archspm.org; Ms. JANELL RASMUSSEN, Deputy Dir., Tel: 651-291-4475; Email: rasmussenj@archspm.org.

Delegate for Consecrated Life—Sr. CAROLYN PUCCIO, C.S.J., Email: puccioc@archspm.org.

Office of Conciliation—VACANT.

Archives and Records Management—MS. ALLISON SPIES, Archivist, Tel: 651-291-4542; Email: spiesa@archspm.org; MS. SEHRI STROM, Records Mgr., Tel: 651-291-4481; Email: stroms@archspm.org.

Administration and Financial Services—MR. THOMAS MERTENS, CFO, Tel: 651-291-4492; Email: mertenst@archspm.org.

Office of Financial Standards and Parish Accounting—Tel: 651-291-4439. MS. MARY JO JUNGWIRTH, Dir. Parish Oper.

Human Resources and Benefits—MS. MARY ELLEN MOE, Dir., Email: moem@archspm.org.

Office of Marriage, Family, & Life—MS. JEAN STOLPESTAD, Dir., Web: www.archspm.org/family.

Worship—Rev. THOMAS MARGEVICIUS, S.T.L., Dir.; MS. LAURINDA IRWIN, Administrative Asst., Email: irwinl@archspm.org.

Communications—TOM HALDEN, Dir., Email: haldent@archspm.org.

Evangelization and Catechesis—MS. CRYSTAL CROCKER, Dir., Email: crockerc@archspm.org.

Archdiocesan Vocation Office—Rev. DAVID BLOOM, Dir., 2260 Summit Ave., St. Paul, 55105. Tel: 651-962-6892; Email: stpaulpriest@10000vocations.org.

Archbishop Harry J. Flynn Catechetical Institute—Web: www.cistudent.com. MS. KELLY WAHLQUIST, Asst. Dir., Tel: 651-962-5028; Email: wahl3194@stthomas.edu.

Institute for Diaconal Formation—Deacon JOSEPH T. MICHALAK JR., Dir., Tel: 651-962-6876; Email: jtmichalak@stthomas.edu.

Ecumenical and Interreligious Affairs—Rev. ERICH RUTTEN, M.A., M.Div., Church of St. Peter Claver, 375 Oxford St. N., St. Paul, 55104.

Center for Mission / Society for the Propagation of the Faith—777 Forest St., St. Paul, 55106-3857. Tel: 651-291-4445; Web: www.centerformission.org. Deacon MICKEY FRIESEN, Dir., Email: friesenm@archspm.org.

Oficina del Ministerio Latino—MS. ESTELA VILLAGRA MANANCERO, Dir., Tel: 651-290-1639; Email: mananceroe@archspm.org.

The Saint Paul Seminary School of Divinity—2260 Summit Ave., St. Paul, 55105. Tel: 651-962-5050; Web: semssp.org. Rev. JOSEPH TAPHORN, Rector-Vice Pres.

Office of Parish and Clergy Services—Deacon STEVEN H. MAIER, Dir., Email: maiers@archspm.org.

Saint John Vianney Seminary—Rev. MICHAEL C. BECKER, Rector, 2115 Summit Ave., #5024, St. Paul, 55105-1095. Tel: 651-962-6825; Email: beck8065@stthomas.edu.

The Catholic Spirit—(Newspaper) Web: www.thecatholicspirit.com. MS. MARIA WIERING, Editor.

Episcopal Vicar for Clergy and Parish Services—Very Rev. MICHAEL TIX, Tel: 651-291-4449; Email: tixm@archspm.org.

Catholic Cemeteries—2105 Lexington Ave. S., Mendota Heights, 55120. Tel: 651-228-9991; Fax: 651-228-9995; Web: www.catholic-cemeteries.org. MS. JOAN GECIK, Dir.

Metropolitan Tribunal—Tel: 651-291-4466; Fax: 651-291-4467; Email: tribunal@archspm.org; Web: archspm.org/departments/metropolitan-tribunal.

Judicial Vicar—Very Rev. MICHAEL C. JOHNSON, J.C.L.

Director of the Tribunal—MS. AMY TADLOCK, J.C.L., Tel: 651-291-4422; Email: tadlocka@archspm.org.

Judges and Auditors—Deacon NATHAN ALLEN, J.D., Tel: 651-291-4465; Email: allenn@archspm.org; MR. DANIEL QUINAN, J.C.L., Tel: 651-291-4548; Email: quinand@archspm.org; MR. MATTHEW KUETTEL, J.C.L., Tel: 651-291-4442; Email: kuettelm@archspm.org; MR. JAMES ZAHLER, J.C.L., Tel: 651-291-4408; Email: zahlerj@archspm.org; MR. RICHARD ALEMAN, Tel: 651-290-1617; Email: alemanr@archspm.org.

Defender of the Bond—MS. MICHELLE GERLACH.

Special Marriage Cases—MS. CATHY POSCH, B.S.

Vicar for Latino Ministry—Rev. JOSEPH A. WILLIAMS, Church of St. Stephen, Minneapolis, 55404. Email: frjoseph@ss-mpls.org.

Archdiocesan Council of Catholic Women—777 Forest St., St. Paul, 55106-3857. Tel: 651-291-4545; Web: www.accwarchspm.org. Rev. DAVID W. KOHNER, Spiritual Advisor; MS. DEBBIE KELLER, Pres., Tel: 651-291-4545; Email: alliec@archspm.org.

Commission on Bio-Medical Ethics—Rev. JOHN P. FLOEDER, Chm., 2260 Summit Ave., Mail #5010, St. Paul, 55105. Tel: 651-962-5029; Email: jpfloeder@stthomas.edu.

Office of Indian Ministry—The Church of Gichitwaa Kateri, 3045 Park Ave. S., Minneapolis, 55409. Tel: 612-824-7606.

Archdiocesan Catholic Committee on Scouting—WILLIAM DAVIES, Chair, Tel: 952-925-1780; Deacon DEL WILKINSON, Chap., Tel: 763-267-7530.

CLERGY, PARISHES, MISSIONS AND PAROCHIAL SCHOOLS

METROPOLITAN ST. PAUL

(RAMSEY COUNTY)

1—CATHEDRAL OF SAINT PAUL (1850)
239 Selby Ave., 55102. Tel: 651-228-1766; Web: www.cathedralsaintpaul.org. Revs. John L. Ubel, Rector; Joseph H. Kuharski, Sacramental Min.; Deacons Ronald G. Schmitz; Phillip B. Stewart.
Additional Worship Site: Church of St. Vincent, 651 Virginia St., 55103.
Catechesis Religious Program—Students 128.

2—ST. ADALBERT (1881) (Polish)
265 Charles Ave., 55103. Tel: 651-228-9002; Email: stadalbert@comcast.net; Web: stadalbertchurch.org. Rev. Minh Vu.
Catechesis Religious Program—Students 183.

3—ST. AGNES (1887) (German)
535 Thomas Ave., 55103. Tel: 651-925-8800; Email: office@churchofsaintagnes.org; Web: www.churchofsaintagnes.org. Rev. James McConville, Parochial Vicar; Deacons Joseph R. Damiani; Nathan E. Allen; Rev. Mark D. Moriarty.
School—St. Agnes School, (Grades PreK-12), 530 Lafond Ave., 55103. Tel: 651-925-8700; Fax: 651-925-8708; Email: info@saintagnesschool.org; Web: www.saintagnesschool.org. Dr. Kevin Ferdinandt, Headmaster. Lay Teachers 54; Students 770.
Catechesis Religious Program—Students 88.

4—ST. ANDREW (1895) Merged with Maternity of the Blessed Virgin, St. Paul.

5—ST. ANDREW KIM (1990) [JC] (Korean)
1435 Midway Pkwy., 55108. Tel: 651-644-1605; Email: andrewkim@andrewkim.us. Rev. Hak Sun (Augustinus) Kim, Parochial Admin.
Catechesis Religious Program—

6—ASSUMPTION (1856) (German)
51 W. Seventh St., 55102. Tel: 651-224-7536; Email: info@assumptionsp.org; Web: assumptionsp.org. Rev. Paul C. Treacy; Deacon James F. Saumweber.
Catechesis Religious Program—261 E. 8th St., 55101. Tel: 651-222-2619. Catechesis Religious Program combined with St. Mary, St. Paul.

7—BLESSED SACRAMENT (1916)
2119 Stillwater Ave. E., 55119-3508.
Tel: 651-738-0677 (Office); Fax: 651-738-6492; Email: jmhoffman@blessedsacramentsp.org; Web: www.blessedsacramentsp.org. Revs. Benny Mekkatt Varghese, C.F.I.C.; Jimmy Puttananickal, C.F.I.C., Parochial Vicar; Deacon Jeremiah N. Saladin.
Catechesis Religious Program—Julia R. Taylor, D.R.E. Students 84.

8—ST. CASIMIR (1892) (Polish)
934 E. Geranium Ave., 55106. Tel: 651-774-0365; Email: office@stcasimirchurch.org; Web: www.stcasimirchurch.org. Revs. Michael Powell, O.M.I.; Ronald Harrer, O.M.I., In Res.
Catechesis Religious Program—
Tel: 651-774-0365, Ext. 101; Email: suevanyo@stcasimirchurch.org. Students 49.

9—ST. CECILIA (1912)
2357 Bayless Pl., 55114. Tel: 651-644-4502; Email: info@stceciliaspm.org; Web: www.stceciliaspm.org. Rev. John Michael Hofstede, (Retired).
Catechesis Religious Program—Students 93.

10—CHURCH OF ST. BERNARD (1890) (German)
Physical Address: 187 Geranium St, 55117.
Tel: 651-488-6733; Fax: 651-489-9203; Email: frivansant@churchofstbernard-stp.org; Web: www.stbernardstpaul.org. Mailing Address: 1160 Woodbridge St., 55117. Revs. Ivan Sant; Saw Joseph, Parochial Vicar.
Catechesis Religious Program—Email: dneira@churchofstbernard-sto.org. David Neira, D.R.E. Students 153.

11—CHURCH OF LUMEN CHRISTI
Office: 2055 Bohland Ave., 55116. Tel: 651-698-5581; Fax: 651-698-9526; Email: pfeela@lumenchristicc.org; Web: www.lumenchristicc.org. Rev. Paul F. Feela, M.A.
Catechesis Religious Program—Phyllis Hamill-Little, D.R.E. Students 98.

12—ST. COLUMBA (1914)
1327 Lafond Ave., 55104. Tel: 651-645-9179; Email: office@stcolumba.org; Web: www.stcolumba.org. Rev. Hoang D. Nguyen; Deacon Thomas Stiles.
Catechesis Religious Program—Students 159.

13—ST. FRANCIS DE SALES (1884) (German)
650 Palace Ave., 55102-3593. Tel: 651-228-1169; Email: sfsjadmin@sf-sj.org; Web: www.sf-sj.org. Revs. Paul C. Treacy, Parochial Admin.; Miguel Jose Velez Nieves, S.E.M.V., Parochial Vicar; Luis Banchs Plaza, Parochial Vicar; Deacon Steven H. Maier.
Catechesis Religious Program—Students 50.

14—ST. GREGORY THE GREAT (1951) Merged See Lumen Christi Catholic Community, St. Paul for records.

15—HOLY CHILDHOOD (1946)
1435 Midway Pkwy., 55108. Tel: 651-644-7495; Email: contact@holychildhoodparish.org; Web: holychildhoodparish.org. Revs. Timothy D. Cloutier, J.C.L.; Joseph Fink, Parochial Vicar; John Berger, In Res.
Catechesis Religious Program—Students 6.

16—HOLY SPIRIT (1936)
515 Albert St. S., 55116. Tel: 651-698-3353; Web: holy-spirit.org. Rev. Daniel C. Haugan; Deacon Joseph T. Michalak Jr.
School—Holy Spirit School, (Grades PreK-8), Web: holy-spirit.org/school-home. Dr. Mary Adrian, Prin. Lay Teachers 25; Students 311.
Catechesis Religious Program—
Fax: menzhuberc@holy-spirit.org. Christopher Menzhuber, Dir. Faith Formation. Students 70.

17—THE IMMACULATE HEART OF MARY (1949) Merged with St. Luke, St. Paul to form St. Thomas More, St. Paul.

18—ST. JAMES (1887) Merged with St. Francis De Sales, St. Paul as of 1/1/2011.

19—ST. JOHN OF ST. PAUL (1886) Merged with St. Pascal Baylon, St. Paul as of 7/1/2013.

20—ST. LEO (1945) Merged See Lumen Christi Catholic Community, St. Paul for records.

21—ST. LOUIS KING OF FRANCE (1868) (French)
506 Cedar St., 55101-2245. Tel: 651-224-3379; Email: markmstlouis@comcast.net; Web: stlouiskingoffrance.org. Revs. John A. Sajdak, S.M.; Joseph Hurtuk, S.M.; Ronald DesRosiers, S.M., In Res., (Retired); Roland Lajoie, S.M., In Res.

22—ST. LUKE (1888) Merged with Immaculate Heart of Mary, St. Paul to form St. Thomas More, St. Paul.

23—ST. MARK (1889)
2001 Dayton Ave., 55104. Tel: 651-645-5717; Email: parishcenter@saintmark-mn.org; Web: www.saintmark-mn.org. Revs. Humberto Palomino, P.E.S.; Mario Castagnola, P.E.S., Parochial Vicar; Adam Keiji Tokashiki, P.E.S., In Res.
School—St. Mark School, (Grades PreK-8), 1983 Dayton Ave., 55104. Tel: 651-644-3380;
Fax: 651-644-1923; Email: schooloffice@markerspride.com; Web: www.markerspride.com. Edgar Alfonzo, Prin. Lay Teachers 15; Students 141.
Catechesis Religious Program—Katy Wehr, Faith Formation Coord. Students 106.

24—ST. MARY (1865)
261 E. 8th St., 55101. Tel: 651-222-2619; Email: office@stmarystpaul.org; Web: stmarystpaul.org. Revs. Benny Mekkatt, C.F.I.C.; Jimmy Puttananickal, C.F.I.C., Parochial Vicar; Anthony Scaria, C.F.I.C., In Res.
Catechesis Religious Program—Shared program with Assumption (St. Paul). Students 113.

25—MATERNITY OF THE BLESSED VIRGIN (1949)
1414 N. Dale St., 55117. Tel: 651-489-8825; Email: info@maternityofmarychurch.org; Web: www.maternityofmarychurch.org. Revs. Timothy D. Cloutier, J.C.L.; Joseph Fink, Parochial Vicar; Deacon Dennis M. Chlebeck.
School—Maternity of Mary/St. Andrew School, (Grades PreK-8), 592 Arlington Ave. W., 55117.
Tel: 651-489-1459; Fax: 651-489-3560; Email: principal@mmsaschool.org; Web: www.mmsaschool.org. Maggie Quast, Prin. Lay Teachers 16; Students 184.
Catechesis Religious Program—Fax: 651-488-4055. Students 120.

26—ST. MATTHEW (1886) (German)
490 Hall Ave., 55107. Tel: 651-457-2334;
Fax: 651-457-1668; Email: administrator@st-matts.org; Web: www.st-matts.org. Rev. Robert M. Kelly, O.P., Parochial Admin.; Deacon Gregg A. Sroder.
See Community of Saints Regional Catholic School, West St. Paul under Elementary Schools, Consolidated, Parochial located in Institution section.
Catechesis Religious Program—Students 22.

27—THE NATIVITY OF OUR LORD (1922)
1900 Wellesley Ave., 55105. Tel: 651-696-5401; Web: www.nativity-mn.org. Revs. Patrick J. Hipwell; Nicholas Hagen, Parochial Vicar; Deacons Donald D. Tienter; Russell A. Kocemba.
School—The Nativity of Our Lord School, (Grades PreK-8), 1900 Stanford Ave., 55105.
Tel: 651-699-1311; Fax: 651-696-5420; Email: school@nativity-mn.org; Web: school.nativity-mn.org. Ms. Kate Wollan, Prin. Lay Teachers 48; Students 768.
Catechesis Religious Program—Tel: 651-696-5454; Fax: 651-696-5458. Students 157.

28—OUR LADY OF GUADALUPE (1931) (Hispanic)
401 Concord Street, 55107. Tel: 651-228-0506; Email: info@olgcatholic.org; Web: www.olgcatholic.org. Revs. Andrew R. Brinkman; Kevin M. Manthey, Sacramental Min.; Deacons Luis E. Rubi; Gregory A. Sroder.
See Community of Saints Regional Catholic School, West St. Paul under Elementary Schools, Consolidated, Parochial located in Institution section.
Catechesis Religious Program—Students 222.

29—ST. PASCAL BAYLON (1946) Receiving parish for St. John of St. Paul.
Mailing Address: 1757 Conway St., 55106.
Tel: 651-774-1585; Email: theresa.ruttger@stpascals.org; Web: www.stpascalbaylon.com. Rev. John J. Mitchell; Deacon Richard J. Moore.
School—St. Pascal Baylon School, (Grades PreK-8), Tel: 651-776-0092; Email: principal@stpascals.org; Web: www.stpascalschool.org. Inna Collier, Prin. Lay Teachers 12; Students 157.
Catechesis Religious Program—Email: kim.roering@stpascals.org. Kim Roering, D.R.E. Students 75.

30—ST. PATRICK (1884)
1095 De Soto St., 55130. Tel: 651-774-8675; Email: stpats15@yahoo.com; Web: www.stpatrickmn.weconnect.com. Rev. Michael Powell, O.M.I.
Catechesis Religious Program—Students 149.

31—ST. PETER CLAVER (1892) (African American)
375 N. Oxford St., 55104. Tel: 651-646-1797; Email: jane.mitchell@spcchurch.org; Web: www.spcchurch.org. Rev. Erich Rutten, M.A., M.Div.; Deacon Fred L. Johnson
Legal Title: Church of Saint Peter Claver
School—St. Peter Claver School, (Grades K-8), 1060 W. Central Ave., 55104. Tel: 651-621-2273;
Fax: 651-647-5394; Email: sspellins@stpclaverschool.org; Web: www.stpclaverschool.org. Terese Shimshock, Prin. Lay Teachers 10; Students 79.
Catechesis Religious Program—Students 98.

32—SACRED HEART (1881) (German)
840 E. Sixth St., 55106. Tel: 651-776-2741. Rev. Timothy L. Norris.
Catechesis Religious Program—Students 103.

33—ST. STANISLAUS (1872) (Czech)
398 Superior St., 55102. Tel: 651-292-0303; Web: ststans.org. Rev. John C. Clay.
Catechesis Religious Program—395 Superior St., 55102. Tel: 651-292-1913; Email: lindsay@ststans.org. Lindsay Lopez, D.R.E. Students 50.

34—ST. THERESE (1926) Merged See Lumen Christi Catholic Community, St. Paul for records.

35—ST. THOMAS MORE
1079 Summit Ave., 55105-2243. Tel: 651-227-7669; Web: www.morecommunity.org. Rev. Warren J. Sazama; Deacon Thomas Dzik.
School—St. Thomas More Catholic School, (Grades PreK-8), 1065 Summit Ave., 55105.
Tel: 651-224-4836; Fax: 651-224-0097; Web: school.morecommunity.org. Patrick Lofton, Prin. Clergy 1; Lay Teachers 17; Students 168; Total Staff 39.
Catechesis Religious Program—Students 69.

36—ST. THOMAS THE APOSTLE (1954) Merged with Blessed Sacrament, St. Paul.

37—ST. VINCENT DE PAUL (1888) [CEM] Merged with Cathedral of Saint Paul.

OUTSIDE METROPOLITAN ST. PAUL

COTTAGE GROVE, WASHINGTON CO., CHURCH OF ST. RITA (1966)
8694 80th St. S., Cottage Grove, 55016.
Tel: 651-459-4596; Fax: 651-459-5364; Email: stritas@saintritas.org; Web: www.saintritas.org. Rev. Ronald Kruel, O.P., Parochial Admin.; Deacons John R. Nicklay; Steve Koop.
Catechesis Religious Program—Email: aschroeder@saintritas.org. Amy Schroeder, D.R.E. Students 217.

LITTLE CANADA, RAMSEY CO., CHURCH OF SAINT JOHN THE EVANGELIST OF LITTLE CANADA (1851) [CEM]
380 Little Canada Rd., Little Canada, 55117.
Tel: 651-484-2708; Web: www.stjohnsoflc.org. Rev. Thomas J. Balluff.
School—Saint John School of Little Canada, (Grades PreK-8), 2621 McMenemy St., Little Canada, 55117.
Tel: 651-484-3038; Email: saintjohnschool@sjolc.org; Web: sjolc.org. Daniel Hurley, Prin. Lay Teachers 18; Students 152.
Catechesis Religious Program—Tel: 651-288-3259; Fax: 651-288-3233. Students 67.

MAHTOMEDI, WASHINGTON CO., ST. JUDE OF THE LAKE (1939)
700 Mathomedi Ave., Mahtomedi, 55115.
Tel: 651-426-3245; Fax: 651-653-3554; Email: parishcouncil@stjudeofthelake.org; Web: www.stjudeofthelake.org. Revs. Cory J. Rohlfing; Paul Basil Kubista, Parochial Vicar.
School—St. Jude of the Lake School, (Grades PreK-5), 600 Mahtomedi Ave., Mahtomedi, 55115.
Tel: 651-426-2562; Fax: 651-653-3662; Email: schoolinfo@stjudeofthelake.org; Web: www.stjudeofthelakeschool.org. Carrie Hackman, Prin. Lay Teachers 10; Students 124.
Catechesis Religious Program—Students 249.

MAPLEWOOD, RAMSEY CO.

1—HOLY REDEEMER (1880) (Italian), Merged See St. Peter, North St. Paul.

2—ST. JEROME (1940)
Church & Office: 380 Roselawn Ave. E., Maplewood, 55117. Tel: 651-771-1209; Fax: 651-771-3466; Email: secretary@stjerome-church.org; Web: www.stjerome-church.org. Rev. Cletus Basekela.
School—St. Jerome School, (Grades PreK-8), 384 E. Roselawn Ave., Maplewood, 55117.
Tel: 651-771-8494; Fax: 651-771-3466; Email: secretary@stjeromeschool.org; Web: stjeromeschool.org. Anne Gattman, Prin. Lay Teachers 11; Students 164.
Catechesis Religious Program—Students 25.

3—PRESENTATION OF THE BLESSED VIRGIN MARY (1946)
1725 Kennard St., Maplewood, 55109.
Tel: 651-777-8116; Fax: 651-777-8743; Email: mail@presentationofmary.org; Web: www.presentationofmary.org. Rev. Thomas J. McKenzie; Deacon Michael D. Powers.
School—Presentation of the Blessed Virgin Mary School, (Grades PreK-8), 1695 Kennard St., Maplewood, 55109. Tel: 651-777-5877;
Fax: 651-777-8283; Web: presentationofmaryschool.org. Nikki Giel, Prin. Lay Teachers 11; Students 195.
Catechesis Religious Program—Students 59.

MENDOTA, DAKOTA CO., ST. PETER (1840) [CEM]
1405 Hwy. 13, P.O. Box 50679, Mendota, 55150.
Tel: 651-452-4550; Fax: 651-456-0646; Email: church@stpetersmendota.org; Web: www.stpetersmendota.org. Rev. Steven B. Hoffman; Deacon Timothy H. Hennessey.
See Faithful Shepherd Catholic School, Eagan under Elementary Schools, Consolidated, Parochial located in the Institution section.
Catechesis Religious Program—Email: kraible@stpetersmendota.org. Kathy Raible, D.R.E. Students 169.

NEW BRIGHTON, RAMSEY CO., ST. JOHN THE BAPTIST (1906) [CEM]
835 2nd Ave., N.W., New Brighton, 55112.
Tel: 651-633-8333; Email: stjohnsnb@pclink.com; Web: www.stjohnnb.com. Revs. Michael C. Skluzacek; Paul J. Shovelain, Parochial Vicar; Deacons Gary F. Schneider; Rodney W. Palmer.
School—St. John the Baptist School, (Grades PreK-8), 845 2nd Ave., N.W., New Brighton, 55112.
Tel: 651-633-1522; Email: barsnessm@stjohnnyb.org; Web: www.stjohnnyb.org. Ann Laird, Prin. Lay Teachers 24; Students 279.
Catechesis Religious Program—Email: balzarinij@stjohnnyb.org. Jessica Balzarini, D.R.E. Students 249.

NORTH ST. PAUL, RAMSEY CO., ST. PETER (1888) [CEM] (Italian)
2600 N. Margaret St., North Saint Paul, 55109.
Tel: 651-777-8304; Fax: 651-777-0497; Email: church@stpetersnsp.org; Web: www.churchofstpeternsp.org. Revs. Ettore Ferrario, F.S.C.B.; Pietro Rossotti, F.S.C.B., Parochial Vicar; Daniele Scorrano, F.S.C.B., Parochial Vicar; Deacon Robert A. Bisciglia.
School—St. Peter School, (Grades PreK-8), 2620 Margaret St. N., North Saint Paul, 55109. Email: adahlman@stpetersnsp.org; Web: www.stpetersnsp.org. Alison Dahlman, Prin. Lay Teachers 13; Students 221.
Catechesis Religious Program—Students 190.

OAKDALE, WASHINGTON CO.

1—GUARDIAN ANGELS (1857) [CEM]
Mailing Address: 8260 4th St. N., Oakdale, 55128.
Tel: 651-738-2223; Fax: 651-738-2453; Email: info@guardian-angels.org; Web: www.guardian-angels.org. Rev. Rodger Bauman; Deacon Mick Humbert.
Child Care—Preschool, Tel: 651-730-7450; Email: nlyons@guardian-angels.org; Web: www.guardian-angels.org/lacp. Lay Teachers 6; Students 60.
Catechesis Religious Program—Students 305.

2—TRANSFIGURATION (1939)
6133 15th St. N., Oakdale, 55128. Tel: 651-501-2209; Web: www.transfigurationmn.org. Rev. John Paul Erickson; Deacon Daniel P. Brewer.
School—Transfiguration School, (Grades PreK-8), 6135 15th St. N., Oakdale, 55128. Tel: 651-501-2220; Fax: 651-501-2258. Andrew Jacobson, Prin. Lay Teachers 15; Students 216.
Catechesis Religious Program—Email:

jkortuem@transfigurationmn.org. Justin Kortuem, D.R.E. Students 121.

ROSEVILLE, RAMSEY CO.

1—CORPUS CHRISTI (1939)
Mailing Address: 2131 Fairview Ave. N., Roseville, 55113-5499. Tel: 651-639-8888; Fax: 651-639-8288; Email: office@churchofcorpuschristi.org; Web: www.churchofcorpuschristi.org. Revs. Marc V. Paveglio, Parochial Admin.; Jonathan J. Kelly, Sacramental Min.; Deacon Glenn D. Skuta.
Catechesis Religious Program—Students 120.

2—SAINT ROSE OF LIMA (1939)
2048 N. Hamline Ave., Roseville, 55113.
Tel: 651-645-9389; Web: www.saintroseoflima.net. Revs. Marc V. Paveglio; Jonathan J. Kelly, Sacramental Min.; Deacon Glenn D. Skuta.
School—Saint Rose of Lima School, (Grades PreK-8), 2072 Hamline Ave. N., Roseville, 55113.
Tel: 651-646-3832; Fax: 651-647-6437; Email: sslaikeu@mysaintrose.net; Web: mysaintrose.net. Sean Slaikeu, Prin. Lay Teachers 17; Students 123.
Catechesis Religious Program—Email: dmcpherson@saintroseoflima.net. Deb McPherson, D.R.E. Students 96.

SHOREVIEW, RAMSEY CO., ST. ODILIA (1960) [CEM]
3495 N. Victoria St., Shoreview, 55126.
Tel: 651-484-6681; Fax: 651-484-0780; Email: info@stodilia.org; Web: www.stodilia.org. Revs. Phillip J. Rask; Michael Peter Daly, Parochial Vicar; Deacons James F. Saumweber; William J. Carroll, Latino Ministry.
School—St. Odilia School, (Grades PreK-8),
Tel: 651-484-3364; Email: schooloffice@stodilia.org; Web: www.stodiliaschool.org. Mr. Brian Ragatz, Prin. Lay Teachers 36; Students 614.
Catechesis Religious Program—Brenda McLennan, Youth Formation; Lucy Arimond, Adult Formation. Students 499.

WEST ST. PAUL, DAKOTA CO.

1—ST. JOSEPH (1942)
Mailing Address: 1154 Seminole Ave., West St. Paul, 55118. Tel: 651-457-2781; Fax: 651-451-1272; Email: frcreagan@churchofstjoseph.org; Web: www.churchofstjoseph.org. Revs. Michael Creagan; Timothy Wratkowski, Parochial Vicar; Mark Daniel Pavlak, Weekend Mass Support; Deacons Thomas P. Michaud Sr.; Gerald A. Scherkenbach, J.C.L.
School—St. Joseph School, (Grades PreK-8), 1138 Seminole Ave., West St. Paul, 55118.
Tel: 651-457-8550; Fax: 651-457-0780; Email: office@stjosephwsp.org; Web: www.stjosephwsp.org. Greg Wesely, Prin. Lay Teachers 27; Students 383.
Catechesis Religious Program—Tel: 651-457-8841. Students 360.

2—ST. MICHAEL (1868)
337 Hurley Ave. E., West St. Paul, 55118. Mailing Address: c/o Church of St. Rita, 8694 80th St. S., Cottage Grove, 55116. Tel: 651-459-4596; Email: stritas@saintritas.org. Rev. Richard A. Banker.
Catechesis Religious Program—

WHITE BEAR LAKE, RAMSEY CO.

1—ST. MARY OF THE LAKE (1881) [CEM]
4690 Bald Eagle Ave., White Bear Lake, 55110.
Tel: 651-429-7771; Email: contactus@stmarys-wbl.org; Web: www.stmarys-wbl.org. Rev. Ralph W. Talbot Jr.
Church: 4741 Bald Eagle Ave., White Bear Lake, 55110.
Catechesis Religious Program—Email: kfeidt@stmarys-wbl.org. Karlene Feidt, D.R.E. Students 377.

2—ST. PIUS X (1954)
3878 Highland Ave., White Bear Lake, 55110.
Tel: 651-429-5337; Fax: 651-429-5339; Email: questions@churchofstpiusx.org; Web: www.churchofstpiusx.org. Revs. Joseph Jerome Bambenek; Desmond Murtala Alhassan, In Res.; Deacon Timothy R. Harrer.
Catechesis Religious Program—Email: sgutowski@churchofstpiusx.org. Students 86.

WOODBURY, WASHINGTON CO., SAINT AMBROSE OF WOODBURY (1998)
Office: 4125 Woodbury Dr., Woodbury, 55129-9627.
Tel: 651-768-3030; Fax: 651-714-9257; Email: greg.hereford@saintambroseofwoodbury.org; Web: www.saintambroseofwoodbury.org. Revs. Peter J. Williams; Nicholas Froehle, Parochial Vicar; Deacons Lawrence E. Amell; William Riordan.
School—Saint Ambrose of Woodbury School, (Grades PreK-8), Tel: 651-768-3000; Email: betsy.osterhaushand@saintambroseofwoodbury.org; Web: saintambroseschool.org. Ms. Betsy Hand, Prin. Lay Teachers 39; Students 721.
Catechesis Religious Program—Email: patti.watkins@saintambroseofwoodbury.org. Patti Watkins, D.R.E. Students 1,097.

METROPOLITAN MINNEAPOLIS

(HENNEPIN COUNTY)

1—ST. ALBERT THE GREAT (1935)
2836 33rd Ave. S., Minneapolis, 55406.
Tel: 612-724-3643; Email: info@saintalbertthegreat.org; Web: www.saintalbertthegreat.org. Revs. Joseph P. Gillespie, O.P.; Herb Hayek, O.P., In Res.; Robert Kelly, O.P., In Res.; Cornelius A. Kilroy, O.P., In Res. Res.: 2833 32nd Ave. S., Minneapolis, 55406.
See Risen Christ Catholic School, Minneapolis under Elementary Schools, Consolidated, Parochial located in the Institution section.
Catechesis Religious Program—Email: j.heikkila@saintalbertthegreat.org. Janelle Heikkila, D.R.E. Students 36.

2—ALL SAINTS (1916) (Polish)
435 4th St., N.E., Minneapolis, 55413.
Tel: 612-379-4996; Web: www.fsspminneapolis.org. Revs. Gerard Saguto, F.S.S.P.; Alex Stewart, F.S.S.P., Parochial Vicar.
See Pope John Paul II Catholic School, Minneapolis under Elementary Schools, Consolidated, Parochial located in the Institution section.
Catechesis Religious Program— See Church of All Saints. Students 180.

3—ST. ANNE (1884) Merged See Church of St. Anne-St. Joseph Hien.

4—CHURCH OF ST. ANNE - ST. JOSEPH HIEN (1884/1987) (Vietnamese)
2627 Queen Ave. N., Minneapolis, 55411.
Tel: 612-529-0503; Email: sasjhparish@gmail.com; Web: gxannagiusehien.net. Revs. Louis Ha Pham, C.R.M.; Alphonse Tri Vu, C.R.M., Parochial Vicar.
Catechesis Religious Program—Students 427.

5—ANNUNCIATION (1922)
509 W. 54th St., Minneapolis, 55419.
Tel: 612-824-0787; Fax: 612-824-9915; Email: info@annunciationmsp.org; Web: www.annunciationmsp.org. Rev. Brian J. Park; Deacon Sean M. Curtan.
School—Annunciation School, (Grades PreK-8), 525 W. 54th St., Minneapolis, 55419-1818.
Tel: 612-823-4394; Fax: 612-824-0998; Web: www.annunciationmsp.org/school. Jennifer Cassidy, Prin. Lay Teachers 24; Students 432.
Catechesis Religious Program—
Tel: 612-824-9993, Ext. 251. Students 104.

6—ST. ANTHONY OF PADUA (1849) Merged into Holy Cross, Minneapolis on 7/1/2013.

7—ASCENSION (1890)
Mailing Address: 1723 Bryant Ave. N., Minneapolis, 55411. Tel: 612-529-9684; Fax: 612-529-7618; Email: webmail@ascensionmpls.org; Web: ascensionmpls.org. Rev. Dale J. Korogi.
School—Ascension School, (Grades K-8), 1726 Dupont Ave. N., Minneapolis, 55411.
Tel: 612-521-3609; Web: www.ascensionschoolmn.org. Benito Matias, Prin. Lay Teachers 24; Students 341.
Catechesis Religious Program— Shared program with Our Lady of Victory (Minneapolis) and St. Bridget (Minneapolis). Tel: 612-521-7454;
Fax: 612-529-3343. Students 194.

8—ST. AUSTIN (1937) Merged with St. Bridget, Minneapolis.

9—THE BASILICA OF ST. MARY CO-CATHEDRAL (1907)
Mailing Address: P.O. Box 50010, Minneapolis, 55405-0010. Rev. John M. Bauer.
Office: 88 N. 17th St., Minneapolis, 55403-1295.
Tel: 612-333-1381; Email: bsm@mary.org; Web: mary.org.
Catechesis Religious Program—Tel: 612-317-3473. Students 200.

10—ST. BONIFACE (1858) (German)
629 Second St., N.E., Minneapolis, 55413.
Tel: 612-379-2761; Fax: 612-676-1532; Email: boniface1858@usfamily.net; Web: www.stbonifacempls.org. Rev. Biju Pattasseril, CFIC, Parochial Admin.
See Pope John Paul II Catholic School, Minneapolis under Elementary Schools, Consolidated, Parochial located in the Institution section.
Catechesis Religious Program— This is a shared program with Holy Cross, Minneapolis.
Tel: 612-379-2451. Students 51.

11—ST. BRIDGET (1915)
3811 Emerson Ave. N., Minneapolis, 55412.
Tel: 612-529-7779; Fax: 612-529-8451; Email: info@stbridgetnorthside.com; Web: stbridgetnorthside.com. Revs. Thomas Santa, C.Ss.R., Parochial Admin.; Paul L. Jarvis, Parochial Vicar; Deacon Richard J. Heineman.
Church of St. Austin, (Worship Site) 4050 Upton Ave. N., Minneapolis, 55412.
Catechesis Religious Program— See Ascension (Minneapolis) - Shared program.

12—ST. CHARLES BORROMEO (1938)
2739 Stinson Blvd., N.E., St. Anthony, 55418-3124.
Tel: 612-781-6529; Email: stchbinfo@stchb.org; Web: www.stchb.org. Revs. Troy D. Przybilla; David Blume, In Res.; Deacon Stephen M. Najarian.
School—St. Charles Borromeo School, (Grades PreK-8), 2727 Stinson Blvd., N.E., Minneapolis, 55418-3124. Danny Kieffer, Prin. Lay Teachers 18; Students 308.
Catechesis Religious Program—Students 86.

13—CHRIST THE KING (1938) [JC]
Church & Office: 5029 Zenith Ave. S., Minneapolis, 55410. Tel: 612-920-5030; Fax: 612-926-0283; Email: parishoffice@ctkmpls.org; Web: www.ctkmpls.org. Rev. Herb Hayek, O.P.
See Carondelet Catholic School under Elementary Schools, Consolidated, Parochial located in the Institution section.
Catechesis Religious Program—Students 214.

14—ST. CLEMENT (1902) Merged into Holy Cross, Minneapolis on 7/1/2013.

15—SS. CYRIL AND METHODIUS (1891) (Slovak)
1315 2nd St., N.E., Minneapolis, 55413-1905.
Tel: 612-379-9736; Email: cyril1891@aol.com; Web: scyril.org. Revs. Daniel F. Griffith, J.D., Parochial Admin.; Fernando Ortega, Parochial Vicar; Deacon Clarence J. Shallbetter.
Catechesis Religious Program—Students 101.

16—ST. FRANCES CABRINI (1946)
1500 Franklin Ave., S.E., Minneapolis, 55414-3697.
Tel: 612-339-3023; Email: admin@cabrinimn.org; Web: www.cabrinimn.org. Rev. Paul G. Moudry.
Catechesis Religious Program—Students 52.

17—CHURCH OF GICHITWAA KATERI (2008) (Native American) (Native American Quasi-Parish)
Church & Office: 3045 Park Ave. S., Minneapolis, 55407-1517. Tel: 612-824-7606; Fax: 844-272-9071; Email: phillipss@archspm.org; Web: katerimpls.org. Revs. Douglas Allen Ebert, Parochial Admin.; Stanley V. Sledz, Sacramental Min., (Retired); Mr. Shawn Phillips, Parish Life Coord.
Catechesis Religious Program—Students 32.

18—ST. HEDWIG (1914) (Polish), Merged canonically, not civilly, into Holy Cross, Minneapolis on 7/1/13.

19—ST. HELENA (1913)
3201 E. 43rd St., Minneapolis, 55406-3858.
Tel: 612-729-7344; Fax: 612-724-8695; Email: church@sainthelena.us; Web: www.sainthelena.us. Mailing Address: 3204 E. 43rd St., Minneapolis, 55406. Rev. Richard R. Villano.
School—St. Helena School, (Grades PreK-8), 3200 E. 44th St., Minneapolis, 55406. Tel: 612-729-9301; Fax: 612-729-6016; Email: school@sainthelenaschool.us; Web: sainthelenaschool.us. Mr. Paul Dieltz, Prin. Lay Teachers 13; Students 156.
Catechesis Religious Program—Tel: 612-729-7321. Students 54.

20—HOLY CROSS (1886) (Polish)
1621 University Ave., N.E., Minneapolis, 55413.
Tel: 612-789-7238; Fax: 612-789-5769; Email: info@ourholycross.org; Web: ourholycross.com. Revs. Spencer J. Howe, Parochial Admin.; Byron S. Hagan, Parochial Vicar; Stanislaw Poszwa, Parochial Vicar; Earl C. Simonson, Pastor Emeritus, (Retired); Deacon John J. Belian.
St. Hedwig—(Worship Site) 129 29th Ave., N.E., St. Anthony, 55418.
St. Clement, (Worship Site) 901 24th Ave., N.E., Minneapolis, 55418.
See Pope John Paul II Catholic School, Minneapolis under Elementary Schools, Consolidated, Parochial located in the Institution section.
Catechesis Religious Program—Tel: 612-789-9168. Students 50.

21—HOLY NAME (1916)
3637 11th Ave. S., Minneapolis, 55407.
Tel: 612-724-5465; Fax: 612-724-5466; Email: jstephan@churchoftheholyname.org; Web: www.churchoftheholyname.org. Rev. Leo J. Schneider, Parochial Admin.
See Risen Christ Catholic School, Minneapolis under Elementary Schools, Consolidated, Parochial located in the Institution section.
Catechesis Religious Program—Students 75.

22—HOLY ROSARY/SANTO ROSARIO (1878)
Physical Address: 2400 18th Ave. S., Minneapolis, 55404. Tel: 612-724-3651; Fax: 612-728-8944; Email: holyrosary2424@gmail.com; Web: www.holyrosaryop.com. Mailing Address: 2424 18th Ave. S., Minneapolis, 55404. Rev. Gerald Stookey, O.P.
See Risen Christ Catholic School, Minneapolis under Elementary Schools, Consolidated, Parochial located in the Institution section.
Catechesis Religious Program—Email: jcuzcotenezaca@gmail.com. Juan Cuzco-Tenezaca, D.R.E. Students 376.
Convent—1614 E. 24th St., Minneapolis, 55404.

23—CHURCH OF THE INCARNATION (1909)
3817 Pleasant Ave., Minneapolis, 55409-1228.
Tel: 612-822-2101; Email: contact@inc-scj.org; Web: www.inc-scj.org. Rev. Kevin M. McDonough; Deacon Carl Valdez.
See Risen Christ Catholic School, Minneapolis under Elementary Schools, Consolidated, Parochial located in the Institution section.
Catechesis Religious Program—Students 214.

24—ST. JOAN OF ARC (1946)
4537 3rd Ave. S., Minneapolis, 55419.
Tel: 612-823-8205; Fax: 612-825-7028; Email:

contact@stjoan.com; Web: www.saintjoanofarc.org. Revs. James R. DeBruycker; James Cassidy, Parochial Vicar.
Catechesis Religious Program—Students 560.
25—ST. JOSEPH HIEN (1987) [JC] (Vietnamese), Closed. See Church of St. Anne-St. Joseph Hien, Minneapolis.
26—ST. LAWRENCE (1887)
1203 5th St., S.E., Minneapolis, 55414.
Tel: 612-331-7941; Email: info@umncatholic.org; Web: www.umncatholic.org. Rev. Jon Vander Ploeg, Pastor & Dir. Newman Ctr.
Catechesis Religious Program—
27—ST. LEONARD OF PORT MAURICE (1941) (African American)
3953 Clinton Ave. S., Minneapolis, 55409. Mailing Address: 3949 Clinton Ave. S., Minneapolis, 55409.
Tel: 612-825-5811; Email: slpm3949@msn.com; Web: stleonardmn.org. Rev. Leo J. Schneider.
Catechesis Religious Program—Students 23.
28—ST. OLAF (1941) [JC]
215 S. 8th St., Minneapolis, 55402.
Tel: 612-332-7471; Fax: 612-332-3412; Email: vklima@saintolaf.org; Web: www.saintolaf.org. Revs. Patrick A. Kennedy; Michael J. Krenik, Parochial Vicar; Mark H. Wehmann, Parochial Vicar.
Catechesis Religious Program—Students 17.
29—OUR LADY OF LOURDES (1877) (French)
One Lourdes Pl., Minneapolis, 55414.
Tel: 612-379-2259; Web: www.lourdesmpls.org. Revs. Daniel F. Griffith, J.D.; David Haschka, S.J., Parochial Vicar; Deacon Thomas J. Winninger.
Catechesis Religious Program—Students 23.
30—OUR LADY OF MOUNT CARMEL (1910) (Italian)
701 Fillmore St., N.E., Minneapolis, 55413.
Tel: 612-623-4019; Email: olmc@olmcmpls.org; Web: www.olmcmpls.org. Rev. Paul G. Moudry.
See Pope John Paul II Catholic School, Minneapolis under Elementary Schools, Consolidated, Parochial located in the Institution section.
Catechesis Religious Program— Consolidated with All Saints, Minneapolis. Students 16.
31—OUR LADY OF PEACE (1991)
5426 12th Ave., S., Minneapolis, 55417.
Tel: 612-824-3455; Fax: 612-823-5102; Email: parishadmin@olpmn.org; Web: www.olpmn.org. Rev. Joah Ellis.
School—Our Lady of Peace School, (Grades PreK-8), 5435 11th Ave. S., Minneapolis, 55417.
Tel: 612-823-8253; Fax: 612-824-7328; Email: schooladmin@olpmn.org; Web: school.olpmn.org. Paul Berry, Prin. Lay Teachers 24; Students 173.
Catechesis Religious Program—Email: jbiedrzycki@olpmn.org. Jon Biedrzycki, D.R.E. Students 122.
32—OUR LADY OF PERPETUAL HELP, Closed. For inquiries for parish records contact the chancery.
33—OUR LADY OF VICTORY (1945)
5155 Emerson Ave. N., Minneapolis, 55430.
Tel: 612-529-7788. Rev. Terrence M. Hayes.
Catechesis Religious Program— See Ascension (Minneapolis) - Shared program.
34—ST. PHILIP (1906) [CEM] Merged with Ascension Parish, Minneapolis.
35—CHURCH OF ST. STEPHEN OF MINNEAPOLIS (1885)
Mailing Address: 2211 Clinton Ave., Minneapolis, 55404. Tel: 612-767-2430; Fax: 612-767-2439; Email: info@ststephenscatholic.org; Web: www.ststephenscatholic.org. Revs. Joseph A. Williams; Michael Peter Daly, Latino Vocations.
See Risen Christ Catholic School, Minneapolis under Elementary Schools, Consolidated, Parochial located in the Institution section.
Catechesis Religious Program—Email: hguzman@ststephenscatholic.org. Hector Guzman, D.R.E. Students 400.
36—ST. THOMAS THE APOSTLE (1908)
2914 W. 44th St., Minneapolis, 55410.
Tel: 612-922-0041; Email: info@stthomasmpls.org; Web: www.stthomasmpls.org. Rev. Michael A. Reding.
Catechesis Religious Program— Supports the consolidated Carondelet Catholic School, Minneapolis. Email: bnolan@stthomasmpls.org. William Nolan, D.R.E. Students 278.
37—VISITATION (1946) Merged with Annunciation, Minneapolis.

OUTSIDE METROPOLITAN MINNEAPOLIS

BLAINE, ANOKA CO., ST. TIMOTHY'S (1943)
Mailing Address: 707 89th Ave., N.E., Blaine, 55434.
Tel: 763-784-1329; Fax: 763-784-0652; Email: info@churchofsttimothy.com; Web: www.churchofsttimothy.com. Rev. Joseph Whalen; Deacons Thomas M. Quayle; Joseph J. Frederick.
Catechesis Religious Program—Students 354.
BLOOMINGTON, HENNEPIN CO.
1—ST. BONAVENTURE (1959)
901 E. 90th St., Bloomington, 55420.
Tel: 952-854-4733; Fax: 952-851-9690; Email: office@saintbonaventure.org; Web: www.saintbonaventure.org. Revs. Richard Kaley, O.F.M.-Conv.; Edmund Goldbach, O.F.M.Conv., In Res.; Camillus Gott, O.F.M.Conv., In Res.; Deacons Jon A. DeLuney; Micahel Redfearn.
Catechesis Religious Program—Tel: 952-854-4753; Email: faithformation@saintbonaventure.org. Students 129.
2—ST. EDWARD (1967)
9401 Nesbitt Ave. S., Bloomington, 55437.
Tel: 952-835-7101; Fax: 952-835-0156; Email: receptionist@stedwardschurch.org; Web: www.stedwardschurch.org. Rev. Richard A. Banker; Deacon James F. DeShane.
Catechesis Religious Program—Students 188.
3—NATIVITY OF THE BLESSED VIRGIN MARY (1949)
9900 Lyndale Ave. S., Bloomington, 55420-4733.
Tel: 952-881-8671; Fax: 952-881-8692; Email: parishoffice@nativitybloomington.org; Web: www.nativitybloomington.org. Rev. Nels H. Gjengdahl; Deacon John M. Shearer.
School—Nativity of the Blessed Virgin Mary School, (Grades PreK-8), 9901 E. Bloomington Fwy., Bloomington, 55420. Tel: 952-881-8160;
Fax: 952-881-3032; Email: nativity@nativitybloomington.org; Web: school.nativitybloomington.org. Mindy Reeder, Prin. Lay Teachers 24; Students 361.
Catechesis Religious Program—Students 89.
BROOKLYN CENTER, HENNEPIN CO., ST. ALPHONSUS (1959)
7025 Halifax Ave. N., Brooklyn Center, 55429.
Tel: 763-561-5100; Fax: 763-561-0336; Email: parishoffice@mystals.org; Web: www.stalsmn.org. Revs. Donald Willard, C.Ss.R.; Tony Judge, C.Ss.R., Parochial Vicar; Aaron Meszaros, C.Ss.R., Parochial Vicar; Thanh Nguyen, C.Ss.R., Pastoral Min.; Matthew Bonk, C.Ss.R., In Res.; Patrick Keyes, C.Ss.R., In Res.; Tuan Pham, C.Ss.R., In Res.; Thomas Santa, C.Ss.R., In Res.; Bro. Bruce Davidson, C.Ss.R., In Res.; Deacon Michael C. Wurdock.
School—St. Alphonsus School, (Grades PreK-8), 7031 Halifax Ave. N., Brooklyn Center, 55429.
Tel: 763-561-5101; Fax: 763-503-3368; Email: schooloffice@mystals.org; Web: www.stalsmnschool.org. Kari Staples, Prin. Lay Teachers 13; Students 193.
Catechesis Religious Program—4111 71st Ave. N., Brooklyn Center, 55429. Email: youthministry@mystals.org. Students 460.
BROOKLYN PARK, HENNEPIN CO.
1—ST. GERARD MAJELLA (1970)
9600 Regent Ave. N., Brooklyn Park, 55443.
Tel: 763-424-8770; Email: info@st-gerard.org; Web: www.st-gerard.org. Rev. Thomas Santa, C.Ss.R.
Catechesis Religious Program—Students 292.
2—ST. VINCENT DE PAUL (1855) [CEM]
9100 93rd Ave. N., Brooklyn Park, 55445-1407.
Tel: 763-425-2210; Web: www.saintvdp.org. Revs. Dennis Zehren; Paul Baker, Parochial Vicar; Deacon Lawrence W. Lawinger.
School—St. Vincent de Paul School, (Grades PreK-8), 9050 93rd Ave. N., Brooklyn Park, 55445.
Tel: 763-425-3970; Fax: 763-425-2674; Email: schoolinfo@saintvdp.org; Web: school.saintvdp.org. Lisa Simon, Prin. Lay Teachers 26; Students 490.
Catechesis Religious Program—Students 620.
BURNSVILLE, DAKOTA CO.
1—CHURCH OF THE RISEN SAVIOR (1970)
1501 E. County Rd. 42, Burnsville, 55306.
Tel: 952-431-5222; Email: admin@risensavior.org; Web: www.risensavior.org. Revs. Thomas Krenik; Luis Banchs Plaza, Parochial Vicar.
Catechesis Religious Program—Students 407.
2—MARY, MOTHER OF THE CHURCH (1965)
3333 Cliff Rd. E., Burnsville, 55337.
Tel: 952-890-0045; Email: receptionist@mmotc.org; Web: mmotc.org. Revs. James M. Perkl; Timothy C. Rudolphi, Parochial Vicar; Deacon James R. Pufahl.
Catechesis Religious Program—Students 267.
COLUMBIA HEIGHTS, ANOKA CO., IMMACULATE CONCEPTION (1923)
4030 Jackson St., N.E., Columbia Heights, 55421.
Tel: 763-788-9062; Email: info@immac-church.org; Web: www.iccsonline.org. Rev. James E. Peterson; Deacon Larry Palkert.
School—Immaculate Conception School, (Grades PreK-8), Tel: 763-788-9065; Web: school.iccsonline.org. Jane Bona, Prin. Lay Teachers 14; Students 166.
Catechesis Religious Program—Email: mnawrocki@immac-church.org. Mary Nawrocki, D.R.E. Students 85.
COON RAPIDS, ANOKA CO., CHURCH OF THE EPIPHANY (1964) [CEM]
1900 111th Ave., N.W., Coon Rapids, 55433.
Tel: 763-755-1020; Email: church@epiphanymn.org; Web: www.epiphanymn.org. Revs. Thomas W. Dufner; Kyle Patrick Kowalczyk, Parochial Vicar; Deacons Kim M. Jensen; Bruce H. Maltzen.
School—Church of the Epiphany School, (Grades PreK-8), 11001 Hanson Blvd., N.W., Coon Rapids, 55433. Tel: 763-754-1750; Email: schoolinfo@epiphanymn.org; Web: www.epiphanyschoolmn.org. Ann Coone, Prin. Lay Teachers 28; Students 363.
Catechesis Religious Program—Tel: 763-862-4355; Email: jfink@epiphanymn.org. Jill Fink, D.R.E. Students 327.
CRYSTAL, HENNEPIN CO., ST. RAPHAEL (1951)
7301 Bass Lake Rd., Crystal, 55428.
Tel: 763-537-8401; Fax: 763-537-4878; Email: gmetzger@straphaelcrystal.org; Web: www.straphaelcrystal.org. Revs. Michael L. Rudolph; Robert J. Altier, Parochial Vicar.
School—St. Raphael School, (Grades PreK-8),
Tel: 763-504-9450; Fax: 763-504-9460; Web: www.srsmn.org. Ryan Zgutowicz, Prin. Lay Teachers 20; Students 160.
Catechesis Religious Program—
Tel: 763-537-8401, Ext. 211; Fax: 763-537-4878. Students 128.
EAGAN, DAKOTA CO.
1—ST. JOHN NEUMANN (1977)
4030 Pilot Knob Rd., Eagan, 55122.
Tel: 651-454-2079; Email: fr.ebert@sjn.org; Web: sjn.org. Revs. Douglas Allen Ebert; Toulee (Peter) Ly, Parochial Vicar; Deacon Martin G. Meyer.
See Faithful Shepherd Catholic School under Elementary Schools, Consolidated, Parochial located in the Institution section.
Catechesis Religious Program—Students 717.
2—ST. THOMAS BECKET (1989)
4455 S. Robert Tr., Eagan, 55123. Tel: 651-683-9808; Email: kmaza@st.thomasbecket.org; Web: www.stbeagan.org. Rev. Timothy Wozniak; Deacon Mickey Friesen.
See Faithful Shepherd Catholic School under Elementary Schools, Consolidated, Parochial located in the Institution section.
Catechesis Religious Program—Students 329.
EDEN PRAIRIE, HENNEPIN CO., PAX CHRISTI (1981)
12100 Pioneer Trl., Eden Prairie, 55347-4208.
Tel: 952-941-3150; Email: pax@paxchristi.com; Web: www.paxchristi.com. Revs. J. Michael Byron, S.T.D.; William A. Murtaugh, Parochial Vicar; Deacons Terrence G. Beer; Charles A. Bobertz; Alphonse Schroeder.
Catechesis Religious Program—Students 590.
EDINA, HENNEPIN CO.
1—OUR LADY OF GRACE (1946)
5071 Eden Ave., Edina, 55436. Mailing Address: P.O. Box 223, Edina, 55436. Tel: 952-929-3317;
Fax: 952-929-4612; Email: robertdurham@olgparish.org; Web: www.olgparish.org. Revs. Kevin Finnegan; Matthew John Northenscold, Parochial Vicar.
School—Our Lady of Grace School, (Grades K-8), 5051 Eden Ave., Edina, 55436. Tel: 952-929-5463; Email: info@olg.org; Web: www.olgschool.net. Maureen Trenary, Prin. Lay Teachers 51; Students 652.
Catechesis Religious Program—Students 436.
2—ST. PATRICK (1857)
6820 St. Patrick's Ln., Edina, 55439.
Tel: 952-941-3164; Fax: 952-941-7371; Email: office@stpatrick-edina.org; Web: www.stpatrick-edina.org. Revs. Albert P. Backmann, Parochial Admin., (Retired); Jerome W. Fehn, In Res.; Deacon Anthony M. Pasko.
Catechesis Religious Program—Students 355.
FRIDLEY, ANOKA CO., ST. WILLIAM (1963)
6120 5th St., N.E., Fridley, 55432. Tel: 763-571-5600; Web: chofstwilliams.com. Rev. David T. Ostrowski.
Catechesis Religious Program—Students 108.
GOLDEN VALLEY, HENNEPIN CO.
1—GOOD SHEPHERD (1946)
145 Jersey Ave. S., Golden Valley, 55426.
Tel: 763-544-0416; Fax: 763-544-9896; Email: info@goodshepherdgv.org; Web: www.goodshepherdgv.org. Rev. Luke C. Marquard; Deacon Eric M. Gunderson.
School—Good Shepherd School, (Grades K-6),
Tel: 763-545-4285; Email: schoolinfo@gsgvschool.org; Web: www.gsgvschool.org. Mike McGinty, Prin. Lay Teachers 19; Students 265.
Catechesis Religious Program—Students 91.
2—ST. MARGARET MARY (1946)
2323 Zenith Ave. N., Golden Valley, 55422.
Tel: 763-588-9466; Fax: 763-588-0040; Email: myparish@smm-gv.org; Web: www.smm-gv.org. Rev. Thomas Rayar.
Catechesis Religious Program—Students 69.
HAM LAKE, ANOKA CO., CHURCH OF SAINT PAUL (1981)
1740 Bunker Lake Blvd., N.E., Ham Lake, 55304.
Tel: 763-757-6910; Fax: 763-757-6920; Email: contact@churchofsaintpaul.com; Web: www.churchofsaintpaul.com. Rev. James T. Livingston; Deacon Timothy M. Zinda.
Catechesis Religious Program—Tel: 763-757-1148. Students 296.
LINO LAKES, ANOKA CO., ST. JOSEPH OF THE LAKES (1891) [CEM]
171 Elm St., Lino Lakes, 55014. Tel: 651-784-3015;
Fax: 651-784-3699; Email:

office@saintjosephsparish.org; Web: www.saintjosephsparish.org. Rev. Michael F. Anderson; Deacon Thomas A. Konkel

Church of St. Joseph of Rice Lake

Catechesis Religious Program—Students 723.

NEW HOPE, HENNEPIN CO., ST. JOSEPH (1858) [CEM]
8701 36th Ave. N., New Hope, 55427.
Tel: 763-544-3352; Email: drademacher@stjosephparish.com; Web: www.stjosephparish.com. Rev. Terrence Rassmussen, Parochial Admin.; Deacon Robert A. Bramwell.

Catechesis Religious Program—Students 290.

Saint Joseph, (Worship Site) 13015 Roackford Rd., Plymouth, 55441.

PLYMOUTH, HENNEPIN CO., ST. MARY OF THE LAKE (1935)
105 Forestview Ln. N., Plymouth, 55441.
Tel: 763-545-1443; Email: info@smlplymouth.org; Web: www.smlplymouth.org. Rev. Curtis F. Lybarger.

Catechesis Religious Program—Students 193.

RICHFIELD, HENNEPIN CO.

1—THE CHURCH OF THE ASSUMPTION/LA IGLESIA DE LA ASUNCION (1876)
Mailing Address: 305 E. 77th St., Richfield, 55423.
Tel: 612-866-5019; Fax: 612-866-5274; Email: ryan@assumptionrichfield.org; Web: www.assumptionrichfield.org. Rev. Michael Kueber; Deacon Peter Loving.
See Blessed Trinity Catholic School of Richfield Minnesota under Elementary Schools, Consolidated, Parochial located in the Institution section.

Catechesis Religious Program—Students 310.

2—ST. PETER (1943)
6730 Nicollet Ave. S., Richfield, 55423.
Tel: 612-866-5089; Fax: 612-866-5080; Email: stpeters@stpetersrichfield.org; Web: www.stpetersrichfield.org. Rev. Gerald Dvorak; Deacon Mark D. Johanns.
See Blessed Trinity Catholic School of Richfield, Minnesota under Elementary Schools, Consolidated, Parochial located in the Institution section.

Catechesis Religious Program—Students 60.

3—ST. RICHARD (1952)
7540 Penn Ave. S., Richfield, 55423.
Tel: 612-869-2426; Web: www.strichards.com. Rev. Mark L. Pavlik; Deacon Robert Schnell.
See Blessed Trinity Catholic School of Richfield Minnesota under Elementary Schools, Consolidated, Parochial located in the Institution section.

Catechesis Religious Program—Students 60.

ROBBINSDALE, HENNEPIN CO., SACRED HEART (1910)
4087 W. Broadway, Robbinsdale, 55422.
Tel: 763-537-4561; Email: cshadmin@shrmn.org; Web: www.shrmn.org. Rev. Bryan J. B. Pedersen, M.Div.; Deacon James W. Ramsey.

School—Sacred Heart Catholic School, (Grades PreK-8), 4050 Hubbard Ave. N., Robbinsdale, 55422.
Tel: 763-537-1329; Fax: 763-537-1486; Email: info@shcsr.org; Web: www.sacredheartschoolrobbinsdale.org. Karen Bursey, Prin. Lay Teachers 16; Students 189.

Catechesis Religious Program—Email: bbrouillard@shrmn.org. Bunny Brouillard, D.R.E. Students 295.

ST. LOUIS PARK, HENNEPIN CO.

1—HOLY FAMILY (1926)
5900 W. Lake St., St. Louis Park, 55416.
Tel: 952-929-0113; Fax: 952-915-1474; Email: staff@hfcmn.org; Web: www.hfcmn.org. Revs. Joseph R. Johnson; Marcus F. Milless, Sacramental Min.; Deacon James Meyer.

School—Holy Family Academy, (Grades PreK-8), 5925 W. Lake St., St. Louis Park, 55416-2019.
Tel: 952-925-9193; Fax: 952-925-5298; Email: info@hfamn.org; Web: www.hfamn.org. Mr. Jim Grogan, Prin. Lay Teachers 18; Students 190.

Catechesis Religious Program—Students 87.

2—MOST HOLY TRINITY (1943) Merged with Our Lady of Grace, Edina.

OUTSIDE TWIN-CITY METROPOLITAN AREA

ALBERTVILLE, WRIGHT CO., ST. ALBERT (1902) [CEM]
11400 57th St., N.E., Albertville, 55301-0127. Mailing Address: P.O. Box 127, Albertville, 55301-0127. Tel: 763-497-2474; Fax: 763-497-7678; Email: stalbertmn@gmail.com; Web: www.churchofstalbert.org. Revs. Peter M. Richards; Joseph Arthur Zabinski, Parochial Vicar; Deacons Steven C. Dupay; Paul M. Ravnikar.

Catechesis Religious Program—Email: stalbertmnfaithformation@gmail.com. Jean Wold, D.R.E. Students 111.

ANNANDALE, WRIGHT CO., ST. IGNATIUS (1882) [CEM]
35 Birch Street E., Annandale, 55302. Mailing Address: P.O. Box 126, Annandale, 55302.
Tel: 320-274-8828; Fax: 320-274-3961; Email: st.ignatius.mn@gmail.com; Web: www.stignatiusmn.com. Revs. John D. Meyer; Andrew B. Stueve, Parochial Vicar.

Catechesis Religious Program—
Tel: 320-274-8828, Ext. 24;
Tel: 320-274-8828, Ext. 33. Students 242.

ANOKA, ANOKA CO., CHURCH OF ST. STEPHEN (1856) [CEM]
525 Jackson St., Anoka, 55303. Tel: 763-421-2471; Email: info@ststephenchurch.org; Web: www.ststephenchurch.org. Revs. Jon Bennet Tran; Matthew Quail, Parochial Vicar; Matthew Shireman, Parochial Vicar; Deacons Charles A. Waugh; Ramon Garcia Degollado, Hispanic Ministry.

School—Church of St. Stephen School, (Grades PreK-8), 506 Jackson St., Anoka, 55303.
Tel: 763-421-3236; Fax: 763-712-7433; Email: schoolweb@ststephenchurch.org; Web: ststephenschool.org. Diane Morri, Prin. Lay Teachers 22; Students 366.

Catechesis Religious Program—Students 471.

BAYPORT, WASHINGTON CO., ST. CHARLES (1943) [CEM] [JC]
409 N. 3rd St., Bayport, 55003. Tel: 651-439-4511; Fax: 651-430-9717; Email: office@stcb.comcastbiz.net; Web: www.stcharlesbayport.com. Rev. Mark J. Joppa.
See St. Croix Catholic School, Stillwater under Elementary Schools, Consolidated, Parochial located in the Institution section.

Catechesis Religious Program—Students 63.

BELLE CREEK, GOODHUE CO., ST. COLUMBKILL (1860) [JC] Merged with Holy Trinity, Goodhue on 7/1/2013.

BELLE PLAINE, SCOTT CO., OUR LADY OF THE PRAIRIE (1972) [CEM 2]
200 E. Church St., Belle Plaine, 56011.
Tel: 952-873-6564; Fax: 952-873-6717; Email: parish@ourladyoftheprairie.com; Web: ourladyoftheprairie.com. Rev. Brian T. Lynch; Deacon Robert T. Raleigh.

School—Our Lady of the Prairie School, (Grades PreK-6), Email: school@ourladyoftheprairie.com; Web: school.ourladyoftheprairie.com. Wendy Alessio, Prin. Lay Teachers 5; Students 58.

Catechesis Religious Program—Students 154.

BELLECHESTER, GOODHUE CO., ST. MARY (1859) [CEM] Merged with Holy Trinity, Goodhue on 7/1/2013.

BUFFALO, WRIGHT CO., ST. FRANCIS XAVIER (1888) [CEM 2]
223 19th St., N.W., Buffalo, 55313-5042.
Tel: 763-684-0075; Fax: 763-684-4771; Email: travis.nelson@stfxb.org; Web: www.stfxb.org. Rev. Nathaniel Meyers; Deacon Paul B. Buck.

Rectory—300 1st Ave., N.W., Buffalo, 55313.

School—St. Francis Xavier School, (Grades K-8), 219 19th St., N.W., Buffalo, 55313-5042.
Tel: 763-684-0075; Fax: 763-684-4771; Email: alisa.louwagie@stfxb.org; Web: school.stfxb.org. Alisa Louwagie, Prin. Lay Teachers 23; Students 244.

Catechesis Religious Program—Tel: 763-489-9224; Email: debbie.gladitsch@stfxb.org. Debbie Gladitsch, Dir. Faith Formation & Youth Min. Students 290.

CANNON FALLS, GOODHUE CO., ST. PIUS V (1856) [CEM]
410 W. Colvill Ave., Cannon Falls, 55009.
Tel: 507-263-2578; Email: spvparish@gmail.com; Web: www.stpiusvcf.org. Rev. Terry P. Beeson; Deacon Kevin M, Downie.

Catechesis Religious Program—Email: spvcfyouth@gmail.com. Cindy Meyers, D.R.E. Students 164.

CARVER, CARVER CO., ST. NICHOLAS (1868) [CEM 2]
412 W. Fourth St., Carver, 55315. Mailing Address: P.O. Box 133, Carver, 55315. Tel: 952-448-2345; Fax: 952-368-0502; Email: jodeestnicholas@embarqmail.com; Web: www.stnicholascarver.org. Revs. William Deziel; Edison Galarza, O.C.C.S.S., Parochial Vicar.

Catechesis Religious Program—Students 50.

CEDAR LAKE, SCOTT CO., ST. PATRICK OF CEDAR LAKE TOWNSHIP (1856) [CEM]
24425 Old Hwy. 13 Blvd., Jordan, 55352.
Tel: 952-492-6276; Email: admin@stpandc.mn.org; Web: www.stpandc.mn.org. Rev. Michael J. Miller.

Catechesis Religious Program—Tel: 952-492-5723. Students 122.

Mission—St. Catherine of Spring Lake Township (1865) [CEM] 4500 220th St. E., Prior Lake, 55372. Tel: 952-447-2180.

CEDAR, ANOKA CO., ST. PATRICK (1894) [CEM]
19921 Nightingale St., N.W., Oak Grove, 55011-9204. Tel: 763-753-2011; Fax: 763-753-9803; Email: stpats@st-patricks.org; Web: www.st-patricks.org. Rev. Allan Paul Eilen; Deacon George P. Stahl.

Catechesis Religious Program—Students 487.

CENTERVILLE, ANOKA CO., ST. GENEVIEVE (1854) [CEM]
7087 Goiffon Rd., Centerville, 55038.
Tel: 651-429-7937; Fax: 651-653-0071; Email: info@stgens.org; Web: www.stgen.org. Rev. Gregory L. Esty.

Catechesis Religious Program—Tel: 651-426-1818. Students 215.

St. Genevieve, (Worship Site) 6995 Centerville Rd., Centerville, 55038.

CHANHASSEN, CARVER CO., ST. HUBERT (1865) [CEM] (German)
8201 Main St., Chanhassen, 55317.
Tel: 952-934-9106; Email: webmaster@sthubert.org; Web: www.sthubert.org. Revs. Rolf R. Tollefson; Aric Aamodt, Parochial Vicar; Deacons Patrick Hiri; Jerry Little.

School—St. Hubert School, (Grades PreK-8),
Tel: 952-934-6003; Fax: 952-906-1229; Email: kari.zobel@sthubert.org; Web: school.sthubert.org. Thomas Donlon, Prin.; Connie Klingelhutz, Librarian. Lay Teachers 36; Students 653.

Catechesis Religious Program—Students 449.

CHASKA, CARVER CO., GUARDIAN ANGELS (1858) [CEM]
215 W. 2nd St., Chaska, 55318. Tel: 952-227-4000; Email: info@gachaska.org; Web: www.gachaska.org. Revs. William Deziel; Edison Galarza, O.C.C.S.S., Parochial Vicar; Deacon John E. Cleveland.

School—Guardian Angels School, (Grades PreK-8), 217 W. Second St., Chaska, 55318. Tel: 952-227-4010 ; Email: gaangels@gachaska.org; Web: school.gachaska.org. Sue Lovegreen, Prin. Lay Teachers 9; Students 69.

Catechesis Religious Program—Email: nmaxwell@gachaska.org. Neal Maxwell, D.R.E. Students 219.

CLEARWATER, WRIGHT CO., ST. LUKE (1870) [CEM]
17545 Huber Ave. N.W., Clearwater, 55320-0249.
Tel: 320-558-2124; Email: admin@churchofstlukes.com; Web: www.churchofstlukes.com. Rev. Dennis J. Backer.

Catechesis Religious Program—Students 155.

CLEVELAND, LE SUEUR CO., CHURCH OF THE NATIVITY (1865) [CEM]
200 W. Main, P.O. Box 187, Cleveland, 56017.
Tel: 507-243-3166; Email: office@maryschurches.com; Web: www.maryschurches.com. Revs. Christopher L. Shofner; James J. Stiles, Parochial Vicar; James F. Adams, Parochial Vicar.

Catechesis Religious Program—Email: lynn.kluntz@hotmail.com. Lynn Kluntz. Students 97.

COATES, DAKOTA CO., ST. AGATHA (1870) [CEM]
Office: 3700 160th St. E., Rosemount, 55068.
Tel: 651-437-7498; Web: saintagatha.org. Rev. Richard J. Mahoney, (Retired).

Catechesis Religious Program—Students 9.

COLOGNE, CARVER CO., ST. BERNARD (1859) [CEM]
212 Church St., E., Cologne, 55322.
Tel: 952-466-2031; Email: busadmin@st-bernard-cologne.org; Web: www.st-bernard-cologne.org. Rev. Gregory E. Abbott.

Catechesis Religious Program—Julie Kleindl, Faith Formation; Kara Wickenhauser, Faith Formation. Students 50.

CORCORAN, HENNEPIN CO., ST. THOMAS THE APOSTLE (1896) [CEM 4] [JC4]
20,000 County Rd. 10, Corcoran, 55340.
Tel: 763-420-2385; Email: selsen@saintsppta.org; Web: www.saintsppta.org. Revs. Glen T. Jenson; Kevin P. Magner, Parochial Vicar; Deacon Michael P. Nevin.

Catechesis Religious Program— Shared program with Saints Peter and Paul, Loretto. Students 122.

DAYTON, HENNEPIN CO., ST. JOHN THE BAPTIST (1862) [CEM 2]
18380 Columbus St., Dayton, 55327.
Tel: 763-428-2828; Fax: 763-428-6462; Email: sjbchurch@yahoo.com; Web: www.sjbdayton.org. Mailing Address: P.O. Box 201, Dayton, 55327-0201. Rev. Timothy J. Yanta; Deacon Sherman H. Otto.

Catechesis Religious Program—Email: sarah.sjbchurch@gmail.com. Sarah Moylan, D.R.E. Students 56.

DEEPHAVEN, HENNEPIN CO., ST. THERESE (1946)
18323 Minnetonka Blvd., Deephaven, 55391.
Tel: 952-473-4422; Email: parish@st-therese.org; Web: www.st-therese.org. Rev. Leonard Andrie.

School—St. Therese School, (Grades PreK-8), 18325 Minnetonka Blvd., Deephaven, 55391.
Tel: 952-473-4355; Email: school@st-therese.org; Web: www.st-therese.org/school. Lauren Caton, Prin. Lay Teachers 15; Sisters 3; Students 153.

Catechesis Religious Program—Students 346.

DELANO, WRIGHT CO.

1—THE CHURCH OF SAINT MAXIMILIAN KOLBE, [CEM 3]
204 S. River St., Delano, 55328. Tel: 763-972-2077; Web: www.delanocatholic.com. Rev. Nathan LaLiberte; Deacons Bruce L. Bowen; Joseph M. Kittok.

School—Saint Maximilian Kolbe School, (Grades PreK-6), 235 S. Second St., Delano, 55328.
Tel: 763-972-2528; Web: stmaxkolbeschool.org. P.O. Box 470, Delano, 55328-0470. Mary Ziebell, Interim Prin. Lay Teachers 11; Students 89.

Catechesis Religious Program—Students 326.

2—ST. JOSEPH (1902) [CEM] (Polish), Merged with St. Peter, Delano to form The Church of Saint Maximilian Kolbe, Delano.

3—ST. MARY OF CZESTOCHOWA (1884) [CEM]
1867 95th St., S.E., Delano, 55328. Tel: 952-955-1139 ; Email: stboniface-stmarypastor@gmail.com; Web: stboniface-stmary.org. Rev. Joseph-Quoc T. Vuong.

Catechesis Religious Program—Students 48.

4—ST. PETER (1865) [CEM 2] (German), Merged with

St. Joseph, Delano to form The Church of Saint Maximilian Kolbe, Delano.

ELYSIAN, LE SUEUR CO., ST. ANDREW (1894)
Church & Mailing Address: 305 Park Ave., N.E., Box 261, Elysian, 56028. Tel: 507-362-4311; Fax: 507-362-4339; Email: holyt7@frontiernet.net. Rev. Michael W. Ince.
Catechesis Religious Program—Students 37.

EXCELSIOR, HENNEPIN CO., ST. JOHN THE BAPTIST (1903) [CEM]
680 Mill St., Excelsior, 55331-3272.
Tel: 952-474-8868; Fax: 952-444-3474; Email: stjohns@stjohns-excelsior.org; Email: parishadmin@stjohns-excelsior.org; Web: www.stjohns-excelsior.org. Rev. Alex Bernard Carlson.
School—St. John the Baptist Catholic Montessori School, (Grades PreK-8), 638 Mill St., Excelsior, 55331. Tel: 952-474-5812; Email: school@stjohns-excelsior.org. Nicholas Fonte, Prin. Lay Teachers 5; Students 59.
Catechesis Religious Program—Email: tgruber@stjohns-excelsior.org. Taylor Gruber, D.R.E. Students 139.

FARIBAULT, RICE CO.
1—DIVINE MERCY CATHOLIC CHURCH (2002) [CEM 2]
139 Mercy Dr., Faribault, 55021. Tel: 507-334-2266; Email: bwagner@divinemercy.cc; Web: divinemercy.cc. Mailing Address: 4 Second Ave., S.W., Faribault, 55021-6029. Revs. Kevin T. Kenney; Brandon Michael Theisen, Parochial Vicar.
School—Divine Mercy Catholic School, (Grades PreK-5), 15 Third Ave., S.W., Faribault, 55021.
Tel: 507-334-7706; Fax: 507-332-2669; Email: info@dmcs.cc; Web: www.dmcs.cc. Ms. Gina Ashley, Prin. Lay Teachers 18; Students 279.
Catechesis Religious Program—
Tel: 507-334-2266, Ext. 16/17; Email: thunt@divinemercy.cc. Terri Hunt, D.R.E. Students 146.
2—IMMACULATE CONCEPTION (1856) Merged with Sacred Heart and St. Lawrence, Faribault to form Divine Mercy Catholic Church, Faribault.
3—ST. LAWRENCE (1869) (German), Merged with Sacred Heart and Immaculate Conception, Faribault to form Divine Mercy Catholic Church, Faribault.
4—SACRED HEART, (French—German), Merged with St. Lawrence and Immaculate Conception, Faribault to form Divine Mercy Catholic Church, Faribault.

FARMINGTON, DAKOTA CO., CHURCH OF ST. MICHAEL (1854) [CEM]
Mailing Address: 22120 Denmark Ave., Farmington, 55024. Tel: 651-463-3360; Fax: 651-463-2339; Email: info@stmichael-farmington.org; Web: www.stmichael-farmington.org. Rev. Benjamin Little; Deacon Russell D. Shupe.
Catechesis Religious Program—Email: lshupe@stmichael-farmington.org. Laura Shupe, Dir. Children's Faith Formation. Students 414.

FOREST LAKE, WASHINGTON CO., ST. PETER (1904) [CEM]
1250 S. Shore Dr., Forest Lake, 55025.
Tel: 651-982-2200; Fax: 651-982-2220; Email: pastor@stpeterfl.org; Web: www.stpeterfl.org. Revs. Daniel J. Bodin; Benjamin Wittnebel, Parochial Vicar; Deacons Gary Houle; Ralph M. L'Allier; Terrence Moravec.
School—St. Peter School, (Grades PreK-7),
Tel: 651-982-2215; Email: jmorehead@school.stpeterfl.org; Web: www.school.stpeterfl.org. Mr. James Morehead, Prin. Lay Teachers 22; Students 253.
Catechesis Religious Program—Students 444.

GOODHUE, GOODHUE CO., THE CHURCH OF THE HOLY TRINITY, Receiving parish for St. Mary's, Bellechester and St. Columbkill, Goodhue.
211 4th St. N., P.O. Box 275, Goodhue, 55027-0275.
Tel: 651-923-4472; Email: holytrinitygoodhue@gmail.com; Web: www.holytrinitygoodhue.org. Revs. Randal J. Kasel, Parochial Admin.; Thomas E. McCabe, Parochial Vicar. In Res.
Worship Sites—
St. Mary's Church—221 Chester Ave., Bellechester, 55027. Tel: 651-923-4305.
St. Columbkill Church, 36483 Co. 47 Blvd., P.O. Box 275, Goodhue, 55027. Tel: 651-258-4307.
Holy Trinity Church, Tel: 651-923-4472.
Catechesis Religious Program—Students 127.

HAMEL, HENNEPIN CO., ST. ANNE (1879) [CEM]
200 Hamel Rd. Box 256, Hamel, 55340-0256.
Tel: 763-478-6644; Fax: 763-478-9141; Email: office@saintannehamel.org; Web: www.saintannehamel.org. Revs. Corey T. Belden; Kevin P. Magner, Parochial Vicar.
Catechesis Religious Program—Email: dre@saintannehamel.org. Laura Reither, D.R.E. Students 60.

HAMPTON, DAKOTA CO., ST. MATHIAS (1900) [CEM]
23315 Northfield Blvd., Hampton, 55031.
Tel: 651-437-9030; Fax: 651-437-3427; Email: parishoffice@stmathias.com; Web: www.stmathias.com. Rev. Cole T. Kracke.
Catechesis Religious Program— See St. John the Baptist, Vermillion shared program. Email: sr.tresa@sjb-school.org. Sr. Tresa Margret, D.R.E.

HANCOCK TOWNSHIP, CARVER CO., ASSUMPTION, Closed. For inquiries for parish records contact the chancery.

HASSAN TOWNSHIP, HENNEPIN CO., ST. WALBURGA (1857) Merged For inquiries for parish records please see Mary Queen of Peace, Rogers.

HASTINGS, DAKOTA CO., ST. ELIZABETH ANN SETON (1987) [CEM] [JC]
2035 W. Fifteenth St., Hastings, 55033.
Tel: 651-437-4254; Email: info@seasparish.org; Web: www.seasparish.org. Revs. David R. Hennen; Michael Barsness, Parochial Vicar.
School—St. Elizabeth Ann Seton School, (Grades PreK-8), 600 Tyler St., Hastings, 55033.
Tel: 651-437-3098; Fax: 651-438-3377; Email: tsullivan@seas-school.org; Web: www.seas-school.org. Tim Sullivan, Prin. Lay Teachers 18; Students 291.
Catechesis Religious Program—Email: jskaife@seasparish.org. Jill Skaife, D.R.E. Students 241.

HEIDELBERG, LE SUEUR CO., ST. SCHOLASTICA (1856) [CEM] Merged with St. Wenceslaus, New Prague.

HOPKINS, HENNEPIN CO.
1—ST. JOSEPH'S (1922) [CEM] Merged with St. John the Evangelist, Hopkins to form The Parish of Saint Gabriel the Archangel of Hopkins, Minnesota.
2—THE PARISH OF SAINT GABRIEL THE ARCHANGEL (1950)
Mailing Address: 6 Interlachen Rd., Hopkins, 55343. Tel: 952-935-5536; Fax: 952-938-2724; Web: www.stgabrielhopkins.org. Rev. James C. Liekhus; Deacon Darrel T. Branch
Legal Name: The Parish of Saint Gabriel the Archangel of Hopkins, Minnesota
Worship Sites—
St. Gabriel the Archangel, St. John Campus—
St. Gabriel the Archangel, St. Joseph Campus, 1310 Main St., Hopkins, 55343.
See Notre Dame Academy, Minnetonka under Elementary Schools, Consolidated, Parochial located in the Institution section.
Catechesis Religious Program—Cindy Novak, Children's Ministry. Students 207.

HUGO, WASHINGTON CO., ST. JOHN THE BAPTIST (1902) [CEM] Merged with St. Genevieve, Centerville.

INVER GROVE HEIGHTS, DAKOTA CO., CHURCH OF ST. PATRICK (1856) [CEM]
3535 72nd St., E., Inver Grove Heights, 55076.
Tel: 651-455-6624; Web: churchofstpatrick.com. Rev. Brian J. Fier; Deacon John E. Vomastek.
Catechesis Religious Program—Email: tneuman@churchofstpatrick.com. Teresa Neuman, D.R.E. Students 261.

JORDAN, SCOTT CO., ST. JOHN THE BAPTIST (1858) [CEM] [JC]
313 E. 2nd St., Jordan, 55352. Tel: 952-492-2640; Fax: 952-492-5683; Email: office@sjbjordan.org; Web: www.sjbjordan.org. Rev. Neil Edward Bakker.
School—St. John the Baptist School, (Grades PreK-6), 215 Broadway St. N., Jordan, 55352.
Tel: 952-492-2030; Fax: 952-492-3211. Courtney Bierlein, Prin. Lay Teachers 11; Students 101.
Catechesis Religious Program—Email: sjbjordanff@gmail.com. Tina Goetz, D.R.E. Students 190.

KENYON, GOODHUE CO., ST. MICHAEL (1944) [CEM]
108 Bullis St., Kenyon, 55946. Tel: 507-789-6120; Email: stmichaels@kmwb.net; Web: stmichaelskenyon.wordpress.com. Revs. Kevin T. Kenney; Brandon Michael Theisen, Parochial Vicar; Deacon Newell R. McGee.
Catechesis Religious Program—Email: faithformation@kmwb.net. Annette Kraft, D.R.E. Students 90.

KILKENNY, LE SUEUR CO., ST. CANICE (1858) [CEM] Merged with Most Holy Redeemer, Montgomery.

LAKE ST. CROIX BEACH, WASHINGTON CO., ST. FRANCIS OF ASSISI (1938)
16770 13th St. S., Lake St. Croix Beach, 55043.
Tel: 651-436-7817; Fax: 651-436-6524; Email: office@stfrancislscbmn.org; Web: www.stfrancislscbmn.org. Rev. Mark J. Underdahl, Email: frmark@stfrancislscbmn.org.
Catechesis Religious Program—Students 120.

LAKEVILLE, DAKOTA CO., ALL SAINTS (1877) [CEM]
Mailing Address: 19795 Holyoke Ave., Lakeville, 55044. Tel: 952-469-4481; Fax: 952-469-5752; Email: info@allsaintschurch.com; Web: www.allsaintschurch.com. Revs. Thomas Wilson; Chad VanHoose, Parochial Vicar; Deacons James Marschall; George Nugent.
Rectory—19738 Hazel Nut Ave., Lakeville, 55044.
School—All Saints School, (Grades K-8),
Tel: 952-469-3332; Email: school@allsaintschurch.com; Web: school.allsaintschurch.com. Lay Teachers 25; Students 348.
Catechesis Religious Program—Email: kfideler@allsaintschurch.com. Students 830.

LE CENTER, LE SUEUR CO.
1—CHURCH OF ST. HENRY (1859) [CEM]
38807 261st Ave., Le Center, 56057. Web: www.stmarysthenry.org. Mailing Address: 165 N. Waterville Ave., Le Center, 56057. Revs. Christopher L. Shofner; James F. Adams, Parochial Vicar; James J. Stiles, Parochial Vicar.
Catechesis Religious Program— See St. Mary, Le Center shared program. Email: jeanrb@frontier.com. Jean Boothby, D.R.E.
2—ST. MARY (1899) [CEM]
165 N. Waterville Ave., Le Center, 56057.
Tel: 507-357-6633; Fax: 507-357-4838; Email: gloriagw@frontier.com; Web: www.stmarysthenry.org. Revs. Christopher L. Shofner; James J. Stiles, Parochial Vicar; James F. Adams, Parochial Vicar.
Catechesis Religious Program— Shared program with St. Henry, Le Sueur. Email: jeanrb@frontier.com. Jean Boothby, D.R.E. Students 270.

LE SUEUR, LE SUEUR CO., ST. ANNE (1852) [CEM 2]
217 N. 3rd St., Le Sueur, 56058. Tel: 507-665-3811; Email: stanneschurchoffice@gmail.com; Web: www.stanneslesueur.org. Revs. Christopher L. Shofner; James F. Adams, Parochial Vicar; James J. Stiles, Parochial Vicar.
School—St. Anne School, (Grades PreK-5), 511 N. 4th St., Le Sueur, 56058. Tel: 507-665-2489; Email: info@stanneslesueur.org. Diane M. Lee, Prin. Lay Teachers 10; Students 124.
Catechesis Religious Program—Email: lbecker@stanneslesueur.org. Lauri Becker, D.R.E. Students 95.

LEXINGTON, LE SUEUR CO., ST. JOSEPH (1903) [CEM] Merged with St. Wenceslaus, New Prague.

LINDSTROM, CHISAGO CO., ST. BRIDGET OF SWEDEN (1948)
13060 Lake Blvd., Lindstrom, 55045.
Tel: 651-257-2474; Fax: 651-257-1498; Email: kkornowski@stbridgetofsweden.org; Web: www.stbridgetofsweden.org. Mailing Address: P.O. Box 754, Lindstrom, 55045. Rev. David W. Kohner.
Catechesis Religious Program—Students 196.

LONG LAKE, HENNEPIN CO., ST. GEORGE (1916) [CEM]
133 N. Brown Rd., Long Lake, 55356-9560.
Tel: 952-473-1247; Fax: 952-404-0129; Email: stgeorge@msn.com; Web: www.stgeorgelonglake.org. Rev. Mark R. Juettner; Deacon Bruce L. Bowen.
Catechesis Religious Program—Christina Ruiz, D.R.E. Students 83.

LONSDALE, RICE CO., IMMACULATE CONCEPTION (1903) [CEM 2]
116 Alabama St., S.E., Lonsdale, 55046-0169.
Tel: 507-744-2829; Email: icparish@lonstel.com; Web: churchoftheimmaculateconception.net. Mailing Address: 202 Alabama St., S.E., Lonsdale, 55046. Rev. Nicholas William VanDenBroeke.
See Holy Cross LNMV Catholic School, Webster under Elementary Schools, Consolidated, Parochial located in the Institution section.
Catechesis Religious Program— See St. Nickolaus, New Market shared program. Email: kathyc@holycrossschool.net. Kathy Chlan, D.R.E.

LORETTO, HENNEPIN CO., SS. PETER AND PAUL (1867) [CEM]
145 Railway St. E., Loretto, 55357. Mailing Address: P.O. Box 96, Loretto, 55357. Tel: 763-479-0535; Fax: 763-479-4383; Email: selsen@saintsppta.org; Web: www.saintsppta.org. Revs. Glen T. Jenson; Kevin P. Magner, Parochial Vicar.
Rectory—175 Loretto St., Loretto, 55357.
Catechesis Religious Program— See St. Thomas the Apostle, Corcoran shared program.

MAPLE GROVE, HENNEPIN CO., ST. JOSEPH THE WORKER (1870)
Mailing Address: 7180 Hemlock Ln., Maple Grove, 55369. Tel: 763-425-6505; Fax: 763-425-6587; Web: www.sjtw.net. Rev. Michael Sullivan; Deacons Kevin J. O'Connor; John T. Wallin.
Catechesis Religious Program—Students 741.

MAPLE LAKE, WRIGHT CO., ST. TIMOTHY (1882) [CEM 3]
8 Oak Ave. N., Maple Lake, 55358. Tel: 320-963-3726; Fax: 320-963-2008; Email: parishoffice@churchofsttimothy.org; Web: www.churchofsttimothy.org. Revs. John D. Meyer; Andrew B. Stueve, Parochial Vicar; Deacon Ron Freeman.
School—St. Timothy School, (Grades PreK-8), 215 Division St. E., Maple Lake, 55358.
Tel: 320-963-3417; Fax: 320-963-8804; Email: schooloffice@churchofsttimothy.org; Web: school.churchofsttimothy.org. Dawn McCabe, Prin. Lay Teachers 13; Students 121.
Catechesis Religious Program—Students 181.

MARYSBURG, LESUEUR CO., IMMACULATE CONCEPTION OF MARYSBURG (1857) [CEM]
27528 Patrick St., Madison Lake, 56063.
Tel: 507-243-3166; Email: office@maryschurches.com; Web: www.maryschurches.com. Revs. Christopher L. Shofner; James F. Adams, Parochial Vicar; James J. Stiles, Parochial Vicar.

Catechesis Religious Program— Combined with Nativity Church, Cleveland, MN. Email: lynn.kluntz@hotmail.com. Lynn Kluntz, D.R.E. Students 77.

MARYSTOWN, SCOTT CO., ST. MARY OF THE PURIFICATION (1855) [CEM] Merged see Sts. Joachim & Anne, Shakopee.

MIESVILLE, DAKOTA CO., ST. JOSEPH (1873) [CEM]
23955 Nicolai Ave. E., Hastings, 55033-9650.
Tel: 651-437-3526; Fax: 651-437-3506; Email: stjosephm@embarqmail.com; Web: www.stjosephmiesville.com. Rev. Terry P. Beeson.
Catechesis Religious Program—Students 107.

MINNETONKA, HENNEPIN CO., IMMACULATE HEART OF MARY (1946)
13505 Excelsior Blvd., Minnetonka, 55345.
Tel: 952-935-1432; Email: jbauer@ihm-cc.org; Web: ihm-cc.org. Rev. John M. Bauer.
See Notre Dame Academy, Minnetonka under Elementary Schools, Consolidated, Parochial located in the Institution section.
Catechesis Religious Program—Students 94.

MONTGOMERY, LE SUEUR CO., MOST HOLY REDEEMER (1881) [CEM 2] Receiving parish for St. Canice, Kilkenny.
Mailing Address: 206 Vine Ave., W., Montgomery, 56069. Tel: 507-364-7981; Fax: 507-364-8660; Email: hredeemer@frontiernet.net; Web: www.hredeemerparish.org. Rev. Victor Valencia; Deacon Jason A. Myhre.
School—Most Holy Redeemer School, (Grades PreK-8), 205 Vine Ave., W., Montgomery, 56069.
Tel: 507-364-7383; Fax: 507-364-5964; Email: info@mosthrs.org; Web: mosthrs.org. George Vondracek, Prin. Lay Teachers 7; Students 88.
Catechesis Religious Program—Students 96.
St. Canice, (Worship Site) 183 W. Maple St., Kilkenny, 56052.

MONTICELLO, WRIGHT CO., ST. HENRY (1904) [CEM]
1001 E. 7th St., Monticello, 55362. Tel: 763-295-2402 ; Email: info@sthenrycatholic.com; Web: www.sthenrycatholic.info. Rev. Tony VanderLoop; Deacon Michael A. Medley.
Catechesis Religious Program—Tel: 763-271-3079. Students 386.

MOUND, HENNEPIN CO., OUR LADY OF THE LAKE (1909) [CEM]
2385 Commerce Blvd., Mound, 55364.
Tel: 952-472-1284; Email: reurich@ourladyofthelake.com; Web: www.ourladyofthelake.com. Rev. Anthony O'Neill; Deacon Delvin L. Wilkinson.
School—Our Lady of the Lake School, (Grades PreK-8), 2411 Commerce Blvd., Mound, 55364.
Tel: 952-472-8228; Fax: 952-843-5693; Email: cfranck@schoololl.com; Web: school.ourladyofthelake.com. Becky Kennedy, Prin. Lay Teachers 12; Students 129.
Catechesis Religious Program—Email: khejna@ourladyofthelake.com. Kathy Hejna, D.R.E. Students 219.

NEW MARKET, SCOTT CO., SAINT NICKOLAUS (1893) [CEM]
51 Church St., New Market, 55054.
Tel: 952-461-2403; Email: jberry@stncc.net; Web: www.stncc.net. Rev. Patrick Thomas Barnes.
See Holy Cross LNMV Catholic School, Lonsdale under Elementary Schools, Consolidated, Parochial located in the Institution section.
Catechesis Religious Program— Shared program with Most Holy Trinity, Veseli and Immaculate Conception, Lonsdale. Students 257.

NEW PRAGUE, SCOTT CO., ST. WENCESLAUS (1857) [CEM]
215 Main St. E., New Prague, 56071-1837.
Tel: 952-758-3225; Fax: 952-758-2960; Email: info@npcatholic.org; Web: www.npcatholic.org. Revs. Eugene J. Theisen, Parochial Vicar; Kevin I. Clinton; Deacon Robert C. Wagner.
Worship Sites—
St. John Campus—20687 Hub Dr., New Prague, 56071. Tel: 952-758-4642.
St. Scholastica Campus, 31525 181st Ave., New Prague, 56071.
School—St. Wenceslaus School, (Grades PreK-8), 227 Main St. E., New Prague, 56071. Tel: 952-758-3133; Fax: 952-758-2958; Web: swsaints.org. Kimberly Doyle, Prin. Clergy 1; Lay Teachers 19; Students 217.
Catechesis Religious Program—Email: laura.schoenecker@npcatholic.org. Laura Schoenecker, D.R.E. Students 387.

NEW TRIER, DAKOTA CO., ST. MARY (1856) [CEM]
8433 239th St. E., New Trier, 55031.
Tel: 651-437-5546; Email: info@stmarysnewtrier.com; Web: stmarysnewtrier.com. Rev. Cole T. Kracke.
Catechesis Religious Program— Share Faith Formation, St. Mathias, Hampton.

NORTH BRANCH, CHISAGO CO., ST. GREGORY THE GREAT (1874) [CEM]
38725 Forest Blvd., North Branch, 55056.
Tel: 651-674-4056; Email: info@stgregorynb.org; Web: www.stgregorynb.org. Mailing Address: P.O. Box 609, North Branch, 55056. Rev. Mark Shane Stoppel-Wasinger.
Catechesis Religious Program— Shared Faith Formation, Sacred Heart, Rush City.
Tel: 651-674-7382. Students 106.

NORTHFIELD, RICE CO.
1—ANNUNCIATION (1863) [CEM]
4996 Hazelwood Ave., Northfield, 55057-4255.
Tel: 952-652-2625; Email: secretary-ac@integra.net. Rev. Dennis Dempsey.
Catechesis Religious Program—Students 35.
2—ST. DOMINIC (1869) [CEM]
104 Linden St. N., Northfield, 55057.
Tel: 507-645-8816; Fax: 507-645-8818; Email: secretary@churchofstdominic.org; Web: www.churchofstdominic.org. Mailing Address: 216 N. Spring St., Northfield, 55057-1431. Rev. Dennis Dempsey; Deacon Steven J. Moses.
Rectory—116 Linden St. N., Northfield, 55057.
School—St. Dominic School, (Grades PreK-8),
Tel: 507-645-8136; Email: office@schoolofstdominic.org; Web: schoolofstdominic.org. Vicki Kalina Marvin, Prin. Lay Teachers 14; Students 154.
Catechesis Religious Program—Email: maramangan@churchofstdominic.org. Mara Mangan, D.R.E. Students 300.

NORWOOD, CARVER CO., ASCENSION CATHOLIC CHURCH (1859) [CEM 2]
323 Reform St., N., Norwood, 55368.
Tel: 952-467-3351; Email: busadmin@ascensionnya.org; Web: www.ascensionnya.org. Rev. Gregory E. Abbott.
Catechesis Religious Program—Julie Kleindl, Faith Formation; Kara Wickenhauser, Faith Formation; Chris George, Adult Formation. Students 120.

PINE ISLAND, GOODHUE CO., ST. MICHAEL (1878) [CEM]
451 5th St., S.W., Pine Island, 55963-0368.
Tel: 507-356-4280; Fax: 507-356-2080; Email: stmichaeloffice@bevcomm.net; Web: stpaulstmichael.com. Revs. Randal J. Kasel; Thomas E. McCabe, Parochial Vicar.
Catechesis Religious Program—Students 71.

PRIOR LAKE, SCOTT CO., ST. MICHAEL (1912) [CEM 2]
16311 Duluth Ave., S.E., Prior Lake, 55372.
Tel: 952-447-2491; Fax: 952-447-2489; Email: info@stmichael-pl.org; Web: www.stmichael-pl.org. Rev. Thomas J. Walker, J.D.; Deacon Richard J. Roy
Legal Title: Church of St. Michael of Prior Lake
School—St. Michael Catholic School, (Grades PreK-8), 16280 Duluth Ave., S.E., Prior Lake, 55372.
Tel: 952-447-2124; Fax: 952-447-2132 (Primary); Email: info@saintmpl.org; Web: saintmpl.org. Mary Yamoah, Prin. Lay Teachers 18; Students 310.
Catechesis Religious Program—Email: tbeer@stmichael-pl.org. Students 751.

RAMSEY, ANOKA CO., ST. KATHARINE DREXEL (2004) (Quasi-Parish)
7101 143rd Ave., N.W., Ste. G, Ramsey, 55303. Email: info@stkdcc.org; Web: www.stkdcc.org. Rev. Paul A. Jaroszeski; Deacon Randall J. Bauer.
Catechesis Religious Program—Email: tbauer@stkdcc.org. Troy Bauer, Pastoral Assoc., Youth Ministries. Students 130.

RED WING, GOODHUE CO., CHURCH OF ST. JOSEPH (1865) [CEM]
435 W. 7th St., Red Wing, 55066. Tel: 651-388-1133; Email: parish@stjosephredwing.org; Web: www.stjosephredwing.org. Mailing Address: 426 8th St., W., Red Wing, 55066. Revs. Thomas M. Kommers; Thomas McCabe, Sunday Spanish Mass; Deacon Patrick W. Evans.
Catechesis Religious Program—Email: lmyers@stjosephredwing.org. Lori Ann Myers, D.R.E. Students 139.

ROGERS, HENNEPIN CO.
1—ST. MARTIN (1912) Merged For inquiries for parish records contact The Catholic Church of Mary Queen of Peace, Rogers.
2—THE CATHOLIC CHURCH OF MARY QUEEN OF PEACE, Rev. Michael C. Kaluza; Deacon Joseph Smith.
Worship Sites—
St. Martin Church—21304 Church Ave., Rogers, 55374. Tel: 763-428-2585; Fax: 763-428-3460; Email: parishoffice@mqpcatholic.org; Web: mqpcatholic.org.
St. Walburga Church, 12020 Fletcher Ln., Rogers, 55374.
School—Mary, Queen of Peace School, (Grades PreK-5), 21201 Church Ave., Rogers, 55374.
Tel: 763-428-2355; Fax: 763-428-2062; Email: mqpschooloffice@mqpcatholic.org. Michael Gerard, Prin., Email: mgerard@mqpcatholic.org. Lay Teachers 14; Students 87.
Catechesis Religious Program—Students 268.

ROSEMOUNT, DAKOTA CO., ST. JOSEPH (1865) [CEM 2]
13900 Biscayne Ave., Rosemount, 55068.
Tel: 651-423-4402; Email: maggie.roth@stjosephcommunity.org; Web: www.stjosephcommunity.org. Rev. Paul A. Kammen; Deacons Stephen J. Boatwright; Gordon B. Bird.
Rectory—13889 Blanca Ct., Rosemount, 55068.
School—St. Joseph School, (Grades PreK-8),
Tel: 651-423-1658; Email: kelly.roche@stjosephcommunity.org. Kelly Roche, Prin. Lay Teachers 13; Students 235.
Catechesis Religious Program—Students 592.

RUSH CITY, CHISAGO CO., SACRED HEART (1870) [CEM]
415 W. 5th St., Rush City, 55069. Mailing Address: P.O. Box 45, Rush City, 55069. Tel: 320-358-4370; Fax: 866-779-1580; Email: sacredheart@q.com; Web: www.sacredheartrcmn.org. Rev. Mark Shane Stoppel-Wasinger.
Church: 425 Field Ave., S., Rush City, 55069.
Catechesis Religious Program—Students 49.

ST. BENEDICT, SCOTT CO., ST. BENEDICT, [CEM] [JC] Merged with St. Wenceslaus, New Prague.

ST. BONIFACIUS, HENNEPIN CO., ST. BONIFACE (1859) [CEM]
4025 Main St., St. Bonifacius, 55375. Mailing Address: P.O. Box 68, St. Bonifacius, 55375.
Tel: 952-446-1054; Email: stbonifaceoffice@mchsi.com; Web: stboniface-stmary.org. Rev. Joseph-Quoc T. Vuong.
Catechesis Religious Program—Students 65.

ST. MICHAEL, WRIGHT CO., ST. MICHAEL (1857) [CEM 2]
11300 Frankfort Pkwy., N.E., St. Michael, 55376.
Tel: 763-497-2745; Fax: 763-497-5273; Email: jbonham@stmcatholicchurch.org; Web: www.stmcatholicchurch.org. Revs. Peter M. Richards; Joseph Arthur Zabinski, Parochial Vicar; Deacons Steven C. Dupay; Paul M. Ravnikar; Greg J. Steele.
School—St. Michael Catholic School, (Grades PreK-8), 14 Main St. N., Saint Michael, 55376.
Tel: 763-497-3887; Fax: 763-497-9159; Email: jhaller@stmcatholicschool.org; Web: www.stmcatholicschool.org. Jenny Haller, Prin. Lay Teachers 24; Students 468.
Catechesis Religious Program—Students 417.

ST. PAUL PARK, WASHINGTON CO., ST. THOMAS AQUINAS (1884) [CEM]
920 Holley Ave., St. Paul Park, 55071.
Tel: 651-459-2131; Fax: 651-459-8756; Email: mluedtke1@st-thomas-aquinas.com; Web: www.st-thomas-aquinas.com. Rev. J. Anthony Andrade.
Catechesis Religious Program—Students 80.

ST. THOMAS, LE SUEUR CO., ST. THOMAS (1858) Merged with St. Anne, Le Sueur.

SAVAGE, SCOTT CO., ST. JOHN THE BAPTIST (1854) [CEM]
Mailing Address: 4625 W. 125th St., Savage, 55378-1357. Tel: 952-890-9465; Fax: 952-890-3006; Email: pastor@stjohns-savage.org; Web: www.stjohns-savage.org. Revs. Donald E. DeGrood; Tim Sandquist, Parochial Vicar; Deacon Robert Scott Durham.
School—St. John the Baptist School, (Grades PreK-8), 12508 Lynn Ave. S., Savage, 55378.
Tel: 952-890-6604; Fax: 952-890-9481; Email: psingewald@stjohns-savage.org; Web: www.stjohns-savage.org/school/school-home. Phil Singewald, Prin. Lay Teachers 25; Students 404.
Catechesis Religious Program—Students 386.

SHAFER, CHISAGO CO., THE CHURCH OF SAINT FRANCIS XAVIER (1884)
25267 Redwing Ave., Shafer, 55074.
Tel: 651-465-7345; Fax: 651-465-6632; Web: www.stjosephtaylorfalls.org. Mailing Address: 540 River St., P.O. Box 234, Taylors Falls, 55084. Rev. John M. Drees, Parochial Admin.; Deacon Michael Martin Jr.
Catechesis Religious Program—Students 10.

SHAKOPEE, SCOTT CO.
1—STS. JOACHIM AND ANNE (1865) [CEM] [JC] Receiving parish for St. Mark, Shakopee, St. Mary of the Purification, Shakopee & St. Mary, Shakopee.
2700 17th Ave. E., Shakopee, 55379.
Tel: 952-445-1319; Web: www.ssjacs.org. Revs. Erik Carl Martin Lundgren; Paul Matthew Haverstock, Parochial Vicar.
School—Shakopee Area Catholic School (1895) (Grades PreK-8), Tel: 952-445-3387;
Fax: 952-445-7256; Web: www.sacsschools.org. Julie Moran, Prin. Lay Teachers 44; Students 653; Total Staff 77.
Catechesis Religious Program—Kathleen Dierberger, D.R.E. K-5. Students 297.
Worship Sites—
Church of St. Mark—350 Atwood St. S., Shakopee, 55379.
Church of St. Mary of the Purification, 15850 Marystown Rd., Shakopee, 55379.
Church of St. Mary, 535 Lewis St. S., Shakopee, 55379.
2—ST. MARK (1856) [JC2] (German), Merged see Sts. Joachim and Anne, Shakopee.
3—ST. MARY (1865) Merged with St. Mark to form Sts. Joachim and Anne, Shakopee.

SHIELDSVILLE, RICE CO., ST. PATRICK, SHIELDSVILLE (1856) [CEM]
7525 Dodd Rd., Shieldsville, 55021.
Tel: 507-334-6002; Email:

spshieldsville@qwestoffice.net; Web: www.spshieldsville.org. Rev. Victor Valencia.
Catechesis Religious Program—Tracy Velishek, D.R.E. Students 12.
SOUTH ST. PAUL, DAKOTA CO.
1—ST. AUGUSTINE (1896) Merged with Holy Trinity, South St. Paul.
2—HOLY TRINITY (1918)
Mailing Address: 749 6th Ave. S., South St. Paul, 55075. Tel: 651-455-1302 (Office); Fax: 651-455-7600 ; Email: bulletin@holytrinitys.org; Web: www.holytrinitysspmn.org. Revs. John P. Echert, S.S.L.; Robert J. Grabner, In Res.; Deacon Ronald M. Smisek.
School—Holy Trinity School, (Grades PreK-8), 745 6th Ave. S., South St. Paul, 55075. Tel: 651-455-8557 ; Fax: 651-455-9696; Email: secretary@holytrinitys.org; Web: www.holytrinityssp.org. Dawn Kincs, Prin. Lay Teachers 13; Students 147.
Catechesis Religious Program—Tel: 651-455-6004; Email: reled@holytrinityssp.org. John Balk, D.R.E. Students 82.
3—ST. JOHN VIANNEY (1946) [CEM]
840 19th Ave. N., South St. Paul, 55075.
Tel: 651-451-1863; Email: info@sjvssp.org; Web: www.sjvssp.org. Mailing Address: 789 17th Ave. N., South St. Paul, 55075. Rev. Antony Skaria, C.F.I.C.; Deacon Scott K. Wright.
See Community of Saints Regional Catholic School, West St. Paul under Elementary Schools, Consolidated, Parochial located in the Institutions section.
Catechesis Religious Program—Jill Vujovich-Laabs, D.R.E. Students 61.
STILLWATER, WASHINGTON CO.
1—ST. MARY (1865) [JC] (German)
423 S. Fifth St., Stillwater, 55082. Tel: 651-439-1270; Fax: 651-439-7045; Email: info@costm.org; Web: www.stmarystillwater.org. Revs. Michael J. Izen; John Powers, Parochial Vicar.
See St. Croix Catholic School, Stillwater under Elementary Schools, Consolidated, Parochial located in the Institution section.
Catechesis Religious Program— Shared Faith Formation, St. Michael, Stillwater. Students 47.
2—CHURCH OF ST. MICHAEL (1853) [JC]
611 S. Third St., Stillwater, 55082-4908.
Tel: 651-439-4400; Fax: 651-430-3271; Email: info@costm.org; Web: www.stmichaelstillwater.org. Revs. Michael J. Izen; John Powers, Parochial Vicar.
See St. Croix Catholic School, Stillwater under Elementary Schools, Consolidated, Parochial located in the Institution section.
Catechesis Religious Program—St. Croix Valley Faith Formation, Stillwater, 55082.
Tel: 651-351-3175; Web: www.sccff.net. Students 271.
TAYLORS FALLS, CHISAGO CO., ST. JOSEPH'S (1873)
490 Bench St., Taylors Falls, 55084. Mailing Address: 540 River St., P.O. Box 234, Taylors Falls, 55084. Tel: 651-465-7345; Email: stjosephstfrancis@outlook.com; Web: www.stjosephtaylorsfalls.org. Rev. John M. Drees; Deacon Michael Martin Jr.
Catechesis Religious Program—Students 63.
UNION HILL, LE SUEUR CO., ST. JOHN THE EVANGELIST, [CEM] Merged with St. Wenceslaus, New Prague.
VERMILLION, DAKOTA CO., ST. JOHN THE BAPTIST (1881) [CEM]
106 Main St. W., Vermillion, 55085. Mailing Address: 23315 Northfield Blvd., Hampton, 55031.
Tel: 651-437-9030; Fax: 651-437-3427; Email: parishoffice@stmathias.com; Web: www.stjohns-vermillion.com. Rev. Cole T. Kracke.
School—St. John the Baptist School, (Grades PreK-4), 111 W. Main St., Vermillion, 55085. Mailing Address: P.O. Box 50, Vermillion, 55085.
Tel: 651-437-2644; Fax: 651-437-9006; Email: office@sjb-school.org; Web: sjb-school.org. Rita Humbert, Prin. Lay Teachers 7; Students 86.
Catechesis Religious Program— Shared program with St. Mathias, Hampton. Email: srtresa@sjb-school.org. Sr. Tresa Margret, D.R.E. Students 189.
VESELI, RICE CO., MOST HOLY TRINITY (1874) [CEM 2]
4939 Washington St., Veseli, 55046.
Tel: 507-744-2823; Fax: 507-744-4163; Email: mhtveseli@gmail.com; Web: www.mhtveseli.com. Rev. John G. Lapensky.
See Holy Cross LNMV Catholic School, Lonsdale under Elementary Schools, Consolidated, Parochial located in the Institution section.
Catechesis Religious Program— See St. Nicklaus, New Market shared program.
VICTORIA, CARVER CO., ST. VICTORIA (1856) [CEM]
8228 Victoria Dr., Victoria, 55386. Tel: 952-443-2661 ; Fax: 952-443-3866; Email: rortman@stvictoria.org; Web: www.stvictoria.net. Rev. Robert L. White; Deacon Ray Ortman.
Rectory—8356 Victoria Dr., Victoria, 55386.
Catechesis Religious Program—Email: eklinker@stvictoria.org. Emily Klinker, D.R.E. Students 551.
WACONIA, CARVER CO., ST. JOSEPH CATHOLIC COMMUNITY (1859) [CEM]
41 E. 1st St., Waconia, 55387. Tel: 952-442-2384; Fax: 952-442-3719; Email: churchoffice@stjosephwaconia.org; Web: www.stjosephwaconia.org. Rev. Stan P. Mader; Deacon James W. Bauhs.
School—St. Joseph Catholic School, (Grades PreK-8), Tel: 952-442-4500; Email: schooloffice@stjosephwaconia.org; Web: school.stjosephwaconia.org. Bruce Richards, Prin., Tel: 952-442-3716. Lay Teachers 15; Students 181.
Catechesis Religious Program—Students 309.
WATERTOWN, CARVER CO., IMMACULATE CONCEPTION (1863) [CEM]
Mailing Address: P.O. Box 548, Watertown, 55388. Tel: 952-955-1458; Email: iccwatertown@gmail.com. Rev. James William Devorak.
Catechesis Religious Program—Email: iccwreled@gmail.com. Theresa Washburn, D.R.E. Students 160.
WATERVILLE, LE SUEUR CO., HOLY TRINITY (1892) [CEM]
506 Common St., Waterville, 56096.
Tel: 507-362-4311; Email: holyt7@frontiernet.net. Rev. Michael W. Ince.
Catechesis Religious Program—Students 67.
WAVERLY, WRIGHT CO., ST. MARY (1884) [CEM] [JC3]
607 Maple Ave., P.O. Box 278, Waverly, 55390.
Tel: 763-658-4319; Web: stmarys-waverly.net. Rev. Kenneth L. O'Hotto.
Catechesis Religious Program—Students 201.
WAYZATA, HENNEPIN CO.
1—ST. BARTHOLOMEW (1916)
630 E. Wayzata Blvd., Wayzata, 55391.
Tel: 952-473-6601; Email: stbarts@st-barts.org; Web: www.st-barts.org. Rev. Michael Van Sloun; Deacon Richard P. Witucki.
School—St. Bartholomew School, (Grades PreK-6), Tel: 952-473-6189; Email: stbartsschool@st-barts.org; Web: st-bartsschool.org. Patrick Fox, Prin. Lay Teachers 11; Students 143.
Catechesis Religious Program—Students 286.
2—HOLY NAME OF JESUS (1865) [CEM]
155 County Rd. 24, Wayzata, 55391.
Tel: 763-473-7901; Fax: 763-745-3480; Email: email@hnoj.org; Web: www.hnoj.org. Revs. Stephen D. Ulrick; Bryce Evans, Parochial Vicar; Deacon Dennis G. Hanson.
School—Holy Name of Jesus School, (Grades PreK-6), Tel: 763-473-3675; Email: mlaurent@hnoj.org; Web: www.hnoj.org/school. Martha Laurent, Prin., Tel: 763-745-3485. Lay Teachers 28; Students 313.
Catechesis Religious Program—Students 1,032.
ZUMBROTA, GOODHUE CO., ST. PAUL (1900) [CEM] [JC]
749 S. Main St., Zumbrota, 55992-1608.
Tel: 507-732-5324; Fax: 507-732-5347; Email: stpauls@hcinet.net; Web: www.stpaulstmichael.com. Revs. Randal J. Kasel; Thomas E. McCabe, Parochial Vicar.
Catechesis Religious Program—Students 17.

Chaplains of Public Institutions

ST. PAUL. *Children's Hospital*. Rev. Michael G. Monogue.
St. Joseph's-HealthEast Hospital,
Tel: 651-232-3611 (Spiritual Care Dept.). Rev. Biju Pattasseril, CFIC, Email: frbijum@usfamily.net.
Ramsey County Correctional Facilities. Served by Jesuit Novitiate.
Regions Hospital, 640 Jackson St., 55101. Revs. Ronald Harrer, O.M.I., Jimmy Mathew Puttananickal, O.M.I.
United Hospitals, Inc.. Rev. Michael G. Monogue.
MINNEAPOLIS. *Abbot-Northwestern Hospital*, 3617 38th Ave. S., Minneapolis, 55066. Rev. Sebastien Bakatu.
Fairview University Medical Center. Rev. Vaughn Treco.
Hennepin County Medical Center, 2421 Third Ave. S., Minneapolis, 55404. Rev. Marcus F. Milless.
Veterans Administration Medical Center, 1 Veterans Dr., Minneapolis, 55417. Revs. William Brenna, Damien Schill.
EDINA. *Fairview-Southdale Hospital*, 6401 France Ave. S., Edina, 55435. Rev. Jerome W. Fehn.
COON RAPIDS. *Mercy Hospital*, 4050 Coon Rapids Blvd., Coon Rapids, 55433. Rev. Peter Yakubu Ali.
HASTINGS. *Hennepin County Adult Detention Center*. Rev. David Haschka, S.J.
Regina Medical Center. Vacant.
LINO LAKES. *Minnesota Correctional Facility*. (Shared Ministry) Vacant, 1121 E. 46th St., Minneapolis, 55407.
MAPLEWOOD. *St. John's Hospital*, 1575 Beam Ave., Maplewood, 55109. Rev. Leo J. Schneider(Lutheran).
NEW HOPE. *St. Therese Care Center & Residence*, 8000 Bass Lake Rd., New Hope, 55428. Attended by the Church of St. Therese, Deephaven.
ROBBINSDALE. *North Memorial Hospital*, 3300 Oakdale Ave. N., Robbinsdale, 55422. Rev. Bruno Chizoba Nwachukwu.
SHAKOPEE. *Women's State Reformatory*. Vacant.
ST. LOUIS PARK. *Park Nicollet Methodist Hospital*, 6500 Excelsior Blvd., St. Louis Park, 55426. Rev. Jerome W. Fehn.
STILLWATER. *Minnesota State Prison*. (Shared Ministry) Vacant.

Leave of Absence:
Revs.—
Barrett, David A.
Conlin, Daniel C., J.C.D.
Gallatin, Joseph G.
Hughes, Peter M.
Johnson, Lawrence R.
Joseph, Thomas J.
Keating, Michael J.
Pish, Robert H.
Wenthe, Christopher T.

On Duty Outside the Archdiocese:
Revs.—
Anderson, Jake E., St. John Paul II Newman Center, Univ. of Nebraska at Omaha
Burns, James P., Pres., St. Mary's Univ. of Minnesota
Jones, Colin Daniel, Graduate Education, Pontifical North American College, Rome
Koop, Evan S., Graduate Education, Pontifical North American College, Rome
Schaffer, Gregory J., Jesucristo Resucitado, Apartado 272, Puerto Ordaz, Estado Bolivar Venezuela 8050.

Military Chaplains:
Revs.—
Blake, Lawrence R., Active military service.
Creagan, Michael
Fehn, Jerome W.
Magnuson, Sean R.

Retired: Mail for retired priests may be sent to: Archdiocesan Catholic Center, 777 Forest St., St. Paul, MN 55106-3857.
Revs.—
Adrian, Stephen J., (Retired)
Arms, Michael M., (Retired)
Backmann, Albert P., (Retired)
Beckman, Martin A., (Retired)
Bowers, Ronald J., J.C.D., (Retired)
Brambilla, Charles A., (Retired)
Brandes, John F., (Retired)
Bury, Harold J., (Retired)
Campbell, Theodore C., (Retired)
Carroll, Roger, (Retired)
Custodio, Rinaldo B., (Retired)
Dandurand, Douglas E., Ph.D., (Retired)
Dease, Dennis J., (Retired)
Doffing, Gordon M., (Retired)
Donahue, John G., (Retired)
Ehmke, Matthew, (Retired)
Erlander, Michael, (Retired)
Evenson, Dennis D., (Retired)
Fitzgerald, Thomas P., (Retired)
Fitzpatrick, John P., (Retired)
Fitzpatrick, Robert J., (Retired)
Forliti, John E., (Retired)
Friberg, Daniel, (Retired)
Fried, Francis L., (Retired)
Gamber, William K., (Retired)
Goman, Ralph J., (Retired)
Grafsky, George J., (Retired)
Grieman, Gerald G., (Retired)
Griffin, Patrick E., (Retired)
Gutierrez, Jose, (Retired)
Hackenmueller, Jerome B., (Retired)
Hart, Robert B., (Retired)
Hazel, Robert L., (Retired)
Herrmann, James, (Retired)
Hessian, Roger J., (Retired)
Himmelsbach, James R., (Retired)
Hofstede, John Michael, (Retired)
Huar, Ralph F., (Retired)
Hubbard, Lawrence E., (Retired)
Hunstiger, Thomas, (Retired)
Keane, Robert E., (Retired)
Keiser, Jerome F., (Retired)
Kenney, William J., (Retired)
Kinney, George R., (Retired)

Kittock, Francis R., (Retired)
Klaers, Marvin J., (Retired)
LaCanne, Stephen J., M.Div., N.A.C.C., (Retired)
LaVan, Kenneth G., (Retired)
Lepak, Roy C., (Retired)
Long, John M., (Retired)
Ludescher, Kenneth F., (Retired)
Mahoney, Richard J., (Retired)
Malone, John M., (Retired)
Martin, William F., (Retired)
Maslowski, Stanley J., (Retired), P.O. Box 28338, Saint Paul, 55128
McDonough, Thomas R., (Retired)
Meyer, Frederick C., (Retired)
Monaghan, Robert T., (Retired)
Monsour, Raymond G., (Retired)
Montero Pazimo, Hugo L., (Retired)
Nolan, Timothy F., (Retired)
Notebaart, James C., (Retired)
Nygaard, Robert C., (Retired)
O'Brien, Thomas F.A., (Retired)
O'Gara, Stephen R., (Retired)
O'Rourke, Bryan A., (Retired)
Parkos, John F., (Retired)
Paron, William J., (Retired)
Piche, Donald J., (Retired)
Pierre, Kenneth J., (Retired)
Pouliot, Eugene A., (Retired)
Pouliot, Francis A., (Retired)
Reidy, James E., (Retired)
Ryan, Patrick J., (Retired)
Sauber, Arnold M., (Retired)
Savundra, Edwin, (Retired)
Schoenberger, James T., (Retired)
Schwartz, Robert M., (Retired)
Shallbetter, Martin, (Retired)
Siebenaler, John M., (Retired)
Siebenaler, Leonard, (Retired)
Siebenaler, Martin, (Retired)
Sieg, Thomas H., (Retired)
Simonson, Earl C., (Retired)
Sipe, Robert J., (Retired)
Skrypek, Gregory A., (Retired)
Sledz, Stanley V., (Retired)
Slusser, Michael S., (Retired)
Smith, David W., (Retired)
Sochacki, Walter L., (Retired)
Stolzman, William F., (Retired)
Tasto, Harold J., (Retired)
Tatel, Orlando G., (Retired)
Thompson, Dennis S., (Retired)
Thoomkuzhy, George T.V., (Retired)
Valit, Robert L., (Retired)
Wampach, Frank J., (Retired)
Welch, Gregory T., (Retired)
Welzbacher, George, (Retired)
Whittier, William O., (Retired)
Wittman, Peter C., (Retired)
Wolnik, James G., (Retired).

Permanent Deacons:
Allen, Nathan E., Metropolitan Tribunal; St. Agnes, St. Paul
Amell, Lawrence E., (Diocese of Superior) St. Ambrose, Woodbury
Babcock, George H., (Retired)
Barrett, Ervin F., (Retired)
Bauer, Randall J., St. Katharine Drexel, Ramsey
Bauhs, James W., St. Joseph, Waconia
Beck, William E., (Retired), Resides outside the Archdiocese
Becker, Donald L., (Retired)
Bednarczyk, Peter, St. Stephen, Anoka
Beer, Terrence G., Pax Christi, Eden Prairie
Belian, John J., Holy Cross, Minneapolis
Bellavance, Peter G., (Resides outside the Archdiocese)
Bird, Gordon B., St. Joseph, Rosemount
Bisciglia, Robert A., St. Peter, North Saint Paul
Bisek, Jerome H., (Retired)
Bliss, Bertrum T., (Diocese of St. Cloud)
Boatwright, Stephen J., St. Joseph, Rosemount
Bobertz, Charles A., (Diocese of St. Cloud) Pax Christi, Eden Prairie
Boisclair, A. Richard, (Retired)
Bowen, Bruce L., St. Maximilian Kolbe, Delano; St. George, Long Lake
Bramwell, Robert A., St. Joseph, New Hope
Branch, Darrel T., St. Gabriel the Archangel, Hopkins
Brewer, Daniel P., Transfiguration, Oakdale
Buck, Paul B., St. Francis, Buffalo
Carroll, William J., (Archdiocese of Mexico City) St. Odilia, Shoreview
Chlebeck, Dennis M., Maternity of Mary, St. Paul
Christensen, Harlan L., (Leave of Absence)
Ciresi, Jerome D., (Retired)
Clasen, James L., Franciscan Health Community, St. Paul
Cleveland, John E., Guardian Angels, Chaska
Courrier, Darrel O., (Resides outside the Archdiocese)
Curtan, Sean M., Annunciation, Minneapolis
D'Heilly, Peter A., (Retired)
Damiani, Joseph R., St. Agnes, St. Paul
DeLuney, Jon A., St. Bonaventure, Bloomington
DeShane, James F., St. Edward, Bloomington
Devine, Gerald L., (Retired)
Dewitte, Michael R., Corrections Ministry
Dolan, Thomas E., (Retired)
Dols, Bernard R., (Retired)
Downie, Kevin M., St. Pius, Cannon Falls
Dupay, Steven C., (Diocese of St. Cloud) St. Michael, St. Michael; St. Albert, Albertville
Durham, Robert Scott, St. John the Baptist, Savage
Dzik, Thomas W., St. Thomas More, St. Paul
Erpenbach, William L., (Retired)
Evans, Patrick W., St. Joseph, Red Wing
Fidler, Donald F.
Frederick, Joseph J., St. Timothy, Blaine
Freeman, Ronald L., St. Timothy, Maple Lake
Friesen, Michael F., Center for Mission; St. Thomas Becket, Eagan
Gannon, Daniel A., (Diocese of La Crosse) The St. Paul Seminary
Garcia Degollado, Ramon, St. Stephen, Anoka
Glover, Guy R., (Retired)
Gruber, Leonard L., (Retired)
Gunderson, Eric M., Good Shepherd, Golden Valley
Hamilton, Donald L., (Retired)
Hanson, Dennis G., Holy Name of Jesus, Wayzata
Harrer, Timothy R., St. Pius X, White Bear Lake
Heiman, William L., (Leave of Absence)
Heineman, Richard J., St. Bridget, Minneapolis
Helmeke, Timothy D., (Retired)
Hennessey, Timothy H., St. Peter, Mendota
Hirl, Patrick J., St. Hubert, Chanhassen
Hoffman, Gary J., (Retired)
Holst, David W., (Retired)
Houle, Gary J., St. Peter, Forest Lake
Huibregtse, David J., (Retired)
Humbert, Michael A., Guardian Angels, Oakdale
Ingwell, David M.
Janes, Edward R., (Retired)
Jaques, Martin, (Retired), (Resides Outside the Archdiocese)
Jenney, William E., (Retired), (Archdiocese of Dubuque)
Jensen, Kim M., Epiphany, Coon Rapids
Jents, Kevin C., (Retired)
Johanns, Mark D., St. Peter, Richfield
Johnson, Fred L., St. Peter Claver, St. Paul
Kasbohm, Thomas F., (Retired)
Kelly, Robert P., (Retired)
Kenney, Joseph G., (Retired)
Kirchoffner, Daniel D., (Retired)
Kittok, Joseph M., St. Maximilian Kolbe, Delano
Klish, Richard M., (Retired), (Resides Outside the Archdiocese)
Kocemba, Russell A., Nativity of Our Lord, St. Paul
Konkel, Thomas A., St. Joseph, Lino Lakes
Koop, Steven E., St. Rita, Cottage Grove
L'Allier, Ralph M., St. Peter, Forest Lake
Langlois, Thomas P., (Retired)
Lawinger, Lawrence W., Dir. of Diaconate, St. Vincent de Paul, Brooklyn Park
Lee, Joseph C., (Retired)
Little, Gerald G., St. Hubert, Chanhassen
Loving, Peter, (Archdiocese of Galveston-Houston), Assumption, Richfield
Maier, Steven H., Dir. of Parish & Clergy Svcs., St. Francis de Sales; St. Paul
Maltzen, Bruce H., (Diocese of St. Cloud), Epiphany, Coon Rapids
Marschall, James J., All Saints, Lakeville
Martin, Michael Jr., St. Joseph, Taylors Falls; St. Francis Xavier, Franconia
Masla, John A., (Retired), (Diocese of Sacramento)
McDonald, James F., (Retired)
McGee, Newell R., St. Michael, Kenyon
McLaughlin, James E., (Retired)
McPherson, Joseph T., (Retired)
Medley, Michael A., St. Henry, Monticello
Meyer, James V., Holy Family, St. Louis Park
Meyer, Martin G., St. John Neumann, Eagan
Michalak, Joseph T. Jr., Dir. of Institute for Diaconal Formation, Holy Spirit, St. Paul
Michaud, Thomas P. Jr., St. Joseph, West St. Paul
Michaud, Thomas P. Sr., (Retired)
Moore, Richard J., St. Pascal Baylon, St. Paul
Moravec, Terrence D., St. Peter, Forest Lake
Moses, Steven J., St. Dominic, Northfield
Myhre, Jason A., (Diocese of New Ulm) Most Holy Redeemer, Montgomery
Najarian, Stephen M., St. Charles Borromeo, Minneapolis
Nevin, Michael P., St. Thomas the Apostle, Corcoran
Nicklaus, Alan P., All Saints, Lakeville
Nicklay, John R., St. Rita, Cottage Grove
Nistler, James, (Retired)
Nowak, David, (Leave of Absence)
O'Connor, Kevin J., St. Joseph the Worker, Maple Grove
O'Connor, Robert F., (Retired)
Ochiagha, Ifeangi J., (Leave of Absence)
Ortman, Raymond C., St. Victoria, Victoria
Otto, Sherman H., St. John the Baptist, Dayton
Palkert, Lawrence L., Immaculate Conception, Columbia Heights
Palmer, Rodney W., St. John the Baptist, New Brighton
Pashby, Richard E., (Retired)
Pasko, Anthony M., St. Patrick, Edina
Powers, Michael D., Presentation of the Blessed Virgin Mary, Maplewood
Price, James T., (Retired)
Pufahl, James R., Mary, Mother of the Church, Burnsville
Quayle, Thomas M., St. Timothy, Blaine
Rajcich, George M., (Resides Outside the Archdiocese)
Raleigh, Robert T., Our Lady of the Prairie, Belle Plaine
Ramsey, James W., Sacred Heart, Robbinsdale
Ravnikar, Paul M., St. Michael, St. Michael and St. Albert, Albertville
Redfearn, Michael, St. Bonaventure, Bloomington
Reed, John A., (Resides Outside the Archdiocese)
Reinhardt, James W., Holy Family, St. Louis Park
Riordan, William, Dir. of Clergy Personnel, St. Ambrose, Woodbury
Roy, Richard J., St. Michael, Prior Lake
Rubi, Luis E., Our Lady of Guadalupe, St. Paul; St. Matthew. St. Paul; St. Michael, West St. Paul
Rynda, Gerald T., (Diocese of La Crosse)
Saladin, Jeremiah N., Blessed Sacrament, St. Paul
Salchert, John J., (Retired), (Diocese of St. Cloud)
Saumweber, James F., Assumption, St. Paul; St. Odilia, Shoreview
Scherer, Terrance P., (Retired)
Scherkenbach, Gerald A., St. Joseph, West St. Paul
Schmitz, Joseph F., (Retired)
Schmitz, Ronald G., Cathedral of St. Paul
Schneider, Gary F., St. John the Baptist, New Brighton
Schnell, Robert L., St. Richard, Richfield
Schramer, Joseph J., (Retired)
Schroeder, Allan A., (Retired)
Schroeder, Alphonse L., Pax Christi, Eden Prairie
Shallbetter, Clarence J., Ss. Cyril & Methodius, Minneapolis
Shambour, Leonard J., (Retired)
Shearer, John M., Nativity of the Blessed Virgin, Bloomington
Shoberg, Mylo, (Retired), On Leave of Absence
Shupe, Russell D., St. Michael, Farmington
Skuta, Glenn D., St. Rose of Lima, Roseville; Corpus Christi, St. Paul
Smisek, Ronald M., Holy Trinity, South St. Paul
Smith, Joseph P., Mary Queen of Peace, Rogers
Sroder, Gregory A., St. Matthew, St. Paul; Our Lady of Guadalupe, St. Paul; St. Michael, West St. Paul
Stahl, George P., St. Patrick, Oak Grove
Steele, Gregory J., (Diocese of St. Cloud) St. Michael, St. Michael
Stewart, Phillip B., Leo C. Byrne Residence; Cathedral of St. Paul
Stiles, Thomas G., St. Columba, St. Paul
Stromen, Sherman E., (Retired)
Tangney, Francis J., (Retired)
Tatone, Paul M., (Retired)
Thell, Francis J., Corrections Ministry
Thoennes, Michael J., (Resides Outside the Archdiocese)
Thornton, James L., (Retired)
Tienter, Donald D., Nativity of the Lord, St. Paul
Tschann, Paul E., Leave of Absence
Urbanski, Roger G., (Retired)
Valdez, Carl R., Sagrado Corazon de Jesus, & Incarnation, Minneapolis
Vomastek, John E., St. Patrick, Inver Grove Heights
Wagner, James M., (Retired)
Wagner, Robert C., St. Wenceslaus, New Prague
Walchuk, Christopher, (Diocese of Winona-Rochester)
Wallin, John T., St. Joseph the Worker, Maple Grove
Warhol, Robert W., (Retired)
Warne, Maynard E., (Retired)
Waugh, Charles A., St. Stephen, Anoka
Weiland, John D., (Retired)
Wesley, R. Daniel, Corrections Ministry
Wierschem, Joseph G., (Retired)
Wilkinson, Delvin L., Our Lady of the Lake, Mound
Winn, Michael, (Leave of Absence)
Winninger, Thomas J., Our Lady of Lourdes, Minneapolis
Witucki, Richard P., St. Bartholomew, Wayzata
Wright, Scott K., St. John Vianney, South St. Paul
Wurdock, Michael C., St. Alphonsus, Brooklyn Center

Yang, Naokao P., Cathedral of St. Paul

Zinda, Timothy M., St. Paul's, Ham Lake.

INSTITUTIONS LOCATED IN DIOCESE

[A] SEMINARIES, ARCHDIOCESAN

ST. PAUL. *St. John Vianney Seminary*, 2115 Summit Ave., #5024, 55105. Tel: 651-962-6825; Fax: 651-962-6835; Email: sjv@stthomas.edu; Web: www.vianney.net. Revs. Michael C. Becker, Rector & Pres.; Abraham George; Paul Gitter; Andrew M. Jaspers; Jonathan J. Kelly; Joseph H. Kuharski; John Whitlock; Susan Barrett, Seminary Admin.; Mr. John Daniewicz, Dir., Academic Formation; Mary Frame, Admin. Asst.; Dede Leininger, Event Coord.; Tizoc Rosales, Dir., Devel. Priests 7; Students 98; Total Staff 5.

The Saint Paul Seminary (1894) School of Divinity of the University of St. Thomas, 2260 Summit Ave., 55105. Tel: 651-962-5050; Fax: 651-962-5790; Web: www.stthomas.edu/sod. Rev. Msgrs. Aloysius R. Callaghan, S.T.L., J.C.D., Rector & Vice Pres. Emeritus; Steven Rohlfs, Spiritual Dir.; Revs. Scott M. Carl, S.S.L., Vice Rector; John P. Floeder, Dean, Seminarians; John Gallas, Formator & Adj., Theology; Jeffrey H. Huard, Dir., Spiritual Formation; John A. Klockeman, Asst. Dir.., Spiritual Direction & Dir., Archbishop Flynn Catechetical Institute; Allen Kuss, Dir., Pastoral Formation; Thomas Margevicius, S.T.L., Instructor, Liturgical Theology & Homiletics and Dir., Worship; Joseph Taphorn, Rector & Vice Pres.-Elect; Kevin Zilverberg, S.S.L., S.T.B., Prof.; Deacons Daniel Gannon, J.D., Dir., Institute for Ongoing Clergy Formation; Joseph T. Michalak Jr., Dir., Inst. for Diaconate Formation; Sr. Katarina Schuth, O.S.F., Ph.D., Prof.; Mr. Thomas Fisch, Ph.D., Prof.; Mr. John Froula, Ph.D., Prof.; Mr. Stephen A. Hipp, S.T.D., Prof.; Mr. David Jenkins, D.Mus., Dir., Liturgical Music; Mr. N. Curtis LeMay, Dir., Archbishop Ireland Memorial Library; Mr. Paul Ruff, Asst. Dir., Human Formation; Mr. Tom Ryan, Vice Pres., Institutional Advancement; Deborah Savage, Ph. D., Prof.; Mr. William Stevenson, Ph.D., Prof.; Mr. Kenneth D. Synder, Ph.D., Dean; Dr. Christopher Thompson, Ph.D., Prof.; Mr. Christian D. Washburn, Ph.D., Prof.

The Saint Paul Seminary Deacons 3; Priests 10; Seminarians 83; Students 154; Total Staff 30; School of Divinity Lay Students 71; Clergy / Religious Teachers 5.

[B] SEMINARIES, RELIGIOUS, OR SCHOLASTICATES

ST. PAUL. *Jesuit Novitiate*, 1035 Summit Ave., 55105-3034. Tel: 651-224-5593; Fax: 651-224-4734; Email: UMInovitiate@jesuits.org. Revs. Gregory J. Hyde, S.J., Supr.; William M. O'Brien, S.J., Dir.; Lawrence Ober, S.J., Socius; Bro. Ralph Cordero, S.J., Minister-Socius

Legal Title: Jesuit Novitiate of Saint Alberto Hurtado Novices 17; Priests 3; Total Staff 4; Clergy / Religious Teachers 1.

[C] COLLEGES AND UNIVERSITIES

ST. PAUL. *St. Catherine University* (1905) (Grades Associate-Doctorate), 2004 Randolph Ave., 55105. Tel: 651-690-6525; Email: president@stkate.edu; Web: www.stkate.edu. ReBecca Koenig Roloff, M.B.A., Pres.; Lynda Szymanski, Interim Provost; Andrew Melendres, Sr. Vice Pres. Enrollment Mngmt. & Student Affairs; Angela Riley, Vice Pres. Finance & CFO; Beth Halloran, Vice Pres.; Pat Pratt-Cook, Vice Pres.; Tarshia Stanley, Dean, School of Humanities, Arts & Sciences; Michelle Wieser, Interim Dean, School of Business; Lisa Dutton, Interim Dean, Health Sciences; Kim Dinsey-Read, Interim Dean, Nursing; Kate Barrett, OTD, Dir. Myser Initiative on Catholic Identity; Anne Weyandt, J.D., Ed.D., Assoc. Prof. Liberal Arts; Emily Asch, Librarian. Lay Teachers 498; Students 4,859; Total Staff 552; Clergy / Religious Teachers 1.

**University of St. Thomas* (1885) (Grades Associate-Doctorate), 2115 Summit Ave., 55105. Tel: 651-962-5000; Fax: 651-962-6504; Email: gmzitzer@stthomas.edu; Web: www.stthomas.edu. Alvin Abraham, Dean, Dougherty Family College; Kathlene Campbell-Dean, Dean, School of Education; Dr. Corrine Carvahlo, Interim Dean, School of Social Work; Edmund Clark, Vice Pres. IT Services & CIO; Allan Cotrone, Vice Pres. Enrollment Mgmnt.; Rev. Dennis J. Dease, Pres. Emeritus; Stephen Fritz, Athletics Dir.; Sara E. Goss Methner, Gen. Counsel; Ms. Karen Lange, Vice Pres. Student Affairs; Dr. Stefanie A. Lenway, Dean, Opus College of Business; Kymm (Pollack) Martinez, Chief Mktg. Officer; Amy McDonough, Chief of Staff; Richard G. Plumb, Exec. Vice Pres. & Provost.; Rob Riley, Vice Provost, Academic Affairs; Ken Snyder, Interim Academic Dean, The Saint Paul Seminary School of Divinity; Rev. Larry Snyder, Vice Pres. Mission; Dr. Julie H. Sullivan, Pres.; Rev. Joseph Taphorn, Vice Pres. & Rector, The Saint Paul Seminary School of Divinity; Michelle Thom, Assoc. Vice Pres. HR; Erik J. Thurman, Vice Pres. Devel. & Alumni Rels.; Artika Tyner, Asst. Vice Pres. Diversity for Business Affairs & Inclusion; Mark Vangsgard, Vice Pres. Business Affairs & CFO; Robert K. Vischer, Dean, School of Law; Dr. Donald Weinkauf, Dean, School of Engineering; Yohuru Williams, Dean, College of Arts & Sciences. Priests 36; Sisters 2; Students 10,035; Total Faculty & Staff 1,909.

MINNEAPOLIS. **University of St. Thomas*, 1000 La Salle Ave., Minneapolis, 55403. Tel: 651-962-5000.

[D] HIGH SCHOOLS, ARCHDIOCESAN

MENDOTA HEIGHTS. *Saint Thomas Academy*, (Grades 7-12), 949 Mendota Heights Rd., Mendota Heights, 55120-1496. Tel: 651-454-4570; Fax: 651-454-4574; Web: www.cadets.com. Matthew Mohs, Prin. Lay Teachers 51; Students 607.

[E] HIGH SCHOOLS, PRIVATE

ST. PAUL. *Cretin-Derham Hall*, 550 S. Albert St., 55116. Tel: 651-690-2443; Fax: 651-696-3394; Email: rjohnson@c-dh.org; Web: www.cretinderhamhall.org. Mona Passman, Prin. Lay Teachers 92; Students 1,028.

MINNEAPOLIS. *Cristo Rey Jesuit High School*, 2924 4th Ave. S., Minneapolis, 55408. Tel: 612-545-9700; Email: accounting@cristoreytc.org; Web: www.cristoreytc.org. Erin Healy, Prin. Lay Teachers 29; Students 503.

DeLaSalle High School, One DeLaSalle Dr., Minneapolis, 55401. Tel: 612-676-7600; Fax: 612-676-7691; Email: principal@delasalle.com; Web: www.delasalle.com. James Benson, Prin. Lay Teachers 52; Students 750.

Totino-Grace High School, 1350 Gardena Ave., N.E., Fridley, 55432-5899. Tel: 763-571-9116; Fax: 763-571-9118; Email: cheri.broadhead@totinograce.org; Web: www.totinograce.org. Cheri Broadhead, Prin. Lay Teachers 59; Students 697.

EDINA. **Chesterton Academy*, 5300 France Ave. S., Edina, 55410. Tel: 952-378-1779; Fax: 952-406-8739; Email: info@chestertonacademy.org; Web: www.chestertonacademy.org. David Beskar, Headmaster. Lay Teachers 18; Students 168.

FARIBAULT. *Bethlehem Academy*, (Grades 6-12), 105 Third Ave. S.W., Faribault, 55021. Tel: 507-334-3948; Fax: 507-334-3949; Email: cardinals@bacards.org; Web: www.bacards.org. Charles Briscoe, Prin. Lay Teachers 20; Students 276.

MAPLEWOOD. *Hill-Murray School*, (Grades 6-12), 2625 Larpenteur Ave. E., Maplewood, 55109-5098. Tel: 651-777-1376; Fax: 651-748-2444; Email: eherman@hill-murray.org; Web: www.hill-murray.org. Erin Herman, Prin. Lay Teachers 67; Students 851.

MENDOTA HEIGHTS. *Convent of the Visitation School* (1873) (Grades PreK-12), 2455 Visitation Dr., Mendota Heights, 55120. Tel: 651-683-1700; Fax: 651-454-7144; Email: info@vischool.org; Web: www.visitation.net. Rene Gavic, Head of School. Grades PreK-6 are co-ed. Day school for girls grades 7-12. Lay Teachers 67; Students 581.

RICHFIELD. *Academy of Holy Angels*, 6600 Nicollet Ave. S., Richfield, 55423-2462. Tel: 612-798-2600; Fax: 612-798-2610; Email: hfoley@ahastars.org; Web: www.academyofholyangels.org. Heidi Foley, Prin. Lay Teachers 52; Students 650.

ST. LOUIS PARK. *Benilde-St. Margaret's School* (1907) (Grades 7-12), 2501 Hwy. 100 S., St. Louis Park, 55416. Tel: 952-927-4176; Fax: 952-920-8889; Email: sskinner@bsmschool.org; Web: www.bsmschool.org. Dr. Susan Skinner, Prin. Lay Teachers 97; Students 1,166.

VICTORIA. *Holy Family Catholic High School* (2000) 8101 Kochia Ln., Victoria, 55386. Tel: 952-443-4659; Fax: 952-443-1822; Email: communications@hfchs.org; Web: www.hfchs.org. Kathleen Brown, Prin. Lay Teachers 29; Students 400.

[F] ELEMENTARY SCHOOLS, CONSOLIDATED, PAROCHIAL

ST. PAUL. *Highland Catholic School*, (Grades PreK-8), 2017 Bohland Ave., 55116. Tel: 651-690-2477; Fax: 651-699-1869; Email: j.schmidt@highlandcatholic.org; Web: www.highlandcatholic.org. Jane Schmidt, Ed.S., Prin. Serving the parishes of Lumen Christi Catholic Community. Lay Teachers 31; Students 505.

MINNEAPOLIS. *Carondelet Catholic School*, (Grades PreK-8), Main Office: 3210 W. 51st St., Minneapolis, 55410. Tel: 612-927-8673; Fax: 612-927-7426; Email: skerr@carondelet-mpls.org; Web: www.carondeletcatholicschool.com. Rev. Michael A. Reding, Admin.; Sue Kerr, Prin. Lay Teachers 32; Students 394.

St. John Paul II Catholic Preparatory School, (Grades K-8), 1630 Fourth St., N.E., Minneapolis, 55413. Tel: 612-789-8851; Fax: 612-789-8773; Email: office@johnpaulprep.org; Web: johnpaulprep.org. Rev. Kevin Finnegan, Admin.; Mrs. Tricia Menzhuber, Prin. Serving the parishes of St. Cyril, Holy Cross, All Saints, Our Lady of Lourdes, St. Boniface, Our Lady of Mt. Carmel and St. Lawrence. Lay Teachers 11; Students 124.

Risen Christ Catholic School (1993) (Grades K-8), 1120 E. 37th St., Minneapolis, 55407. Tel: 612-822-5329; Fax: 612-729-2336; Email: info@risenchristschool.org; Web: risenchristschool.org. Rev. Joseph P. Gillespie, O.P., Admin.; Kathy Yates, Prin. Founded by the parishes of Holy Name, Holy Rosary, Incarnation, St. Albert the Great and St. Stephen. Lay Teachers 23; Students 339.

EAGAN. *Faithful Shepherd Catholic School*, (Grades PreK-8), 3355 Columbia Dr., Eagan, 55121. Tel: 651-406-4747; Fax: 651-406-4743; Email: schooloffice@fscsmn.org; Web: www.fscsmn.org. Rev. Steven B. Hoffman, Admin.; Ms. Sheila Hendricks, Prin. Serving the parishes of St. Peter, St. John Neumann and St. Thomas Becket. Lay Teachers 29; Total Enrollment 459.

MAPLE GROVE. **Ave Maria Academy*, (Grades PreK-8), 7000 Jewel Ln. N., Maple Grove, 55311. Tel: 763-494-5387; Email: info@avemariaacademy.org. Mrs. Katie Danielson, Prin. Lay Teachers 16; Students 194.

MINNETONKA. *Notre Dame Academy*, (Grades PreK-8), 13505 Excelsior Blvd., Minnetonka, 55345. Tel: 952-358-3500; Fax: 952-935-2031; Email: info@nda-mn.org; Web: www.nda-mn.org. Ginger Vance, Prin.; Rev. James C. Liekhus, Canonical Admin. Lay Teachers 16; Students 225.

RICHFIELD. *Blessed Trinity Catholic School of Richfield, Minnesota* (1994) (Grades PreK-8), 6720 Nicollet Ave. S, Richfield, 55423. Tel: 612-869-5200 ; Fax: 612-767-2191; Email: school@btcsmn.org; Email: principal@btcsmn.org; Web: www.btcsmn.org. Rev. Michael Kueber, Admin.; Patrick O'Keefe, Prin. Serving the parishes of Assumption, St. Peter's and St. Richard's. Lay Teachers 16; Students 235.

STILLWATER. *St. Croix Catholic School*, (Grades PreK-8), 621 S. Third St., Stillwater, 55082. Tel: 651-439-5581; Fax: 651-439-8360; Email: srmaryjuliana@stccs.org; Web: www.stcroixcatholic.org. Rev. Michael J. Izen, Admin.; Sr. Mary Aquinas Halbmaier, Prin. Serving the parishes of St. Charles, Bayport; St. Mary, Stillwater; St. Michael, Stillwater. Lay Teachers 25; Students 304.

WEBSTER. *Holy Cross Catholic School*, (Grades PreK-8), 6100 37th St. W., Webster, 55088. Tel: 952-652-6100; Fax: 952-652-6102; Email: info@holycrossschool.net; Web: www.holycrossschool.net. Rev. Patrick Thomas Barnes, Admin.; Dr. Constance Krocak, Ed.D., Prin. Serving the parishes of Lonsdale, New Market & Veseli. Lay Teachers 11; Students 103.

WEST ST. PAUL. *Community of Saints Regional Catholic School*, (Grades PreK-8), 335 Hurley St. E., West St. Paul, 55118. Tel: 651-457-2510; Fax: 651-457-5049; Email: bkramer@communityofsaints.org; Web: www.communityofsaints.org. Rev. Steve Adrian, Admin.; Bridget Kramer, Prin. Serving the parishes of St. Michael, West St. Paul; Saint Matthew, St. Paul; Saint John Vianney, South St. Paul and Our Lady of Guadalupe, St. Paul. Lay Teachers 14; Students 219.

**Elizabeth Ann Seton Montessori School* Merged with St. Agnes School's Pre-K Program. 140 Thompson Ave. E., #160, West St. Paul, 55118.

WHITE BEAR LAKE. *Frassati Catholic Academy*, (Grades PreK-8), 4690 Bald Eagle Ave., White Bear Lake, 55110. Tel: 651-429-7771; Fax: 651-429-9539; Email: pgallivan@frassatiwbl.org; Web: www.frassatiwbl.org. Patrick Gallivan, Prin. Lay Teachers 16; Students 260.

[G] GENERAL HOSPITALS

ST. PAUL. **HealthEast St. Joseph's Hospital* (1853) 45 W. 10th St., 55102. Tel: 651-232-3000; Email: tgnelson@healtheast.org. Deb Rodahl, Vice Pres. St Joseph's Opers.; Revs. Tim Nelson, Vice Pres. Spiritual Well Being; Brian K. Gutzmann, M.Div., A.P.C.-B.C.C., Dir. Spiritual Care. Bed Capacity:

Licensed 401; Staffed 230 425; Priests 2; Tot Asst. Annually 12,000; Total Staff 1,600; Total Assisted 17,000.

St. Mary's Health Clinics (1992) 1884 Randolph Ave., 55105-1700. Tel: 651-287-7700; Fax: 651-690-7014; Email: info@stmarysclinics.org; Web: www.stmaryshealthclinics.org. Sue Gehlsen, Interim Exec. Dir. Sisters 1; Total Staff 19; Neighborhood Clinics 7; Patients Visits Annually 4,447; Volunteers 225.

HASTINGS. *Regina Hospital* Regina Hospital, part of Allina Heath. 1175 Nininger Rd., Hastings, 55033. Tel: 651-404-1000; Fax: 651-404-1460; Email: pamela.kochendorfer@allina.com; Web: www.allinahealth.org/Regina-Hospital/. Tom Thompson, Pres.; Deacon Michael A. Humbert, Spiritual Care; Joanne Peters, Contact Person. Bed Capacity 57; Tot Asst. Annually 53,831; Total Staff 374.

SHAKOPEE. *St. Francis Regional Medical Center* (1938) 1455 St. Francis Ave., Shakopee, 55379-3380. Tel: 952-428-3000; Tel: 952-428-2401; Fax: 952-428-3820; Email: kathy.tyler@allina.com; Web: www.stfrancis-shakopee.com. Dr. Monte Johnson, Interim Pres.; Kyle Vlach, Chap. Sponsored by Sisters of St. Benedict, Duluth, MN. Bed Capacity 93; Nurses 304; Tot Asst. Annually 143,950; Total Staff 906.

[H] HOMES FOR AGED

ST. PAUL. *Holy Family Residence*, 330 Exchange St. S., 55102. Tel: 651-227-0336; Fax: 651-227-7321; Email: msstpaul@littlesistersofthepoor.org; Web: www.littlesistersofthepoor.org. Sisters Maria Francis Pale, Supr. & Pres.; Mary Elizabeth Anderson, Vice Pres. & Admin.; Mrs. Amber Decheine, Business Mgr.; Sr. Michael Anthony Hargan, Trustee; Jeanie Greene, Contact Person. Aged Residents 73; Bed Capacity 73; Little Sisters of the Poor 9; Tot Asst. Annually 118; Apartments 32; Total Staff (All Facilities) 130.

**Our Lady of Peace* (1936) 2076 St. Anthony Ave., 55104. Tel: 651-789-5031; Fax: 651-789-0690; Email: joes@ourladyofpeacemn.org; Web: www.ourladyofpeacemn.org. Joseph Stanislav, Pres. & CEO. Tot Asst. Annually 490; Total Staff 90.

MINNEAPOLIS. *Benedictine Health Center of Minneapolis*, 618 E. 17th St, Minneapolis, 55404. Tel: 612-879-2800; Email: steve.jobe@bhshealth.org. Steve Jobe, Admin. Bed Capacity 95; Tot Asst. Annually 350; Total Staff 180.

DEEPHAVEN. *St. Therese of Deephaven Senior Living* dba Deephaven Woods Senior Living, 18025 Minnetonka Blvd., Deephaven, 55391. Tel: 952-288-2187; Fax: 952-746-8578; Email: lbird2@fairview.org. Rev. Leonard Andrie, Contact Person. Bed Capacity 78; Tot Asst. Annually 87; Total Staff 50.

HASTINGS. *Regina Senior Living* dba Regina Care Center & Regina Assisted Living, 1175 Nininger Rd., Hastings, 55033. Tel: 651-480-4333; Fax: 651-404-1286; Email: shelley.solberg@bhshealth.org; Web: www.reginaseniorliving.org. Shelley Solberg, Admin.; Donna Loomis, Contact Person. Bed Capacity 131; Total Staff 101.

RED WING. *Benedictine Living Center of Red Wing* dba Saint Crispin Living Community, 135-213 Pioneer Rd., Red Wing, 55006. Tel: 651-388-1234; Email: jake.goering@bhshealth.org. Jake Goering, Admin. & CEO. Bed Capacity 119; Tot Asst. Annually 59,445; Total Staff 196.

SHAKOPEE. *St. Gertrude's Health and Rehabilitation Center*, 1850 Sarazin St., Shakopee, 55379. Tel: 952-233-4400; Fax: 952-233-4476; Email: rick.meyer@bhshealth.org; Web: www.stgertrudesshakopee.org. Dick Mulerone, Chm.; Rick Meyer, CEO; Kevin Rymanowski, Treas. Bed Capacity 105; Total Staff 313; Total Resident Days Annually 36,384.

The Gardens at St. Gertrudes Assisted Living.

[I] MONASTERIES AND RESIDENCES OF PRIESTS AND BROTHERS

ST. PAUL. *Congregation of the Sons of the Immaculate Conception*, 261 8th St. E., 55101. Tel: 651-222-2619; Fax: 651-224-1190; Email: antonyts@live.in. Revs. Benny Mekkatt Varghese, C.F.I.C., Supr., North American Delegation; Antony Skaria, C.F.I.C., Supr.; Jimmy Puttananickal, C.F.I.C.

Sacred Heart Rectory, 840 6th St. E., 55106-4543. Tel: 651-776-2741; Fax: 651-776-2759; Email: leoh.sacredheart@gmail.com; Email: timothy_norris@hotmail.com. Rev. Timothy L. Norris.

MINNEAPOLIS. *St. Albert the Great Priory*, 2833 32nd Ave. S., Minneapolis, 55406. Tel: 612-724-3644; Email: j.gillespie@saintalbertthegreat.org. Revs. James A. Spahn, O.P.; Vincent Davila, O.P., Cyndic; Cornelius A. Kilroy, O.P.; Joseph P. Gillespie, O.P.; Patrick Tobin, O.P., Ph.D.; Scott Steinkerchner, O.P.; Paul J. Johnson, O.P.; Herbert C. Hayek, O.P.; James-Peter Trares, O.P.; Gerald Stookey, O.P., Prior; Robert M. Kelly, O.P., Lector. Order of Preachers (Dominicans). Province of St. Albert the Great. Total in Residence 11.

Markoe House Jesuit Community, 2900 11th Ave. S., #1015-1019, Minneapolis, 55407. Tel: 414-698-6949; Email: markoe.jesuits@yahoo.com. Revs. Richard J. Fichtinger, S.J.,; David Haschka, S.J.; Matthew L. Linn, S.J.; John M. Paul, S.J.; Paul Lickteig, S.J.; Warren Sazama, S.J.; Bro. Aaron A. Bohr I, S.J., Youth Min. *Pro Ecclesia Sancta Residence. SEMV Residence.*

BLOOMINGTON. *St. Bonaventure Friary*, 901 E. 90th St., Bloomington, 55420. Tel: 952-854-4731; Email: richardk@saintbonaventure.org. Revs. Edmund Goldbach, O.F.M.Conv.; Camillus Gott, O.F.M.-Conv.; Richard Kaley, O.F.M.Conv.; Matthew Malek, O.F.M.Conv.; Bro. Jeffrey Hines, O.F.M.-Conv.

BROOKLYN CENTER. *Redemptorist Fathers of Hennepin County*, 7025 Halifax Ave. N., Brooklyn Center, 55429-1394. Tel: 763-561-5100; Fax: 763-561-0336; Email: parishoffice@mystals.org; Web: www.redemptoristsdenver.org. Revs. Matthew Bonk, C.Ss.R., Missionary; Tony Judge, C.Ss.R., Parochial Vicar; Patrick Keyes, C.Ss.R., Rector; Thanh Nguyen, C.Ss.R., Assoc. Pastor; Tuan Pham, C.Ss.R., Missionary; Thomas Santa, C.Ss.R., MIssionary; Donald Willard, C.Ss.R., Pastor; Bro. Bruce Davidson, C.Ss.R., Missionary; Rev. Aaron Meszaros, C.Ss.R., Assoc. Pastor.

LAKE ELMO. CARMELITE HERMITAGE OF THE BLESSED VIRGIN MARY (1987) 8249 DeMontreville Tr. N., Lake Elmo, 55042-9545. Tel: 651-779-7351; Fax: 651-779-7351; Email: carmelbvm@gmail.com; Web: www.carmelitehermitage.org. Revs. Elijah Schwab, O.Carm., Admin.; John M. Burns, O.-Carm., Prior; Patrick Peter Peach, O.Carm., Librarian. Carmel of the Blessed Virgin Mary. Brothers 4; Priests 3.

PRIOR LAKE. *St. Joseph Cupertino Friary*, 16385 St. Francis Ln., Prior Lake, 55372. Tel: 952-447-2182; Email: director@franciscanretreats.net; Web: www.franciscanretreats.net. Bro. Bob Roddy, O.F.-M.Conv., Vicar; Revs. James Van Dorn, O.F.M.-Conv., Guardian; Steven J. McMichael, O.F.M.Conv.; Xavier Goulet, O.F.M.Conv.

[J] CONVENTS AND RESIDENCES FOR SISTERS

ST. PAUL. *Franciscan Sisters of St. Paul* (1863) 225 Frank St., 55106. Tel: 651-495-1922; Email: jreetz@csjstpaul.org. 1884 Randolph Ave., 55105. Sr. Mary Lucy Scheffler, O.S.F., Supr. Sisters 5.

St. Mary's Mission House (1894) 265 Century Ave., 55125. Tel: 651-738-9704; Email: sspcdelegateoffice@usfamily.net; Web: www.clavermissionarysisters.org. Sr. Genevieve Kudlik, S.S.P.C., Supr. Missionary Sisters of St. Peter Claver. Sisters 15.

Monastery of the Visitation (1873) 2455 Visitation Dr., Mendota Heights, 55120. Tel: 651-683-1700; Fax: 651-454-7144; Email: denvil@vischool.org. Sisters Mary Denise Villaume, V.H.M., Supr.; Brigid Marie Keefe, Sec. Visitation Nuns 3.

St. Paul's Monastery, 2675 Benet Rd., 55109-4808. Tel: 651-777-8181; Fax: 651-773-5124; Email: srpaula@stpaulsmonastery.org; Web: www.osb.org/spm. Sisters Paula Hagen, O.S.B., Prioress; Mary Lou Dummer, O.S.B., Sub Prioress. Benedictine Sisters of Pontifical Jurisdiction. Sisters 34.

Sisters of St. Joseph of Carondelet (1851) 1884 Randolph Ave., 55105-1700. Tel: 651-690-7000; Fax: 651-690-7039; Email: nfyksen@csjstpaul.org; Web: www.csjstpaul.org. Sisters Susan Hames, C.S.J., Prov. Leadership Team; Suzanne Herder, C.S.J., Prov. Leadership Team; Catherine Steffens, C.S.J., Prov. Leadership Team. Ministry in the fields of Education; Health; Social Services; Spirituality. Sisters of Province 161; Total Staff 83.

Province Leadership Team: Sisters Katherine Rossini, C.S.J.; Margaret Gillespie, C.S.J.; Jean Wincek, C.S.J. Carondelet Center; St. Joseph School of Music; Editorial Development Associates; Good Ground Press; St. Mary's Health Clinics; Youth & Family Center, Inc.; Sisters of St. Joseph of Carondelet Ministries Foundation, St. Paul Province; Learning in Style; St. Catherine University; Minnesota Center for Health Care Ethics; Wisdom Ways: A Resource Center for Spirituality; St. Joseph Worker Program; Sarah's, an Oasis for Women; Celeste's Dream.

MINNEAPOLIS. *Visitation Monastery of Minneapolis*, 1527 Fremont Ave. N., Minneapolis, 55411. Tel: 612-521-6113; Email: vmonastery@aol.com; Web: www.visitationmonasteryminneapolis.org. Sr. Karen Mohan, V.H.M., Supr. Sisters 8.

DEEPHAVEN. *Franciscan Clarist Congregation, F.C.C.*, Vimala Province, Convent of St. Therese House, 17931 Minnetonka Blvd., Deephaven, 55391-3322. Tel: 952-473-4771; Email: tresamargret37@gmail.com. Sr. Tresa Margret, Regl. Supr. Sisters 15; Total in Residence 15.

LAKE ELMO. *Carmel of Our Lady of Divine Providence* (1952) 8251 De Montreville Tr. N., Lake Elmo, 55042-9547. Tel: 651-777-3882; Email: carmelbvm@gmail.com. Mother Marie-Ange of the Eucharistic Heart, Prioress; Rev. John M. Burns, O.Carm., Chap. Discalced Carmelite Nuns. Novices 3; Professed 11; Sisters 13.

[K] SECULAR INSTITUTES

ST. PAUL. *Missionaries of the Kingship of Christ*, 8951 Thomas Ln., Woodbury, 55125. Tel: 651-501-3640; Email: woodburyjane@aol.com; Web: www.simrc.org. Susan Larkin, Pres. Secular Institute of Pontifical Right for women and men founded in Italy in 1919.

[L] RETREAT HOUSES AND CENTERS OF SPIRITUALITY

ST. PAUL. *Benedictine Center - St. Paul's Monastery*, 2675 Benet Rd., 55109. Tel: 651-777-7251; Fax: 651-773-5124; Email: info@benedictinecenter.org; Web: www.benedictinecenter.org. Sam Rahberg, Dir. Total Staff 4.

Maryhill (1790) 1800 Graham Ave. #309, 55116. Tel: 651-696-2970; Email: societydhm@gmail.com; Web: www.dhmna.org. Marilyn Smith, Contact Person. Sponsored by Society of the Daughters of the Heart of Mary. Daughters of the Heart of Mary 2; Total in Residence 1.

BUFFALO. *Christ the King Retreat Center* (1952) 621 First Ave. S., Buffalo, 55313. Tel: 763-682-1394; Fax: 763-682-3453; Email: christtheking@kingshouse.com; Web: www.kingshouse.com. Revs. James Deegan, O.M.I., Dir.; Raymond R. Kirtz, O.M.I.; Lon Konold, O.M.I.; Robert Morin, O.M.I.; Richard Sudlik, O.M.I.; Aloysius Svobodny, O.M.I.; Bro. Daniel Bozek, O.M.I. Brothers 1; Priests 7; Total in Residence 6; Total Staff 38.

LAKE ELMO. *Jesuit Retreat House* (1948) 8243 Demontreville Tr. N., Lake Elmo, 55042-9545. Tel: 651-777-1311; Fax: 651-777-1312; Email: demontreville@aol.com. Rev. Patrick M. McCorkell, S.J., Dir. Total in Residence 1; Total Staff 10.

MARINE ON ST. CROIX. *Christian Brothers Retreat Center*, 15525 St. Croix Tr. N., Marine on St. Croix, 55047. Tel: 651-433-2486; Fax: 651-433-5755; Email: dunrovin@dunrovin.org; Web: www.dunrovin.org. Jerome Meeds, Pres. Bed Capacity 65; Total in Residence 9; Total Staff 22; Total Assisted 4,000.

PRIOR LAKE. *Franciscan Retreats and Spirituality Center* (1956) 16385 Saint Francis Ln., Prior Lake, 55372. Tel: 952-447-2182; Email: director@franciscanretreats.net; Web: www.franciscanretreats.net. Revs. Steven J. McMichael, O.F.M.Conv.; James Van Dorn, O.F.M.Conv., Assoc. Dir. & Guardian; Bro. Bob Roddy, O.F.M.-Conv., Retreat Dir.; Rev. Xavier Goulet, O.F.M.-Conv. Brothers 1; Priests 3; People Served 1,700; Staff 9.

[M] HOMES FOR DISABLED

ST. PAUL. *Our House of Minnesota, Inc. I* (1975) 1846 Dayton Ave., 55104. Tel: 651-644-6650. Bed Capacity 6; Tot Asst. Annually 6; Total Staff 22.

Office:Tel: 615-646-1104; Fax: 615-646-1104. Dennis Holman, Admin.

Our House of Minnesota, Inc. II (1975) 1846 Portland, 55104. Tel: 651-644-2411. Bed Capacity 6; Tot Asst. Annually 6; Staff 22.

Office:Tel: 615-646-1104; Fax: 615-646-1104. Dennis Holman, Admin.

[N] ASSOCIATIONS OF THE FAITHFUL

ST. PAUL. THE COMPANIONS OF CHRIST (1992) 2137 Marshall Ave., 55104. Tel: 651-642-5933; Email: frtonyoneill@gmail.com; Web: www.CompanionsOfChrist.org. Rev. Anthony O'Neill, Mod. Total Membership 29.

FRANCISCAN BROTHERS OF PEACE, Queen of Peace Friary, 1289 Lafond Ave., 55104-2035. Tel: 651-646-8586; Fax: 651-646-9083; Email: franciscan@brothersofpeace.org; Web: www.brothersofpeace.org. Bros. Dominic Michael Hart, F.B.P.; John Mary Kaspari, F.B.P.; Joseph Katzmarek, F.B.P.; Pio King, F.B.P.; Paschal Listi, F.B.P.; Antonio Pagba, F.B.P.; Conrad Richardson, F.B.P., Community Servant; James Voeller, F.B.P.; Seraphim Wirth, F.B.P., Vicar. Novices 2; Postulants 1; Total in Residence 12; Total Staff 1.

WEST ST. PAUL. COMMUNITY OF CHRIST THE REDEEMER, 110 Crusader Ave. W., West St. Paul, 55118. Tel: 651-451-6123; Fax: 651-451-6145; Email: info@ccredeemer.org; Web: www.ccredeemer.org. Mr. Gordon C. DeMarais, Pres.

[O] CAMPS AND COMMUNITY CENTERS

MCGREGOR. *Catholic Youth Camps, Inc.*, Administrative Offices: 2233 Hamline Ave., Ste. B1, Roseville, 55113. Tel: 651-636-1645; Email: office@cycamp.org; Web: www.cycamp.org. Camp location: 19590 520th Ln., McGregor, 55760. Natalie King, Exec. Dir. Students 18; Total Staff 20; Total Assisted 650.

[P] NEWMAN CENTERS

MINNEAPOLIS. *Newman Center at St. Lawrence*, 1203 5th St., S.E., Minneapolis, 55414.
Tel: 612-331-7941; Email: info@umncatholic.org; Web: www.umncatholic.org. Rev. Jon Vander Ploeg, Dir. Total Staff 3.

[Q] MISCELLANEOUS LISTINGS

ST. PAUL. *Francophone African Chaplaincy*, 629 2nd St., N.E., Minneapolis, 55413. Tel: 763-269-0017; Email: joomalanga05@gmail.com. 777 Forest St., 55106.

Growing in Faith Capital Campaign, 777 Forest St., 55106. Tel: 651-291-4405; Email: thuentec@archspm.org. Mr. Joseph Kueppers, Chancellor.

Minnesota Conference of Catholic Bishops, 475 University Ave. W., 55103. Tel: 651-227-8777;
Fax: 651-227-2675; Email: info@mncatholic.org; Web: www.mncatholic.org. Jason A. Adkins Esq., Exec. Dir. M.C.C.B. is a Minnesota Corporation, the purpose of which is to promote the general welfare of the people of the State of Minnesota. All Catholic Bishops of the State of Minnesota constitute Ex Officio the Board of Directors. Total Staff 7.

Nativity of Our Lord Endowment Fund, 1900 Wellesley Ave., 55105. Tel: 651-696-5401;
Fax: 651-696-5458; Email: info@nativity-mn.org; Web: www.nativity-mn.org. Laura Barr, Admin. Total Assisted 5,000.

Sisters of St. Joseph of Carondelet Ministries Foundation, St. Paul Province, 1884 Randolph Ave., 55105. Tel: 651-690-7026; Fax: 651-690-7039; Email: rscorpio@csjministriesfoundation.org; Web: www.csjministriesfoundation.org. Ralph Scorpio, Exec. Dir.

MINNEAPOLIS. *Catholic Charities of Saint Paul & Minneapolis*, 1200 2nd Ave. S., Minneapolis, 55403. Tel: 612-204-8500; Email: tim.marx@cctwincities.org; Web: www.cctwincities.org. Tim Marx, CEO. Tot Asst. Annually 20,000; Total Staff 642.

Catholic Eldercare, Inc. (1982) 817 Main St., N.E., Minneapolis, 55413. Tel: 612-379-1370;
Fax: 612-362-2486; Email: info@catholiceldercare.org; Web: www.catholiceldercare.org. Dan Johnson, Pres. & CEO. Total Staff 350; Total Assisted 439.

Skilled Nursing Facility, Tel: 612-379-1370;
Fax: 612-379-2486; Web: www.catholiceldercare.org. Bed Capacity 150; Lay Staff 272; Total Staff 272; Total Assisted 150.

MainStreet Lodge Assisted Living, 909 Main St., N.E., Minneapolis, 55413. Tel: 612-362-2450;
Fax: 612-362-2449; Web: www.catholiceldercare.org. Lay Staff 19; Total Staff 19; Units 51; Total Assisted 54.

Catholic Eldercare By Day, Tel: 612-362-2405;
Fax: 612-362-2401; Web: www.catholiceldercare.org. Lay Staff 8; Assisted 39; Staff 11.

Rivervillage East Assisted Living, 2919 Randolph St. N.E., Minneapolis, 55418. Tel: 612-605-2500;
Fax: 612-605-2404; Web: www.catholiceldercare.org. Lay Staff 39; Total Staff 39; Units 70; Total Assisted 72.

**Catholic Eldercare Community Foundation, Inc.*, 817 Main St., N.E., Minneapolis, 55413.
Tel: 612-379-1370; Email: info@catholiceldercare.org; Web: www.catholiceldercare.org. Dan Johnson, Pres.

Catholic Single Adults Club of the Twin Cities (1958) P.O. Box 581321, Minneapolis, 55458-1321.
Tel: 651-368-5003; Email: drcpb@earthlink.net. Carl Berstrom, Chairperson, Leadership Com. Members 40.

Cristo Rey Corporate Work Study Program - Twin Cities, 2924 - 4th Ave. S., Minneapolis, 55408.
Tel: 612-545-9700; Email: kesiahkolbow@cristoreytc.org. Jeb Myers, Pres.; Kesiah Kolbow, Dir.

The Islander Foundation, 1 De La Salle Dr., Minneapolis, 55401. Tel: 612-867-6887; Email: nicholas@islanderfoundation.org. Douge M. Schildgen, Coord.; Nicholas Grue, Coord.; Mary McLaren, Sec. Staff 1.

Queen Anne Communities, 2627 Queen Ave. N., Minneapolis, 55411. Tel: 612-529-0503;
Fax: 612-529-5860; Email: sasjhparish@gmail.com. Rev. Louis Pham Ha.

Sagrado Corazon de Jesus, 3817 Pleasant Ave., Minneapolis, 55409. Tel: 612-874-7169;
Fax: 612-822-7928; Email: sagradocorazonl@msn.com. Rev. Kevin M. McDonough, Pres.; Bradley Capouch, Vice Pres.; Deacon Carl Valdez, Sec.; Victor Guillen, Treas.

Youth and Family Center Inc. (1986) 4405 E. Lake St., Minneapolis, 55406. Tel: 612-722-9612; Email: youthandfamilycenter@gmail.com. Sisters Martha Merriman, C.S.J., Dir.; Betty Wurm, C.S.J., Dir. Counseling Center. Total Staff 2; Clergy / Religious Teachers 2; Total Assisted 22.

APPLE VALLEY. *Twin Cities Cursillo*, 15797 Highview Dr., Apple Valley, 55124. Tel: 952-891-1029; Email: patcroke@aol.com. Patrick J. Croke, Treas.

BLAINE. **The Way of the Shepherd*, (Grades PreK-8), 13200 Central Ave., N.E., Blaine, 55434.
Tel: 763-862-9110; Fax: 763-390-2675; Email: administrator@wayoftheshepherd.org; Web: www.wayoftheshepherd.org. Fran Erling, Contact Person. Lay Teachers 8; Students 111.

EAGAN. **The Laboure Society, Inc.*, 1365 Corporate Center Curve, Ste. 104, Eagan, 55121.
Tel: 651-452-1160; Fax: 651-964-3273; Email: info@labouresociety.org. John Flanagan, Exec. Dir.

HASTINGS. *Regina Foundation*, 1175 Nininger Rd., Hastings, 55033. Tel: 651-404-1104;
Tel: 651-404-1454; Fax: 651-404-1275; Email: brandi.poellinger@allina.com; Web: www.allinahealth.org/Regina-Hospital/Foundation. Cindy Hoffmann, Chm.; Joe Harris, Vice Chm.; Ken LaCroix, Sec./Treas.; Joanne Peters, Admin. Asst.

Regina Healthcare, Inc., 1175 Nininger Rd., Hastings, 55033. Tel: 651-404-1451;
Fax: 651-404-1460; Email: pamela.kochendorfer@allina.com. Lynn Moratzka, Chair; Leon Endres, Treas.

INVER GROVE HEIGHTS. *Catholic Finance Corporation* (2000) 5826 Blackshire Path, Inver Grove Heights, 55076. Tel: 651-389-1070; Fax: 651-389-1071; Email: info@catholicfinance.org; Web: www.catholicfinance.org. Alan J. Erickson, Mng. Dir.; Amanda Braith, Mgr. Office Opers.

MAPLEWOOD. *The Hill-Murray Foundation*, 2625 Larpenteur Ave. E., Maplewood, 55109.
Tel: 651-777-1376; Fax: 651-748-2444; Email: jhansen@hill-murray.org. Mr. James Hansen, Pres.

Maple Tree Monastery Childcare Center, 2625 Benet Rd., Maplewood, 55109. Tel: 651-770-0766;
Fax: 651-777-2408; Email: jschlauch2@aol.com; Email: mapletreeccc@gmail.com. Sisters Paula Hagen, O.S.B., Prioress - St. Paul Monastery; Catherine Nehotte, Bd. Pres.; Jennie Schlauch, Prin. Lay Staff 29; Students 70; Total Staff 30; Clergy / Religious Teachers 1; Bd. Members 5; Total Assisted 74.

MINNETONKA. **Aim Higher Foundation*, 2610 University Ave. W. Ste. 525, Minnetonka, 55114.
Tel: 612-819-6711; Email: info@aimhigherfoundation.org; Email: jhoughton@aimhigherfoundation.org; Web: aimhigherfoundation.org. Jean Houghton, Pres. Staff 3.

NEW PRAGUE. *First Avenue Properties of New Prague*, 215 Main St. E, New Prague, 56071.
Tel: 952-758-3920; Email: Peter.Guzulaitis@npcatholic.org. David B. Bruzek, Pres.

OSSEO. *Benedictine Senior Living at Steeple Pointe*, 625 Central Ave., Osseo, 55369. Tel: 763-425-4440;
Fax: 763-391-0747; Email: kristel.lastine@bhshealth.org. Kristel Lastine, Admin. Bedrooms 59; Total Assisted 59.

PLYMOUTH. *Catholic Services Appeal Foundation of the Saint Paul and Minneapolis Area*, 12805 Hwy. 55, Ste. 210, Plymouth, 55441. Tel: 612-294-6622; Email: beaudryj@csafspm.org. John Norris, Pres.

ST. ANTHONY. *St. Charles Borromeo Endowment Fund Trust*, 2420 St. Anthony Blvd., St. Anthony, 55418. Tel: 612-781-6529; Email: tpomeroy@stchb.org. 2739 Stinson Blvd., St. Anthony, 55418. Rev. Troy D. Przybilla. Staff 1.

WEST ST. PAUL. NET MINISTRIES, INC., 110 Crusader Ave. W., West St. Paul, 55118-4427.
Tel: 651-450-6833; Fax: 651-450-9984; Email: ministry@netusa.org; Web: www.netusa.org. Mr. Mark Berchem, Pres. Retreatants 95; Total Staff 75; Volunteers 200.

Saint Paul's Outreach, Inc., 5814 Blackshire Path, Inver Grove Heights, 55076. Tel: 651-451-6114; Email: info@spo.org; Web: www.spo.org. Most Rev. Andrew H. Cozzens, S.T.D., Chm. Bd.; Mr. Gordon C. DeMarais, Pres. Tot Asst. Annually 22,000; Total Staff 158.

Twin Cities TEC of the Archdiocese of St. Paul-Minneapolis, Minnesota, Inc., (Twin Cities TEC): 337 Hurley Ave. E., West St. Paul, 55118.
Tel: 651-281-0085; Email: retreats@twincitiestec.org; Web: www.twincitiestec.org. Jeffrey Campeau, Exec. Dir. Total Staff 1; Total Assisted 500.

RELIGIOUS INSTITUTES OF MEN REPRESENTED IN THE ARCHDIOCESE

For further details refer to the corresponding bracketed number in the Religious Institutes of Men or Women section.

[0200]—*Benedictine Monks* (St. John's Abbey)—O.S.B.
[0330]—*Brothers of the Christian Schools* (Midwest Prov.)—F.S.C.
[0270]—*Carmelite Fathers and Brothers (Carmelite Hermitage of the Blessed Virgin Mary)*—O.Carm.
[]—*Carmelites of Mary Immaculate* (Sacred Heart Province); (Kerala, India)—C.M.I.
[]—*The Congregation of the Mother of the Redeemer* (Carthage, MO)—C.R.M.
[]—*Congregation of the Sons of the Immaculate Conception* (Woodbridge, Ontario)—C.F.I.C.
[0480]—*Conventual Franciscans* (Prov. of Our Lady of Consolation)—O.F.M.Conv.
[0520]—*Franciscan Friars* (St. Louis); (Prov. of Sacred Heart)—O.F.M.
[0690]—*Jesuit Fathers and Brothers*—S.J.
[0780]—*Marist Fathers* (American Prov.)—S.M.
[]—*Misioneros Oblatos de los Corazones Santisimos* (Ecuador)—O.C.C.S.S.
[]—*Oblates of Mary Immaculate* (Washington, DC; U.S. Prov.)—O.M.I.
[0430]—*Order of Preachers (Dominicans)* (Prov. of St. Albert the Great)—O.P.
[1205]—*Priestly Fraternity of the Missionaries of St. Charles Borromeo* (Boston, MA)—F.S.C.B.
[]—*Priestly Fraternity of St. Peter Society of Apostolic Life* (Elmhurst, PA)—F.S.S.P.
[]—*Pro Ecclesia Sancta* (Lima, Peru)—P.E.S.
[1070]—*Redemptorist Fathers* (Denver Prov.)—C.SS.R.
[]—*Servants of the Holy Eucharist of the Blessed Virgin Mary* (Puerto Rico)—S.E.M.V.
[]—*Society of Christ* (Lombard, IL)—S.CH.

RELIGIOUS INSTITUTES OF WOMEN REPRESENTED IN THE ARCHDIOCESE

[0230]—*Benedictine Sisters of Pontifical Jurisdiction* St. Paul, St. Joseph, Duluth, MN; Watertown, SD)—O.S.B.
[]—*Congregation of Our Lady of Sion* (Toronto, ON)—N.D.S.
[3710]—*Congregation of the Sisters of St. Agnes*—C.S.A.
[3832]—*Congregation of the Sisters of St. Joseph* (Created from merger of several C.S.J. Provinces)—C.S.J.
[1780]—*Congregation of the Sisters of the Third Order of St. Francis of Perpetual Adoration* (Eastern Region)—F.S.P.A.
[1830]—*Contemplative Sisters of the Good Shepherd*—C.G.S.
[0810]—*Daughters of the Heart of Mary*—D.H.M.
[0420]—*Discalced Carmelite Nuns*—O.C.D.
[1070-03]—*Dominican Sisters* Congregation of the Most Holy Rosary (Sinsinawa, WI)—O.P.
[1070-07]—*Dominican Sisters Congregation of St. Cecilia* (Diocese of Nashville, TN)—O.P.
[1070-13]—*Dominican Sisters Congregation of the Most Holy Rosary* (Adrian, MI)—O.P.
[]—*Dominican Sisters of Mary Mother of the Eucharist* (Diocese of Lansing)—O.P.
[]—*Franciscan Clarist Congregation* (Deephaven, MN)—F.C.C.
[1310]—*Franciscan Sisters of Little Falls, Minnesota*—O.S.F.
[1485]—*Franciscan Sisters of St. Paul, MN*—O.S.F.
[]—*Guadalupan Sisters* (Congregacion de Hermanas de La Salle); (Mexico)—H.G.S.
[1870]—*Handmaids of the Heart of Jesus Sisters* (New Ulm, MN)—A.C.J.
[]—*Immaculate Heart of Mary Mother of Christ* (Nigeria)—I.H.M.
[2340]—*Little Sisters of the Poor*—L.S.P.
[]—*Missionaries of Charity* (St. Louis, MO)—M.C.
[3990]—*Missionary Sisters of St. Peter Claver*—S.S.P.C.
[]—*Pro Ecclesia Sancta* (Lima, Peru)—P.E.S.
[2970]—*School Sisters of Notre Dame* (Central Pacific Prov.)—S.S.N.D.
[1680]—*Schools Sisters of St. Francis*—O.S.F.
[3590]—*Servants of Mary (Servite Sisters)* (Ladysmith, WI)—O.S.M.
[0430]—*Sisters of Charity of the Blessed Virgin Mary* (Dubuque, IA)—B.V.M.
[1530]—*Sisters of St. Francis of the Congregation of Our Lady of Lourdes, Sylvania, Ohio*—O.S.F.
[1570]—*Sisters of St. Francis of the Holy Family* (Dubuque, IA)—O.S.F.
[3840]—*Sisters of St. Joseph of Carondelet*—C.S.J.
[3930]—*Sisters of St. Joseph of the Third Order of St. Francis*—S.S.J.-T.O.S.F.
[1830]—*The Sisters of the Good Shepherd* (Prov. of Mid-North America)—R.G.S.
[]—*Sisters of the Living Word* (Arlington Heights, IL)—S.L.W.
[3320]—*Sisters of the Presentation of the B.V.M.* (Dubuque, IA; Aberdeen, SD)—P.B.V.M.
[1720]—*Sisters of the Third Order Regular of St.*

Francis of the Congregation of Our Lady of Lourdes (Rochester, MN)—O.S.F.
[4190]—*Visitation Nuns*—V.H.M.

ARCHDIOCESAN CEMETERIES

ST. PAUL. *Calvary*
The Catholic Cemeteries, 2105 Lexington Ave., S., Mendota Heights, 55120. Tel: 651-228-9991; Fax: 651-228-9995; Email: info@catholic-cemeteries.org; Web: www.catholic-cemeteries.org. Ms. Joan Gacik, Dir.
MINNEAPOLIS. *St. Anthony & St. Mary*
MENDOTA HEIGHTS. *Resurrection*
NEW HOPE. *Assumption & Gethsemane*

PARISH CEMETERIES

ALBERTVILLE. *St. Albert Cemetery*, 11400 57th St., N.E., P.O. Box 127, Albertville, 55301. Tel: 763-497-2474; Fax: 763-497-7678; Email: stalbertmn@gmail.com; Web: www.churchofstalbert.org. Rev. Peter M. Richards, Contact Person
ANNANDALE. *St. Ignatius Cemetery*, P.O. Box 126, Annandale, 55302. Tel: 320-274-8828; Fax: 320-274-3961; Email: bonnie@stignatiusmn.com. Rev. John D. Meyer, Contact Person
ANOKA. *Calvary Cemetery/Church of St. Stephen*, 525 Jackson St., Anoka, 55303. Tel: 763-421-2471; Fax: 763-421-4230; Email: info@ststephenchurch.org. Rev. Jon Bennet Tran, Contact Person
BAYPORT. *St. Michael Cemetery*, 409 Third St., Bayport, 55003. Tel: 651-439-4511; Fax: 651-430-9717; Email: office@stcb.comcastbiz.net; Web: www.stcharlesbayport.com. Rev. Mark J. Joppa, Contact Person
BELLE PLAINE. *Sacred Heart Cemetery*, 200 E. Church St., Belle Plaine, 56011. Tel: 952-873-6564; Fax: 952-873-6717; Email: parish@ourladyoftheprairie.com. Rev. Brian T. Lynch, Contact Person
Saint Peter and Paul Cemetery, 200 E. Church St., Belle Plaine, 56011. Tel: 952-873-6564; Fax: 952-873-6717; Email: parish@ourladyoftheprairie.com. Rev. Brian T. Lynch, Contact Person
BROOKLYN PARK. *St. Vincent de Paul Cemetery*, 9100 93rd Ave. N., Brooklyn Park, 55445. Tel: 763-425-2210; Fax: 763-425-7898; Email: churchinfo@saintvdp.org. Rev. Dennis Zehren, Contact Person
BUFFALO. *St. Mark's Cemetery*, 223 19th St., N.W., Buffalo, 55313. Tel: 763-684-0075; Fax: 763-684-4771; Email: nate.meyers@stfxb.org. Rev. Nathaniel Meyers, Contact Person
Saint Francis Xavier Cemetery, Mailing Address: 223 19th St. N.W., Buffalo, 55313. Tel: 763-684-0075; Fax: 763-684-4771; Email: nate.meyers@stfxb.org. Rev. Nathaniel Meyers, Contact Person
BURNSVILLE. *St. John the Baptist Catholic Cemetery*, 4625 W. 125th St., Savage, 55378. Tel: 952-890-9465; Email: pastor@stjohns-savage.org. Rev. Donald E. DeGrood, Contact Person
CANNON FALLS. *St. Pius V Cemetery*, 410 Colvill St. W., Cannon Falls, 55009. Tel: 507-263-2578; Fax: 507-263-8005; Email: spvparish@gmail.com. Rev. Terry P. Beeson, Contact Person
CARVER. *St. Nicholas Cemetery*, 412 W. 4th St., Carver, 55315. Mailing Address: P.O. Box 133, Carver, 55315. Tel: 952-448-2345; Fax: 952-368-0502; Email: stnicholas@embarqmail.com. Rev. William Deziel, Contact Person
CENTERVILLE. *St. Genevieve Cemetery*, 7087 Goiffon St., Centerville, 55038. Tel: 651-429-7937; Fax: 651-653-0071; Email: info@stgens.org. Rev. Gregory L. Esty, Contact Person. St. John the Baptist Cemetery in Hugo now under the care of the Church of St. Genevieve.
CHANHASSEN. *St. Hubert Cemetery*, 8201 Main St., Chanhassen, 55317. Tel: 952-934-9106; Fax: 952-934-8209; Email: webmaster@sthubert.org. Rev. Rolf R. Tollefson, Contact Person
CHASKA. *Guardian Angels Cemetery*, 215 W. 2nd St., Chaska, 55318. Tel: 952-227-4000; Fax: 952-227-4050; Email: info@gachaska.org. Rev. William Deziel, Contact Person
CLEARWATER. *St. Luke Cemetery*, 17545 Huber Ave., N.W., Clearwater, 55320. Tel: 320-558-2124; Email: admin@churchofstlukes.com. Rev. Dennis J. Backer, Contact Person
CLEVELAND. *Calvary Cemetery*, 165 Waterville Ave. N., Le Center, 56057. Tel: 507-243-3166; Fax: 507-357-4838; Email: gloriagw@frontier.com. Rev. Christopher L. Shofner, Contact Person
COLOGNE. *St. Bernard Cemetery*, 212 Church St. E., Cologne, 55322. Tel: 952-466-2031; Email: busadmin@st-bernard-cologne.org. Rev. Stan P. Mader, Contact Person
COON RAPIDS. *Epiphany Cemetery*, 1900 111th Ave. N.W., Coon Rapids, 55433. Tel: 763-862-4300; Fax: 763-862-4303; Email: jmackey@epiphanymn.org; Web: www.epiphanymn.org. Rev. Thomas W. Dufner, Contact Person
CORCORAN. *St. Jean de Chantel Cemetery*, 20000 County Rd. 10, Corcoran, 55340. Tel: 763-420-2385; Email: frjenson@saintsppta.org. Rev. Glen T. Jenson, Contact Person
Old St. Thomas Cemetery, 21420 93rd Ave. N., Corcoran, 55340. Tel: 763-479-0535; Email: bsullivan@saintsppta.org. 20000 County Rd. 10, Corcoran, 55340. Rev. John Gallas, Contact Person
St. Thomas the Apostle Cemetery, 20000 County Rd. 10, Corcoran, 55340. Tel: 763-420-2385; Fax: 763-420-4710; Email: frjenson@saintsppta.org. Rev. Glen T. Jenson, Contact Person
DAYTON. *St. John the Baptist Cemetery*, 18380 Columbus St., P.O. Box 201, Dayton, 55327. Tel: 763-428-2828; Fax: 763-428-6462; Email: sjbchurch@yahoo.com. Rev. Timothy J. Yanta, Contact Person
Old St. John the Baptist Cemetery, 18380 Columbus St., P.O. Box 201, Dayton, 55327. Tel: 763-428-2828; Fax: 763-428-6462; Email: sjbchurch@yahoo.com. Rev. Timothy J. Yanta, Contact Person
DELANO. *Calvary Cemetery*, 204 S. River St., Delano, 55328. Tel: 763-972-2077; Fax: 763-972-6177; Email: fr.nathan@delanocatholic.com. Rev. Nathan LaLiberte, Contact Person
St. Joseph Cemetery, 204 S. River St., Delano, 55328. Tel: 763-972-2077; Fax: 763-972-6177; Email: fr.nathan@delanocatholic.com. Rev. Nathan LaLiberte, Contact Person
St. Mary of Czestochowa Cemetery, 1867 95th St., S.E., Delano, 55328. Tel: 952-955-1139; Email: stbonifacepastor@gmail.com. Rev. Joseph-Quoc T. Vuong, Contact Person
St. Peter Cemetery, P.O. Box 470, Delano, 55328. Tel: 763-972-2077; Email: cemetery@delanocatholic.com. Rev. Nathan LaLiberte, Contact Person
EXCELSIOR. *Resurrection Cemetery*, 680 Mill St., Excelsior, 55331. Tel: 952-474-8868; Fax: 952-444-3474; Email: stjohns@stjohns-excelsior.org; Web: www.stjohns-excelsior.org/parish/Resurrection-Cemetery. Rev. Alex Bernard Carlson, Contact Person
FARIBAULT. *Calvary Cemetery*, 4 Second Ave. S.W., Faribault, 55021. Tel: 507-334-2266; Fax: 507-334-3895; Email: bwagner@divinemercy.cc. Rev. Kevin T. Kenney, Contact Person
St. Lawrence Cemetery, 4 2nd Ave., S.W., Faribault, 55021. Tel: 507-334-2266; Fax: 507-334-3895; Email: bwagner@divinemercy.cc. Rev. Kevin T. Kenney, Contact Person
St. Patrick Cemetery, 7525 Dodd Rd., Faribault, 55021. Tel: 507-334-6002; Fax: 507-334-1960; Email: spshieldsville@qwestoffice.net; Web: www.spshieldsville.org. Rev. Victor Valencia, Contact Person
FARMINGTON. *St. Michael Cemetery*, 22120 Denmark Ave., Farmington, 55024. Tel: 651-463-3360; Fax: 651-463-2339; Email: info@stmichael-farmington.org; Web: www.stmichael-farmington.org. Rev. Benjamin Little, Contact Person
GOODHUE. *St. Mary Cemetery*, 308 4th St. N, Goodhue, 55027. Tel: 651-923-4472; Email: holytrinitygoodhue@gmail.org. Rev. Randal J. Kasel, Admin.
FOREST LAKE. *Calvary Cemetery*, 1250 S. Shore Dr., Forest Lake, 55025. Tel: 651-982-2200; Email: pastor@stpeterfl.org. Rev. Daniel J. Bodin, Contact Person
HAMEL. *St. Anne Cemetery*, 200 Hamel Rd., P.O. Box 256, Hamel, 55340. Tel: 763-478-6644; Fax: 763-478-9141; Email: office@saintannehamel.org. Rev. Corey T. Belden, Contact Person
HAMPTON. *St. Mary Cemetery*, 8433 239th St. E., Hampton, 55031. Tel: 651-437-5546; Email: info@stmarysnewtrier.com; Web: www.stmarysnewtrier.com. Rev. Cole T. Kracke, Contact Person
St. Mathias Cemetery, 23315 Northfield Blvd., Hampton, 55031. Tel: 651-437-9030; Fax: 651-437-3427; Email: parishoffice@stmathias.com. Rev. Cole T. Kracke, Contact Person
HASTINGS. *St. Elizabeth Ann Seton Cemetery*, 2035 15th St. W., Hastings, 55033. Tel: 651-437-4254; Fax: 651-438-2948; Email: info@seasparish.org; Web: www.seasparish.org. Rev. David R. Hennen, Contact Person
INVER GROVE HEIGHTS. *St. Patrick Cemetery*, 3535 72nd St. E., Inver Grove Heights, 55076. Tel: 651-455-6624; Email: bfier@churchofstpatrick.com. Rev. Brian J. Fier, Contact Person
JORDAN. *St. John the Baptist Cemetery*, 313 2nd St. E., Jordan, 55352. Tel: 952-492-2640; Fax: 952-492-5683; Email: office@sjbjordan.org. Rev. Neil Edward Bakker, Contact Person
Saint Catherine Cemetery, 24425 Old Hwy. 13, Jordan, 55352. Tel: 952-492-6276; Fax: 952-492-6290; Email: admin@stpandc.mn.org. Rev. Michael J. Miller, Contact Person
Saint Patrick Cemetery, 24425 Old Hwy. 13 Blvd., Jordan, 55352. Tel: 952-492-6276; Fax: 952-492-6290; Email: admin@stpandc.mn.org. Rev. Michael J. Miller, Contact Person
KENYON. *St. Edwards of Richland*, 108 Bullis St., Kenyon, 55946. Tel: 507-789-6120; Email: stmichaels@kmwb.net. Rev. Kevin T. Kenney, Contact Person
KILKENNY. *St. Canice Cemetery*, 206 Vine Ave W, Montgomery, 56069. Tel: 507-364-7981; Fax: 507-364-8660; Email: hredeemer@frontiernet.net. Rev. Victor Valencia, Contact Person. Now under the care of Most Holy Redeemer, Montgomery.
LAKEVILLE. *All Saints Cemetery*, 19795 Holyoke Ave., Lakeville, 55044. Tel: 952-469-4481; Fax: 952-469-5752; Email: info@allsaintschurch.com. Rev. Thomas Wilson, Contact Person
LE CENTER. *St. Mary's Calvary Cemetery*, 165 N. Waterville Ave., Le Center, 56057. Tel: 507- 357-6633; Fax: 507-357-4838; Email: gloriagw@frontier.com. Rev. Christopher L. Shofner, Contact Person
LE SUEUR. *St. Anne Cemetery*, 217 N. 3rd St., Le Sueur, 56058. Tel: 507-665-3811; Fax: 507-665-2995; Email: stanneschurchoffice@gmail.com. Rev. Christopher L. Shofner, Contact Person
Calvary Cemetery, 217 N. 3rd St., Le Sueur, 56058. Tel: 507-665-3811; Fax: 507-665-2995; Email: stanneschurchoffice@gmail.com. Rev. Christopher L. Shofner, Contact Person
St. Thomas Cemetery, 217 N. 3rd St., Le Sueur, 56058. Tel: 507-665-3811; Fax: 507-665-2995; Email: stanneschurchoffice@gmail.com; Web: www.stanneslesueur.org. Rev. Christopher L. Shofner, Contact Person
LINO LAKES. *St. Joseph Cemetery*, 171 Elm St., Lino Lakes, 55014. Tel: 651-784-3015; Fax: 651-784-3699; Email: office@saintjosephsparish.org; Web: www.mystjoes.org. Rev. Michael F. Anderson, Contact Person
LITTLE CANADA. *Saint John's Church of Little Canada Cemetery*, 380 Little Canada Rd., Little Canada, 55117. Tel: 651-484-2708; Fax: 651-484-0567; Email: pastor@stjohnsoflc.org. Rev. Thomas J. Balluff, Contact Person
LONG LAKE. *St. George Cemetery*, 133 N. Brown Rd., Long Lake, 55356. Tel: 952-473-1247; Fax: 952-404-0129; Email: stgeorge@msn.com. Rev. Mark R. Juettner, Contact Person
LONSDALE. *Calvary Cemetery*, Tel: 507-744-2829; Fax: 507-744-2826; Email: icparish@lonstel.com. Rev. Nicholas William VanDenBroeke, Contact Person
MADISON LAKE. *Marysburg Cemetery*, 27528 Patrick St., Madison Lake, 56063. Tel: 507-243-3166; Email: office@maryschurches.com; Web: www.maryschurches.com. Rev. Christopher L. Shofner, Contact Person
MAPLE GROVE. *St. Patrick's Cemetery*, 20000 County Rd. 10, Corcoran, 55340. Tel: 763-420-2385; Email: frjenson@saintsppta.org. Rev. Glen T. Jenson, Contact Person
MAPLE LAKE. *St. Timothy Cemetery*, 8 Oak Ave. N., Maple Lake, 55358. Tel: 320-963-3726; Fax: 320-963-2008; Email: parishoffice@churchofsttimothy.org. Rev. John D. Meyer, Contact Person
MEDINA. *Sts. Peter and Paul Cemetery*, 145 Railway St. E., P.O. Box 96, Loretto, 55357. Tel: 763-479-0535; Fax: 763-479-4383; Email: frjenson@saintsppta.org. Rev. Glen T. Jenson, Contact Person
MENDOTA. *St. Peter Cemetery*, 1405 Hwy. 13, Mendota, 55150. Tel: 651-452-4550; Email: church@stpetersmendota.org; Web: www.stpetersmendota.org. P.O. Box 50679, Mendota, 55150. Rev. Steven B. Hoffman, Contact Person
MIESVILLE. *St. Joseph Cemetery*, 23955 Nicolai Ave. E., Hastings, 55033. Tel: 651-437-3526; Email: stjosephm@embarqmail.com; Web: www.stjosephmiesville.com. Rev. Terry P. Beeson, Contact Person
MINNEAPOLIS. *St. Joan of Arc Memorial Garden*, 4537 3rd Ave. S., Minneapolis, 55419. Tel: 612-823-8205; Fax: 612-825-7028; Email: dheaney@stjoan.com; Web: www.saintjoanofarc.org. Rev. James R. DeBruycker, Contact Person
MINNETONKA. *St. Margaret's Cemetery*, 6 Interlachen Rd., Hopkins, 55343. Tel: 952-935-5536; Fax: 952-938-2724; Email: receptionistchurch@stgabrielhopkins.org. Rev. James C. Liekhus, Contact Person
MONTGOMERY. *Calvary Cemetery*, 206 Vine Ave. W., Montgomery, 56069. Fax: 507-364-8660; Email: hredeemer@frontiernet.net. Rev. Victor Valencia, Contact Person
St. John's Cemetery, 206 Vine Ave. W., Montgomery, 56069. Tel: 507-364-7981; Fax: 507-364-8660;

Email: hredeemer@frontiernet.net. Rev. Victor Valencia, Contact Person

MONTICELLO. *St. Henry Cemetery*, 1001 7th St. E., Monticello, 55362. Tel: 763-295-2402; Email: info@sthenrycatholic.com. Rev. Tony VanderLoop, Contact Person

Legal Title: Church of Saint Henry Cemetery

MOUND. *Our Lady of the Lake Cemetery*, Mailing Address: 2385 Commerce Blvd., Mound, 55364. Tel: 952-472-1284; Fax: 952-843-5667; Email: reurich@ourladyofthelake.com. Rev. Anthony O'Neill, Contact Person

NEW BRIGHTON. *St. John the Baptist Cemetery*, 835 2nd Ave. N.W., New Brighton, 55112. Tel: 651-633-8333; Fax: 651-633-7404; Email: stjohnsnb@pclink.com. Rev. Michael C. Skluzacek, Contact Person

NEW MARKET. *St. Nicholas Cemetery*, 51 Church St., Elko/New Market, 55054. Tel: 952-461-2403; Fax: 952-461-2423; Email: jberry@stncc.net. Rev. Patrick Thomas Barnes, Contact Person

NEW PRAGUE. *St. Benedict Cemetery*, Mailing Address: 215 Main St. E., New Prague, 56071. Tel: 952-758-3225; Fax: 952-758-2960; Email: info@npcatholic.org. Rev. Kevin I. Clinton, Contact Person

St. John the Evangelist Cemetery, Mailing Address: 215 Main St. E., New Prague, 56071. Tel: 952-758-3225; Fax: 952-758-2960; Email: info@npcatholic.org. Rev. Kevin I. Clinton, Contact Person

St. Joseph Cemetery, 215 Main St. E., New Prague, 56071. Fax: 952-758-2960; Email: info@npcatholic.org. Rev. Kevin I. Clinton, Contact Person

St. Scholastica Cemetery, Mailing Address: 215 Main St. E., New Prague, 56071. Fax: 952-758-2960; Email: info@npcatholic.org. Rev. Kevin I. Clinton, Contact Person

St. Wenceslaus Cemetery, 215 E. Main St., New Prague, 56071. Tel: 952-758-3225; Fax: 952-758-2960; Email: info@npcatholic.org. Rev. Kevin I. Clinton, Contact Person

NORTH BRANCH. *St. Joseph Cemetery*, 38725 Forest Blvd. N., P.O. Box 609, North Branch, 55056. Tel: 651-674-4056; Fax: 651-277-4563; Email: info@stgregorynb.org. Rev. Mark Shane Stoppel-Wasinger, Contact Person

NORTH SAINT PAUL. *St. Mary's Cemetery*, 2600 Margaret St. N., North Saint Paul, 55109. Tel: 651-777-8304; Fax: 651-777-0497; Email: info@churchofstpetersnsp.org. Rev. Ettore Ferrario, F.S.C.B., Contact Person

NORTHFIELD. *Annunciation of Hazelwood Cemetery*, 4996 Hazelwood Ave., Northfield, 55057. Tel: 952-652-2625; Email: secretary-ac@integra.com. Rev. Dennis Dempsey, Contact Person

Calvary Cemetery, 216 Spring St. N., Northfield, 55057. Tel: 507-645-8816; Fax: 507-645-8818; Email: secretary@churchofstdominic.org. Rev. Dennis Dempsey, Contact Person

NORWOOD. *Ascension Cemetery*, 323 Reform St. N., Norwood, 55368. Tel: 952-467-3351; Email: busadmin@ascensionnya.org. Rev. Stan P. Mader, Contact Person

St. Patrick's Cemetery, 323 Reform St. N., Norwood, 55368. Tel: 952-467-3351; Email: busadmin@ascensionnya.org. Rev. Gregory E. Abbott, Contact Person

OAK GROVE. *St. Patrick of Cedar Creek Cemetery*, 19921 Nightingale St. N.W., Oak Grove, 55011. Tel: 763-753-2011; Fax: 763-753-9803; Email: stpats@st-patricks.org. Rev. Allan Paul Eilen, Contact Person

OAKDALE. *Guardian Angels Cemetery*, 8260 4th St. N., Oakdale, 55128. Tel: 651-738-2223; Fax: 651-738-2453; Email: info@guardian-angels.org; Web: guardian-anagels.org. Rev. Rodger Bauman, Contact Person

PINE ISLAND. *St. Michael Cemetery*, 451 5th St., S.W., Pine Island, 55963. Tel: 507-356-4280; Fax: 507-356-2080; Email: stmichaeloffice@bevcomm.net. Rev. Randal J. Kasel, Contact Person

PLYMOUTH. *St. Joseph Cemetery*, 8701 36th Ave. N., New Hope, 55427. Tel: 763-544-3352; Fax: 763-544-3435; Email: lkotecki@stjosephparish.com. Rev. Terrence Rassmussen, Contact Person

PRIOR LAKE. *St. Michael Cemetery*, 16311 Duluth Ave. S.E., Prior Lake, 55372. Tel: 952-447-2491; Fax: 952-447-2489; Email: info@stmichael-pl.org; Web: www.stmichael-pl.org. Rev. Thomas J. Walker, J.D., Contact Person

RED WING. *Calvary Cemetery*, 426 W. 8th St., Red Wing, 55066. Tel: 651-388-1133; Email: parish@stjosephredwing.org. Rev. Thomas M. Kommers, Contact Person

RICHFIELD. *Assumption Cemetery*, 305 E. 77th St., Richfield, 55423. Tel: 612-866-5019; Fax: 612-866-5274; Email: maria@assumptionrichfield.org. Rev. Michael Kueber, Contact Person

ROGERS. *St. Martin Cemetery*, 21304 Church Ave., Rogers, 55374. Tel: 763-428-2585; Fax: 763-428-3460; Email: parishoffice@mqpcatholic.org; Web: mqpcatholic.org. Rev. Michael C. Kaluza, Contact Person

St. Walburga Cemetery, 21304 Church Ave., Rogers, 55374. Tel: 763-428-2585; Fax: 763-428-3460; Email: parishoffice@mqpcatholic.org; Web: mqpcatholic.org. Rev. Michael C. Kaluza, Contact Person

ROSEMOUNT. *St. Joseph Cemetery*, 13900 Biscayne Ave., Rosemount, 55068. Tel: 651-423-4402; Fax: 651-888-5685. Rev. Paul A. Kammen, Contact Person

RUSH CITY. *Calvary Cemetery*, 425 Field Ave., P.O. Box 45, Rush City, 55069. Tel: 320-358-4370; Fax: 866-779-1580; Email: sacredheart@q.com. Rev. Mark Shane Stoppel-Wasinger, Contact Person

SHAFER. *St. Francis Xavier Cemetery*, 540 River St., P.O. Box 234, Taylors Falls, 55084. Fax: 651-465-6632; Email: stjosephstfrancis@outlook.com; Web: www.stjosephtaylorsfalls.org. Rev. John M. Drees, Contact Person

SHAKOPEE. *St. Mary of the Purification Cemetery*, 2700 17th Ave. E., Shakopee, 55379. Tel: 952-445-1319; Fax: 952-445-0511; Email: frlundgren@ssjacs.org. Rev. Erik Carl Martin Lundgren, Contact Person

ST. BONIFACIUS. *St. Boniface Cemetery*, 4025 Main St., P.O. Box 68, St. Bonifacius, 55375. Tel: 952-446-1054; Email: stbonifaceoffice@mchsi.com. Rev. Joseph-Quoc T. Vuong, Contact Person

ST. MICHAEL. *St. Michael Cemetery*, 11300 Frankfort Pkwy N.E., St. Michael, 55376. Tel: 763-442-6831; Fax: 763-497-2745; Email: djtcctbj@gmail.com; Web: www.stmcatholicchurch.org. Rev. Peter M. Richards, Contact Person

ST. PAUL PARK. *St. Thomas Aquinas Cemetery*, 920 Holley Ave., St. Paul Park, 55071. Tel: 651-459-2131; Fax: 651-459-8756. Rev. J. Anthony Andrade, Contact Person

VERMILLION. *St. Agatha Cemetery*, 3700 160th St. E., Rosemount, 55068. Tel: 651-699-0660. Rev. Richard J. Mahoney, Contact Person, (Retired)

St. John the Baptist Cemetery, 23315 Northfield Blvd., Hampton, 55031. Tel: 651-437-9030; Fax: 651-437-3427; Email: parishoffice@stmathias.com. Rev. Cole T. Kracke, Contact Person

VESELI. *St. John's Cemetery*, 4939 Washington N., Veseli, 55046. Tel: 507-744-2823; Email: mhtveseli@gmail.com. Rev. John G. Lapensky, Contact Person

Most Holy Trinity Cemetery, 4939 Washington N., Veseli, 55046. Tel: 507-744-2823; Fax: 507-744-4413; Email: mhtveseli@gmail.com. Rev. John G. Lapensky, Contact Person

VICTORIA. *St. Victoria Cemetery*, 8228 Victoria Dr., Victoria, 55386. Tel: 952-443-2661; Fax: 952-443-3866; Email: mcatino@stvictoria.org. Rev. Robert L. White, Contact Person

WACONIA. *St. Joseph Cemetery*, 41 E. 1st St., Waconia, 55387. Tel: 952-442-2384; Fax: 952-442-3719; Email: churchoffice@stjosephwaconia.org. Rev. Stan P. Mader, Contact Person

WATERTOWN. *Immaculate Conception Cemetery*, 109 Angel Ave., N.W., PO Box 548, Watertown, 55388. Tel: 952-955-1458; Email: iccw@frontiernet.net; Web: www.iccwatertown.org. Rev. James William Devorak, Contact Person

WATERVILLE. *Calvary Cemetery*, 506 Common St., Waterville, 56096. Tel: 507-362-4311; Email: HolyT7@frontiernet.net. Rev. Michael W. Ince, Contact Person

WAVERLY. *St. Mary Cemetery*, 607 Elm St., P.O. Box 278, Waverly, 55390. Tel: 763-658-4319; Fax: 763-658-3519. Rev. Kenneth L. O'Hotto, Contact Person

WAYZATA. *Holy Name of Jesus Cemetery*, 155 County Rd. 24, Wayzata, 55391. Tel: 763-473-7901; Fax: 763-745-3488; Email: email@hnoj.org; Web: www.hnoj.org. Rev. Stephen D. Ulrick, Contact Person

WHITE BEAR LAKE. *St. Mary of the Lake Cemetery*, 4690 Bald Eagle Ave., White Bear Lake, 55110. Tel: 651-429-7771; Fax: 651-429-9539; Email: contactus@stmarys-wbl.org. Rev. Ralph W. Talbot Jr., Contact Person

ZUMBROTA. *St. Paul Cemetery*, 749 Main St., Zumbrota, 55992. Tel: 507-732-5324; Email: stpauls@hcinet.net. Rev. Randal J. Kasel, Contact Person

NECROLOGY

† Moudry, Richard Paul, (Retired), Died Jun. 17, 2018
† Fleming, Martin Michael P., (Retired), Died May. 18, 2018
† Hamel, Robert Frederick, (Retired), Died Apr. 21, 2018
† La Fontaine, Paul A., (Retired), Died Dec. 10, 2018
† Roach, Francis Joseph, (Retired), Died Jun. 14, 2018

An asterisk (*) denotes an organization that has established tax-exempt status directly with the IRS and is not covered by the USCCB Group Ruling.

Diocese of St. Petersburg

(Dioecesis Sancti Petri in Florida)

Most Reverend

GREGORY L. PARKES, J.C.L.

Fifth Bishop of St. Petersburg; ordained June 26, 1999; appointed Bishop of Pensacola-Tallahassee March 20, 2012; ordained and installed June 5, 2012; appointed Fifth Bishop of St. Petersburg November 28, 2016; installed January 4, 2017. *Office: P.O. Box 40200, St. Petersburg, FL 33743-0200.*

Most Reverend

ROBERT N. LYNCH

Retired Fourth Bishop of St. Petersburg; ordained May 13, 1978; appointed Fourth Bishop of St. Petersburg December 5, 1995; consecrated and installed January 26, 1996; retired November 28, 2016. *Office: P.O. Box 40200, St. Petersburg, FL 33743-0200.*

ESTABLISHED JUNE 17, 1968.

Square Miles 3,177.

Comprises the Counties of Citrus, Hernando, Hillsborough, Pasco and Pinellas in the State of Florida.

For legal titles of parishes and diocesan institutions, consult the Pastoral Center.

Pastoral Center: P.O. Box 40200, St. Petersburg, FL 33743-0200. Tel: 727-344-1611; Fax: 727-345-2143.

Web: www.dosp.org

Email: communicate@dosp.org

STATISTICAL OVERVIEW

Personnel	
Bishop	1
Retired Bishops	1
Abbots	1
Priests: Diocesan Active in Diocese	93
Priests: Diocesan Active Outside Diocese	3
Priests: Retired, Sick or Absent	68
Number of Diocesan Priests	164
Religious Priests in Diocese	96
Total Priests in Diocese	260
Extern Priests in Diocese	76
Ordinations:	
Diocesan Priests	3
Transitional Deacons	3
Permanent Deacons in Diocese	115
Total Brothers	15
Total Sisters	118
Parishes	
Parishes	74
With Resident Pastor:	
Resident Diocesan Priests	60
Resident Religious Priests	10
Without Resident Pastor:	
Administered by Priests	4
Missions	6
Professional Ministry Personnel:	
Brothers	5
Sisters	93
Welfare	
Catholic Hospitals	4
Total Assisted	739,479
Health Care Centers	7
Total Assisted	49,122
Homes for the Aged	15
Total Assisted	1,150
Day Care Centers	12
Total Assisted	831
Specialized Homes	4
Total Assisted	61
Special Centers for Social Services	67
Total Assisted	14,906
Educational	
Diocesan Students in Other Seminaries	21
Total Seminarians	21
Colleges and Universities	2
Total Students	17,140
High Schools, Diocesan and Parish	4
Total Students	1,945
High Schools, Private	3
Total Students	1,425
Elementary Schools, Diocesan and Parish	25
Total Students	8,535
Elementary Schools, Private	2
Total Students	840
Non-residential Schools for the Disabled	2
Total Students	165
Catechesis/Religious Education:	
High School Students	2,189
Elementary Students	14,400
Total Students under Catholic Instruction	46,660
Teachers in the Diocese:	
Priests	1
Scholastics	8
Brothers	4
Sisters	17
Lay Teachers	1,064
Vital Statistics	
Receptions into the Church:	
Infant Baptism Totals	3,011
Minor Baptism Totals	127
Adult Baptism Totals	625
Received into Full Communion	476
First Communions	4,263
Confirmations	3,475
Marriages:	
Catholic	595
Interfaith	285
Total Marriages	880
Deaths	3,037
Total Catholic Population	479,082
Total Population	3,237,046

Former Bishops—Most Revs. CHARLES B. MCLAUGHLIN, D.D., ord. June 6, 1941; appt. Titular Bishop of Risinium and Auxiliary of Raleigh, Jan. 13, 1964; appt. First Bishop of St. Petersburg, May 8, 1968; installed June 17, 1968; died in office, Dec. 14, 1978; W. THOMAS LARKIN, D.D., ord. May 15, 1947; Second Bishop of St. Petersburg; appt. April 24, 1979; ord. Bishop, May 27, 1979; installed June 28, 1979; retired Nov. 28, 1988; died Nov. 4, 2006.; JOHN C. FAVALORA, D.D., S.T.L., Third Bishop of St. Petersburg; ord. Dec. 20, 1961; appt. Bishop of Alexandria, June 16, 1986; ord. and installed July 29, 1986; appt. Third Bishop of St. Petersburg, March 7, 1989; installed May 16, 1989; appt. third Archbishop of Miami Nov. 3, 1994; installed Dec. 20, 1994; retired April 20, 2010.; ROBERT N. LYNCH, D.D., Bishop Emeritus of St. Petersburg, ord. May 13, 1978; appt. Fourth Bishop of St. Petersburg Dec. 5, 1995; ord. and installed Jan. 26, 1996; retired Nov. 28, 2016.

Diocesan Offices

Pastoral Center—6363 Ninth Ave. N., St. Petersburg, 33710. Tel: 727-344-1611; Fax: 727-345-2143. *Mailing Address: P.O. Box 40200, St. Petersburg, 33743-0200.*

Tribunal—6363 Ninth Ave. N, Saint Petersburg, 33710. Tel: 727-341-6858; Tel: 727-341-6859; Fax: 727-374-0206. Address all Rogatory commissions and matrimonial matters to the Tribunal.

WBVM 90.5 FM, Inc.—717 S. Dale Mabry Hwy., Tampa, 33609. Tel: 813-289-8040.

Office of the Bishop

Office of the Bishop—Most Rev. GREGORY L. PARKES; MRS. MALISSA AARONSON, Exec. Sec.

Diocesan Curia

Vicar General—Rev. Msgr. ROBERT F. MORRIS, V.G.; MRS. LUCIA GUYER, Exec. Sec.

Moderator of the Curia—Rev. Msgr. ROBERT F. MORRIS, V.G.

Chancellor—Deacon RICK WELLS, J.C.L.; MRS. MARIA T. GONZALEZ, Exec. Sec.; MRS. LISA MOBLEY, Archivist & Notary.

Victim Assistance Coordinator—MR. JOHN LAMBERT, L.C.S.W., Tel: 866-407-4505 (Toll Free); Email: jl@dosp.org.

Secretary for Administration—MR. FRANK V. MURPHY III; MRS. LUCIA GUYER, Exec. Sec.

Director of Ministry to Priests—Rev. Msgr. MICHAEL G. MUHR, M.Div., M.A.

The Tribunal—

Judicial Vicar—Very Rev. JOSEPH L. WATERS, J.C.L., J.V.

Coordinator of Tribunal Services—MR. DAVID RIDENOUR, J.D., J.C.L.

Tribunal Staff—

Judges—Rev. Msgrs. ROBERT C. GIBBONS, J.D., J.C.L.; RONALD AUBIN, J.C.L.; Rev. FRANCIS MUTESAASIRA LUBOWA, J.C.L.; Deacon RICK WELLS, J.C.L.; Very Revs. JOSEPH L. WATERS, J.C.L., J.V.; C. TIMOTHY CORCORAN III, J.D., V.F.; Rev. ALEXANDER PADILLA II, J.C.L.

Promoters of Justice—Rev. Msgr. DACIAN DEE, J.C.D., (Retired); MR. DAVID RIDENOUR, J.D., J.C.L.

Defenders of the Bond—Rev. Msgr. DACIAN DEE, J.C.D., (Retired); Rev. WILLIAM J. SWENGROS, J.C.D.; MR. DAVID RIDENOUR, J.D., J.C.L.

Notaries—MRS. MARY SUE OLIVER; MS. ANA RIVERA; MRS. KIM PACANA.

College of Consultors—Rev. Msgrs. ROBERT F. MORRIS,

V.G.; ROBERT C. GIBBONS, J.D., J.C.L.; RONALD AUBIN, J.C.L.; Revs. ARTHUR PROULX; JOHN TAPP; Very Rev. JAMES B. JOHNSON, V.F.; Rev. CRAIG MORLEY.

Vocations Office—Revs. CARL J. MELCHIOR JR., Dir.; JUSTIN PASKERT, Assoc. Dir.; KYLE SMITH, Assoc. Dir.; ANTHONY J. USTICK, Assoc. Dir.; MRS. HEIDI VARLEY, Asst. Dir.

Permanent Diaconate Office—Deacons JOHN ALVAREZ, Dir.; JAMES GREVENITES, Asst. Dir.; PETER ANDRE, Supvr. Practicums; MRS. SUE HUERTAS, Administrative Asst.

Vicar for Religious—Sr. MARLENE WEIDENBORNER, O.S.F., Dir.

Department of Christian Formation

Sea, Apostleship of the—

Tampa Port Ministry-Seafarers Center—1912 Eastport Dr., Tampa, 33610. Tel: 813-234-8693; Fax: 813-238-5060. Deacon KEVIN DWYER, Chap.

Charismatic Renewal—

English—VACANT.

Spanish Speaking Spiritual Moderator—VACANT; WINSTON GUEVARA, Pres. Charismatic Commission.

Cursillo, English—Deacon DAVID G. LESIEUR, Cursillo, English & Spiritual Advisor, 15520 North Blvd., Tampa, 33613; TOM DOYLE, Lay Dir., Email: tom@ststephencatholic.org.

Cursillo, Spanish—Rev. RAFAEL E. MARTOS, Spiritual Advisor, Tel: 813-681-9115; FERNANDO GUERRERO, Lay Dir., Tel: 813-545-5374.

Ecumenical and Inter-Religious Affairs—Rev. ROBERT J. SCHNEIDER, Dir., St. Cecelia Church, 820 Jasmine Way, Clearwater, 33756. Tel: 727-447-3494; Deacon JAMES GREVENITES, Asst. Dir., St. Raphael Church, 1376 Snell Isle Blvd., N.E., St. Petersburg, 33704. Tel: 727-821-7989.

Multicultural Ministry—Rev. GILBERTO QUINTERO, Sec. Multicultural Ministries; MR. CARLOS FLORES, Assoc. Dir. Hispanic Ministries.

Our Lady of Good Counsel Camp—Very Rev. JAMES B. JOHNSON, V.F., Dir., 8888 E. Gobbler Dr., Floral City, 34436. Tel: 352-726-2198; Email: goodcounselcamp@aol.com.

Propagation of the FaithRev. PAUL KOCHU, Dir.; MRS. CAROLYN MARHEFKA, Sec.

Worship, Office of—MR. DOUGLAS REATINI, Dir.; MRS. SYLVIA SANCHEZ, Assoc. Dir.

Catholic Schools Office—MR. CHRIS PASTURA, Supt.; DR. MARK MAJESKI, Assoc. Supt.; DR. ANN DAVIS, Assoc. Supt.; MRS. TONI JOHNSTON, Administrative Asst.; MS. DEBORAH MOORE, Administrative Asst.

Evangelization, Formation, Youth and Family Life—MR. BRIAN A. LEMOI, Exec. Dir.; MRS. KATHY FILIPPELLI, Dir. Faith Formation - Children & Adults; MRS. DIANE KLEDZIK, Dir. Marriage & Family Life; MR. RYAN PHELAN, Dir. Youth & Young Adult Ministry; MRS. CHERYL LAFRAZIA, Administrative Asst.; MS. DIANE MONTEMURRO, Administrative Asst.; MS. DEBBIE ALEXANDER, Asst. Dir. Marriage Preparation; MS. DALE BROWN, Dir. Lay Pastoral Ministry Inst.; MS. LEONA PESZKA, Admin./Prog. Asst., Lay Pastoral Ministry Inst.

Father William F. Balfe Memorial Library—Located at: Bishop McLaughlin High School, 13651 Hays Rd., Spring Hill, 34610.

Scouting Office, Girls—Rev. Msgr. ANTON DECHERING, Dir., (Retired), 1600 54th Ave. S., St. Petersburg, 33712. Tel: 727-867-3663; MRS. GRETCHEN TARROU, Diocesan Chair, Tel: 727-439-9164; MRS. LAURIE DEVER, Diocesan Vice Chair, Email: rjlkdever@gmail.com.

Scouting Office, Boys—Deacon EDWARD ANCTIL, Diocesan Chap., Tel: 813-626-7588; MR. PHIL RAYMOND, Diocesan Chm., Tel: 813-482-5117.

Department of Christian Service

Communications Office—MRS. TERESA L. PETERSON, Exec. Dir.; MS. MARIA MERTENS, Communications Coord.

Diocesan Radio - WBVM 90.5 FM—MR. JOHN MORRIS, Station Mgr., Mailing Address: 717 S. Dale Mabry Hwy., Tampa, 33609. Tel: 813-289-8040; Tel: 800-223-9286 (800-223-WBVM); Fax: 813-282-3580.

Prison and Jail Ministry—Deacon PETER ANDRE, Dir.; MRS. HEIDI SUMNER, Sec., Tel: 727-344-1611, Ext. 5414; Tel: 727-344-1611, Ext. 5415.

Life, Justice and Advocacy Ministry—MRS. SABRINA BURTON-SCHULTZ, Dir., Tel: 727-344-1611, Ext. 5325; MS. DIANE MONTEMURRO, Administrative Asst.; MRS. MEGAN BUCKLER, CRS Coord.

Department of Administration

Department of Administration—MR. FRANK V. MURPHY III, Sec. for Admin.; MRS. LUCIA GUYER, Exec. Sec.

Calvary Catholic Cemetery and Miserere Guild—MR. TERRY YOUNG, Dir. Cemeteries; Rev. CHARLES LEKE, Chap.

Finance and Accounting—MR. PHIL SIGNORE, Exec. Dir.; MS. KELLY BUI, Admin. Asst.; MS. STEPHANIE BOYLE, Controller; MRS. JEANNE AGE, Dir. Accounting Svcs.; MS. MELISSA ARMSTRONG, Construction Accounting Assoc.; MRS. MARGARET BECKER, Mgr., Financial Systems Admin.; MR. THOMAS HIERONYMUS, Dir. Parish & School Accounting; MR. ROBERT ROGERS, Accounting Mgr.; MRS. SUSAN HALES, Financial Reporting & Analysis Mgr.; MS. TERRI WILES, Accounts Payable Assoc.; MS. MARIA-INES LOYDI, Accounts Receivable Assoc.; MS. SUSAN VICE, Systems Implementation Specialist; MS. KATHLEEN KING, Lead Processing Specialist; MS. DEBRA BURNETT, Processing Specialist; MS. MICHELLE MARKIEVICH, Processing Specialist.

Diocesan Finance Council—Rev. Msgrs. ROBERT F. MORRIS, V.G.; JOSEPH A. PELLEGRINO; Very Rev. RICHARD JANKOWSKI; Rev. GEORGE C. CORRIGAN, O.F.M.; CHRISTOPHER MCDONNELL; MR. MICHAEL CARRERE; MR. CHRIS SCHELLMAN; MRS. NANCY RIDENOUR; MR. FRANK V. MURPHY III; MR. GERALD P. GIGLIA; MR. CHAU H. DUONG; MR. THOMAS MORIARTY; MRS. LAURA E. PRATHER.

Insurance and Risk Management—MRS. VALERIE BURNS.

Real Estate and Planning—MR. ROBERT HUTCHINSON.

Information Technology—MR. MARK MOFFITT, Dir.; MR. RAY MILLER, Enterprise Information Systems; MR. RICARDO ARCELAY, Systems Admin.; MR. ROB SMITH, Support Technician.

Office of Construction Management—MR. HUNG PHAM, Exec. Dir.

Human Resources—MR. JOSEPH LOEBER, Exec. Dir.; MR. MICHAEL CRAIG, Dir. Safe Environment; MRS. FAITH ESCHENFELDER, Sec.; MRS. ELLEN HALLORAN, Fingerprinting Coord.; MRS. VALERIE BURNS, Coord. Retirement Svcs.; MRS. LISA BAGGETT, Benefits Admin.; MS. TAMMIE LAURITO, Coord. Payroll Reporting.

Internal Services Administration—MS. ANGIE PETERSON, Mgr.; MR. JOE BONCZEK, Asst.; MR. AL BEMIS, Maintenance; MS. NANCY FLANIGAN, Receptionist; MS. PEGGY MILAM, Receptionist; MS. LAURIE FLEMING, Hospitality.

Office of Stewardship and Development—MS. MEEGAN WRIGHT, Exec. Dir.; MS. JEANNE SMITH, Assoc. Dir.

The Catholic Foundation—MS. MEEGAN WRIGHT, Exec. Dir.

Pastoral Offices and Consultative Bodies to the Diocesan Curia

Presbyteral Council—

Officers—Most Rev. GREGORY L. PARKES, Pres.; Rev. Msgrs. ROBERT F. MORRIS, V.G., Vice Pres.; ROBERT C. GIBBONS, J.D., J.C.L., Chm.; Very Rev. LEONARD PLAZEWSKI, V.F., Sec.

Ex Officio Members—Rev. Msgrs. ROBERT F. MORRIS, V.G.; MICHAEL G. MUHR, M.Div., M.A., Dir., Ministry to Priests; Very Revs. JOSEPH L. WATERS, J.C.L., J.V.; RICHARD JANKOWSKI, West Central Deanery; KRZYSZTOF GAZDOWICZ, V.F., East Central Deanery; C. TIMOTHY CORCORAN III, J.D., V.F., North Central Deanery; JOHN F. MCEVOY, V.F., Southeast Deanery; THOMAS ANASTASIA, V.F., Southwest Deanery; JAMES B. JOHNSON, V.F., Northern Deanery; LEONARD PLAZEWSKI, V.F., South Central Deanery; LEONARD G. PIOTROWSKI, V.F., Central Deanery; JOHN BLUM, V.F., Southern Deanery; Rev. GARY DOWSEY, Dir., Priestly Growth & Enrichment Commission.

Elected Pastors—Rev. Msgrs. ROBERT C. GIBBONS, J.D., J.C.L.; JOSEPH A. PELLEGRINO; MICHAEL G. MUHR, M.Div., M.A.; Revs. ROBERT J. SCHNEIDER; JOHN TAPP.

Elected Parochial Vicars—Revs. JOHN B. LIPSCOMB; CURTIS V. CARRO; FELIPE GONZALEZ; JUSTIN PASKERT; BRADLEY REED; ANTHONY J. USTICK.

Elected Retired Incardinated Member—Rev. Msgr. BRENDAN MULDOON, (Retired).

Appointed Members—Revs. CRAIG MORLEY; ARTHUR J. PROULX, V.F.

Personnel Board—Rev. ROBERT J. SCHNEIDER; Very Rev. JOSEPH L. WATERS, J.C.L., J.V.; Rev. Msgr. ROBERT F. MORRIS, V.G.; Very Rev. LEONARD G. PIOTROWSKI, V.F.; Revs. CARL J. MELCHIOR JR.; STEVEN CHUCK DORNQUAST; Very Rev. RICHARD JANKOWSKI; Revs. GILBERTO QUINTERO; JOHN TAPP.

Priestly Growth and Enrichment Commission—Revs. GARY DOWSEY, Chm.; ALLAN TUPA; STEVEN CHUCK DORNQUAST; CURTIS V. CARRO; CRAIG MORLEY; JOHN B. LIPSCOMB; KEVIN MACKIN, O.F.M. Ex Officio: Rev. Msgr. MICHAEL G. MUHR, M.Div., M.A.; Rev. CARL J. MELCHIOR JR.

Diocesan Legal Counsel—DiVito, Higham & Vasti, P.A., 4514 Central Ave., St. Petersburg, 33711-1041. Tel: 727-321-1201; Fax: 727-321-5181. MR. JOSEPH A. DIVITO; FREDERICK A. HIGHAM JR.; PETER VASTI.

Diocesan Review Board—MRS. SUE BRETT, Chm., Tel: 727-384-0730; Fax: 727-344-4060.

Organizations Serving the Diocese

Pension Plan For Employees of the Entities of the Diocese of St. Petersburg—

Pension Plan Administrator—Gabriel, Roeder, Smith & Co., One E. Broward Blvd., Ste. 505, Fort Lauderdale, 33301-1872. Tel: 954-527-1616; Fax: 954-525-0083.

Catholic Charities, Diocese of St. Petersburg, Inc.—

Central Services—1213 16th St., N., St. Petersburg, 33705. Tel: 727-893-1314; Fax: 727-893-1307; Web: www.ccdosp.org. MR. FRANK V. MURPHY III, Pres.

Pious Foundations

Catholic Education Foundation, Inc.—6363 Ninth Ave. N., St. Petersburg, 33710. Tel: 727-344-1611. *Mailing Address: P.O. Box 40200, St. Petersburg, 33743-0200.*

Catholic Formation, Inc.—MR. FRANK V. MURPHY III, 6363 Ninth Ave. N., Saint Petersburg, 33710.

Emmaus Foundation, Inc.— dba Catholic Foundation of the Diocese of St. Petersburg*6363 Ninth Ave. N., St. Petersburg, 33710.* Tel: 727-344-1611. *Mailing Address: P.O. Box 40200, St. Petersburg, 33743-0200.*

Organizations of the Catholic Faithful

Catholic Daughters of the Americas—

Tel: 212-877-3041 (National Office). MS. MICHELE BOWMAN, State Regent, Email: michelebowman227@gmail.com.

Diocesan Council of Catholic Women—Rev. THEODORE COSTELLO, Diocesan Moderator, Tel: 727-797-2375.

Family of St. Jerome, "Familiae Sancti Hieronymi"—MR. JAN G. HALISKY, P.A., Praeses Generalis, 507 S. Prospect Ave., Clearwater, 33756.

Knights of Columbus—Rev. TIMOTHY P. CUMMINGS, Diocesan Chap., Tel: 352-726-1670.

Knights of Peter Claver—St. Peter Claver, Tampa Council #379 Grand Knight THOREAU NELLUM, Tel: 813-681-3010; Web: kofpc.org (National); Email: obcm@aol.com.

Knights of Peter Claver Ladies Auxiliary—St. Peter Claver, Tampa Court #379 LOETTE CUPID, Tel: 813-870-2540; Email: loettec@ymail.com; Web: kofpc.org (National).

Marian Servants of Divine Providence—MRS. ADRIENNE T. NOVOTNY, M.Ed., Contact Person, 702 S. Bayview Ave., Clearwater, 33759. Tel: 727-799-4003.

Our Lady's Tridentine Mass Society—MR. JAN G. HALISKY, P.A., Representative, 507 S. Prospect Ave., Clearwater, 33756.

Society of St. Vincent de Paul—

**Central Council of St. Petersburg Diocese—4556 Manhattan Ave., Ste. A, Tampa, 33611.* Tel: 813-831-5100. Very Rev. JOHN F. MCEVOY, V.F., Spiritual Advisor, Tel: 813-645-1302; MR. MARVIN ROPERT, Exec. Dir., Tel: 813-839-9325; MS. NANCY JONES, Pres.

**Hernando Citrus St. Vincent de Paul Society District Council*—MR. JAMES YESKE, Pres., Tel: 352-688-8396.

**West Hillsborough District Council*—MS. NANCY JONES, Pres., Tel: 813-251-8678.

**East Hillsborough District Council*—MR. TOM DAMBLY, Pres., Tel: 813-956-7754.

**Pasco District Council*—MS. JANICE LATTUCA, Pres., Tel: 727-372-8908.

**South Pinellas District Council*—MR. JOHN GERDES, Pres., Tel: 813-909-3152; MR. PATRICK SULLIVAN, Pres., Special Works Pres., Tel: 727-867-9452; MICHAEL J. RAPOSA, CEO.

**Upper Pinellas District Council*—MR. BOB SORRELL, Pres., Tel: 727-559-2315.

CLERGY, PARISHES, MISSIONS AND PAROCHIAL SCHOOLS

CITY OF ST. PETERSBURG

(PINELLAS COUNTY)

ST. PETERSBURG

1—CATHEDRAL OF ST. JUDE THE APOSTLE (1950) 5815 5th Ave. N., 33710. Tel: 727-347-9702; Fax: 727-343-8370; Web: www.cathedralalive.org/.

Revs. Arthur J. Proulx, V.F., Rector; Alexander Padilla II, J.C.L., Parochial Vicar; Deacons John Carter, Parish Life Coord.; John Fox.
School—Cathedral of St. Jude the Apostle School, (Grades PreSchool-8),
600 58th St. N., 33710. Clergy 4; Lay Teachers 25; Students 385.
Catechesis Religious Program—Students 115.
2—BLESSED TRINITY (1960) 1600 54th Ave. S., 33712. Tel: 727-867-3663; Fax: 727-864-2679; Web: btsp.org. Rev. Wayne C. Genereux; Deacons William Lovelace, Dir. Faith Formation; John Schaefer, Spiritual Advisor/Care Svcs.; Lionel Roberts; Vincent Sclarani, Music Min.; Aimee Holley, Pastoral Assoc.; Eileen Plasse, Pastoral Assoc.
See St. Paul Interparochial School, St. Petersburg under Elementary Schools, Interparochial located in the Institution section.
Catechesis Religious Program—Students 23.
3—HOLY CROSS (1965) 7851 54th Ave. N., 33709. Tel: 727-546-3315; Email: holycross7851@gmail.com; Web: holycrossrcc.com. Rev. Emery Longanga; Deacon Richard Zeitler.
Catechesis Religious Program—
Tel: 727-546-9654; Email: faithformation@holycrossrcc.com. Joseph Havelka, D.R.E. Students 51.
4—HOLY FAMILY (1956) 200 78th Ave., N.E., 33702-4416. Tel: 727-526-5783; Fax: 727-521-2545; Email: hfkathy@tampabay.rr.com. Rev. Craig Morley; Deacons Peter Andre, Support Svcs. Mgr.; Ted Fahrendorf.
Schools—Holy Family Early Childhood Center—
Tel: 727-525-8489; Email: nmeyers@holyfamilycatholicschool.com. Nina Meyers, Dir. ECC 1 - PreK Lay Teachers 15; Students 82.
Holy Family School, (Grades K-8),
250 78th Ave. N.E., 33702-4416. Tel: 727-526-8194; Fax: 727-527-6567; Email: jdesrosiers@holyfamilycatholicschool.com; Email: principal@holyfamilycatholicschool.com; Web: www.holyfamilycatholicschool.com. Mrs. Abigail Rudderham, Prin. Lay Teachers 15; Students 183.
Catechesis Religious Program—Linda Johnston, Dir. Faith Formation. Students 143.
5—ST. JOSEPH (1926) Mailing Address: 2624 Union St. S., 33712. Tel: 727-822-2153; Fax: 727-823-5820; Email: stjoseph@stjosephstpete.org; Web: stjosephstpete.org. Rev. Stephan Brown, S.V.D.; Mr. Derek Wright, Business Mgr.
Catechesis Religious Program—Mrs. Lemi Vanwanzeele, D.R.E. Students 53.
6—ST. MARY OUR LADY OF GRACE (1921) 515 Fourth St. S., 33701. Tel: 727-896-2191; Fax: 727-895-6279; Web: www.stmaryolg.org. Revs. Damian Amantia, T.O.R.; James Morman, T.O.R., Parochial Vicar; Deacon Michael Menchen.
Catechesis Religious Program—Students 3.
**Daystar Life Center, Inc.*—
226 6th St., S., 33701.
7—ST. PAUL (1929) 1800 12th St. N., 33704.
Tel: 727-822-3481; Email: parishoffice@stpaulstpete.com. Rev. Msgr. Robert C. Gibbons, J.D., J.C.L.; Rev. Jonathan Stephanz, Parochial Vicar.
School—St. Paul School, (Grades PreK-8),
1900 12th St. N., 33704. Tel: 727-823-6144;
Fax: 727-896-0609; Web: www.stpaul1930.org. Sr. Joan Carberry, O.S.F., Asst. Prin. Clergy 1; Lay Teachers 20; Sisters 2; Students 327.
See St. Paul Children's Center under Pre Schools and Day Care Centers located in the Institution section.
Catechesis Religious Program—
Fax: 727-822-1754. Students 125.
Mission—The Mercy of God Polish Mission
1358 20th Ave. N., 33704. Email: polskamisjastpete@gmail.com.
8—ST. RAPHAEL (1961) 1376 Snell Isle Blvd., N.E., 33704. Tel: 727-821-7989; Email: straphaels@st-raphaels.com; Web: www.st-raphaels.com. Rev. Timothy H. Sherwood; Rev. Msgr. J. Bernard Caverly, Pastor Emeritus, (Retired); Rev. Kevin Mackin, O.F.M., Parochial Vicar; Deacon James Grevenites, Business Mgr. In Res., Rev. Jose G. Gonzalez, (Retired).
School—St. Raphael School, (Grades PreK-8),
Tel: 727-821-9663, Ext. 2111; Email: srsoffice@st-raphaels.com; Web: www.straphaelschool.net. Ms. Kathy Bogataj, Prin. Lay Teachers 19; Students 221.
Catechesis Religious Program—Lynn Edmonds, D.R.E.; Karen Gendron, Dir. Youth Min. Students 360.
9—TRANSFIGURATION (1959) Mailing Address: 4000 43rd St. N., 33714. Tel: 727-525-0262; Email: office@transfigparish.org. Rev. Carlos J. Rojas, Admin.
Catechesis Religious Program—
Email: reled@transfigparish.org. Mercedes Cedeno, Coord. Faith Formation. Students 0.

OUTSIDE THE CITY OF ST. PETERSBURG

BEVERLY HILLS, CITRUS CO., OUR LADY OF GRACE (1964)
6 Roosevelt Blvd., Beverly Hills, 34465.
Tel: 352-746-2144; Fax: 352-746-6892; Email: ourladyofgracecc@embarqmail.com; Web: www.ourladyofgracefl.org. Rev. Erwin Belgica; Rev. Msgr. Cesar Petilla, Parochial Vicar.
Catechesis Religious Program—Email: olgfaithformation@embarqmail.com. Susan Salisbury, D.R.E. Students 49.

BRANDON, HILLSBOROUGH CO., CHURCH OF THE NATIVITY (1960) [JC]
705 E. Brandon Blvd., Brandon, 33511.
Tel: 843-681-4608; Email: dirfinop@nativitycatholicchurch.org; Web: nativitycatholicchurch.org. Rev. John Tapp; Rev. Msgr. James C. Lara, Pastor Emeritus, (Retired); Revs. Felipe Gonzalez; Belisario Riveros; Deacons Mark Taylor, M.D.; Robert Harris; Elix Castro.
Res.: 805 Westbrook, Brandon, 33511.
School—Church of the Nativity School, (Grades PreK-8), Tel: 813-689-3395; Email: ncsprincipal@nativitycatholicschool.org; Web: www.nativitycatholicschool.org. Maureen Ringley, Prin.; Bill Amrhein, Vice Prin.; Jennifer Seebaran, Vice Prin. Lay Teachers 52; Students 623.
Catechesis Religious Program—Tel: 813-689-9101; Email: pam@nativitycatholicchurch.org. Pamela Emery, D.R.E. Students 1,055.

BROOKSVILLE, HERNANDO CO., ST. ANTHONY THE ABBOT (1892)
20428 Cortez Blvd., Brooksville, 34601-5601.
Tel: 352-796-2096; Email: parishoffice@stantchurch.org; Web: www.stanthonytheabbot.org. Rev. Paul Pecchie; Deacons Manuel Carreiro; Michael Ruffner.
Catechesis Religious Program—(Grades PreK-6), Email: dre@stantchurch.org. Mrs. Miriam Melfy, D.R.E. Students 85.

CITRUS SPRINGS, CITRUS CO., ST. ELIZABETH ANN SETON (1976)
1401 W. Country Club Blvd., Citrus Springs, 34434.
Tel: 352-489-4889; Email: steas@tampabay.rr.com; Web: www.stelizabethcs.org. Rev. Sojan Punakkattu; Rev. Msgr. George Cummings, Pastor Emeritus, (Retired).
Office & Mailing Address: 1460 W. St. Elizabeth Pl., Citrus Springs, 34434.
Catechesis Religious Program—Students 48.

CLEARWATER, PINELLAS CO.
1—ALL SAINTS (1987)
2801 Curlew Rd., Clearwater, 33761.
Tel: 727-789-1025; Email: allsaintsclearwater@gmail.com; Web: www.allsaintsclearwater.org. Rev. Alan Weber; Deacons Jack Lyons; Scott Huang.
See Guardian Angels Interparochial School, Clearwater under Elementary Schools, Interparochial located in the Institution section.
Catechesis Religious Program—Students 64.
2—ST. BRENDAN (1978)
245 Dory Passage, Clearwater, 33767.
Tel: 727-443-5485; Email: stbrendan@stbrendancatholic.org; Web: www.stbrendancatholic.org. Rev. Eric Hunter, V.F.; Rev. Msgr. Michael F. Devine, Pastor Emeritus, (Retired); Deacon James Gibson, Pastoral Assoc.
See St. Cecelia Interparochial School, Clearwater under Elementary Schools, Interparochial located in the Institution section.
Catechesis Religious Program—Karen Werner, RCIA Dir.
3—ST. CATHERINE OF SIENA (1976)
1955 S. Belcher Rd., Clearwater, 33764.
Tel: 727-531-7721; Fax: 727-531-7723; Email: scoscontact@gmail.com; Web: www.scosparish.org. Rev. Msgr. Robert Morris, V.G.; Revs. John J. Marino, O.F.M., Parochial Admin.; Charles Leke, (In Res.); Deacons Rick Wells, J.C.L.; Francisco Martinez-Pacini; Joseph Zucchero; Sisters Kathleen Beatty, S.S.J., Pastoral Assoc.; Rosamunda Massawe, C.D.N.K., Pastoral Assoc.
See St. Cecelia Interparochial School, Clearwater under Elementary Schools, Interparochial located in the Institution section.
Catechesis Religious Program—Email: chinery@scosparish.org; Email: briand@scosparihs.org. Elizabeth Chinery, D.R.E.; Sherri Briand, Dir. Youth Min. Students 166.
4—ST. CECELIA (1924)
820 Jasmine Way, Clearwater, 33756.
Tel: 727-447-3494; Email: office@stceceliachurch.org. Rev. Robert J. Schneider; Rev. Msgrs. Aiden Foynes, Pastor Emeritus, (Retired); Patrick Irwin, Pastor Emeritus, (Retired); Rev. Jacinto Vera Mejia, C.Ss.R., Parochial Vicar; Rev. Msgr. Michael Carruthers, Parochial Vicar; Deacons Eusebio Torres; John Ustick.
See St. Cecelia Interparochial School, Clearwater under Elementary Schools, Interparochial located in the Institution section.
Catechesis Religious Program—Email: dre@stceceliachurch.org. Beth Barringer, D.R.E. Students 517.
5—LIGHT OF CHRIST (1966)
2176 Marilyn St., Clearwater, 33765.
Tel: 727-441-4545; Email: info@locchurch.org; Web: www.locchurch.org. Rev. Bill D. Wilson Jr.
See St. Cecelia Interparochial School, Clearwater under Elementary Schools, Interparochial located in the Institution section.
Child Care—Pre-School, Tel: 727-442-4797. Mrs. Rebecca Daschbach, Dir. Lay Teachers 4; Students 60.
Catechesis Religious Program—Tel: 727-442-7081; Email: svv@locchurch.org. Sr. Veronica Visceglia, S.S.N.D., D.R.E. Students 380.
6—ST. MICHAEL THE ARCHANGEL (1981)
2281 State Rd. 580, Clearwater, 33763.
Tel: 727-797-2375; Fax: 727-791-8287; Email: smaclw@verizon.net. Very Rev. Gregg Tottle, V.F.; Rev. Ted Costello, Parochial Vicar; Deacon Paul Koppie; Sisters Therese Carolan, Pastoral Assoc.; Therese Dugan, S.N.D., Pastoral Assoc.
Catechesis Religious Program—Email: kwhite1948@aol.com. Mrs. Katie White, D.R.E. Students 27.

CRYSTAL RIVER, CITRUS CO., ST. BENEDICT (1953)
Mailing Address: 455 S. Suncoast Blvd., Crystal River, 34429. Tel: 352-795-4478; Tel: 352-795-4479; Email: stbens@tampabay.rr.com; Web: stbenedictcrystalriver.org. Rev. Ryszard Stradomski; Deacon Fred Oberst.
Catechesis Religious Program—Students 65.
Daystar Life Center of Citrus County—6751 W. Gulf to Lake Hwy., Crystal River, 34429.

DADE CITY, PASCO CO.
1—ST. RITA (1912) (Hispanic)
14404 14th St., Dade City, 33523. Tel: 352-567-2894; Email: saintritafl@gmail.com; Web: www.stritaparich.org. Revs. Dayan Machado; Carlos Borgos; Deacon Irvin Lau.
Catechesis Religious Program—Yuri Pena, M.H.M.L., D.R.E.; Sr. Norma Cime, M.H.M.L., D.R.E. Students 500.
2—SACRED HEART (1888) [CEM]
32145 Saint Joe Rd., Dade City, 33525.
Tel: 352-588-3641; Fax: 352-588-5299; Email: office@sacredheartdadecity.org; Web: www.sacredheartdadecity.org. Very Rev. Krzysztof Gazdowicz, V.F.; Ms. Claire Obordo, Pastoral Assoc.
Catechesis Religious Program—Email: dre@sacredheartdadecity.org. Mrs. Judy Bires, D.R.E. Students 63.
Child Care—Sacred Heart Child Care Center, 32245 Saint Joe Rd., Dade City, 33525. Tel: 352-588-4060; Email: director@sacredheartecc.com; Web: www.sacredheartecc.com. Ms. Lucinda O'Quinn, Dir. Students 142.

DUNEDIN, PINELLAS CO., OUR LADY OF LOURDES (1959)
750 San Salvador Dr., Dunedin, 34698.
Tel: 727-733-3606; Fax: 727-733-8305; Email: frgary@ourladydunedin.org; Web: ourladydunedin.org. Revs. Gary Dowsey; Victor Amorose, Parochial Vicar; Robert Smith.
School—Our Lady of Lourdes School, (Grades PreK-8), 730 San Salvador Dr., Dunedin, 34698.
Tel: 727-733-3776; Fax: 727-733-4333; Email: frontdesk@myoll.com; Web: www.myoll.com. Dr. Anne Penny, Prin. Lay Teachers 20; Students 239.
Catechesis Religious Program—Tel: 813-733-0872; Fax: 813-733-8305; Email: maryann@ourladydunedin.org. Sarah Davis, Dir. Evangelization & Lifelong Faith Formation; Michael J. Raposa, RCIA Coord. Students 138.

GULFPORT, PINELLAS CO., MOST HOLY NAME OF JESUS (1960)
5800 15th Ave. S., Gulfport, 33707.
Tel: 727-347-9989; Email: pats@mostholyname.org; Web: mostholyname.org. Rev. Francis Mutesaasira Lubowa, J.C.L., Admin.
Catechesis Religious Program—Email: dre@mostholyname.org. Fran Marinari, D.R.E.; Brianna Sims, Youth Min. Students 75.

HOLIDAY, PASCO CO., ST. VINCENT DE PAUL (1969)
4843 Mile Stretch Dr., Holiday, 34690.
Tel: 727-938-1794; Fax: 727-938-1975; Email: frbillsss@svdpfl.com. Revs. William Fickel, S.S.S.; Dominic Long, Parochial Vicar; Deacon Frank Longo. In Res., Rev. Peter Van Tuong Nguyen, S.S.S.
Catechesis Religious Program—Tel: 727-938-1001; Email: svdpfaithformation@yahoo.com. Jane Etzel, D.R.E. Students 105.

HOMOSASSA, CITRUS CO., ST. THOMAS THE APOSTLE (1987)
7040 S. Suncoast Blvd., Homosassa, 34446.
Tel: 352-628-7000; Email: stthom@embarqmail.com; Web: www.stthomashomosassa.com. Revs. Jose Glenn Diaz, Admin.; Jose C. Colina, In Res.
Res.: 18 Beverly Ct., Homosassa, 34446.
Tel: 352-503-6260.
Catechesis Religious Program—Email:

stthom3@embarqmail.com. Alicia Kaltneckar, C.R.E. Students 23.

HUDSON, PASCO CO., ST. MICHAEL THE ARCHANGEL (1971) Revs. James Ruhlin; Pastor Mafikiri; Deacon Eugene Beil.

Res.: 8014 State Rd. #52, Hudson, 34667.

Tel: 727-868-5276; Fax: 727-862-9187; Email: office@saintmichaelchurch.org; Web: www.saintmichaelchurch.org.

Catechesis Religious Program—Email: balvarez@saintmichaelchurch.org. Barbara Alvarez, D.R.E. Students 139.

INDIAN ROCKS BEACH, PINELLAS CO., ST. JEROME (1956) Mailing Address: 10895 Hamlin Blvd., Largo, 33774. Tel: 727-595-4610; Email: pastor@stjeromeonline.org; Web: www.stjeromeonline.org. Rev. Thomas Morgan; Rev. Msgr. Brendan Muldoon, Pastor Emeritus, (Retired); Rev. Robert Cadrecha, Parochial Vicar; Deacon Frederick Kunder; Sr. Lucia Brady, O.S.C., Pastoral Assoc.; Thomas Kurt, Dir. Music Min.

Child Care—Early Childhood Center, Tel: 727-596-9491; Fax: 727-596-8953. Denise Roach, Dir.

Catechesis Religious Program—Tel: 727-595-3100. Patrick Glim, D.R.E.; Joseph Plesko, D.R.E. Students 125.

INVERNESS, CITRUS CO., OUR LADY OF FATIMA (1955) Mailing Address: 550 U.S. Hwy. 41 S., Inverness, 34450. Tel: 352-726-1670; Fax: 352-344-8384; Email: debbiefatima550@yahoo.com; Web: www.ourladyoffatimainv.org. Revs. Timothy P. Cummings; Claudius Mpuya Mganga, Parochial Vicar; Deacons Stephen Kurylowicz; Nick Nowak.

Res.: 518 Desota Ave., Inverness, 34450.

Catechesis Religious Program—Email: annettefatima550@yahoo.com. Annette Tremante, D.R.E. Students 83.

LAND O'LAKES, PASCO CO., OUR LADY OF THE ROSARY (1952)

2348 Collier Pkwy., P.O. Box 1229, Land O'Lakes, 34639. Tel: 813-949-4565; Fax: 813-948-1981; Email: office@ladyrosary.org; Web: www.ladyrosary.org. Rev. Msgr. Ronald Aubin, J.C.L.; Rev. Elixavier Castro; Deacons Augustin Ortiz; Kenneth Anderson; Frank DeSanto; William T. Ditewig, Ph.D.

Catechesis Religious Program—Tel: 813-949-2699; Email: youngdisciples@ladyrosary.org. Mike Buckler, Dir. Youth Min.; Matthew Irwin, Dir. Young Disciples. Students 650.

LARGO, PINELLAS CO.

1—ST. MATTHEW (1985)

Tel: 727-393-1288; Email: info@stmat.org; Web: www.stmat.org. Very Rev. Thomas J. Anastasia, V.F.; Deacon Anthony Quattrocki.

Catechesis Religious Program—Email: faithformation@stmat.org. Mr. Philip Coit, D.R.E. Students 43.

Mission—Holy Martyrs of Vietnam, 9099 90th Ave. N., Largo, 33777. Tel: info@stmat.org. Rev. Gioan Nguyen Vu Viet.

2—ST. PATRICK (1958)

2121 16th Ave., S.W., Largo, 33770.

Tel: 727-584-2318; Email: bhug@stpatricklargo.org; Web: stpatricklargo.org. Revs. Dominic Corona; Jonathan Emery, Parochial Vicar; Deacon Richard Brady.

School—St. Patrick School, (Grades PreK-8), 1501 Trotter Rd., Largo, 33770. Tel: 727-581-4865; Fax: 727-581-7842; Email: kgalley@stpatrickcatholic.org; Web: www.stpatrickcatholic.org. Keith Galley, Prin. Clergy 1; Lay Teachers 18; Students 165.

Catechesis Religious Program—Sr. Kathleen Luger, D.R.E. Students 65.

LECANTO, CITRUS CO., ST. SCHOLASTICA (1987)

4301 W. Homosassa Tr., Lecanto, 34461.

Tel: 352-746-9422; Fax: 352-746-2335; Email: mychurch@stscholastica.org; Web: www.stscholastica.org. Very Rev. James B. Johnson, V.F.; Rev. Jose Tejada; Deacons Robert Smith; Samuel Hunt.

Catechesis Religious Program—Email: tholland@stscholastica.org. Theresa Holland, D.R.E. Students 37.

LUTZ, HILLSBOROUGH CO., ST. TIMOTHY (1985)

17512 Lakeshore Rd., Lutz, 33558-4802.

Tel: 813-968-1077; Email: carrie.rush@sainttims.org; Web: www.sainttims.org. Very Rev. Kenneth Malley, V.F.; Revs. John B. Lipscomb, Parochial Vicar; Louis Turcotte, Parochial Vicar; Deacons Peter J. Burns, Pastoral Min.; Jerry L. Crall; Glenn Smith; Edward LaRose.

See Most Holy Redeemer Interparochial School, Tampa under Elementary Schools, Interparochial located in the Institution section.

Catechesis Religious Program—Tel: 813-961-1716. Justin Lantz, Youth Min.; Peggy Cloutier, Dir. Faith Formation. Students 713.

MASARYKTOWN, PASCO CO., ST. MARY, OUR LADY OF SORROWS (1931)

Mailing Address: 18810 U.S. Hwy. 41, Masaryktown, 34604. Tel: 352-796-2792; Fax: 352-544-0398; Email: sacerdos@bellsouth.net; Web: www.saintmaryols.com. Rev. Thomas L. Madden, V.F.

Catechesis Religious Program—Patricia Pratt, A.R.E. Students 11.

NEW PORT RICHEY, PASCO CO.

1—OUR LADY QUEEN OF PEACE (1913)

5340 High St., New Port Richey, 34652.

Tel: 727-849-7521; Fax: 727-849-4814; Email: office@ladyqueenofpeace.org; Web: ladyqueenofpeace.org. Revs. Sebastian Earthedath, M.S.T.; Joseph Kalarickal, M.S.T., Parochial Vicar; Saji James, M.S.T., Parochial Vicar; Deacon Roger F. Lind.

Catechesis Religious Program—Tel: 727-842-9396; Email: faithformation@ladyqueenofpeace.org. Sally McMullen, D.R.E.

2—ST. THOMAS AQUINAS (1980)

8320 Old C.R. #54, New Port Richey, 34653-6415.

Tel: 727-372-8600; Fax: 727-372-5712; Email: bulletin@stanpr.org; Web: www.stanpr.org. Revs. Eric Peters; George Varkey, M.S.T.

Child Care—St. Thomas Early Childhood Development Center, Tel: 727-376-2330; Fax: 727-372-5712; Email: staecc@aol.com. Alicia Mumma, Dir.

Catechesis Religious Program—Email: suesferra@aol.com. Sue Sferra, Faith Formation Team Leader. Students 400.

PALM HARBOR, PINELLAS CO., ST. LUKE THE EVANGELIST (1985)

2757 Alderman Rd., Palm Harbor, 34684-1700. Rev. Paul Kochu; Deacons Joe Reid, Pastoral Assoc.; Michael Waldron.

Child Care—St. Luke Early Childhood Center, Tel: 727-787-2914; Fax: 727-786-8648; Email: stlecc@gte.net. Kathleen Mitchell, Dir.

See Guardian Angels Interparochial School, Clearwater under Elementary Schools, Interparochial located in the Institution section.

Catechesis Religious Program—Tel: 727-787-2845; Fax: 727-786-8648. Students 271.

PINELLAS PARK, PINELLAS CO., SACRED HEART (1955) 7809 46th Way, Pinellas Park, 33781.

Tel: 727-541-4447; Fax: 727-541-2073; Email: shcc7809@gmail.com. Revs. Kevin Yarnell, Admin.; Vijaya Polamarasetty, O.C.C., Parochial Vicar; Deacons David Sirrianna; Chris Jensen.

Catechesis Religious Program—Email: religiouseducation@sacredheartcatholic.org. Kim Paczynski, D.R.E. & Liturgy Dir. Students 98.

PLANT CITY, HILLSBOROUGH CO., ST. CLEMENT (1912) 1104 N. Alexander St., Plant City, 33563.

Tel: 813-752-8251; Email: info@stclementpc.org; Web: www.stclementpc.org. Revs. Michael T. O'Brien; Pedro Zapata, Parochial Vicar; Deacons Manuel Santiago, (Retired); Neil Legner.

Catechesis Religious Program—Email: cathy@stclementpc.org. Cathy Rosales, D.R.E. Students 520.

PORT RICHEY, PASCO CO., ST. JAMES THE APOSTLE (1984)

8400 Monarch Dr., Port Richey, 34668.

Tel: 727-869-3130; Email: office@stjamesportrichey.org; Web: stjamesportrichey.org. Very Rev. Michael Cormier, V.F.; Deacons Mark Manko; James Minary.

Catechesis Religious Program—Email: faith.formation@stjamesportrichey.org. Deacon Mark Manko, D.R.E. Students 83.

RIDGE MANOR, HERNANDO CO., ST. ANNE (1960)

4142 Treiman Blvd., Hwy. 301, Ridge Manor, 33523. Tel: 352-583-2550; Email: stanne@embarqmail.com. Rev. John S. Hays.

Res.: 35135 Whispering Oaks Blvd., Ridge Manor, 33523.

Catechesis Religious Program—Students 22.

RIVERVIEW, HILLSBOROUGH CO., RESURRECTION (1983) Mailing Address: 6819 Krycul Ave., Riverview, 33578. Tel: 813-677-2175; Email: resurrectioncatholic@yahoo.com. Rev. Eugeniusz Gancarz; Deacon Pedro Leon.

Child Care—Resurrection Early Childhood Center, (Ages 3-4) Tel: 813-672-0077. Ivonne Roldan-Cortes, Dir.

Catechesis Religious Program—Tina Ver Pault, D.R.E. Students 221.

RUSKIN, HILLSBOROUGH CO., ST. ANNE (1956)

106 11th Ave., N.E., Ruskin, 33570-3625.

Tel: 813-645-1714; Email: office@saintanneruskin.org; Web: www.saintanneruskin.org. Very Rev. John F. McEvoy, V.F.; Rev. William M. Santhouse, Parochial Vicar; Deacons Dale Bacik; Edward Smith; Vernon Schmitz; Patrick Frye; Patti Marzilli, Business Mgr.; Linda Parkansky, Min. & Liturgy Coord.

Catechesis Religious Program—Email: choffmann@saintanneruskin.org. Carissa Hoffmann, D.R.E. Students 359.

ST. PETE BEACH, PINELLAS CO., ST. JOHN VIANNEY (1948)

445 82nd Ave., St. Pete Beach, 33706.

Tel: 727-360-1147; Email: info@sjvcc.org. Very Rev. John Blum, V.F.; Rev. Justin Freeman, O. de M., Parochial Vicar; Deacons Joseph Grote; Richard Santello.

School—St. John Vianney School, (Grades PreK-8), 500 84th Ave., St. Pete Beach, 33706.

Tel: 727-360-1113; Fax: 727-367-8734; Email: rromano@sjvcc.org; Web: www.sjvcs.org. Gina Code, Prin. Lay Teachers 20; Students 232.

Catechesis Religious Program—Email: fboyle@sjvcc.org. Frank Boyle, D.R.E. Students 102.

SAFETY HARBOR, PINELLAS CO., ESPIRITU SANTO (1960) 2405 Philippe Pkwy., Safety Harbor, 34695.

Tel: 727-726-8477; Email: terry@espiritusanto.cc; Web: www.espiritusanto.cc. Very Rev. Leonard G. Piotrowski, V.F.; Rev. Bradley Reed, Parochial Vicar; Sr. Donna Daniels, S.N.D., Coord. Pastoral Svcs.; Deacons Vincent Alterio, Pastoral Assoc.; Dominic P. Friscia, Pastoral Assoc.; John Alvarez, Pastoral Assoc.; Greg Nash, Pastoral Assoc.; Steven Girardi, Pastoral Assoc.

School—Espiritu Santo School, (Grades PreK-8), 2405A Philippe Pkwy., Safety Harbor, 34695-2047.

Tel: 727-812-4650; Fax: 727-812-4658; Email: mmansour@escschool.org; Web: www.escschool.org. Veronica Slain, Prin. Lay Teachers 51; Students 415.

Catechesis Religious Program—Tel: 727-812-4656. Students 663.

SAN ANTONIO, PASCO CO., ST. ANTHONY OF PADUA (1883) [CEM]

32852 Rhode Island Ave., P.O. Box 875, San Antonio, 33576. Tel: 352-588-3081; Email: adminassistant@saopccfl.org; Email: business@saopccfl.org; Web: saopccfl.org. Revs. Garry Welsh; Henry J. Riffle, Pastor Emeritus, (Retired); Kyle Smith, In Res.

Catechesis Religious Program—Students 103.

SEFFNER, HILLSBOROUGH CO., ST. FRANCIS OF ASSISI (1987)

4450 C.R. 579, Seffner, 33584. Tel: 813-681-9115; Fax: 813-689-4148; Email: sfaseffner@tampabay.rr.com; Web: stfrancisсс.com. P.O. Box 1218, Seffner, 33583. Rev. Edison Bernavaz; Deacon Richard Beaudry. In Res., Rev. James McAteer, I.C., (Retired).

Catechesis Religious Program—Judy Erlendssaon, D.R.E. Students 149.

SEMINOLE, PINELLAS CO.

1—BLESSED SACRAMENT (1959)

11565 66th Ave. N., Seminole, 33772.

Tel: 727-391-4661; Fax: 727-391-5638; Web: blessedsacramentonline.org/. Revs. G. Richard Pilger, I.C.; James Gordon, I.C., Pastor Emeritus.

School—Blessed Sacrament School, (Grades PreK-8), 11501 66th Ave. N., Seminole, 33772.

Tel: 727-391-4060; Fax: 727-391-5638; Email: bclark@bscschool.com; Web: www.bscschool.com. Mrs. Rebecca Clark, Prin.

Florida Catholic Conference Accrediation Lay Teachers 22; Students 220.

Catechesis Religious Program—Email: faithformationbscseminole@gmial.com. Students 137.

2—ST. JUSTIN MARTYR (1987)

Mailing Address: 10851 Ridge Rd., Seminole, 33778. Tel: 727-397-3312; Email: pwaloga@stjustinmartyr.net; Web: www.stjustinmartyr.net. Rev. Gerald Hendry, Parochial Admin.

Catechesis Religious Program—Bob Metz, Dir., Faith Formation. Students 80.

SPRING HILL, HERNANDO CO.

1—ST. FRANCES XAVIER CABRINI (1980)

Mailing Address: 5030 Mariner Blvd., Spring Hill, 34609. Tel: 352-683-9666; Fax: 352-688-2660; Email: info@stfrances.org; Web: www.stfrances.org. Very Rev. Richard Jankowski; Rev. Jose George, Parochial Vicar; Deacons Roland Desjardins; Gregorio Lugo; Edward Smith; Robert Anderson; Tom Casey; Frank Chiapetta.

Catechesis Religious Program—Tel: 352-686-9954; Email: scollinsworth@stfrances.org. Sherri Collinsworth, D.R.E. Students 557.

2—SAINT JOAN OF ARC (1988)

13485 Spring Hill Dr., Spring Hill, 34609.

Tel: 352-688-0663; Email: jchrchca@tampabay.rr.com; Web: www.stjoanofarcfl.com. Rev. Patrick M. Rebel; Deacons Jose Cruz; Fred LaPiana.

Catechesis Religious Program—Mary Jo Waggoner, D.R.E. Students 95.

3—ST. THERESA (1968)

1107 Commercial Way, Spring Hill, 34606.

Tel: 352-683-2849; Email: joanie@saint-theresa.org; Web: www.saint-theresa.org. Revs. Bruce King, I.C.; Paul Stiene, I.C., Parochial Vicar; James McAteer, I.C., In Res., (Retired); Deacons James McMahon; Victor Gonzalez; Jose Rios, (Retired).

Catechesis Religious Program—Mary Chapman, Dir. Faith Formation. Students 128.

SUN CITY CENTER, HILLSBOROUGH CO., PRINCE OF PEACE (1970)

Mailing Address: 702 Valley Forge Blvd., Sun City Center, 33573-5353. Tel: 813-634-2328;

Fax: 813-633-6670; Email: maureen@popcc.org; Web: www.popcc.org. Revs. Joel Kovanis; Augustine Mailadiyil; Maureen Vilcheck, Business Mgr.
Res.: 1002 Fordham Dr., Sun City Center, 33573.
Catechesis Religious Program—Email: michelle@popcc.org. Michelle Szczeoanski, D.R.E. Students 65.
Mission—Our Lady of Guadalupe Mission (1989) 16650 U.S. 301 S., Wimauma, 33598.
Tel: 813-633-2384; Email: missionguadalupe@gmail.com. Rev. Gilberto Quintero, Admin.

TAMPA, HILLSBOROUGH CO.

1—BLESSED SACRAMENT (1959)
7001 12th Ave. S., Tampa, 33619-4601.
Tel: 813-626-2984; Fax: 813-626-2842; Email: office@blessedsacramentcatholic.org. Rev. Kazimierz Domek.
Res.: 1205 Windermere Way, Tampa, 33619-4601.
Catechesis Religious Program—Students 141.

2—CHRIST THE KING (1941)
821 S. Dale Mabry Hwy., Tampa, 33609.
Tel: 813-876-5841; Fax: 813-873-2426; Web: www.ctk-tampa.org/. Very Rev. Leonard Plazewski, V.F.; Rev. Curtis V. Carro, Parochial Vicar; Deacons Paul Haber; Ronald Fly.
School—Christ the King School, (Grades PreK-8), 3809 Morrison Ave., Tampa, 33629.
Tel: 813-876-8770; Fax: 813-879-0315; Email: ntanis@cks-school.org; Web: www.cks-school.org. Nick Tanis, Prin. Clergy 1; Lay Teachers 37; Students 529.
Catechesis Religious Program—Tel: 813-870-2509. Casey Kiser, Coord. Faith Formation (PreK-5); Alexis Redig, Coord. Middle School Min. & Formation; Melissa Mulson, Coord. Middle School Min. & Formation. Students 553.

3—EPIPHANY OF OUR LORD (1963)
2510 E. Hanna Ave., Tampa, 33610.
Tel: 813-234-8693; Fax: 813-238-5060; Email: epiphany_tampa2@yahoo.com; Web: epiphanytampa.weebly.com/. Mailing Address: P.O. Box 11246, Tampa, 33680. Revs. Edwin Palka; Ignatius Tuoc, Pastor Emeritus, (Retired).
Catechesis Religious Program—Tel: 813-238-1751. Students 120.
Missions—St. Joseph Vietnamese Mission—Rev. Chien X. Dihn, S.V.D., Admin.
Immaculate Conception Haitian Catholic Mission, Rev. Pierre A Dorvil, S.M.M., Priest in Charge.

4—INCARNATION (1962)
8220 W. Hillsborough Ave., Tampa, 33615.
Tel: 813-885-7861; Email: secretary@icctampa.org; Web: www.icctampa.org. 5124 Gateway Dr., Tampa, 33615. Revs. Michael Suszynski; Francisco Hernandez, Parochial Vicar; Brian C. Fabiszewski, Parochial Vicar; Deacons Ramon Rodriguez; Matthew Shirina.
School—Incarnation School, (Grades PreK-8), 5111 Webb Rd., Tampa, 33615. Tel: 813-884-4502;
Fax: 813-885-3734; Email: icsmmood@icstampa.org; Web: icstampa.org. Marrie McLaughlin, Prin.; Elaine Zambito, Admin. Lay Teachers 26; Students 265.
Catechesis Religious Program—(Grades PreK-5), Tel: 813-884-3624; Email: dff@icctampa.org. Students 350.

5—ST. JOSEPH (1896)
3012 W. Cherry St., Tampa, 33607.
Tel: 813-877-5729; Email: stjosephtpa@gmail.com; Web: www.stjosephchurchtampa.org. Rev. Nelson Restrepo; Deacon Jorge Suarez.
Catechesis Religious Program—Tel: 813-877-5729; Email: levantatesjc@gmail.com. Julia Valdes, D.R.E. Students 190.

6—ST. LAWRENCE (1959)
5225 N. Himes Ave., Tampa, 33614-6623.
Tel: 813-875-4040; Fax: 813-876-0491; Email: info@stlawrence.org; Web: www.stlawrence.org. Very Rev. Daniel R. Kayajan, C.S.C., V.F.; Rev. Steven Chuck Dornquast, Parochial Vicar; Deacons Crispin Stout, Admin., Pastoral Progs.; Gregory Lambert; Julio Vazquez. In Res., Revs. Edward C. Keating, O.F.M., (Retired); Lawrence Ahyuwa.
School—St. Lawrence School, (Grades PreK-8), 5223 N. Himes Ave., Tampa, 33614. Patricia Freund, Prin. Lay Teachers 35; Students 509.
Catechesis Religious Program—Students 200.

7—ST. MARK THE EVANGELIST (1996)
Mailing Address: 9724 Cross Creek Blvd., Tampa, 33647. Tel: 813-907-7746; Email: JDePiero@stmarktampa.org. Rev. David DeJulio; Deacons Scott Paine; Jose Moronta; Moises Guitierrez.
Catechesis Religious Program—Email: faithformation@stmarktampa.org. Laura Rivera, D.R.E. Students 893.

8—ST. MARY (1966)
15520 North Blvd., Tampa, 33613. Tel: 813-961-1061 ; Fax: 813-961-3782; Email: office@stmarytampa.org; Web: www.stmarytampa.org. Very Rev. C. Timothy Corcoran III, J.D., V.F.; Deacons John Iadanza; James Manzi; David G. Lesieur. In Res., Rev. Luis Chito Valenciano.
604 Shellcracker Ct., Tampa, 33613.
Catechesis Religious Program—Tel: 813-963-2079; Fax: 813-968-7218. Mrs. Mary Anne Malone, D.R.E. Students 150.
Mission—Santa Maria, 14004 N. 15th St., Tampa, 33613-3554. Tel: 813-263-6979; Email: jgimenez@stmarytampa.org. Rev. Ramon Hernandez, Sacramental Min., (Retired).

9—MARY HELP OF CHRISTIANS (1929)
Mailing Address: 6400 E. Chelsea St., Tampa, 33610.
Tel: 813-626-7588; Email: parish@mhctampa.org; Web: www.mhctampa.org. Revs. Steve Dumais; Benjamin Kim, S.B.D., Parochial Vicar; Deacon Edmond Anctil.
Catechesis Religious Program—Students 52.

10—MOST HOLY REDEEMER (1937)
10110 Central Ave. N., Tampa, 33612-7402.
Tel: 813-933-2859; Email: office@mhrtampa.org; Web: www.mhrtampa.org. Revs. Anthony Coppola; Jonathan Loverita, J.C.L., Parochial Vicar; Deacons Joseph Krzanowski; Kevin Dwyer; Ronald Rojas.
Catechesis Religious Program—Students 80.

11—OUR LADY OF PERPETUAL HELP (1890) [JC] (Hispanic—Haitian)
1711 11th Ave., Tampa, 33605. Tel: 813-248-5701; Fax: 813-241-4128; Email: olph@tampabay.rr.com; Web: olphtampa.org. Revs. Hector Cruz; Kenneth Ridgeway, S.M., In Res.; Raymond Coolong, S.M., In Res.; Paul Morrissey, S.M., In Res.
Catechesis Religious Program—Students 31.

12—ST. PATRICK (1958) [JC]
4518 S. Manhattan Ave., Tampa, 33611.
Tel: 813-839-5337; Email: info@stpatricktampa.org. Revs. Salvator Stefula, T.O.R.; Stanley Holland, T.O.R., Parochial Vicar; Deacon Ben Hooks.
Catechesis Religious Program—

13—ST. PAUL (1963)
Mailing Address: 12708 N. Dale Mabry Hwy., Tampa, 33618-2802. Tel: 813-961-3023; Fax: 813-962-8780; Email: parishcommunications@stpaulchurch.com; Web: www.stpaulchurch.com. Revs. William J. Swengros, J.C.D.; George Gyasi, Parochial Vicar; Robert G. Romaine; Deacons Carlos Celaya; Raymond Dever; Michael Maloney, Business Mgr.
Catechesis Religious Program—Email: ccayon@stpaulchurch.com. Carmen Cayon, D.R.E. Students 793.

14—ST. PETER CLAVER (1893) (African American)
1203 N. Nebraska Ave., Tampa, 33602-3044.
Tel: 813-223-7098; Email: stpeterclaver@gmail.com; Web: spclavertampa.wix.com/spcchurch. Rev. Hugh Chikawe.
Res.: 3708 N. 12th St., Tampa, 33603.
School—St. Peter Claver School, (Grades PreK-8), 1401 Governor St., Tampa, 33602-3044.
Tel: 813-224-0865; Fax: 813-223-6726; Email: mbabatunde@spccs.org; Email: mbraithwaite@spccs.org; Web: stpeterclavercatholicschool.org. Sr. Maria Goretti Babatunde, S.S.M.A., Prin. Lay Teachers 30; Students 209.
Catechesis Religious Program—Sr. Maria Babatyunde, D.R.E. Students 9.

15—SACRED HEART (1860)
Mailing Address: P.O. Box 1524, Tampa, 33601.
Tel: 813-229-1595; Fax: 813-221-2350; Email: jwilliams@sacredheartfla.org; Web: sacredheartfla.org. 509 N. Florida Ave., Tampa, 33602. Revs. George C. Corrigan, O.F.M.; Zachary Elliott, O.F.M., Parochial Vicar; Salim Joseph, O.F.M., Parochial Vicar; Larry Cabrera, Business Mgr.; Sean Fitzsimmons-Brown, Dir. Liturgical Ministries & Music.
Catechesis Religious Program—Email: bferreris@sacredheartfla.org. Barbara Ferreris, Dir. Faith Formation. Students 282.

TARPON SPRINGS, PINELLAS CO., ST. IGNATIUS OF ANTIOCH (1889)
715 E. Orange St., Tarpon Springs, 34689.
Tel: 727-937-4050; Email: kcreamer@ignatius.net; Web: www.st.ignatius.net. Mailing Address: P.O. Box 1306, Tarpon Springs, 34688-1306. Rev. Msgr. Joseph A. Pellegrino; Rev. Kyle Bell, Parochial Vicar; Deacons Samuel Moschetto; John Edgerton; Rev. Kevin Molloy, In Res.
See Guardian Angels Interparochial School, Clearwater under Elementary Schools, Interparochial located in the Institution section.
Child Care—St. Ignatius Early Childhood Center (1984) 725 E. Orange St., Tarpon Springs, 34689. Mrs. Sharon Stokely, Dir.
Catechesis Religious Program—Email: fmorin@ignatius.net. Mrs. Fran Morin, D.R.E. Students 399.

TEMPLE TERRACE, HILLSBOROUGH CO., CORPUS CHRISTI (1958)
Mailing Address: 9715 N. 56th St., Temple Terrace, 33617. Tel: 813-988-1593; Fax: 813-985-3583; Email: pshaneyfelt@spiritualhome.org; Web: www.spiritualhome.org. Rev. Michael R. Smith.
School—Corpus Christi School, (Grades PreK-8), Tel: 813-988-1722; Email: kkearney@cccstt.org; Web: cccstt.org. Kelly Kearney, Prin. Lay Teachers 19; Students 193.
Catechesis Religious Program—Lily Hughson, D.R.E. Students 434.

TRINITY, PASCO, CO., ST. PETER THE APOSTLE (2008)
12747 Interlaken Rd., Trinity, 34655.
Tel: 727-264-8968; Fax: 727-264-8969; Email: office@sptatrinity.org; Email: faithform@spta.org; Email: youth@sptatrinity.org; Email: finance@sptatrinity.org; Web: www.sptatrinity.org. Rev. Msgr. Dennis E. Hughes, V.F.; Deacon James Paterson
Legal Name: St. Peter the Apostle Catholic Church in Trinity, Inc.
Catechesis Religious Program—Gyda M. DePeppe, D.R.E. Students 163.

VALRICO, HILLSBOROUGH CO., ST. STEPHEN (1987)
10118 St. Stephen Cir., Riverview, 33569.
Tel: 813-689-4900; Email: FrDermot@ststephencatholic.org; Web: www.ststephencatholic.org. Revs. Dermot Dunne; Timothy Williford, Parochial Vicar; Deacons Edward Dodenhoff; Daniel Gratkowski.
Church: 5049 Bell Shoals Rd., Valrico, 33596.
School—St. Stephen Catholic School, (Grades PreK-8), 10424 St. Stephen Cir., Riverview, 33569.
Tel: 813-741-9203; Fax: 813-741-9622; Email: lumoh@sscsfl.org; Web: www.sscsfl.org. Linda Umoh, Prin. Lay Teachers 20; Students 315.
Catechesis Religious Program—10424 St. Stephen Cir., Riverview, 33569. Tel: 813-671-4434; Email: Rosie@ststephencatholic.org. Rosie Bridges, D.R.E. Students 1,000.

ZEPHYRHILLS, PASCO CO., ST. JOSEPH CATHOLIC CHURCH (1912)
5316 11th St., Zephyrhills, 33542. Tel: 813-782-2813; Email: info@stjosephzephyrhills.org. Revs. Allan Tupa; Mathew K. Abraham, A.L.C.P., Parochial Vicar; Beverly Burgess, Business Mgr.
Catechesis Religious Program—Students 77.

On Duty Outside the Diocese:
Rev. Msgr.—
Toups, David L.
Revs.—
Boyle, Ryan C., J.C.L.
Clement, Philip Dac
Scott, Philip.

Retired:
Rev. Msgrs.—
Caverly, J. Bernard, (Retired)
Cippel, John A., (Retired)
Cooke, Colman M., Ph.D., (Retired)
Cummings, George, (Retired)
Daly, Desmond, (Retired)
Dechering, Anton, (Retired)
Dee, Dacian, J.C.D., (Retired)
Devine, Michael F., (Retired)
Diez, Antonio, (Retired)
DuBois, William, (Retired)
Earner, Thomas, (Retired)
Foynes, Aiden, (Retired)
Garcia, Avelino R., (Retired)
Irwin, Patrick, (Retired)
Lara, James C., (Retired)
McCahon, Joseph F., (Retired)
Muldoon, Brendan, (Retired)
Mullen, Austin, (Retired)
Neff, John, (Retired)
Revs.—
Andrews, Gregory J., (Retired)
Argentino, Ralph J., (Retired)
Bucaria, James A., Ph.D., (Retired)
D'Antonio, John A., V.F., (Retired)
Dionne, Francis, (Retired)
Gonzalez, Jose G., (Retired)
Goudreau, Paul, (Retired)
Hernandez, Ramon, (Retired)
Kane, John, (Retired)
Lamp, Edward, (Retired)
Lawlor, Brendan, (Retired)
Lettre, Raymond, (Retired)
Lorden, Demetrio, (Retired)
Lydon, Michael, (Retired)
Marecki, Ronald, (Retired)
Merkel, James, (Retired)
Mizener, Paul, (Retired)
Monteleone, Jacob, (Retired)
Morton, Vincent, (Retired)
Murphy, John C., (Retired)
Rahill, Patrick, (Retired)
Riffle, Henry J., (Retired)
Spillett, Thomas, (Retired)
Tuoc, Ignatius, (Retired)
Vera, Jude, (Retired).

Permanent Deacons:
Alterio, Vincent
Alvarez, John
Anctil, Edmond
Anderson, Kenneth
Anderson, Robert
Andre, Peter
Arno, Michael
Bacik, Dale
Beaudry, Richard
Beil, Eugene
Bevvino, Frank, (On Duty Outside of Diocese)
Brady, Richard
Burns, Peter J.
Cardona, David
Carreiro, Manuel
Carter, John
Casey, Tom
Castro, Elix
Celaya, Carlos
Chiappetta, Frank
Conway, Scott, (On Duty Outside of Diocese)
Crall, Jerry
Cruz, Jose
DeSanto, Frank
Desjardins, Roland
Dever, Raymond
Diaz, William
Ditewig, William T., Ph.D.
Dodenhoff, Edward
Dunphy, Melvin
Dwyer, Kevin
Edgerton, John
Evans, Forrest, (On Duty Outside the Diocese)
Fahrendorf, Ted
Fernandes, Rudolph, (On Duty Outside of Diocese)
Fly, Ronald
Fox, John
Friscia, Dominic
Frye, Patrick
Gibson, James
Girardi, Steven
Gonzalez, Victor
Gorman, William
Gould, Stanley
Gratkowski, Daniel
Grevenites, James
Grote, Joseph
Gutierrez, Moises
Haber, Paul
Harris, Robert
Henriquez, Francisco
Holmes, Michael, (On Duty Outside the Diocese)
Hooks, Ben
Huang, Scott
Hunt, Samuel
Iadanza, John
Jensen, Chris
Johanning, Kenneth
Julian, Frank
Kijonka, Anthony
Koppenaal, John, (On Duty Outside the Diocese)
Koppie, Paul
Krzanowski, Joseph
Kunder, Frederick
Kurylowicz, Stephen
Lambert, Gregory
LaPiana, Fred
LaRose, Edward
Lau, Irvin
Legner, Neil
Leon, Pedro
Lesieur, David G.
Lind, Roger F.
Longo, Frank
Lovelace, William
Lugo, Gregorio
Lyons, John
Maldonado, Pablo
Manko, Mark
Martin, Ted
Martinez-Pacini, Francisco
McGory, Gerald
McMahon, James
Medeiros, Joseph
Menchen, Michael
Minary, James
Montayre, Maximo
Moronta, Jose
Moschetto, Samuel
Nagle, Richard Jr.
Nash, Greg
Nowak, Joseph
Oberst, Fred
Orth, Kevin, (On Duty Outside the Diocese)
Ortiz, Augustin
Paine, Scott
Paterson, James
Pignataro, Angelo
Polcari, Joseph
Poole, Gregory
Quattrocki, Anthony
Reid, Joseph
Rios, Jose
Rivera, Jose
Roberts, Lionel
Rodriguez, Manuel
Rodriguez, Ramon
Rojas, Ronald
Ruffner, Michael
Ryba, Michael
Santello, Richard
Schaefer, John
Schmitz, Vernon
Shirina, Matthew
Sirrianna, David
Small, Vincent
Smith, Edward
Smith, Edward G.
Smith, Glenn
Smith, Robert
Snyder, Dennis, (On Duty Outside the Diocese)
Solorzano, Jose
Stout, Crispin
Suarez, Jorge
Taylor, Mark, M.D.
Thomas, Alan, O.F.M.
Tibbets, Albert
Torres, Eusebio
Ustick, John
Vance, Ronald, (On Duty Outside the Diocese)
Vasquez, Julio
Waldron, Michael
Wells, Rick, J.C.L.
Westwater, James
Zeitler, Richard
Zucchero, Joseph.

INSTITUTIONS LOCATED IN DIOCESE

[A] COLLEGES

SAINT LEO. *Saint Leo University*, (Grades Bachelors-Masters), 33701 State Rd. 52, St. Leo, 33574. Tel: 352-588-8200; Tel: 352-588-8894; Fax: 352-588-8917; Email: eileen.dunbar@saintleo.edu; Web: www.saintleo.edu. MC2004 P.O. Box 6665, Saint Leo, 33574-6665. Dr. William J. Lennox Jr., Pres.; Revs. Kyle Smith, Dir., Univ. Min.; Michael Cooper, S.J., S.T.D., Asst. Prof. Religion. An Independent and Catholic Coeducational Liberal Arts University
Saint Leo University, Inc.
Saint Leo University Educational Fund, Inc. Clergy 1; Lay Teachers 224; Priests 1; Students 13,095; Total Enrollment 13,095.

[B] HIGH SCHOOLS, DIOCESAN

ST. PETERSBURG. *St. Petersburg Catholic High School, Inc.*, 6333 9th Ave. N., 33710. Tel: 727-344-4065; Fax: 727-343-9311; Email: info@spchs.org; Web: spchs.org. Mr. Ross Bubolz, Prin.; Mrs. Lori Wright, Media Center Coord.; Mrs. Kathryn Brasseur, Coord. of Youth Ministry; Rev. Anthony J. Ustick, Chap. Lay Teachers 28; Sisters of the Third Franciscan Order (Syracuse, NY) 1; Students 304; Salesians of St. John Bosco (New Rochelle, NY) 4.

CLEARWATER. *Clearwater Central Catholic High School, Inc.* (1962) 2750 Haines Bayshore Rd., Clearwater, 33760. Tel: 727-531-1449; Fax: 727-535-7034; Email: jdeputy@ccchs.org; Web: www.ccchs.org. John Venturella, Pres.; James Deputy, Prin.; Enrique Garza, Asst. Prin.; Mrs. Leanne Knoop, Dean; Lauren Spatola, Dean. Lay Teachers 36; Students 563.

SPRING HILL. *Bishop McLaughlin Catholic High School, Inc.* (2003) 13651 Hays Rd., Spring Hill, 34610. Tel: 727-857-2600; Fax: 727-857-2610; Email: sspencer@bmchs.com; Web: www.bmchs.com. Mrs. Camille Jowanna, Prin. Lay Teachers 20; Students 300.

TAMPA. *Tampa Catholic High School, Inc.* (1962) 4630 N. Rome Ave., Tampa, 33603. Tel: 813-870-0860; Fax: 813-877-9136; Email: enrollment@tampacatholic.org; Web: www.tampacatholic.org. Mr. Robert Lees, Prin. Congregation of Christian Brothers (New Rochelle, NY) 3; Clergy 1; Lay Teachers 67; Students 752.

[C] HIGH SCHOOLS, PRIVATE

TAMPA. *Academy of the Holy Names* (1881) (Grades PreK-12), 3319 Bayshore Blvd., Tampa, 33629. Tel: 813-839-5371; Fax: 813-839-3924; Email: araimo@holynamestpa.org; Web: www.holynamestpa.org. Mr. Arthur Raimo, Pres.; Stephanie Nitchals, Prin. High School
Academy of the Holy Names of Florida, Inc. Lay Teachers 45; Students 464.

Cristo Rey Tampa High School at Mary Help of Christians, Inc., 6400 E. Chelsea St., Tampa, 33610. Tel: 813-621-8300; Email: cspano@cristoreytampa.org; Web: www.cristoreytampa.org. Revs. Franco Pinto, Dir.; Steve Ryan, S.D.B., Provincial Asst.; Joseph Hannon, S.D.B., Teacher/Counselor. Cristo Rey Tampa High School, part of the replicable model of the Cristo Rey Network(R), opened in August 2016 to serve youth from economically-challenged families and provide a life-changing opportunity of an affordable Catholic, college preparatory education and real-world work experience. Lay Teachers 11; High School Students 162; Estimated Number of Catholics 104; Clergy/Religious Teachers 1; Total Students 162; Staff 32.

Jesuit High School, 4701 N. Himes Ave., Tampa, 33614. Tel: 813-877-5344; Fax: 813-872-1853; Email: info@jesuittampa.org; Web: www.jesuittampa.org. Revs. Paul Deutsch, S.J., Rector; Richard C. Hermes, S.J., Pres.; Barry Neuburger, Prin.; Ted Beil, Librarian; Rev. Jay Hooks, Chap.
Jesuit High School of Tampa, Inc., FKA
St. Louis Catholic, Benevolent and Educational Association, Inc.
Jesuit High School Foundation, Inc. Lay Teachers 66; Priests 6; Students 807; Clergy/Religious Teachers 10.

[D] ELEMENTARY SCHOOLS, INTERPAROCHIAL

CLEARWATER. *St. Cecelia Interparochial School*, (Grades PreK-8), 1350 Court St., Clearwater, 33756. Tel: 727-461-1200; Fax: 727-446-9140; Email: scsoffice@st-cecelia.org; Web: www.st-cecelia.org. Ms. Valerie Wostbrock, Prin.; Elaine Deja, Librarian; Sheila Dale, Contact Person & Admin. Asst. Serving Light of Christ, St. Brendan, St. Catherine of Siena and St. Cecelia. Lay Teachers 34; Students 472.

Guardian Angels Catholic School, (Grades PreK-8), 2270 Evans Rd., Clearwater, 33763. Tel: 727-799-6724; Fax: 727-724-9018; Email: mstalzer@gacsfl.com; Web: www.gacsfl.com. Mary Stalzer, Prin. & Contact Person. Serving All Saints, St. Ignatius, St. Luke and St. Michael the Archangel. Lay Teachers 26; Students 243.

[E] ELEMENTARY SCHOOLS, DIOCESAN

ST. PETERSBURG. *Catholic Academies - Diocese of St. Petersburg, Inc.*, P.O. Box 40200, 33743-0200. Tel: 727-344-1611; Fax: 727-345-3086.
Catholic School System - Diocese of St. Petersburg, Inc., P.O. Box 40200, 33743-0200. Tel: 727-344-1611; Fax: 727-345-3086.

LECANTO. *Saint John Paul II Catholic School*, (Grades PreK-8), 4341 W. Homosassa Tr., Lecanto, 34461. Tel: 352-746-2020; Fax: 352-746-3448; Email: office@sjp2.us; Web: www.sjp2.us. John Larkin, Prin.; Donna Osborne, Admin. Asst. A Ministry of the Catholic School System - Diocese of St. Petersburg, Inc. Lay Teachers 21; Students 191.

LUTZ. *Mother Teresa of Calcutta Catholic School* (1954) (Grades K-8), 17524 Lakeshore Rd., Lutz, 33558. Tel: 813-933-4750; Fax: 813-933-3181; Email: office@mtctampa.org; Web: www.mtctampa.org. Mr. Johnnathan Combs, Prin.; Mrs. Jackie St. Charles, Asst. Prin. A Ministry of the Catholic School System - Diocese of St. Petersburg, Inc. Lay Teachers 25; Students 415.

PINELLAS PARK. *Sacred Heart Catholic School*, (Grades PreK-8), 7951 46th Way N., Pinellas Park, 33781. Tel: 727-544-1106; Fax: 727-544-1737; Email: ryevich@shsaints.org. Mr. Robert Yevich, Prin. A Ministry of the Catholic Academies - Diocese of St. Petersburg, Inc. Lay Teachers 23; Students 262.

PORT RICHEY. *Bishop Larkin Catholic School*, (Grades PreK-8), 8408 Monarch Dr., Port Richey, 34668. Tel: 727-862-6981; Fax: 727-869-9893; Email: office@bishoplarkin.org. Sr. Regina Ozuzu, H.H.C.J., Prin. A Ministry of the Catholic School System - Diocese of St. Petersburg, Inc. Lay Teachers 20; Sisters 2; Students 245.

SAN ANTONIO. *St. Anthony Catholic School* (1884) (Grades K-8), 12155 Joe Herrmann Dr., San Antonio, 33576. Tel: 352-588-3041; Fax: 352-588-3142; Email: salice@stanthonyschoolfl.org; Email: denisemckenna@stanthonyschoolfl.org; Web: www.stanthonyschoolfl.org. P.O. Box 847, San Antonio, 33576-0847. Sr. Alice Ottapurackal, F.S.S.E., Prin.; Betty Will, Librarian. A Ministry of the Catholic School System - Diocese of St. Petersburg, Inc.; Catholic School System, DOSP, System. Clergy 2; Lay Teachers 16; Sisters 2; Students 209.

SPRING HILL. *Notre Dame Catholic School*, (Grades PreK-8), 1095 Commercial Way, Spring Hill, 34606. Tel: 352-683-0755; Fax: 352-683-3924; Email: notredame@ndcsfl.org; Web: www.ndcsfl.org. Ms. Florence Buono, Prin. A Ministry of the

Catholic School System - Diocese of St. Petersburg, Inc. Lay Teachers 20; Students 245.

TAMPA. *St. Joseph Catholic School*, (Grades PreK-8), 2200 N. Gomez Ave., Tampa, 33607. Tel: 813-879-7720; Email: bbudd@sjstampa.org; Web: www.stjosephtampa.org. Mrs. Brenda Budd, Prin. A Ministry of the Catholic Academies - Diocese of St. Petersburg, Inc. Clergy 1; Lay Teachers 23; Students 290.

[F] ELEMENTARY SCHOOLS, PRIVATE

TAMPA. *Academy of the Holy Names* (1881) (Grades PreK-12), 3319 Bayshore Blvd., Tampa, 33629. Tel: 813-839-5371; Fax: 813-839-1486; Email: ewise@holynamestpa.org; Web: www.holynamestpa.org. Mr. Arthur Raimo, Pres.; Mrs. Bridgid Fishman, Prin. Elementary School; Stephanie Nitchals, Prin. High School
Academy of the Holy Names of Florida, Inc. Clergy 1; Lay Teachers 90; Sisters of the Holy Names of Jesus and Mary (U.S.-Ontario Provinces) 6; Students 950.

Villa Madonna School, (Grades K-8), (Early Childhood Care Program, Grades 3-8) 315 W. Columbus Dr., Tampa, 33602. Tel: 813-229-1322; Fax: 813-223-4812; Web: www.villamadonnaschool.com. Sr. Mary Jackson, F.M.A., Prin.; Mrs. Vicki Fabiano, Librarian
Salesian Sisters of Tampa, Inc. Clergy 5; Lay Teachers 37; Daughters of Mary Help of Christians/Salesian Sisters 5; Students 332.

[G] PRESCHOOLS AND DAY CARE CENTERS

ST. PETERSBURG. *St Paul Children's Center*, 1800 12th St. N., 33704. Tel: 727-822-3481; Fax: 727-822-1754; Email: toni@stpaulstpete.com. Mrs. Toni Johnston, Dir. 2 months through 2 yrs. Lay Teachers 6.

CLEARWATER. *Light of Christ (Early Childhood Center)* (1985) Ages 2-5, Extended Care. 2176 Marilyn St., Clearwater, 33765. Tel: 727-442-4797; Fax: 727-489-1903; Email: rad@locchurch.org. Mrs. Rebecca Daschbach, Dir. Lay Teachers 10; Students 60.

DADE CITY. *Sacred Heart Early Childhood Center* Infant-PreK, Extended Care. 32245 Saint Joe Rd., Dade City, 33525. Tel: 352-588-4060; Fax: 352-588-4871; Email: sheccleo@embarqmail.com. Ms. Lucinda O'Quinn, Admin. Lay Teachers 28; Students 109.

LAND O'LAKES. *Our Lady of the Rosary Early Childhood Center - Mary's House - ECC*, 2348 Collier Pkwy., P.O. Box 1229, Land O Lakes, 34639. Tel: 813-948-5999; Email: MarysHouse@Ladyrosary.org; Web: www.ladyrosary.org. Corrine Ertl, Admin.; Rev. Msgr. Ronald Aubin, J.C.L., Pastor. Clergy 1; Lay Teachers 10; Students 165.

LARGO. *St. Jerome Early Childhood Center* (1990) Ages 2-4. 10895 Hamlin Blvd., Largo, 33774. Tel: 727-596-9491; Fax: 727-596-8953; Email: preschool@stjeromeecc.org; Web: stjeromeearlychildhoodcenter.org. Denise Roach, Dir.; Rev. Thomas Morgan, Pastor. Children 70; Lay Teachers 4; Students 70; Total Staff 10.

LUTZ. *St. Timothy Catholic Early Childhood Learning Center*, 17512 Lakeshore Rd., Lutz, 33558. Tel: 813-960-4857; Fax: 813-961-9429; Email: daisy.cintron@sainttims.org; Web: www.sainttims.org. Ms. Daisy Cintron, M.Ed., Dir.; Very Rev. Kenneth Malley, V.F. Lay Teachers 6; Students 89.

NEW PORT RICHEY. *St. Thomas Aquinas Early Childhood Center*, 8320 Old CR 54, New Port Richey, 34653. Tel: 727-376-2330; Fax: 727-376-2330; Email: staecc@aol.com; Web: staecc.stanpr.org. Alicia Mumma, Admin.; Kari Glenny, Sec.; Rev. Eric Peters, Pastor. Lay Teachers 4; Students 89; Assistants 4.

PALM HARBOR. *St. Luke Early Childhood Center* Ages 2-4, Extended Care. 2757 Alderman Rd., Palm Harbor, 34684. Tel: 727-787-2914; Fax: 727-786-8648; Email: stlecc@gmail.com. Kathleen Mitchell, Dir.; Rev. Paul Kochu. Lay Teachers 10; Students 75.

TAMPA. *St. Paul Child Enrichment* (1981) Ages 2-5. 12708 N. Dale Mabry Hwy., Tampa, 33618-2802. Tel: 813-264-3314; Fax: 813-962-8780; Email: maguiar@stpaulchurch.com. Mrs. Martha Aguiar, Dir.; Rev. William J. Swengros, J.C.D. Children 115; Lay Teachers 14.

TARPON SPRINGS. *St. Ignatius Early Childhood Center* Ages 2-5. 725 E. Orange St., Tarpon Springs, 34689-1306. Tel: 727-937-5427; Fax: 727-722-9000; Email: sstokely@ignatius.net; Web: www.siecc.net. Mrs. Sharon Stokely, Dir.; Rev. Msgr. Joseph A. Pellegrino. Clergy 14; Students 102.

[H] SCHOOLS FOR EXCEPTIONAL CHILDREN

PINELLAS PARK. *Morning Star Catholic School - Pinellas Park, Inc.* (1969) (Grades 1-12), 4661 80th Ave. N., Pinellas Park, 33781. Tel: 813-544-6036; Fax: 813-546-9058; Email: info@morningstarschool.org; Web: www.morningstarschool.org. Mrs. Susan Conza, Prin. Lay Teachers 15; Students 84.

TAMPA. *Morning Star Catholic School - Tampa, Inc.* (1958) (Grades 1-8), 210 E. Linebaugh Ave., Tampa, 33612. Tel: 813-935-0232; Tel: 813-932-2321; Fax: 813-932-2321; Email: eodom@morningstartampa.org; Web: www.morningstartampa.org. Eileen Odom, Prin.; Alina Lopez, Librarian. Clergy 5; Lay Teachers 9; Students 80.

[I] SCHOOLS FOR THEOLOGICAL AND SPIRITUAL TRAINING

ST. PETERSBURG. *Father William F. Balfe Memorial Library*, 13651 Hays Rd., Spring Hill, 34610. Rev. Msgr. Robert Morris, V.G., Exec. Diocesan Library.

CLEARWATER. *The Cenacle of Our Lady of Divine Providence*, 702 S. Bayview Ave., Clearwater, 33759. Tel: 727-724-9505; Email: cenacleschool@divineprovidence.org; Web: www.divineprovidence.org. 711 S. Bayview Ave., Clearwater, 33759. Alicia Goodwin, Dir. School of Spiritual Direction; Public Association of the Faithful. Lay Teachers 1; Total Enrollment 125; Total Staff 7.

[J] CATHOLIC CHARITIES

ST. PETERSBURG. *Catholic Charities Housing, Inc.*, 1213 16th St. N., 33705. Tel: 727-893-1314; Fax: 727-893-1307; Email: cch@ccdosp.org; Web: www.ccdosp.org. Mr. Frank V. Murphy III, Pres.; Mr. Mark Dufva, Exec. Dir.
Catholic Charities - Alicia Arms, Inc.
Catholic Charities - Arbor Villas, Inc.
Catholic Charities - The Palms at University, Inc.

Catholic Charities, Diocese of St. Petersburg, Inc., 1213 16th St. N., 33705. Tel: 727-893-1313; Fax: 727-893-1307; Email: catholic.charities@ccdosp.org; Web: www.ccdosp.org. Mr. Frank V. Murphy III, Pres.; Mr. Mark Dufva, Exec. Dir. Tot Asst. Annually 15,000; Total Staff 200; Personnel 151.

Jeff Forbes Center - Administrative Offices, 1213 16th St. N., 33705. Tel: 727-893-1313; Fax: 727-893-1307; Email: catholic.charities@ccdosp.org; Web: www.ccdosp.org. Mr. Frank V. Murphy III, Pres.; Mr. Mark Dufva, Exec. Dir. Tot Asst. Annually 15,000; Total Staff 200.

Services Provided, Email: catholic.charities@ccdosp.org; Web: www.ccdosp.org. Life Ministry: Elder: Respite Programs for Caregivers of Memory Loss Clients, Parish based Volunteer Support. Family Services: Resettlement & Immigration Assistance, Mobile Medical Unit for Farm Workers, Pregnancy & Parenting Support. Project Rachel, Adoption, Pathways to Self-Sufficiency, St. Andre Free Clinic; Shelter Ministry: HIV Services: Permanent & Transitional Housing & Voucher Program. Farm Worker Services: Full Service for Migrant Farm Workers including 122 apartments. Homeless Services: Prevention, Housing Counseling, Respite, Emergency, Permanent & Transitional Housing. Elder: HUD 202 Very Low-Income Senior Housing, HUD 202 Service Co-ordination. Affordable Housing: Homebuyer Education & Housing Counseling & Foreclosure Prevention. Benedict Haven, Bethany Family Apartments, Catholic Charities Family Housing, Pinellas Hope, Pasco County Women's Shelter, Pinellas Village, Veterans Transition in Place.

Catholic Charities Community Development Corp., 1213 16th St. N., 33705. Tel: 727-893-1313; Fax: 727-893-1307; Email: cccdc@ccdosp.org; Web: www.ccdosp.org. Mr. Frank V. Murphy III, Pres.

Catholic Charities - St. Benedict Housing, Inc., 1213 16th St. N., 33705.

LARGO. *Catholic Charities - Pinellas Village, Inc.*, 8384 Bayou Boardwalk, Seminole, 33777.

NEW PORT RICHEY. *Catholic Charities - Palm Island, Inc.*, 6423 Illinois Ave., New Port Richey, 34653. Tel: 727-557-4779.

[K] GENERAL HOSPITALS

ST. PETERSBURG. *St. Anthony's Hospital, Inc.*, 1200 7th Ave. N., 33705. Tel: 727-825-1103; Fax: 727-825-1223; Email: john.mullet@baycare.org; Email: marfln@juno.com; Web: www.stanthonys.com. Rev. John Mullet, M.Div., M.A., Dir. Pastoral Care; Mr. Robert Sherman, Dir. Foundation; Rev. Al Hall, Chap. (Baptist); Mardie Chapman, Chap. (United Church of Christ); Jose Furtado, Chap.; Reid Isenhart, Chap. (Presbyterian); Jerome Massimino, O.F.M., Chap.; Sr. Mary McNally, O.S.F. Franciscan Sisters of Allegany.
St. Anthony's Hospital, Inc.
St. Anthony's Ancillary Services, Inc.
St. Anthony's Professional Buildings and Services, Inc.
St. Anthony's Health Care Foundation, Inc. Bed Capacity 344; Tot Asst. Annually 56,024; Total Staff 1,200.

TAMPA. *St. Joseph's Hospital, Inc.* (1934) 3001 W. Martin Luther King Blvd., Tampa, 33607. Tel: 813-356-7310; Tel: 813-870-4000; Fax: 813-872-2936; Fax: 813-870-4639; Email: arlene.mcgannon@baycare.org; Web: www.sjbhealth.org. Jennifer Paquette, Dir.; Karen Cappello, Mgr.; Jill Mallott, Admin.; Jan Hoyt, Pastoral Associate; Revs. Lawrence Ahyuwa, Chap.; Kenneth Gerth, M.C.C.J., Chap.; George Maliekal, Chap.; Lawrence Mulinda, Chap.; Augustine Okwuzu, Chap.; Victor Bartolotta, Chap.; Anthony Britten-Campbell, Chap.; Bee Kirk, Chap.; Anne Butcher, Chap.; Robert White, Chap.; Sonia Alvarado, Chap.; John Aransi, Chap. (Pentecostal); George Francis, Chap. (Baptist); Molly Mary Garnett, Chap. (Presbyterian); Susan Hill, Chap. (Presbyterian); Tina Imperato, Chap.; Kelvin Price, Chap. (A.M.E.); Linda Scrofani, Chap.; Angel Sullivan, Chap. (Am. Baptist, U.S.A.); Briana Whaley, Chap. (Cooperative Baptist). Catholic Health Ministries.
St. Joseph's Hospital, Inc.
St. Joseph's Ancillary Services, Inc.
St. Joseph's Community Care, Inc.
St. Joseph's Enterprises, Inc.
St. Joseph's Health Care Center, Inc.
St. Joseph's Hospital of Tampa Foundation, Inc.
St. Joseph's Specialty Services, Inc.
John Knox Village of Tampa Bay, Inc.
Franciscan Properties, Inc.
San Damiano Enterprises, Inc. Bed Capacity 1,006; Tot Asst. Annually 247,694; Total Staff 6,059; Inpatient Admissions 54,993; Emergency Room Visits 235,136; Outpatient Visits 336,136; Pastoral Care Volunteers 25; Eucharistic Ministers 23; Physicians 1,200.

[L] RETIREMENT AND HEALTH CARE CENTERS

ST. PETERSBURG. *Bon Secours St. Petersburg Home Care Services Inc.*, 10901 Roosevelt Blvd., Ste. 200, 33716. Tel: 727-577-7990; Fax: 727-576-6138; Email: michelle_barlow@bshsi.org; Web: bonsecours.com/st-petersburg. Karen Reich, CEO. Sisters of Bon Secours(Serves Pinellas & Pasco Counties).

**Bon Secours-Maria Manor Nursing Care Center, Inc.*, 10300 4th St. N., 33716. Tel: 727-568-1000; Fax: 727-576-1447; Email: kathleen_walsh@bshsi.org; Email: kip_corriveau@bshsi.org; Web: bonsecours.com/st-petersburg. Karen Reich, CEO; Kip Corriveau, Dir.; Kathleen Walsh, Admin. Sisters of Bon Secours. Bed Capacity 274; Tot Asst. Annually 360; Total Staff 400; Residents Year Round 260.

CLEARWATER. *La Clinica Guadalupana, Inc.* (1995) 1020 Lakeview Rd., Clearwater, 33756. Tel: 727-462-5424; Fax: 727-462-8117; Email: lifeknight@mindspring.com. Dr. Jay E. Carpenter, M.D., Pres. Religious 2; Tot Asst. Annually 3,500; Volunteers 20.

[M] RETIREMENT HOUSING

ST. PETERSBURG. *Blessed Trinity Housing, Inc.* dba Trinity House, 5701 16th St. S., 33705. Tel: 727-865-7590; Fax: 727-867-1701; Email: trinityhousemgr@spm.net. Nanci Huffer, Mgr. Residents 76; Total Staff 4.

Holy Cross Housing dba Casa Santa Cruz, 7825 54th Ave. N., 33709. Tel: 727-541-2631; Fax: 727-547-6741; Email: sjacobs@ccdosp.org. Mr. Joseph A. DiVito, Registered Agent. Total in Residence 76; Total Staff 5.

Transfiguration Housing, Inc., 4021 45th St. N., 33714. Tel: 727-914-8912; Fax: 727-914-8919. Yvonn Lopez-Cortez, Asst. Mgr.

CLEARWATER. *St. Michael's Housing, Inc.* dba Casa Miguel (1984) 2285 State Rd., #580, Clearwater, 33763. Tel: 727-797-8551; Fax: 727-797-8736; Email: jlungaro@ccdosp.org. Mrs. JoAnn Lungaro, Admin. Independent Living. Residents 82; Total Staff 5.

HUDSON. *Bethlehem Housing, Inc.* dba Bethlehem House, 8010 State Rd. 52, Hudson, 34667. Tel: 727-819-2861; Fax: 727-869-2781; Email: bethlehem.house@verizon.net. Virginia Seamster, Mgr. Residents 60; Total Staff 3.

PLANT CITY. *St. Clement Housing, Inc.*, 1102 N. Alexander St., Plant City, 33563. Tracey Brown, Housing Mgr.

TAMPA. *Blessed Sacrament Housing, Inc.* dba Blessed Sacrament Manor, 6801 12th Ave. S., Tampa, 33619. Tel: 813-620-0221; Fax: 813-620-0473; Email: jagosto@ccdosp.org. John Agosto, Housing Mgr. Total Staff 2; Clients 74.

Christ the King Housing II, Inc. dba Kings Arms, 4125 N. Lincoln Ave., Tampa, 33607. Tel: 813-873-0234; Fax: 813-871-2061; Email: k.

arms@verizon.net. Nancy Gonzalez, Mgr. Total in Residence 90; Total Staff 3.

Christ the King Housing, Inc. dba Kings Manor, 2946 W. Columbus Dr., Tampa, 33607.
Tel: 813-875-0139; Fax: 813-876-2182; Email: browen@ccdosp.org. Betsy Rowen, Admin. Residents 115; Total Staff 5.

Epiphany Housing of Tampa, Inc. dba Epiphany Arms, 2508 E. Hanna Ave., Tampa, 33610.
Tel: 813-232-2693; Fax: 813-232-2984; Email: epiphanyarms@carteretmgmt.com. Residents 81; Total Staff 11.

St. Lawrence Housing, Inc., 4815 N. MacDill Ave., Tampa, 33614-6898. Tel: 813-877-5800;
Fax: 813-877-5882; Email: Yajairad@spm.net. Rev. Msgr. Michael G. Muhr, M.Div., M.A., Pres. Total in Residence 80; Total Staff 5.

St. Lawrence Housing II, Inc., c/o 5225 N. Himes Ave., Tampa, 33614. Tel: 813-875-4040;
Fax: 813-876-0491. Rev. Msgr. Michael G. Muhr, M.Div., M.A.

St. Patrick's Housing Corporation dba Patrician Arms, 4516 S. Manhattan Ave., Tampa, 33611.
Tel: 813-835-8227; Fax: 813-835-7918; Email: blendstrom@ccdosp.org. Total in Residence 82; Total Staff 3.

St. Patrick's Housing Corporation II dba Patrician Arms II, 4514 S. Manhattan Ave., Tampa, 33611.
Tel: 813-443-5761; Fax: 813-443-5821. Total in Residence 79; Total Staff 4.

[N] SENIOR CENTERS

LARGO. *Bethlehem Centre, Inc.*, 10895 Hamlin Blvd., Largo, 33774. Tel: 727-596-9394;
Fax: 727-596-8953; Email: Bethlehem.Centre@gmail.com. Joanne Biamonte, Dir. Senior Center offering programs in Fitness, Exercise, Social, Educational, Music, Art, and Religious Nature on Tuesday, Wednesday, and Friday. Hot luncheon is available on Tuesday (Oct.-March). Tot Asst. Annually 275; Total Staff 1; Total Assisted Per Week 125.

[O] MONASTERIES AND RESIDENCES OF PRIESTS AND BROTHERS

ST. PETERSBURG. *St. Anthony Friary* Franciscan Residence and Retirement Community. 357 2nd St. N., 33701. Tel: 727-822-7917;
Fax: 727-821-8067; Email: hnp@hnp.org. Revs. Kevin Tortorelli, Pastoral Min./Coord.; James Nero, Assoc. Pastor; Mario Di Lella, O.F.M., (Retired); Gerald M. Dolan, O.F.M., (Retired); William Bried, O.F.M.; John Hogan; William McConville; John J. Marino, O.F.M.; Thomas P. Jones, O.F.M.; Thomas K. Murphy, O.F.M.; John Anglin, O.F.M.; Eric Carpine, O.F.M.; Kevin Mackin, O.F.M.; Neil O'Connell, O.F.M.; John McDowell, O.F.M.; Joseph Hertel, O.F.M.; Raymond Mann, O.F.M.; Jerome Massimino, O.F.M.; Bernerd Splawski, O.F.M.; Anthony Carrozzo, O.F.M.; Robert G. Young, O.F.M.; Vincent Laviano, O.F.M.; Kevin Downey, O.F.M.; Edward Flanagan, O.F.M.; James F. Toal, O.F.M., (Retired); Adam Szufel, O.F.M.; Bros. Michael Madden, O.F.M.; William Mann, O.F.M., (Retired); Alan Thomas, O.F.M., (Retired); Valerian Vaverchak, O.F.M., (Retired); Karl Koenig, (Retired)

St. Anthony Friary (St. Petersburg) Franciscan Friars-Holy Name Province, Inc. Total in Residence 32.

Missionaries of Africa (1868) 5757 7th Ave. N., 33710-7112. Tel: 727-343-1001; Email: jeangorilla@aol.com; Web: www.missionariesofafrica.org. Revs. Roger A. LaBonte, M.Afr., (Retired), (Retired); Jean Claude Robitaille, M.Afr., Local Supr.; Joseph Elmo Hebert, M.Afr., Coord., (Retired); John Joseph Braun, M.Afr., (Retired), (Retired); Roger Bisson, M.Afr., Ministry, (Retired); Richard Archambault, M.Afr., (Retired); George Markwell, M.Afr., (Retired); Bro. Martin Chapper, M.Afr., (Retired), (Retired). USA Sector Brothers 1; Priests 7.

St. Peter Nolasco Residence (1984) 5650 7th Ave. N., 33710-7112. Tel: 727-345-4766; Fax: 727-347-5345; Email: josepheddy@orderofmercy.org; Web: www.orderofmercy.org. Revs. Joseph Eddy, O.de.M., Local Supr.; Daniel Bowen, O.de.M.; Kenneth Breen, O.de.M.; Oscar Kozyra, O.de.M.; Michael E. Perry, O.de.M.

Fathers of Our Lady of Mercy, Inc. Total in Residence 5; Total Staff 5.

CLEARWATER BEACH. *St. Paul Friary*, 50 Somerset St., Clearwater Beach, 33767-1543. Tel: 727-443-7351. Revs. Stephen Galambos, O.F.M.; Francis Paolo, O.F.M.; Bros. Mark Brown, O.F.M.; Juniper O'Connor, O.F.M.

PINELLAS PARK. *Priests of the Sacred Heart*, 6701 82nd Ave. N., Pinellas Park, 33781. Tel: 727-541-2661;
Fax: 727-547-0408. Most Rev. Joseph Potocnak, S.C.J., (Retired); Revs. Frank Burshnick, S.C.J., (Retired); Paul Grizzelle-Reid, S.C.J., (Retired); Ralph Intranuovo, S.C.J., (Retired); Patrick Lloyd, S.C.J., (Retired); Steve Pujdak, S.C.J., House Treas., (Retired); Gregory Speck, S.C.J.; Bros. Michael Fette, S.C.J., (Retired); Gabriel Kersting, S.C.J., (Retired). Total in Residence 11; Total Staff 2.

SAINT LEO. *St. Leo Abbey* (1889) P.O. Box 2350, St. Leo, 33574. Tel: 352-588-8624; Fax: 352-588-5217; Web: www.saintleoabbey.org. Rt. Rev. Isaac Camacho, O.S.B., Abbot; Revs. David Steinwachs, O.S.B., Prior; Felix Augustin, O.S.B.; Joseph Paek, O.S.B.; Very Rev. Clement Rees, O.S.B.; Rev. Robert Velten, O.S.B. Brothers 7; Priests 5; Internal Oblates 2; Novices & Juniors 3.

ST. PETE BEACH. *Franciscan Friary*, 555 - 68th Ave., St. Pete Beach, 33706. Tel: 727-367-2408; Email: rwells@dosp.org. Rev. Bernardas Talaisis.

TAMPA. *Salesians of Don Bosco*, Mary Help of Christians Center, 6400 E. Chelsea St., Tampa, 33610. Tel: 813-626-6191; Fax: 813-621-5251; Email: frstevesdb@aol.com; Web: www.mhctampa.org. Rev. Stephen Ryan, S.D.B., Contact Person.

[P] CONVENTS AND RESIDENCES FOR SISTERS

ST. PETERSBURG. *St. Anthony of Padua Convent*, 1332 7th Ave. N., 33705-1409. Tel: 727-498-8709;
Tel: 727-954-3981; Email: marfln@juno.com. Sisters Marita Flynn, O.S.F., Contact Person; Margaret Foley, O.S.F., Registrar, St. Anthony's Hosp.; Mary McNally, O.S.F. Franciscan Sisters of Allegany (Allegany, NY). Sisters 3; Total in Residence 3.

ST. LEO. *Holy Name Monastery* (1889) 33201 State Hwy. 52, St. Leo, 33574. Tel: 352-588-8320;
Fax: 352-588-8319; Email: holyname@saintleo.edu; Web: www.benedictinesistersoffl.org. Sr. Roberta Bailey, O.S.B., Prioress. Motherhouse and Novitiate of the Benedictine Sisters of Florida.

Benedictine Sisters of Florida Sisters 14.

TAMPA. *St. Clare Convent*, 2924 W. Curtis St., Tampa, 33614-7102. Tel: 813-870-4272; Email: sistercathycahill@gmail.com. Sr. Catherine Cahill, O.S.F., Sec. Franciscan Sisters of Allegany (Allegany, NY). Sisters 5.

St. Elizabeth Convent, 3000 N. Perry Ave., Tampa, 33603-5345. Tel: 813-229-1978; Fax: 813-228-9066; Email: tuckeryellen@gmail.com; Web: www.alleganyfranciscans.org. Sr. Mary Ellen Tucker, O.S.F., Supr. Franciscan Sisters of Allegany. Sisters 11; Total in Residence 11; Total Staff 7.

Franciscan Convent, 3006 Perry Ave., Tampa, 33603-5345. Tel: 813-229-2492; Email: jeanneosf@aol.com. Sr. Jeanne Williams, O.S.F., Contact Person. Franciscan Sisters of Allegany. Sisters 2; Total in Residence 2.

Surfside Condos - Franciscan Sisters of Allegany, NY, 15462 Gulf Blvd., #1003, Madeira Beach, 33708. Tel: 727-898-9501; Email: joanc1230@tampabay.rr.com; Email: congsecretary@fsallegany.org. Sr. Joan Carberry, O.S.F., Contact Person. Sisters 10.

Villa Madonna Convent, 315 W. Columbus Dr., Tampa, 33602. Tel: 813-229-1322; Email: SECTampaVM19@gmail.com; Email: secsecretary19@gmail.com; Email: eagles@villamadonnaschool.com; Web: www.villamadonnaschool.com. Sr. Mary Jackson, F.M.A., Supr. Salesian Sisters of Tampa, Inc. dba Villa Madonna School Sisters 6; Total in Residence 6; Total Staff 6.

[Q] RETREAT CENTERS

CLEARWATER. *Retreat Ministry of the Marian Servants of Divine Providence*, 702 S. Bayview Ave., Clearwater, 33759. Tel: 727-799-4003; Email: retreats@divineprovidence.org; Web: www.divineprovidence.org. 711 S. Bayview Ave., Clearwater, 33759. Alicia Goodwin, Contact Person. Public Association of the Faithful.

LUTZ. *Bethany Center, Inc.*, 18150 Bethany Center Dr., Lutz, 33558. Tel: 813-960-6300; Fax: 813-960-6303 ; Web: www.bethanycenterfl.org. Mr. Greg Kieler, Dir.; Rev. John B. Lipscomb, Spiritual Advisor/ Care Svcs.

SAINT LEO. *Saint Leo Abbey Retreat Center* (1975) 33601 State Rd. 52, P.O. Box 2350, St. Leo, 33574. Tel: 352-588-8631; Email: saintleoretreat@saintleo.edu; Web: www.saintleoabbey.org. Dianna Roby, Business Mgr.; Bros. Tate Rupp, O.S.B., Youth Retreats; Stanislaw Sullivan, O.S.B., Guest Master. Total Staff 6.

TAMPA. *Franciscan Center, Retreat House*, 3010 N. Perry Ave., Tampa, 33603-5345. Tel: 813-229-2695 ; Fax: 813-228-0748; Email: info@franciscancentertampa.org; Web: www.franciscancentertampa.org. Sr. Anne Dougherty, O.S.F., D.Min., Pres. & CEO; Sharon Joller, Mktg. Dir.; Ora-Leigh Harris, Event Coord.; Ron Rampersad, Kitchen Mgr.; Christina Strain, Admin.; Karen Davies-Chaieb, Admin. Franciscan Sisters of Allegany. Total Staff 8.

Mary Help of Christians Center (1928) 6400 E. Chelsea St., Tampa, 33610-5628.
Tel: 813-626-6191; Fax: 813-626-6191; Email: center@mhctampa.org; Web: www.mhctampa.org. Revs. Stephen Ryan, S.D.B., Dir.; Steve Dumais, Pastor; Michael Chubirko, S.D.B.; Benjamin Kim, S.B.D.; Bruce Craig, S.D.B.; Sidney Figlia, S.D.B.; Paul Grauls, S.D.B.; John Masiello, S.D.B.; Jeremiah Reen, S.D.B.; Kenneth Rodes, S.D.B.; Raul Acosta Zunini, S.D.B.; Bros. Michael Brinkman, S.D.B.; David Iovacchini, S.D.B.; Georges Marquis, S.D.B.; Bob Metell, S.D.B.; Joe Tortorici, S.D.B.

[R] PRIVATE ASSOCIATIONS OF THE CHRISTIAN FAITHFUL

CLEARWATER. COMMUNITY OF THE MARIAN SERVANTS OF DIVINE PROVIDENCE (1981) 711 S. Bayview Ave., Clearwater, 33759. Tel: 727-797-7412; Email: info@divineprovidence.org; Web: www.divineprovidence.org. Diane F. Brown, Dir. Public Association of the Faithful.

Our Lady of Divine Providence House of Prayer,
Tel: 727-797-7412; Email: info@divineprovidence.org.

[S] SUMMER CAMPS

ST. PETERSBURG. *Our Lady of Good Counsel Camp* (1948) 8888 E. Gobbler Dr., Floral City, 34436.
Tel: 352-726-2198; Tel: 352-270-8831;
Fax: 352-726-3212; Email: goodcounselcamp@aol.com; Web: goodcounselcamp.org. 4301 W. Homosassa Tr., Lecanto, 34461. Very Rev. James B. Johnson, V.F., Dir.

TAMPA. *Mary Help of Christians Camp*, 6400 Chelsea St., Tampa, 33610. Tel: 813-626-6191;
Fax: 813-626-5251; Email: frstevesdb@aol.com; Web: www.mhctampa.org. Rev. Stephen Ryan, S.D.B., Contact Person.

[T] CAMPUS MINISTRY

ST. PETERSBURG. *Eckerd College - Catholic Campus Ministry*, c/o 2624 Union St. S., 33712.
Tel: 727-822-2153; Fax: 727-823-5820. Rev. Stephan Brown, S.V.D., Chap. Total in Residence 1.

TAMPA. *Catholic Student Center, University of South Florida* (1967) 13005 N. 50th St., Temple Terrace, 33617-1022. Tel: 813-988-3727; Email: director@catholicusf.org; Email: office@catholicusf.org; Web: www.catholicusf.org. Rev. Justin Paskert, Dir.; Deacon Frank Julian.

University of Tampa - Catholic Student Organization, c/o The University of Tampa, 401 W. Kennedy Blvd., Box 10-F, Tampa, 33606.
Tel: 813-257-3665; Fax: 813-258-7214. Rev. Justin Paskert, Dir.

[U] MISCELLANEOUS

ST. PETERSBURG. *Benedict Haven, Inc.*, 210 72nd Ave. N., 33702. Tel: 727-525-5205; Email: catholic.charities@ccdosp.org; Web: www.ccdosp.org. Catholic Charities, Diocese of St. Petersburg / Benedict Haven, 1213 16th St. N., 33705. Mr. Frank V. Murphy III, Pres.; Mr. Mark Dufva, Exec.

Catholic Charities Community Dev. Corp., 1213 16th St. N., 33705. Tel: 727-893-1313;
Fax: 727-893-1307; Email: catholic.charities@ccdosp.org; Web: www.ccdosp.org. Mr. Frank V. Murphy III, Pres.; Mr. Mark Dufva, Exec. Dir. Tot Asst. Annually 15,000; Total Staff 151.

Diocese of St. Petersburg, Inc., 6363 9th Ave. N., 33710.

DOSP USF Housing, Inc., P.O. Box 40200, 33743-0200.

Good News Ministries of Tampa Bay, Inc., 7403 Restful Water Way, Riverview, 33569.
Tel: 888-932-3248; Email: dir-admin@gnm.org; Web: gnm.org; Web: marriagevocation.net; Web: gnm.org-es.org. 5474 Williams Rd., Ste. 2B, Tampa, 33610. Mrs. Terry Modica, CEO; Mr. Ralph Modica, Chm. Full Time, paid 5; Tot Asst. Annually 1,000,000; Volunteers 25.

Magnificat Inc., Lower Pinellas Deanery Chapter of the Diocese of St. Petersburg, Florida, 3228 13th St. N., 33704. Tel: 727-542-0418; Email: magnificatofstpetersburg@gmail.com.

Partners with Haiti, Inc., 1800 12th St. N., 33704.
Tel: 727-822-3481; Fax: 727-822-1754. Rev. Msgr. Robert C. Gibbons, J.D., J.C.L.

Pastoral Center, 6363 9th Ave. N., 33710.
Tel: 727-344-1611; Fax: 727-345-2143. Deacon Rick Wells, J.C.L., Chancellor. For detailed information on the following listings contact the Chancery Office.

Allegany Community Out Reach Grant Fund, Inc.

Catholic Media Ministry, Inc.

Christopher Assurance, Inc.

The Congregation of the Sisters of St. Clare (Florida), Inc., 625 Court St., 2nd Fl., Clearwater, 33756.

Allegany Franciscan Ministries, Inc.
Regis Manor, Inc.
WBVM, 90.5 FM, Inc., Clearwater.
Catholic Charities Community Development, Corp.
Catholic Charities Foundation of Tampa Bay, Inc.
The Greater Tampa Catholic Lawyers Guild, Inc., P.O. Box 1816, Tampa, 33601.
Franciscan Center of Tampa, FL, Inc., 3010 Perry Ave., Tampa, 33603. Tel: 813-229-2695; Fax: 813-228-0748; Email: info@franciscancentertampa.org; Web: www.franciscancentertampa.org. Sr. Anne Dougherty, O.S.F., D.Min., CEO.
Savings and Loan Trust.
Employee Benefit Trust.

BELLAIR. *Mantle of Mary, Inc.*, 845 Indian Rocks Rd., Belleair, 33756. Tel: 727-446-0939; Email: mpublishing2@gmail.com; Web: www.mantlepublishing.com. Carol Marquardt, Pres., Founder.

BRANDON. *Partners with La Victoria, Inc.*, 705 E. Brandon Blvd., Brandon, 33511-5443. Tel: 813-681-4608; Email: zim.stoten@gmail.com; Web: www.pwlv.org. Rev. John Tapp, Pastor.
**Sun Coast Catholic Ministries, Inc.*, 2716 Broadway Center Blvd., Brandon, 33510.

CLEARWATER. *Allegany Franciscan Ministries, Inc.* (1997) 33920 U.S. Hwy. 19 N., Ste. 269, Palm Harbor, 34684. Tel: 727-507-9668; Fax: 727-507-8557; Email: ecoogan@afmfl.org; Web: www.afmfl.org. Eileen Coogan, CEO. Total Staff 9.

OLDSMAR. **Digital Disciple Corporation*, 3905 Tampa Rd., #24, Oldsmar, 34677. Tel: 727-744-4684; Email: ccerveny@digitaldisciple.network. Sr. Caroline Cerveny, S.S.J.-T.O.S.F., Pres.

PALM HARBOR. **Living His Life Abundantly International, Inc.*, 36181 E. Lake Rd., Ste. 320, Palm Harbor, 34685. Tel: 813-854-1518; Tel: 800-558-5452; Fax: 813-891-1267; Email: info@womenofgrace.com; Web: www.womenofgrace.com. Johnnette S. Benkovic, Pres.

TAMPA. **Renew Haiti, Inc.*, 821 Dale Mabry Hwy., Tampa, 33609. Tel: 813-876-5841; Email: haiti@ctk-tampa.org; Web: www.renew-haiti.org. Very Rev. Leonard Plazewski, V.F., Head of Board.
Tampa Magnificat, 2617 W. Prospect Rd., Tampa, 33629. Tel: 813-390-6611; Email: tampamagnificat@gmail.com; Web: tampamagnificat.org. Patricia M. Eddy, Coord.

VALRICO. **Knanya Catholic Congress of Central Florida, Inc.*, 2620 Washington, Valrico, 33594. Tel: 813-681-6189; Fax: 813-230-8031; Email: jillikal@aol.com.

RELIGIOUS INSTITUTES OF MEN REPRESENTED IN THE DIOCESE

For further details refer to the corresponding bracketed number in the Religious Institutes of Men or Women section.

[0310]—*Congregation of Christian Brothers* (New Rochelle, NY)—C.F.C.
[]—*Congregation of Marians of the Immaculate Conception* (Stockbridge, MA)—M.I.C.
[0220]—*Congregation of the Blessed Sacrament* (Cleveland, OH)—S.S.S.
[0520]—*Franciscan Friars* (New York, NY; Dublin, Ireland)—O.F.M.
[]—*Franciscan Province of Our Lady of Guadalupe*—O.F.M.
[]—*Holy Spirit Fathers*—A.L.C.P.
[0300]—*Institute of Charity* (Peoria, IL)—I.C.
[0780]—*Marist Fathers* (Washington, D.C.)—S.M.
[0850]—*Missionaries of Africa* (Washington, DC)—M.Afr.
[0380]—*Missionary Society of St. Thomas the Apostle*—M.S.T.
[0870]—*Montfort Missionaries*—S.M.M.
[0970]—*Order of Our Lady of Mercy* (Cleveland, OH)—O.deM.
[0200]—*Order of St. Benedict* (St. Leo, FL)—O.S.B.
[1130]—*Sacred Heart Fathers and Brothers* (Hales Corner, WI)—S.C.J.
[1190]—*Salesians of St. John Bosco* (New Rochelle, NY)—S.D.B.
[0690]—*Society of Jesus* (New Orleans, LA; Chicago, IL; Boston, MA)—S.J.
[0420]—*Society of the Divine Word* (Techny, IL; Bay St. Louis, MS)—S.V.D.
[0560]—*Third Order Regular of Saint Francis* (Pittsburgh, PA; Etlers, PA)—T.O.R.

RELIGIOUS INSTITUTES OF WOMEN REPRESENTED IN THE DIOCESE

[0230]—*Benedictine Sisters of Florida* (St. Leo, FL)—O.S.B.
[3110]—*Congregation of Our Lady of Retreat in the Cenacle* (Lake Ronkonkoma, NY)—R.C.
[]—*Congregation of the Servants of Jesus, the High Priest* (Dong Nai, Vietnam)—S.J.P.
[0850]—*Daughters of Mary Help of Christians* (Haledon, NJ)—F.M.A.
[0960]—*Daughters of Wisdom* (Islip, NY)—D.W.
[1180]—*Franciscan Sisters of Allegany, New York*—O.S.F.
[1460]—*Franciscan Sisters of St. Elizabeth* (Parsippany, NJ)—F.S.S.E.
[1260]—*Handmaids of the Holy Child Jesus* (Nigeria)—H.H.C.J.
[]—*Hermanas Franciscanas de La Imaculada*—H.F.I.
[]—*Hermit: Consecrated Virgin* (St. Petersburg, FL)—HER.C.V.
[]—*Missionary Daughters of the Blessed Mother of the Light* (Yucatan, Mexico)—M.H.M.L.
[D]—*Our Lady of Kilimanjaro* (Tanzania, Africa)—C.D.N.K.
[2970]—*School Sisters of Notre Dame* (Baltimore, MD; Chicago, IL; Wilton Prov.)—S.S.N.D.
[1070-03]—*Sinsinawa Dominicans* (Sinsinawa, WI)—O.P.
[]—*Sisters of Charity of the Blessed Virgin* (Dubuque, IA)—B.V.M.
[1930]—*Sisters of Holy Cross* (Montreal, Canada)—C.S.C.
[2990]—*Sisters of Notre Dame* (Chardon, OH)—S.N.D.
[3000]—*Sisters of Notre Dame de Namur* (Ohio Province)—S.N.D.de.N.
[1490]—*Sisters of Saint Francis of the Neuman Communities* (Syracuse)—O.S.F.
[3893]—*Sisters of Saint Joseph of Chestnut Hill, Philadelphia*—S.S.J.
[3750]—*Sisters of St. Chretienne* (Wrentham, MA)—S.S.Ch.
[3770]—*Sisters of St. Clare* (Dublin, Ireland)—O.S.C.
[3930]—*Sisters of St. Joseph, Third Order of St. Francis*—S.S.J.-T.O.S.F.
[]—*Sisters of St. Michael the Archangel* (Toronto, Canada)—S.S.M.A.
[1990]—*Sisters of the Holy Names of Jesus and Mary* (Albany, NY)—S.N.J.M.
[2350]—*Sisters of the Living Word* (Arlington, IL)—S.L.W.
[2160]—*Sisters, Servants of the Immaculate Heart of Mary* (Scranton, PA)—I.H.M.
[4190]—*Visitation of Holy Mary* (Wheeling, WV)—V.H.M.

DIOCESAN CEMETERIES

CLEARWATER. *Miserere Guild, Inc.* dba Calvary Catholic Cemetery, 5233 118th Ave. N., Clearwater, 33760. Tel: 727-572-4355; Fax: 727-592-9241. Mr. Terry Young, Dir.; Rev. Charles Leke, Chap.

NECROLOGY

† Mulligan, Edward, (Retired), Died Aug. 3, 2018
† Wal, Edward, Transfiguration, St. Petersburg, Died Oct. 21, 2018

An asterisk (*) denotes an organization that has established tax-exempt status directly with the IRS and is not covered by the USCCB Group Ruling.

Diocese of Salina

(Dioecesis Salinensis)

Most Reverend

GERALD L. VINCKE

Bishop of Salina; ordained June 12, 1999; appointed Bishop of Salina June 13, 2018; installed August 22, 2018. *Office: 103 N. Ninth, P.O. Box 980, Salina, KS 67402-0980.*

Chancery Office: 103 N. Ninth, P.O. Box 980, Salina, KS 67402-0980. Tel: 785-827-8746; Fax: 785-827-6133.

Email: chancery@salinadiocese.org

Web: www.salinadiocese.org

Square Miles 26,685.

Formerly Diocese of Concordia.

Established August 2, 1887.

See transferred to Salina December 23, 1944.

(New boundaries established by Apostolic Letters dated July 1, 1897).

Bounded on the west by Colorado, on the north by Nebraska, on the east by the east lines of Washington, Riley, Geary and Dickinson Counties, and on the south by the south lines of Dickinson, Saline, Ellsworth, Russell, Ellis, Trego, Gove, Logan and Wallace Counties in the State of Kansas.

For legal titles of parishes and diocesan institutions, consult the Chancery Office.

STATISTICAL OVERVIEW

Personnel	
Bishop	1
Priests: Diocesan Active in Diocese	34
Priests: Diocesan Active Outside Diocese	1
Priests: Retired, Sick or Absent	18
Number of Diocesan Priests	53
Religious Priests in Diocese	17
Total Priests in Diocese	70
Extern Priests in Diocese	2
Ordinations:	
Diocesan Priests	1
Transitional Deacons	1
Permanent Deacons in Diocese	18
Total Brothers	1
Total Sisters	92
Parishes	
Parishes	86
With Resident Pastor:	
Resident Diocesan Priests	30
Resident Religious Priests	8
Without Resident Pastor:	
Administered by Priests	45
Administered by Lay People	3
Professional Ministry Personnel:	
Brothers	3
Sisters	7
Lay Ministers	88
Welfare	
Catholic Hospitals	1
Total Assisted	36,771
Homes for the Aged	2
Total Assisted	228
Educational	
Diocesan Students in Other Seminaries	11
Total Seminarians	11
High Schools, Diocesan and Parish	5
Total Students	573
Elementary Schools, Diocesan and Parish	11
Total Students	1,729
Catechesis/Religious Education:	
High School Students	945
Elementary Students	1,838
Total Students under Catholic Instruction	5,096
Teachers in the Diocese:	
Priests	3
Lay Teachers	232
Vital Statistics	
Receptions into the Church:	
Infant Baptism Totals	624
Minor Baptism Totals	53
Adult Baptism Totals	90
Received into Full Communion	126
First Communions	785
Confirmations	771
Marriages:	
Catholic	179
Interfaith	98
Total Marriages	277
Deaths	532
Total Catholic Population	37,891
Total Population	331,051

Former Bishops—Rt. Revs. RICHARD SCANNELL, D.D., cons. in Nashville, Tenn., Nov. 30, 1887; transferred to Omaha, Jan. 30, 1891; died Jan. 8, 1916; JOHN J. HENNESSY, D.D., Apostolic Administrator, 1891-98, Bishop of Wichita; THADDEUS BUTLER, D.D., Bishop-elect; died July 17, 1897; JOHN F. CUNNINGHAM, D.D., cons. Sept. 21, 1898; died June 23, 1919; Most Revs. FRANCIS J. TIEF, D.D., cons. March 30, 1921; retired and appointed Titular Bishop of Nisa, June 11, 1938; died Sept. 22, 1965; FRANK A. THILL, D.D., cons. Oct. 28, 1938; transferred to Salina, Dec. 23, 1944; died May 21, 1957; FREDERICK W. FREKING, D.D., J.C.D., cons. Nov. 30, 1957; transferred to LaCrosse, Dec. 30, 1964; CYRIL J. VOGEL, D.D., ord. Bishop, June 17, 1965; died Oct. 4, 1979; DANIEL W. KUCERA, O.S.B., Ph.D., D.D., ord. May 26, 1949; appt. Titular Bishop of Natchez and Auxiliary Bishop of Joliet, June 6, 1977; cons. July 21, 1977; appt. Bishop of Salina, March 11, 1980; installed May 7, 1980; transferred to Archbishop of Archdiocese of Dubuque, Feb. 23, 1984; retired Oct. 16, 1995; GEORGE K. FITZSIMONS, D.D., ord. March 18, 1961; appt. Titular Bishop of Pertusa and Auxiliary Bishop of Kansas City-St. Joseph May 27, 1975; Episcopal ord. July 3, 1975; appt. Bishop of Salina March 22, 1984; installed May 29, 1984; retired Oct. 21, 2004; died July 28, 2013.; PAUL S. COAKLEY, ord. May 21, 1983; appt. Bishop of Salina Oct. 21, 2004; ord. and installed Dec. 28, 2004; appt. Archbishop of Oklahoma City Dec. 16, 2010; installed Feb. 11, 2011.; EDWARD J. WEISENBURGER, ord. Dec. 19, 1987; appt. Bishop of Salina Feb. 6, 2012; ord. and installed May 1, 2012; appt. Bishop of Tucson Oct. 3, 2017; installed Nov. 29, 2017.

Chancery Office—103 N. Ninth, P.O. Box 980, Salina, 67402-0980. Tel: 785-827-8746; Fax: 785-827-6133.

Chancellor & Moderator of the Curia—Mailing Address: P.O. Box 980, Salina, 67402-0980. Rev. KEITH WEBER, Email: keith.weber@salinadiocese.org.

Vicar General—Rev. FRED GATSCHET.

Vicar for Clergy—Rev. RICHARD DAISE.

Vice Chancellor—MR. COREY LYON, J.C.L.

Prenuptial Paperwork Services—MR. COREY LYON, J.C.L., Mailing Address: P.O. Box 980, Salina, 67402-0980.

Diocesan Finance Officer—MR. KYLE HAUGH, CPA; MRS. JENNIFER HOOD, CPA, Asst. Finance Officer & Business Mgr., Mailing Address: P.O. Box 980, Salina, 67402-0980.

Diocesan Tribunal—103 N. Ninth, P.O. Box 980, Salina, 67402-0980. Tel: 785-827-8746; Fax: 785-827-6133.

Judicial Vicar-Officialis—Rev. Msgr. BARRY E. BRINKMAN, J.C.L., J.V.

Defender of the Bond—Rev. Msgr. JAMES E. HAKE, J.C.L., (Retired).

Diocesan Judges & Auditor—MR. COREY LYON, J.C.L.; Revs. PETER O'DONNELL, J.C.L.; DANIEL L. SCHEETZ, J.C.L., (Retired).

Notary—Sr. CAROLYN JUENEMANN, C.S.J.

Procurator and Advocate—Rev. RANDALL D. WEBER, J.C.L.

Diocesan Finance Council—MR. KYLE HAUGH, CPA, Chm.; JAN MARKS; BETH SHEARER, C.F.R.E.; MRS. JENNIFER HOOD, CPA; TIM WERTH; MR. TROY SOUKUP; MR. RON GFELLER; MR. DAVID DREILING; MR. NORMAN KELLY; MITZI RICHARDS; JORDAN WEBB; DOUG STEIN; AMY STONEBRAKER; Most Rev. GERALD L. VINCKE.

College of Consultors—Rev. Msgr. JAMES E. HAKE, J.C.L., (Retired); Revs. FRED GATSCHET; KEITH WEBER; MICHAEL ELANJIMATTATHIL, C.M.I.; FRANK COADY; KEVIN WEBER; JOSEPH KIEFFER; Rev. Msgr. BARRY E. BRINKMAN, J.C.L., J.V.; Most Rev. GERALD L. VINCKE.

Personnel Board—Rev. Msgr. BARRY E. BRINKMAN, J.C.L., J.V., Chm. & Ex Officio; Revs. DONALD D. ZIMMERMAN, (Retired); GALE HAMMERSCHMIDT; MICHAEL ELANJIMATTATHIL, C.M.I., (India). Ex Officio: Revs. KEITH WEBER; FRED GATSCHET; Most Rev. GERALD L. VINCKE.

Priests' Council—Revs. JOSEPH KIEFFER; DANA CLARK; KEVIN WEBER; RICHARD DAISE; MICHAEL ELANJIMATTATHIL, C.M.I.; KEITH WEBER; Rev. Msgr. BARRY E. BRINKMAN, J.C.L., J.V.; Revs. GALE HAMMERSCHMIDT; DONALD ZIMMERMAN; FRED GATSCHET; JARETT KONRADE; NICHOLAS PARKER; FRANK COADY. Ex Officio: Rev. Msgr. JAMES E. HAKE, J.C.L., (Retired); Most Rev. GERALD L. VINCKE.

Office of Priestly Vocations—Revs. GALE HAMMERSCHMIDT, Co Dir.; KEVIN WEBER, Co Dir. Vocations Board: Revs. KEVIN WEBER; CARLOS RUIZ SANTOS; Sr. BARBARA ELLEN APACELLER, C.S.J.; MR. RICK BINDER; Revs. GALE HAMMERSCHMIDT; JARETT KONRADE; NICHOLAS PARKER; Most Rev. GERALD L. VINCKE.

Diocesan Offices and Directors

Art and Architecture Commission—MR. KYLE HAUGH, CPA, Chm.; Rev. Msgr. JAMES E. HAKE, J.C.L., Vice Chm., (Retired); Revs. FRANK COADY; DONALD D. ZIMMERMAN, (Retired); KEVIN WEBER; MRS. JENNIFER HOOD, CPA; DAVID LARSON; JEFF EASTER; BETH SHEARER, C.F.R.E. Ex Officio: Rev. KEITH WEBER; Most Rev. GERALD L. VINCKE.

Priests' Continuing Formation Committee—Revs. RICHARD DAISE, Chm.; FRANK COADY; BRIAN LAGER; DANA CLARK; Most Rev. GERALD L. VINCKE.

Catholic Charities Board—MICHELLE L. MARTIN, CEO & Exec. Dir.; MRS. JOYCE RATCLIFF; MARC ZIEGLER; CASY ZIEGLER, Sec.; JOANN NEWTON, Treas.; VIC BAIER, Sec.; DEBBIE BAIER; RYAN ROSAUER; SHANNON ROSAUER; FRENCHIE BUCKNER; JENNIFER SCHAULIS, Pres.; DAN SCHIPPERS, Vice Pres.; RITA

KEATING; MARK RITTER; DOREEN SIMPSON. Ex Officio: Rev. JEROME L. MORGAN; Most Rev. GERALD L. VINCKE.

Catholic Charities of Northern Kansas—1500 S. 9th St., P.O. Box 1366, Salina, 67401. Tel: 785-825-0208; Fax: 785-826-9708. MICHELLE L. MARTIN, CEO & Exec. Dir., Email: mmartin@ccnks.org; ERIC FRANK, Dir. Devel.; CARLISLE BERGQUIST, M.A., L.C.M.F.T., Therapist; JEANIE WARNER, Mktg. & Data Mgr.; PEGGY CRIPPEN, PMI/Adoption Case Worker; DIANA DE LA TORRE, Front Office Asst.; BERTA LOPEZ, Salina Office Mgr.; JUAN C. SEQURA DE LUNA, Immigration Asst.; CLAUDETTE HUMPHREY, Dir. Financial Stabilization; CECILIA SMITH, Finance Mgr.; JILL SMITH-BARKER, Outreach/Disaster Relief Mgr.; CARA IVEY, Volunteer Coord.

Immigration—KAREN Q. COUCH, Immigration Attorney.

Catholic Charities Outreach Office - Hays—JEANNE RIEDEL, Office Mgr.; AMANDA ROME, Social Svc. Case Mgr.; GWEN HODGES, M.S.W., L.S.C.S.W., Counseling, 112 E. 12th St., Hays, 67601. Tel: 785-625-2644; Tel: 877-625-2644; Fax: 785-625-6497.

Catholic Charities Outreach Office - Manhattan—323 Poyntz, Ste. 102, Manhattan, 66502. Tel: 785-323-0644; Email: ccmanhattan@ccnks.org. HELEN MATTHEWS, Office Mgr.; JESSICA PALEN, PMI/Adoption/Therapist; DARA STEPHENS, Mobile Outreach Coord.

Catholic Community Annual Appeal—Mailing Address: P.O. Box 980, Salina, 67402-0980. Fax: 785-827-6133.

Office of Catholic Formation—Sr. BARBARA ELLEN APACELLER, C.S.J., Dir., 103 N. Ninth, P.O. Box 825, Salina, 67402. Tel: 785-827-8746; Fax: 785-827-6133.

Coordinator of Office of Catholic Formation—Sr. BARBARA ELLEN APACELLER, C.S.J., Email: barbcsj@salinadiocese.org.

Director of Religious Education—Sr. BARBARA ELLEN APACELLER, C.S.J., Email: barbcsj@salinadiocese.org.

Secretary & Audio Visuals—JULIE BILSON.

Superintendent of Schools—DR. NICK COMPAGNONE, Email: ministry@salinadiocese.org; Web: www.salinadiocese.com.

Executive Secretary for Religious Education & Schools—KAREN TAYLOR.

Director Adult Faith Formation—Rev. FRANK COADY, Email: liturgy@salinadiocese.org.

Office of Deacons—Mailing Address: P.O. Box 980, Salina, 67402. Email: liturgy@salinadiocese.org. Rev. NICHOLAS PARKER, Dir.

Associate Director of Deacons—Rev. NICHOLAS PARKER.

Audiovisual—JULIE BILSON, Email: avlibrary@salinadiocese.org.

Office of Family Life—Email: familylife@salinadiocese.org. MR. COREY LYON, J.C.L., Dir.

Office of New Evangelization—Rev. STEVEN HEINA, Moderator, P.O. Box 908, Salina, 67402-0980.

Catholic Youth Organization and Youth Ministry—Sr. BARBARA ELLEN APACELLER, C.S.J., Mailing Address: P.O. Box 980, Salina, 67402.

Cursillo—Rev. DAMIAN RICHARDS, Spiritual Dir., St. John the Baptist Parish, 622 E. Main, Beloit, 67420; CHRISTIAN LUTZ, Contact Person, 501 E. 8th St., Hays, 67601. Tel: 785-259-5168.

Holy Childhood, Pontifical Association—Rev. STEVEN HEINA, Dir., P.O. Box 980, Salina, 67402.

Office of Liturgy—Rev. FRANK COADY, Dir., Mailing Address: P.O. Box 980, Salina, 67402. Tel: 785-827-8746; Fax: 785-827-6133; Email: liturgy@salinadiocese.org.

Newspaper—The Register of the Roman Catholic Diocese of Salina, Inc. KAREN BONAR, Editor; MRS. JENNIFER HOOD, CPA, Business Mgr., Email: newspaper1@salinadiocese.org. Mailing Address: P.O. Box 1038, Salina, 67402.

Propagation of the FaithRev. STEVEN HEINA, Dir., P.O. Box 980, Salina, 67402. Tel: 785-827-8746; Email: propfaith@salinadiocese.org.

Rural Life Conference—Sacred Heart Parish, 585 N. French, Colby, 67701. Tel: 785-462-2179; Fax: 785-460-6613. Rev. RICHARD DAISE, Dir., Email: richarddaise@sbcglobal.net.

Diocesan Rural Life Commission—Rev. RICHARD DAISE, Moderator; TOM MURPHY, Pres.; PETER LORENZ, Vice Pres.; GREG STEPHENS; JANICE KRUSE, Treas.; GEORGE GASSMAN; ROSANN FELDER; Sr. CARMELLA THIBAULT, C.S.J.; Rev. BRIAN LAGER, Sec.; JO MURPHY; JUSTINE DLABAL; FRANCIS GOECKEL; ARTHUR BEFORT; Most Rev. GERALD L. VINCKE.

Salina Diocesan Clergy Health and Retirement Association, Inc.—103 N. Ninth, P.O. Box 980, Salina, 67402-0980. Board of Trustees: MR. KYLE HAUGH, CPA, Chm.; Revs. ALVIN WERTH, (Retired); JOSEPH KIEFFER; RICHARD DAISE; HENRY BAXA, At Large, (Retired); DAVID METZ; DONALD ZIMMERMAN, At Large. Ex Officio: Rev. Msgr. BARRY E. BRINKMAN, J.C.L., J.V.; MRS. JENNIFER HOOD, CPA; BETH SHEARER, C.F.R.E.; Rev. FRED GATSCHET; Most Rev. GERALD L. VINCKE.

Salina Diocesan Council of Catholic Women (S.D. CC.W.)—Rev. DARYL OLMSTEAD, Moderator, St. Boniface, Box 87, Tipton, 67485.

Boy Scouts—Rev. BRIAN LAGER, P.O. Box 100, Plainville, 67663-0100.

Girl Scouts—Sr. BARBARA ELLEN, C.S.J., Dir., Mailing Address: P.O. Box 825, Salina, 67402-0825.

Office of Priestly Vocations—Revs. GALE HAMMERSCHMIDT, Co Dir.; KEVIN WEBER, Co Dir.

Lay Review Board-Diocesan Committee Regarding Alleged Cases of Child Sexual Abuse—MRS. SHERRIE KELLY, Chair; MR. COREY LYON, J.C.L., Moderator; MRS. NANCY MAIN; DR. GEORGE JERKOVICH; MRS. MONICA WOOLSONCROFT; MR. GUY STEIER; MICHAEL MARSHALL; MRS. MELISSA SHORT ESHLEMAN. Ex Officio: Deacon STEVEN H. FRUEH, Diocesan Assistance Coord.; MRS. MARIA CHENEY; Revs. BILL SURMEIER; KEITH WEBER; Rev. Msgr. JAMES E. HAKE, J.C.L., (Retired); Most Rev. GERALD L. VINCKE.

Office of Safety and Security—MR. COREY LYON, J.C.L., Moderator, Email: corey.lyon@salinadiocese.org.

To Report Abuse—Tel: 785-825-0865; Email: reportabuse@salinadiocese.org. MRS. MARIA CHENEY, Diocesan Assistance Coord., Mailing Address: P.O. Box 2984, Salina, 67402. Tel: 785-827-8746.

Hispanic Ministry Committee—Revs. CARLOS RUIZ SANTOS, Dir.; KEVIN WEBER; Rev. Msgr. BARRY E. BRINKMAN, J.C.L., J.V.; Revs. DONALD ZIMMERMAN; ANDREW ROCKERS; JOHN SCHMEIDLER, O.F.M.Cap.; GALE HAMMERSCHMIDT; Most Rev. GERALD L. VINCKE. All Mexican Missionary Sisters currently working in the diocese.

Respect Life—

Moderator—Rev. HENRY BAXA, (Retired), St. Edward Parish Rectory, 1827 Q St., Belleville, 66935. Tel: 785-527-5559; Email: stedward1925@gmail.com. Coordinator: MR. COREY LYON, J.C.L., Email: respectlife@salinadiocese.org.

Office of Stewardship & Development—BETH SHEARER, C.F.R.E., Dir., Chancery Office, P.O. Box 980, Salina, 67402-0980. Email: beth.shearer@salinadiocese.org.

Office of Hispanic Ministry—Mailing Address: Chancery Office, P.O. Box 980, Salina, 67402-0980. Rev. CARLOS RUIZ SANTOS, Dir.

Office of Information Technology—MR. JEFF EASTER, Dir.

Catholic Community Foundation Board—BETH SHEARER, C.F.R.E., Dir.; MR. KYLE HAUGH, CPA; MR. JERRY PATTERSON; MRS. JENNIFER HOOD, CPA; FRIEDA MAI WEIS; Revs. LARRY LETOURNEAU, (Retired); RICHARD DAISE; DONALD ZIMMERMAN; NORLENE LETOURNEAU.

CLERGY, PARISHES, MISSIONS AND PAROCHIAL SCHOOLS

CITY OF SALINA

(SALINE COUNTY)

1—SACRED HEART CATHEDRAL PARISH (1876) [JC] Revs. Nicholas Parker; Justin Palmer; Deacons Jorge Rivera; Mark Roberti.
Church: 118 N. Ninth St., 67401. Tel: 785-823-7221; Email: sacredheart@shcathedral.com; Web: www.shcathedral.com.
Catechesis Religious Program—Email: pa@shcathedral.com English Religious Education; Email: aaranda12@hotmail.com Spanish Religious Education. Nancy Jaquay, D.R.E., R.C.I.A. & Pastoral Assoc.; Mirna Aranda, Spanish D.R.E. Students 314.
Mission—St. Joseph, Brookville, 118 N. 9th, 67401.

2—ST. ELIZABETH ANN SETON PARISH (1982) [JC]
1000 Burr Oak Ln., 67401. Tel: 785-825-5282; Email: office@stesalina.org; Web: www.stesalina.org. Rev. Keith Weber.
Rectory—1061 Burr Oak Ln., 67401.
Tel: 785-825-4413.
Catechesis Religious Program—Melanie Melander, D.R.E.; Luci Larson, D.R.E. Students 177.

3—ST. MARY QUEEN OF THE UNIVERSE PARISH (1959) [JC]
230 E. Cloud St., 67401. Tel: 785-827-5575; Email: kathy@stmsalina.org; Web: stmsalina.org. Revs. Kevin Weber; Andy Hammeke.
Rectory—324 Albert, 67401.
School—St. Mary Queen of the Universe Parish School, (Grades PreK-6), 304 E. Cloud St., 67401. Tel: 785-827-4200; Fax: 785-827-7765; Email: kcochran@stmarysalina.org. Dr. Nick Compagnone, Prin. Lay Teachers 31; Students 295.
Catechesis Religious Program—Nancy Sherffius, D.R.E. Students 162.
Mission—St. Patrick Parish, 800 Block Spring St., Gypsum, 67448.

OUTSIDE THE CITY OF SALINA

ABILENE, DICKINSON CO., ST. ANDREW PARISH (1874) [CEM]
311 S. Buckeye Ave., Abilene, 67410.
Tel: 785-263-1570; Email: stachurch@eaglecom.net; Web: www.standrewparishabilene.org. Rev. Donald Zimmerman.
Rectory—201 S.W. 4th. Tel: 785-263-7094.
School—St. Andrew Parish School, (Grades PreK-5), Tel: 785-263-2453; Email: standrews@sasabilene.com; Web: standrewsabilene.com. Christina Bacon, Prin.; Rev. Abraham Panthalanickal. Clergy 1; Lay Teachers 8; Students 112.
Catechesis Religious Program—Shannon Woods, D.R.E. Students 131.

ANGELUS, SHERIDAN CO., ST. PAUL PARISH (1887) [CEM] (German), Attended by St. Joseph Parish, Oakley.
12001 S. Rd. 130 W., Angelus, 67738.
Tel: 785-671-3828; Email: stpauls@st-tel.net. Mailing Address: c/o St. Joseph Parish, 625 Freeman Ave., Oakley, 67748. Revs. Donald F. Pfannenstiel; Luke Thielen.

Catechesis Religious Program—Tel: 785-443-2728; Email: ostmeyerjaj@yahoo.com. Amanda Ostmeyer, D.R.E. Students 36.

ANTONINO, ELLIS CO., OUR LADY HELP OF CHRISTIANS PARISH (1905) Attended by St. Fidelis Friary.
695 210th Ave., Antonino, 67601. Tel: 785-735-9456; Email: beforte@hfetmpm.org. Rev. Earl Befort, O.F.M.Cap.
Res.: St. Fidelis Friary, 900 Cathedral Ave., Victoria, 67671.

ATWOOD, RAWLINS CO., SACRED HEART PARISH (1879) [CEM] [JC3] Rev. Gnanasekar Kulandai, H.G.N.
Res.: 508 N. Railroad Ave., Atwood, 67730.
Tel: 785-626-3335; Email: church508@yahoo.com.
Catechesis Religious Program—Loretta A. Studer, Office Mgr. & D.R.E. Students 28. ASSUMPTION OF MARY PARISH.
Mission—St. John Nepomucene.

AURORA, CLOUD CO., ST. PETER PARISH (1880) [JC] Attended by St. John the Baptist Parish, Clyde.
112 Kansas Ave., Aurora, 67417-0009.
Tel: 785-446-3474; Tel: 785-446-3793; Email: stjohn@nckcn.com. 204 N. High, Clyde, 66938. Rev. Steven Heina.
Catechesis Religious Program—(Attending Concordia for Rel. Educ.) Students 5.

BEARDSLEY, RAWLINS CO., ST. JOHN NEPOMUCENE PARISH (1910) [CEM] (Czech)
7048 Rd. 12, Atwood, 67730. Tel: 785-626-3335; Fax: 785-626-3431; Email: church508@yahoo.com. Mailing Address: c/o Sacred Heart Parish, 508 N. Railroad Ave., Atwood, 67730. Rev. Gnanasekar Kulandai, H.G.N.
Church: Atwood, 67730.
Catechesis Religious Program—8970 Rd. 3, McDonald, 67745. Tel: 785-538-2519; Email: jensabatka@outlook.com. Jennifer Sabatka, D.R.E. Students 19.

BELLEVILLE, REPUBLIC CO., ST. EDWARD PARISH (1901) [CEM]
1827 Q St., P.O. Box 99, Belleville, 66935.
Tel: 785-527-5559; Email: stedward6810@nckcn.com. Rev. David Metz; Deacon Steven F. Heiman; Rev. Henry Baxa, (Retired).
Catechesis Religious Program—Sacred Hearts Center, 1813 Q St., Belleville, 66935.
Tel: 785-527-5819. Tynan Dowell, D.R.E. Students 81.

BELOIT, MITCHELL CO., ST. JOHN THE BAPTIST PARISH (1869) [CEM]
622 E. Main, Beloit, 67420. Tel: 785-738-2851; Fax: 785-738-3410; Email: sjparish@nckcn.com. Revs. Damian Richards; David Michael, H.G.N.
Res.: 701 E. Court St., Beloit, 67420.
Tel: 785-738-2851; Email: sjparish@nckcn.com; Web: www.stjohnsbeloit.org.
School—St. John the Baptist Parish School, (Grades PreK-12), Tel: 785-738-3941; Email: mkee@gostj.com; Web: www.gostjohns.com. Revs. Damian Rich-

ards; David Michael, H.G.N. Religious Teachers 3; Lay Teachers 25; Students 165.
High School—St. John the Baptist Parish High School, (Grades 7-12), Tel: 785-738-2942; Email: mkee@gostj.com; Web: www.gostjohns.com. Revs. Damian Richards; David Michael, H.G.N. High School Students 75.
Catechesis Religious Program—Jennifer Hewitt, D.R.E. Students 124.
Missions—Mankato, Esbon, Glasco, Smith Center—
St. Mary Parish, 301 E. 1st, Box 554, Glasco, 67445.
Sacred Heart Parish, S. Grantt: Box 13, Esbon, 66941-0013.
St. Theresa Parish, 722 N. Commercial, Box 265, Mankato, 66956-0265.
St. Mary Parish, 403 W. Hwy 36, Box 263, Smith Center, 66967-0263.

BIRD CITY, CHEYENNE CO., ST. JOSEPH PARISH (1911) [JC]
203 N. Bird Ave., Bird City, 67731.
Tel: 785-332-2680; Email: olph@nwkansascatholics.com. Mailing Address: c/o St. Francis Parish, 625 River St., P.O. Box 1170, St. Francis, 67756. Revs. Andrew Rockers, Admin.; Joseph Asirvatham, H.G.N., Parochial Vicar.

BROOKVILLE, SALINE CO., ST. JOSEPH PARISH (1884) [CEM] Attended by Sacred Heart Cathedral, Salina.
110 W. 3rd, Brookville, 67425. Tel: 785-823-7221; Email: sacredheart@shcathedral.com. Mailing Address: 118 N. 9th, 67401. Revs. Nicholas Parker; Justin Palmer.
Catechesis Religious Program—Students 8.

CATHARINE, ELLIS CO., ST. CATHERINE PARISH (1892) [CEM 2] (German)
Mailing Address: P.O. Box 18, Catharine, 67627-0018. Tel: 785-650-1746; Email: stonehill@ruraltel.net. 1681 St. Joseph St., Catharine, 67627. Rev. Earl Befort, O.F.M.Cap.; Glenda Schuetz, Parish Life Coord.
Catechesis Religious Program—

CAWKER CITY, MITCHELL CO., SAINTS PETER AND PAUL PARISH (1878) [CEM] (German), Attended by St. Boniface Parish, Tipton.
308 Gambrinus, Cawker City, 67430.
Tel: 785-373-4455; Email: boniface@wtciweb.com. c/o St. Boniface Parish, P.O. Box 87, Tipton, 67485-0087. Revs. Daryl Olmstead; Joseph Asirvatham, H.G.N.
Catechesis Religious Program—1202 Holly, Cawker City, 67430. Tel: 785-781-4211; Email: lisa_larocque@yahoo.com. Lisa LaRocque, D.R.E. Students 13.

CHAPMAN, DICKINSON CO., ST. MICHAEL PARISH (1883) [CEM]
P.O. Box 217, Chapman, 67431-0217.
Tel: 785-922-6509; Email: smichael-chapman@sbcglobal.net; Web: smchapmanparish.org. 210 E. 6th St., Chapman, 67431. Rev. John Wolesky, Priest Supvr.; Marita Campbell, Parish Life Coord. Now a mission parish of Immaculate Conception Parish, Solomon.
Catechesis Religious Program—Laurie McLaughlin, D.R.E. Students 77.

CLAY CENTER, CLAY CO., SAINTS PETER AND PAUL PARISH (1879) [CEM]
730 Court St., Clay Center, 67432. Tel: 785-632-5011 ; Email: sspp@eaglecom.net. Rev. Randall D. Weber, J.C.L.; Deacons Walter Slingsby; Michael Robinson.
Catechesis Religious Program—Tel: 785-632-3204. Cyndy Schwensen, D.R.E. Students 135.
Mission—St. Anthony Parish, 612 W. 4th, Miltonvale, 67466.

CLIFTON, WASHINGTON CO., ST. MARY OF THE ASSUMPTION PARISH, [CEM] (French—German), Attended by St. John the Baptist Parish, Clyde.
213 Clifton St., Clifton, 66937. Tel: 785-446-3474; Email: stjohn@nckcn.com. Mailing Address: c/o St. John the Baptist, 204 N. High, Clyde, 66938. Rev. Steven Heina.
Catechesis Religious Program—Tel: 785-348-5404; Email: peacetew@hotmail.com. Therese Leiszler, D.R.E. Students 23.

CLYDE, CLOUD CO., ST. JOHN THE BAPTIST PARISH (1880) [CEM] (French—German)
204 N. High, Clyde, 66938. Tel: 785-446-3474; Email: stjohn@nckcn.com. Rev. Steven Heina; Brenda Koch, Pastoral Assoc.
Catechesis Religious Program—Tel: 785-446-2600; Email: mnobert2@yahoo.com. Megan Norbert, C.R.E. Students 89.
Missions—St. Mary of the Assumption Parish—213 Clifton St., Clifton, 66937.
St. Peter Parish, 112 Kansas Ave., Aurora, 67417-0009.

COLBY, THOMAS CO., SACRED HEART PARISH (1886) [CEM]
585 N. French Ave., Colby, 67701. Tel: 785-462-2179; Email: parish@sacredheartcolby.com; Web: www.sacredheartcolby.com. Rev. Richard Daise.
School—Sacred Heart Parish School, (Grades PreK-5), Tel: 785-460-2813; Email: school@sacredheartcolby.com; Web: sacredheartcolby.com. Mrs. Alice Ziegler, Prin.; Rev. Richard Daise. Clergy 1; Lay Teachers 12; Students 130.
Catechesis Religious Program—Fax: 785-460-6613. Students 186.

COLLYER, TREGO CO., ST. MICHAEL PARISH (1893) [CEM] [JC] (German)
Mailing Address: 708 Ainsie Ave., Collyer, 67631.
Tel: 785-743-2330; Email: ctkstm@ruraltel.net. 412 N. 9th, WaKeeney, 67672. Rev. Charles Steier.
Catechesis Religious Program—Tel: 785-769-4423; Email: tlwalt62@gmail.com. Laura Walt, D.R.E.

CONCORDIA, CLOUD CO., OUR LADY OF PERPETUAL HELP PARISH (1887) [CEM 2] (French)
307 E. Fifth, P.O. Box 608, Concordia, 66901-2213.
Tel: 785-243-1099; Email: olph@olphconcordia.org; Web: www.olphconcordia.org. Rev. David Metz.
Res.: 420 Kansas, P.O. Box 608, Concordia, 66901.
Catechesis Religious Program—Yolinda Meyer, D.R.E. Students 225.

CUBA, REPUBLIC CO., ST. ISIDORE PARISH (1873) [CEM] (Czech), Attended by St. Edward Parish, Belleville.
603 Linden, Cuba, 66935. Tel: 785-527-5559; Email: stedward6810@nckcn.com. Mailing Address: c/o St. Edward Parish, P.O. Box 99, Belleville, 66935-0099. Rev. David Metz.
Catechesis Religious Program—

DAMAR, ROOKS CO., ST. JOSEPH PARISH (1912) [CEM] (French), Attended by Immaculate Heart of Mary Parish, Hill City.
Mailing Address: P.O. Box 68, Damar, 67632.
Tel: 785-839-4343; Email: sjdamar@ruraltel.net. 100 N. Main, Damar, 67632. Rev. Henry Saw Lone.
Catechesis Religious Program—Tel: 785-421-7052; Email: tanyahamel@usd281. Tanya Hamel, D.R.E. Students 23.

DELPHOS, OTTAWA CO., ST. PAUL PARISH, [CEM] Merged Canonically with Immaculate Conception Parish, Minneapolis.

DORRANCE, RUSSELL CO., ST. JOSEPH PARISH (1902) [CEM] (German—Irish), Attended by St. Wenceslaus Parish, Wilson.
1011 Lincoln, Dorrance, 67490. Tel: 785-658-3361; Email: swchurch@wtciweb.com. Mailing Address: c/o St. Wenceslaus Parish, P.O. Box 528, Wilson, 67490. Rev. Mathew Chacko, C.M.I.

DOWNS, OSBORNE CO., ST. MARY PARISH (1903) Attended by St. Boniface, Tipton.
1312 Prentiss St., P. O. Box 221, Downs, 67437.
Tel: 785-454-3722; Email: jkneihous@ruraltel.net. Mailing Address: P.O. Box 221, Downs, 67437. Revs. Daryl Olmstead; Leo Blasi.
Catechesis Religious Program—Tel: 785-454-3990; Email: rcgoheen@ruraltel.net. Cheryl Goheen, D.R.E. Students 40.

ELLIS, ELLIS CO., ST. MARY PARISH (1870) [CEM]
703 Monroe, Ellis, 67637-2231. Tel: 785-726-4522; Email: stmary@gbta.net; Web: stmarysofellis.org/. Rev. Dana Clark; Sr. Doris M. Flax, C.S.J., Pastoral Assoc.
School—St. Mary Parish School, (Grades PreK-6), 605 Monroe St., Ellis, 67637. Tel: 785-726-3185; Fax: 785-726-3166; Email: apfeifer@stmarysellis.net. April Pfeifer, Prin.; Shelly Hensley, Librarian. Lay Teachers 11; Students 78.
Catechesis Religious Program—Lucia Bain, D.R.E. Students 100.
Convent—603 Monroe, Ellis, 67637.
Tel: 785-726-4696; Email: stmary@gbta.net.

ELLSWORTH, ELLSWORTH CO., ST. BERNARD PARISH (1909)
911 Kansas St., Ellsworth, 67439. Tel: 785-472-3136; Email: stbernards@att.net; Web: www.stbsti.com. Rev. Joshua Werth.
Catechesis Religious Program—Karen Kratzer, Youth Min.; Angie Ptacek, Youth Min. Students 72.
Mission—St. Ignatius Loyola Parish, P.O. Box 5, Kanopolis, 67454-0005.

ELMO, DICKINSON CO., ST. COLUMBA PARISH, [CEM] Attended by St. John the Evangelist Parish, Herington.
890 Main, Hope, 67451. Tel: 785-258-2013; Email: fatherpeter7756@gmail.com; Web: highway4catholics.org. c/o St. John the Evangelist Parish, 712 N. Broadway, Herington, 67449. Rev. Peter O'Donnell, J.C.L.; Deacon Richard J. Kramer.

ESBON, JEWELL CO., SACRED HEART PARISH (1887) [CEM] Attended by St. Theresa Parish, Mankato.
South Grant St., Esbon, 66941. Tel: 785-378-3913; Email: stheresa422@gmail.com. P.O. Box 265, Mankato, 66956. Revs. Damian Richards; David Michael, H.G.N.
Catechesis Religious Program—Students 7.

FORT RILEY, GEARY CO., FORT RILEY CATHOLIC COMMUNITY
Garrison Chaplain's Office, 2560 Trooper Dr., Fort Riley, 66442. Tel: 785-240-1443; Email: anthonykazarnowicz@yahoo.com. Revs. Anthony Kazarnowicz, Chap., 118 Scott Pl., Apt. B, Fort Riley, 66442; Curtis L. Kondik, Chap.
Catechesis Religious Program—Email: peaceprayer16@hotmail.com. Roxanne G. Martinez, D.R.E. Students 140.

GLASCO, CLOUD CO., ST. MARY PARISH (1878) [CEM]
301 E 1st St., Glasco, 67445. Tel: 785-738-2851; Email: sjparish@nckcn.com. Mailing Address: c/o St. John the Baptist Parish, 622 E. Main St., Beloit, 67420. Revs. Damian Richards; David Michael, H.G.N.

GOODLAND, SHERMAN CO., OUR LADY OF PERPETUAL HELP PARISH (1887)
307 W. 13th, Goodland, 67735. Tel: 785-890-7205; Email: olph@nwkansascatholics.com. Revs. Andrew Rockers, Admin.; Joseph Asirvatham, H.G.N., Parochial Vicar.

GORHAM, RUSSELL CO., ST. MARY HELP OF CHRISTIANS (1894) [CEM]
135 - 3rd St., P.O. Box 135, Gorham, 67640.
Tel: 785-637-5241; Email: st_marys@gorhamtel.com. Rev. Michael Elanjimattathil, C.M.I.

GRAINFIELD, GOVE CO., ST. AGNES PARISH (1910) [JC] (German), Attended by MIssion to Sacred Heart Parish, Park, KS.
266 Cedar, P.O. Box 156, Grainfield, 67737.
Tel: 785-673-4684; Tel: 785-673-4255; Email: stagneschurch256@gmail.com; Web: www.govecountycatholicparishes.org. Rev. James Maruthukunnel Thomas, C.M.I.
Catechesis Religious Program—Cammie Heier, D.R.E. Students 29.

GREENLEAF, WASHINGTON CO., SACRED HEART PARISH (1890) [CEM] Attended by St. John the Baptist, Hanover.
601 E Main St., P.O. Box 62, Greenleaf, 66943.
Tel: 785-337-2289; Email: wcccpastor1@yahoo.com; Web: washcountycc.net. Mailing Address: c/o St. John the Baptist, 114 S. Church St., P.O. Box 395, Hanover, 66945. Revs. Joseph Kieffer; Soossaimari Rathinam, H.G.N.

GRINNELL, GOVE CO., IMMACULATE CONCEPTION OF THE BLESSED VIRGIN MARY PARISH (1896) [CEM] (German), Attended by Sacred Heart, Park.
P.O. Box 69, Grinnell, 67738. Tel: 785-824-3221; Email: imcgrinn@st-tel.net; Web: www.govecountycatholicparishes.org. 308 Monroe, Grinnell, 67738. Rev. James Maruthukunnel Thomas, C.M.I.
Catechesis Religious Program—Tel: 785-824-3344; Email: lcmense@gmail.com. Christy Mense, C.R.E. Students 9.

GYPSUM, SALINE CO., ST. PATRICK PARISH, Attended by Immaculate Conception of the Blessed Mary Parish, Solomon.
3599 N. Field Rd., P.O. Box 337, Solomon, 67480-0337. Tel: 785-655-2221; Email: daylenetracy@msn.com. 800 Spring St., Gypsum, 67448. Revs. Kevin Weber; Andrew Hammeke; Daylene Tracy, Parish Life Coord. Now a mission parish of St. Mary Queen of the Universe Parish, Salina.

HANOVER, WASHINGTON CO., ST. JOHN THE BAPTIST PARISH (1868) [CEM] (Bohemian)
114 S. Church St., Box 395, Hanover, 66945.
Tel: 785-337-2289; Email: wcccpastor1@yahoo.com; Web: www.washcountycc.net. Revs. Joseph Kieffer; Soossaimari Rathinam, H.G.N.
School—St. John the Baptist Parish School, (Grades 1-8), Tel: 785-337-2368; Email: trundle@stjohnshanover.com. Timothy Rundle, Prin. Lay Teachers 7; Students 87.
Catechesis Religious Program—Kathy Zarybnicky, D.R.E. Students 144.
Missions—Sacred Heart Parish—Box 62, Greenleaf, 66943.
St. Augustine Parish, 410 B St., Washington, 66968.

HAYS, ELLIS CO.
1—IMMACULATE HEART OF MARY PARISH (1967) [JC]
1805 Vine, Hays, 67601. Tel: 785-625-7339; Email: skisner@ihm-church.com; Web: www.ihm-church.com. Rev. Msgr. Barry E. Brinkman, J.C.L., J.V.; Deacon David Kisner.
School—Holy Family Elementary Grade School, (Grades PreSchool-6), 1800 Milner, Hays, 67601-3796. Tel: 785-625-3131; Fax: 785-625-2098; Email: rwentling@hfehays.org; Web: www.hfehays.org. Rachel Wentling, Prin.; Rev. Msgr. Barry E. Brinkman, J.C.L., J.V.; Janice Collins, Librarian. Lay Teachers 22; Students 312.
Catechesis Religious Program—Email: deacondave@ihm-church.com. Mr. Rick Binder, Youth Dir.; Sr. Beverly Carlin, RCIA, Adult Formation & Liturgy. Students 259.
2—ST. JOSEPH PARISH (1876) [JC]
215 W. 13th St., P.O. Drawer 1000, Hays, 67601.
Tel: 785-625-7356; Email: stjoseph@stjoehays.com; Web: www.stj-church.com. Revs. Fred Gatschet; Anthony Tony Kulandaijesu; Kevin Rupp, Liturgy Dir.; Tony Dreiling, Business Mgr.
See Holy Family Grade School, Hays under Grade Schools, Inter-Parochial located in the Institution section.
See Thomas More Prep Marian High School, Hays

under High Schools Inter-Parochial located in the Institution section.
Catechesis Religious Program—Email: stjdre@stjoehays.com. Becky Newell, D.R.E. Students 69.
Mission—Comeau Catholic Campus Center, 506 W. 6th, Hays, 67601.
3—ST. NICHOLAS OF MYRA PARISH (1983)
2901 E. 13th, Hays, 67601. Tel: 785-628-1446; Email: rfweigel@eaglecom.net; Web: stn-church.com. Rev. Jarett Konrade.
Catechesis Religious Program—Bill Meagher, C.R.E.; Mandy Meagher, C.R.E. Students 289.
Mission—St. Francis of Assisi Parish, 883 Moscow St., Munjor, 67601.
HERINGTON, DICKINSON CO., ST. JOHN THE EVANGELIST PARISH, [CEM]
712 N. Broadway, Herington, 67449.
Tel: 785-258-2013; Email: fatherpeter7756@gmail.com. Rev. Peter O'Donnell, J.C.L.; Deacon Richard J. Kramer.
Catechesis Religious Program—Tel: 785-983-4481; Email: angiedre813@gmail.com. Angie Stika, D.R.E. & Dir. Youth Ministry. Students 44.
Missions—St. Phillip Parish—114 S. Main, Hope, 67449.
St. Columba Parish, 712 N Broadway, Herington, 67449.
HERNDON, RAWLINS CO., ASSUMPTION OF MARY PARISH (1880) [CEM] (German), Attended by Sacred Heart Parish, Atwood.
541 Palermo Ave., Herndon, 67739.
Tel: 785-626-3335; Fax: 785-626-3431; Email: church508@yahoo.com. Mailing Address: c/o Sacred Heart Parish, 508 N. Railroad Ave., Atwood, 67730. Rev. Gnanasekar Kulandai, H.G.N.

Catechesis Religious Program—Loretta A. Studer, D.R.E. Students 3.
HILL CITY, GRAHAM CO., IMMACULATE HEART OF MARY PARISH (1958)
110 N. 10th Ave., Hill City, 67642. Tel: 785-421-2535 ; Email: maryheart@ruraltel.net. Rev. Henry Saw Lone.
Catechesis Religious Program—2600 P Ter., Bogue, 67625. Tel: 785-737-3092; Email: bwkeith@ruraltel.net. Wendy Keith, D.R.E. Students 69.
Mission—St. Joseph's Church, 107 N. Oak, Damar, Rooks Co. 67632. Tel: 785-839-4343; Email: sjdamar@ruraltel.net. Donna Benoit, Contact Person.
HOLYROOD, ELLSWORTH CO., ST. MARY PARISH (1886) Attended by St. Wenceslaus Parish, Wilson.
202 S. Frank St., Holyrood, 67490. Tel: 785-658-3361 ; Email: swchurch@wtciweb.com. Mailing Address: c/o St. Wenceslaus Parish, Box 528, Wilson, 67490. Rev. Mathew Chacko, C.M.I.
HOPE, DICKINSON CO., ST. PHILLIP PARISH, Attended by St. John Parish, Herington.
114 Main, Hope, 67451. Tel: 785-258-2013; Email: fatherpeter7756@gmail.com; Web: highway4catholics.org. Mailing Address: c/o St. John Parish, 712 N. Broadway, Herington, 67449. Rev. Peter O'Donnell, J.C.L.; Deacon Richard J. Kramer.
Church: Hope, 67451. Tel: 785-366-7353.
Catechesis Religious Program—Students 11.
HOXIE, SHERIDAN CO., ST. FRANCES CABRINI PARISH (1948) [CEM] Rev. Vincent Thu Laing.
Res.: 924 N. 17th, Box 38, Hoxie, 67740.
Tel: 785-675-3300; Email: sfrances@ruraltel.net; Web: www.hoxieseguinparishes.org.
Catechesis Religious Program—Briget Koster, Rel. Educ. Coord.; Amanda Tremblay, Youth Min. Coord. & Parish Spiritual Life. Twinned with St. Martin's, Seguin, Hoxie. Students 85.
Mission—St. Martin of Tours Parish, Box 38, Seguin, TX 67740-0038.
JAMESTOWN, CLOUD CO., ST. MARY'S (1873) Closed. For sacramental records contact Our Lady of Perpetual Help, Concordia.
JUNCTION CITY, GEARY CO., ST. FRANCIS XAVIER PARISH (1867) [CEM]
218 N. Washington, P.O. Box 399, Junction City, 66441. Tel: 785-238-2998; Email: office@saintxparish.org; Web: www.saintxparish.org. Rev. Kyle Berens; Deacon Edward Souza; Karlie Brown, Dir., Evangelization.
Schools—St. Francis Xavier Parish School—(Grades PreK-12), 200 N. Washington St., Junction City, 66441. Tel: 785-238-2841; Fax: 785-238-5021; Email: office@saintxparish.org; Web: www.saintxrams.org. Mr. Shawn Augustine, Prin. (Elementary and High School); Rebecca Cronander, Librarian. Lay Teachers 13; Students 79.
High School, (Grades 9-12), Rev. Kyle Berens, Supt.; Mr. Shawn Augustine, Prin. Lay Teachers 15; Students 40.
Catechesis Religious Program—Email: stxavier@abba.kscoxmail.com. Kurt Leistner, D.R.E.; Sandy Leistner, D.R.E. Students 182.
KANOPOLIS, ELLSWORTH CO., ST. IGNATIUS LOYOLA PARISH (1947) [JC] (Mexican), Attended by St. Bernard Parish, Ellsworth.
127 N. Missouri, Kanopolis, 67454.
Tel: 785-472-4628; Email: stbernards@att.net. Rev. Joshua Werth.
Catechesis Religious Program—911 N. Kansas, Ellsworth, 67439. Tel: 785-472-3136; Email: kratzerk@bartoncc.edu; Email: alumcreek13@gmail.com. Karen Kratzer, Youth Min.; Angie Ptacek, Youth Min. Students 13.
LEOVILLE, DECATUR CO., IMMACULATE CONCEPTION OF THE BLESSED VIRGIN MARY PARISH (1885) [CEM] Attended by Sacred Heart Parish, Oberlin.
Highway 23, Leoville, 67757. Tel: 785-475-3103; Email: catholic@ruraltel.net. c/o Sacred Heart Parish, 210 E. Washington, Oberlin, 67749. Rev. Mark Berland.
Catechesis Religious Program—Tel: 785-454-3103. Mindy Fleckenstein, D.R.E. Students 25.
LINCOLN, LINCOLN CO., ST. PATRICK PARISH (1870) [CEM 2]
206 N. Fifth, Box 327, Lincoln, 67455.
Tel: 785-524-4823; Email: stpat327@gmail.com. Rev. Mark Wesely.
Catechesis Religious Program—Tel: 785-436-2405; Email: doras@wilsonstatebank.net. Dora Schroeder, D.R.E. Students 67.
LOGAN, PHILLIPS CO., ST. JOHN THE EVANGELIST PARISH (1878) [CEM] Attended by Saints Philip & James Parish, Philipsburg.
Mailing Address: 203 E. Main, P.O. Box 128, Logan, 67646-0128. Tel: 785-689-4299; Email: stjohn1@ruraltel.net. Rev. George Chalbhagam, C.M.I., (India).
Catechesis Religious Program—Email: chalbhagamcmi@yahoo.co.in. Terra Brown, D.R.E. Students 24.
MANHATTAN, RILEY CO.
1—ST. ROBERT BELLARMINE PARISH - ST. ISIDORE CATHOLIC STUDENT CENTER (1963)
711 Denison Ave., Manhattan, 66502.
Tel: 785-539-7496; Email: stisidores@stisidores.com; Web: www.stisidores.com. Revs. Gale Hammerschmidt; Ryan McCandless.
2—SEVEN DOLORS OF THE BLESSED VIRGIN MARY PARISH (1880)
221 S Juliette St., Manhattan, 66502.
Tel: 785-565-5000; Email: office@sevendolors.com; Web: www.sevendolors.com. Revs. Kerry Ninemire; Carlos Ruiz Santos; Deacons Ron Lehman; Edward Souza. In Res., Rev. Merlin Kieffer, (Retired).
Res. & Rectory: 624 Pierre St., Manhattan, 66502.
School—Manhattan Catholic Schools, (Grades PreK-8), 306 S. Juliette Ave., Manhattan, 66502-6297. Tel: 785-565-5050; Fax: 785-565-5055; Email: shulshoff@manhattancatholicschools.org; Web: www.manhattancatholicschools.org. Scott Hulshoff, Prin.; Carrie Ellis, Librarian. Lay Teachers 23; Students 265.
Catechesis Religious Program—Email: reoffice@sevendolors.com. Debra Price, D.R.E.; Maria McAnerney, Dir., Youth Min. Students 181.
Mission—St. Patrick Parish, 16th & Walnut, Ogden, 66517.
3—ST. THOMAS MORE PARISH (1981)
2900 Kimball Ave., Manhattan, 66502.
Tel: 785-776-5151; Email: stm@stmmanhattan.com; Web: stmmanhattan.com. Rev. Frank Coady; Deacons Wayne Talbot, Pastoral Assoc.; Lawrence Erpelding; Buzz Harris.
Catechesis Religious Program—Email: kthru6@stmmanhattan.com; Email: youthmin@stmmanhattan.com. Josefina Gantt, D.R.E.; Rick Smith, Youth Min. Students 439.
MANKATO, JEWELL CO., ST. THERESA PARISH (1949) [CEM] Attended by St. John, Beloit.
422 N. Commercial, Box 265, Mankato, 66956-0265. Tel: 785-378-3939; Email: stheresa422@gmail.com. Revs. Damian Richards; David Michael, H.G.N.
Catechesis Religious Program—Students 5.
MILTONVALE, CLOUD CO., ST. ANTHONY PARISH (1910) Attended by Saints Peter and Paul Parish, Clay Center.
614 W. 4th St., Miltonvale, 67466. Tel: 785-632-5011; Fax: 785-632-3914; Email: sspp@eaglecom.net. Mailing Address: c/o Saints Peter and Paul Parish, 730 Court St., Clay Center, 67432. Rev. Randall D. Weber, J.C.L.
MINNEAPOLIS, OTTAWA CO., IMMACULATE CONCEPTION OF THE BLESSED VIRGIN MARY PARISH (1985)
Mailing Address: 216 Cherry St., Box 167, Minneapolis, 67467. Tel: 785-392-2079; Email: iccmkansas@gmail.com. Rev. Mark Wesely.
Catechesis Religious Program—Jackie Martinez, D.R.E. Students 43.
Mission—St. Patrick Parish, 206 N. 5th, Lincoln, 67455-0327.
MORROWVILLE, WASHINGTON CO., SAINTS PETER AND PAUL PARISH (1887) [CEM] Merged Canonically with St. Augustine's Parish, Washington.
MUNDEN, REPUBLIC CO., ST. GEORGE PARISH (1887) [CEM] (Czech), Attended by St. Edward Parish, Belleville.
105 W. Myrza, Munden, 66959. Tel: 785-527-5559; Email: stedward6810@nckcn.com. Mailing Address: c/o St. Edward Parish, 1827 Q St., Belleville, 66935. Rev. David Metz.
Catechesis Religious Program—Tynan Dowell, D.R.E.
MUNJOR, ELLIS CO., ST. FRANCIS OF ASSISI PARISH (1876) [CEM]
883 Moscow St., Munjor, 67601. Tel: 785-625-5314; Email: office@stfrancis-church.com; Web: www.stfrancis-church.com. Rev. Jarett Konrade; Mrs. Lilly Binder, Pastoral Assoc.
Catechesis Religious Program—Tel: 785-259-2762. Joseph Pfannenstiel, C.R.E. Students 25.
NEW ALMELO, NORTON CO., ST. JOSEPH PARISH (1874) [CEM] Attended by St. Francis of Assisi Parish, Norton.
28035 St. John St., New Almelo, 67645-9742.
Tel: 785-567-4875; Email: stjosephcc@ruraltel.net. Rev. Jose G. Kumblumkal, C.M.I.; Roberta Bruinekool, Contact Person.
Catechesis Religious Program—Shelly Wahlmeier, D.R.E. Students 23.
NORTON, NORTON CO., ST. FRANCIS OF ASSISI PARISH (1878) Rev. Jose G. Kumblumkal, C.M.I.
Res.: 108 S. Wabash, Box 148, Norton, 67654.
Tel: 785-877-2234; Email: stfranci@ruraltel.net; Web: www.stfrancisassisi.org.
Catechesis Religious Program—Suzi Brooks, D.R.E. Students 78.
Mission—St. Joseph's Church, 28035 St. John St., New Almelo, Norton Co. 67652. Tel: 785-567-4875; Email: stjosephcc@ruraltel.net.
OAKLEY, LOGAN CO., ST. JOSEPH PARISH (1890) [CEM]
625 Freeman Ave., Oakley, 67748. Tel: 785-671-3828 ; Tel: parish@sjoakley.org. Revs. Donald F. Pfannenstiel; Luke Thielen; Deacons Dennis Engel; Michael Brungardt.
School—St. Joseph Parish School, (Grades K-5), 725 Freeman Ave., Oakley, 67748. Tel: 785-671-4451; Fax: 785-671-3919; Email: principal@sjoakley.org; Web: sjoakley.org. Rebecca Scheck, Prin. Clergy 7; Lay Teachers 9; Priests 1; Students 82.
Catechesis Religious Program—St. Joseph Parish Annex, Tel: 785-672-2432; Email: kbhemmert@st-tel.net. Barbara Hemmert, D.R.E. Students 160.
Mission—St. Paul.
OBERLIN, DECATUR CO., SACRED HEART PARISH (1888) [JC]
210 E. Washington, Oberlin, 67749.
Tel: 785-475-3103; Email: catholic@ruraltel.net. Rev. Mark Berland.
Catechesis Religious Program—Krickit Ketterl, D.R.E. Students 29.
OGDEN, RILEY CO., ST. PATRICK PARISH (1859) [CEM] Attended by Seven Dolors of the Blessed Virgin Mary Parish, Manhattan.
16th & Walnut, Ogden, 66517. Tel: 785-565-5000; Email: office@sevendolors.com. Mailing Address: c/o Seven Dolors of the Blessed Virgin Mary Parish, 731 Pierre St., Manhattan, 66502. Revs. Kerry Ninemire; Carlos Ruiz Santos.
Res.: P.O. Box A, Ogden, 66517. Tel: 785-565-5090.
OSBORNE, OSBORNE CO., ST. ALOYSIUS GONZAGA PARISH (1881) [CEM]
203 N. Elm, P.O. Box 267, Osborne, 67473.
Tel: 785-346-5582; Email: stal@ruraltel.net. Revs. Daryl Olmstead, 308 Gambrinus, Tipton, 67485. Tel: 785-373-4455; Leo Blasi.
Catechesis Religious Program—Brenda Henke, D.R.E. Students 4.
Mission—St. Mary's, 1312 Prentice, Downs, Osborne Co. 67437. Tel: 785-454-3551.
PARK, GOVE CO., SACRED HEART PARISH (1898) [CEM] (German)
202 S. Cottonwood, P.O. Box 78, Park, 67751.
Tel: 785-673-4684; Email: shcpark@ruraltel.net; Web: www.govecountycatholicparishes.org. Rev. James Maruthukunnel Thomas, C.M.I.
Catechesis Religious Program—Terese Selensky, D.R.E.; Denise Wittman, D.R.E.; Frina Kaiser, D.R.E.; Esther Thielen, D.R.E. Students 61.
Missions—St. Agnes—266 Cedar, Box 156, Grainfield, 67737.
Immaculate Conception of the Blessed Virgin Mary, 3rd & Monroe, P.O. Box 69, Grinnell, 67738.
PFEIFER, ELLIS CO., HOLY CROSS, Closed. For sacramental records contact St. Fidelis, Victoria. Rev. John Schmeidler, O.F.M.Cap., Admin.
PHILLIPSBURG, PHILLIPS CO., SAINTS PHILIP AND JAMES PARISH (1875)
690 S. 7th, Phillipsburg, 67661. Tel: 785-543-5367; Email: sspjchurch@sbcglobal.net; Web: www.phillipsburgcatholic.org. Rev. George Chalbhagam, C.M.I., (India).
Catechesis Religious Program—Kim Ellenberger, D.R.E. Students 39.
Mission—St. John the Evangelist, Logan, Phillips Co.. Tel: 785-689-4299.

PLAINVILLE, ROOKS CO., SACRED HEART PARISH (1890) [CEM]
206 N. Washington, P.O. Box 100, Plainville, 67663. Tel: 785-434-4658; Email: shcparish@shcplainville.org. Rev. Brian Lager.
School—Sacred Heart Parish School, (Grades PreK-6), Tel: 785-434-2157; Email: principal@shcplainville.org; Web: shcplainville.org. Laura Foss, Prin.; Rev. Brian Lager. Lay Teachers 9; Students 84.
Catechesis Religious Program—Email: shchurch@ruraltel.net. Deidre Jones, C.R.E. Students 58.
Mission—St. Thomas Parish, 722 Main St., Stockton, 67669.

RUSSELL, RUSSELL CO., ST. MARY QUEEN OF ANGELS PARISH (1886) [CEM]
Mailing Address: 415 S. Windsor St., Russell, 67665. Tel: 785-483-2871; Email: smqoa@ruraltel.net; Web: www.stmaryrussell.com. Rev. Michael Elanjimattathil, C.M.I., (India).
Catechesis Religious Program—Email: smqoare@ruraltel.net. Bonita Ney, D.R.E. Students 131.

ST. FRANCIS, CHEYENNE CO., ST. FRANCIS OF ASSISI PARISH (1912) [JC] (German)
625 S. River St., P.O. Box 1170, St. Francis, 67756. Tel: 785-332-2680; Email: olph@nwkansascatholics.com. 307 W. 13th St., Goodland, 67735. Revs. Andrew Rockers, Admin.; Joseph Asirvatham, H.G.N., Parochial Vicar.

SCHOENCHEN, ELLIS CO., ST. ANTHONY PARISH (1877) [CEM] Attended by St. Joseph Parish, Hays.
215 W. 13th, Schoenchen, 67667. Tel: 785-735-9456; Email: beforte@hfetmpm.org. Mailing Address: 900 Cathedral Ave., Victoria, 67671. Rev. Earl Befort, O.-F.M.Cap.
Res.: 215 W. 13th, Hays, 67601. Tel: 785-628-9214; Fax: 785-625-7394.

SEGUIN, SHERIDAN CO., ST. MARTIN PARISH (1910) [CEM] Attended by St. Frances Cabrini Parish, Hoxie. Religious education twinned with St. Francis Cabrini, Hoxie, KS.
540 14th St., Seguin, 67740. Tel: 785-675-3300; Email: sfrances@ruraltel.net. Mailing Address: c/o St. Francis Cabrini Parish, P.O. Box 38, Hoxie, 67740. Rev. Vincent Thu Laing.

SELDEN, SHERIDAN CO., SACRED HEART PARISH (1906) [CEM]
205 S. Mission, Box 75, Selden, 67757.
Tel: 785-386-4496; Email: sacredheart@ruraltel.net. Rev. Mark Berland.
Catechesis Religious Program—Dolores Juenemann, D.R.E. Students 23.

SHARON SPRINGS, WALLACE CO., HOLY GHOST PARISH (1907) (German)
403 N. Main St., Box 190, Sharon Springs, 67758-0190. Tel: 785-890-7205; Email: roxym.bussen@gmail.com. Mailing Address: c/o Our Lady of Perpetual Help Parish, 307 W. 13th, Goodland, 67735. Revs. Andrew Rockers, Admin.; Joseph Asirvatham, H.G.N., Parochial Vicar.

SMITH CENTER, SMITH CO., ST. MARY PARISH (1959) Attended by St. John the Baptist, Beloit.
403 W. Hwy 36, Smith Center, 66967.
Tel: 785-282-6888; Email: stheresa422@gmail.com. P.O. Box 265, Mankato, 66956. Revs. Damian Richards; David Michael, H.G.N.
Catechesis Religious Program—Box 263, Smith Center, 66967-0263. Tel: 785-378-3939; Email: sjpastor@nckcn.com. Mrs. Stacey Rempe, D.R.E. Students 34.

SOLOMON, DICKINSON CO., IMMACULATE CONCEPTION OF THE BLESSED VIRGIN MARY PARISH (1886) [CEM]
3599 N. Field Rd., P.O. Box 337, Solomon, 67480.
Tel: 785-655-2221; Email: daylenetracy@msn.com; Web: immaculateconceptionsolomon.org. Rev. John Wolesky; Daylene Tracy, Parish Life Coord.
Catechesis Religious Program—Tel: 785-294-0577; Email: stephanietiernan@yahoo.com. Stephanie Tiernan, D.R.E. Students 28.
Mission—St. Michael Parish, 210 E. 6th, P.O. Box 217, Chapman, Dickinson Co. 67431.
Tel: 785-922-6509; Email: smichael-chapman@sbcgobal.net. Marita Campbell, Contact Person.

STOCKTON, ROOKS CO., ST. THOMAS PARISH (1878) [CEM] (German), Attended by Sacred Heart Parish, Plainville.
722 Main St., Stockton, 67669. Tel: 785-434-4658; Email: shcparish@shcplainville.org. Mailing Address: c/o Sacred Heart Church, P.O. Box 100, Plainville, 67663-0100. Revs. Brian Lager; Soossaimari Rathinam, H.G.N., Parochial Vicar.
Catechesis Religious Program—Email: shchurch@ruraltel.net. Jessica Billinger, C.R.E. Students 34.

TIPTON, MITCHELL CO., ST. BONIFACE PARISH (1874) [CEM]
308 Gambrinus, P. O. Box 87, Tipton, 67485-0087.
Tel: 785-373-4455; Email: boniface@wtciweb.com. Revs. Daryl Olmstead; Joseph Asirvatham, H.G.N., 203 N. Elm, Osborne, 67473. Tel: 785-346-5582.
High School—St. Boniface Parish High School,
Tel: 785-373-5835; Email: boniface@wtciweb.com. Gery Hake, Prin.; Marilyn Ohnsat, Sec. Lay Teachers 6; Priests 1; High School Students 25.
Catechesis Religious Program—Tel: 785-373-5835; Email: stacehake_tcs@yahoo.com. Stacie Hake, D.R.E. Students 53.
Missions—SS. Peter & Paul—1202 Holly, P.O. Box 25, Cawker City, Mitchell Co. 67430.
St. Aloysius, 230 N. Elm, P.O. Box 267, Osborne, 67473.
St. Mary's, 1312 Prentiss, P.O. Box 221, Downs, 67437.

VICTORIA, ELLIS CO., THE BASILICA OF ST. FIDELIS (1876) [CEM] (German—Russian) Rev. John Schmeidler, O.F.M.Cap.
Church Office: 601 10th St., Victoria, 67671.
Tel: 785-735-2777; Fax: 785-735-2779; Email: fidelis@ruraltel.net; Web: www.stfidelischurch.com.
Res.: 900 Cathedral Ave., Victoria, 67671.
Tel: 785-735-9456; Fax: 785-735-9455.
Catechesis Religious Program—Tel: 785-735-9244; Email: sfreled@ruraltel.net. Shirley Brungardt, D.R.E. Students 190.

VINCENT, ELLIS CO., ST. BONIFACE PARISH (1904) [CEM] (German—Russian), Attended by St. Fidelis Parish, Victoria.
Vincent Ave., Victoria, 67671. Tel: 785-735-2777;
Tel: 785-735-9456; Fax: 785-735-2779; Email: fidelis@ruraltel.net; Web: www.stbonifacevincent.com. c/o St. Fidelis Parish, 601 10th St., Victoria, 67671. Rev. John Schmeidler, O.F.M.Cap.

WAKEENEY, TREGO CO., CHRIST THE KING PARISH (1933) [CEM]
412 N. Ninth St., WaKeeney, 67672.
Tel: 785-743-2330; Email: ctkstm@ruraltel.net. Rev. Charles Steier.
Catechesis Religious Program—Tel: 785-769-3094; Email: vkfx@ruraltel.net. Verna Flax, D.R.E. Students 80.
Mission—St. Michael Parish.

WALKER, ELLIS CO., ST. ANN PARISH (1904) [CEM] (German—Russian), Attended by St. Fidelis Parish, Victoria.
Walker Ave., Walker, 67674. Tel: 785-735-2777;
Fax: 785-735-2779; Email: fidelis@ruraltel.net. Mailing Address: c/o St. Fidelis Parish, 601 10th St., Victoria, 67671. Rev. John Schmeidler, O.F.M.Cap.

WASHINGTON, WASHINGTON CO., ST. AUGUSTINE PARISH (1946) [JC]
410 B St., Washington, 66968. Tel: 785-325-3147; Email: staugustinesecretary@gmail.com; Web: washcountycc.net. Revs. Joseph Kieffer; Soossaimari Rathinam, H.G.N.
Res.: St. John the Baptist Church, 114 S. Church St., P.O. Box 395, Hanover, 66945. Tel: 785-337-2289; Email: wcccpastor@yahoo.com.
Catechesis Religious Program— Twinned with SS. Peter & Paul, Morrowville and Sacred Heart, Greenleaf. Crystal L'Ecuyer, C.R.E. Students 102.

WILSON, ELLSWORTH CO., ST. WENCESLAUS PARISH (1882) [CEM] (Czech)
2811 Ave. D., Wilson, 67490. Tel: 785-658-3361; Email: swchurch@wtciweb.com. P.O. Box 528, Wilson, 67490-0528. Rev. Mathew Chacko, C.M.I.
Catechesis Religious Program—Mary Kratky, D.R.E. Students 46.
Missions—St. Joseph—P.O. Box 528, Dorrance, Russell Co. 67490.
St. Mary Parish, Holyrood, Ellsworth Co. 67450.

On Duty Outside the Diocese:
Rev.—
Awotwi, Charles K., Military Archdiocese.

Retired:
Rev. Msgr.—
Hake, James, J.C.L., (Retired), 1815 Highland Ave., 67401
Revs.—
Dallen, James, (Retired), W. 818 21st Ave., Spokane, WA 99203
Dlabal, Norbert, (Retired), 118 N. 9th, 67401
Flax, Myron, O.F.M.Cap., (Retired), 900 Cathedral Ave., Victoria, 67671
Gibson, Beryl, (Retired), 501 3rd St., Phillipsburg, 67661
Grennan, James, (Retired), 403 Barton St., Russell, 67665
Hoover, James, (Retired), 13th and Washington, P.O. Box 279, Concordia, 66901
Kieffer, Merlin, (Retired), 618 Pierre, Manhattan, 66502
Letourneau, Larry, (Retired), 655 Georgetown Ct., Unit A, 67401
Long, Melvin, (Retired), P.O. Box 4350, Palm Springs, CA 92263-4350
Meitl, Roger K., (Retired), 6550 E. 45th St. N. #210, Bel Aire, 67226
Metro, LeRoy, (Retired), 1068 Burr Oak Ln., 67401
Morgan, Jerome, (Retired), P.O. Box 980, 67401
Petrovsky, Felix, O.F.M.Cap., (Retired)
Scheetz, Daniel L., J.C.L., (Retired), 1531 N. Elm St., Russell, 67665
Surmeier, William J., PsyD., L.C.P.C., (Retired), 200 E. 25th St., Hays, 67601
Torrez, Basil, (Retired), P.O. Box 214, Collyer, 67631
Werth, Alvin, (Retired), 501 W. 37th, #11, Hays, 67601
Zimmerman, Donald D., (Retired), 2844 Kelly Dr., Manhattan, 66502.

Permanent Deacons:
Deacons—
Brungardt, Michael
Chaput, Terry, (Retired)
Engel, Dennis
Erpelding, Lawrence
Frueh, Steven H.
Harris, Buzz
Heiman, Steve
Kisner, David
Koerner, Tom, (Retired)
Kramer, Dick
Lehman, Ron
Rivera, Jorge
Roberti, Mark
Robinson, Michael
Schrick, Thomas
Slingsby, Walter
Souza, Edward
Talbot, Wayne
Urban, Steve
Vrbas, Mark
Watford, Scott.

INSTITUTIONS LOCATED IN DIOCESE

[A] HIGH SCHOOLS, INTER-PAROCHIAL

SALINA. *Sacred Heart Junior-Senior High School* (1908) (Grades 7-12), 234 E. Cloud, 67401.
Tel: 785-827-4422; Fax: 785-827-8648; Email: john@sacredheartknights.org; Web: www.sacredheartknights.org. John Krajicek, Prin.; Revs. Andy Hammeke, Chap.; Kevin Weber, Pastor-Mod.; Susan Goodman, Librarian. Religious Teachers 1; Lay Teachers 20; Students 200.

HAYS. *Thomas More Prep-Marian Jr/Sr High School* (1908) (Grades 7-12), 1701 Hall, Hays, 67601.
Tel: 785-625-6577; Fax: 785-625-3912; Email: meitnerc@tmpmarian.org; Web: www.tmp-m.org. Chad Meitner, Prin.; Bob Leikam, Prin.; Rev. Msgr. Barry E. Brinkman, J.C.L., J.V., Pastor-Mod. A six-year Catholic High School (grades 7-12), with college preparatory programs conducted under the auspices of local Catholic parishes.
Thomas More Prep-Marian High Inc. Lay Teachers 27; Priests 1; Students 273; Total Staff 85.
Endowment Foundation of Thomas More Prep-Marian, Inc. Jeff Brull, Advancement Dir.
Thomas More Prep-Marian Alumni Assoc., 1701 Hall, Hays, 67601. Tel: 785-625-9434; Email: alumni@tmpmarian.org; Web: www.tmp-m.org. Rev. Earl Befort, O.F.M.Cap., Chap.

[B] HOSPITALS

MANHATTAN. **Ascension Via Christi Hospital Manhattan, Inc.*, 1823 College Ave., Manhattan, 66502. Tel: 785-776-2841; Email: Robert.Copple@ascension.org; Web: www.viachristi.org. Robert Copple, Pres. Bed Capacity 94; Tot Asst. Annually 36,771; Total Staff 486.

[C] HOMES FOR AGED

HAYS. *Ascension Living Via Christi Village*, 2225 Canterbury, Hays, 67601. Tel: 785-628-3241; Fax; 785-628-3310; Email: Betsy.Schwien@ascension.org; Web: www.ascension.org. Betsy Schwien, CEO; Rev. Harvey Dinkel, O.F.M.-Cap., M.A., M.S., Chap. Total Staff 175; Assisted Living Units 39; Long Term Care 96; Total Assisted 228.

MANHATTAN. *Via Christi Village Manhattan, Inc.* (1990) Subsidiary of Via Christi Villages, Inc.; Subsidiary of Ascension Health Senior Care. 2800 Willow Grove Rd., Manhattan, 66502.
Tel: 785-539-7671; Fax: 785-539-9125; Email:

marissa.pultz@ascension.org; Email: cheyenne.strunk@ascension.org; Web: www.viachristi.org/villages. Cheyenne Strunk, Exec. Dir. Residents 43; Total Staff 160; Skilled Nursing 93.

[D] MONASTERIES AND RESIDENCES OF PRIESTS AND BROTHERS

VICTORIA. *St. Fidelis Friary*, 900 Cathedral Ave., Victoria, 67671. Tel: 785-735-9456; Fax: 785-735-9455; Email: hpdinkel@ruraltel.net. Revs. John Schmeidler, O.F.M.Cap., Pastor, Guardian; Earl Befort, O.F.M.Cap.; Harvey Dinkel, O.F.M.Cap., M.A., M.S.; Myron Flax, O.F.M.-Cap., (Retired); Felix Petrovsky, O.F.M.Cap., (Retired); Gilmary Tallman, O.F.M.Cap.; Earl Meyer, O.F.M.Cap.; Bro. Joseph McGlynn, O.F.M.-Cap. Total in Residence 9.

[E] CONVENTS AND RESIDENCES FOR SISTERS

CONCORDIA. *Sisters of St. Joseph of Concordia*, P.O. Box 279, Concordia, 66901. Tel: 785-243-2149; Fax: 785-243-4741; Email: csjcenter@csjkansas.org; Web: www.csjkansas.org. 215 Court St., Concordia, 66901. Sr. Jean Rosemarynoski, C.S.J., Pres., Nazareth Motherhouse for the Sisters of St. Joseph; Contact Person; Rev. James Hoover, Chap., (Retired). Sisters 92; Professed Sisters 91; Total in Community 92.

[F] RETREAT CENTERS

CONCORDIA. *Manna House of Prayer*, 323 E. Fifth St., Box 675, Concordia, 66901. Tel: 785-243-4428; Fax: 785-243-4321; Email: retreatcenter@mannahouse.org; Web: www.mannahouse.org. Sr. Betty Suther, C.S.J., Admin. Total in Residence 6; Total Staff 10.

VICTORIA. *Capuchin Center for Spiritual Life*, 900 Cathedral Ave., Victoria, 67671. Tel: 785-735-9393; Fax: 785-735-9455; Email: ccsl@ruraltel.net. Rev. John Schmeidler, O.F.M.Cap., Dir.

[G] CAMPUS MINISTRY

HAYS. *Comeau Catholic Campus Center*, Office: 506 W. Sixth, Hays, 67601. Tel: 785-625-7396; Email: comeauccc@yahoo.com. Revs. Fred Gatschet, Chap.; Jarett Konrade, Campus Min. Total Staff 2.

MANHATTAN. *St. Robert Bellarmine Parish - St. Isidore Catholic Student Center*, 711 Denison Ave., Manhattan, 66502. Tel: 785-539-7496; Email: stisidores@stisidores.com; Web: www.stisidores.com. Revs. Gale Hammerschmidt; Ryan McCandless. Total Staff 7.

[H] MISCELLANEOUS

SALINA. *St. Joseph Annex, Inc.*, 401 W. Iron, 67401. Tel: 785-827-8746, Ext. 12; Fax: 785-827-6133; Email: kyle.haugh@salinadiocese.org. P.O. Box 980, 67402-0980. Mr. Kyle Haugh, CPA, CEO.

Marymount Memorial Educational Trust Fund, 103 N. 9th St., 67401-2503. Tel: 785-827-8746, Ext. 12; Fax: 785-827-6133; Email: kyle.waugh@salinadiocese.org. P.O. Box 980, 67402-0980. Kyle Waugh, CEO.

The Register of the Roman Catholic Diocese of Salina, Inc., 103 N. Ninth St., 67401-2503. Tel: 785-827-8746; Email: newspaper1@salinadiocese.org. P.O. Box 980, 67402-0980. Karen Bonar, Editor.

Roman Catholic Diocese of Salina Deposit and Loan Inc., 103 N. Ninth St., 67401-2503. Tel: 785-827-8746, Ext. 12; Fax: 785-827-6133; Email: kyle.haugh@salinadiocese.org. P.O. Box 980, 67402-0980. Mr. Kyle Haugh, CPA, CEO.

Roman Catholic Diocese of Salina St. Joseph Fund, Inc., 103 N. 9th St., 67401-2503. Tel: 785-827-8746, Ext. 12; Email: kyle.haugh@salinadiocese.org. P.O. Box 980, 67402-0980. Mr. Kyle Haugh, CPA, CEO.

Sacred Heart Junior-Senior Endowment Fund, Inc., 234 E. Cloud, 67401-6436. Tel: 785-825-4011; Fax: 785-827-8648; Email: melissaa@sacredheartknights.org; Web: www.sacredheartknights.org. John Krajicek, Prin.

Salina Catholic Diocese Education Endowment, Inc., 103 N. Ninth St., 67401-2503. Tel: 785-827-8746; Fax: 785-827-6133; Email: kyle.haugh@salinadiocese.org. P.O. Box 980, 67402-0980. Mr. Kyle Haugh, CPA, CEO.

Salina Catholic Diocese Gift & Annuity Fund, Inc., 103 N. Ninth St., 67401-2503. Tel: 785-827-8746, Ext. 12; Fax: 785-827-6133; Email: kyle.haugh@salinadiocese.org. P.O. Box 980, 67402-0980. Mr. Kyle Haugh, CPA, CEO.

Salina Catholic Diocese Seminary Burses, Inc., 103 N. Ninth St., 67401-2503. Tel: 785-827-8746; Fax: 785-827-6133; Email: chancery@salinadiocese.org. P.O. Box 980, 67402-0980. Mr. Kyle Haugh, CPA, CEO.

Salina Diocesan Clergy Health and Retirement Association, Inc., 103 N. 9th St., 67401-2503. Tel: 785-827-8746, Ext. 12; Fax: 785-827-6133; Email: kyle.haugh@salinadiocese.org. Diocese of Salina, P.O. Box 980, 67402-0980. Mr. Kyle Haugh, CPA, CEO.

Vocatio of Salina, Tel: 785-539-7496; Email: ghammerschmidt@salinadiocese.org. Rev. Gale Hammerschmidt, Mod.

CONCORDIA. *Nazareth Convent & Academy Corporation*, P.O. Box 279, Concordia, 66901. Tel: 785-243-2149; Fax: 785-243-4741; Email: csjcenter@csjkansas.org; Web: www.csjkansas.org. 215 Court St., Concordia, 66901. Rev. James Hoover, Chap., (Retired); Sr. Jean Rosemarynoski, C.S.J., Pres.

Neighborhood Initiatives, Inc., P.O. Box 279, Concordia, 66901. Tel: 785-243-2149; Fax: 785-243-4741; Email: sisterjean@csjkansas.org. 215 Court St., Concordia, 66901. Sr. Jean Rosemarynoski, C.S.J., Pres.

RELIGIOUS INSTITUTES OF MEN REPRESENTED IN THE DIOCESE

For further details refer to the corresponding bracketed number in the Religious Institutes of Men or Women section.

[0470]—*The Capuchin Friars* (Province of Mid-America)—O.F.M.Cap.

[0275]—*Carmelites of Mary Immaculate* (Provincial House - Kochi, India)—C.M.I.

[]—*Heralds of Good News* (Mary Queen of Apostles Province, Tamil Nadu, India)—H.G.N.

RELIGIOUS INSTITUTES OF WOMEN REPRESENTED IN THE DIOCESE

[3832]—*Congregation of the Sisters of St. Joseph*—C.S.J.

[]—*Consecrated Hermitess*.

[]—*Missionary Sisters of the Eucharistic Heart of Christ the King*.

[]—*The Missionary Sisters of the Most Holy Redeemer and St. Bridget*.

[3830-15]—*Sisters of St. Joseph*—C.S.J.

NECROLOGY

† Hough, Roger W., (Retired), Died Mar. 4, 2018
† Werth, Loren J., (Retired), Died Jul. 30, 2018

An asterisk (*) denotes an organization that has established tax-exempt status directly with the IRS and is not covered by the USCCB Group Ruling.

Diocese of Salt Lake City

(Dioecesis Civitatis Lacus Salsi)

Most Reverend

OSCAR AZARCON SOLIS

Bishop of Salt Lake City; ordained April 28, 1979; appointed Titular Bishop of Urci and Auxiliary Bishop of Los Angeles December 11, 2003; ordained February 10, 2004; appointed Bishop of Salt Lake City January 10, 2017; installed March 7, 2017. *Office: 27 C St., Salt Lake City, UT 84103-2397.*

Diocesan Offices and Organizations: 27 C St., Salt Lake City, UT 84103-2397. Tel: 801-328-8641; Fax: 801-328-9680.

Web: www.dioslc.org

ESTABLISHED AS A VICARIATE-APOSTOLIC ON NOV. 23, 1886.

Square Miles 84,990.

Erected a Diocese on January 27, 1891.

Originally comprised all Utah and the Counties of Eureka, Lander, Lincoln, White Pine, Nye, Elko and Clark in the State of Nevada. By Apostolic Constitution dated March 27, 1931, the Nevada section was separated from the Salt Lake Diocese and incorporated in the Reno Diocese. The name was changed to Diocese of Salt Lake City on March 31, 1951.

Comprises the State of Utah.

Patron of the Diocese of Salt Lake City: St. Mary Magdalene.

For legal titles of parishes and diocesan institutions, consult the Chancery Office.

STATISTICAL OVERVIEW

Personnel	
Bishop	1
Priests: Diocesan Active in Diocese	34
Priests: Diocesan Active Outside Diocese	1
Priests: Retired, Sick or Absent	15
Number of Diocesan Priests	50
Religious Priests in Diocese	8
Total Priests in Diocese	58
Extern Priests in Diocese	17
Permanent Deacons in Diocese	85
Total Brothers	1
Total Sisters	24
Parishes	
Parishes	49
With Resident Pastor:	
Resident Diocesan Priests	33
Resident Religious Priests	3
Without Resident Pastor:	
Administered by Priests	13
Missions	20
Professional Ministry Personnel:	
Sisters	2
Lay Ministers	55
Welfare	
Day Care Centers	16
Total Assisted	585
Special Centers for Social Services	3
Total Assisted	319,000
Other Institutions	1
Total Assisted	46,120
Educational	
Diocesan Students in Other Seminaries	8
Total Seminarians	8
High Schools, Diocesan and Parish	3
Total Students	1,534
Elementary Schools, Diocesan and Parish	13
Total Students	3,531
Catechesis/Religious Education:	
High School Students	1,998
Elementary Students	8,240
Total Students under Catholic Instruction	15,311
Teachers in the Diocese:	
Priests	1
Sisters	2
Lay Teachers	382
Vital Statistics	
Receptions into the Church:	
Infant Baptism Totals	2,462
Minor Baptism Totals	377
Adult Baptism Totals	153
Received into Full Communion	568
First Communions	2,749
Confirmations	2,373
Marriages:	
Catholic	346
Interfaith	61
Total Marriages	407
Deaths	497
Total Catholic Population	316,110
Total Population	3,161,105

Former Bishops—Rt. Revs. LAWRENCE SCANLAN, D.D., ord. June 24, 1868; appt. Vicar-Apostolic of Utah, Jan. 25, 1887; cons. Titular Bishop of Larandum, June 29, 1887; named first Bishop of Salt Lake, Jan. 30, 1891; died May 10, 1915; JOSEPH S. GLASS, C.M., D.D., LL.D., ord. Aug. 15, 1897; cons. Aug. 24, 1915; died Jan. 26, 1926; JOHN J. MITTY, D.D., ord. Dec. 22, 1906; cons. Sept. 8, 1926; made Coadjutor Archbishop of San Francisco, cum jure successionis, Feb. 4, 1932; Titular Archbishop of Egina; succeeded to the See, March 5, 1935; died Oct. 15, 1961; Most Revs. JAMES E. KEARNEY, D.D., ord. Sept. 19, 1908; appt. July 4, 1932; cons. Oct. 28, 1932; appt. Bishop of Rochester, July 31, 1937; installed Nov. 11, 1937; died Jan. 12, 1977; LEO J. STECK, D.D., ord. June 8, 1924; appt. Auxiliary Bishop of Salt Lake, March 3, 1948; cons. Titular Bishop of Ilium, May 20, 1948; died June 19, 1950; DUANE G. HUNT, D.D., LL.D., ord. June 27, 1920; appt. Aug. 6, 1937; cons. Oct. 28, 1937; appt. assistant at the Pontifical Throne; appt. May 25, 1946; died March 31, 1960; JOSEPH LENNOX FEDERAL, D.D., ord. Dec. 8, 1934; appt. Auxiliary Bishop of Salt Lake City, Feb. 5, 1951; cons. April 11, 1951; made Coadjutor Bishop of Salt Lake City, May 8, 1958; succeeded to the See, March 31, 1960; retired April 22, 1980; died Aug. 31, 2000; WILLIAM KEITH WEIGAND, D.D., ord. May 25, 1963; appt. Sept. 3, 1980; ord. Bishop, Nov. 17, 1980; transferred to the See of Sacramento; installed Jan. 27, 1994; GEORGE H. NIEDERAUER, Ph.D., ord. April 30, 1962; appt. Bishop of Salt Lake City Nov. 3, 1994; ord. Jan. 25, 1995; appt. Archbishop of San Francisco Dec. 15, 2005; installed Feb. 15, 2006; died May 2, 2017.; JOHN C. WESTER, ord. May 15, 1976; appt. Bishop of Salt Lake City Jan. 8, 2007; installed March 14, 2007; appt. Archbishop of Santa Fe April 27, 2015.

Diocesan Pastoral Center—27 C St., Salt Lake City, 84103-2397. Tel: 801-328-8641; Fax: 801-328-9680.

Office of the Bishop—Tel: 801-328-8641; Fax: 801-328-9680. MARYLIN ACOSTA, Exec. Asst.

Administrative Assistant to the Bishop—Rev. Msgr. J. TERRENCE FITZGERALD, P.A., (Retired).

Vicar General, Vicar for Clergy and Moderator of the Curia—Rev. Msgr. COLIN F. BIRCUMSHAW, Tel: 801-328-8641.

Chancellor—Deacon GEORGE W. READE, Tel: 801-328-8641, Ext. 315; TONI GLENN, Asst., Tel: 801-328-8641, Ext. 345.

Vice Chancellor—Very Rev. LANGES J. SILVA, J.C.D., Tel: 801-328-8641, Ext. 312.

Diocesan Offices

Archives—GARY TOPPING, Ph.D., Dir., Tel: 801-328-8641, Ext. 346.

Campus Ministry—VACANT, Tel: 801-328-8641.

Catholic Community Services—PETER CORROON, Pres.; BRADFORD R. DRAKE, Exec. Dir., 745 E. 300 S., Salt Lake City, 84102. Tel: 801-977-9119, Ext. 1222; Fax: 801-977-8227.

Catholic Foundation of Utah—JENIFER B. GIBBONS, Pres.; JENNIFER L. CARROLL, Exec. Dir., Tel: 801-328-8641, Ext. 306.

Catholic Relief Services—JEAN HILL, Tel: 801-328-8641, Ext. 336.

Catholic Schools Offices—MARK LONGE, Supt., Tel: 801-328-8641, Ext. 315; Sr. CATHERINE KAMPHAUS, C.S.C., Assoc. Supt., Tel: 801-328-8641, Ext. 330.

Cemetery–Mount Calvary—JOHN CURTICE, Dir.; LINDA QUINTANA, Sec., Tel: 801-355-2476; Fax: 801-328-3294.

Chancery—Deacon GEORGE W. READE, Chancellor, Tel: 801-328-8641, Ext. 364; TONI GLENN, Asst., Tel: 801-328-8641, Ext. 345.

College of Consultors—Rev. Msgrs. COLIN F. BIRCUMSHAW; J. TERRENCE FITZGERALD, P.A., (Retired); Very Rev. MARTIN L. DIAZ; Revs. JOHN S. EVANS; JOHN E. NORMAN; Very Rev. LANGES J. SILVA, J.C.D.; Revs. GUSTAVO VIDAL; KENNETH L. VIALPANDO.

Deans—Revs. FRANCISCO PIRES, Salt Lake Deanery; OSCAR MARTIN PICOS, Southwestern Deanery; DAVID J. BITTMENN, Wasatch Deanery; ALBERT KILEO, A.L.C.P., Eastern Deanery; ERIK J. RICHTSTEIG, Northern Deanery.

Permanent Diaconate—Deacon ROBERT H. HARDY, Dir., Tel: 801-328-8641, Ext. 327.

Diaconate Formation—Deacon DREW M. PETERSEN JR., Dir., Tel: 801-328-8641, Ext. 337; Rev. ELEAZAR SILVA GALVAN, Dir. Academics, Tel: 801-328-8941.

Diocesan Stewardship and Development—KARIN HURLEY, Dir., Tel: 801-328-8641, Ext. 328.

Diocesan Office for Persons with Disabilities—DOLORES LOPEZ, Tel: 801-328-8641, Ext. 333.

Diocesan Pastoral Council—

Ecumenical Commission—Rev. Msgr. JOSEPH M. MAYO, (Retired); Very Revs. LANGES J. SILVA, J.C.D.; MARTIN L. DIAZ; Rev. CHRISTOPHER P. GRAY.

Engaged Encounter—FRANK PEDROZA; JOANN PEDROZA, Tel: 801-214-8220.

Family Life-Natural Family Planning—VEOLA MARTINEZ-BURCHETT, Tel: 801-328-8641, Ext. 324.

Finance Council—Rev. Msgr. COLIN F. BIRCUMSHAW; Revs. CLARENCE J. SANDOVAL; JOHN S. EVANS; MARY KAY GRIFFIN, CPA; JEAN BRILL; MARK LONGE; JEFF STOKES; KATHIE BROWN ROBERTS, Esq.; Deacon GEORGE W. READE; NANCY ESSARY; MS. JOAN LOFFREDO, CPA, Staff Liaison.

Finance Office—MS. JOAN LOFFREDO, CPA, CFO, Tel: 801-328-8641, Ext. 309; DEBRA CANDELARIA, Sec., Tel: 801-328-8641, Ext. 310.

Government Liaison—JEAN HILL, Tel: 801-328-8641, Ext. 336.

Hispanic Ministry—MARIA-CRUZ GRAY, Dir., Tel: 801-

328-8641, Ext. 361; Sandra Maxwell, Sec., Tel: 801-328-8641, Ext. 332.

Liaison for Hispanic Priests—Rev. Javier G. Virgen, Tel: 801-328-8641, Ext. 358.

Holy Childhood Association—Deacon George W. Reade, Dir., Tel: 801-328-8641, Ext. 315.

Liturgy Office—Ruth Dillon, Dir., Tel: 801-328-8641, Ext. 363; Tel: 801-328-8641, Ext. 322; Trisha Norcross, Sec., Tel: 801-328-8641, Ext. 323.

Liturgical Commission—Rev. Samuel Dinsdale, Tel: 801-487-1000.

Correctional Institution Ministry—Rev. James E. Blaine, Chap. Utah State Prison, (Retired), Mailing Address: P.O. Box 142, American Fork, 84003. Tel: 385-233-1657; Deacon Joaquin Mixco, Coord. Jail Ministry for Salt Lake Valley, Tel: 801-913-5703; Rev. Manuel de Jesus Ceron, Ventura, Central Utah Correctional Facility, Gunnison. Tel: 435-896-5593.

Board For Ongoing Formation of Priests—Clergy Continuing Education, Rev. Msgr. Colin F. Bircumshaw. Team: Very Rev. Martin L. Diaz, Chm.; Revs. Eleazar Silva Galvan; Francisco Pires; Kenneth L. Vialpando; Samuel Dinsdale; Reynato Rodillas; Fernando R. Velasco Castro.

Native American Ministry—Dolores Lopez, Tel: 801-328-8641, Ext. 333.

Newspaper—Intermountain Catholic Marie Mischel, Editor, Tel: 801-328-8641, Ext. 340; Vacant, Assoc. Editor, Tel: 801-328-8641, Ext. 341; Arthur Heredia, Business Mgr., Tel: 801-328-8641, Ext. 356; Cris Paulsen, Advertising Rep. & Mktg. Dir., Tel: 801-328-8641, Ext. 339; Laura Vallejo, Staff Writer, Tel: 801-328-8641, Ext. 351; Vacant, Graphic Designer, Tel: 801-328-8641.

Peace and Justice Commission—Jean Hill, Dir., Tel: 801-328-8641, Ext. 336.

Presbyteral Council—Very Rev. Martin L. Diaz, Pres.; Vacant, Vice Pres.; Rev. John S. Evans, Sec.

Priests' Mutual Benefit Society (Retirement)—Board of Directors: Rev. Msgrs. Colin F. Bircumshaw, Pres. & Ex Officio; Joseph M. Mayo, Sec. & Treas., (Retired); Very Rev. Martin L. Diaz; Rev. Msgr. Robert J. Bussen, (Retired); Revs. John S. Evans; Andrzej Skrzypiec; Ms. Joan Loffredo, CPA, CFO.

Priests' Personnel Board—Rev. Msgrs. Colin F. Bircumshaw; J. Terrence Fitzgerald, P.A., (Retired); Joseph M. Mayo, (Retired); Rev. Javier G. Virgen; Very Rev. Langes J. Silva, J.C.D.; Revs. Kenneth L. Vialpando; Francisco Pires; Omar Ontiveros; Clarence J. Sandoval.

Real Estate Office—Deacon George W. Reade, Tel: 801-328-8641, Ext. 315; Toni Glenn, Asst., Tel: 801-328-8641, Ext. 345.

Religious Education—Susan Northway, Dir., Tel: 801-328-8641, Ext. 326.

Sisters' Council—Executive Team: Sisters Genevra Rolf, C.S.C., Episcopal Liaison for Women Rel.; Catherine Kamphaus, C.S.C., Pres.; Mary Ann Pajakowski, C.S.C., Sec.

Society for the Propagation of the FaithDeacon George W. Reade, Dir., Tel: 801-328-8641, Ext. 315; Toni Glenn, Asst., Tel: 801-328-8641, Ext. 345.

Skaggs Tuition Assistance Program for Catholic Schools—Sr. Genevra Rolf, C.S.C., Tel: 801-328-8641, Ext. 334; Kathleen McMahon, Tel: 801-328-8641, Ext. 347.

Tribunal—

Judicial Vicar—Very Rev. Langes J. Silva, J.C.D., Tel: 801-328-8641, Ext. 312.

Secretary and Notary—Virginia Rodriguez, Tel: 801-328-8641, Ext. 316.

Promoter of Justice—Rev. Msgr. J. Terrence Fitzgerald, P.A., (Retired).

Defenders of the Bond—Rev. Msgr. Joseph M. Mayo, (Retired); Mrs. Deborah Barton, J.C.L.

Judges—Very Rev. Langes J. Silva, J.C.D.; Rev. Msgr. John A. Renken, J.C.D., S.T.D., M.C.L.

Victim Assistance Coordinator and Safe Environment—Sandy Growe, Tel: 801-328-8641, Ext. 344.

Vocation Office—Rev. Joseph D. Delka, Dir., Tel: 801-328-8941, Ext. 110; Deacon Sunday S. Espinoza, Assoc. Dir.; Rev. Christopher P. Gray, Assoc. Dir., Tel: 801-328-8641, Ext. 358.

Youth and Young Adult Ministry—Junuee Castro, Dir., Tel: 801-328-8641, Ext. 313.

CLERGY, PARISHES, MISSIONS AND PAROCHIAL SCHOOLS

SALT LAKE CITY

(Salt Lake County)

1—Cathedral of the Madeleine LLC 202 (1866)
331 E. S. Temple St., 84111. Tel: 801-328-8941; Email: mdiaz@utcotm.org; Web: utcotm.org. Very Rev. Martin L. Diaz; Rev. Joseph D. Delka; Deacons Drew Petersen; John Kranz.
School—Madeleine Choir School, (Grades PreK-8), 205 E. 1st Ave., 84103. Tel: 801-323-9850; Fax: 801-323-0581; Email: gglenn@utmcs.org; Web: www.utmcs.org. Mr. Gregory A. Glenn, M.A., Admin. Lay Teachers 41; Students 405.
Catechesis Religious Program—Fax: 801-364-6504. Students 326.
Good Samaritan Program—Patricia Wesson, Prog. Dir. Number Served 170,000.

2—Saint Ambrose LLC 214 (1948)
2315 Redondo Ave., 84108. Tel: 801-485-5610; Email: paroff@xmission.com; Web: www.stambroseslc.com. Rev. Andrzej Skrzypiec, Email: sandrzej@comcast.net; Deacons John Bash; George W. Reade.
School—J. E. Cosgriff Memorial School, (Grades PreK-8), 2335 Redondo Ave., 84108.
Tel: 801-486-3197; Fax: 801-484-8270; Email: bhunt@cosgriff.org; Web: www.cosgriff.org. Mrs. Elizabeth Hunt, Prin.; Jennifer Shrum, Librarian. Lay Teachers 24; Preschool 91; Students 307.
Catechesis Religious Program—Tel: 801-485-9324; Fax: 801-484-1065. Students 406.

3—Saint Ann LLC 215 (1917)
2119 S. 400 E., 84115-2872. Tel: 801-487-1000; Email: omaro1975@gmail.com. Rev. Omar Ontiveros.
School—Saint Ann LLC 215 School, (Grades PreSchool-8), 430 E. 2100 S., 84105.
Tel: 801-486-0741; Fax: 801-486-0742; Email: sredle@ksaschool.org; Email: rose@utahweb.com; Web: www.ksaschool.org. Shirley Redle, Prin. Clergy 1; Lay Teachers 13; Students 137.
Catechesis Religious Program—Tel: 801-243-3174; Email: maxgreenbean@msn.com. Students 120.

4—Saint Catherine of Siena Catholic Newman Center LLC 218 (1981)
170 S. University St., 84102. Tel: 801-359-6066; Email: office@stcatherineslc.org; Web: stcatherineslc.org. Revs. Jacek Buda; Marcin Szymanski; Lukasz Misko, O.P., Campus Min.
Catechesis Religious Program—Students 96.

5—Our Lady of Guadalupe LLC 208 (1944) (Hispanic)
Mailing Address: 257 N. 700 W., 84116.
Tel: 801-364-2019; Email: ologsecretary@gmail.com. 715 W. 300 North, 84116. Rev. Jose Fidel Barrera-Cruz; Deacon Moises Ruiz, Sacramental Min.
Res.: 323 Argyle Ct. 84116
Catechesis Religious Program—Tel: 801-755-6079; Email: trujillobeatriz65@gmail.com. Beatriz Trujillo, D.R.E. & Coord. Students 675.

6—Our Lady of Lourdes LLC 211 (1913) [CEM]
1085 E. 700 S. St., 84102. Tel: 801-322-3330; Email: sandy@callingallfriends.com; Web: lourdes-slc.org. Rev. J. J. Schwall.
School—Our Lady of Lourdes LLC 211 School, (Grades K-8), 1065 E. 700 S. St., 84102.
Tel: 801-364-5624; Fax: 801-364-0925; Email: tbergquist@lourdesschool.org; Email: gpoteracki@lourdesschool.org; Web: lourdesschool.org. Mrs. Christine Bergquist, Prin. Lay Teachers 16; Students 176.
Catechesis Religious Program—Students 10.

7—Our Lady of Perpetual Help LLC 261 (1994) (Other) (Vietnamese Parish)
4360 W. 5415 S., Kearns, 84118. Tel: 801-968-8981; Email: oloph2018@gmail.com. Rev. Tai Nguyen.
Church & Res.: 5415 S. 4360 W., 84118.
Catechesis Religious Program—Students 173.

8—Saint Patrick LLC 241 (1892)
Mailing Address: 1058 W. 400 S., 84104-1261.
Tel: 801-596-7233; Email: stpatoffice@comcast.net. Rev. Anastasius Iwuoha; Deacon Sefo A. Manu.
Res.: 1072 W. 400 S., 84104-1261.
Catechesis Religious Program—

9—Sacred Heart LLC 210 (1917)
948 S. 2nd East St., 84111. Tel: 801-363-8632; Email: sacredheart210@gmail.com. 174 E. 900 South, 84111. Rev. Eleazar Silva Galvan.
Catechesis Religious Program—174 E. 900 S., 84111. Tel: 801-694-4073; Email: charocer4@gmail.com. Charo Alcocer, D.R.E. Students 80.

10—Saint Thomas More Catholic Church LLC 248 (1981)
Mailing Address: 3015 E. Creek Rd., Cottonwood Heights, 84093-6575. Rev. John S. Evans; Deacons Mark E. Solak; John Keyser; Rev. Dominic Briese, O.P., In Res.
Res. & Parish Center: 3047 E. Creek Rd., Cottonwood Heights, 84093-6575. Tel: 801-942-5285; Email: parish@stmutah.org; Web: www.stmutah.org.
Catechesis Religious Program—Email: tami@stmutah.org. Tami Bernstein, D.R.E. Students 149.

11—Saint Vincent de Paul LLC 250 (1925)
1375 E. Spring Ln., 84117. Tel: 801-272-9216; Email: parishoffice@stvincents-school.org. Rev. John E. Norman; Rev. Msgr. M. Francis Mannion, Pastor Emeritus, (Retired); Deacon David Osman.
School—Saint Vincent de Paul LLC 250 School, (Grades PreK-8), 1385 E. Spring Ln., 84117.
Tel: 801-277-6702; Fax: 801-424-0450; Email: ggreen@stvincents-school.org. Gary Green, Prin. Lay Teachers 17; Students 290.
Catechesis Religious Program—Tel: 801-527-2037. Students 44.

SUBURBAN SALT LAKE CITY

1—Blessed Sacrament LLC 201 (1972)
9757 S. 1700 E., Sandy, 84092. Tel: 801-571-5517; Email: sjackson@blessedsacschool.org; Web: blessedsacramentsandy.parishesonline.com. Rev. Samuel Dinsdale; Deacons Marcel Soklaski; Billy Martin; Sharon Jackson, Pastoral Assoc.
School—Blessed Sacrament LLC 201 School, (Grades PreSchool-8),
1745 E. 9800 S., Sandy, 84092. Tel: 801-572-5311; Fax: 801-572-0251; Email: bpenn@blessedsacschool.org; Web: www.blessedsacschool.org. Bryan Penn, Prin. Lay Teachers 17; Students 202.
Catechesis Religious Program—
Email: smartin@blessedsacschool.org. Sharon Martin, D.R.E. Students 59.
Station—Our Lady of the Snows
Alta.

2—Saint Francis Xavier LLC 222 (1955)
4501 W. 5215 S., Kearns, 84118. Tel: 801-968-2123; Email: sainfrancisxavier@sfxkearns.org; Web: sfxkearns.org. Rev. Eugenio Yarce; Deacon Douglas C. Biediger.
See St. Francis Xavier Regional School, Kearns under Elementary Schools, Regional located in the Institution section.
Catechesis Religious Program—
Tel: 801-968-2123, Ext. 153. Students 800.

3—Immaculate Conception LLC 206 (1890)
Mailing Address: 8892 W. State Hwy., P.O. Box 151, Copperton, 84006. Tel: 801-569-2706; Email: icpcopperton@gmail.com. Rev. David Trujillo, Admin.; Greg Schindler, Asst. Admin.; Mrs. Christy Kelley, D.R.E.; Mrs. Heidi Madill, Business Mgr.
Catechesis Religious Program—Students 6.

4—Saint Joseph the Worker LLC 232 (1964)
7405 S. Redwood Rd., West Jordan, 84084.
Tel: 801-255-8902; Email: office@sjtwchurch.org; Web: www.sjtwchurch.org. Rev. Javier G. Virgen; Deacon Sunday S. Espinoza.
Catechesis Religious Program—
Tel: 801-251-1236; Email: ccd@sjtwchurch.org. Mrs. Melissa Castellano, D.R.E. Students 153.

5—Saint Jude LLC (1975) [CEM] (Maronite)
4893 Wasatch St., Murray, 84107. Tel: 801-268-2820; Email: Father.Joubran@hotmail.com; Web: www.stjudemaroniteutah.org. Rev. Joubran Boumerhi.
Catechesis Religious Program—
Fax: 801-268-2620. Waddell Goins, D.R.E. Students 2.

6—Saint Martin de Porres LLC 236 (1982)
Mailing Address: 4976 Valois Cir., Taylorsville, 84119. Tel: 801-968-2369. 4914 S. 2200 West, Taylorsville, 84129. Rev. Jan Bednarz.
Catechesis Religious Program—
Tel: 801-209-8945; Email: carolmom50@yahoo.com. Caroline Costello, D.R.E. Students 83.

7—Our Lady of Lourdes LLC 209 (1916) [CEM]
2840 S. 9000 W., P.O. Box 38, Magna, 84044.
Tel: 801-508-1595; Fax: 801-508-7027; Email: ololmagna@gmail.com. Rev. Lourduraj Gally Gregory.
Catechesis Religious Program—
2864 S. 9000 W., Magna, 84044. Students 120.

8—Saints Peter and Paul LLC 243 (1972)
3560 W. 3650 S., West Valley City, 84120.
Tel: 801-966-5111; Email: stpeterpaul@live.com. Revs. Francisco Pires; Jorge Roldan; Deacons George J. Sluga; Constantine Campos; Joaquin Mixco.
Catechesis Religious Program—
Tel: 801-966-5111, Ext. 202; Fax: 801-966-0114. Students 550.

9—Saint Therese of the Child Jesus LLC 246 (1925) (Spanish)
7832 S. Allen St., Midvale, 84047. Tel: 801-255-3721; Email: stthereses.parish@gmail.com; Web: www.sthererse.org. Rev. Jose Alberto Barrera; Deacons Stanley L. Stott; Rubel J. Salaz.
Res.: 7860 S. Allen St., Midvale, 84047.
Catechesis Religious Program—Students 378.

OUTSIDE SALT LAKE CITY

American Fork, Utah Co., Saint Peter LLC 242 (1969)
634 N. 600 E., American Fork, 84003.
Tel: 801-756-7771; Email: stpeters6@yahoo.com;

Web: www.stpetersamericanfork.parishesonline.com. 622 N. 600 East, American Fork, 84003.
Catechesis Religious Program—Tel: 801-756-2747. Students 153.
Station—Eagle Mountain.

BOUNTIFUL, DAVIS CO., SAINT OLAF LLC 239 (1943)
276 E. 1700 South, Bountiful, 84010.
Tel: 801-295-3621; Email: marcie@saintolaf.net; Web: stolafut.org. Rev. Reynato Rodillas; Deacon Scott Dodge.
School—Saint Olaf LLC 239 School, (Grades K-8), 1793 S. Orchard Dr., Bountiful, 84010.
Tel: 801-295-5341; Fax: 801-295-5915; Email: saintolaf@saintolaf.net; Web: stolafs.org. Mrs. Kathy Dorich, Librarian. Lay Teachers 18; Students 154.
Catechesis Religious Program—Students 99.

BRIGHAM CITY, BOX ELDER CO., SAINT HENRY LLC 225 (1950)
380 S. 2nd E., P.O. Box 872, Brigham City, 84302.
Tel: 435-723-2941; Email: sthenrys@comcast.org. Rev. Patrick Reuse, S.J.; Deacons Kary Meyersick; Andy Hunnel.
Catechesis Religious Program—Tel: 435-723-1215. Students 153.
Mission—Santa Ana, 760 W. 600 N., Tremonton, Box Elder Co. 84337.

CEDAR CITY, IRON CO., CHRIST THE KING LLC 203 (1936)
Mailing Address: 690 S. Cove Dr., Cedar City, 84720. Deacons Carlos Mendez; Denny Davies.
Res.: 680 S. Cove Dr., Cedar City, 84720.
Tel: 435-586-8298; Email: ctk@skyviewmail.com.
Catechesis Religious Program—Email: ctkdre@gmail.com. Nancy K. Lefort, D.R.E. Students 150.
Missions—St. Gertrude—Panguitch, 84759.
St. Sylvester, Escalante, Garfield Co. 84726.
Stations—St. Dominic—Bryce Canyon, Garfield Co. 84717.
Duck Creek Village, Kane Co. 84762.

CENTRAL VALLEY, SEVIER CO., SAINT ELIZABETH LLC 220 (1947)
815 N. SR 118, Central Valley, 84754.
Tel: 435-896-5539; Email: stecatholicparish@gmail.com. Rev. Manuel Ceron Valdez.
Res.: 76 S. 200 W., Richfield, 84701.
Catechesis Religious Program—Students 6.
Missions—St. Anthony of the Desert—North on Sandcreek Rd., Torrey, Wayne Co. 84775.
St. Jude, 160 E. Center St., Ephraim, Sanpete Co. 84627.
San Juan Diego Mission, 25 W. Center St., Gunnison, Sanpete Co. 84634.
Station—Central Utah Correctional Facility, [JC] Gunnison. Tel: 801-528-6000; Fax: 801-528-6259.

DRAPER, SALT LAKE CO., SAINT JOHN THE BAPTIST LLC 252 (1999)
300 E. 11800 S., Draper, 84020. Tel: 801-984-7101; Fax: 801-984-7114; Email: office@sjb-parish.org; Web: www.sjb-parish.org. Rev. Richard T. Sherman; Deacon Paul Graham.
School—Saint John the Baptist LLC 252 School, (Grades PreK-12), Fax: 801-984-7122; Email: nikkiward@sjbelementary.org. Clergy 1; Lay Teachers 30; Students 570.
Catechesis Religious Program—Email: rachelholt@sjb-parish.org; Email: teraniepelch@sjb-parish.org. Rachel Holt, D.R.E.; Teranie Pelch, RCIA Coord. Students 232.

EAST CARBON, CARBON CO., GOOD SHEPHERD LLC 204 (1947)
Mailing Address: c/o Notre Dame de Lourdes, 185 N. Carbon Ave., East Carbon, 84520. Tel: 435-637-1846; Fax: 435-637-6338; Email: notredame@emerytelcom.net. 201 Center St., East Carbon, 84520. Rev. Rafael A. Murillo.
Res.: 205 N. Carbon Ave., Price, 84501.
Catechesis Religious Program—Tel: 435-630-0815; Email: ndbills@sisna.com. Catherine Kane, D.R.E.
Mission—St. Michael, 140 N. Long St., Green River, Emery Co. 84525.

EUREKA, JUAB CO., SAINT PATRICK LLC 257 (1885) Rev. Jose Gregorio Rausseo Gomez.
Res.: P.O. Box 387, Payson, 84651. Email: utah@paysonsanandres.org.
Catechesis Religious Program—

HELPER, CARBON CO., SAINT ANTHONY OF PADUA CATHOLIC CHURCH LLC 216 (1944) [JC]
5 S. Main, Helper, 84526-1533. Tel: 435-472-5661; Tel: 435-472-8367; Email: santhony@emerytelcom.net. Rev. Albert Kileo, A.L.C.P.
Catechesis Religious Program—Tel: 435-472-8367. Pam Felice, D.R.E. Students 43.

KANAB, KANE CO., SAINT CHRISTOPHER LLC 219 (1953)
39 W. 200 S., Kanab, 84741. Tel: 435-644-3414; Email: stccc@kanab.net. Rev. Oscar Martin Picos.

LAYTON, DAVIS CO., SAINT ROSE OF LIMA LLC 245 (1948)
210 S. Chapel St., P.O. Box 557, Layton, 84041. Rev. Clarence J. Sandoval; Deacons John C. Weis, (Retired); Manuel Trujillo; Bernardo Villar.
Res.: 280 S. Chapel St., Layton, 84041.
Tel: 801-546-2541; Email: church@stroseut.org.
Catechesis Religious Program—Tel: 801-544-5425; Email: kevin.cummings@stroseut.org. Kevin Cummings, D.R.E. Students 279.

LOGAN, CACHE CO., SAINT THOMAS AQUINAS LLC 247 (1941)
725 S. 250 E., Hyde Park, 84318. Tel: 435-752-1478; Email: stthomas2006@gmail.com. Rev. Fernando Velasco, Admin.; Deacon Jim Miller; Sr. Marilyn Mark, O.S.B., Liturgy Dir.
Res.: 573 E. 2050 N., North Logan, 84341.
Catechesis Religious Program—Students 226.
Mission—Utah State University, St. Jerome Newman Center, 795 N. 800 E., Logan, Cache Co. 84321. Tel: 435-753-7670.

MILFORD, BEAVER CO., SAINT BRIDGET LLC 217 (1948)
Mailing Address: 210 S. 1st W., P.O. Box 785, Milford, 84751. Tel: 435-387-2732; Email: r_montoro@hotmail.com. Rev. Roberto Montoro.
Res.: 96 S. Center, P.O. Box 924, Delta, 84624.
Catechesis Religious Program—Students 75.
Missions—St. John Bosco—96 S. Center, P.O. Box 924, Delta, Millard Co. 84624.
Holy Family, 445 S. 200 E., P.O. Box 292, Fillmore, Millard Co. 84631. Tel: 801-835-6449.

MOAB, GRAND CO., SAINT PIUS X LLC 244 (1955) Rev. Rowland Nwokocha.
Res.: 122 W. 400 N., P.O. Box 636, Moab, 84532.
Tel: 435-259-5211; Email: piusx@frontiernet.net.
Catechesis Religious Program—Students 10.
Mission—Sacred Heart, Hwy. 46/Main, LaSal, San Juan Co. 84530.

MONTICELLO, SAN JUAN CO., SAINT JOSEPH LLC 229 (1935) [JC]
385 S. Main, P.O. Box 518, Monticello, 84535.
Tel: 801-259-5211; Email: piusx@frontiernet.net. Rev. Rowland Nwokocha.
Station—Blanding.

OGDEN, WEBER CO.

1—HOLY FAMILY LLC 205 (1979)
1100 E. 5550 S., Ogden, 84403. Tel: 801-479-1112; Email: hfcc@hfutah.org; Web: holyfamilycatholicchurch.org. Rev. William F. Wheaton; Deacon Douglas B. Smith.
Catechesis Religious Program—Email: hfcre@hfutah.org. Carl Leuschner, D.R.E. Students 94.

2—SAINT JAMES THE JUST LLC 226 (1966)
495 N. Harrison Blvd., Ogden, 84404.
Tel: 801-782-5393; Email: stjames_secretary@comcast.net. Rev. Erik J. Richtsteig; Deacons Kenneth W. Murphy; Steve Neveraski; Herschel Hester; Robert W. Bambrick.
Catechesis Religious Program—Email: stjames_dre@comcast.net; Email: stjames_secretary@comcast.net. Elizabeth Atkins, D.R.E.; Terri Ward, D.R.E. (Pre-School). Students 145.

3—SAINT JOSEPH LLC 230 (1875)
514 24th St., Ogden, 84401. Tel: 801-399-5627; Email: FrMSciumbato@dioslc.org; Web: www.stjosephogden.org/home. Revs. Michael R. Sciumbato; Stephen Tilley; Charles T. Cummins; Deacons Howard Schuyler; Dan Essary; Keith W. Norrell; Honorio Moreno.
See St. Joseph Regional School, Ogden under Elementary Schools, Regional located in the Institution section.
Catechesis Religious Program—Tel: 801-621-3602; Fax: 801-621-3602; Email: reprogram3602@msn.com (English); Email: mariagandara55@msn.com (Spanish). Students 631.
Mission—St. Florence, 6481 E. Hwy. 39, Huntsville, Weber Co. 84317.

4—SAINT MARY LLC 237 (1957)
Mailing Address: 4050 S. 3900 W., West Haven, 84401. Tel: 801-621-7961; Fax: 801-394-1244; Email: Office@Stmarysutah.org; Web: www.StMarysutah.org. Rev. Gustavo Vidal; Deacons Jack Clark; Thom Rodgers.
Catechesis Religious Program—Tel: 801-391-8655; Email: Safeenvir@stmarysutha.org. Joe Rodrigues, D.R.E. Students 459.

OREM, UTAH CO., ST. FRANCIS OF ASSISI LLC 221 (1892) [CEM]
Mailing Address: 65 E. 500 N., Orem, 84057-4030.
Tel: 801-221-0750; Email: parish@oremstfrancis.org. Revs. David J. Bittmenn; Rogelio Felix-Rosas; Deacons Julio Palomino; Vincente Vasquez.
Res.: 1661 N. 500 E., Orem, 84057-4030.
Catechesis Religious Program—
Tel: 801-221-0750, Ext. 16; Fax: 801-221-0759. Students 1,129.

PARK CITY, SUMMIT CO., SAINT MARY OF THE ASSUMPTION LLC 238 (1881)
1505 W. White Pine Canyon Rd., Park City, 84060.
Tel: 435-649-9676; Email: info@stmarysparkcity.com; Web: www.stmarysparkcity.com. Revs. Christopher P. Gray; Ariel Durian, Parochial Vicar; Deacons Tom Tosti; Robert H. Hardy.
Mission—St. Lawrence, 1st West Center, Heber City, Wasatch Co. 84032. Linda Miller, Admin.

PAYSON, UTAH CO., SAN ANDRES LLC 212 (1986) Rev. Jose Gregorio Rausseo Gomez.
Church & Mailing Address: 315 E. 100 N., P.O. Box 387, Payson, 84651. Email: utsanandres@gmail.com.
Catechesis Religious Program—Students 250.
Mission—San Isidro, Elberta, 84626.

PRICE, CARBON CO., NOTRE DAME DE LOURDES LLC 207 (1918)
185 N. Carbon Ave., Price, 84501. Tel: 435-637-1846; Fax: 435-637-6338; Email: notredame@emerytelcom.net. Rev. Rafael A. Murrillo.
Res.: 205 N. Carbon Ave., Price, 84501.
Catechesis Religious Program—Tel: 435-630-0815; Email: ndbills@sisna.com. Catherine Kane, D.R.E. Students 160.
Mission—San Rafael, 1716 S. Hwy. 10, Huntington, Emery Co. 84528.

RIVERTON, SALT LAKE CO., SAINT ANDREW CATHOLIC CHURCH LLC 233 (2006)
11835 S. 3600 W., Riverton, 84065.
Tel: 801-253-6030; Email: secretary@standrewut.com; Web: www.standrewut.com. Rev. Marco T. Lopez; Deacon Michael E. Bulson.
School—Saint Andrew Catholic School LLC Series 233, (Grades PreK-8), Tel: (801) 253-6000; Email: info@standrewut.org; Web: www.standrewut.org. Erin Carrabba, Prin. Clergy 1; Lay Teachers 18; Students 193.
Catechesis Religious Program—Tel: 801-253-6031; Email: dre@standrewut.com. Mariana Rodriguez, D.R.E. Students 171.

ROOSEVELT, DUCHESNE CO., SAINT HELEN LLC 224 (1940) [CEM]
433 E. 200 N., P.O. Box 415, Roosevelt, 84066.
Tel: 436-722-2975; Email: sainthelencatholic@gmail.com. Rev. Arokia Dass David.
Catechesis Religious Program—Students 26.
Missions—Holy Spirit—Duchesne, Duchesne Co.
Blessed Kateri Tekakwitha, Fort Duchesne, Uintah Co.

ST. GEORGE, WASHINGTON CO., ST. GEORGE LLC 223 (1955)
Mailing Address: 259 W. 200 N., P.O. Box 188, St. George, 84771. Tel: 435-673-2604; Fax: 435-688-2704; Email: saintgeorgecatholic@hotmail.com; Web: www.saintgeorgecatholics.com. Revs. Oscar Martin Picos; Sebastien Sasa; Deacons Rigoberto Aquirre; Rogaciano Tellez.
Catechesis Religious Program—Bishop Scanlan Bldg., 157 N. 200 W., St. George, 84770. Students 485.
Missions—San Pablo—Beryl, Iron Co. 84714. Saturdays 6pm.
Saint Paul Catholic Center, 171 S. Main, Hurricane, 84737. Every Sunday 12:30pm.
Station—Zion National Park, St. George. (Lodge) Sunday 8am.

TOOELE, TOOELE CO., ST. MARGUERITE LLC 235 (1910)
15 S. 7th St., Tooele, 84074. Tel: 435-882-3860; Email: stmarguerite1910@gmail.com. Rev. Kenneth L. Vialpando.
School—St. Marguerite LLC 235 School, (Grades PreK-8), Tel: 435-882-0081; Email: tkirkbride@stmargschool.org@stmargschool.org; Web: stmargschool.org. Trisha Kirkbride, Prin. Lay Teachers 14; Students 153.
Catechesis Religious Program—Students 123.

VERNAL, UINTAH CO., SAINT JAMES THE GREATER LLC 227 (1923) [JC]
138 N. 100 West St., Vernal, 84078.
Tel: 435-789-3016; Email: stjamesvernal@gmail.com. Rev. Showri Rayalu Kalva.
Catechesis Religious Program—Tel: 435-789-3034. Students 91.

WENDOVER, TOOELE CO., SAN FELIPE LLC 251 (2000) (Spanish)
606 E. Aria Blvd., P.O. Box 1270, Wendover, 84083.
Tel: 435-406-9610; Email: info@sanfelipecatholicchurch.com. Rev. Oscar Manuel Hernandez-Hernandez, Admin.
Catechesis Religious Program—Students 203.

Chaplains of Public Institutions

SALT LAKE CITY. *Adult Detention Complex*,
Tel: 801-743-5500.
County Youth Detention Center, Tel: 801-261-2060.
Decker Lake Youth Detention Center,
Tel: 801-954-9200. Deacon Manuel Trujillo.
Veterans Administration Hospital, 500 Foothill Dr., 84113. Tel: 801-582-1565. Rev. Bruce R. Clapham.
Wasatch Youth Center, Tel: 801-265-5860.

DRAPER. *Utah State Prison*, P.O. Box 142, American Fork, 84003. Tel: 801-576-7827. Rev. James E. Blaine, (Retired), Tel: 801-576-7485.

GUNNISON. *Central Utah Correctional Facility*, Tel: 435-528-6000. Rev. Manuel de Jesus Ceron Valdez.

On Duty Outside the Diocese:
Rev.—
Frez, Joseph S., Diocese of Broken Bay, Australia.

Retired:
Rev. Msgrs.—
Bussen, Robert J., (Retired)
Daz, Rudolph A., (Retired)
Fitzgerald, J. Terrence, P.A., (Retired)
Mannion, M. Francis, (Retired)
Mayo, Joseph M., (Retired)
Moore, Terence M., Ph.D., (Retired)
Winterer, Michael J., (Retired)
Revs.—
Blaine, James E., (Retired)
Carley, Patrick F., (Retired)
Curnutte, William G., (Retired)
Diaz, Hernando, (Retired)
Ha, Dominic Thuy Dang, (Retired)
Herba, Stanislaw, (Retired)
Hope, Donald E., (Retired)
Van Massenhove, David L., (Retired).

Permanent Deacons:
Aquirre, Rigoberto, St. George, St. George
Bambrick, Robert W., St. James the Just, Ogden
Bash, John, St. Ambrose, Salt Lake City
Bassett, Willis, Christ Prince of Peace, Hill AFB
Becerra-Bejar, Jose, Saint Peter, American Fork
Biediger, Douglas C., St. Francis Xavier, Kearns
Bulson, Michael E., St. Andrew, Riverton
Campos, Constantine, Sts. Peter and Paul, West Valley City
Clark, Jack, St. Mary, West Haven
Conniff, John, (Retired)
Cormier, Joe H., (Retired), (Out of Diocese)
Corrao, Thomas P., St. Joseph, Monticello
Cortez, Carlos, Our Lady of Lourdes, Magna
Cummings, Owen, (Outside of Diocese)
Davies, Denny, Christ the King, Cedar City
Dillon, Dale R.
Dodge, Scott, St. Olaf, Bountiful
Espinoza, Sunday S., St. Joseph the Worker, West Jordan
Essary, Dan, St. Joseph, Ogden
Farrell, Eugene, (Retired)
Flaim, Mansueto, St. Marguerite. Tooele
Garcia, James D., (Retired)
Glodowski, Robert J., (Retired)
Goette, Juan, St. Peter, American Fork
Gorman, Jack, (Retired)
Graham, Paul, St. John the Baptist, Draper
Gray, Forrest, (Retired)
Hardy, Robert H., Diaconate Dir., St. Mary of the Assumption, Park City
Hester, Herschel, St. James the Just, Ogden
Huffman, Rick, St. Marguerite, Tooele
Hunnel, Dwayne A., St. Henry, Brigham City
Johansson, Otto, San Felipe, Wendover
Johnson, Lynn R., (Retired), Cathedral - Bishop
Keyser, John, St. Thomas More, Salt Lake City
Klein, Richard H., (Outside the Diocese)
Kranz, John, Cathedral, Salt Lake City
Langner, Russell, (Retired)
Lopez, Anthony J., (Retired)
Manu, Sefo A., St. Patrick, Salt Lake City
Marrufo, Guillermo, St. Therese of the Child Jesus, Midvale
Martin, Billy, Blessed Sacrament, Sandy
Mendez, Carlos, Christ the King, Cedar City
Mendez, Guillermo, Cathedral, Salt Lake City
Merino, Reynaldo Q., (Retired)
Meyersick, Karl E., St. Henry, Brigham City
Miller, James P., St. Thomas Aquinas, Hyde Park
Mixco, Joaquin, Sts. Peter and Paul, West Valley City
Montano, Fernando, St. Elizabeth, Central Valley
Moreno, Honorio, St. Joseph, Ogden
Mota, Hector, Jail Ministry
Murphy, Kenneth W., (Retired)
Neveraski, Steve, St. James the Just, Ogden
Norrell, Keith W., St. Joseph, Ogden
Osman, David, St. Vincent de Paul, Murray
Padilla, Duane, St. Andrew, Riverton
Palm, Lowell, (Retired)
Palomino, Julio, St. Francis of Assisi, Orem
Petersen, Drew M. Jr., Cathedral of the Madeleine, Salt Lake City; Dir. of Formation
Reade, George W., St. Ambrose, Salt Lake City; Chancellor
Rodgers, Thomas A., St. Mary, West Haven
Rodriguez, Mario A., (Out of Diocese)
Ruiz, Moises, Our Lady of Guadalupe, Salt Lake City
Salaz, Rubel J., St. Therese, Midvale
Sanchez, Mel J., (Retired)
Schuyler, Howard, St. Joseph, Ogden; St. Florence, Huntsville
Sluga, George J., St. Peter & Paul, West Valley City
Smith, Douglas B., Holy Family, Ogden
Soklaski, Marcel, Blessed Sacrament, Sandy
Solak, Mark E., St. Thomas More, Sandy
Solorzano, Armando, Sacred Heart, Salt Lake City
Spencer, Noel, (Retired)
Stewart, Thomas J., (Retired)
Stott, Stanley L., St. Therese, Midvale
Tellez, Rogaciano, St. George, St. George
Thaeler, John S., Christ Prince of Peace, Hill AFB
Toro, German A., San Andres, Payson
Tosti, Tom, St. Mary of the Assumption, Park City
Trudell, William J., (Out of Diocese)
Trujillo, Manuel, St. Rose of Lima, Layton, UT; Jail Ministry
Vasquez, Vincente, St. Francis of Assisi, Orem
Velez, Manuel Ceron, Sacred Heart, Salt Lake City
Villar, Bernardo, St. Rose of Lima, Layton
Waiss, Terrance, St. Florence, Huntsville
Weis, John C., (Retired).

INSTITUTIONS LOCATED IN DIOCESE

[A] HIGH SCHOOLS, DIOCESAN

SALT LAKE CITY. *Judge Memorial Catholic High School* (1921) 650 S. 1100 E., 84102. Tel: 801-363-8895; Fax: 801-236-2923; Email: plambert@judgememorial.com; Web: www.judgememorial.com. Patrick Lambert, Prin. Day School. (Coed) Lay Teachers 61; Students 593; Total Staff 30.

DRAPER. *Juan Diego Catholic High School, Skaggs Catholic Center, LLC* (1999) 300 E. 11800 S., Draper, 84020. Tel: 801-984-7650; Fax: 801-984-7601; Email: drgaleycolosimo@skaggscatholiccenter.org; Web: www.jdchs.org. Dr. Gabriel Colosimo, Prin.; Sharon Philips, Librarian. Religious Teachers 1; Lay Teachers 53; Total Enrollment 770; Total Staff 78.

OGDEN. *St. Joseph Catholic High School*, 1790 Lake St., Ogden, 84401. Tel: 801-394-1515; Email: clayjones@stjosephutah.com; Web: www.stjosephutah.com. Clay Jones, Prin. Lay Teachers 17; Students 173.

[B] ELEMENTARY SCHOOLS, REGIONAL

KEARNS. *St. Francis Xavier Regional School*, (Grades PreSchool-8), 4501 W. 5215 S., Kearns, 84118. Tel: 801-966-1571; Fax: 801-966-1639; Email: mrozsahegyi@stfxcs.org; Web: stfrancisxavierschool.org. Marianne Rozsahegyi, Prin.; Mrs. Kathleen Kilby, Librarian. Lay Teachers 15; Students 249.

OGDEN. *St. Joseph Catholic Elementary School* (1877) (Grades PreSchool-8), 2980 Quincy Ave., Ogden, 84403. Tel: 801-393-6051; Fax: 801-393-6086; Email: nessary@stjosephutah.com; Web: www.stjosephutah.com/es. Rev. Eric Richsteig; Nancy Essary, Prin.; Paige Laubacher, Librarian. Lay Teachers 28; Students 394; Total Staff 48.

[C] FOUNDATIONS

SALT LAKE CITY. *Catholic Foundation of Utah* (1984) 27 C St., 84103. Tel: 801-456-9306; Email: jennifer.carroll@dioslc.org; Web: www.catholicfoundationofutah.org. Jennifer L. Carroll, Exec. Dir.; Jenifer Gibbons, Pres.

[D] CONVENTS, MONASTERIES AND RESIDENCES FOR SISTERS

SALT LAKE CITY. **Carmel of the Immaculate Heart of Mary Monastery* (1952) 5714 Holladay Blvd., 84121. Tel: 801-277-6075; Fax: 801-277-4263; Email: carmelsl@xmission.com; Web: www.carmelslc.org. Mother Therese Bui, O.C.D., Prioress. Sisters 12.

Our Lady of Lourdes Convent, 675 S. 1100 E., 84102. Tel: 801-583-1204; Email: sbrennan@cscsisters.org. Madeleine Clayton, Supr. Sisters of the Holy Cross 2.

DRAPER. *Congregation of the Sisters of the Holy Cross, Vivian Skaggs Armstrong Convent* (1998) 554 E. 11800 S., Draper, 84020. Tel: 801-501-8349; Email: celinedounies@sjbelementary.org; Email: patrice6250@gmail.com; Email: lsantos@cscsisters.org. Sr. Suzanne Brennan, C.S.C., Treas.

Sisters of the Holy Cross, Inc. Sisters 3.

PARK CITY. *Congregation of the Sisters of the Holy Cross*, 3221 Homestead Rd., Park City, 84098. Tel: 435-655-7980; Email: sbrennan@cscsisters.org. Sr. Suzanne Brennan, C.S.C., Treas.

Sisters of the Holy Cross, Inc. Sisters 3.

[E] NEWMAN CENTERS

SALT LAKE CITY. *University of Utah, Newman Center* (St. Catherine of Siena Catholic Newman Center) 170 S. University St., 84102. Tel: 801-359-6066; Email: office@stcatherineslc.org; Web: www.stcatherineslc.org. Rev. Lukasz Misko, O.P., Campus Min. Total Staff 3.

EPHRAIM. *St. Jude Catholic Center*, 160 E Center, Ephraim, 84627. Tel: 435-283-6242; Email: stecatholicparish@gmail.com. Rev. Manuel de Jesus Ceron Valdez, Pastor; Deacon Fernando Montano, Deacon.

OGDEN. *Weber State University, Newman Center*, 3738 Custer Ave., Ogden, 84403. Tel: 801-399-9531; Email: JudyFranquelin@aol.com. Rev. Charles T. Cummins, Dir. Total in Residence 1; Total Staff 1.

[F] CATHOLIC SOCIAL SERVICES

SALT LAKE CITY. *Catholic Community Services of Utah*, 745 E. 300 S., 84102. Tel: 801-977-9119; Fax: 801-977-8227; Fax: 801-977-9224; Email: jlazaro@ccsutah.org; Web: www.ccsutah.org. Peter Corroon, Brd. Pres.; Bradford R. Drake, Exec. Dir. Tot Asst. Annually 27,560; Total Staff 100; Meals Served at the St. Vincent de Paul Center 261,501.

Northern Utah Joyce Hansen Hall Food Bank, St. Martha's Baby Layette Project, Bridging the Gap, 2504 F. Ave., Ogden, 84401. Tel: 801-394-5944; Fax: 801-621-8468; Web: www.ccsnorthernutah.org. Mailing Address: 2504 F Ave., Ogden, 84401.

Homeless Services - St. Vincent de Paul Dining Hall, Bishop K. Weigand Homeless Resource Center, 437 W. 200 S., 84104. Tel: 801-363-7710; Fax: 801-595-8532; Email: mmelville@ccsutah.org. Deacon George W. Reade, Chancellor. Tot Asst. Annually 10,547; Total Staff 8.

Refugee Resettlement, Immigration Services, Refugee Fostercare, 745 E. 300 S., 84102. Tel: 801-977-9119; Fax: 801-977-9224; Email: abatar@ccsutah.org. Deacon George W. Reade, Chancellor. Tot Asst. Annually 2,282; Total Staff 60.

Holy Cross Ministries, 860 E. 4500 S., Ste. 204, 84107. Tel: 801-261-3440; Fax: 801-261-3390; Email: agardner@hcmutah.org; Web: www.holycrossministries.org. Emmie Gardner, Dir. Outreach Program, Health Education, Seniors, Children, Women, Immigration Legal Services, Bi-Lingual Counseling, Parish Health, Afterschool, School Readiness & Summer Programs. Tot Asst. Annually 4,311; Total Staff 27.

[G] MISCELLANEOUS

SALT LAKE CITY. *Catholic Diocese of Salt Lake City Capital Development Corporation*, 27 C St., 84103. Tel: 801-328-8641; Email: toni.glenn@dioslc.org. Deacon George W. Reade, Chancellor.

Catholic Diocese of Salt Lake City Real Estate Corporation, 27 C St., 84103. Tel: 801-328-8641; Email: toni.glenn@dioslc.org. Deacon George W. Reade, Chancellor.

Ministries of the Catholic Diocese of Salt Lake City LLC, 27 C St., 84103. Tel: 801-328-8641; Email: toni.glenn@dioslc.org. Deacon George W. Reade, Chancellor.

DRAPER. *Skaggs Catholic Center LLC*, 300 E. 11800 S., Draper, 84020. Tel: 801-984-7600; Tel: 801-984-7654; Fax: 801-984-7601; Email: jocendagorta@skaggscatholiccenter.org. Jo Cendagorta, Dir.; Patrick Reeder, Prin. Day Care 233; Students 352; High School Students 766; Elementary School Students 571; Pre K Enrollment 41; Faculty 24; Staff 49.

OGDEN. *Give Me A Chance, Inc.*, 2913 Grant Ave., Ogden, 84401-3614. Tel: 801-627-2235; Fax: 801-621-4169; Email: srarthurg@yahoo.com; Web: www.givemeachanceutah.org. Sr. Arthur Gordon, D.C., Dir.

RELIGIOUS INSTITUTES OF MEN REPRESENTED IN THE DIOCESE

For further details refer to the corresponding bracketed number in the Religious Institutes of Men or Women section.

[]—*Apostolic Life Community Priests in the Opus Spiritus Sanctu*—A.L.C.P.

[0690]—*Jesuit Fathers* (California Prov.)—S.J.

[0430]—*Order of Preachers (Dominicans)* (Western Province)—O.P.

RELIGIOUS INSTITUTES OF WOMEN REPRESENTED IN THE DIOCESE

[0230]—*Benedictine Sisters of Pontifical Jurisdiction*—O.S.B.

[1920]—*Congregation of the Sisters of the Holy Cross*—C.S.C.

[0760]—*Daughters of Charity of St. Vincent de Paul* (Province of the West)—D.C.
[0420]—*Discalced Carmelite Nuns*—O.C.D.
[]—*Sisters for Christian Community*—S.F.C.C.

DIOCESAN CEMETERIES

SALT LAKE CITY. *Mount Calvary Catholic*, 275 U St., 84103. Tel: 801-355-2476; Email: john.curtice@dioslc.org. John Curtice, Dir.

NECROLOGY

† Elliott, Patrick H., (Retired), Died Nov. 29, 2018
† Govorchin, Vincent, (Retired), Died Jul. 25, 2018
† Hart, John B., (Retired), Died Jul. 27, 2018

An asterisk (*) denotes an organization that has established tax-exempt status directly with the IRS and is not covered by the USCCB Group Ruling.

Diocese of San Angelo

(Dioecesis Angeliana)

Most Reverend

MICHAEL J. SIS

Bishop of San Angelo; ordained July 19, 1986; appointed Bishop of San Angelo December 12, 2013; consecrated and installed January 27, 2014. *Mailing Address: P.O. Box 1829, San Angelo, TX 76902.*

Most Reverend

MICHAEL D. PFEIFER, O.M.I.

Retired Bishop of San Angelo; ordained December 21, 1964; consecrated and installed Bishop of San Angelo July 26, 1985; retired December 12, 2013. *P.O. Box 659432, San Antonio, TX 78265.*

ESTABLISHED OCTOBER 16, 1961.

Square Miles 37,433.

Comprises 29 Counties in the State of Texas as follows: Andrews, Brown, Callahan, Coke, Coleman, Concho, Crane, Crockett, Ector, Glasscock, Howard, Irion, Kimble, McCulloch, Martin, Menard, Midland, Mitchell, Nolan, Pecos, Reagan, Runnells, Schleicher, Sterling, Sutton, Taylor, Terrell, Tom Green and Upton.

For legal title of parishes and diocesan institutions, consult the Chancery Office.

The Chancery: P.O. Box 1829, San Angelo, TX 76902. Tel: 325-651-7500; Fax: 325-651-6688.

Web: www.sanangelodiocese.org

STATISTICAL OVERVIEW

Personnel	
Bishop	1
Retired Bishops	1
Priests: Diocesan Active in Diocese	39
Priests: Diocesan Active Outside Diocese	1
Priests: Retired, Sick or Absent	8
Number of Diocesan Priests	48
Religious Priests in Diocese	7
Total Priests in Diocese	55
Extern Priests in Diocese	14
Ordinations:	
Diocesan Priests	2
Permanent Deacons	15
Permanent Deacons in Diocese	83
Total Brothers	5
Total Sisters	19
Parishes	
Parishes	45
With Resident Pastor:	
Resident Diocesan Priests	34
Resident Religious Priests	2
Without Resident Pastor:	
Administered by Priests	8
Administered by Deacons	1
Missions	21
Professional Ministry Personnel:	
Brothers	5
Sisters	19
Lay Ministers	43
Welfare	
Day Care Centers	1
Total Assisted	45
Special Centers for Social Services	7
Total Assisted	11,605
Educational	
Diocesan Students in Other Seminaries	8
Total Seminarians	8
Elementary Schools, Diocesan and Parish	3
Total Students	945
Catechesis/Religious Education:	
High School Students	2,143
Elementary Students	7,500
Total Students under Catholic Instruction	10,596
Teachers in the Diocese:	
Sisters	2
Lay Teachers	89
Vital Statistics	
Receptions into the Church:	
Infant Baptism Totals	1,527
Minor Baptism Totals	273
Adult Baptism Totals	117
Received into Full Communion	214
First Communions	1,948
Confirmations	1,403
Marriages:	
Catholic	272
Interfaith	85
Total Marriages	357
Deaths	928
Total Catholic Population	85,741
Total Population	793,328

Former Bishops—Most Revs. THOMAS J. DRURY, D.D., LL.D., ord. June 2, 1935; appt. Oct. 16, 1961; cons. and installed Jan. 24, 1962; transferred to Corpus Christi, July 19, 1965; died July 22, 1992; THOMAS TSCHOEPE, D.D., ord. May 30, 1943; appt. Bishop Jan. 12, 1966; cons. March 9, 1966; transferred to Dallas, Aug. 27, 1969; died Jan. 24, 2009; STEPHEN A. LEVEN, D.D., ord. June 10, 1928; cons. Feb. 8, 1956, Auxiliary of San Antonio; appt. to San Angelo Oct. 22, 1969; retired April 16, 1979; died June 28, 1983; JOSEPH A. FIORENZA, ord. May 29, 1954; appt. Sept. 4, 1979; ord. and installed Oct. 25, 1979; transferred to Galveston-Houston, Dec. 18, 1984; MICHAEL D. PFEIFER, O.M.I., (Retired), ord. Dec. 21, 1964; appt. Bishop of San Angelo May 31, 1985; cons. and installed July 26, 1985; retired Dec. 12, 2013.

Vicar General—Very Rev. SANTIAGO D. UDAYAR, Ed.D., J.C.L.

Chancery Office—804 Ford, San Angelo, 76905. Tel: 325-651-7500; Fax: 325-651-6688. *Mailing Address: Box 1829, San Angelo, 76902.* Office Hours: Mon.-Fri. 9-12 & 1-5.

Chancellor—MR. MICHAEL WYSE.

Diocesan Tribunal—Mailing Address: P.O. Box 1829, San Angelo, 76902.

Judicial Vicar—Very Rev. TOM BARLEY, J.C.L., Judge, Mailing Address: P.O. Box 1829, San Angelo, 76902.

Judges—MR. THOMAS C. BURKE, J.C.L.; Rev. Msgr. LARRY J. DROLL, J.C.L.; Very Rev. RODNEY WHITE, J.C.L.

Defensores Vinculi—Very Revs. SANTIAGO D. UDAYAR, Ed.D., J.C.L.; MARK WOODRUFF; Rev. CARLOS DAVANTES, J.C.L.

Promoter of Justice for Priest Cases—Very Rev. TOM BARLEY, J.C.L.

Promoter of Justice for Marriage Cases—MR. THOMAS C. BURKE, J.C.L.

Case Managers/Ecclesiastical Notaries—JEAN G. GULLY; MARY ELLEN PAYTON.

Diocesan Consultors—Rev. Msgr. LARRY J. DROLL, J.C.L.; Revs. HUBERT WADE; MICHAEL RODRIGUEZ; Rev. Msgrs. ROBERT BUSH; FREDERICK NAWARSKAS; Very Revs. TOM BARLEY, J.C.L.; SANTIAGO D. UDAYAR, Ed.D., J.C.L.

Priests' Personnel Board—Very Revs. SANTIAGO D. UDAYAR, Ed.D., J.C.L., Chm.; RODNEY WHITE, J.C.L.; Rev. Msgr. FREDERICK NAWARSKAS; Revs. PATRICK AKPANOBONG; RYAN ROJO; MR. MICHAEL WYSE, Ex Officio.

Presbyteral Council—Very Rev. SANTIAGO D. UDAYAR, Ed.D., J.C.L., Ex Officio; Rev. PATRICK AKPANOBONG, Chm.; Rev. Msgrs. ROBERT BUSH; LARRY J. DROLL, J.C.L.; FREDERICK NAWARSKAS; Revs. FELIX ARCHIBONG; BERNARDITO GETIGAN; BALA ANTHONY GOVINDU; NILO NALUGON; EMILIO SOSA; MR. MICHAEL WYSE, Ex Officio.

Office for Religious—Sr. ELSA GARCIA, C.D.P., Dir.

Diocesan Offices and Directors

Diocesan Finance Officer—STEVE MCKAY, CPA.

Campaign for Human Development—MR. MICHAEL WYSE.

Catholic Relief Services—Rev. DAVID HERRERA.

Communications Office—MR. BRIAN BODIFORD.

Continuing Education of the Clergy—Rev. Msgr. LARRY J. DROLL, J.C.L.

Cursillos de Cristiandad—LUISA RAYOS, (English); MR. FRANCISCO ESTRADA, (Spanish).

Deans—Very Revs. TOM BARLEY, J.C.L., San Angelo Deanery; RODNEY WHITE, J.C.L., Midland-Odessa Deanery; Rev. Msgr. FREDERICK NAWARSKAS, Abilene Deanery.

Diocesan Liturgical Commission—MRS. LORI HINES.

Immigration Services—NELLY DIAZ, (Abilene, San Angelo).

Mission Council—MIKE CANON, Chm.; Rev. FRANCIS ONYEKOZURU, Moderator.

Newspaper—West Texas Angelus MR. BRIAN BODIFORD, Editor.

Evangelization and Catechesis—Ministries - Catechesis, Evangelization, Family Life, Youth, Young Adult, Campus Ministry Sisters HILDA MAROTTA, O.S.F., Dir.; ADELINA GARCIA, O.S.F., Assoc. Dir.; JOYCE DETZEL, C.D.P., Assoc. Dir.

Permanent Deacon Director—Deacon FEDERICO MEDINA JR.

Permanent Deacon Formation—Deacon FEDERICO MEDINA JR.

Prison Ministry Coordinator—Deacon MICHAEL MEDINA.

Pro-Life—MR. JERRY MICHAEL PETERS.

Priests' Pension Plan—Board of Directors: Rev. EMILIO SOSA, Chm.; Very Rev. TOM BARLEY, J.C.L., Sec.;

Rev. PATRICK AKPANOBONG; Very Rev. SANTIAGO D. UDAYAR, Ed.D., J.C.L.; Rev. TERRY BRENON.
Propagation of the FaithMR. MICHAEL WYSE.
Rural Life—Deacon FLOYD SCHWARTZ, Dir.
Schools—MS. JOAN WILMES, Supt.
Vicar for Priests—Rev. Msgr. LARRY J. DROLL, J.C.L.
Victim Assistance Coordinator—MRS. LORI HINES.
Vocations Office—Rev. MICHAEL A. RODRIGUEZ, Dir.

CLERGY, PARISHES, MISSIONS AND PAROCHIAL SCHOOLS

CITY OF SAN ANGELO

(TOM GREEN COUNTY)

1—CATHEDRAL OF THE SACRED HEART (1884)
20 E. Beauregard Ave., 76903-5929.
Tel: 325-658-6567; Email: sanangelo.cathedral@sanangelodiocese.org. Very Rev. Steven Hicks, Rector; Rev. Josh Gray, Parochial Vicar; Deacon Steven Zimmerman.
Catechesis Religious Program—Email: szimmerman@sanangelodiocese.org. Students 141.
Endowment—Sacred Heart Cathedral-Parish Educational Endowment Fund, Inc.,
Tel: 915-658-6567.

2—HOLY ANGELS (1961)
2202 Rutgers Ave., 76904. Tel: 325-944-8967; Email: sanangelo.holyangels@sanangelodiocese.org. Revs. Charles C. Greenwell, Ed.D.; Balachandra Nagipogu, (India) Parochial Vicar; Deacons Harry J. Pelto Sr.; Walter Hammons II; Leslie Maiman.
Church: 2309 A & M Ave., 76904. Tel: 325-949-7286.
School—Angelo Catholic School, (Grades 3-8), 2315 A & M Ave., 76904. Tel: 325-949-1747;
Fax: 325-942-1547; Email: btrojcak@angelocatholicschool.org; Email: llopez@angelocatholicschool.org; Web: www.angelocatholicschool.org/. Becky Trojcak, Prin. Lay Teachers 12; Students 127.
Catechesis Religious Program—Tel: 325-942-8192; Email: lhines@sanangelodiocese.org. Mrs. Lori Hines, D.R.E., (Grades PreK-12). Students 298.

3—ST. JOSEPH (1942) (Hispanic)
301 W. 17th, 76903. Tel: 325-653-5006; Email: sanangelo.stjoseph@sanangelodiocese.org; Web: www.stjosephsanangelo.org. Revs. Bala Anthony Govindu; Felix Archibong; Deacons Abel Fernandez; Antero Gonzalez.
Catechesis Religious Program—Vickie Rivero, C.R.E. Students 446.

4—ST. MARGARET (1965)
2619 Era St., 76905. Tel: 325-651-4633; Email: sanangelo.stmargaret@sanangelodiocese.org. Very Rev. Santiago D. Udayar, Ed.D., J.C.L.
Catechesis Religious Program—Marie Vasquez, C.R.E. (Elementary). Students 5.

5—ST. MARY'S (1930) (Hispanic)
11 W. Ave. N., 76903. Tel: 325-655-6278; Email: sanangelo.stmary@sanangelodiocese.org. Rev. Joey Faylona; Deacons Michael Lopez; Marc Mata.
Catechesis Religious Program—Silvia Alvarez, D.R.E. Students 495.

OUTSIDE THE CITY OF SAN ANGELO

ABILENE, TAYLOR CO.

1—ST. FRANCIS OF ASSISI (1906) (Hispanic)
826 Cottonwood St., Abilene, 79601.
Tel: 325-672-6695; Email: stfrancisabilene@gmail.com. Rev. Isidore Ochiabuto, (Nigeria); Deacon Marc P. Main.
Catechesis Religious Program—Rosa Castillo, D.R.E. Students 185.

2—HOLY FAMILY (1976)
5410 Buffalo Gap Rd., P.O. Box 5970, Abilene, 79606. Tel: 325-692-1820; Email: mail@holyfamilyabilene.org. Rev. Msgr. Frederick Nawarskas; Rev. Mamachan Joseph, C.M.I., Parochial Vicar; Deacons Gerald Schwalb; Gary Rhodes; Daniel Vaughan.
Catechesis Religious Program—Dr. Robert Moore, D.R.E. Students 355.

3—SACRED HEART (1891)
837 Jeanette St., Abilene, 79602-2410.
Tel: 325-677-7951; Email: abilene.sacredheart@sanangelo.diocese.org. Rev. Msgr. Robert Bush; Rev. Bernard L. Gully, In Res.; Deacons Arturo Casarez; Dwain Hennessey.
Catechesis Religious Program—Email: jgumpala@sanangelodiocese.org. Sr. Jyothi Gumpula, C.S.A., D.R.E. Students 202.
Mission—Sts. Joachim and Ann, [CEM] N. 1st St. & Cherry St., Clyde, Callahan Co. 79510.
SACRED HEART PERPETUAL ADORATION CHAPEL, 1541 S. 8th St., Abilene, 79602.

4—ST. VINCENT PALLOTTI (1963) (Mexican-American)
2525 Westview Dr., Abilene, 79603-2138.
Tel: 325-672-1794; Fax: 325-754-8491; Email: abilene.stvincent@sanangelodiocese.org. Rev. Emilio Sosa.
Catechesis Religious Program—Students 181.
Mission—Our Mother of Mercy, 1300 S. Locust, P.O. Box 206, Merkel, Taylor Co. 79536.
Tel: 325-928-5239.

ANDREWS, ANDREWS CO., OUR LADY OF LOURDES (1958)
201 N.E. Ave. K, Andrews, 79714. Tel: 432-523-4215; Tel: 432-523-4968; Fax: 432-523-5070; Email: andrews@sanangelodiocese.org; Email: ollandrews@valornet.com. Rev. Joseph Ogbonna, (South Africa).
Catechesis Religious Program—Patricia Alaniz, C.R.E. Students 414.
Mission—Our Lady of Lourdes, Web: www.ollandrews.com.

BALLINGER, RUNNELS CO., ST. MARY STAR OF THE SEA (1885)
605 N. 5th St., Ballinger, 76821. Tel: 325-365-2687; Email: ballinger@sanangelodiocese.org. Rev. Yesuratnam Mulakaleti; Deacon David Workman.
Res.: 608 N. 6th St., Ballinger, 76821-4836.
Catechesis Religious Program—Caroline Toliver, C.R.E. Students 120.
Missions—St. James—215 N. Washington, Bronte, Coke Co. 76933.
Our Lady of Guadalupe, 601 W. 10th, Robert Lee, Coke Co. 76945.

BIG LAKE, REAGAN CO., ST. MARGARET OF CORTONA (1949) [JC]
107 E. 1st. St., Big Lake, 76932. Tel: 325-884-3221; Email: biglake@sanangelodiocese.org. Rev. Prem S. Thumma.
Church & Office: 100 N. Mississippi St., Big Lake, 76932.
Catechesis Religious Program—Trish Soto, D.R.E.; Sarah Rodriguez, C.R.E. Students 141.
Missions—St. Thomas—110 Hwy. 67, Rankin, 79778.
St. Francis, 201 W. 5th, Iraan, Pecos Co. 79744.

BIG SPRING, HOWARD CO., HOLY TRINITY PARISH
1009 Hearn St., Big Spring, 79720.
Tel: 432-714-4930; Email: bigspring@sanangelodiocese.org. Mailing Address: P.O. Box 951, Big Spring, 79721. Rev. Serafin P. Avenido Jr., (Philippines); Deacon Juan Arguello.
Catechesis Religious Program—Email: jl2jacobo@aol.com. Joe Jacobo, D.R.E. Students 220.

BRADY, MCCULLOCH CO., ST. PATRICK'S (1876) [JC]
406 S. Bridge, P.O. Box 1188, Brady, 76825.
Tel: 325-597-2324; Email: brady@sanangelodiocese.org; Web: www.stpatricksbrady.org. Rev. Bhaskar Mendem, (India); Deacon Robert Selvera.
Rectory—201 S. Pecan St., Brady, 76825.
Catechesis Religious Program—Belinda Gonzales, D.R.E. Students 36.
Mission—St. Francis Xavier, Melvin, McCullogh Co.

BROWNWOOD, BROWN CO., ST. MARY'S (1896) [JC] (Hispanic)
1103 Main St., Brownwood, 76801. Tel: 325-646-7455 ; Tel: 325-646-9630; Fax: 325-646-6643; Email: brownwood@sanangelodiocese.org; Web: www.sm1familybwd.org. Mailing Address: 1101 Booker St., Brownwood, 76801. Rev. Francis Njoku, (Africa); Deacon John Specht.
Res.: 1105 Main Ave., Brownwood, 76801.
Catechesis Religious Program—Juana Gonzalez, C.R.E. (K-5); Sady Cady, C.R.E. (6-12). Students 224.

CARLSBAD, TOM GREEN CO., ST. THERESE (1957)
11774 Beaumont, Carlsbad, 76934-0416.
Tel: 325-465-8062; Email: carlsbad@sanangelodiocese.org; Email: sthcarlstx@frontier.com. P.O. Box 416, Carlsbad, 76934. Very Rev. Santiago D. Udayar, Ed.D., J.C.L.

COLEMAN, COLEMAN CO., SACRED HEART (1892) (Anglo—Hispanic)
303 E. College, Coleman, 76834. Tel: 325-625-5773; Email: scrdhrt@web-access.net; Web: www.sacredheartchurchcoleman.org. Rev. Laurent Mvondo, (Cameroon); Deacon Ray M. Nunez.
Catechesis Religious Program—201 San Saba, Coleman, 76834. Students 56.

COLORADO CITY, MITCHELL CO., ST. ANN'S (1943) (Hispanic)
2005 Walnut St., Colorado City, 79512.
Tel: 325-728-3252; Email: coloradocity@sanangelodiocese.org. Rev. Michael Udegbunam.
Res.: 107 E. 21st St., Colorado City, 79512. Email: stannccty@att.net.
Catechesis Religious Program—Janie Davila, D.R.E. Students 144.
Mission—St. Joseph (1924) 403 S. Hinson, Loraine, Mitchell Co. 79532.

CRANE, CRANE CO., GOOD SHEPHERD (1943)
810 S. Virginia, P.O. Box 1294, Crane, 79731.
Tel: 432-558-2718; Fax: 432-558-7917; Email: crane@sanangelodiocese.org. Rev. Kumar Jujjuvarapu, (India) Parochial Vicar; Deacons Julio Carrasco, (Retired); Apolonio Gutierrez; Felix Segura.
Res.: 1109 S. Virginia St., P.O. Box 1294, Crane, 79731. Tel: 432-558-7497; Email: abmvondo@yahoo.com.
Catechesis Religious Program—Teresa Figueroa, C.R.E. Students 221.
Missions—St. Isidore—4614 S. Frank, Coyanosa, Pecos Co.. Tel: 432-652-8216; Fax: 432-652-3875.
Our Lady of Lourdes, 103 Merrill Ave., Imperial, Pecos Co.

EDEN, CONCHO CO., ST. CHARLES (1927) [JC] (Mexican—German)
302 Moss St., P.O. Box 575, Eden, 76837.
Tel: 325-869-8311; Email: eden@sanangelodiocese.org. Rev. Albert Ezenaya; Deacon Joe Lopez.
Rectory—302 Allen St., Eden, 76837.
Catechesis Religious Program—Email: jlopez@sanangelodiocese.org. Students 25.
Missions—Our Lady of Guadalupe—12196 County Rd. 6009, Millersview, Concho Co. 76862.
St. Phillip Mission, 11937 Co. Rd. 5511, P.O. Box 711, Eola, Concho Co. 76937.

ELDORADO, SCHLEICHER CO., OUR LADY OF GUADALUPE (1924) [CEM] [JC] (Hispanic)
901 Divide St., Hwy 277, Eldorado, 76936.
Tel: 325-853-2663; Email: eldorado@sanangelodiocese.org. 824 N. Divide St., Eldorado, 76936. Rev. Joseph Vathalloor, C.M.I., (India); Deacons Michael Kahlig; Victor Belman.
Res.: P.O. Box 211, Eldorado, 76936.
Catechesis Religious Program—Sylvia Belman, C.R.E.; Valerie Sanchez, D.R.E. Students 97.
Missions—Immaculate Conception—P.O. Box 36, Knickerbocker, Tom Green Co. 76939.
Tel: 325-944-2820.
St. Peter's, 324 N. Commerce, P.O. Box 471, Mertzon, Irion Co. 76941. Tel: 325-835-2000.

FORT STOCKTON, PECOS CO.

1—ST. AGNES (1953) [CEM] [JC] Merged with St. Joseph, Ft. Stockton to form Our Lady of Guadalupe, Ft. Stockton.

2—ST. JOSEPH'S (1875) [CEM] [JC] Merged with St. Agnes, Ft. Stockton to form Our Lady of Guadalupe, Ft. Stockton.

3—OUR LADY OF GUADALUPE
403 S. Main, P.O. Box 1488, Fort Stockton, 79735.
Tel: 432-336-5027; Email: fortstockton@sanangelodiocese.org. Rev. Lorenzo Hatch; Deacons Luis Villarreal; Reuben Reyes; Daniel Holguin Jr.
Catechesis Religious Program—Rena Ibarra, D.R.E. Students 490.

JUNCTION, KIMBLE CO., ST. THERESA OF THE CHILD JESUS (1959) [JC]
114 S. 7th St., P.O. Box 486, Junction, 76849.
Tel: 325-446-3393; Email: junction@sanangelodiocese.org. Rev. Innocent Eziefule.
Res.: South 7th & Oak St., P.O. Box 486, Junction, 76849. Tel: 325-446-3393; Email: junction@sanangelodiocese.org.
Catechesis Religious Program—Reginald Stapper, D.R.E. Students 50.

MCCAMEY, UPTON CO., SACRED HEART (1935)
710 S. Burleson, P.O. Box 1320, McCamey, 79752.
Tel: 432-652-8216; Email: mccamey@sanangelodiocese.org. Rev. Kumar Jujjuvarapu, Parochial Vicar; Deacons Julio Carrasco, (Retired); Felix Segura.
Catechesis Religious Program—Students 57.
Missions—St. Isidore—Corner of Sarabee & Battle, Coyanosa, Pecos Co. 79730.
Our Lady of Lourdes, 103 Merrille Ave., Imperial, Pecos Co. 79743.

MENARD, MENARD CO., SACRED HEART (1873) [JC]
609 Ellis St., P.O. Box 788, Menard, 76859.
Tel: 325-396-4906; Email: menard@sanangelodiocese.org. Rev. Mamachan Joseph, C.M.I.
Catechesis Religious Program—Annamarie Valdez, D.R.E. Students 25.

MIDLAND, MIDLAND CO.

1—ST. ANN'S (1896)
1906 W. Texas Ave., Midland, 79701-6564.
Tel: 432-682-6303; Fax: 432-684-4528; Email: parish@stannsparish.us; Web: www.stannsparish.us. Rev. Msgr. Larry J. Droll, J.C.L.; Rev. Rojo Ryan; Maya DeAnda, Business Mgr.; Sr. Elsa Garcia, C.D.P., Social Ministries Coord.; Kristin Atkinson, Coord. of Religious Ed.; Amy Jurewicz, Parish Accountant; Leonor Spencer, Spanish Ministry Coord.
School—St. Ann's School, (Grades PreK-8), 2000 W. Texas Ave., Midland, 79701. Tel: 432-684-4563; Fax: 432-687-2468; Email: jwilmes@stanns.us; Web: www.stanns.us. Ms. Joan Wilmes, Admin.; Mr. Fernando Ochoa, Admin. Lay Teachers 36; Students 493; Clergy / Religious Teachers 17.

Catechesis Religious Program—Email: midland.stann@sanangelodiocese.org. Kristin Atkinson, C.R.E.; Alison Pope, Youth Min.; Perla Garcia, Youth Min. Students 493.

2—OUR LADY OF GUADALUPE (1960) (Hispanic)
1401 E. Garden Ln., Midland, 79701.
Tel: 432-682-2581; Email: midland.olg@sanangelodiocese.org. Revs. David Herrera; Reginald Anthony Odima; Deacons Jesse Guajardo; Ricardo Torres; Ignacio Villa.
Catechesis Religious Program—Janie Garivay, D.R.E. Students 579.

3—SAN MIGUEL ARCANGEL CHURCH (1984) (Hispanic)
1100 Camp St., Midland, 79701. Tel: 432-570-0952; Email: midland.sanmiguel@sanangelodiocese.org; Web: www.sanmiguelchurch.com. Rev. Patrick Akpanobong; Deacons Victor Lopez; Michael LaMonica; Alex Perez; Sador Sotelo
Legal Title: Our Lady of San Juan.
Catechesis Religious Program—Tel: 432-620-9546. Mary Lopez, C.R.E. Students 294.

4—ST. STEPHEN'S (1982)
4601 Neely Ave., Midland, 79707. Tel: 432-520-7394; Email: midland.ststephen@sanangelodiocese.org. Very Rev. Rodney White, J.C.L.; Timothy Hayter, Parochial Vicar; Rev. Freddy Martin Pérez; Deacons Leonard Hendon Jr.; Luis Mata Sr.; Lorenzo Salazar; Fidel Saldivar.
Rectory—4613 Neely Ave., Midland, 79707.
Catechesis Religious Program—Gretchen Lara, D.R.E. Students 600.

MILES, RUNNELS CO., ST. THOMAS (1962) [JC]
P.O. Box 306, Miles, 76861. Tel: 325-468-3171; Email: st.thomas_miles@wcc.net. Rev. Ariel R. Lagunilla; Very Rev. Tom Barley, J.C.L., In Res.; Deacon Frankie D. Aguirre.
Catechesis Religious Program—Email: miles@sanangelodiocese.org. Michelle Halfmann, D.R.E.; Patricia Hohensee, D.R.E. Students 81.

ODESSA, ECTOR CO.

1—ST. ANTHONY (1948) (Hispanic)
1321 W. Monahans St., Odessa, 79761.
Tel: 432-337-2213; Fax: 432-333-3631; Email: odessa.stanthony@sanangelodiocese.org. 907 S. Dixie Blvd., Odessa, 79761. Revs. Frank Chavez; Anthony Franco; Deacons Alex Sosa; Flavio Franco.
Catechesis Religious Program—Email: evillegas@sanangelodiocese.org. Sr. Elizabeth P. Villegas, O.N.D., D.R.E. (Religious Education classes combined with St. Joseph, Odessa) Students 328.

2—ST. ELIZABETH ANN SETON (1982)
7601 N. Grandview, Odessa, 79765.
Tel: 432-367-4657; Fax: 432-367-0700; Email: office@setonparishodessa.org. Very Rev. Mark Woodruff; Timothy Hayter, Parochial Vicar; Deacons Gary Brooks; Salvador Primera.
Catechesis Religious Program—Email: ccd@setonparishodessa.org; Email: youth@setonparishodessa.org. Marilyn Kay Hemann, D.R.E. (Elementary); Johnny Aldas, C.R.E. (Jr. & Sr. High School). Students 624.

3—HOLY REDEEMER (1961) (Hispanic)
2633 Conover, Odessa, 79763. Tel: 432-580-4295; Fax: 432-332-6631; Email: hrccredeemer15@gmail.com. Revs. Juan Fernando Bonilla Sanchez, M.S.P.; Juan Cortez, Parochial Vicar; Deacons Andrew Davis; Antonio Gonzales; Edward Gonzalez; Manuel Luevano; Orlando Mendoza.
Catechesis Religious Program—Tel: 432-332-9231; Tel: 432-337-2084. Sr. Rosalia B. Sabud, O.N.D., D.R.E.; Anita T. Diaz, C.R.E. Students 723.
Mission—Our Lady of San Juan Mission, 905 Edgeport Dr., Odessa, 79765. Tel: 432-362-2017; Fax: 432-339-2002.

4—ST. JOSEPH (1948) (Hispanic)
907 S. Dixie Blvd., Odessa, 79761. Tel: 432-337-2213; Fax: 432-333-3631; Email: odessa.stjoseph@sanangelodiocese.org. Revs. Frank Chavez; Anthony Franco; Deacons Flavio Franco; Alex Sosa.
Res.: 1321 W. Monahans, Odessa, 79763. Web: www.Stjosephanthonychurches.org.
Catechesis Religious Program—Tel: 432-334-6478; Email: evillegas@sanangelodiocese.org. Sr. Elizabeth P. Villegas, O.N.D., D.R.E. Students 815.
Missions—St. Martin de Porres—2821 E. Hammett, Odessa, Ector Co. 79766.
St. Anthony, 1321 W. Monahans, Odessa, 79763. Email: odessa.stanthony@sanangelodiocese.org.

5—ST. MARY'S CHURCH (1938) [CEM]
612 E. 18th St., Odessa, 79761. Tel: 432-332-5334; Email: odessa.stmary@sanangelodiocese.org. Rev. Bernard Getigan.
School—St. Mary's Central Catholic School, (Grades PreK-8), 1703 N. Adams, Odessa, 79761.
Tel: 432-337-6052; Fax: 432-332-2942; Email: stmaryschool@sanangelodiocese.org; Web: smccsodessa.org. Benjamin Villarreal, Prin.; Ann Lustgarden, Librarian. Lay Teachers 24; Sisters 3; Students 237.
Catechesis Religious Program—Students 349.

OLFEN, RUNNELS CO., ST. BONIFACE (1901) [CEM]
1118 County Rd. 234, Rowena, 76875.
Tel: 325-442-2893; Email: olfen@sanangelodiocese.org. Rev. Ariel R. Lagunilla.
Catechesis Religious Program—Waldeen Halfmann, D.R.E. Students 26.

OZONA, CROCKETT CO., OUR LADY OF PERPETUAL HELP (1929) (Hispanic)
1715 Martinez St., P.O. Box 1069, Ozona, 76943.
Tel: 325-392-3353; Fax: 325-392-3720; Email: ozona@sanangelodiocese.org. Rev. Hilary A. Ihedioha, (Nigeria).
Res.: 1711 Martinez St., P.O. Box 1069, Ozona, 76943.
Catechesis Religious Program—Margaret Longoria, C.R.E. Students 183.
Mission—Good Shepherd, 104 Main (Hwy 290), Sheffield, Pecos Co. 79781. Email: sheffield@sanangelodiocese.org.

ROWENA, RUNNELS CO., ST. JOSEPH'S (1906) [CEM] (German—Czech)
506 Edwards St., P.O. Box 96, Rowena, 76875.
Tel: 325-442-3521; Email: rowena@sanangelodiocese.org. Rev. Ariel R. Lagunilla; Deacons Frankie D. Aguirre; Charlie Evans; Alan Pelzel.
Res.: 501 Bennie St., P.O. Box 96, Rowena, 76875.
Tel: 325-442-3521; Email: rowena@sanangelodiocese.org.
Catechesis Religious Program—Email: kjhoelscher5@gmail.com. Karen Hoelscher, D.R.E. Students 29.

ST. LAWRENCE, GLASSCOCK CO., ST. LAWRENCE (1948) [CEM] (German)
2400 FM 2401, Garden City, 79739.
Tel: 432-397-2300; Email: stlawrence@sanangelodiocese.org. Rev. Chinnapureddy Pagidela, (India); Deacons Joel Gutierrez; Floyd Schwartz.
Catechesis Religious Program—Email: kristinhalf@gmail.com. Kristin Halfmann, D.R.E.; Irma Alvarado, D.R.E.; Carmen Rios Amador, D.R.E. Students 198.
Missions—St. Thomas—Midkiff, Upton Co..
Tel: 432-535-2266.
Catechesis Religious Program—Students 16.
St. Paschal Baylona, P.O. Box 271, Sterling City, Sterling Co. 76951-0271.
Catechesis Religious Program—Students 30.

SANDERSON, TERRELL CO., ST. JAMES CHURCH (1916) (Hispanic)
209 E. Hackberry, P.O. Box 520, Sanderson, 79848.
Tel: 432-336-5027. Rev. Lorenzo Hatch; Thelma Calzada, Bookkeeper.
Catechesis Religious Program—Jose Fuentes Jr., D.R.E. Students 44.

SONORA, SUTTON CO., ST. ANN'S (1927) (Hispanic)
311 W. Plum St., P.O. Box 1397, Sonora, 76950.
Tel: 325-387-2278; Email: sonora@sanangelodiocese.org. Rev. Terence V. Brenon.
Res.: 105 Oakwood, Box 1397, Sonora, 76950.
Tel: 325-387-2278; Email: sonora@sanangelodiocese.org.
Catechesis Religious Program—Delia Samaniego, D.R.E. Students 200.

STANTON, MARTIN CO., ST. JOSEPH'S (1881) (Mexican-American)
405 N. Convent St., P.O. Box 846, Stanton, 79782-0846. Tel: 432-756-3743; Email: stanton@sanangelodiocese.org. Rev. Patrick Akpanobong; Rev. Msgr. Timothy Schwertner, Sacramental Priest; Deacons Ernie Sanchez, (Retired); Clemente Villa, Pastoral Min./Coord., Cell: 432-212-8602.
Catechesis Religious Program—Email: floress@crcom.net. Santiago Flores, D.R.E. Students 128.
Mission—St. Isidore, [CEM] Lenorah, Martin Co..
Catechesis Religious Program—Students 17.

SWEETWATER, NOLAN CO.

1—HOLY FAMILY (1885) (Hispanic), Merged with Immaculate Heart of Mary, Sweetwater to form Holy Spirit Church Sweetwater.

2—HOLY SPIRIT PARISH (2013) (Hispanic)
511 W. Alabama, P.O. Box 847, Sweetwater, 79556.
Tel: 325-235-3318; Email: immaculatemary@suddenlinkmail.com. Rev. Nilo Nalugon; Deacons W. W. Butler; David Mendez.
Res.: 507 Crane St., Sweetwater, 79556.
Tel: 915-235-3318 (Office); Email: immaculatemary@suddenlinkmail.com.
Catechesis Religious Program—Email: tiglesias@sanangelodiocese.org. Sr. Luisita Iglesias, O.N.D., D.R.E. Students 259.

3—IMMACULATE HEART OF MARY, Merged with Holy Family, Sweetwater to form Holy Spirit Church, Sweetwater.

WALL, TOM GREEN CO., ST. AMBROSE (1941) [CEM]
8602 Loop 570, P.O. Box 228, Wall, 76957.
Tel: 325-651-7551; Email: wall@sanangelodiocese.org; Web: www.saint-ambrose.org. Rev. Joseph Choutapalli; Deacons Allan Lange; Daniel Shannahan, Youth Min.
Catechesis Religious Program—Marisol O'Leary, C.R.E., 2132 White Rock Rd., 76904; Kim Schwartz, C.R.E.; Michele Rohmfeld, D.R.E.; Krystal Braden, C.R.E., 13105, 76904. Students 237.
Mission—Holy Family, 18370 Bledsoe Rd., Mereta, Tom Green Co. 76940. Tel: 325-468-3101.

WINTERS, RUNNELS CO., OUR LADY OF MT. CARMEL (1962) (Hispanic)
119 W. College, Winters, 79567. Tel: 325-939-0968; Email: winters@sanangelodiocese.org. Rev. Laurent Mvondo, (Cameroon).
Catechesis Religious Program—Maryanne Woffenden, C.R.E. Students 34.

Chaplains of Public Institutions

SAN ANGELO. *Angelo State University*, 2451 Dena Dr., 76904. Tel: 325-949-8033. Rev. Francis Onyekozuru.

ABILENE. *Abilene Christian University, Hardin-Simmons University, McMurry University*, Sacred Heart Church, 837 Jeanette, Abilene, 79602.
Tel: 325-676-5434. Cristen Macke.

MIDLAND/ODESSA. *University of Texas Permian Basin, Odessa College, Midland College*, 1049 N. Ave. I, Odessa, 79763. Lisa Martinez.

Military Chaplains:
Rev.—
Covos, Ruben, 417 Tuskegee Blvd., Bldg 417, Dover AFB, DE 19902.

Retired:
Rev. Msgrs.—
Bridges, James P., (Retired), 2603 Wyldewood Dr., Midland, 79707
Voity, Maurice, S.T.L., (Retired), 5 Maya, Port Saint Lucie, FL 34952
Zientek, Benedict, (Retired), P.O. Box 2447, Brenham, 77834
Revs.—
Knickerbocker, Knick, (Retired), P.O. Box 129, London, 76854
Manimala, Thomas, (Retired), Manimala House Vilankkanur, P.O. 670 582, Kannur Dt, India
Regan, Richard J., (Retired), 1001 Society Hill Blvd., Cherry Hill, NJ 08003. Tel: 432-264-2936
Rodriguez, Gilbert, (Retired), P.O. Box 61152, 76906
Wade, Hugh, (Retired), 609 N. 6th St., Ballinger, 76821.

Permanent Deacons:
Aguirre, Frankie D., St. Joseph, Rowena; St. Boniface, Olfen; St. Thomas, Miles
Arguello, Juan, Holy Trinity, Big Spring
Belman, Victor, Our Lady of Guadalupe, Eldorado
Boniface, Olfen, St. Thomas, Miles
Brady, Bill, (Inactive), (Outside of Diocese)
Brooks, Gary, St. Elizabeth Ann Seton, Odessa; St. Elizabeth Ann Seton, Odessa
Butler, Bill, (Retired)
Camarillo, Alfred Sr., Holy Redeemer, Odessa
Carrasco, Julio, (Retired), (Retired)
Casarez, Art, Sacred Heart, Abilene
Evans, Charlie, St. Joseph, Rowena
Fernandez, Abel, St. Joseph, San Angelo
Franco, Flabio, St. Joseph, Odessa
Gonzales, Antonio, (Retired)
Gonzalez, Antero, St. Joseph, San Angelo
Greene, Fred, (Retired)
Guajardo, Jesse, Our Lady of Guadalupe, Midland
Gutierrez, Apolonio, (Retired)
Hammons, Walter II, Holy Angels, San Angelo
Hendon, Leonard Jr., St. Stephen, Midland
Hennessey, Dwain, Sacred Heart, Abilene
Hinojos, Paul, (Retired), (Retired)
Holguin, Daniel Jr., Our Lady of Guadalupe, Fort Stockton
Ibarra, Roy, (In Service Outside the Diocese)
Kahlig, Michael, St. Peter, Mertzon
Lambert, Charles, Holy Family, Abilene
LaMonica, Michael, San Miguel Arcangel, Midland
Lange, Allan, St. Ambrose, Wall
Lange, Stanley, St. Thomas, Miles
Lopez, Joseph, St. Charles, Eden
Lopez, Michael, St. Mary, San Angelo
Lopez, Victor, San Miguel Arcangel, Midland
Luevano, Manuel, Holy Redeemer, Odessa
Main, Marc P., St. Francis of Assisi, Abilene
Martinez, Enrique, (Retired)
Mata, Luis Sr., St. Stephen, Midland
Mata, Marc, St. Mary, San Angelo
Medina, Federico Jr., Sacred Heart Cathedral, San Angelo
Medina, Michael, St. Joseph, Stanton
Mendez, Hector, St. Mary, Odessa
Moreno, Robert, Our Lady of Guadalupe, Midland
Napoles, Jesus, St. Ann, Midland
Nunez, Reynaldo, Sacred Heart, Coleman
Ortiz, Jesse, St. Mary, Odessa

Pelto, Harry J. Sr., Holy Angels, San Angelo
Pena, Daniel, (Retired)
Perez, Alex, San Miguel Arcangel, Midland
Primera, Salvador, St. Elizabeth Ann Seton, Midland
Ramirez, Victor, St. Vincent Pallotti, Abilene
Reyes, Reuben, Our Lady of Guadalupe, Fort Stockton
Rhodes, Gary, Holy Family, Abilene
Salazar, Lorenzo, St. Stephen, Midland
Saldivar, Fidel, St. Stephen, Midland
Sanchez, Claudio, (In Service Outside of Diocese)
Sanchez, Ernie, (Retired), (Retired)
Schwalb, Gerald, Holy Family, Abilene
Segura, Felix, Sacred Heart, McCamey
Selvera, Robert, St. Patrick, Brady
Shannahan, Daniel, St. Ambrose, Wall
Sosa, Alex, St. Joseph, Odessa
Sotelo, Sador, San Miguel Arcangel, Midland
Specht, John, St. Mary, Brownwood
Torres, Ricardo, Our Lady of Guadalupe, Midland
Vasquez, Jesse, (In Service Outside Diocese)
Vaughan, Daniel, Holy Family, Abilene
Villa, Clemente Jr., St. Joseph, Stanton
Villa, Ignacio, Our Lady of Guadalupe, Midland
Villarreal, Luis, Our Lady of Guadalupe, Fort Stockton
Workman, David, St. Mary Star of the Sea, Ballinger
Zimmerman, Steven, Sacred Heart Cathedral, San Angelo.

INSTITUTIONS LOCATED IN DIOCESE

[A] MONASTERIES AND RESIDENCES OF PRIESTS & BROTHERS

CHRISTOVAL. *Hermits of the Blessed Virgin Mary of Mount Carmel* (1991) 7637 Allen Rd., P.O. Box 337, Christoval, 76935-0337. Tel: 325-896-2249; Fax: 325-896-2265; Email: stellamaris@carmelitehermits.org; Web: www.CarmeliteHermits.org. Revs. Fabian Maria Rosette, O.Carm., Prior; Martin Hubbs, O.Carm., Subprior. Mt. Carmel Hermitage Novices 1; Postulants 2; Solemnly Professed 4; Hermits 7.

[B] CONVENTS AND RESIDENCES FOR SISTERS

SAN ANGELO. *School Sisters of St. Francis*, 110 Crestwood Dr., 76903. Tel: 325-651-2403; Email: garcia.adelina@gmail.com. Sr. Hilda Marotta, O.S.F., Contact Person. Sisters 2.

CHRISTOVAL. *Carmelite Nuns of the Ancient Observance* (1989) Monastery of Our Lady of Grace, 6202 CO Rd. 339, Christoval, 76935-3023. Tel: 325-853-1722 ; Fax: 325-853-1722; Email: desertcarmel@carmelnet.org; Web: carmelnet.org/christoval/christoval.htm. Sr. Mary Grace Erl, O.-Carm., Vicar Prioress

Carmelite Nuns of the Diocese of San Angelo, TX Sisters 7.

[C] CHARITABLE ORGANIZATIONS

ABILENE. *St. Vincent De Paul Society*, 1241 Walnut, Abilene, 79601. Tel: 325-677-6871; Fax: 325-672-0623; Email: svdpabilenestore@gmail.com. Deacon Marc P. Main, Member. Total Staff 3; Total Assisted 12,000.

St. Vincent De Paul Thrift Store.

BIG SPRING. *St. Vincent De Paul Society* Food Distribution. P.O. Box 549, Big Spring, 79720. Tel: 432-270-5029; Email: bshtconf@yahoo.com. Erlinda Rios, Dir. Families 1,480; Individuals 3,500.

MIDLAND. *St. Vincent De Paul Society* (1985) 1906 W. Texas Ave., Midland, 79701. Tel: 432-684-3887; Email: midland.stann@sanangelodiocese.org. Kevin Harrington, Dir.

ODESSA. *Catholic Charities Community Services Odessa, Inc.*, 2500 Andrews Hwy., Odessa, 79761. Tel: 432-332-1387; Fax: 432-332-3240; Email: executivedirector@ccodessa.org. Tot Asst. Annually 655; Total Staff 2.

STANTON. *St. Vincent De Paul Society*, P.O. Box 846, Stanton, 79782. Tel: 432-756-3743; Fax: 432-756-3756. 405 N. Convent St., Stanton, 79782. Email: Stanton@sanangelodiocese.org. Deacon Clemente Villa Jr., Pastoral Coord.

[D] SCHOOLS

ODESSA. *Holy Cross Catholic High School*, (Grades 9-10), 7601 N. Grandview Ave., Odessa, 79710-1252. Tel: 432-701-0741; Email: cgonzalez@holycrosschs.org. P.O. Box 51252, Odessa, 79710. Carolyn Gonzalez, Head of School.

[E] CAMPUS MINISTRY

SAN ANGELO. *Catholic Newman Center*, 2451 Dena Dr., 76904. Tel: 325-949-8033; Email: sanangelo.newmancenter@sanangelodiocese.org; Web: www.catholicram.org. Rev. Francis Onyekozuru, Campus Min. & Director; Ms. Kimberly Hollingsworth, Sec.; Ms. Jesenia Navejas, Sec. Total Staff 3.

[F] MISCELLANEOUS

SAN ANGELO. *The Catholic Charitable Foundation for the Roman Catholic Diocese of San Angelo*, 804 Ford St., 76905. P.O. Box 1824, 76902. Tel: 325-651-7500; Email: smckay@sanangelodiocese.org. Len Mertz, Chm.

Christ the King Retreat Center, 802 Ford, 76905. Tel: 325-651-5352; Tel: 325-651-5358; Fax: 325-651-5667; Email: ckrc@sanangelodiocese.org. Mr. Thomas C. Burke, J.C.L., Dir. Total Staff 25.

Franciscan Resource Center, 133 W. Concho, Ste. 108, 76903. Tel: 325-651-2403; Email: frcsanangelo@gmail.com. Sr. Adelina Garcia, O.S.F., Contact Person.

Magnificat-San Angelo Chapter, Inc., 3937 Inglewood Dr., 76904. Email: roxyadame1965@gmail.com. Roxanne Adame, Contact Person.

RELIGIOUS INSTITUTES OF MEN REPRESENTED IN THE DIOCESE

For further details refer to the corresponding bracketed number in the Religious Institutes of Men or Women section.

[]—*Carmelites of Mary Immaculate* (St. Joseph Province, Kottayam, India)—C.M.I.

[]—*Carmelites of Mary Immaculate* (St. Joseph Province, Thiruvanathapuram, India)—C.M.I.

[0270]—*Curia Generalizia dei Carmelitani* (Roma, Italy)—O.Carm.

[]—*Missionary Servants of the Word* (Mexico)—M.S.P.

[0910]—*Oblates of Mary Immaculate* (Southern American Prov.)—O.M.I.

[1060]—*Society of the Most Precious Blood* (Kansas City Prov.)—C.PP.S.

RELIGIOUS INSTITUTES OF WOMEN REPRESENTED IN THE DIOCESE

[0320]—*Carmelite Nuns of the Ancient Observance*—O.Carm.

[1010]—*Congregation of Divine Providence of San Antonio, Texas*—C.D.P.

[]—*Institute of Coadjutors of the Social Apostolate* (Mexico)—I.C.A.S.

[]—*Oblates of Notre Dame, Philippines*—O.N.D.

[1680]—*School Sisters of St. Francis*—O.S.F.

An asterisk (*) denotes an organization that has established tax-exempt status directly with the IRS and is not covered by the USCCB Group Ruling.

Archdiocese of San Antonio

(Archidioecesis Sancti Antonii)

Most Reverend

GUSTAVO GARCIA-SILLER, M.SP.S.

Archbishop of San Antonio; ordained June 22, 1984; appointed Auxiliary Bishop of Chicago and Titular See of Esco January 24, 2003; consecrated March 19, 2003; appointed Archbishop of San Antonio October 14, 2010; installed November 23, 2010; Pallium conferred June 20, 2011. *Pastoral Center, 2718 W. Woodlawn Ave., San Antonio, TX 78228-5124.* Tel: 210-734-2620; Tel: 210-734-1664; Fax: 210-734-0708.

Archdiocesan Pastoral Center / Chancery: 2718 W. Woodlawn Ave., San Antonio, TX 78228. Tel: 210-734-2620; Fax: 210-734-0231.

Web: www.archsa.org

Most Reverend

THOMAS J. FLANAGAN, D.D.

Auxiliary Bishop Emeritus of San Antonio; ordained June 10, 1956; appointed Auxiliary Bishop of San Antonio and Titular Bishop of Bavagaliana January 5, 1998; consecrated February 16, 1998; retired December 15, 2005. *Res.: 80 Peter Baque Rd., San Antonio, TX 78209.* Tel: 210-826-7721. *Mailing Address: 2718 W. Woodlawn Ave., San Antonio, TX 78228-5124.*

Most Reverend

MICHAEL J. BOULETTE

Auxiliary Bishop of San Antonio; ordained March 19, 1976; appointed Titular Bishop of Hieron and Auxiliary Bishop of San Antonio January 23, 2017; consecrated March 20, 2017. *Pastoral Center, 2718 W. Woodlawn Ave., San Antonio, TX 78228-0410.*

ESTABLISHED AUGUST 28, 1874.

Square Miles 23,180.

Created an Archbishopric, August 3, 1926.

The San Antonio Archdiocese comprises Atascosa, Bandera, Bexar, Comal, Edwards, Frio, Gillespie, Gonzales, Guadalupe, Karnes, Kendall, Kerr, Kinney, McMullen (that part of McMullen County north of the Nueces River), Medina, Real, Uvalde, Val Verde and Wilson.

For legal titles of parishes and archdiocesan institutions, consult the Pastoral Center.

STATISTICAL OVERVIEW

Personnel	
Archbishops	1
Auxiliary Bishops	1
Retired Bishops	1
Priests: Diocesan Active in Diocese	103
Priests: Diocesan Active Outside Diocese	7
Priests: Retired, Sick or Absent	52
Number of Diocesan Priests	162
Religious Priests in Diocese	188
Total Priests in Diocese	350
Extern Priests in Diocese	19
Ordinations:	
Diocesan Priests	3
Transitional Deacons	4
Permanent Deacons	12
Permanent Deacons in Diocese	330
Total Brothers	72
Total Sisters	618
Parishes	
Parishes	138
With Resident Pastor:	
Resident Diocesan Priests	75
Resident Religious Priests	53
Without Resident Pastor:	
Administered by Priests	11
Missions	34
New Parishes Created	1
Professional Ministry Personnel:	
Brothers	11
Sisters	188

Welfare	
Catholic Hospitals	5
Total Assisted	1,166,882
Health Care Centers	3
Homes for the Aged	8
Total Assisted	1,731
Residential Care of Children	3
Total Assisted	2,189
Day Care Centers	16
Specialized Homes	3
Total Assisted	3,476
Special Centers for Social Services	7
Total Assisted	261,933
Residential Care of Disabled	1
Total Assisted	1,695
Other Institutions	1
Total Assisted	88
Educational	
Seminaries, Diocesan	1
Students from This Diocese	21
Students from Other Diocese	48
Seminaries, Religious	4
Total Seminarians	21
Colleges and Universities	5
Total Students	18,445
High Schools, Diocesan and Parish	3
Total Students	1,040
High Schools, Private	6
Total Students	1,900
Elementary Schools, Diocesan and Parish	24
Total Students	7,435
Elementary Schools, Private	4
Total Students	1,100
Catechesis/Religious Education:	
High School Students	4,018
Elementary Students	11,660
Total Students under Catholic Instruction	45,619
Teachers in the Diocese:	
Priests	6
Brothers	10
Sisters	15
Lay Teachers	1,016
Vital Statistics	
Receptions into the Church:	
Infant Baptism Totals	5,079
Minor Baptism Totals	741
Adult Baptism Totals	432
Received into Full Communion	550
First Communions	6,301
Confirmations	5,205
Marriages:	
Catholic	1,518
Interfaith	48
Total Marriages	1,566
Deaths	3,881
Total Catholic Population	804,754
Total Population	2,762,857

Former Bishops—Rt. Revs. ANTHONY DOMINIC PELLICER, D.D., ord. Aug. 15, 1850; cons. Dec. 8, 1874; died April 14, 1880; JOHN C. NERAZ, D.D., ord. Feb. 19, 1854; cons. May 8, 1881; died Nov. 15, 1894; JOHN ANTHONY FOREST, D.D., ord. April 12, 1863; cons. Oct. 28, 1895; died March 11, 1911; Most Revs. JOHN W. SHAW, D.D., Coadjutor Bishop of San Antonio; appt. Feb. 7, 1910; cons. Titular Bishop of Castabala, April 14, 1910; succeeded to the See of San Antonio, March 11, 1911; made assistant at the Pontifical Throne, Sept., 1916; promoted to the See of New Orleans, Jan. 25, 1918; died Nov. 2, 1934; ARTHUR JEROME DROSSAERTS, D.D., LL.D., Bishop of San Antonio; appt. July 18, 1918; cons. Dec. 8, 1918; named Archbishop, Aug. 3, 1926; Pallium conferred February 16, 1927; assistant at the Pontifical Throne, Aug. 19, 1934; died Sept. 8, 1940; ROBERT E. LUCEY, S.T.D., Bishop of Amarillo; appt. Feb. 10, 1934; cons. May 1, 1934; promoted to the Archepiscopal See of San Antonio, Jan. 23, 1941; assistant to Pontifical Throne April 1959; retired June 4, 1969; died Aug. 1, 1977; FRANCIS J. FUREY, Titular Bishop of Temnus and Auxiliary of Philadelphia; appt. Aug. 24, 1960; cons. Dec. 22, 1960; promoted to Coadjutor and Apostolic Administrator "sede plena" of San Diego, July 25, 1963; succeeded March 6, 1966; promoted to Archepiscopal See of San Antonio, June 4, 1969; installed Aug. 6, 1969; Pallium conferred, Dec. 15, 1969; died April 23, 1979; PATRICK F. FLORES, D.D., ord. May 26, 1956; appt. Titular Bishop of Italica and Auxiliary of San Antonio March 18, 1970; cons. May 5, 1970; appt. Bishop of El Paso April 4, 1978; installed May 29, 1978; promoted Archiepiscopal See of San Antonio Aug. 28, 1979; installed Oct. 13, 1979; retired Dec. 29, 2004; died Jan. 9, 2017.; JOSE H. GOMEZ, S.T.D., ord. Aug. 15, 1978; appt. Auxiliary Bishop of Denver and Titular See of Belali Jan. 23, 2001; ord. March 26, 2001; appt. Archbishop of San Antonio Dec. 29, 2004; installed Feb. 15, 2005; Pallium conferred June 29, 2005; appt. Coadjutor Archbishop of Los Angeles April 6, 2010.

Office of the Archbishop—PABLO GARCIA, Personal Asst. to Archbishop, Email: pablo.garcia@archsa.org; LINDA RAMIREZ, Exec. Asst. to Archbishop, Email: linda.ramirez@archsa.org; YENISSE ROMAN RAMIREZ, Exec. Asst. to Archbishop & Archives for the Office of Archbishop, Email: yenisse.roman@archsa.org.

Office of the Chancellor—Tel: 210-734-1976. Sr. JANE ANN SLATER, C.D.P., Email: janeann.slater@archsa.org; YOLANDA REBELES, Administrative Asst., Email: yolanda.rebeles@archsa.org.

Vicars General—Most Rev. MICHAEL L. BOULETTE, D.D., D.Min., V.G., Tel: 210-734-1676; Fax: 210-734-2774; Very Rev. LAWRENCE J. CHRISTIAN, E.V., Tel: 210-734-2620; Fax: 210-734-0780.

Assistant to the Moderator of the Curia—Rev. MARTIN J. LEOPOLD, J.C.L., Tel: 210-734-1674; Email: mleopold@archsa.org.

Archives & Records Management Office—
Tel: 210-734-1959; Email: archive@archsa.org. ELVIRA SANCHEZ KISSER, Dir., Tel: 210-734-1956; Email: elvira.kisser@archsa.org; JACLYN GEORGES, Processing Archivist, Tel: 210-734-1947; Email: jaclyn.georges@archsa.org; JOAN JAROSEK, Archive Project Cataloger, Tel: 210-734-2620, Ext. 1101; Email: joan.jarosek@archsa.org.

Archdiocesan Office of Stewardship and Development—JULIE SEGUIN, Dir., Tel: 210-734-1907; Email: developmentoffice@archsa.org.

Annual Appeal, Grants—CECILE MONTANEZ, Dir., Tel: 210-734-1991; Email: cecile.montanez@archsa.org.

St. John/Assumption Seminary—2600 W. Woodlawn, San Antonio, 78228-5196. Tel: 210-734-5137; Fax: 210-734-5137; Email: assumptionseminary@archsa.org; Web: www.assumptionseminary.org. Very Rev. JAIME E. ROBLEDO, P.S.S., Rector/Pres.

Vice Rector of Formation—Rev. RENATO LOPEZ, P.S.S.

Vice Rector of Admissions—Rev. SERVANDO GUERRERO.

Executive Administrative Assistant—MRS. MELANIE CASTILLO.

Office Manager—MR. JOSE CASTANEDA.

Vocation Office—2600 W. Woodlawn Ave., San Antonio, 78228-5196. Tel: 210-735-0553; Email: vocations@archsa.org. Rev. JONATHAN W. FELUX, Dir.; Sr. ANA CECILIA MONTALVO, F.Sp.S., Asst. Dir.; ANA BOJORQUEZ, Administrative Asst.; SHARON MENEZES, Administrative Asst.

Catholic Community Foundation—111 Barilla Pl., Ste. 101, San Antonio, 78209. STEPHEN OSWALD, CEO/Pres., Tel: 210-732-2157; Email: steve.oswald@ccftx.org; RACHEL BABCOCK, Exec. Asst., Email: rachel.babcock@ccftx.org.

Episcopal Vicar and Interfaith Relations—Very Rev. LAWRENCE J. CHRISTIAN, E.V., Tel: 210-734-1676; Email: lawrence.christian@archsa.org.

Archdiocesan Tribunal—Tel: 210-734-2620, Ext. 1135; Tel: 210-734-1696; Fax: 210-734-1987.

Judicial Vicar—Rev. Msgr. CHARLES J. CHAFFMAN, J.C.D., Ph.D.

Adjutant Judicial Vicar—Rev. TONY VILANO, J.C.L.

Director—ANASTACIO J. HINOJOSA, M.A.

Judges—Very Rev. Msgr. TERENCE NOLAN, J.C.L.; Rev. Msgrs. JAMES HENKE, (Retired); JAMES JANISH; Revs. EMMET CAROLAN, (Retired); KRIKOR GREGORY CHAHIN, J.C.D.; RONALD F. WALTERS, O.F.M., J.C.L.; MARTIN J. LEOPOLD, J.C.L.; Sr. JANICE GROCHOWSKY, C.S.J., J.C.L.

Defenders of the Bond—Revs. TONY VILANO, J.C.L.; KRIKOR GREGORY CHAHIN, J.C.D.; RONALD F. WALTERS, O.F.M., J.C.L.; MARTIN J. LEOPOLD, J.C.L.; JOSE RAMON PEREZ; Sr. JANICE GROCHOWSKY, C.S.J., J.C.L.

Approved Advocates—ANASTACIO J. HINOJOSA, M.A.

Case Coordinator Auditors—ADRIANA FERRARO SEAWRIGHT, M.S.W.; IRENE KING; TERESA GONZALES.

Intake and Tribunal Archives Coordinator—COLETTE BROWN.

Notaries/Secretary—PAMELA MANDEVILLE; MARISSA AMADOR.

Due Process: Councils of Conciliation and Arbitration—

Diocesan Administration

Administrative Services Department—Rev. MARTIN J. LEOPOLD, J.C.L., Dir., Tel: 210-734-2620; Tel: 210-734-1674.

Archdiocesan Chief Financial Officer—RUBEN HINOJOSA, Tel: 210-734-1605; Fax: 210-734-2774; Email: ruben.hinojosa@archsa.org.

Archdiocesan Controller—DELIA THOMAS, Tel: 210-734-1677; Fax: 210-734-2774; Email: delia.thomas@archsa.org.

Office of Construction—RANDY KELL, Mgr., Tel: 210-734-1942; Tel: 210-630-7495; Email: randy.kell@archsa.org.

Office of Risk Management—LOGAN UNDERDOWN, Dir., Tel: 210-431-3465; Tel: 800-831-9107 (Toll Free); Fax: 210-431-7742; Email: logan.underdown@archsa.org.

Archdiocesan Finance Council—MARY OSWALD; ROSEMARY ELIZALDE; MATTHEW SPIESS; MICHAEL BARRY; JACK LIGON; LISA SIMS; SARAH GONZALES.

Building Committee—JIM RODRIGUEZ; STEVE PERSYN; ANTHONY CENTENO JR.; LOGAN UNDERDOWN; RANDY KELL; GARY HEIMER.

Lay Pension Plan Committee—RUBEN HINOJOSA; JOHN SPRENCEL, Chm.; DELIA THOMAS; VICTORIA ESPARZA; Rev. MARTIN J. LEOPOLD, J.C.L. Correspondence: RUBEN HINOJOSA, Tel: 210-734-1605; Email: ruben.hinojosa@archsa.org.

Archdiocesan Cemeteries Office—ISMAEL GALVAN, Exec. Dir., Mailing Address: 746 Castroville Rd., San Antonio, 78237. Tel: 210-432-8134; Email: ismael.galvan@archsa.org.

Lay Pension Office—LYDIA WASHINGTON, Tel: 210-734-1633; Email: lydia.washington@archsa.org.

Parish and School Accounting—LAURA TORRES, Sr. Accountant, Tel: 210-734-1983; Email: laura.torres@archsa.org.

Human Resources—VICTORIA ESPARZA, Tel: 210-734-2620, Ext. 1324; Email: victoria.esparza@archsa.org.

Information Technology—MR. JOHN TROLLINGER, Tel: 210-734-2620, Ext. 1320.

Print Service Center—Tel: 210-734-2620, Ext. 1501. RICOH.

Mail Room—Tel: 210-734-1631; Fax: 210-734-0231. RICOH.

Department of Clergy and Consecrated Life—Very Rev. JAMES P. FISCHLER, C.I.C.M., Dir. & Vicar for Clergy, Tel: 210-734-2620; Fax: 210-734-1957; MARTHA ROSS, Administrative Asst., Tel: 210-734-1672.

Office for Religious—Sr. ELIZABETH ANN VASQUEZ, S.S.C.J., Dir., Tel: 210-734-1639; Tel: 210-734-1957; CLAUDIA GARZA, Administrative Asst., Tel: 210-734-1658.

Office of Diaconate and Formation—Deacon MICHAEL PAWELEK, Dir.; MARTHA CANTU, Administrative Asst., Tel: 210-734-2620; Fax: 210-734-1957.

Deans—Metropolitan Area: Very Revs. STEVEN A. GAMEZ, V.U., North; KEVIN P. FAUSZ, C.M., V.U., Central; MIKE HORAN, V.U., Northwest; PATRICK O'BRIEN, V.U., Northeast; MICHAEL A. BOUZIGARD, S.J., V.U., Western; RYAN CARNECER, C.I.C.M., V.U., Southwest; EDVIN RODRIGUEZ, V.U., Southeast; Rev. Msgr. PATRICK J. RAGSDALE, V.U., North Central. Rural Area: Very Revs. DENNIS JARZOMBEK, V.F., Floresville; JOHN NOLAN, V.F., Fredericksburg; VARGHESE ANTONY, (India) V.F., Hondo; PRASANNA KUMAR MESE, (India) V.F., Pleasanton; CARLOS B. VELAZQUEZ, V.F., Seguin; ADRIAN M. ADAMIK, V.F., Uvalde.

Archdiocesan Presbyteral Council—Most Revs. GUSTAVO GARCIA-SILLER, M.Sp.S., D.D.; MICHAEL J. BOULETTE, D.D., D.Min., V.G.; Very Rev. Msgrs. TERENCE NOLAN, J.C.L.; FRANCISZEK KURZAJ; Rev. Msgr. PATRICK J. RAGSDALE, V.U.; Very Rev. Msgr. MICHAEL YARBROUGH, At Large; Very Revs. KEVIN P. FAUSZ, C.M., V.U., Chm.; LAWRENCE J. CHRISTIAN, E.V.; MICHAEL A. BOUZIGARD, S.J., V.U.; MIKE HORAN, V.U.; PATRICK O'BRIEN, V.U.; PRASANNA KUMAR MESE, (India) V.F.; RYAN CARNECER, C.I.C.M., V.U.; EDVIN RODRIGUEZ, V.U.; STEVEN A. GAMEZ, V.U.; DENNIS JARZOMBEK, V.F.; JOHN NOLAN, V.F.; VARGHESE ANTONY, (India) V.F.; ADRIAN M. ADAMIK, V.F.; JAMES P. FISCHLER, C.I.C.M.; CARLOS B. VELAZQUEZ, V.F.; JAIME E. ROBLEDO, P.S.S.; Revs. MARTIN J. LEOPOLD, J.C.L.; TONY VILANO, J.C.L.; ANTHONY O. CUMMINS; DAVID GARCIA, At Large; LEOPOLDO G. PEREZ, O.M.I., S.T.D., M.Div., Education; Sr. JANE ANN SLATER, C.D.P., Chancellor.

Priests Personnel Board—Most Revs. GUSTAVO GARCIA-SILLER, M.Sp.S., D.D.; MICHAEL J. BOULETTE, D.D., D.Min., V.G.; Very Revs. JAMES P. FISCHLER, C.I.C.M.; ADRIAN M. ADAMIK, V.F.; VARGHESE ANTONY, (India) V.F.; PRASANNA KUMAR MESE, (India) V.F.; MICHAEL A. BOUZIGARD, S.J., V.U.; RYAN CARNECER, C.I.C.M., V.U.; KEVIN P. FAUSZ, C.M., V.U.; STEVEN A. GAMEZ, V.U.; MIKE HORAN, V.U.; DENNIS JARZOMBEK, V.F.; JOHN NOLAN, V.F.; PATRICK O'BRIEN, V.U.; EDVIN RODRIGUEZ, V.U.; CARLOS B. VELAZQUEZ, V.F.; Rev. MARTIN J. LEOPOLD, J.C.L.

College of Consultors—Most Rev. MICHAEL J. BOULETTE, D.D., D.Min., V.G.; Very Rev. Msgrs. TERENCE NOLAN, J.C.L.; FRANCISZEK KURZAJ; Very Revs. KEVIN P. FAUSZ, C.M., V.U.; GILBERTO VALLEJO, V.F.; Revs. DAVID GARCIA; ANTHONY O. CUMMINS, (Retired); TONY VILANO, J.C.L.

Vicar for Retired Priests—Rev. ANTHONY O. CUMMINS, (Retired), P.O. Box 1736, Boerne, 78006. 8520 Cross Mountain Trail, #1202, San Antonio, 78255. Email: frtony.cummins@gmail.com.

Office of Catholic Schools—

Superintendent—MARTHA WEST, Tel: 210-734-2620, Ext. 1225; Web: sacatholicschools.org; Email: marti.west@archsa.org.

Associate Superintendent—CYNTHIA LUNA, Tel: 210-734-2620, Ext. 1234; Email: cindy.luna@archsa.org.

Administrative Assistant—LOURDES ESPINOZA, Tel: 210-734-2620, Ext. 1231; Email: lourdes.espinoza@archsa.org.

Director of Counseling and Student Services—VERONICA BALL, Tel: 210-734-2620, Ext. 1516; Email: veronica.ball@archsa.org.

Director of Enrichment Programs—VERONICA MONTALVO, Tel: 210-734-2620, Ext. 1039; Email: veronica.montalvo@archsa.org.

Director of Policy and Compliance—ILIANA DAILY, Tel: 210-734-2620, Ext. 1514; Email: iliana.daily@archsa.org.

Associate Counselor—DR. REBECCA GARZA, Tel: 210-734-2620, Ext. 1252; Email: rebecca.garza@archsa.org.

Director of Recruitment & Enrollment—DENE HUMMON, Tel: 210-734-2620, Ext. 1257; Email: dene.hummon@archsa.org.

Early Childhood Instructional Support Specialist—LAURA ORTIZ, Tel: 210-734-2620, Ext. 1242; Email: laura.ortiz@archsa.org.

Director of School Finance—MONICA BUSTILLOS, Tel: 210-734-2620, Ext. 1262; Email: monica.bustillos@archsa.org.

Staff Accountant—ELSA ASTORGA, Tel: 210-734-2620, Ext. 1271; Email: elsa.astorga@archsa.org.

CYO Athletics—JASON ALVAREZ, Dir., Tel: 210-734-1627; Email: jason.alvarez@archsa.org.

Hope for the Future—Tuition Assistance and School Grants. AMY HONE, Dir., Tel: 210-734-1642; Email: amy.hone@archsa.org; JESSICA RIVERA, Assoc. Dir. Devel., Tel: 210-734-1618; Email: jessica.rivera@archsa.org; DENISE MATCEK LIEDTKA, Assoc. Dir. Mktg. & Communications, Tel: 210-734-1943; Email: denise.liedtka@archsa.org.

Department of Communications—JORDAN MCMORROUGH, Dir., Tel: 210-734-1634; Fax: 210-734-2939; Email: jmcmorrough@archsa.org; PAULA TRIGO-GALAN, Communication Asst., Tel: 210-734-1988; Email: paula.trigo-galan@archsa.org.

Catholic Television of San Antonio (CTSA), Channel 15—YESENIA RAMIREZ, Tel: 210-734-2620, Ext. 1113; Tel: 210-734-1915; Fax: 210-734-2939; Email: yesenia.ramirez@archsa.org.

Today's Catholic Newspaper—MR. JORDAN B. MCMORROUGH, Editor, Tel: 210-734-1634; Fax: 210-734-2939; Email: jmcmorrough@archsa.org.

Department for Pastoral Ministries—Mailing Address: 2718 W. Woodlawn, San Antonio, 78228-5124. JOAN MARTINEZ, M.A.P.M., Dept. Head, Tel: 210-734-1624; Email: joan.martinez@archsa.org; LORRAINE ROSE, Administrative Asst. Supvr., Tel: 210-734-1638; Email: lorraine.rose@archsa.org.

Office for Pastoral Secretariats—Mailing Address: 2718 W. Woodlawn, San Antonio, 78228-5124. Rev. HELIODORO LUCATERO, Ph.D., Dir., Secretariat for Liturgy & Christian Prayer, Tel: 210-734-1912; Email: heliodoro.lucatero@archsa.org; GLORIA F. ZAPIAIN, M.A., Dir., Secretariat for Evangelization, Catechesis, Faith Formation, & Ministry for Persons with Special Needs for Catechesis, Tel: 210-734-1960; Email: gloria.zapiain@archsa.org; MRS. LIZETT FARIAS, M.A.P.M., Dir., Secretariat for Christian Community: Laity, Marriage, Family Life & Youth, Tel: 210-734-1646; Email: lizett.farias@archsa.org; MR. AARON A. CASTILLO, Dir., Secretariat for Mission: Life, Justice, Peace & Outreach, and Young Adults, Tel: 210-734-1955; Email: aaron.castillo@archsa.org.

Office for Events and Gatherings—Mailing Address: 2718 W. Woodlawn, San Antonio, 78228-5124. JUAN CARLOS RODRIGUEZ, Dir., Tel: 210-734-1632; Email: juancarlos.rodriguez@archsa.org.

Office for Liturgies and Trainings—GRACE RODRIGUEZ, Mgr., Tel: 210-734-1643; Email: grace.rodriguez@archsa.org.

Office for Parish Life—Mailing Address: 2718 W. Woodlawn, San Antonio, 78228-5124. RICARDO J. LUZONDO, M.D., Dir., Tel: 305-934-5387; Email: ricardo.luzondo@archsa.org.

Academy for Lay Ecclesial Ministry—Mailing Address: 2718 W. Woodlawn, San Antonio, 78228-5124. PETER DUCTRUM, M.A., M.Div., Dir., Tel: 210-734-5188; Email: peter.ductram@archsa.org.

Office for Pastoral Care Ministries—Mailing Address: 2718 W. Woodlawn, San Antonio, 78228-5124. JOAN MARTINEZ, M.A.P.M., Interim Dir., Tel: 210-734-1624; Email: joan.martinez@archsa.org.

Campus Ministry—Mailing Address: 2718 W. Woodlawn, San Antonio, 78228-5124.
Tel: 830-486-5509. VERONICA YBARRA, Dir., Email: veronica.ybarra@archsa.org. UTSA, UTSA Downtown, Our Lady of the Lake University, University of the Incarnate Word, St. Mary's University, Texas A&M-San Antonio, Texas Lutheran University-Seguin, Schreiner University-Kerrville, Trinity University, Southwest Texas Junior College-Uvalde; Alamo Community Colleges: San Antonio College, St. Phillip, Palo Alto, Northwest Vista, Northeast Lakeview. St. Anthony Catholic Student Center at U.T.S.A.: Sr. CLARICE SUCHY, S.T.J., Coord., Mailing Address: 14523 Roadrunner Way, San Antonio, 78249. Tel: 210-299-9594; Email: clarice.suchy@archsa.org.

Criminal Justice Ministry—Mailing Address: 2718 W. Woodlawn, San Antonio, 78228-5124. Tel: 210-734-1980. Deacon ROBERT J. LEIBRECHT, Dir., Email: robert.leibrecht@archsa.org.

Hospital Ministry—Mailing Address: 2718 W. Woodlawn, San Antonio, 78228-5124. Tel: 210-415-5552. MRS. ELIZABETH RAMIREZ, Dir., Email: elizabeth.ramirez@archsa.org.

Deaf Ministry—Mailing Address: 2718 W. Woodlawn, San Antonio, 78228-5124. Tel: 210-734-1636. MRS. ANGELA MAUER, Dir., Email: angela.mauer@archsa.org.

Mission Awareness—Mailing Address: 2718 W. Woodlawn, San Antonio, 78228-5124. Tel: 210-734-1913. MS. SARA KATHERINE GARCIA, Coord., Email: sara.garcia@archsa.org.

Office of Victim Assistance and Safe Environment—MR. STEVE MARTINEZ, L.C.S.W., L. S.O.T.P., Dir., Email: smartinez@archsa.org; NORMA ALVARADO, Admin. Asst., 135 Barilla Pl., San Antonio, 78209. Tel: 210-734-7786; Tel: 877-700-1888 (Toll Free); Email: ovase@archsa.org.

Catholic Charities, Archdiocese of San Antonio, Inc.—J. ANTONIO FERNANDEZ, Pres. & CEO, 202 W. French, San Antonio, 78212-5818. Tel: 210-222-1294; Fax: 210-227-0217.

Catholic Counseling and Consultation Center—LESLIE ELLENBOGEN, L.C.S.W., Dir., 231 W. Commerce St., San Antonio, 78205. Tel: 210-377-1133; Fax: 210-377-1230.

St. Peter and Joseph's Home—(See Protective Institutions).

Seton Home—(See Protective Institutions).

Refugee Services—PAULA WALKER, 202 W. French Pl., San Antonio, 78212-5818. Tel: 210-222-1294; Fax: 210-242-3174.

Caritas Legal Service—1801 W. Cesar Chavez Blvd., San Antonio, 78207. Tel: 210-433-3256; Fax: 210-433-0851. EVELYN HURON.

Diocesan Offices And Directors

Catholic Center for Charismatic Renewal—1707 S. Flores, San Antonio, 78204. Tel: 210-226-7545; Fax: 210-212-9330; Email: info@cccr.net. Rev. ROBERT E. HOGAN, B.B.D., M.Div., M.A., Assoc. Liaison.

Catholic Lawyers Guild—Rev. MARTIN J. LEOPOLD, J.C.L., Spiritual Moderator, Mailing Address: 2718 W. Woodlawn Ave., San Antonio, 78228-5124. Tel: 210-734-2620.

Catholic Physicians Guild—Rev. LEOPOLD PEREZ, O.M.I., 285 Oblate Dr., San Antonio, 78216. Tel: 210-457-7714; Web: www.cathmeda.org.

Censores Librorum—VACANT.

Movimiento Familiar Cristano and Marriage Encounter—2718 W. Woodlawn Ave., San Antonio, 78228. Tel: 210-651-0645; Email: mfccsafeste@hotmail.com. Regional Directors: JULIO ALARCON; MARIA ALARCON.

Black Catholic Apostolate—CAROL WHITE, 1819 Nevada, San Antonio, 78203. Tel: 210-532-5358; Cell: 210-387-6095; Email: cwhite@archsa.org.

Cursillo Movement (Spanish)—804 Ruiz St., San Antonio, 78207. Tel: 210-227-8258. Rev. JAIME RENTERIA-TORRES, M.N.M., Spiritual Advisor; ANA F. ESPARZA, Lay Dir.

Archdiocesan Union of Holy Name Society—MARJORIE PETRI, Mailing Address: P.O. Box 5789, San Antonio, 78201-0789. Tel: 210-828-2675; Email: mpetriql@gmail.com.

Respect Life Program—2718 W. Woodlawn Ave., San Antonio, 78228. Tel: 210-734-1960. GLORIA F. ZAPIAIN, M.A., Email: gloria.zapiain@archsa.org.

CLERGY, PARISHES, MISSIONS AND PAROCHIAL SCHOOLS

CITY OF SAN ANTONIO

1—CATHEDRAL OF SAN FERNANDO (1731) (Hispanic) Mailing Address: 231 W. Commerce, 78205-2718. Tel: 210-227-1297; Email: info@sfcathedral.org; Email: lsanchez@sfcathedral.org; Web: www.sfcathedral.org. Very Rev. Victor Valdez, Rector; Revs. Rafal Duda, Parochial Vicar; Tomichan Moonnanapillil, MSFS, Parochial Vicar; Juan Carlos Tejada; Deacons Joseph Marroquin; Roger Macias; Jesse Nunez; Roger H. Morales. In Res., Rev. Raymond Schuster, (Retired).
Catechesis Religious Program—Email: lmandujano@sfcathedral.org. Lupita Mandujano, D.R.E. Students 101.
Mission—San Francesco di Paola (Italian) 205 Piazza Italia, Bexar Co. 78207. Tel: 210-227-0548; Fax: 210-226-5086. Very Rev. Victor Valdez.

2—ST. AGNES (1923) (Hispanic) 829 Ruiz St., 78207. Tel: 210-227-8258; Email: Ninfa.delgado@stagneschurchsa.org; Web: www.stagneschurchsa.org. 804 Ruiz St., 78207. Rev. Jaime Renteria-Torres, M.N.M.
Catechesis Religious Program—Tel: 210-227-8258; Email: glasmary@hotmail.com. Sr. Maria Teresa Gonzalez, D.R.E. Students 208.

3—ST. ALPHONSUS (1925) (Hispanic) 2004 Chihuahua St., 78207. Tel: 210-433-9365; Email: st.alphonsus@sbcglobal.net. 1202 S. Zarzamora St., 78207. Very Rev. Michael A. Bouzigard, S.J., V.U., Admin.; Deacon Trinidad Gutierrez.
Catechesis Religious Program—Tel: 210-432-3176. Students 109.

4—ST. ANN (1912) (Hispanic) 210 St. Ann St., 78201. Tel: 210-734-6687; Email: office@stanncatholicchurch.com; Web: www.stanncatholicchurch.com. Very Rev. Lawrence J. Christian, E.V.
Catechesis Religious Program—Sr. Blanca Hinojosa, H.C.G., D.R.E. Students 247.

5—ST. ANTHONY PARISH 14523 Roadrunner Way, 78249-1515. Tel: 210-699-9594; Fax: 210-699-9572; Email: jason.martini@archsa.org; Email: clarice.suchy@archsa.org. Rev. Jason Martini, Admin.; Sr. Clarice Suchy, S.T.J., Campus Min. Coord.

6—ST. ANTHONY MARY CLARET (1988) 6150 Roft Rd., 78253. Tel: 210-688-9033; Fax: 210-688-3575; Email: saclaret@saclaret.com; Web: www.samcsa.com. Revs. Jan Piotr Klak, Ph.L., S.T.L.; Brian Garcia, Parochial Vicar; Deacons Gerald Campa; Jerome P. Kozar.
Catechesis Religious Program—Email: reoffice@saclaret.com. Michelle Reynolds, D.R.E.; Jennifer Rupert, RCIA Coord. Students 1,119.

7—ST. ANTHONY OF PADUA (1957) 102 Lorenz Rd., 78209. Tel: 210-824-1743; Email: secretary@stanthonydepadua.org; Web: www.stanthonydepadua.org. Jose Castillo, Music Min.; Rev. Kevin Shanahan, M.S.C.; Deacons Gilbert Wiessler; Joe Borrego.
Catechesis Religious Program—Email: sonyas@stanthonydepadua.org. Sonya Sanchez, D.R.E. Students 236.

8—BASILICA OF THE NATIONAL SHRINE OF THE LITTLE FLOWER, OUR LADY OF MT. CARMEL AND ST. THERESE PARISH (1926) (Hispanic) 824 Kentucky Ave., 78201. Tel: 210-735-9126; Fax: 210-735-1389; Email: scantu@littleflowerbasilica.org; Email: frluisbelmonteocd@littleflowerbasilica.org; Web: www.littleflowerbasilica.org. 1715 N. Zarzamora, 78201. Revs. Luis Gerardo Belmonte-Luna, O.C.D.; Marion J. Bui, O.C.D., Parochial Vicar; Deacons Antonio G. Rodriguez; Jimmy Garza, (Retired). In Res., Revs. Henry Bordeaux, O.C.D.; Emmanuel Javert Nnadozie, O.C.D.
Res.: 906 Kentucky Ave., 78201-6097.
School—Basilica of the National Shrine of the Little Flower, Our Lady of Mt. Carmel and St. Therese Parish School, (Grades PreK-8), 905 Kentucky Ave., 78201. Tel: 210-732-9207; Fax: 210-732-3214; Email: jcastro@littleflowerschool.net; Web: www.littleflowercatholicschool.org. Jackie Castro, Prin.; Lynette Mendoza, Librarian. Lay Teachers 17; Sisters 1; Students 157.
Catechesis Religious Program—Tel: 210-735-9126, Ext. 110; Email: dre@littleflowerbasilica.org. Cameron Galvan, D.R.E. Students 166.

9—ST. BENEDICT (1958) (Polish—Hispanic) 4535 Lord Rd., 78220. Tel: 210-648-0123; Email: st_benedict_church@sbcglobal.net; Web: stbenedictchurchsa.org. Rev. Juan Carlos Bello-Carrillo, T.O.R.; Deacon Timothy E. Tucker.
Catechesis Religious Program—Tel: 210-648-4632; Email: lord4535@att.net. Joyce Broussard, D.R.E. Students 135.

10—BLESSED SACRAMENT (1956) 600 Oblate Dr., 78216. Tel: 210-824-3381; Email: resparza@blessedsacrament.church; Web: www.blessedsacrament.church. Rev. Christopher Munoz; Deacon Frank Martinez.
School—Blessed Sacrament School, (Grades PreK-8), Email: michael.fierro@blessedschool.com; Web: www.blessedschool.com. Mr. Michael Fierro, Prin. Religious Teachers 1; Lay Teachers 19; Students 190.
Catechesis Religious Program—Students 125.

11—ST. BONAVENTURE (1959) (Hispanic) 1918 Palo Alto Rd., 78211. Tel: 210-922-1685; Email: stbonaventure@satx.rr.com; Web: www.catholicearth.com/sb-sa. Rev. Jean-Oscar Nlandu; Deacons Fidel Hinojosa, (Retired); Amador Gonzalez, (Retired); Luis L. Arredondo; Christopher Von Allmen.
Catechesis Religious Program—Tel: 210-922-1882. Gabrielle Zapata, D.R.E. Students 538.

12—ST. BRIGID (1972) Mailing Address: 6907 Kitchener St., 78240. Tel: 210-696-0896; Email: VirgCrawford@stbrigidcc.org; Web: www.stbrigidcc.org. Rev. Stuart Juleen; Deacons Thomas Billimek; Juan Espinosa; Harold Decuir; Donald V. Bradley Jr.; Ernest Roy Amo; Ruben Davila.
Res.: 6903 Kitchener St., 78240. Email: ParishOffice@stbrigidcc.org.
Catechesis Religious Program—Sr. Dorothy Moczygemba, C.S.S.F., D.R.E. Students 505.

13—ST. CECILIA (1919) (Hispanic) 125 W. Whittier St., 78210-2897. Tel: 210-533-7109; Email: pastor@stceciliasa.org; Web: www.stceciliasa.org. Very Rev. Edvin Rodriguez, V.U.; Deacon Carlos Marquez Jr.
Catechesis Religious Program—Sr. Maria I. Corona, P.C.I., D.R.E. Students 196.
Mission—Purisima Concepcion 807 Mission Rd., Bexar Co. 78210. Email: sfernandoc@aol.com. Rev. David Garcia, Admin.

14—CHRIST THE KING (1928) (Hispanic) 2623 Perez St., 78207. Tel: 210-433-6301; Email: christ.church26@sbcglobal.net; Web: ctksatx.com. Very Rev. Mike Horan, V.U.
Catechesis Religious Program—Tel: 210-433-3640; Email: ctksare@gmail.com. Juan Arriola, D.R.E. Students 153.

15—ST. CLARE (1959) (Hispanic) 7701 Somerset Rd., 78211. Tel: 210-924-5252; Email: rsamour@att.net; Web: www.stclaresatx.net. Rev. Richard Samour; Deacon Gilbert M. Maldonado.
Catechesis Religious Program—Tel: 210-924-5252, Ext. 304. Maria Delores M. Marek, D.R.E. Students 78.

16—DIVINE PROVIDENCE (1981) (Hispanic) 5667 Old Pearsall Rd., 78242-2335. Tel: 210-623-3970; Email: dpcatholic@gmail.com; Web: dpusa.org. Very Rev. Ryan Carnecer, C.I.C.M., V.U.; Deacons Ricardo De La Garza; Jose A. Suniga; Mrs. Elvira Stephenson, Business Mgr.; Mrs. Roselea Llano, Registrar.

17—ST. DOMINIC (1971) 5919 Ingram Rd., 78228. Tel: 210-435-6211; Email: stdominicparish@att.net; Email: stdominics@att.net. Rev. Phillip D. Henning, V.U.; Deacons Wayne Archer; Scott Imburgia; Ray Gonzalez; Joe Vidaurri.

18—ST. ELIZABETH ANN SETON (1961) Rev. Msgr. Conor McGrath; Deacon Lee Jan.
Res.: 8500 Cross Mountain Tr., 78255. Tel: 210-698-1941; Email: martha@seaschurch.com; Web: www.seaschurch.com.
Catechesis Religious Program—Heidi Neuenfeldt, D.R.E. Students 794.

19—ST. FRANCIS OF ASSISI (1980) Mailing Address: 4201 De Zavala Rd., 78249-2000. Tel: 210-492-4600; Fax: 210-492-8128; Email: receptionist@sfasat.org; Web: sfasat.org. Revs. Tony Vilano, J.C.L.; Krzysztof Pawlowski; Sr. Rose Kruppa, C.D.P., Pastoral Assoc.; Deacons Tom Franklin, (Retired); James H. Hewson; Michael A. Portele; Eugene A. Festa, (Retired).
Res.: 14219 Golden Woods, 78249.
Catechesis Religious Program—Larry Perry, Dir. Faith Formation; Miriam Flores, D.R.E.; Monica Harness, Youth Min. Students 475.

20—ST. GABRIEL (1958) (Hispanic) Rev. Joaquin J. Rojas, M.N.M., (Mexico).
Res.: 747 S.W. 39th St., 78237. Tel: 210-433-3689; Fax: 210-433-0546; Email: saintgabrielchurch@sbcglobal.net.
Catechesis Religious Program—Tel: 210-433-3354. Virginia Ibarra, D.R.E. Students 105.

21—ST. GERARD MAJELLA (1911) Revs. James E. Shea, C.Ss.R.; Robert H. Lindsey, C.Ss.R.; Deacon Jose L. Ocampo; Mr. Rick McLaughlin, Music Dir. In Res., Revs. Francis Han Pham, C.Ss.R.; Alton Carr, C.Ss.R.
Church Office: 1523 Iowa St., 78203. Tel: 210-533-0161 (Church Office); Fax: 210-533-0558; Email: info@saintgerardchurch.org.
Res.: 1617 Iowa St., 78203.
Catechesis Religious Program—Email: sjones@saintgerardchurch.org. Shirley Jones, D.R.E. Students 85.

22—ST. GREGORY'S (1955) 700 Dewhurst Rd., 78213. Tel: 210-342-5271; Email: stgregthegreat@yahoo.com; Web: stgregorys.net. Rev. Rudy Carrola; Deacons Fred Campos Jr.; Joe Lopez; Carlos R. Cerna.
School—St. Gregory's School, (Grades PreK-8),

Tel: 210-342-0281; Email: daniel.martinez@stgregorys.net; Web: www.stgregorysa.org. Mr. Daniel Martinez, Prin. Lay Teachers 31; Students 419.
Catechesis Religious Program—
Tel: 210-342-3826; Fax: 210-342-0245. Gloria Silva, C.R.E. Students 243.
23—ST. HELENA (1974)
14714 Edgemont St., 78247. Tel: 210-653-3316; Email: estherc@sthelena.org; Web: www.sthelena.org. Rev. Lenin Naffate, (Mexico) V.U.; Deacons Paul Gustowski; John Murphy.
Res.: 14527 Angora St., 78247.
Catechesis Religious Program—Corrie Solis, D.R.E. Students 435.
24—ST. HENRY (1904) (Hispanic)
1619 S. Flores St., 78204. Tel: 210-225-6877; Email: sthenrys@sbcglobal.net; Web: www.sthenrysatx.org. Rev. Robert E. Hogan, B.B.D., M.Div., M.A.; Bros. Sean Stilson, Parochial Vicar; Ruben Garza, Pastoral Assoc.; Deacon Joseph L. De Leon, Ph.D.
Catechesis Religious Program—
Tel: 210-227-1585. Sr. Sheeja Kannanthara, D.R.E. Students 95.
25—HOLY FAMILY (1963) (Hispanic)
152 Florencia, 78228-5899. Tel: 210-433-8216; Email: valdezlorenzo79@yahoo.com; Email: pastor@holyfamilysa.com; Web: www.saholyfamily.com. Rev. Patrick Seitz; Deacon Lorenzo Valdez.
Catechesis Religious Program—
Tel: 210-433-8216 (Ext 17 or 23). Ester Mango, C.R.E. Students 108.
26—HOLY NAME (1961) (Polish—Hispanic)
3814 Nash Blvd., 78223. Tel: 210-333-5020; Email: holynameadmin@holynameusa.org; Email: aford@holynameusa.org; Web: www.holynameusa.org. Rev. Martin Parayno, O.S.B., (Philippines); Deacons Reynaldo Hinojosa Sr.; Daniel Kearns, (Retired); Roberto R. Ruiz, (Retired); Joe Avila; Jun Sorio, Music Min.; Allan Ford, Parish Office Mgr,; Rev. Jose Nestor Lachica, In Res.
School—Holy Name School, (Grades PreK-8),
Tel: 210-333-7356; Fax: 210-333-7693; Email: jtiller@hncstx.org; Web: www.hncstx.org. Jennifer Tiller, Admin. Lay Teachers 12; Students 208.
Catechesis Religious Program—
Email: ibickel@holynameusa.org. Irma Bickel, D.R.E. Students 264.
27—HOLY REDEEMER (1901) [CEM] (African American)
1819 Nevada, 78203. Tel: 210-532-5358; Email: kevin.fausz@archsa.org. Very Rev. Kevin P. Fausz, C.M., V.U.
Catechesis Religious Program—
Email: rene.brooks@outlook.com. Rene Brooks, D.R.E. Students 39.
28—HOLY ROSARY (1948) (Hispanic)
159 Camino Santa Maria, 78228. Tel: 210-433-3241; Email: jthompson@hrosary.com; Web: www.holyrosarysa.org. Rev. John Thompson; Deacons Francisco Sandoval; Albert Sanchez.
Catechesis Religious Program—
Email: ereyes@hrosary.com. Bro. Esteban Reyes, D.R.E. Students 75.
29—HOLY SPIRIT (1964)
Mailing Address: P.O. Box 460729, 78246-0729.
Tel: 210-341-1395; Fax: 210-341-8438; Email: frantonio@holyspiritsa.org; Email: socialmedia@holyspiritsa.org; Web: www.holyspiritsa.org. 8134 Blanco Rd., 78216. Very Rev. Antonio Gonzalez; Rev. Francisco Quezada, Parochial Vicar; Deacons Warren A. Wilkins; Evan Wittig; Thomas Tucker; Peter R. Olivares.
Parish Office: 758 W. Ramsey, 78216.
School—Holy Spirit School, (Grades PreK-8),
770 W. Ramsey Rd., 78216. Tel: 210-349-1169;
Fax: 210-349-1247; Email: info@hscssa.org; Web: www.hscssa.org. Margaret Webb, Prin. (PreK3-8) Clergy 7; Lay Teachers 38; Students 444.
30—HOLY TRINITY (1987)
20523 Huebner Rd., 78258-3915.
Tel: 210-497-4200, Ext. 307; Email: gloria@holytrinitysat.org; Web: www.holytrinitysat.org. Very Rev. Msgr. Michael Yarbrough; Revs. Daniel Villarreal; Michael English; Deacons Jerry Micek; Michael Cleary; John B. Eichelberger; David R. Seguin; Dickie Yzaguirre.
Res.: 18018 Crystal Knoll, 78258.
Catechesis Religious Program—
Tel: 210-497-4145; Fax: 210-497-3041; Email: kristin@holytrinitysat.org. Kristen Casas, C.R.E.; Eric Mejia, Asst. C.R.E. Students 1,242.
31—IMMACULATE CONCEPTION (1933) (Hispanic)
314 Merida St., 78207. Tel: 210-225-2986;
Fax: 210-225-2987; Web: issygarcia@aol.com. Rev. Isidore Garcia, O.M.I.
Catechesis Religious Program—Herlinda Barrentos, D.R.E. Students 69.
32—IMMACULATE HEART OF MARY (1912) (Hispanic)
617 S. Santa Rosa Blvd., 78204. Tel: 210-226-8268; Email: admin@ihmsatx.org; Web: ihmsatx.org. Revs. Gabriel Ruiz, C.M.F.; Thomas Thennadiyil, C.M.F.; Deacons Jorge Bonilla-Valentin; Alfonso Cervantes; Revs. Mark Clarke, C.M.F., In Res.; Len Brown, C.M.F., In Res.; Nnamdi Ebem, C.M.F., In Res.; Bejamin Romero, C.M.F., In Res.
Catechesis Religious Program—
Tel: 210-224-8829; Tel: 210-251-4826; Email: dre@ihmsatx.org. Mary Salas, D.R.E. Students 112.
33—ST. JAMES THE APOSTLE (1954) (Hispanic)
907 W. Theo Ave., 78225. Tel: 210-922-2136; Cell: 210-712-4098; Email: stjamestheapostlesa@gmail.com; Web: www.stjamestheapostlesa.org. Rev. Joseph Kandeor, M.S.P.; Deacons Ernest Moran; Jesse P. Alcala.
School—St. James the Apostle School, (Grades PreK-8),
Tel: 210-924-1201; Email: sr.debbie.walker@stjamesschoolsa.org; Web: www.stjamesschoolsa.org. Sr. Debbie Walker, Prin. Religious Teachers 2; Lay Teachers 23; Students 355.
Catechesis Religious Program—
Tel: 210-922-4061. Mary Toscano, D.R.E. Students 448.
34—ST. JOHN BERCHMANS (1910) (Hispanic)
1147 Cupples Rd., 78226. Tel: 210-434-3247; Email: accounting@stjohnberchmans.com. Rev. Fidele O. Dikete, V.U.; Deacon Jesus Rodriguez.
School—St. John Berchmans School, (Grades PreK-8),
Tel: 210-433-0411; Email: sjb.info@sjbsa.com; Web: www.sjbschool-sa.com. Nora Garcia, Prin.; Mrs. Ariana Hopcus, Librarian; Mrs. Sandy Salazar, Sec. Lay Teachers 15; Students 201.
Catechesis Religious Program—
Fax: 210-432-0431; Email: rosydre@yahoo.com. Ms. Rosalinda Rodriguez, D.R.E. Students 160.
35—ST. JOHN NEUMANN (1977)
Mailing Address: 6680 Crestway Dr., 78239.
Tel: 210-654-1643; Fax: 210-654-8031; Email: pa@sjnsa.org; Web: www.sjnsa.org. Rev. Alex Pereida; Deacons Stephen Kerr, Sacramental Min.; Larry Lindsey, Sacramental Min.; Mrs. Blanca Loza Rocha, Pastoral Assoc.
Catechesis Religious Program—Blanca Loza Rocha, D.R.E. Students 216.
36—ST. JOHN THE EVANGELIST (1956)
4603 St. John's Way, 78212. Tel: 210-738-2201; Email: st-john@sbcglobal.net. Rev. Isak Keyman-Ige; Deacon Thomas Villalon.
Catechesis Religious Program—Yolanda Gutierrez, L.M.S.W., C.R.E. Students 152.
37—ST. JOSEPH (Downtown) (1868) [CEM]
623 E. Commerce St., 78205. Tel: 210-227-0126; Email: mariomsss@aol.com; Email: marioanthony48@yahoo.com. Rev. Mario Marzocchi, S.S.S.; Deacon Vincent Schell.
Catechesis Religious Program—Beatrice Bailey, D.R.E. Students 55.
38—ST. JOSEPH SPOUSE OF THE VIRGIN MARY (South San) (1935) (Hispanic)
535 New Laredo Hwy., 78211-1900.
Tel: 210-924-4383; Email: stjosephss.frontoffice@gmail.com; Web: www.stjosephss.com. Rev. Alberto Colin; Deacons Genaro Herrera; Guadalupe De Luna.
Catechesis Religious Program—Students 176.
39—ST. JUDE (1954) (Hispanic) Rev. Roney M. Cardoso, O.S.A.; Deacons Bartolo Ramos; Felipe Barajas.
Res.: 130 S. San Augustine Ave., 78237.
Tel: 210-432-8044; Email: stjudeninaguajardo@yahoo.com.
Catechesis Religious Program—
Tel: 210-432-1582; Email: stjude.religioused@yahoo.com. Lisa Martinez, D.R.E. Students 362.
Mission—Santa Maria Goretti
Bexar Co.
40—ST. LAWRENCE (1959) (Hispanic)
236 E. Petaluma Blvd., Bldg. 4, 78221.
Tel: 210-924-4401; Fax: 210-924-4075; Email: stlawrpastoral7@hotmail.com; Web: www.stlawrencesa.org. Rev. Jose Ramon Perez-Martinez; Deacons Nestor Huizar Jr.; Charles F. Pope Sr.; Alicia Ortiz, Business Mgr.
Catechesis Religious Program—
Tel: 210-924-6470; Email: stlawreedu@sbcglobal.net. Mary Zavala, C.R.E. Students 414.
41—ST. LEO (1919) Rev. Frank Macias; Deacons Gerald Gonzalez; Thomas Torres, (Retired); Robert M. Caldwell Jr.; Robert Paiz Ibarra; J. Mark Luther.
Office: 4401 S. Flores, 78214. Tel: 210-533-9108; Email: stleoschurch@yahoo.com; Web: www.saintleoschurch.net.
Res.: 148 W. Hafer, 78214.
Catechesis Religious Program—
Email: terrisanch@yahoo.com. Teresa Sanchez, D.R.E. Students 414.
42—ST. LEONARD'S (1966) (Hispanic)
8510 S. Zarzamora, 78224-2099. Tel: 210-924-6000; Email: stleonard@att.net; Web: www.stleonardsa.org. Rev. Eduardo Martinez, Admin.; Deacons Rey Ybarra; Alfred J. Gaona.
Catechesis Religious Program—
Tel: 210-924-6000, Ext. 5; Email: jlstleonard1@gmail.com. Jessy Lizarraga-Lira, D.R.E. Students 330.
43—ST. LUKE (1959)
4603 Manitou, 78228-1889. Tel: 210-433-2777; Email: office@stlukecatholic.org; Web: www.saintlukeparish.com. Revs. Eric Ritter; Alejandro del Bosque, L.C.; Deacons Jose Escamilla; Richard Gonzalez; Jack Don Nichols; Robert Torres.
Res.: 6014 Horizon, 78228.
School—St. Luke School, (Grades PreK-8),
Tel: 210-434-2011; Email: debbie.rodriguez@stlukecatholic.org; Web: www.stlukecatholic.org. Mrs. Mary Helen Cover, Prin. Clergy 2; Lay Teachers 31; Students 489.
Catechesis Religious Program—Rick Olivarez, C.R.E. Students 506.
44—ST. MARGARET MARY (1955) (Hispanic) Rev. Jimmy David Drennan; Deacons Gerardo Mechler; Zeke Moczygemba; Jose Almanza, (Retired); Gabriel J. Rosas, (Retired); Francisco Lafuente.
Res.: 1314 Fair Ave., 78223. Tel: 210-532-6309;
Fax: 210-532-6333; Email: stmargaretmaryinsatx@yahoo.com; Web: www.stmmcc.org.
Catechesis Religious Program—
Email: rubiolinda80@gmail.com. Linda Rubio, D.R.E. Students 213.
Mission—St. Catherine
2202 Hicks, Bexar Co. 78210.
45—ST. MARK THE EVANGELIST (1976)
1602 Thousand Oaks Dr., 78232-2398.
Tel: 210-494-1606; Fax: 210-494-4957; Email: dhamlin@stmarkevangelist.com; Web: stmarkevangelist.com. Rev. Msgr. Kevin E. Ryan; Dorothea G. Hamlin, Pastoral Admin.; Pamela Raines, Devel. Dir.; Robert Martinez, Pastoral Assoc.; Deacons Steven Marques; Gilbert S. Hernandez; Raul Adam; Larry Brisiel; Hipolito Huerta; Gary Marks, Dir. Music.
Catechesis Religious Program—
Tel: 210-494-7434. Elizabeth Herring, D.R.E.; Frank Peacher, D.R.E. (High School); Anne Kemper, Coord. C.C.D. Children; Paul Vance, Adult Faith Formation. Students 725.
46—ST. MARTIN DE PORRES (1964) (Hispanic)
1730 Dahlgreen Ave., 78237. Tel: 210-432-5203; Email: sporres1730@gmail.com. Revs. Joaquin J. Rojas, M.N.M., (Mexico); Mauricio Chavez-Guerrero, M.N.M.; Antonio Lopez-Macias, Parochial Vicar; Deacon Benito Resendiz; Olga Terrazas, Business Mgr.
Catechesis Religious Program—
Tel: 210-436-2071. Students 342.
47—ST. MARY (1852) [CEM]
202 N. St. Mary's St., 78205. Tel: 210-226-8381; Email: stmarysa78205@gmail.com. Revs. John J. Gordon, O.M.I.; Edward Hauf, O.M.I.
48—ST. MARY MAGDALEN (1940) (Hispanic) Rev. William H. Combs, B.B.D., B.B.D.; Deacons David Zamora; Arturo Lozano. In Res., Revs. George T. Montague, S.M.; Robert E. Hogan, B.B.D., M.Div., M.A.
Office: 1710 Clower St., 78201. Tel: 210-735-5269; Email: smm@stmarymagdalensa.org; Web: stmm.info.
Res.: 1701 Alametos St., 78201.
School—St. Mary Magdalen School, (Grades PreK-8),
1700 Clower St., 78201. Tel: 210-735-1381;
Fax: 210-735-2406; Email: william.daily@stmmsa.og; Web: www.stmmsa.org. William Daily, Prin.; Roberta Gujardo, Librarian. Clergy 1; Lay Teachers 25; Sisters 1; Students 409.
Catechesis Religious Program—
Tel: 210-735-5284. Mrs. Francis Portillo, D.R.E. Students 496.
49—ST. MATTHEW CATHOLIC CHURCH (1968)
10703 Wurzbach Rd., 78230. Tel: 210-478-5000; Email: kay@stmatts.org; Web: stmatts.org. Revs. Dennis Arechiga; Abel Ruiz; Deacons Tom Fox; Alonzo Guzman; Rafael Lara; Michael F. Nealis; Oscar Vela Jr.; John Ochiagha; Scott Sowell; Rev. Msgr. Juan Alfaro, In Res., (Retired); Rev. James L. Empereur, S.J.
School—St. Matthew's School, (Grades PreK-8),
Tel: 210-478-5099; Email: office@stmatts.org. Jennifer Grenardo, Prin. Lay Teachers 49; Students 690.
Catechesis Religious Program—
Tel: 210-478-5010; Email: SrTherese@stmatts.org. Sr. Therese Gleitz, D.R.E. Students 877.
50—ST. MICHAEL (1866) [CEM] (Hispanic)
418 Indiana, 78210. Tel: 210-532-3707; Email: stmichaelrcc78210@yahoo.com. Very Rev. Kevin P. Fausz, C.M., V.U.; Rev. Miguel Moreno, Parochial Vicar.
Catechesis Religious Program—Rosemary Davila, D.R.E. Students 55.
51—OUR LADY OF GOOD COUNSEL (1952) (Hispanic)

1204 Castroville Rd., 78237. Tel: 210-432-0873; Email: olgcsa@yahoo.com. Rev. Jose Ramon Perez.
Catechesis Religious Program—
Tel: 210-432-6430. Students 102.

52—OUR LADY OF GRACE (1938)
223 E. Summit Ave., 78212. Tel: 210-734-7285; Email: diane.wyrick@olgsa.org; Web: www.olgsa.org. Revs. Martin J. Leopold, J.C.L.; Agustin Estrada, Parochial Vicar.
Res.: 237 E. Summit Ave., 78212.
Catechesis Religious Program—
Email: kim.olivarez@olgsa.org. Kimberly Olivarez, D.R.E. Students 346.

53—OUR LADY OF GUADALUPE (1911) (Hispanic)
1321 El Paso St., 78207. Tel: 210-226-4064; Email: guadalupesat@yahoo.com. Very Rev. Michael A. Bouzigard, S.J., V.U.; Rev. Mark McKenzie, S.J., Parochial Vicar; Deacon Ruben Felan.
*Catechesis Religious Program—*Maria Del Rosario Funakoshi, D.R.E. Students 79.

54—OUR LADY OF PERPETUAL HELP (1913) (Hispanic)
618 S. Grimes St., 78203. Tel: 210-532-7031; Email: secretary.olphsa@gmail.com. Very Rev. Kevin P. Fausz, C.M., V.U.; Deacon Charles Gamez.
Catechesis Religious Program—
Email: dre.olphsa@gmail.com. Students 108.

55—OUR LADY OF SORROWS (1915) (Hispanic)
3107 N. St. Mary's St., 78212. Tel: 210-732-6295; Email: olsorrows.1915@gmail.com; Web: www.ourladyofsorrows-sa.org. Revs. Martin J. Leopold, J.C.L.; Marian Piekarczyk, S.D.S., Spiritual Advisor/Care Svcs.; Deacons Jesse Fraga; Denis F. Perez, Admin. In Res.
*Catechesis Religious Program—*Students 64.

56—OUR LADY OF THE ANGELS (1947) (Hispanic)
1214 Stonewall St., 78211. Tel: 210-924-6591; Fax: 210-924-6593; Email: ourlady1214@gmail.com; Web: www.olasa.org. Rev. William Kraus, OFM CAP; Deacons Albert Ramirez; Jose F. Moreno; Bro. Donald Rank.
Catechesis Religious Program—
Tel: 210-532-9344; Email: srpatriciaoladre@gmail.com. Sr. Maria Patricia Gonzalez, H.C.G., D.R.E. Students 211.

57—ST. PATRICK (1895) (Hispanic)
1114 Willow St., 78208. Tel: 210-226-5223; Email: stpatrickwillow@hotmail.com; Web: www.saintpatricks.net. Rev. Johanes Teguh Raharjo, C.I.C.M.
*Catechesis Religious Program—*Students 143.

58—ST. PAUL (1954) (Hispanic)
1201 Donaldson Ave., 78228. Tel: 210-733-7152; Email: mgonzales@saintpaulsa.org; Web: www.saintpaulsa.org. 350 Sutton Dr., 78228. Rev. Msgr. Charles J. Chaffman, J.C.D., Ph.D.; Deacons Agustin Arismendez; Carl Weekly; Norman Kutschenreuter; Jennifer Smyrl, Pastoral Assoc.; Virginia Valenzuela, Pastoral Assoc.; Michelle Weekley, Pastoral Assoc.
School—St. Paul School, (Grades PreK-8),
307 John Adams, 78228. Tel: 210-732-2741;
Fax: 210-732-7702; Email: mary.crow@stpaulroyals.org. Mrs. Mary I. Crow, Prin. Lay Teachers 12; Religious 2; Students 196.
Community Center—
Tel: 210-736-0055; Fax: 210-738-9600; Email: mdavila@saintpaulsa.org. Mary Davila, Business Mgr.
Child Care—Learning Center
Tel: 210-738-8715; Fax: 210-738-8403. Josie Gonzalez, Dir. (Daycare) Children 99.
Catechesis Religious Program—
Email: rarismendez@saintpaulsa.org. Rosie Arismendez, D.R.E. Students 185.

59—ST. PETER PRINCE OF THE APOSTLES (1923)
111 Barilla Pl., 78209. Tel: 210-822-3367; Email: stppa@sbcglobal.net; Web: www.stpeterprinceoftheapostles.org. Revs. Martin J. Leopold, J.C.L.; Agustin Estrada, Parochial Vicar; Deacons Robert Kusenberger; Richard De Hoyos; John Paul Benage; Lora Balusik, Business Mgr.
School—St. Peter Prince of the Apostles School, (Grades K-8),
112 Marcia Pl., 78209. Tel: 210-824-3171;
Fax: 210-822-4504; Email: becky.pawelek@stpeterprince.org; Web: www.stpeterprince.org. Gabriel Duarte, Prin. Religious Teachers 2; Lay Teachers 16; Students 137.
Catechesis Religious Program—
Email: spfaithformation@sbcglobal.net. Students 184.

60—ST. PHILIP OF JESUS (1914) (Hispanic)
150 E. Lambert, 78204. Tel: 210-226-5024; Email: stphilipofjesus78204@gmail.com; Web: www.stphilipofjesus.org. 142 E. Lambert, 78204. Rev. Robert E. Hogan, B.B.D., M.Div., M.A.; Bro. Sean Stilson, Parochial Vicar; Deacons Jose Sanchez, (Retired); Gilbert C. De La Portilla; Myron Benavides.
*Catechesis Religious Program—*Students 142.

61—ST. PIUS X (1957)
3303 Urban Crest, 78209. Tel: 210-824-0139;
Fax: 210-829-5125; Email: stpiusx@stpiusxsa.org; Web: www.stpiusxsa.org. 3907 Harry Wurzbach Rd., 78209. Very Rev. Patrick O'Brien, V.U., Admin.; Deacons Daniel T. McShane; Jose A. Santos.
School—St. Pius X School, (Grades PreK-8),
7734 Robin Rest Dr., 78209. Tel: 210-824-6431;
Fax: 210-824-7454; Email: spxschool@stpiusxsa.org. Mrs. Jane Zarate, Prin. Lay Teachers 28; Students 253.
*Catechesis Religious Program—*Stephanie Kristek, Dir. Faith Formation. Students 135.

62—PRINCE OF PEACE (1980)
7893 N. Grissom Rd., 78251. Tel: 210-681-8330; Email: communications@princeofpeacecatholic.org; Web: www.princeofpeacecatholic.org. Revs. Rodolfo Caballero, S.T.L., Ph.D.; Praveen Lakkisetti, Parochial Vicar; Deacons Agripino Sanabria; Robert G. Correa; Richard Juarez; Heriberto Eddie Limas Sr.; Timothy McCarthy.
Catechesis Religious Program—
Tel: 210-681-5063. Barbara Forde, D.R.E. Students 931.

63—RESURRECTION OF THE LORD (1981)
7990 W. Military Dr., 78227. Tel: 210-675-1471; Email: ecabrera1@satx.rr.com; Email: rojypeter@rediffmail.com. Revs. Binoj Jose, H.G.N.; Roji Peter, H.G.N.; Deacons Jose Angel Martinez; George Salazar Sr.
Res.: 7151 Cypress Grove, 78227.
*Catechesis Religious Program—*Students 327.

64—ST. ROSE OF LIMA (1981)
9883 Marbach Rd., 78245. Tel: 210-675-1920;
Fax: 210-675-6067; Email: stroseoflima78245@gmail.com; Web: stroseoflima.church. Very Rev. Steven A. Gamez, V.U.; Rev. Johnson Le, Parochial Vicar; Deacons John W. Gearhart; Antonio Lira; Rafael Lopez-Negroni.
Catechesis Religious Program—
Email: saintrose_re@yahoo.com. Sr. Abigail Toledo, D.R.E. Students 1,167.

65—SACRED HEART (1899) (Hispanic)
2114 W. Houston St., 78207-3496.
Tel: 210-227-5059, Ext. 203; Email: frfredshsa@gmail.com. Revs. Frederic Mizengo, C.I.C.M., (Congo); Roy Quiogue, C.I.C.M.; Deacon Rudy Rodriguez.
Catechesis Religious Program—
Tel: 210-227-9763. Irene Ybarra, D.R.E. Students 240.

66—SAN FRANCISCO DE LA ESPADA (1731) (Hispanic)
10040 Espada Rd., 78214. Tel: 210-627-2064;
Fax: 210-627-2059; Email: espadacabrini@gmail.com. Revs. Andres Gallegos; Nicholas Baxter, O.F.M.
Res.: 5710 Arlitt Dr., 78222.
Catechesis Religious Program—
Tel: 210-627-2962. Sonia Valero, D.R.E., Tel: 210-781-3311. Students 170.
Mission—St. Frances Cabrini
1606 San Casimiro, Bexar Co. 78214.

67—SAN JOSE Y SAN MIGUEL (1720) (Hispanic)
701 E. Pyron Ave., 78214. Tel: 210-922-0543;
Fax: 210-932-2271; Email: sanjoseinsatx@yahoo.com; Web: www.missionsanjosechurh.org. Rev. Claudio Rogelio Martinez, O.F.M.; Deacons Frank J. Chip Perry; George Wunderlich.
Catechesis Religious Program—
Email: sunigajrfrancisco@hotmail.com. Francisco Suniga Jr., C.R.E. Students 73.

68—SAN JUAN CAPISTRANO (1731) (Hispanic)
Mailing Address: P.O. Box 14308, 78214-0308.
Tel: 210-534-3161; Email: padregalvin@priest.com. Rev. James Gerard Galvin, (Scotland) (Retired).
Res.: 9101 Graf Rd., 78214.
Church: 78214.
*Catechesis Religious Program—*Students 95.
Mission—St. Ann
Southton, Bexar Co.

69—SAN JUAN DE LOS LAGOS SHRINE (1952) (Hispanic)
3231 El Paso St., 78207-4607. Tel: 210-433-9722;
Fax: 210-433-9526; Email: sanjuanshrine@att.net; Web: sanjuanshrinesa.org. Rev. Ricardo V. Guerra, O.M.I.; Deacon Albert Salinas.
Res.: 2918 El Paso St., 78207.
Catechesis Religious Program—
Tel: 210-433-2411. Students 116.

70—SANTO NINO DE CEBU (1993) (Filipino)
Mailing Address: 5655 Rigsby Ave., 78222.
Tel: 210-648-1705; Fax: 210-648-5365; Email: santo.nino.sa@gmail.com. Rev. Arnold Ibarra; Deacon Arsenio Reyes Jr., Liturgy Dir.; Regina Pino, Parish Council Chair.
*Catechesis Religious Program—*Mrs. Jetrina Salazar-Licon, D.R.E. Students 87.

71—SHRINE OF ST. PADRE PIO OF PIETRELCINA (2001)
Mailing Address: 20770 US Hwy. 281N, Ste. 108 PMB 611, 78258. Tel: 210-497-6101; Email: stpadrepio@sbcglobal.net; Web: www.shrineofpadrepio.com. 3843 Bulverde Pkwy., 78259. Rev. Msgr. Patrick J. Ragsdale, V.U.; Rev. Krikor Gregory Chahin, J.C.D.; Deacons Kevin Kanter; Oscar Perez; Kenneth Gottardy; Richard F. Neville Jr.; John Patrick McGarrity; Clinton A. Couch.
Shrine—Shrine of St. Padre Pio.

72—ST. STEPHEN (1965) (Hispanic), Closed. For inquiries for parish records contact the chancery.

73—ST. THOMAS MORE (1964)
4411 Moana Dr., 78218. Tel: 210-655-5070; Email: stmparish@live.com. Rev. Tomy Thomas, H.G.N., (India); Deacon Timothy M. Tate Sr.
School—St. Thomas More School, (Grades PreK-8),
4427 Moana Dr., 78218. Tel: 210-655-2882;
Fax: 210-655-9603; Email: kgutierrez@stmcs62.org; Web: www.st-thomas-more-school.org. Mrs. Kimberly A. Gutierrez, Prin. Lay Teachers 12; Students 104.
*Catechesis Religious Program—*Elizabeth Rodriguez, C.R.E. Students 41.

74—ST. TIMOTHY'S (1953) (Hispanic)
1515 Saltillo St., 78207. Tel: 210-434-2391; Email: sttimothycatholic@yahoo.com. Deacons Antonio Caballero; Hector Ledesma.
*Catechesis Religious Program—*Frances Gonzalez, D.R.E. Students 109.

75—VIETNAMESE MARTYRS CATHOLIC CENTER (1976)
1240 Holbrook, 78218. Tel: 210-646-0726; Email: francispham@yahoo.com; Web: www.vietsa.org. Rev. Francis Han Pham, C.Ss.R.
*Catechesis Religious Program—*Students 112.

76—ST. VINCENT DE PAUL (1961)
4222 S.W. Loop 410, 78227-4495. Tel: 210-674-1200;
Fax: 210-674-1640; Email: MySVDPparish@gmail.com; Web: www.MySVDPparish.org. Revs. Hugo O. Maese, M.Sp.S.; Armando Hernandez, M.Sp.S., Parochial Vicar; Lucille O'Barr, Business Mgr.; Gilbert Aldrete Jr., Music Min.; Deacon Apolonio Eduardo Garcia.
Catechesis Religious Program—
Tel: 210-674-4291; Email: MySVDPparish.RE@gmail.com. Josie Dobroski, C.R.E. Students 281.

OUTSIDE THE CITY OF SAN ANTONIO

BANDERA, BANDERA CO., ST. STANISLAUS (1855) [CEM] [JC] (Polish)
311 7th St., Box 757, Bandera, 78003-0757.
Tel: 830-460-4712; Email: ststanis@sbcglobal.net; Web: www.ststanislausbandera.com. Very Rev. Msgr. Franciszek Kurzaj.
*Catechesis Religious Program—*Joan Schmidt, C.R.E. Students 133.
Mission—St. Victor's Chapel, 10514 Park Rd. 37, Lakehills, Bandera Co. 78063.

BOERNE, KENDALL CO., ST. PETER THE APOSTLE (1866) (German)
202 W. Kronkosky St., Boerne, 78006.
Tel: 830-816-2233; Fax: 830-249-6175; Email: Pastoraloffice@Stpetersboerne.com; Email: Terise@stpetersboerne.com. Rev. Norman Ermis; Deacons Paul Rayburg; Ken Nickel; Michael Matteson; Terise Bransford, Pastoral Admin.; Joe Cortez III, Dir. Music, Liturgy.
*Catechesis Religious Program—*Email: Terise@stpetersboerne.com. Julia Cortez, Elementary Faith Formation Coord.; Laura Balderama Contreras, Assoc.; Lacey Sorrell, Youth Min. (Middle School & High School); Bert Hernandez, Youth Min. High School Confirmation; Michelle Pechacek, Youth Min. Middle School Edge Prog.; Marjorie Saur, Good Shepherd Coord.; Darcy Maciolek, RCIA & Faith Formation for Adults. Students 930.

BRACKETTVILLE, KINNEY CO., ST. MARY MAGDALEN (1875) [CEM] Rev. James N. Ikeatuegwu, Admin.; Deacons James Bader; Richard Lawrence.
301 S. Ann St., Box 95, Brackettville, 78832.
Tel: 830-563-2487; Email: stmarymag@sbcglobal.net.
*Catechesis Religious Program—*Students 101.
Mission—St. Blaise, Spofford Junction, Kinney Co.

CANYON LAKE, COMAL CO., ST. THOMAS THE APOSTLE (1967)
180 St. Thomas Dr., Canyon Lake, 78133.
Tel: 830-964-3497; Email: stthomas@gvtc.com; Email: stthomas@canyonlake.org. Deacons Clifford Hall; Robert J. Leibrecht.
*Catechesis Religious Program—*Email: drestt@gvtc.com. A'Laura Vrana, D.R.E.; Beate Buescher, Good Shepherd Coord. Students 108.

CASTROVILLE, MEDINA CO., ST. LOUIS (1844) [CEM] (Alsatian) Revs. James Fischler, C.I.C.M.; Sonny Aryanto, C.I.C.M.; Deacons Louis P. Bernal; Richard P. Hoedebecke.
Res.: 610 Madrid, Castroville, 78009.
Tel: 830-931-2826; Email: rectory@stlouischurchcastroville.org.
School—St. Louis School, (Grades PreK-5),
Tel: 830-931-3544; Email: karen.rothe@saintlouiscs.org; Web: saintlouis.org. Ms. Karen Rothe, Prin. Lay Teachers 10; Students 135.
*Catechesis Religious Program—*Tel: 830-423-6156; Email: ddrtex1629@gmail.com. Deborah Ruiz, D.R.E. Students 354.
Mission—St. Francis of Assisi (Medina Lake Chapel), Mico, Medina Co.

CESTOHOWA, KARNES CO., NATIVITY OF THE BLESSED VIRGIN MARY (1873) [CEM] (Polish)
300 FM 3191 Cestohowa, Falls City, 78113.
Tel: 830-745-2633; Email: nbvm@hughes.net. Rev. Andrzej Waszczenko, S.D.S., (Poland).
Catechesis Religious Program—Sheri Jurgajtis, D.R.E. Students 31.

CHARLOTTE, ATASCOSA CO., ST. ROSE OF LIMA (1909) (Hispanic)
333 Madero Ave., P.O. Box 69, Charlotte, 78011.
Tel: 830-277-1242; Fax: 830-274-1242; Email: st.roselima1@gmail.com. Rev. Jozef Glabinski, Admin.
Catechesis Religious Program—Tel: 830-480-4319. Rosa Juarez, D.R.E. Students 101.
Mission—St. Joseph, 703 Congress St., P.O. Box 297, Tilden, McMullen Co. 78072.

COMFORT, KENDALL CO., SACRED HEART (1949)
Mailing Address: P.O. Box 599, Comfort, 78013-0599. Tel: 830-995-3708; Email: sacredheart@hctc.net. 114 N. Hwy. 87, Comfort, 78013. Rev. Martin Garcia-Avila; Deacon David Burkart.
Office: 510 Broadway, Comfort, 78013.
Res.: 104 Daniel St., Comfort, 78013.
Tel: 830-995-3501.
Catechesis Religious Program—Students 158.

CONVERSE, BEXAR CO., ST. MONICA (1959)
Mailing Address: 501 North St., P.O. Box 1209, Converse, 78109. Revs. Alejandro del Bosque, L.C.; Mauricio Lopez, Parochial Vicar.
Res.: 8902 Willmon Way, 78239. Tel: 210-658-3816; Email: parish@saintmonicaconverse.net; Web: www.saintmonicaconverse.net.
School—St. Monica Catholic School, (Grades PreK-8), 515 North St., Converse, 78109.
Tel: 210-658-6701; Fax: 210-658-6945; Email: kgeyer@saintmonica.net; Email: office@saintmonica.net; Web: www.saintmonica.net. Mrs. Kristy Geyer, Prin. Lay Teachers 22; Students 312.
Catechesis Religious Program—Tel: 210-658-7920. Janice Van Slambrouck, D.R.E. Students 456.

D'HANIS, MEDINA CO., HOLY CROSS (1847) [CEM]
P.O. Box 426, D'Hanis, 78850. Email: holycrossdhanis@gmail.com; Web: holycross-dhanis.org. 310 FM 2200 S., D'Hanis, 78850.
Tel: 830-363-7269. Rev. Anthony Bonela.
Mission—Immaculate Heart of Mary, 213 County Rd. 743, Yancey, Medina Co. 78886.

DEL RIO, VAL VERDE CO.
1—ST. JOSEPH (1927) [CEM]
510 Wernett St., P.O. Box 1429, Del Rio, 78841-1429.
Tel: 830-775-4753; Fax: 830-774-7128; Email: dalilah@stjosephdelrio.com; Web: www.stjosephdelrio.com. Revs. Jaime Paniagua; Sady Nelson Santana, Parochial Vicar; Deacons Efrain Santana; Raymundo Mendoza; Manuel R. Limones; Klaus Wilheim; Marco Escobar; Emiliano Pina.
Catechesis Religious Program—Tel: 830-775-5200. Esther G. Cardenas, D.R.E.; Louis Rios, Coord.; Mrs. Cristina Rios, Coord. Students 669.
2—OUR LADY OF GUADALUPE (1906) (Hispanic)
505 Cuellar St., Del Rio, 78840. Tel: 830-775-3713; Email: alogon20@outlook.com. Revs. Carlos Oscar Velazquez-Lazaro, M.N.M.; Martin Alonso Bustos Gonzalez, M.N.M.; Deacons Adrian Falcon; Juan Padilla.
Res.: 509 Garza St., Del Rio, 78840.
Catechesis Religious Program—Tel: 830-775-2178. Students 193.
Mission—San Juan Diego Chapel, 523 Jeffery Dr., V V Park Estates, Del Rio, Valverde Co. 78840.
3—SACRED HEART (1895) [CEM]
P. O. Box 1503, Del Rio, 78841. Tel: 830-775-2143; Email: sacredheartcatholic@stx.rr.com. 307 E. Losoya St., Del Rio, 78840. Rev. Pius Ezeigbo; Deacons David B. Scarbo; Edgardo Amaro; Robert Sanchez.
Res.: 411 Spring St., P.O. Box 1503, Del Rio, 78841-1503.
School—Sacred Heart School, (Grades PreK-8), 209 E. Greenwood, Del Rio, 78840. Tel: 830-775-3274; Fax: 830-774-2836; Email: schooloffice@shsdelrio.org; Web: www.shsdelrio.org. Araceli Faz, Prin. Lay Teachers 16; Students 160.
Catechesis Religious Program—Students 201.
Mission—Mary, Queen of the Universe, Comstock, Valverde Co.

DEVINE, MEDINA CO., ST. JOSEPH'S (1897) [CEM]
108 S. Washington Dr., Devine, 78016.
Tel: 830-663-2244; Email: st-patrick@sbcglobal.net. Rev. Tu T. Nguyen.
Catechesis Religious Program—Students 202.
Missions—St. Augustine—Moore, Frio Co. 78057.
Our Lady of Mt. Carmel, Bigfoot, Frio Co. 78005.

DILLEY, FRIO CO., ST. JOSEPH'S (1899) (Hispanic)
114 E. Frio, P.O. Box N, Dilley, 78017.
Tel: 830-965-2080; Email: rubgar101@hotmail.com. Rev. Ruben Garcia, B.A., M.Div.
Catechesis Religious Program—Steve Lozano, D.R.E. Students 178.
Mission—St. Mary, Dilley, Frio Co.

ELMENDORF, BEXAR CO., ST. ANTHONY (1896) [CEM]
Mailing Address: 16505 Kilowatt Rd., P.O. Box 248, Elmendorf, 78112. Tel: 210-635-8539;
Tel: 210-635-8308; Fax: 210-635-8644; Email: stanthonysofc@gmail.com; Email: stanthonys635@gmail.com; Email: stanthonyspastor@gmail.com; Web: www.stanthonyelmendorf.com. Rev. Andrew Kafara, (Poland); Deacons Michael Vrzalik; Zafirin Moczygemba.
Catechesis Religious Program—Tel: 210-834-1482; Email: mary.jo.1967@gmail.com. Mary Jo Johnson, D.R.E. Students 129.
Mission—Our Lady of Perpetual Help, [CEM] Saspamco, Bexar Co.

FALLS CITY, KARNES CO., HOLY TRINITY (1902) [CEM] (Polish)
Mailing Address: Box 158, Falls City, 78113.
Tel: 830-254-3539; Fax: 830-254-3530; Email: holytrinityfc@sbcglobal.net. Rev. Grzegorz Sawicki, S.D.S., (Poland).

FLORESVILLE, WILSON CO., SACRED HEART (1882) [CEM]
1009 Trail St., Floresville, 78114. Tel: 830-393-6117; Email: church@churchsh.org; Web: www.churchsh.org. Rev. Jorge Campos-Covarrubias; Deacons Scott Donaho; Doroteo Chavarria; Ralph E. Guerra; Juan A. Bosquez.
School—Sacred Heart School, (Grades PreK-5), 1007 Trail St., Floresville, 78114. Tel: 830-393-2117; Fax: 830-393-6968; Email: hilary.reile@shsfloresville.org; Web: www.shsfloresville.org. Hilary Reile, Prin. Religious Teachers 1; Lay Teachers 16; Students 100.
Catechesis Religious Program—Email: flosacredheartchurch@gmail.com. Gracie Trevino, D.R.E. Students 245.

FREDERICKSBURG, GILLESPIE CO., ST. MARY'S (1846) [CEM] (German)
307 W. Main St., Fredericksburg, 78624-9523.
Tel: 830-997-9523; Email: info@stmarysmail.com; Web: church.stmarysfbg.com. Very Rev. John Nolan, V.F.; Rev. Jean Baptiste Magbia Zabusu, Parochial Vicar; Deacons Gregorio Martinez Jr.; Francisco De La Torre; Patrick Klein; Brian Anthony Lewis.
Res.: 309 W. San Antonio St., Fredericksburg, 78624. Email: lreeh@stmarysmail.com; Web: www.stmarysfbg.com.
Church: 304 W. San Antonio St., Fredericksburg, 78624.
School—St. Mary's School, (Grades K-8),
Tel: 830-997-3914; Email: lreeh@stmarysmail.com; Web: school.stmarysfbg.com. John Mein, Prin. Lay Teachers 21; Students 260.
Catechesis Religious Program—Email: athomas@stmarysmail.com. Students 565.
Mission—Our Lady of Guadalupe, Fredericksburg, Gillespie Co.

GONZALES, GONZALES CO., ST. JAMES (1885) [CEM]
417 N. College St., Gonzales, 78629.
Tel: 830-672-2945; Email: catholic@stx.rr.com; Web: ccgaw.org. Revs. Stanislaw Fiuk, (Poland); Michael E. Peinemann, Parochial Vicar; Deacons Alfonso Moreno; Terrence Brennan; John Klapuch.
Missions—Sacred Heart—426 St. John, Gonzales, Gonzales Co. 78629. Rev. Paul A. Raaz, (Retired).
St. Patrick, U.S. Hwy. 90 A, Waelder, Gonzales Co. 78959.
Stations—Texan Nursing and Rehab—Gonzales.
Hill Country Nursing and Rehab, Gonzales.

HARPER, GILLESPIE CO., ST. ANTHONY (1908) [CEM]
Mailing Address: P.O. Box 309, Harper, 78631.
Tel: 830-864-4026; Fax: 830-864-4379; Email: Stanthony1@windstream.net; Web: Stanthonyharper.org. Rev. Martin Garcia-Avila, Admin.; Deacon Curtis Klein.
Res.: 163 N. Third St., Harper, 78631.
Catechesis Religious Program—Students 49.

HELOTES, BEXAR CO., OUR LADY OF GUADALUPE (1942) [CEM]
13715 Riggs Rd., Helotes, 78023. Mailing Address: P.O. Box 639, Helotes, 78023. Tel: 210-695-8791; Email: olgmail@olghelotes.org; Email: mburns@olghelotes.org; Web: www.olghelotes.org. Very Rev. Msgr. Carlos Davalos, V.U.; Revs. Anthony Male, (India) Parochial Vicar; Danny Nyang'au, Parochial Vicar; Deacons Daniel D. Quaderer; William Thornberry; Leonard T. Cortinaz; Ernest G. Zepeda; Rodolfo Mendez Jr.; Kathy Tragos, Pastoral Assoc.
Catechesis Religious Program—Email: dpeaks@olghelotes.org. Danna Peaks-Sullivan, D.R.E.; Angela Quintanilla, Youth Min. (Middle School); Jason Keck, Youth Min. Students 494.

HOBSON, KARNES CO., ST. BONIFACE (1901) [CEM] (German—Polish)
358 CR 220, Hobson, 78117. Tel: 830-780-3559; Email: boniface@hughes.net. Rev. Andrzej Waszczenko, S.D.S., (Poland).
Catechesis Religious Program—Brenda Orszulak, D.R.E. Students 18.

HONDO, MEDINA CO., ST. JOHN THE EVANGELIST (1892) [CEM]
Mailing Address: 2102 Ave. J, Hondo, 78861.
Tel: 830-741-2236; Fax: 830-426-3339; Email: vpimentel@stjohnevangelist.com. Rev. Binoj Jose Elukkunnel, H.G.N., (India); Vangie Pimentel, Admin.
Catechesis Religious Program—Tel: 830-741-2284; Email: sfernandez@stjohnevangelist.org. Sylvia Fernandez, D.R.E. Students 420.

JOURDANTON, ATASCOSA CO., ST. MATTHEW'S (1912) [CEM]
Mailing Address: P.O. Box 670, Jourdanton, 78026.
Tel: 830-769-3687; Email: stmatthew@wireweb.net. 1608 Campbell Ave., Jourdanton, 78026. Rev. Kazimierz Oleksy, S.D.S., (Poland).
Catechesis Religious Program—Students 143.
Mission—St. Ignatius, 101 W. Ave. F, Christine, Atascosa Co. 78012.

KARNES CITY, KARNES CO., ST. CORNELIUS (1917) Rev. Stanislaw P. Marciniak.
Res.: 605 E. Calvert St., Karnes City, 78118.
Tel: 830-780-3947; Email: stcornelius3947@sbcglobal.net.
Catechesis Religious Program—Tel: 830-780-3949. Jimmy Lopez, C.R.E. Students 113.
Mission—St. Elizabeth, Fashing, Atascosa Co.

KENEDY, KARNES CO., OUR LADY QUEEN OF PEACE (1959) [CEM]
Mailing Address: P.O. Box 89, Kenedy, 78119.
Tel: 830-583-2417; Email: stanthonyscc@yahoo.com; Email: janssenshirl@yahoo.com. Rev. Norbert H. Herman, (Poland).
Res.: 605 Karnes St., Kenedy, 78119. Email: kenedyolqop@yahoo.com.
Catechesis Religious Program—Ms. Diana Aguirre Martinez, C.R.E. Students 90.

KERRVILLE, KERR CO., NOTRE DAME (1911)
Mailing Address: 909 Main St., Kerrville, 78028.
Tel: 830-257-5961; Email: frdavid@notredamechurch.cc; Web: www.notredamechurch.cc. Rev. David Wagner, Admin.; Deacons Alfredo Jimmy Bill Jr.; Raul M. Gutierrez; Juan A. Martinez; Sonny Kaufhold.
Res.: 959 Main St., Kerrville, 78028.
School—Notre Dame School, (Grades PreK-8), 907 Main St., Kerrville, 78028. Tel: 830-257-6707; Fax: 830-792-4370; Email: debbie.mossman@notredameschool.cc; Web: www.notredameschool.cc. Sandi Killo, Prin. Lay Teachers 19; Students 130.
Catechesis Religious Program—Tel: 830-896-4233. Students 268.

KIRBY, BEXAR CO., ST. JOAN OF ARC (1971)
2829 Ackermann Rd., 78219-2100. Tel: 210-661-5277; Email: sjoakirby@yahoo.com. Rev. Heliodoro Lucatero, Ph.D.; Deacons Robert Galan Jr.; Gilbert P. Rivera, (Retired); Wilfredo (Todd) Dapilmoto, (Retired).
Res.: 4906 Wheatland, 78219.
Catechesis Religious Program—Students 228.

KOSCIUSZKO, WILSON CO., ST. ANN'S (1898) [CEM] (Polish)
8161 FM 541-E, Stockdale, 78160-6554.
Tel: 830-745-2541; Fax: 830-745-2434; Email: stannskos@gmail.com; Web: www.stannskos.com. Rev. Damian Jaje, S.D.S., Admin.
Catechesis Religious Program—Students 28.

LA VERNIA, WILSON CO., ST. ANN (1917) [CEM]
14151 U.S. Hwy. 87 W., La Vernia, 78121.
Tel: 830-779-3131; Email: office@stannlv.org. Very Rev. Dennis Jarzombek, V.F.; Rev. Wanjiru Ndung'u, Parochial Vicar; Deacons Israel Bocanegra; Wesley Rist.
Catechesis Religious Program—Tel: 210-287-1745. Shannon Kosub, D.R.E. Students 453.

LACOSTE, MEDINA CO., OUR LADY OF GRACE (1911) [CEM]
15825 Bexar St, P.O. Box 39, LaCoste, 78039.
Tel: 830-985-3357; Email: olgrace@earthlink.net. Rev. Paul Cleary; Deacon Joseph C. Boland.
Catechesis Religious Program—Tel: 830-985-3355; Email: olgdre@earthlink.net. Linda B. Johnson, D.R.E. Students 302.
Mission—St. John Vianney, 12703 Cinco de Mayo, Bexar Co. 78252.

LOSOYA, BEXAR CO., EL CARMEN CATHOLIC CHURCH (1813) [CEM] (Hispanic) (Our Lady of Mt. Carmel)
18555 Leal Rd. (Losoya), 78221. Tel: 210-626-2333; Email: olomtcarmel@gmail.com; Email: frpuenteolomtcarmel@gmail.com. Rev. Jose Francisco Puente-Flores; Deacon Jose Hernandez.
Catechesis Religious Program—Tel: 210-482-0086. Rosa Nunez, D.R.E.; Maria Celia Aldrich, D.R.E. Students 178.

LYTLE, ATASCOSA CO., ST. ANDREW (1904) [CEM]
14831 Main St., Lytle, 78052. Very Rev. Varghese Antony, (India) V.F.
Catechesis Religious Program—Students 279.
Missions—St. John Bosco—500 5th St., Natalia, Medina Co. P.O. Box 326, Lytle, 78052.
Immaculate Conception, 800 Diaz St., P.O. Box 326, Coal Mine, Atascosa Co. 78052.

MACDONA, BEXAR CO., OUR LADY QUEEN OF HEAVEN

(1994) (Hispanic)
Mailing Address: P.O. Box 94, Macdona, 78054-0094. Tel: 210-622-3282; Email: tello_65@yahoo.com.mx. Rev. Oscar Tello-Curiel.
Res.: 11150 Macdona-LaCoste Rd., Atascosa, 78002. Email: OLQH11150@aol.com.
Catechesis Religious Program—Betty Arredondo, D.R.E. Students 159.

MARTINEZ, BEXAR CO., ST. JEROME (1925) [CEM]
7955 Real Rd., 78263-3003. Tel: 210-648-2694; Email: st.jerome@stjeromesatx.org. Rev. Scott Janysek.
Catechesis Religious Program—Email: dre@stjeromesatx.org. Kristin Rumfield, D.R.E.; Jessica Lubianski, Youth Min. Students 217.

NEW BRAUNFELS, COMAL CO.
1—HOLY FAMILY (1964)
245 S. Hidalgo, New Braunfels, 78130.
Tel: 830-609-5320; Email: holyfamily@satx.rr.com; Email: rfrancois@msf-america.org. Rev. Ralainirina Francois Rakotovoavy, M.S.F.
Catechesis Religious Program—Tel: 830-608-9615. Angie Kiesling, D.R.E. Students 386.
2—OUR LADY OF PERPETUAL HELP (1926)
138 W. Austin St., New Braunfels, 78130.
Tel: 830-625-3534; Email: olphnb1@att.net. Very Rev. Camillo Botello Jr., M.S.F., V.F.; Deacon Ralph Brock.
Catechesis Religious Program—Tel: 830-629-4506. Students 88.
Mission—St. John, 210 House St., New Braunfels, Comal Co. 78130.
3—SS. PETER AND PAUL (1845) [CEM 2]
386 N. Castell St., New Braunfels, 78130.
Tel: 830-625-4531; Fax: 830-606-5461; Email: church@sppnb.org; Web: sppnb.org. Revs. Carlos Oscar Velazquez-Lazaro, M.N.M.; Krzysztof Bytomski, Parochial Vicar; Deacons Fred Fey; Ben Wehman, (Retired); William Schroeder; Ernest Mendez, (Retired); Robert Gorman; Rusty W. Brandt.
School—SS. Peter and Paul School, (Grades PreK-8), 315 N. Seguin, Ste. 300, New Braunfels, 78130.
Tel: 830-625-1077; Fax: 830-606-6916; Email: jburas@sppnb.org. Janet Buras, Prin.; Rebecca Matschek, Librarian. Religious Teachers 2; Lay Teachers 31; Students 380.
Catechesis Religious Program—
Tel: 830-625-4531, Ext. 201; Email: billsmith@sppnb.org. Bill Smith, D.R.E. Students 1,335.
Mission—St. Joseph, Comal, Comal Co.. Email: frcarlos@sppnb.org.

NIXON, GONZALES CO., ST. JOSEPH'S (1915) [CEM]
207 S. Washington Ave., Nixon, 78140-2920.
Tel: 830-582-1127; Fax: 830-582-1108; Email: stjosephnixontx@yahoo.com. Rev. Kuriakose P. Ouseph, (India); Deacon John Moreno.
Catechesis Religious Program—Tel: 830-534-1136. Floencia Cisneros, D.R.E. Students 84.

PANNA MARIA, KARNES CO., IMMACULATE CONCEPTION OF THE BLESSED VIRGIN MARY (1854) [CEM] (Polish)
P.O. Box 9, Panna Maria, 78144. Tel: 830-780-2748; Email: pan1854@yahoo.com. 13879 N. FM 81, Panna Maria, 78144. Rev. Wieslaw Iwaniec.
Catechesis Religious Program—Tel: 361-649-6231; Email: glmoczy@agristar.net. Lisa Moczygemba, D.R.E. Students 25.
Mission—St. Helena, Helena, Karnes Co.

PEARSALL, FRIO CO., IMMACULATE HEART OF MARY (1891) [CEM] [JC]
422 W. Brazos, P.O. Box AK, Pearsall, 78061.
Tel: 830-334-4046; Email: ihm@prontonet.net; Web: ihmptx.org. Rev. Jesus Camacho; Deacons Marcus Salazar; Roberto Villarreal.
Catechesis Religious Program—Rebecca Ramirez, D.R.E. Students 270.

PLEASANTON, ATASCOSA CO.
1—ST. ANDREW (1913) [CEM] [JC3] (Hispanic)
626 Market St., Pleasanton, 78064-2747.
Tel: 830-569-3356; Email: standrewcc@sbcglobal.net. Very Rev. Prasanna Kumar Mese, (India) V.F., Admin.; Deacons Adam Garza; Bennie Garcia Jr.; Kurt G. Warnken.
Catechesis Religious Program—Deborah Shows, D.R.E. Students 340.
Mission—Sacred Heart, Campbell and St. Francis St., Campbellton, Atascosa Co. 78008.
2—ST. LUKE-LOIRE (1859)
3930 FM 536, Pleasanton, 78064. Tel: 830-393-6021; Email: stlukeloire@gmail.com. Rev. Thaddeus Tabak, S.D.S., (Poland).
Catechesis Religious Program—Danielle Pascarella, D.R.E. Students 50.
Mission—Our Lady of Guadalupe, [CEM] [JC2] 170 Hackberry St., Leming, Loire Co. 78050.

POTEET, ATASCOSA CO., ST. PHILIP BENIZI (1897) [CEM] (Hispanic)
P.O. Box 348, Poteet, 78065. Tel: 830-742-3796; Email: alelocicm1@aol.com. 274 Avenue H, Poteet, 78065. Rev. Albert Lelo, C.I.C.M.
Catechesis Religious Program—Rudy Gonzales, D.R.E. Students 262.

POTH, WILSON CO., BLESSED SACRAMENT (1910) [CEM]
Mailing Address: P.O. Box 339, Poth, 78147.
Tel: 830-484-3302; Email: bless@gvec.net. Rev. Grzegorz Szewczyk, S.D.S., (Poland); Deacons Alan Crosby; Michael Velasquez.
Res.: 488 W. Westmeyer, Poth, 78147.
Catechesis Religious Program—Tel: 830-484-3303. Rebecca Raabe, D.R.E. Students 253.

ROCKSPRINGS, EDWARDS CO., SACRED HEART OF MARY (1900) [JC] (Hispanic)
P.O. Box 887, Rocksprings, 78880. Tel: 830-682-2165 ; Fax: 830-682-6165; Email: sacredheartmary@swtexas.net. Very Rev. Adrian M. Adamik, V.F.
Missions—St. Mary Magdalen—311 E. Third St., Camp Wood, Real Co. 78833. Tel: 830-234-3366.
St. Raymond of Pennafort, 2nd St. and Mountain St., Leakey, Real Co. 78873. Tel: 830-279-5860. Deacon Ruben Navarro.

RUNGE, KARNES CO., ST. ANTHONY'S (1901) [CEM 2] (Polish)
Mailing Address: P.O. Box 188, Runge, 78151.
Tel: 830-239-4146; Email: stanthonyscc@yahoo.com. 809 N. Helena, Runge, 78151. Rev. Norbert H. Herman, (Poland).
Res.: 101 W. Arenoso St., Runge, 78151.
Catechesis Religious Program—Tel: 713-294-2815; Email: contreras.irene@yahoo.com. Irene Contreras, C.R.E. Students 50.

ST. HEDWIG, BEXAR CO., ANNUNCIATION OF THE BLESSED VIRGIN MARY (1855) [CEM] (Polish)
14011 FM 1346, P.O. Box 100, St. Hedwig, 78152.
Tel: 210-667-1232; Email: annunciationbvm@hotmail.com. Rev. Boleslaw Zadora, S.D.S., (Poland); Deacon Richard T. Coronado.
Catechesis Religious Program—Email: rappmund@cs.com. Deanna Sanchez, D.R.E. Students 110.

SABINAL, UVALDE CO., ST. PATRICK'S (1884) [CEM]
501 N. Orange St., Sabinal, 78881. Mailing Address: P.O. Box 117, Sabinal, 78881. Rev. Michael Ajewole, M.S.P.
Catechesis Religious Program—Students 22.
Missions—St. Joseph—Knippa, Uvalde Co.
St. Mary, Vanderpool, Bandera Co.

SCHERTZ, GUADALUPE CO., CHURCH OF THE GOOD SHEPHERD (1972)
Mailing Address: P.O. Box 929, Schertz, 78154.
Tel: 210-658-4350; Fax: 210-658-7051; Email: gsoffice@satx.rr.com; Web: www.goodshepherdschertz.com. 1065 E. Live Oak Rd., Schertz, 78154. Rev. Octavio A. Muguerza; Cathy Wilkes, Admin.; Deacons Harvey Balcer; Elmer Fernandez.
Catechesis Religious Program—Tel: 210-314-5735; Email: dregs@satx.rr.com. Ms. Marsha Whitener-Valdez, D.R.E. Students 227.
Mission—Immaculate Conception, 213 N. Barnett St., Marion, Guadalupe Co. 78124.

SEGUIN, GUADALUPE CO.
1—ST. JAMES (1873) [CEM]
510 S. Camp St., Seguin, 78155. Tel: 830-379-1796; Email: info@saintjamescc.org. Rev. Msgr. Dennis Darilek; Very Rev. Gregory J. Nevlud, V.F., Parochial Vicar.
School—St. James School, (Grades PreK-8), 507 S. Camp St., Seguin, 78155. Tel: 830-379-2878; Fax: 830-379-0047; Email: ccummins@sjcstx.org; Web: www.sjcstx.org. Dr. Cindy Cummins, Prin.; Shelly Marek, Librarian. Lay Teachers 18; Students 190.
Catechesis Religious Program—Tel: 830-379-7689. Sr. Cal Leopold, O.S.F., D.R.E.; Joey Gutierrez, Youth Min. Students 145.
2—OUR LADY OF GUADALUPE (1908) [CEM] (Hispanic)
409 W. Krezdorn, Seguin, 78155-4429.
Tel: 830-379-4338; Email: olgseg@satx.rr.com; Web: www.SeguinOLG.com. Revs. David Tonary, M.S.F., (Canada); Aloysius Irawan, MSF; Bro. Rolland Kapsner, M.S.F.; Deacons Nick L. Carrillo; Joe Flores.
Catechesis Religious Program—Tel: 830-379-2818; Email: dtonary1@satx.rr.com. Glenda Moreno, D.R.E. Students 435.
Mission—St. Joseph, 5093 Redwood Rd., Redwood, Guadalupe Co. 78666.

SELMA, BEXAR CO., OUR LADY OF PERPETUAL HELP (1897) [CEM] (German)
16075 N. Evans Rd., Selma, 78154-3824.
Tel: 210-651-6913; Fax: 210-651-5272; Email: info@olph.org. Revs. Jeffrey Pehl; Frank Garcia, Parochial Vicar; Deacons Bill Hartman; Louis Heimer; Barry Scheel; Jesse Mata; Kenneth Mamot; Annabelle Hernandez, Parish Admin.
Child Care—Child Development Center, Students 106.
School—Our Lady of Perpetual Help School, (Grades K-8), Tel: 210-651-6811, Ext. 124; Email: wohln@olphselma.org. Clergy 1; Lay Teachers 23; Students 379.
Catechesis Religious Program—Jaclyn Ruli, Rel. Coord.; Amy Rubio, Youth Min. Coord. Students 810.

SMILEY, GONZALES CO., ST. PHILIP BENIZI (1963) (Hispanic)
102 Morey, Smiley, 78159. 207 S. Washington Ave., Nixon, 78140. Tel: 830-582-1127; Fax: 830-582-1108; Email: stjosephnixontx@yahoo.com. Rev. Kuriakose P. Ouseph, (India); Deacon John J. Moreno.
Catechesis Religious Program—Tel: 830-534-1136. Floencia Cisneros, D.R.E. Students 31.

SOMERSET, BEXAR CO., ST. MARY'S (1920) [CEM] (Hispanic)
19711 N. Dixon Rd., Somerset, 78069. Email: stmarys.somerset.tx@gmail.com; Web: www.stmcstx.org. Rev. Alex Pereida; Deacon Robert Cruz.
Catechesis Religious Program—Mrs. Sylvia Cruz, D.R.E. Students 106.

SPRING BRANCH, COMAL CO. (HONEY CREEK), ST. JOSEPH - HONEY CREEK (1876) [CEM]
25781 Hwy. 46 W., Spring Branch, 78070-3613.
Tel: 830-980-2268; Email: suet@stjhc.church. Rev. Francis McHugh, (Ireland); Deacons Glendower Bliss III; Jesus Mireles; Michael Pawelek.
Catechesis Religious Program—Sue Torres, Dir. Faith Formation. Students 738.

STOCKDALE, WILSON CO., ST. MARY (1895) [CEM]
Box 535, Stockdale, 78160. Tel: 830-996-3415; Email: stmarys@gvec.net. 1201 W. St. Mary's St., Stockdale, 78160. Very Rev. Dennis Jarzombek, V.F.; Deacon Benjamin Gimenez Jr.
Catechesis Religious Program—Students 101.

STONEWALL, GILLESPIE CO., ST. FRANCIS XAVIER (1945) [CEM] (German—Hispanic)
400 St. Francis St., P.O. Box 209, Stonewall, 78671-3717. Tel: 830-644-2368; Fax: 830-644-2068; Email: stfrancisx@beecreek.net. Very Rev. John Nolan, V.F.; Rev. Jean Baptiste Magbia Zabusu, Parochial Vicar.
Catechesis Religious Program—Tel: 830-997-0783; Email: kdbaethge@gmail.com. Kim Baethge, D.R.E. Students 53.

UVALDE, UVALDE CO., SACRED HEART (1883) [CEM] (Hispanic)
408 Fort Clark St., Uvalde, 78801. Tel: 830-278-3448 ; Fax: 830-278-2835; Email: secretary_shc@att.net. Very Rev. Eduardo D. Morales, V.U.; Deacons Hector V. Garcia, (Retired); Kenneth Dirksen; Gilbert Salazar, (Retired); Daniel A. Ibarra; Federico Flores.
School—Sacred Heart School, (Grades PreK-6), 401 W. Leona St., Uvalde, 78801. Janice Estrada, Prin. Religious Teachers 1; Lay Teachers 7; Students 75.
Catechesis Religious Program—Tel: 830-278-4846; Email: cecilia.martz_shc@att.net. Mrs. Cecilia Martinez, D.R.E. Students 617.

VON ORMY, BEXAR CO.
1—ST. PETER THE FISHERMAN (1990) (Hispanic)
17534 N. State Hwy. 16, Von Ormy, 78073.
Tel: 830-276-4985; Email: peter.fisherman.cc@gmail.com. Rev. James M. Kotara; Deacon Richard Wells.
Catechesis Religious Program—Tel: 830-276-8778. Mary Cohrs, D.R.E. Students 90.
2—SACRED HEART (1935) (Hispanic)
13466 IH 35 S., P.O. Box 722, Von Ormy, 78073-0722. Tel: 210-622-3457; Email: sacredheart78073@hotmail.com. Rev. Oscar Tello-Curiel; Deacon Carlos Rodriguez.
Res.: 11150 Macdona-LaCoste Rd., Atascosa, 78002.
Catechesis Religious Program—Loretta Flores, D.R.E. Students 179.

KOREAN APOSTOLATE

BOERNE, KENDALL CO., KOREAN MARTYRS CATHOLIC CHURCH (1982) (Korean)
7655 Curres Creek, Boerne, 78015.
Tel: 210-698-3877; Email: KMCCSA.Sec@gmail.com; Web: www.KMCCSA.org. Rev. Chongman John the Baptist Lee.

OLD SPANISH MISSIONS

SAN ANTONIO, BEXAR CO., OLD SPANISH MISSIONS, (aka Las Misiones)
c/o Pastoral Center, 7711 Madonna, 78216.
Tel: 210-357-5601; Email: oldspanishmissions@archsa.org. Mailing Address: P.O. Box 7804, 78207. Rev. David Garcia, Dir.; Ms. Diana Aguirre Martinez, Dir.
Missions—Purisima Concepcion—807 Mission Rd., 78210. Rev. David Garcia, Admin.
San Francisco de la Espada, 10040 Espada Rd., 78214.
San Jose, 701 E. Pyron Rd., 78214.
San Juan Capistrano, 9101 Graf Rd., 78214.
Vacant

Chaplains of Public Institutions

SAN ANTONIO. *Audie Murphy VA Hospital*, 7400 Merton Minter Blvd., 78229. Tel: 210-617-5308. Vacant.
Baptist Memorial Hospital, 111 Dallas St., 78205. Tel: 210-222-8431. Mrs. Elizabeth Ramirez.

Brooke Army Medical Center, Tel: 210-916-1105; Tel: 210-916-2172; Fax: 210-916-1169.
Res.: 3851 Roger Brooke Blvd., Bldg. 3600, Fort Sam Houston, 78234.
Tel: 210-916-4141 (After 4:30pm & Weekends).
St. Luke's Baptist Hospital; University Hospital, 4502 Medical Dr., 78229. Tel: 210-680-2635 (Res.).
Methodist Hospital, 7700 Floyd Curl, 78229.
Tel: 210-692-4030. Rev. Marian Piekarczyk, S.D.S.
Nix Hospital, 414 Navarro, 78205. Sr. Stephanie Morales, F.M.I.
San Antonio State Hospital, 6711 S. New Braunfels, 78223. Tel: 210-532-8811. Rev. Paul Anekwe.
Santa Rosa Hospital System, 519 W. Houston, 78207. Tel: 210-704-2021. Rev. Roy Quiogue, C.I.C.M.
Southwest General Hospital, Tel: 210-921-2000. Deacon Leon Mueller.
KERRVILLE. *Veterans' Administration Hospital*, Kerrville. Tel: 830-896-2020. Sr. Jane McKenzie, O.S.F.

Special Assignment:
Revs.—
Foster, John Mary, M.D.M., P.O. Box 1759, New Braunfels, 78133. Tel: 830-629-5042
Hunt, Henry Clay III, Prison Min., 535 New Laredo Hwy., 78211
Raphel, Tomy, Hospital Min., 3107 N. St. Mary's St., 78212
Venegas, Dennis, Hospital Min., 223 E. Summit, 78212.

Graduate Studies:
Very Rev.—
Vallejo, Gilberto, V.F., Universidad Pontificia de México, CD de México, México.
Rev.—
Anguiano, Jesus, St. Mary's Seminary and University, Baltimore, MD.

Military Chaplains:
Revs.—
Eke, Rafael E., U.S. Army
Gonzalez, George G., Chap. Major, 4707 Winged Foot Way, Columbus, GA 31909-8006
Hernandez, Alfred Ricardo, Col. Catholic Chap., 9028 Privilege Point, Converse, 78109. Tel: 210-566-3523
Nee, Eugene O., PSC 50 Box 667, APO, AE 09494
Tellez, Jairo A., Major, U.S.A.F., Air Police CMR 480, Box 3029, APO, AE 09128.

On Leave:
Revs.—
Betancourt-Salazar, Cesar
Duran, Jorge
Gallegos, Valentine Jr.
Hernandez, Antonio X.
Kammerer, James
Lopez, Mauricio A., (Colombia)
Pavlicek, Edward A. Jr.
Sandoval, Luis
Seiwert, James K.

Retired:
Most Revs.—
Flanagan, Thomas J., D.D., (Retired), Tel: 210-826-7721
Pfeifer, Michael D., O.M.I., (Retired), 334 W. Kings Hwy., 78212. Tel: 210-736-1685
Yanta, John W., D.D., (Retired), 5015 Bayonne, 78228
Rev. Msgrs.—
Alfaro, Juan, (Retired), St. Matthews, 10703 Wurzbach Rd., 78230
Bily, Lambert S., #1401, (Retired)
Cashin, James, (Retired)
Cronin, Patrick, #301, (Retired)
Fater, Douglas, (Retired), 20110 Horizon Way, 78258. Tel: 210-490-6390
Flanagan, Patrick J., (Retired), 3843 Barrington #204A, 78217. Tel: 210-599-4900
Goertz, Alois J., (Retired), Padua Place Nursing Home, 80 Peter Baque Rd., 78209. Tel: 210-698-0175
Henke, James, (Retired), 11929 FM 340, Shiner, 77984
Hubertus, Albert, #1002, (Retired)
Marron, Patrick L., (Retired), P.O. Box 206, Fischer, 78623-9998
Martinez, Leonel, (Retired)
McKenna, Enda, #1301, (Retired)
O'Gorman, Michael B., (Retired), 226 Pinewood, 78216. Tel: 210-829-5068
Palmer, Thomas, (Retired), Padua Place, 80 Peter Baque Rd., 78209. Tel: 210-826-7721
Wagner, John A., #202, (Retired)
Wesselsky, Emil J., #1201, (Retired)
Revs.—
Barlow, James P., (Retired), 17 Carolwood Dr., 78213
Collins, William, M.S.C., (Retired), 123 W. Laurel St., 78212. Tel: 210-226-5514
Conway, James, (Retired), Casa de Padres Retirement Center, 8520 Cross Mountain Tr., #1201, 78255. Tel: 210-260-2482
Cummins, Anthony O., (Retired), P.O. Box 1736, Boerne, 78006. Tel: 830-230-5587
Dakin, Kenneth M., (Retired), P.O. Box 3026, Canyon Lake, 78133. Tel: 830-964-3816
de la Rose, Jose, (Retired), 4212 Medical Dr., #1608, 78229
DeGerolami, Michael, (Retired), 2420 McCullough #107, 78212
Galvin, James Gerard, (Scotland) (Retired), 1314 McKinley Ave., 78210
Heitkamp, Samuel, (Retired), 764 Fredericksburg Rd., New Braunfels, 78130-6014. Tel: 830-632-5490
Johnston, Robert F., (Retired), 837 Village Sq., Palm Springs, CA 92262. Tel: 760-322-3236
Makothakat, John M., Ph.D., S.T.D., J.C.D., (Retired), 285 Oblate Dr., 78216. Tel: 210-341-1366
Maurer, Carl R., #402, (Retired)
McKenna, Peter, (Retired), 1 7 Jocleyn, Dundalk, Ireland A91DH
Ochoa, Einer, (Retired), 5825 Elmwood Rd., San Bernardino, CA 92401-3201
Pena, Richard, (Retired), 1614 W. Houston St., 78207
Raaz, Paul A., (Retired), 1804 CR 355, Shiner, 77984
Schuster, Raymond, (Retired), 231 W. Commerce St., 78205. Tel: 210-227-1297
Sieczynski, Jerzy, (Retired), 202 Carter St., 78207
Stiles, Wallis J., V.F., (Retired), Padua Place, 80 Peter Baque Rd., 78209
Villanueva, Jose Antonio, (Retired), Casa de Padres, 8520 Cross Mountain Tr., #202, 78255. Tel: 210-698-0175
Wiera, Stefan, Ph.D., (Retired), 13003 Southton Run, 78223. Carolan, Emmet, 1402.

Permanent Deacons:
Abat, Jacques, (Retired), St. Monica, San Antonio
Adam, Raul, (Retired), St. Mark the Evangelist, San Antonio
Alcala, Jesse, St. James, San Antonio
Archer, Wayne, St. Dominic, San Antonio
Arismendez, Agustin, St. Paul, San Antonio
Arredondo, Luis L., St. Bonaventure, San Antonio
Avila, Joe, Our Lady of Guadalupe, San Antonio
Bader, James W., St. Mary Magdalen, Brackettville
Balcer, Harvey J., Good Shepherd, Schertz
Benage, John Paul, St. Peter Prince of the Apostles, San Antonio
Benavides, Myron, St. Philip of Jesus, San Antonio
Bernal, Louis P., St. Louis, Castroville
Bill, Alfredo P. Jr., Notre Dame, Kerrville
Billimek, Thomas E., St. Brigid, San Antonio
Bliss, Glendower III, St. Joseph, Honey Creek
Bocanegra, Israel, St. Ann, La Vernia
Boland, Joseph C., Our Lady of Grace, La Coste
Borrego, Joe T., St. Anthony of Padua, San Antonio
Bosquez, Juan A., Sacred Heart, Floresville
Bradley, Donald V., St. Brigid, San Antonio
Brandt, Rusty W., Sts. Peter & Paul, New Braunfels
Bravo, Ernesto G., (Retired), St. Peter the Fisherman, Von Ormy
Brennan, Terrence, St. James, Gonzales
Brisiel, Lawrence C. Sr., St. Mark Evangelist, San Antonio
Brock, Ralph, Our Lady of Perpetual Help, New Braunfels
Burkart, David, Sacred Heart, Comfort
Caldwell, Robert M. Jr., St. Leo, San Antonio
Campa, Gerard, St. Anthony Mary Claret, San Antonio
Campos, Fred Jr., St. Gregory the Great, San Antonio
Cantu, Guadalupe, Our Lady Queen of Peace, Kenedy
Carrillo, Nick L., Our Lady of Guadalupe, Seguin
Cepero, Victor, San Fernando, San Antonio
Cerna, Carlos R., St. Gregory the Great
Cervantes, Alfonso, Immaculate Heart of Mary, San Antonio
Charron, Paul, St. Thomas More, San Antonio
Cleary, Michael, Holy Trinity, San Antonio
Contreras, Lorenzo, Our Lady Queen of Heaven, Macdona
Coronado, Richard T., Annunciation of B.V.M., St. Hedwig
Correa, Robert G., Prince of Peace, San Antonio
Cortinaz, Leonard T., Our Lady of Guadalupe, Helotes, TX
Couch, Clinton A., Shrine of St. Padre Pio of Pietrelcina, San Antonio
Crosby, Alan, Blessed Sacrament, Poth
Cuellar, Pedro Luz, St. Matthew, San Antonio
De Hoyos, Richard, St. Peter Prince, San Antonio
De La Garza, Ricardo, Divine Providence, San Antonio
De La Portilla, Gilbert C., St. Philip of Jesus, San Antonio
De La Torre, Francisco, St. Mary's, Fredericksburg
De Leon, Joseph L., Ph.D., St. Henry, San Antonio
De Luna, Guadalupe, St. Joseph South Side, San Antonio
Delgado, Juan Jose, St. Patrick, San Antonio
Dirksen, Kenneth, Sacred Heart, Uvalde
Dooley, Sean W., St. Monica, Converse
Drumm, Michael Sr., St. Ann La Vernia, TX
Duggan, Dennis, St. Mark the Evangelist, San Antonio
Eichelberger, John B., Holy Trinity, San Antonio
Escamilla, Jose, St. Luke, San Antonio
Espinosa, Juan, St. Brigid, San Antonio
Falcon, Adrian, Our Lady of Guadalupe, Del Rio
Felan, Ruben, St. Stephen, San Antonio
Ferguson, Edward T., Diocese of Dallas
Fernandez, Elmer, Good Shepherd, Schertz
Festa, Eugene A., St. Francis of Assisi, San Antonio
Fey, Fred, Sts. Peter & Paul, New Braunfels
Flores, Federico, Sacred Heart, Uvalde
Fox, Thomas J., St. Matthew's, San Antonio
Galan, Robert Jr., St. Joan of Arc, Kirby
Gallardo, Frank, Our Lady of Grace, San Antonio
Gaona, Alfred J., St. Leonard, San Antonio
Garcia, Apolonio Eduardo, (Retired), St. Vincent de Paul, San Antonio
Garcia, Arturo, St. Lawrence, San Antonio
Garcia, Bennie, St. Andrew, Pleasanton
Garcia, Candelario, St. Patrick, San Antonio
Garcia, Hector, Sacred Heart, Uvalde
Garcia, Julio III, San Fernando Cathedral, San Antonio
Garcia, Victor, St. James, Seguin
Garza, Adam, St. Andrew, Pleasanton
Garza, Ernesto, St. Matthew, San Antonio
Garza, James, St. James, Seguin
Garza, Robert M., St. Luke, San Antonio
Gearhart, John W., St. Rose of Lima, San Antonio
Gonzales, Ramon Jr., St. Joseph S.S., San Antonio
Gonzalez, Gerald, St. Leo, San Antonio
Gonzalez, Richard, St. Luke, San Antonio
Gorman, Robert, Sts. Peter & Paul, New Braunfels
Gottardy, Kenneth, St. Padre Pio, San Antonio
Guerra, Ralph E., Sacred Heart, Floresville
Gustowski, Paul, St. Helena's, San Antonio
Gutierrez, Raul M., Notre Dame, Kerrville
Gutierrez, Trinidad, St. Alphonsus, San Antonio
Guzman, Alonzo, St. Matthew, San Antonio
Hall, Clifford R., St. Thomas, Canyon Lake
Hartman, William H., Our Lady of Perpetual Help, Selma
Heimer, Louis H., Our Lady of Perpetual Help, Selma
Hernandez, Elieser
Hernandez, Gilbert S., St. Mark the Evangelist, San Antonio
Hernandez, Jose D., Basilica of O.L. Mt. Carmel, San Antonio
Hewson, James H., St. Francis Assisi, San Antonio
Hinojosa, Reynaldo G. Sr., Holy Name, San Antonio
Hobbs, John R., St. Ann, San Antonio
Hoedebecke, Richard P., St. Louis, Castroville
Hoelscher, Wilbur L., St. Matthew's, San Antonio
Houle, Thomas W., St. Matthew, San Antonio
Huerta, Hipolito, St. Mark the Evangelist, San Antonio
Huizar, Nestor Jr., St. Lawrence, San Antonio
Ibarra, Daniel A., Sacred Heart, Uvalde
Ibarra, Robert Paiz, St. Leo the Great, San Antonio
Imburgia, Scott, St. Dominic, San Antonio
Jimenez, Edward G. Jr., St. Jerome, San Antonio
Jimenez, Raymond F., Mission Concepcion, San Antonio
Juarez, Ricardo, Prince of Peace, San Antonio
Kanter, Kevin, St. Padre Pio of Pietrelcina, San Antonio
Karam, Jack, St. Monica, Converse
Kaufold, Harold Sonny, Notre Dame, Kerrville
Kerr, Stephen, St. John Neumann, San Antonio
Klalpuch, John, St. James, Gonzales
Klein, Patrick, (Retired), St. Mary, Fredericksburg
Kozar, Jerome P., St. Anthony Mary Claret, San Antonio
Kusenberger, Robert, St. Peter Prince of Apostles, San Antonio
Kutschenreuter, Norman, St. Matthew's, San Antonio
Lafuente, Francisco, St. Margaret Mary, San Antonio
Lammons, Charles, St. Jerome, San Antonio
Lara, Rafael, St. Matthew, San Antonio
Ledesma, Hector Sr., St. Timothy, San Antonio

Leibrecht, Robert J., St. Thomas the Apostle, Canyon Lake
Lewis, Brian Anthony, St. Mary, Fredricksburg
Limones, Manuel R., St. Joseph, Del Rio
Lindsey, James L., Holy Name, San Antonio
Lira, Antonio, St. Rose of Lima, San Antonio
Lopez, Jose L., St. Gregory the Great, San Antonio
Lopez-Negroni, Rafael, St. Rose of Lima, San Antonio
Lozano, Arturo, St. Mary Magdalen, San Antonio
Lucio, Jesus Jr., St. Martin de Porres, San Antonio
Luther, J. Mark, St. Leo, San Antonio
Macias, C. Roger Jr., San Fernando, San Antonio
Maldonado, Gilbert M., St. Clare, San Antonio
Mamot, Kenneth, O.L. Perpetual Help, Selma
Marques, Steven J., St. Mark the Evangelist, San Antonio
Marquez, Carlos Jr., St. Thomas More, San Antonio
Marroquin, Joseph, San Fernando Cathedral
Martinez, Frank, Blessed Sacrament, San Antonio
Martinez, Gregorio Jr., St. Mary, Fredericksburg
Martinez, Jose Angel, Resurrection of the Lord, San Antonio
Martinez, Juan A., Notre Dame, Kerrville
Mata, Jesus Jr., Our Lady of Perpetual Help, Selma
Matteson, Michael, St. Peter the Apostle, Boerne
Maxwell, Donald Jr., Sts. Peter & Paul, New Braunfels
McCarthy, Timothy, Prince of Peace, San Antonio
McGarrity, John Patrick, Shrine of St. Padre Pio, San Antonio
McShane, Daniel T., St. Pius X, San Antonio
Mechler, Gerardo A., St. Margaret Mary, San Antonio
Mendez, Rodolfo Jr., O. L. Guadalupe, Helotes
Mendoza, Raymundo V., St. Joseph, Del Rio
Mireles, Jesus, St. Joseph Honey Creek, Spring Branch
Moczygemba, Zafirin, St. Margaret Mary, San Antonio
Moran, Ernest, St. James the Apostle, San Antonio
Moreno, Alfonso, Sacred Heart, Gonzales
Moreno, John J., St. Philip's, Smiley
Moreno, Jose F., Our Lady of Angels, San Antonio
Murphy, John, St. Helena, San Antonio
Navarro, Ruben W., St. Raymond Pennafort, Leakey
Nealis, Michael F., St. Matthew, San Antonio
Neville, Richard F. Jr., St. Padre Pio, San Antonio
Nichols, Jack Don, St. Luke, San Antonio
Nickel, Kenneth F., St. Peter the Apostle, Boerne
Nunez, Jesse, St. Henry, San Antonio
Ocampo, Jose L., St. Gerard, San Antonio
Ochiagha, John, St. Matthew, San Antonio
Olivares, Peter R., St. Leonard, San Antonio
Overbay, Gary, St. Raymond Pennafort, Leaky
Padilla, Juan R., O.L., Guadalupe, Del Rio
Pawelek, Michael, St. Joseph, Spring Branch
Perez, Denis F., Our Lady of Grace, San Antonio
Perez, Miguel Jr., St. Joseph, Devine
Perez, Oscar, Shrine of St. Padre Pio, San Antonio
Perry, Frank J. Chip, San Jose Mission, San Antonio
Portele, Michael A., St. Francis of Assisi, San Antonio
Quaderer, Daniel D., Our Lady of Guadalupe, Helotes
Rambaran, Cliff, Sacred Heart, Comfort
Ramirez, Albert, Our Lady of Angels, San Antonio
Rayburg, Paul M., St. Peter the Apostle, Boerne
Resendiz, Benito, St. Martin de Porres, San Antonio
Reyes, Arsenio Jr., Santo Nino de Cebu, San Antonio
Rist, Wesley Raymond, St. Ann, La Vernia
Rodriguez, Alberto R., St. Cecilia, San Antonio
Rodriguez, Antonio G., Basilica of the National Shrine of the Little Flower
Rodriguez, Carlos, Sacred Heart of Jesus, Von Ormy
Rodriguez, Jesus, St. John Berchmans, San Antonio
Rodriguez, Roy A., St. James the Apostle, San Antonio
Rodriguez, Santiago, San Jose Mission, San Antonio
Ruiz, Roberto R., Holy Name, San Antonio
Rutkowski, Carl, St. Stanislaus, Bandera
Salazar, George Sr., Resurrection of the Lord, San Antonio
Salazar, Gilberto, Sacred Heart, Uvalde
Salazar, Marcus, Immaculate Heart of Mary, Pearsall
Salinas, Alberto, San Juan DeLos Lagos, San Antonio
Salinas, Samuel Jr., St. Ann, San Antonio
Sanchez, Albert, St. Paul, San Antonio
Sandoval, Jose F., Holy Rosary, San Antonio
Santana, Efrain, St. Joseph, Del Rio
Santos, Jose A., St. Pius X, San Antonio
Scarbo, David B., Sacred Heart, Del Rio
Scheel, Barry Lee, Our Lady Perpetual Help, Selma
Schell, Vincent, St. Joseph (Downtown), San Antonio
Seguin, David R., Holy Trinity, San Antonio
Suniga, Jose A., Divine Providence, San Antonio
Tate, Timothy M. Sr., St. Thomas More, San Antonio
Thornberry, William, Our Lady of Guadalupe, Helotes
Torres, George R., St. Joseph, Devine
Torres, Joseph R., Holy Redeemer, San Antonio
Trujillo, Nicolas E., St. James, Seguin
Tucker, Thomas, St. John Neumann, San Antonio
Tucker, Timothy E., St. Benedict, San Antonio
Urteaga, Fermin, St. Jerome, Martinez
Vela, Oscar Jr., St. Matthew, San Antonio
Villalon, Thomas A., St. John Evangelist, San Antonio
Villanueva, Luis, St. Joseph, Devine
Villareal, Ricardo, Holy Spirit, San Antonio
Villarreal, Roberto, Immaculate Heart of Mary, Pearsall
Von Allmen, Christopher, St. Bonaventure, San Antonio
Weekley, Carl, St. Paul, San Antonio
Wells, Richard, St. Peter The Fisherman, Von Ormy
Wilkins, Warren A., Holy Spirit, San Antonio
Wittig, Evan, Holy Spirit, San Antonio
Wunderlich, George, San Jose y Miguel Mission, San Antonio
Ybarra, Hermengildo Rey, St. Leonard, San Antonio
Yzaguirre, Raul R., Holy Trinity, San Antonio
Zamora, David, St. Mary Magdalen, San Antonio
Zepeda, Ernest G., Our Lady of Guadalupe, Helotes.

INSTITUTIONS LOCATED IN DIOCESE

[A] SEMINARIES, ARCHDIOCESAN

SAN ANTONIO. *Assumption Seminary* aka Assumption-St. John's Seminary, 2600 W. Woodlawn Ave., 78228-5196. Tel: 210-734-5137; Fax: 210-734-2324; Email: assumptionseminary@archsa.org; Web: www.assumptionseminary.org. Very Rev. Jaime E. Robledo, P.S.S., Rector; Revs. Renato Lopez, P.S.S., Vice Rector, Formation; Servando Guerrero, Vice Rector, Admin.; Michael Davis, Devel. Dir.; Mr. Jose Castaneda, Business Mgr.; Revs. Luis Cornelli, P.S.S., Faculty; Anthony J. Pogorelc, P.S.S., Faculty; Marcos Ramos, O.P., Faculty; Sr. Dianne Heinrich, C.D.P., Faculty; Mr. Martin Martinez, Faculty; Revs. Nam J. Kim, P.S.S., Faculty; Vincent Bui, P.S.S., Faculty

The Seminary of the Assumption of the Blessed Virgin Mary-St. John of San Antonio, TX Religious Teachers 9; Lay Staff 2; Lay Teachers 1; Priests 8; Seminarians 71; Sisters 1.

Office of Diaconate Ministry and Formation, Pastoral Center, 2718 W. Woodlawn, 78228-5124. Tel: 210-734-2620; Fax: 210-734-1957; Email: mike.pawelek@archsa.org; Email: martha.cantu@archsa.org. Deacon Michael Pawelek, Dir. Clergy 337; Students 78.

[B] SEMINARIES, RELIGIOUS OR SCHOLASTICATES

SAN ANTONIO. *Blessed Mario Borzaga Formation Community* (Theology) 222 Oblate Dr., 78216. Tel: 210-248-9087; Email: rsalas@omiusa.org. Revs. Raul Salas, O.M.I., Supr.; Ronald Framboise, O.M.I., Assoc. Dir.; Raymond Mwangala, O.M.I., Assoc. Dir.; Revs. David Ullrich, O.M.I., Dir.; Jose Ponce, O.M.I., Dir.; Paul Selvaraj, O.M.I.; Hector Kalaluka. Missionary Oblates of Mary Immaculate, United States Province. Clergy 5; Religious Teachers 1; Priests 5; Students 14; Scholastic Brothers 14.

Congregation of Holy Cross - Formation Community (1989) Brother Charles Andersen Residence, 320 Brahan Blvd., 78215-1020. Tel: 210-843-9070; Email: bmwcsc@yahoo.com. Bro. Michael Winslow, C.S.C., Dir. Brothers 4; Religious Teachers 1; Students 1.

MSF Formation Community, 104 Cas Hills Dr., 78213. Tel: 210-344-9145; Fax: 210-344-9146; Email: paula.garza@archsa.org; Web: www.msf-america.org. Rev. Francois Rakotovoavy. Priests 1.

San Damiano Friary, Initial House of Formation, 1104 Kentucky Ave., 78201. Tel: 210-734-4962; Email: sandamianobooks@gmail.com. Revs. Gary W. Johnson, O.F.M.Conv., Guardian & Formation Dir.; Andrew Martinez, O.F.M.Conv., Formation Dir.; Friars Phillip Ley, O.F.M.Conv.; Timothy Unser, O.F.M.Conv.; Rev. Bryan Hajovsky, O.F.M. Conv., Chap.; Friar Peter Lee, O.F.M.Conv. Conventual Franciscan Friars. Religious Teachers 6; Professed 10; Students 12; Temporary Professed 8.

[C] COLLEGES AND UNIVERSITIES

SAN ANTONIO. *St. Mary's University of San Antonio, Texas* (1852) (Grades Bachelors-Doctorate), 1 Camino Santa Maria, Office of the President - Box 72, 78228-8572. Tel: 210-436-3722; Fax: 210-431-2226; Fax: 210-436-3325 (Alumni Relations); Email: tmengler@stmarytx.edu; Web: www.stmarytx.edu. Thomas Mengler, J.D., Pres.; Rosalind Alderman, Ph.D., Admin.; Rev. Timothy Eden, S.M., Admin.; Richard Kimbrough, Admin.; Aaron Tyler, Ph.D., Admin.; Tim Bessler, Ph.D., Dean of Students and Asst. Provost; Dr. Winston Erevelles, Ph.D., Dean School of Science, Engineering and Technology; Christopher Frost, Dean, Arts, Humanities & Social Sciences; Mr. Stephen Sheppard, J.D., J.S.D., Dean School of Law; Dr. Tanja Singh, D.B.A., Dean, Bill Greehey School of Business; Caroline Byrd, Interim Dir. Louis J. Blume Academic Library; Robert Hu, Ph.D., Dir. Law Library; Dr. Grace Walle, F.M.I., Chap. Law School; Revs. Conrad J. Kaczkowski, S.M., Ph.D., Prof., (Retired); George T. Montague, S.M., Prof.; John A. Leies, S.M., S.T.D.; W. Franz Schorp, S.M. Conducted by the Society of Mary.(Coed) Brothers 4; Religious Teachers 23; Lay Teachers 385; Priests 6; Sisters 1; Students 3,648.

The Mexican American Catholic College (1972) 3115 W. Ashby Pl., 78228-5104. Tel: 210-732-2156; Tel: 866-893-6222; Fax: 210-732-9072; Email: macc@maccsa.org; Web: www.maccsa.org. Arturo Chavez, Ph.D., Pres. & CEO; Rev. Len Brown, C.M.F., Vice Pres.; Very Rev. Lawrence J. Christian, E.V., Chm.; Ms. Alma Alvarado, Dean of Students; Ms. Laura Graham, Dir. Cont. Ed.; Clemencia Barrera, Dir. HR & Finance; Ms. Lodie Mueller, Coord. E.S.L.; Juanita Garcia, Librarian; Revs. Edward Owens, Assoc. Prof.; Benjamin Romero-Arrieta, C.M.F., Assoc. Prof. Religious Teachers 16; Lay Teachers 16; Religious 3; Students 388; Staff 25.

Oblate School of Theology (1903) (Grades Bachelors-Doctorate), (Coed) (Graduate Theology) 285 Oblate Dr., 78216-6693. Tel: 210-341-1366; Fax: 210-341-4519; Email: info@ost.edu; Web: www.ost.edu. Rev. Ronald Rolheiser, O.M.I., Ph. D., S.T.D., Pres.; Mr. Rene Espinosa, Exec.; Dr. Scott Woodward, D.Min., Dean, Vice Pres. Academic Affairs; John Marden, Admin.; Mr. Pedro Cantu, Dir. Physical Plant; K.T. Cockerell, Dir.; Victoria Luna, Dir.; Dr. Rose A. Marden, D.Min., Dir.; Brenda Reyna, Dir.; Noemy Colon, Registrar; Mat Martin, Archivist; Julia Hinojosa, Admin.; Laurence Gonzalez, Admin.; Sr. Deborah Fuchs, Spiritual Advisor. Conducted by the Missionary Oblates of Mary Immaculate. Priests 13; Sisters 8; Students 162; Lay Professors 10.

Faculty: Revs. Ken Hannon, O.M.I., Ph.D.; John M. Makothakat, Ph.D., S.T.D., J.C.D., (Retired); James Myers, P.S.S., Dir. Ministry to Ministers & Intl. Priests Prog.; Joseph LaBelle, O.M.I., S.T.D., Prof.; Robert E. Wright, O.M.I., Ph.D., Co-Dir. M.Div. Prog.; Wayne A. Cavalier, O.P., M.R.E., Ph. D., Dir. Min. Prog.; Bryan Silva, O.M.I., Psy.D.; Roger H. Keeler, (Canada) M.Th., J.C.D., Ph.D.; Cliff Knighten, M.Div., M.A., Dir. Spec. Prog.; Mrs. Bonnie Le Melle Abadie, Dir. Lay Ministry; Mrs. Rita Velasquez, Asst. Dir. Lay Ministry; Sisters Susan Pontz, S.S.C.M., Ed.D., IT Dir.; Addie Lorraine Walker, S.S.N.D., Ph.D., Prof.; Linda Bolinsky, D.Min., S.S.M.; Rev. John J. Markey, O.P., Dir.; Dr. Greg Zuschlag, Ph.D., Prof.; Renata Furst, Ph.D., Asst. Prof. Scripture & Spirituality; Sr. Linda Gibler, O.P., Assoc. Academic Dean; Maria Garcia, M.S., Library Dir.; Dr. Victor Carmona, Ph.D.; Rose Mary Lopez, Dir.; Steven Chase, Prof.; Rodolfo Luna, Prof.; Rev. Francis Santucci, O.M.I., S.T.D., Prof.

**Our Lady of the Lake University*, (Grades Bachelors-Doctorate), 411 S.W. 24th, 78207-4689. Tel: 210-434-6711; Fax: 210-431-4055; Email: iperez@ollusa.edu; Web: www.ollusa.edu. Diane E. Melby, Ed.D., Pres.; Gloria Urrabazo, Vice Pres. Mission & Ministry. Sponsored by Congregation of Divine Providence. Religious Teachers 2; Lay Teachers 208; Sisters 2; Students 3,212.

University of the Incarnate Word, (Grades Bachelors-Doctorate), 4301 Broadway, 78209. Tel: 210-829-6000; Fax: 210-829-3901; Email: douge@uiwtx.edu; Email: mlgarci2@uiwtx.edu; Web: www.uiw.edu. Thomas Evans, Pres.; Jakob Rinderknecht, Chm. Pastoral Institute; Dr. Kathleen Light, Ph.D., Provost; Donna Denise Staudt, Assoc. Provost; Dean, School of Ed.; Marisol Scheer, Registrar; Dr. Forrest Aven, Dean, HEB School of Business Admin.; Dr. Carlos Garcia, Dean, School of Math, Science & Engineering; Dr. Mary Hoke, Dean, School of Nursing & Health Professionals; David Maize, Dean; Vincent Porter, Dean, School of Extended Studies; Kevin B. Vichcales, Ph.D., Dean, Humanities, Arts, & Social Sciences Provost; Sharon Welkey, Dean, School of

Media & Design; Timothy Wingert, Interim Dean of Optometry; Annette Thompson, Dir. Human Resources; Elisabeth F. Villarreal, Dir. Campus Min.; Edith Cogdell, C.P.A., Comptroller; Margaret Garcia, Dir.; Sr. Kathleen Coughlin, C.C.V.I.; Douglas B. Endsley, M.B.A., C.P.A.; Marcos Fragoso; Dr. David Jurenovich, Ph.D.; Dr. Cyndi Wilson Porter. Brothers 1; Religious Teachers 2; Priests 1; Sisters 2; Students 10,226; Lay Faculty 760.

[D] HIGH SCHOOLS, ARCHDIOCESAN

SAN ANTONIO. *Antonian College Preparatory High School*, 6425 West Ave., 78213. Tel: 210-344-9265; Fax: 210-344-9267; Email: tpetersen@antonian.org; Web: www.antonian.org. Mr. Timothy Petersen, Prin.; Rev. Mark Clarke, C.M.F., Chap.; Maggie Hernandez, Librarian. (Coed) Lay Teachers 50; Priests 1; Students 721.

St. Gerard Catholic High School & Regional Middle School, (Grades 6-12), 521 S. New Braunfels Ave., 78203. Tel: 210-533-8061; Fax: 210-533-3697; Email: mmendez@stgerardsa.org; Email: srico@stgerardsa.org; Email: lmaltos@stgerardsa.org; Web: www.stgerardsa.org. Michelle Mendez, Prin. Religious Teachers 1; Lay Teachers 13; Sisters 1; Students 108.

NEW BRAUNFELS. *St. John Paul II Catholic High School*, 6720 FM 482, New Braunfels, 78132. Tel: 830-643-0802; Fax: 830-643-0806; Email: ailiff@johnpaul2chs.org; Web: www.johnpaul2chs.org. Andrew Iliff, Prin.; Sandee Phelan, Librarian. Religious Teachers 2; Lay Teachers 25; Students 220.

[E] HIGH SCHOOLS, REGIONAL

KERRVILLE. *Our Lady of the Hills Regional Catholic High School* (2002) 235 Peterson Farm Rd., Kerrville, 78028. Tel: 830-895-0501; Fax: 830-895-3470; Email: olh@ourladyofthehills.org; Web: www.ourladyofthehills.org. Mrs. Therese Schwarz, Prin.; Ann Branton, Librarian. Religious Teachers 2; Lay Teachers 15; Students 103.

[F] HIGH SCHOOLS, PRIVATE

SAN ANTONIO. *St. Anthony Catholic High School*, 3200 McCullough Ave., 78212-3099. Tel: 210-832-5600; Fax: 210-832-5615; Email: kvidaurr@uiwtx.edu; Web: www.sachs.org. Kristina Vidaurri, Prin.; Douglas B. Endsley, M.B.A., C.P.A. Lay Teachers 40; Students 300.

Central Catholic High School, 1403 N. St. Mary's St., 78215-1785. Tel: 210-225-6794; Fax: 210-227-9353; Email: pgarro@cchs-satx.org; Email: swalswick@cchs-satx.org; Web: www.cchs-satx.org. Paul Garro, Pres.; Stephen Walswick, Prin. Brothers 4; Religious Teachers 2; Lay Teachers 48; Priests 3; Students 605.

Healy Murphy Center, Inc., (Grades PreK-12), 618 Live Oak St., 78202. Tel: 210-223-2944; Fax: 210-224-1033; Email: dwatson@healymurphy.org; Web: www.healymurphy.org. Douglas J. Watson, Exec. Dir.; Stanton Lawrence, Prin. High school, GED, and child development center for youth in crisis. Lay Teachers 17; Nurses 1; Sisters 3; Students 400; Counselors 2; Childhood Development Department: Ages 6 wks - 5 yrs 110.

Holy Cross of San Antonio, (Grades 6-12), 426 N. San Felipe, 78228. Tel: 210-433-9395; Fax: 210-433-1666; Email: stanley.culotta@holycross-sa.org; Email: rene.escobedo@holycross-sa.org; Web: www.holycross-sa.org. Bro. Stanley Culotta, C.S.C., Pres.; Dr. Rene Escobedo, Prin. Brothers of Holy Cross. Brothers 4; Religious Teachers 1; Lay Teachers 17; Priests 1; Students 282.

Incarnate Word High School, 727 E. Hildebrand Ave., 78212-2598. Tel: 210-829-3102; Fax: 210-832-2140; Email: strilka@uiwtx.edu; Web: www.incarnatewordhs.org. David Udovich, Interim Prin.; Mary Ann delaGarza, Vice Prin.; Yanira Cruz, Librarian. Brothers 1; Lay Teachers 46; Sisters 2; Students 444.

Providence Catholic School, (Grades 6-12), 1215 N. St. Mary's St., 78215-1737. Tel: 210-224-6651; Fax: 210-224-6214; Email: agarcia@providencehs.net; Web: www.providencecatholicschool.net. Ms. Alicia Garcia, Prin.; Elsie Denoux, Vice Prin. Lay Teachers 31; Sisters 1; Students 256.

[G] ELEMENTARY SCHOOLS, ARCHDIOCESAN

SAN ANTONIO. *Rolling Hills Catholic School*, (Grades PreK-8), 21140 Gathering Oak, 78260. Tel: 210-497-0323; Fax: 210-497-5192; Email: frontoffice@rollinghillscatholic.org; Web: www.rollinghillscatholic.org. Mr. Jonathan Kiesler, Prin. Lay Teachers 16; Students 107.

[H] ELEMENTARY SCHOOLS, PRIVATE

SAN ANTONIO. *St. Anthony School*, (Grades PreK-8), 205 W. Huisache Ave., 78212. Tel: 210-732-8801; Fax: 210-732-5968; Email: pramirez@stanthonysa.org; Web: www.stanthonysa.org. Patricia Ramirez, Prin.; Rev. Martin J. Leopold, J.C.L.; Kathy Guerra, Librarian. Lay Teachers 31; Priests 1; Students 320.

St. John Bosco School (1944) (Grades K-8), 5630 W. Commerce St., 78237. Tel: 210-432-8011; Fax: 866-214-8083; Email: fmasuojbc@aol.com. Mrs. Roxanne LeBlanc, Prin.; Mrs. Rosa Martinez, Librarian. Institute of the Daughters of Mary Help of Christians (Salesian Sisters of St. John Bosco). Day School 3k- 8 Religious Teachers 4; Lay Teachers 17; Sisters 10; Students 272.

St. John Bosco Child Development Center, Tel: 210-432-1686; Fax: 866-214-8083. Mrs. Sandra Guerrero, Dir. Students 65; Staff 24.

Mount Sacred Heart School, Inc., (Grades K-8), 619 Mount Sacred Heart Rd., 78216. Tel: 210-342-6711 ; Fax: 210-342-4032; Email: vbeck@mountsacredheart.org; Web: www.mountsacredheart.com. Sharon Longoria, Prin. Lay Teachers 30; Sisters 2; Students 265.

PLEASANTON. *Our Lady of Grace Catholic School* dba Our Lady of Grace Catholic School-Pleasanton, (Grades PreK-5), 626 Market St., Pleasanton, 78064. Tel: 830-569-8073; Fax: 830-569-8065; Email: jgeyer@olgapleasanton.org; Web: www.olgcstx.org. Jeanette Geyer, Prin. Lay Teachers 8; Students 73; Staff 14.

[I] GENERAL HOSPITALS

SAN ANTONIO. *The Children's Hospital of San Antonio - Christus Health*, 333 N. Santa Rosa St., 78207. Tel: 210-321-8004; Tel: 210-704-4899; Email: dennis.gonzales@christushealth.org; Web: www.christussantarosa.org. Mailing Address: 100 N.E. Loop 410, Ste. 800, 78216. Dr. Charles Hankins, Pres.; Ms. Cris Daskevich, CEO; Dr. Dennis Gonzales, Regl. Vice Pres., Mission Integration. Owned and operated by Christus, Santa Rosa Health Care Corp. Licensed Beds 249; Tot Asst. Annually 165,761; Total Staff 1,200.

Christus Santa Rosa Health Care Corporation, 100 N.E. Loop 410, Ste. 800, 78216. Tel: 210-321-8004; Tel: 210-704-2739; Email: dennis.gonzales@christushealth.org; Web: www.christussantarosa.org. Dean Alexander, CEO; Dr. Dennis Gonzales, Regl. Vice Pres. Mission Integration; Michael Hyde, Dir.; Margaret Jones, Dir. Spiritual Care; Sr. Michele O'Brien, C.C.V.I., Dir. Health related activities Bed Capacity 739; Priests 5; Sisters 8; Tot Asst. Annually 500,000; Total Staff 3,400.

Christus Santa Rosa Hospital - Alamo Heights, 403 Treeline Park Dr., 78209. Mailing Address: 100 N.E. Loop 410, Ste. 800, 72816. Tel: 210-294-8001; Tel: 210-704-2739; Email: dennis.gonzales@christushealth.org. Dr. Dennis Gonzales, Regl. Vice Pres., Mission Integration; LaNell Scott, Admin. Bed Capacity 36; Tot Asst. Annually 6,029; Total Staff 132.

Christus Santa Rosa Hospital, Westover Hills Owned & operated by Christus Santa Rosa Health Care Corp. 11212 Hwy. 151, 78251. Mailing Address: 100 N.E. Loop 410, Ste. 800, 78216. Tel: 210-321-8004; Tel: 210-703-8988; Email: dennis.gonzales@christushealth.org; Web: www.christussantarosa.org. Dean Alexander, Pres.; Dr. Dennis Gonzales, Regl. Vice Pres., Mission Integration; Michael Hyde, Dir. Bed Capacity 150; Tot Asst. Annually 90,000; Total Staff 671.

Christus Santa Rosa Hospital - Medical Center, 2827 Babcock Rd., 78229. Tel: 210-321-8004; Tel: 210-705-6190; Email: dennis.gonzales@christushealth.org; Web: www.christussantarosa.org. Mailing Address: 100 N.E. Loop 410, Ste. 800, 78216. Dr. Ian Thompson, Pres.; Dr. Dennis Gonzales, Regl. Vice Pres., Mission Integration. Bed Capacity 172; Tot Asst. Annually 37,396; Total Staff 500.

NEW BRAUNFELS. *Christus Santa Rosa Hospital - New Braunfels*, 600 N. Union Ave., New Braunfels, 78130. Mailing Address: 100 N.E. Loop 410, Ste. 800, 78216. Tel: 210-321-8004; Tel: 830-606-2183; Email: dennis.gonzales@christushealth.org; Web: www.christussantarosa.org. Jim Wesson, Pres.; Dr. Dennis Gonzales, Regl. Vice Pres., Mission Integration. Owned and operated by Christus, Santa Rosa Health Care Corp. Bed Capacity 132; Tot Asst. Annually 75,072; Total Staff 389.

[J] PROTECTIVE INSTITUTIONS

SAN ANTONIO. *St. Peter & St. Joseph Children's Home* (1891) 919 Mission Rd., 78210. Tel: 210-533-1203; Fax: 210-533-6199; Email: ggonzalez@ccaosa.org; Web: www.stpjhome.org. Cecilia Santos, Sec. Bed Capacity 147; Staff 175; Total Assisted 1,153.

Seton Home, 1115 Mission Rd., 78210. Tel: 210-533-3504; Fax: 210-533-3467; Email: info@setonhomesa.org; Web: www.setonhomesa.org. Thelma Gutierrez, Exec. Bed Capacity 85; Tot Asst. Annually 238; Total Staff 113; Total Assisted 85.

Visitation House Ministries, 945 W. Huisache, 78201. Tel: 210-735-6910; Fax: 210-738-8794; Email: cynthia.bossard@amormeus.org; Web: www.visitationhouseministries.org. P.O. Box 12074, 78212. Sr. Yolanda Tarango, C.C.V.I., Dir. Operated by the Sisters of Charity of the Incarnate Word of San Antonio, TX.A nonprofit corporation chartered under the laws of the State of Texas; Provides a two year transitional housing program for homeless women and children and learning center for women. Bed Capacity 22; Tot Asst. Annually 75; Total Staff 9.

BOERNE. *Children's Inn*, 316 W. Highland Dr., Ste. 200, Boerne, 78006-2534. Email: children@gvtc.com. Sr. Kathleen Kean, S.S.J., Co-Dir. Provides foster care for children and young adults with special needs in a holistic setting. Religious Teachers 1; Nurses 1; Residents 5; Students 1; Total Assisted 7.

[K] DAY CARE CENTERS AND KINDERGARTENS

SAN ANTONIO. *St. Anthony Day Care Learning Center*, 1707 Centennial Blvd., 78211. Tel: 210-924-4443; Fax: 210-924-4469; Email: salc@satx.rr.com. Sisters Mary Ann Domagalski, M.S.S.A., Admin.; Lucelia Sanchez, M.S.S.A., Dir.

Organization name: Missionary Servants of St. Anthony Children 100; Religious Teachers 1; Lay Staff 14; Sisters 2; Students 75.

Blessed Sacrament Academy, (Grades Day Care-PreSchool), 1135 Mission Rd., 78210. Tel: 210-532-5363, Ext. 126; Fax: 210-532-2149; Email: okorenek@bsasa.org; Web: www.blessedsacramentacademysa.org. Sr. M. Odilia Korenek, I.W.B.S., Exec. Dir. & Pres.; Carol Silva, Dir. Religious Teachers 2; Students 105.

Blessed Sacrament Parents Academy, 1135 Mission Rd., 78210. Tel: 210-532-0894; Fax: 210-532-6698; Email: klozano@bsasa.org. Sr. M. Odilia Korenek, I.W.B.S., CEO; Katherine Lozano, Dir. Lay Teachers 3; Students 600; Support Staff 6.

Child Development Center, 1135 Mission Rd., 78210. Tel: 210-532-5363; Fax: 210-532-2149; Web: www.blessedsacramentacademysa.org. Carol Silva, Dir. Religious Teachers 1; Lay Teachers 14; Sisters of the Incarnate Word and Blessed Sacrament 3; Students 135.

Carmelite Learning Center aka Carmelite Sister DCJ, 2006 Martin Luther King Dr., 78203. Tel: 210-533-0651; Fax: 210-533-3910; Email: carmelitelearningcenter@gmail.com. Ms. Narlie Hebert, Prin. Attended from St. Gerard. Religious Teachers 2; Day Care 73; Lay Staff 16; Carmelite Sisters of the Divine Heart of Jesus 8; Students 75.

Immaculate Conception Kindergarten and Nursery, 2407 W. Travis St., 78207. Tel: 210-226-3934; Fax: 210-226-3934; Email: perpetualdaycare@att.net. Sr. Maria de Lourdes Quiroga, Dir. Religious Teachers 2; Lay Staff 10; Sisters 4; Students 51.

[L] HOMES FOR AGED

SAN ANTONIO. *Casa De Padres*, 8520 Cross Mountain Tr. #100, 78255. Tel: 210-698-0175; Fax: 210-698-5318; Email: casadepadres@gmail.com. Mrs. Tara Castro, Dir., Tel: 210-698-0175; Tel: 830-981-9192; Rev. Msgrs. Lambert S. Bily, (Retired), No. 1401; Patrick Cronin, (Retired), 8520 Cross Mountain Tr., #1402, 78255. No. 301; Albert Hubertus, (Retired), Tel: 210-698-8682. No. 1101; Enda McKenna, (Retired); John A. Wagner, (Retired), Tel: 210-698-1332. No. 202; Emil J. Wesselsky, (Retired), No. 1201; Revs. James Conway, (Retired), No. 1302; Carl R. Maurer, (Retired), 8520 Cross Mt. Tr., #402, 78255. No. 402; Jose Antonio Villanueva, (Retired), No. 202; Emmet Carolan, (Retired); Anthony Cummins, (Retired). Independent Living for Retired Priests of the San Antonio Archdiocese. Bed Capacity 18; Tot Asst. Annually 13; Staff 3. In Res. Very Rev. Msgr. Terence Nolan, J.C.L., Tel: 201-698-0349. No. 701.

St. Francis Nursing Home and Independent Living, 630 W. Woodlawn, 78212. Tel: 210-736-3177; Fax: 210-738-2221; Email: st.francis@sbcglobal.net. Sisters Helen Haladyna, S.O.L.S., Pres. of Corp.; Samuela Komperda, Admin.; Rev. William McNamara, Chap. Seraphic Sisters of Our Lady of Sorrows.Home for the Aged and Convalescents. Bed Capacity 143; Priests 1; Sisters 15; Total Staff 150.

Incarnate Word Retirement Community, 4707 Broadway, 78209. Tel: 210-829-7561; Fax: 210-828-0020; Email: Paul.Harrison@iwretire.org; Web: www.IwRetire.org. Paul Harrison, Exec. Dir. For lay persons also. Bed Capacity 295; Tot Asst. Annually 1,200; Total in Residence 315; Outreach Program 850; Staff 275.

Marianist Residence: Skilled Nursing, 520 Fordham Ln., 78228-4800.

Tel: 210-436-3771 (Nurses' Station); Fax: 210-433-6005; Email: mogradysm@gmail.com. Bros. Michael O'Grady, S.M., Dir.; James Jaeckle, S.M., Sub Dir., Health Care Oper.; Revs. Gerald Chinchar, In Res.; Bernard Lee, S.M., In Res.; John A. Leies, S.M., S.T.D. Home for Infirm Marianist Brothers and Priests. Bed Capacity 16; Priests 5; Religious 9; Total Staff 41; Total Assisted 37.

McCullough Hall Nursing Center, Inc. (1992) (Incorporated 2003) 603 S.W. 24th St., 78207-4696. Tel: 210-435-7711; Fax: 210-433-6600; Email: hdanklefs@mchall.org. Hilary Danklefs, Admin.; Sr. Mary Bordelon, C.D.P., Contact Person. Bed Capacity 51; Staff 49; Total Assisted 51.

Oblate Madonna Residence, 5722 Blanco Rd., 78216. Tel: 210-341-2350; Fax: 210-340-3732; Email: cpond@omiusa.org. Revs. Charles Banks, O.M.I., Supr.; Ronald Carignan, O.M.I.; John Collet, O.M.I.; Leo Dummer, O.M.I.; Jack Franko, O.M.I.; Joseph LaBelle, O.M.I., S.T.D.; Michael Levy, O.M.I.; Francis Montalbano, O.M.I.; Roberto Pena, O.M.I.; Cornelius Scanian, O.M.I.; Harry Schuckenbrock, O.M.I.; Richard Sheehan, O.M.I.; Edward Vrazel, O.M.I.; Robert Wright, O.M.I.; Gerald Brunet, O.M.I., (Retired); William Davis, O.M.I., (Retired); William E. Zapalac, O.M.I., (Retired); Bro. Valmond LeClerc, O.M.I.; Rev. James Miller, O.M.I. Missionary Oblates of Mary Immaculate. Home for retired Priests and Brothers. Bed Capacity 39; Brothers 1; Priests 25; Total Staff 36; Assisted Living 9.

Missionary Servants of St. Anthony dba Padua Place, 80 Peter Baque Rd., 78209-1805. Tel: 210-826-7721 ; Fax: 210-826-7791; Email: PP8061@sanantonio.twcbc.com. Ms. Mary Quintero, Dir.; Sr. Mary Ann Domagalski, M.S.S.A., Admin. Home for infirm and retired Priests and Brothers. Bed Capacity 17; Priests 20; Tot Asst. Annually 22; Bishops 2. In Res. Most Rev. Thomas J. Flanagan, D.D., V.G., (Retired); Rev. Msgrs. John Brennan, (Retired); Leonel Martinez, (Retired); Thomas Palmer, (Retired); Revs. Henry Heese, (Retired); Wallis J. Stiles, V.F., (Retired); James Wuerth, M.S.F.; Rev. Patrick O'Connor, M.S.C.; Rev. Msgrs. James Cashin, (Retired); Alois J. Goertz, (Retired); Arnold Anders; John A. Wagner, (Retired); Revs. James Beegan, M.S.F.; Simon Brzozowski, O.M.I.; Arthur Ockwood, M.S.F., (Retired).

KENEDY. *John Paul II Nursing Home*, 209 S. 3rd St., Kenedy, 78119. Tel: 830-583-9841; Fax: 830-583-9458; Email: johnpaul2nh@yahoo.com; Email: sragnesbochenek@gmail.com. Sr. Agnes Bochenek, S.O.L.S., Admin. Residents 50; Seraphic Sisters of Our Lady of Sorrows 9; Total Staff 55.

[M] MONASTERIES AND RESIDENCES OF PRIESTS AND BROTHERS

SAN ANTONIO. *Casa Maria Marianist Community*, St. Mary's University, One Camino Santa Maria, #18, 78228-8518. Tel: 210-436-3066; Fax: 210-431-4216; Email: msullivan@stmarytx.edu. Revs. Timothy Eden, S.M.; James Tobin, S.M.; Bros. Dennis Bautista, S.M., Tel: 210-436-3775; Michael Sullivan, S.M., Tel: 210-436-3258; Brian Zampier, S.M.

Casa San Juan Marianist Community, 1701 Alametos, 78201. Tel: 210-667-6751; Fax: 210-738-0698; Email: GMontague@stmarytx.edu. Rev. George T. Montague, S.M., Dir.

Central Catholic Marianist Community, 1403 N. St. Mary's St., 78215-1785. Tel: 210-225-1112; Fax: 210-227-9353; Email: j.mueller25@hotmail.com. Revs. James Mueller, S.M., Dir. of Religious Community; Gerald Haby, S.M., (Retired). Brothers 4; Priests 3.

De Mazenod House (Faculty Residence) 7707 Madonna Dr., 78216. Tel: 210-349-8572; Fax: 210-349-8572; Email: fsantucci@omiusa.org. Revs. Francis Santucci, O.M.I., S.T.D., Supr.; Raymond John Marek, O.M.I., Business Mgr.; Ken Hannon, O.M.I., Ph.D.; David Munoz, O.M.I.; Bryan Silva, O.M.I., Psy.D.; Warren Brown, O.M.I. *US Province of the Missionary Oblates of Mary Immaculate.* Priests 6.

Discalced Carmelite Fathers of San Antonio, 906 Kentucky Ave., 78201-6097. Tel: 210-735-9127, Ext. 100; Tel: 210-735-9126, Ext. 100; Fax: 210-738-0818; Email: scantu@littleflowerbasilica.org; Email: frluisbelmonteocd@littleflowerbasilica.org; Web: www.littleflowerbasilica.org. Revs. Luis G. Belmonte Luna, O.C.D., Supr.; Marion J. Bui, O.C.D., Vicar; Emmanuel Javert Nnadozie, O.C.D.; Bonaventure Sauer, O.C.D.; Henry Bordeaux, O.C.D. Priests 5; Professed 5.

Dominican Community of San Juan Macias aka San Juan Macias Community, 822 Chevy Chase Dr., 78209. Tel: 210-233-9772; Email: sjmpriiory@gmail.com; Email: waycav@aol.com. Revs. Wayne A. Cavalier, O.P., M.R.E., Ph.D., Supr.; John J. Markey, O.P., Prof.; Marcos Ramos, O.P., Prof.; Leobardo Almazan, O.P. Priests 4.

Holy Cross Community, 426 N. San Felipe St., 78228. Tel: 210-434-3801; Fax: 210-438-1068; Email: stanley.culotta@holycross-sa.org; Web: www.holycross-sa.org. Bro. Stanley Culotta, C.S.C., Dir. Brothers 2. *Bro. Charles Andersen Residence*, 320 Brahan Blvd., 78215. Tel: 210-223-9117; Email: croteau_roger@yahoo.com. Bro. Michael Winslow, C.S.C., Dir. Bed Capacity 6; Brothers 4; Priests 1; Tot Asst. Annually 5; Total Staff 5.

Holy Rosary Marianist Community, 159 Camino Santa Maria, 78228-4997. Cell: 314-497-3437; Email: cjohnson@sm-usa.org. Bros. Charles Johnson, S.M., Dir.; Esteban Reyes-Duran, Dir. Religious Educ.; Mark Motz, S.M., Vocation Dir.; Revs. Raymundo Dominguez; John Thompson.

Holy Trinity Fathers, 401 Squires Row, 78213. Tel: 210-781-4945; Email: thdymowski@gmail.com. Revs. Thomas Dymowski, O.SS.T; J. Edward Owens, O.SS.T., Member. Closer to a formation house.

Hospital Ministry House, 6111 Walking Gait, 78240. Tel: 210-437-0147; Email: nbrown16@satx.rr.com. Rev. Nicholas Brown, S.C.J., Chap.

Ligustrum Marianist Community, 253 W. Ligustrum Dr., 78228-4020. Tel: 210-433-9114; Email: rvilla4@stmarytx.edu; Email: rvela3@stmarytx.edu. Revs. Richard Villa, S.M., Dir.; Rudy Vela, S.M.; William J. Meyer, S.M., D.Min.; Bro. Thomas Suda, S.M. Priests 3.

Marianist Residence, St. Mary's University, 520 Fordham Ave., 78228-4800. Tel: 210-436-3745; Fax: 210-433-6099; Email: mogradysm@gmail.com. Bro. Michael O'Grady, S.M., Dir., Tel: 210-436-3745; Revs. Conrad J. Kaczkowski, S.M., Ph.D., Prof., (Retired); Gerald Chinchar, In Res.; Timothy Dwyer, S.M., In Res.; Bernard Lee, S.M., In Res.; H. James Bartlett, S.M.; J. Donald Cahill, S.M.; Anthony Jansen, S.M., Tel: 210-436-3777; John A. Leies, S.M., S.T.D., Tel: 210-436-3227; John J. Manahan, S.M.; Joseph G. Rasky, S.M.; W. Franz Schorp, S.M., Tel: 210-431-2259. Brothers 28; Priests 12.

Marianist Vocation Ministry, 159 Camino Santa Maria, 78228-4901. Tel: 210-436-3245; Email: cjohnson@sm-usa.org; Web: marianist.com/vocations. Bro. Michael O'Grady, S.M., Dir.

Missionaries of the Sacred Heart Sectional Headquarters of the Irish Province for California and Southern States. 123 W. Laurel St., 78212-4667. Tel: 210-226-5514; Fax: 210-226-5725; Email: laurelmsc@sbcglobal.net. Revs. Kevin Shanahan, M.S.C., Supr.; William Collins, M.S.C., (Retired); Michael Fitzgibbon, M.S.C.; James A. Harnan, M.S.C.; Jeremiah McCarthy, M.S.C.; Michael O'Brien, M.S.C.; Patrick O'Connor, M.S.C. *Religious Activities Office*, 123 W. Laurel, 78212. Tel: 210-226-5514; Email: bcol436690@aol.com. Rev. Bill Collins, Member.

Missionary Oblates of Mary Immaculate aka San Antonio USP Support Office, US Province Support Office, 327 Oblate Dr., 78216-6602. Tel: 210-349-1475; Fax: 210-349-7411; Email: inoyola@omiusa.org; Web: www.omiusa.org. Revs. Richard Hall, O.M.I., Supr.; James Chambers, O.M.I., Treas. US Province Support Office–liaison for Washington DC Provincial Office.*Oblate Vocation Office*, 5712 Blanco Rd., Bldg. 42, 78216-6602. Tel: 210-349-1475; Tel: 210-340-0036; Fax: 210-349-7411; Email: vocations@omiusa.org; Web: www.omiusa.org. Rev. Richard Hall, O.M.I., Southwest Area Vocation Dir. 302 Oblate Dr., 78216. Revs. James Chambers, O.M.I.; Ronald Rolheiser, O.M.I., Ph.D., S.T.D.

North American Redemptorist Theology Residence, Inc., 1523 Iowa St., 78203.

Oblate Benson Residence, 334 W. Kings Hwy., 78212. Tel: 210-370-3923; Email: rhall@omiusa.org. Revs. Richard Hall, O.M.I., Supr.; Pat Guidon, O.M.I., Dir.; Leopoldo G. Perez, O.M.I., S.T.D., M.Div.; John G. Castro, O.M.I.; David Uribe, O.M.I.; Thomas Ovalle, O.M.I., Tel: 210-732-8771. Missionary Oblates of Mary Immaculate - Southwest Area. Priests 6.

Presentation Brothers, 631 Oak Knoll Dr., 78228. Tel: 210-255-1412; Email: fpm1802@juno.com; Web: www.presentationbrothers.com. Bros. Francis Schafer, F.P.M., Provincial Supr.; Michael McGrath, F.P.M., Community Leader; Ralph Toodle, F.P.M., Vocation Dir.; James Needham, F.P.M.; Francis Sebo, F.P.M. Brothers 4.

The Redemptorists/San Antonio, 1617 Iowa St., 78203. Tel: 210-533-0161; Fax: 210-533-0558; Email: info@saintgerardchurch.org. 1523 Iowa St., 78203. Revs. James E. Shea, C.Ss.R., Supr., 1523 Iowa St., 78203; Alton Carr, C.Ss.R., 1523 Iowa St., 78203; Robert H. Lindsey, C.S.s.R.; Francis Han Pham, C.Ss.R., 1523 Iowa St., 78203; Robert A. Ruhnke, C.Ss.R., Fax: 210-534-1280; Bro. Charles Fucik, C.Ss.R. (Province of Denver).

San Damiano Friary, 1104 Kentucky Ave., 78201. Tel: 210-734-4962; Email: sandamianobooks@gmail.com. Revs. Gary W. Johnson, O.F.M.Conv., Guardian & Formation Dir.; Andrew Martinez, O.F.M.Conv., Formation Dir.; Friars Peter Lee, O.F.M.Conv.; Philip Ley, O.F.M.Conv.; Rev. Bryan Hajovsky, O.F.M. Conv., Chap.; Bro. Tim Unser, O.F.M.Conv., Librarian. Conventual Franciscan Friars.

Woodlawn Marianist Community, 3303 W. Woodlawn Ave., Marianist Community, 78228. Tel: 210-436-0182; Fax: 210-436-0188; Email: sdowning07@gmail.com. Revs. Sean Downing, Dir.; Lawrence Doersching, S.M.; Bro. Timothy Pieprzyca, S.M. Brothers 1; Priests 2.

FALLS CITY. *Salvatorian Fathers Community of Texas*, 211 W. Meyer St., P.O. Box 158, Falls City, 78113. Tel: 830-254-3539; Fax: 830-254-3530; Email: greg@sds.pl. Revs. Grzegorz Sawicki, S.D.S., (Poland) Supr.; Damian Jaje, S.D.S., (Poland); Josef Musiol, S.D.S., (Poland); Kazimierz Oleksy, S.D.S., (Poland); Marian Piekarczyk, S.D.S.; Grzegorz Szewczyk, S.D.S., (Poland); Thaddeus Tabak, S.D.S., (Poland); Andrzej Waszczenko, S.D.S., (Poland); Boleslaw Zadora, S.D.S., (Poland); Dariusz Ziebowicz, S.D.S., (Poland); Marcin Pawel Czyz, S.D.S.

[N] CONVENTS AND RESIDENCES FOR SISTERS

SAN ANTONIO. *Missionary Servants of St. Anthony*, 100 Peter Baque Rd., 78209-1805. Tel: 210-824-4553; Fax: 210-824-4554; Email: PBmssa29@sanantonio.twcbc.com. Sr. Mary Ann Domagalski, M.S.S.A., Supr. Motherhouse and Novitiate of the Missionary Servants of St. Anthony; St. Anthony Retreat Center; St. Anthony Learning Center; Padua Place.

Missionary Servants of St. Anthony Sisters 2.

Blessed Sacrament Convent, 227 Keller St., 78204. Tel: 210-223-5013; Fax: 210-444-0779; Tel: 210-433-9365; Cell: 361-548-5920. Sisters Patricia Rodriguez, H.M.S.S., Local Supr.; Lucia Sanchez; Maria Medina, Sec. Mercedarian Sisters of the Blessed Sacrament. Sisters 8.

Blessed Sacrament and Incarnate Word Convent, 1135 Mission Rd., 78210. Tel: 210-534-8005; Fax: 210-534-8005; Email: okorenek@bsasa.org. Sr. Stephanie Marie Martinez, I.W.B.S., Supr. Sisters of the Incarnate Word and Blessed Sacrament of Victoria, TX. Sisters 5.

St. Brigid's Convent, 5118 Loma Linda Dr., 78201. Tel: 210-733-0701; Tel: 210-738-1472; Fax: 210-785-2820; Email: sbc@brigidines.us; Web: www.brigidine.org.au. Sisters Teresa Carter, C.S.B., Co-Leader; Mary Teresa Cullen, C.S.B., Co-Leader; Margaret Doyle, C.S.B., Co-Leader. Area House.; Address matters connected with congregation to the Co-Leaders. Sisters 12.

Brigid's Place A day retreat center.

Carmelite Sisters of the Divine Heart of Jesus (DCJ), 2006 Martin Luther King Dr., 78203. Tel: 210-533-0651; Fax: 210-533-3910; Email: sister.barbara@yahoo.com. Sr. M. Barbara Leary, Supr. Carmelite Sisters of the Divine Heart of Jesus. Sisters 8.

Congregation of Divine Providence Generalate, 515 S.W. 24th St., 78207. Tel: 210-434-1866; Fax: 210-568-1050; Email: generalate@cdptexas.org; Web: www.cdptexas.org. Sisters Pearl Ceasar, Supr.; Mary Bordelon, C.D.P., Rel. Order Leader; Lourdes Leal, C.D.P., Rel. Order Leader; Anita Brenek, Rel. Order Leader; Patricia Regan, Treas.; Charlotte Kitowski, Archivist. Sisters 121.

Cordi-Marian Missionary Sisters, Cordi-Marian Villa, 11624 Culebra Rd. #501, 78253. Tel: 210-798-8220; Fax: 210-798-8225; Email: sr_roseann@yahoo.com; Web: cordimarian.org. Sr. Celina Martin, M.C.M., Local Supr. / Retreat Center; Rev. Virginio Vasquez, C.M.F., Chap. Convent, Provincial House, Retirement and Retreat Center. Sisters 20.

Cordi-Marian Missionary Sisters Convent Formation House (1921) 2902 Morales St., 78207. Tel: 210-433-5064; Fax: 210-433-5064; Email: mcalicia@aol.com. Sr. Alicia Macias, M.C.M., Supr. & Formation Provider. Sisters 3.

Daughters of Charity Residence, 7603 Somerset Rd., 78211. Tel: 210-927-2795; Email: denise.larock@doc.org; Web: daughtersofcharity.org. 3026 Golden Ave., 78211. Sr. Denise La Rock, D.C., Sister Servant. Daughters of Charity of St. Vincent de Paul, Province of St. Louis Sisters 5.

The Daughters of St. Paul Convent, 9318 Wind Dancer, 78251. Tel: 210-569-0500; Email: SanAntonio@paulinemedia.com. Sr. Maria Elizabeth Borobia, F.S.P., Supr. Sisters 3.

Eucharistic Franciscan Missionary Sisters, 558 Cumberland, 78204. Tel: 210-224-7993; Email:

lupevilla720@hotmail.com. Sr. Maria Guadalupe Villasenor, M.E.F., Supr. Sisters 2.

Hermanas Catequistas Guadalupanas Convent, 4110 S. Flores St., 78214. Tel: 210-532-9344; Fax: 210-532-9344; Email: guadalupanasregionaldelegation@yahoo.com. Sr. Maria Martha Ruiz, H.C.G., Supr. Sisters 11.

Hermanas Josefinas, 2622 W. Summit Ave., 78228. Tel: 210-737-0584; Fax: 210-737-0584; Email: coronadohj@hotmail.com. Sr. Crispina Paraguirre, Regl. Delegate. Sisters 2.

Casa Santa Maria de Guadalupe, 2622 W. Summit Ave., 78228. Tel: 210-737-0584; Email: coronadojh@hotmail.com. Christina Pannaguirre, Dir. Sisters 3.

Communidad de la Cesarita, 511 Shadwell, 78228. Tel: 210-737-0584; Email: coronadohj@hotmail.com. Sisters Maria Rivera, Supr.; Cristina Parraguerra, Asst. Sisters 9.

Casa San Jose (Retired Sisters) 402 John Adams Dr., 78228. Tel: 210-732-1973; Email: coronadohj@hotmail.com. Sr. Guadalupe Mondragon, Supr. Sisters 8.

Incarnate Word Generalate (1869) 4503 Broadway, 78209-6297. Tel: 210-828-2224; Fax: 210-828-9741; Email: carolyn.psencik@amormeus.org; Web: www.amormeus.org. Sr. Teresa Maya, C.C.V.I., Congregation Leader. General Administration of the Congregation of Sisters of Charity of the Incarnate Word. Sisters 270; Adult Baptisms (18 & Older) 276; Total in U.S. Province 140.

Headwaters at Incarnate Word, Inc., 4503 Broadway, 78209. Tel: 210-828-2224, Ext. 280; Fax: 210-828-9741; Email: pamela.ball@headwaters-iw.org; Web: www.headwaters-iw.org. Alex Antram, Exec. Dir.; Pamela Ball, Assoc. Dir. Sisters 1.

Women's Global Connection, 4503 Broadway, 78209. Tel: 210-828-2224, Ext. 297; Email: wgc.lisauribe@gmail.com; Email: wgc.tamarramencey@gmail.com; Email: wgc.mabuck@gmail.com; Email: wgc.nicolefoy@gmail.com; Web: www.womensglobalconnection.org. Lisa Uribe, Dir. Sisters 3.

Incarnate Word Retirement Community Inc., U.S. Province, 4707 Broadway, 78209-6215. Tel: 210-829-7561 (Retirement Center); Fax: 210-828-0020; Email: steve.fuller@iwretire.org; Web: www.iwretire.org. Mr. Steven Fuller, CEO; Alma Cosme, Dir. Community Rels.; Linda Williams, Admin. Extended Care; Bernie Prendergast, Asst. Coord. Extended Care. Sisters 68; Total in Residence 315.

Institute of the Daughters of Mary Help of Christians, Province of Mary Immaculate, 6019 Buena Vista St., 78237-1700. Tel: 210-432-0089; Tel: 210-432-0090; Fax: 210-432-4016; Email: sr.rruizfma@gmail.com; Web: www.salesiansisterswest.org. Sr. Rosann Ruiz, F.M.A., Prov. Salesian Sisters of St. John Bosco. Sisters 89.

St. James Convent, 402 Nunes, 78225. Tel: 210-533-9659; Fax: 210-924-0201; Email: tsironifma@gmail.com; Email: srdebwalk@gmail.com. Sr. Theresa Sironi, F.M.A., Supr. Daughters of Mary Help of Christians (Salesian Sisters of St. John Bosco). Sisters 4.

St. John Bosco Convent, 5630 W. Commerce St., 78237-1313. Tel: 210-432-8008; Fax: 866-214-8083; Email: fmasuojbc@stjohnbosco-satx.org. Sr. Martina Ponce, Supr. Daughters of Mary Help of Christians. Sisters 10.

St. Joseph's Convent - S.S.N.D., 2372 W. Southcross, 78211-1898. Tel: 210-923-2364; Fax: 210-923-2364; Email: dmsiebenmorgen@ssndcp.org. Sr. Dolores Marie Siebenmorgen, Coord. Sisters 6.

Marianist Sisters Residence, 235 W. Ligustrum Dr., 78228. Tel: 210-433-5501; Fax: 210-433-0300; Email: provincialfmiusa@gmail.com; Web: www.marianistsisters.org. Sisters Gretchen Trautman, F.M.I., Prov.; Lavon Kampf, F.M.I., Dir. of Sisters. Centralhouse of the Congregation of the Daughters of Mary Immaculate. Marianist Sisters, (Community Dayton, OH). Annunciation House, Kettering, OH. Sisters 13.

McCullough Hall Nursing Center, Inc., 603 S.W. 24th St., 78207-4696. Tel: 210-435-7711; Fax: 210-433-6600; Email: hdanklefs@mchall.org. Hilary Danklefs, Admin.; Sr. Mary Bordelon, C.D.P., Contact Person. Capacity 51; Sisters 33; Lay Persons 12; Staff 49; Total Assisted 51.

Missionary Catechists of Divine Providence Central House and Admin. Offices St. Andrew's Convent, 2318 Castroville Rd., 78237. Tel: 210-432-0113; Fax: 210-432-1709; Email: mainoffice@mcdp.org; Web: mcdp.org. Sisters Guadalupe Ramirez, M.C.D.P., Supr.; Mary John Trevino, M.C.D.P., Treas. Sisters 31.

Missionary Sisters of Our Lady of Perpetual Help (M.P.S.), 2822 Wade St., 78210. Tel: 210-532-3546; Email: garzamps@yahoo.com. Sr. Magdalena Noguez, M.P.S., Contact Person. Sisters 6.

Monastery of the Discalced Carmelite Nuns, 6301 Culebra Rd., 78238-4909. Tel: 210-680-1834; Fax: 210-680-3106; Email: carmelsat@yahoo.com; Web: www.carmelsanantonio.org. Mother Therese Leonard, O.C.D., Prioress. Sisters 8.

Our Lady of the Lake Convent Center, 603 S.W. 24th St., 78207. Tel: 210-434-1866; Fax: 210-431-9965; Email: sfllange@gmail.com. Sisters Frances Lorene Lange, C.D.P., Pastoral Min. / Coord.; Madeline Zimmerer, C.D.P., Pastoral Min. / Coord. Sisters of Divine Providence.Home for retired Sisters of Divine Providence. Sisters 123; Professed Sisters 121.

O.L.L. Convent Home for Retired Sisters of Divine Providence Sisters Frances Lorene Lange, C.D.P., Coord.; Madeline Zimmerer, C.D.P., Coord.

Presentation Province Center, 8931 Callaghan Rd., 78230. Tel: 210-979-8879; Email: sectypbvmus@gmail.com; Web: www.pbvmunion.org. P.O. Box 100785, 78201-8785. Sr. Joan Sullivan, P.B.V.M., Provincial of U.S. Province. Congregation: Union of Sisters of the Presentation of the Blessed Virgin Mary Sisters 1; Total in U.S. Province 78.

Presentation Sisters, 8931 Callaghan Rd., 78230-4570. Tel: 210-342-2503; Email: pbvmsat@mail.com; Web: www.pbvmunion.org. Sr. Consilio O'Keefe, P.B.V.M., Supr. Residence of the Community of the Union of the Sisters of the Presentation of the B.V.M. Sisters 9.

Presentation Sisters, 415 Arbor Pl., 78207. Tel: 210-223-4916; Email: pbvmsisters@yahoo.com; Web: www.pbvmunion.org. Sr. Sharon Altendorf, P.B.V.M., Supr. Congregation: Union of Sisters of the Presentation of the Blessed Virgin Mary Sisters 2.

Provincial Offices of the Sisters of the Sacred Heart of Jesus of St. Jacut, 11931 Radium St., 78216-2714. Tel: 210-344-7203; Fax: 210-341-0721; Email: nmknezek@hotmail.com. Sr. Cornelia M. Knezek, Prov. Sisters of the Sacred Heart of Jesus of St. Jacut Sisters 28.

Convent: St. Joseph Community, 1014 Spent Wing, 78213. Tel: 210-375-7248; Email: nmknezke@hotmail. Sr. Nell Marie Knezke, Supr. Sisters 3. *Convent*, 818 Firefly, 78216. Tel: 210-349-6689; Tel: 210-344-7203; Email: nmknezek@hotmail.com. Sr. Cornelia M. Knezek, Prov. Sisters 4.

Convent: Holy Spirit Convent, 10802 Silhouette Dr., 78216. Tel: 210-344-4777; Email: nmknezke@hotmail.com. Sr. Nell Marie Knezke, Supr. Sisters 6.

Convent: Casa Ste. Emile, 302 Harriet Dr., 78216. Tel: 210-822-9844; Email: nmknezek@hotmail.com. Sr. Nell Marie Knezek, Supr. Sisters 4.

Convent: Santa Maria Community, 10803 Silhouette Dr., 78216. 11931 Radium, 78216. Tel: 210-340-1872; Tel: 210-344-7203; Email: nmknezek@hotmail.com. Sr. Cornelia M. Knezek, Prov. Sisters 5.

Convent: Beth Rachamim Community, 1203 Viewridge, 78213. 11931 Radium, 78216. Tel: 210-308-0257; Tel: 210-344-7203; Email: nmknezek@hotmail.com. Sr. Cornelia M. Knezek, Prov. Sisters 3.

Religious of Mary Immaculate Convent, 719 Augusta St., 78215. Tel: 210-226-0025; Tel: 210-223-8163; Email: villamarmi@yahoo.com; Web: villamariaresidence.com. Sr. Monica Gomez, R.M.I., Local Supr. Religious of Mary Immaculate Sisters. Sisters 5.

School Sisters of Notre Dame, 3735 Twisted Oaks Dr., 78217. Tel: 210-435-3234; Cell: 210-454-3682; Email: sbmssnd@yahoo.com; Web: www.ssnd.org. Sisters Barbara Masch, S.S.N.D., Correspondent; Carla Lusch, S.S.N.D.; Judy Scheffler, Teacher. Sisters 3.

Seraphic Sisters of Our Lady of Sorrows Convent, 621 W. Woodlawn Ave., 78212. Tel: 210-734-3364; Email: sisters@seraphicsisters.org. Sr. Gabriela Rog, O.L.S., Supr. Sisters 5.

The Sisters of Perpetual Adoration Convent, 2403 W. Travis St., 78207. Tel: 210-228-0092; Fax: 210-226-3934; Email: sistersofperpetualadorationtx@gmail.com. Sr. Estela Garcia, Supr. Sisters 9.

Sisters of the Holy Spirit and Mary Immaculate, 300 Yucca St., 78203-2318. Tel: 210-533-5149; Fax: 210-533-3434; Email: holyspirit@shsp.org; Web: www.shsp.org. Sr. Geraldine Klein, S.H.Sp., Gen. Supr. Motherhouse of the Sisters of the Holy Spirit and Mary Immaculate. Sisters 67.

St. Teresa's Convent, 206 Beechwood, 78216. Tel: 210-532-7303; Email: clarice.suchy@gmail.com; Web: www.teresiansisters.org. Sr. Amelia Ibarra, S.T.J., Coord. Society of St. Teresa of Jesus 4.

Ursuline Residence, 515 S.W. 24th St., 78207. Tel: 210-454-2382; Email: sresh_2000@yahoo.com. Sr. Elizabeth Hatzenbuehler, O.S.U. Sisters 3.

BOERNE. *St. Scholastica Monastery* aka Benedictine Sisters (Congregation of Benedictine Sisters), 216 W. Highland, Boerne, 78006. Tel: 830-249-2645; Tel: 830-816-8504; Fax: 830-249-1365; Email: sahrosb@gvtc.com; Email: devcbs@yahoo.com; Web: www.boernebenedictines.org. Sr. Frances Briseno, O.S.B., Prioress. Benedictine Sisters, Monastery, and Novitiate.

Benedictine Sisters (Congregation of Benedictine Sisters) Sisters 15.

UVALDE. *Society of St. Teresa of Jesus* (Teresian Sisters) 466 Encino, Uvalde, 78801. Tel: 830-278-6724; Email: avilesstj@yahoo.com; Web: teresians.org. Sr. Dolores Aviles, S.T.J., Coord. Sisters 3.

[O] RETREAT HOUSES

SAN ANTONIO. *Oblate Renewal Center*, Mailing Address: 5700 Blanco Rd., 78216-6615. Tel: 210-349-4173; Fax: 210-349-4281; Email: orc@ost.edu; Web: www.ost.edu/oblate_renewal_center.htm. Mr. K.T. Cockrell, Dir. of Retreats & Events Svcs.; Sr. Deborah Fuchs, Spiritual Adviser / Care Svcs.

BOERNE. *Omega Retreat Center* (1982) 316 W. Highland Dr., Ste. 100, Boerne, 78006. Tel: 830-816-8470 (San Antonio); Tel: 830-249-3894 (Boerne); Email: finbmc@gmail.com; Web: www.benedictineministries.org. Karen Herrin, Business Mgr.

CASTROVILLE. *Moye Retreat Center*, 600 London St., Castroville, 78009. Tel: 830-931-2233; Email: dbippert@cdptexas.org; Email: moyecenter@cdptexas.org; Web: www.moyecenter.org. Donna Bippert, Coord.; Sr. Mary Bordelon, C.D.P., Contact Person. Under the direction of the Sisters of Divine Providence.Center for Retreats, Renewal, and Conferences. Sisters 1.

[P] CATHOLIC CHARITABLE ORGANIZATIONS AND CLINICS

SAN ANTONIO. *Catholic Charities, Archdiocese of San Antonio Inc.*, 202 W. French Pl., 78212. Tel: 210-222-1294; Email: afernandez@ccaosa.org; Web: www.ccaosa.org. Mr. J. Antonio Fernandez, CEO. Guadalupe Community Center, San Antonio Birth Doulas, Guadalupe Home, St. PJ's Children's Home, Seton Home, Family and Children Services, Counseling Services, Project Rachel, Refugee Services, Retired Senior Volunteer Program (RSVP), Foster Grandparent Program, Caritas Legal Services, Guardianship and Wills, Volunteer Income Tax Assistance (VITA) Tot Asst. Annually 260,000; Total Staff 179.

Administration, 202 W. French Pl., 78212. Tel: 210-222-1294; Fax: 210-227-0217; Email: info@ccaosa.org; Web: www.ccaosa.org. J. Antonio Fernandez, Pres. & CEO.

Caritas Legal Services, 110 Bandera Rd., 78228. Tel: 210-433-3256; Fax: 210-223-3980; Email: ehuron@ccaosa.org.

Catholic Charities Counseling Services, 231 W. Commerce, 78205. Tel: 210-377-1133; Fax: 210-377-1230; Email: lellenbogen@ccaosa.org; Web: ccaosa.org. Kari Stewart, Dir. See Curia Section - Department of Social & Community Services. Total Staff 5.

Guadalupe Community Center, 1801 W. Cesar Chavez Blvd., 78207. Tel: 210-226-6178; Fax: 210-226-9188; Email: lnemeth@ccaosa.org. Elizabeth Nemeth, Exec.

Guadalupe Home, 202 W. French Pl., 78212. Tel: 210-476-0707; Email: sseaney@ccaosa.org. Bed Capacity 11; Tot Asst. Annually 52; Total Staff 8.

Refugee Services, 202 W. French Pl., 78212. Tel: 210-222-1294; Fax: 210-242-3174; Email: pwalker@ccaosa.org. Paula Torisk, Dir.

San Antonio Birth Doulas, 4522 Fredericksburg Rd., #A-47, Balcones Heights, 78201. Tel: 210-222-0988; Email: sdeleon@ccaosa.org. Suzanne DeLeon, Exec.; Chevonne Davis, Doulas Coord. Tot Asst. Annually 475; Total Staff 3.

Daughters of Charity Services of San Antonio, 7607 Somerset Rd., 78211. Tel: 314-733-8000; Email: jimpicciche@ascension.org; Web: www.dcssa.org. Joseph R. Impicciche, Exec Vice Pres. Tot Asst. Annually 12,000; Total Staff 150.

This corporation operates centers at five locations:

DePaul Family Center, 7607 Somerset, 78211. Tel: 210-334-2300; Fax: 210-922-0332; Email: catalina.berry@dcssa.org. Catalina Berry, Dir. Sisters 2; Tot Asst. Annually 3,000; Total Staff 20.

El Carmen Wellness Center, 18555-1 Leal Rd., 78221. 7603 Somerset Rd., 78211. Tel: 210-626-1745; Email: catalina.berry@dcssa.org; Email: Irma.Vargas@doc.org; Web: www.dcssa.org. Sr. Irma Vargas, Contact Person. Total Staff 3.

La Mision Family Health Care, 19780 U.S. Hwy. 281 S., 78221. Tel: 210-626-0600;

Fax: 210-626-1174; Email: margarita.arroyo@dcssa.org; Email: anne.spears@dcssa.org; Web: www.dcssa.org. Veronica Segura, CEO. Tot Asst. Annually 12,000; Total Staff 25.

DePaul Children's Center, 3050 Golden Ave., 78211. Tel: 210-334-2311; Fax: 210-334-2344; Email: ellen.kron@doc.org. Sr. Ellen Kron, D.C., Exec. Children's Development.

DePaul - Wesley Children's Center, 1418 Fitch St., 78211. Tel: 210-334-2390; Fax: 210-927-4030; Email: ellen.kron@doc.org. Sr. Ellen Kron, D.C., Exec. Child Development Center.

[Q] FOUNDATIONS, ENDOWMENTS AND TRUSTS

SAN ANTONIO. *Casa de Padres Endowment Fund*, Mailing Address: 2718 W. Woodlawn, 78228. Tel: 210-734-2620; Fax: 210-734-0708; Email: ruben.hinojosa@archsa.org. Most Rev. Gustavo Garcia-Siller, M.Sp.S., D.D.

The Catholic Community Foundation for the Roman Catholic Church of the Archdiocese of San Antonio aka Catholic Community Foundation, 111 Barilla Pl., Ste. 101, 78209. Tel: 210-732-2157; Tel: 210-732-2153; Fax: 210-828-5826; Email: steve.oswald@ccftx.org; Web: www.ccftx.org. Stephen Oswald, CEO; Rachel Babcock, Contact Person.

Catholic Fraternity Fund, LLC (An affiliated entity of the Catholic Community Fund) 111 Barilla Pl., Ste. 101, 78209. Tel: 210-732-2157; Email: steve.oswald@ccftx.org; Web: www.catholicfund.us. Stephen Oswald, CEO.

Friends of Santa Rosa Foundation dba Friends of Christus Santa Rosa Foundation, 100 N.E. Loop 410, Ste. 706, 78216. Tel: 210-321-8004; Tel: 210-704-3349; Email: Michele.OBrien@amormeus.org; Web: www.friendsfoundation.org. John E. Bel, Pres.; Sr. Michele O'Brien, C.C.V.I., Dir.

Historical Centre Foundation (2000) 231 W. Commerce, 78205. Tel: 210-227-1297; Email: hcfed@sfcathedral.org; Web: historicalcentrefoundation.org. Mr. Louis Sanchez, Interim Exec.; Amelia G. Nieto; Very Rev. Victor Valdez, Rector.

Holy Spirit Sisters' Trust, 300 Yucca St., 78203-2318. Tel: 210-533-5149; Fax: 210-533-3434; Email: holyspirit@shsp.org. Sr. Geraldine Klein, S.H.Sp., Pres. Sisters of the Holy Spirit.

Mary Jane Ihle Clark Endowment Fund for Ministry to Persons with Disabilities, 2718 W. Woodlawn, 78228. Tel: 210-734-2620; Fax: 210-734-2774; Email: ruben.hinojosa@archsa.org. Most Rev. Gustavo Garcia-Siller, M.Sp.S., Ordianry.

National Foundation for Mexican-American Vocations, 2718 W. Woodlawn, 78228. Tel: 210-734-2620; Fax: 210-734-0231; Email: ruben.hinojosa@archsa.org; Web: www.archsa.org/vocations. Rev. Jonathan W. Felux, Vocation Office. A nonprofit organization to financially help Mexican American Seminarians.

Providence Trust, 515 S.W. 24th St., 78207. Tel: 210-434-1866; Fax: 210-434-6640; Email: ramonabezner@gmail.com. Sisters Ramona Bezner, C.D.P., Trustee; Diane Heinrich, C.D.P., Trustee; Anita Brenk, C.D.P., Trustee. Congregation of Divine Providence, Inc. Charitable Trust.

San Antonio Catholic Worker House of Hospitality, 626 Nolan St., 78202. Tel: 210-224-7736; Email: info@sa-catholicworker.org; Web: www.sa-catholicworker.org. Chris Plauche, Dir.

**Santa Rosa Children's Hospital Foundation* dba Children's Hospital of Santa Rosa, 100 N.E. Loop 410, Ste. 706, 78216. Tel: 210-704-2800; Tel: 210-704-3349; Email: Michele.OBrien@amormeus.org. John E. Bel, Pres.; Sr. Michele O'Brien, C.C.V.I., Dir.

Seton Home Endowment Fund, Mailing Address: 2718 W. Woodlawn, 78228. Tel: 210-734-2620; Fax: 210-734-2774; Email: ruben.hinojosa@archsa.org. Most Rev. Gustavo Garcia-Siller, M.Sp.S., D.D.

BOERNE. *Benedictine Sisters Charitable Trust One*, 216 W. Highland Dr., Boerne, 78006. Tel: 210-219-5514 ; Tel: 830-816-8504, Ext. 105; Fax: 210-348-6745; Email: snmika2010@gmail.com; Email: sahrosb@gvtc.com. Sr. Susan Mika, O.S.B., Trustee.

Benedictine Sisters Charitable Trust Two, 216 W. Highland, Boerne, 78006. Tel: 830-816-8504; Fax: 830-249-1365; Email: sahrosb@gvtc.com. Sr. Sylvia Ahr, O.S.B., Trustee.

HELOTES. *Virgen de Guadalupe Foundation*, 3308 Broadway, Ste. 401, 78209. P.O. Box 1728, Helotes, 78023. Tel: 830-388-3009; Email: adriancoronado@aol.com; Email: vgradio@aol.com; Web: www.VGR1380.com. Adrian Coronado, Pres.

[R] SHRINES

SAN ANTONIO. *Basilica of the National Shrine of the Little Flower*, 1715 N. Zarzamora, 78201. Tel: 210-735-9126; Fax: 210-735-1389; Email: sdehoyos@littleflowerbasilica.org; Email: scantu@littleflowerbasilica.org; Email: amigeon@littleflowerbasilica.org; Web: www.littleflowerbasilica.org. Mailing Address: 824 Kentucky Ave., 78201. Rev. Luis Belmonte-Luna, Rector; Susan Cantu, Exec.; Anna Migeon, Dir. This entity includes the National Shrine of the Little Flower Restoration Project.

Oblate Lourdes Grotto Shrine of the Southwest, Tepeyac de San Antonio, 5712 Blanco Rd., 78216. Revs. Saturnino Lajo, O.M.I., Ministries Dir., Spanish Services; Thomas Ovalle, O.M.I., Dir.

Our Lady of Czestochowa, Grotto Shrine and Convent, 138 Beethoven St., 78210. Tel: 210-337-8193 (Convent); Email: serzeznik@gmail.com; Web: www.seraphicsisters.org. Sr. Emilia Rzeznik, O.L.S., Supr. Seraphic Franciscan Sisters of Our Lady of Sorrows. Sisters 5.

[S] MISCELLANEOUS

SAN ANTONIO. **ACTS Missions*, 7711 Madonna Dr., 78216. Tel: 210-342-1077; Email: dalaniz@actsmissions.org; Web: www.actsmissions.org. Deborah Alaniz, Exec. Dir.

**The Alexander House Apostolate*, Mailing Address: P.O. Box 592107, 78259. Tel: 210-858-6195; Fax: 210-490-8869; Email: info@thealexanderhouse.org; Web: www.thealexanderhouse.org. Gregory Alexander, CEO; Julie Alexander, Co-Founder & Dir.

Archdiocesan Union of Holy Name Societies, 115 Springwood, 78216. Tel: 210-828-2675; Email: mpetriql@gmail.com. Marjorie Petri, Pres.

The Archdiocese of San Antonio Capital Campaign Inc., 2718 W. Woodlawn Ave., 78228. Tel: 210-734-1907; Email: julie.seguin@archsa.org; Web: www.ontheway-andale.org. Most Rev. Gustavo Garcia-Siller, M.Sp.S., D.D., Pres.; Rev. Martin J. Leopold, J.C.L., Vice Pres.

Brothers of the Beloved Disciple A private association of the faithful. 1701 Alametos, 78201. Tel: 210-667-6751; Fax: 210-738-0698; Email: GMontague@stmarytx.edu; Web: www.brothersofthebeloveddisciple.com. Revs. George T. Montague, S.M., Supr.; William H. Combs, B.B.D., B.B.D.; Robert E. Hogan, B.B.D., M.Div., M.A.; John Bentley, Member; Bros. Ruben Garza, Member; Sean Stilson, Member. Brothers 1; Priests 5.

Catholic Cemeteries of the Archdiocese of San Antonio, 746 Castroville Rd., 78237. Tel: 210-438-8134; Fax: 210-438-8128; Email: catherine.kramer@archsa.org. Catherine Kramer, Business Mgr.

Catholic Physicians Guild of San Antonio, 202 W. French Pl., 78212. Tel: 210-579-0716; Email: info@cathmedsa.org. Clark Kardys, Pres.

Christus Continuing Care dba Christus Homecare, 100 N.E. Loop 410, Ste. 800, 78216. Tel: 210-785-5200; Fax: 210-785-5490; Email: dean.alverson@ChristusHealth.org; Web: www.christushomecare.org. Dean Alverson, CEO. Bed Capacity 16; Tot Asst. Annually 3,470; Staff 15.

Christus Santa Rosa Family Health Center, 11130 Christus Hills, 78251. Mailing Address: 100 N.E. Loop 410, Ste. 800, 78216. Tel: 210-321-8004; Tel: 210-704-2739; Email: dennis.gonzales@christushealth.org; Web: www.christussantarosa.org. Dr. Dennis Gonzales, Regl. Vice Pres., Mission Integration; Dr. Jose R. Hinojosa, Dir. Family Health Ctr.

Cordi-Marian Education Center (2003) 2902 Morales St., 78207. Tel: 210-433-5064; Email: mcmalicia@aol.com. Sr. Alicia Macias, M.C.M., Supr.

CYO Athletics, 2718 W. Woodlawn Ave., 78228. Tel: 210-734-2620; Fax: 210-734-9112; Email: jason.alvarez@archsa.org; Web: www.archsa.org/cyo. Jason Alvarez, Dir.; Deacon Jose Hernandez, Assoc. Sports Coord. Yearly Youth Sports Participants 5,000.

Daughters of Mary Help Development Office aka Department of Mission Advancement, Daughters of Mary Help of Christians Office of Mission Advancement, 6019 Buena Vista St., 78237-1700. Tel: 210-431-4999; Fax: 210-431-0944; Email: sswdevelopment@sbcglobal.net; Web: salesiansisterswest.org. Sr. Bernadette Mota, F.M.A., Dir. Promotes the apostolic works of both the Daughters of Mary Help of Christians (Salesian Sisters) and VIDES-USA (Volunteers International for Development, Education, and Service).

Eucharistic Adoration of San Antonio, Inc., Mailing Address: P.O. Box 691006, 78269-1006. Tel: 210-558-8802; Fax: 512-366-9787; Email: adore24@aol.com; Email: CorcoranTexas@gmail.com; Email: sanctusangelicus@yahoo.com; Web: www.adore24.org. Mary Therese Corcoran, Pres. & Exec. Dir.

Federation of Catholic Parent Teacher Clubs of the Archdiocese of San Antonio, c/o Catholic Schools Office, 2718 W. Woodlawn, 78228. Tel: 210-734-2620; Web: pgonzaba@satx.rr.com; Web: www.archsa.org. Priscilla Gonzaba, Pres. Volunteer.

Friends of St. Clare, 2718 W. Woodlawn, 78228. Tel: 210-734-2620, Ext. 1103; Email: eloch@archsa.org. Hector M. Guzman Jr., Pres.

House of Mercy Gift Shop, Inc., 1201 Donaldson Ave., 78228. Tel: 210-736-0055, Ext. 101; Email: mdavila@saintpaulsa.org. Mary Davila, Business Mgr.

**La Promesa Foundation* aka Guadalupe Radio Network, 3308 Broadway, Ste. 401, 78209. Tel: 210-579-9844; Fax: 210-821-5052; Email: lenoswald@grnonline.com; Web: www.grnonline.com. Leonard Oswald, Pres.

Madonna Center, Inc., 1906 Castroville Rd., 78237. Tel: 210-432-2374; Fax: 210-432-2389; Email: info@madonnacentersa.org; Web: madonnacentersa.org. Roger Caballero, Dir. Family Strengthening Services, Casework, Early Head Start, Pre School and After School Care, Seniors Socialization and Wellness Programs. Emergency Food Pantry, Summer Education and Recreation Programs.

Marian Center of San Antonio, Mailing Address: P.O. Box 831001, 78283-1001. Tel: 210-225-6279; Fax: 210-225-0044; Email: mariancenterofsa@hotmail.com; Web: mariancenterofsa.com. Ms. Therese H. Palacios, Pres.

Marian Community of Reconciliation aka Fraternas Societies of Apostolic Life 2715 Marlborough Dr., 78230. Tel: 210-541-0635; Email: ppollack@fraternas.org. Patricia J. Pollack, Supr.

Mary Help Network (ADMA), Mary Help Network (ADMA), 6019 Buena Vista St., 78237. Tel: 210-432-0804; Fax: 210-436-7719; Email: srmponce@gmail.com; Web: salesiansisterswest.org. Sr. Martina Ponce, Dir.

St. Mary's Holdings, Inc., c/o St. Mary's University, 1 Camino Santa Maria, 78228. Tel: 210-436-3727; Fax: 210-431-4210; Email: pdebartolo@stmarytx.edu; Email: calonzo@stmarytx.edu. Mrs. Peggy DeBartolo, Vice Pres.

MCSP, Inc. dba Youth Sports, Inc., 714 E. Theo Ave., 78210. Tel: 210-477-8900; Fax: 210-477-8914; Email: info@mcsportspark.org. Mr. Erik Markus, Dir.

Merced Housing Texas, 212 W. Laurel St., 78212. Tel: 210-281-0234; Fax: 210-281-0238; Email: merced@mercedhousingtexas.org; Web: www.mercedhousingtexas.org. Susan R. Sheeran, Pres. Founded by a consortium of religious orders to provide quality, affordable, service enriched housing for the economically poor, to strengthen families and promote healthy communities.

St. Monica's Guild (1929) 7711 Robin Rest Dr., 78209. Tel: 210-657-1326. Mrs. Celeste Barron, Contact Person. A social, civic, and charitable group.

Oblate Missions, 323 Oblate Dr., 78216-6629. Tel: 210-736-1685, Ext. 141; Fax: 210-736-1314; Email: contact@oblatemissions.org; Web: www.oblatemissions.org. Revs. David Uribe, O.M.I., Exec.; Saturnino Lajo, O.M.I., Chap., Dir.; Arthur Flores, O.M.I., V.U., Dir. Clergy 3; Employees 37.

Pilgrim Center of Hope - Evangelization Ministry (1993) 7680 Joe Newton, 78251. Tel: 210-521-3377; Fax: 210-521-0288; Email: ministry@pilgrimcenterofhope.org; Web: www.pilgrimcenterofhope.org. Deacon Tom Fox, Dir.; Mrs. Mary Jane Fox, Co-Dir.

Presentation Ministry Center, 2003 Ruiz St., 78207. Tel: 210-663-6055; Email: pbvmcenter@yahoo.com. Mrs. Stacey Merkt, Dir. Administrators 1.

Project Rachel of San Antonio, 110 Bandera Rd., 78228. Tel: 210-342-4673; Email: rachel@anewchoice.org; Web: www.projectrachelsanantonio.org. Karla Quinones, Dir. Tot Asst. Annually 51; Total Staff 2; Total Assisted 350.

Religious of Mary Immaculate (Pontifical) Villa Maria, 719 Augusta St., 78215. Tel: 210-226-0025; Tel: 210-223-8163; Email: villamarmi@yahoo.com; Web: www.religiosasdemariainmaculada.org. Sr. Monica Gomez, R.M.I., Local Supr. Apostolic Work: Counseling & guidance of young women of good moral conduct of any race or religion. Girls 20; Sisters 5.

San Antonio Community Law Center, 322 W. Woodlawn Ave., 78212. 201 Gladiola Ln., 78213. Tel: 210-271-9595; Fax: 210-734-4410; Email: sacommunitylawcenter@netzero.net. Bro. William Dooling, C.S.C., Dir. Provides legal assistance to the working poor, children, and underserved.

San Antonio Inter-Community Finance Office aka SAIFO, 11931 Radium Dr., 78216. Tel: 210-341-8884; Fax: 210-341-0721; Email:

kmoylan@saifo.com. Kimberly Moylan, Dir. of Finance.

Servants of Jesus and Mary, S.A., 5734 Quail Canyon, 78249. Tel: 210-691-0684; Email: milaabellra@hotmail.com; Web: www.servantsofjesusandmary.ning.com. Milagros Abellera, Pres.

Socially Responsible Investment Coalition, 285 Oblate Dr., 78216. Tel: 210-344-6778; Email: afalkenberg@sric-south.org; Web: www.sric-south.org. Ms. Anna Falkenberg, Exec. Dir.

VIDES Volunteers International Development Education and Solidarity, 6019 Buena Vista St., 78237-1700. Tel: 210-373-9532; Fax: 210-435-1919; Email: director@vides.us; Web: www.vides.us. Sr. Mary Gloria Mar, F.M.A., Dir.

The World Apostolate of Fatima, 719 Wayside, 78213. Tel: 210-344-9810; Email: johndeliasatexas@att.net. Rev. Mauricio Lopez, Mod.

BOERNE. *Benedictine Ministries Corporation*, 316 W. Highland Dr., Boerne, 78006. Tel: 830-816-8470; Fax: 830-249-1365; Email: finbmc@gmail.com; Web: benedictineministries.org. Karen Herrin, Business Mgr.

INGRAM. *St. Peter Upon the Water, A Center For Spiritual Direction and Formation*, 234 Indian Creek Rd., Ingram, 78025. Tel: 830-367-5959; Fax: 830-367-3774; Email: michael.boulette@archsa.org. Most Rev. Michael J. Boulette, D.D., D.Min., V.G., Dir.

MOUNTAIN HOME. *Tecaboca - A Marianist Center For Spiritual Renewal*, 5045 Junction Hwy. 27, Mountain Home, 78058. Tel: 830-866-3425; Fax: 830-866-3781; Email: director@tecaboca.com; Web: www.tecaboca.com. Kay Tally-Foos, Exec. Dir. Operated by Marianist Province of the U.S. Summer Catholic Camps for boys, girls and families; year round retreats and school programs.

RELIGIOUS INSTITUTES OF MEN REPRESENTED IN THE ARCHDIOCESE

For further details refer to the corresponding bracketed number in the Religious Institutes of Men or Women section.

[0140]—*The Augustinians* (Prov. of Castile)—O.S.A.
[0200]—*Benedictine Monks*—O.S.B.
[0600]—*Brothers of the Congregation of Holy Cross*—C.S.C.
[0360]—*Claretian Missionaries* (Western Prov.)—C.M.F.
[]—*Congregation of Maronite Lebanese Missionaries*—M.L.M.
[0220]—*Congregation of the Blessed Sacrament*—S.S.S.
[1330]—*Congregation of the Mission*—C.M.
[0630]—*Congregation of the Missionaries of the Holy Family*—M.S.F.
[1130]—*Congregation of the Priests of the Sacred Heart*—S.C.J.
[0470]—*Capuchin Franciscan Friars*—O.F.M.Cap.
[0260]—*Discalced Carmelite Fathers*—O.C.D.
[0520]—*Franciscan Friars* (Sacred Heart Prov.)—O.F.M.
[0585]—*Heralds of the Good News* (India)—H.G.N.
[0690]—*Jesuit Fathers and Brothers* (New Orleans Prov.)—S.J.
[]—*Missionaries of the Nativity of Mary* (Mexico)—M.N.M.
[1110]—*Missionaries of the Sacred Heart*—M.S.C.
[]—*Missionaries of the Holy Spirit*—Ms.Sp.S.
[0854]—*Missionary Society of St. Paul of Nigeria*—M.S.P.
[0860]—*Missionhurst Congregation of the Immaculate Heart of Mary*—C.I.C.M.
[0910]—*Oblates of Mary Immaculate*—O.M.I.
[0480]—*Order of Friars Minor Conventual Franciscans*—O.F.M.Conv.
[0430]—*Order of Preachers (Dominican)* (New Orleans Prov.)—O.P.
[1310]—*Order of the Most Holy Trinity and of the Captives*—O.SS.T.
[]—*Presentation Brothers*—F.P.M.
[1070]—*Redemptorist Fathers*—C.Ss.R.
[0760]—*Society of Mary (Marianists)*—S.M.
[1290]—*Society of St. Sulpice*—P.S.S.
[1200]—*Society of the Divine Savior*—S.D.S.

RELIGIOUS INSTITUTES OF WOMEN REPRESENTED IN THE ARCHDIOCESE

[0100]—*Adorers of the Blood of Christ*—A.S.C.
[0230]—*Benedictine Sisters of the Pontifical Jurisdiction*—O.S.B.
[1810]—*Bernardine Sisters of the Third Order of St. Francis*—O.S.F.
[0360]—*Carmelite Sisters of the Divine Heart of Jesus*—D.C.J.
[]—*Catechetical Sisters of Arogyamatha*—C.S.A.
[]—*Congregation of Dinaservanasabaha - Servants of the Poor* (India)—D.S.S.
[1010]—*Congregation of Divine Providence of San Antonio, Texas*—C.D.P.
[0460]—*Congregation of Sisters of Charity of the Incarnate Word*—C.C.V.I.
[3735]—*Congregation of St. Brigid*—C.S.B.
[1170]—*Congregation of St. Felix of Cantalice (Felician Sisters)*—C.S.S.F.
[0870]—*Congregation of the Daughters of Mary Immaculate (Marianist Sisters)*—F.M.I.
[2200]—*Congregation of the Incarnate Word and Blessed Sacrament*—I.W.B.S.
[0725]—*Cordi-Marian Missionary Sisters*—M.C.M.
[0760]—*Daughters of Charity of St. Vincent de Paul*—D.C.
[0850]—*Daughters of Mary Help of Christians (Salesians)*—F.M.A.
[]—*Daughters of Mary Mother of Mercy*—D.M.M.M.
[0950]—*Daughters of St. Paul*—F.S.P.
[1070-03]—*Dominican Sinsinawa WI*—O.P.
[1070-19]—*Dominican Sisters*—O.P.
[1150]—*Eucharistic Franciscan Missionary Sisters*—M.E.F.
[1900]—*Hermanas Catequistas Guadalupanas*—H.C.G.
[1910]—*Hermanas Josefinas*—H.J.
[2590]—*Hermanas Mercedarias Del Santisimo Sacramento*—H.M.S.S.
[]—*Hijas del Espiritu Santo*—F.Sps.
[2470]—*Maryknoll*—M.M.
[]—*Misionarios Del Nino Jesus de la Salud*—M.N.J.S.
[]—*Mission of Divine Mercy*—M.D.M.
[2770]—*Missionaries of Jesus, Mary and Joseph*—M.J.M.J.
[2690]—*Missionary Catechists of Divine Providence, San Antonio, Texas*—M.C.D.P.
[2890]—*Missionary Servants of St. Anthony*—M.S.S.A.
[]—*Missionary Sisters of Mary Immaculate*—M.S.M.I.
[]—*Missionary Sisters of Our Lady of Perpetual Help*—M.P.S.
[0420]—*Order of Discalced Carmelite Nuns*—O.C.D.
[]—*Pax Christi Institute*—P.C.I.
[3460]—*Religious of Mary Immaculate*—R.M.I.
[2970]—*School Sisters of Notre Dame*—S.S.N.D.
[1690]—*School Sisters of the Third Order of St. Francis*—O.S.F.
[]—*Seraphic Franciscan Sisters of Our Lady of Sorrows*—O.L.S.
[]—*Sisters for Christian Community*—S.F.C.C.
[3195]—*Sisters of Perpetual Adoration*—A.P.G.
[3360]—*Sisters of Providence St. Mary of the Woods*—S.P.
[3780]—*Sisters of St. Cyril and Methodius*—S.S.C.M.
[1705]—*Sisters of St. Francis of Assisi of Milwaukee*—O.S.F.
[1570]—*Sisters of St. Francis of the Holy Family* (Dubuque, IA)—O.S.F.
[]—*Sisters of St. Joseph* (Philadelphia, PA)—S.S.J.
[2050]—*Sisters of the Holy Spirit and Mary Immaculate*—S.H.Sp.
[3320]—*Sisters of the Presentation of the B.V.M.*—P.B.V.M.
[3670]—*Sisters of the Sacred Heart of Jesus*—S.S.C.J.
[2150]—*Sisters Servants of the Immaculate Heart of Mary*—I.H.M.
[2160]—*Sisters Servants of the Immaculate Heart of Mary*—I.H.M.
[4020]—*Society of St. Theresa of Jesus*—S.T.J.
[4110]—*Ursuline Nuns (Roman Union)*—O.S.U.

ARCHDIOCESAN CEMETERIES

SAN ANTONIO. *Holy Cross*, 17501 Nacogdoches, 78266. Tel: 210-651-6011; Fax: 210-651-5241; Email: Teresa.Gariepy@archsa.org. Teresa Gariepy, Business Mgr.

San Fernando No. 1, 1100 S. Colorado, 78207. Tel: 210-432-2303; Fax: 210-432-3254; Email: Richard.Corpus@archsa.org. Mailing Address: 746 Castroville Rd., 78237. Richard Corpus, Business Mgr.

San Fernando No. 2, 746 Castroville Rd., 78237. Tel: 210-432-2303; Fax: 210-432-3254; Email: Richard.Corpus@archsa.org. Richard Corpus, Business Mgr.

San Fernando No. 3 (Roselawn), 1735 Cupples Rd., 78226. Tel: 210-432-2364; Fax: 210-432-4346; Email: ismael.galvan@archsa.org. Mailing Address: 746 Castroville Rd., 78237. Ismael Galvan, Dir.

PRIVATE RELIGIOUS ORDER CEMETERY

SAN ANTONIO. *Resurrection Cemetery*, 11624 Culebra Rd., Bldg. 7, 78253. Tel: 210-798-8220, Ext. 10; Fax: 210-798-8225; Email: resurrection@cordi-marian.org; Web: www.cordi-marian.org. Richard Ruiz, Gen. Mgr.

NECROLOGY

† Rubaj, Leon B., (Retired), Died Oct. 1, 2018

An asterisk (*) denotes an organization that has established tax-exempt status directly with the IRS and is not covered by the USCCB Group Ruling.

Diocese of San Bernardino

Most Reverend

GERALD R. BARNES

Bishop of San Bernardino; ordained December 20, 1975; appointed Titular Bishop of Montefiascone and Auxiliary of San Bernardino January 28, 1992; ordained March 18, 1992; succeeded to the See, December 28, 1995; installed as Second Bishop of San Bernardino March 12, 1996. *Office: 1201 E. Highland Ave., San Bernardino, CA 92404-4641.*

Diocesan Pastoral Center: 1201 E. Highland Ave., San Bernardino, CA 92404-4641. Tel: 909-475-5300; Fax: 909-475-5155.

Web: www.sbdiocese.org

Email: sbdiocese@sbdiocese.org

ESTABLISHED NOVEMBER 6, 1978.

Square Miles 27,293.

Comprises the Counties of San Bernardino and Riverside.

Legal Title: The Roman Catholic Bishop of San Bernardino, a Corporation Sole (Churches, Rectories, Halls, Catechetical Centers, etc.).

STATISTICAL OVERVIEW

Personnel	
Bishop	1
Retired Bishops	1
Priests: Diocesan Active in Diocese	58
Priests: Diocesan Active Outside Diocese	3
Priests: Retired, Sick or Absent	37
Number of Diocesan Priests	98
Religious Priests in Diocese	119
Total Priests in Diocese	217
Extern Priests in Diocese	62
Ordinations:	
Transitional Deacons	3
Permanent Deacons	10
Permanent Deacons in Diocese	125
Total Brothers	13
Total Sisters	95
Parishes	
Parishes	92
With Resident Pastor:	
Resident Diocesan Priests	25
Resident Religious Priests	38
Without Resident Pastor:	
Administered by Priests	26
Administered by Deacons	1
Administered by Lay People	2
Missions	8
Pastoral Centers	5
Professional Ministry Personnel:	
Brothers	4
Sisters	17
Lay Ministers	99
Welfare	
Catholic Hospitals	2
Total Assisted	354,386
Specialized Homes	5
Total Assisted	184,193
Special Centers for Social Services	10
Total Assisted	31,211
Educational	
Seminaries, Diocesan	1
Students from This Diocese	11
Diocesan Students in Other Seminaries	21
Seminaries, Religious	1
Total Seminarians	32
High Schools, Diocesan and Parish	2
Total Students	971
High Schools, Private	1
Total Students	558
Elementary Schools, Diocesan and Parish	25
Total Students	5,476
Elementary Schools, Private	2
Total Students	491
Catechesis/Religious Education:	
High School Students	11,772
Elementary Students	27,100
Total Students under Catholic Instruction	46,400
Teachers in the Diocese:	
Priests	2
Sisters	1
Lay Teachers	561
Vital Statistics	
Receptions into the Church:	
Infant Baptism Totals	3,830
Minor Baptism Totals	5,199
Adult Baptism Totals	348
Received into Full Communion	685
First Communions	13,720
Confirmations	8,029
Marriages:	
Catholic	1,617
Interfaith	144
Total Marriages	1,761
Deaths	2,858
Total Catholic Population	1,740,655
Total Population	4,580,670

Former Bishop—Most Rev. PHILLIP F. STRALING, D.D., ord. March 19, 1959; appt. Bishop of San Bernardino July 18, 1978; cons. Nov. 6, 1978; transferred to See of Reno, June 29, 1995; retired June 21, 2005.

Auxiliary Bishop Emeritus—Most Rev. RUTILIO J. DEL RIEGO.

Diocesan Pastoral Center—1201 E. Highland Ave., San Bernardino, 92404-4641. Tel: 909-475-5300; Fax: 909-475-5155. Office Hours: Mon.-Fri. 8:30 am-4:30 pm.

All correspondence should be addressed to the Diocesan Pastoral Center unless otherwise noted.

Office of the Bishop—Email: bishopsoffice@sbdiocese.org.

Executive Office Administrator to the Bishop—MS. EDNA PRECIADO, Tel: 909-475-5113; Fax: 909-475-5109; Email: epreciado@sbdiocese.org.

Episcopal Master of Ceremonies/Special Assistant to the Bishop—MR. RICHARD C. HERBST, Tel: 909-475-5124; Fax: 909-474-4902; Email: rherbst@sbdiocese.org.

Office of the Vicar General—Very Rev. Msgr. GERARD M. LOPEZ, S.T.L., V.G., Vicar Gen., Dir. Priest Personnel & Mod. of the Curia, Tel: 909-475-5120; Fax: 909-475-5109; Email: glopez@sbdiocese.org.

Associate Director—Rev. ERIK L. ESPARZA, J.C.L., Tel: 909-475-5122; Fax: 909-475-5109; Email: eesparza@sbdiocese.org.

Office Administrator to Vicar General/Director of Priest Personnel—MS. YOLANDA LEAR, Tel: 909-475-5123; Fax: 909-475-5109; Email: ylear@sbdiocese.org.

Office Administrator to Associate Director of Priest Personnel—MS. CYNTHIA C. ORTEGA, Tel: 909-475-5107; Fax: 909-475-5109; Email: ccortega@sbdiocese.org.

Coordinator of Victim Assistance Ministry—Sr. ROSALINE O'CONNOR, R.S.M., Tel: 909-855-2296; Fax: 909-475-5109; Email: roconnor@sbdiocese.org.

Office of Episcopal Vicars—Riverside Metropolitan Area Pastoral Region: Very Rev. RAFAEL A. PARTIDA, E.V. Riverside Pastoral Region: Very Rev. RAFAEL A. PARTIDA, E.V. San Bernardino Pastoral Region: Very Rev. ROMEO N. SELECCION, M.S., E.V.

Office Administrator to the Episcopal Vicars and the Auxiliary Bishop Emeritus—MRS. LILIANA B. MENDEZ-CHAVEZ, Tel: 909-475-5117; Fax: 909-475-5109; Email: lmendez-chavez@sbdiocese.org.

Vicars Forane—Hemet: Very Rev. ANTHONY C. DAO, V.F., Tel: 951-676-4403. High Desert: Very Rev. CANICE NWIZU, V.F., Tel: 760-246-7083. Low Desert: Very Rev. ALEX GAMINO, V.F., Tel: 760-347-3507. Riverside: Very Rev. GENEROSO T. SABIO, M.S.C., V.F., Tel: 951-683-0800. San Bernardino: Very Rev. LEONARD D. DEPASQUALE, I.M.C., V.F., Tel: 909-884-0104. West End: Very Rev. BENEDICT C. NWACHUKWU-UDAKU, V.F., Tel: 909-899-1049.

Chief Financial Officer—MS. LAURA J. CLARK, Tel: 909-475-5150; Fax: 909-475-5156.

Executive Secretary—MS. ROSALBA VALDEZ, Tel: 909-475-5150; Email: rvaldez@sbdiocese.org.

Office of the Chancellor—Sr. SARA KANE, C.S.J., Chancellor, Tel: 909-475-5100; Fax: 909-475-5109; Email: chancellor@sbdiocese.org.

Office Administrator—MRS. MARTHA JIMENEZ, Tel: 909-475-5100; Fax: 909-475-5109; Email: mjimenez@sbdiocese.org.

Vice Chancellor, Apostolic and Ethnic Affairs—MRS. MARIA H. ECHEVERRIA, Tel: 909-475-5140; Fax: 909-474-4916; Email: mecheverria@sbdiocese.org.

Administrative Assistant—YOLANDA MADRID, Tel: 909-475-5142; Fax: 909-474-4916; Email: ymadrid@sbdiocese.org.

Vice Chancellor, Ecclesial Services—Deacon F. MICHAEL JELLEY, Tel: 909-475-5119; Fax: 909-474-4906; Email: mjelley@sbdiocese.org.

Office Manager—NORMA VERDUGO, Tel: 909-475-5160; Fax: 909-474-4906.

Legal Counsel—MR. WILFRID C. LEMANN, Fullerton, Lemann, Schaefer and Dominick LLP, 215 N. "D" St., San Bernardino, 92401-1701. Tel: 909-889-3691; Fax: 909-888-5119.

Canonical Services (Tribunal)—Tel: 909-475-5320; Fax: 909-474-4914; Email: canonicalservices@sbdiocese.org.

Judicial Vicar—Very Rev. DAVID ANDEL, J.C.L., J.V., Email: dandel@sbdiocese.org.

Adjutant Judicial Vicar—Rev. BONIFACIO N. VELASQUEZ, F.M.M., J.C.D., Email: bvelasquez@sbdiocese.org.

Defender of the Bond—Bro. MANUEL E. RUIZ, O.de. M., J.C.L., Email: ruizm@sbdiocese.org.

Promoter of Justice—MRS. MARLA V. PRUNEDA, J.C.L.

Judges—Rev. Msgr. DONALD S. WEBBER, J.C.L., (Retired); Very Rev. DAVID ANDEL, J.C.L., J.V.; Rev. Msgr. PHILIP A. BEHAN, J.C.L., (Retired); Rev. GEORGE GONZALES, (Indult), (Retired); Deacon SCOTT HUNSICKER, J.C.L., (Retired); Revs. ERIK L. ESPARZA, J.C.L.; BONIFACIO N. VELASQUEZ, F.M.M., J.C.D.; MR. STEPHEN H.

OSBORN, J.D., J.C.L., (Retired); MRS. MARLA V. PRUNEDA, J.C.L.

Assessors—M. MAGDALENA CANTU-ROMO, Th.M., M.A., M.S., L.M.F.T., Email: mcanturomo@sbdiocese.com; Rev. TONG BA NGUYEN, Email: tnguyen@sbdiocese.org.

Diocesan Notaries—GINA GRADIAS-PENMAN, Email: ggradias@sbdiocese.org; IRENE MARTINEZ, Email: imartinez@sbdiocese.org; JARELI JACOBO, Email: jjacobo@sbdiocese.org.

Bishop's Advisors and Advisory Boards

College of Consultors—Most Revs. GERALD R. BARNES, D.D.; RUTILIO J. DEL RIEGO; Very Rev. Msgr. GERARD M. LOPEZ, S.T.L., V.G.; Very Rev. RAFAEL A. PARTIDA, E.V.; Rev. Msgr. TOM WALLACE; Very Revs. ROMEO N. SELECCION, M.S., E.V.; DAVID ANDEL, J.C.L., J.V.; Rev. Msgr. THOMAS J. BURDICK; Very Rev. DENNIS L. LEGASPI.

Diocesan Curia—Most Rev. GERALD R. BARNES, D.D.; Very Rev. Msgr. GERARD M. LOPEZ, S.T.L., V.G.; Very Revs. RAFAEL A. PARTIDA, E.V.; ROMEO N. SELECCION, M.S., E.V.; Sr. SARA KANE, C.S.J.; Deacon F. MICHAEL JELLEY; MRS. MARIA H. ECHEVERRIA; MS. LAURA J. CLARK; Sr. MARY CHILEE OKOKO, D.M.M.M.; MR. JOHN H. ANDREWS; Very Rev. DAVID ANDEL, J.C.L., J.V.; MS. MARIA H. SEDANO; MRS. LAURA LOPEZ; MRS. MARY F. JANSEN.

Presbyteral Council—Ex Officio Members: Most Rev. GERALD R. BARNES, D.D., Pres.; Very Rev. Msgr. GERARD M. LOPEZ, S.T.L., V.G.; Very Revs. ROMEO N. SELECCION, M.S., E.V.; RAFAEL A. PARTIDA, E.V. Appointed Members: Very Revs. GENEROSO T. SABIO, M.S.C., V.F.; LEONARD D. DEPASQUALE, I.M.C., V.F.; BENEDICT C. NWACHUKWU-UDAKU, V.F.; CANICE NWIZU, V.F.; ALEX GAMINO, V.F.; ANTHONY C. DAO, V.F.; Rev. ELISEO NAPIERE, M.S.P. Elected Members: Revs. ERIK L. ESPARZA, J.C.L.; MANUEL CARDOZA; MICHAEL ONWUEMELIE, C.S.Sp.; Very Rev. JAMES MCLAUGHLIN, V.F.; Revs. JAMES M. GIBSON, C.R.; ALBERT R. UTZIG, S.S.C.; CRISTOBAL SUBOSA; CLETUS IMO; Rev. Msgrs. HOWARD A. LINCOLN; THOMAS J. BURDICK; DONALD S. WEBBER, J.C.L.

Council for Consecrated Life—Most Rev. GERALD R. BARNES, D.D.; Sisters PATRICIA ANN PHILLIPS, S.H.C.J.; MARY FRANCES COLEMAN, R.S.M.; THERESA MAHER, C.P.P.S.; PATRICIA HAIRE, C.S.J.; MARIA JENNIFER NGUYEN, L.H.C.; JUDINE JACOBS, S.M.I.C.; HORTENSIA DEL VILLAR, S.A.C.; GENEVA BERNS, O.S.F.; Revs. PAUL MURTAGH, SS.CC.; BIJU THOMAS MANDAPATHIL, S.V.D.

Ministerial Personnel and Placement Board—Ex Officio: Most Rev. GERALD R. BARNES, D.D.; Very Rev. Msgr. GERARD M. LOPEZ, S.T.L., V.G.; Very Revs. RAFAEL A. PARTIDA, E.V.; ROMEO N. SELECCION, M.S., E.V.; Deacon F. MICHAEL JELLEY; Rev. ERIK L. ESPARZA, J.C.L. Elected Members: Revs. EDMUND GOMEZ; TIMOTHY TRUONG DO; JAMES OROPEL; Ms. KIRSTEN R. THORSTAD; Deacon LUIS SANCHEZ; Rev. Msgr. THOMAS J. BURDICK.

Bishop's Advisory Commissions—

Commission on the Status of Women in Church and Society—MRS. MARIA H. ECHEVERRIA, Chm., 1201 E. Highland Ave., San Bernardino, 92404-4641. Tel: 909-475-5140.

Commission for Ministry for Families of Gay and Lesbian Catholics—1201 E. Highland Ave., San Bernardino, 92404. Tel: 909-475-5125. VACANT, Chm.

Diocesan Liturgical Commission—MRS. CLARE COLELLA, Chm., Tel: 909-475-5335.

Ecumenical Office—Revs. GREGORY ELDER, Chm., St. Martha Church, 37200 Whitewood Rd., Murrieta, 92563. Tel: 951-698-8180; Fax: 951-698-7353; MANUEL CARDOZA, 6885 Del Rosa Ave., San Bernardino, 92404. Tel: 909-884-6375; Fax: 909-884-8976; MR. DAVID C. OKONKWO, Tel: 909-475-5194; Fax: 909-475-5343.

Bishop's Advisory Committees—

Diocesan Building Committee—Tel: 909-475-5310; Email: building@sbdiocese.org. Very Rev. RAFAEL A. PARTIDA, E.V., Chm.

Diocesan Review Committee—MR. GERARDO J. LOPEZ, Chm., Tel: 909-475-5120.

Finance Council—MS. LAURA J. CLARK, CFO, Tel: 909-475-5150; Fax: 909-475-5457; MR. BRUCE SATZGER, Chm.

Budget Committee—MR. BRUCE SATZGER, Chm.

Catholic Foundation Trustees—MR. MICHAEL VANDERPOOL, Chm.

Financial Review Committee—MR. BRUCE SATZGER, Chm.

Investment Committee—MR. MICHAEL VANDERPOOL, Chm.

Diocesan Offices

Accounting Services—Tel: 909-475-5480; Fax: 909-475-5489; Email: accounting@sbdiocese.org. PEGGY KOSTER, Office Dir., Tel: 909-475-5482; Email: pkoster@sbdiocese.org.

Apostolic and Ethnic Affairs—MRS. MARIA H. ECHEVERRIA, Vice Chancellor & Dept. Dir., Tel: 909-475-5140; Fax: 909-474-4916; Email: mecheverria@sbdiocese.org.

Administrative Secretary—YOLANDA MADRID, Tel: 909-475-5142; Fax: 909-474-4916; Email: ymadrid@sbdiocese.org.

Apostolic Groups & Movements in the Diocese—Please contact the office of Mrs. Maria H. Echeverria, Vice Chancellor, for all lay organizations.

Asociacion Escuela de la Cruz—
Catholic Committee on Scouting—
Catholic Daughters of the Americas—
Catholic Men's Fellowship—
Couples for Christ—
Cursillo in Christianity—
Filipino Movement—
Spanish Movement—
Vietnamese Movement—
El Shaddai—
Encuentro Matrimonial Mundial—
Engaged Encounter (English)—
Engaged Encounter (Spanish)—
Equestrian Order of the Holy Sepulchre of Jerusalem—
Escuela de Evangelizacion Nazareth (E.D.E.N.)—
Fellowship of Catholic Christian Women (FCCW)—
Foundation for Family and Life (FFL) for Couples for Christ (CFC)—
Italian Catholic Federation—
Jovenes Para Cristo—
Knights of Columbus—
Knights of Peter Claver—
Ladies Auxiliary, Knights of Peter Claver—
Magnificat (English and Spanish)—
Marriage Encounter (English)—
Marriage Enrichment—
Movimiento Familiar Cristiano Catolico—
Prevencion y Rescate—
Retrouvaille (English)—
Retrouvaille (Spanish)—
Serra International—
Society of St. Vincent de Paul—
Su Misericordia—
Talleres de Oracion y Vida—
World Apostolate of Fatima (Blue Army)—

Archives—Tel: 909-475-5397; Fax: 909-474-4907; Web: sites.google.com/site/sbdarchivesoffice/. PETER BRADLEY, Archivist, Tel: 909-475-5399; Email: pbradley@sbdiocese.org.

Statistical Research Specialist—ANGELICA ALBA, Tel: 909-475-5143; Email: aalba@sbdiocese.org.

Document Management Specialist—VICTOR MENDEZ, Tel: 909-475-5396; Email: vmendez@sbdiocese.org.

Asian / Pacific Ministry—Sr. MARIA JENNIFER NGUYEN, L.H.C., Dir., Tel: 909-475-5348; Fax: 909-474-4916; Email: mjnguyen@sbdiocese.org.

The following ministries can be contacted through the Office of Asian/Pacific Islander Ministry:
Chamorro Ministry—
Filipino Ministry—
Indonesian Ministry—
Korean Ministry—
Samoan Ministry—
Tongan Ministry—
Vietnamese Ministry—

Campus Ministry—Tel: 909-475-5450; Fax: 909-475-5155. MRS. MARY F. JANSEN, Dir. Campus Ministry & Campus Min. Univ. Redlands, Tel: 909-475-5450; Email: mjansen@sbdiocese.org; Sr. MARIA ASOPESIO IOSEFO, S.M.S.M., Campus Min., Cal State Univ., San Bernardino. Tel: 909-537-7337; Fax: 909-537-7339; Email: miosefo@sbdiocese.org; Revs. CYRIACUS OGU, Campus Min., Riverside Community College, Tel: 951-682-8751; Email: cogu@sbdiocese.org; ALWYN B. ANFONE, Campus Min., Univ. of Calif., Riverside, Tel: 951-682-8751; Email: anfone@sbdiocese.org.

Catechetical Ministry—Tel: 909-475-5452; Fax: 909-475-5457; Email: catechetical@sbdiocese.org. MARIA G. COVARRUBIAS, Office Dir., Tel: 909-475-5452; Email: mcovarrubias@sbdiocese.org; SUSANA SOTO, Admin. Sec., Email: ssoto@sbdiocese.org; TERESA ROCHA, Low Desert/Hemet Vicariate Coord., Tel: 909-475-5386; Email: trocha@sbdiocese.org; KARINA GOMEZ, West End/Riverside Vicariate Coord., Tel: 909-475-5388; Email: kgomez@sbdiocese.org; RAY ALMANZA, San Bernardino/High Desert Vicariate Coord., Tel: 909-475-5384; Email: ralmanza@sbdiocese.org; MARIO MARTINEZ, Marriage Initiative Coord., Tel: 909-475-5385; Email: mmartinez@sbdiocese.org.

Catholic Cemeteries—Tel: 909-475-5300; Fax: 909-474-5109. Rev. Msgr. GERARD M. LOPEZ, S.T.L., V.G., Pastoral Dir.

Catholic Mutual Group—Rezek Centre, 2101 N. Waterman Ave., Third Fl., San Bernardino, 92404. Tel: 909-886-6001; Fax: 909-883-9311. TAMAR BRINKERHOFF, Regl. Mgr., Email: tbrinkerhoff@catholicmutual.org; RUBEN A. LUNA, CPCU, Asst. Claims/Risk Mgr., Email: rluna@catholicmutual.org; ANNE RUBIO, Regl. Svcs. Office Sec., Email: arubio@catholicmutual.org.

Catholic Schools—Tel: 909-475-5437; Fax: 909-475-5477; Email: catholicschools@sbdiocese.org. SAMUEL TORRES, Supt.; MARIBEL ARGUELLES, Assoc. Supt.; AUSTIN CONLEY III, Dir. Advancement for Catholic Schools; VICTORIA KENNEDY, Office Supvr.; MARIA DE JESUS RAMIREZ, Administrative Asst.

Charismatic Renewal—Tel: 909-475-5365; Fax: 909-474-4919; Email: crc@sbdiocese.org; Web: www.ocrsb.org. MARINA CARRION, Office Dir., Tel: 909-475-5366; Email: mcarrion@sbdiocese.org; ANITA MUNOZ, Prog. Coord., Tel: 909-475-5371; Email: amunoz@sbdiocese.org; EVERARDO HUERTA, English Facilitator, Tel: 909-475-5367; Email: ehuerta@sbdiocese.org; REBECCA AVALOS, Administrative Sec., Tel: 909-475-5368; Email: ravalos@sbdiocese.org.

Child and Youth Protection—Tel: 909-475-5125; Fax: 909-475-5126. ELDER SAMANIEGO, Interim Dir., Tel: 909-475-5129; Email: esamaniego@sbdiocese.org; JOHANNA SANCHEZ, Administrative Sec., Tel: 909-475-5128; Email: jsanchez@sbdiocese.org; MARTHA I. BARAJAS, Office Coord., Tel: 909-475-5300; Email: mbarajas@sbdiocese.org.

Construction and Real Estate—Tel: 909-475-5310; Fax: 909-474-4913; Email: ocre@sbdiocese.org. DAVID MEIER, Dir., Tel: 909-475-5305; Email: dmeier@sbdiocese.org; CARLEEN TUCKER, Property Mgr., Email: ctucker@sbdiocese.org; MICHAEL VARGAS, Property Mgr. Estimator, Email: mvargas@sbdiocese.org; ALBERTO MACIAS TOVAR, Property Maintenance, Email: atovar@sbdiocese.org; NORMAN TURNER, Office Coord., Email: nturner@sbdiocese.org; CINDY LOMELI, Administrative Sec., Email: clomeli@sbdiocese.org; AMBER TORRES, Administrative Sec., Email: atorres@sbdiocese.org.

Continuing Formation of Priests—Tel: 909-475-5456; Fax: 909-474-4906. DR. JOSE ANTONIO MEDINA, Office Dir., Tel: 909-475-5456; Email: jmedina@sbdiocese.org; MARIA CRISTINA MENDEZ, Administrative Sec. II, Tel: 909-475-5163; Email: mcmendez@sbdiocese.org.

Diaconate Formation—Tel: 909-475-5163; Fax: 909-474-4906. Deacon EDWARD CLARK, Office Dir., Tel: 909-475-5162; Email: eclark@sbdiocese.org; MARIA CRISTINA MENDEZ, Administrative Sec. II, Tel: 909-475-5163; Email: mcmendez@sbdiocese.org.

Ecclesial Services—Tel: 909-475-5160; Fax: 909-474-4906. Deacons F. MICHAEL JELLEY, Vice Chancellor, Vicar for Deacons and Dept. Dir., Tel: 909-475-5119; Email: mjelley@sbdiocese.org; LUIS SANCHEZ, Assoc. Dir., Tel: 909-475-5459; Email: luissanchez@sbdiocese.org.

Office Manager—NORMA VERDUGO, Tel: 909-475-5161; Email: nverdugo@sbdiocese.org.

Emergency Operations Collaborative (EOC)—Tel: 909-475-5411; Tel: 909-475-5333 (Emergency Response). ANN MARIE GALLANT, EOC Dir., Email: agallant@sbdiocese.org.

Evangelization and Adult Faith Formation—Tel: 909-475-5195; Fax: 909-475-5155; Email: evanaff@sbdiocese.org. PAULINA ESPINOSA, Dir., Tel: 909-475-5197; Email: pespinosa@sbdiocese.org; MARIA PETRUSEK, Coord., Tel: 909-475-5196; Email: mpetrusek@sbdiocese.org; LAURA ROSALES, Administrative Sec., Email: lrosales@sbdiocese.org.

Valley Missionary Program—Rev. ARTURO QUEZADA, S.T., Spiritual Dir., 52565 Oasis Palm Ave., Coachella, 92236. Tel: 760-398-9277; Tel: 760-398-9278; Fax: 760-398-9281; Email: vmpcoachella@hotmail.com.

Facilities Services—Tel: 909-475-5315; Fax: 909-475-5319. DERRICK SERVIN, Office Coord., Email: dservin@sbdiocese.org; RAMON ARREZOLA, Facilities Coord., Email: rarrezola@sbdiocese.org; ADAM MEIER, Facility Maintenance, Email: ameier@sbdiocese.org; CHRISTINE CAMACHO, Facilities Asst., Email: ccamacho@sbdiocese.org; MARIA CHAVIRA, Receptionist, Email: mchavira@sbdiocese.org.

Financial Affairs—Tel: 909-475-5150; Fax: 909-475-5156; Email: financialaffairs@sbdiocese.org. MS. LAURA J.

CLARK, CFO & Dept. Dir., Email: lclark@sbdiocese.org; MS. ROSALBA VALDEZ, Exec. Sec., Email: rvaldez@sbdiocese.org.

Hispanic Affairs—Tel: 909-475-5360; Fax: 909-474-4916; Email: hispanicaffairs@sbdiocese.org. PETRA ALEXANDER, Dir., Tel: 909-475-5363; Email: palexander@sbdiocese.org; SONIA SANCHEZ, Sec., Tel: 909-475-5362; Email: smsanchez@sbdiocese.org.

Human Resources—Tel: 909-475-5170; Fax: 909-475-5189; Email: humanresources@sbdiocese.org. VIRGINIA TURNER, Senior Dir., Tel: 909-475-5172; Email: vturner@sbdiocese.org; SINIA BUSTAMANTE, Assoc. Dir., Tel: 909-475-5177; Email: sbustamante@sbdiocese.org; DAVID ACOSTA, Employee Rels. Mgr., Tel: 909-475-5179; Email: dacosta@sbdiocese.org; WENDY AGUILERA, Benefits Mgr., Tel: 909-475-5171; Email: waguilera@sbdiocese.org; PAULA GARCIA, Fingerprint Clerk, Tel: 909-475-5175; Email: pgarcia@sbdiocese.org; NOEMI GRACE, H.R. Coord., Tel: 909-475-5178; Email: ngrace@sbdiocese.org; MARTIN LOUREIRO, H.R. Coord., Tel: 909-475-5174; Email: mloureiro@sbdiocese.org; GEORGINA MEZA, Administrative Sec., Tel: 909-475-5176; Email: gmeza@sbdiocese.org.

Information Technology Services—Tel: 909-475-5400 ; Fax: 909-475-5357; Email: informationtechnologyservices2@sbdiocese.org. EUGENE GHINEA, Office Dir., Tel: 909-475-5401; Email: eghinea@sbdiocese.org; TERESA PEREZ, Administrative Asst., Tel: 909-475-5415; Email: tperez@sbdiocese.org; STEPHEN BROWN JR., Network Admin., Tel: 909-475-5419; Email: sbrown@sbdiocese.org; ERIC KUSKE, Database Admin./Mgr., Tel: 909-475-5403; Email: ekuske@sbdiocese.org; ANTHONY DEVLIN, IT Support Tech., Tel: 909-475-5418; Email: adevlin@sbdiocese.org; DEREK BROWN, Video Conf. Tech., Tel: 909-475-5415; Email: dbrown@sbdiocese.org; CHRISTIAN GALLEGOS, Mail Room Supvr., Tel: 909-475-5405; Email: cgallegos@sbdiocese.org; LINDA TERAN, Mailroom Clerk, Tel: 909-475-5412; Email: lteran@sbdiocese.org; CHRISTINA GARZA, Mailroom Clerk, Tel: 909-475-5413; Email: cgarza@sbdiocese.org.

Ministry of Educational Services—Tel: 909-475-5450; Fax: 909-475-5155; Email: MES@sbdiocese.org. MRS. MARY F. JANSEN, Dept. Dir., Email: mjansen@sbdiocese.org; DOLORES MARTINEZ, Administrative Asst., Email: dmartinez@sbdiocese.org.

Ministry Formation Institute—Tel: 909-475-5375; Fax: 909-474-4920; Email: mfi@sbdiocese.org. MS. MARIA H. SEDANO, Dept. Dir., Tel: 909-475-5387; Email: msedano@sbdiocese.org; STEVE HALLIGAN, CMFP English Coord., Tel: 909-475-5382; Email: shalligan@sbdiocese.org; MARIA ANTONIA AMAO, CMFP Spanish Coord., Email: mariaamao@sbdiocese.org; ELIZABETH CORTEZ, PMFP Coord. Riverside Region, Tel: 909-475-5377; Email: ecortez@sbdiocese.org; CRISTINA CASTILLO, PMFP Coord. San Bernardino Program, Tel: 909-475-5574; Email: ccastillo@sbdiocese.org; DAISY ROSAS, Administrative Asst., Email: drosas@sbdiocese.org; ELYANA FERNANDEZ, Office Asst., Email: e.fernandez@sbdiocese.org; RAFAEL DAVILA, Sec., Email: rdavila@sbdiocese.org.

Ministry of Life, Dignity and Justice—Tel: 909-475-5475; Fax: 909-474-4926. Sr. CHILEE OKOKO, D.M.M.M., Dept. Dir., Tel: 909-475-5478; Email: srchilee@sbdiocese.org; JOSEFINA GADZINSKI, Administrative Sec., Tel: 909-475-5476; Email: jgadzinski@sbdiocese.org.

Advocacy and Justice for Immigrants Programs—ABRAHAM JOVEN, Dir., Tel: 909-475-5351; Email: ajoven@sbdiocese.org; JANINE DE LA TORRE, Administrative Sec., Tel: 909-475-5469; Email: janinedelatorre@sbdiocese.org.

Community Services and Outreach Programs—Tel: 909-475-5465; Fax: 909-474-4923; Email: socialconcerns@sbdiocese.org. Sr. HORTENSIA DEL VILLAR, S.A.C., Dir., Tel: 909-475-5468; Email: hdelvillar@sbdiocese.org; MARIA EVA HERNANDEZ, Administrative Sec., Tel: 909-475-5467; Email: mehernandez@sbdiocese.org.

Catholic Campaign for Human Development—Sr. HORTENSIA DEL VILLAR, S.A.C., Dir., Tel: 909-475-5468; Fax: 909-475-5473; Email: hdelvillar@sbdiocese.org.

Education and Formation Programs—JOSE LUIS ELIAS, Dir., Tel: 909-475-5466; Email: jelias@sbdiocese.org; MARIA EVA HERNANDEZ, Administrative Sec., Tel: 909-475-5467; Email: mehernandez@sbdiocese.org.

Respect Life and Pastoral Care Programs—Tel: 909-475-5351; Fax: 909-474-4923; Email: respect&care@sbdiocese.org. MARY HUBER, Dir., Tel: 909-475-5352; Email: mhuber@sbdiocese.org; JANINE DE LA TORRE, Administrative Sec., Tel: 909-475-5469; Email: janinedelatorre@sbdiocese.org.

Restorative Justice Programs—Tel: 909-475-5479; Fax: 909-474-4927. MARCIANO AVILLA, Dir., Tel: 909-475-5479; Email: mavilla@sbdiocese.org; ANNA HAMILTON, Assoc. Dir., Tel: 909-475-5474; Email: ahamilton@sbdiocese.org; Sr. ROSARIO CORONADO, E.E.P., High Desert Coord., Tel: 760-261-3013; Email: mcoronado@sbdiocese.org; VIANNEY SANDOVAL, Office Asst., Tel: 909-475-5472; Email: v.sandoval@sbdiocese.org.

Media—Tel: 909-475-5400; Fax: 909-475-5357. MR. JOHN H. ANDREWS, Dept. Dir., Tel: 909-475-5421; Email: jandrews@sbdiocese.org; TERESA PEREZ, Administrative Asst., Tel: 909-475-5415; Email: tperez@sbdiocese.org.

Ministry to Catholics of African Decent—Tel: 909-475-5194; Fax: 909-475-4979. MR. DAVID C. OKONKWO, Dir., Email: cadministry@sbdiocese.org.

Catholics of African Descent Board—1201 E. Highland Ave., San Bernardino, 92404-4641. Tel: 909-475-5194; Fax: 909-475-5155.

Nigerian Igbo Catholic Ministry—

Igbo Catholic Women Organization Ministry—

Ministry With Young Catholics—Tel: 909-475-5167; Fax: 909-474-4921; Email: myo@sbdiocese.org. EDGARDO JUAREZ, Dir., Tel: 909-475-5166; Email: ejuarez@sbdiocese.org; REYNA TINAJERO, Administrative Sec., Tel: 909-475-5167; Email: rtinajero@sbdiocese.org; GUADALUPE ABREO ROMERO, Youth Prog. Coord., Tel: 909-475-5168; Email: gromero@sbdiocese.org; BERENICE VILLA, Youth Prog. Coord., Tel: 909-475-5169; Email: bvilla@sbdiocese.org; BRENDA NORIEGA, Young Adults Prog. Coord., Tel: 909-475-5361; Email: bnoriega@sbdiocese.org; Sr. MARIA EVA PLASCENCIA, E.E.P., High Desert Coord., Tel: 951-380-2990; Email: meplascencia@sbdiocese.org.

Mission—Mailing Address: 1201 E. Highland Ave., San Bernardino, 92404. Tel: 909-475-5130; Fax: 909-475-4909; Email: missions@sbdiocese.org. Rev. Msgr. TOM M. WALLACE, Dir., Tel: 909-475-5130; Email: twallace@sbdiocese.org; TAMMY GRIFFIN, Admin. Sec., Tel: 909-475-5133; Email: tgriffin@sbdiocese.org.

Mission Advancement—Tel: 909-475-5460; Fax: 909-474-4908. JULIO CHAVEZ, Oper. Mgr., Tel: 909-475-5462; Email: jchavez@sbdiocese.org; DAVID DOLORES, DDF Annual Appeal Coord., Tel: 909-475-5463; Email: ddolores@sbdiocese.org; ELISABET GAONA, Administrative Sec., Tel: 909-475-5444; Email: egaona@sbdiocese.org.

Mission Integration—Tel: 909-475-5108; Fax: 909-474-4906. Sr. LINDA NICHOLSON, C.S.J., Dir., Email: lnicholson@sbdiocese.org.

Native American Ministry—Rev. EARL HENLEY, M.S.C., Dir., 23600 Soboba Rd., P.O. Box 1027, San Jacinto, 92581. Tel: 951-487-1160; Fax: 951-654-2086 (Call First); Email: ehenley@sbdiocese.org; Sr. MARIANNA TORRANO, R.S.C.J., Superior, Tel: 951-654-7899; Email: mtorrano@rscj.org.

Parish Assistance—Tel: 909-475-5490; Fax: 909-475-5307; Email: parishassistance@sbdiocese.org. URSULA HINKSON, Dir., Tel: 909-475-5153; Email: uhinkson@sbdiocese.org; CAROLINE BEATTY, Assoc. Dir., Tel: 909-475-5492; Email: cbeatty@sbdiocese.org; LAURA KEYSER, Auditor, Tel: 909-475-5493; Email: lkeyser@sbdiocese.org; ANGIE GALLARDO, Sr. Accountant, Tel: 909-475-5494; Email: agallardo@sbdiocese.org; CLAUDIA AGUAYO, Administrative Sec./Bookkeeper, Tel: 909-475-5496; Email: caguayo@sbdiocese.org; CHRISTOPHER SANDOVAL, Accounting Clerk, Tel: 909-475-5495; Email: csandoval@sbdiocese.org.

Pastoral Planning and Transitions—Tel: 909-475-5146 ; Fax: 909-474-4903; Email: pastoralplanning@sbdiocese.org; Web: www.pastoralplanningministry.com. MRS. LAURA LOPEZ, Dept. Dir., Tel: 909-475-5147; Email: llopez@sbdiocese.org.

Director of Transitions—MARCO ELIAS, Dir., Tel: 909-475-5118; Email: melias@sbdiocese.org; CHRIS VITAL, Planning Asst., Tel: 909-475-5145; Email: cvital@sbdiocese.org.

Payroll Services—Tel: 909-475-5188; Fax: 909-475-5183; Email: payroll2@sbdiocese.org. MRS. TRANG PHAM, C.P.P., Office Dir., Tel: 909-475-5182; Email: tpham@sbdiocese.org; NORMA NEGRETE, Assoc. Dir., Tel: 909-475-5191; Email: nnegrete@sbdiocese.org; GLORIA YANEZ, Payroll Specialist, Tel: 909-475-5186; Email: gyanez@sbdiocese.org; MICHELLE HERNANDEZ, Payroll Specialist, Tel: 909-475-5191; Email: mhernandez@sbdiocese.org.

Religious and Consecrated Life—Tel: 909-475-5345; Fax: 909-474-4906; Email: consecratedlife@sbdiocese.org. Sr. MARY FRANCES COLEMAN, R.S.M., Vicar for Rel., Tel: 909-475-5342; Email: mfcoleman@sbdiocese.org; NORMA VERDUGO, Office Mgr., Tel: 909-475-5161; Email: nverdugo@sbdiocese.org.

Seminarians—Saint Junipero Serra House of Formation, 12725 Oriole Ave., Grand Terrace, 92313. Tel: 909-783-0260; Fax: 909-783-0223. Very Rev. JORGE A. GARCIA, Rector, Email: jgarcia@sbdiocese.org; GLORIA OROZCO, Facilities Mgr., Email: gorozco@sbdiocese.org; Revs. EMMANUEL UKAEGBU-ONUOHA, Spiritual Dir., Email: eonuoha@sbdiocese.org; JOSE A. SANZ, D.L.P., Academic Dean; Most Rev. RUTILIO J. DEL RIEGO, Dir. Pastoral Formation & Auxiliary Bishop Emeritus, Email: rdelriego@sbdiocese.org.

Vicar for Priests—Tel: 909-475-5161; Fax: 909-474-4906; Email: vicar-for-priests@sbdiocese.org. Rev. Msgr. TOM WALLACE, Vicar for Priests, Tel: 909-475-5130; Email: twallace@sbdiocese.org; MARIA CRISTINA MENDEZ, Administrative Sec., Tel: 909-475-5163; Email: mcmendez@sbdiocese.org.

Vicar for Retired Priests—Tel: 909-475-5130; Fax: 909-474-4906. Rev. Msgr. TOM M. WALLACE, Vicar for Retired Priests, Email: twallace@sbdiocese.org; Sr. MARY FRANCES COLEMAN, R.S.M., Vicar for Retired Priests, Tel: 909-475-5342; Email: mfcoleman@sbdiocese.org; NORMA VERDUGO, Office Mgr., Tel: 909-475-5161; Email: nverdugo@sbdiocese.org.

Vocations—12716 Oriole Ave., Grand Terrace, 92313. Tel: 909-783-1305; Fax: 909-783-0223; Email: vocations@sbdiocese.org. Sr. SARAH SHREWSBURY, O.S.C., Office Dir., Email: sshrewsbury@sbdiocese.org; REYNA MONARREZ, Sec., Email: rmonarrez@sbdiocese.org.

Worship Office—Tel: 909-475-5335; Fax: 909-474-4915; Email: worship@sbdiocese.org. Sr. JEREMY GALLET, S.P., Dir., Tel: 909-475-5336; Email: jgallet@sbdiocese.org; GRACY IBARRA, Administrative Asst., Tel: 909-475-5337; Email: gibarra@sbdiocese.org; CHRISTOPHER ESTRELLA, Coord., Liturgical Music, Email: cestrella@sbdiocese.org; ADRIANA FRANCO, Liturgy Formation & Site Coord., Email: afranco@sbdiocese.org; YESICA JIMENEZ, Sr. Coord., Formation, Email: yjimenez@sbdiocese.org.

CLERGY, PARISHES, MISSIONS AND PAROCHIAL SCHOOLS

CITY OF SAN BERNARDINO

(SAN BERNARDINO COUNTY)

1—OUR LADY OF THE ROSARY CATHEDRAL (1927)
2525 N. Arrowhead Ave., 92405. Tel: 909-883-8991; Fax: 909-882-2061; Email: olrosary.sb@sbdiocese.org. Mailing Address: 265 W. 25th St., 92405. Revs. Duong Nguyen; Alexander Sila, S.V.D., Parochial Vicar; Deacons Thomas Dewhirst; Michael F. Jelley.

School—Holy Rosary Academy, (Grades PreK-8), 2620 N. Arrowhead Ave., 92405. Tel: 909-886-1088; Fax: 909-475-5263; Email: holyrosary.ocs@sbdiocese.org; Web: www.holyrosaryacademyandpreschool.org. Ms. Cheryll Austin, Prin.; Margie Jasso, Librarian. Participating Parishes: Our Lady of the Rosary Cathedral, San Bernardino; Our Lady of the Assumption, San Bernardino; St. Catherine of Siena, Rialto; Our Lady of Guadalupe, San Bernardino; St. Catherine of Alexandria, Riverside; St. Adelaide, Highland; St. Anthony, Our Lady of the Lake, Lake Arrowhead; Our Lady of the Immaculate Conception, Colton; St. Joseph the Worker, Loma Linda; St. James, Perris; St. Francis de Sales, Riverside. Lay Teachers 8; Students 166; Total Staff 16; Clergy / Religious Teachers 8.

Catechesis Religious Program—Email: mhavins@sbdiocese.org. Ms. Monica Havins, D.R.E. Students 12.

2—ST. ANTHONY (1948)
1640 Western Ave., 92411-1300. Tel: 909-887-3810; Fax: 909-880-0982; Email: stanthony.sb@sbdiocese.org. Revs. Paul Appiah-Kubi, S.V.D.; Pavol Sochulak, S.V.D., In Res.; Deacons Michael Bellinder; Mario Gutierrez.

Catechesis Religious Program—Ms. Sophia Navarrete, Sec. Students 469.

3—ST. BERNARDINE CHURCH (1862)
531 N. F. St., 92410-3109. Tel: 909-884-0104; Fax: 909-885-4634; Email: stbernardine.sb@sbdiocese.org. Very Rev. Leonard D. DePasquale, I.M.C., V.F., Admin.; Deacons Alfonso Martinez; Edwin Esttrella.

Catechesis Religious Program—Email: youth.

stbernardine.sb@sbdiocese.org. Rosie Aguirre, D.R.E. Students 270.

4—OUR LADY OF GUADALUPE (1925) (Hispanic)
Tel: 909-888-0044; Fax: 909-888-4428; Email: olg.sb@sbdiocese.org. Revs. Pedro E. Amezcua, C.O.R.C.; Christian Francisco Vera Cabrera, C.O.R.C., Parochial Vicar; Deacon Daniel Taylor.
Catechesis Religious Program—Alma Salazar, C.R.E. (Spanish); Olga Saenz, C.R.E. (English). Students 415.

5—OUR LADY OF HOPE CATHOLIC COMMUNITY, INC. (2006)
6885 Del Rosa Ave., 92413-3860. Tel: 909-884-6375; Fax: 909-885-8976; Email: olofhopeparish@sbdiocese.org. Revs. Manuel Cardoza; Toan Pham, Parochial Vicar; Deacon Eric Vilchis.
Del Rosa Avenue Worship Site—6885 Del Rosa Ave., 92404.
Valencia Avenue Worship Site—1000 Valencia Ave., 92410.
Catechesis Religious Program—Tel: 909-885-7472; Email: laguilar@sbdiocese.org. Ms. Laura Aguilar, Contact Person. Students 590.

6—OUR LADY OF THE ASSUMPTION (1954)
796 W. 48th St., 92407-3594. Tel: 909-882-2931; Fax: 909-883-4851; Email: olassumption.sb@sbdiocese.org. Rev. Rogelio Gonzalez, Admin.; Deacons Daniel O'Camb; Mark Weber.
School—Our Lady of the Assumption School, (Grades PreK-8), Tel: 909-881-2416; Fax: 909-886-7892; Email: olassumption@sbdiocese.org; Web: olabruins.com. Mrs. Susan Long, Prin. Participating Parishes: St. Anthony, San Bernardino; Holy Rosary Cathedral, San Bernardino; St. Catherine of Siena, Rialto; St. Frances Xavier Cabrini, Yucaipa. Lay Teachers 10; Students 177.
Catechesis Religious Program—Email: kestrella@olasb.org. Estrella Kathleen, C.R.E. Students 184.

OUTSIDE THE CITY OF SAN BERNARDINO

ADELANTO, SAN BERNARDINO CO., CHRIST THE GOOD SHEPHERD (1962)
17900 Jonathan St., Adelanto, 92301.
Tel: 760-246-7083; Fax: 760-246-4603; Email: cgshepherd.adelanto@sbdiocese.org; Web: www.christthegoodshepherd-ca.org. Very Rev. Canice Nwizu, V.F., Admin.; Deacon Santos Aguilera.
Catechesis Religious Program—Angelica Campos, D.R.E.; Ms. Dolores Flores, C.R.E. Students 160.

ALTA LOMA, SAN BERNARDINO CO., ST. PETER & ST. PAUL (1970)
9135 Banyan St., Alta Loma, 91737-2338.
Tel: 909-987-9312; Fax: 909-980-9404; Email: stpeterstpaul.altaloma@sbdiocese.org; Web: www.stpeterstpaul.com. Revs. Henry M. Sseriiso, I.M.C.; Juan Sandoval-Ochoa, Parochial Vicar; Deacons John Barna; Robert A. Beidle.
Catechesis Religious Program—Jennifer Campbell, D.R.E. Students 286.

ANZA, RIVERSIDE CO., SACRED HEART (1988)
56250 Hwy. 371, P.O. Box 390118, Anza, 92539-0118. Rev. Alphonsus Ngwaogu; Deacon Francisco Meza.
Catechesis Religious Program—Ms. Lynnette Smith, C.R.E. Students 46.

APPLE VALLEY, SAN BERNARDINO CO., OUR LADY OF THE DESERT (1974)
18386 Corwin Rd., Apple Valley, 92307-2328.
Tel: 760-242-4427; Fax: 760-242-1195; Email: oldesertapplevalley@sbdiocese.org. Revs. Delwyn Haroldson, C.R.; James M. Gibson, C.R., Parochial Vicar; Henry A. Ruszel, C.R., In Res., (Retired).
Catechesis Religious Program—Ms. Sylvia Fath, Dir, of Catechetical Min. Students 294.

BARSTOW, SAN BERNARDINO CO., ST. JOSEPH (1914)
505 E. Mountain View St., Barstow, 92311-2924.
Tel: 760-256-5891; Fax: 760-256-8307; Email: parishoffice@stjosephbarstow.com. Revs. Remigius Owuamanam; Gabriel Ezeh, S.M.M.M., Parochial Vicar; Michael Okafor, S.M.M.M., Parochial Vicar; Deacons Donald Burgett, (Retired); Joseph Moorman.
Catechesis Religious Program—Email: csepulveda@sbdiocese.org. Cecilia Sepulveda, D.R.E. Students 151.
Missions—St. Madeline Sophie Barat—83395 Trona Rd., Trona, 93562. Tel: 760-372-4717; Fax: 760-372-4717; Email: stmadeleinesophieba@sbdiocese.org.
Our Lady of the Desert, 57457 State Hwy. 127, Baker, San Bernardino Co. 92309. Tel: 760-733-4308.

BEAUMONT, RIVERSIDE CO., SAINT KATERI TEKAKWITHA CATHOLIC COMMUNITY, INC. (2006)
1234 Palm Ave., Beaumont, 92223.
Tel: 951-845-2849; Fax: 951-845-3446; Email: stkateritekakwitha@sbdiocese.org; Web: www.stkateritekakwitha.org. Very Rev. Dennis L. Legaspi; Revs. Stephen C. Porter, S.T.L., Parochial Vicar; Dominic Vu, Parochial Vicar; Ba Tong Nguyen, In Res.; Deacons Mark Hodnick; Armando Luevano Jr.
Banning Worship Site, 157 W. Nicolet St., Banning, 92220. Teletype: 951-849-2434; Fax: 951-849-8698.
Catechesis Religious Program—Tel: 951-849-2434; Email: irodriguez@sbdiocese.org. Ms. Irene Rodriguez, D.R.E. Students 283.

BIG BEAR LAKE, SAN BERNARDINO CO., ST. JOSEPH (1931)
42242 N. Shore Dr., Big Bear Lake, 92315.
Tel: 909-866-3030; Fax: 909-866-5087; Email: stjoseph.bigbear@sbdiocese.org. P.O. Box 1709, Big Bear Lake, 92315-1709. Rev. Paul Smith, C.R., Admin.; Deacons James Webber; Brooke Wagner.
Catechesis Religious Program—Email: bwagner@sbdiocese.org. Deacon Brooke Wagner, D.R.E. Students 144.

BLOOMINGTON, SAN BERNARDINO CO., ST. CHARLES BORROMEO (1939) (Hispanic)
11342 Spruce St., Bloomington, 92316.
Tel: 909-877-0792; Fax: 909-877-4304; Email: stcharlesborromeo@sbdiocese.org; Web: www.stcharlesborromeoca.com. Rev. Pavol Sochulak, S.V.D., Interim Admin.
Catechesis Religious Program—Elizabeth Cervantes, Contact Person. Students 480.

BLYTHE, RIVERSIDE CO., ST. JOAN OF ARC (1920)
875 E. Chanslorway, Blythe, 92225.
Tel: 760-922-3261; Fax: 760-922-5279; Email: stjoanofarchinblythe@sbdiocese.org. Rev. Henry Licznerski, C.R.; Deacon Hikyung (H.K.) Han.
Catechesis Religious Program—Ms. Norma Castillo, C.R.E. Students 227.

CATHEDRAL CITY, RIVERSIDE CO., ST. LOUIS (1948)
68633 C St., Cathedral City, 92234.
Tel: 760-328-2398; Fax: 760-770-4598; Email: stlouis.cathedralcity@sbdiocese.org. Revs. Luis Guido; Anthony Ibegbunam, Parochial Vicar.
Catechesis Religious Program—Email: rnunez@sbdiocese.org. Raquel Nunez, C.R.E. Students 516.

CHINO HILLS, SAN BERNARDINO CO., ST. PAUL THE APOSTLE (1986)
14085 Peyton Dr., Chino Hills, 91709-1610.
Tel: 909-465-5503; Fax: 909-465-1683; Email: stpaultheapostle.chinohills@sbdiocese.org; Web: www.sptacc.org. Very Rev. Romeo N. Seleccion, M.S., E.V.; Revs. Joseph Piloten, M.S., Parochial Vicar; Michael L. Sturn, Parochial Vicar; Deacons Tony Moralez; Gary Quinn.
School—St. Paul the Apostle Preschool, (Grades PreK-PreK), Tel: 909-325-8950; Fax: 909-465-1683; Email: cstutzman@sbdiocese.org. Ms. Christina Stutzman, Prin. Participating Parishes: St. Paul the Apostle, Chino Hills; St. Margaret Mary, Chino; St. Oscar Romero, Eastvale. Lay Teachers 3; Students 25; Total Staff 4.
Catechesis Religious Program—Email: vramirez@sptacc.org; Email: ealcantara@sptacc.org; Email: cebbit@sptacc.org. Edric Alcantara, C.R.E.; Ms. Concha Ebbit, C.R.E. (Spanish); Vera Ramirez, C.R.E. (English). Students 1,502.

CHINO, SAN BERNARDINO CO.

1—ST. MARGARET MARY (1947)
12686 Central Ave., Chino, 91710-3508.
Tel: 909-591-7400; Fax: 909-461-4548; Email: stmargaretmary@sbdiocese.org. Revs. Michael Miller, Admin.; Eulices Godinez, Parochial Vicar; Deacon John Anthony Cruz.
School—St. Margaret Mary School, (Grades PreK-8), 12664 Central Ave., Chino, 91710. Tel: 909-591-8419 ; Fax: 909-591-6960; Email: smms.ocs@sbdiocese.org; Web: www.smms-chino.org. Mr. Waylynn Senn, Prin.; Sr. Kathleen Cleary, O.S.F., Librarian. Participating Parishes: St. Margaret Mary, Chino; St. Paul the Apostle, Chino Hills; St. Elizabeth Ann Seton, Ontario; Our Lady of Guadalupe, Chino; Our Lady of Lourdes, Montclair; Sacred Heart, Rancho Cucamonga; San Secondo D'Asti, Guasti; St. George, Ontario; St. Joseph, Upland. Lay Teachers 16; Religious 1; Students 358; Total Staff 37.
Catechesis Religious Program—Email: nkeegan@sbdiocese.org. Ms. Nancy Keegan, C.R.E. Students 624.

2—OUR LADY OF GUADALUPE (1902) (Hispanic)
5048 D St., Chino, 91710. Tel: 909-263-1826; Fax: 909-591-9404; Email: olg.chino@sbdiocese.org; Web: ourladyofguadalupechino.com. Revs. Edmund Gomez; Raul Perez, Parochial Vicar; Deacon Anthony Brenes-Rios.
Catechesis Religious Program—Email: rrosales@sbdiocese.org. Mr. Rolando Rosales, D.R.E. Students 623.

COACHELLA, RIVERSIDE CO., OUR LADY OF SOLEDAD (1923) (Hispanic)
52525 Oasis Palm Ave., Coachella, 92236.
Tel: 760-398-5577; Fax: 760-501-0039; Email: olsoledad.coachella@sbdiocese.org. Rev. Guy Wilson, S.T.; Deacons Fernando Heredia; Sergio Vasquez; Jose Israel Garcia, (Retired).
Catechesis Religious Program—Doris Marquez, C.R.E. (English); Maria Duarte, C.R.E. (Spanish). Students 1,003.
Mission—San Felipe de Jesus, 67305 Hwy. 86, Thermal, Riverside Co. 92274.

COLTON, SAN BERNARDINO CO.

1—IMMACULATE CONCEPTION (1943)
1106 N. La Cadena Dr., Colton, 92324.
Tel: 909-825-5110; Fax: 909-825-0912; Email: immaculateconception.colton@sbdiocese.org; Web: www.coltoncatholic.net. Revs. Bonifacio N. Velasquez, F.M.M., J.C.D.; Nelson Angel Bonilla, F.M.M., Parochial Vicar; Deacon Leonard Castanon.
Catechesis Religious Program—Mr. Salvador Madrigal, D.R.E. Students 374.

2—SAN SALVADOR (1852) (Hispanic)
169 W. L St., Colton, 92324-3446. Tel: 909-825-3481; Fax: 909-825-4473; Email: sansalvador.colton@sbdiocese.org. Rev. Moises Henriquez de Paz; Deacon Mark Martinez.
Catechesis Religious Program—Mr. Salvador Madrigal, D.R.E.; Jose A. Gonzalez, D.R.E. Students 210.

CORONA, RIVERSIDE CO.

1—CORPUS CHRISTI (1994)
3760 N. McKinley St., Corona, 92879-1956.
Tel: 951-272-9043; Fax: 951-272-6821; Email: corpuschristi.corona@sbdiocese.org; Web: www.corpuschristicorona.com. Revs. Gerald C. De Luney; Sergio Renteria-Sanchez, Parochial Vicar.
Catechesis Religious Program—Ms. Maria Veronica Sell, C.R.E. Students 1,379.

2—ST. EDWARD (1896)
417 W. Grand Blvd., Corona, 92882.
Tel: 951-549-6000; Fax: 951-549-6009; Email: stedward.corona@sbdiocese.org; Web: www.stedwardcorona.com. Mailing Address: 610 W. 5th St., Corona, 92882. Revs. Hector Magallon, Admin.; Carlos G. Garduno, C.O.R.C., Parochial Vicar.
School—St. Edward School, (Grades PreK-8), 500 S. Merrill St., Corona, 92882. Tel: 951-737-2530; Fax: 951-737-1074; Email: stedward.ocs@sbdiocese.org; Web: www.stedward1947.com. Mr. Nathan Arnold, Prin.; Ms. Heidi Morgan, Librarian. St. Oscar Romero, Eastvale; St. Andrew Kim, Corona; St. Frances of Rome, Wildomar; St. Francis de Sales, Riverside; St. Paul the Apostle, Chino Hills; St. Edward, Corona; St. Matthew, Corona; St. Mary Magdalene, Corona; Corpus Christi, Corona; St. Mel, Norco; The Shrine of the Presentation, Corona; St. Thomas, Riverside; St. Catherine of Alexandria, Riverside. Lay Teachers 29; Religious 1; Students 271; Clergy / Religious Teachers 1.
Catechesis Religious Program—
Tel: 951-549-6000, Ext. 203; Email: mmena@sbdiocese.org. Maria Cecilia Mena, C.R.E. Students 189.

3—ST. MARY MAGDALENE (1989)
8540 Weirick Rd., Corona, 92883-4995.
Tel: 951-277-1801; Fax: 951-277-2104; Email: secretary@smmcorona.org; Web: www.smmcorona.org. Revs. Joseph Than Van Liem, C.M.C.; Basil Toan Quang Doan, Parochial Vicar; Deacon Armando Hernandez.
Catechesis Religious Program—Email: mmiller@smmcorona.org; Email: sacramentos@smmcorona.com. Margaret Miller, C.R.E. (English); Lydia Mendoza, C.R.E. (Spanish). Students 229.

4—ST. MATTHEW (1973)
2140 W. Ontario Ave., Corona, 92882-5651.
Tel: 951-737-1621; Fax: 951-737-9715; Email: stmatthew.corona@sbdiocese.org; Web: www.stmatthewcorona.org. Revs. Hieu Trong Nguyen, S.V.D.; Hien Pham, S.V.D., Parochial Vicar.
Catechesis Religious Program—Email: raguilera@sbdiocese.org. Raquel Aguilera, D.R.E. Students 556.

5—SAINT OSCAR ROMERO CATHOLIC COMMUNITY, INC.
6905 Harrison Ave., Corona, 92880.
Tel: 951-893-1522. Mailing Address: 14395 Chandler St., Eastvale, 92880. Rev. Patrick V. Kirsch; Deacons Donnie Geaga; Victor Tiambeng.

CRESTLINE, SAN BERNARDINO CO., ST. FRANCES XAVIER CABRINI (1946)
P.O. Box 3817, Crestline, 92325-3817.
Tel: 909-338-2303; Fax: 909-338-2383; Email: stfrancesxaviercabrini.crestline@sbdiocese.org; Web: www.stfrancesxcabriniparish.com. Rev. Neil D. Fuller, S.V.D., Admin.; Deacon Rick Bassford.
Catechesis Religious Program—Ms. Suzanne Munoz, Contact Person.

DESERT HOT SPRINGS, RIVERSIDE CO., ST. ELIZABETH OF HUNGARY (1946)
66-700 Pierson Blvd., Desert Hot Springs, 92240-3740. Tel: 760-251-9268; Fax: 760-329-6760; Email: stelizabethofhungary.dhs@sbdiocese.org; Web: www.stelizabethdhs.org. Rev. Khan D. Ngo, Admin.; Deacon Victor Gonzalez.
Catechesis Religious Program—Email:

pbalderrama@sbdiocese.org. Patricia Balderrama, C.R.E. Students 152.

FONTANA, SAN BERNARDINO CO.

1—ST. GEORGE (1954)
17895 San Bernardino Ave., Fontana, 92335-6155.
Tel: 909-877-1531; Fax: 909-877-6531; Email: stgeorge.fontana@sbdiocese.org. Revs. Deebar Yonas, S.V.D.; Biju Thomas, In Res.; Deacon Alfredo Vargas.
Catechesis Religious Program—
Tel: 909-877-3935, Ext. 103. Maria de Jesus Ramirez, C.R.E. Students 398.

2—SAINT JOHN XXIII CATHOLIC COMMUNITY, INC. (2006)
7650 Tamarind Ave., Fontana, 92336.
Tel: 909-822-4732; Fax: 909-822-0620; Email: stjohnxxiii@sbdiocese.org. Revs. Cletus Imo, Admin.; Tomas Guillen, Parochial Vicar; Jacob Thomas Vettathu, M.S., Parochial Vicar; Deacons Nelson Glass; Abel Zamora.
Rialto Worship Center—222 E. Easton St., Rialto, 92376. Tel: 909-421-7030; Fax: 909-421-1374.
School—Resurrection Academy, (Grades PreK-8), 17434 Miller Ave., Fontana, 92336-2223.
Tel: 909-822-4431; Fax: 909-822-0617; Email: resurrection.ocs@sbdiocese.org; Web: www.resurrectionacademy.net. Mrs. Madeleine Thomas, Prin. St. John XXIII; St. Joseph, Fontana; St. Mary's Fontana; St. George, Fontana. Lay Teachers 15; Students 198.
Catechesis Religious Program—Mrs. Guadalupe Huerta, C.R.E. (Spanish); Ms. Rose Ladore, C.R.E. (English). Students 384.

3—ST. JOSEPH (1930)
17080 Arrow Blvd., Fontana, 92335-3807.
Tel: 909-822-0566; Fax: 909-829-1739; Email: stjoseph.fontana@sbdiocese.org; Web: www.stjosephfontana.com. Revs. Efrain Villalobos, M.S.P.; Juan Escobedo, Parochial Vicar; Deacon Greg Moore.
Catechesis Religious Program—Email: cm.stjoseph.fontana@sbdiocese.org. Maria Valadez, Contact Person. Students 481.

4—ST. MARY (1939)
16550 Jurupa Ave., Fontana, 92337-7452.
Tel: 909-822-5670; Fax: 909-357-4688; Email: stmary.fontana@sbdiocese.org. Revs. Albert R. Utzig, S.S.C.; Suresh Manickam, H.G.N., Parochial Vicar; Brendan O'Sullivan, S.S.C., In Res.; Deacon Carlos Morales.
Catechesis Religious Program—Tel: 909-822-4570. Paty Ruiz, D.R.E. Students 481.

GRAND TERRACE, SAN BERNARDINO CO., CHRIST THE REDEEMER (1981)
12745 Oriole Ave., Grand Terrace, 92313-6133.
Tel: 909-783-3811; Fax: 909-783-4683; Email: christtheredeemer.grandterrace@sbdiocese.org; Web: ctrgt.org. Rev. Anthony C. Waturuocha, Admin.; Deacons Paul Ahan; Jose Herrera.
Catechesis Religious Program—Students 164.

HEMET, RIVERSIDE CO.

1—HOLY SPIRIT (1991)
26340 Soboba St., P.O. Box 5268, Hemet, 92544.
Tel: 951-927-8544; Fax: 951-927-8546; Email: holyspirithemet@sbdiocese.org. Rev. Michael Onwuemelie, C.S.Sp.; Deacons A.R. McDaniel; Manuel Ramirez.
Catechesis Religious Program—Josephine Chagolla, C.R.E. Students 204.

2—OUR LADY OF THE VALLEY (1946)
780 S. State St., Hemet, 92543-7163.
Tel: 951-929-6131; Fax: 951-929-8009; Email: olv.hemet@sbdiocese.org; Web: www.olvhemet.org. Revs. Cornelius T. McQuillan, C.S.Sp.; Daniel Abba, Parochial Vicar; Paul Hoang, Parochial Vicar; Deacon John Langmead.
Catechesis Religious Program—Mr. Gustavo Lemus, C.R.E. Students 739.

HESPERIA, SAN BERNARDINO CO., HOLY FAMILY PARISH (1963)
9974 I Ave., Hesperia, 92345-5482.
Tel: 760-244-9180; Fax: 760-244-1959; Email: holyfamily.hesperia@sbdiocese.org; Web: www.holyfamilyhd.org. Revs. Manuel Jadraque Jr.; Reginald Ibe, Parochial Vicar; Deacon Marcial Ampuero.
Catechesis Religious Program—Email: marcial.a@hfchesperia.org. Deacon Marcial Ampuero, D.R.E. Students 916.

HIGHLAND, SAN BERNARDINO CO., ST. ADELAIDE (1956)
27457 E. Baseline St., Highland, 92346-3206.
Tel: 909-868-8669; Fax: 909-862-1603; Email: stadelaide.highland@sbdiocese.org; Web: www.stadelaidehighland.com. Very Rev. Romeo N. Seleccion, M.S., E.V., Priest Mod.; Rev. Alex Rodarte, Priest Min.; Mr. Fernando Solorio, Pastoral Coord.; Deacon Victor A. Barrion.
School—St. Adelaide School, (Grades PreK-8), 27487 E. Base Line Rd., Highland, 92346.
Tel: 909-862-5851; Fax: 909-862-2877; Email: stadelaide.ocs@sbdiocese.org; Web: www.stadelaideacademy.org. Mrs. Barbara A. Malouf, Prin. Participating Parishes: St. Adelaide, Highland; St. John Bosco, Highland; Holy Name of Jesus, Redlands; St. Catherine, Rialto; St. Joseph the Worker, Loma Linda; Holy Rosary, San Bernardino; Our Lady of Hope, San Bernardino; Our Lady of the Assumption, San Bernardino. Lay Teachers 13; Students 180; Total Staff 21.
Catechesis Religious Program—Email: lramirez@sbdiocese.org; Email: ralvarado@sbdiocese.org. Lorena Ramirez, D.R.E.; Mrs. Rosa Isela Alvarado, C.R.E. Students 380.
Mission—St. John Bosco, 28991 Merris St., East Highland, San Bernardino Co. 92346.

IDYLLWILD, RIVERSIDE CO., QUEEN OF ANGELS (1942)
54525 N. Circle Dr., P.O. Box 1106, Idyllwild, 92549-1106. Tel: 951-659-2708; Fax: 951-659-0208; Email: queenofangels.idyllwild@sbdiocese.org. Rev. Charles M. Miller.
Catechesis Religious Program—Ms. Rita Millward, Sec.

INDIO, RIVERSIDE CO., OUR LADY OF PERPETUAL HELP (1937)
45299 Deglet Noor St., Indio, 92201.
Tel: 760-347-3507; Fax: 760-347-8367; Email: olph.indio@sbdiocese.org; Web: www.olphindio.org. 82470 Bliss Ave. Bldg.2, Indio, 92201. Very Rev. Alex Gamino, V.F.; Rev. Edwin Logrono, Parochial Vicar; Deacons Brijido Rodriguez; Jeronimo Lugo; Mark Padilla.
School—Our Lady of Perpetual Help School, (Grades K-8), 82-470 Bliss Ave., Indio, 92201.
Tel: 760-347-3786; Fax: 760-347-7207; Email: olphindio.ocs@sbdiocese.org; Web: www.olphschoolindio.com. Mrs. Diane T. Arias, Prin. Participating Parishes: Our Lady of Perpetual Help, Indio Our Lady of Soledad, Coachella St. Francis of Assisi, La Quinta. Lay Teachers 15; Students 200.
Catechesis Religious Program—Ms. Evangelina Soto, C.R.E. Students 536.

JOSHUA TREE, SAN BERNARDINO CO., ST. CHRISTOPHER OF THE DESERT (1961) [JC] Closed. Sacramental records at St. Mary of the Valley, Yucca Valley.

LA QUINTA, RIVERSIDE CO., ST. FRANCIS OF ASSISI (1974)
47225 Washington St., La Quinta, 92253.
Tel: 760-564-1255; Fax: 760-564-0763; Email: stfrancisofassisi.laquinta@sbdiocese.org. Revs. James McLaughlin; Peter Phan, Parochial Vicar; Deacons David Hockwalt; Jaime Rosas; John Scanlon.
Catechesis Religious Program—
Tel: 760-564-1255, Ext. 208; Email: mphelps@sbdiocese.org. Myrna Phelps, C.R.E. Students 449.

LAKE ARROWHEAD, SAN BERNARDINO CO., OUR LADY OF THE LAKE (1938)
27627 Rim of the World Dr., Lake Arrowhead, 92352. Tel: 909-337-2333; Fax: 909-337-5041; Email: ollake.lakearrowhead@sbdiocese.org. Mailing Address: P.O. Box 1929, Lake Arrowhead, 92352-1929. Rev. Michel Osuch, C.R.; Deacon Michael Juback.
Catechesis Religious Program—
Tel: 909-337-2333, Ext. 140. Ms. Genese Horan, C.R.E.; Ms. Shauna Smith, C.R.E. Students 229.

LENWOOD, SAN BERNARDINO CO., ST. PHILIP NERI (LENWOOD) (1979)
25333 Third St., Barstow, 92311. Tel: 760-253-5412; Fax: 760-253-3191; Email: stphilipneribarstow@sbdiocese.org. 505 E. Mountain View St., Barstow, 92311. Revs. Remigius Owuamanam; Gabriel Ezeh, S.M.M.M., Parochial Vicar; Michael Okafor, S.M.M.M., Parochial Vicar; Deacon Joseph Moorman.
Catechesis Religious Program—Veronica Maria Saiz, Contact Person. Students 37.

LOMA LINDA, SAN BERNARDINO CO., ST. JOSEPH THE WORKER (1944)
10816 Mt. View Ave., Loma Linda, 92354.
Tel: 909-796-2605; Fax: 909-796-0755; Email: stjosephtheworker.lomalinda@sbdiocese.org; Web: www.stjosephlomalinda.org. Rev. Noel Cruz, M.S.
Catechesis Religious Program—Email: msandoval@sbdiocese.org. Mark R. Sandoval, C.R.E. Students 99.

LUCERNE VALLEY, SAN BERNARDINO CO., ST. PAUL (1963)
8973 Mesa, Lucerne Valley, 92356.
Tel: 760-242-4427; Fax: 760-242-1195; Email: stpaul.lucernevalley@sbdiocese.org. Mailing Address: 18386 Corwin Rd., Apple Valley, 92307. Revs. Delwyn Haroldson, C.R.; James M. Gibson, C.R., Parochial Vicar; Henry A. Ruszel, C.R., In Res., (Retired).
Catechesis Religious Program—Ms. Sylvia Fath, D.R.E. Students 2.

MECCA, RIVERSIDE CO., SANCTUARY OF OUR LADY OF GUADALUPE (1964) (Hispanic)
65100 Dale Kiler Rd., P.O. Box 218, Mecca, 92254.
Tel: 760-396-2717; Fax: 760-396-0047; Email: olgshrinemecca@sbdiocese.org. Rev. Francisco Valdovinos-Ruiz; Deacon Luis Ayala.
Catechesis Religious Program—
Tel: 760-396-2717, Ext. 112. Noemi Mejia, C.R.E. Students 455.

MONTCLAIR, SAN BERNARDINO CO., OUR LADY OF LOURDES (1955)
10191 Central Ave., Montclair, 91763-3801.
Tel: 909-626-7278; Fax: 909-626-0562; Email: ollourdes.montclair@sbdiocese.org. Revs. Anton Nyo, M.S., Parochial Vicar; Jacob Thomas Vettathu, M.S., Pastor.
School—Our Lady of Lourdes School, (Grades PreK-8), 5303 Orchard St., Montclair, 91763.
Tel: 909-625-5034; Fax: 909-625-5034; Email: ourladyoflourdes.ocs@sbdiocese.org; Web: www.ollschool.com. 2252 N. Albright Ave., Montclair, 91763. Beverly Diaz de Leon, Prin. Participating Parishes: St. Paul the Apostle, Chino Hills; St. Elizabeth Ann Seton, Ontario; Our Lady of Guadalupe, Ontario; St. Anthony, Upland; St. Peter and St. Paul, Alta Loma; Sacred Heart, Rancho Cucamonga; St. Margaret Mary, Chino. Lay Teachers 10; Students 197; Total Staff 10.
Catechesis Religious Program—Mrs. Yoselin Chisel Romero, D.R.E. Students 436.

MORENO VALLEY, RIVERSIDE CO.

1—ST. CHRISTOPHER (1957)
25075 Cottonwood Ave., Moreno Valley, 92553-0397.
Tel: 951-924-1968; Fax: 951-247-6477; Email: stchristopher.morenovalley@sbdiocese.org; Web: www.stchristophermv.org. Revs. Antonio Abuan, M.S., Interim Admin.; Joseph P. Thuruthel, M.S., Parochial Vicar; Deacon Manuel Rivas.
School—St. Christopher Preschool, (Grades PreK-PreK), Tel: 951-571-8347; Fax: 951-571-8348; Email: stchristopher.ocs@sbdiocese.org; Web: www.stcpreschool.com. Eleanor Manucal, Prin. Participating Parishes: St. Christopher, Moreno Valley. Lay Teachers 3; Students 25; Total Staff 4.
Catechesis Religious Program—Rosa Maria Ramos, Contact Person. Students 1,909.

2—ST. PATRICK (1989)
10915 Pigeon Pass Rd., Moreno Valley, 92557.
Tel: 951-485-6673; Fax: 951-485-3834; Email: stpatrick@sbdiocese.org; Web: www.stpatrickmv.org. Very Rev. Rafael A. Partida, E.V.; Revs. Johnny Dang, Parochial Vicar; Mark E. Kotlarczyk, Parochial Vicar; Deacons Jose Serrano; Ernest Lara; Ernesto Ocampo.
Rectory—22589 Mountain View Rd., Moreno Valley, 92557.
Catechesis Religious Program—
Tel: 951-485-6673, Ext. 113; Email: ggutierrez@sbdiocese.org. Christina Robbins, C.R.E. (English); Ms. Diana Palma, C.R.E. Students 905.

MURRIETA, RIVERSIDE CO., ST. MARTHA (1992)
37200 Whitewood Rd., Murrieta, 92563-5040.
Tel: 955-169-8818; Fax: 951-698-7353; Email: stmartha.murrieta@sbdiocese.org; Web: www.stmarthamurr.com. Very Rev. Rafael A. Partida, E.V., Priest Mod.; Revs. Joseph T. Ellison, (Mexico) Priest Min.; Gregory Elder, Priest Min.; Javier Escobar, Priest Min.; Ms. Kirsten R. Thorstad, Pastoral Coord.; Deacons Porfirio Diaz; Christopher Ciraulo; Wilfredo Vita.
Catechesis Religious Program—Angela Valencia, C.R.E. Students 1,006.

NEEDLES, SAN BERNARDINO CO., ST. ANN (1887)
Mailing Address: P.O. Box 190, Needles, 92363-0190.
Tel: 760-326-2721; Fax: 760-326-3068; Email: stannneedles@sbdiocese.org. Rev. Amaro Saumell III.
Office: 218 D St., Needles, 92363. Email: hlcox@sbdiocese.org.
Catechesis Religious Program—Ms. Sharon Bowling, Sec. Students 21.

NORCO, RIVERSIDE CO., ST. MEL (1959)
4140 Corona Ave., Norco, 92860-0700.
Tel: 951-737-7144; Fax: 951-735-8332; Email: stmel.norco@sbdiocese.org; Web: www.stmelsnorco.org. Revs. Gerardo Mendoza; Athanasius Ezealla, Parochial Vicar.
Catechesis Religious Program—Tel: 951-737-8140. Emily Guilherme, D.R.E. Students 486.

ONTARIO, SAN BERNARDINO CO.

1—ST. ELIZABETH ANN SETON (1980)
2713 S. Grove Ave., Ontario, 91761-6931.
Tel: 909-947-2956; Fax: 909-923-2946; Email: stelizabethannseto.ontario@sbdiocese.org; Web: www.seascc-ont.org. Revs. Cristobal Subosa; Martinianus C. Chileke, Parochial Vicar; Deacon Octavio Echeverria.
Catechesis Religious Program—
Tel: 909-947-2956, Ext. 27; Email: rquinn@seascc-ont.org. Rhodora Quinn, Faith Formation Assoc. Students 358.

2—ST. GEORGE (1905)
505 N. Palm Ave., Ontario, 91762. Tel: 909-983-2637; Fax: 909-395-9707; Email: stgeorge.ontario@sbdiocese.org; Web: www.stgoergeontario.org. Revs. Trung Mai, S.V.D., Admin.; Bihn Le, Parochial Vicar; Deacons Luis Sanchez; Bernardo Esparza; Jimmy Vu.
School—St. George School, (Grades K-8), 322 W. D St., Ontario, 91762. Tel: 909-984-9123;

Fax: 909-984-0921; Email: stgeorge.ocs@sbdiocese.org; Web: www.stgeorgeontario.com. Mr. Andrew Ramirez, Prin. Participating Parishes: St. Anthony, Upland; St. Joseph, Upland; Our Lady of Lourdes, Montclair; St. Margaret Mary, Chino; St. Elizabeth Ann Seaton, Ontario. Lay Teachers 13; Students 268; Total Staff 36; Clergy / Religious Teachers 2.
Catechesis Religious Program—Mrs. Gina Solomon, C.R.E. Students 604.

3—OUR LADY OF GUADALUPE (1948) (Hispanic)
710 S. Sultana Ave., Ontario, 91761-2554.
Tel: 909-983-2904; Fax: 909-984-1541; Email: olg.ontario@sbdiocese.org. Revs. Roberto Cristobal Flores, S.V.D.; Yos Kurniawan Sodanango, Parochial Vicar.
Catechesis Religious Program—Email: mmolina@sbdiocese.org. Martha Molina, C.R.E. Students 637.

4—SAN SECONDO D'ASTI (1926) (Italian)
250 N. Turner Ave., Ontario, 91761.
Tel: 909-390-0011; Fax: 909-390-9919; Email: sansecondodasti.guasti@sbdiocese.org; Web: www.sansecondodasti.org. P.O. Box 1056, Guasti, 91743. Rev. Stanley I. Onwuegbule, Admin.
Catechesis Religious Program—Email: ssda@sbdiocese.org. Mrs. Alma Zendejas, D.R.E. Students 176.

PALM DESERT, RIVERSIDE CO.

1—CHRIST OF THE DESERT (1928) (Newman Center)
73441 Fred Waring Dr., Palm Desert, 92260-2286.
Tel: 760-346-0089; Fax: 760-340-2245; Email: christofthedesert@sacredheartpalmdesert.com. Rev. Msgr. Howard A. Lincoln. All catechetical needs are done at Sacred Heart Church in Palm Desert.

2—SACRED HEART (1956)
43775 Deep Canyon Rd., Palm Desert, 92260-3164.
Tel: 760-346-6502; Fax: 760-773-4873; Email: sacredheart.pd@sbdiocese.org; Web: www.sacredheartpalmdesert.com. Rev. Msgr. Howard A. Lincoln.
School—Sacred Heart School, (Grades K-8),
Tel: 760-346-3513; Fax: 760-773-0673; Email: sacredheartpd.ocs@sbdiocese.org; Web: sacredheartpalmdesert.com. Alan Bruzzio, Prin. Lay Teachers 33; Students 641.
Catechesis Religious Program—Deacon Charlie Stanton, D.R.E. Students 234.

PALM SPRINGS, RIVERSIDE CO.

1—OUR LADY OF GUADALUPE (1912) (Cahuilla Indian)
204 S. Calle El Segundo, Palm Springs, 92262.
Tel: 760-325-5809; Fax: 760-325-9031; Email: olg.palmsprings@sbdiocese.org; Web: www.olgps.org. Revs. David K. Foxen, M.S.C.; Juan R. Romero, Parochial Vicar. No religious Education Program everything is done at Our Lady of Solitude.

2—OUR LADY OF SOLITUDE (1928) [JC] (Hispanic)
151 W. Alejo Rd., Palm Springs, 92262-5666.
Tel: 760-325-3816; Fax: 760-325-5316; Email: olsolitude.ps@sbdiocese.org. Revs. David K. Foxen, M.S.C.; Juan R. Romero, Parochial Vicar, (Retired).
Catechesis Religious Program—Tel: 760-325-9816; Email: ljaquez@sbdiocese.org; Email: eoveth9@gmail.com. Mr. Oveth Espino, D.R.E. Students 332.

3—ST. THERESA (1948)
2800 E. Ramon Rd., Palm Springs, 92264-7996.
Tel: 760-323-2669; Fax: 760-322-8581; Email: parishoffice@sbdiocese.org; Web: www.sttheresaps.com. Rev. John P. Kavcak, M.S.C.; Deacon Pablo J. Benavides Jr.
School—St. Theresa School, (Grades PreK-8), 455 S. Compadre, Palm Springs, 92262-7996.
Tel: 760-327-4919; Fax: 760-327-4429; Web: www.stsps.org. Michael Keno, Prin. Participating Parishes: Our Lady of Guadalupe Parish, Palm Springs; Our Lady of Solitude Parish, Palm Springs; St. Elizabeth of Hungary, Desert Hot Springs; Sacred Heart, Palm Desert. Lay Teachers 16; Students 196; Total Staff 16.
Catechesis Religious Program—Tel: 760-323-3669. Erika Gonzalez, C.R.E.; Yolanda Lopez, C.R.E. Students 311.

PERRIS, RIVERSIDE CO., ST. JAMES (1907)
269 W. Third St., Perris, 92570-2073.
Tel: 951-657-2380; Fax: 951-943-7290; Email: stjames.perris@sbdiocese.org. Revs. Eliseo Napiere, M.S.P.; Jose A. Orozco, Parochial Vicar; Deacon Ricardo Uribe.
School—St. James School, (Grades K-8), 250 W. Third St., Perris, 92570-2005. Tel: 951-657-5226; Fax: 951-657-1793; Email: stjames.ocs@sbdiocese.org; Web: www.stjamescs.com. Mr. Thomas Strickland, Prin. Participating Parishes: st. Vincent Ferrer, Sun City; St. Frances of Rome, Wildomar; St. Christopher, Moreno Valley. Lay Teachers 11; Students 141.
Catechesis Religious Program—240 S. B St., Perris, 92570. Tel: 951-940-5219; Fax: 951-940-5192; Email: tdejesussalas@sbdiocese.org. Teresita de Jesus Salas, C.R.E. Students 1,528.
Convent—230 W. B St., Perris, 92570.

PHELAN, SAN BERNARDINO CO., SAINT JUNIPERO SERRA (1989)
8820 Sheep Creek Rd., Phelan, 92371-2570.
Tel: 760-868-4342; Fax: 760-868-2171; Email: stjuniperoserra.phelan@sbdiocese.org; Web: ww.stserraphelan.org. Rev. Joachim Lechukwu, (Nigeria) Admin.; Deacons Thomas Miller; Frank Alaniz.
Catechesis Religious Program—
Tel: 760-868-4342, Ext. 42; Email: ctorres@sbdiocese.org. Claudia Torres, D.R.E. Students 147.

RANCHO CUCAMONGA, SAN BERNARDINO CO.

1—OUR LADY OF MOUNT CARMEL (1905)
10079 Eighth St., Rancho Cucamonga, 91730.
Tel: 909-987-2717; Fax: 909-987-3818; Email: olmtcarmel.rc@sbdiocese.org. Very Rev. Romeo N. Seleccion, M.S., E.V., Interim Admin.; Deacons Donald Norris; Guadalupe Ramirez.
Catechesis Religious Program—
Tel: 909-987-2717, Ext. 21; Email: egarcia.olmtcarmel.rc@sbdiocese.org. Mrs. Esthela Garcia, C.R.E. Students 267.

2—SACRED HEART (1953)
12704 Foothill Blvd., Rancho Cucamonga, 91739-9795. Tel: 909-899-1049; Fax: 909-899-3229; Email: sacredheart.rc@sbdiocese.org. Very Rev. Benedict C. Nwachukwu-Udaku, V.F.; Revs. Julian Chikezie Okoroanyanwu, Parochial Vicar; Edward J. Molumby, S.T., In Res.; Deacons Edward Clark; Antonio Hernandez.
School—Sacred Heart School, (Grades K-8), 12676 Foothill Blvd., Rancho Cucamonga, 91739.
Tel: 909-899-1049, Ext. 400; Fax: 909-899-0413; Email: sacredheartrc.ocs@sbdiocese.org; Web: shsrcbulldogs.webs.com. Dr. Danielle Espinoza, Prin. Participating Parishes: St. Peter and St. Paul, Alta Loma; St. Charles Borromeo, Bloomington; Our Lady of Mt. Carmel, Montclair; St. Jostph, Fontana. Lay Teachers 15; Students 324.
Catechesis Religious Program—Email: cecilia.f@sacredheartrc.org. Cecelia Fornelli, C.R.E. Students 1,062.

REDLANDS, SAN BERNARDINO CO., THE HOLY NAME OF JESUS CATHOLIC COMMUNITY, INC. (2006)
115 W. Olive Ave., Redlands, 92373-5245.
Tel: 909-793-2469; Fax: 909-335-1719; Email: theholynameofjesus.redlands@sbdiocese.org. Revs. Erik L. Esparza, J.C.L., Priest Moderator; Yovanny Acosta, Priest Min.; Hau Q. Vu, Priest Min.; Deacons Stephen Serembe, Pastoral Coord.; Michael Bellinder; Ayed Khader; Antonio Mejico; Jesse Robles.
Columbia Worship Site—1205 Columbia St., Redlands, 92373-5245.
School—Sacred Heart Academy, (Grades PreK-8), 215 S. Eureka St., Redlands, 92373.
Tel: 909-792-3958; Fax: 909-792-7292; Email: sacredheartred.ocs@sbdiocese.org; Web: www.sharedlands.org. Mrs. Angela C. Williams, Prin. Participating Parishes: The Holy Name of Jesus Catholic Community, Redlands; Our Lady of the Assumption, San Bernardino; St. Frances Xavier Cabrini, Yucaipa. Lay Teachers 18; Students 280.
Catechesis Religious Program—Email: kgrozak@sbdiocese.org. Karen Grozak, D.R.E. Students 523.

RIALTO, SAN BERNARDINO CO., ST. CATHERINE OF SIENA (1949)
339 N. Sycamore Ave., Rialto, 92376-5943.
Tel: 909-875-1360; Fax: 909-875-2822; Email: stcatherineofsiena.rialto@sbdiocese.org. Revs. Briccio Tamoro, S.V.D.; Richard Casillas, S.V.D., Parochial Vicar; Deacon Gonzalo Sotelo.
School—St. Catherine of Siena School, (Grades PreK-8), 335 N. Sycamore Ave., Rialto, 92376.
Tel: 909-875-7821; Email: cougars_1956@yahoo.com; Web: www.stcatherinerialto.com. Beverly Winn, Prin. Participating Parishes: St. Catherine or Siena, Rialto; San Salvador, Colton; Immaculate Conception, Colton; St. John XXIII, Fontana/Rialto; St. Anthony; St. Charles Borromeo, Bloomington; St. George, Fontana; Sacred Heart Rancho Cucamonga; St. Adelaide, Highland; The Holy Name of Jesus, Redlands. Lay Teachers 9; Students 145; Total Staff 11.
Catechesis Religious Program—
Tel: 909-875-1360, Ext. 122. Rosalie Vilchis, C.R.E. Students 660.

RIVERSIDE, RIVERSIDE CO.

1—ST. ANDREW KIM KOREAN COMMUNITY (1989)
4750 Challen Ave., Riverside, 92503.
Tel: 951-264-0661; Fax: 951-352-4900; Email: st_kindaekon@msn.com. Rev. Sunguk Paul Yang, M.S.C.
Catechesis Religious Program—Ms. Monica Song, Contact Person. Students 36.

2—ST. ANDREW NEWMAN CENTER (1971) Serving Riverside Community College & University of California at Riverside.
105 W. Big Springs Rd., Riverside, 92507-4737.
Tel: 909-682-8751; Fax: 951-682-3513; Email: newman.riv@sbdiocese.org. Revs. Cyriacus Ogu, Admin.; Alwyn B. Anfone, Parochial Vicar.
Catechesis Religious Program—
Tel: 951-682-8751, Ext. 13; Email: mdyall@sbdiocese.org. Ms. Mary A. Dyall, Contact Person. Students 115.

3—ST. ANTHONY (1923)
3074 Madison St., Riverside, 92504-4478.
Tel: 951-352-8393; Fax: 951-352-8816; Email: stanthony.riv@sbdiocese.org. Revs. Clemente Perez-Tellez; L. Omar Reyes, Parochial Vicar; Deacon Carlos Augustin Rosado.
Catechesis Religious Program—Lilia Gonzalez, D.R.E. Students 162.

4—ST. CATHERINE OF ALEXANDRIA (1946)
3680 Arlington Ave., Riverside, 92506.
Tel: 951-781-9855; Fax: 951-781-3061; Email: stcatherineofalexandria.riv@sbdiocese.org. 7005 Brockton Ave., Riverside, 92506. Very Rev. Generoso T. Sabio, M.S.C., V.F.; Revs. Sesinando Cajucom Jr., M.S.C., Parochial Vicar; Sagayaraj Emmanuel, M.S.C., Parochial Vicar; Adrianus Budhi, M.S.C., In Res.; Deacons John De Gano; Richard Heames.
School—St. Catherine of Alexandria School, (Grades K-8), 7025 Brockton Ave., Riverside, 92506.
Tel: 951-684-1091; Fax: 951-684-4936; Email: elandin@stcatherine-riverside.org; Web: www.stcofa1.org. Enrique Landin, Prin. Participating Parishes: Corpus Christi, Corona; St. Andrew Newman Center, Riverside; St. Anthony, Riverside; St. Catherine of Alexandria, Riverside; St. Christopher, Moreno Valley; St. Edward, Corona; St. Francis de Sales, Riverside; St. Charles Borromeo, Bloomington. Lay Teachers 15; Students 256; Total Staff 29; Clergy / Religious Teachers 4.
Catechesis Religious Program—
Tel: 951-781-9855, Ext. 25; Email: owiseman@stcofa.org. Olivia G. Wiseman, D.R.E. Students 533.

5—ST. FRANCIS DE SALES (1886)
4268 Lime St., Riverside, 92501-3868.
Tel: 951-686-4004; Fax: 951-686-3948; Email: stfrancisdesales.riv@sbdiocese.org; Web: www.stfrancisdesales-riverside.com. Rev. Louis Abdoo, I.M.C.; Deacon Joseph Marino.
School—St. Francis de Sales School, (Grades K-8), 4205 Mulberry St., Riverside, 92501.
Tel: 951-683-5083; Fax: 951-683-0249; Email: ngibson@sbdiocese.org; Web: www.sfdslions.com. Ms. Trenna Meins, Prin.; Mrs. Norma Gibson. Participating Parishes: St. Charles Borromeo, Bloomington; St. Margaret Mary, Chino; Our Lady of the Immaculate Conception, Colton; St. Edward, Corona; St. Matthew, Corona; Sacred Heart, Jurupa Valley; St. Joseph, St. Mary, Christ the Redeemer, St. Joseph the Worker, Loma Linda; St. Mel, Norco; St. James, Perris; St. Catherine of Siena, Rialto; Our Lady of Guadalupe. Lay Teachers 23; Dominican Sisters of Houston, TX 1; Students 125; Total Staff 26; Clergy / Religious Teachers 2.
Catechesis Religious Program—Email: jlewis@sbdiocese.org. Julia Lee-Lewis, D.R.E. Students 197.

6—ST. JOHN THE EVANGELIST (1956)
3980 Opal St., Riverside, 92509-7297.
Tel: 951-684-6864; Fax: 951-684-3115; Email: stjohntheevangelist@sbdiocese.org. Rev. Porfirio Romo, M.S.P.; Deacon Paul Von Ins; Sr. Gabriela Gutierrez.
Catechesis Religious Program—Sylvia Boyd, D.R.E. Students 656.
Mission—Our Lady of Guadalupe, 2518 Hall Ave., Riverside, Riverside Co. 92509.

7—OUR LADY OF GUADALUPE SHRINE (1929) (Hispanic)
2858 Ninth St., Riverside, 92507-4957.
Tel: 951-684-0279; Fax: 951-684-0390; Email: olgshrine.riv@sbdiocese.org. Revs. Alfonso Duran-Ortega, O.de.M.; L. Omar Reyes, Parochial Vicar.
Catechesis Religious Program—Tel: 951-683-1123. Sara Garcia, C.R.E. Students 207.

8—OUR LADY OF PERPETUAL HELP (1955)
5250 Central Ave., Riverside, 92504-1825.
Tel: 951-689-8921; Fax: 951-689-3619; Email: olph.riv@sbdiocese.org. Rev. Miguel R. Ceja, Admin.; Deacons Nam Bui; Bernardo Hernandez.
Rectory—6390 Lionel Ct., Riverside, 92504.
School—Our Lady of Perpetual Help School, (Grades PreK-8), Participating parishes: Corpus Christi, Corona; Our Lady of the rosary Cathedral, San Benrardino; Queen of Angels, Riverside; St. Patrick, Moreno Valley; St. Andrew Newman Center, Riverside; St. John the Evangelist, Riverside; St. Thomas the Apostle, Riverside; St. Catherine of Alexandria, Riverside; St. Mel, Norco. 6866 Streeter Ave., Riverside, 92504-2299. Tel: 951-689-2125; Fax: 951-689-9354; Email: olphriverside.ocs@sbdiocese.org; Web: olphriverside.com. Mrs. Ann R. Meier, Prin. Lay Teachers 10; Students 189; Total Staff 24.
Catechesis Religious Program—
Tel: 909-689-9821, Ext. 23. Ms. Mary Fisher, C.R.E. (English); Ms. Eva Jaimes, C.R.E. (Spanish); Sr. Hang Le, C.R.E. (Vietnamese). Students 645.

9—QUEEN OF ANGELS (1949)

4824 Jones Ave., Riverside, 92505-1499.
Tel: 951-689-3674; Email: queenofangelsriv@sbdiocese.org. Revs. Beni Leu, S.V.D., Admin.; Duy John Tran, S.V.D., Parochial Vicar; Predheep Sathiyanathan, Parochial Vicar.
Catechesis Religious Program—
Tel: 951-687-3674, Ext. 121. Rosa Maria Gouveia, D.R.E.; Ms. Mariana Flores, C.R.E. Students 747.

10—SACRED HEART (1945)
9935 Mission Blvd., Riverside, 92509.
Tel: 951-685-5058; Fax: 951-685-1056; Email: sacredheartriv@sbdiocese.org. Rev. Andres Garcia-Chavez.
Catechesis Religious Program—Email: marielenamurillo@sbdiocese.org. Mrs. Marielena Murillo, C.R.E. Students 216.

11—ST. THOMAS THE APOSTLE (1903)
3774 Jackson St., Riverside, 92503-4359.
Tel: 951-689-1131; Fax: 951-354-7402; Email: stthomastheapostle.riv@sbdiocese.org; Web: www.st-thomas-riverside.com. Rev. Frank T. Dicristina; Deacon Paul Myers.
School—St. Thomas School, (Grades K-8), 9136 Magnolia Ave., Riverside, 92503. Tel: 951-689-1981; Fax: 951-689-1985; Email: stasriverside@gmail.com; Web: www.stasriverside.com. Dian Pizurie, Prin. Participating Parishes: O.L.P.H. - Riverside; St. Thomas the Apostle - Riverside; Queen of Angels - Riverside; St. Christopher - Moreno Valley; St. Catherine of Alexandria - Riverside. Lay Teachers 12; Students 163; Total Staff 18.
Catechesis Religious Program—Email: maceves@sbdiocese.org. Marisol Aceves Cordova, C.R.E. (Spanish); Ms. Dana Lyn Robles, C.R.E. (English). Students 364.

RUNNING SPRINGS, SAN BERNARDINO CO., ST. ANNE IN THE MOUNTAINS (1963)
Mailing Address: P.O. Box 2400, Running Springs, 92382-2400. Tel: 909-867-2832; Fax: 909-867-2450; Email: stanne.runningsprings@sbdiocese.org; Web: mountaincatholic.org. Rev. Michal Osuch, C.R.
Office: 30480 Fredalba Rd., Running Springs, 92382.
Catechesis Religious Program— Combined with Our Lady of the Lake, Lake Arrowhead. Terri MacDonald, Contact Person.

SAN JACINTO, RIVERSIDE CO.
1—ST. ANTHONY (1890)
630 S. Santa Fe Ave., San Jacinto, 92583-4012.
Tel: 951-654-7911; Fax: 951-654-2309; Email: stanthony.sjc@sbdiocese.org. Revs. Hector Vasquez, Admin.; Abil Raj Pannerserlvam, H.G.N., Parochial Vicar; Deacon Fernando Vera.
School—St. Hyacinth Academy, (Grades PreK-8), 275 S. Victoria Ave., San Jacinto, 92583.
Tel: 951-654-2013; Fax: 951-654-5644; Email: sha.ocs@sbdiocese.org; Web: www.shaeagles.org. Mrs. Grace Lacsamana, Prin. Participating Parishes: Our Lady of the Valley, Hemet; Holy Spirit, Hemet. Lay Teachers 16; Students 215; Total Staff 16.
Catechesis Religious Program—Email: atorrez@sbdiocese.org. Alvino Torrez, C.R.E. Students 549.

2—ST. JOSEPH MISSION (1888) (Native American)
23600 Soboba Rd., San Jacinto, 92581-1027.
Tel: 951-654-2086; Email: stjoseph.sanjacinto@sbdiocese.org. P.O. Box 1027, San Jacinto, 92583. Rev. Earl Henley, M.S.C.; Deacon Andrew Orosco.
School—St. Jude Mission School, (Grades K-6), 23600 Soboba Rd., P.O. Box 399, San Jacinto, 92581.
Tel: 951-213-1276; Fax: 951-487-8822; Email: stjudesoboba@aol.com. Ann Peace, Contact Person. Lay Teachers 2; Sisters 2; Students 10; Total Staff 6; Clergy / Religious Teachers 2.
Catechesis Religious Program—Tel: 951-485-6673. Deacon Andrew Orosco, D.R.E. Students 30.
Chapels—Our Lady of the Snows Chapel—Cahuilla Indian Reservation, Anza, 92539. Tel: 951-763-5636.
St. Rose of Lima Chapel, Tel: 909-659-2708. Rev. Earl Joseph Henley, M.S.C.
St. Mary Chapel, Morongo Indian Reservation (11231 Mission Rd.), Banning, 92220.
Tel: 951-849-2434; Fax: 951-849-8698. Mailing Address: 157 W. Nicolet St., Banning, 92220. Rev. Earl Joseph Henley, M.S.C.
St. Michael Chapel, Pechanga Indian Reservation, Temecula, 92592. Rev. Earl Joseph Henley, M.S.C.
Sacred Hearts of Mary and Jesus Chapel, Torres-Martinez Indian Reservation, Thermal, 92274. Rev. Earl Joseph Henley, M.S.C.

SUN CITY, RIVERSIDE CO., ST. VINCENT FERRER (1965)
27931 Murrieta Rd., Sun City, 92586-2320.
Tel: 951-679-4531; Fax: 951-679-7521; Email: stvincentferrer@sbdiocese.org; Web: www.mystvincentferrer.org. Revs. Frederick A. Costales, M.S., Pastor & Supr.; Rizal Acosta, Parochial Vicar; Deacons Patrick Necerato; Efren Ramirez.
Catechesis Religious Program—Email: mwedeking@sbdiocese.org. Mary Wedeking, D.R.E. Students 639.

TEMECULA, RIVERSIDE CO., ST. CATHERINE OF ALEXANDRIA (1979)
41875 C St., Temecula, 92592-3029.
Tel: 951-676-4403; Fax: 951-695-6659; Email: stcatherineofalexandria.temecula@sbdiocese.org; Web: www.stcatherineofalexandria.net. Very Rev. Anthony C. Dao, V.F.; Rev. Johnny Dang, Parochial Vicar; Deacons Efren Ramirez; James Kincaid.
Catechesis Religious Program—Yolanda Ortiz, D.R.E.; Maria Barth, C.R.E. (Spanish); Letha Heylmun, C.R.E.; Ms. Sharla Ortiz, C.R.E. (English). Students 774.

TWENTYNINE PALMS, SAN BERNARDINO CO., BLESSED SACRAMENT (1940)
6785 Sage Ave., Twentynine Palms, 92277.
Tel: 760-367-3343; Fax: 760-367-0543; Email: blessedsacrament29palms@sbdiocese.org; Web: www.blessedsacramentchurch29palms.com. Rev. Eliseus Uju.
Catechesis Religious Program—Leanne Duncan, D.R.E.; Elaine Ashfield, C.R.E. Students 80.

UPLAND, SAN BERNARDINO CO.
1—ST. ANTHONY (1974)
2110 N. San Antonio Ave., Upland, 91784.
Tel: 909-985-2803; Fax: 909-982-8643; Email: stanthony.upland@sbdiocese.org; Web: www.stanthonyupland.org. Revs. Gerald Vidad; Michael J. Fredericks, Parochial Vicar; Deacons Antonio Hernandez; Robert A. Beidle; Richard Simpson; Isaias Palma.
Catechesis Religious Program—Ms. Lori Muniz, D.R.E. Students 202.

2—ST. JOSEPH (1922)
877 N. Campus Ave., Upland, 91786-3930.
Tel: 909-981-8110; Fax: 909-982-8991; Email: stjoseph.upland@sbdiocese.org. Revs. Timothy Truong Do, Admin.; Carlos Martinez; Deacons Mark Lopez; Luc Morisset; Roberto Villatoro.
School—St. Joseph School, (Grades K-8), 905 N. Campus Ave., Upland, 91786. Tel: 909-920-5185; Fax: 909-920-5190; Email: stjosephupland.ocs@sbdiocese.org; Web: www.stjosephupland.org. Mrs. Sandra Alamo-Ng, Prin. St. Peter and St. Paul, Alta Loma; St. Anthony, Upland; Sacred Heart, Rancho Cucamonga; St.Elizabeth Ann Seton; Ontario, St. George, Ontario; Our Lady of Lourdes, Montclair; Our Lady of Mt.Carmel, RanchoCucamonga; San Secondo D'Aasti, Guasti. Lay Teachers 11; Students 324; Total Staff 30.
Catechesis Religious Program—
Tel: 909-981-8110, Ext. 29. Debbi Aud, C.R.E. Students 261.
Convent—Sisters of the Presentation of the Blessed Virgin Mary (P.B.V.M.), 925 N. Campus Ave., Upland, 91786. Tel: 909-982-2686. Sr. Sheila Reen, Contact Person. Sisters 4.

VICTORVILLE, SAN BERNARDINO CO.
1—HOLY INNOCENTS (1991)
13230 El Evado Rd., Victorville, 92392.
Tel: 760-955-6010; Fax: 760-955-2100; Email: holyinnocentes.victorville@sbdiocese.org. Revs. Patrick Travers, SS.CC.; Geoffrey Eboh, Parochial Vicar.
Catechesis Religious Program—Email: jbarrera@sbdiocese.org. Juana M. Barrera, D.R.E. Students 735.

2—ST. JOAN OF ARC (1922)
15512 Sixth St., Victorville, 92395-3200.
Tel: 760-245-7674; Fax: 760-245-7077; Email: stjoanofarc.victorville@sbdiocese.org; Web: stjoanhd.org. Revs. Ciro Libanati; Jude Lourdhuraj Durairaj, Parochial Vicar; Deacon Manuel Gomez.
Catechesis Religious Program—Tel: 760-245-4904; Email: alombardo@sbdiocese.org. Ms. Alicia Lombardo, C.R.E. Students 350.

WILDOMAR, RIVERSIDE CO., ST. FRANCES OF ROME (1887)
21591 Lemon St., Wildomar, 92595-8410.
Tel: 951-674-6881; Fax: 951-674-6443; Email: office@sfrome.com; Web: www.sfrome.com. Revs. James F. Gayta Oropel; Francis A. Grant, Parochial Vicar; Deacons Joseph Franco; Raymond B. Moon.
School—St. Frances of Rome Preschool, (Grades PreK-PreK), Tel: 909-475-5435; Web: sfrome.com/parish-preschool. Victoria Kennedy, Contact Person. St. Frances of Rome Catholic Church, Wildomar. Lay Teachers 4; Students 10; Total Staff 4.
Catechesis Religious Program—
Tel: 951-674-6881, Ext. 224; Email: jpablin@sbdiocese.org. Leticia Pablin, C.R.E. Students 876.

WINCHESTER, RIVERSIDE CO., ST. MOTHER TERESA OF CALCUTTA CATHOLIC COMMUNITY, INC. (2006)
34750 Whisper Hts., Winchester, 92596.
Tel: 951-325-7707; Fax: 951-325-2306; Email: smtoc.winchester@sbdiocese.org; Web: www.btocchurch.org. 31579 Wintners Pointe Ct., Winchester, 92596. Rev. Msgr. Thomas J. Burdick; Rev. Ken T. Vu, Parochial Vicar; Deacons Jose Ibarra; Frank Merarcardante
Legal Name: Blessed Teresa of Calcutta Catholic Community, Inc.
Catechesis Religious Program—Tel: 951-676-4403; Email: daxline@btocchurch.org. Diane Axline, C.R.E. Students 509.

WRIGHTWOOD, SAN BERNARDINO CO., OUR LADY OF THE SNOWS (1946)
975 Lark Rd., Wrightwood, 92397. Tel: 760-868-4342 ; Fax: 760-868-2171; Email: olsnows.phelan@sbdiocese.org; Web: www.olswrightwood.org. Rev. Joachim Lechukwu, (Nigeria) Admin.; Deacon Tom Miller.
Catechesis Religious Program—
Tel: 760-868-4342, Ext. 42. Claudia Torres, C.R.E. Students 9.

YUCAIPA, SAN BERNARDINO CO., ST. FRANCES XAVIER CABRINI (1948)
12687 California St., Yucaipa, 92399-4405.
Tel: 909-797-2533; Fax: 909-790-5803; Email: stfrancesxaviercabrini.yucaipa@sbdiocese.org; Web: www.stfrancesxcabrinichurch.org. Rev. Santos L. Ortega, V.F.; Deacons Peter S. Bond; Daniel D. Hudec; Francisco Herrera.
Catechesis Religious Program—Virginia Velazquez, C.R.E. Students 341.

YUCCA VALLEY, SAN BERNARDINO CO., ST. MARY OF THE VALLEY (1953)
7495 Church St., Yucca Valley, 92284-3247.
Tel: 760-365-2287; Fax: 760-369-0622; Email: stmaryofthevalley.yuccavalley@sbdiocese.org; Web: www.stmaryofthevalley.com. Rev. Mark Bertelli; Deacon Glen Miller.
Catechesis Religious Program—Email: acervantes@sbdiocese.org. Araceli Cervantes, C.R.E. Students 134.

Chaplains of Public Institutions

SAN BERNARDINO. *St. Bernardine Medical Center*, 2101 N. Waterman Ave., 92404. Tel: 909-883-8711; Fax: 909-881-4531; Email: wileen.hernandez@dignityhealth.org. Rev. Msgr. Antonio Sudario, (Philippines) Chap., Rev. Joel Kelley, O.S.B., Chap.
Patton State Hospital, 3102 E. Highland Ave., Patton, 92369. Tel: 909-425-7429. Rev. Ignatius H. Rodrigues, (Retired), Steve Gomez.
San Bernardino Community Hospital, 1805 Medical Center Dr., 92411. Tel: 909-887-6333. Rev. Celestine Mbanu, (Nigeria).

APPLE VALLEY. *St. Mary Medical Center*, 18300 Hwy. 18, Apple Valley, 92307-0404. Tel: 760-242-2311; Email: judy.wagner@stjoe.org; Web: www.stmaryapplevalley.com. Sr. Mary Jo Piccione, S.P., Chap., Judy Wagner, M.A., M.S., L.B.S.W., C.C.L.S., Vice. Pres.

BLYTHE. *Chuckawalla Valley State Prison*, P.O. Box 2289, Blythe, 92226. Tel: 760-922-5300, Ext. 644. Rev. Ikechukwu Titus Ibeh.
Ironwood State Prison, 19005 Wileys Well Rd., P.O. Box 1968, Blythe, 92226. Tel: 760-921-3000. Rev. Alex C. Nnaukwu, Chap.

CHINO. *California Institution for Men*, 14901 Central Ave., P.O. Box 128, Chino, 91708.
Tel: 909-597-1821; Email: freburuche@yahoo.com. Rev. Eugene Eburuche, S.M.M.M., Sr. Elizabeth O'Keefe, R.S.H.M.

COLTON. *Arrowhead Regional Medical Center*, 400 N. Pepper, Colton, 92324. Tel: 909-580-1000. Rev. Miguel A. Urrea.

CORONA. *California Institution for Women*, 16756 Chino-Corona Rd., Corona, 91720.
Tel: 909-597-1771; Email: maryloyola.Yettke@cdcr.ca.gov. Dr. Maryloyola Yettke, Chap.

FONTANA. *Kaiser Permanente Hospital*, 9961 Sierra Ave., Fontana, 92335. Tel: 909-829-5850. Rev. Pierre L. Deglaire, C.S.Sp., Chap.

LOMA LINDA. *Jerry L. Pettis Memorial Veterans Hospital*, 11201 Benton St., Loma Linda, 92357.
Tel: 909-825-7084, Ext. 310; Email: leonard.mestas@va.gov. Revs. Ignacio M. Estrada, S.V.D., Chap., Leonard Mestas, Chap.
Loma Linda University Medical Center, 11234 Anderson St., Loma Linda, 92354.
Tel: 909-558-4000, Ext. 44367. Revs. Romanus Ike, Chap., James Onyenani, Chap.

MORENO VALLEY. *Riverside University Health System Regional Medical Center*, 56520 Cactus Ave., Moreno Valley, 92555. Tel: 951-486-4334. Rev. Eduardo Aguirre.

MURRIETA. *Loma Linda University Medical Center*, 28062 Baxter Rd., Murrieta, 92563.
Tel: 951-445-7341. Rev. Joseph T. Ellison, (Mexico).

NORCO. *California Rehabilitation Center*, 5th St. & Western, P.O. Box 1841, Norco, 91760.
Tel: 909-737-2683, Ext. 4305; Email: tharder@cdcr.ca.gov. Mr. Terry Harder.

RIVERSIDE. *Riverside Community Hospital*, 4445 Magnolia Ave., Riverside, 92501.
Tel: 909-788-3000. Rev. Adrianus Budhi, M.S.C.

TWENTY NINE PALMS. *Marine Corps Base*, Twenty-Nine Palms Marine Corps Base, Immaculate Heart of Mary Catholic Community, P.O. Box 788200, Twentynine Palms, 92278-8200. Tel: 760-830-6456 ; Fax: 760-830-4491. Rev. Jovito B. Roldan, J.C.L., Chap.

VICTORVILLE. *Federal Corrections Institute*, 13777 Air Expwy. Blvd., Victorville, 92394.
Tel: 760-530-5000, Ext. 5400. Rev. Innocent Emechete.

Special or Other Diocesan Assignments:
Revs.—
Barry, Michael, SS.CC., Mary's Mercy Center
Cao, John Mary Vu, C.M.C., Chap., Shrine of the Presentation
Palomares, Jesus, S.T., Chap., Valley Missionary Program
Rodriguez, Allen D., S.T., Chap., Holy Spirit Missionary Cenacle.

Retired:
Rev. Msgrs.—
Behan, Philip A., J.C.L., (Retired), 27250 Murrieta Rd., Spc. 285, Sun City, 92586
Corciulo, Cosimo, (Retired), 316 Mount Shasta Dr., Norco, 92860
Encinares, Cesar E., (Philippines) (Retired), 550 W. 5th St., Unit 212, 92401
Ryan, John, (Retired), 934 N. Dearborn, Redlands, 92374
Webber, Donald S., J.C.L., (Retired), 26634 Amhurst Ct., Sun City, 92586
Revs.—
Barker, Jack, K.C.H.S., (Retired), 23345 Bishop Rd., Murrieta, 92562
Baseford, Paul, (Retired), 485 Foxenwood Dr., Santa Maria, 93455
Chavez, Arturo, (Retired), 26071 St. Mary, Sun City, 92586
Connor, Vincent, (Retired), 23277 Sand Canyon Cir., Corona, 92883
Das Neves, Antonio C., (Retired), 28228 Paseo Grande Dr., Sun City, 92586
Devine, Charles F., (Retired), 1744 Santo Domingo Way, Hemet, 92545
DiLeo, Anthony, (Retired), 43981 Northgate Ave., Temecula, 92592
Donat, Robert J., (Retired), 5412 Calle de Arboles, Torrance, 90505
Gil, Paul R., (Retired), 1201 E. Highland Ave., 92404
Gonzales, George, (Retired), 24266 Barton Rd. Unit #7, Loma Linda, 92354
Guillen-Santoyo, Patricio, (Retired), Pacifica Senior Living Hillsborough, 11918 Central Ave. Apt. 245, Chino, 91710
Hindman, John, (Retired), 4222 Lionhead Ave., Riverside, 92503
Humphrys, Richard A., (Retired), c/o 326 W. Fourth St., Perris, 92570-3400
Jenkins, Kenneth F., (Retired), P.O. Box 720, Palm Desert, 92261
Kiefer, William J., (Retired), 27920 Niagara Ct., Sun City, 92586
Kopec, Chester C., O.P., (Retired), 4320 Columbia Ave., Riverside, 92501
Kurilec, Robert E., (Retired), 7743 Grundy St., Pensacola, FL 32507
Leahy, Maurice J., (Retired), Chicago, IL 60643. 9222 S. Oakley, Chicago, IL 60643
Lowe, Frank E., (Retired), 1385 Passage St., Palm Springs, 92261
McGuiness, Edward J., (Retired), Nazareth House, 6333 Rancho Mission Rd., San Diego, 92108
McNally, Michael R., (Retired), P.O. Box 3802, 92413-3802
O'Donnell, Edmond Ned, (Retired), P.O. Box 1405, Upland, 91786
Ochetti, Jerome, (Retired), 1051 Golden Rain St., Upland, 91786
Patron, Charles A., (Retired), 7868 Milliken Ave., #484, Rancho Cucamonga, 91730
Rasquinha, G. Ignatius, (Retired), Ingleside Lodge, 55747 Mountain View Trail, Yucca Valley, 92284
Rodrigues, Ignatius H., (Retired), 1728 N. Forest Oaks Dr., Beaumont, 92223
Rusk, Ron L., (Retired), 110 Roosevelt, Banning, 92222
Schultz, Charles F. Jr., S.T.D., (Retired), 1201 E. Highland Ave., 92404
Wagner, John F., (Retired), 44684 Lorraine Dr., Temecula, 92592.

Permanent Deacons:
Aguilera, Santos, Adelanto
Ahan, Paul, Grand Terrace
Alaniz, Frank, (Retired)
Amador, Robert, (Retired)
Ampuero, Marcial, Hesperia
Ayala, Luis, Mecca
Badena, Miguel, (Inactive)
Baltodano, Eduardo Antonio Jr., Temecula
Barna, John, Alta Loma
Barrion, Victor A., Highland
Bassford, Rick, Crestline
Beidle, Robert A., Alta Loma
Bellinder, Michael, San Bernardino
Benavides, Pablo J. Jr., Palm Springs
Bettencourt, John, (Retired)
Bond, Peter S., Yucaipa
Brenes-Rios, Anthony, Chino
Bui, Nam, Riverside
Burgett, Donald, (Retired)
Campbell, Gerald, (Retired)
Castanon, Leonard, Colton
Ciraulo, Christopher, Murrieta
Clark, Edward, Rancho Cucamonga
Clinton, Jack, (Retired)
Cover, Richard, (Retired)
Cruz, John Anthony, Chino
DeGano, John, Riverside
Dewhirst, Thomas, San Bernardino
Diaz, Porfirio, Murrieta
Echeverria, Octavio, Ontario
Esparza, Bernardo, Ontario
Estrella, Edwin, San Bernardino
Franco, Joseph, Wildomar
Garcia, Jose Israel, (Retired)
Geaga, Donnie, Eastvale
Glass, Nelson, Fontana/Rialto
Gomez, Manual, Victorville
Gonzalez, Victor, Desert Hot Springs
Gutierrez, Mario, San Bernardino
Han, Hikyung (H.K.), Blythe
Harmon, Glenn R., (Retired)
Heames, Richard, (Retired)
Henke, Jack, (Retired)
Heredia, Fernando, Coachella
Hernandez, Antonio, Rancho Cucamonga
Hernandez, Bernardo, Riverside
Hernandez, Jose Armando, Corona
Herrera, Francisco, Yucaipa
Herrera, Jose, Grand Terrace
Hockwalt, David, La Quinta
Hodnick, Mark, Beaumont
Hudec, Daniel D., Yucaipa
Hunsicker, Scott, J.C.L., (Retired)
Ibarra, Jose, Winchester
Jelley, Michael F., San Bernardino
Jimenez, Austin, Ontario
Juback, Michael, Lake Arrowhead
Khader, Ayed, Redlands
Kilbourn, Austin, (Retired)
Kim, John, M.D., (Inactive)
Kincaid, James, Temecula
Langmead, John, (Retired)
Lara, Ernest, Moreno Valley
Lawson, John, Temecula
Lopez, Mark, Upland
Luevano, Armando Jr., Beaumont
Lugo, Jerry, Indio
Malkowski, Dennis, (Retired)
Marino, Joseph, Riverside
Martinez, Alfonso, San Bernardino
Martinez, Mark, Colton
Martinez, Pat, (Retired)
McDaniel, Alvin, (Retired)
Mejico, Antonio, Redlands
Melton, Harold, (Retired)
Mercadante, Frank, Winchester
Mercado, Jesus, Cathedral City
Meza, Francisco, Anza
Miller, Glenn, Yucca Valley
Miller, Thomas, Phelan
Mirci, Philip, (Inactive)
Moon, Raymond B., Wildomar
Moore, Greg, Fontana
Moorman, Joseph, Barstow
Morales, Carlos, Fontana
Moralez, Tony, Chino Hills
Morisset, Luc, Upland
Myers, Paul, (Retired)
Necerato, Patrick, Sun City
Neufell, James A., (Retired)
Norris, Donald, Rancho Cucamonga
Ocampo, Ernesto, Moreno Valley
Olivas, Manuel, (Retired)
Orosco, Andrew, Native American Ministry
Ortiz, Joe, (Retired)
Padilla, Mark, Indio
Palma, Isaias, Upland
Partida, Ralph Jr., (Retired)
Phillips, Robert, (Retired)
Pimentel, Simon, (Retired)
Quinn, Gary, Ontario, Chino Hills
Ramirez, Efren, Sun City
Ramirez, Guadalupe, Rancho Cucamonga
Ramirez, Manuel, Hemet
Rivas, Manuel, Moreno Valley
Robles, Jesse, Redlands
Rodriguez, Brijido, Indio
Rosado, Carlos Augustin, Riverside
Rosas, Jaime, La Quinta
Sanchez, Luis, Ontario
Scanlon, John, La Quinta
Sepulveda, Ralph, (Retired)
Serembe, Stephen, Redlands
Serrano, Jose, Moreno Valley
Servin, Armando, Temecula
Shalhoub, William J., (Retired)
Shellem, Bill, (Retired)
Simpson, Richard, Upland
Skora, John, (Retired)
Sotelo, Gonzalo, Rialto
Stanton, Charlie, (Retired)
Taylor, Daniel, (Retired)
Tiambeng, Victor, Eastvale
Uribe, Ricardo, Perris
Vargaz, Alfredo, Fontana
Vasquez, Sergio, Coachella
Vela, Joe, (Retired)
Vera, Fernando, San Jacinto
Vilchis, Eric, San Bernardino
Villatoro, Roberto, Upland
Vita, Wilfredo, Murrieta
Von Ins, Paul, Riverside
Von Voight, Fred, (Retired)
Vu, Toan, Ontario
Wagner, Brooke, Big Bear Lake
Weber, James, Big Bear Lake
Weber, Mark, San Bernardino
Zamora, Abel, Fontana/Rialto.

INSTITUTIONS LOCATED IN DIOCESE

[A] SEMINARIES, RELIGIOUS OR SCHOLASTICATES

GRAND TERRACE. *Saint Junipero Serra House of Formation* (1985) 12725 Oriole Ave., Grand Terrace, 92313. Tel: 909-783-0260;
Fax: 909-783-0223; Email: jgarcia@sbdiocese.org. Revs. Emmanuel Ukaegbu-Onuoha, Dir. of Spiritual Formation; Jose A. Sanz, D.L.P., Dir. of Academics; Very Most Revs. Rutilio Del Riego, D.L.P., Dir. of Pastoral Formation; Jorge A. Garcia, Rector. Religious Teachers 4; Priests 4; Seminarians 14; Sisters 4; Students 35.

[B] HIGH SCHOOLS, DIOCESAN

SAN BERNARDINO. *Aquinas High School* Participating Parishes: Holy Rosary, San Bernardino; Our Lady of Assumption, San Bernardino; St. Adelaide, Highland; St. George, Fontana; St. Catherine of Siena, Rialto; St. Joseph, Fontana 2772 Sterling Ave., 92404. Tel: 909-886-4659; Fax: 909-886-7717; Email: aquinashs.ocs@sbdiocese.org; Web: www.aquinashs.net. Christopher Barrows, Prin.; Dr. Jim Brennan, Pres. Lay Teachers 35; Daughters of Mary Mother of Mercy Congregation (DMMM) 1; Students 518; Total Staff 36.

RIVERSIDE. *Notre Dame High School* Participating Parishes: St. Catherine of Alexandria, Riverside; St. Francis de Sales, Riverside; St. Edward, Corona; St. Thomas the Apostle, Riverside; St. James, Perris; St. Mel, Norco. 7085 Brockton Ave., Riverside, 92506. Tel: 951-275-5896;
Fax: 951-781-9020; Email: mluttringer@ndhsriverside.org; Web: www.ndhsriverside.org. Matthew Luttringer, Prin.; Mrs. Lydia Dashkovitz, Librarian. Lay Teachers 29; Priests 1; Students 508; Total Staff 30.

[C] HIGH SCHOOLS, PRIVATE

PALM DESERT. **Xavier College Preparatory* Participating Parishes: Sacred Heart Church, Palm Desert; St. Theresa, Palm Springs; Our Lady of Perpetual Help, Indio. 34-200 Cook St., Palm Desert, 92211. Tel: 760-601-3900; Fax: 760-601-3901; Email: calling@xavierprep.org; Web: xavierprep.org. Mr. Chris Alling, Prin. Lay Teachers 47; Students 574; Total Staff 48.

[D] ELEMENTARY SCHOOLS, PRIVATE

TEMECULA. *Saint Jeanne de Lestonnac School*, (Grades PreK-8), Participating Parishes: St. Martha, Murrieta; St. Catherine of Alexandria, Temecula; Blessed Teresa of Calcutta, Winchester 32650 Avenida Lestonnac, Temecula, 92592. Tel: 951-587-2505; Fax: 951-587-2515; Email: stjeannedelestonnac.ocs@sbdiocese.org; Email: ernestineodn@gmail.com; Web: www.sjdls.com. Mrs. Kristen Mora, Prin.; Mrs. Sue Fitzgerald, Librarian. Lay Teachers 28; Company of Mary 3; Students 476; Staff 32.

[E] HOMES FOR SENIOR CITIZENS

SAN BERNARDINO. *St. Bernardine Plaza Corporation*, 550 W. Fifth St., 92401. Tel: 909-888-0153; Fax: 909-381-1589; Email: stbern2@la.twcbc.com. 1201 E. Highland Ave., 92404. Ms. Laura J. Clark, CFO. Total Staff 5; Units 150.

[F] GENERAL HOSPITALS AND CLINICS

SAN BERNARDINO. *St. Bernardine Medical Center*, 2101 N. Waterman Ave., 92404. Tel: 909-883-8711; Fax: 909-881-4531; Email: Robert.Sahagian@DignityHealth.org; Web: www.stbernardinemedicalcenter.org. Douglas Kleam, Pres. Bed Capacity 342; Tot Asst. Annually 183,973; Total Staff 1,672.

St. Bernardine Medical Center Foundation, 2101 N. Waterman Ave., 92404. Tel: 909-881-4516; Email: Robert.Sahagian@DignityHealth.org; Web: www.supportstbernardine.org. Dan Murphy, Vice Pres. & Exec. Dir. Employees 4.

San Bernardino Community Hospital, 1805 Medical Center Dr., 92411. Tel: 909-887-6333; Email: cmbanu@sbdiocese.org; Web: locations.dignityhealth.org. Rev. Celestine Mbanu, (Nigeria) Chap. Bed Capacity 343; Tot Asst. Annually 8,000; Total Staff 4.

APPLE VALLEY. *St. Joseph Health, St. Mary*, 18300 Hwy. 18, Apple Valley, 92307. Tel: 760-242-2311; Fax: 760-242-2994; Email: judy.wagner@stjoe.org; Web: www.stmaryapplevalley.com. Judy Wagner, M.A., M.S., L.B.S.W., C.C.L.S., Vice Pres., Mission Services; Erika Corle, Asst. Bed Capacity 212; Sisters 132; Tot Asst. Annually 170,413; Total Staff 1,700.

[G] ALCOHOL AND DRUG REHABILITATION CENTERS

VICTORVILLE. *St. John of God Health Care Services*, 13333 Palmdale Rd., P.O. Box 2457, Victorville, 92393. Tel: 760-241-4917; Fax: 760-241-8911; Email: gbarnes@sjghcs.org. Gregory Barnes, Admin. & Exec. Dir. Sponsored by the Brothers of St. John of God.Alcohol and Drug Rehabilitation Program. Bed Capacity 64; Brothers 3; Patients Asst Anual. 920; Total Staff 32.

[H] CATHOLIC SOCIAL SERVICE ORGANIZATIONS

SAN BERNARDINO. *Catholic Charities San Bernardino & Riverside Counties*, Administration Office, 1450 N. D St., 92405. Tel: 909-388-1239; Fax: 909-384-1130; Email: info@ccsbriv.org; Web: ccsbriv.org. Ken F. Sawa, M.S.W., L.C.S.W., CEO, Exec. Vice Pres.; Jesse R. Gonzalez, Dir. Admin. Tot Asst. Annually 31,211; Total Staff 76; Poverty Alleviation Centers 10; Immigrant Assistance/Refuge Assistance Centers 6.

**Mary's Mercy Center, Inc.*, 641 Roberds Ave., P.O. Box 7563, 92411. Tel: 909-889-2558; Fax: 909-386-7704; Email: mmcinc@msn.com; Web: marysmercycenter.org. Michael J. Hein, Vice Pres. Tot Asst. Annually 3,360; Veronica's Home 160; Mary's Table 3,200; Staff 21.

INDIO. **Martha's Village & Kitchen, Inc.*, 83-791 Date Ave., Indio, 92201. Tel: 760-347-4741, Ext. 114; Fax: 760-347-9551; Email: lbarrack@marthasvillage.org; Web: www.marthasvillage.org. Linda Barrack, Pres. & C.E.O. A member of Father Joe's Villages. Tot Asst. Annually 6,000; Total Staff 60.

[I] MONASTERIES AND RESIDENCES OF PRIESTS AND BROTHERS

APPLE VALLEY. *Congregation of the Resurrection, CR*, 875 E. Chanslorway, Blythe, 92225. Tel: 760-922-3261; Fax: 760-922-5279; Email: stjoanofarcinblythe@hotmail.com. Revs. James M. Gibson, C.R.; Delwyn Haroldson, C.R.; Henry Licznerski, C.R.; Michal Osuch, C.R.; Paul Smith, C.R.; Henry A. Ruszel, C.R., (Retired). P.O. Box 1929, Lake Arrowhead, 92359. Tel: 909-337-2333; Fax: 909-337-5041. Rev. Michal Osuch, C.R. P.O. Box 1709, Big Bear Lake, 92315. Tel: 909-866-3030 ; Fax: 909-866-5087. Rev. Paul Smith, C.R.

Hospitaller Brothers of St. John of God, 18467 Chapay Ln., Apple Valley, 92307. Tel: 760-885-8527. Bros. Edward Francis McEnroe, Prior; Thaddeus Bui, Prior; Eric Hoffer, O.H. Brothers 3; Tot Asst. Annually 3,500; Poverty Alleviation Centers 1; Centers for Rehabilitation of Drug Abusers 1.

CORONA. *Confraternity of Operarios Del Reino De Cristo, C.O.R.C.*, 605 W. 5th St., Corona, 92882. Tel: 951-549-6000; Fax: 951-549-6009. Revs. Hector Magallon, Admin.; Juan Francisco Abonce Zepeda, C.O.R.C., Regl. Supr.; Christian F. Vera Cabrera, Parochial Vicar; Carlo G. Garduno Garay, C.O.R.C., Parochial Vicar; Pedro Enrique Amezcua Nunez, C.O.R.C., Pastor.

Shrine of Presentation, 1775 S. Main St., Corona, 92882. Tel: 951-737-4125; Email: felixluancmc@yahoo.com; Web: www.medangcon.net. Revs. Felix Luan, Pres.; Tan (Francis) Ta, Vice Pres.; Andrew Mary Sang Linh Do, C.M.C. Shrine of Presentation (Den Thanh Me Dang Con).

GRAND TERRACE. *Diocesan Laborer Priests, DLP*, Blessed Junipero Serra House of Formation, 12725 Oriole Ave., Grand Terrace, 92313. Tel: 909-783-0260; Fax: 909-783-0223; Email: serrahouse@hotmail.com. Rev. Jose A. Sanz, D.L.P., Dir. of Seminarians; Most Rev. Rutilio J. del Riego, Auxiliary Bishop Emeritus.

HEMET. *Congregation of the Holy Spirit*, Casa Laval Retirement Community, 309 E. Whitter Ave., P.O. Box 3509, Hemet, 92546-3509. Tel: 951-312-2603; Fax: 951-929-7865; Email: jgaglione@aol.com. Revs. Joseph B. Gaglione, C.S.Sp., Supr., (Retired); Michael Onwuemelie, C.S.Sp., Pastor.

Congregation of the Sacred Hearts of Jesus and Mary, SS.CC., Western U.S. Province, Hemet House of Prayer, 32481 Sage Rd., Hemet, 92544. Tel: 951-767-9303; Email: pcrowley@sbdiocese.org. Revs. Patrick Fanning, Novice Master; Jeremiah Holland, SS.CC., Asst. Novice Master; Patrick J. Crowley, SS.CC., Regional Vicar; Patrick Travers, SS.CC., Pastor; Paul Murtagh, SS.CC.; Martin O'Loghlen, SS.CC.; Michael Barry, SS.CC.

LUCERNE VALLEY. *The Cistercian Congregation of the Holy Family, St. Joseph Monastery*, 21010 Lucerne Valley Cutoff, P.O. Box 960, Lucerne Valley, 92356-0960. Tel: 760-666-0203; Email: xitostjoseph@gmail.com. Revs. M. Anthony Hanh Si Pham, O.Cist., Supr.; M. Justin Cong Huu Ho, O.Cist.; M. Timothy Qui Van Than, O.Cist.; Bros. M. Peter-Binh Quynh Dang Pham, O.Cist.; M. Francis of Assisi Phu Quoc Nguyen, O.Cist.; Bonaventure Dong Van Pham, O.Cist.; M. Peter Khanh Minh Ngoc Pham, O.Cist.; Stephan Hoa Van Nguyen, O.Cist.; Revs. M. Robert Canh X Lai; M. Antony Nguyen.

MORENO VALLEY. *Missionaries of Our Lady of La Salette, MS*, 25075 Cottonwood Ave., Moreno Valley, 92553. Tel: 951-924-1968; Fax: 951-247-6477; Email: fredcostales@sbdiocese.org. Revs. Clarence Gesbert Saldua, M.S., Admin.; Antonio Abuan, M.S., Admin.; Frederick A. Costales, M.S., Supr., Vincent Ferrer Parish, Menifee; Very Rev. Romeo N. Seleccion, M.S., E.V., Episcopal Vicar; Revs. Joseph Peethuruthel, M.S., Parochial Vicar; Jacob Thomas Vettathu, M.S., Parochial Vicar, Our Lady of Lourdes Parish, Montclair; Joseph Christian Pilotin, M.S., Parochial Vicar, St. Paul the Apostle Parish, Chino Hills, CA, St. Paul the Apostle Parish, Chino Hills; Rizal Acosta, Parochial Vicar; Noel Cruz, M.S., Pastor.

REDLANDS. *Discalced Carmelites, OCD*, P.O. Box 8067, Redlands, 92375. Tel: 909-792-1047; Fax: 909-798-3497; Email: elcarmelorh@gmail.com; Web: wwwdiscalcedcarmelitefriars.com. Revs. Adam Gregory Gonzales, O.C.D., Prov.; Thomas Reeves, Dir. / Supr.; Bro. Juan Torres; Rev. Bernard Perkins, O.C.D.

[J] CONVENTS AND RESIDENCES FOR SISTERS

BIG BEAR LAKE. *Society Devoted to the Sacred Heart, S.D.S.H.*, 896 Cienega Rd., P.O. Box 1795, Big Bear Lake, 92315. Tel: 909-866-5696; Fax: 909-866-5650; Email: sdshbigbear@gmail.com. Sisters Michelle Bittner, Contact Person; Rachael Gleason, S.D.S.H.; Rose Amoranto, S.D.S.H.; Hannah Barnett, S.D.S.H.; Joan Games, S.D.S.H.; Laura Bradford. Sisters 6.

CALIMESA. *Missionary Sisters of the Immaculate Conception* (SMIC) 1271 Nugget Ct., Calimesa, 92320. Fax: 909-795-8128; Email: judinefran@aol.com. Sisters Judine Jacobs, S.M.I.C., Religious, Volunteer at: Carol's Kitchen; Blessed Kateri Tekakawitha Church; Cabazon Community Center; Banning Community Center.; Frances Karovic, S.M.I.C., Volunteer Parish Health Ministry at Saint Kateri Tekakwitha Church, Member of Ethics Committee at St. Bernardine's Hospital in San Bernardino, CA. Sisters 2; Sisters (Madonna of Desert Community) 2.

REDLANDS. *Sisters of Mercy, U.S. Province*, U. S. Province, Provincial House, 1075 Bermuda Dr., Redlands, 92374. Tel: 909-798-4747; Fax: 909-798-5300; Email: roconnor-sm@sbdiocese.org; Web: www.sistersofmercy.ie. Sr. Rosaline O'Connor, R.S.M., Prov. Leader. Total in U.S. Province 39.

TEMECULA. *Congregation of Kkottongnae Brothers and Sisters of Jesus* (CKSJ) 37885 Woodchuck Rd., Temecula, 92592. Tel: 951-302-3400; Fax: 951-302-3400; Email: kkotjun@hanmail.net. Sr. He Gyung Bartholomew, Dir. Sisters 3.

Sisters of the Company of Mary Our Lady, Convent, 32650 Avenida Lestonnac, Temecula, 92592. Tel: 951-587-2504; Fax: 951-587-2515; Email: leticiasalzar@mac.com; Web: sjdls.com. Sr. Ernestine Velarde, O.D.N., School Pres. Sisters 8.

Vina de Lestonnac Retirement Center-Convent, 39300 De Portola Rd., Temecula, 92592. Tel: 951-302-2800; Fax: 951-303-1985; Email: USRegionsec@odnusa.org. Sr. Elvira Rios, O.D.N., Supr. Total in Residence 9.

[K] DIOCESAN CORPORATIONS

SAN BERNARDINO. **Caritas Telecommunications Corporation*, 1201 E. Highland Ave., 92404. Tel: 909-475-5415; Fax: 909-475-5357; Email: jandrews@sbdiocese.org; Web: www.sbdiocese.org. Mr. John H. Andrews, Dir.

Catholic Education Foundation of the Diocese of San Bernardino, 1201 E. Highland Ave., 92404. Tel: 909-475-5300; Email: lclark@sbdiocese.org. Ms. Laura J. Clark, CFO; Austin Conley III, Dir. of Advancement, Office of Catholic Schools.

The Catholic Foundation, 1201 E. Highland Ave., 92404. Tel: 909-475-5150; Fax: 909-475-5156; Email: lclark@sbdiocese.org. Ms. Laura J. Clark, CFO.

Diocesan Development Fund, Inc., 1201 E. Highland Ave., 92404. Tel: 909-475-5150; Fax: 909-475-5156; Email: lclark@sbdiocese.org. Ms. Laura J. Clark, CFO.

Diocese of San Bernardino Cemetery Corp., Inc., 1201 E. Highland Ave., 92404. Tel: 909-475-5150; Fax: 909-475-5156; Email: cemeteries@sbdiocese.org. Ms. Laura J. Clark, CFO; Rev. Msgr. Gerard M. Lopez, S.T.L., V.G., Pastoral Dir.

Diocese of San Bernardino Education & Welfare Corporation, 1201 E. Highland Ave., 92404-4641. Tel: 909-475-5150; Fax: 909-457-5156; Email: lclark@sbdiocese.org. Ms. Laura J. Clark, CFO.

Diocese of San Bernardino Land Development Corporation, 1201 E. Highland Ave., 92404. Tel: 909-475-5150; Fax: 909-475-5156; Email: lclark@sbdiocese.org. Ms. Laura J. Clark, CFO.

Saint Junipero Serra House of Formation, Inc., 1201 E. Highland Ave., 92404. Tel: 909-475-5150; Fax: 909-475-5156; Email: lclark@sbdiocese.org. Ms. Laura J. Clark, CFO.

SAN JACINTO. *Kateri Tekakwitha Fund*, P.O. Box 302, San Jacinto, 92581-0302. Tel: 951-654-7899; Fax: 951-654-2086; Email: mtorrano@rscj.org. Sr. Marianna Torrano, R.S.C.J., Sec. & CFO.

[L] CAMPS & RETREATS

BIG BEAR LAKE. *Sacred Heart Retreat Camp*, 896 Cienega Rd., P.O. Box 1795, Big Bear Lake, 92315. Tel: 909-866-5696; Fax: 909-866-5650; Email: office@sacredheartretreatcamp.com; Web: www.sacredheartretreatcamp.com. Sisters Rachael Gleason, S.D.S.H., Dir.; Michelle Bittner, Supr. Total in Residence 9; Total Staff 13.

REDLANDS. *El Carmelo Retreat House*, 926 E. Highland Ave., P.O. Box 8067, Redlands, 92375. Tel: 909-792-1047; Fax: 909-798-3497; Email: elcarmelorh@gmail.com; Web: www.elcarmelo.org. Rev. Adam Gregory Gonzales, O.C.D., Prov. Brothers 1; Priests 3; Sisters 4; Total in Residence 3; Total Staff 20.

RIVERSIDE. *Divine Word Seminary - Divine Word Retreat Center*, 11316 Cypress Ave., Riverside, 92505. Tel: 951-689-4858; Fax: 951-785-0327; Email: pschmidt@sbdiocese.org. Revs. Donald O'Connor, S.V.D., Admonitor; Edmund Afagbegee, S.V.D., Dir.; Paul L. Schmidt, S.V.D., Rector; Long Van Nguyen, S.V.D., Vice Rector. Brothers 1; Priests 11; Total in Residence 12; Total Staff 9.

SVD House, SVD House, 30823 Mission St., Highland, 92346-6345. Tel: 909-748-6561. Revs. Joseph P. Scott, S.V.D.; Sony Sebastian, S.V.D., Prov. Supr.

RUNNING SPRINGS. *St. Anne in the Mountains Catholic Church and Retreat Center*, 30480 Fredalba Rd, P.O. Box 2400, Running Springs, 92382. Tel: 909-867-2832; Fax: 909-867-4250; Email: stanneinthemountains@aol.com; Web: www.mountaincatholic.org. Terri MacDonald, Contact Person; Ms. Francine Coyne, Asst.

TEMECULA. *Vina de Lestonnac Ministry Center* -

Retreat, 39300 De Portola Rd., Temecula, 92592. Tel: 951-302-5571; Fax: 951-302-2830; Email: vinadelestonnac@odnusa.org. 16791 E. Main St., Tustin, 92780. Debbie Fanzo, Dir.; Ms. Tina Volz, Retreat Coord.

Lestonnac Chalet - Retreat, 24719 San Moritz Dr., Crestline, 92325. Tel: 714-541-3125; Email: lestonnacretreat@odnusa.org. 16791 E. Main St., Tustin, 92780. Sr. Elvira Rios, O.D.N., Sec.

[M] NEWMAN CENTERS

SAN BERNARDINO. *Catholic Newman Club at California State University, San Bernardino*, 1201 E. Highland Ave., 92404. Tel: 909-537-7337; Fax: 909-537-7339; Email: miosefo@sbdiocese.org; Web: sites.google.com/site/sbdiocesecampusministry. Sr. Maria Asopesio Iosefo, S.M.S.M., Campus Minister.

Catholic Newman Club at University of Redlands, 1201 E. Highland Ave., 92404. Tel: 909-475-5450; Fax: 909-475-5155; Email: mjansen@sbdiocese.org. Mrs. Mary F. Jansen, Campus Minister.

RIVERSIDE. *St. Andrew Newman Center*, 105 W. Big Springs Rd., Riverside, 92507. Tel: 951-682-8751; Fax: 951-682-3513; Email: newman.riv@sbdiocese.org; Web: sanccatholic.org. Revs. Cyriacus Ogu, Admin.; Alwyn B. Anfone, Parochial Vicar. Serving Riverside City-College and University of California at Riverside.

[N] MISCELLANEOUS

SAN BERNARDINO. *Ministerio Biblico Verbo Divino (MBVD)*, Mailing Address: P.O. Box 1610, 92402. 555 N. E St., 92401. Tel: 909-383-9030; Fax: 909-383-4987; Email: mbvdsb@gmail.com; Web: www.verbodivino.org. Rev. Joseph P. Scott, S.V.D., Pres. & Contact Person.

**Wordnet, Inc.*, 532 N. "D" St., 92401-1304. Tel: 909-383-4333; Fax: 909-383-4347; Email: exdir@wordnet.tv; Web: wordnet.tv. Sr. Patricia Ann Phillips, S.H.C.J., Exec. Dir.; Rev. Sony Sebastian, S.V.D., Exec. Producer; Sr. Jeanne Harris, O.P., Communications Dir.; Dolores Onkingco, Dir. Finance; Joann Martinez, Database Mgr.; Rev. Biju Thomas Mandapathil, S.V.D., Assoc. Dir. Brothers 1; Lay Staff 2; Priests 3; Sisters 2.

RIVERSIDE. *Misioneros Laicos del Verbo Divino*, 4093 Tyler St., Riverside, 92503. Tel: 951-359-8900; Email: mfloresmlvd@mail.com. Ms. Mariana Flores, Admin.

[O] CLOSED OR MERGED PARISHES

SAN BERNARDINO. *St. Anne* (1938) Closed 2006. For sacramental records, contact Our Lady of Hope, Tel: 909-884-6375.

Christ the King (1934) Closed 2006. For sacramental records, contact Our Lady of Hope, Tel: 909-884-6375.

Our Lady of Fatima (1952) Closed 2006. For sacramental records, contact Our Lady of Hope, Tel: 909-884-6375.

St. Theresa Parish Closed 1992. For sacramental records, contact Diocesan Archives.

ALBERHILL. *Blessed Sacrament Parish* Closed 1965. For sacramental records, contact Diocesan Archives.

AMBOY. *St. Raymond Parish* Closed 1970. For sacramental records, contact Diocesan Archives.

BANNING. *Precious Blood* (1890) Closed 2006. For sacramental records, contact Saint Kateri Tekakwitha, Tel: 951-849-2434.

BEAUMONT. *Sacred Heart Parish* Closed 1965. For sacramental records, contact Saint Kateri Tekakwitha, Tel: 951-849-2434.

San Gorgonio (1908) Closed 2006. For sacramental records, contact Saint Kateri Tekakwitha, Tel: 951-849-2434.

EAGLE MOUNTAIN. *St. Augustine* Closed 2001. For sacramental records, contact Diocesan Archives.

FONTANA. *Church of the Resurrection* (1953) Closed 2006. For sacramental records, contact Saint John XXIII, Tel: 909-822-4732.

HIGHGROVE. *Our Lady of Guadalupe* Closed 1981. For sacramental records, contact Christ the Redeemer, Tel: 909-475-5399.

JOSHUA TREE. *St. Christopher of the Desert* Closed 2010. For sacramental records, contact St. Mary of the Valley Parish, Tel: 760-365-2287.

LUDLOW. *St. Michael Parish* Closed 1962. For sacramental records, contact Diocesan Archives.

ORO GRANDE. *St. Cecilia Parish* Closed 1975. For sacramental records, contact St. Joan of Arc, Victorville, Tel: 760-245-7674.

REDLANDS. *St. Mary* (1941) Closed 2006. For sacramental records, contact The Holy Name of Jesus, Tel: 909-793-2469.

Sacred Heart (1894) Closed 2006. For sacramental records, contact The Holy Name of Jesus, Tel: 909-793-2469.

RIALTO. *St. Thomas More* (1961) Closed 2006. For sacramental records, contact Saint John XXIII, Tel: 909-822-4732.

RIVERSIDE. *St. Ignatius Parish* Closed 1972. For sacramental records, contact Our Lady of Guadalupe Shrine, Tel: 951-684-0279.

THOUSAND PALMS. *St. Philip the Apostle* (1991) Closed 2007. For sacramental records, contact Diocesan Archives.

RELIGIOUS INSTITUTUES OF MEN REPRESENTED IN THE DIOCESE.

For further details refer to the corresponding bracketed number in the Religious Institutes of Men or Women section.

[0140]—*Order of St. Augustine*—O.S.A.
[0380]—*Comboni Missionaries of the Sacred Heart of Jesus*—M.C.C.J.
[]—*Confraternity of Operarios del Reino de Cristo*—C.O.R.C.
[]—*Congregation of Kkottongnae Brothers of Jesus*—C.K.B.J.
[0865]—*Congregation of the Mother of the Redeemer*—C.R.M.
[0650]—*Congregation of the Holy Spirit*—C.S.Sp.
[1080]—*Congregation of the Resurrection*—C.R.
[1140]—*Congregation of the Sacred Hearts of Jesus and Mary* (Western Prov.)—SS.CC.
[0390]—*Consolata Missionaries*—I.M.C.
[]—*Diocesan Laborer Priests*—D.L.P.
[0260]—*Discalced Carmelite Friars* (Western Prov.)—O.C.D.
[0855]—*Fraternidad Misionera de Maria*—F.M.M.
[0585]—*Heralds of Good News*—H.G.N.
[0670]—*Hospitaller Brothers of St. John of God*—O.H.
[]—*Misioneros Servidores de la Palabra*—M.S.P.
[0720]—*Missionaries of Our Lady of La Salette*—M.S.
[1110]—*Missionaries of the Sacred Heart*—M.S.C.
[]—*Missionaries of the Sacred Heart* (Philippines)—M.S.C.
[0840]—*Missionary Servants of the Most Holy Trinity*—S.T.
[]—*Missionary Society of the Phillipines*—M.S.P.
[0340]—*Order of Cistercians*—O.Cist.
[0970]—*Order of Our Lady of Mercy*—O.de.M.
[0200]—*Order of St. Benedict*—O.S.B.
[0370]—*Society of St. Columbian*—S.S.C.
[0420]—*Society of the Divine Word* (Western Prov.)—S.V.D.
[]—*Sons of Mary Mother of Mercy*—S.M.M.M.

RELIGIOUS INSTITUTES OF WOMEN REPRESENTED IN THE DIOCESE

[]—*Congregation of Kkottongnae Sisters of Jesus*—C.K.S.J.
[3260]—*Congregation of Sisters of the Precious Blood*—C.PP.S.
[2549]—*Congregation of the Sisters of Mercy* (U.S. Prov.)—R.S.M.
[0885]—*Daughters of Mary Mother of Mercy*—D.M.M.M.
[1070-12]—*Dominican Sisters of Mission San Jose*—O.P.
[]—*Franciscan Sisters of the Heart of Jesus* Pakistan—C.J.H.
[]—*Hermanas del Divino Pastor*—H.D.P.
[]—*Hermanas Evangelizadoras Eucaristicas de los Pobres*—E.E.P.
[]—*Hermanas Misioneras Servidoras de la Palabra* Mexico—H.M.S.P.
[2390]—*Lovers of the Holy Cross*—L.H.C.
[2420]—*Marist Missionary Sisters*—S.M.S.M.
[1845]—*Missionary Guadalupanas of the Holy Spirit*—M.G.Sp.S.
[2790]—*Missionary Servants of the Most Blessed Trinity*—M.S.B.T.
[]—*Missionary Sisters of Mary*—M.S.M.
[2760]—*Missionary Sisters of the Immaculate Conception of the Mother of God*—S.M.I.C.
[]—*Oblates of Santa Marta*—O.S.M.
[3130]—*Our Lady of Victory Missionary Sisters*—O.L.V.M.
[4070]—*Religious of the Sacred Heart*—R.S.C.J.
[3465]—*Religious of the Sacred Heart of Mary*—R.S.H.M.
[1680]—*School Sisters of St. Francis* Milwaukee—O.S.F.
[]—*Sisters for Christian Community*—S.F.C.C.
[0470]—*Sisters of Charity of the Incarnate Word*—C.C.V.I.
[3360]—*Sisters of Providence of St. Mary of-the-Woods*—S.P.
[0230]—*Sisters of St. Benedict Monastery*—O.S.B.
[1540]—*Sisters of Saint Francis* Clinton, Iowa—O.S.F.
[1680]—*Sisters of St. Francis* Rochester, MN—O.S.F.
[3770]—*Sisters of St. Clare*—O.S.C.
[3840]—*Sisters of St. Joseph of Carondolet*—C.S.J.
[0700]—*Sisters of the Company of Mary Our Lady*—O.D.N.
[1850]—*Sisters of the Guardian Angel*—S.A.C.
[4050]—*Society Devoted to the Sacred Heart*—S.D.S.H.
[4060]—*Society of the Holy Child Jesus*—S.H.C.J.
[3320]—*Union of Sisters of the Presentation of the B.V.M.* (U.S. Province)—P.B.V.M.

DIOCESAN CEMETERIES

COLTON. *Our Lady Queen of Peace Catholic Cemetery*, Mailing Address: 1201 E. Highland Ave., 92404-4641. Tel: (909) 475-5300; Fax: 909-474-4910; Email: mail@sbcatholiccemeteries.org; Web: sbcatholiccemeteries.org. 3510 Washington St., Colton, 92324. Rev. Msgr. Gerard M. Lopez, S.T.L., V.G., Pastoral Dir.; Ms. Laura J. Clark, Contact Person

NECROLOGY

† Gorman, John, (Retired), Died May. 15, 2018
† Marx, Louis N., Guasti, CA; San Secondo d'Asti, Died Apr. 13, 2018
† Moore, James, (Retired), Died May. 3, 2018

An asterisk (*) denotes an organization that has established tax-exempt status directly with the IRS and is not covered by the USCCB Group Ruling.

Diocese of San Diego

(Dioecesis Sancti Didaci)

Most Reverend

ROBERT W. MCELROY

Bishop of San Diego; ordained April 12, 1980; appointed Titular Bishop of Gemellae in Byzacena and Auxiliary Bishop of San Francisco July 6, 2010; ordained September 7, 2010; appointed Bishop of San Diego March 3, 2015; ordained April 15, 2015; installed April 15, 2015. *Office: 3888 Paducah Dr., San Diego, CA 92117.*

Mailing Address: P.O. Box 85728, San Diego, CA 92186-5728. Tel: 858-490-8200; Fax: 858-490-8272. . *Pastoral Center: 3888 Paducah Dr., San Diego, CA 92117.*

Web: www.sdcatholic.org

Email: rvaldivia@sdcatholic.org

Most Reverend

ROBERT H. BROM, D.D.

Bishop Emeritus of San Diego; ordained December 18, 1963; appointed Bishop of Duluth March 25, 1983; consecrated and installed May 23, 1983; appointed Coadjutor Bishop of San Diego April 22, 1989; succeeded to the See July 10, 1990; retired September 18, 2013. *Office: P.O. Box 85728, San Diego, CA 92186-5728.* Tel: 858-490-8200.

Most Reverend

JOHN P. DOLAN

Auxiliary Bishop of San Diego; ordained July 1, 1989; appointed Titular Bishop of Uchi Maius and Auxiliary Bishop of San Diego April 19, 2017; installed June 8, 2017. *Pastoral Center: 3888 Paducah Dr., San Diego, CA 92117.*

ESTABLISHED JULY 11, 1936.

Square Miles 8,852.

Comprises the Counties of Imperial and San Diego in the State of California.

Legal Titles: The Roman Catholic Bishop of San Diego, a Corporation Sole–(Churches, Rectories, Halls, Catechetical Centers, etc.) Diocese of San Diego.
For legal titles of parishes and diocesan institutions, consult the Diocesan Office.

STATISTICAL OVERVIEW

Personnel	
Bishop	1
Auxiliary Bishops	1
Retired Bishops	2
Abbots	1
Retired Abbots	1
Priests: Diocesan Active in Diocese	100
Priests: Diocesan Active Outside Diocese	1
Priests: Diocesan in Foreign Missions	2
Priests: Retired, Sick or Absent	50
Number of Diocesan Priests	153
Religious Priests in Diocese	81
Total Priests in Diocese	234
Extern Priests in Diocese	49
Ordinations:	
Diocesan Priests	3
Religious Priests	1
Permanent Deacons	4
Permanent Deacons in Diocese	135
Total Brothers	29
Total Sisters	207
Parishes	
Parishes	97
With Resident Pastor:	
Resident Diocesan Priests	78
Resident Religious Priests	13
Without Resident Pastor:	
Administered by Priests	6
Missions	14
Professional Ministry Personnel:	
Brothers	29
Sisters	207
Lay Ministers	163
Welfare	
Catholic Hospitals	2
Total Assisted	417,515
Health Care Centers	2
Total Assisted	2,600
Homes for the Aged	2
Total Assisted	421
Day Care Centers	1
Total Assisted	600
Specialized Homes	3
Total Assisted	6,200
Special Centers for Social Services	6
Total Assisted	130,900
Residential Care of Disabled	1
Total Assisted	90
Educational	
Diocesan Students in Other Seminaries	8
Total Seminarians	8
Colleges and Universities	3
Total Students	9,299
High Schools, Diocesan and Parish	3
Total Students	2,746
High Schools, Private	3
Total Students	1,772
Elementary Schools, Diocesan and Parish	40
Total Students	10,141
Elementary Schools, Private	4
Total Students	979
Non-residential Schools for the Disabled	1
Total Students	413
Catechesis/Religious Education:	
High School Students	9,050
Elementary Students	19,489
Total Students under Catholic Instruction	53,897
Teachers in the Diocese:	
Brothers	5
Sisters	12
Lay Teachers	1,464
Vital Statistics	
Receptions into the Church:	
Infant Baptism Totals	7,314
Minor Baptism Totals	918
Adult Baptism Totals	361
Received into Full Communion	596
First Communions	8,316
Confirmations	5,204
Marriages:	
Catholic	1,445
Interfaith	231
Total Marriages	1,676
Deaths	3,144
Total Catholic Population	1,391,278
Total Population	3,484,311

Former Bishops—Most Revs. CHARLES F. BUDDY, D.D., S.T.D., Ph.D., ord. Sept. 19, 1914; appt. First Bishop of San Diego, Oct. 31, 1936; cons. Dec. 21, 1936; named Asst. at Pontifical Throne, Jan. 12, 1964; died March 6, 1966; FRANCIS J. FUREY, D.D., Ph.D., LL.D., ord. March 15, 1930; appt. Auxiliary Bishop of Philadelphia, Aug. 17, 1960; cons. Dec. 22, 1960; succeeded to the See of San Diego, March 6, 1966; transferred to Archbishop of San Antonio, June 4, 1969; died April 23, 1979; LEO T. MAHER, D.D., Bishop of San Diego; ord. Dec. 18, 1943; First Bishop of Santa Rosa; appt. Feb. 21, 1962; cons. April 5, 1962; transferred to San Diego, Aug. 27, 1969; retired July 10, 1990; died Feb. 23, 1991; ROBERT H. BROM, ord. Dec. 18, 1963; appt. Bishop of Duluth March 25, 1983; cons. and installed May 23, 1983; appt. Coadjutor Bishop of San Diego April 22, 1989; succeeded to the See July 10, 1990; retired Sept. 18, 2013.; CIRILO B. FLORES, D.D., ord. June 8, 1991; appt. Auxiliary Bishop of Orange Jan. 5, 2009; cons. March 19, 2009; appt. Coadjutor Bishop of San Diego Jan. 4, 2012; succeeded to the See Sept. 18, 2013; died Sept. 6, 2014.

Pastoral Center—3888 Paducah Dr., San Diego, 92117. Mailing Address: P.O. Box 85728, San Diego, 92186-5728. Tel: 858-490-8200; Fax: 858-490-8272; Web: www.sdcatholic.org. Office Hours: Mon.-Fri. 8:30-4:30.

Chancellor—Tel: 858-490-8232. MARIA OLIVIA (MARIOLY) GALVAN.

Moderator of the Curia—Most Rev. JOHN P. DOLAN.

Vice Moderator of the Curia—RODRIGO VALDIVIA, J.C.L.

Judicial Vicar—Very Rev. Msgr. STEVEN F. CALLAHAN, J.C.L.

Diocesan Tribunal

Adjutant Judicial Vicar—Rev. EDWARD P. MCNULTY, J.C.L.

Promoter of Justice—Rev. DAVID N. CROISETIERE.

Defenders of the Bond—Rev. Msgr. DANIEL J. DILLABOUGH, J.C.L.; Revs. AGUSTIN OPALALIC, J.C.D.; MICHAEL RAVENKAMP, S.J., J.C.L.

Diocesan Judges—MS. ANNA AMATO, J.C.L.; RODRIGO VALDIVIA, J.C.L.; Rev. Msgr. MARK A. CAMPBELL, J.C.L.

Tribunal Auditors—MS. BARBARA KEARNS; Deacon ROBERT FITZMORRIS.

Notary—LETICIA MENDOZA.

Diocesan Offices and Directors

Archivist—Contact: Chancellor's Office. Tel: 858-490-8208.

Catholic Charities—Mailing Address: P.O. Box 121831, San Diego, 92112-1831. Tel: 619-231-2828. DR. APPASWAMY "VINO" PAJANOR, Exec. Dir.

Cemetery Committee—Very Rev. Msgr. DENNIS MIKULANIS, Dir., Holy Cross Cemetery, 4470 Hilltop Dr., San Diego, 92102. Tel: 619-264-3127.

Censores Librorum—Very Rev. Msgr. RICHARD DUNCANSON, S.T.D.; BERNADEANE CARR, S.T.L.

Child and Youth Protection—RODRIGO VALDIVIA, J.C.L.

Civil Affairs—WILLIAM NOLAN, Esq., Tel: 858-490-8277.

Stewardship—MANNY AGUILAR, Dir., Tel: 858-490-8294.

Information Technology—MATTHEW DOLAN, Dir., Tel: 858-490-8329.

Construction Services—DANIEL RANCOURT, Dir., Tel: 858-490-8215.

Ethnic and Intercultural Communities—
Tel: 858-490-8306. Very Rev. MICHAEL PHAM, Dir.

Ecumenical and Interreligious Affairs—Very Rev. Msgr. DENNIS MIKULANIS, Dir., 17252 Bernardo Center Dr., Rancho Bernardo, 92128-2086. Tel: 858-487-4314.

Evangelization & Catechetical Ministry—MARIA OLIVIA (MARIOLY) GALVAN, Dir., Tel: 858-490-8232.

Family Life & Spirituality—Tel: 858-490-8299. LAURA MARTIN-SPENCER, Dir.; RICARDO MARQUEZ, Ph.D., Dir.

Finance—MARK A. FISHER, Finance Officer, Tel: 858-490-8316; SHIRLEY PAJANOR, Controller, Tel: 858-490-8207.

Institute for Adult Education and Formation for Ministry—BERNADEANE CARR, S.T.L., Dir., Tel: 858-490-8212.

Schools—JOHN GALVAN, Dir., Tel: 858-490-8240; MATTHEW CORDES, Assoc. Dir., Tel: 858-490-8240; JULIE CANTILLON, Assoc. Dir., Tel: 858-490-8244.

Youth Ministry—GERARDO ROJAS, Dir., Tel: 858-490-8260.

Young Adult Ministry—PATRICK RIVERA, Dir., Tel: 858-490-8261.

Human Resources—ROBERTA ESPINOSA, Dir., Tel: 858-490-8282.

Liturgy and Spirituality—NOREEN MCINNES, Dir., Tel: 858-490-8290.

Missions—Tel: 858-490-8250. Rev. JON P. KIRBY, S.V.D., Dir.; Sr. EVA RODRIGUEZ, S.J.S., Assoc. Dir.

Permanent Diaconate—VACANT, Dir.; JOSE ERNESTO GONZALEZ, Assoc. Dir., Tel: 858-490-8239.

Priests—Rev. MICHAEL MURPHY, Dir., 655 C Ave., Coronado, 92118-3167. Tel: 619-437-4846; Fax: 619-437-1572.

Priestly Formation - St. Francis Center—Very Rev. MATTHEW D. SPAHR, Dir., Tel: 619-291-7446; Fax: 619-291-7011.

Office of Life, Peace and Justice—Most Rev. JOHN P. DOLAN, Dir., Tel: 858-490-8310; ROBERT EHNOW, Ph.D., Assoc. Dir. Restorative Justice, Tel: 858-490-8375; MARIA LOURDES VALENCIA, Assoc. Dir. Culture of Life, Tel: 858-490-8323.

Southern Cross-(Diocesan Newspaper)—Rev. CHARLES FULD, Editor, (Retired), Tel: 858-490-8279.

Priestly Vocations—Tel: 619-291-7446. Rev. LAURO MINIMO, Dir.

Women Religious—Tel: 858-490-8289. Sr. KATHLEEN WARREN, O.S.F., Dir.

Advisory Bodies

Clergy Personnel Board—Most Rev. JOHN P. DOLAN; Revs. MINH Q. DO; PETER ESCALANTE; Very Rev. EMILIO A. MAGANA; Rev. RAYMOND G. O'DONNELL; Very Rev. MATTHEW D. SPAHR; Rev. NEMESIO SUNGCAD.

College of Consultors—Very Rev. Msgr. STEVEN F. CALLAHAN, J.C.L.; Very Rev. EFRAIN BAUTISTA; Rev. Msgr. EDWARD BROCKHAUS, (Retired); Most Rev. JOHN P. DOLAN; Revs. MANUEL EDIZA; PETER ESCALANTE; MICHAEL F. MURPHY; Very Rev. MICHAEL PHAM; Rev. ANTHONY SAROKI; Very Rev. MATTHEW D. SPAHR.

Finance Council—Very Rev. Msgr. STEVEN F. CALLAHAN, J.C.L.; MS. CHERYL BLACKWELL; Rev. Msgr. MARK A. CAMPBELL, J.C.L.; MS. CARINA COLEMAN; MRS. SUSAN CARTER; Rev. Msgr. DANIEL J. DILLABOUGH, J.C.L.; MR. PETER KRUSE; MR. MARK LINDSAY; MR. MARK NEILSON; MR. BRIAN RILEY; MR. STEVEN SHEA; MS. ANN STECK; Deacon JIM F. VARGAS, O.F.S.; MR. WILLIAM WARD.

Vicars Forane—Very Revs. EDMUNDO ZARATE-SUAREZ, Cathedral; PETER M. MCGUINE, El Cajon; BRUCE J. ORSBORN, Oceanside; MARK EDNEY, El Centro; EFRAIN BAUTISTA, South Bay; MATTHEW D. SPAHR, Mission; NICHOLAS P. CLAVIN, Escondido.

Miscellaneous

Apostleship of the Sea—JOSEPH BARTEL, Dir., Tel: 619-702-4703; Rev. JAMES BOYD, Chap., Tel: 858-292-1822.

Hispanic Charismatic Renewal Center (Carismatica Hispana)—PAULA BARAJAS, Coord.; LUIS BARAJAS, Coord., 521 E. 8th St., National City, 91950. Tel: 619-929-1950.

Cursillo—Rev. GILBERT J. GENTILE, S.J., Spiritual Advisor; DANIEL PERWICH, Lay Dir., Tel: 619-347-6485.

Filipino—RAMON DELA CRUZ, Lay Dir., Tel: 858-484-6131; LUZ MONTEMAYER, Asst. Lay Dir., Tel: 619-267-7006; VACANT, Spiritual Advisor.

Hispanic—JOSE PAQUE, Pres. Secretariat, Tel: 619-572-6358; Deacon AGUSTIN CASTRO, Spiritual Advisor.

Vietnamese—Rev. MICHAEL X. TRAN, Spiritual Dir.; RACHELLE P. NGUYEN, Lay Dir., Tel: 619-602-2857.

Missionary Childhood Association—Mailing Address: P.O. Box 82386, San Diego, 92138-2386.
Tel: 858-490-8250. Sr. EVA RODRIGUEZ, S.J.S., Assoc. Dir.

Propagation of the FaithMailing Address: P.O. Box 82386, San Diego, 92186-2386. Tel: 858-490-8250. Rev. JON P. KIRBY, S.V.D., Dir.

Victim Assistance Coordinator—Tel: 858-490-8353. VACANT.

CLERGY, PARISHES, MISSIONS AND PAROCHIAL SCHOOLS

CITY OF SAN DIEGO

(SAN DIEGO COUNTY)

1—SAINT JOSEPH CATHEDRAL CATHOLIC PARISH (1874)
1535 Third Ave., 92101-3192. Tel: 619-239-0229; Email: info@sdcathedral.org. Very Rev. Patrick J. Mulcahy; Revs. Clement Iorliam, In Res.; Michael X. Tran, In Res.
Catechesis Religious Program—Students 111.

2—ASCENSION CATHOLIC PARISH (1980)
11292 Clairemont Mesa Blvd., 92124.
Tel: 858-279-2735; Fax: 858-279-1023; Email: office@ascension-sd.org; Web: www.ascension-sd.org. Rev. Edwin Tutor; Deacons Jim Scull; Adam Curtis.
Catechesis Religious Program—Email: marilyn@ascension-sd.org. Marilyn Timmons, D.R.E. Students 160.

3—BLESSED SACRAMENT CATHOLIC PARISH (1938)
4540 El Cerrito Dr., 92115. Tel: 619-582-5722; Email: jyin@blessedsacrament-sandiego.org; Web: www.blessedsacrament-sandiego.org. Rev. Jose Goopio, S.V.D.; Deacons A. Anthony Albers; Herbert Kelsey.
Catechesis Religious Program—
Tel: 619-582-5722, Ext. 124. Students 60.

4—CHRIST THE KING CATHOLIC PARISH (1938)
29 N. 32nd St., 92102. Tel: 619-231-8906; Email: ctksandiego@gmail.com. Rev. Tommie Jennings, M.A.
Catechesis Religious Program—Students 117.

5—GOOD SHEPHERD CATHOLIC PARISH (1970)
8200 Gold Coast Dr., 92126-3699.
Tel: 858-271-0207 Parish Office; Fax: 858-271-0748; Email: goodshepherd@goodshepherdparish.net; Web: www.goodshepherdparish.net. Very Rev. Michael Pham; Revs. Victor T. Maristela; Nathan McWeeney.
School—Good Shepherd Catholic Parish School, (Grades PreSchool-8), 8160 Gold Coast Dr., 92126. Tel: 858-693-1522; Fax: 858-693-3439; Email: gsoffice@goodshepherdcatholic.net; Web: www.gscs-online.org. Ladonna Lambert, Prin.; Miranda Espejo, Librarian. Lay Teachers 11; Students 172.
Catechesis Religious Program—Email: glenn@goodshepherdparish.net. Glenn Valois, D.R.E. Students 1,159.

6—HOLY FAMILY CATHOLIC PARISH (1942)
1957 Coolidge St., 92111-7098.
Tel: 858-277-0404, Ext. 101; Email: church@oneholyfamily.org; Web: oneholyfamily.org. Rev. Peter Vu Lam.
Child Care—Preschool, Kathie Morgen, Dir.
Catechesis Religious Program—Tel: 858-268-0557. Students 200.

7—HOLY SPIRIT CATHOLIC PARISH (1952)
2725-55th St., 92105-5094. Tel: 619-262-2435; Fax: 619-262-8718; Email: info@holyspiritsd.org; Web: www.holyspiritsd.org. Revs. Dickens Remy; Phien Van Pham.
Catechesis Religious Program—Email: religioused@holyspiritsd.org. Elodia Castillo, D.R.E. Students 126.

8—THE IMMACULATA CATHOLIC PARISH (1958)
5998 Alcala Park, USD Campus, 92110-2492.
Tel: 619-574-5700; Email: parish1@sandiego.edu; Web: www.theimmaculata.org. Very Rev. Matthew D. Spahr.
Catechesis Religious Program—Tel: 619-574-5702; Fax: 619-574-5703. Students 203.

9—IMMACULATE CONCEPTION CATHOLIC PARISH (1849) [CEM]
2540 San Diego Ave., 92110-2840. Tel: 619-295-4141; Email: parish@immaculate-conception-sandiego.org. Very Rev. Michael Sinor; Deacon Robert H. Fitzmorris.
Catechesis Religious Program—Students 10.

10—ST. JEROME (1985) Closed. For inquiries for parish records contact the chancery.

11—ST. MAXIMILIAN KOLBE MISSION (1971) (Polish)
1735 Grand Ave., 92109. Tel: 858-272-7655; Email: pastor@polishmission.org. Rev. Czeslaw Rybacki, S.Ch.
Catechesis Religious Program—Tel: 619-668-0485.

12—MISSION SAN DIEGO DE ALCALA CATHOLIC PARISH (1769) (California's First Mission)
10818 San Diego Mission Rd., 92108-2429.
Tel: 619-283-7319; Email: receptionist@missionsandiego.org. Revs. Peter Escalante; William A. Springer; William Zondler; Deacon Ernest Grosso.
Catechesis Religious Program—Tel: 619-624-0900; Fax: 619-624-0019. Students 230.

13—OUR LADY OF ANGELS CATHOLIC PARISH (1906)
656 24th St., 92102-2911. Tel: 619-239-1231. Rev. Agustin Opalalic, J.C.D.
Catechesis Religious Program—Sr. Gloria Galvan, D.R.E. Students 429.

14—OUR LADY OF GUADALUPE CATHOLIC PARISH SAN DIEGO (1919)
1770 Kearny Ave., 92113-1128. Tel: 619-233-3838; Email: jauthersj@olgsd.org; Email: vtoscano@olgsd.org; Web: olgsd.org. Revs. John P. Auther, S.J.; Neal J. Wilkinson, S.J.
School—Our Lady's School, (Grades K-8), 650 24th St., 92102. Tel: 619-233-8888; Fax: 619-501-2951. Noel Bishop, Prin. Please see Our Lady's School under Our Lady of Guadalupe. Lay Teachers 16; Students 205.
Catechesis Religious Program—Students 355.

15—OUR LADY OF MT. CARMEL CATHOLIC PARISH SAN DIEGO (1976)
13541 Stoney Creek Rd., 92129. Tel: 858-484-1070; Email: ourlady@olmc-sandiego.org; Web: olmcsandiego.org. Revs. Anthony Saroki; Ignatius Kipchirchir; Deacons Noel Rivera; Manny Porciuncula; Juan Faus.
Catechesis Religious Program—Students 443.

16—OUR LADY OF REFUGE CATHOLIC PARISH (1977)
4226 Jewell St., 92109. Tel: 858-274-9670; Email: marissa@ourladyofrefuge.net; Web: www.ourladyofrefugesandiego.net. Rev. David N. Croisetiere; Deacon Salvador Huitron.
Catechesis Religious Program—Tel: 858-274-2959. Vicky Jimenez, D.R.E. Students 56.

17—OUR LADY OF THE ROSARY CATHOLIC PARISH (1925) (Italian)
1629 Columbia St., 92101. Tel: 619-234-4820; Fax: 619-234-3445; Email: parish@olrsd.org. Revs. Joseph Tabigue, C.R.S.P.; Louis M. Solcia, C.R.S.P.; Albino Vecina, C.R.S.P.
Catechesis Religious Program—Violet Huscher, Coord. Students 90.

18—OUR LADY OF THE SACRED HEART CATHOLIC PARISH (1911)
4177 Marlborough Ave., 92105-1412.
Tel: 619-280-0515. Revs. Jose Goopio, S.V.D.; Vinh Daniel Nguyen.
Child Care—Preschool, Tel: 619-284-0124. Enid Dixon, Dir.
School—Our Lady of the Sacred Heart Catholic Parish School, (Grades PreK-8), 4106 42nd St., 92105. Tel: 619-284-1715; Fax: 619-284-8332; Email: mainoffice@skda-sd.org. Alfonso Magana, Prin.; Mary Hutchings, Librarian. Lay Teachers 12; Students 168.
Catechesis Religious Program—Tel: 619-283-9262; Email: adatennison@yahoo.com. Ada Tennison, D.R.E. Students 360.

19—OUR MOTHER OF CONFIDENCE CATHOLIC PARISH (1964)
3131 Governor Dr., 92122. Tel: 858-453-0222; Email: frontdesk@omcsandiego.org; Web: www.omcsandiego.org. Rev. Msgr. Mark A. Campbell, J.C.L.; Rev. Romeo Smith Jr., In Res.; Deacons William Klopchin; Scott Wall.
Catechesis Religious Program—Tel: 858-453-3554. Sr. Angela Therese Meram, D.R.E., Pastoral Assoc.; Ian Mascarenhas, Youth Min. Students 200.

20—SACRED HEART CATHOLIC PARISH SAN DIEGO (1911)
4776 Saratoga Ave., 92107-9990. Tel: 619-224-2746; Email: ParishOffice@sacredheartob.org. Rev. Thomas Kiely; Deacon Mark Wieczorek.
Child Care—Preschool, 4895 Saratoga Ave., 92107. Tel: 619-222-7252; Fax: 619-222-2836; Email: shaobpreschool2@gmail.com; Web: www.sacredheartpreschool.org. Suzette Wydra, Dir. Lay Teachers 25; Students 130.
Catechesis Religious Program—Tel: 619-255-3500. Cathleen Hornsby, D.R.E. Students 147.

21—SAINT AGNES CATHOLIC PARISH (1908)
1140 Evergreen St., 92106. Tel: 619-223-2200;

Email: sesdon@earthlink.net. Rev. Donald E. Coleman.
Catechesis Religious Program—Tel: 619-223-9748; Fax: 619-223-4725. Students 93.

22—SAINT ANNE CATHOLIC PARISH (2008)
2337 Irving Ave., 92113. Tel: 619-239-8253, Ext. 111; Tel: 619-239-8253, Ext. 122; Email: mjimenez.stanne@gmail.com; Email: st.annepastorssecretary@gmail.com; Web: stannessandiego.org. Revs. John Lyons, F.S.S.P.; Christopher Mahowald, F.S.S.P.; Anthony Dorsa.
Catechesis Religious Program—Students 84.

23—SAINT BRIGID CATHOLIC PARISH (1940)
4735 Cass St., 92109-2698. Tel: 858-483-3030; Email: info@saintbrigidparish.org; Web: www.saintbrigidparish.org. Very Rev. Msgr. Steven F. Callahan, J.C.L.; Rev. Sebastian Bukenya; Deacons Michael Daniels; Chris Hulburt.
Catechesis Religious Program—Tel: 858-483-3032; Email: gayle@saintbrigidparish.org. Gayle Heyman, D.R.E. Students 264.

24—SAINT CATHERINE LABOURE CATHOLIC PARISH (1964)
4124 Mt. Abraham Ave., 92111. Tel: 858-277-3133; Email: office@stcatherinelaboure.net; Web: www.stcatherinelaboure.net. Rev. Brian Hayes, J.C.L.
Res.: 4026 Mt. Abraham Ave., 92111.
Catechesis Religious Program—Tel: 858-275-0587; Tel: 858-277-3738; Email: kkeith@stcatherinelaboure.net; Email: youth@stcatherinelaboure.net. Kathy Keith, Rel. Educ. Coord.; Rafael Quevedo, D.R.E. (Youth Program). Students 27.

25—SAINT CHARLES BORROMEO CATHOLIC PARISH (1946)
2802 Cadiz St., 92110-4870. Tel: 619-225-8157; Email: office@saintcharlespl.com; Web: www.saintcharlespl.com. Rev. John Amsberry.
School—Saint Charles Borromeo Catholic Parish School, (Grades PreK-8), 2808 Cadiz St., 92110. Tel: 619-223-8271; Fax: 619-223-2695; Email: office@saintcharlesacademy.com. Christopher Moeller, Prin. Lay Teachers 12; Students 226.
Catechesis Religious Program—Students 61.

26—SAINT CHARLES CATHOLIC PARISH (1946)
990 Saturn Blvd., 92154. Tel: 619-423-0242; Web: saintcharles.org. Very Rev. Emilio A. Magana; Revs. Burt Boudoin; Roland Kelso, In Res.; Deacons Howard Mick Dennison; Ken Montoya; Sam Martinez, (Retired); David Lewis.
School—Saint Charles Catholic Parish School, (Grades K-8), 929 18th St., 92154. Tel: 619-423-3701; Fax: 619-423-5331; Email: principal@saintcharlesschool.com; Web: saintcharlesschool.com. Mrs. Sylvia Benning, Prin. Lay Teachers 12; Students 200.
Catechesis Religious Program—Tel: 619-575-2240. Students 335.

27—SAINT COLUMBA CATHOLIC PARISH (1955)
3327 Glencolum Dr., 92123. Tel: 858-277-3863; Email: stcolumbarectory@gmail.com; Web: www.stcolumbasandiego.com. Revs. Edward McNulty; Hak Jun Hong; Deacon H. William Vasquez Jr.
Child Care—Preschool, Tel: 858-279-0161. Trish Gilsdorf, Dir.
School—Saint Columba Catholic Parish School, (Grades PreK-8), Tel: 858-279-1882; Email: lglenwinkel@yahoo.com; Email: principal@stcolumbaschool.org; Web: stcolumbaschool.org. Lay Teachers 9; Students 159; Religious Teachers 10.
Catechesis Religious Program—Tel: 858-277-3861. Students 111.

28—SAINT DIDACUS CATHOLIC PARISH (1926)
4772 Felton St., 92116. Tel: 619-284-3472; Email: mainoffice@stdidacuschurch.org; Web: www.stdidacuschurch.org. Rev. Enrique Fuentes; Deacons Dino Serafino; Marco Antonio Huizar.
Child Care—Preschool, Tel: 619-284-8730, Ext. 307. Rose Witt, Dir.
School—Saint Didacus Catholic Parish School, (Grades PreSchool-8), 4630 34th St., 92116. Tel: 619-284-8730; Fax: 619-284-1764; Email: principal@stdidacusparishschool.org; Web: www.stdidacusparishschool.org. Christine Dean, Prin. Lay Teachers 14; Students 213.
Catechesis Religious Program—Elena Platas, D.R.E. Students 160.

29—SAINT GREGORY THE GREAT CATHOLIC PARISH (1985)
11451 Blue Cypress Dr., 92131. Tel: 858-653-3540; Fax: 858-653-3550; Email: information@stgg.org; Web: www.stgg.org. Very Rev. Nicholas P. Clavin; Deacons Ronald H. Diem; Doug Pingel.
School—St. Gregory the Great Catholic School, (Grades PreSchool-8), 15315 Stonebridge Pkwy., 92131. Tel: 858-397-1290; Fax: 858-397-1294; Email: office@stggcs.org; Web: www.stggcs.org. Maeve O'Connell, Prin.; Darlene Howard, Asst. Prin. Lay Teachers 14; Students 225.
Catechesis Religious Program—Tel: 858-653-3594. Students 858.

30—SAINT JOHN THE EVANGELIST (1913)
1638 Polk Ave., 92103. Tel: 619-291-1660; Email: office@sjesandiego.org; Web: www.sjesandiego.org. Revs. Kevin P. Casey, S.J.; Tommie Jennings, M.A., In Res.
Legal Name: Saint John the Evangelist Catholic Parish San Diego
Catechesis Religious Program—Email: aaron@sjesandiego.org. Aaron Bianco, S.T.D., D.R.E. Students 65.

31—SAINT JUDE SHRINE OF THE WEST CATHOLIC PARISH (1946) [CEM]
3785 Boston Ave., 92113-3210. Tel: 619-264-2195; Email: info@stjudesd.com; Web: www.stjudesd.com. 1129 South 38th St., 92113-3210. Revs. Jose Edmundo Zarate-Suarez; Antonio Morales; Romeo Velos, C.S.; Deacons Manuel Rodriguez; John Ellis.
Catechesis Religious Program—Tel: 619-264-4795; Fax: 619-264-2198. Rosa Murguia, Coord. Students 496.

32—SAINT MARY MAGDALENE CATHOLIC PARISH (1953)
1945 Illion St., 92110. Tel: 619-276-1041; Fax: 619-276-0144; Email: frsteve@stmarymagonline.org; Email: frminh@stmarymagonline.org. Revs. Stephen P. McCall; Minh Q. Do; William Headley, In Res., (Retired); Anthony C. May, In Res., (Retired); Deacon Ralph Skiano.
Child Care—Preschool, Tel: 619-276-6545, Ext. 226. Amy Igou, Dir.
School—Saint Mary Magdalene Catholic Parish School, (Grades PreK-8), Tel: 619-276-6545; Fax: 619-276-5359; Email: info@schoolofthemadeleine.com; Web: www.schoolofthemadeleine.com. Mrs. Jean Coleman, Prin. Administrators 2; Aides 17; Lay Teachers 30; Students 600; Staff 4.
Catechesis Religious Program—Tel: 619-276-1248; Email: religioused@stmarymagonline.org. Sofia Segocia, D.R.E. Students 180.

33—SAINT MICHAEL CATHOLIC PARISH SAN DIEGO (1957)
2643 Homedale St., 92139. Tel: 619-470-1977; Email: msalamat@stmichaelsandiego.org; Web: www.stmichaelsandiego.org. Revs. Manuel Ediza; Rolando Gabutera; Deacons Jim Aquino; Gustavo Magana; Carl Shelton.
Child Care—Preschool, Tel: 619-472-5437; Fax: 619-470-5231. Miss Lucy Zamorano, Dir.
School—Saint Michael Catholic Parish San Diego School, (Grades PreSchool-8), 2637 Homedale St., 92139. Tel: 619-470-4880; Fax: 619-470-1050; Email: mjohnson@stmichaelsandiego.org; Web: www.smasandiego.org. Mrs. Mary Johnson, Prin. Lay Teachers 10; Students 109.
Catechesis Religious Program—Students 431.

34—SAINT PATRICK CATHOLIC PARISH SAN DIEGO (1921)
3585 30th St., 92104-4142. Tel: 619-295-2157; Fax: 619-297-3346; Web: www.stpatrickschurchsd.com. Revs. Carlos Medina, O.S.A., Admin.; Philip Yang; Kirk Davis, O.S.A., In Res.; Michael McFadden, O.S.A., In Res.
School—Saint Patrick Catholic Parish San Diego School, (Grades PreSchool-8), 3014 Capps St., 92104-4222. Tel: 619-297-1314; Email: secretary@stpatrick.sdcoxmail.com. Mr. Daniel O'Neal, Prin.; Mr. Hernan Valdivia, Prin. Lay Teachers 11; Students 175.
Catechesis Religious Program—Email: religioused@gmail.com. Mrs. Eneida Scoby, D.R.E.
Chapel—St. Augustine High School Chapel, 3266 Nutmeg St., 92104-5151.

35—SAINT RITA CATHOLIC PARISH (1941)
5124 Churchward St., 92114-3797. Tel: 619-264-3165; Email: connie@stritaschurchsd.org; Web: stritasd.weconnect.com. Rev. Armando P. Escurel.
Child Care—Preschool, Tel: 619-264-8831. Vicky Torres, Dir.
School—Saint Rita Catholic Parish School, (Grades PreK-8), 5165 Imperial Ave., 92114. Tel: 619-264-0109; Email: principal@stritassd.org; Web: www.stritassd.org. Gina Olsen, Prin.; Ruberta Castro, Librarian. Lay Teachers 10; Students 189.
Catechesis Religious Program—Tel: 619-264-4399; Email: margaretsfcc@aol.com. Sr. Margaret Castro, D.R.E. Students 237.

36—SAINT THERESE CATHOLIC PARISH (1956)
6400 Saint Therese Way, 92120-3018. Tel: 619-582-3716; Email: susan@sttheresesparish.org; Web: www.sttheresesparish.org. Rev. Peter Bosque.
Child Care—Preschool, Tel: 619-583-1493. Susan Conley, Dir.
School—St. Therese Academy, (Grades PreSchool-8), Tel: 619-583-6270; Fax: 619-583-5721; Email: msperrazzo@sta-sd.org. Mark Sperrazzo, Prin. Lay Teachers 19; Sisters 3; Students 350.
Catechesis Religious Program—Tel: 619-286-4605. Students 200.

37—SAINT THERESE OF CARMEL CATHOLIC PARISH (1985)
Church: 4355 Del Mar Trails Rd., 92130. Tel: 858-481-3232; Email: parishoffice@stocsd.org; Web: www.stocsd.org. Rev. Chris Tozzi; Deacons John Fanelle; Philip Hardjadinata.
Catechesis Religious Program—Breah Paradowski, Coord. Faith Formation; Toni Colombo, D.R.E.; Melissa Colombo, Youth Min.; Jennifer Fry, Coord. Students 550.

38—SAINT VINCENT DE PAUL CATHOLIC PARISH (1910)
4077 Ibis St., 92103-1899. Tel: 619-299-3880; Fax: 619-299-9509. Rev. Alexander De Paulis.
Child Care—Preschool, Tel: 619-296-2261. Yolanda Aliaga, Dir.
School—Saint Vincent de Paul Catholic Parish School, (Grades K-8), Tel: 619-296-2222; Email: srkathleen@svscatholic.org. Lay Teachers 13; Students 237; Religious Teachers 1.
Catechesis Religious Program—Students 45.

39—SAN RAFAEL CATHOLIC PARISH (1974)
17252 Bernardo Center, 92128. Tel: 858-487-4314; Fax: 858-487-1498; Email: office@sanrafaelparish.org; Web: www.sanrafaelparish.org. Very Rev. Msgr. Dennis Mikulanis; Rev. Showri Nagothu; Deacon Robert Holgren; Therese Bulat, Music Min.; Cheryl Danzl, Office Mgr.; Jackie Kramer, Sacristan & Wedding Coord.; Maria Ohlendorf, Business Mgr.
Catechesis Religious Program—Email: religioused@sanrafaelparish.org; Email: youthministry@sanrafaelparish.org. Christopher O'Donnell, D.R.E.; Quyen Skiano, C.R.E.; Lailani Gachalian, Youth Min. Students 409.

OUTSIDE THE CITY OF SAN DIEGO

ALPINE, SAN DIEGO CO., QUEEN OF ANGELS CATHOLIC PARISH (1950)
2569 Victoria Dr., Alpine, 91901-3662. Tel: 619-445-2145; Fax: 619-445-9682; Email: parish@queenofangels.org; Web: www.queenofangels.org. Rev. Timothy Deutsch.
Catechesis Religious Program—Email: katrina@queenofangels.org. Katrina Thornton, D.R.E. Students 73.

BONITA, SAN DIEGO CO., CORPUS CHRISTI CATHOLIC PARISH (1984)
450 Corral Canyon Rd., Bonita, 91902-4072. Tel: 619-482-3954. Very Rev. Efrain Bautista; Rev. Claro Ortiz; Deacons Wil Hollowell; Raul Millan; Alan Pangilinan.
Child Care—Preschool, 480 Corral Canyon Rd., Bonita, 91902. Araceli Ongyan, Dir. Clergy / Religious Teachers 13.
Catechesis Religious Program—Tel: 619-482-3953; Email: reled@corpuschristicatholic.org. Michael Wickham, D.R.E. Students 1,188.

BORREGO SPRINGS, SAN DIEGO CO., SAINT RICHARD CATHOLIC PARISH (1954) [CEM]
611 Church Ln., Borrego Springs, 92004-1128. Tel: 760-767-5701; Email: pastor@strichardborrego.com. P.O. Box 1128, Borrego Springs, 92004. Rev. Fernando Maldonado.
Catechesis Religious Program—Students 92.
Mission—Christ the King Catholic Mission, 3811 Del Mar Dr., Salton Sea Beach, Imperial Co. 92274.

BRAWLEY, IMPERIAL CO.

1—SACRED HEART CATHOLIC PARISH BRAWLEY (1908)
402 S. Imperial Ave., Brawley, 92227. Tel: 760-679-3505; Email: sh@brawleycatholic.org; Email: aa@brawleycatholic.org; Web: www.brawleycatholic.org. Revs. Edward Horning; Andrew Kunambi; Deacon Donald L. Spinney.
Child Care—Preschool, 428 S. Imperial Ave., Brawley, 92227. Tel: 760-344-2662; Email: office@sacredheartschoolbrawley.org; Web: www.sacredheartschoolbrawley.org. Susie Wood, Dir. Administrators 1; Lay Teachers 1; Students 12.
School—Sacred Heart Catholic Parish Brawley School, (Grades K-8), 428 S. Imperial Ave., Brawley, 92227. Tel: 760-344-2662; Fax: 760-344-1910; Email: office@sacredheartschoolbrawley.org; Web: www.sacredheartschoolbrawley.org. Mrs. Annalisa Burgos, Prin.
Legal Title: Sacred Heart School. Lay Teachers 7; Students 69.
Catechesis Religious Program—Students 95.

2—SAINT MARGARET MARY CATHOLIC PARISH (1934)
620 S. Cesar Chavez St., Brawley, 92227. Tel: 760-550-9830; Email: smm@brawleycatholic.org; Web: www.brawleycatholic.org. Revs. Edward Horning; Andrew Kunambi.
Catechesis Religious Program—Tel: 760-344-6515; Fax: 760-344-7598. Students 329.

CALEXICO, IMPERIAL CO., OUR LADY OF GUADALUPE CATHOLIC PARISH CALEXICO (1907) (Mexican)
124 E. Fifth St., Calexico, 92231. Tel: 760-357-1822; Email: olgcalexico@hotmail.com. Revs. Jose A. Sosa, Sch.P.; Manuel Sanahuja; Deacon Refugio Gonzalez.
Child Care—Preschool, Jazel Sanchez, Dir.
School—Our Lady of Guadalupe Academy, (Grades PreSchool-8), 535 Rockwood Ave., Calexico, 92231.

Tel: 760-357-1986; Fax: 760-357-3282; Email: mmeza@olgacademy.com. Sr. Maria Elvia Gonzalez, S.J.S., Prin.; Silvia Chavarin, Librarian. Lay Teachers 23; Students 447; Clergy / Religious Teachers 5.
Catechesis Religious Program—Sr. Bertha Maria Meza, S.J.S., D.R.E. Students 350.

CALIPATRIA, IMPERIAL CO., SAINT PATRICK CATHOLIC PARISH CALIPATRIA (1919)
133 E. Church St., P.O. Box 238, Calipatria, 92233.
Tel: 760-502-6348; Fax: 760-502-6347; Email: stpatrickcalipatria@gmail.com; Email: stpatrickoffice@gmail.com; Web: www.stpatricks-catholic-church-of-calipatria-ca-business.site. Rev. Reynaldo Roque.
Catechesis Religious Program—Tel: 760-502-6350. Students 70.
Mission—Immaculate Heart of Mary, 19 Sixth St., Niland, 92257. Tel: 760-359-3730; Email: a_sadorra@yahoo.com. Augustine Sadorra.

CARLSBAD, SAN DIEGO CO.
1—SAINT ELIZABETH SETON CATHOLIC PARISH (1977)
6628 Santa Isabel St., Carlsbad, 92009-5148.
Tel: 760-438-3393; Email: janiceh@seschurch.org; Web: www.seschurch.org. Rev. Michael Robinson; Deacon Jerry Heitschmidt.
Catechesis Religious Program—Tel: 760-607-5014; Fax: 760-438-3438; Email: reled-ses@gmail.com. Larry Broding, D.R.E. Students 606.
2—SAINT PATRICK CATHOLIC PARISH CARLSBAD (1943)
3821 Adams St., Carlsbad, 92008-0249.
Tel: 760-729-2866; Email: webmaster@stpatrickcarlsbad.com; Web: www.stpatrickcarlsbad.com. Revs. William F. Rowland, C.J.M.; Juan Castillo, C.J.M.; Ricardo Juarez Frausto, C.J.M.; Deacons Miguel Enriquez; Michael Frazee; Richard Pomphrey; Edward Moser.
School—Saint Patrick Catholic Parish Carlsbad School, (Grades K-8), Saint Patrick Catholic School 3820 Pio Pico Dr., Carlsbad, 92008.
Tel: 760-729-1333; Fax: 760-729-4643; Email: dnelson@stpaddys.org; Web: www.stpaddys.org. Brian Sestito, Vice Prin.; Denise Nelson, Prin. Lay Teachers 26; Students 465.
Catechesis Religious Program—Tel: 760-729-8442. Students 689.

CAMPO, SAN DIEGO CO., SAINT ADELAIDE OF BURGUNDY CATHOLIC PARISH
1347 Dewey Pl., P.O. Box 369, Campo, 91906.
Tel: 619-478-1017; Email: stadelaide@att.net. Rev. Ignatius Dibeashi.
Catechesis Religious Program—Students 12.
Mission—St. Mary Magdalene, 44686 Calexico Ave., Jacumba, San Diego Co. 91934.

CHULA VISTA, SAN DIEGO CO.
1—MATER DEI CATHOLIC PARISH (2004)
1571 Magdalena Ave., Chula Vista, 91921.
Tel: 619-656-3735; Email: parish@materdeicv.org; Web: www.materdeicv.org. P.O. Box 212047, Chula Vista, 91921. Rev. Jovencio D. Ricafort; Deacon Fred Swingle III.
Catechesis Religious Program—Tel: 619-656-3740; Fax: 619-656-2939; Email: rep@materdeicv.org. Students 509.
2—MOST PRECIOUS BLOOD CATHOLIC PARISH (1957)
1245 4th Ave., Chula Vista, 91911-3012.
Tel: 619-422-2100; Fax: 619-422-1375; Email: mpbchurch@gmail.com; Web: www.preciousbloodchurch.com. Revs. Silverio Espenilla; Niranjan Kanmury, In Res.; Deacons Rolando Bonggat; Ruben Pelina.
Catechesis Religious Program—Tel: 619-422-2159; Email: mpbwcc@hotmail.com. Sr. Camille Crabbe, C.V.I., D.R.E. Students 279.
3—OUR LADY OF GUADALUPE CATHOLIC PARISH CHULA VISTA (1945)
345 Anita St., Chula Vista, 91911-4198.
Tel: 619-422-3977; Email: olguadalupecv@yahoo.com. Revs. Ramiro Chan; Feliere Louise; Deacons Raul Hernandez; Guillermo Valdivia.
Catechesis Religious Program—Tel: 619-422-1887. Students 400.
4—SAINT PIUS X CATHOLIC PARISH CHULA VISTA (1955)
1120 Cuyamaca Ave., Chula Vista, 91911-3506.
Tel: 619-420-9193; Email: bookkeeper@stpiusx.org. Revs. Jay T. Bananal; Corey Tufford; Deacons Peter Johnson; Patrick Wright.
Child Care—Preschool, Maria Lira, Dir.
School—Saint Pius X Catholic Parish Chula Vista School, (Grades K-8), 37 E. Emerson St., Chula Vista, 91911. Tel: 619-422-2015; Fax: 619-422-0048; Email: info@spxcv.org. John Turskey, Prin. Lay Teachers 12; Students 245; Religious Teachers 12.
Catechesis Religious Program—
Tel: 619-420-9193, Ext. 104/105; Email: plopez@saintpiusx.org. Paul Lopez, D.R.E. Students 360.
5—SAINT ROSE OF LIMA CATHOLIC PARISH (1913)
293 H St., Chula Vista, 91910-4703.
Tel: 619-427-0230; Email: parish@strosecv.com; Web: www.strosecv.com. Rev. Miguel Campos, Sch. P.; Deacons Gerardo Marquez; Charles Frice; John Gabbard; Juan Buenrostro.
Child Care—Preschool, 278 Alvarado St., Unit 2, Chula Vista, 91910. Glenda Martinez, Dir.
School—Saint Rose of Lima Catholic Parish School, (Grades PreK-8), 278 Alvarado St., Unit 2, Chula Vista, 91910. Tel: 619-422-1121; Fax: 619-422-8007; Email: school@strosecv.com; Web: www.strosecv.com. Mr. Jeff Saavedra, Prin. Lay Teachers 14; Students 345.
Catechesis Religious Program—Tel: 619-426-6717. Sr. Patricia Weldon, D.R.E. Students 425.

CORONADO, SAN DIEGO CO., SACRED HEART CATHOLIC PARISH CORONADO (1897)
655 C Ave., Coronado, 92118-2229.
Tel: 619-435-3167; Email: sacredheart@sacredheartcor.org; Web: www.sacredheartcor.org. Rev. Michael F. Murphy; Most Rev. Neal Buckon, In Res., (Retired); Rev. Msgr. Donal C. Sheahan, In Res., (Retired); Deacons Robert E. Griffin Jr.; Kevin Murray; Frank Osgood; Frederico Drachenberg.
School—Sacred Heart Catholic Parish Coronado School, (Grades PreK-8), 706 C Ave., Coronado, 92118. Tel: 619-437-4431; Fax: 619-437-1559; Email: school@sacredheartcoronado.org; Web: www.sacredheartcoronado.org. Mr. Peter Harris, Prin. Lay Teachers 11; Students 250.
Catechesis Religious Program—
Tel: 619-435-3167, Ext. 302. Students 197.

DESCANSO, SAN DIEGO CO., OUR LADY OF LIGHT CATHOLIC PARISH (1935)
9136 Riverside Dr., Descanso, 91916.
Tel: 619-445-3620; Email: office@ourladyoflight.church; Web: ourladyoflight.church. Rev. Steven Larion.
Catechesis Religious Program—Email: Gloria@ourladyoflight.church. Gloria White, D.R.E. Students 17.

EL CAJON, SAN DIEGO CO.
1—THE CHURCH OF SAINT LUKE CATHOLIC PARISH (1985)
1980 Hillsdale Rd., El Cajon, 92019.
Tel: 619-442-1697; Email: parishoffice@thechurchofstluke.org. Rev. Ronald Cochran; Deacons Dennie C. Nickell; Allan Williams; Jerry Stenovec.
Catechesis Religious Program—Email: passoc@thechurchofstluke.org. Jane Alfano, D.R.E. Students 156.
2—HOLY TRINITY CATHOLIC PARISH (1903)
405 Ballard St., El Cajon, 92019-2123.
Tel: 619-444-9425; Email: admin@holytrinityelcajon.org; Web: www.holytrinityelcajon.org. Revs. Eddie Ruiz; Reynald Evangelista; Deacon Timothy Treadwell.
Child Care—Preschool, Tel: 619-444-1052. Debbie Edelbrock, Dir.
School—Holy Trinity Catholic Parish School, (Grades PreK-8), 509 Ballard St., El Cajon, 92019-2125. Tel: 619-444-7529; Fax: 619-444-3721; Email: principal@holytrinityhawks.com; Web: www.holytrinityschoolelcajon.com. Francine Moss, Prin. Lay Teachers 16; Students 171.
Catechesis Religious Program—Email: admin@holytrinityelcajon.org. Students 380.
3—OUR LADY OF GRACE CATHOLIC PARISH (1954)
2766 Navajo Rd., El Cajon, 92020-2183.
Tel: 619-469-0133; Web: www.olg-church.org. Rev. Peter McGuine; Deacon John Sawaya.
School—Our Lady of Grace Catholic Parish School, (Grades K-8), Tel: 619-466-0055; Web: www.olg.org. Mrs. Susan Hause, Prin. Lay Teachers 16; Students 260.
Catechesis Religious Program—Tel: 619-466-5656; Email: gkruzel@olg-church.org; Web: www.olg-church.org/learn/faith-formation. Georgene Kruzel, Pastoral Min./Coord. Students 199.
4—SAINT KIERAN CATHOLIC PARISH (1958)
1510 Greenfield Dr., El Cajon, 92021-3511.
Tel: 619-588-6881; Email: secretary@stkierans.sdcoxmail.com; Web: www.stkieran.com. Rev. Ben Davison; Deacon D. Frank Reilly.
Child Care—Preschool, Erin Marshall, Dir.
School—Saint Kieran Catholic Parish School, (Grades PreSchool-8), 1347 Camillo Way, El Cajon, 92021. Tel: 619-588-6398; Fax: 619-588-6382; Email: pprovo@saintkierancatholicschool.org. Mrs. Patricia Provo, Prin. Lay Teachers 14; Students 165; Religious Teachers 1.
Catechesis Religious Program—Students 59.
5—SAINT LOUISE DE MARILLAC CATHOLIC PARISH (1944)
2005 Crest Dr., El Cajon, 92021-4309.
Tel: 619-749-7908; Fax: 619-486-6934; Email: frscotty@aol.com; Email: stlouisecrest@cox.net. Rev. Scott A. Burnia; Deacon Kevin Helfers.
Catechesis Religious Program—Students 6.

EL CENTRO, IMPERIAL CO.
1—OUR LADY OF GUADALUPE CATHOLIC PARISH EL CENTRO (1946)
153 E. Brighton Ave., El Centro, 92243.
Tel: 760-352-5535; Email: olgec@hotmail.com; Email: churchlady@elcentrocatholic.org. Revs. Ron Mark Edney; Gerardo Gomez Zapien; Deacons Domingo Enriquez; Sergio Hernandez.
Catechesis Religious Program—
Tel: 760-352-5535, Ext. 212. Francisco Cabrera, Coord. Faith Formation. Students 537.
Mission—Sacred Heart, 40 E. Main, Heber, Imperial Co. 92249.
2—SAINT MARY CATHOLIC PARISH EL CENTRO (1907) [JC]
795 LaBrucherie, El Centro, 92243.
Tel: 760-352-4211; Email: churchlady@elcentrocatholic.org. Revs. Ron Mark Edney; Gerardo Gomez Zapien; David Sereno, In Res.; Deacons Domingo Enriquez; Sergio Hernandez.
Child Care—Preschool, Norma Grady, Dir.
School—Saint Mary Catholic Parish El Centro School, (Grades PreSchool-8), 700 S. Waterman Ave., El Centro, 92243. Tel: 760-352-7285; Email: receptionist@elcentrostmarys.org; Email: adminassistant@elcentrostmarys.org. Sr. Katia Chavez, S.J.S., Prin.; Diana Vasquez, Librarian. Lay Teachers 9; Sister Servants of the Blessed Sacrament 2; Students 214; Religious Teachers 5.
Catechesis Religious Program—
Tel: 760-353-8260 (K-8); Tel: 760-353-7280 (9-12). Students 580.

ENCINITAS, SAN DIEGO CO., SAINT JOHN THE EVANGELIST (1946)
1001 Encinitas Blvd., Encinitas, 92024-2828.
Tel: 760-753-6254; Email: admin@saintjohnencinitas.org; Web: saintjohnencinitas.org. Revs. James Bahash; Robert Kibaki
Legal Name: Saint John the Evangelist Catholic Parish Encinitas
Child Care—Preschool, Annette Conrad, Dir.
School—Saint John the Evangelist School, (Grades PreSchool-8), 1003 Encinitas Blvd., Encinitas, 92024. Tel: 760-944-8227; Fax: 760-944-8939. Mr. Dan Schuh, Prin. Lay Teachers 25; Students 486.
Catechesis Religious Program—Tel: 760-436-0664. Students 682.

ESCONDIDO, SAN DIEGO CO.
1—CHURCH OF ST. TIMOTHY CATHOLIC PARISH (1985)
2960 Canyon Rd., Escondido, 92025-7402.
Tel: 760-489-1200; Email: info@sttimothychurch.com. Rev. Fernando Ramirez; Deacon John Depner.
Catechesis Religious Program—Email: Kevin@sttimothychurch.com. Kevin Kennedy, D.R.E. Students 176.
2—CHURCH OF THE RESURRECTION CATHOLIC PARISH (1970) [JC]
1445 Conway Dr., Escondido, 92027.
Tel: 760-747-2322; Email: info@resurrectionchurch.org; Web: www.resurrectionchurch.org. Revs. Kenneth Del Priore; Abel Barajas; Deacons Edwin Gonzales Montoya; Michael Partida; Gilbert Villegas.
Catechesis Religious Program—
Tel: 760-747-2322, Ext. 201. Students 648.
Comunidad Hispana—Fax: 760-747-7090.
3—SAINT MARY CATHOLIC PARISH ESCONDIDO (1890)
1170 S. Broadway Ave., Escondido, 92025-5815.
Tel: 760-745-1611; Email: reception@stmaryp.org; Web: www.stmaryp.org. Revs. Scott Herrera; Manuel Gutierrez del Toro; Gabriel Afeti; Deacons Amador Duran; James Kostick; Mitch Renix; Andres Sanchez.
Child Care—Preschool, 130 E. 13th Ave., Escondido, 92025. Web: www.stmaryp.org/st-mary-preschool. Ms. Joanne Strantz, Dir. Students 27.
School—St. Mary School, (Grades K-8), 130 E. 13th Ave., Escondido, 92025. Tel: 760-743-3431; Email: office@stmesc.org; Email: principal@stmesc.org; Web: www.stmesc.org. Amanda Johnston, Prin. Lay Teachers 11; Students 156.
Catechesis Religious Program—Email: esaucedo@stmaryp.org. Enedina Saucedo, D.R.E. Students 973.

FALLBROOK, SAN DIEGO CO., SAINT PETER THE APOSTLE CATHOLIC PARISH (1946)
450 S. Stage Coach Ln., Fallbrook, 92028.
Tel: 760-689-6204; Email: office@stpeter-fallbrook.org; Web: www.stpeter-fallbrook.org. Rev. Ramon Marrufo; Deacon Daniel Rosas.
Child Care—Preschool, Gisela Gutierrez, Dir.
School—St. Peter the Apostle Catholic School, (Grades PreSchool-8), Tel: 760-689-6250;
Fax: 760-689-6240; Web: www.spacschool.com. Lay Teachers 12; Students 140.
Catechesis Religious Program—Students 540.

HOLTVILLE, IMPERIAL CO., SAINT JOSEPH CATHOLIC PARISH HOLTVILLE (1911)
560 Maple Ave., Holtville, 92250. Tel: 760-356-2147; Email: saintjosephocm@gmail.com. Rev. Jose Alfredo Moreno.
Catechesis Religious Program—Tel: 760-356-5738; Email: saintjospehocm@gmail.com. Maria Baca, D.R.E. Students 241.

IMPERIAL, IMPERIAL CO., SAINT ANTHONY OF PADUA

CATHOLIC PARISH IMPERIAL (1948)
211 W. Sixth St., Imperial, 92251. Tel: 760-355-1347; Fax: 760-545-1050; Email: stanparish@sbcglobal.net. Rev. Alexander Aquino.
Catechesis Religious Program—Tel: 760-355-1304. Maria Fugett, Catechetical Min. Dir. Students 262.

JACUMBA, SAN DIEGO CO., ST. MARY MAGDALENE (1947)
See separate listing. A mission of St. Adelaide of Burgundy, Campo.
Tel: 619-478-1017; Email: stadelaide@att.net; Web: www.stadelaideparish.com. Rev. Ignatius Dibeashi.

JAMUL, SAN DIEGO CO., SAINT PIUS X CATHOLIC PARISH JAMUL (1956)
14107 Lyons Valley Rd., P.O. Box 369, Jamul, 91935-0369. Tel: 619-669-0085; Fax: 619-669-0087; Email: parishoffice@stpiusxjamul.com; Web: www.stpiusxjamul.com. Rev. Hignio Garcia.
Catechesis Religious Program—Students 40.

JULIAN, SAN DIEGO CO., SAINT ELIZABETH OF HUNGARY CATHOLIC PARISH (1949)
2814 B St., P.O. Box 366, Julian, 92036-0366.
Tel: 760-765-0613; Email: office@stelizabethjulian.org. Rev. William A. Kernan.
Catechesis Religious Program—Students 1.

LA JOLLA, SAN DIEGO CO.
1—ALL HALLOWS CATHOLIC PARISH (1959)
6602 La Jolla Scenic Dr. S., La Jolla, 92037-5799.
Tel: 858-459-6074; Email: allhallowsparish@gmail.com. Rev. Raymond G. O'Donnell.
School—All Hallows Catholic Parish School, (Grades K-8), 2390 Nautilus, La Jolla, 92037.
Tel: 858-459-6074; Fax: 858-200-0081; Email: mainoffice@allhallows.com; Web: www.allhallowsacademy.com. Mary Skeen, Prin. Aides 5; Lay Teachers 17; Students 225.
Catechesis Religious Program—Catherine Adams, D.R.E. Students 40.

2—MARY, STAR OF THE SEA CATHOLIC PARISH (1906)
7669 Girard Ave., La Jolla, 92037-4480.
Tel: 858-454-2631; Email: marystarofthesea@marystarlajolla.org; Web: beta.co-optx.com/agape-connect/Sites/MSOS/. Rev. James Rafferty.
Church: 7713 Girard Ave., La Jolla, 92037-4480.
Tel: 858-454-2631; Email: marystarofthesea@san.rr.com.
School—Stella Maris Academy, (Grades K-8), 7654 Herschel Ave., La Jolla, 92037. Tel: 858-454-2461; Fax: 858-454-4913; Email: info@stellamarisacademy.org; Web: www.stellamarisacademy.org. Patricia Lowell, Prin. Lay Teachers 20; Students 161.
Catechesis Religious Program—Tel: 858-551-8359. Donna Widmer, D.R.E.; Martin Magana, D.R.E. Students 284.

LA MESA, SAN DIEGO CO., SAINT MARTIN OF TOURS CATHOLIC PARISH (1921)
7710 El Cajon Blvd., La Mesa, 91942-6932.
Tel: 619-465-5334; Email: info@saintmartinoftours.cc; Web: www.stmartinoftoursparish.org. Revs. Elmer Mandac; Danilo Valdepenas, In Res.; Deacon Allen Rosker.
Child Care—Preschool, 7714 El Cajon Blvd., La Mesa, 91942. Tel: 619-698-8462.
School—Saint Martin of Tours Catholic Parish School, (Grades PreSchool-8), 7708 El Cajon Blvd., La Mesa, 91942-6932. Tel: 619-466-3241; Fax: 619-466-0285; Email: info51@stmartinacademy.org; Web: www.stmartinacademy.org. Antoinette Dimuzio, Prin. Lay Teachers 18; Students 278.
Catechesis Religious Program—Tel: 619-698-8434. Christine Davis, D.R.E. Students 200.

LAKESIDE, SAN DIEGO CO.
1—SAINT KATERI TEKAKWITHA NATIONAL INDIAN PARISH (1982) [CEM] [JC3]
1054 Barona Rd., Lakeside, 92040-1502.
Tel: 619-443-3412; Email: bktparish@aol.com; Web: www.bktparish.com. Rev. Herman Manuel, S.V.D.; Edward Nolan, Pastoral Coord.
Catechesis Religious Program—Tel: 619-445-8333. Natalie Nostos, D.R.E. Students 34.
Missions—Assumption of BVM—Lakeside, San Diego Co. 92040.
Nativity of BVM, Alpine, San Diego Co.
Immaculate Conception of BVM, El Cajon, San Diego Co.

2—OUR LADY OF PERPETUAL HELP (1947)
13208 Lakeshore Dr., Lakeside, 92040.
Tel: 619-443-1412; Email: karen.woollard@olphchurch.org. Revs. Ronald J. Buchmiller; Joseph Khuyen Van Lai; Deacons Dennis O'Neil; Mark Silva; Patrick Root
Legal Name: Our Lady of Perpetual Help Catholic Parish Lakeside
Catechesis Religious Program—Tel: 619-443-5110; Email: patrick.rivera@olphchurch.org. Patrick Rivera, D.R.E. Students 150.

LEMON GROVE, SAN DIEGO CO., SAINT JOHN OF THE CROSS CATHOLIC PARISH (1939)
8086 Broadway, Lemon Grove, 91945-2598.
Tel: 619-466-3209; Web: www.sjcparish.com. Revs. Peter Navarra; Nelson Vencilao; Long Nguyen, In Res.; Deacon James Robert Stanley.
Child Care—Preschool, Tel: 619-466-8624, Ext. 103. Idania Walters, Dir.
School—Saint John of the Cross Catholic Parish School, (Grades PreK-8), 8175 Lemon Grove Way, Lemon Grove, 91945. Tel: 619-466-8624; Fax: 619-466-3732; Email: ainiguez@sjcparish.com; Web: www.stjohncross.org. Mr. Gregory Krumm, Prin.; Mrs. Rosa Olea, Librarian. Lay Teachers 15; Students 287; Religious Teachers 1.
Catechesis Religious Program—Tel: 619-461-2681. Jessie Ramirez, D.R.E. Students 859.
Convent—8171 Lemon Grove Way, Lemon Grove, 91945. Sisters of Mercy of the Blessed Sacrament 6.

NATIONAL CITY, SAN DIEGO CO.
1—SAINT ANTHONY OF PADUA (1910) (Hispanic)
Mailing Address: 410 W. 18th St., National City, 91950. Tel: 619-477-4520; Email: stanthonyofpadua@sbcglobal.net. Rev. Jose Edmundo Zarate-Suarez; Deacon Braulio Gutierrez
Legal Name: Saint Anthony of Padua Catholic Parish National City
Res.: 2837 J Ave., National City, 91950.
Tel: 619-477-4520; Email: stanthonyofpadua@sbcglobal.net.
Catechesis Religious Program—Martha Mendoza, D.R.E. Students 274.

2—SAINT MARY CATHOLIC PARISH NATIONAL CITY (1926)
Mailing Address: 426 E. Seventh St., National City, 91950-2322. Tel: 619-474-1501; Fax: 619-474-1502; Email: secretary@stmarynationalcity.com; Email: frontdesk@stmarynationalcity.com; Email: 19neman51@gmail.com. Rev. Nemesio Sungcad.
Catechesis Religious Program—707 "E" Ave., National City, 91950. Students 164.

NILAND, IMPERIAL CO., IMMACULATE HEART OF MARY,
See separate listing. No longer a parish; now a mission of St. Patrick, Calipatria.
19 6th St., Niland, 92257. Tel: 760-502-6348. Rev. Reynaldo Roque.

OCEANSIDE, SAN DIEGO CO.
1—MISSION SAN LUIS REY CATHOLIC PARISH (1798)
4070 Mission Ave., Oceanside, 92057-6497.
Tel: 760-757-3250; Web: www.sanluisreyparish.org. Revs. Vincent Mesi, O.F.M.; Francisco Alejo, O.F.M.; Oscar Mendez.
Res.: 4050 Mission Ave., Oceanside, 92057-6497.
Catechesis Religious Program—Email: zavalaed@sanluisreyparish.org. Elena Zavala, D.R.E. Students 763.
Mission—Mission San Luis Rey De Francia.

2—SAINT MARGARET CATHOLIC PARISH (1977)
4300 Oceanside Blvd., Oceanside, 92056-2999.
Tel: 760-941-5560; Email: ccd@oceanside4christ.com; Web: www.oceanside4christ.com. Rev. Cavana Wallace; Deacon Charles Navarrete.
Catechesis Religious Program—Email: ccd@oceanside4christ.com. Pam Talbot, D.R.E. Students 219.

3—SAINT MARY, STAR OF THE SEA CATHOLIC PARISH (1937)
609 Pier View Way, Oceanside, 92054-2861.
Tel: 760-722-1688; Fax: 760-722-2653; Email: barbie-stmarys@hotmail.com; Web: www.stmarystars.org. Revs. Gerardo Fernandez; Charles Ceaser Maria Antony Louis, In Res.
Child Care—Preschool, Tel: 760-722-7475. Debbie Shapiro, Dir.
School—Saint Mary, Star of the Sea Catholic Parish School, (Grades PreSchool-8), 515 Wisconsin Ave., Oceanside, 92054. Tel: 760-722-7259; Fax: 760-722-0862; Email: info@stmarystars.com; Web: stmarystars.com. Angela Willburn, Prin. Lay Teachers 20; Students 300.
Catechesis Religious Program—515 Pier View Way, Oceanside, 92054. Students 450.

4—SAINT THOMAS MORE CATHOLIC PARISH (1985)
1450 S. Melrose Dr., Oceanside, 92056.
Tel: 760-758-4100, Ext. 100; Email: parishoffice@stmoside.org. Rev. Michael Ratajczak; Deacons Thomas A. Goeltz; John Fredette.
Res.: 1358 Fern Pl., Vista, 92081.
Catechesis Religious Program—Email: debbief@stmoside.org. Debbie Fredette, D.R.E. Students 57.

PALA, SAN DIEGO CO., MISSION SAN ANTONIO DE PALA CATHOLIC PARISH (1816)
3015 Pala Mission Rd., Pala, 92059-0070.
Tel: 760-742-3317; Email: manahan.rey@gmail.com; Web: www.missionsanantonio.org. P.O. Box 70, Pala, 92059. Revs. Reynaldo Manahan; Oscar Lopez Guevarra; Deacon Carlos Monsalvo.
Catechesis Religious Program—
Tel: 760-742-3317, Ext. 112; Email: dcncarlos@missionsanantonio.org. Students 107.
Chapels—Rincon Indian Reservation, St. Bartholomew—
La Jolla Indian Reservation, Our Lady of Refuge.
Pauma Indian Reservation, St. James.

POWAY, SAN DIEGO CO.
1—SAINT GABRIEL CATHOLIC PARISH (1973)
13734 Twin Peaks Rd., Poway, 92064.
Tel: 858-748-5348; Web: www.saintgabrielschurch.com. Very Rev. Michel Froidurot; Revs. Patrick J. Murphy; Harold Tindall, In Res., (Retired); Deacons Ricardo Elizondo; Michael Fish.
Catechesis Religious Program—Email: dre@saintgabrielschurch.com. Mary Romag, D.R.E. Students 539.

2—SAINT MICHAEL CATHOLIC PARISH POWAY (1959)
15546 Pomerado Rd., Poway, 92064-2404.
Tel: 858-487-4755; Fax: 858-487-5937; Email: stmikes@smpoway.org; Web: www.smpoway.org. Revs. Melchisedech Monreal; David Exner; Deacons John Charron; Terry Hannify.
Child Care—Preschool, 15542 Pomerado Rd., Poway, 92064. Tel: 858-485-1303. Lori Romero, Dir. Lay Teachers 3; Students 42.
School—St. Michael's School, (Grades K-8), Tel: 858-485-1303; Fax: 858-485-5059. Kathleen Mock, Prin. Lay Teachers 39; Students 499.
Catechesis Religious Program—Tel: 858-485-1392; Email: kellis@smpoway.org. Kelli Salceda, D.R.E. Students 505.

RAMONA, SAN DIEGO CO., IMMACULATE HEART OF MARY CATHOLIC PARISH (1947)
537 E St., Ramona, 92065. Tel: 760-789-0583; Web: www.ihmramona.org. Rev. Eduardo Bernardino; Deacons Andres Escobedo; William Turner.
Catechesis Religious Program—Tel: 760-789-6151; Email: t2holy@gmail.com. Tammy Mansir, D.R.E. Students 204.

RANCHO SANTA FE, SAN DIEGO CO., CHURCH OF THE NATIVITY CATHOLIC PARISH (1985)
6309 El Apajo Rd., Rancho Santa Fe, 92067.
Tel: 858-756-1911; Web: nativitycatholic.org. P.O. Box 8770, Rancho Santa Fe, 92067-8770. Rev. Msgr. Richard F. Duncanson, S.T.D.; Deacon James Walsh.
School—Church of the Nativity Catholic Parish School, (Grades PreSchool-8), Tel: 858-756-6763; Email: mzures@nativitymail.org; Web: www.thenativityschool.org. Mr. Paul Parker, Prin. Lay Teachers 20; Students 199.
Catechesis Religious Program—Tel: 858-756-9562. Mrs. Patti Smiley, Elementary R.E. Coord.; Mike James, Youth Min. Students 335.

SAN MARCOS, SAN DIEGO CO., SAINT MARK CATHOLIC PARISH (1963) [CEM]
1147 Discovery St., San Marcos, 92078-1313.
Tel: 760-744-1540; Email: veronica@stmarksrcc.org; Web: stmarksrcc.org. Very Rev. Bruce J. Orsborn; Revs. Derek Twilliger; Bernardo Lara.
Catechesis Religious Program—Tel: 760-744-1130. Students 2,041.
Mission—2557 Sarver Ln., San Marcos, San Diego Co. 92069.

SAN YSIDRO, SAN DIEGO CO., OUR LADY OF MT. CARMEL CATHOLIC PARISH SAN YSIDRO (1927)
2020 Alaquinas Dr., San Ysidro, 92173-2107.
Tel: 619-428-1415; Fax: 619-428-5626; Email: olmcsy@gmail.com; Web: www.ourladyofmountcarmel-sy.org. Revs. Jose Castillo; Jose Whittingham; Deacons Jose Luis Medina; Raul Gonzalez.
School—Our Lady of Mt. Carmel Catholic Parish San Ysidro School, (Grades 1-8), 4141 Beyer Blvd., San Ysidro, 92173-2133. Tel: 619-428-2091; Fax: 619-428-8324; Email: FrontOffice@olmc.school. Sr. Eva Lujano, S.J.S., Prin.; Ma. Eugenia Villareal, Librarian. Lay Teachers 12; Sister Servants of the Blessed Sacrament 3; Students 236; Religious Teachers 2.
Catechesis Religious Program—109 Seaward Ave., San Ysidro, 92173. Students 407.

SANTA YSABEL, SAN DIEGO CO., SANTA YSABEL INDIAN MISSION CATHOLIC PARISH (1818) [CEM]
23013 Hwy. 79, Santa Ysabel, 92070-1010.
Tel: 760-765-0810; Email: missionsantaysabel1818@yahoo.com. P.O. Box 129, Santa Ysabel, 92070-0129. Rev. William A. Kernan.
Mission—St. Francis of Assisi, Hwy. 79 & Stage Rd., Warner Springs, San Diego Co. 92086.
Catechesis Religious Program—Nancy Garbo, D.R.E. Students 14.

SANTEE, SAN DIEGO CO., GUARDIAN ANGELS CATHOLIC PARISH (1962)
9310 Dalehurst Rd., Santee, 92071-1010.
Tel: 619-448-1213; Fax: 619-448-2980; Email: par.sec@ga.sdcoxmail.com; Web: www.guardianangelssantee.org. Rev. André Ramos.
Child Care—Preschool, Tel: 619-596-3281; Email: preschool@ga.sdcoxmail.com. Joyce Keup, Dir. Students 38; Clergy / Religious Teachers 4.
Catechesis Religious Program—9310 Dalehurst, Santee, 92071. Tel: 619-596-3282; Email: mcprsm@ga.sdcoxmail.com. Sr. Mary Potter, R.S.M., D.R.E. Students 286.

SOLANA BEACH, SAN DIEGO CO., SAINT JAMES CATHOLIC PARISH (1911)
625 S. Nardo Ave., Solana Beach, 92075-2398.

Tel: 858-755-2545; Email: Info@stjames-stleo.com; Web: www.stjamesandleo.org. Revs. Gerard Lecomte; John H. Howard, C.J.M., Pastor Emeritus; Deacons Peter Hodsdon; Albert P. Graff.
Child Care—Preschool, Laura Kuhn, Dir.
School—St. James Academy, (Grades PreSchool-8), 623 S. Nardo Ave., Solana Beach, 92075.
Tel: 858-755-1777; Fax: 858-755-3124; Email: principal@saintjamesacademy.com; Web: saintjamesacademy.com. Christine Lang, Prin. Lay Teachers 19; Students 208; Religious Teachers 2.
Catechesis Religious Program—
Tel: 858-755-2545, Ext. 106; Email: psmith@stjames-stleo.com; Email: jdiaz@stjames-stleo.com. Pamela Smith, D.R.E.; Jannet Diaz, D.R.E. Students 265.
Mission—St. Leo, 936 Genevieve, Solana Beach, San Diego Co. 92075. Sr. Zita Toto, O.L.C., Coord.
Catechesis Religious Program—Jannet Diaz, D.R.E. (Spanish). Students 160.

SPRING VALLEY, SAN DIEGO CO., SANTA SOPHIA CATHOLIC PARISH (1956)
9800 San Juan St., Spring Valley, 91977.
Tel: 619-463-6629; Email: info@santasophia.org; Web: www.santasophia.org. Rev. Devdas Masillamony.
Child Care—Preschool, Victoria Simanek, Dir.
School—Santa Sophia Catholic Parish School, (Grades PreSchool-8), 9806 San Juan St., Spring Valley, 91977. Tel: 619-463-0488; Fax: 619-668-5469; Email: santasophiaacademyoffice@gmail.com; Web: http://santasophiaacademy.org/. Karen Laaperi, Prin., ssaklaaperi@hotmail.com. Aides 4; Lay Teachers 12; Students 228.
Catechesis Religious Program—Tel: 619-668-5459; Email: sscmopadlo@gmail.com. Bernadette Padlo, Dir. Students 305.

VALLEY CENTER, SAN DIEGO CO., SAINT STEPHEN CATHOLIC PARISH (1981)
31020 Cole Grade Rd., Valley Center, 92082-1015.
Tel: 760-749-3324; Web: www.st-stephenvc.org. P.O. Box 1015, Valley Center, 92082. Rev. Luke Jauregui; Deacons Charles Embury; Gilbert Salinas; John Tobin.
Catechesis Religious Program—Tel: 760-749-3352; Fax: 760-749-6608. MArcal Lopez, D.R.E.; John Navarette, Youth Min. Students 552.

VISTA, SAN DIEGO CO., SAINT FRANCIS OF ASSISI CATHOLIC PARISH (1941)
525 W. Vista Way, Vista, 92083-5974.
Tel: 760-945-8000; Email: jweiss@stfrancis-vista.org; Web: www.stfrancis-vista.org. Revs. Ruben Arceo, S.J.; Roldan Nunez; Ricardo Juarez Frausto, C.J.M., In Res,; Sr. Madeline Fitzgerald, O.S.C.; Deacons Loi Hoang; Ronald Arnold; Pedro Enciso; Juan Santillan.
Child Care—Preschool, Tel: 760-630-7964. Jennifer Paino, Dir.
School—Saint Francis of Assisi Catholic Parish School, (Grades PreSchool-8), Tel: 760-630-7960; Email: info@sfs-vista.org. Elizabeth Joseph, Prin. Lay Teachers 9; Students 301.
Catechesis Religious Program—Email: SGuillen@stfrancis-vista.org. Stacy Guillen, D.R.E. Students 746.

WESTMORLAND, IMPERIAL CO., SAINT JOSEPH CATHOLIC PARISH WESTMORLAND (1939)
300 N. Center St., Westmorland, 92281.
Tel: 760-679-3505; Email: aa@brawleycatholic.org; Web: www.brawleycatholic.org. Mailing Address: 402 S. Imperial Ave., Brawley, 92227. Revs. Edward Horning; Andrew Kunambi.
Catechesis Religious Program—Students 25.

WINTERHAVEN, IMPERIAL CO., SAINT THOMAS INDIAN MISSION CATHOLIC PARISH (1780)
350 Piacho Rd., P.O. Box 1176, Winterhaven, 92283-1176. Tel: 760-572-0283; Web: www.stthomasindianmission.org. Rev. George Decasa.
Catechesis Religious Program—Students 16.

Chaplains of Public Institutions

Hospitals

SAN DIEGO.
Kaiser Permanente Medical Center,
Tel: 619-528-5188. Rev. Danilo Valdepenas, Chap.
Rady Children's Hospital, Tel: 858-576-1700. Rev. Raymundus Wea, S.V.D.
Scripps Hospital, Tel: 858-626-4123. Rev. Romeo Smith Jr., Chap.
Scripps Mercy Hospital, Tel: 619-260-7020. Revs. Lawrence Agi, Clement Iorliam.
Sharp Memorial Hospital, Tel: 858-939-3475. Rev. Raymundus Wea, S.V.D.
UCSD Medical Center, Tel: 619-657-7000. Rev. Clement Iorliam, Chap.

CHULA VISTA.
Scripps Mercy Hospital, 435 H St., Chula Vista, 91910. Tel: 619-691-7000; Fax: 619-691-7522; Web: www.scrippshealth.org. Rev. Reynald Evangelista, Chaplain, Mark Weber, Chap.

LA JOLLA.
UCSD Thornton Hospital. Rev. Tom Jose Kuzhippalayil, S.D.B.
Veterans Administration Hospital, La Jolla.
Tel: 858-552-8585. Rev. B. Jeffrey Blangiardi, S.J.

LA MESA.
Sharp Grossmont Hospital, Tel: 619-465-0711. Rev. Danilo Valdepenas, Chap.

OCEANSIDE.
Tri City Hospital, 4002 Vista Way, Oceanside, 92049.
Tel: 760-940-7954. Rev. Robert Kibaki, A.J., Chap.

Detention Ministries

SAN DIEGO.
East Mesa Detention Facility, 446 Alta Rd., 92158.
Tel: 619-661-2669.
Geo West Regional Detention Facility. Contact: Office for Social Ministry, (858) 490-8375.
Tel: 619-232-9221.
George F. Bailey Detention Facility. Contact: Joe Gersztyn, Tel: 619-987-1614 Tel: 619-661-2620.
Kearny Mesa Juvenile Detention Facility,
Tel: 858-694-4500. Rob Moscato, Chap., Tel: 858-405-7964.
Metropolitan Correction Center, Tel: 619-232-4311. Rev. Edgar Serrano, Chap., Tel: 619-232-4311, Ext. 1463.
R.J. Donovan Correctional Facility,
Tel: 619-661-6500. Deacon Miguel Enriquez, Chap.
San Diego Central Jail, Tel: 619-615-2737. Tom Erpelding, Chap., Tel: 619-696-6526.
San Diego Correction Facility, Federal. Contact: Office for Life, Peace & Justice, Tel: (858) 490-8375.

BRAWLEY.
Calipatria State Prison, Brawley. Deacon Refugio Gonzalez, Tel: 769-348-7000, Ext. 6139.

CHULA VISTA.
South Bay Detention Facility, Tel: 619-691-4818. Contact: Office for Life, Peace & Justice, Tel: 858-490-8375.

EL CENTRO.
El Centro Juvenile Hall, 324 Applestill Rd., El Centro, 92243. Tel: 760-339-6229; Email: icprob@co.imperial.ca.us. Contact: Office for Life, Peace & Justice, Tel: 858-490-8375.
Imperial County Jail, 328 Applestill Rd., El Centro, 92243. Tel: 760-339-6369. Deacon Marcos Lopez, Tel: 760-455-0584Contact: Office for Life, Peace & Justice, Tel: 858-490-8375.

IMPERIAL.
Centinela State Prison, Tel: 760-337-7900. Deacon Marcos Lopez, Chap., Tel: 760-337-7900, Ext. 6472.

SANTEE.
Las Colinas Women's Detention Facility, 451 Riverview Pkwy., Santee, 92071. Tel: 619-258-3176 . Jenny Quimpo, Tel: 619-972-9714.

VISTA.
Vista Detention Facility, 325 Melrose Dr., Ste. 200, Vista, 92083. Tel: 760-940-4473. Diane Otto, 325 Melrose Dr., Ste. 200, Vista, 92083. Tel: 760-730-0251.

State Conservation Camps

SAN DIEGO.
Rainbow Conservation Camp, 8215 Rainbow Heights Rd., Fallbrook, 92028. Tel: 760-728-7034; Web: www.cdcr.ca.gov. Deacon Carlos Monsalvo, Chap., Tel: 760-803-9970.

Ports

SAN DIEGO.
Port of San Diego, 1760 Water St., 92101.
Tel: 619-702-4703. Rev. James Boyd, Chap., Tel: 858-292-1822, Joseph Bartel.
San Diego Airport, 2802 Cadiz St., 92110-4813.
Tel: 619-225-8157. Rev. John Amsberry.

On Duty Outside the Diocese:
Revs.—
Eggleston, Earl
Moraga, Cecilio, (Missionary Work)
Stanonik, Anthony.

Unassigned:
Revs.—
Foley, Patrick
Tran, Michael X.

Special or Other Diocesan Assignments:
Rev.—
Tamayo, Eric.

Retired:
Most Revs.—
Brom, Robert H., D.D., (Retired), P.O. Box 85728, 92128
Chavez, Gilbert E., D.D., (Retired), 2020 Alaquinas Dr., San Ysidro, 92173
Rev. Msgrs.—
Bolger, William, (Retired), 7350 Golfcrest Pl., #3006, 92119
Bourgeois, Lloyd, (Retired), 11640 San Salvador Rd., 92128
Brockhaus, Edward, (Retired), 2920 Union St., #201, 92103
Carroll, Joseph A., (Retired), 33 16th St., 92101
Chylewski, Anthony, (Retired), 15646 Vista Vicente Dr., Ramona, 92065
Cuddihy, William, (Retired), 12274 Lomica Dr., 92128
Dolan, Neal T., (Retired), 17376 Hillero Ct., 92128
Elliott, William, (Retired), 17446 Plaza Cerado, #68, 92128
Fawcett, Henry F., (Retired), 620 State St., #218, 92101
Finnerty, Joseph L., (Retired), 17842 Sintonte Dr., 92128
Gallagher, Michael J., (Retired), 9320 Earl St., #20, La Mesa, 91942
Giesing, Anthony, (Retired), 4863 Glacier Ave., 92120
Kirk, Raymond, (Retired), 26634 Amhurst Ct., Sun City, 92586
Lechner, Roger A., (Retired), 28890 Lilac Rd., Sp. 89, Valley Center, 92082
Mullarkey, Patrick J., (Retired), 6333 Rancho Mission Rd., 92108
O'Sullivan, Jeremiah, (Retired), 6333 Rancho Mission Rd., 92108
Portman, John R., (Retired), 1775 Diamond St., #1-303, 92109
Purcell, Lawrence M., S.T.D., (Retired), 624 Calle Paula, Solana Beach, 92075
Sheahan, Donal C., (Retired), 655 C Ave., Coronado, 92118
Shipley, William, (Retired), 2450 Crandall Dr., 92111
Revs.—
Byrne, George, (Retired), P.O. Box 600524, 92160
Collier, Joseph, (Retired), 27250 Murrietta Rd., #285, Sun City, 92586
Conwill, Giles, (Retired), P.O. Box 366, Morrow, GA 30260
Corcoran, Brian, (Retired), 238 Vista Montana Rd., 92054
Dempsey, Nicholas, (Retired), 8520 Old Stonefield Chase, 92127
Dunkley, George, (Retired)
Dunn, Stephen, (Retired), P.O. Box 287, Palm Springs, 92263
Fuld, Charles, (Retired), 10480 Rancho Carmel Dr., 92128
Gold, William, (Retired), 1893 Fire Mountain Rd., Oceanside, 92054
Hebert, Ronald, (Retired), 8712 N. Magnolia Ave., Spc. 96, Santee, 92071
Holland, Kilian, (Retired), P.O. Box 2543, New Smyrna Beach, FL 32169
Krouse, Dennis, (Retired), P.O. Box 2991, Spring Valley, 91979
May, Anthony C., (Retired), 1945 Illion St., 92110
Moreno, Jorge, (Retired), P.O. Box 436099, San Ysidro, 92143
O'Connor, Dennis, (Retired), 1102 Pacific Beach Dr., #E, 92109
Ortiz, Michael, (Retired), 510 Camino de la Reina, #136, 92108
Perozich, Richard L., (Retired), 2747 S. Kihei Rd., A-201, Kihei, HI 96753
Poulsen, James N., (Retired), 7710 El Cajon Blvd., La Mesa, 91941
Rapp, Bernard A., (Retired), 6333 Rancho Mission Rd., 92108
Sostrich, John L., (Retired), 125 Inspiration Blvd., #209, Eastland, TX 76448
Stevenson, William, (Retired), 5707 Adobe Falls Rd., Unit D, 92120
Tindall, Harold, (Retired), P.O. Box 897, Poway, 92074
Vesga, Mario, (Retired), 293 H St., Chula Vista, 91910
Villarreal, Manuel, (Retired), 3458 Hillside Ln., Fallbrook, 92028
White, Robert, (Retired).

Permanent Deacons:
Albers, A. Anthony, (Retired), Blessed Sacrament, San Diego
Allen, Ronald, Seattle, WA
Amicone, Nicholas, Ormond Shores, FL
Aquino, Jaime, San Diego
Arnold, Raymond, (Retired), Redding, CA
Arnold, Ronald, St. Francis of Assisi, Vista
Barretto, Robert, Alburquerque, NM
Beiner, Robert, St. John the Evangelist, Encinitas
Bell, L. Ferris, (Retired), Lancaster, PA
Bennett, David, St. Mark, San Marcos
Blackmon, Lyle, St. Mary Star of the Sea, Oceanside
Bonggat, Rolando, (Retired), Chula Vista
Booth, Robert, St. John the Evangelist, San Diego
Bucon, Mark, La Jolla

Bueno, Luiz, St. John of the Cross, Lemon Grove
Buenrostro, Juan, St. Rose of Lima, Chula Vista
Burns, Jeffrey, San Diego
Byrne, Patrick J., Pueblo, CO
Carpizo, Magno, (Retired), San Diego
Castro, Agustin, Resurrection, Escondido
Charron, John, St. Michael, Poway
Clarke, William G., (Retired), Lakeside
Collins, Michael, Nampa, ID
Curtis, Adam, Ascension, San Diego
Daniels, Michael, St. Brigid, San Diego
Davidson, Paul, Oceanside
Dean, Bennett, (Retired), Murrieta, CA
Del Rio, Jose Luis, San Diego
Delano, Joseph, (Retired), Marlborough, MA
Dennison, Howard Mick, (Retired), Imperial Beach
Depner, John, St. Timothy, Escondido
DePozo, Daniel, (Retired), Henderson, NV
Diem, Ronald H., St. Gregory the Great, San Diego
Donarski, Conrad, Spring Hill, TN
Drachenberg, Frederico, Sacred Heart, Coronado
Duran, Amador, St. Mary, Escondido
Early, John Michael, (Retired), Escondido
Ekhaml, Robert T., (Retired), San Diego
Elizondo, Ricardo, St. Gabriel, Poway
Ellis, John A., St. Jude Shrine of the West, San Diego
Embury, Charles, St. Stephen, Valley Center
Enciso, Pedro, (Retired), Vista
Enriquez, Domingo, Our Lady of Guadalupe, El Centro
Enriquez, Miguel, St. Patrick, Carlsbad
Escobedo, Andres, Immaculate Heart of Mary, Ramona
Fanelle, John, St. Therese of Carmel, San Diego
Faus, Juan, Our Lady of Mt. Carmel, San Diego
Fickes, Dale, Gig Harbor, WA
Fish, Michael, St. Gabriel, Poway
Fitzmorris, Robert H., Immaculate Conception, San Diego
Frazee, Michael, St. Patrick, Carlsbad
Fredette, John, St. Thomas More, Oceanside
Frice, Charles, St. Rose of Lima, Chula Vista
Gabbard, John, St. Rose of Lima Chula Vista
Goeltz, Thomas A., St. Thomas More, Oceanside
Gonzalez, Raul, Our Lady of Mt. Carmel, San Ysidro
Gonzalez, Refugio, Our Lady of Guadalupe, Calexico
Graff, Albert P., (Retired), La Jolla
Griffin, Robert E. Jr., Sacred Heart, Coronado
Grosso, Ernest, Mission San Diego de Alcala, San Diego
Guess, Harry Jr., Hermitage, TN
Gullotta, Daniel, Vail, AZ
Gutierrez, Braulio, St. Anthony of Padua, National City
Hardick, Richard, St. Augustine High School, San Diego
Heitschmidt, Jerry, St. Elizabeth Seton, Carlsbad
Hernandez, Raul, Our Lady of Guadalupe, Chula Vista
Hernandez, Sergio, Our Lady of Guadalupe, El Centro
Hitch, James, (Retired), Bonita
Hoang, Loi, St. Francis of Assisi, Vista
Hodsdon, Peter, St. James, Solana Beach
Holgren, Robert, Our Lady of Mt. Carmel, San Diego
Hollowell, Christopher Wil, Corpus Christi, Bonita
Huitron, Salvador, Our Lady of Refuge, San Diego
Huizar, Marco Antonio, St. Didacus, San Diego
Hulburt, Robert, St. Brigid, San Diego
Hunt, Samuel, (Retired), Homosassa, FL
Jensen, Don, St. Peter the Apostle, Fallbrook
Jiron, Guillermo, El Paso, TX
Johnson, Peter, St. Pius X, Chula Vista
Kabbany, Antoine, St. Jakob Melkite Community
Kapral, Vince, Santa Sophia, Spring Valley
Keeley, James, (Retired), San Diego
Kelsey, Herbert, Blessed Sacrament, San Diego
Klopchin, William, (Retired), San Diego
Korty, William, Parker, CO
Kostick, James, (Retired), Escondido
Kutler, Harold, (Retired), Oceanside
Leach, David, (Retired), Carlsbad
Lewis, David, St. Charles, San Diego
Litke, Lane, St. Pius X, Chula Vista
Lopez, Marcos, St. Margaret Mary, Brawley
Lozoya, Margarito, (Retired), Chula Vista
Magana, Gustavo, San Diego
Maria, Michael, La Mesa
Marquez, Gerardo, St. Rose of Lima, Chula Vista
Martinez, David, St. Catherine Laboure, San Diego
Martinez, Seodello A., (Retired), San Diego
McDaniel, Alvin, (Retired), Hemet, CA
Medina, Jose Luis, Our Lady of Mt. Carmel, San Ysidro
Melrose, Richard, Bellevue, NE
Mercardante, Frank, Temecula
Millan, Raul, Corpus Christi, Bonita
Miller, James, Logan, UT
Monsalvo, Carlos, Mission San Antonio de Pala, Pala
Montoya, Edwin Gonzales, Resurrection, Escondido
Montoya, Kenneth, (Retired), San Diego
Moore, Joseph, St. Joseph Cathedral, San Diego
Moser, Edward, St. Patrick, Carlsbad
Moya, Alberto, St. Anthony of Padua, Imperial
Mueller, Robert, St. Francis of Assisi, Vista
Murray, Kevin, Sacred Heart, Coronado
Navarrete, Charles, St. Margaret, Oceanside
Nguyen, Peter, (Retired), San Diego
Nickell, Dennie, (Retired), El Cajon
O'Neil, Dennis, Our Lady of Perpetual Help, Lakeside
O'Riordan, Stephen, Our Lady of the Rosary, San Diego
Osgood, Franklin B., (Retired), Coronado
Pangilinan, Alan, Corpus Christi, Bonita
Partida, Michael, Resurrection, Escondido
Pelina, Ruben, Most Precious Blood, Chula Vista
Perez, Dominador, St. Mary of the Sea, Oceanside
Pomphrey, Richard, St. Patrick, Carlsbad
Porciuncula, Manuel, (Retired), San Diego
Powers, Daniel, Charleston, SC
Reilly, Frank, St. Kieran, El Cajon
Rennix, Mitchell, St. Mary, Escondido
Rivera, Noel, Our Lady of Mt. Carmel, San Diego
Robbins, Ralph, (Retired), San Marcos
Rodriguez, Manuel, St. Jude Shrine of the West, San Diego
Root, Patrick, Our Lady of Perpetual Help, Lakeside
Rosas, Daniel, St. Peter the Apostle, Fallbrook
Rosker, Allen, St. Martin of Tours, La Mesa
Salinas, Gilbert, St. Stephen, Valley Center
Sanchez, Andres, St. Mary, Escondido
Santen, Joseph R., Mooresville, NC
Santillan, Juan, St. Francis of Assisi, Vista
Santoyo, Juan Francisco, (Retired), La Mesa
Sawaya, John, Our Lady of Grace, El Cajon
Scull, James, Ascension, San Diego
Serafini, Dino, St. Didacus, San Diego
Shelton, Carl, (Retired), San Diego
Shockley, Gordon E., (Retired), San Antonio, TX
Silvia, Mark, Our Lady of Perpetual Help, Lakeside
Skiano, Ralph, St. Mary Magdalene, San Diego
Skupnik, Raymond, Seal Beach, CA
Smyth, Gregory, (Retired), Chula Vista
Spinney, Donald L., Sacred Heart, Brawley
Stanley, James, St. John of the Cross, Lemon Grove
Stenovec, Gerald, St. Luke, El Cajon
Swingle, Fred III, Mater Dei, Chula Vista
Thompson, Ward, Lone Tree, IA
Thornton, Fred, Queen of Angels, Alpine
Threatt, Marvin, (Retired), Spring Valley
Tobin, John, St. Stephen, Valley Center
Treadwell, Timothy, Holy Trinity, El Cajon
Trumble, John, (Retired), Las Vegas, NV
Turcich, John, St. Pius X, Jamul
Turner, William, Immaculate Heart of Mary, Ramona
Vaillancourt, Leonard, Latham, NY
Valdivia, Guillermo, Our Lady of Guadalupe, Chula Vista
Vargas, Jim F., O.F.S., Mary Star of the Sea, La Jolla
Vasquez, H. William Jr., Mission San Diego de Alcala & St. Columba, San Diego
Villafana, Martin, (Retired), San Diego
Villegas, Gilbert, Chula Vista
Wall, Scott, Our Mother of Confidence, San Diego
Walsh, James, Nativity, Rancho Santa Fe
Warren, David, St. Joseph Cathedral, San Diego
Wieczorek, Mark, Sacred Heart, San Diego
Williams, Allan, St. Luke, El Cajon
Wright, Patrick, St. Therese, San Diego
Yeatts, Bernard, (Retired), San Diego.

INSTITUTIONS LOCATED IN DIOCESE

[A] SEMINARIES, DIOCESAN

SAN DIEGO. *St. Francis De Sales Center* aka House of Priestly Formation, 1667 Santa Paula Dr., 92111. Tel: 619-291-7446; Fax: 619-291-7011; Email: mmunz@sdcatholic.org; Web: www.sdcatholic.org. Revs. Lauro Minimo, Vocation Dir.; Gilbert J. Gentile, S.J., Spiritual Dir.; Very Rev. Matthew D. Spahr, Dir. of Priestly Formation. For priests and priestly formation. Priests 3; Students 15.

[B] HIGHER EDUCATION

SAN DIEGO. *University of San Diego* (1949) 5998 Alcala Park, 92110-2492. Tel: 619-260-4600; Email: cathyjohnson@sandiego.edu; Web: www.sandiego.edu. James T. Harris, Pres.; Rev. Msgr. Daniel J. Dillabough, J.C.L., Vice Pres. Mission & Ministry. Religious Teachers 7; Lay Teachers 424; Priests 4; Sisters 2; Students 8,905; Total University Full-time Faculty 427; Law Students 781; Undergraduate Students 5,711; Graduate Students 1,911.

University Ministers: Michael Lovette-Colyer, Asst. Vice Pres. Dir. Univ. Min.; Amy Gualtieri, Sacristan; Mary Kruer, Assoc. Univ. Min.; Maria Gaughan, Asst. Univ. Min.; Mark Peters, Assoc. Univ. Min.; Sr. Virginia Rodee, R.S.C.J., Asst. Vice Pres. for Mission; Annette Welsh, Assoc. Univ. Min.; Revs. Michael White, C.S.Sp., Univ. Chap.; Gino Correa, O.F.M., Univ. Chap.; Martin Latiff, M.C., Univ. Chap.; Julia Campagna, Assoc. Univ. Min.

Faculty: Rev. William Headley, Prof., (Retired); Sisters Mary Hotz; Terri Monroe, R.S.C.J.; Tobi Tondi, S.H.C.J.

Msgr. John Portman Chair of Roman Catholic Systematic Theology, Tel: 619-260-7844; Fax: 619-260-2260; Web: www.sandiego.edu/theo/about/portman.

Frances G. Harpst Center for Catholic Thought and Culture Jeffrey M. Burns, Dir., Tel: 619-260-7936; Web: www.sandiego.edu/cctc.

Center for the Study of Latino/Latina Catholicism, Tel: 619-260-4525; Fax: 619-260-2260; Web: www.sandiego.edu/cas/latino-cath. Dr. Orlando Espin, Dir.

Center for Christian Spirituality, Tel: 619-260-4784; Fax: 619-260-7905; Web: www.sandiego.edu/ccs. Erin Bishop, Dir.

Pastoral Care and Counseling Program, Tel: 619-260-4784; Fax: 619-260-7905.

ESCONDIDO. **John Paul the Great Catholic University*, 220 W. Grand Ave., Escondido, 92025. Tel: 858-653-6740; Fax: 858-653-3791; Email: LConnolly@jpcatholic.com; Web: www.jpcatholic.edu. Derry (Jeremiah) Connolly, Ph.D., Pres. Lay Teachers 40; Priests 3; Students 340; Religious Teachers 3.

OCEANSIDE. *Franciscan School of Theology*, 4050 Mission Ave., Oceanside, 92057. Tel: 760-547-1800; Fax: 760-547-1807; Email: mjhiggins@fst.edu; Web: www.fst.edu. Rev. Michael J. Higgins, T.O.R., Pres.; Friar Garrett Galvin, O.F.M., Vice Pres.; Kimberly Renna, Vice Pres.; Carl Adkins, Librarian. Brothers 2; Religious Teachers 8; Lay Teachers 4; Priests 5; Students 54.

[C] HIGH SCHOOLS, PRIVATE

SAN DIEGO. *Academy of Our Lady of Peace* (1882) 4860 Oregon St., 92116. Tel: 619-297-2266; Fax: 619-297-2473; Email: llek@aolp.org; Email: jhooper@aolp.org; Web: www.aolp.org. Lauren Lek, Head of School; Jessica Hooper, Asst. Head of School; Siobhan DeVore, Librarian. (Girls) Religious Teachers 7; Lay Teachers 50; Students 750.

St. Augustine High School (1922) 3266 Nutmeg St., 92104-5199. Tel: 619-282-2184; Fax: 619-282-1203; Email: kevenson@sahs.org; Web: www.sahs.org. James Horne, Prin.; Edwin Hearn, Pres.; Revs. Kirk Davis, O.S.A., Chap. Campus Min.; Mark Menegatti, O.S.A.; Bros. Max Villeneuve, O.S.A.; Barnaby Johns, O.S.A.; Deacon Richard Hardick; Jason Alcoser, Librarian. Conducted by The Augustinians.(Boys); (For information concerning the monastery see separate listing under Monasteries). Administrators 7; Religious Teachers 2; Deacons 1; Lay Teachers 54; Priests 2; Students 734.

SAN MARCOS. *Saint Joseph Academy* (Co-Ed) 500 Las Flores Dr., San Marcos, 92078. Tel: 760-305-8505; Fax: 760-305-8466; Email: office@saintjosephacademy.org; Web: www.saintjosephacademy.org. Anthony Biese, Headmaster. Lay Teachers 30; Students 288.

[D] HIGH SCHOOLS, DIOCESAN

SAN DIEGO. *Cathedral Catholic High School*, 5555 Del Mar Heights Rd., 92130. Tel: 858-523-4000; Fax: 858-523-4097; Email: kcalkins@cathedralcatholic.org; Email: slaaperi@cathedralcatholic.org; Web: www.cathedralcatholic.org. Mr. Stevan Laaperi, Pres.; Kevin Calkins, Prin. Religious Teachers 4; Lay Teachers 110; Priests 4; Students 1,622.

CALEXICO. *Vincent Memorial Catholic High School*, 525 W. Sheridan, Calexico, 92231. Tel: 760-357-3461; Fax: 760-357-0902; Email: vmoffice@vmchs.com; Web: vmchs.com. Sr. Guadalupe Hernandez, S.J.S., Prin. (Coed). Conducted by Sisters Servants of the Blessed Sacrament. Lay Teachers 16; Sisters 1; Students 262.

CHULA VISTA. *Mater Dei Catholic High School*, 1615 Mater Dei Dr., Chula Vista, 91913. Tel: 619-423-2121; Fax: 619-423-6910; Email: mdietz@materdeicatholic.org; Web: www.materdeicatholic.org. Mr. John Rey, CPA, Pres.; Frank Stingo, Prin.; Sarah Hickman, Librarian. (Coed) Lay Teachers 50; Priests 1; Students 862.

[E] ELEMENTARY SCHOOLS DIOCESAN

SAN DIEGO. *St. Katherine Drexel Academy*, (Grades K-8), 4551 56th St., 92115. Tel: 619-582-3862; Fax: 619-265-9310; Email: mainoffice@skda-sd.org. Mrs. Anne Egan, Prin. Lay Teachers 8; Students 150.

CHULA VISTA. *Mater Dei Juan Diego Academy*, (Grades PreK-6), 1615 Mater Dei Dr., Chula Vista, 91913. Tel: 619-423-2121; Email: info@mdjda.org; Web: www.mdjda.org. Leticia Oseguera, Prin.; Cristina Torres, Admin. Lay Teachers 13; Students 272.

[F] ELEMENTARY SCHOOLS PRIVATE

SAN DIEGO. *Nativity Prep Academy*, (Grades 6-8), 2755 55th St., 92105. Tel: 619-544-9455; Fax: 619-501-1734; Email: info@nativityprep.org; Web: www.nativityprep.org. Brendan Sullivan, Pres.; Elijah Bonde, Prin.; Xochitl Alvarez, Dir. Graduate Support Program; Bill Sullivan, Dir. Admissions & High School Placement; Lisa Welch, Dir. Philanthropy; Diana Junge, Bus. Mgr. Lay Teachers 7; Students 64.

Nazareth School, (Grades PreSchool-8), 10728 San Diego Mission Rd., 92108. Tel: 619-641-7987; Fax: 619-280-4652; Email: principal@nazarethschool.org; Web: www.nazarethschool.org. Dr. Colleen Mauricio, Prin.; Georgina Barragan, Dir., Preschool. Lay Teachers 17; Students 307.

Notre Dame Academy, (Grades PreSchool-8), 4345 Del Mar Trails Rd., 92130. Tel: 858-509-2300; Fax: 858-509-5915; Email: ndaadministration@ndasd.org; Web: www.ndasd.org. Sr. Marie Pascale Clisson, U.C.S.C., Prin.; Ursula Segura, Dir., Preschool, Tel: 858-509-2300. Religious Teachers 3; Lay Teachers 38; Sisters 3; Students 320.

SAN MARCOS. *St. Joseph Academy*, (Grades PreK-12), (Co-Ed) 500 Las Flores Dr., San Marcos, 92078. Tel: 760-305-8505; Fax: 760-305-8466; Email: office@saintjosephacademy.org; Web: www.saintjosephacademy.org. Anthony Biese, Headmaster

Sierra Madre Academy. Lay Teachers 20; Students 288.

[G] SPECIAL SCHOOLS

SAN DIEGO. *Mater Dei Juan Diego Adult Center*, 1615 Mater Dei Dr., Chula Vista, 91913. Tel: 619-423-2121; Email: nbartels@mdchs.net. Nancy Bartels, Dir. Lay Teachers 5; Students 325.

EL CAJON. *St. Madeleine Sophie's Center*, 2119 E. Madison Ave., El Cajon, 92019-1111. Tel: 619-442-5129; Fax: 619-442-9651; Email: demerson@stmsc.org; Web: www.stmsc.org. Debra Turner-Emerson, CEO. Lay Teachers 125; Tot Asst. Annually 600; Total Staff 135; Enrollment 413.

[H] PROTECTIVE INSTITUTIONS

SPRING VALLEY. *Noah Homes* (1983) 12526 Campo Rd., Spring Valley, 91978. Tel: 619-660-6200; Fax: 619-660-1481; Email: m.nocon@noahhomes.org; Web: www.noahhomes.org. Molly Nocon, Chief Exec. Dir. Bed Capacity 90; Tot Asst. Annually 90; Total Staff 100.

[I] HOSPITALS

SAN DIEGO. *Scripps Mercy Hospital* (1890) 4077 Fifth Ave., 92103. Tel: 619-294-8111; Fax: 619-686-3530; Email: Ybarra.Miriam@scrippshealth.org; Web: www.scrippshealth.org. Tom Gammiere, Chief Exec.; Sr. Mary Gallagher, R.S.M., Mgr. Spiritual Care & Dir. Mission Integration; Mark Zangrando, Sr. Dir. Mission Integration; Revs. Gerald Swanson, Chap. (Baptist); Lawrence Agi; Michael Harkay, Chap.; Ann Albrecht, Chap.; Sr. Carol Pack, S.S.S., Chap. Bed Capacity 655; Patients Asst Anual. 206,426; Tot Asst. Annually 322,587; Total Staff 3,375.

Scripps Mercy Chula Vista, 435 H St., Chula Vista, 91910. Tel: 619-691-7000. Mark Weber, B.C.C., Chap.; Rev. Emmanuel Ochigbo. Bed Capacity 183; Patients Asst Anual. 94,928; Staff 1,140.

[J] HOMES FOR SENIOR CITIZENS

SAN DIEGO. *Cathedral Plaza*, 1551 Third Ave., 92101. Tel: 619-234-0093; Fax: 619-234-5168; Email: cathedral@cathedralplaza.sd.coxmail.com. Bobbi Pentchev, Resident Mgr.; Tim Althoff, Supvr. Maintenance

Cathedral Plaza Development Corp., A California Nonprofit Corporation Total Staff 6; Apartments 221; In Residence 253; Total Assisted 172.

Guadalupe Plaza, 4142 42nd St., 92105. Tel: 619-584-2414; Fax: 619-584-2886; Email: lily@royalpropertymgmt.com. Lily Warner, Contact Person

Guadalupe Plaza Development Corp., A California Nonprofit Corporation Apartments 126; In Residence 146.

St. John's Plaza, 8150 Broadway, Lemon Grove, 91945. Tel: 619-466-5354; Fax: 619-466-6643; Email: stjohnsplaza@sjp.sdcoxmail.com. Malinda Himango, Resident Mgr.

Calexico Plaza Development Corp., A California Nonprofit Corporation Total in Residence 104; Total Staff 4; Residences 99.

Nazareth House of San Diego, Inc., 6333 Rancho Mission Rd., 92108. Tel: 619-563-0480; Fax: 619-624-9215; Email: marie@nazarethhouse.sd.org; Web: www.nazarethhouse.sd.org. Sr. Marie McCormack, C.S.N., Admin. Retired Priests Residential and Assisted Living Capacity 145; Priests 11; Sisters of Nazareth of San Diego 5.

[K] MONASTERIES AND RESIDENCES OF PRIESTS AND BROTHERS

SAN DIEGO. *Augustinian Community* (1922) 3180 University Ave., Ste. 255, 92104. Tel: 619-282-2028 ; Fax: 619-282-2233; Email: osa-west@sbcglobal.net. Revs. Gary Sanders, O.S.A., Prior; Thomas W. Behan, O.S.A.; Jerome F. Bevilacqua, O.S.A.; Robert W. Gavotto, O.S.A., Chap.; Harry M. Neely, O.S.A.; Raymond Elam, O.S.A.; John Grace, O.S.A.; Mark Menegatti, O.S.A.; Ronnie Custorio, O.S.A.; Carlos Medina, O.S.A. *Augustinian Provincialate* (1981) 3180 University Ave., Ste. 255, 92104-2045. Tel: 619-235-0247; Fax: 619-231-2814; Email: osa-west@sbcglobal.net. Very Rev. Kevin C. Mullins, O.S.A., Prior Provincial.

OCEANSIDE. *Old Mission San Luis Rey* (1798) 4050 Mission Ave., Oceanside, 92057-6402. Tel: 760-757-3651; Fax: 760-757-4613; Email: kathleen@sanluisrey.org; Web: www.sanluisrey.org. Kathleen Flanagan, Exec. Dir.; Friar John Kiesler, O.F.M., Dir.; Juan Jose Jauregui, Asst. Formation Dir.; Revs. Vincent Mesi, O.F.M.; Francisco Alejo, O.F.M. Franciscan Friars. Priests 13.

Prince of Peace Abbey, 650 Benet Hill Rd., Oceanside, 92058-1253. Tel: 760-967-4200; Fax: 760-967-8711; Email: princeabby@aol.com; Web: www.princeofpeaceabbey.org. Rt. Rev. Charles Wright, O.S.B., Abbot Emeritus, (Retired); Revs. Sharbel Ewen, O.S.B., Abbot; Basil Mattingly, O.S.B.; Michel Pham, O.S.B.; Paul Farrelly, O.S.B.; Stephanos Pedrano, O.S.B.; Bros. Peter Aslin, O.S.B.; Joseph Black, O.S.B.; Anselm Clark, O.S.B.; Blaise Heuke, O.S.B.; Peter Khoa Le, O.S.B.; Benedict Menezes, O.S.B.; Raphael Meyer, O.S.B.; Mario Quizon, O.S.B.; Daniel Sokol, O.S.B.; Meinrad Taylor, O.S.B.; David Cobos, O.S.B.; Noel Greenawalt, O.S.B.; Philip Poutous, O.S.B.; Emmanuel Tran, O.S.B.; Damien Evangelista, O.S.B.; Bede Clark, O.S.B. Benedictine Fathers. Brothers 16; Priests 6.

SOLANA BEACH. *The Eudists - Congregation of Jesus and Mary*, 744 Sonrisa St., Solana Beach, 92075-2407. Fax: 858-755-0046; Email: jhhcjm@eudistsusa.org; Email: accounting@eudistsusa.org; Email: spirituality@eudistsusa.org; Web: www.eudistsusa.org. Revs. William F. Rowland, C.J.M., Supr.; John H. Howard, C.J.M., Treas.

[L] CONVENTS AND RESIDENCES FOR SISTERS

SAN DIEGO. *Carmelite Monastery of San Diego, California* (Discalced) Cloistered Contemplative Nuns 5158 Hawley Blvd., 92116-1934. Tel: 619-280-5425; Fax: 619-280-3775; Email: carmelsd@sbcglobal.net; Web: www.carmelsandiego.com. Sr. Michaela Gresko, Prioress. Sisters 14.

Community of the Holy Spirit (1970) 1263 Robinson Ave., #25, 92103. Tel: 619-692-0659; Email: lutz93@cox.net. Sr. Linda Lutz, Dir. Sisters 12.

Congregation of the Sisters of Nazareth, 6333 Rancho Mission Rd., 92108. Tel: 619-563-0480; Fax: 619-516-4038; Email: marie@nazarethhousesd.org. Sr. Marie McCormack, C.S.N., Supr. Sisters 5.

Daughters of Divine Charity, 6036 Camino Rico, 92120. Tel: 619-287-1320; Email: almaisa.ny@gmail.com. Sr. Valdecina Santos-Silva, F.D.C. Sisters 3.

Dominican Sisters of Adrian, 17565 Caminito Canasto, 92127. Tel: 619-255-4238; Email: kclausen2@cox.net. Sr. Joan Kowalski, O.P., Contact Person. Sisters 1.

Institute de L'Union-Chretienne de Saint Chammound, 4345 Del Mar Trails Rd., 92130. Tel: 858-509-2300; Email: slong@ndasd.org. Sr. Marie Pascale Clisson, U.C.S.C., Contact Person. Sisters 3.

Missionaries of Charity (1950) 3877 Boston Ave., 92113-3218. Tel: 619-263-9566; Email: kwarren@sdcatholic.org. Sr. Anne Marie Durano, M.C., Supr. Sisters 20.

Religious of Jesus and Mary, 1510 Third Ave., 92101. Tel: 619-234-0556; Email: amagner@rjmusa.org. Sr. Rosemary Nicholson, R.J.M., Supr. Sisters 4.

School Sisters of Notre Dame, 1997 Magdalene Way, 92110. Tel: 619-276-5830; Email: jweisma1@san.rr.com. Sr. Mary Ann Owens, S.S.N.D., Contact Person. Sisters 4.

Sisters of Mercy US Province (1831) 4702 Norma Dr., 92115. Tel: 619-417-0293; Email: alwrsm@gmail.com. Sr. Rosaline O'Connor, R.S.M., Prov. Sisters 9.

Sisters of Providence, St. Mary-of-the-Woods, 6665 Canyon Rim Row, #216, 92111. Tel: 562-325-1256; Email: doreenlai@yahoo.com.sg. Sisters Doreen Lai, Dir.; Dawn Tomaszewski, Supr. Sisters 1.

Sisters of Social Service, 3525 Third Ave., 92103-4908. Tel: 619-295-1896; Email: SistersSocialService@gmail.com. Sr. Michelle Walsh, S.S.S., Gen. Supr. Sisters 3.

Sisters of St. Francis (Philadelphia) (1855) 6333 Rancho Mission Rd., 92108. Tel: 619-563-0480. Sr. Mary Kiely, O.S.F., Outreach in Educ. at Father Joe's Villages in San Diego. Sisters 1.

Sisters of St. Joseph of Carondelet, 1033 Hayes Ave., 92103. Tel: 619-295-2887; Fax: 619-297-2473; Email: doan@aolp.org. Sr. Susan Jabro, C.S.J., Prov. Sisters 13.

Sisters of St. Joseph of Orange, 440 S. Batavia St., 92868. Tel: 714-633-8121; Email: sr.ellen.jordan@csjorange.org; Web: www.csjorange.org. Sr. Ellen Jordan, C.S.J., Contact Person. Sisters 1.

Society of the Holy Child Jesus, 6243 Caminito Telmo, 92111. Tel: 619-231-7788; Email: americanprovince@shcj.org. Carroll Juliano, Prov. Sisters 2.

Trinitarians of Mary, 6702 Del Cerro Blvd., 92120. Tel: 619-667-3942; Fax: 619-667-3942; Email: trinitariansofmary@gmail.com. Sr. Lillie Diaz, T.M., Major Supr. Sisters 5.

BONITA. *Sister Servants of the Blessed Sacrament* (1904) 3173 Winnetka Dr., Bonita, 91902. Tel: 619-267-0720; Fax: 619-267-0920; Email: lmbarba@sisterservantssjs.org. Sr. Maria Paz Uribe, S.J.S., Provincial Supr. Sisters 48.

CHULA VISTA. *Franciscan Missionaries of Our Lady of Peace* (1941) 575 E St., #20, Chula Vista, 91910. Tel: 619-691-9008; Fax: 619-425-7514; Email: mareaport@hotmail.com. P.O. Box 432453, San Ysidro, 92143-2453. Sisters Gabriela Chavez MTP, Maj. Supr.; Maria Espinoza, Outreach Coord. Sisters 1.

Religious of the Incarnate Word (1625) 153 Rainier Ct., Chula Vista, 91911. Tel: 619-869-7337; Email: incarword.ca@gmail.com. Mother Loreley Ifran, C.V.I., Supr. 5 in Chula Vista, 4 in El Centro 9; Total number of Sisters in organization 375.

EL CENTRO. *Our Lady of Victory Missionary Sisters*, 142 E. Octillo Dr., El Centro, 92243. Tel: 760-352-1263; Email: info@olvm.org. Sr. Mary Jo Nelson, Pres. Sisters 3.

FALLBROOK. *Hermanas del Corazon de Jesus Sacramentado*, 133 Alvarado Ct., Fallbrook, 92028. Tel: 760-645-3372; Fax: 760-645-3372; Email: hcjsfbrk@aol.com; Email: 3holycruz@hotmail.com. Sr. Ruth Irene Becerra Leyva, H.C.J.S., Major Supr. Sisters 2.

IMPERIAL BEACH. *Medical Missionaries of Mary*, 997 Ocean Ln., Apt. 4, Imperial Beach, 91932. Cell: 619-495-7290; Email: mmmpaulaz@gmail.com; Web: www.mmmworldwide.org. Sr. Paula Smith, M.M.M. Sisters 1.

LEMON GROVE. *Mercedarian Sisters of the Blessed Sacrament*, 8171 Lemon Grove Way, Lemon Grove, 91945. Tel: 619-460-4271; Fax: 619-460-1060; Email: mdoloresm@sbcglobal.net. Sr. Rosario Vega, H.M.S.S., Regl. Supr. Sisters 4.

SAN YSIDRO. *Dominican Sisters, Tacoma WA*, 1879 Via Las Tonadas, San Ysidro, 92173. Tel: 619-428-1629 ; Email: dominicans@tacomaop.org. Sr. Roseanne Cordova. Sisters 2.

Sisters Servants of the Blessed Sacrament, 3173 Winnetka Dr., Bonita, 91902. Tel: 619-267-0720; Fax: 619-600-1061; Email: provincial@usasjs.org; Web: www.usasjs.org. Sr. Lilia M. Barba, S.J.S., Prov. Sisters 26.

VISTA. *Sisters of St. Clare (O.S.C.)*, 1171 Via Santa Paulo, Vista, 92081. Tel: 760-295-0611; Email: madfitz@icloud.com. Sr. Madeline Fitzgeral, O.S.C., Regl. Coord. Sisters 107.

[M] SOCIAL SERVICES

SAN DIEGO. *Catholic Charities*, 3888 Paducah Dr., 92117. Tel: 619-323-2841; Fax: 619-234-7002; Email: vpajanor@ccdsd.org; Web: www.ccdsd.org. P.O. Box 121831, 92112-1831. Dr. Appaswamy "Vino" Pajanor, Dir. Counseling Services.; Homeless Women's Services. Tot Asst. Annually 10,000; Total Staff 150.

Emergency Services (Main Office), Tel: 619-231-2828; Fax: 619-234-2272.

Pregnancy and Adoption, Tel: 619-231-2828; Fax: 619-234-2272. Patricia Petterson, Ph.D., Dir.

Immigrant Services–San Diego, Tel: 619-287-9454; Fax: 619-234-2272. Dr. Robert Moser, Ph.D., Dir.

La Posada Farm Worker and Homeless Men's

Housing, Carlsbad, Tel: 760-929-2322; Fax: 760-929-8712.

House of Hope–El Centro-Imperial County, Tel: 760-352-1182; Fax: 760-352-5492.

Our Lady of Guadalupe Shelter-Calexico-Imperial County, Tel: 760-357-0894; Fax: 760-357-0895.

Joan of Arc Residence, 1510 Third Ave., 92101. Tel: 619-239-2663; Email: joanofarcresidence@hotmail.com. Sr. Rosemary Nicholson, R.J.M., Admin. Residence for Employed Young Women and College Students 21-60 Years. Capacity 71; Religious 4; Tot Asst. Annually 50; Total Staff 8; Permanent Residents 50.

**S.V.D.P. Management Inc.* dba Father Joe's Villages, 3350 E St., 92102. Tel: 619-446-2100; Fax: 619-446-2129; Email: info@neighbor.org; Web: my.neighbor.org. Deacon Jim F. Vargas, O.F.S., Pres. & CEO. Owns and manages the property for St. Vincent de Paul Village, Inc. Tot Asst. Annually 13,500; Total Staff 400.

**St. Vincent de Paul Village* (1950) 1501 Imperial Ave., 92101. Tel: 619-233-8500; Fax: 619-235-9707; Email: info@neighbor.org; Web: my.neighbor.org. 3350 E St., 92102-3332. Deacon Jim F. Vargas, O.F.S., Pres. & CEO. Housing and supportive services for people experiencing homelessness Tot Asst. Annually 13,500; Total Staff 400.

Franklin Antonio Public Lunch Line (1987) 1501 Imperial Ave., 92101. Tel: 619-233-8500; Fax: 619-235-9707; Email: info@neighbor.org; Web: my.neighbor.org. Ruth Bruland, Chief Program Officer; Deacon Jim F. Vargas, O.F.S., Pres. Daily hot, nutritious meal for men, women and children Tot Asst. Annually 8,500; Total Staff 400.

Housing Programs (1989) 1501 Imperial Ave., 92101. Tel: 619-233-8500; Fax: 619-235-9707; Web: my.neighbor.org; Email: info@neighbor.org. Ruth Bruland, Chief Program Officer; Deacon Jim F. Vargas, O.F.S., Pres. Emergency shelter, transitional housing, rapid rehousing & permanent supportive housing. Bed Capacity 1,600; Tot Asst. Annually 3,000; Total Staff 400.

Therapeutic Childcare Center, 1501 Imperial Ave., 92101. Tel: 619-233-8500; Email: info@neighbor.org; Web: my.neighbor.org. Ruth Bruland, Chief Prog. Officer; Deacon Jim F. Vargas, O.F.S., Pres. state licensed child development center Tot Asst. Annually 450; Total Staff 400.

Chaplaincy Services dba Josue Homes, 1501 Imperial Ave., 92101. Tel: 619-233-8500; Fax: 619-235-9707; Email: info@neighbor.org; Web: my.neighbor.org. Ruth Bruland, Chief Prog. Officer; Deacon Jim F. Vargas, O.F.S., Pres.; Sr. Carmel Lohan, S.M., Chaplaincy Prog. Mgr. Chaplaincy programs include interfaith services, Catholic mass, memorial services, men's conversation groups, women's support groups, meditation, retreats and Bible study. Tot Asst. Annually 450; Total Staff 400.

Addiction Treatment & Education Center (1994) 1501 Imperial Ave., 92101. Tel: 619-233-8500; Fax: 619-235-9707; Email: info@neighbor.org; Web: my.neighbor.org. Ruth Bruland, Chief Program Officer; Deacon Jim F. Vargas, O.F.S., Pres. individual and group addiction treatment for people who are homeless Tot Asst. Annually 500; Total Staff 400.

Day Center for Homeless Adults, 299 17th St., 92101. Tel: 619-233-8500; Email: info@neighbor.org; Web: my.neighbor.org. 1501 Imperial Ave., 92101. Ruth Bruland, Chief Prog. Officer; Deacon Jim F. Vargas, O.F.S., Pres. Provides a safe place to rest during the day, restrooms, laundry, storage, showers, computer lab, phones, and a mailing address. Tot Asst. Annually 6,500; Total Staff 400.

Retail Stores (1950) 3350 E St., 92102. Tel: 619-446-2100; Fax: 619-446-2129; Email: info@neighbor.org; Web: my.neighbor.org/shop. Deacon Jim F. Vargas, O.F.S., Pres.; Donna Snell, Retail Dir.

Mental Health Services, 1501 Imperial Ave., 92101. Tel: 619-233-8500; Email: info@neighbor.org; Web: my.neighbor.org. Ruth Bruland, Chief Prog. Officer; Deacon Jim F. Vargas, O.F.S., Pres. Individual and group therapy to couples, families, single adults, and children. Tot Asst. Annually 700; Total Staff 400.

Affordable Housing, Corporate Office, 3350 E St., 92102. Tel: 619-446-2100; Fax: 619-446-2129; Email: info@neighbor.org; Web: my.neighbor.org. Deacon Jim F. Vargas, O.F.S., Pres. 365 affordable studio, 1-, 2- and 3-bedroom units in 5 buildings. Bed Capacity 365; Tot Asst. Annually 600; Total Staff 400.

Employment & Education Services, 1501 Imperial Ave., 92101. Tel: 619-233-8500; Email: info@neighbor.org; Web: my.neighbor.org. Ruth Bruland, Chief Prog. Officer; Deacon Jim F. Vargas, O.F.S., CEO. phones, fax machines, and printers, computer instruction, resume and job interview preparation, job placement, sector-based training Tot Asst. Annually 1,700; Total Staff 400.

Village Family Health Center Federally Qualified Health Center and Health Care for the Homeless clinic providing primary care, psychiatry, pediatrics, dental care and more 1501 Imperial Ave., 92101. Tel: 619-233-8500; Email: info@neighbor.org; Web: my.neighbor.org. Ruth Bruland, Chief Prog. Officer; Deacon Jim F. Vargas, O.F.S., Pres. Tot Asst. Annually 2,600; Total Staff 400.

Veteran's Services Emergency Shelter & Transitional Housing, mental health and addiction treatment, dental care, meals and alumni group meetings for Veterans of all branches of the military. 1501 Imperial Ave., 92101. Tel: 619-233-8500; Fax: 619-235-9707; Email: info@neighbor.org; Web: my.neighbor.org. Ruth Bruland, Chief Prog. Officer; Deacon Jim F. Vargas, O.F.S., Pres. Tot Asst. Annually 1,600; Total Staff 400.

[N] RETREATS

SAN DIEGO. *Spiritual Ministry Center* (1987) 4822 Del Mar Ave., 92107-3407. Tel: 619-224-9444; Email: spiritmin@rscj.org; Web: www.spiritmin.org. Bunny Flick, Contact Person.

Whispering Winds Catholic Conference Center (1978) Facility: 17606 Harrison Park Rd., Julian, 92036. Tel: 619-464-1479; Fax: 619-464-4491; Email: office@whisperingwinds.org; Web: www.whisperingwinds.org. Office: 4636 Mission Gorge Pl., #203, 92120. Martin Rosales, Exec. Dir. Purpose: Serve over 10,000 guests each year for school, confirmation and parish retreats. Summer family and middle school camps.

DESCANSO. *Camp Oliver*, 8761 Riverside Dr., Descanso, 91916. Tel: 619-445-5945; Fax: 619-445-3326; Email: info@campoliver.org; Web: www.campoliver.org. P.O. Box 206, Descanso, 91916. Trista Brant, Camp Dir. Sisters of Social Service. Residential summer camp for girls & boys, ages 6-12 in July. Available as a retreat facility August to early June. Available for organizations that have their own summer camp program but need a facility. American Camp Association certified.

OCEANSIDE. *Old Mission San Luis Rey Retreat*, 4050 Mission Ave., Oceanside, 92057-6402. Tel: 760-757-3659, Ext. 108; Fax: 760-757-8025; Email: retreats@sanluisrey.org; Web: www.sanluisrey.org. Kathryn De Anda, Dir.

[O] NEWMAN CENTERS

SAN DIEGO. *Newman Center - SDSU*, 5855 Hardy Ave., 92115. Tel: 858-490-8203; Fax: 619-583-8925; Email: office@sdsucatholic.org; Web: www.sdsucatholic.org. Rev. Pedro Rivera, Dir.

University of California at San Diego (Campus Ministry) aka Newman Center Catholic Community at UCSD, 4321 Eastgate Mall, 92121-2102. Tel: 858-452-1957 (Office); Email: cathcom@ucsd.edu; Web: www.catholicucsd.org. Revs. Joaquin Marinez, S.J., Dir.; Manh Tran, Assoc. Dir.; David Vacchi, Pastoral Assoc.; Gabriela Arambulo, Pastoral Assoc.

[P] MISCELLANEOUS

SAN DIEGO. *The St. Augustine Foundation*, 3180 University Ave., Ste. 255, 92104. Email: osa-west@sbcglobal.net. Very Rev. Kevin C. Mullins, O.S.A., Prior Prov.

The Bellesini Foundation, 3180 University Ave., Ste. 255, 92104. Tel: 619-235-0247; Fax: 619-231-2814; Email: osa-west@sbcglobal.net. Very Rev. Kevin C. Mullins, O.S.A. Funding for the education of members of the Order of St. Augustine.

**Catholic Action for Faith and Family*, P.O. Box 910308, 92191. Tel: 858-461-0777; Email: tmckenna@catholicaction.org. Thomas McKenna, Contact Person. An association of Catholics that strives to uphold and defend Christian values inspired by the teachings of the Roman Catholic Church.

Catholic Committee on Scouting, 3350 E St., 92102. Tel: 619-446-2704; Fax: 619-446-2129; Email: ccsbsa@neighbor.org. Rev. Alexander De Paulis, Scout Chap.; Karen Beard, Chm.; Pam Dixon, Coord.

**Catholic Community Foundation of San Diego*, P.O. Box 81023, 92138. Tel: 858-490-8365; Email: grectenwald@sdcatholic.org. Glen Rectenwald, Exec. Dir. Provides a one-stop resource for Catholic philanthropy in the Catholic communities in San Diego and Imperial counties.

Catholic Secondary Education - Diocese of San Diego, Incorporated (2003) 3888 Paducah Dr., P.O. Box 85728, 92186. Tel: 858-490-8301; Fax: 858-490-8272; Email: rvaldivia@sdcatholic.org. Rodrigo Valdivia, J.C.L., Chancellor.

**Children of the Immaculate Heart*, P.O. Box 13954, 92170. Tel: 619-431-5537; Email: officemanager.cih@gmail.com; Email: childrenoftheimmaculateheart@gmail.com; Web: childrenoftheimmaculateheart.org. Grace Williams, CEO.

Christ Child Society, 5418 Baja Dr., 92115. Tel: 619-287-9021; Email: sandiego@nationalchristchild.org. Kathleen Israel, Pres.

Mater Dei Catholic High School Foundation, Inc., 3888 Paducah Dr., P.O. Box 85728, 92186. Tel: 858-490-8310; Fax: 858-490-8348; Email: rvaldivia@sdcatholic.com. Rodrigo Valdivia, J.C.L., Contact Person.

Mater Dei Catholic High School of San Diego Inc., P.O. Box 85728, 92186-5728. Tel: 858-490-8310; Fax: 858-490-8348; Email: rvaldivia@sdcatholic.org. Rodrigo Valdivia, J.C.L., Contact Person.

Mercy Hospital Foundation, San Diego, Scripps Health Foundation, P.O. Box 2669, La Jolla, 92038. Tel: 800-326-3776; Fax: 858-678-6336; Email: braunwarth.mary@scrippshealth.org; Web: www.scrippsfoundation.org. Mary Braunwarth, Senior Dir., Devel.

The Mother Teresa of Calcutta Center, 3835 National Ave., 92113. Tel: 619-662-1484; Fax: 619-662-1268; Email: mtc@motherteresa.org; Web: www.motherteresa.org. Sr. Elizabeth, M.C., Contact Person.

Nazareth School of San Diego, Inc., 10728 San Diego Mission Rd., 92108. Tel: 619-641-7987; Fax: 619-280-4652; Email: Office@nazarethschool.org. Dr. Colleen Mauricio, Prin.

San Diego North County Magnificat - Our Lady of Guadalupe Chapter, 13590 Fall Haven Rd., 92129. Tel: 760-505-6625; Email: rosarylady@cox.net. Rev. John Struzzo, C.S.C., Chap.; Rosemary Geiger, Coord.

The Sisters of Nazareth of San Diego Real Estate Holdings, Inc., 6333 Rancho Mission Rd., 92108. Tel: 619-708-2775; Fax: 619-624-9215; Email: srvera.chan@sistersofnazareth.us. Sr. Vera Chan, Sec.

The Tagaste Foundation, 3180 University Ave., Ste. 255, 92104-2089. Tel: 619-235-0247; Fax: 619-231-2814; Email: osa-west@sbcglobal.net. Very Rev. Kevin C. Mullins, O.S.A., Contact Person. Funding for the support, care and maintenance of the Order of St. Augustine.

**Totus Pro Deo* (All for God) 4698 Alvarado Canyon Rd., Ste. K, 92120. Tel: 619-582-4571; Fax: 619-582-4771; Email: info@allforgod.com; Web: www.allforgod.com. Mrs. Margie Rapp, CEO; Deacon Jim F. Vargas, O.F.S., Dir.

All for God Steubenville So Cal.

EL CAJON. **Catholic Answers, Inc.*, 2020 Gillespie Way, El Cajon, 92020. Tel: 619-387-7200; Fax: 619-387-0042; Email: jennifer@catholic.com; Email: marketing@catholic.com; Web: www.catholic.com. Christopher Check, Pres.

Kraemer Endowment Foundation, Inc. (1992) 2119 E. Madison Ave., El Cajon, 92019-1111. Tel: 858-551-9402; Fax: 858-584-2642; Email: john.seiber@ubs.com; Web: www.stmsc.org. John Seiber, Chm.

ENCINITAS. **Catholic Media Works, Inc.*, P.O. Box 231820, Encinitas, 92023. Tel: 760-635-1122; Email: adebellis@adebellis.com. 3249 Avenida De Sueno, Carlsbad, 92009. Anthony DeBellis, Contact Person. Evangelize the world through media. Carefully select morality-based films & media projects.

ESCONDIDO. **Benedictus*, 8975-7 Lawrence Welk Dr., Escondido, 92026. Tel: 760-500-8565; Email: kostickj@juno.com; Web: www.benedictussd.wordpress.com. Deacon James Kostick, Contact Person.

LA JOLLA. **Friends of the Poor*, 8460 Whale Watch Way, La Jolla, 92037.

OCEANSIDE. *Academy of American Franciscan History*, 4050 Mission Ave., Oceanside, 92057. Tel: 510-548-1755; Fax: 510-549-9466; Email: acadafh@fst.edu; Web: www.aafh.org. Jeffrey M. Burns, Dir. Total Staff 1.

**The Emiliani Project*, 884 Arvita Ct., Oceanside, 92057. Tel: 760-805-3042; Email: missions@emilianiproject.org; Web: emilianiproject.org. Jordan Reece, Contact Person.

POWAY. *The Genesis Initiative* Supports development movie, television and education initiatives. P.O. Box 612, Poway, 92074. Tel: 858-748-3348; Email: info@genesisinitiative.org. Martha Lyles, Contact Person; Dick Lyles, Contact Person.

RELIGIOUS INSTITUTES OF MEN REPRESENTED IN THE DIOCESE

For further details refer to the corresponding bracketed number in the Religious Institutes of Men or Women section.

[]—*Apostles of Jesus*—A.J.

[0140]—*The Augustinians*—O.S.A.

[0200]—*Benedictine Monks*—O.S.B.

[0160]—*Clerics Regular of St. Paul*—C.R.S.P.

[]—*Columban Fathers.*
[0450]—*Congregation of Jesus and Mary*—C.J.M.
[0650]—*Congregation of the Holy Spirit*—C.S.Sp.
[0520]—*Franciscan Friars*—O.F.M.
[0560]—*Franciscans, Third Order Regular*—T.O.R.
[0690]—*Jesuit Fathers and Brothers*—S.J.
[0690]—*Jesuit Fathers and Brothers* (Jesuit West Prov.)—S.J.
[]—*Miles Christi*—M.C.
[]—*Missionaries of Charity Fathers*—M.C.
[0370]—*Missionary Society of Saint Columban*—S.S.C.
[0910]—*Oblates of Mary Immaculate*—O.M.I.
[0260]—*Order of Discalced Carmelites*—O.C.D.
[0430]—*Order of Preachers (Dominicans)*—O.P.
[]—*Piarist Fathers.*
[1065]—*Priestly Fraternity of St. Peter*—F.S.S.P.
[]—*Redemptorists.*
[1190]—*Salesians of Don Bosco*—S.D.B.
[]—*Scalabrinian Missionaries*—C.S.
[]—*Servants of the Risen Christ*—S.R.C.
[1260]—*Society of Christ*—S.Ch.
[0420]—*Society of the Divine Word*—S.V.D.

RELIGIOUS INSTITUTES OF WOMEN REPRESENTED IN THE DIOCESE

[]—*Carmelite Sisters of the Sacred Heart*—C.S.C.
[2020]—*Community of the Holy Spirit*—C.H.S.
[3242]—*Congregation of the Sisters of Nazareth*—C.S.N.
[0790]—*Daughters of Divine Charity*—F.D.C.
[0420]—*Discalced Carmelite Nuns*—O.C.D.
[1070-03]—*Dominican Sisters*—O.P.
[1070-13]—*Dominican Sisters*—O.P.
[1070-20]—*Dominican Sisters*—O.P.
[1070-11]—*Dominican Sisters*—O.P.
[]—*Franciscan Missionaries of Our Lady of Peace*—M.F.P.
[]—*Hermanas del Corazon de Jesus Sacramentado*—H.C.J.S.
[]—*Institute de L'Union-Chretienne de Saint Chaumond*—U.C.S.C.
[2480]—*Medical Missionaries of Mary*—M.M.M.
[2590]—*Mercedarian Sisters of the Blessed Sacrament*—H.M.S.S.
[2710]—*Missionaries of Charity*—M.C.
[]—*Missionary Sisters of the Society of Mary*—S.M.S.M.
[3070]—*North American Unions of Sisters of Our Lady of Charity*—N.A.U.-O.L.C.
[3130]—*Our Lady of Victory Missionary Sisters*—O.L.V.M.
[3450]—*Religious of Jesus and Mary*—R.J.M.
[3449]—*Religious of the Incarnate Word*—C.V.I.
[2970]—*School Sisters of Notre Dame*—S.S.N.D.
[0520]—*Sisters of Charity of Our Lady, Mother of Mercy*—S.C.M.M.
[]—*Sisters for Christian Community*—S.F.C.C.
[2549]—*Sisters of Mercy of Ireland & U.S. Province*—R.S.M.
[2575]—*Sisters of Mercy of The Americas* (West-Midwest)—R.S.M.
[]—*Sisters of Our Lady of Charity of the Good Shepherd*—R.G.S.
[3360]—*Sisters of Providence*—S.P.
[1540]—*Sisters of Saint Francis, Clinton, Iowa*—O.S.F.
[]—*Sisters of Saint Francis, Rochester*—O.S.F.
[1705]—*The Sisters of St. Francis of Assisi*—O.S.F.
[1650]—*Sisters of St. Francis of Philadelphia*—O.S.F.
[3830-03]—*Sisters of St. Joseph* (Orange)—C.S.J.
[3840]—*Sisters of St. Joseph of Carondelet* (Los Angeles, CA; St. Louis, MO)—C.S.J.
[3499]—*Sisters of the Blessed Lady*—S.B.L.
[3260]—*Sisters of the Precious Blood*—C.PP.S.
[4060]—*Society of the Holy Child Jesus*—S.H.C.J.
[4070]—*Society of the Sacred Heart*—R.S.C.J.
[]—*Trinitarians of Mary*—T.M.

DIOCESAN CEMETERIES

SAN DIEGO. *Holy Cross Cemetery and Mausoleum*, 4470 Hilltop Dr., 92102. Tel: 619-264-3127; Fax: 619-264-7852; Email: mario@holycrosssd.com; Web: www.holycrossd.com. Mario Deblasio, Gen. Mgr.; Very Rev. Msgr. Dennis Mikulanis, Dir.

OCEANSIDE. *Old Mission San Luis Rey Cemetery*, 4050 Mission Ave., Oceanside, 92057. Tel: 760-757-3651, Ext. 133; Tel: 760-231-8445; Email: cemeterydirector@sanluisrey.org; Web: www.sanluisrey.org/cemetery. Kathleen Flanagan, Exec. Dir.; Jennifer McClintock, Dir.

PALA. *Pala Indian Missions*, 3015 Pala Mission Rd., P.O. Box 70, Pala, 92059. Tel: 760-742-3317; Fax: 760-742-3040; Email: info@missionsanantonio.org. Rev. Reynaldo Manahan. Six separate Indian burial grounds. No longer open for burials.

NECROLOGY

† Creighton, Edward, (Retired), Died Sep. 9, 2018
† Kulleck, Donald R., (Retired), Died Jan. 12, 2018
† Lyng, Edward F., (Retired), Died Jun. 1, 2018
† Pattison, W. Francis, (Retired), Died Aug. 30, 2018
† Kelly, John Gomes, (Retired), Died Jan. 6, 2018
† Lai, Doan Van, (Retired), Died May. 4, 2017
† Proctor, John G. Jr., (Retired), Died Feb. 27, 2019
† Quinn, John T., (Retired), Died Jan. 16, 2018
† Thompson, J. Noel, (Retired), Died Aug. 2, 2018

An asterisk (*) denotes an organization that has established tax-exempt status directly with the IRS and is not covered by the USCCB Group Ruling.

Archdiocese of San Francisco

(Archidioecesis Sancti Francisci)

Most Reverend

SALVATORE J. CORDILEONE, J.C.D.

Archbishop of San Francisco; ordained July 9, 1982; appointed Auxiliary Bishop of San Diego and Titular Bishop of Natchesium July 5, 2002; ordained August 21, 2002; appointed Bishop of Oakland March 23, 2009; installed May 5, 2009; appointed Archbishop of San Francisco July 27, 2012; installed October 4, 2012. *Office: One Peter Yorke Way, San Francisco, CA 94109-6602.*

The Chancery Office: One Peter Yorke Way, San Francisco, CA 94109-6602.

Web: www.sfarch.org

Email: info@sfarchdiocese.org

Most Reverend

IGNATIUS WANG, J.C.D.

Retired Auxiliary Bishop of San Francisco; ordained July 4, 1959; appointed Titular Bishop of Sitipa and Auxiliary Bishop of San Francisco December 13, 2002; installed January 30, 2003; retired May 16, 2009. *Office: Holy Name of Jesus Church, 1555 39th Ave., San Francisco, CA 94122.*

Most Reverend

WILLIAM J. JUSTICE

Retired Auxiliary Bishop of San Francisco; ordained May 17, 1968; appointed Titular Bishop of Mathara in Proconsulari and Auxiliary Bishop of San Francisco April 10, 2008; ordained May 28, 2008; retired November 16, 2017. *Office: One Peter Yorke Way, San Francisco, CA 94109-6602.*

Most Reverend

ROBERT F. CHRISTIAN, O.P.

Auxiliary Bishop of San Francisco; ordained June 4, 1976; appointed Auxiliary Bishop of San Francisco and Titular Bishop of Giru Marcelli March 28, 2018; installed June 5, 2018. *Chancery Office: One Peter Yorke Way, San Francisco, CA 94109-6602.*

His Eminence

WILLIAM J. LEVADA, S.T.D.

Prefect Emeritus, Congregation for the Doctrine of the Faith; Archbishop Emeritus of San Francisco; ordained December 20, 1961; appointed Titular Bishop of Capri and Auxiliary Bishop of Los Angeles March 29, 1983; Episcopal ordination May 12, 1983; appointed Archbishop of Portland in Oregon July 1, 1986; installed as Archbishop of Portland in Oregon September 21, 1986; appointed Coadjutor Archbishop of San Francisco August 17, 1995; succeeded to See December 27, 1995; appointed Prefect of the Congregation for the Doctrine of the Faith May 13, 2005; departed San Francisco August 15, 2005; Created Cardinal March 24, 2006; retired July 2, 2012. *Office: 322 Middlefield Rd., Menlo Park, CA 94025.*

ESTABLISHED JULY 29, 1853.

Square Miles 1,016.

Code Address: Roman, San Francisco.

Comprises the Counties of San Francisco, San Mateo and Marin in the State of California.

Patrons of the Archdiocese of San Francisco: St. Francis of Assisi, October 4; St. Patrick, March 17.

Legal Title: The Roman Catholic Archbishop of San Francisco, a Corporation Sole.
For legal titles of parishes and archdiocesan institutions, consult the Chancery Office.

STATISTICAL OVERVIEW

Personnel	
Retired Cardinals	1
Archbishops	1
Auxiliary Bishops	1
Retired Bishops	2
Priests: Diocesan Active in Diocese	105
Priests: Diocesan Active Outside Diocese	4
Priests: Diocesan in Foreign Missions	1
Priests: Retired, Sick or Absent	78
Number of Diocesan Priests	188
Religious Priests in Diocese	158
Total Priests in Diocese	346
Extern Priests in Diocese	62
Ordinations:	
Diocesan Priests	1
Religious Priests	4
Transitional Deacons	2
Permanent Deacons in Diocese	83
Total Brothers	25
Total Sisters	565
Parishes	
Parishes	89
With Resident Pastor:	
Resident Diocesan Priests	71
Resident Religious Priests	18
Without Resident Pastor:	
Administered by Priests	4
Missions	11
Pastoral Centers	22
New Parishes Created	1
Closed Parishes	1
Professional Ministry Personnel:	
Brothers	4
Sisters	17
Lay Ministers	98
Welfare	
Catholic Hospitals	3
Total Assisted	398,811
Health Care Centers	4
Total Assisted	4,156
Homes for the Aged	5
Total Assisted	479
Residential Care of Children	1
Total Assisted	80
Day Care Centers	3
Total Assisted	391
Specialized Homes	6
Total Assisted	2,113
Special Centers for Social Services	6
Total Assisted	1,974
Other Institutions	20
Total Assisted	30,577
Educational	
Seminaries, Diocesan	1
Students from This Diocese	14
Students from Other Diocese	54
Total Seminarians	14
Colleges and Universities	2
Total Students	9,216
High Schools, Diocesan and Parish	4
Total Students	3,571
High Schools, Private	10
Total Students	4,524
Elementary Schools, Diocesan and Parish	51
Total Students	14,261
Elementary Schools, Private	8
Total Students	2,279
Catechesis/Religious Education:	
High School Students	2,106
Elementary Students	10,711
Total Students under Catholic Instruction	46,682
Teachers in the Diocese:	
Priests	39
Scholastics	3
Brothers	3
Sisters	11
Lay Teachers	1,422
Vital Statistics	
Receptions into the Church:	
Infant Baptism Totals	4,291
Minor Baptism Totals	275
Adult Baptism Totals	217
Received into Full Communion	360
First Communions	3,979
Confirmations	2,966
Marriages:	
Catholic	653
Interfaith	180
Total Marriages	833
Total Catholic Population	441,736
Total Population	1,776,095

Former Bishops—Rt. Rev. FRANCISCO GARCIA DIEGO Y MORENO, O.F.M., ord. 1808; cons. Bishop of both Californias, Oct. 4, 1840; died in Santa Barbara, April 30, 1846; Most Revs. JOSEPH SADOC ALEMANY, O.P., D.D., cons. Bishop of Monterey, June 30, 1850; appt. first Archbishop of San Francisco, July 29, 1853; resigned and appt. Titular Archbishop of Pelusio, Dec. 28, 1884; died in Valencia, Spain, April 14, 1888; PATRICK WILLIAM RIORDAN, D.D., cons. Titular Archbishop of Cabasa and appt. Coadjutor Archbishop of San Francisco cum jure successionis Sept. 16, 1883; succeeded to Dec. 28, 1884; died in San Francisco, Dec. 27, 1914; GEORGE MONTGOMERY, D.D., cons. Titular Bishop of Tmui and appt. Coadjutor Bishop of Monterey and Los Angeles cum jure successionis April 8, 1894; succeeded to May 6, 1896; appt. Titular Archbishop of Osimo and Coadjutor Archbishop of San Francisco cum jure successionis March 27, 1903; died in San Francisco, Jan. 10, 1907; EDWARD J. HANNA, D.D., cons. Titular Bishop of Titopolis and appt. Auxiliary Bishop of San Francisco Dec. 4, 1912; appt. Archbishop of San Francisco, June 1, 1915; resigned and appt. Titular Archbishop of Gortyna, March 2, 1935; died July 10, 1944; JOHN JOSEPH MITTY, D.D., cons. Bishop of Salt Lake City, June 21, 1926; appt. Coadjutor Archbishop of San Francisco cum jure successionis, Jan. 29, 1932; succeeded to March 2, 1935; died Oct. 15, 1961; JOSEPH T. MCGUCKEN, S.T.D., appt. Auxiliary of Los Angeles, Feb. 4, 1941; cons. Titular Bishop of Sanavo March 19, 1941; appt. Coadjutor Bishop of Sacramento cum jure successionis, Oct. 26, 1955; succeeded to Jan. 14, 1957; appt. Archbishop of San Francisco, Feb. 21, 1962; appt. Assistant at the Pontifical Throne, March 19, 1966; retired Feb. 22, 1977; died Oct. 26, 1983; JOHN R. QUINN, D.D., (Retired), appt. Auxiliary Bishop of San Diego, Oct. 21, 1967; cons. Titular Bishop of Thisiduo, Dec. 12, 1967; transferred to Oklahoma City and Tulsa, Nov. 18, 1971; appt. Archbishop of the Archdiocese of

Oklahoma City, Feb. 6, 1973; appt. Archbishop of San Francisco, April 26, 1977; resigned Dec. 27, 1995; died June 22, 2017.; WILLIAM J. LEVADA, S.T.D., ord. Dec. 20, 1961; appt. Titular Bishop of Capri and Auxiliary Bishop of Los Angeles March 29, 1983; Episcopal ord. May 12, 1983; appt. Archbishop of Portland in Oregon July 1, 1986; installed as Archbishop of Portland in Oregon Sept. 21, 1986; appt. Coadjutor Archbishop of San Francisco Aug. 17, 1995; succeeded to See Dec. 27, 1995; appt. Prefect of Doctrine of the Faith May 13, 2005; created Cardinal March 24, 2006.; GEORGE H. NIEDERAUER, D.D., Ph.D., ord. April 30, 1962; appt. Bishop of Salt Lake City Nov. 3, 1994; Episcopal ordination Jan. 25, 1995; appt. Archbishop of San Francisco Dec. 15, 2005; installed as Archbishop Feb. 15, 2006; retired July 27, 2012; died May 2, 2017.

Chancery and Pastoral Center—One Peter Yorke Way, San Francisco, 94109-6602. Tel: 415-614-5500; Fax: 415-614-5555. Open Mon.-Fri. All applications for dispensations, faculties, etc., and all correspondence should be addressed: Chancery and Pastoral Center.

Office of the Archbishop—

Archbishop—Most Rev. SALVATORE J. CORDILEONE, J.C.D.

Priest Secretary to the Archbishop—Rev. PAUL J. COLEMAN, Tel: 415-614-5609; Fax: 415-614-5601; Email: colemanp@sfarch.org.

Executive Assistant to the Archbishop—KAREN MCLAUGHLIN, J.D., Tel: 415-614-5609; Fax: 415-614-5601; Email: mclaughlink@sfarch.org.

Administrative Assistant, Office of the Archbishop—ROSE MARIE WONG, Tel: 415-614-5604; Email: wongr@sfarch.org.

Auxiliary Bishop—Most Rev. WILLIAM J. JUSTICE, Vicar Gen., Tel: 415-614-5611.

Vicar for Clergy—Rev. RAYMUND REYES, Email: reyesr@sfarch.org.

Manager, Office of the Auxiliary Bishops, Office of the Vicar for Clergy—ANNABELLE C.A. GROH, Tel: 415-614-5611; Fax: 415-614-5613; Email: groha@sfarch.org. Administrative Assistants: SHARON LEE, Tel: 415-614-5614; Email: lees@sfarch.org; MERLE TALENS, Tel: 415-614-5611; Email: talensm@sfarch.org.

Office of the Permanent Diaconate—Deacon MICHAEL J. GHIORSO, Dir., Email: ghiorsom@sfarch.org; PATRICIA JAMESON, Coord., Tel: 415-614-5531; Fax: 415-614-5555; Email: jamesonp@sfarch.org.

Office of Diaconate Formation—Rev. MICHAEL B. SWEENEY, O.P., Dir.; PATRICIA JAMESON, Coord., Tel: 415-614-5615; Fax: 415-614-5555; Email: jamesonp@sfarch.org.

Office of Vocations—Rev. DAVID A. SCHUNK, Tel: 415-614-5683; Email: schunkd@sfarch.org; BETTY RIECHMANN, Administrative Asst., Tel: 415-614-5684; Email: riechmannb@sfarch.org.

Episcopal Vicar for the Spanish Speaking—Rev. MOISES AGUDO, Tel: 415-614-5591; Email: agudom@sfarch.org.

Episcopal Vicar for Filipinos—Very Rev. EUGENE D. TUNGOL, Tel: 415-614-5590; Email: tungole@sfarch.org.

Director of the Office for Consecrated Life—Sr. ROSINA CONROTTO, P.B.V.M., Dir., Tel: 415-614-5535; Email: conrottor@sfarch.org.

Chancellor—Rev. Msgr. C. MICHAEL PADAZINSKI, J.C.D., Tel: 415-614-5619; Fax: 415-614-5696; Email: padazinskim@sfarch.org.

Vice Chancellor and Tribunal Office Manager—ROBERT W. GRAFFIO, J.C.L., Email: graffior@sfarch.org.

College of Consultors—Most Revs. SALVATORE J. CORDILEONE, J.C.D.; WILLIAM J. JUSTICE; Rev. Msgrs. MICHAEL D. HARRIMAN; C. MICHAEL PADAZINSKI, J.C.D.; JAMES T. TARANTINO; Revs. DAVID A. GHIORSO; JOHN J. PIDERIT, S.J., Ph.D.; RAYMUND M. REYES; THOMAS M. HAMILTON; CHARLES PUTHOTA; ANDREW P. SPYROW; MARK D. DOHERTY.

Deans—Revs. THOMAS M. HAMILTON, Deanery 1; CHARITO E. SUAN, Deanery 2; MICHAEL HURLEY, O.P., Deanery 3; BARTHOLOMEW K. LANDRY, C.S.P., Deanery 4; FRANCIS M.M.P. GARBO, (Philippines) Deanery 5; MICHAEL F. QUINN, Deanery 6; CYRIL J. O'SULLIVAN, Deanery 7; ALEX L. LEGASPI, Deanery 8; DIARMUID C. CASEY, C.SS.P., Deanery 9; Rev. Msgrs. JAMES T. TARANTINO, Deanery 10; STEVEN D. OTELLINI, Deanery 11.

Council of Priests—Executive Committee: Revs. THOMAS M. HAMILTON, Chm.; FELIX LIM, Sec.; ANDREW P. SPYROW, Treas.; J. MICHAEL STRANGE, P.S.S., Parliamentarian, (Retired); CYRIL J. O'SULLIVAN, Vice Chair.

Archdiocesan Pastoral Council—Contact: Most Rev. William J. Justice Tel: 415-614-5611; Email: groha@sfarch.org.

Censor Librorum—Rev. JOHN S. KSELMAN, P.S.S., Ph. D.

Vicar General—Most Rev. WILLIAM J. JUSTICE.

Manager, Office of Vicar General—ANNABELLE C.A. GROH, Tel: 415-614-5611.

Assistant to the Vicar General—SHARON LEE, Tel: 415-614-5611.

Administrative Assistant—MERLE TALENS, Tel: 415-614-5611.

Moderator of the Curia—Rev. JOHN J. PIDERIT, S.J., Ph.D.

Executive Assistant—DIANA POWELL, Tel: 415-614-5589; Email: powelld@sfarch.org.

Vicar for Administration—Rev. JOHN J. PIDERIT, S.J., Ph.D.; DIANA POWELL, Exec. Asst., Tel: 415-614-5589; Email: powelld@sfarch.org.

Director, Office of Catholic Identity Assessment and Formation—DR. MELANIE M. MOREY, Tel: 415-614-5520; Email: moreym@sfarch.org.

Office of Child and Youth Protection—Rev. CHARLES PUTHOTA, (India).

Safe Environment Coordinator—TWYLA POWERS, Tel: 415-614-5576; Fax: 415-614-5658; Email: powerst@sfarch.org.

Victim Assistance Coordinator—ROCIO RODRIGUEZ, Tel: 415-614-5506; Fax: 415-614-5658; Email: rodriguez@sfarch.org.

Director of Finance / Chief Financial Officer—MR. JOE PASSARELLO, Tel: 415-614-5511; Email: passarelloj@sfarch.org.

Assistant—SIENA PEREZ, Tel: 415-614-5510; Email: perezs@sfarch.org.

Office of Development—Tel: 415-614-5580; Email: development@sfarch.org. Rev. ANTHONY E. GIAMPIETRO, C.S.B., Ph.D., Interim Dir., Email: giampietroa@sfarch.org.

Development Coordinator & Stewardship Coordinator—FLORIAN ROMERO, Email: romerof@sfarch.org.

Development Assistant—JOCELYN WINKLER, Email: winklerj@sfarch.org.

Archdiocesan Legal Office—Tel: 415-614-5623. MR. LAWRENCE R. JANNUZZI, Esq., Email: jannuzzil@sfarch.org; PAULA F. CARNEY, Esq., Email: carneyp@sfarch.org. Legal Assistant: PHILIP LAM, Email: lamp@sfarch.org.

Office for the Propagation of the Faith - A Pontifical Mission SocietyGENEVIEVE ELIZONDO, Dir., Tel: 415-614-5673; Email: elizondog@sfarch.org.

Missionary Childhood Association - A Pontifical Mission Society—GENEVIEVE ELIZONDO, Dir. & Coord., Tel: 415-614-5670.

Administrative Services—JOSE LEON, Facilities Mgr. for Pastoral Ctr., Email: leonj@sfarch.org; THOMAS HUIJTS, Tel: 415-614-5532; Email: huijtst@sfarch.org.

For Real Estate please contact Real Property Support Corporation (RPSC). Tel: 415-292-0800.

Office of Human Resources—VICKY SALGADO, Dir., Email: salgadov@sfarch.org; MR. PATRICK SCHMIDT, Assoc. Dir., Tel: 415-614-5538; Email: schmidtp@sfarch.org; JANICE WARD, Benefits Mgr., Tel: 415-614-5540; Email: wardj@sfarch.org; LASHONDA PERRY, Benefits Admin., Tel: 415-614-5626; Email: perryl@sfarch.org; SUZANNE NAZARIO, Human Resources Coord., Tel: 415-614-5540; Email: nazarios@sfarch.org; KESHIA KELSEY, Payroll Mgr., Tel: 415-614-5539; Email: kelseyk@sfarch.org.

San Francisco HCSO Coordinator—MS. RONNI DAVIS, Tel: 415-614-5551; Email: davisr@sfarch.org.

Catholic Cemeteries—MONICA WILLIAMS, Mailing Address: P.O. Box 1577, Colma, 94014. Tel: 650-756-2060; Fax: 650-757-0752; Email: mjwilliams@holycrosscemeteries.com; Email: moreinfo@holycrosscemeteries.com.

Archdiocesan Archives—CHRIS DOAN, M.L.S., C.A., Archivist, Tel: 650-328-6502; Email: aasf@stpsu.org.

Office of Ecumenism and Interreligious Affairs—VACANT.

Metropolitan Tribunal and Office of Canonical Affairs—

San Francisco Metropolitan Tribunal—One Peter Yorke Way, San Francisco, 94109-6602. Tel: 415-614-5690; Fax: 415-614-5696.

Judicial Vicar—Rev. Msgr. C. MICHAEL PADAZINSKI, J.C.D.

Adjutant Judicial Vicar—Rev. STEPHEN A. MERIWETHER, J.C.L.

Promoter of Justice—Rev. THUAN V. HOANG, J.C.L.

Defenders of the Bond—Rev. THUAN V. HOANG, J.C.L.; DIANE L. BARR, J.C.D.; ROBERT W. GRAFFIO, J.C.L.

Judges—Rev. Msgr. C. MICHAEL PADAZINSKI, J.C.D., V.G.; Revs. ANGEL N. QUITALIG, J.C.L.; STEPHEN A. MERIWETHER, J.C.L.; KRYSTYNA AMBORSKI, J.C.D.

Tribunal Auditors—JOANN NORRIS; REINA PARADA; JAN SCHACHERN.

Notary and Secretary to the Tribunal—REINA A. PARADA.

Archbishop's Cabinet—Most Revs. SALVATORE J. CORDILEONE, J.C.D.; WILLIAM J. JUSTICE; Rev. Msgr. C. MICHAEL PADAZINSKI, J.C.D.; Rev. JOHN J. PIDERIT, S.J., Ph.D.; MR. JOE PASSARELLO; MR. LAWRENCE R. JANNUZZI, Esq.; MR. MIKE BROWN; MR. JEFFREY BIALEK; DR. NINA K. RUSSO; Rev. CHARLES PUTHOTA, (India).

Department of Pastoral Ministry—Rev. CHARLES PUTHOTA, (India).

Director, Ministry to Spanish Speaking—MRS. CECILIA ARIAS-RIVAS, Tel: 415-614-5573; Fax: 415-614-5658.

Office of Marriage and Family Life—ED HOPFNER, Dir., Tel: 415-614-5547; Fax: 415-614-5658.

Office of Young Adult and Campus Ministry—Tel: 415-614-5595; Fax: 415-614-5658. VACANT.

Office of Ethnic Ministries—VACANT, Dir., Administrative Asst., Tel: 415-614-5575; Tel: 415-614-5574.

African American Ministry—Rev. KENNETH M. WESTRAY, St. Vincent de Paul Church, 2320 Green St., San Francisco, 94123. Tel: 415-922-1010.

Chinese Ministry—Rev. PETER L. ZHAI, S.V.D., Tel: 415-614-5575; Email: zhaip@sfarch.org.

Arab-American Catholic Ministry—Rev. BERNARD B. POGGI, St. Thomas More Church, 1300 Junipero Serra Blvd., San Francisco, 94132. Tel: 415-452-9634.

Polish, Croatian, Slovenian Mission—Rev. TADEUSZ RUSNAK, S.Ch., Nativity Church, 240 Fell St., San Francisco, 94102. Tel: 415-252-5799; Email: trusnak@comcast.net.

Korean Catholic Ministry—St. Michael Korean Church, 32 Broad St., San Francisco, 94112. Tel: 415-333-1194; Fax: 415-333-1196. Rev. JEONG GON KIM.

Tongan Ministry—St. Timothy Church, 1515 Dolan Ave., San Mateo, 94401. Tel: 650-342-2470; Fax: 650-342-8156. Revs. SAIMONE MOALA; KAPIOLANI KAKALA.

Vietnamese Catholic Ministry—Rev. TE VAN NGUYEN, St. Thomas the Apostle Church, 3835 Balboa St., San Francisco, 94121. Tel: 415-387-5545.

Brazilian Ministry—St. Thomas More Church, 1300 Junipero Serra Blvd., San Francisco, 94132. Tel: 415-452-9634. *Saint Raphael Church, 1104 Fifth Ave., San Rafael, 94901.* Tel: 415-454-8141. VACANT.

Burmese Ministry—Rev. FRANCIS THAN HTUN, St. Finn Barr Church, San Francisco, 94112. Tel: 415-333-3627.

Filipino Ministry—Very Rev. EUGENE D. TUNGOL, Church of the Epiphany, 827 Vienna St., San Francisco, 94112.

Hispanic Ministry—Rev. MOISES AGUDO, St. Charles Borromeo Church, 713 S. Van Ness, San Francisco, 94110. Tel: 415-824-1700; MRS. CECILIA ARIAS-RIVAS, Tel: 415-614-5573; Email: ariasrivasc@sfarchdiocese.org.

Haitian Ministry—MR. PIERRE LABOSSIERE, 2822 55th Ave., Oakland, 94605. Email: pierrelabossiere@hotmail.com.

Indonesian Ministry—MR. DODI TJAHJADI, Tel: 408-646-0308.

Irish Ministry—Rev. BRENDAN MCBRIDE, (Ireland) Coord., St. Philip the Apostle Parish, 725 Diamond St., San Francisco, 94114. Tel: 415-282-0141.

Italian Ministry—Rev. Msgr. BRUNO PESCHIERA, Coord. Catholic Ministry, 101 W. Avalon Dr., Pacifica, 94044. Tel: 650-355-8377; Fax: 650-355-0616.

Native American Ministry—MR. ANDY GALVAN, Mission Dolores Basilica, 3321 16th St., San Francisco, 94114. Tel: 415-621-8203, Ext. 15; Email: chocheny@aol.com.

Igbo Nigerian Ministry—Rev. CHARLES ONUBOGU, Our Lady of the Pillar, 400 Church St., Half Moon Bay, 94019. Tel: 650-726-4674. Igbo Mass contacts: St. Paul of the Shipwreck. Tel: 415-468-3434.

Samoan Ministry—MAYA SUISALA, Tel: 866-964-7584, Ext. 20712; Email: maya_suisala@ssa.gov.

Office of Religious Education and Youth Ministry—Sr. CELESTE ARBUCKLE, S.S.S., Dir., Tel: 415-614-5652; Email: arbucklec@sfarchdiocese.org; JANET FORTUNA, Coord. Special Needs, Tel: 415-614-5655; Email: fortunaj@sfarchdiocese.org; Sr. GRACIELA MARTINEZ, O.S.F., Assoc. Dir. Hispanic Ministry & Rel. Educ., Tel: 415-614-5653; Email: martinezg@sfarchdiocese.org; MS. ANELITA REYES, Assoc. Dir. Catechetical Ministries, Tel:

415-614-5651; Email: reyesa@sfarchdiocese.org; VACANT, Assoc. Dir. Youth Ministry & Catechetics, Tel: 415-614-5654.

Ministry of Consolation—ED HOPFNER, Tel: 415-614-5547; Fax: 415-614-5658; Email: hopfnere@sfarchdiocese.org.

Office of Worship—LAURA BERTONE, Dir., Tel: 415-614-5586; Email: bertonel@sfarchdiocese.org.

Department of Catholic Schools—DR. NINA K. RUSSO, Interim Supt. Schools, Tel: 415-614-5596; MR. BRET E. ALLEN, Assoc. Supt. Educational & Professional Leadership, Tel: 415-614-5665; Email: allenb@sfarch.org; PAMELA A. LYONS, Asst. Supt. Faith Formation & Curriculum, Tel: 415-614-5663; DR. MELANIE M. MOREY, Assoc. Supt., Governance & Admin., Tel: 415-614-5520; MR. RODNEY YEE, Mgr. Parish & School Financial Support, Tel: 415-614-5513; MR. GUSTAVO TORRES, Devel. Coord., Alliance of Mission District Catholic Schools, Educator Incentive Grants Prog., Student Scholarship Program., Tel: 415-614-5546; MS. ALICIA WEINMAN, Office Mgr. & PDSO Intl. Student Prog.

Archdiocesan Board of Education—Most Rev. SALVATORE J. CORDILEONE, J.C.D.; Deacon FRED TOTAH, Chm.; MR. STEPHEN FARREN, Vice Chair; MRS. EVALYNNA HO; MRS. MICHELLE JACKSON; MRS. MEGHAN PARENT; MR. VINCENT RIENER; Rev. BRIAN L. COSTELLO; DR. PATRICIA WALTON; MR. SCOTT BIALOUS; Rev. KENNETH M. WEARE, Ph.D.

The Roman Catholic Welfare Corporation of San Francisco—(dissolved April 1, 2008).

Department of Communications—Tel: 415-614-5638. MR. MIKE BROWN, Dir., Email: brownm@sfarch.org; JAN POTTS, Asst. Dir., Email: pottsj@sfarch.org; JOHN GRAY, Communications Mgr., Email: grayj@sfarch.org.

Archdiocesan Publication: "Catholic San Francisco"—Most Rev. SALVATORE J. CORDILEONE, J.C.D.; RICK DELVECCHIO, Editor & Gen. Mgr., Tel: 415-614-5647; Email: delvecchior@sfarch.org.

Office of Human Life and Dignity—
Tel: 415-614-5570. Most Rev. WILLIAM J. JUSTICE, Acting Dir., Tel: 415-614-5571; Fax: 415-614-5568.

Administrative Assistant—CAROLINA PARRALES, Tel: 415-614-5570; Email: parralesc@sfarch.org.

Restorative Justice—JULIO ESCOBAR, Prog. Coord., Tel: 415-614-5638; Email: escobarj@sfarch.org; ALMA ZAMORA, Ministry Coord., Tel: 415-614-5681.

Respect Life, and Project Gabriel—VICKI EVANS, Prog. Coord., Tel: 415-614-5533; Email: evansv@sfarch.org.

Catholic Campaign for Human Development—CAROLINA PARRALES, Prog. Coord., Tel: 415-614-5570; Email: parralesc@sfarch.org. Parish Outreach, Organizing and Immigrant Services: LORENA MELGAREJO, Tel: 415-724-4987; Email: melgarejol@sfarch.org.

Project Rachel—(Post Abortion Counseling) MARY ANN SCHWAB, Prog. Coord., Tel: 415-614-5567.

The Catholic Campaign to end the Use of Death Penalty—CAROLINA PARRALES, Prog. Coord., Tel: 415-614-5570; Email: parralesc@sfarchdiocese.org.

Catholic Relief Services—CAROLINA PARRALES, Prog. Coord., Tel: 415-614-5570; Email: parralesc@sfarchdiocese.org.

CRS Rice Bowl Coordinator—CAROLINA PARRALES, Tel: 415-614-5570.

CLERGY, PARISHES, MISSIONS AND PAROCHIAL SCHOOLS

CITY OF SAN FRANCISCO

(SAN FRANCISCO COUNTY)

1—CATHEDRAL OF ST. MARY (ASSUMPTION) aka St. Mary's Cathedral (1891)
1111 Gough St., 94109. Tel: 415-567-2020; Email: info@stmarycathedralsf.org; Web: www.stmarycathedralsf.org. Revs. Arturo L. Albano; Lawrence Vadakkan, S.B.D.; Deacons Alejandro C. Madero; R. Christoph Sandoval.
Catechesis Religious Program—Students 75.

2—ST. AGNES (1893)
1025 Masonic Ave., 94117. Tel: 415-487-8560; Fax: 415-487-8575; Email: Admin@SaintAgnesSF.com; Web: www.SaintAgnesSF.com. Revs. Raymond Allender, S.J.; Joseph Specht, S.J.; Joseph Spieler, S.J., In Res.; Maureen Beckman, Business Mgr.; Frank Uranich, Music Min.
Catechesis Religious Program—Email: Grace@SaintAgnesSF.com. Grace Salceanu, D.R.E.

3—ALL HALLOWS CHAPEL OF OUR LADY OF LOURDES (1886) Closed. For sacramental records please contact Our Lady of Lourdes, San Francisco.
Chapel—Our Lady of Lourdes.

4—ST. ANNE (1904)
850 Judah St., 94122. Tel: 415-665-1600; Email: info@stanne-sf.org; Web: www.stanne-sf.org. Revs. Daniel Nascimento; Peterson O. Tieng, Parochial Vicar; Most Rev. Daniel F. Walsh, D.D., In Res.; Rev. Peter L. Zhai, S.V.D., In Res.
School—St. Anne School, (Grades PreK-8), 1320 14th Ave., 94122. Tel: 415-664-7977; Fax: 415-661-6904; Email: white@stanne.com; Web: www.stanne.com. Thomas C. White, Prin. (Plus 5 part-time) 26; Preschool 50; Sisters 1; Students 305.
Catechesis Religious Program—
Tel: 415-665-1600, Ext. 38; Fax: 415-665-1603. Students 26.

5—ST. ANTHONY OF PADUA (1893)
3215 Cesar Chavez St., 94110. Tel: 415-647-2704; Fax: 415-647-7282; Email: sanantonio1893@yahoo.com; Web: www.missionparishes.com. Very Rev. Moises R. Agudo.
Chapel—Immaculate Conception Chapel, 3255 Folsom St., 94110.
School—St. Anthony-Immaculate Conception School, (Grades K-8), 299 Precita Ave., 94110.
Tel: 415-648-2008; Fax: 415-648-1825. Ms. Barbara Moodie, Prin. Lay Teachers 6; Students 172.
Catechesis Religious Program—Students 230.

6—ST. BENEDICT PARISH AT ST. FRANCIS XAVIER CHURCH (1913) (Japanese) (Founded 1962 for Deaf and Hearing Impaired).
1801 Octavia, 94109. Tel: 415-567-9855; Email: Zirimenya.Paul@sfarch.org. Revs. Paul Zirimenya; Ghislain C. Bazikila, In Res.
Catechesis Religious Program—Students 12.

7—ST. BONIFACE (1860) (German)
133 Golden Gate Ave., 94102. Tel: 415-863-7515. Revs. Franklin Fong, O.F.M.; John Luat Nguyen, O.F.M. In Res., Revs. Hoang T. Trinh, O.F.M.; John Luat Nguyen, O.F.M.; Bros. Zeno Im; Chris Best, O.F.M.; Henri Djojo; Dick Tandy, O.F.M.; Dennis O. Duffy, O.F.M.; Hajime Okuhara, O.F.M.
Catechesis Religious Program—Students 54.

8—ST. BRENDAN aka St. Brendan the Navigator Church (1929)
29 Rockaway Ave., 94127. Tel: 415-681-4225; Email: saintbrendanchurchsf@gmail.com; Web: www.stbrendanparish.org. Revs. Roger G. Gustafson; Celestine Tyowua; Raymond Tyochemba, In Res.; Paul F. Warren, In Res., (Retired); Ms. Lisa Rosenlund, Business Mgr.
School—St. Brendan School, (Grades K-8), 940 Laguna Honda Blvd., 94127-1239. Tel: 415-731-2665; Fax: 415-731-7207; Email: sbs@stbrendansf.com; Web: www.stbrendansf.com. Ms. Dianne Lakatta, Prin. Lay Teachers 32; Students 311.

9—ST. BRIGID (1863) Closed. For sacramental records please contact St. Vincent de Paul, San Francisco.

10—ST. CECILIA (1917)
2555 17th Ave., 94116. Tel: 415-664-8481. Revs. Rene R. Ramoso; Sebastine Tor Orya Bula, V.C.; Michael Liliedahl. In Res., Rev. Msgr. Floro B. Arcamo, (Retired); Rev. Lodovico Joseph Landi, (Retired).
School—St. Cecilia School, (Grades K-8), 660 Vicente St., 94116. Tel: 415-731-8400; Fax: 415-731-5686; Email: office@stceciliaschool.org; Web: www.stceciliaschool.org. Mrs. Marian Connelly, Prin. Lay Teachers 24; Sisters of the Holy Names of Jesus and Mary 2; Students 606; Clergy / Religious Teachers 1.

11—ST. CHARLES BORROMEO (1887)
713 S. Van Ness Ave., 94110. Tel: 415-824-1700; Fax: 415-824-0844; Email: sancarlosborromeo@sbcglobal.net; Web: www.stcharleschurchsf.com. Revs. Moises Agudo, Admin.; Jorge Arias Salazar, Parochial Vicar; Michael J. Konopik, Parochial Vicar; Deacon Juan Michel.

12—CHURCH OF THE EPIPHANY (1914)
827 Vienna St., 94112. Tel: 415-333-7630; Fax: 415-333-1803; Email: tungol.eugene@sfarch.org; Web: www.epiphanysf.com. Very Rev. Eugene D. Tungol; Revs. Cameron M. Faller; Rolando A. Caverte, In Res., (Retired); Deacons Ramon Zamora; Ven Garcia.
School—School of the Epiphany, (TK-8) 600 Italy Ave., 94112. Tel: 415-337-4030; Fax: 415-337-8583; Email: info@sfepiphany.org; Web: www.sfepiphany.org. Diane Elkins, Prin. Lay Teachers 25; Students 295.
Catechesis Religious Program—
Tel: 415-333-7630, Ext. 15; Email: jpedroza@epiphanysf.com. Oliver Meneses, D.R.E. Students 295.

13—CORPUS CHRISTI (1898)
62 Santa Rosa Ave., 94112. Tel: 415-585-2991; Email: THODUKULAM.THOMAS@SFARCH.ORG. Revs. Thomas Anthony Thodukulan, S.D.B.; Jesse Montes; Edward Liptak, S.D.B.; Aloysius J. Pestun, S.D.B., In Res.; Deacons Alvaro Ortega; Mynor Montepeque.
Catechesis Religious Program—Email: corpuschristisfo@gmail.com. Sr. Elizabeth Villanueva, F.M.A., D.R.E. Students 167.

14—ST. DOMINIC (1873)
2390 Bush St., 94115. Tel: 415-567-7824; Fax: 415-567-1608; Web: www.stdominics.org; Email: info@stdominics.org. Revs. Justin Charles Gable, O.P., Prior; Michael Hurley, O.P.; Isaiah Mary Molano, O.P.; Christopher Wetzel; Bro. Michael James Rivera, Pastoral Assoc.; Deacons Charles McNeil; Dan Rosen; Dino Ornido; Jimmy Salcido. In Res., Revs. Anthony R. Rosevear, O.P., Novice Master; Anselm Ramelow, O.P.; Dismas Sayre; Bro. Gregory R. Lira, O.P.
Catechesis Religious Program—Students 158.

15—ST. EDWARD (1916) Closed. For sacramental records please contact St. Dominic, San Francisco.

16—ST. ELIZABETH (1912) [CEM]
449 Holyoke St., 94134. Tel: 415-468-0820. Rev. Charito E. Suan.
Catechesis Religious Program—490 Goettingen St., 94134. Students 70.

17—ST. EMYDIUS (1913) [CEM]
286 Ashton Ave., 94112. Tel: 415-587-7066; Email: STEMYDIUS@SBCGLOBAL.NET. Revs. William J. Brady; David M. Pettingill, In Res., (Retired).
Catechesis Religious Program—

18—ST. FINN BARR (1926) [CEM]
415 Edna St., 94112. Tel: 415-333-3627; Fax: 415-333-4090; Email: stfinnbarr@yahoo.com; Web: sfbsf.org. Rev. William H. McCain, S.T.L.
School—St. Finn Barr School, (Grades K-8), 419 Hearst Ave., 94112. Tel: 415-333-1800; Fax: 415-333-9397; Email: m.mortonson@stfinnbarr.org; Web: www.stfinnbarr.org. Mele Mortonson, Prin. Lay Teachers 11; Students 242.
Catechesis Religious Program—Email: juliet@stfinnbarr.org. Juliet Samonte, D.R.E. Students 10.

19—ST. FRANCIS OF ASSISI, NATIONAL SHRINE (1849)
610 Vallejo St., 94133. Tel: 415-986-4557; Fax: 415-544-9814; Email: info@shrinesf.org. Very Rev. John DeLaRiva, O.F.M.Cap., Rector.

20—ST. GABRIEL (1941)
2559 40th Ave., 94116. Tel: 415-731-6161; Email: secretary@sgparish.org. Rev. Thomas M. Hamilton. In Res., Revs. John T. Jimenez, (Chap. at Archbishop Riordan High School); Zacharias (Freddie) Thomas, (Chap. at Alma Via of San Francisco); Paul Zirimenya, (Chap. to the Deaf).
Res.: 2535 40th Ave., 94116. Tel: 415-731-6161; Email: hamilton.thomas@sfarch.org; Email: secretary@sgparish.org.
School—St. Gabriel School, 2550 41st Ave., 94116. Tel: 415-566-0314; Fax: 415-566-3223; Email: office@stgabrielsf.com; Web: www.stgabrielsf.com. Mrs. Gina Beal, Prin. Lay Teachers 24; Students 419.
Catechesis Religious Program—Students 380.

21—HOLY CROSS (1887) (Korean), Closed. For inquiries for parish records contact the chancery.

22—HOLY FAMILY CHINESE MISSION aka St. Mary's Chinese Catholic Center–1903 (1921) (Chinese) Now a mission of Old St. Mary's Cathedral/Holy Family Chinese Mission, San Francisco.

23—HOLY NAME OF JESUS (1925)
1555 39th Ave., 94122. Tel: 415-664-8590; Fax: 415-759-4293; Email: hnparishsecretary@gmail.com; Web: holynamesf.org. Revs. Arnold Zamora; Xishou Jin; Most Rev. Ignatius C. Wang, J.C.D., In Res., (Retired).
Res.: 3240 Lawton St., 94122.
School—Holy Name School, 1560 40th Ave., 94122. Tel: 415-731-4077; Fax: 415-731-3328; Web: www.holynamesf.com. Natalie Cirigliano, Prin. Lay Teachers 15; Students 326.
Catechesis Religious Program—Students 36.

24—ST. IGNATIUS (1855)
650 Parker Ave., 94118. Tel: 415-422-2188; Email: grprice@usfca.edu; Email: gbonfiglio@usfca.edu; Email: info@stignatiussf.org; Web: stignatiussf.org. Revs. Gregory R. Bonfiglio, S.J.; Paul D. Devot, S.J.; John A. Coleman, S.J.; Joseph Spieler, S.J.; Deacon Eddy Gutierrez.
Catechesis Religious Program—Tel: 415-422-2195; Email: mjdiamond@usfca.edu; Web: www.stignatiussf.org (click Faith Formation). Mark J. Diamond, Dir. of Parish Faith Formation. Preschool 9; Students 216.

25—ST. JAMES (1888)
1086 Guerrero St., 94110. Tel: 415-824-4232; Email: stjmscath@aol.com. Revs. Shouraiah Pudota; Vincent Musaby'Imana, In Res.
School—St. James School, 321 Fair Oaks St., 94110. Tel: 415-647-8972; Fax: 415-647-0166; Email: stjmscath@aol.com; Web: www.saintjamessf.org. Alex Endo, Prin. Lay Teachers 10; Students 144.
Catechesis Religious Program—Students 23.
Mission—Dominican Sisters of Mission San Jose,

1212 Guerrero St., San Francisco Co. 94110. Tel: 415-824-2052; Email: ica@icaacademy.org. Lisa Graham, Prin.

26—ST. JOHN OF GOD (1967)
1290 Fifth Ave., 94122. Email: aa_sjog@earthlink.net; Web: www.sjog.net. Rev. Narcis L. Kabipi, Admin.
Catechesis Religious Program—Students 12.

27—ST. JOHN THE EVANGELIST (1893)
19 St. Mary's Ave., 94112-1098. Tel: 415-334-4646; Email: saintjohnevangelist@yahoo.com; Web: www.saintJohnEvangelist.org. 98 Bosworth St., 94112. Rev. Agnel De Heredia, Ph.D.
School—St. John School, 925 Chenery St., 94131. Tel: 415-584-8383; Fax: 415-584-8359; Email: principalsj@stjohnseagles.com; Web: www.stjohnseagles.com. Sr. Shirley Garibaldi, O.S.U., Prin. Lay Teachers 20; Students 208; Clergy / Religious Teachers 4.
Catechesis Religious Program—
Tel: 415-334-4646, Ext. 104; Email: saintjohn.re@gmail.com. Mr. Rodrigo Castillo, D.R.E. Students 90.

28—ST. JOSEPH (1861) Closed. For sacramental records please contact St. Patrick, San Francisco.

29—ST. KEVIN (1922)
704 Cortland Ave., 94110. Tel: 415-648-5751;
Fax: 415-648-4441; Email: stkevins70@aol.com; Web: www.stkevinsf.org. Revs. Henryk Noga, S.V.D.; Demetrio Aguilar, S.V.D., In Res.
Catechesis Religious Program—

30—ST. MICHAEL KOREAN CATHOLIC CHURCH (1898) (Korean)
32 Broad St., 94112. Tel: 415-333-1194;
Fax: 415-333-1196; Email: stmichaelinfo@gmail.com. Rev. Jeong Gon Kim.
Catechesis Religious Program—Mr. Kitae Lee, Youth Min. Students 35.

31—MISSION DOLORES BASILICA (1776) [CEM] (Mission San Francisco de Asis),
3321 16th St., 94114. Tel: 415-621-8203;
Fax: 415-621-2294; Email: parish@missiondolores.org. Revs. Francis M.M.P. Garbo, (Philippines); Manuel Curso, In Res., (Retired); Francis Than Htun, In Res.; Stephen A. Meriwether, J.C.L., In Res.; Deacons Vicente Cervantes; Mario Zuniga; Mr. Andy Galvan; Mr. Jerome Lenk, Liturgy Dir.
Catechesis Religious Program—Email: nicaroses31@gmail.com. Maria Rosales-Uribe, D.R.E. Students 46.

32—ST. MONICA (1911) Merged with St. Thomas the Apostle, San Francisco to form St. Monica - St. Thomas the Apostle Parish, San Francisco.

33—ST. MONICA - ST. THOMAS THE APOSTLE PARISH
470 24th Ave., 94121. Tel: 415-751-5275; Email: sakowski.john@sfarch.org. Revs. John J. Sakowski; Kevin Kennedy, Parochial Vicar; Lawrence Gould, S.A.C., In Res.; George Nzungu, In Res.
St. Thomas the Apostle Church, (Worship Site) 3835 Balboa St., 94121.
Schools—St. Monica School—5950 Geary Blvd., 94121. Tel: 415-751-9564; Fax: 415-751-0781; Email: office@stmonicasf.org; Web: stmonicasf.org. Mr. Vincent Sweeters, Prin. Lay Teachers 24; Students 209.
St. Thomas the Apostle School, 3801 Balboa St., 94121. Tel: 415-221-2711; Fax: 415-221-8611. Judy Borelli, Prin. Lay Teachers 34; Students 280.
Catechesis Religious Program—Sr. Noreen O'Connor, C.S.J., D.R.E. Students 55.

34—MOST HOLY REDEEMER (1900)
100 Diamond St., 94114-2414. Tel: 415-863-6259; Email: secretary@mhr.org; Web: www.mhr.org. Rev. Matthew B. Link, C.PP.S.; Michael Poma, Business Mgr.
Catechesis Religious Program—

35—NATIVITY (1902) (Polish—Croatian)
245 Linden St., 94102. Tel: 415-252-5799; Email: parish@sfnativity.org. Rev. Tadeusz Rusnak, S.Ch.
Catechesis Religious Program—Students 6.

36—NOTRE DAME DES VICTOIRES (1856) (French)
566 Bush St., 94108. Tel: 415-397-0113; Web: ndvsf.org. Revs. Juan Gonzalez, S.M.; Etienne Siffert, S.M., In Res., (Retired); Lup Gil Kaatz, RCIA Coord.; Daniel Kaatz, RCIA Coord.; Miriam Kane, Music Min.; Grace Renaud, Music Min.
School—Notre Dame des Victoires School, (Grades K-8), 659 Pine St., 94108. Tel: 415-421-0069;
Fax: 415-421-1440; Email: office@ndvsf.org. Mrs. Sarah Currier, Prin. Lay Teachers 23; Students 277.

37—OLD ST. MARY'S CATHEDRAL & CHINESE MISSION (1854)
660 California St., 94108. Tel: 415-288-3800; Email: frjohn@oldsaintmarys.org; Web: www.oldsaintmarys.org. Revs. John Ardis; Thomas A. Tavella, C.S.P.; Joseph Scott, C.S.P.; Deacon Simon Tsui, Pastoral Assoc. In Res., Revs. Richard Chilson, C.S.P., (Retired); Thomas J. Dove, C.S.P., (Retired); Vincent P. Manalo, C.S.P.; Thomas F. Foley, C.S.P.; Terrance Ryan, C.S.P.; John E. Hurley, C.S.P.; Michael Evernden, C.S.P.; Bartholomew K. Landry, C.S.P.
Schools—St. Mary School & Chinese Catholic Center—836 Kearny St., 94108. Tel: 415-929-4690;
Fax: 415-929-4699; Web: www.stmaryschoolsf.org.
Chinese Language School, 838 Kearny St., 94108. Tel: 415-929-4694. Deacon Simon Tsui, Prin., St. Mary's Language School.
Holy Family Association—Tel: 415-929-4696;
Fax: 415-929-4698. Juliana Chung, Chair.
Catechesis Religious Program—
Mission—Holy Family Chinese Mission.

38—OUR LADY OF FATIMA BYZANTINE CATHOLIC CHURCH (1954)
5920 Geary Blvd., 94121. Tel: 415-752-2052; Email: kennedy.kevin@sfarch.org; Web: www.byzantinecatholic.org. Rev. Kevin Kennedy; Deacon Kyrill Bruce E. Pagacz.
Res.: 170 24th Ave., 94121.

39—OUR LADY OF GUADALUPE, Closed. For sacramental records please contact SS. Peter and Paul, San Francisco.

40—OUR LADY OF LOURDES (1942)
1715 Oakdale Ave., 94124. Tel: 415-285-3377. Revs. Daniel E. Carter, Email: dancrter@aol.com; Andrew Ibegbulem, Parochial VIcar.
Catechesis Religious Program—Joint program with St. Paul of the Shipwreck. Students 103.
Mission—All Hallows Chapel, 1440 Newhall St., San Francisco Co. 94124.

41—ST. PATRICK (1851)
756 Mission St., 94103. Tel: 415-421-3730; Email: information@stpatricksf.org. Revs. Roberto A. Andrey; Linh T. Nguyen; Deacon Ferdinand Mariano. In Res., Revs. Anthony E. McGuire, (Retired); Raphael L. Laizer.
Catechesis Religious Program—Nenette Murata, D.R.E. Students 90.

42—ST. PAUL (1880)
221 Valley St., 94131. Tel: 415-648-7538;
Fax: 415-648-4740; Email: stpaulssf@gmail.com; Email: jamie@stpaulsf.org; Web: www.stpaulsf.org. Revs. Mario P. Farana; Joseph A. Bradley, In Res.
Child Care—St. Paul Littlest Angel Pre-School, Tel: 415-824-5437; Fax: 415-824-5430; Email: littlestangelpreschool@gmail.com. Ms. Peg Kayser, Prin. Students 35.
School—St. Paul School, 1690 Church St., 94131. Tel: 415-648-2055; Fax: 415-648-1920. Mrs. Katie Kiss, Prin. Lay Teachers 10; Students 222.
Catechesis Religious Program—Dorothy Vigna, D.R.E. Students 58.
Convent—Novitiate of the Missionaries of Charity, 312 29th St., 94131. Tel: 415-647-1889.

43—ST. PAUL OF THE SHIPWRECK (1915)
1122 Jamestown Ave., 94124. Tel: 415-468-3434; Email: spswoffice@aol.com; Web: www.stpauloftheshipwreck.org. Revs. Daniel E. Carter; Andrew Ibegbulem, Parochial Vicar; Sr. Estela Martinez Padilla, M.F.P., Pastoral Assoc.; Deacons Larry Chatmon; Sergio Gomez.
Catechesis Religious Program—Students 103.

44—ST. PETER (1867)
1200 Florida St., 94110. Tel: 415-282-1652; Email: stpeterparish@yahoo.com; Web: www.stpetersf.com. Revs. Moises Agudo; Michael J. Konopik, Parochial Vicar; Jorge Arias Salazar, Parochial Vicar; Rev. Msgrs. John F. Rodriguez, In Res., (Retired); Jose A. Rodriguez, In Res., (Retired).
School—St. Peter School, (Grades K-8), 1266 Florida St., 94110. Tel: 415-647-8662; Fax: 415-647-4618; Email: info@sanpedro.org; Web: www.stpeterssf.org. Sandra Jimenez, Prin. Lay Teachers 13; Students 252.
Catechesis Religious Program—Students 345.

45—SS. PETER AND PAUL (1884) (Italian)
Sts Peter & Paul: 666 Filbert St., 94133.
Tel: 415-421-0809; Email: gibbons@stspeterpaul.sanfrancisco.ca.us; Web: www.salesiansspp.org. Revs. Gael E. Sullivan, S.D.B., Admin.; Jose Lucero, S.D.B., Parochial Vicar; Albert Mengon, S.D.B., Parochial Vicar; Ernest Martinez, In Res.; Armand Oliveri, S.D.B., In Res., (Retired).
School—Saints Peter and Paul School, (Grades PreK-8), 660 Filbert St., 94133. Tel: 415-421-5219;
Fax: 415-421-1831; Email: lharris@sspeterpaulsf.org; Web: sspeterpaulsf.org. Dr. Lisa Harris, Ed.D., Prin. Lay Teachers 26; Salesian Sisters 5; Students 244.
Catechesis Religious Program—Students 231.

46—ST. PHILIP THE APOSTLE (1910)
725 Diamond St., 94114. Tel: 415-282-0141; Email: info@saintphilipparish.org; Web: www.saintphilipparish.org. Rev. Stephen H. Howell; Mrs. Sandra Kearney, Pastoral Assoc.; Rio Stefanus, Fin. & Business Mgr. In Res., Revs. Brendan McBride, (Ireland); Patrick J. Summerhays, In Res.
School—St. Philip the Apostle School, (Grades PreK-8), 665 Elizabeth St., 94114. Tel: 415-824-8467;
Fax: 415-282-0121; Email: info@saintphilipschool.org; Web: www.saintphilipschool.org. Ms. Mary McKeever, Prin. Lay Teachers 12; Students 251.
Catechesis Religious Program—Students 9.

47—SACRED HEART (1885) Closed. For inquiries for parish records contact the chancery.

48—STAR OF THE SEA (1894)
4420 Geary Blvd., 94118. Tel: 415-751-0450; Email: admin@starparish.com; Web: starparish.com. Revs. Joseph Illo; Mark V. Taheny, Parochial Vicar; John Fewel, Parochial Asst.; John Mary Chung, In Res.; Mathias Wambua, In Res.
School—Star of the Sea School, (Grades PreSchool-8), 360 9th Ave., 94118. Tel: 415-221-8558;
Fax: 415-221-7118; Email: tpoon@staroftheseasf.com; Web: www.staroftheseasf.com. Mr. Terrence Hanley, Prin. Clergy 2; Lay Teachers 12; Students 137.
Catechesis Religious Program—
Tel: 415-751-0450, Ext. 22. Claire Herrick, Dir. of Evangelization & Catechesis. Students 44.

49—ST. STEPHEN (1950)
601 Eucalyptus Dr., 94132-1526.
Tel: 415-681-2444, Ext. 1; Fax: 415-681-7843; Email: info@SaintStephenSF.org; Web: www.SaintStephenSF.org. Mailing Address: 451 Eucalyptus Dr., 94132. Revs. Anthony P. LaTorre; Manuel Abad.
School—St. Stephen School, 401 Eucalyptus Dr., 94132. Tel: 415-664-8331; Fax: 415-242-5608; Web: ststephenschoolsf.org. Mrs. Sharon McCarthy Allen, Prin. Lay Teachers 19; Students 280.
Catechesis Religious Program—
Tel: 415-681-2444, Ext. 4; Email: faithformation@saintstephensf.org. Mary Molly Mullaney, D.R.E. Students 27.

50—ST. TERESA (1880)
1490 19th St., 94107. Tel: 415-285-5272; Email: info@stteresasf.org; Web: stteresasf.org. Mailing Address: 390 Missouri St., 94107-2820. Revs. Michael A. Greenwell, O.Carm.; Michael E. Kwiecien, O.Carm.; Deacon Martin Schurr.
Catechesis Religious Program—Anna Rose Schelstrate, D.R.E. Students 36.

51—ST. THOMAS MORE (1950)
1300 Junipero Serra Blvd., 94132. Tel: 415-452-9634; Email: felipe.marvin@sfarch.org; Email: marvzinsf@gmail.com. Revs. Marvin Paul Felipe, S.D.B., (Philippines); Bernard B. Poggi; Very Rev. Canon Andrew R. Johnson; Deacons Khaled Abu-Alshaer; Arthur Sanchez.
Catechesis Religious Program—Students 26.

52—ST. THOMAS THE APOSTLE (1922) Merged with St. Monica, San Francisco to form St. Monica - St. Thomas the Apostle Parish, San Francisco.

53—ST. VINCENT DE PAUL (1901)
2320 Green St., 94123. Tel: 415-922-1010; Email: westray.ken@sfarch.org; Web: svdpsf.org. Rev. Kenneth M. Westray; Rev. Msgr. Harry G. Schlitt, In Res., (Retired); Rev. Michael Strange, P.S.S., In Res.
School—St. Vincent de Paul School, 2350 Green St., 94123. Tel: 415-346-5505; Fax: 415-346-0970; Web: svdpsf.com. Mrs. Marguerite Pini, Prin. Lay Teachers 20; Students 243.
Catechesis Religious Program—Students 8.

54—VISITACION, CHURCH OF THE (1907)
655 Sunnydale Ave., 94134. Tel: 415-494-5517;
Fax: 415-494-5513; Email: info@visitacionchurch.org; Web: www.visitacionchurch.org. Rev. Thuan V. Hoang, J.C.L. In Res., Rev. Victorio R. Balagapo, (Retired).
School—Our Lady of the Visitacion, (Grades K-8), 785 Sunnydale Ave., 94134. Tel: 415-239-7840;
Fax: 415-239-2559; Email: heverhart@olvsf.org; Email: mluk@olvsf.org; Web: www.olvsf.org. Mrs. Hannah Everhart, Prin.; Mr. Michael Luk, Asst. Prin. Clergy 8; Lay Teachers 15; Daughters of Charity of St. Vincent de Paul 2; Students 250.
Catechesis Religious Program—Includes Our Lady of Guadalupe Mission Program. Students 130.
Mission—Our Lady of Guadalupe, 285 Alvarado St., Brisbane, San Mateo Co. 94005.

OUTSIDE THE CITY OF SAN FRANCISCO

BELMONT, SAN MATEO CO.

1—IMMACULATE HEART OF MARY (1947)
1040 Alameda de las Pulgas, Belmont, 94002.
Tel: 650-593-6157; Email: office@ihmbelmont.org; Web: ihmbelmont.org. Rev. Mark Mazza; Deacons Steven Hackett; Henry Jacquemet; Leon Kortenkamp.
School—Immaculate Heart of Mary School, 1000 Alameda de las Pulgas, Belmont, 94002.
Tel: 650-593-4265; Fax: 650-593-4342; Email: ihmoffice@ihmschoolbelmont.org; Web: www.ihmschoolbelmont.org. Mrs. Teri Grosey, Prin. Lay Teachers 11; Students 233.
Catechesis Religious Program—Mrs. Julie Britton-Kanzaki, C.R.E., Dir. Faith Formation. Students 181.

2—ST. MARK (1965)
325 Marine View Ave., Belmont, 94002.
Tel: 650-591-5937; Email: st_markschurch@yahoo.com; Web: www.saintmarks.us. Rev. Msgr. James T.

Tarantino. In Res., Rev. Martin S. Njoalu; Deacon Gerard F. Quinn.
Catechesis Religious Program—Tel: 650-591-7072; Email: sm.faithform@yahoo.com. Students 69.

BURLINGAME, SAN MATEO CO.

1—ST. CATHERINE OF SIENA (1908)
1310 Bayswater Ave., Burlingame, 94010.
Tel: 650-344-6884; Email: stcsiena@yahoo.com; Web: stcsiena.org. Revs. John A. Ryan; Toan X. Nguyen, Parochial Vicar; P. Gerard O'Rourke, In Res., (Retired).
School—St. Catherine of Siena School, (Grades K-8), 1300 Bayswater Ave., Burlingame, 94010.
Tel: 650-344-7176; Fax: 650-344-7426; Email: office@stcatherineofsiena.net; Web: www.stcos.com. Sr. Antonella Manca, M.S.C., Prin. Lay Teachers 21; Sisters 5; Students 308; Clergy / Religious Teachers 2.

2—OUR LADY OF ANGELS (1926)
1721 Hillside Dr., Burlingame, 94010.
Tel: 650-347-7768; Email: parishoffice@olaparish.org; Web: ola.community. Revs. Michael Mahoney, O.F.M.Cap.; Brian McKenna, O.F.M.Cap.; James Stump, O.F.M.Cap., Parochial Vicar; Eugene M. Ludwig, O.F.M.Cap., In Res.
School—Our Lady of Angels School, 1328 Cabrillo Ave., Burlingame, 94010. Tel: 650-343-9200; Fax: 650-343-5260. Amy Costa, Prin. Lay Teachers 19; Students 311; Religious Teachers 1.
Child Care—Preschool, 1341 Cortez Ave., Burlingame, 94010. Tel: 650-343-3115; Email: olapreschool@yahoo.com. Lysette Cukar, Dir.; Daniel Martin, Co-Dir. Lay Teachers 8; Students 52.
Catechesis Religious Program—Tel: 650-347-3671; Email: schoolofreligion@olaparish.org. Ms. Johna Maychrowitz, D.R.E.; Chris Mariano, Youth Min. & Dir. Confirmation, Tel: 650-343-5809. Students 310.

COLMA, SAN MATEO CO., HOLY ANGELS (1914)
107 San Pedro Rd., Colma, 94014.
Tel: 650-755-0478, Ext. 100; Email: ning2allen@yahoo.com. Revs. Alex L. Legaspi; J. Manuel Estrada; Antonio G. Petilla, In Res., (Retired); Deacons Lernito Prudenciado; Joseph Ramos.
School—Holy Angels School, 20 Reiner St., Colma, 94014. Tel: 650-755-0220; Fax: 650-755-0258; Email: srleonarda@aol.com; Email: stangonan@holyangelscolma.org; Web: www.holyangelscolma.com. Sr. Leonarda Montealto, O.P., Prin. Lay Teachers 17; Sisters 7; Students 214; Clergy / Religious Teachers 2.
Catechesis Religious Program—Tel: 650-992-5539; Email: holyangelsccd@hotmail.com. Sr. Anita Torres, P.B.V.M., C.R.E. Students 248.

DALY CITY, SAN MATEO CO.

1—ST. ANDREW (1968) (Filipino)
1571 Southgate Ave., Daly City, 94015.
Tel: 650-756-3222; Email: Lahey.Piers@sfarch.org. Rev. Piers M. Lahey.
Rectory—One Ridgefield Ave., Daly City, 94015. Email: standrew1968@att.net.
Catechesis Religious Program—Tel: 650-991-2937; Email: noels@standrew-dalycity.org. Ms. Michele Bussey, D.R.E. Students 150.

2—OUR LADY OF MERCY (Westlake) (1954)
One Elmwood Dr., Daly City, 94015.
Tel: 650-755-2727; Email: olmcatholicchurch@gmail.com; Web: olmcath.org. Revs. Domingo Orimaco; Gabriel Wankar, Parochial Vicar; Rey V. Culaba, C.S.S.R., In Res.; Sr. Virginia Barcelona, R.V.M., Pastoral Assoc.; Deacons Michael J. Ghiorso; Marcos M. Cobillas.
School—Our Lady of Mercy School, 7 Elmwood Dr., Daly City, 94015. Tel: 650-756-3395; Fax: 650-756-5872; Web: www.olmbulldogs.com. Mr. Jeffrey Burgos, Prin. Lay Teachers 32; Students 400.
Catechesis Religious Program—Tel: 650-992-5769; Fax: 650-756-3457. Sr. Rosabel Sare, D.R.E. Students 185.
Convent—Religious of the Virgin Mary, Our Lady of Mercy, 15 Elmwood Dr., Daly City, 94015.

3—OUR LADY OF PERPETUAL HELP (1925)
60 Wellington Ave., Daly City, 94014.
Tel: 650-755-9786; Email: olphrectory@gmail.com; Web: www.olphparishdc.org. Revs. Augusto E. Villote; Manuel D. Igrobay, Parochial Vicar.
School—Our Lady of Perpetual Help School, 80 Wellington Ave., Daly City, 94014. Tel: 650-755-4438 ; Fax: 650-755-7366; Email: info@olphdc.org; Web: www.olphdc.org. Corrine Muscat, Prin. Lay Teachers 9; Students 183.
Catechesis Religious Program—Tel: 650-755-4010; Email: padre_ba@yahoo.com. Students 190.

EAST PALO ALTO, SAN MATEO CO., ST. FRANCIS OF ASSISI (1951)
1425 Bay Rd., East Palo Alto, 94303.
Tel: 650-322-2152; Fax: 650-322-7319. Rev. Lawrence C. Goode; Deacon Louis Dixon. In Res., Rev. Msgr. John R. Coleman, (Retired); Rev. Gabriel Flores.
Catechesis Religious Program—Tel: 650-325-6236; Fax: 650-322-7319. Students 614.

FAIRFAX, MARIN CO., ST. RITA (1930)
100 Marinda Dr., Fairfax, 94930. Tel: 415-456-4815; Email: saintritafairfax@att.net; Web: www.SaintRitaChurch.org. Rev. Kenneth M. Weare, Ph.D.
Catechesis Religious Program—Mrs. Carol Bennetts, D.R.E. Students 52.

FOSTER CITY, SAN MATEO CO., ST. LUKE (1970)
1111 Beach Park Blvd., Foster City, 94404.
Tel: 650-345-6660; Fax: 650-345-8167; Email: saintlukefc@gmail.com; Web: saintlukefc.org. Rev. Jonathan Paala; Deacons Mar Tano; Paul Lucia, Parish Mgr.
Res.: 1388 Halibut St., Foster City, 94404.
Catechesis Religious Program—Tel: 650-574-9191; Fax: 650-573-7409. Students 140.

GREENBRAE, MARIN CO., ST. SEBASTIAN (1951)
373 Bon Air Rd., Greenbrae, 94904.
Tel: 415-461-0704; Email: sebastian94904@yahoo.com. Revs. William H. Thornton; Jerry Murphy, Parochial Vicar; Paul E. Perry, In Res.; Deacons David Previtali; William Turrentine.
Catechesis Religious Program—Students 37.

HALF MOON BAY, SAN MATEO CO., OUR LADY OF THE PILLAR (1868) [CEM]
400 Church St., Half Moon Bay, 94019.
Tel: 650-726-4650; Email: office@ourladyofthepillar.org. Revs. Jose M. Corral; Charles Onubogu, In Res.
Catechesis Religious Program—Tel: 650-726-5587. Students 125.
Missions—St. Anthony—[CEM] 696 North St., Pescadero, San Mateo Co. 94060.
Our Lady of Refuge, 146 Sears Ranch Rd., La Honda, San Mateo Co. 94020.

LAGUNITAS, MARIN CO., ST. CECILIA (1937)
450 W. Cintura Ave., P.O. Box 289, Lagunitas, 94938. Tel: 415-488-9799; Email: stcecilia.lagunitas@yahoo.com; Email: stcecilia.lagunitas@gmail.com; Web: www.stcecilia-lagunitas.org. Rev. Cyril J. O'Sullivan.
Catechesis Religious Program—Mrs. Carol Bennetts, D.R.E.; Margaret Farley, D.R.E. Students 19.
Mission—St. Mary (1867) 4100 Nicasio Valley Rd., Nicasio, Marin Co. 94946. Email: stmary.nicasio@yahoo.com; Email: stmary.nicasio@gmail.com; Web: www.stmary-nicasio.org.

LARKSPUR, MARIN CO., ST. PATRICK (1915)
401 Magnolia, Larkspur, 94939. Tel: 415-924-0600; Email: parish@stpatricksmarin.org; Web: www.stpatricksparish.com. Mailing Address: 114 King St., Larkspur, 94939. Rev. Msgr. C. Michael Padazinski, J.C.D.
School—St. Patrick School, (Grades K-8), 120 King St., Larkspur, 94939. Tel: 415-924-0501; Fax: 415-924-3544; Email: contact@stpatricksmarin.org; Web: stpatricksmarin.org. Angela Hadsell, Prin. Lay Teachers 21; Students 252.
Catechesis Religious Program—
Tel: 415-924-0600, Ext. 15; Email: l_gramlich@stpatricksmarin.org; Email: n_mcauliffe@stpatricksmarin.org. Lisa Gramlich, D.R.E.; Nicole McAuliffe, D.R.E. Students 141.

MENLO PARK, SAN MATEO CO.

1—ST. ANTHONY (1951)
3500 Middlefield Rd., Menlo Park, 94025.
Tel: 650-366-4692; Email: stanthonycatholicparish@live.com. Revs. Fabio E. Medina; Jose Eduardo Mendoza; Max Torres, Operations Mgr.
Catechesis Religious Program—Tel: 650-365-6071. Asusena Aguilar, D.R.E. Students 315.
Clothing Distribution Center—Free clothing for men & women.
Mission—San Jose Obrero, 400 Heller St., Redwood City, San Mateo Co. 94063.

2—THE CHURCH OF THE NATIVITY (1877)
210 Oak Grove Ave., Menlo Park, 94025. Cell: 650-323-7914; Fax: 650-323-3231; Email: nativityparish@sbcglobal.net; Web: www.nativitymenlo.org. Rev. Msgr. Steven D. Otellini; Rev. Patrick J. Driscoll, Parochial Vicar; Deacon Dominick Peloso.
School—Nativity Catholic School, (Grades PreK-8), 1250 Laurel St., Menlo Park, 94025.
Tel: 650-325-7304; Fax: 650-325-3841; Email: info@nativityschool.com; Web: www.nativityschool.com. Lay Teachers 12; Students 218.
Catechesis Religious Program—Tel: 650-853-1009. Mrs. Monica Hickam, D.R.E. Students 98.

3—ST. DENIS (1853; Restored, 1961)
2250 Avy Ave., Menlo Park, 94025. Web: www.stdenisparish.org; Cell: 415-686-9951; Email: wpodell@aol.com. Rev. W. Paul O'Dell.
Mission—Our Lady of the Wayside (1902) 930 Portola Rd., Portola Valley, San Mateo Co. 94028. Tel: 650-854-5976; Email: odell.paul@sfarch.org. In Res., Rev. Msgr. Jose A. Rodriguez, (Retired).
Catechesis Religious Program—
Tel: 650-854-5976, Ext. 102. Lucy Soltau, D.R.E. & Youth Min. Students 215.

4—ST. RAYMOND (1950)
1100 Santa Cruz Ave., Menlo Park, 94025.
Tel: 650-323-1755; Fax: 650-561-3755; Email: office@straymondmp.org; Web: www.straymondmp.org. Rev. Carl Schlichte, Admin.; Deacon Tom Kelly. In Res., Revs. Dominic DeLay; Michael Carey; Eugene W. Sousa, O.P.; Allen Robert Duston, O.P.; Xavier M. Lavagetto, O.P.; Patrick O'Neil, O.P.; Emmanuel F. Taylor, O.P.
Res.: 1231 Arbor Rd., Menlo Park, 94025.
School—St. Raymond School, (Grades PreK-8), 1211 Arbor Rd., Menlo Park, 94025. Tel: 650-322-2312; Fax: 650-322-2910; Web: www.straymond.org. Ms. Valerie Mattei, Prin. Lay Teachers 30; Sisters 2; Students 291; Clergy / Religious Teachers 1.
Catechesis Religious Program—Mrs. Jennifer Sanchez, D.R.E. Students 180.

MILL VALLEY, MARIN CO., OUR LADY OF MT. CARMEL (1910)
3 Oakdale Ave., Mill Valley, 94941.
Tel: 415-388-4190; Email: officeolmc@gmail.com; Web: www.mountcarmelmv.org. Rev. Patrick T. Michaels.
Catechesis Religious Program—17 Buena Vista, Mill Valley, 94941. Students 130.

MILLBRAE, SAN MATEO CO., ST. DUNSTAN (1940)
1133 Broadway, Millbrae, 94030. Tel: 650-697-4730; Email: glynn.joseph@sfarch.org; Web: saintdunstanchurch.org. Revs. Joseph Glynn, C.S.Sp.; Diarmuid C. Casey, C.S.Sp., Parochial Vicar; Brendan Hally, C.S.Sp., Parochial Vicar; Alwyn Furtado, C.S.Sp., In Res.; Deacon RIchard Cepriano.
School—St. Dunstan School, 1150 Magnolia Ave., Millbrae, 94030. Tel: 650-697-8119; Fax: 650-697-9295; Email: ccalaunan@st-dunstan.org; Web: st-dunstan.org. Mr. James Spray Jr., Prin. Lay Teachers 18; Students 202.
Catechesis Religious Program—Tel: 650-697-7451; Email: stdunstanccd@att.net. Sherre Leone, D.R.E. Students 125.

NOVATO, MARIN CO.

1—ST. ANTHONY OF PADUA (1968)
1000 Cambridge St., Novato, 94947.
Tel: 415-883-2177; Fax: 415-883-4049; Email: felix_lim@yahoo.com; Web: www.stanthonynovato.org. Revs. Felix Lim; Don Morgan, In Res.; Deacon Joseph Brumbaugh.

2—OUR LADY OF LORETTO (1892)
1806 Novato Blvd., Novato, 94947. Tel: 415-897-2171 ; Email: church@ollnovato.org; Web: www.ollnovato.org. Revs. Brian L. Costello; Erick E. Arauz, Parochial Vicar.
School—Our Lady of Loretto School, 1811 Virginia Ave., Novato, 94945. Tel: 415-892-8621; Fax: 415-892-9631; Web: school.ollnovato.org. Kathleen Kraft, Prin. Lay Teachers 15; Students 194.
Catechesis Religious Program—Tel: 415-897-6714; Email: amy@ollnovato.org. Amy Bjorklund Reeder, D.R.E.; Annie Troy, Youth Min., Confirmation Dir., RCIA & Adult Faith Formation. Students 200; Middle School 55.

OLEMA, MARIN CO., SACRED HEART (1867) [CEM]
10189 State Rte. 1, P.O. Box 70, Olema, 94950.
Tel: 415-663-1139; Fax: 415-663-9660; Email: deavila.rafael@sfarch.org; Email: sacredheart@horizoncable.com. Rev. Rafael Antonio DeAvila.
Catechesis Religious Program—Students 30.
Mission—St. Mary Magdalene, 16 Horseshoe Hill, Bolinas, Marin Co. 94924.

PACIFICA, SAN MATEO CO.

1—GOOD SHEPHERD (1951)
901 Oceana Blvd., Pacifica, 94044. Tel: 650-355-2593 ; Fax: 650-355-1832; Email: good.shepherd.pac@sbcglobal.net; Web: www.gschurchca.org. Rev. Luello N. Palacpac, (Philippines); Deacons Joseph LeBlanc; Ben Salvan; Suzanne Chinn, Pastoral Assoc.
School—Good Shepherd School, (Grades PreK-8), 909 Oceana Blvd., Pacifica, 94044. Tel: 650-359-4544 ; Fax: 650-359-4558; Email: gss.office@goodshepherdschool.us; Web: goodshepherdschool.us. Andreina Gualco, Prin. Lay Teachers 9; Students 150.

2—ST. PETER (1956)
700 Oddstad Blvd., Pacifica, 94044.
Tel: 650-359-6313; Email: stpeterpacifica@comcast.net; Web: www.stpeterpacifica.org. Rev. Jerome P. Foley; Sr. Hilda Sandoval, M.F.P.
Catechesis Religious Program—Tel: 650-359-5000; Email: strhilda@gmail.com. Sr. Hilda Sandoval, M.F.P., D.R.E. Students 165.

PORTOLA VALLEY, SAN MATEO CO., OUR LADY OF THE WAYSIDE (1941) See separate listing. See St. Denis, Menlo Park. Rev. Msgrs. Jose A. Rodriguez, (Retired); John F. Rodriguez, (Retired).

REDWOOD CITY, SAN MATEO CO.

1—ST. MATTHIAS (1961)
1685 Cordilleras Rd., Redwood City, 94062.
Tel: 650-366-9544; Email: info@stmatthiasparish.

org; Web: www.stmatthiasparish.org. Rev. Thomas V. Martin, Admin.; Deacons George A. Salinger; Richard P. Foley; David Rolandelli.
Child Care—St. Matthias Preschool, 533 Canyon Rd., Redwood City, 94062. Tel: 650-367-1320; Fax: 650-366-1049; Web: www.stmatthiasparish.org. Students 61.
Catechesis Religious Program—Email: cff@stmatthiasparish.org. Students 131.

2—OUR LADY OF MOUNT CARMEL (1887)
300 Fulton St., Redwood City, 94062.
Tel: 650-366-3803; Email: parish@mountcarmel.org. Rev. Ulysses L. D'Aquila; Deacon Thomas J. Boyle.
Res.: 347 Grand St., Redwood City, 94062.
School—Our Lady of Mount Carmel School, 301 Grand St., Redwood City, 94062. Tel: 650-366-6127; Fax: 650-366-0902; Web: school.mountcarmel.org. Ms. Teresa Anthony, Prin. Lay Teachers 16; Students 301.
Catechesis Religious Program—Tel: 650-368-8237. Students 387.

3—ST. PIUS (1951)
1100 Woodside Rd., Redwood City, 94061.
Tel: 650-361-1411; Email: saint@pius.org; Web: www.pius.org. Revs. Thomas V. Martin; Teodoro P. Magpayo, S.V.D.; Edgardo Rodriguez. In Res., Revs. Martin Muruli; Gerald D. Coleman, P.S.S., S.T.L., Ph.D., (Retired).
School—St. Pius School, Tel: 650-368-8327; Fax: 650-368-7031; Email: rcarroll@stpiusschool.org; Web: stpiusschool.org. Rita Carroll, Prin. Lay Teachers 16; Students 271.
Catechesis Religious Program—Students 117.

ROSS, MARIN CO., ST. ANSELM (1907)
97 Shady Ln., P.O. Box 1061, Ross, 94957.
Tel: 415-453-2342; Email: info@saintanselm.org; Web: www.saintanselm.org. Rev. Jose Shaji; Deacons Bernard O'Halloran; Edward Cunningham; Robert Yee Meave.
School—St. Anselm School, 40 Belle Ave., San Anselmo, 94960. Tel: 415-454-8667; Fax: 415-454-4730; Web: stanselmschool.com. Kim Orendorff, Prin. Lay Teachers 33; Students 256.
Catechesis Religious Program—Natalie Larraga, D.R.E. Students 143.

SAN BRUNO, SAN MATEO CO.

1—ST. BRUNO (1912)
555 San Bruno Ave. W., San Bruno, 94066.
Tel: 650-588-2121; Email: lupita.stbrunos@gmail.com. Rev. Michael Brillantes; Deacon Ramon De La Rosa.
Catechesis Religious Program—
Tel: 650-588-2121, Ext. 114. Kacey Carey, D.R.E. Students 368.

2—ST. ROBERT (1958)
1380 Crystal Springs Rd., San Bruno, 94066.
Tel: 650-589-2800; Email: reception@Saintroberts.org. Revs. John L. Greene; Tony S. Vallecillo; Deacon John Meyer.
School—St. Robert School, 345 Oak Ave., San Bruno, 94066. Tel: 650-583-5065; Fax: 650-583-1418; Web: saintrobert-school.org. Margo Wright, Prin. Lay Teachers 14; Students 317.
Catechesis Religious Program—Tel: 650-588-0477. Students 243.

SAN CARLOS, SAN MATEO CO., ST. CHARLES (1928)
880 Tamarack Ave., San Carlos, 94070.
Tel: 650-591-7349; Email: Parishoffice@stcharlesparish.org; Web: www.stcharlesparish.org. Revs. David A. Ghiorso; A. Roy Remo; Deacon Ernie von Emster.
School—St. Charles School, (Grades K-8), 850 Tamarack Ave., San Carlos, 94070.
Tel: 650-593-1629; Fax: 650-593-9723; Email: marmando@stcharlesschoolsc.org; Web: stcharlesschoolsc.org. Megan Armando, Prin. Lay Teachers 18; Students 272.
Catechesis Religious Program—Students 347.

SAN MATEO, SAN MATEO CO.

1—ST. BARTHOLOMEW (1955)
600 Columbia Dr., San Mateo, 94402.
Tel: 650-347-0701; Email: stbarts@barts.org. Revs. Michael J. Healy; Rufino J.O. Gepiga, Parochial Vicar.
Res.: 300 Alameda de las Pulgas, San Mateo, 94402. Email: Healy.Michael@sfarch.org.
Catechesis Religious Program—Rachel Smit, D.R.E. Students 254.

2—ST. GREGORY (1941)
2715 Hacienda St., San Mateo, 94403.
Tel: 650-345-8506; Fax: 650-345-9329; Email: pcecc@stgregs-sanmateo.org; Web: saintgregorychurch.org. Revs. Paul Arnoult; Arsenio G. Cirera, (Philippines); Deacons Salvatore Campagna Jr.; Stephen Fox; Robert Leathers.
School—St. Gregory School, 2701 Hacienda St., San Mateo, 94403. Tel: 650-573-0111; Fax: 650-573-6548; Web: stgregs-sanmateo.org. Laura Miller, Prin. Lay Teachers 15; Students 309.
Catechesis Religious Program—Students 380.

3—ST. MATTHEW (1863)
One Notre Dame Ave., San Mateo, 94402.
Tel: 650-344-7622; Fax: 650-344-4830; Email: parish@stmatthewcath.org; Web: www.stmatthew-parish.org. Rev. Msgr. John J. Talesfore; Revs. Dominic Savio Lee, Parochial Vicar; Alvin Yu, Parochial Vicar; Teresita Contreras, Pastoral Assoc. In Res., Most Rev. William J. Justice; Rev. Thomas M. Parenti, (Retired).
School—St. Matthew School, (Grades K-8), 910 S. El Camino Real, San Mateo, 94402. Tel: 650-343-1373; Fax: 650-343-2046; Email: office@stmatthewcath.org; Web: www.stmatthewcath.org. Adrian Peterson, Prin. Lay Teachers 26; Students 615.
Catechesis Religious Program—Students 461.

4—ST. TIMOTHY (1954)
1515 Dolan Ave., San Mateo, 94401.
Tel: 650-342-2468; Email: info@sttims.us; Web: www.sttims.us. Rev. Alner U. Nambatac, (Philippines); Deacons Faiva Po'oi; Fred Totah. In Res., Rev. Kapiolani Kakala.
School—St. Timothy School, Tel: 650-342-6567; Fax: 650-342-5913; Web: www.sttimothyschool.org; Email: dallen@sttimothyschool.org. Ms. Michelle Basile, Prin. Lay Teachers 17; Students 214.
Catechesis Religious Program—Tel: 650-579-0901. Students 203.

SAN RAFAEL, MARIN CO.

1—BLESSED SACRAMENT (1951) Closed. For sacramental records please contact St. Isabella, San Rafael.

2—ST. ISABELLA (Terra Linda) (1961) [CEM]
1 Trinity Way, P.O. Box 6166, San Rafael, 94903.
Tel: 415-479-1560; Email: office@stisabellasparish.org; Web: www.stisabellasparish.org. Revs. V. Mark P. Reburiano; Samuel Musiimenta, Parochial Vicar; Cornelius J. Healy, In Res., (Retired); Deacon Graham Cumming.
School—St. Isabella School, (Grades K-8),
Tel: 415-479-3727; Fax: 415-479-9961; Email: snaretto@stisabellaschool.org; Web: www.stisabellaschool.org. Susan Naretto, Prin. Lay Teachers 19; Students 220.
Catechesis Religious Program—Email: psr@stisabellasparish.org. Ms. Lyn Gatti, D.R.E. Students 300.

3—ST. RAPHAEL (1817)
1104 Fifth Ave., San Rafael, 94901.
Tel: 415-454-8141; Email: Frspyrow@saintraphael.com; Email: kaguilar@saintraphael.com; Web: www.saintraphael.com. Revs. Andrew P. Spyrow; Wade E. Bjerke, Parochial Vicar; Santos Rodriguez, Parochial Vicar; Deacon Eugene B. Smith.
School—St. Raphael School, 1100 Fifth Ave., San Rafael, 94901. Tel: 415-454-4455; Fax: 415-454-5927; Email: office@straphaelschool.com; Web: www.straphaelschool.com. Lydia Collins, Prin. Lay Teachers 13; Students 231; Clergy / Religious Teachers 1.
Catechesis Religious Program—Tel: 415-459-7331; Fax: 415-454-8193. Students 557.
Mission—St. Sylvester, 1115 Point San Pedro Rd., San Rafael, Marin Co. 94901.
Station—San Quentin State Prison, San Quentin, NM. Tel: 415-456-8161.

4—ST. SYLVESTER (1961) Closed. For sacramental records please contact St. Raphael, San Rafael.

SAUSALITO, MARIN CO., ST. MARY STAR OF THE SEA (1881)
180 Harrison Ave., Sausalito, 94965.
Tel: 415-332-1765; Email: frmike@starofthesea.us. Rev. Michael F. Quinn.
Catechesis Religious Program—Email: john@starofthesea.us.

SOUTH SAN FRANCISCO, SAN MATEO CO.

1—ALL SOULS (1913)
315 Walnut Ave., South San Francisco, 94080.
Tel: 650-871-8944; Fax: 650-871-5806; Email: pastor@allsoulsparishssf.org; Email: frmario@allsoulsparishssf.org; Email: secretary@allsoulsparishssf.org; Web: www.allsoulsparishssf.org. Revs. Kazimierz Abrahamczyk; Mario Olea.
Schools—All Souls Preschool—Tel: 650-871-1751. Mrs. Carla Malouf Jisrawi, Dir. Lay Teachers 3; Students 24.
All Souls School, (Grades K-8), 479 Miller Ave., South San Francisco, 94080. Tel: 650-583-3562; Fax: 650-952-1167; Email: info@ssfallsoulsschool.org; Web: www.ssfallsoulsschool.org. Mr. Vincent Riener, Prin. Clergy 2; Lay Teachers 20; Students 276.
Catechesis Religious Program—Tel: 650-873-5356; Email: religiouseducation@allsoulsparishssf.org. Ms. Lourdes Yniguez, D.R.E. Students 370.

2—ST. AUGUSTINE (1970)
3700 Callan Blvd., South San Francisco, 94080.
Tel: 650-873-2282; Email: Staugustinessf@aol.com; Web: Staugustinessf.org. Revs. Raymund M. Reyes; Eduardo Dura; Martin S. Njoalu; Deacons Nestor Fernandez II; Virgil Capetti.

3—MATER DOLOROSA (1961)
307 Willow Ave., South San Francisco, 94080.
Tel: 650-583-4131; Email: frances@mdssf.org; Web: www.mdssf.org. Revs. Rolando S. De la Rosa; Vito J. Perrone, In Res.; Deacons Alex Aragon; Romeo Cruz.
Catechesis Religious Program—Email: cff@mdssf.org. Frances Lidwell, Admin.; Felisa Cepeda, D.R.E. Students 116.

4—ST. VERONICA (1951)
434 Alida Way, South San Francisco, 94080.
Tel: 650-588-1455; Email: churchoffice@stveronicassf.com; Web: www.stveronicassf.com. Rev. Charles Puthota; Deacon Roger Beaudry.
School—St. Veronica School, Tel: 650-589-3909; Fax: 650-589-2826; Web: www.saintveronicassf.org. Kathryn Lucchesi, Prin. Lay Teachers 9; Students 291.
Catechesis Religious Program—
Tel: 650-588-1455, Ext. 305; Email: kguglielmoni@stveronicassf.com. Karen Guglielmoni, Faith Formation Coord. Students 288.

TIBURON, MARIN CO., ST. HILARY (1951)
761 Hilary Dr., Tiburon, 94920-1421.
Tel: 415-435-1122; Email: DianaR@StHilary.Org; Web: www.StHilary.org. Revs. William E. Brown; Andrew W. Ginter, Parochial Vicar.
School—St. Hilary School, 765 Hilary Dr., Tiburon, 94920. Tel: 415-435-2224; Fax: 415-435-5895; Web: www.sainthilaryschool.org. Ms. Marie Bordeleau, Prin. Lay Teachers 23; Students 273.
Catechesis Religious Program—Lisa Veto, D.R.E. Students 134.

TOMALES, MARIN CO., CHURCH OF THE ASSUMPTION (1860) [CEM]
26825 Shoreline Hwy., P.O. Box 82, Tomales, 94971-0082. Tel: 707-878-0028; Email: lopez.juan@sfarch.org. Rev. Juan Manuel Lopez.
Catechesis Religious Program—Tel: 707-878-2208; Email: lopezjuanmanuel585@gmail.com. Students 42.
Mission—St. Helen (1902) Tel: 650-720-1429; Email: lopezjuanmanuel585@gmail.com.

WOODSIDE, SAN MATEO CO., ST. MARCELLA MISSION, Closed. For sacramental records please contact St. Denis, Menlo Park.

Chaplains of Public Institutions

SAN FRANCISCO. *St. Anne's Home*. Vacant.
St. Francis Hospital. Franciscans from St. Boniface Parish.
Kaiser Hospital San Francisco. Rev. Michael E. Kwiecien, O.Carm.
Knights of Malta. The Sovereign Military Order of Malta (Western U.S.A. Association of the Sovereign Military Hospitaller Order of St. John of Jerusalem of Rhodes and of Malta–a Nonprofit Corporation). Rev. Msgr. Steven D. Otellini.
Laguna Honda Home. Trinh T. Hoang, Sr. Dolores Maquire, C.H.F.
St. Mary's Medical Center. Rev. Michael A. Greenwell, O.Carm.
San Francisco Fire Department. Rev. John L. Greene.
San Francisco General Hospital. Revs. Wade E. Bjerke, Xi-shou Jin, Quoc Nguyen, O.F.M.Cap.
San Francisco Police Department. Rev. Michael J. Healy.
San Francisco State Univ., Newman Center. Rev. Marvin Paul Felipe, S.D.B., (Philippines).
Serra Club of San Francisco. Rev. Msgr. Edward P. McTaggart, (Retired).
St. Thomas More Society. (Legal). Rev. Roger G. Gustafson.
Veterans' Hospital, Ft. Miley. Rev. Lawrence Gould, S.A.C., San Francisco.
Young Ladies' Institute. Rev. Thomas M. Hamilton, Grand. Chap.

DALY CITY. *Seton Hospital*. Priests of St. Andrew Parish Rev. Joseph Palathingal.
MARIN. *Serra Club of Marin*.
REDWOOD CITY. *Sequoia Hospital*. Rev. Martin Muruli.
SAN MATEO. *Serra Club of San Mateo*. Vacant.
Sheriff's Honor Camp and Medium Security Facility. Served by Archdiocese and St. Vincent de Paul volunteers, San Mateo District Council.
SAN QUENTIN. *California State Prison*,
Tel: 415-454-1460. Rev. George T. Williams, S.J., Chap.

On Special Assignment:
Rev. Msgr.—
Padazinski, C. Michael, J.C.D., Chancellor & Judicial Vicar
Very Revs.—
Agudo, Moises R., Vicar for Spanish-Speaking
Tungol, Eugene D., Vicar for Filipinos
Revs.—
Hoang, Thuan V., J.C.L., Tribunal, Office of Tyribunal. (Part-time)
Meriwether, Stephen A., J.C.L., Tribunal
Quitalig, Angel N., J.C.L., Tribunal

Schunk, David A., Dir., Vocations
Very Rev. Canon—
Johnson, Andrew R., Office, Devel.

On Duty Outside the Archdiocese:
Rev. Msgr.—
Piechota, Lech, (Vatican City State)
Revs.—
Doherty, Mark D., Studies, Fribourg, Switzerland
Gutierrez, Armando J., Studies, Rome
Hagan, James, Mexico.

Sabbatical:
Rev.—
Suan, Charito E.

Retired:
His Eminence—
Levada, William J., S.T.D., (Retired)
Most Rev.—
Wang, Ignatius C., J.C.D., (Retired)
Rev. Msgrs.—
Arcamo, Floro B., (Retired)
Holleran, J. Warren, S.T.D., (Retired)
McCormick, Maurice M., (Retired)
McKay, James P., (Retired)
McTaggart, Edward P., (Retired)
Pernia, John R., (Retired)
Rodriguez, John F., (Retired), Madrid, Spain
Rodriguez, Jose A., (Retired)
Schlitt, Harry G., (Retired)
Revs.—
Aylward, James W., (Retired)
Balagapo, Victorio R., (Retired)
Bohnert, Edward A., (Retired)
Bravo, Joseph, (Retired)
Brennan, Bernard F., (Retired)
Burns, Thomas J., (Retired)
Caverte, Rolando A., (Retired)
Chung, Anthony, (Retired)
Cloherty, John J., (Retired)
Coleman, Gerald D., P.S.S., S.T.L., Ph.D., (Retired)
Coleman, John K., (Retired)
Curso, Manuel, (Retired)
D'Angelo, Donald S., (Retired)
Decker, Raymond G., (Retired)
Deitch, Richard S., (Retired)
Finegan, Lawrence J., (Retired)
Forner, Craig W., (Retired)
Fredericks, James L., (Retired)
Garcia, James L., (Retired)
Glogowski, John F., (Retired)
Gordon, Joseph A., (Retired)
Greenlaw, Martin F., (Retired)
Healy, Cornelius J., (Retired)
Jocson, Salvador, (Retired)
Landi, Lodovico Joseph, (Retired)
Livingstone, James W., (Retired)
MacDonald, James H., (Retired)
Madden, J. Thomas, (Retired)
Maguire, Daniel J., (Retired)
Martin, Clifford A., (Retired)
McCormick, Kieran J., (Retired)
McElligott, Thomas J., (Retired)
McGuire, Anthony E., (Retired)
Morris, James H., (Retired)
Namocatcat, Felix S., (Retired)
O'Connell, William A., (Retired)
O'Neill, John J., (Retired)
O'Rourke, P. Gerard, (Retired)
Padilla, Aquino, (Retired)
Parenti, Thomas M., (Retired)
Petilla, Antonio G., (Retired)
Pettingill, David M., (Retired)
Pham, Joseph Hung, (Retired)
Phelan, Edward, (Retired)
Raimondi, Michele A., (Retired)
Richard, Joseph E., (Retired)
Riley, Miles O'Brien, (Retired)
Ring, John K., (Retired)
Ring, Vincent D., (Retired)
Rodriguez, Guillermo, (Retired)
Schipper, Carl A., (Retired)
Shipp, Edmund N., (Retired)
Smith, Wilton S., (Retired)
Strange, J. Michael, P.S.S., (Retired)
Trainor, Henry J., (Retired)
Ullery, Kirk J., (Retired)
Walsh, Joseph R., (Retired)
Warren, Paul F., (Retired)
White, Robert Kevin, (Retired)
Young, William W., (Retired)
Zohlen, Ray, (Retired).

Permanent Deacons:
Abu-Alshaer, Khaled, St. Thomas More, San Francisco
Aguilar, Angel, (Retired), St. Timothy, San Mateo
Allen, Charles, St. Teresa, San Francisco
Antillon, Juan, St. Charles Borromeo, San Francisco
Aragon, Alex, Mater Dolorosa, South San Francisco
Beaudry, Roger, St. Veronica, South San Francisco
Boulware, Peter I., (Retired), St. Mary's Cathedral, San Francisco
Boyle, Tom, Our Lady of Mount Carmel, Redwood City
Bromberger, Brian, San Francisco
Bruening, Bill, Our Lady of Perpetual Help, Daly City
Brumbaugh, Joe, St. Anthony of Padua, Novato
Capati, Virgil D., St. Bruno, San Bruno
Cervantes, Vicente, (Retired), Mission Dolores Basilica, San Francisco
Chatmon, Larry, St. Paul of the Shipwreck, San Francisco
Cobillas, Marcos M., Our Lady of Mercy, Daly City
Cruz, Romeo, Mater Dolorosa, South San Francisco
Cumming, Graham, St. Isabella, San Rafael
Cunningham, Ed, St. Anselm, San Anselmo
Curran, Michael, (Retired), St. Dominic, San Francisco
DeLaRosa, Ramon, St. Bruno, San Bruno
Desmond, J. Rory, St. Stephen, San Francisco
Dixon, Louis, St. Francis of Assisi, East Palo Alto
Duffey, Rusty, St. Robert, San Bruno
Fernandez, Nestor II, St. Augustine, South San Francisco
Foley, Richard P., Diaconate Formation Office; St. Matthias
Fox, Stephen, St. Gregory, San Mateo
Friedman, Jerome, (Retired), Nazareth House, San Rafael
Gamarra, David, St. Peter, San Francisco
Garcia, Ven, Epiphany, San Francisco
Ghiorso, Michael J., Our Lady of Mercy, Daly City
Gutierrez, Eddy, St. Ignatius, San Francisco
Hackett, Steven, Immaculate Heart of Mary, Belmont
Haug, James H., Church of the Good Shepherd, Pacifica
Iskander, Fred, (Retired), St. Gregory, San Mateo
Jacquemet, Hank, (Retired), Immaculate Heart of Mary, Belmont
Kelly, Tom, St. Raymond, Menlo Park
Koloamatangi, Benjamin, St. Francis of Assisi Church, East Palo Alto
Kortenkamp, Leon, Diaconate Office
Lavulo, Joe, (Retired), St. Bruno, San Bruno
Leathers, Robert, St. Gregory, San Mateo
LeBlanc, Joe, St. Veronica, South San Francisco
Lucia, Paul, St. Luke, Foster City
McNeil, Chuck, St. Dominic, San Francisco
Meave, Robert Yee, St. Anselm, San Anselmo
Mejia, Jose Abel, St. Timothy, San Mateo
Meyer, John, St. Robert, San Bruno
Mitchell, William, (Retired), Our Lady of Loretto, Novato
Montepeque, Mynor, Corpus Christi, San Francisco
Myers, Jim, St. Isabella, San Rafael
O'Halloran, Bernard, St. Anselm, San Anselmo
Ortega, Alvaro, Corpus Christi, San Francisco
Pagacz, Kyrril Bruce, Our Lady of Fatima Byzantine Catholic Church, San Francisco
Paulino, Antonio, St. Anthony of Padua, San Francisco
Pelimiano, Pete, St. Mary's Cathedral
Peloso, Dominick, Nativity, Menlo Park
Perrigan, Dana, St. Monica, San Francisco
Po'oi, Faiva, St. Timothy, San Mateo
Previtali, David, Saint Sebastian, Greenbrae
Prudenciado, Lernito, Holy Angels, Colma
Quinn, Gerard F., St. Mark, Belmont
Rosen, Dan, St. Dominic, San Francisco
Ruiz, Juan, Holy Angels, Colma
Salinger, George A., St. Matthias, Redwood City
Salvan, Benjamin, Church of the Good Shepherd, Pacifica
Sanchez, Arthur, St. Thomas More, San Francisco
Sandoval, R. Christoph, St. Mary's Cathedral, San Francisco
Santillan, Noel, Church of the Good Shepherd, Pacifica
Schurr, Martin, St. Teresa, San Francisco
Seagren, Charles, St. Raymond, Menlo Park
Sevilla, Wilfredo, Corpus Christi, San Francisco
Smith, Eugene B., St. Raphael, San Raphael
Solan, Peter, St. Monica, San Francisco
Solano, Jose, Colma
Tano, Mar, St. Luke, Foster City
Totah, Fred, St. Timothy, San Mateo
Tsui, Simon, Holy Family Mission, San Francisco
Turrentine, Bill, St. Sebastian, Kentfield
Twitty, Roy, St. Catherine of Sienna, Burlingame
von Emster, Ernie, St. Charles, San Carlos
Younkin, Richard, St. Isabella, San Rafael
Zamora, Ramon, Epiphany, San Francisco
Zuniga, Mario, Mission Dolores, San Francisco.

INSTITUTIONS LOCATED IN DIOCESE

[A] SEMINARIES, ARCHDIOCESAN

MENLO PARK. *St. Patrick's Seminary and University* (1898) Major Seminary of the Archdiocese of San Francisco, under the direction of the Society of St. Sulpice 320 Middlefield Rd., Menlo Park, 94025. Tel: 650-325-5621; Tel: 650-321-5655 (Library); Fax: 650-322-0997; Email: info@stpatricksseminary.org; Web: www.stpatricksseminary.org. Most Reverend Salvatore J. Cordileone, J.C.D., Chancellor
(1891, 1944): The Roman Catholic Seminary of San Francisco Lay Teachers 9; Priests 14; Religious 3; Students 72.

Officers of the Administration: Revs. Gladstone H. Stevens, P.S.S., S.T.L., Ph.D., Pres.-Rector & Vice Chancellor; Professor of Dogmatic Theology; Vincent D. Bui, P.S.S., J.C.L., Dean, Spiritual Life; Instructor, Pastoral Studies, Moral Theology; Anthony Pogorelc, P.S.S., Dir., Field Educ.; Daniel Donohoo, Dean of Men; Dr. Karen Chan, Asst. Prof. Philosophy; Dir., Pre-Theology & Academic Dean.

Resident Faculty: Revs. Inniah Christy T. Arockiaraj, P.S.S., Instructor of Pastoral Studies; Loreto B. Rojas, Instructor of Systematics & Philosophy; Gregory Heidenblut, O.S.A., Instructor, Sacred Scripture; Paul A. Maillet, P.S.S., M.Div., Asst. Prof. Sacred Scripture; Jaime E. Robledo, P.S.S., Instructor, Moral Theology.; George E. Schultze, S.J., Ph.D., Instructor, Moral Theology & Dir. Pastoral Year Program.

Non-Resident Faculty and Staff: Rev. Msgr. Steven D. Otellini, Instructor, Pastoral Studies; Dr. Brian Buckley, Instructor, Philosophy; Mr. Marc Colelli, Vice Pres., Operations; Mrs. Olivia Kirwan, Instructor of Languages; Ms. Erika Delgadillo-Perez, Front Office Mgr.; Mr. David Flores, Human Resources & Fin. Mgr.; Revs. Joseph F. Previtali, Instructor of Dogmatics; Robert McCann, Instructor, Pastoral Studies & Canon Law; Mr. Manvinder Shahi, Registrar; Exec. Asst. to Academic Dean; Rev. Samuel F. Weber, O.S.B., Visiting Prof., Dogmatics; Sr. Margarita Garcia Gonzalez, O.J.S., Food Srvcs. Mgr.; Stephen Cordova, Asst. Prof., Dogmatics; Mrs. Monica Haupt, Dir. English Language Prog.; Dr. Cynthia Hunt, Psych. Counselor; Dr. Charles W. James, S.T.D., Assoc. Prof., Philosophy; Dr. Kristen Kearns, Asst. Prof., ELP; Dr. Jon Kirwan, Asst. Prof., Dogmatic Theology; Dir., Strategic Planning & Accreditation; Mr. David Kriegh, Library Dir.; Ms. Leelamma Sebastian, Assoc. Dir. Pastoral Year & PR Dir.; Mrs. Melissa A. Tamayo, Dir., Admissions & Exec. Asst. to Pres.-Rector.

St. Joseph's-St. Patrick's College Alumni Association, St. Patrick's Seminary, 320 Middlefield Rd., Menlo Park, 94025. Tel: 650-591-3492; Fax: 650-654-3503; Email: murpur@aol.com; Web: www.saintjosephscollege.org. Mr. James P. Murphy, Contact.

[B] SEMINARIES, RELIGIOUS OR SCHOLASTICATES

SAN FRANCISCO. *Capuchin Franciscan Order San Buenaventura Friary*, 750 Anza St., 94118. Tel: 415-387-7005; Email: arwilson@juno.com. Rev. Alan Wilson, O.F.M.Cap, Supr., Assisting at the National Shrine of St. Francis of Assisi.; Very Revs. Harold Snider, O.F.M.Cap., Prov.; John DeLaRiva, O.F.M.Cap., Rector, The National Shrine of St. Francis Assisi; Revs. Quoc Nguyen, O.F.M.Cap., Hospital Chap.; Christopher Kearney, O.F.M.Cap., Archivist; Bro. Mark Ortega, O.F.M.-Cap., (Retired). Brothers 1; Priests 5.

[C] COLLEGES AND UNIVERSITIES

SAN FRANCISCO. **University of San Francisco*, (Grades Bachelors-Doctorate), Established 1855; Chartered by State, 1859. 2130 Fulton St., 94117-1080. Tel: 415-422-5555; Fax: 415-422-2303; Web: www.usfca.edu. Rev. Paul J. Fitzgerald, S.J., Pres.; Dr. Donald E. Heller, Provost & Vice Pres., Academic Affairs; Mr. Peter J. Wilch, Vice Pres., Devel.; Mr. Charles E. Cross, Vice Pres., Business & Finance; Ms. Ellen Ryder, Vice Pres., Mktg. & Communications; Mr. Opinder Bawa, CIO & Vice Pres., Info Technology; Dr. Shirley McGuire, Sr. Vice Provost, Academic Affairs; Dr. Jeff Hamrick, Vice Provost, Inst. Planning, Budget & Effectiveness; Ms. Julie Orio, Vice Provost, Student Life; Dr. Mary Wardell-Ghiararduzzi, Vice Provost, Diversity & Community Engagement; Mr. Michael Beseda, Vice

Provost, Strategic Enrollment; Mr. John D. Trasvina, Dean, School of Law; Dr. Kevin K. Kumashiro, Dean, School of Educ.; Mr. Tyrone H. Cannon, Dean, University Library; Dr. Margaret Baker, Dean, School of Nursing & Health Professions; Dr. Marcelo Camperi, Dean, College of Arts & Sciences; Dr. Elizabeth B. Davis, Dean, School of Mgmt.; Donna J. Davis Esq., Gen. Counsel. Jesuit Fathers. Priests 12; Students 11,018; Lay Faculty 499.

BELMONT. *Notre Dame de Namur University* (1851) 1500 Ralston Ave., Belmont, 94002.
Tel: 650-508-3500; Fax: 650-508-3660; Email: gwhite@ndnu.edu; Web: www.ndnu.edu. Dr. Judith Maxwell Greig, Pres.; Dr. John Lemmon, Interim Provost; Mary Wegmann, Librarian. Sisters of Notre Dame de Namur. Students 1,691; Lay Faculty 238.

[D] HIGH SCHOOLS, ARCHDIOCESAN

SAN FRANCISCO. *Archbishop Riordan High School (Boys)* (1949) 175 Phelan Ave., 94112.
Tel: 415-586-8200; Fax: 415-587-1310; Email: riordan@riordanhs.org; Web: www.riordanhs.org. Andrew Currier, Pres.; Tim Reardon, Prin.; Mr. Daniel Appel, Librarian. Lay Teachers 61; Sisters 1; Students 693; Deacons (Diocesan) 1.

Sacred Heart Cathedral Preparatory (Coed) (1852) 1055 Ellis St., 94109. Tel: 415-775-6626;
Fax: 415-931-6941; Email: rgallagher@shcp.edu; Web: shcp.edu. Bro. Ronald Gallagher, F.S.C., Interim Pres.; Gary Cannon, M.Div., Prin.; Judy Scudder, Librarian; Rev. Rob Carbonneau, C.P., Ph.D., Chap. Sponsored by Daughters of Charity and Christian Brothers. Brothers 5; Lay Teachers 100; Sisters 2; Students 1,330.

KENTFIELD. *Marin Catholic High School*, 675 Sir Francis Drake Blvd., Kentfield, 94904.
Tel: 415-464-3800; Fax: 415-461-7161; Email: tnavone@marincatholic.org; Web: www.marincatholic.org. Tim Navone, Pres.; Mr. Chris Valdez, Prin.; Rev. Msgr. Robert T. Sheeran, S.T.D., Dir., Mission & Ministry, (Retired); Ms. Kate Zamacona, Librarian & Media Specialist. Lay Teachers 44; Priests 1; Sisters 4; Students 775.

SAN MATEO. *Junipero Serra High School (Boys)*, 451 W. 20th Ave., San Mateo, 94403-1385.
Tel: 650-345-8207; Fax: 650-573-6638; Email: padres@serrahs.com; Web: www.serrahs.com. Mr. Lars Lund, Pres.; Barry Thornton, Prin.; Rev. David A. Ghiorso, Chap.; Patrick Vallez-Kelly, Librarian. Lay Teachers 65; Students 825.

[E] HIGH SCHOOLS, PRIVATE

SAN FRANCISCO. *St. Ignatius College Preparatory (Coed)*, Saint Ignatius College Preparatory, 2001 37th Ave., 94116-1165. Tel: 415-731-7500;
Fax: 415-682-5080; Email: info@siprep.org; Web: www.siprep.org. Peter Siggins, Chmn.; Revs. Edward A. Reese, S.J., Pres.; John T. Mitchell, S.J., Supr.; Patrick Ruff, Prin.; William Gotch, Dean Students; Tasia Davis, Dean. Brothers 2; Religious Teachers 5; Lay Teachers 104; Students 1,509.

Immaculate Conception Academy, (Girls) (1883) 3625 24th St., 94110. Tel: 415-824-2052;
Fax: 415-821-4677; Email: ica@icacademy.org; Web: www.icacademy.org. Sr. Diane Aruda, O.P., Pres.; Lisa Graham, Prin. Lay Teachers 24; Sisters 4; Students 381.

Mercy High School (Girls) (1952) 3250 19th Ave., 94132. Tel: 415-334-0525; Fax: 415-334-9726; Email: mercysf@mercyhs.org; Web: www.mercyhs.org. Sr. Carolyn Krohn, R.S.M., Headmistress. Lay Teachers 25; Students 275.

Schools of the Sacred Heart, Convent of the Sacred Heart High School (Girls) (1887) 2222 Broadway, 94115. Tel: 415-563-2900; Fax: 415-929-0553; Email: heart@sacredsf.org; Web: www.sacredsf.org. Ann Marie Krejcarek, Dir.; Rachel Simpson, Head; Amanda Walker, Librarian. Lay Teachers 25; Students 227.

Schools of the Sacred Heart, Stuart Hall High School (2000) (Boys) 1715 Octavia St., 94109.
Tel: 415-345-5811; Fax: 415-931-9161; Email: katie.zepeda@sacredsf.org; Web: www.sacredsf.org. Ann Marie Krejcarek, Pres.; Anthony Farrell, Head; Amanda Walker, Librarian. Lay Teachers 21; Students 223.

ATHERTON. *Sacred Heart Schools, Atherton* (1898) (Grades PreK-12), 150 Valparaiso, Atherton, 94027. Tel: 650-322-1866; Fax: 650-327-7011; Web: www.shschools.org. Mr. Richard Dioli, Dir. of Schools. Religious of the Sacred Heart. Lay Teachers 153; Students 1,160.

BELMONT. *Notre Dame High School (Girls)*, 1540 Ralston Ave., Belmont, 94002. Tel: 650-595-1913;
Fax: 650-595-2116; Email: mosmond@ndhsb.org; Web: www.ndhsb.org. Maryann Osmond, Head of School; Claudia Sarconi, Librarian. Religious Teachers 1; Lay Teachers 49; Students 468.

BURLINGAME. *Mercy High School (Girls)*, 2750 Adeline Dr., Burlingame, 94010-5597. Tel: 650-343-3631;
Fax: 650-343-2316; Web: www.mercyhsb.com. Karen Hanrahan, Head of School; Lauren Conklin, Asst. Head of School, Academics; Summer Dittmer, Asst. Head of School, Student Life; Sarah Murphy, Librarian. Lay Teachers 39; Students 386.

PORTOLA VALLEY. *Woodside Priory School* (Coed, Boarding). 302 Portola Rd., Portola Valley, 94028.
Tel: 650-851-8221; Fax: 650-851-2839; Email: mmager@prioryca.org; Web: www.prioryca.org. Mr. Tim Molak, Head of School; Brian Schlaak, Head of Upper School; Diane Lanctot, Librarian *Benedictine Fathers of the Priory, Inc.* Lay Teachers 55; Priests 3; Students 294.

[F] ELEMENTARY SCHOOLS, ARCHDIOCESAN

SAN FRANCISCO. *St. Brigid Elementary School* (1888) (Grades K-8), 2250 Franklin St., 94109.
Tel: 415-673-4523; Fax: 415-674-4187; Email: office@saintbrigidsf.org; Web: www.saintbrigidsf.org. Sr. Angeles Marin, R.C.M., Prin. Religious Teachers 1; Lay Teachers 16; Students 225; Sisters of the Immaculate Conception 3; Sisters from the Presentation Community 1.

St. Thomas More School (1954) (Grades PreSchool-8), 50 Thomas More Way, 94132. Tel: 415-337-0100 ; Fax: 415-333-2564; Email: marifitz@stmsf.org; Web: www.stthomasmoreschool.org. Marie Fitzpatrick, Prin. Lay Teachers 14; Preschool 38; Students 269.

[G] ELEMENTARY SCHOOLS, PRIVATE

SAN FRANCISCO. *DeMarillac Academy of San Francisco*, (Grades 4-8), 175 Golden Gate Ave., 94102.
Tel: 415-552-5220; Fax: 415-520-6969; Email: theresa_houghton@demarillac.org; Web: www.demarillac.org. Theresa Flynn Houghton, Pres. & CEO; Ms. Chellsea Rivera, Prin. Co-sponsored by Daughters of Charity and De La Salle Christian Brothers. Religious Teachers 1; Lay Teachers 13; Students 119.

Mission Dolores Academy, (Grades K-8), 3371 16th St., 94114. Tel: 415-346-9500; Email: development@mdasf.org. Meredith Essalat, Prin.; Rev. Charles R. Gagan, S.J., Board Member. Lay Teachers 18; Sisters 2; Students 254.

Schools of the Sacred Heart, Convent of the Sacred Heart Elementary School (1887) (Grades K-8), (Girls) 2222 Broadway St., 94115.
Tel: 415-563-2900; Fax: 415-563-0438; Email: heart@sacredsf.org; Web: www.sacredsf.org. Ann Marie Krejcarek, Pres.; Angela Taylor, Head; Amanda Walker, Librarian. Lay Teachers 46; Students 387.

Schools of the Sacred Heart, Stuart Hall For Boys, (Grades K-8), (Boys) 2222 Broadway St., 94115.
Tel: 415-563-2900; Fax: 415-292-3165; Email: heart@sacredsf.org; Web: www.sacredsf.org. Ann Marie Krejcarek, Pres.; Jaime Dominguez, Headmaster; Amanda Walker, Librarian. Schools of the Sacred Heart. Lay Teachers 49; Students 371.

ATHERTON. *Sacred Heart Schools, Atherton* (1906) (Grades PreK-12), (Sacred Heart Schools, Lower and Middle) 150 Valparaiso, Atherton, 94027.
Tel: 650-322-1866; Fax: 650-327-7011; Web: www.shschools.org. Mr. Richard Dioli, Dir. Schools; Francesa Brake, Prin.; Alison Anson, Librarian. Lay Teachers 77; Preschool 69; Students 544.

BELMONT. *Notre Dame Elementary School*, 1200 Notre Dame Ave., Belmont, 94002. Tel: 650-591-2209;
Fax: 650-591-4798; Email: sr.kathryn@nde.org; Web: NDE.org. Sr. Kathryn Keenan, S.N.D., Prin. Religious Teachers 1; Lay Teachers 18; Sisters 1; Students 146.

SAN ANSELMO. *San Domenico School*, (Grades K-12), (Grades K-8, Coed; Grades 9-12, Coed; Boarding & Day Students) 1500 Butterfield Rd., San Anselmo, 94960-1099. Tel: 415-258-1900; Fax: 415-258-1901; Email: cstock@sandomenico.org; Web: www.sandomenico.org. Mrs. Cecily Stock, M.A., J.D., Head of School; Kate Reeser, Prin.; Mrs. Carrie Robley, Middle School Div. Head (Grades 6-8); Mrs. LeaAnne Parlette, Lower School Div. Head (Grades K-5); Mr. Scott Fletcher, Librarian. Clergy 7; Lay Teachers 89; Students 673.

[H] ST. VINCENT DE PAUL SOCIETY

SAN MATEO. **The Society of St. Vincent de Paul, Particular Council of San Mateo County, Inc.* (1931) Main Office, Society of St. Vincent de Paul. 50 N. B St., San Mateo, 94401-3917.
Tel: 650-373-0622; Fax: 650-343-9495; Email: info@svdpsm.org; Web: www.svdpsm.org. Martin Duda, Pres.; Ms. Lorraine M. Moriarty, Exec. Dir. Meals Served 88,000; Total Assisted 25,000.
SVdP's Your Ministry, Tel: 650-589-9039.
Thrift Stores:
40 North B St., San Mateo, 94401.
Tel: 650-347-5101; Fax: 650-244-0543.
1600 El Camino Real, San Bruno, 94066.
Tel: 650-588-5767; Fax: 650-244-0543.
344 Grand Ave., South San Francisco, 94080.
Tel: 650-589-8445; Fax: 650-244-0543.
6256 Top of the Hill (Mission St.), Daly City, 94014.
Tel: 650-992-9271; Fax: 650-244-0543.
2406 El Camino Real, Redwood City, 94063.
Tel: 650-366-6367; Fax: 650-244-0543.
Donation Pickups:
Donation Pick-Ups, San Mateo County, San Francisco County, Santa Clara County,
Tel: 650-871-6844; Fax: 650-244-0543.
SVdP's Catherine Center, 50 N. "B" St., San Mateo, 94401. Tel: 650-838-9800; Fax: 650-838-9847. Safe, supportive housing program for women previously incarcerated.
Vehicle Donation Program, Tel: 800-937-7837;
Fax: 415-977-1070; Web: www.yes-svdp.org.
SVdP's Restorative Justice Ministry, 50 N. B St., San Mateo, 94401. Tel: 650-796-0767;
Fax: 650-343-9495.
SVdP's Peninsula Family Resource Center (PFRC),
Tel: 650-343-4403 Helpline Number;
Fax: 650-343-9495.
SVdP's San Mateo Homeless Help Center, 50 N. B St., San Mateo, 94401. Tel: 650-343-9251;
Fax: 650-343-9495 Mon.-Fri. 10am-12noon.
SVdP's North County Homeless Help Center, 344 Grand Ave., South San Francisco, 94080.
Tel: 650-589-9039;
Fax: 650-244-0543 Mon.-Fri.: 10a.m.-noon; Sat.: 10-11a.m.
SVdP's South County Homeless Help Center, 2600 Middlefield Rd., Redwood City, 94063.
Tel: 650-343-4403 Mon.-Fri. 1pm-2pm.
SVdP's Youth-Service Learning Opportunities,
Tel: 650-589-9039; Fax: 650-244-0543.

SAN RAFAEL. **St. Vincent de Paul Society Marin County District Council* (1946) 820 B St., P.O. Box 150527, San Rafael, 94915. Tel: 415-454-3303;
Fax: 415-454-3406; Email: svdpmarin@vinnies.org; Web: vinnies.org. Richard Gallagher, Pres.; Christine Paquette, Exec. Dir. Meals Served 2,000,000; Staff 15; Total Assisted 16,000.
Affordable Housing (1992) 822 B St., San Rafael, 94901. Tel: 415-454-3303; Fax: 415-454-3406.
Free Dining Room (1981) 820 B St., San Rafael, 94901. Tel: 415-454-3303; Fax: 415-454-3406.
Emergency Help Desk (1992) 822 B. St., San Rafael, 94901. Tel: 415-454-0366; Fax: 415-454-3406.
Rotating Emergency Shelter Team (Rest Program), 822 B St., San Rafael, 94901. Tel: 415-454-3303;
Fax: 415-454-3406.
Vehicle Donations, Tel: 800-322-8284.

[I] DAY NURSERIES

SAN FRANCISCO. *Holy Family Day Home* (1900) 299 Dolores St., 94103. Tel: 415-861-5361;
Fax: 415-703-0125; Email: admin@holyfamilydayhome.org; Web: www.holyfamilydayhome.org. Heather Monado, Exec. Dir.
Holy Family Day Homes of San Francisco Capacity 154; Lay Staff 60; Religious 1.

[J] GENERAL HOSPITALS

SAN FRANCISCO. *St. Mary's Medical Center*, Dignity Health, 450 Stanyan St., 94117. Tel: 415-668-1000;
Fax: 415-750-4893; Email: Robert.Sahagian@DignityHealth.org; Web: www.stmarysmedicalcenter.org. John Allen, Pres.; Rev. Michael A. Greenwell, O.Carm. Sponsored by Sisters of Mercy of the Americas West Midwest Community. Bed Capacity 275; Sisters 8; Tot Asst. Annually 106,952; Total Staff 1,075.
St. Mary's Medical Center Foundation, 450 Stanyan St., 94117. Tel: 415-750-5790; Fax: 415-750-8132; Email: margine.sako@dignityhealth.org; Web: www.supportstmaryssf.org. Margine Sako, Exec. Dir.

[K] SENIOR CITIZEN RESIDENCES

SAN FRANCISCO. *Alexis Apartments of St. Patrick's Parish* (1973) 390 Clementina St., 94103-4138.
Tel: 415-495-3690; Fax: 415-495-3629; Email: alexis@sco.net.
756 Mission St., 94103. Tel: 415-421-3730;
Fax: 415-512-9730. William Wong, Property Mgr. Residents 258; Tot Asst. Annually 230; Total Staff 8.

Home for the Aged of the Little Sisters of the Poor, St. Anne's Home, 300 Lake St., 94118.
Tel: 415-751-6510; Fax: 415-751-1423. Sr. Theresa Robertson, L.S.P., Supr. Bed Capacity 87; Religious 10; Residents 87; Total Staff 109. In Res. Rev. John J. Cloherty, (Retired).

Madonna Residence, 350 Golden Gate Ave., 94102.
Tel: 415-361-5113; Fax: 415-928-5867; Email: smason2@mercyhousing.org; Web: mercyhousing.org. Nonprofit residence for women of low income.

Bed Capacity 72; Tot Asst. Annually 72; Total in Residence 72; Total Staff 7.

SAN RAFAEL. *Nazareth House of San Rafael, Inc.*, 245 Nova Albion Way, San Rafael, 94903. Tel: 415-479-8282; Fax: 415-479-3878; Email: alice@nazarethhousesr.com; Web: www.nazarethsr.org. Bed Capacity 146; Residents 135; Sisters of Nazareth 8; Total Staff 82. In Res. Rev. Msgrs. James P. McKay, (Retired); Maurice M. McCormick, (Retired); Revs. Bernard F. Brennan, (Retired); John J. O'Neill, (Retired); Wilton S. Smith, (Retired); Ray J. Zohlen, (Retired).

[L] RESIDENTIAL GROUP HOMES

SAN FRANCISCO. *The Good Shepherd Gracenter* (1986) 1310 Bacon St., 94134. Tel: 415-337-1938; Fax: 415-586-0355; Email: inquiry@gsgracenter.org; Web: www.gsgracecenter.org. Sr. Marguerite Bartling, CEO. Residential. Bed Capacity 13; Lay Staff 12; Sisters 3; Tot Asst. Annually 78; Total Staff 15; Total Assisted 34.

Mount St. Joseph-St. Elizabeth aka Epiphany Center (1976) 100 Masonic Ave., 94118. Tel: 415-567-8370; Fax: 415-292-5531; Email: sisterbettymarie@theepiphanycenter.org; Email: mrhoades@theepiphanycenter.org; Web: www.theepiphanycenter.org. Sr. Betty Marie Dunkel, D.C., Exec. Dir. Successor Corporation to Mount St. Joseph Home for Girls and St. Elizabeth Infant Hospital. DBA: Epiphany Center Bed Capacity 34; Lay Staff 48; Sisters 1; Tot Asst. Annually 200; Total Staff 49.

Epiphany Center, Tel: 415-567-8370; Fax: 415-346-2356. 1. Comprehensive residential drug treatment with parenting, life skills, and health education groups.; 2. Epiphany In-Home Services for Families at Risk. Individuals Assisted 200.

[M] RETREAT HOUSES

BURLINGAME. *Sisters of Mercy of the Americas West Midwest Community, Inc. Mercy Retreat and Conference Center of Burlingame*, 2300 Adeline Dr., Burlingame, 94010. Tel: 650-340-7474; Fax: 650-340-1229; Email: sistersofmercy@mercywmw.org; Web: mercy-center.org. Suzanne M. Buckley, Dir. Overnight Capacity 90; Daytime Capacity 300.

MENLO PARK. *Vallombrosa Center* (1946) 250 Oak Grove Ave., Menlo Park, 94025. Tel: 650-325-5614; Fax: 650-325-0908; Web: www.vallombrosa.org. Rev. Patrick O'Neil, O.P., Dir. *Vallombrosa Center, Conference and Retreat Center of the Archdiocese of San Francisco* Priests 1; Daytime Served 120; Overnight Served 100; Staff 9.

SAN RAFAEL. *Santa Sabina Center* (1939) 25 Magnolia, San Rafael, 94901. Tel: 415-457-7727; Fax: 415-457-2310; Email: info@santasabinacenter.org; Web: www.santasabinacenter.org. Sr. Margaret Diener, O.P., Dir. Dominican Sisters Retreat and Conference Center.

[N] MONASTERIES AND RESIDENCES OF PRIESTS AND BROTHERS

SAN FRANCISCO. *St. Dominic Priory* (1876) 2390 Bush St., 94115-3124. Tel: 415-567-7824; Fax: 415-931-3360; Fax: 415-567-1608 (Parish); Web: www.stdominics.org. Revs. Michael Hurley, O.P., Pastor; Anthony R. Rosevear, O.P., Novice Master & Vicar; Justin Charles Gable, O.P.; Isaiah Mary Molano, O.P., Sub-Prior; James J. Moore, O.P.; Anselm Ramelow, O.P.; Joseph Mary Sergott, O.P.; Bros. Gregory R. Lira, O.P.; Daniel Thomas. Brothers 2; Novices 6; Priests 8.

Jesuit Community at St. Ignatius College Preparatory, Jesuit Community at St. Ignatius College Preparatory, 2001 37th Ave., 94116-1165. Tel: 415-731-7500; Email: jmitchell@siprep.org; Web: www.siprep.org. Revs. Edward Reese, S.J., Pres.; Charles R. Gagan, S.J., Exec.; John T. Mitchell, S.J., Supr.; Ronald C. Clemo, S.J., Sacramental Min.; Donald B. Sharp, S.J., S.T.D., Sacramental Min., (Retired); A. Francis Stiegeler, S.J., Faculty; Bros. Daniel C. Corona, S.J., Subminister; Douglas E. Draper, S.J., Admin.; Rev. Joseph D. Fessio, S.J., Editor; Bros. Arthur W. Lee, S.J., Member; Hermenegildo V. Potestades, S.J., Registered Nurse; Rev. Joaquin Jose Sumpaico, S.J., Member. Brothers 4; Priests 8.

Loyola House Jesuit Community (Corporate Title: Jesuit Community at University of San Francisco) 2600 Turk Blvd., 94118-4347. Tel: 415-422-4200; Fax: 415-422-5651; Web: www.usfca.edu/jesuit. Revs. Paul J. Fitzgerald, S.J., Pres., Univ. of San Francisco; Stephen A. Privett, S.J., Chancellor; Arturo Araujo, S.J., Assoc. Prof., Art & Architecture; Geoffrey R. Dillon, S.J., Prof., Educ./Dept.; Clinical-Field Dir., Teacher Ed. Dept.; Project Dir. Learn Belize; Paul D. Devot, S.J., Assoc. Pastor, St. Ignatius Church; Vincent Hansdak, S.J.; Albert A. Grosskopf, S.J., Catholic Divorce Min.; R. Daniel Kendall, S.J., Prof., Theology; Gerdenio S. Manuel, S.J., Prof., Pscyhology, Dir. St. Ignatius Institute; Dennis C. Recio, S.J., Asst. Prof., English, St. Ignatius Institute; Donal Godfrey, S.J., Assoc. Dir. Univ. Ministry; Antoni J. Ucerler, S.J., Dir., Research & Assoc. Prof., Center for the Pacific Rim; Matthew J. Motyka, S.J., Prof. Romance Languages; John A. Coleman, S.J., Assoc. Pastor St. Ignatius Church; Gregory R. Bonfiglio, S.J., Pastor, St. Ignatius Church; Timothy Godfrey, S.J., Prof., School of Nursing & Rector; Ralph Metts, S.J., Minister; Paolo Gamberini, S.J., Asst. Prof., Theology; Cathal Doherty, S.J., Asst. Prof., Theology; Benhur Navarro Abril, S.J., Grad. Student; Stephen Nzyoki Nduti, S.J., Grad. Student, School of Ed.; Amalabuna Albert Kineni, S.J., Grad Student, Educ. Leadership; Thomas A. Renshaw, S.J., Grad Student, Educ. Leadership; M. Joseph Savariappan, S.J., Doctoral Student; Tarimo Aquiline, S.J., Assoc. Prof., Theology & Religious Studies. Priests 23.

Marist Center of the West Society of Mary, U.S. Province (Marist) 625 Pine St., 94108-3210. Tel: 415-398-3543; Fax: 415-781-4937; Email: randyh@maristsociety.org. Revs. Rene Iturbe, S.M., Supr.; Bruce J. Lery, S.M., Chap.; Mr. Jack Ridout, Dir., Vocations; Revs. Phillip d'Auby, S.M., (Retired); Dennis Steik, S.M., (Retired); Bro. Joseph Grima, S.M., (Retired); Revs. Alfred Puccinelli, S.M., (Retired); Etienne Siffert, S.M., (Retired). Brothers 1; Priests 6.

Salesian Provincial Residence, 1100 Franklin St., 94109. Tel: 415-441-7144; Fax: 415-441-7155; Email: suosec@aol.com. Revs. Ted Montemayor, S.D.B., Prov.; Thomas Prendiville, S.D.B., Vice Prov.; Tho Bui, S.D.B., Prov. Treas.; Jerry Wertz, S.D.B. Brothers 1; Priests 6. In Res. Revs. Larry Lorenzoni, S.D.B., (Retired); Richard Presenti, S.D.B.; Chuyen Nguyen, S.D.B.; Bro. Lawrence King, S.D.B., Archivist.

San Buenaventura Friary, 750 Anza St., 94118. Tel: 415-387-7005; Email: arwilson@juno.com. Residence of Capuchin Provincial House, Burlingame, CA.

BURLINGAME. *Capuchin Provincial House* (1991) 1345 Cortez Ave., Burlingame, 94010. Tel: 650-344-8321 ; Fax: 650-342-5664; Email: finance@olacapuchins.org; Web: www.olacapuchins.org. Very Rev. Harold Snider, O.F.M.Cap., Prov.; Revs. Donal Burke, O.F.M.Cap., Devel. Dir.; Miguel Angel Ortiz, O.F.M.Cap., Prov. Sec.; Bro. Alexander Escalera, O.F.M.Cap., Spiritual Asst. to SFO; Rev. Richard Lopes, O.F.M.Cap., Hospital Chap. *Capuchin Franciscan Seminarians Foundation*, 1345 Cortez Ave., Burlingame, 94010. Tel: 650-344-8321; Fax: 650-342-5664; Email: finance@olacapuchins.org. Michael Smith, Chm. *Capuchin Franciscan General Needs Foundation*, 1345 Cortez Ave., Burlingame, 94010. Tel: 650-344-8321; Fax: 650-342-5664; Email: finance@olacapuchins.org. Walter Bankovich, Chm. *Capuchin Franciscan Mission Foundation*, 1345 Cortez Ave., Burlingame, 94010. Tel: 650-344-8321; Fax: 650-342-5664; Email: finance@olacapuchins.org. Walter Bankovich, Chm. *Capuchin Franciscan Foundation for Retired Friars*, 1345 Cortez Ave., Burlingame, 94010. Tel: 650-344-8321; Fax: 650-342-5664; Email: finance@olacapuchins.org. Michael Smith, Chm.

PORTOLA VALLEY. *Woodside Priory*, 302 Portola Rd., Founders Hall, Portola Valley, 94028-7897. Tel: 650-851-8221; Tel: 650-851-6133; Fax: 650-851-2839; Email: mmager@prioryca.org; Web: www.prioryca.org. Revs. Martin J. Mager, O.S.B., Supr.; Maurus B. Nemeth, O.S.B.; Rt. Rev. Matthew K. Leavy, O.S.B., Campus Min. *Benedictine Fathers of the Priory, Inc.* Priests 3.

[O] CONVENTS AND RESIDENCES FOR SISTERS

SAN FRANCISCO. *Carmelite Monastery of Cristo Rey, Discalced Carmelite Nuns* (1927) 721 Parker Ave., 94118-4227. Tel: 415-387-2640; Email: prioress@cmcrnuns.org. Sisters 13.

Discalced Carmelite Nuns of Berkeley, Inc., 721 Parker Ave., 94118-4227. Tel: 415-387-2640; Email: prioress@cmcrnuns.org. Mother Elizabeth Ramirez, O.C.D., Sec. Sisters 12.

Franciscan Missionaries of Our Lady of Peace (1941) Tel: 415-587-3729; Fax: 415-587-3729. *Our Lady of Guadalupe Convent* (1989) 46 Harrington St., 94112. Tel: 415-587-3729; Fax: 415-587-3729; Email: camberos.eva1990@yahoo.com. Sr. Eva Camberos, M.F.P., Supr. Sisters in Archdiocese 3.

Mercy Place (Sisters of Mercy-Burlingame), 826 30th Ave., 94121-3522. Tel: 415-876-4303. Sisters 5.

Monastery of Perpetual Adoration, Nuns of Perpetual Adoration, 771 Ashbury St., 94117-4013. Tel: 415-566-2743; Fax: 415-564-4469; Email: mpador@aol.com. Mother Rosalba Vargas, A.P., Supr. In Formation 3; Cloistered Nuns 9.

Sisters of Social Service, 1850 Ulloa St., 94116. Tel: 415-681-9219; Email: arbucklec@sfarch.org; Web: www.socialservicesisters.org. Sr. Celeste Arbuckle, S.S.S., Contact Person. Sisters 3.

Sisters of St. Francis - Mt. Alverno Marian Residence, 1330 Brewster Ave., Redwood City, 94062-1312. Tel: 650-369-1725; Fax: 650-369-0845; Email: blohm@sndden.org. Claire Blohm, Chief Fin. Officer. Sisters in Archdiocese 7.

Sisters of St. Joseph of Orange, Email: jmrmmcsj@sbcglobal.net.

Sisters of St. Joseph of Orange (1912) 1737 Silliman St., 94134. Tel: 415-585-0159; Fax: 415-585-0159; Email: csjsf@comcast.net. Sisters 2.

Sisters of the Good Shepherd (1932) 1310 Bacon St., 94134. Tel: 415-586-2822; Fax: 415-586-0355; Email: Ischille@gspmna.org. Sisters 6.

Sisters of the Presentation San Francisco (1854 - CA; 1775 - Ireland) 281 Masonic Ave., 94118-4416. Tel: 415-422-5001; Fax: 415-422-5026; Email: syu@pbvmsf.org; Web: www.presentationsisterssf.org. Sr. Michele Anne Murphy, P.B.V.M., Pres. Sisters 60; Sisters in Archdiocese of San Francisco 46.

Verbum Dei Missionary Fraternity (1963) 3365-3373 19th St., 94110. Tel: 415-282-3005; Fax: 415-282-3005; Email: areacouncil@verbumdeiusa.org; Web: www.verbumdeiusa.org. Sr. Rosalia Meza, Prov. (Institute of Consecrated Life, Rome, Italy); Prayer and ministry of the Word, working with youth, young adults & adults. Sisters 24.

ATHERTON. *Religious of the Sacred Heart-Oakwood*, 140 Valparaiso Ave., Atherton, 94027-4403. Tel: 650-323-8343; Fax: 650-326-2251. Sr. Clare Pratt, R.S.C.J., Community Life Dir. Retirement Center for elderly Religious of the Sacred Heart. Sisters 49; Sisters in Archdiocese 69.

BURLINGAME. *Sisters of Mercy of the Americas West Midwest Community, Inc.*, 2300 Adeline Dr., Burlingame, 94010-5599. Tel: 650-340-7474; Fax: 650-340-1299; Email: sistersofmercy@mercywmw.org; Web: www.sistersofmercy.org/west-midwest. Sisters Susan Sanders, R.S.M., Pres.; Ana Maria Pineda, R.S.M., Vice Pres.; Maria Klosowski, R.S.M., Leadership Team; Margaret Mary Hinz, R.S.M., Leadership Team; Margaret Maloney, R.S.M., Leadership Team; Rebecca Vandenbosch, CFO. Sisters 531; Associates 603.

DALY CITY. *Daughters of Charity of St. Vincent de Paul* (1633) 2000 Sullivan Ave., Daly City, 94015-2202. Tel: 650-991-6715; Fax: 650-991-6055; Email: docsmc@sbcglobal.net. Sr. Arthur Gordon, D.C., Supr. Sisters in Archdiocese 12.

Quinhon Missionary Sisters of the Holy Cross (1988 - USA; 1926 - Vietnam) 298 Southgate Ave., Daly City, 94015. Tel: 650-755-7231; Email: sistersmtgqndc@yahoo.org; Email: josephinedao3@yahoo.com. Sisters Catherine Huong Nguyen, Student; Angeline Tran, PreK Teacher. Sisters 3.

Religious of the Virgin Mary, Our Lady of Mercy Convent, 15 Elmwood Dr., Daly City, 94015. Tel: 650-992-5769. Sr. Nicolina P. Estivez, R.V.M. Sisters Residing in Archdiocese 5.

MENLO PARK. *Corpus Christi Monastery* (1921) 215 Oak Grove Ave., Menlo Park, 94025-3272. Tel: 650-322-1801; Fax: 650-322-6816; Email: dominicannun@nunsmenlo.org; Web: www.nunsmenlo.org. Sr. Maria Christine, O.P., Prioress. Nuns of the Order of Preachers. Cloistered Religious 12.

PACIFICA. *Missionaries of Charity* (1982) (India) 164 Milagra Dr., Pacifica, 94044. Tel: 650-355-3091. Sisters 11.

Noviciate (1982) 312 29th St., 94131. Tel: 415-647-1889. Novices 19; Sisters 4.

Queen of Peace (1984) 55 Sadowa St., 94112. Tel: 415-586-3449. Sisters 5.

REDWOOD CITY. *Daughters of St. Paul*, 3079 Oak Knoll Dr., Redwood City, 94062. Tel: 650-368-3184; Email: redwoodoffice@paulinemedia.com; Web: www.pauline.org. Sr. Domenica Vitello, F.S.P, Supr. Sisters 5.

Sisters of Saint Francis - Mount Alverno, 1330 Brewster Ave., Redwood City, 94062-1312. Tel: 650-369-1725; Fax: 650-369-0845; Email: marylitell@franciscanway.org. Sr. Mary Litell, Provincial. Sisters 50.

Trinity Community, 1506 Roosevelt Ave., Redwood City, 94061. Tel: 650-339-1240; Email: srdorothym@aol.com. Sr. Dorothy McCormack, O.S.F. Sisters of St. Francis. Sisters 2.

SAN RAFAEL. *Carmelite Monastery of the Mother of God, Discalced Carmelite Nuns*, 530 Blackstone Dr., San Rafael, 94903. Tel: 415-479-6872; Fax: 415-491-4964; Email: sram@motherofgodcarmel.org. Sr. Anna Marie Vanni, O.C.D., Prioress. Sisters 7.

Dominican Sisters of San Rafael Generalate & Convent (1850) 1520 Grand Ave., San Rafael, 94901-2236. Tel: 415-453-8303; Fax: 415-453-8367; Email: maureen.mcinerney@sanrafaelop.org; Web: sanrafaelop.org. Sr. Maureen McInerney, O.P., Prioress Gen. Sisters 69; Total in Archdiocese 59; Total in Community 69.

Dominican Convent, 1540 Grand Ave., San Rafael, 94901-2236. Tel: 415-454-9221; Email: maureen.mcinerney@sanrafaelop.org. Sr. Maureen McInerney, O.P., Prioress. Sisters 15.

Jane d'Aza Convent, 60 Locust Ave., San Rafael, 94901-2237. Tel: 415-453-4784; Email: maureen.mcinerney@sanrafaelop.org. Sr. Maureen McInerney, O.P., Prioress. Sisters 3.

Our Lady of Lourdes Convent, 77 Locust Ave., San Rafael, 94901-2237. Tel: 415-457-3171; Email: maureen.mcinerney@sanrafaelop.org. Sr. Maureen McInerney, O.P., Prioress. Sisters 19.

San Domenico Convent, 1500 Butterfield Rd., San Anselmo, 94960-1057. Tel: 415-453-9172; Email: maureen.mcinerney@sanrafaelop.org. Sr. Maureen McInerney, O.P., Prioress. Sisters 3.

St. Margaret Convent, 40 Locust Ave., San Rafael, 94901-2237. Tel: 415-458-2952; Email: maureen.mcinerney@sanrafaelop.org. Sr. Maureen McInerney, O.P., Prioress. Sisters 5.

St. Dominic Convent, 2517 Pine St., 94115-2609. Tel: 415-567-8282; Email: maureen.mcinerney@sanrafaelop.org. Sr. Maureen McInerney, O.P., Prioress. Sisters 7.

St. Rose Convent, 2515 Pine St., 94115-2609. Tel: 415-441-2685; Email: maureen.mcinerney@sanrafaelop.org. Sr. Maureen McInerney, O.P., Prioress. Sisters 3.

[P] CATHOLIC CHARITIES

SAN FRANCISCO. *Catholic Charities CYO of the Archdiocese of San Francisco*, Administrative Office: 990 Eddy St., 94109. Tel: 415-972-1200; Fax: 415-972-1201; Email: moreinfo@catholiccharitiessf.org; Web: www.catholiccharitiessf.org. Jeffrey V. Bialik, Exec. Dir.; Dorothy Cartahenz, Exec. Asst.; Keith Spindle, Dir., Administrative Svcs. & CFO; Kathy Brown, Dir., Advancement; Tere Brown, Dir., Prog. Opers.; Kent Eagleson, Dir., Youth Residential Svcs.; Marilyn Lovelace-Grant, Dir. Human Resources. Total Staff 42.

Board of Directors: Most Rev. Salvatore J. Cordileone, J.C.D., Chm.; Simon Manning, Pres.; Ann Gray Miller, Sec.; Jeffrey V. Bialik, Exec. Dir.; Joe Boerio; Theodore Borromeo; Gregory Bullian; Kathleen Cardinal; Martha Brigham; Timothy Connors; Hugo Kostelni; David Hultman; Jerilyn Gelt; Herbert W. Foedisch Jr.; Steven Kane; Maura A. Markus; Sharon McCarthy-Allen; Kathleen McEligot, Treas.; Robert P. McGrath; Sr. Maureen McInerney, O.P.; Stephen Molinelli; Michael Pautler; D. Paul Regan; Mike Selfridge; George Sundby; Dr. Pierre Theodore; Rev. Kenneth M. Westray; Lori H. Whitney; Mr. Peter J. Wilch.

Directors Emeritus: Nicholas Andrade; John E. Cahill Jr.; Deborah Dasovich; Jeffrey Fenton; Jack Fitzpatrick; Bernard P. Hagan Sr.; Cecilia Herbert; Nanette Lee Miller; William T. Ring; Rita Semel; Maureen O'Brien Sullivan.

Aging Support Services:

Catholic Charities Adult Day Services San Francisco, 50 Broad St., 94112. Tel: 415-452-3500; Fax: 415-452-3505; Email: pclement@catholiccharitiessf.org; Web: www.catholiccharitiessf.org. Patty Clement-Cihak, Prog. Dir., Aging Support Svcs. Tot Asst. Annually 50; Total Staff 7.

Catholic Charities Adult Day Services San Mateo County, 787 Walnut St., San Carlos, 94070. Tel: 650-592-9325; Fax: 650-592-2316; Email: csantoni@catholiccharitiessf.org; Web: www.catholiccharitiessf.org. Carmen Santoni, Program Mgr. Tot Asst. Annually 71; Total Staff 6.

Catholic Charities OMI Senior Center, 65 Beverly St., 94132. Tel: 415-334-5550; Fax: 415-334-5554; Email: rmendez@catholiccharitiessf.org; Web: www.catholiccharitiessf.org. Rosa Mendez, Program Dir.

Behavioral Health Services:

Catholic Charities Behavioral Health Services San Francisco, 2559 40th Ave., 94116. Tel: 415-564-7882; Email: dross@catholiccharitiessf.org; Web: www.catholiccharitiessf.org. Dave Ross, Ph.D., Program Dir., Behavioral Health Svcs.

Catholic Charities Behavioral Health Services San Mateo County, 36 37th Ave., San Mateo, 94403. Tel: 650-295-2160; Fax: 650-286-1141; Email: dross@catholiccharitiessf.org; Web: www.catholiccharitiessf.org. Dave Ross, Ph.D., Program Dir., Behavioral Health Svcs.

Children & Youth Services:

Catholic Charities Boys' & Girls' Homes, 823 Euclid Ave., 94118. Tel: 415-221-3443; Fax: 415-387-1627; Email: sdouglas@catholiccharitiessf.org; Web: www.catholiccharitiessf.org. Scheron Douglas, Prog. Supvr.

Catholic Charities Canal Family Support, 50 Canal St., San Rafael, 94901. Tel: 415-454-8596; Fax: 415-485-3185; Email: cgarcia@catholiccharitiessf.org; Web: www.catholiccharitiessf.org. Carlos Garcia, Prog. Dir. Tot Asst. Annually 162; Total Staff 6.

Catholic Charities CYO Athletics, 1728 Ocean Ave., #229, 94112. Tel: 415-988-7652; Fax: 415-988-7060; Email: cclendinen@catholiccharitiessf.org; Web: www.catholiccharitiessf.org. Courtney Johnson-Clendinen, Division Dir., Children & Youth Svcs.

Catholic Charities CYO Camp/Retreat Center/Outdoor Environmental Education, 2136 Bohemian Hwy., Occidental, 95465. Tel: 707-874-0200; Fax: 707-874-0230; Email: rgarcia@catholiccharitiessf.org; Web: www.catholiccharitiessf.org. Ricardo Garcia, Dir., CYO Camp & Retreat Center. Tot Asst. Annually 4,237; Total Staff 32.

Catholic Charities CYO Transportation, 699 Serramonte Blvd., Ste. 210, Daly City, 94015. Tel: 650-757-2110; Fax: 650-758-1425; Email: mrea@catholiccharitiessf.org; Web: www.catholiccharitiessf.org. Marty Rea, Gen. Mgr. Tot Asst. Annually 30,000; Total Staff 33.

Catholic Charities Maureen & Craig Sullivan Youth Services, 801 Jessie St., 94103. Tel: 415-863-1171, Ext. 100; Fax: 415-863-1114; Email: lrossi@catholiccharitiessf.org; Web: www.catholiccharitiessf.org. Liliana Carnero Rossi, Ph. D., Prog. Dir. Tot Asst. Annually 130; Total Staff 5.

Catholic Charities St. Vincent's School for Boys, 1 St. Vincent Dr., San Rafael, 94903. Tel: 415-507-2000; Fax: 415-491-0842; Email: dgallagher@catholiccharitiessf.org; Email: mcarter@catholiccharitiessf.org; Web: www.catholiccharitiessf.org. Dan Gallagher, Div. Dir., St. Vincent's. Tot Asst. Annually 107; Total Staff 71.

Catholic Charities Treasure Island Child Development Center, 850 Avenue D, Bldg. 502, 94130. Tel: 415-801-4745; Email: kautumn@catholiccharitiessf.org; Web: www.catholiccharitiessf.org. Kathie Autumn, Div. Dir., Housing Support Svcs. Tot Asst. Annually 308; Total Staff 13.

Homelessness and Housing Services:

Catholic Charities 10th & Mission Family Housing, 1390 Mission St., 94103. Tel: 415-863-1141; Fax: 415-861-2873; Email: glippert@catholiccharitiessf.org; Web: www.catholiccharitiessf.org. Geofrey Lippert, Contact Person. Tot Asst. Annually 424; Total Staff 6.

Catholic Charities Assisted Housing & Health, 990 Eddy St., 94109. Tel: 415-972-1344; Fax: 415-972-1339; Email: ebrown@catholiccharitiessf.org; Web: www.catholiccharitiessf.org. Erick Brown, Prog. Dir. Tot Asst. Annually 573; Total Staff 5.

Catholic Charities Derek Silva Community, 20 Franklin St., 94102. Tel: 415-553-8700; Fax: 415-575-3739; Email: kfauteux@catholiccharitiessf.org; Web: www.catholiccharitiessf.org. Kevin Fauteux, Ph.D., M.S.N., Prog. Dir. Tot Asst. Annually 72; Total Staff 4.

Catholic Charities Edith Witt Senior Community, 1390 Mission St., 94103. Tel: 415-503-0816; Fax: 415-861-2873; Email: aayala@catholiccharitiessf.org; Web: www.catholiccharitiessf.org. Ana Ayala, Prog. Dir.

Catholic Charities Homelessness Prevention, 990 Eddy St., 94109. Tel: 415-972-1310; Fax: 415-972-1339; Email: jcartagena@catholiccharitiessf.org; Web: www.catholiccharitiessf.org. Jose Cartagena, Prog. Mgr. Tot Asst. Annually 939; Total Staff 6.

Catholic Charities Leland House, 141 Leland Ave., 94134. Tel: 415-405-2000; Fax: 415-337-1137; Email: sgodt@catholiccharitiessf.org; Web: www.catholiccharitiessf.org. Stephanie J. Godt, Prog. Mgr. Tot Asst. Annually 46; Total Staff 36.

Catholic Charities Peter Claver Community, 1340 Golden Gate, 94115. Tel: 415-749-3800; Fax: 415-569-3153; Email: tsagun@catholiccharitiessf.org; Web: www.catholiccharitiessf.org. Tonja Sagun, Prog. Mgr. Tot Asst. Annually 35; Total Staff 28.

Catholic Charities Rita da Cascia Community, 1652 Eddy St., #8, 94115. Tel: 415-202-0941; Fax: 415-202-0937; Email: ehammerle@catholiccharitiessf.org; Web: www.catholiccharitiessf.org. Ellen Hammerle, Ph.D., Div. Dir., Health Support Svcs. Tot Asst. Annually 230; Total Staff 10.

Catholic Charities St. Joseph's Family Center, 899 Guerrero St., 94110. Tel: 415-550-4478; Fax: 415-550-4479; Email: jlandaverde@catholiccharitiessf.org; Web: www.catholiccharitiessf.org. Jose Landaverde, Prog. Mgr. Tot Asst. Annually 101; Total Staff 12.

Catholic Charities Star Community Home, 4350 Geary Blvd., 94118. Tel: 415-379-9571; Fax: 415-379-9688; Email: llopez@catholiccharitiessf.org; Web: www.catholiccharitiessf.org. Lucia Lopez, Prog. Mgr. Tot Asst. Annually 99; Total Staff 8.

Catholic Charities Treasure Island Supportive Housing, P.O. Box 78037, 94107. Tel: 415-743-0018; Email: ngoncalves@catholiccharitiessf.org; Email: tevans@catholiccharitiessf.org; Web: www.catholiccharitiessf.org. Nella Goncalves, Div. Dir., Housing Support Svcs. Tot Asst. Annually 424; Total Staff 6.

Refugee and Immigrant Services:

Catholic Charities Refugee & Immigrant Services San Francisco, 990 Eddy St., 94109. Tel: 415-972-1200; Fax: 415-972-1360; Email: fgonzalez@catholiccharitiessf.org; Web: www.catholiccharitiessf.org. Francisco Gonzalez, Prog. Dir. Tot Asst. Annually 1,002; Total Staff 6.

Catholic Charities Refugee & Immigrant Services San Mateo County, 36 37th Ave., San Mateo, 94403. Tel: 650-295-2160; Fax: 650-295-1321; Email: dotero@catholiccharitiessf.org; Web: www.catholiccharitiessf.org. Diana Otero, Prog. Dir. Tot Asst. Annually 1,001; Total Staff 8.

[Q] NEWMAN CENTERS

SAN FRANCISCO. *Catholic Student Association of UCSF* (1967) 1290 Fifth Ave., 94122-2649. Tel: 415-566-5610; Fax: 415-566-5073; Email: stjohnofgod-sf@sbcglobal.net; Web: www.sjog.net.

Newman Center, San Francisco State University, St. Thomas More Church, 1300 Junipero Serra Blvd., 94132-2913. Tel: 415-452-9634; Fax: 415-452-9653; Email: stmchurch2002@aol.com; Web: www.STMChurch.com. Rev. Marvin Paul Felipe, S.D.B., (Philippines) Chap.

[R] PERSONAL PRELATURES

SAN FRANCISCO. *Prelature of the Holy Cross and Opus Dei* (1982) 765 14th Ave., 94118. Tel: 415-386-0431; Fax: 415-752-7177; Web: www.opusdei.org. Priests 2; Total Staff 45; Total Assisted 200.

Menlough Study Center, 1160 Santa Cruz Ave., Menlo Park, 94025. Tel: 650-327-1675. Rev. Msgr. James A. Kelly.

[S] MISCELLANEOUS LISTINGS

SAN FRANCISCO. *Alliance of Mission District Catholic Schools (AMDCS)*, 1 Peter York Way, 94109. Tel: 415-614-5546; Fax: 415-614-5546; Email: torresg@sfarch.org; Web: www.sfarchdiocese.org/amdcs. Mr. Gustavo Torres, Admin. & Devel. Coord., Alliance, Mission District Cath. Schools, Archdiocesan Grants Prog.

**American Auxiliary of Paris Foreign Missions*, 425 California St., Ste. 2500, 94104.

St. Anthony Foundation (1950) 150 Golden Gate Ave., 94102. Tel: 415-241-2600; Fax: 415-440-7770; Email: info@stanthonysf.org; Web: www.stanthonysf.org. Barry J. Stenger, Exec. Dir.; Bro. Chris Best, O.F.M., Chap.; Patricia Gallagher, Dir., Devel & Outreach. A nonprofit, charitable corporation assisting the homeless and low-income. Priests 1; Staff 140.

Archdiocesan Council of Catholic Women, One Peter Yorke Way, 94109-6602. Tel: 415-614-5500; Fax: 415-353-5555. A. Cathleen Mibach, Pres.

The Archdiocese of San Francisco Parish and School Juridic Persons Real Property Support Corporation, 1301 Post St., Ste. 102, 94109. Tel: 415-292-0800; Fax: 415-292-0805. John Christian, Dir.

The Archdiocese of San Francisco Parish, School and Cemetery Juridic Persons Capital Assets Support Corporation, 1301 Post St., Ste. 103, 94109-6667. Tel: 415-292-3600; Email: kennedya@adsfcasc.org. Mr. Richard P. Hannon, Dir.

St. Benedict Parish for Deaf and Hearing Impaired at St. Francis Xavier Church, 1801 Octavia, 94109. Tel: 415-567-9855; Tel: 415-567-0438 (TDD); Tel: 415-255-5868 (Video Phone); Fax: 415-567-0916; Email: stbenz1801@gmail.com; Web: www.sfdeafcatholics.org. Masses for the Deaf & Hard of Hearing.In Res. Rev. Ghislain C. Bazikila.

California Handicapables, Inc. (1965) 1274 30th Ave., 94122. Tel: 415-566-2331. Miss Nadine Calligiuri, Founder; John O'Keeffe. To give shut-ins and handicapped people of all faiths an opportunity for monthly Mass, lunch and general fellowship. We generally meet the third Saturday of every month at St. Mary's Cathedral, San Francisco. Please call for more information.

Caritas Business Services, 203 Redwood Shores Pkwy., Ste. 800, Redwood City, 94065. Tel: 650-551-6631; Fax: 650-551-6532; Email: wahidchoudhury@dochs.org; Web: www.dochs.org. Wahid Choudhury, Controller.

Catholic Charismatic Renewal (CCR) (1982) One Peter Yorke Way, 94109. Tel: 415-614-5500; Fax: 415-614-5522; Web: sfspirit.com. Revs. Raymund M. Reyes, Liaison; Jose M. Corral, Liaison to Spanish Speaking; Angel N. Quitalig, J.C.L., Assoc. Liaison; Deacon Ernie von Emster, Assoc. Liaison.

Catholic Kolping Society (1887) 440 Taraval St., 94116. Tel: 415-381-3989. Lisa Brinkmann, Pres.; Catherine Vennemeyer, Treas.

Catholic Scouting, Tel: 415-614-5652; Fax: 415-614-5658.

The Christopher Missions Foundation, 101 Montgomery St., Ste. 1900, 94104. Tel: 415-306-3788; Fax: 415-432-6201.

Congregation of the Holy Family of Blessed Mariam Thresia, India, 3112 Turk Blvd., 94118. Tel: 415-666-3237; Email: chfsfo@yahoo.com; Web: www.blessedmariamthresia.org.

Daughters of Carmel (Congregation of Putri Karmel) St. Cecilia Convent, 2550-18th Ave., 94116. Tel: 415-242-4625. Sr. Maria Theofila, P.Karm., Pres.

Equestrian Order of the Holy Sepulchre of Jerusalem - Northwestern Lieutenancy, 8 Lenox Way, 94127. Tel: 415-682-4228. H.E. Mary Currivan O'Brien, L.G.C.H.S.

Father Raphael Piperni Charitable Trust, 1100 Franklin St., 94109. Tel: 415-441-7144; Fax: 415-441-7155; Email: suosec@aol.com. Rev. Tho Bui, S.D.B., Admin. (The FRPC (R) Trust).

ICA San Francisco Work Study, Inc., 3625 24th St., 94110. Tel: 415-824-2052. Mr. Tim Szarnicki, CEO & Dir.

Legion of Mary (1921) 1425 Bay Rd., East Palo Alto, 94303. Tel: 650-322-2152; Fax: 650-322-7319; Email: sfofassisi@sbcglobal.net. Rev. Lawrence C. Goode, Spiritual Dir., San Francisco Senatus.

The Megan Furth Memorial Fund, 3371 16th St., 94114. Tel: 415-346-9500. Rev. Charles Gagan, S.J., Pres.

**Mercy Housing California*, 1360 Mission St., Ste. 300, 94103. Tel: 415-355-7100; Fax: 415-355-7101; Email: jdolin@mercyhousing.org; Web: www.mercyhousing.org. Housing development for low-income families, elderly, and singles.

Mercy Family Plaza, c/o Mercy Housing California, 1360 Mission St., Ste. 300, 94103. Tel: 415-355-7100; Fax: 415-355-7101. Thirty-six affordable units for families.

M.H.R. AIDS Support Group, 100 Diamond St., 94114-2414. Tel: 415-863-6259, Ext. 10; Fax: 415-552-8786; Email: mhr@mhr-asg.com; Web: www.mhr-asg.com.

St. Paul High School Alumnae Assoc., 221 Valley St., 94131. Tel: 415-648-7538; Email: sphsalumnae@yahoo.com. Marilyn Highlander-Pool, Pres. Not-for-profit charitable outreach.

Pauline Books & Media, 935 Brewster Ave., Redwood City, 94063. Tel: 650-369-4230; Fax: 650-369-4390; Email: redwood@paulinemedia.com; Web: www.pauline.org. Sr. Mary Domenica Vitello, F.S.P., Supr. Daughters of St. Paul. Sisters 5.

Philip Rinaldi Charitable Trust, 1100 Franklin St., 94109. Tel: 415-441-7144; Fax: 415-441-7155; Email: suosec@aol.com. Rev. Tho Bui, S.D.B., Admin. For the care of needy youth and for the formation needs of Salesians of St. John Bosco.

The Ricci Institute for Chinese-Western Cultural History, University of San Francisco, 2130 Fulton St., LM280, 94117-1080. Tel: 415-422-6401; Fax: 415-422-2291; Email: ricci@usfca.edu; Web: www.usfca.edu/ricci. Rev. Antoni J. Ucerler, S.J., Dir.; Xiaoxin Wu, Ed.D., Admin. Dir.; Mark Mir, Research Fellow & Chinese Library Cataloguer; May Lee, Prog. Asst.; Stephen Ford, Editorial Asst.; Krislyn Tanaka, Assoc. Researcher.

St. Rose Corporation, 2501 Pine St., 94115. Tel: 415-440-9568; Email: patricia.boss@sanrafaelop.org.

Officers of the Board: Sr. Carla Kovack, O.P., Chair; Joan Elliot, Sec.; Sisters Patricia Boss, O.P., CFO; Anne Bertain, O.P., Dir.; Susannah Malarkey, O.P., Dir.; Jean Marie Fernandez, R.G.S., Dir.; Robert Drucker, Dir.; Tony Farrell, Dir.

Seeds of Life - Verbum Dei (2013) 31448 Hwy. 33, Tracy, 95304. Mailing Address: 3365 19th St., 94110. Tel: 209-637-3404; Email: seedsoflife@verbumdeiusa.org; Web: seeds.verbumdeiusa.org. Sr. Ellen Hess, V.D.M.F., Contact Person.

Shrine of St. Jude Thaddeus, 2390 Bush St., 94115. Tel: 415-931-5919; Fax: 415-593-0350; Email: info@stjude-shrine.org; Web: www.stjude-shrine.org. Rev. James J. Moore, O.P., Dir.; Stedman Matthew, Chief Admin. Officer; Rosa Pinto, Office Mgr.

Sisters of the Presentation Community Support Trust Fund, 2340 Turk Blvd., 94118. Tel: 415-422-5001; Tel: 415-722-9577; Email: pchiesa@pbvmsf.org. Nanette Lee Miller, Trustee, Chairperson; Kathy Atkinson, Trustee; Sisters Patricia Boss, O.P., Trustee; Linda Ann Cahill, D.C., Trustee; Pamela Chiesa, P.B.V.M., M.A., M.B.A., Trustee; Patricia Anne Cloherty, P.B.V.M., Trustee; Mary Connolly, Trustee; Sr. Patricia Creedon, R.S.M., Trustee; Fred Najjar, Trustee. Trust used for the religious and charitable needs of the Sisters of the Presentation of the Blessed Virgin Mary.

BURLINGAME. *St. Conrad Center for Ministry and Studies* (2013) 1534 Arch St., Berkeley, 94708. Email: finance@olacapuchins.org. 1345 Cortez Ave., Burlingame, 94010. Tel: 650-344-8321; Fax: 650-342-5664. Very Rev. Harold Snider, O.F.-M.Cap., CEO.

Music at Kohl Mansion, Inc., 2750 Adeline Dr., Burlingame, 94010. Tel: 650-762-1130; Fax: 650-343-8464; Email: director@musicatkohl.org; Web: www.musicatkohl.org. To develop and promote public knowledge and appreciation of musical arts by sponsoring chamber music concerts and other public performances of music, as well as music education activities.

San Buenaventura Center for Ministry and Studies (2013) 750 Anza St., 94118. 1345 Cortez Ave., Burlingame, 94010. Tel: 650-344-8321; Fax: 650-344-5664; Email: finance@olacapuchins.org. Very Rev. Harold Snider, O.F.M.Cap., CEO.

DALY CITY. *Vincentian Service Corps West*, 25 San Fernando Way, Ste. B, Daly City, 94015-2065. Tel: 650-755-1633; Fax: 650-755-1637; Email: vsc@vscwest.org; Email: Sistertrangdc@vscwest.org; Web: www.vscwest.org. Sisters Margaret McDonnell, D.C., Chairperson; Trang Truong, D.C., Dir.

MENLO PARK. *The Benedict XVI Institute for Sacred Music and Divine Worship*, 320 Middlefield Rd., Menlo Park, 94025.

REDWOOD CITY. *The Catholic Worker Community* (1975) 545 Cassia St., Redwood City, 94063. Tel: 650-366-4415. Lawrence P. Purcell, Dir. A foster home for teenagers.

**St. Francis Center of Redwood City*, 151 Buckingham Ave., Redwood City, 94063. Tel: 650-365-7829; Fax: 650-365-7829; Email: SChristina@aol.com; Web: www.stfrancisrwc.org. Sr. Christina Heltsley, O.P., Exec. Dir.

PORTOLA VALLEY. *St. Stephen Hungarian Catholic Mission*, 302 Portola Rd., Portola Valley, 94028.

SAN RAFAEL. **Center Interfaith Housing*, 164 N. San Pedro Rd., San Rafael, 94903. Tel: 415-492-9340; Fax: 415-492-1340.

Mission Holding Corporation (1995) 1520 Grand Ave., San Rafael, 94901-2236. Tel: 415-453-8303; Fax: 415-453-8367; Email: maureen.mcinerney@sanrafaelop.org; Web: sanrafaelop.org. Governing Board: Sisters Maureen McInerney, O.P., Pres.; Susan Allbritton, O.P., Sec.; Abby Newton, O.P.; Mary Kieffer, O.P.; Carla Kovack, O.P.

The Sisters of Nazareth of San Rafael Real Estate Holdings, Inc., 245 Nova Albion Way, San Rafael, 94903. Tel: 415-479-8282; Fax: 415-479-6413.

Sisters of the Third Order of St. Dominic Support Charitable Trust Fund, 1520 Grand Ave., San Rafael, 94901-2236. Tel: 415-453-8303; Fax: 415-453-8367; Email: maureen.mcinerney@sanrafaelop.org; Web: sanrafaelop.org. Sisters Maureen McInerney, O.P., Chmn.; Patricia Boss, O.P., CFO; Susan Allbritton, O.P., Sec.; Jeffrey V. Bialik, Trustee; Sisters Darylynn Costa, O.P., Trustee; Patricia Creedon, R.S.M., Trustee; Bernice Garcia, O.P., Trustee; Ingrid Sheets, Trustee; Mal Visbal, Trustee; Mr. Tan N. Vo, Trustee. Trust used for the religious and charitable needs of the Sisters of the Third Order of St. Dominic, Congregation of the Most Holy Name.

Sisters of the Third Order of St. Dominic, Congregation of the Most Holy Name, Support Charitable Trust Fund.

SOUTH SAN FRANCISCO. *The Contemplatives of Saint Joseph*, 377 Willow Ave., South San Francisco, 94080-1446. Tel: 267-500-4155; Fax: 650-871-1685; Email: cosj@att.net; Web: www.cosjmonastery.com. Revs. Vito J. Perrone, Supr.; Joseph Homick, Member. A public clerical association of the Christian faithful.

[T] CLOSED INSTITUTIONS

SAN FRANCISCO. *All Hallows Church* For sacramental records please contact Our Lady of Lourdes, 1715 Oakdale Ave., San Francisco 94124, Tel: 415-285-3377; Fax: 415-285-2191.

St. Brigid Church For sacramental records please contact St. Vincent de Paul, 2320 Green St., San Francisco 94123, Tel: 415-992-1010; Fax: 415-922-7203.

St. Edward the Confessor Church For sacramental records please contact St. Dominic, 2390 Bush St., San Francisco, 94115, Tel: 415-567-7854; Fax: 415-567-1608.

St. Francis of Assisi Church For sacramental records please contact SS. Peter and Paul, 666 Filbert St., San Francisco, 94133, Tel: 415-421-0809; Fax: 415-421-0217.

Holy Cross Korean Church For sacramental records please contact Chancery Office, One Peter Yorke Way, San Francisco, 94109, Tel: 415-614-5500; Fax: 415-614-5555.

Immaculate Conception Church For sacramental records please contact St. Anthony of Padua, 3215 Cesar Chavez St., San Francisco, 94110, Tel: 415-647-2704; Fax: 415-647-7282.

St. Joseph Church For sacramental records please contact St. Patrick, 756 Mission St., San Francisco, 94103, Tel: 415-421-0547; 512-9730.

Our Lady of Guadalupe Church For sacramental records please contact SS. Peter and Paul, 666 Filbert St., San Francisco, 94133, Tel: 415-421-0809; Fax: 415-421-0217.

Sacred Heart Church For sacramental records please contact the Chancery Office, One Peter Yorke Way, San Francisco, 94109.

SAN RAFAEL. *Blessed Sacrament Church* For sacramental records please contact St. Isabella, One Trinity Way, San Rafael, 94901, Tel: 415-479-1560; Fax: 415-479-8303.

St. Sylvester Church For sacramental records please contact St. Raphael, 1104 Fifth Ave., San Rafael, 94901, Tel: 415-453-2314; Fax: 415-453-5402.

WOODSIDE. *St. Marcella Mission* For sacramental records please contact St. Denis, 2250 Avy Ave., Menlo Park, 94025, Tel: 650-854-5976; Fax: 650-854-3754.

RELIGIOUS INSTITUTES OF MEN REPRESENTED IN THE ARCHDIOCESE

For further details refer to the corresponding bracketed number in the Religious Institutes of Men or Women section.

[]—*Apostolic Life Community of Priests* Moshe, Tanzania.
[0200]—*Benedictine Monks* (Hungary)—O.S.B.
[0330]—*Brothers of the Christian Schools* (Prov. of San Francisco)—F.S.C.
[0470]—*The Capuchin Franciscans* (Irish Prov.)—O.F.M.Cap.
[0480]—*Conventual Franciscans*—O.F.M.Conv.
[0520]—*Franciscan Friars* (Santa Barbara Prov.)—O.F.M.
[0650]—*Holy Ghost Fathers*—C.S.Sp.
[0690]—*Jesuit Fathers and Brothers* (California Prov.)—S.J.
[0780]—*Marist Fathers and Brothers* (United States Prov.)—S.M.
[]—*Order of Carmelites*—O.Carm.
[0430]—*Order of Preachers (Dominicans)* (Western Prov.)—O.P.
[0897]—*Paris Foreign Mission Society*—M.E.P.
[1030]—*Paulist Fathers*—C.S.P.
[1190]—*Salesian Don Bosco*—S.D.B.
[1260]—*Society of Christ* (Chicago Prov.)—S.Chr.
[1290]—*Society of the Priests of Saint Sulpice* (American Prov.)—P.S.S.

RELIGIOUS INSTITUTES OF WOMEN REPRESENTED IN THE ARCHDIOCESE

[1310]—*Congregation of the Franciscan Sisters of Little Falls, MN.*
[]—*Congregation of the Holy Family of Blessed Mariam Thresia, India.*
[3242]—*Congregation of the Sisters of Nazareth*—C.S.N.
[]—*Daughters of Carmel* (Putri Karmel).
[0730]—*Daughters of Charity of Canossa*—F.D.C.C.
[0760]—*Daughters of Charity of St. Vincent de Paul* (Prov. of the West)—D.C.
[0880]—*Daughters of Mary and Joseph*—D.M.J.
[0850]—*Daughters of Mary Help of Christians*—F.M.A.
[0420]—*Discalced Carmelite Nuns*—O.C.D.
[1050]—*Dominican Contemplative Nuns*—O.P.
[1070-13]—*Dominican Sisters*—O.P.
[1070-04]—*Dominican Sisters of San Rafael*—O.P.
[]—*Dominican Sisters of the Philippines.*
[]—*Franciscan Missionaries, Our Lady of Peace*—M.F.P.
[]—*Las Hermanas Misioneras*—M.S.C.Gpe.
[2340]—*Little Sisters of the Poor*—L.S.P.
[2390]—*Lovers of the Holy Cross Sisters*—L.H.C.
[2710]—*Missionary Sisters of Charity*—M.C.
[]—*Missionary Sisters of the Sacred Side*—M.S.C.
[3190]—*Nuns of the Perpetual Adoration of the Blessed Sacrament*—A.P.
[]—*Oblates Sisters of Jesus the Priest*—O.S.J.
[0950]—*Pious Society Daughters of St. Paul*—F.S.P.
[]—*Religious of the Sacred Heart of Jesus*—R.S.C.J.
[]—*Religious of the Virgin Mary*—R.V.M.
[0430]—*Sisters of Charity of the Blessed Virgin Mary*—B.V.M.
[2575]—*Sisters of Mercy of the Americas* West Midwest Community. (Omaha, NE)—R.S.M.

[3000]—*Sisters of Notre Dame de Namur* (Prov. of CA)—S.N.D.deN.
[4080]—*Sisters of Social Service of Los Angeles, Inc.*—S.S.S.
[]—*Sisters of St. Dominic of Mission San Jose*—O.P.
[1630]—*Sisters of St. Francis of Penance and Christian Charity*—O.S.F.
[3840]—*Sisters of St. Joseph of Carondelet* (Los Angeles Prov.)—C.S.J.
[3930-03]—*Sisters of St. Joseph of Orange*—C.S.J.O.
[1830]—*The Sisters of the Good Shepherd*—R.G.S.
[1960]—*Sisters of the Holy Family* (San Francisco, CA)—S.H.F.
[1990]—*Sisters of the Holy Names of Jesus and Mary* (Provs. of CA; Oregon; Washington)—S.N.J.M.
[2130]—*Sisters of the Immaculate Conception* (Prov. of Madrid)—R.C.M.
[3320]—*Sisters of the Presentation of the B.V.M.*—P.B.V.M.
[1890]—*Society of Helpers*—H.H.S.
[3330]—*Union Sisters of the Presentation of the Blessed Virgin Mary*—P.B.V.M.
[4110]—*Ursuline Nuns (Roman Union)*—O.S.U.
[]—*Verbum Dei Missionary Fraternity*.

ARCHDIOCESAN CEMETERIES AND MAUSOLEUMS

SAN FRANCISCO. *Holy Cross Cemetery and Mausoleum*, P.O. Box 1577, Colma, 94014. Tel: 650-756-2060; Fax: 650-757-0752; Email: moreinfo@holycrosscemeteries.com.

MENLO PARK. *Holy Cross*, P.O. Box 1577, Colma, 94014. Tel: 650-323-6375; Fax: 650-757-0752; Email: moreinfo@holycrosscemeteries.com.

SAN RAFAEL. *Mount Olivet*, 270 Ranchitos Rd., San Rafael, 94903. Email: moreinfo@holycrosscemeteries.com.

An asterisk (*) denotes an organization that has established tax-exempt status directly with the IRS and is not covered by the USCCB Group Ruling.

Diocese of San Jose in California

(Dioecesis Sancti Josephi in California)

Most Reverend

OSCAR CANTU, S.T.D.

Bishop of San Jose; ordained May 21, 1994; appointed Auxiliary Bishop of San Antonio and Titular Bishop of Dardano June 2, 2008; appointed Bishop of Las Cruces February 28, 2013; appointed Coadjutor Bishop of San Jose July 11, 2018; Succeeded to See May 1, 2019.

ZELUS DOMUS TUAE COMEDIT ME

Diocese of San Jose: 1150 N. First St., Ste. 100, San Jose, CA 95112. Tel: 408-983-0100; Fax: 408-983-0295.

Web: www.dsj.org

Email: chancellor@dsj.org

Most Reverend

PATRICK J. MCGRATH, D.D., J.C.D.

Bishop Emeritus of San Jose; ordained June 7, 1970; appointed Auxiliary Bishop of San Francisco and Titular Bishop of Allegheny December 6, 1988; Episcopal ordination January 25, 1989; appointed Coadjutor Bishop of San Jose June 29, 1998; succeeded to See November 27, 1999; retired May 1, 2019.

Most Reverend

PIERRE DUMAINE, D.D., PH.D.

Bishop Emeritus of San Jose; ordained June 15, 1957; appointed Auxiliary Bishop of San Francisco and Titular Bishop of Sarda April 28, 1978; Episcopal ordination June 29, 1978; appointed Bishop of San Jose January 27, 1981; installed as Bishop of San Jose March 18, 1981; retired November 27, 1999. *Chancery Office: Diocese of San Jose, 1150 N. First St., Ste. 100, San Jose, CA 95112.*

ESTABLISHED JANUARY 27, 1981.

Square Miles 1,300.

The Diocese of San Jose comprises the County of Santa Clara in the State of California.

Patrons of the Diocese of San Jose: St. Joseph, Husband of Mary, March 19; St. Clare of Assisi, August 11.

Legal Title: The Roman Catholic Bishop of San Jose, a Corporation Sole.
For legal titles of parishes and diocesan institutions, consult the Chancery Office.

STATISTICAL OVERVIEW

Personnel	
Bishop	1
Retired Bishops	2
Priests: Diocesan Active in Diocese	93
Priests: Diocesan Active Outside Diocese	4
Priests: Retired, Sick or Absent	55
Number of Diocesan Priests	152
Religious Priests in Diocese	165
Total Priests in Diocese	317
Extern Priests in Diocese	28
Ordinations:	
Diocesan Priests	3
Transitional Deacons	2
Permanent Deacons	3
Permanent Deacons in Diocese	37
Total Brothers	62
Total Sisters	306
Parishes	
Parishes	49
With Resident Pastor:	
Resident Diocesan Priests	44
Resident Religious Priests	4
Missions	3
Pastoral Centers	2
Professional Ministry Personnel:	

Brothers	1
Sisters	36
Lay Ministers	144
Welfare	
Homes for the Aged	1
Total Assisted	100
Residential Care of Children	1
Day Care Centers	1
Special Centers for Social Services	1
Total Assisted	41,000
Educational	
Diocesan Students in Other Seminaries	9
Total Seminarians	9
Colleges and Universities	1
Total Students	8,768
High Schools, Diocesan and Parish	1
Total Students	1,741
High Schools, Private	5
Total Students	5,320
Elementary Schools, Diocesan and Parish	27
Total Students	8,248
Elementary Schools, Private	2
Total Students	382
Catechesis/Religious Education:	

High School Students	3,693
Elementary Students	9,573
Total Students under Catholic Instruction	37,734
Teachers in the Diocese:	
Priests	38
Sisters	3
Lay Teachers	1,538
Vital Statistics	
Receptions into the Church:	
Infant Baptism Totals	5,110
Minor Baptism Totals	296
Adult Baptism Totals	314
Received into Full Communion	348
First Communions	5,167
Confirmations	3,639
Marriages:	
Catholic	706
Interfaith	159
Total Marriages	865
Deaths	1,736
Total Catholic Population	635,000
Total Population	1,948,715

Former Bishop—Most Revs. PIERRE DUMAINE, D.D., Ph.D., (Retired), ord. June 15, 1957; appt. Auxiliary Bishop of San Francisco and Titular Bishop of Sarda, April 28, 1978; Episcopal ordination June 29, 1978; appt. Bishop of San Jose Jan. 27, 1981; installed as Bishop of San Jose March 18, 1981; retired Nov. 27, 1999; PATRICK J. MCGRATH, D.D., J.C.D., ord. June 7, 1970; appt. Auxiliary Bishop of San Francisco and Titular Bishop of Allegheny Dec. 6, 1988; Episcopal ordination Jan. 25, 1989; appt. Coadjutor Bishop of San Jose June 29, 1998; succeeded to See Nov. 27, 1999; retired May 1, 2019.

Diocese of San Jose—1150 N. First St., Ste. 100, San Jose, 95112. Tel: 408-983-0100; Fax: 408-983-0295; Web: www.dsj.org.

Vicar General and Moderator of the Curia—Rev. Msgr. FRANCIS V. CILIA, V.G., Tel: 408-983-0154; Fax: 408-983-0242.

Vicar General, Office for Special Projects—Very Rev. BRENDAN MCGUIRE, V.G., Tel: 408-983-0198; Fax: 408-983-0242.

Lay Retirement Board—Rev. Msgr. FRANCIS V. CILIA, V.G.; JOSEPH BAUER; MARTIN CHARGIN; STEVE DUFFY; LINDA GRECO, Ex Officio; JOSEPH GUERRA; MARY LYONS; ROSALIE MARTY; BRIAN MOONEY, Ex Officio; CHARLES TULLY; ROBBIE OCAMPO; MICHAEL LEE; REA VALLARTA.

Chancellor—LINDA TULLY, Tel: 408-983-0144; Fax: 408-983-0147.

Vicar for Clergy—Rev. Msgr. FRANCIS V. CILIA, V.G., Tel: 408-983-0154; Fax: 408-983-0242.

Judicial Vicar—Rev. ANDRES C. LIGOT, J.C.D.

Delegate to Religious—Sr. ROSALIE PIZZO, S.N.D.deN, Tel: 408-983-0123; Fax: 408-983-0121.

Chief Development Officer—JOSEPH NAYLOR, Tel: 408-983-0244; Fax: 408-983-0290.

Bishop's Cabinet—Most Rev. OSCAR CANTU, S.T.D.; Rev. Msgr. FRANCIS V. CILIA, V.G.; Very Rev. BRENDAN MCGUIRE, V.G.; Revs. JOSEPH BENEDICT, S.T.D.; JUSTIN LE; JOHN HURLEY, C.S.P.; JENNIFER BELTRAMO; LINDA GRECO; BRIAN MOONEY; JOSEPH NAYLOR.

College of Consultors—Most Rev. OSCAR CANTU, S.T.D.; Rev. Msgr. FRANCIS V. CILIA, V.G.; Revs. HECTOR BASANEZ; JOSEPH BENEDICT, S.T.D.; THUC SI HO; ANDRES LIGOT, J.C.D.; Very Rev. BRENDAN MCGUIRE, V.G.

Council of Priests—Most Rev. OSCAR CANTU, S.T.D., Pres.; Rev. CHRISTOPHER BENNETT, Chm.; Rev. Msgr. FRANCIS V. CILIA, V.G., Ex Officio; Revs. TITO JESUS CARTAGENAS JR.; ANGELO DAVID; MICHAEL D. HENDRICKSON; KEVIN P. JOYCE, (Retired); ENZIE LAGATTUTA; JUSTIN LE; ANDRES LIGOT, J.C.D.; Very Rev. BRENDAN MCGUIRE, V.G., Ex Officio; Revs. ANDREW C. NGUYEN; GERALD NWAFOR, (Nigeria); MATTHEW D. STANLEY; WALTER SUAREZ.

Council of Religious—Sr. ROSALIE PIZZO, S.N.D.deN, Chm.; Bro. WILLIAM BOLTS, S.M.; Mother MARIE BON SECOURS CASABADAN, S.S.V.M.; Rev. VINCENT DUONG, S.J.; Sisters ROSHEEN GLENNON, C.S.J.; MOLLY NEVILLE, S.N.J.M.; Rev. MARIO J. PRIETTO, S.J.; Sisters MICHELE RANDALL, D.C.; GEMMA WILSON, P.B.V.M.; MARILYN WILSON, B.V.M.

Deans—Revs. V. WARWICK JAMES, Deanery 2; JOSEPH M. BENEDICT, S.T.D., Deanery 3; Rev. Msgr. WILFREDO S. MANRIQUE, J.C.L., Deanery 4; Revs. GREGORY C. KIMM, Deanery 5; ROBERT A. FAMBRINI, S.J., Deanery 6; CHRISTOPHER BENNETT, Deanery 7.

Ecumenical and Interreligious Affairs—Rev. JOSE RUBIO, S.T.D., Dir. & Delegate to Eastern Rite Churches.

San Jose Chinese Catholic Mission—Revs. CARLOS ALBERTO OLIVERA, Pastor; PAUL J. GODA, S.J., Chap., Cantonese Comm.

Catholic Charities—Catholic Charities of Santa Clara County GREGORY R. KEPFERLE, CEO.

Propagation of the Faith-Holy Childhood Association-Catholic Relief ServicePAUL MINER, Dir., Tel: 408-983-0158.

Roman Catholic Welfare Corporation—Most Rev. OSCAR CANTU, S.T.D., Pres.; Rev. Msgr. FRANCIS V. CILIA, V.G., Vice Pres.; LINDA TULLY, Sec.; BRIAN MOONEY, Treas.; JENNIFER BELTRAMO.

Roman Catholic Seminary Corporation—Most Rev. OSCAR CANTU, S.T.D., Pres.; Rev. Msgr. FRANCIS V. CILIA, V.G., Vice Pres.; LINDA TULLY, Sec.; Rev. ANDRES LIGOT, J.C.D.; BRIAN MOONEY, Treas.

The Valley Catholic (Diocesan Newspaper)—Diocese of San Jose: 1150 N. First St., Ste. 100, San Jose, 95112. Tel: 408-983-0262. LIZ SULLIVAN, Editor, Tel: 408-983-0228; ROSALINDA ZEPEDA, Business Mgr.

Diocesan Tribunal—Diocese of San Jose, 1150 N. First St., Ste. 100, San Jose, 95112. Tel: 408-983-0219.

Judicial Vicar—Rev. ANDRES C. LIGOT, J.C.D.

Adjutant Judicial Vicar—Rev. NOEL SANVICENTE, J.C.D.

Judges—Revs. SAJU JOSEPH, J.C.L.; ANDRES LIGOT, J.C.D.; NOEL SANVICENTE, J.C.D.

Defender of the Bond—Rev. ROBERT E. HAYES, J.C.L.

Case Instructor—Tel: 408-983-0224. ZAIRA MARTINEZ-ROBLES.

Administrative Assistant and Notary—Sr. SOFIA BERRONES, M.C.D.P., Tel: 408-983-0219.

Finance Office—BRIAN MOONEY, CFO; JOHN HOFFMAN, Controller; IAN ABELL, Dir. Facilities & Risk Mgmt.; LEI WANG, Facilities Inspector & Coord.; VACANT, Compliance Officer.

Finance Council—MICHAEL HOPE, Chm.; KEVIN BEDOLLA; GEORGE DELUCCHI; STEVE DUFFY; NANCY ERBA; TROY JONES; TIM NONDORF; ROGER QUINLAN; DONALD WAITE.

Building Committee—Rev. Msgr. FRANCIS V. CILIA, V.G.; Rev. CHRISTOPHER BENNETT; IAN ABELL, Chm.; DAN BROWN; CHRIS CIECHANOWSKI; PAUL HOUGH SR.; PAUL LAWSON; BRIAN MOONEY; PATRICK PFEIFFER; KIMBERLY SHIELDS; RAMIRO TORRES.

Stewardship & Development Office—JOSEPH NAYLOR, Chief Devel. Officer, Tel: 408-983-0244; Fax: 408-983-0290.

Department of Cemeteries—Tel: 650-428-3730. DENNIS FAIRBANK, Interim Dir.

Vicar for Clergy—Rev. Msgr. FRANCIS V. CILIA, V.G., Tel: 408-983-0154.

Director of Deacon Life—Deacon DONALD SIFFERMAN.

Diocesan Clergy Personnel Board—Most Rev. OSCAR CANTU, S.T.D., Ex Officio; Rev. Msgr. FRANCIS V. CILIA, V.G., Chm. & Ex Officio; Rev. RITCHE S. BUEZA; Rev. Msgrs. WILFREDO S. MANRIQUE, J.C.L.; JOSEPH J. MILANI, (Retired); EUGENE P. O'DONNELL, (Retired); Revs. ANDREW C. NGUYEN; WALTER SUAREZ; KATHY SCHLOSSER; LUPITA VITAL.

Ongoing Formation of Clergy—Rev. Msgr. FRANCIS V. CILIA, V.G., Ex Officio; Revs. JOSEPH BENEDICT, S.T.D.; RITCHE S. BUEZA; ANDREW C. NGUYEN; Rev. Msgr. FRANCISCO RIOS; Deacons RICK HAECKEL; DONALD SIFFERMAN, Ex Officio.

Priests' Retirement Board—Rev. Msgrs. EUGENE P. O'DONNELL, Chm., (Retired); J. PATRICK BROWNE, (Retired); FRANCIS V. CILIA, V.G., Ex Officio; TERRENCE J. SULLIVAN, (Retired); BRIAN MOONEY, Ex Officio; Revs. JOSEPH BENEDICT, S.T.D.; ROBERT E. HAYES, J.C.L.; ERNESTO ORCI; RICK RODONI; GEORGE DELUCCHI; TIM NONDORF.

Vocation Office—Rev. RITCHE S. BUEZA, Dir.

Vocation Assessment Team—Rev. RITCHE S. BUEZA, Ex Officio; Rev. Msgr. FRANCIS V. CILIA, V.G., Ex Officio; Revs. HAO DINH; GENEROSO GERONIMO, (Philippines); GERARDO MENCHACA; Sr. ROSALIE PIZZO, S.N.D.deN; Rev. MATTHEW D. STANLEY; DOROTHY CARLSON; BERNIE PERCELL; DR. THOMAS PLANT.

Deacon Formation—Tel: 408-983-0256. Deacons PHILLIP FLOWERS, Dir.; DONALD SIFFERMAN, Dir. Deacon Life.

Permanent Diaconate Admissions and Evaluations Board—Deacon PHILLIP FLOWERS, Dir.; Rev. Msgr. FRANCIS V. CILIA, V.G., Ex Officio; Revs. JOSEPH BENEDICT, S.T.D.; RITCHE S. BUEZA; GERARDO MENCHACA; ANTHONY MANCUSO; ROBERT MCKAY, (South Africa) Ph.D.; IRMA ALARCON DE RANGEL, Dir. Adv. Lay Leaders; LINDA CUNHA-RICCHIO; Deacon THO LE; SANDY SIFFERMAN.

Office of the Chancellor—LINDA TULLY, Chancellor, Tel: 408-983-0144.

Diocesan Archives and Records Management—685 E. Brokaw Rd., San Jose, 95112. Tel: 408-320-1831. ROBERT MARCH.

Human Resources Office—LINDA GRECO, Chief Human Resources Officer, Tel: 408-983-0149.

Department of Catholic Schools—JENNIFER BELTRAMO, Supt. Schools; KIMBERLY SHIELDS, Assoc. Supt. Schools; DR. TARA ROLLE, Assoc. Supt, Drexel Schools; CHYRISE KING, Assoc. Supt., Mktg. & Enrollment.

Office for Evangelization—Rev. JOHN HURLEY, C.S.P., Vicar, Tel: 408-983-0182.

Director for Faith Formation—ROBERT RODRIGUES, Tel: 408-983-0138.

Hispanic Apostolate—LUPITA VITAL, Dir., Tel: 408-983-0133; SANDRA TORRES, Assoc. Dir., Tel: 408-983-0112.

Director for Hispanic Youth and Young Adults—LUPITA VITAL, Tel: 408-983-0133.

Youth and Young Adult Ministry—GIANG STEVE DO, Dir., Tel: 408-983-0122; ROBBIE OCAMPO, Assoc. Dir., Tel: 408-983-0207.

Missions Office—Rev. Msgr. FRANCIS V. CILIA, V.G., Dir., Tel: 408-983-0154.

Director of Liturgy—CHRISTOPHER WEMP, Tel: 408-983-0136.

Director of Social Justice Ministries—PAUL MINER, Dir., Tel: 408-983-0158.

Detention Ministry—Sr. MARYANN CANTLON, C.S.J., Dir. Detention/Restorative Justice Min., Tel: 408-983-0131.

Human Concerns Commission—PAUL MINER, Liaison, Tel: 408-983-0158.

Liturgical Commission—CHRISTOPHER WEMP, Liaison, Tel: 408-983-0136.

Pastoral Resource Committee for Ministry to Gay and Lesbian Catholics—Rev. G. ROBERT LEGER, (Retired), Tel: 408-245-5554.

Respect Life Program—PAUL MINER, Liaison, Tel: 408-983-0158.

Institute for Leadership in Ministry—Tel: 408-983-0111. IRMA ALARCON DE RANGEL, Dir.

Office for the Protection of Children and Vulnerable Adults—ANTHONY GONZALEZ, Tel: 408-983-0113; Tel: 408-983-0141 (Emergency Line); Fax: 408-983-0203.

Victim Assistance Coordinator—GRISELDA CERVANTEZ, Tel: 408-983-0225 (Emergency Line); Fax: 408-983-0203.

Safe Environment Coordinator—LY HELGESON, Tel: 408-983-0248.

CLERGY, PARISHES, MISSIONS AND PAROCHIAL SCHOOLS

CITY OF SAN JOSE

1—CATHEDRAL BASILICA OF ST. JOSEPH (1849) (Hispanic—Latino) (Mexican National Church)
80 S. Market St., 95113. Tel: 408-283-8100; Email: cbsjoffice@gmail.com. Revs. Joseph M. Benedict, S.T.D.; Jeff Fernandez, Parochial Vicar; Hector Villela-Huerta, (Mexico) Parochial Vicar; Deacon Gregorio Ortiz.
Catechesis Religious Program—Students 321.

2—ST. ANTHONY (1982)
20101 McKean Rd., 95120. Tel: 408-997-4800; Fax: 408-997-4801; Email: churchstanthony@dsj.org; Web: churchstanthony.com. Rev. Lawrence Hendel.
Old Church: 21800 Bertram Rd., New Almaden, 95120.
Catechesis Religious Program—Students 48.

3—ST. BROTHER ALBERT CHMIELOWSKI POLISH CATHOLIC PASTORAL MISSION (1986) (Polish)
10250 Clayton Rd., 95127-4336. Tel: 408-251-8490; Email: office@saintalbert.us; Web: www.saintalbert.us. Revs. Slawomir Murawka, S.Chr., In Res.; Jan Fiedurek, S.Chr.
Catechesis Religious Program—Students 76.

4—CHRIST THE KING dba Parroquia Cristo Rey (1997)
5284 Monterey Rd., 95111. Tel: 408-362-9958; Email: ideluna@dsj.org. Revs. Luis Vargas; Truyen Nguyen, Parochial Vicar; Deacon Joseph The Hoang.
Res.: 75 Cyclamen St., 95111.
Catechesis Religious Program—Students 407.

5—ST. CHRISTOPHER (1951)
1576 Curtner Ave, 95125. Tel: 408-269-2226; Email: loretta.pfaff@stchrissj.org; Web: www.saintchris.com. Msgr. Allen Center, 2278 Booksin Ave., 95125. Revs. Christopher Bennett; Paolo Gobbo, Parochial Vicar; Khoa Vu, Parochial Vicar; Deacons Richard Noack; Bruce Zorio.
School—St. Christopher School, (Grades K-8), Tel: 408-723-7223; Email: info@stchris.us; Web: www.stchris.us. Sally Douthit. Lay Teachers 60; Students 600.
Catechesis Religious Program—

6—CHURCH OF THE TRANSFIGURATION (1965)
Mailing Address: 4325 Jarvis Ave., 95118.
Tel: 408-264-3600; Fax: 408-264-3600; Email: transfiguration@dsj.org; Web: www.sanjosetransfig.com. Rev. Tito Jesus Cartagenas Jr.; Paula Ramos, Faith Formation Dir.
Catechesis Religious Program—Students 40.

7—FIVE WOUNDS PORTUGUESE NATIONAL CHURCH (1914) (Portuguese)
1375 E. Santa Clara St., 95116. Tel: 408-292-2123; Email: info@fivewoundschurch.org; Web: www.fivewoundschurch.org. Rev. Antonio Silveira.
Catechesis Religious Program—Mr. Joseph Khanh Russo, D.R.E. Students 94.
IMMACULATE HEART OF MARY ORATORY
Email: rueda@dsj.org; Web: institute-christ-king.org/sanjose-home. Rev. Canon Rafael Ueda, Chap.

8—ST. FRANCES CABRINI (1955)
15333 Woodard Rd., 95124. Tel: 408-879-1120; Email: frhendrickson@sfcabrini.org; Web: sfcabrini.org. Revs. Michael D. Hendrickson; Gabriel Lee, Parochial Vicar; Daniel C. Urcia, Ed.D., In Res.
School—St. Frances Cabrini School, (Grades PreSchool-8),
15325 Woodard Rd., 95124. Tel: 408-377-6545; Fax: 408-377-8491; Email: info@sfcschool.org; Web: www.sfcschool.org. Jane Daigle, Prin. Clergy 1; Lay Teachers 38; Students 620.
Catechesis Religious Program—

9—ST. FRANCIS OF ASSISI (1997)
5111 San Felipe Rd., 95135. Tel: 408-223-1562; Fax: 408-223-1759; Email: mstanley@dsj.org; Web: www.sfoasj.com. Revs. Matthew D. Stanley; Michael Syjueco, Parochial Vicar; Lieu Vu, Parochial Vicar; Deacons Willy Agbayani; Silvanus Offorjebe; Andrzej Sobczyk.

10—HOLY CROSS (1906) (Italian)
580 E. Jackson St., 95112. Tel: 408-294-2440; Email: holycross.sanjose@gmail.com; Web: www.holycrosssj.com. Revs. Leonardo Rocha, C.S.; Henri-Claude Testamar, C.S., Parochial Vicar.
Catechesis Religious Program—
Email: rochoa@dsj.org. Bro. Raul Ochoa, C.S., D.R.E. Students 250.

11—HOLY FAMILY (1905)
4848 Pearl Ave., 95136. Tel: 408-265-4040; Email: holyfamilysj@dsj.org; Web: holyfamilysanjose.org. Revs. Andrew V. Nguyen; Celso Singson, Parochial Vicar; Deacon Raymond Gans.
School—Holy Family School, (Grades PreK-8),
4850 Pearl Ave., 95136. Tel: 408-978-1355; Fax: 408-978-0290; Email: office@hfsj.org; Web: www.holyfamilyschoolsj.com. Maeve Hannon, Prin.; Terri Lanoie, Librarian. Lay Teachers 18; Students 331.
Catechesis Religious Program—

12—HOLY KOREAN MARTYRS (2005) (Korean)
1523 McLaughlin Ave., 95122. Tel: 408-734-9721; Fax: 669-231-4137; Email: sjkcm@sbcglobal.net; Web: www.sjkoreancatholic.org. Revs. Taehoon Ko; Young Sam Kim, Parochial Vicar.
Catechesis Religious Program—

13—HOLY SPIRIT (1963)
1200 Redmond Ave., 95120. Tel: 408-997-5101; Email: pwarne@dsj.org; Web: www.holyspiritchurch.org. Very Rev. Brendan McGuire, V.G.; Rev. Edgar Elamparo I, Parochial Vicar; Penny Warne, Pastoral Assoc.; Merry Reardon, Pastoral Assoc.
School—Holy Spirit School, A Drexel School, (Grades PreSchool-8),
1198 Redmond Ave., 95120. Tel: 408-268-0794; Fax: 408-268-5281; Email: mchristensen@dsj.org; Web: www.holyspirit-school.org. Mrs. Maureen Christensen, Prin.; Mr. Greg Vohs, Vice Prin.; Claudia Jones, Admin. Lay Teachers 26; Students 453.

14—ST. JOHN VIANNEY (1952)
4609 Hyland Ave., 95127. Tel: 408-258-7832, Ext. 22; Tel: lestrada@dsj.org. Mailing Address: 4600 Hyland Ave., 95127. Rev. Steven P. Brown; Rev. Msgr. Jeronimo Gutierrez, Parochial Vicar; Deacon Raul Mendoza; Luis Estrada, Admin.
Rectory—
4607 Alum Rock Ave., 95127.
School—St. John Vianney School, (Grades PreK-8), 4601 Hyland Ave., 95127. Tel: 408-258-7677; Fax: 408-258-5997; Email: school@sjvsj.org; Web: www.sjvsj.org. Mrs. Laura Seminatore, Prin. Lay Teachers 27; Sisters of the Presentation of the B.V.M. 1; Students 440.
Catechesis Religious Program—English & Spanish language catechetical programs.

15—ST. JULIE BILLIART (1974)
6410 Cottle Rd., 95123. Tel: 408-629-3030; Email: office@stjulies.org; Email: info@stjulies.org; Web: www.stjulies.org. Mailing Address: 366 St. Julie Dr., 95119. Revs. Angelo David; Pedro Perez-Sencion, Parochial Vicar; Sharon Aeria, Pastoral Associate.
Catechesis Religious Program—
Tel: 408-629-3030, Ext. 102; Email: faithformation@stjulies.org. Yolanda Toulet, D.R.E. Students 463.

16—ST. LEO THE GREAT (1923)
88 Race St., 95126. Tel: 408-293-3503; Email:

stleosanjose@yahoo.com; Web: www.stleochurchsj.org. Revs. Enzie Lagattuta; Eric Piczon, Parochial Vicar; Rev. Msgr. Matthew Koo, In Res., (Retired); Rev. Randy S. Valenton, In Res.
School—St. Leo the Great School, (Grades PreK-8), Tel: 408-293-4846; Email: ctorrisi@stleosj.org. Matt Komar, Prin. Lay Teachers 15; Students 245.
Catechesis Religious Program—

17—ST. MARIA GORETTI (1961)
2980 Senter Rd., 95111. Tel: 408-363-2300; Email: smgparish@smgsj.org; Web: www.smgsj.org. Revs. Justin Le; Jonathan Cuarto, Parochial Vicar; Dat Luong, Parochial Vicar; Pedro Tejeda, Parochial Vicar; Deacons Jaime Garcia; Anthony Pham.
Catechesis Religious Program—

18—ST. MARTIN OF TOURS (1914)
200 O'Connor Dr., 95128. Tel: 408-294-8953; Email: stmartinoftours@icloud.com. Revs. Saju Joseph, J.C.L.; Generoso Geronimo, (Philippines) Parochial Vicar.
School—St. Martin of Tours School, (Grades K-8), 300 O'Connor Dr., 95128. Tel: 408-287-3630; Email: mmcenery@dsj.org; Web: www.stmartinsj.org. Deborah Gisi-Rodriguez, Prin.; Ashely Lopez, Librarian. Lay Teachers 23; Students 348.
Catechesis Religious Program—

19—ST. MARY OF THE ASSUMPTION (1975) (Croatian) (Croatian Mission)
901 Lincoln Ave., 95126. Tel: 408-279-0279; Email: dgveric@dsj.org. Rev. Drago Gveric, O.F.M.
Catechesis Religious Program—Students 67.
Croatian Franciscan Fathers Corporation—
Franciscan Fathers—

20—MOST HOLY TRINITY (1961)
2040 Nassau Dr., 95122. Tel: 408-729-0101; Email: sghogan@mht-church.org. Revs. Robert A. Fambrini, S.J.; Vincent Duong, S.J., Parochial Vicar; Andrew Garcia, S.J., Parochial Vicar; Duc Vu, S.J., Parochial Vicar; Deacons Ruben Solorio; Dung Quoc Tran.
School—Most Holy Trinity School, A Drexel School, (Grades PreK-8),
Tel: 408-729-3431; Email: JMcIntyre@dsj.org. Jaime McIntyre, Prin.; Becki Diaz, Contact Person. Lay Teachers 14; Students 192.

21—OUR LADY OF GUADALUPE (1962) (Hispanic)
2020 E. San Antonio St., 95116. Tel: 408-258-7057; Email: olgparishsj@gmail.com. Revs. Gerardo Menchaca; Rolando Santoianni, I.V.E., (Argentina) Parochial Vicar; Kevin P. Joyce, In Res., (Retired).
Catechesis Religious Program—Ms. Connie Torres, D.R.E. Students 365.

22—OUR LADY OF LA VANG PARISH (1871) (Vietnamese)
389 E. Santa Clara St., 95112. Tel: 408-291-6280; Tel: 408-294-8120; Email: mtolibas@dsj.org. Mailing Address: 25 N. 14th St., Ste. 540, 95112. Revs. Peter Loi Huynh; Andrew C. Nguyen, Parochial Vicar; Peter Luc The Phan, Parochial Vicar; Deacon Tho Le.
Vietnamese Ministry—
Tel: 408-291-6280; Fax: 408-291-6289.
School—St. Patrick School, A Drexel School, (Grades K-8),
51 N. 9th St., 95112. Tel: 408-283-5858;
Fax: 408-283-5852; Email: oislas@dsj.org; Email: mhaupt@dsj.org; Email: mangeles@dsj.org; Web: www.stpatrickschool.org. Olga Islas, Prin.; Sr. Christena Papavera, Librarian. Sponsored by the Daughters of Charity. Lay Teachers 15; Students 246.

23—OUR LADY OF REFUGE
2165 Lucretia Ave., 95122. Tel: 408-715-2278; Email: llmiranda@dsj.org; Web: ourladyofrefugesj.org. Revs. Hugo Marcel Rojas; Anthony Tan Nguyen, Parochial Vicar; Sisters Silvia Frias, M.E.S.S.T., Pastoral Associate; Catherine Phuong Dang, L.H.C., D.R.E.
Catechesis Religious Program—
Mission—Santee Mission
1382 Tami Lee Dr. #4, Santa Clara Co. 95122.

24—QUEEN OF APOSTLES (1960)
4911 Moorpark Ave., 95129. Tel: 408-253-7560; Email: office@qofa.org; Web: www.qofa.org. Revs. Thuc Si Ho; Reynaldo Sarmiento, Parochial Vicar; Deacon Brian McKenna.
School—Queen of Apostles School, (Grades PreK-8), 4950 Mitty Way, 95129. Tel: 408-252-3659;
Fax: 408-873-2645; Email: guel@qofa-school.org; Web: www.qofa-school.org. Martin Chargin, Prin.; Mary Ann Sandau, Librarian. Lay Teachers 18; Students 313.
Catechesis Religious Program—

25—SACRED HEART OF JESUS (1920) (Hispanic)
325 Willow St., 95110. Tel: 408-292-0146; Email: hjimenez@dsj.org; Web: www.sacredheartsanjose.org. Revs. Walter Suarez Lopez; Andrey Garcia, Parochial Vicar; Ritche S. Bueza, In Res.
Catechesis Religious Program—

26—SANTA TERESA (1967)
794 Calero Ave., 95123. Tel: 408-889-3303; Email: info@santateresachurch.com; Web: santateresachurch.com. Rev. George Aranha; Deacon Steven Herrera.
Catechesis Religious Program—
Email: nancy@santateresachurch.com; Email: lynda@santateresachurch.com. Nancy Royal, Pastoral Assoc. and Faith Formation Dir.; Lynda DeManti, Pastoral Assoc. and RCIA Coord. Students 94.

27—ST. THOMAS OF CANTERBURY (1967)
1522 McCoy Ave., 95130. Tel: 408-378-1595;
Fax: 408-378-1215; Email: frdave@stthomassj.org; Web: www.stthomassj.org. Rev. David Mercer.
Res.: 2546 Neville Ave., 95130.
Catechesis Religious Program—
Email: vschwoob@dsj.org. Students 58.

28—ST. VICTOR (1961)
3150 Sierra Rd., 95132. Tel: 408-251-7055; Email: admin@stvictorchurch.org; Web: www.stvictorchurch.org. Mailing Address: 3108 Sierra Road, 95132. Revs. Mark Gazzingan; Allen Navarro, Parochial Vicar; John Offor, (Nigeria) Parochial Vicar; Deacon Carl Bugarin; Sr. Sara King, Pastoral Associate.
School—St. Victor School, (Grades PreK-8),
Tel: 408-251-1740; Fax: 408-251-1492; Email: pwolf@dsj.org. Patricia Wolf, Prin.; Joan Passalaqua, Librarian; Maria Victoria Hinkle, Admin.; Rosanne Huey, Business Mgr. Clergy 1; Lay Teachers 15; Students 200.
Catechesis Religious Program—St. Victor Catechetical Ministry.

OUTSIDE THE CITY OF SAN JOSE

ALVISO, SANTA CLARA CO., OUR LADY, STAR OF THE SEA (1984)
1385 Michigan Ave., Alviso, 95002.
Tel: 408-263-2121; Email: starofthesea.dsj@sbcglobal.net. Mailing Address: P.O. Box 426, Alviso, 95002-0426. Rev. Hector Basanez.
Catechesis Religious Program—Students 163.

CAMPBELL, SANTA CLARA CO., ST. LUCY (1947)
2350 Winchester Blvd., Campbell, 95008.
Tel: 408-378-2464; Email: stlucyparishoffice@dsj.org; Web: www.stlucy-campbell.org. Revs. Mark Arnzen; Steve Kim, Parochial Vicar; Deacon Harry Collins.
School—St. Lucy School, (Grades PreK-8), 76 Kennedy Ave., Campbell, 95008. Tel: 408-871-8023; Fax: 408-378-4945; Email: principal@stlucyschool.org. Susan Grover, Prin. Lay Teachers 16; Students 312.
Catechesis Religious Program—

CUPERTINO, SANTA CLARA CO., ST. JOSEPH OF CUPERTINO (1913)
10110 N. De Anza Blvd., Cupertino, 95014.
Tel: 408-252-7653; Fax: 408-252-5263; Email: sjcparish@stjoscup.org; Web: www.stjoscup.org. Revs. Gregory C. Kimm; Athanasius Kikoba, (Uganda) Parochial Vicar; Edsil Ortiz, Parochial Vicar; Deacon Ronald Hansen.
School—St. Joseph of Cupertino School, (Grades PreK-8), 10120 N. DeAnza Blvd., Cupertino, 95014.
Tel: 408-252-6441; Fax: 408-252-9771; Email: mlee@dsj.org; Web: www.sjcschool.org. Michael Lee, Prin. Lay Teachers 14; Students 270; Clergy / Religious Teachers 1.
Catechesis Religious Program—Email: catmin@stjoscup.org. Tam Tran, D.R.E. Students 144.

GILROY, SANTA CLARA CO., ST. MARY (1865) [CEM]
11 First St., Gilroy, 95020. Tel: 408-847-5151; Email: dpelliccione@dsj.org; Web: smpgilroy.org. Revs. Robert S. Brocato; Jose Rubio, S.T.D., Parochial Vicar; Johannes Busch, Parochial Vicar; Deacon Pat Allen.
School—St. Mary School, (Grades K-8), 7900 Church St., Gilroy, 95020-4499. Tel: 408-842-2827;
Fax: 408-847-7679; Email: kkramer@dsj.org; Email: pgreteman@dsj.org; Web: www.stmarygilroy.org. Pamela Greteman, Prin. Lay Teachers 23; Sisters 1; Students 252.
Catechesis Religious Program—7950 Church St., Gilroy, 95020. Email: bzarka@dsj.org. Barbara Zarka, D.R.E. Students 873.

LOS ALTOS, SANTA CLARA CO.
1—ST. NICHOLAS, Merged with St. William, Los Altos to form St. Nicholas and St. William Catholic Parish, Los Altos.
2—ST. NICHOLAS AND ST. WILLIAM CATHOLIC PARISH (1947)
473 Lincoln Ave., Los Altos, 94022.
Tel: 650-948-2158; Tel: 650-559-2080; Email: finance257@dsj.org; Web: www.stnicholasandstwilliam.org. Revs. John Poncini; Anthony Uytingco, Parochial Vicar; Deacon Charles Corbalis; Carol Thornton, Liturgy Dir.; Lidia Fiandeiro, Business Mgr.
Res.: 611 S. El Monte Ave., Los Altos, 94022.
School—St. Nicholas School, (Grades K-8), 12816 S. El Monte Ave., Los Altos Hills, 94022.
Tel: 650-941-4056; Email: jpopolizio@stnicholaslah.com; Web: www.stnicholaslah.com. Jan Popolizio, Prin.; Stacy French, Vice Prin. Lay Teachers 17; Students 255; Clergy / Religious Teachers 1.
Catechesis Religious Program—Email: ccampbell@dsj.org; Tel: 650-948-2158, Ext. 2209. Catherine Campbell, D.R.E. Students 317.
3—ST. SIMON (1955)
1860 Grant Rd., Los Altos, 94024.
Tel: 650-967-8311, Ext. 10; Fax: 650-967-8876; Email: rectory@stsimon.org; Web: www.stsimon.org. Revs. V. Warwick James; Maurice Igboerika, (Nigeria) Parochial Vicar; Mendie Nguyen, Parochial Vicar; Michael J. Burns, In Res., (Retired).
School—St. Simon School, (Grades PreK-8), 1840 Grant Rd., Los Altos, 94024. Tel: 650-968-9952;
Fax: 650-988-9308; Email: rroth@stsimon.org. Mr. Ryan Roth, Prin.; Mrs. Laura Potter. Clergy 1; Lay Teachers 31; Students 490.
Catechesis Religious Program—Email: mhnguyen@stsimon.org. Sr. Mary-Han Nguyen, D.R.E. Students 286.
4—ST. WILLIAM, Merged with St. Nicholas, Los Altos to form St. Nicholas and St. William Catholic Parish.

LOS GATOS, SANTA CLARA CO., ST. MARY OF THE IMMACULATE CONCEPTION (1912)
219 Bean Ave., Los Gatos, 95030. Tel: 408-354-3726; Email: rrodoni@stmaryslg.org; Email: mjaraya@stmaryslg.org; Web: stmaryslg.org. Revs. Rick Rodoni; Biju Varghese, (India) Parochial Vicar.
School—St. Mary of the Immaculate Conception School, (Grades K-8), 30 Lyndon Ave., Los Gatos, 95030. Tel: 408-354-3944; Fax: 408-395-9151; Email: jjohnston@stmaryslg.org; Web: www.smslg.org. James Johnston, Prin.; Sheila Chavez, Librarian. Lay Teachers 18; Students 237.

MILPITAS, SANTA CLARA CO.
1—ST. ELIZABETH (1968)
750 Sequoia Dr., Milpitas, 95035. Tel: 408-262-8100; Email: elizabethchurch@comcast.net; Web: www.stelizabethmilpitas.org. Revs. Francisco Miramontes; Vincent Tinh Thanh Dang, Parochial Vicar; Deacon John Vu.
Catechesis Religious Program—Students 526.
2—ST. JOHN THE BAPTIST (1877)
279 S. Main St., Milpitas, 95035. Tel: 408-262-2546; Email: mgonzalo@dsj.org; Web: www.sjbparish.org. Rev. Msgr. Wilfredo S. Manrique, J.C.L.; Revs. Eduardo Obero, Parochial Vicar; Andres C. Ligot, J.C.D., In Res.
School—St. John the Baptist School, (Grades PreSchool-8), 360 S. Abel St., Milpitas, 95035.
Tel: 408-262-8110; Fax: 408-262-0814; Email: info@sjbs.org; Web: www.sjbs.org. Christopher Brazil, Prin.; Jaclyn George, Librarian. Lay Teachers 10; Students 199; Clergy / Religious Teachers 3.
Catechesis Religious Program—Email: cbrazil@sjbs.org; Email: mollat@sjbparish.org. Christopher Brazil, D.R.E.; Cory Mollat, D.R.E. Students 132.

MORGAN HILL, SANTA CLARA CO., ST. CATHERINE OF ALEXANDRIA (1909)
17400 Peak Ave., Morgan Hill, 95037.
Tel: 408-779-3959; Email: office@stca.org; Web: www.stca.org. Revs. Sergio Ovando, S.T.D.; Neil Francis Kalaw, Parochial Vicar; Rev. Msgr. Francisco Rios, Parochial Vicar; Deacons Juan Aquino; Phillip Flowers; Erik Haeckel.
School—St. Catherine of Alexandria School, (Grades K-8), 17500 Peak Ave., Morgan Hill, 95037.
Tel: 408-779-9950; Fax: 408-779-9928; Email: fesparza@stcatherinemh.org; Web: www.stcatherinemh.org. Fabienne Esparza, Prin.; Linda Knox, Vice Prin. Lay Teachers 13; Students 319.
Catechesis Religious Program—

MOUNTAIN VIEW, SANTA CLARA CO.
1—ST. ATHANASIUS (1959)
160 N. Rengstorff Ave., Mountain View, 94043.
Tel: 650-961-8600, Ext. 102; Email: Athanasius@comcast.net; Web: stathanasiusparish.com. Revs. Oscar Tabujara; Paul-Cuong Phan, Parochial Vicar; Deacon Leonel Mancilla.
Catechesis Religious Program—Email: lmancilla@dsj.org. Students 146.
2—ST. JOSEPH (1901)
582 Hope St., Mountain View, 94041.
Tel: 650-967-3831; Email: dbayona@dsj.org; Web: sjpmv.org. Revs. Engelberto Gammad, J.C.D.; Thierry Geris, Parochial Vicar.
School—St. Joseph School, A Drexel School, (Grades K-8), 1120 Miramonte Ave., Mountain View, 94040.
Tel: 650-967-1839; Fax: 650-691-1530; Email: anowell@dsj.org. Anne Nowell, Prin. Lay Teachers 16; Students 276.
Catechesis Religious Program—

PALO ALTO, SANTA CLARA CO.
1—ST. ALBERT THE GREAT (1961) Merged with St. Thomas Aquinas Parish.
2—OUR LADY OF THE ROSARY (1959) Merged with St. Thomas Aquinas Parish.
3—ST. THOMAS AQUINAS (1901)
3290 Middlefield Rd., Palo Alto, 94306.
Tel: 650-494-2496; Email: emikalonis@dsj.org; Web: www.paloaltocatholic.org. Revs. Estanislao Mikalonis; Michael Gazzingan, (Philippines) Parochial Vicar; Anthony Tuong Nguyen, Parochial Vicar; Severo Kuupuo, (Ghana) In Res.; John Hester, In Res., (Retired); Deacon Daniel Hernandez.
School—St. Elizabeth Seton Catholic Community School, (Grades PreK-8), 1095 Channing Ave., Palo

Alto, 94301. Tel: 650-326-9004; Fax: 650-326-2949; Email: info@setonpaloalto.org; Web: www.setonpaloalto.org. Evelyn Rosa, Prin.; Celia Rodriguez, Librarian. Sponsored by the Daughters of Charity. Lay Teachers 20; Students 280.
Catechesis Religious Program—Email: susan.olsen@dsj.org. Susan Olsen, D.R.E.; Maria de Jesus Gutierrez, D.R.E.; Christopher Mardesich, D.R.E. Students 33.

SANTA CLARA, SANTA CLARA CO.

1—ST. CLARE (1777)
941 Lexington St., Santa Clara, 95050.
Tel: 408-248-7786; Fax: 408-248-8150; Email: stclareparish@dsj.org; Web: www.stclareparish.org. Mailing Address: 725 Washington St., Santa Clara, 95050-4935. Revs. Tadeusz Terembula; Prosper Molengi, Parochial Vicar.
School—St. Clare School, A Drexel School, (Grades K-8), Tel: 408-246-6797; Email: office@stclareschool.org; Web: www.stclareschool.org. Madeline Rader, Prin. Clergy 1; Lay Teachers 11; Students 279.
Catechesis Religious Program—Email: prascon@dsj.org. Paty Rascon, Catechetical Coord. & Hispanic Ministry Coord. Students 90.

2—ST. JUSTIN (1951)
2655 Homestead Rd., Santa Clara, 95051.
Tel: 408-248-1094; Tel: 408-296-1193; Web: www.stjustin.org. Revs. Christopher Bransfield; Gerald Nwafor, (Nigeria) Parochial Vicar; James Okafor, (Nigeria) In Res.
School—St. Justin School, (Grades PreK-8), Tel: 408-248-1094; Email: schooloffice@stjustinschool.org; Web: www.stjustinschool.org. Karen Suty, Prin. Lay Teachers 18; Students 310.
Catechesis Religious Program—

3—ST. LAWRENCE, THE MARTYR (1959)
1971 Saint Lawrence Dr., Santa Clara, 95051.
Tel: 408-296-3000; Fax: 408-296-3100; Email: parish@saintlawrence.org; Web: www.saintlawrence.org. Revs. Ernesto Orci; Joseph Page, Parochial Vicar; Richard Hilliard, In Res.
School—Saint Lawrence Elementary & Middle School, (Grades PreK-8), 1977 St. Lawrence Dr., Santa Clara, 95051. Tel: 408-296-2260; Fax: 408-615-1343; Email: gwholley@slemsorg; Email: mlopez@slems.org; Web: www.saintlawrence.org/school. Laura Gremett, Prin.; Martin Procaccio, Prin. Lay Teachers 20; Students 288.
Catechesis Religious Program—Email: edepaz@saintlawrence.org. Eleanor De Paz, D.R.E. Students 189.

4—OUR LADY OF PEACE (1961)
2800 Mission College Blvd., Santa Clara, 95054.
Tel: 408-988-4585; Email: info@olop-shrine.org; Web: www.olop-shrine.org. Revs. Brian Dinkel, I.V.E.; Jonathan Yu Dumlao, I.V.E., Parochial Vicar; Willian Montalvo, I.V.E., Parochial Vicar; Thomas Paul Steinke, I.V.E., Parochial Vicar.
Catechesis Religious Program—Tel: 408-988-7648; Email: adut.edu@olop-shrine.org; Email: olopccd@servidoras.org. Sr. Maria Nikopoia, S.S.V.M.; Mother Maria Bon Secours, S.S.V.M., D.R.E.; Sr. Maria de Foy, S.S.V.M., Dir. Children's Rel. Educ. Students 833.

5—SAN JOSE CHINESE CATHOLIC MISSION (2012) (Chinese) (Cantonese Catholic Community)
725 Washington St., Santa Clara, 95050-4966.
Tel: 408-758-8917; Email: aolivera@dsj.org; Web: sjccm.com. Revs. Carlos Alberto Olivera; Paul J. Goda, S.J., Chap., Cantonese Community.
Catechesis Religious Program—

SARATOGA, SANTA CLARA CO.

1—CHURCH OF THE ASCENSION (1964)
Mailing Address: 12033 Miller Ave., Saratoga, 95070. Tel: 408-725-3939; Email: jgalang@dsj.org; Web: www.churchoftheascension.net. Revs. Jose Galang; Noel Sanvicente, J.C.D., In Res.
Catechesis Religious Program—Email: aliebmann@dsj.org. Ms. Ann Liebmann, Youth Catechetical & Prog. Dir. Students 68.

2—SACRED HEART (1951)
13716 Saratoga Ave., Saratoga, 95070.
Tel: 408-867-3634; Email: c.orasin@sacredheartsaratoga.org; Web: www.sacredheartsaratoga.org. Revs. Gary Thomas; Robert McKay, (South Africa) Ph.D., Parochial Vicar; Deacon Donald Sifferman.
School—Sacred Heart School, (Grades PreK-8), 13718 Saratoga Ave., Saratoga, 95070.
Tel: 408-867-9241; Fax: 408-867-9242; Email: webmaster@sacredheartsaratoga.org; Web: school.sacredheartsaratoga.org. Tom Pulchny, Prin. Lay Teachers 17; Students 265.
Child Care—Pre-School, Lay Teachers 3; Students 14.
Catechesis Religious Program—

STANFORD, SANTA CLARA CO., CATHOLIC COMMUNITY AT STANFORD (1997)
Mailing Address: Old Union, 3rd Floor, Stanford University, P.O. Box 20301, Stanford, 94309.
Tel: 650-725-0080; Email: admin@stanfordcatholic.org; Web: http://web.stanfordcatholic.org. Revs. Xavier Lavagetto, O.P.; Dominic DeLay, O.P., Parochial Vicar; Robert Glynn, S.J., Chap.; Deacon John Kerrigan.
Catechesis Religious Program—Students 95.

SUNNYVALE, SANTA CLARA CO.

1—CHURCH OF THE RESURRECTION (1963)
1399 Hollenbeck Ave., Sunnyvale, 94087.
Tel: 408-245-5554; Email: maryclare@resparish.org; Web: www.resparish.net. Mailing Address: 725 Cascade Dr., Sunnyvale, 94087. Revs. John Doanh Phong Nguyen, S.J.; Arthur Yabes, S.V.D., Parochial Vicar; Andrzej Salapata, (Poland) In Res.; Deacon Michael Haas.
School—Church of the Resurrection Elementary School, A Drexel School, (Grades PreSchool-8), 1395 Hollenbeck Ave., Sunnyvale, 94087.
Tel: 408-245-4571; Email: marie.reid@rescatholicschool.org; Email: school@rescatholicschool.org; Web: http://rescatholicschool.org/. Jacqueline T. Wright, Prin. Lay Teachers 18; Sisters 1; Students 224.
Catechesis Religious Program—Students 117.

2—ST. CYPRIAN (1961)
195 Leota Ave., Sunnyvale, 94086. Tel: 408-739-8506; Email: info@saintcyprian.org; Web: www.saintcyprian.org. Mailing Address: 1133 W. Washington Ave., Sunnyvale, 94086. Revs. Vincent Pineda; Martin Chukwunenye Ezeador, In Res.
Catechesis Religious Program—

3—ST. MARTIN (1916)
590 Central Ave., Sunnyvale, 94086.
Tel: 408-736-3724; Email: stmartinparishsv@yahoo.com; Web: www.saintmartinparish.org. Revs. Roberto Gomez; Hao Dinh, Parochial Vicar; Ed Samy, In Res., (Retired); Deacon Dung Quoc Tran.
Catechesis Religious Program—593 Central Ave., Sunnyvale, 94086. Tel: 408-736-3725; Email: ncordova@dsj.org. Nancy Cordova, Dir. Faith Formation. Students 98.

Chaplains of Public Institutions

SAN JOSE. *Catholic Scouting*. Rev. Paul A. Soukup, S.J., Tel: 408-554-4124.
Detention Ministry for Juveniles. Rev. Daniel C. Urcia, Ed.D., Tel: 408-983-0134.
Notre Dame Club of San Jose/Silicon Valley. Very Rev. Brendan McGuire, V.G.
O'Connor Hospital. Revs. Andrzej Salapata, (Poland) Chap., Randy S. Valenton, Chap.
Santa Clara County Jail. Rev. Daniel C. Urcia, Ed.D.
Santa Clara County Women's Facility. Sr. Maryann Cantlon, C.S.J.
Santa Clara Valley Medical Center. Revs. Kevin Ballard, S.J., Andrzej Salapata, (Poland), Thomas E. Splain, S.J., Randy S. Valenton, Sr. Donna Marie Moses, OP.

STANFORD. *Stanford Medical Center*. Rev. Samuel Oppong.

Special Assignment:
Rev. Msgr.—
Cilia, Francis V., V.G., Vicar Gen., Mod. of the Curia & Assoc. Vicar for Clergy
Very Rev.—
McGuire, Brendan, V.G., Vicar Gen. for Special Projects
Revs.—
Benedict, Joseph, S.T.D., Ongoing Formation of Clergy
Bueza, Ritche S., Dir. Vocations & Vicar Filipino Min.
Carson, Michael, Assoc. Dir. for Native American Affairs, USCCB, Washington, DC
Dinh, Hao, Vicar for Vietnamese Ministry
Geronimo, Generoso, (Philippines) Vicar for Priests
Hayes, Robert E., J.C.L., Judicial Vicariate, Defender of the Bond
Hurley, John, C.S.P., Vicar for Evangelization
Kim, Joseph, Theological Studies, Rome
Kim, Steve, Campus Minister, St. Francis High School (part-time)
Ligot, Andres C., J.C.D., Judicial Vicar
Mancuso, Anthony, Interim Pres. and Chap., St. Francis High School
O'Toole, Barry, L.C., Hospital Ministry
Ovando, Sergio, S.T.D., Chair of Faith Formation Commission
Pedigo, Jon, S.T.L., Dir. Advocacy and Community Engagement, Catholic Charities
Rubio, Jose, S.T.D., Dir. Ecumenical & Interreligious Affairs & Delegate Eastern Rite Churches
Salapata, Andrzej, (Poland) Hospital Ministry
Sanvicente, Noel, J.C.D., Adjutant Judicial Vicar, Judicial Vicariate
Suarez, Walter, Vicar Hispanic Min.
Urcia, Daniel C., Ed.D., Chap., Restorative Justice Ministry
Valenton, Randy S., Hospital Ministry
Vanthu, Joseph N., Dir. Vietnamese Catholic Center, (Retired).

On Duty Outside the Diocese:
Revs.—
Carson, Michael, Assoc. Dir. Native American Affairs, USCCB
Kim, Joseph, Theological Studies, Rome
Royston, Basil G., D.Min., Archdiocese of Guadalajara, Mexico.

On Leave of Absence:
Rev. Msgr.—
Nguyen, Hien Minh, J.C.D.
Revs.—
Abrego, Martin
Benas, Randy
Gray, Robert
Hernandez, Enrico
Rojas, Roberto.

Retired:
Most Rev.—
DuMaine, R. Pierre, (Retired)
Rev. Msgrs.—
Andre, Ludwig, (Retired)
Browne, J. Patrick, (Retired)
Coleman, John, (Retired)
Do, Dominic Dinh, (Retired)
Koo, Matthew, (Retired)
Larkin, Alexander C., (Retired)
Milani, Joseph J., (Retired)
Mitchell, Michael J., (Retired)
O'Donnell, Eugene P., (Retired)
Perata, Stephen, (Retired)
Sandersfeld, John, (Retired)
Sullivan, Terrence J., (Retired)
Walsh, James, (Retired)
Revs.—
Bonsor, Jack, (Retired)
Burns, Michael J., (Retired)
Davis, Terence, (Retired)
Derry, Daniel, (Retired)
Duong, Paul, (Retired)
Hester, John, (Retired)
Joyce, Kevin P., (Retired)
Kilcoyne, Patrick, (Retired)
LaRocca, Jack, (Retired)
Leger, G. Robert, (Retired)
Leininger, William, (Retired)
Lopez, Abel, J.C.L., (Retired)
Mancha, George, (Retired)
Manding, Benito O., (Retired)
McMahon, Walter M., (Retired)
Moran, Robert, (Retired)
Morgan, W. Donald, (Retired)
Neary, Mark, (Retired)
Pegnam, William, (Retired)
Percell, Lawrence, (Retired)
Rich, Joseph, (Retired)
Samy, Ed, (Retired)
Saso, Michael, (Retired)
Segovia, Norman, (Retired)
Tinh, Joseph Nguyen, (Retired)
Traverso, Leonard, (Retired)
Vanthu, Joseph N., (Retired)
Weisbeck, Paul, (Retired).

Permanent Deacons:
Agbayani, Willy, Restorative Justice, Liturgical Min., St. Francis of Assisi
Allen, Pat, St. Mary, Gilroy
Alvarez, Joseph, (Retired)
Aquino, Juan, St. Catherine of Alexandria
Bugarin, Carl, St. Victor
Collins, Harry, (Retired)
Corbalis, Charles, St. Nicholas and St. William
Flowers, Phillip, St. Catherine of Alexandria
Gans, Raymond, Holy Family
Garcia, Jamie, St. Maria Goretti
Haas, Michael, Church of the Resurrection
Haeckel, Eric, St. Catherine of Alexandria
Hansen, Ronald, St. Joseph of Cupertino
Hernandez, Daniel, St. Thomas Aquinas
Herrera, Steven, Santa Teresa, San Jose; Immersion Trip Coord.
Ho, Joseph Nhut, (Retired)
Hoang, Joseph The, Christ the King; Catholic Charities
Hoffman, Lou, (Retired)
Huynh, Joseph N., (Retired)
Kerrigan, John, Catholic Comm. at Stanford
Le, Tho, Our Lady of La Vang
Malone, Robert, Residing Outside the Diocese
Mancilla, Leonel, St. Athanasius
McCarty, Philip, St. Leo the Great
McKenna, Brian, Queen of Apostles
Mendoza, Raul, St. John Vianney

Noack, Richard, St. Christopher
Nojadera, Bernard V., USCCB, Washington, DC
Offorjebe, Sunny, St. Francis of Assisi
Ortiz, Gregorio, Cathedral Basilica of St. Joseph
Perez, Vicente, (Retired)
Pham, Anthony, Restorative Justice, Liturgical Min., St. Maria Goretti
Sifferman, Donald, Sacred Heart, Saratoga; Children's Hospital, Stanford
Sobczyk, Andrzej, St. Francis of Assisi
Solorio, Ruben, Most Holy Trinity
Tran, Dung Quoc, Most Holy Trinity; Vietnamese Catholic Center
Vu, John, St. Elizabeth
Zorio, Bruce, St. Christopher.

INSTITUTIONS LOCATED IN DIOCESE

[A] SHRINES

SANTA CLARA. *Shrine of Our Lady of Peace*, 2800 Mission College Blvd., Santa Clara, 95054. Tel: 408-988-4585; Fax: 408-988-0679; Email: info@olop-shrine.org. Rev. Brian Dinkel, I.V.E., Dir.

Our Lady of Peace Gift Shop, Tel: 408-980-9825; Fax: 408-988-2488.

[B] COLLEGES AND UNIVERSITIES

SANTA CLARA. *Santa Clara University*, 500 El Camino Real, Santa Clara, 95053-0001. Tel: 408-554-4000; Tel: 408-554-4160; Fax: 408-554-2700; Email: surveyrequests@scu.edu; Web: www.scu.edu. Revs. Michael E. Engh, S.J., Pres.; William J. Rewak, S.J., Chancellor; Michael Crowley, Vice Pres.; Dr. Dennis Jacobs, Provost & Vice Pres., Academic Affairs; James Lyons, Vice Pres., Univ. Rels.; Michael Sexton, Vice Pres., Enrollment Mgmt.; Molly McDonald, Admin.; John Ottoboni, Admin.; Caryn Beck-Dudley, Dean; Lisa Kloppenberg, Dean; Rev. Kevin O'Brien, S.J., Dean; Dr. Debbie Tahmassebi, Dean; Dr. Sabrina Zirkel, Dean; Renee Baumgartner, Dir.; Don Heider, Dir.; Thane Kreiner, Dir.; Revs. Dorian Llywelyn, S.J., Dir.; John R. Treacy, S.J., Chap.; Jennifer Nutefall, Librarian. Clergy 73; Students 8,642; Clergy / Religious Teachers 23.

Jesuit School of Theology of Santa Clara University (Society of Jesus)A graduate school of Santa Clara University, located in Berkeley, CA. (Please see the Diocese of Oakland for full listing.); Mission Santa Clara. Founded in 1777. University established in 1851 and chartered by the State in 1855. Lay Teachers 529; Students 8,422; Priest Teachers 29.

Jesuit Community, 500 El Camino Real, Santa Clara, 95053-1600. Tel: 408-554-4124; Fax: 408-554-4795; Email: jblaettler@scu.edu. Revs. Arthur F. Liebscher, S.J., Rector Jesuit Community; Samuel P. Bellino, S.J.; James R. Blaettler, S.J.; Constant Bossou, S.J.; Luis F. Calero, S.J.; Paul G. Crowley, S.J.; Fady El Chidiac, S.J.; Michael E. Engh, S.J.; Mark Fusco, S.J.; Andrew J. Garavel, S.J.; Paul J. Goda, S.J.; Paul P. Mariani, S.J.; John P. Mossi, S.J.; Alfred E. Naucke, S.J.; Thao N. Nguyen, S.J.; Peter G. Pabst, S.J.; Dennis R. Parnell, S.J.; Charles T. Phipps, S.J.; William J. Rewak, S.J.; Robert W. Scholla, S.J.; Dennis C. Smolarski, S.J.; Paul A. Soukup, S.J.; Salvatore A. Tassone, S.J.; John R. Treacy, S.J.; Maria Joseph Israel, S.J.; Gerald Robinson, S.J.; Michael A. Zampelli, S.J.; J. Kevin Waters, S.J.; Bros. Jeffrey R. Allen, S.J.; Mr. Thomas C. Bracco, S.J.; Mr. Edward Ngo, Member; Barbara J. Murray, Librarian

Jesuit Community at Santa Clara University, Inc. Priests 29.

[C] HIGH SCHOOLS, DIOCESAN

SAN JOSE. *Archbishop Mitty High School* (Coed) 5000 Mitty Ave., 95129. Tel: 408-252-6610; Email: brosnan@mitty.com; Web: www.mitty.com. Mr. Timothy Brosnan, Pres.; Kate Caputo, Prin. Lay Teachers 116; Students 1,741; Total Staff 190.

[D] HIGH SCHOOLS, PRIVATE

SAN JOSE. *Bellarmine College Preparatory*, 960 W. Hedding St., 95126. Tel: 408-294-9224; Fax: 408-294-1894; Email: tdelcarlo@bcp.org; Web: www.bcp.org. Kristina Luscher, Prin.; Chris Meyercord, Pres.; Rev. Gerald T. Wade, S.J., Chancellor; Tana Perotin, Librarian; Revs. Mario J. Prietto, S.J., Supr. & Contact; Richard E. Cobb, S.J.; Michael Moodie, S.J.; Robert J. Shinney, S.J.; Most Rev. Carlos A. Sevilla, S.J. Society of Jesus. Lay Teachers 112; Priests 5; Students 1,640; Clergy / Religious Teachers 2.

**Cristo Rey San Jose High School*, 1389 E. Santa Clara St., 95116. Tel: 408-293-0425; Fax: 408-293-5607; Email: peter.pabst@cristoreysj.org; Web: www.cristoreysanjose.org. Dr. Margaret Higgins, Pres.; Rev. Peter G. Pabst, S.J., Chancellor; Joe Dazols Albers, Prin. Society of Jesus Lay Teachers 40; Students 451; Clergy / Religious Teachers 1.

Notre Dame High School, 596 S. Second St., 95112. Tel: 408-294-1113; Fax: 408-293-9779; Email: mbriley@ndsj.org; Web: www.ndsj.org. Mary Beth Riley, Prin.; Amy Huang, Dir. Digital Learning & Resources. Sisters of Notre Dame de Namur. Lay Teachers 61; Students 639; Total Staff 88; Clergy / Religious Teachers 1.

Presentation High School, 2281 Plummer Ave., 95125. Tel: 408-264-1664; Fax: 408-264-2043; Email: lblythe@presentationhs.org; Web: www.presentationhs.org. Rev. Rick Rodoni, Chap.; Mrs. Katherine Georgiev, Prin. Sisters of the Presentation. Lay Teachers 70; Students 830; Total Staff 101.

MORGAN HILL. *Saint John XXIII College Prep*, 2350 Winchester Blvd., Campbell, 95008-4098. Tel: 408-378-2464; Email: skim@dsj.org. Rev. Steve Kim, Contact Person.

MOUNTAIN VIEW. *St. Francis High School*, 1885 Miramonte Ave., Mountain View, 94040. Tel: 650-968-1213; Fax: 650-968-3241; Email: dianewilson@sfhs.com; Web: www.sfhs.com. Katie Peekell, Prin.; Rev. Anthony J. Mancuso, Ed.D., Pres.; Mr. Simon Raines, Dir.; Rev. Steve Kim, Chap.; Ann Lane, Librarian. Brothers of Holy Cross. Lay Teachers 104; Priests 2; Students 1,760; Total Staff 172.

[E] MIDDLE SCHOOLS, PRIVATE

SAN JOSE. *Sacred Heart Nativity School*, (Grades 6-8), 310 Edwards, 95110. Tel: 408-993-1293; Fax: 408-993-0675; Email: development@shnativity.org; Web: www.shnativity.org. Lorraine Shepherd, Prin.; Deacon Ruben Solorio, Pres. Clergy 1; Lay Teachers 8; Students 105; Total Staff 19.

CAMPBELL. *Canyon Heights Academy, Inc.*, (Grades PreSchool-8), 775 Waldo Rd., Campbell, 95008. Tel: 408-370-6727; Email: mrichardson@chamail.net; Web: www.canyonheightsacademy.com. Margaret Richardson, Ed.D., Head of School; Fr. Anthony Sortino, Chap. Lay Teachers 25; Students 277; Clergy / Religious Teachers 1.

[F] CATHOLIC CHARITIES OF THE DIOCESE OF SAN JOSE

SAN JOSE. *Catholic Charities of Santa Clara County* Services Divisions: Advocacy & Community Engagement; Behavioral Health Svcs.; Children, Youth & Family Devel.; Economic Devel. Svcs.; Emergency Programs & Housing Svcs.; Refugee Svcs. 2625 Zanker Rd., 95134. Tel: 408-468-0100; Fax: 408-944-0275; Email: info@catholiccharitiesscc.org; Web: www.catholiccharitiesscc.org. Gregory R. Kepferle, CEO; Margaret Williams, CAO & CFO; Susan Lucas-Taylor, CDO; Lin Velasquez, CHRO; Sara Reyes, Sr. Div. Dir. Children, Youth & Family Devel.; Elia Latif, Div. Dir. Economic Devel. Svcs.; Brady Umfleet, Div. Dir. Behavioral Health Svcs.; Candace Chen, Div. Dir. Refugee Foster Care; Lindsey Caldwell, Div. Dir. Emergency Progs. & Housing Svcs.; Rev. Jon Pedigo, S.T.L., Div. Dir. Advocacy & Community Engagement; Caroline Ocampo, Dir. Communications & Public Affairs. Tot Asst. Annually 38,000; Total Staff 544.

Advocacy & Community Engagement, 2625 Zanker Rd., 95134. Tel: 408-468-0100; Email: info@catholiccharitiesscc.org.

Handicapables, Tel: 408-468-0100.

Parish Partnerships, Tel: 408-468-1011.

Step Up Silicon Valley, Tel: 408-468-0100.

Volunteers, Tel: 408-468-0100.

Behavioral Health Services, 2625 Zanker Rd., 95134. Tel: 408-468-0100; Email: info@catholiccharitiesscc.org.

Older Adult Wellness Center, Tel: 408-468-0100.

Restorative Justice Center, Tel: 408-468-0100.

Youth & Family Wellness Center, Tel: 408-468-0100.

Children, Youth & Family Development, 2625 Zanker Rd., 95134. Tel: 408-468-0100; Email: info@catholiccharitiesscc.org.

Adult Day Care Services, 2625 Zanker Rd., 95134. Tel: 408-468-0100.

Bridges of Hope, Tel: 408-468-0100.

CORAL (Communities Organizing Resources to Advance Learning), Tel: 408-283-6150.

Family Resource Centers, Tel: 408-468-0100.

Franklin McKinley's Children's Initiative, Tel: 408-283-6150.

Long Term Care Ombudsman, Tel: 408-944-0567.

Probation Gang Resistance & Intervention Program, Tel: 408-468-0100.

Senior Community Services, Tel: 408-468-0100.

Washington United Youth Center, Tel: 408-938-6731.

Youth Empowerment for Success, Tel: 408-283-6150.

Economic Development Services, 2625 Zanker Rd., 95134. Tel: 408-468-0100; Email: info@catholiccharitiesscc.org.

Car Donation, Tel: 866-565-5912.

Disaster Recovery Services, Tel: 408-468-0100.

Employment Services, Tel: 408-468-0100.

Home Care Aide Certification & Placement Services, Tel: 408-468-0100.

Immigration Legal Services, Tel: 408-468-0100.

Refugee & Immigration Integration, Tel: 408-468-0100.

Responsible Landlord English Initiative, Tel: 408-283-6150.

Emergency Program & Housing Services, 2625 Zanker Rd., 95134. Tel: 408-468-0100; Email: info@catholiccharitiesscc.org.

Housing Sharing, Tel: 408-468-0100.

Supportive Housing Services, Tel: 408-468-0100.

Refugee Services, 2625 Zanker Rd., 95134. Tel: 408-468-0100; Email: info@catholiccharitiesscc.org.

Refugee Resettlement, Tel: 408-468-0100.

Refugee Foster Care, Tel: 408-468-0100.

[G] HOTEL, SENIOR CITIZENS RESIDENCE

SAN JOSE. *Giovanni Center, Inc.*, 85 S. Fifth St., 95112. Tel: 408-288-7436; Fax: 408-288-7264; Email: jeannedarc@jsco.net. Joshua Fass, Property Mgr. A California nonprofit charitable, public-benefit, housing project for low-income elderly. Sponsored by the Roman Catholic Bishop of San Jose, a corporation sole. Lay Staff 3; Residents 30; Units 24.

Jeanne d'Arc Manor, 85 S. Fifth St., 95112. Tel: 408-288-7421; Fax: 408-288-7264; Email: jeannedarc@jsco.net. Joshua Fass, Property Mgr. Housing project for low-income elderly and disabled. Sponsored by the Roman Catholic Bishop of San Jose, A Corporation Sole. Lay Staff 10; Residents 110; Units 87.

[H] HOMES FOR THE AGED

MOUNTAIN VIEW. *Villa Siena*, 1855 Miramonte Ave., Mountain View, 94040. Tel: 650-961-6484; Fax: 650-961-6254; Email: cbernard@villa-siena.org; Web: www.villa-siena.org. Mrs. Corine Bernard, Exec. Dir.; Sr. Janet Barrett, D.C., Pres. & Bd. Chm. Daughters of Charity of St. Vincent de Paul.Residential Care and Skilled Nursing Facility. Residents 100; Total Staff 90; In Nursing Care 20; Nursing Staff 30; Professed Sisters 3.

[I] RETREATS

LOS ALTOS. *Jesuit Retreat Center of Los Altos*, 300 Manresa Way, Los Altos, 94022. Tel: 650-917-4000 ; Web: www.jrclosaltos.org. Revs. Robert J. Fabing, S.J., Dir.; Kevin Leidich, S.J., Supr.; Chi V. Ngo, S.J., Dir.; Andrew Rodriguez, S.J., Pastoral Min./ Coord.; Robert Glynn, S.J., In Res.; Russell J. Roide, S.J., In Res. Priests 6.

[J] MONASTERIES AND RESIDENCES OF PRIESTS AND BROTHERS

SAN JOSE. *Carmelite Monastery, Novitiate*, P.O. Box 3420, 95156-3420. Tel: 408-251-1361; Fax: 408-251-1854; Email: geraldtwerner@aol.com. 12455 Clayton Rd., 95127. Revs. James Geoghegan, O.C.D.; Robert Barcelos, O.C.D., Novice Master; John Colm Stone, O.C.D.; Patrick Sugrue, O.C.D.; Paul Koenig; Very Rev. Gerald Werner, O.C.D., Prior. Brothers 2; Priests 6.

CUPERTINO. *The Marianist Center*, 22683 Alcalde Rd., Cupertino, 95014. Tel: 408-207-4800; Fax: 408-255-9006; Email: somervillej1@gmail.com. Revs. Robert Hackel, S.M.; Joseph Hartzler, S.M.; Robert Hughes, S.M.; Raymond Malley, S.M.; John Putka, S.M.; Stephen Tutas, S.M.; Bros. William Bolts, S.M.; Thomas Deasy, S.M.; Thomas Farnsworth, S.M.; Robert Hoppe, S.M.; Howard Hughes, S.M.; James Leahy, S.M.; Robert Metzger, S.M.; Stanley Murakami, S.M.; Michael Murphy, S.M.; John Samaha, S.M.; John Schlund, S.M.; Ed Shiras, S.M.; John Somerville, S.M., Dir.; Frank Spaeth, S.M.; LeRoy Viera, S.M.; Jim Vorndran, S.M.; Vincent Wayer, S.M. Marianist Center. Brothers 17; Priests 6; Total in Residence 23. *The Alcalde House*, 22683 Alcalde Rd., Cupertino, 95014-3903. Tel: 408-207-4808; Fax: 408-255-9006; Email: somervillej1@gmail.com. Bro. Jack Somerville, Dir. Brothers 1; Total in Residence 1. *The Bordeaux House*, 22683 Alcalde Rd., Cupertino, 95014. Tel: 408-207-4800; Fax: 408-255-9006; Email: somervillej1@gmail.com. Bro. Vincent Wayer, S.M. Brothers 3; Total in Residence 4. Living In Other Residences: Bro. Robert Juenemann, S.M., Avila House, 618 Crestmoor Dr., 95129. Tel: 408-861-0560.

LOS ALTOS. *Maryknoll*, 23000 Cristo Rey Dr., Los

Altos, 94024. Tel: 650-386-4342; Fax: 650-386-4377 ; Email: maryknolllosaltos@maryknoll.org; Web: www.maryknollsociety.org. Most Rev. J. Quinn Weitzel, M.M.; Revs. William M. Boteler, M.M.; Robert J. Carleton, M.M.; John Conway, M.M.; Robert Coyne, M.M.; Marvin Deutsch, M.M.; Joseph Hermes, M.M.; Stephen Judd, M.M., Dir.; Joseph A. Klecha, M.M.; Thomas Marti, M.M.; John Moynihan, M.M.; Bryce Nishimura, M.M.; Philip F. Sheerin, M.M.; John Soltis, M.M.; Bros. Joseph Dowling, M.M.; Edward Redmond, M.M.; Venard Ruane, M.M.; Leo V. Shedy, M.M. Maryknoll Residence for Priests and Brothers. Brothers 3; Priests 10; Bishops 1.

LOS GATOS. *USA West Province, Society of Jesus*, 300 College Ave, Los Gatos, 95030-7009.
Tel: 503-226-6977; Fax: 503-228-6741; Email: uweprovince@jesuits.org; Web: www.jesuitswest.org. P.O. Box 519, Los Gatos, 95031-0519. Very Rev. Scott Santarosa, S.J., Prov.; Revs. Alfred E. Naucke, S.J., Prov. Sec.; Michael Bayard, S.J., Socius; John M. Martin, S.J., Treas.; Glen Butterworth, S.J., Tertian; Christopher Nguyen, S.J., Vocation Dir.; Christopher Weekly, S.J., Asst. for Parish & Spiritual Ministries; Theodore Gabrielli, S.J., Asst. for International Ministries; Michael Gilson, S.J., Asst. for Secondary & Pre-Secondary Education; Anthony E. Sholander, S.J., Delegate for Formation & Asst. for Planning; Ignatius Ohno, S.J., Delegate for Sr. Jesuits; Robert R. Ballecer, S.J.; Victor M. Cancino, S.J.; Thomas J. Carroll, S.J.; Joseph V. Dao, S.J.; Roberto Carlos Duran, S.J.; Edward S. Fassett, S.J.; Mr. Thomas J. Flowers, S.J.; Fred J. Green, S.J.; Robert B. Grimaldi, S.J.; Lawrence P. Herrera, S.J.; Scott M. Lewis, S.J.; John J. McLain, S.J.; Bartholomew J. Murphy, S.J.; Wafik H. Nasry, S.J.; J. Alejandro Olayo Mendez, S.J.; Stephen F. Pisano, S.J.; Mark A. Ravizza, S.J.; Richard J. Schneck, S.J.; Thomas P. Sherman, S.J.; Peter K. Siu, S.J.; Thomas H. Smolich, S.J.; Daniel T. Spotswood, S.J.; Marc P. Valadao, S.J.

USA West Province, Society of Jesus; Society of Jesus, Oregon Province, Portland, OR; The Pioneer Educational Society, Spokane, WA; Montana Catholic Missions, SJ; The Society of Jesus, Alaska; Jesuit Seminary Association; California Jesuit Missionaries; Our Lady of the Oaks dba Jesuit Retreat Center of the Sierra. Brothers 23; Priests 288; Scholastics 71.

Sacred Heart Jesuit Center, Provincial Office, P.O. Box 519, Los Gatos, 95031. Tel: 408-884-1700;
Fax: 408-884-1701; Email: jprivett@jesuits.org. Revs. John Privett, S.J., Supr.; Richard Case, S.J., Asst. Supr.; John M. Martin, S.J., Treas.; Denis Collins, S.J., Retreat Dir.; Joseph J. Fice, S.J., Retreat and Spiritual Dir.; Thomas G. Allender, S.J.; Joseph T. Angilella, S.J.; Kenneth Baker, S.J.; Kevin Ballard, S.J.; Arnold Beezer, S.J.; Paul Bernadicou, S.J.; E. Louis Bishop, S.J.; Richard Brown, S.J.; Michael J. Buckley, S.J.; Peter Burns, S.J.; Bernard J. Bush, S.J.; George A. Carroll, S.J.; Thomas Connolly, S.J.; James Conyard, S.J.; Michael Cook, S.J.; Bernard Coughlin, S.J.; George J. Dumais, S.J.; Robert James Egan, S.J.; James W. Felt, S.J.; Thomas P. Finsterbach, S.J.; L. Paul Fitterer, S.J.; Robert Fitts, S.J.; John F. Foster, S.J.; Thomas W. Foster, S.J.; Thomas W. Franxman, S.J.; William J. Fulco, S.J.; Thomas Gallagher, S.J.; Reynold J. Gatto, S.J.; Gerald Gordon, S.J.; Albert Grosskopf, S.J.; Leo J. Hombach, S.J.; James R. Laudwein, S.J.; Jerold W. Lindner, S.J.; Andrew Maddock, S.J.; Terrence L. Mahan, S.J.; Ernest R. Martinez, S.J.; Robert B. Mathewson, S.J.; Joseph W. Morris, S.J.; Armand M. Nigro, S.J.; Charles R. Olsen, S.J.; Louis A. Peinado, S.J.; Charles Peterson, S.J.; Thomas G. Piquado, S.J.; L. Michael Pope, S.J.; J. Daniel Powers, S.J.; Jamie J. Rasura, S.J.; James Reichmann, S.J.; Thomas J. Reilly, S.J.; John Ridgway, S.J.; Anastacio S. Rivera, S.J.; Lawrence Robinson, S.J.; Richard Rolfs, S.J.; James Rude, S.J.; James V. Schall, S.J.; Robert Schlim, S.J.; Francis R. Smith, S.J.; Thomas E. Splain, S.J.; Patrick Stewart, S.J.; Peter J. Togni, S.J.; Frederick P. Tollini, S.J.; Bernard Tyrrell, S.J.; Gary Uhlenkott, S.J.; Anthony P. Via, S.J.; Silvano P. Votto, S.J.; Carlton E. Whitten, S.J.; Thomas G. Williams, S.J.; Bros. Michael Bennett, S.J.; Justin A. DeChance, S.J.; William C. Farrington, S.J.; John E. Keck, S.J.; Thomas Koller, S.J.; James Lee, S.J.; Frederick Mercy, S.J.; Charles J. Onorato, S.J.; Daniel J. Peterson, S.J.; Theodore C. Rohrer, S.J.

California Province of the Society of Jesus dba Sacred Heart Jesuit Center Brothers 10; Priests 73.

SANTA CLARA. *Casa San Inigo, Jesuit Residence*, 1075 Benton St., Santa Clara, 95050-4801.
Tel: 408-642-1406; Email: ctilley@jesuits.org. Revs. Charles J. Tilley, S.J., Community Coord.; Samuel P. Bellino, S.J.; Peter G. Pabst, S.J.; Bro. Jeffrey R. Allen, S.J. Brothers 1; Priests 3.

The Institute of the Incarnate Word (IVE), 2800 Mission College Blvd., Santa Clara, 95054.
Tel: 408-988-4585; Email: bdinkel@dsj.org. Revs. Brian Dinkel, I.V.E.; Jonathan Yu Dumlao, I.V.E.; Willian Montalvo, I.V.E.; Thomas Paul Steinke, I.V.E. Priests 4.

Jesuit Community Please see listing under Santa Clara University, located under Colleges and Universities. 500 El Camino Real, Santa Clara, 95053. Tel: 408-554-4124; Fax: 408-554-4795; Email: jblaettler@jesuits.org. Rev. James R. Blaettler, S.J., Min. to Jesuit Community. Brothers 1; Priests 27.

[K] CONVENTS AND RESIDENCES FOR SISTERS

SAN JOSE. *Community of the Holy Spirit*, 1275 Naglee Ave., 95126. Tel: 408-275-1710. Sr. Jolene M. Schmitz, C.H.S., Contact. Sisters 1.

Daughters of Charity of St. Vincent de Paul, O'Connor Sisters Home, 350 O'Connor Dr., 95128.
Tel: 408-862-9377; Email: srmrandall@doc1633.org. Sr. Julie Kubasak, D.C., Prov. Sisters 6.

Eucharistic Missionaries of the Most Holy Trinity, 815 S. Daniel Way, 95128. Tel: 408-243-3157; Email: giselamesst@hotmail.com. Mother Maria Gisela N. Enriquez, M.E.S.S.T., Supr. Sisters 4.

La Salle Sisters, 3867 Silver Creek Rd., 95121-1969.
Tel: 408-238-9351; Email: thuha87@yahoo.com; Email: atdo@scu.edu; Web: thelasallesisters.org. Sisters Thuha Nguyen, L.S.S, Supr.; Anhloan Do, L.S.S., Dir.; Olivia Thanh Vu, L.S.S., Sec.; Magdalene BachTuyet Nguyen, L.S.S., Librarian; Theresa Thu Ha Nguyen, L.S.S., Contact Person. Sisters 14.

Quinhon Missionary Sisters of the Holy Cross, 368 Neilson Ct., 95111. Tel: 408-362-9719;
Tel: 408-362-0148; Email: cdang@dsj.org; Web: http://www.mtgqn.org. Sr. Magdalena Duong, Supr. Sisters 8.

Sinsinawa Dominican Congregation of the Most Holy Rosary, 2024 McDaniel Ave., #2, 95128.
Tel: 408-298-4050; Email: virginia@pflugler.org. Sr. Virginia Pfluger, O.P., Local Contact. Sisters 1.

Sisters of Mercy of Americas (Burlingame), 1600 Petersen Ave., #40, 95129. Tel: 408-500-5441;
Fax: 408-550-9983; Email: eloros@global.net. Sr. Laura Reicks, Regional Pres. Sisters 3.

CUPERTINO. *Blessed Virgin Missionaries of Carmel (B.V.M.C.)*, 10130 N. De Anza Blvd., Cupertino, 95014. Tel: 408-257-1022; Email: srkristine2010@gmail.com. Sr. Gloria P. Solis, B.V.M.C., Supr. Sisters 3.

LOS ALTOS HILLS. *Daughters of Charity of St. Vincent de Paul, Seton Provincialate*, 26000 Altamont Rd., Los Altos Hills, 94022. Tel: 650-941-4490;
Fax: 650-949-8883; Email: srjkubasak@doc1633.org; Web: www.daughtersofcharity.com. Sr. Julie Kubasak, D.C., Prov. Sisters 51; Total in Province 102; Total in Diocese 51.

Immaculate Heart Monastery of the Poor Clares, 28210 Natoma Rd., Los Altos Hills, 94022-3320.
Tel: 650-948-2947; Email: tatiana@promessi.com; Web: http://poorclareslosaltos.org. Mother Maura Heinen, P.C.C., Abbess. Sisters 25.

LOS GATOS. *Sisters of the Holy Names of Jesus & Mary*, P.O. Box 907, Los Gatos, 95031-0907.
Tel: 408-395-0259; Email: kondreyco@snjmuson.org; Web: www.snjmusontario.org. Sisters Maureen Delaney, S.N.J.M., Prov. Supr. & Contact; Mary Breiling, S.N.J.M., Leadership Team; Guadalupe Guajardo, S.N.J.M., Leadership Team; Margaret Kennedy, S.N.J.M., Leadership Team; Rita Rohoe, S.N.J.M., Leadership Team. Sisters of the Holy Names of Jesus and Mary US-Ontario Province.Other sisters reside in communities in Campbell, San Jose, Saratoga, and Sunnyvale. Sisters 125.

MILPITAS. *The Congregation of the Augustinian Recollect Sisters in California*, 307 Moretti Ln., Milpitas, 95035. Tel: 408-262-3536;
Tel: 408-416-7501; Email: marcegono@sjbs.org; Web: www.augustinianrecollect.org.ph. Myrna Arcegono Sr., Supr. Sisters 4.

SANTA CLARA. *Carmelite Monastery of the Infant Jesus, Discalced Carmelite Nuns*, 1000 Lincoln St., Santa Clara, 95050. Tel: 408-296-8412;
Fax: 408-248-4846; Email: santaclaracarmel@sbcglobal.net; Web: www.members.aol.com/santaclaracarmel. Sr. Irene of Jesus and Mary, O.C.D., Prioress. Sisters 9.

Institute of the Servants of the Lord and the Virgin of Matara, 2800 Mission College Blvd., Santa Clara, 95054. Tel: 408-829-6860; Email: c.ourladyofpeace@servidoras.org; Web: www.ssvmusa.org. Mother Marie Notre Dame de Bon Secours Casadaban, S.S.V.M. Sisters 9.

Sisters of Charity of the Blessed Virgin Mary, 1220 Tasman Dr. #571, Sunnyvale, 94089.
Tel: 408-220-5150; Web: www.bvmcong.org. Sr. Marilyn Wilson, B.V.M., Contact Person. Sisters 4.

SARATOGA. *Dominican Sisters of St. Catherine of Siena*, 14735 Aloha Ave., Saratoga, 95070.
Tel: 408-898-3967; Email: sasnyderop@aol.com. Sr. Susan Snyder, O.P., Prioress.

[L] MISCELLANEOUS LISTINGS

SAN JOSE. *Caritas Housing Corporation*, 1400 Parkmoor Ave., Ste. 190, 95126. Tel: 408-550-8300; Fax: 408-550-8339; Email: info@charitieshousing.org; Web: www.charitieshousing.org. Dan Wu, Exec. Dir.

The Catholic Community Foundation of Santa Clara County, 777 N. First St., Ste. 490, 95112.
Tel: 408-995-5219; Fax: 408-995-5865; Email: info@cfoscc.org; Web: www.cfoscc.org. Mary Quilici Aumack, Exec. Dir.

Charities Housing Development Corporation of Santa Clara County, 1400 Parkmoor Ave., Ste. 190, 95126. Tel: 408-550-8300; Fax: 408-550-8339; Email: info@charitieshousing.org; Web: www.charitieshousing.org. Dan Wu, Exec. Dir. Total Staff 60.

Christ Child Society of San Jose, 19825 Oakhaven Dr., Saratoga, 95070. Tel: 408-446-5522; Email: 2parkersmp@sbcglobal.net. Pamela Parker, Pres.

Hope Charities Housing Corporation, 1400 Parkmoor Ave., Ste. 190, 95126. Tel: 408-550-8300;
Fax: 408-550-8339; Email: info@charitieshousing.org; Web: www.charitieshousing.org. Dan Wu, Exec. Dir.

St. Joseph Financial Services (2018) 1150 N. First St., Ste. 100, 95112. Tel: 707-933-7111; Email: dawn.williams@stjsf.org; Web: www.stjsf.org. Dawn Williams, CEO.

**La Salle Community Center*, 248 Kirk Ave., 95127-2220. Tel: 408-684-4701; Tel: 408-708-4139; Email: anhloanls@gmail.com; Web: www.thelasallesisters.org. Sr. Anhloan Do, L.S.S., Dir. Preschool 43; Total in Community 3.

Roman Catholic Seminary Corporation of San Jose, 1150 N. First St., Ste. 100, 95112.
Tel: 408-983-0154; Fax: 408-983-0242; Email: cilia@dsj.org. Rev. Msgr. Francis V. Cilia, V.G., Vice Pres. & Contact Person.

San Antonio Charities, 1400 Parkmoor Ave., Ste. 190, 95126. Tel: 408-550-8300; Fax: 408-550-8339; Email: info@charitieshousing.org; Web: www.charitieshousing.org. Dan Wu, Exec. Dir.

San Jose Cathedral Foundation (A nonprofit, charitable, public-benefit California corporation.) 80 S. Market St., 95113. Tel: 408-283-8100;
Fax: 408-283-8110; Email: tzuccaro@dsj.org; Web: www.stjosephcathedral.org. Rev. Joseph M. Benedict, S.T.D., Exec. Dir.

San Jose English Cursillo, P.O. Box 6648, 95150-6648. Mr. Chris Basanese, Lay Dir.

SJSU Catholic Newman Center, 300 S. 10th St., 95112.

Stoney Pine Charities Housing Corporation, 1400 Parkmoor Ave., Ste. 190, 95126. Tel: 408-550-8300; Fax: 408-550-8339; Email: info@charitieshousing.org; Web: www.charitieshousing.org. Dan Wu, Exec. Dir.

Sunset Charities Housing Corporation, 1400 Parkmoor Ave., Ste. 190, 95126. Tel: 408-550-8300; Fax: 408-550-8339; Email: info@charitieshousing.org; Web: www.charitieshousing.org. Dan Wu, Exec. Dir.

Vietnamese Catholic Center, 2849 S. White Rd., 95148. Tel: 408-983-0144; Email: jvanthu@dsj.org; Web: www.dsj.org. Rev. Joseph N. Vanthu, Dir., (Retired).

Vietnamese Youth and Culture Association, La Salle Vietnam House, 1103 Maxey Ct., 95132.
Tel: 408-926-4665; Email: frerephong@gmail.com; Web: www.lasan.org. Bros. Fortunat Phong, F.S.C., Dir.; Valery Nguyen Van Anh, F.S.C.; Cosmas Vu Van Tuan, F.S.C. Brothers of the Christian Schools (San Francisco Prov.). Students 150; Clergy / Religious Teachers 3.

CUPERTINO. *St. Joseph Cupertino Retirement Residence*, 10130 N. DeAnza Blvd., Cupertino, 95014. Tel: 408-257-1022; Fax: 408-257-3272; Email: mmitchell@dsj.org. Rev. Msgr. Michael J. Mitchell, Dir., (Retired). Priests 6; Total Staff 3.

EAST PALO ALTO. *Rosalie Rendu Inc.*, 1760 Bay Rd. #24, East Palo Alto, 94303-1674. Tel: 650-473-9522 ; Tel: 650-949-8868; Fax: 650-949-8864; Email: jday@doc1633.org. Mailing Address: 26000 Altamont Rd., Los Altos Hills, 94022. Sr. Julie Kubasak, D.C., CEO.

LOS ALTOS. *Jesuit Institute for Family Life*, 300 Manresa Way, Los Altos, 94022. Tel: 650-948-4854 ; Fax: 650-948-0640; Email: rfabing@jesuit.org; Web: www.elretiro.org. Rev. Robert J. Fabing, S.J., Dir.

LOS ALTOS HILLS. *Daughters of Charity Ministry Services Corporation*, 26000 Altamont Rd., Los Altos Hills, 94022-4317. Tel: 650-949-8868;
Fax: 650-949-8864; Email: jday@doc1633.org. Sr. Julie Kubasak, D.C., Pres.

Ministry Services of the Daughters of Charity of St.

Vincent de Paul, 26000 Altamont Rd., Los Altos Hills, 94022. Tel: 650-949-8868; Email: jday@doc1633.org. Sr. Julie Kubasak, D.C., Pres.

Vincentian Marian Youth, 26000 Altamont Rd., Los Altos Hills, 94022. Tel: 650-941-4490; Fax: 650-949-8883; Email: jday@doc1633.org. Sr. Julie Kubasak, D.C., Visitatrix.

LOS GATOS. *California Jesuit Missions*, P.O. Box 519, Los Gatos, 95031-0519. Tel: 408-884-1612; Fax: 408-884-1601; Email: uweprovince@jesuits.org; Web: www.jesuitswest.org. Rev. Theodore Gabrielli, S.J., Dir.

Jesuit Seminary Association, P.O. Box 519, Los Gatos, 95031-0519. Tel: 408-884-1600; Fax: 408-884-1621; Email: uweprovince@jesuits.org; Web: www.jesuitswest.org. Rev. John M. Martin, S.J., Treas.

USA West Province, Society of Jesus Irrevocable Aged-Infirm Fund Charitable Trust, P.O. Box 519, Los Gatos, 95031-0519. Tel: 408-884-1600; Fax: 408-884-1601; Email: UWETreasurer@jesuits.org. Very Rev. Scott Santarosa, S.J., Trustee.

USA West Province, Society of Jesus Irrevocable Apostolic Fund Charitable Trust, P.O. Box 519, Los Gatos, 95031-0519. Tel: 408-884-1600; Fax: 408-884-1601; Email: uwetreasurer@jesuits.org. Very Rev. Scott Santarosa, S.J., Trustee.

USA West Province, Society of Jesus Irrevocable Formation Fund Charitable Trust, P.O. Box 519, Los Gatos, 95031-0519. Tel: 408-884-1600; Fax: 408-884-1601; Email: uwetreasurer@jesuits.org. Very Rev. Scott Santarosa, S.J., Trustee.

USA West Province, Society of Jesus Irrevocable Foundations Fund Charitable Trust, P.O. Box 519, Los Gatos, 95031-0519. Tel: 408-884-1600; Fax: 408-884-1601; Email: uwetreasurer@jesuits.org. Very Rev. Scott Santarosa, S.J., Trustee.

MENLO PARK. *Roman Catholic Communications Corporation* dba Catholic Telemedia Network, 324 Middlefield Rd., Menlo Park, 94025. Tel: 650-326-7850; Fax: 650-326-4605; Email: ronald@ctnba.org. Most Revs. Patrick J. McGrath, D.D., J.C.D., Chm.; Michael C. Barber, S.J., Vice Chm.; Ronald J. Loiacono, Exec. Dir.

Roman Catholic Communications Corporation of the Bay Area.

MORGAN HILL. *Learning and Loving Education Center*, 16890 Church St., #16, Morgan Hill, 95037. Tel: 408-776-1196; Fax: 408-776-1130; Email: edctr@earthlink.net; Email: christahanson@earthlink.net; Web: www.learningandloving.org. Christa Hanson, Exec. Dir.

Serra International Region 11, District 31, 1282 Shasta Ave., 95126. Tel: 831-227-9134; Email: dianaseixas@aol.com. Diana Seixas, Dist. 31 Gov.

MOUNTAIN VIEW. *Holy Trinity Community North America - Silicon Valley Region*, 4216 Silver Water Way, Sacramento, 95742. Tel: 408-833-5044; Email: erick.yo@gmail.com; Web: htcna.org/. 5010 Birkdale Way, 95138. Paulus Usong, Exec.

Villa Siena Foundation, 1855 Miramonte Ave., Mountain View, 94040. Tel: 650-961-6484; Fax: 650-961-6254; Email: foundation@villa-siena.org; Web: villa-siena.org. Mrs. Corine Bernard, Exec. Dir.

SANTA CLARA. *Catholic Professionals*, P.O. Box 6346, 95150. Tel: 408-491-9229; Email: cpbcinfo@gmail.com; Web: sjcatholicprofessionals.com. Rev. Msgr. John Sandersfeld, (Retired); Mawuko Nyviadzi, Pres.

IVE West Coast Trust, 2800 Mission College Blvd., Santa Clara, 95054. Tel: 408-988-4585; Email: bdinkel@dsj.org. Rev. Brian Dinkel, I.V.E., Contact Person.

Jesuit Volunteer Corps., 500 El Camino Real, Santa Clara, 95050. Tel: 408-241-4200; Fax: 408-241-4201; Email: lstrubeck@jesuitvolunteers.org; Web: www.jesuitvolunteers.org. Ms. Laura Strubek, Admin.

Saint Joseph Academy (Homeschool Cooperative) 2800 Mission College Blvd., Santa Clara, 95054. Tel: 650-716-7704; Email: sr.angeles@servidoras.org. Sr. Angeles Garcias, Prin. Lay Teachers 7; Students 49; Clergy / Religious Teachers 4.

The Roman Catholic Welfare Corporation of San Jose, 1150 N. First St., Ste. 100, 95112. Tel: 408-983-0154; Email: cilia@dsj.org. Rev. Msgr. Francis V. Cilia, V.G., Vice Pres.

Theological Studies, Inc., Kenna Hall 323, 500 El Camino Real, Santa Clara, 95053. Tel: 408-554-4542; Email: tseditor@scu.edu; Web: www.theologicalstudies.net. Rev. Paul G. Crowley, S.J., Editor; Ms. April Flowers, Business Mgr. Total Staff 7.

RELIGIOUS INSTITUTES OF MEN REPRESENTED IN THE DIOCESE

For further details refer to the corresponding bracketed number in the Religious Institutes of Men or Women section.

[0330]—*Brothers of the Christian Schools*—F.S.C.
[]—*Congregation of the Mission - Vincentians*—C.M.
[0260]—*Discalced Carmelite Friars*—O.C.D.
[]—*Franciscan Friars Province of Most Holy Redeemer* (Croatia)—O.F.M.
[0305]—*Institute of Christ the King Sovereign Priest*.
[0685]—*Institute of Incarnate Word* (Argentina)—I.V.E.
[0690]—*Jesuit Fathers and Brothers (Society of Jesus)* (Jesuits West Prov.)—S.J.
[]—*Legionaries of Christ*—L.C.
[0760]—*Marianists (Society of Mary)*—S.M.
[0800]—*Maryknoll (Catholic Foreign Mission Society of America, Inc.)*—M.M.
[1210]—*Missionaries of St. Charles - Scalabrinians (Province of St. John Baptist)*—C.S.
[0430]—*Order of Preachers (Province of the Most Holy Name of Jesus-Western Dominican Province)*—O.P.
[1030]—*Paulist Fathers*—C.S.P.
[1260]—*Society of Christ (Society of Christ for Polonia)*—S.Ch.

RELIGIOUS INSTITUTES OF WOMEN REPRESENTED IN THE DIOCESE

[]—*Blessed Virgin Missionaries of Carmel*—B.V.M.C.
[]—*Caritas Sisters of Jesus*—C.S.J.
[2020]—*Community of the Holy Spirit*—C.H.S.
[]—*Congregation of the Augustinian Recollects*—A.R.
[1070-12]—*Congregation of the Queen of the Holy Rosary (Dominican Sisters)*—O.P.
[0760]—*Daughters of Charity of St. Vincent De Paul*—D.C.
[0420]—*Discalced Carmelite Nuns*—O.C.D.
[1070-25]—*Dominican Sisters of St. Catherine of Siena*.
[]—*Dominican Sisters of St. Rose of Lima*—O.P.
[]—*Eucharistic Missionaries of the Most Holy Trinity* (Mexico)—M.E.S.S.T.
[1270]—*Franciscan Hospitaller Sisters of the Immaculate Conception*—F.H.IC.
[3625]—*Institute of the Servants of the Lord and the Virgin of Matara*—S.S.V.M.
[]—*LaSalle Sisters* (Vietnam)—L.S.
[2470]—*Maryknoll Sisters of St. Dominic*—M.M.
[2690]—*Missionary Catechists of Divine Providence*—M.C.D.P.
[3760]—*Order of St. Clare (Immaculate Heart Monastery of Poor Clares)*—P.C.C.
[]—*Qui Nhon Missionary Sisters of the Holy Cross* (Vietnam)—L.H.C.
[2970]—*School Sisters of Notre Dame*—S.S.N.D.
[1070-03]—*Sinsinawa Dominican Congregation of the Most Holy Rosary*—O.P.
[0430]—*Sisters of Charity of the Blessed Virgin Mary*—B.V.M.
[0990]—*Sisters of Divine Providence*—C.D.P.
[2516]—*Sisters of Mercy (Ireland)*—R.S.M.
[2570]—*Sisters of Mercy of the Americas (Regional Community of Burlingame)*—R.S.M.
[3000]—*Sisters of Notre Dame de Namur*—S.N.D.deN.
[3840]—*Sisters of St. Joseph of Carondelet* (Province of Los Angeles)—C.S.J.
[3850]—*Sisters of St. Joseph of Chambery*—C.S.J.
[1990]—*Sisters of the Holy Names of Jesus and Mary (California Province)*—S.N.J.M.
[3320]—*Sisters of the Presentation of the Blessed Virgin Mary*—P.B.V.M.

DIOCESAN CEMETERIES AND MAUSOLEUMS

SAN JOSE. *Calvary Catholic Cemetery*, 2650 Madden Ave., 95116. Tel: 408-258-2940; Fax: 833-428-3733; Email: cemeteryinfo@dsj.org; Web: www.ccdsj.org. Dennis Fairbank, Dir. (Santa Clara Co.).

LOS ALTOS. *Gate of Heaven*, 22555 Cristo Rey Dr., Los Altos, 94024. Tel: 650-428-3730; Fax: 650-428-3733 ; Email: cemeteryinfo@ccdsj.org; Web: www.ccdsj.org. Dennis Fairbank, Dir.

NECROLOGY

† Browne, Dennis, (Retired), Died Aug. 27, 2018
† Kidney, Timothy, (Retired), Died Oct. 13, 2018

An asterisk (*) denotes an organization that has established tax-exempt status directly with the IRS and is not covered by the USCCB Group Ruling.

Archdiocese of Santa Fe

(Archidioecesis Sanctae Fidei)

Most Reverend

JOHN C. WESTER

Archbishop of Santa Fe; ordained May 15, 1976; appointed Auxiliary Bishop of San Francisco and Titular Bishop of Lamiggiga June 30, 1998; ordained September 18, 1998; appointed Bishop of Salt Lake City January 8, 2007; installed March 14, 2007; appointed Archbishop of Santa Fe April 27, 2015; installed June 4, 2015. *Catholic Center: 4000 St. Joseph Pl., N.W., Albuquerque, NM 87120.*

Most Reverend

MICHAEL J. SHEEHAN, S.T.L., J.C.D.

Retired Archbishop of Santa Fe; ordained July 12, 1964; consecrated and installed as First Bishop of Lubbock June 17, 1983; appointed Apostolic Administrator of Santa Fe April 6, 1993; installed as Eleventh Archbishop of Santa Fe September 21, 1993; retired April 27, 2015. *Res.: Catholic Center, 4000 St. Joseph Pl., N.W., Albuquerque, NM 87120.*

Archdiocese of Santa Fe Catholic Center: 4000 St. Joseph Pl., N.W., Albuquerque, NM 87120.* Tel: 505-831-8100.

ESTABLISHED IN 1850.

Square Miles 61,142.

Created an Archbishopric in 1875.

Solemnly consecrated to the Immaculate Heart of Mary on October 7, 1945.

Comprises the Counties of Colfax, Curry, DeBaca, Guadalupe, Harding, Los Alamos, Mora, Quay, Roosevelt, San Miguel, Santa Fe, Socorro, Taos, Torrance and Union with a part of Bernalillo, Sandoval, Rio Arriba and Valencia Counties.

Patron of the Archdiocese: St. Francis of Assisi.

For legal titles of parishes and archdiocesan institutions, consult the Chancery Office.

STATISTICAL OVERVIEW

Personnel	
Archbishops	1
Retired Archbishops	1
Abbots	3
Priests: Diocesan Active in Diocese	92
Priests: Diocesan Active Outside Diocese	5
Priests: Retired, Sick or Absent	50
Number of Diocesan Priests	147
Religious Priests in Diocese	73
Total Priests in Diocese	220
Extern Priests in Diocese	24
Ordinations:	
Diocesan Priests	4
Transitional Deacons	3
Permanent Deacons	17
Permanent Deacons in Diocese	210
Total Brothers	86
Total Sisters	87
Parishes	
Parishes	93
With Resident Pastor:	
Resident Diocesan Priests	79
Resident Religious Priests	13
Without Resident Pastor:	
Administered by Lay People	1
Missions	226
Pastoral Centers	4
Professional Ministry Personnel:	
Brothers	5
Sisters	23
Lay Ministers	232
Welfare	
Catholic Hospitals	1
Total Assisted	556,445
Health Care Centers	1
Total Assisted	1,102
Day Care Centers	1
Total Assisted	80
Specialized Homes	1
Total Assisted	158
Special Centers for Social Services	7
Total Assisted	579,381
Residential Care of Disabled	1
Total Assisted	16
Educational	
Diocesan Students in Other Seminaries	23
Students Religious	2
Total Seminarians	25
Colleges and Universities	1
Total Students	361
High Schools, Diocesan and Parish	1
Total Students	640
High Schools, Private	1
Total Students	466
Elementary Schools, Diocesan and Parish	14
Total Students	2,696
Catechesis/Religious Education:	
High School Students	4,853
Elementary Students	11,992
Total Students under Catholic Instruction	21,033
Teachers in the Diocese:	
Sisters	3
Lay Teachers	301
Vital Statistics	
Receptions into the Church:	
Infant Baptism Totals	3,114
Minor Baptism Totals	411
Adult Baptism Totals	213
Received into Full Communion	298
First Communions	3,947
Confirmations	2,768
Marriages:	
Catholic	679
Interfaith	90
Total Marriages	769
Deaths	3,284
Total Catholic Population	325,389
Total Population	1,298,548

Former Archbishops—Most Revs. J. B. LAMY, cons. Nov. 24, 1850; created first Archbishop, 1875; resigned July 18, 1885; died Feb. 13, 1888; J. B. SALPOINTE, D.D., cons. Bishop of Doryla and Vicar Apostolic of Arizona, June 20, 1869; appt. Coadjutor of Santa Fe "cum jure successionis", April, 22, 1884; promoted to the Titular Archiepiscopal See of Anazarba, Oct. 11 of same year; succeeded to the See of Santa Fe, July 18, 1885; resigned Jan. 7, 1894 Titular Archbishop of Tomi; died July 15, 1898; P. L. CHAPELLE, cons. Nov. 1, 1891; Archbishop of Santa Fe, Jan. 7, 1894; transferred to New Orleans, Dec. 1, 1897; died Aug. 9, 1905; PETER BOURGADE, D.D., cons. May 1, 1885 Bishop of Thaumacum and Vic. Ap. of Arizona; Bishop of Tucson, May 8, 1897; transferred to Santa Fe, Jan. 7, 1899; died May 17, 1908; J. B. PITAVAL, D.D., cons. Titular Bishop of Sora and Auxiliary of Santa Fe, July 25, 1902; promoted to the See of Santa Fe, Jan. 3, 1909; resigned Feb., 1918; appt. Titular Archbishop of Amida, July 29, 1918; died May 23, 1928; ALBERT T. DAEGER, O.F.M., D.D., cons. May 7, 1919; died Dec. 2, 1932; RUDOLPH ALOYSIUS GERKEN, D.D., cons. Bishop of Amarillo, April 26, 1927; appt. Archbishop of Santa Fe, June 2, 1933; installed as Archbishop of Santa Fe, Aug. 23, 1933; died March 2, 1943; EDWIN V. BYRNE, D.D., cons. Bishop of Ponce, P.R.; transferred to Diocese of San Juan, P.R.; promoted to Archbishop of Santa Fe, June 15, 1943; died July 25, 1963; JAMES P. DAVIS, D.D., cons. Bishop of San Juan, P.R., Oct. 6, 1943; promoted to Archbishop, April 30, 1960; transferred to Archdiocese of Santa Fe, Jan. 3, 1964; retired Oct. 1974; died March 4, 1988; ROBERT F. SANCHEZ, cons. 10th Archbishop of Santa Fe, July 25, 1974; resigned April 6, 1993; died Jan. 20, 2012.; MICHAEL J. SHEEHAN, D.D., S.T.L., J.C.D., ord. July 12, 1964; cons. and installed as First Bishop of Lubbock June 17, 1983; appt. Apostolic Administrator of Santa Fe April 6, 1993; installed as Eleventh Archbishop of Santa Fe Sept. 21, 1993; retired April 27, 2015.

All offices are located at the Archdiocese of Santa Fe Catholic Center, 4000 St. Joseph Pl., N.W., Albuquerque, NM 87120. Tel: 505-831-8100, unless otherwise indicated.

Office of the Archbishop

Vicar General—4000 St. Joseph's Pl., N.W., Albuquerque, 87120. Very Rev. GLENNON F. JONES, V.G.

Episcopal Vicar—5901 St. Joseph Dr., N.W., Albuquerque, 87120. Rev. Msgr. LAMBERT J. LUNA.

Episcopal Vicar for Doctrine and Life—4000 St. Joseph's Pl., N.W., Albuquerque, 87120. Very Rev. MICHAEL T. DEMKOVICH, O.P.

Secretary to the Archbishop—MS. DOLORES CORDOVA, Tel: 505-831-8120.

Office of the Chancellor

Chancellor—MR. THOMAS P. MACKEN, Esq.

Archivist and Artistic Patrimony—MS. BERNADETTE LUCERO, 223 Cathedral Pl., Santa Fe, 87501. Tel: 505-983-3811.

Attorney for the Archdiocese—MR. JUAN L. FLORES, 302 8th St., N.W., Ste. 200, Albuquerque, 87103. Tel: 505-938-7770; Fax: 505-938-7781.

Communications-Media—MRS. CELINE RADIGAN, Dir., Tel: 505-831-8180.

Ecumenical Commission and Interreligious Affairs—Rev. Msgr. BENNETT J. VOORHIES, Dir., 4000 St. Joseph Pl., N.W., Albuquerque, 87120. Tel: 505-831-8243; Fax: 505-831-8206.

General Services—MR. DAVID QUEZADA, Exec. Dir., 4000 St. Joseph Pl., N.W., Albuquerque, 87120. Tel: 505-831-8100.

Madonna Retreat and Conference Center—ESTHER-MARIE NAGIEL, Dir., 4040 St. Joseph Pl., N.W., Albuquerque, 87120. Tel: 505-831-8196.

Newspaper, Archdiocesan "People of God"—Most Rev. JOHN C. WESTER, Publisher; MRS. CELINE RADIGAN, Editor, 4000 St. Joseph Pl., N.W., Albuquerque, 87120. Tel: 505-831-8180.

Parish Bulletin Service, "The Catholic Communicator"—JENNY CHILSON, Mailing Address: P.O. Box 93244, Albuquerque, 87199-3244. Tel: 505-856-0333; Fax: 505-822-5589.

Human Resources—MS. CATHY SALCIDO, Dir., Tel: 505-831-8130.

Immaculate Heart of Mary Retreat and Conference Center—MR. JEFF SNODGRASS, Dir., Tel: 505-988-1975.

Canonical Services Division

Judicial Vicar—Very Rev. OSCAR W. COELHO, J.C.L., Tel: 505-831-8177.

College of Consultors—Most Rev. JOHN C. WESTER; Rev. Msgr. LAMBERT J. LUNA, Episcopal Vicar; Very Rev. JOHN CANNON; Rev. ADAM LEE ORTEGA Y ORTIZ; Very Rev. GLENNON F. JONES, V.G., Vicar Gen.; Rev. Msgr. DOUGLAS A. RAUN.

Council of Men and Women Religious—VACANT.

Holy Childhood Association—See Mission Office Svcs.

Mission OfficeRev. ARKAD BICZAK, Dir. Propagation of the Faith; Holy Childhood; Catholic Relief Svcs., John XXIII Catholic Community, 4831 Tramway Ridge Dr., N.E., Albuquerque, 87111. Tel: 505-293-0088.

Office of Religious—4000 St. Joseph Pl., N.W., Albuquerque, 87120. Tel: 505-831-8158; Fax: 505-831-8115. Very Rev. GLENNON F. JONES, V.G., Vicar for Rel., Email: gjones@archdiosf.org.

Pastoral Planning—MICHELLE MONTEZ, Exec. Dir., 4000 St. Joseph Pl., N.W., Albuquerque, 87120. Tel: 505-831-8221; Fax: 505-831-8206; Email: planning@archdiosf.org.

Permanent Diaconate Program—4000 St. Joseph Pl., N.W., Albuquerque, 87120. Tel: 505-831-8229. Deacon ANDRES CARRILLO, Dir.

Pilgrimage for Vocations—Rev. EDMUND SAVILLA, Dir., Ascension Parish, 2150 Raymac Rd., S.W., Albuquerque, 87105. Tel: 505-877-8550.

Presbyteral Council of the Archdiocese of Santa Fe—Most Rev. JOHN C. WESTER, Pres. (Ex Officio); Very Rev. GLENNON F. JONES, V.G., Vicar for Clergy (Ex Officio Member); Rev. Msgr. LAMBERT J. LUNA, Episcopal Vicar (Ex Officio Member); Very Rev. CLARENCE MAES, Chm.; Revs. DOMINIC BERNARD PIERSON, Vice Chm.; MICHAEL NIEMCZAK, Sec. (At Large Member); Very Revs. PATRICK SCHAFER, O.F.M.; STEPHEN C. SCHULTZ, Member; OSCAR W. COELHO, J.C.L.; ROB YAKSICH; JOHN CANNON; CHARLES UGOCHUKWU, (Nigeria); JAMES MARSHALL; MICHAEL T. DEMKOVICH, O.P.; Revs. LAWRENCE R. BRITO; DANIEL GUTIERREZ; HOI TRAN; FRANCISCO ALANIS, O.S.B.; EMMANUEL IZUKA, (Nigeria); LARRY BERNARD, O.F.M.; JUAN MENDEZ, Retired Priest Delegate, (Retired); THOMAS J. MAYEFSKE, (Minister to Priests), (Retired); DONATUS ONYEKE, C.S.Sp., (Nigeria) Delegate for Relg.

Propagation of the FaithSee Mission Office.

Vicars Forane (Deans)—Very Revs. JOHN CANNON, Santa Fe Deanery; CLARENCE MAES, Albuquerque-Deanery A; STEPHEN C. SCHULTZ, Albuquerque - Deanery B; PATRICK SCHAFER, O.F.M., Albuquerque Deanery C; JAMES MARSHALL, Southwest Deanery; GLENNON F. JONES, V.G., Northwest Deanery; ROB YAKSICH, Northeast Deanery; CHARLES UGOCHUKWU, (Nigeria) Southeast Deanery.

Tribunal—Tel: 505-831-8177; Fax: 505-831-8151.

Judicial Vicar—Very Rev. OSCAR W. COELHO, J.C.L.

Adjutant Judicial Vicars—Revs. RONALD J. BOWERS, J.C.D., (Retired); JEROME A. PLOTKOWSKI, J.C.L., (Retired).

Promoter of Justice—Rev. Msgr. JEROME MARTINEZ Y ALIRE, J.C.L.

Defenders of the Bond—Rev. GABRIEL PAREDES, J.C.L.; Rev. Msgr. JEROME MARTINEZ Y ALIRE, J.C.L.; Most Rev. MICHAEL JARBOE SHEEHAN, S.T.L., J.C.D., (Retired); Rev. SOTERO SENA.

Associate Judges—Rev. JEROME A. PLOTKOWSKI, J.C.L., (Retired); Rev. Msgr. JEROME MARTINEZ Y ALIRE, J.C.L.; Revs. KEVIN W. NIEHOFF, O.P., J.C.L.; RONALD WALTERS, O.F.M., J.C.L.; RONALD J. BOWERS, J.C.D., (Retired); Deacon GEORGE SANDOVAL, Ph.D.; MARY ANN EKLUND, Ph.D.

Notaries—MR. JOSEPH SINICO; MS. LOUELLEN N. MARTINEZ.

Delegate for Matrimonial Dispensations—Very Rev. OSCAR W. COELHO, J.C.L.

Appeal Court—Tel: 505-831-8177.

Vocations—Tel: 505-831-8143. Very Rev. JOHN B. TRAMBLEY II, Dir.; MS. JENNIFER CORY WOODCOX, Office Mgr.; Rev. MICHAEL NIEMCZAK, Asst. Dir.

Finance Division

Executive Director of Finance—MR. TONY SALGADO, CPA, Tel: 505-831-8132.

Annual Catholic Appeal Foundation—Archdiocesan Annual Appeal Campaign Tel: 505-831-8155. MRS. KARIN WRASMAN, Dir.

The Catholic Foundation of the Archdiocese of Santa Fe—MR. EDWARD LARRANAGA, Exec. Dir., 4333 Pan American Frwy., N.E., Ste. D, Albuquerque, 87107. Tel: 505-872-2901; Fax: 505-872-2905. Nonprofit Corporation for financial support of Archdiocese of Santa Fe.

Finance Council—Most Rev. JOHN C. WESTER, Pres.; Very Rev. GLENNON F. JONES, V.G., Vicar for Clergy; Rev. Msgr. LAMBERT J. LUNA, Episcopal Vicar; Rev. ROBERT LANCASTER; MR. GIG BRUMMEL; MR. STAN SLUDER; MR. JAMES MAGOVERN; MRS. VIRGINIA SCHROEDER; MS. JENNIFER CANTRELL, CPA, Chairperson; MR. WILLIAM F. RASKOB III.

Property Managers and Construction Contract Coord.—Tel: 505-831-8397. MR. THOMAS P. MACKEN, Esq., Exec. Dir.

Pastoral Ministries

Executive Director—MICHELLE MONTEZ, 4000 St. Joseph Pl., N.W., Albuquerque, 87120. Tel: 505-831-8151.

Catholic Campaign for Human Development—ANNE AVELLONE, Coord., 4000 St. Joseph Pl., N.W., Albuquerque, 87120. Tel: 505-831-8167.

Catholic Committee on Scouting—(Boy Scouts and Girl Scouts) FRED UNSWORTH, Chm.; Deacon DAVID LITTLE, Spiritual Advisor.

Catholic Schools Office—SUSAN M. MURPHY, M.A., Supt., Tel: 505-831-8172.

Catholic Charities—JAMES GANNON, Dir., 6001 Marble, N.E., Albuquerque, 87110. Tel: 505-724-4670.

Cursillo Movement—Deacon ANDRES CARRILLO, Spiritual Dir.

People Living With Disabilities—Tel: 505-831-8174. Deacon ROBERT VIGIL, Dir.; KAREN MITCHELL, Coord. for Deaf Circle & Disabilities.

Evangelization—MICHELLE MONTEZ, Exec. Dir., Tel: 505-831-8221.

Formation for Christian Service—Deacon KEITH DAVIS, Dir., Tel: 505-831-8187.

Hospital Ministry—Sr. STELLA SANTINA NNEJI, D.M.M.M., Coord. Hospital Chaplaincy Svcs., Tel: 505-831-8347.

Prison & Detention Ministry—Deacon ROBERT VIGIL, Dir., Tel: 505-831-8174. Coordinator for Prison & Jail Ministry: Rev. CHRIS KERSTIAN, O.F.M. Coordinators for Threshold Program: Tel: 505-831-8174. Deacon ROBERT VIGIL; HERMAN DELGADO, Mentor Coord.; JOSEPHINE WAR, Mentee Coord.

Archdiocesan Network for Catholic Legislative Advocacy—ANNE AVELLONE, Tel: 505-831-8167.

Liturgical Commission—Most Rev. JOHN C. WESTER, Pres.; MS. BARBARA GUENTHER, Chm., 4000 St. Joseph Pl., N.W., Albuquerque, 87120. Tel: 505-831-8194.

Marriage and Family Life Office—MRS. BETH LUKES, Dir., Tel: 505-831-8117.

Ministry to Spanish Speaking—MS. ROCIO GONZALEZ, Dir., Tel: 505-831-8152.

African American Ministry—MS. BRENDA DABNEY, Pt. Coord., Tel: 505-831-8167.

Native American Ministry—SHIRLEY ZUNI, Dir., Tel: 505-831-8126.

Newman Centers—

ALBQ: Aquinas Newman Center—Rev. MICHAEL DEPALMA, Dir., Univ. of New Mexico, 1815 Lomas Rd., N.E., Albuquerque, 87106. Tel: 505-247-1095.

LAS VEGAS: Newman Center—Rev. GEORGE SALAZAR, Coord., Highlands University, 811 Sixth St., Las Vegas, 87701. Tel: 505-425-9295.

PORTALES: St. Thomas Moore Newman Center—Very Rev. CHARLES UGOCHUKWU, (Nigeria) Chap., Mailing Address: Eastern New Mexico University, P.O. Box 2253, Portales, 88130. Tel: 505-356-5615.

SANTA FE—VACANT.

SOCORRO: St. Patrick Newman Center—Deacon NICHOLAS KELLER, 801 School of Mines Rd., Socorro, 87801. Tel: 575-838-2084.

Office of Worship—Tel: 505-831-8128. DAMARIS THILLET, Dir.

RCIA—VACANT, Tel: 505-831-8194.

Religious Education—Sr. MARY EDNA PEARL ESQUIBEL, C.S.S.F., Dir., Tel: 505-831-8127. 4000 St. Joseph Pl., N.W., Albuquerque, 87120. Tel: 505-831-8128.

Schools of Lay Ministry Formation—

Albuquerque Deanery A,B,C & SW, "Emmaus Journey"—4000 St. Joseph Pl., N.W., Albuquerque, 87120. Tel: 505-831-8187. Deacon KEITH DAVIS.

Northwest Deanery - Camino de Fe—JOANNE DUPONT-SANDOVAL, Coord., Mailing Address: P.O. Box 429, Truchas, 87578. Tel: 505-689-2404.

Santa Fe Deanery - Jornada de Fe—JOEL HOPKO, Coord., 11 Chusco Rd., Santa Fe, 87508. Tel: 505-466-8412.

Spanish School of Ministry—MS. ROCIO GONZALEZ, Dir., Tel: 505-831-8152; BEATIZ QUEZADA, Coord. Albuquerque Area, Tel: 505-831-8147; IRAM IVARBOL, Coord. Portales Area, Tel: 505-831-8147.

St. Vincent de Paul Council—Deacon THOMAS M. TYNAN, Spiritual Dir., 1520 Sara Rd., S.E., Rio Rancho, 87124. Tel: 505-892-1511.

Social Justice—ANNE AVELLONE, Tel: 505-831-8167.

Youth and Young Adult Ministry—BERNADETTE JARAMILLO, Dir., Tel: 505-831-8145.

Ministry Resource Center—Deacon KEITH DAVIS, Dir., Tel: 505-831-8187.

Victim Assistance Coordinator—ANNETTE M. KLIMKA, Tel: 505-831-8144; Email: aklimka@archdiosf.org.

CLERGY, PARISHES, MISSIONS AND PAROCHIAL SCHOOLS

CITY OF SANTA FE

(SANTA FE COUNTY)

1—THE CATHEDRAL BASILICA OF ST. FRANCIS OF ASSISI (1610) [CEM]
131 Cathedral Pl., Santa Fe, 87501-2127.
Tel: 505-982-5619; Email: rector@cbsfa.org. P.O. Box 2127, Santa Fe, 87501. Revs. Adam Lee Ortega y Ortiz, Rector; Christopher James Hallada; Tia Pham; Deacons William Kollasch; Juan Martinez.
Catechesis Religious Program—Sr. Anna Maria Lozano, M.C.S.H., D.R.E. Students 249.

2—ST. ANNE CATHOLIC CHURCH (1942) [JC]
511 Alicia St., Santa Fe, 87501. Tel: 505-983-4430; Email: cmtz1611@aol.com. Rev. Larry R. Brito; Deacons Enrique M. Montoya; Andy Dimas.
Catechesis Religious Program—Students 150.

3—CRISTO REY PARISH (1939) [JC]
1147 Cristo Rey St., Santa Fe, 87501.
Tel: 505-983-8528; Email: office@cristoreyparish.org; Web: www.cristoreyparish.org. Mailing Address: 1120 Canyon Rd., Santa Fe, 87501. Rev. Adam Lee Ortega y Ortiz.
Mission—*Our Lady of Guadalupe*, La Canada de los Alamos, Santa Fe, Santa Fe Co. 87501.
Catechesis Religious Program—Elementary Grades Twinned with Cathedral Basilica.

4—ST. JOHN THE BAPTIST-SANTA FE (1953)
1301 Osage Ave., Santa Fe, 87505. Tel: 505-983-5034 ; Email: administration@sjtbcc.com; Web: www.sjtbcc.net. Rev. James Sanchez; Deacons Andres Carrillo; Jack Conrad; Andy Lopez.
Catechesis Religious Program—Students 116.

5—SAN ISIDRO (1835) [CEM 2] (Hispanic)
3552 Agua Fria St., Santa Fe, 87507.
Tel: 505-471-0710; Email: sanisidro4@gmail.com; Web: sanisidroparish.org. Very Rev. John Cannon; Deacons Michael Salazar; Anthony Trujillo; Theodore Branch.
Catechesis Religious Program—Tel: 505-920-0569. Sr. Juanita Gonzalez, D.R.E. Students 317.
Mission—*San Jose*, La Cienega, Santa Fe Co.

6—SANTA MARIA DE LA PAZ CATHOLIC COMMUNITY (1990)
11 College Ave., Santa Fe, 87508-9225.
Tel: 505-473-4200; Email: smdlp@smdlp.org. Revs. Daniel M. Balizan; Earl Rohleder, Sacramental Min., (Retired); Michael Niemczak; Tommy Martinez, Business Mgr.; Sr. Magdalena Casas, D.L.J.C., Dir. Hispanic Ministry & Evangelization; Deacons Juan M. Rodriguez, (Retired); Dennis Snyder; Eloy Gallegos; John Cordova; Brenda Weimer, Liturgy Dir.
Catechesis Religious Program—Teresa Felix, D.R.E.; Bernadette C. Bach, Dir. RCIA; Tommy Baca, Youth Min. Students 205.

7—SHRINE OF OUR LADY OF GUADALUPE-SANTA FE (1882) [CEM] [JC] (Hispanic)
417 Agua Fria St., Santa Fe, 87501.

Tel: 505-983-8868; Email: dgarcia@archdiosf.org. Rev. Dennis M. Garcia, J.C.L.; Deacons Gilbert Valdez, Pastoral Assoc.; Jose Luis Burrola, Pastoral Assoc.; Thomas Stith, Pastoral Assoc.
Catechesis Religious Program—Tel: 505-988-3336. Monica Hernandez, C.R.E. Students 378.
Missions—San Ysidro—
Our Lady of Sorrows, Rio en Medio, Santa Fe Co.. Tel: 505-982-5588.

OUTSIDE THE CITY OF SANTA FE

ABIQUIU, RIO ARRIBA CO., ST. THOMAS APOSTLE (1745) [CEM 5] (Hispanic)
1 Church Plaza, P.O. Box 117, Abiquiu, 87510.
Tel: 505-685-4462; Email: stthomasapostle@windstream.net. Rev. Valentine Phu Ngoc Au.
Catechesis Religious Program—Briana Velasquez, D.R.E. Students 27.
Missions—San Miguel Archangel—Canones, Rio Arriba Co.
San Antonio, Medanales, Rio Arriba Co.
San Pedro, Youngsville, Rio Arriba Co.
San Juan Bautista, Coyote, Rio Arriba Co.
Santa Teresa, Mesa de Poleo, Rio Arriba Co.
Santo Nino, Capulin, Rio Arriba Co.
Nuestra Senora de Guadalupe, Gallina, Rio Arriba Co.

ALBUQUERQUE, BERNALILLO CO.

1—ST. ANNE-ALBUQUERQUE (1929)
1400 Arenal Rd., S.W., 87105. Tel: 505-877-3121; Email: st.anne.abq@gmail.com. Rev. Irby C. Nichols; Deacons Paul LeFebre; Juan Barajas; Victoriano Ceballos-Moreno.
Catechesis Religious Program—Tel: 505-877-0581. Brenda Romero, D.R.E. Students 209.
Mission—Morada de San Jose, 2100 La Vega Rd., S.W., Bernalillo Co. 87105.

2—ST. CHARLES BORROMEO (1934) [JC]
1818 Coal Pl., S.E., 87106. Tel: 505-242-3462; Email: office@stcharlesbabq.org. Rev. Vincent Dominguez; Deacons John Rasinski; Paul Dung Van Nguyen.
School—St. Charles Borromeo School, (Grades PreK-8), 1801 Hazeldine Ave., S.E., 87106.
Tel: 505-243-5788; Fax: 505-764-8842; Email: phorton@stcharlesabq.org. Lay Teachers 14; Students 100.
Catechesis Religious Program—Students 83.

3—CHURCH OF THE ASCENSION (1962) [CEM 2]
2150 Raymac Rd., S.W., 87105. Tel: 505-877-8550. Rev. Edmund Savilla; Deacon Leon Jones.
Catechesis Religious Program—Tel: 505-877-8144. Anna Villegas, D.R.E.; Rachel Baca, D.R.E. Students 82.

4—ST. EDWIN (1965) (Hispanic)
2105 Barcelona, S.W., 87105. Tel: 505-877-2967; Email: office@stedwinabq.com. Rev. Peter Muller, O.-Praem.
Catechesis Religious Program—Students 91.

5—ST. FRANCIS XAVIER-ALBUQUERQUE (1928) [JC] (Hispanic)
820 Broadway Blvd., S.E., 87102. Tel: 505-243-5201; Email: SFXavier_abq19@archdiosf.org. Rev. Francis Bijoy, O.Praem., Admin.
Catechesis Religious Program—Tel: 505-515-1862; Tel: 505-261-2066. Christa Varela, D.R.E.; Dalila Rascon, D.R.E., Spanish. Students 60.

6—HOLY FAMILY-ALBUQUERQUE (1953) (Hispanic)
562 Atrisco Dr., S.W., P.O. Box 12127, 87195.
Tel: 505-842-5426; Email: holyfamilychurch@quest.net. Very Rev. Patrick Schafer, O.F.M.; Rev. Jose Luis Peralta-Andrade; Deacons Santos Abeyta; Constantino Avalos-Sanchez; Eddie Blea.
Catechesis Religious Program—Tel: 505-842-5448; Email: holyfamilychurch505@yahoo.com. Karen Mitchell, D.R.E. Students 300.

7—HOLY GHOST (1953)
833 Arizona St. S.E., 87108. Tel: 505-265-5957; Fax: 505-265-5958; Web: holyghost.weconnect.com. Very Rev. Hyginus Chuks Anuta; Deacon Ricardo Chavez.
School—Holy Ghost School, (Grades PreK-8), (Elementary and Middle School 6201 Ross S.E., 87108. Tel: 505-256-1563; Fax: 505-262-9635; Email: contact@hgcsabq.com; Web: www.holyghostcatholicschool.com. Dr. Noreen Copeland, Ph.D., Prin. Lay Teachers 19; Students 226.
Catechesis Religious Program—
Tel: 505-265-1975 (Spanish); Email: hgministeriosesp@gmail.com. Marlene Torres, Hispanic Min. Coord. Students 150.

8—IMMACULATE CONCEPTION-ALBUQUERQUE aka Immaculate Conception Church (1883) (Hispanic)
619 Copper Ave., N.W., 87102. Tel: 505-247-4271; Web: ICCABQ.ORG. Revs. Warren J. Broussard, S.J.; Jason Lalonde; Richard W. McGowan, S.J., In Res.; Robert L. Sullivan, S.J., In Res.; Joseph Vanderholt, S.J., In Res.; Deacon George Sandoval, Ph.D.
School—St. Mary Catholic School, (Grades PreK-8), 224 Seventh St., N.W., 87102. Tel: 505-242-6271; Fax: 505-242-4837; Email: support@stmarys.me; Web: www.stmarys.me. Jacqueline Terrazas, Prin. Lay Teachers 28; Students 322.
Catechesis Religious Program—Joy Dinaro, D.R.E.; Sr. Teresa Aparicio, O.L.V.M., D.R.E., Spanish. Students 101.

9—SAINT JOHN XXIII CATHOLIC COMMUNITY (1984)
4831 Tramway Ridge Dr., N.E., 87111.
Tel: 505-293-0088; Fax: 505-293-7276; Email: pastor@johnxxiiicc.org; Web: www.johnxxiiicc.org. Revs. Arkad Biczak; Sean M. Garrity, C.S.B., Parochial Vicar; Charles T. Dougherty, C.P., Sacramental Min.; Deacons John Russo; Alex Trujillo, (Retired); Clara Maestas, Business Mgr.
Res.: 4749 Danube Dr., N.E., 87111.
Catechesis Religious Program—Tel: 505-293-7756. Jude D. Fournier, D.R.E. Students 363.

10—ST. JOSEPH ON THE RIO GRANDE (1986)
5901 St. Joseph's Dr., N.W., 87120.
Tel: 505-839-7952; Email: SJRG_abq53@archdiosf.org. Rev. Msgr. Lambert J. Luna; Rev. William McNichols, Sacramental Min.; Deacons Bert Dohle; George Miller; Robert Barretto.
Catechesis Religious Program—Tel: 505-244-2154; Fax: 505-833-1920. Students 317.

11—ST. JUDE THADDEUS (1968)
Mailing Address: 5712 Paradise Blvd., N.W., 87114. Tel: 505-898-0826 (Church); Tel: 505-897-4006; Fax: 505-792-9810; Email: stjude@stjudenm.org. Rev. Tien-Tri Nguyen; Deacons Faustin Archuleta; Salvador Mercado.
Catechesis Religious Program—Yvette Serna, D.R.E. Students 900.

12—NATIVITY OF THE BLESSED VIRGIN MARY (1936) [CEM] [JC2]
9502 Fourth St., N.W., 87114. Tel: 505-898-5253; Email: NBVM_abq02@archdiosf.org; Web: www.n-bvm.org. Rev. Nathan Libaire; Deacons Leonard Martinez; Juan Ortiz; Michael Illerbrun; Ralph Vigil.
Catechesis Religious Program—Students 6.
Mission—Our Lady of Mount Carmel, 7807 Edith, Bernalillo Co. 87114.

13—OUR LADY OF FATIMA (1949) [JC]
4020 Lomas Blvd., N.E., 87110. Tel: 505-265-5868; Email: OLOFatima_abq9@archdiosf.org; Web: www.fatimachurchabq.org. Very Rev. Stephen C. Schultz; Deacon Bill Ennis.
School—Our Lady of Fatima School, (Grades PreK-8), Tel: 505-255-6391; Email: pdehaas@fatimaschoolabq.com; Web: www.fatimaschoolabq.com. Paula DeHass, Prin. Lay Teachers 12; Students 108; Religious Teachers 1.
Catechesis Religious Program—Students 55.

14—OUR LADY OF GUADALUPE-ALBUQUERQUE (1954) (Hispanic)
1860 Griegos, N.W., 87107. Tel: 505-345-4596; Email: olog9108@gmail.com. Rev. Joe Vigil; Deacons George W. Valverde; Manuel Cabrera; Manuel Montoya; Anna Gomez Rubio, Office Mgr., Office Mgr.
Catechesis Religious Program—Tel: 505-344-7153. Jessica Bruciaga, D.R.E. (English & Hispanic Community). Students 181.

15—OUR LADY OF LAVANG (1986) [JC] (Vietnamese)
1015 Chelwood Park N.E., 87112. Tel: 505-275-3079; Email: htran@archdiosf.org; Web: Lavangabq.org. Rev. Hoi Tran.
Catechesis Religious Program—Students 197.

16—OUR LADY OF MOST HOLY ROSARY (1950) (Hispanic)
5415 Fortuna Rd., N.W., 87105. Tel: 505-836-5011; Email: hrparish@holyrosaryabq.org. Rev. Graham R. Golden, O.Praem.; Deacons Frank Perez; Keith Davis; Joseph Silva; James Owens, O.Praem., Pastoral Assoc.; Ms. Barbara Guenther, Pastoral Assoc.; Norma Vivian, Pastoral Assoc.; Louise Nielsen, Pastoral Assoc.
Res.: 5825 Coors S.W., 87121.

17—OUR LADY OF THE ANNUNCIATION (1959)
2532 Vermont, N.E., 87110. Tel: 505-298-7553; Email: contact@annunciationparishabq.org; Web: annunciationparishabq.org. Rev. Msgr. Bennett J. Voorhies; Rev. June N. Ramos, Parochial Vicar; Deacons Victor J. Bachechi; Lawrence Anthony Rivera; Patrick Sena.
School—Our Lady of the Annunciation School, (Grades PreK-8), 2610 Utah N.E., 87110.
Tel: 505-299-6783; Fax: 505-299-2182; Email: hwillets@annunciationparishabq.org. Mrs. Cindy Shields, Prin.; Amy McCarty, Vice Prin. Lay Teachers 30; Students 425.
Catechesis Religious Program—Tel: 505-296-0411. Mrs. Leslie Monette, D.R.E. Students 201.

18—OUR LADY OF THE ASSUMPTION-ALBUQUERQUE (1954)
811 Guaymas Pl., N.E., 87108-2398.
Tel: 505-256-9818; Fax: 505-256-3131; Web: www.olacs.org. Revs. Edward C. Domme; Michael Cimino, Parochial Vicar; Deacons Jim Delgado; John Granato; Maurice Graff.
Res.: 8030 Fruit Ave., N.E., 87108-2324.
Tel: 505-255-5727.
School—Our Lady of the Assumption-Albuquerque School, (Grades PreK-8), 815 Guaymas Pl., N.E., 87108-2331. Tel: 505-256-3167; Fax: 505-232-0282; Email: office@olacs.org; Email: rsanchez@olacs.org. Rebecca Sanchez, Prin.; Faith Johnston, Librarian. Lay Teachers 16; Students 168.
Catechesis Religious Program—Students 144.

19—PRINCE OF PEACE CATHOLIC COMMUNITY (2000)
12500 Carmel Ave., N.E., 87122. Tel: 505-856-7657; Email: popabq@icloud.com; Web: www.popabq.org. Rev. Michael J. Shea; Deacon Steve Fraker, Pastoral Assoc.; Mr. Joe Sena, Business Mgr.
Catechesis Religious Program—Robert Shields, Catechetical Leader. Students 168.

20—QUEEN OF HEAVEN (1952)
5311 Phoenix, N.E., 87110. Tel: 505-881-1772; Email: qhoffice@qofhabq.com. Rev. Fernando A. Saenz; Deacons Ruben Barela, RCIA Coord.; Larry Cleveland, Liturgy Dir.; Pilar Garcia, Youth Min.; Stephen Sais.
School—Queen of Heaven School, (Grades PreK-8), 5303 Phoenix Ave., N.E., 87110. Tel: 505-881-2484; Fax: 505-837-1123. Mary Catherine Keating, Prin. Lay Teachers 13; Students 100.

21—RISEN SAVIOR CATHOLIC COMMUNITY (1979)
7701 Wyoming, N.E., 87109. Tel: 505-821-1571; Email: hope@risensaviorcc.org; Web: www.risensaviorcc.org. Revs. Timothy A. Martinez; Thomas Noesen, O.P.; Deacons Mark Bussemeier; Timothy Parker; Manuel Garcia; Kevin Newman, Liturgist.
Catechesis Religious Program—Mary Parker, D.R.E. (Children) & Dir. PreSchool; Carrie Anaya, D.R.E. (Youth); Sr. Annette Lucero, O.P., Dir. Community Catechesis. Students 322.

22—SACRED HEART-ALBUQUERQUE (1903) [JC]
412 Stover Ave., S.W., 87102. Tel: 505-242-0561; Email: sacredheartnm@comcast.net; Web: www.barelas.org. Rev. Rick Zerwas; Deacon Robert Vigil.
Catechesis Religious Program—Brenda Sais, D.R.E. Students 65.

23—SAN FELIPE DE NERI (1706) (Hispanic)
2005 N. Plaza, N.W., 87104. Tel: 505-243-4628; Email: apavlak@sanfelipedeneri.org; Web: www.sanfelipedeneri.org. P.O. Box 7007, 87194. Rev. Andrew J. Pavlak; Deacons Jose Lucero; Maurice Menke; Tom Perez; Robert Morrow.
School—San Felipe de Neri School, (Grades PreK-8), 2000 Lomas Blvd., N.W., 87104. Tel: 505-242-2411; Email: apowledge@sanfelipedenerischool.org; Web: sanfelipedenerischool.org/. Mrs. Ashley Powledge, Prin. Lay Teachers 14; Students 126.
Catechesis Religious Program—Walter Lujan, D.R.E. Students 120.
Mission—San Jose de los Duranes, 2110 Los Luceros Rd., N.W., Bernalillo Co. 87104.

24—SAN IGNACIO (1916) (Hispanic)
1300 Walter St., N.E., 87102. Tel: 505-243-4287; Email: SanIgnacio_abq23@archdiosf.org. Rev. Andrew J. Pavlak, Canonical Pastor; Deacon Robert Morrow.
Res.: 1226 Walter, N.E., 87102.
Catechesis Religious Program—Students 22.

25—SAN JOSE-ALBUQUERQUE (1938) [CEM]
2401 Broadway, S.E., 87102-5009. Tel: 505-242-3658; Email: sanjoseparish@msn.com. Rev. Gabriel Paredes, J.C.L.; Deacons Edgar Torres; Raul Talavera.
Catechesis Religious Program—Sr. Mariza Lopez, Fd.C.C., D.R.E., English. Students 639.

26—SANGRE DE CRISTO (1972)
8901 Candelaria, N.E., 87112. Tel: 505-293-2327; Email: sangredecristocatholicchurch@gmail.com. Rev. Thomas Kayammakal, (India).
Catechesis Religious Program—Students 33.

27—SANTUARIO SAN MARTIN DE PORRES (1979) (Hispanic)
8321 Camino San Martin, S.W., 87121.
Tel: 505-836-4676; Email: sanmartin31@aol.com. Very Rev. Oscar W. Coelho, J.C.L.; Rev. Jerome A. Plotkowski, J.C.L., (Retired); Deacons Cresencio Salinas; Ken Trujillo; Oscar Marquez.
Catechesis Religious Program—Lourdes Morachiz, Spanish D.R.E. Students 673.

28—SHRINE OF ST. BERNADETTE (1959)
11401 Indian School Rd. NE, 87112.
Tel: 505-298-7557; Email: info@ssbnm.org; Web: www.ShrineofSt.Bernadette.com. 11509 Indian School Rd. NE, 87112. Rev. Leo L. Padget; Deacons Joe Santana; Terry Palmer; William Barry.
Res.: 1800 Martha St. N.E., 87112.
Catechesis Religious Program—Tel: 505-247-6830. Levi Romero, D.R.E. Students 281.

29—SHRINE OF THE LITTLE FLOWER ST. THERESE OF THE INFANT JESUS PARISH (1947) (Shrine Dedicated 1955)
300 Mildred, N.W., 87107. Tel: 505-344-8050; Email: sttheresechurch@yahoo.com; Web: www.littleflower.uni.cc. Rev. Vincent P. Chavez; Deacons Michael Wesley; Thomas Baca.
School—St. Therese Catholic School, (Grades PreK-8), 311 Shropshire N.W., 87107. Tel: 505-344-4479; Fax: 505-345-6210; Email: d.illerbrun@stschool.org;

Web: www.sttheresesschoolabq.org. Donna Illerbrun, Prin. Lay Teachers 17; Students 208.
Catechesis Religious Program—Rosa Aragon, D.R.E. Students 119.

30—ST. THOMAS AQUINAS UNIVERSITY PARISH (1950) (Serving the University of New Mexico)
1815 Las Lomas Rd. NE, 87106-3803.
Tel: 505-247-1094; Email: lobocatholic.org@gmail.com. Rev. Michael DePalma.
Res.: 1806 Sigma Chi Rd., N.E., 87106-3803.
Catechesis Religious Program—Dora Montoya, D.R.E. Students 33.

ANTON CHICO, GUADALUPE CO., SAN JOSE-ANTON CHICO (1857) [CEM] [JC5] (Hispanic)
1081 Iglesia Rd., P.O. Box 99, Anton Chico, 87711.
Tel: 575-427-1164; Email: sanjose@plateautel.net. Rev. George Salazar, Canonical Pastor; Lugardita Romo, Parish Life Coord.
Catechesis Religious Program—Tel: 505-427-4114. Students 21.
Missions—Dilia, Guadalupe Co.
Dahlia, Guadalupe Co.
Tecolotito, San Miguel Co.
Sangre de Cristo (1834) Plaza de Arriba.

ARROYO SECO, TAOS CO., LA SANTISIMA TRINIDAD (1834) [CEM] [JC4] (Spanish)
498 Hwy. 150, P.O. Box 189, Arroyo Seco, 87514.
Tel: 575-776-2273; Email: trinityparish@qwestoffice.net. Rev. Angelo Marquez; Deacons Romolo Arellano; Larry Torres.
Catechesis Religious Program—P.O. Box 66, Arroyo Seco, 87514. Viola Espinoza, D.R.E. Students 118.
Missions—*Nuestra Senora de Dolores*—Upper Plaza, Arroyo Hondo, Taos Co. 87513.
San Antonio de Padua, Valdez Plaza, Valdez, Taos Co. 87580.
Santo Nino de Atocha, Santo Nino Rd., Las Colonias, Taos Co. 87529.
San Cristobal, San Cristobal, Taos Co.

BELEN, VALENCIA CO., OUR LADY OF BELEN (1793) [CEM] [JC]
101 A N. 10th St., Belen, 87002. Tel: 505-861-0969; Email: lobchurch@ourladyofbelen.org. Revs. Clement Niggel; Albert Mutebi; Deacons Michael Montoya; Manuel Trujillo; Jerry Baca.
School—*St. Mary's School*, (Grades K-8),
Tel: 505-864-0484; Email: mgood@stmarysbelen.com; Web: www.stmarysbelen.com. Melodie Good, Prin. Lay Teachers 12; Students 187; Religious Teachers 1.
Catechesis Religious Program—Tel: 505-864-7869. Therese Salazar, D.R.E. Students 373.
Missions—*Our Lady of Guadalupe*—Los Chavez, Valencia Co.
San Francisco Xavier, Jarales, Valencia Co.
San Isidro, Pueblitos, Valencia Co.
Cristo Rey, Bosque, Valencia Co.

BERNALILLO, SANDOVAL CO., OUR LADY OF SORROWS-BERNALILLO (1699) [CEM 2] (Indian—Hispanic)
301 S. Camino del Pueblo, P.O. Box 607, Bernalillo, 87004. Tel: 505-867-5252; Email: frclarence@olosbern.com. Very Rev. Clarence Maes; Rev. Francisco Carabajal, Parochial Vicar; Deacons Jose de Jesus Cervantes; Gonzalo Calderon; Dan Kennedy; Eric Buenavente.
Catechesis Religious Program—Students 438.
Missions—43 San Antonio, Placitas, Sandoval Co. 87043.
1416 Hwy. 313, Algodones, Sandoval Co. 87001.
300 Parrot Blvd., Sandia Indian Pueblo, Sandoval Co. 87004.

CERRILLOS, SANTA FE CO., ST. JOSEPH-CERRILLOS (1850) [CEM 4]
7th First St., P.O. Box 98, Cerrillos, 87010.
Tel: 505-471-1562; Email: st-josephs@live.com. Revs. Daniel M. Balizan; Bruce Hausfeld, Sacramental Min.; Bryant Hausfeld, Sacramental Min.; Tommy Martinez, Business Mgr.
Catechesis Religious Program—Students 4.
Missions—*San Francisco de Asis*—State Rd. 14, Golden, Santa Fe Co. 87047. Tel: 505-473-4200; Email: pastor@smdlp.org.
Nuestra Senora de los Remedios, State Rd. 41, Galisteo, Santa Fe Co. 87540.

CHAMA, RIO ARRIBA CO., ST. PATRICK-CHAMA (1964) [JC] (Hispanic—Anglo)
352 Pine St., Hwy. 29, P.O. Box 36, Chama, 87520-0036. Tel: 575-756-2926; Email: st.patrickparish@elvallecatolico.org. Rev. Ted Butler; Deacons Harold Gallegos; Joseph Valdez.
Catechesis Religious Program—Tel: 575-588-7473; Email: DRE@elvallecatolico.org. Joan Dudley, D.R.E. Students 75.
Missions—*Santo Nino de Atocha*—Hwy. 84 & State Rd. 310, Cebolla, Rio Arriba Co. 87518.
San Juan Nepomuceno, County Rd. 295, Canjilon, Rio Arriba Co. 87515.

CHIMAYO, RIO ARRIBA CO., HOLY FAMILY-CHIMAYO (1955) [CEM] [JC2] (Hispanic)
10 Private Dr. 1440, P.O. Box 235, Chimayo, 87522.
Tel: 505-351-4360; Web: www.holychimayo.us. Revs. Julio Gonzalez, S.F.; Jose Maria Blanch, S.F.; James Suntum, S.F.; Luis Gomez Lopez.
Catechesis Religious Program—Students 30.
Missions—*Holy Rosary*—Truchas, Rio Arriba Co.
San Jose de Gracia, Trampas, Taos Co.
Santo Domingo, Cundiyo, Rio Arriba Co.
San Antonio, Cordova, Rio Arriba Co.
Sagrado Corazon, Rio Chiquito, Rio Arriba Co.
Santo Tomas, Ojo Sarco, Rio Arriba Co.
San Miguel Archangel, El Valle, Taos Co.
Shrine—*Santuario de Chimayo*, Chimayo, Rio Arriba Co. 87522.

CIMARRON, COLFAX CO., IMMACULATE CONCEPTION CHURCH-CIMARRON (1864) [JC] (Hispanic—Mexican)
440 W. 18th St., Cimarron, 87714-9705.
Tel: 575-376-2553; Fax: 575-376-2553; Email: iccparishoffice@yahoo.com. P.O. Box 75, Cimarron, 87714. Rev. Benoit Trieu Van Vu.
Catechesis Religious Program—Students 48.
Missions—*St. Mel*—200 Willow Creek, Eagle Nest, Colfax Co. 87718.
Holy Angels, 34 Westridge Rd., Angel Fire, 87710.
San Antonio, Black Lake, Colfax Co.

CLAYTON, UNION CO., ST. FRANCIS XAVIER-CLAYTON (1937) [JC]
115 N. First St., Clayton, 88415. Tel: 575-374-8894; Email: stfrancisxavier@plateautel.net. Rev. Joel O. Bugas; Deacon P. Louis Montoya; Theresa Gard, Business Mgr.; Hayley Encinias, Dir.
Catechesis Religious Program—Andrea Naranjo, D.R.E. & RCIA Coord. Students 70.
Missions—*Our Lady of Guadalupe*—Des Moines, Union Co.
St. Joseph, Folsom, Union Co.
Sacred Heart, Moses, Union Co.

CLOVIS, CURRY CO.

1—OUR LADY OF GUADALUPE-CLOVIS (1945) [CEM 2] [JC2]
108 N. Davis St., Clovis, 88101. Tel: 575-763-4445; Email: ologclovis@yahoo.com. Revs. Eli Valadez; Christopher Martinez; Deacons Bob Pullings; Daniel Chavez; Steve Garcia.
Catechesis Religious Program—Tel: 575-762-7343. Cecilia Moore, D.R.E. (Grades K-8); Deacon Steve Garcia, RCIA Prog. Students 543.
Mission—*San Jose*, Box 122, Texico, Curry Co. 88135.

2—SACRED HEART-CLOVIS (1906)
921 Merriwether St., Clovis, 88101.
Tel: 575-763-6947; Email: sacredheartclovis@gmail.com. Rev. Leon Vigil; Deacons Juan A. Rodriguez; Michael A. Rowley.
Catechesis Religious Program—Students 309.
Mission—Melrose, Curry Co. 88124.

CORRALES, SANDOVAL CO., SAN YSIDRO (1966) [CEM]
5015 Corrales Rd., P.O. Box 182, Corrales, 87048.
Tel: 505-898-1779; Email: SY_corrales36@archdiosf.org. Rev. James McGowan; Deacon Thomas Burns.
Catechesis Religious Program—Tel: 505-620-3675. Ken Cantwell, D.R.E. Students 70.

DIXON, RIO ARRIBA CO., ST. ANTHONY-DIXON (1929) [CEM 3]
Private Dr. 1114 SR 75, Dixon, 87527-0039.
Tel: 505-579-4389; Email: standixon@valornet.com; Web: www.stanthonydixon.parishesonline.com. P.O. Box 39, Dixon, 87527. Rev. Simeon F. Wimmershoff.
Catechesis Religious Program—Students 12.
Missions—*Nuestra Senora de Guadalupe*—Velarde, Rio Arriba Co.
Nuestra Senora de los Dolores, Pilar, Taos Co.
San Jose, Lyden, Rio Arriba Co.

EL RITO, RIO ARRIBA CO., SAN JUAN NEPOMUCENO (1832) [CEM] [JC9] (Spanish)
1191 Main St., P.O. Box 7, El Rito, 87530.
Tel: 575-581-4714; Email: sjnparish@gmail.com. Rev. Joseph Van Tao Nguyen.
Catechesis Religious Program—Students 36.
Missions—Gen. Del., La Madera, Rio Arriba Co. 87539.
Gen. Del., Las Tablas, Taos Co. 87539.
Gen. Del., Ojo Caliente, Rio Arriba Co. 87549.
Gen. Del., Petaca, Taos Co. 87539.
Gen. Del., Servilleta, Taos Co. 87539.
Gen. Del., Vallecitos, Rio Arriba Co. 87581.
Gen. Del., Canon de Vallecitos, Rio Arriba Co. 87581.
Gen. Del., Tres Piedras, Taos Co. 87579.
P.O. Box 7, Placitas, Rio Arriba Co. 87530.

ESPANOLA, RIO ARRIBA CO., SACRED HEART-ESPANOLA (1950) [CEM 2] (Hispanic)
908 Calle Rosario, P.O. Box 69, Espanola, 87532.
Tel: 505-753-4225; Email: sacredheart@windstream.net. Rev. Dominic Bernard Pierson; Deacons Christopher Gilbert; Alex Valdez.
Catechesis Religious Program—Sr. Annunciata Mary Ekezie, I.H.M., (Nigeria) D.R.E. Students 90.
Missions—*San Jose*—Hernandez, Rio Arriba Co.
San Antonio, El Guache, Rio Arriba Co.
Our Lady of Guadalupe, Guachupanque, Rio Arriba Co.
San Francisco, El Duende, Rio Arriba Co.

FORT SUMNER, DE BACA CO., ST. ANTHONY OF PADUA-FORT SUMNER (1958) [CEM] (Hispanic)
443 W. Richard Ave., P.O. Box 370, Fort Sumner, 88119. Tel: 575-355-2320; Email: stanthonyfortsumnerparish@yahoo.com. Rev. Sotero A. Sena; Deacon Edward Sena.
Catechesis Religious Program—Students 47.

ISLETA PUEBLO, BERNALILLO CO., ST. AUGUSTINE (1613) [CEM] (Native American)
TR 35, #71, P.O. Box 849, Isleta Pueblo, 87022.
Tel: 505-869-3398; Email: StAugustine_Isleta21@archdiosf.org. Rev. George Pavamkott, O.Praem., (India).
Catechesis Religious Program—Students 115.

JEMEZ PUEBLO, SANDOVAL CO., SAN DIEGO MISSION (1608) [CEM] [JC4] (Native American—Spanish)
475 Mission Rd., Jemez Pueblo, 87024.
Tel: 575-834-7300; Email: larbernard@cybermesa.com. P.O. Box 79, Jemez Pueblo, 87024-0079. Rev. Larry Bernard, O.F.M.
Catechesis Religious Program—Tel: 505-967-5016. Bonnie Fragua Johnson, D.R.E. Students 70.
Missions—*Our Lady of Guadalupe*—Canon, Sandoval Co.
Santo Toribio, Ponderosa, Sandoval Co.
San Ysidro, San Ysidro, Sandoval Co.
Santa Ana, Santa Ana, Sandoval Co.
Our Lady of the Assumption Zia Pueblo, Zia, Sandoval Co.

JEMEZ SPRINGS, SANDOVAL CO., OUR LADY OF THE ASSUMPTION-JEMEZ SPRINGS (1947) [CEM]
Mailing Address: P.O. Box 10, Jemez Springs, 87025.
Tel: 575-829-4138. Rev. Pio Dang Xuan Ba, s.P.
Catechesis Religious Program—

LA JOYA, SOCORRO CO., OUR LADY OF SORROWS-LA JOYA (1830) [CEM 6] (Spanish)
Mailing Address: 19 Calle de la Iglesia, P.O. Box 32, La Joya, 87028. Tel: 505-864-4461;
Tel: 505-864-4170 (Rectory); Fax: 505-864-4461; Email: parishoffice@olslajoya.nm.org; Web: www.olslajoyanm.org. Rev. Tobechukwu P. Oluoha, OSA, (Nigeria); Deacon Felix Barela.
Catechesis Religious Program—Ronnie Sinclair, D.R.E. Students 34.
Missions—*San Antonio*—Abeytas, Socorro Co.
San Jose, Contreras, Socorro Co.
San Isidro, Las Nutrias, Socorro Co.
San Juan, Veguita, Socorro Co.
San Antonio, Sabinal, Socorro Co.

LAS VEGAS, SAN MIGUEL CO.

1—IMMACULATE CONCEPTION-LAS VEGAS (1885) [CEM]
811 Sixth St., Las Vegas, 87701. Tel: 505-425-7791; Email: icchurch2000@yahoo.com. Revs. George Salazar; Jason Pettigrew; Deacon Ernest Chavez, Rel Edu. Coord. (High School).
Catechesis Religious Program—Tel: 505-454-0685. Darlene Chavez, Rel. Educ. Coord. (Elementary). Students 340.
Mission—*Los Vigiles (Our Lady of Refuge)*, Las Vegas, San Miguel Co. 87701.

2—OUR LADY OF SORROWS CHURCH-LAS VEGAS (1851) [CEM 2] [JC2] (Hispanic)
403 Valencia St., Las Vegas, 87701.
Tel: 505-454-1469; Email: olos-sc@outlook.com. Rev. George Robert Yaksich; Deacon Reyes L. Sanchez.
Catechesis Religious Program—Tel: 505-425-6823. Deacon Reyes L. Sanchez, D.R.E. Students 114.
Missions—*Nuestra Senora de Guadalupe*—HC 68, Box 11, Sapello, San Miguel Co. 87745.
Tel: 505-425-8084.
San Isidro, HC 32, Box 26, Trujillo, San Miguel Co. 87701. Tel: 505-641-5367.
Holy Family, Garita. Box 1020, Variadero, San Miguel Co. 88421. Tel: 505-641-5339.
Santo Nino, HC 69, Box 4, Rociada Abajo, San Miguel Co. 87742. Tel: 505-425-8251.
Santo Nino, Montezuma. El Porvenir Rte., Box 63, Gallinas, San Miguel Co. 87731. Tel: 505-425-6015.
Chapels—*Christ the King*—2609 Encino St., Las Vegas, 87701. Tel: 505-425-6894.
San Jose, Hot Springs.
San Antonio, Box 90, El Porvenir, 87731.
Tel: 505-425-8010.
San Ignacio, HC 68, Box 15, San Ignacio, 87745.
Tel: 505-425-3092; Tel: 505-454-1139.
Our Lady of Sorrows, Anton Chico Rte., Box 39, Tecolote, 87701. Tel: 505-421-5599.
San Geronimo, Mineral Hill Rte., Box 310, San Geronimo, 87701. Tel: 505-425-3011.
San Antonio, P.O. Box 85, Los Montoyas, 87701.
Tel: 505-425-3405.
Lourdes.
San Jose, HC 69, Box 12A, Rociada, 87742.
Tel: 505-425-2809.
San Rafael, c/o Chris & Loretta, Baca HC 31 Mirasol, Las Vegas, 87701. Tel: 505-425-9640.
Santo Nino de Atocha, Anton Chico Rte., Box 20, Las Vegas, 87701. Tel: 505-425-8014.
Ojitos Frios.
Manuelitas.
Santo Nino, Tel: 505-454-0409.

LOS ALAMOS, LOS ALAMOS CO., IMMACULATE HEART OF

MARY (1946)
Mailing Address: 3700 Canyon Rd., Los Alamos, 87544. Tel: 505-662-6193; Email: ihm@ihmcc.org; Web: ihmcc.org. Very Rev. Glennon F. Jones, V.G.; Deacons Ray Alcouffe; Michael Irving; Donato Lucero; James O'Hara; John Sutton; Greg Smithhisler, Liturgy Dir.
Res.: 3694 Canyon Rd., Los Alamos, 87544. Email: ihm@ihmcc.org; Web: www.ihmcc.org.
Catechesis Religious Program—3580 Canyon Rd., Los Alamos, 87544. Tel: 505-662-7773; Fax: 505-662-7333. Caren Stephens, D.R.E.; Cathy Kohlrust, Youth Dir. & Adult Formation. Students 420.
Mission—St. Joseph, 196 Meadow, White Rock, Los Alamos Co. 87547.

LOS LUNAS, VALENCIA CO., SAN CLEMENTE (1961) [CEM 2] [JC]
244 Luna, P.O. Box 147, Los Lunas, 87031.
Tel: 505-865-7385. Very Rev. James Marshall; Rev. Francisco Alanis, O.S.B., Parochial Vicar, San Juan Diego; Deacons Jim Snell, Business Mgr.; Robert Burkhard; Paul Baca; Hector Avitia; Charles E. Schwenn.
Catechesis Religious Program—Tel: 505-865-9370. Students 536.
Missions—San Antonio—Los Lentes, Valencia Co.
San Juan Diego, P.O. Box 3320, Los Lunas, 87031. Tel: 505-866-0443; Email: sanjuandiego@qwestoffice.net.

LOS OJOS, RIO ARRIBA CO., SAN JOSE-LOS OJOS (1883) [CEM] [JC2] (Hispanic)
State Rd. 514 #101, P.O. Box 6, Los Ojos, 87551.
Tel: 575-588-7473; Email: sjsncc@elvallecatolico.org; Web: www.elvallecatolico.org. Rev. Ted Butler.
Catechesis Religious Program—Tel: 301-887-3410. Joan Dudley, D.R.E. Students 50.
Stations—Ensenada.
La Puente.
Plaza Blanca.

MORA, MORA CO., ST. GERTRUDE THE GREAT (1851) [CEM] [JC9] (Hispanic)
#12 County Rd. A-033, P.O. Box 599, Mora, 87732.
Tel: 575-387-2336; Email: stgertrudes.aa@gmail.com. Rev. Paul Grala, S.O.L.T., Parochial Vicar; Deacon Cristobal Eloy Roybal.
Catechesis Religious Program—Students 160.
Missions—San Jose—Le Doux, Mora Co.
Nuestra Senora del Carmel, El Carmen, Mora Co.
Santa Rita, Lucero, Mora Co.
San Santiago Alto del Talco, Alto del-Talco, Mora Co.
San Isidro, Ojo Feliz, Mora Co.
El Santo Nino de Atocha, Buena Vista, Mora Co.
San Acacio, Golondrinas, Mora Co.
Sacred Heart of Jesus, Rainsville, Mora Co.
San Antonio de Padua, Chacon, Mora Co.
Immaculate Heart of Mary, Holman, Mora Co.
San Antonio de Padua, Cleveland, Mora Co.
Nuestra Senora de Guadalupe, Guadalupita, Mora Co.
El Santo Nino de Atocha, Monte Aplanado, Mora Co.
Santa Teresita del Nino Jesus, Turquillo, Mora Co.
San Rafael, La Cueva, Mora Co.
San Jose, Canoncito, Mora Co.

MORIARTY, TORRANCE CO., ESTANCIA VALLEY CATHOLIC PARISH aka Our Lady of Mount Carmel (1972) [CEM 3]
1400 A 3rd St., S., P.O. Box 129, Moriarty, 87035.
Tel: 505-832-6655; Fax: 505-832-6057; Email: parishoffice@evcpnm.org; Web: www.evcpnm.org. Revs. Robert Lancaster; John Kimani, Parochial Vicar; Deacons Juan S. Lucero; Kenneth Peccatiello; Lincoln Richey.
Res.: 1400 B 3rd St., S., Moriarty, 87035.
Catechesis Religious Program—
Tel: 505-832-6655, Ext. 212; Email: formation@evcpnm.org. Tamara Magoffe, Catechetical Leader, Rel. Formation & Youth Min. Students 154.
Missions—Sts. Peter & Paul—101 S. Ninth St., Estancia, Torrance Co. 87016.
San Antonio, 8566 Hwy. 55 W., Tajique, 87016.
St. Elizabeth Ann Seton, 85 Hwy. 344, Edgewood, 87015.

MOUNTAINAIR, TORRANCE CO., ST. ALICE (1946) [CEM 5] [JC] (Hispanic)
301 S Roosevelt St., P.O. Box 206, Mountainair, 87036. Tel: 505-847-2291; Email: stalicemtn@q.com. Rev. Malachy Obiejesi, (Nigeria); Deacon Alton Adams.
Res.: 209 W. 3rd St., Mountainair, 87036.
Tel: 505-847-2291; Email: stalicemtn@q.com.
Catechesis Religious Program—Yvonne Garcia, Catechetical Leader. Students 60.
Missions—San Lorenzo—Abo, Torrance Co.
St. Vincent de Paul, Punta de Agua, Torrance Co.
Nuestra Senora de Dolores, Manzano, Torrance Co.
St. Anthony, Torreon, Torrance Co.
Our Lady of Sorrows, Willard, Torrance Co.

PECOS, SAN MIGUEL CO., ST. ANTHONY OF PADUA-PECOS (1862) [CEM 5]
10 St. Anthony's Loop, HC 74 Box 23, Pecos, 87552. Tel: 505-757-6345; Email: saint.anthonys.pecos@gmail.com. Rev. Chike Uba, Admin.
Catechesis Religious Program—Tel: 505-757-6305. Students 88.
Missions—Nuestra Senora de La Luz—Canoncito, Santa Fe Co.
Santo Nino, Las Colonias, San Miguel Co.
Nuestra Senora de Guadalupe, Glorieta, Santa Fe Co.
Sagrada Familia, Rowe, San Miguel Co.
Nuestra Senora de Guadalupe, El Macho, San Miguel Co.

PENA BLANCA, SANDOVAL CO., NUESTRA SENORA DE GUADALUPE - PENA BLANCA (1877) [CEM 3] (Hispanic—Native American)
816 Hwy. 22, P.O. Box 1270, Pena Blanca, 87041.
Tel: 505-465-2226; Email: OLOG_penablanca57@archdiosf.org. Rev. Michael Garcia; Deacon Joe Segura.
Catechesis Religious Program—Students 122.
Missions—St. Bonaventure—Indian Pueblo Cochiti, Sandoval Co.
San Felipe, Indian Pueblo San Felipe, Sandoval Co.
Santo Domingo, Indian Pueblo Santo Domingo, Sandoval Co.
Santa Barbara, Sile, Sandoval Co.
San Miguel, La Bajada, Sandoval Co.

PENASCO, TAOS CO., SAN ANTONIO DE PADUA (1866) [CEM]
14079 N. Hwy. 75, P.O. Box 460, Penasco, 87553-0460. Tel: 575-587-2111; Fax: 575-587-2188; Email: josefarodriguezsadp@gmail.com. Rev. Simeon F. Wimmershoff.
Catechesis Religious Program—15081 N. Hwy. 75, Penasco, 87553. Tel: 575-587-2216. Joyce Kilgore, D.R.E. Students 64.
Missions—Santa Cruz Mission—Chamisal, Taos Co.
Sagrado Corazon Mission, Rio Lucio, Taos Co.
Nuestra Senora de los Dolores Mission, Vadito, Taos Co.
San Lorenzo Mission, Picuris Indian Pueblo, Taos Co.
San Juan Nepomuceno Mission, Llano San Juan, Taos Co.
Nuestra Senora de la Asuncion Mission, Placita, Taos Co.
Santa Barbara Mission, Rodarte, Taos Co.

PERALTA, VALENCIA CO., OUR LADY OF GUADALUPE-PERALTA (1970) [CEM] (Hispanic)
3674 Hwy. 47, P.O. Box 10, Peralta, 87042.
Tel: 505-869-2189; Email: ologoffice@yahoo.com. Rev. Emmanuel Izuka, (Nigeria); Deacon Edward Espinosa.
Catechesis Religious Program—Tel: 505-869-6993; Fax: 505-869-6996. Monica Casias-McKay, Faith Formation Coord. Students 184.
Mission—Sangre de Cristo, Valencia, Valencia Co.
Station—Valencia, Peralta.

POJOAQUE, SANTA FE CO., NTRA. SRA. DE GUADALUPE DEL VALLE DE POJOAQUE (1959) [CEM 2] (Spanish—Native American)
9 Grazing Elk Dr., Santa Fe, 87506-7140.
Tel: 505-455-2472; Email: ologpojoaque@gmail.com. Rev. Msgr. Jerome Martinez y Alire, J.C.L.; Deacons John Archuleta; Pedro Garcia; Daniel Valdez; Reuben Roybal; Greg Romero.
Catechesis Religious Program—Tel: 505-455-2267. Donna Martinez, D.R.E. Students 175.
Missions—Sagrado Corazon de Jesus—Nambe, Santa Fe Co.
San Antonio de Padua, El Rancho, Santa Fe Co.
San Francisco de Asis, Nambe Indian Pueblo, Santa Fe Co.

PORTALES, ROOSEVELT CO., ST. HELEN (1952)
1600 S. Ave. O, Portales, 88130. Tel: 575-356-4241. Very Rev. Charles Ugochukwu, (Nigeria); Deacon Roberto Herrera.
Mission—Thomas More Center, 1608 W. 17th St., Portales, Roosevelt Co. 88130.

QUESTA, TAOS CO., ST. ANTHONY-QUESTA (1841) [CEM 6]
10 Church Plaza, P.O. Box 200, Questa, 87556.
Tel: 575-586-0470; Email: sanantoniodelrio@hotmail.com. Rev. Andrew Ifele; Deacons Marcus J. Rael; Jose Leroy Lucero.
Catechesis Religious Program—Parish Center: 2453 St. Hwy 522, Questa, 87556. Tel: 575-586-0649. Ceina Sally Lucero, D.R.E. Students 96.
Missions—Our Lady of Guadalupe—Cerro, Taos Co.
St. Edwin, Red River, Taos Co.
Sagrado Corazon, Costilla, Taos Co.
Santo Nino, Amalia, Taos Co.

RANCHOS DE TAOS, TAOS CO., SAN FRANCISCO DE ASIS (1936) [CEM] (Hispanic)
60 St. Francis Plaza, P.O. Box 72, Ranchos De Taos, 87557-0072. Tel: 575-758-2754; Email: sanfranciscoranchos@gmail.com. Rev. Dino Candelaria.
Catechesis Religious Program—Jennifer Archuleta, D.R.E. Students 110.
Missions—Ntra. Sra. de San Juan de Los Lagos—Talpa, Taos Co.
Ntra. Sra. del Carmel, Llano Quemado, Taos Co.
San Isidro, Los Cordovas, Taos Co.

RATON, COLFAX CO., ST. PATRICK - ST. JOSEPH (1891) [CEM] [JC]
105 Buena Vista St., Raton, 87740.
Tel: 575-445-9763; Fax: 575-445-7026; Email: stspatjoe@bacavalley.com. Rev. William Woytavich; Deacon Thomas Alderette.
Catechesis Religious Program—104 Buena Vista St., Raton, 87740. Tel: 575-445-9563. Vickie Castellini-Blaisure, D.R.E.; Brad Long, RCIA Coord. Students 118.

RIBERA, SAN MIGUEL CO., SAN MIGUEL DEL VADO (1804) [CEM] [JC7] (Hispanic—Native American)
Hwy. 3, P.O. Box 507, Ribera, 87560.
Tel: 575-421-2780; Email: sanmiguel@plateautel.net. Rev. Moses Nwankwo, (Nigeria).
Catechesis Religious Program—Students 23.
Missions—San Isdro Labrador Mission—[CEM] [JC] San Isidro Norte, San Miguel Co.
San Jose Mission, [CEM] [JC] San Jose, San Miguel Co.
San Juan Nepomuceno Mission, [CEM] [JC] San Juan, San Miguel Co.
Santa Rita Mission, [CEM] [JC] Santa Rita, San Miguel Co.
San Antonio de Padua, [CEM] [JC] El Pueblo, San Miguel Co.
Our Lady of the Rosary Misson, [CEM] [JC] La Lagunita, San Miguel Co.
Nuestra Senora de Guadalupe Mission, [CEM] [JC] San Isidro Sur, San Miguel Co.

RIO RANCHO, SANDOVAL CO.
1—CHURCH OF THE INCARNATION (2003)
2309 Monterrey Rd., NE, Rio Rancho, 87144.
Tel: 505-771-8331; Email: claire@ccincarnation.org; Web: incarnation.church. Rev. Leo W. Ortiz; Deacons George Meyerson, Pastoral Assoc.; Norbert Archibeque; Jerome Paszkiewicz; Louis Bernal; Mark Buie.
Catechesis Religious Program—Josemaria Balderas, D.R.E. Students 265.

2—ST. JOHN VIANNEY CHURCH (1997)
1001 Meteor Ave. N.E., Rio Rancho, 87124.
Tel: 505-892-4449; Email: info@sjvnm.org; Web: www.sjvnm.org. Rev. Scott Mansfield; Deacon Stephen S. Rangel.
Catechesis Religious Program—Edwina Herrera, D.R.E. Students 226.

3—ST. THOMAS AQUINAS (1974)
1502 Sara Rd., S.E., Rio Rancho, 87124.
Tel: 505-892-1511; Fax: 505-892-1511, Ext. 107; Email: pastor@stanm.org; Web: stanm.org. Rev. Msgr. Douglas A. Raun; Rev. Scott McKee; Deacons Roger Ayers; David Little, Dir. Adult Ministries; Frank Smith; Thomas M. Tynan; Leroy Sanchez; Edward Leyba.
School—St. Thomas Aquinas School, (Grades PreK-8), 1100 Hood Rd., S.E., Rio Rancho, 87124.
Tel: 505-892-3221; Fax: 505-892-3350; Email: principal@stasnm.net; Web: www.stasnm.org. Sr. Anne Louise Abascal, M.P.F., Prin. Lay Teachers 24; Religious 2; Students 409.
Catechesis Religious Program—Tel: 505-892-1497; Email: cre@stanm.org. Sr. Roseanne Fernandez, D.R.E.

ROY, HARDING CO., HOLY FAMILY-ST. JOSEPH (1918) [CEM 4] (Hispanic)
515 St. George Ln., Roy, 87743. Tel: 575-485-9633; Email: holyfamilyroy@yahoo.com. P.O. Box 37, Roy, 87743. Rev. Robert Peccatiello.
Catechesis Religious Program—Students 25.
Missions—Bueyeros, Harding Co.
Gallegos, Harding Co.
Sabinoso, San Miguel Co.

SAN JUAN PUEBLO, RIO ARRIBA CO. (INDIAN PUEBLO), SAN JUAN BAUTISTA (1598)
185 Popay Ave., P.O. Box 1075, Ohkay Owingeh, 87566. Tel: 505-852-4179. Revs. Jose Herrera, Admin.; Robert Bustamante; Deacons John Bird; Michael Salazar; Gregory Aguilar.
Catechesis Religious Program—Tel: 505-852-2270; Fax: 505-852-9719. Sr. Mariana Nwankwo, D.R.E. Students 265.
Missions—San Antonio—Alcalde, Rio Arriba Co.
San Pablo, Chamita, Rio Arriba Co.
San Rafael, El Guique, Rio Arriba Co.
San Miguel, Ranchitos, Rio Arriba Co.
San Francisco, [CEM] Estaca, Rio Arriba Co.
Sagrada Familia, Alcalde, Rio Arriba Co. 87511.
San Diego, Tesuque, 87574.
San Idelfonso, San Idelfonso Pueblo, 87501.
Santa Clara, Santa Clara Pueblo, Rio Arriba Co., NM 87532.
St. Anne, Alcalde, Rio Arriba Co. 87511.
Shrine—Our Lady of Lourdes, Pilgrimage shrine.

SANTA CRUZ, SANTA FE CO., HOLY CROSS (1695) [CEM] (Hispanic)
1332 Holy Cross St., P.O. Box 1228, Santa Cruz, 87567-1228. Tel: 505-753-3345; Email:

holycrossadm@yahoo.com. Revs. Javier Gutierrez, S.F.; John Plans, S.F., Parochial Vicar.
School—Holy Cross School, (Grades PreK-12), Tel: 505-753-4644; Fax: 505-216-0653; Email: holycrosscadm@yahoo.com. Mrs. Terry Ann Lopez, Prin.; Katharine Gutierrez, Librarian. Lay Teachers 7; Students 93.
Catechesis Religious Program—Tel: 505-216-5001. Betty Andrade, D.R.E. (Elementary); Salomon Velasquez, D.R.E. (Junior & Senior High); Sunny Velasquez, D.R.E. (Junior & Senior High). Students 321.
Missions—La Sangre de Cristo—Cuarteles, Santa Fe Co., NM 87567.
Nacimiento de Santo Nino Jesus, La Puebla, Santa Fe Co., NM 87522. La Puebla, Santa Fe Co., NM 87522.
San Isidro, Mesilla, 88046.
San Pedro, San Pedro, Santa Fe Co., NM 87533.
Santo Nino de Atocha, Santo Nino, Santa Fe Co., NM 87533.

SANTA ROSA, GUADALUPE CO., ST. ROSE OF LIMA (1907) [CEM] (Hispanic)
439 Third St., Santa Rosa, 88435. Tel: 575-472-3724; Email: luciaf11@hotmail.com. Rev. Christopher Denzell Bernabe; Deacon Marvin M. Marquez.
Catechesis Religious Program—Tel: 505-472-3992. Sr. Ann Kaufmann, D.R.E. Students 150.
Missions—Nuestra Senora Del Refugio—Church Rd., Puerto de Luna, Guadalupe Co.
San Ignacio, San Ignacio Rd., San Ignacio, Guadalupe Co.
San Isidro, 439 S. 3rd St., Borica, Guadalupe Co.
Santo Nino, Cuervo, Guadalupe Co.
San Jose, Colonias, Guadalupe Co.
Holy Family, Pintada, Guadalupe Co.
Our Lady of Sorrows, Milagro, Guadalupe Co.

SOCORRO, SOCORRO CO., SAN MIGUEL (1615) [CEM 8] [JC] (Native American—Hispanic)
403 El Camino Real, N.W., Socorro, 87801. Tel: 575-835-2891; Tel: 575-835-2891; Email: smiguel@sdc.ord. Rev. John Anasiudu; Deacons Miguel Ybarra; Nicholas Keller.
Catechesis Religious Program—Bernadette Zamora, D.R.E. Students 17.
Missions—La Sagrada Familia—Lemitar, Socorro Co.
San Lorenzo, Polvadera, Socorro Co.
San Jose, Luis Lopez, Socorro Co.
San Antonio, San Antonio, Socorro Co.
San Antonio, Alamillo, Socorro Co.
St. Mary Magdalene, Magdalena, Socorro Co.
San Juan Bautista, Kelly, Socorro Co.
Santa Rita, Riley, Socorro Co.

SPRINGER, COLFAX CO., ST. JOSEPH (1882) [JC] (Hispanic)
605 Fifth St., P.O. Box 516, Springer, 87747. Tel: 575-483-2775; Email: stjosephicc@hotmail.com. Rev. Benoit Trieu Van Vu; Deacon Edward Olona.
Catechesis Religious Program—Marcella Jensen, D.R.E. Students 15.
Missions—Our Lady of Mt Carmel Mission—Palo Blanco, Colfax Co.
San Isidro Mission, Tinaja, Colfax Co.

TAOS, TAOS CO., NUESTRA SENORA DE GUADALUPE-TAOS (1801) [CEM] (Spanish)
205 Don Fernando St., Taos, 87571. Tel: 575-758-9208; Email: olgtaos@yahoo.com. Rev. Daniel Gutierrez; Deacons Donald Martinez; Jerry Quintana.
Catechesis Religious Program—Tel: 575-776-4764. Students 141.
Mission—St. Jerome, Taos Pueblo, Taos, Taos Co. 87571.
Chapels—St. Teresa—
Nuestra Senora De Dolores, Witt Rd., Canon, Taos, 87571.
Immaculate Conception, Ranchitos Rd., Taos, 87571.
San Antonio, La Loma Plaza, Taos, 87571.

TIERRA AMARILLA, RIO ARRIBA CO., SANTO NINO-TIERRA AMARILLA (1966) [JC] (Hispanic)
1 County Rd. 323, P.O. Box 160, Tierra Amarilla, 87575. Tel: 575-588-7473; Fax: 575-588-7239; Email: sjsncc@elvallecatolico.org; Web: www.elvallecatolico.org. Rev. Ted Butler.
Catechesis Religious Program—Twinned with San Jose, Los Ojos.

TIJERAS, BERNALILLO CO., HOLY CHILD (1962) [CEM 9] [JC2]
19 Camino del Santo Nino, P.O. Box 130, Tijeras, 87059. Tel: 505-281-2297; Email: holychildparish@aol.com; Web: holychildparishnm.org. Rev. Mark E. Granito; Deacons Larry Carmony; Maurice Rodriguez; Randy Rodriguez.
School—Holy Child Catholic School, (Grades PreK-8), Tel: 505-281-3077; Email: jmartinez456@comcast.net; Web: www.holychildcatholicschool.org. Lay Teachers 11; Students 80.
Catechesis Religious Program—Connie Rogers, D.R.E. Students 60.
Missions—Holy Child—Carnuel, Bernalillo Co.
San Juan de Nepumoceno, Chilili, Bernalillo Co.
San Isidro, Escobosa, Bernalillo Co.
San Antonio, 11991 N. Hwy. 14, San Antonio, Bernalillo Co. 87008.
San Isidro, Sedillo, Bernalillo Co.
San Lorenzo, 55 Canoncito Rd., Cedar Crest, Bernalillo Co. 87008.
Senor de Mapimi, San Antonito.

TOME, VALENCIA CO., IMMACULATE CONCEPTION-TOME (1739) [CEM] (Spanish)
7 Church Loop, P.O. Box 100, Tome, 87060-0100. Tel: 505-865-7497; Email: secy@immaculateconceptiontome.com; Web: www.immaculateconceptiontome.org. Rev. Jose A. Hernandez.
Catechesis Religious Program—7 Church Loop, Juan Diego Hall, Tel: 505-865-4220. Martha Sanchez, D.R.E. Students 147.
Mission—Immaculate Conception Casa Colorado, State Hwy. 304 S., Belen, Valencia Co. 87002.

TUCUMCARI, QUAY CO., ST. ANNE-TUCUMCARI (1910) [JC]
306 W. High St., Tucumcari, 88401. Tel: 575-461-2515; Email: stannestucumcari@gmail.com. Rev. John Paul Afuecheta.
Catechesis Religious Program—Tel: 575-461-2525. Nancy Arias, D.R.E. Students 176.
Missions—St. Anthony—Logan, Quay Co.
Sacred Heart, Nara Visa, Quay Co.
Our Lady of Guadalupe, San Jon, Quay Co.
St. Joan of Arc, Montoya, Quay Co. 88401.

VAUGHN, GUADALUPE CO., ST. MARY (1936) [JC] (Hispanic)
376 W. 8th St., P.O. Box 276, Vaughn, 88353. Tel: 575-584-2924; Email: stmarys@plateautel.net. Rev. Christopher Denzell Bernabe.
Catechesis Religious Program—P.O. Box 128, Vaughn, 88353. Tel: 575-584-2696. Linda Montoya, D.R.E. Students 2.
Missions—Encino, Torrance Co.
Duran, Torrance Co.
Pastura, Guadalupe Co.
Pinos Wells, Torrance Co.

VILLANUEVA, SAN MIGUEL, OUR LADY OF GUADALUPE-VILLANUEVA (1830) [CEM 6] (Hispanic)
4 Our Lady of Guadalupe, P.O. Box 39, Villanueva, 87583. Tel: 575-421-2548; Fax: 575-421-2548; Email: nsdeguadalupe@plateautel.net. Rev. Moses Nwankwo, (Nigeria).
Catechesis Religious Program—Lana Gallegos, D.R.E. Students 40.
Missions—Sena, San Miguel Co.
Cerrito, San Miguel Co.
Gonzales Ranch, San Miguel Co.
Leyba, San Miguel Co.
Aurora, San Miguel Co.

WAGON MOUND, MORA CO., SANTA CLARA (1882) [CEM] (Hispanic)
501 Nolan St., Wagon Mound, 87752. Rev. Terrence Brennan, (Retired); Deacon Charlie Duran.
Res.: 805 Calhoun Ave., Wagon Mound, 87752.
Catechesis Religious Program—Students 8.
Missions—Ocate, Mora Co.
Los Hueros, Mora Co.
Los Le Febres, Mora Co.
Watrous, Mora Co.

PILGRIMAGE SHRINES

SANTA FE
SHRINE OF OUR LADY OF GUADALUPE
417 Agua Fria St., Santa Fe, 87501. Tel: 505-983-8868; Email: olog_sf73@archdiosf.org. Rev. Dennis M. Garcia, J.C.L.

ALBUQUERQUE
SHRINE OF ST. BERNADETTE
11509 Indian School Rd., N.E., 87112. Tel: 505-247-6829; Email: lpadget@archdiosf.org; Web: www.ShrineofStBernadette.com. Rev. Leo L. Padget.
SHRINE OF THE LITTLE FLOWER/ST. THERESE OF THE INFANT JESUS
300 Mildred, N.W., 87107. Tel: 505-344-8050; Fax: 505-345-3248; Email: sttheresechurch@yahoo.com. Rev. Vincent P. Chavez.

CHIMAYO
SANTUARIO DE CHIMAYO, Attended by Holy Family, Chimayo
15 Santuario Dr., Chimayo, 87522. Tel: 505-351-4360 ; Email: holyfamily@cybermesa.com; Web: www.holychimayo.us. Rev. Julio Gonzales, S.F., Spiritual Advisor.

ISLETA PUEBLO
SHRINE OF SAINT KATERI TEKAKWITHA, Attended by St. Augustine.
71 Tribal Rd. 35, Isleta Pueblo, 87022. Tel: 505-869-3398; Email: gpavamkott@archdiosf.org. Mailing Address: P.O. Box 849, Isleta Pueblo, 87022. Rev. George Pavamkott, O.Praem., (India).

Priests Serving Private and Public Institutions

SANTA FE. *Christus St. Vincent Regional Medical Center*. Rev. Donatus Onyeke, C.S.Sp., (Nigeria) Chap.
Hospital. Sr. Stella Santina Nneji, D.M.M.M., Coord. Hospital Ministry.
New Mexico State Penitentiary.
ALBUQUERQUE. *Lovelace Hospital*. Rev. Edgar Sanchez.
Presbyterian Hospital. Rev. Thomas Pulickal, O. Praem.
Prison Ministry. Rev. Chris Kerstian, O.F.M., Coord., Deacon Robert Vigil, Dir. Outreach.
University Hospital. Rev. Benjamin O. Onwumelui, (Nigeria).
V.A. Hospital. Rev. Bijoy Francis, O.Praem.
Westside Hospitals. Rev. Robert Campbell, O.Praem.
LAS VEGAS. *State Hospital*. Rev. George SalazarAttended by Immaculate Conception Parish.
LOS LUNAS. *Correctional Facility (State)*. Deacon Robert Vigil.

On Duty Outside the Archdiocese:
Rev.—
Whorton, Jeffrey.

Retired:
Most Rev.—
Sheehan, Michael Jarboe, S.T.L., J.C.D., (Retired)
Rev. Msgrs.—
Bolman, Anthony P., (Retired)
Eggert, Francis X., (Retired)
Gomez, Leo, (Retired), (GLP)
Hebert, J. Gaston, (Retired)
Lucero, Leo, (Retired)
Olona, Richard, (Retired)
Revs.—
Bowers, Ronald J., J.C.D., (Retired)
Brasher, C. John, (Retired)
Brennan, Terrence, (Retired)
Brown, Charles, (Retired)
Bui, Joseph Tin Manh, (Retired)
Carney, John F., (Retired)
Conway, John, (Retired)
Falbo, Samuel, (Retired)
Furfaro, Virgil, (Retired)
Garcia, Millan, (Retired)
Jakobiak, Arthur, (Retired)
Jaramillo, Luis, (Retired)
Johnson, Gerald, (Retired)
Malley, Francis, (Retired)
Mayefske, Thomas J., (Retired), (Diocese of Green Bay)
Mendez, Juan, (Retired)
Mitchell, Douglas J., (Retired)
Mondragon, Antonio, (Retired)
Moore, Augustine J., Ph.D., (Retired)
Mueller, Jerome D., O.F.M., (Retired)
Plotkowski, Jerome A., J.C.L., (Retired)
Pretto-Ferro, Franklin D., (Retired)
Prieto, Frank, (Retired)
Rohleder, Earl, (Retired)
Romero, Anthony E., (Retired)
Rubio-Boitel, Fernando, (Retired)
Sanchez, Steven A., (Retired)
Schulz, Ronald, (Retired), (Diocese of Palm Beach, FL)
Shedlock, John, (Retired)
Vance, James L., (Retired)
Young, William E. Jr., (Retired).

Permanent Deacons:
Abeyta, Santos, Holy Family, Albuquerque
Adams, Alton, St. Alice, Mountainair
Aguilar, Gregory, Santa Clara Pueblo, Tewa Missions
Alcouffe, Raymond, Immaculate Heart of Mary, Los Alamos
Alderette, Thomas, St. Patrick/St. Joseph, Raton
Aragon, Raphael (Ray) P., St. Anne, Tucumcari
Archibeque, Norbert, Church of the Incarnation, Rio Rancho
Archuleta, Faustin, St. Jude Thaddeus, Albuquerque
Archuleta, John, Nuestra Senora de Guadalupe, Pojoaque
Archunde, Gregory, (Outside the Archdiocese)
Arellano, Romolo, La Santisima Trinidad, Arroyo Seco
Arquero, Albert, (Retired)
Avalos-Sanchez, Constantino, Holy Family, Albuquerque
Avitia, Hector, San Clemente, Los Lunas
Ayala, Jose, St. Anne, Albuquerque
Ayers, Roger, St. Thomas, Rio Rancho
Baca, Jerry, Our Lady of Belen, Belen
Baca, Paul, San Clemente, Los Lunas
Baca, Rudolph, (Retired)

Baca, Thomas, St. Therese Parish and Shrine, Albuquerque
Baca, Tomas, (Outside the Archdiocese)
Bachechi, Victor, Annunciation, Albuquerque
Barajas, Juan, St. Anne, Albuquerque
Barela, Ruben, Queen of Heaven, Albuquerque
Barkocy, Kevin, Prince of Peace, Albuquerque
Barry, William, St. Bernadette, Albuquerque
Beare, Harry, (Retired), Albuquerque
Beaudette, James, (Retired)
Bernal, Louis, Church of Incarnation, Rio Rancho
Bird, John, St. John the Baptist, Ohkay Owingeh Pueblo
Blea, Edward, Holy Family, Albuquerque
Branch, Theodore, San Isidro, Santa Fe
Broussard, Peter, (Outside the Archdiocese)
Buenaventa, Eric, Our Lady of Sorrows, Bernalillo
Buie, Mark, Incarnation, Rio Rancho
Burkhard, Robert, San Clemente, Los Lunas
Burns, Thomas, (Retired), San Ysidro, Corrales
Burrola, Jose Luis, Our Lady of Guadalupe, Santa Fe
Bussemeier, Mark, Risen Savior, Albuquerque
Cabrera, Juan, Our Lady of Guadalupe, Albuquerque
Calderon, Gonzalo, Our Lady of Sorrows, Bernalillo
Campos, Peter, Immaculate Conception, Las Vegas, New Mexico
Carbajal, James, (Outside of Archdiocese)
Carmony, Larry, Holy Child, Tijeras
Carrillo, Andres, St. John the Baptist, Santa Fe; Dir., Permanent Diaconate
Casaus, Luis, (Retired)
Ceballos-Moreno, Victoriano, St. Anne, Albuquerque
Centenera, Leandro, Prince of Peace, Albuquerque
Cervantes, Jose de Jesus, Our Lady of Sorrows, Bernalillo
Chavez, Andrew, (Retired)
Chavez, Daniel, Our Lady of Guadalupe, Clovis
Chavez, Ernest, Immaculate Conception, Las Vegas
Chavez, Ricardo, Holy Ghost, Albuquerque
Cleveland, Larry, Queen of Heaven, Albuquerque
Contreras, Donald, St. Thomas Aquinas University Parish, Albuquerque
Cordova, John, Santa Maria De La Paz, Santa Fe
Cupps, Donald, (Outside of Archdiocese)
Davis, Keith, Our Lady of the Most Holy Rosary, Albuquerque
Delgado, James P., Our Lady of the Assumption, Albuquerque
Dimas, Juan (Andy), St. Anne, Santa Fe
Do, Tien Bui, Our Lady of Lavang, Albuquerque
Dohle, Albert, St. Joseph on the Rio, Albuquerque
Duran, Charles, Santa Clara, Wagon Mound
Eklund, Bruce, (Retired)
Ennis, William, Our Lady of Fatima, Albuquerque
Escandon, Jose, (Retired), Albuquerque
Espinosa, Edward, Our Lady of Guadalupe, Peralta
Esquibel, A. Edwin, La Joya (On Leave)
Fraker, Steven, Prince of Peace, Albuquerque
Gagnon, Fabian, (Retired)
Gallegos, Eloy, Santa Maria de la Paz, Santa Fe
Gallegos, Manuel Heraldo, St. Patrick-St. Joseph, Chama
Gallegos, Martin Jr., St. John the Baptist, Santa Fe
Garcia, Joseph, St. John the Baptist, Santa Fe
Garcia, Manuel, Risen Savior, Albuquerque
Garcia, Nestor, (Retired)
Garcia, Pedro, Nuestra Senora de Guadalupe, Pojoaque
Garcia, Pilar, Queen of Heaven, Albuquerque
Garcia, Stephan, Our Lady of Guadalupe, Clovis
Gilbert, Christopher, Sacred Heart, Espanola
Graff, Maurice, Our Lady of Assumption, Albuquerque
Grajeda, Raul, (On Leave)
Granato, John, Our Lady of the Assumption, Albuquerque
Greivel, Rene, St. Joseph on the Rio Grande, Albuquerque
Henderson, Gregorio, (Outside the Archdiocese)
Hernandez, Louis, St. Charles Borromeo, Albuquerque
Herrera, Diego A., (Retired)
Herrera, Joseph, (Retired)
Herrera, Roberto, St. Helen, Portales
Hietpas, Gerald M., (Retired)
Hoefler, William C., (Retired)
Illerbrun, Michael, Nativity of the Blessed Virgin Mary, Albuquerque
Irving, Michael, (Outside the Archdiocese)
Jiron, Robert, (Retired)
Johnson, Charles V., (Retired)
Jones, Leon, Church of the Ascension, Albuquerque
Keller, Nicholas, San Miguel, Socorro
Kenny, Daniel, Our Lady of Sorrows, Bernalillo
Kollasch, William, St. Francis Cathedral Basilica, Santa Fe
Krepps, John, Immaculate Heart of Mary, Los Alamos, NM
LeFebre, Paul, St. Anne, Albuquerque
Leonard, Mark, (Outside the Archdiocese)
Lewis, James R. "Bob", (Retired)
Leyba, Edward, St Thomas, Rio Rancho
Little, David, St. Thomas, Rio Rancho
Lopez, Andrew, St. John the Baptist, Santa Fe
Lopez, Demetrio, (Retired)
Lopez, Jose O., Holy Family, Chimayo
Lucero, Donato, (Retired)
Lucero, Jose E., (Retired)
Lucero, Juan S., Estancia Valley Parish, Moriarty
Lucero, Leroy, St. Anthony, Questa
Maloney, Kevin, (Outside the Archdiocese)
Marquez, Mark Marvin, St. Rose of Lima, Santa Rosa
Marquez, Oscar, (On Leave)
Martinez, Donald J., Our Lady of Guadalupe, Taos
Martinez, Eloy, (Retired)
Martinez, Jose Leroy, (Retired)
Martinez, Juan G., San Miguel del Vado, Ribera
Martinez, Juan R., St. Francis Cathedral, Santa Fe
Martinez, Leonard, Nativity, Albuquerque
Medina, Jesus, Our Lady of the Most Holy Rosary, Albuquerque
Menke, Maurice, San Felipe, Albuquerque
Mercado, Salvador, St. Jude, Albuquerque
Meyerson, George, Incarnation, Rio Rancho
Miller, George, St. Joseph on the Rio Grande, Albuquerque
Montano, Marcus, Sacred Heart, Albuquerque
Montoya, Enrique M., St. Anne, Santa Fe
Montoya, Manuel, Our Lady of Guadalupe, Albuquerque
Montoya, Michael, Our Lady of Belen, Belen
Montoya, P. Louis, St. Francis Xavier, Clayton
Morrison, Charles, St. Anne, Tucumcari
Morrow, Robert, San Ignacio, Albuquerque
Nguyen, Dung (Paul), St. Charles, Albuquerque
O'Hara, James, Immaculate Heart of Mary, Los Alamos, NM
Olona, Edward, St. Joseph, Springer
Ortiz, Juan, Nativity of the Blessed Virgin Mary, Albuquerque
Ortwerth, Paul, (Retired)
Pacheco, Charles, (Retired)
Padilla, Enrique, Prince of Peace, Albuquerque
Palmer, Terry, St. Bernadette, Albuquerque
Parker, Timothy, Risen Savior, Albuquerque
Paszkiewicz, Jerome, Church of the Incarnation, Rio Rancho
Peccatiello, Kenneth, Estancia Valley, Moriarty
Perez, Frank, Our Lady of the Most Holy Rosary, Albuquerque
Perez, Tomas, San Felipe de Neri, Albuquerque
Pullings, Harold, Our Lady of Guadalupe, Clovis
Quintana, Jerry, Our Lady of Guadalupe, Taos
Rael, Felimon, (Retired)
Rael, Marcus, St. Anthony, Questa
Rangel, Stephen S., St. John Vianney, Rio Rancho
Rasinski, John, St. Charles Borromeo, Albuquerque
Richey, Lincoln, Estancia Valley, Moriarty
Rivera, Lawrence Anthony, Our Lady of the Annunciation, Albuquerque, NM
Rodriguez, Juan, (Retired)
Rodriguez, Juan A., Sacred Heart, Clovis
Rodriguez, Maurice, Holy Child, Tijeras
Rodriguez, Randall, Holy Child, Tijeras
Romero, Greg, Nuestra Senora de Guadalupe, Pojoaque
Romero, Jerome, (On Leave)
Roseborough, Donald, Immaculate Conception, Albuquerque
Rowley, Michael, Sacred Heart, Clovis
Roybal, Christobal, St. Gertrude, Mora
Roybal, Reuben, Nuestra Senora de Guadalupe, Pojoaque
Roybal, Richard, St. Anthony, Pecos
Russell, Robert Davis, (Outside the Archdiocese)
Russo, John L., John XXIII Catholic Community, Albuquerque
Sais, Stephen, Queen of Heaven, Albuquerque
Salazar, Ernest, Holy Cross, Santa Cruz
Salazar, Michael, San Isidro-San Jose, Santa Fe
Salazar, Miguel, St. John the Baptist, Ohkay Owingeh Pueblo
Salazar, Phillip, (Outside the Archdiocese)
Salazar, Samuel, (On Leave)
Salinas, Cresencio, San Martin De Porres, Albuquerque
Sanchez, Leroy, St. Thomas Aquinas, Rio Rancho
Sanchez, Norbert C., (Retired)
Sanchez, Reyes, Our Lady of Sorrows, Las Vegas
Sanchez, Robert, Our Lady of Belen, Belen
Sandoval, George, Ph.D., Immaculate Conception, Albuquerque
Santana, Joe, St. Bernadette, Albuquerque
Schwenn, Charles E., San Clemente, Los Lunas
Sedillo, Michael, Immaculate Conception, Cimarron
Segura, Jose, Our Lady of Guadalupe, Pena Blanca
Sena, Edward, St. Anthony of Padua, Fort Sumner
Sena, Patrick, Our Lady of the Annunciation, Albuquerque
Sheehan, Dan, (Retired)
Silva, Joseph, Our Lady of the Most Holy Rosary, Albuquerque
Sinatra, Kenneth, (Retired)
Smith, Frank, St. Thomas, Rio Rancho
Snell, Jimmie, San Clemente, Los Lunas; Dir. of Diaconate Formation
Stith, Thomas, Our Lady of Guadalupe, Santa Fe
Sutton, John, Immaculate Heart of Mary, Los Alamos, NM
Talavera, Raul, San Jose, Albuquerque
Toquinto, Jesus, (Outside the Archdiocese)
Torres, Christopher, Immaculate Conception, Las Vegas
Torres, Edgar, San Jose, Albuquerque
Torres, Larry, Holy Trinity, Arroyo Seco
Trujillo, Alex, (Retired)
Trujillo, Anthony, San Isidro - San Jose, Santa Fe
Trujillo, Kenneth, San Martin de Porres, Albuquerque
Trujillo, Manuel, Our Lady of Belen, Belen, NM
Tuma, Eugene, (Retired)
Tynan, Thomas M., St. Thomas Aquinas, Rio Rancho
Valdez, Alex, Sacred Heart, Espanola
Valdez, Gilbert, Our Lady of Guadalupe, Santa Fe
Valdez, Jose, Nuestra Senora de Guadalupe, Pojoaque
Valdez, Joseph, St. Patrick-St. Joseph, Chama
Valkenburgh, Thomas Van, (Retired)
Valverde, George W., (On Leave)
Vigil, Ralph, Nativity of the Blessed Virgin Mary, Albuquerque
Vigil, Robert, Sacred Heart, Albuquerque
Welch, Robert, (Retired)
Wesley, Michael, St. Therese, Albuquerque
Wicker, Byron, (Retired)
Ybarra, Miguel, San Miguel, Socorro.

INSTITUTIONS LOCATED IN DIOCESE

[A] HIGH SCHOOLS, ARCHDIOCESAN AND PAROCHIAL

ALBUQUERQUE. *St. Pius X High School*, 5301 St. Joseph Dr., N.W., 87120. Tel: 505-831-8400; Fax: 505-831-8413; Email: eolguin@spxabq.org; Web: www.saintpiusx.com. Barbara Rothweiler, Prin.; Very Rev. John B. Trambley II, Pres.; Jennifer Hillsey, Librarian. Deacons 2; Lay Teachers 52; Priests 1; Sisters 1; Students 638; Clergy/Religious Teachers 2.

[B] HIGH SCHOOLS, PRIVATE

SANTA FE. *St. Michael's High School*, (Grades 7-12), (Coed Day School) 100 Siringo Rd., Santa Fe, 87505. Tel: 505-983-7353; Fax: 505-982-8722; Email: spatten@smhs.me; Web: www.stmichaelsff.org. Sam Govea, Prin. Lay Teachers 38; Students 497.

[C] ELEMENTARY REGIONAL SCHOOL

SANTA FE. *Santo Nino Regional Catholic School*, (Grades PreK-6), 23 College Ave., Santa Fe, 87508. Tel: 505-424-1766; Fax: 505-473-1441; Email: snrcs@santoninoregional.org; Web: www.santoninoregional.org. Mr. Dirk Steffens, Prin. Lay Teachers 19; Students 232; Clergy/Religious Teachers 1.

[D] GENERAL HOSPITALS

SANTA FE. **CHRISTUS St. Vincent Regional Medical Center*, 455 St. Michael's Dr., Santa Fe, 87505. Tel: 505-983-3361; Fax: 505-913-5210; Email: ContactUs@stvin.org; Web: www.christushealth.org. Mrs. Lillian Montoya, CEO. Bed Capacity 200; Tot Asst. Annually 255,000; Total Staff 500.

[E] SPECIAL HOSPITALS AND SANATORIA FOR INVALIDS

SANTA FE. *Villa Therese Catholic Clinic*, 219 Cathedral Pl., Santa Fe, 87501. Tel: 505-983-8561; Fax: 505-982-7863; Email: execdirector@vtccsf.org; Email: limberpine@aol.com; Web: www.vtccsf.org. Victoria Otero, Dir. Tot Asst. Annually 2,000; Total Staff 2.

[F] SHELTER CARE HOMES

ALBUQUERQUE. *Good Shepherd Center, Inc.*, 218 Iron St., S.W., 87103. Tel: 505-243-2527; Fax: 505-247-2207; Email: gsc@gscnm.org. Mailing Address: P.O. Box 749, 87103. Stephanie Vigil,

Pres. Direct Service Agency for the Homeless. Bed Capacity 60; Tot Asst. Annually 170,068; Total Staff 10.

[G] CARE HOMES FOR PHYSICALLY AND MENTALLY HANDICAPPED

ALBUQUERQUE. *Casa Angelica* (1967) 5629 Isleta Blvd., S.W., 87105. Tel: 505-877-5763; Fax: 505-873-2786 ; Email: lturner@casaangelica.org; Web: www. casaangelica.org. Louise Turner, Admin. Home for developmentally disabled children and young adults. Bed Capacity 16; Lay Staff 52; Residents 16; Sisters 1; Total Staff 56; Total Assisted 16.

[H] MONASTERIES AND RESIDENCES OF PRIESTS AND BROTHERS

ABIQUIU. *Monastery of Christ in the Desert* (1964) 1305 Forest Service Rd. 151, Abiquiu, 87510. P.O. Box 270, Abiquiu, 87510. Tel: 575-613-4233; Fax: 419-831-9113; Email: cidguestmaster@christdesert.org; Web: www. christdesert.org. Rt. Revs. Caedmon Holmes, Subprior; Philip Lawrence, O.S.B., Abbot; Revs. Christian Leisy, O.S.B.; Bernard Cranor, O.S.B.; Benedict McCaffree, O.S.B., Prior; Joseph Gabriel Cuismano, O.S.B.; Luis Regalado, O.S.B.; Mayeal Thu Van Tran, O.S.B.; Thomas Benedict Baxter, O.S.B.; Simeon Cook, O.S.B.; Andrew Dzung An Nguyen, O.S.B.; Gregory Vu, O.S.B.; John-Paul Mario, O.S.B.; Fernando Hool Salazar, O.S.B.; Jeffrey Steele, O.S.B.; Joseph Kuchta Chylinski, O.S.B. Novices 12; Postulants 8; Priests 16; Professed 56; Solemnly Professed 48; Total in Community 102.

ALBUQUERQUE. *Community of the Franciscans of the Renewal San Juan Diego Friary*, 404 San Mateo Blvd., N.E., 87108. Tel: 505-990-3001; Fax: 505-990-0187; Email: cfrgensec@franciscanfriars.com; Web: www.cfrnewmexico.com. Revs. Joachim Joseph Bellavance, C.F.R., Supr.; Anthony Marie Baetzold, C.F.R.; Juan Diego Sutherland, C.F.R.; Bro. Vittorio Jean Marie Pesce, C.F.R.; Revs. Daniel Marie Williamson, C.F.R., Vicar, Vicar; Ignatius Shin.

Santa Maria de la Vid Abbey, 5825 Coors Blvd., S.W., 87121-6700. Tel: 505-873-4399; Fax: 505-873-4667; Email: norbertines@norbertinecommunity.org; Web: www.norbertinecommunity.org. Very Rev. Robert E. Campbell, O.Praem.; Rt. Rev. Joel P. Garner, O.-Praem., Abbot; Revs. Eugene Gries, O.Praem., Prior; Bijoy Francis Valayil, O.Praem., (India); George Pavamkott, O.Praem., (India); Peter Muller, O.Praem.; Graham R. Golden, O.Praem.; Thomas Pulikal, O.Praem., (India); Stephen A. Gaetner, O.Praem.; Deacon James Owens, O.-Praem., Treas. Canons Regular of Premontre (Norbertine Community).Sponsor of the Norbertine Spirituality Center. Brothers 1; Priests 9.

The Province of Our Lady of Guadalupe (1985) 1204 Stinson, S.W., 87121-3440. Tel: 505-831-9199; Fax: 505-831-9577; Email: ofmprovsec@aol.com; Email: fronw@aol.com; Web: www.olgofm.org. Mailing Address: P.O. Box 12315, Albuquerqe, 87195-0315. Very Rev. Jack Clark Robinson, O.F.M., Prov.; Bros. Efren Quintero, O.F.M., Sec.; Bruce Michalek, O.F.M., Dir.; George Ward, O.F.M., Asst. Treas.; Rev. Ronald Walters, O.F.M., J.C.L., Treas.; Very Rev. Patrick Schafer, O.F.M., Councillor; Bros. Richardo Garcia, O.F.M.; Bart Wolf, O.F.M.; Gordon Boykin, O.F.M.; Michael Burns, O.F.M.; Revs. Erasmo Romero, O.F.M., Vocation Dir.; Emeric Nordmeyer, O.F.M., (Retired); Richard Rohr, O.F.M.; Hilaire Valiquette, O.F.M.
Franciscan Indian Missions
Franciscan Mission Center
The Province of Our Lady of Guadalupe of the Order of Friars Minor, Inc.
Southwest Franciscan Missions Brothers 15; Priests 28.

Villa Mathias, Inc., 901 Bro. Mathias Pl., N.W., P.O. Box 389, 87103. Tel: 505-243-4238; Fax: 505-764-9721; Email: brogsullivan@aol.org. Bro. Gerard Sullivan, B.G.S., Prior. Brothers 3.

JEMEZ SPRINGS. *Our Lady of Lourdes*, P.O. Box 10, Jemez Springs, 87025-0010. Tel: 575-829-3004; Fax: 575-829-3706; Email: servants@theservants.org; Web: www.theservants.org. Very Rev. David T. Fitzgerald, s.P., Servant Gen. & Father Servant; Rev. Pio Dang Xuan Ba, s.P., Admin.; Bros. Bernard Scollon, s.P.; John Paul Pelletier, s.P. Brothers 3; Priests 2. *Formation House*,
Tel: 505-829-3720; Fax: 505-829-3706.

PECOS. *Our Lady of Guadalupe Abbey*, 16 Guadalupe Ln., P.O. Box 1080, Pecos, 87552-1080. Tel: 505-757-6415; Fax: 505-757-2285; Email: guestmaster@pecosmonastery.org; Web: www. pecosmonastery.org. Revs. Symeon Galazka; Aidan Gore, O.S.B. Oliv.; Colman Heffern, O.S.B. Oliv.; Robert Lussier, O.S.B. Oliv.; Andrew Miles, O.S.B.; Bros. Bruno Boyko, O.S.B. Oliv.; John M. Davies, O.S.B. Oliv.; Francis Dawson, O.S.B. Oliv.; Joseph Janeczko, O.S.B. Oliv.; Jaboc Kozel, O.S.B. Oliv.; James M. Marron, O.S.B. Oliv.; Sr. Helen Vasquez, O.S.B. Oliv. (Olivetan Benedictine Monks) Brothers 6; Priests 5; Sisters 1.

[I] CONVENTS AND RESIDENCES FOR SISTERS

SANTA FE. *Discalced Carmelite Monastery* (1945) 49 Mount Carmel Rd., Santa Fe, 87505-0352. Tel: 505-983-7232; Email: vocation@carmelofsantafe.org; Web: www. carmelofsantafe.org. Mother Marie Bernadette Bennett, Prioress. Novices 2; Sisters 8; Solemn Professed Nuns 6.

ALBUQUERQUE. *Cristo Rey Provincial House*, 5625 Isleta Blvd., S.W., 87105. Tel: 505-873-2854; Fax: 505-873-0678; Email: fdccalb@yahoo.com; Web: www.canossiansisters.org. Sr. Anna Maria Serafini, Provincial. Canossian Daughters of Charity. Sisters 15.

RIO RANCHO. *Felician Sisters of the Southwest United States of America*, 4210 Meadowlark Ln., S.E., Rio Rancho, 87124-1021. Tel: 505-892-8862; Fax: 505-891-3893; Email: smchristopher@feliciansisters.org; Web: www. feliciansistersna.org. Sr. Mary Christopher Moore, C.S.S.F., Prov. Sisters 19.

[J] RETREAT HOUSES

SANTA FE. *Immaculate Heart of Mary Retreat and Conference Center*, 50 Mount Carmel Rd., Santa Fe, 87505. Tel: 505-988-1975; Fax: 505-988-3963; Email: jsnodgrass@archdiosf.org. Mr. David Quezada, Exec. Dir.; Mr. Jeff Snodgrass, Dir.

ALBUQUERQUE. *Madonna Retreat and Conference Center*, 4040 St. Joseph Pl., N.W., 87120. Tel: 505-831-8196; Fax: 505-831-8103; Email: madonnacenter@archdiosf.org; Web: www. retreatabq.org. Mr. David Quezada, Exec. Dir.; Esther-Marie Nagiel, Dir. Total in Residence 5; Total Staff 7.

PECOS. *Our Lady of Guadalupe Olivetan Benedictine Abbey*, 16 Guadalupe Ln., P.O. Box 1080, Pecos, 87552. Tel: 505-757-6415; Fax: 505-757-2285; Email: guestmaster@pecosmonastery.org; Web: www.pecosmonastery.org. Rev. Aidan Gore, O.S.B. Oliv., Abbot.

[K] NEWMAN CENTERS

ALBUQUERQUE. **Faith and Justice Center Inc.*, 619 Copper Ave., N.W., 87102. Tel: 505-247-4271; Email: wbroussard@iccabq.org. Rev. Warren J. Broussard, S.J., Dir.

St. Thomas Aquinas University Parish (1950) 1815 Las Lomas Rd., N.E., 87106. Tel: 505-247-1094; Fax: 505-247-2933; Email: mdepalma@archdiosf.org; Web: www.lobocatholic.org. Rev. Michael DePalma, Parish Pastor. Priests 1; Total in Residence 1; Total Staff 4.

**Trinity House Catholic Worker*, 1925 Five Points Rd., S.W., 87105. Tel: 505-842-5697; Email: trinityhousesecw@gmail.com. Swami Omkata, Dir.

LAS VEGAS. *Highlands University Newman Center*, 909 8th St., Las Vegas, 87701. Mailing Address: 811 - 6th St., Las Vegas, 87701. Tel: 505-425-7791; Fax: 505-425-6991; Email: icchurch2000@yahoo.com. Rev. George Salazar, Campus Min. Attended by Immaculate Conception Parish, Las Vegas.

PORTALES. *University Catholic Center - St. Thomas More Chapel*, E.N.M.U., 1614 W. 17th St., Portales, 88130. Tel: 575-356-4241; Fax: 575-359-1721; Email: emmabritton. sthelens@gmail.com. Very Rev. Charles Ugochukwu, (Nigeria) Chap. Total Staff 1.

SOCORRO. *St. Patrick Newman Center*, 801 School of Mines Rd., Socorro, 87801. Tel: 575-835-8650; Email: agalleoo@nmt.edu. Deacon Nicholas Keller, Dir.

[L] MISCELLANEOUS LISTINGS

SANTA FE. *St. Michael's High School Foundation*, 100 Siringo Rd., Santa Fe, 87505. P.O. Box 22563, Santa Fe, 87502. Tel: 505-988-2264; Fax: 505-955-8921; Email: mayers@smhs.me; Web: stmikesfoundation.org/. Mrs. Tara Block Archuleta, Pres.; Maureen Ayers, Exec.

ALBUQUERQUE. *Annual Catholic Appeal Foundation of the Archdiocese of Santa Fe*, 4000 St. Joseph Pl., N.W., 87120. Tel: 505-831-8155; Fax: 505-831-8111 ; Email: kwrasman@archdiosf.org; Web: www. acaarchdiosf.org. Mrs. Karin Wrasman, Dir.

Anselm Weber Fund, 1204 Stinson St., S.W., P.O. Box 12315, 87195-0315. Tel: 505-877-6394; Email: treasolg@comcast.net. Rev. Ronald Walters, O.F.M., J.C.L., Corp. Teas.

Archbishop's School Fund, 4000 St. Joseph Pl., N.W., 87120. Tel: 505-831-8172; Fax: 505-831-8107; Email: smurphy@archdiosf.org. Susan M. Murphy, M.A., Supt.

Archdiocesan Priests Retirement Fund, Inc., 5024 4th St., N.W., 87107. Tel: 505-503-8637; Fax: 505-343-1463; Email: jen@jcantrellcpa.com. Rev. Dennis M. Garcia, J.C.L., Pres.

Archdiocese of Santa Fe D&L Fund, 4000 St. Joseph Pl., N.W., 87120. Tel: 505-831-8132; Fax: 505-831-8115; Email: tsalgado@asfcca.org. Mr. Tony Salgado, CPA, Exec.

Archdiocese of Santa Fe Real Estate Corporation, 4000 St. Joseph Pl., N.W., 87120. Tel: 505-831-8397; Email: tmacken@archdiosf.org. Mr. Thomas P. Macken, Esq., Chancellor.

Archdiocese of Santa Fe Real Estate Trust, 4000 St. Joseph Pl., N.W., 87120. Tel: 505-831-8397; Fax: 505-831-8228; Email: tmacken@archdiosf.org. Mr. Thomas P. Macken, Esq., Chancellor.

**St. Bernadette Institute of Sacred Art* (1993) P.O. Box 8249, 87198. Tel: 505-717-5157; Fax: 505-271-8467; Email: stbernadetteinst@gmail.com; Web: www. stbernadetteinstitute.com. Dan Paulos, Dir., Email: sbi@nmia.com. Sponsors and supports Catholic art and artists.

The Brothers of the Good Shepherd, 901 Brother Mathias Pl., N.W., P.O. Box 389, 87102-7103. Tel: 505-243-4238; Fax: 505-764-9721; Email: brogsullivan@aol.com; Web: www.sjog-na.org. Bro. Gerard Sullivan, B.G.S., Prior. Brothers 3.

Caritas Deus Inc., 412 Iron St., S.W., P.O. Box 749, 87103. Tel: 505-243-2527; Fax: 505-247-2207; Email: brosean68@gmail.com. Bro. Sean McIsaac, Dir. Property management nonprofit corporation.

Catholic Charismatic Center (1978) 1412 Fifth St., N.W., 87102. Tel: 505-247-0397; Fax: 505-843-9147 ; Email: abqcatholiccharismaticcenter@gmail.com; Web: www.asqccc.org. Sr. Anthony Birdsall, D.L.J.C., Dir. Total in Residence 2; Total Staff 3.

The Catholic Foundation of the Archdiocese of Santa Fe (1991) 4333 Pan American Fwy., N.E., Ste. D, 87107. Tel: 505-872-2901; Fax: 505-872-2905; Email: ed@thecatholicfoundation.org; Web: www. thecatholicfoundation.org. Mr. Edward Larranaga, Pres. Total Staff 5.

Charity Unlimited, 901 Brother Mathias Pl., N.W., P.O. Box 389, 87103. Tel: 505-243-4238; Fax: 505-764-9721; Email: brogsullivan@aol.com. Bro. Gerard Sullivan, B.G.S., Prior. Property management nonprofit corporation.

Dominican Ecclesial Institute (D.E.I.) (1996) 4060 St. Josephs Pl., N.W., Ste. 210, 87125. Tel: 505-243-0525; Fax: 505-414-7724; Email: director@deiabq.org; Web: www.deiabq.org. Ian Wood, Dir. Total Staff 2.

Fraternidad Piadosa de Nuestro Padre Jesus Nazareno, 4000 St. Joseph Pl., N.W., 87120. Tel: 505-259-0254; Tel: 505-345-7397; Email: joselucero@comcast.net. Deacon Jose E. Lucero, Spiritual Advisor.

St. Joseph Fertility Care Center (1976) 4000 St. Joseph Pl., N.W., Lourdes Hall, #130, 87120. Tel: 505-831-8222; Fax: 505-831-8223; Email: angel@fertilitycare.net. Angelique N. Garcia, Pres.

St. Pius X High School Foundation, Inc., 5301 St. Joseph Dr., N.W., 87120. Tel: 505-831-8423; Fax: 505-831-8438; Email: bwallace@spxabq.org; Web: www.saintpiusx.com. Barbara Rothweiler, Prin. Nonprofit corporation for the financial support of St. Pius X High School.

Roger Huser Fund, 1204 Stinson St. S.W., P.O. Box 12315, 87195-0315. Tel: 505-877-6394; Email: fronw186@gmail.com. Rev. Ronald Walters, O.F.M., J.C.L., Treas.

Santa Maria de la Vid Abbey, 5825 Coors Blvd., S.W., 87121-6700. Tel: 505-873-4399; Fax: 505-873-4667; Email: norbertines@norbertinecommunity.org; Web: www.norbertinecommunity.org. Rt. Rev. Joel P. Garner, O.Praem., Abbot. Total in Residence 13; Total Staff 4.

JEMEZ SPRINGS. *EDSA Charitable Trust*, 18161 Hwy. 4, Jemez Springs, 87025. P.O. Box 489, Jemez Springs, 87025. Tel: 575-829-3720; Email: xuanba236@gmail.com. Rev. Pio Dang Xuan Ba, s. P., Admin.

Fitzgerald Charitable Trust, 18161 Hwy. 4, Jemez Springs, 87025. Tel: 575-829-3586; Fax: 575-829-3706; Email: xuanba236@gmail.com; Web: www.theservants.org. Rev. Pio Dang Xuan Ba, s.P., Admin.

RIO RANCHO. *St. Felix Pantry, Inc.*, 4020 Barbara Loop S.E., Rio Rancho, 87124-1023. Tel: 505-891-8075; Fax: 505-891-8075; Email: smangela@stfelixpantry.org. Sr. Mary Angela Parkins, C.S.S.F., Pres. Total Staff 145; Total Assisted Per Month 4,000.

RELIGIOUS INSTITUTES OF MEN REPRESENTED IN THE ARCHDIOCESE

For further details refer to the corresponding bracketed number in the Religious Institutes of Men or Women section.

[0200]—*Benedictine Monks* (Pecos; Abbey of Christ in the Desert, Abiquiu)—O.S.B.

[0330-1]—*Brothers of Christian Schools*—F.S.C.

[0900]—*Canons Regular of Premontre* (Norbertine Fathers and Brothers of Santa Maria de la Vid Abbey, Albuquerque, NM)—O.Praem.
[0170]—*Congregation of St. Basil* (Toronto, Canada)—C.S.B.
[0650]—*Congregation of the Holy Spirit* (Nigeria)—C.S.S.P.
[1000]—*Congregation of the Passion* (South River, NJ)—C.P.
[0520]—*Franciscan Friars* (Our Lady of Guadalupe)—O.F.M.
[0535]—*Franciscan Friars of the Renewal* (Bronx, NY)—C.F.R.
[0670]—*Hospitaller Brothers of St. John of God*—O.H.
[0800]—*Maryknoll* (Maryknoll, NY)—M.M.
[0200-2]—*Oliventan Benedictines* (Our Lady of Guadalupe Abbey, Pecos, NM)—O.S.B. Oliv.
[0430]—*Order of Preachers-Dominicans* (St. Albert the Great Province)—O.P.
[0140]—*Order of St. Augustine of Nigeria* (Prov. of Nigeria, Plateau State)—O.S.A.
[1230]—*Servants of the Paraclete* (Jemez Springs, NM)—s.P.
[0690]—*Society of Jesus* (New Orleans Prov., Missouri Prov.)—S.J.
[0975]—*Society of Our Lady of the Most Holy Trinity* (Corpus Christi, TX)—S.O.L.T.
[0640]—*Sons of the Holy Family* (Silver Spring, MD)—S.F.

RELIGIOUS INSTITUTES OF WOMEN REPRESENTED IN THE ARCHDIOCESE

[0200]—*Benedictine Sisters* (Pecos and Abiquiu, NM)—O.S.B.
[0730]—*Canossian Daughters of Charity* (Albuquerque, NM)—Fd.C.C.
[1070-09]—*Congregation of St. Catherine of Siena* (Racine, WI)—O.P.
[3832]—*Congregation of the Sisters of St. Joseph*—C.S.J.
[1780]—*Congregation of the Sisters of the Third Order of St. Francis of Perpetual Adoration* (La Crosse, WI)—F.S.P.A.
[0885]—*Daughters of Mary Mother of Mercy* (Umuahia, Abia State, Nigeria)—D.M.M.M.
[0420]—*Discalced Carmelite Nuns* (Santa Fe, NM)—O.C.D.
[0965]—*Disciples of the Lord Jesus Christ* (Prayer Town, TX)—D.L.J.C.
[1070-14]—*Dominican Sisters* (Grand Rapids, MI)—O.P.
[1070-13]—*Dominican Sisters* (Adrian, MI)—O.P.
[1115]—*Dominican Sisters of Peace* (Columbus, OH)—O.P.
[1170]—*Felician Sisters* (Congregation of Sisters of St. Felix of Cantalice)—C.S.S.F.
[2183]—*Immaculate Heart of Mary Mother of Christ* (Onitsha, Anambra State, Nigeria)—I.H.M.
[]—*Missionary Catechists of the Sacred Heart of Jesus and Mary* (Victoria, TX)—M.C.S.H.
[]—*Missionary Sisters of the Blessed Sacrament* (Ughelli Delta State, Nigeria)—M.S.B.S.
[3130]—*Our Lady of Victory Missionary Sisters* (Huntington, IN)—O.L.V.M.
[3430]—*Religious Teachers Filippine* (St. Lucy Filippine Province, Morristown, NJ)—M.P.F.
[]—*Sisters for Christian Community* (Cincinnati, OH)—S.F.C.C.
[0440]—*Sisters of Charity of Cincinnati, Ohio* (Mt. St. Joseph, OH)—S.C.
[1805]—*Sisters of St. Francis of the Neumann Communities* (Syracuse, NY)—O.S.F.
[2360]—*Sisters of Loretto at the Foot of the Cross* (Littleton, CO)—S.L.
[2575-2]—*Sisters of Mercy of the Americas* (Cumberland, RI)—R.S.M.
[2575]—*Sisters of Mercy of the Americas* (Omaha, NE)—R.S.M.
[1705]—*The Sisters of St. Francis of Assisi* (Milwaukee, WI)—O.S.F.
[1630]—*Sisters of St. Francis of Penance and Christian Charity* (Sacred Heart & Holy Name Provinces, Stella Niagara, NY)—O.S.F.
[1640]—*Sisters of St. Francis of Perpetual Adoration* (St. Joseph Province, Colorado Springs, CO)—O.S.F.
[3830-1]—*Sisters of St. Joseph* (Boston, MA)—C.S.J.
[0260]—*Sisters of the Blessed Sacrament for Indians and Colored People* (Bensalem, PA)—S.B.S.
[3670]—*Sisters of the Sacred Heart of Jesus of Saint Jacut* (San Antonio, TX)—S.S.C.J.
[1720]—*Sisters of the Third Order Regular of St. Francis of the Congregation of Our Lady of Lourdes* (Rochester, MN)—O.S.F.
[2150-60]—*Sisters, Servants of the Immaculate Heart of Mary* (Scranton, PA)—I.H.M.
[3105]—*Society of Our Lady of the Most Holy Trinity* (Skidmore, TX)—S.O.L.T.

ARCHDIOCESAN CEMETERIES

ALBUQUERQUE. *Catholic Cemetery Association*, 1900 Edith Blvd. S.W., 87120. Tel: 505-248-1532; Email: ldetommaso@asfcca.org. Leah DeTommaso, Exec. Dir., Tel: 505-248-1532. Diocesan Cemeteries, Rosario (Santa Fe), Mt. Calvary (Albuquerque) and Gate of Heaven (Albuquerque).

NECROLOGY

† Chavez, Patrick Jose, (Retired), Died Nov. 18, 2018
† Farris, Daniel Lee, (Retired), Died Nov. 23, 2018
† Zotter, Thomas A., (Retired), Died Sep. 30, 2018

An asterisk (*) denotes an organization that has established tax-exempt status directly with the IRS and is not covered by the USCCB Group Ruling.

Diocese of Santa Rosa in California

(Dioecesis Sanctae Rosae in California)

Most Reverend

ROBERT FRANCIS VASA

Bishop of Santa Rosa in California; ordained May 22, 1976; appointed Bishop of Baker November 19, 1999; consecrated and installed January 26, 2000; appointed Coadjutor Bishop of Santa Rosa in California January 24, 2011; installed March 6, 2011; succeeded June 30, 2011.

Most Reverend

DANIEL F. WALSH, D.D.

Retired Bishop of Santa Rosa in California; ordained March 30, 1963; appointed Titular Bishop of Tigia and Auxiliary of San Francisco September 24, 1981; appointed Bishop of Reno-Las Vegas June 9, 1987; installed August 6, 1987; appointed Bishop of Las Vegas March 21, 1995; installed June 28, 1995; appointed Bishop of Santa Rosa in California on April 4, 2000; installed May 22, 2000; retired June 30, 2011.

Chancery Office: 985 Airway Ct., Santa Rosa, CA 95403. Tel: 707-566-3300; Fax: 707-542-9702. . *Mailing Address: P.O. Box 1297, Santa Rosa, CA 95402-1297.*

Web: www.srdiocese.org

ESTABLISHED FEBRUARY 21, 1962.

Square Miles 11,711.

Comprises six Counties in the State of California-viz., Del Norte, Humboldt, Lake, Mendocino, Napa and Sonoma.

Legal Titles: "The Roman Catholic Bishop of Santa Rosa, a Corporation Sole" and "The Roman Catholic Welfare Corporation of Santa Rosa."
For legal titles of parishes and diocesan institutions, consult the Chancery Office.

STATISTICAL OVERVIEW

Personnel	
Bishop	1
Retired Bishops	1
Priests: Diocesan Active in Diocese	36
Priests: Diocesan Active Outside Diocese	4
Priests: Retired, Sick or Absent	27
Number of Diocesan Priests	67
Religious Priests in Diocese	11
Total Priests in Diocese	78
Extern Priests in Diocese	11
Permanent Deacons in Diocese	50
Total Brothers	26
Total Sisters	20
Parishes	
Parishes	40
With Resident Pastor:	
Resident Diocesan Priests	36
Resident Religious Priests	4
Missions	22
Pastoral Centers	2
Professional Ministry Personnel:	
Brothers	16
Sisters	20
Lay Ministers	16
Welfare	
Catholic Hospitals	4
Total Assisted	398,545
Health Care Centers	1
Total Assisted	160,963
Residential Care of Children	1
Total Assisted	90
Special Centers for Social Services	2
Total Assisted	19,555
Educational	
Diocesan Students in Other Seminaries	6
Total Seminarians	6
High Schools, Diocesan and Parish	2
Total Students	782
High Schools, Private	4
Total Students	835
Elementary Schools, Diocesan and Parish	8
Total Students	1,679
Elementary Schools, Private	1
Total Students	88
Catechesis/Religious Education:	
High School Students	1,418
Elementary Students	6,691
Total Students under Catholic Instruction	11,499
Teachers in the Diocese:	
Priests	1
Lay Teachers	266
Vital Statistics	
Receptions into the Church:	
Infant Baptism Totals	2,475
Minor Baptism Totals	278
Adult Baptism Totals	109
Received into Full Communion	171
First Communions	2,921
Confirmations	1,951
Marriages:	
Catholic	423
Interfaith	58
Total Marriages	481
Deaths	743
Total Catholic Population	196,378
Total Population	981,888

Former Bishops—Most Revs. LEO T. MAHER, D.D., ord. Dec. 18, 1943; appt. First Bishop of Santa Rosa, Feb. 21, 1962; cons. April 5, 1962; translated San Diego, Aug. 27, 1969; died Feb. 23, 1991; MARK J. HURLEY, D.D., Ph.D., J.C.B., LL.D., ord. Sept. 23, 1944; appt. Titular Bishop of Thunusuda and Auxiliary of San Francisco, Oct. 12, 1967; cons. Jan. 4, 1968; translated Santa Rosa, Nov. 9, 1969; appt. member of the Vatican Secretariat for Non-Believers, consultor to the Congregation for Catholic Education; resigned as Bishop of Santa Rosa, April 15, 1986; died Feb. 5, 2001; JOHN T. STEINBOCK, D.D., ord. May 1, 1963; Titular Bishop of Midila and Auxiliary Bishop of Orange; appt. May 29, 1984; translated Santa Rosa, March 31, 1987; translated Fresno, Nov. 25, 1991; died Dec. 5, 2010; G. PATRICK ZIEMANN, D.D., ord. April 29, 1967; appt. Titular Bishop of Obba and Auxiliary Bishop of Los Angeles, Dec. 29, 1986; ord. Bishop, Feb. 23, 1987; appt. Bishop of Santa Rosa, July 14, 1992; resigned as Bishop of Santa Rosa, July 21, 1999; died Oct. 22, 2009.; DANIEL F. WALSH, D.D., ord. March 30, 1963; appt. Titular Bishop of Tigia and Auxiliary of San Francisco Sept. 24, 1981; appt. Bishop of Reno-Las Vegas June 9, 1987; installed Aug. 6, 1987; appt. Bishop of Las Vegas March 21, 1995; installed June 28, 1995; appt. Bishop of Santa Rosa in California on April 4, 2000; installed May 22, 2000; retired June 30, 2011.

Chancery Office—985 Airway Court, Santa Rosa, 95403. Tel: 707-566-3300; Fax: 707-542-9702. *Mailing Address: P.O. Box 1297, Santa Rosa, 95402-1297*. Office Hours: Mon.-Fri. 8:30-4:30All applications for dispensations, faculties, etc., and all correspondence should be addressed to the Chancery Office.

Vicar General—Rev. Msgr. DANIEL P. WHELTON, Mailing Address: P.O. Box 1297, Santa Rosa, 95402. Email: dwhelton@srdiocese.org.

Deans—Revs. DENIS A. O'SULLIVAN, Sonoma-North Deanery; ANDRES QUERIJERO, O.C.D., Mendocino/Lake Deanery; ALVIN M. VILLARUEL, Sonoma South Deanery; ELISEO AVENDANO, Napa Deanery; FRANCIS GAYAM, (India) Humboldt/Del Norte Deanery.

Chancellor—Rev. Msgr. DANIEL P. WHELTON, Mailing Address: P.O. Box 1297, Santa Rosa, 95402. Email: dwhelton@srdiocese.org.

Moderator of the Curia—Rev. Msgr. DANIEL P. WHELTON, Mailing Address: P.O. Box 1297, Santa Rosa, 95402. Email: lpeter@srdiocese.org.

Director of Clergy Personnel—Rev. Msgr. DANIEL P. WHELTON, Mailing Address: P.O. Box 1297, Santa Rosa, 95402. Email: dwhelton@srdiocese.org.

Vicar for Priests—Rev. Msgr. DANIEL P. WHELTON.

Diocesan Finance Officer—DAVID ADAMS, Mailing Address: P.O. Box 1297, Santa Rosa, 95402. Tel: 707-566-3317; Email: dadams@srdiocese.org.

Secretary to the Bishop—LYNNE PETER, Tel: 707-566-3325; Fax: 707-566-3310; Email: lpeter@srdiocese.org.

Diocesan Tribunal—Mailing Address: P.O. Box 1297, Santa Rosa, 95402-1297. Tel: 707-566-3370; Fax: 707-566-3385.

Judicial Vicar—Rev. FERGAL MCGUINNESS, J.C.L., Mailing Address: P.O. Box 1297, Santa Rosa, 95402.

Adjutant Judicial Vicar—Rev. ABEL MENA, J.C.L.

Promoter of Justice—Rev. Msgr. DANIEL P. WHELTON.

Defender of the Bond—Rev. DAVID SHAW, (Retired).

Diocesan Judges—Rev. Msgrs. JAMES P. GAFFEY, Ph. D., (Retired); JOHN J. BRENKLE, (Retired); Rev. ABEL MENA, J.C.L.

Advocates—Rev. WILLIAM P. DONAHUE; Deacons RAY NOLL, Ph.D.; JOSEPH OLSEN JR.

Tribunal Auditor—Sr. MARY VIANNEY, M.S.S.R.

Notaries—Rev. Msgr. DANIEL P. WHELTON; LYNNE PETER; Sr. MARY ROSE MANK, M.S.S.R.

Presbyteral Council—All priests in active ministry in the Diocese of Santa Rosa are members of the

Presbyteral Council along with: Revs. ALVIN VILLARUEL; FRANCIS GAYAM, (India); ANDRES QUERIJERO, O.C.D.; ELISEO AVENDANO; DENIS A. O'SULLIVAN; Rev. Msgr. DANIEL P. WHELTON, J.C.L., V.G., Vicar Gen. - Ex Officio.

College of Consultors—Rev. Msgr. DANIEL P. WHELTON, Vicar Gen.; Revs. ALVIN VILLARUEL; FRANCIS GAYAM, (India); ANDRES QUERIJERO, O.C.D.; DENIS A. O'SULLIVAN; ELISEO AVENDANO.

Parish Priest Consultors—Revs. FRANCIS GAYAM, (India); ANDRES QUERIJERO, O.C.D.; ELISEO AVENDANO; DENIS A. O'SULLIVAN; ALVIN M. VILLARUEL; Rev. Msgr. DANIEL P. WHELTON, J.C.L., V.G.

Clergy Personnel Board—Revs. FRANK EPPERSON; OSCAR DIAZ; DENIS A. O'SULLIVAN; Rev. Msgr. DANIEL P. WHELTON.

Diocesan Finance Council—Most Rev. ROBERT F. VASA; Rev. Msgr. DANIEL P. WHELTON; Revs. BALASWAMY GOVINDU; ALVIN M. VILLARUEL; STEPHEN IMBODEN; DOUGLAS BOILEAU; JOSEPH BARRERA; DANIEL CATONE; EVERT FERNANDEZ; ANNA HICKEY; PHIL MYERS; MARTIN MCCORMICK; DAN PRINCE; DAN GALVIN II; DAVID ADAMS; KIM SAMPIETRO.

Diocesan Building Committee—ED RONCHELLI; JOHN SCHULTZ; JOSEPH PANDOLFO; DAVID ADAMS; Rev. Msgr. DANIEL P. WHELTON, J.C.L., V.G.; KELLY RIGHETTI.

Diocesan Review Board—DR. ALISA LIGUORI, Ph.D.; DR. MARY KILLEEN LYONS, Ph.D.; Deacon JOHN STORM; RICHARD ORTIZ; GEORGE BERG. Consultants: DAN GALVIN II; JULIE SPARACIO, Dir. Office for the Protection of Children & Youth; HON. CHARLOTTE WALTER WOODARD, (Retired); DANIEL HANLON, (Retired); Rev. Msgr. DANIEL P. WHELTON, Promoter of Justice.

Priests Pension Board—Revs. GERARD GORMLEY; SAMUEL MOSES BROWN; WILLIAM P. DONAHUE; DAVID SHAW, (Retired); SEAN ROGERS; Rev. Msgr. DANIEL P. WHELTON.

Communications & Evangelization Committee—Most Rev. ROBERT F. VASA; Rev. RAUL LEMUS; Deacon GARY MOORE; DENNIS PURIFICACION, Ed.D.; JUDY BARRETT; MARK BRUMLEY; MICHELE DAVIS; JOHN GALTON; GREG HARDER; CHRISTOPHER LYFORD; Sr. MARY ROSE MANK, M.S.S.R.; STEPHEN MORRIS; DR. LINDA NORMAN, Ph.D.; VALERIE PRESTEN.

Diocesan Offices and Directors

Advancement—985 Airway Ct., Santa Rosa, 95403. Tel: 707-566-3396; Fax: 707-542-9702; Cell: 707-280-3592. *Mailing Address: P.O. Box 1297, Santa Rosa, 95402.* RUSS FERREIRA.

Director of the Office for the Protection of Children and Youth—JULIE SPARACIO, 985 Airway Ct., Santa Rosa, 95403. Tel: 707-566-3308. Mailing Address: P.O. Box 1297, Santa Rosa, 95402-1297.

Attorney for the Diocese—DANIEL J. GALVIN III, Shapiro, Galvin, Shapiro & Moran, 640 Third St., 2nd Fl., Santa Rosa, 95404. Tel: 707-544-5858; Fax: 707-544-6702.

Boy Scouts—985 Airway Ct., Santa Rosa, 95403. Tel: 707-566-3343. STEPHEN MORRIS.

Catholic Charities, Central Administrative Office—LEN MARABELLA, Ph.D., Exec. Dir., 987 Airway Ct., Santa Rosa, 95403. Tel: 707-528-8712; Fax: 707-575-4910. Mailing Address: P.O. Box 4900, Santa Rosa, 95402-4900.

Catholic Community Foundation—985 Airway Ct., Santa Rosa, 95403. Tel: 707-566-3344; Fax: 707-544-3360. *Mailing Address: P.O. Box 1297, Santa Rosa, 95402-1297.* Rev. Msgr. DANIEL P. WHELTON; DAVID ADAMS; JOSEPH BARRERA; VALERIE PRESTEN; JOHN MOYNIER; DR. LINDA NORMAN, Ph.D.; Revs. ALVIN M. VILLARUEL; BALASWAMY GOVINDU; Most Rev. ROBERT F. VASA; RUSS FERREIRA; DOUGLAS BOILEAU; Sr. CARITAS MARIE, M.S.S.R.; DANIEL CATONE; RICHARD CUNEO; DAN GALVIN II.

Cemeteries—ANGELA SCHEIHING, Assoc. Dir., 2930 Bennett Valley Rd., Santa Rosa, 95404. Tel: 707-546-6290; Fax: 707-546-2773. Mailing Address: P.O. Box 2098, Santa Rosa, 95405.

Continuing Clergy Formation—Rev. Msgr. DANIEL P. WHELTON.

Communications—CHRISTOPHER LYFORD, 24 Ursuline Rd., Santa Rosa, 95403. Tel: 707-566-3302; Fax: 707-546-4239. Mailing Address: P.O. Box 1297, Santa Rosa, 95402-1297.

Custodian of Records—Rev. Msgr. DANIEL P. WHELTON, 985 Airway Ct., Santa Rosa, 95403. Tel: 707-566-3312. Mailing Address: P.O. Box 1297, Santa Rosa, 95402-1297.

Catholic Restorative Justice Ministries—24A Ursuline Rd., Santa Rosa, 95403. Tel: 707-544-9080; Fax: 707-544-9081. Deacon JOHN STORM, Dir.

Director of Seminarians—985 Airway Ct., Santa Rosa, 95403. Tel: 707-545-7610. *Mailing Address: P.O. Box 1297, Santa Rosa, 95402.* Rev. FRANK EPPERSON.

Ecumenical and Interreligious Affairs—Mailing Address: P.O. Box 1297, Santa Rosa, 95402. Tel: 707-566-3300; Fax: 707-542-9702.

Hispanic Ministry—Rev. OSCAR DIAZ, Dir., 303 Stony Point Rd., Santa Rosa, 95482. Tel: 707-544-7272; Fax: 707-544-2901.

Catholic Cursillo Movement & Movimento Cursillisto of the Diocese of Santa Rosa—Mailing Address: P.O. Box 1297, Santa Rosa, 95402. MARY PETERSON, Tel: 707-495-3095; Deacon SERGIO OROZCO; DEBBIE SIMONSON, Tel: 904-463-1070.

Movimiento Familiar Cristiano—Mailing Address: 343 Freeway Dr., Napa, 94558. Tel: 707-254-9878 . ALEJANDRO GONZALEZ; ANA GONZALEZ; Rev. MARIO VALENCIA.

Stewardship, Appeals & CCF—925 Airway Ct., Santa Rosa, 95403. Tel: 707-566-3344; Fax: 707-542-9702. *Mailing Address: P.O. Box 1297, Santa Rosa, 95402.* Sr. CARITAS MARIE, M.S.S.R.

Movimiento Carismatico—Rev. CARLOS ORTEGA, Dir., St. Aloysius Parish, P.O. Box 66, Point Arena, 95468. Tel: 707-882-1734.

Santa Rosa Diocesan Council of Catholic Women—Mailing Address: P.O. Box 1297, Santa Rosa, 95402. CINDY CUNNINGHAM.

Newspaper—North Coast Catholic CHRISTOPHER LYFORD, Mailing Address: P.O. Box 1297, Santa Rosa, 95402-1297. Tel: 707-566-3302; Fax: 707-546-4239.

Permanent Diaconate—Deacons PETER MATHEWS; GARY MOORE.

Propagation of the FaithMailing Address: P.O. Box 1297, Santa Rosa, 95402-1297. Tel: 707-539-5377; Email: garyfmoore@gmail.com. Deacon GARY MOORE, Contact Person.

Religious Education—24 Ursuline Rd., Santa Rosa, 95403. Tel: 707-566-3313; Fax: 707-542-9702. DENNIS PURIFICACION, Ed.D., Dir.

Family Life—Mailing Address: P.O. Box 1297, Santa Rosa, 95402. Tel: 707-566-3305; Fax: 707-542-9702 . Deacon DAVE GOULD; CARLIN GOULD.

Schools—Office: 985 Airway Ct., Santa Rosa, 95403. Tel: 707-566-3311. *Mailing Address: P.O. Box 1297, Santa Rosa, 95402.* DR. LINDA NORMAN, Ph. D., Supt. of Schools.

Youth and Young Adult Ministry—STEPHEN MORRIS, Dir., Mailing Address: P.O. Box 1297, Santa Rosa, 95402. Cell: 310-849-2342; Fax: 707-566-3320.

Vocations—Rev. RAUL LEMUS, Mailing Address: P.O. Box 1297, Santa Rosa, 95402. Tel: 707-495-6750; Fax: 707-542-9702.

CLERGY, PARISHES, MISSIONS AND PAROCHIAL SCHOOLS

CITY OF SANTA ROSA

(SONOMA COUNTY)

1—PASTOR OF ST. EUGENE CATHEDRAL OF SANTA ROSA, A CORPORATION SOLE (1950) [CEM]
2323 Montgomery Dr., 95405. Tel: 707-542-6984; Email: office@steugenes.com; Web: www.steugenes.com. Revs. Frank Epperson; Daniel Roa; Jeffrey Keyes, In Res.; Deacons Russ Bowden; Michael Heinzelman; Gary Moore.
School—Cathedral of St. Eugene School, (Grades PreSchool-8), 300 Farmers Ln., 95405. Tel: 707-545-7252; Fax: 707-545-2594; Email: office@steugenesch.org; Web: www.steugenesch.org. Mrs. Barbara Gasparini, Prin. Clergy 1; Lay Teachers 15; Students 283.
Catechesis Religious Program—Students 85.

2—PASTOR OF HOLY SPIRIT CATHOLIC CHURCH OF SANTA ROSA, A CORPORATION SOLE (1964)
1244 St. Francis Rd., 95409. Tel: 707-539-4495; Fax: 707-539-3343; Email: holy-spirit@sbcglobal.net; Web: WWW.holyspirit-sr.org. Rev. Ron Serban.
Catechesis Religious Program—Megan O'Neill, D.R.E. Students 154.

3—PASTOR OF RESURRECTION CATHOLIC CHURCH OF SANTA ROSA, A CORPORATION SOLE (1967)
303 Stony Point Rd., 95401. Tel: 707-544-7272; Email: fr.oscardc@gmail.com. Revs. Oscar Diaz; Jose Gonzalez; Deacon Stephen Ellis.
Catechesis Religious Program—Terri Muir Small, D.R.E. Students 100.

4—PASTOR OF ST. ROSE OF LIMA CATHOLIC CHURCH OF SANTA ROSA, A CORPORATION SOLE (1877)
398 10th St., 95401. Tel: 707-542-6448; Fax: 707-542-3359; Email: church@stroseonline.org; Web: stroseonline.org. Revs. Denis A. O'Sullivan; Gabriel Barrera; Samuel Moses Brown, In Res.
School—St. Rose of Lima School, (Grades PreSchool-8), 4300 Old Redwood Hwy., 95403. Tel: 707-545-0379; Fax: 707-545-7150; Email: stroseschool@sonic.net; Web: www.strosecatholicschool.org. Kathy Ryan, Prin.; Carla Flaherty, Librarian. Clergy 2; Lay Teachers 16; Students 267.
Catechesis Religious Program—Sr. Olive Murphy, R.S.M., C.R.E. Students 713.

5—PASTOR OF STAR OF THE VALLEY CATHOLIC CHURCH OF SANTA ROSA, A CORPORATION SOLE (1981)
495 White Oak Dr., 545 White Oak Dr., 95409. Tel: 707-539-6262; Email: sov@sonic.net; Web: www.starofthevalley.org. Rev. Msgr. James E. Pulskamp, V.G.

OUTSIDE CITY OF SANTA ROSA

AMERICAN CANYON, NAPA CO., PASTOR OF HOLY FAMILY CATHOLIC CHURCH OF AMERICAN CANYON, A CORPORATION SOLE (1994)
402 Donaldson Way, American Canyon, 94503. Tel: 707-645-9331; Fax: 707-731-1637; Email: holyfamily.amcan@gmail.com. 91 Antonina Ave., Ste. D, American Canyon, 94503. Rev. Frederick K.A. Kutubebi; Deacons Victor Leach; Michael Simmons.
Catechesis Religious Program—Deacon Vic Leach, D.R.E. Students 31.

ARCATA, HUMBOLDT CO., PASTOR OF ST. MARY CATHOLIC CHURCH OF ARCATA, A CORPORATION SOLE (1883) [CEM]
1690 Janes Rd., Arcata, 95521. Tel: 707-822-7696; Email: stmarysarcata@gmail.com; Web: stmarysarcata.com. Revs. Francis Gayam, (India); Andrew Pacheco, Parochial Vicar; Deacons John Gai; Jon Pedicino, Ph.D.
Catechesis Religious Program—Patricia Heavilin, D.R.E. Students 40.
Missions—St. Joseph—340 Greenwood Ave., Blue Lake.
St. Kateri Tekakwitha, Kateri Ln., Hoopa, 95546. c/o St. Mary's Parish, 1690 Janes Rd., Arcata, 95521.
Legal Title: Pastor of St. Kateri Tekakwitha Catholic Mission of Hoopa, a Corporation Sole.

BOYES HOT SPRINGS, SONOMA CO., PASTOR OF ST. LEO THE GREAT CATHOLIC CHURCH OF BOYES HOT SPRINGS, A CORPORATION SOLE (1966)
601 W. Agua Caliente Rd., Sonoma, 95476. Tel: 707-996-8422; Fax: 707-996-3984; Email: office@stleosonoma.org; Web: stleosonoma.org. P.O. Box 666, Boyes Hot Springs, 95416. Rev. Jojo Puthussery, M.F., (India).
Catechesis Religious Program—Nancy Gibson, D.R.E.; Rosa Chavez, D.R.E. Students 163.

CALISTOGA, NAPA CO., PASTOR OF OUR LADY OF PERPETUAL HELP CATHOLIC CHURCH OF CALISTOGA, A CORPORATION SOLE (1915)
901 Washington St., Calistoga, 94515. Tel: 707-942-6894; Email: olphcalistoga@att.net; Web: olphcalistoga.org. Rev. Angelito Peries.
Catechesis Religious Program—Students 115.

CLEARLAKE, LAKE CO., PASTOR OF OUR LADY QUEEN OF PEACE CATHOLIC CHURCH OF CLEARLAKE, A CORPORATION SOLE (1967)
14435 Uhl Ave., Clearlake, 95422. Tel: 707-994-6618; Email: qopcc@sonic.net; Web: www.qopclearlake.org. P.O. Box 460, Clearlake, 95423. Rev. Adam Kotas, Admin.
Catechesis Religious Program—Julie Swehla, D.R.E. Students 102.
Mission—Queen of the Rosary, Lucerne, 95458.

CLOVERDALE, SONOMA CO., PASTOR OF ST. PETER CATHOLIC CHURCH OF CLOVERDALE, A CORPORATION SOLE (1917)
491 S. Franklin St., Cloverdale, 95425. Tel: 707-894-2535; Fax: 707-894-9603; Email: sp-olmc@outlook.com. Rev. David Galeana; Daisy Rauda, Sec.
Catechesis Religious Program—Students 139.
Mission—Our Lady of Mt. Carmel, Asti.

COTATI, SONOMA CO., PASTOR OF ST. JOSEPH CATHOLIC CHURCH OF COTATI, A CORPORATION SOLE (1913)
150 St. Joseph Way, Cotati, 94931-4117. Tel: 707-795-4807; Fax: 707-795-7851; Email: pbrolemus@gmail.com; Web: www.sjccotati.org. Rev. Raul Lemus; Rev. Msgr. Daniel P. Whelton, In Res.; Deacon Phillip Salazar.
Catechesis Religious Program—Norma Suarez, D.R.E. Students 260.

CRESCENT CITY, DEL NORTE CO., PASTOR OF JOSEPH CATHOLIC CHURCH OF CRESCENT CITY, A CORPORATION SOLE (1869) [CEM]
319 E St., Crescent City, 95531. Tel: 707-465-1762; Email: sjccc707@yahoo.com; Web: www.sjccc.net. Rev. Gregory Villaescusa; Deacons Aadam Trask, RCIA Coord.; Juan Gamez, Dir. of Hispanic Min.
Catechesis Religious Program—Students 73.
Mission—St. Robert and Ann, Mild Rd., Klamath, 95548.

EUREKA, HUMBOLDT CO.
1—PASTOR OF ST. BERNARD CATHOLIC CHURCH OF EUREKA, A CORPORATION SOLE (1864) [CEM]
615 H St., Eureka, 95501. Tel: 707-442-6466; Email: office@saintbernards.org. Rev. Bernard D'Sa, S.F.X., Admin.; Deacons Dance Farrell; Frank Weber.
Catechesis Religious Program—Melanie Broswick, D.R.E. Students 33.
Mission—St. Joseph, 201 Henderson St., Eureka, 95501.
2—PASTOR OF SACRED HEART CATHOLIC CHURCH OF EUREKA, A CORPORATION SOLE (1963)
2085 Myrtle Ave., Eureka, 95501. Tel: 707-443-8429; Email: sacredheartoffice@suddenlinkmail.com. Rev. Bernard D'Sa, S.F.X., Admin.; Deacon Anthony Viegas.
Catechesis Religious Program—Melanie Broswick, C.R.E. Students 84.
FERNDALE, HUMBOLDT CO., PASTOR OF ASSUMPTION OF OUR LADY CATHOLIC CHURCH OF FERNDALE, A CORPORATION SOLE (1878) [CEM]
546 Berding St., P.O. Box 1097, Ferndale, 95536.
Tel: 707-786-9551; Email: assump@suddenlink.net. Rev. Mario Laguros, (Philippines).
Catechesis Religious Program—Susan Regli, D.R.E. Students 18.
Mission—St. Patrick, St Patrick Mission, Petrolia, 95558.
FORT BRAGG, MENDOCINO CO., PASTOR OF OUR LADY OF GOOD COUNSEL CATHOLIC CHURCH, A CORPORATION SOLE (1890)
255 S. Harold St., Fort Bragg, 95437.
Tel: 707-964-0229; Email: olgcinfb@gmail.com. Rev. Andres Querijero, O.C.D.
Catechesis Religious Program—Students 174.
FORTUNA, HUMBOLDT CO., PASTOR OF ST. JOSEPH CATHOLIC CHURCH OF FORTUNA, A CORPORATION SOLE (1909) [CEM]
820 14th St, P.O. Box 420, Fortuna, 95540.
Tel: 707-725-1148; Email: stjosephchurch@suddenlink.net; Web: stjoeparish.org. Rev. Edildberto Ramon; Deacons Thomas Silva; Francisco Nunez; Rafael Meraz; Craig Brown; Abraham Castillo.
Res.: 2312 Newburg Rd., Fortuna, 95540.
Catechesis Religious Program—2292 Newburg Rd., Fortuna, 95540. Students 212.
Mission—St. Patrick, Loleta.
GARBERVILLE, HUMBOLDT CO., PASTOR OF OUR LADY OF THE REDWOODS CATHOLIC CHURCH OF GARBERVILLE, A CORPORATION SOLE (1950)
515 Maple Ln., P.O. Box 115, Garberville, 95542.
Tel: 707-923-7864. Rev. Mario Laguros, (Philippines).
GUERNEVILLE, SONOMA CO., PASTOR OF ST. ELIZABETH CATHOLIC CHURCH OF GUERNEVILLE, A CORPORATION SOLE (1916)
14095 Woodland Dr., Guerneville, 95446-9553.
Tel: 707-869-2107; Email: churchelizabeth@comcast.net. Rev. Luis M. Penaloza.
Missions—St. Catherine—Chapel Dr., Monte Rio, 95462. Woodland Dr., Guerneville, 95446.
Legal Title: Pastor of St. Catherine of Siena Catholic Mission of Monte Rio, a Corporation Sole.
St. Colman, Cazadero Hwy., Cazadero, 95421.
Legal Title: Pastor of St. Coleman Catholic Mission of Cazadero, a Corporation Sole.
HEALDSBURG, SONOMA CO., PASTOR OF ST. JOHN THE BAPTIST CATHOLIC CHURCH OF HEALDSBURG, A CORPORATION SOLE (1884)
208 Matheson St., Healdsburg, 95448.
Tel: 707-433-5536; Fax: 707-433-1813; Email: mlhjones.sjc@gmail.com; Web: www.stjohnshealdsburg.org. Revs. Sean Rogers; Peter Nawanekezie, In Res.; Deacon Malcom Barrack.
School—St. John the Baptist Catholic School, (Grades PreSchool-8), 217 Fitch St., Healdsburg, 95448. Tel: 707-433-2758; Fax: 707-433-0353; Email: james.brandt@sjshbg.org; Web: sjshbg.org. James Brandt, Prin. Lay Teachers 17; Students 209.
Catechesis Religious Program—Email: scrotty.sjc@gmail.com. Mrs. Suzanne Crotty, D.R.E. Students 185.
HOOPA, HUMBOLDT CO., PASTOR OF ST. KATERI TEKAKWITHA CATHOLIC MISSION OF HOOPA, A CORPORATION SOLE (1955)
Pine Creek Road & St. Kateri Ln., Hoopa, 95546.
Tel: 707-822-7696; Email: stmarysarcata@gmail.com; Web: stmarysarcata.com. Mailing Address: 1690 Janes Rd., Arcata, 95521. Revs. Francis Gayam, (India); Andrew Pacheco, Parochial Vicar; Deacon Ken Bond.
LAKEPORT, LAKE CO., PASTOR OF ST. MARY IMMACULATE CATHOLIC CHURCH OF LAKEPORT, A CORPORATION SOLE (1871) [CEM]
801 N. Main St., Lakeport, 95453. Tel: 707-263-4401; Email: admin@stmaryslakeport.com. Rev. Mario Valencia.
Catechesis Religious Program—Judith Salmeron, D.R.E. Students 143.
Mission—St. Peter, [CEM] Kelseyville.
MCKINLEYVILLE, HUMBOLDT COUNTY, PASTOR OF CHRIST THE KING CATHOLIC CHURCH OF MCKINLEYVILLE, A CORPORATION SOLE (1967)
Mailing Address: 1951 McKinleyville Ave., P.O. Box 2367, McKinleyville, 95519. Tel: 707-839-2911; Email: ctkparish@att.net. Revs. Francis Gayam, (India); Andrew Pacheco, Parochial Vicar.
Res.: 1690 Janes Rd., Arcata, 95521.
Catechesis Religious Program—Students 18.
Mission—Holy Trinity, Hector St., Trinidad, 95570.
MENDOCINO, MENDOCINO CO., PASTOR OF ST. ANTHONY CATHOLIC CHURCH OF MENDOCINO, A CORPORATION SOLE (1864) [CEM]
10700 Lansing St., P.O. Box 665, Mendocino, 95460.
Tel: 707-937-5808; Fax: 707-937-2406; Web: stanthonysofmendocino.com. Rev. Louis J. Nichols.
Mission—Blessed Sacrament, P.O. Box 28, Elk, 95432. Tel: 707-877-3275; Email: dcong1061@gmail.com.
Legal Title: Pastor of Blessed Sacrament Catholic Mission of Elk, a Corporation Sole.
MIDDLETOWN, LAKE CO., PASTOR OF ST. JOSEPH CATHOLIC CHURCH OF MIDDLETOWN, A CORPORATION SOLE (1894)
21396 Hwy 175, Middletown, 95461.
Tel: 707-987-3676; Email: stjoseph11@att.net. P.O. Box 1350, Middletown, 95461. Rev. James McSweeney.
Catechesis Religious Program—Students 38.
Mission—Our Lady of the Lake, Loch Lomond.
Station—Our Lady of the Pines, Forest Lake.
NAPA, NAPA CO.
1—PASTOR OF ST. APOLLINARIS CATHOLIC CHURCH OF NAPA, A CORPORATION SOLE (1957)
3700 Lassen St., Napa, 94558. Tel: 707-257-2555; Fax: 707-257-3552; Email: stasparishsec@gmail.com; Web: www.stapollinarisparish.org. Revs. Balaswamy Govindu; David Jenuwine, Parochial Vicar; Deacons Francis Dahl; Joel Momsen; John Dermody; Peter Mathews.
School—St. Apollinaris School, (Grades PreK-8), Tel: 707-224-6525; Fax: 707-224-5400; Email: acardwell.adminsec@gmail.com; Web: www.stapollinaris.com. Olivia Brazil, Prin. Lay Teachers 10; Students 302.
Catechesis Religious Program—Tel: 707-255-7200; Email: fatimapmorcon@gmail.com. Ms. Fatima Jiminez, D.R.E. Students 250.
2—PASTOR OF ST. JOHN THE BAPTIST CATHOLIC CHURCH OF NAPA, A CORPORATION SOLE (1858) Revs. Ismael Mora; Patrick Stephenson, (Retired); Thomas Kyallo, (Kenya); Deacons Sergio Velazquez; Joel Tapia; Stan Thompson-Short; Jaime Tafolla; Joe Oberting.
Res.: 960 Caymus St., Napa, 94559.
Tel: 707-226-9379; Tel: 707-226-9379, Ext. 14; Fax: 707-254-9262; Email: frontdesk@saintjohnscatholic.org.
School—St. John the Baptist School, (Grades K-8), 983 Napa St., Napa, 94559. Tel: 707-224-8388; Fax: 707-224-0236; Email: schoolinfo@sjtbcschool.org; Web: school.stjohnscatholic.org. Olivia Brazil, Prin.; Melanie Oberting, Librarian. Lay Teachers 12; Students 140.
Catechesis Religious Program—Linda Zepeda, D.R.E.; Wayne Beasley, D.R.E.; Olga Vazquez, D.R.E.; Eustolia Valazquez, C.R.E. (Spanish); Teresa Olguin, C.R.E. (Spanish); Edna Solorio, Confirmation Coord. & Youth Min. Students 706.
Station—State Hospital, St. Luke's Chapel, Imola.
3—PASTOR OF ST. THOMAS AQUINAS CATHOLIC CHURCH OF NAPA, A CORPORATION SOLE aka St. Thomas Aquinas Catholic Church (1964)
2725 Elm St., Napa, 94558-6029. Tel: 707-255-2949; Email: stthomas_napa@att.net; Web: www.stthomasaquinasnapa.com. Deacon James Eckert, Ordinary; Revs. Abel Mena, J.C.L.; Gary Sumpter, In Res.; Deacon Jesse DeLuna.
Catechesis Religious Program—Students 279.
OCCIDENTAL, SONOMA CO., PASTOR OF ST. PHILIP CATHOLIC CHURCH OF OCCIDENTAL, A CORPORATION SOLE (1903) [CEM]
3730 Bohemian Hwy., P.O. Box 339, Occidental, 95465. Tel: 707-874-3812; Fax: 707-874-9201; Email: philip.teresa@yahoo.com; Web: stphilipstteresa.org. Rev. Fergal McGuinness, J.C.L.
Mission—St. Teresa, [CEM] Bodega.
PETALUMA, SONOMA CO.
1—PASTOR OF ST. JAMES CATHOLIC CHURCH OF PETALUMA, A CORPORATION SOLE (1964)
125 Sonoma Mt. Pkwy., Petaluma, 94954.
Tel: 707-762-4256; Fax: 707-762-4044; Email: mimi@stjamespetaluma.com. Revs. Michael A. Culligan; Lawrence Mutiso; Deacons Ray Noll, Ph.D.; Randy Kokke.
Catechesis Religious Program—Students 336.
2—PASTOR OF ST. VINCENT DE PAUL CATHOLIC CHURCH OF PETALUMA, A CORPORATION SOLE (1857)
35 Liberty St., Petaluma, 94952.
Tel: 707-762-4278, Ext. 12; Email: wpdonah@gmail.com. Revs. Williams Donahue; Ramon Pons; Deacons James Carr; John Norris.
School—St. Vincent de Paul School, (Grades K-8), Howard & Union Sts., Petaluma, 94952.
Tel: 707-762-6426; Fax: 707-762-6791; Email: info@svelem.org; Web: www.svelem.org. Katie Salmassian, Prin.; DeAnn Sarlatte, Prin. Clergy 1; Lay Teachers 16; Students 150.
High School—St. Vincent de Paul High School, 849 Keokuk, Petaluma, 94952. Tel: 707-763-1032; Fax: 707-763-9448; Email: pdaly@svhs-pet.org; Web: www.svhs-pet.org. Patrick W. Daly, Prin. Lay Teachers 25; Students 240.
Catechesis Religious Program—Rose Marie Woodruff, D.R.E. Students 551.
POINT ARENA, MENDOCINO CO., PASTOR OF ST. ALOYSIUS CATHOLIC CHURCH OF POINT ARENA, A CORPORATION SOLE (1889) [CEM]
70 School St., P.O. Box 66, Point Arena, 95468.
Tel: 707-882-1734; Email: ortgarcar@hotmail.com. Rev. Carlos Ortega; Deacon Sergio Orozco.
Catechesis Religious Program—Students 15.
Mission—Mary, Star of the Sea, Gualala.
ROHNERT PARK, SONOMA CO., PASTOR OF ST. ELIZABETH CATHOLIC CHURCH OF ROHNERT PARK, A CORPORATION SOLE (1981)
4595 Snyder Ln., Rohnert Park, 94928.
Tel: 707-585-3708; Email: stelizseton@sbcglobal.net. Rev. Thomas K. Diaz; Deacon Joseph Olsen.
Catechesis Religious Program—Students 91.
SAINT HELENA, NAPA CO., PASTOR OF ST. HELENA CATHOLIC CHURCH OF ST. HELENA, A CORPORATION SOLE (1887) Church; (1866) Parish [CEM]
1340 Tainter St., St. Helena, 94574.
Tel: 707-963-1228; Fax: 707-963-2894; Email: info@sthelenacatholic.com; Web: www.sthelenacatholic.com. Rev. Manuel Chavez; Deacon Bruce Miroglio.
Catechesis Religious Program—Students 106.
SEBASTOPOL, SONOMA CO., PASTOR OF ST. SEBASTIAN CATHOLIC CHURCH OF SEBASTOPOL, A CORPORATION SOLE (1898)
7983 Covert Ln., Sebastopol, 95472.
Tel: 707-823-2208; Email: info@stseb.org; Web: www.stseb.org. Rev. Gerard Gormley.
Catechesis Religious Program—Students 126.
SONOMA, SONOMA CO., PASTOR OF ST. FRANCIS SOLANO CATHOLIC CHURCH OF SONOMA, A CORPORATION SOLE (1878) [CEM]
469 Third St. W., Sonoma, 95476. Tel: 707-996-6759; Email: sfrancis_solano@sbcglobal.net. Rev. Alvin Vilaruel; Deacon Dave Gould.
School—St. Francis Solano School, (Grades K-8), 342 W. Napa St., Sonoma, 95476. Tel: 707-996-4994; Fax: 707-996-2662; Email: stf.schooloffice@saintfrancissolano.org. Debbie Picard, Prin. Lay Teachers 16; Students 188.
Catechesis Religious Program—Sarah Wilson, D.R.E. Students 264.
UKIAH, MENDOCINO CO., PASTOR OF ST. MARY OF THE ANGELS CATHOLIC CHURCH OF UKIAH, A CORPORATION SOLE (1887)
900 S. Oak St., Ukiah, 95482. Tel: 707-462-1431; Web: stmaryschurchukiah.com. Revs. Anthaiah Madanu, Admin.; Jose Isaac Alejandro de la Cruz, Parochial Vicar.
School—St. Mary of the Angels School, (Grades K-8), 991 S. Dora St., Ukiah, 95482. Tel: 707-462-3888; Fax: 707-462-6014; Email: principal@smsukiah.org; Web: www.stmarysukiah.org. Mary Leittem-Thomas, Prin. Lay Teachers 15; Students 189.
Catechesis Religious Program—Students 380.
Missions—St. Francis Mission—Center St., Hopland, 95482. Email: stmukiahservice@gmail.com.
St. Elizabeth Seton, School Rd., Philo, 95466. Email: stmukiahacctng@gmail.com.
WILLITS, MENDOCINO CO., PASTOR OF ST. ANTHONY OF PADUA CATHOLIC CHURCH OF WILLITS, A CORPORATION SOLE (1903)
61 W. San Francisco Ave., Willits, 95490.
Tel: 707-459-2252; Email: stanthonywillits@att.net. Rev. Arogyriah Bandanadam.
Mission—Our Lady, Queen of Peace, [CEM] Covelo, Mendocino Co..
Catechesis Religious Program—Students 66.
WINDSOR, SONOMA CO., PASTOR OF OUR LADY OF GUADALUPE CATHOLIC CHURCH OF WINDSOR, A CORPORATION SOLE (1969)
8400 Old Redwood Hwy., Windsor, 95492.
Tel: 707-837-8962; Fax: 707-837-9157; Email: officeolg@gmail.com; Web: olgwindsor.org. Rev. Michaelraj Philominsamy; Deacon Todd Graveson.
Catechesis Religious Program—Students 445.
YOUNTVILLE, NAPA CO., PASTOR OF ST. JOAN OF ARC CATHOLIC CHURCH OF YOUNTVILLE, A CORPORATION SOLE (1920)
6404 Washington St., P.O. Box 2009, Yountville, 94599. Tel: 707-944-2461; Email: stjoanofarc01@aol.com. Rev. Eliseo Avendano; Deacon Charles Cancilla.
Catechesis Religious Program—Lilia Manzo, D.R.E. Students 130.
Mission—Holy Family, Rutherford.

Chaplains Of Public Institutions

IMOLA. *Napa State Hospital*, Imola, 94558. Deacon Joseph McDonnell, Chap.

PETALUMA. *U.S. Coast Guard Training Center*.

YOUNTVILLE. *Veterans Administration Home, St. Michael Chapel*. Rev. Noelani M. Sheckler-Smith, Chap.Served by the St. Joan of Arc Parish, Yountville.

On Duty Outside the Diocese:
Revs.—
Baptista, Diego
Lewandowski, Krzysztof
Rioux, Ray.

Retired:
Rev. Msgrs.—
Brady, Gerard J., (Retired)
Brenkle, John J., (Retired)
Fahey, Gerard, (Retired)
Gaffey, James P., Ph.D., (Retired)
Revs.—
Allen, Loren, (Retired)
Benjamin, Robert, (Retired)
Blake, Robert, (Retired)
Canny, Stephen, (Retired)
Castro, Robert, (Retired)
Cloney, Michael W., (Retired)
Coddaire, Louis, (Retired)
Crews, John S., Ed.D., (Retired)
Diaz De Leon, Juan Ramon, (Retired)
Griffin, John, (Retired)
Ittiyappara, Mathew, (Retired)
Kalil, Gordon, (Retired)
Logan, Gary, (Retired)
Lombardi, Gary, (Retired)
MacPherson, Stephen E.C., (Retired)
Martin, John J., (Retired)
McCormick, John, (Retired)
Metcalf, Andrew, (Retired)
Shaw, David, (Retired)
Stephenson, Patrick, (Retired)
Sumpter, Gary, (Retired)
Talcott, Peter, (Retired).

Permanent Deacons:
Barnes, Patrick, Petaluma
Barrack, Malcolm, Healdsburg
Barrack, Malcom, Healdsburg
Bond, Ken, Arcata
Bowden, Russ, Santa Rosa
Brown, Craig, Fortuna
Cancilla, Charles, (Archdiocese of San Francisco), Yountville
Carr, James, Petaluma
Castillo, Abraham, (Inactive)
Dahl, Francis, Napa
De Los Santos, Ruben, (Retired)
DeLuna, Jesse, Napa
Dermody, John, Napa
Eckert, Jim, Napa
Ellis, Stephen, Santa Rosa
Farrell, Dance, Eureka
Fernandez, Jesus, (Retired)
Gai, John, Arcata
Gamez, Juan, Crescent City
Gould, Dave, Sonoma
Graveson, Todd, Windsor
Heinzelman, Michael, Santa Rosa
Hercher, Jim, (Retired), Santa Rosa
Hogan, Roger, (Ministry outside the Diocese)
Jacobs, Jeff, (Ministry Outside the Diocese)
Justus, Steven, (Retired)
Kokke, Randy, Petaluma
Leach, Victor, American Canyon
Madrigal, Jesus, Anderson
Martin, Harry, (Retired), Cloverdale
Mathews, Peter, Napa
Meraz, Rafael, Fortuna
Miroglio, Bruce, Saint Helena
Momsen, Joel, (Inactive)
Moody, William, (Ministry outside the Diocese)
Moore, Gary, Santa Rosa
Nangle, Tom, Petaluma
Noll, Ray, Ph.D., Petaluma
Norris, John, Petaluma
Nunez, Francisco, Fortuna
Oberting, Joe, Napa
Olsen, Joseph, (Retired)
Orozco, Sergio, Point Area
Pedicino, Jon, Ph.D., Arcata
Ramirez, Arturo, (Ministry outside the Diocese)
Robinson, David, (Ministry outside the Diocese)
Salazar, Phillip, (Archdiocese of Santa Fe), Cotati
Silva, Thomas, Fortuna
Simmons, Michael, American Canyon
Stanton, Charlie, (Ministry outside the Diocese)
Storm, John, Santa Rosa
Tafolla, Jaime, Napa
Tapia, Joel, Napa
Thompson-Short, Stan, Napa
Torrado, Miguel, (Ministry outside the Diocese)
Trask, Aadam, Crescent City
Velazquez, Sergio, Napa
Vera, Juventino, Sebastopol
Viegas, Anthony, Eureka
Vilotti, Dan, Ukiah
Weber, Frank, Eureka
Woodruff, W. Everett, (Retired).

INSTITUTIONS LOCATED IN DIOCESE

[A] HIGH SCHOOLS, DIOCESAN

SANTA ROSA. *Cardinal Newman High School*, 50 Ursuline Rd., 95403. Tel: 707-546-6470; Fax: 707-544-8502; Email: info@cardinalnewman.org; Web: cardinalnewman.org. Laura Held, Pres.; Graham Rutherford, Dean; Bernadette Calhoun, Dean; Richard Herrmann, Dean; Rev. Samuel Moses Brown, D.R.E. Religious Teachers 5; Lay Teachers 41; Priests 2; Sisters 1; Students 569.

[B] HIGH SCHOOLS, PRIVATE

NAPA. *Justin-Siena High School*, 4026 Maher St., Napa, 94558. Tel: 707-255-0950; Fax: 707-255-0334; Email: dholquin@justin-siena.org; Web: justin-siena.org. Mr. David Holquin, Pres.; Robert Bailey, Admin.; Heidi Harrison, Admin. Brothers 1; Lay Teachers 50; Students 555.
**Justin-Siena High School Corporation, Inc.*
**Justin-Siena High School Foundation, Inc.*

[C] SCHOOLS, PRIVATE

NAPA. *Kolbe Academy & Trinity Prep*, (Grades K-12), 2055 Redwood Rd., Napa, 94558. Tel: 707-258-9030; Fax: 707-258-9031; Email: office@kolbetrinity.org; Email: jbertolini@kolbetrinity.org; Web: www.kolbetrinity.org. John Bertolini, Headmaster; Rev. Gary Sumpter, Chap., (Retired). Civil incorporation: Trinity Education Center, Inc. Clergy 1; Religious Teachers 1; Lay Teachers 25; Students 117.

EUREKA. **St. Bernard's Catholic School*, (Grades 7-12), 222 Dollison St., Eureka, 95501. Tel: 707-443-2735 ; Fax: 707-443-4723; Email: info@saintbernards.us; Web: saintbernards.us. Paul Shanahan, Pres./Prin.; Mike Grummert, Vice Prin.; Deacon Dance Farrell, D.R.E. Deacons 2; Lay Teachers 22; Students 220.

[D] CATHOLIC CHARITIES

SANTA ROSA. *Catholic Charities of the Diocese of Santa Rosa*, 987 Airway Ct., 95403. P.O. Box 4900, 95402. Tel: 707-528-8712; Fax: 707-595-1269; Email: info@srcharities.org; Web: srcharities.org. Len Marabella, Ph.D., Exec.; Allan Kelly, Business Mgr.; Angie Moeller, Dir.; Maria Solarez, Dir.; Marilyn Stuart, Dir. Tot Asst. Annually 9,707; Total Staff 170.

Administrative Services Center, 987 Airway Ct., 95403. Tel: 707-528-8712; Fax: 707-843-3538; Email: hr2@srcharities.org; Web: www.srcharities.org. Len Marabella, Ph.D., Exec. Dir.; Allan Kelly, Business Mgr.; Angie Moeller, Dir. Advancement & Grants, Email: donorrelations@srcharities.org; Maria Solarez, Dir. Human Resources; Marilyn Stuart, Dir. Accounting & Finance. Tot Asst. Annually 19,572.

Nightingale Napa, 1950 Jefferson St., Napa, 94559. Tel: 707-819-2165; Email: crebullida@srcharities.org. Jennielynn Holmes, Dir.

Napa County:

Rainbow House, 1219 Jefferson St. #2, Napa, 94559. Tel: 707-224-4403; Fax: 707-224-2889; Email: crebullida@srcharities.org. Jennielynn Holmes, Dir. Bed Capacity 43; Tot Asst. Annually 66; Total Staff 3.

Sonoma County:

Alzheimer's Respite/Resource Center, 987 Airway Ct., 95403. Tel: 707-528-8712; Fax: 707-843-3538; Email: mosmon@srcharities.org; Web: www.srcharities.org. Michele Osmon, Prog. Dir., Senior Svcs. Tot Asst. Annually 42; Total Staff 7.

Family Support Center, 465 A St., 95401. Tel: 707-542-5426. P.O. Box 4900, 95402. Fax: 707-843-3816; Email: fscfrontdesk@srcharities.org. Jennielynn Holmes, Dir. Tot Asst. Annually 500; Total Staff 50.

Homeless Services Center Nightingale at Brookwood/Samuel L. Jones Hall, 600 Morgan St., 95401. Tel: 707-525-0226. P.O. Box 4900, 95402. Email: smerridagrant@srcharities.org. Jennielynn Holmes, Prog. Dir. Tot Asst. Annually 2,100; Total Staff 10.

Housing Services, 465 A St., 95401. P.O. Box 4900, 95401. Tel: 707-542-5426; Fax: 707-843-3816; Email: fscfrontdesk@srcharities.org. Jennielynn Holmes, Prog. Dir. Tot Asst. Annually 500; Total Staff 20.

Immigration and Resettlement Services, 987 Airway Ct., 95403. Tel: 707-578-6000; Fax: 707-843-3538; Email: iladd@srcharities.org. Karen Shimizu, Prog. Dir. Tot Asst. Annually 5,076; Total Staff 14.

Parish/Community Services, 987 Airway Ct., 95403. Tel: 707-528-8712; Fax: 707-843-3538; Email: kshimizu@srcharities.org. Karen Shimizu, Prog. Dir. Tot Asst. Annually 20,000; Total Staff 32.

Coach 2 Career, 465 A St., 95401. P.O. Box 4900, 95401. Tel: 707-542-5426; Fax: 707-843-3816; Email: fscfrontdesk@srcharities.org. Jennielynn Holmes, Prog. Dir., Email: jholmes@srcharities.org.

Coordinated Entry, 465 A St., 95401. Tel: 866-542-5480; Fax: 707-843-3816; Email: kwhite@srcharities.org. Jennielynn Holmes, Prog. Dir. Tot Asst. Annually 500; Total Staff 6.

I'm Home Alone, 987 Airway Ct., 95403. Tel: 707-528-8712; Fax: 707-843-3538; Email: mosmon@srcharities.org. Karen Shimizu, Dir. of Opers.; Michele Osmon, Admin. Tot Asst. Annually 64; Total Staff 38.

Restyle Marketplace, 1001 W. College Ave., 95401. Tel: 707-284-1700; Email: ksilva@srcharities.org. Jennielynn Holmes, Dir. Tot Asst. Annually 1,000; Total Staff 3.

[E] GENERAL HOSPITALS

SANTA ROSA. *Santa Rosa Memorial Hospital*, 1165 Montgomery Dr., 95405. Tel: 707-546-3210; Fax: 707-547-4685; Email: katy.hillenmeyer@stjoe.org; Web: www.stjoesonoma.org. Todd Salnas, Pres.; Rev. Peter Nwanekezie, Priest Chap. St. Joseph Health Ministry, Renton, WA. Bed Capacity 329; Employees 2,081; Tot Asst. Annually 263,268; Total Staff 2,081.

EUREKA. *St. Joseph Hospital of Eureka* aka St. Joseph Health, Humboldt, 2700 Dolbeer St., Eureka, 95501. Tel: 707-445-8121; Fax: 707-269-3897; Email: EMT@stjoe.org; Web: www.stjosepheureka.org. Roberta Luskin-Hawk, M.D., CEO; Julie Malvey, Vice Pres.
Legal Name: Providence St. Joseph Health Bed Capacity 153; Tot Asst. Annually 54,797; Total Staff 1,170.

FORTUNA. *Redwood Memorial Hospital* aka St. Joseph Health, Humboldt, 3300 Renner Dr., Fortuna, 95540. Tel: 707-725-3361; Fax: 707-725-7212; Email: EMT@stjoe.org; Web: www.redwoodmemorial.org. Roberta Luskin-Hawk, M.D., CEO; Julie Malvey, Vice Pres.
Legal Name: Providence St. Joseph Health Bed Capacity 35; Tot Asst. Annually 17,989; Total Staff 230.
Redwood Memorial Foundation, 330 Renner Dr., Fortuna, 95540.

NAPA. *Queen of the Valley Medical Center*, 1000 Trancas St., Napa, 94558. Tel: 707-252-4411; Fax: 707-257-3633; Email: Maria.Curtis@stjoe.org; Web: www.thequeen.org. Revs. Valentine Ibeh, Chap.; Frederick K.A. Kutubebi, Priest Chap. Sisters of St. Joseph of Orange, California. Bed Capacity 208; Priests 2; Tot Asst. Annually 160,963; Total Staff 1,532.

PETALUMA. *Petaluma Valley Hospital*, 400 N. McDowell Blvd., Petaluma, 94954. Tel: 707-778-1111; Email: Tyler.Hedden@stjoe.org; Web: www.stjoesonoma.org. Mr. Tyler Hedden, Exec. St. Joseph Health Ministry. Bed Capacity 80; Tot Asst. Annually 62,491; Total Staff 383.

[F] RESIDENTIAL TREATMENT CENTERS

SONOMA. *Hanna Boys Center*, 17000 Arnold Dr., Sonoma, 95476. Tel: 707-996-6767; Fax: 707-996-4742; Email: jyankovich@hannacenter.org; Web: www.hannacenter.org. Mike Ruyle, Prin.; Brian Farragher, Dir.; Rev. Gregory McGivern, Chap.; Celeste Cook, Librarian. Serving at-risk boys, ages 13 to 18 years, who have a history of adversity in their lives. Our program helps youth recover and to build resilience through core values, nurturing of the mind, the body and the spirit, guiding their growth to become productive, healthy, and compassionate young men.
Hanna Boys Center Clergy 4; Religious Teachers 3; Priests 1; Students 90; Total Staff 110; School Staff 25.

[G] CAMPS AND COMMUNITY CENTERS

DUNCAN MILLS. *St. Joseph Camp*, 22776 Moscow Rd., P.O. Box 198, Duncan Mills, 95430-0198. Tel: 707-865-0169 Lodge;

Tel: 707-865-2135 Caretaker; Fax: 707-865-1025; Email: jstice@dlsi.org Caretaker. Bro. Richard Lemberg, F.C.S., Dir. Brothers of the Christian Schools.

[H] NEWMAN CENTERS

ARCATA. *Newman Community, Humboldt State University*, 700 Union St., Arcata, 95521.
Tel: 707-822-6057; Email: rfosnaugh@hsunewmancenter.com; Web: www.hsunewmancenter.com. Revs. Francis Gayam, (India) Pastor; Andrew Pacheco, Pastoral Assoc.; Deacon Kenneth M. Bond, Sacramental Min.

PENNGROVE. *Newman Center at Sonoma State University*, 1798 E. Cotati Ave., Penngrove, 94951. P.O. Box 1297, 95402. Tel: 936-203-0572; Email: ratorczynski@gmail.com. Rev. Robert Torczynski, Chap.

[I] HOUSES OF PRAYER AND RETREAT HOUSES

SANTA ROSA. *Angela Center*, 400 Angela Dr., 95403. 9248 Lakewood Dr., Windsor, 95492. Email: angelacenter@gmail.com. Sisters Christine Van Swearingen, O.S.U., Dir.; Dianne Baumunk, O.S.U., Prog. Dir. Bed Capacity 38.

NAPA. *Christian Brothers Retreat and Conference Center*, 4401 Redwood Rd., P.O. Box 3720, Napa, 94558. Tel: 707-252-3810; Tel: 707-252-3703;
Tel: 707-252-3899; Fax: 707-252-7046; Email: confctr@dlsi.org; Web: www.christianbrosretreat.com. Mary Jane Hagan, Conference Center Mgr.; Bro. Donald Johanson, F.S.C., Prov.

OAKVILLE. *Carmelite House of Prayer*, 20 Mount Carmel Dr., P.O. Box 347, Oakville, 94562.
Tel: 707-944-2454; Email: ocdoakville@gmail.com. Rev. Mark Kissner, Prior. Religious 4.

[J] MONASTERIES AND RESIDENCES FOR PRIESTS AND BROTHERS

NAPA. *De La Salle Institute/Provincial Office*, 4401 Redwood Rd., Napa, 94558-9708.
Tel: 707-252-0222; Fax: 707-252-0407; Email: brdonald@dlsi.org; Web: www.delasalle.org. Bro. Donald Johanson, F.S.C., Prov. Brothers of the Christian Schools.*Lasallian Education Corporation*, 4401 Redwood Rd., Napa, 94558.
Tel: 707-252-3844; Fax: 707-252-7046; Email: brdonald@dlsi.org. Bro. Donald Johanson, F.S.C., Prov. *District of San Francisco Christian Brothers Charitable Trust*, 4401 Redwood Rd., Napa, 94558-9708. Tel: 707-252-0222; Fax: 707-252-0407; Email: brdonald@dlsi.org. Bro. Donald Johanson, F.S.C., Prov. *Lasallian Education Fund*, 4401 Redwood Rd., Napa, 94558-9708.
Tel: 707-252-3800; Fax: 707-252-7046; Email: bromarkfsc@dlsi.org. Bros. Donald Johanson, F.S.C., Chm.; Mark Murphy, F.S.C., Chm.
Holy Family Community, 4405 Redwood Rd., Napa, 94558-9708. Tel: 707-252-3713; Tel: 707-252-3787; Email: vkenneth@dlsi.org; Web: www.delasalle.org. Bro. Victor Kenneth, F.S.C., Bro. Dir. Brothers of the Christian Schools. Brothers 16.
Provincialate Community, 4403 Redwood Rd., Napa, 94558. Tel: 707-252-0222; Fax: 707-252-7046; Email: scampbel@dlsi.org. Bros. Stanislaus Campbell, F.S.C., Dir.; Donald Johanson, F.S.C., Prov.; James Joost, F.S.C., Prov. Asst. Brothers of the Christian Schools. Brothers 11.

OAKVILLE. *Carmelite House of Prayer*, 20 Mount Carmel Dr., P.O. Box 347, Oakville, 94562.
Tel: 707-944-2454; Email: ocdoakville@gmail.com; Web: oakvillecarmites.org. Revs. Mark Kissner, Prior; Matthew Williams, Subprior; Christopher La Rocca, Member; James Zakowicz, Member. Discalced Carmelite Friars. Religious 4.

[K] CONVENTS AND RESIDENCES FOR SISTERS

SANTA ROSA. *The Marian Sisters of Santa Rosa, MSSR*, Regina Pacis Convent, 2257 Hoen Ave., 95405.
Tel: 707-326-7593; Email: srteresachriste@mariansisters.com; Web: www.mariansisters.com. Mother Teresa Christe Johnson, M.S.S.R., Supr. Sisters 14.
Provincialate of Ursuline Nuns, 400 Angela Dr., 95403. 9248 Lakewood Dr., Windsor, 95492.
Tel: 650-755-9897; Cell: 707-484-7841; Email: stister2@aol.com; Email: cvs535@gmail.com. Sr. Shirley Ann Garibaldi, O.S.U., Prov., Tel: 650-346-9897. Ursulines of the Roman Union - Western Province. Sisters 15.

WHITETHORN. *Our Lady of the Redwoods Abbey*, 18104 Briceland-Thorn Rd., Whitethorn, 95589.
Tel: 707-986-7419; Fax: 707-986-1176; Email: kdevico@redwoodsabbey.org; Web: www.redwoodsabbey.org. Sr. Kathleen De Vico, O.C.S.O., Abbess. Cistercian Nuns of the Strict Observance. Priests 1; Sisters 11.

WINDSOR. *Ursuline Residence*, 9248 Lakewood Dr., Windsor, 95492. Cell: 707-484-7841; Email: cvs535@aol.com. 400 Angela Dr., 95403. Sr. Christine Van Swearingen, O.S.U., Treas. Ursuline Western Province Sisters 1.

[L] MISCELLANEOUS

SANTA ROSA. **Angela Merici and John Henry Newman Foundation, Inc.*, 50 Ursuline Rd., 95403. c/o Cardinal Newman High School, 50 Ursuline Rd., 95403. Tel: 707-546-6470, Ext. 105;
Fax: 707-544-8502; Email: trogdon@cardinalnewman.org; Email: held@cardinalnewman.org. Laura Held, Pres. For the benefit of Cardinal Newman High School, Santa Rosa, California.
**Catholic Community Foundation*, P.O. Box 1297, 95402. 985 Airway Ct., 95403. Tel: 707-566-3344;
Fax: 707-566-3360; Email: srcaritasmarie@srdiocese.org. Sr. Caritas Marie, M.S.S.R., Dir.
Catholic Youth Organization, P.O. Box 1297, 95402-1297. Mike Griffin, Commissioner; Rich Ruybalid, Pres.
Ursuline Sisters Supplemental Care Fund Trust, 400 Angela Dr., 95403. 9248 Lakewood Dr., Windsor, 95492. Tel: 415-586-0680; Email: patbyrneduggan@aol.com. Sr. Christine Van Swearingen, O.S.U., Trustee.
Pastor of Vietnamese Martyrs Catholic Church of Santa Rosa, A Corporation Sole, 2652 Stony Point Rd., 95407. Tel: 707-293-7992; Email: vietcatholicsantarosa@gmail.com. Rev. Chinh Nguyen, Admin.
Pastor of Vietnamese Martyrs Catholic Church of Santa Rosa, A Corporation Sole.

NAPA. *Lasallian Christian Brothers Foundation, Inc.*, 4401 Redwood Rd., Napa, 94558.
Tel: 707-252-3800; Email: bromarkfsc@dlis.org. Bros. Mark Murphy, F.S.C., Vice Pres.; Donald Johanson, F.S.C., Chm.
**Life Legal Defense Foundation*, Mary Riley, P.O. Box 2105, Napa, 94558. Tel: 707-224-6675;
Fax: 707-224-6676; Email: info@lldf.org; Email: mary@lldf.org; Web: lifelegaldefensefoundation.org. Mary Riley, Vice Pres., Operations.

RELIGIOUS INSTITUTES OF MEN REPRESENTED IN THE DIOCESE

For further details refer to the corresponding bracketed number in the Religious Institutes of Men or Women section.

[0330]—*Brothers of the Christian Schools* (San Francisco Prov.)—F.S.C.
[0280]—*Carthusian Order*—O.Cart.
[0350]—*Cistercian Order of the Strict Observance*—O.C.S.O.
[0260]—*Discalced Carmelite Friars* (Anglo-Irish Prov.)—O.C.D.
[0420]—*Divine Word Missionaries*—S.V.D.
[]—*Missionaries of Faith* (India)—M.F.
[]—*Society of St. Francis Xavier* (India)—S.F.X.
[1060]—*Society of the Precious Blood*—C.PP.S.

RELIGIOUS INSTITUTES OF WOMEN REPRESENTED IN THE DIOCESE

[0670]—*Cistercian Nuns of the Strict Observance*—O.C.S.O.
[]—*Congregation of the Sisters of Mercy*—R.S.M.
[1070-04]—*Dominican Sisters*—O.P.
[2575]—*Institute of the Sisters of Mercy of the Americas*—R.S.M.
[]—*Marian Sisters of Santa Rosa*—M.S.S.R.
[0430]—*Sisters of Charity of the Blessed Virgin Mary* (Dubuque, IA)—B.V.M.
[4090]—*Sisters of Social Service*—S.S.S.
[1570]—*Sisters of St. Francis* (Dubuque, IA)—O.S.F.
[3830-03]—*Sisters of St. Joseph*—C.S.J.
[4110]—*Ursuline Nuns* (Western Prov.)—O.S.U.

DIOCESAN CEMETERIES

SANTA ROSA. *Calvary Catholic*, 2930 Bennett Valley Rd., 95404. Tel: 707-546-6290; Email: calvarysantarosa@sbcglobal.net. P.O. Box 2098, 95405. Angela Scheihing, Contact Person

PETALUMA. *Calvary Catholic*, 304 Magnolia Ave., Petaluma, 94953. Tel: 707-762-8462; Email: calvarysantarosa@sbcglobal.net. Angela Scheihing, Contact Person

SAINT HELENA. *Holy Cross*, 2121 Spring St., St. Helena, 94574. Tel: 707-963-1703; Email: calvarysantarosa@sbcglobal.net. Angela Scheihing, Contact Person

SONOMA. *St. Francis Solano*, 550 E. Napa St., Sonoma, 95476. Tel: 707-546-6290; Email: calvarysantarosa@sbcglobal.net. Angela Scheihing, Contact Person

NECROLOGY

† Hynes, William, (Retired), Died May, 21, 2018

An asterisk (*) denotes an organization that has established tax-exempt status directly with the IRS and is not covered by the USCCB Group Ruling.

Diocese of Savannah

(Dioecesis Savannensis)

Most Reverend

GREGORY J. HARTMAYER, OFM CONV.

Bishop of Savannah; ordained May 5, 1979; appointed Bishop of Savannah July 19, 2011; ordained and installed October 18, 2011. *Catholic Pastoral Center, 2170 E. Victory Dr., Savannah, GA 31404-3918.*

Catholic Pastoral Center, 2170 E. Victory Dr., Savannah, GA 31404-3918. Tel: 912-201-4100; Fax: 912-201-4101.

Web: www.diosav.org

Email: communications@diosav.org

Most Reverend

J. KEVIN BOLAND, D.D.

Bishop Emeritus of Savannah; ordained June 14, 1959; appointed Bishop of Savannah February 7, 1995; ordained and installed April 18, 1995; retired July 19, 2011.

Square Miles 37,038.

Established as Diocese of Savannah July 19, 1850. Name changed to Diocese of Savannah-Atlanta Jan. 5, 1937; Redesignated Nov. 8, 1956.

Comprises 90 Counties in the southern part of the State of Georgia.

Patrons of the Diocese: I. St. John the Baptist; II. Our Lady of Perpetual Help. This diocese was solemnly consecrated to the Sacred Heart of Jesus, May 7, 1872, and on Dec. 8, 1943, it was solemnly consecrated to the Immaculate Heart of Mary.

For legal titles of parishes and diocesan institutions, consult the Chancery.

STATISTICAL OVERVIEW

Personnel	
Bishop	1
Retired Bishops	1
Priests: Diocesan Active in Diocese	59
Priests: Diocesan Active Outside Diocese	2
Priests: Retired, Sick or Absent	25
Number of Diocesan Priests	86
Religious Priests in Diocese	18
Total Priests in Diocese	104
Extern Priests in Diocese	17
Ordinations:	
Diocesan Priests	2
Transitional Deacons	2
Permanent Deacons	11
Permanent Deacons in Diocese	84
Total Brothers	6
Total Sisters	76
Parishes	
Parishes	57
With Resident Pastor:	
Resident Diocesan Priests	40
Resident Religious Priests	13
Without Resident Pastor:	
Administered by Priests	4
Missions	21
Professional Ministry Personnel:	
Brothers	2
Sisters	22
Welfare	
Catholic Hospitals	1
Total Assisted	200,000
Special Centers for Social Services	15
Total Assisted	300,000
Educational	
Diocesan Students in Other Seminaries	19
Total Seminarians	19
High Schools, Diocesan and Parish	3
Total Students	446
High Schools, Private	3
Total Students	1,092
Elementary Schools, Diocesan and Parish	13
Total Students	3,076
Elementary Schools, Private	1
Total Students	178
Non-residential Schools for the Disabled	1
Total Students	53
Catechesis/Religious Education:	
High School Students	957
Elementary Students	5,700
Total Students under Catholic Instruction	11,521
Teachers in the Diocese:	
Priests	12
Brothers	3
Sisters	5
Lay Teachers	502
Vital Statistics	
Receptions into the Church:	
Infant Baptism Totals	1,251
Minor Baptism Totals	239
Adult Baptism Totals	141
Received into Full Communion	243
First Communions	1,604
Confirmations	1,361
Marriages:	
Catholic	232
Interfaith	111
Total Marriages	343
Deaths	649
Total Catholic Population	75,603
Total Population	2,934,000

Former Bishops—Rt. Revs. FRANCIS X. GARTLAND, D.D., first bishop; ord. Aug. 5, 1832; appt. Bishop of Savannah July 23, 1850; cons. Nov. 10, 1850; died Sept. 20, 1854; JOHN BARRY, D.D., ord. Sept. 24, 1825; elected Admin. See of Savannah, Sept. 1854; appt. See of Savannah Jan. 9, 1857; cons. Aug. 2, 1857; died Nov. 21, 1859; AUGUSTIN VEROT, P.S.S., D.D., ord. Sept. 20, 1828; cons. Titular Bishop of Danaba April 25, 1858; installed Vic. Ap. of Florida June 3, 1858; appt. to See of Savannah July 14, 1861; appt. Bishop of St. Augustine March 11, 1870; died June 10, 1876; His Eminence IGNATIUS CARDINAL PERSICO, O.F.M. Cap., D.D., ord. Jan. 24, 1846; appt. Coadjutor Vic. Ap. Bombay and Titular Bishop of Gratianopolis March 8, 1854; cons. June 4, 1854; appt. Vic. Ap. Thibet Dec. 19, 1856; resigned June 24, 1860; appt. to See of Savannah March 11, 1870; resigned Aug. 25, 1872; appt. Titular Bishop of Bolina June 23, 1874; appt. Coadjutor Bishop of Aquino, Sora, e Pontecorvo, Italy July 15, 1878; succeeded Bishop of Aquino, Sora, e Pontecorvo, Italy; resigned March 1887; appt. Roman Curia and Titular Archbishop of Tamiathis March 14, 1887; appt. Sec. Cong. for the Oriental Churches March 20, 1889; appt. Sec. Cong. of the Propagation of the Faith June 13, 1891; elevated to Cardinal Jan. 16, 1893; appt. Cardinal-Priest of San Pietro in Vincoli Jan. 19, 1893; appt. Prefect Congregation for Indulgences and Relics May 30, 1893; died Dec. 7, 1895; Rt. Revs. WILLIAM H. GROSS, C.Ss.R., D.D., ord. March 21, 1863; appt. Bishop of Savannah Feb. 14, 1873; cons. April 27, 1873; promoted to Oregon City Feb. 1, 1885; died Nov. 14, 1898; THOMAS A. BECKER, D.D., ord. June 18, 1859; appt. Bishop of Wilmington March 3, 1868; cons. Aug. 16, 1868; transferred to See of Savannah March 26, 1886; installed May 16, 1886; died July 29, 1899; BENJAMIN J. KEILEY, D.D., ord. Dec. 31, 1873; appt. Bishop of Savannah April 2, 1900; cons. June 3, 1900; resigned Feb. 13, 1922; appt. Titular Bishop of Scillium March 24, 1922; died June 17, 1925; Most Revs. MICHAEL J. KEYES, S.M., D.D., ord. June 21, 1907; appt. Bishop of Savannah July 8, 1922; cons. Oct. 18, 1922; resigned & appt. Titular Bishop of Areopolis and Assistant at the Pontifical Throne Sept. 23, 1935; died July 31, 1959; GERALD P. O'HARA, D.D., J.U.D., appt. Titular Bishop of Heliopolis and Auxiliary Bishop of Philadelphia April 26, 1929; cons. May 20, 1929; appt. to See of Savannah, Nov. 16, 1935; installed Jan. 15, 1936; appt. Official to Romania May 21, 1946; resigned Official to Romania July 5, 1950; granted personal title of Archbishop Savannah-Atlanta July 12, 1950; appt. Ap. Nuncio to Ireland Nov. 27, 1951; appt. Ap. Delegate to Great Britain, June 8, 1954; resigned See of Savannah; appt. Titular Archbishop of Pessinus Nov. 11, 1959; died July 16, 1963; THOMAS J. MCDONOUGH, D.D., J.C.D., ord. May 26, 1938; appt. Titular Bishop of Thaenae and Auxiliary Bishop of St. Augustine, March 10, 1947; cons. April 30, 1947; transferred to Savannah as Auxiliary Jan. 2, 1957; Admin. to Savannah Nov. 11, 1959; succeeded to See March 2, 1960; installed April 27, 1960; appt. Archbishop of Louisville, March 1, 1967; installed May 2, 1967; resigned Sept. 29, 1981; died Aug. 4, 1998; GERARD L. FREY, D.D., ord. April 2, 1938; appt. Bishop of Savannah May 31, 1967; cons. and installed Aug. 8, 1967; transferred to See of Lafayette Nov. 7, 1972; retired May 13, 1989; died Aug. 16, 2007; RAYMOND W. LESSARD, D.D., S.T.D., J.C.L., ord. Dec. 16, 1956; appt. Bishop of Savannah March 5, 1973; cons. and installed April 27, 1973; resigned Feb. 7, 1995; died Jan. 3, 2016; J. KEVIN BOLAND, ord. June 14, 1959; appt. Bishop of Savannah Feb. 7, 1995; ord. and installed April 18, 1995; retired July 19, 2011; appt. Admin. of Savannah until Oct. 18, 2011.

Chancellor—Very Rev. PABLO MIGONE, Tel: 912-201-4113.

Vicar General—Very Rev. DANIEL F. FIRMIN, J.C.L., V.G., Tel: 912-201-4126.

Chancery—Catholic Pastoral Center, 2170 E. Victory Dr., Savannah, 31404-3918. Tel: 912-201-4100; Fax: 912-201-4101. Very Rev. DANIEL F. FIRMIN, J.C.L., V.G., Tel: 912-201-4110; Fax: 912-201-4081.

Safe Environment/Immigration—Catholic Pastoral Center, 2170 E. Victory Dr., Savannah, 31404-3918. Tel: 912-201-4074. JOAN B. ALTMEYER.

Director of Finance—LAWRENCE P. SAUNDERS, Catholic Pastoral Center, 2170 E. Victory Dr., Savannah, 31404-3918. Tel: 912-201-4123; Fax: 912-201-4127.

Diocesan Tribunal—Catholic Pastoral Center, 2170 E. Victory Dr., Savannah, 31404-3918. Tel: 912-201-4134; Fax: 912-201-4099.

Judicial Vicar—Very Rev. J. GERARD SCHRECK, J.C.D., J.V., V.F.

Tribunal Judges—Very Revs. J. GERARD SCHRECK, J.C.D., J.V., V.F.; DANIEL F. FIRMIN, J.C.L., V.G.

Defender of the Bond—Very Revs. JEREMIAH J. MCCARTHY, J.C.L., J.V., V.F.; DOUGLAS K. CLARK, S.T.L., V.F.

Tribunal Director—DR. DAVID CASTRONOVO, J.D., J.C.D.

Case Assessors & Notaries—DRUCILLA MENDEZ; BERNADINE REGO.

Notary—KATHRYN E. PEREIRA.

Promoter of Justice—Rev. THOMAS HEALY, (Retired).

Censor Librorum—Very Rev. DOUGLAS K. CLARK, S.T.L., V.F.

Archivist & Records Manager—KATHRYN E. PEREIRA, Catholic Pastoral Center, 2170 E. Victory Dr., Savannah, 31404-3918. Tel: 912-201-4070.

Legal Counsel—Catholic Pastoral Center, 2170 E. Victory Dr., Savannah, 31404-3918. Tel: 912-201-4100. ROBERT PACE.

Finance Council—S. SCOTT VOYNICH, Chm.; Most Rev. GREGORY J. HARTMAYER, O.F.M.Conv.; Very Revs. DANIEL F. FIRMIN, J.C.L., V.G.; SCOTT WINCHEL, V.F.; ROBERT W. SCHIVERA; JACK MARKLEY; CELESTE C. SHEAROUSE; KAY FORD; DR. FRANCIS P. ROSSITER JR.; CLARENCE A. DAVIS; DONALD THOMPSON. Staff: LAWRENCE P. SAUNDERS; LIAM J. O'CONNOR; ROBERT PACE; MARY ALICE NADEAU; MAUREEN COATES; PAUL NOTT.

Investment Committee—Most Rev. GREGORY J. HARTMAYER, O.F.M.Conv.; DONALD THOMPSON, Chm.; KAY FORD; JACK MARKLEY.

Clergy Personnel—Very Revs. DANIEL F. FIRMIN, J.C.L., V.G.; PABLO MIGONE; J. GERARD SCHRECK, J.C.D., J.V., V.F.; JACEK SZUSTER, V.F.; RAYMOND G. LEVREAULT, V.F.; DOUGLAS K. CLARK, S.T.L., V.F.; TIMOTHY P. MCKEOWN, V.F.; SCOTT WINCHEL, V.F.; JEREMIAH J. MCCARTHY, J.C.L., J.V., V.F.

Human Resources/Director of Operations—JO ANN GREEN.

Deans—

Savannah Deanery—Very Rev. J. GERARD SCHRECK, J.C.D., J.V., V.F., 222 E. Harris St., Savannah, 31401-4699. Tel: 912-233-4709.

Augusta Deanery—Very Rev. JACEK SZUSTER, V.F., 720 Telfair St., P.O. Box 2446, Augusta, 30903-2446. Tel: 706-722-7774.

Albany Deanery—Very Rev. RAYMOND G. LEVREAULT, V.F., 421 Edgewood Lane, Albany, 31707. Tel: 229-273-3446.

Columbus Deanery—Very Rev. JEREMIAH J. MCCARTHY, J.C.L., J.V., V.F., 2000 Kay Cir., Columbus, 31907-3229. Tel: 706-561-8678.

Macon Deanery—Very Rev. SCOTT WINCHEL, V.F., St. Joseph Church, 830 Poplar St., Macon, 31201. Tel: 478-745-1631.

Statesboro Deanery—Very Rev. DOUGLAS K. CLARK, S.T.L., V.F., 221 John Paul Ave., Statesboro, 30458-5076. Tel: 912-681-6726.

Valdosta-Brunswick Deanery—Very Rev. TIMOTHY P. MCKEOWN, V.F., St. Francis Xavier, 405 Howe St., Brunswick, 31520-7526. Tel: 912-265-3249.

College of Consultors—Rev. Msgr. JOHN A. KENNEALLY, V.G., V.F.; Very Revs. DOUGLAS K. CLARK, S.T.L., V.F.; JEREMIAH J. MCCARTHY, J.C.L., J.V., V.F.; DANIEL F. FIRMIN, J.C.L., V.G.; Rev. FREDY A. ANGEL; Very Rev. ALLAN J. MCDONALD, V.F.; Rev. PATRICK A. OTOR, M.S.P.; Very Revs. TIMOTHY P. MCKEOWN, V.F.; PABLO MIGONE; J. GERARD SCHRECK, J.C.D., J.V., V.F.

Presbyteral Council—Very Revs. SCOTT WINCHEL, V.F., Chm.; TIMOTHY P. MCKEOWN, V.F., Vice Chm.; Rev. BENJAMIN DALLAS, Sec./Treas.

Diocesan Offices and Directors

Newspaper—The Southern Cross MICHAEL JOHNSON, Editor, Catholic Pastoral Center, 2170 E. Victory Dr., Savannah, 31404-3918. Tel: 912-201-4054; Fax: 912-201-4101; Email: editor@diosav.org.

Director of Communications—BARBARA KING, Catholic Pastoral Center, 2170 E. Victory Dr., Savannah, 31404-3918. Tel: 912-201-4052; Fax: 912-201-4101; Email: communications@diosav.org.

Director of Catholic Education/Superintendent of Schools—MICHELLE KROLL, Catholic Pastoral Center, 2170 E. Victory Dr., Savannah, 31404-3918. Tel: 912-201-4122.

Director of Black Catholic Ministry—Rev. ROBERT E. CHANEY, Catholic Pastoral Center, 2170 E. Victory Dr., Savannah, 31404-3918. Tel: 912-201-4077; Fax: 912-201-4101; Email: af-am-ministry@diosav.org.

Director of Catholic Charities of Savannah—Sr. PATRICIA BROWN, S.S.M.N., 2170 E. Victory Dr., Savannah, 31404-3918. Tel: 912-201-4068; Fax: 912-201-4101.

Director of Construction & Properties—Catholic Pastoral Center, 2170 E. Victory Dr., Savannah, 31404-3918. Tel: 912-201-4066; Fax: 912-201-4101; Email: pnott@diosav.or. PAUL NOTT.

Director of Family Life—Catholic Pastoral Center, 2170 E. Victory Dr., Savannah, 31404-3918. Tel: 912-201-4058; Email: familylife@diosav.org. JAYNE STEFANIC.

Director of Hispanic Ministry—LIDIA NIEDERKORN, Catholic Pastoral Center, 2170 E. Victory Dr., Savannah, 31404-3918. Tel: 912-201-4067.

Director of Permanent Diaconate—Deacon KELLEY G. CULVER, 4447 Whisperwood Dr., Martinez, 30907. Tel: 706-855-9893.

Director of Evangelization—ANN PINCKNEY, Catholic Pastoral Center, 2170 E. Victory Dr., Savannah, 31404-3918. Tel: 912-201-4041; Fax: 912-201-4101; Email: apinckney@diosav.org.

Director of Stewardship and Development—Catholic Pastoral Center, 2170 E. Victory Dr., Savannah, 31404-3918. Tel: 912-201-4050. MAUREEN COATES.

Director of the Catholic Foundation of South Georgia—LIAM J. O'CONNOR, Catholic Pastoral Center, 2170 E. Victory Dr., Savannah, 31404-3918. Tel: 912-201-4061.

Delegate for Consecrated Life—Sr. MARGARET DOWNING, R.S.M., 5381 Pine Needle Dr., Columbus, 31907-1804. Tel: 443-827-5631.

Director of Vocations—Very Rev. PABLO MIGONE, 2170 E. Victory Dr., Savannah, 31404-3918. Tel: 912-201-4113.

Director of Youth & Young Adult Ministry—2170 E. Victory Dr., Savannah, 31404-3918. Tel: 912-201-4057. AMY ELKINS.

Apostleship of the Sea—Mailing Address: P.O. Box 877, Tybee Island, 31328. Tel: 912-655-6302. Rev. RICHARD YOUNG.

Campaign for Human Development—Sr. PATRICIA BROWN, S.S.M.N., Catholic Pastoral Center, 2170 E. Victory Dr., Savannah, 31404-3918. Tel: 912-201-4058.

Associate Director of Campus Ministry—2170 E. Victory Dr., Savannah, 31404-3918. Tel: 912-201-4056. ABIGAIL BYRON-GOSLIN.

Georgia Southern University at Armstrong Campus—KRYSTYNA SWIERCZWSKI, Campus Min.; Rev. JASON P. ADAMS, Chap., Tel: 912-201-4056; Email: savannahccm@diosav.org; Web: www.newmanconnection.com/locations/detail/armstrong-atlantic-state-university/seek-catholic-campus-ministry. Facebook; Instagram. Affiliated with St. James Catholic Church 8412 Whitefield Ave., Savannah, GA 31406. Tel: 912-355-3132.

Albany State University—Tel: 229-669-4202; Web: www.newmanconnection.com/locations/detail/albany-state-university/catholic-campus-ministry. TERRIE ALBY, Campus Min., Email: tlalby@yahoo.com; Rev. CHRISTOPHER ORTEGA, Chap. Affiliated with Saint Teresa's Catholic Church, 421 Edgewood Lane, Albany, GA 31707. Tel: 229-439-2302.

Andrew College—Bro. JASON MUHLENKAMP, G.H.M., Campus Min. Coord., Email: jmuhlenkamp@glenmary.org; Web: www.newmanconnection.com/locations/detail/4479. Affiliated with Holy Family Church, 533 Arlington Ave., P.O. Box 425, Blakely, GA 39823. Tel: 229-723-3339.

Augusta State University—Rev. VERNON KNIGHT, Chap., Tel: 706-733-6627, Ext. 203; Email: augustaccm@diosav.org; Web: www.newmanconnection.com/locations/detail/4381. Facebook; Instagram. Affiliated with St. Mary's on the Hill Church, Annunciation House, 2561 Central Ave., Augusta, GA 30904. Tel: 706-733-6627, Ext. 203.

College of Coastal Georgia—MARUSOL SOLER; LAURIE JONES, Tel: 912-201-4056; Email: campusministry@diosav.org; Web: www.newmanconnection.com/locations/detail/2052. Affiliated with St. Francis Xavier Church, Christian Formation Center, 1116 Richmond St., Brunswick, GA 31520. Tel: 912-264-6805, Ext. 12.

Columbus State University—Rev. EMANUEL VASCONCELOS, O.F.M.Conv., Chap., Tel: 706-561-8676; Email: columbusccm@diosav.org; Web: www.newmanconnection.com/locations/detail/columbus-state-university/catholic-campus-ministry-st.-anne-catholic-church. Facebook; Instagram. Affiliated with St. Anne Catholic Church, 2000 Kay Circle, Columbus, GA 31907. Tel: 706-561-8676.

Georgia Southern University—COREY KIEFFER, FOCUS Team Dir., Email: corey.kieffer@focus.org; Rev. JOHN R. JOHNSON, Chap., Tel: 912-681-6726, Ext. 204; Email: gsufocus@gmail.com; Email: southernccm@diosav.org; Web: www.newmanconnection.com/locations/detail/georgia-southern-university/st.-matthew-parish-and-newman-center. Facebook; Instagram. Affiliated with St. Matthew Catholic Church, 221 John Paul Ave., Statesboro, GA 30458. Tel: 912-681-6726; Email: dclark5735@gmail.com.

Mercer University—Rev. JOHN WRIGHT, Chap., Tel: 478-745-1631, Ext. 125; Email: jwright@diosav.org; Email: mercerccm@diosav.org; Web: www.newmanconnection.com/locations/detail/mercer-university/catholic-newman-ministry. Facebook. Affiliated with Saint Joseph Catholic Church, 830 Poplar St., Macon, GA 31201. Tel: 478-745-1631.

Savannah College of Art and Design—KRYSTYNA SWIERCZWSKI, Campus Min.; Very Rev. PABLO MIGONE, Chap., Tel: 912-201-4056; Email: savannahccm@diosav.org; Web: www.newmanconnection.com/locations/detail/savannah-college-of-art-and-design/creed-savannah-catholic-campus-ministry. Facebook; Instagram. Affiliated with Cathedral of St. John the Baptist, 222 E. Harris St., Savannah, GA 31404. Tel: 912-233-4709. Sacred Heart Catholic Church, 1707 Bull St., Savannah, Ga 31404. Tel: 912-232-0792.

Savannah State University—KRYSTYNA SWIERCZWSKI, Campus Min.; Deacon HOSEA BENNETT, Chap., Tel: 912-201-4056; Email: savannahccm@diosav.org; Web: www.newmanconnection.com/locations/detail/2899. Affiliated with St. James Catholic Church, 8412 Whitefield Ave., Savannah, GA 31406. Tel: 912-355-3132.

Valdosta State University—BETHANIE BASS, Campus Min.; Rev. DAWID A. KWIATKOWSKI, Chap., Valdosta State University Catholic Center, 1524 N. Oak St., Valdosta, 31602. Tel: 229-561-4456; Email: bbass@stjohnschl.org; Web: www.newmanconnection.com/locations/detail/valdosta-state-university/st.-john-the-evangelist. Facebook; Instagram. Affiliated with St. John the Evangelist Church, 800 Gornto Rd., Valdosta, GA 31602. Tel: 229-244-2430.

Catholic Relief Services—Sr. PATRICIA BROWN, S.S.M.N., Catholic Pastoral Center, 2170 E. Victory Dr., Savannah, 31404-3918. Tel: 912-201-4058.

Council of Catholic Women—KATE HAASE, 6 Sea Eagle Ct., Savannah, 31411. Tel: 912-604-9669; Email: kthaze@me.com.

Diocesan Worship Commission—Very Rev. DOUGLAS K. CLARK, S.T.L., V.F., Pastor, 221 John Paul Ave., Statesboro, 30458-5016. Tel: 912-681-6726; Email: dclark@diosav.org.

Diocesan Scout Chairman—JAMIE ANDERSON.

Diocesan Catholic Scouting—AMY ELKINS, Catholic Pastoral Center, 2170 E. Victory Dr., Savannah, 31404. Tel: 912-201-4057.

Diocesan Scout Chaplain—Rev. JASON P. ADAMS, St. James Parish, 8412 Whitefield Ave., Savannah, 31406. Tel: 912-355-1523.

Ecumenism and Interreligious Affairs—Rev. MICHAEL J. KAVANAUGH, Dir., St. Peter the Apostle Church, 7020 Concord Rd., P.O. Box 30859, Savannah, 31419. Tel: 912-897-5156; Email: mkavanaug@diosav.org.

Georgia Catholic Conference—Archdiocese of Atlanta, 2401 Lake Park Dr., Smyrna, 30080. Tel: 440-920-7367; Fax: 440-920-7341. FRANCIS J. MULCAHY, Esq., M.T.S., Exec. Sec.

Mission Cooperative Appeal—Very Rev. DANIEL F. FIRMIN, J.C.L., V.G., Catholic Pastoral Center, 2170 E. Victory Dr., Savannah, 31404-3918. Tel: 912-201-4110; Fax: 912-201-4081.

Propagation of the FaithANN PINCKNEY, Catholic Pastoral Center, 2170 E. Victory Dr., Savannah, 31404-3918. Tel: 912-201-4041; Fax: 912-201-4101; Email: apinckney@diosav.org.

Victim Assistance Coordinator—ROSEMARY DOWNING, Tel: 912-201-4073.

CLERGY, PARISHES, MISSIONS AND PAROCHIAL SCHOOLS

CITY OF SAVANNAH

(CHATHAM COUNTY)

1—CATHEDRAL OF ST. JOHN THE BAPTIST (1873)
222 E. Harris St., 31401-4699. Tel: 912-233-4709; Fax: 912-233-8229; Email: csjbsav@aol.com. Very Rev. J. Gerard Schreck, J.C.D., J.V., V.F., Rector; Rev. Msgr. William O. O'Neill, In Res., (Retired); Very Rev. Pablo Migone, In Res.; Rev. Thomas J. Peyton, In Res., (Retired); Deacon Dewain Smith.
Catechesis Religious Program—Janee Przybyl, D.R.E. Total Enrollment 13.

2—ST. BENEDICT THE MOOR (1874) (African American)
441 E. Broad St, 31401. Tel: 912-232-7147; Fax: 912-238-0184; Email: stbenedict@bellsouth.net; Web: stbenedicttmcc.org. Mailing Address: 556 E. Gordon St., 31401. Rev. Romanus Obiora Ezeugwu, M.S.P.
, Sharon Carson, D.R.E. Total Enrollment 22.

3—ST. FRANCES XAVIER CABRINI (1968)
11500 Middleground Rd., 31419. Tel: 912-925-4725; Email: sfcc.office@cabrini-sav.org; Web: cabrini-sav.org. Rev. Gabriel Cummings.

4—ST. JAMES (1956)
8412 Whitfield Ave., 31406-6198. Tel: 912-355-1523; Fax: 912-353-7226; Email: bmacaulay@stjamessav.com; Web: www.stjamessav.com. Very Rev. Daniel F. Firmin, J.C.L., V.G.; Revs. Samuel Aniekwe, Parochial Vicar; Jason P. Adams, Parochial Vicar.
School—St. James School, (Grades PreK-8), Tel: 912-355-3132; Fax: 912-355-1996; Email: srlisa@sjcs-savannahga.org; Web: www.stjameschargers.com. Sr. Lisa A. Golden, I.H.M., Prin. Lay Teachers 30; Students 383; Clergy / Religious Teachers 3.
Mission—Our Lady of Good Hope, Isle of Hope, Chatham Co.

5—MOST BLESSED SACRAMENT (1920)
1003 E. Victory Dr., 31405-2499. Tel: 912-356-6980; Email: parish@mbschurch.org; Web: www.mbschurch.org. Revs. Brett A. Brannen; John Tran; Deacon Gerald R. Clark.
Res.: 909 E. Victory Dr., 31405-2499.
School—Most Blessed Sacrament School, (Grades PreK-8), Tel: 912-356-6987; Fax: 912-356-6988; Email: aswanger@bss-savannah.org; Web: bss-savannah.org. Mrs. Lynn Brown, Prin. Clergy 2; Lay Teachers 42; Students 427.

6—MOST PURE HEART OF MARY (1907) Closed. For inquiries for parish records contact the chancery.

7—STS. PETER AND PAUL (1980) (Vietnamese)
3115 Victory Dr., 31404-4598. Tel: 912-354-4014; Email: kimsnguyen@juno.com. Rev. Kim Son Nguyen.

8—ST. PETER THE APOSTLE CHURCH (1993)
Mailing Address: 7020 Concord Rd., P.O. Box 30859, 31410. Tel: 912-897-5156; Email: lwilharm@spacsav.net; Web: saintpetertheapostle.com. Rev. Michael J. Kavanaugh; Very Rev. Msgr. P. James Costigan, V.F.
Res.: 302 Bryson Dr., 31410.
School—St. Peter the Apostle Catholic School, (Grades PreK-8), Tel: 912-897-5224; Fax: 912-897-0801; Email: school@saintpetertheapostle.com; Web: school.saintpetertheapostle.com. Mr. Joe Thomas, Prin. Lay Teachers 18; Students 213; Clergy / Religious Teachers 1.

9—RESURRECTION OF OUR LORD (2000)
112 Fell St., 31415-1828. Tel: 912-232-5258; Email: rbrtgen@aol.com; Web: resurrection.diosav.net. Rev. Robert E. Chaney; Deacon Hosea Bennett.

10—SACRED HEART OF JESUS (1880)
1707 Bull St., 31401. Tel: 912-232-0792; Fax: 912-236-0065; Email: secretary@sacredheartsavannah.org; Web: www.sacredheartsavannah.org. Revs. John J. Lyons, V.F.; Paul Gutting; Sr. Pauline O'Brien, M.F.I.C., Pastoral Assoc.; Deacon Robert Larcher.
Res.: 102 E. 57th St., 31405-3326.
Catechesis Religious Program—Veronica Campbell, D.R.E. Total Enrollment 93.

OUTSIDE THE CITY OF SAVANNAH

ALBANY, DOUGHERTY CO., ST. TERESA (1875)
421 Edgewood Ln., Albany, 31707. Tel: 229-439-2302; Email: stteresasfront@bellsouth.net; Web: stteresaschurch.org. Very Rev. Raymond G. Levreault, V.F.; Revs. Paul C. Ladda, Parochial Vicar; Oscar Juan Mendoza, Parochial Vicar; Christopher Ortega, Parochial Vicar; Deacons John C. Dallas; Michael Leach.
School—St. Teresa School, (Grades PreK-11), 417 Edgewood Ln., Albany, 31707-3991. Tel: 229-436-0134; Fax: 229-436-0135; Email: frontoffice@stteresas.org; Web: stteresas.org. Susie Hatcher, Prin. Lay Teachers 27; Students 146.
Catechesis Religious Program—Deacon Michael Leach, D.R.E.; Lori Leach, D.R.E. Total Enrollment 340.
St. Clare's Evangelization-Community Center—2005 Martin Luther King Dr., P.O. Box 4123, Albany, 31706-4123. Tel: 229-883-2566; Fax: 229-883-9116; Email: stclarescenter@att.net. Sr. Maura Molloy, M.F.I.C., Dir.
Neighbors in Need—2005 Martin Luther King Dr., P.O. Box 4123, Albany, 31706-3001. Tel: 229-883-2872; Email: neighbors-in-need@mediacombb.net. Tina Appollonio, Dir.

AMERICUS, SUMTER CO., ST. MARY (1891)
332 S. Lee St., Americus, 31709-3916. Tel: 229-924-3495; Email: stmaryamericus@gmail.com; Web: www.stmaryamericus.com. Rev. Francis Gillespie, S.J.; Deacon Bernie Bosse, RCIA Coord.
Catechesis Religious Program—Ron Akerman, D.R.E. Total Enrollment 65.

AUGUSTA, RICHMOND CO.

1—CHURCH OF THE MOST HOLY TRINITY (1810)
Mailing Address: 720 Telfair St, P.O. Box 2446, Augusta, 30903-2446. Tel: 706-722-4944; Fax: 706-722-7774; Email: helen@themostholytrinity.org. Very Rev. Jacek Szuster, V.F.; Deacons Elmore J. Butler; Kent Plowman.
Res.: 2347 Redwood Dr., Augusta, 30904.
School—Immaculate Conception Catholic School, (Grades PreK-12), Tel: 706-722-9964; Email: principal@icaugusta.org; Web: www.icaugusta.org. Mrs. Allison Palfy, Prin. Clergy 1; Lay Teachers 10; Students 53.

2—ST. JOSEPH (1954)
2607 Lumpkin Rd., Augusta, 30906-3222. Tel: 706-798-1920; Email: stjoesaug@aol.com; Web: stjoesch.org. Revs. Mark N. Van Alstine; Sooho Lee, Parochial Vicar; Juan Carlos Castillo Mayorga, Parochial Vicar; Deacons Gregory L. Bernard; James Lloyd; Tom Valois.
Catechesis Religious Program—Annette Eyrich, D.R.E. Total Enrollment 264.

3—ST. MARY ON THE HILL (1917)
1420 Monte Sano Ave., Augusta, 30904-5394. Tel: 706-733-6627; Fax: 706-733-4887; Email: smoth@knology.net. Revs. Mark J. Ross; Vernon Knight, Parochial Vicar; Michael Hull; Deacons Don McArdle; Anthony E. Wagner; Albert J. Sullivan Jr.; Kenneth R. Maleck; Jason Lanham.
School—St. Mary on the Hill School, (Grades K-8), 1220 Monte Sano Ave., Augusta, 30904-5394. Tel: 706-733-6193; Fax: 706-737-7985; Email: smcs@knology.net; Web: www.stmaryssaints.org. Mrs. Laura Webster, Prin. Lay Teachers 42; Students 445.
Chapels—Aquinas Chapel—1920 Highland Ave., Augusta, 30904. Tel: 706-736-5516; Fax: 706-736-2678.
Adoration Chapel.

BAINBRIDGE, DECATUR CO., ST. JOSEPH'S (1887)
1207 Randolph St., Bainbridge, 39819-0192. Tel: 229-243-9146; Email: sjcatholichurch@gmail.com; Web: stjoebainbridge.diosav.net. 822 Ramsay St., P.O. Box 192, Bainbridge, 39819. Rev. Victor M. Canela, S.T.
Mission—Church of the Incarnation, 5541 Hwy. 91, Donalsonville, Seminole Co. 39845.

BLAKELY, EARLY CO., HOLY FAMILY (1965)
517 Arlington Ave., P.O. Box 425, Blakely, 39823-0425. Tel: 229-723-3339; Email: mkerin@glenmary.org. Rev. Michael Kerin.
Mission—St. Luke, P.O. Box 491, Cuthbert, Randolph Co. 39840.

BRUNSWICK, GLYNN CO., ST. FRANCIS XAVIER (1884)
405 Howe St., Brunswick, 31520-7526. Tel: 912-265-3249; Email: annbuebel@bellsouth.net. Very Rev. Timothy P. McKeown, V.F.; Rev. Christopher Hassel; Deacons Lawrence Guyer; Ntungwa Maasha.
Rectory: 729 Union St., Brunswick, 31520-8018.
School—St. Francis Xavier School, (Grades PreK-8), 1121 Union St., Brunswick, 31520. Tel: 912-265-9470; Fax: 912-265-9950; Email: tmermann@sfxcs.org; Web: www.sfxcs.org. Dr. Terrence Mermann, Prin. Lay Teachers 20; Students 200; Clergy / Religious Teachers 1.
Catechesis Religious Programs—Deacon Lawrence Guyer, D.R.E. Total Enrollment 27.
Christian Formation Center, 1116 Richmond St., Brunswick, 31520. Tel: 912-264-6805; Fax: 912-264-6885. Students 135.
Mission—Nativity of Our Lady, 1000 N. Way St., Darien, McIntosh Co. 31305.
St. Francis Center - CSS—520 E. Mary St., Valdosta, 31601. Tel: 229-242-8656; Fax: 229-244-2752; Email: sfc520@att.net. 800 Gornto Rd., Valdosta, 31602. Sr. Nuala Mulleady, M.F.I.C., Dir.

CLAXTON, EVANS CO., ST. CHRISTOPHER (1958)
400 S. River St., Claxton, 30417-2150. Tel: 912-739-3913; Cell: 478-955-5854; Email: saintchristopher@bellsouth.net; Web: www.stchristopherclaxton.com. Revs. John R. Johnson; Vicente Terrazas, Parochial Vicar; Deacon James Spacher.
Missions—Holy Cross—90 W. Bacon St., Pembroke, Bryan Co. 31321.
Our Lady of Guadalupe, 3879 S. Berry Rd., Sand Hill, 30427.
Catechesis Religious Program—Alfredo Vicente, D.R.E. Total Enrollment 100.
Mission—St. Jude, 911 N. Veterans Blvd., Glennville, Tattnall Co. 30427-0772.

COLUMBUS, MUSCOGEE CO.

1—ST. ANNE (1961)
2000 Kay Cir., Columbus, 31907-3229. Tel: 706-561-8678; Fax: 706-565-4845; Email: office@stanneweb.com; Web: stannecsg.com. Very Rev. Jeremiah J. McCarthy, J.C.L., J.V., V.F.; Revs. Thomas Brian O'Shaughnessy, Parochial Vicar; Joseph Buencamino, Parochial Vicar; Deacons Robert Herrmann; Edgar L. Ensley Jr.; John R. Quillen.
School—St. Anne-Pacelli Catholic School, (Grades PreK-12), 2020 Kay Cir., Columbus, 31907. Tel: 706-561-8232; Fax: 706-563-0211; Email: inforequest@sasphs.net; Web: beaviking.com. Ronie Collins, Pres.; Mrs. Jocelyn Smith, Prin. Lay Teachers 52; Students 686; Clergy / Religious Teachers 3.
Catechesis Religious Program—Email: szimmermann@stanneweb.com. Suzanne Zimmermann, D.R.E. Total Enrollment 202.
St. Anne Community Outreach—1820 Box Rd., Columbus, 31907-3254. Tel: 706-568-1592; Fax: 706-568-1699; Email: outreach@sasphs.net; Web: stannecsg.com/outreach.html. Katherine (Katie) Byers, Dir.; Katrina Oliver, Asst. Dir. Tot Asst. Annually 11,776; Volunteers 309; Staff 3.

2—ST. BENEDICT THE MOOR CATHOLIC CHURCH (1958) (African American)
2930 Thomas St., Columbus, 31906-0714. Mailing Address: 2935 9th St., Columbus, 31906-0714. Tel: 706-323-8300; Fax: 706-324-2641; Email: stbenedict07@knology.net; Web: stbenedictthemoorcolumbus.org. Rev. Charles A. Atuah, M.S.P.
Catechesis Religious Program—Gail Buffong, D.R.E.
St. Benedict Outreach Program—Email: bedcas45@yahoo.com. Beverly Casimier, Dir. Tot Asst. Annually 319.

3—HOLY FAMILY (1835) [JC]
320 12th St., Columbus, 31901. Tel: 706-323-6908; Email: holyfamily706@bellsouth.net; Web: holyfamilycolumbus.com. Revs. Daniel P. O'Connell; Finbarr P. Stanton, In Res., (Retired).
Res.: 1001 Brookwood Ave., Columbus, 31906.
Catechesis Religious Program—Students 114.
Holy Family Social Services Outreach Program—Tel: 706-322-0098; Fax: 706-323-2043; Email: holyfamily6706@gmail.com; Web: holyfamilycolumbus.com. Gretchen Whaley-Wong, Dir. Tot Asst. Annually 5,499.

4—OUR LADY OF LOURDES (1958)
1953 Torch Hill Rd., Columbus, 31903. Tel: 706-689-5720; Email: lourdesoffice21@gmail.com. Rev. Nicholas Mansell.
Mission—St. Mary Magdalen, 232 S. Broad St., Buena Vista, Marion Co. 31803. Fr. Robert Benko.

CORDELE, CRISP CO., ST. THERESA (1931)
807 Third St. S., Cordele, 31015-1705. Tel: 229-273-3446; Email: churchofthelittleflower@gmail.com. Rev. Paulinus Chikelue Okpala, Parochial Admin.

DOUGLAS, COFFEE CO., ST. PAUL'S (1938)
Mailing Address: 4178 U.S. Hwy. 441 S., Douglas, 31533-5732. Tel: 912-384-3560; Email: saintpaul@windstream.net. Rev. Paul A. O'Connell; Bertha Capetillo, Pastoral Assoc.; Deacon Ron Milkas.
Res.: 623 Briarwood Rd., Douglas, 31533.
Missions—St. William—807 S. Merrimac, Fitzgerald, Ben Hill Co. 31750-0801. Deacon William Drexler.
Holy Family, Willacoochee, Atkinson Co.

DUBLIN, LAURENS CO., IMMACULATE CONCEPTION (1911)
1559 U.S. Hwy. 441 N., Dublin, 31021. Tel: 478-272-0266; Email: iccdublin@immaculate-conception-church.net; Web: www.immaculate-conception-church.net. Revs. Stephen J. Pontzer; Jacob N. Almeter, Parochial Vicar.
Catechesis Religious Program—Leanna Magluilo, D.R.E. Total Enrollment 60.
Rectory—331 Shadow Pond Rd., Dublin, 31021.
Mission—St. William, 301 S. Smith St., Sandersville, Washington Co. 31082. Tel: 478-552-3352.

EASTMAN, DODGE CO., ST. MARK (1989)
1687 Hawkinsville Hwy., Eastman, 31023-4241. Tel: 478-272-0266; Email: iccdublin@immaculate-conception-church.net. Mailing Address: 1559 Hwy

441 N, Dublin, 31021. Revs. Stephen J. Pontzer; Jacob N. Almeter, Parochial Vicar.

FORT VALLEY, PEACH CO., ST. JULIANA'S CATHOLIC CHURCH
804 Martin Luther King Jr. Dr., P.O. Box 1022, Fort Valley, 31010. Email: stjulianacc804@gmail.com. Rev. Carlos E. Pinzon, O.F.M.; Deacon Kenneth P. Hutnick.

GROVETOWN, COLUMBIA CO., ST. TERESA OF AVILA (1968)
4921 Columbia Rd., Grovetown, 30813-5237.
Tel: 706-863-4956; Fax: 706-863-5001; Email: info@st-teresa.com; Web: www.st-teresa.com. Revs. Walter Y. (Mike) Ingram, V.F.; Michael E. Roverse, Parochial Vicar; Gonzalo Meza, Parochial Vicar; Peter Hung Nguyen, Parochial Vicar; Deacons William L. Johnson; Kerry C. Diver; Joseph S. Soparas; Robert J. Kepshire.
Catechesis Religious Program—Tel: 706-863-0252; Email: ffoffice@st-teresa.com; Web: st-teresa.com/childrens-faith-formation. Miriam Martin, D.R.E. Students 720.

HAZLEHURST, JEFF DAVIS CO., GOOD SHEPHERD (1967)
259 Baxley Hwy, Hazlehurst, 31513.
Tel: 912-366-0238; Email: restrada@diosav.org; Web: goodshepherdsaintrose.com. Mailing Address: P.O. Box 330, Baxley, 31515-0330. Rev. Rafael A. Estrada.
Missions—St. Rose of Lima—1520 City Circle Rd., Baxley, Appling Co. 31513.
St. Raymond, 1929 6A - Hwy. 32 W., Alma, 31510.

HINESVILLE, LIBERTY CO., ST. STEPHEN, FIRST MARTYR (1980)
399 Woodland Ave., Hinesville, 31313-2719.
Tel: 912-876-4364; Email: sscc399@clds.net. Rev. Adam J. Kasela; Deacon Douglas Delzeith.

JESUP, WAYNE CO., ST. JOSEPH (1964)
1048 E. Cherry St., Jesup, 31546. Tel: 912-427-9239; Email: stjoejesup@bellsouth.net; Web: stjosephsjesup.org. Rev. Keith O'Neill, O.F.M.Conv., Parochial Admin.
Res.: 1055 E. Plum St., Jesup, 31546-4012.
Catechesis Religious Program—Laura Bradt, D.R.E. Total Enrollment 38.

KATHLEEN, HOUSTON CO., ST. PATRICK (1969)
2410 GA Hwy. 127, Kathleen, 31047-2820.
Tel: 478-987-4213; Email: saintpat@stpatrickga.org. Rev. Eric R. Filmer; Deacons James Roberge, Pastoral Assoc.; Ralph H. McAtee, (Retired).
Rectory: 208 Wingfield Way, Kathleen, 31047.

MACON, BIBB CO.
1—HOLY SPIRIT (1968)
4074 Chambers Rd., Macon, 31206-4702.
Tel: 478-788-6386; Fax: 478-788-2837; Email: pastor@holyspiritmacon.org; Web: www.holyspiritmacon.org. Rev. David A. Koetter.

2—ST. JOSEPH (1841)
830 Poplar St., Macon, 31201-2093.
Tel: 478-745-1631; Email: church@st-joseph.cc; Web: stjosephmacon.wordpress.com. Very Rev. Scott Winchel, V.F.; Rev. John Wright; Deacons Donald R. Coates; Thomas J. Eden.
School—St. Joseph School, (Grades PreK-6), 905 High St., Macon, 31201. Tel: 478-742-0636; Fax: 478-746-7685; Email: alex.porto@sjsmacon.org; Web: www.sjsmacon.org. Mr. Alex Porto, Prin. Lay Teachers 29; Students 215.
Catechesis Religious Program—Mrs. Candia Michela, D.R.E. Total Enrollment 195.

3—ST. PETER CLAVER (1915)
131 Ward St., Macon, 31204-3193. Tel: 478-743-1454; Email: bettyemiddlebrooks@yahoo.com. Revs. William McIntyre, O.F.M.; John Coughlin; Deacons James B. Hubbard; Reginald Russell. Order of Franciscan Friars
School—St. Peter Claver Catholic School, (Grades PreK-8), 133 Ward St., Macon, 31204-3193. Tel: 478-743-3985; Fax: 478-743-0054; Email: info@spccatholicschool.org; Web: www.spccatholicschool.org. Sr. Cheryl Ann Hillig, D.C., Prin. Lay Teachers 17; Sisters 2; Students 172.
Catechesis Religious Program—Bettye Middlebrooks, D.R.E.; Edgar Cabrera, D.R.E. Total Enrollment 97.

MCRAE, TELFAIR CO., HOLY REDEEMER (1968)
17 Telfair Ave., McRae, 31055-1625.
Tel: 478-272-0266; Email: iccdublin@immaculate-conception-church.net. Mailing Address: 1559 Hwy 441 N, Dublin, 31021. Revs. Stephen J. Pontzer; Jacob N. Almeter, Parochial Vicar.

MONTEZUMA, MACON CO., ST. MICHAEL MISSION CATHOLIC CHURCH
P.O. Box 1022, Fort Valley, 31030. Email: stjulianacc804@gmail.com. 718 N. Dooly St., Montezuma, 31063. Rev. Carlos E. Pinzon, O.F.M.; Deacon Kenneth P. Hutnick.

MOULTRIE, COLQUITT CO., IMMACULATE CONCEPTION (1978)
1132 Second St. SE, Moultrie, 31768.
Tel: 229-985-6550; Email: icmoult@moultriega.net. Rev. Alfonso Gutierrez; Deacon Brian Rollock.
Res.: 202 Hillcrest Ave., Moultrie, 31768. Web: www.iccmoultrie.org.
Mission—St. John Vianney, P.O. Box 391, Camilla, Mitchell Co. 31730-0391. Tel: 229-336-8685.

PINE MOUNTAIN, HARRIS CO., CHRIST THE KING CHURCH (2006)
6700 GA Hwy. 354, P.O. Box 899, Pine Mountain, 31822. Tel: 706-663-0090; Email: ctkpinemountain@att.net; Web: www.christthekingpinemountain.org. Rev. John R. Madden.
Catechesis Religious Program—Kelly Brooks, D.R.E. Total Enrollment 57.

PORT WENTWORTH, CHATHAM CO., OUR LADY OF LOURDES (1940)
501 S. Coastal Hwy., (GA Hwy. 25), Port Wentworth, 31407-4056. Tel: 912-667-0602; Email: ololchurch@comcast.net. Revs. Thomas J. Murphy; Luis Fonseca; Sr. Georgette Cunniff, M.F.I.C., D.R.E.

RAY CITY, ST. ANTHONY OF PADUA CATHOLIC CHURCH
2530 Garner Rd., Ray City, 31645. Tel: 229-455-5554; Email: santonyga@outlook.com; Web: www.anthonyofpaduaga.org. Rev. Fredy A. Angel; Deacons Raymond E. Brown; Steven Mancuso, D.R.E.

RICHMOND HILL, BRYAN CO., ST. ANNE (1955)
10550 Ford Ave., P.O. Box 648, Richmond Hill, 31324-0648. Tel: 912-756-3343; Email: admin@stannerh.org; Web: www.stannerh.org. Very Rev. Allan J. McDonald, V.F.; Rev. Andrew Larkin, Parochial Vicar; Deacons Paul Gutting; Ray Moreau.
Res.: 312 Victor's Ct., Richmond Hill, 31324-0601.

SPRINGFIELD, EFFINGHAM CO., ST. BONIFACE CHURCH (1987)
1952 GA Hwy. 21 S., Springfield, 31329-5207.
Tel: 912-754-7473; Fax: 912-754-1201; Email: parishoffice@sbcatholic.com; Email: secretary@sbcatholic.com; Web: www.sbcatholic.com. Rev. Martino Ba Thong Nguyen; Deacon Richard Rafter.

ST. MARY'S, CAMDEN CO., OUR LADY STAR OF THE SEA (1969)
106 E. Dillingham St., St. Marys, 31558.
Tel: 912-882-4718; Email: office@weareolss.org. Rev. Mariusz K. Fuks; Deacons Joseph Bezy; Tim Hughes; Henry Nieves.
Mission—St. Francis of Assisi, 700 Kingsland Dr, Folkston, Charlton Co. 31537. Tel: 912-496-3219.
Catechesis Religious Program—CCD, Email: religioused@weareolss.org. Tim Hughes, D.R.E.; Rhonda Hughes, D.R.E. Students 148.

ST. SIMONS ISLAND, GLYNN CO., ST. WILLIAM (1968)
2300 Frederica, St. Simons Island, 31522-1965.
Tel: 912-638-2647; Fax: 912-638-7577; Email: stwilliamschurch@comcast.net; Web: www.stwill.net. Rev. Msgr. John A. Kenneally, V.G., V.F.; Rev. Jim Holloway, Substitute Clergy, (Retired); Deacon George F. Ruehling III; Mrs. Barbara Pelletier, Wedding Coord./Sacristan; Mrs. Lois Richter, Organist; Ms. Jan Roberts, Admin.; Mr. Jim Spaeder, Parish Engineer; Mrs. Kate Hamer, Music Min.; Nancy Power, D.R.E.; Mrs. Stacey Bristol, Sec.
Catechesis Religious Program—Nancy Power, D.R.E. Total Enrollment 112.

STATESBORO, BULLOCH CO., ST. MATTHEW (1944)
221 John Paul Ave., Statesboro, 30458-5016.
Tel: 912-681-6726; Email: mcannady@saintmatthewsparish.com; Web: www.saintmatthewsparish.com. Rev. Douglas K. Clark, S.T.L.; Deacons John O'Malley; Michael J. McGrath.

SWAINSBORO, EMANUEL CO., HOLY TRINITY (1957)
928 W. Main St., Swainsboro, 30401-5502.
Tel: 478-237-6783; Email: holytrinity.swainsboro@gmail.com. Rev. Gordian Iwuji.
Mission—Holy Family, 1110 S. Lewis St., P.O. Box 65, Metter, Candler Co. 30439. Tel: 912-685-5811; Email: holyfamily@pineland.net.

SYLVANIA, SCREVEN CO., OUR LADY OF THE ASSUMPTION (1957)
121 Ridgecrest Dr., Sylvania, 30467-1840.
Tel: 912-564-2312; Email: nov45@aol.com; Email: llussier@diosav.org. Rev. Louis Lussier, O.S.Cam.
Res.: 118 Ridgecrest Dr., Sylvania, 30467-1840.
Mission—St. Bernadette, 441 North Ave., Millen, Jenkins Co. 30442.
Chapel—St. Joseph Chapel, Bay Branch.

THOMASVILLE, THOMAS CO., ST. AUGUSTINE (1936)
211 N. Pinetree Blvd., Thomasville, 31792-3973.
Tel: 229-226-3624; Email: staugustinethomasville@gmail.com; Web: www.staugustinethomasville.weebly.com. Rev. Godfred Boachie-Yiadom; Deacon John Blaha.
Catechesis Religious Program—Miguel Gutierrez, D.R.E. Total Enrollment 92.
Mission—St. Elizabeth Seton Church, 1500 11th Ave., N.W., Cairo, 39828-4007.

THUNDERBOLT, CHATHAM CO., NATIVITY OF OUR LORD, Closed. For inquiries for parish records contact the chancery.

TIFTON, TIFT CO., OUR DIVINE SAVIOUR (1953)
1205 Love Ave., P.O. Box 212, Tifton, 31793-0201.
Tel: 229-382-4600; Email: ods@friendlycity.net. 211 E. 12th St., Tifton, 31794. Rev. Peter Oyenugba, M.S.P.
Rectory—2001 N. Central Ave., Tifton, 31794.
Mission—St. Ann, 9007 U.S. Hwy. 82 E., Alapaha, Berrien Co. 31622. Email: ODS@friendlycity.net.
Catechesis Religious Program—Jackie Beals, D.R.E. Total Enrollment 222.

TYBEE ISLAND, CHATHAM CO., ST. MICHAEL'S CATHOLIC CHURCH (1891)
802 Lovell Ave., Tybee Island, 31328-0001.
Tel: 912-786-4505; Fax: 912-786-4166; Email: office@saintmichaelstybee.org; Web: www.saintmichaelstybee.org. Rev. Gerald Ragan, V.F.
Catechesis Religious Program—Susan Weber, D.R.E. Total Enrollment 13.

VALDOSTA, LOWNDES CO., ST. JOHN THE EVANGELIST (1927)
800 Gornto Rd., Valdosta, 31602-1699.
Tel: 229-244-2430; Email: stjohns@stjohnevang.org. Revs. Brian R. LaBurt; Dawid A. Kwiatkowski; Deacons David Lasseter; Columbus Carter; Peter Falkenhausen; Paul Worth; James Burns.
Res.: 2404 Berkley Dr., Valdosta, 31602-1699.
School—St. John Catholic School, (Grades PreK-8), Tel: 229-244-2556; Fax: 229-244-0865. Mr. Vito Pellitteri, Prin. Lay Teachers 18; Students 140; Staff 7.
Catechesis Religious Program—Susan Kramer, D.R.E. Total Enrollment 190.
Mission—San Jose, 421 W. Marion Ave., Lake Park, Lowndes Co. 31636.

VIDALIA, TOOMBS CO., SACRED HEART (1967)
3119 North St. E., Vidalia, 30474. Tel: 912-537-7709; Fax: 912-537-4691; Email: sacredheartvidalia@gmail.com; Web: www.sacredheartvidalia.org. Rev. Benjamin Dallas; Deacon Joseph P. Claroni.
Mission—St. Andrew the Apostle, 138 Industrial Blvd., Reidsville, 30453.
Catechesis Religious Program—Star Cruz, D.R.E.

WARNER ROBINS, HOUSTON CO., SACRED HEART (1945)
Mailing Address: 300 S. Davis Dr. Ste 300, Warner Robins, 31088. Tel: 478-923-0124; Fax: 478-328-3078; Email: secretary@sacredheartwr.com; Email: development@sacredheartwr.com; Web: sacredheartwr.org. Very Rev. Msgr. Fred J. Nijem, V.F.; Rev. Kevin O'Keefe; Deacons James A. Hunt; Ronald Simons.
School—Sacred Heart School, (Grades PreK-8), 300 S. Davis Dr., Bldg. 100, Warner Robins, 31088.
Tel: 478-923-9668; Fax: 478-923-5822; Email: shsprincipal2016@gmail.com; Web: www.shswr.org. Rev. Al Chromy, Prin. Lay Teachers 18; Students 192.
Sacred Heart Christian Service Center—136 Northview Ave., Warner Robins, 31088.
Tel: 478-929-3897; Fax: 478-328-3078; Email: csc@sacredheartwr.com. 300 S. Davis Dr., Bldg. 300, Warner Robins, 31088. Gregory K. Schliekelman, Dir.
Catechesis Religious Program—Tonya Soriano, D.R.E. Total Enrollment 397.

WAYCROSS, WARE CO., ST. JOSEPH'S (1960)
2011 Darling Ave., Waycross, 31501-1846.
Tel: 912-283-7700; Email: sjcwaycross@att.net. Rev. Robert A. Cushing.
Res.: 809 Blackshear Ave., Waycross, 31501.
Catechesis Religious Program—Lacey Gruver, D.R.E. Total Enrollment 143.

WAYNESBORO, BURKE CO., SACRED HEART (1961)
115 S. Liberty St., P.O. Box 1100, Waynesboro, 30830-4548. Tel: 706-554-2535; Email: sacredheartwaynesboro@yahoo.com. Rev. Patrick A. Otor, M.S.P.; Deacons Paul DeVito; Brian Goodman.
Mission—St. Joan of Arc, P.O. Box 175, Louisville, Jefferson Co. 30434. Tel: 478-625-3433; Fax: 478-625-3433.
Catechesis Religious Program—Caroline LaBauve, D.R.E.

On Duty Outside the Diocese:
Rev. Msgr.—
Schreck, Christopher J., S.T.B., S.S.L., Ph.D., S.T.D., Pontifical College Josephinum, 7625 N. High St., Columbus, OH 43235-1498. Tel: 614-885-5585
Rev.—
Pachence, Ronald A., University of San Diego, 5998 Alcala Park, San Diego, CA 92110. Tel: 619-260-4784.

On Leave of Absence:
Revs.—
Angell, Stephen J.
Donahue, Timothy C.
Ferguson, Justin R.
Killips, Aaron
Schraufnagel, Steven.

Retired:
Most Rev.—
Boland, Kevin J., D.D., (Retired), Catholic Pastoral Center, 2170 E. Victory Dr., 31404. Tel: 912-201-4100
Rev. Msgrs.—
LeFrois, Marvin, (Retired), 800 Gornto Rd., Valdosta, 31602-1699. Tel: 912-253-0041
O'Neill, William O., (Retired), 222 E. Harris St., 31401. Tel: 912-484-5828
Revs.—
Arnoldt, David L., (Retired), 6 Bransford Pl., Augusta, 31909. Tel: 706-650-9222
Cerrone, Michael J., (Retired), 24745 Foothill Dr., Salinas, CA 93908. Tel: 972-358-9833
Gergel, Stephen J., (Retired), 116 Lake Manor Dr., Kingsland, 31548-5639. Tel: 912-576-2716
Gonzalez, George A., (Retired), 4707 Winged Foot Way, Columbus, 31909
Greenway, George G., (Retired), 220 Villager Dr., Saint Simons Island, 31522-5331. Tel: 912-634-6272
Hart, Richard M., (Retired), P.O. Box 5733, Augusta, 30916. Tel: 478-718-3886
Healy, Thomas, (Retired), P.O. Box 3084, Augusta, 30914
Higgins, Francis C., (Retired), 2117 E. 41st St., 31404. Tel: 912-236-9267
Holloway, James, (Retired), 500 Ocean Blvd., #7, Saint Simons Island, 31522. Tel: 912-634-2171
Keohane, Donal, (Retired), St. Martin of Tours, 11967 Sunset Blvd., Los Angeles, CA 90049. Tel: 310-476-7403
Kumbalaprampil, Xavier, (Retired), Kumbalaparambil House, P.O. AIMS Ponekkara, Cochin - 682041, India. Tel: 91-484-280-2268
Lamb, Wes, (Retired), 2002 GA Hwy. 21 S., Springfield, 31329
Leahy, William, (Retired), 244 Tower St., Folkston, 31537. Tel: 912-496-3372
Lubinsky, Michael, (Retired), 231 W. Montgomery X Rds., 31406
Markham, John C., (Retired), 2609 Henry St., Unit A-6, Augusta, 30904. Tel: 706-231-1863
Minch, Richard, (Retired), 112 Katie Dr., Rincon, 31326. Tel: 912-826-0783
Nellis, Thomas, (Retired), 22 Greenwood Ave., Statesboro, 30458
O'Brien, Patrick, (Retired), 103 Winchester Dr., 31410. Tel: 912-898-7504
O'Keeffe, Michael, (Retired), Blessed Trinity Church, 5 S.E. 17th St., Ocala, FL 34471
Patterson, Frank, (Retired), 3421 Pontiac Dr., Columbus, 31907. Tel: 706-568-3643
Peyton, Thomas J., (Retired), 222 E. Harris St., 31401
Quang, John, (Retired), 47339 Timberland St., Belleville, MI 48111. Tel: 734-975-1309
Ryan, Timothy K., (Retired), 1000 Applewood Dr., Apt. 233, Roswell, 30076. Cell: 678-852-3684
Stanton, Finbarr P., (Retired), 320 12th St., Columbus, 31901. Cell: 229-854-0670.

Permanent Deacons:
Andruzzi, Louis J.
Arcand, Dennis A.
Daly, Michael F.
Fetterman, Richard F.
Foster, George H.
Goodman, Arnold
Halbur, Richard A.
McAtee, Ralph H., (Retired)
Mongan, Patrick F.
Morales-Morales, Reinaldo
Murphy, Michael.

INSTITUTIONS LOCATED IN DIOCESE

[A] HIGH SCHOOLS, DIOCESAN

AUGUSTA. *Aquinas High School*, (Grades 9-12), 1920 Highland Ave., Augusta, 30904-5305.
Tel: 706-736-5516; Fax: 706-736-2678; Email: mlewis@aquinashigh.org; Web: www.aquinashigh.org. Michelle Kroll, Supt.; Mrs. Maureen Lewis, Prin. Religious Teachers 1; Deacons 1; Lay Teachers 20; Students 231.

[B] HIGH SCHOOLS, PRIVATE

SAVANNAH. *Benedictine Military School*, 6502 Seawright Dr., 31406-2752. Tel: 912-644-7000; Fax: 912-356-3527; Email: jacob.horne@bcsav.net; Email: frank.ziemkiewicz@bcsav.net; Web: www.thebc400.com. Rev. Frank Ziemkiewicz, Headmaster; Very Rev. Jean-Luc Zadroga, Prior; Bros. Matthew Hershey, Teacher; Timothy J. Brown, O.S.B., Librarian; Revs. David Klecker, Teacher; John Paul Heiser, Teacher; Ronald P. Gatman, O.S.B., Campus Min. Boys 393; Clergy 6; Religious Teachers 4; Lay Teachers 55; Religious 8; Students 393.
St. Vincent's Academy, 207 E. Liberty St., 31401-3577. Tel: 912-236-5508; Fax: 912-236-7877; Email: maryanne.hogan@savga.net; Web: www.svaga.net. Mrs. Mary Anne Hogan, Prin. Sisters of Mercy of the Americas. Girls 300; Lay Teachers 34; Students 300.

MACON. *Mount de Sales Academy*, (Grades 6-12), 851 Orange St., Macon, 31201. Tel: 478-751-3240; Fax: 478-751-3241; Email: alivingston@mountdesales.net; Web: www.mountdesales.net. Mr. David Held, Pres.; Dr. Michael Franklin, Prin. (Upper); Kari Alderman, Prin. (Middle). Independent school affiliated with the Sisters of Mercy of the Americas. Lay Teachers 56; Students 577.

[C] SERVICES TO FAMILIES

SAVANNAH. *St. Joseph's Hospital, Inc.*, 11705 Mercy Blvd., 31419. Tel: 912-819-3415; Email: beattym@sjchs.org; Web: www.sjchs.org. Mr. Paul P. Hinchey, Pres. & CEO; Sr. Margaret Beatty, Vice Pres., Mission Svcs.; Revs. Rodolfo P. Roxas, Chap., (Retired); Matthew Ericksen, Chap.; Joseph A. Smith, Chap. Sisters of Mercy, South Central Community Bed Capacity 305; Tot Asst. Annually 94,123; Total Staff 1,270.

MACON. *Family Advancement Ministries*, 538 Orange St., Macon, 31201-2073. Tel: 478-746-9803; Fax: 478-745-0847; Email: grolfes.fam@gmail.com; Web: familyadvancementministries.org. Mrs. Gigi Rolfes, Dir. Social Services; utility/rental assistance and educational support for families with young children. Tot Asst. Annually 3,550; Total Staff 6.

[D] MONASTERIES AND RESIDENCES OF PRIESTS

SAVANNAH. *The Benedictine Priory*, 6502 Seawright Dr., 31406. Tel: 912-356-3520; Fax: 912-356-3527; Email: jean-luc.zadroga@bcsav.net. Rev. Frank Ziemkiewicz, Headmaster; Very Rev. Jean-Luc Zadroga, Prior; Rev. Ronald P. Gatman, O.S.B., Subprior; Bros. Timothy Brown, O.S.B., In Res.; Matthew Hershey, In Res.; Rev. David Klecker, In Res. Dependent Priory of St. Vincent Archabbey, Latrobe, PA.

[E] CONVENTS AND RESIDENCES FOR SISTERS

SAVANNAH. *Carmelite Monastery* (1958) 11 W. Back St., 31419-3219. Tel: 912-925-8505; Tel: 912-925-8506; Email: olconfidence@yahoo.com; Web: carmelofsavannah.org. Sr. Mary Elizabeth Angaine, Prioress. Nuns 12.
Mercy Convent, 11801 McAuley Dr., 31419-1709.
Tel: 912-925-3800; Fax: 912-925-3823; Email: mshumard@mercysc.org. Ms. Maureen Shumard, Admin. Retired Sisters of Mercy. Sisters 9.

[F] MISCELLANEOUS

SAVANNAH. *Catholic Charities of South Georgia*, 2170 E. Victory Dr., 31404-3918. Tel: 912-201-4100; Fax: 912-201-4101; Email: pmbrown@diosav.org; Web: www.diosav.org/catholiccharities. Sr. Patricia Brown, S.S.M.N., Dir. Total Staff 1.
The Catholic Foundation of South Georgia, 2170 E. Victory Dr., 31404-3918. Tel: 912-201-4100; Email: loconnor@diosav.org; Web: www.diosav.org/catholicfdn-southga. Liam J. O'Connor, Exec. Dir.; Robert W. Schivera, Chm.
Foundation for Priestly Vocations, Inc., 1003 E. Victory Dr., 31405. Tel: 706-513-4660; Email: bbrannen@diosav.org. Rev. Brett A. Brannen, Contact Person.
Social Apostolate of Savannah, 502 E. Liberty St., 31401. P. O. Box 8703, 31412. Tel: 912-233-1877; Fax: 912-651-3638; Email: socapsa@aol.com. Ms. Latacia Avila, Dir. Tot Asst. Annually 8,405; Staff 5.

AUGUSTA. *Alleluia Catholic Fellowship*, 2110 Richards St., P.O. Box 6805, Augusta, 30916-6805.
Tel: 706-798-1882; Fax: 706-560-2759; Email: danalmeter@hotmail.com; Web: www.yeslord.com. Dan Almeter, Moderator.
Catholic Social Services of Augusta, 811 12th St., Augusta, 30901-2749. Tel: 706-364-0208;
Tel: 706-722-3661; Fax: 706-722-4758; Email: director@cssaugusta.com; Web: www.cssaugusta.com. Sr. Janet Roddy, M.F.I.C., Dir. Tot Asst. Annually 8,444; Total Staff 12.

BRUNSWICK. *Society of St. Vincent de Paul (Glynn County)*, 1217 Newcastle St., Brunswick, 31520-7534. Tel: 912-262-6027; Email: dheinecke@bellsouth.net. Michael Moravec, Pres.

FORTSON. *Deacons in Ministry, Inc.*, 144 Crater Dr., Fortson, 31808. Tel: 800-745-4416; Email: yahula1@charter.net; Email: pmissions@charter.net; Web: www.parishmission.net. Deacon Robert Herrmann, Contact Person.

[G] CLOSED INSTITUTIONS

SAVANNAH. *Archives & Records Management Office*, 2170 E. Victory Dr., 31404. Tel: 912-201-4070. The following parish, school or institutional records may be found at the above address unless otherwise indicated. Notations to sacramental records of closed parishes held by the Archives & Records Management Office should be directed there and specify the parish name. The location of records periodically changes. Inquiries for records of parishes, schools or institutions not on this list should be directed to the above address.
Cathedral Day School (Savannah).
Immaculate Conception Parish (Augusta).
Marist School (Savannah).
Most Pure Heart of Mary School / St. Mary School (Savannah).
Nativity of Our Lord Parish (Thunderbolt).
Notre Dame Academy (Savannah).
Our Lady of Lourdes School (Columbus).
Pius X (Savannah).
Sacred Heart Parish (Augusta).
Sacred Heart Interparochial School (Savannah).
Sacred Heart School (Augusta).
Sacred Heart School (Savannah).
St. Anthony Svhool (Savannah).
St. Benedict School (Savannah).
St. John Vianney Minor Seminary (Savannah).
St. Joseph School (Waycross).
St. Michael School (Tybee Island).
St. Patrick Parish (Augusta).
St. Patrick Parish (Savannah).
St. Vincent Grammar School (Savannah).

RELIGIOUS INSTITUTES OF MEN REPRESENTED IN THE DIOCESE
For further details refer to the corresponding bracketed number in the Religious Institutes of Men or Women section.
[0200]—*Benedictine Monks* (St. Vincent Archabbey)—O.S.B.
[0240]—*Camillian Fathers & Brothers*—O.S.Cam.
[0480]—*Conventual Franciscans* (Provs. of Our Lady of Consolation & Our Lady of the Angels)—O.F.M.Conv.
[0520]—*Franciscan Friars* (Holy Name Province)—O.F.M.
[0570]—*Glenmary Home Missioners* (Glendale, OH)—G.H.M.
[0690]—*Jesuit Fathers & Brothers*—S.J.
[0854]—*Missionaries of St. Paul*—M.S.P.
[0840]—*Missionary Servants of Most Holy Trinity* (Dublin)—S.T.
[0780]—*Society of Mary*—S.M.
[0975]—*Society of Our Lady of the Most Holy Trinity*—S.O.L.T.

RELIGIOUS INSTITUTES OF WOMEN REPRESENTED IN THE DIOCESE
[1780]—*Congregation of the Sisters of the Third Order of St. Francis of Perpetual Adoration*—F.S.P.A.
[0760]—*Daughters of Charity of St. Vincent De Paul* (Emmitsburg, MD)—D.C.
[0420]—*Discalced Carmelite Nuns*—O.C.D.
[1360]—*Missionary Franciscan Sisters of the Immaculate Conception*—M.F.I.C.
[]—*Sisters for Christian Community*—S.F.C.C.
[2575]—*Sisters of Mercy of the Americas* (Baltimore, Burlingame, Erie)—R.S.M.
[3950]—*Sisters of Saint Mary of Namur*—S.S.M.N.
[3893]—*Sisters of St. Joseph* (Chestnut Hill, PA)—S.S.J.
[3840]—*Sisters of St. Joseph of Carondelet* (St. Louis, MO)—C.S.J.
[0260]—*Sisters of the Blessed Sacrament*—S.B.S.
[2170]—*Sisters, Servants of the Immaculate Heart of Mary*—I.H.M.

DIOCESAN CEMETERIES

SAVANNAH. *Savannah Catholic Cemetery* Catholic Cemetery, Catholic Pastoral Center, 1720 Wheaton St., 31404. 2170 E. Victory Dr., 31404.
Tel: 912-201-4100; Email: pdnott@diosav.org; Web: diosav.org/constructionandproperties-cemetery. Paul Nott, Dir. & Construction & Properties

AUGUSTA. *Most Holy Trinity Cemetery*, 720 Telfair St., P.O. Box 2446, Augusta, 30903. Tel: 706-722-4944; Email: helen@themostholytrinity.org. Very Rev. Jacek Szuster, V.F.

ST. PAUL'S PARISH, DOUGLAS. *Holy Family Mission, Willacoochee*, 126 Holy Family Rd., Willacoochee, 31650. Tel: 912-384-3560; Email: saintpaul@windstream.net. 4178 U.S. Hwy. 441 S., Douglas, 31535. Rev. Paul A. O'Connell. Attached to Holy Family Mission, Willacoochee, a mission of St. Paul's Parish, Douglas.

SYLVANIA. *St. Joseph, Bay Branch*, Bay Branch Rd., Sylvania, 30467. 121 Ridgecrest Dr., Sylvania, 30467. Tel: 912-564-2312; Email: nov45@aol.com. Rev. Louis Lussier, O.S.Cam.

An asterisk (*) denotes an organization that has established tax-exempt status directly with the IRS and is not covered by the USCCB Group Ruling.

Diocese of Scranton

(Dioecesis Scrantonensis)

Most Reverend

JOSEPH C. BAMBERA, D.D., J.C.L.

Bishop of Scranton; ordained November 5, 1983; appointed Bishop of Scranton February 23, 2010; installed April 26, 2010.

Chancery Office: 300 Wyoming Ave., Scranton, PA 18503. Tel: 570-207-2216; Fax: 570-207-2236.

Web: www.dioceseofscranton.org

Most Reverend

JOSEPH F. MARTINO, D.D., HIST. E.D.

Bishop Emeritus of Scranton; ordained December 18, 1970; appointed Titular Bishop of Cellae in Mauretania and Auxiliary Bishop of Philadelphia January 24, 1996; consecrated March 11, 1996; appointed Bishop of Scranton July 25, 2003; resigned August 31, 2009. *Res.: Regina Coeli Residence for Priests, 685 York Rd., Warminster, PA 18974.* Tel: 267-608-8557.

Most Reverend

JAMES C. TIMLIN, D.D.

Bishop Emeritus of Scranton; ordained July 16, 1951; appointed Titular Bishop of Gunugo and Auxiliary Bishop of Scranton August 3, 1976; consecrated September 21, 1976; succeeded to See of Scranton April 24, 1984; installed June 7, 1984; resigned July 25, 2003. *Res.: Villa St. Joseph, 1600 Green Ridge St., Dunmore, PA 18509.* Tel: 570-343-6170.

Most Reverend

JOHN M. DOUGHERTY, D.D.

Auxiliary Bishop Emeritus of Scranton; ordained June 15, 1957; appointed Titular Bishop of Sufetula and Auxiliary Bishop of Scranton February 7, 1995; Episcopal ordination received March 7, 1995; resigned August 31, 2009. *Office: 300 Wyoming Ave., Scranton, PA 18503.* Tel: 570-558-4309.

ESTABLISHED MARCH 3, 1868.

Square Miles 8,847.

Comprises the Counties of Luzerne, Lackawanna, Bradford, Susquehanna, Wayne, Tioga, Sullivan, Wyoming, Lycoming, Pike and Monroe in Pennsylvania.

For legal titles of parishes and diocesan institutions, consult the Chancery Office.

STATISTICAL OVERVIEW

Personnel	
Bishop	1
Retired Bishops	3
Priests: Diocesan Active in Diocese	103
Priests: Diocesan Active Outside Diocese	8
Priests: Retired, Sick or Absent	103
Number of Diocesan Priests	214
Religious Priests in Diocese	35
Total Priests in Diocese	249
Extern Priests in Diocese	20
Ordinations:	
Diocesan Priests	2
Permanent Deacons in Diocese	91
Total Brothers	5
Total Sisters	378
Parishes	
Parishes	118
With Resident Pastor:	
Resident Diocesan Priests	92
Resident Religious Priests	5
Without Resident Pastor:	
Administered by Priests	16
Administered by Deacons	2
Administered by Religious Women	1
Administered by Lay People	2
Missions	17
Closed Parishes	2
Professional Ministry Personnel:	
Sisters	1
Lay Ministers	1
Welfare	
Catholic Hospitals	2
Total Assisted	178,000
Homes for the Aged	7
Total Assisted	568
Residential Care of Children	1
Total Assisted	20
Day Care Centers	3
Total Assisted	80
Specialized Homes	3
Total Assisted	381
Special Centers for Social Services	85
Total Assisted	137,750
Residential Care of Disabled	99
Total Assisted	368
Educational	
Diocesan Students in Other Seminaries	11
Total Seminarians	11
Colleges and Universities	4
Total Students	15,465
High Schools, Diocesan and Parish	4
Total Students	1,160
High Schools, Private	1
Total Students	726
Elementary Schools, Diocesan and Parish	16
Total Students	3,366
Elementary Schools, Private	1
Total Students	70
Catechesis/Religious Education:	
High School Students	1,412
Elementary Students	10,471
Total Students under Catholic Instruction	32,681
Teachers in the Diocese:	
Priests	4
Sisters	18
Lay Teachers	366
Vital Statistics	
Receptions into the Church:	
Infant Baptism Totals	2,151
Minor Baptism Totals	157
Adult Baptism Totals	90
Received into Full Communion	177
First Communions	2,235
Confirmations	1,979
Marriages:	
Catholic	489
Interfaith	189
Total Marriages	678
Deaths	4,053
Total Catholic Population	227,459
Total Population	1,092,929

Former Bishops—Rt. Revs. WILLIAM O'HARA, D.D., ord. Dec. 21, 1842; First Bishop; cons. July 12, 1868; died Feb. 3, 1899; MICHAEL J. HOBAN, D.D., ord. May 22, 1880; Second Bishop; cons. Coadjutor, March 22, 1896; succeeded to See, Feb. 3, 1899; died Nov. 13, 1926; Most Revs. THOMAS C. O'REILLY, D.D., Third Bishop; ord. June 4, 1898; elected Dec. 19, 1927,; cons. Feb. 16, 1928; installed March 8, 1928; died March 25, 1938; WILLIAM J. HAFEY, D.D., Fourth Bishop; ord. June 16, 1914; appt. First Bishop of Raleigh, April 6, 1925; cons. June 24, 1925; transferred to Scranton as Coadjutor cum jure successionis and Apostolic Administrator, Oct. 2, 1937; succeeded to See, March 25, 1938; died May 12, 1954; JEROME D. HANNAN, D.D., Fifth Bishop; ord. May 22, 1921; appt. August 17, 1954; cons. Sept. 21, 1954; died Dec. 15, 1965; J. CARROLL MCCORMICK, D.D., Sixth Bishop; ord. July 10, 1932; appt. Titular Bishop of Ruspae and Auxiliary of Philadelphia, Jan. 11, 1947; cons. April 23, 1947; appt. Bishop of Altoona-Johnstown, June 25, 1960; transferred to the See of Scranton, March 4, 1966; installed May 25, 1966; retired Feb. 15, 1983; died Nov. 2, 1996; JOHN J. O'CONNOR, D.D., Seventh Bishop; ord. Dec. 15, 1945; appt. Titular Bishop of Cuzola and Auxiliary Bishop to the Military Vicar April 24, 1979; cons. May 27, 1979; appt. Bishop of Scranton, May 10, 1983; installed June 29, 1983; transferred to the See of New York, Jan. 31, 1984; died May 3, 2000; JAMES C. TIMLIN, D.D., (Retired), Eighth Bishop; ord. July 16, 1951; appt. Titular Bishop of Gunugo and Auxiliary Bishop of Scranton Aug. 3, 1976; cons. Sept. 21, 1976; succeeded to See of Scranton April 24, 1984; installed June 7, 1984; resigned July 25, 2003; JOSEPH F. MARTINO, D.D., Hist. E.D., (Retired), Ninth Bishop; ord. Dec. 18, 1970; appt. Titular Bishop of Cellae in Mauretania and Auxiliary Bishop of Philadelphia Jan. 24, 1996; cons. March 11, 1996; appt. Bishop of Scranton July 25, 2003; resigned Aug. 31, 2009.

Vicar General & Moderator of the Curia—Rev. Msgr. THOMAS M. MULDOWNEY, V.G., Tel: 570-207-2269.

Chancery Office—300 Wyoming Ave., Scranton, 18503-1279. Tel: 570-207-2216; Fax: 570-207-2236.

Regional Episcopal Vicars—Revs. CYRIL D. EDWARDS, V.E., Northern Pastoral Region, Tel: 570-342-4881; GLENN E. MCCREARY, V.E., Western Pastoral Region, Tel: 570-546-3900; RICHARD E. CZACHOR, V.E., Eastern Pastoral Region, Tel: 570-629-4572; JOHN V. POLEDNAK, V.E., Southern Pastoral Region, Tel: 570-457-3502; Tel: 570-650-0954.

Chancellor—MS. LINDA E. PRICE, J.C.L., Tel: 570-207-2216; Fax: 570-207-2236.

Diocesan Financial Office—Tel: 570-207-2237. ROBERT J. MILLER, Dir.; EILEEN BARTOLI, Asst. Dir. Finance.

Diocesan Tribunal—300 Wyoming Ave., Scranton, 18503-1279. Tel: 570-207-2246; Fax: 570-207-2274. Direct all inquiries concerning marriage nullity, dispensations and permissions to this office.

Judicial Vicar & Episcopal Vicar for Matrimonial Processes—Rev. ANTHONY J. GENEROSE, J.V., V.E., J.C.L.

Coordinator—JOSEPH V. FOX.

Judges—Rev. Msgr. PATRICK J. PRATICO, J.C.D.; Revs. BRIAN J.W. CLARKE, J.C.L.; THOMAS J. PETRO, J.C.L.; MS. LINDA E. PRICE, J.C.L.

Defenders of the Bond—Rev. Msgr. JOSEPH G. QUINN, J.D., J.C.L.; Revs. JAMES J. WALSH, J.C.L.; EDUARD SHESTAK, J.C.L., S.T.D.

Promoter of Justice—Rev. Msgr. FRANCIS J. MARINI, J.D., J.C.O.D.

Auditor—JOSEPH V. FOX.

Procurator/Advocates—JOSEPH V. FOX; Rev. JAMES BAKER, J.C.L.; EDWARD CONDON, J.C.D.; MATTHEW ORZOLEK, J.C.L.; MR. JAY CONZEMIUS, J.C.L.

Notaries—JOSETTE JORDAN; JUDY MYERSKI.

Diocesan Finance Council—Rev. Msgr. THOMAS M. MULDOWNEY, V.G., Ex Officio; Rev. GERALD W. SHANTILLO; JOHN DEVINE; JOHN H. GRAHAM;

JAMES E. O'BRIEN JR., Esq.; CARLON E. PREATE; PAUL WOELKERS; JAMES BEBLA; ROBERT J. MILLER, Ex Officio; Sr. THERESE O'ROURKE, I.H.M.; JOSEPH A. O'BRIEN, Esq.

Diocesan Consultors—Revs. JEFFREY J. WALSH, V.E.; RICHARD J. CIRBA; JOSEPH G. ELSTON; Rev. Msgr. THOMAS M. MULDOWNEY, V.G.; Revs. RICHARD E. CZACHOR, V.E.; JOHN M. LAPERA; RICHARD J. POLMOUNTER.

Deans—Rev. Msgr. NEIL J. VAN LOON, Scranton; Revs. DAVID P. CAPPELLONI, Dunmore; JOHN M. LAPERA, Clarks Summit; GERARD M. MCGLONE, V.F., Carbondale; PHILLIP J. SLADICKA, Pittston; J. DUANE GAVITT, Wilkes-Barre; JOSEPH J. PISANESCHI, Kingston; MICHAEL J. PICCOLA, Hazleton; RICHARD W. BECK, Honesdale; MICHAEL F. QUINNAN, Stroudsburg; ANDREW S. HVOZDOVIC, Sayre; BERT S. KOZEN, Williamsport.

Presbyteral Council—Rev. Msgrs. THOMAS M. MULDOWNEY, V.G.; NEIL J. VAN LOON; Revs. BRIAN J.T. CLARKE, J.C.L.; SAMUEL J. FERRETTI; MICHAEL M. BRYANT; JOHN S. TERRY; RICHARD J. CIRBA; RICHARD E. CZACHOR, V.E.; CYRIL D. EDWARDS, V.E.; JOHN M. LAPERA; GLENN E. MCCREARY, V.E.; JOHN V. POLEDNAK, V.E.; RICHARD J. POLMOUNTER; GREGORY A. REICHLEN; ROBERT J. SIMON; JEFFREY J. WALSH, V.E.; Rev. Msgrs. JOHN J. BENDIK, (Retired); MICHAEL J. DELANEY; Revs. ANDREW S. HVOZDOVIC; LOUIS T. KAMINSKI; WILLIAM J.P. LANGAN; GREGORY F. LOUGHNEY; GERARD M. MCGLONE, V.F.; EDWARD L. MICHELINI; EUGENE A. NOLAN, S.J.; JAMES J. WALSH, J.C.L.

Diocesan Building Commission—All plans for building should be sent to Chancery Office, 300 Wyoming Ave., Scranton, PA 18503-1279. JOHN HENNEMUTH; Rev. PATRICK L. ALBERT; JAMES DEVERS; Rev. JOSEPH D. VERESPY; JOHN POCIUS; THOMAS CONSIDINE. Ex Officio: Rev. Msgr. THOMAS M. MULDOWNEY, V.G.; ROBERT J. MILLER; FRANK M. SEMANSKI; JAMES BEBLA.

Episcopal Vicar for Clergy—Rev. JEFFREY J. WALSH, V.E., 300 Wyoming Ave., Scranton, 18503-1279. Tel: 570-591-5006; Fax: 570-591-5028.

Diocesan Review Board—Rev. Msgr. THOMAS M. MULDOWNEY, V.G.; Rev. JAMES PRICE, C.P.; LISA JANOSKI Esq.; FRANK MAJAIKES, M.S.; Sr. MARY HELEN NUGENT, R.S.M.; EUGENE TALARICO, Esq.; MRS. MARY BETH PACUSKA, R.N., M.S.N.; JOSEPH A. O'BRIEN, Esq.

Diocesan Offices and Directors

Catholic Campaign for Human Development—Diocesan Pastoral Center, 330 Wyoming Ave., Scranton, 18503. Tel: 570-207-2213. KATY WINDELS, Coord., Service & Social Justice.

Campus Ministry—MARY ANNE MALONE, Dir., Mailing Address: Diocesan Pastoral Center, 330 Wyoming Ave., Scranton, 18503. Tel: 570-207-2213, Ext. 1100.

Catholic Charismatic Renewal—Mailing Address: P.O. Box 3306, Scranton, 18505. Rev. AUGUST A. RICCIARDI, Spiritual Moderator, Tel: 570-457-5900; ROBERT VALIANTE, Liaison to Bishop; KAREN MCLAIN, Conference Coord., Tel: 570-344-2214.

Catholic Relief Services—Rev. Msgr. THOMAS M. MULDOWNEY, V.G., 300 Wyoming Ave., Scranton, 18503-1279. Tel: 570-207-2216.

Catholic Social Services—MARY THERESA MALANDRO, Diocesan Sec., Catholic Human Svcs. & CEO, Catholic Social Svcs., 300 Wyoming Ave., Scranton, 18503. Tel: 570-207-3808, Ext. 1020; Fax: 570-591-5012.

Board of Governance—Rev. JOHN C. LAMBERT; DAVID HAAS; WILLIAM SHERGALIS; JOSEPH H. KNECHT; Deacon J. PATRICK MCDONALD; Sr. ANN WALSH, I.H.M.; VINCENT SPLENDIDO.

Natural Family Planning Coordinator—330 Wyoming Ave., Scranton, 18503. Tel: 570-207-2213. JEN HOUSEL, Dir. Family Life & Community/Office for Parish Life.

Cemeteries—DOMINIC RINALDI, Diocesan Dir. Catholic Cemeteries, Tel: 570-207-2238.

Censor Librorum—Rev. CHARLES P. CONNOR, Ph.D., S.T.L., Mt. St. Mary's Seminary, 16300 Old Emmitsburg Rd., Emmitsburg, MD 21727. c/o 300 Wyoming Ave., Scranton, 18503.

Cursillo Movement—Rev. PHILLIP J. SLADICKA, Spiritual Mod., Queen of the Apostles Parish, 715 Hawthorne St., Avoca, 18641. Tel: 570-457-3412.

Diocesan Commission on Ecumenism and Inter-Faith Matters—Rev. Msgr. VINCENT J. GRIMALIA, Coord., (Retired), 80 E. Northampton St., Apt. 105, Wilkes-Barre, 18701. Tel: 570-829-1471.

Diocesan Secretary for Property & Risk Management—FRANK M. SEMANSKI, 300 Wyoming Ave., Scranton, 18503. Tel: 570-558-4310; Fax: 570-558-4311.

Diocesan Historian—Rev. CHARLES P. CONNOR, Ph.D., S.T.L., Mt. St. Mary's Seminary, 16300 Old Emmitsburg Rd., Emmitsburg, MD 21727. Tel: 570-207-2216. 300 Wyoming Ave., Scranton, 18503.

Diocesan Office for Communications—330 Wyoming Ave., Scranton, 18503-1272. Tel: 570-207-2219; Tel: 800-246-0288; Fax: 570-207-2281. ERIC DEABILL, Exec. Dir.

Diocesan Safe Environment Coordinator—KATHLEEN BOLINSKI, 300 Wyoming Ave., Scranton, 18503. Tel: 570-207-1453; Fax: 570-207-1457.

Diocesan Office of Development—300 Wyoming Ave., Scranton, 18503-1279. Tel: 570-207-2250; Fax: 570-207-1835. JAMES BEBLA, Diocesan Sec.; CHRISTOPHER E. SHEPERIS, Dir. Devel. Oper.

Diocesan Appeal Office—300 Wyoming Ave., Scranton, 18503. JAMES BEBLA, Dir., Tel: 570-207-2250; VACANT, Mgr. Devel. & Alumni Rels., Tel: 570-207-2250, Ext. 1027; Fax: 570-207-1835.

Diocesan Grant Writer—300 Wyoming Ave., Scranton, 18503. Tel: 570-207-2250. SANDRA SNYDER.

Diocese of Scranton Catholic Community Foundation—JAMES BEBLA, Dir., 300 Wyoming Ave., Scranton, 18503-1279. Tel: 570-207-2250; Fax: 570-207-1835.

Diocese of Scranton Scholarship Foundation—JAMES BEBLA, Dir., 300 Wyoming Ave., Scranton, 18503-1279. Tel: 570-207-2250; Fax: 570-207-1835.

Coordinator for Ecumenism & Interfaith Relations—Rev. Msgr. VINCENT J. GRIMALIA, Dir., (Retired), 80 E. Northampton St., Wilkes-Barre, 18701. Tel: 570-829-1471.

Office for Parish Life—Diocesan Pastoral Center, 330 Wyoming Ave., Scranton, 18503. Tel: 570-207-2213 . CHRISTOPHER TIGUE, Dir, C.Y.O.

Diocesan Secretary for Parish Life—330 Wyoming Ave., Scranton, 18503. Tel: 570-207-2213, Ext. 1148. CATHERINE J. BUTEL.

Director for Word & Lifelong Faith Formation—330 Wyoming Ave., Scranton, 18503. Tel: 570-207-2213, Ext. 1100. MARY ANNE MALONE.

Consultant for Youth and Campus Ministry—330 Wyoming Ave., Scranton, 18503. Tel: 570-207-2213. FRED MERCADANTE.

Coordinator for Youth/Young Adult Ministry—330 Wyoming Ave., Scranton, 18503. Tel: 570-207-2213. SHANNON KOWALSKI.

Director for Worship—330 Wyoming Ave., Scranton, 18503. Tel: 570-207-2213, Ext. 1158. DAVID BALOGA.

Coordinator for RCIA—Rev. ROBERT J. SIMON.

Director for Service and Social Concerns—330 Wyoming Ave., Scranton, 18503. Tel: 570-207-2213, Ext. 1130. KATY WINDELS.

Coordinator for Diocesan Missions and Director for Pontifical Missions—300 Wyoming Ave., Scranton, 18503. Tel: 570-207-2259, Ext. 1155. Rev. BRIAN J.T. CLARKE, J.C.L.

Coordinator for Pilgrimages—Rev. ANDREW S. HVOZDOVIC.

Director for Community and Family Development—330 Wyoming Ave., Scranton, 18503. Tel: 570-207-2213, Ext. 1104. JEN HOUSEL.

Coordinator for Ecumenical and Interfaith Relations—Rev. Msgr. VINCENT J. GRIMALIA, (Retired).

Coordinator for Lay Ministry Formation—330 Wyoming Ave., Scranton, 18503. Tel: 570-207-2213, Ext. 1157. KITTY SCANLAN.

Coordinator for Pastoral Council Development—330 Wyoming Ave., Scranton, 18503. Tel: 570-207-2213, Ext. 1131. ANN MARIE CAWLEY.

Events Coordinator, Diocesan Pastoral Center—330 Wyoming Ave., Scranton, 18503. Tel: 570-207-2213, Ext. 1105; Tel: 570-591-5005. SUSAN BURKE.

Ministry with the Deaf Persons with Disabilities—VACANT.

Chaplain for the Deaf—Rev. JOSEPH G. ELSTON, Chap., 330 Wyoming Ave., Scranton, 18503-1272. Tel: 570-207-2213, Ext. 1101.

Diocesan Pro-Life Office—Diocesan Pastoral Center, 330 Wyoming Ave., Scranton, 18503-1279. Tel: 570-207-2213, Ext. 1130. KATY WINDELS, Contact Person.

Formation for Servant Leadership—CATHERINE J. BUTEL, Diocesan Sec., Tel: 570-207-2213, Ext. 1148.

Pontifical Mission Societies—300 Wyoming Ave., Scranton, 18503. Tel: 570-207-2259. Rev. BRIAN J.T. CLARKE, J.C.L.

Property & Risk Management Office—300 Wyoming Ave., Scranton, 18503. FRANK M. SEMANSKI, Sec., Tel: 570-207-2232; Fax: 570-558-4302; ED CARLIN, Property Assets Dir., Tel: 570-207-2237, Ext. 1029; THOMAS CONSIDINE, Risk Mgmt. Dir., Tel: 570-558-4310.

Consecrated Life Office—VACANT.

Hispanic Ministry Outreach—Revs. JOHN C. RUTH, Coord. Hispanic Min. Lackawanna County, St. Patrick Parish, Scranton. Tel: 570-344-2679; GREGORY F. LOUGHNEY, Coord. Hispanic Min. Monroe County, c/o Most Holy Trinity Parish, Cresco. Tel: 570-595-3100; FIDEL TICONA, C.S.C., Hispanic Ministry, Mailing Address: c/o St. Nicholas Parish, Wilkes-Barre, 18701. Tel: 570-823-7736; VICTOR LEON, O.S.J., c/o Annunciation Parish, Hazleton. Tel: 570-454-0212; SEAN G. CARPENTER, St. Maximilian Kolbe Parish, Pocono Pines. Tel: 570-646-6424.

Holy Childhood Association—300 Wyoming Ave., Scranton, 18503. Tel: 570-207-2259. Rev. BRIAN J.T. CLARKE, J.C.L.

Legion of Mary—Contact: MARY BOLCAVAGE, Pres. Scranton Curia, Tel: 570-876-1136; VACANT, Spiritual Dir.

Liturgical Commission—VACANT.

Marriage Encounter—Contact: DIANE ZINDELL; ED ZINDELL, 14 Evergreen Dr., Jermyn, 18433. Tel: 570-876-1610.

D.C.C.M.—Rev. JAMES E. MCGAHAGAN, Chap., (Retired).

D.C.C.W.—Rev. JAMES E. MCGAHAGAN, Chap., (Retired).

Newspaper—The Catholic Light *330 Wyoming Ave., Scranton, 18503-1279.* Tel: 570-207-2229; Fax: 570-207-2271. ERIC DEABILL, Editor.

Parish Pastoral Planning—Rev. JOHN M. LAPERA, Consultant, St. Gregory, 330 N. Abington Rd., Clarks Green, 18411. Tel: 570-587-4808.

Diocesan Television Station-CTV—ERIC DEABILL, Exec. Dir.; JAMES BRENNAN, Mgr., Diocesan Pastoral Center, 330 Wyoming Ave., Scranton, 18503-1272. Tel: 570-207-2213.

Permanent Diaconate Office—Rev. Msgr. DAVID A. BOHR, S.T.D., Diocesan Sec. for Clergy Formation & Dir. Continuing Educ. for Priests, 300 Wyoming Ave., Scranton, 18503. Tel: 570-207-2269.

Pilgrimages—Rev. ANDREW S. HVOZDOVIC, Diocesan Dir., Epiphany Parish, 304 S. Elmer Ave., Sayre, 18840. Tel: 570-888-9641.

Priests' Purgatorial Society—Rev. JEFFREY J. WALSH, V.E., Episcopal Vicar for Clergy, 300 Wyoming Ave., Scranton, 18503-1279. Tel: 570-591-5006.

Priests' Retirement Advisory Board—JAMES R. BURKE; Rev. Msgr. THOMAS M. MULDOWNEY, V.G.; ROBERT J. MILLER; Revs. DAVID CAPPELONI; RICHARD E. CZACHOR, V.E.; JOHN J. KILPATRICK, (Retired); SCOTT P. STEROWSKI.

Propagation of the Faith300 Wyoming Ave., Scranton, 18503. Tel: 570-207-2259. Rev. BRIAN J.T. CLARKE, J.C.L., Dir.

Catholic School System Board Members—Revs. JOHN V. POLEDNAK, V.E.; GLENN E. MCCREARY, V.E.; CYRIL D. EDWARDS, V.E.; JOHN J. VICTORIA; RICHARD E. CZACHOR, V.E.; JOSEPH D. VERESPY; DR. GREGORY BASTING, Holy Cross; MR. JAMES REDINGTON, Holy Redeemer; DR. CAROL LATZANICH, Notre Dame; MAGGIE ROCHE, St. John Neumann; MR. JEFFREY N. LYONS, Prin. (High School); MR. JAMES A. JONES, Prin. (Elem. School); MRS. KATHLEEN DEWAN, Holy Cross; PAUL H. ROONEY JR., Notre Dame; JOSEPH A. O'BRIEN, Esq., Attorney; MR. BENJAMIN TOLERICO, Prin. Holy Cross High School; MRS. DOREEN DOUGHERTY, Prin., All Saints Academy.

Retirement Fund for Religious—Rev. Msgr. THOMAS M. MULDOWNEY, V.G., Vicar Gen.

Schools—JASON MORRISON, Diocesan Sec. & COO, Catholic Educ., Tel: 570-207-2251; MICHELLE LONG, Asst. Supt. Schools, 300 Wyoming Ave., Scranton, 18503. Tel: 570-207-2251; KATHLEEN GILMARTIN, Asst. Supt., Tel: 570-207-2251; DANIELLE E. RAKE, Dir. Enrollment & Mktg., Tel: 570-207-2251; Cell: 570-702-2666.

Scouts of America—Most Holy Trinity Parish, 236 Rte. 390, Cresco, 18326. Tel: 570-595-3100. Rev. GREGORY F. LOUGHNEY, Chap.

Victim Assistance Coordinator—300 Wyoming Ave., Scranton, 18503. Tel: 570-862-7551. MRS. MARY BETH PACUSKA, R.N., M.S.N., Email: mary-beth-pacuska@dioceseofscranton.org.

VIRTUS—KATHLEEN BOLINSKI, Safe Environment Prog. Coord., 300 Wyoming Ave., Scranton, 18503. Tel: 570-207-1453; Fax: 570-207-1457.

Diocesan Office for Continuing Education for Clergy—Rev. Msgr. DAVID A. BOHR, S.T.D., Dir., 300 Wyoming Ave., Scranton, 18503. Tel: 570-207-2269.

Diocesan Office for Clergy Formation—Rev. Msgr.

DAVID A. BOHR, S.T.D., Diocesan Sec., Tel: 570-207-2269.

Vocations—300 Wyoming Ave., Scranton, 18503. Rev. DONALD J. WILLIAMS, Dir. Vocations & Seminarians, Tel: 570-207-2216, Ext. 1013; DOMINICK COSTANTINO, Vocation Prog. Coord., Tel: 570-207-2216, Ext. 1069.

CLERGY, PARISHES, MISSIONS AND PAROCHIAL SCHOOLS

CITY OF SCRANTON

(LACKAWANNA COUNTY)

1—ST. PETER'S CATHEDRAL (1853) [CEM 2]
315 Wyoming Ave., 18503. Tel: 570-344-7231; Fax: 570-344-4749; Email: info@stpeterscathedral.org; Web: www.stpeterscathedral.org. Rev. Msgr. Dale R. Rupert, M.A.; Deacon Edward R. Shoener. In Res., Most Rev. Joseph C. Bambera, D.D., J.C.L., Bishop of Scranton; Rev. Msgr. Thomas M. Muldowney, V.G.; Rev. Jeffrey J. Walsh, V.E.
Convent—333 Wyoming, 18503.

2—ST. ANN'S BASILICA PARISH (1901)
1250 St. Ann St., 18504. Revs. Francis Landry, C.P.; Sibi Padinjaredath, C.P.; Joseph R. Jones, C.P.
Catechesis Religious Program—Students 160.

3—ST. ANTHONY OF PADUA (1913) (Italian), Closed. For inquiries for parish records please see Holy Rosary, Scranton. (part of Mary Mother of God Parish, Scranton).

4—ST. CLARE (1967) Merged Restructured with St. Paul Scranton as of June 2009. All information for St. Clare has been incorporated into St. Paul, Scranton.

5—ST. DAVID'S (1946) Closed. For all inquiries see St. Patrick's, Scranton.

6—DIVINE MERCY (1875) [CEM] Restructured with Immaculate Conception, St. John the Baptist, Taylor; St. Mary Czestochowa, Moosic & St. Joseph, Minooka.
312 Davis St., 18505. Rev. Francis L. Pauselli.
Worship Site: St. Joseph Church.
Catechesis Religious Program—Students 268.

7—ST. FRANCIS OF ASSISI (1920) (Italian) Consolidated, additional worship site of St. Paul of the Cross Parish.
c/o 1217 Prospect Ave., 18505. Tel: 570-343-6420; Fax: 570-343-3664. Rev. Scott P. Sterowski.

8—HOLY FAMILY (1891) [CEM] Closed. For inquiries for parish records please see St. Peter's Cathedral, 315 Wyoming Ave., Scranton, PA 18503 (Tel: 570-344-7231).

9—HOLY NAME OF JESUS (1938) Closed. Additional worship site of St. John Neumann, Scranton.

10—HOLY ROSARY (1871) Closed. Restructured with St. Joseph, Scranton and St. Anthony of Padua, Scranton, both now closed. Worship site of Mary, Mother of God Parish, Scranton.

11—IMMACULATE CONCEPTION (1967) Restructured with Christ the King, Dunmore, now closed. Revs. Patrick J. McLaughlin; Joseph F. Sica; Deacon J. Patrick McDonald.
Res.: 801 Taylor Ave., 18510.
Catechesis Religious Program—Students 256.

12—ST. JOHN THE EVANGELIST (1886) Closed. For inquiries for parish records please contact St. Paul of the Cross Parish, Scranton (Tel: 570-343-6420).

13—ST. JOSEPH'S (1894) [CEM] (Lithuanian), Closed. See Mary, Mother of God Parish, Scranton for sacramental records.

14—ST. JOSEPH'S (1875) [CEM] Merged and restructured with Immaculate Conception & St. Mary of Czestochowa, Greenwood. For inquiries for parish records please contact Divine Mercy, Scranton.

15—ST. LUCY'S (1901) (Italian) Merged with SS. Peter & Paul, Scranton. Rev. Samuel J. Ferretti; Deacon Carmine Mendicino.
Res.: 949 Scranton St., 18504. Web: stlucy-church.org.
Catechesis Religious Program—Students 61.

16—ST. MARY CZESTOCHOWA (1904) [CEM] (Polish), Closed. For inquiries for parish records, contact Divine Mercy, Scranton (Tel: 570-344-1724).

17—ST. MARY OF THE ASSUMPTION (1854) [CEM 2] (German), Closed. For inquiries for parish records, please see St. John Neumann, Scranton (Tel: 570-344-6159).

18—MARY, MOTHER OF GOD PARISH, [CEM 2]
316 William St., 18508. Tel: 570-342-4881; Email: frcyedwards@gmail.com; Email: mmog.secretary@gmail.com; Web: www.marymotherofgodparish.org. Revs. Cyril D. Edwards, V.E.; Martin J. Gaiardo, Pastoral Assoc., (Retired); Sr. Therese Dougherty, RCIA Coord.; Deacon Jan F. Mroz.
Worship Site: Holy Rosary Church.
Catechesis Religious Program—Students 340.

19—ST. MICHAEL'S (1914) (Lithuanian)
1703 Jackson St., 18504. Tel: 570-961-1205; Email: fsspscranton@gmail.com; Web: stmichaelsrcc. Rev. Simon Harkins, F.S.S.P.

20—NATIVITY OF OUR LORD, Merged and restructured with Holy Name of Jesus, Scranton & St. Mary of the Assumption, Scranton. Primary worship site of Saint John Neumann. Inquiries for parish records, please contact Saint John Neumann, Scranton (Tel: 570-344-6159).

21—ST. PATRICK (1870)
1403 Jackson St., 18504. Tel: 570-344-2679; Email: stpatrick_scr@yahoo.com. Revs. Richard E. Fox; John C. Ruth, In Res.
Catechesis Religious Program—Students 308.
Chapel—Scranton, Immaculate Heart of Mary, 1605 Oram St., 18504.

22—ST. PAUL (1887) Merged with St. Clare, Scranton. Rev. Msgrs. Neil J. Van Loon, V.E.; William J. Feldcamp, Pastor Emeritus, (Retired); Deacon John Hanni. In Res., Rev. Donald J. Williams.
Res.: 1510 Penn Ave., 18509. Tel: 570-961-1549; Fax: 570-961-0335; Email: info@stpaulscranton.org.
Catechesis Religious Program—Students 150.

23—SAINT PAUL OF THE CROSS, SCRANTON (1885) [CEM] (Polish) Former Sacred Hearts of Jesus & Mary, St. John the Evangelist & St. Francis of Assisi Parishes.
1217 Prospect Ave., 18505. Tel: 570-343-6420; Email: sacredhearts@epix.net. Rev. Scott P. Sterowski.

24—SS. PETER AND PAUL (1910) [CEM] (Polish) Linked with St. Lucy, Scranton.
1309 W. Locust St., 18504. Tel: 570-343-7015; Email: secretary.sspp@gmail.com. Revs. Samuel J. Ferretti; Alvaro de Oliveira Joaquim, O.S.J.; Deacon Carmine Mendicino.
Catechesis Religious Program—Students 20.

25—SACRED HEARTS OF JESUS AND MARY, Merged with St. John the Evangelist & St. Francis of Assisi, Scranton. See Saint Paul of the Cross, Scranton (Tel: 570-343-6420). Worship site for St. Paul of the Cross, Scranton.

26—SAINT JOHN NEUMANN, SCRANTON (1903) Merger of Holy Name of Jesus, St. Mary of the Assumption, Scranton & Nativity of Our Lord, Scranton.
633 Orchard St., 18505. Tel: 570-344-6159; Email: mbryant@stjnparish.org. Revs. Michael Bryant; Ryan P. Glenn; Deacon Albert V. Giacometti. In Res., Rev. William B. Pickard, (Retired).
Worship Sites—
Nativity of Our Lord Church—Lackawanna Co. 18505.
Holy Name of Jesus Church, 1414 E. Elm St., 18505.
Catechesis Religious Program—Students 153.

27—ST. VINCENT DE PAUL (1925) Closed. For inquiries for parish records contact Mary, Mother of God, Scranton. Merged with St. Joseph, Scranton, Holy Rosary, Scranton & St. Anthony of Padua, Scranton.

OUTSIDE THE CITY OF SCRANTON

ARCHBALD, LACKAWANNA CO.

1—CHRIST THE KING PARISH
429 Church St., Archbald, 18403. Tel: 570-876-1701; Fax: 570-876-3617; Web: www.christthekingparisharchbaldeynon.org. Revs. Paul C. Fontanella; Dominic Obour.
Worship Sites—
St. Thomas Aquinas Church—
St. Mary of Czestochowa Church, 417 Main St., Eynon, 18403.
Catechesis Religious Program—Combined with St. Mary of Czestochowa, Eynon. Students 471.

2—ST. THOMAS AQUINAS (1858) [CEM] Merged with St. Mary of Czestochowa, Eynon. Primary worship site of Christ the King Parish, Archbald.
429 Church St., Archbald, 18403. Tel: 570-876-1701; Fax: 570-876-3617; Email: st.tom@comcast.net. Rev. Christopher S. Sahd.

ASHLEY, LUZERNE CO.

1—HOLY ROSARY (1900) (Slovak), Closed. For inquiries for parish records please see St. Leo's, Ashley (Tel: 570-825-6669).

2—ST. LEO (1887)
33 Manhattan St., Ashley, 18706. Tel: 570-825-6669; Email: saintlhrc@gmail.com. Revs. Vincent H. Dang; Thomas J. O'Malley, Pastor Emeritus, (Retired).
Catechesis Religious Program—Students 20.

ATHENS, BRADFORD CO., ST. JOSEPH (1852) Merged with St. John the Evangelist, South Waverly & Epiphany, Sayre. For inquiries for parish records, contact Epiphany, Sayre (Tel: 570-888-9641).

AVOCA, LUZERNE CO.

1—ST. MARY (1871) [CEM] Merged
715 Hawthorne St., Avoca, 18641. Rev. Phillip J. Sladicka. with Sts. Peter & Paul, Avoca. Worship site of Queen of the Apostles Parish, Avoca.

2—SS. PETER AND PAUL (1909) [CEM] (Polish), Closed. For inquiries for parish records please see Queen of the Apostles, Avoca (Tel: 570-457-3412).

3—QUEEN OF THE APOSTLES PARISH
715 Hawthorne St., Avoca, 18641. Tel: 570-457-3412; Fax: 570-457-2483; Email: staff@queenoftheapostles.com. Rev. Phillip J. Sladicka; Deacon James A. Rose.
Worship Site: St. Mary's Church, 715 Hawthorne St., Avoca, 18641.
Catechesis Religious Program—Students 128.

BASTRESS, LYCOMING CO., IMMACULATE CONCEPTION OF THE BLESSED VIRGIN MARY (1847) [CEM] (German)
c/o 118 Kendall Ave., Jersey Shore, 17740.
Tel: 570-745-3301; Email: icsloffice@comcast.net. Immaculate Conception of the B.V.M. Parish, 5973 Jacks Hollow Rd., Williamsport, 17702. Rev. Bert S. Kozen. Linked with St. Luke, Jersey Shore.
Catechesis Religious Program—Students 125.
Convent—Mother of the Eucharist, 6100 Jacks Hollow Rd., Williamsport, 17702. Tel: 570-745-3334. Sr. Joan May, C.N., Guardian.

BEAR CREEK, LUZERNE CO.

1—ST. CHRISTOPHER (1962) Closed. Merged with Holy Saviour, Wilkes-Barre (Tel: 570-823-4988). (Now St. Andre Bessette Parish).

2—ST. ELIZABETH (1938)
5700 Bear Creek Blvd., Bear Creek, 18602.
Tel: 570-472-3061; Fax: 570-472-3503. Rev. Thomas J. Maloney, Sacramental Min., (Retired); Mr. Anthony Butel, Parish Life Coord.
Catechesis Religious Program—Students 58.
Mission—St. Mark, Thornhurst, Luzerne Co.

BENTLEY CREEK, BRADFORD CO., ST. ANN'S (1843) [CEM] Merged with Epiphany, Sayre. For inquiries for parish records please see Epiphany, Sayre (Tel: 570-888-9641).

BLAKESLEE, MONROE CO., CHRIST THE KING (1976) Closed. For inquiries for parish records please see St. Maximilian Kolbe, Pocono Pines (Tel: 570-888-9641).

BLOSSBURG, TIOGA CO.

1—ST. JOHN NEUMANN, Closed. For inquiries for parish records, please see Holy Child, Mansfield (Tel: 570-662-3568).

2—ST. MARY'S (1874) [CEM 3] (Polish), Closed. For inquiries for parish records contact Holy Child, Mansfield. Worship site for Holy Child Parish, Mansfield.

BRODHEADSVILLE, MONROE CO., OUR LADY QUEEN OF PEACE (1968)
1402 Rte. 209, P.O. Box 38, Brodheadsville, 18322.
Tel: 610-681-6137; Email: churchoffice@qopchurch.org; Web: www.qopchurch.org. Rev. Michael F. Quinnan; Deacons Ralph E. Weichand; Joseph P. Rodgers; Robert A. O'Connor Jr.
Catechesis Religious Program—Jacqueline Douglas, D.R.E. Students 540.

CANADENSIS, MONROE CO., ST. BERNADETTE (1967) Closed. Merged with St. Mary of the Mount, Mt. Pocono, and St. Ann, Tobyhanna. For inquiries, contact Most Holy Trinity, Cresco.
Res.: 1365 Rte. 390, Canadensis, 18325.
Mission—Our Lady of Fatima, Closed. State Park, Promised Land, Monroe Co.

CANTON, BRADFORD CO., ST. MICHAEL aka St. Johns - St. Michaels Church (1853) [CEM]
106 N. Washington St., Canton, 17724.
Tel: 570-673-5253; Email: stmichaelparish@frontiernet.net; Web: stmichaelscanton.org. Rev. Joseph P. Kutch.
Worship Site: St. Michael Church, 107 N. Washington St., Canton, 17724.
Catechesis Religious Program—Students 43.
Missions—St. John Nepomucene—[CEM] 133 Exchange St., Troy, Bradford Co. 16947. Email: stmichaelparish@frontiernet.net. Mailing Address: 106 N. Washington St., Canton, 17724.
St. Aloysius, Green St. & Division Alley, Ralston, Lycoming Co. 17763.

CARBONDALE, LACKAWANNA CO.

1—OUR LADY OF MT. CARMEL (1882) [CEM] (Italian) Linked with St. Rose of Lima, Carbondale.
15 Fallbrook St., Carbondale, 18407. Revs. James Price, C.P.; Paul C. Fontanella.
Catechesis Religious Program—Combined program wit St. Rose of Lima, Carbondale.

2—ST. ROSE OF LIMA (1832) [CEM 2] Merged with St. Michael, Simpson & linked with Our Lady of Mt. Carmel, Carbondale. Revs. James Price, C.P.; Paul C. Fontanella; Deacon Edward Casey.
Res.: 6 N. Church St., Carbondale, 18407.
Tel: 570-282-2991; Fax: 570-282-7580; Email: strose@echoes.net; Web: www.strosecarbondale.weconnect.com.
Catechesis Religious Program—Kathryn Yaklic, D.R.E. Students 303.

CARVERTON, LUZERNE CO., ST. FRANCES CABRINI (1947) Linked with St. Therese, Shavertown PA.
585 Mt. Olivet Rd., Kingston Twp., Wyoming, 18644-9333. Tel: 570-696-3737; Email: sfcbs@comcast.net. Rev. James J. Paisley.
Catechesis Religious Program—Students 47.

Mission—Blessed Sacrament, Closed. Centermoreland, Luzerne Co.

CLARKS GREEN, LACKAWANNA CO., ST. GREGORY (1974)
330 N. Abington Rd., Clarks Green, 18411.
Tel: 570-587-4808; Email: churchofstgreg@gmail.com; Web: thechurchofstgregory.com. Rev. John M. Lapera; Deacon Robert P. Sheils Jr.
Catechesis Religious Program—Students 603.

CLARKS SUMMIT, LACKAWANNA CO., OUR LADY OF THE SNOWS (1911)
301 S. State St., Clarks Summit, 18411.
Tel: 570-586-1741; Fax: 570-586-2504; Email: info@olsparish.net; Web: www.olsparish.net. Rev. Msgr. Joseph G. Quinn, J.D., J.C.L.; Rev. Babu Muttickal; Deacon Leo L. Lynn.
Catechesis Religious Program—Students 499.
Mission—St. Benedict, Newton, Lackawanna Co.

CONYNGHAM, LUZERNE CO., ST. JOHN BOSCO (1964)
2 Charles Ave., P.O. Box 919, Conyngham, 18219.
Tel: 570-788-1997; Fax: 570-788-6667; Email: stjb@ptd.net. Mailing Address: 573 State Rte. 93, Conyngham, 18219. Rev. Richard J. Polmounter; Deacon Maurice J. Cerasaro Jr.
Catechesis Religious Program—Carla Bednar, D.R.E. Students 420.

CRESCO, MONROE CO., MOST HOLY TRINITY PARISH
236 Rte. 390, Cresco, 18326. Tel: 570-595-3100; Fax: 570-595-3200; Email: mht-poconos@outlook.com; Email: bamfinance@gmail.com; Web: www.mht-poconos.org. Rev. Gregory F. Loughney; Jaime Restrepo; Rev. Msgr. Arthur J. Kaschenbach, Pastor Emeritus, (Retired); Deacons Alan S. Baranski; Jose L. Mendoza.
Catechesis Religious Program—Msgr. McHugh School: 212 Rte. 390, Cresco, 18326. Students 140.

DALLAS, LUZERNE CO., GATE OF HEAVEN (1951) Linked with Our Lady of Victory, Harveys Lake.
40 Machell Ave., Dallas, 18612. Rev. Daniel A. Toomey; Deacon Thomas M. Cesarini.
Catechesis Religious Program—Students 192.

DALTON, LACKAWANNA CO., OUR LADY OF THE ABINGTONS (1967) Linked with St. Patrick, Nicholson.
700 W. Main St., Dalton, 18414. Tel: 570-563-1622; Email: spolachurch@gmail.com; Web: www.spolachurch.weebly.com. Revs. Arbogaste Satoun; John J. Kilpatrick, Pastor Emeritus, (Retired); Deacon Paul J. Brojack.
Catechesis Religious Program—Students 46.

DICKSON CITY, LACKAWANNA CO.
1—ST. THOMAS THE APOSTLE, Closed. For inquiries for parish records please see Visitation of the Blessed Virgin Mary.
2—VISITATION OF THE BLESSED VIRGIN MARY (1890) [CEM] (Polish)
619 Dundaff St., Dickson City, 18519.
Tel: 570-489-2091; Email: vbvm@comcast.net; Web: vbvm.org. Mailing Address: 1090 Carmalt St., Dickson City, 18519. Rev. Msgr. Patrick J. Pratico, J.C.D.
Catechesis Religious Program—Students 123.

DORRANCE, LUZERNE CO., OUR LADY HELP OF CHRISTIANS (1948) [CEM] (Polish) Linked with St. Jude, Mountaintop.
3529 St. Mary's Rd.,, Wapwallopen, 18660-1901.
Tel: 570-868-5855; Email: stmarysdorrance@gmail.com. Revs. Joseph J. Evanko; Stephen A. Krawontka.
Catechesis Religious Program—Students 104.

DRUMS, LUZERNE CO., CHURCH OF THE GOOD SHEPHERD (1940)
Mailing Address: 87 S. Hunter Hwy., West Hazleton, 18202. Tel: 570-788-3141; Fax: 570-788-2916; Email: gsch@ptd.net. Rev. Connell A. McHugh.
Res.: 553 Putnam St., West Hazleton, 18202.
Catechesis Religious Program—Students 170.

DUNMORE, LACKAWANNA CO.
1—ALL SAINTS (1905) (Slovak), Closed. Merged with Our Lady of Mount Carmel, Dunmore (Tel: 570-346-7429).
2—SS. ANTHONY & ROCCO PARISH, (Italian)
303 Smith St., Dunmore, 18512. Rev. David P. Cappelloni.
Worship Sites—
St. Anthony of Padua, Dunmore—208 Smith St., Dunmore, 18512.
St. Rocco, Dunmore, 122 Kurtz St., Dunmore, 18512.
Catechesis Religious Program—Students 192.
Convent—Religious Teachers Filippini, 118 Kurtz St., Dunmore, 18510. Tel: 570-343-1422; Fax: 570-346-3099.
3—ST. ANTHONY OF PADUA (1894) (Italian), Closed. Restructured with St. Rocco, Dunmore to form SS. Anthony & Rocco, Dunmore. Also parish worship site for SS. Anthony & Rocco (Tel: 570-344-1209).
4—ST. CASIMIR, (Polish), Closed. Merged with Our Lady of Mount Carmel, Dunmore (Tel: 570-346-7429).
5—CHRIST THE KING (1949) Closed. For inquiries for parish records please see Immaculate Conception Parish, Scranton (Tel: 570-961-5211).
6—ST. MARY OF MOUNT CARMEL, Merged with All Saints and St. Casimir, Dunmore. See Our Lady of Mount Carmel Parish, Dunmore (Tel: 570-346-7429).
7—OUR LADY OF MOUNT CARMEL PARISH (1856) [CEM 2] Merger of All Saints, St. Casimir & St. Mary of Mt. Carmel Parishes.
322 Chestnut St., Dunmore, 18512.
Tel: 570-346-7429; Fax: 570-346-0523; Email: stmarysdunmore@aol.com; Web: www.olmcdunmore.org. Rev. John A. Doris; Andrew Fazio Sr., Pastoral Min./Coord.
Legal Title: St. Mary of Mount Carmel.
School—Saint Mary of Mount Carmel Elementary School, (Grades PreK-8), 325 Chestnut St., Dunmore, 18512. Tel: 570-346-4429; Email: cjslcd@gmail.com. Kathleen Hubert, Prin.
Catechesis Religious Program—Lisa Murphy, C.C.D. Coord. Students 664.
8—ST. ROCCO'S (1905) (Italian), Merged with St. Anthony of Padua, Dunmore to form SS. Anthony & Rocco, Dunmore. Additional worship site for SS. Anthony & Rocco.

DUPONT, LUZERNE CO., SACRED HEART OF JESUS (1902) [CEM] (Polish)
215 Lackawanna Ave., Dupont, 18641.
Tel: 570-654-3713; Email: shojesuschurch@gmail.com; Web: www.sacredheartdupont.com. Rev. Thomas J. Petro, J.C.L.
Catechesis Religious Program—Students 130.

DURYEA, LUZERNE CO.
1—HOLY ROSARY (1893) (Polish), Closed. For inquiries see Nativity of Our Lord Parish, Duryea. Also worship site for Nativity of Our Lord, Duryea.
2—ST. JOSEPH (1909) [CEM] (Lithuanian), Merged with Sacred Heart of Jesus, Duryea. For inquiries for parish records, contact Nativity of Our Lord Parish, Duryea, Tel: 570-457-3502.
3—NATIVITY OF OUR LORD PARISH (1893) [CEM] (Polish)
127 Stephenson St., Duryea, 18642. Rev. John V. Polednak, V.E.; Deacon Andre F. Kubacinski.
Catechesis Religious Program—Students 130.
4—SACRED HEART OF JESUS (1889) (German), Merged with Nativity of Our Lord Parish, Duryea. Additional worship site for Nativity of Our Lord Parish, Duryea.

DUSHORE, SULLIVAN CO.
1—ST. BASIL THE GREAT (1838) Closed. See Immaculate Heart of Mary, Dushore. Parish worship site for Immaculate Heart of Mary Parish, 101 Churchill St.
2—IMMACULATE HEART OF MARY PARISH (1838) [CEM]
1 St. Francis Dr., Mildred, 18632. Rev. Thomas J. Major.
Worship Sites—
St. Basil the Great—Dushore, Sullivan Co.
St. Francis of Assisi, Eagles Mere, Sullivan Co.
St. Francis of Assisi, Mildred, Sullivan Co.
S. Philip and James Church-St. John Neumann Shrine, Sugar Ridge.
St. Francis Xavier, Overton, Closed. For inquiries for parish records please contact Immaculate Heart of Mary Parish, Dushore.
Sacred Heart, Laporte, Closed. For inquiries for parish records please contact Immaculate Heart of Mary Parish, Dushore.
Catechesis Religious Program—Students 148.

EAST STROUDSBURG, MONROE CO.
1—ST. JOHN'S CHURCH (1986)
5171 Milford Rd., East Stroudsburg, 18302.
Tel: 570-223-9144; Fax: 570-223-9146; Email: stjohnda18@gmail.com; Web: www.churchofstjohn.com. Rev. Gregory A. Reichlen; Deacon Max Francois.
Catechesis Religious Program—Tel: 570-223-0888; Email: stjohnre28@gmail.com. Ana Lisa Kolakowski. Students 175.
2—ST. MATTHEW (1902)
178 Ridgeway St., East Stroudsburg, 18301.
Tel: 570-421-2342; Fax: 570-421-8414; Email: rectory@ptd.net. Revs. Gerald W. Shantillo; John J. Chmil; Jaime Restrepo; Deacons Jose Oscar Langlois; Svetko Jurjevic; Kevin L. Scheirer.
Res.: 200 Brodhead Ave., East Stroudsburg, 18301.
Catechesis Religious Program—Students 341.

ELKLAND, TIOGA CO., ST. THOMAS THE APOSTLE (1907)
111 First St., Elkland, 16920. Tel: 814-258-5121; Fax: 814-258-5122; Email: ststhomascatherine@stny.rr.com. Revs. David W. Bechtel, Admin.; John M. Kita.
Catechesis Religious Program—Students 8.
Mission—St. Catherine of Siena, 146 Lincoln St., Westfield, Tioga Co. 16950.

ELMHURST, LACKAWANNA CO., ST. EULALIA (1950)
214 Blue Shutters Rd., Roaring Brook Twp., 18444.
Tel: 570-842-7656; Fax: 570-842-7193; Email: office@sainteulalias.com; Web: www.sainteulalias.com. Rev. Msgr. John W. Jordan; Mrs. Ellen Dermody, Pastoral Assoc.; Elizabeth Strasburger, D.R.E.; Scott Coates, Music Min.
Catechesis Religious Program—Students 352.

EXETER, LUZERNE CO.
1—ST. ANTHONY OF PADUA (1928) (Italian), Closed. For inquiries for parish records contact Saint Barbara Parish, Exeter (Tel: 570-654-2103). Parish worship site for Saint Barbara Parish.
2—SAINT BARBARA PARISH
224 Memorial St., Exeter, 18643. Tel: 570-654-2103; Fax: 570-655-3313; Email: stanthonyexeter@comcast.net. Rev. Michael E. Finn, V.F.; Deacons William A. Dervinis; Walter G. Janoski.
Res.: 28 Memorial Ave., Exeter, 18643.
Worship Sites—
St. Anthony of Padua—Exeter.
St. Cecilia, 1700 Wyoming Ave., Exeter, 18643.
3—ST. CECILIA (1900) [CEM] Additional worship site for Saint Barbara Parish, Exeter (Tel: 570-654-2103).
1670 Wyoming Ave., Exeter, 18643.
Tel: 570-654-2103; Email: stanthonyexter@comcast.net. Rev. Michael E. Finn, V.F.; Deacons William A. Dervinis; Walter G. Janoski.
Res.: 1700 Wyoming Ave., Exeter, 18643.
4—ST. JOHN THE BAPTIST (1898) (Polish), Closed. For inquiries for parish records, contact St. Barbara Parish, Exeter (Tel: 570-654-2103).

EYNON, LACKAWANNA CO.
1—ST. MARY OF CZESTOCHOWA (1915) (Polish), Merged with St. Mary of Vilna, Eynon & St. Thomas Aquinas, Archbald. For inquiries for parish records, contact Christ the King Parish, Archbald, PA.
Residence, Res.: 417 Main St., Eynon, 18403.
Tel: 570-876-1701.
2—ST. MARY OF VILNA, (Lithuanian), Closed. For inquiries for parish records, contact Christ the King Parish, Archbald, PA.

FAIRMOUNT SPRINGS, LUZERNE CO., ST. MARTHA (1966) Merged with St. Mary, Our Lady of Perpetual Help, Mocanaqua & Corpus Christi, Glen Lyon to form Holy Spirit Parish, Mocanaqua. Additional worship site for Holy Spirit, Mocanaqua.
Mailing Address: c/o 150 Main St., Mocanaqua, 18655. Rev. Louis T. Kaminski.
Church: 260 Bonnieville Rd., Stillwater, 17878.
Catechesis Religious Program—Students 29.

FOREST CITY, SUSQUEHANNA CO.
1—ASCENSION PARISH, Linked with St. Katharine Drexel Parish, Pleasant Mount.
612 Hudson St., Forest City, 18421.
Tel: 570-785-3838. Rev. Brian J.T. Clarke, J.C.L.
Worship Site: St. Joseph, 741 Delaware St., Forest City, 18421.
2—ST. JOSEPH (1904) (Slovenian), Merged with Sacred Heart of Jesus, Forest City. Worship site for Ascension Parish, Forest City.
741 Delaware St., Forest City, 18421.
3—SACRED HEART OF JESUS (1904) (Polish), Closed. Merged with St. Agnes, Forest City and linked with St. Katharine Drexel, Pleasant Mount. Rev. Brian J.T. Clarke, J.C.L.
Res.: 612 Hudson St., Forest City, 18421.
Tel: 570-785-3838; Email: rccfc@nep.net.

FREELAND, LUZERNE CO.
1—ST. ANTHONY, Closed. For inquiries for parish records please see Our Lady of the Immaculate Conception, Freeland (Tel: 570-636-3035).
2—ST. CASIMIR, Closed. For inquiries for parish records please see Our Lady of the Immaculate Conception, Freeland (Tel: 570-636-3035).
3—ST. JOHN NEPOMUCENE, Closed. For inquiries for parish records please see Our Lady of the Immaculate Conception, Freeland (Tel: 570-636-3035).
4—OUR LADY OF THE IMMACULATE CONCEPTION (1862) [CEM]
898 Centre St., Freeland, 18224. Tel: 570-636-3035; Fax: 570-636-1743; Email: secretary@ourladyfreeland.org. Rev. Michael J. Kloton.
Catechesis Religious Program—Students 100.

FRIENDSVILLE, SUSQUEHANNA CO.
1—SAINT BRIGID PARISH
17 Cottage St., P.O. Box 75, Friendsville, 18818.
Tel: 570-553-2288; Fax: 570-553-2975. Rev. Casimir M. Stanis; Deacon Kenneth S. Brennan.
Worship Site: St. Francis Xavier, Friendsville, 726 Main St., Friendsville, 18818.
Catechesis Religious Program—Students 46.
Mission—St. Augustine, 295 Church Rd., Brackney, Susquehanna Co. 18812.
2—ST. FRANCIS XAVIER (1831) [CEM 3] Merged with St. Thomas the Apostle, Little Meadows & St. Joseph, St. Joseph. Worship site for Saint Brigid Parish, Friendsville.
17 Cottage St., P.O. Box 75, Friendsville, 18818.
Tel: 570-553-2288; Fax: 570-553-2975; Email: sfxc@epix.net; Web: www.ourparishcommunity.com. Rev. Casimir M. Stanis; Deacon Kenneth S. Brennan.
Mission—St. Patrick, Closed Irish Hill, Rte. 3033, Middletown, Susquehanna Co.
3—ST. JOSEPH (1829) [CEM 2] [JC] Closed. For

inquiries for parish records please see Saint Brigid Parish, Friendsville.

GLEN LYON, LUZERNE CO.

1—ST. ADALBERT, Merged with St. Denis & St. Michael's, Glen Lyon to form Corpus Christi. For parish records please contact Holy Spirit Parish, Mocanaqua. Parish Office: 31 S. Market St., Glen Lyon.

2—CORPUS CHRISTI (2001) (Merging of St. Adalbert, St. Denis & St. Michael's, Glen Lyon & St. Mary's, Wanamie. For inquiries for parish records, contact Corpus Christi.) Linked with Holy Spirit, Mocanaqua.
31 S. Market St., Glen Lyon, 18617.
Tel: 570-736-6372; Fax: 570-736-6232; Email: hsparish@pa.metrocast.net. Rev. Louis T. Kaminski.
Catechesis Religious Program—Students 90.

3—ST. DENIS, Closed. Merged with Corpus Christi, Glen Lyon (Tel: 570-736-6372).

4—ST. MARY (Wanamie) (1906) (Lithuanian), Closed. For inquiries for parish records, contact Corpus Christi, Glen Lyon (Tel: 570-736-6372).

5—ST. MICHAEL, Closed. Merged with Corpus Christi, Glen Lyon. For inquiries for parish records contact Holy Spirit, Mocanaqua, PA.

GOULDSBORO, WAYNE CO., ST. RITA (1975)
512 Main St., P.O. Box 537, Gouldsboro, 18424.
Tel: 570-842-4995; Fax: 570-842-5429; Email: strcgouldsboro@gmail.com; Web: www.stritaspa.org. Rev. Kevin P. Mulhern, Sacramental Min., (Retired); Mr. Anthony Butel, Parish Life Coord.
Catechesis Religious Program—Students 33.
Mission—St. Anthony of Padua, Closed Newfoundland, Wayne Co.

GREAT BEND, SUSQUEHANNA CO., ST. LAWRENCE (1872) [CEM] Linked with St. Martin of Tours, Jackson; St. John the Evangelist, Susquehanna. It is a worship site of Most Holy Trinity Parish, Susquehanna.
380 Franklin St., Great Bend, 18821. Rev. David W. Cramer.
Catechesis Religious Program—Students 72.
Mission—St. John the Apostle, [CEM] Closed New Milford, Susquehanna Co.

HANOVER TOWNSHIP, WASHINGTON CO., EXALTATION OF THE HOLY CROSS (1917) [CEM] (Polish) Linked with St. Robert Bellarmine, Wilkes-Barre.
420 Main Rd., Hanover Township, 18706-6094.
Tel: 570-823-6242; Email: exhc@aol.com; Web: www.exhc.org. Rev. Richard J. Cirba.
Catechesis Religious Program—Students 75.

HARDING-FALLS, LUZERNE CO., CHURCH OF THE HOLY REDEEMER aka Corpus Christi Parish (1952) Merged with Immaculate Conception Church, West Pittston. For inquiries for parish records see Corpus Christi Parish, West Pittston. Additional worship site of Corpus Christi.

HARLEIGH, LUZERNE CO., SACRED HEART OF JESUS (1903) Closed. For inquiries for parish records please see Queen of Heaven Parish, Hazleton (Tel: 570-454-8797).

HARVEYS LAKE, LUZERNE CO., OUR LADY OF VICTORY (1969) Linked with Gate of Heaven, Dallas.
16 Second St., Harveys Lake, 18618. Rev. Daniel A. Toomey.
Catechesis Religious Program—Students 109.

HAWLEY, WAYNE CO., BLESSED VIRGIN MARY, QUEEN OF PEACE (1852) [CEM]
314 Chestnut Ave., Hawley, 18428. Rev. Richard W. Beck; Deacon Matthew G. Lorent.
Catechesis Religious Program—Students 245.
Mission—St. Veronica, Lake Wallenpaupack, Pike Co.

HAZLETON, LUZERNE CO.

1—ANNUNCIATION, HAZLETON (1855) [CEM]
122 S. Wyoming St., Hazleton, 18201.
Tel: 570-454-0212; Email: stgabes@ptd.net. Revs. Mariusz Beczek, O.S.J.; Victor Leon, O.S.J.; Daniel L. Schwebs, O.S.J.
Worship Site: St. Gabriel.
Catechesis Religious Program—Students 274.

2—CHURCH OF THE MOST PRECIOUS BLOOD (1885) (Italian)
131 E. Fourth St., Hazleton, 18201. Revs. Anthony J. Generose, J.V., V.E., J.C.L.; Louis Grippi, Pastor Emeritus.
Catechesis Religious Program—Students 284.
Convent—221 E. Fourth St., Hazleton, 18201. Sr. Bernadette Borelli, D.M., Supr.

3—SS. CYRIL & METHODIUS, HAZLETON (1882) [CEM] (Slovak), Merged with St. Stanislaus, Hazleton. Revs. Michael J. Piccola; Joseph Dang; Deacon Leonard G. Kassick.
Res.: P.O. Box 2099, Hazleton, 18201.
Worship Site: St. Joseph, 604 N. Laurel St., Hazleton, 18201.
Catechesis Religious Program—Students 51.
Mission—St. Ladislaus, Closed.

4—ST. GABRIEL, Merged with Our Lady of Mount Carmel and Holy Trinity (German), Hazleton. Worship site of Annunciation, Hazelton.

5—HOLY ROSARY (1916) (Italian)
240 S. Poplar St., Hazleton, 18201. Rev. Brian J.W. Clarke, J.C.L.; Deacon Vincent M. Oberto.
Catechesis Religious Program—Students 114.

6—HOLY TRINITY (1887) [CEM 2] (German), Closed. For inquiries for parish records contact Annunciation Parish, Hazleton.

7—HOLY TRINITY (1907) [CEM] (Slovak), Closed. Merged with St. Joseph (Slovak), Hazleton. For inquiries for parish records please see SS. Cyril & Methodius, Hazelton (Tel: 570-454-0881).

8—ST. JOSEPH (1882) [CEM] (Slovak), Merged with St. Stanislaus and Holy Trinity (Slovak), Hazelton. For inquiries for parish record please contact SS. Cyril & Methodius, Hazleton. Worship site for SS. Cyril & Methodius, Hazleton.

9—OUR LADY OF GRACE (1910) [CEM] (Italian), Closed. Worship site for Queen of Heaven, Hazelton. For inquiries for parish records please contact Queen of Heaven, Hazelton (Tel: 570-454-8797).

10—OUR LADY OF MOUNT CARMEL (1905) (Tyrolese), Closed. Merged with Holy Trinity (Slovak), Hazleton (now closed). For inquiries for parish records please see SS. Cyril & Methodius Parish, Hazleton (Tel: 570- 454-0881).

11—SS. PETER AND PAUL (1887) (Lithuanian), Closed. For inquiries for parish records please see Holy Name of Jesus Parish, West Hazleton (Tel: 570-454-3933).

12—QUEEN OF HEAVEN, HAZLETON, [CEM] Merged with Sacred Heart of Jesus, Harleigh, St. Mary, Lattimer & St. Nazarius, Pardeesville.
750 N. Vine St., Hazleton, 18201. Tel: 570-454-8797; Email: olg2@ptd.net; Email: mrsjayb@verizon.net. Revs. Anthony J. Generose, J.V., V.E., J.C.L.; Neftali Sena; Deacon Robert A. Roman.
Worship Site: Our Lady of Grace, Hazleton, Luzerne Co.
Catechesis Religious Program—Students 47.

13—ST. STANISLAUS (1893) [CEM] (Polish), Closed. For inquiries for parish records please see SS. Cyril & Methodius Parish, Hazleton (Tel: 570-454-0881).

HONESDALE, WAYNE CO., ST. JOHN THE EVANGELIST (1842) [CEM 3] Merged with St. Joseph, White Mills.
150 Terrace St., Honesdale, 18431.
Tel: 570-253-4561; Fax: 570-253-1058; Email: stjohnshonesdale@gmail.com; Web: honesdalecatholic.com. 414 Church St., Honesdale, 18431. Rev. William J.P. Langan.
Worship Sites—
St. Bernard—Beach Lake.
St. John the Evangelist.
St. Joseph, Rileyville.
St. Mary Magdalene, 416 Church St., Honesdale, 18431.
Catechesis Religious Program—Mrs. Anastasia Legg, D.R.E. Students 65.

HUDSON, LUZERNE CO., ST. JOSEPH'S (1889) [CEM] (Polish), Closed. Merged with Sacred Heart, Plains and SS Peter and Paul, Plains.

HUGHESTOWN, LUZERNE CO., BLESSED SACRAMENT (1945) Merged with St. Mary, Help of Christians, Pittston. For inquiries for parish records please see Our Lady of the Eucharist Parish, Pittston (Tel: 570-654-0263).

INKERMAN, LUZERNE CO., ST. MARK (1900) Closed. For inquiries for parish records please contact St. Maria Goretti, Laflin.

JACKSON, SUSQUEHANNA CO., ST. MARTIN OF TOURS (1940) Linked with St. Lawrence, Great Bend & St. John the Evangelist, Susquehanna. it is a worship site of Most Holy Trinity Parish, Susquehanna.
Mailing Address: 15 E. Church St., Susquehanna, 18847. Tel: 570-853-4634; Fax: 570-853-3356. Rev. David W. Cramer.
Catechesis Religious Program—Students 40.
Convent—Capuchin Sisters of Nazareth St. Joseph Convent, 8175 State Rte. 492, Jackson, 18825.
Mission—St. Paul, Closed. Starrucca, Wayne Co.

JERMYN, LACKAWANNA CO.

1—SACRED HEART OF MARY (1889) [CEM] Merged with Sacred Heart of Jesus, Mayfield. Worship site for Sacred Heart of Jesus & Mary Parish, Jermyn. For inquiries for parish records please contact Sacred Hearts of Jesus & Mary, Jermyn (Tel: 570-876-1061).

2—SACRED HEARTS OF JESUS & MARY, JERMYN (1889) [CEM] Merged with Sacred Heart of Jesus, Mayfield. Rev. Shane L. Kirby, V.E., S.T.L., J.C.L.; Deacon Patrick J. Massino.
Res.: 624 Madison Ave., Jermyn, 18433-1697.
Worship Site: Sacred Heart of Mary Church, Jermyn, Lackawanna Co.
Catechesis Religious Program—Students 70.

JERSEY SHORE, LYCOMING CO., ST. LUKE (1902) linked with Immaculate Conception of the Blessed Virgin Mary, Bastress.
Mailing Address: c/o Immaculate Conception, 5973 Jacks Hollow Rd., Williamsport, 17702. Rev. Bert S. Kozen.
Res.: 118 Kendall Ave., Jersey Shore, 17740.
Catechesis Religious Program—Students 98.

JESSUP, LACKAWANNA CO.

1—ST. JAMES (1899) [CEM] Closed. Merged with Queen of Angels Parish, Jessup.

2—ST. MARY'S ASSUMPTION (1904) [CEM] (Italian), Closed. For inquiries for parish records contact Queen of Angels Parish, Jessup (Tel: 570-489-2252).

3—QUEEN OF ANGELS PARISH
320 First Ave., Jessup, 18434. Tel: 570-489-2252; Email: stjames-jessup@hotmail.com. Mailing Address: 605 Church St., Jessup, 18434. Rev. Gerard M. McGlone, V.F.; Deacon Gerard L. Carpenter.
Worship Site: St. Michael, 320 First Ave., Jessup, 18434.
Catechesis Religious Program—Students 268.

KINGSTON, LUZERNE CO.

1—ST. HEDWIG (1901) [CEM] (Polish), Closed. For inquiries for parish records please see St. Ignatius Loyola, Kingston (Tel: 570-288-6446).

2—ST. IGNATIUS LOYOLA, KINGSTON (1885) [CEM] Merged with St. Mary's Annunciation, Kingston.
339 N. Maple Ave., Kingston, 18704.
Tel: 570-288-6446; Fax: 570-288-0463; Email: siloffice@aol.com; Web: stignatiuspa.com. Rev. Msgr. David L. Tressler; Rev. Joseph Mosley; Deacon John E. O'Connor.
Worship Site: St. Ann's, Kingston. Tel: 570-288-5919.
Catechesis Religious Program—Students 275.

3—ST. MARY'S ANNUNCIATION (1902) (Lithuanian), Closed. For inquiries for parish records, please see St. Ignatius Loyola, Kingston (Tel: 570-288-6446).

LAFLIN, LUZERNE CO., ST. MARIA GORETTI (1967)
42 Redwood Dr., Laflin, 18702. Tel: 570-655-8956; Fax: 570-655-1746; Email: 42redwood@comcast.net; Web: www.stmariagoretti-laflin.org. Rev. James J. Walsh, J.C.L.; Deacon Michael S. Imbrogno.
Catechesis Religious Program—Michelle Pinto, D.R.E. Students 120.

LAKE ARIEL, WAYNE CO., ST. THOMAS MORE (1941) [CEM]
105 Gravity Rd., P.O. Box 188, Lake Ariel, 18436.
Tel: 570-698-5584; Fax: 570-698-8468; Email: stthomasstmary@echoes.net. Rev. Stephen J. Stavoy.
Catechesis Religious Program—Students 133.
Mission—St. Mary, Ledgedale, Wayne Co.

LAKE SILKWORTH, LUZERNE CO., OUR LADY OF MOUNT CARMEL (1923) [CEM]
2011 State Rte. 29, Hunlock Creek, 18621-4303.
Tel: 570-477-5040; Email: olmchc@gmail.com. Rev. Alex J. Roche.
Catechesis Religious Program—Students 95.

LAKE WINOLA, WYOMING CO., ST. MARY OF THE LAKE (1986) Linked with Nativity B.V.M., Tunkhannock.
1872 Dalton Rd., P.O. Box 1, Lake Winola, 18657.
Tel: 570-836-3275; Email: stmaryofthelake@frontier.com. Rev. Patrick L. Albert; Deacon Raymond A. Pieretti.
Res.: 99 E. Tioga St., Tunkhannock, 18657.
Catechesis Religious Program—Students 52.

LARKSVILLE, LUZERNE CO., ST. ANTHONY OF PADUA (1908) Closed. For inquiries for parish records please see St. John the Baptist, Larksville, Plymouth (Tel: 570-779-9620).

LATTIMER, LUZERNE CO., ST. MARY'S LATTIMER, (Italian), Closed. Merged with St. Nazarius, Pardeesville, now closed, Our Lady of Grace, Hazleton and Sacred Heart of Jesus, Harleigh. For inquiries for parish records please contact Queen of Heaven, Hazelton (Tel: 570-454-8797).

LITTLE MEADOWS, SUSQUEHANNA CO., ST. THOMAS THE APOSTLE (1887) Closed. For inquiries for parish records please see Saint Brigid Parish, Friendsville (Tel: 570-553-2288).

LORDS VALLEY, PIKE CO., ST. JOHN NEUMANN (1976) Linked with St. Ann, Shohola.
705 Rte. 739, Hawley, 18428. Tel: 570-775-6791; Email: sjnfin@ptd.net. Rev. Thomas J. Major; Deacons John Nash; Henry J. Ernst.
Catechesis Religious Program—Students 62.
Mission—Good Shepherd, Route 402, Blooming Grove, 18428.

LUZERNE, LUZERNE CO.

1—ST. ANN'S (1924) (Lithuanian), Closed. For inquiries for parish records please see Holy Family, Luzerne (Tel: 570-287-6600).

2—HOLY FAMILY (1999)
574 Bennett St., Luzerne, 18709. Tel: 570-287-6600; Fax: 570-283-0706; Email: hfamparish@comcast.net; Web: www.holyfamilyluzerne.org. Rev. Walter Jenkins, C.S.C., Admin.
Catechesis Religious Program—Students 70.

3—ST. JOHN NEPOMUCENE (1907) (Slovak), Closed. For inquiries for parish records please see Holy Family, Luzerne (Tel: 570-287-6600).

4—SACRED HEART CHURCH (1893) (German), Closed. For inquiries for parish records contact Holy Family, Luzerne (Tel: 570-287-6600).

MANSFIELD, TIOGA CO., HOLY CHILD (1953) Merged with St. John Neumann, Blossburg. Rev. Bryan B. Wright.
Res.: 237 S. Main St., Mansfield, 16933.
Worship Sites—

Holy Child Church—240 S. Main St., Mansfield, 16933.
St. Mary of Czestochowa Church, 138 St. Mary's St., Blossburg, 16912.
Catechesis Religious Program—Students 65.
Mission—St. Mary, Closed. Center St., Tioga, Tioga Co. 16946.

MATAMORAS, PIKE CO., ST. JOSEPH (1892) Linked with St. Patrick, Milford.
309 Ave. F, Matamoras, 18336. Rev. Joseph J. Manarchuck.
Catechesis Religious Program—Students 107.
Mission—Holy Family, Cemetery Rd., Mill Rift, Pike Co. 18340.

MAYFIELD, LACKAWANNA CO., SACRED HEART OF JESUS (1904) [CEM] (Polish), Closed. For inquiries for parish records please see Sacred Hearts of Jesus & Mary, Jermyn (Tel: 570-876-1061).

MESHOPPEN, WYOMING CO., ST. JOACHIM (1873) [CEM] Merged with St. Mary's Assumption, Wyalusing. Worship site for Our Lady of Perpetual Help, Wyalusing.
Mailing Address: Our Lady of Perpetual Help Parish, 245 State St., Wyalusing, 18853. Rev. Joseph J. Manarchuck.
Res.: Meshoppen, 18630.
Mission—St. Bonaventure, [CEM] Closed.

MILDRED, SULLIVAN CO., ST. FRANCIS OF ASSISI (1894) Merged with St. Basil, Dushore. For inquiries for parish records, contact Immaculate Heart of Mary, Dushore (Tel: 570-928-8865). Worship site for Immaculate Heart of Mary Parish, Dushore.
Missions—St. Francis of Assisi—Eagles Mere, Sullivan Co.
Sacred Heart, Closed.

MILFORD, PIKE CO.
1—ST. PATRICK (1946) linked with St. Joseph, Matamoras. Rev. Joseph J. Manarchuck; Deacon Thomas M. Spataro.
Catechesis Religious Program—Students 168.
2—ST. VINCENT DE PAUL (1976)
101 St. Vincent Dr., Milford, 18337-9672.
Tel: 570-686-4545; Fax: 800-565-1762; Email: stvoff@ptd.net; Email: svdfrjb@ptd.net; Web: stvdepaulchurch.org. Rev. John B. Boyle; Deacons Joseph A. LaCorte; Joseph A. D'Aiello; Brian Drury.

MOCANAQUA, LUZERNE CO.
1—ASCENSION OF THE LORD, (Slovak), Closed. For parish records & information see Holy Saint Parish.
Mailing Address: c/o 150 Main St., Mocanaqua, 18655.
2—ST. MARY, OUR LADY OF PERPETUAL HELP (1904) [CEM] (Polish), Merged Rev. Louis T. Kaminski. with Ascension, Mocanaqua and St. Martha, Fairmount Springs. Worship site for Holy Spirit Parish, Mocanaqua.
Parish Office: 31 S. Market St., Glen Lyon, 18617.
Res.: 150 Main St., Mocanaqua, 18655.
Tel: 570-736-6372; Fax: 570-736-6232; Email: hsparish@pa.metrocast.net.

MONTDALE, LACKAWANNA CO.
1—CORPUS CHRISTI (1942) Merged with St. Pius X, Royal. Worship site for St. John Vianney Parish, Montdale, Scott Twp. For inquiries for parish records, please contact St. John Vianney, Montdale (Tel: 570-254-9502).
2—ST. JOHN VIANNEY (1942) Merged with St. Pius X, Royal. Rev. Michael J. Kirwin; Deacon Edwin L. Salva Sr.
Res.: 704 Montdale Rd., Scott Twp., 18447.
Tel: 570-254-9502; Fax: 570-254-6233; Email: ccrc402@comcast.net; Web: www.stjvp.org.
Worship Sites—
Corpus Christi Church, Scott Twp.—
St. Pius X Church, Royal.
Catechesis Religious Program—JoAnn Wilbur, D.R.E. Students 185.

MONTOURSVILLE, LYCOMING CO., OUR LADY OF LOURDES (1942)
800 Mulberry St., Montoursville, 17754. Rev. Michael S. McCormick.
Catechesis Religious Program—Students 193.

MONTROSE, SUSQUEHANNA CO., HOLY NAME OF MARY (1898) [CEM]
278 S. Main St., Montrose, 18801. Rev. Philip S. Rayappan.
Catechesis Religious Program—Students 220.

MOSCOW, LACKAWANNA CO., ST. CATHERINE OF SIENA (1861)
P.O. Box 250, Moscow, 18444. Rev. Robert J. Simon.
Catechesis Religious Program—Students 365.

MOUNT POCONO, MONROE CO., ST. MARY OF THE MOUNT (1909) Closed. Merged with St. Bernadette, Canadensis and St. Ann, Tobyhana. For inquiries see Most Holy Trinity Parish, Cresco.

MOUNTAIN TOP, LUZERNE CO., ST. JUDE (1953) Linked with Our Lady Help of Christians, Dorrance.
420 S. Mountain Blvd., Mountain Top, 18707.
Tel: 570-474-6315, Ext. 221; Email: mglenn@stjc.org; Web: www.stjc.org. Revs. Joseph J. Evanko; Stephen A. Krawontka; Deacons Eugene J. Kovatch; James T. Atherton.
School—St. Jude Elementary School, (Grades PreK-8), 422 S. Mountain Blvd., Mountain Top, 18707.
Tel: 570-474-5803; Fax: 570-403-6159; Email: efischer@sjspa.org. Sr. Ellen Fischer, S.C.C., Prin.
Catechesis Religious Program—Students 550.

MUNCY, LYCOMING CO., RESURRECTION (1941)
75 Musser Ln., Muncy, 17756. Tel: 570-546-3900; Email: resurrection@windstream.net; Web: www.resurrectiononline.net. Rev. Glenn E. McCreary, V.E.
Catechesis Religious Program—Students 130.

NANTICOKE, LUZERNE CO.
1—SAINT FAUSTINA KOWALSKA PARISH (1894) [CEM] (Polish), Merged with St. Stanislaus, St. Francis of Assisi, Holy Child and St. Mary of Czestochowa, Nanticoke. Rev. James R. Nash; Deacons Thaddeus Wadus; Florian G. Gyza.
Res.: 520 S. Hanover St., Nanticoke, 18634-2799.
Worship Sites—
Holy Trinity Church—Nanticoke, Luzerne Co.
St. Mary Czestochowa Church, 1030 S. Hanover St., Nanticoke, 18634.
Catechesis Religious Program—Students 159.
2—ST. FRANCIS OF ASSISI (1872) [CEM] Closed. For inquiries for parish records please see Saint Faustina Kowalska Parish, Nanticoke.
3—HOLY CHILD (1942) (Polish), Closed. For inquiries for parish records please see Saint Faustina Kowalska Parish, Nanticoke.
4—HOLY TRINITY (1894) Merged with Holy Child, St. Francis of Assisi, St. Stanislaus, St. Joseph and St. Mary of Czestochowa, Nanticoke. Worship site for St. Faustina Kowalska Parish, Nanticoke.
5—ST. JOSEPH (1888) [CEM] Closed. For inquiries for parish records please see Saint Faustina Kowalska Parish, Nanticoke.
6—ST. MARY OF CZESTOCHOWA (1901) [CEM] (Polish), Merged with Holy Trinity, Holy Child, St. Francis of Assisi, St. Stanislaus and St. Joseph, Nanticoke. Worship site for St. Faustina Kowalska Parish, Nanticoke.
Mailing Address: c/o Saint Faustina Kowalska Parish, 520 S. Hanover St., Nanticoke, 18634.
7—ST. STANISLAUS (1875) [CEM] (Polish), Closed. For inquiries for parish records see Saint Faustina Kowalska Parish, Nanticoke.

NICHOLSON, WYOMING CO., ST. PATRICK (1888) [CEM] Linked with Our Lady of the Abingtons, Dalton.
205 Main St., P.O. Box 409, Nicholson, 18446.
Tel: 570-942-6602; Email: spolachurch@gmail.com; Web: www.spolachurch.weebly.com. Rev. Arbogaste Satoun; Deacon Paul J. Brojack.
Catechesis Religious Program—Students 38.

OLD FORGE, LACKAWANNA CO.
1—ST. LAWRENCE O'TOOLE (1895) Closed. Worship site for Prince of Peace, Old Forge (Tel: 570-457-5900).
2—ST. MARY (1897) (Italian), Closed. Worship site for Prince of Peace Parish, Old Forge (Tel: 570-457-5900).
3—ST. MICHAEL (1905) (Polish), Closed. For inquiries for parish records please see Prince of Peace Parish, Old Forge (Tel: 570-457-5900).
4—PRINCE OF PEACE PARISH, OLD FORGE (1895)
123 W Grace St., Old Forge, 18518.
Tel: 570-457-5900; Fax: 570-457-5896; Email: ofparishes@comcast.net. Rev. August A. Ricciardi.
Worship Sites—
St. Mary Church—
St. Lawrence O'Toole Church, 620 S. Main St., Old Forge, 18518.
Catechesis Religious Program—Students 205.
5—ST. STANISLAUS, Closed. For inquiries for parish records please see Prince of Peace Parish, Old Forge (Tel: 570-457-5900).

OLYPHANT, LACKAWANNA CO.
1—HOLY CROSS PARISH (1875) [CEM] Merger of St. Patrick, Holy Ghost (Slovak), Olyphant and St. Michael the Archangel, Olyphant. Linked with Blessed Sacrament, Throop.
200 Delaware Ave., Olyphant, 18447.
Tel: 570-489-0752; Email: sphg@verizon.net. Rev. Msgr. Michael J. Delaney.
Worship Site: St. Patrick Church.
Catechesis Religious Program— Total combined with St. Michael the Archangel, Olyphant & Holy Ghost, Olyphant. Students 221.
2—HOLY GHOST (1888) (Slovak), Closed. For inquiries for parish records see Holy Cross Parish, Olyphant (Tel: 570-489-0752).
3—ST. MICHAEL THE ARCHANGEL (1909) [CEM] (Polish), Closed. For inquiries for parish records see Holy Cross Parish, Olyphant (Tel: 570-489-0752).
4—ST. PATRICK (1875) Closed. For inquiries for parish records please see Holy Cross Parish, Olyphant. Worship site for Holy Cross Parish (Tel: 570-489-0752).

PARDEESVILLE, LUZERNE CO., ST. NAZARIUS (1966) (Italian), Closed. For inquiries for parish records please see Queen of Heaven Parish, Hazleton (Tel: 570-454-8797).

PECKVILLE, LACKAWANNA CO., SACRED HEART OF JESUS (1946)
1101 Willow St., Peckville, 18452. Rev. Msgr. Peter P. Madus, (Retired).
Catechesis Religious Program—Students 177.

PITTSTON, LUZERNE CO.
1—ST. CASIMIR'S (1890) (Lithuanian), Closed. For inquiries for parish records please see St. John the Evangelist, Pittston (Tel: 570-654-0053).
2—ST. JOHN THE BAPTIST (1892) [CEM 2] (Slovak), Closed. For inquiries for parish records please see St. John the Evangelist, Pittston (Tel: 570-654-0053).
3—ST. JOHN THE EVANGELIST (1854) [CEM] Linked with St. Joseph Marello, Pittston
35 William St., Pittston, 18640. Tel: 570-654-0053; Email: angelsofsje@aol.com; Web: www.stjohnspittston.com. Rev. Joseph G. Elston; Jackson Pinhero; Rev. John J. Kulavich, In Res., (Retired); Sr. Kieran Williams, I.H.M., Pastoral Assoc.; Deacon David E. Marx.
Res.: 237 William St., Pittston, 18640.
Catechesis Religious Program—JoAnne McHale, D.R.E. Students 168.
4—ST. JOSEPH (1909) (Polish), Closed. For inquiries for parish records please see St. John the Evangelist, Pittston (Tel: 570-654-0053).
5—ST. JOSEPH MARELLO PARISH, (Italian)
237 William St., Pittston, 18640. Tel: 570-654-6902; Fax: 570-655-5448. Revs. Jackson Pinheiro, O.S.J.; John D. Shearer, O.S.J.; Deacon Santo Agolino.
Worship Site: Our Lady of Mt. Carmel Church, Pittston, Luzerne Co.
Catechesis Religious Program—Students 250.
6—ST. MARY'S ASSUMPTION (1863) (German), Closed. For inquiries for parish records please see Our Lady of the Eucharist Parish, Pittston (Tel: 570-654-0263).
Mailing Address: 535 N. Main St., Pittston, 18640.
7—ST. MARY, HELP OF CHRISTIANS (1851) [CEM] Closed. Worship site of Our Lady of the Eucharist Parish, Pittston (Tel: 570-654-0263).
535 N. Main St., Pittston, 18640.
8—OUR LADY OF MT. CARMEL (1904) [CEM] (Italian) Merged with St. Rocco, Pittston and part of St. Joseph Marello Parish, Pittston. Parish worship site of St. Joseph Marello Parish (Tel: 570-654-6902).
9—OUR LADY OF THE EUCHARIST PARISH, [CEM 2]
535 N. Main St., Pittston, 18640. Tel: 570-654-0263; Email: olepittston@gmail.com; Web: www.eucharist-pittston.org. Rev. Jeffrey J. Walsh, V.E., Sacramental Min.; Sr. Mary Ann Cody, I.H.M., Parish Life Coord.
Worship Site: St. Mary, Help of Christians Church.
Catechesis Religious Program—Students 77.
10—ST. ROCCO (1919) [CEM] (Italian), Closed. For inquiries for parish records contact the chancery. For inquiries for parish records contact St. Joseph Marello Parish, Pittston (Tel: 570-654-6902).

PLAINS, LUZERNE CO.
1—SS. PETER AND PAUL (1898) [CEM] (Polish), Merged with Sacred Heart, Plains and St. Joseph, Hudson. Rev. John C. Lambert.
Res.: 13 Hudson Rd., Plains, 18705.
Catechesis Religious Program—Students 146.
2—SACRED HEART (1883) Merged with St. Joseph's, Hudson & SS. Peter and Paul, Plains (Tel: 570-825-6663).

PLEASANT MOUNT, WAYNE CO.
1—ST. JAMES (1887) For inquiries for parish records please see St. Katharine Drexel, 361 Great Bend Tpke., Pleasant Mount, PA (Tel: 570-785-3838). Worship site for St. Katharine Drexel.
2—ST. KATHARINE DREXEL PARISH (1887) Merger of St. James, Pleasant Mount & St. Juliana, Rock Lake. Linked with Ascension Parish, Forest City.
612 Hudson St., Forest City, 18421. P.O. Box 53, Pleasant Mount, 18453. Rev. Brian J.T. Clarke, J.C.L.
Worship Sites—
St. James Church—361 Great Bend Tpke., Pleasant Mount, 18453.
St. Juliana Church, Creamton Dr., Rte. 247, Rock Lake, PA 18453.
Catechesis Religious Program—Students 4.
Missions—St. Cecilia—Closed.
Assumption of the B.V.M., Closed.

PLYMOUTH, LUZERNE CO.
1—ALL SAINTS PARISH (1885) [CEM 3] Merger of Nativity B.V.M., St. Stephen and St. Vincent de Paul, Plymouth.
66 Willow St., Plymouth, 18651. Tel: 570-779-5323; Email: allsaints66@comcast.net; Web: www.allsaintsplymouth.com. Rev. Jacek J. Bialkowski.
Worship Site: Nativity B.V.M. Church, Plymouth, Luzerne Co.
Catechesis Religious Program—Students 145.
2—ST. JOHN THE BAPTIST (1899) (Polish), Merged with St. Anthony of Padua, Larksville and SS. Cyril and Methodius, Edwardsville. Rev. Gerald J. Gurka, 126

Nesbitt St., Larksville, 18651. Tel: 570-779-9620; Fax: 570-779-7652; Deacon Frank H. Hine.
3—ST. STEPHEN (1886) (Slovak), Closed. For Parish records see All Saints, Plymouth (Tel: 570-779-5323).
4—ST. VINCENT DE PAUL (1872) [CEM] Closed. For Parish records see All Saints, Plymouth (Tel: 570-779-5323).
101 Church St., Plymouth, 18651.
POCONO PINES, MONROE CO.
1—ST. MAXIMILIAN KOLBE (1985) Merged with Christ the King, Blakeslee (closed) and Our Lady of the Lake, Pocono Pines to become St. Maximilian Kolbe Parish. Rev. Sean G. Carpenter; Deacons Frank Gisoldi; Thomas V. Amoroso.
Res.: 5112 Pocono Crest Rd., P.O. Box O, Pocono Pines, 18350.
Worship Site: Our Lady of the Lake Church.
Catechesis Religious Program—Students 134.
2—OUR LADY OF THE LAKE (1985) Merged with Christ the King, Blakeslee, closed. For inquiries for parish records please contact St. Maximilian Kolbe, Pocono Pines. Worship site for St. Maximilian Kolbe Parish, Pocono Pines (Tel: 570-646-6424).
ROCK LAKE, WAYNE CO., ST. JULIANA (1838) Merged with St. Katharine Drexel, Pleasant Mount & linked with Sacred Heart & St. Joseph, Forest City. For inquiries for parish records, see St. Katharine Drexel, Pleasant Mount (Tel: 570-785-3838).
ROYAL, SUSQUEHANNA CO., ST. PIUS X (1967) Merged with Corpus Christi, Montdale. Worship site for St. John Vianney Parish. Rev. Michael J. Kirwin; Deacon Edwin L. Salva Sr.
Res.: 3615 State Rte 106, Clifford Township, 18470.
Office & Mailing Address: c/o St. John Vianney Parish, 704 Montdale Rd., Scott Twp., 18447.
SAYRE, BRADFORD CO., EPIPHANY PARISH (1888) See separate listing.
304 S. Elmer Ave., Sayre, 18840.
Tel: 570-888-9641, Ext. 2; Email: epiphanyparishoffice304@gmail.com; Web: thechurchoftheepiphany.com. Revs. Andrew S. Hvozdovic; Jose Kuriappilly.
School—Epiphany Elementary School, (Grades PreK-6), 627 Stephenson St., Sayre, 18840.
Tel: 570-888-5802; Fax: 570-888-2362; Email: kkathleen902@gmail.com. Sr. Kathleen Kelly, I.H.M., Prin. Students 107.
Catechesis Religious Program—Students 132.
Mission—Our Lady of Perpetual Help, Ridgebury, Bradford Co.
SHAVERTOWN, LUZERNE CO., ST. THERESE (1926) Linked with St. Frances Cabrini Church, Wyoming, PA.
64 Davis St., Shavertown, 18708. Tel: 570-696-1144; Email: jpaisley@sttherese-shavertown.com; Web: stthereses-shavertown.com. Rev. James J. Paisley.
Catechesis Religious Program—Students 466.
SHOHOLA, PIKE CO., ST. ANN'S (1928) [CEM] Linked with St. John Neumann, Lords Valley.
Mailing Address: 125 Richardson Ave., Shohola, 18458. Tel: 570-832-4275; Email: stann@ptd.net; Web: www.stannshohola.org. Rev. Edward J. Casey; Deacon Joseph Connelly.
Res.: 123 Richardson Ave., Shohola, 18458.
Catechesis Religious Program—Mary Bajda, D.R.E. Students 87.
Missions—St. Mary of the Assumption—Lackawaxen, Pike Co.
Sacred Heart of Jesus, Greeley, Pike Co.
SIMPSON, LACKAWANNA CO., ST. MICHAEL (1903) [CEM] (Polish), Merged with St. Rose of Lima Parish, Carbondale (Tel: 570-282-2991). Worship site for St. Rose of Lima.
6 N. Church St., Carbondale, 18407.
Tel: 570-282-2991; Email: strose@echoes.net; Web: www.strosecarbondale.weconnect.com. Rev. James Price, C.P.
Res.: 46 Midland St., Simpson, 18407.
SOUTH WAVERLY, BRADFORD CO., ST. JOHN THE EVANGELIST (1902) Closed. For inquiries for parish records please see Epiphany Parish, Sayre (Tel: 570-888-9641).
SOUTH WILLIAMSPORT, LYCOMING CO., ST. LAWRENCE (1931) Linked with St. Boniface, Williamsport.
821 W. Central Ave., Williamsport, 17702.
Tel: 570-326-1544; Fax: 570-326-6746; Email: stboniface@comcast.net; Web: stlawrencecatholic.com. Mailing Address: 326 Washington Blvd., Williamsport, 17701. Revs. William Corcoran; James Tracy; Rev. Msgr. Stephen D. McGough, Pastor Emeritus, (Retired).
Catechesis Religious Program—Students 171.
STROUDSBURG, MONROE CO., ST. LUKE (1968)
818 Main St., Stroudsburg, 18360. Rev. Carmen J. Perry; Deacons Thomas W. Hogan Jr.; Philip F. Zimich.
Res.: 906 Main St., Stroudsburg, 18360.
Catechesis Religious Program—Students 400.
SUGAR NOTCH, LUZERNE CO.
1—HOLY FAMILY PARISH (1901) [CEM] Consolidation.
828 Main St., Sugar Notch, 18706. Tel: 570-822-8983 ; Email: hfsc828@ptd.net. Rev. Joseph R. Kakareka.
Catechesis Religious Program—Students 33.
2—SS. PETER AND PAUL CHAPEL (1847) (Lithuanian), Closed. For inquiries for parish records please see Holy Family Parish, Sugar Notch (Tel: 570-822-8983).
SUSQUEHANNA, SUSQUEHANNA CO., ST. JOHN THE EVANGELIST (1847) [CEM] Linked with St. Lawrence, Great Bend & St. Martin of Tours, Jackson. It is now the primary worship site of the newly consolidated Most Holy Trinity Parish, Susquehanna.
15 E. Church St., Susquehanna, 18847.
Tel: 570-853-4634; Email: jointoffice3@gmail.com. Rev. David W. Cramer.
Catechesis Religious Program—Students 100.
SWOYERSVILLE, LUZERNE CO.
1—ST. ELIZABETH ANN SETON PARISH (1895) [CEM] (Slovak)
116 Hughes St., Swoyersville, 18704.
Tel: 570-287-6624; Email: setonpa@aol.com; Web: www.setonpa.com. Rev. Joseph J. Pisaneschi; Deacon John B. Ziegler.
Worship Site: Holy Trinity Church.
Catechesis Religious Program—Students 174.
2—HOLY NAME OF JESUS (1905) Closed. Merged with St. Mary of Czestochowa and Holy Trinity, Swoyersville. For inquires for parish records contact St. Elizabeth Ann Seton Parish, Swoyersville (Tel: 570-287-6624).
3—HOLY TRINITY (1895) Merged with Holy Name/St. Mary, Swoyersville. Renamed St. Elizabeth Ann Seton Parish. Worship site for St. Elizabeth Ann Seton Parish.
4—ST. MARY OF CZESTOCHOWA (1909) Closed. Merged with Holy Name of Jesus, Swoyersville. For inquires for parish records contact St. Elizabeth Ann Seton Parish, Swoyersville (Tel: 570-287-6624).
TANNERSVILLE, MONROE CO., OUR LADY OF VICTORY (1968)
327 Cherry Lane Rd., P.O. Box 195, Tannersville, 18372. Tel: 570-629-4575; Email: victory2@ptd.net; Web: olvchurch.com. Rev. Richard E. Czachor, V.E.
Catechesis Religious Program—Students 270.
TAYLOR, LACKAWANNA CO.
1—IMMACULATE CONCEPTION (1898) Closed. For inquiries contact Divine Mercy Parish, Scranton.
312 Davis St., 18505. Tel: 570-344-1724.
2—ST. JOHN THE BAPTIST (1904) (Slovak), Closed. For inquiries contact Divine Mercy Parish, Scranton.
312 Davis St., 18505. Tel: 570-344-1724.
THROOP, LACKAWANNA CO.
1—ST. ANTHONY, Merged with St. Bridget and St. John to form Blessed Sacrament Parish, Throop. Linked with Holy Cross, Olyphant (Tel: 570-489-1963).
2—BLESSED SACRAMENT PARISH (1911) [CEM] (Polish) Merger of St. Anthony's, St. Bridget's and St. John the Baptist, Throop. Linked with Holy Cross, Olyphant.
215 Rebecca St., Throop, 18519. Rev. Msgr. Michael J. Delaney.
Worship Site: St. Anthony Church, Throop, Lackawanna Co.
Catechesis Religious Program—Students 85.
3—ST. BRIDGET'S (1916) Closed. For inquiries for parish records please see Blessed Sacrament Parish, Throop (Tel: 570-489-1963).
4—ST. JOHN THE BAPTIST (1905) [CEM] (Slovak), Closed. For inquiries for parish records please contact Blessed Sacrament Parish, Throop (Tel: 570-489-1963).
TOBYHANNA, MONROE CO., ST. ANN (1923) [CEM 2] Merged with St. Mary of the Mount, Mount Pocono & St. Bernadette, Canadensis. Worship site for Most Holy Trinity Parish, Cresco.
Mailing Address: 236 Rte. 390, Cresco, 18326. Revs. John B. Boyle; Gregory F. Loughney.
Res.: Main St., P.O. Box 188, Tobyhanna, 18466-0188.
Worship Site: Msgr. McHugh Elementary School—212 Rte 390, Cresco, 18326.
Catechesis Religious Program—Students 674.
TOWANDA, BRADFORD CO., SS. PETER AND PAUL (1841) [CEM 3]
106 Third St., Towanda, 18848. Rev. Edward L. Michelini.
Catechesis Religious Program—Students 129.
Mission—Immaculate Conception, Closed.
TUNKHANNOCK, WYOMING CO., NATIVITY OF BLESSED VIRGIN MARY (1884) [CEM 2] Linked with St. Mary of the Lake, Lake Winola.
99 E. Tioga St., P.O. Box 186, Tunkhannock, 18657-0186. Tel: 570-836-3275; Email: nativitybvmchurch@frontier.com, Rev. Patrick L. Albert; Deacon Raymond A. Pieretti.
Catechesis Religious Program—Students 176.
WAYMART, WAYNE CO., ST. MARY (1915) [CEM]
242 Carbondale Rd., P.O. Box 160, Waymart, 18472. Tel: 570-488-6440; Email: stmarysway@echoes.net. Rev. Joseph S. Sitko, Sacramental Min., (Retired); Deacon Edward T. Kelly, Parish Life Coord.
Catechesis Religious Program—Students 43.
Mission—St. Patrick, Closed.
WELLSBORO, TIOGA CO., ST. PETER'S (1879) [CEM 2]
47 Central Ave., Wellsboro, 16901. Rev. David W. Bechtel.
Catechesis Religious Program—Students 180.
Mission—Sacred Heart, Closed.
WEST HAZLETON, LUZERNE CO.
1—ST. FRANCIS OF ASSISI (1940) Closed. For inquiries for parish records please see Holy Name of Jesus Parish, West Hazleton (Tel: 570-454-3933).
2—HOLY NAME OF JESUS PARISH
213 W. Green St., West Hazleton, 18202.
Tel: 570-454-3933; Fax: 570-454-8326; Email: holynameparish@ptd.net. Rev. Peter J. O'Rourke. In Res., Rev. Msgr. Arthur J. Kaschenbach, (Retired).
Worship Site: Transfiguration Church.
Catechesis Religious Program—Students 55.
3—TRANSFIGURATION (1907) [CEM] (Polish), Closed. For inquiries for parish records please see Holy Name of Jesus Parish, West Hazleton. Worship site for Holy Name of Jesus Parish, West Hezleton (Tel: 570-454-3933).
WEST PITTSTON, LUZERNE CO.
1—CORPUS CHRISTI PARISH (1910)
605 Luzerne Ave., West Pittston, 18643.
Tel: 570-654-2753; Fax: 570-654-9244; Email: ccrectory@CorpusChristiNEPA.com; Web: www.corpuschristinepa.com. Rev. Msgr. John J. Sempa, V.F.; Deacon James R. Meizanis; Rev. Michael S. Drevitch, In Res.
Immaculate Conception West Pittston & Church of the Holy Redeemer
Worship Sites—
Holy Redeemer—2435 State Route 92, Falls.
Immaculate Conception.
Catechesis Religious Program—Students 273.
2—IMMACULATE CONCEPTION (1910) Closed. For inquiries for parish records please see Corpus Christi Parish, West Pittston. Worship site for Corpus Christi Parish, West Pittston.
WEST WYOMING, LUZERNE CO.
1—SAINT MONICA PARISH (1953)
363 W. 8th St., West Wyoming, 18644. Rev. Peter A. Tomczak; Deacon William G. Jenkins.
Worship Sites—
Our Lady of Sorrows Church, West Wyoming.
Catechesis Religious Program—Students 132.
2—OUR LADY OF SORROWS (1953) Closed. For inquiries for parish records please see Saint Monica Parish, West Wyoming. Worship site for Saint Monica Parish, West Wyoming (Tel: 570-693-1991).
WESTON, LUZERNE CO., SACRED HEART (1888) [CEM]
554 Main St., P.O. Box A, Weston, 18256. Rev. Patrick D. McDowell.
Catechesis Religious Program—Students 10.
WHITE HAVEN, LUZERNE CO., ST. PATRICK (1874) [CEM]
521 Northumberland St., White Haven, 18661. Rev. Michael J. Kloton; Sr. Jane Gaughan, I.H.M., Coord. Parish Svcs.
Office: 411 Allegheny St., White Haven, 18661.
Catechesis Religious Program—Students 125.
WHITE MILLS, WAYNE CO., ST. JOSEPH (1968) Closed. For inquiries for parish records please contact St. John the Evangelist, Honesdale (Tel: 570-253-4561).
WILKES-BARRE, LUZERNE CO.
1—ST. ALOYSISUS (1899) Closed. For inquiries for parish records please contact St. Robert Bellarmine, Wilkes-Barre. Worship site for St. Robert Bellarmine, Wilkes-Barre (Tel: 570-823-3791).
2—ST. ANDRE BESSETTE PARISH
Mailing Address: 668 N. Main St., Wilkes-Barre, 18705. Tel: 570-823-4988; Fax: 570-823-5932; Email: ccnewb@live.com; Web: standrebessettewb.com. Rev. Kenneth M. Seegar.
3—ST. ANDREW PARISH (1920) Merger of St. Patrick and St. Boniface, Wilkes-Barre (now closed). Revs. Joseph A. Kearney, Sacramental Min., (Retired); James E. McGahagan, Pastor Emeritus, (Retired); Deacon William F. Behm, Parish Life Coord.
Res.: 316 Parrish St., Wilkes-Barre, 18702.
Tel: 570-823-1948; Tel: 570-823-8330; Email: stbonstpat@verizon.net; Web: standrewwilkesbarre.org.
Worship Site: St. Patrick Church, Wilkes-Barre.
Catechesis Religious Program—Judy Flaherty, D.R.E.; Karen Legge, D.R.E. Students 24.
4—ST. BENEDICT PARISH (1882) Merger of Blessed Sacrament, St. Dominic and St. Francis, Wilkes-Barre.
155 Austin Ave., Wilkes-Barre, 18705. Rev. Joseph A. Kearney, (Retired); Deacon Donald J. Crane.
Worship Site: St. Dominic Church, Wilkes Barre, Luzerne Co.
Catechesis Religious Program—Students 152.
5—BLESSED SACRAMENT (1917) [CEM] Closed. For inquiries for parish records please see St. Benedict Parish, Wilkes-Barre (Tel: 570-822-8871).
6—ST. BONIFACE (1896) (German), Closed. For inquiries for parish records please contact St. Andrew Parish, Wilkes-Barre (Tel: 570-823-1948).

7—ST. CASIMIR (1889) [CEM] (Lithuanian), Closed. For inquiries for parish records please contact St. Robert Bellarmine Parish, Wilkes-Barre (Tel: 570-823-3791).

8—ST. DOMINIC (1882) Closed. For inquiries for parish records please contact St. Benedict Parish, Wilkes-Barre (Tel: 570-822-8871). Worship site for St. Benedict Parish, Wilkes-Barre.

9—ST. FRANCIS OF ASSISI (1913) (Lithuanian), Closed. For inquiries for parish records please contact St. Benedict Parish, Wilkes-Barre (Tel: 570-822-8871).

10—HOLY ROSARY (1906) (Italian), Closed. For inquiries for parish records please see St. Andrew Parish, Wilkes-Barre (Tel: 570-823-1948).

11—HOLY SAVIOUR (1895) Closed. For inquiries for parish records please contact St. Andre Bessette Parish, Wilkes-Barre. Worship site for St. Andre Bessette Parish, Wilkes-Barre (Tel: 570-823-4988).

12—HOLY TRINITY (1893) [CEM 2] (Lithuanian), Closed. For inquiries for parish records please see Our Lady of Hope Parish, Wilkes-Barre (Tel: 570-824-7832).

13—ST. JOHN THE BAPTIST (1924) (Slovak), Closed. For inquiries for parish records see St. Benedict, Wilkes-Barre (Tel: 570-822-8871).

14—ST. JOHN THE EVANGELIST (1927) Merged with Sacred Heart of Jesus, Wilkes-Barre. See St. Andre Bessette Parish for records (Tel: 570-823-4988).

15—ST. JOSEPH (Georgetown) (1898) Closed. For inquiries for parish records please see Our Lady of Hope Parish, Wilkes-Barre (Tel: 570-824-7832).

16—ST. JOSEPH (1927) (Slovak), Closed. For inquiries for parish records please contact Our Lady of Fatima Parish, Wilkes-Barre (Tel: 570-823-4168).

17—ST. MARY OF THE IMMACULATE CONCEPTION (1845) [CEM] Closed. For inquiries for parish records please contact Our Lady of Fatima Parish, Wilkes-Barre. Worship site for Our Lady of Fatima Parish, Wilkes-Barre (Tel: 570-823-4168).

18—MATERNITY OF THE BLESSED VIRGIN MARY (1885) [CEM 2] (Polish), Closed. For inquiries for parish records please contact Our Lady of Hope Parish, Wilkes-Barre. Worship site for Our Lady of Hope Parish, Wilkes-Barre (Tel: 570-824-7832).

19—ST. NICHOLAS (1856) [CEM 2] (German)
226 S. Washington St., Wilkes-Barre, 18701-2897. Tel: 570-823-7736; Tel: 570-823-5842; Fax: 570-823-0256; Email: stnicholas@stnicholasrc.org. Revs. Joseph D. Verespy; Fidel Ticona, C.S.C.; Rev. Msgr. Joseph G. Rauscher, Pastor Emeritus, (Retired); Michael Golubiewski.
Catechesis Religious Program—Mr. James McDermott, D.R.E. Students 249.
Convent—254 S. Washington St., Wilkes-Barre, 18701. Sr. Immacolata Scargoni, S.C.C.

20—OUR LADY OF FATIMA PARISH, Merger of St. Mary of the Immaculate Conception, St. Joseph (Slovak) and St. Therese, Wilkes-Barre.
134 S. Washington St., P.O. Box 348, Wilkes-Barre, 18701. Rev. J. Duane Gavitt; Deacon Leo R. Thompson.
Worship Site: St. Mary of the Immaculate Conception.
Catechesis Religious Program—Students 94.

21—OUR LADY OF HOPE PARISH (1885) [CEM 2] (Polish) Merger of Holy Trinity, St. Joseph and Maternity of the B.V.M., Wilkes-Barre.
40 Park Ave., Wilkes-Barre, 18702. Rev. John S. Terry; Deacon Joseph F. DeVizia. In Res., Rev. Richard G. Ghezzi.
Worship Site: Maternity of the Blessed Virgin Mary Church, Wilkes-Barre, Luzerne Co.
Catechesis Religious Program—Students 45.

22—ST. PATRICK (1920) Closed. For inquiries for parish records please contact St. Andrew, Wilkes-Barre. Worship site for St. Andrew Parish, Wilkes-Barre (Tel: 570-823-1948).

23—ST. ROBERT BELLARMINE PARISH aka St. Aloysius Church (1899) Linked with Exaltation of the Holy Cross, Hanover Twp.
143 W. Division St., Wilkes-Barre, 18706. Tel: 570-823-3791, Ext. 2; Email: stalschurch@staloysiuswb.com. Rev. Richard J. Cirba; Deacon Raymond J. Lenahan.
Worship Site: St. Aloysius Church, Wilkes-Barre, Luzerne Co.
Catechesis Religious Program—Students 204.

24—SACRED HEART (1896) [CEM] Closed. For inquiries for parish records please contact St. Andre Bessette Parish, Wilkes-Barre (Tel: 570-823-4988).

25—ST. STANISLAUS KOSTKA (1908) [CEM] (Polish), Closed. Worship site for St. Andre Bessette Parish, Wilkes-Barre (Tel: 570-823-4988).

26—ST. THERESE (1929) Closed. For inquiries for parish records please contact Our Lady of Fatima Parish, Wilkes-Barre (Tel: 570-823-4168).

WILLIAMSPORT, LYCOMING CO.

1—ST. ANN (1959)
1220 Northway Rd., Williamsport, 17701. Rev. John J. Victoria; Deacon Stephen Frye.
Catechesis Religious Program—Students 117.
Mission—Assumption of the B.V.M., Closed. For records see St. Ann, Williamsport Cascade, Lycoming Co.

2—ANNUNCIATION, Closed. For inquiries see St. Joseph the Worker Parish, Williamsport (Tel: 570-323-9456). Worship site for St. Joseph the Worker.
702 W. 4th St., Williamsport, 17701.

3—ASCENSION (1907) Closed. For inquiries contact St. Joseph the Worker Parish, 711 W. Edwin St., Williamsport, PA (Tel: 570-323-9456).

4—ST. BONIFACE (1853) (German) Linked with St. Lawrence, South Williamsport.
326 Washington Blvd., Williamsport, 17701. Tel: 570-326-1544; Fax: 570-326-6746; Email: stboniface@comcast.net; Web: stbonifacecatholic.com. Rev. William Corcoran; Rev. Msgr. Stephen D. McGough, Pastor Emeritus, (Retired); Rev. James Tracy.

5—HOLY ROSARY (1915) (Polish), Closed. For inquiries for parish records please contact St. Joseph the Worker, Williamsport (Tel: 570-323-9456).

6—ST. JOSEPH THE WORKER (1865) [CEM]
711 W. Edwin St., Williamsport, 17701. Tel: 570-323-9456; Fax: 570-323-3728; Email: office@sjwparish.com; Web: sjwparish.com. Rev. Brian F. Van Fossen; Deacon Stephen Frye; Ms. Makenzie Conner, Youth Min.; Mrs. Lauren Cooley, Stewardship Coord.; Mrs. Molly Eisley, Adult Faith Formation; James Foran, D.R.E.
Rectory—1000 Woodmont Ave., Williamsport, 17701.
Annunciation Church, 702 W. 4th St., Williamsport, 17701.

7—MATER DOLOROSA (1908) (Italian), Closed. For records see St. Joseph the Worker Parish, Williamsport (Tel: 570-323-9456).

WYALUSING, BRADFORD CO.

1—ST. MARY OF THE ASSUMPTION (1950) Merged Linked with St. Joachim, Meshoppen. Worship site for Our Lady of Perpetual Help, Wyalusing.

2—OUR LADY OF PERPETUAL HELP PARISH, Merger of St. Mary of the Assumption, Wyalusing and St. Joachim, Meshoppen.
245 State St., Wyalusing, 18853. Rev. Peter Tran, Admin.
Worship Sites—
St. Joachim Church—Sterling St., Meshoppen.
St. Mary of the Assumption Church, Wyalusing, Bradford Co.
Catechesis Religious Program—Students 18.
Mission—St. Anthony, Closed. Stowell, Wyoming Co.

WYOMING, LUZERNE CO., ST. JOSEPH'S (1914) [CEM] (Polish), Closed. For inquiries for parish records please contact Saint Monica Parish, West Wyoming.

Chaplains of Public Institutions

DALLAS. *State Correctional Institution*, Dallas, 18612. Tel: 570-675-1101.

EAST STROUDSBURG. *East Stroudsburg State University*, 200 Prospect St., East Stroudsburg, 18301. Tel: 570-422-3525; Fax: 570-422-3410. Rev. Gerald W. Shantillo.

LA PLUME. *Keystone College*. Rev. Msgr. Joseph G. Quinn, J.D., J.C.L.
Clarks Summit. Tel: 570-586-1741.

MUNCY. *Muncy Prison*, Muncy. Tel: 570-546-3900. Rev. Glenn E. McCreary, V.E., Chap.
Resurrection, 75 Musser Ln., Muncy, 17756.

WILKES-BARRE. *Geisinger Wyoming Valley Hospital*, Wilkes-Barre. Tel: 570-822-9561. Rev. Joseph A. Kearney, (Retired)
St. Benedict, 155 Austin Ave., Wilkes-Barre, 18705.

WILLIAMSPORT. *Lycoming College*, 700 College Pl., Box 149, Williamsport, 17701. Tel: 570-321-4111. Rev. John J. Victoria.

On Special or Other Diocesan Assignment:
Rev. Msgr.—
Grimalia, Vincent J., Diocesan Coord. for Ecumenical and Interreligious Affairs, (Retired), St. Luke's Villa, 80 E. Northampton St., Wilkes-Barre, 18701. Tel: 570-829-1471
Revs.—
Elston, Joseph G., Chap. Ministry for the Deaf, 529 Stephenon St., Duryea, 18642. Pastor, St. John the Evangelist/ St. Joesph Marello Parish, Pittston; Chaplain, Marywood University
Ghezzi, Richard G., Chap., Little Flower Manor & St. Therese Residence, 40 Park Ave., Wilkes-Barre, 18201. Tel: 570-824-7832; Tel: 570-824-7833. St. Luke's Villa, 80 E. Northampton St., Wilkes-Barre, 18701.

On Duty Outside the Diocese:
Rev. Msgr.—
Rossi, Walter R., Rector, 400 Michigan Ave., N.E., Washington, DC 20017. Tel: 202-526-8300
Revs.—
Connor, Charles P., Ph.D., S.T.L., 16300 Old Emmitsburg Rd., Emmitsburg, MD 21727
Doherty, Daniel J., S.S., St. Charles Villa, 603 Maiden Choice Ln., Baltimore, MD 21228. Tel: 410-864-4005; Tel: 410-747-1211. 5400 Roland Ave., Baltimore, MD 21210
Kirby, Shane L., V.E., S.T.L., J.C.L., Villa Stritch, Via della Nocetta, 63, 00164 Rome, Italy
Melnick, John E., c/o St. Mary-St. Anthony Parish, 615 N. 7th St., Kansas City, KS 66101. Tel: 913-371-1408
Munkelt, Richard A., 1360 Pleasant Valley Way, West Orange, NJ 07052. Tel: 201-319-1765
Pilon, Jean-Pierre G., St. Mary's Church, P.O. Box 599, Campbellford, ON Canada K0L 1L0. Tel: 705-653-1093
Tudgay, Jeffrey D., The Catholic University of America, Curley Hall, 620 Michigan Ave., Washington, DC 20064
Washington, Christopher T., J.C.D., S.T.D., Apostolic Nunciature in Lithuania, c/o Apostolic Nunciature in the U.S., 3339 Massachusetts Ave., N.W., Washington, DC 20008.

Military Chaplains:
Revs.—
Fullerton, Daniel, Chap. CHC, USN, USS Essex LH02, Unit 100150, Box 1, Fpo, AP 96643
Hochreiter, Robert S., Chap., Col., U.S.A.F., 2270 White House Cove, Newport News, VA 23602. Tel: 757-874-8602
Kelly, Brian F., Chap., Cap., U.S.N., 7183 Willett Cir., Carlsbad, CA 92011. Tel: 858-577-1333.

Unassigned or Leave of Absence:
Rev. Msgr.—
Crynes, J. Peter
Very Rev.—
Poplawski, John F., V.F.
Revs.—
Altavilla, Philip A.
Boylan, Martin M.
Clay, Christopher R.
Drevitch, Michael S.
Ensey, Eric S.
Flanagan, Austin E.
Harris, Michael B.
Hawley, Gerard L.
Honhart, Mark A.
Kelly, Gregory W.
Kilpatrick, Andrew W.
Kita, John M.
Leonard, Albert P.
Meighan, Joseph F.
Motsay, Russell E.
O'Bell, John C.
Paulish, W. Jeffrey
Perrins, Samuel T.
Roberts, Marshall M.
Sahd, Christopher S.
Shoback, Thomas P.
Terrera, Carlos Bernardo
Vito, Alfred J.
Wasilewski, Marek, M.Id.
Wilson, Joseph B.
Young, Vincent J.
Ziebacz, Wieslaw M.

Retired:
Most Revs.—
Dougherty, John M., D.D., (Retired), 1600 Green Ridge St., Dunmore, 18509. Tel: 570-241-5064. Auxiliary Bishop Emeritus of Scranton
Martino, Joseph F., D.D., Hist. E.D., (Retired), 685 York Rd., Warminster, 18974. Tel: 267-608-8557. Bishop Emeritus of Scranton
Timlin, James C., D.D., (Retired), 1600 Green Ridge St., 18509. Tel: 570-343-6170. Bishop Emeritus of Scranton
Rev. Msgrs.—
Banick, Thomas V., (Retired), 1342 Jefferson Ave., Dunmore, 18509. Tel: 570-343-5462
Beeda, Francis J., (Retired), 200 S. Meade St., Rm. 204, Wilkes-Barre, 18702. Tel: 570-822-3554
Bendik, John J., (Retired), Villa St. Joseph, 1600 Green Ridge St., Dunmore, 18509. Tel: 570-881-9564
Bergamo, John A., J.C.L., (Retired), 236 Rte. 390, Cresco, 18326. Tel: 570-460-5270
Esseff, John A., (Retired), 1600 Green Ridge St., Dunmore, 18509. Tel: 570-941-0986
Feldcamp, William J., (Retired), 1600 Green Ridge St., 18509. Tel: 570-561-8876
Kaschenbach, Arthur J., (Retired), Holy Name of Jesus Rect., 213 W. Green St., West Hazleton, 18201. Tel: 570-454-3933
Kelly, Joseph P., M.S.W., (Retired), Villa St. Joseph, 1600 Green Ridge St., Dunmore, 18509. Tel: 570-417-3072
Kulik, Alexander T., (Retired), 1600 Green Ridge St., 18509. Tel: 570-341-8881
Madus, Peter P., (Retired), 1600 Green Ridge St., Dunmore, 18509. Tel: 570-698-6667

McAndrews, Donald A., (Retired), 1600 Green Ridge St., 18509. Tel: 570-207-5586
McGarry, James J., (Retired), Holy Family Residence, 2500 Adams Ave., 18509
McGough, Stephen D., (Retired), P.O. Box 42, Williamsport, 17701
Rauscher, Joseph G., (Retired), Villa St. Joseph, 1600 Green Ridge St., Dunmore, 18509. Tel: 570-417-2193
Siconolfi, Constantine V., (Retired), 207 Karen Dr., 18505. Tel: 570-343-1001
Ward, William P., (Retired), 1600 Green Ridge St., 18509. Tel: 570-341-1558

Revs.—
Adonizio, Joseph J., (Retired), 154 Rock St., Pittston, 18640. Tel: 570-654-8032
Albosta, John T., (Retired), Villa St. Joseph, 1600 Green Ridge St., Dunmore, 18509. Tel: 570-267-4405
Alco, James J., (Retired), 68 West 8th St., Apt. B, Wyoming, 18644
Campbell, William D., (Retired), Little Flower Manor, 200 S. Meade St., Rm. 212, Wilkes-Barre, 18702
Cappeloni, Thomas A., (Retired), 27 E. 23rd St., Hazleton, 18202
Carr, Eugene R., (Retired), Villa St. Joseph, 1600 Green Ridge St., Dunmore, 18509. Tel: 570-371-7642
Cipriano, Joseph F., (Retired), Allied Srvs. Skilled Nursing & Rehab. Ctr., 303 Smallacombe Dr., Clarks Summit, 18411. Tel: 570-961-0328
Cortese, Patrick S., (Retired), Fritzengertown Senior Living, 159 S. Old Tpke. Rd., Drums, 18222
Culnane, William R., (Retired), 1600 Green Ridge St., 18509-2197. Tel: 570-677-5749
Cummings, Charles J., (Retired), 1600 Green Ridge St., Dunmore, 18509. Tel: 570-220-2070
Deviney, Raymond L., (Retired), Little Flower Manor, 200 S. Meade St., Wilkes-Barre, 18702. Tel: 570-823-6131
Dormer, David J., (Retired), 499 Evergreen Ln., Catawissa, 17820. Tel: 570-441-7496; Tel: 570-441-7496
Gaiardo, Martin J., (Retired), 499 Mulberry St., Apt. 1216, 18503. Tel: 570-347-4826
Gallia, Andrew R., (Retired), 620 Clark St., Rear, Old Forge, 18518. Tel: 570-457-3423
Greskiewicz, Joseph A., (Retired), 1600 Green Ridge St., Dunmore, 18509
Grippe, Louis A., (Retired), 359 Parsonage St., Pittston, 18640
Gunning, Eugene L., (Retired), P.O. Box J, Newfoundland, 18445. Tel: 570-881-2368
Horanzy, Joseph M., (Retired), 1600 Green Ridge St., Dunmore, 18509. Tel: 570-479-0446
Hudak, Thomas R., (Retired), 100 Greenbush St., 18508. Tel: 570-333-0486
Jeffrey, George A., (Retired), 1600 Green Ridge St., Dunmore, 18509. Tel: 570-814-2745
Karle, William J., (Retired), Highland Park Senior Living, 874 Schechter Dr., Wilkes-Barre Twp., 18702. Tel: 570-970-4600
Kearney, Joseph A., (Retired), 44 Calvin St., Wilkes Barre, 18705. Tel: 570-301-3735
Kilpatrick, John J., (Retired), 1600 Green Ridge St., Dunmore, 18509. Tel: 570-344-2154
Kizis, Kenneth G., (Retired), Little Flower Manor, 200 S. Meade St., Wilkes-Barre, 18702
Kulavich, John J., (Retired), 35 William St., Pittston, 18640. Tel: 570-653-0053
Langan, Vincent F., (Retired), Villa St. Joseph, 1600 Green Ridge St., Dunmore, 18509. Tel: 570-423-9556
Litcheck, Michael P., (Retired), St. Therese Assisted Living, 260 S. Meade St., Rm 17, Wilkes-Barre, 18702. Tel: 570-208-5346
Lyman, Edward P., (Retired), Villa St. Joseph, 1600 Green Ridge St., Dunmore, 18509. Tel: 570-614-8461
Maloney, Thomas J., (Retired), 1867 Stag Run, Pocono Lake, 18347. Tel: 570-646-1716
Manno, John K., (Retired), 1338 Elliott St., Williamsport, 17701. Tel: 570-337-1163
Marchetti, Michael H., (Retired), 2181 N.E. 67th St., Apt. 623, Fort Lauderdale, FL 33308. Tel: 570-947-8234
McGahagan, James E., (Retired), 63 Lockhart St., Wilkes-Barre, 18702. Tel: 570-825-7906
McHale, John F., (Retired), 11233B Snowflake Ct., Columbia, MD 21044. Tel: 410-992-4053
McKernan, Leo J., (Retired), Blandina Apartments - D, 68 W. Eighth St., Wyoming, 18644
Menghini, Peter D., (Retired), Allied Terrace, 100 Terrace Ln., Rm 319, 18505
Motsay, Joseph R., (Retired), 3645 N. Stirrup Dr., Beverly Hills, FL 34465
Mulhern, Kevin P., (Retired), 322 Chestnut St., Dunmore, 18512. Tel: 570-346-7479
Mullen, Paul M., (Retired), Mercy Center, P.O. Box 370, Dallas, 18612. Tel: 570-675-2131
O'Malley, Thomas J., (Retired), St. Mary's Villa Residence, 1 Pioneer Pl., Elmhurst, 18444. Tel: 570-842-5274
Obaza, Theodore L., (Retired), St. Therese Residence, 200 S. Meade St., Wilkes-Barre, 18702. Tel: 570-823-6131
Oldfield, Albert E., (Retired), 260 S. Meade St., Wilkes-Barre, 18702. Tel: 570-823-6131
Petruska, William M., (Retired), 78 Aberdeen Rd., Bld D, Moscow, 18444. Tel: 619-787-1184
Pickard, William B., Maryhouse Catholic Worker, (Retired), 55 E. 3rd St., New York, NY 10003. Tel: 212-777-9617
Rable, Cyril J., (Retired), Little Flower Manor, 200 South Meade St., Wilkes-Barre, 18702. Tel: 570-823-6131
Rafferty, Michael J., (Retired), 1600 Green Ridge St., 18509. Tel: 570-961-3723
Sarnecki, Thomas G., (Retired), 10036 63rd Ave., N. Bld. 5, Unit 18, St. Petersburg, FL 33708. Tel: 727-800-6650
Sinnott, Andrew R., (Retired), 400 N. Gates Ave., Apt. 2, Kingston, 18704
Sitko, Joseph S., (Retired), 684 Homestead St., Simpson, 18407. Tel: 570-282-0375
Turi, John J., (Retired), Villa St. Joseph, 1600 Green Ridge St., Dunmore, 18509
Urban, Anthony M., (Retired), 635 Church St., Swoyersville, 18704. Tel: 570-283-1763
Weber, Joseph O., (Retired), Holy Family Residence, 2500 Adams Ave., 18509
Yenkevich, Daniel J., (Retired), 846 Gibbons St., 18505. Tel: 570-961-0196
Zavacki, Richard A., (Retired), St. Luke's Villa, 80 E. Northampton St., Rm 109, Wilkes-Barre, 18701
Zipay, Michael J., (Retired), 1600 Green Ridge St., Dunmore, 18509.

INSTITUTIONS LOCATED IN DIOCESE

[A] SEMINARIES, RELIGIOUS

PITTSTON. *St. Joseph's Oblate Seminary*, 1880 Hwy. 315, Pittston, 18640. Tel: 570-654-7542; Fax: 570-654-8621; Email: provincial@osjoseph.org. Revs. Joseph D. Sibilano, O.S.J., Facility Dir. & Rector; Raymond Tabon, O.S.J.; Alvaro de Oliveira Joaquim, O.S.J., Dir. Portuguese Community; John D. Shearer, O.S.J., Vocation Dir.

[B] COLLEGES AND UNIVERSITIES

SCRANTON. *Marywood University*, (Grades Associate-Masters), 2300 Adams Ave., 18509.
Tel: 570-340-6053; Tel: 570-348-6211;
Fax: 570-340-6014; Email: persico@marywood.edu; Email: mbaron@marywood.edu; Web: www.marywood.edu. Sr. Mary Persico, I.H.M., Pres.; Dr. Renee Zehel, Vice Pres. for Univ. Advancement; Dr. Frances M. Zauhar, Dean, College of Liberal Arts & Sciences; Ann Boland-Chase, M.A., Vice Pres. for Enrollment Management and Student Success; James J. Sullivan, Dean, Professional Studies; Atty. Mary Theresa G. Paterson, Sec., Univ. & Gen. Counsel; Tammy McHale, Vice Pres. for Business Affairs and Treas.; Susan Turell, Provost; Ross Novak, Dean of Students; Lori Swanchak, Interim Dean, Health/Human Services. Sisters, Servants of the Immaculate Heart of Mary Religious Teachers 6; Lay Teachers 154; Sisters 13; Students 2,879.

The University of Scranton, (Grades Associate-Doctorate), (Society of Jesus) 18510.
Tel: 570-941-7400; Fax: 570-941-4097; Email: info@scranton.edu; Web: www.scranton.edu. Rev. Kevin P. Quinn, S.J., Pres.; Dr. Joseph H. Dreisbach, Assoc. Provost, Intl. Educ.; Patricia L. Tetreault, Assoc. Vice Pres. Human Resources; Mr. Edward J. Steinmetz, Sr. Vice Pres., Finance & Admin.; Mr. Gerald C. Zaboski, Vice Provost, Enrollment Mgmt. & External Affairs; Dr. Robert W. Davis Jr., Chief of Staff; Susan Bowen, CEO; Dr. Brian Conniff, Dean, College of Arts & Sciences; Dr. Michael Mensah, Dean, Kania School of Mgmt.; Julie Ferguson, Registrar; Dr. Debra A. Pellegrino, Dean, Panuska College of Professional Studies; Dr. Thomas Smith, Dir. Counseling Center; Dr. Anitra McShea, Vice Provost, Student Formation; Mr. Charles E. Kratz, Dean, Library; Robert B. Farrell Esq., Gen. Counsel; Gary R. Olsen, Vice Pres., Univ. Advancement; Revs. John J. Begley, S.J., Prof., Theology; Timothy J. Cadigan, S.J., Prof., Biology; Ryan Maher, S.J., Pres., Scranton Preparatory School; Richard G. Malloy, S.J., Univ. Chap.; Herbert B. Keller, S.J., Rector, Scranton Prep; John J. Levko, S.J., Prof., Mathematics; Leonard A. Martin, S.J., St. Mary's Byzantine Catholic Church, Scranton.; Bernard R. McIlhenny, S.J.; Ronald H. McKinney, S.J., Prof., Philosophy; J. Patrick Mohr, S.J., Prof., Philosophy; James D. Redington, S.J., Jesuit Fellow in Jesuit Center; Eugene A. Nolan, S.J., Min.; Daniel Sweeney, S.J., Prof. Political Science; Ryan Sheehan, Esq., Interim Exec. Dir., The Jesuit Center; Helen Wolf, Ph.D., Exec. Dir. Campus Ministries. Lay Teachers 285; Priests 14; Students 5,422.

DALLAS. *Misericordia University*, (Grades Associate-Masters), 301 Lake St., Dallas, 18612.
Tel: 570-674-6314; Email: csomers@misericordia.edu; Web: www.misericordia.edu. Mr. Thomas Botzman, Ph.D., Pres.; Ms. Kathleen A. Foley, B.S., M.S., Vice Pres.; Ms. Susan Helwig, Vice Pres. Instl. Advancement; Dr. Barbara Loftus, Vice Pres. Planning, Assessment & Research; Sr. Jean Messaros, R.S.M., Vice Pres. Mission Integration; Rev. Alex J. Roche, Chap. Conference for Mercy Higher Education Mid-Atlantic Region Division, Dallas, PA. Religious Teachers 1; Students 2,830; Sisters Teaching 3.

Administration: Mr. Thomas Botzman, Ph.D., Pres.; Mr. Eric Nelson, Vice Pres. of Finance & Admin.; Dr. Charles Brody, Vice Pres. of Academic Affairs; Ms. Susan Helwig, Vice Pres. Instl. Advancement; Sr. Jean Messaros, R.S.M., Vice Pres. Mission Integration; Mrs. Jane Dessoye, M.S., Enrollment Mgr.; Mr. Joseph Redington, Registrar; Bernadette Rushmer, Dir., Career Svcs.; Sr. Cynthia March, R.S.M., Dir. Counseling Svcs.; Mr. Val Apanovich, Dir. Information Technology; Dr. Barbara Loftus, Vice Pres. Planning, Assessment & Research; Mrs. Martha Stevenson, Dir., Library Svcs.; Ms. Kathleen A. Foley, B.S., M.S., Dean of Students; Mr. Ronald Hromisin, C.P.A., Controller; Mr. James Roberts, Dir. Mktg. & Public Rels.

WILKES-BARRE. **King's College*, (Grades Bachelors-Masters), Wilkes-Barre, 18711. Tel: 570-208-5899; Fax: 570-208-5809; Web: www.kings.edu. Brothers 2; Lay Teachers 139; Priests 11; Students 2,321.

Officers of the College: Rev. John J. Ryan, C.S.C., Pres.; Joseph Evan, Provost & Vice Pres. Academic Affairs; Ms. Janet Mercincavage, Vice Pres. Student Affairs; Frederick A. Pettit, E.S.Q., Vice Pres. Instl. Advancement; Mr. Corry Unis, Vice Pres. Enrollment Mgmt.; Rev. Thomas P. Looney, C.S.C., College Chap. & Dir. Campus Ministry; Barry H. Williams, J.D., C.P.A., Dean, William J. McGowan School of Business; Mr. Paul J. Moran, Assoc. Vice Pres. & Chief Info. Officer; Mr. Daniel T. Cebrick, Registrar; Mr. Brian Cook, M.S., N.C.C., C.P.C., Dir. Counseling Ctr.; Mr. James J. Anderson, Exec. Dir. Admissions. Holy Cross Community. Holy Cross Community Revs. Genaro P. Aguilar, C.S.C., Alumni Chaplain; Anthony R. Grasso, C.S.C., Prof. English; Richard C. Hockman, C.S.C.; Daniel J. Issing, C.S.C., Asst. Prof. Theology; Charles J. Kociolek, C.S.C., Assoc. Dir. Academic Advisement; Brent A. Kruger, Part-time Faculty; Thomas P. Looney, C.S.C., College Chap. & Dir. Campus Ministry; Walter Jenkins, C.S.C., Supr. Holy Cross Community; Stephen C. Pepper, C.S.C., Assoc. Campus Minister; John J. Ryan, C.S.C., Pres.; Eric Schimmel, C.S.C., Dir. McGowan Hispanic Outreach Prog.; Bros. Stephen J. LaMendola, C.S.C., Academic Liaison, Educ. Dept.; James H. Miller, C.S.C., Assoc. Prof. Theatre; John R. Kratz, Dir. Academic Advisement. In Res. Rev. Joseph J. Long, C.S.C., (Retired).

[C] HIGH SCHOOLS, DIOCESAN

SCRANTON. *Holy Cross High School*, 501 E. Drinker St., Dunmore, 18512. Tel: 570-346-7541;
Tel: 570-346-7542; Fax: 570-348-1070; Email: btolerico@hchspa.org. Rev. Cyril D. Edwards, V.E., Chap.; Mr. Benjamin Tolerico, Prin.; Cathy Chiumento, Vice Pres. Lay Teachers 28; Priests 1; Sisters 2.

EAST STROUDSBURG. *Notre Dame Jr. / Sr. High School*, (Grades 7-12), (member of the Notre Dame Regional School System of the Diocese of Scranton, Inc.) 60 Spangenburg Ave., East Stroudsburg, 18301. Tel: 570-421-0466; Fax: 570-476-0629; Email: principal@ndhigh.org. Rev. Msgr. John A. Bergamo, J.C.L., Chap., (Retired); Mr. Jeffrey N. Lyons, Prin.; Mrs. Patricia Burke, Librarian; Debra Krogulski, D.R.E. Lay Teachers 23; Priests 1.

WILKES-BARRE. *Holy Redeemer High School* (member of the Holy Redeemer Regional School System of the Diocese of Scranton, Inc.) 159 S. Pennsylvania Blvd., Wilkes-Barre, 18701. Tel: 570-829-2424; Fax: 570-829-4412. Rev. Joseph G. Elston, Chap. & Dean, Students; Mr. Michael Reese, Interim Prin.; Cathy Chiumento, Prin. Lay Teachers 40; Priests 1; Sisters 4.

WILLIAMSPORT. *Saint John Neumann Regional*

Academy High School Campus, (Grades 7-12), (member of the Saint John Neumann Regional School System of the Diocese of Scranton, Inc.) 901 Penn St., Williamsport, 17701. Tel: 570-323-9953; Fax: 570-321-7146. Mr. Richard Cummings, Prin.; Rev. Bert S. Kozen, Chap. & D.R.E.; Shawn Moore, D.R.E.; Mr. Eugene Kurzejweski, Admin.

[D] HIGH SCHOOLS, PRIVATE

SCRANTON. **Scranton Preparatory School*, 1000 Wyoming Ave., 18509. Tel: 570-941-7737; Fax: 570-941-6118; Web: www.scrantonprep.com. Rev. Ryan Maher, S.J., Pres.; Matthew R. Bernard, Prin.; Kathleen Ciccotti, Librarian. Society of Jesus. Lay Teachers 65; Priests 2; Students 829; Jesuit Scholastic 1.

Faculty: Angelo J. Rizzo, S.J., Jesuit Scholastic.

[E] DIOCESAN ELEMENTARY SCHOOLS

SCRANTON. *All Saints Academy*, (Grades PreK-8), (member of the Holy Cross Regional School System of the Diocese of Scranton, Inc.) 1425 Jackson St., 18504. Tel: 570-343-8114; Fax: 570-343-0378. Mrs. Doreen Dougherty, Prin.; Catherine Mineo, Librarian. Lay Teachers 19; Sisters 1.

Saint Clare/Saint Paul Elementary School (Main Campus), (Grades 3-8), (member of the Holy Cross Regional School System of the Diocese of Scranton, Inc.) 1527 Penn Ave., 18509. Tel: 570-343-7880; Tel: 570-343-4485; Fax: 570-343-0069. Doug Workman, Prin.; Sr. Rosella Saluato, I.H.M., Librarian.

Saint Clare/Saint Paul Elementary School (Primary Campus), (Grades PreK-2), (member of the Holy Cross Regional School System of the Diocese of Scranton, Inc.) 2215 N. Washington Ave., 18509. Tel: 570-343-2790; Fax: 570-343-4905. Doug Workman, Prin.; Sr. Rosella Saluato, I.H.M., Librarian. Lay Teachers 21; Priests 2; Sisters 3.

NativityMiguel Scranton, (Grades 5-8), 1 Knox Rd., (Lower Level of Temple Hesed), 18505. Robert H. Angeloni, Pres., Tel: 570-955-5176; Fax: 570-955-5707; Sr. Josephine Cioffi, I.H.M., Prin.; Carmela Smith, Dir. Opers.

CLARKS GREEN. *Our Lady of Peace Elementary School*, (Grades K-8), (member of the Holy Cross Regional School System of the Diocese of Scranton, Inc.) 410 N. Abington Rd., Clarks Green, 18411. Tel: 570-587-4152; Fax: 570-586-5393; Email: olpeaceschool@comcast.net. Mrs. Colleen Jumper, Prin.; Mrs. Carol Harrison, Librarian.

CRESCO. *Monsignor McHugh Elementary School*, (Grades PreK-8), (member of the Notre Dame Regional School System of the Diocese of Scranton, Inc.) 212 Rte. 390, Cresco, 18326. Tel: 570-595-7463; Fax: 570-595-9639; Email: mmsprincipal@monsignormchugh.org. Mrs. Becca Torregrosso, Prin.; Elizabeth DeRoo, Librarian. Lay Teachers 14; Priests 1.

DUNMORE. *Saint Mary of Mount Carmel Elementary School*, (Grades PreK-8), (member of the Holy Cross Regional School System of the Diocese of Scranton, Inc.) 325 Chestnut St., Dunmore, 18512. Tel: 570-346-4429; Tel: 570-346-4560; Fax: 570-346-3016; Email: cjslcd@gmail.com. Mrs. Cathy Sosnowski, Prin.

DURYEA. *Holy Rosary Elementary School*, (Grades PreK-8), (member of the Holy Redeemer Regional School System of the Diocese of Scranton, Inc.) 125 Stephenson St., Duryea, 18642. Tel: 570-457-2553; Fax: 570-457-3537; Email: mskutack@holyrosaryduryea.org. Mrs. Candice Lee, Prin.

EAST STROUDSBURG. *Notre Dame Elementary School*, (Grades PreK-6), (member of the Notre Dame Regional School System of the Diocese of Scranton, Inc.) 60 Spangenburg Ave., East Stroudsburg, 18301. Tel: 570-421-3651; Fax: 570-422-6935; Email: principal@ndelementary.org. Sr. Mary Alice Kane, I.H.M., Prin.; Mrs. Barbara Camlet, Librarian. Lay Teachers 13; Sisters 2.

EXETER. *Wyoming Area Catholic Elementary School*, (Grades PreK-8), (member of the Holy Redeemer Regional School System of the Diocese of Scranton, Inc.) 1690 Wyoming Ave., Exeter, 18643. Tel: 570-654-7982; Tel: 570-655-8082; Fax: 570-654-0605; Email: erishcoff@wacsh.com. Mrs. Eileen Rishcoff, Prin. Lay Teachers 12.

HAZLETON. *Holy Family Academy*, (Grades PreK-8), (member of the Holy Redeemer Regional School System of the Diocese of Scranton, Inc.) 601 N. Laurel St., Hazleton, 18201. Tel: 570-455-9431; Fax: 570-455-2847; Email: principal@holyfamilyacademy.info. Mr. Jason Tribbet, Interim Prin.; Zelda Ondish, Librarian. Lay Teachers 15.

JESSUP. *La Salle Academy*, (Grades 4-8), (member of the Holy Cross Regional School System of the Diocese of Scranton, Inc.) 309 First Ave., Jessup, 18434. Tel: 570-489-2010; Fax: 570-489-3887; Email: emm59@aol.com. Mrs. Ellen M. Murphy, Prin. Lay Teachers 20.

KINGSTON. *Good Shepherd Academy*, (Grades PreK-8), (member of the Holy Redeemer Regional School System of the Diocese of Scranton, Inc.) 316 N. Maple Ave., Kingston, 18704. Tel: 570-718-4724; Fax: 570-718-4725; Email: jjones@gsapa.org. Mr. James A. Jones, Prin.; Mr. Stan Pavlick, Asst. Prin.

MOUNTAINTOP. *Saint Jude Elementary School*, (Grades PreK-8), (member of the Holy Redeemer Regional School System of the Diocese of Scranton, Inc.) 422 S. Mountain Blvd., Mountain Top, 18707. Tel: 570-474-5803; Fax: 570-403-6159. Sr. Ellen Fischer, S.C.C., Prin.

SAYRE. *Epiphany Elementary School*, (Grades PreK-8), (member of the Holy Cross Regional School System of the Diocese of Scranton, Inc.) 627 Stevenson St., Sayre, 18840. Tel: 570-888-5802; Fax: 570-888-2362; Email: epiphany-school@hotmail.com. Sr. Kathleen Kelly, I.H.M., Prin. Religious Teachers 3; Lay Teachers 11; Priests 1; Sisters 2; Students 87.

TOWANDA. *Saint Agnes Elementary School*, (Grades PreK-6), (member of the Holy Cross Regional School System of the Diocese of Scranton, Inc.) 102 Third St., Towanda, 18848. Tel: 570-265-6803; Fax: 570-265-3065. Chad Shrawder, Prin. Lay Teachers 10.

WILKES-BARRE. *Saint Nicholas/Saint Mary Elementary School*, (Grades PreK-8), (member of the Holy Redeemer Regional School System of the Diocese of Scranton, Inc.) 242 S. Washington St., Wilkes-Barre, 18701. Tel: 570-823-8089; Fax: 570-823-1402. Christopher Tigue, Prin.; Sandy Sipsky, Librarian. Lay Teachers 22.

WILLIAMSPORT. *Saint John Neumann Regional Academy*, (Grades PreK-6), (Elementary Campus) (Member of the Saint John Newmann Regional School System of the Diocese of Scranton, Inc.) 710 Franklin St., Williamsport, 17701. Tel: 570-326-3738; Tel: 570-326-7385. Mrs. Susan Kaiser, Prin.

[F] PRESCHOOLS AND CHILD CARE CENTERS

CLARKS GREEN. *St. Gregory Early Childhood Center*, 330 N. Abington Rd., Clarks Summit, 18411. Tel: 570-587-4808; Fax: 570-586-4515; Email: churchofstgreg@gmail.com. Rev. John M. Lapera, Dir. Lay Teachers 4; Priests 1.

MILFORD. *Happy Faces Preschool at St. Vincent de Paul*, 101 St. Vincent Dr., Milford, 18337-9672. Tel: 570-686-1867; Tel: 570-686-4545; Fax: 800-565-1762; Email: stvincentdepaul@pikeonline.net. Denise Spinetta, Dir.

MOSCOW. *St. Catherine Preschool* (1985) P.O. Box 250, Church St., Moscow, 18444. Tel: 570-848-1258. Lisa Sgobba, Dir.

[G] RENEWAL CENTERS

NANTICOKE. *Holy Family Spiritual Renewal Center* (1996) 151 Old Newport St., Nanticoke, 18634-1300. Tel: 570-735-2599; Fax: 570-735-2599; Email: mjmhudak@verizon.net. Michael J. Hudak, Co-Dir. Total Staff 2; Total Assisted 4.

[H] GENERAL HOSPITALS

MUNCY. *Muncy Valley Hospital*, 215 E. Water St., Muncy, 17756. Tel: 570-546-8282; Fax: 570-546-4150; Web: www.susquehannahealth.org. Ronald Reynolds, Chief Admn. Officer. Capacity 158; Patients Asst Anual. 99,850; Total Staff 317.

WILLIAMSPORT. *Divine Providence Hospital of the Sisters of Christian Charity*, 1100 Grampian Blvd., Williamsport, 17701. Tel: 570-320-7833; Fax: 570-320-7820; Email: apaul@susquehannahealth.org; Web: www.susquehannahealth.org. Robert Kane, Pres.; Rev. Fidelis Ekemgba, Chap.; Sisters Christina Marie Cables, S.C.C., Coord.; Ann Marie Paul, S.C.C, Dir. of Mission Integration. Bed Capacity 70; Patients Asst Anual. 215,033; Total Staff 418.

Sisters of Christian Charity Healthcare Corporation, 1100 Grampian Blvd., Williamsport, 17701. Tel: 570-320-7658; Email: tajacobs@scceast.org; Web: www.susquehannahealth.org. Sr. Teresa Ann Jacobs, S.C.C., Dir., Sponsorship Svcs.

[I] SPECIAL HOSPITALS

SCRANTON. *St. Joseph's Center* (1888) 2010 Adams Ave., 18509. Tel: 570-342-8379; Fax: 570-342-6080; Email: kkowalchick@stjosephscenter.org; Web: www.stjosephscenter.org. Sr. Maryalice Jacquinot, I.H.M., Pres. & CEO. Bed Capacity 145; Patients Asst Anual. 155; Tot Asst. Annually 155; Total Staff 600.

[J] SPECIAL EDUCATION SCHOOLS

SCRANTON. *Lourdesmont Behavioral Health Services* (1889) 326 Adams Ave., 18503. Tel: 570-348-6100; Fax: 314-381-7102; Email: cmcquaid@gspmna.org. Sr. Mary Carolyn McQuaid, Treas.

Good Shepherd Youth & Family Services of NEPA Sisters of the Good Shepherd 1.

[K] HOMES FOR AGED

SCRANTON. *Home for Aged of the Little Sisters of the Poor, Holy Family Residence* (1907) 2500 Adams Ave., 18509. Tel: 570-343-4065; Fax: 570-346-1196; Email: scmothersuperior@littlesistersofthepoor.org. Sr. Theresa Louisa Wooching, L.S.P., Pres.; Rev. E. Francis Kelly, Chap. Aged Residents 52; Little Sisters of the Poor 9; Tot Asst. Annually 91; Residents in Independent Living Apartments 23.

DALLAS. *Mercy Center Nursing Unit, Inc.*, 301 Lake St., P.O. Box 370, Dallas, 18612. Tel: 570-675-2131; Fax: 570-674-7606; Email: derikson@mcnu.org; Web: www.mcnu.org. Sr. Sara Sweeney, R.S.M., Admin.; Sheila Heck, Dir. of Nursing; Rev. Richard Rojas, Chap. Bed Capacity 140; Total Staff 209; Total Assisted 221.

MOSCOW. *St. Mary's Villa Nursing Home* (1962) 516 St. Mary's Villa Rd., Elmhurst Twp., 18444. Tel: 570-842-7621; Fax: 570-842-2953; Email: lkanarr@stmarysvilla.com. Linda Kanarr, CEO/Admin. Covenant Health Inc., Tewksbury, MA. Bed Capacity 112; Residents 112; Total Staff 200; Total Assisted 65.

St. Mary's Villa Residence (1999) One Pioneer Pl., Elmhurst Twp., 18444. Tel: 570-842-5274; Fax: 570-842-3472; Email: lkanarr@stmarysvilla.com. Koryn Gallagher, Admin. Covenant Health Inc., Tewksbury, MA Residents 64; Total Staff 45.

WILKES-BARRE. *Little Flower Manor of the Diocese of Scranton*, 200 S. Meade St., Wilkes-Barre, 18702. Tel: 570-823-6131; Fax: 570-823-5171. John T. Howells, Exec. Dir.; Rev. Richard G. Ghezzi, Chap. Aged Residents 133; Sisters 4; Total Staff 230.

St. Therese Residence, 260 S. Meade St., Wilkes-Barre, 18702. Tel: 570-823-6131; Fax: 570-208-0143. Brenda Casciano, Admin.; Rev. Richard G. Ghezzi, Chap. Residents 60; Total Staff 41.

Saint Luke's Villa, 80 E. Northampton St., Wilkes-Barre, 18701. Tel: 570-826-1031. John T. Howells, Exec. Dir.; Rev. Msgr. Vincent J. Grimalia, Chap., (Retired). Tot Asst. Annually 126; Total Staff 108.

[L] MONASTERIES AND RESIDENCES OF PRIESTS AND BROTHERS

SCRANTON. *Saint Ann's Passionist Monastery* (1909) Part of the Congregation of the Passion - St. Paul of the Cross Province 1233 St. Ann St., 18504. Tel: 570-347-5691; Fax: 570-347-9387; Email: info@stannsmonasterybasilica.org; Web: http://stannsmonasterybasilica.org/. Revs. John J. Connor, C.P., Asst. Supr.; Francis Landry, C.P., Pastor; Very Rev. Richard Burke, C.P., Rector; Revs. Vincent Boney, C.P.; Edward Buchheit, C.P.; Siby John, C.P.; Bro. Andre Mathieu, C.P.; Rev. Thomas McCann, C.P.; Bro. Joseph Rogers, C.P.; Rev. Lee Havey, C.P.; Mr. Cristian Martinez Montalvo; Bro. Jonathan Pabon Tirado; Mr. Luis Guivas Gerena; Revs. Mark Ward; Robert Carbonneau. Brothers 3; Total Number in Temporary Vows 2; Total in Community 13.

ELMHURST. *Priestly Fraternity of St. Peter (F.S.S.P.), North American District Headquarters* (1991) Priestly Fraternity of St. Peter, 450 Venard Rd., S. Abington Twp., 18411. Tel: 570-842-4000; Fax: 570-319-9770; Email: info@fssp.com; Web: www.fssp.com. Revs. Zachary Akers, F.S.S.P., Dir. Devel.; Gerard Saguto, F.S.S.P., Dist. Supr.; Simon Harkins, F.S.S.P., District Bursar. Priests 119; Seminarians 71; Transitional Deacons 5.

LACEYVILLE. *Franciscan Missionary Hermits of St. Joseph* (1998) 85 Joseph Dr., Laceyville, 18623. Tel: 570-869-2918. Rev. Pio Mandato, F.M.H.J.

PITTSTON. *Holy Spouses Province of the Oblates of St. Joseph*, East Coast Central Office: 1880 Hwy. 315, Pittston, 18640. Tel: 570-654-7542; Fax: 570-654-8621. Very Rev. Paul A. McDonnell, O.S.J., Prov. Supr. Brothers 3; Priests 24; Temporary Professed 1.

[M] DIOCESAN RESIDENCE FOR RETIRED PRIESTS

DUNMORE. *Villa St. Joseph*, 1600 Green Ridge St., Dunmore, 18509. Tel: 570-343-4791; Email: michelle-brislin@dioceseofscranton.org. Michelle Brislin, Admin.; Most Rev. John M. Dougherty, D.D., V.G., Auxiliary Bishop Emeritus, (Retired); Rev. Msgr. David A. Bohr, S.T.D., Rector, Tel: 570-343-4791; Fax: 570-343-3040; Revs. Michael J. Zipay, (Retired); Vincent F. Langan, (Retired); Rev. Msgr. John J. Bendik, (Retired); Rev. John T. Albosta, (Retired); Joseph M. Boles, Died Apr. 15, 2018; Revs. Eugene R. Carr, (Retired); Joseph F. Cipriano, (Retired); William R. Culnane, (Retired); Rev. Msgrs. John A. Esseff, (Retired); William J. Feldcamp, (Retired); Revs. Joseph A. Greskiewicz,

(Retired); Joseph M. Horanzy, (Retired); George Jeffrey; Rev. Msgr. Joseph P. Kelly, M.S.W., (Retired); Rev. John J. Kilpatrick, (Retired); Rev. Msgr. Alexander T. Kulik, (Retired); Revs. Edward P. Lyman, (Retired); Joseph J. Mattey, (Retired); Rev. Msgrs. Donald A. McAndrews, (Retired); James J. McGarry, (Retired); Revs. Thomas J. O'Malley, (Retired); Michael J. Rafferty, (Retired); Rev. Msgr. Joseph G. Rauscher, (Retired); Most Rev. James C. Timlin, D.D., (Retired); Rev. John J. Turi, (Retired); Rev. Msgr. William P. Ward, (Retired). In Res. Most Rev. James C. Timlin, D.D., (Retired), Tel: 570-343-6170; Rev. Msgrs. David A. Bohr, S.T.D., Rector, Tel: 570-558-1453; John A. Esseff, (Retired), Tel: 570-941-0986; William J. Feldcamp, (Retired), Tel: 570-561-8876; Joseph P. Kelly, M.S.W., (Retired), Tel: 570-417-3072; Alexander T. Kulik, (Retired), Tel: 570-344-2142; Rev. Edward P. Lyman, (Retired), (Retired); Rev. Msgrs. Donald A. McAndrews, (Retired); James J. McGarry, (Retired), Tel: 570-344-4395; William P. Ward, (Retired), Tel: 570-341-1558; Revs. John T. Albosta, (Retired); William D. Campbell, (Retired), Tel: 570-344-7865; Eugene R. Carr, (Retired), Tel: 570-371-7642; Joseph F. Cipriano, (Retired), Tel: 570-961-0328; William R. Culnane, (Retired), Tel: 570-677-5749; Joseph A. Greskiewicz, (Retired), Tel: 570-814-6639; Joseph M. Horanzy, (Retired), Tel: 570-479-0446; George A. Jeffrey, (Retired), Tel: 570-814-2745; John J. Kilpatrick, (Retired), Tel: 570-344-2154; Kenneth G. Kizis, (Retired), Tel: 570-342-7406; Joseph J. Mattey, (Retired); Thomas J. O'Malley, (Retired); Cyril J. Rable, (Retired), Tel: 570-344-2113; Michael J. Rafferty, (Retired), Tel: 570-961-3723; John J. Turi, (Retired); Rev. Msgr. Joseph G. Rauscher, (Retired), (Retired), Email: 570-417-2193.

[N] CONVENTS AND RESIDENCES FOR SISTERS

SCRANTON. *Immaculate Heart of Mary Center* (1971) 2300 Adams Ave., 18509. Tel: 570-342-6850; Fax: 570-346-5439; Email: communications@sistersofihm.org; Web: www.sistersofihm.org. Sisters Ellen Maroney, I.H.M., Pres., Tel: 570-346-5425; Mary Ellen Higgins, Vice Pres.; Ann Marie Lynott, I.H.M., Assoc. Admin. of I.H.M. Center, Tel: 570-346-5408; M. Francine Fasolka, I.H.M., Dir. Communications, Tel: 570-346-5404; Ms. Debbie Worlinsky, Dir. of Finance, Tel: 570-346-5406; Sr. Ann Monica Bubser, I.H.M., Dir. Devel., Tel: 570-346-5431; Ms. Jane O'Neill, Dir. I.H.M. Assoc. Program, Tel: 570-963-2480; Sisters Rose Marie Mozzachio, I.H.M., Dir. I.H.M. Center EEI, Tel: 570-346-5429; Donna Korba, I.H.M., Dir. Justice & Peace & Integrity of Creation, Tel: 570-346-5411; Minnette Susan Welding, I.H.M., Dir. Vocations, Tel: 570-346-5414; Mary Ann Adams, I.M.H., Dir. Ministry Resources, Tel: 570-346-5401; Mary Elaine Anderson, Dir. of Candidates & Novices; Kathleen Clancy, I.H.M., Dir. of IHM Welcoming Space; Elizabeth Pearson, Congregational Archivist; Theresa Jordan, Councilor; Nancy DeCesare, Councilor; Mary Reap, I.H.M., Ph.D., Councilor; M. Francine Fasolka, Dir. of Communications; Mary Slavinskas, Dir. of Heartworks; Eleace King, Dir. of ESL; Jean Coughlin, I.H.M., IHM Campus Admin. Sisters, Servants of the Immaculate Heart of Mary. Sisters 2; Professed Sisters 340.

Pascucci Family Our Lady of Peace Residence, 2300 Adams Ave., 18509. Tel: 570-346-5423; Fax: 570-346-5418; Email: coughlinj@sistersofihm.org. Sisters Mary Kathleen Faliskie, I.H.M., Asst. Admin., Tel: 570-346-5422; Jean Coughlin, I.H.M., Admin., Tel: 570-346-5421; Kate McCarron Sr., Admin. Sisters, Servants of the Immaculate Heart of Mary 100.

DALLAS. *Sisters of Mercy of the Americas, Mid-Atlantic Community*, 301 Lake St., P.O. Box 369, Dallas, 18612-0369. Tel: 570-675-2048; Fax: 570-675-9051; Email: ddellaporta@mercymidatlantic.org; Web: www.mercymidatlantic.org. Sr. Patricia Vetrano, R.S.M., Pres. Sisters 927.

TUNKHANNOCK. *Capuchin Sisters of Nazareth*, Mother of God Convent, 215 Wellwood Dr., Tunkhannock, 18657. Tel: 570-836-2737; Email: heatherbetts@dioceseofscranton.org. Sr. Theresa May, Supr.

[O] RETREAT HOUSES

MOUNT POCONO. *Villa Our Lady Retreat House*, 245 Meadowside Rd., Mount Pocono, 18344-9714. Tel: 570-839-7217; Fax: 570-839-1027; Email: jeanan44@ptd.net; Web: www.villaourlady.com. Sisters Jean Anthony Rodgers, O.S.F., Admin.; Maria James Riedel, O.S.F., Asst. Admin. & Supr. Bernardine Sisters 4.

SOUTH ABINGTON TOWNSHIP. *St. Gabriel's Retreat Center*, 631 Griffin Pond Rd., South Abington Township, 18411. Tel: 570-586-4957; Fax: 570-587-3314; Email: kporter@epix.net. Religious of the Passion of Jesus Christ; Passionist Nuns (Contemplative).

[P] CAMPS AND COMMUNITY CENTERS

WILKES-BARRE. *Catholic Youth Center*, 36 S. Washington St., Wilkes-Barre, 18701. Tel: 570-823-6121; Fax: 570-823-0175; Email: wvcyc@epix.net. Rev. John S. Terry, Dir.; Mr. Mark Soprano, Exec. Dir.

[Q] MISCELLANEOUS LISTINGS

SCRANTON. *African Sisters Education Collaborative (ASEC)* (2006) Marywood University, Immaculate Mary House, 2300 Adams Ave., 18509. Tel: 570-961-4700; Fax: 570-340-6085; Email: executivedirector@asec-sldi.org; Web: www.asec-sldi.org. Sisters Mary Cecilia Draru, Exec. Dir. of ASEC; Mary Atuu; Jennifer Akello.

**Aid to the Church in Russia*, 300 Wyoming Ave., 18503-1279. Tel: 570-207-2216; Fax: 570-207-2236. Rev. Msgr. Thomas M. Muldowney, V.G., Vicar Gen.

St. Ann's Foundation, 1239 St. Ann's St., 18504. Tel: 570-347-5691; Fax: 570-347-9387. Very Rev. Richard Burke, C.P., Exec. Dir.

St. Anthony's Haven, 409-411 Olive St., 18509. Tel: 570-342-1295, Ext. 204; Fax: 570-342-0985; Email: ghallinan@cssresidential.org. Men's & Women's Shelter.

St. James Manor, 600 Wyoming Ave., 18509. Tel: 570-342-1295, Ext. 202; Fax: 570-342-0985. Supportive Housing Program.

St. Francis of Assisi Kitchen, 500 Penn Ave., 18509. Tel: 570-342-5556; Fax: 570-963-8832; Web: www.stfranciskitchen.com. Rev. Msgr. Joseph P. Kelly, M.S.W., Dir., (Retired).

Friends of the Poor (1984) Jackson Terrace, 148 Meridian Ave., 18504. Tel: 570-348-4429; Fax: 570-207-1516; Email: friendsofthepoor@fotp-ihm.org; Web: www.fotp-ihm.org. Ms. Meghan Loftus, CEO; Sr. Ann Walsh, I.H.M., Asst. Dir.

I.H.M. Congregation Charitable Trust (1986) 2300 Adams Ave., 18509. Tel: 570-342-6850; Fax: 570-346-5439; Email: jordant@sistersofihm.org. Sr. Ellen Maroney, I.H.M., Pres. Congregation of the Sisters, Servants of the Immaculate Heart of Mary.

Sisters of IHM Foundation, IHM Center, 2300 Adams Ave., 18509. Tel: 570-346-5431; Email: bubsera@sistersofihm.org; Web: www.sistersofihm.org. Sr. Ann Monica Bubser, I.H.M., Exec.

DALLAS. *Mercy Consultation Center*, 3560 Memorial Hwy., P.O. Box 370, Dallas, 18612. Tel: 570-675-2284; Fax: 570-675-4390; Email: mercyconsul3@epix.net. Sr. Mary Helen Nugent, Dir.

NANTICOKE. *People of God Community of Northeastern PA* (1984) 151 Old Newport St., Nanticoke, 18634-1300. Tel: 570-735-2599; Fax: 570-735-2679; Email: jimmyg@epix.net. James Gialanella, Pres.

PITTSTON. *The Gabriel House*, 13 William St., Pittston, 18640. Tel: 570-602-9796; Fax: 570-602-8396; Email: bkuprionas@csswb.org. Transitional housing facility for women and women with young children.

WILKES-BARRE. *Project REMAIN*, 215 High St., Apt. 100, Wilkes-Barre, 18701. Tel: 570-829-5373. Sr. Imelda Sherrett, R.S.M., Dir. Service for the elderly and the needy residents in the High Rises.

Project Remain Outreach dba John B. McGlynn Center, Boulevard Townhomes, 72 Midland Ct., Wilkes-Barre, 18702. Tel: 570-824-8891; Fax: 570-970-1079. Sr. Miriam Francis Stadulis, R.S.M., Dir. Outreach to low income families in the housing projects.

St. Vincent De Paul Kitchen, 39 E. Jackson St., Wilkes-Barre, 18701. Tel: 570-829-7796; Fax: 570-208-9182; Email: amccawley@csswb.org. Mary Theresa Vautrinot, Exec. Dir.; Mike Cianciotta, Project Dir.

RELIGIOUS INSTITUTES OF MEN REPRESENTED IN THE DIOCESE

For further details refer to the corresponding bracketed number in the Religious Institutes of Men or Women section.

[1000]—*Congregation of the Passion* (Union City, NJ)—C.P.
[0690]—*Jesuit Fathers and Brothers* (Maryland Prov.)—S.J.
[0930]—*Oblates of St. Joseph* (Asti, Italy)—O.S.J.
[1065]—*Priestly Fraternity of St. Peter*—F.S.S.P.
[0610]—*Priests of the Congregation of Holy Cross* (Wilkes-Barre, PA)—C.S.C.

RELIGIOUS INSTITUTES OF WOMEN REPRESENTED IN THE DIOCESE

[1810]—*Bernardine Sisters of the Third Order of St. Francis*—O.S.F.
[0330]—*Carmelite Sisters of the Aged and Infirm*—O.Carm.
[2980]—*Congregation of Notre Dame*—C.N.D.
[0890]—*Daughters of Our Lady of Mercy*—D.M.
[]—*Dominican Sisters of Sparkhill.*
[2575]—*Institute of the Sisters of Mercy of the Americas*—R.S.M.
[]—*Little Sisters of Mary Immaculate of Gulu* (Uganda)—L.S.M.I.G.
[]—*Little Sisters of St. Francis*—L.S.O.F.
[2340]—*Little Sisters of the Poor*—L.S.P.
[3170]—*Religious of the Passion of Jesus Christ*—C.P.
[3430]—*Religious Teachers Filippini*—M.P.F.
[0660]—*Sisters of Christian Charity*—S.C.C.
[3780]—*Sisters of Saints Cyril and Methodius*—SS.C.M.
[3840]—*Sisters of St. Joseph of Carondelet*—C.S.J.
[1830]—*Sisters of the Good Shepherd*—R.G.S.
[2160]—*Sisters, Servants of the Immaculate Heart of Mary*—I.H.M.

DIOCESAN CEMETERIES

SCRANTON. *Cathedral*, 1708 Oram St., 18504. Tel: 570-207-2209; Fax: 570-558-4311; Email: dominic-rinaldi@dioceseofscranton.org; Email: Cathedral-cem@dioceseofscranton.org; Email: kbeck@dioceseofscranton.org; Email: mbarrett@dioceseofscranton.org. 300 Wyoming Ave., 18503. Dominic Rinaldi, Dir.

Diocesan Cemeteries Office, 300 Wyoming Ave., 18503. Tel: 570-558-4310; Fax: 570-558-4311; Email: dominic-rinaldi@dioceseofscranton.org. Dominic Rinaldi, Dir.

CARVERTON. *Mount Olivet*, 612 Mt. Olivet Rd., Carverton, 18644. Tel: 570-696-3636; Tel: 570-558-4310; Fax: 570-696-4705; Email: dominic-rinaldi@dioceseofscranton.org; Email: jgabriesheski@dioceseofscranton.org; Email: mmikolosko@dioceseofscranton.org. Mailing Address: 300 Wyoming Ave., 18503. Dominic Rinaldi, Dir.

DRUMS. *Calvary*, Rte. 309, 49 S. Hunter Hwy., P.O. Box 485, Drums, 18222. Tel: 570-788-2150; Fax: 570-708-2938; Email: dominic-rinaldi@dioceseofscranton.org; Email: Calvary-cem@dioceseofscranton.org; Email: mfoley@dioceseofscranton.org; Email: tzellner@dioceseofscranton.org. Dominic Rinaldi, Dir.

MOSCOW. *St. Catherine*, Main St., Rte. 435, P.O. Box 114, Moscow, 18444. Tel: 570-842-8411; Fax: 570-842-8406; Email: Dominic-Rinaldi@dioceseofscranton.org. Dominic Rinaldi, Dir.

OLD FORGE. *Holy Cross*, Oak & Keyser Ave., Old Forge, 18518. Tel: 570-347-9251; Fax: 570-347-4354

WILLIAMSPORT. *Resurrection*, 4323 Lycoming Mall Dr., P.O. Box 12, Montoursville, 17754. Tel: 570-368-2727; Fax: 570-368-2727

NECROLOGY

† Louis, John H., S.T.L., J.C.D., (Retired), Died Apr. 26, 2018
† Yarrish, Bernard E., S.T.L., (Retired), Died Jun. 6, 2018
† Blake, William B., (Retired), Died Nov. 29, 2018
† Boles, Joseph M., (Retired), Died Apr. 15, 2018
† Hazzouri, Alex J., (Retired), Died Nov. 15, 2018
† Hughes, Ronald J., (Retired), Died Jul. 17, 2018
† Kelleher, Robert J., (Retired), Died Mar. 15, 2018

Archdiocese of Seattle

Archidioecesis Seattlensis

Most Reverend

JAMES PETER SARTAIN, D.D., S.T.L.

Archbishop of Seattle; ordained July 15, 1978; appointed Bishop of Little Rock January 4, 2000; consecrated and installed March 6, 2000; appointed Bishop of Joliet May 16, 2006; installed June 27, 2006; appointed Archbishop of Seattle September 16, 2010; installed December 1, 2010. *Chancery: 710 9th Ave., Seattle, WA 98104.* Tel: 206-382-4886; Fax: 206-382-3495.

Chancery Office: 710 9th Ave., Seattle, WA 98104. Tel: 206-382-4560

Web: www.seattlearchdiocese.org

Email: info@seattlearch.org

Most Reverend

PAUL D. ETIENNE, D.D., S.T.L.

Coadjutor Archbishop of Seattle; ordained June 27, 1992; appointed Bishop of Cheyenne October 19, 2009; installed December 9, 2009; appointed Archbishop of Anchorage October 4, 2016; installed November 9, 2016; appointed Coadjutor Archbishop of Seattle April 29, 2019; installed June 7, 2019. *Chancery Office: 710 9th Ave., Seattle, WA 98104.*

Most Reverend

ALEXANDER J. BRUNETT, PH.D.

Archbishop Emeritus of Seattle; ordained July 13, 1958; appointed Bishop of Helena April 19, 1994; consecrated and installed July 6, 1994; appointed Archbishop of Seattle October 28, 1997; installed December 18, 1997; retired September 16, 2010. *Office: 710 9th Ave., Seattle, WA 98104.* Tel: 206-382-4886; Fax: 206-382-3495.

Most Reverend

EUSEBIO L. ELIZONDO, M.SP.S.

Auxiliary Bishop of Seattle; ordained August 18, 1984; appointed Auxiliary Bishop of Seattle and Titular Bishop of Acholla May 12, 2005; ordained June 6, 2005. *Office: 710 9th Ave., Seattle, WA 98104.* Tel: 206-274-3112.

Most Reverend

DANIEL H. MUEGGENBORG

Auxiliary Bishop of Seattle; ordained July 14, 1989; appointed Titular Bishop of Tullia and Auxiliary Bishop of Seattle April 6, 2017; installed May 31, 2017. *Office: 710 9th Ave., Seattle, WA 98104.*

Square Miles 28,731.

Established May 31, 1850. Name Changed to Seattle, September 11, 1907.

Created Archdiocese, June 23, 1951.

Comprises the Counties of Clallam, Clark, Cowlitz, Grays Harbor, Island, Jefferson, King, Kitsap, Lewis, Mason, Pacific, Pierce, San Juan, Skagit, Skamania, Snohomish, Thurston, Wahkiakum and Whatcom in the State of Washington.

Legal Title: "Corporation of the Catholic Archbishop of Seattle."
For legal titles of parishes and archdiocesan institutions, consult The Chancery.

STATISTICAL OVERVIEW

Personnel	
Archbishops	2
Retired Archbishops	1
Auxiliary Bishops	2
Abbots	1
Priests: Diocesan Active in Diocese	100
Priests: Diocesan Active Outside Diocese	2
Priests: Retired, Sick or Absent	76
Number of Diocesan Priests	178
Religious Priests in Diocese	95
Total Priests in Diocese	273
Extern Priests in Diocese	28
Ordinations:	
Diocesan Priests	3
Transitional Deacons	3
Permanent Deacons in Diocese	106
Total Brothers	15
Total Sisters	305
Parishes	
Parishes	145
With Resident Pastor:	
Resident Diocesan Priests	99
Resident Religious Priests	14
Without Resident Pastor:	
Administered by Priests	20
Administered by Deacons	3
Administered by Lay People	9
Missions	25
Professional Ministry Personnel:	
Sisters	18
Lay Ministers	346
Welfare	
Catholic Hospitals	13
Total Assisted	1,859,821
Health Care Centers	2
Total Assisted	12,517
Homes for the Aged	16
Total Assisted	3,290
Day Care Centers	1
Total Assisted	112
Specialized Homes	13
Total Assisted	939
Special Centers for Social Services	175
Total Assisted	98,967
Educational	
Diocesan Students in Other Seminaries	19
Total Seminarians	19
Colleges and Universities	2
Total Students	8,846
High Schools, Diocesan and Parish	5
Total Students	2,464
High Schools, Private	6
Total Students	3,661
Elementary Schools, Diocesan and Parish	57
Total Students	14,412
Elementary Schools, Private	5
Total Students	894
Non-residential Schools for the Disabled	73
Total Students	1,149
Catechesis/Religious Education:	
High School Students	4,920
Elementary Students	23,200
Total Students under Catholic Instruction	59,565
Teachers in the Diocese:	
Priests	39
Scholastics	5
Brothers	6
Sisters	20
Lay Teachers	1,713
Vital Statistics	
Receptions into the Church:	
Infant Baptism Totals	4,923
Minor Baptism Totals	617
Adult Baptism Totals	329
Received into Full Communion	343
First Communions	5,566
Confirmations	4,074
Marriages:	
Catholic	757
Interfaith	348
Total Marriages	1,105
Deaths	2,475
Total Catholic Population	582,247
Total Population	5,810,850

Former Bishops—Rt. Revs. A. M. A. BLANCHET, cons. Bishop of Walla Walla, Sept. 27, 1846; transferred to Nesqually, May 31, 1850; resigned 1879; made Bishop of Ibora; died Feb. 25, 1887; AEGIDIUS JUNGER, D.D., cons. Oct. 28, 1879; died Dec. 26, 1895; Most Revs. EDWARD JOHN O'DEA, D.D., cons. Bishop of Nesqually, Sept. 8, 1896; See transferred to Seattle, Sept. 11, 1907; died Dec. 25, 1932; GERALD SHAUGHNESSY, S.M., S.T.D., appt. Bishop of Seattle July 1, 1933; cons. Sept. 19, 1933; died May 18, 1950; THOMAS A. CONNOLLY, D.D., cons. Aug. 24, 1939; succeeded, May 18, 1950; retired Feb. 25, 1975; died April 18, 1991; RAYMOND G. HUNTHAUSEN, D.D., ord. June 1, 1946; appt. Bishop of Helena, Montana, July 8, 1962; cons. Aug. 30, 1962; appt. Archbishop of Seattle, Feb. 25, 1975; installed May 22, 1975; retired Aug. 21, 1991; died July 22, 2018.; THOMAS J. MURPHY, D.D., S.T.D., ord. April 12, 1958; appt. Bishop of Great Falls, July 5, 1978; appt. Coadjutor Archbishop of Seattle, May 26, 1987; succeeded to See Aug. 21, 1991; died June 26, 1997; ALEXANDER J. BRUNETT, Ph.D., D.D., ord. July 13, 1958; appt. Bishop of Helena, Montana April 19, 1994; cons. July 6, 1994; appt. Archbishop of Seattle Oct. 28, 1997; installed Dec. 18, 1997; retired Sept. 16, 2010.

Chancery Office—Office of the Archbishop, 710 9th Ave., Seattle, 98104. Tel: 206-382-4886.

Vicar General—Most Rev. EUSEBIO L. ELIZONDO, M.Sp.S., J.C.L., 710 9th Ave., Seattle, 98104. Tel: 206-274-3112.

Vicar General and Moderator of the Curia—710 9th Ave., Seattle, 98104. Tel: 206-274-3142. Most Rev. DANIEL H. MUEGGENBORG.

Chancellor—MS. MARY E. SANTI, J.C.L., 710 9th Ave., Seattle, 98104. Tel: 206-264-2089; Fax: 206-274-3110.

Vice Chancellor—Please send all prenuptial files to Chancellor's Office. Tel: 206-654-4655; Fax: 206-274-3110. MR. BEN ALTENHOFEN.

Executive Assistant to the Archbishop—MS. ANGELA KISON, Tel: 206-382-4525.

Executive Assistant to Auxiliary Bishop Elizondo—MS. FATIMA MALDONADO, Tel: 206-274-3112.

Executive Assistant to Auxiliary Bishop Mueggenborg—VACANT, Tel: 206-274-3142.

Presbyteral Council—Most Revs. EUSEBIO L. ELIZONDO, M.Sp.S., J.C.L.; DANIEL H. MUEGGENBORG; Very Revs. TODD O. STRANGE; GERALD BURNS; VINCENT M. GILMORE; TIMOTHY W. ILGEN; BRYAN A. OCHS; Rev. PHILIP H. RAETHER; Very Revs. ANTHONY E. BAWYN, J.C.D.; MICHAEL G. RYAN; Revs. HANS M. OLSON, Council Chm.; KURT NAGEL; Very Revs. K. SCOTT CONNOLLY; JAMES NORTHROP; Rev. MICHAEL J. MCDERMOTT; Very Revs. CAL R. CHRISTIANSEN; DAVID H. YOUNG; GARY M. ZENDER; Revs. TUAN NGUYEN; STEVEN SALLIS; PAUL M. WECKERT, O.S.B.; BRYAN DOLEJSI; THOMAS M. LUCAS, S.J.; THOMAS L. VANDENBERG, (Retired).

College of Consultors—Revs. TUAN NGUYEN; MICHAEL

J. McDermott; Very Rev. David T. Mulholland; Revs. Hans M. Olson; Bryan Dolejsi; Paul A. Magnano; Steven Sallis; Kurt Nagel; Thomas L. Vandenberg, (Retired).

Deans—Very Revs. K. Scott Connolly, Northern; Gerald Burns, Pierce; Vincent M. Gilmore, Snohomish; Timothy W. Ilgen, South Sound; Rev. Philip H. Raether, North Seattle; Very Revs. Todd O. Strange, Eastside; Michael G. Ryan, South Seattle; James Northrop, South King; David H. Young, Olympic; Bryan A. Ochs, Southern.

Metropolitan Tribunal

Judicial Vicar—Very Rev. Anthony E. Bawyn, J.C.D., 710 9th Ave., Seattle, 98104. Tel: 206-382-4830; Fax: 206-382-2071.

Director—Sr. Carolyn A. Roeber, O.P., J.D., J.C.L., Ph.D.

Adjunct Judicial Vicars—Most Rev. Eusebio L. Elizondo, M.Sp.S., J.C.L.; Rev. Paul R. Pluth, J.C.L.

Judges—Very Rev. Anthony E. Bawyn, J.C.D.; Rev. Daniel Andree, C.Ss.R., J.C.D.; Mr. James L. Brooks, M.Ed.; Rev. James Eblen, S.T.L., Ph.D., (Retired); Most Rev. Eusebio L. Elizondo, M.Sp. S., J.C.L.; Rev. Paul R. Pluth, J.C.L.; Ms. Lynda Robitaille, J.C.D.; Sr. Carolyn A. Roeber, O.P., J.D., J.C.L., Ph.D.

Defenders of the Bond—Sr. Beverly K. Dunn, S.P., J.C.D.; Ms. Karen S. Giffin, M.Min.; Ms. Roberta Small, J.C.L.; Ms. Elizabeth Staal, D.Min.

Notaries—Ms. Christina Machnik; Ms. Ligia Mahoney.

Archdiocesan Councils and Commissions

Parish Revolving Fund Commission—Mr. Dennis J. O'Leary, Exec. Dir. of Chancery, 710 9th Ave., Seattle, 98104. Tel: 206-382-4834; Fax: 206-382-4583.

Archdiocesan Building Commission—710 9th Ave., Seattle, 98109. Tel: 206-382-4851; Fax: 206-382-4266. Mr. Dennis J. O'Leary, Exec. Dir. of Chancery; Mr. Dennis Lehtinen, Chm.

Archdiocesan Finance Council—710 9th Ave., Seattle, 98104. Tel: 206-382-4529; Fax: 206-274-3199. Mr. Joe Schick, CFO; Mr. Dave Boitano, Chair.

Archdiocesan Offices and Directors

Accounting Services—Ms. Mary Jo Gillis, Controller, 710 9th Ave., Seattle, 98104. Tel: 206-382-4377; Fax: 206-903-4624; Mr. Tom Grechis, Asst. Controller, Tel: 206-382-4287.

Administration and Finance, Office of—710 9th Ave., Seattle, 98104. Tel: 206-382-4529; Fax: 206-274-3199. Mr. Joe Schick, CFO.

Archives and Records Management—710 9th Ave., Seattle, 98104. Tel: 206-382-4352; Fax: 206-382-4840. Mr. Seth Dalby, Dir.

Associated Catholic Cemeteries—710 9th Ave., Seattle, 98104. Tel: 206-524-1451; Fax: 206-525-9628. Mr. Richard Peterson, Dir.

Benefits Services—Ms. Geralyn Mirante-Marley, Dir., 710 9th Ave., Seattle, 98104. Tel: 206-382-4286; Fax: 206-382-3493.

Campaign for Human Development—Mr. J. L. Drouhard, Dir., 710 9th Ave., Seattle, 98104. Tel: 206-382-4869; Fax: 206-382-3487.

Campus Ministry—710 9th Ave., Seattle, 98104. Tel: 206-382-4562; Fax: 206-903-4627. Deacon Eric Paige, Exec. Dir.

Catholic Relief Services—710 9th Ave., Seattle, 98104. Tel: 206-382-4582; Tel: 800-869-7028 (Toll Free); Fax: 206-264-2084. Ms. Kelly Hickman, Asst. Dir.

Office of Catholic Schools—710 9th Ave., Seattle, 98104. Tel: 206-382-4861; Tel: 800-473-5651 (Toll Free); Fax: 206-654-4651. Ms. Kristin Dixon, Supt. Catholic Schools.

Catholic Youth Organization Athletics—710 9th Ave., Seattle, 98104. Tel: 206-274-3128; Fax: 206-903-4627. Mr. Scott Bailey, Dir.

Catholic Youth Organization Camps—710 9th Ave., Seattle, 98104. Tel: 425-829-5644; Fax: 206-903-4627. Mr. Shaune Randles, Dir.

Chancery Operations—Mr. Dennis J. O'Leary, Exec. Dir. Chancery, 710 9th Ave., Seattle, 98104. Tel: 206-382-4289; Fax: 206-382-4583.

Communications, Office of—710 9th Ave., Seattle, 98104. Tel: 206-382-4862; Tel: 800-473-5641 (Toll Free); Fax: 206-382-3487. Vacant.

Magazine "Northwest Catholic"—Tel: 206-382-4870; Tel: 800-473-5641; Fax: 206-382-3487. Mr. Kevin Birnbaum, Interim Editor.

Criminal Justice Ministry Services—710 9th Ave., Seattle, 98104. Tel: 206-382-4847; Fax: 206-382-2069. Mr. Joe Cotton.

Cultural and Ethnic Faith Formation—710 9th Ave., Seattle, 98104. Tel: 206-654-4644; Tel: 800-950-4970 (Toll Free); Fax: 206-264-2084. Mr. Carlos Carillo, Dir.

Deacon Services—Deacon Frank DiGirolamo, Dir. Deacons, 710 9th Ave., Seattle, 98104. Tel: 206-382-1477; Fax: 206-654-4654.

Discipleship—710 9th Ave., Seattle, 98104. Tel: 206-382-4852; Fax: 206-382-2069. Ms. Erica Cohen Moore, Dir.

Due Process—Very Rev. Anthony E. Bawyn, J.C.D., Contact, 710 9th Ave., Seattle, 98104. Tel: 800-950-4965 (Toll Free); Tel: 206-382-3484.

Evangelization, Formation and Discipleship—710 9th Ave., Seattle, 98104. Tel: 206-382-4864. Deacon Eric Paige, Exec. Dir.

Hispanic/Latino Ministry Services—710 9th Ave., Seattle, 98104. Tel: 206-382-4846; Tel: 800-465-6862, Ext. 4825 (Toll Free); Fax: 206-382-2069. Mr. Edwin Ferrera, Dir.

Human Resources—Ms. Mary E. Santi, J.C.L., Exec. Dir., 710 9th Ave., Seattle, 98104. Tel: 206-382-4570; Tel: 800-261-4749 (Toll Free); Fax: 206-382-4267.

Inclusion Ministry—710 9th Ave., Seattle, 98104. Tel: 206-382-4852; Fax: 206-382-2069. Ms. Erica Cohen Moore.

Information Technology & Services—Mr. Kirk Altenhofen, Exec. Dir., 710 9th Ave., Seattle, 98104. Tel: 206-382-4282; Fax: 206-382-4840.

Library Media Center—Ms. Lisa Hillyard, 710 9th Ave., Seattle, 98104. Tel: 206-382-4883; Tel: 800-869-7027 (Toll Free); Fax: 206-382-3487.

Liturgy—710 9th Ave., Seattle, 98104. Tel: 206-654-4652; Tel: 800-473-5657 (Toll Free); Fax: 206-903-4612. Ms. Jennifer Day, Coord.

Missionary Childhood Association—710 9th Ave., Seattle, 98104. Tel: 206-382-4582; Tel: 800-869-7028 (Toll Free); Fax: 206-264-2084. Ms. Kelly Hickman, Asst. Dir.

Missions—710 9th Ave., Seattle, 98104. Tel: 206-382-4580; Tel: 800-869-7028 (Toll Free); Fax: 206-264-2084. Mr. J. L. Drouhard, Dir.

Multicultural Ministries—710 9th Ave., Seattle, 98104. Tel: 206-382-4828; Tel: 800-465-6862 (Toll Free); Fax: 206-382-2069. Deacon Carl Chilo, Dir. Multicultural Communities.

Parish and School Faith Formation—710 9th Ave., Seattle, 98104. Tel: 206-654-4644; Tel: 800-950-4970 (Toll Free); Fax: 206-264-2084. Mr. Carlos Carillo, Dir.

Parish Financial Services—Mr. Scott Bader, Dir., 710 9th Ave., Seattle, 98104. Tel: 206-382-7316; Tel: 800-768-7986 (Toll Free); Fax: 206-382-4279.

Parish Stewardship—Mr. Steve Homiack, Dir., 710 9th Ave., Seattle, 98104. Tel: 206-903-4619; Tel: 866-381-2033 (Toll Free); Fax: 206-903-4610.

Pastoral Care—710 9th Ave., Seattle, 98104. Tel: 206-382-4847; Tel: 800-465-6862 (Toll Free); Fax: 206-654-4654. Mr. Joe Cotton, Dir.

Pastoral Planning and Research—Mr. Dennis J. O'Leary, Exec. Dir., Tel: 206-382-4832; Tel: 800-327-5295 (Toll Free); Fax: 206-274-3161; Ms. Mary Beth Celio, Dir. Research, 710 9th Ave., Seattle, 98104. Tel: 206-382-4272.

Payroll Services Office—710 9th Ave., Seattle, 98104. Tel: 206-274-7667. Mr. Jeremy Package, Payroll Svcs. Mgr.

Planned Giving—710 9th Ave., Seattle, 98104. Tel: 206-274-3117; Tel: 800-752-5902 (Toll Free); Fax: 206-903-4610. Charisse Valtinson.

Catholic Archdiocese of Seattle Clergy Medical Plan Veba Trust—Most Rev. J. Peter Sartain, D.D., S.T.L.; Very Rev. Anthony E. Bawyn, J.C.D., Chm. Trustees; Ms. Geralyn Mirante-Marley, Benefits Dir., Tel: 206-382-4286.

Priests' Pension Plan—Most Rev. J. Peter Sartain, D.D., S.T.L.; Very Rev. Anthony E. Bawyn, J.C.D., Chm. Trustees; Ms. Geralyn Mirante-Marley, Benefits Dir., Tel: 206-382-4286.

Propagation of the Faith, Society for theMr. J.L. Drouhard, Dir., 710 9th Ave., Seattle, 98104. Tel: 206-382-4580; Tel: 800-869-7028 (Toll Free); Fax: 206-382-3487.

Society for St. Peter the Apostle—Mr. J. L. Drouhard, Dir., 710 9th Ave., Seattle, 98104. Tel: 206-382-4580; Tel: 800-869-7028 (Toll Free); Fax: 206-382-3487.

Property and Construction Services—Mr. Edward Foster, Dir., 710 9th Ave., Seattle, 98104. Tel: 206-382-4851; Tel: 800-809-4923 (Toll Free); Fax: 206-382-4266.

Religious Communities—710 9th Ave., Seattle, 98104. Tel: 206-382-4829; Fax: 206-274-3161. Vacant.

Religious Education—710 9th Ave., Seattle, 98104. Tel: 206-654-4644; Tel: 800-950-4970 (Toll Free); Fax: 206-264-2084. Mr. Carlos Carillo, Dir.

Seminarian Services—Rev. Bryan Dolejsi, Dir., 710 9th Ave., Seattle, 98104. Tel: 206-382-4880; Tel: 800-809-4919; Fax: 206-654-4654.

Stewardship and Development Department—710 9th Ave., Seattle, 98104. Tel: 206-382-4563; Fax: 206-903-4610. Deacon Pierce Murphy, Exec. Dir.

Vicar for Clergy, Office of—710 9th Ave., Seattle, 98104. Tel: 206-382-7317; Tel: 800-809-4919 (Toll Free); Fax: 206-654-4654. Very Rev. Gary M. Zender.

Chief of Staff—Mr. Nicholas Schoen, Tel: 206-382-2060.

Pastoral Outreach Coordinator—Ms. Denise Aubuchon, Tel: 206-382-4592; Tel: 800-446-7762 (Toll Free); Email: hotline@seattlearch.org.

Vocations—Rev. Bryan Dolejsi, Dir., 710 9th Ave., Seattle, 98104. Tel: 206-387-4880; Fax: 206-654-4654.

Young Adult Ministry—710 9th Ave., Seattle, 98104. Tel: 206-382-4963; Fax: 206-903-4627. Ms. Megan Pepin, Dir.

Youth Ministry—710 9th Ave., Seattle, 98104. Tel: 206-274-3175; Fax: 206-903-4627. Ms. Daria Lobato, Dir.

CLERGY, PARISHES, MISSIONS AND PAROCHIAL SCHOOLS

CITY OF SEATTLE

(King County)

1—St. James Cathedral (1904)
804 Ninth Ave., 98104. Tel: 206-622-3559; Fax: 206-622-5303; Email: mlaughlin@stjames-cathedral.org; Web: www.stjames-cathedral.org. Very Rev. Michael G. Ryan; Rev. David A. Brant, In Res., (Retired).
Station—St. Ignatius Chapel, Seattle University, 901 12th St., 98122.

2—St. Alphonsus (1901)
5816 15th Ave., N.W., 98107. Tel: 206-784-6464; Email: parishinfo@stalseattle.org; Web: stalseattle.org/parish. Rev. Richard Klepac.
School—St. Alphonsus School, (Grades PreSchool-8), Tel: 206-782-4363. Matthew Eisenhauer, Prin. Lay Teachers 16; Students 235.
Catechesis Religious Program—Students 40.

3—St. Andrew Kim Personal Parish
11700 1st Ave., N.E., 98125-4714. Tel: 206-362-2278; Fax: 206-362-2492; Email: standrewkim.us@gmail.com. Revs. John the Baptist Kwang Chol Hong; Andrew Seung Hyun Lee, Parochial Vicar.
Catechesis Religious Program—Students 217.

4—St. Anne (1908)
1411 1st Ave. W., 98119. Tel: 206-282-0223; Fax: 206-217-9541; Email: info@stanneseattle.org. Rev. Oliver Duggan, Mod.; Very Rev. Anthony E. Bawyn, J.C.D., Parish Priest; Mr. Ron Ryan, Pastoral Coord.
School—St. Anne School, (Grades PreSchool-8), 101 W. Lee St., 98119. Tel: 206-282-3538; Fax: 206-284-4191. Mary Sherman, Prin. Lay Teachers 20; Students 258.
Catechesis Religious Program—Students 170.

5—Assumption (1924)
6201 33rd Ave. N.E., 98115. Tel: 206-522-7674; Fax: 206-522-6308; Email: info@assumptionseattle.com. Rev. Oliver Duggan.
School—Assumption School, (Grades PreK-8), 6220 32nd Ave., N.E., 98115-7233. Tel: 206-524-7452; Fax: 206-524-6757. Christina Viega McGill, Prin. Lay Teachers 28; Students 540.
Catechesis Religious Program—Students 30.

6—St. Benedict (1906)
1805 N. 49th St., 98103. Tel: 206-635-0843; Fax: 206-632-2167; Email: parish@stbens.net; Web: www.stbens.net. Revs. Philip H. Raether, Priest Mod.; Bryan Dolejsi, Parish Priest; Marti Lundberg, Pastoral Coord.
Res.: 1700 N. 49th St., 98103.
School—St. Benedict School, (Grades PreK-8), 4811 Wallingford Ave. N., 98103. Tel: 206-633-3375; Fax: 206-632-3236. Mr. Brian Anderson, Prin.; Susan Lisi, Librarian. Lay Teachers 19; Students 208.
Catechesis Religious Program—Students 45.

7—St. Bernadette (1958)
1028 S.W. 128th St., 98146. Tel: 206-242-7370; Fax: 206-812-3142; Email: shellyc@saintbernadette.net; Web: www.saintbernadette.net. Mailing

Address: 861 S.W. 126th St., 98146. Very Rev. Michael H. Wright.
School—St. Bernadette School, (Grades PreK-8), Tel: 206-244-4934; Fax: 206-244-4943. Carol Diaz Mendoza, Prin. Lay Teachers 15; Students 203.
Catechesis Religious Program—Students 30.

8—BLESSED SACRAMENT (1908)
5041 Ninth Ave., N.E., 98105. Tel: 206-547-3020; Fax: 206-547-6371; Email: info@bspwa.org. Revs. John Marie Bingham, O.P.; Jordan Bradshaw, O.P., Parochial Vicar; Roberto Corral, O.P., Parochial Vicar; Mark Manzano, O.P., Parochial Vicar; Thomas Aquinas Pickett, O.P., Parochial Vicar; Francis Le, O.P., In Res.; James Thompson, O.P., In Res.
Catechesis Religious Program—Web: www.blessed-sacrament.org. Students 170.

9—ST. BRIDGET (1968) [CEM]
Mailing Address: 4900 N.E. 50th St., 98105.
Tel: 206-523-8787; Fax: 206-528-7511; Email: parishoffice@stbridgetchurch.org; Web: www.stbridgetchurch.org. Rev. Kyle C. Manglona, Admin.
Res.: 5000 50th Ave., N.E., 98105.
Catechesis Religious Program—Tel: 206-523-9760. Students 160.

10—ST. CATHERINE OF SIENA (1929)
814 N.E. 85th, 98115. Tel: 206-524-8800. Rev. Patrick Sherrard, Admin.
School—St. Catherine of Siena School, (Grades PreSchool-8), 8524 8th Ave. N.E., 98115.
Tel: 206-525-0581; Fax: 206-985-0253. Pamela Schwarz, Prin. Lay Teachers 17; Students 249.
Catechesis Religious Program—Students 80.

11—CHRIST OUR HOPE PARISH (2009)
1902 2nd Ave., 98101-1155. Tel: 206-448-8826; Email: mail@christourhopeseattle.org. Rev. William Heric, Admin.
Mission—Plymouth Congregational Church Chapel, 1217 6th Ave., 98101.

12—CHRIST THE KING (1930)
405 N. 117th St., 98133. Tel: 206-362-1545;
Fax: 206-364-8325; Email: parish@ckseattle.org. Rev. Armando Guzman; Deacon Joseph Sifferman.
School—Christ the King School, (Grades PreSchool-8), 415 N. 117th St., 98133. Tel: 206-364-6890. Anne Brand, Prin. Lay Teachers 16; Students 175.
Catechesis Religious Program—Students 289.

13—ST. EDWARD (1906)
Mailing Address: 4212 S. Mead St., 98118.
Tel: 205-722-7888; Fax: 206-722-7895; Web: www.stedwardparish.net. Revs. Felino Paulino; Calixto Alex Pablo, Parochial Vicar; Very Rev. Armando S. Perez, Parochial Vicar; Rev. Showreelu Simham, Parochial Vicar; Deacons Jose DeLeon; Sagato Pele; Asipeli Tuifua.
Res.: 4213 S. Orcas, 98118.
School—St. Edward School, (Grades PreK-8), 4200 S. Mead St., 98118. Tel: 206-725-1774;
Fax: 206-725-4569. Mary Lundeen, Prin. Lay Teachers 9; Sisters 1; Students 145.
Catechesis Religious Program—Students 67.

14—ST. FRANCIS OF ASSISI (1929)
15226 21st Ave. S.W., Burien, 98166.
Tel: 206-242-4575; Fax: 206-242-1957; Email: parishoffice@stfoa.org. Mailing Address: P.O. Box 929, Seahurst, 98062-0929. Rev. Richard K. Hayatsu; Deacon Theman Pham.
Res.: 15236 21st Ave., S.W., 98166.
School—St. Francis of Assisi School, (Grades K-8), P.O. Box 870, Seahurst, 98062. Tel: 206-243-5690;
Fax: 206-433-8593. Rosemary Leifer, Prin.; Mary DeMarre, Librarian. Lay Teachers 33; Students 472.
Catechesis Religious Program—Students 140.

15—ST. GEORGE (1903)
5306 13th Ave. S., 98108. Tel: 206-762-7744;
Fax: 206-762-4207; Email: info@stgeorgeparish.com. Revs. Felino Paulino; Calixto Alex Pablo, Parochial Vicar; Very Rev. Armando S. Perez, Parochial Vicar; Rev. Showreelu Simham, Parochial Vicar; Deacons Sagato Pele; Jose DeLeon; Asipeli Tuifua.
School—St. George School, (Grades PreSchool-8), 5117 13th Ave. S., 98108. Tel: 206-762-0656;
Fax: 206-763-3220. Monica Wingard, Prin. Lay Teachers 15; Students 250.
Catechesis Religious Program—Students 45.

16—HOLY FAMILY (1921)
9622 20th Ave., S.W., 98106. Tel: 206-767-6220;
Fax: 206-767-0374; Email: office@hfseattle.org; Web: www.hfseattle.org. Revs. Jose M. Alvarez; Armando Red, Parochial Vicar; Deacon Abel Magana.
School—Holy Family School, (Grades PreSchool-8), 9615 20th Ave., S.W., 98106. Tel: 206-767-6640;
Fax: 206-767-9466. Michael Bacigalupi, Prin. Lay Teachers 15; Students 137.
Catechesis Religious Program—Students 220.

17—HOLY ROSARY (1907)
4139 42nd Ave., S.W., 98116. Tel: 206-935-8353; Email: parishoffice@holyrosaryseattle.org; Web: www.holyrosaryseattle.org. Rev. Matthew T. Oakland.
School—Holy Rosary School, (Grades PreK-8), 4142 42nd Ave., S.W., 98116. Tel: 206-937-7255;
Fax: 206-937-2610; Web: www.holyrosaryws.org. Anna Horton, Prin.; Sue Harris, Librarian. Lay Teachers 37; Students 439.
Catechesis Religious Program—
Tel: 206-935-8353, Ext. 203; Email: Evangelization@HolyRosarySeattle.org. Students 60.

18—IMMACULATE CONCEPTION (1891)
820 18th Ave., 98122. Tel: 206-322-5970;
Fax: 206-322-9417; Email: office@icseattle.org. Revs. Maurice Mamba Ngalamulume, Admin.; Negusse Fesseha Keleta, (Eritrea) In Res.; Deacons Gregory McNabb, Pastoral Assoc.; Joseph Connor.
Catechesis Religious Program—Students 15.

19—ST. JOHN THE EVANGELIST (1917)
121 N. 80th St., 98103. Tel: 206-782-2810; Email: parishoffice@stjohnsea.org; Web: www.stjohnsea.org. Rev. Crispin Okoth.
School—St. John School, (Grades PreK-8), 120 N. 79th St., 98103. Tel: 206-783-0337; Email: ddamelio@stjohnsea.org; Web: www.st-johnsea.org. Bernadette O'Leary, Prin.; Merrick Bodmer, Librarian. Clergy 3; Lay Teachers 30; Students 540.
Catechesis Religious Program—Email: jrudden@stjohnsea.org. Julia Rudden, D.R.E. Students 605.

20—ST. JOSEPH (1907)
732 18th Ave. E., 98112. Tel: 206-324-2522;
Fax: 206-329-5698; Web: www.stjosephparish.org. Revs. John Whitney, S.J.; Julian Climaco, S.J., Parochial Vicar; Deacon Stephen Wodzanowski, Pastoral Assoc.
School—St. Joseph School, (Grades K-8), 700 18th Ave. E., 98112. Tel: 206-329-3260; Fax: 206-324-7773 . Patrick Fennessy, Prin. Lay Teachers 42; Sisters 1; Students 625.
Catechesis Religious Program—Students 125.

21—ST. MARGARET OF SCOTLAND (1910)
3221 14th Ave. W., 98119. Tel: 206-282-1804; Email: pastor@st-margaret-church.org; Web: www.st-margaret-church.org. Rev. Andrzej Galant, S.Ch.
Catechesis Religious Program—Students 95.

22—ST. MARY (1899)
611 20th Ave. S., 98144. Tel: 206-324-7100; Email: stmarysparish@hotmail.com; Web: www.saintmarysseattle.org. Rev. Felino Paulino, Priest Mod.; Very Rev. Armando S. Perez, Parish Priest; Mr. Olaf Valderrabano, Pastoral Coord.
Catechesis Religious Program—Students 128.

23—ST. MATTHEW (1954)
1240 N.E. 127th St., 98125. Tel: 206-363-6767;
Fax: 206-362-4863; Email: office@stmatthewseattle.org; Web: www.stmatthewseattle.org. Rev. Khanh D. Nguyen.
School—St. Matthew School, (Grades PreK-8), 1230 N.E. 127th St., 98125. Tel: 206-362-2785;
Fax: 206-440-9476. Karen Herlihy, Prin. Lay Teachers 14; Students 208.
Catechesis Religious Program—Students 55.

24—NORTH AMERICAN MARTYRS PERSONAL PARISH (2008)
5816 15th Ave. N.W., 98107. Tel: 206-641-6504; Email: nam@fssp.com; Web: www.northamericanmartyrs.org. Mailing Address: 12546 B 5th Ave. N.E., 98125. Revs. Joseph Heffernan, F.S.S.P.; Adrian Debow, Parochial Vicar; Caleb Insco, F.S.S.P., Parochial Vicar.

25—OUR LADY OF FATIMA (1952)
3218 W. Barrett St., 98199. Tel: 206-283-1456; Email: lsmith@olfatima.org. 3307 W. Dravus St., 98199. Rev. Philip H. Raether; Deacon Ronald H. Allen.
School—Our Lady of Fatima School, (Grades K-8), 3301 W. Dravus St., 98199. Tel: 206-283-7031;
Fax: 206-299-3202; Email: info@olfatima.org; Web: www.school.olfatima.org. Nicholas Ford, Prin.; Mollie Overa, Librarian. Lay Teachers 21; Students 268.
Catechesis Religious Program—Tel: 206-352-4586. Students 95.

26—OUR LADY OF GUADALUPE (1960)
7000-35th Ave., S.W., 98126. Tel: 206-935-0358; Email: parishoffice@olgseattle.org; Web: www.olgseattle.org. Rev. John Walmesley.
School—Our Lady of Guadalupe School, (Grades PreK-8), 3401 S.W. Myrtle, 98126. Tel: 206-935-0651 ; Fax: 206-938-3695; Email: info@guadalupeschool.org; Web: www.guadalupe-school.org. Donna Ramos, Prin.; Loretta Kramer, Librarian. Lay Teachers 19; Students 253.
Catechesis Religious Program—Students 48.

27—OUR LADY OF LOURDES (1892)
10243 12th Ave. S., 98168. Tel: 206-735-7598; Email: office.stoll@gmail.com. 4415 S. 140th St., Tukwila, 98168. Very Rev. James Northrup; Rev. Francis Mau Van Ho, S.D.D., Parochial Vicar.
Catechesis Religious Program—Students 235.

28—OUR LADY OF MOUNT VIRGIN (1911)
1531 Bradner Pl. S., 98144. Tel: 206-324-8521;
Fax: 206-324-0405; Email: info@mountvirgin.org. Revs. Hung T. Nguyen; Patrick J. Twohy, S.J., Parochial Vicar (Native American Community); Deacon Joseph Yuen, (Chinese Community).
Catechesis Religious Program—Students 36.

29—OUR LADY OF THE LAKE (1929)
8900 35th Ave., N.E., 98115. Tel: 206-523-6776; Email: tsmith@ollseattle.org; Web: www.ollparishseattle.org. 3517 N.E. 89th St., 98115. Rev. Timothy Clark, Admin.; Deacon Dennis T. Duffell.
School—Our Lady of the Lake School, (Grades K-8), 3520 N.E. 89th St., 98115. Tel: 206-525-9980;
Fax: 206-523-2858. Vince McGovern, Prin.; Deb Werner, Librarian. Lay Teachers 17; Students 199.
Catechesis Religious Program—Students 292.

30—ST. PATRICK (1918)
2702 Broadway E., 98102. Tel: 206-329-2960;
Fax: 206-329-2961; Email: office@stpatrickseattle.org; Web: www.stpatrickseattle.org. Very Rev. Michael G. Ryan, Mod.; Rev. Patrick S. Clark, Parish Priest, (Retired); Ms. JoAnn Choi, Pastoral Coord.
Catechesis Religious Program—Students 45.

31—ST. PAUL (1953)
5600 S. Ryan St., 98178. Tel: 206-725-2050;
Fax: 206-722-3946. Revs. Felino Paulino; Calixto Alex Pablo, Parochial Vicar; Very Rev. Armando S. Perez, Parochial Vicar; Rev. Showreelu Simham, Parochial Vicar; Deacons Jose DeLeon; Sagato Pele; Asipeli Tuifua.
School—St. Paul School, (Grades PreSchool-8), 10001 57th Ave. S., 98178. Tel: 206-725-0780;
Fax: 206-725-0781. Lay Teachers 12; Students 148.
Catechesis Religious Program—Students 16.

32—ST. PETER (1931)
2807 15th Ave. S., 98144. Tel: 206-324-2290;
Fax: 206-324-4020; Email: stpeterseattle@broadstripe.net. Revs. Felino Paulino; Calixto Alex Pablo, Parochial Vicar; Very Rev. Armando S. Perez, Parochial Vicar; Rev. Showreelu Simham, Parochial Vicar.
Catechesis Religious Program—Students 54.

33—SACRED HEART OF JESUS (1889)
205 2nd Ave. N., 98109. Tel: 206-284-4680;
Fax: 206-284-3161; Email: info@sacredheartseattle.com; Web: www.sacredheartseattle.com. Revs. Richard Luberti, C.Ss.R.; Denis Ryan, C.Ss.R., Parochial Vicar; William M. Cleary, C.Ss.R., In Res.; Lyle E. Konen, C.Ss.R., In Res.; William Peterson, C.Ss.R., In Res.; Binh Ta, C.Ss.R., In Res.; Timothy Watson, C.Ss.R., In Res.

34—ST. THERESE (1926)
3416 E. Marion St., 98122. Tel: 206-325-2711;
Fax: 206-329-8373; Email: office@st-therese.cc; Web: www.saintthereseparish.org. Rev. Maurice Mamba Ngalamulume, Admin.; Deacon Gregory McNabb, Pastoral Assoc.
School—St. Therese School, (Grades PreK-8), 900-35th Ave., 98122. Tel: 206-324-0460;
Fax: 206-324-8464. Mr. Matthew DeBoer, Prin. Lay Teachers 12; Students 128.
Catechesis Religious Program—Students 123.

35—VIETNAMESE MARTYRS PERSONAL PARISH (2010)
6801 S. 180th St., Tukwila, 98188. Tel: 206-325-5626 ; Fax: 206-324-5849; Email: vmpadmin@vmpwa.org. Revs. Thanh X. Dao; Francis Mien, In Res., (Retired); Anthony Lan Tran, In Res., (Retired); Deacon Mau Nguyen.

OUTSIDE THE CITY OF SEATTLE

ABERDEEN, GRAYS HARBOR CO., ST. MARY (1885)
306 E. Third St., Aberdeen, 98520. Tel: 360-532-8300 ; Fax: 360-538-9987; Email: stmary@ghcatholic.org. Revs. Francis Arulappan, H.G.N., Admin.; Victor Raj Anas Dass, H.G.N., Parochial Vicar; Vinner Raj Simeon Raj, H.G.N., Parochial Vicar.
Res.: 320 E. Third St., Aberdeen, 98520.
School—St. Mary School, (Grades PreSchool-8), 518 N. H St., Aberdeen, 98520. Tel: 360-532-1230;
Fax: 360-532-1209. Nicole Franson, Prin. Lay Teachers 15; Students 151.
Catechesis Religious Program—
Tel: 360-532-8300, Ext. 110. Students 156.
Mission—St. Paul, P.O. Box 332, Westport, Grays Harbor Co. 98585.

ANACORTES, SKAGIT CO., ST. MARY (1910)
4001 St. Mary's Dr., Anacortes, 98221.
Tel: 360-293-2101; Email: admin@stmaryanacortes.org; Web: www.stmaryanacortes.org. Rev. Mel Strazicich; Deacon Cary Parnell.
Catechesis Religious Program—Tel: 360-293-2101. Students 89.

ARLINGTON, SNOHOMISH CO., IMMACULATE CONCEPTION (1890)
1200 E. Fifth St., P.O. Box 69, Arlington, 98223-0069. Tel: 360-435-8565; Fax: 360-435-9732; Email: icc-sjv@comcast.net; Web: www.stillycatholic.org. Rev. Ramon Santa Cruz.
Catechesis Religious Program—
Tel: 360-435-8565, Ext. 13; Email: kkichlinedre@comcast.net. Kathleen Kichline, D.R.E. Students 157.
Mission—St. John Mary Vianney, 1150 Riddle St., Darrington, Snohomish Co. 98241.

AUBURN, KING CO., HOLY FAMILY (1904)
505 17th St., S.E., Auburn, 98002. Tel: 253-833-5130; Fax: 253-833-3421; Email: cbanning@holyfamilyauburn.org. Rev. R. Roy C. Baroma.
School—Holy Family School, (Grades PreK-8), Tel: 253-833-8688; Fax: 253-833-9311. Daniel Hill, Prin. Lay Teachers 15; Students 196.
Catechesis Religious Program—Students 382.

BAINBRIDGE ISLAND, KITSAP CO., ST. CECILIA (1950)
1310 Madison Ave. N., Bainbridge Island, 98110. Tel: 206-842-3594; Fax: 206-842-6988; Email: secretary@saintcparish.org; Web: www.saintcparish.org. Rev. ` Mark M. Kiszelewski.
School—St. Cecilia School, (Grades PreSchool-8), Tel: 206-842-2017; Email: info@saintceciliaschool.org; Web: www.saintceciliaschool.org. Susan Kilbane, Prin.
Catechesis Religious Program—
Tel: 206-842-3594, Ext. 102. Students 40.

BATTLE GROUND, CLARK CO., SACRED HEART (1877) [CEM]
Mailing Address: 1603 N. Parkway Ave., P.O. Box 38, Battle Ground, 98604. Tel: 360-687-4515; Fax: 360-687-3322; Email: info@sacredheartbg.org; Web: www.sacredheartbg.org. Rev. Aloysius G. Ssensamba, Admin.
Catechesis Religious Program—Email: debbie@sacredheartbg.org. Deborah Adams, D.R.E. Students 72.
Mission—St. Joseph the Worker, 200 W. Jones St., Yacolt, Clark Co. 98675. Email: d.wilson@sacredheartbg.org.

BELLEVUE, KING CO.
1—ST. LOUISE (1960)
141 156th Ave., S.E., Bellevue, 98007. Tel: 425-747-4450; Fax: 425-214-5380; Email: info@stlouise.org. Very Rev. Gary M. Zender; Rev. Fabian MacDonald, Parochial Vicar; Deacons William Haines Jr.; Samuel Basta.
School—St. Louise School, (Grades K-8), 133 156th Ave., S.E., Bellevue, 98007. Tel: 425-746-4220; Fax: 425-644-3294; Web: www.stlouiseschool.org. Dan Fitzpatrick, Prin.; Mary Carson, Librarian. Lay Teachers 45; Students 442.
Catechesis Religious Program—
Tel: 425-747-4450, Ext. 5464. Students 40.
2—ST. MADELEINE SOPHIE (1968)
4400 130th Place S.E., Bellevue, 98006-2014. Tel: 425-747-6770, Ext. 100; Email: Parishoffice@stmadsophie.org; Web: www.stmadeleine.org. Revs. James D. Picton, J.D., J.C.L.; Donald Perea, Parochial Vicar; Deacon Bruno Bahk.
School—St. Madeleine Sophie School, (Grades PreK-8), c/o St. Madeleine Sophie Parish, 4400 130th Pl. S.E., Bellevue, 98006-2014. Tel: 425-747-6770, Ext. 201; Email: schooloffice@stmadsophie.org; Web: www.smsbellevue.org. Mr. Dan Sherman, Prin. Lay Teachers 18; Students 175.
Catechesis Religious Program—
Tel: 425-747-6770, Ext. 124; Email: maggie@stmadsophie.org; Email: akareta@stmadsophie.org; Email: elaine@stmadsophie.org; Email: ann@stmadsophie.org. Maggie Rader, Whole Community Catechsis; Ann Kareta, RCIA & Marriage Preparation; Elaine Low, Baptism Preparation; Ann LaBeck, Confirmation. Students 300.
3—SACRED HEART (1946)
9460 N.E. 14th St., Bellevue, 98004. Tel: 425-454-9536; Fax: 425-450-3909; Email: lpaulsen@sacredheart.org; Web: www.sacredheart.org. Revs. James O. Johnson Jr., Priest Mod.; John C. Madigan, Parish Priest, (Retired); Deacon Samuel Basta, Pastoral Coord.
School—Sacred Heart School, (Grades K-8), 9450 N.E. 14th St., Bellevue, 98004. Tel: 425-451-1773; Fax: 425-450-3918. David Burroughs, Prin. Lay Teachers 37; Students 407.
Catechesis Religious Program—Students 281.

BELLINGHAM, WHATCOM CO.
1—ASSUMPTION (1889)
2116 Cornwall Ave., Bellingham, 98225. Tel: 360-733-1380; Email: parishoffice@assumption.org; Web: www.assumption.org. Very Rev. K. Scott Connolly; Deacon Lawrence Kheriaty.
School—Assumption School, (Grades PreK-8), Tel: 360-733-6133; Email: theoffice@school.assumption.org; Web: www.school.assumption.org. Don Anderson, Prin. Lay Teachers 18; Students 205.
Catechesis Religious Program—Students 87.
2—SACRED HEART (1905) [JC]
1115 14th St., Bellingham, 98225. Tel: 360-734-2850; Fax: 360-734-0947; Email: melissa.johnson@shbham.org. Rev. Cody Ross, Admin.
Catechesis Religious Program—Students 90.
Station—Newman Campus Ministry, 714 N. Garden St., Bellingham, 98225.

BLACK DIAMOND, KING CO., ST. BARBARA (1910)
32416 6th Ave., P.O. Box 189, Black Diamond, 98010. Tel: 360-886-2229; Fax: 360-886-2617; Email: office@stbarbarachurch.org; Web: www.stbarbarachurch.org. Rev. David Rogerson.
Catechesis Religious Program—Students 102.

BOTHELL, KING CO., ST. BRENDAN (1949)
10051 N.E. 195th St., Bothell, 98011-2931. Tel: 425-483-9400; Fax: 425-486-9735; Web: saintbrendan.org. Very Rev. Nicholas F. Wichert.
School—St. Brendan School, (Grades K-8), 10049 N.E. 195th St., Bothell, 98011. Tel: 425-483-8300; Fax: 425-483-2839; Email: secretary@school.saintbrendan.org; Web: school.saintbrendan.org. Catherine Shumate, Prin.; Joyceanne Michaels, Librarian. Lay Teachers 18; Students 216.
Catechesis Religious Program—Students 267.

BOTHELL, SNOHOMISH CO., ST. ELIZABETH ANN SETON (1983)
3216 180th St. S.E., Mill Creek, 98012-6534. Tel: 425-481-0303; Fax: 425-485-8510. Mailing Address: P.O. Box 12429, Mill Creek, 98082-0429. Revs. Jose Gerardo Alberto, M.Sp.S.; Jose de Jesus Sanchez, M.Sp.S., Parochial Vicar; Jose Ugalde, M.Sp.S., Parochial Vicar.
Catechesis Religious Program—Tel: 425-481-9358; Web: www.easbothell.org. Stephanie Moran, D.R.E. Students 758.

BREMERTON, KITSAP CO.
1—HOLY TRINITY (1964)
4215 Pine Rd. N.E., Bremerton, 98310. Tel: 360-377-7674; Fax: 360-377-6181; Email: mail@holytrinitymail.org. Mailing Address: P.O. Box 910, Tracyton, 98393. Very Rev. Derek J. Lappe, Priest Mod.; Revs. Dennis Sevilla, Parish Priest, (Retired); Jack Buckalew, Parish Priest, (Retired); Deacons Henry Miner; John Amlag; Veronica Kelly, Pastoral Coord.
Catechesis Religious Program—Tel: 360-479-9525. Students 177.
2—OUR LADY, STAR OF THE SEA (1902)
1513-6th St., Bremerton, 98337. Fax: 360-479-1468; Email: info@starofthesea.net; Web: www.starofthesea.net; Tel: 360-479-3777. Very Rev. Derek J. Lappe; Deacons William Hamlin; James Decker.
School—Our Lady, Star of the Sea School, 1516-5th St., Bremerton, 98337. Tel: 360-373-5162. Jeanette Wolfe, Prin. Lay Teachers 11; Students 200.
Catechesis Religious Program—Students 178.

BUCKLEY, PIERCE CO., ST. ALOYSIUS (1892)
211 W. Mason Ave., Buckley, 98321. Tel: 360-829-6515; Fax: 360-829-5190; Email: office@saint-aloysius-catholic-church.org. Revs. Anthony K. A. Davis, Admin.; Clarence Jones, Parochial Vicar; Deacon Raymond Daigh.
Catechesis Religious Program—Tel: 360-829-9958. Students 45.
Mission—Our Lady of Lourdes (1894) [CEM] Wilkeson, Pierce Co.

BURLINGTON, SKAGIT CO., ST. CHARLES (1885)
935 Peterson Rd., Burlington, 98233. Tel: 360-757-0128; Fax: 360-757-0418; Email: stcharles@stcharles0burlington-wa.org. Revs. Thomas McMichael; Jeffrey Moore, Parochial Vicar; Very Rev. Paul A. Magnano, Parish Priest; Deacon Antonio Cavazos.
Catechesis Religious Program—Students 113.

CAMAS, CLARK CO., ST. THOMAS AQUINAS (1870) [CEM]
324 N.E. Oak, Camas, 98607. Tel: 360-834-2126; Email: office@stthomascamas.org. Revs. Gary F. Lazzeroni; Michael Dion, Parochial Vicar.
Catechesis Religious Program—
Tel: 360-834-2126, Ext. 2. Students 205.
Mission—Our Lady Star of the Sea, P.O. Box 901, Stevenson, Skamania Co. 98648. Deacon William Townsend.

CASTLE ROCK, COWLITZ CO., ST. MARY (1910)
120 Powell Rd., Castle Rock, 98611-0960. Tel: 360-274-7404; Fax: 360-274-7328; Email: smcc58@cni.net. Mailing Address: 701 26th Ave., Longview, 98632. Very Rev. Bryan A. Ochs; Rev. Sebastin Sebastian, Parochial Vicar.
Catechesis Religious Program—Students 36.

CENTRALIA, LEWIS CO., ST. MARY (1910)
225 N. Washington Ave., Centralia, 98531. Tel: 360-748-4953; Fax: 360-748-3149; Email: office@wlpcatholic.org; Web: www.wlpcatholic.org. Mailing Address: 157 S.W. 6th St., Chehalis, 98532. Revs. Jacob M. Maurer; Christopher Hoiland, Parochial Vicar; Deacons Loren Lane; Arturo Ramirez.
Catechesis Religious Program—Email: adriana@wlpcatholic.org; Email: darlene@wlpcatholic.org. Adriana Garibay, D.R.E.; Darlene Mackey, D.R.E. Students 20.

CHEHALIS, LEWIS CO., ST. JOSEPH (1888)
682 S.W. Cascade Ave., Chehalis, 98532. Tel: 360-748-4953; Fax: 360-748-3149; Web: www.wlpcatholic.org. Mailing Address: 157 S.W. 6th St., Chehalis, 98532. Revs. Jacob M. Maurer; Christopher Hoiland, Parochial Vicar; Deacons Loren Lane; Arturo Ramirez.
School—St. Joseph School, (Grades PreSchool-8), 123 S.W. 6th St., Chehalis, 98532. Tel: 360-748-0961; Fax: 360-748-8502. Lay Teachers 10; Students 150.
Catechesis Religious Program—Email: adriana@wlpcatholic.org; Email: darlene@wlpcatholic.org. Adriana Garibay, D.R.E.; Darlene Mackey, D.R.E. Students 125.

COVINGTON, KING CO., ST. JOHN THE BAPTIST (1990)
25810 156th Ave., S.E., Covington, 98042. Tel: 253-630-0701; Fax: 253-630-3174; Email: office@sjtbcc.org; Web: www.sjtbcc.org. Rev. James P. Coyne.
Catechesis Religious Program—Students 402.

DES MOINES, KING CO., ST. PHILOMENA (1927)
1790 S. 222nd St., Des Moines, 98198. Tel: 206-878-8709; Fax: 206-824-3480; Email: parishoffice@stphil.com. Revs. Stephen Woodland; Gilberto Mora Tapia, Parochial Vicar; Deacon Gerald Graddon.
School—St. Philomena School, (Grades K-8), 1815 S. 220th, Des Moines, 98198. Tel: 206-824-4051; Fax: 206-878-8646. Lay Teachers 12; Students 225.
Catechesis Religious Program—Tel: 206-824-5582. Students 247.

DUVALL, KING CO., HOLY INNOCENTS (1914)
26526 N.E. Cherry Valley Rd., P.O. Box 850, Duvall, 98019. Tel: 425-788-1400; Email: office@holyinn.org. Revs. James O. Johnson Jr.; Raphael D. Mkuzi, Parochial Vicar; Deacon Mirek Sztajno.
Catechesis Religious Program—Jennie Caldwell, D.R.E. Students 142.

EDMONDS, SNOHOMISH CO., HOLY ROSARY (1940)
760 Aloha St., P.O. Box 206, Edmonds, 98020-0206. Tel: 425-778-3122; Fax: 425-672-4909; Web: www.holyrosaryedmonds.org. Very Rev. Vincent M. Gilmore, Admin.; Deacons Raymond Biersbach; Craig Lundberg.
School—Holy Rosary School, (Grades PreSchool-8), 770 Aloha St., P.O. Box 206, Edmonds, 98020. Tel: 425-778-3197; Fax: 425-771-8144. Susan Venable, Prin.; Carlotta Rojas, Librarian. Lay Teachers 17; Sisters 1; Students 252.
Catechesis Religious Program—Tel: 425-778-3122. Students 271.

ELMA, GRAYS HARBOR CO., ST. JOSEPH (1890) [CEM]
501 W. Main St., P.O. Box 3027, Elma, 98541. Tel: 360-482-3190; Fax: 360-482-3107; Email: office.twosaints@gmail.com. Rev. Charles Banduku, Admin.; Deacon F. Thomas Hawkins.
Catechesis Religious Program—Students 38.
Mission—St. John, Broadway and Church St., Montesano, Grays Harbor Co. 98563.

ENUMCLAW, KING CO., SACRED HEART OF JESUS (1888) [CEM]
1614 Farrelly St., Enumclaw, 98022. Tel: 360-825-3759; Fax: 360-825-6832; Email: brenda@sacredheartenumclaw.org; Web: www.sacredheartenumclaw.org. Revs. Anthony K. A. Davis, Admin.; Clarence Jones, Parochial Vicar; Deacons Raymond Daigh; George Mounce III.
Catechesis Religious Program—Students 225.
Station—Crystal Mountain, Crystal Mountain Chapel.

EVERETT, SNOHOMISH CO.
1—IMMACULATE CONCEPTION (1904)
2619 Cedar St., Everett, 98201. Tel: 425-349-7014; Fax: 425-349-7015; Email: goldstein@ic-olph.org; Web: www.ic-olph.org. Revs. Joseph F. Altenhofen; Francis Le, O.P., Parochial Vicar; Deacon Dennis Kelly.
Res.: 2509 Hoyt Ave., Everett, 98201.
Church: 2501 Hoyt Ave., Everett, 98201.
School—Immaculate Conception School, (Grades PreSchool-8), 2508 Hoyt Ave., Everett, 98201. Tel: 425-349-7777; Fax: 425-349-7048. Kathy Wartelle, Prin. Lay Teachers 28; Students 255.
Catechesis Religious Program—Students 152.
2—ST. MARY MAGDALEN (1957)
8517 7th Ave., S.E., Everett, 98208. Tel: 425-353-1211; Fax: 425-348-0458; Web: www.smmparish.org. Revs. Hans M. Olson; Titus E. G. Bayani, Parochial Vicar; Deacon David P. Alcorta.
School—St. Mary Magdalen School, (Grades PreK-8), 8615 7th Ave., S.E., Everett, 98208. Tel: 425-353-7559; Fax: 425-356-2687; Email: Info@stmarym.org; Web: www.stmarym.org. Zack Cunningham, Prin.; Laura Mellahan, Librarian. Lay Teachers 25; Students 400.
Catechesis Religious Program—Students 510.
Mission—St. John, 829 3rd St., Mukilteo, Snohomish Co. 98275.
3—OUR LADY OF PERPETUAL HELP (1891) [CEM]
Mailing Address: 2619 Cedar St., Everett, 98201. Tel: 425-349-7014; Fax: 425-349-7015. Revs. Joseph F. Altenhofen; Francis Le, O.P., Parochial Vicar; Deacon Dennis Kelly.
Res.: 2509 Hoyt Ave., Everett, 98201.
Church: 2617 Cedar St., Everett, 98201.
Catechesis Religious Program—Students 232.

FEDERAL WAY, KING CO.
1—ST. THERESA (1924)
3939 S.W. 331st, Federal Way, 98023.

Tel: 253-838-5924; Fax: 253-838-0300; Email: linda.demarce@sttheresafw.org. Revs. Richard K. Hayatsu, Mod.; Jean Pierre Kasonga, Parochial Vicar; Gilberto Mora Tapia, Parochial Vicar; Deacon Tom O'Loughlin; Linda M. DeMarce, Pastoral Coord.
Catechesis Religious Program—Students 275.
2—ST. VINCENT DE PAUL (1961)
30525 8th Ave. S., Federal Way, 98003.
Tel: 253-839-2320; Email: info@stvincentparish.org; Web: stvincentparish.org. Very Rev. William McKee; Deacon Juan Lezcano.
School—St. Vincent De Paul School, (Grades K-8), 30527 8th Ave. S., Federal Way, 98003.
Tel: 253-839-3532; Fax: 253-946-1247. Wanda Stewart, Prin.; Urdene Rickard, Librarian. Lay Teachers 15; Students 255.
Catechesis Religious Program—John Simpson, D.R.E., Adult Faith & Family Formation; Brita Jaingue, D.R.E.,Youth Min.; Jame Nguyen, D.R.E., Children's Min.; Katie Goodson, D.R.E., Lay Min. and Evangelization. Students 277.
FERNDALE, WHATCOM CO., ST. JOSEPH (1893)
5781 Hendrickson Ave., Ferndale, 98248.
Tel: 360-384-3651; Fax: 360-384-1879; Email: administration@stjosephferndale.org. Rev. Francis Thumbi, Admin.
Catechesis Religious Program—Tel: 360-384-8818. Students 250.
Missions—St. Anne—Blaine, Whatcom Co. 98230.
St. Joachim (Indian Reservation), Bellingham.
FIFE, PIERCE CO.
1—ST. MARTIN OF TOURS (1947)
2303-54th Ave. E., Fife, 98424. Tel: 253-922-7882; Email: office@stmartinoftoursfife.com. Revs. Michael Radermacher; Anh B. Tran, Parochial Vicar; Deacon Patrick Kelley.
School—All Saints at St. Martin of Tours, (Grades K-8), 2323 54th Ave. E., Fife, 98424. Tel: 253-922-5360; Fax: 253-922-6746; Web: www.allsaintspuyallup.org. Amy Orm, Prin.
Catechesis Religious Program—Tel: 253-922-6858. Students 91.
2—ST. PAUL CHONG HASANG PERSONAL PARISH
1316 62nd Ave. E., Fife, 98424-1312.
Tel: 253-896-4489; Fax: 253-896-9468. Revs. Lino Hyun-Gyu Kim; Tae Chul Lee, Parochial Vicar.
FORKS, CLALLAM CO., ST. ANNE PARISH (1930)
511 5th Ave., P.O. Box 2359, Forks, 98331.
Tel: 360-374-9184; Email: stanneforks@centurylink.net. Revs. Zevier Arockiam, H.G.N., Admin.; Francis Arulappan, H.G.N., Parochial Vicar; Vinner Raj Simeon Raj, H.G.N., Parochial Vicar.
Catechesis Religious Program—Tel: 360-374-6405. Students 37.
Mission—St. Thomas the Apostle, Clallam Bay, Clallam Co.
FRIDAY HARBOR, SAN JUAN CO., ST. FRANCIS (1860) [CEM]
425 Price St., Friday Harbor, 98250.
Tel: 360-378-2910; Email: stfrancisfh@centurytel.net; Web: stfrancissji.org. Mailing Address: P.O. Box 1489, Friday Harbor, 98250. Revs. Watson Paramasivan, Admin.; Rajasekar Savarimuthu, Parochial Vicar.
Res.: 370 Marguerite, P.O. Box 1489, Friday Harbor, 98250. Tel: 360-378-0189.
Catechesis Religious Program—Students 26.
Stations—St. Francis-Eastsound—956 N. Beach Rd., Eastsound, 98245.
St. Francis-Lopez Island Community, Center Church, Davis Bay Rd., Lopez Island.
GIG HARBOR, PIERCE CO., ST. NICHOLAS (1931)
Mailing Address: 3510 Rosedale St. N.W., Gig Harbor, 98335-1818. Tel: 253-851-8850; Email: office@stnicholascc.org; Web: www.stnicholascc.org. Rev. Mark A. Guzman; Deacons Mikhail S. Alnajjar; Dale Fickes.
Res.: 3504 Coho St., Gig Harbor, 98335.
School—St. Nicholas School, (Grades PreK-8), 3555 Edwards St., Gig Harbor, 98335. Tel: 253-858-7632; Fax: 253-858-1597. Amy Unruh, Prin. Lay Teachers 16; Students 144.
Catechesis Religious Program—Tel: 253-851-9040. Students 149.
HOQUIAM, GRAYS HARBOR CO., OUR LADY OF GOOD HELP (1906)
200 L St., Hoquiam, 98550. Tel: 360-532-8300;
Fax: 360-538-9987; Email: olgh@ghcatholic.org. Mailing Address: 306 E. 3rd St., Aberdeen, 98520. Revs. Francis Arulappan, H.G.N., Admin.; Vinner Raj Simeon Raj, H.G.N., Parochial Vicar; Victor Raj Anas Dass, H.G.N., Parochial Vicar.
Res.: 208 L St., Hoquiam, 98550.
Mission—Our Lady of the Olympics.
ISSAQUAH, KING CO., ST. JOSEPH (1962)
220 Mt. Park Blvd., S.W., P.O. Box 200, Issaquah, 98027. Tel: 425-392-5516; Fax: 425-392-2722; Email: office@sjcissaquah.org; Web: www.sjcissaquah.org. Very Rev. Todd O. Strange; Deacon Patrick Moynihan, The Haitian Project.
Schools—Issaquah Campus—(Grades PreK-4), 220 Mt. Park Blvd., S.W., Issaquah, 98027.
Tel: 425-313-9129; Fax: 425-313-7296. Peg Johnston, Prin. Lay Teachers 27; Students 355.
Snoqualmie Campus, (Grades PreSchool-3), 38645 S.E. Newton St., Snoqualmie, 98065.
Tel: 425-888-9130. Peg Johnston, Prin.
Catechesis Religious Program—Amy Field, D.R.E. Students 425.
KELSO, COWLITZ CO., IMMACULATE HEART OF MARY (1910)
2200 Allen St., Kelso, 98626-5004. Tel: 360-423-3650 ; Fax: 360-423-4165; Email: ihom@cni.net. Mailing Address: 2571 Nichols Blvd., Longview, 98632. Very Rev. Bryan A. Ochs; Rev. Sebastin Sebastian, Parochial Vicar.
Catechesis Religious Program—
KENT, KING CO., HOLY SPIRIT PARISH (1890) [CEM]
327 2nd Ave. S., Kent, 98032. Tel: 253-859-0444; Web: www.holyspiritkent.org. Mailing Address: 310 3rd Ave. S., Kent, 98032. Rev. Raymond Cleaveland, Admin.
Catechesis Religious Program—Students 133.
KIRKLAND, KING CO.
1—HOLY FAMILY (1915)
7045 120th Ave., N.E., Kirkland, 98033.
Tel: 425-822-0295; Fax: 425-827-0648; Web: www.hfkparish.org. Revs. Kurt Nagel; Chad Green, Parochial Vicar.
School—Holy Family School, (Grades PreSchool-8), 7300 120th Ave., N.E., Kirkland, 98033.
Tel: 425-827-0444; Fax: 425-827-0150; Web: www.hfkschool.org. Jacqueline Degel, Prin. Lay Teachers 21; Students 265.
Catechesis Religious Program—Students 478.
2—ST. JOHN MARY VIANNEY (1971)
12600 84th Ave., N.E., Kirkland, 98034.
Tel: 425-823-0787; Email: mberard@sjvkirkland.org; Web: www.sjvkirkland.org. Rev. Vu Phong Tran.
Res.: 12614 84th Ave., N.E., Kirkland, 98034.
Catechesis Religious Program—Students 134.
LA CONNER, SKAGIT CO., SACRED HEART (1875)
404 Douglas St., P.O. Box 757, La Conner, 98257-0757. Tel: 360-466-3967; Email: sacredheartlaconner@gmail.com. Revs. Thomas McMichael; Jeffrey Moore, Parochial Vicar; Very Rev. Paul A. Magnano, Parish Priest; Deacon Antonio Cavazos.
Catechesis Religious Program—Students 65.
LACEY, THURSTON CO., SACRED HEART OF JESUS (1923)
812 Bowker St. S.E., Lacey, 98503-1210.
Tel: 360-491-0890; Fax: 360-456-1028; Email: staff@3hearts.org; Web: www.sacredheartlacey.com. Mailing Address: P.O. Box 3805, Lacey, 98509-3805. Very Rev. Timothy W. Ilgen; Deacons Terry Barber; Rey Ronquillo; Ronald San Nicolas.
Catechesis Religious Program—Students 428.
LAKE STEVENS, SNOHOMISH CO., HOLY CROSS PARISH (2004)
6915 State Rte. 92, P.O. Box 746, Lake Stevens, 98258. Tel: 360-691-2636; Email: admin@hccclakestevens.org; Web: www.holycrossparish.ws. Rev. Joseph DeFolco.
Catechesis Religious Program—Lee Ann Balbirona, D.R.E. Students 125.
LAKEWOOD, PIERCE CO.
1—ST. FRANCES CABRINI (1952)
5505 108th St., S.W., Lakewood, 98499.
Tel: 253-588-2141; Fax: 253-582-5351; Web: www.cabrini.us. Rev. Paul J. Brunet; Deacons George Mounce III; Joe Lehman.
School—St. Frances Cabrini School, (Grades PreSchool-8), 5621 108th St., S.W., Lakewood, 98499. Tel: 253-584-3850. Stephanie Van Leuven, Prin. Lay Teachers 15; Students 238.
Catechesis Religious Program—Students 266.
2—ST. JOHN BOSCO (1968)
10508 112 St., S.W., Lakewood, 98498.
Tel: 253-582-1028; Fax: 253-584-0633; Web: www.stjbosco.org. Rev. Marc L. Powell.
Catechesis Religious Program—Students 175.
Mission—Immaculate Conception, Nisqually & Main, Steilacoom, Pierce Co. 98388.
LANGLEY, ISLAND CO., ST. HUBERT (1938)
Mailing Address: 804 3rd St., P.O. Box 388, Langley, 98260-0388. Tel: 360-221-5383; Email: sthubert@whidbey.com. Rev. Richard J. Spicer.
Res.: 815 Saratoga Rd., Langley, 98260.
Catechesis Religious Program—Students 33.
LONGVIEW, COWLITZ CO., ST. ROSE DE VITERBO (1928)
701 26th Ave., Longview, 98632. Tel: 360-425-4660; Fax: 360-577-5820; Email: info@strose-longview.org; Web: www.stroselongview.catholicweb.com. Very Rev. Bryan A. Ochs; Rev. Sebastin Sebastian, Parochial Vicar; Deacon Fred Johnson.
School—St. Rose de Viterbo School, (Grades PreSchool-8), 720 26th Ave., Longview, 98632.
Tel: 360-577-6760; Fax: 360-577-3689; Web: www.strose-school.org. Chester Novitt, Prin. Lay Teachers 16; Students 135.
Catechesis Religious Program—Tel: 360-425-4660. Students 215.
Mission—St. Catherine, Cathlamet.
LYNDEN, WHATCOM CO., ST. JOSEPH (1897)
205 Twelfth St., Lynden, 98264. Tel: 360-354-2334; Fax: 360-354-5889; Email: info@stjoseph-stpeter.org. Rev. Francisco J. Cancino, Admin.
Catechesis Religious Program—Students 242.
Mission—St. Peter, [CEM 3] 6210 Mt. Baker Hwy., Deming, Whatcom Co. 98244.
LYNNWOOD, SNOHOMISH CO., ST. THOMAS MORE (1962)
6511-176th St., S.W., Lynnwood, 98037.
Tel: 425-743-2929; Fax: 425-743-3652; Email: cathyb@stmp.org; Web: www.stmp.org. Rev. Stephen Okumu; Deacon Clark Goecker.
Res.: 17414 64th Ave. W., Lynnwood, 98037.
School—St. Thomas More School, (Grades PreSchool-8), Tel: 425-743-4242; Fax: 425-745-8367. Teresa Fewel, Prin.; Tessa Watters, Librarian. Lay Teachers 21; Students 260.
Catechesis Religious Program—Students 189.
MARYSVILLE, SNOHOMISH CO., ST. MARY (1888) [CEM]
4200 88th St., N.E., Marysville, 98270.
Tel: 360-653-9400; Fax: 360-658-7439; Email: stmaryoffice@stmary-stanne.org; Web: www.stmary-stanne.org. Rev. Peter Mactutis.
Catechesis Religious Program—
Tel: 360-658-9400, Ext. 103 (Youth);
Tel: 360-653-9400, Ext. 104 (Elementary). Students 400.
Mission—St. Anne, (Tulalip Indian Reservation) 7213 Totem Beach Rd., Tulalip, Snohomish Co. 98271.
MERCER ISLAND, KING CO., ST. MONICA (1958)
4301 88th Ave., S.E., Mercer Island, 98040.
Tel: 206-232-2900; Fax: 206-232-7875; Email: parishoffice@stmonicami.org; Web: www.stmonica.cc. Rev. Patrick Freitag; Deacons Larry McDonald; Frank DiGirolamo.
School—St. Monica School, (Grades PreK-8), 4320 87th, S.E., Mercer Island, 98040. Tel: 206-232-5432; Fax: 206-275-2874; Email: info@stmonicasea.org; Web: stmonicasea.org. Marybeth Bohm, Prin. Clergy 1; Lay Teachers 19; Students 150.
Catechesis Religious Program—Tel: 206-232-9829; Fax: 206-232-3321. Students 103.
MONROE, SNOHOMISH CO., ST. MARY OF THE VALLEY (1902)
601 W. Columbia St., Monroe, 98272.
Tel: 360-794-8945; Fax: 360-805-0201; Email: smvm@stmaryvalley.org. Mailing Address: P.O. Box 279, Monroe, 98272-0279. Rev. Phillip A. Bloom.
Catechesis Religious Program—Students 119.
MOUNT VERNON, SKAGIT CO.
1—IMMACULATE CONCEPTION (1899)
400 N. 15th St., Mount Vernon, 98273.
Tel: 360-336-6622; Fax: 360-336-5203; Email: icc@icc-mv.org; Web: www.iccmv.org. Revs. Thomas McMichael; Jeffrey Moore, Parochial Vicar; Very Rev. Paul A. Magnano, Parish Priest; Deacon Antonio Cavazos.
School—Immaculate Conception Regional School, (Grades PreSchool-8), 1321 E. Division St., Mount Vernon, 98274. Tel: 360-428-3912;
Fax: 360-424-8838; Email: admissions@icrsweb.org; Web: www.icrsweb.org. Gwen Rodrigues, Prin. Lay Teachers 13; Students 219.
Catechesis Religious Program—Regli Wilson, D.R.E. (Hispanic). Students 222.
2—SKAGIT VALLEY CATHOLIC CHURCHES
215 N. 15th St., Mount Vernon, 98273.
Tel: 360-336-6622; Fax: 360-336-5203; Email: pastor@icc-mv.org; Web: www.svcc.us. Rev. Martin Bourke.
MOUNTLAKE TERRACE, SNOHOMISH CO., ST. PIUS X (1955)
22301 58th Ave. W., Mountlake Terrace, 98043.
Tel: 425-775-7545; Fax: 425-778-0413; Email: stpiusxparish@frontier.com. Very Rev. Cal R. Christiansen; Rev. Raymond Heffernan, In Res., (Retired); Deacon Derrel Craig.
School—St. Pius X School, (Grades PreSchool-8), 22105 58th W., Mountlake Terrace, 98043.
Tel: 425-778-9861; Fax: 425-776-2663; Web: www.stpx.org. Mr. Clinton Parker, Prin. Lay Teachers 13; Students 165.
Catechesis Religious Program—Students 130.
OAK HARBOR, ISLAND CO., ST. AUGUSTINE (1939)
185 N. Oak Harbor St., P.O. Box 1319, Oak Harbor, 98277. Tel: 360-675-2303; Email: information@staugustineoh.org. Rev. Paul R. Pluth, J.C.L.
Res.: 180 N.W. 1st Ave., Oak Harbor, 98277.
Catechesis Religious Program—
Tel: 360-675-2303, Ext. 25. Students 160.
Mission—St. Mary, 207 N. Main, P.O. Box 1443, Coupeville, Island Co. 98239.
OCEAN SHORES, GRAYS HARBOR CO., ST. JEROME (1969)
15 Patrick Way, Ocean Shores, 98569.
Tel: 360-289-2838; Email: stjerome@ghcatholic.org. Mailing Address: 306 E. Third St., Aberdeen, 98520-4007. Revs. Francis Arulappan, H.G.N., Admin.; Vinner Raj Simeon Raj, H.G.N., Parochial Vicar; Victor

Raj Anas Dass, H.G.N., Parochial Vicar; Stephen Roman, In Res., (Retired).
Catechesis Religious Program—Students 55.
OLYMPIA, THURSTON CO., ST. MICHAEL (1848) [CEM]
1208 11th Ave., S.E., P.O. Box 766, Olympia, 98507.
Tel: 360-754-4667; Fax: 360-754-0628; Email: office@saintmichaelparish.org; Web: www.saintmichaelparish.org. Very Rev. James E. Lee; Rev. Louis Cunningham; Deacons Robert Rensel; John Bergford.
School—St. Michael School, (Grades K-8), 1204 11th Ave., S.E., Olympia, 98501. Tel: 360-754-5131; Fax: 360-753-6090; Web: www.stmikesolympia.org. Connor Geraghty, Prin. Lay Teachers 16; Students 277.
Catechesis Religious Program—P.O. Box 766, Olympia, 98507. Students 614.
PE ELL, LEWIS CO., ST. JOSEPH (1894) [CEM 2]
417 N. Main, Pe Ell, 98572. Tel: 360-942-3000. Mailing Address: P.O. Box 31, Raymond, 98577. Rev. Zevier Arockiam, H.G.N.; Deacon Loren Lane.
Catechesis Religious Program—Students 24.
Mission—Holy Family, State Hwy. 6, Frances, Pacific Co. 98572.
PORT ANGELES, CLALLAM CO., QUEEN OF ANGELS (1891)
209 W. 11th St., Port Angeles, 98362.
Tel: 360-452-2351; Email: qasj@olypen.com; Web: www.queenofangelsparish.org. Revs. Dennis E. Robb; Leonardo Pestano, Parochial Vicar; Deacons Peter Flatley; Donald Tillitson.
School—Queen of Angels School, (Grades PreSchool-8), 1007 S. Oak, Port Angeles, 98362.
Tel: 360-457-6903; Fax: 360-457-6866; Web: www.qofaschool.org. Mike Juhas, Prin.; Ceci Kimball, Librarian. Lay Teachers 14; Students 135.
Catechesis Religious Program—Students 47.
PORT ORCHARD, KITSAP CO., ST. GABRIEL (1942)
1150 Mitchell Ave., Port Orchard, 98366-4416.
Tel: 360-876-2762; Fax: 360-876-6085; Email: judyricciardi@stgabrielpo.org. Rev. Phuong V. Hoang; Deacon John Ricciardi.
Catechesis Religious Program—Tel: 360-876-2834. Students 376.
Mission—Prince of Peace (1970) N.E. 1171 Sand Hill Rd., P.O. Box 517, Belfair, Mason Co. 98528.
PORT TOWNSEND, JEFFERSON CO., ST. MARY STAR OF THE SEA (1859) [CEM]
1335 Blaine St., Port Townsend, 98368.
Tel: 360-385-3700; Fax: 360-379-1989; Web: www.stmaryss.com. Rev. Peter Adoko-Enchill; Deacon Bill Swanson.
Catechesis Religious Program—Tel: 360-385-1662. Students 50.
POULSBO, KITSAP CO., ST. OLAF (1968)
18943 Caldart Ave., N.E., Poulsbo, 98370.
Tel: 360-779-4291; Email: michelleann@stolafschurch.org. Very Rev. David H. Young.
Catechesis Religious Program—Students 100.
Mission—St. Peter, 910 South St., Suquamish, Kitsap Co. 98392.
PUYALLUP, PIERCE CO.
1—ALL SAINTS (1899)
204 6th Ave., S.W., Puyallup, 98371.
Tel: 253-845-7521; Fax: 253-845-3105; Email: allsaints@allsaintsparish.com. Revs. Michael Radermacher; Anh B. Tran, Parochial Vicar; Deacon David Jones, Pastoral Assoc.
School—All Saints School, (Grades PreSchool-8), Puyallup Campus: 504 2nd St. S.W., Puyallup, 98371. Tel: 253-845-5025; Fax: 253-435-9841; Web: www.allsaintspuyallup.org. Fife Campus: 2323 54th Ave. E., Fife, 98424. Tel: 253-922-5360. Amy Orm, Prin. Lay Teachers 20; Students 291.
Catechesis Religious Program—Students 251.
2—HOLY DISCIPLES (1996)
10425 187th St. E., Puyallup, 98374.
Tel: 253-875-6630; Email: info@holydisciples.org; Web: www.holydisciples.org. Rev. Matthew L. O'Leary.
Catechesis Religious Program—Web: www.holydisciples.org. Students 224.
Mission—Our Lady of Good Counsel, 229 Antonie Ave. N., Eatonville, Pierce Co. 98328.
RAYMOND, PACIFIC CO., ST. LAWRENCE (1904)
1112 Blake St., P.O. Box 31, Raymond, 98577.
Tel: 360-942-3000; Fax: 360-942-3000. Rev. Zevier Arockiam, H.G.N.
Catechesis Religious Program—Students 34.
REDMOND, KING CO., ST. JUDE (1978) [CEM]
10526 166th Ave., N.E., Redmond, 98052.
Tel: 425-883-7685; Email: kristas@stjude-redmond.org. Revs. James O. Johnson Jr.; Raphael D. Mkuzi, Parochial Vicar.
Res.: 16621 N.E. 106th St., Redmond, 98052.
Catechesis Religious Program—Students 297.
RENTON, KING CO.
1—ST. ANTHONY (1901)
416 S. 4th St., Renton, 98057. Tel: 425-255-3132; Email: info@st-anthony.cc; Web: www.st-anthony.cc. Mailing Address: 314 S. 4th St., Renton, 98057. Rev. Jack D. Shrum; Xavier Sengol Bazil, H.G.N., Parochial Vicar; Deacons Teodoro Rodriguez; Lamar Reed; Josh Schaan, Pastoral Assoc.
School—St. Anthony School, (Grades PreK-8), 336 Shattuck Ave. S., Renton, 98057. Tel: 425-255-0059; Fax: 425-235-6555; Email: Cantu@sasr.org; Web: www.sasr.org. Michael Cantu, Prin. Lay Teachers 25; Sisters 1; Students 452.
Catechesis Religious Program—Students 432.
2—ST. STEPHEN THE MARTYR (1966)
13055 S.E. 192nd St., Renton, 98058.
Tel: 253-631-1940; Email: bettymencke@gmail.com. Rev. Edward Goodwin White; Jaya Kumar Embeti, Parochial Vicar; Deacon Carl Chilo.
Res.: 19309 133rd Ave., S.E., Renton, 98058.
Catechesis Religious Program—Tel: 253-631-6175. Students 989.
SAMMAMISH, KING CO., MARY, QUEEN OF PEACE (1987)
1121 228th Ave., S.E., Sammamish, 98075.
Tel: 425-391-1178; Email: office@mqp.org; Web: www.mqp.org. Rev. Kevin F.X. Duggan; Deacon Jack Luz.
Catechesis Religious Program—Students 696.
SEAVIEW, PACIFIC CO., ST. MARY (1965)
1310 48th St., P.O. Box 274, Seaview, 98644-0274.
Tel: 360-642-2002; Fax: 360-642-7100; Email: stmaryoffice@stmary-stanne.org. Rev. Zevier Arockiam, H.G.N.; Deacons E. Jerome Sadler; Dick Wallace.
Catechesis Religious Program—Students 7.
Station—McGowan.
SEDRO-WOOLLEY, SKAGIT CO., IMMACULATE HEART OF MARY (1890)
719 Ferry St., Sedro Woolley, 98284.
Tel: 360-855-0077; Fax: 360-855-2282; Email: iheart@ihm-sw.org. Revs. Thomas McMichael; Jeffrey Moore, Parochial Vicar; Very Rev. Paul A. Magnano, Parish Priest; Deacon Antonio Cavazos.
Catechesis Religious Program—Students 46.
Mission—St. Catherine, 239 Limestone, Concrete, Skagit Co. 98237.
SEQUIM, CLALLAM CO., ST. JOSEPH (1916)
121 E. Maple, P.O. Box 1209, Sequim, 98382.
Tel: 360-683-6076; Fax: 360-683-4674; Email: qasj@olypen.com. Revs. Dennis E. Robb; Leonardo Pestano, Parochial Vicar; Deacons Rob Lebrecgue; Peter Flatley; Donald Tillitson.
Catechesis Religious Program—Students 79.
SHELTON, MASON CO., ST. EDWARD (1892) [JC]
601 W. C St., P.O. Box 758, Shelton, 98584.
Tel: 360-426-6134; Email: stedoffice@hctc.com; Web: www.saintedwardsshelton.org. Rev. Paul A. Kaech.
Catechesis Religious Program—Students 216.
SHORELINE, KING CO.
1—ST. LUKE (1955)
322 N. 175th St., Shoreline, 98133.
Tel: 206-546-2451; Fax: 206-546-0328; Email: parishcenter@stlukecp.org; Web: www.stlukecp.org. Revs. Bradley R. Hagelin; Colin Parrish, Parochial Vicar.
School—St. Luke School, (Grades K-8), 17533 St. Luke Pl. N., Shoreline, 98133. Tel: 206-542-1133; Fax: 206-546-8693. Mr. Christopher Sharp, Prin.; Jennifer Feucht, Librarian. Lay Teachers 20; Students 365.
Catechesis Religious Program—Students 120.
2—ST. MARK (1954)
18033 15th Pl., N.E., Shoreline, 98155.
Tel: 206-364-7900; Fax: 206-367-3919; Email: office@saintmarkshoreline.org; Web: www.saintmarkshoreline.org. Rev. Joseph P. Mitchell, Admin.
School—St. Mark School, (Grades K-8),
Tel: 206-364-1633; Web: www.stmss.org. Kathryn Palmquist-Keck, Prin. Lay Teachers 10; Students 161.
Catechesis Religious Program—Students 28.
SNOHOMISH, SNOHOMISH CO., ST. MICHAEL (1886)
1512 Pine Ave., Snohomish, 98290.
Tel: 360-568-0821; Fax: 360-568-6426; Email: administrator@stmichaelsnohomish.org. Rev. Milhton Scarpetta; Deacons Gene Vanderzanden; Pierce Murphy.
Catechesis Religious Program—Students 254.
SNOQUALMIE, KING CO., OUR LADY OF SORROWS (1929)
39025 S.E. Alpha St., P.O. Box 909, Snoqualmie, 98065. Tel: 425-888-2974; Fax: 425-888-7098; Email: staff@olos.org; Web: www.olos.org. Rev. Duc Cong Nguyen; Deacon Winfred Clapham.
Catechesis Religious Program—Students 142.
Mission—St. Anthony, P.O. Box 175, Carnation, King Co. 98014.
Station—St. Bernard's Chapel, Snoqualmie Summit.
STANWOOD, SNOHOMISH CO., ST. CECILIA (1908)
26900 78th Ave., N.W., P.O. Box 1002, Stanwood, 98292. Tel: 360-629-3737; Fax: 360-629-6127; Email: secretary@saintccc.org; Web: www.stceciliastanwood.org. Rev. Raymond Bueno, Parochial Vicar.
Catechesis Religious Program—Tel: 360-629-4425. Students 142.
SUMNER, PIERCE CO., ST. ANDREW (1921)
1401 Valley Ave. E., Sumner, 98390.
Tel: 253-863-2253; Email: parishoffice@standrewsumner.org; Web: www.standrewsumner.org. Very Rev. Gerald Burns; Rev. Francis Arulappan, H.G.N., Parochial Vicar; Deacon Eric Paige.
Mission—SS. Cosmas and Damian, 213 W. Leber St., P.O. Box 215, Orting, Pierce Co. 98360.
Tel: 360-893-3154; Email: bulletins@standrewsumner.org.
SWINOMISH, ST. PAUL (1867) (Native American)
17456 Pioneer Pkwy., La Conner, 98257. Mailing Address: 4001 St. Mary's Dr., Anacortes, 98221.
Tel: 360-293-2101; Email: admin@stmaryanacortes.org. Revs. Thomas McMichael; Jeffrey Moore, Parochial Vicar; Very Rev. Paul A. Magnano, Parish Priest.
TACOMA, PIERCE CO.
1—ST. ANN (1924)
7025 S. Park Ave., Tacoma, 98408. Tel: 253-472-1360; Email: stanntacoma@gmail.com; Web: www.trparishes.org. Revs. Tuan Nguyen; Jim Harbaugh, S.J., Parochial Vicar; Dwight P. Lewis, In Res.
Rectory—7001 S. Park Ave., Tacoma, 98408.
Catechesis Religious Program—Tel: 253-472-1360. Students 100.
2—ST. CHARLES BORROMEO (1956)
7112 S. 12th St., Tacoma, 98465. Tel: 253-564-5185; Email: parishinfo@stcharlesb.org; Web: www.stcharlesb.org. Revs. Michael J. McDermott; Justin Ryan; Deacon Mark Shine.
School—St. Charles Borromeo School, (Grades PreK-8), Daniel Hill, Prin.; Mrs. Kim Hart, Librarian. Lay Teachers 30; Students 519.
Catechesis Religious Program—
Tel: 253-564-5185, Ext. 3036; Email: jclark@stcharlesb.org. Jodi Clark, D.R.E. Students 234.
3—HOLY CROSS (1915)
5510 N. 44th St., Tacoma, 98407. Tel: 253-759-3368; Fax: 253-759-6126; Email: georgina@holycrosstacoma.org. Very Rev. David T. Mulholland; Rev. Ronald W. Knudsen, Parish Priest, (Retired).
Catechesis Religious Program—Tel: 253-759-3491. Students 37.
4—HOLY ROSARY (1891)
424 S. 30th St., Tacoma, 98402. Tel: 253-383-4549; Fax: 253-383-4540; Email: parish@holyrosarytacoma.org. Revs. Michael Radermacher, Mod.; Martin Bourke, Parish Priest; Deacons Jim Fish, Pastoral Min./Coord.; Michael Teskey.
School—Holy Rosary Bilingual Academy, (Grades PreK-8), 504 S. 30th St., Tacoma, 98402.
Tel: 253-272-7012; Fax: 253-404-1804; Email: office@holyrosarybilingual.org; Web: www.holyrosarybilingual.org. Katie Dempsey, Prin. Employees 24; Lay Teachers 11; Students 200.
Catechesis Religious Program—Students 21.
5—ST. JOHN OF THE WOODS (1924)
9903 24th Ave., E., Tacoma, 98445.
Tel: 253-537-8551; Email: susteskey@gmail.com; Web: www.trparishes.org. Revs. Tuan Nguyen; Jim Harbaugh, S.J., Parochial Vicar.
Catechesis Religious Program—Tel: 253-531-7110. Students 63.
6—ST. JOSEPH (1911) (Slovak)
602 S. 34th St., Tacoma, 98418. Tel: 253-472-2489; Fax: 253-473-1201; Email: parish@saintjosephtacoma.org. Rev. Michael J. Stinson, F.S.S.P.
7—ST. LEO THE GREAT (1879)
710 S. 13th St., Tacoma, 98405. Tel: 253-272-5136; Fax: 253-272-6285; Email: admin@stleoparish.org. Revs. Matthew Holland, Admin.; Alan Yost, S.J., Parochial Vicar.
Catechesis Religious Program—Students 165.
8—OUR LADY, QUEEN OF HEAVEN (1893)
14601 A St. S., Tacoma, 98444. Tel: 253-537-3252; Email: kimberlyp@ourladyqueenofheaven.org; Web: www.ourladyqueenofheaven.org. Rev. John J. Wilkie.
Catechesis Religious Program—Students 225.
9—ST. PATRICK (1891)
1123 N. J St., Tacoma, 98403. Tel: 253-383-2783; Web: www.saintpats.org. 1001 N. J St., Tacoma, 98403. Email: parish@saintpats.org. Very Rev. David T. Mulholland; Deacon William Eckert.
School—St. Patrick School, (Grades PreK-8), 1112 N. G St., Tacoma, 98403. Tel: 253-272-2297; Fax: 253-383-2003; Email: school@saintpats.org; Web: www.saintpats.org. Chris Gavin, Prin. Lay Teachers 25; Students 355.
Catechesis Religious Program—Students 175.
10—SS. PETER & PAUL (1892) (Polish)
3422 Portland Ave., Tacoma, 98404.
Tel: 253-507-5861; Fax: 253-627-7848; Email: stspeterpaultacoma@comcast.net. Rev. Eugeniusz Bolda, S.Ch.
11—ST. RITA OF CASCIA (1922) (Italian)
1403 S. Ainsworth Ave., Tacoma, 98405.

Tel: 253-627-4851; Email: office@stritastacoma.org; Web: www.stritastacoma.org. Very Rev. David T. Mulholland.
Catechesis Religious Program—Students 23.
12—SACRED HEART (1912)
4520 McKinley Ave., Tacoma, 98404.
Tel: 253-472-7738; Fax: 253-475-0071; Email: sh-tacoma@live.com. Revs. Tuan Nguyen; J. Patrick McDermott, Parochial Vicar; Jim Harbaugh, S.J., Parochial Vicar; Deacon Mauricio Anaya.
Catechesis Religious Program—Students 210.
13—VISITATION (1892)
3314 S. 58th St., Tacoma, 98409. Tel: 253-473-4960; Fax: 253-474-8378; Email: admin@visitationchurch.org. Revs. Michael Radermacher, Priest Mod.; Martin Bourke, Parish Priest; Deacons Jim Fish, Pastoral Coord.; Michael Teskey.
School—Visitation School, (Grades PreSchool-8), 3306 S. 58th St., Tacoma, 98409. Tel: 253-474-6424; Fax: 253-474-6718; Web: www.visitationschool.net. Thomas Jay, Prin. Lay Teachers 13; Students 134.
Catechesis Religious Program—Students 89.
TOLEDO, LEWIS CO., ST. FRANCIS XAVIER (1838) [CEM]
139 Spencer Rd., Toledo, 98591. Tel: 360-864-4126; Fax: 360-864-4135; Email: stfrancis@toledotel.com; Web: www.wlpcatholic.org. Revs. Jacob M. Maurer; Christopher Hoiland, Parochial Vicar.
Catechesis Religious Program—Students 18.
TUKWILA, KING CO., ST. THOMAS (1912)
4415 S. 140th St., Tukwila, 98168. Tel: 206-242-5501 ; Fax: 206-244-9387; Email: office.stoll@gmail.com. Very Rev. James Northrup; Rev. Francis Mau Van Ho, S.D.D., Parochial Vicar.
Catechesis Religious Program—Tel: 206-242-8189. Students 80.
VANCOUVER, CLARK CO.
1—HOLY REDEEMER (2000)
17010 N.E. 9th St., Vancouver, 98684.
Tel: 360-885-7780; Fax: 360-944-7560; Email: edb@holyredeemervanc.org; Web: www.holyredeemervanc.org. Mailing Address: P.O. Box 871417, Vancouver, 98687-1417. Rev. Thomas Nathe.
Catechesis Religious Program—Students 420.
2—ST. JOHN THE EVANGELIST (1868) [CEM]
8701 N.E. 119 St., Vancouver, 98662.
Tel: 360-573-3325; Fax: 360-573-3344; Email: office@stjohnvancouver.org; Web: www.stjohnvancouver.org. Rev. Thomas Belleque; Deacon Adolfo Carbajal.
Catechesis Religious Program—Email: saclife@stjohnvancouver.org. Roberta Casanova, D.R.E. Students 500.
3—ST. JOSEPH (1952)
400 S. Andresen Rd., Vancouver, 98661.
Tel: 360-696-4407; Fax: 360-696-3959; Email: carriem@stjoevan.org. Mailing Address: 6600 Highland Dr., Vancouver, 98661. Revs. Gary F. Lazzeroni; Michael Dion, Parochial Vicar; Deacon Scott Aikin.
School—St. Joseph School, (Grades K-8), 6500 Highland Dr., Vancouver, 98661. Tel: 360-696-2586; Fax: 360-696-0977; Web: www.stjoevanschool.org. Joe Manning, Prin. Lay Teachers 27; Students 315.
Catechesis Religious Program—Students 122.
4—OUR LADY OF LOURDES (1958)
Mailing Address: 4723 N.W. Franklin St., Vancouver, 98663. Tel: 360-695-1366;
Fax: 360-695-0610; Email: lisa@ollparish.org. Rev. Richard McCallister; Deacons David Robinson; Tim Shamrell.
Res.: 5007 N.W. Franklin St., Vancouver, 98663.
School—Our Lady of Lourdes School, (Grades PreSchool-8), 4701 N.W. Franklin St., Vancouver, 98663. Tel: 360-696-2301; Fax: 360-696-6700. Holly Rogers, Prin. Lay Teachers 18; Students 265.
Catechesis Religious Program—Email: katelyn@ollparish.org; Email: chiara@ollparish.org. Katelyn Steinke, D.R.E., Director of Faith Formation; Chiara Marcy, D.R.E., Youth Ministry. Students 200.
5—THE PROTO-CATHEDRAL OF ST. JAMES THE GREATER (1836) [CEM]
218 W. 12th St., Vancouver, 98660.
Tel: 360-693-3052; Email: office@protocathedral.org; Web: www.protocathedral.org. Rev. William R. Harris.
Catechesis Religious Program—Students 102.
VASHON, KING CO., ST. JOHN VIANNEY (1964)
16100 115th Ave. S.W., Vashon, 98070.
Tel: 206-567-4149; Email: office@vashonsjv.org; Web: www.stjohnvianneyvashon.com. Mailing Address: P.O. Box 308, Vashon, 98070. Rev. David L. Mayovsky.
Catechesis Religious Program—Email: vashonsjv@centurytel.net. Mary Lawrence, D.R.E., Faith Formation/RCIA. Students 64.
WOODINVILLE, KING CO., SAINT TERESA OF CALCUTTA (2004)
17856 N.E. Woodinville Duvall Rd., Woodinville, 98077. Tel: 425-806-8096; Email: frschuster@saintteresacalcutta.org; Web: www.saintteresacalcutta.org. Rev. Frank Schuster.
Catechesis Religious Program—Robert Phelan, D.R.E. Students 173.
WOODLAND, COWLITZ CO., ST. PHILIP (1950) [CEM]
430 Bozarth, Box 2169, Woodland, 98674.
Tel: 360-225-8308; Fax: 360-225-8866; Email: churchoffice@stphilipwoodland.com. Revs. Thomas Belleque, Priest Mod.; Raphael D. Mkuzi, Parochial Vicar; Deacon Jack Roscoe, Pastoral Coord.
Catechesis Religious Program—Students 127.
Missions—St. Joseph—136 S. 4th St., Kalama, Cowlitz Co. 98625.
St. Mary of Guadalupe (1888) [CEM] 1520 N. 65th Ave., Ridgefield, Clark Co. 98642.
YELM, THURSTON CO., ST. COLUMBAN (1960)
506 1st St. S., Yelm, 98597. Tel: 360-458-3031; Email: pat@sc-sp.org; Web: www.saintcolumbanyelm.org. Rev. Dean Mbuzi, Admin.
Catechesis Religious Program—Tel: 360-458-2360. Students 145.
Mission—St. Peter, Sussex & Keithan St., Tenino, 98598. Tel: 360-264-2124; Email: loretta@sc-sp.org. St. Columban 506 1st St. S., Yelm, 98598.

Chaplains of Public Institutions

SEATTLE. *Federal Detention Center*. Rev. Timothy Watson, C.Ss.R., Chap.
First Hill Hospital Ministry. Very Rev. Bryan L. Hersey, c/o 804 9th Ave., 98104, Rev. Reynaldo T. Yu.
King County Jail. Shannon O'Donnell, Pastoral Care Min.
King County Juvenile Facility. Mr. Joe Cotton.
Northwest Detention Center. Rev. Isidro Lepez, S.J.
U.S. Public Health Hospital. Attended by St. Peter Church, Seattle.
Veterans Administration Medical Center.
ABERDEEN. *Stafford Creek Correction Center*. Karin Ciani, Pastoral Care Min.
BELFAIR. *Mission Creek Correction Center for Women*. Janine Schott, Pastoral Care Min.
BUCKLEY. *Rainier School*. Vacant.
CLALLAM BAY. *Clallam Bay Correction Center*. Rev. Francis Arulappan, H.G.N.
EVERETT. *Snohomish County Jail*. Rev. Jay DeFolco, Chap.
FORKS. *Clearwater / Olympic Correction Center*. Rev. Francis Arulappan, H.G.N., Chap.
GIG HARBOR. *Washington Corrections Center for Women*. Mary Rutter, Pastoral Care Min.
KENT. *Regional Justice Center*. Rev. Richard Gallagher, Catholic Chap., (Retired), Mary Rutter, Pastoral Care Min.
LITTLE ROCK. *Cedar Creek Correction Center*. Deacon John Elshaw.
MONROE. *Monroe Correctional Complex*. Gloria Kempton, Pastoral Min.
ORTING. *U.S. Soldiers' Home*. Attended by St. Andrew Church, Sumner.
PORT ORCHARD. *Washington Veterans Home Hospital*. VacantAttended by St. Gabriel Church, Port Orchard.
SHELTON. *Washington Corrections Center*, P.O. Box 900, Shelton, 98584. Deacon Robert Rensel, Pastoral Care Min.
SNOQUALMIE. *Echo Glen Children's Center*. Deacon Mirek Sztajno.
TACOMA. *Pierce County Jail*. Kay Bowen.
Veterans Admin. Medical Center.
VANCOUVER. *Larch Correction Center*. Mr. Jeff Ripp, Pastoral Care Min.
Veterans Administration Hospital. Attended from Archdiocese of Portland in Oregon.
Washington State School for the Blind. Attended from St. James Church, Vancouver.
Washington State School for the Deaf. Attended from St. John Church, Vancouver.

Special Assignment:
Very Revs.—
Bawyn, Anthony E., J.C.D., Judicial Vicar, 710 9th Ave., 98104
Zender, Gary M., Vicar for Clergy, 710 9th Ave., 98104
Rev.—
Dolejsi, Bryan, Dir. Vocations, 710 9th Ave., 98104.

On Duty Outside the Archdiocese:
Rev.—
Larrivee, Leo J., S.S., c/o 710 9th Ave., 98104.

Retired:
Revs.—
Angelovic, Michael, (Retired), 424 N. 85th St., #410, 98103
Bailey, James L. "Larry", (Retired)
Batterberry, Michael J., (Retired), 4700 S.W. Dash Point Rd., #G4, Federal Way, 98023
Belisle, Ronald H., (Retired)
Bowman, John, (Retired), 6544 40th Ave., N.E., 98115
Brant, David A., (Retired), 804 9th Ave., 98104
Buckalew, Jack, (Retired), P.O. Box 910, Tracyton, 98393
Bulger, John, (Retired), 54 Mitchell St., Pittson, PA 18640
Camuso, Robert, (Retired), 2570 27th Ave. W., 98199
Clark, Patrick S., (Retired), 2702 Broadway E., 98102
Connole, Marlin J., (Retired), 2863 Sundance Cir. E., Palm Springs, CA 92262
Dalton, James, (Retired), 22757 Hull Rd., Mount Vernon, 98274
Dickey, Bryon A., (Retired)
Douglas, Gordon W., (Retired), 3212 40th Ave. W., 98199
Eblen, James, S.T.L., Ph.D., (Retired), 131 Bellevue Ave. E., #203, 98102
Fox, Sean P., (Retired), 4700 S.W. Dash Point Rd., #G1, Federal Way, 98023
Gallagher, Richard, (Retired), 4700 S.W. Dashpoint Rd., Unit E3, Federal Way, 98023
Gese, David, (Retired), 1506 149th St. Court S. #2, Spanaway, 98387
Godley, Patrick, (Retired), Cliff Rd., Ballyheigue, County Kerry AZ Ireland
Gonzalez, Emelio R., (Retired), 13974 Avon Allen Rd., Mount Vernon, 98273
Haycock, Anthony J., (Retired), St. Mary, c/o 710 9th Ave., 98104
Haydock, Kenneth, (Retired), 12505 Greenwood Ave. N., #A204, 98133
Heffernan, Raymond, (Retired), P.O. Box 1489, Friday Harbor, 98250
Heneghan, Jarlath, (Retired), 4700 SW Dash Point Rd., #G3, Federal Way, 98023
Jonientz, Bernard, (Retired), 375 Union Ave., S.E., #B, Renton, 98059
Knudsen, Ronald W., (Retired)
Kramis, Joseph, (Retired), 2309 E. Main, #141, Puyallup, 98372
Larson, Jan, (Retired), 321 S.E. Orchard Dr., #11, North Bend, 98045
Laverty, Seamus, (Retired)
Ludvik, John L., (Retired)
Madigan, John C., (Retired), 760 Aloha St., Edmonds, 98020
Mayovsky, Gerald L., (Retired), 4700 S.W. Dash Point Rd., #E1, Federal Way, 98023
McLaughlin, John, (Retired), 1930 S.E. Oakview Dr., Chehalis, 98532
McMullan, John, (Retired), 6703 Pampus Dr., Orlando, FL 32819
Mien, Francis, (Retired), 1230 E. First St., 98122
Moran, Kevin, (Retired), 4700 S.W. Dash Point Rd., #G2, Federal Way, 98023
O'Brien, Roger, (Retired), 7328 196th St., S.W., #203, Lynnwood, 98036
O'Callaghan, Thomas, (Retired), P.O. Box 346, Suquamish, 98392
O'Neil, Michael, (Retired), 908 E. Ember Cir., Mesa, AZ 85208
Olvida, Victor A., (Retired)
Palluck, M. Charles, (Retired), 35229 S.E. Kinsey St., #203, Snoqualmie, 98065
Park, Thomas R., (Retired), P.O. Box 5737, Tacoma, 98415
Pastro, Vincent, (Retired)
Peterson, C. Vincent, (Retired), 9433 Olympus Beach Rd., N.E., Bainbridge Island, 98110
Quinn, Thomas, (Retired), Lislea, Aclare, Po, County Sligo Ireland
Raschko, Michael, Ph.D., (Retired), 1614 Summit, #502, 98122
Renggli, John J., (Retired), 4700 Dash Point Rd., #E4, Federal Way, 98023
Rink, George, (Retired), 1828 S.W. 318th Pl., Unit D, Federal Way, 98023
Ritter, Patrick, (Retired)
Roman, Stephen, (Retired), St. Jerome Church, P.O. Box 190, Ocean Shores, 98569
Rowan, Stephen, (Retired), P.O. Box 51029, 98115
Sauer, Timothy J., (Retired)
Sevilla, Dennis, (Retired), 7555 Hawkstone Ave. S.W., Port Orchard, 98367
Smith, Roger J., (Retired), P.O. Box 880, Morton, 98356
Suss, Thomas J., (Retired), 13047 W. Blue Sky Dr., Sun City, AZ 85375
Szeman, Stephen J., (Retired), 7045 120th Ave., N.E., Kirkland, 98033
Tolang, Jaime, (Retired), Immaculate Conception, 820 18th Ave., 98122
Tran, Anthony Lan, (Retired), 6841 S. 180th St., 98188
Treacy, William, (Retired), Treacy Levine Center, 24880 Brotherhood Rd., Mount Vernon, 98274

Vandenberg, Thomas L., (Retired), 31080 9th Ave. S., Federal Way, 98003
Ward, Richard J., (Retired), 4700 S.W. Dash Pt. Rd. #G4, Federal Way, 98023. St. James Cathedral, 804 9th Ave., 98104
Weisenberger, Gary, (Retired), 3008 N. Narrows Dr., #C 101, Tacoma, 98407
Williams, James, J.C.L., (Retired), 14423 4th CRT St., 98168
Woodman, Gerald, (Retired), P.O.Box 2169, Woodland, 98674
Yanez, Horacio V., (Retired).

Permanent Deacons:
Aikin, Scott
Alcorta, David P.
Allen, Daniel
Allen, Ronald H.
Amlag, John
Anaya, Mauricio
Bahk, Bruno
Barber, Terry
Basta, Samuel
Batstone, William
Bergford, John
Biersbach, Raymond, (Extern)
Carbajal, Adolfo
Cavazos, Antonio
Chilo, Carl
Chin, Kwok
Clapham, Winfred
Combs, Richard, (Extern)
Connor, Joseph
Craig, Derrel
Cummins, Donald, (Extern)
Daigh, Raymond, a
Decker, James
DeLeon, Jose
Denby, Marshall
DiGirolamo, Frank
Duffell, Dennis T.
Dunne, Joseph
Eckert, William
Elshaw, John
Fickes, Dale, (Extern)
Fish, Jim
Flatley, Peter
Goecker, Clark, (Extern)
Gorman, Lawrence
Graddon, Gerald
Greer, Jeffrey
Haines, William Jr.
Hamlin, William
Hawkins, F. Thomas
Hoover, Delbert
Jesmer, Lawrence
Johnson, Frederick
Jones, David
Jung, Deuk
Kelley, Patrick
Kelly, Dennis
Kheriaty, Lawrence
Kim, Duk
Labrecque, Richard, (Extern)
Lane, Loren
Lehman, Joe
Lezcano, Juan
Lundberg, Craig
Luz, Jack, (Extern)
Magaña, Abel
Magnuson, Jack
Marcell, Terrance
McDonald, Lawrence
McGlone, Stephen
McGuire, Rodney
McNabb, Joseph III
Miner, Henry, (Extern)
Mounce, George III
Moynihan, Patrick
Murdy, Don
Murphy, Pierce, (Extern)
Myer, Philip
Nguyen, Phillip
Nicholas, Joseph, (Extern)
O'Loane, Philip
O'Loughlin, Tom
Olsen, David
Paige, Eric
Pardo, Anselmo
Parnell, Cary
Parsons, Eamon D.
Pele, Sagato
Pentony, Michael J.
Pham, Theman
Ramirez, Arturo, (Extern)
Rapp, David
Reed, Lamar
Rensel, Robert
Ricciardi, John
Riggio, Michael
Rodriguez, Teodoro
Ronquillo, Rey
Roscoe, John, (Extern)
Rupno, Robert
Sadler, E. Jerome, (Extern)
San Nicolas, Ronald, (Extern)
Shamrell, Tim
Shine, Mark
Shriver, Joseph
Sifferman, Joseph
Snider, Lloyd
Swanson, Carl, (Extern)
Sztajno, Mirek
Teskey, Michael
Tillitson, Donald
Townsend, William
Tuifua, Asipeli
Vanderzanden, Gene
Wallace, Dick
Warfield, T. Jackson
Wodzanowski, Stephen
Yang, Joua Pao
Yuen, Joseph
Zellmer, Gary, (Extern)
Zuanich, Matthew.

INSTITUTIONS LOCATED IN DIOCESE

[A] COLLEGES AND UNIVERSITIES

SEATTLE. *Seattle University*, (Grades Bachelors-Doctorate), 901 12th Ave., 98122-1090. Tel: 206-296-6000; Fax: 206-296-6200; Web: www.seattleu.edu. Revs. Stephen V. Sundborg, S.J., Pres.; Thomas M. Lucas, S.J., Rector; David Anderson, S.J.; Jerry Cobb, S.J.; Peter B. Ely, S.J., Vice Pres. Mission Ministry; Robert Grimm, S.J.; Patrick Kelly, S.J.; David J. Leigh, S.J.; Patrick J. Howell, S.J.; Thomas R.E. Murphy, S.J.; Ignatius F. Ohno, S.J.; Trung Pham, S.J.; Frank B. Savadera, S.J.; Josef V. Venker, S.J.; Eric J. Watson, S.J.; Bro. James Selinsky, S.J.; Rev. L. John Topel, S.J. Lay Teachers 742; Priests 17; Students 7,405.

LACEY. *Saint Martin's University* (1895) (Grades Bachelors-Masters), 5000 Abbey Way, S.E., Lacey, 98503. Tel: 360-491-4700; Fax: 360-459-4124; Email: admissions@stmartin.edu; Web: www.stmartin.edu. Roy F. Heynderickx, Ph.D., Pres.; Molly E. Smith, Ph.D., Provost & Vice Pres. Academic Affairs; Revs. Benedict L. Auer, O.S.B., (Retired); Bede Classick, O.S.B., Treas.; Gerard D. Kirsch, O.S.B., Faculty, History; Killian Malvey, O.S.B., Faculty, English & Religious Studies; Rt. Rev. Neal G. Roth, O.S.B., Chancellor; Rev. George J. Seidel, O.S.B.; Bros. Luke Devine, O.S.B., Assoc. Campus Min.; Boniface Lazzari, O.S.B., Faculty, Spanish; Aelred Woodard, O.S.B., Faculty, Religious Studies. Order of St. Benedict Master's Comprehensive University.Resident and non-resident students. Brothers 3; Lay Teachers 70; Priests 5; Students 1,700.

[B] HIGH SCHOOLS, ARCHDIOCESAN

SEATTLE. *Bishop Blanchet High School* (1954) (Coed) 8200 Wallingford Ave. N., 98103. Tel: 206-527-7711; Fax: 206-527-7712; Email: pskinner@bishopblanchet.org; Web: www.bishopblanchet.org. Antonio DeSapio, Pres.; Sam Procopio, Prin. Lay Teachers 68; Priests 1; Sisters 1; Students 945.

O'Dea High School (1923) (Boys) 802 Terry Ave., 98104-1238. Tel: 206-622-6596; Fax: 206-340-4110; Email: jdwalker@odea.org; Web: www.odea.org. James Walker, Prin. Lay Teachers 35; Students 485.

Pope John Paul II High School, 5608 Pacific Ave. S.E., Lacey, 98503-1258. Tel: 360-438-7600; Fax: 360-438-7607; Email: principal@popejp2hs.org; Web: www.popejp2hs.org. Ronald E. Edwards, Pres.; Therese Allin, Prin.

BURIEN. *John F. Kennedy Catholic High School* (1966) (Coed) 140 S. 140th, Burien, 98168. Tel: 206-246-0500; Fax: 206-242-0831; Web: www.kennedyhs.org. Mr. Michael L. Prato, Pres.; Nancy Bradish, Prin.; Rev. Bryan Dolejsi; Jen Parker-Haas, Librarian. Lay Teachers 63; Priests 1; Students 845.

VANCOUVER. *St. Elizabeth Ann Seton Catholic High School*, 811 N.E. 112th Ave., #200, Vancouver, 98684. Tel: 360-258-1932; Fax: 360-258-1936. Patricia Roscoe, Pres.; Dr. Robert Rusk, Prin. Teachers 9.

[C] HIGH SCHOOLS, PRIVATE

SEATTLE. *Holy Names Academy* (1880) (Girls) 728 21st Ave. E., 98112. Tel: 206-323-4272; Fax: 206-323-5254; Email: eswift@holynames-sea.org; Web: www.holynames-sea.org. Ms. Elizabeth Swift, Head, School & Prin.; Anna Sebree, Librarian. Congregation of the Sisters of the Holy Names of Jesus and Mary. Lay Teachers 52; Sisters 4; Students 690.

**Seattle Nativity School*, P.O. Box 20730, 98102. 2800 S. Massachusetts St., 98144. Tel: 206-494-4708; Web: www.seattlenativity.org. Rev. Jeff McDougall, S.J., Pres.; Edward Nelson, Prin.

Seattle Preparatory School (1891) (Coed) 2400-11th Ave. E., 98102. Tel: 206-324-0400; Fax: 206-577-2198; Email: mreid@seaprep.org; Web: www.seaprep.org. Mr. Kent Hickey, Pres.; Erin Luby, Prin.; Liz Borgen, Librarian. Lay Teachers 69; Priests 1; Students 719.

BELLEVUE. *Forest Ridge School of the Sacred Heart* (1907) (Grades 5-12), (Girls) 4800 139th Ave., S.E., Bellevue, 98006. Tel: 425-641-0700; Fax: 425-643-3881; Email: mpierotti@forestridge.org; Web: www.forestridge.org. Julie Grasseschi, Dir.; Sarah Ellison, Librarian. Lay Teachers 61; Religious of the Sacred Heart 1; Students 344.

EVERETT. *Archbishop Thomas J. Murphy High School* (Coed) 12911 39th Ave., S.E., Everett, 98208-6159. Tel: 425-379-6363; Fax: 425-385-2875; Web: www.am-hs.org. Steve Schmutz, Pres.; Alex Crane, Prin.; Deborah Hitchcock, Librarian. Lay Teachers 44; Students 500.

SAMMAMISH. *Eastside Catholic School* (Coed) 232 228th Ave., S.E., Sammamish, 98074. Tel: 425-295-3000; Fax: 425-392-5160; Web: www.eastsidecatholic.org. Gil Picciotto, Pres.; Barbara Swann, Prin. Lay Teachers 76; Priests 1; Students 930.

TACOMA. *Bellarmine Preparatory School* (1928) (Coed) 2300 S. Washington, Tacoma, 98405. Tel: 253-752-7701; Fax: 253-761-3505; Web: www.bellarmineprep.org. Robert Modarelli, Pres.; Cindy Davis, Prin.; Revs. John D. Fuchs, S.J., Supr.; Alejandro Baez, S.J., In Res.; Gerard E. Chapdelaine, S.J., In Res.; Eugene P. Delmore, S.J., In Res.; Jerry Graham, S.J., In Res.; Jim Harbaugh, S.J., In Res.; Peter Henriot, S.J., In Res.; Matthew Holland, S.J., In Res.; Stephen C. Lantry, S.J., In Res.; Isidro Lepez, S.J., In Res.; Frederick P. Mayovsky, S.J., In Res.; Joseph O. McGowan, S.J., In Res.; Robert Niehoff, S.J., In Res.; Alan Yost, S.J., In Res. Sponsored by the Jesuits West Province of the Society of Jesus. Deacons 1; Lay Teachers 67; Students 850; Clergy / Religious Teachers 1.

[D] ELEMENTARY SCHOOLS, PRIVATE

SEATTLE. *Villa Academy*, (Grades PreK-8), (Coed) 5001 N.E. 50th St., 98105. Tel: 206-524-8885; Fax: 206-523-7131; Email: jmilroy@thevilla.org; Web: www.thevilla.org. John K. Milroy, Head of School. Lay Teachers 40; Students 415.

LACEY. *Holy Family School*, (Grades PreSchool-8), 2606 Carpenter Rd., S.E., Lacey, 98503. Tel: 360-491-7060; Fax: 360-456-3725; Email: office@holyfamilylacey.com; Web: holyfamilylacey.com. P.O. Box 3700, Lacey, 98509. Monica Davis, Prin. Lay Teachers 10; Students 100.

[E] CATHOLIC COMMUNITY SERVICES OF THE ARCHDIOCESE OF SEATTLE

SEATTLE. *Advocacy and Caring for Children*, 100 23rd Ave. S., 98144. Tel: 206-328-5973; Fax: 206-328-4835; Email: acc@ccsww.org; Web: www.advocacyandcaringforchildren.org. Patty Shepherd-Barnes, Pres.; Helen Santucci, Vice Pres.

Catholic Charities Foundation of Western Washington, 100 23rd Ave. S., 98144-2302. Tel: 206-328-5696; Fax: 206-328-5699; Email: peterb@ccsww.org. Mr. Michael Reichert, Pres.

Catholic Community Services of Western Washington, 100 23rd Ave. S., 98144-2302. Tel: 206-328-5696; Fax: 206-328-5699; Email: info@ccsww.org; Web: www.ccsww.org. Michael L. Reichert, Pres.

Whatcom Family Center, 1133 Railroad Ave., Ste. 100, Bellingham, 98225-5054. Tel: 360-676-2164; Fax: 360-676-2144; Email: info@ccsww.org. Will Rice, Vice Pres.

Hope House, 207 Kentucky St., Bellingham, 98225. Tel: 360-676-2164; Email: info@ccsww.org. Will Rice, Vice Pres.

CCS NW Immigration Services, 300 S. 1st St., Ste. C, Mount Vernon, 98273. Tel: 360-416-7095; Email: info@ccsww.org. Will Rice, Vice Pres.

Skagit Family Center, 614 Peterson Rd., Burlington, 98233-3126. Tel: 360-856-3054; Fax: 360-676-2144; Email: info@ccsww.org. Will Rice, Vice Pres.

Skagit Farmworker Center, 2727 E. College Way,

Mount Vernon, 98273. Tel: 360-899-9085; Email: info@ccsww.org. Will Rice, Vice Pres.
Snohomish Family Center, 1918 Everett Ave., Everett, 98201-3607. Tel: 425-257-2111; Fax: 425-257-2120; Email: info@ccsww.org. Will Rice, Vice Pres.
Sebastian Place, 1925 196th St., S.W., Lynnwood, 98036. Tel: 425-293-0557; Email: info@ccsww.org. Will Rice, Vice Pres.
King County Family Centers & Randolph Carter Family and Learning Center, 100 23rd Ave. S., 98144-2302. Tel: 206-323-6336; Fax: 206-324-4835 ; Email: info@ccsww.org. Bill Hallerman, Vice Pres. & Agency Dir.
Aloha Inn, 1911 Aurora Ave. N., 98109. Tel: 206-283-6070; Email: info@ccsww.org. Bill Hallerman, Vice Pres.
Native American Men's House, 322 23rd Ave. E., 98112. Tel: 206-749-4180; Email: info@ccsww.org. Bill Hallerman, Vice Pres.
Bridge Shelter, 1923 3rd Ave., 98101. Tel: 206-956-9563; Email: info@ccsww.org. Bill Hallerman, Vice Pres.
Coming Home Program, 1902 2nd Ave., 98101. Tel: 206-956-9561; Email: info@ccsww.org. Bill Hallerman, Vice Pres.
CReW, 1902 2nd Ave., 98101. Tel: 206-956-9570; Email: info@ccsww.org. Bill Hallerman, Vice Pres.
Kent Community Engagement, 1225 W. Smith St., Kent, 98032. Tel: 253-850-2503; Email: info@ccsww.org. Bill Hallerman, Vice Pres.
Parke Studios, 1902 2nd Ave., 98101. Tel: 206-956-9561; Email: info@ccsww.org. Bill Hallerman, Vice Pres.
Lazarus Center, 2329 Rainier Ave. S., 98144. Tel: 206-323-6341; Fax: 206-623-6191; Email: info@ccsww.org. Bill Hallerman, Vice Pres.
Mary McClinton Center, Tel: 206-256-9865.
Matt Talbot Center, 2313 3rd Ave., 98121. Tel: 206-256-9865; Email: info@ccsww.org. Bill Hallerman, Vice Pres.
Michael's Place, 1307 E. Spring St., 98122. Tel: 206-726-5688; Email: info@ccsww.org. Bill Hallerman, Vice Pres.
Monica's Village Place I Programs, 140 23rd Ave. S., 98144. Tel: 206-323-7130; Email: info@ccsww.org. Bill Hallerman, Vice Pres.
Spirit Journey, 12794 78th Ave. S., 98178. Tel: 206-715-7514; Email: info@ccsww.org. Bill Hallerman, Vice Pres.
Pregnancy & Parenting Support, 4250 S. Mead St., 98118. Tel: 206-445-5669; Email: info@ccsww.org. Bill Hallerman, Vice Pres.
Sacred Heart Shelter, 232 Warren Ave. N., 98109-4815. Tel: 206-285-7489; Fax: 206-285-9556; Email: info@ccsww.org. Bill Hallerman, Vice Pres.
Solanus Casey Center, 804 9th Ave., 98104. Tel: 206-223-0907; Email: info@ccsww.org. Bill Hallerman, Vice Pres.
St. Martin de Porres Shelter, 1561 Alaskan Way S., 98134. Tel: 206-323-6341; Fax: 206-328-5666; Email: info@ccsww.org. Bill Hallerman, Vice Pres.
Village Spirit Center for Community Change and Healing, 140 23rd Ave. S., 98144. Tel: 206-328-4470; Fax: 206-328-4869; Email: info@ccsww.org. Bill Hallerman, Vice Pres.
Women's Wellness Center, 1900 2nd Ave., 98101-1102. Tel: 206-256-0665; Email: info@ccsww.org. Bill Hallerman, Vice Pres.
Youth Tutoring Program, 1700 21st Ave. S., Ste. 101, 98144. Tel: 206-328-5953; Email: info@ccsww.org. Bill Hallerman, Vice Pres.
New Bethlehem, 11920 N.E. 80th St., Kirkland, 98033. Tel: 425-679-0350; Email: info@ccsww.org. Bill Hallerman, Vice Pres.
East King County Family Center, 11061 N.E. 2nd St., Bellevue, 98004. Tel: 425-213-1963; Email: info@ccsww.org. Bill Hallerman, Vice Pres.
South King County Family Center, 1229 W. Smith St., Kent, 98035. Tel: 253-854-0077; Fax: 253-850-2503; Email: info@ccsww.org. Bill Hallerman, Vice Pres.
Katherine's House, 1229 W. Smith St., Kent, 98035. Tel: 253-856-7716; Email: info@ccsww.org. Bill Hallerman, Vice Pres.
Rita's House, 1229 W. Smith St., Kent, 98035. Tel: 253-883-5271; Email: info@ccsww.org. Bill Hallerman, Vice Pres.
Federal Way Day Center, 33505 13th Pl., S. D, Federal Way, 98003. Tel: 253-893-7898; Email: info@ccsww.org. Bill Hallerman, Vice Pres.
Catholic Community Services Southwest Family Centers & Tahoma Family Center, 1323 S. Yakima Ave., Tacoma, 98405-4457. Tel: 253-383-3697; Fax: 253-572-3193; Email: info@ccsww.org. Denny Hunthausen, Vice Pres. & Agency Dir.
Nativity House Shelter, 702 S. 14th St., Tacoma, 98405. Tel: 253-502-2780; Email: info@ccsww.org. Denny Hunthausen, Vice Pres.
Family Housing Network, 5050 S. Tacoma Way, Tacoma, 98409. Tel: 253-471-5340; Fax: 253-471-5343; Email: info@ccsww.org. Denny Hunthausen, Vice Pres.
Tahoma Indian Center & Bridges Village, 1809 E. 31st St., Tacoma, 98404. Tel: 253-593-2707; Fax: 253-593-2608; Email: info@ccsww.org. Denny Hunthausen, Vice Pres.
Adult Behavioral Health, 403 W. State St., Aberdeen, 98520. Tel: 360-612-3839; Email: info@ccsww.org. Denny Hunthausen, Vice Pres.
Benedict House, 250 S. Cambrian Ave., Bremerton, 98312-4102. Tel: 360-377-6136; Tel: 360-627-9697; Email: info@ccsww.org. Denny Hunthausen, Vice Pres.
Thurston County Family Center, 604 Devoe St., S.E., Olympia, 98501. Tel: 360-753-3340, Ext. 122; Fax: 360-753-2295; Email: info@ccsww.org. Denny Hunthausen, Vice Pres.
St. Mike's Tikes Early Learning Center, 1208 11th Ave. S.E., Olympia, 98501-1601. Tel: 360-586-1585 ; Email: info@ccsww.org. Denny Hunthausen, Vice Pres.
Drexel House, 604 Devoe St., S.E., Olympia, 98501. Tel: 360-753-3340, Ext. 127; Fax: 360-753-2295; Email: info@ccsww.org. Denny Hunthausen, Vice Pres.
Volunteer Services, 129 Decatur St., N.W., Olympia, 98502-5220. Tel: 844-851-9380; Email: info@ccsww.org. Denny Hunthausen, Vice Pres.
Volunteer Services, 3525 7th Ave., Olympia, 98502. Tel: 360-584-6815; Fax: 253-502-2670; Email: info@ccsww.org. Denny Hunthausen, Vice Pres.
Grays Harbor Family Center, 410 N. "H" St., Aberdeen, 98520-0284. Tel: 360-637-8563; Fax: 360-637-9016; Email: info@ccsww.org. Denny Hunthausen, Vice Pres.
Clark/Skamania Family Center, 9300 N.E. Oakview Dr., Ste. B, Vancouver, 98662-6157. Tel: 360-567-2211; Fax: 360-567-2212; Email: info@ccsww.org. Denny Hunthausen, Vice Pres.
Cowlitz/Wahkiakum Family Center, 676 26th Ave., Longview, 98632-1816. Tel: 360-577-2200; Fax: 360-577-2205. Denny Hunthausen, Vice Pres.
Catholic Community Services Northwest Recovery Centers / CCS Recovery Center - Bellingham, 515 Lakeview Dr., Bellingham, 98225. Tel: 360-676-2187; Fax: 360-676-2762; Email: info@ccsww.org. Donna Wells, Dir., CCS N.W. Recovery Center.
CCS Recovery Center - Skagit, 614 Peterson Rd., Burlington, 98233. Tel: 360-757-0131; Fax: 360-757-0136; Email: info@ccsww.org. Donna Wells, Dir.
CCS Recovery Center - Everett, 2610 Wetmore Ave., Everett, 98201. Tel: 425-258-5270; Fax: 425-258-5270; Email: info@ccsww.org. Donna Wells, Dir.
CCS Recovery Center - Marysville, 1227 2nd St., Marysville, 98270. Tel: 360-651-2366; Fax: 360-653-3119; Email: info@ccsww.org. Donna Wells, Dir.
Family Behavioral Health System - Tukwila, 631 Strander Blvd., Ste. A, Tukwila, 98188. Tel: 253-850-2500; Fax: 253-850-2530; Email: info@ccsww.org. Mary Stone-Smith, Vice Pres.
Family Behavioral Health System - Northend, 5410 N. 44th St., Tacoma, 98407. Tel: 253-759-9544; Tel: 800-566-9053; Fax: 253-759-9512; Email: info@ccsww.org. Mary Stone Smith, Vice Pres. & System Dir.
Family Behavioral Health System - St. Patrick's Tacoma, 1001 N. "J" St., Tacoma, 98403. Tel: 253-761-3890; Fax: 253-830-6243; Email: info@ccsww.org. Mary Stone-Smith, Vice Pres.
Family Behavioral Health System - Aberdeen, 224 W. Wishkan St., Aberdeen, 98520. Tel: 360-532-9050; Fax: 360-532-0577; Email: info@ccsww.org. Mary Stone-Smith, Vice Pres.
Family Behavioral Health System - Bremerton, 2625 Wheaton Way, Ste. B, Bremerton, 98310. Tel: 360-792-2020; Tel: 888-649-6732; Fax: 360-478-6993; Email: info@ccsww.org. Mary Stone-Smith, Vice Pres.
Family Behavioral Health System - Olympia, 1011 10th Ave., S.E., Olympia, 98501. Tel: 360-878-8248; Tel: 888-322-7156; Fax: 360-489-0402; Email: info@ccsww.org. Mary Stone-Smith, Vice Pres.
Family Behavioral Health System - Shelton, 601 W. Franklin St., Ste. T202, Shelton, 98554. Tel: 360-878-8248; Fax: 360-489-0402; Email: info@ccsww.org. Mary Stone-Smith, Vice Pres.
Family Behavioral Health System - Vancouver, 9300 N.E. Oak View Dr., Vancouver, 98662. Tel: 360-567-2211; Tel: 800-388-6378; Fax: 360-567-2212; Email: info@ccsww.org. Mary Stone-Smith, Vice Pres.
Family Behavioral Health - Westside, 7610 40th St., Stes. 100/300/400, University Place, 98466. Tel: 253-830-6242; Fax: 253-433-3106; Email: info@ccsww.org. Mary Stone-Smith, Vice Pres.
Family Behavioral Health - Yelm, 715 Yelm Ave. E., Ste. 8, Yelm, 98597. Tel: 360-878-8248; Fax: 360-489-0402; Email: info@ccsww.org. Mary Stone-Smith, Vice Pres.
Family Behavioral Health System - Oregon, 1904 S.E. Division St., Portland, OR 97202. Tel: 503-517-8663; Fax: 503-943-4994; Email: info@ccsww.org. Mary Stone-Smith, Vice Pres.
Catholic Community Services Long Term Care System, 1323 Yakima Ave., Tacoma, 98405-4457. Tel: 877-870-1582; Tel: 253-502-2734; Fax: 253-272-6356; Email: info@ccsww.org. Peter Nazzal, Vice Pres. & Long Term Care System Dir.
Long-Term Care System - Aberdeen, 218 S. M St., Aberdeen, 98520-6141. Tel: 360-637-8784; Fax: 360-637-9016; Email: info@ccsww.org. Peter Nazzal, Vice Pres.
Long-Term Care System - Bellingham, 1742 Iowa St., Bellingham, 98229-4702. Tel: 800-219-0335; Tel: 360-758-6163; Fax: 360-756-5847; Email: info@ccsww.org. Peter Nazzal, Vice Pres.
Long-Term Care System - Bremerton, 285 5th St., Ste. 3, Bremerton, 98337-1804. Tel: 800-642-8019; Tel: 360-792-2066; Fax: 360-792-2054; Email: info@ccsww.org. Peter Nazzal, Vice Pres.
Long-Term Care System - Chehalis, 1570 N. National Ave., Ste. 211, Chehalis, 98532-2219. Tel: 800-642-8021; Tel: 360-345-1100; Fax: 360-345-1101; Email: info@ccsww.org. Peter Nazzal, Vice Pres.
Long-Term Care System - Everett, 1001 N. Broadway, Ste. A-12, Everett, 98201-1582. Tel: 800-562-4663; Tel: 425-212-9571; Fax: 425-789-1152; Email: info@ccsww.org. Peter Nazzal, Vice Pres.
Long-Term Care System - Kent, 835 Central Ave. N., Ste. D-113, Kent, 98032. Tel: 800-722-3479; Tel: 253-850-2528; Fax: 253-589-0272; Email: info@ccsww.org. Peter Nazzal, Vice Pres.
Long-Term Care System - Lakewood, 5705 Main St., S.W., Lakewood, 98499-6508. Tel: 253-722-5070; Fax: 253-589-0272; Email: info@ccsww.org. Peter Nazzal, Vice Pres.
Long Term Care Center Longview, 923 Fir St., Longview, 98632-1816. Tel: 800-925-7186; Tel: 360-200-5070; Fax: 360-577-2125; Email: info@ccsww.org. Peter Nazzal, Vice Pres.
Long-Term Care System - Port Angeles, 701 E. Front St., Port Angeles, 98362. Tel: 360-417-5420; Tel: 855-582-2700; Fax: 360-417-5434; Email: info@ccsww.org. Peter Nazzal, Vice Pres.
Long-Term Care System - Shelton, 1716 Olympic Hwy. N., Shelton, 98584-0947. Tel: 800-642-8026; Tel: 360-427-2230; Fax: 360-427-2233; Email: info@ccsww.org. Peter Nazzal, Vice Pres.
Long Term Care System - Tumwater, 5109 Capitol Blvd., S.E., Ste. D, Tumwater, 98501. Tel: 800-783-8193; Fax: 360-586-2930; Email: info@ccsww.org. Peter Nazzal, Vice Pres.
Long-Term Care System - Vancouver, 5411 E. Mill Plain Blvd., Ste. 22, Vancouver, 7046 98661-7046. Tel: 360-213-1023; Tel: 360-738-6163; Fax: 360-360-1024; Email: info@ccsww.org. Peter Nazzal, Vice Pres.

[F] CATHOLIC HOUSING SERVICES OF THE ARCHDIOCESE OF SEATTLE

SEATTLE. *Archdiocesan Housing Authority* dba Catholic Housing Services of Western Washington, 100 23rd Ave. S., 98144. Tel: 206-328-5731; Fax: 206-328-5743; Email: info@ccsww.org. Michael L. Reichert, Pres.; Chris Jowell, Vice Pres.; Rob Van Tassell, Dir.; Marcia Jaeger, Dir.
Chancery Place Apartments, 910 Marion St., Ste. 105, 98104. Tel: 206-343-9415; Fax: 206-343-0680; Email: info@ccsww.org. Chris Jowell, Vice Pres.
Francis Place, 1122 Cornwall Ave., Bellingham, 98225. Tel: 360-671-3529; Fax: 360-734-0410; Email: info@ccsww.org. Chris Jowell, Vice Pres.
Dorothy Day House, 106 Bell St., 98121. Tel: 206-374-4364; Fax: 206-374-8611; Email: info@ccsww.org. Chris Jowell, Vice Pres.
Frederic Ozanam House, 801 9th Ave., 98104. Tel: 206-441-4606; Fax: 206-441-5764; Email: info@ccsww.org. Chris Jowell, Vice Pres.
Josephinum Apartments, 1902 2nd Ave., 98101. Tel: 206-448-8500; Fax: 206-956-9561; Email: info@ccsww.org. Chris Jowell, Vice Pres.
Katharine's Place, 3512 S. Juneau St., 98118. Tel: 206-722-0717; Fax: 206-722-3534; Email: info@ccsww.org. Chris Jowell, Vice Pres.
Noel House at Bakhita Gardens, 118 Bell St., 98121. Tel: 206-441-3210; Fax: 206-441-0350; Email: info@ccsww.org. Chris Jowell, Vice Pres.
Patrick Place Apartments, 4251 Aurora Ave. N., 98103. Tel: 206-737-9258; Fax: 206-632-0920; Email: info@ccsww.org. Chris Jowell, Vice Pres.
Rose of Lima at Bakhita Gardens, 118 Bell St., 98121. Tel: 206-456-3100; Fax: 206-456-3487; Email: info@ccsww.org. John Hickman, Vice Pres.; Chris Jowell, Dir.
Santa Teresita del Nino Jesus, 2427 Holden St.,

98106. Tel: 206-767-2005; Fax: 206-767-1967; Email: info@ccsww.org. John Hickman, Vice Pres.; Chris Jowell, Dir.

Spruce Park Apartments, 155 21st Ave., 98122. Tel: 206-322-0450; Fax: 206-328-6637; Email: info@ccsww.org. John Hickman, Vice Pres.; Chris Jowell, Dir.

St. Martin's on Westlake, 2008 Westlake Ave., 98121. Tel: 206-340-0410; Fax: 206-682-8843; Email: info@ccsww.org. Chris Jowell, Vice Pres.

Traugott Terrace, 2317 3rd Ave., 98121. Tel: 206-267-3023; Fax: 206-267-3027; Email: info@ccsww.org. John Hickman, Vice Pres.; Chris Jowell, Dir.

La Casa de San Jose, 2419 Continental Pl., Mount Vernon, 98273. Tel: 360-424-3883; Fax: 360-424-3503; Email: info@ccsww.org. John Hickman, Vice Pres.; Chris Jowell, Dir.

Wintonia Apartments, 1431 Minor Ave., 98101. Tel: 206-467-1878; Fax: 206-467-7679; Email: info@ccsww.org. John Hickman, Vice Pres.; Chris Jowell, Dir.

Sumner Commons, 6100 154th Ave. Ct. E., Sumner, 98390. Tel: 253-826-5199; Fax: 253-826-2781; Email: info@ccsww.org. Chris Jowell, Vice Pres.

La Casa de San Juan Diego, 125 S. Pekin Rd., Woodland, 98674. Tel: 360-225-9872; Fax: 360-841-8679; Email: info@ccsww.org. Chris Jowell, Vice Pres.

Women's Referral Center, 2030 3rd Ave., 98121. Tel: 206-441-3210; Fax: 206-441-0350; Email: info@ccsww.org. John Hickman, Vice Pres.; Chris Jowell, Dir.

Champion House, 1800 145th Pl., S.E., Bellevue, 98007. Tel: 425-644-4344; Fax: 425-644-9867; Email: info@ccsww.org. Chris Jowell, Vice Pres.

Maurice G. Elbert House, 16000 N.E. 8th St., Bellevue, 98008. Tel: 425-747-5111; Fax: 425-641-3141; Email: info@ccsww.org. John Hickman, Vice Pres.; Chris Jowell, Dir.

Max Hale Center, 285 5th St., Ste. 1, Bremerton, 98337. Tel: 360-792-2117; Email: info@ccsww.org. John Hickman, Vice Pres.; Chris Jowell, Dir.

Franciscan Apartments, 15237 21st Ave., S.W., Burien, 98166. Tel: 206-431-8001; Fax: 206-431-1254; Email: info@ccsww.org. John Hickman, Vice Pres.; Chris Jowell, Dir.

Tumwater Apartments, 5701 6th Ave., S.W., Tumwater, 98501. Tel: 360-352-4321; Fax: 360-352-3557; Email: info@ccsww.org. John Hickman, Vice Pres.; Chris Jowell, Dir.

Kincaid Housing/Kincaid Court Apartments, 6210 Parker Rd. E., Sumner, 98390-2645. Tel: 253-863-8818; Fax: 253-826-1006; Email: info@ccsww.org. John R. Hickman, Vice Pres.; Chris Jowell, Dir.

Washington Grocery Building, 1133 Railroad Ave., Bellingham, 98225. Tel: 360-738-8234; Fax: 360-738-8290; Email: info@ccsww.org. Chris Jowell, Dir.

Pioneer Court Housing/Pioneer Court Apartments, 507 W. Stewart Ave., #104, Puyallup, 98371-9402. Tel: 253-848-0874; Fax: 253-826-1006; Email: info@ccsww.org. Chris Jowell, Vice Pres.

Monte Cristo Hotel Apartments, 2929 Hoyt Ave., #111, Everett, 98201. Tel: 425-258-9503; Fax: 425-258-9602; Email: info@ccsww.org. John Hickman, Vice Pres.; Chris Jowell, Dir.

Emmons Apartments, 1010 S. 8th St., Tacoma, 98405. Tel: 253-274-5710; Fax: 253-779-8300; Email: info@ccsww.org. John Hickman, Vice Pres.; Chris Jowell, Dir.

Sunrise Court Housing/Sunrise Court Apartments, 110 140th St. S., Tacoma, 98444-6931. Tel: 253-537-2429; Fax: 253-536-7148; Email: info@ccsww.org. John R. Hickman, Vice Pres.; Chris Jowell, Dir.

Matsusaka Townhomes, 810A S. 13th St., Tacoma, 98405. Tel: 253-593-2120; Fax: 253-272-8143; Email: info@ccsww.org. John Hickman, Vice Pres.; Chris Jowell, Dir.

Villa San Juan Bautista, 2613 Crooks Hill Rd., Centralia, 98531. Tel: 360-807-6285; Fax: 360-330-1464; Email: info@ccsww.org. Chris Jowell, Dir.

Redmond Elderly Housing Association/Emma McRedmond Manor, 7960 169th Ave., N.E., Redmond, 98053. Tel: 425-869-2424; Fax: 425-558-5526; Email: info@ccsww.org. John R. Hickman, Vice Pres.; Chris Jowell, Dir.

AHA-Pierce County Association/Norm Fournier Court, 112 127th St. S., Tacoma, 98444-5000. Tel: 253-531-5087; Fax: 253-536-7148; Email: info@ccsww.org. John R. Hickman, Vice Pres.; Chris Jowell, Dir.

Halcyon Foundation, 1200 134th Ave., N.E., Bellevue, 98005. Tel: 425-644-4344; Fax: 425-644-9867; Email: info@ccsww.org. Chris Jowell, Vice Pres.

[G] CHILD CARE SERVICES

SEATTLE. *Providence Mount St. Vincent Child Care*, 4831 35th Ave., S.W., 98126-2799. Tel: 206-938-6784; Fax: 206-938-8999.

[H] HOSPITALS AND HEALTH CARE SYSTEMS

SEATTLE. *Providence Health & Services*, 1801 Lind Ave. S.W., Renton, 98057-9016. Tel: 425-525-3355; Fax: 425-525-5038; Email: cindy.strauss@providence.org. Cynthia G. Strauss, Sec.

Providence Health System-California, Tel: 425-525-3355; Fax: 425-525-5038.

Providence Health & Services-Oregon, Tel: 425-525-3355; Fax: 425-525-5038.

Providence Health & Services-Washington, Tel: 425-525-3355; Fax: 425-525-5038.

CENTRALIA. *Providence Centralia Hospital*, 914 S. Scheuber Rd., Centralia, 98531. Tel: 360-736-2803; Fax: 360-330-8614; Web: www.providence.org. *Providence Health System dba Providence Centralia Hospital* Bed Capacity 128; Patients Asst Anual. 259,121; Total Staff 722.

EVERETT. *Providence General Foundation*, 916 Pacific Ave., Everett, 98201. Tel: 425-258-7500; Fax: 425-258-7507. Randy Petty, Exec. Dir.

Providence Regional Medical Center Everett, 1321 Colby Ave., Everett, 98201. Tel: 425-261-2000; Fax: 425-261-4051; Web: www.washington.providence.org/hospitals/regional-medical-center/. Preston M. Simmons, FACHE; D.W. Donovan, Vice Pres. Mission Integration & Spiritual Care. Bed Capacity 501; Patients Asst Anual. 214,672; Total Staff 3,129.

FEDERAL WAY. *St. Francis Hospital of Federal Way*, 34515 9th Ave. S. (M.S. 21-01), Federal Way, 98003-6761. Tel: 253-835-8100 King County; Tel: 253-944-8100 Pierce County; Fax: 253-952-7988; Web: www.chifranciscan.org. Tony McLean, Pres. Sisters of St. Francis of Philadelphia. Bed Capacity 134; Patients Asst Anual. 144,493; Total Staff 938.

GIG HARBOR. *St. Anthony Hospital*, 11567 Canterwood Blvd., N.W., Gig Harbor, 98332. Tel: 253-857-1431. Dianna Kielian, Senior Vice Pres. Mission; David Schultz. Bed Capacity 80; Tot Asst. Annually 65,978; Staff 536.

OLYMPIA. *Providence St. Peter Hospital*, c/o Providence Centralia Hospital, 413 Lilly Rd., N.E., Olympia, 98506-5166. Tel: 360-491-9480; Fax: 360-493-7268. Medrice Coluccio, Chief Exec.

Sisters of Providence - Mother Joseph Province Bed Capacity 390; Patients Asst Anual. 322,497; Total Staff 2,244.

Providence St. Peter Foundation, 413 Lilly Rd., N.E., Olympia, 98506-5116. Tel: 360-493-7980; Fax: 360-493-4631. Sr. Anita Butler, S.P., Contact Person; Nancy Riordan, Exec. Dir., Foundation.

SUMNER. *Catholic Pastoral Care-Hospital Tacoma Ministry*, 1401 Valley Ave. E., Sumner, 98390. Tel: 253-363-2253. Rev. David Gese, Chap., (Retired), 1506 149th St., Ct. S, #2, Spanaway, 98387.

TACOMA. *CHI Franciscan Health*, 1145 Broadway Plaza, Ste. 1200 (MS07-00), Tacoma, 98402. Tel: 253-680-4016; Fax: 253-680-4056. Dianna Kielian, Contact Person.

St. Clare Hospital, 11315 Bridgeport Way, S.W. (M.S. 41-01), Lakewood, 98499. Tel: 253-985-1711; Fax: 253-512-2833; Web: www.fhshealth.org. Syd Bersante, Pres.; Dianna Kielian, Senior Vice Pres., Mission. Sisters of St. Francis of Philadelphia. Bed Capacity 106; Patients Asst Anual. 104,785; Total Staff 711.

St. Joseph Medical Center, 1717 S. J St., P.O. Box 2197, Tacoma, 98405-2197. Tel: 253-426-4101; Fax: 253-426-6880; Web: www.chifranciscan.org. Syd Bersante, Pres.; Rev. Dennis Sevilla, (Retired). Sisters of St. Francis of Philadelphia. Patients Asst Anual. 457,474; Total Staff 3,339.

VANCOUVER. **PeaceHealth - System Services Center*, 1115 S.E. 164th Ave., Vancouver, 98683. Tel: 360-729-1000; Email: sbrewer@peacehealth.org; Web: www.peacehealth.org. Liz Dunne, Pres. & CEO; Dianna Kielian, Exec. PeaceHealth* holds its own not-for-profit tax-exempt status with the IRS. Total Staff 800.

PeaceHealth - Peace Island Medical Center, 1117 Spring St., Friday Harbor, 98250. 1115 S.E. 164th Ave., Dept. 314, Vancouver, 98683. Tel: 360-729-1000; Tel: 360-387-2141; Email: sbrewer@peacehealth.org; Web: www.peacehealth.org. Liz Dunne, Pres.; Dianna Kielian, Exec. Bed Capacity 10; Tot Asst. Annually 3,692; Total Staff 05.

PeaceHealth - St. John Medical Center, 1615 Delaware St., Longview, 98632. 1115 S.E. 164th Ave., Dept. 314, Vancouver, 98683. Tel: 360-729-1000; Tel: 360-414-2000; Email: sbrewer@peacehealth.org; Web: www.peacehealth.org. Liz Dunne, Pres.; Dianna Kielian, Exec. Sisters of St. Joseph of Peace and PeaceHealth. Bed Capacity 346; Tot Asst. Annually 63,097; Total Staff 1,510.

PeaceHealth - St. Joseph Medical Center, 2901 Squalicum Pkwy., Bellingham, 98225. 1115 S.E. 164th Ave., Dept. 314, Vancouver, 98683. Tel: 360-729-1000; Tel: 360-734-5400; Email: sbrewer@peacehealth.org; Web: www.peacehealth.org. Liz Dunne, Pres.; Dianna Kielian, Exec. Sisters of St. Joseph of Peace and PeaceHealth. Bed Capacity 255; Tot Asst. Annually 81,485; Total Staff 2,665.

PeaceHealth - Southwest Medical Center, 400 N.E. Mother Joseph Pl., Vancouver, 98664. 1115 S.E. 164th Ave., Dept. 314, Vancouver, 98683. Tel: 360-729-1000; Tel: 360-514-2000; Email: sbrewer@peacehealth.org; Web: www.peacehealth.org. Liz Dunne, Pres.; Dianna Kielian, Exec. Bed Capacity 450; Tot Asst. Annually 95,626; Total Staff 3,249.

PeaceHealth - United General Medical Center, 2000 Hospital Dr., Sedro Woolley, 98284. Email: sbrewer@peacehealth.org; Web: www.peacehealth.org. 1115 S.E. 164th Ave., Vancouver, 98683. Tel: 360-729-1000; Tel: 360-856-6021. Liz Dunne, Pres.; Dianna Kielian, Exec. Bed Capacity 25; Tot Asst. Annually 12,901; Staff 320.

[I] NURSING HOMES

SEATTLE. *Providence Health and Services - Washington* dba Providence Mt. St. Vincent, 4831 35th Ave., S.W., 98126. Tel: 206-937-3700; Fax: 206-938-8999; Email: charlene.boyd@providence.org; Web: washington.providence.org. Ms. Charlene Boyd, Admin.

Sisters of Providence - Mother Joseph Province Bed Capacity 215; Sisters 3; Tot Asst. Annually 750; Total Staff 500; Apartments 109.

Providence Mount St. Vincent Foundation, 4831 35th Ave., S.W., 98126. Tel: 206-938-8994; Fax: 206-938-8999; Email: cscollins@providence.org. Pat Welch, Bd. Pres.; Molly Swain, Exec. Dir. Bed Capacity 335; Residents 316; Total Staff 500; Total Assisted 980.

ISSAQUAH. *Providence Marianwood*, 3725 Providence Point Dr., S.E., Issaquah, 98029. Tel: 425-391-2800; Fax: 425-391-5440; Web: www.providencemarianwood.org. Sisters of Providence Health System. Bed Capacity 120; Tot Asst. Annually 876; Total Staff 175.

Providence Marianwood Foundation, 3725 Providence Point Dr., S.E., Issaquah, 98029. Tel: 425-391-2895. Sr. Anita Butler, S.P., Contact Person; Jenna Higgins.

OLYMPIA. *Providence Mother Joseph Care Center*, 3333 Ensign Rd., N.E., Olympia, 98506. Tel: 360-493-4900; Fax: 360-493-4000. Rev. David Bates, M.Div., Chap.; Kate Gormally, Admin. Patients Asst Anual. 900; Total Staff 210.

[J] HOSPICES

EVERETT. *Providence Hospice and Home Care of Snohomish County*, 2731 Wetmore Ave., #500, Everett, 98201. Tel: 425-261-4800; Fax: 425-261-4725; Web: www.providence.org/phhc. Total Staff 223; Served 5,717.

Providence Hospice & Home Care of Snohomish Co. Foundation, 2731 Wetmore Ave., #500, Everett, 98201. Tel: 425-261-4805; Fax: 425-261-4850; Email: cwittren@providence.org. Connie Wittren, Devel. Dir.

OLYMPIA. *Providence Sound HomeCare and Hospice*, 3432 South Bay Rd., N.E., Olympia, 98506. Tel: 800-869-7062; Tel: 360-459-8311; Fax: 360-493-4657; Web: www.providence.org. Catherine Kozian, Dir., Hospice. Patients Asst Anual. 6,800; Total Staff 208.

[K] RESIDENCES FOR ELDERLY, DISABLED, OR LOW INCOME

SEATTLE. *Heritage House at The Market*, 1533 Western Ave., 98101. Tel: 206-382-4119; Fax: 206-382-0201; Email: marika.chadella@providence.org. Total Staff 35; Total Assisted 64.

Providence ElderPlace, 4515 Martin Luther King Jr. Way S., Ste. 100, 98108. Tel: 206-320-5325; Fax: 206-320-5326; Email: susan.tuller@providence.org; Web: http://washington.providence.org/senior-care/elderplace. Susan Tullerq, Exec. Dir.

Providence Mount St. Vincent, 4831 35th Ave. S., 98126. Tel: 206-937-3700; Fax: 206-938-8999; Email: charlene.boyd@providence.org; Web: www.providence.org/themount. Bed Capacity 335; Residents 316; Total Staff 500; Total Assisted 780.

Providence Peter Claver House, 7101 38th Ave. S., 98118. Tel: 206-721-6265; Fax: 206-721-1327; Email: duong.nguyen@providence.org. Duong Nguyen, Housing Dir. Tot Asst. Annually 79; Total Staff 5; Units 79.

Providence Vincent House, 1423 First Ave., 98101.

Tel: 206-682-9307; Fax: 206-682-0548. Residents 61; Total Staff 4.

CENTRALIA. *Providence Blanchet House*, 1700 Providence Pl., Centralia, 98531. Tel: 360-330-8748; Fax: 360-330-8795.

Providence Rossi House, 1700 Providence Pl., Centralia, 98531. Tel: 360-330-8748; Fax: 360-330-8795.

CHEHALIS. *Providence Place*, 350 S.E. Washington Ave., Chehalis, 98532. Tel: 360-740-7518; Fax: 360-740-6504. Residents 60.

OLYMPIA. *Providence St. Francis House*, 3415 12th Ave., Olympia, 98506. Tel: 360-493-5700; Fax: 360-493-5801.

Sunshine House, 413 N. Lilly Rd., Olympia, 98506-5166. Tel: 360-493-7900; Fax: 360-493-5569; Email: ed.micas@providence.org; Web: www.providence.org/swsa/patient_resources/sun shine.htm.

Providence Health System, WA Total Staff 8; Total Assisted 95,000.

[L] SOCIAL SERVICES

SEATTLE. **L'Arche Noah Sealth of Seattle*, P.O. Box 22023, 98122-0023. Tel: 206-325-9434; Fax: 206-568-0367; Email: info@larcheseattle.org; Web: www.larcheseattle.org. Very Rev. Michael G. Ryan, Contact Person.

Providence Regina House, 8201 10th Ave. S., #6, 98108. Tel: 206-763-9204; Fax: 206-633-3525. Jack Jannack, Mgr.

Sojourner Place, 5071 8th Ave., N.E., 98105. Tel: 206-545-4200; Fax: 206-633-3525. Sisters of Providence - Mother Joseph Province. Residents 11; Staff 4.

[M] MONASTERIES AND RESIDENCES OF PRIESTS AND BROTHERS

SEATTLE. *Arrupe Jesuit Community at Seattle University*, 924 East Cherry St., 98122-4341. Tel: 206-296-6340; Fax: 206-296-6399. Revs. David Anderson, S.J.; Jerry Cobb, S.J.; Quentin Dupont, S.J.; Peter B. Ely, S.J.; Robert Grimm, S.J.; Patrick J. Howell, S.J.; Patrick Kelly, S.J.; David J. Leigh, S.J.; Thomas M. Lucas, S.J.; Matthew Ma, S.J.; Thomas R.E. Murphy, S.J.; Colleens Dinladzer Nsame, S.J.; Ignatius F. Ohno, S.J.; Doug Pduti, S.J.; Trung Pham, S.J.; Frank B. Savadera, S.J.; Stephen V. Sundborg, S.J.; L. John Topel, S.J.; James Taiviet Tran, S.J.; Patrick J. Twohy, S.J.; Josef V. Venker, S.J.; Eric J. Watson, S.J.; William M. Watson, S.J.; Bro. James Selinsky, S.J.; Mr. Lucas Sharma, S.J.

Jesuit House, Seattle, 621 17th Ave. E., 98112. Tel: 206-324-0329. Revs. Jeff McDougall, S.J., Supr.; Charles Barnes, S.J.; Julian Climaco, S.J.; Ryan Rallanka, S.J.; John Rashford, S.J.; John Whitney, S.J.; Mr. James Antonio, S.J.

Maryknoll Fathers & Brothers, 958-16th Ave. E., 98112. Tel: 206-322-8831; Fax: 206-324-6909; Email: seattle@maryknoll.org; Web: www.maryknoll.us. Mrs. Annapatrice Johnson, Dir.

The Redemptorist Society of Washington, 205 2nd Ave. N., 98109. Tel: 206-284-4680; Fax: 203-284-3161; Email: info@sacredheartseattle.com. Revs. Daniel Andree, C.Ss.R., J.C.D.; William M. Cleary, C.Ss.R.; Lyle E. Konen, C.Ss.R.; Richard Luberti, C.Ss.R.; William Peterson, C.Ss.R.; Denis Ryan, C.Ss.R.; Binh Ta, C.Ss.R.; Timothy Watson, C.Ss.R.

LACEY. *St. Martin's Abbey*, 5000 Abbey Way, S.E., Lacey, 98503-7500. Tel: 360-491-4700; Tel: 360-438-4440 (Abbot); Fax: 360-438-4441; Email: thabbot@stmartin.edu; Web: www.stmartin.edu. Rt. Revs. Neal G. Roth, O.S.B., Abbot; Adrian J. Parcher, O.S.B., V.I. Abbot; Rev. Peter Tynan, O.S.B., Campus Min.; Bros. Nicolaus G. Wilson, O.S.B., Prior; Ramon Newell, O.S.B., Subprior; Mark Bonneville, O.S.B., Treas.; Rev. Bede Classick, O.S.B., Treas., St. Martin Univ.; Bro. Edmund Ebbers, O.S.B., Oblate Dir.; Revs. Paul M. Weckert, O.S.B., Vocation Dir.; Gerard D. Kirsch, O.S.B., Archivist; Bros. Luke Devine, O.S.B., Prof.; Boniface Lazzari, O.S.B., Prof.; Aelred Woodard, O.S.B., Member; Revs. Killian Malvey, O.S.B., Prof.; George J. Seidel, O.S.B., Prof.; Very Rev. Justin D. McCreedy, O.S.B., Member; Rev. Marion (Qui-Thac) Nguyen, O.S.B., Member; Bro. Bede Nicol, O.S.B., Guestmaster; Rev. Edward R. Receconi, O.S.B., Member; Bros. Damien-Joseph Brandon Rappuhn, O.S.B., Asst. Guestmaster; Michael Ferman, O.S.B., Novice. Order of St. Benedict, University and Novitiate. Brothers 9; Novices 1; Priests 11; Solemnly Professed 8.

[N] CONVENTS AND RESIDENCES FOR SISTERS

SEATTLE. *St. Joseph's Residence*, 4800 37th Ave., S.W., 98126. Tel: 206-937-4600; Fax: 206-923-4001 (8:30am-8:30pm); Email: jacqueline.fernandes@providence.org. Sr. Jacqueline Fernandes, S.P., Supr. & Admin. Sisters of Providence 36; Dominican Sisters of Tacoma 11; Sisters (Daughters of Mary) 2; Sisters (Carmelites) 1; Dominican Sisters of Adrian 3; Benedictine Sisters 1.

**Lovers of the Holy Cross of Go Vap*, 20013 120th Ave. S.E., Kent, 98031-1654. Tel: 253-478-3162; Email: sotheresa@hotmail.com. Sr. Thao Duong, General Supr. Rep. Sisters 18.

Sisters of St. Joseph of Peace, 1104 21st Ave. E., 98112. Tel: 206-324-1529; Web: csjp.org. Sisters 4.

Sisters of St. Joseph of Peace, Our Lady Province, Charitable Trust, 1663 Killarney Way, P.O. Box 248, Bellevue, 98009-0248. Tel: 425-467-5400; Fax: 425-462-9760; Web: www.csjp.org. Sr. Sheila Lemieux, C.S.J.P., Congregation Leader.

BELLEVUE. *St. Mary's Residence and Novitiate*, 1663 Killarney Way, Bellevue, 98004. Tel: 425-467-5400 ; Fax: 425-462-9760; Web: www.csjp.org. P.O. Box 1763, Bellevue, 98009-1763. Sr. Judy Johnson, C.S.J.P., Admin. Sisters of St. Joseph of Peace 26.

St. Mary's Western U.S. Office for Sisters of St. Joseph of Peace, 1663 Killarney Way, Bellevue, 98004. Tel: 425-467-5499; Fax: 425-462-9760; Email: lhanson@csjp-olp.org; Web: www.csjp.org. Mailing Address: P.O. Box 248, Bellevue, 98009-0248. Sr. Sheila Lemieux, C.S.J.P., Congregational Leader. Sisters of St. Joseph of Peace. Sisters 54.

LACEY. *St. Placid Priory*, 500 College St., N.E., Lacey, 98516. Tel: 360-438-1771; Fax: 360-438-9236; Email: stplacid@stplacid.org; Email: smcdonald@stplacid.org; Web: www.stplacid.org. Sr. Sharon McDonald, O.S.B., Prioress. Includes The Priory Spirituality Center and The Priory Store. Novices 1; Postulants 1; Sisters of St. Benedict 10.

RENTON. *Sisters of Providence, Mother Joseph Province*, 1801 Lind Ave., S.W., #9016, Renton, 98057-9016. Tel: 425-525-3386; Fax: 425-525-3984; Web: www.sistersofprovidence.net. Sr. Judith Desmarais, S.P., Prov. Supr.

Providence Archives, 4800 37th Ave., S.W., 98126-2724. Tel: 206-937-4600; Fax: 206-923-4001; Email: archives@providence.org; Web: www.providence.org/phs/archives. Loretta Greene, Archivist; Peter Schmid, Visual Resources Archivist.

Sisters of Providence Retirement Trust, 1801 Lind Ave., S.W., #9016, Renton, 98057. Tel: 425-525-3729; Email: jennifer.hall@providence.org. Sr. Anita Butler, S.P., Chair & Contact Person.

SHAW ISLAND. *Our Lady of the Rock Priory* (Cloistered) P.O. Box 425, Shaw Island, 98286. Tel: 360-468-2321; Fax: 360-468-2319; Web: olrmonastery.org. Rev. Mother Therese Critchley, O.S.B., Supr. Benedictine Nuns. Professed Nuns 7.

SHORELINE. *St. Joseph's Carmelite Monastery (Cloistered)*, 2215 N.E. 147th, Shoreline, 98155. Tel: 206-363-7150; Fax: 206-365-7335; Email: seattlecarm@comcast.net. Sr. Maria Valla, O.C.D., Prioress. Discalced Carmelites 11; In Formation 4.

TACOMA. *III Order of St. Dominic*, Tacoma Dominican Center, 935 Fawcett Ave. S., Tacoma, 98402. Tel: 253-272-9688; Fax: 253-272-8790; Email: dominicans@tacomaop.org; Web: www.tacomaop.org. Sr. Sharon Casey, O.P., Pres. (Congregation of St. Thomas Aquinas), Sisters of Saint Dominic of Tacoma Charitable Trust - Tacoma Dominican Center. Sisters 46.

Sister of St. Francis of Philadelphia, St. Ann Retirement Convent, 6602 S. Alaska St., Tacoma, 98408. Tel: 253-474-8319; Tel: 253-475-0791; Fax: 253-474-0734; Email: stann@stannconvent.org. *Serra House*, 6602 S. Alaska St., Tacoma, 98408. Tel: 253-474-8026. *Hermitage Place*, 6602 S. Alaska St., Tacoma, 98408. Tel: 253-474-9803. *Olympus House*, 6602 S. Alaska St., Tacoma, 98408. Tel: 253-474-8573. *Marian House*, 6802 47th St. W., Tacoma, 98466. Tel: 253-564-1816.

[O] RETREAT HOUSES, CONFERENCE CENTERS AND CAMPS

SEATTLE. *Camp Don Bosco*, 710 9th Ave., 98104. Tel: 206-382-4562 Contact CYO:; Email: cyo@seattlearch.org; Web: www.seattlearchdiocese.org/camping.

Camp Gallagher, c/o 710 9th Ave., 98104. Email: cyo@seattlearch.org; Web: www.seattlearchdiocese.org/camping.

Camp Hamilton, 710 9th Ave., 98104. Tel: 206-382-4562; Email: cyo@seattlearch.org; Web: www.seattlearchdiocese.org/camping.

FEDERAL WAY. *The Archbishop Alex J. Brunett Retreat and Faith Formation Center at the Palisades*, 4700 S.W. Dash Point Rd., #100, Federal Way, 98023. Tel: 206-748-7998; Fax: 206-382-3482; Email: palisades@seattlearch.org; Web: www.seattlearchdiocese.org/palisades. Patrick Sharkey, Dir.

[P] CAMPUS MINISTRY

SEATTLE. *Saint Martin's University (Lacey)*, 5000 Abbey Way., S.E., Lacey, 98503-7500. Tel: 360-412-6155; Email: acarlin@stmartin.edu. Angela Carlin, Dir. Campus Min.; Susan Leyster, Dir., Service Immersion; Rev. Peter Tynan, O.S.B., Chap. Campus Ministry.

Seattle University Campus Ministry, 901 12th Ave., P.O. Box 222000, 98122-1090. Tel: 206-296-6075; Fax: 206-296-6097; Email: campusministry@seattleu.edu; Web: www.seattleu.edu/campusministry/.

University of Washington, Catholic Newman Center, 4502 20th Ave., N.E., 98105. Tel: 206-527-5072; Web: www.uwnewman.org. Rev. Jordan Bradshaw, O.P., Chap.

Western Washington University-Newman Center, 714 A. N. Garden St., Bellingham, 98225. Tel: 360-410-0218; Web: westerncatholic.org. Rev. Cody Ross, Chap. Catholic Campus Ministry.

TACOMA. *Pacific Lutheran University Catholic Student Ministry*, 12180 Park Ave. S., Tacoma, 98447. Tel: 253-531-6900; Email: catholic@plu.edu.

University of Puget Sound Catholic Campus Fellowship, 1500 N. Warner St., Tacoma, 98416. Tel: 253-879-3374; Email: ccm@ups.edu.

[Q] MISCELLANEOUS

SEATTLE. *Called To Serve As Christ Campaign Fund*, P.O. Box 14964, 98114. 710 Ninth Ave., 98114-9919.

Catholic Seafarer's Ministry (formerly: Catholic Seamen's Club) 3568 W. Marginal Way, 98106. Tel: 206-441-4773; Fax: 206-441-8059; Email: dahra@cscseattle.org. Rev. Anthony J. Haycock, Chap., (Retired). Total Assisted 6,083.

Sea-Tac Airport, Tel: 206-441-4773. Deacon Michael Riggio, Dir.

Cursillo Movement, P.O. Box 68803, 98168-0803. Tel: 206-304-0594. Jose Blakely, Dir.

The Food Bank at St. Mary's, 611 20th Ave. S., 98144. Tel: 206-324-7100, Ext. 21; Fax: 206-324-0500; Email: alison@thefbsm.org.

St. Francis House, 169 12th Ave., 98122. Tel: 206-621-0945; Fax: 206-621-0945; Email: st.francis@live.com. Kathleen McKay, Dir. Third Order of St. Francis.

Fulcrum Foundation, 910 Marion St., 98104. Tel: 206-219-5826; Fax: 206-219-5810; Email: info@fulcrumfoundation.org; Web: www.fulcrumfoundation.org. 710 9th Ave., 98104. Mrs. Julie Coleman, Exec.

**Intercommunity Housing Ferndale*, 2505 3rd Ave., Ste. 204, 98121. Tel: 206-838-5700; Fax: 206-838-5705; Email: intercommunity@mercyhousing.org; Web: www.mercyhousing.org.

**Intercommunity Peace & Justice Center*, 1216 N.E. 65th St., 98115. Tel: 206-223-1138; Fax: 206-223-1139; Email: ipjc@ipjc.org; Web: www.ipjc.org. Patricia Bowman, Exec.

**Mercy Housing Northwest*, 6930 Martin Luther King Jr. Way S., 98118. Tel: 206-838-5700; Fax: 206-838-5705; Web: www.mercyhousing.org. Bill Rumpf, Pres.

**My Catholic Faith Ministries*, P.O. Box 24866, Federal Way, 98093. Tel: 888-765-9269; Fax: 888-623-0042; Email: info@mycatholicfaith.org; Web: www.mycatholicfaith.org. Tom Curran, Exec. Dir.

Sacred Story Institute, 1401 E. Jefferson, Ste. 405, 98122. Tel: 206-302-7630.

South Seattle Catholic Schools, 4212 S. Mead, 98118. Tel: 206-722-7888; Fax: 206-722-7895.

**Sterling Senior Housing*, 2505 Third Ave., Ste. 204, 98121. Tel: 206-838-5700. Paul Chiocco, Contact Person.

Washington State Catholic Conference, 710 9th Ave., 98104. Tel: 206-301-0556; Fax: 206-301-0558; Email: wscc@thewscc.org. Joseph Sprague, Exec.

EDMONDS. *Edmonds Dominicans, Holy Angels Alumnae Assoc.*, 942 N.W. 60th, 98107. Tel: 206-782-1181; Tel: 206-546-6561; Fax: 206-789-2498.

SNOHOMISH. **Healing the Culture*, 605 2nd St., Ste. 218, Snohomish, 98290. Tel: 360-243-3811; Email: mail@healingtheculture.com. Camille Pauley, CEO.

SUMNER. *Pierce County Deanery*, 1401 Valley Ave. E., Sumner, 98390. Tel: 253-863-2254; Email: admin@piercecountydeanery.org. Very Rev. Gerald Burns, Dean; Christine Kolbrick, Admin.

RELIGIOUS INSTITUTES OF MEN REPRESENTED IN THE ARCHDIOCESE

For further details refer to the corresponding bracketed number in the Religious Institutes of Men or Women section.

[0200]—*Benedictine Monks* (Lacey, WA)—O.S.B.

[0260]—*Discalced Carmelite Fathers and Brothers* (Western Prov.)—O.C.D.

[]—*Dominican Fathers and Brothers, Order of Preachers*—O.P.
[]—*Domus Dei Clerical Society of Apostolic Life*—S.D.D.
[0690]—*Jesuit The Society of Jesus* (West Prov.)—S.J.
[0800]—*Maryknoll*—M.M.
[0660]—*Missionaries of the Holy Spirit*—M.Sp.S.
[1065]—*Priestly Fraternity of St. Peter*—F.S.S.P.
[1070]—*Redemptorist Fathers & Brothers*—C.Ss.R.
[1250]—*Society of Christ* (American-Canadian Prov.)—S.Ch.
[0975]—*Society of Our Lady of the Most Holy Trinity*—S.O.L.T.

RELIGIOUS INSTITUTES OF WOMEN REPRESENTED IN THE ARCHDIOCESE

[1070-13]—*Adrian Dominican Sisters*—O.P.
[0180]—*Benedictine Nuns of the Primitive Observance*—O.S.B.
[]—*Blessed Sacrament Sisters of Charity*—B.S.S.C.
[]—*Carmelite Sisters of Our Lady - Carm.*—O.L.
[]—*Daughters of Mary*—D.M.
[0420]—*Discalced Carmelite Nuns of the order of Our Blessed Lady of Mount Carmel*—O.C.D.
[]—*Franciscan Sisters of Perpetual Adoration.*
[]—*Lovers of the Holy Cross of Vietnam*—L.H.C.
[]—*Missionary Sisters of the Rosary of Fatima*—M.R.F.
[2519]—*Religious Sisters of Mercy of Alma* (Alma, MI)—R.S.M.
[2970]—*School Sisters of Notre Dame*—S.S.N.D.
[0430]—*Sisters of Charity of the Blessed Virgin Mary*—B.V.M.
[3000]—*Sisters of Notre Dame*—S.N.D.
[]—*Sisters of Our Lady of Perpetual Help*—S.O.L.P.H.
[3105]—*Sisters of Our Lady of the Most Holy Trinity*—S.O.L.T.
[3350]—*Sisters of Providence*—S.P.
[]—*Sisters of St. Benedict, St. Placid Priory*—O.S.B.
[]—*Sisters of St. Dominic, Congregation of St. Thomas Aquinas* (Tacoma, WA)—O.P.
[1650]—*Sisters of St. Francis of Philadelphia*—O.S.F.
[3840]—*Sisters of St. Joseph of Carondelet* (California Prov. & St. Louis Prov.)—C.S.J.
[3890]—*Sisters of St. Joseph of Peace*—C.S.J.P.
[1990]—*Sisters of the Holy Names of Jesus and Mary* (U.S. & Ontario Province)—S.N.J.M.
[]—*Society of the Sacred Heart*—R.S.C.J.
[]—*Sisters of the Lovers of the Holy Cross of Go Vap of Vietnam*—L.H.C.

ARCHDIOCESAN CEMETERIES

Associated Catholic Cemeteries: Central Office 910 7th Ave., 98104. Tel: 206-522-0996

SEATTLE.

Calvary Cemetery, 5041 35th Ave., N.E., 98105. Tel: 206-522-0996; Fax: 206-525-9628; Email: richp@mycatholiccemetery.org; Web: www.mycatholiccemetery.org. Richard Peterson, Dir.

FEDERAL WAY.

Gethsemane Cemetery, 37600 Pacific Hwy. S., Federal Way, 98003. Tel: 253-838-2240; Fax: 253-874-5910; Email: richp@mycatholiccemetery.org; Web: www.mycatholiccemetery.org. Richard Peterson, Dir.

KENT.

St. Patrick Cemetery, 20400 Orillia Rd., Kent, 98032. Tel: 253-838-2240; Fax: 253-874-5910; Email: richp@mycatholiccemetery.org; Web: www.mycatholiccemetery.org. c/o 37600 Pacific Hwy. S., Federal Way, 98003. Richard Peterson, Dir.

SHORELINE.

Holyrood Cemetery, 205 N.E. 205th St., Shoreline, 98155. Tel: 206-363-8404; Fax: 206-365-6580; Email: richp@mycatholiccemetery.org; Web: www.mycatholiccemetery.org. Richard Peterson, Dir.

NECROLOGY

† Hunthausen, Raymond G., Archbishop Emeritus of Seattle, Died Jul. 22, 2018
† Basso, Richard, (Retired), Died Oct. 6, 2018
† Jennings, John A., (Retired), Died Oct. 7, 2018
† Naumes, Matthew, (Retired), Died Aug. 13, 2018
† Tran, Phuong Duc, (Retired), Died May. 30, 2018
† Wagner, Michael, Tacoma, WA, Holy Rosary and Visitation, Died May. 2, 2018

An asterisk (*) denotes an organization that has established tax-exempt status directly with the IRS and is not covered by the USCCB Group Ruling.

Diocese of Shreveport

(Dioecesis Sreveportuensis in Louisiana)

(VACANT SEE)

Chancery Office: 3500 Fairfield Ave., Shreveport, LA 71104. Tel: 318-868-4441; Fax: 318-868-4469.

Web: www.dioshpt.org

ESTABLISHED AND CREATED A DIOCESE JUNE 16, 1986.

Comprises the Counties (parishes) of Bienville, Bossier, Caddo, Claiborne, DeSoto, East Carroll, Jackson, Lincoln, Morehouse, Ouachita, Red River, Richland, Sabine, Union, Webster and West Carroll.

For legal titles of parishes and diocesan institutions, consult the Chancery Office.

STATISTICAL OVERVIEW

Personnel	
Priests: Diocesan Active in Diocese	19
Priests: Retired, Sick or Absent	10
Number of Diocesan Priests	29
Religious Priests in Diocese	18
Total Priests in Diocese	47
Extern Priests in Diocese	3
Ordinations:	
Diocesan Priests	1
Transitional Deacons	1
Permanent Deacons in Diocese	34
Total Brothers	2
Total Sisters	25
Parishes	
Parishes	27
With Resident Pastor:	
Resident Diocesan Priests	11
Resident Religious Priests	12
Without Resident Pastor:	
Administered by Priests	4
Missions	10
Professional Ministry Personnel:	
Brothers	1
Sisters	3
Lay Ministers	28
Welfare	
Health Care Centers	3
Total Assisted	257,285
Homes for the Aged	1
Total Assisted	282
Day Care Centers	2
Total Assisted	126
Specialized Homes	1
Total Assisted	367
Special Centers for Social Services	22
Total Assisted	21,583
Educational	
Diocesan Students in Other Seminaries	6
Total Seminarians	6
High Schools, Diocesan and Parish	2
Total Students	717
Elementary Schools, Diocesan and Parish	4
Total Students	1,119
Catechesis/Religious Education:	
High School Students	453
Elementary Students	1,837
Total Students under Catholic Instruction	4,132
Teachers in the Diocese:	
Lay Teachers	144
Vital Statistics	
Receptions into the Church:	
Infant Baptism Totals	409
Minor Baptism Totals	42
Adult Baptism Totals	41
Received into Full Communion	89
First Communions	409
Confirmations	374
Marriages:	
Catholic	91
Interfaith	58
Total Marriages	149
Deaths	301
Total Catholic Population	41,615
Total Population	812,200

Former Bishop—Most Revs. WILLIAM B. FRIEND, ord. May 7, 1959; appt. Titular Bishop of Pomaria and Auxiliary Bishop of Alexandria-Shreveport Aug. 31, 1979; ord. Bishop Oct. 30, 1979; appt. Bishop of Alexandria-Shreveport Nov. 23, 1982; installed Jan. 11, 1983; appt. Bishop of Shreveport June 16, 1986; retired Dec. 20, 2006; died April 2, 2015.; MICHAEL G. DUCA, J.C.L., ord. April 29, 1978; appt. Bishop of Shreveport April 1, 2008; ord. May 19, 2008; appt. Bishop of Baton Rouge June 26, 2018; installed Aug. 24, 2018 .

Diocesan Administrator—Very Rev. PETER B. MANGUM, J.C.L., J.V.

Moderator of the Curia—Very Rev. ROTHELL PRICE, J.C.L.

Vicars Forane—Very Rev. Msgr. EARL V. PROVENZA, V.F., Western Deanery, (Retired); Very Rev. FRANK COENS, O.F.M., V.F., Eastern Deanery.

Chancery Office—Catholic Center, 3500 Fairfield Ave., Shreveport, 71104. Tel: 318-868-4441; Fax: 318-868-4469; Email: chancellorsoffice@dioshpt.org.

Chancellor—MR. RANDY G. TILLER.

Judicial Vicar—Very Rev. PETER B. MANGUM, J.C.L., J.V.

Adjutant Judicial Vicar—Very Rev. ROTHELL PRICE, J.C.L.

Ecclesiastical Notary—MR. RANDY G. TILLER, Chancellor, Email: rtiller@dioshpt.org.

Moderator of the Tribunal—VERONICA LACOUR, Email: vlacour@dioshpt.org.

Judges—Very Revs. PETER B. MANGUM, J.C.L., J.V., Diocesan Admin.; ROTHELL PRICE, J.C.L., Moderator of the Curia; PETER FAULK, J.C.L., J.V., Assoc. Judge & Ponems (Diocese of Alexandria).

Defenders of the Bond—Rev. PHILIP F. MICHIELS, (Retired); Sr. LYNN MCKENZIE, O.S.B., J.D., J.C.L.

Promoter of Justice—Sr. LYNN MCKENZIE, O.S.B., J.D., J.C.L.

Advocates—Rev. JAMES FERGUSON, J.C.L., (Diocese of Alexandria).

Corporate Council—Very Revs. PETER B. MANGUM, J.C.L., J.V., Diocesan Admin.; ROTHELL PRICE, J.C.L., Moderator of the Curia; MR. RANDY G. TILLER, Chancellor.

College of Consultors—Very Revs. PETER B. MANGUM, J.C.L., J.V.; ROTHELL PRICE, J.C.L.; FRANK COENS, O.F.M., V.F.; Very Rev. Msgr. EARL V. PROVENZA, V.F., (Retired); Revs. JOSEPH AMPATT; JERRY J. DAIGLE JR.; KARL J. DAIGLE; TIMOTHY C. HURD; MATTHEW TYLER LONG; RICHARD NORSWORTHY; MARK WATSON.

Presbyteral Council—Very Rev. PETER B. MANGUM, J.C.L., J.V., Diocesan Admin.; Revs. JOSEPH AMPATT; JERRY J. DAIGLE JR.; KARL J. DAIGLE; RICHARD NORSWORTHY.

Ex Officio Members—Very Rev. Msgr. EARL V. PROVENZA, V.F., (Retired); Very Revs. FRANK COENS, O.F.M., V.F.; ROTHELL PRICE, J.C.L., Moderator of the Curia.

Finance Council - Ex Officio Members—Very Revs. PETER B. MANGUM, J.C.L., J.V., Diocesan Admin.; ROTHELL PRICE, J.C.L., Moderator of the Curia; MR. RANDY G. TILLER, Chancellor; Rev. MATTHEW TYLER LONG; NONA DAILEY; LAWRENCE W. PETTIETTE JR.; MARGARET GREEN; TOMMY COCKRELL; MATTHEW J. COUVILLION; ELIZABETH PIERRE.

Priests' Retirement Board—Very Rev. ROTHELL PRICE, J.C.L., Moderator of the Curia; Revs. LAVERNE PIKE THOMAS, (Retired); JOSEPH A. MARTINA JR.; TIMOTHY C. HURD; JAMES R. MCLELLAND, (Retired); MR. DOMINIC MAINIERO; MR. EDDIE J. RICHARD; MR. KENNETH L. VINCENT.

The Catholic Foundation of North-Central Louisiana, Inc.—Contact the Catholic Center for information. Tel: 318-868-4441; Fax: 318-868-4469.

Diocesan Offices and Directors

Black Catholic Commission—Very Rev. ROTHELL PRICE, J.C.L., Moderator of the Curia.

Business Affairs—MRS. JILL BRANIFF, CPA, Catholic Center, 3500 Fairfield Ave., Shreveport, 71104. Tel: 318-868-4441; Fax: 318-868-4609.

Campaign for Human Development—Very Rev. ROTHELL PRICE, J.C.L., Moderator of the Curia.

Campus Ministry—(See Youth and Young Adult Ministry).

Catechesis & Religious Formation—MR. RANDY G. TILLER, Acting Dir. & Chancellor, Fax: 318-868-4469.

Catholic Charities—Catholic Charities, 331 E. 71st St., Shreveport, 71106. Tel: 318-865-0200; Fax: 318-865-0230. MEG GOORLEY, Exec. Dir.

Catholic Relief Services—Very Rev. ROTHELL PRICE, J.C.L., Moderator of the Curia.

Cemeteries—MR. RANDY G. TILLER, Chancellor.

Church Vocations—Very Rev. ROTHELL PRICE, J.C.L., Ex Officio.

Clergy Continuing Formation Director—Rev. MATTHEW TYLER LONG.

Communications—MR. JOHN MARK WILLCOX, Dir., 3500 Fairfield Ave., Shreveport, 71104. Tel: 318-868-4441; Fax: 318-868-4609.

Development Director—MR. JOHN MARK WILLCOX, Catholic Center, 3500 Fairfield Ave., Shreveport, 71104. Tel: 318-868-4441; Fax: 318-868-4609.

Diocesan Publications—MRS. JESSICA RINAUDO, Editor, Catholic Center, 3500 Fairfield Ave., Shreveport, 71104. Tel: 318-868-4441; Fax: 318-868-4609.

Ecumenism and Interreligious Affairs—St. Pius

Parish, 4300 N. market St., Shreveport, 71107. Tel: 318-222-2165. Rev. JOSEPH A. MARTINA JR.

Facility Manager, Catholic Center—MR. EDWARD HYDRO, Catholic Center, 3500 Fairfield Ave., Shreveport, 71104. Tel: 318-868-4441; Fax: 318-868-4605.

Fairview House (Residence for Clergy)—1000 Fairview, Shreveport, 71104. Tel: 318-868-4441; Fax: 318-868-4605.

Greco Institute—Catholic Center, 3500 Fairfield Ave., Shreveport, 71104. Tel: 318-868-4441; Fax: 318-868-4456.

Hispanic Ministry—MRS. ROSALBA QUIROZ, Dir., Catholic Center, 3500 Fairfield Ave., Shreveport, 71104. Tel: 318-868-4441; Fax: 318-868-4578; Rev. ALOYS JOST, O.F.M., Hispanic Ministry - Eastern Deanery, Res.: St. Thomas Aquinas Friary, 810 Carey Ave., Ruston, 71270.

Holy Childhood—Sr. CAROL SHIVELY, O.S.U., Contact Person, Catholic Center, 3500 Fairfield Ave., Shreveport, 71104. Tel: 318-868-4441; Fax: 318-868-5057.

Human Resources—Deacon MICHAEL STRAUB, Dir., 3500 Fairfield Ave., Shreveport, 71104. Tel: 318-868-4441; Fax: 318-868-4609.

Information Systems Management—MS. PATRICIA PILLORS, Dir., Catholic Center, 3500 Fairfield Ave., Shreveport, 71104. Tel: 318-868-4441; Fax: 318-868-4456.

Jail-Prison Ministry—Contact: Dianne Rachal, Dir. of Worship.

Diocesan Liturgy Commission—KIM LONG; JOHN GUERRIERO; CAROL PAGA; Revs. TIMOTHY C. HURD; MARK WATSON; Deacon MICHAEL WHITEHEAD; Rev. MICHAEL THANG'WA, F.M.H., (Kenya); MR. AARON WILSON; Very Rev. PETER B. MANGUM, J.C.L., J.V.; GWEN STUART; JO KAUFMAN; MRS. DIANNE RACHAL, Ex Officio.

Marriage and Family Life—MRS. CAROL GATES, Tel: 318-221-5296; Email: cgates@sjbcathedral.org.

Mission Director—Very Rev. ROTHELL PRICE, J.C.L., Moderator of the Curia.

Mission Effectiveness—MR. RANDY G. TILLER, Dir., Catholic Center, 3500 Fairfield Ave., Shreveport, 71104. Tel: 318-868-4441; Fax: 318-868-4469.

Permanent Deacon Formation Program—Deacon CLARY NASH, Dir., 3500 Fairfield Ave., Shreveport, 71104. Tel: 318-868-4441; Fax: 318-868-4578.

Propagation of the FaithVery Rev. ROTHELL PRICE, J.C.L., Moderator of the Curia.

Resource Center (Library)—MS. KATE RHEA.

Respect Life—Contact the Chancery Tel: 318-868-4441.

Schools—Sisters CAROL SHIVELY, O.S.U., Supt.; ANN MIDDLEBROOKS, S.E.C., Assoc. Supt., Catholic Center, 3500 Fairfield Ave., Shreveport, 71104. Tel: 318-868-4441; Fax: 318-868-5057.

Child Nutrition Program—3500 Fairfield Ave., Shreveport, 71104. Tel: 318-868-4441; Fax: 318-868-5057.

Catholic Scouting—Rev. DARIUSZ PAWLOWSKI, Chap., Mailing Address: Chancery, 3500 Fairfield Ave., Shreveport, 71104. Tel: 318-868-4441; Fax: 318-868-4469.

St. Vincent de Paul Society—Mailing Address: P.O. Box 3911, Shreveport, 71133-3911. Tel: 318-780-7755. MR. JIM BEADLES, Contact Person.

Victim Assistance Coordinator—MS. GLENNDA LAWSON, Tel: 318-294-1031.

Worship—MRS. DIANNE RACHAL, Dir., Catholic Center, 3500 Fairfield Ave., Shreveport, 71104. Tel: 318-868-4441; Fax: 318-868-4578.

Youth and Young Adult Ministry—Catholic Center, 3500 Fairfield Ave., Shreveport, 71104. Tel: 318-868-4441; Fax: 318-868-4469. MR. RANDY G. TILLER, Chancellor.

CLERGY, PARISHES, MISSIONS AND PAROCHIAL SCHOOLS

CITY OF SHREVEPORT

(CADDO PARISH)

1—ST. JOHN BERCHMANS CATHEDRAL (1902)
939 Jordan St., 71101-4391. Tel: 318-221-5296; Email: cgates@sjbcathedral.org; Web: www.sjbcathedral.org. Very Rev. Peter B. Mangum, J.C.L., J.V., Rector; Rev. Duane Trombetta, Parochial Vicar; Deacon John Basco.
School—St. John Berchmans Cathedral School, (Grades PreK-8), 947 Jordan St., 71101.
Tel: 318-221-6005; Fax: 318-425-0648; Web: www.sjbcathedralschool.org. Jennifer Deason, Prin. Lay Teachers 20; Students 227.
Catechesis Religious Program—Students 70.

2—ST. ELIZABETH ANN SETON (1984)
522 E. Flournoy-Lucas Rd., 71115-3802.
Tel: 318-798-1887; Email: stelizabethannse@seasshreveport.com; Web: www.seasShreveport.com. Revs. Timothy C. Hurd; Joseph Ampatt, Parochial Vicar; Deacons John Lynch; Homer Tucker; Michael Whitehead.
Catechesis Religious Program—Students 181.

3—HOLY TRINITY (1856)
315 Marshall St., 71101. Tel: 318-221-5990; Email: rprice@dioshpt.org; Email: gyoungblood@dioshpt.org; Web: www.holytrinity-shreveport.com. Very Rev. Rothell Price, J.C.L.; Deacons Daniel LeMoine, Sacramental Min.; Jorge Martinez, Liturgy Dir.; Gwendolyn Youngblood, Business Mgr.
Catechesis Religious Program—

4—ST. JOSEPH (1949)
211 Atlantic Ave., 71105. Tel: 318-865-3581; Email: mlong@stjosephchurch.net. Revs. Matthew Tyler Long; Biju Kuriakose, Parochial Vicar; Fidel Mondragon, Parochial Vicar; Deacons Bruce Pistorius; William Roche; Freeman Ligon.
School—St. Joseph School, (Grades PreK-8), 1210 Anniston Ave., 71105. Tel: 318-865-3585;
Fax: 318-868-1859. Judith McGimsey, Prin. Lay Teachers 31; Students 351.
Catechesis Religious Program—Students 188.

5—ST. MARY OF THE PINES (1973)
1050 Bert Kouns Industrial Loop, 71118-3499.
Tel: 318-687-5121; Web: www.stmops.org. Revs. Michael Thang'wa, F.M.H., (Kenya); John Paul Crispin, F.M.H., (Kenya) Parochial Vicar; Deacon Clary Nash, Community Coord., Sacred Heart.
Catechesis Religious Program—Students 104.
Mission—Sacred Heart of Jesus, Mailing Address: 4736 Lyba St., P.O. Box 19467, 71149-0467.
Tel: 318-635-2121; Email: deaconnash@comcast.net.

6—OUR LADY OF THE BLESSED SACRAMENT (1923) (African American)
1558 Buena Vista St., 71101-2448. Tel: 318-222-3790; Email: olbschurchsport@gmail.com; Web: olbschurchsport.org. Rev. Jean Bosco Uwamungu, (Rwanda); Deacon Charles Thomas.
Catechesis Religious Program—Students 24.

7—OUR LADY OF THE HOLY ROSARY (1952) Closed. For inquiries for parish records contact the chancery.

8—ST. PIUS X (1955)
4300 N. Market St., 71107-2953. Tel: 318-222-2165; Email: stpiusxsec@bellsouth.net. Rev. Joseph A. Martina Jr.; Deacon Jeff Chapman.
Child Care—Child Development Center,
Tel: 318-425-2192; Fax: 318-675-0132. Students 52.
Catechesis Religious Program—Students 49.

9—ST. THERESA, Consolidated with St. John Berchmans Cathedral.

OUTSIDE THE CITY OF SHREVEPORT

BASTROP, MOREHOUSE PARISH

1—ST. JOSEPH (1943) [CEM]
217 Harrington Ave., Bastrop, 71220.
Tel: 318-281-4327; Email: sjccbastrop@gmail.com. Rev. Joseph Kuzichalil; Deacon Marc Vereen.
Catechesis Religious Program—Students 25.

2—OUR LADY HELP OF CHRISTIANS, Consolidated with St. Joseph, Bastrop.

BENTON, BOSSIER PARISH, ST. JUDE (1964)
4700 Palmetto Rd., Benton, 71006. Tel: 318-746-2508; Fax: 318-742-4526; Email: mwise@suddenlinkmail.com; Web: www.stjudebossier.org. Rev. Karl J. Daigle; Deacons Larry Craig Mills; Steve Lehr; Michael Wise; Burton Ainsworth, Prison Min.
Res.: 101 Magnolia Chase, Benton, 71006.
Catechesis Religious Program—Christine Sloan, D.R.E. Students 228.

BOSSIER CITY, BOSSIER PARISH

1—CHRIST THE KING (1939)
425 McCormick St., Bossier City, 71111-4692.
Tel: 318-221-0238; Email: ctkbossier@christthekingbossier.org. Revs. Mark Watson; Rigoberto Betancurt, Parochial Vicar; Deacon Ricardo Rivera.
Catechesis Religious Program—Students 25.

2—MARY, QUEEN OF PEACE (1999)
7738 Barksdale Blvd., Bossier City, 71112.
Tel: 318-752-5971. Rev. Nicholas Owino Onyach, O.F.M.; Deacon Michael Straub.
Res.: 2101 Hope St., Bossier City, 71112.
Catechesis Religious Program—Students 98.
Mission—St. George, 3076 Hwy. 155, Coushatta, 71019-0937.

GRAMBLING, LINCOLN PARISH, ST. BENEDICT THE BLACK (1966) (African American)
471 Main St., Grambling, 71245-3088.
Tel: 318-247-6734. Rev. George Thirumangalam.
Catechesis Religious Program—Students 4.

HODGE, JACKSON PARISH, ST. LUCY (1935) [CEM]
1100 S. 2nd St., P.O. Box 100, Hodge, 71247-0100.
Tel: 318-259-2326; Email: stlucych@bellsouth.net. Rev. George Thirumangalam; Deacon Terry Walsworth, Pastoral Admin.
Res.: 1104 S. 2nd St., P.O. Box 100, Hodge, 71247-0100.
Catechesis Religious Program—(Grades PreK-2), Students 18.

LAKE PROVIDENCE, EAST CARROLL PARISH, ST. PATRICK (1870) [CEM]
207 Scarborough St., P.O. Box 351, Lake Providence, 71254-0351. Tel: 318-559-2876; Email: stpatrickchurchoffice@gmail.com. Rev. Joseph Kallookalam, C.M.I., (India).
Catechesis Religious Program—Students 41.

MANSFIELD, DESOTO PARISH, ST. JOSEPH (1907) [CEM 4]
305 Jefferson St., P.O. Box 760, Mansfield, 71052-0760. Tel: 318-872-1158; Email: stjoseph@nwcable.net. Rev. James Moran, C.O.; Deacon William L. Kleinpeter.
Catechesis Religious Program—Fax: 318-872-1161. Students 107.
Mission—St. Ann's Chapel, 2260 Hwy. 171, Stonewall, DeSoto Parish 71078.

MANY, SABINE PARISH, ST. JOHN THE BAPTIST (1871) [CEM]
1130 E. San Antonio Ave., Many, 71449-3226.
Tel: 318-256-5680; Email: office@stjohnmany.org; Web: stjohnmany.org. Rev. Francis Kamau, F.M.H., (Kenya); Deacon Michael Sullivan.
Catechesis Religious Program—Students 65.
Mission—St. Terence, 44847 Hwy. 191, Many, 71449.

MINDEN, WEBSTER PARISH, ST. PAUL (1942)
410 Fincher Rd., P.O. Box 799, Minden, 71058-0799.
Tel: 318-377-5364; Fax: 318-377-5394; Email: vkuntz@bellsouth.net. Rev. Sebastian Kallarackal, C.M.I., (India).
Catechesis Religious Program—Students 50.
Missions—Blessed Sacrament—2688 Military Rd., Ringgold, Bienville Parish 71068.
St. Margaret, 600 E. 2nd St., Homer, Claiborne Parish 71040.
Chapel—Chapel of Ease Sacred Heart, 304 Gaisser St., Springhill, Webster Parish 71075. (Contact chancery for information.).

MONROE, OUACHITA PARISH

1—JESUS THE GOOD SHEPHERD (1958)
2510 Emerson St., Monroe, 71201-2699.
Tel: 318-325-7549; Email: secretary@jgschurch.org. Rev. David Keith Garvin; Deacons Tom Deal; Christopher Domingue.
Priest's Residence—800 Marquette St., Monroe, 71201.
School—Jesus the Good Shepherd School, (Grades PreK-6), 900 Good Shepherd Ln., Monroe, 71201.
Tel: 318-325-8569; Fax: 318-325-9730; Email: lpatrick@jesusgoodshepherd.org. Lisa Patrick, Prin.; Lynda Cookston, Librarian. Lay Teachers 25; Students 341.
Catechesis Religious Program—Students 72.

2—ST. JOSEPH (1956) Closed. For inquiries for parish records contact the chancery.

3—LITTLE FLOWER OF JESUS (1940) (African American)
600 S. 16th St., Monroe, 71201. Tel: 318-322-1224; Fax: 318-322-1261; Email: hlittleflowerc@comcast.net; Web: www.littleflowercatholicchurch.org. Rev. Adrian Fischer, O.F.M.; Deacon Verdine Williams.
Res.: 616 S. 16th St., Monroe, 71201.
Tel: 318-324-9706.
School—Little Flower of Jesus School, 610 S. 16th St., Monroe, 71201. Tel: 318-322-7379. Mrs. Deborah S. Marshall, Dir. Preschool. Lay Teachers 16; Students 80.
Catechesis Religious Program—Mrs. Genevieve Armstrong, D.R.E. Students 20.

4—ST. MATTHEW (1851) [CEM]
121 Jackson St., Monroe, 71201. Tel: 318-323-8878. Rev. Mark E. Franklin; Deacon Scott Brandle.
Catechesis Religious Program—Students 11.

5—OUR LADY OF FATIMA (1952) [JC]
3205 Concordia, P.O. Box 4136, Monroe, 71211-4136.
Tel: 318-325-7595; Email: office@olfmonroe.org. Revs. Paul Thundurparampil; Job Edathinatt Scaria, C.M.I., (India) Parochial Vicar.
Rectory—207 Sheridan, Monroe, 71201.
School—Our Lady of Fatima School, (Grades PreK-6), 3202 Franklin St., Monroe, 71201.
Tel: 318-387-1851; Fax: 318-387-7593; Email: office@olfmonroe.org. Dr. Carynn Wiggins, Prin. Lay Teachers 17; Students 211.
Catechesis Religious Program—
Mission—St. Lawrence, 357 Swartz School Rd., Monroe, 71203. Tel: 318-343-1618; Email: edathinatt@hotmail.com.

OAK GROVE, WEST CARROLL PARISH, SACRED HEART (1947)
201 Purvis St., P.O. Box 419, Oak Grove, 71263-0419. Tel: 318-559-2876; Email: sacredheartccoffice@gmail.com; Web: stpatricksacredheart.com. Rev. Joseph Kallookalam, C.M.I., (India); Deacon David Nagem.

Catechesis Religious Program—Students 35.

RAMBIN, DESOTO PARISH, ST. MARY, Consolidated with St. Joseph, Mansfield.

RAYVILLE, RICHLAND PARISH, SACRED HEART (1920) 716 Francis St., Rayville, 71269. Tel: 318-728-2445; Email: philippazhayakari@yahoo.com. Rev. Philip Pazhayakari, C.M.I., (India) Ph.D.
Catechesis Religious Program—Tel: 318-728-2445. Students 8.
Mission—St. Theresa, 420 Main St., Delhi, Richland Parish 71232.

RUSTON, LINCOLN PARISH, ST. THOMAS AQUINAS (1941) 813 Carey Ave., Ruston, 71270-4915. Tel: 318-255-2870; Email: stacbulletin@suddenlinkmail.com; Web: stthomasaquinasruston.com. Rev. Tony Posadas; Bro. Michael Ward, O.F.M., Campus Min.; Deacons John J. Serio; Oscar Hannibal; Robert Ransom.
Catechesis Religious Program—Students 135.

VIVIAN, CADDO PARISH, ST. CLEMENT (1945) 819 N. Pine, Vivian, 71082-3354. Tel: 318-375-2789; Email: whitecotton1234@gmail.com. Rev. Joseph A. Martina Jr.; Deacon Orlando Batongbakal.
Catechesis Religious Program—Students 13.

WEST MONROE, OUACHITA PARISH, ST. PASCHAL (1940) [CEM] 711 N. 7th St., West Monroe, 71291-4211. Tel: 318-323-1631; Email: cstpaschalsre@comcast.net; Web: StPaschalChurch.org. Very Rev. Frank Coens, O.F.M., V.F.; Deacon Timothy Cotita.
Catechesis Religious Program—Students 90.
Mission—Our Lady of Perpetual Help, 600 Water St., Farmerville, Union Parish 71241.

ZWOLLE, SABINE PARISH, ST. JOSEPH (1881) [CEM 3] 307 Hammond St., Zwolle, 71486-0008. Tel: 318-645-6155; Email: loveladys@bellsouth.net. P.O. Box 8, Zwolle, 71486. Rev. Richard Norsworthy. Res.: 303 Hammond St., Zwolle, 71486.
Catechesis Religious Program—Students 249.
Mission—St. Ann, [CEM] 5272 Hwy. 482, Noble, Sabine Parish 71462.

Retired:
Very Rev. Msgr.—
Provenza, Earl V., V.F., (Retired)
Revs.—
Kennedy, John D., (Retired)
Lombard, Richard J., (Retired)
McLelland, James R., (Retired)
Michiels, Philip F., (Retired)
Puthuppally, Joseph, (Retired)
Scully, Patrick A., (Retired)
Thomas, LaVerne Pike, (Retired)
Williams, Kenneth, (Retired).

Permanent Deacons:
Ainsworth, Burton
Basco, John
Batongbakal, Orlando
Brandle, Scott
Chapman, Jeff
Cotita, Timothy
Deal, Tom
Domingue, Christopher
Goss, William II
Hannibal, Oscar
Kleinpeter, William L.
Lehr, Steve
LeMoine, Daniel
Ligon, W. Freeman
Lynch, John
Martinez, Jorge
Mills, Larry Craig
Morris, Ronald J., (Retired)
Nagem, David
Nash, Clary
Pistorius, Bruce
Ransom, Robert
Rivera, Ricardo
Roche, William
Serio, John J.
Straub, Michael
Sullivan, Michael
Thomas, Charles
Tucker, Homer
Vereen, Marc
Walsworth, Terry
Whitehead, Michael
Williams, Verdine
Wise, Michael.

INSTITUTIONS LOCATED IN DIOCESE

[A] HIGH SCHOOLS, DIOCESAN

SHREVEPORT. *Loyola College Prep*, 921 Jordan St., 71101-4390. Tel: 318-221-2675; Fax: 318-226-6334; Email: office@loyolaprep.org; Web: www.loyolaprep.org. Mr. John LeBlanc, Prin.; Very Rev. Peter B. Mangum, J.C.L., J.V., Chap. Lay Teachers 35; Students 422.

MONROE. *St. Frederick High School*, (Grades 7-12), 3300 Westminster Ave., Monroe, 71201-3299. Tel: 318-323-9636; Fax: 318-323-7456; Email: warriors@stfrederickhigh.org; Web: www.stfrederickhigh.org. Dr. Carynn Wiggins, Prin.; Rev. Jerry J. Daigle Jr., Chap. Religious Teachers 1; Employees 35; Lay Teachers 28; Students 295.

[B] GENERAL HOSPITALS

SHREVEPORT. *CHRISTUS Health Northern Louisiana* dba CHRISTUS Health Shreveport - Bossier (1907) (1907) 1453 E. Bert Kouns Industrial Loop, 71105. Tel: 318-681-5000; Fax: 318-681-5475 (Admin.); Email: kim.kelsch@christushealth.org; Web: christushealthsb.org. Isaac Palmer, CEO; Judy Deshotels, Vice Pres.; Revs. Felix Alaribe, Dir.; Thomas John Vadakemuriyil, C.M.I., (India) Chap.; Mr. Jan Leffers, Chap.; Mary Preziosi, Chap. Bed Capacity 220; Tot Asst. Annually 199,447; Total Staff 1,149.

COUSHATTA. *CHRISTUS Coushatta Health Care Center*, 1635 Marvel St., Coushatta, 71019. Tel: 318-932-2000; Fax: 318-932-2198; Email: kim.kelsch@christushealth.org; Web: www.christuscoushatta.org. Isaac Palmer, CEO; Brandon Hillman, Admin. CHRISTUS Health Northern Louisiana. Bed Capacity 25; Tot Asst. Annually 24,838; Total Staff 216.

MONROE. *St. Francis Medical Center, Inc.*, 309 Jackson Street, Monroe, 71210. Tel: 318-966-4000; Fax: 318-966-4142; Email: kristin.wolkart@fmolhs.org; Web: www.stfran.com. P.O. Box 1901, Monroe, 71210-1901. Kristin Wolkart, Pres. & CEO; Rev. Philip Chacko Theempalangattu, (India) Chap. Bed Capacity 367; Franciscan Missionaries of Our Lady 1; Tot Asst. Annually 33,000; Total Staff 1,776; Staff 1,776.
St. Francis Medical Center Foundation, Inc., 309 Jackson St., Monroe, 71201. Tel: 318-966-7732; Fax: 318-966-4142; Email: Aimee.Kane@fmolhs.org. Kristin Wolkart, Contact Person.

[C] HOMES FOR AGED

MONROE. *CHRISTUS St. Joseph Home*, 2301 Sterlington Rd., P.O. Box 6057, Monroe, 71211-6057. Tel: 318-323-3426; Fax: 318-387-7157; Email: kim.kelsch@christushealth.org. Christopher Karam, CEO; Anna Warren, Admin. Operated by CHRISTUS Health Monroe. Sisters 1; Total Staff 140; Licensed Capacity Nursing Care 130; Assisted Living 60; Total Assisted 282.

[D] SPECIAL CENTERS FOR SOCIAL SERVICES & ASSISTANCE

SHREVEPORT. *St. Catherine Community Center*, 7109 Henderson Ave., 71106-7109. Tel: 318-868-4441; Fax: 318-868-4469; Email: lsutton@dioshpt.org. Mailing Address: c/o Randy Tiller, 3500 Fairfield Ave., 71104. Ms. Linda Sutton, Sec.

LAKE PROVIDENCE. **LCWR Region V Lake Providence Collaborative Ministries*, 106 Ingram St., Lake Providence, 71254. Tel: 318-559-3747; Email: liturgist44@hotmail.com. Sr. Bernadette Barrett, S.H.Sp., Coord. Tutoring, employment skills development, community organizing, and senior citizen programs. Direct assistance. Staff 1.

[E] CONVENTS AND RESIDENCES FOR SISTERS

SHREVEPORT. *Motherhouse of the Daughters of the Cross in America* Contact the Chancery. 3500 Fairfield Ave., 71104. Tel: 318-868-4441; Email: jbraniff@dioshpt.org. Sr. Maria Smith, Supr. Sisters 2.

[F] NEWMAN CENTERS

GRAMBLING. *Student Center*, 471 Main St., Grambling, 71245-3088. Tel: 318-247-6734 (Office); Fax: 318-247-6288; Email: stbenedict471@gmail.com. David Ponton, Campus Min.

MONROE. *Catholic Campus Ministry at the University of Louisiana at Monroe* (formerly Northeast Louisiana University) 911 University Ave., Monroe, 71211-7250. Tel: 318-343-4897; Fax: 318-343-4812; Email: edathinatt@hotmail.com. P.O. Box 7250, Monroe, 71211-7250. Revs. Paul Thundurparampil, Pastor; Job Edathinatt Scaria, C.M.I., (India) Campus Min.

RUSTON. *E. Donn Piatt Catholic Student Center at Louisiana Tech University*, 600 Thornton St., Ruston, 71270-4946. Tel: 318-251-0793; Email: acts.latech.edu@gmail.com; Web: www.stac-acts.com. Rev. Tony Posadas, Pastor; Bro. Michael Ward, O.F.M., Campus Min.

[G] MISCELLANEOUS

SHREVEPORT. *Magnificat-Nowela Chapter*, 7724 Tampa Way, 71105. Email: rwhite@dioshpt.org; Email: balistre@bellsouth.net. P.O. Box 4293, 71134. Linda Balistrella, Coord.

RELIGIOUS INSTITUTES OF MEN REPRESENTED IN THE DIOCESE

For further details refer to the corresponding bracketed number in the Religious Institutes of Men or Women section.

[0275]—*Carmelites of Mary Immaculate (India)*—C.M.I.
[0950]—*Congregation of the Oratory of Pontifical Rite* (Oratorians)—C.O.
[0520]—*Franciscan Friars* (Prov. of St. John the Baptist)—O.F.M.
[]—*Franciscan Missionaries of Hope* (Kenya)—FMH.

RELIGIOUS INSTITUTES OF WOMEN REPRESENTED IN THE DIOCESE

[0470]—*Congregation of the Sisters of Charity of the Incarnate Word, Houston, Texas*—C.C.V.I.
[0770]—*Daughters of the Cross*—D.C.
[1380]—*Franciscan Missionaries of Our Lady*—O.S.F.
[1430]—*Franciscan Sisters of Our Lady of Perpetual Help*—O.S.F.
[3120]—*Sisters of Our Lady of Sorrows*—O.L.S.
[]—*Sisters of the Destitute* India.
[]—*Sisters of the Eucharistic Covenant*—S.E.C.
[2050]—*Sisters of the Holy Spirit and Mary Immaculate*—S.H.Sp.
[4120-03]—*Ursuline Nuns of the Congregation of Paris*—O.S.U.

DIOCESAN CEMETERIES

SHREVEPORT. *St. Joseph*, Catholic Center, 3500 Fairfield Ave., 71104. Tel: 318-868-4441; Fax: 318-868-4609; Email: lsutton@dioshpt.org. 2100 Texas St., shreveport, 71101. Mr. Randy G. Tiller, Contact Person; Mr. Edward Hydro, Contact Person

NECROLOGY

† LaCaze, J. Carson, Shreveport, LA, Cathedral of St. John Berchmans, Died Jul. 7, 2018

An asterisk (*) denotes an organization that has established tax-exempt status directly with the IRS and is not covered by the USCCB Group Ruling.

Diocese of Sioux City

(Dioecesis Siopolitana)

Most Reverend

R. WALKER NICKLESS

Bishop of Sioux City; ordained August 4, 1973; appointed Bishop of Sioux City November 10, 2005; Episcopal ordination January 20, 2006. *Chancery: Administrative Offices, 1821 Jackson St., P.O. Box 3379, IA 51102-3379.* Tel: 712-255-7933; Fax: 712-233-7598.

Most Reverend

LAWRENCE D. SOENS, D.D.

Bishop Emeritus of Sioux City; ordained May 6, 1950; appointed Bishop of Sioux City June 15, 1983; consecrated and installed August 17, 1983; retired November 28, 1998. *Mailing Address: P.O. Box 3379, Sioux City, IA 51102-3379.* Fax: 712-233-7598.

Chancery: Administrative Offices, 1821 Jackson St., P.O. Box 3379, Sioux City, IA 51102-3379. Tel: 712-255-7933; Fax: 712-233-7598.

Web: www.scdiocese.org

Email: bishopnickless@scdiocese.org

ESTABLISHED JANUARY 15, 1902.

Square Miles 14,518.

Corporate Title: "The Diocese of Sioux City."

Comprises 24 Counties in the northwest part of Iowa, west of Winnebago, Hancock, Wright, Hamilton and Story Counties, and north of Harrison, Shelby, Audubon, Guthrie and Dallas Counties.

For legal titles of parishes and diocesan institutions, consult the Chancery.

STATISTICAL OVERVIEW

Personnel	
Bishop	1
Retired Bishops	1
Priests: Diocesan Active in Diocese	44
Priests: Diocesan Active Outside Diocese	4
Priests: Retired, Sick or Absent	57
Number of Diocesan Priests	105
Religious Priests in Diocese	2
Total Priests in Diocese	107
Extern Priests in Diocese	3
Ordinations:	
Religious Priests	1
Transitional Deacons	3
Permanent Deacons	5
Permanent Deacons in Diocese	54
Total Sisters	52
Parishes	
Parishes	73
With Resident Pastor:	
Resident Diocesan Priests	33
Without Resident Pastor:	
Administered by Priests	40
New Parishes Created	1
Closed Parishes	13
Professional Ministry Personnel:	
Sisters	8
Lay Ministers	28
Welfare	
Catholic Hospitals	3
Total Assisted	341,359
Homes for the Aged	3
Total Assisted	410
Special Centers for Social Services	6
Total Assisted	3,273
Educational	
Diocesan Students in Other Seminaries	9
Total Seminarians	9
Colleges and Universities	1
Total Students	1,229
High Schools, Diocesan and Parish	7
Total Students	1,392
Elementary Schools, Diocesan and Parish	16
Total Students	4,610
Catechesis/Religious Education:	
High School Students	1,730
Elementary Students	5,006
Total Students under Catholic Instruction	13,976
Teachers in the Diocese:	
Priests	5
Sisters	1
Lay Teachers	539
Vital Statistics	
Receptions into the Church:	
Infant Baptism Totals	1,097
Minor Baptism Totals	76
Adult Baptism Totals	44
Received into Full Communion	88
First Communions	1,306
Confirmations	1,253
Marriages:	
Catholic	230
Interfaith	110
Total Marriages	340
Deaths	1,054
Total Catholic Population	84,539
Total Population	446,614

Former Bishops—Most Revs. PHILIP J. GARRIGAN, D.D., ord. June 11, 1870; appt. March 21, 1902; cons. May 25, 1902; died Oct. 14, 1919; EDMOND HEELAN, D.D., ord. June 24, 1890; cons. April 8, 1919; died Sept. 20, 1948; JOSEPH M. MUELLER, D.D., ord. June 14, 1919; cons. Oct. 16, 1947; died Aug. 9, 1981; FRANK H. GRETEMAN, D.D., ord. Dec. 8, 1932; appt. Titular Bishop of Vissalsa April 14, 1965; cons. May 26, 1965; appt. Bishop of Sioux City Oct. 20, 1970; installed Dec. 9, 1970; retired Aug. 17, 1983; died March 21, 1987; LAWRENCE D. SOENS, D.D., (Retired), ord. May 6, 1950; appt. Bishop of Sioux City June 15, 1983; installed Aug. 17, 1983; retired Nov. 28, 1998; DANIEL N. DINARDO, D.D., ord. July 16, 1977; appt. Coadjutor Bishop of Sioux City Aug. 19, 1997; Episcopal ord. Oct. 7, 1997; appt. Bishop of Sioux City Nov. 28, 1998; appt. Coadjutor Bishop of Galveston-Houston Jan. 16, 2004; installed March 26, 2004; appt. Coadjutor Archbishop Dec. 29, 2004; created Cardinal Priest Nov. 24, 2007.

Vicar General and Moderator of the Curia—Very Rev. BRADLEY C. PELZEL, V.G.; Very Rev. Msgr. KEVIN C. MCCOY, S.T.D., V.G., Mailing Address: P.O. Box 3379, Sioux City, 51102-3379.

Chancery—Administrative Offices, 1821 Jackson St., P.O. Box 3379, Sioux City, 51102-3379. Tel: 712-255-7933; Fax: 712-233-7598.

Chancellor—Deacon DAVID A. LOPEZ, Ph.D., Mailing Address: P.O. Box 3379, Sioux City, 51102. Tel: 712-233-7512.

Vice Chancellor, Special Assistant to the Bishop and Director Pastoral Planning—Very Rev. BRENT C. LINGLE, Mailing Address: P.O. Box 3379, Sioux City, 51102-3379. Tel: 712-233-7534. Cathedral of the Epiphany, 1000 Douglas St., Sioux City, 51105.

Diocesan Tribunal—Address all prenuptial files and marriage nullity process materials to: *P.O. Box 3379, Sioux City, 51102-3379.* Tel: 712-233-7533; Fax: 712-233-7588.

Judicial Vicar—Rev. Msgr. R. MARK DUCHAINE, J.C.L., 1825 Jackson St., P.O. Box 3379, Sioux City, 51102-3379.

Adjutant Judicial Vicar—Rev. MICHAEL J. ERPELDING, J.C.L.

Promoter of Justice—Very Rev. Msgr. KEVIN C. MCCOY, S.T.D., V.G.

Defenders of the Bond—Very Rev. Msgr. KEVIN C. MCCOY, S.T.D., V.G.; Rev. Msgr. MICHAEL D. SERNETT, J.C.D., V.G., (Retired).

Judges—Rev. Msgr. R. MARK DUCHAINE, J.C.L.; Revs. MICHAEL J. ERPELDING, J.C.L.; PAUL-LOUIS ARTS, M.S., (Retired); JEROME P. COSGROVE, M.S., (Retired); MR. EUGENE J. ULSES, J.C.L.

Notary—TERRI NIEDERGESES.

Diocesan Finance Council—Most Rev. R. WALKER NICKLESS, Pres.; Very Rev. BRADLEY C. PELZEL, V.G.; Very Rev. Msgr. KEVIN C. MCCOY, S.T.D., V.G. Directors: MR. STEVE LENSING; MR. JIM GRETEMAN; Rev. ROGER J. LINNAN, (Retired); MR. JEFFREY R. MOHRHAUSER; MR. RANDY KRAMER; DR. MICHAEL JUNG; MR. JAMES COSGROVE; MS. KAREN WALDSCHMITT; MRS. THERESA GOLIBER.

Diocesan Legal Counsel—MR. MIKE ELLWANGER, (Rawlings, Nieland, Probasco, Killinger, Ellwanger, Jacobs, Mohrhauser, Law Firm, Sioux City). Refer all legal matters to The Chancery.

Presbyteral Council—Most Rev. R. WALKER NICKLESS; Very Rev. BRADLEY C. PELZEL, V.G.; Very Rev. Msgr. KEVIN C. MCCOY, S.T.D., V.G.; Very Rev. CRAIG A. COLLISON, V.F., Chm.; Rev. DR. TIMOTHY A. FRIEDRICHSEN, Vice Chm.; Very Rev. TERRY A. RODER, V.F., Sec./Treas.; Revs. BRIAN C. HUGHES; THOMAS J. HART, (Retired); ROGER J. LINNAN, (Retired); Very Rev. DOUGLAS M. KLEIN, V.F.; Revs. SHANE A. DEMAN; STEVEN W. BRODERSEN, (Retired); BRUCE LAWLER; Very Rev. MARK J. STOLL, J.C.L., V.F., Recording Sec.

Diocesan Consultors—Very Rev. BRADLEY C. PELZEL, V.G.; Very Rev. Msgr. KEVIN C. MCCOY, S.T.D., V.G.; Very Revs. CRAIG A. COLLISON, V.F.; TERRY A. RODER, V.F.; Revs. BRIAN C. HUGHES; SHANE A. DEMAN.

Deans—Very Revs. DOUGLAS M. KLEIN, V.F., Northwest Deanery; CRAIG A. COLLISON, V.F., Northeast Deanery; TERRY A. RODER, V.F.,

Southwest Deanery; MARK J. STOLL, J.C.L., V.F., Southeast Deanery.

Diocesan Offices and Directors

Board of Education—Most Rev. R. WALKER NICKLESS; MRS. PATTY LANSINK; MR. BRAD MAGILL; MR. PETE HAEFS, Chm.; MRS. CINDY EDGE; Revs. MERLIN J. SCHRAD; SIBY PUNNOOSE; MICHAEL J. KOHN CRONIN; MRS. THERESA ENGEL; MRS. SHARYL BRUNING; MS. MARY FISCHER; MR. MIKE MCGOWAN.

Monsignor Lafferty Tuition Foundation Board—Most Rev. R. WALKER NICKLESS; Very Rev. BRADLEY C. PELZEL, V.G.; Very Rev. Msgr. KEVIN C. MCCOY, S.T.D., V.G.; MR. MATT GRETEMAN; MR. MICHAEL MURPHY; Rev. MERLIN J. SCHRAD; MRS. DAWN PROSSER; MRS. PATTY LANSINK; MR. AARON GRETEMAN; MRS. SHERRY NILLES; MR. MARK ELY; MRS. ADRIENNE COLLINS; MRS. AMANDA WOODALL; MR. JACK HOLTON; MR. BRIAN MCCLAIN.

Building Commission—Rev. BRIAN C. HUGHES; Very Rev. BRENT C. LINGLE; Rev. ANDREW GALLES; MR. BRAD MOLLET.

Catholic School Foundation of the Diocese of Sioux City—Very Rev. DAVID A. HEMANN; Most Rev. R. WALKER NICKLESS, Pres., 1821 Jackson St., Sioux City, 51105; Very Rev. BRADLEY C. PELZEL, V.G.; Very Rev. Msgr. KEVIN C. MCCOY, S.T.D., V.G.; MR. CHARLES KELLEN, Chm.; Rev. SHANE A. DEMAN; MRS. LIZ DETERMAN; MR. JOHN STEFFES; MR. JIM ROSSITER; MR. RANDY SCHMITZ; MR. DAN FLATTERY; MR. LEON HEIDER; MR. DENNIS BOYLE; MRS. PATTY LANSINK.

Archives—1821 Jackson St., P.O. Box 3379, Sioux City, 51102-3379. Tel: 712-233-7525. CECILIA LOPEZ.

Catholic Youth Organization—Rev. RANDY L. SCHON, Mailing Address: P.O. Box 658, Cherokee, 51012-0658.

Censor Librorum—VACANT.

Catholic Charities—MRS. AMY BLOCH, L.I.S.W., C.A.D.C., 1601 Military Rd., Sioux City, 51103. Tel: 712-252-4547. Fort Dodge Office: 3 N. 17th St., Fort Dodge, 50501. Tel: 515-576-4156. Carroll Office: 409 1/2 W. 7th St., Carroll, 51401. Tel: 712-792-9597. Storm Lake Office: 1709 Richland St., Storm Lake, 50588. Tel: 712-792-9597. Algona Office: Court House Annex, 109 W. State St., Algona, 50511. Tel: 515-295-8840. Spencer Office: 1111 4th Ave. W, Spencer, 51301. Tel: 712-580-4320.

Continuing Education for Priests—Rev. SHANE A. DEMAN.

Council of Catholic Women—Rev. JAMES J. TIGGES, Moderator, (Retired), St. Mary Church, 311 4th St. N., Humboldt, 50548-1647. Tel: 515-332-2856.

Department of Formation and Ministry—Very Rev. BRENT C. LINGLE, Coord.; Deacons DAVID A. LOPEZ, Ph.D., Dir. Deacon Formation; TIMOTHY MURPHY, Dir., Deacon Personnel, 1607 N. West St., Carroll, 51401-1498. Tel: 712-792-0513; MR. FRED SHELLABARGER, Dir., Evangelization, Discipleship and Family Life; MRS. KARA KARDELL, Asst. Dir. Youth and Young Adult Ministry; MS. BRIANA ROBERTS, Coord. Hispanic Ministry; MR. DARBY YOUNG, Asst. Dir. Marriage & Family Life; MRS. PATTY LANSINK, Supt. Catholic Schools; MRS. KELLY KOHOUT, Dir. Education Svcs.; MRS. STACIA THOMPSON, Coord. Enrollment & Outreach.

Office of Worship—Very Rev. BRENT C. LINGLE.

Episcopal Representative for Religious—Sr. JANET MAY, O.S.F., Sec./Treas. & Liaison to the Bishop.

Holy Childhood Association—Very Rev. BRENT C. LINGLE, Mailing Address: P.O. Box 3379, Sioux City, 51102-3379.

Liturgy Commission—Very Rev. BRENT C. LINGLE.

Office of "The Catholic Globe"—MRS. JOANNE FOX, Editor, 1825 Jackson St., P.O. Box 5079, Sioux City, 51102-5079. Tel: 712-255-2550. Editorial Office; Circulation.

Office of Catholic Education—1821 Jackson, P.O. Box 3379, Sioux City, 51102-3379. Tel: 712-233-7589. MRS. PATTY LANSINK, Supt.

Priests' Personnel Board—Most Rev. R. WALKER NICKLESS, Chm.; Very Rev. BRADLEY C. PELZEL, V.G.; Very Rev. Msgr. KEVIN C. MCCOY, S.T.D., V.G.; Very Rev. DOUGLAS M. KLEIN, V.F.; Rev. BRIAN C. HUGHES; Very Rev. CRAIG A. COLLISON, V.F.

Priests' Pension Plan - Board of Trustees—Most Rev. R. WALKER NICKLESS, Chm.; Very Rev. BRADLEY C. PELZEL, V.G.; Very Rev. Msgr. KEVIN C. MCCOY, S.T.D., V.G.; Revs. DANIEL M. GREVING; JOHN J. MCGUIRK, (Retired); THOMAS J. TOPF, (Retired); Deacon RICHARD L. BILLINGS, Chm.; MR. ALLEN REYNOLDS; MR. DAVID FLATTERY; MR. THOMAS P. GRIMSLEY; MRS. MARGARET FUENTES; MR. JEFFREY R. MOHRHAUSER; Rev. BRUCE A. LAWLER.

Propagation of the Faith, Association of the Holy Childhood, Catholic Students' Mission CrusadeVery Rev. BRENT C. LINGLE, 1821 Jackson St., P.O. Box 3379, Sioux City, 51102-3379.

Office of Communications—Mailing Address: P.O. Box 3379, Sioux City, 51102-3379. Tel: 712-233-7513. MS. SUSAN O'BRIEN, Dir. Communications & Devel.

St. Joseph Education Society—(Diocesan Seminarian Board). *Mailing Address: P.O. Box 3379, Sioux City, 51102-3379*. Tel: 712-233-7512. Deacon DAVID A. LOPEZ, Ph.D.

Victim Assistance Coordinator—ANGIE MACK, Mercy Child Advocacy Center. Tel: 712-279-5610; Tel: 866-435-4397 (Toll Free); Email: macka@mercyhealth.com.

Safe Environment Coordinator—DAN ELLIS, Tel: 712-233-7517; Email: dane@scdiocese.org.

Vocations—Rev. SHANE A. DEMAN, P.O. Box 3379, Sioux City, 51102. Tel: 712-233-7523.

CLERGY, PARISHES, MISSIONS AND PAROCHIAL SCHOOLS

CITY OF SIOUX CITY

(WOODBURY COUNTY)

1—CATHEDRAL OF THE EPIPHANY (1867)
1000 Douglas St., 51105-1399. Tel: 712-255-1637; Email: info@sccathedral.org; Web: www.sccathedral.org. Very Rev. Brent C. Lingle, Rector; Revs. Mauro Sanchez, Parochial Vicar; Jeremy J. Wind, Parochial Vicar; Very Rev. Bradley C. Pelzel, V.G., In Res.; Deacons Bruce Chartier; Jorge L. Fernandez; David A. Lopez, Ph.D.; Tom Morgan; James H. Sands.
St. Boniface Church—
St. Joseph Church.
See Bishop Heelan Catholic Schools under Inter-Parochial Schools located in the Institution section.
Catechesis Religious Program—Students 374.

2—BLESSED SACRAMENT (1922) Closed. with St. Michael to form Holy Cross.

3—ST. BONIFACE (1887) [JC] (German), Merged with Cathedral of the Epiphany, Sioux City.

4—ST. CASIMIR (1915) (Lithuanian), Closed. For inquiries for parish records contact the chancery.

5—ST. FRANCIS OF ASSISI (1907) (Polish), Closed. For inquiries for parish records contact the chancery.

6—HOLY CROSS CATHOLIC PARISH
2223 Indian Hills Dr., 51108.

7—IMMACULATE CONCEPTION (1905) [JC] Merged with Nativity Parish to form Mater Dei Parish, Sioux City.

8—ST. JOSEPH (1887) [JC] Closed. Merged with Cathedral of the Epiphany, Sioux City.

9—ST. MICHAEL (1906) [JC] Closed. Merged with Holy Cross, Sioux City.

10—MATER DEI CATHOLIC PARISH (1966)
4243 Natalia Way, 51106-4099. Tel: 712-276-4821; Email: lcchurch@cableone.net; Email: office@scnativity.org; Web: www.materdeisc.org. 1212 Morningside Ave., 51106. Revs. Daniel J. Rupp; Andrew Galles; Deacons Dennis Brockhaus; Kevin Poss.
Immaculate Conception Church—
Church of the Nativity of our Lord Jesus Christ.
See Bishop Heelan Catholic Schools under Inter-Parochial Schools located in the Institution section.
Catechesis Religious Program—Email: cre@scnativity.org. Mrs. Linda Bracht, D.R.E.; Mrs. Mary Lehr, D.R.E. Students 223.

11—SACRED HEART (1907) [JC]
5000 Military Rd., 51103-1564. Tel: 712-233-1652. Very Rev. Terry A. Roder, V.F.
See Bishop Heelan Catholic Schools under Inter-Parochial Schools located in the Institution section.
Catechesis Religious Program—Michelle Rethman, D.R.E. Students 130.

OUTSIDE SIOUX CITY

AKRON, PLYMOUTH CO., ST. PATRICK (1888) [CEM]
650 Dakota St., P.O. Box 317, Akron, 51001-0317. Tel: 712-551-1501. Rev. Paul D. Bormann; Deacon Richard Port, Contact Person.
Catechesis Religious Program—Students 67.

ALGONA, KOSSUTH CO., ST. CECELIA (1880) [CEM]
P.O. Box 633, Algona, 50511-0633. Tel: 515-295-3435 ; Email: stcecelia@fivesaintscommunity.com; Web: www.fivesaintscommunity.com. Very Rev. Edward M. Girres, V.F.; Rev. Sunny Dominic, Parochial Vicar; Deacon Bill Black; Mr. Brad Magill.
School—Seton Elementary School Building/Bishop Garrigan Catholic Schools, (Grades K-6).
Catechesis Religious Program—

ALTON, SIOUX CO., ST. MARY'S (1870) [CEM] (German)
609 10th St., Alton, 51003. Tel: 712-756-4224; Email: altonsmc@midlands.net. Rev. Daniel M. Greving; Deacon Daniel Goebel.
School—Spalding Catholic, (Grades PreK-2), Consolidation of Alton, Hospers and Granville.
Catechesis Religious Program—Cluster of St. Mary, St. Anthony's, and St. Joseph's. Students 19.

ANTHON, WOODBURY CO., ST. JOSEPH'S (1890) [CEM]
400 E. Randolph St, Anthon, 51004.
Tel: 712-373-5573; Email: bkanthon@scdiocese.org. P.O. Box 285, Anthon, 51004. Rev. Msgr. Raymond Duchaine.
Catechesis Religious Program—Mrs. Charlene Boyer, C.R.E. Students 42.

ARCADIA, CARROLL CO., ST. JOHN THE BAPTIST (1875) [CEM] (German)
610 S. Gault St, Arcadia, 51430. Tel: 712-689-2595; Email: stjohnarcadia@gmail.com; Web: christthekingcatholiccommunity.org. P.O. Box 23, Arcadia, 51430-0023. Revs. Kevin M. Richter; Brian H. Feller, Parochial Vicar; John J. Gerald, (India) Parochial Vicar; Shinoj Jose, Parochial Vicar; Very Rev. Mark J. Stoll, J.C.L., V.F., Parochial Vicar; Revs. Richard R. Remmes, Sacramental Min., (Retired); Timothy R. Schott, Sacramental Min., (Retired).
Catechesis Religious Program—Robin Lawler, D.R.E. Students 13.

ARMSTRONG, EMMET CO., ST. MARY'S (1892) [CEM] [JC]
404 Fifth Ave., P.O. Box 437, Armstrong, 50514-9301. Tel: 712-864-3160; Tel: 712-362-5851; Email: stpatssec@qwestoffice.net; Web: www.stpatstmary.com. Rev. Merlin J. Schrad.
Catechesis Religious Program—Students 28.

ASHTON, OSCEOLA CO., ST. MARY'S CATHOLIC CHURCH (1880) [CEM] Closed. Merged with St. Andrew, Sibley.

AUBURN, SAC CO., ST. MARY'S (1893) [JC] (German), Closed. Merged with St. Mary, Lake City.

AYRSHIRE, PALO ALTO CO., SACRED HEART, Closed. Merged with Holy Family, Ayrshire.

BANCROFT, KOSSUTH CO., ST. JOHN THE BAPTIST (1891) [CEM] [JC]
204 S. Summit St., P.O. Box 195, Bancroft, 50517-0195. Tel: 515-885-2462; Email: blessedtrinity@wctatel.net; Web: www.blesstrinity.org. Rev. Steven J. McLoud; Deacon Philip Doocy, (Retired).
Catechesis Religious Program—Students 93.

BARNUM, WEBSTER CO., ST. JOSEPH'S (1891) [CEM] Closed. For inquiries for parish records contact Holy Trinity Parish of Webster County, Fort Dodge.

BODE, KOSSUTH CO., ST. JOSEPH (1876) [CEM]
Mailing Address: 1023 Hwy. 169, Bode, 50519.
Tel: 515-379-1062; Email: stjoechurch@hotmail.com. Very Rev. Edward M. Girres, V.F.
Catechesis Religious Program—Students 2.

BOONE, BOONE CO., SACRED HEART (1868) [CEM]
915 12th St., Boone, 50036-2295. Tel: 515-432-1971; Fax: 515-432-1975; Email: parishsecretary@shboone.com; Web: www.sacredhrt.org. Rev. Brian C. Hughes; Deacons David Brown; Darwin Messerly; Scott Steffen.
Catechesis Religious Program—Kathy Steffen, D.R.E. Students 103.
School—Sacred Heart School, 1111 Marshall St., Boone, 50036.
ST. JOHN.
Endowment—Friends of Sacred Heart School, 115 E. Lincoln Way, Ste. 200, Jefferson, 50129.

BREDA, CARROLL CO., ST. BERNARD'S (1880) [CEM]
304 N. 2nd St., Breda, 51436. Tel: 712-673-2582; Fax: 712-673-2239; Email: stbernard@westianet.net; Web: christthekingcatholiccommunity.org. P.O. Box 39, Breda, 51436-0039. Very Rev. Mark J. Stoll, J.C.L., V.F.; Rev. Timothy R. Schott, Sacramental Min., (Retired); Deacon Tim Murphy, D.R.E.
Res.: 206 N. 2nd St., Breda, 51436. Tel: 712-673-2351 ; Email: stbernard@westianet.net.
Parish is a member of the consolidated K-12 Kuemper Catholic School System, Carroll, IA. Please refer to Kuemper Catholic School System under Inter-Parochial Schools in the Institution section.
Catechesis Religious Program—1607 N. West St., Carroll, 51401. Tel: 712-792-9244. Students 5.

CARROLL, CARROLL CO.
1—HOLY SPIRIT (1964) [JC] Merged with St. Lawrence, Carroll to form St. John Paul II, Carroll.
2—ST. JOHN PAUL II CATHOLIC PARISH, [JC]
1607 N. West St., Carroll, 51401-1498.
Tel: 712-792-9244; Email: stjp2carroll@gmail.com. Revs. Kevin M. Richter; Brian H. Feller; Deacon Tim Murphy, D.R.E.
3—ST. LAWRENCE, Merged with Holy Spirit to form St. John Paul II, Carroll.

CHARTER OAK, CRAWFORD CO., ST. BONIFACE (1883) [CEM] (German—Irish), Closed. Now an oratory of St. Rose of Lima, Denison,.

CHEROKEE, CHEROKEE CO., IMMACULATE CONCEPTION (1870) [CEM 2]
709 W. Cedar St., P.O. Box 658, Cherokee, 51012-0658. Tel: 712-225-4606; Email: iccherokee@gmail.

com. Rev. Jeffrey A. Schleisman; Deacon Leroy Rupp.
Catechesis Religious Program—Laurie Dreier, D.R.E. Students 163.
CHURDAN, GREENE CO., ST. COLUMBKILLE (1886) [CEM] (German—Irish), Merged and now a oratory under St. Joseph, Jefferson.
CLARE, WEBSTER CO., ST. MATTHEW'S (1886) [CEM] Closed. For inquiries for parish records contact Holy Trinity Parish of Webster County, Fort Dodge.
COON RAPIDS, CARROLL CO., ANNUNCIATION (1891) [CEM]
724 Elm St, Coon Rapids, 50058-0076.
Tel: 712-999-2823; Email: cranchurch@gmail.com. P.O. Box 76, Coon Rapids, 50058. Revs. Kevin M. Richter; Brian H. Feller; Shinoj Jose; Deacon Louis Meiners.
Res.: 702 Elm St., P.O. Box 76, Coon Rapids, 50058-0076.
Catechesis Religious Program— (Linked with St. Joseph, Dedham & St. Elizabeth Seton, Glidden) Paulette McDonough, D.R.E. Students 59.
DANBURY, WOODBURY CO., ST. MARY'S (1897) [CEM] (German)
604 Peach St, Danbury, 51019. Tel: 712-364-2718; Email: ballr@scdiocese.org. P.O. Box 331, Danbury, 51019. Rev. Richard D. Ball.
School—Danbury Elementary aka Danbury Catholic, (Grades PreK-6), Tel: 712-883-2244; Email: dcathsecretary@gmail.com; Web: www.danburycatholic.org. Mrs. Amy Seuntjens, Prin. Aides 2; Lay Teachers 5; Students 63.
Catechesis Religious Program—Students 16.
DAYTON, WEBSTER CO., CHRIST THE KING (1950) [CEM] Closed. For inquiries for parish records contact Holy Trinity Parish of Webster County, Fort Dodge.
DEDHAM, CARROLL CO., ST. JOSEPH'S (1892) [CEM]
502 Main St., Dedham, 51440. Tel: 712-792-9244; Email: bkdedham@scdiocese.org; Web: dedhamiowa.com/community/stjosephchurch.html. Mailing Address: 1607 N. West St., Carroll, 51401-1498. Revs. Kevin M. Richter; Brian H. Feller, Parochial Vicar; Shinoj Jose, Parochial Vicar; Deacon Louis Meiners.
School—Kuemper Catholic School System, (Grades K-12).
DENISON, CRAWFORD CO., ST. ROSE OF LIMA (1872) [CEM]
916 2nd Ave S, P.O. Box 280, Denison, 51442-0280.
Tel: 712-263-2152; Email: strose@monarctech.net. Revs. Randy L. Schon; Cuong Hung Nguyen, S.V.D.
Sacred Heart—Secondary church under Denison St. Rose of Lima.
School—St. Rose of Lima School, Tel: 712-263-5408. Lay Teachers 7; Students 78.
Catechesis Religious Program—Students 172.
ST. BONIFACE, Charter Oak Charter Oak.
ST. MARY - DOW CITY.
DOW CITY, CRAWFORD CO., ST. MARYS (1947) (German—Irish), Closed. Merged with St. Rose of Lima, Denison.
DUNCOMBE, WEBSTER CO., ST. JOSEPH'S (1880) [CEM] Closed. For inquiries for parish records contact Holy Trinity Parish of Webster County, Fort Dodge.
EARLY, SAC CO., SACRED HEART (1882) [CEM]
501 Church St, Early, 50535. Tel: 712-273-5577; Email: shchurch@evertek.net. Revs. Dr. Timothy A. Friedrichsen; Michael J. Kohn Cronin, Parochial Vicar; Deacons Paul M. Kestel; Kenneth Lindquist; Mark Prosser; Rick Rohr; Michael Higgins.
Catechesis Religious Program—Denise Pickhinke, D.R.E. Students 19.
EMMETSBURG, PALO ALTO CO.
1—HOLY FAMILY (1856) [CEM] (Irish)
2003 S. Broadway, P.O. Box 322, Emmetsburg, 50536-0322. Tel: 712-852-3187; Email: hfp@e-irish.org; Email: bkemmetsburg@scdiocese.org. Rev. William A. Schreiber.
School—Emmetsburg Catholic School, (Grades PreK-8), 1903 Broadway St., Emmetsburg, 50536. Tel: 712-852-3464; Fax: 712-852-3464; Email: kwuebker@e-irish.org; Email: jhyslop@e-irish.org; Web: www.emmetsburgcatholic.org. Mrs. Jean Hyslop, Prin. Clergy 1; Lay Teachers 13; Students 124.
Catechesis Religious Program—Students 73.
SACRED HEART - AYRSHIRE.
SACRED HEART - RUTHVEN.
2—ST. THOMAS, Closed. For sacramental records contact Holy Family, Emmetsburg.
ESTHERVILLE, EMMET CO., ST. PATRICK'S (1891) [CEM]
903 Central Ave., P.O. Box 383, Estherville, 51334-0383. Tel: 712-362-5851; Email: stpatssec@qwestoffice.net; Web: www.stpatstmary.com. Rev. Merlin J. Schrad; Deacon John S. Rudd.
Catechesis Religious Programs—Kathy Cornwall, D.R.E.
Duhigg Center, 902 Central Ave., P.O. Box 383, Estherville, 51334. Tel: 712-362-4172. Students 159.
FONDA, POCAHONTAS CO., OUR LADY OF GOOD COUNSEL (1884) [CEM]
521 N Main St., Fonda, 50540. Tel: 712-288-6480; Email: olgcfonda@gmail.com. P.O. Box 339, Fonda, 50540-0339. Very Rev. Craig A. Collison, V.F.
Catechesis Religious Program—Dana Erickson, D.R.E. Students 92.
ST. COLUMBKILLE - VARINA.
FORT DODGE, WEBSTER CO.
1—CORPUS CHRISTI (1856) [JC] Closed. For inquiries for parish records contact Holy Trinity Parish of Webster County, Fort Dodge.
2—HOLY ROSARY (1946) [JC] Closed. For inquiries for parish records contact Holy Trinity Parish of Webster County, Fort Dodge.
3—HOLY TRINITY PARISH OF WEBSTER COUNTY (2006)
2220 4th Ave. N., Fort Dodge, 50501.
Tel: 515-955-6077; Fax: 515-955-8473; Email: holytrinityparish@fdcatholic.com; Web: www.holytrinitywci.org. Very Rev. Msgr. Kevin C. McCoy, S.T.D., V.G.; Rev. Patrick M. Behm, Parochial Vicar; Deacons Daniel F. Carney; Joseph Coleman; Rick Salocker; Edward Albright.
See St. Edmond Catholic School, Inc., Fort Dodge under Inter-Parochial Schools located in the Institution Section.
Catechesis Religious Program—Mary Salocker, D.R.E. Students 31.
4—SACRED HEART (1897) [JC] Closed. For inquiries for parish records contact Holy Trinity Parish of Webster County, Fort Dodge.
GILMORE CITY, POCAHONTAS CO., ST. JOHN'S (1889) [CEM] Closed. Merged with St. Mary, Humboldt.
GLIDDEN, CARROLL CO., ST. ELIZABETH SETON (1977)
226 W. 6th St., Glidden, 51443. Tel: 712-673-2582; Web: christthekingcatholiccommunity.org. P.O. Box 513, Glidden, 51443-0513. Very Rev. Mark J. Stoll, J.C.L., V.F.; Rev. Timothy R. Schott, V.F., Sacramental Min., (Retired); Deacons Gregory Sampson; Gary Schon.
Catechesis Religious Program—Tel: 712-659-3051. Students 79.
GRAETTINGER, PALO ALTO CO., IMMACULATE CONCEPTION (1891) [CEM]
305 N. Cameron Ave., Graettinger, 51342.
Tel: 712-852-3187; Email: hfp@e-irish.org. P.O. Box 322, Emmetsburg, 50536. Rev. William A. Schreiber.
Res.: 903 Central Ave., P.O. Box 383, Estherville, 51334. Tel: 712-362-5851; Fax: 712-362-5852; Email: stpatssec@qwestoffice.net.
Catechesis Religious Program—503 W. Olive St., Graettinger, 51342. Students 58.
GRAND JUNCTION, GREENE CO., ST. BRIGID'S (1873) [CEM] (Irish), Merged and now a secondary church of St. Joseph, Jefferson.
GRANVILLE, SIOUX CO., ST. JOSEPH (1886) [CEM]
Mailing Address: 528 Elm St., P.O. Box 127, Granville, 51022. Tel: 712-727-3551; Email: christec@mtcnet.net. Rev. Daniel M. Greving; Deacon Daniel Goebel.
Res.: 609 10th St., Alton, 51003.
Catechesis Religious Program—Tami List, D.R.E. Pilgrim cluster held at St. Mary's, Alton. Students 87.
HALBUR, CARROLL CO., ST. AUGUSTINE'S (1904) [CEM]
320 W. 2nd St., Halbur, 51444. Tel: 712-673-2582; Email: stbernard@westianet.net; Web: christthekingcatholiccommunity.org. P.O. Box 13, Halbur, 51444-0013. Very Rev. Mark J. Stoll, J.C.L., V.F.; Deacons Gregory Sampson; Tim Murphy, D.R.E.
Parish is a member of the consolidated K-12 Kuemper Catholic School System, Carroll, IA. Please refer to Kuemper Catholic School System under Inter-Parochial Schools in the Institution section.
Holy Angels - Roselle.
Catechesis Religious Program—1607 N. West St., Carroll, 51401. Tel: 712-792-9244; Web: christthekingcatholiccommunity.org. Students 19.
HARTLEY, O'BRIEN CO., ST. JOSEPH'S
260 N. 4th Ave., Hartley, 51346. Tel: 712-930-3423; Email: hogant@scdiocese.org. P.O. Box 817, Spencer, 51301-0817. Rev. Timothy J. Hogan.
ST. CECILIA.
SACRED HEART.
HAWARDEN, SIOUX CO., ST. MARY'S (1887) [JC]
1125 Avenue L, Hawarden, 51023-0271.
Tel: 712-551-1501; Email: bormannp@scdiocese.org; Email: stmarydre@gohitec.com; Web: www.stmaryshawarden.org. Rev. Paul D. Bormann.
Catechesis Religious Program—Students 290.
HOLSTEIN, IDA CO., OUR LADY OF GOOD COUNSEL (1884) [CEM]
513 Mueller St., Holstein, 51025-9802.
Tel: 712-368-4755; Email: olgcholstein@hotmail.com. Rev. Jeffrey A. Schleisman; Rev. Msgrs. Kenneth A. Seifried, In Res., (Retired); Ken Seifried, (Retired).
Catechesis Religious Program—Students 52.
HORNICK, WOODBURY CO., ST. PHILIP'S (1900) Closed. For inquiries for parish records contact the chancery.
HOSPERS, SIOUX CO., ST. ANTHONY'S (1877) [CEM]
500 Elm St., Hospers, 51238-0086. Tel: 712-752-8784 ; Email: stacc@nethtc.net; Web: pilgrimcluster.org. P.O. Box 86, Hospers, 51238. Rev. Daniel M. Greving; Deacon Daniel Goebel.
Res.: c/o St. Mary, 609 10th St., Alton, 51003.
Catechesis Religious Program—Tami List, D.R.E. Students 6.
HUMBOLDT, HUMBOLDT CO., ST. MARY'S (1878) [CEM]
311 4th St. N., Humboldt, 50548-1647.
Tel: 515-332-2856; Web: www.humboldtareacc.org. Very Rev. Daniel C. Guenther, V.F.
School—St. Mary's School, Tel: 515-332-2134; Email: cedge@stmaryhumboldt.org; Web: www.stmaryhumboldt.org. Very Rev. Daniel C. Guenther, V.F. Clergy 6; Lay Teachers 10; Students 2,019.
Catechesis Religious Program—Students 149.
IDA GROVE, IDA CO., SACRED HEART (1878) [CEM]
800 N. Main, P.O. Box 203, Ida Grove, 51445-1297.
Tel: 712-364-4418; Email: igrectory@frontiernet.net. Rev. Richard D. Ball; Deacon Mike Stover, Pastoral Min./Coord.
Catechesis Religious Program—Students 129.
JEFFERSON, GREENE CO., ST. JOSEPH'S (1875)
503 N. Chestnut St., Jefferson, 50129-1507.
Tel: 515-386-2638; Email: joejeff@netins.net. Rev. John J. Gerald, (India).
Catechesis Religious Program—501 N. Locust, Jefferson, 50129. Students 80.
ST. BRIGID.
ST. COLUMBKILLE.
KINGSLEY, PLYMOUTH CO., ST. MICHAEL'S (1888) [CEM]
208 Brandon St., P.O. Box 99, Kingsley, 51039-0099.
Tel: 712-378-2722; Fax: 712-378-2021; Email: stmichael@wiatel.net; Web: westforkcatholiccommunity.org. Rev. Msgr. Raymond Duchaine.
Catechesis Religious Program—Barbara Sitzmann, D.R.E. Students 114.
LAKE CITY, CALHOUN CO., ST. MARY'S (1894) [CEM] [JC]
205 N. Lloyd St., P.O. Box 131, Lake City, 51449-0131. Tel: 712-464-3395; Email: catholic@windstream.net; Web: calhouncatholic.org. Rev. Lynn A. Bruch; Deacon Robert Lenz.
Catechesis Religious Program—Julie Storr, D.R.E. Students 82.
ST. JOSEPH.
LARCHWOOD, LYON CO., ST. MARY (1898) (German—Dutch)
1030 Blaine Ave, P.O. Box 37, Larchwood, 51241-0037. Tel: 712-477-2273; Email: holymarycluster@yahoo.com; Web: holymarycluster.webs.com. Rev. Francis S. Makwinja.
Res.: 1413 Holder St., P.O. Box 37, Larchwood, 51241-0037.
Catechesis Religious Program—Students 142.
LAURENS, POCAHONTAS CO., SACRED HEART (1893) [CEM] Closed. Merged with Resurrection of Our Lord, Pocahontas.
LE MARS, PLYMOUTH CO.
1—ALL SAINTS ROMAN CATHOLIC CHURCH (2014) [CEM] [JC] (German)
605 Plymouth St., N.E., Le Mars, 51031.
Tel: 712-546-5223; Fax: 712-546-8346; Email: allsaints@premieronline.net. Revs. Bruce Lawler; Matthew Solyntjes; Deacons Thomas Henrich; Paul Gengler.
Res.: 109 6th Ave. S.W., Le Mars, 51031.
School—Gehlen Catholic School, 709 Plymouth St., S.E., Le Mars, 51031. Tel: 712-546-4181; Fax: 712-546-9384; Email: lnussbaum@gehlencatholic.org; Web: www.gehlencatholic.org. Rev. Bruce Lawler, Pres.; Jeff Alesch, Prin.; Mrs. Lorie A. Nussbaum, Prin. Lay Teachers 39; Students 525.
Endowment—All Saints Endowment Fund.
Catechesis Religious Program—Cecilia Henrich, Diocesan D.R.E. Students 255.
Missions—St. Joseph at Ellendale—23533 K22, Merrill, Plymouth Co. 51038.
St. Joseph's.
2—ASSUMPTION CHURCH (1890) [CEM 2] Closed. For inquiries for parish records contact the chancery.
LEDYARD, KOSSUTH CO., SACRED HEART (1887) [CEM] [JC]
205 Logan St., Ledyard, 50556-0067.
Tel: 515-885-2462; Email: mclouds@scdiocese.org; Web: www.blesstrinity.org. P.O. Box 195, Bancroft, 50517. Rev. Steven J. McLoud.
Res.: 204 S. Summit Ave., P.O. Box 195, Bancroft, 50517.
Catechesis Religious Program—Twinned with St. John's, Bancroft. Students 10.
LIDDERDALE, CARROLL CO., HOLY FAMILY (1914) [CEM] (German), Closed. For inquiries see St. John Paul II Parish, Carroll.
LIVERMORE, HUMBOLDT CO., SACRED HEART (1881) [CEM]
14 4th Ave., P.O. Box 32, Livermore, 50558-886.
Tel: 515-379-2508; Email: sacredheartlivermore@hotmail.com. Very Rev. Daniel C. Guenther, V.F.

Catechesis Religious Program—Krystin Olson, D.R.E. Students 31.

LOHRVILLE, CALHOUN CO., ST. JOSEPH'S (1885) [CEM] (Irish), Closed. with and now an oratory of St. Mary, Lake City.

MADRID, BOONE CO., ST. MALACHY'S (1923) [JC]
405 Gerald St., Madrid, 50156-1464.
Tel: 515-795-2613; Tel: 515-795-2731; Email: stmalachymadrid@outlook.com; Web: www.stmalachys-madrid.com. 207 Gerald St., Madrid, 50156. Rev. Brian C. Hughes; Deacon Verne Burke, Email: vernob@outlook.com.
Catechesis Religious Program—Kelley Grothus, D.R.E. Students 179.

MALLARD, PALO ALTO CO., ST. MARY'S (1889) Closed. For inquiries for parish records contact the chancery.

MANILLA, CRAWFORD CO., SACRED HEART (1887) [CEM] Closed. Merged with and now a worship site of St. Rose of Lima, Denison.

MANNING, CARROLL CO., SACRED HEART (1916) [CEM] (German)
203 Sue St., Manning, 51455-1399.
Tel: 712-263-2152; Email: mclouds@scdiocese.org; Email: strose@monarctech.net; Web: www.monarctech.net. P.O. Box 280, Denison, 51442. Revs. Randy L. Schon; Cuong Hung Nguyen, S.V.D.
Res.: 1008 2nd Ave S, Denison, 51442.
Catechesis Religious Program—Students 117.

MANSON, CALHOUN CO., ST. THOMAS (1885) [CEM 2]
P.O. Box 131, Lake City, 51449. Tel: 712-464-3395; Web: www.calhouncatholic.org. 1100 8th St., Manson, 50563-0099. Rev. Lynn A. Bruch; Deacon Robert Lenz.
Catechesis Religious Program—Students 85.
ST. MARY - POMEROY.

MAPLE RIVER, CARROLL CO., ST. FRANCIS OF ASSISI (1904) [CEM] (German), Closed. For inquiries for parish records contact Our Lady of Mt. Carmel parish in Mt. Carmel, IA.

MAPLETON, MONONA CO., ST. MARY'S (1894) [CEM 2]
Mailing Address: 703 Heisler St., Mapleton, 51034.
Tel: 712-882-1780; Email: ballr@scdiocese.org; Email: mapletonparishcoordinator@gmail.com. Rev. Richard D. Ball.
Catechesis Religious Program—Students 41.

MARCUS, CHEROKEE CO., HOLY NAME (1877) [CEM]
102 N. Elm, Marcus, 51035. Tel: 712-225-4606; Email: mccarthyw@scdiocese.org. P.O. Box 366, Marcus, 51035-0366. Rev. William A. McCarthy; Deacon Jerry Bertrand, D.R.E.
Catechesis Religious Program—Students 110.

MARYHILL, CHEROKEE CO., VISITATION OF THE B.V.M. (1895) [CEM] Closed. For inquiries for Parish records please contact Immaculate Conception, Cherokee.

MILFORD, DICKINSON CO., ST. JOSEPH'S (1884) [CEM]
1305 Okoboji Ave., Milford, 51351-1232.
Tel: 712-338-2274; Fax: 712-338-2191; Email: info@stjosephmilford.org; Web: www.stjosephmilford.org. Rev. Timothy A. Johnson.
Res.: 1413 Okoboji Ave., Milford, 51351.
Catechesis Religious Program—Sharon Mayer, D.R.E. Students 161.

MOORLAND, WEBSTER CO., OUR LADY OF GOOD COUNSEL (1902) [CEM] Closed. For inquiries for parish records contact Holy Trinity Parish of Webster County, Fort Dodge.

MOUNT CARMEL, CARROLL CO., OUR LADY OF MT. CARMEL (1869) [CEM] (German)
19481 140th St, Breda, 51436. Tel: 712-673-2582; Email: marks@scdiocese.org; Web: christthekingcatholiccommunity.org. 206 N. 2nd St., P.O. Box 39, Breda, 51436-0039. Very Rev. Mark J. Stoll, J.C.L., V.F.; Rev. Timothy R. Schott, Sacramental Min., (Retired); Deacon Tim Murphy, D.R.E.
Parish is a member of newly consolidated K-12 Kuemper Catholic School System, Carroll, IA. Please refer to Kuemper Catholic School System under Inter-Parochial Schools in the Institution section.
Catechesis Religious Program—1607 N. West St., Carroll, 51401. Tel: 712-792-9244. Students 8.

MOVILLE, WOODBURY CO., IMMACULATE CONCEPTION (1892)
419 Jones St., P.O. Box 802, Moville, 51039-0802.
Tel: 712-873-3644; Fax: 712-873-3931; Email: icmoville@wiatel.net; Web: www.westforkcatholiccommunity.org. Rev. Msgr. Raymond Duchaine.
Res.: 403 Jones St., P.O. Box 802, Moville, 51039-0802.
Catechesis Religious Program—Angela Duffy, D.R.E. Students 106.

NEPTUNE, PLYMOUTH CO., ST. JOSEPH (Hinton) (1884) [CEM] (German), Closed. For inquiries for parish records please contact Assumption Church, Merrill.

ODEBOLT, SAC CO., ST. MARTIN'S (1877) [CEM]
400 Hansen Blvd., P.O. Box 500, Odebolt, 51458.
Tel: 712-668-2690; Email: stmartinodebolt@hotmail.com. Rev. Joseph A. Dillinger; Deacon Byron Stone.
Catechesis Religious Program—Julia Mogensen, D.R.E. Students 57.

OGDEN, BOONE CO., ST. JOHN'S (1896) [CEM] Closed. and now an oratory of Sacred Heart, Boone.

ONAWA, MONONA CO., ST. JOHN (1900)
1009 13th St., Onawa, 51040-1508.
Tel: 712-423-1004; Email: michaele@scdiocese.org; Email: stjohnparishhall@msn.com. Rev. Michael J. Erpelding, J.C.L.; Deacon Joseph Scurlock.
Catechesis Religious Program—Colleen Maule, D.R.E. Students 93.
Mission—St. Bernard, Blencoe, Monona Co.

OTO, WOODBURY CO., ST. MARY'S ROMAN CATHOLIC CHURCH (1868) Closed. Merged with St. Mary, Mapleton.

OYENS, PLYMOUTH CO., ST. CATHERINE'S (1900) [CEM] Closed. Merged with St. Mary's Parish, Remsen.

POCAHONTAS, POCAHONTAS CO., CHURCH OF THE RESURRECTION (1973) [CEM]
16 S.W. 2nd St., Pocahontas, 50574.
Tel: 712-335-3242; Email: prparish@gmail.com. Very Rev. Craig A. Collison, V.F.
Catechesis Religious Program—Students 50.

POMEROY, CALHOUN CO., ST. MARY'S (1881) [CEM] Closed. Merged with St. Thomas, Manson.

REMSEN, PLYMOUTH CO., ST. MARY'S (1885) [CEM]
121 E. 4th St., P.O. Box 509, Remsen, 51050.
Tel: 712-786-1437; Email: smparish@midlands.net. Rev. William A. McCarthy; Deacon Rick Roder.
School—St. Mary's Schools, 321 Fulton St., Remsen, 51050. Tel: 712-786-1160; Fax: 712-786-1167; Email: doumal@rsmschools.org. Mr. Les Douma, Prin.; Ms. Mary Riedemann, Librarian. Lay Teachers 11; Students 165.
See St. Mary's High School, Remsen under Inter-Parochial Schools located in the Institution Section.
Catechesis Religious Program—Students 47.
ST. CATHERINE - OYENS.

ROCK RAPIDS, LYON CO., HOLY NAME (1890) [CEM] (Irish)
1108 S. Carroll St., Rock Rapids, 51246-9529.
Tel: 712-472-3248; Email: holymarycluster@yahoo.com; Email: bkrockrapids@scdiocese.org. Rev. Francis S. Makwinja.
Pastor's Res.: St. Mary Rectory, 1413 Holder St., Larchwood, 51241.
Catechesis Religious Program—Students 88.

ROCK VALLEY, SIOUX CO., ST. MARY'S (1895) [CEM]
St. Mary's Catholic Church, 1821 14th St., Rock Valley, 51247. Tel: 712-476-2060; Email: smrv@premieronline.net; Web: www.stmarysrockvalley.org. Very Rev. Douglas M. Klein, V.F.
Catechesis Religious Program—Students 142.

ROCKWELL CITY, CALHOUN CO., ST. FRANCIS OF ASSISI (1899) [CEM] (German)
744 Main St., Rockwell City, 50579.
Tel: 712-464-3395; Web: calhouncatholic.org. P.O. Box 131, Lake City, 51449. Rev. Lynn A. Bruch; Deacon Robert Lenz.
Catechesis Religious Program—Students 62.

ROLFE, POCAHONTAS CO., ST. MARGARET'S (1895) [CEM] Closed. For inquiries for parish records contact the chancery.

ROSELLE, CARROLL CO., HOLY ANGELS (1874) [CEM] Closed. Now a worship site of St. Augustine, Halbur.

ROYAL, CLAY CO., ST. LOUIS (1923) Closed. Merged with Sacred Heart, Spencer.

RUTHVEN, PALO ALTO CO., SACRED HEART (1889) [CEM] Closed. Merged with Holy Family, Emmetsburg.

SAC CITY, SAC CO., ST. MARY'S (1892) [CEM] (German—Irish)
600 S. 12th St., Sac City, 50583. Tel: 712-662-7240; Email: dillingerj@scdiocese.org. Rev. Joseph A. Dillinger; Deacon B. (Butch) Stone.
Catechesis Religious Program—Students 79.

ST. BENEDICT, KOSSUTH CO., ST. BENEDICT'S (1877) [CEM] Closed. Merged with St. Joseph, Wesley.
School—Seton Elementary, Consolidation of St. Cecelia, Algona, St. Benedict and St. Joseph, Wesley.

SALIX, WOODBURY CO., ST. JOSEPH'S (1869) [CEM] [JC]
510 Tipton St, P.O. Box 270, Salix, 51052.
Tel: 712-946-5635; Email: stjoseph@longlines.com; Web: www.stjoessalix.com. Rev. Michael J. Erpelding, J.C.L.
Catechesis Religious Program—Kathy Jo Mitchell, D.R.E. Students 76.

SANBORN, O'BRIEN CO., ST. CECILIA'S (1882) Closed. and now an oratory of St. Joseph, Hartley.

SCHALLER, SAC CO., ST. JOSEPH'S (1891) [CEM] Closed. Merged with St. Mary, Storm Lake.

SCRANTON, GREENE CO., ST. PAUL'S (1926) Closed. For inquiries for parish records contact the chancery.

SHELDON, O'BRIEN CO., ST. PATRICK'S (1873) [CEM] (Irish)
310 10th St., Sheldon, 51201-1530.
Tel: 712-234-3220; Email: punnooses@scdiocese.org; Web: sheldonstpats.org. Rev. Siby Punnoose.
St. Mary - Ashton.
School—1020 4th Ave., Sheldon, 51201.
Tel: 712-324-3181.
Catechesis Religious Program—Paulette Karolczak, D.R.E. Students 137.

SIBLEY, OSCEOLA CO., ST. ANDREW'S (1896) [CEM]
716 Eighth St., Sibley, 51249-0130.
Tel: 712-754-2739; Email: standrewsibley@premieronline.net; Web: hwy60catholiccluster.org. P.O. Box 97, Sibley, 51249. Rev. Siby Punnoose; Christy Funk, Sec.
Catechesis Religious Program— (Clustered with St. Mary, Ashton) Christy Funk, D.R.E. Students 95.

SIOUX CENTER, SIOUX CO., CHRIST THE KING (2010)
501 2nd Ave., S.W., Sioux Center, 51250.
Tel: 712-722-3011; Email: smrv@premieronline.net; Web: www.christthekingsc.org. Very Rev. Douglas M. Klein, V.F.
Catechesis Religious Program—Robyn VanVenrooij, D.R.E. Students 198.

SIOUX RAPIDS, BUENA VISTA CO., ST. JOSEPH (1886) [CEM] Closed. Merged with St. Mary, Storm Lake.

SPENCER, CLAY CO., SACRED HEART (1882)
1111 4th Ave. W., P.O. Box 817, Spencer, 51301-0817. Tel: 712-262-3047; Email: qtjhz@aim.com; Web: www.spencersacredheart.com. Rev. Timothy J. Hogan.
School—Sacred Heart School, (Grades PreK-6), Tel: 712-262-6428; Email: rolberding@spencersacredheart.com. Lay Teachers 12; Students 173.
Catechesis Religious Program—Email: mmaurer@spencersacredheart.com. Mollie Maurer, D.R.E. Students 200.

SPIRIT LAKE, DICKINSON CO., ST. MARY'S (1914) [CEM]
1005 Hill Ave., P.O. Box 354, Spirit Lake, 51360-0354. Tel: 712-336-1742; Email: kellyp@scdiocese.org; Email: secretary@stmarysspiritlake.org; Web: www.stmarysspiritlake.org. Rev. Paul Kelly.
Catechesis Religious Program—Students 155.

STORM LAKE, BUENA VISTA CO., ST. MARY'S (1872) [CEM]
Third & Seneca Sts., Storm Lake, 50588-1106.
Tel: 712-732-3110; Email: parish@stormlakecatholic.com. 300 E. Third St., Storm Lake, 50588-2554. Revs. Dr. Timothy A. Friedrichsen; Michael J. Kohn Cronin, Parochial Vicar; Deacons Mark Prosser; Paul M. Kestel; Rick Rohr; Kenneth Lindquist; Michael Higgins.
St. Joseph Church.
School—Elementary & High School, (Grades K-12), Tel: 712-732-3110; Email: cpudenz@stormlakecatholic.com; Web: www.stormlakecatholic.com. Rev. Dr. Timothy A. Friedrichsen, Pres. Lay Teachers 33; Students 310.
Catechesis Religious Program—Kathleen Eckerman, D.R.E. Students 289.

SUTHERLAND, O'BRIEN CO., SACRED HEART (1883) [CEM] Closed. Now an oratory of St. Joseph, Hartley.

TEMPLETON, CARROLL CO., SACRED HEART (1882) [CEM]
202 S. 5th Ave., Templeton, 51463.
Tel: 712-673-2582; Email: stbernard@westianet.net; Web: christthekingcatholiccommunity.org. P.O. Box 104, Templeton, 51463-0104. Very Rev. Mark J. Stoll, J.C.L., V.F.; Deacons Gregory Sampson; Tim Murphy, D.R.E.
Parish is a member of the consolidated K-12 Kuemper Catholic School System, Carroll, IA. Please refer to Kuemper Catholic School System under Inter-Parochial Schools in the Institution section.
Catechesis Religious Program—1607 N. West St., Carroll, 51401. Tel: 712-792-9244. Students 6.

VAIL, CRAWFORD CO., ST. ANN'S (1878) [CEM]
P.O. Box 280, Denison, 51442. Tel: 712-263-2152; Email: strose@monarctech.net. 102 5th Ave, Vail, 51465. Revs. Randy L. Schon; Cuong Hung Nguyen, S.V.D.
See Kuemper Catholic School System, Carroll under Inter-Parochial Schools located in the Institution section.
Catechesis Religious Program—Students 36.

VARINA, POCAHONTAS CO., ST. COLUMBKILLE'S (1882) [CEM] Closed. Now an oratory of Our Lady of Good Counsel, Fonda.

WALL LAKE, SAC CO., ST. JOSEPH'S (1878) (German)
102 W. 5th St., P.O. Box 130, Wall Lake, 51466.
Tel: 712-662-7240; Email: dillingerj@scdiocese.org. Rev. Joseph A. Dillinger; Deacon B. (Butch) Stone.
Res.: 600 S. 12th St., Sac City, 50583.
Catechesis Religious Program—Students 161.

WESLEY, KOSSUTH CO., ST. JOSEPH'S (1891) [CEM]
405 East St. S., Wesley, 50483-0038.
Tel: 515-679-4279; Email: bkwesley@scdiocese.org; Web: www.blesstrinity.org. P.O. Box 38, Wesley, 50483. Rev. Steven J. McLoud.
High School—Bishop Garrigan High School, (Grades 7-12), 1224 N. McCoy, Algona, 50511.
Tel: 515-295-3521; Email: petersonc@bishopgarrigan.org.
Catechesis Religious Program—St. Cecelia Faith Formation: 715 E. North St., Algona, 50511.

Tel: 515-295-3435; Email: joycev@netamumail.com. Joyce Van Haastert, D.R.E. Students 10.

WEST BEND, PALO ALTO CO., SS. PETER AND PAUL (1888) [CEM]
205 N. Broadway, West Bend, 50597.
Tel: 515-887-3333; Email: sspp@ncn.net. P.O. Box 16, West Bend, 50597-0316. Very Rev. Edward M. Girres, V.F.; Rev. Sunny Dominic, Parochial Vicar; Deacons Bill Black; Brad Magill.
Catechesis Religious Program—Ann Langel, D.R.E. Students 54.

WHITTEMORE, KOSSUTH CO., ST. MICHAEL'S (1889) [CEM]
613 3rd St, P.O. Box 337, Whittemore, 50598-0337.
Tel: 515-884-2680; Email: stmwhitt@ncn.net; Web: www.fivesaintscommunity.com. Very Rev. Edward M. Girres, V.F.; Rev. Sunny Dominic; Deacons Joseph Straub, (Retired); William Black, Pastoral Min./ Coord.
Res.: P.O. Box 633, Algona, 50511-0633.
Tel: 515-295-3435.
Catechesis Religious Program—See separate listing at St. Cecelia, Algona. Students 15.

WILLEY, CARROLL CO., ST. MARY'S (1882) [CEM]
205 Olympic Ave., Willey, 51401. Tel: 712-792-9244; Email: stjp2carroll@gmail.com. c/o St. John Paul II Parish: 1607 N. West St., Carroll, 51401. Rev. Kevin M. Richter.
Rectory—421 E. Bluff, Carroll, 51401.
Please see Kuemper Catholic School System under Inter-Parochial Schools located in the Institution Section.
Catechesis Religious Program—Students 38.

Chaplains of Public Institutions

SIOUX CITY. *Holy Spirit Retirement Home*. Rev. Dennis W. Meinen, (Retired).
Mercy Medical Center. Revs. Anthony Nwudah, Augustine "Gus" Peter.
Woodbury County Jail. Deacon Joseph Twidwell Jr.
CARROLL. *St. Anthony Regional Hospital*.
FORT DODGE. *Marian Home and Village*. Deacon Daniel F. Carney.
Trinity Regional Hospital. Deacon Joseph Coleman.
ROCKWELL CITY. *Calhoun County State Reformatory, Minimum Security for Men*. Rev. Lynn A. Bruch.

On Duty Outside the Diocese:
Revs.—
Barrett, Miles J., Cdr., 11 Eider Ln., North Cape May, NJ 08204
Esquiliano, J. David
Kurzak, John F., 4328 Proctor Pl., San Diego, CA 92116. Tel: 210-380-3165
Vit, William J. Jr., (Archdiocese for the Military Services, USA).

Leave of Absence:
Revs.—
Hewitt, Matthew A.
Lona, Frank E.

Retired:
Rev. Msgrs.—
Donahoe, Thomas, (Retired), 916 3 Williams Dr., Fort Dodge, 50501. Tel: 515-573-8612. Fort Dodge, IA
Seifried, Kenneth A., (Retired), Holstein, IA
Sernett, Michael D., J.C.D., V.G., (Retired), Pocahontas, IA

Revs.—
Arts, Paul-Louis, M.S., (Retired), Scottsdale, AZ
Bertrand, Armand J., (Retired), Sioux City, IA
Boekelman, Timothy J., (Retired), Carroll, IA
Boes, Clair L., (Retired), Rockwell City, IA
Boes, Marvin, (Retired), Sioux City, IA
Brodersen, Steven W., (Retired), Carroll, IA
Bruch, James A., (Retired), Ogden, IA
Burns, Laurence J., (Retired), Sioux City, IA
Cosgrove, Jerome P., M.S., (Retired), Sioux City, IA
Currans, Clement W., (Retired), Emmetsburg, IA
Eisele, Paul F., (Retired), Le Mars, IA
Fangman, Robert M., (Retired), Carroll, IA
Farrell, Emmett L., (Retired), San Diego, CA
Feierfeil, Gerald F., (Retired), Sioux City, IA
Flanagan, Thomas J., (Retired), Milford, IA
Fransco, Peter J., (Retired), Ruthven, IA
Hart, Thomas J., (Retired), Humboldt, IA
Hartz, Gerald A., (Retired), Bakersfield, CA
Higgins, Francis E., (Retired)
Hoffman, Andrew W., Carroll, IA
Kollasch, Merle F., (Retired), Bode, IA
Koster, Dale F., (Retired), Carroll, IA
Leiting, Robert L., (Retired), Carroll, IA
Linnan, Roger, (Retired), Sioux City, IA
McAlpine, Harry D., (Retired), Sioux City, IA
McCarty, Lawrence L., V.F., (Retired), Manson, IA
McGuirk, John J., (Retired), Sioux City, IA
Meinen, Dennis W., (Retired), Sioux City, IA
Murray, Eugene, (Retired), Marcus, IA
Nguyen, Phillip Hieu Van, (Retired), Sioux City, IA
O'Kane, Patrick J., (Retired), Omaha, NE
Pick, Anthony, (Retired), Slayton, MN
Ramaeker, Victor, (Retired), Algona, IA
Reicks, Allan A., (Retired), Carroll, IA
Reiff, Dale E., (Retired), Carroll, IA
Remmes, Richard R., (Retired), Arcadia, IA
Ries, Richard S., (Retired), Sibley, IA
Schott, Timothy R., (Retired), Carroll, IA
Sefcik, Dennis L., (Retired), Pocahontas, IA
Sitzmann, Eugene E., (Retired), Cherokee, IA
Sitzmann, Richard A., (Retired), Sioux City, IA
Smith, James R., (Retired), Storm Lake, IA
Snyder, Gary B., (Retired), Carroll, IA
Stapenhorst, Verne P., (Retired), Mesquite, NV
Thomas, John M., (Retired), Algona, IA
Tiedeman, Edmund H., (Retired), Fonda, IA
Tigges, James J., (Retired), Fort Dodge, IA
Topf, Thomas J., (Retired), Sioux City, IA
Vakulskas, John A. Jr., (Retired), Okoboji, IA
Walsh, Patrick, (Retired), Sioux City, IA
Yetmar, Charles J., (Retired), Tel: 515-955-7260. Fort Dodge, IA.

Permanent Deacons:
Albright, Edward, Holy Trinity, Fort Dodge
Bertrand, Gerald L., Holy Name, Marcus; St. Mary Remsen
Billings, Richard, Sacred Heart, Sioux City
Black, William, St. Cecelia, Algona; St Michael, Whittemore; St. Joseph, Bode; Ss. Peter and Paul, West Bend
Brockhaus, Dennis, Mater Dei, Sioux City
Brown, David, Sacred Heart, Boone
Burke, Verne, St. Malachy, Madrid; Sacred Heart, Boone
Carney, Daniel F., Holy Trinity, Fort Dodge
Chartier, Bruce, Cathedral of the Epiphany, Sioux City
Coleman, Joseph, Holy Trinity, Fort Dodge
Doocy, Philip F., (Retired)
Fernandez, Jorge L., Cathedral of the Epiphany, Sioux City
Forrest, Ronald M., (Retired)
Gallagher, Jeffrey F., (Retired)
Gengler, Paul, All Saints, Le Mars
Goebel, Daniel, St. Joseph, Granville; St. Mary, Alton; St. Anthony, Hospers
Hand, Michael J., Sacred Heart, Sioux City
Henrich, Thomas, All Saints, Le Mars
Higgins, Michael, Sacred Heart, Early; St. Mary, Storm Lake
Kallsen, Richard, Holy Cross, Sioux City
Karpuk, Fred P., Holy Cross, Sioux City
Kestel, Paul M., Sacred Heart, Early; St. Mary, Storm Lake
Lenz, Robert D., St. Mary Church, Lake City; St. Thomas , Manson; St. Francis, Rockwell City
Lindquist, Ken, Sacred Heart, Early; St. Mary, Storm Lake
Lopez, David A., Ph.D., Cathedral of the Epiphany, Sioux City
Maguire, Don, St. Cecelia, Algona; St. Michael, Whittemore; St. Joseph, Bode; Ss. Peter and Paul, West Bend
McGill, Brad, St. Cecelia, Algona; St. Michael, Whittemore; St. Joseph, Bode; Ss. Peter and Paul, West Bend
Meiners, Louis, St. Joseph, Dedham; Annunciation, Coon Rapids; St. Elizabeth Seton, Glidden
Messerly, Darwin, Sacred Heart, Boone; St. Malachy, Madrid
Morgan, Tom, Cathedral of the Epiphany, Sioux City
Murphy, Tim, St. John Paul II, Carroll
Penton, David, St. Cecelia, Algona; St. Michael, Whittemore; St. Joseph, Bode; Ss. Peter and Paul, West Bend
Port, Richard, St. Patrick, Akron; St. Mary, Hawarden
Poss, Kevin, Mater Dei, Sioux City
Prenger, Dave, St. John Paul II, Carroll
Prosser, Mark, St. Mary, Storm Lake; Sacred Heart, Early
Reicks, Jerry, (Retired)
Roder, Rick, St. Mary, Remsen; Holy Name, Marcus
Rohr, Richard, St. Mary, Storm Lake; Sacred Heart, Early
Rudd, John S., St. Patrick's, Estherville; St Mary, Armstrong
Rupp, J. LeRoy, Immaculate Conception, Cherokee; Our Lady of Good Counsel, Holstein
Salocker, Rick, Holy Trinity, Fort Dodge
Sampson, Gregory, St. Bernard, Breda; Our Lady of Mount Carmel, Mount Carmel; St. John, Arcadia; St. Augustine, Halbur; Sacred Heart, Templeton; St. Elizabeth Seton, Glidden
Sands, James H., Cathedral of the Epiphany, Sioux City
Schon, Gary, (Retired)
Scurlock, Joseph, (Retired)
Sitzman, Larry K., Holy Cross, Sioux City
Steffen, Scott, Sacred Heart, Boone; St. Malachy, Madrid
Stone, Byron, St. Joseph, Wall Lake; St. Mary, Sac City; St. Martin, Odebolt
Stover, Michael, Sacred Heart, Ida Grove; St. Mary, Danbury; St. Mary, Mapleton
Streit, Gerald B., (Retired)
Sullivan, Eldon, (Retired)
Tigges, Dale, Holy Cross, Sioux City.

INSTITUTIONS LOCATED IN DIOCESE

[A] COLLEGES AND UNIVERSITIES

SIOUX CITY. *Briar Cliff University*, 3303 Rebecca St., 51104-2324. Tel: 712-279-5321; Fax: 712-279-5410; Email: bernice.metz@briarcliff.edu; Web: www.briarcliff.edu. Rachelle Karstens, Pres.; Deidre Engel, Registrar. Sisters of St. Francis of the Holy Family of Dubuque, Iowa.Liberal Arts University. Lay Teachers 67; Sisters 4; Students 1,229; Lay Administrators & Staff 115.

[B] INTER-PAROCHIAL SCHOOLS

SIOUX CITY. *Bishop Heelan Catholic Schools*, (Grades PreK-12), 50 13th St., 51102-1439.
Tel: 712-252-1350; Fax: 712-252-9086; Email: timm.funk@bishopheelan.org; Web: www.bishopheelan.org. Mr. Timm Funk, Pres.; Mr. Chris Bork, Prin. Serving the parishes of Master Dei, Cathedral, Holy Cross, and Sacred Heart. Religious Teachers 1; Lay Teachers 132; Priests 1; Sisters 1; Students 1,574; Total Staff 45.
Bishop Heelan High School, 1231 Grandview Blvd., 51103. Tel: 712-252-0573; Fax: 712-252-4897; Email: Chris.Bork@bishopheelan.org; Web: www.bishopheelan.org. Mr. Chris Bork, Prin.; Sr. Colane Recker, Librarian. Lay Teachers 45; Priests 1; Sisters 1; Students 487.
Holy Cross School-Blessed Sacrament Center, 3030 Jackson St., 51104. Tel: 712-277-4739; Fax: 712-258-3698; Email: liz.rickert@bishopheelan.org. Michael Sweeney, Prin.; Pam Wilmes, Librarian. Consolidated with St. Michael Center Lay Teachers 21; Students 227.
St. Michael, (Grades PreK-2), 4105 Harrison, 51108. Tel: 712-239-1090; Fax: 712-239-8546; Email: molly.hegarty@bishopheelan.org; Web: www.bishopheelan.org. Michael Sweeney, Prin.; Pam Wilmes, Librarian. Consolidated with Blessed Sacrament. Lay Teachers 11; Students 110.
Sacred Heart, (Grades PreK-8), 5010 Military Rd., 51103. Tel: 712-233-1624; Fax: 712-233-1469; Email: connealyk@bishopheelan.org; Web: www.bishopheelan.org. Kate Connealy, Prin.; Julie Walding, Librarian. Lay Teachers 30; Students 345; Total Staff 35.
Mater Dei School Immaculate Conception Center, (Grades PreK-4), 3719 Ridge Ave., 51106.
Tel: 712-276-6216; Fax: 712-274-1221; Email: fischerm@bishopheelan.org; Web: www.bishopheelan.org. Ms. Mary Fischer, Prin.; Mrs. Vicky Samuelson, Librarian. Lay Teachers 16; Students 233.
Mater Dei School Nativity Center, (Grades 5-8), 4243 Natalia Way, 51106-4099. Tel: 712-274-0268; Fax: 712-274-0377; Email: fischerm@bishopheelan.org; Web: www.bishopheelan.org. Ms. Mary Fischer, Prin.; Ashley Hanson, Librarian. Consolidated with Immaculate Conception Parish. Lay Teachers 12; Total Enrollment 142.

ALGONA. *Bishop Garrigan Schools*, 1224 N. McCoy St., Algona, 50511. Tel: 515-295-3521; Email: millerl@bishopgarrigan.org; Email: petersonc@bishopgarrigan.org. Lynn Miller, Pres.; Kristie Hough, Prin.; Christina Peterson, Prin. Serving the parishes at Algona, Bancroft, St. Benedict, Bode, Emmetsburg, Humboldt, Livermore, Wesley, West Bend, and Whittemore. Religious Teachers 1; Lay Teachers 40; Priests 3; Students 520.

CARROLL. *Kuemper Catholic School System*, (Grades PreK-12), 116 S. East St., Carroll, 51401.
Tel: 712-792-3313; Fax: 712-792-8073; Email: jjsteffes@kuemper.org; Web: www.kuemper.org. Mr. John Steffes, Pres. Grades PreK-8 Religious Teachers 2; Lay Teachers 87; Students 1,153.
Holy Spirit Center, (Grades PreK-5), 116 S. East St., Carroll, 51401. Tel: 712-792-3313;

Fax: 712-792-8073. Ted Garringer, Prin. PreK-5th Grade.

St. Lawrence Center, (Grades 6-8), 1519 N. West St., Carroll, 51401. Tel: 712-792-2123;
Fax: 712-792-3365. Ted Garringer, Prin. 6th-8th Grade.

Kuemper Catholic High School, 201 S. Clark St., Carroll, 51401. Tel: 712-792-3610;
Tel: 712-792-3569; Fax: 712-792-8072;
Fax: 712-792-8070. Mr. Pete Haefs, Prin. 9th-12th Grade. Lay Teachers 85.

FORT DODGE. *St. Edmond Catholic School, Inc.*, (Grades PreK-12), 2220 4th Ave. N., Fort Dodge, 50501. Tel: 515-955-6077; Fax: 515-955-8473; Email: gibbm@st-edmond.pvt.k12.is.us; Web: www.st-edmond.pvt.k12.ia.us. Mrs. Mary Gibb, Pres.; Linda Mitchell, Prin.; Mr. Thomas Miklo, Dir. Devel. Clergy 5; Religious Teachers 10; Lay Teachers 55; Priests 2; Students 590.

GRANVILLE. *Spalding Catholic Schools, Inc.* Spalding Catholic, (Grades PreK-6), 908 6th Ave., P.O. Box 436, Alton, 51003. Tel: 712-756-4532;
Tel: 712-756-4528; Email: contact@spaldingcatholic.org; Web: www.spaldingcatholic.org. Rev. Daniel M. Greving, Pres.; Mr. Joe Mueting, Prin.; Deacon Daniel Goebel, Deacon. Serving the parishes of Granville; Alton and Hospers. Clergy 2; Religious Teachers 2; Lay Teachers 9; Priests 1; Students 57.

LE MARS. *Gehlen Catholic School* (1875) (Grades PreK-12), 709 Plymouth St., N.E., Le Mars, 51031.
Tel: 712-546-4181; Fax: 712-546-9384; Email: lnussbaum@gehlencatholic.org; Web: www.gehlencatholic.org. Revs. Bruce Lawler, Pres.; Matthew Solyntjes, Chap.; Jeff Alesch, Prin. (7-12); Mrs. Lorie A. Nussbaum, Prin. (PreK-6). Religious Teachers 1; Lay Teachers 41; Students 515.

REMSEN, *St. Mary's High School*, 523 Madison, P.O. Box 500, Remsen, 51050. Tel: 712-786-1433;
Fax: 712-786-2499; Email: burkeyj@rsmschools.org; Web: www.rsmschools.org. Jeffrey Burkey, Prin. Religious Teachers 1; Lay Teachers 13; Students 72.

STORM LAKE. *St. Mary's School*, (Grades PreK-12), 300 E. Third Street, Storm Lake, 50588.
Tel: 712-732-4166; Fax: 712-732-4590; Email: djones@stmarys-storm.pvt.k12.ia.us; Email: rberg@stmarys-storm.pvt.k12.ia.us; Web: www.stormlakecatholic.com. Ryan Berg, Prin.; Diane Jones, Prin. (PreK-5). Serving St. Mary's. Clergy 4; Lay Teachers 32; Priests 2; Students 301.

[C] GENERAL HOSPITALS

SIOUX CITY. *Mercy Medical Center - Sioux City*, 801 Fifth St., 51101. Tel: 712-279-2011;
Fax: 712-284-7227; Email: daniecha@mercyhealth.com; Web: www.mercysiouxcity.com. Rev. Kristy May, Chap., United Church of Christ; Anthony Nwudah, Chap., Catholic Priest; Mrs. Mary Kay Daniels, Chap., Catholic; JoAnn Simons, Chap., Evangelical Church in America; Ms. Beth Hughes, Pres.; Ms. Colleen Walters, Vice Pres.; Ms. Mary Hendriks, Dir. Trinity Health, Catholic Health Ministries Bed Capacity 464; Tot Asst. Annually 232,837; Total Staff 1,174; Total Assisted 232,837.

CARROLL. *St. Anthony Regional Hospital*, 311 S. Clark St., P.O. Box 628, Carroll, 51401.
Tel: 712-792-3581; Fax: 712-792-3119; Email: esmith@stanthonyhospital.org; Web: www.StAnthonyHospital.org. Edward H. Smith Jr., Pres. & CEO; Rev. Kevin M. Richter. Bed Capacity 79; Patients Asst Anual. 69,488; Total Staff 86.

ESTHERVILLE. *Avera Holy Family* aka Avera Holy Family Hospital, 826 N. Eighth St., Estherville, 51334. Tel: 712-362-2631; Fax: 712-362-2636; Email: info@avera-holyfamily.org; Web: www.averaholyfamily.org. Ms. Deb Herzberg, Pres. Sisters of the Presentation of the B.V.M. of Aberdeen, S.D., & Benedictine Sisters of Sacred Heart Monastery, Yankton, S.D.. Bed Capacity 25; Tot Asst. Annually 39,034; Total Staff 230.

Holy Family Hospital Foundation.,
Tel: 712-362-2631; Fax: 712-362-2636. Bed Capacity 25; Tot Asst. Annually 37,588; Total Staff 219.

[D] HOMES FOR THE AGED

SIOUX CITY. *Holy Spirit Retirement Home*, 1701 W. 25th St., 51103. Tel: 712-252-2726; Email: patt@holyspiritretirementhome.org; Web: www.holyspiritretirementhome.com. Rev. Dennis W. Meinen, Chap., (Retired). Total in Residence 150; Total Staff 140; Total Assisted 235.

CARROLL. *St. Anthony Nursing Home* (1963) 406 E. Anthony St., Carroll, 51401. Tel: 712-792-3581;
Fax: 712-792-3119; Email: esmith@stanthonyhospital.org. Edward H. Smith Jr., Pres. & CEO; Peg Scheidt, Dir. Pastoral Care. Residents 78; Total Staff 83.

FORT DODGE. *The Marian Home*, 2400 Sixth Ave. N., Fort Dodge, 50501-3542. Tel: 515-576-1138;
Fax: 515-576-5099; Email: ehalverson@marianhome.com; Web: www.marianhome.com. Mr. Eric Halverson, Admin. Guests 97; Total in Residence 181; Total Staff 125.

[E] CONVENTS AND RESIDENCES FOR SISTERS

SIOUX CITY. *Monastery of the Discalced Carmelite Nuns*, 2901 S. Cecelia St., 51106-3299.
Tel: 712-276-1680; Fax: 712-276-5966; Email: carmelitesiouxc@gmail.com; Web: www.siouxcitycarmel.org. Mother Joseph of Jesus, O.C.D., Prioress. Novices 1; Sisters 8; Solemn Professed 7.

[F] SECULAR INSTITUTES

MILFORD. *Opus Spiritus Sancti* (1950) 1305 Okoboji Ave., Milford, 51351. Tel: 712-338-2274; Email: flanagandrtj12@gmail.com. Rev. Thomas J. Flanagan, Contact Person, (Retired).

[G] MISCELLANEOUS

SIOUX CITY. *The Catholic Schools Foundation of the Diocese of Sioux City* (1968) 1821 Jackson St., 51105. Tel: 712-255-7933; Fax: 712-233-7598; Email: susano@scdiocese.org; Web: www.scdiocese.org. Ms. Susan O'Brien, Dir.

Holy Spirit Retirement Home Foundation, Inc., 1701 W. 25th St., 51103. Tel: 712-252-2726;
Fax: 712-293-1953; Email: raneee@holyspiritretirementhome.com. Most Rev. R. Walker Nickless, Pres.; Ranee Ehrich, Dir.; Lisa Lowe, Admin.

Monsignor Lafferty Tuition Foundation, 1821 Jackson St., 51105. Tel: 712-255-7933;
Fax: 712-233-7598; Email: pattyl@scdiocese.org; Web: scdiocese.org. Mrs. Patty Lansink, Supt.

ALGONA. *Friends of Garrigan High School, Inc.*, Friends of Garrigan High School, 1224 N. McCoy St., Algona, 50511. Tel: 515-295-3521;
Tel: 515-395-3525; Email: laubenthalm@bishopgarrigan.org. Lynn Miller, Supt. High School 150.

CARROLL. *Kuemper Catholic School Foundation, Inc.* (1985) 116 S. East St., Carroll, 51401.
Tel: 712-792-3313; Fax: 712-792-8073; Email: cksundrup@kuemper.org; Web: www.kuemper.org. Sharon Olerich, Devel. Dir.

Orchard View, Inc., 421 S. Clark St., Carroll, 51401.
Tel: 712-792-2042; Fax: 712-794-5522; Email: esmith@stanthonyhospital.org; Web: www.StAnthonyHospital.org. Edward H. Smith Jr., Pres. & CEO. Franciscan Sisters of Perpetual Adoration. Total in Residence 51.

FORT DODGE. *Saint Edmond Catholic School Foundation*, 2220 4th Ave. N., Fort Dodge, 50501.
Tel: 515-955-6077; Fax: 515-955-8473; Email: frkevin@fdcatholic.com; Web: www.st-edmond.pvt.k12.ia.us. Mrs. Mary Gibb, Pres.; Tom Miklo, Devel. Dir.

Holy Trinity Parish Cemetery Improvement Society, 2220 4th Ave N., Fort Dodge, 50501.
Tel: 515-955-6077; Fax: 515-955-8473; Email: bobh@fdcatholic.com. Very Rev. Msgr. Kevin C. McCoy, S.T.D., V.G., Contact Person.

Holy Trinity Parish Foundation of Webster County, 2220 4th Ave N., Fort Dodge, 50501.
Tel: 515-955-6077; Fax: 515-955-8473; Email: frkevin@fdcatholic.com. Very Rev. Msgr. Kevin C. McCoy, S.T.D., V.G.

The Marian Home Foundation, 2400 6th Ave. N., Fort Dodge, 50501. Tel: 515-576-1138;
Fax: 515-576-5099; Email: ehalverson@marianhome.com. Mr. Eric Halverson, Admin.

GRANVILLE. *Spalding Catholic Schools Foundation, Inc.*, 908 6th Ave., P.O. Box 436, Alton, 51003.
Tel: 712-756-4532; Email: danpgoebel@gmail.org; Web: www.Spaldigcatholic.org. Dan Goebel, Sec.

POCAHONTAS. *Magnificat - NW Iowa Chapter* (2014) 1104 1st Ave., N.W., Pocahontas, 50574.
Tel: 712-335-4393; Email: magnificatnwia@gmail.com. Julie Storr, Contact Person.

STORM LAKE. *St. Mary's Foundation of Storm Lake, Iowa*, 300 E. 3rd St., P.O. Box 1106, Storm Lake, 50588. Tel: 712-732-3110; Fax: 712-732-8173; Email: dprosser@stormlakecatholic.com; Email: parish@stormlakecatholic.com; Web: www.stormlakecatholic.com. Rev. Dr. Timothy A. Friedrichsen.

WEST BEND. *Shrine of the Grotto of the Redemption*, 208 1st Ave. N.W., P.O. Box 376, West Bend, 50597. Tel: 515-887-2371; Fax: 515-887-2372; Email: grottocoordinator@gmail.com; Web: www.westbendgrotto.com. Andrew Milam, Dir.; Rev. Sunny Dominic, Rector.

RELIGIOUS INSTITUTES OF WOMEN REPRESENTED IN THE DIOCESE

For further details refer to the corresponding bracketed number in the Religious Institutes of Men or Women section.

[1780]—*Congregation of the Sisters of the Third Order of St. Francis of Perpetual Adoration* (Central Prov.)—F.S.P.A.

[0420]—*Discalced Carmelite Nuns*—O.C.D.

[]—*Opus Spiritus Sancti*—O.S.S.

[]—*The Order of St. Benedict*—O.S.B.

[]—*Servants of Mary*—O.S.M.

[]—*Sisters For Christian Community*—S.F.C.C.

[2575]—*Sisters of Mercy of the Union in USA Comm.* Cedar Rapids—O.S.F.

[1570]—*Sisters of St. Francis of the Holy Family*—O.S.F.

[1540]—*Sisters of St. Francis, Clinton, IA*—O.S.F.

[3320]—*Sisters of the Presentation of the B.V.M.* Dubuque, IA & Aberdeen, SD—P.B.V.M.

[]—*Sisters of the Society of Our Lady of the Most Holy Trinity*—S.O.L.T.

DIOCESAN CEMETERIES

SIOUX CITY. *Calvary Cemetery*, Office: 1821 Jackson St., P.O. Box 3379, 51102-3379. Tel: 712-233-7511;
Fax: 712-233-7598; Email: audreyk@scdiocese.org; Email: waltp@scdiocese.org. Very Rev. Bradley C. Pelzel, V.G., Vicar

LEMARS. *Calvary Cemetery*, 605 Plymouth St., N.E., LeMars, 51031. Tel: 712-546-5223;
Fax: 712-546-8346; Email: allsaints@premieronline.net. Steve De Rocher, Admin.; Annette Kuiken, Contact Person

NECROLOGY

† Adams, Edmond F., (Retired), Died Oct. 22, 2018
† Grendler, Albert O., (Retired), Died Aug. 6, 2018
† Larkin, Michael T., (Retired), Died May. 15, 2018
† Ries, Donald C., (Retired), Died Sep. 11, 2018

Diocese of Sioux Falls

(Dioecesis Siouxormensis)

Most Reverend

PAUL J. SWAIN

Bishop of Sioux Falls; ordained to priesthood May 27, 1988, Diocese of Madison; appointed Bishop of Sioux Falls August 31, 2006; Episcopal ordination October 26, 2006. *Chancery Office: 523 N. Duluth Ave., Sioux Falls, SD 57104.*

Catholic Chancery Office: 523 N. Duluth Ave., Sioux Falls, SD 57104. Tel: 605-334-9861; Fax: 605-988-3804.

Web: sfcatholic.org

Email: malthoff@sfcatholic.org

ESTABLISHED NOVEMBER 12, 1889.

Square Miles 35,091.

Comprises those parts of South Dakota lying east and north of the Missouri River.

For legal titles of parishes and diocesan institutions, consult the Chancery Office.

STATISTICAL OVERVIEW

Personnel	
Bishop	1
Priests: Diocesan Active in Diocese	84
Priests: Diocesan Active Outside Diocese	4
Priests: Retired, Sick or Absent	32
Number of Diocesan Priests	120
Religious Priests in Diocese	9
Total Priests in Diocese	129
Extern Priests in Diocese	3
Ordinations:	
Diocesan Priests	1
Transitional Deacons	2
Permanent Deacons in Diocese	39
Total Brothers	1
Total Sisters	215
Parishes	
Parishes	119
With Resident Pastor:	
Resident Diocesan Priests	67
Resident Religious Priests	1
Without Resident Pastor:	
Administered by Priests	48
Professional Ministry Personnel:	
Brothers	2
Sisters	9
Lay Ministers	102
Welfare	
Catholic Hospitals	12
Total Assisted	1,160,287
Health Care Centers	9
Homes for the Aged	3
Total Assisted	343
Special Centers for Social Services	8
Educational	
Diocesan Students in Other Seminaries	21
Total Seminarians	21
Colleges and Universities	2
Total Students	1,751
High Schools, Diocesan and Parish	3
Total Students	975
Elementary Schools, Diocesan and Parish	21
Total Students	3,638
Elementary Schools, Private	1
Total Students	187
Catechesis/Religious Education:	
High School Students	1,844
Elementary Students	7,652
Total Students under Catholic Instruction	16,068
Teachers in the Diocese:	
Priests	1
Sisters	1
Lay Teachers	337
Vital Statistics	
Receptions into the Church:	
Infant Baptism Totals	1,369
Minor Baptism Totals	55
Adult Baptism Totals	43
Received into Full Communion	165
First Communions	1,564
Confirmations	1,316
Marriages:	
Catholic	313
Interfaith	164
Total Marriages	477
Deaths	850
Total Catholic Population	110,386
Total Population	570,605

Former Bishops—Rt. Revs. MARTIN MARTY, O.S.B., D.D., ord. Sept. 14, 1856; appt. Bishop of Tiberias, Aug. 8, 1879; appt. Vicar Apostolic of Dakota, Aug. 12, 1879; consecrated Feb. 1, 1880; Bishop of Sioux Falls, 1889; transferred to St. Cloud, MN, 1894; died Sept. 19, 1896; THOMAS O'GORMAN, D.D., ord. Nov. 5, 1865; appt. Jan. 24, 1896; consecrated April 19, 1896; died Sept. 18, 1921; Most Revs. BERNARD J. MAHONEY, D.D., ord. Feb. 27, 1904; appt. May 22, 1922; consecrated June 29, 1922; died March 20, 1939; WILLIAM O. BRADY, S.T.D., D.D., appt. Bishop of Sioux Falls, June 10, 1939; consecrated Aug. 24, 1939; appt. Coadjutor of St. Paul, June 21, 1956; succeeded to the See, Oct. 11, 1956; died Oct. 1, 1961; LAMBERT A. HOCH, D.D., ord. May 30, 1928; Bishop of Bismarck; appt. Jan. 23, 1952; consecrated March 25, 1952; transferred to Sioux Falls, Nov. 27, 1956; retired June 13, 1978; died June 27, 1990; PAUL V. DUDLEY, D.D., ord. June 2, 1951; ord. Auxiliary Bishop of Archdiocese of St. Paul/Minneapolis, Jan. 25, 1977; appt. Bishop of Sioux Falls Sept. 26, 1978; installed Dec. 13, 1978; retired March 21, 1995; died Nov. 20, 2006; ROBERT J. CARLSON, ord. May 22, 1970; appt. Titular Bishop of Aviocala and Auxiliary Bishop of Saint Paul and Minneapolis Nov. 22, 1983; cons. Jan. 11, 1984; appt. Coadjutor Bishop of Sioux Falls Jan. 13, 1994; Succeeded to the See March 21, 1995; appt. Bishop of Saginaw Dec. 29, 2004; appt. Archbishop of St. Louis April 21, 2009.

Office of the Bishop—Most Rev. PAUL J. SWAIN.

Vicar General—Very Rev. CHARLES L. CIMPL, 523 N. Duluth Ave., Sioux Falls, 57104.

Moderator of the Curia—VACANT, 523 N. Duluth Ave., Sioux Falls, 57104.

Episcopal Vicar for Clergy—VACANT.

Catholic Chancery Office—Bishop Hoch Catholic Pastoral Center, 523 N. Duluth Ave., Sioux Falls, 57104. Tel: 605-334-9861; Fax: 605-334-2092. Refer all official business to this address.

Chancellor—MR. MATTHEW ALTHOFF, 523 N. Duluth Ave., Sioux Falls, 57104. Tel: 605-988-3704.

Vice Chancellor—MR. JEROME KLEIN, Tel: 605-988-3745.

Vocations—523 N. Duluth Ave., Sioux Falls, 57104. Tel: 605-988-3772. Revs. SHAUN THOMAS HAGGERTY, Dir.; JORDAN SAMSON, Assoc. Dir.

Deacon Formation—523 N. Duluth Ave., Sioux Falls, 57104. Tel: 605-988-3715. Deacon JOHN P. DEVLIN.

Marriage Tribunal—523 N. Duluth Ave., Sioux Falls, 57104. Tel: 605-988-3757.

Judicial Vicar—Very Rev. GREGORY TSCHAKERT, J.C.L.

Tribunal Judges—Revs. RODNEY FARKE, (Retired); KENNETH J. KOSTER; JOHN LANTSBERGER; Very Rev. CHARLES L. CIMPL.

Defenders of the Matrimonial Bond—Very Rev. GREGORY TSCHAKERT, J.C.L.; Sisters LYNN MARIE WELBIG, J.C.L., Ph.D.; KATHLEEN BIERNE, P.B.V.M., J.C.L.; Rev. JIM FRIEDRICH; THERESA A. WYBURN, J.C.L.; AMANDA M. ZURFACE, Judge & Defender of the Bond; Rev. JONATHAN VENNER.

Matrimonial Tribunal—MRS. HEATHER J. EICHHOLZ, J.C.L.

Auditor—Sr. KATHLEEN BIERNE, P.B.V.M., J.C.L.

Advocate Ad Casum—VACANT.

Notary of Matrimonial Tribunal—MERCEDES SUPIK, Ecclesiastical Notary.

Office of Planning—(See Delegate of Discipleship & Evangelization).

Safe Environment—RIHANNON DELLE, Coord.

Administration and Parish Services—

Delegate and Finance Officer—MR. MICHAEL BANNWARTH, 523 N. Duluth Ave., Sioux Falls, 57104. Tel: 605-988-3759; Fax: 605-988-3746.

Information Technology—MRS. DAWN WOLF, Dir.

Human Resources—MRS. TWILA ROMAN, Delegate.

Cemeteries and Property Management—VACANT.

Liturgy, Faith Formation, and Catholic Education—

Office of Discipleship, Evangelization and Parish Services—523 N. Duluth Ave., Sioux Falls, 57104. MR. DARYL THURINGER, Delegate.

Marriage, Family and Respect Life—523 N. Duluth Ave., Sioux Falls, 57104. Tel: 605-988-3776. MRS. EMILY LEEDOM, Dir.

Master of Ceremonies—Rev. DARIN SCHMIDT.

Catholic Schools—523 N. Duluth, Sioux Falls, 57104. Tel: 605-988-3761. (See Delegate of Discipleship & Evangelization).

Adult Discipleship & Evangelization—DR. CHRISTOPHER BURGWALD, S.T.D., Dir., 523 N. Duluth Ave., Sioux Falls, 57104. Tel: 605-988-3770.

Youth Discipleship & Evangelization—523 N. Duluth Ave., Sioux Falls, 57104. Tel: 605-988-3767. MR. ERIC GALLAGHER, Dir.; MS. BECCA ECKREN, Coord.

Office of Worship—VACANT.

Marian Apostolate—Rev. Msgr. CHARLES MANGAN, J.C.L.

Communications and Social Ministries—

Delegate and Vice Chancellor—MR. JEROME KLEIN, 523 N. Duluth Ave., Sioux Falls, 57104. Tel: 605-988-3789.

Catholic Family Services—MR. JEROME KLEIN, Dir.; DR. MARCIE MORAN, Clinical Dir., 523 N. Duluth Ave., Sioux Falls, 57104. Tel: 605-988-3775.

Communications Office - "Bishop's Bulletin"—Rev. MICHAEL GRIFFIN, Bishop's Bulletin Exec. Editor; MR. GENE YOUNG, Bishop's Bulletin Mng. Editor,

523 N. Duluth Ave., Sioux Falls, 57104. Tel: 605-988-3789.

Parish and Diocesan Advancement—

Delegate and President of the Catholic Community Foundation for Eastern South Dakota—MARK CONZEMIUS, 523 N. Duluth Ave., Sioux Falls, 57104. Tel: 605-988-3788.

Operations, Catholic Family Sharing Appeal—MRS. MELINDA NORTH, Vice Pres. & Dir. Catholic Family Sharing Appeal.

Planned Giving—ANDREW BARTELL, J.D., J.C.L., Dir.

Diocesan Consultors—Very Revs. CHARLES L. CIMPL; JAMES P. MORGAN; GREGORY TSCHAKERT, J.C.L.; Revs. PAUL A. RUTTEN; EDWARD J. PIERCE, (Retired); TERENCE ANDERSON; ANDREW DICKINSON.

Consilium Administrationis—Most Rev. Bishop, Vicar General, Chancellor.

Presbyteral Council—Very Rev. CHARLES L. CIMPL; Rev. TERENCE ANDERSON; Very Rev. JAMES P. MORGAN; Revs. DANA ROBERT CHRISTENSEN; PAUL A. RUTTEN; THOMAS ANDERSON; Very Rev. GREGORY TSCHAKERT, J.C.L.; Revs. ANDREW DICKINSON; RODNEY FARKE, (Retired); JOSEPH FORCELLE; TERRY L. WEBER.

Diocesan Offices and Directors

Apostleship of Prayer—Mailing Address: 523 N. Duluth Ave., Sioux Falls, 57105.

Building Commission—MR. MATTHEW ALTHOFF, Chancellor; MR. MICHAEL BANNWARTH, Finance Officer, Catholic Chancery Office, 523 N. Duluth Ave., Sioux Falls, 57104.

Social Outreach—MR. JEROME KLEIN, 523 N. Duluth Ave., Sioux Falls, 57104. Tel: 605-988-3745.

Censor Librorum—DR. CHRISTOPHER BURGWALD, S.T.D., 523 N. Duluth Ave., Sioux Falls, 57104.

Cursillo—Rev. RODNEY FARKE, (Retired), 1700 8th St. S., Brookings, 57006.

Diocesan Archivist—MR. MATTHEW ALTHOFF, Chancellor, 523 N. Duluth Ave., Sioux Falls, 57104. Tel: 605-334-9861.

Ecumenical Commission—VACANT.

Newman Apostolate—VACANT.

Permanent Diaconate Council—901 N. Tahoe Tr., Sioux Falls, 57110-5779. Deacon JOSEPH TWIDWELL JR.

Priest Personnel Committee—Very Rev. CHARLES L. CIMPL, Vicar Gen.; Revs. JOHN LANTSBERGER; JOHN W. SHORT; MICHAEL WENSING; PAUL A. RUTTEN; JORDAN SAMSON; DANIEL H. SMITH.

Propagation of the FaithVACANT.

Search—523 N. Duluth Ave., Sioux Falls, 57104. Tel: 605-334-9861.

Spanish-Speaking Apostolate—Mailing Address: St. Mary's Parish, P.O. Box 589, Clear Lake, 57226-0589. Rev. JOHN J. HELMUELLER.

Teens Encounter Christ—523 N. Duluth Ave., Sioux Falls, 57104. Tel: 605-334-9861.

Victim Assistance Coordinator—MRS. TWILA ROMAN, Tel: 605-988-3741; Email: troman@sfcatholic.org.

CLERGY, PARISHES, MISSIONS AND PAROCHIAL SCHOOLS

CITY OF SIOUX FALLS

(MINNEHAHA COUNTY)

1—CATHEDRAL OF SAINT JOSEPH PARISH (1880) [JC]
521 Duluth Ave., 57104. Tel: 605-336-7390; Email: cathedral@sfcatholic.org. Very Rev. James P. Morgan, Rector; Revs. Darin Schmidt, Parochial Vicar; Timothy Smith, Parochial Vicar; Deacon William Radio.
Catechesis Religious Program—Students 106.

2—CHRIST THE KING PARISH OF MINNEHAHA COUNTY (1949)
1501 W. 26th St., 57105. Tel: 605-332-5477; Email: ctkchurch@midconetwork.com. Revs. Richard Fox; James Zimmer, In Res.; Deacons Leon Cantin, (Retired); James Boorman.
See Christ the King Elementary School, Sioux Falls under Inter-Parochial Schools located in the Institution section.
Catechesis Religious Program—Students 83.

3—HOLY SPIRIT PARISH OF MINNEHAHA COUNTY (1988)
3601 E. Dudley Ln., 57103. Tel: 605-371-2320; Email: holyspiritsf@holyspiritsf.org; Web: www.holyspiritsf.org. Very Rev. Charles L. Cimpl; Rev. Tyler Mattson, Parochial Vicar.
Res.: 4008 Lisanne, 57103.
Catechesis Religious Program—Students 457.

4—SAINT KATHARINE DREXEL PARISH OF MINNEHAHA COUNTY (2004)
Mailing Address: 1800 S. Katie Ste. 1, 57106.
Tel: 605-275-6870; Email: church.stkatharinedrexel@midconetwork.com; Web: www.stkdsfsd.org. Rev. Gregory Tschakert, J.C.L.; Deacon Dennis Seiner.
Catechesis Religious Program—Students 272.

5—SAINT LAMBERT PARISH OF MINNEHAHA COUNTY (1958)
1000 S. Bahnson Ave., 57103. Tel: 605-336-8808; Email: stlambertparish@sfcatholic.org; Web: stlambertparish.org. Revs. Shaun Thomas Haggerty; Joseph Scholten, Parochial Vicar; Deacon Roger R. Heidt.
Res.: 3901 E. 16th St., 57103.
See St. Lambert Elementary, Sioux Falls under Inter-Parochial Schools located in the Institution section.
Catechesis Religious Program—Tel: 605-338-4728; Email: ebauman@sfcatholic.org. Ellen Bauman, D.R.E.; Lori Stowell, Liturgy Dir. Students 446.

6—IMMACULATE HEART OF MARY PARISH OF MINNEHAHA COUNTY (1947)
2109 S. Fifth Ave., 57105. Tel: 605-332-6391; Email: stmarysf@midco.net. Rev. David A. Desmond; Deacon Henry Knapp.
See St. Mary, Sioux Falls under Inter-Parochial Schools located in the Institution section.
Catechesis Religious Program—Students 169.

7—SAINT MICHAEL PARISH OF MINNEHAHA COUNTY (1979) [JC]
1600 S. Marion Rd., 57106. Tel: 605-361-1600; Email: info@stmichaelsfsd.org. Revs. Terry L. Weber; Tom Hartman, Parochial Vicar; Deacon John P. Devlin.
See St. Michael Elementary School, Sioux Falls under Inter-Parochial Schools located in the Institution section.
Catechesis Religious Program—Students 491.

8—OUR LADY OF GUADALUPE PARISH OF MINNEHAHA COUNTY (1996) [JC]
217 N Sherman Ave, 57103-1410. Tel: 605-338-8126; Email: olgparish@sfcatholic.org. Rev. Kristopher Cowles.
Res.: 1220 E. 8th St., 57103-1702.
Catechesis Religious Program—Students 196.

9—SAINT THERESE PARISH OF MINNEHAHA COUNTY (1917)
901 N. Tahoe Tr., 57110. Tel: 605-338-2433; Web: www.sttheresesf.org. Rev. Kevin O'Dell.
Res.: 1301 N. Dubuque Ave., 57110-6450.
Catechesis Religious Program—Students 172.

OUTSIDE THE CITY OF SIOUX FALLS

ABERDEEN, BROWN CO.

1—SAINT MARY PARISH OF BROWN COUNTY, [CEM]
409 2nd Ave., N.E., Aberdeen, 57401.
Tel: 605-229-4422; Email: info@stmaryabr.com. Revs. Michael Griffin; Andrew Thuringer, Parochial Vicar; Deacon Peter Mehlaff.
School—Saint Mary Parish of Brown County School, See separate listing under Inter-Parochial Schools in the Institution section.
Catechesis Religious Program—Students 175.

2—SACRED HEART PARISH OF BROWN COUNTY (1882) [CEM]
502 2nd Ave., S.E., Aberdeen, 57401.
Tel: 605-225-7065; Email: sacredheartaberdeen@gmail.com. Revs. Mark Lichter; Patrick Grode; Mark Axtmann, In Res.
Res. & Church: 409 3rd. Ave., S.E., Aberdeen, 57401.
See Roncalli Schools, Aberdeen under Inter-Parochial Schools located in the Institution section.
Catechesis Religious Program—Students 216.

ALEXANDRIA, HANSON CO., SAINT MARY OF MERCY PARISH OF HANSON COUNTY (1880) [CEM]
220 5th St, Alexandria, 57311. Tel: 605-239-4578; Web: parishesonline.com/find/st-mary-of-mercy. P.O. Box 158, Alexandria, 57311. Rev. Dana Robert Christensen.
Catechesis Religious Program—Students 128.

ARLINGTON, KINGSBURY CO., SAINT JOHN THE EVANGELIST PARISH OF KINGSBURY COUNTY (1907) Served from DeSmet.
Mailing Address: 301 S. Main St., Arlington, 57212.
Tel: 605-854-3564; Fax: 605-854-9961; Email: catholickingsbury@gmail.com. Rev. Richard Baumberger.
Catechesis Religious Program—Students 53.

ARMOUR, DOUGLAS CO., SAINT PAUL THE APOSTLE PARISH OF DOUGLAS COUNTY (1886)
206 1st St., Armour, 57313. Tel: 605-724-2191; Email: stpaul@unitelsd.com. Rev. Cathal Gallagher.
Catechesis Religious Program—Jim Werkmeister, D.R.E. Students 65.

ARTESIAN, SANBORN CO., SAINT CHARLES BORROMEO PARISH OF SANBORN COUNTY (1908) [JC] Attended by
541 W 2nd Ave, Artesian, 57314. Tel: 605-796-4666; Fax: 605-796-4666; Email: frjim@santel.net. P.O. Box 266, Woonsocket, 57385. Rev. Jim Friedrich.
Catechesis Religious Program—Students 17.

AURORA, BROOKINGS CO., ST. WILLIAM (1881) [CEM] Merged into and became a part of Our Lady of Good Counsel Parish, Elkton.

BERESFORD, UNION CO., ST. TERESA OF AVILA PARISH OF UNION COUNTY aka St. Teresa (1885) [CEM]
901 S. Third St., P.O. Box 472, Beresford, 57004.
Tel: 605-763-2028; Email: stteresa@bmtc.net. Rev. David Roehrich.
Catechesis Religious Program—Students 105.

BIG BEND, HUGHES CO., SAINT CATHERINE PARISH OF HUGHES COUNTY (1950) [CEM] Attended by Fort Thompson.
SD Hwy 34 and Cut Across Rd. 4 Miles S. on W. Bend Rd., Big Bend, 57346. Tel: 605-473-5335; Email: pastteam@gwtc.net. P.O. Box 47, Fort Thompson, 57339-0047. Revs. Christianus Hendrick, S.C.J.; Mark Mastin, S.C.J.; Deacon Steven A. McLaughlin.
Catechesis Religious Program—Students 23.

BIG STONE CITY, GRANT CO., SAINT CHARLES BORROMEO PARISH OF GRANT COUNTY (1882) [CEM]
106 3rd Ave., P.O. Box 68, Big Stone City, 57216.
Tel: 605-862-8485; Email: bigstone.stcharles@sfcatholic.org. Rev. David Garza, Parish Admin.
Catechesis Religious Program—Students 19.

BOWDLE, EDMUNDS CO., SAINT AUGUSTINE PARISH OF EDMUNDS COUNTY (1894) [CEM]
3023 S. 3rd Ave., Box 310, Bowdle, 57428-0310.
Tel: 605-285-6466; Email: staug@venturecomm.net. Rev. Kevin Doyle.
Catechesis Religious Program—Students 30.

BRANDON, MINNEHAHA CO., RISEN SAVIOR PARISH OF MINNEHAHA COUNTY (1979) [JC]
301 N. Splitrock Blvd., Brandon, 57005-0080.
Tel: 605-582-6902; Fax: 605-582-3993; Email: secretary@risensaivorbrandon.com; Web: risensaviorbrandon.com. P.O. Box 80, Brandon, 57005. Rev. David Krogman.
Res.: 312 9th Ave. N., Brandon, 57005.
Catechesis Religious Program—Students 322.

BRIDGEWATER, MCCOOK CO., SAINT STEPHEN PARISH OF MCCOOK COUNTY (1883) [CEM] Attended by St. Mary of Mercy, Alexandria.
P.O. Box 49, Bridgewater, 57319. Tel: 605-239-4578; Email: maryofmercy@triotel.net; Web: parishesonline.com/find/st-stephen-church-57319.
351 N Juniper St, Bridgewater, 57319. Revs. Dana Robert Christensen; Jonathan Venner, In Res.
Catechesis Religious Program—Students 14.

BRITTON, MARSHALL CO., SAINT JOHN DE BRITTO PARISH OF MARSHALL COUNTY (1888) [JC]
812 8th St., Britton, 57430. Tel: 605-448-5379; Email: britton.stjohndebritto@sfcatholic.org. P.O. Box 108, Britton, 57430-0108. Rev. Albert Cizewski.
Catechesis Religious Program—Students 50.

BROOKINGS, BROOKINGS CO., SAINT THOMAS MORE PARISH OF BROOKINGS COUNTY (1904) [CEM]
1700 8th St. S., Brookings, 57006. Tel: 605-692-4361; Email: info@stmbrookings.org; Web: www.stmbrookings.org. Rev. Terence Anderson.
Catechesis Religious Program—Students 493.

BRYANT, HAMLIN CO., SAINT MARY PARISH OF HAMLIN COUNTY (1881) [CEM] Attended by St. Michael, Clark.
209 S. Broadway, Bryant, 57221. Tel: 605-854-9961; Email: catholickingsbury@gmail.com. P.O. Box 15, DeSmet, 57231-0015. Rev. Richard Baumberger.
Catechesis Religious Program—Students 32.

CANTON, LINCOLN CO., SAINT DOMINIC PARISH OF LINCOLN COUNTY
Mailing Address: 800 E. Walnut, Canton, 57013.
Tel: 605-764-5640; Email: stdominiccanton@gmail.com; Web: www.parishesonline.com/find.st-dominic-church-57013. Rev. John Rader.
Res.: 809 E. Walnut, Canton, 57013.
Catechesis Religious Program—Students 81.

CASTLEWOOD, HAMLIN CO., SAINT JOHN THE EVANGELIST PARISH OF HAMLIN COUNTY (1885) [JC] Attended by Kranzburg.
201 E Merrill St, Castlewood, 57223.
Tel: 605-886-9166; Fax: 605-886-2715; Email: elindner@sfcatholic.org. P.O. Box 166, Kranzburg, 57245. Rev. Kenneth J. Koster.
Catechesis Religious Program—Students 46.

CENTERVILLE, TURNER CO., GOOD SHEPHERD PARISH OF TURNER COUNTY (1888) [JC] Attended by Beresford.
411 Wisconsin, Centerville, 57014. Tel: 605-763-2028 ; Email: stteresa@bmtc.net. Mailing Address: P.O. Box 472, Beresford, 57004-0472. Rev. David Roehrich.
Catechesis Religious Program—Students 46.

CHAMBERLAIN, BRULE CO., SAINT JAMES PARISH OF BRULE COUNTY (1891) [JC]
400 S. Main St., Chamberlain, 57325.
Tel: 605-734-2144; Email: sjcatholic@midstatesd.net. Rev. Andrew Swietochowski; Deacons Maurice Barrett; James Bregel.
Catechesis Religious Program—Students 118.

CLARK, CLARK CO., SAINT MICHAEL PARISH OF CLARK COUNTY (1887) [CEM]
112 N. Idaho, P.O. Box 28, Clark, 57225.
Tel: 605-532-3855; Email: office@cfhcatholics.org; Web: www.parishesonline.com. Rev. Daniel H. Smith.
Catechesis Religious Program—Shannon Huber, D.R.E. Students 32.

CLEAR LAKE, DEUEL CO., SAINT MARY PARISH OF DEUEL COUNTY (1900)
408 Third St. W., Clear Lake, 57226.
Tel: 605-874-2080; Email: triparish@itctel.com. P.O. Box 589, Clear Lake, 57226-0589. Rev. John J. Helmueller.
Catechesis Religious Program—Students 65.

COLMAN, MOODY CO., SAINT PETER PARISH OF MOODY COUNTY (1905) [CEM] Attended by SS. Simon & Jude, Flandreau.
200 N. Allen St, Colman, 57017. Tel: 605-997-2610; Email: simonjude@iw.net. Mailing Address: c/o Ss. Simon & Jude, 105 S. Bates St., Flandreau, 57028. Rev. Douglas Binsfeld.
Catechesis Religious Program—Students 65.

DAKOTA DUNES, UNION CO., SAINT TERESA OF CALCUTTA OF UNION COUNTY (1999)
995 N. Sioux Point Rd., Dakota Dunes, 57049.
Tel: 605-235-1942; Web: www.secatholics.org. Revs. Joseph Vogel; Steven Robert Jones, Sacramental Min.; Deacon Joseph Twidwell Jr.
Catechesis Religious Program—Julie Eakin, D.R.E. Students 105.

DANTE, CHARLES MIX CO., ASSUMPTION OF THE BLESSED VIRGIN MARY PARISH OF CHARLES MIX COUNTY (1909) [CEM]
416 Haines St, Dante, 57329. Tel: 605-384-5155; Email: wagner.stjohn@sfcatholic.org. Mailing Address: P.O. Box 305, Wagner, 57380. Rev. Robert Wullweber.
Catechesis Religious Program—Students 83.

DE SMET, KINGSBURY CO., SAINT THOMAS AQUINAS PARISH OF KINGSBURY (1901) [CEM]
512 SW 3rd St., De Smet, 57231. Tel: 605-854-9961; Email: catholickingsburgy@gmail.com. P.O. Box 15, De Smet, 57231-0015. Rev. Richard Baumberger.
Res.: 203 Harvey Dunn Ave., De Smet, 57231.
Catechesis Religious Program—Students 59.

DELL RAPIDS, MINNEHAHA CO., SAINT MARY PARISH OF MINNEHAHA COUNTY (1898) [CEM]
608 E. 8th St., Dell Rapids, 57022. Tel: 605-428-3990 ; Email: stmaryadmin@stmarydellrapids.org; Web: www.stmarydellrapids.org. Rev. John Lantsberger.
Schools—Saint Mary Parish of Minnehaha County School—(Grades PreK-6), Tel: 605-428-3459; Web: drstmary.org. Rev. John Lantsberger, Supt.; Deb Kallhoff, Prin. Lay Teachers 12; Students 139.
Saint Mary Parish of Minnehaha County School, (Grades 7-12), Tel: 605-428-5591; Web: stmarycatholicschools.org. Casey Michel, Prin. aka St. Mary Junior/Senior High School Lay Teachers 9; Students 28.
Catechesis Religious Program—Students 167.

DIMOCK, HUTCHINSON CO., SAINTS PETER AND PAUL PARISH OF HUTCHINSON COUNTY (1885) [CEM]
146 W. 1st St., Dimock, 57331. Tel: 605-928-3883; Email: carolweber@sacredheart.org. Rev. David Stevens.
Catechesis Religious Program—Students 50.

DUNCAN, BUFFALO CO., ST. PLACIDUS (1887) [CEM] Merged into and became a part of St. Joseph Parish, Wessington Springs.

EDEN, MARSHALL CO., SACRED HEART PARISH OF MARSHALL COUNTY (1917) [CEM]
114 S 2nd St, Eden, 57232. Tel: 605-486-4702; Email: sheden@venturecomm.net. P.O. Box 15, Eden, 57232. Rev. Brian Simon, Admin.
Catechesis Religious Program—Students 24.

ELK POINT, UNION CO., SAINT JOSEPH PARISH OF UNION COUNTY (1901) [CEM] Attended by St. Peter, Jefferson.
605 E. Main St., Elk Point, 57025. Tel: 605-356-2693; Fax: 605-356-3284; Email: stjoseph@iw.net; Email: stjoseph@secatholics.org; Web: secatholics.org. P.O. Box 340, Elk Point, 57025-0340. Revs. Joseph Vogel; Steven Robert Jones, Sacramental Min.
Catechesis Religious Program—Students 189.

ELKTON, BROOKINGS CO., OUR LADY OF GOOD COUNSEL PARISH OF BROOKINGS COUNTY (1879) [CEM] Attended by Flandreau.
202 W 7th St, Elkton, 57026-0337. Tel: 605-997-2610 ; Email: simonjude@iw.net. Mailing Address: 105 S. Bates, Flandreau, 57028. Rev. Douglas Binsfeld.
Res.: Box E, Elkton, 57026.
Catechesis Religious Program—Students 91.

EMERY, HANSON CO., SAINT MARTIN PARISH OF HANSON COUNTY (1891) [CEM] Attended by St. Mary of Mercy, Alexandria.
342 3rd Ave., P.O. Box 312, Emery, 57332.
Tel: 605-239-4578; Email: maryofmercy@triotel.net; Web: parishesonline.com/find/st-martin-church-57332. Rev. Dana Robert Christensen.
Catechesis Religious Program—Students 54.

EPIPHANY, HANSON CO., EPIPHANY PARISH OF HANSON COUNTY (1896) [CEM] Attended by Howard.
107 Jackson, Epiphany, 57321. Tel: 605-772-4543; Email: stagatha@alliancecom.net. P.O. Box 100, Howard, 57349. Rev. Chester Murtha.
Catechesis Religious Program—Students 23.

ESTELLINE, HAMLIN CO., SAINT FRANCIS DE SALES PARISH OF HAMLIN COUNTY (1884) [CEM] Attended by Clear Lake.
1201 Eva Ave, Estelline, 57234. Tel: 605-874-2080; Email: triparish@itctel.com. P.O. Box 589, Clear Lake, 57226. Rev. John J. Helmueller.
Catechesis Religious Program—Students 34.

ETHAN, DAVISON CO., HOLY TRINITY (1889) [CEM] Merged into and became a part of Sts. Peter & Paul Parish, Dimock.

EUREKA, MCPHERSON CO., SAINT JOSEPH PARISH OF MCPHERSON COUNTY (1896) Attended by Herreid.
602 2nd St., P.O. Box 184, Eureka, 57437.
Tel: 605-284-5190; Email: stjoseph@valleytel.net. Rev. Thomas Clement.
Catechesis Religious Program—Students 21.

FARMER, HANSON CO., ST. PETER (1889) Closed. For inquiries for parish records contact the chancery.

FAULKTON, FAULK CO., SAINT THOMAS THE APOSTLE PARISH OF FAULK COUNTY (1903) [CEM]
206 10th Ave. S., P.O. Box 394, Faulkton, 57438.
Tel: 605-598-6590; Email: stthomas@venturecomm.net. Rev. Christopher Hughes; Deacon Arvid Holsing.
Church: 1013 Court St., Faulkton, 57438.
Catechesis Religious Program—Dawn Melius, D.R.E. Students 84.

FLANDREAU, MOODY CO., SAINTS SIMON AND JUDE PARISH OF MOODY COUNTY (1882) [CEM]
105 S. Bates St., Flandreau, 57028.
Tel: 605-997-2610. Rev. Douglas Binsfeld.
Catechesis Religious Program—Students 103.

FLORENCE, CODINGTON CO., BLESSED SACRAMENT PARISH OF CODINGTON COUNTY (1889) [CEM]
803 6th St, Florence, 57235. Tel: 605-532-3855; Email: office@cfhcatholics.org; Web: www.parishesonline.com. P.O. Box 28, Clark, 57225. Rev. Daniel H. Smith.

Catechesis Religious Program—Pat Callan, D.R.E. Students 41.

FORT THOMPSON, BUFFALO CO., SAINT JOSEPH PARISH OF BUFFALO COUNTY (1889) [CEM]
817 SD Hwy. 47, P.O. Box 47, Fort Thompson, 57339.
Tel: 605-245-2350; Email: pastteam@gwtc.net. Revs. Christianus Hendrick, S.C.J.; Mark Mastin, S.C.J.; Sr. Charles Palm, Admin.; Deacon Steven A. McLaughlin.
Catechesis Religious Program—Students 63.

GARRETSON, MINNEHAHA CO., SAINT ROSE OF LIMA PARISH OF MINNEHAHA COUNTY (1898) [CEM]
705 3rd St., Garretson, 57030. Tel: 605-594-3750. P.O. Box 0, Garretson, 57030. Rev. Jeffrey Thomas Norfolk; Deacon Donald Wagner.
Catechesis Religious Program—Students 102.

GARY, DEUEL CO., SAINT PETER PARISH OF DEUEL COUNTY (1900) Attended by Clear Lake.
612 Herrick St., Gary, 57237. Tel: 605-874-2080; Fax: 605-874-1333; Email: triparish@itctel.com. P.O. Box 589, Clear Lake, 57226. Rev. John J. Helmueller.
Catechesis Religious Program—Students 9.

GEDDES, CHARLES MIX CO., SAINT ANN PARISH OF CHARLES MIX COUNTY (1902) [CEM] [JC] Attended by Platte.
Mailing Address: 303 5th St, P.O. Box 137, Geddes, 57342. Tel: 605-337-3710; Tel: 605-337-2465; Fax: 605-337-2542; Email: office.stanngeddes@sfcatholic.org. Rev. Mathew Vazhappilly, C.M.I., (India). In Res., Rev. Roger Geditz, (Retired).
Catechesis Religious Program—Joe Tegethoff, D.R.E. Students 23.

GETTYSBURG, POTTER CO., SACRED HEART PARISH OF POTTER COUNTY aka Sacred Heart Parish (1905) [CEM]
203 E. Garfield Ave., P.O. Box 285, Gettysburg, 57442. Tel: 605-765-2161; Email: sacred@venturecomm.net; Web: GetSHC.org. Rev. Jerome Kopel.
Catechesis Religious Program—308 N. East Street, Gettysburg, 57442. Tel: 605-765-2359; Email: sacredheartre@venturecomm.net. Students 109.

GRENVILLE, DAY CO., SAINT JOSEPH PARISH OF DAY COUNTY (1885) [CEM] Attended by Eden Parish
22 St Joseph St, Grenville, 57239. Tel: 605-486-4702; Email: sheden@venturecomm.net. P.O. Box 191, Grenville, 57239. Rev. Brian Simon, Admin.
Catechesis Religious Program—Students 5.

GROTON, BROWN CO., SAINT ELIZABETH ANN SETON PARISH OF BROWN COUNTY (1883) (formerly St. John the Baptist).
803 1st St. N., P.O. Box 407, Groton, 57445.
Tel: 605-397-2775; Email: seas@nvc.net. Rev. Michael D. Kelly.
Catechesis Religious Program—Students 94.

GROVER, CODINGTON CO., ST. PETER (1901) Merged into and became a part of St. Henry Parish, Henry.

HARROLD, HUGHES CO., ST. JOHN THE EVANGELIST, [CEM] Merged into and became a part of St. Mary Parish, Highmore.

HARRISBURG, LINCOLN CO., SAINT JOHN PAUL II PARISH OF LINCOLN COUNTY (2017)
220 S. Cliff Ave, Ste. 126, Harrisburg, 57032.
Tel: 605-988-3750; Email: office1@jp2sd.org. P.O. Box 65, Harrisburg, 57032-0065. Rev. John L. Rutten; Deacon Glenn Ridder.

HARTFORD, MINNEHAHA CO., ST. GEORGE PARISH OF MINNEHAHA COUNTY aka St. George Catholic Church (1882) [CEM]
408 S. Western Ave., P.O. Box 577, Hartford, 57033.
Tel: 605-528-3902; Email: rdissing@stgeorgehartford.com; Email: dre@stgeorgehartford.com; Email: frpaulking@sfcatholic.org; Web: www.stgeorgehartford.com. Rev. Paul Stephen King.
Res.: 300 W. Mickelson, Hartford, 57033.
Catechesis Religious Program—*St. George Center*, 408 S. Western Ave., Hartford, 57033. Students 230.

HECLA, BROWN CO., ST. ANTHONY OF PADUA (1904) [JC] Merged into and became a part of St. John de Britto Parish, Britton.

HENRY, CODINGTON CO., SAINT HENRY PARISH OF CODINGTON COUNTY (1882) [CEM] Attended by Blessed Sacrament, Florence.
605 4th St, Henry, 57243. Tel: 605-532-3855; Email: office@cfhcatholics.org; Web: www.parishesonline.com. P.O. Box 28, Clark, 57225. Rev. Daniel H. Smith.
Catechesis Religious Program—Sarah Wanner, D.R.E. Students 32.

HERREID, CAMPBELL CO., SAINT MICHAEL PARISH OF CAMPBELL COUNTY (1895) [CEM]
106 2nd Ave. W., P.O. Box 37, Herreid, 57632.
Tel: 605-437-2614; Email: stmichaels@valleytel.net. Rev. Thomas Clement.
Catechesis Religious Program—Students 30.

HIGHMORE, HYDE CO., SAINT MARY PARISH OF HYDE COUNTY (1906) [CEM]
311 Parker Ave., P.O. Box 457, Highmore, 57345.
Tel: 605-852-2733; Email: stmaryshighmore@yahoo.com. Rev. Paul Josten.
Catechesis Religious Program—Students 56.

HOSMER, EDMUNDS CO., HOLY TRINITY (1912) [CEM] Merged into and became part of St. Augustine Parish, Bowdle.

HOVEN, POTTER CO., SAINT ANTHONY PARISH OF POTTER COUNTY (1887) [CEM] Rev. Kevin Doyle.
Res.: 546 Main St., Box 98, Hoven, 57450.
Tel: 605-948-2451; Email: stanthony@venturecomm.net; Web: saintanthonyofpadua.wordpress.com.
Catechesis Religious Program—Mailing Address: P.O. Box 339, Bowdle, 57428. Students 53.

HOWARD, MINER CO., SAINT AGATHA PARISH OF MINER COUNTY (1882) [CEM]
202 W Washington Ave, Howard, 57349.
Tel: 605-772-4543; Email: stagatha@alliancecom.net. P.O. Box 100, Howard, 57349. Rev. Chester Murtha.
Catechesis Religious Program—Students 96.

HUMBOLDT, MINNEHAHA CO., SAINT ANN PARISH OF MINNEHAHA COUNTY (1912) [CEM] Rev. Robert V. Krantz; Sr. Jane Schoenfelder, O.S.B.
Res.: 204 S. Jefferson, P.O. Box 195, Humboldt, 57035. Tel: 605-363-3330; Email: stpatmontrose@siouxvalley.net.
Catechesis Religious Program—Students 69.

HUNTIMER, MINNEHAHA CO., SAINT JOSEPH THE WORKMAN PARISH OF MINNEHAHA COUNTY (1889) [CEM]
46408 245th St., Colton, 57018. Tel: 605-594-3750; Email: stroseoflima@alliancecom.net. P.O. Box O, Garretson, 57030. Rev. Jeffrey Thomas Norfolk.
Catechesis Religious Program—Students 65.

HURON, BEADLE CO., HOLY TRINITY PARISH OF BEADLE COUNTY (1999) [CEM]
Mailing Address: 425 21st St. S.W., Huron, 57350.
Tel: 605-352-2203; Email: hthuron@hur.midco.net; Web: HolyTrinityHuron.org. Rev. Michael Schneider; Deacons William Kappler; Roger Puthoff.
Res.: 425 20th St., S.W., Huron, 57350.
School—Holy Trinity Parish of Beadle County School, (Grades PreK-6), Tel: 605-352-9344; Email: michelle.schoenfelder@k12.sd.us; Web: holytrinity.k12sd.us. Mrs. Michelle Schoenfelder, Prin. Lay Teachers 13; Students 151.
Catechesis Religious Program—Students 161.

IDYLWILDE, TURNER CO., SAINT BONIFACE PARISH OF TURNER COUNTY (1885) [CEM] Attended by St. George, Scotland.
28703 444th Ave., Idylwilde, 57043.
Tel: 605-583-4318. P.O. Box 449, Scotland, 57059. Rev. Randy Phillips.
Catechesis Religious Program—Students 54.

IPSWICH, EDMUNDS CO., HOLY CROSS PARISH OF EDMUNDS COUNTY (1886) [CEM]
20 6th St., Ipswich, 57451. Tel: 605-426-6967; Email:

ipswich.holycross@sfcatholic.org. P.O. Box 67, Ipswich, 57451-0067. Rev. Russell Homic.
Catechesis Religious Program—Students 98.

IROQUOIS, KINGSBURY CO., ST. PAUL (1914) [CEM] Merged into and became a part of St. Thomas Aquinas Parish, De Smet.

JEFFERSON, UNION CO., SAINT PETER PARISH OF UNION COUNTY (1867) [CEM]
402 Main St, Jefferson, 57038. Tel: 605-966-5716; Email: stpeters@longlines.com; Email: stpeter@secatholics.org. P.O. Box 188, Jefferson, 57038-0188. Revs. Joseph Vogel; Steven Robert Jones, Sacramental Min.
Res.: 105 E Dakota St, P.O. Box 188, Jefferson, 57038-0188.
Child Care—Preschool, P.O. Box 98, Jefferson, 57038-0098. Tel: 605-966-5746. Students 21.
Catechesis Religious Program—(Combined with St. Joseph, Elk Point) Students 58.

KIMBALL, BRULE CO., SAINT MARGARET PARISH OF BRULE COUNTY (1884) [CEM]
417 S. Elm, Kimball, 57355. Tel: 605-778-6420; Email: stmargarets@midstatesd.net. P.O. Box 137, Kimball, 57355-0137. Rev. Andrew Swietochowski.
Child Care—Preschool, Students 32; Teachers 2.
Catechesis Religious Program—Students 118.

KRANZBURG, CODINGTON CO., HOLY ROSARY PARISH OF CODINGTON COUNTY (1879) [CEM]
202 Minnesota Ave. N.E., P.O. Box 166, Kranzburg, 57245. Tel: 605-647-2187. Rev. Kenneth J. Koster.
Catechesis Religious Program—Students 107.

LAKE ANDES, CHARLES MIX CO., SAINT MARK PARISH OF CHARLES MIX COUNTY (1904) [CEM]
251 N. 3rd, Lake Andes, 57356. Tel: 605-724-2191; Email: stpaul@unitelsd.com. Mailing Address: 206 1st St., Armour, 57313. Rev. Cathal Gallagher.
Catechesis Religious Program—Students 36.

LAKE CITY, MARSHALL CO., ST. JOSEPH (1919) [CEM] Merged into and became a part of Sacred Heart Parish, Eden.

LENNOX, LINCOLN CO., SAINT MAGDALEN PARISH OF LINCOLN COUNTY, [CEM]
417 E. 6th Ave, P.O. Box 136, Lennox, 57039.
Tel: 605-647-2187; Email: info@ststmagdalenlennox.org; Web: stmagdalenlennox.parishesonline.com. Rev. John Rader.
Catechesis Religious Program—Lisa Mikkelsen, D.R.E. Students 111.

LEOLA, MCPHERSON CO., OUR LADY OF PERPETUAL HELP PARISH OF MCPHERSON COUNTY (1891) [CEM] Attended by Holy Cross, Ipswich.
1000 N Main, Leola, 57456. Tel: 605-426-6967; Email: leola.olph@sfcatholic.org. P.O. Box 67, Ipswich, 57451-0067. Rev. Russell Homic.
Res.: 20 6th St., Ipswich, 57451.
Catechesis Religious Program—Students 24.

LESTERVILLE, YANKTON CO., ST. JOHN THE BAPTIST PARISH OF YANKTON COUNTY (1904) [CEM] Attended by St. Wenceslaus, Tabor.
700 1st St., Lesterville, 57040. Tel: 605-463-2336; Fax: 605-463-2518; Email: stwenceslaus@hcinet.net. Mailing Address: 205 N. Lidice, Tabor, 57063. Rev. Anthony Urban.
Catechesis Religious Program—Students 42.

MADISON, LAKE CO., SAINT THOMAS AQUINAS PARISH OF LAKE COUNTY (1881) [CEM]
321 N. Van Eps Ave., Madison, 57042.
Tel: 605-256-2304. Rev. DeWayne Kayser.
School—Saint Thomas Aquinas Parish of Lake County School, (Grades PreK-5), 401 N. Van Eps Ave., Madison, 57042. Tel: 605-256-4419; Fax: 605-256-4419; Web: st-thomas.k12.sd.us. Cate Luvaas, Prin. Lay Teachers 13; Students 81.
Catechesis Religious Program—Students 149.

MARION, TURNER CO., OUR LADY OF PERPETUAL HELP PARISH OF TURNER COUNTY (1880) [CEM] Merged with St. Christina Parish of Turner County.

MARTY, CHARLES MIX CO., SAINT PAUL PARISH OF CHARLES MIX COUNTY (1913) [CEM] (Native American)
102 Church Dr, Marty, 57361. Tel: 605-384-3234; Email: stpaulsparish@hcinet.net. P.O. Box 266, Marty, 57361-0266. Rev. Cathal Gallagher.
Catechesis Religious Program—Students 18.

MAYFIELD, YANKTON CO., ST. COLUMBA (1902) [CEM] Merged with St. Boniface Parish, Idylwilde.

MELLETTE, SPINK CO., ALL SAINTS PARISH OF SPINK COUNTY (1944) [CEM] Attended by St. Bernard, Redfield.
Mailing Address: 23 S 1st Ave, Box 46, Mellette, 57461-0046. Tel: 605-887-3414; Email: Mellette.allsaints@sfcatholic.org. Rev. Thomas Anderson.
Catechesis Religious Program—Students 38.

MILBANK, GRANT CO., SAINT LAWRENCE PARISH OF GRANT COUNTY (1882) [CEM]
113 S. 6th St., Milbank, 57252. Tel: 605-432-9122; Email: stlawrencemilbank@gmail.com; Web: www.stlawrencemilbank.org. Rev. Gary K. DeRouchey; Deacon Chet Cordell.
Res.: 101 S. 6th St., Milbank, 57252.
School—Saint Lawrence Parish of Grant County School, (Grades PreK-6), Tel: 605-432-5673; Web: stlawrence.k12.sd.us. Ms. Brenda Anderson, Prin.; Rev. Gary K. DeRouchey, School Admin. Clergy 1; Lay Teachers 11; Students 124.
Catechesis Religious Program—Students 154.

MILLER, HAND CO., SAINT ANN PARISH OF HAND COUNTY (1884) [CEM] Rev. Paul Josten.
Res.: 709 E. 4th St., P.O. Box 198, Miller, 57362.
Tel: 605-853-2207; Email: stann1962@mncomm.com; Web: www.stannmiller.com.
Catechesis Religious Program—Students 106.

MITCHELL, DAVISON CO.

1—HOLY FAMILY PARISH OF DAVISON COUNTY (1880) [JC]
222 N. Kimball St., Mitchell, 57301.
Tel: 605-996-3639; Email: holyfamily@mitchelltelecom.net; Web: www.holyfamilymitchell.com. Revs. Ken Lulf; Barry Reuwsaat; Deacon Joseph Graves.
Catechesis Religious Program—1510 W. Elm, Mitchell, 57301. Students 283.

2—HOLY SPIRIT PARISH OF DAVISON COUNTY (1962) [CEM]
1401 W. Cedar Ave., Mitchell, 57301.
Tel: 605-996-7424; Email: secretary@holyspiritmitchell.org. Rev. John W. Short; Deacon Nick Baus.
Catechesis Religious Program— See Holy Family for details. Students 107.

MOBRIDGE, WALWORTH CO., SAINT JOSEPH PARISH OF WALWORTH COUNTY (1912) [JC]
518 2nd Ave., W., Mobridge, 57601.
Tel: 605-845-2100. Rev. William Hamak.
Catechesis Religious Program—Students 112.

MONTROSE, MCCOOK CO., SAINT PATRICK PARISH OF MCCOOK COUNTY (1904) [CEM]
211 S. Church, P.O. Box 158, Montrose, 57048.
Tel: 605-363-5068; Fax: 605-363-3856; Email: stpatmontrose@siouxvalley.net. Rev. Robert V. Krantz.
Catechesis Religious Program—Students 132.

MOUNT VERNON, DAVISON CO., ST. MICHAEL (1900) Merged into and became a part of St. John Parish, Plankinton.

NEW EFFINGTON, ROBERTS CO., SACRED HEART (1913) Merged into and became a part of St. John the Baptist Parish, Rosholt.

ONAKA, FAULK CO., ST. JOHN THE BAPTIST (1906) [CEM] Merged into and became a part of St. Anthony of Padua, Hoven.

ONIDA, SULLY CO., SAINT PIUS X PARISH OF SULLY COUNTY (1959) [CEM] Attended by Sacred Heart, Gettysburg.
102 6th St., P.O. Box 13, Onida, 57564-0013.
Tel: 605-258-2336; Email: stpiusx@venturecomm.net; Web: stpiusxonida.org. Rev. Jerome Kopel.
Catechesis Religious Program—Email: stpiusxre@live.com. Students 34.

ORIENT, FAULK CO., ST. JOSEPH (1884) [CEM] Merged into and became a part of St. Thomas the Apostle Parish, Faulkton.

PARKER, TURNER CO., SAINT CHRISTINA PARISH OF TURNER COUNTY (1881) [CEM]
Mailing Address: 360 W 1st St, P.O. Box 610, Parker, 57053. Tel: 605-297-4983; Email: stchristina@iw.net; Web: www.parishesonline.com/find/st-christina-catholic- church. Rev. Thomas Fitzpatrick.
Catechesis Religious Program—Students 56.

PARKSTON, HUTCHINSON CO., SACRED HEART PARISH OF HUTCHINSON COUNTY (1887) [CEM 2]
411 W. Main St., P.O. Box 460, Parkston, 57366.
Tel: 605-928-3676. Rev. David Stevens; Deacon Barry Wagner.
Catechesis Religious Program—Students 149.

PIERRE, HUGHES CO.

1—BLESSED KATERI TEKAKWITHA, Closed. For inquiries for parish records contact the chancery.

2—SAINTS PETER AND PAUL PARISH OF HUGHES COUNTY (1882) [CEM]
304 N. Euclid, Pierre, 57501. Tel: 605-224-2483; Email: sspeterandpaulcatholic@gmail.com. Rev. J. Joseph Holzhauser.
School—Saints Peter and Paul Parish of Hughes County School, (Grades K-5), Tel: 605-224-7185; Web: stjosephpierre.k12.sd.us. Mrs. Darlene Braun, Prin. Lay Teachers 15; Students 187.
Catechesis Religious Program—Students 400.

PLANKINTON, AURORA CO., SAINT JOHN PARISH OF AURORA COUNTY (1881)
308 E. 3rd St., Plankinton, 57368. Tel: 605-942-7125; Email: office@pfcatholics.org. P.O. Box 430, Plankinton, 57368-0430. Rev. Robert Edward Lacey.
Catechesis Religious Program—Teachers 122.

PLATTE, CHARLES MIX CO., SAINT PETER THE APOSTLE PARISH OF CHARLES MIX COUNTY (1904) [CEM]
317 Ohio Ave., Platte, 57369. Tel: 605-337-3710; Email: secretary@stpeterplattesd.org. Rev. Grant Lacey; Deacon Joseph Tegethoff.
Catechesis Religious Program—Students 44.

POLO, HAND CO., SAINT LIBORIUS PARISH OF HAND COUNTY (1904) [CEM] Attended by St. Thomas the Apostle Parish, Faulkton.
17985 354th Ave., Orient, 57467. Tel: 605-598-6590; Email: stthomaspastor@venturecomm.net; Email: stliborius@venturecomm.net. Rev. Christopher Hughes.
Catechesis Religious Program—Students 31.

PUKWANA, BRULE CO., ST. ANTHONY (1891) Merged into and became a part of St. James Parish, Chamberlain.

RAMONA, LAKE CO., SAINT WILLIAM OF VERCELLI PARISH OF LAKE COUNTY (1899) Attended by St. Agatha, Howard.
120 W. 3rd St., Howard, 57054. Tel: 605-772-5564; Fax: 605-772-5179; Email: stagatha@alliancecom.net. P.O. Box 100, Howard, 57349-0100. Rev. Chester Murtha.
Catechesis Religious Program—

REDFIELD, SPINK CO., SAINT BERNARD PARISH OF SPINK COUNTY (1884) [CEM] Rev. Thomas Anderson.
Res.: 213 E. 6th Ave., Redfield, 57469-1249.
Tel: 605-472-1482; Email: sbernard@abe.midco.net; Web: www.stbernardredfield.org.
Catechesis Religious Program—Students 135.

REVILLO, GRANT CO., ANNUNCIATION PARISH OF GRANT COUNTY (1889) [CEM] Attended by St. Lawrence, Milbank.
301 5th St, P.O. Box 128, Revillo, 57259.
Tel: 605-862-8485; Email: revillo.annunciation@sfcatholic.org. Rev. David Garza, Parish Admin.
Catechesis Religious Program—Students 14.

ROSCOE, EDMUNDS CO., SAINT THOMAS APOSTLE PARISH OF EDMUNDS COUNTY (1885) [JC] Attended by Ipswich.
605 N. Andrwe St., Roscoe, 57471. Tel: 605-426-6967; Email: stthomas@sfcatholic.org. P.O. Box 67, Ipswich, 57451-0067. Rev. Russell Homic.
Catechesis Religious Program—Students 34.

ROSHOLT, ROBERTS CO., SAINT JOHN THE BAPTIST PARISH OF ROBERTS COUNTY (1911) [CEM]
218 W. Dakota St., P.O. Box 45, Rosholt, 57260.
Tel: 605-537-4583. Rev. Gregory L. Frankman.
Catechesis Religious Program—Students 38.

SALEM, MCCOOK CO., SAINT MARY, HELP OF CHRISTIANS PARISH OF MCCOOK COUNTY (1885) [CEM]
240 N. Idaho, P.O. Box 308, Salem, 57058.
Tel: 605-425-2600; Email: stmaryadm@triotel.net; Web: www.salemcatholic.org. Rev. Martin E. Lawrence.
School—St. Mary School, (Grades K-8), 205 W. Essex Ave., P.O. Box 40, Salem, 57058. Tel: 605-425-2607; Web: stmarysschoolsalem.weebly.com. Linda Merkwan, Prin. Clergy 1; Lay Teachers 4; Students 45.
Catechesis Religious Program—Students 51.

SCOTLAND, BON HOMME CO., SAINT GEORGE PARISH OF BON HOMME COUNTY (1906) [CEM]
930 3rd St, Scotland, 57059. Tel: 605-583-4318; Email: stgchrch@gwtc.net. P.O. Box 449, Scotland, 57059. Rev. Randy Phillips.
Catechesis Religious Program—Students 30.

SELBY, WALWORTH CO., SAINT ANTHONY PARISH OF WALWORTH COUNTY (1900) Attended by Herreid.
Mailing Address: 7209 5th Ave., P.O. Box 231, Selby, 57472. Tel: 605-649-6338; Fax: 605-437-2505; Email: stmichaels@valleytel.net. Rev. Thomas Clement.
Catechesis Religious Program—Students 34.

SENECA, FAULK CO., ST. BONIFACE (1903) Merged into and became part of St. Thomas the Apostle, Faulkton.

SIGEL, YANKTON CO., ST. AGNES (1885) [CEM] Merged with St. John the Baptist Parish, Lesterville.

SISSETON, ROBERTS CO.

1—SAINT KATERI TEKAKWITHA PARISH OF ROBERTS COUNTY (1962) [CEM 2]
619 N. Main Ave., Sisseton, 57262. Tel: 605-698-7414 ; Email: sissetoncath.office@gmail.com; Web: www.nesdcatholics.org. Mailing Address: 120 E. Chestnut, Sisseton, 57262. Rev. Jerome Ranek.
Catechesis Religious Program—Michelle Skarnagel, D.R.E. (Combined with St. Peter, Sisseton). Students 3.

2—SAINT PETER PARISH OF ROBERTS COUNTY (1899) [CEM]
525 E. Chestnut St., Sisseton, 57262.
Tel: 605-698-7414; Email: sissetoncath.office@gmailcom; Web: www.nesdcatholics.org. Mailing Address: 120 E. Chestnut, Sisseton, 57262. Rev. Jerome Ranek.
Catechesis Religious Program—Students 46.

SPENCER-FARMER, MCCOOK CO., ST. JOHN NEUMANN (1999) Merged into and became a part of Epiphany Parish, Epiphany.

SPRINGFIELD, BON HOMME CO., SAINT VINCENT DE PAUL PARISH OF BON HOMME COUNTY, Attended by Tyndall.
1203 Wood St, Springfield, 57062. Tel: 605-589-3504; Email: stleochurch@hcinet.net. P.O. Box 47, Tyndall, 57066-0047. Rev. Joseph Forcelle.
Catechesis Religious Program— Attend at St. Leo, Tyndall.

STEPHAN, HYDE CO., IMMACULATE CONCEPTION PARISH

OF HYDE COUNTY (1886) [CEM] [JC] Attended by Ft. Thompson.
Mailing Address: 206 Crow Creek Loop, Stephan, 57346. Tel: 605-852-2215; Email: pastteam@gwtc.net. Revs. Christianus Hendrick, S.C.J.; Mark Mastin, S.C.J.; Deacon Steven A. McLaughlin.
Catechesis Religious Program—
STICKNEY, AURORA CO., SAINT MARY PARISH OF AURORA COUNTY (1908) [CEM] Attended by Plankinton.
400 Main St., Stickney, 57375. Tel: 605-942-7125; Email: office@pfcatholics.org. P.O. Box 430, Plankinton, 57368-0430. Rev. Robert Edward Lacey.
Catechesis Religious Program—Students 17.
TABOR, BON HOMME CO., SAINT WENCESLAUS PARISH OF BON HOMME COUNTY (1872) [CEM]
205 N. Lidice St., Tabor, 57063. Tel: 605-463-2336; Email: stwenceslaus@hcinet.net. Rev. Anthony Urban.
Catechesis Religious Program—Students 222.
TEA, LINCOLN CO., SAINT NICHOLAS PARISH OF LINCOLN COUNTY (1905) [JC]
140 W. Brian St., P.O. Box 116, Tea, 57064.
Tel: 605-498-5792; Email: info@stnicholastea.org. Rev. Thomas Fitzpatrick.
Res.: 200 W. Brian St., P.O. Box 116, Tea, 57064.
Catechesis Religious Program—Students 256.
TRIPP, HUTCHINSON CO., HOLY ROSARY, Merged into and became a part of Sacred Heart Parish, Parkston. Email: sacredheart@santel.net.
TURTON, SPINK CO., SAINT JOSEPH PARISH OF SPINK COUNTY (1888) [CEM] [JC]
201 E Linden St, Turton, 57477. Tel: 605-397-8448; Email: mtroske@nvc.net; Email: frmichaelkelly@sfcatholic.org. P.O. Box 407, Groton, 57445. Rev. Michael D. Kelly; Deacon Gordon Richard.
Catechesis Religious Program—Students 32.
TYNDALL, BON HOMME CO., SAINT LEO THE GREAT PARISH OF BON HOMME COUNTY (1890) [CEM]
100 E. 20th Ave., Tyndall, 57066. Tel: 605-589-3504; Email: stleochurch@hcinet.net. P.O. Box 47, Tyndall, 57066-0047. Rev. Joseph Forcelle.
Catechesis Religious Program—Students 104.
Station—Springfield Correctional Facility, Springfield. Tel: 605-369-2201.
VEBLEN, MARSHALL CO., ST. JOHN NEPOMUCENE (1907) [CEM] Merged into and became a part of St. Peter Parish, Sisseton.
VERMILLION, CLAY CO., SAINT AGNES PARISH OF CLAY COUNTY (1860) [CEM 2] [JC]
416 S. Walker St., Vermillion, 57069.
Tel: 605-624-4478; Email: saintagneschurch@msn.com. Rev. John Fischer; Deacons Timothy Tracy; Dennis Davis.
School—Saint Agnes Parish of Clay County School, (Grades PreK-5), 909 E. Lewis St., Vermillion, 57069. Tel: 605-624-4144; Fax: 605-624-6239; Web: stagnes.k12.sd.us. Mrs. Darla Hamm, Prin.; Kathy Crowley, Librarian. Lay Teachers 11; Students 144.
Catechesis Religious Program—Micky Rasmussen, D.R.E. Students 192.
WAGNER, CHARLES MIX CO., SAINT JOHN THE BAPTIST PARISH OF CHARLES MIX COUNTY (1903) [CEM]
107 SW High Ave., Wagner, 57380.
Tel: 605-384-5518; Email: wagner.stjohn@sfcatholic.org; Web: stjohnthebaptistcatholicchurch.weebly.com. P.O. Box 637, Wagner, 57380. Rev. Robert Wullweber; Deacon Albert J. Kocer, (Retired).
Catechesis Religious Program—Students 78.
WAKONDA, CLAY CO., SAINT PATRICK PARISH OF CLAY COUNTY (1904) [CEM 2] Attended by Newman Center, Vermillion.
209 Iowa St, Wakonda, 57073-0386.
Tel: 605-763-2028; Email: stteresa@bmtc.net. P.O. Box 472, Beresford, 57004-0472. Rev. David Roehrich.
Catechesis Religious Program—Students 33.
WATERTOWN, CODINGTON CO.
1—HOLY NAME OF JESUS PARISH OF CODINGTON COUNTY (1955) [JC]
1009 Skyline Dr., Watertown, 57201.
Tel: 605-886-2628; Email: tlb.holyname@midconetwork.com. Rev. Michael Wensing.
Catechesis Religious Program—Mary Triplet, D.R.E. Students 294.
2—IMMACULATE CONCEPTION PARISH OF CODINGTON COUNTY (1887) [CEM]
103 SE 3rd St, Watertown, 57201. Tel: 605-886-4049; Email: office@icparishwatertown.org. Revs. Paul A. Rutten; Brian Eckrich, Parochial Vicar.
Res.: 119 4th St., S.E., Watertown, 57201.
Catechesis Religious Program—Students 245.
WAUBAY, DAY CO., IMMACULATE CONCEPTION PARISH OF DAY COUNTY (1894) [CEM] Attended by Webster.
Mailing Address: 1101 E. 1st St., Webster, 57274.
Tel: 605-345-3447; Fax: 605-345-4871; Email: ctkparish@ctkwebster.org; Web: www.icwaubay.org/home. 1045 Main St, Waubay, 57273. Rev. Melvin T. Kuhn.
Catechesis Religious Program—Students 26.
WAVERLY, CODINGTON CO., ST. JOSEPH (1889) [CEM] Merged into and became a part of Holy Rosary Parish, Kranzburg.
WEBSTER, DAY CO., CHRIST THE KING PARISH OF DAY COUNTY (1884) [CEM]
1101 E. 1st St., Webster, 57274. Tel: 605-345-3447. Rev. Melvin T. Kuhn; Michael Wambach.
Catechesis Religious Program—Students 115.
WESSINGTON SPRINGS, JERAULD CO., SAINT JOSEPH PARISH OF JERAULD COUNTY (1906) [JC]
507 Barrett Ave. N., Wessington Springs, 57382.
Tel: 605-539-9569; Email: frjim@santel.net. P.O. Box 348, Wessington Springs, 57382. Revs. Jim Friedrich; Paul Nereparampil, C.M.I., (India) In Res.
Catechesis Religious Program—Students 50.
WESSINGTON, BEADLE CO., ST. JOSEPH, Merged into and became a part of St. Ann Parish, Miller.
WESTPORT, BROWN CO., SACRED HEART PARISH OF WESTPORT (1889) [CEM]
16 W 2nd Ave, Westport, 57481. Tel: 605-229-1011; Email: aquinasnewman@nvc.net. 310 SE 15th Ave, Aberdeen, 57401-7505. Rev. Jordan Samson.
Catechesis Religious Program—Students 30.
WHITE LAKE, AURORA CO., SAINT PETER PARISH OF AURORA COUNTY (1883) [CEM] Attended by Plankinton
101 S. Ellis, White Lake, 57383. Tel: 605-249-2700; Email: office@pfcatholics.org. P.O. Box 277, White Lake, 57383-0277. Rev. Robert Edward Lacey.
Catechesis Religious Program—Students 55.
WHITE, BROOKINGS CO., SAINT PAUL PARISH OF BROOKINGS COUNTY (1898) [JC]
102 W 5th St, P.O. Box 617, White, 57276-0617.
Tel: 605-692-9461. Rev. Andrew Dickinson.
Catechesis Religious Program—Students 50.
WILMOT, ROBERTS CO., ST. MARY (1886) [CEM] Merged into and became a part of St. Lawrence Parish, Milbank.
WOONSOCKET, SANBORN CO., SAINT WILFRID PARISH OF SANBORN COUNTY (1884) [CEM]
203 N. 2nd Ave., P.O. Box 266, Woonsocket, 57385.
Tel: 605-796-4666; Cell: 605-933-9042; Email: stwilfrids@santel.net; Web: www.santel.net/~stwilfrid. Rev. Jim Friedrich.
Catechesis Religious Program—Students 51.
WORTHING, LINCOLN CO., ST. EDWARD (1908) [CEM] Merged into and became a part of St. Magdalen Parish Lennox.
YANKTON, YANKTON CO.
1—SAINT BENEDICT PARISH OF YANKTON COUNTY (1993) [JC] Revs. Scott S. Traynor; D'Cruz Nicholas, Parochial Vicar; Deacons Ronald Kachena; Jack Dahlsied.
Res.: 1500 St. Benedict Dr., Yankton, 57078.
Tel: 605-664-6214; Email: stbenedictyankton@gmail.com.
Catechesis Religious Program—Students 179.
2—SACRED HEART PARISH OF YANKTON COUNTY (1871) [CEM]
509 Capitol St., Yankton, 57078. Tel: 605-665-3655; Email: sacredheart@yanktoncatholic.org. Revs. Larry Regynski; D'Cruz Nicholas, Parochial Vicar.
See Sacred Heart School under Interparochial Schools located in the Institution section.
Catechesis Religious Program—Dr. Tim Mulhair, D.R.E.; Camille Massing, D.R.E. Students 145.

Chaplains of Public Institutions

SIOUX FALLS. *Minnehaha County Correctional Centers*. Vacant.
South Dakota State Penitentiary. Rev. Jeffrey Thomas Norfolk, Chap. [P-266345].
Veteran's Hospital. (Vacant).
FLANDREAU. *Government Indian School*. Attended by SS. Simon & Jude, Flandreau.
SPRINGFIELD. *Mike Durfee Correctional Facility*. Attended by St. Leo, Tyndall.
YANKTON. *Federal Prison Camp*. (Vacant).
Mickelson Center for the Neurosciences. (Vacant).

Retired:
Rev. Msgrs.—
Andraschko, James, (Retired), 3701 E. Peony Pl., 57103
Barnett, Stephen, (Retired), 2416 S. Sherman Ave., 57105
Burian, Ed, (Retired), 1021 Avenue K, Hawarden, IA 51023
Doyle, James Michael, (Retired), 2913 Ridgeview Way, 57105
Hermann, Carlton P., (Retired), 505 Burgess Rd., Yankton, 57078-1819
Mahowald, Richard J., P.A., (Retired), 4510 S. Prince of Peace Pl., 57103
Wagner, Joseph, (Retired), 3920 Barrington St., San Antonio, TX 78217
Revs.—
Axtmann, David, (Retired), P.O. Box 284, Highmore, 57345-0284
Barber, Hal L., (Retired), P.O. Box 387, Parker, 57053
Brady, John, (Retired), 509 Broadway, Yankton, 57078
Bream, James I., (Retired), 4915 S. Glenview Rd., 57108
Duman, Charles J., (Retired), 500 S. Ohlman St., Mitchell, 57301
Farke, Rodney, (Retired), 1926 Laurel Ln., Brookings, 57006
Geditz, Roger, (Retired), P.O. Box 136, Geddes, 57342
Holtzman, Jerome, (Retired), 77 Paradise Dr., Watertown, 57201
Imming, Donald, (Retired), 30 Walker St., Vermillion, 57069
Janes, David A., (Retired), 1003 N. Dakota St., #8, Aberdeen, 57401
Meier, Denis, (Retired), 8728 Benet Pl., 100 28th Ave, S.E. # 212, Watertown, 57201
Moris, Daniel Lee, (Retired), 4554 Galtier St., Shoreview, MN 55126
Osborn, William, (Retired), P.O. Box 132, Colman, 57017
Pathiyamoola, Paul, (Retired), Box 312, Emery, 57332-0312
Pierce, Edward J., (Retired), 1108 W. 57th St., #203B, 57108
Puthenkulathil, Joseph, (India) (Retired), P.O. Box 237, Marion, 57043-0237
Ramos, A. W., (Retired), 523 N. Duluth Ave., 57104
Rasmussen, John, (Retired), P.O. Box 456, Elk Point, 57025-0456
Riedman, John, (Retired), 501 North Buckboard Dr., Kerrville, TX 78028
Ternes, Gary J., J.C.L., (Retired), 9401 S. Lyndale Ave. #204, Bloomington, MN 55402
Thury, Gerald, (Retired), 27121 408th Ave., Dimock, 57331
Vinslauski, Robert B., (Retired), P.O. Box 122, Ramona, 57054-0122.

Permanent Deacons:
Barnier, Thane, St. Therese, Sioux Falls
Barrett, Maurice, St. James, Chamberlain
Barry, James T. (Tim), Ed.D., (Out of Diocese)
Baus, Nick, Holy Spirit, Mitchell
Boorman, James, Christ the King, Sioux Falls
Bregel, James, St. James, Chamberlain; St. Margaret, Kimball
Cantin, Leon, (Retired), (Retired)
Conrads, Michael, (Retired)
Cordell, Chester, St. Lawrence, Milbank; Native American Ministry, Marvin, SD
Counter, Ralph, (Retired)
Davis, Dennis, St. Agnes, Vermillion
Devlin, John P., St. Michael, Sioux Falls
Dickes, Timothy, Cathedral of St. Joseph, Sioux Falls
Frankman, William, (Retired)
Graves, Joseph, Holy Family, Mitchell
Hayes, James M., (Out of Diocese)
Heidt, Roger, Chancery Office; St. Lambert, Sioux Falls
Holsing, Arvid, St. Thomas the Apostle, Faulkton
Huntington, Michael, (Retired)
Jetty, Alfred Bud, (Retired), Chamberlain
Kachena, Ronald, St. Benedict, Yankton
Kappler, William, Holy Trinity, Huron
Knapp, Henry J., St. Mary's, Sioux Falls
McLaughlin, Steven A., Lower Brule Team Ministry, Fort Thompson
Mehlhaff, Peter, St. Mary, Aberdeen
Pardew, Harold, (Retired)
Puthoff, Roger, Holy Trinity, Huron
Radio, William, Cathedral of St. Joseph, Sioux Falls
Richard, Gordon, St. Joseph, Turton
Ridder, Glenn, St. John Paul II, Harrisburg
Seiner, Dennis, St. Katharine Drexel, Sioux Falls
Slason, Stillman W., (Retired)
Tracy, Timothy, St. Agnes, Vermillion
Twidwell, Joseph Jr., Blessed Teresa of Calcutta, Dakota Dunes
Wagner, Barry, Sacred Heart, Parkston
Wagner, Donald, St. Rose of Lima, Garretson
Walden, James I., (Retired)
Wambach, Micheal A., Christ the King, Webster
Wathen, Jerome F., (Retired).

INSTITUTIONS LOCATED IN DIOCESE

[A] COLLEGES AND UNIVERSITIES

ABERDEEN. *Presentation College* (1951) 1500 N. Main St., Aberdeen, 57401. Tel: 605-225-1634; Fax: 605-229-8330; Email: presidentsoffice@presentation.edu; Web: www.presentation.edu. Margaret Huber, Pres.; Rev. Joseph Sheehan, O.Carm., Chap. Sisters of the Presentation of the B.V.M.Campus also located at Fairmont, MN Lay Teachers 50; Priests 1; Sisters 2; Students 821.

YANKTON. *Mount Marty College*, 1105 W. 8th St., Yankton, 57078. Tel: 605-668-1514;
Fax: 605-668-1357; Email: admissions@mtmc.edu; Web: www.mtmc.edu. Mr. Marcus B. Long, Pres.; Joanna Mueller, Asst. Pres.; Jordan Foos, Dir. Campus Min.; Rev. Valerian Odermann, O.S.B., Chap.; Sandra Brown, Librarian. Benedictine Sisters of Sacred Heart Monastery. Religious Teachers 12; Students 821.89.

Mount Marty College - Watertown Location, 3100 S.W. 9th Ave., Ste. 200, P.O. Box 1385, Watertown, 57201. Tel: 605-886-6777;
Fax: 605-668-1618; Email: watertown@mtmc.edu. Mr. Marcus B. Long, Pres.; Sr. Rosemarie Maly, O.S.B., Dir.; Cristina Gordon, Dir.; Jordan Foos, Asst. Dir., Campus Ministry; Joanna Mueller, Asst. to Pres.; Sandra Brown, Librarian. Benedictine Sisters of Sacred Heart Monastery. Clergy 2; Sisters 1; Students 109.

[B] EDUCATION CENTERS, PRIVATE

CHAMBERLAIN. *St. Joseph Indian School*, 1301 N. Main St., P.O. Box 89, Chamberlain, 57325.
Tel: 605-234-3300; Fax: 605-234-3483; Email: mytrell@stjo.org; Web: www.stjo.org. Mike Tyrell, Pres.; Kathleen Whitebird, Prin.; Rev. Anthony Kluckman, S.C.J., Chap. Lay Teachers 21; Priests 1; Students 180.

[C] INTER-PAROCHIAL SCHOOLS

SIOUX FALLS. *Sioux Falls Catholic School System*, (Grades PreK-12), 3100 W. 41st St., 57105.
Tel: 605-336-6241; Fax: 605-575-3345; Email: kgroos@sfcss.org; Web: sfcss.org. Mr. Kyle Groos, Pres.; Ms. Brenda Mitzel, Dir., Instruction. Religious Teachers 1; Lay Teachers 164; Students 2,655.

O'Gorman High School, 3201 S. Kiwanis Ave., 57105. Tel: 605-336-3644; Fax: 605-336-9272; Email: jmahoney@sfcss.org; Web: sfcss.org. Mrs. Joan Mahoney, Prin.; Rev. Joseph Scholten, Chap. Religious Teachers 1; Lay Teachers 48; Priests 1; Students 802.

O'Gorman Catholic Junior High, (Grades 7-8), 3100 W. 41st St., 57105. Tel: 605-988-0546;
Fax: 605-336-9839; Email: wcharron@sfcss.org; Web: sfcss.org. Wade Charron, Prin.; Rev. Lance Matson, Chap. Religious Teachers 1; Lay Teachers 23; Students 354.

St. Mary Elementary, (Grades PreK-6), 2001 S. 5th Ave., 57105. Tel: 605-334-9881; Fax: 605-334-9224 ; Email: mshields@sfcss.org; Web: sfcss.org. Michelle Shields, Prin.; Rev. David A. Desmond, Pastor. Religious Teachers 2; Lay Teachers 22; Students 367.

Holy Spirit Elementary, (Grades PreK-6), 4309 S. Bahnson Ave., 57103. Tel: 605-371-1481;
Fax: 605-371-1483; Email: rmanning@sfcss.org; Web: sfcss.org. Regan Manning, Prin.; Very Rev. Charles L. Cimpl, Pastor. Religious Teachers 1; Lay Teachers 24; Students 354.

Christ the King Elementary School, (Grades PreK-6), 1801 S. Lake Ave., 57105. Tel: 605-338-5103;
Fax: 605-335-1231; Email: jkolbeck@sfcss.org; Web: sfcss.org. Ms. Julie Kolbeck, Prin.; Rev. Richard Fox, Pastor. Religious Teachers 1; Lay Teachers 10; Students 131.

St. Lambert Elementary School, (Grades PreK-6), 1000 S. Bahnson Ave., 57103. Tel: 605-338-7042;
Fax: 605-336-8727; Email: cdavis@sfcss.org. Colleen Davis, Prin.; Rev. Shaun Thomas Haggerty, Pastor. Religious Teachers 1; Lay Teachers 9; Students 162.

St. Michael Elementary School, (Grades PreK-6), 1610 S. Marion Rd., 57106. Tel: 605-361-0021;
Fax: 605-361-0094; Email: lhuemoeller@sfcss.org. Lisa Huemoeller, Prin. Lay Teachers 21; Students 272.

St. Katherine Drexel Elementary, (Grades PreK-6), 1800 S. Katie Ave., Ste. 2, 57106.
Tel: 605-275-6994; Fax: 605-275-6996; Email: scharron@sfcss.org. Ms. Stacy Charron, Prin.; Rev. Gregory Tschakert, J.C.L., Pastor. Religious Teachers 1; Lay Teachers 10; Students 183.

ABERDEEN. *Aberdeen Catholic Schools Education Office*, 1400 N. Dakota St., Aberdeen, 57401.
Tel: 605-226-2100; Fax: 605-226-0616; Email: vickiehaiar@aberdeenroncalli.org; Web: www.aberdeenroncalli.org. Tim Weisz, Pres. Lay Teachers 40; Students 518.

Roncalli Primary School, (Grades PreK-2), 419 N.E. 1st. Ave., Aberdeen, 57401. Tel: 605-225-3460; Email: info@aberdeenroncalli.org. Ms. Paula Florey, Prin.; Sandy Andera, Librarian. Lay Teachers 10; Students 164.

Roncalli Elementary School, (Grades 3-6), 501 S.E. 3rd. Ave., Aberdeen, 57401. Tel: 605-229-4100;
Fax: 605-229-4101; Email: info@aberdeenroncalli.org. Ms. Paula Florey, Prin.; Sandy Andera, Librarian. (Elementary) Lay Teachers 14; Students 162.

Roncalli High School, (Grades 7-12), 1400 N. Dakota St., Aberdeen, 57401. Tel: 605-225-7440;
Fax: 605-226-0616; Email: info@aberdeenroncalli.org; Web: www.aberdeenroncalli.org. Mr. Ed Mitzel, Prin.; Cathy McNeary, Librarian. Lay Teachers 25; Priests 2; Students 217.

MITCHELL. *John Paul II School*, (Grades PreK-6), 1510 W. Elm Ave., Mitchell, 57301. Tel: 605-996-2365;
Fax: 605-995-0378; Email: robin.cahoy@k12sd.us; Web: johnpaul2.org. Mrs. Robin Cahoy, Prin.; Jackie Rezac, Librarian. Lay Teachers 14; Priests 3; Students 160; Total Enrollment 160.

WATERTOWN. *Watertown Catholic School Corporation*, (Grades PreK-6), 109 3rd St., S.E., Watertown, 57201. Tel: 605-886-3883; Fax: 605-886-0199; Email: carol.dagel@k12.sd.us. Mrs. Carol Dagel, Prin.; Kathy Stewart, Librarian. Lay Teachers 14; Students 220.

YANKTON. *Sacred Heart School*, (Grades PreK-8), 1500 St. Benedict Dr., Ste. 200, Yankton, 57078-6884.
Tel: 605-665-5841; Fax: 605-689-3900; Email: laura.m.haberman@k12.sd.us; Email: sherry.rockne@k12.sd.us; Web: www.yanktonsacredheartschool.org. Laura Haberman, Prin. (PK-4); Dr. Tim Mulhair, Prin. (5-8). Clergy 3; Lay Teachers 27; Students 223; Total Enrollment 330.

[D] GENERAL HOSPITALS

SIOUX FALLS. *Avera McKennan*, 1325 S. Cliff Ave., P.O. Box 5045, 57117-5045. Tel: 605-322-8000;
Fax: 605-322-7822; Email: david.flicek@avera.org; Web: www.averamckennan.org. David Flicek, Pres.; Rev. David Krogman, Chap. Sponsored by Sisters of the Presentation of the B.V.M. of Aberdeen, S.D., and Benedictine Sisters of Sacred Heart Monastery, Yankton, S.D. Bed Capacity 505; Tot Asst. Annually 308,328; Total Staff 4,305.

Avera McKennan aka Avera Prince of Peace, 4513 Prince of Peace, 57103. Tel: 605-322-5600;
Fax: 605-322-5622; Email: justin.hinker@avera.org. Justin Hinker, Admin. Sponsored by the Sisters of the Presentation of the BVM of Aberdeen, South Dakota and the Benedictine Sisters of Sacred Heart Monastery, Yankton, SD.; Avera McKennan d/b/a Avera Prince of Peace Bed Capacity 174; Tot Asst. Annually 464; Total Staff 297.

Avera McKennan dba Avera Behavioral Health Center, 4400 W. 69th St., 57108.
Tel: 605-322-4005; Fax: 605-322-4009; Email: thomas.otten@avera.org. David Flicek, Pres. Sponsored by Sisters of the Presentation of the B.V.M. of Aberdeen, S.D. and Benedictine Sisters of Sacred Heart Monastery, Yankton, S.D.Avera McKennan d/b/a Avera Behavioral Health Center Tot Asst. Annually 105,200; Total Staff 313; Staffed Beds 347.

ABERDEEN. *Avera St. Luke's*, 305 S. State St., Aberdeen, 57401. Tel: 605-622-5000;
Fax: 605-622-5127; Email: todd.forkel@avera.org; Web: www.averastlukes.org. Todd Forkel, Pres.; Rev. Mark Axtmann, Chap. Sponsored by Sisters of the Presentation of the B.V.M. of Aberdeen, SD, and Benedictine Sisters of Sacred Heart Monastery, Yankton, SD. Bed Capacity 99; Tot Asst. Annually 300,000; Total Staff 1,050.

Avera St. Luke's dba Avera Mother Joseph Manor Retirement Community, 1002 N. Jay St., Aberdeen, 57401. Tel: 605-622-5850;
Fax: 605-622-5851; Email: tom.snyder@avera.org. Tom Snyder, Admin. Sponsored by the Sisters of the Presentation of the BVM of Aberdeen, South Dakota, and the Benedictine Sisters of Sacred Heart Monastery, Yankton, SD; Avera St. Luke's d/b/a Avera Mother Joseph Manor Retirement Community Residents 81; Total Staff 143; Units for Apartment Living 58; Assisted Living Beds 34.

DELL RAPIDS. *Avera McKennan* dba Avera Dells Area Hospital, 909 N. Iowa Ave., Dell Rapids, 57022.
Tel: 605-428-5431; Fax: 605-428-3906; Email: Scott.Hargens@avera.org. Scott Hargens, Admin. Sponsored by Sisters of the Presentation of the B.V.M. of Aberdeen, S.D., and Benedictine Sisters of Sacred Heart Monastery, Yankton, S.D.; Avera McKennan d/b/a Avera Dells Area Hospital Bed Capacity 23; Tot Asst. Annually 190; Total Staff 64.

DE SMET. *Avera Queen of Peace* aka Avera De Smet Memorial Hospital, 306 S.W. Prairie Ave., P.O. Box 160, De Smet, 57231. Tel: 605-854-6100;
Fax: 605-854-6105; Email: stephanie.reasy@avera.org. Stephanie Reasy, Admin. Sponsored by the Sisters of the Presentation of the BVM of Aberdeen, South Dakota, and the Benedictine Sisters of Sacred Heart Monastery, Yankton, SD.; Avera Queen of Peace d/b/a Avera De Smet Memorial Hospital Bed Capacity 6; Tot Asst. Annually 12,954; Total Staff 32.

EUREKA. *Avera St. Luke's* dba Avera Eureka Health Care Center, 202 J Ave., P.O. Box 40, Eureka, 57437. Tel: 605-284-2145; Fax: 605-284-2011; Email: carmen.weber@avera.org; Web: www.averastlukes.org. Carmen Weber, Admin. Sponsored by Sisters of Presentation of the B.V.M of Aberdeen, SD & Benedictine Sisters of Sacred Heart Monastery, Yankton, SD.Avera St. Luke's d/b/a Avera Eureka Health Care Center Bed Capacity 56; Tot Asst. Annually 2; Total Staff 73.

GETTYSBURG. *Avera Gettysburg*, 606 E. Garfield, Gettysburg, 57442. Tel: 605-765-2488;
Fax: 605-765-2704; Email: robert.scheckler@avera.org. Robert Scheckler, Admin. Sponsored by the Sisters of the Presentation of the BVM of Aberdeen, South Dakota, and the Benedictine Sisters of Sacred Heart Monastery, Yankton, SD Bed Capacity 10; Tot Asst. Annually 500; Total Staff 81.

MILBANK. *Avera McKennan* dba Milbank Area Hospital Avera, 301 Flynn Dr., Milbank, 57252.
Tel: 605-432-4538; Fax: 605-432-5412; Email: natalie.gauer@avera.org. Natalie Gauer, Admin. Sponsored by the Sisters of the Presentation of the BVM of Aberdeen, South Dakota, and the Benedictine Sisters of Sacred Heart Monastery, Yankton, SD.; Avera McKennan d/b/a Milbank Area Hospital Avera Bed Capacity 25; Tot Asst. Annually 41,000; Total Staff 65.

MITCHELL. *Avera Queen of Peace*, 525 N. Foster, Mitchell, 57301. Tel: 605-995-2000;
Fax: 605-995-2441; Email: thomas.clark@avera.org; Web: www.averaqueenofpeace.org. Thomas Clark, Regl. Pres. Sponsored by Sisters of the Presentation of the B.V.M., Aberdeen, SD, and Benedictine Sisters of Sacred Heart Monastery, Yankton, SD. Bed Capacity 67; Tot Asst. Annually 170,600; Total Staff 530.

Avera Queen of Peace dba Avera Brady Health & Rehabilitation, Avera Brady Assisted Living, 500 S. Ohlman, Mitchell, 57301. Tel: 605-996-7701;
Fax: 605-995-6134; Email: julie.hoffman@avera.org. Julie Hoffmann, Admin. Sponsored by Sisters of the Presentation of the B.V.M., Aberdeen, SD, and Benedictine Sisters of Sacred Heart Monastery, Yankton, SD.; Avera Queen of Peace d/b/a Avera Brady Health & Rehab; Avera Queen of Peace d/b/a Avera Brady Assisted Living Sisters 1; Tot Asst. Annually 248; Total Staff 132; Skilled Nursing Care Units 84; Assisted Living 25.

Avera Queen of Peace dba Bishop Hoch Villa, 500 S. Ohlman St., Mitchell, 57301. Tel: 605-996-7701;
Fax: 605-995-6134; Email: Julie.Hoffmann@avera.org. Julie Hoffmann, Admin. Sponsored by Sisters of the Presentation of the B.V.M. of Aberdeen, S.D., and Benedictine Sisters of Sacred Heart Monastery, Yankton, S.D.; Avera Queen of Peace d/b/a Bishop Hoch Villa.

PARKSTON. *St. Benedict Health Center* dba Avera St. Benedict Health Center, 401 W. Glynn Dr., Parkston, 57366. Tel: 605-928-3311;
Fax: 605-928-7368; Email: rita.blasius@avera.org; Web: www.averastbenedict.org. Rita Blasius, Pres. Sponsored by the Sisters of the Presentation of the BVM of Aberdeen, South Dakota, and the Benedictine Sisters of Sacred Heart Monastery, Yankton, SD.; St. Benedict Health Center d/b/a Avera St. Benedict Health Center Bed Capacity 99; Tot Asst. Annually 23,929; Total Staff 222.

PIERRE. *Avera St. Mary's*, 801 E. Sioux Ave., Pierre, 57501. Tel: 605-224-3303; Fax: 605-224-3423; Email: karen.gallagher@avera.org. Todd Forkel, CEO; Karen Gallagher, Dir. Includes: Maryhouse Residential Nursing Facility and Parkwood Retirement Apartments. Sponsored by Sisters of the Presentation of the B.V.M. of Aberdeen, S.D., and Benedictine Sisters of Sacred Heart Monastery, Yankton, S.D. Bed Capacity 60; Tot Asst. Annually 152,300; Total Staff 550.

TYNDALL. *St. Michael's Hospital*, 410 W. 16th Ave., Tyndall, 57066. Tel: 605-589-2100;
Fax: 605-589-2115; Email: cdeurmier@avera.org. Carol Deurmier, CEO. Bed Capacity 25; Tot Asst. Annually 7,204; Total Staff 80.

WESSINGTON SPRINGS. *Avera Queen of Peace* dba Avera Weskota Memorial Medical Center, 604 N.E. 1st

St., Wessington Springs, 57382. Tel: 605-539-1201; Fax: 605-539-4580; Email: stephanie.reasy@avera.org. Stephanie Reasy, Admin. Sponsored by the Sisters of the Presentation of the BVM of Aberdeen, South Dakota, and the Benedictine Sisters of Sacred Heart Monastery, Yankton, SD.; Avera Queen of Peace d/b/a Avera Weskota Memorial Medical Center Bed Capacity 16; Tot Asst. Annually 702; Total Staff 28.

YANKTON. *Sacred Heart Health Services* dba Avera Sacred Heart Hospital, 501 Summit, Yankton, 57078. Tel: 605-668-8000; Fax: 605-668-4412; Email: mark.miller@avera.org. Douglas Ekeren, Pres. & CEO. Sponsored by Sisters of the Presentation of the B.V.M. of Aberdeen, SD and Benedictine Sisters of Sacred Heart Monastery, Yankton, SD. Bed Capacity 99; Tot Asst. Annually 36,914; Total Staff 557.

Sacred Heart Health Services dba Avera Sister James Nursing Homes, 2111 W. 11th, Yankton, 57078. Tel: 605-668-8900; Fax: 605-668-8939; Email: mark.miller@avera.org. Douglas Ekeren, Pres. Sponsored by the Sisters of the Presentation of the BVM of Aberdeen, South Dakota, and the Benedictine Sisters of Sacred Heart Monastery, Yankton, SD.; Sacred Heart Health Services d/b/a Avera Majestic Bluffs.

[E] HOMES FOR AGED

MILBANK. *St. William's Care Center*, 103 N. Viola St., Milbank, 57252. Tel: 605-432-5811; Fax: 605-432-3187; Email: sr_marydsmp@yahoo.com. Sr. Mary Walker, Admin. Conducted by Daughters of St. Mary of Providence, Milbank. Bed Capacity 60; Total Staff 100; Total Assisted 95.

[F] CONVENTS AND RESIDENCES FOR SISTERS

SIOUX FALLS. *Perpetual Adoration Sisters of the Blessed Sacrament*, 707 W. 4th St., 57104. Tel: 605-336-2374; Fax: 605-357-7290; Email: adoratrices@msn.com. Sr. Caridad Morales, A.P., Supr. Novices 2; Sisters 9.

ABERDEEN. *Presentation Convent*, 1500 N. 2nd St., Aberdeen, 57401. Tel: 605-229-8419; Fax: 605-229-8412; Email: jklein@presentationsisters.org; Web: www.presentationsisters.org. Sr. Janice Klein, Pres. Motherhouse and Novitiate of the Sisters of the Presentation of the B.V.M. Sisters 62; Final Professed Sisters 62.

ALEXANDRIA. *Monastery of Our Mother of Mercy and St. Joseph Discalced Carmelite Nuns*, 221 W. 5th St., P.O. Box 67, Alexandria, 57311-0067. Tel: 605-239-4382; Fax: 605-239-4676; Email: malthoff@sfcatholic.org. Mother Mary Elias of the Immaculate Conception, O.C.D., Prioress; Rev. Dana Robert Christensen, Chap.

Discalced Carmelite Nuns of Alexandria, South Dakota, Inc. Solemnly Professed Sisters 7; First Professed 3.

MARTY. *Motherhouse Oblate Sisters of the Blessed Sacrament*, St. Sylvester's Convent: 103 Church Ln., P.O. Box 204, Marty, 57361. Tel: 605-384-3305 ; Fax: 605-384-3575; Email: osbs@cme.com. Sr. Miriam Shindelar, O.S.B.S., Community Leader. Professed Sisters 4.

MITCHELL. *Sisters of St. Francis of Our Lady of Guadalupe*, 1417 W. Ash Ave., Mitchell, 57301. Tel: 605-996-1410; Email: sistersofstfrancis@mit.midco.net. Sr. M. Loretta Von Rueden, Sister Leader. Private Assn. of the Faithful. Professed Sisters 3.

WATERTOWN. *Mother of God Monastery*, 110 28th Ave., S.E., Watertown, 57201-8419. Tel: 605-882-6633; Fax: 605-882-6658; Email: prioress@watertownbenedictines.org; Web: watertownbenedictines.org. Sr. Terri Hoffman, Prioress. The Benedictine Sisters of Mother of God Monastery Sisters 48.

YANKTON. *Sacred Heart Monastery*, 1005 W. 8th St., Yankton, 57078-3389. Tel: 605-668-6000; Fax: 605-668-6153; Email: mwentzlaff@mtmc.edu; Web: yanktonbenedictines.org. Sr. Maribeth Wentzlaff, O.S.B., Prioress. Motherhouse and Novitiate of the Benedictine Sisters. Sisters 79.

[G] NEWMAN CENTERS

ABERDEEN. *Saint Thomas Aquinas Newman Center*, 310 S.E. 15th Ave., Aberdeen, 57401. Tel: 605-229-1011; Email: aquinasnewman@nvc.net; Web: nsunewman.com. Rev. Jordan Samson, Dir.

Northern State University, 310 S.E. 15th Ave., Aberdeen, 57401. Tel: 605-229-1011; Fax: 605-226-3274; Email: aquinasnewman@nvc.net. Rev. Jordan Samson, Dir.; Megan Schulz, Campus Min.

BROOKINGS. *Pope Pius XII Newman Center*, 1321 8th St., Brookings, 57006. Tel: 605-692-9461; Fax: 605-692-9461; Email: ccpoffice@brookings.net; Web: www.piusxiinewman.com. Box 730, Brookings, 57006-0730. Rev. Andrew Dickinson, Dir.

MADISON. *Dakota State University* Attended by St. Thomas Parish, Madison. 321 N. Van Eps Ave., Madison, 57042. Tel: 606-256-2304; Email: cburgwald@sfcatholic.org. Dr. Christopher Burgwald, S.T.D., Contact Person.

VERMILLION. *Saint Thomas More Newman Center*, 320 E. Cherry St., Vermillion, 57069. Tel: 605-624-2697; Email: newmanpc@coyotes.usd.edu. Rev. Steven Robert Jones, Dir.

University of South Dakota, 320 E. Cherry St., Vermillion, 57069. Tel: 605-624-2697; Fax: 605-624-4145; Email: newmanpc@coyotes.usd.edu. Rev. Jeffrey Thomas Norfolk.

[H] MISCELLANEOUS LISTINGS

SIOUX FALLS. *Avera Health*, 3900 W. Avera Dr., 57108-5721. Tel: 605-322-4700; Fax: 605-322-4799; Email: contactus@avera.org; Web: www.avera.org. Mr. Bob Sutton, Pres. Sponsored by the Sisters of the Presentation of the B.V.M., Aberdeen, SD, and the Benedictine Sisters of Sacred Heart Monastery, Yankton, SD.

Benedictine Volunteers, Inc., 110 S.E. 28th Ave. #60, Watertown, 57201. Tel: 605-886-4159; Email: prioress@dailypost.com; Web: benedictinevolunteers.com. Sr. Terri Hoffman, Prioress.

The Berakhah House, 400 N. Western Ave., 57104. Tel: 605-334-9861; Fax: 605-334-2092; Email: malthoff@sfcatholic.org. 523 N. Duluth Ave., 57104. Mr. Matthew Althoff, Chancellor.

Bishop Dudley Hospitality House, 101 N. Indiana Ave., 57103. Tel: 605-332-3176; Tel: 605-809-8424; Email: info@bdhh.org. Chad Campbell, Dir. Total Staff 3.

The Catholic Community Foundation for Eastern South Dakota, 523 N. Duluth Ave., 57104. Tel: 605-988-3795; Fax: 605-988-3746; Email: mconzemius@sfcatholic.org; Web: www.sfcatholic.org. Mark Conzemius, Pres.

Catholic Member Corporation, 523 N. Duluth Ave., 57104. Tel: 605-334-9861; Email: malthoff@sfcatholic.org. Mr. Matthew Althoff, Chancellor.

Catholic Property Corporation, 523 N. Duluth Ave., 57104. Tel: 605-334-9861; Email: malthoff@sfcatholic.org. Mr. Matthew Althoff, Chancellor.

City of Sioux Falls Catholic Schools Property Corporation, 523 N. Duluth Ave., 57104. Tel: 605-988-3759; Fax: 604-334-2092; Email: mbannwar@sfcatholic.org; Web: www.sfcatholic.org. Mr. Matthew Althoff, Chancellor.

Diocese of Sioux Falls Outreach Ministry Property Corporation, 523 N. Duluth Ave., 57104. Tel: 605-988-3700; Fax: 605-334-0292; Email: malthoff@sfcatholic.org. Most Rev. Paul J. Swain, Pres.; Very Rev. Charles L. Cimpl; Mr. Matthew Althoff, Sec. & Treas.

St. Francis House, 1301 E. Austin St., 57103. Tel: 605-334-3879; Fax: 605-575-3999; Email: director@stfrancishouse.com. Julie Becker, Exec. Dir. Bed Capacity: Males 40; Females 6; Families 7.

Holy Spirit School Permanent Trust, 3601 E. Dudley Ln., 57103. Tel: 605-371-2320; Fax: 605-371-1957; Email: holyspiritsf@holyspiritsf.org. Very Rev. Charles L. Cimpl, Contact Person.

St. Joseph Catholic Housing, Inc., Catholic Chancery Office, 523 N. Duluth Ave., 57104. Tel: 605-334-9861; Fax: 605-988-3746; Email: mbannwar@SFCatholic.org. Mr. Matthew Althoff, Chancellor.

Little Flower of Jesus School Foundation, Inc., 901 N. Tahoe Tr., 57110-5779. Tel: 605-338-2433; Fax: 605-339-2203; Email: office@sttheresesf.org. Rev. Kevin O'Dell, Pastor.

St. Matthew Stewardship, Inc., 523 N. Duluth Ave., 57104. Tel: 605-988-3759; Fax: 605-988-3746; Email: mbannwar@sfcatholic.org; Web: www.sfcatholic.org. Mr. Matthew Althoff, Chancellor.

Native Hope, Inc., 112 S. Main St., P.O. Box 600, Chamberlain, 57325. Tel: 888-999-2108; Email: trisha.burke@nativehope.com. Trisha Burke, Contact Person.

Parish Deposit & Loan Fund Trust (2015) 523 N. Duluth Ave., 57104-2714. Tel: 605-334-9861; Email: mbannwar@sfcatholic.org. Mr. Matthew Althoff, Sec.

Pension Plan for Priests of the Diocese of Sioux Falls Trust, 523 N. Duluth Ave., 57104. Tel: 605-334-9861; Fax: 605-334-2092; Email: malthoff@sfcatholic.org; Web: www.sfcatholic.org. Mr. Matthew Althoff, Chancellor.

Retired Priests Medical Benefits Plan Trust for the Diocese of Sioux Falls, 523 N. Duluth Ave., 57104. Tel: 605-334-9861; Email: malthoff@sfcatholic.org. Mr. Matthew Althoff, Chancellor.

Sioux Falls Catholic School Foundation, 3100 W. 41st St., 57105. Tel: 605-575-3362; Fax: 605-575-3345; Email: mkaten@sfcss.org; Web: sfcss.org. Most Reverend Paul J. Swain, Trustee. Total Staff 2.

The Sioux Falls Equestrian Order of the Holy Sepulchre of Jerusalem, 523 N. Duluth Ave., 57104. Tel: 605-338-0769; Email: jscleary@sio.midco.net. Shawn Cleary, Pres.

The South Dakota Catholic Physicians Guild (2014) 2809 W. 33rd St., Apt. 8, 57105-4336. Dr. David Stevens, Pres.

ABERDEEN. *The Presentation Sisters Heritage Trust*, 1500 N. 2nd, Aberdeen, 57401. Tel: 605-229-8419; Fax: 605-229-8412; Email: jklein@presentationsisters.org; Web: www.presentationsisters.org. Sr. Janice Klein, P.B.V.M., Pres. Sponsored by: Sisters of the Presentation of the Blessed Virgin Mary of Aberdeen, South Dakota.

**Aberdeen Catholic Foundation, Inc.*, 13 SE. 2nd Ave., Ste. 6, Aberdeen, 57401. Tel: 605-218-0072; Email: david.vetch@acf.network. David Vetch, Dir.

IRENE. *Broom Tree Retreat and Conference Center*, 29827 446th St., Irene, 57039. Tel: 605-263-1040; Fax: 605-263-1043; Email: ksees@sfcatholic.org. Rev. Joseph Vogel, Dir.; Mrs. Kris Sees, Admin. Dir.

MILBANK. *Blue Cloud Abbey Retirement Trust*, 116 S. Main St., P.O. Box 1013, Milbank, 57252. Tel: 812-357-6752; Email: mcmullen@tnics.com. Rev. John McMullen, O.S.B., Treas.

Asociacion Benedictina de Coban Resurrection Priory Dependent on Blue Cloud Abbey. 116 S. Main St., P.O. Box 1013, Milbank, 57252-1013. Tel: 605-398-9200. Rev. John McMullen, O.S.B., Treas.

MITCHELL. *Mitchell Foundation for Catholic Education*, 1510 W. Elm, Mitchell, 57301. Tel: 605-999-9127; Fax: 605-995-0378; Email: mfce@mit.midco.net; Web: www.mitchellfce.com. Nicole Fuhrer, Dir. Devel.

WATERTOWN. *St. Ann's Corporation*, 100 28th Ave. S.E., Watertown, 57201. Tel: 605-886-9177; Fax: 605-882-3193; Email: prioress@dailypost.com. Sr. Nancy Zemcuznikov, O.S.B., Admin.

Benet Place (Independent Senior Apartments) 100 28th Ave., S.E., Watertown, 57201. Tel: 605-886-9177; Fax: 605-882-3193. Units 38; Staff 10.

Benet Place Assisted Living, 90 28th Ave., S.E., Watertown, 57201. Tel: 605-882-8555; Fax: 605-882-8556. Units 16; Staff 15.

The Benedictine Sisters Foundation of Watertown, 110 28th Ave., S.E., Watertown, 57201. Tel: 605-882-6633; Fax: 605-882-6658; Email: prioress@dailypost.com; Web: watertownbenedictines.org. Sr. Terri Hoffman, Prioress.

Holy Name Foundation, Inc., 1009 Skyline Dr., Watertown, 57201. Tel: 605-886-2628; Fax: 605-886-2142; Email: frmichaelwensing@sfcatholic.org. Rev. Michael Wensing, Contact Person.

Immaculate Conception School Foundation, Inc., 309 2nd Ave., S.E., Watertown, 57201. Tel: 605-886-3883; Fax: 605-886-0199; Email: office@icparishwatertown.org. Rev. Paul A. Rutten, Contact Person.

Retirement Trust, Mother of God Monastery, 110 28th Ave., S.E., Watertown, 57201. Tel: 605-882-6633; Fax: 605-882-6658; Email: prioress@dailypost.com; Web: watertownbenedictines.org. Sr. Terri Hoffman, Prioress.

YANKTON. *Benedictine Center, Inc.*, 1005 W. 8th, Yankton, 57078. Tel: 605-668-6000; Fax: 605-668-6153; Email: mwentzlaff@mtmc.edu. Sr. Maribeth Wentzlaff, O.S.B., Prioress.

Benedictine Health Foundation, Inc., 1000 W. 4th, Ste. 14, Yankton, 57078. Tel: 605-668-8310; Email: BHF@SHHServices.com. Frannie Kieffer, Exec. Dir.

The House of Mary Shrine, Inc., Lewis & Clark Lake, Box 455, Yankton, 57078-0455. Tel: 605-668-0121; Email: thehouseofmaryshrine@gmail.com. Jean Weller, Pres. Bd. of Directors.

Yankton Catholic Community Foundation, 509 Capital St., Yankton, 57078. Tel: 605-665-3655, Ext. 3; Email: yccfo@yanktoncatholic.org. Kelly Kathol, Dir.

RELIGIOUS INSTITUTES OF MEN REPRESENTED IN THE DIOCESE

For further details refer to the corresponding bracketed number in the Religious Institutes of Men or Women section.

[0275]—*Carmelites of Mary Immaculate*—C.M.I.

[1130]—*Congregation of the Priests of the Sacred Heart* (Hales Corners, WI)—S.C.J.

[0270]—*Order of Carmelites* (Middletown, NY)—O.Carm.

[0200]—*Order of St. Benedict* (Richardton, ND)—O.S.B.

RELIGIOUS INSTITUTES OF WOMEN REPRESENTED IN THE DIOCESE

[0230]—*Benedictine Sisters of Pontifical Jurisdiction* (Yankton, Watertown, SD)—O.S.B.

[0940]—*Daughters of St. Mary of Providence*—D.S.M.P.

[0420]—*Discalced Carmelite Nuns of the Monastery of Our Mother of Mercy* (Alexandria, SD)—O.C.D.

[3010]—*Oblate Sisters of the Blessed Sacrament*—O.S.B.S.

[3190]—*Perpetual Adoration Sisters of the Blessed Sacrament*—A.P.

[]—*Sisters of the Divine Savior*.

[3320]—*Sisters of the Presentation of the B.V.M.*—P.B.V.M.

[1720]—*Sisters of the Third Order Regular of St. Francis of the Congregation of Our Lady of Lourdes*—O.S.F.

INTER-PAROCHIAL CEMETERIES

SIOUX FALLS. *St. Michael Cemetery*, 3001 N. Cliff Ave., 57104. Tel: 605-338-3376; Fax: 605-338-4270; Email: djohnson@sfcatholic.org. Dan Johnson, Exec. Dir.

An asterisk (*) denotes an organization that has established tax-exempt status directly with the IRS and is not covered by the USCCB Group Ruling.

Diocese of Spokane

(Dioecesis Spokanensis)

Most Reverend

THOMAS A. DALY

Bishop of Spokane; ordained May 9, 1987; appointed Auxiliary Bishop of San Jose and Titular Bishop of Tabalta March 16, 2011; Episcopal ordination May 25, 2011; appointed Bishop of Spokane March 12, 2015; installed May 20, 2015. *Chancery, 1023 W. Riverside Ave., P.O. Box 1453, Spokane, WA 99210-1453.*

Most Reverend

WILLIAM S. SKYLSTAD, D.D.

Bishop Emeritus of Spokane; ordained May 21, 1960; appointed Bishop of Yakima February 22, 1977; consecrated and installed May 12, 1977; transferred to Spokane April 17, 1990; succeeded to the See April 27, 1990; retired June 30, 2010.

Chancery: 1023 W. Riverside Ave., Spokane, WA 99210. Mailing Address: P.O. Box 1453, Spokane, WA 99210-1453

ESTABLISHED DECEMBER 17, 1913.

Square Miles 24,356.

Solemnly consecrated to the Immaculate Heart of Mary on December 8, 1948.

Corporate Title: "The Catholic Bishop of Spokane, a Corporation Sole."

Comprises the following Counties in the State of Washington: Okanogan, Ferry, Stevens, Pend Oreille, Lincoln, Spokane, Adams, Whitman, Franklin, Walla Walla, Columbia, Garfield and Asotin.

For legal titles of parishes and diocesan institutions, consult the Chancery.

STATISTICAL OVERVIEW

Personnel	
Bishop	1
Retired Bishops	1
Priests: Diocesan Active in Diocese	46
Priests: Diocesan Active Outside Diocese	3
Priests: Retired, Sick or Absent	26
Number of Diocesan Priests	75
Religious Priests in Diocese	28
Total Priests in Diocese	103
Extern Priests in Diocese	5
Permanent Deacons in Diocese	45
Total Brothers	4
Total Sisters	99
Parishes	
Parishes	80
With Resident Pastor:	
Resident Diocesan Priests	36
Resident Religious Priests	5
Without Resident Pastor:	
Administered by Priests	39
Missions	2
Pastoral Centers	1
Professional Ministry Personnel:	
Brothers	3
Sisters	14
Lay Ministers	53
Welfare	
Catholic Hospitals	6
Total Assisted	1,797,338
Homes for the Aged	2
Total Assisted	469
Residential Care of Children	1
Total Assisted	20
Day Care Centers	1
Total Assisted	217
Specialized Homes	3
Total Assisted	1,145
Special Centers for Social Services	14
Total Assisted	304,105
Residential Care of Disabled	2
Total Assisted	21
Other Institutions	13
Total Assisted	2,667
Educational	
Seminaries, Diocesan	1
Students from This Diocese	2
Students from Other Diocese	14
Diocesan Students in Other Seminaries	2
Total Seminarians	4
Colleges and Universities	1
Total Students	7,563
High Schools, Diocesan and Parish	1
Total Students	84
High Schools, Private	2
Total Students	1,026
Elementary Schools, Diocesan and Parish	13
Total Students	3,173
Catechesis/Religious Education:	
High School Students	591
Elementary Students	3,126
Total Students under Catholic Instruction	15,567
Teachers in the Diocese:	
Priests	2
Scholastics	2
Brothers	2
Lay Teachers	239
Vital Statistics	
Receptions into the Church:	
Infant Baptism Totals	1,278
Minor Baptism Totals	138
Adult Baptism Totals	93
Received into Full Communion	172
First Communions	1,450
Confirmations	1,563
Marriages:	
Catholic	203
Interfaith	54
Total Marriages	257
Deaths	636
Total Catholic Population	148,612
Total Population	874,187

Former Bishops—Most Revs. A. F. SCHINNER, D.D., cons. Bishop of Superior, July 25, 1905; resigned from that See, Jan. 15, 1913; appt. first Bishop of Spokane, March 18, 1914; resigned Dec. 17, 1925, and made Titular Bishop of Sala; died Feb. 7, 1937; CHARLES D. WHITE, D.D., ord. Sept. 24, 1910; appt. Dec. 20, 1926; cons. Feb. 24, 1927; died Sept. 25, 1955; BERNARD J. TOPEL, D.D., Ph.D., appt. Coadjutor Bishop Aug. 9, 1955; cons. Sept. 21, 1955; succeeded to the See Sept. 25, 1955; retired April 11, 1978; died Oct. 22, 1986; LAWRENCE H. WELSH, D.D., ord. May 26, 1962; appt. Bishop of Spokane Nov. 7, 1978; cons. and installed Dec. 14, 1978; resigned April 17, 1990; appt. Auxiliary of St. Paul-Minneapolis, Nov. 5, 1991; died Jan. 13, 1999; WILLIAM S. SKYLSTAD, D.D., ord. May 21, 1960; appt. Bishop of Yakima February 22, 1977; cons. and installed May 12, 1977; transferred to Spokane April 17, 1990; succeeded to the See April 27, 1990; retired June 30, 2010.; BLASE J. CUPICH, S.T.D., ord. Aug. 16, 1975; appt. Bishop of Rapid City July 7, 1998; ord. and installed Sept. 21, 1998; appt. Bishop of Spokane June 30, 2010; installed Sept. 3, 2010; appt. Archbishop of Chicago Sept. 20, 2014; installed Nov. 18, 2014; Elevated to Cardinal Nov. 19, 2016.

Vicar General—Very Rev. DARRIN CONNALL, Mailing Address: P.O. Box 1453, Spokane, 99210. Tel: 509-358-7305; Email: dconnall@dioceseofspokane.org.

Vicar for Finance—Rev. BRIAN MEE, Mailing Address: P.O. Box 1453, Spokane, 99201. Tel: 509-358-7333; Email: bmee@dioceseofspokane.org.

Vicar for Priests—Rev. PATRICK KERST, 505 W. St. Thomas More Way, Spokane, 99208. Tel: 509-466-0220; Email: pkerst@dioceseofspokane.org.

Chancellor—Rev. MARK F. PAUTLER, J.C.L., (Retired), Mailing Address: P.O. Box 1453, Spokane, 99210-1453. Tel: 509-358-7339; Email: mpautler@dioceseofspokane.org.

Archivist—Mailing Address: P.O. Box 1453, Spokane, 99210-1453. Tel: 509-358-7340; Email: mscole@dioceseofspokane.org. Rev. MICHAEL J. SAVELESKY.

Diocesan Tribunal—Mailing Address: P.O. Box 1453, Spokane, 99210-1453. Tel: 509-358-7336; Fax: 509-693-3313; Email: tribunal@dioceseofspokane.org.

Judicial Vicar—Rev. MARK F. PAUTLER, J.C.L., (Retired).

Adjutant Judicial Vicar—VACANT.

Promoter of Justice—Rev. TYRONE J. SCHAFF, (Retired).

Defenders of the Bond—Rev. Msgr. JOHN M. STEINER; Rev. JOSE LUIS MILLAN.

Executive Assistant—MARY COLE.

Presbyteral Council—President: Most Rev. THOMAS A. DALY; Revs. KEVIN OILAND, Chm.; PAUL HERIC, Vice Chair; JOSEPH BELL; MICHAEL BLACKBURN, O.F.M.; VICTOR M. BLAZOVICH; JAMES MURPHY, S.J.; JEFFREY CORE; JOACHIM L. HIEN, (Retired); MICHAEL KWIATKOWSKI; JEFFREY LEWIS; MATTHEW NICKS; LUTAKOME NSUBUGA; KYLE RATUISTE; MIGUEL GUSTAVO RUIZ-JUAREZ; BRIAN SATTLER; LUCAS E. TOMSON; ALEJANDRO ZEPEDA; PAUL VEVIK. Ex Officio: Very Rev. DARRIN CONNALL; Revs. PATRICK KERST; BRIAN MEE.

College of Consultors—Very Rev. DARRIN CONNALL; Revs. PATRICK KERST; BRIAN MEE; JOSEPH BELL; MIGUEL GUSTAVO RUIZ-JUAREZ; MATTHEW NICKS; JEFFREY LEWIS.

Priest Personnel Board - Presider—Most Rev. THOMAS A. DALY; Revs. PATRICK KERST, Ex Officio; VICTOR M. BLAZOVICH; JEFFREY CORE; JOSEPH M. WEITENSTEINER, (Retired); JOSE LUIS MILLAN; LUCAS E. TOMSON.

Deans—Revs. PAUL VEVIK, (North Spokane Deanery); KYLE RATUISTE, (South Spokane Deanery); JEFFREY CORE, (East Spokane Deanery); BRIAN SATTLER, (Northern Deanery); PAUL HERIC, (Western Deanery); ALEJANDRO ZEPEDA, (Southern Deanery); LUCAS E. TOMSON, (Palouse Deanery).

Diocesan Offices and Directors

Office of Evangelization—BRIAN KRAUT, Mailing Address: P.O. Box 1453, Spokane, 99210-1453. Tel: 509-358-7314; Email: bkraut@dioceseofspokane.org.

Fiscal Services Office—MERRILIN FULTON, Mailing Address: P.O. Box 1453, Spokane, 99210-1453. Tel: 509-358-7323; Email: mfulton@dioceseofspokane.org.

Office of Stewardship & Development—Mailing Address: P.O. Box 1453, Spokane, 99210-1453. Tel: 509-358-8000. CHRIS KRESLINS, Email: ckreslins@dioceseofspokane.org.

Catholic Administration Services—Mailing Address: P.O. Box 1453, Spokane, 99210-1453. Tel: 509-358-7323. MERRILIN FULTON, Email: mfulton@dioceseofspokane.org.

Nazareth Guild—12 E. 5th Ave., Spokane, 99202. Mailing Address: P.O. Box 76, Spokane, 99210-1453. Tel: 509-744-3259. ALEXANDRA LEE, Email: alee@dioceseofspokane.org.

Office of Human Resources and Child and Youth Protection—Mailing Address: P.O. Box 1453, Spokane, 99210-1453. VICTORIA LOVELAND, Tel: 509-358-7338; Email: vloveland@dioceseofspokane.org; DUANE SCHAFER, Ph.D., Tel: 509-358-4283; Email: dfschafer@dioceseofspokane.org.

Computer & Technology Services—Mailing Address: P.O. Box 1453, Spokane, 99210-1453. Tel: 509-358-7346. MARY GREEN, Email: mgreen@dioceseofspokane.org.

Catholic Schools—Mailing Address: P.O. Box 1453, Spokane, 99210-1453. Tel: 509-358-7330. KATIE RIECKERS, Email: krieckers@dioceseofspokane.org.

Office of Communications—Mailing Address: P.O. Box 1453, Spokane, 99210-1453. Tel: 509-358-7340. MITCHELL PALMQUIST, Email: mpalmquist@dioceseofspokane.org.

Office of Respect Life—Mailing Address: P.O. Box 1453, Spokane, 99210-1453. Tel: 509-385-5251. MICHAEL DUMAIS, Coord., Email: mdumais@dioceseofspokane.org.

Charismatic Renewal (Bilingual)—Mailing Address: 1517 E. 33rd, Spokane, 99203. Tel: 509-747-7213. Rev. MIGUEL MEJIA, Email: mmejia@dioceseofspokane.org.

Ecumenical Relations—Mailing Address: P.O. Box 1453, Spokane, 99210-1453. Tel: 509-358-7305. Most Rev. WILLIAM S. SKYLSTAD, D.D., (Bishop Emeritus), Email: wskylstad@dioceseofspokane.org.

Vietnamese Catholic Community—Mailing Address: 2227 N. Cedar, Spokane, 99205. Tel: 509-714-2942. Rev. VINCENT VAN DAO NGUYEN, Chap., Vietnamese Catholic Community of the Diocese of Spokane, Email: vdao@dioceseofspokane.org.

Vocations—Mailing Address: 429 E. Sharp Ave., Spokane, 99202-1837. Tel: 509-313-7100; Email: vocations@dioceseofspokane.org; Web: www.spokanevocations.org. Very Rev. DANIEL J. BARNETT, Dir.

Director of Deacon Formation—VACANT.

Director of Deacons—Mailing Address: 503 N. Walnut Rd., Spokane Valley, 99206. Tel: 509-993-4425. Deacon KELLY STEWART, Email: kstewart@dioceseofspokane.org.

Catholic Committee on Scouting—MR. ROBERT (BOB) SMEE, Chm., Tel: 509-534-5176; Email: rwsmee@msn.com; Deacon DANIEL GLATT, Chap., Tel: 509-747-7213; Email: dglatt@dioceseofspokane.org.

Bishop White Seminary—Mailing Address: 429 E. Sharp Ave., Spokane, 99202-1837. Tel: 509-313-7100; Email: info@bishopwhitesem.org; Web: www.bishopwhitesem.org. Very Rev. DANIEL J. BARNETT, Rector.

Social Ministries/Catholic Charities—12 E. 5th Ave., Spokane, 99202. Mailing Address: Catholic Charities of Eastern Washington, P.O. Box 2253, Spokane, 99210. Tel: 509-358-4250. ROB MCCANN, Ph.D., Pres. & CEO, Email: rmccann@ccspokane.org.

Censor Liborum—Mailing Address: P.O. Box 1453, Spokane, 99210-1453. Tel: 509-358-7300; Email: mscole@dioceseofspokane.org. Rev. MICHAEL J. SAVELESKY.

Continuing Education of Priests—Mailing Address: 429 E. Sharp Ave., Spokane, 99202. Tel: 509-313-7100. Very Rev. DANIEL J. BARNETT, Email: dbarnett@dioceseofspokane.org.

Detention Ministry—1517 E. 33rd Ave., Spokane, 99203. Tel: 509-747-7213. Rev. MIGUEL MEJIA, Coord., Email: mmejia@dioceseofspokane.org.

Catholic Cemeteries of Spokane— dba Holy Cross Funeral & Cemetery Services*Mailing Address: P.O. Box 18006, Spokane, 99228-0006.* Tel: 509-467-5496; Fax: 509-467-6649; Email: info@holycrossofspokane.org; Web: holycrossofspokane.org. RICK MCLEAN, Dir.

Immaculate Heart Retreat Center—Mailing Address: 6910 S. Ben Burr Rd., Spokane, 99223. Tel: 509-448-1224; Email: ihrc@ihrc.net; Web: www.ihrc.net. Deacon JOHN RUSCHEINSKY, Dir., Email: jruscheinsky@dioceseofspokane.org.

Society for the Propagation of the FaithMailing Address: P.O. Box 1453, Spokane, 99210. Tel: 509-358-7300. Rev. BRIAN MEE, Email: bmee@dioceseofspokane.org.

Victims Assistance Coordinator—Mailing Address: P.O. Box 1453, Spokane, 99210-1453. Tel: 509-353-0442. ROBERTA SMITH, Email: rvsmith@dioceseofspokane.org.

CLERGY, PARISHES, MISSIONS AND PAROCHIAL SCHOOLS

CITY OF SPOKANE

(SPOKANE COUNTY)

1—CATHEDRAL OF OUR LADY OF LOURDES (1881)
1115 W. Riverside Ave., 99201. Tel: 509-358-4290; Email: cberry@dioceseofspokane.org; Web: www.SpokaneCathedral.com. Very Rev. Darrin Connall; Rev. Kyle Ratuiste, Parochial Vicar; Deacons James Kestell, Pastoral Assoc.; John Ruscheinsky, Pastoral Assoc. In Res., Rev. Msgr. Robert A. Pearson, (Retired); Rev. Eugene Tracy, (Retired).
Catechesis Religious Program—Students 45.

2—ST. ALOYSIUS (1890)
330 E. Boone Ave., 99202. Tel: 509-313-7004; Web: www.stalschurch.org. Revs. Tom Lamanna; Jerry Graham, Parochial Vicar; Mr. Donald Weber, Parish Admin.
School—St. Aloysius School, (Grades K-8), 611 E. Mission Ave., 99202. Tel: 509-489-7825; Fax: 509-487-0975; Email: kkelly@dioceseofspokane.org; Web: Stalsschool.com. Ms. Angie Krauss, Prin. Lay Teachers 19; Students 305.
Child Care—Montessori Education Center, Tel: 509-489-7825. Marta Shollenberger, Dir. Lay Teachers 2; Students 30.
Catechesis Religious Program—Michele Lassiter, D.R.E. Students 71.

3—ST. ANN (1902)
2116 E. First Ave., 99202. Tel: 509-535-3031; Email: info@stannsspokane.org. Rev. Patrick Baraza; Dr. Craig Bartmess, Ph.D., Parish Life Coord.
Legal Title: St. Ann Parish-Spokane.
Catechesis Religious Program—Jolie Montevario, D.R.E. Students 45.

4—ST. ANTHONY (1909)
2320 N. Cedar St., 99205. Tel: 509-327-1162. Revs. Jose Luis Millan; Vincent Van Dao Nguyen, Chap.; Deacon James Schwarzer.
See Trinity School, Spokane under Interparochial Grade Schools located in the Institution section.
Educare Center—2315 N. Cedar St., 99205. Tel: 509-327-9369. Ms. Amber Lynde, Dir. Lay Teachers 18; Students 167.
Catechesis Religious Program—Email: cberube@dioceseofspokane.org. Sr. Consuela Berube, D.R.E. Students 32.

5—ASSUMPTION OF THE BLESSED VIRGIN MARY (1958)
3624 W. Indian Trail Rd., 99208. Tel: 509-326-0144; Email: wthomas@dioceseofspokane.org; Web: www.assumptionspokane.org. Rev. Timothy Hays; Deacon Kelly Stewart.
School—Assumption Parish Catholic School, (Grades PreK-8), 3618 W. Indian Trail Rd., 99208. Tel: 509-328-1115; Fax: 509-328-7872; Email: tromano@assumptioncatholic.org; Web: www.assumptioncatholic.org. T.J. Romano, Prin., Email: tromano@assumptioncatholic.org. Lay Teachers 11; Students 243.
Catechesis Religious Program—Jane Weigelt, Sacramental Prep., Email: jweigelt@dioceseofspokane.org. Students 247.

6—ST. AUGUSTINE (1914)
428 W. 19th Ave., 99203. Tel: 509-747-4421; Email: staugustine@dioceseofspokane.org; Web: staugustinespokane.com. Rev. Brian Mee; Deacons Scott Brockway; Allen Peterson.
Catechesis Religious Program—Tel: 509-747-7972; Email: imullner@dioceseofspokane.org. Ivana Mullner, D.R.E. Students 97.

7—ST. CHARLES (1950)
4515 N. Alberta St., 99205. Tel: 509-327-9573; Web: www.stcharlesspokane.com. Rev. Sean Thomson, Admin.
School—St. Charles Catholic School, (Grades PreK-8), Tel: 509-327-9575; Email: office@stcharlesspokane.com; Web: www.stcharlesspokane.com. Heather Schlaich. Lay Teachers 12; Students 147; Clergy / Religious Teachers 1.
Catechesis Religious Program—Students 14.

8—ST. FRANCIS OF ASSISI (1915)
1104 W. Heroy Ave., 99205. Tel: 509-325-1321; Email: amturney@dioceseofspokane.org. Rev. Michael Blackburn, O.F.M.
Res.: 4420 N. Jefferson, 99205.
Catechesis Religious Program—Tammie Fabien, D.R.E. Students 19.

9—ST. FRANCIS XAVIER (1906)
545 E. Providence Ave., P.O. Box 7179, 99207. Tel: 509-487-6363; Email: office@sfxspokane.org; Email: pastor@sfxspokane.org; Web: www.facebook.com/sfxspokane. Rev. David Gaines; Deacon Roy Buck.

10—ST. JOHN VIANNEY (1949)
503 N. Walnut Rd., Spokane Valley, 99206. Tel: 509-926-5428; Email: admin@sjvchurch.org; Web: www.sjvchurch.org. P.O. Box 141125, Spokane Valley, 99214-1125. Rev. Kevin Oiland; Deacon Nick Senger, Prin.
School—St. John Vianney Catholic School, (Grades PreK-8), 501 N. Walnut Rd., 99206. Tel: 509-926-7987; Fax: 509-891-9030; Email: jolson@sjvspokane.org; Web: st.johnvianney.com. Lay Teachers 10; Students 119.
Catechesis Religious Program—Rita Cosby, D.R.E. Students 52.

11—ST. JOSEPH (1890)
1503 W. Dean Ave., 99201. Tel: 509-328-4841; Email: stjoeondean@aol.com. Rev. Jose Luis Millan; Deacons José Torres; Harley Salazar; Sr. Irene Knopes, S.N.J.M., Admin.
See Trinity School, Spokane under Interparochial Grade Schools located in the Institution section.
Catechesis Religious Program—Gail Wallace, D.R.E. Students 95.

12—ST. MARY (1913)
304 S. Adams Rd., Spokane Valley, 99216. Tel: 509-928-3210; Web: stmarysspokane.com. Revs. Jeffrey Core; Michael L. Ishida, Parochial Vicar; Deacons Daniel Glatt; Mike Miller.
School—St. Mary School, (Grades PreK-8), 14601 E. 4th Ave., 99216. Tel: 509-924-4300; Email: cweiler@stmarysspokane.org; Web: www.stmarysspokane.com. Laurie Nauditt, Prin. Lay Teachers 17; Students 251; Clergy / Religious Teachers 16.
Catechesis Religious Program—Marie Bricher, D.R.E. Students 92.

13—MARY QUEEN (1957)
3423 E. Carlisle Ave., 99217-7208. Tel: 509-483-4384 ; Email: maryqueen@dioceseofspokane.org. Rev. Paul Vevik; Deacon Donald Whitney.

14—OUR LADY OF FATIMA (1956)
1517 E. 33rd Ave., 99203. Tel: 509-747-7213; Email: olf@fatimaspokane.com; Web: www.fatimaspokane.com. Revs. Miguel Mejia; Patrick Hartin, Senior Priest, (Retired).
Catechesis Religious Program—Email: mmejia@dioceseofspokane.org.

15—ST. PASCHAL (1916)
2523 N. Park Rd., Spokane Valley, 99214-1125. Tel: 509-926-5428; Email: admin@sjvchurch.org; Web: sjvchurch.org. P.O. Box 141125, Spokane Valley, 99214. Rev. Kevin Oiland.
Educare Center—Lay Teachers 2; Students 70.

16—ST. PATRICK (1893)
5025 N. Nelson St., 99217. Mailing Address: 505 W. St. Thomas More Way, 99208. Tel: 509-487-1325; Web: www.stpatrickspokane.org. Rev. David Gaines, Admin.
Res.: 5021 N. Nelson St., 99217-6161.
Catechesis Religious Program—Janet Provinsal, D.R.E.
Convent—Missionaries of Charity, 5008 N. Lacey St., 99217. Tel: 509-487-6363. Rev. Brian Sattler, Chap. Sisters 3.

17—ST. PETER (1956)
3520 E. 18th Ave., 99223-3814. Tel: 509-534-2227; Email: stpeter@dioceseofspokane.org; Web: stpeterspokane.org. Revs. Jeffrey Lewis; Michael D. Venneri, Senior Priest, (Retired); Deacons Nick Senger; Victor Lopez.
Catechesis Religious Program—Michelle Oresky, D.R.E. & Youth Min. Students 80.

18—SACRED HEART (1911)
219 E. Rockwood Blvd., 99202. Tel: 509-747-5810;

Email: office@shparishspokane.org; Web: shparishspokane.org. Rt. Rev. Msgr. Kevin A. Codd; Deacon Brian Ernst.

Catechesis Religious Program—Sr. Gabrielle Marie, D.R.E.; Maria Haxton, D.R.E. Students 7.

19—ST. THOMAS MORE (1957)
505 W. St. Thomas More Way, 99208.
Tel: 509-466-3811; Fax: 509-466-4701; Web: www.parish.thomasmorespokane.org. Rev. Patrick Kerst; Deacons Doug Banks, Prin.; Thomas Heavey.

School—St. Thomas More School, (Grades PreK-8), 515 W. St. Thomas More Way, 99208. Web: www.school.thomasmorespokane.org. Lay Teachers 13; Students 263; Educare Enrollment 93; Clergy / Religious Teachers 1.

Catechesis Religious Program—Mrs. Valerie Barnes, D.R.E. Students 65.

OUTSIDE THE CITY OF SPOKANE

BREWSTER, OKANOGAN CO., SACRED HEART (1958)
214 S. 5th St., P.O. Box 548, Brewster, 98812.
Tel: 509-689-2931. Rev. Pedro Bautista Peraza; Deacons José Aparicio; Bonifacio Arebalo.

Catechesis Religious Program—Ms. Jessica Garcia, D.R.E. Students 104.

CHENEY, SPOKANE CO., ST. ROSE OF LIMA (1881)
460 N. Fifth St., Cheney, 99004. Tel: 509-235-6229; Email: msine@dioceseofspokane.org; Web: stroseoflimacheney.org. Rev. Paul Heric, Admin.

Catechesis Religious Program—Peter Guthrie, Diocesan D.R.E. Students 37.

CHEWELAH, STEVENS CO., ST. MARY OF THE ROSARY (1885) [CEM]
502 E. Main Ave., P.O. Box 26, Chewelah, 99109.
Tel: 509-935-8028; Web: chewelahcatholic.org. Rev. Stephen Booth.
508-A Main St., Chewelah, 99109. Res.: P.O. Box 26, Chewelah, 99109.

Catechesis Religious Program—Students 30.

CLARKSTON, ASOTIN CO., HOLY FAMILY (1914) [CEM]
1102 Chestnut St., Clarkston, 99403.
Tel: 509-758-6102; Email: holyfamily@dioceseofspokane.org; Web: hfparish.com. Rev. Richard Root.
Res.: 1007 12th St., Clarkston, 99403.
Church: 1107 Chestnut St., Clarkston, 99403.

School—Holy Family School, (Grades K-6), 1002 Chestnut St., Clarkston, 99403. Tel: 509-758-6621; Fax: 509-758-7025; Email: ssray@holyfamilyclarkston.com. Sharon Hunt, Prin. Lay Teachers 8; Students 135; Clergy / Religious Teachers 1.

Child Care—Educare Preschool, Tel: 509-758-2737; Email: rroot@dioceseofspokane.org. Sharon Hunt, Prin. Students 45.

Catechesis Religious Program—Mrs. Sharon Clizer, D.R.E. Students 121.

CLAYTON, STEVENS CO., ST. JOSEPH, Closed. For inquiries for parish records contact the chancery.

COLBERT, SPOKANE CO., ST. JOSEPH (1910)
3720 E. Colbert Rd., Colbert, 99005.
Tel: 509-466-4991; Email: office@stjosephcolbert.org; Web: stjosephcolbert.org. Rev. Brian Sattler; Deacon Joseph Schroeder.

Rectory—3720A E. Colbert Rd., Colbert, 99005.
Tel: pastor@stjosephcolbert.org.

Catechesis Religious Program—Joshua Haxton, Youth Min.; Kathy Catron, D.R.E. Students 48.

COLFAX, WHITMAN CO., ST. PATRICK (1878)
1018 S. Main St., Colfax, 99111. Tel: 509-397-3921; Email: stpatrickcolfax@gmail.com. Rev. Albert Grasher.

Catechesis Religious Program—Linda Marler, D.R.E. Students 41.

COLTON, WHITMAN CO., ST. GALL (1893) [CEM]
P.O. Box 108, Colton, 99113. Rev. Joseph Sullivan.
See Guardian Angel-St. Boniface School, Colton under Interparochial Grade Schools located in the Institution section.

COLVILLE, STEVENS CO., IMMACULATE CONCEPTION (1861)
320 N. Maple, Colville, 99114.
Tel: 509-684-6223, Ext. 6; Email: info@myparishfamily.org. Rev. Kenneth T. St. Hilaire.

Catechesis Religious Program—Marilyn Beaudry, D.R.E. Students 42.

CONNELL, FRANKLIN CO., ST. VINCENT (1964)
220 S. Dayton St., Connell, 99326. Mailing Address: P.O. Box 1030, Connell, 99326. Tel: 509-234-2262; Email: secSt.vincent2015@gmail.com; Web: nfranklincatholic.com. Rev. Miguel Gustavo Ruiz-Juarez.
Res.: 212 S. Ephrata, Connell, 99326.

Catechesis Religious Program—Enrique Lopez, D.R.E. Students 200.

COULEE DAM, OKANOGAN CO., ST. BENEDICT, Closed. For sacramental records, contact St. Henry's, Grand Coulee (Diocese of Yakima).

CURLEW, FERRY CO., ST. PATRICK MISSION (1907)
Mission of Immaculate Conception Republic WA
9 Church St., Curlew, 99118. Tel: 509-775-3935; Email: rsemple@dioceseofspokane.org; Web: www.myparishfamily.org. Mailing Address: P.O. Box 333, Republic, 99166. Rev. Richard Semple, Admin.

DAVENPORT, LINCOLN CO., IMMACULATE CONCEPTION (1893) [CEM]
1310 Adams St., Davenport, 99122.
Tel: 509-725-1761; Email: rfloch@dioceseofspokane.org. Rev. W. Roy Floch.

Catechesis Religious Program—

DAYTON, COLUMBIA CO., ST. JOSEPH (1890)
112 S. First St., Dayton, 99328-0003.
Tel: 509-382-2311; Email: stjosephdayton@dioceseofspokane.org. P.O. Box 0003, Dayton, 99328. Rev. Steven Werner.

Catechesis Religious Program—Melissa Gemmell, D.R.E. Students 10.

DEER PARK, SPOKANE CO., ST. MARY PRESENTATION (1912) [CEM]
602 E. 6th St., P.O. Box 749, Deer Park, 99006.
Tel: 509-276-2948; Email: stmarypresentation@gmail.com; Web: www.stmaryspresentation.org. Rev. Thomas Connolly; Deacon Perry Pearman.
Res.: 427 E. 7th Ave., Deer Park, 99006.

Catechesis Religious Program—Mrs. Margie Booth, D.R.E. Students 39.

ELTOPIA, FRANKLIN CO., ST. PAUL THE APOSTLE (1964)
14181 Glade Rd., P.O. Box 268, Eltopia, 99330.
Tel: 509-297-4371. Rev. Miguel Gustavo Ruiz-Juarez.

Catechesis Religious Program—Angie Manterola, D.R.E. Students 65.

Mission—San Juan Diego (Basin City), 440 Bailie Blvd., Basin City, 99343. Tel: 509-234-2262; Fax: 509-234-2262; Email: st.paulcatholicchurch1964@gmail.com; Web: nfranklincatholic.com.

Catechesis Religious Program—Students 40.

FORD, STEVENS CO., ST. PHILIP BENIZI (1912)
5247 Hubert Rd., Ford, 99013. Tel: 509-725-1761. Mailing Address: 1310 Adams St., Davenport, 99122-9454. Rev. W. Roy Floch.

Catechesis Religious Program—Students 5.

HARRINGTON, LINCOLN CO., ST. FRANCIS OF ASSISI (1906)
206 Coal Creek Rd., Harrington, 99134-0166.
Tel: 509-725-1761; Email: rfloch@dioceseofspokane.org. c/o Immaculate Conception Parish, 1310 Adams St., Davenport, 99122-9454. Rev. W. Roy Floch.

Catechesis Religious Program—

INCHELIUM, FERRY CO., ST. MICHAEL'S MISSION
21 St. Michael's Way, Inchelium, 99138.
Tel: 509-720-3815; Email: josephfortier@gmail.com. P.O. Box 122, Inchelium, 99138. Revs. Jake Morton, S.J.; Joseph Fortier, S.J.

Catechesis Religious Program—Students 35.

IONE, PEND OREILLE CO., ST. BERNARD
302 N. 8th Ave., P.O. Box 731, Ione, 99139.
Tel: 509-447-4231; Email: pocoparishes@gmail.com. Rev. Victor M. Blazovich.

Catechesis Religious Program—Erin Kinney, D.R.E., Email: ekinney@dioceseofspokane.org. Students 17.

KELLER, FERRY CO., ST. ROSE OF LIMA
P.O. Box 187, Keller, 99140. Tel: 509-722-4592. Revs. Jake Morton, S.J.; Joseph Fortier, S.J.

KETTLE FALLS, STEVENS CO., SACRED HEART OF JESUS (1906)
Mailing Address: 320 N. Maple St., Colville, 99114.
Tel: 509-684-6223; Email: info@myparishfamily.org. Rev. Kenneth T. St. Hilaire.

LA CROSSE, WHITMAN CO., ST. JOSEPH (1906)
308 E. 2nd St., Lacrosse, 99143. Tel: 509-397-3921; Email: stpatrickcolfax@gmail.com. Mailing Address: 1018 S. Main St., Colfax, 99111. Rev. Albert Grasher.

Catechesis Religious Program—Mrs. Mary Bertrard, D.R.E.

LIND, ADAMS CO., ST. AMBROSE (1920) Closed. For records please contact St. Agnes, Ritzville.

MEDICAL LAKE, SPOKANE CO., ST. ANNE (1889) [CEM]
708 E. Lake St., P.O. Box 125, Medical Lake, 99022.
Tel: 509-723-1459. Rev. Dale Tuckerman, Admin.

Catechesis Religious Program—Jessica Spracklen, D.R.E. Students 22.

METALINE FALLS, PEND OREILLE CO., ST. JOSEPH (1950)
406 Park St., P.O. Box 417, Metaline Falls, 99153.
Tel: 509-446-2651; Email: pocoparishes@gmail.com. Rev. Victor M. Blazovich, Web: pocoparishes.org.

Catechesis Religious Program—Erin Kinney, D.R.E.

NESPELEM, OKANOGAN CO., SACRED HEART MISSION (1915) [CEM]
209 9th St., P.O. Box 70, Nespelem, 99155.
Tel: 509-634-4249; Email: njam52@hotmail.com. Rev. Jake Morton, S.J.

Catechesis Religious Program—Nancy Armstrong-Montes, D.R.E. Students 20.

NEWPORT, PEND OREILLE CO., ST. ANTHONY (1908)
612 W. First St., P.O. Box C, Newport, 99156.
Tel: 509-447-4231; Email: pocoparishes@gmail.com. Rev. Victor M. Blazovich.

Catechesis Religious Program—Sasha Tefft, D.R.E., Email: stefft@dioceseofspokane.org. Students 10.

NINE MILE FALLS, STEVENS CO., OUR LADY OF THE LAKE (2002)
6122 Hwy 291, P.O. Box 447, Nine Mile Falls, 99026.
Tel: 509-313-6701; Web: maroni.com/olotl. Rev. Timothy R. Clancy, S.J.; Deacon Craig Blomgren.

Catechesis Religious Program—Cindy Blomgren, D.R.E., Tel: 509-464-0131; Email: ccblomgren@yahoo.com. Students 15.

NORTHPORT, STEVENS CO., PURE HEART OF MARY (1898)
720 W. South Ave., Northport, 99157.
Tel: 509-684-6223; Email: info@myparishfamily.org. Mailing Address: 320 N. Maple St., Colville, 99114. Rev. Kenneth T. St. Hilaire.

OAKESDALE, WHITMAN CO., ST. CATHERINE OF ALEXANDRIA
4th & Steptoe, Oakesdale, 99158. Tel: 509-285-6672. Rev. David Kruse.

ODESSA, LINCOLN CO., ST. JOSEPH (1905)
208 N. Alder, P.O. Box 106, Wilbur, 99159.
Tel: 509-647-2380; Email: stagnesritzville@gmail.com. Rev. Rory Pitstick

Legal Title: St. Joseph Catholic Parish - Odessa.

Catechesis Religious Program—Tel: 509-659-0437.

OKANOGAN-OMAK, OKANOGAN CO., OUR LADY OF THE VALLEY (1976)
2511 Elmway, Okanogan, 98840. Tel: 509-422-5049; Email: lnsubuga@dioceseofspokane.org; Web: okvalleycatholicparishes.org. Rev. Lutakome Nsubuga; Alondra Rivera, Sec.

Catechesis Religious Program—Suzanne Craig, D.R.E. Students 57.

OMAK, OKANOGAN CO.

1—ST. JOSEPH (1945)
530 Jackson St., Omak, 98841. Tel: 509-826-6401; Email: jedgertonm@gmail.com. Mailing Address: 323 Edmonds St., Omak, 98841. Rev. Jake Morton, S.J.

Catechesis Religious Program—

2—ST. MARY'S MISSION (1886) [CEM]
20 Mission Rd., Omak, 98841. Tel: 509-826-6401. Mailing Address: 323 Edmonds St., Omak, 98841. Rev. Jake Morton, S.J.

Catechesis Religious Program—(Combined with Paschal Sherman Indian School).

OROVILLE, OKANOGAN CO., IMMACULATE CONCEPTION (1898)
1715 Main St., P.O. Box 308, Oroville, 98844.
Tel: 509-476-2110; Email: lnsubuga@dioceseofspokane.org. Rev. Lutakome Nsubuga; Charlene Stiles, Business Mgr.

Catechesis Religious Program—Maria Viveros, D.R.E. Students 40.

OTHELLO, ADAMS CO., SACRED HEART (1956)
616 E. Juniper St., Othello, 99344. Tel: 509-488-5653; Email: sacredheart@dioceseofspokane.org. Rev. Alejandro Zepeda; Deacons Antonio Beraza; Joel Pruneda; Jesus Rodelo.

Catechesis Religious Program—Anna Salmeron, D.R.E. Students 401.

OTIS ORCHARDS, SPOKANE CO., ST. JOSEPH (1892)
Mailing Address: 4521 N. Arden Rd., Otis Orchards, 99027-9358. Tel: 509-926-7133; Email: info@stjoeparish.org; Web: stjoeparish.org. Rev. Mike Kwiatkowski; Deacon Gonzalo Chalo Martinez.
Res.: 1879 N. Holl Blvd., Liberty Lake, 99016.

Catechesis Religious Program—Teresa McCann, D.R.E. Students 100.

PASCO, FRANKLIN CO., ST. PATRICK (1909)
1320 W. Henry, Pasco, 99301.
Tel: 509-547-8841, Ext. 119; Email: llopez@dioceseofspokane.org; Web: www.stpatspasco.org. Revs. Robert D. Turner; Jose Maldonado; Deacons Victor Ortega; Luis Ramos; Abraham Valdovinos; Antonio Rodriguez; Gary Franz; Robert Kalinowski; Sr. Francis Marie Seale, Children's Center Dir.; Brian Rebar, Youth Min. In Res., Rev. Msgr. Pedro Ramirez, (Retired); Rev. Rex Familiar.

School—St. Patrick School aka St. Patrick Catholic School - Pasco, (Grades K-8), 1016 N. 14th Ave., Pasco, 99301. Tel: 509-547-7261; Email: principal@stpatspasco.org; Web: stpatspasco.org/school. Kris Peugh, Prin. Lay Teachers 13; Students 190.

Catechesis Religious Program—
Tel: 509-547-8841, Ext. 114. Raquel Aguilera, Diocesan D.R.E. Students 900.

POMEROY, GARFIELD CO., HOLY ROSARY (1878) [CEM]
634 High St., Pomeroy, 99347-9702.
Tel: 509-843-3801. Rev. Steven Werner.

Catechesis Religious Program—Rev. Katie Landkammer, D.R.E. Students 28.

PULLMAN, WHITMAN CO., SACRED HEART (1913)
440 N.E. Ash St., Pullman, 99163. Tel: 509-332-5312; Email: sacredheartpullman@frontier.com; Web: www.sacredheartpullman.org. Rev. Steven L. Dublinski, V.G.; Deacon James Evermann.

Catechesis Religious Program—Tel: 509-332-4402. Theresa Paul, D.R.E., Email: tpaul@dioceseofspokane.org. Students 122.

REARDAN, LINCOLN CO., ST. MICHAEL (1907)
455 W. Cottonwood St., Reardan, 99029.
Tel: 509-723-1459; Email: llavoie@dioceseofspokane.

org; Web: www.westplainscatholicparishes.org. P.O. Box 125, Medical Lake, 99022. Rev. Dale Tuckerman, Admin.
Catechesis Religious Program—Joanne Schultz, D.R.E. Students 11.

REPUBLIC, FERRY CO., IMMACULATE CONCEPTION (1898)
261 E. 7th St., P.O. Box 333, Republic, 99166. Tel: 509-775-3935; Email: Ferrycatholic@gmail.com. Rev. Richard Semple.
Res.: 270 E. 7th St., P.O. Box 333, Republic, 99166. Email: rsemple@dioceseofspokane.org. Students 2.
Catechesis Religious Program—

RITZVILLE, ADAMS CO., ST. AGNES (1915)
404 E. Fifth Ave., Ritzville, 99169. Tel: 509-659-0437 ; Email: stagnesritzville@gmail.com. Rev. Rory Pitstick, Admin.
Legal Title: St. Agnes Catholic Parish - Ritzville.
Catechesis Religious Program—Students 3.

ROCKFORD, SPOKANE CO., ST. JOSEPH (1901)
138 S. River St., Rockford, 99030. Tel: 509-928-3210; Email: stmary@dioceseofspokane.org. Mailing Address: P.O. Box 54, Rockford, 99030. Rev. Jeffrey Core.

ROSALIA, WHITMAN CO., HOLY ROSARY (1892)
622 N. Plaza Ave., P.O. Box 8, Rosalia, 99170. Tel: 509-998-0209; Email: msavelesky@dioceseofspokane.org. Rev. Michael J. Savelesky.
Res.: 5103 N. Stevens, 99205.
Catechesis Religious Program—

ST. JOHN, WHITMAN CO., OUR LADY OF PERPETUAL HELP (1960)
403 West Liberty, P.O. Box 325, St. John, 99171. Tel: 509-998-0209; Email: msavelesky@dioceseofspokane.org. Rev. Michael J. Savelesky, Email: msavelesky@dioceseofspokane.org.
Res.: 5103 N. Stevens, 99205.
Catechesis Religious Program—

SPRAGUE, LINCOLN CO., MARY QUEEN OF HEAVEN (1885) [CEM]
103 E Alder St., Sprague, 99032. Tel: 509-723-1459; Email: llavoie@dioceseofspokane.org. P.O. Box 125, Medical Lake, 99022. Rev. Dale Tuckerman, Admin.

SPRINGDALE, STEVENS CO., SACRED HEART (1911)
110 S. 2nd St., Springdale, 99173. Tel: 509-935-8028; Email: sbooth@dioceseofspokane.org. Mailing Address: P.O. Box 26, Chewelah, 99109. Rev. Stephen Booth.

TEKOA, WHITMAN CO., SACRED HEART (1893) [CEM]
822 N Washington St., P.O. Box 957, Tekoa, 99033. Tel: 509-284-3001; Email: dkruse@dioceseofspokane.org. Rev. David Kruse, Admin.
Res.: 429 E. Sharp Ave., 99201. Tel: 509-688-5784; Email: sthomson@dioceseofspokane.org.
Catechesis Religious Program—Joe Heffron, Coord.; MaryJo Heffron, Coord. Students 8.

TONASKET, OKANOGAN CO., HOLY ROSARY
S. Whitcomb Ave. & E. 1st St., Tonasket, 98855. Tel: 509-476-2110; Email: lnsubuga@dioceseofspokane.org. P.O. Box 308, Oroville, 98844. Rev. Jose Jaime Maldonado-Reyna; Charlene Stiles, Business Mgr.
Catechesis Religious Program—Marta Wisdom, D.R.E. Students 45.

TWISP, OKANOGAN CO., ST. GENEVIEVE (1907) [JC]
403 Burgar St., P.O. Box 6, Twisp, 98856. Tel: 509-997-4201; Web: www.methowcatholic.com. Rev. Pedro Bautista Peraza; Deacon Bill Wehmeyer.
Catechesis Religious Program—Sarah Salmon, Rel. Educ. Coord. Students 25.

UNIONTOWN, WHITMAN CO., ST. BONIFACE (1882) [CEM]
205 S. St. Boniface St., Uniontown, 99179. Tel: 509-229-3548; Email: stgbcc@gmail.com; Web: www.saintbonifaceandsaintgall.org. P.O. Box 108, Colton, 99113. Rev. Joseph Sullivan.
See Guardian Angel-St. Boniface School, Colton under Interparochial Grade Schools located in the Institution section.

USK, PEND OREILLE CO.
1—ST. JUDE (1941)
111 River Rd., P.O. Box 385, Usk, 99180. Tel: 509-447-2685; Email: pocoparishes@gmail.com; Web: www.pocoparishes.org. Rev. Victor M. Blazovich, Web: pocoparishes.org.
Res.: 612 W. First St., P.O. Box C, Newport, 99156. Tel: 509-447-4231.
2—OUR LADY OF SORROWS
1981 LeClerc Creek Rd., Cusick, 99119. Tel: 509-447-4231; Email: pocoparishes@gmail.com. P.O. Box C, Newport, 99156. Rev. Victor M. Blazovich.

VALLEY, STEVENS CO., HOLY GHOST (1914) [CEM]
3083 Hemlock St., Valley, 99181. Tel: 509-935-8028; Web: chewelahcatholic.org. P.O. Box 26, Chewelah, 99109. Rev. Stephen Booth.
Station—St. Joseph, 3150 Church Rd., Valley, Stevens Co., St. Joseph 99181.

WAITSBURG, WALLA WALLA CO., ST. MARK (1888)
405 W. 5th St., Waitsburg, 99361. Tel: 509-382-2311. Mailing Address: P.O. Box 0003, Dayton, 99328-0003. Rev. Steven Werner.
Catechesis Religious Program—

WALLA WALLA, WALLA WALLA CO.
1—ASSUMPTION OF THE BLESSED VIRGIN MARY (1953)
2098 E. Alder St., Walla Walla, 99362. Tel: 509-525-3310, Ext. 2. Revs. Matthew Nicks; Esteban F. Soler, I.V.E., Parochial Vicar; Curtis Seidel, Chap.; Deacon Jim Barrow.
Catechesis Religious Program—408 W. Poplar St., Walla Walla, 99362. Tel: 509-525-3310, Ext. 4; Email: redirector@wwcatholic.com. Ms. Maddi Baird, D.R.E. Students 33.
See Walla Walla Catholic School System, Walla Walla under High Schools, Interparochial located in the Institution section.
2—ST. FRANCIS OF ASSISI (1915)
722 W. Alder St., Walla Walla, 99362. Tel: 509-525-3310, Ext. 1; Email: stfrancis@wwcatholic.com; Web: wallawllacatholicparishes.org/. Revs. Matthew Nicks; David Gaines, Parochial Vicar; Esteban F. Soler, I.V.E., Parochial Vicar; Tyler Smedley, Chap.; Deacon Jim Barrow.
Catechesis Religious Program—Sr. Margarita Hernandez, S.P., D.R.E., Tel: 509-529-5141; Email: redirector@wwcatholic.com. Students 22.
3—ST. PATRICK (1859)
408 W. Poplar St., Walla Walla, 99362. Tel: 509-525-3310, Ext. 3; Email: stpatrick@wwcatholic.com. Revs. Matthew Nicks; Esteban F. Soler, I.V.E., Parochial Vicar; Curtis Seidel, Chap.; Deacons Olegario Reyes; James Barrow; Maclobi Robles.
Catechesis Religious Program—Tel: 509-525-3310, Ext. 4; Email: redirector@wwcatholic.com. Ms. Maddi Baird, D.R.E. Students 186.

WASHTUCNA, ADAMS CO., HOLY TRINITY (1967) Closed. For inquiries for parish records contact St. Paul, Eltopia.

WELLPINIT, STEVENS CO., SACRED HEART (1943) [CEM]
6156 Ford-Wellpinit Rd., Wellpinit, 99040. Tel: 509-725-1761. Mailing Address: 1310 Adams St., Davenport, 99122-9454. Rev. W. Roy Floch.

WESTEND, STEVENS CO., OUR LADY OF LOURDES (1938)
6242 W. End Rd., Fruitland, 99129. Tel: 509-725-1761. Mailing Address: 1310 Adams St., Davenport, 99122-9454. Rev. W. Roy Floch.
Catechesis Religious Program—

WILBUR, LINCOLN CO., SACRED HEART (1900)
605 S.W. Alder, P.O. Box 106, Wilbur, 99185. Tel: 509-647-2380; Email: stagnesritzville@gmail.com. Rev. Rory Pitstick, Admin.
Legal Title: Sacred Heart Catholic Parish - Wilbur.
Catechesis Religious Program—Email: rpitstick@dioceseofspokane.org.

Chaplains of Public Institutions

WALLA WALLA. *Washington State Penitentiary*. Served by priests of Walla Walla.

Hospital Chaplains:
Revs.—
Hernandez, Jose Luis, Providence Sacred Heart Medical Center & Children's Hospital, Spokane
Obiske, Bonaventure, Providence Holy Family Hospital, Spokane.

Leave of Absence:
Rev.—
Amah, Peter O.

Military Services:
Revs.—
Peak, James, US Army
Poole, Richard C., US Air Force.

Retired:
Rev. Msgrs.—
Pearson, Robert A., (Retired), 1115 W. Riverside Ave., 99201
Ramirez, Pedro, (Retired), 1320 W. Henry, Pasco, 99301
Steiner, John, (Retired), 221 E. Rockwood Blvd., #302, 99202
Revs.—
Baronti, David, (Retired), Honduras
Borchardt, Edgar, (Retired)
Caswell, Thomas C., (Retired), 1729 W. Bridge Ave., 99201
Eis, Charles R., (Retired), 9202 Irvington Ave., San Diego, CA 92123-3129
Hartin, Patrick, (Retired), 1517 E. 33rd Ave., 99223
Hien, Joachim L., (Retired), 3231 W. Boone Ave., Unit 721, 99201
Kuhns, James, (Retired), 1627 E. 33rd, 99203
Lorge, Felix P., (Retired), 12011 S. Player Dr., 99223
MacMahon, Patrick, (Retired), Ireland
McNeese, Robert J., (Retired), 3511 E. Carroll Ln., 99223
Pautler, Mark F., J.C.L., (Retired), 221 E. Rockwood Blvd., #202, 99202
Savelesky, Michael, Ph.D., (Retired), 5103 N. Stevens, 99205
Schaff, Tyrone J., (Retired), P.O. Box 13247, Spokane Valley, 99213
Skok, Charles, (Retired), 34 E. 8th Ave., 99202
Tracy, Eugene, (Retired), 1115 W. Riverside Dr., 99201
Venneri, Michael D., (Retired), 3520 E. 18th Ave., 99223
Weitensteiner, Joseph M., (Retired), P.O. Box 8087, 99203.

Permanent Deacons:
Aparicio, José, Sacred Heart, Brewster
Arebalo, Bonifacio, Sacred Heart, Brewster
Banks, Douglas, St. Thomas More, Spokane
Barrow, Jim, St. Francis & St. Patrick, Walla Walla
Beraza, Antonio, Sacred Heart, Othello
Blaine, Jim, (Retired), Spokane Valley
Blomgren, Craig, Our Lady of the Lake, Suncrest
Bradley, T. Patrick, (Retired)
Brockway, Scott, St. Augustine, Spokane
Buck, Roy, St. Francis Xavier, Spokane
Byrne, John, (Retired), Our Lady of Fatima, Spokane
Dalecki, Robert, (On Leave of Absence)
Dudinsky, David, (Retired), St. Francis of Assisi, Spokane
Dunlap, Kenneth, (Retired), Spokane
Ernst, Brian, Sacred Heart, Spokane
Evermann, James, Sacred Heart, Pullman
Franz, Gary, St. Patrick, Pasco
Glatt, Daniel, St. Mary, Spokane Valley
Heavey, Thomas, St. Thomas More, Spokane
Kalinowski, Robert, (Retired)
Kestell, James, Cathedral of Our Lady of Lourdes, Spokane
Lopez, Victor, St. Peter, Spokane
Martinez, Gonzalo Chalo, St. Joseph, Otis Orchards
Miller, Michael D., St. Mary, Spokane Valley
Ortega, Victor, St. Patrick, Pasco
Pearman, Perry, St. Mary Presentation, Deer Park
Peterson, Allen, St. Augustine, Spokane
Phelps, Andrew, (Retired), Spokane
Pruneda, Joel, Sacred Heart, Othello
Ramos, Luis, St. Patrick, Pasco
Reyes, Olegario, St. Patrick, Walla Walla
Reyna, Ramiro, St. Vincent, Connell
Ritchie, Dan, (Retired), Spokane
Rodelo, Jesus, Sacred Heart, Othello
Rodriguez, Antonio, St. Patrick, Pasco
Ruscheinsky, John, Immaculate Heart Retreat Center & Cathedral of Our Lady of Lourdes, Spokane
Schaefer, Edward, (On Leave)
Schroeder, Joseph, St. Joseph, Colbert
Schwarzer, James, St. Anthony, Spokane
Senger, Nick, St. Peter, Spokane
Stewart, Kelly, Assumption of the Blessed Virgin Mary, Spokane Valley
Torres, José, St. Joseph, Spokane
Valdovines, Abraham, St. Patrick, Pasco
Wehmeyer, Bill, St. Genevieve, Twisp
Westover, John, (Retired), Ohio
Whitney, Donald, Mary Queen, Spokane.

INSTITUTIONS LOCATED IN DIOCESE

[A] SEMINARIES, DIOCESAN

SPOKANE. *Bishop White Seminary*, 429 E. Sharp Ave., 99202. Tel: 509-313-7100; Email: tferguson@bishopwhitesem.org; Email: info@bishopwhitesem.org; Web: www.bishopwhitesem.org. Very Rev. Daniel J. Barnett, Rector; Rev. Patrick Baraza, Vice Rector & Dean of Men; Dr. Michael Tkacz, Ph.D., Dir. Intellectual Formation; Most Rev. William S. Skylstad, D.D., Dean; Revs. Eugene Tracy, Dean, (Retired); Joachim Hien, Dean, (Retired). Clergy 3; Religious Teachers 3; Faculty 3; Students 16.

[B] COLLEGES AND UNIVERSITIES

SPOKANE. *Gonzaga University* dba Jesuit Community at Gonzaga, 323 E. Boone Ave., 99202. Tel: 509-313-6076; Fax: 509-313-6086; Email: rorholmm@gonzaga.edu. 502 E. Boone, 99258. Revs. Timothy R. Clancy, S.J.; Paul M. Cochran,

S.J.; Thomas Colgan, S.J.; Kevin Connell, S.J.; Michael J. Connolly, S.J.; Stephen M. Hess, S.J.; Kenneth R. Krall, S.J.; Stephen R. Kuder, S.J.; Patrick J. Lee, S.J.; Robert Lyons, S.J.; Joseph Nguyen; Brad Reynolds, S.J.; Quan Tran, S.J.; James K. Voiss, S.J.; Daniel Nevares; Revs. JK Adams, Educator; Kelechi Ahamefula, Doctoral Student; Dzao Vu, Educator; Rev. Jerry Graham, Pastor; Thomas Lamanna, Pastor. College of Arts and Sciences, and Schools of Law, Engineering, Education, Business Administration, Graduate School. Professional Studies Education conducted by the Fathers of the Society of Jesus. Clergy 8; Students 7,563; Lay Faculty 457.

The Ministry Institute dba Mater Dei Ministry Institute (at Gonzaga University) E. 405 Sinto Ave., 99202-1849. Tel: 509-313-5765; Fax: 509-313-5766; Email: bartletts@gonzaga.edu. Nathaniel Greene, Pres.; Shonna Bartlett, Prog. Dir.; Diane Imes, Admin. Dir. Religious Teachers 2; Lay Teachers 6; Priests 6; Sisters 6; Students 13; Lay Administrators 4; Full-time Enrollment 3.

[C] HIGH SCHOOLS, INTERPAROCHIAL

WALLA WALLA. *Walla Walla Catholic School System* dba DeSales Catholic High School, (Grades PreK-12), 919 E. Sumach St., Walla Walla, 99362. Tel: 509-525-3030; Fax: 509-527-0361; Email: wwcs@thewwcs.com; Email: desales@thewwcs.com; Email: jlesko@thewwcs.com; Web: www.wallawallacatholicschools.com. John Lesko, Prin., Assumption; Revs. Matthew Nicks, Pres.; Curtis Seidel, Chap. Religious Teachers 1; Lay Teachers 22; Students 314; Elementary Students 221; High School Students 93.

[D] HIGH SCHOOLS, PRIVATE

SPOKANE. *Gonzaga Preparatory School*, E. 1224 Euclid Ave, 99207. Tel: 509-483-8511; Fax: 509-483-3124; Email: mdougherty@gprep.com; Web: www.gprep.com. Michael Dougherty, Pres.; Ms. Cindy Reopelle, Prin. Religious Teachers 1; Lay Teachers 60; Jesuit Scholastics 1; Students 865; Jesuit Priests 2.

PASCO. *Tri Cities Prep, A Catholic High School*, 9612 St. Thomas Dr., Pasco, 99301. Tel: 509-546-2465; Fax: 509-546-2490; Email: blee@tcprep.org; Email: pbutler@tcprep.org. Mr. Brett Powers, Prin. Lay Teachers 14; Students 152.

[E] INTERPAROCHIAL GRADE SCHOOLS

SPOKANE. *All Saints Catholic School- Primary Building*, (Grades PreK-8), K-4th at Primary Building; Pre-K and 5th-8th at Middle Building 3510 E. 18th Ave., 99223. Tel: 509-534-1098, Ext. 215; Fax: 509-534-1529; Email: ljohnson@allsaintsspokane.net; Web: allsaintsspokane.org. Dr. Lori Johnson, Prin. Clergy 1; Lay Teachers 12; Students 170.

All Saints Catholic School - Middle Building, (Grades K-4), 1428 E. 33rd Ave., 99203. Tel: 509-624-5712; Fax: 509-624-7752; Email: ljohnson@allsaintsspokane.net. Dr. Lori Johnson, Prin. Serving St. Peter, St. Ann, and Our Lady of Fatima Parishes. Clergy 1; Lay Teachers 15; Students 208.

Cataldo Catholic School, (Grades PreK-8), 455 W. 18th Ave., 99203. Tel: 509-624-8759; Fax: 509-624-8763; Email: office@cataldo.org; Web: www.cataldo.org. Mr. Zack Cunningham, Prin. Serving St. Augustine, Sacred Heart, and Cathedral of Our Lady of Lourdes Parishes. Lay Teachers 25; Students 368.

Trinity School, (Grades PreK-8), 2315 N. Cedar, 99205. Tel: 509-327-9369; Fax: 509-328-4128; Email: information@trinityspokane.com; Web: trinityspokane.org. Mrs. Sandra Nokes, Prin.; Ms. Nancy Likarish, Librarian. Serving St. Anthony and St. Joseph Parishes. Clergy 2; Religious Teachers 1; Lay Teachers 10; Students 260; Personnel 20.

COLTON. *Guardian Angel-St. Boniface School*, (Grades K-8), 306 Steptoe, Colton, 99113. Tel: 509-229-3579; Email: gasbschool@colton-wa.com; Web: gasbschool.org. P.O. Box 48, Colton, 99113. Lori Becker, Prin.; Holly Meyer, Librarian. Serving St. Gall and St. Boniface Parishes. Clergy 1; Religious Teachers 1; Lay Teachers 4; Students 16.

WALLA WALLA. *Assumption Elementary School*, (Grades PreK-8), 2066 E. Alder St., Walla Walla, 99362. Tel: 509-525-9283; Fax: 509-527-0848; Email: jlesko@wallawallacatholicschools.com; Email: wwcs@thewwcs.com; Web: www.wallawallacatholicschools.com. Rev. Matthew Nicks, Pres.; John Lesko, Prin. Serving Assumption, St. Francis of Assisi, and St. Patrick Parishes. Lay Teachers 20; Students 221.

[F] GENERAL HOSPITALS

SPOKANE. *Providence Holy Family Hospital (Providence Health & Services-Washington)*, N. 5633 Lidgerwood St., 99208. Tel: 509-482-0111; Email: SHMC@providence.org; Web: www.holy-family.org. Peg Currie, COO / Chief Nursing Officer. Bed Capacity 197; Tot Asst. Annually 197,097; Total Staff 1,061; Chaplains 7.

Providence Sacred Heart Medical Center & Children's Hospital (Providence Health & Services-Washington), W. 101 8th Ave., 99204. Tel: 509-474-3040; Fax: 509-474-3153; Email: PSHMC.information@providence.org; Web: WWW.SHMC.org. Peg Currie, COO, Providence Health Care. Bed Capacity 719; Tot Asst. Annually 629,861; Total Staff 4,565; Chaplains 18.

CHEWELAH. *Providence St. Joseph's Hospital (of Chewelah) (Providence Health & Services-Washington)*, 500 E. Webster, Chewelah, 99109. Tel: 509-935-8211; Fax: 509-935-5205; Email: Kelley.Robertson@providence.org; Web: www.providence.org/stjosephs. 982 E. Columbia Ave., Colville, 99114. Ronald G. Rehn, DHA, CMPE, Chief Exec.; Kelly Corcoran, Dir. Bed Capacity 25; Tot Asst. Annually 32,064; Total Staff 182.

COLVILLE. *Providence Mount Carmel Hospital (Providence Health & Services-Washington)*, 982 E. Columbia Ave., Colville, 99114. Tel: 509-685-5100; Fax: 509-685-2080; Email: Kelley.Robertson@providence.org; Web: www.providence.org/mountcarmel. Ronald G. Rehn, DHA, CMPE, Chief Exec.; Kelly Corcoran, Dir. Bed Capacity 25; Tot Asst. Annually 88,316; Total Staff 322.

PASCO. *Our Lady of Lourdes Hospital at Pasco*, 520 Fourth Ave., Pasco, 99301-2568. Tel: 314-733-8000 ; Email: jimpicciche@ascension.org; Web: www.ascension.org. 11775 Borman Dr., 2nd Fl., Saint Louis, MO 63146. Mr. Joseph Impicciche, Exec. Bed Capacity 127; Sisters of St. Joseph of Carondelet 2; Tot Asst. Annually 400,000; Total Staff 950.

WALLA WALLA. *Providence St. Mary Medical Center* (Part of Providence Health & Services) 401 W. Poplar, Walla Walla, 99362. Tel: 509-897-3320; Fax: 509-897-5950; Email: frank.erickson@providence.org; Web: www.providence.org/stmary. P.O. Box 1477, Walla Walla, 99362. Mrs. Susan Blackburn, COO. Sisters of Providence. Bed Capacity 92; Tot Asst. Annually 450,000; Total Staff 1,300; Volunteers 107.

[G] PROTECTIVE INSTITUTIONS

Catholic Social Service

SPOKANE.

St. Anne's Children and Family Center, 25 W. 5th Ave., 99204. Mailing Address: P.O. Box 2253, 99210-2253. Tel: 509-232-1111; Fax: 509-232-1118 (Childcare Center); Email: dmiller@ccspokane.org; Web: www.stanneskids.com; Web: www.cceasternwa.org. Dietra Miller, Dir. For children 1 month through 8 years of age. Students 217; Staff 48; Total Assisted 217.

Bernadette Place, 925 N. A St. #2, P.O. Box 2253, 99210-2253. Tel: 509-326-2023; Email: loriley@ccspokane.org; Web: www.cceasternwa.org. Robert J. McCann, Ph.D., CEO. Affordable housing for persons with disabilities and special needs. Bed Capacity 9; Tot Asst. Annually 9; Total Staff 1; Total Assisted 9.

Catholic Charities of Spokane aka Catholic Charities Eastern Washington, 12 E. Fifth Ave., 99202. Tel: 509-358-4250; Fax: 509-358-4259; Email: sbrotherton@ccspokane.org; Web: www.cceasternwa.org. P.O. Box 2253, 99210-2253. Robert J. McCann, Ph.D., CEO. Tot Asst. Annually 72,920; Total Staff 328.

House of Charity, 32 W. Pacific, 99201. Tel: 509-624-7821; Fax: 509-742-3463; Email: hschleigh@ccspokane.org; Web: www.cceasternwa.org. P.O. Box 2253, 99210-2253. Heather Schleigh, Dir. Shelter, sleeping program, services and transitional housing for homeless men and women Tot Asst. Annually 176,290; Total Staff 37.

St. Margaret's Shelter, 101 E. Hartson Ave., P.O. Box 2253, 99210-2253. Tel: 509-624-9788; Fax: 509-624-1461; Email: sstadelman@ccspokane.org; Web: www.cceasternwa.org. Sharon Stadelman, Dir. Emergency and transitional shelter for women & children. Bed Capacity 36; Tot Asst. Annually 261; Total Staff 28.

Morning Star Boys' Ranch, 4511 S. Glenrose Rd., 99203. Tel: 509-448-0202; Fax: 509-448-1413; Email: msbr@msbranch.org; Web: morningstarboysranch.org. P.O. Box 8087, 99203. John Hindman, Exec. Dir.; Kate McCaslin, COO. Total Staff 70; Children in Residence 18; Total Assisted 20.

Providence Adult Day Health (Providence Health & Services-Washington), 6018 N. Astor, 99208. Tel: 509-482-2475; Fax: 509-482-2490; Email: oscar.haupt2@providence.org; Web: washington.providence.org. Mr. Oscar Haupt, Business Mgr. Purpose: to provide adult day health programs, including rehab & nursing, to the elderly and disabled. Tot Asst. Annually 13,894; Total Staff 17; Clients 154.

Summit View, 820 N. Summit Blvd., 99201. P.O. Box 2253, 99210-2253. Tel: 509-327-9524; Email: loriley@ccspokane.org; Web: www.cceasternwa.org. Glori Houston, Dir. of Housing. 27 units of housing for families. Total Apartments 27.

Transitional Programs for Women dba Transitions, 3128 N. Hemlock, 99205. Tel: 509-328-6702; Tel: 509-455-4249; Tel: 509-496-0396; Tel: 509-325-2959; Tel: 509-747-9222; Fax: 509-325-9877; Email: info@help4women.org; Email: erice-sauer@help4women.org; Email: styler-babkirk@help4women.org; Email: pnolan@help4women.org; Email: amanning@help4women.org; Email: jborgan@help4women.org; Web: www.help4women.org. Edie A. Rice-Sauer, Exec. Dir. Bed Capacity 247; Tot Asst. Annually 1,775; Total Staff 40.

Miryam's House, 3128 N. Hemlock St., 99205. Tel: 509-747-9222; Fax: 509-747-7261; Email: amanning@help4women.org; Web: www.help4women.com. Edie A. Rice-Sauer, Exec. Transitional housing residential program and supportive services for women in transition. Tot Asst. Annually 60; Total Staff 3.

Transitional Living Center, 3128 N. Hemlock, 99205. Tel: 509-325-2959; Tel: 509-328-6702; Fax: 509-325-9877; Email: erice-sauer@help4women.org; Email: amanning@help4women.org; Web: www.help4women.org. Edie A. Rice-Sauer, Dir. Housing for homeless women & children.

Transitions Bed Capacity 55; Tot Asst. Annually 90; Total Staff 6.

Transitions New Leaf Bakery Cafe, 3104 W. Ft. George Wright Dr., 99204. Tel: 509-496-0396; Fax: 509-325-9877; Email: jborgan@help4women.org. Edie Rice Sauer, Exec. Dir.; Jamie Borgan, Prog. Dir. Staff 4; Total Assisted 100.

Transitions Educare, 3128 N. Hemlock, 99205. Tel: 509-325-2959; Fax: 509-325-8319; Email: erice-sauer@help4women.org. Edie A. Rice-Sauer, Exec. Staff 4; Total Assisted Families 35.

Women's Hearth, 920 W. Second Ave., 99201. Tel: 509-455-4249; Fax: 509-456-3531; Email: styler-babkirk@help4women.org; Web: www.help4women.org. Susan Tyler-Babkirk, Prog. Dir. & Contact Person. A safe place for women at risk. Tot Asst. Annually 1,449; Total Staff 6.

CHEWELAH.

Providence DominiCare, 110 S. 3rd St. E., Chewelah, 99109. Tel: 509-935-4925; Fax: 509-935-4082; Email: joan.sisco@providence.org; Web: washington.providence.org. P.O. Box 1070, Chewelah, 99109. Joan Sisco, Exec. Dir. A home care/personal care service in Stevens, Ferry & Pend Oreille Counties. Tot Asst. Annually 5,500; Total Staff 25.

COLVILLE.

The Rhodena, 230 S. Wynne, Colville, 99114. Tel: 509-459-6183; Fax: 509-358-4259; Email: ghouston@ccspokane.org; Web: www.cceasternwa.org. P.O. Box 2253, 99210-2253. Glori Houston, Dir. A six unit affordable housing complex for families living in Colville, WA. Tot Asst. Annually 6; Total Staff 15.

DAYTON.

Project Timothy: Christian Service Center, 247 E. Main St., Dayton, 99328. Tel: 509-382-2943; Email: tschlachter@hotmail.com; Web: projecttimothy.org. Rev. Steven Werner. Sponsored by St. Joseph Catholic Parish - Dayton Total Families 557; Total Assisted 1,357.

St. Vincent de Paul Store, 247 E. Main, Dayton, 99328. Tel: 509-382-4146; Email: jobobpat@hotmail.com. Mr. Skeeter Reis, Pres.; Bob Patras, Vice Pres.; Lydia C. Buettner, Treas. Total Assisted 753.

WALLA WALLA.

Catholic Charities Walla Walla, 408 W. Poplar, Walla Walla, 99362. Tel: 509-525-0572; Fax: 509-525-0576; Email: tmeliah@ccspokane.org. Mailing Address: P.O. Box 2253, 99210-2253. Tim Meliah, Dir. Tot Asst. Annually 233; Total Staff 4.

[H] SENIOR CITIZEN HOUSING

SPOKANE. *Cathedral Plaza Apartments*, W. 1120 Sprague Ave., 99201. Tel: 509-747-6777; Email: dbyrd@ccspokane.org; Web: www.cceasternwa.org. Mailing Address: P.O. Box 2253, 99210-2253. Glori Houston, Dir. Capacity 150; Staff 5; Total Assisted 150.

The Delaney, Mailing Address: P.O. Box 2253, 99210-2253. Tel: 509-747-5081; Email: delaney@ccspokane.org; Web: www.cceasternwa.org. Glori Houston, Dir. Capacity 84; Staff 3; Total Assisted 84.

Fahy Garden Apartments, W. 1411 Dean Ave.,

99201. Tel: 509-326-6759; Fax: 509-323-5205; Email: fahys@ccspokane.org; Web: www.cceasternwa.org. Mailing Address: P.O. Box 2253, 99210-2253. Glori Houston, Dir. Capacity 31; Staff 5; Total Assisted 31.

Fahy West Apartments, W. 1523 Dean Ave., 99201. Tel: 509-326-6759; Fax: 509-323-5205; Email: fahys@ccspokane.org; Web: www.cceasternwa.org. Mailing Address: P.O. Box 2253, 99210-2253. Glori Houston, Dir. Capacity 55; Staff 5; Total Assisted 55.

The O'Malley Apartments, E. 707 Mission Ave., 99202. Tel: 509-487-1150; Fax: 509-487-1189; Email: omalley@ccspokane.org; Web: www.cceasternwa.org. Mailing Address: P.O. Box 2253, 99210-2253. Glori Houston, Dir. Capacity 99; Tot Asst. Annually 99; Staff 5.

Rockwood Lane, 221 E. Rockwood Blvd., 99202. Tel: 509-838-3200; Fax: 509-838-1688; Email: pbutler@ccspokane.org; Web: www.cceasternwa.org. Mailing Address: P.O. Box 2253, 99210-2253. Glori Houston, Property Mgr. Capacity 106; Tot Asst. Annually 106; Staff 10.

Senior Service - Senior Nutrition, 12 E. 5th Ave, P.O. Box 2253, 99210-2253. Tel: 509-459-6175; Email: tcarroll@ccspokane.org; Web: www.cceasternwa.org. Tom Carroll, Dir. Staff 3; Total Assisted 3,109.

CLARKSTON. *Austen Manor*, 1222 Chestnut St., Clarkston, 99403. Tel: 509-751-9640; Fax: 509-751-9610; Email: austenmanor@ccspokane.org; Web: www.cceasternwa.org. Mailing Address: P.O. Box 2253, 99210-2253. D.J. Joepino, Property Mgr. Capacity 30; Total Staff 2; Total Assisted 30.

PULLMAN. *Pioneer Square*, 220 S.E. Kamiaken St., Pullman, 99163. Tel: 509-332-1106; Fax: 509-332-2516; Email: pioneersquare@ccspokane.org; Web: www.cceasternwa.org. Mailing Address: P.O. Box 2253, 99210-2253. Glori Houston, Dir. Capacity 45; Total Staff 2; Total Assisted 45.

WALLA WALLA. *Garden Court/Mike Foye*, 420 W. Alder St., Walla Walla, 99362. P.O. Box 2253, 99210-2253. Tel: 509-529-4706; Email: ghouston@ccspokane.org; Web: www.cceasternwa.org. Glori Houston, Dir. of Housing. Capacity 45; Tot Asst. Annually 45; Staff 4.

[I] HOMES FOR AGED

SPOKANE. *Emilie Court Assisted Living (Providence Health & Services-Washington)*, 34 E. 8th Ave., 99202-1202. Tel: 509-474-2550; Fax: 509-474-2618; Email: charlene.longworth@providence.org; Web: www.emiliecourt.org. Charlene Longworth, Admin. Bed Capacity 60; Tot Asst. Annually 59; Total Staff 50.

Providence St. Joseph Care Center (Providence Health & Services-Washington) (A Non-profit Corporation) 17 E. 8th Ave., 99202. Tel: 509-474-5678; Tel: 509-474-7924; Email: Marcia.ross@providence.org. Robert Hellrigel, CEO. Sisters of Providence-Mother Joseph Province. Bed Capacity 113; Tot Asst. Annually 410; Total Staff 189; Chaplains 1.

[J] MONASTERIES AND RESIDENCES OF PRIESTS AND BROTHERS

SPOKANE. *Regis Community*, N. 1107 Astor St., 99202. Tel: 509-313-6014; Fax: 509-313-6086; Email: rorholmm@gonzaga.edu. Rev. John V. Murphy, S.J., Pastoral Min./Coord., (Retired); Mr. Paul Grubb, Province Vocation Promoter; Revs. John Izzo, Dir. of Ignatian Way Project; Robert Erickson; Joseph Fortier, S.J.; John O'Leary, S.J., (Retired); George (Max) Oliva; James Torrens; Frank Case, S.J.; Peter J. Byrne, S.J. Bea House.

[K] CONVENTS AND RESIDENCES FOR SISTERS

SPOKANE. *Holy Names Foundation*, 1960 N. Holy Names Ct., 99224. Tel: 503-675-7123; Fax: 503-675-7138; Email: VCummings@snjmuson.org. Sr. Maureen Delaney, Prov. Support for educational activities of Sisters of the Holy Names of Jesus and Mary.

Missionaries of Charity, 5008 N. Lacey St., 99217. Tel: 509-487-3963; Email: jsiira@dioceseofspokane.org. Mother Rose Poor, Supr. Sisters 3.

Monastery of St. Clare dba Poor Clare Nuns, 4419 N. Hawthorne St., 99205-1399. Tel: 509-327-4479; Fax: 509-327-5171; Email: stclare800@gmail.com; Web: www.calledbyjoy.com. Sr. Marcia Kay LaCour, O.S.C., Abbess. Papal Enclosure Novitiate.

Franciscan Monastery of St. Clare Professed Cloistered Nuns 5.

Sisters of the Holy Names, 1960 N. Holy Names Ct., 99224. Tel: 503-675-7123; Fax: 503-675-7138; Email: vcummings@snjmuson.org. Viki Cummings. Sisters of the Holy Names of Jesus and Mary (U.S. Ontario Province). Sisters 30.

NEWPORT. *Carmelite Sisters of Mary*, 2892 Hwy. 211, Newport, 99156. Tel: 509-292-0978; Email: carmelitesrsofmary@ifiber.tv. Sr. Leslie L. Lund, Prioress, Email: carmelitesrsofmary@ifiber.tv. Sisters 2; Hermitages 6.

[L] ASSOCIATIONS OF THE FAITHFUL

SPOKANE. *Sisters of Mary, Mother of the Church*, 4624 E. Jamieson Rd., 99223. Tel: 509-448-9890; Email: sistermarybeth@yahoo.com; Web: www.sistersofmarymc.org. Mother Kathryn Joseph, S.M.M.C., Supr.; Sr. Marybeth, S.M.M.C., Business Mgr. Members 10.

[M] RETREAT HOUSES

SPOKANE. *Immaculate Heart Retreat Center*, 6910 S. Ben Burr Rd., 99223. Tel: 509-448-1224; Fax: 509-448-1623; Email: ihrc@ihrc.net; Web: www.ihrc.net. Deacon John Ruscheinsky, Dir.

KAIROS House of Prayer, 1714 W. Stearns Rd., 99208. Tel: 509-466-2187; Email: mscole@dioceseofspokane.org. Sisters M. Florence Leone Poch, O.S.F., Coord.; Rita Beaulieu. Provides a place called to a prayerful, reflective environment for people of all faiths. Spiritual accompaniment is available.

Spiritual Exercises in Everyday Life (SEEL), 330 E. Boone Ave., 99202. Tel: 509-313-5898; Fax: 509-313-5892; Email: seelspokane@gmail.com. Jennifer Doolittle, Dir.

[N] NEWMAN CENTERS

CHENEY. *Catholic Newman Center at Eastern Washington University*, 837 Elm St., Cheney, 99004. Tel: 509-235-8402; Email: newmanewu@gmail.com; Web: www.ewucatholics.org. Peter Guthrie, Dir.; Rev. Paul Heric, Pastor.

PULLMAN. *St. Thomas More Catholic Student Center - Washington State University* aka Newman Center, 820 N.E. B St., Pullman, 99163-4025. Tel: 509-332-6311; Email: catholiccougs@gmail.com; Web: www.catholiccougs.org. Rev. Lucas E. Tomson, Pastor. Employees 5; Adult Baptisms (18 & Older) 2; Infant Baptisms (up to age 7) 5; Catholic Marriages 1; Estimated Number of Catholics 250; Number Received Into Full Communion 13.

[O] MISCELLANEOUS

SPOKANE. *Catholic Charities Foundation*, 12 E. 5th Ave., 99202. Tel: 509-358-4250; Fax: 509-358-4259; Email: abyrd@ccspokane.org. P.O. Box 2253, 99210-2253. Ann Marie Byrd, Dir.

Family to Family (2017) 505 W. St. Thomas More Way, 99208. Tel: 509-466-0740; Email: ftfguatemala@gmail.com; Web: familytofamilyguatemala.com. Mrs. Miriam Devaney, Admin.

Holy Names Music Center, 3910 W. Custer Dr., 99224. Tel: 509-326-9516; Fax: 509-326-7155; Email: music@hnmc.org; Web: www.hnmc.org. Suzanne Bjork, Admin. Sponsored by Sisters of the Holy Names, Washington Province. Lay Teachers 35; Sisters 4; Students 500.

Immaculate Heart Retreat Center Foundation, 6910 S. Ben Burr Rd., 99223-1819. Tel: 509-448-1224; Fax: 509-448-1623; Email: ihrc@ihrc.net. Deacon John Ruscheinsky, Dir.

Kateri Northwest Ministry Institute, 330 E. Boone Ave., 99202. Tel: 509-313-7024; Fax: 509-313-5892; Email: katerinmi@gmail.com; Email: kateri@katerinmi.org; Web: www.katerinmi.org. P.O. Box 4693, 99220. Rev. Michael Fitzpatrick, S.J., Dir.; Jenny Edgren, Office Mgr. Kateri Northwest Ministry Institute is a Jesuit-affiliated formation program dedicated to the development of all ministries needed for reservation- and urban-based Indian Catholic church communities of the Northwest. Forming church communities to be fully Native and fully Catholic, Kateri Northwest Ministry Institute endeavors to build up and support Native people and those working among Native Americans, empowering the people to assume leadership roles within their own church communities.

**L'Arche Spokane*, 703 E. Nora Ave., 99207-2455. Tel: 509-483-0438; Fax: 509-483-0460; Email: info@larcheofspokane.org; Web: www.larcheofspokane.org. Malia Walden, Office Mgr.; Maurine Barrett, Dir. & Community Leader. Total Assisted 12.

Nazareth Guild, 12 E. 5th Ave., 99202. Tel: 509-744-3257; Tel: 509-744-3259; Email: dbattaglia@dioceseofspokane.org; Email: alee@dioceseofspokane.org; Web: nazarethguild.org. P.O. Box 76, 99210. Alexandra Lee, Dir.; Debbie Battaglia, Business Mgr.

Our Lady of La Vang Center (2016) 2227 N. Cedar St., 99205. Tel: 509-328-1467; Email: vdao@dioceseofspokane.org. 2320 N. Cedar St., 99205. Rev. Vincent Van Dao Nguyen, Pastor.

Providence Health Care (Providence Health & Services-Washington), 101 W. 8th Ave., Mother Gamelin Center, 99204. Tel: 509-474-7126; Fax: 509-474-7324; Email: lori.staley@providence.org; Email: Patricia.petersen@providence.org. Ms. Elaine Couture, CEO. Providence Health Care is an integrated healthcare delivery network made up of: Providence Sacred Heart Medical Center and Children's Hospital, Providence Holy Family Hospital, Providence Mount Carmel Hospital, Providence St. Joseph's Hospital, Providence Adult Day Health, Providence DominiCare, and Providence Physician Services.

Providence Medical Research Center, 105 W. 8th Ave., Ste. 6050W, 99204. Tel: 509-474-4345; Tel: 509-474-4345; Fax: 509-474-4325; Email: Joy.Durham@providence.org; Email: Lori.Staley@providence.org. Ms. Elaine Couture, CEO.

Serra Club of Spokane, P.O. Box 31535, 99223-3025. Tel: 509-468-6774; Email: dominis60@gmail.com; Web: www.serraclubofspokane.com. Steve Domini, Pres.

The Catholic Foundation of Eastern Washington, 1023 W. Riverside Ave., 99210. Tel: 509-358-7334; Email: mtracy@dioceseofspokane.org; Web: www.spokanecatholicfoundation.com. P.O. Box 1484, 99210. Sr. Mary E. Tracy, S.N.J.M., Exec. Dir.

DAYTON. *St. Mark Waitsburg and St. Joseph Dayton Catholic Parish Foundation*, 112 S. 1st St., Dayton, 99328. Tel: 509-382-2311; Email: stjosephdayton@dioceseofspokane.org. P.O. Box 0003, Dayton, 99328-0003. Rev. Steven Werner.

POMEROY. *Holy Rosary Catholic Church Foundation of Garfield County*, 634 High St., Pomeroy, 99347. Tel: 509-843-3801; Email: holyrosarypomeroy@dioceseofspokane.org. Rev. Steven Werner.

RELIGIOUS INSTITUTES OF MEN REPRESENTED IN THE DIOCESE

For further details refer to the corresponding bracketed number in the Religious Institutes of Men or Women section.

[0520]—*Franciscan Friars* (Santa Barbara Prov.)—O.F.M.

[0690]—*Jesuit Fathers and Brothers*—S.J.

RELIGIOUS INSTITUTES OF WOMEN REPRESENTED IN THE DIOCESE

[1780]—*Congregation of the Sisters of the Third Order of St. Francis of Perpetual Adoration*—F.S.P.A.

[1070-03]—*Dominican Sisters*—O.P.

[1180]—*Franciscan Sisters of Allegany, New York*—O.S.F.

[3760]—*Order of St. Clare*—O.S.C.

[]—*Sisters for Christian Community Eastern Washington Area Communication.*

[3350]—*Sisters of Providence*—S.P.

[1650]—*The Sisters of St. Francis of Philadelphia*—O.S.F.

[3840]—*Sisters of St. Joseph of Carondelet*—C.S.J.

[1990]—*Sisters of the Holy Names of Jesus and Mary*—S.N.J.M.

DIOCESAN CEMETERIES

SPOKANE. *Catholic Cemeteries of Spokane*, 7200 N. Wall St., 99208. P.O. Box 18006, 99228. Tel: 509-467-5496; Fax: 509-467-6649; Email: info@holycrossofspokane.org; Web: www.holycrossofspokane.org. Rick McLean, Dir.

Holy Cross Funeral and Cemetery Center, 7200 N. Wall St., 99208. P.O. Box 18006, 99228. Tel: 509-467-5496; Fax: 509-467-6649; Email: info@holycrossofspokane.org; Web: www.holycrossofspokane.org. Rick McLean, Dir.

St. Joseph Funeral and Cemetery Center, 17825 E. Trent Ave., 99216. P.O. Box 18006, 99228. Tel: 509-467-5496; Fax: 509-467-6649; Email: info@holycrossofspokane.org; Web: www.holycrossofspokane.org. Rick McLean, Dir.

Mary Queen of Peace Funeral and Cemetery Center, 6910 S. Ben Burr Rd., 99223. P.O. Box 18006, 99228. Tel: 509-467-5496; Fax: 509-467-6649; Email: info@holycrossofspokane.org; Web: www.holycrossofspokane.org. Rick McLean, Dir.

NECROLOGY

† Haspedis, George, (Retired), Died Nov. 3, 2018

An asterisk (*) denotes an organization that has established tax-exempt status directly with the IRS and is not covered by the USCCB Group Ruling.

Diocese of Springfield-Cape Girardeau

(Dioecesis Campifontis-Capitis Girardeauensis)

Most Reverend

EDWARD M. RICE

Bishop of Springfield-Cape Girardeau; ordained January 3, 1987; appointed Auxiliary Bishop of Saint Louis and Titular Bishop of Sufes December 1, 2010; ordained January 13, 2011; appointed Bishop of Springfield-Cape Girardeau April 26, 2016; installed June 1, 2016. *The Catholic Center, 601 S. Jefferson Ave., Springfield, MO 65806-3143.*

Most Reverend

JOHN J. LEIBRECHT, D.D., PH.D.

Bishop Emeritus of Springfield-Cape Girardeau; ordained March 17, 1956; appointed Bishop of Springfield-Cape Girardeau October 23, 1984; consecrated December 12, 1984; retired January 24, 2008. *Res.: 1152 W. Camino Alto St., Springfield, MO 65810.* Tel: 417-987-0884; Email: jleibrecht@mchsi.com.

Chancery Office: The Catholic Center, 601 S. Jefferson Ave., Springfield, MO 65806-3143. Tel: 417-866-0841; Fax: 417-866-1140.

Web: www.dioscg.org

Email: treidy@dioscg.org

ESTABLISHED AUGUST 24, 1956.

Square Miles 25,719.

Comprises the following Counties in the State of Missouri: Barry, Barton, Bollinger, Butler, Cape Girardeau, Carter, Cedar, Christian, Dade, Dallas, Dent, Douglas, Dunklin, Greene, Howell, Iron, Jasper, Laclede, Lawrence, McDonald, Madison, Mississippi, New Madrid, Newton, Oregon, Ozark, Pemiscot, Polk, Reynolds, Ripley, Scott, Shannon, Stoddard, Stone, Taney, Texas, Wayne, Webster and Wright.

For legal titles of parishes and diocesan institutions, consult The Catholic Center.

STATISTICAL OVERVIEW

Personnel	
Bishop	1
Retired Bishops	1
Abbots	1
Retired Abbots	1
Priests: Diocesan Active in Diocese	41
Priests: Retired, Sick or Absent	27
Number of Diocesan Priests	68
Religious Priests in Diocese	55
Total Priests in Diocese	123
Extern Priests in Diocese	11
Ordinations:	
Diocesan Priests	2
Religious Priests	1
Permanent Deacons	3
Permanent Deacons in Diocese	27
Total Brothers	45
Total Sisters	54
Parishes	
Parishes	66
With Resident Pastor:	
Resident Diocesan Priests	35
Resident Religious Priests	10
Without Resident Pastor:	
Administered by Priests	21
Missions	18
Pastoral Centers	4
Professional Ministry Personnel:	
Sisters	9
Lay Ministers	74
Welfare	
Catholic Hospitals	8
Total Assisted	1,000,000
Health Care Centers	85
Total Assisted	2,700,000
Homes for the Aged	1
Total Assisted	250
Day Care Centers	1
Total Assisted	33
Specialized Homes	1
Total Assisted	200
Educational	
Diocesan Students in Other Seminaries	11
Total Seminarians	11
High Schools, Diocesan and Parish	3
Total Students	990
Elementary Schools, Diocesan and Parish	23
Total Students	3,567
Catechesis/Religious Education:	
High School Students	962
Elementary Students	2,781
Total Students under Catholic Instruction	8,311
Teachers in the Diocese:	
Brothers	1
Sisters	5
Lay Teachers	356
Vital Statistics	
Receptions into the Church:	
Infant Baptism Totals	620
Minor Baptism Totals	71
Adult Baptism Totals	125
Received into Full Communion	172
First Communions	1,059
Confirmations	762
Marriages:	
Catholic	221
Interfaith	36
Total Marriages	257
Deaths	540
Total Catholic Population	64,974
Total Population	13,583,859

Former Bishops—Most Revs. CHARLES H. HELMSING, D.D., cons. as Titular Bishop of Axomis and Auxiliary Bishop of Archdiocese of St. Louis, April 19, 1949; appt. Bishop of Springfield-Cape Girardeau, Aug. 24, 1956; transferred to Diocese of Kansas City-St. Joseph, Jan. 27, 1962; retired Aug. 17, 1977; died Dec. 20, 1993; IGNATIUS J. STRECKER, D.D., appt. April 7, 1962; cons. June 20, 1962; transferred to Archdiocese of Kansas City in Kansas, Sept. 10, 1969; retired Sept. 8, 1993; died Oct. 16, 2003; His Eminence WILLIAM CARDINAL BAUM, S.T.D., appt. Feb. 18, 1970; cons. April 6, 1970; transferred to Archdiocese of Washington D.C., May 9, 1973; elevated to Cardinal, May 24, 1976; appt. Prefect, Congregation for Catholic Education in the Vatican, Jan. 15, 1980; Major Penitentiary, appt. April 6, 1990.; retired Nov. 22, 2001; died July 23, 2015; BERNARD CARDINAL LAW, D.D., ord. May 21, 1961; appt. Bishop of Springfield-Cape Girardeau, Oct. 22, 1973; cons. Dec. 5, 1973; appt. Archbishop of Boston, Jan. 23, 1984; elevated to Cardinal, May 25, 1985; resigned Dec. 13, 2002; appt. Archpriest of St. Mary Major Basilica, Rome, Italy May 27, 2004; retired Nov. 21, 2011; died Dec. 20, 2017.; Most Revs. JOHN J. LEIBRECHT, D.D., Ph.D., ord. March 17, 1956; appt. Bishop of Springfield-Cape Girardeau Oct. 23, 1984; cons. Dec. 12, 1984; retired Jan. 24, 2008.; JAMES V. JOHNSTON JR., ord. June 9, 1990; appt. Bishop of Springfield-Cape Girardeau Jan. 24, 2008; ord. March 31, 2008; appt. Bishop of Kansas City-Saint Joseph Sept. 15, 2015; ord. Nov. 4, 2015.

Vicar General—Rev. Msgr. THOMAS E. REIDY, V.G.

Chancery Office—The Catholic Center, 601 S. Jefferson Ave., Springfield, 65806-3143. Tel: 417-866-0841; Fax: 417-866-1140.

Chancellor—Rev. Msgr. THOMAS E. REIDY, V.G.

Vice Chancellor—Rev. THOMAS P. KIEFER, J.C.L.

Regional Priest Moderators—Region I: Rev. JOHN (J.) F. FRIEDEL, M.A., M.Div. Region II: VACANT. Region III: Rev. MARK J. BINDER. Region IV: Rev. MICHAEL V. MCDEVITT, M.A., M.Div. Region V: VACANT. Region VI: Rev. JAMES J. UNTERREINER. Region VII: Rev. JOHN M. HARTH. Region VIII: VACANT. Region IX: VACANT.

Office of Administration

Catholic Foundation Of The Diocese Of Springfield-Cape Girardeau—Most Rev. EDWARD M. RICE, Pres.; Rev. Msgr. THOMAS E. REIDY, V.G., Vice Pres.; MS. JANET L. SMITH, Sec. Treas.

Development and Properties—DR. EUGENE AUG, Ph.D., Dir.

Diocesan Development Fund—DR. EUGENE AUG, Ph.D., Dir. Devel. & Properties; Most Rev. EDWARD M. RICE; Revs. DAVID N. COON; MARK J. BINDER; MRS. LESLIE A. EIDSON; MS. JANET L. SMITH; TAMMY STANDER; MARC TRUBY; PAM WESBECHER; RON WESBECHER.

Finance—MS. JANET L. SMITH, Dir.

Financial Council—MS. JANET L. SMITH, Dir. Finance; DR. EUGENE AUG, Ph.D., Diocesan Dir., Devel. & Properties; MR. LARRY G. GRINSTEAD; MR. TOM BARR; MR. CHRIS CHURCHWELL; MR. LOUIS GRIESEMER; MR. STAN IRWIN; MRS. ANN SAUNDERS.

Planned Giving—DR. EUGENE AUG, Ph.D., Coord.

Office of Education

Catholic Schools—DR. EUGENE AUG, Ph.D., Interim Supt. Schools.

Office of Communications, Media & Publications—MRS. LESLIE A. EIDSON, Dir.

Newspaper, Diocese of Springfield-Cape Girardeau—"The Mirror"; quarterly Spanish newspaper, "Rostros" MRS. LESLIE A. EIDSON, Editor; MRS. ANGIE TOBEN, Circulation & Administrative Asst.

Ecumenism—Rev. Msgr. THOMAS E. REIDY, V.G.; MR. NICHOLAS C. LUND-MOLFESE, M.A., J.D.

Office of Ministry

Campus Ministries—Revs. JOHN (J.) F. FRIEDEL, M.A., M.Div., Diocesan Dir. & Chap. Missouri Southern State Univ., Tel: 417-623-8643; FRANCISCO JAVIER, C.M.F., Missouri State Univ. Campus Min., Tel: 417-865-0802; Sr. MICHELLE NGUYEN, C.M.R., Pastoral Assoc., Missouri State Univ. Campus Min., Tel: 417-865-0802; Deacon THOMAS J. SCHUMER, Southeast Missouri State Univ. Campus Min., Tel: 573-335-3899; Rev. PATRICK I. NWOKOYE, Ph.D., Southeast Missouri State Univ. Campus Min. & Priest Chap.

Diaconate (Permanent)—Rev. DAVID F. HULSHOF, M.A., Dir.; Deacon WALTER L. BIRI, Asst. Dir.

Diocesan Director of Continuing Formation of Clergy—Rev. Msgr. THOMAS E. REIDY, V.G.

Family Ministries—MR. NICHOLAS C. LUND-MOLFESE, M.A., J.D.

Diocesan Council on Family Ministries—MR. NICHOLAS C. LUND-MOLFESE, M.A., J.D. Region I: Rev. JOHN (J.) F. FRIEDEL, M.A., M.Div. Region II: Rev. DAVID BAUNACH. Region III: VACANT. Region IV: VACANT. Region V: Rev. SHOBY MATHEW CHETTIYATH. Region VI: VACANT. Region VII: Rev. DAVID N. COON; ROB BUNGER; KIM BUNGER; CHRIS DITTMER; NATALIE DITTMER; ALAN ESSNER; DENISE ESSNER. Region VIII: VACANT. Region IX: VACANT.

Natural Family Planning—MR. NICHOLAS C. LUND-MOLFESE, M.A., J.D.

Rite of Christian Initiation of Adults—Co Directors: Rev. DAVID J. DOHOGNE; MRS. LYNN MELENDEZ.

Hispanic Ministries—MRS. MILAGROS CALVETTI, Dir.

Social Ministries, Evangelization, and Formation—MR. NICHOLAS C. LUND-MOLFESE, M.A., J.D., Dir.

**Catholic Charities of Southern Missouri, Inc.—St. Anne Campus, 424 E. Monastery St., Springfield, 65807.* Tel: 417-720-4213; Fax: 417-866-1140; Email: ccsomo@ccsomo.org. MRS. MAURA A. TAYLOR, Exec. Dir.

Office of Child and Youth Protection—WILLIAM J. HOLTMEYER JR., M.S., N.C.C., L.P.C., C.E.A.P., Q-SAP.

Victim Assistance Coordinator—JUDY A. ST. JOHN, L.P.C., N.C.C., Tel: 573-587-3139; Email: vacl@dioscg.org.

Tribunal—

Judicial Vicar—Rev. THOMAS P. KIEFER, J.C.L.

Adjutant Judicial Vicar—Rev. VINCENT E. BERTRAND, J.C.L.

Coordinator—Rev. MICHAEL P. JOYCE, C.M.

Auditor—Rev. Msgr. THOMAS E. REIDY, V.G.

Judges—Revs. VINCENT E. BERTRAND, J.C.L.; THOMAS P. KIEFER, J.C.L.; Rev. Msgr. THOMAS E. REIDY, V.G.

Promoter of Justice—Rev. MICHAEL P. JOYCE, C.M.

Advocates for the Petitioners—Parish Priests, deacons, and pastoral ministers.

Advocates for the Respondent—Revs. MICHAEL V. MCDEVITT, M.A., M.Div.; DAVID F. HULSHOF, M.A.; RICK L. JONES, M.Div., L.P.C.

Defender of the Bond—VACANT.

Notary—MRS. LINDA MURPHY.

Vicar For The Religious—Rev. Msgr. THOMAS E. REIDY, V.G.

Vocations-Seminarians—Rev. SCOTT M. SUNNENBERG, Dir. Vocations/Seminarians.

Youth Ministry—MRS. LYNN MELENDEZ.

Catholic Scouting—Rev. PATRICK I. NWOKOYE, Ph.D., Diocesan Chap., Tel: 573-335-3899; MR. JOHN NEWTON, Assoc. Diocesan Chap., Tel: 417-866-0841.

Camp Re-NEW-All—MRS. KIM SELLERS, Camp Dir.; MS. MEAGAN MOORE, Camp Dir.; MS. MARY BLACK, Camp Dir.

Office of Worship

Office of Worship—Rev. DAVID J. DOHOGNE, Dir.

Liturgical Commission—Rev. DAVID J. DOHOGNE, Dir. Office of Worship.

Priests' Eucharistic League Confraternity of The Most Blessed Sacrament—Rev. MICHAEL V. MCDEVITT, M.A., M.Div., Dir.

Officials And Committees

Catholic Relief Services—Rev. Msgr. THOMAS E. REIDY, V.G.

Cemeteries—Rev. Msgr. THOMAS E. REIDY, V.G.

Censor—Rev. ALLAN L. SAUNDERS.

Health Affairs—MR. NICHOLAS C. LUND-MOLFESE, M.A., J.D., Dir.

Project Rachel (Post Abortion Ministry)—KIM BRAYMAN, Coord.

Missionary Apostolate - Society for the Propagation of the FaithRev. GLENN A. EFTINK, Tel: 573-722-3504.

National Shrine Of The Immaculate Conception—Rev. Msgr. THOMAS E. REIDY, V.G., Dir.

Priests' Mutual Benefit Society—Rev. Msgr. THOMAS E. REIDY, V.G., Exec. Sec.; Revs. FERGUS MONAGHAN; NORMAND G. VARONE, (Retired); LEWIS E. HEJNA; MICHAEL V. MCDEVITT, M.A., M.Div.; DAVID F. HULSHOF, M.A.; ALLAN L. SAUNDERS; JOHN M. HARTH.

Pro-Life Director—MR. NICHOLAS C. LUND-MOLFESE, M.A., J.D.

Diocesan Consultative Groups

Diocesan Consultors—Revs. JOHN (J.) F. FRIEDEL, M.A., M.Div.; THOMAS P. KIEFER, J.C.L.; Rev. Msgr. THOMAS E. REIDY, V.G.; Revs. HENRY GRODECKI, C.M.; ALLAN L. SAUNDERS; DAVID F. HULSHOF, M.A.; DAVID J. DOHOGNE.

Presbyteral Council—Revs. COLBY J. ELBERT; DANIEL ROBLES; JOSEPH WEIDENBENNER; SHERMAN B. WALL, O.M.I.; GASPAR MASILAMANI, C.M.F; WILLIAM M. HODGSON; JOSEPH KELLY; CHARLES DUNN; DAVID N. COON; THOMAS P. KIEFER, J.C.L. Appointed Member: Rev. Msgr. THOMAS E. REIDY, V.G.

Diocesan Pastoral Council—Most Rev. EDWARD M. RICE.

Diocesan School Board—DR. EUGENE AUG, Ph.D., Interim Supt.; Rev. WILLIAM M. HODGSON; JULIA GRIESEMER-BENTLEY; MRS. BECKI ESSNER; Bro. DAVID ANTHONY MIGLIORINO, O.S.F.; LAURA JUSTISS; VALDIS ZALITE; BLAKE ZAPLETAL; MRS. CHERYL HALL; SONDRA HULSHOF; TINA SIDES.

Diocesan Lay Endowment Board—Rev. DAVID F. HULSHOF, M.A., Chm.; STEPHEN ADAMS; GREG ECK; RITA LUECKENOTTE; MRS. LYNN MELENDEZ; RITA OTRADOVC.

Catholic Organizations And Movements

Charismatic Prayer Groups—MRS. MILAGROS CALVETTI.

Cursillo Movement—SHARON ESSNER; Rev. WILLIAM M. HODGSON.

Secretariat for Cursillo—Rev. WILLIAM M. HODGSON, Diocesan Chap.

St. Francis de Sales Association—Rev. Msgr. THOMAS E. REIDY, V.G., Chap.; Rev. GLENN A. EFTINK.

Diocesan Council of Catholic Women (DCCW)—Tel: 573-979-7599. Rev. JAMES J. UNTERREINER, Diocesan Spiritual Moderator; JOYCE LUTEN, Dir. At-Large.

Apostolates And Commissions

Apostolate to the Deaf—Rev. DAVID L. MILLER, Dir., Tel: 417-532-4811.

State Office

Diocesan Delegates To The Missouri Catholic Conference—

Public Policy Committee—MR. NICHOLAS C. LUND-MOLFESE, M.A., J.D.; MARYANN MITTS.

CLERGY, PARISHES, MISSIONS AND PAROCHIAL SCHOOLS

CITY OF SPRINGFIELD

(GREENE COUNTY)

1—CATHEDRAL OF ST. AGNES (1908) [CEM] [JC]
533 S. Jefferson Ave., 65806. Tel: 417-831-3565; Fax: 417-865-0367; Email: stagnesfrontdesk@gmail.com; Web: www.saintagnescathedral.org. Revs. Lewis E. Hejna; Joseph Stoverink; Patrick M. Mac The Tran, C.M.C.; Sr. Elizabeth Ann Weiler, A.S.C., Min. of Care.
School—Cathedral of St. Agnes School, (Grades 1-8), 531 S. Jefferson Ave., 65806. Tel: 417-866-5038; Fax: 417-866-2906; Email: lpaulsell@scspk12.org; Web: www.scspk12.org. Ms. Lindsay Paulsell, Prin. Aides 4; Lay Teachers 16; Students 188; Counselor 1.
Catechesis Religious Program—Students 37.

2—ST. ELIZABETH ANN SETON (1981) [CEM]
2200 W. Republic Rd., 65807. Tel: 417-887-6472; Email: parishinfo@seaschurch.org; Web: www.seaschurch.org. Rev. Msgr. Thomas E. Reidy, V.G.; Rev. Colby J. Elbert; Sisters Pat Hall, RCIA Coord.; Bernadette Goessling, S.S.N.D., RCIA Coord.; Deacon Thomas M. Brewer, RCIA Dir.
School—St. Elizabeth Ann Seton School, (Grades 1-8), Tel: 417-887-6056; Fax: 417-887-2189; Email: chall@scspk12.org; Web: www.scspk12.org. Mrs. Cheryl Hall, Prin. Aides 7; Lay Teachers 30; Students 230.
Catechesis Religious Program—Students 394.

3—HOLY TRINITY (1966) [JC]
2818 E. Bennett, 65804. Tel: 417-883-3440; Fax: 417-883-0072; Email: tkile@holytrinityspringfield.com; Web: www.holytrinity-catholic.com. Rev. J. Fergus Monaghan; Mary Gray, Music Coord.; Rev. Jerome Amaechi, In Res.
Catechesis Religious Program—Students 131.

4—IMMACULATE CONCEPTION (1868) [JC]
3555 S. Fremont, 65804. Tel: 417-887-0600; Fax: 417-887-0027; Email: staff@ic-parish.org; Web: www.ic-parish.org. Rev. Thomas P. Kiefer, J.C.L.
Res.: 3535 S. Fremont, 65804.
School—Immaculate Conception School, (Grades 1-8), 3555A S. Fremont, 65804. Tel: 417-881-7000; Fax: 417-881-7087; Email: tcoleman@scspk12.org. Teresa Coleman, Prin. Aides 11; Lay Teachers 27; Students 507.
Catechesis Religious Program—Students 70.

5—ST. JOSEPH (1892) [JC]
1115 N. Campbell Ave., 65802. Tel: 417-865-1112; Fax: 417-865-7488; Email: stjosephspmo@yahoo.com; Web: www.stjosephspmo.org. Rev. Karl Barmann, O.S.B.; Deacon Mathey F. Fletcher.
School—St. Joseph School, (Grades 1-8), 515 W. Scott, 65802. Tel: 417-866-0667; Fax: 417-866-2862; Email: bjohnson@stjosephcatholicacademy.org; Web: www.stjosephcatholicacademy.org. Bonnie Johnson, Prin. Aides 1; Lay Teachers 11; Students 67; Counselor 1.
Catechesis Religious Program—Students 69.

6—SACRED HEART (1882) [JC]
Mailing Address: 1609 N. Summit, 65803.
Tel: 417-869-3646; Fax: 417-869-2218; Email: sheartch@sbcglobal.net; Web: www.sacredheartch.org. Rev. Gasper Masilamoni, C.M.F.; Jim Farrar; Andrew Peters, Music Dir. In Res., Rev. Joseph A. Orthel.
Catechesis Religious Program—Students 233.

CITY OF CAPE GIRARDEAU

(CAPE GIRARDEAU COUNTY)

1—CATHEDRAL OF ST. MARY OF THE ANNUNCIATION (1868) [CEM] [JC]
Mailing Address: 615 William St., Cape Girardeau, 63703. Tel: 573-335-9347; Fax: 573-335-0649; Email: smparish@stmarycathedral.net; Web: www.stmarycathedral.net. Rev. Allan L. Saunders; Victor Anokwute.
Res.: 629 William St., Cape Girardeau, 63703.
School—Cathedral of St. Mary of the Annunciation School, (Grades 1-8), 210 S. Sprigg, Cape Girardeau, 63703. Tel: 573-335-3840; Email: christineostendorf@stmarycape.org. Christine Ostendorf, Prin. Aides 2; Clergy 3; Lay Teachers 17; Students 216.
Catechesis Religious Program—Brenda Kuhn, D.R.E. Students 293.
Old St. Vincent's—(Chapel of Ease).

2—ST. VINCENT DE PAUL (1836)
1913 Ritter Dr, Cape Girardeau, 63701.
Tel: 573-335-7667; Fax: 573-335-0034; Email: contactus@svparish.com; Web: www.svcape.com. Revs. Rick L. Jones, M.Div., L.P.C.; Alexander Nwagwu; Deacons Robbie R. Huff; Thomas J. Schumer; Mark Kiblinger.
Res.: 741 N. Forest, Cape Girardeau, 63701.
School—St. Vincent de Paul School, (Grades 1-8), 1919 Ritter Dr., Cape Girardeau, 63701.
Tel: 573-334-9594; Fax: 573-334-0425; Email: kglastetter@svcape.eduk12.net. Mrs. Kay Glastetter, Prin. Aides 10; Lay Teachers 27; Religious 1; Students 417.
Catechesis Religious Program—Students 116.

OUTSIDE THE CITIES OF SPRINGFIELD AND CAPE GIRARDEAU

ADVANCE, STODDARD CO., ST. JOSEPH (1905) [CEM]
33921 State Highway 91, Advance, NC 63730. Rev. Glenn A. Eftink.
Res.: P.O. Box 640, Advance, 63730.
Catechesis Religious Program—Students 23.

AURORA, LAWRENCE CO., HOLY TRINITY (1906) [CEM]
Hwy. 60 & Carnation Rd. (22383 Lawrence 1180), P.O. Box 533, Aurora, 65605. Tel: 417-678-2403; Fax: 417-678-2551; Email: htcc482@outlook.com. Paul Pudhota.
Catechesis Religious Program—Students 38.

BENTON, SCOTT CO., ST. DENIS (1840) [CEM]
P.O. Box 127, Benton, 63736. Tel: 573-545-3864; Email: stdenisparishoffice@yahoo.com; Web: saintdenisbenton.weebly.com. 135 N Winchester, Benton, 63736. Rev. Bala Swamy Govindu.
School—St. Denis School, (Grades 1-8), 105 N. Winchester, P.O. Box 189, Benton, 63736.
Tel: 573-545-3017; Fax: 573-545-9185; Email:

karenpowers650@yahoo.com; Web: stdenisbenton.eduk12.net. Mrs. Karen Powers, Prin. Aides 1; Lay Teachers 9; Students 104.
Catechesis Religious Program—Students 8.
BILLINGS, CHRISTIAN CO., ST. JOSEPH (1879) [CEM]
320 N.W. Washington Ave., P.O. Box 100, Billings, 65610. Tel: 417-744-2490; Fax: 417-744-2490; Email: stjosephbillinmo@aol.com. Rev. Augustine R. Njuu, A.J.
Catechesis Religious Program—Students 87.
BOLIVAR, POLK CO., SACRED HEART (1946) [CEM]
1405 W. Fair Play St., Bolivar, 65613.
Tel: 417-326-5596; Fax: 417-326-5596; Email: shoffice@windstream.net; Web: www.sacredheartbolivar.org. Rev. Scott M. Sunnenberg.
Catechesis Religious Program—Students 64.
Mission—St. Catherine of Siena, P.O. Box 42, Humansville, Polk Co. 65674.
BRANSON, TANEY CO., OUR LADY OF THE LAKE (1922)
203 Vaughn Dr., Branson, 65616. Tel: 417-334-2928; Fax: 417-334-6883; Email: OLLBranson@suddenlinkmail.com; Web: www.ladyofthelakeparish.org. Revs. David F. Hulshof, M.A.; Joseph Kelly; Deacons Daniel Vaughn; Richard Harden; David Wright, Business Mgr.; Mrs. Pat Hutcheson, D.R.E.
BUFFALO, DALLAS CO., ST. WILLIAM (1946)
404 S Locust St, Buffalo, 65622. Rev. David L. Miller; Deacon Michael Fritz.
Res.: P.O. Box 518, Buffalo, 65622.
Catechesis Religious Program—Students 11.
CARTHAGE, JASPER CO., ST. ANN (1872)
1156 Grand Ave, Carthage, 64836-2832.
Tel: 417-358-1841; Email: stannschurch@sbcglobal.net; Web: www.stannschurchcarthage.org. 908 Clinton St, Carthage, 64836. Revs. J. Friedel; Charles Dunn; Jose Marino Novoa; Deacon James V. Walter.
Res.: 517 E. 10th St., Carthage, 64836.
School—St. Ann School, (Grades PreK-6), 1156 Grand, Carthage, 64836. Tel: 417-358-2674; Fax: 417-358-8976; Email: mcortez@stannscarthage.com. Mikelle Cortez, Prin. Lay Teachers 9; Priests 1; Students 72.
CARUTHERSVILLE, PEMISCOT CO., SACRED HEART (1892)
605 Ward Ave., Caruthersville, 63830.
Tel: 573-333-4301; Fax: 573-333-4301; Email: sacredheart63830@outlook.com; Web: sacredheartsemo.org. Dominic Ibok; Ms. Erika Garcia; Deacon James Darter.
Catechesis Religious Program—
CASSVILLE, BARRY CO., ST. EDWARD
Mailing Address: P.O. Box 492, Cassville, 65625.
Tel: 417-847-4948; Fax: 417-847-4947; Email: stedwardcassville@gmail.com; Web: stewardcatholicchurch.org. 107 W. 17th St., Cassville, 65625. Revs. Rahab Isidor; David Baunach.
Office: 101 W. 17th St., Cassville, 65625.
Res.: 1802 Y Hwy., P.O. Box 492, Cassville, 65625.
Catechesis Religious Program—Students 31.
CHAFFEE, SCOTT CO., ST. AMBROSE (1907) [CEM]
418 S. 3rd St., Chaffee, 63740. Tel: 573-887-3953; Fax: 573-887-3953; Email: frtochtropga@yahoo.com. Rev. Randolph G. Tochtrop.
Res.: 318 S. 3rd St., Chaffee, 63740.
School—St. Ambrose School, (Grades 1-8), 419 S. 3rd St., Chaffee, 63740. Tel: 573-887-6711; Fax: 573-887-6711; Email: stalenderle@gmail.com; Web: guardianangel.eduk12.net. Ms. Laura Enderle, Prin. Lay Teachers 6; Students 59.
Catechesis Religious Program—Students 56.
CHARLESTON, MISSISSIPPI CO., ST. HENRY (1873)
304 Court St., Charleston, 63834. Tel: 573-683-2114; Email: connie@sainthenry.org; Web: www.sthenrychurch.org. Rev. David J. Dohogne.
School—St. Henry School, (Grades 1-8), 306 Court St., Charleston, 63834. Tel: 573-683-6218; Fax: 573-683-4124; Email: principal@sainthenry.org. Amy Galemore, Prin. Lay Teachers 6; Students 54.
Catechesis Religious Program—
CONWAY, LACLEDE CO., SACRED HEART (1908) [CEM]
310 S. Spruce St., P.O. Box 8, Conway, 65632.
Tel: 417-589-6782; Email: sheart@centurytel.net. Rev. Mark J. Binder; Deacons James Soptick; Michael Fritz.
Catechesis Religious Program—Students 24.
DEXTER, STODDARD CO., SACRED HEART (1889)
103 E. Market St., Dexter, 63841-1732.
Tel: 573-624-7333; Fax: 573-642-4076; Email: dexter.sacred.heart@gmail.com. 115 E. Market St., Dexter, 63841. Rev. William W. Hennecke Jr.
Church: 102 E. Castor, Dexter, 63841.
Catechesis Religious Program—Students 67.
DONIPHAN, RIPLEY CO., ST. BENEDICT (1859) [CEM]
306 Kegler, Doniphan, 63935. Tel: 573-996-3301; Email: stb1849@windstream.net; Web: stbenedictdoniphan.com. Revs. Michael McDevitt, Admin., (Retired); Simon M. Enudu.
Catechesis Religious Program—Sandra Kennon, C.R.E. Students 22.
EL DORADO SPRINGS, CEDAR CO., ST. ELIZABETH OF HUNGARY (1946) [CEM]
609 S. Main, El Dorado Springs, 64744.
Tel: 417-876-3216; Email: mtienhoa@yahoo.com. Rev. Mark M. Hoa Le, C.M.C.
Catechesis Religious Program—Students 23.
Mission—St. Peter the Apostle, 222 N. Hwy. J, P.O. Box 583, Stockton, Cedar Co. 65785.
Tel: 417-276-5588.
FORSYTH, TANEY CO., OUR LADY OF THE OZARKS (1964)
Mailing Address: 951 Swan Valley Dr., Forsyth, 65653. Tel: 417-546-5208; Email: ourladyoftheozarks@yahoo.com; Web: www.ourladyoftheozarks.org. Revs. David F. Hulshof, M.A.; Joseph Kelly; Sr. Charlotte Flarlong, S.S.N.D., Pastoral Assoc.; Deacons Richard Harden; Daniel Vaughn.
Catechesis Religious Program—Students 3.
FREDERICKTOWN, MADISON CO., ST. MICHAEL THE ARCHANGEL (1827) [CEM]
Tel: 573-783-2182; Fax: 573-783-5230; Email: stmic@charter.net; Web: www.stmichaelfredericktown.com. Rev. John S. Braun.
Catechesis Religious Program—Students 40.
GLENNONVILLE, DUNKLIN CO., ST. TERESA (1905) [CEM]
40694 State Hwy. JJ, Campbell, 63933-9148.
Tel: 573-328-4544; Fax: 573-328-4544. Rev. William W. Hennecke Jr.
School—St. Teresa School, (Grades 1-8), 40468 State Hwy. JJ, Campbell, 63933-9148. Tel: 573-328-4197; Fax: 573-328-4197; Email: klynn@gmail.com; Web: stteresa.eduk12.net. Kim Lynn, Prin. Lay Teachers 6; Students 65; Aides 1.
Catechesis Religious Program—Students 9.
HOUSTON, TEXAS CO., ST. MARK (1952)
117 E. South Oak Crest, Houston, 65483.
Tel: 417-967-3589; Email: stmarkchurch@centurytel.net. Rev. Rayappa Chinnabathini.
Catechesis Religious Program—Students 31.
Missions—St. Vincent de Paul—12552 Bell Rd., Roby, 65557.
St. John The Baptist, 222 W. Hwy. 32, Licking, 65542.
IRONTON, IRON CO., STE. MARIE DU LAC (1878) [CEM]
350 S. Main St., Ironton, 63650. Tel: 573-546-2611; Email: stmariedu@gmail.com. Rev. James J. Untereiner.
Catechesis Religious Program—
Missions—Our Lady of Sorrows—Lesterville, Reynolds Co.
St. Philip Benizi, Viburnum, Iron Co.
JACKSON, CAPE GIRARDEAU CO., IMMACULATE CONCEPTION (1850) [CEM]
208 S. Hope St., Ste. 101, Jackson, 63755.
Tel: 573-243-3182; Email: pastor@icjacksonmo.com; Web: www.icjacksonmo.com. Rev. John M. Harth; Jerry Ganiel, Music Coord.; Deacons Walter L. Biri; Alvin Stoverink.
School—Immaculate Conception School, (Grades 1-8), 300 S. Hope St., Jackson, 63755.
Tel: 573-243-5013; Fax: 573-243-7216; Email: mcampbell@icsjackson.com; Web: icsjackson.eduk12.net. Michele Campbell, Prin. Aides 2; Lay Teachers 18; Students 209.
Catechesis Religious Program—Meg Garner, Youth Min. Students 126.
JOPLIN, JASPER CO.
1—ST. MARY (1938) [JC]
Mailing Address: 3035 S. Central Rd., Joplin, 64804.
Tel: 417-623-3333; Fax: 417-623-4015; Email: church@stmarysparishjoplin.com; Web: www.maryjoplin.parishesonline.com. Rev. Joseph Weidenbenner.
School—St. Mary School, (Grades 1-8), 3025 S. Central City Rd., Joplin, 64804. Tel: 417-623-1465; Fax: 417-553-7887; Email: ahamlet@jacss.org. Ms. Ann Hamlet, Prin. Aides 3; Lay Teachers 16; Students 170.
Catechesis Religious Program—Students 65.
2—ST. PETER THE APOSTLE (1877) [JC]
812 S. Pearl Ave., Joplin, 64801-4396.
Tel: 417-623-8643; Fax: 417-623-0866; Email: stpetersjoplin@yahoo.com; Web: saintpetertheapostlejoplin.com. Revs. J. Friedel; Charles Dunn; Jose Marino, C.M.F.
School—St. Peter the Apostle School, (Grades 6-8), 931 S. Byers Ave., Joplin, 64801-4396.
Tel: 417-624-5605; Fax: 417-624-6254; Email: twelch@jacss.org. Mrs. Tracey Welch, Prin. Lay Teachers 8; Sisters 1; Students 76.
Catechesis Religious Program—Students 39.
KELSO, SCOTT CO., ST. AUGUSTINE (1878)
201 S. Messmer, P.O. Box 26, Kelso, 63758.
Tel: 573-264-4106; Tel: 573-264-4724; Email: parishoffice4106@gmail.com; Web: www.stakelso.org. Rev. Michael J. Casteel.
School—St. Augustine School, (Grades 1-8), 230 S. Hwy. 61, P.O. Box 97, Kelso, 63758-0097.
Tel: 573-264-4644; Fax: 573-264-1475; Web: stakelso.eduk12.net/. Sarah Cato, Prin. Clergy 1; Lay Teachers 13; Students 169.
Catechesis Religious Program—
KENNETT, DUNKLIN CO., ST. CECILIA (1923)
1226 College St., P.O. Box 306, Kennett, 63857. Rev. Daniel Robles.
Catechesis Religious Program—Students 91.
KIMBERLING CITY, STONE CO., OUR LADY OF THE COVE (1960)
20 Kimberling Blvd., P.O. Box 548, Kimberling City, 65686. Tel: 417-739-4700; Fax: 417-739-1782; Email: ourladyofthecove@yahoo.com; Web: www.ourladyofthecove.org. Rev. Joji Vincent, O.S.B., Admin.; Deacon Gregg Erickson.
Catechesis Religious Program—Mary Lippert, Dir. P.S.R. Students 73.
LAMAR, BARTON CO., ST. MARY (1904) [CEM]
200 E. 17th St., Lamar, 64759. Tel: 417-682-2492; Email: pteter51@gmail.com. Rev. Patrick A. Teter.
Catechesis Religious Program—Students 29.
LEBANON, LACLEDE CO., ST. FRANCIS DE SALES (1870) [CEM]
345 Grand St., Lebanon, 65536. Tel: 417-532-4811; Fax: 417-532-8847; Email: lebanoncatholic@gmail.com; Web: www.fidnet.com/~stfrank/index.html. Rev. David L. Miller.
Catechesis Religious Program—Students 90.
Chapel—Bennett Springs, Sportman's Chapel.
LEOPOLD, BOLLINGER CO., ST. JOHN (1856) [CEM]
103 W. Main St., Leopold, 63760. Mailing Address: P.O. Box 83, Leopold, 63760. Tel: 573-238-3300; Fax: 573-238-2450; Email: cindythele@hotmail.com; Web: www.stjohnscatholiccemetery.org. Rev. David N. Coon; Daniel Seiler, Music Dir.; Nick Elfrink, D.R.E.; Tonya Gott, Youth Min.; Cindy Thele.
Catechesis Religious Program—Students 135.
Mission—St. Anthony, [CEM] Hwy. AB, Leopold, 63760.
MALDEN, DUNKLIN CO., ST. ANN (1890)
Mailing Address: c/o St. Teresa Parish, 40694 State Hwy. JJ, Campbell, 63933. Tel: 573-328-4544; Email: teresann@catholicweb.com. Rev. William W. Hennecke Jr.
Church: 304 N. Douglas St., Malden, 63863.
Catechesis Religious Program—Students 3.
MANSFIELD, WRIGHT CO., IMMACULATE HEART OF MARY (1943)
PO Box 468, Mansfield, 65704. Tel: 417-924-3779; Email: pwightman@centurylink.net. 354 N Roote Ave, Mansfield, 65704. Leo Arockiasamy, Admin.; Rev. Paul Wightman, O.M.I.
Res.: Rte. 6, Box 6700, Ava, 65608.
Catechesis Religious Program—Students 19.
Missions—St. Leo the Great—R.R. 6, Box 6700, Ava, Douglas Co. 65608. Tel: 417-683-5249; Email: stleoschurchava@gmail.com.
St. William, P.O. Box 367, Gainesville, Ozark Co. 65655. Tel: 417-679-4804.
MARSHFIELD, WEBSTER CO., HOLY TRINITY (1892)
515 E. Washington, Marshfield, 65706-1865.
Tel: 417-859-2228; Email: htmparish@centurytel.net. Rev. Mark J. Binder; Deacons James Soptick; Michael Fritz.
Res.: 125 N. Locust, Marshfield, 65706.
Catechesis Religious Program—Students 55.
MONETT, BARRY CO., ST. LAWRENCE (1891) [CEM]
405 7th St., Monett, 65708. Tel: 417-235-3286; Fax: 800-998-9780; Email: stlawrence1892@gmail.com; Web: stlawbiblestudy.wix.com/stlawrencemonett. Revs. Rahab Isidor; David Baunach.
Res.: 503 7th St., Monett, 65708.

School—St. Lawrence School, (Grades 1-6), 407 7th St., Monett, 65708. Tel: 417-235-3721; Fax: 417-235-3721; Email: virsik12@gmail.com. Mrs. Vicki Irsik, Prin. Aides 1; Lay Teachers 6; Students 68.
Catechesis Religious Program—Students 207.
MOUNT VERNON, LAWRENCE CO., ST. SUSANNE (1939)
720 W Sloan St, Hwy V, Mount Vernon, 65712. Rev. Chori Seraiah.
Catechesis Religious Program—Students 44.
Mission—St. Patrick, 51 N. H Hwy., Greenfield, 65661. Tel: 417-637-2542; Email: stpatrickcatholicchurch@yahoo.com. P.O. Box 364, Greenfield, 65661. Bobbi Moseley, Parish Life Coord.
MOUNTAIN GROVE, WRIGHT CO., SACRED HEART (1893)
302 E. State St., Mountain Grove, 65711.
Tel: 417-926-3803; Email: sacredheartmtngrove@gmail.com. Leo Arockiasamy, Admin.; Rev. Paul Wightman, O.M.I.; Deacon Joseph Kurtenbach, Parish Life Coord.
Catechesis Religious Program—Students 18.
Mission—St. Michael, Cabool, Texas Co.
MOUNTAIN VIEW, HOWELL CO., ST. JOHN VIANNEY (1951)
808 State Rd. Y, Mountain View, 65548.
Tel: 417-934-2649; Email: sjvmtnview1959@gmail.com. Rajarao Gona.
Catechesis Religious Program—

Mission—St. Sylvester, Eminence, Shannon Co.

NEOSHO, NEWTON CO., ST. CANERA (1871) [JC]
504 S. Washington St., Neosho, 64850.
Tel: 417-451-3411; Email: stcanera@sbcglobal.net; Web: www.canera.org. 507 S. Wood St., Neosho, 64850. Samson Dorival.
Catechesis Religious Program—Students 122.
Mission—Nativity of Our Lord, 227 Sulphur St., Noel, McDonald Co. 64854. Tel: 417-475-3144; Email: office@nativitychurch.us.

NEW HAMBURG, SCOTT CO., ST. LAWRENCE (1847) [CEM]
Mailing Address: P.O. Box 247, Benton, 63736-8159.
Tel: 573-545-3317; Fax: 573-545-3317; Email: casteel_23@yahoo.com; Web: splawrencechurchnewhamburg.weebly.com. 1017 State Hwy. A, Benton, 63736. Rev. Bala Swamy Govindu.
Church: 1001 State Hwy. A, Benton, 63736-0247.
Catechesis Religious Program—Students 52.

NEW MADRID, NEW MADRID CO., IMMACULATE CONCEPTION (1789)
607 Davis St., New Madrid, 63869.
Tel: 573-748-5183; Fax: 573-748-7718; Email: icnm1789@gmail.com; Web: icnewmadrid.com. Dominic Ibok, Admin.; Deacon James Darter.
Res.: 605 Davis St., New Madrid, 63869.
School—Immaculate Conception School, (Grades 1-8), 560 Powell, New Madrid, 63869.
Tel: 573-748-5123; Fax: 573-748-5150; Email: icsoffice@yahoo.com; Web: https://icssaints.eduk12.net/. Ms. Lynette Fowler, Prin. Aides 1; Lay Teachers 6; Students 71.
Catechesis Religious Program—Students 11.

NIXA, CHRISTIAN CO., ST. FRANCIS OF ASSISI (2004)
844 S. Gregg Rd., P.O. Box 1920, Nixa, 65714.
Tel: 417-725-1975; Email: office@stfrancisnixa.org; Web: stfrancisnixa.org. Rev. Msgr. Thomas E. Reidy, V.G.; Revs. Colby J. Elbert; Michael V. McDevitt, M.A., M.Div., In Res.
Catechesis Religious Program—Students 67.

ORAN, SCOTT CO., GUARDIAN ANGEL (1892) [CEM 2]
604 Church St., P.O. Box 158, Oran, 63771.
Tel: 573-262-3210; Fax: 573-262-3210; Email: kbfarms1@hotmail.com; Web: www.guardianangelchurch.net. Rev. Randolph G. Tochtrop.
School—Guardian Angel School, (Grades 1-8), 514 Church St., Oran, 63771. Tel: 573-262-3583; Email: kkluesnerga@gmail.com. Katrina Kluesner, Prin. Aides 1; Lay Teachers 8; Students 89.
Catechesis Religious Program—Students 49.

OZARK, CHRISTIAN CO., ST. JOSEPH THE WORKER (1961)
1796 N. State Hwy. NN, Ozark, 65721.
Tel: 417-581-6328; Fax: 417-581-4957; Email: priest@sjwozark.org; Web: www.saintjosephozark.org. Rev. Jose Thundathil Antoney, C.M.I.; Deacon Horacio Quiles.
Catechesis Religious Program—Students 135.

PIEDMONT, WAYNE CO., ST. CATHERINE OF SIENA (1873)
109 Piedmont Ave., Piedmont, 63957.
Tel: 573-223-4924; Cell: 573-247-0277; Email: stcatherinepiedmont@gmail.com; Web: stcatherineofsiena.us. Rev. Daniel J. Hirtz.
Catechesis Religious Program—Students 12.
Missions—St. George—Tel: 573-323-8576.
Our Lady of Sorrows, Williamsville, Wayne Co.

PIERCE CITY, LAWRENCE CO., ST. MARY (1883) [CEM 2]
200 Front St., Pierce City, 65723. Tel: 417-476-2827; Fax: 417-476-5827; Email: st_marys@live.com. Rev. Matthew J. Rehrauer.
School—St. Mary School, (Grades 1-8), 202 Front St., Pierce City, 65723. Tel: 417-476-2824;
Fax: 417-476-2824; Email: judy.harper@stmaryspiercecity.org. Judy Harper, Prin. Clergy 1; Lay Teachers 6; Students 88.
Catechesis Religious Program—Students 66.

POPLAR BLUFF, BUTLER CO., SACRED HEART (1891) [CEM]
825 Vine St., Poplar Bluff, 63901. Tel: 573-785-9635; Tel: 573-785-2069; Email: shparish@socket.net. 123 N. 8th St., Poplar Bluff, 63901. Revs. Michael McDevitt, Admin., (Retired); Simon M. Enudu; Deacon David O. Farris.
School—Sacred Heart School, (Grades 1-8),
Tel: 573-785-5836; Fax: 573-785-3908; Email: gribbinsmonique@gmail.com; Web: sacredheartpb.eduk12.net. Ms. Monique Gribbins, Prin. Aides 3; Clergy 3; Lay Teachers 9; Students 154.
Catechesis Religious Program—Students 43.

PORTAGEVILLE, NEW MADRID CO., ST. EUSTACHIUS (1902)
210 W. Fourth St., Portageville, 63873.
Tel: 573-379-5247; Email: eustachius@sbcglobal.net. Rev. Daniel Robles.
Res.: 200 W. Fourth St., Portageville, 63873.
School—St. Eustachius School, (Grades 1-8), 214 W. Fourth St., Portageville, 63873. Tel: 573-379-3525; Fax: 573-379-3843; Email: steustachiusschool@yahoo.com. Mrs. Patricia Rone, Prin. Aides 3; Lay Teachers 7; Students 81.
Catechesis Religious Program—Students 12.

PULASKIFIELD, BARRY CO., SS. PETER AND PAUL (1892) [CEM]
P.O. Box 208, Pierce City, 65723-0208.
Tel: 417-476-2463; Email: stspp1892@gmail.com. 2951 Farm Rd 2040, Pierce City, 65723-0208. Paul Pudhota, Parochial Admin.
Catechesis Religious Program—Students 13.

SALEM, DENT CO., SACRED HEART (1880)
602 W. Butler, Salem, 65560. Tel: 573-729-4291; Email: sacredheartsalem@gmail.com. Rev. Michael Q. Do.
Catechesis Religious Program—Students 62.
Mission—Christ the King, P.O. Box 177, Bunker, Reynolds Co. 63629.
Chapel—Montauk, St. Jude.

SARCOXIE, NEWTON CO., ST. AGNES (1870) [CEM]
P.O. Box 218, Pierce City, 65723-0218. 26952 Cherry Rd, Sarcoxie, 64862. Tel: 417-476-2827; Email: stagnessp@gmail.com. Rev. Matthew J. Rehrauer.
Catechesis Religious Program—Students 4.

SCOTT CITY, SCOTT CO., ST. JOSEPH (1911) [CEM]
Mailing Address: 201 S. Messmer, Scott City, 63780.
Tel: 573-264-4106; Fax: 573-264-4106; Email: parishoffice4106@gmail.com; Web: stjosephsc.org. 604 Sycamore St., Scott City, 63780. Rev. Michael J. Casteel.
School—St. Joseph School, (Grades 1-8), 606 Sycamore, Scott City, 63780. Tel: 573-264-2600;
Fax: 573-264-1325; Email: stjoeinsc@charter.net. Betty Spalding, Prin. Aides 2; Lay Teachers 4; Students 32.
Catechesis Religious Program—

SENECA, NEWTON CO., ST. MARY (1884) [CEM]
1209 Wyandotte St, Seneca, 64865. Rev. Patrick A. Teter.
Res.: P.O. Box 1169, Seneca, 64865.
Catechesis Religious Program—Students 24.

SHELL KNOB, BARRY CO., HOLY FAMILY (1978)
24036 FR 1255, P.O. Box 229, Shell Knob, 65747.
Tel: 417-858-2518; Fax: 417-858-6029; Email: catholicchur772@centurytel.net. Revs. Rahab Isidor; David Baunach.
Catechesis Religious Program—Students 2.

SIKESTON, SCOTT CO., ST. FRANCIS XAVIER (1892)
245 W Front St, Sikeston, 63801. Tel: 573-471-2447; Fax: 573-471-9820; Email: parishoffice@stfxsikeston.org; Email: fatherdavid@stfxsikeston.org; Web: stfxsikeston.org. Rev. David J. Dohogne.
School—St. Francis Xavier School, (Grades 1-8), 106 N. Stoddard, Sikeston, 63801. Tel: 573-471-0841;
Fax: 573-475-9847; Email: principal@stfxsikeston.org; Web: sfxschool.eduk12.net. Mrs. Debbie Pollock, Prin. Aides 3; Lay Teachers 11; Students 121.
Catechesis Religious Program—

VERONA, LAWRENCE CO., SACRED HEART (1874) [CEM]
Mailing Address: P.O. Box 533, Aurora, 65605-0533.
Tel: 417-678-2403; Fax: 417-678-2551; Email: sacredheart.veronachurch@gmail.com. 212 N 2nd St, Verona, 65769. Revs. Rahab Isidor; David Baunach.
Church: Adams & Second St., Verona, 65769.
Catechesis Religious Program—Students 190.

WEBB CITY, JASPER CO., SACRED HEART (1908)
909 N. Madison Ave., Webb City, 64870.
Tel: 417-673-2044, Ext. 101; Fax: 866-249-9190; Email: sacredheartsecretary@gmail.com; Web: sacredheartwebbcity.org. PO Box 470, Webb City, 64870-0470. Revs. John (J.) F. Friedel, M.A., M.Div.; Francisco (Paco) J. Gordillo Villamil.

WEST PLAINS, HOWELL CO., ST. MARY (1902)
Mailing Address: P.O. Box 67, West Plains, 65775.
Tel: 417-256-2556; Email: stmarychurchwestplains@gmail.com. Rev. Shoby Mathew Chettiyath.
Res.: 1551 Bill Virdon Blvd., West Plains, 65775.
Catechesis Religious Program—Students 69.
Mission—Sacred Heart, Thayer, Oregon Co.

WILLOW SPRINGS, HOWELL CO., SACRED HEART (1897) [CEM]
1050 W. Bus Hwy. 60-63, Willow Springs, 65793.
Tel: 417-469-2447. Rev. Sherman B. Wall, O.M.I.; Deacon G. Alan Bandy.
Catechesis Religious Program—Students 16.
Mission—St. Joseph, White Church, Howell Co.

Chaplains of Public Institutions

SPRINGFIELD. *Mercy Hospital Springfield* dba St. John's Hospital, Tel: 417-820-2000.
Springfield Hospital Ministry. Rev. Jerome Amaechi, Chap.
U.S. Medical Center, 1900 W. Sunshine, 65802.
Tel: 417-862-7041, Ext. 1669. Rev. Msgr. Thomas E. Reidy, V.G., Tel: 417-887-6472, Revs. Colby J. Elbert, Chap., Michael V. McDevitt, M.A., M.Div., Deacon Mathey F. Fletcher.

CHARLESTON. *Southeast Correctional Center*, Charleston. Tel: 573-683-4409.

FORDLAND. *Ozark Correctional Center*, Fordland.
Tel: 417-767-4491. Rev. Mark J. Binder, Chap.

JOPLIN. *Joplin Hospital Ministry*, Joplin.
Tel: 417-781-2727.

LICKING. *South Central Correctional Center*,
Tel: 573-674-4470. Rev. Rayappa Chinnabathini.

POPLAR BLUFF. *Poplar Bluff Hospital Ministry*. Rev. William M. Hodgson, Tel: 573-785-9635.

On Duty Outside the Diocese:
Revs.—
Straus, Brian, University of St. Mary of the Lake, Mundelein, IL
Williams, Andrew, University of St. Mary of the Lake, Mundelein, IL.

Leave of Absence:
Revs.—
Carr, Gary M., 5610 Village Royale Ln., Apt. B, Saint Louis, 63128
Manso, Bobby
Nundwe, Saviour
Skrzypek, Jaroslaw Z., J.C.L.
Wenani, Kizito.

Retired:
Rev. Msgrs.—
Eftink, Edward M., Ph.D., (Retired), Lutheran Nursing Home, 2825 Bloomfield Rd., Rm. 21-D, Cape Girardeau, 63703. Tel: 417-861-8520
Orf, Raymond V., (Retired), 10 Archbishop May Dr., St. Louis, 63119. Tel: 314-968-4913
Rolwing, Richard C., (Retired), 378 Etherton Dr., Cape Girardeau, 63703. Tel: 573-335-3206
Revs.—
Boyer, Mark G., M.A., M.Div., M.R.E., (Retired), 1140 E. Stanford St., 65807-2058
Clavin, M. Oliver, (Retired), 2268 E. Mirabeau St., 65804
Landewe, Robert A., (Retired), Springfield Villa, 1100 E. Montclair St., 65807-5095. Tel: 417-350-3760
Lutz, Frederick J., (Retired), 2268 E. Mirabeau St., 65804
Marquart, Ernest J., (Retired), Park Place Assisted Living, 1211 N. Ash St., Mountain View, 65548. Tel: 417-261-1181
McDevitt, Michael, (Retired), 1042 W. Butterfield Dr., Nixa, 65714
McLoughlin, Paul J., (Retired), 4355 S. National, Apt 206, 65810
Monaghan, Justin D., (Retired), 3421 S. Stonebrook Ct., Joplin, 64804
Morciniec, Peter J., (Retired), Springfield Villa, 1100 E. Montclair St., 65807-5095
Varone, Normand G., (Retired), 383 Etherton Dr., Cape Girardeau, 63703
Wilk, Mitchell S., (Retired), 363 Etherton Dr., Cape Girardeau, 63703-7577
Wissman, J. Patrick, (Retired), 1521 W. Chestnut St., Bolivar, 65613.

Permanent Deacons:
Bandy, G. Alan, Sacred Heart, Willow Springs
Biri, Walter L., Immaculate Conception, Jackson
Brewer, Thomas M., St. Elizabeth Ann Seton, Springfield
Carrol, Kevin, Immaculate Conception, Springfield
Darter, James, Sacred Heart, Caruthersville; Immaculate Conception, New Madrid
Ellman, Edward V.
Erickson, Gregg, Our Lady of the Cove, Kimberling City
Farrar, James, Sacred Heart, Springfield
Farris, David O., Sacred Heart, Poplar Bluff
Fletcher, Mathey F., St. Joseph, Springfield
Fritz, Michael, Sacred Heart, Conway
Harden, Richard, Our Lady of the Lake, Branson
Huff, Robbie R., St. Vincent de Paul, Cape Girardeau
Keefe, Patrick J., St. Mary, West Plains
Keller, William J., Cathedral of St. Agnes, Springfield
Kiblinger, Mark, St. Vincent de Paul, Cape Girardeau
Kurtenbach, Joseph, Sacred Heart, Mountain Grove
Long, James E. Jr., Immaculate Conception, Jackson
Quiles, Horacio, St. Joseph the Worker, Ozark
Schumer, Thomas J., St. Vincent de Paul, Cape Girardeau; Catholic Campus Ministry at Southeast Missouri State University
Soptick, James, Holy Trinity, Marshfield
Steffes, Gary D., St. Francis of Assisi, Nixa
Stoverink, Alvin, Immaculate Conception, Jackson
Vaughn, Daniel, Our Lady of the Lake, Branson
Vrooman, David

Walter, James V., St. Anne, Carthage

Wand, Mark A., Cathedral of St. Agnes, Springfield.

INSTITUTIONS LOCATED IN DIOCESE

[A] SEMINARIES, RELIGIOUS, OR SCHOLASTICATES

AVA. *Assumption Novitiate (Trappists)*, R.R. 5, Box 1056, Ava, 65608-9142. Tel: 417-683-5110; Fax: 417-683-5658; Email: frmaryalberic@hughes.net; Web: assumptionabbey.org. Rev. Alberic Maisog, O.C.S.O., Supr.; Rt. Rev. Cyprian Harrison, O.C.S.O., Abbot.

CARTHAGE. *The Congregation of the Mother of the Redeemer*, 1900 Grand Ave., Carthage, 64836. Tel: 417-358-7787; Fax: 417-358-9508; Email: cmc@dongcong.net; Web: dongcong.us. Rev. Paul M. Tai Tran, C.M.C., Prov. Religious Teachers 33; Students 40.

[B] HIGH SCHOOLS, DIOCESAN

SPRINGFIELD. *Springfield Catholic High School* (Coed) 2340 S. Eastgate, 65809-2832. Tel: 417-887-8817; Fax: 417-885-1165; Email: jskahan@scspk12.org; Web: www.scspk12.org. Mrs. Jeanne Skahan, Prin.; Sr. Cecilia Ann Rezac, Dir.; Revs. Colby J. Elbert, Chap.; Joseph Stoverink, Chap. Religious Teachers 1; Lay Teachers 32; Priests 1; Students 392; Counselors 2.

Springfield Catholic School System, 2340 S. Eastgate Ave., 65809-2832. Tel: 417-865-5567; Fax: 417-865-5278; Email: srceciliaann@scspk12.org; Web: www.scspk12.org. Sr. Cecilia Ann Rezac, Dir.

CAPE GIRARDEAU. *Notre Dame Regional High School*, 265 Notre Dame Dr., Cape Girardeau, 63701-8517. Tel: 573-335-6772; Fax: 573-335-3458; Email: brotherdavid@notredamecape.org; Web: www.notredamehighschool.org. Bro. David Anthony Migliorino, O.S.F., Prin.; Revs. Michael J. Casteel, Chap.; John M. Harth, Chap. Co-Instructional Regional High School Brothers 1; Lay Teachers 42; Students 502; Counselors 3.

JOPLIN. *St. Mary*, (Grades PreK-5), 3025 S. Central City Rd., Joplin, 64804. Tel: 417-623-1465; Fax: 417-553-7887; Email: jlown@jacss.org; Web: www.jacss.org. Ms. Joanne Lown, Prin. Aides 2; Religious Teachers 1; Lay Teachers 16; Students 158.

McAuley Catholic High School, 930 Pearl Ave., Joplin, 64801. Tel: 417-624-9320; Fax: 417-626-8334; Email: twelch@jacss.org; Web: www.jacss.org. Mrs. Tracey Welch, Prin.; Rev. Charles Dunn, Chap. Lay Teachers 13; Students 85; Counselors 2.

St. Peter the Apostle Middle School, (Grades 6-8), 931 Byers, Joplin, 64801. Tel: 417-624-5605; Fax: 417-624-6254; Email: twelch@jacss.org; Web: www.jacss.org. Mrs. Tracey Welch, Prin. Lay Teachers 8; Sisters 1; Students 68.

[C] CATHOLIC CHARITIES

SPRINGFIELD. **Catholic Charities of Southern Missouri, Inc.*, St. Anne Campus, 424 E. Monastery St., 65807. Tel: 417-720-4213; Fax: 417-720-4216; Email: info@ccsomo.org; Web: www.ccsomo.org. Mrs. Maura A. Taylor, Exec. Dir. Tot Asst. Annually 5,000; Total Staff 100.

[D] GENERAL HOSPITALS

SPRINGFIELD. *Mercy Hospital Springfield*, 1235 E. Cherokee, 65804. Tel: 417-820-3612; Fax: 417-820-8730; Email: Marynell.Ploch@Mercy.Net; Web: www.mercy.net. Susan Hannasch, Counsel. Member of Mercy Health. Bed Capacity 866; Tot Asst. Annually 35,863; Total Staff 368.

CAPE GIRARDEAU. **Saint Francis Medical Center*, 211 Saint Francis Dr., Cape Girardeau, 63703-8399. Tel: 573-331-3000; Fax: 573-331-5310 (Administration); Email: sfmc@sfmc.net; Web: www.sfmc.net. Maryann Reese, CEO; Rev. Patrick I. Nwokoye, Ph.D., Chap.; Sisters Maureen Elfrink; Jane Ann Kiefer. Owned and operated by a lay board with Diocesan sponsorship. Bed Capacity 308; Sisters 2; Tot Asst. Annually 204,614; Total Staff 100; Inpatients 12,014; Outpatients 192,600.

**Saint Francis Foundation*, 211 St. Francis Dr., Cape Girardeau, 63703. Tel: 573-331-5133; Fax: 573-331-5031.

**Saint Francis Healthcare System (formerly known as St. Francis Hospital of Franciscan Sisters)*, 211 Saint Francis Dr., Cape Girardeau, 63703. Tel: 573-331-3000 (Main); Fax: 573-331-5009 (Administration); Email: sfmc@sfmc.net. Maryann Reese, CEO. Bed Capacity 289.

AURORA. *Mercy Hospital Aurora*, 500 Porter Ave., Aurora, 65605. Tel: 417-678-7800; Fax: 417-678-7840; Email: Marynell.Ploch@mercy.net; Web: www.mercy.net. Suzanne Gamet, Admin. Bed Capacity 25; Tot Asst. Annually 32,290; Total Staff 137; Inpatients 860; Outpatients 31,430.

CARTHAGE. *Mercy Hospital Carthage*, 3125 Dr. Russell Smith Way, Carthage, 64836. Tel: 417-358-8121; Email: Marynell.Ploch@Mercy.Net; Web: www.mercy.net. Scott Watson, Admin. Bed Capacity 25; Tot Asst. Annually 7,989; Total Staff 97.

CASSVILLE. *Mercy Hospital Cassville*, 94 S. Main St., Cassville, 65625. Tel: 417-847-6000; Fax: 417-847-6083; Email: Marynell.Ploch@mercy.net; Web: www.mercy.net. Suzanne Gamet, Admin. Bed Capacity 18; Tot Asst. Annually 33,728; Total Staff 113; Inpatient 292; Outpatient 33,436.

JOPLIN. *Mercy Hospital Joplin*, 100 Mercy Way, Joplin, 64804. Tel: 417-781-2727; Email: Marynell.Ploch@mercy.net; Web: mercy.net. Susan Hannasch, Counsel. Bed Capacity 240; Inpatient 9,174; Outpatient 109,221.

LEBANON. **Mercy Hospital Lebanon*, 100 Hospital Dr., Lebanon, 65536. Tel: 417-533-6100; Fax: 417-533-6021; Email: Marynell.Ploch@Mercy.Net; Web: www.mercy.net. Mercy Corp Paralegal-Legal Dept., 14528 S. Outer 40 Rd., Ste. 100, Chesterfield, 63017. Susan Hannasch, Gen. Counsel. Bed Capacity 62; Tot Asst. Annually 62,399; Total Staff 69.

MOUNTAIN VIEW. *Mercy St. Francis Hospital*, 100 W. U.S. Hwy. 60, Mountain View, 65548. Tel: 417-934-7000; Email: Marynell.Ploch@mercy.net; Web: www.mercy.net. Susan Hannasch, Counsel. Daughters of St. Francis of Assisi and Sisters of Mercy (Managed by Mercy Health Springfield Communities) Bed Capacity 25; Sisters 2; Tot Asst. Annually 25,443; Total Staff 98; Inpatient 228; Outpatient 25,215.

The Sister Cornelia Blasko Foundation, Inc., 100 W. Hwy. 60, P.O. Box 82, Mountain View, 65548. Tel: 417-934-7090; Email: Marynell.Ploch@Mercy.Net. Susan Hannasch, Reg. Gen. Counsel.

[E] SPECIAL HOSPITALS

SPRINGFIELD. *Mercy Hospital Springfield*, 1100 E. Montclair, 65807. Tel: 417-820-8500; Fax: 417-820-8547; Email: Marynell.Ploch@Mercy.Net. Rev. Timothy Toohey, Chap.; Mark Lungnecker, Admin. Skilled Care of Long Term Nursing Home, for the Aged and Chronically Ill. Bed Capacity 120; Tot Asst. Annually 120; Total Staff 256.

[F] MONASTERIES AND RESIDENCES OF PRIESTS AND BROTHERS

SPRINGFIELD. *Claretians Missionaries' Residence-Villa Claret*, 1530 N. Summit Ave., 65803. Tel: 417-869-0075; Email: pastor.shc.sgf@gmail.com. Revs. Gaspar Masilamani, C.M.F, Chap.; Francisco Javier Reyes; Bro. Manuel Benavides, C.M.F.

AVA. *Assumption Abbey (Trappist)*, Rte. 5, Box 1056, Ava, 65608. Tel: 417-683-5110; Fax: 417-683-5658; Email: frmaryalberic@hughes.net; Web: www.assumptionabbey.org. Rev. Thaddeus Nguyen, O.Cist., Supr.; Rt. Rev. Cyprian Harrison, O.C.S.O., Abbot Emeritus; Revs. Alberic Maisog, O.C.S.O., Priest; Leon Brockman, O.C.S.O.; Basil Nguyen, O.Cist.; Peter Vu, O.Cist.; Bros. Francis Flaherty, O.C.S.O.; Alphonse Hua; Ambrose Hung; Gabriel Nghia. Brothers 5; Priests 4; Superior 1; Abbot Emeritus 1.

Our Lady of the Angels Friary, RR. 5, Box 1042, Ava, 65608. Tel: 417-683-4303.

CARTHAGE. *Congregation of the Mother Redeemer*, 1900 Grand Ave., Carthage, 64836. Tel: 417-358-7787; Fax: 417-358-9508; Email: cmc@dongcong.net; Web: dongcong.us. Revs. Paul M. Tai Tran, C.M.C., Prov. Min.; Polycarp M. DucThuan Nguyen, C.M.C., Treas.; Francis M. Hung Long Tran, C.M.C., Sec.; Vincent Thanh Au, Novice Master; Peter M. Khuong Tran, C.M.C., Asst. II; Thanh (Philip M.) Do, C.M.C., Asst. III; (Timothy M.) MyViet Tran, C.M.C., Asst. IIII; Andrew M. Nguyen Hong An, C.M.C.; Isidore M. Dinh Thanh Bac, C.M.C.; Albert M. P. Kim Ban, C.M.C.; Bros. Justin M. Xuan Binh, C.M.C.; John M. Tu Quang Bui, C.M.C.; Michael M. Trung Dan, C.M.C.; (Josaphat M.) Cuong Manh Do, C.M.C.; Rev. (Bartholomew M.) Hoa Thai Do, C.M.C.; Bro. (Maximilian M.) Loc the Do, C.M.C.; Rev. (Michael M.) Quang Van Do, C.M.C.; Bro (Pio Pietrelcina M.) Tu Thien Lam, C.M.C.; Bro. (Martin M.) Minh Le, C.M.C.; Revs. Simon M. Diem Phuc Le, C.M.C.; Aloysius M. Tran Liem, C.M.C.; Bro. (Sylvester M.) Thuong Quy Lu, C.M.C.; Revs. (Francis Xavier M.) Tri Van Luong, C.M.C.; (John Damascene M.) Vuong Duc Ngo, C.M.C.; Raymond M. Dien Nguyen, C.M.C.; Bros. (John Vianney M.) Huy Duc Nguyen, C.M.C.; John XXIII M. Su Giao Nguyen, C.M.C.; (John Baptist M.) Duc Hien Nguyen, C.M.C.; (Thomas M.) Hoc Nguyen, C.M.C.; Anthony M. Dan Huu Nguyen, C.M.C.; (George M.) Dyllan Huynh Nguyen, C.M.C.; John Paul II M. Phi Long Nguyen, C.M.C.; (Stanislaus M.) An Ngoc Nguyen, C.M.C.; Rev. Patrick M. Ngoc Nguyen, C.M.C.; Bros. (Junipero Serra M.) Nhon Thanh Nguyen, C.M.C.; Peter M. Thieu Nguyen, C.M.C.; (Titus M.) Si Tien Nguyen, C.M.C.; (Barnabas M.) Anh Khai Tran Nguyen, C.M.C.; (Justin M.) Ky Tri Nguyen, C.M.C.; (Francis M.) Thuan Duc Pham, C.M.C.; (Benedict M.) Quy Duy Pham, C.M.C.; (Augustine M.) An Hong Pham, C.M.C.; Rev. Bartholomew M. Van Minh Pham, C.M.C.; Bros. (Matthew M.) Tan Nhat Pham, C.M.C.; Joseph M. Tho Pham, C.M.C.; Revs. (Aloysius M.) Tran Ngoc Thoai, C.M.C.; John M. Hien Duc Tran, C.M.C.; Bros. Stephen M. Chu Du Tran, C.M.C.; (Bernadine M.) Hien Khac Tran, C.M.C.; Luke M. Nam Phuong Tran, C.M.C.; Thomas M. Nguyen L. Truong, C.M.C.; Matthew M. Kim Vu, C.M.C.; (Gabriel M.) Thuan Trung Vu, C.M.C.; Revs. Louis Dang Duc Anh, C.Ss.R.; Joseph Cao Phuong Ky, S.S.; Joseph Huy Chuong Doan; Joseph Do Ba Ai; James Do Ba Cong; Rochus Vu Dinh Hoat. Brothers 37; Priests 33; Collaborator 3. *Mater Dei Building*, 1900 Grand Ave., Carthage, 64836. Tel: 417-358-7787; Fax: 417-358-9508. (Home for retired priests). In Res. Revs. Joseph Cao Phuong Ky, S.S.; Joseph Do Ba Ai; James Do Ba Cong; James Thuc Van Truong, O.S.B.; Joseph Huy Chuong Doan; Rochus Vu Dinh Hoat. (Not members of the Congregation of the Mother Co-Redemptrix). Home for Retired Priest Rev. Louis Dang Duc Anh, C.Ss.R.

MARIONVILLE. *The Society of Our Mother of Peace, Sons of Our Mother of Peace*, Mary the Font Solitude, 6150 Antire Rd., High Ridge, 63049. Tel: 636-677-3235; Fax: 636-253-8344; Email: marythefont@gmail.com. Revs. Placid Guste, S.M.P., Supr.; John R. Hansen, S.M.P., Prov.; Macarius Etim

The Society of Our Mother of Peace, Sons of Our Mother of Peace - Queen of Heaven Solitude Members 3.

[G] CONVENTS AND RESIDENCES FOR SISTERS

SPRINGFIELD. *Congregation of Mary Queen*, 625 S. Jefferson Ave., 65806. Tel: 417-869-9842; Email: cmrusa@hotmail.com; Web: www.trinhvuong.org. Sr. Jacinta Tran, Supr. Sisters 7.

Little Portion Franciscans, 2122 W. Village Ter., 65810. Tel: 417-766-2220; Email: srcecilia@att.net. Sisters 2.

AVA. *Nazareth Hermitage*, R.R. 5, Box 1122, Ava, 65608. Tel: 417-683-2401. Rev. Leon Brockman, O.C.S.O., Chap. Brothers 1; Priests 1; Sisters 4.

MARIONVILLE. *The Society of Our Mother of Peace, Daughters of Our Mother of Peace*, 12494 Hwy. T, Marionville, 65705-7121. Tel: 417-744-2011; Email: sfatqueenofheaven@yahoo.com. Sisters Mary Fidelis Lane, S.M.P., Supr.; Mary Grace Sabas, Evangelization; Regina Bastarache, S.M.P., Coord. of Evangelization

The Society of Our Mother of Peace, Daughters of Our Mother of Peace, Queen of Heaven Solitude Sisters 4.

[H] RETREAT HOUSES

AVA. *Assumption Abbey* (Trappist) RR. 5, Box 1056, Ava, 65608. Tel: 417-683-5110; Fax: 417-683-5658; Email: avaguesthouse@hughes.net; Web: www.assumptionabbey.org. Rev. Alberic Maisog, O.C.S.O.

MARIONVILLE. *The Society of Our Mother of Peace, Daughters of Our Mother of Peace*, 12494 Hwy. T, Marionville, 65705. Tel: 417-744-2011; Email: sfatqueenofheaven@yahoo.com. Sisters Mary Fidelis Lane, S.M.P., Dir.; Mary Grace Sabas, Evangelization; Regina Bastarache, S.M.P., Coord. of Evangelization; Mary Monica Bonete, S.M.P.

The Society of Our Mother of Peace, Daughters of Our Mother of Peace, Queen of Heaven Solitude.

[I] SHRINES

CARTHAGE. *Shrine of Immaculate Heart of Mary*, 1900 Grand Ave., Carthage, 64836. Tel: 417-358-8580; Fax: 417-358-9508; Email: heartofmaryshrine@yahoo.com; Web: www.dongcong.net/khiettam. Rev. Raymond M. Nguyen Dien, C.M.C., Dir.

[J] NEWMAN CENTERS

SPRINGFIELD. *Catholic Campus Ministry O'Reilly Catholic Student Center, Missouri State University, Drury University, Ozarks Technical Community College*, 847 S. Holland, 65806-3513. Tel: 417-865-0802; Fax: 417-865-0895; Email:

jreyes@ccm847.org; Web: www.ccm847.org. Rev. Francisco Javier Reyes, Dir.; Sr. Michelle Nguyen, C.M.R., Pastoral Assoc.

CAPE GIRARDEAU. *Catholic Campus Ministry Southeast Missouri State University, Newman Center*, 512 N. Pacific, Cape Girardeau, 63701-4712. Tel: 573-335-3899; Fax: 573-334-0088; Email: deacontom@ccmin.org; Web: www.ccmin.org. Rev. Patrick I. Nwokoye, Ph.D., Chap.; Deacon Thomas J. Schumer, Dir.

BRANSON. *Catholic Campus Ministry* (College of the Ozarks) 203 Vaughn Dr., Branson, 65616. Tel: 417-334-2928; Fax: 417-334-6883; Email: frdavefh@gmail.com; Web: OLLBranson.com. Rev. David F. Hulshof, M.A., Chap.

JOPLIN. *Catholic Campus Ministry, Missouri Southern State University*, 812 S. Pearl Ave., Joplin, 64801-4336. Tel: 417-623-8643; Email: jfriedel@dioscg.org. Rev. John (J.) F. Friedel, M.A., M.Div., Dir.

[K] MISCELLANEOUS

SPRINGFIELD. **Mercy Clinic Springfield Communities*, Mercy Corp Paralegal - Legal Dept., 14528 S. Outer 40 Rd., Ste. 100, Chesterfield, 63017. Tel: 417-820-2000; Email: Marynell.Ploch@mercy.net; Web: www.mercy.net. 1965 S. Fremont St., Ste. 200, 65804. Stuart Stangeland, COO.

Mercy Health Foundation Springfield, 3231 S. National Ave., 65807. 3265 S. National Ave., 65807. Tel: 417-820-6111; Email: Marynell.Ploch@mercy.net. Susan Hannasch, Counsel.

Mercy Health Springfield Communities, 1235 E. Cherokee, 65804. Tel: 417-820-3612; Fax: 417-820-8730; Email: Marynell.Ploch@Mercy.Net. Philip Wheeler, Senior Vice Pres.- Gen. Counsel.

Mercy Research, 1235 E. Cherokee St., 65804. Tel: 417-841-0244; Fax: 417-841-0252; Email: Marynell.Ploch@Mercy.Net. Susan Hannasch, Gen. Counsel.

Queen of Angels Day Care Center, 625 S. Jefferson, 65806. Tel: 417-832-0852; Email: queenofangels.abc@gmail.com; Web: www.trinhvuong.org. Sr. Faustina Le, Dir. Religious Teachers 4; Students 28.

CARTHAGE. *Office of the Immaculate Heart of Mary Shrine*, 1749 Grand Ave., Carthage, 64836. Tel: 417-358-8580; Fax: 417-358-9508; Web: www.dongcong.net/khiettam.

JOPLIN. *Mercy Health Foundation Joplin*, 3016 McClelland Blvd., Joplin, 64804. Tel: 417-208-3609 ; Email: Marynell.Ploch@Mercy.Net. Miranda Lewis, Dir.

Mercy Health Southwest Missouri/Kansas Communities, 2817 St. John's Blvd., Joplin, 64804. Tel: 417-781-2727; Fax: 417-625-2910; Email: Marynell.Ploch@Mercy.Net. Philip Wheeler, Senior Vice Pres.- Gen. Counsel.

**Mercy Village Joplin, Inc.*, 1148 W. 28th St., Joplin, 64804. Tel: 417-623-7123; Fax: 417-623-7223. Sherryl Weeks.

RELIGIOUS INSTITUTES OF MEN REPRESENTED IN THE DIOCESE

For further details refer to the corresponding bracketed number in the Religious Institutes of Men or Women section.

[]—*Apostles of Jesus*—A.J.
[0275]—*Carmelites of Mary Immaculate*—C.M.I.
[0340]—*Cistercian Fathers*—O.Cist.
[1330]—*Congregation of the Mission Western Province*—C.M.
[]—*Congregation of the Mother Redeemer*—C.R.M.
[0515]—*Franciscan Brothers of the Third Order Regular*—O.S.F.
[0585]—*Heralds of Good News*—H.G.N.
[0360]—*Missionary Sons of the Immaculate Heart of Mary (Claretians)*—C.M.F.
[0870]—*Montfort Missionaries*—S.M.M.
[0910]—*Oblates of Mary Immaculate (Oblates)* (United States Prov.)—O.M.I.
[0350]—*Order of Cistercians of the Strict Observance (Trappist)*—O.C.S.O.
[0200]—*Order of St. Benedict (Benedictines)*—O.S.B.
[1070]—*Redemptorist Fathers*—C.Ss.R.
[]—*The Society of Our Mother of Peace*—S.M.P.
[1290]—*Society of the Priests of Saint Sulpice*—S.S.

RELIGIOUS INSTITUTES OF WOMEN REPRESENTED IN THE DIOCESE

[0100]—*Adorers of the Blood of Christ*—A.S.C.
[0230]—*Benedictine Sisters of the Pontifical Jurisdiction* (St. Joseph, MN)—O.S.B.
[0397]—*Congregation of Mary, Queen*—C.M.R.
[2840]—*Congregation of the Poor Clare Missionary Sisters*—M.C.
[0460]—*Congregation of the Sisters of Charity of the Incarnate Word* (San Antonio)—C.C.V.I.
[0725]—*Cordi-Marian Missionary Sisters Congregation*—M.C.M.
[0920]—*Daughters of St. Francis of Assisi* (Lacon, Illinois)—D.S.F.
[1240]—*Franciscan Sisters, Daughters of the Sacred Hearts of Jesus and Mary* (Wheaton)—O.S.F.
[2080]—*Home Mission Sisters of America (Glenmary)*—G.H.M.S.
[]—*Little Portion Franciscans*—O.S.F.
[2400]—*Marian Sisters of the Diocese of Lincoln*—M.S.
[]—*Nazareth Hermitage.*
[2970]—*School Sisters of Notre Dame* (Central Pacific)—S.S.N.D.
[0430]—*Sisters of Charity of the Blessed Virgin Mary* (Dubuque)—B.V.M.
[1010]—*Sisters of Divine Providence* (San Antonio, TX)—C.D.P.
[2575]—*Sisters of Mercy of the Americas* (West Midwest Community)—R.S.M.
[2575]—*Sisters of Mercy of the Americas* (South Central Community)—R.S.M.
[3840]—*Sisters of St. Joseph of Carondelet* (Los Angeles)—C.S.J.
[1970]—*Sisters of the Holy Family of Nazareth*—C.S.F.N.
[]—*The Society of Our Mother of Peace*—S.M.P.
[4110]—*Ursuline Nuns (Roman Union)* (St. Louis, MO)—O.S.U.

An asterisk (*) denotes an organization that has established tax-exempt status directly with the IRS and is not covered by the USCCB Group Ruling.

Diocese of Springfield in Illinois

(Dioecesis Campifontis in Illinois)

Most Reverend

THOMAS J. PAPROCKI

Bishop of Springfield in Illinois; ordained May 10, 1978; appointed Auxiliary Bishop of Chicago and Titular Bishop of Vulturara January 24, 2003; consecrated March 19, 2003; installed as ninth Bishop of Springfield in Illinois June 22, 2010. *Office: Catholic Pastoral Center, 1615 W. Washington St., Springfield, IL 62702-4757.*

Catholic Pastoral Center: 1615 W. Washington St., Springfield, IL 62702-4757. Tel: 217-698-8500; Fax: 217-698-0802.

ERECTED JULY 29, 1853.

Square Miles 15,139.

Formerly Diocese of Quincy.

See Transferred to Alton, January 9, 1857. To Springfield, October 26, 1923.

Comprises the following Counties of Illinois: Adams, Bond, Brown, Calhoun, Cass, Christian, Clark, Coles, Crawford, Cumberland, Douglas, Edgar, Effingham, Fayette, Greene, Jasper, Jersey, Macon, Macoupin, Madison, Menard, Montgomery, Morgan, Moultrie, Pike, Sangamon, Scott and Shelby.

For legal titles of parishes and diocesan institutions, consult the Chancery Office.

STATISTICAL OVERVIEW

Personnel	
Bishop	1
Priests: Diocesan Active in Diocese	73
Priests: Diocesan Active Outside Diocese	5
Priests: Retired, Sick or Absent	26
Number of Diocesan Priests	104
Religious Priests in Diocese	34
Total Priests in Diocese	138
Extern Priests in Diocese	13
Ordinations:	
Diocesan Priests	5
Transitional Deacons	1
Permanent Deacons in Diocese	53
Total Brothers	18
Total Sisters	475
Parishes	
Parishes	129
With Resident Pastor:	
Resident Diocesan Priests	58
Resident Religious Priests	8
Without Resident Pastor:	
Administered by Priests	63
Welfare	
Catholic Hospitals	8
Total Assisted	743,271
Homes for the Aged	1
Total Assisted	26,280
Residential Care of Children	1
Total Assisted	19
Day Care Centers	1
Total Assisted	100
Special Centers for Social Services	11
Total Assisted	323,508
Residential Care of Disabled	1
Total Assisted	95
Educational	
Diocesan Students in Other Seminaries	21
Total Seminarians	21
Colleges and Universities	1
Total Students	1,294
High Schools, Diocesan and Parish	1
Total Students	208
High Schools, Private	6
Total Students	1,972
Elementary Schools, Diocesan and Parish	37
Total Students	7,806
Elementary Schools, Private	1
Total Students	56
Catechesis/Religious Education:	
High School Students	324
Elementary Students	1,908
Total Students under Catholic Instruction	13,589
Teachers in the Diocese:	
Priests	25
Sisters	25
Lay Teachers	869
Vital Statistics	
Receptions into the Church:	
Infant Baptism Totals	1,399
Minor Baptism Totals	113
Adult Baptism Totals	103
Received into Full Communion	239
First Communions	1,717
Confirmations	2,014
Marriages:	
Catholic	290
Interfaith	185
Total Marriages	475
Deaths	1,595
Total Catholic Population	125,999
Total Population	1,137,696

Former Bishops—Rt. Revs. HENRY DAMIAN JUNCKER, D.D., ord. 1834; cons. April 28, 1857; died Oct. 2, 1868; PETER JOSEPH BALTES, D.D., ord. 1853; cons. Jan. 23, 1870; died Feb. 15, 1886; JAMES RYAN, D.D., ord. 1871; cons. May 1, 1888; died July 2, 1923; Most Revs. JAMES A. GRIFFIN, D.D., ord. 1909; cons. Feb. 25, 1924; died Aug. 5, 1948; WILLIAM A. O'CONNOR, D.D., ord. 1927; cons. March 7, 1949; installed March 17, 1949; retired July 22, 1975; died Nov. 14, 1983; JOSEPH A. MCNICHOLAS, D.D., ord. 1949; cons. March 25, 1969; installed Sept. 3, 1975; died April 17, 1983; DANIEL L. RYAN, D.D., J.C.L., ord. May 3, 1956; ord. Titular Bishop of Surista in Mauritania and Auxiliary to the Bishop of Joliet in Illinois, Sept. 30, 1981; appt. Bishop of Springfield in Illinois, Nov. 22, 1983; installed Jan. 18, 1984; retired Oct. 19, 1999; died Dec. 31, 2015; GEORGE J. LUCAS, ord. May 24, 1975; appt. Bishop of Springfield in Illinois Oct. 19, 1999; ord. and installed Dec. 14, 1999; appt. Archbishop of Omaha June 3, 2009.

Bishop's Administrative Team—Rev. Msgr. DAVID J. HOEFLER, V.G., M.Div., Vicar Gen. & Moderator of the Curia; Very Rev. CHRISTOPHER A. HOUSE, S.T.L., J.C.L., V.J., Dept. Canonical & Pastoral Svcs.; MR. JOHN J. MAXWELL, CPA, Dept. Fin. Svcs.; PATRICIA KORNFELD, Dept. Personnel Svcs.; Very Rev. BRIAN C. ALFORD, Dept. Vocational Svcs.; MICHAEL CHRISTIE, Evangelical & Catechetical Svcs.; MR. STEVEN ROACH, Dept. Community Svcs.

Chancellor—Very Rev. CHRISTOPHER A. HOUSE, S.T.L., J.C.L., V.J.

Executive Secretary—JOAN REED.

Vicars Forane—

Alton Deanery—Very Rev. JEFFREY H. GOECKNER, V.F.

Decatur Deanery—Very Rev. JOSEPH M. MOLLOY, V.F.

Effingham Deanery—Very Rev. R. DEAN PROBST, J.C.L., V.F.

Jacksonville Deanery—Very Rev. THOMAS C. MEYER, V.F.

Litchfield Deanery—Very Rev. ALBERT F. ALLEN, V.F.

Quincy Deanery—Rev. Msgr. LEO ENLOW, V.F.

Springfield Deanery—Very Rev. JEFFERY A. GRANT, V.F.

Diocesan Curia—

All diocesan agencies and councils are located at the Catholic Pastoral Center, unless otherwise indicated. *Catholic Pastoral Center, 1615 W. Washington St., Springfield, 62702-4757.* Tel: 217-698-8500; Fax: 217-698-0802.

Office of the Bishop—Most Rev. THOMAS JOHN PAPROCKI; CHERYL KNUDSON, Exec. Sec.; MR. PATRICK HUTT. (Executive Assistant to the Bishop, Episcopal Master of Ceremony for the Bishop, Priest Secretary and Project Leader for Special Projects).

Moderator of the Curia/Office of the Vicar General—Rev. Msgr. DAVID J. HOEFLER, V.G., M.Div., Vicar Gen. & Moderator of the Curia; JOAN REED, Exec. Sec.; Bro. ANTHONY JOSEPH MCCOY, F.S.C., Assoc. Exec. Sec.; RUTH STAAB, Receptionist for Catholic Pastoral Center, Special Projects & Central Supply.

Chaplain, Courage Apostolate—Rev. JAMES E. ISAACSON, S.J.C.

Delegate for Extern Priests—Rev. Msgr. DAVID J. HOEFLER, V.G., M.Div.

Delegate for Senior Priests—Rev. Msgr. DAVID L. PETERS, (Retired).

Liaison for Prison Ministries—Rev. DANIEL L. WILLENBORG, Liaison.

Ministry to Priests Team—Most Rev. THOMAS JOHN PAPROCKI; Rev. Msgr. DAVID J. HOEFLER, V.G., M.Div.; Very Revs. BRIAN C. ALFORD; THOMAS C. MEYER, V.F.; SETH A. BROWN; Revs. THOMAS HAGSTROM; JOSEPH T. HAVRILKA; STEPHEN A. THOMPSON; ALLEN M. KEMME; JAMES PALAKUDY, S.A.C.

Theological Consultant to the Diocesan Curia—Very Rev. SETH A. BROWN.

Delegate for Strategy and Logistics—MICHAEL CHRISTIE.

Villa Maria Catholic Life Conference and Retreat Center—1903 E. Lake Shore Dr., Springfield, 62712-5514. Tel: 217-529-2213; Fax: 217-241-2485; Web: villa.dio.org. Deacon GREGORY MAYNERICH, Dir., Email: gmaynerich@dio.org.

Commission for Priests' Benefits—Rev. Msgr. DAVID J. HOEFLER, V.G., M.Div., Ex Officio; Revs. DANIEL J. BERGBOWER; GERALD L. BUNSE, M.Div.; Very Rev. JEFFERY A. GRANT, V.F.; Rev. Msgr. THOMAS P. HOLINGA; Rev. ALLEN M. KEMME; Rev. Msgrs. MICHAEL R. KUSE, (Retired); DAVID L. PETERS, Ex Officio, (Retired). Consultant: Deacon WILLIAM E. KESSLER, Consultant.

Priests' Personnel Board—Most Rev. THOMAS JOHN PAPROCKI; Very Revs. BRIAN C. ALFORD; SETH A. BROWN; Revs. GERALD BUNSE; JOHN C. BURNETTE; BERNARD THOMAS DONOVAN; PAT G. JAKEL; T. JOSEPH HAVRILKA; HYLAND SMITH; Rev. Msgr. DAVID J. HOEFLER, V.G., M.Div., Ex Officio; Very Rev. CHRISTOPHER A. HOUSE, S.T.L., J.C.L., V.J., Consultant.

Department for Canonical and Pastoral Services—Very Rev. CHRISTOPHER A. HOUSE, S.T.L., J.C.L., V.J., Chancellor & Dir.

Office of the Chancellor/Director of Policy Development—Very Rev. CHRISTOPHER A. HOUSE,

S.T.L., J.C.L., V.J., Chancellor; Joan Reed, Exec. Sec.

Chaplain, Equestrian Order of the Holy Sepulchre of Jerusalem—Very Rev. Christopher A. House, S.T.L., J.C.L., V.J., Chancellor.

Chaplain, Catholic Physicians Guild/Catholic Medical Association—Rev. Msgr. David S. Lantz.

Delegate for Healthcare Professionals—Deacon William E. Kessler.

Delegate for Legal Professionals—Rev. John H. Nolan.

Diocesan Ecumenical and Interreligious Officer—Rev. Scott A. Snider.

Liaison for Priests—Rev. Kevin Michael Laughery, J.C.L.

Vicar for Religious—Very Rev. Seth A. Brown.

Office for Archives and Records Management—Katherine Oubre, Dir.; Phillip (P.J.) Oubre, Archives Asst.; Patrick Keen, Project Archival Technician.

Office for Divine Worship and the Catechumenate—Rev. Daren J. Zehnle, J.C.L., Dir.; Vicki Walker, Sec.

Office for Tribunal Services—Very Rev. Christopher A. House, S.T.L., J.C.L., V.J., Judicial Vicar; Rev. Kevin M. Laughery, J.C.L., Judge; Very Rev. R. Dean Probst, J.C.L., V.F., Judge; Revs. Daren J. Zehnle, J.C.L., Adjutant Judicial Vicar; Pawel Augustyniak, J.C.L., Judge; Arthur Anderson, O.F.M., Promoter of Justice & Defender of the Bond Ad Hoc; Becky Donaldson, Office Mgr. & Notary.

Department for Vocational Services—Very Rev. Brian C. Alford, Dir.

Office for Vocations—Very Rev. Brian C. Alford, Dir.

Office for the Diaconate—Deacon David G. Sorrell, Dir.; Joan Reed, Exec. Sec.; Deacon Gregory Maynerich, Assoc. Dir. Ongoing Formation & Ministry.

Office for Vicar for Priests—Very Rev. Brian C. Alford, Vicar.

Office for Vicar for Religious—Very Rev. Seth A. Brown.

Department for Evangelical and Catechetical Services—Michael Christie, Dir.

Center for Discipleship and Stewardship—524 E. Lawrence Ave., Springfield, 62703. Katie Price, Dir.; Rev. Charles A. Edwards, Consultant.

Office for Campus Ministry—Newman Ctr., 500 Roosevelt Ave., Charleston, 61920. Tel: 217-348-0188; Fax: 217-348-8964. Mr. Roy Lanham, M.A., Dir., Email: rlanham@eiunewman.org.

Office for Catechesis—Christine Malmevik, Dir.; Cynthia Gallo Callan, Exec. Sec.

Office for Catholic Schools—Brandi Borries, Supt.; Lori Casson, Sec.

"Catholic Times" Diocesan Newspaper—Vacant, Editor; Cathy Furkin, Exec. Sec.; Laura Weakley, Office Mgr.; William Callan, Layout & Design Mgr.; Carole House, Layout/Design Asst.; Diane Schlindwein, Assoc. Editor.

Office for Communications—Vacant, Dir.; Michael Hoerner, Assoc. Dir. Web Devel., Social Media & Technical Advisor; Cathy Furkin, Exec. Sec.

Office for Information Technology—Dan Gauwitz, Dir.

Office for Marriage and Family Life—Carlos Tejeda, Dir.

Office for the Missions—Deacon Patrick O'Toole, Dir., Email: missions@dio.org.

Office for Youth and Young Adult Ministry—Kyle Holtgrave, Dir.; Cynthia Gallo Callan, Administrative Asst.

Department for Financial Services—Mr. John J. Maxwell, CPA, Dir.

Office for Finances—Mr. John J. Maxwell, CPA, Dir.; Joseph Zerletich, Parish Financial Accountant; Janet Vespa, Controller; Christina Maher, ACSA & Parish Reporting Support Staff; Heather McMillen, Accountant; Bobbie Ozanic, ACSA Coord. & Sec.

Diocese of Springfield in Illinois Deposit and Loan Fund—Most Rev. Thomas John Paprocki, Trustee; Mr. John J. Maxwell, CPA, Contact Person; Rev. Msgr. David J. Hoefler, V.G., M.Div., Contact Person.

Loan Committee—Rev. Msgr. David J. Hoefler, V.G., M.Div.; Patrick Ketchum; Leo A. Lenn; Mr. John J. Maxwell, CPA; John Staudt; Janet Vespa.

Deposit and Loan Investment Committee—James Davis; Timothy Healy; J. Michael Houston. Consultors: Mr. John J. Maxwell, CPA; Mr. Shaun Riedell; Janet Vespa.

Office for Development—Mr. Shaun Riedell, Dir.; Bobbi Ozanic, Office Asst.

Foundation for the People of the Roman Catholic Diocese of Springfield in Illinois Board of Directors—Most Rev. Thomas John Paprocki, Pres.; Rev. Msgr. David J. Hoefler, V.G., M.Div., Vice Pres.; Mr. John J. Maxwell, CPA, Treas.; Mr. Shaun Riedell, Sec.; Brandi Borries, Member. Consultant: Janet Vespa.

Foundation for the People of the Roman Catholic Diocese of Springfield in Illinois Advisory Board Members—Michael Bickhaus; Michael Durbin; John Gibbons; Rance Higgins; Very Rev. Thomas C. Meyer, V.F.; Mrs. Marlene Mulford; Christopher Niemann; Thomas C. Pavlik Jr.; Jeff Stauffer; Polly Wand.

Office for Insurance and Benefits—Patrick Ketchum, Dir.; Michael Kelly, Assoc. Dir.; Laura Weakley, Insurance Assoc., Fax: 217-698-8282 (Confidential for Insurance Issues).

Diocesan Health Insurance Program Committee—Brandi Borries; Michael Christie; Rev. Msgr. David J. Hoefler, V.G., M.Div.; Patrick Ketchum, Chair; Michael Kelly; Patricia Kornfeld; Mr. John J. Maxwell, CPA; Audra Schultz; Janet Vespa; Laura Weakley; Julie Yost.

Lay Employees' Pension Plan Administrative Committee—Brandi Borries; Michael Christie, Chm.; Mr. John J. Maxwell, CPA, Treas.; Thomas Frier; Rev. Msgr. David J. Hoefler, V.G., M.Div.; Patrick Ketchum, Sec.; Michael Kelly; Patricia Kornfeld; Janet Vespa; Laura Weakley. Consultant: Jerald T. Barkmeier.

Office for Property, Buildings and Cemeteries—Gregory Fleck, Dir.; Brad Fisher, Cemetery Assoc.

Maintenance—Doug Crocher, Facilities Mgr.; Ryan McCarty, Maintenance; John Doedtman, Maintenance.

Commission for Buildings and Property—Very Rev. Christopher A. House, S.T.L., J.C.L., V.J., Member; Rev. Msgr. David J. Hoefler, V.G., M.Div., Consultant; Ann M. Carr; Gerald L. Glaus Sr.; Deacon Dominic Palazzolo; Thomas C. Pavlik Jr., Chm. Members: Gregory Fleck; Mr. John J. Maxwell, CPA.

Cemetery Advisory Board—Revs. Thomas Hagstrom; Joseph T. Havrilka; Linda Medlock; Deacon John O'Brien; Gregory Fleck, Member; Brad Fisher, Consultant.

Department for Personnel Services—Patricia Kornfeld, Dir.

Office for Human Resources—Patricia Kornfeld, Dir.; Debbie Maynerich, Administrative Asst.

Office for Safe Environment—Vacant, Dir. & Victim Asst. Min.; Debbie Maynerich, Administrative Asst.

Department for Community Services—Mr. Steven E. Roach, M.S., Exec. Dir.

Chaplain, Catholic Medical Association—Rev. Msgr. David S. Lantz.

Diocesan Campaign for Justice and Hope—Donna Moore.

Office for Catholic Charities—(Central Administration) Steven E. Roach, M.S., Exec. Dir., 1625 W. Washington, Springfield, 62702. Tel: 217-523-9201; Fax: 217-523-5624; Amber Cerveny, Devel. Coord.; Elaine Perine, CPA, Dir. Finance & Admin.; Amy Maher, Dir. Oper.

Corporate Board Members—Most Rev. Thomas John Paprocki, Pres.; Rev. Msgr. David J. Hoefler, V.G., M.Div.; Very Rev. Christopher A. House, S.T.L., J.C.L., V.J.; Mr. John J. Maxwell, CPA.

Corporate Board Directors—Larry Clark, Chm.; Susan Breheny; Reginald Coleman, Ex Officio; R. Thomas Cullen; Rev. John Doctor, O.F.M.; James M. Graham; Deacon William E. Kessler; Clare McCulla; Mrs. Marlene Mulford; Chris Peterson, Dir.; Richard Gibson, Dir.; Robert Schultz, Treas.; Sr. Jomary Trstensky, O.S.F., M.H.A., M.S.N.; Andy Watson, Vice Chm.; John C. Webster, Sec.

Office for Pro-Life Activities & Special Ministries—Donna Moore, Dir.; Karla A. Crews, Assoc. Dir., Spec. Needs Ministry; Christine Lansaw, Assoc. Dir. Deaf Ministry.

Black Catholic Commission—Victoria Dhabalt Compton; Cathy Gwynn-Hines; Johnetta Jordan; Leroy Jordan; Donna Moore, Ex Officio; Mrs. Renee Saunches; Lorna Simon; Sr. Mary Jean Traeger, O.P.

Immigration Commission—Ed Cardenes, Chm.; Bozi Kieke; Donna Moore; Elaine Perine, CPA; Steven E. Roach, M.S.; Laura Wolfe, Sec.

Diocesan Committee for Hispanic Ministry (Comite Diocesano de Ministerio Hispano)—Penny Clay; Luptya Cantu; Revs. Paul A. Habing; Kevin Mann, S.J.C.; Sr. Ofelia Quiroz-Martinez, M.A.G.; Donna Moore; Mrs. Doris Nordin; Carlos Tejeda; Rev. Daniel L. Willenborg.

Diocesan Campaign for Justice and Hope Allocation Committee—Donna Moore, Dir.; Steven E. Roach, M.S., Ex Officio; Neide Steiner; Judy Unger, (Alton Deanery); Ken Handley, (Decatur Deanery); Edward Smith, (Decatur Deanery); Deacons Eugene V. Uptmor Jr., (Effingham Deanery); Michael P. Ellerman, (Jacksonville Deanery); Joseph Kaufmann, (Jacksonville Deanery); Deacon Raymond L. Roth Jr., (Litchfield Deanery); Elaine Bekoin-Minor, (Springfield Deanery); Terry Tuttle, (Springfield Deanery).

Councils

Diocesan Finance Council—Most Rev. Thomas John Paprocki; Very Rev. Albert F. Allen, V.F.; Rev. Michael B. Haag; James Davis; William L. Hahn; Robin G. Hake; Linda Harchanick; Timothy Healy; Deacon William E. Kessler; J. Michael Houston; Dan McGuire; John Staudt; Kenneth Vogt; Gregory Fleck. Consultants: Rev. Msgr. David J. Hoefler, V.G., M.Div.; Mr. John J. Maxwell, CPA; Mr. Shaun Riedell; Janet Vespa.

Presbyteral Council—Most Rev. Thomas John Paprocki, Pres.; Rev. Steven M. Arisman; Very Rev. Albert F. Allen, V.F.; Revs. Mariadas Chatla; Christopher J. Comerford; Rev. Msgr. Leo J. Enlow, V.F.; Very Revs. Jeffrey H. Goeckner, V.F.; Jeffery A. Grant, V.F.; Rev. Thomas Hagstrom; Rev. Msgr. David J. Hoefler, V.G., M.Div., Ex Officio & Vice Chm.; Very Rev. Christopher A. House, S.T.L., J.C.L., V.J., Chancellor, Sec., Treas. & Ex Officio; Rev. Robert Johnson; Very Revs. Thomas C. Meyer, V.F.; Joseph M. Molloy, V.F.; Rev. Msgr. James D. O'Shea, (Retired); Rev. Martin Smith; Very Rev. R. Dean Probst, J.C.L., V.F.; Revs. Scott A. Snider, Chm.; John M. Titus; Donald L. Wolford; Very Rev. Brian C. Alford, Ex Officio.

College of Consultors—Very Revs. Brian C. Alford; Seth A. Brown; Revs. Joseph P. Carlos, O.F.M.; Christopher J. Comerford; Rev. Msgr. David J. Hoefler, V.G., M.Div.; Rev. William Jeffry Holtman, O.F.S.; Very Rev. Christopher A. House, S.T.L., J.C.L., V.J., Sec.; Revs. Hyland Smith; Stephen A. Thompson.

Diocesan Pastoral Council—Margaret Antenan; Betty Bailey; Megan Breheny-Bennett; Michael Christie, Chm.; Sr. M. Margaretta Dalton, F.S.G.M.; Rev. Charles A. Edwards; Patty Fitzpatrick; Deacon James J. Ghiglione; Dale Hilgenbrinck; Rev. Msgr. David J. Hoefler, V.G., M.Div.; Very Rev. Christopher A. House, S.T.L., J.C.L., V.J.; Nicole Lohman; George Menard; David Michael; Kathy Philips, Sec.; Linda Rull; Sr. Rene Simonelic; Rev. Stephen A. Thompson; Elaine Wagner; Zach Wichmann, Vice Chm.

CLERGY, PARISHES, MISSIONS AND PAROCHIAL SCHOOLS

CITY OF SPRINGFIELD

(Sangamon County)

1—Cathedral of the Immaculate Conception (1928) [JC]

524 E. Lawrence Ave., 62703. Tel: 217-522-3342; Email: lduffey@cathedral.dio.org. Very Rev. Christopher A. House, S.T.L., J.C.L., V.J.; Revs. Michael Friedel, Parochial Vicar; Wayne Stock, Parochial Vicar; Deacons Irvin (Larry) Smith, Dir. of Nulity & Assistance; Thomas Scott Keen, D.R.E.

2—St. Agnes (1889)

245 N. Amos Ave., 62702. Tel: 217-793-1330; Email: sac245@comcast.net. Revs. Robert J. Jallas, V.F.; Pawel Augustyniak, J.C.L., Parochial Vicar; Deacon Roy Harley.

School—St. Agnes School, (Grades PreSchool-8), 251 North Amos Ave., 62702. Tel: 217-793-1370; Email: info@stagnescatholicschool.org; Web: stagnescatholicschool.org. Rachel Cunningham, Prin. Clergy 1; Lay Teachers 28; Students 307.

Catechesis Religious Program—Students 87.

3—St. Aloysius (1928) [JC]

2119 N. 20th St., 62702. Tel: 217-544-4554; Web: www.saintaloysius.org. Rev. Clinton Honkomp, O.P., Email: fr.honkomp@yahoo.com; Deacon Dominic Anthony Palazzolo.

School—St. Aloysius School, (Grades PreSchool-8), 2125 N. 21st St., 62702. Tel: 217-544-4553; Email: angie.daniels@saintaloysius.org; Web: saintaloysius.org. Clergy 1; Lay Teachers 16; Students 156.

Catechesis Religious Program—

4—Blessed Sacrament (1924)

1725 S. Walnut Ave., 62704. Tel: 217-528-7521;

Email: mantenan@bsps.org. Very Rev. Jeffery A. Grant, V.F.; Rev. Ronnie Lorillo; Deacons David R. Erdmann; Thomas G. Burns.
School—Blessed Sacrament School, (Grades PreK-8), 748 West Laurel, 62704. Tel: 217-522-7534; Fax: 217-522-7542; Email: hoffmann@bssbruins.org; Web: www.bssbruins.org. Lay Teachers 31; Students 525; Clergy / Religious Teachers 2.
Catechesis Religious Program—Students 56.

5—CHRIST THE KING (1963)
1930 Barberry Dr., 62704. Tel: 217-546-3527; Email: church@ctkparish.com. Rev. Joseph G. Ring.
School—Christ the King School, 1920 Barberry Dr., 62704. Tel: 217-546-2159; Fax: 217-546-0291; Email: fahey@ctkcougars.com; Web: www.ctkcougars.com. Lay Teachers 30; Students 367.
Catechesis Religious Program— (Elementary) Students 62.

6—ST. FRANCES CABRINI (1948)
1020 N. Milton Ave., 62702. Tel: 217-522-8555; Email: parishoffice@stcabrini.dio.org; Web: www.stcabrini.dio.org. Rev. Scott Thelander, S.J.C.
Catechesis Religious Program—Catherine Becker, Dir. Faith Formation. Students 5.

7—ST. JOSEPH (1875)
1345 N. Sixth St., 62702. Tel: 217-544-7426; Email: parish@stjoseph.dio.org. Rev. Manuel P. Cuizon, C.R.S., (Philippines) Admin.; Deacon Lawrence H. Day; Sisters Mary Ellen Backes, O.S.U., Pastoral Assoc. Evangelization; Martha Marie Kirbach, O.P., Pastoral Assoc. Pastoral Care.
Res.: 1300 N. 5th St., 62702. Tel: 217-528-6717.
Catechesis Religious Program—Sr. Mary Ellen Backes, O.S.U., D.R.E. Students 17.

8—ST. KATHARINE DREXEL (2001)
Mailing Address: 722 S. 12th St., 62703.
Tel: 217-523-4501; Email: pastor@kdrexel.org. Revs. James E. Isaacson, S.J.C.; Kevin Mann, S.J.C., Parochial Vicar; Trenton Rauck, Parochial Vicar.
Sacred Heart Church: 730 S. 12th St., 62703.
St. Patrick Church: 1720 S. Grand Ave. East, 62703.
Catechesis Religious Program—Students 39.

9—LITTLE FLOWER (1947) [JC]
800 Stevenson Dr., 62703. Tel: 217-529-1606; Fax: 217-529-1649; Email: pax@littleflowerchurch.net; Web: littleflowerchurch.net. Rev. Allen M. Kemme; Rev. Msgr. John R. Ossola, Pastor Emeritus, (Retired).
School—Little Flower School, (Grades PreK-8), 900 Stevenson Dr., 62703. Tel: 217-529-4511; Fax: 217-529-0405; Email: office@little-flower.org; Web: little-flower.org. Dr. William Moredock, Prin. Lay Teachers 16; Students 199.
Catechesis Religious Program—Ali Orr, D.R.E. Students 38.

10—ST. PATRICK, Merged with Sacred Heart of Jesus, Springfield to form St. Katharine Drexel, Springfield.For inquiries for parish records, contact the Diocesan Office for Archives and Records Management.

11—SS. PETER AND PAUL (1859) (German), Closed. For inquiries for parish records, contact the Diocesan Office for Archives and Records Management.

12—SACRED HEART OF JESUS (1884) (German), Merged with St. Patrick, Springfield to form St. Katharine Drexel, Springfield.For inquiries for parish records, contact the Diocesan Office for Archives and Records Management.

OUTSIDE THE CITY OF SPRINGFIELD

ALEXANDER, MORGAN CO., VISITATION B.V.M. (1909) [CEM]
506 Rte. 36, Alexander, 62601. Tel: 217-488-3545; Fax: 217-488-3545; Email: quadpastoralunit@gmail.com; Web: www.quadpastoralunit.com. Mailing Address: P.O. Box 20, New Berlin, 62670. Very Rev. Seth A. Brown.
Church: Old U.S. 36, Alexander, 62601.
Catechesis Religious Program—414 Wyatt, Franklin, 62638. Students 3.

ALTAMONT, EFFINGHAM CO., ST. CLARE (1874) [CEM] (German)
216 N. Ninth St., Altamont, 62411.
Tel: 618-483-5346; Email: office@stclarealtamont.dio.org. Rev. Christudasan Kurisadima, Admin.
Catechesis Religious Program—Students 55.
Mission—St. Mary, St. Elmo, Fayette Co.

ALTON, MADISON CO.

1—ST. MARY'S (1858) [CEM]
Mailing Address: 519 E. 4th St., Alton, 62002.
Tel: 618-465-4284; Fax: 618-463-4637; Email: laurie@stmarysalton.com; Web: www.stmarysalton.com. Revs. Jeremy Paulin; John Luong, O.M.V.; Paul Nguyen, Pastoral Assoc.; Deacon James Schwartzkopf, R.C.I.A. Coord.; Ron Abraham, Music Min. In Res., Rev. David Beauregard, O.M.V.
Res.: 525 E. Fourth St., Alton, 62002.
Schools—St. Mary's School—(Grades PreSchool-8), 536 E. 3rd St., Alton, 62002. Tel: 618-465-8523; Tel: 681-465-9719; Fax: 618-465-4725; Web: www.smsalton.com. Alex Pulido, Prin. Lay Teachers 22; Preschool 43; Students 303; Sisters of St. Francis of the Martyr St. George 2.
Middle School, (Grades PreSchool-8), 1015 Milton Rd., Alton, 62002.
Catechesis Religious Program—Rev. John Wykes, O.M.V., D.R.E. Students 74.

2—ST. MATTHEW (1947) Closed. For inquiries for parish records, contact the Diocesan Office for Archives and Records Management.

3—ST. PATRICK (1883) Closed. For inquiries for parish records, contact the Diocesan Office for Archives and Records Management.

4—SS. PETER AND PAUL (1855) [JC]
717 State St., Alton, 62002. Tel: 618-465-4221; Email: info@ssppalton.com; Web: www.ssppalton.com. Rev. Jason P. Stone; Chrissy Lewis, Business Mgr.
School—Ss. Peter and Paul School, (Grades PreK-8), 801 State St., Alton, 62002. Tel: 618-465-8711; Fax: 618-465-6405; Email: hcvngh@yahoo.com; Web: www.sspsch.com. Mr. Harry Cavanaugh, Prin.; Angela Bormon, Librarian; Becky Williams, Librarian. Lay Teachers 12; Students 58.
Catechesis Religious Program—Students 10.

ARCOLA, DOUGLAS CO., ST. JOHN THE BAPTIST (1865) [JC]
204 S. Pine St., Arcola, 61910. Tel: 217-268-3766; Fax: 217-268-3545; Email: johnbaptist@consolidated.net. Mailing Address: 205 S. Locust St., P.O. Box 133, Arcola, 61910. Rev. Angel Sierra; Margaret Thompson, Sec.
Catechesis Religious Program—Parish School of Religion, Maria Miller, D.R.E. Students 101.

ARENZVILLE, CASS CO., ST. FIDELIS (1853) (German—Irish)
215 W. Fifth St., Beardstown, 62618.
Tel: 217-371-4713; Email: staalf4@casscomm.com. Mailing Address: 240 E. Myrtle St., Virginia, 62691. Very Rev. Thomas C. Meyer, V.F.; Revs. Braden Maher, Parochial Vicar; Rafal Pyrchla, Parochial Vicar; Deacon Paul Koch.
Res.: 453 E. State St., Jacksonville, 62650.
Church: 601 W. North St., Arenzville, 62611.
Catechesis Religious Program—

ASHLAND, CASS CO., ST. AUGUSTINE (1875) [CEM]
320 N. Saratoga, Ashland, 62612. Tel: 217-476-8856; Email: sta@casscomm.com; Web: www.staugustineashland.org. Rev. Daren J. Zehnle, J.C.L.
Catechesis Religious Program—Tanya Wallbaum, D.R.E. Students 31.

ASSUMPTION, CHRISTIAN CO., ASSUMPTION B.V.M. (1857) [CEM]
301 St. Peter St., Assumption, 62510.
Tel: 217-226-3536; Email: stmarybvm1857@aim.com. Rev. Marianna Sathuluri, (India) Parochial Admin.; Deacon John O'Brien.
Catechesis Religious Program—Tel: 217-226-3205. Students 30.

ATHENS, MENARD CO., HOLY FAMILY (1903) [CEM]
309 N. Springfield Rd., Athens, 62613.
Tel: 217-632-7118; Email: stpeter234@sbcglobal.net; Web: hfa.dio.org. Mailing Address: 711 S. 6th St., Petersburg, 62675. Rev. Msgr. Thomas P. Holinga.
Res.: 212 Washington St., Petersburg, 62675.
Tel: 217-632-0151.
Catechesis Religious Program—Lisa Reeves, Admin. Religious Education Program merged with St. Peter Church. Students 17.

AUBURN, SANGAMON CO.

1—ST. BENEDICT (1880) [JC] Merged with Sacred Heart, Divernon and St. Mary, Pawnee to form Holy Cross, Auburn. For inquiries for parish records, contact Holy Cross, Auburn.

2—HOLY CROSS (2006)
125 E. Washington St., Auburn, 62615-0168.
Tel: 217-438-6222; Email: hcp@royell.org. P.O. Box 168, Auburn, 62615. Rev. James Palakudy, S.A.C.
St. Benedict Church, 128 E. Washington St., Auburn, 62615.
Catechesis Religious Program—Students 70.

BARRY, PIKE CO., HOLY REDEEMER (1954) [JC] Closed. For inquiries for parish records, contact St. Mary, Pittsfield.

BATCHTOWN, CALHOUN CO., ST. BARBARA (1910) [CEM] Merged with St. Mary, Brussels and St. Joseph, Meppen to form Blessed Trinity, Brussels. For inquiries for parish records, contact Blessed Trinity, Brussels.

BEARDSTOWN, CASS CO., ST. ALEXIUS (1853) [CEM]
215 W. 5th St., Beardstown, 62618.
Tel: 217-371-4713; Email: staalf4@casscomm.com. 240 E. Myrtle St., Virginia, 62691. Very Rev. Thomas C. Meyer, V.F.; Revs. Braden Maher, Parochial Vicar; Rafal Pyrchla, Parochial Vicar; Deacon Paul Koch.
Res.: 453 E. State St., Jacksonville, 62650.
Catechesis Religious Program—Students 227.

BELLEVIEW, CALHOUN CO., ST. AGNES (1900) [CEM] Merged with St. Anselm, Kampsville, St. Norbert, Hardin and St. Michael, Michael to form St. Francis of Assisi, Hardin. For inquiries for parish records, contact St. Francis of Assisi, Hardin.

BELTREES, JERSEY CO., ST. MICHAEL (1877) [CEM] Closed. For inquiries for parish records, contact St. Ambrose, Godfrey.

BENLD, MACOUPIN CO., ST. JOSEPH (1915)
218 E. Central Ave., Benld, 62009. Tel: 217-839-3456; Email: simonjude3456@gmail.com; Web: macoupincatholicchurch.com. Mailing Address: 304 N. Macoupin, Gillespie, 62033. Rev. Michael B. Haag; Deacon Dennis W. Baker; Ms. Rosemary Messner, Music Min.
Church: 310 W. Central Ave., Benld, 62009.
Catechesis Religious Program—Ms. Karla Huddlestun, D.R.E. Students 17.

BETHALTO, MADISON CO., OUR LADY QUEEN OF PEACE (1945)
132 Butcher St., P.O. Box 100, Bethalto, 62010.
Tel: 618-377-6519; Email: church@olqpbethalto.org. Rev. Thomas R. Liebler.
School—Our Lady Queen of Peace School, (Grades PreK-8), 618 N. Prairie, Bethalto, 62010.
Tel: 618-377-6401; Email: olqpeve@hotmail.com. Eve Remiszewski, Prin. Lay Teachers 14; Students 135.
Catechesis Religious Program—Students 41.

BETHANY, MOULTRIE CO., ST. ISIDORE (1864) [CEM]
364 CR 2000 N, Bethany, 61914. Tel: 217-864-3467; Email: sarisman@dio.org. Mailing Address: c/o Our Lady of the Holy Spirit, 400 Whitetail Cr., Mt. Zion, 62549. Rev. Steven M. Arisman.
Res.: c/o Our Lady of the Holy Spirit, 400 Woodland Ln., Mt. Zion, 62549. Email: mtzolhs@comcast.net; Web: www.mtzolhs.org.
Catechesis Religious Program—Mandy Hoffman, D.R.E. Students 6.

BISHOP CREEK, EFFINGHAM CO., ST. ALOYSIUS (1865) [CEM] Closed. For inquiries for parish records, contact St. Isidore the Farmer, Dieterich.

BLACK JACK, MADISON CO., ST. JOHN THE BAPTIST, Closed. For inquiries for parish records, contact the Diocesan Office for Archives and Records Management.

BLUFFS, SCOTT CO., ST. PATRICK (1871) Closed. For inquiries for parish records, contact St. Mark, Winchester.

BRIGHTON, MACOUPIN CO., ST. ALPHONSUS (1868) [CEM] (German)
920 N. Main St., Brighton, 62012. Tel: 618-372-3352; Email: office@sap-brighton.org; Web: www.sap-brighton.org. Rev. William F. Kesser, Parochial Admin.; Susan Matsche, Sec.
Res.: 918 N. Main St., Brighton, 62012.
Catechesis Religious Program—Chastity Brockway. Students 25.

BROCTON, EDGAR CO., ST. THOMAS AQUINAS (1899) Closed. For inquiries for parish records, contact St. Mark, Winchester.

BRUSSELS, CALHOUN CO.

1—BLESSED TRINITY (2005)
111 E. Main, P.O. Box 38, Brussels, 62013-0038.
Tel: 618-883-2400; Fax: 618-883-2511. Rev. Don J. Roberts; Deacon Michael B. Hagen.
Res.: Meppen Ln., Meppen, 62013. Tel: 618-883-2309
School—St. Mary School, 105 East Main, P. O. Box 39, Brussels, 62013. Tel: 618-883-2124. Rebecca Lorts, Prin. Lay Teachers 7; Students 55.
Catechesis Religious Program—

2—ST. MARY (1851) [CEM] Merged with St. Barbara, Batchtown and St. Joseph, Meppen to form Blessed Trinity, Brussels. For inquiries for parish records, contact Blessed Trinity, Brussels.

BUFFALO, SANGAMON CO., ST. JOSEPH (1882) Closed. For inquiries for parish records please see Resurrection Parish, Illiopolis.

BUNKER HILL, MACOUPIN CO., ST. MARY (1854) [CEM] Closed. For inquiries for parish records, contact the Diocesan Office for Archives and Records Management.

CAMP POINT, ADAMS CO., ST. THOMAS (1860)
109 E. Spring St., P.O. Box 252, Camp Point, 62320.
Tel: 217-593-6685; Email: stthomascp@gmail.com; Web: www.stthomascp.org. Rev. Stephen A. Thompson; Deacon Michael P. Ellerman.
Res.: 401 W. North St., Mount Sterling, 62353-0252. Tel: 217-773-3233.
Parish Hall:—103 E. Spring St., Camp Point, 62320.
Catechesis Religious Program—Students 33.

CARLINVILLE, MACOUPIN CO.

1—SS. MARY & JOSEPH (1996) [JC] SS. Mary & Joseph was formed by the merger of St. Mary's of the Immaculate Conception & St. Joseph.
2010 E. First S. St., P.O. Box 647, Carlinville, 62626.
Tel: 217-854-7151; Email: secretaryssmjc@gmail.com; Web: www.macoupincatholicchurch.com. Rev. Michael B. Haag; Deacon Dennis W. Baker; Ms. Karla Huddlestun, D.R.E.

2—ST. MARY'S OF THE IMMACULATE CONCEPTION, Closed. For inquiries for parish records, contact the Diocesan Office for Archives and Records Management.

CARROLLTON, GREENE CO., ST. JOHN THE EVANGELIST (1858) [CEM]
414 Third St., Carrollton, 62016. Tel: 217-942-3551; Email: mchatla@dio.org. Revs. Mariadas Chatla, Admin.; Henry Schmidt, Pastor Emeritus, (Retired); Deacon Charles Theivagt.
School—St. John the Evangelist School, (Grades PreK-8), 426 Third St., Carrollton, 62016-1319.
Tel: 217-942-6814; Fax: 217-942-5274; Email: lschnettgoecke@stjohnscarrollton.org. Julie Lake, Prin. Clergy 1; Lay Teachers 12; Students 161.
Catechesis Religious Program—Students 5.

CASEY, CLARK CO., ST. CHARLES BORROMEO (1878)
300 E. Jefferson St., Casey, 62420. Tel: 217-826-2845 ; Email: stmarysmarshall@hotmail.com; Email: mckchurches@weebly.com. Mailing Address: 414 S. 6th St., Marshall, 62441. Rev. Augustine Koomson, Admin.
Catechesis Religious Program—Ms. Karla Huddlestun, D.R.E. Students 17.

CHANDLERVILLE, CASS CO., ST. BASIL, Merged with St. Luke, Virginia. For inquiries for parish records, contact St. Luke, Virginia.

CHARLESTON, COLES CO., ST. CHARLES BORROMEO (1873)
921 E. Madison St., Charleston, 61920.
Tel: 217-345-3332; Email: office@saintcharleschurch.org. Rev. Hyland Smith; Deacon William Jeffrey Beals, Pastoral Assoc.
Catechesis Religious Program—Deacon William Jeffrey Beals, D.R.E. Students 90.

CHATHAM, SANGAMON CO., ST. JOSEPH THE WORKER (1920)
700 E. Spruce St., Chatham, 62629.
Tel: 217-483-3772; Fax: 217-483-4581; Email: stjos@comcast.net; Web: www.stjoschatham.org. Rev. John H. Nolan; Deacon Gregory Maynerich; Sr. Judith Pfile, O.P., Pastoral Assoc.
Res.: 1812 Turtle Creek Dr., Chatham, 62629.

COFFEEN, MONTGOMERY CO., ST. JOHN THE BAPTIST (1898) [CEM] [JC] Closed. For inquiries for parish records please see St. Agnes, Hillsboro.

COLLINSVILLE, MADISON CO., SS. PETER AND PAUL (1855) [CEM] (Italian)
207 Vandalia St., Collinsville, 62234.
Tel: 618-345-4343; Email: aauer@saintspeter-paul.org; Web: www.saintspeter-paul.org. Rev. John P. Beveridge; Deacons James R. Hill; Fernando Solomon, O.P.Miss.
Res.: 200 Westview St., Collinsville, 62234.
School—SS. Peter and Paul School, (Grades PreK-8), 210 N. Morrison Ave., Collinsville, 62234.
Tel: 618-344-5450; Fax: 618-344-5536; Web: www.sspeter-paulschool.org. Lay Teachers 17; Students 192.
Catechesis Religious Program—Email: dj@saintspeter-paul.org. Deacon James J. Ghiglione, D.R.E. Students 50.

DALTON CITY, MOULTRIE CO., SACRED HEART (1891) Closed. For inquiries for parish records, contact the Diocesan Office for Archives and Records Management.

DECATUR, MACON CO.
1—HOLY FAMILY (1959) [JC]
2400 S. Franklin St., Decatur, 62521.
Tel: 217-423-6223; Email: holyfamilychurch1@comcast.net; Web: www.decaturholyfamily.com. Very Rev. Joseph M. Molloy, V.F.
Convent—Holy Family Convent, 2450 S. Franklin St., Decatur, 62521. Sisters 2.
School—Holy Family School, (Grades PreSchool-8), Tel: 217-423-7049; Fax: 217-423-0137; Email: dalexander@hfcschool.org; Web: www.hfcschool.org. Debbie Alexander, Prin. Lay Teachers 20; Preschool 39; Springfield Dominican Sisters 1; Students 181.
Catechesis Religious Program—Students 47.
2—ST. JAMES (1877) [JC] Merged with St. Patrick, Decatur to form Saints James and Patrick Parish, Decatur. For inquiries for parish records contact Saints James and Patrick Parish, Decatur.
3—SAINTS JAMES AND PATRICK PARISH (2007) [CEM]
407 E. Eldorado St., Decatur, 62523.
Tel: 217-429-5363 (Office); Tel: 217-428-7733 (Office) ; Fax: 217-429-8206; Email: office@ssjpparish.com; Web: www.ssjpparish.org. Rev. John C. Burnette; Anita Olson, Office Mgr.; Carla Hahn, Finance Sec.; Mrs. Sue Miller, Min. Scheduler; Mr. Tom Prior, Outreach; Mrs. Robin Canary, Sec.
School—St. Patrick School, (Grades PreK-8), 412 N. Jackson, Decatur, 62523. Tel: 217-423-4351; Email: sweetj@ssjpparish.com; Web: www.decaturstpatrick.org. Jan Sweet, Prin. Lay Teachers 14; Students 146.
Catechesis Religious Program—Students 49.
4—OUR LADY OF LOURDES (1958) [JC]
3850 Lourdes Dr., Decatur, 62526. Tel: 217-877-4404 ; Email: frrick@ololchurch.com. Rev. Richard W. Weltin.
School—Our Lady of Lourdes School, (Grades PreSchool-8), 3950 Lourdes Dr., Decatur, 62526-1799. Tel: 217-877-4408; Fax: 217-872-3655; Email: joe@ololchurch.com. Lay Teachers 18; Students 234.
Catechesis Religious Program—Barb Hertl, D.R.E., Tel: 217-791-3015. Students 99.
5—ST. PATRICK (1853) [JC] Merged with St. James, Decatur to form Saints James and Patrick Parish, Decatur. For inquiries for parish records contact Saints James and Patrick Parish, Decatur.
6—ST. THOMAS THE APOSTLE (1925)
2160 N. Edward St., Decatur, 62526.
Tel: 217-877-4146. Rev. Richard W. Weltin; Rev. Msgr. James D. O'Shea, (Retired); Deacon Kevin Richardson.
Res.: 3850 Lourdes Dr., Decatur, 62526.
Catechesis Religious Program—Students 12.

DIETERICH, EFFINGHAM CO.
1—IMMACULATE CONCEPTION (1905) [CEM] Closed. For inquiries for parish records, contact St. Isidore the Farmer, Dieterich.
2—ST. ISIDORE THE FARMER CHURCH (2004) [CEM]
19812 E. 1000th Ave., Dieterich, 62424.
Tel: 217-925-5579; Fax: 217-925-5879; Email: office@stisidore.dio.org; Web: stisidore.weconnect.com. Rev. William J. Rooney, O.F.M.
Catechesis Religious Program—Students 288.

DIVERNON, SANGAMON CO., SACRED HEART (1905) [CEM] Merged with St. Benedict, Auburn and St. Mary, Pawnee to form Holy Cross, Auburn. For inquiries for parish records, contact Holy Cross, Auburn.

EAST ALTON, MADISON CO., ST. KEVIN (1959) Merged with St. Bernard, Wood River to form Holy Angels, Wood River. For inquiries for parish records, contact Holy Angels, Wood River.

EDGEWOOD, EFFINGHAM CO., ST. ANNE (1865) [CEM] (German)
408 Broad St., Edgewood, 62426. Tel: 618-483-5346; Email: office@stclarealtamont.dio.org. Mailing Address: 216 N. Ninth, Altamont, 62411. Rev. Christudasan Kurisadima, Admin.
Catechesis Religious Program—Tel: 614-238-4513. Students 4.

EDWARDSVILLE, MADISON CO.
1—ST. BONIFACE (1869) [CEM] (German)
110 N. Buchanan St., Edwardsville, 62025.
Tel: 618-656-6450; Email: stbchurch@st-boniface.com; Web: www.st-boniface.com. Very Rev. Jeffrey H. Goeckner, V.F.; Rev. Robert Paul Johson; Deacon Daniel L. Corbett.
Res.: 326 N. Buchanan St., Edwardsville, 62025.
Child Care—Preschool, Tel: 618-692-9315. Students 61.
School—St. Boniface School, (Grades K-8), 128 N. Buchanan St., Edwardsville, 62025.
Tel: 618-656-6917; Email: stbschool@st-boniface.com. Mrs. Laura Kretzer, Prin. Clergy 1; Lay Teachers 16; Students 213.
Catechesis Religious Program—Students 270.
2—ST. MARY (1842) [CEM] [JC]
1802 Madison Ave., Edwardsville, 62025.
Tel: 618-656-4857; Email: office@stmaryedw.org. Rev. Daniel J. Bergbower.
School—St. Mary School, (Grades PreK-8),
Tel: 618-656-1230; Email: wepkingdk@stmaryedw.org. Mrs. Diane Wepking, Prin. Clergy 1; Lay Teachers 14; Students 174.
Catechesis Religious Program—Students 145.

EFFINGHAM, EFFINGHAM CO.
1—ST. ANTHONY OF PADUA (1858) [CEM]
101 E. Virginia, P.O. Box 764, Effingham, 62401.
Tel: 217-347-7129; Email: bulletin@stanthony.com. Revs. Charles A. Edwards; Mark Walker Tracy; Deacon Joseph A. Emmerich.
School—St. Anthony of Padua School, St. Anthony Grade School, 405 N. Second St., Effingham, 62401.
Tel: 217-347-0419; Fax: 217-347-2749; Email: vmurphy@stanthony.com; Web: stanthony.com. Clergy 2; Lay Teachers 29; Students 404.
High School—St. Anthony of Padua High School, St. Anthony High School, 304 E. Roadway Ave., Effingham, 62401. Tel: 217-342-6969;
Fax: 217-342-6997; Email: jsemple@stanthony.com. Lay Teachers 19; Priests 3; Students 208.
Catechesis Religious Program—Students 26.
2—SACRED HEART (1892) [JC]
405 S. Henrietta, P.O. Box 870, Effingham, 62401.
Tel: 217-347-7177; Email: shchurch@sheff.org; Web: www.sheff.org. Rev. Michal Rosa.
School—Sacred Heart School, (Grades K-8),
Tel: 217-342-4060; Email: v.wenthe@sheff.org. Mrs. Vicki Wenthe, Admin. Lay Teachers 15; Students 238.
Catechesis Religious Program—Students 106.

FARMERSVILLE, MONTGOMERY CO., ST. MARY (1876) [CEM] [JC]
310 Nobbie St., Farmersville, 62533.
Tel: 217-227-3349; Email: aallen@dio.org. Very Rev. Albert F. Allen, V.F., Admin.; Rev. Gerald L. Bunse, M.Div., Pastor Emeritus; Deacon Patrick J. O'Toole.

FIELDON, JERSEY CO., ST. MARY (1850) [CEM]
306 N. Washington, Jerseyville, 62052.
Tel: 618-498-3416; Email: hgchurch@gtec.com. Revs. Stephen J. Pohlman; Martin Smith, Parochial Vicar; Deacon John J. Bretz.
Res.: 506 S. State St., Jerseyville, 62052.
Catechesis Religious Program—Clustered with Holy Ghost, Jerseyville. Students 5.

FRANKLIN, MORGAN CO., SACRED HEART OF JESUS (1886) [CEM]
414 Wyatt, Franklin, 62638. Tel: 217-488-3545;
Fax: 217-488-3545; Email: quadpastoralunit@gmail.com; Web: quadpastoralunit.com. Mailing Address: P.O. Box 20, New Berlin, 62670. Very Rev. Seth A. Brown.
Catechesis Religious Program—Students 23.

GILLESPIE, MACOUPIN CO., SS. SIMON AND JUDE (1879) [CEM]
304 N. Macoupin St., Gillespie, 62033.
Tel: 217-839-3456; Email: simonjude3456@gmail.com; Web: macoupincatholicchurch.com. Rev. Michael B. Haag; Deacon Dennis W. Baker; Ms. Rosemary Messner, Music Min.
Catechesis Religious Program—Ms. Karla Huddlestun, D.R.E. Students 34.

GIRARD, MACOUPIN CO., ST. PATRICK (1887)
745 W. Center St., P.O. Box 105, Girard, 62640.
Tel: 217-299-3007; Email: Stpat-sec@royell.org; Web: www.stpatgirard.com. Rev. James Palakudy, S.A.C.
Catechesis Religious Program—Terri Joslin, D.R.E. Students 29.

GLEN CARBON, MADISON CO., ST. CECILIA (1926)
155 N. Main St., Glen Carbon, 62034-1625.
Tel: 618-288-3200; Fax: 618-288-3292; Email: office@stcparish.org; Web: www.stcparish.org. Very Rev. Donald Patrick Gibbons; Deacon Jerry L. Cato.
Catechesis Religious Program—St. Cecilia Family Life Center, Tel: 618-288-5523; Email: faithformation@stcparish.org. Paula Raffaelle, D.R.E. Students 170.

GODFREY, MADISON CO., ST. AMBROSE (1947) [JC]
820 W. Homer M. Adams Pkwy., Godfrey, 62035.
Tel: 618-466-2921; Email: office@saintambroseparish.org; Web: www.saintambroseparish.org. Rev. Steven A. Janoski; Deacons William E. Kessler; Thomas W. Wilkinson Sr.; Jay William Wackerly Sr.
Res.: 3307 Morkel Dr., Godfrey, 62035.
Tel: 618-466-6408.
School—St. Ambrose School, (Grades K-8), 822 W. Homer M. Adams Pkwy., Godfrey, 62035.
Tel: 618-466-4216; Email: jheil@stambrosegodfrey.org; Web: www.stambrosegodfrey.org. Lay Teachers 19; Students 261.
Catechesis Religious Program—Students 40.

GRAFTON, JERSEY CO., ST. PATRICK (1871)
11 N. Evans, P.O. Box 218, Grafton, 62037.
Tel: 618-786-3512; Fax: 618-786-2027; Email: stpatricks@gtec.com. Revs. Stephen J. Pohlman; Martin Smith, Parochial Vicar; Deacon John J. Bretz.
Res.: 506 S. State St., Jerseyville, 62052.
Res.: 306 N. Washington St., Jerseyville, 62052.
Catechesis Religious Program—Students 10.

GRANITE CITY, MADISON CO.
1—ST. ELIZABETH (1871) [CEM] [JC]
2300 Pontoon Rd., Granite City, 62040.
Tel: 618-877-3300, Ext. 4; Fax: 618-877-9800; Email: secretary@stelizabethparish.net. Rev. Zachary T. Edgar.
Res.: 3235 Edgewood, Granite City, 62040.
School—St. Elizabeth School, (Grades PreK-8),
Tel: 618-877-3300, Ext. 127. Lay Teachers 12; Students 215; Clergy / Religious Teachers 1.
Child Care—St. Elizabeth Preschool,
Tel: 618-877-3300, Ext. 124.
Catechesis Religious Program—Laura Black, D.R.E. Students 37.
2—HOLY FAMILY (1988) [CEM] [JC]
2606 Washington Ave., Granite City, 62040-4810.
Tel: 618-877-7158; Email: eboyer@holyfamilycatholicgc.org; Web: holyfamilycatholicgc.org. Rev. William Jeffry Holtman, O.F.S.; Deacon Neil Wayne Suermann.
School—Holy Family School, (Grades 1-8), 1900 St. Clair Ave., Granite City, 62040. Tel: 618-877-5500; Email: holyfamsch@yahoo.com; Web: holyfamilyhawks.net. Mrs. Margaret Pennell, Prin. Lay Teachers 12; Students 177.
Catechesis Religious Program—Email: paxfamdiak@charter.net. Mrs. Nancy Diak, D.R.E. Students 22.

GRANTFORK, MADISON CO., ST. GERTRUDE (1872) [CEM]
202 N. Locust St., Grantfork, 62249.
Tel: 618-669-2391; Email: icstn2011@gmail.com; Web: www.icstnstg.org. Mailing Address: P.O. Box 410, Pierron, 62273. Rev. Paul Bonk.
Catechesis Religious Program—Tel: 618-675-3662. Kim Lewis, C.R.E.; Brenda Knackstedt, C.R.E. Students 31.

GREEN CREEK, EFFINGHAM CO., ST. MARY HELP OF CHRISTIANS (1860) [CEM] (German)
20057 N. 1525th St., Effingham, 62401.

Tel: 217-844-2062; Fax: 217-844-2062; Email: kimgreencreek@consolidated.net. Revs. Sunder Ery; Suresh Sambaturu, Parochial Vicar.
Catechesis Religious Program—Students 39.
GREENFIELD, GREENE CO., ST. MICHAEL (1880) [CEM]
411 Sheffield, Greenfield, 62044. Tel: 217-368-2176; Email: mchatla@dio.org. Rev. Mariadas Chatla, Parochial Admin.; Deacon Charles Theivagt.
Catechesis Religious Program—Martha Rawe, D.R.E. Students 12.
GREENUP, CUMBERLAND CO., CHRIST THE KING (1937)
110 E. Lincoln, Greenup, 62428. Tel: 217-826-2845; Email: stmarysmarshall@hotmail.com. Mailing Address: 414 S 6th St., Marshall, 62441. Rev. Augustine Koomson, Parochial Admin.
Catechesis Religious Program—Tel: 217-923-3523; Email: akoomson@dio.org. Karla Huddleston, D.R.E. Students 28.
GREENVILLE, BOND CO., ST. LAWRENCE (1868) [CEM]
512 S. Prairie St., P.O. Box 401, Greenville, 62246.
Tel: 618-664-9149; Email: stlawgrnvl@att.net. Rev. Alan Hunter, Admin.; Lisa Coleman, Sec.
Res.: 518 S. Prairie St., Greenville, 62246.
Catechesis Religious Program—Debbie Klincar, D.R.E. Students 87.
GRIGGSVILLE, PIKE CO., HOLY FAMILY, Closed. For details for parish records see St. Mary, Pittsfield.
HAGAMAN, MACOUPIN CO., ST. CATHERINE (1905) Closed. For inquiries for parish records, contact the Diocesan Office for Archives and Records Management.
HARDIN, CALHOUN CO.
1—ST. FRANCIS OF ASSISI (2005) [CEM]
304 French St., P.O. Box C, Hardin, 62047.
Tel: 618-576-2628; Fax: 618-576-9448; Email: stfrancisom@gmail.com; Web: www.sfacalhoun.com. Rev. Don J. Roberts; Deacon Mike Hagen Sr.
Res.: 35 Kiel Dr., Meppen, 62013.
School—St. Norbert School, (Grades PreK-8), 401 Vineyard St., P.O. Box 525, Hardin, 62047.
Tel: 618-576-2514; Fax: 618-576-8074; Email: stnorbertschool@snswolves.com; Email: rfriedel@snswolves.com. Aides 5; Clergy 1; Lay Teachers 5; Students 75.
Catechesis Religious Program—Email: sfaparishcre@gmail.com. Maria Carmody, D.R.E. Students 129.
2—ST. NORBERT (1872) [CEM] Merged with St. Agnes, Belleview, St. Anselm, Kampsville and St. Michael, Michael to form St. Francis of Assisi, Hardin. For inquiries for parish records, contact St. Francis of Assisi, Hardin.
HIGHLAND, MADISON CO., ST. PAUL (1844) [JC]
1412 Ninth St., Highland, 62249. Tel: 618-654-2339; Web: www.stpaulhighland.org. Revs. Pat G. Jakel; Adam Prichard, Parochial Vicar; Rev. Msgr. David L. Peters, Pastor Emeritus, (Retired); Deacon David S. Bohnenstiehl.
School—St. Paul School, (Grades PreK-8), 1416 Main St., Highland, 62249. Tel: 618-654-7525; Fax: 618-654-8795. Kathy Sherman, Prin. Lay Teachers 18; Students 229.
Catechesis Religious Program—1420 Ninth St., Highland, 62249. Tel: 618-654-2339, Ext. 216. Ron Knapp, D.R.E. Students 146.
HILLSBORO, MONTGOMERY CO., ST. AGNES (1840) [CEM]
216 E. Tremont St., P.O. Box 98, Hillsboro, 62049.
Tel: 217-532-5288; Email: agnesone_chris@consolidated.net; Web: stagneshillsboro.com. Rev. Daniel L. Willenborg; Deacon Leland B. Johns.
Parish Office: 212 E. Tremont St., P.O. Box 98, Hillsboro, 62049.
Catechesis Religious Program—Students 111.
HUME, EDGAR CO., ST. MICHAEL (1876)
206 N. Pine St., Villa Grove, 61956.
Tel: 217-832-8352; Email: villagrove.hume@gmail.com; Web: sacredheartandstmicheal.com. Mailing Address: St. Mary's Church, 205 Center St., Hume, 61932. Rev. Aloysius Okey Ndeanaefo.
Catechesis Religious Program—Students 6.
ILLIOPOLIS, SANGAMON CO., RESURRECTION PARISH (1866) [CEM] [JC]
410 Anne St., P.O. Box 47, Illiopolis, 62539.
Tel: 217-486-3851; Email: resurrectionparish1@comcast.net. Rev. Fredrick Mbiere
Legal Title: Visitation Parish.
Res.: 112 N. 6th St., P.O. Box 590, Riverton, 62561-0590.
Catechesis Religious Program—Students 19.
ISLAND GROVE, JASPER CO., ST. JOSEPH (1874) [CEM] Closed. For inquiries for parish records, contact St. Isidore the Farmer, Dieterich.
JACKSONVILLE, MORGAN CO., OUR SAVIOUR (1851) [CEM 2]
500 E. State St., Jacksonville, 62650. Mailing Address: 453 E. State St., Jacksonville, 62650.
Tel: 217-245-6184; Fax: 217-245-6185; Email: osparish1@mchsi.com; Web: www.oursaviourparish.org. Very Rev. Thomas C. Meyer, V.F.; Revs. Braden Maher, Parochial Vicar; Rafal Pyrchla, Parochial Vicar.
School—Our Saviour School, (Grades K-8), 455 E. State St., Jacksonville, 62650. Tel: 217-243-8621; Email: svandevelde@oss-shamrocks.com; Web: oursaviourshamrocks.com. Stephanie VanDeVelde, Prin. Lay Teachers 23; Students 320.
Catechesis Religious Program—Tel: 217-245-7633. Students 90.
JERSEYVILLE, JERSEY CO.
1—ST. FRANCIS XAVIER (1857) [CEM] [JC] (Irish—German)
506 S. State St., Jerseyville, 62052-0260.
Tel: 618-498-3518; Email: stfrancisxavier@gtec.com. Revs. Stephen J. Pohlman; Martin Smith, Parochial Vicar; Deacon John J. Bretz.
School—St. Francis/Holy Ghost School, (Grades PreK-8), 412 S. State St., Jerseyville, 62025.
Tel: 618-498-4823; Email: janet.goben@sfhg.org. Mrs. Janet Goben, Prin. Lay Teachers 23; Students 316.
Catechesis Religious Program— Twinned with Holy Ghost, Jerseyville, IL. Tel: 618-498-2665. Danielle Schroeder, D.R.E. Students 385.
2—HOLY GHOST (1883) [JC] (German)
306 N. Washington St., Jerseyville, 62052.
Tel: 618-498-3416; Email: hgchurch@gtec.com. Revs. Stephen J. Pohlman; Martin Smith, Parochial Vicar; Deacon John J. Bretz.
Res.: 506 S. State, Jerseyville, 62052.
See St. Francis/Holy Ghost School, Jerseyville under St. Francis Xavier, Jerseyville for details.
Catechesis Religious Program— Twinned with St. Francis, Jerseyville. Students 110.
KAMPSVILLE, CALHOUN CO., ST. ANSELM (1877) [CEM] Merged with St. Agnes, Belleview, St. Norbert, Hardin and St. Michael, Michael to form St. Francis of Assisi, Hardin. For inquiries for parish records, contact St. Francis of Assisi, Hardin.
KINCAID, CHRISTIAN CO., ST. RITA (1920)
30 St. Rita Ct., P.O. Box 439, Kincaid, 62540.
Tel: 217-237-2333; Email: strita1@consolidated.net. Rev. Msgr. David S. Lantz; Deacon James Robert Baxter.
Catechesis Religious Program—Cindy Tilley, D.R.E. Students 27.
LIBERTY, ADAMS CO., ST. BRIGID (1860) [CEM]
706 N. Main St., P.O. Box 228, Liberty, 62347.
Tel: 217-645-3444; Email: churchbej@gmail.com; Web: stbrigidedwardjoseph.weebly.com. Rev. Jeffrey E. Stone.
Rectory—806 N. Main St., Liberty, 62347-0228.
Catechesis Religious Program—Students 56.
LILLYVILLE, CUMBERLAND CO., SACRED HEART (1877) [CEM] (German)
127 County Road 100 E, P.O. Box 68, Sigel, 62462.
Tel: 217-844-3371; Email: sery@dio.org. Revs. Sunder Ery; Suresh Sambaturu, Parochial Vicar.
Res.: 20057 N. 1525th St., Effingham, 62401.
Tel: 217-844-3371; Cell: 217-343-1766.
Catechesis Religious Program—Tel: 217-844-2312. Students 58.
LITCHFIELD, MONTGOMERY CO., HOLY FAMILY (1988) [CEM] Formerly St. Mary, founded in 1857 & St. Aloysius founded in 1883.
410 S. State St., P.O. Box 8, Litchfield, 62056.
Tel: 217-324-2776; Fax: 217-324-2868; Email: holyfamily@consolidated.net; Web: www.holyfamilylitchfield.org. 411 S. Jackson St., Litchfield, 62056. Rev. Daniel L. Willenborg; Deacon Sean A. Caveny.
Res.: 216 E. Tremont St., P.O. Box 98, Hillsboro, 62049. Tel: 217-532-5288; Fax: 217-532-2631.
Catechesis Religious Program—Tel: 217-556-3365; Tel: 217-710-0098. Students 61.
LIVINGSTON, MADISON CO., SACRED HEART (1913) [CEM]
188 Livingston Ave., P.O. Box 458, Livingston, 62058. Tel: 618-637-2211. Rev. George Radosevich, Tel: 618-635-8490.
Res.: 322 E. Main St., Staunton, 62088.
Catechesis Religious Program—Combined with St. Michael Parish, Staunton.
LOVINGTON, MOULTRIE CO., ST. MARY, Closed. For inquiries for parish records, contact St. Isidore, Bethany.
MACON, MACON CO., ST. STANISLAUS (1866) Closed. For inquiries for parish records, contact the Diocesan Office for Archives and Records Management.
MADISON, MADISON CO., ST. MARY AND ST. MARK (2002) [JC]
1621 10th St., Madison, 62060. Tel: 618-452-5180; Email: stmary.church@ymail.com. Rev. William Jeffry Holtman, O.F.S.; Deacon Neil Wayne Suermann.
Rectory—Holy Family Catholic Church, 2606 Washington Ave., Granite City, 62040.
Catechesis Religious Program—Mrs. Nancy Diak, D.R.E. Students 9.
MARINE, MADISON CO., ST. ELIZABETH (1856) [CEM]
120 N. Windmill St., P.O. Box 457, Marine, 62061.
Tel: 618-887-4535; Email: stelizabeth@att.net. Rev. Paul A. Habing.
Catechesis Religious Program—Sr. Linda Mary Delonais, Pastoral Assoc. Faith Formation.
MARSHALL, CLARK CO., ST. MARY (1847) [CEM]
414 S. 6th St., Marshall, 62441. Tel: 217-826-2845; Email: stmarysmarshall@hotmail.com. Rev. Augustine Koomson, Parochial Admin.
Catechesis Religious Program—Christy Peters, D.R.E. Students 60.
MARYVILLE, MADISON CO., MOTHER OF PERPETUAL HELP (1938)
200 N. Lange, Maryville, 62062. Tel: 618-344-6464; Email: secretary@mph.dio.org; Web: mph.dio.org. Rev. T. Joseph Havrilka.
Res.: 510 E. Perry St., Maryville, 62062.
Catechesis Religious Program—Students 57.
MATTOON, COLES CO., IMMACULATE CONCEPTION (1856) [CEM]
320 N. 21st St., Mattoon, 61938. Tel: 217-235-0539; Fax: 217-235-0593; Email: immaculate@mchsi.com; Web: www.mattoonimmaculateconception.org. Rev. John M. Titus; Deacon Eugene V. Uptmor Jr.
Catechesis Religious Program—Students 100.
MEDORA, MACOUPIN CO., ST. JOHN THE EVANGELIST (1914) (German)
203 N. Main St., Medora, 62063. Tel: 618-372-3352; Email: office@sap-brighton.org; Web: www.sap-brighton.org. Mailing Address: 920 N. Main St., Brighton, 62012. Rev. William F. Kessler, Parochial Admin.; Susan Matsche, Sec.
Res.: c/o St. Alphonsus Church, 918 N. Main St., Brighton, 62012.
Catechesis Religious Program—Chastity Brockway, C.R.E. Clustered with St. Alphonsus, Brighton. Students 1.
MENDON, ADAMS CO., ST. EDWARD (1890) [CEM]
218 S. State Rd., Mendon, 62351. Tel: 217-645-3444; Email: churchbej@gmail.com; Web: www.stbrigidedwardjoseph.weebly.com. Mailing Address: P.O. Box 228, Liberty, 62347. Rev. Jeffrey E. Stone.
Res.: 806 N. Main St., Liberty, 62347. Email: sbtparishoffice@sbcglobal.net.
Church: 214 S. State Rd., Mendon, 62351.
Catechesis Religious Program—Students 72.
MEPPEN, CALHOUN CO., ST. JOSEPH (1864) [CEM] Merged with St. Barbara, Batchtown and St. Mary, Brussels to form Blessed Trinity, Brussels. For inquiries for parish records, contact Blessed Trinity, Brussels.
MICHAEL, CALHOUN CO., ST. MICHAEL (1864) [CEM] (Irish), Merged with St. Agnes, Belleview, St. Norbert, Hardin and St. Anselm, Kampsville to form St. Francis of Assisi, Hardin. For inquiries for parish records, contact St. Francis of Assisi, Hardin.
MONTROSE, EFFINGHAM CO., ST. ROSE OF LIMA (1879) [CEM]
301 N. Springcreek Rd., P.O. Box 68, Montrose, 62445. Tel: 217-924-4337; Fax: 217-924-4312; Email: strosechurch@mmtcnet.com. Revs. Joseph P. Carlos, O.F.M.; Kenneth Rosswog, O.F.M.
Catechesis Religious Program—Tel: 217-924-4626. Lisa Probst, D.R.E. Students 59.
MORRISONVILLE, CHRISTIAN CO., ST. MAURICE (1870) [CEM]
706 E. 4th St., P.O. Box 45, Morrisonville, 62546.
Tel: 217-526-3363; Email: aallen@dio.org. Very Rev. Albert F. Allen, V.F., Admin.; Rev. Gerald L. Bunse, M.Div., Pastor Emeritus; Deacon Patrick O'Toole.
Res.: 310 Nobbe St., Farmersville, 62533. Email: jbunse1951@aol.com.
Catechesis Religious Program—Students 47.
MOUNT OLIVE, MACOUPIN CO.
1—ASCENSION (1886) [CEM] (Croatian), Consolidated with Holy Trinity to form Blessed Pope John Paul II, Mount Olive. For inquiries for parish records, contact St. John Paul II, Mount Olive.
2—HOLY TRINITY (1912) [CEM] (Slovak), Consolidated with Ascension to form Blessed Pope John Paul II, Mount Olive. For inquiries for parish records, contact St. John Paul II, Mount Olive.
3—SAINT JOHN PAUL II (2011)
705 E. Main St., Mount Olive, 62069.
Tel: 217-999-4981; Email: bjpii@madisontelco.com. Rev. Thomas Hagstrom; Deacon Thomas S. Lucia.
Catechesis Religious Program—Linda Hasquin, D.R.E. Students 12.
MOUNT STERLING, BROWN CO., HOLY FAMILY (1864) [CEM]
401 W. North St., P.O. Box 252, Mount Sterling, 62353. Tel: 217-773-3233; Email: sthompson@smseagle.org. Rev. Stephen A. Thompson; Deacon Michael P. Ellerman.
School—St. Mary, (Grades PreSchool-8), 408 W. Washington, Mount Sterling, 62353.
Tel: 217-773-2825; Fax: 217-773-2399; Email: tmckeown@smseagle.org; Web: www.smseagle.org. Melissa Obert, Prin. Lay Teachers 7; Students 83; Clergy / Religious Teachers 1.
MOUNT ZION, MACON CO., OUR LADY OF THE HOLY SPIRIT (1974)

400 Woodland Cir., Mt. Zion, 62549.
Tel: 217-864-3467; Fax: 217-864-3091; Email: mtzolhs@comcast.net; Web: www.mtzolhs.org. Rev. Steven M. Arisman.

MOWEAQUA, SHELBY CO., ST. FRANCES DE SALES (1895) [JC]
231 E. Watten St., Moweaqua, 62550.
Tel: 217-226-3536; Email: stmarybvm1857@aim.com. Mailing Address: 301 St. Peter St., Assumption, 62510. Rev. Marianna Sathuluri, (India) Parochial Admin.; Deacon John O'Brien.
Catechesis Religious Program—Tel: 217-226-3205. Students 6.

MURRAYVILLE, MORGAN CO., ST. BARTHOLOMEW (1884) [CEM] Closed. For inquiries for parish records, contact Our Savior, Jacksonville.

NEOGA, CUMBERLAND CO., ST. MARY OF THE ASSUMPTION (1897) [CEM] [JC] (German)
Mailing Address: P.O. Box 68, Sigel, 62462.
Tel: 217-844-3371; Email: sery@dio.org. Revs. Sunder Ery; Suresh Sambaturu, Parochial Vicar.
Res.: 20057 N. 125th St., Effingham, 62401.
Fax: 217-844-2309.
Church: 670 Walnut Ave., Neoga, 62447.
Tel: 217-895-2166; Email: stmary@rr1.net; Web: www.fourparishes.com.
Catechesis Religious Program—Eric Thompson, D.R.E. Students 49.

NEW BERLIN, SANGAMON CO., SACRED HEART OF MARY (1858) [CEM]
404 E. Birch, P.O. Box 20, New Berlin, 62670.
Tel: 217-488-3545; Fax: 217-488-3545; Email: quadpastoralunit@gmail.com; Web: quadpastoralunit.com. Very Rev. Seth A. Brown.
Catechesis Religious Program—Students 31.

NEW DOUGLAS, MADISON CO., ST. UBALDUS (1872) [CEM] Closed. For inquiries for parish records, contact Sacred Heart, Livingston.

NEWTON, JASPER CO., ST. THOMAS THE APOSTLE (1873) [CEM 3]
404 W. Jourdan St., P.O. Box 225, Newton, 62448.
Tel: 618-783-8741; Email: stthomaschurch@psbnewton.com; Web: stthomasnewton.net. Very Rev. R. Dean Probst, J.C.L., V.F.; Deacon Larry Miller; Linda M. Hemrich, Sec.; Mrs. Jill Bierman, Admin.
Res.: 501 W. Jourdan St., P.O. Box 225, Newton, 62448.
School—St. Thomas the Apostle School, (Grades K-8), 306 W. Jourdan St., Newton, 62448.
Tel: 618-783-3517; Fax: 618-783-2224; Email: jillbierman@stthomassaints.com; Web: www.stthomassaints.com. Mrs. Jill Bierman, Prin. Clergy 1; Lay Teachers 9; Students 154.
Catechesis Religious Program—Pete Pasero, D.R.E. Students 178.

NIANTIC, MACON CO., ST. ANN (1889) [JC] Closed. For inquiries for parish records please see Resurrection Parish, Illiopolis.

NOKOMIS, MONTGOMERY CO., ST. LOUIS (1870) [CEM]
311 S. Elm St., Nokomis, 62075-1310.
Tel: 217-563-7146; Email: parish@slsk8.org; Web: www.slsk8.org. Very Rev. Albert F. Allen, V.F.
School—St. Louis School, (Grades PreK-8), 509 E. Union, Nokomis, 62075. Tel: 217-563-7445;
Fax: 217-563-7450; Web: www.stlouis-nokomis.k12.il.us. Elaine Wagner, Prin. Clergy 1; Lay Teachers 10; Students 78.
Catechesis Religious Program—Students 27.

NORTH ARM, EDGAR CO., ST. ALOYSIUS (1817) [CEM]
18925 E. 1350th Rd., P.O. Box 577, Paris, 61944.
Tel: 217-466-3355; Email: pat.catanzariti@stmaryschurchparis.org. Rev. Valery Burusu.
Res.: 117 E. Edgar St., P.O. Box 577, Paris, 61944.
Catechesis Religious Program—Combined with St. Mary's, Paris.

OBLONG, CRAWFORD CO., OUR LADY OF LOURDES (1954)
506 W. Missouri St., Oblong, 62449.
Tel: 618-544-7526; Email: crawford_catholics@rocketmail.com. Mailing Address: 207 E. Walnut St., Robinson, 62454. Rev. James A. Flach.
Catechesis Religious Program—Courtney Ferris, D.R.E. Students 9.

OCONEE, SHELBY CO., SACRED HEART (1872) [CEM]
201 N. Walnut St., P.O. Box 45, Oconee, 62553.
Tel: 217-539-4325; Email: shparish@frontiernet.net. Rev. Rodney A. Schwartz.
Res. & Rectory: 303 S. Locust, P.O. Box 440, Pana, 62557.
Catechesis Religious Program—Students 17.

PALMYRA, MACOUPIN CO., HOLY ROSARY (1954) Closed. For inquiries for parish records, contact the Diocesan Office for Archives and Records Management.

PANA, CHRISTIAN CO., ST. PATRICK (1858) [CEM]
303 S. Locust St., P.O. Box 440, Pana, 62557.
Tel: 217-562-5396; Email: panastpats@gmail.com. Rev. Rodney A. Schwartz.
Res.: 6 E. Fifth St., P.O. Box 440, Pana, 62557.
Fax: 217-562-2308.
School—Sacred Heart, (Grades PreK-8), 3 E. 4th St., Pana, 62557. Tel: 217-562-2425; Fax: 217-562-2942; Email: diese@consolidated.net; Web: www.shspana.com. Theresa Trader, Prin. Clergy 1; Lay Teachers 10; Students 171.
Catechesis Religious Program—Tel: 217-562-2308. Students 104.

PANAMA, BOND CO., SACRED HEART (1916) [JC] Closed. For inquiries for parish records please see St. Agnes, Hillsboro.

PARIS, EDGAR CO., ST. MARY (1849) [CEM]
528 N. Main St., P.O. Box 577, Paris, 61944.
Tel: 217-466-3355; Email: pat.catanzariti@stmaryschurchparis.org. Rev. Valery Burusu, Admin.
Catechesis Religious Program—Students 39.

PAWNEE, SANGAMON CO., ST. MARY (1899) [CEM] Merged with St. Benedict, Auburn and Sacred Heart, Divernon to form Holy Cross, Auburn. For inquiries for parish records, contact Holy Cross, Auburn.

PETERSBURG, MENARD CO., ST. PETER (1868) [CEM]
711 S. 6th St., Petersburg, 62675. Tel: 217-632-7118; Email: stpeter234@sbcglobal.net; Web: spp.dio.org. Rev. Msgr. Thomas P. Holinga.
Res.: 212 Washington, Petersburg, 62675.
Catechesis Religious Program—Lisa Reeves, Admin. Students 46.

PIERRON, MADISON AND BOND COS., IMMACULATE CONCEPTION (1892) [CEM]
991 Main St., P.O. Box 410, Pierron, 62273.
Tel: 618-669-2391; Email: icstn2011@gmail.com; Web: www.icstnstg.org. Rev. Paul Bonk.
Res.: 971 Main St., P.O. Box 410, Pierron, 62273.
Catechesis Religious Program—Students 30.

PITTSFIELD, PIKE CO., ST. MARY (1852) [CEM] [JC]
226 E. Adams, Pittsfield, 62363. Tel: 217-285-4321; Fax: 217-285-9400; Email: stmarymark@gmail.com; Web: www.stmaryspittsfield.dio.org. Rev. Mark A. Schulte; Deacon Michael (Kim) Scott.
Catechesis Religious Program—Tel: 217-285-6702; Email: religiousedstmarys@gmail.com. Gloria Heinen, D.R.E. Students 25.

POCAHONTAS, BOND CO., ST. NICHOLAS (1871) [CEM]
401 E. State St., Pocahontas, 62275.
Tel: 618-669-2391; Email: icstn2011@gmail.com; Web: www.icstnstg.org. Rev. Paul Bonk.
Catechesis Religious Program—Students 7.

QUINCY, ADAMS CO.

1—ALL SAINTS (1999) [JC] Merged with St. Boniface, Quincy and St. Mary (Immaculate Conception), Quincy to form Blessed Sacrament, Quincy. For inquiries for parish records, contact the Diocesan Office for Archives and Records Management.

2—ST. ANTHONY OF PADUA (1859) [CEM]
2223 St. Anthony Rd., Quincy, 62305.
Tel: 217-222-5996; Email: secretary@stanthonypadua.org; Web: www.stanthonypadua.org. Rev. Bernard Thomas Donovan; Deacon Harry L. Cramer.
School—St. Dominic Catholic Elementary School, (Grades PreK-8), 4100 Columbus Rd., Quincy, 62305. Tel: 217-224-0041; Fax: 217-224-0042; Web: www.stdominicquincy.org. Mrs. Susan Kelley, Prin. Lay Teachers 14; Students 170.
Catechesis Religious Program—Email: dre@stanthonypadua.org. Bonnie Nytes, D.R.E. Students 205.

3—BLESSED SACRAMENT (2006)
1119 S. Seventh St., Quincy, 62301.
Tel: 217-222-2759; Fax: 217-222-6463; Email: blessedsac@blessedscs.org. Rev. Christopher J. Comerford; Deacon Terrence J. Ellerman, D.R.E.; Linda Ohnemus, Business Mgr.; Steve Buckman, Music Min.; Sally Kroner, Office Sec.
School—Blessed Sacrament School, (Grades PreSchool-8), 1115 S. 7th, Quincy, 62301.
Tel: 217-228-1477; Email: principal@blessedscs.org; Web: www.blessedscs.org. Clergy 2; Lay Teachers 15; Preschool 38; Students 198.
Catechesis Religious Program—Tel: 217-222-2758. Students 275.

4—ST. BONIFACE (1837) [JC] Merged with All Saints, Quincy and St. Mary (Immaculate Conception), Quincy to form Blessed Sacrament, Quincy. For inquiries for parish records, contact the Diocesan Office for Archives and Records Management.

5—ST. DOMINIC (1977) [JC] Merged with St. Anthony of Padua, Quincy. For inquiries for parish records, contact the Diocesan Office for Archives and Records Management.

6—ST. FRANCIS SOLANUS (1860) [JC]
1721 College Ave., Quincy, 62301. Tel: 217-222-2898; Email: church@stfrancissolanus.com; Web: stfrancissolanus.com. Revs. Donald Blaeser, O.F.M.; Robert Barko, O.F.M., Parochial Vicar; Deacon Wayne R. Zimmerman.
School—St. Francis Solanus School, (Grades PreK-8), 1720 College Ave., Quincy, 62301.
Tel: 217-222-4077; Fax: 217-222-5049; Email: school@stfrancissolanus.com. Mr. Michael Holbrook, D.R.E. Lay Teachers 23; Students 300.
Catechesis Religious Program—Students 60.

7—ST. JOHN THE BAPTIST (1880) (German), Merged with St. Rose of Lima, Quincy to form All Saints, Quincy. Records at Blessed Sacrament, Quincy. For inquiries for parish records, contact the Diocesan Office for Archives and Records Management.

8—ST. JOSEPH (1867) [CEM]
1435 E. 1500 St., Liberty, 62305. Tel: 217-434-8442; Email: stjoe@adams.net. P.O. Box 228, Liberty, 62347. Rev. Jeffrey E. Stone.
Catechesis Religious Program—Students 23.

9—ST. MARY (IMMACULATE CONCEPTION) (1867) [JC] Merged with All Saints, Quincy and St. Boniface, Quincy to form Blessed Sacrament, Quincy. For inquiries for parish records, contact the Diocesan Office for Archives and Records Management.

10—ST. PETER (1839) [JC]
2600 Maine St., Quincy, 62301. Tel: 217-222-3155; Email: church@cospq.org. Rev. Msgr. Leo J. Enlow, V.F.; Rev. Aaron Kuhn, Parochial Vicar; Deacons Robert M. Lundberg; Jeffrey Wolf. St. Peter Parish of Quincy Illinois
School—St. Peter School, (Grades PreK-8), 2500 Maine St., Quincy, 62301. Tel: 217-223-1120;
Fax: 217-223-1173; Email: c.venvertloh@cospq.org; Web: www.stpeterschool.com. Mrs. Cindy Venvertloh, Prin. Clergy 2; Lay Teachers 24; Students 422.
Catechesis Religious Program—Students 56.

11—ST. ROSE OF LIMA PARISH (1892) (Irish)
1009 N. 8th St., Quincy, 62301. Tel: 217-222-2511;
Fax: 217-222-2511; Email: saintrosequincy@att.net; Web: www.saintrosequincy.org. Rev. Arnaud Devillers, F.S.S.P.
Catechesis Religious Program—Students 50.

RAMSEY, FAYETTE CO., ST. JOSEPH (1870) [CEM] (German—Irish)
126 E. Main, P.O. Box 455, Ramsey, 62080.
Tel: 618-423-2424; Email: st.josephschurch_ramsey@yahoo.com. Rev. Scott A. Snider, Admin.
Res.: 118 E. Main, P.O. Box 455, Ramsey, 62080.
Catechesis Religious Program—Students 17.

RAYMOND, MONTGOMERY CO., ST. RAYMOND (1874) [CEM]
306 S. McElroy, P.O. Box 349, Raymond, 62560.
Tel: 217-229-4435; Email: aallen@dio.org. Very Rev. Albert F. Allen, V.F., Admin.; Rev. Gerald L. Bunse, M.Div., Pastor Emeritus; Deacon Patrick J. O'Toole.
Catechesis Religious Program—Students 12.

RIVERTON, SANGAMON CO., ST. JAMES (1871)
112 N. Sixth St., P.O. Box 590, Riverton, 62561-0590.
Tel: 217-629-7717; Email: stjamesrctry@gcctv.com. Rev. Raphael Paul DeMoreno; Deacon James G. Bollman; Terry Willis, Sec.
Catechesis Religious Program—Deborah Fleck, D.R.E. Students 30.

ROBINSON, CRAWFORD CO., ST. ELIZABETH aka St. Elizabeth of Hungary Catholic Church (1907)
207 E. Walnut St., Robinson, 62454.
Tel: 618-544-7526; Email: crawford_catholics@rocketmail.com. Rev. James A. Flach, Parochial Admin.
Catechesis Religious Program—Fax: 618-544-9327. Courtney Ferris, D.R.E. Students 107.

ROCHESTER, SANGAMON CO., ST. JUDE (1976)
633 S. Walnut St., P.O. Box 47, Rochester, 62563-0047. Tel: 217-498-9197; Fax: 217-498-7180; Email: balford@dio.org; Email: bscoggins@stjude.dio.org. Very Rev. Brian C. Alford; Deacons Thomas A. Walker; Raymond L. Roth Jr.
Catechesis Religious Program—Students 146.

ST. ELMO, FAYETTE CO.

1—ST. BONAVENTURE (1843) [CEM] (Irish—German), Closed. For inquiries for parish records, contact St. Clare, Altamont.

2—ST. MARY (1904) (German)
610 W. Cumberland Rd., St. Elmo, 62458.
Tel: 618-483-5346; Email: office@stclarealtamont.dio.org. Mailing Address: 216 N. Ninth, Altamont, 62411. Rev. Christudasan Kurisadima, Admin.
Catechesis Religious Program—Students 4.

ST. JACOB, MADISON CO., ST. JAMES (1894)
503 Washington St., St. Jacob, 62281.
Tel: 618-667-6571; Email: stjerome@stjeromeparish.org; Web: www.stjeromeparish.org. Mailing Address: St. Jerome Parish, 511 S. Main St., Troy, 62294-1812. Rev. Kevin Michael Laughery, J.C.L.
Catechesis Religious Program—

SHELBYVILLE, SHELBY CO., IMMACULATE CONCEPTION (1862)
1431 State Hwy. 128, P.O. Box 233, Shelbyville, 62565. Tel: 217-774-3434; Email: icchurch@consolidated.net. Rev. Marianna Sathuluri, (India) Parochial Admin.
Catechesis Religious Program—Students 39.

SHERMAN, SANGAMON CO., ST. JOHN VIANNEY (1931) [CEM]
902 St. John Dr., P.O. Box 229, Sherman, 62684.
Tel: 217-523-3816; Email: ssaladino@sjv.dio.org. Rev. George Philip Nellikunnel, S.A.C.; Deacon Benedict P. Hoefler.

Res.: 712 Lost Tree Dr., Sherman, 62684. Email: parish@sjv.dio.org; Web: sjv.dio.org.
Catechesis Religious Program—Jennifer Grebner, D.R.E.; Stacie Henderson, D.R.E. Students 167.

SHIPMAN, MACOUPIN CO., ST. DENIS (1876) [CEM] Closed. For inquiries for parish records, contact the Diocesan Office for Archives and Records Management.

SHUMWAY, EFFINGHAM CO., ANNUNCIATION (1879) [CEM]
P.O. Box 96, Shumway, 62461. Cell: 217-690-2640; Web: www.stmarysshumway.org. Revs. Charles A. Edwards; Mark Walker Tracy, Parochial Vicar.

SIGEL, SHELBY CO., ST. MICHAEL THE ARCHANGEL (1867) [CEM] (German)
200 N. Church St., P.O. Box 68, Sigel, 62462.
Tel: 217-844-3371; Email: sigelstmichaelchurch@gmail.com. Rev. Sunder Ery.
Res.: 20057 N. 1525th St., Effingham, 62401.
Tel: 217-844-2062; Fax: 217-844-2309; Web: www.fourparishes.com.
School—St. Michael the Archangel School, 200 N. Church St., P.O. Box 8, Sigel, 62462.
Tel: 217-844-2231; Email: nbniemerg80@gmail.com; Web: www.ssmcs.org. Rev. Sunder Ery, Supt.; Mr. Nick Niemerg, Prin. Lay Teachers 12; Students 163.
Catechesis Religious Program—Students 34.

STAUNTON, MACOUPIN CO., ST. MICHAEL THE ARCHANGEL (1875) [JC2]
428 E. North St., Staunton, 62088-0240.
Tel: 618-635-3140; Email: stmikeof@madisontelco.com; Web: www.stmichaelsstaunton.com. P.O. Box 240, Staunton, 62088. Rev. George Radosevich.
Res.: 322 E. Main, Staunton, 62088-0240.
Tel: 618-635-8490.
Church: 415 E. Main St., Staunton, 62088-1451.
Catechesis Religious Program—Students 136.

STE. MARIE, JASPER CO., ST. MARY (1837) [CEM] [JC] (French—German)
112 W. Embarras St., P.O. Box 68, Ste. Marie, 62459.
Tel: 618-455-3155; Email: stmaryschurch@psbnewton.com. Very Rev. R. Dean Probst, J.C.L., V.F.
Catechesis Religious Program—Students 50.

STONINGTON, CHRISTIAN CO., HOLY TRINITY (1879) (Irish—German)
308 N. Pine, P.O. Box 257, Stonington, 62567.
Tel: 217-325-3697; Email: holytrinity1879@outlook.com. Rev. Msgr. David S. Lantz, Email: dlantz@sjv.dio.org; Deacon James Robert Baxter.
Res.: 108 N. Elm St., P.O. Box 257, Stonington, 62567. Email: holytrinity@consolidated.net.
Catechesis Religious Program—Students 24.

SULLIVAN, MOULTRIE CO., ST. COLUMCILLE (1892)
516 W. Jackson St., Sullivan, 61951.
Tel: 217-235-0539; Email: st.columcillesullivan@gmail.com. Mailing Address: 320 N. 21st St., Mattoon, 61938. Revs. John M. Titus; John E. Sohm, Pastor Emeritus, (Retired).
Catechesis Religious Program—Students 27.

TAYLORVILLE, CHRISTIAN CO., ST. MARY (1845)
116 W. Adams St., P.O. Box 470, Taylorville, 62568.
Tel: 217-824-8178; Email: Dlantz@dio.org. Rev. Msgr. David S. Lantz; Deacon James Robert Baxter.
School—St. Mary School, (Grades PreK-6), 422 S. Washington, Taylorville, 62568. Tel: 217-824-6501; Email: crobertson@st-maryschool.com. Clergy 1; Lay Teachers 7; Students 149.
Catechesis Religious Program—Carole Harrison, D.R.E. Students 59.
Missions—Holy Trinity—108 N. Pine, Stonington, 62567. Tel: 217-325-3697; Email: holytrinity1879@outlook.com.
St. Rita, 30 St. Rita, Kincaid, 62540.
Tel: 217-237-2333; Email: strita1@consolicated.net.

TEUTOPOLIS, EFFINGHAM CO., ST. FRANCIS OF ASSISI (1839) [CEM]
203 E. Main St., P.O. Box 730, Teutopolis, 62467-0730. Tel: 217-857-6404; Email: stfrancischurch@mchsi.com; Web: www.stfrancischurch.com. Revs. Joseph P. Carlos, O.F.M.; Kenneth Rosswog, O.F.M., Parochial Vicar; Mr. Daniel Williams, Music Min.
Catechesis Religious Program—Tel: 217-857-6477. Mr. Dan Niemerg, D.R.E.; Mrs. Maria Kingery, Youth Min.; Ms. Emilie Esker, RCIA Coord. Students 569.

TROY, MADISON CO., ST. JEROME (1870) [CEM 2]
511 S. Main St., Troy, 62294. Tel: 618-667-6571; Email: stjerome@stjeromeparish.org. Rev. Kevin Michael Laughery, J.C.L.
Res.: 64 Westbrooke, Troy, 62294. Web: www.stjeromeparish.org.
School—St. John Neumann, (Grades K-8), 142 Wilma Dr., Maryville, 62062. Tel: 618-345-7230; Fax: 618-345-4350; Email: office@sjncrusaders.org; Web: www.sjncrusaders.org. Lay Teachers 17; Students 223.
Catechesis Religious Program—Sr. Linda Mary Delonais, Pastoral Assoc. Faith Formation. Students 171.

TUSCOLA, DOUGLAS CO., FORTY MARTYRS (1865)
201 E. Van Allen St., Tuscola, 61953.
Tel: 217-253-4412; Email: fortymartyrs@gmail.com. Mailing Address: 110 E. Van Allen St., P.O. Box 440, Tuscola, 61953. Rev. Angel Sierra; Deb Kleiss, Sec.

VANDALIA, FAYETTE CO., MOTHER OF DOLORS (1850) [CEM]
322 N. Seventh St., P.O. Box 377, Vandalia, 62471.
Tel: 618-283-0214; Email: motherofdolors@nwcable.net; Web: motherofdolors.com. Rev. Scott A. Snider.
Catechesis Religious Program—Students 59.

VENICE, MADISON CO., ST. MARK (1871) Closed. For inquiries for parish records, contact the Diocesan Office for Archives and Records Management.

VILLA GROVE, DOUGLAS CO., SACRED HEART (1906)
206 N. Pine, Villa Grove, 61956. Tel: 217-832-8352; Email: villagrove.hume@gmail.com; Web: sacredheartandstmicheal.com. Rev. Aloysius Okey Ndeanaefo.
Church: 212 N. Pine, Villa Grove, 61956.
Catechesis Religious Program—Students 35.

VIRDEN, MACOUPIN CO., SACRED HEART (1914) (Slovak) St. Catherine's (1866) Merged in 1978.
722 N. Springfield St., Virden, 62690.
Tel: 217-965-4545; Email: secretary@sacredheart.dio.org; Web: www.sacredheartvirden.com. Rev. James Palakudy, S.A.C.; Deacon Ricky Joe Schnetzler Sr.
Res.: 125 E. Washington St., P.O. Box 168, Auburn, 62615. Tel: 217-438-6196.
Catechesis Religious Program—Rebecca Yemm, D.R.E. Students 37.

VIRGINIA, CASS CO., ST. LUKE (1840)
240 E. Myrtle St., Virginia, 62691. Tel: 217-371-4713 ; Email: staalf4@casscomm.com. Very Rev. Thomas C. Meyer, V.F.; Revs. Braden Maher, Parochial Vicar; Rafal Pyrchla, Parochial Vicar.
Catechesis Religious Program—Students 9.

WAVERLY, MORGAN CO., ST. SEBASTIAN (1856) [CEM]
265 E. Elm St., Waverly, 62692. Tel: 217-488-3545; Email: quadpastoralunit@gmail.com; Web: quadpastoralunit.com. P.O. Box 20, New Berlin, 62670. Very Rev. Seth A. Brown.
Catechesis Religious Program—414 Wyatt, Franklin, 62638. Clustered with Sacred Heart, Franklin. Students 3.

WHITE HALL, GREENE CO., ALL SAINTS (1883)
Mailing Address: 167 Ross St., White Hall, 62092.
Tel: 217-942-3551; Tel: 217-374-2056; Email: lschnettgoecke@stjohnscarrollton.org. Revs. Mariadas Chatla, Parochial Admin.; Henry Schmidt, Pastor Emeritus, (Retired); Deacon Charles Theivagt.
Res.: 414 Third St., Carrollton, 62016.
Church: S. Main St., White Hall, 62092.
Catechesis Religious Program—Gina Edwards, D.R.E. Students 28.

WILSONVILLE, MACOUPIN CO., HOLY CROSS (1926) Closed. For inquiries for parish records, contact the Diocesan Office for Archives and Records Management.

WINCHESTER, SCOTT CO., ST. MARK (1860) [CEM]
108 E. Pearl St., Winchester, 62694.
Tel: 217-285-4321; Fax: 217-285-9400; Email: stmarymark@gmail.com. Mailing Address: 226 E. Adams, Pittsfield, 62363. Rev. Mark A. Schulte; Deacon Michael (Kim) Scott.
Catechesis Religious Program—Students 8.

WITT, MONTGOMERY CO., ST. BARBARA (1905) [CEM] Closed. For inquiries for parish records please see St. Louis, Nokomis.

WOOD RIVER, MADISON CO.
1—ST. BERNARD (1919) Merged with St. Kevin, Alton to form Holy Angels, Wood River. For inquiries for parish records, contact Holy Angels, Wood River.
2—HOLY ANGELS (2005)
345 E. Acton Ave., Wood River, 62095.
Tel: 618-254-0679; Fax: 618-254-2690; Email: holyangelswr@yahoo.com. Rev. Donald L. Wolford.
Catechesis Religious Program—Students 38.

Chaplains of Public Institutions

SPRINGFIELD. *University of Illinois at Springfield*, 1345 N. 6th St., 62702. Rev. Kevin Mann, S.J.C., Dir. of Campus Ministry, Chap.

ALTON. *Alton State Hospital*. Attended by the Catholic Churches in Alton. Vacant.

HILLSBORO. *Graham Correctional Center*, R.R. #1, Hwy. 185, P.O. Box 499, Hillsboro, 62049.
Tel: 217-532-6961. Rev. Daniel L. Willenborg, Chap.

JACKSONVILLE. *Illinois School for the Deaf*, 125 S. Webster, Jacksonville, 62650. Tel: 217-245-6184; Email: osparish1@mchsi.com. Attended by Our Savior Parish.
Illinois School for the Visually Impaired, 453 E. State St., Jacksonville, 62650. Tel: 217-245-6184; Email: osparish1@mchsi.com. Attended by Our Savior Parish.
Jacksonville Correctional Center. Very Rev. Thomas C. Meyer, V.F., Chap.

MOUNT STERLING. *Western Illinois Correctional Center*, 2500 Rt. 99 S., Mount Sterling, 62353.
Tel: 217-773-4441. Deacon Michael P. Ellerman, Chap.

QUINCY. *Illinois Veterans' Home*, 1901 N. 18th, Quincy, 62301. Tel: 217-224-0591; Email: dblickhan@dio.org. Rev. Donald L. Blickhan, Chap., (Retired).

TAYLORVILLE. *Taylorville Correctional Center*, Rt. 29 S., P.O. Box 1000, Taylorville, 62658.
Tel: 217-824-4004. Rev. Daniel L. Willenborg, Chap.

VANDALIA. *Vandalia Correctional Center*, Rt. 51 N., P.O. Box 550, Vandalia, 62471. Tel: 618-283-4170. Rev. Daniel L. Willenborg, Chap.

Special or Other Diocesan Assignment:
Rev. Msgrs.—
Hoefler, David J., V.G., M.Div., 1615 W. Washington St., 62702-4757
Steffen, Kenneth Charles, J.C.L., M.A., M.Div., D.Min., St. Francis Hospital, 1215 Franciscan Drive, P.O. Box 1215, Litchfield, 62056-1215
Revs.—
Bagyo, Samuel Jr., St. James Monastery, 2500 St. James Road, 62707
Sotiroff, Stephen T., 1 Franciscan Way, P.O. Box 9020, Alton, 62002-9020
Bro.—
Zawadzki, Adam, O.P.Miss., Dominican House of Studies, 1011 Alton Ave., Madison, 62060.

On Duty Outside the Diocese:
Rev. Msgr.—
Renken, John, 130 Springhurst Ave., Ottawa, ON Canada K1S0E5
Revs.—
Bohorquez, Carlos M., 375 AMW/HC, 320 Ward Dr., Bldg. 1620, Scott Air Force Base, 62225
Friedel, Michael, Pontifical North American College, Vatican City State, 00120
Gallenbach, Thomas E., (Retired), 7075 Del Ray, Las Vegas, NV 89117. Tel: 702-254-5488 (Home); Tel: 702-363-1902 (Office)
Harman, Peter C., S.T.B., S.T.L., S.T.D., Vatican City State 00120
Kala, Paul, Missionary Society of St. Theresa, P.O. Box 579, Wa, U/W/R, Ghana
Rankin, Dominic, Pontifical North American College, 00120, Vatican City State.

Absent on Leave:
Revs.—
Brey, Christopher J.
DeGrand, Robert L.
Dennis, Thomas J.
Harmon, Barry
Kerber, Joseph P.
Schmidt, David.

Retired:
Rev. Msgrs.—
Kuse, Michael R., (Retired), 2837 Harrison Street, Quincy, 62301
O'Shea, James D., (Retired), 1729 Dial Ct., 62704-3501
Ossola, John R., (Retired), St. Joseph's Home of Springfield, 3306 S. 6th St. Rd., 62707. Tel: 217-529-5596
Peters, David L., (Retired), 14 Kaeser Ct., Highland, 62249
Very Rev.—
Neuman, James L., V.F., (Retired), 126 Lakewood Dr., Hillsboro, 62049
Revs.—
Anschutz, Larry L., (Retired), 207 W. 7th N., Mount Olive, 62069
Blickhan, Donald L., (Retired), 624 S. 21st St., Quincy, 62301
Brunette, Larry H., (Retired), 2 Itasca Pl., Unit 324, Itasca, 60143
Carberry, John P., (Retired), 1707 N. 12th St., Fifer-A. Rm. 113-A, Quincy, 62301
Chiola, Richard L., Ph.D., (Retired), 2926 Victoria Dr., 62704
Dahlby, Charles, (Retired), 139 Stardust Dr., Sherman, 62684
Donohoe, Peter, (Retired), 714 Douglas Pl., Alton, 62002
Gallenbach, Thomas E., (Retired), 7075 Del Ray, Las Vegas, NV 89117
Kennedy, John, (Retired), 411 Spring Lake Dr., Quincy, 62305-1051
Kraft, Philip G., (Retired), P.O. Box 7492, 62791
Meyer, Bernard A., (Retired), 4725 W. Quincy Ave., #207, Denver, CO 80236
Nelson, Charles T., (Retired), 26 Pearl St., Winchester, 62694
Porter, Robert N., (Retired), 203 Elizabeth Dr., Litchfield, 62056-1786

Schlangen, Louis, (Retired), 1905 N. 2800th Ave., Loraine, 62349
Schmidt, Carl, (Retired), 509 N. Main St., Effingham, 62401
Schmidt, Henry, (Retired), 414 Third St., Carrollton, 62016
Simburger, R. Joseph, (Retired), P.O. Box 462, Albers, 62215
Sohm, John E., (Retired), P.O. Box 464, Sullivan, 61938
Spriggs, Robert W., (Retired), 50 Starfish Dr., #104, Hilton Head Island, SC 29928
Sullivan, Kevin B., (Retired), 920 E. Devonshire Ave., Unit 4030, Phoenix, AZ 85104
Zimmerman, David, (Retired), 2601 Montvale Dr., Apt. 319, 62704.

Permanent Deacons:
Deacons—
Baker, Dennis W., Ss. Mary and Joseph, Carlinville; Ss. Simon and Jude, Gillespie; St. Joseph, Benld
Baxter, James Robert, St. Mary, Taylorville; Holy Trinity, Stonington; St. Rita, Kincaid
Beals, William Jeffrey, St. Charles Borromeo, Charleston
Bohnenstiehl, David S., St. Paul, Highland
Bollman, James G., St. James, Riverton
Burns, Thomas G., Blessed Sacrament, Springfield
Cato, Jerry L., St. Cecilia, Glen Carbon
Caveny, Sean A., Holy Family, Litchfield
Corbett, Daniel L., (Retired)
Cramer, Harry L., St. Anthony of Padua, Quincy
Crosby, Robert F., St. Jacob, St. James; St. Jerome, Troy
Day, Lawrence H., St. Joseph, Springfield
Dodge, James W., St. Aloysius, Springfield
Ellerman, Michael P., Holy Family, Mt. Sterling; St. Thomas, Camp Point
Ellerman, Terrence J., Blessed Sacrament, Quincy
Emmerich, Joseph A., Annunciation, Shumway; St. Anthony, Effingham
Erdmann, David R., Blessed Sacrament, Springfield
Esselman, John M., Leave of Absence
Ghiglione, James J., Ss. Peter & Paul, Collinsville
Hagen, Michael B., Blessed Trinity, Brussels; St. Francis of Assisi, Hardin
Harley, Roy, St. Agnes, Springfield
Hill, James R., SS. Peter and Paul, Collinsville
Hoefler, Benedict P., St. John Vianney, Sherman
Johns, Leland B., St. Agnes, Hillsboro
Kay, John Douglas, Sacred Heart, Effingham
Keen, Thomas Scott, Cathedral of the Immaculate Conception, Springfield
Kessler, William E., St. Ambrose, Godfrey
Koch, Paul, St. Alexius, Beardstown; St. Fidelis, Arenzville
Laabs, Allison (Al) C., Christ the King, Springfield
Lucia, Thomas S., St. John Paul II, Mt. Olive
Lundberg, Robert M., St. Peter, Quincy
Magerl, Roch A., St. Peter, Petersburg; Holy Family, Athens
Maynerich, Gregory
Melton, James Michael, Mother of Perpetual Help, Maryville
Murphy, John M.
O'Brien, John, (Retired)
O'Toole, Patrick J., St. Mary, Farmersville; St. Maurice, Morrisonville, St. Raymond, Raymond
Palazzolo, Dominic Anthony, St. Aloysius, Springfield
Parquette, Gregory, St. Katharine Drexel, Springfield
Richardson, Kevin, St. Thomas the Apostle, Decatur
Roth, Raymond L. Jr., St. Jude, Rochester
Rupp, James, (Leave of Absence)
Schnetzler, Ricky Joe Sr., Sacred Heart, Virden
Schwartzkopf, James, St. Mary, Alton
Scott, Michael (Kim), St. Mark, Winchester; St. Mary, Pittsfield
Smith, Irvin (Larry), Cathedral of the Immaculate Conception, Springfield
Sorrell, David G.
Suermann, Neil Wayne, Holy Family, Granite City; St. Mary and St. Mark, Madison
Theivagt, Charles, St. John the Evangelist, Carrollton; All Saints, White Hall; St. Michael, Greenfield
Uptmor, Eugene V. Jr., Immaculate Conception, Mattoon
Wackerly, Jay William Sr., St. Ambrose, Godfrey
Walker, Thomas A., St. Jude, Rochester
Wilkinson, Thomas W. Sr., St. Ambrose, Godfrey
Wolf, Kenneth, St. Peter, Quincy
Zimmerman, Wayne R., St. Francis Solanus, Quincy.

INSTITUTIONS LOCATED IN DIOCESE

[A] SEMINARIES, RELIGIOUS OR SCHOLASTICATES

GODFREY. *Immaculate Heart of Mary Novitiate*, 4300 Levis Ln., Godfrey, 62035. Tel: 618-466-2233; Email: pmcgee@omiusa.org. Bro. Patrick McGee, Dir.; Rev. Frank Kuczera, Vicar. Religious Teachers 2; Novices 3; Priests 1; Students 3.

[B] COLLEGES AND UNIVERSITIES

QUINCY. *Quincy University* (1860) 1800 College Ave., Quincy, 62301. Tel: 800-688-4295; Tel: 217-228-5432; Email: admissions@quincy.edu; Email: qualumni@quincy.edu; Email: communityrelations@quincy.edu; Web: www.quincy.edu. Mr. Phillip Conover, Pres.; Rev. John Doctor, O.F.M., Vice Pres. Mission & Ministry & Univ. Chap.; Dr. Teresa Reed, Vice Pres.; Bro. Terrence Santiapillai, O.F.M., Reference & Archive Asst., Brenner Library. Franciscan Friars, Sacred Heart Province. Brothers 1; Lay Teachers 51; Priests 2; Students 1,171.

[C] HIGH SCHOOLS, PRIVATE

SPRINGFIELD. *Sacred Heart-Griffin* (1895) 1200 W. Washington St., 62702. Tel: 217-787-1595; Fax: 217-787-9856; Email: rapacz@shg.org; Web: www.shg.org. Sr. Katherine O'Connor, O.P., Pres.; Kara Rapacz, Prin.; Mr. Robert Brenneisen, Asst. Prin.; Jennifer Bettis, Dir. Advancement; Leslie Seck, Dir.; Mr. Thomas Fiaush, Business Mgr.; Rev. Wayne Stock, Chap.; Rachel Bielby, Librarian. Springfield Dominican Sisters. Lay Teachers 43; Sisters 2; Students 608.

ALTON. *Marquette Catholic High School* (1927) 219 E. 4th St., Alton, 62002. Tel: 618-463-0580; Fax: 618-465-4029; Email: scrafton@marquettecatholic.org; Web: marquettecatholic.com. Michael Slaughter, Prin. Lay Teachers 35; Sisters 1; Students 415.

DECATUR. *St. Teresa High School* (1930) 2710 N. Water St., Decatur, 62526. Tel: 217-875-2431; Fax: 217-875-2436; Email: stadmin@st-teresahs.org; Web: stteresa.org. Dr. Kenneth C. Hendriksen, CEO; Mr. Larry Day, Prin.; Laura Brosamr Senger, B.S., M.S., Librarian. Religious Teachers 1; Lay Teachers 26; Students 227.

GLEN CARBON. **Father McGivney Catholic High School*, 7190 Bouse Rd., Glen Carbon, 62034. Tel: 618-855-9010; Fax: 618-855-9011; Email: principal@mcgivneygriffins.com; Email: jlombardi@mcgivneygriffins.com; Web: www.mcgivneygriffins.com. Very Rev. Jeffrey H. Goeckner, V.F., Pres.; Doug Villhard, Bd. Chm.; Mr. Joseph Lombardi, Prin.; Emily Joellenbeck, Dir.; Mrs. Lindsey Jones, Sec. Lay Teachers 19; Students 201.

JACKSONVILLE. *Routt Catholic High School* (1902) 500 E. College Ave., Jacksonville, 62650. Tel: 217-243-8563; Fax: 217-243-3138; Email: nroscetti@routtcatholic.com; Web: www.routtcatholic.com. Nick Roscetti, Prin. Lay Teachers 16; Students 129; Part-time Teachers 7.

QUINCY. *Quincy Notre Dame High School*, 1400 S. 11th, Quincy, 62301-7252. Tel: 217-223-2479; Fax: 217-223-0023; Email: mmcdowell@quincynotredame.org; Web: www.quincynotredame.org. Mark McDowell, Prin. Lay Teachers 29; Students 392.

[D] ELEMENTARY SCHOOLS, PRIVATE

SPRINGFIELD. *Saint Patrick Catholic Grade School* (1910) (Grades PreK-5), 1800 S. Grand Ave. E., 62703. Tel: 217-523-7670; Fax: 217-523-0760; Email: gmahoney@st-patrick.org. Jeff Hamrick, Bd. Chairperson; Lori Loveless, Prin. Lay Teachers 5; Sisters 1; Students 56.

[E] THE CATHOLIC CHARITIES OF THE DIOCESE OF SPRINGFIELD IN ILLINOIS

SPRINGFIELD. *Catholic Charities of Springfield*, 120 S. 11 St., 62702. Tel: 217-523-4551; Email: maher@cc.dio.org; Web: www.cc.dio.org. Amy Maher, Dir. Guests 176,862; Tot Asst. Annually 20,179; Total Staff 12.

Crisis Assistance & Advocacy and Holy Family Food Pantry, 120 S. 11th St., 62703. Tel: 217-523-4551; Fax: 217-523-8425; Email: buttell_spfld@cc.dio.org; Web: www.cc.dio.org. Mark Buttell, Dir. Tot Asst. Annually 17,885; Total Staff 12.

St. Clare's Health Clinic, 700 N. 7th St., Ste. A, 62702. Tel: 217-523-1474; Fax: 217-523-0194; Email: stclares@cc.dio.org; Web: www.cc.dio.org. Mark Buttell, Dir. Total Staff 3; Total Assisted 2,669.

St. John's Breadline, 430 N. Fifth St., 62702. Tel: 217-528-6098; Fax: 217-528-3605; Email: buttell_spfld@cc.dio.org; Web: www.cc.dio.org. Mark Buttell, Dir. Total Staff 8; Meals Served Annually 187,984.

ALTON. *Madison County Catholic Charities*, 3512 McArthur Blvd., Alton, 62002. Tel: 618-462-0634; Fax: 618-462-3209; Email: brown_ccmc@cc.dio.org; Web: www.cc.dio.org. Denise Brown, Area Dir. Tot Asst. Annually 13,744; Total Staff 8.

BEARDSTOWN. *St. Anne Residence*, 309 E. Ninth St., Beardstown, 62618. Tel: 800-745-5194; Fax: 217-323-3228; Email: wessing@cc.dio.org; Web: www.cc.dio.org. Mr. Steven E. Roach, M.S., Exec. Dir. Residents 23; Tot Asst. Annually 23; Total Staff 1.

CARLINVILLE. *Carlinville Catholic Charities* (1990) 525 W. Second S., Carlinville, 62626. Tel: 217-854-4511 ; Fax: 217-854-8049; Email: kelly_cccarl@cc.dio.org; Web: www.cc.dio.org. John Kelly, Area Dir. Tot Asst. Annually 22,300; Total Staff 9.

DECATUR. *Catholic Charities of Decatur* (1944) 247 W. Prairie Ave., Decatur, 62523. Tel: 217-428-3458; Fax: 217-428-4415; Email: rademacher_dec@cc.dio.org; Web: www.cc.dio.org. Marie Rademacher, Area Dir. Tot Asst. Annually 47,980; Total Staff 29.

Catholic Charities of Decatur, 247 W. Prairie Ave. (Main Office), Decatur, 62523. Tel: 217-428-3458; Fax: 217-428-4415; Email: rademacher_dec@cc.dio.org. Marie Rademacher, Dir. Tot Asst. Annually 47,122; Total Staff 29.

EFFINGHAM. *Effingham Catholic Charities*, 1502 E. Fayette, P.O. Box 1017, Teutopolis, 62467. Tel: 217-857-1458; Fax: 217-857-1481; Email: srcarol_ceff@cc.dio.org; Web: www.cc.dio.org. Sr. Carol Beckermann, O.S.F., Area Dir. Total Staff 17.

GRANITE CITY. *Madison County Catholic Charities* (1942) 2266 Madison Ave., Granite City, 62040. Tel: 618-877-1184; Fax: 618-798-4287; Email: brown_ccmc@cc.dio.org; Web: www.cc.dio.org. Office: 1821 Edison Ave., Granite City, 62040. Denise Brown, Area Dir. Tot Asst. Annually 3,017; Total Staff 4.

MATTOON. *Mattoon Catholic Charities* (1996) 4217 Dewitt Ave., Mattoon, 61938. Tel: 217-235-0420; Fax: 217-235-0425; Email: albin_matt@cc.dio.org; Web: www.cc.dio.org. Debbie Albin, Area Dir. Tot Asst. Annually 46,143; Total Staff 16.

QUINCY. *Quincy Catholic Charities*, 620 Maine St., Quincy, 62301. Tel: 217-222-0958; Fax: 217-222-8737; Email: bruns_qcc@cc.dio.org; Web: www.cc.dio.org. Jackie Bruns, Area Dir. Tot Asst. Annually 25,443; Total Staff 13.

WOOD RIVER. *Society of St. Vincent de Paul (Diocesan Central Council)*, 345 E. Acton Ave., Wood River, 62095. Tel: 618-254-0679; Email: mwkwr@aol.com. Marie Kladar, Pres. Total Staff 1.

[F] CHILDREN'S HOMES

ALTON. *Catholic Children's Home*, 1400 State St., Alton, 62002. Tel: 618-465-3594; Fax: 618-465-4023; Email: info@catholicchildrenshome.com; Web: www.catholicchildrenshome.com. Kim Speidel, Prin.; Mr. Steven Roach, Exec. Dir.; Michael Montez, Admin. Residents 19; Students 33; Total Staff 47.

[G] GENERAL HOSPITALS

SPRINGFIELD. *St. John's Hospital* (1875) 800 E. Carpenter St., 62769. Tel: 217-544-6464; Fax: 217-535-3989; Email: ej.kuiper@hshs.org; Email: stacie.reichensperger@hshs.org; Web: www.st-johns.org. E. J. Kuiper, Pres.; Stacie Reichensperger, Dir., Mission Integration & Spiritual Care Svcs. Bed Capacity 439; Students 123; Tot Asst. Annually 197,800; Total Staff 2,969.

St. John's College, Department of Nursing, Tel: 217-544-6464, Ext. 45165; Fax: 217-757-6870. Charlene Aaron, Ph.D., R.N., Chancellor. Students 123.

ALTON. *OSF HealthCare Saint Anthony's Health Center* (1925) 1 Saint Anthony's Way, Alton, 62002-0340. Tel: 618-465-2571; Fax: 618-465-4569; Email: robert.brandfass@osfhealthcare.org; Web: www.osfhealthcare.org. Ajay P. Pathak, Pres.; Rev. Stephen T. Sotiroff, Chap. Two Campuses: OSF Saint Anthony's Health Center and OSF Saint Clare's Hospital Bed Capacity 140; Tot Asst. Annually 92,969; Total Staff 804.

DECATUR. *St. Mary's Hospital*, 1800 E. Lake Shore Dr., Decatur, 62521. Tel: 217-464-2473; Fax: 217-464-1616; Email: frnick.husain@hshs.org; Email: Amy.Bulpitt@hshs.org; Web: www.stmarysdecatur.com. Rev. Msgr. David J. Hoefler, V.G., M.Div., Vicar. Bed Capacity 355; Sisters 2; Total Staff 1,037.

EFFINGHAM. *St. Anthony's Memorial Hospital*, 503 N. Maple St., Effingham, 62401. Tel: 217-342-2121; Fax: 217-347-4829; Email: saecommunications@hshs.org; Web: www.stanthonyshospital.org. Ms. Theresa Rutherford, Pres. & CEO; Rev. Ralph Zetzl, O.F.M., Chap. Bed

Capacity 133; Tot Asst. Annually 147,784; Total Staff 918.

GREENVILLE. **HSHS Holy Family Hospital, Inc.*, 200 Healthcare Dr., Greenville, 62246.
Tel: 618-690-3401; Email: brian.nall@hshs.org. Brian Nall, Pres. & C.E.O. Bed Capacity 42; Tot Asst. Annually 38,348; Total Staff 232.

HIGHLAND. *HSHS St. Joseph's Hospital*, 12866 Troxler Ave., Highland, 62249. Tel: 618-651-2600; Fax: 618-651-2533; Email: Amy.Bulpitt@hshs.org; Web: www.stjosephshighland.org. John A. Ludwig, Pres. & CEO. Bed Capacity 25; Hospital Sisters of the Third Order of St. Francis 2; Tot Asst. Annually 1,258; Total Staff 264.

LITCHFIELD. *St. Francis Hospital*, 1215 Franciscan Dr., P.O. Box 1215, Litchfield, 62056.
Tel: 217-324-2191; Fax: 217-324-3081; Email: Vickie.Morris@hshs.org; Web: www.stfrancis-litchfield.org. Joanne VanLeer, Mission Leader. Bed Capacity 25; Hospital Sisters of the Third Order of St. Francis 1; Tot Asst. Annually 66,033; Total Staff 300; Staff 255.

SHELBYVILLE. **HSHS Good Shepherd Hospital, Inc.*, 200 S. Cedar St., Shelbyville, 62565.
Tel: 217-774-3961; Email: aaron.puchbauer@hshs.org; Email: Jean.Hudson@hshs.org. Aaron Puchbauer, Pres. & C.E.O. Bed Capacity 30; Tot Asst. Annually 387; Total Staff 152.

[H] SPECIAL CARE INSTITUTIONS

SPRINGFIELD. *Brother James Court* (1975) 2508 St. James Rd., 62707. Tel: 217-747-5901;
Fax: 217-747-5971; Email: administrator@brotherjamescourt.com; Web: www.brotherjamescourt.com. Sonia Bartels, Admin. Franciscan Brothers of the Holy Cross.Residence for Mentally Retarded Male Adults. Bed Capacity 99; Residents 91; Tot Asst. Annually 95; Total Staff 108.

[I] HOMES FOR AGED

SPRINGFIELD. *St. Joseph's Home* (1903) 3306 S. Sixth St. Rd., 62703. Tel: 217-529-5596;
Fax: 217-529-8590; Email: mbergman@saintjosephshome.org; Web: www.saintjosephshome.org. Maxine Bergman, Admin.; Rev. Msgr. John R. Ossola, Chap. Residence for the Elderly & Nursing Home. Bed Capacity 84; Residents 72; Sisters 6; Tot Asst. Annually 26,280; Total Staff 143.

[J] MONASTERIES AND RESIDENCES OF PRIESTS AND BROTHERS

SPRINGFIELD. *Franciscan Brothers of the Holy Cross* (1862) (America 1928) St. James Monastery, 2500 Saint James Rd., 62707-9736. Tel: 217-528-4757; Cell: 217-652-1829; Fax: 217-528-4824; Email: br.stephen@franciscanbrothers.net; Web: www.franciscanbrothers.net. Bro. Stephen Bissler, F.F.S.C., Supr. Represented in the Arch/Dioceses of: Springfield, IL; St. Louis, MO Total in Residence 9.

Our Lady of Angels Friary, Our Lady of Angels Friary at Greccio, 4849 La Verna Rd., 62707. Our Lady of Angels Friary at Greccio, P.O. Box 2153, 62705. Tel: 217-522-9822; Email: chart@thefriars.org. Revs. John Sullivan, O.F.M.; Charles Hart, O.F.M.; Andre Schludecker, O.F.M.; Dennis Koopman; Bro. Earl Benz, O.F.M. Franciscan Province of the Sacred Heart. Brothers 1; Priests 4.

MADISON. *Dominican Missionaries for the Deaf Apostolate* aka Mark Seven - DePaul House of Studies, 1011 Alton Ave., Madison, 62060.
Tel: 317-432-0484; Email: solomonf@dominicanmissionaries.org; Email: Adamzawadzki@Dominicanmissioniaries.org; Web: www.DominicanMissionaries.org. Bro. Adam Zawadzki, O.P.Miss., Prior; Deacon Fernando Solomon, O.P.Miss., Vicar. Clergy 3; Novices 8; Solemnly Professed 6; Total in Residence 20.

QUINCY. *St. Francis Solanus Friary* (1860) 1721 College Ave., Quincy, 62301. Tel: 217-222-2898;
Fax: 217-222-3020; Email: church@stfrancissolanus.com; Web: www.stfrancissolanus.com. Revs. Donald Blaeser, O.F.M.; Robert Barko, O.F.M. Priests 2.

Holy Cross Friary, 724 N. 20th St., Quincy, 62301.
Tel: 217-223-9920; Fax: 217-223-9992; Email: doctojo@quincy.edu. Revs. John Doctor, O.F.M., Supr.; Irenaeus Kimminau, O.F.M., Sacramental Min., (Retired); John Ostdiek, O.F.M., Sacramental Min.; James Wheeler, O.F.M., Sacramental Min.; Joseph Zimmerman, O.F.M., Sacramental Min., (Retired); Albert Merz, Business Mgr.; Bro. Terence Santiapillai, O.F.M., Asst. Librarian/Archives, Quincy Univ.; William Spencer, Sabbatical. Brothers 1; Priests 7.

TEUTOPOLIS. *St. Francis Assisi Friary* (1839) 203 E. Main St., P.O. Box 730, Teutopolis, 62467-0730.
Tel: 217-857-6404; Fax: 217-857-1031; Email: stfrancischurch@mchsi.com. Revs. Joseph P. Carlos, O.F.M., Admin.; William J. Rooney, O.F.M.; Kenneth Rosswog, O.F.M.; Ralph Zetzl, O.F.M. Priests 4.

[K] CONVENTS AND RESIDENCES FOR SISTERS

SPRINGFIELD. *Dominican Sisters of Springfield, Il*, Sacred Heart Convent, 1237 W. Monroe St., 62704-1680. Tel: 217-787-0481; Fax: 217-787-8169; Email: sragemma@spdom.org; Web: www.springfieldop.org. Sisters Rebecca Ann Gemma, O.P., Prioress Gen.; Barbara Blesse, O.P., Vicaress Gen.; Judith Hilbing, O.P., Prioress; Rev. Peter Witchousky, O.P., Chap. Motherhouse of the Springfield Dominican Sisters. Motherhouse and Novitiate of the Dominican Sisters of Springfield, Illinois. Sisters in the Congregation 181; In Motherhouse 92.

St. Francis Convent (1844, Congregation); (1875, Province) 4849 LaVerna Rd., 62707. P.O. Box 19431, 62794-9431. Tel: 217-522-3386;
Fax: 217-522-2483; Email: jschneider@hsosf-usa.org; Web: www.hospitalsisters.org. Sisters Maureen O'Connor, O.S.F., M.B.A., M.S.N., Prov. Supr.; Christa Ann Struewing, O.S.F., Community Life Leader; Revs. Andre Schludecker, O.F.M., Chap.; Dennis Koopman, Chap. Hospital Sisters of St. Francis Sisters 48. *St. Francis Convent*, 2101 Shabbona, 62702. Tel: 217-789-4936; Email: moconnor@hsosf-usa.org; Web: www.hospitalsisters.org. Sr. Maureen O'Connor, O.S.F., M.B.A., M.S.N., Prov.
Legal Title: Hospital Sisters of St. Francis Sisters 3. *St. Francis Convent*, 4145 Sunderland Dr., Decatur, 62526. Tel: 217-877-2278; Email: rmenachery@hsosf-usa.org; Web: www.hospitalsisters.org. Sr. Rosily Menachery, O.S.F., Rel. Order Leader
Legal Title: Hospital Sisters of St. Francis. Sisters 2. *St. Francis Convent*, 52 Fairview, 62711. Web: www.hospitalsisters.org. P.O. Box 19431, 62794-9431. Tel: 217-522-3386; Email: moconnor@hsosf-usa.org. Sr. Maureen O'Connor, O.S.F., M.B.A., M.S.N., Prov.
Legal Title: Hospital Sisters of St. Francis. St. Francis Convent, 2717 Arrowhead, 62702.
Tel: 217-528-6492; Email: rmenachery@hsosf-usa.org; Web: www.hospitalsisters.org. Sr. Rosily Menachery, O.S.F., Rel. Order Leader
Legal Title: Hospital Sisters of St. Francis Sisters 2.

Hospital Sisters of St. Francis-USA, Inc., 4849 LaVerna Rd., 62707. Tel: 217-522-3386;
Fax: 217-522-2695; Email: jschneider@hsosf-usa.org; Web: www.hospitalsisters.org. P.O. Box 19431, 62794-9431. Sr. Janice Schneider, O.S.F., Treas. Sisters 48.

Missionary Sisters of the Sacred Heart of Jesus "Ad Gentes", 260 N. Amos Ave., 62702.
Tel: 217-331-4983; Email: ofelia.quiroz@gmail.com. Sisters Ofelia Quiroz-Martinez, M.A.G., Supr.; Eloisa Torralba Aquino, M.A.G., Subprior. Sisters 2.

Monastery of Mary the Queen, Dominican Nuns-Order of Preachers, Monastery of Mary the Queen, 1237 W. Monroe St., 62704. Tel: 217-787-0481;
Fax: 217-787-8169; Email: srannamarie@gmail.com; Web: opnunsil.org. Sr. Anna Pierre, Prioress. Nuns 25.

Ursuline Convent (1857) Ursuline Convent, 4849 LaVerna Rd., P.O. Box 670, 62705-0670.
Tel: 217-492-5940; Email: tdcapeosu@yahoo.com. Sr. Theresa Davey, O.S.U., Prioress. Sisters 6.

ALTON. *St. Clare's Villa*, 915 E. 5th St., Alton, 62002. 915 E. 5th St. 412, Alton, 62002. Cell: 314-397-3382; Email: mmccullacdp@gmail.com; Web: www.cdpsisters.org. Sr. Mary McCulla, C.D.P., Provincial Asst. Sisters 3.

St. Francis Convent (1923) 1 Franciscan Way, P.O. Box 9020, Alton, 62002-9020. Tel: 618-463-2750;
Fax: 618-465-5064; Email: vocations@altonfranciscans.org; Email: secretariat@altonfranciscans.org; Web: www.altonfranciscans.org. Mother M. Maximilia Um, F.S.G.M., Prov. Supr.; Rev. Stephen T. Sotiroff, Chap. Novices 7; Postulants 3; Sisters 117; Final Professed 91; Junior Professed 16.

Ursuline Convent of the Holy Family of the Ursuline Nuns of the Roman Union, 823 Danforth St., Alton, 62002. Tel: 618-462-4771; Fax: 618-433-1631; Email: susan.kienzler@gmail.com. Sr. Susan Kienzler, O.S.U., Prioress. Sisters 14.

[L] NEWMAN CENTERS

CARLINVILLE. *Blackburn College Newman Club*, 2010 E. 1st South St., P.O. Box 647, Carlinville, 62626.
Tel: 217-854-7151; Email: mhaag@dio.org. Deacon Dennis W. Baker, Contact Person. Students 200; Chaplains 2.

CHARLESTON. *Eastern Illinois University Newman Catholic Center*, 500 Roosevelt Ave., Charleston, 61920. Tel: 217-348-0188; Email: newman@eiunewman.org; Web: www.eiunewman.org. Rev. Hyland Smith, Chap.; Mr. Roy Lanham, M.A., Dir.; Mrs. Doris Nordin, Campus Min.; Emily Rogers, Campus Min.

DECATUR. *Millikin University Newman Catholic Community*, Campus: 1184 W. Main St., Decatur, 62522. Tel: 217-429-5363; Fax: 217-429-8206; Email: office@ssjpparish.com; Web: www.munewman.org. Revs. John C. Burnette, Chap.; Steven M. Arisman, Chap.; Mr. Tom Prior, Campus Min.

EDWARDSVILLE. *Southern Illinois University Catholic Campus Ministry* aka Southern Illinois University Edwardsville Catholic Campus Ministry, The Center for Spirituality & Sustainability, 81 Circle Dr., P.O. Box 1059, Edwardsville, 62026.
Tel: 618-650-3205; Fax: 618-650-3264; Email: roblack@siue.edu; Web: www.siuenewmancatholic.com. Robin Black-Rubenstein, Dir. Total Staff 3.

JACKSONVILLE. *Illinois College Newman Catholic Community*, 1101 W. College Ave., Jacksonville, 62650. 453 E. State St., Jacksonville, 62650.
Tel: 217-245-6184; Fax: 217-245-6185; Email: osparish1@mchsi.com. Very Rev. Thomas C. Meyer, V.F., Chap.

MacMurray College Newman Catholic Community, c/o 453 E. State St., Jacksonville, 62650.
Tel: 217-245-6184; Fax: 217-245-6185; Email: tmeyer@dio.org. Rev. Braden Maher, Chap.

TEUTOPOLIS. **Newman Connection, Inc.*, 902 W. Main St., Teutopolis, 62467. Tel: 866-815-2034; Email: mniebrugge@newmanconnection.com; Web: www.newmanconnection.com. Matthew Zerrusen, Pres.; William Zerrusen, Exec. Dir.; Michele Niebrugge, Treas. & Exec. Asst.; Mr. Roy Lanham, M.A., Diocesan Representative; Rev. Robert Lampitt, Dir.; Randy Pifher, Dir., Outreach; Gregory Schweitz, Dir., Serra Rep.; Rev. Tony Stephens, C.P.M., Dir.

[M] MISCELLANEOUS LISTINGS

SPRINGFIELD. *Catholic Care Center, Inc.*, Catholic Pastoral Center, 1615 W. Washington St., 62702.
Tel: 217-698-8500, Ext. 195; Fax: 217-698-0802; Email: gfleck@dio.org; Web: www.dio.org. Mr. Leo A. Lenn, Pres.; Gregory K.J. Fleck, Exec. Sec. & Dir.; Mr. John J. Maxwell, CPA, Treas. & Dir.; Steven E. Roach, M.S., Dir.; Rev. Msgr. David J. Hoefler, V.G., M.Div., Diocesan Admin.

Catholic Living Communities NFP, 1625 W. Washington St., 62702. Tel: 217-523-9201; Email: roach@cc.dio.org. Mr. Steven Roach, Contact Person.

Diocesan Care Management, Inc., Catholic Pastoral Center, 1615 W. Washington St., 62702.
Tel: 217-698-8500, Ext. 195; Fax: 217-698-0802; Email: gfleck@dio.org; Web: www.dio.org. Rev. Msgr. David J. Hoefler, V.G., M.Div., Pres. & Dir.; Mr. John J. Maxwell, CPA, Treas. & Dir.; Gregory K.J. Fleck, Exec. Sec. & Dir.

Dominican Sisters of Springfield in Illinois Charitable Trust (1998) Sacred Heart Convent, 1237 W. Monroe, 62704-1680. Tel: 217-787-0481;
Fax: 217-787-8169; Email: sragemma@spdom.org; Web: www.springfieldop.org. Dan Anderson, Treas.

FLC Corporation NFP, 4849 LaVerna Rd., 62707-9780. Email: jschneider@hsosf-usa.org. P.O. Box 19431, 62794-9431. Tel: 217-522-3386;
Fax: 217-522-2695. Sr. Janice Schneider, O.S.F., Treas.

Foundation for the People of the Diocese of Springfield in Illinois, 1615 W. Washington, 62702. Tel: 217-698-8500, Ext. 114;
Fax: 217-698-0802; Email: sriedell@dio.org. Most Rev. Thomas John Paprocki, Ordinary
The Foundation for the People of the Roman Catholic Diocese of Springfield in Illinois.

Hospital Sisters Health System (1978) 4936 LaVerna Rd., P.O. Box 19456, 62794-9456.
Tel: 217-523-4747; Email: Amy.Bulpitt@hshs.org. Mary Starmann-Harrison, Pres. & CEO; Ann M. Carr.

Hospital Sisters Mission Outreach Corporation, 4930 LaVerna Rd., 62705. Tel: 217-525-8843;
Fax: 217-523-4742; Email: gwinson@mission-outreach.org; Web: www.mission-outreach.org. P.O. Box 1665, 62705-1665. Georgia Winson, Exec. Dir.

Hospital Sisters of St. Francis Foundation, Inc. (1984) 4936 LaVerna Rd., P.O. Box 19456, 62794-9456. Tel: 217-523-4747; Fax: 217-523-0542; Email: daniel.mccormack@hshs.org. Daniel McCormack, Pres.

Hospital Sisters Services, Inc. (1983) 4936 LaVerna Rd., P.O. Box 19456, 62794-9456.
Tel: 217-523-4747; Fax: 217-523-0542; Email: Amy.Bulpitt@hshs.org. Mary Starmann-Harrison, Pres.; Ann M. Carr, Treas.

Jubilee Farm, NFP, 6760 Old Jacksonville Rd., New Berlin, 62670-6747. Tel: 217-787-6927; Email: jubilee.farm@comcast.net; Web: www.jubileefarm.info. Sr. Sharon Zayac, O.P., Exec. Dir.

Leadership Conference of Women Religious, 1237 W.

Monroe, 62704. Tel: 217-787-0481; Fax: 217-787-8169; Email: sragemma@spdom.org. Sisters Betsy Pawlicki, O.P., Chairperson; Joyce Sahnabarger, O.S.F., Vice-Chair; Joanne Bierl, M.M.M., Sec.; Janice Schneider, O.S.F., Treas.
Sponsored Activity: Project IRENE.

Legion of Mary, 400 N. Whitetail Cir., Mt. Zion, 62549-1409. C/O Jan Mudd, 925 Woodland Dr., Mt. Zion, 62549. Tel: 217-864-3467; Email: olbssecretary@hotmail.com. Janice Mudd, Pres.

St. Martin De Porres Center, Inc., 1725 S. Grand Ave., E., 62703. Tel: 217-528-2851; Email: jreed@dio.org. John Brahler, Contact Person.

Priests' Purgatorial Society Catholic Pastoral Center 1615 W. Washington, 62702. Tel: 217-698-8500; Fax: 217-698-0802; Email: dhoefler@dio.org. Rev. Msgr. David J. Hoefler, V.G., M.Div., Contact Person.

**Springfield Developmental Center Ltd.* (1976) 4595 LaVerna Rd., 62707. Tel: 217-525-8271; Fax: 217-525-5801; Email: director@spflddevcenter.org; Email: officemanager@spflddevcenter.org. Kathryn Clark, Dir. Franciscan Brothers of the Holy Cross.Developmental Training Program for Developmentally Disabled Adults. Lay Staff 14; Clients 70.

Theresian Foundation, Inc., 1237 W. Monroe St., 62704. Tel: 217-726-5484; Email: 5dimensions@att.net; Web: www.theresians.org. Victoria S. Schmidt, Exec. Dir. Theresian Foundation exists to provide financial sustainability for Theresians International.

Theresians International, Inc. aka Sacred Heart Convent, 1237 W. Monroe St., 62704. Tel: 217-726-5484; Email: 5dimensions@att.net; Web: www.theresians.org. Victoria S. Schmidt, Exec. Dir. Theresians International is a Catholic organization open to all Christian women with members in eight countries. Total in Community 2,000.

Villa Maria - Catholic Life Center (Retreat and Conference Center) 1903 E. Lake Shore Dr., 62712-5514. Tel: 217-529-2213; Email: gmaynerich@dio.org; Web: villa.dio.org.

Weber House - Weber Care Corporation, 2520 St. James Rd., 62707. Tel: 217-522-8406; Fax: 217-522-8406; Email: bakerconni2520@att.net. Bro. John Francis Tyrrell, F.F.S.C., Pres.; Constance Baker, Prog. Coord. & QSP. Bed Capacity 8.

ALTON. *St. Francis Day Care Center*, 710 College Ave., P.O. Box 9020, Alton, 62002-9020. Tel: 618-463-2766; Email: secretariat@altonfranciscans.org. Sr. M. Theresita Hearon, F.S.G.M., Dir. Day Care Center Religious Teachers 5; Sisters 5; Students 100; Total Staff 29; Assisted Daily 100.

EFFINGHAM. *Effingham Ministries, Inc.*, 512 E. Hendelmeyer, Effingham, 62401. Tel: 217-347-0415; Email: Mhingtgen@mercyhousing.org; Web: www.mercyhousing.org. Melissa Clayton, Vice Pres.

QUINCY. *Ladies of Charity of Quincy*, 510 S. 4th St., Quincy, 62301. Tel: 217-222-6359; Email: locquincy11@yahoo.com. Jane Haas, Pres.

Priestly Fraternity of St. Peter, 1009 N. 8th St., Quincy, 62301-1845. Tel: 217-222-2511; Email: saintrosequincy@att.net; Web: www.saintrosequincy.org. Rev. Arnaud Devillers, F.S.S.P.

VANDALIA. **Our Sorrowful Mothers Ministry*, 331 N. 7th St., Vandalia, 62471. Email: osmm@sbcglobal.net. Rev. Scott A. Snider, Chap.

RELIGIOUS INSTITUTES OF MEN REPRESENTED IN THE DIOCESE

For further details refer to the corresponding bracketed number in the Religious Institutes of Men or Women section.

[]—*Canons Regular of St. John Cantius*—S.J.C.
[]—*Dominican Missionaries for the Deaf* (Apostolate, San Antonio)—O.P. Miss.
[0510]—*Franciscan Brothers of the Holy Cross*—F.F.S.C.
[0520]—*Franciscan Friars* (Sacred Heart Province)—O.F.M.
[0800]—*Maryknoll*—M.M.
[0910]—*Oblates of Mary Immaculate* (Central Province)—O.M.I.
[0940]—*Oblates of the Virgin Mary*—O.M.V.
[0430]—*Order of Preachers (Dominicans)*—O.P.
[1065]—*The Priestly Fraternity of St. Peter*—F.S.S.P.
[0990]—*Society of the Catholic Apostolate*—S.A.C.

RELIGIOUS INSTITUTES OF WOMEN REPRESENTED IN THE DIOCESE

[0100]—*Adorers of the Blood of Christ* (Ruma, IL; Wichita, KS)—A.S.C.
[1730]—*Congregation of the Sisters of the Third Order of St. Francis* (Oldenburg, IN)—O.S.F.
[1710]—*Congregation of the Third Order of St. Francis of Mary Immaculate, Joliet, IL*—O.S.F.
[1060]—*Dominican Contemplative Sisters*—O.P.
[1070-10]—*Dominican Sisters*—O.P.
[1430]—*Franciscan Sisters of Our Lady of Perpetual Help*—O.S.F.
[1770]—*Hospital Sisters of Third Order of St. Francis*—O.S.F.
[]—*Missionary Sisters of the Sacred Heart of Jesus "Ad Gentes"*—M.A.G.
[2970]—*School Sisters of Notre Dame* (St. Louis, MO)—S.S.N.D.
[0990]—*Sisters of Divine Providence* (St. Louis Prov.)—C.D.P.
[1580]—*Sisters of St. Francis of the Immaculate Conception*—O.S.F.
[1600]—*Sisters of St. Francis of the Martyr St. George*—F.S.G.M.
[4110]—*Ursuline Nuns (Roman Union)* (Central Prov.)—O.S.U.
[14120]—*Ursuline Sisters Mount Saint Joseph*—O.S.U.

DIOCESAN CEMETERIES

SPRINGFIELD. *Calvary Cemetery Association*
Calvary Cemetery, Springfield Linda Medlock, Cemetery Mgr.

CARLINVILLE. *Calvary Cemetery Association*, 53 White Tail Dr., Carlinville, 62626. Tel: 217-825-8584.
New Calvary Cemetery, Carlinville Jeff Link, Cemetery Mgr.
Old Calvary Cemetery, Carlinville Jeff Link, Cemetery Mgr.

DECATUR. *Calvary Cemetery Association*, 407 E. Eldorado St., Decatur, 62523. Tel: 217-429-5363; Email: jburnette@dio.org.
Calvary Cemetery, Decatur Rev. John C. Burnette, Cemetery Mgr.

EDWARDSVILLE. *Calvary Cemetery Association*, 2606 Washington Ave., Granite City, 62040. Tel: 618-877-7158; Email: jholtman@dio.org.
Calvary Cemetery, Edwardsville Rev. William Jeffry Holtman, O.F.S.

LITCHFIELD. *Holy Cross Cemetery Association*, P.O. Box 8, Litchfield, 62056. Tel: 217-324-2776; Email: dwillenborg@dio.org.
Holy Cross Cemetery, Litchfield Very Rev. James L. Neuman, V.F., Cemetery Mgr., (Retired)

MOUNT STERLING. *Catholic Cemetery Association*, 401 W. North St., P.O. Box 252, Mount Sterling, 62353. Tel: 217-773-3233; Email: sthompson@dio.org.
Mt. Sterling Catholic Cemetery Rev. Stephen A. Thompson, Cemetery Mgr.

QUINCY. *Catholic Cemetery Association*, 1730 N. 18th St., Quincy, 62301.
Calvary Cemetery, Quincy, 1730 N. 18th St., Quincy, 62301. Tel: 217-223-3390
St. Peter Cemetery, Quincy, 1730 N. 18th St., Quincy, 63201. Tel: 217-223-3390
St. Boniface Cemetery, Quincy, 1730 N. 18th St., Quincy, 62301. Tel: 217-223-3390

NECROLOGY

† Auda, Lawrence J., (Retired), Died Jul. 7, 2018
† Savoree, John M., (Retired), Died Sep. 18, 2018
† Trojcak, Ronald, Died Apr. 4, 2018

An asterisk (*) denotes an organization that has established tax-exempt status directly with the IRS and is not covered by the USCCB Group Ruling.

Diocese of Springfield in Massachusetts

(Dioecesis Campifontis)

Most Reverend

MITCHELL T. ROZANSKI

Bishop of Springfield in Massachusetts; ordained November 24, 1984; appointed Titular Bishop of Walla Walla and Auxiliary Bishop of Baltimore July 3, 2004; consecrated August 24, 2004; appointed Bishop of Springfield in Massachusetts June 19, 2014; installed August 12, 2014. *Chancery Office: P.O. Box 1730, Springfield, MA 01102-1730.*

Most Reverend

TIMOTHY A. MCDONNELL

Bishop Emeritus of Springfield in Massachusetts; ordained June 1, 1963; appointed Titular Bishop of Semina and Auxiliary Bishop of New York October 30, 2001; consecrated December 12, 2001; appointed Bishop of Springfield in Massachusetts March 9, 2004; installed April 1, 2004; retired June 19, 2014. *Mailing Address: Saint Joseph Rectory, 414 North St., Pittsfield, MA 01201-4674.*

ESTABLISHED JUNE 14, 1870.

Square Miles 2,822.

Comprises the Counties of Berkshire, Franklin, Hampden and Hampshire in the State of Massachusetts.

For legal titles of parishes and diocesan institutions, consult the Chancery Office.

Chancery Office: P.O. Box 1730, Springfield, MA 01102-1730. Tel: 413-732-3175; Fax: 413-737-2337.

Web: www.diospringfield.org

Email: mail@diospringfield.org

STATISTICAL OVERVIEW

Personnel	
Bishop	1
Retired Bishops	1
Priests: Diocesan Active in Diocese	81
Priests: Diocesan Active Outside Diocese	5
Priests: Diocesan in Foreign Missions	1
Priests: Retired, Sick or Absent	43
Number of Diocesan Priests	130
Religious Priests in Diocese	54
Total Priests in Diocese	184
Extern Priests in Diocese	13
Ordinations:	
Diocesan Priests	2
Transitional Deacons	3
Permanent Deacons in Diocese	100
Total Brothers	14
Total Sisters	262
Parishes	
Parishes	79
With Resident Pastor:	
Resident Diocesan Priests	67
Resident Religious Priests	5
Without Resident Pastor:	
Administered by Priests	5
Administered by Deacons	2
Missions	7
Pastoral Centers	1
Closed Parishes	1
Professional Ministry Personnel:	
Sisters	21
Lay Ministers	13
Welfare	
Catholic Hospitals	1
Total Assisted	200,121
Health Care Centers	1
Total Assisted	5,601
Homes for the Aged	5
Total Assisted	450
Special Centers for Social Services	9
Total Assisted	76,328
Other Institutions	1
Total Assisted	124
Educational	
Diocesan Students in Other Seminaries	9
Total Seminarians	9
Colleges and Universities	2
Total Students	1,531
High Schools, Diocesan and Parish	2
Total Students	408
Elementary Schools, Diocesan and Parish	12
Total Students	2,573
Catechesis/Religious Education:	
High School Students	2,588
Elementary Students	5,988
Total Students under Catholic Instruction	13,097
Teachers in the Diocese:	
Priests	2
Sisters	9
Lay Teachers	279
Vital Statistics	
Receptions into the Church:	
Infant Baptism Totals	1,474
Minor Baptism Totals	105
Adult Baptism Totals	96
Received into Full Communion	397
First Communions	1,477
Confirmations	1,328
Marriages:	
Catholic	315
Interfaith	54
Total Marriages	369
Deaths	3,098
Total Catholic Population	199,289
Total Population	828,667

Former Bishops—Most Revs. PATRICK THOMAS O'REILLY, D.D., cons. Sept. 25, 1870; died May 28, 1892; THOMAS DANIEL BEAVEN, D.D., cons. Oct. 18, 1892; died Oct. 5, 1920; THOMAS M. O'LEARY, D.D., cons. Sept. 8, 1921; died Oct. 10, 1949; CHRISTOPHER J. WELDON, D.D., cons. March 24, 1950; retired Oct. 15, 1977; died March 19, 1982; JOSEPH F. MAGUIRE, D.D., (Retired), cons. Auxiliary Bishop of Boston, Feb. 2, 1972; installed Bishop of Springfield, Nov. 4, 1977; retired Dec. 27, 1991; died Nov. 23, 2014.; JOHN A. MARSHALL, D.D., cons. Bishop of Burlington, Jan. 25, 1972; installed Bishop of Springfield, Feb. 18, 1992; died July 3, 1994; THOMAS LUDGER DUPRE, D.D., J.C.D., (Retired), ord. May 23, 1959; appt. Auxiliary Bishop of Springfield and Titular Bishop of Hodelm April 19, 1990; cons. May 31, 1990; appt. Bishop of Springfield March 14, 1995; installed May 8, 1995; resigned Feb. 11, 2004; died Dec. 30, 2016.; TIMOTHY A. MCDONNELL, ord. June 1, 1963; appt. Titular Bishop of Semina and Auxiliary Bishop of New York Oct. 30, 2001; cons. Dec. 12, 2001; appt. Bishop of Springfield in Massachusetts March 9, 2004; installed April 1, 2004; retired June 19, 2014.

Office of the Bishop—76 Elliot St., P.O. Box 1730, Springfield, 01102-1730. Tel: 413-452-0803; Fax: 413-452-0804; Email: bishop@diospringfield.org.

Notary—STACY DIBBERN.

Vicar General and Moderator of the Curia—Rev. Msgr. CHRISTOPHER D. CONNELLY, J.C.L., 65 Elliot St., P.O. Box 1730, Springfield, 01102-1730.

Chancery Office—76 Elliot St., P.O. Box 1730, Springfield, 01102. Tel: 413-732-3175; Fax: 413-737-2337.

Chancellor and Vicar for Canonical Affairs—76 Elliot St., P.O. Box 1730, Springfield, 01102. Tel: 413-452-1805; Fax: 413-737-2337. Rev. Msgr. DANIEL P. LISTON, J.C.L.

Vice-Chancellor—Rev. ROBERT W. THRASHER, J.C.D., (Retired).

Judicial Vicar—Rev. Msgr. JOHN J. BONZAGNI, M.Ed., J.C.L., J.D.

Episcopal Vicars—Rev. Msgrs. MICHAEL SHERSHANOVICH, Berkshire Vicariate; RONALD G. YARGEAU, Franklin-Hampshire Vicariate, (Retired); DANIEL P. LISTON, J.C.L., Hampden East Vicariate; HOMER P. GOSSELIN, Hampden Central and Hampden West Vicariate.

Vicars for the Clergy—Revs. CHRISTOPHER A. MALATESTA; ROBERT A. GENTILE JR.

Vicar for Religious—65 Elliot St., P.O. Box 1730, Springfield, 01102-1730. Tel: 413-452-0609. VACANT.

Diocesan Tribunal—65 Elliot St., P.O. Box 1730, Springfield, 01102. Tel: 413-452-0664; Fax: 413-747-8482. Rev. Msgr. JOHN J. BONZAGNI, M.Ed., J.C.L., J.D., Judicial Vicar/Attorney at Law.

Judges—Rev. Msgrs. DANIEL P. LISTON, J.C.L.; CHRISTOPHER D. CONNELLY, J.C.L.; JOHN J. BONZAGNI, M.Ed., J.C.L., J.D.; Rev. JOHN G. LESSARD-THIBODEAU, J.C.L.

Promoter of Justice—Rev. JOHN G. LESSARD-THIBODEAU, J.C.L.

Defender of the Bond—Revs. JOHN P. MCDONAGH, J.C.L.; MICHAEL PIERZ, J.C.L.

Instructor Procurator-Advocate—Rev. Msgr. JUAN GARCIA; Deacons WILLIAM F. KERN, J.D.; JAMES MC ELROY, J.D.

Psychological Consultants—Rev. J. DONALD R. LAPOINTE, S.T.L., L.I.C.S.W., (Retired); Rev. Msgr. GEORGE A. FARLAND, M.Ed., CAS Psychology; DAVID ARMSTRONG, L.I.C.S.W.

Auditors—Deacons GARY DOANE; LEO COUGHLIN; JOHN ANTAYA; THEODORE T. TUDRYN; PAUL BRIERE; DAVID CULLITON; Rev. JOHN HURLEY; Deacon BRUCE ZITER.

Notaries—MS. MARIE DUSSAULT; CARMEN MARTINEZ.

Presbyteral Council—Most Rev. MITCHELL T. ROZANSKI; Rev. Msgrs. CHRISTOPHER D. CONNELLY, J.C.L., Vicar Gen.; DANIEL P. LISTON, J.C.L., Chancellor; Revs. DANIEL S. PACHOLEC; DAVID AUFIERO; MATTHEW ALCOMBRIGHT; PIOTR PAWLUS; CHRISTOPHER J. WAITEKUS; YERICK MENDEZ; ROBERT S. WHITE, C.S.S., B.A., S.T.L.; DOUGLAS MCGONGLE; Revs. JONATHAN REARDON; WILLIAM A. TOURIGNY; JOHN J. BRENNAN; PIOTR CALIK; MICHAEL F. BERNIER; WARREN J. SAVAGE; THOMAS M. SHEA, (Retired); MARK S. STELZER, Ph.D.

Deans—Revs. KENNETH J. TATRO, Hampden West Deanery; FRANCIS E. REILLY, Hampshire Deanery; TIMOTHY J. CAMPOLI, Franklin Deanery; CHRISTOPHER A. MALATESTA, Berkshire Deanery; ROBERT A. GENTILE JR., Greater Holyoke Deanery; Rev. Msgr. GEORGE A. FARLAND, M.Ed., Springfield Deanery; Revs. WILLIAM A. TOURIGNY, Hampden Central Deanery; JOHN K. SHEAFFER, Hampden East Deanery.

Diocesan Consultors—Rev. Msgrs. CHRISTOPHER D. CONNELLY, J.C.L.; HOMER P. GOSSELIN; JOHN J. BONZAGNI, M.Ed., J.C.L., J.D.; DANIEL P. LISTON, J.C.L.; Revs. CHRISTOPHER A. MALATESTA; WAYNE C. BIERNAT; DAVID M. DARCY; MARK M. MENGEL, S.S.C.; PIOTR PAWLUS; CHRISTOPHER J. WAITEKUS; DANIEL B. BRUNTON, (Retired).

Bishop's Commission for Clergy—Most Rev. MITCHELL T. ROZANSKI; Rev. Msgrs. CHRISTOPHER D. CONNELLY, J.C.L.; DAVID J. JOYCE, (Retired); JOHN J. BONZAGNI, M.Ed., J.C.L., J.D.; DANIEL P. LISTON, J.C.L.; Revs. JOHN A. ROACH, (Retired); CHRISTOPHER A. MALATESTA; MATTHEW ALCOMBRIGHT; PIOTR CALIK; ROBERT A. GENTILE JR.; GARY M. DAILEY; MICHAEL J. WOOD JR.; DAVID M. DARCY; BRIAN F. MCGRATH; FRANCIS E. REILLY; JOHN K. SHEAFFER.

Bishop's Cabinet—Rev. Msgrs. CHRISTOPHER D. CONNELLY, J.C.L.; JOHN J. BONZAGNI, M.Ed., J.C.L., J.D., Attorney at Law.; DANIEL P. LISTON, J.C.L.; WILLIAM F. LABROAD JR.; PATRICIA FINN MCMANAMY, L.I.C.S.W.; KATHRYN BUCKLEY-BRAWNER; MARK DUPONT; GINA M. CZERWINSKI; CATHERINE FARR; PERO RIVERA MORAN; DANIEL BAILLARGEON, Ph.D.

Diocesan Diaconate Council—Most Rev. MITCHELL T. ROZANSKI; Deacon LEO COUGHLIN, Dir.; Rev. Msgr. JOHN J. BONZAGNI, M.Ed., J.C.L., J.D., Advisor; Deacons PEDRO RIVERA-MORAN; FRANCIS RYAN; WILLIAM TOLLER; DAVID BERGERON; DONALD HIGBY; DANIEL ROMANELLO. Wives: KAY BUCCI; JEANNE WAINRIGHT.

Diocesan Diaconate Formation Board—Deacons LEO COUGHLIN, Dir.; ROGER CARRIER, Supvr.; THOMAS LYNCH; ANGEL PEREZ; Sr. MELINDA PELLERIN, S.S.J.; MARION M. JOHNSON; CAROLYN GROVES.

Diocesan Commission for the Liturgy—65 Elliot St., P.O. Box 1730, Springfield, 01102-1730. Tel: 413-452-0839. Revs. GEOFFREY J. DEEKER, C.S.S.; WARREN J. SAVAGE; Deacon ROGER CARRIER.

Finance Officer—WILLIAM F. LABROAD JR., 65 Elliot St., P.O. Box 1730, Springfield, 01102. Tel: 413-732-3175.

Diocesan Offices and Directors

Apostolate to the Handicapped—Sr. JOAN MAGNANI, S.S.J., Dir.; Rev. JOHN HURLEY, Chap., Holy Name Rectory, 323 Dickinson St., Springfield, 01108. Tel: 413-532-0713 (Voice and TTY); Fax: 413-322-7065.

Building Commission—65 Elliot St., P.O. Box 1730, Springfield, 01102-1730. Rev. JEFFREY A. BALLOU, Chm.

Building Consultant—65 Elliot St., P.O. Box 1730, Springfield, 01102. Tel: 413-452-0695. RUSSELL SPRAGUE.

Campaign for Human Development—KATHRYN BUCKLEY-BRAWNER, Dir., 65 Elliot St., P.O. Box 1730, Springfield, 01102. Tel: 413-452-0697; Fax: 413-746-3421.

Counseling Office—PATRICIA FINN MCMANAMY, L.I.C.S.W., Dir., Tel: 413-452-0624.

Catholic Charities Agency—KATHRYN BUCKLEY-BRAWNER, Dir., 65 Elliot St., P.O. Box 1730, Springfield, 01102-1730. Tel: 413-452-0606.

Annual Catholic Appeal—65 Elliot St., Springfield, 01101. Tel: 413-452-0670; Email: k.harrington@diospringfield.org. *Mailing Address: P.O. Box 1730, Springfield, 01102.* KATHLEEN HARRINGTON, Mgr.

Catholic Relief Services—KATHRYN BUCKLEY-BRAWNER, 65 Elliot St., P.O. Box 1730, Springfield, 01102. Tel: 413-732-3175.

Cemeteries—JOSEPH KOSTEK, Pres. Cemeteries, 65 Elliot St., Springfield, 01101-1730. Tel: 413-782-0349; Fax: 413-785-5449. Gate of Heaven Cemetery, 421 Tinkham Rd., Springfield, 01129. Tel: 413-782-4731. Saint Michael's Cemetery, 1601 State St., Springfield, 01109. Tel: 413-733-0695. St. Aloysius Cemetery, 1601 State St., Springfield, 01109. St. Benedict Cemetery, Liberty St., Springfield, 01104. Tel: 413-782-4731. St. Matthew Cemetery, 366 Springfield St., Springfield, 01109. Tel: 413-733-0659. St. Mary Cemetery, 203 Southampton Rd., Westfield, 01085. Tel: 413-568-7775. St. Rose Cemetery, Lyman St., South Hadley, 01075. Tel: 413-782-4731. Notre Dame Cemetery, Lyman St., South Hadley, 01075. Calvary Cemetery, Northampton St., Holyoke, 01040. Tel: 413-782-4731. Precious Blood Cemetery, Willimansett St., South Hadley, 01075. Tel: 413-782-4731.

Censor Librorum—Rev. MARK S. STELZER, Ph.D.

Clergy Counseling Service—Rev. Msgr. GEORGE A. FARLAND, M.Ed., Sacred Heart Rectory, 395 Chestnut St., Springfield, 01104. Tel: 413-732-3721.

Communications and Public Relations—MARK DUPONT, Dir., Tel: 413-452-0648; Tel: 413-737-4744; Fax: 413-747-0273. 65 Elliot St., P.O. Box 1730, Springfield, 01102-1730.

Catholic Communications Corporation—MARK DUPONT, Pres., 65 Elliot St., P.O. Box 1730, Springfield, 01102-1730. Tel: 413-737-4744; Fax: 413-747-0273.

Services—

Chalice of Salvation (Televised Mass)—Bro. TERRENCE A. SCANLON, C.P., Exec. Dir., 65 Elliot St., P.O. Box 1730, Springfield, 01102-1730. Tel: 413-452-0642.

Real to Reel (Television News Magazine)—MARK DUPONT, Exec. Producer, 65 Elliot St., P.O. Box 1730, Springfield, 01102-1730. Tel: 413-452-0648.

The Catholic Mirror (Magazine)—REBECCA DRAKE, Editor, 65 Elliot St., P.O. Box 1730, Springfield, 01102-1730. Tel: 413-452-0636.

Continuing Education for Priests—Elms College, 291 Springfield St., Chicopee, 01013. Tel: 413-265-2575 . Rev. WARREN J. SAVAGE, Chm.

Office of Faith Formation—65 Elliot St., P.O. Box 1730, Springfield, 01102-1730. Tel: 413-452-0677. GINA M. CZERWINSKI, Dir.

Cursillo Movement—Rev. Msgr. DAVID J. JOYCE, Dir. English-Speaking Cursillo Movement, (Retired), 65 Elliot St., P.O. Box 1730, Springfield, 01102-1730. Tel: 413-732-3175; MARY VAZQUEZ, Spanish-Speaking Cursillo Movement, Tel: 413-535-0163.

Diocesan Office of Black Catholic Ministry—MARION M. JOHNSON, Administrative Dir., St. Michael's Cathedral Rectory, 260 State St., Springfield, 01103. Tel: 413-781-3656; Email: marionmarie@rcn.com; Web: www.diospringfield.org/ministries/bc.html.

Diocesan Office for Communications—MARK DUPONT, 65 Elliot St., P.O. Box 1730, Springfield, 01102-1730. Tel: 413-737-4744; Fax: 413-747-0273.

Education—DANIEL BAILLARGEON, Ph.D., Supt. of Schools; DR. GAIL FURMAN, Consultant, 65 Elliot St., P.O. Box 1730, Springfield, 01102-1730. Tel: 413-452-0830; Fax: 413-452-0817.

Fiscal Affairs—WILLIAM F. LABROAD JR., Finance Officer, 65 Elliot St., P.O. Box 1730, Springfield, 01102-1730. Tel: 413-452-0687; Fax: 413-785-5449.

Holy Childhood Association—Rev. J. DONALD R. LAPOINTE, S.T.L., L.I.C.S.W., (Retired).

Holy Family League of Charity—c/o Office of Catholic Charities, P.O. Box 1730, Springfield, 01102-1730. Tel: 413-732-3175.

Human Resources—65 Elliot St., P.O. Box 1730, Springfield, 01102-1730. Tel: 413-452-0683. CATHERINE FARR, Dir.

Payroll and Benefits Coordinator—ANNETTE PLOURDE, Tel: 413-452-0691.

Notary—ANNETTE PLOURDE.

Diocesan Cori and Virtus Coordinator—65 Elliot St., P.O. Box 1730, Springfield, 01102-1730. Tel: 413-452-0696. LI LING WALLER.

Massachusetts Catholic Conference—Most Rev. MITCHELL T. ROZANSKI; Rev. Msgr. CHRISTOPHER D. CONNELLY, J.C.L.; Sr. ANNETTE MCDERMOTT, S.S.J.; JOHN EGAN ESQ., 65 Elliot St., P.O. Box 1730, Springfield, 01102-1730. Tel: 413-732-3175.

Ministry to the Deaf—Rev. MATTHEW ALCOMBRIGHT.

Newman Apostolate and Campus Ministry—Revs. JOHN P. MCDONAGH, J.C.L., Dir. Campus Ministry, Newman Center; GARY M. DAILEY, Dir., Newman Center, 472 N. Pleasant St., Amherst, 01002. Tel: 413-549-0300.

Office for the Protection of Children and Youth—MS. PATRICIA FINN MCMANAMY, L.I.C.S.W., Dir., 65 Elliot St., P.O. Box 1730, Springfield, 01102-1730. Tel: 413-452-0624.

Office of Social Concerns—PATRICIA FINN MCMANAMY, L.I.C.S.W., Dir., 65 Elliot St., P.O. Box 1730, Springfield, 01102-1730. Tel: 413-452-0615.

Pastoral Ministry—Mailing Address: 65 Elliot St., P.O. Box 1730, Springfield, 01102-1730. Tel: 413-732-3175.

Permanent Diaconate—Deacon LEO COUGHLIN, Dir., 65 Elliot St., P.O. Box 1730, Springfield, 01102-1730. Tel: 413-452-0674; Fax: 413-747-0273.

Ministry to Retired Priests—65 Elliot St., P.O. Box 1730, Springfield, 01102-1730. Rev. JOHN A. ROACH, Vicar for The Retired, (Retired).

Wellness Coordinator—65 Elliot St., P.O. Box 1730, Springfield, 01102-1730. Tel: 413-452-0697. SUSAN WEHNER.

Pro-Life Commission—TIMOTHY BIGGINS, Chm., 65 Elliot St., P.O. Box 1730, Springfield, 01102-1730. Tel: 413-732-3175.

Propagation of the FaithRev. J. DONALD R. LAPOINTE, S.T.L., L.I.C.S.W., Dir., (Retired), 65 Elliot St., P.O. Box 1730, Springfield, 01102-1730. Tel: 413-452-0675.

Refugee Resettlement Program/Immigration Services—Catholic Charities Agencies, Inc., 65 Elliot St., P.O. Box 1730, Springfield, 01102-1730. Tel: 413-452-0606.

Southeast Asian Apostolate—Rev. PETER HA DINH DANG, Dir., St. Paul the Apostle Church, 235 Dwight Rd., Springfield, 01108. Tel: 413-737-4422; Fax: 413-746-8378.

Catholic Latino Ministry—Deacon PEDRO RIVERA-MORAN, Dir.; LUCY RAMOS, Exec. Sec., 65 Elliot St., P.O. Box 1730, Springfield, 01102-1730. Tel: 413-452-0631; Email: hispanicmin@diospringfield.org.

The Saint Thomas More Society—Deacon WILLIAM KERN, Esq., Pres.

Bishop Marshall Center—MS. MARGOT MORAN, Dir., St. Michael's Cathedral, 260 State St., Springfield, 01105. Tel: 413-732-2301.

Springfield Catholic Women's Club—Co Presidents: KATHRYN SEWARD; CAROL BURKE, Mailing Address: Diocese of Springfield, P.O. Box 1730, Springfield, 01102-1730.

Victim Assistance Coordinator—PATRICIA FINN MCMANAMY, L.I.C.S.W.

Vocations—65 Elliot St., P.O. Box 1730, Springfield, 01102-1730. Tel: 413-452-0816; Fax: 413-452-0817. Co Directors: Revs. MATTHEW ALCOMBRIGHT; MICHAEL J. WOOD JR.

Office of Youth Ministry—65 Elliot St., P.O. Box 1730, Springfield, 01101-1730. Tel: 413-452-0677. GINA M. CZERWINSKI, Dir. Catechetics & Youth Formation.

CLERGY, PARISHES, MISSIONS AND PAROCHIAL SCHOOLS

CITY OF SPRINGFIELD

(HAMPDEN COUNTY)

1—ST. MICHAEL'S CATHEDRAL (1847)
254 State St., 01103. Tel: 413-781-3656; Email: scrivener@diospringfield.org; Web: stmichaelscathedralspfld.org. Mailing Address: 260 State St., 01103. Rev. Msgr. Christopher D. Connelly, J.C.L., Rector; Sr. Eileen Sullivan, S.S.J., Outreach Min.; Deacons Leo Coughlin; Angel Perez; Jose Rivera, Pastoral Assoc.; Ms. Dolly Garzon, Pastoral Assoc.

Catechesis Religious Program—Lynn Dubreuil, D.R.E. Students 118.

Mission—St. Francis Chapel, 254 Bridge St., Hampden Co. 01102-1730. Tel: 413-452-0631.

2—ALL SOULS (1908) (Spanish)
449 Plainfield St., 01107. Tel: 413-736-0076; Fax: 413-731-0962; Email: blessedsacramentchurch@comcast.net. Mailing Address: 445 Plainfield St., 01007. Rev. Jose Siesquen Flores, (Peru) Admin.; Deacon Jose Rivera.

Catechesis Religious Program—

3—ST. ALOYSIUS (1873) (French), Merged with St. Matthew, Springfield, to form St. Jude, Indian Orchard.

4—BLESSED SACRAMENT (1953) (Hispanic)
445 Plainfield St., 01107. Tel: 413-736-2167;

Fax: 413-731-0962; Email: blessedsacramentchurch@comcast.net. Rev. Jose Siesquen Flores, (Peru) Admin.; Deacons Genaro Medina; Kevin McCarthy.
Catechesis Religious Program—Nilda Resto, D.R.E. Students 205.

5—St. Catherine of Siena (1961)
1023 Parker St., 01129. Tel: 413-783-8619; Email: parishoffice@stcatherine.us. Rev. Jacques Coly, Admin.; Deacon John Antaya.
Catechesis Religious Program—Students 121.

6—Holy Cross (1949)
219 Plumtree Rd., 01118. Tel: 413-783-4111;
Fax: 413-783-4112; Email: hrrectory@gmail.com. Mailing Address: 221 Plumtree Rd., 01118. Rev. David M. Darcy; Deacon William Toller.
Catechesis Religious Program—175 Eddywood St., 01118. Tel: 413-372-6239; Email: hcc.cathy@gmail.com. Cathy Daniel, D.R.E. Students 59.

7—Holy Family (1901) (African American—Hispanic), Closed. Merged into St. Michael's Cathedral with records being kept at St. Michael's Cathedral, Springfield.

8—Holy Name (1909)
323 Dickinson St., 01108. Tel: 413-733-5823;
Fax: 413-788-6481. Rev. Mark M. Mengel, S.S.C., Admin.; Sr. Melinda Pellerin, S.S.J., Pastoral Min.; Mary Reale, Finance Mgr.
Catechesis Religious Program—
Tel: 413-733-5823, Ext. 123. Claudine Bouchard Collins, C.R.E. Students 101.

9—Immaculate Conception (1905) (Polish)
25 Parker St. (Indian Orchard), 01151.
Tel: 413-543-3627; Fax: 413-543-4301; Email: iccmoffice@gmail.com. Rev. Stanislaw Sokol; Deacon Donald Philip, Admin.
Catechesis Religious Program—Students 38.

10—St. Joseph's (1873) (French), Closed. For inquiries for parish records please contact St. Michael's Cathedral, Springfield.

11—Mary Mother of Hope Parish (2010)
840 Page Blvd., 01104. Tel: 413-739-0546;
Fax: 413-733-6155; Email: marymotherofhope@comcast.net. Rev. Michael J. Wood Jr. In Res., Rev. Donatus Ironuma.
Catechesis Religious Program—Tel: 413-736-1622; Fax: 413-736-9299. Lee Lyon, D.R.E. Students 260.
Office of the Ministry of the Deaf—Tel: 413-241-3193; Tel: 413-739-0456, Ext. 7 (Voice);
Teletype: 413-391-7340 (TTY); Email: cathdeafmin@diospringfield.org.

12—St. Mary's (1948) Merged with Our Lady of Hope, Springfield to form Mary Mother of Hope Parish, Springfield. All records located at Mary Mother of Hope Parish, Springfield.

13—Our Lady of Hope (1906) Closed. Merged with St. Mary's, Springfield to form Mary Mother of Hope Parish, Springfield. All records located at Mary Mother of Hope Parish, Springfield.

14—Our Lady of Mt. Carmel (1907) (Italian)
123 William St., 01105. Tel: 413-734-5433;
Fax: 413-731-0680; Email: mountcarmelrectoryoffice@gmail.com. Revs. Robert S. White, C.S.S., B.A., S.T.L.; Paolo Bagattini, C.S.S., Parochial Vicar; Sr. Elizabeth A. Matuszek, S.S.J., Pastoral Assoc.
Catechesis Religious Program—Tel: 413-204-7789; Email: divenuto4@aol.com; Web: www.olmcspfld.com. Students 73.

15—Our Lady of the Rosary (1917) [JC] (Polish), Closed. For records see Immaculate Conception Parish, Springfield. Rev. Stanislaw Sokol.

16—Our Lady of the Sacred Heart (1929)
407 Boston Rd., 01109. Tel: 413-782-8041;
Fax: 413-783-9150; Email: olshspringfield@gmail.com. Mailing Address: 51 Rosewell St., 01109. Rev. Ryan Rooney; Deacons Odell Daniel; Angel Diaz.
Res.: 417 Boston Rd., 01109.
Catechesis Religious Program—Sharon Sabourin, D.R.E. Students 68.

17—St. Patrick's (1961)
1900 Allen St., 01118-1820. Tel: 413-783-6201;
Fax: 413-783-7787; Email: stpatspringfield@aol.com; Web: www.saintpatricks-springfield.org. Rev. Msgr. Daniel P. Liston, J.C.L.; Deacon George Kozach; Sr. Paula Robillard, S.S.J., D.R.E.

18—St. Paul the Apostle (1960)
235 Dwight Rd., 01108. Tel: 413-737-4422; Email: stpaulchurch235@gmail.com. Rev. Peter Ha Dinh Dang; Deacons Francis D. Rogers; Ly X. Cao; Khanh Tran.
Catechesis Religious Program—Tel: 413-386-7633. Hai Vu, D.R.E. Students 142.

19—Sacred Heart (1872)
387 Chestnut St.. Tel: 413-732-3721;
Fax: 413-733-5731; Email: shc395@aol.com. Mailing Address: 395 Chestnut St., 01104. Rev. Msgr. George A. Farland, M.Ed.; Deacon William Kern, Esq.
Catechesis Religious Program—Students 173.

20—St. Thomas Aquinas (1908) (French—Vietnamese), Closed. For inquiries for sacramental records contact Blessed Sacrament, Springfield.

OUTSIDE THE CITY OF SPRINGFIELD

Adams, Berkshire Co.

1—St. John Paul II Parish
21 Maple St., P.O. Box 231, Adams, 01220-0231.
Tel: 413-743-0577; Fax: 413-743-4665; Email: bjpparish@yahoo.com. Rev. Steven G. Montesanti; Deacon Gregory Lafreniere.
Catechesis Religious Program—Nicholas Petropulos, D.R.E.; Steven Melito, D.R.E. Students 86.

2—Notre Dame des Sept Douleurs (1882) (French), Merged with St. Thomas Aquinas, Adams to form Notre Dame des Sept Douleurs and St. Thomas Aquinas, Adams.

3—Notre Dame des Sept Douleurs and St. Thomas Aquinas (1998) Merged with St. Stanislaus Kostka, Adams to form St. John Paul II, Adams.

4—St. Stanislaus Kostka (1902) [CEM] (Polish), Merged with Notre Dame des Sept Douleurs, Adams and St. Thomas Aquinas, Adams to form St. John Paul II, Adams.

5—St. Thomas Aquinas (1875) Merged with Notre Dame des Sept Douleurs, Adams to form Notre Dame des Sept Douleurs and St. Thomas Aquinas, Adams.

Agawam, Hampden Co.

1—All Saints (2001) Closed. For inquiries for parish records contact Sacred Heart, Feeding Hills.

2—St. John the Evangelist (1946)
833 Main St., Agawam, 01001. Tel: 413-786-8105;
Fax: 413-455-3100; Email: sje.parishsecretary@gmail.com. Rev. Michael Pierz, J.C.L., Admin.; Mary Scannell, Pastoral Min.
Catechesis Religious Program—Tel: 413-455-3215; Email: reled@stjohnagawam.org. Students 250.

3—St. Theresa of the Child Jesus (1883) Merged with Saint Anthony Mission to form All Saints, Agawam. For inquiries for parish records please see Sacred Heart, Feeding Hills.

Amherst, Hampshire Co., St. Brigid's (1872) [CEM]
122 N. Pleasant St., P.O. Box 424, Amherst, 01004-0424. Tel: 413-256-6181; Email: stbrigidamherst@gmail.com. Rev. John T. Smegal.
Catechesis Religious Program—Students 99.

Belchertown, Hampshire Co., St. Francis of Assisi (1926)
24 Jabish St., Belchertown, 01007.
Tel: 413-323-6272, Ext. 1; Email: francisatbtown@gmail.com; Web: www.stfrancisbelchertown.com. Mailing Address: 10 Park St., P.O. Box 612, Belchertown, 01007. Rev. John K. Sheaffer.
Catechesis Religious Program—Email: carolyn.groves@gmail.com. Dr. Carolyn Vogt Groves, D.R.E.; Melissa Hurst, C.R.E. Students 264.

Bondsville, Hampden Co.

1—St. Adalbert's (1910) Closed. Sacramental Records at Saint Thomas Parish, Palmer.

2—St. Bartholomew's (1878) [JC] Closed. Merged with St. Thomas the Apostle, Palmer. All records will be transferred to St. Thomas the Apostle, Palmer.

Brimfield, Hampden Co., St. Christopher's (1953)
20 Sturbridge Rd., Rte. 20, Brimfield, 01010.
Tel: 413-245-7274; Email: stchrisbrimfield@gmail.com. Mailing Address: P.O. Box 387, Brimfield, 01010. Rev. John J. Brennan.
Rectory—16 Sturbridge Rd., Rte. 20, P.O. Box 387, Brimfield, 01010-0387.
Catechesis Religious Program—Students 80.
Mission—St. Monica, Wales, Hampden Co.. (Closed).

Cheshire, Berkshire Co., St. Mary of the Assumption (1926) [JC]
159 Church St., Cheshire, 01225. Tel: 413-743-2110; Email: office@saintmaryscatholic.org; Web: saintmaryscatholic.org. Rev. Matthew Guidi; Deacon Robert Hitter.
Catechesis Religious Program—Tel: 413-743-5423; Fax: 413-743-5423; Email: mtamosfarm@roadrunner.com. Students 83.
Mission—North American Martyrs Chapel / Shrine of St. Kateri Tekawitha, 151 Old State Rd., Lanesborough, 01237.

Chicopee, Hampden Co.

1—St. Anne's (1912)
30 College St., Chicopee, 01020. Tel: 413-532-7503;
Fax: 413-532-5970; Email: stannesec@aol.com. Rev. John E. Connors; Deacon Romeo Hebert.
Catechesis Religious Program—Tel: 413-533-8038. Students 122.

2—St. Anthony of Padua (1926) (Polish)
56 St. Anthony St., Chicopee, 01013.
Tel: 413-538-9475; Fax: 413-538-9859; Email: pastor@stanthonychicopee.com; Web: www.stanthonychicopee.com. Rev. Jacek Leszczynski.
Catechesis Religious Program—Edward Potyrala, D.R.E. Students 147.

3—Assumption (1885) (French), Closed. Merged with Holy Name of Jesus, Chicopee. All records kept at Holy Name of Jesus, Chicopee.

4—St. George's (1893) (French), Closed. Merged into Holy Name of Jesus, Chicopee. All records kept at Holy Name of Jesus, Chicopee.

5—Holy Name of Jesus (1838) [CEM]
94 Springfield St., Chicopee, 01013.
Tel: 413-594-8700; Email: holynamechicopee@aol.com. Mailing Address: 104 Springfield St., Chicopee, 01013. Rev. William A. Tourigny; Deacon David Southworth.
Catechesis Religious Program—Students 40.

6—St. Mary's (1939) Closed. Merged into St. Anthony of Padua, Chicopee. All records kept at St. Anthony of Padua, Chicopee.

7—Nativity of the Blessed Virgin Mary (1897) [JC] (French), Closed. Merged into St. Anthony of Padua, Chicopee. All records kept at St. Anthony of Padua, Chicopee.

8—St. Patrick's (1872) [CEM] (Irish), Closed. Merged into Holy Name of Jesus, Chicopee. All records kept at Holy Name of Jesus, Chicopee.

9—St. Rose de Lima (1909) [CEM] (French)
600 Grattan St., Chicopee, 01020. Tel: 413-536-4558;
Fax: 413-534-9130; Email: frbill@sterose.org. Mailing Address: 15 Chapel St., Chicopee, 01020. Rev. William A. Tourigny; Rev. Msgr. John F. Myslinski, Weekend Ministry; Deacon Michael Trznadel.
School—St. Joan of Arc, (Grades PreK-8), 587 Grattan St., Chicopee, 01020. Tel: 413-533-1475;
Fax: 413-533-1418; Email: businessoffice@sjachicopee; Web: sjachicopee.org. Paula Jenkins, Prin.; Irene Ruel, Librarian. Lay Teachers 17; Students 206.
Catechesis Religious Program—Email: cindee@sterose.org. Cynthia Gagnon, D.R.E. Students 99.

10—St. Stanislaus Basilica (1891) [CEM] (Polish)
570 Front St., Chicopee, 01013. Tel: 413-594-6669; Email: contact@ststansbasilica.org. Mailing Address: 40 Cyman Dr., Chicopee, 01013. Revs. Joseph Bayne, O.F.M. Conv.; Paul Miskiewicz, O.F.M. Conv., Parochial Vicar; Mieczyslaw Wilk, O.F.M. Conv., Parochial Vicar; Bro. Michael Duffy, O.F.M. Conv., Prof.; Deacon Joseph Peters.
Res.: 566 Front St., Chicopee, 01013.
School—St. Stanislaus Basilica School, (Grades PreK-8), 534 Front St., Chicopee, 01013.
Tel: 413-592-5135; Fax: 413-598-0187; Email: ststanis@st.stanislaus.mec.edu; Web: st.stanislaus.mec.edu. Sr. Cecelia Haier, F.S.S.J., Prin.; Karen Shea, Vice Prin. Clergy 1; Lay Teachers 25; Sisters 1; Students 293.
Catechesis Religious Program—
Tel: 413-594-6669, Ext. 129. Sr. M. Andrea Ciszewski, F.S.S.J., D.R.E.; Mrs. Karen Ford, Confirmation Coord. Students 95.

Dalton, Berkshire Co., St. Agnes (1907)
489 Main St., Dalton, 01226. Tel: 413-684-0125; Email: cmalatesta@saintagnescc.com; Web: stagnescc.com. Rev. Christopher A. Malatesta; Deacons George Morrell; Richard Radzick.
School—St. Agnes School, (Grades PreK-8), 30 Carson St., Dalton, 01226. Tel: 413-684-3143;
Fax: 413-684-3124; Email: jstankiewicz@saintagnescc.com; Web: stagnescc.com. James Stankiewicz, Headmaster. Lay Teachers 16; Students 148.
Catechesis Religious Program—513 Main St., Dalton, 01226. Tel: 413-684-1803; Email: lstankiewicz@saintagnescc.com. Lisa Stankiewicz, D.R.E. Students 410.
Chapel—St. Patrick Chapel, 43 Church St., Hinsdale, 01235.

East Longmeadow, Hampden Co., St. Michael's (1894)
110 Maple St., East Longmeadow, 01028. Mailing Address: 128 Maple St., East Longmeadow, 01028.
Tel: 413-525-4253; Email: stmichaelsparishel@gmail.com. Rev. Wayne C. Biernat; Sisters Mary McGeer, S.S.J., Pastoral Assoc.; Betty Broughan, S.S.J., Pastoral Assoc.
Res.: 108 Maple St., East Longmeadow, 01028.
Catechesis Religious Program—Mailing Address: 53 Somers Rd., East Longmeadow, 01028.

Easthampton, Hampshire Co.

1—Immaculate Conception (1871) [CEM] Merged with Sacred Heart, Easthampton and Our Lady of Good Counsel, Easthampton to form Our Lady of the Valley, Easthampton.

2—Our Lady of Good Counsel (1906) (French), Merged with Sacred Heart, Easthampton and Immaculate Conception, Easthampton to form Our Lady of the Valley, Easthampton.

3—Our Lady of the Valley (2010)
33 Adams St., Easthampton, 01027.
Tel: 413-527-9778; Fax: 413-527-9353; Email: olveasthampton@gmail.com. Revs. Douglas McGonagle; John Gawienowski, Parochial Vicar.
School—Our Lady's Child Care Center, 35 Pleasant St., Easthampton, 01027. Tel: 413-527-6133;
Fax: 413-527-0517; Email: ourladyccc@charter.net.

Perri Taylor, Dir. (Child Care). Lay Teachers 20; Students 100.
Catechesis Religious Program—40 Franklin St., Easthampton, 01027. Caroline Growhoski, Rel. Ed. Coord.
4—SACRED HEART (1909) [CEM] (Polish), Closed. Merged with Immaculate Conception, Easthampton and Our Lady of Good Counsel, Easthampton to form Our Lady of the Valley, Easthampton.
FEEDING HILLS, HAMPDEN CO., SACRED HEART (1946)
1065 Springfield St., Feeding Hills, 01030.
Tel: 413-786-8200; Fax: 413-786-7802; Email: office@sacredheartfeedinghills.org; Web: www.sacredheartfeedinghills.org. Mailing Address: 1061 Springfield St., Feeding Hills, 01030. Rev. Steven S. Amo.
Res.: 1103 Springfield St., Feeding Hills, 01030.
Catechesis Religious Program—Lisa Raffia, D.R.E. Students 278.
FLORENCE, HAMPSHIRE CO., ANNUNCIATION (1878) Closed. Now a chapel of Saint Elizabeth Ann Seton, Northampton. All records transferred to Saint Elizabeth Ann Seton, Northampton.
GRANBY, HAMPSHIRE CO., IMMACULATE HEART OF MARY (1951)
256 State St., Granby, 01033. Tel: 413-467-9821; Fax: 413-467-2988; Email: parish@ihmgranby.org. Rev. Charles H. Kuzmeski.
Catechesis Religious Program—Tel: 413-467-3566; Email: faithformation@ihmgranby.org. Students 142.
GREAT BARRINGTON, BERKSHIRE CO., ST. PETER'S (1864) [CEM]
213 Main St., Great Barrington, 01230.
Tel: 413-528-1157; Email: st.petergb12@gmail.com. Mailing Address: 16 Russell St., Great Barrington, 01230. Rev. William P. Murphy; Deacons Richard Magenis; Edward Shaw.
Catechesis Religious Program—Students 64.
GREENFIELD, FRANKLIN CO.
1—BLESSED SACRAMENT (1960) [CEM]
221 Federal St., Greenfield, 01301.
Tel: 413-773-3311; Fax: 413-773-5785; Email: blsacrament@gmail.com; Web: blessedsacramentgreenfieldma.org. Mailing Address: 182 High St., Greenfield, 01301. Rev. Timothy J. Campoli; Deacons John Leary; George Nolan.
Catechesis Religious Program—Tel: 413-774-2918; Email: lltilton2@gmail.com. Laurie Tilton, D.R.E.
2—HOLY TRINITY (1868)
133 Main St., Greenfield, 01301-3209.
Tel: 413-774-2884; Email: office.holytrinity@crocker.com. Rev. Timothy J. Campoli; Deacons Channing L. Bete Jr.; Paul F. DeCarlo.
Catechesis Religious Program—Students 66.
3—SACRED HEART (1912) [CEM] (Polish), Closed. Merged with St. Mary, Turner Falls & St. Ann, Turner Falls to form Our Lady of Peace, Turner Falls.
HADLEY, HAMPSHIRE CO.
1—HOLY ROSARY (1916) (Polish), Merged with St. John, Hadley, to form Most Holy Redeemer, Hadley.
2—ST. JOHN'S (1915) Merged with Holy Rosary, Hadley, to form Most Holy Redeemer, Hadley.
3—MOST HOLY REDEEMER (1998) [CEM]
120 Russell St., Hadley, 01035-0375.
Tel: 413-584-1326; Email: mhrchurch@yahoo.com. P.O. Box 375, Hadley, 01035. Rev. Piotr Pawlus.
Catechesis Religious Program—Students 60.
HAMPDEN, HAMPDEN CO., ST. MARY'S (1951) [CEM]
27 Somers Rd., Hampden, 01036. Tel: 413-566-8843; Email: stmarys@razuma.com; Web: www.stmaryshampden.org. Rev. Timothy J. Murphy.
Catechesis Religious Program—Tel: 413-567-8742. Mrs. Angelane Welker, D.R.E. Students 83.
HATFIELD, HAMPSHIRE CO.
1—HOLY TRINITY (1916) [CEM] (Polish), Merged with St. Joseph, Hatfield to form Our Lady of Grace, Hatfield. For inquiries for parish records please see Our Lady of Grace, Hatfield.
2—ST. JOSEPH (1899) Merged with Holy Trinity, Hatfield to form Our Lady of Grace, Hatfield.
3—OUR LADY OF GRACE PARISH (2010)
15 School St., P.O. Box 34, Hatfield, 01038.
Tel: 413-247-9079; Fax: 413-247-9080; Email: ourladyofgracehatfield@yahoo.com. Rev. Robert J. Coonan; Deacon Mark Kolasinski.
Res.: 11 School St., Hatfield, 01038.
Catechesis Religious Program—Students 98.
HAYDENVILLE, HAMPSHIRE CO.
1—ST. MARY'S (1889) [CEM] Closed. Merged with St. Catherine's, Leeds to form Our Lady of the Hills, Haydenville.
2—OUR LADY OF THE HILLS (2007) [CEM]
173 Main St., Haydenville, 01039-9768.
Tel: 413-268-7212; Email: olothparish@gmail.com. Rev. Richard A. Bondi.
HINSDALE, BERKSHIRE CO., ST. PATRICK'S (1868) Closed. Now a chapel under St. Agnes, Dalton.
HOLYOKE, HAMPDEN CO.
1—BLESSED SACRAMENT (1913)
1945 Northampton St., Holyoke, 01040.
Tel: 413-532-0713; Fax: 413-322-7065; Email: blsachol@comcast.net. Rev. Robert A. Gentile Jr. In Res., Rev. Richard A. Riendeau, (Retired).
School—Blessed Sacrament School, (Grades K-8), 21 Westfield Rd., Holyoke, 01040. Tel: 413-536-2236; Fax: 413-534-0795; Email: officebss@comcast.net. Anne L. O'Connor, Prin. Lay Teachers 15; Sisters of St. Joseph 2; Students 205.
Catechesis Religious Program—Kelly Gauthier, D.R.E.
Mission—Holyoke Soldier's Home Chapel, 110 Cherry St., Holyoke, Hampden Co. 01040.
Tel: 413-532-9475.
2—HOLY CROSS (1905) Merged with Mater Dolorosa, Holyoke to form Our Lady of the Cross, Holyoke. Parish records are located at Our Lady of the Cross.
3—HOLY FAMILY (1949) Closed. For inquiries for parish records please see Blessed Sacrament, Holyoke.
4—IMMACULATE CONCEPTION (1905) [JC]
54 N. Summer St., Holyoke, 01040-6279.
Tel: 413-532-5784; Fax: 413-532-8852; Email: icparish@outlook.com. Rev. Yerick Mendez, Admin.; Deacons Frederick Pelletier; Jose Correa.
Catechesis Religious Program—Students 42.
5—ST. JEROME (1854) [CEM]
181 Hampden St., Holyoke, 01040. Tel: 413-532-6381 ; Email: st_jerome@comcast.net. Mailing Address: 169 Hampden St., Holyoke, 01040-4597. Rev. Mark S. Stelzer, Ph.D., Admin.
Catechesis Religious Program—Students 65.
6—MATER DOLOROSA (1896) [CEM] (Polish), Merged with Holy Cross Holyoke to form Our Lady of the Cross, Holyoke. Parish records are located at Our Lady of the Cross.
7—OUR LADY OF GUADALUPE (2001) [CEM 3] [JC]
427 Maple St., Holyoke, 01040. Tel: 413-532-4282; Fax: 413-532-2182; Email: ourladyofguadalupe@gmail.com. Mailing Address: 435 Maple St., Holyoke, 01040. Rev. Yerick Mendez, Admin.; Deacons Jose Correa; Pedro Rivera-Burgos.
Catechesis Religious Program—Students 37.
8—OUR LADY OF PERPETUAL HELP (1890) (French), Merged with Sacred Heart to form Our Lady of Guadalupe, Holyoke.
9—OUR LADY OF THE CROSS (2011)
Holy Cross Ave., Holyoke, 01040. Tel: 413-532-5661; Fax: 413-532-7889; Email: parish@ourladyofthecross.com. Mailing Address: 15 Maple St., Holyoke, 01040. Rev. Albert Scherer, O.F.-M.Conv.
Res.: St. John Paul II Friary, 23 Sycamore St., Holyoke, 01041-4698.
School—Mater Dolorosa School, (Grades PreK-8), 25 Maple St., Holyoke, 01040. Tel: 413-532-2831; Fax: 413-532-8588; Email: mrs.rex@materdolorosaschool.org; Web: www.materdolorosaschool.org. Linda Rex, Prin. Lay Teachers 17; Students 211.
Catechesis Religious Program—Tel: 413-532-7889. Students 30.
10—OUR LADY OF THE ROSARY (1886) Closed. For inquiries for parish records contact the chancery.
11—PRECIOUS BLOOD (1869) Closed. For inquiries for parish records contact Our Lady of Guadalupe, Holyoke.
12—SACRED HEART (1876) Merged with Our Lady of Perpetual Help to form Our Lady of Guadalupe, Holyoke.
HOUSATONIC, BERKSHIRE CO.
1—ALL SAINTS (1913) (Polish), Closed. For inquiries for parish records contact Blessed Teresa of Calcutta, Housatonic.
2—SAINT TERESA OF CALCUTTA PARISH aka Corpus Christi Church (2009)
1085 Main St., Housatonic, 01236. Tel: 413-274-3443 ; Email: st.teresa9@gmail.com. Mailing Address: P.O. Box 569, Housatonic, 01236-0569. Rev. William P. Murphy; Deacon Edward Shaw.
Catechesis Religious Program—Students 72.
3—CORPUS CHRISTI (1899) [CEM] Closed. Merged. See Blessed Teresa of Calcutta, Housatonic.
HUNTINGTON, HAMPSHIRE CO., ST. THOMAS (1886) [CEM] Closed. Merged with Our Lady of the Rosary, Russell & St. John Mission, Chester to form Holy Family Parish, Russell. All records located at Holy Family Parish, Russell.
LANESBORO, BERKSHIRE CO., NORTH AMERICAN MARTYRS (1969) A Mission of St. Mary of the Assumption Parish, Cheshire.
LEE, BERKSHIRE CO., ST. MARY'S (1857) [CEM]
140 Main St., Lee, 01238. Tel: 413-243-0275; Fax: 413-243-1926; Email: lcsmchurch@gmail.com. Mailing Address: 40 Academy St., Lee, 01238. Revs. Brian F. McGrath; Daniel Cymer, Parochial Vicar.
School—St. Mary's School, (Grades PreK-8), 115 Orchard St., Lee, 01238. Tel: 413-243-1079; Fax: 413-243-1022; Email: jmasten@stmaryslee.org; Web: stmaryslee.org. Jennifer Masten, Prin.; Paula Salinetti, Librarian. Lay Teachers 14; Students 132.
Catechesis Religious Program—
Tel: 413-243-1079, Ext. 8. Students 87.
Missions—St. Mary of the Lakes—Otis, Berkshire Co.
Saint Joseph, Stockbridge, Berkshire Co. 01263.
LEEDS, HAMPSHIRE CO., ST. CATHERINE'S (1911) [JC] Closed. Merged with St. Mary, Haydenville to form Our Lady of the Hills, Haydenville.
LENOX DALE, BERKSHIRE CO., ST. VINCENT DE PAUL (1904)
29 Crystal St., Lenox Dale, 01242-0259.
Tel: 413-637-0157; Email: stvincentlenoxdale@gmail.com. P.O. Box 259, Lenox Dale, 01242. Rev. Msgr. John J. Bonzagni, M.Ed., J.C.L., J.D.; Deacons John E. Zick; Daniel Romanello.
LENOX, BERKSHIRE CO., ST. ANN (1891) [CEM]
134 Main St., Lenox, 01240. Tel: 413-637-0157; Email: stannlenox@verizon.net; Web: stannlenox.org. Rev. Msgr. John J. Bonzagni, M.Ed., J.C.L., J.D.; Deacons John E. Zick; Daniel Romanello.
Catechesis Religious Program—Tel: 413-637-4027; Fax: 413-637-2945; Email: stannccd2@gmail.com. Students 127.
LONGMEADOW, HAMPDEN CO., ST. MARY'S (1936)
509 Longmeadow St., Longmeadow, 01106. Mailing Address: 519 Longmeadow St., Longmeadow, 01106. Tel: 413-567-3124; Email: parishoffice@stmarylong.org. Revs. Christopher J. Waitekus; Michael Kokoszka; Deacon Donald J. Higby. In Res., Rev. John P. McDonagh, J.C.L.
Priest's Res./Rectory: 10 Hopkins Pl., Longmeadow, 01106.
School—St. Mary's School, (Grades PreK-8), 56 Hopkins Pl., Longmeadow, 01106. Tel: 413-567-0907; Fax: 413-567-7695; Email: stmarysacademy@comcast.net. Joan MacDonald, Prin.; Diane McDonald, Librarian. Lay Teachers 18; Students 240.
Catechesis Religious Program—Tel: 413-567-3420; Fax: 413-567-0264. Students 608.
LUDLOW, HAMPDEN CO.
1—CHRIST THE KING (1948) (Polish)
41 Warsaw Ave., Ludlow, 01056. Tel: 413-583-2630; Email: ctkludlow@gmail.com. Rev. Raymond A. Soltys.
Catechesis Religious Program—Students 270.
2—SAINT ELIZABETH PARISH (2010) (Previously St. John the Baptist 1904)
191 Hubbard St., Ludlow, 01056. Tel: 413-583-3467; Email: klawrence@stelizabethludlow.org; Email: lgroux@stelizabethludlow.org; Web: www.stelizabethludlow.org. Mailing Address: 181 Hubbard St., Ludlow, 01056. Rev. Msgr. Homer P. Gosselin; Rev. Norman B. Bolton, In Res., (Retired); Deacons Thomas Rickson; Normand Grondin; Keith Davies.
School—St. Elizabeth Parish School aka St. John The Baptist School, (Grades PreK-8), 217 Hubbard St., Ludlow, 01056. Tel: 413-583-8550; Fax: 413-589-0544; Email: sjbsoffice@gmail.com; Web: sjbludlow.org. Mrs. Shelly Rose, Prin. Lay Teachers 15; Students 209; Clergy / Religious Teachers 1.
Catechesis Religious Program—Tel: 413-583-4204. Michele Witowski, D.R.E. Students 363.
3—ST. JOHN THE BAPTIST (1904) (French), Merged with St. Mary, Ludlow to form Saint Elizabeth Parish. All records kept at Saint Elizabeth Parish, Ludlow.
4—ST. MARY (1968) Closed. Merged with St. John the Baptist, Ludlow to form Saint Elizabeth Parish, Ludlow. All records kept at Saint Elizabeth Parish, Ludlow.
5—OUR LADY OF FATIMA (1948) (Portuguese)
438 Winsor St., Ludlow, 01056. Tel: 413-583-2312; Fax: 413-547-0207; Email: fatima7687@charter.net. Rev. Vitor Oliveira; Deacon Antonio Gois.
Catechesis Religious Program—Students 167.
MILLERS FALLS, FRANKLIN CO., ST. JOHN'S (1898) Closed. For inquiries for parish records contact Our Lady Peace, Turners Falls.
MONSON, HAMPDEN CO., ST. PATRICK'S (1878) [CEM]
22 Green St., P.O. Box 473, Monson, 01057.
Tel: 413-267-3622; Email: stpatmon@aol.com. Rev. John J. Brennan; Deacons Gary Doane; Bernard Pellissier.
Catechesis Religious Program—Students 94.
NORTH ADAMS, BERKSHIRE CO.
1—ST. ANTHONY OF PADUA (1903) (Italian), Closed. Merged. See St. Elizabeth of Hungary, North Adams.
2—SAINT ELIZABETH OF HUNGARY PARISH (2009)
70 Marshall St., North Adams, 01247. Rev. Dariusz P. Wudarski; Deacons George Galli; Bruce Ziter.
Catechesis Religious Program—Kate Annichiarico, D.R.E. (Elementary); Connie Therrien, D.R.E. (H.S.). Students 155.
3—ST. FRANCIS (1863) [CEM] Closed. Merged. See St. Elizabeth of Hungary, North Adams.
4—HOLY FAMILY (1997) Merged with Our Lady of Incarnation, North Adams, to form Our Lady of Mercy, North Adams.

5—NOTRE DAME (1875) Closed. For inquiries for parish records contact the chancery.
6—OUR LADY OF MERCY (1997) Closed. See St. Elizabeth of Hungary, North Adams.
7—OUR LADY OF MERCY SHRINE (1997) Merged with Holy Family, North Adams, and Our Lady of the Incarnation, North Adams.
8—OUR LADY OF THE INCARNATION (1955) Merged with Holy Family, North Adams, to form Our Lady of Mercy, North Adams.

NORTHAMPTON, HAMPSHIRE CO.
1—BLESSED SACRAMENT (1899) Closed. Merged with Saint Elizabeth Ann Seton Parish, Northampton. All records to Saint Elizabeth Ann Seton Parish, Northampton.
2—SAINT ELIZABETH ANN SETON (2010) (French)
99 King St., Northampton, 01060. Tel: 413-584-7310; Fax: 413-584-4788; Email: peggyconstant@saintelizabethannseton.net. Mailing Address: 87 Beacon St., Florence, 01062. Revs. Francis E. Reilly; Barrent C. Pease.
Catechesis Religious Program—Students 220.
Chapel—Our Lady of the Annunciation, 87 Beacon St., Florence, 01062.
3—ST. JOHN CANTIUS (1904) (Polish), Closed. Merged with Saint Elizabeth Ann Seton Parish, Northampton. All records to Saint Elizabeth Ann Seton Parish, Northampton.
4—ST. MARY OF THE ASSUMPTION (1866) [CEM] (Irish), Closed. Merged with Saint Elizabeth Ann Seton Parish, Northampton. All records to Saint Elizabeth Ann Seton Parish, Northampton.

NORTHFIELD, FRANKLIN CO., ST. PATRICK (1973) [CEM]
82 Main St., Northfield, 01360. Tel: 413-498-2728; Email: stpatricksrcc@gmail.com. Mailing Address: 80 Main St., Northfield, 01360-1022. Rev. Thomas Lisowski; Deacon David Culliton.
Catechesis Religious Program—Students 10.

ORANGE, FRANKLIN CO., ST. MARY (1903)
19 Congress St., Orange, 01364. Tel: 978-544-2900; Email: office@stmaryolr.org; Web: www.stmaryorange.online. Rev. Shaun O'Connor.
Catechesis Religious Program—Students 23.

PALMER, HAMPDEN CO., ST. THOMAS THE APOSTLE (1864) [CEM] Merged with St. Bartholomew's, Bondsville. Rev. Richard M. Turner.
Res.: 1076 Thorndike St., Palmer, 01069. Tel: 413-283-5091.
Catechesis Religious Program—Tel: 413-283-5651. Students 90.

PITTSFIELD, BERKSHIRE CO.
1—ST. CHARLES (1893)
89 Briggs Ave., Pittsfield, 01201. Tel: 413-442-7470; Fax: 413-445-5267; Email: stcharlespittsfield@gmail.com; Web: www.stcharlespittsfield.org. Rev. Msgr. Michael Shershanovich, Admin.
Catechesis Religious Program—100 Briggs Ave., Pittsfield, 01201. Tel: 413-442-0591; Email: faithformation@gmail.com. Gwen Shaughnessy, D.R.E.
2—ST. FRANCIS (1960) Closed. For inquiries for parish records contact St. Joseph, Pittsfield.
3—HOLY FAMILY (1912) (Polish), Closed. For inquiries for parish records contact St. Joseph, Pittsfield.
4—ST. JOSEPH'S (1849) [CEM]
414 North St., Pittsfield, 01201. Tel: 413-445-5789; Email: michelemadden@berkshire.rr.com; Email: msgrmike@berkshire.rr.com. Rev. Msgr. Michael Shershanovich; Most Rev. Timothy A. McDonnell, In Res.
Catechesis Religious Program—Students 140.
5—ST. MARK'S (1913)
400 West St., Pittsfield, 01201. Tel: 413-447-7510. Rev. Christopher Fedoryshyn, Admin.
6—ST. MARY THE MORNING STAR (1915) Closed. For inquiries for parish records contact St. Joseph, Pittsfield.
7—NOTRE DAME (1868) Closed. Sacramental Records at Saint Joseph, Pittsfield.
8—OUR LADY OF MT. CARMEL (1903) (Italian), Closed. For inquiries for parish records contact St. Joseph, Pittsfield.
9—SACRED HEART (1919)
196 Elm St., Pittsfield, 01201. Tel: 413-443-6960; Fax: 413-442-9649; Email: pinkchurch@aol.com. Mailing Address: 191 Elm St., Pittsfield, 01201-6588. Rev. Michael F. Bernier; Deacons James A. Hager, Pastoral Min.; Robert Esposito.
Catechesis Religious Program—Tel: 413-442-5564. Students 247.
10—ST. TERESA (1926) Closed. For inquiries for parish records contact St. Joseph, Pittsfield.

RUSSELL, HAMPDEN CO.
1—HOLY FAMILY PARISH (2010) [JC]
5 Main St., P.O. Box 405, Russell, 01071-0405. Tel: 413-862-4418; Email: holyfamily.parish@aol.com. Rev. Ronald F. Sadlowski; Deacon David Baillargeon.
Catechesis Religious Program—Deborah Bogoff, D.R.E. Students 54.
2—OUR LADY OF THE ROSARY (1969) Closed. Merged with St. Thomas, Huntington & St. John Mission, Chester to form Holy Family Parish, Russell. All records located at Holy Family Parish, Russell.

SHEFFIELD, BERKSHIRE CO., OUR LADY OF THE VALLEY (1901) [CEM]
99 Maple Ave., P.O. Box 515, Sheffield, 01257. Tel: 413-229-3028; Email: deaconmulholland@gmail.com. Rev. Bruce Teague, Admin., (Retired).
Catechesis Religious Program—Students 30.
Missions—Immaculate Conception—Main St., Mill River, Berkshire Co. 01244.
Our Lady of the Hills, Beartown Rd., Monterey, Berkshire Co. 01245.

SHELBURNE FALLS, FRANKLIN CO., ST. JOSEPH'S (1883)
34 Monroe Ave., Shelburne Falls, 01370. Tel: 413-625-6405; Email: st.josephccsf@comcast.net. Rev. William H. Lunney; Deacon Thomas Rabbitt.
Catechesis Religious Program—Students 14.
Missions—St. John the Baptist—Colrain, Franklin Co. 01340.
St. Christopher, Charlemont, Franklin Co. 01339.

SOUTH DEERFIELD, FRANKLIN CO.
1—HOLY FAMILY PARISH (2008)
29 Sugarloaf St., South Deerfield, 01373. Tel: 413-665-3254; Fax: 413-665-0303; Email: holyfamily12@verizon.net; Web: www.holyfamilysd.org. Rev. Jonathan Reardon; Deacon Rodney Patten.
Catechesis Religious Program—Students 65.
Mission—St. Marks, Delabarre Ave., Conway, 01341.
2—ST. JAMES (1895) Closed. Merged see Holy Family, South Deerfield.
3—ST. STANISLAUS B. AND M. (1908) [CEM] Closed. Merged see Holy Family, South Deerfield.

SOUTH HADLEY, HAMPSHIRE CO.
1—ST. PATRICK'S (1878)
30 Main St., South Hadley, 01075. Tel: 413-532-2850; Email: stpatrickssh@comcast.net. Rev. James Nolte; Deacon David Bergeron.
Catechesis Religious Program—Email: stpatdre@outlook.com. Susan Napolitano, D.R.E.
2—ST. THERESA OF LISIEUX (1946)
9 East Parkview Dr., South Hadley, 01075-2103. Tel: 413-532-3228; Fax: 413-540-0964; Email: parishsecretarystl@gmail.com. Rev. Michael J. Twohig.
Catechesis Religious Program—
Tel: 413-532-3228, Ext. 120. Patricia Monroe, D.R.E. Students 65.

SOUTHWICK, HAMPDEN CO., OUR LADY OF THE LAKE (1951)
224 Sheep Pasture Rd., P.O. Box 1150, Southwick, 01077. Tel: 413-569-0161; Fax: 413-569-0081; Email: ollake7@aol.com. Rev. Henry L. Dorsch; Deacon David Przybylowski.
Catechesis Religious Program—Lynda Daniele, D.R.E. Students 148.

STOCKBRIDGE, BERKSHIRE CO., ST. JOSEPH'S (1922) [CEM] Closed. Now a mission of St. Mary, Lee.

THORNDIKE, HAMPDEN CO., ST. MARY'S (1876) Closed. For inquiries for parish records contact the chancery.

THREE RIVERS, HAMPDEN CO.
1—ST. ANNE'S (1882) [CEM] (French), Closed. Merged with SS. Peter and Paul to form Divine Mercy Parish, Three Rivers. All records kept at Divine Mercy Parish, Three Rivers.
2—DIVINE MERCY PARISH
2267 Main St., Three Rivers, 01080. Tel: 413-283-6030; Email: stspeterpaulanne@gmail.com. Mailing Address: P.O. Box 157, Three Rivers, 01080. Rev. Stefan J. Niemczyk.
Catechesis Religious Program—Joan Brigham, D.R.E. Students 89.
3—SS. PETER AND PAUL (1903) [CEM] (Polish), Closed. Merged with St. Anne's to form Divine Mercy Parish, Three Rivers. All records kept at Divine Mercy Parish, Three Rivers.

TURNERS FALLS, FRANKLIN CO.
1—ST. ANNE (1884) [CEM] (French), Closed. Merged with Sacred Heart, Greenfield & St. Mary, Turner Falls to form Our Lady of Peace, Turner Falls.
2—ST. MARY'S (1872) [CEM] Closed. Merged with Sacred Heart, Greenfield & St. Anne, Turner Falls to form Our Lady of Peace, Turner Falls.
3—OUR LADY OF CZESTOCHOWA (1909) [CEM] (Polish)
84 K St., Turners Falls, 01376. Tel: 413-863-4748; Email: olczestochowa@gmail.com; Web: ChroniclesofCzestochowa.wordpress.com. Rev. Sean O'Mannion.
Catechesis Religious Program—Students 102.
4—OUR LADY OF PEACE (2006)
80 Seventh St., Turners Falls, 01376. Tel: 413-863-2585; Fax: 413-863-8978; Email: frstan@ourladyofpeacetf.com; Web: www.ourladyofpeace.weconnect.com. Rev. Stanley J. Aksamit; Deacon Joseph Bucci.
Rectory—90 Seventh St., Turners Falls, 01376. Email: church@ourladyofpeacetf.com.
Catechesis Religious Program—Tel: 413-863-4015; Email: 1952gary@comcast.net. Carol Holubecki, D.R.E. Students 123.

WARE, HAMPSHIRE CO.
1—ALL SAINTS (1860) [CEM] [JC2]
17 North St., Ware, 01082. Tel: 413-967-4963; Email: allsaintschurch17@gmail.com; Web: allsaintsware.org. Rev. Piotr S. Calik.
Catechesis Religious Program—Ms. Roberta Lojko, D.R.E. Students 90.
2—ST. MARY'S (1905) [CEM] (Polish)
60 South St., Ware, 01082. Tel: 413-967-5913; Fax: 413-967-4679; Email: smcrectory@comcast.net; Web: www.stmarysware.org. Rev. Jeffrey A. Ballou.
Catechesis Religious Program—Students 101.
3—OUR LADY OF MT. CARMEL (1871) (French), Closed. For inquiries for sacramental records contact All Saints, Ware.

WEST SPRINGFIELD, HAMPDEN CO.
1—ST. FRANCES XAVIER CABRINI PARISH (2009) Closed. For inquiries for sacramental records please contact St. Thomas the Apostle Parish, West Springfield.
2—IMMACULATE CONCEPTION (1877) Closed. Merged see St. Frances Xavier Cabrini, West Springfield.
3—ST. LOUIS DE FRANCE (1895) (French), Closed. Merged see St. Frances Xavier Cabrini, West Springfield.
4—ST. THOMAS THE APOSTLE (1900) [CEM]
63 Pine St., West Springfield, 01089. Tel: 413-739-4779; Fax: 413-739-1608; Email: stthomassecretary@comcast.net; Web: www.stthomaswestspringfield.org. Mailing Address: 47 Pine St., West Springfield, 01089. Revs. Kenneth J. Tatro; David R. Raymond; Deacons James H. Marcus; Joseph W. Kielbasa Jr.; Gerald Solitario.
School—St. Thomas the Apostle School, (Grades PreK-8), 75 Pine St., West Springfield, 01089. Tel: 413-739-4131; Fax: 413-731-8768; Email: phottinssj@comcast.net. Sr. Patricia Hottin, S.S.J., Prin. Lay Teachers 32; Sisters of St. Joseph 4; Students 310.
Catechesis Religious Program—89 Pine St., West Springfield, 01089.

WEST STOCKBRIDGE, BERKSHIRE CO., ST. PATRICK'S (1871) [CEM]
30 Albany Rd., West Stockbridge, 01266. Tel: 413-232-4427. Rev. Msgr. John J. Bonzagni, M.Ed., J.C.L., J.D.; Deacon John E. Zick.
Church: 134 Main St., Lenox, 01240.
Catechesis Religious Program—Students 6.

WESTFIELD, HAMPDEN CO.
1—ST. CASIMIR'S (1915) Merged with St. Peter's, Westfield to form St. Peter and St. Casimir, Westfield.
2—HOLY TRINITY (1903) (Polish)
335 Elm St., Westfield, 01085. Tel: 413-568-1506; Fax: 413-572-2533; Email: htoffice@comcast.net; Web: www.holytrinitywestfield.com. Rev. Rene L. Parent, M.S.; Deacon Charles Wainwright.
Catechesis Religious Program—Students 63.
3—ST. MARY'S (1862)
30 Bartlett St., Westfield, 01085. Tel: 413-562-5477; Web: www.stmarysofwestfield.com. Rev. John F. Tuohey, Parochial Vicar; Deacons Roger Carrier; Pedro Rivera; Rev. Matthew Alcombright.
Schools—St. Mary Elementary School—(Grades K-8), 35 Bartlett St., Westfield, 01085. Tel: 413-568-2388; Fax: 413-568-7460; Email: jjensen-derrig@stmsaints.org. Juli Jensen-Derrig, Prin. Lay Teachers 16; Students 223.
St. Mary Pre Kindergarten, 23 Bartlett St., Westfield, 01085. Tel: 413-568-2388. Juli Jensen-Derrig, Prin. Lay Teachers 2; Students 30.
St. Mary Pre-School, 23 1/2 Bartlett St., Westfield, 01085. Tel: 413-568-2388. Juli Jensen-Derrig, Prin. Students 12.
High School—St. Mary High School, 27 Bartlett St., Westfield, 01085. Tel: 413-568-5692; Fax: 413-562-3501. Mr. Matthew Collins, Prin. Lay Teachers 16; Students 65.
Catechesis Religious Program—Office of Rel. Educ., 86 Mechanic St., Westfield, 01085. Mrs. Joanne Bagge, D.R.E.; Mrs. Kay Mowatt, D.R.E. Students 476.
4—OUR LADY OF THE BLESSED SACRAMENT (1910)
127 Holyoke Rd., Westfield, 01085. Mailing Address: P.O. Box 489, Westfield, 01086-0489. Tel: 413-562-3450; Email: olbsoffice@aol.com; Web: diospringfield.org/olbs. Rev. Daniel S. Pacholec; Deacon Paul Federici, Dir. Faith Formation.
Rectory—85 Ridgeview Terrace, Westfield, 01085.
Catechesis Religious Program—Email: olbsccd@aol.com. Sheila Conroy, Coord., Elementary Educ.; Lisa Laferriere, Coord., Middle/High School Educ. Students 239.
5—ST. PETER AND ST. CASIMIR (2003)
24 State St., Westfield, 01085. Tel: 413-568-5421; Fax: 413-562-3879; Email: sspetetcas@comcast.net. Mailing Address: 22 State St., Westfield, 01085. Rev. William H. Wallis; Deacon Paul Briere.
Catechesis Religious Program—32 State St., Westfield, 01085.
6—ST. PETER'S (1913) Merged with St. Casimir, Westfield to form St. Peter and St. Casimir, Westfield.

WILBRAHAM, HAMPDEN CO., ST. CECILIA'S (1951)
42 Main St., Wilbraham, 01095.
Tel: 413-596-4232, Ext. 101; Email: administrator@saintceciliawilbraham.org; Web: www.saintceciliawilbraham.org. Mailing Address: 7 Maple St., Wilbraham, 01095. Rev. Daniel J. Boyle; Sr. Mary McCue, S.N.D., Pastoral Min, Tel: 413-596-4232, Ext. 105; Deacons James Ziemba; Andrew Nowicki.
Catechesis Religious Program—Email: cff@saintceciliawilbraham.org. Students 649.

WILLIAMSTOWN, BERKSHIRE CO.
1—SS. PATRICK AND RAPHAEL (1997)
63 Southworth St., Williamstown, 01267-2414.
Tel: 413-458-4946, Ext. 11; Email: saintspatrickandraphael@gmail.com; Web: www.williamstowncatholics.org. Mailing Address: 54 Southworth St., Williamstown, 01267. Rev. Michael C. Lillpopp.
Catechesis Religious Program—53 Southworth St., Williamstown, 01267. Debbie Cameron, D.R.E. Students 55.
2—ST. PATRICK'S (1887) Merged with St. Raphael, Williamstown, to form SS. Patrick and Raphael, Williamstown.
3—ST. RAPHAEL (1891) Merged with St. Patrick, Williamstown, to form SS. Patrick and Raphael, Williamstown.

Chaplains of Public Institutions

SPRINGFIELD. *Baystate Medical Center*, Office of Pastoral Ministry at Baystate, 01199. Rev. Fidelis Lemchi.
Mercy Medical Center. Rev. Donatus Ironuma, Chap.
Olympus Specialty Hospital, Sacred Heart Rectory, 395 Chestnut St., 01104. Tel: 413-732-3721.

CHICOPEE. *Hampden County Women's Correctional Center*. Rev. Jose A. Bermudez, Chap.

GREENFIELD. *Franklin County Jail & House of Correction*. Rev. Jose A. Bermudez, Chap.

HOLYOKE. *Soldiers' Home*, Holyoke. Tel: 413-532-0713. Pastoral services provided by Blessed Sacrament Parish.

NORTHAMPTON. *Veterans Administration Hospital*, 421 N. Main St., Northampton, 01060.
Tel: 413-584-4040. Rev. Lionel E. Bonneville, (Retired).

PITTSFIELD. *Berkshire Medical Center*,
Tel: 413-447-2000. Rev. Peter Naranjo, Chap., 725 North St., Pittsfield, 01201
One County Rte. 13, Chatham Center, NY 12184-9639. Tel: 413-392-4516.

WESTFIELD. *Western Massachusetts Hospital*, Westfield. Tel: 413-562-3450. Served by Our Lady of the Blessed Sacrament Parish.

On Duty Outside the Diocese:
Revs.—
Bombardier, Paul A., 441 Fellsway Way, Medford, 02155
Furman, Frank, Graduate studies, Rome
Longe, James W., Military
Marchese, Joseph P., Chestnut Hill, 02167. Chap.
Parzynski, Tomasz P., St. John Neumann Parish, Miami, FL
Silwa, Ryan, Silverstream Priory, Ireland.

Absent on Leave:
Revs.—
Glover, Mark, in Residence at Sacred Heart Rectory, 395 Chestnut St., 01104
Lawlor, Francis, in residence at Sacred Heart Rectory, 395 Chestnut St., 01104
Tran, Quynh Dinh.

Retired:
Rev. Msgrs.—
Garcia, Juan F., (Peru) (Retired), Holy Cross Rectory, 221 Plumtree Rd., 01118
Joyce, David J., (Retired), Holy Name Rectory, 323 Dickinson St., 01108
Sniezyk, Richard S., (Retired), 112 S.W. 15th St., Cape Coral, FL 33991
Walsh, Francis E., (Retired), 23-25 Bachelor Walk O'Connell Bridge, Dublin, Ireland
Yargeau, Ronald G., (Retired), P.O. Box 184, Erving, 01344
Revs.—
Benoit, Adrian J., (Retired), 281 Chauncey Walker St., #153, Belchertown, 01007
Bolton, Norman B., (Retired), 191 Hubbard St., Ludlow, 01056
Bonneville, Lionel E., (Retired), 47 Fenway Dr., 01119
Brunton, Daniel B., (Retired), 30 Barlett St., Westfield, 01085
Creane, Anthony, (Retired), 5300 Washington St., Apt. 1205, Hollywood, FL 33201
Crombie, Francis H., (Retired), 1336 Enfield St., Apt. 305, Enfield, CT 06082
Cullen, Anthony F., (Retired), 40 Cromwell St., Swansea, United Kingdom SA1 6EK
Cyr, William F., (Retired), St. John Paul II Rectory, P.O. Box 231, Adams, 01220
DiMascola, Charles J., (Retired), 110 Vernon St., Greenfield, 01301
Gallerini, Philip G., (Retired), Warwick, RI
Gilbertson, Lee C., (Retired), 29 Shoreline Dr., Belfast, ME 04915
Gonet, Charles F., (Retired), 1365 Northampton St., Holyoke, 01040
Gregory, Peter A., (Retired), 199 Lenox Ave., Pittsfield, 01201
Hoar, Leo James, (Retired), 164 Stonehenge Dr., Brewster, 02631
Honan, Eugene D., (Retired), 131 River Rd., Huntington, 01050
Joyce, James K., (Retired), Devonshire Estates, 329 Pittsfield Rd., Apt. 228, Lenox, 01240
Kennedy, Francis M., (Retired), P.O. Box 677, Southampton, 01073
Lapointe, J. Donald R., S.T.L., L.I.C.S.W., (Retired), P.O. Box 1433, Northampton, 01061
Lavoie, Merle L., (Retired), 114 College Hwy., Southampton, 01073
Lis, John S., (Retired), 833 Main St., Agawam, 01001
Noiseux, Donald A., (Retired), 110 Vernon St., Greenfield, 01301
O'Connor, Vincent M., (Retired), 110 Monastery Ave., West Springfield, 01089
Riendeau, Richard A., (Retired), 1945 Northampton St., Holyoke, 01040
Roach, John A., (Retired), 19 N. Green River, P.O. Box 132, Colrain, 01340
Rousseau, William C., (Retired), 50 Cardinal Dr., Agawam, 01001
Scahill, James J., (Retired), P.O. Box 2445, Westerly, RI 02891
Shea, Thomas M., (Retired), 164 Dickinson Hill Rd, P.O. Box 82, Russell, 01071
Sipitowski, James A., (Retired), P.O. Box 118, Westfield, 01085
Soranno, Joseph M., (Retired), P.O. Box 2445, Westerly, RI 02891
Teague, Bruce, (Retired), P.O. Box 390189, Cambridge, 02139
Thrasher, Robert W., J.C.D., (Retired), 221 Plumtree Rd., 01118
Twardzik, Michael W.T., (Retired), 40 Elizabeth St., Dansville, NY 14437.

Permanent Deacons:
Antaya, John, St. Catherine of Sienna, Springfield
Badame, Joseph, (Retired), 9541 W. Carol Ave., Peoria, AZ 85345
Baillargeon, David, (Unassigned)
Baldasaro, Pasqual, St. Joseph, Pittsfield
Bergeron, David, St. Patrick, S. Hadley
Bergeron, Leo, (Retired)
Bete, Joseph Channing, Holy Trinity, Greenfield
Bledsoe, John, V.F., St. Patrick, South Hadley
Brawner, William, (Unassigned)
Briere, Paul, Blessed Sacrament, Westfield
Bucci, Joseph, Our Lady of Peace, Turners Falls
Campion, Gerald, Mother of Hope, Springfield
Cao, Ly X., St. Paul, Springfield
Carrier, Roger, St. Mary, Westfield
Cary, Herbert L., (Retired)
Conroy, James, St. Thomas, West Springfield
Correa, Jose, Our Lady of Guadalupe, Holyoke
Coughlin, Leo, St. Michael's Cathedral, Springfield
Culliton, David, St. Patrick, Northfield
Daniel, Odell, Our Lady of the Sacred Heart, Springfield
Davies, Keith, St. Elizabeth, Ludlow
DeCarlo, Paul F., Holy Trinity, Greenfield
Diaz, Celso B., (On Duty Outside the Diocese)
Digan, Robert, St. Mary, Lee
Digiacomo, Enzo, St. Anthony, Springfield (Maronite)
Doane, Gary, St. Thomas, Palmer
Duval, Robert L., (Retired), St. Elizabeth, Ludlow
Esposito, Robert, Sacred Heart, Pittsfield
Faber, Edward H., (Retired), Hanward Hill E., East Longmeadow, 01028. St. John the Baptist, Ludlow
Farrell, Robert, Our Lady of Mt. Carmel, Springfield
Federici, Paul, Our Lady of the Blessed Sacrament, Westfield
Fleury, Bernard J., (Retired), 244 Main Rd., Westhampton, 01027. Annunciation, Florence, MA
Fox, John, Divine Mercy, Three Rivers
Galli, George, St. Elizabeth of Hungary, N. Adams
Garde, Joseph, (Retired)
Gois, Antonio, Our Lady of Fatima, Ludlow
Grondin, Normand, St. Elizabeth, Ludlow
Hager, James A., Sacred Heart, Pittsfield
Hannoush, Norman, St. Anthony, Springfield (Maronite)
Herbert, Romeo, St. Anne, Chicopee
Higby, Donald, St. Mary, Longmeadow
Hitter, Robert, St. Mary, Cheshire
Hodges, Michael, Holy Name, Springfield
Kaiser, L. Joseph, (Retired)
Keator, George, St. Ann, Lenox
Kern, William, Sacred Heart, Springfield
Kielbasa, Joseph W. Jr., St. Thomas the Apostle, West Springfield
Kolasinski, Mark, Our Lady of Grace, Hatfield
Kozach, George, St. Patrick Church, Springfield
Lafreniere, Gregory, St. John Paul II
Leary, John, Blessed Sacrament, Greenfield
Lingham, Michael, (Retired)
Lynch, Thomas, Newman Catholic Center, UMASS, Amherst
Magenis, Richard, St. Peter, Great Barrington
Marcus, James H., St. Maron Maronite Church, Torrington, CT
Mazzariello, Paul, Hampden Co. Correctional Facility
Mc Elroy, James, J.D., St. Mary, Lee
McCarthy, Kevin, Blessed Sacrament, Springfield
Medina, Genaro Sr., All Souls, Latino Ministry, Springfield
Meyer, Edward, (Retired)
Miller, Lucien M., Campus Ministry, University of Massachusetts, Amherst
Mireault, Leon, (Retired)
Monat, Noe, (Retired)
Morrell, George, St. Agnes, Dalton
Mulholland, Sean, St. Marks, Pittsfield
Mutti, Al, Mary Mother of Hope, Springfield
Nolan, George, Blessed Sacrament, Greenfield
O'Brien, John P., (On Duty Outside the Diocese)
Patten, Rodney, Holy Family, S. Deerfield
Pelletier, Frederick J., (Retired), Immaculate Conception, Holyoke
Pellissier, Bernard, (Retired)
Pennell, Wendell, Blessed Sacrament, Holyoke
Perez, Angel, St. Michael's Cathedral, Springfield
Perkins, Michael, (Unassigned)
Peters, Joseph, St. Stanislaus, Chicopee
Phillip, Donald, Immaculate Conception, Indian Orchard
Picard, David, St. John the Evangelist, Agawam
Przybylowski, David, Our Lady of the Lake, Southwick
Rabbitt, Thomas, St. Joseph, Shelburne Falls
Radzick, Richard, St. Agnes, Dalton
Rael, Lincoln C., (Retired), 47 Nonotuck St., Holyoke, 01040
Ratte, Arthur E., (Retired)
Rickson, Thomas, St. Elizabeth, Ludlow
Rivera, Jose, All Souls, Springfield
Rivera, Jose, St. Michael's Cathedral, Springfield
Rivera-Burgos, Pedro, Our Lady of Guadalupe, Holyoke
Rivera-Moran, Pedro
Rogers, Francis D., (Retired), St. Paul the Apostle, Springfield
Romanello, Daniel, St. Ann, Lenox
Ryan, Francis, Sts. Patrick & Raphael, Williamstown
Sanmiguel, Lino, St. Anthony of Padua, Chicopee
Santiago-Martinez, Adalberto, Our Lady of Guadalupe, Holyoke
Shaw, Edward, Blessed Teresa of Calcutta, Housatonic
Smith, Joseph P., (Retired)
Solitario, Gerald, St. Thomas the Apostle, W. Springfield
Southworth, David, St. Mary, Longmeadow
St. George-Sorel, Gilbert, St. Mary, Ware
Talbot, Richard, (Retired)
Toller, William, Holy Cross, Springfield
Tran, Khanh, St. Paul, Springfield
Trova, Spencer, St. Charles, Pittsfield
Trznadel, Michael, Holy Family, South Deerfield
Tudryn, Theodore, Holy Family, South Deerfield
Vernard, John, Holy Name, Springfield
Wainwright, Charles, Holy Trinity, Westfield
Wallen, Paul, (Retired), Springfield, MA
Zick, John E., St. Anne, Lenox
Ziemba, James, St. Cecilia, Wilbraham
Ziter, Bruce, St. Elizabeth of Hungary, North Adams.

INSTITUTIONS LOCATED IN DIOCESE

[A] COLLEGES AND UNIVERSITIES

CHICOPEE. *College of Our Lady of the Elms*, 291 Springfield St., Chicopee, 01013. Tel: 413-265-2293 ; Fax: 413-265-2346; Email: breauw@elms.edu; Email: russettg@elms.edu; Email: longleyk@elms.edu; Web: www.elms.edu. Dr. Harry Dumay, Pres.; Dr. Walter C. Breau, Vice Pres.; Mrs. Katie Longley, Treas.; Mr. Gary Russett, Business Mgr.; Anthony Fonseca, Dir. Alumnae Library; Most Rev. Mitchell T. Rozanski. Sisters of St. Joseph. Brothers 1; Lay Teachers 74; Priests 2; Professors 78; Sisters 1; Students 1,531; Total Staff 158.

[B] HIGH SCHOOLS, DIOCESAN

CHICOPEE. *Pope Francis Preparatory School*, 99 Wendover Rd., 01118. Tel: 833-999-7673; Email: askus@popefrancisprep.org; Web: www.popefrancisprep.org. Dr. Paul Harrington Jr., Head of School. Religious Teachers 2; Lay Teachers 38; Sisters 1; Students 336.

PITTSFIELD. *St. Joseph Central High School*, 22 Maplewood Ave., Pittsfield, 01201.
Tel: 413-447-9121; Fax: 413-443-7020; Web: www.stjoehigh.org. Dr. Amy Gelinas, Ed.D., Prin.; Sr. Jean Bostley, Librarian. Sisters of St. Joseph. School closed 6/19/17 Lay Teachers 16; Sisters 1; Students 80; Total Staff 28.

[C] ELEMENTARY SCHOOLS, DIOCESAN

SPRINGFIELD. *Saint Michael's Academy*, (Grades PreK-8), 153 Eddywood St., 01118. Tel: 413-782-5246; Fax: 413-782-8137; Email: a.obrien@smaspringfield.org; Web: www.smaspringfield.org. Ann Dougal. Lay Teachers 29; Students 473.

ADAMS. *St. Stanislaus Kostka School*, (Grades PreK-8), 108 Summer St., Adams, 01220. Tel: 413-734-1091; Email: saintstans2014@gmail.com; Web: saintstansadams.org. Linda Reardon, Prin. Clergy 1; Lay Teachers 14; Felician Sisters 1; Students 107.

[D] GENERAL HOSPITALS

SPRINGFIELD. *CHE - The Mercy Hospital, Inc.*, 271 Carew St., Box 9012, 01102-9012.
Tel: 413-748-9000; Fax: 413-781-7217; Web: www.mercycares.com. Rev. Stanley Kim, M.Div., BCC, Spiritual Care Dir.; Dr. Scott Wolf, Dir.; Robert Baral, Chap.; Lynn Cochran, Chap.; Anne Frieze, Chap.; Rev. Donatus Ironuma, Chap.; Bob Martin, Chap.; Marianne Power, Chap. Bed Capacity 251; Tot Asst. Annually 200,000; Sisters of Providence 2; Total Staff (Mercy Hospital) 1,600.

Brightside, Inc. Private, Nonprofit Agency. 1233 Main St., Holyoke, 01040. Tel: 413-539-2480;
Fax: 413-827-4250; Fax: 413-539-2496; Email: mariezygmont@sphs.com; Web: www.mercycares.com. Dr. Scott Wolf, DO, CEO, Admin.; Mark Paglia, Dir. Outpatient Svcs. Sisters of Providence. Total Staff 55; Family Home Based Therapy Assisted Annually 650.

Providence Behavioral Health Hospital, 1233 Main St., Holyoke, 01040. Tel: 413-536-5111;
Fax: 413-539-2992. Lorraine Peterson, Chap.; Judith Grupenhoff, Spiritual Care Youth Specialist. Bed Capacity 131; Total Staff 460; Spiritual Care Department 2.

TURNERS FALLS. *Farren Care Center, Inc.*, 340 Montague City Rd., Turners Falls, 01376.
Tel: 413-774-3111; Fax: 413-774-7049; Email: jim.clifford@sphs.com; Web: www.mercycares.com. Sher Sweet, Chap.; Nancy Godbot, Admin.; Judith Grupenhoff. Bed Capacity 122; Tot Asst. Annually 121; Total Staff 187.

[E] FAMILY SERVICES

SPRINGFIELD. *Diocesan Office of Child and Youth Protection*, 65 Elliot St., P.O. Box 1730, 01102-1730. Tel: 413-732-3175; Tel: 413-452-0624; Fax: 413-452-0678; Email: cconnelly@diospringfield.org; Web: www.diospringfield.org/MC.html. Ms. Patricia Finn McManamy, L.I.C.S.W., Dir. Tot Asst. Annually 200; Total Staff 2.

HOLYOKE. *Providence Ministries for the Needy, Inc.* dba Providence Ministries Service Network, 40 Brightside Dr., Holyoke, 01040. Tel: 413-536-9109; Fax: 413-536-1137; Email: SRudder@provministries.org; Web: www.provministries.org. Mr. James Wall, Pres.; Mr. Kevin Ross, Vice Pres.; Mrs. Shannon Rudder, Exec.; Ms. Joanne Beauregard, Treas.; Sisters Mary Caritas Geary, S.P., Sec.; Senga Fulton, S.P., Trustee; Margaret McCleary, S.P., Trustee; Mr. Jeff Hayden, Trustee; Mr. Paul Malouin, Trustee; Mr. Ed McCarron, Trustee; Ms. Ruth Roy, Trustee. Sponsored by the Sisters of Providence of Holyoke, MA. Tot Asst. Annually 79,000; Total Staff 15.

Broderick House, 56 Cabot St., Holyoke, 01041.
Tel: 413-533-5909; Email: Srudder@provministries.org; Web: www.provministries.org. Mrs. Shannon Rudder, Exec. SRO (single room occupancy), permanent housing for low income sober men. Bed Capacity 24; Tot Asst. Annually 24.

Margaret's Pantry, 56 Cabot St., Holyoke, 01040.
Tel: 413-538-8026; Email: brendal@provministries.org. 40 Brightside Dr., Holyoke, 01040. Brenda Lamadeline, Contact Person. Provides emergency food to families and individuals. Tot Asst. Annually 8,000; Total Staff 1.

McCleary Manor, 40 Brightside Dr., Holyoke, 01041. Tel: 413-536-9109; Fax: 413-536-1137; Email: srudder@provministries.org; Web: www.provministries.org. Mrs. Shannon Rudder, Exec. Single room occupancy, permanent sober housing for low income single males. Bed Capacity 25; Tot Asst. Annually 25.

St. Jude's Clothing Center, 56 Cabot St., Holyoke, 01040. Tel: 413-538-8026; Email: brendal@provministries.org; Web: www.provministries.org. 40 Brightside Dr., Holyoke, 01040. Brenda Lamagdeline, Contact Person. Distributes clothing and household items to the poor. Tot Asst. Annually 4,000; Total Staff 1.

Loreto House, 51 Hamilton St., Holyoke, 01041.
Tel: 413-533-5909; Email: srudder@provministries.org; Web: www.provministries.org. Mrs. Shannon Rudder, Exec. A single room occupancy transitional housing site for men in recovery or homeless. Bed Capacity 30; Tot Asst. Annually 60; Total Staff 5.

Kate's Kitchen, 51 Hamilton St., Holyoke, 01040. 40 Brightside Dr., Holyoke, 01040. Tel: 413-532-0233; Email: srudder@provministries.org; Web: www.provministries.org. Dalton Clark, Contact Person. A community kitchen which provides one meal daily to anyone in need. Capacity 150; Tot Asst. Annually 55,000; Total Staff 25.

foodWorks@Kate's Kitchen, 51 Hamilton St., Holyoke, 01040. Tel: 413-536-9121; Email: rwebb@provministries.org; Email: dclarke@provministries.org; Email: srudder@provministries.org; Web: www.provministries.org. Mrs. Shannon Rudder, Exec. 12 week culinary training program for low income/homeless adults. Capacity 12.

TURNERS FALLS. *Montague Catholic Social Ministries, Inc.* (1994) 43 Third St., Turners Falls, 01376.
Tel: 413-863-4804; Fax: 413-863-4844; Email: heather@mcsmcommunity.org; Email: laura@mcsmcommunity.org; Web: mcsmcommunity.org. Heather Wood, Dir. Purpose: To be a resource to children and families in the areas of parent education, family literacy, positive conflict resolution, communication skills, and community building; to assist in providing information and referral, the formation of community partnerships and neighborhood development and to facilitate parish concerns and social justice efforts. Montague Catholic Social Ministries nurtures connections, resilience and self-sufficiency in Franklin County families through preventative strength-based support, education, leadership development and empowerment. Tot Asst. Annually 4,265; Total Staff 9; Total Assisted 6,328.

[F] HOMES FOR AGED

SPRINGFIELD. *St. Luke's Home* (1916) 85 Spring St., 01105. Tel: 413-736-5494; Fax: 413-746-5075. Barbara Tadeo, Admin. Residents 84; Staff 30.

HOLYOKE. *Mary's Meadow, Inc.*, 12 Gamelin St., Holyoke, 01040. Tel: 413-536-7511;
Fax: 413-536-7917; Email: kpopko@sisofprov.org; Web: www.mercycares.com/marys-meadow. c/o Sisters of Providence Ministry Corp., 5 Gamelin St., Holyoke, 01040. Sisters Kathleen Popko, S.P., Pres.; Senga Fulton, S.P., Treas.; Mary Caritas Geary, S.P., Sec.; Geraldine Noonan, S.P., Bd. of Trustee; Ms. Jill Keough, Bd. of Trustee; Ms. Margaret Lenihan, Bd. of Trustee; Mr. Kenneth Spafford, Bd. of Trustee; Mr. Michael Tremble, Bd. of Trustee. Bed Capacity 40; Tot Asst. Annually 320; Total Staff 90.

Providence Place, Inc., 5 Gamelin St., Holyoke, 01040. Tel: 413-534-9700; Fax: 413-534-9782; Email: rpelland@providenceplace.org; Web: providenceplace.org. Sr. Kathleen Popko, S.P., Pres.; Richard Pelland, Exec. Dir.; Sisters Senga Fulton, S.P., Treas.; Mary Caritas Geary, S.P., Sec.; Geraldine Noonan, S.P., Bd. of Trustee; Ms. Jill Keough, Bd. of Trustee; Ms. Margaret Lenihan, Bd. of Trustee; Mr. Kenneth Spafford, Bd. of Trustee; Mr. Michael Tremble, Bd. of Trustee. Sisters of Providence. Total in Residence 140; Total Staff 66.

Beaven Kelly Home (1909) 25 Brightside Dr., Holyoke, 01040. Tel: 413-532-4892; Fax: 413-535-2355. Lori Hannah, Admin; Rev. Carol Smith. Residents 122; Staff 130.

LENOX. *Mount Carmel Care Center, Inc.*, 320 Pittsfield Rd., Lenox, 01240. Tel: 413-637-2660;
Fax: 413-637-3085; Email: gmercier@mcccl.org; Email: aranolde@mcccl.org; Email: gchamberlin@mcccl.org; Web: www.mountcarmelcarecenter.org. Mr. George Mercier, Admin. Bed Capacity 69; Total Staff 94.

[G] MONASTERIES AND RESIDENCES OF PRIESTS AND BROTHERS

STOCKBRIDGE. *Congregation of Marian Fathers of The Immaculate Conception of the Most Blessed Virgin Mary*, Eden Hill, 2 Prospect Hill Rd., Stockbridge, 01262. Tel: 413-298-1101; Fax: 413-298-0207; Email: provincial@marian.org; Web: www.thedivinemercy.org; Web: www.marian.org. Bro. John Bryda, M.I.C.; Rev. Daniel P. Cambra; Very Rev. Kazimierz Chwalek, M.I.C.; Revs. Kenneth Dos Santos, M.I.C.; Richard Drabik, M.I.C.; Mark Fanders; Rev. Michael Gaitley, M.I.C.; Bro. Kenneth Galisa, M.I.C.; Revs. Andrzej Gorczyca, M.I.C.; David Gunter, M.I.C.; Walter Gurgul, M.I.C.; Victor Incardona, M.I.C.; David Lord, M.I.C.; Bro. John Luth, M.I.C.; Revs. Seraphim Michalenko, M.I.C.; Martin Rzeszutek, M.I.C.; Robert Vennetti, M.I.C. *Provincial Office*,
Tel: 413-298-1101; Fax: 413-298-0207; Email: provincial@marian.org. Very Rev. Kazimierz Chwalek, M.I.C., Prov. Supr.; Rev. Donald Callaway, M.I.C., Vicar Prov. *The National Shrine of The Divine Mercy*, Tel: 413-298-3931;
Fax: 413-298-3910; Email: dmshrine@marian.org; Web: www.thedivinemercy.org/shrine. Revs. Anthony Gramlich, M.I.C., Rector; Kenneth Dos Santos, M.I.C., Prov. Sec. *Association of Marian Helpers, Marian Helpers Center*, Tel: 413-298-3691 ; Fax: 413-298-3583; Email: info@marian.org; Web: www.marian.org. Mr. Kevin Dougherty, Exec. Dir. Marian Helpers Center; Rev. Christopher Alar, M.I.C., Dir. Marian Helpers Center; Bro. Andrew Maczynski, M.I.C., Promoter of Marian Missions. *John Paul II Institute of Divine Mercy*,
Tel: 866-895-3236; Email: jpii@marian.org; Email: questions@thedivinemercy.org; Web: www.thedivinemercy.org/jpii. Rev. Seraphim Michalenko, M.I.C., Dir. Emeritus. *Marian Fathers of the Immaculate Conception of the B.V.M., Inc.*,
Tel: 413-298-1101; Email: provincial@marian.org. *Marian Services Corporation*, Tel: 413-298-3931; Email: shrine@marian.org. Rev. Kenneth Dos Santos, M.I.C., Priest. *National Shrine of the Divine Mercy Corporation*, Tel: 413-298-3931; Email: shrine@marians.org. *Marian Helpers Corporation. Marian Real Estate Trust. Marian Endowment Trust. Marian Education and Training Trust*,
Tel: 413-298-3931; Email: shrine@marians.org. *Marian Charitable Annuity Trust. Marian Continuing Care Trust*, Tel: 413-298-3931; Email: shrine@marians.org. Rev. Kenneth Dos Santos, M.I.C., Priest.

Lay Outreach of the Province:

Eucharistic Apostles of the Divine Mercy (EADM), Eden Hill, Stockbridge, 01262. Tel: 877-380-0727; Email: eadm@marian.org; Web: www.thedivinemercy.org. Dr. Bryan Thatcher, M.D., Dir.

Mother of Mercy Messengers (MOMM), Eden Hill, Stockbridge, 01262. Tel: 830-634-0727; Email: eadm@marian.org; Web: www.thedivinemercy.org/eadm. Dave Maroney, Dir.; Joan Maroney, Dir., Tel: 877-380-0727; Web: www.thedivinemercy.org/momm.

Healthcare Professionals for Divine Mercy, Eden Hill, Stockbridge, 01262. Tel: 877-380-0727; Email: marie@nursesfordivinemercy.org; Web: www.thedivinemercy.org/healthcare. Marie Romagnano, R.N., B.S.N., Dir.

[H] CONVENTS AND RESIDENCES FOR SISTERS

SPRINGFIELD. *Congregation of the Sisters of St. Joseph of Springfield* (1883) 577 Carew St., 01104.
Tel: 413-536-0853; Email: mail@ssjspringfield.com; Web: www.ssjspringfield.org. Sisters Joan Ryzewicz, Pres.; Angela Deady, Vice Pres. The Congregation of the Sisters of St. Joseph of Springfield. Administrative Offices of the Sisters of St. Joseph of Springfield. Sisters 189; Total Staff 15.

HOLYOKE. *Daughters of the Heart of Mary Provincial Residence* (1791) 1339 Northampton St., Holyoke, 01040-1958. Tel: 413-533-6681; Fax: 413-533-4217; Email: dhmprovadm@gmail.com; Web: www.dhmna.org. Mona Balicki, Prov. Sec. Sisters 1; Total in Residence 1; Total Staff 3.

Franciscan Missionary Sisters of Assisi Vice-Provincial House and Formation House, 1039 Northampton St., Holyoke, 01040-1320.

Tel: 413-532-8156; Fax: 413-534-7741; Email: fmsausa@comcast.net; Web: www.sistersofassisi.org. Sr. Regina Mulenga, S.F.M.A., Vice Prov. Supr.

Franciscan Missionary Sisters of Assisi - Saint Francis Convent - Vice Provincial House and Formation House Sisters 14.

Marian Center, Inc., 1365 Northampton St., Holyoke, 01040. Tel: 413-534-4502; Fax: 413-534-7353; Email: mnajimy@aol.com. Sr. Miriam Najimy, D.H.M., Supr. Total in Residence 13; Total Staff 50.

Sisters of Providence (1873) 5 Gamelin St., Holyoke, 01040. Tel: 413-536-7511; Fax: 413-536-7917; Email: kpopko@sisofprov.org; Web: www.sisofprov.org. Sisters Kathleen Popko, S.P., Pres.; Mary Caritas Geary, S.P., Vice Pres.; Senga Fulton, S.P., Sec. Motherhouse of the Sisters of Providence.

Legal Holdings and Titles: Sisters of Providence, Inc.; The Hillside at Providence, Inc.; Hillside Residence, Inc. Sisters 30.

TYRINGHAM. *Order of the Visitation of Holy Mary*, Monastery of the Visitation, 14 Beach Rd., Tyringham, 01264. Tel: 413-243-3995; Fax: 413-243-3543; Email: vistyr@aol.com; Web: www.vistyr.org. P.O. Box 432, Tryingham, 01264. Mother Mariam Rose, V.H.M., Supr. Order of the Visitation of Holy Mary 16.

WEST SPRINGFIELD. *Monastery of the Mother of God, Dominican Nuns (Contemplative)*, 1430 Riverdale St., West Springfield, 01089-4698. Tel: 413-736-3639; Fax: 413-736-0850; Email: monasteryws@comcast.net; Email: srmbursarws@yahoo.com. Sr. Mary of the Immaculate Heart, O.P., Prioress. Adoration to the Blessed Sacrament Chapel. Solemnly Professed Nuns 12.

[I] RETREAT HOUSES AND CHRISTIAN LIFE CENTERS

WESTFIELD. *Genesis Spiritual Life and Conference Center, Inc.*, 53 Mill St., Westfield, 01085. Tel: 413-562-3627; Fax: 413-572-1060; Email: genesis@genesisspiritualcenter.org; Web: www.genesisspiritualcenter.org. Liz Walz, Exec. Dir. Retreats, workshops and spiritual guidance designed to promote health of body, mind and spirit. Also, host day and overnight conferences. Total in Residence 2; Total Staff 16.

[J] SPANISH APOSTOLATES

SPRINGFIELD. *Catholic Latino Ministry*, 65 Elliot St., P.O. Box 1730, 01102-1730. Tel: 413-452-0631; Email: a.lopez@diospringfield.org. Mr. Andres Lopez, Dir.; Lucy Ramos, Asst. Dir.

[K] BUREAU FOR EXCEPTIONAL CHILDREN AND ADULTS

HOLYOKE. *Bureau for Exceptional Children and Adults Inc.* (1972) 537 Northampton St., Box 1039, Holyoke, 01041. Tel: 413-538-7450; Fax: 413-536-5691; Email: frjohn@jerichobeca.org. Sr. Joan Magnani, S.S.J., Dir. Lay Staff 5; Sisters 1.

[L] YOUTH SERVICES

GOSHEN. *Holy Cross Camp Grounds*, 108 Cape St., Goshen, 01032. Mailing Address: 489 Main St., Dalton, 01226. Tel: 413-684-0125; Fax: 413-684-0734; Email: cmalatesta@saintagnescc.com; Web: www.campholycross.org. Rev. Christopher A. Malatesta. Religious Teachers 1; Students 1,500; Total Staff 1.

[M] NEWMAN APOSTOLATES AND CAMPUS MINISTRIES

SPRINGFIELD. *American International College*, P.O. Box 1730, 01102. Tel: 413-452-0837; Tel: 413-205-3090; Email: j.mcdonagh@diospringfield.org. Campus Outreach, Lee Hall 30, 01109. Rev. John P. McDonagh, J.C.L., Chap.

Newman Apostolates and Campus Ministries, 65 Elliot St., P.O. Box 1730, 01102-1730. Tel: 413-452-0837; Email: j.mcdonagh@diospringfield.org. Rev. John P. McDonagh, J.C.L., Coord.

Campus Outreach in Higher Education, 65 Elliot St., P.O. Box 1730, 01102-1730. Tel: 413-452-0837; Email: j.mcdonagh@diospringfield.org. Rev. John P. McDonagh, J.C.L., Coord.

Springfield College Campus Ministry, 263 Alden St., Springfield College, 01109-3797. Tel: 413-452-0837 ; Email: j.mcdonagh@diospringfield.org. 263 Alden St., Spiritual Life, 01109-3797. Rev. John P. McDonagh, J.C.L., Campus Min., Tel: 413-452-0837.

Western New England University, Germain Campus Center, 1215 Wilbraham Rd., Rm. 247, 01119-2684. Tel: 413-782-1628; Fax: 413-585-2752; Email: sheilahanifan@comcast.net. Ms. Sheila Hanifin, Coord. of Spiritual Life, Tel: 413-567-1322; Rev. Norman B. Bolton, (Retired), 181 Hubbard St., Ludlow, 01056. Tel: 413-572-5567.

AMHERST. *Amherst College*, Cardigan Center for Religious Life, P.O. Box 2277, Amherst, 01002. Tel: 860-558-0986; Email: rcarrier@amherst.edu. 38 Woodside Ave., Amherst, 01002-5000. Deacon Roger Carrier, Deacon.

Center for Religious Life.

University of Massachusetts, Newman Center, 472 N. Pleasant St., Amherst, 01002-1739. Tel: 413-549-0300; Fax: 413-548-9182; Email: g.dailey@diospringfield.org; Web: www.newmanumass.org. Revs. Gary Dailey, Dir. & Chap.; Robert Miskell, Assoc. Dir.; Virginia Webb, Dir. Devel.; Deacon Thomas Lynch, Deacon on Staff.

CHICOPEE. *College of Our Lady of the Elms College*, 291 Springfield St., Chicopee, 01013. Tel: 413-265-2289 ; Fax: 413-594-6699; Email: allanc@elms.edu; Email: breauw@elms.edu; Email: longleyk@elms.edu; Email: russettg@elms.edu; Web: www.elms.edu. Rev. Mark S. Stelzer, Ph.D., Chap., Our Lady of the Elms, 35 Gaylord St., Chicopee, 01013. Tel: 413-265-2590, Ext. 3591; Sr. Carol Allan, S.S.J., Dir. Campus Ministry; Eileen Kirk, Asst. Dir. Campus Ministry, Tel: 413-265-2468.

LONGMEADOW. *Bay Path University*, 588 Longmeadow St., Longmeadow, 01106. St. Mary's Church, 519 Longmeadow St., Longmeadow, 01106. Tel: 413-452-0837; Email: j.mcdonagh@diospringfield.org. Rev. John P. McDonagh, J.C.L. Diocese of Springfield, Campus Outreach.

NORTH ADAMS. *Massachusetts College of Liberal Arts* Served by St. Elizabeth of Hungary, North Adams St. Elizabeth of Hungry Parish, 70 Marshall St., North Adams, 01247-0868. Tel: 413-663-5316; Email: stelizabethbulletin@yahoo.com. Rev. Dariusz P. Wudarski, Chap.

NORTHAMPTON. *Smith College*, St. Elizabeth Ann Seton Parish Office, 87 Beacon St., Northampton, 01062. Tel: 413-584-7310, Ext. 104; Email: freilly@saintelizabethannseton.net. Rev. Francis E. Reilly. Served by St. Elizabeth Seton Ann Parish, Northampton, MA.

PITTSFIELD. *Berkshire Community College*, 400 West St., Pittsfield, 01201-3194. Tel: 413-447-7510; Email: j.mcdonagh@diospringfield.org. Rev. David Aufiero. Served by St. Mark's.

SOUTH HADLEY. *Mount Holyoke College*, Office of the Chaplain, Eliot House, Mt. Holyoke College, 50 College St., South Hadley, 01075. Tel: 413-538-2054; Fax: 413-538-2787; Email: ammcderm@mtholyoke.edu. Sr. Annette McDermott, S.S.J., Rel. Advisor, Tel: 413-532-3228, Ext. 11; Rev. Michael J. Twohig, Sacramental Min. Served by St. Theresa de Lisieux Parish, South Hadley.

WESTFIELD. *Westfield State University*, Alfred and Amelia Ferst Interfaith Center, 577 Western Ave., Westfield, 01085. Tel: 413-572-5567; Fax: 413-562-3613; Email: wsavage@westfield.ma.edu. Rev. Warren J. Savage; Deacons Roger Carrier, Asst. Newman Club Advisor; James Conroy, Chap.

WILLIAMSTOWN. *Williams College*, Diocese of Springfield, P.O. Box 1730, 65 Elliot St., 01102-1730. 38 Chapin Hall Dr., Williamstown, 01267. Tel: 413-597-2483; Fax: 413-597-3955; Email: gary.caster@williams.edu. Rev. Gary C. Caster, Catholic Chap. Served by St. Patrick's.

[N] MISCELLANEOUS

SPRINGFIELD. *The Foundation of the Roman Catholic Diocese of Springfield, Massachusetts, Inc.*, 65 Elliot St., P.O. Box 1730, 01102-1730. Tel: 413-452-0687; Fax: 413-785-5449; Email: william.labroad@diospringfield.org; Web: www.diospringfield.org. William F. LaBroad Jr., Financial Officer.

The Friends of the Sisters of St. Joseph of Springfield, Inc. (2016) 577 Carew St., 01104. Tel: 413-536-0853; Email: mail@ssjspringfield.com. Sr. Joan Ryzewicz, Pres.

Mercy LIFE, Inc., 2112 Riverdale St., Ste. 1, West Springfield, 01089. Tel: 413-748-7223; Fax: 413-493-2024; Web: www.mercycares.com. Joseph Larkin, R.N., Exec. Dir.

Sisters of Providence Health System, Inc., 271 Carew St., 01104. Tel: 413-748-9000; Fax: 413-781-7217; Web: www.mercycares.com.

CHICOPEE. *Elms College Foundation, Inc.*, 291 Springfield St., Chicopee, 01013. Tel: 413-265-2372 ; Fax: 413-265-2346; Email: longleyk@elms.edu; Email: russettg@elms.edu. Mrs. Katie Longley, Treas.

The Friends of the Elms College, Inc., 291 Springfield St., Chicopee, 01013. Tel: 413-265-2372; Fax: 413-265-2346; Email: breauw@elms.edu; Email: longleyk@elms.edu; Email: russettg@elms.edu. Dr. Walter C. Breau, Admin.

Mary's House of Prayer, 202 E. Main St., Chicopee, 01020. Tel: 413-452-0886; Email: maryshouse@diospringfield.org. Rev. J. Donald R. Lapointe, Dir.

EASTHAMPTON. *Bethlehem House, Inc.*, 33 Knipfer Ave., Easthampton, 01027. Tel: 413-262-8517; Tel: 413-527-2861; Email: bethlehem_house@verizon.net. P.O. Box 1393, Easthampton, 01027. Ms. Pamela Hibbard, Dir.

HOLYOKE. *Sisters of Providence Endowment Trust*, 5 Gamelin St., Holyoke, 01040. Tel: 413-536-7511, Ext. 2551; Fax: 413-536-7917; Email: kpopko@sisofprov.org. Sisters Senga Fulton, S.P., Trustee; Mary Martin de Porres Grise, S.P., Trustee; Kathleen Popko, S.P., Trustee.

Sisters of Providence Ministry Corporation, 5 Gamelin St., Holyoke, 01040. Tel: 413-536-7511; Fax: 413-536-7917; Email: kpopko@sisofprov.org. Sisters Kathleen Popko, S.P., Pres.; Mary Caritas Geary, S.P., Vice Pres.; Senga Fulton, S.P., Sec.; Mr. John Dowd Jr., Dir.; Mr. Dennis Fitzpatrick, Dir.; Ms. Diane LaCosse, Dir.; Mr. James Wall, Dir.

Genesis Spiritual Life and Conference Center, Inc.; Providence Ministries for the Needy, Inc.; Providence Place, Inc.; Mary's Meadow at Providence Place, Inc.; Mount St. Vincent Care Center

Mount St. Vincent's Care Center (1972) 35 Holy Family Rd., Holyoke, 01040-2758. Tel: 413-532-3246; Fax: 413-532-0309; Email: kpopko@sisofprov.org. Eriko Umana, Admin.; Jacek Muszynski, Spiritual Care Coord. Total Staff 130; Persons Under Care 122.

Sisters of Providence Retirement and Continuing Care Trust, 5 Gamelin St., Holyoke, 01040. Tel: 413-536-7511, Ext. 2551; Fax: 413-536-7917; Email: kpopko@sisofprov.org. Sisters Mary Caritas Geary, S.P., Trustee; Margaret McCleary, S.P., Trustee; Ruth McGoldrick, S.P., Trustee. Retirement and Continuing Care Trust.

The Hillside at Providence, Inc., 5 Gamelin St., Holyoke, 01040. Tel: 413-536-7511, Ext. 2551; Fax: 413-536-7971; Email: kpopko@sisofprov.org. Sisters Kathleen Popko, S.P., Pres.; Senga Fulton, S.P., Treas.; Mary Caritas Geary, S.P., Sec.

Hillside Residence, Inc., 5 Gamelin St., Holyoke, 01040. Tel: 413-536-7511; Fax: 413-536-7917; Email: kpopko@sisofprov.org. Sisters Kathleen Popko, S.P., Pres.; Senga Fulton, S.P., Vice Pres.; John Wesolowski, Treas.; Sr. Mary Caritas Geary, S.P., Clerk.

PALMER. *Apostolate of the Suffering, Inc.*, 1915 Ware St., Palmer, 01069-9560. Tel: 413-283-4529; Web: www.sodcvs.org/eng; Email: maryfarm@comcast.net. Bro. Robert J. Letasz, S.O.D.C., Pres. & Dir.; Stasia A. Bronner, Admin.; Rev. Daniel B. Brunton, Spiritual Dir., (Retired).

RELIGIOUS INSTITUTES OF MEN REPRESENTED IN THE DIOCESE

For further details refer to the corresponding bracketed number in the Religious Institutes of Men or Women section.

[]—*The Association of Marian Helpers of Stockbridge, MA.*

[0740]—*Congregation of Marians of the Immaculate Conception*—M.I.C.

[1000]—*Congregation of the Passion* (Union City, NJ)—C.P.

[0480]—*Conventual Franciscans*—O.F.M.Conv.

[0720]—*The Missionaries of Our Lady of La Salette*—M.S.

[1280]—*Stigmatine Fathers and Brothers*—C.S.S.

RELIGIOUS INSTITUTES OF WOMEN REPRESENTED IN THE DIOCESE

[0810]—*Daughters of the Heart of Mary*—D.H.M.

[1050]—*Dominican Contemplative Nuns*—O.P.

[1170]—*Felician Sisters*—C.S.S.F.

[1330]—*Franciscan Missionary Sisters of Assisi*—S.F.M.A.

[1470]—*Franciscan Sisters of St. Joseph*—F.S.S.J.

[1180]—*Franciscan Sisters of the Allegany, New York*—O.S.F.

[]—*Missionary Sisters of Our Lady of Africa.*

[]—*Oblate Sisters of the Most Holy Eucharist*—O.S.S.E.

[0570]—*Sisters of Charity Seton Hill*—S.C.

[3000]—*Sisters of Notre Dame de Namur*—S.N.D.deN.

[3340]—*Sisters of Providence*—S.P.

[3830-16]—*Sisters of St. Joseph*—S.S.J.

[3850]—*Sisters of St. Joseph of Chambery*—C.S.J.

[0150]—*Sisters of the Assumption*—S.A.S.V.

[4190]—*Visitation Nuns*—V.H.M.

DIOCESAN CEMETERIES

SPRINGFIELD. *St. Benedict Cemetery*, Liberty St., 01104. Tel: 413-782-0341; Fax: 413-782-5450; Web: www.diospringfield.org. Mailing Address: Springfield Diocesan Cemeteries, Inc., 421 Tinkham Rd., 01129. Rev. Msgr. Daniel P. Liston, J.C.L., Chancellor

Gate of Heaven, 421 Tinkham Rd., 01129. Tel: 413-782-0341; Fax: 413-782-5450; Email: j.kostek@diospringfield.org; Web: www.

diospringfield.org. Rev. Msgr. Daniel P. Liston, J.C.L., Chancellor

St. Matthew Cemetery, 366 Springfield St., 01109. Mailing Address: Springfield Diocesan Cemeteries, Inc., 421 Tinkham Rd., 01129. Tel: 413-782-0341; Fax: 413-782-5450; Web: www.diospringfield.org. Mr. Joseph Kostik, Pres.

St. Michael's Cemetery, 1601 State St., 01109. Tel: 413-782-0349; Fax: 413-782-5450; Web: www.diospringfield.org. 421 Tinkham Rd., 01129. Mr. Joseph Kostik, Pres.

HOLYOKE. *Calvary Cemetery*, Office: Northampton St., Holyoke, 01040. Tel: 413-782-0341; Fax: 413-782-5450; Web: www.diospringfield.org. Rev. Msgr. Daniel P. Liston, J.C.L., Chancellor

INDIAN ORCHARD. *St. Aloysius Cemetery*, Office: Berkshire Ave., Indian Orchard, 01151. Mailing Address: Springfield Diocesan Cemeteries, Inc., 1601 State St., 01109. Tel: 413-782-0341; Fax: 413-782-5450; Web: www.diospringfield.org. Mr. Joseph Kostik, Pres.

SOUTH HADLEY. *Notre Dame Cemetery*, Springfield Diocesan Cemeteries, Inc., 63 Lyman St., South Hadley, 01075. Tel: 413-420-0001; Fax: 413-420-0004; Email: j.kostek@diospringfield.org; Web: www.diospringfield.org. Mr. Joseph Kostik, Dir.

Precious Blood Cemetery, Willimansett St., South Hadley, 01075. 63 Lyman St., South Hadley, 01075. Tel: 413-420-0001; Fax: 413-420-0004; Email: j.kostek@diospringfield.org; Web: www.diospringfield.org. Mr. Joseph Kostik, Pres.

St. Rose Cemetery, Rts. 33 & 202, South Hadley, 01075. Tel: 413-420-0001; Fax: 413-420-0004; Email: jkostek@diospringfield.org; Web: www.diospringfield.org. Springfield Diocesan Cemeteries, Inc., 63 Lyman St., South Hadley, 01075. Mr. Joseph Kostik, Pres.

WESTFIELD. *St. Mary Cemetery*, 203 Southampton Rd., Westfield, 01085. Tel: 413-568-7775; Fax: 413-568-2727; Web: www.diospringfield.org. Mr. Joseph Kostik, Pres.

NECROLOGY

† Begley, Thomas B., (Retired), Died Dec. 2, 2018
† Bombardier, Dennis P., (Retired), Died Apr. 22, 2018
† Chwalek, John C., (Retired), Died Mar. 9, 2018
† Dean, John T., (Retired), Died Feb. 24, 2018
† Fitzgerald, Edward T., (Retired), Died May. 8, 2018
† Foley, Daniel R., (Retired), Died Mar. 11, 2018
† Greenway, George G., (Retired), Died Jul. 23, 2018
† O'Connor, Matthew J., (Retired), Died Dec. 24, 2016
† Plasse, Eugene J., (Retired), Died Oct. 13, 2018
† Sullivan, Francis X., (Retired), Died Dec. 24, 2016
† Sullivan, John L., (Retired), Died Sep. 26, 2018

An asterisk (*) denotes an organization that has established tax-exempt status directly with the IRS and is not covered by the USCCB Group Ruling.

Diocese of Steubenville

(Dioecesis Steubenvicensis)

Most Reverend

JEFFREY MARC MONFORTON

Bishop of Steubenville; ordained June 25, 1994; appointed Bishop of Steubenville July 3, 2012; installed September 10, 2012. *Chancery Office: 422 Washington St., P.O. Box 969, Steubenville, OH 43952-5969.*

Most Reverend

GILBERT I. SHELDON, D.D., D.MIN.

Bishop Emeritus of Steubenville; ordained February 28, 1953; appointed Auxiliary and Titular Bishop of Taparura April 20, 1976; consecrated June 11, 1976; appointed to Steubenville January 28, 1992; installed April 2, 1992; retired August 6, 2002.

ESTABLISHED 1944.

Square Miles 5,913.

Comprises these thirteen Counties in the State of Ohio: Athens, Belmont, Carroll, Gallia, Guernsey, Harrison, Jefferson, Lawrence, Meigs, Morgan, Monroe, Noble and Washington.

For legal titles of parishes and diocesan institutions, consult the Chancery Office.

Chancery Office: 422 Washington St., P.O. Box 969, Steubenville, OH 43952-5969. Tel: 740-282-3631; Fax: 740-282-3327.

Web: www.diosteub.org

Email: bgreer@diosteub.org

STATISTICAL OVERVIEW

Personnel	
Bishop	1
Retired Bishops	1
Priests: Diocesan Active in Diocese	40
Priests: Diocesan Active Outside Diocese	3
Priests: Retired, Sick or Absent	29
Number of Diocesan Priests	72
Religious Priests in Diocese	30
Total Priests in Diocese	102
Extern Priests in Diocese	5
Ordinations:	
Diocesan Priests	1
Transitional Deacons	1
Permanent Deacons in Diocese	15
Total Brothers	8
Total Sisters	86
Parishes	
Parishes	52
With Resident Pastor:	
Resident Diocesan Priests	51
Without Resident Pastor:	
Administered by Priests	1
Missions	3
Closed Parishes	2
Professional Ministry Personnel:	
Sisters	2
Lay Ministers	1
Welfare	
Catholic Hospitals	1
Total Assisted	275,541
Special Centers for Social Services	1
Total Assisted	29,579
Residential Care of Disabled	1
Total Assisted	49
Educational	
Diocesan Students in Other Seminaries	9
Total Seminarians	9
Colleges and Universities	1
Total Students	3,028
High Schools, Diocesan and Parish	3
Total Students	338
Elementary Schools, Diocesan and Parish	9
Total Students	1,362
Catechesis/Religious Education:	
High School Students	367
Elementary Students	1,072
Total Students under Catholic Instruction	6,176
Teachers in the Diocese:	
Sisters	1
Lay Teachers	183
Vital Statistics	
Receptions into the Church:	
Infant Baptism Totals	243
Minor Baptism Totals	48
Adult Baptism Totals	43
Received into Full Communion	109
First Communions	313
Confirmations	512
Marriages:	
Catholic	56
Interfaith	43
Total Marriages	99
Deaths	393
Total Catholic Population	31,320
Total Population	499,460

Former Bishops—Most Revs. JOHN KING MUSSIO, D.D., J.C.D., named First Bishop of Steubenville; ord. for Archdiocese of Cincinnati Aug. 15, 1935; appt. First Bishop of Steubenville March 16, 1945; cons. May 1, 1945; retired Oct. 11, 1977; died April 15, 1978; ALBERT H. OTTENWELLER, D.D., S.T.L., named Second Bishop of Steubenville; ord. June 19, 1943; appt. Titular Bishop of Perdices and Auxiliary of Toledo April 17, 1974; cons. May 29, 1974; appt. Second Bishop of Steubenville Oct. 11, 1977; installed Nov. 22, 1977; retired April 2, 1992; died Sept. 23, 2012.; GILBERT I. SHELDON, D.D., D.Min., (Retired), named Third Bishop of Steubenville.; ord. Feb. 28, 1953; appt. Auxiliary and Titular Bishop of Taparura April 20, 1976; cons. June 11, 1976; appt. Third Bishop of Steubenville Jan. 28, 1992; installed April 2, 1992; retired Aug. 6, 2002; R. DANIEL CONLON, D.D., J.C.D., Ph.D., ord. Jan. 15, 1977; named Fourth Bishop of Steubenville May 22, 2002; cons. and installed Aug. 6, 2002; appt. Bishop of Joliet May 17, 2011; installed July 14, 2011.

Vicar General—Mailing Address: 422 Washington St., P.O. Box 969, Steubenville, 43952-5969. Tel: 740-282-3631. Rev. JAMES M. DUNFEE, M.A., S.T.L., Email: jdunfee@diosteub.org.

Executive Assistant to the Bishop—JAMES PIAZZA, Mailing Address: 422 Washington St., P.O. Box 969, Steubenville, 43952-5969. Tel: 740-282-3631; Email: jpiazza@diosteub.org.

Executive Secretary to the Bishop—Mailing Address: 422 Washington St., P.O. Box 969, Steubenville, 43952-5969. Tel: 740-282-3631. DEBORAH COOK, Email: dcook@diosteub.org.

Episcopal Vicar for Pastoral Planning & Personnel—Very Rev. THOMAS A. CHILLOG, M.Div., Mailing Address: 422 Washington St., P.O. Box 969, Steubenville, 43952-5969. Tel: 740-282-3631; Email: tchillog@diosteub.org.

Chancellor—Mailing Address: 422 Washington St., P.O. Box 969, Steubenville, 43952-5969. Tel: 740-282-3631; Fax: 740-282-3327. Rev. BRADLEY W. GREER, M.A., S.T.B., Email: bgreer@diosteub.org.

Diocesan Offices and Directors

Diocesan Archivist—Mailing Address: 422 Washington St., P.O. Box 969, Steubenville, 43952-5969. Tel: 740-282-3631. EMILY TEACHOUT, Email: eteachout@diosteub.org.

Diocesan Finance Office—Mailing Address: P.O. Box 969, Steubenville, 43952-5969. Tel: 740-282-3631. PATRICK HENRY, CFO.

Diocesan Finance Council—Most Rev. JEFFREY M. MONFORTON, D.D., S.T.B., S.T.L., S.T.D., Pres.; Rev. JAMES M. DUNFEE, M.A., S.T.L., Chm. Council Members: GREGORY J. AGRESTA; PATRICK HENRY; MARK BRADLEY; JAMES PIAZZA; THOMAS H. HISRICH; SUSAN TOLBERT; Rev. Msgr. JOHN C. KOLESAR, V.F.

Diocesan Tribunal—Mailing Address: 422 Washington St., P.O. Box 969, Steubenville, 43952-5969. Tel: 740-282-3631.

Judicial Vicar—Very Rev. WILLIAM D. CROSS, M.Div., J.C.L.

Auditors—Very Rev. THOMAS A. CHILLOG, M.Div.; Rev. DANIEL HEUSEL, M.Div., J.C.L.

Notaries—Rev. DANIEL HEUSEL, M.Div., J.C.L.; COLLEEN BAHEN.

Defenders of the Bond—Rev. Msgr. GERALD E. CALOVINI, V.F.; Very Rev. THOMAS A. CHILLOG, M.Div.; Rev. DANIEL HEUSEL, M.Div., J.C.L.

Director of the Tribunal & Notary—COLLEEN BAHEN.

Judges—Most Rev. GILBERT I. SHELDON, D.D., D.Min., (Retired); Rev. JAMES M. DUNFEE, M.A., S.T.L.; Rev. Msgr. KURT H. KEMO, J.C.L., M.Div.; Rev. VINCENT J. HUBER, M.Ed., S.T.B., (Retired).

Information & Technology—Mailing Address: 422 Washington St., P.O. Box 969, Steubenville, 43952-5969. Tel: 740-282-3631. MARTIN B. THOMPSON, Dir.

Diocesan Deaneries and Deans

Deans—Revs. ANTHONY R. BATT, Mother of Hope Deanery; THOMAS F. HAMM JR., Nativity of Mary Deanery; Very Rev. WILLIAM D. CROSS, M.Div.,

J.C.L., Presentation Deanery; Rev. TIMOTHY J. SHANNON, Visitation Deanery.

Child and Youth Protection—Mailing Address: 422 Washington St., P.O. Box 969, Steubenville, 43952-5969. Tel: 740-282-3631; Fax: 740-282-3327. Rev. JAMES M. DUNFEE, M.A., S.T.L., Contact Person, Email: jdunfee@diosteub.org.

Child Protection Review Board—Rev. JAMES M. DUNFEE, M.A., S.T.L. Members: Judge FRANK A. FREGIATO; DR. JOSEPH DIPALMA; DAN FRY, Esq.; SANDRA L. NICHOLOFF, Esq.; Deacon PAUL WARD; JAMES PIAZZA; MICHELE SANTIN.

Presbyteral Council—Revs. TIMOTHY J. HUFFMAN; DAVID L. GAYDOSIK; ROBERT A. GALLAGHER; JOHN F. MUCHA; Rev. Msgr. DONALD E. HORAK, (Retired); Revs. MARK A. MOORE; JAMES M. DUNFEE, M.A., S.T.L.; Very Rev. THOMAS A. CHILLOG, M.Div., Chm.; Rev. WILLIAM WAGNER, O.R.C.

College of Consultors—Very Rev. THOMAS A. CHILLOG, M.Div.; Revs. THOMAS A. NELSON; JOHN F. MUCHA; MARK A. MOORE; DAVID L. GAYDOSIK; JAMES M. DUNFEE, M.A., S.T.L.

Priests Personnel Board—Rev. Msgr. J. MICHAEL CAMPBELL, Senior Clergy; Revs. JAMES M. DUNFEE, M.A., S.T.L., Middle Age Clergy; THOMAS A. NELSON, Southern Area; MICHAEL GOSSETT, Younger Clergy; JOHN F. MUCHA, Central Area; ANTHONY R. BATT, Northern Area; Very Rev. THOMAS A. CHILLOG, M.Div., Ex Officio.

Facilities & Property Management—Mailing Address: P.O. Box 969, Steubenville, 43952-5969. Tel: 740-282-3631; Fax: 740-282-3327. SCOTT YARMAN, Dir.

Diocesan Building Commission—SCOTT YARMAN, Contact Person; GEORGE CATTRELL; MICHAEL HOMOL; JOHN HUMPE; TIM PESTIAN; JAMES PIAZZA; JAMES SNINCHAK; MARK VIOLA.

Diocesan Director of Cemeteries—Rev. Msgr. JOHN C. KOLESAR, V.F., Mailing Address: 221 Hanna Ave., Adena, 43901. Tel: 740-546-3463.

Campus Ministry—Rev. MARK A. MOORE, Mailing Address: 38 N. College St., Athens, 45701. Tel: 740-592-2711; Email: mmoore@diosteub.org.

Censores Librorum—Rev. JAMES M. DUNFEE, M.A., S.T.L.; ALAN SCHRECK, Ph.D.

Office of Christian Formation and Schools—Deacon PAUL WARD, Dir./Supt. Schools, Mailing Address: P.O. Box 969, Steubenville, 43952-5969. Tel: 740-282-3631; Fax: 740-282-3327.

Diocesan Communications—Mailing Address: P.O. Box 969, Steubenville, 43952. Tel: 740-282-3631; Fax: 740-282-3238. DINO ORSATTI, Dir.

Publication, "Steubenville Register"—Mailing Address: 422 Washington St., P.O. Box 969, Steubenville, 43952-5969. Tel: 740-282-3631; Fax: 740-282-3238. Most Rev. JEFFREY M. MONFORTON, D.D., S.T.B., S.T.L., S.T.D., Pres. & Publisher; DINO ORSATTI, Editor.

Office of Civil Law—THOMAS S. WILSON ESQ., Mailing Address: P.O. Box 969, Steubenville, 43952-5969. Tel: 740-282-3631; Fax: 740-282-3327.

Continuing Education of Priests—Rev. PAUL HREZO, Coord., Mailing Address: Christ Our Light Parish, 701 Gomber Ave., Cambridge, 43725. Tel: 740-432-7609.

Diocesan Director of Ecumenism—Rev. THOMAS F. HAMM JR., Mailing Address: St. Louis Catholic Church, 91 State St., Gallipolis, 45631. Tel: 740-446-0669.

Diocesan Office of Worship—Mailing Address: P.O. Box 969, Steubenville, 43952-5969. Tel: 740-282-3631. Rev. BRADLEY W. GREER, M.A., S.T.B., Interim Dir.

Health Panel of the Clergy—Very Rev. THOMAS A. CHILLOG, M.Div., Contact Person, Mailing Address: P.O. Box 969, Steubenville, 43952-5969. Tel: 740-282-3631.

Diocesan Office of Human Resources—Mailing Address: P.O. Box 969, Steubenville, 43952-5969. Tel: 740-282-3631; Fax: 740-282-1409. SHANNON MINCH-HUGHES, Dir.

Catholic Rural Life—Rev. DAVID L. GAYDOSIK, Mailing Address: 334 S. Main St., Woodsfield, 43793. Tel: 740-472-0187; Fax: 740-472-0182.

Office of Catholic Charities and Social Concerns—Catholic Campaign for Human Devel.; Hispanic Ministry; Samaritan House. MICHELE SANTIN, Dir.; RUTH ANN TURNER, Social Svcs. Coord., Mailing Address: P.O. Box 969, Steubenville, 43952-5969. Tel: 740-282-3631; Tel: 800-339-7890; Fax: 740-282-3327.

Sacred Heart Center of Hope—Mailing Address: P.O. Box 969, Steubenville, 43952-5969. Tel: 740-282-3631. Sr. KATHERINE CALDWELL, T.O.R., Mission & Prog. Developer.

Marriage, Family and Respect Life—JOSEPH SCHMIDT, Dir., Mailing Address: 409 Second St., Ste. D, Marietta, 45750. Tel: 740-516-9270; Email: jschmidt@diosteub.org; Web: www.diosteub.org/family.

Priests' Retirement Board—Mailing Address: Triumph of the Church, P.O. Box 908, Steubenville, 43962. Tel: 740-264-6177. Rev. THOMAS R. NAU, Chm.

Propagation of the FaithMailing Address: 307 Seventh St., P.O. Box 331, Beverly, 45715. Tel: 740-984-2555. Rev. TIMOTHY J. KOZAK, Asst. Dir.

RCIA—Rev. THOMAS F. HAMM JR., Dir., Mailing Address: 85 State St., Gallipolis, 45631. Tel: 740-732-4576; Tel: 740-446-0669.

Office of Stewardship and Development—Mailing Address: P.O. Box 969, Steubenville, 43952-5969. Tel: 740-282-3631; Tel: 740-317-5678; Fax: 740-282-3327. Sr. MARY BRIGID CALLAN, Dir., Email: mcallan@diosteub.org.

Diocesan/Parish Share Campaign—Rev. JAMES M. DUNFEE, M.A., S.T.L., Dir.; Sr. MARY BRIGID CALLAN, Assoc. Dir.; MARTIN B. THOMPSON, Assoc. Dir., Tel: 740-282-3631.

Delegate for Priests—Very Rev. THOMAS A. CHILLOG, M.Div., Mailing Address: P.O. Box 969, Steubenville, 43952-5969. Tel: 740-282-3631.

Delegate for Religious—Rev. Msgr. J. MICHAEL CAMPBELL, Mailing Address: Basilica of St. Mary of the Assumption, 506 Fourth St., Marietta, 45750. Tel: 740-373-3643.

Vicar for Retired Priests—Rev. JOHN MUCHA, Mailing Address: 68210 Neola Ave., Bridgeport, 43912. Tel: 740-635-0408.

Victim Assistance Coordinator—Mailing Address: P.O. Box 969, Steubenville, 43952. Tel: 740-282-3631; Fax: 740-282-3327. Rev. JAMES M. DUNFEE, M.A., S.T.L., Contact, Email: jdunfee@diosteub.org.

Office of Vocations—Mailing Address: Diocese of Steubenville, P.O. Box 969, Steubenville, 43952. Tel: 740-264-0868; Fax: 740-282-3327. Rev. MICHAEL GOSSETT, Dir., Email: mgossett@diosteub.org. Assistant Directors: Revs. DANIEL HEUSEL, M.Div., J.C.L., Mailing Address: 3745 Tallman Ave., Bellaire, 43906. Tel: 740-676-0051; Email: dheusel@diosteub.org; JONAS SHELL, Mailing Address: 38 N. College St., Athens, 45701. Tel: 740-593-7822; Email: jshell@diosteub.org.

Diocesan Council of Catholic Women—Rev. TIMOTHY P. MCGUIRE, Moderator; JOANNE KOLANSKI, Pres., Mailing Address: 46919 Columbia St., St. Clairsville, 43950. Tel: 740-695-1617; Cell: 740-312-8356; Email: jkolanski51@comcast.net.

CLERGY, PARISHES, MISSIONS AND PAROCHIAL SCHOOLS

CITY OF STEUBENVILLE

(JEFFERSON COUNTY)

1—ST. ANTHONY OF PADUA, [JC] Closed. For inquiries for parish records contact Triumph of the Cross, Steubenville.

2—HOLY FAMILY, [JC]
2608 Hollywood Blvd., 43952. Tel: 740-264-2825; Fax: 740-264-9348; Email: rectory@holyfamilyweb.org. Rev. Msgr. Gerald E. Calovini, V.F.; Deacons Stephen F. Miletic; Edward G. Kovach; Drake McCalister.
Please see Catholic Central High School, Bishop John King Mussio Central Junior High School & Bishop John King Mussio Central Elementary School located in the Institution section.

3—HOLY NAME CATHEDRAL, [JC] Closed June 8, 2014 for renovation. See Triumph of the Cross Parish for more information.
411 S. 5th St., 43952. Tel: 740-264-6177; Email: totcmailbox@comcast.net. P.O. Box 908, 43952. Revs. Thomas R. Nau; Ryan Gray, Parochial Vicar; Deacons Richard G. Adams; Randall Redington.
Please see Catholic Central High School, Bishop John King Mussio Central Junior High School & Bishop John King Mussio Central Elementary Schools located in the Institution section.

4—HOLY ROSARY, [JC] Closed. For inquiries for parish records contact Triumph of the Cross, Steubenville.

5—IMMACULATE HEART OF MARY CHAPEL, Closed. For inquiries for parish records contact the chancery.

6—OUR LADY OF NORTH AMERICA MARTYRS, Closed. For inquiries for parish records please see St. Peter's, Steubenville.

7—ST. PETER'S, [JC]
425 N. Fourth St., 43952. Tel: 740-282-7612; Email: office@stpetersteub.com; Web: www.stpetersteub.com. Revs. Timothy J. Huffman; Bradley W. Greer, M.A., S.T.B., Parochial Vicar; Deacon Thomas F. Maedke.
Please see Catholic Central High School, Bishop John King Mussio Central Junior High School & Bishop John King Mussio Central Elementary School located in the Institution section.

8—ST. PIUS X, [JC] Closed. For inquiries for parish records contact Triumph of the Cross, Steubenville.

9—SERVANTS OF CHRIST THE KING, Closed. For inquiries for parish records contact Triumph of the Cross, Steubenville.

10—ST. STANISLAUS, [JC] Closed. For inquiries for parish records contact Triumph of the Cross, Steubenville.

11—TRIUMPH OF THE CROSS
204 Rosemont Ave, P.O. Box 908, 43952. Tel: 740-264-6177; Fax: 740-266-2844; Email: totcmailbox@comcast.net; Web: www.triumphofthecross.org. Revs. Thomas R. Nau; Ryan Gray; Deacons Randall Redington; Richard G. Adams.
Catechesis Religious Program—Barbara VanBeveren, D.R.E.
Please see Catholic Central High School, Bishop John King Mussio Central Junior High School & Bishop John King Mussio Central Elementary School located in the Institution section.

OUTSIDE THE CITY OF STEUBENVILLE

ADENA, JEFFERSON CO., ST. CASIMIR CHURCH, [CEM]
221 Hanna Ave., Adena, 43901. Tel: 740-546-3463; Email: stcadena@frontier.com. Rev. Msgr. John C. Kolesar, V.F.; Sr. Jeanne Vucic, Pastoral Assoc.
Catechesis Religious Program—Tel: 740-546-4380; Email: jvucic1@frontier.com. Sr. Jeanne Vucic, D.R.E.; Mrs. Shirley Pastre, D.R.E. Students 9.

AMSTERDAM, JEFFERSON CO., ST. JOSEPH, [CEM]
7457 State Hwy. 152, Richmond, 43944.
Tel: 740-765-4142; Email: jmccoy@diosteub.org. Rev. John J. McCoy Jr.
Church: 333 N. Main St., Amsterdam, 43903.

ATHENS, ATHENS CO.

1—CHRIST THE KING UNIVERSITY PARISH
141 Mill St., Athens, 45701. Tel: 740-592-2711; Email: wserbonich@athenscatholic.org; Web: www.athenscatholic.org. Mailing Address: 75 Stewart St, Athens, 45701-2925. Revs. Mark A. Moore; Thomas A. Nelson, Parochial Vicar; Deacon Daniel P. Murray.
Catechesis Religious Program—Nancy Denhart, D.R.E. Students 95.

2—ST. PAUL CHURCH, [CEM]
75 Stewart St., Athens, 45701. Tel: 740-592-2711; Email: wserbonich@athenscatholic.org; Web: www.athenscatholic.org. 38 N. College St., Athens, 45701. Revs. Mark A. Moore; Thomas A. Nelson, Parochial Vicar; Deacon Daniel P. Murray.
Catechesis Religious Program—Students 46.
Chapel—Guysville, St. John.

BARNESVILLE, BELMONT CO., ASSUMPTION, [CEM]
306 W. Main St., Barnesville, 43713.
Tel: 740-425-2181; Email: assymptionandstmarychurches@yahoo.com. Rev. David Cornett.
Catechesis Religious Program—Students 46.

BARTON, BELMONT CO., OUR LADY OF ANGELS, Closed. For inquiries for parish records see St. Joseph, Bridgeport.

BELLAIRE, BELMONT CO.

1—ST. JOHN, [JC]
415 37th St, Bellaire, 43906. Tel: 740-676-0051; Fax: 740-671-9776; Email: stjohns3745@comcast.net; Web: www.bnspcatholic.org. Mailing Address: 3745 Tallman Ave., Bellaire, 43906. Rev. Daniel Heusel, M.Div., J.C.L.
School—St. John Central Grade School, (Grades PreK-8), 3625 Guernsey St., Bellaire, 43906.
Tel: 740-676-4932; Fax: 740-676-4934; Email: jarett.kuhns@omeresa.net. Mr. Jarett Kuhns, Prin. Lay Teachers 14; Students 96.

2—ST. MICHAEL'S, [CEM] [JC] Closed. For inquiries for parish records please see St. John, Bellaire.

BELLE VALLEY, NOBLE CO., CORPUS CHRISTI, [CEM]
221 Main St, 1036 Belford St., Belle Valley, 43717.
Tel: 740-732-4129; Email: ststephencc@roadrunner.com. P.O. Box 286, Caldwell, 43724. Revs. Wayne E. Morris; Chester J. Pabin.

BEVERLY, WASHINGTON CO., ST. BERNARD, [CEM]
307 Seventh St., P.O. Box 331, Beverly, 45715.
Tel: 740-984-2555; Email: contact@StBernardBeverly.org; Web: StBernardBeverly.org. Rev. Timothy J. Kozak; Rev. Msgr. Robert J. Kawa, Pastor Emeritus, (Retired).

BLAINE, BELMONT CO., ALL SAINTS, Closed. For inquiries for parish records please see St. Joseph, Bridgeport.

BRIDGEPORT, BELMONT CO.

1—ST. ANTHONY OF PADUA, [JC]
630 Main St., Bridgeport, 43912. Tel: 740-635-0283; Email: bridgeportparishes@comcast.net. Rev. John Mucha.

Church: 68210 Neola Ave., Bridgeport, 43912. Email: jmucha@diosteub.org.
2—St. Joseph, [JC]
68210 Neola Ave, Bridgeport, 43912.
Tel: 740-635-0408; Fax: 740-635-1166; Email: jmucha@diosteub.org. Rev. John Mucha.
Res.: 630 Main St., Bridgeport, 43912.
Brilliant, Jefferson Co., Our Lady of Fatima, Closed. Sacramental records are located at St. Agnes, Mingo Junction.
Buchtel, Athens Co., St. Patrick, Consolidated with St. Andrew to form St. Mary of the Hills, Nelsonville.
Burkhart, Monroe Co., St. Joseph's, [CEM 2] Closed. For inquiries for parish records please contact St. Sylvester, Woodsfield.
Byesville, Guernsey Co., Holy Trinity, [CEM] Closed. For inquiries for parish records please contact Christ our Light, Cambridge.
Cadiz, Harrison Co., St. Teresa
143 E. South St., Cadiz, 43907. Tel: 740-942-2211; Email: harrcntcath@frontier.net. Rev. Frederick C. Kihm.
Caldwell, Noble Co.
1—Immaculate Conception, [CEM]
14700 Fulda Rd., Caldwell, 43724. Tel: 740-732-4129 ; Email: ststephencc@roadrunner.com. P.O. Box 286, Caldwell, 43724. Revs. Wayne Morris; Chester J. Pabin.
Res.: 43700 Fulda Rd., Caldwell, 43724.
2—St. Stephen, [CEM]
1036 Belford St., P.O. Box 286, Caldwell, 43724.
Tel: 740-732-7412; Email: ststephencc@roadrunner.com. Revs. Wayne E. Morris; Chester J. Pabin.
Cambridge, Guernsey Co.
1—St. Benedict, Closed. For inquiries for parish records see Christ Our Light, Cambridge.
2—Christ Our Light Parish, [CEM 3]
701 Gomber Ave., Cambridge, 43725.
Tel: 740-432-7609; Email: col_office@catholicweb.com. Rev. Paul Hrezo, Admin.
School—St. Benedict School, (Grades K-8), 220 N. 7th St., Cambridge, 43725. Tel: 740-432-6751; Fax: 740-432-4511; Email: lynn.padden@omeresa.net; Web: www.stbenedictschool.net. Mrs. Jane Rush, Prin. Clergy 2; Lay Teachers 13; Franciscan Sisters of Christian Charity 4; Students 110.
Catechesis Religious Program—Students 70.
SS. Peter and Paul, 136 E. High Ave., Lore City, 43755.
Carlisle, Noble Co., St. Michael, [CEM]
44935 Carlisle Rd., P.O. Box 286, Caldwell, 43724.
Tel: 740-732-4129; Email: ststephencc@roadrunner.com. Revs. Wayne Morris; Chester J. Pabin.
Res.: 43700 Fulda Rd., P.O. Box 286, Caldwell, 43724. Tel: 740-734-4129; Email: ststephencc@roadrunner.com.
Church: 43925 County Rd. 43, Caldwell, 43724.
Carrollton, Carroll Co., Our Lady of Mercy
748 Roswell Rd., S.W., P.O. Box 155, Carrollton, 44615. Tel: 330-627-4664, Ext. 100; Email: info@olmcarrollton.org; Web: www.olmcarrollton.org. Rev. Anthony R. Batt.
Catechesis Religious Program—Students 61.
Chesapeake, Lawrence Co., St. Ann
310 Third Ave., Chesapeake, 45619.
Tel: 740-867-4434; Email: stannchurch1@frontier.com; Web: stannchurch.weebly.com. Rev. Charles Moran.
Catechesis Religious Program—Students 25.
Churchtown, Washington Co., St. John the Baptist, [CEM]
17784 State Rte. 676, Marietta, 45750.
Tel: 740-896-3566; Fax: 740-896-3567; Email: stjohnchurchtown@yahoo.com; Web: www.stjohnchurchtown.com. Rev. Timothy Davison, Pastoral Assoc.
School—St. John Central Grade School, (Grades PreK-8), Tel: 740-896-2697; Email: mschwendeman39@gmail.com. Deacon Paul Ward, Pastoral Min. / Coord. Lay Teachers 13; Students 125.
Colerain, Belmont Co., St. Frances Cabrini
U.S. Rte. 250, P.O. Box 38, Colerain, 43916.
Tel: 740-635-9933; Email: stfrancab@comcast.net. Rev. Timothy P. McGuire.
Dillonvale, Jefferson Co., St. Adalbert, [CEM]
39 Smithfield St., Dillonvale, 43917.
Tel: 740-546-3463; Email: stcadena@frontier.com. c/o 221 Hanna Ave., Adena, 43901. Rev. Msgr. John C. Kolesar, V.F.
Catechesis Religious Program—Rosemary Zelek, D.R.E.; James Piazza, D.R.E. Students 15.
Fairpoint, Belmont Co., St. Joseph, Closed. For inquiries for parish records please contact St. Mary, St. Clairsville.
Flushing, Belmont Co., St. Paul's, [CEM] Closed. For inquiries for parish records contact St. Mary, St. Clairsville.
Gallipolis, Gallia Co., St. Louis, [CEM]
85 State St., Gallipolis, 45631. Tel: 740-446-0669; Fax: 740-446-9859; Email: stlouis85@att.net. Rev. Thomas F. Hamm Jr.
Glouster, Athens Co., Holy Cross, [CEM]
Mailing Address: 110 E. Washington St., Nelsonville, 45764. Tel: 740-767-3068; Email: holycross@nelsonvilletv.com. Mailing Address: 31 Republic Ave, Glouster, 45732. Rev. Msgr. Donald E. Horak, Admin., (Retired).
Church: Corner of Madison & Republic Avenues, Glouster, 45732.
Harriettsville, Noble Co., St. Henry, [CEM]
36575 Church St., Lower Salem, 45745.
Tel: 740-896-2207; Email: olm.churchlowell@gmail.com. Mailing Address: 5001 Lowell Hill Rd., Lowell, 45786. Rev. Timothy J. Shannon.
Hopedale, Harrison Co., Sacred Heart, [JC]
209 Cross St., Hopedale, 43976. Tel: 740-942-2211; Email: fkihm@diosteub.org. Rev. Frederick C. Kihm.
Res. & Mailing Address: 143 E. South St., Cadiz, 43907. Email: harrcntcath@frontier.net.
Church: 205 Cross St., Hopedale, 43976.
Ironton, Lawrence Co.
1—St. Joseph Parish, [JC]
905 S. Fifth St., P.O. Box 499, Ironton, 45638.
Tel: 740-532-0712; Email: stjoelaw@roadrunner.com. Revs. David L. Huffman; Matthew W.J. Gossett.
Catechesis Religious Program—315 S. 6th St., Ironton, 45638. Jane Rudmann, D.R.E. Students 58.
2—St. Lawrence Parish, [JC]
905 S. Fifth St., P.O. Box 499, Ironton, 45638-0499.
Tel: 740-532-0561; Email: stjoelaw@roadrunner.com. Revs. David L. Huffman; Matthew W.J. Gossett.
School—St. Lawrence Central Grade School, (Grades PreK-6), 315 S. 6th St., Ironton, 45638.
Tel: 740-532-5052; Fax: 740-532-5082; Email: jcm-1@sbcglobal.net; Web: irontoncatholicschools.org. Mr. Paul Mollett, Prin.; Mr. James Christopher Monte, Prin.; Kathy Kratzenberg, Librarian. Lay Teachers 10; Students 99.
High School—St. Joseph Central High School, (Grades 7-12), 912 S. 6th St., Ironton, 45638.
Tel: 740-532-0485; Fax: 740-532-3699; Email: chris.monte@irontoncatholicschools.org; Web: irontoncatholicschools.com. Rev. David L. Huffman. Lay Teachers 12; Students 96.
Convent—615 Center St., Ironton, 45638.
Lafferty, Belmont Co., St. Mary, [CEM] Closed. For inquiries for parish records please contact St. Mary, St. Clairsville.
Little Hocking, Washington Co., St. Ambrose, [CEM]
5080 School House Rd., Little Hocking, 45742.
Tel: 740-423-7422; Email: rgallagher@diosteub.org; Web: stambroseohio.org. Rev. Robert A. Gallagher.
Catechesis Religious Program—Students 40.
Lore City, Guernsey Co., SS. Peter and Paul, [CEM] Closed. Now an oratory of Christ Our Light, Cambridge.
Lowell, Washington Co., Our Lady of Mercy, [CEM]
5001 Lowell Hill Rd., Lowell, 45744.
Tel: 740-896-2207; Email: olm.churchlowell@gmail.com. Rev. Timothy J. Shannon.
Malvern, Carroll Co., St. Francis Xavier (1848) [CEM]
P.O. Box 275, Minerva, 44657. Tel: 330-868-4498; Email: smstgabriel@frontier.com. Rev. Victor Cinson.
Church: 125 Carrollton St., Malvern, 44644.
Tel: 330-868-4498; Email: smstgabriel@frontier.com; Web: stgabriel-stfrancis.org.
Catechesis Religious Program—Students 4.
Marietta, Washington Co., Basilica of St. Mary of the Assumption, [CEM 2]
506 Fourth St., Marietta, 45750. Tel: 740-373-3643; Fax: 740-376-2956; Web: www.stmarysmarietta.org. Very Rev. Msgr. John Michael Campbell; Rev. Joshua Erickson, Parochial Vicar.
School—Basilica of St. Mary of the Assumption School, (Grades PreK-8), 320 Marion St., Marietta, 45750. Tel: 740-374-8181; Fax: 740-374-8602; Email: mollyfrye@stmaryscatholic.org; Web: stmarys.k12.oh.us. Susan Rauch, Prin.; Molly Frye, Prin. Lay Teachers 21; Students 156.
Marietta College Campus Ministry, 506 Fourth St., Marietta, 45750. Email: mcampbell@diosteub.org.
Catechesis Religious Program—Students 90.
Martins Ferry, Belmont Co., St. Mary, [CEM]
20 N. Fourth St., Martins Ferry, 43935.
Tel: 740-633-1416; Email: stmarymf@sbcglobal.net. Rev. Thomas Marut.
School—St. Mary Central, (Grades PreK-8), 24 N. Fourth St., Martins Ferry, 43935. Tel: 740-633-5424; Fax: 740-633-5462; Email: maryc.nichelson@omeresa.net; Web: www.smcmartinsferry.weebly.com. Mary Carolyn Nichelson, Prin. Aides 2; Lay Teachers 9; Preschool 30; Students 120.
Maynard, Belmont Co., St. Stanislaus, Closed. For inquiries for parish records please contact St. Mary, St. Clairsville.
McConnelsville, Morgan Co., St. James
257 E. Bell Ave., McConnelsville, 43756. Web: StJamesMcConnelsville.org. P.O. Box 331, Beverly, 45715. Tel: 740-984-2555; Email: contact@StJamesMcConnelsville.org. Revs. Timothy J. Kozak; Paul Walker, Pastor Emeritus, (Retired).
Miltonsburg, Monroe Co., St. John the Baptist, [CEM 2]
35560 Miltonsburg-Calais Rd., Woodsfield, 43793.
Tel: 740-472-0187; Email: dgaydosik@diosteub.org. Mailing Address: 334 S. Main St., Woodsfield, 43793. Rev. David L. Gaydosik.
Minerva, Carroll Co., St. Gabriel the Archangel
400 West High, P.O. Box 275, Minerva, 44657.
Tel: 330-868-4498; Email: smstgabriel@frontier.com. Rev. Victor Cinson.
Catechesis Religious Program—Students 69.
Mingo Junction, Jefferson Co.
1—St. Agnes, [JC]
Mailing Address: 204 St. Clair Ave., Mingo Junction, 43938-1047. Tel: 740-535-1491; Email: offices@stagnesmingo.org; Web: www.stagnesmingo.org. Rev. James M. Dunfee, M.A., S.T.L.; Deacon Paul D. Ward.
Catechesis Religious Program—Twinned with Triumph of the Cross, Steubenville. Students 10.
2—Annunciation, Closed. Parish records can be found at St. Agnes Church, Mingo Junction.
3—St. Bernadette, Closed. Sacramental records are located at St. Agnes, Mingo Junction.
Morges, Carroll Co., St. Mary, [CEM]
8012 Bachelor Rd, P.O. Box 690, Waynesburg, 44688. Tel: 330-627-4664; Email: atozzi@neo.rr.com. Rev. Anthony R. Batt.
Neffs, Belmont Co., Sacred Heart, Closed. See St. John, Bellaire.
Nelsonville, Athens Co., St. Mary of the Hills, Consolidated with St. Andrew, Nelsonville and St. Patrick, Buchtel to form St. Mary of the Hills.
31 Republic Ave., Glouster, 45732. Tel: 740-767-3068 ; Email: stmary@nelsonvilletv.com. Rev. Msgr. Donald E. Horak, Admin., (Retired).
Pine Grove, Lawrence Co., St. Mary, [CEM]
905 S. Fifth St., P.O. Box 499, Ironton, 45638-0499.
Tel: 740-532-0712; Email: stjoelaw@roadrunner.com. Revs. David L. Huffman; Matthew W.J. Gossett.
Piney Fork, Jefferson Co., St. Therese, Closed. For inquiries for Sacramental records please see St. Casimir, Adena.
Pomeroy, Meigs Co., Sacred Heart, [CEM] Sacramental records are at Christ the King University Parish, Athens.
161 Mulberry Ave., Pomeroy, 45769.
Tel: 740-992-5898; Tel: 740-592-2711; Fax: 740-593-8602; Email: wserbonich@athenscatholic.org; Web: www.sacredheartpomeroy.com. Mailing Address: 75 Stewart St., Athens, 45701. Revs. Mark A. Moore; Thomas A. Nelson, Parochial Vicar; Deacon Daniel P. Murray.
Powhatan Point, Belmont Co., St. John Vianney, Closed. Merged into St. Mary, Shadyside.
Richmond, Jefferson Co., St. John Fisher
7457 St. Hwy. 152, Richmond, 43944.
Tel: 740-765-4142; Email: jmccoy@diosteub.org. Rev. John J. McCoy Jr.
St. Clairsville, Belmont Co., St. Mary's
218 W. Main St., St. Clairsville, 43950.
Tel: 740-695-9993; Tel: 740-695-2076; Email: office@stmaryschurchstc.com; Web: www.stmaryschurchstc.com. Mailing Address: 212 W. Main St., St. Clairsville, 43950. Very Rev. Thomas A. Chillog, M.Div.; Rev. Matthew W.J. Gossett; Deacon Charles J. Schneider.
Res.: 230 W. Main St., St. Clairsville, 43950.
School—St. Mary Central Grade School, (Grades PreSchool-8), 226 W. Main St., St. Clairsville, 43950. Tel: 740-695-3189; Fax: 740-695-3851; Email: nannette.kennedy@omeresa.net; Web: stmarycentral.com. Mrs. Nannette Kennedy, Prin. Clergy 2; Lay Teachers 12; Students 163.
Catechesis Religious Program—Email: DRE@stmaryschurchstc.com. Michal Zabrecky, D.R.E. Students 105.
Shadyside, Belmont Co., St. Mary's (1946)
350 E. 40th St., Shadyside, 43947. Tel: 740-676-0051 ; Fax: 740-671-9776; Web: bnspcatholic.org. c/o 3745 Tallman Ave., Bellaire, 43906. Rev. Daniel Heusel, M.Div., J.C.L.
Catechesis Religious Program—Students 16.
Smithfield, Jefferson Co., Our Lady, Queen of Peace, [JC] Closed. For inquiries for Sacramental records please see St. Casimir, Adena.
Temperanceville, Belmont Co., St. Mary's, [CEM]
55699 Marietta St, Barnesville, 43713.
Tel: 740-425-2181; Email: assumptionandstmarychurches@yahoo.com. Mailing Address: 306 W. Main St., Barnesville, 43713. Rev. David Cornett.
Tiltonsville, Jefferson Co., St. Joseph (1917)
Mailing Address: P.O. Box 8, Tiltonsville, 43963-

0008. Tel: 740-859-4018; Email: sj-sl@comcast.net; Web: stjosephstlucyparishes.org. Very Rev. William D. Cross, M.Div., J.C.L.
Res.: 204 Mound St., Tiltonsville, 43963-1017.
Catechesis Religious Program— (Combined with St. Lucy, Yorkville) Students 7.

TORONTO, JEFFERSON CO.

1—ST. FRANCIS OF ASSISI, [JC]
409 Grant St., Toronto, 43964. Tel: 740-537-4433; Email: sfsjtoronto@sbcglobal.net; Web: www.sfsjtoronto.com. Mailing Address: 1225 N. River Ave., Toronto, 43964. Rev. Thomas A. Vennitti.
Catechesis Religious Program—Judy Koehnlein, D.R.E. Students 27.

2—ST. JOSEPH'S, [JC]
1225 N. River Ave., Toronto, 43964.
Tel: 740-537-4433; Email: sfsjtoronto@sbcglobal.net; Web: www.sfsjtoronto.com. Rev. Thomas A. Vennitti.
Catechesis Religious Program—Judy Koehnlein, D.R.E. Students 9.

VINCENT, WASHINGTON CO., ST. AMBROSE, Consolidated with St. Ambrose, Little Hocking.

WINTERSVILLE, JEFFERSON CO.

1—BLESSED SACRAMENT, [JC]
852 Main St., Wintersville, 43953-3870.
Tel: 740-264-0868; Email: mail@wintersvilleparishes.org; Web: www.wintersvilleparishes.org. Rev. Msgr. Kurt H. Kemo, J.C.L., M.Div.; Revs. Michael Gossett; Vincent J. Huber, M.Ed., S.T.B., In Res., (Retired); Deacons Mark A. Erste; Dr. Thomas E. Graham. Merged with Our Lady of Lourdes, Wintersville.
Please see Catholic Central High School, Bishop John King Mussio Central Junior High School and Bishop John King Mussio Elementary School located in the Institution section.
Catechesis Religious Program— Merged with Steubenville Catholic Faith Formation Program. Barbara VanBeveren, DRE. Students 24.

2—OUR LADY OF LOURDES, [JC]
1521 Bantam Ridge Rd., Wintersville, 43953.
Tel: 740-264-0868; Email: mail@wintersvilleparishes.org; Web: www.wintersvilleparishes.org. Mailing Address: 852 Main St, Wintersville, 43953. Rev. Msgr. Kurt H. Kemo, J.C.L., M.Div.; Rev. Michael Gossett; Deacons Mark A. Erste; Dr. Thomas E. Graham. Merged with Blessed Sacrament, Wintersville.
Please see Catholic Central High School, Bishop John King Mussio Central Junior High School & Bishop John King Mussio Central Elementary School located in the Institution section.

WOODSFIELD, MONROE CO., ST. SYLVESTER, [CEM]
332 S Main St, Woodsfield, 43793. Tel: 740-472-0187; Email: dgaydosik@diosteub.org; Web: www.monroecountycatholic.org. Mailing Address: 334 S Main St, Woodsfield, 43793. Rev. David L. Gaydosik.
Res.: 38867 Briar Ridge Rd., Woodsfield, 43793.
School—Central Grade School, (Grades PreSchool-8), 119 Wayne St., Woodsfield, 43793.
Tel: 740-472-0321; Fax: 740-472-1994; Email: nsss_rguiler@seovec.org. Robyn Guiler, Prin. Clergy 2; Lay Teachers 11; Students 117.
Catechesis Religious Program—Students 4.

YORKVILLE, JEFFERSON CO., ST. LUCY'S
P.O. Box 8, Tiltonsville, 43963-0008.
Tel: 740-859-4018; Fax: 740-859-6041; Email: sj-sl@comcast.net; Web: stjosephstlucyparishes.org. Very Rev. William D. Cross, M.Div., J.C.L.

DIOCESAN MISSIONS

BLOOMINGDALE, JEFFERSON CO., ST. THOMAS MORE MISSION, Closed. Sacramental records are located at St. John Fisher, Richmond.

CHAUNCEY, ATHENS CO., ST. JUDE MISSION, Closed. Sacramental records are located at St. Paul Church, Athens.

CRESCENT, BELMONT CO., ST. ELIZABETH MISSION, Closed. Sacramental records are located at St. Stanislaus Church, Maynard.

FREEPORT, HARRISON CO., ST. MATTHIAS MISSION
143 E. South St., Cadiz, 43907. Tel: 740-942-2211; Email: harrcntcath@frontier.net. Rev. Frederick C. Kihm.
Church: 11 5 W. Main St, Freeport, 43973.

HAMMONDSVILLE, JEFFERSON CO., NATIVITY OF OUR LORD MISSION, Closed. Sacramental records are located at St. Joseph Church, Toronto.

JEWETT, HARRISON CO., OUR LADY OF PERPETUAL HELP MISSION, Closed. Sacramental records located at 1435 E. South St., Cadiz, OH 43907.

SARDIS, MONROE CO., ST. JOHN BOSCO MISSION, [CEM]
37325 Fifth Ave., Sardis, 43946. Tel: 740-472-0187; Email: dgaydosik@diosteub.org. 334 S. Main St., Woodsfield, 43793. Rev. David L. Gaydosik.

TAPPAN LAKE, HARRISON CO., CHRIST THE KING SUMMER MISSION, Closed. Sacramental records are located at: 143 E. South St., Cadiz 43907. Tel: 740-942-2211.

TUPPER PLAINS, MEIGS CO., OUR LADY OF LORETTO CHURCH, Closed. Sacramental records are located at Sacred Heart Church, Pomeroy.

On Duty Outside the Diocese:
Rev. Msgr.—
Wippel, John, Ph.D., S.T.L., M.A., 8101 Connecticut Ave., Chevy Chase, MD 20815. Tel: 301-593-9345; Tel: 202-319-6648
Revs.—
Calabrese, Charles L., 5729 Ridgerock Rd., Fort Worth, TX 76132. Tel: 817-945-9401
Maxfield, Edward A. Jr., S.T.B., S.T.L., Casa Santa Maria, Piazza della Pilotta, 1, 00187, Rome, Italy.

Retired:
Most Rev.—
Sheldon, Gilbert I., D.D., D.Min., (Retired), Steubenville, OH
Rev. Msgrs.—
Boehm, James A., (Retired), 1266 Norberry Ct., #21, Cranberry Township, PA 16066-5116
Coyne, George R., (Retired), 67330 Ebbert Rd., S. Unit 2, Saint Clairsville, 43950. Tel: 740-296-5038
Froehlich, Mark J., (Retired), 67261 Lakeview Ave., Belmont, 43718
Gaughan, Patrick E., (Retired), 7700 Redman Ln., Reynoldsburg, 43068. Tel: 614-447-0668
Giannamore, Anthony J., (Retired), 709 Brockton Pl. E., Sun City Center, FL 33573. Tel: 813-633-3553
Horak, Donald E., (Retired), 24 Marietta Ave., Athens, 45701. Tel: 740-249-4339
Kawa, Robert J., (Retired), 912 Ferry St., Apt. B1, Beverly, 45715
Myers, William R., (Retired), 3505 Calumet Rd., Apt 2B, Ludlow Falls, 45339. Tel: 937-719-3235
Pasquinelli, Frederick A., (Retired), Harbour Senior Living of South Hills, 1320 Greentree Rd., Rm. 209, Pittsburgh, PA 15220. Tel: 412-592-3644
Petronek, Thomas C., (Retired), 1810 National Rd., B3-109, Wheeling, WV 26003
Revs.—
Borer, Robert D., (Retired), 421 Huston Hills Dr., Cambridge, 43725. Tel: 740-435-0105
Cencula, Leonard T., (Retired), 1127 Euclid Ave., Apt. 1009, Cleveland, 44115. Tel: 740-632-4624
Deasio, August J., M.A., (Retired), 935 Yellow Mills Rd., Shortsville, NY 14548. Tel: 716-289-3074
DiRenzo, Michael J., (Retired), 2731 Englewood Dr., Melbourne, FL 32940. Tel: 321-253-3303
Graven, Thomas J., (Retired), P.O. Box 603, Huntington, WV 25710. Tel: 304-736-7937
Heinz, Walter E., (Retired), 5700 Bayshore Rd., Lot 244, Palmetto, FL 34221. Tel: 701-541-5029
Holler, Martin J., (Retired), 75 Stewart St., Athens, 45701. Tel: 740-592-2289
Huber, Vincent J., M.Ed., S.T.B., (Retired), P.O. Box 2613, Wintersville, 43953. Tel: 740-317-4939
Magary, Thomas A., (Retired), 4339 Steuben Woods Dr., 43953. Tel: 740-296-1898
Martinosky, Joseph A., (Retired), 2340 Airport Dr., Rm. 204, Columbus, 43219. Tel: 614-416-6172
Mascolino, Charles E., (Retired), 164 Vireo Dr., Wintersville, 43953. Tel: 740-266-9032
Massucci, Joseph D., (Retired), 840 Warrington Place, Dayton, 45419-3646
Reischman, Virgil, (Retired), 50300 State Rte. 145, Woodsfield, 43793. Tel: 740-472-5627
Safraniec, Joseph N., (Retired), St. Francis Way, Eagan, MN 55123-1167. Tel: 651-405-6705
Saprano, Samuel, (Retired), 930 Debbie Ct., Dayton, 45414. Tel: 937-609-3099
Tornes, Dale F., (Retired), P.O. Box 1226, Uniontown, 44685. Tel: 740-541-8129
Tuttle, Richard J., (Retired), 108 Crystal Cove, Kissimmee, FL 34759. Tel: 863-853-2985
Walker, Paul, (Retired), 43 N. 9th St., Apt. 411, Mc Connelsville, 43756. Tel: 740-651-7404; Tel: 740-651-5070.

Permanent Deacons:
Adams, Richard G., 660 Ross Park Blvd., 43952. Tel: 740-283-4564
Dr. Carson, Donald Scott, 173 Grosvenor St., Athens, 45701. (2016)
Cerrato, Dominic, 2910 Bisbee Dr., Joliet, IL 60432. Tel: 740-944-1846. (On Duty Outside the Diocese)
Erste, Mark A., 330 Muskett Rd., Bloomingdale, 43910. Tel: 740-944-1653
Dr. Graham, Thomas E., 178 Anthony Dr., Wintersville, 43953. (2016)
Kovach, Edward G., 1109 Ridge Ave., 43952. (2016)
Maedke, Thomas F., 491 Westwood Dr., 43952. Tel: 740-381-2115
Miletic, Stephen F., 131 Crawford Ave., 43952. Tel: 740-264-9477
Miravalle, Mark, 315 High St., Hopedale, 43976. Tel: 740-444-4407; Tel: 740-283-3771 (FUS); Tel: 740-697-2277
Murray, Daniel P., 7779 LeMaster Rd., Athens, 45701. Tel: 740-797-9017
Pettie, Paul, 1591 San Carlos St., St. Augustine, FL 32080-5480. Tel: 904-471-4541. (Inactive)
Poyo, Ralph, 1106 Jackson Pl., 43952. Tel: 740-314-5528
Redington, Randall, 401 Rosemont Ave., 43952. Tel: 740-266-7255
Schneider, Charles J., 38675 National Rd., Bethesda, 43719. (2016)
Ward, Paul D., 3129 Glendwell Ave., 43952. (2016)
Weisand, Lee V., 115 Marshall Rd., Marietta, 45750. Tel: 740-374-1400.

INSTITUTIONS LOCATED IN DIOCESE

[A] COLLEGES AND UNIVERSITIES

STEUBENVILLE. *Franciscan University of Steubenville*, (Grades Associate-Masters), 1235 University Blvd., 43952. Tel: 740-283-3771;
Fax: 740-283-6472; Email: admissions@franciscan.edu; Web: www.franciscan.edu. Rev. Sean Sheridan, T.O.R., Pres.; William Gorman, COO; Richard Rollino, Vice Pres. of Finance; Mr. David M. Skiviat, Vice Pres. Finance & Admin.; Dr. Daniel R. Kempton, Vice Pres., Academic Affairs; Mr. Brenan Pergi, Vice Pres. Human Res.; Mr. David Schmiesing, Vice Pres. Student Life; Mr. Joel Recznik, Vice Pres., Enrollment Mgmt.; Mr. Michael Hernon, Vice Pres. Advancement; Mrs. Kimberly Sponseller, Exec. Dir., Mktg & Comm.; Mr. Daniel Miles, Exec. Asst. to the Pres.; Nancy Oliver, Dir.; Amy Leoni, Librarian; Revs. Brian Cavanaugh, T.O.R., Assoc. in Information Technology; Nathan Malavolti, T.O.R., VP Pastoral Care & Evangelization; Donald S. Frinsko, T.O.R., Theology Prog.; Dominic Scotto, T.O.R., Adjunct Prof. in Theology; Joseph Yelenc, T.O.R., Biology Prof.; Gregory Plow, T.O.R., Dir. Priestly Discernment Prog.; Matthew Russick, T.O.R., Campus Min., Austrian Prog.; Shawn Roberson, T.O.R., Univ. Chap.; Richard Martignetti, O.F.M.; Jonathan McElhone; John Shanahan, T.O.R., Local Min. & Pastoral Assoc.; Seraphim Beshoner, T.O.R., Asst. Dir. Priestly Discernment Prog. & Asst. Univ. Chap.; Bros. John Paul McMahon, T.O.R., House Treas.; David Dodd, Pastoral Assoc.; Nathan Meckey, T.O.R., Pastoral Assoc. Brothers 3; Clergy 6; Religious Teachers 6; Lay Teachers 220; Priests 13; Sisters 9; Students 2,518.

[B] HIGH SCHOOLS, CENTRAL

STEUBENVILLE. *Catholic Central High School*, (Grades 9-12), 320 West View, 43952. Tel: 740-264-5538;
Fax: 740-264-5443; Email: tcostello@steubenvillecatholiccentral.org; Web: www.steubenvillecatholicschools.org. Thomas Costello, Prin.; Mrs. Judith Lucas, Admin. Lay Teachers 20; Priests 1; Students 224; Chaplain 1.

BELLAIRE. *St. John Central High School*, 3625 Guernsey St., Bellaire, 43906. Tel: 740-676-4932;
Fax: 740-676-4934; Email: jarett.kuhns@omeresa.net; Web: sjcirish.org. Mr. Jarett Kuhns, Prin. Religious Teachers 1; Lay Teachers 14; Sisters 1; Students 30.

[C] JUNIOR-SENIOR CENTRAL HIGH SCHOOLS

IRONTON. *St. Joseph Central*, (Grades 7-12), 912 S. Sixth St., Ironton, 45638. Tel: 740-532-0485;
Fax: 740-532-3699; Email: chris.monte@irontoncatholicschools.org. Mr. James Christopher Monte, Prin. Religious Teachers 1; Lay Teachers 11; Students 87; Total Staff 13.

[D] CENTRAL JUNIOR HIGH SCHOOLS

STEUBENVILLE. *Bishop John King Mussio Central Junior High School*, (Grades 7-8), 320 W. View Ave., Ste. 2, 43952. Tel: 740-346-0028;
Fax: 740-346-0070; Email: santinone@bishopmussiojh.org; Web: www.steubenvillecatholicschools.org. Theresa Danaher, Prin. Lay Teachers 11; Students 108.

[E] ELEMENTARY SCHOOLS, CENTRAL

STEUBENVILLE. *Bishop John King Mussio Central Elementary School*, (Grades PreK-6), 100 Etta Ave., 43952. Tel: 740-264-2550; Fax: 740-266-2843; Email: tdanaher@bishopmussiojh.org; Web: www.steubenvillecatholicschools.org. Theresa Danaher, Prin. Religious Teachers 2; Lay Teachers 26; Students 392.

[F] GENERAL HOSPITALS

STEUBENVILLE. *Trinity Health System*, Administration, 4000 Johnson Rd., 43952. Tel: 740-264-8360; Tel: 740-264-8110; Fax: 740-264-8108; Email: jgratzmiller@trinityhealth.com; Web: www.trinityhealth.com. Rev. Thomas R. Nau, Chap. Bed Capacity 500; Nurses 381; Tot Asst. Annually 5,608,000; Total Staff 1,590; LPNs 22; Admissions 8,064; Outpatients 232,141; Emergency Room 35,183; Births 490; Nurse Anesthetists 19.

Trinity Medical Center, West, Administration, 4000 Johnson Rd., 43952. Tel: 740-264-8000; Fax: 740-264-8108; Email: jgratzmiller@trinityhealth.com; Web: www.trinityhealth.com. Rev. Thomas R. Nau, Chap.

Trinity Medical Center, East, Administration, 380 Summit Ave., 43952. Tel: 740-264-8000; Fax: 740-264-8108; Email: jgratzmiller@trinityhealth.com. Sr. Nancy Ferguson, O.S.F., Dir.

Trinity Health System Foundation, 380 Summit Ave., 43952. Tel: 740-283-7791; Fax: 740-283-7538 ; Email: jedmiston@trinityhealth.com. Rev. Thomas R. Nau, Chap.

[G] RESIDENTIAL CARE FACILITY

CARROLLTON. *St. John Villa*, 701 Crest St., N.W., P.O. Box 457, Carrollton, 44615. Tel: 330-627-9789; Fax: 330-627-4826; Email: swilliamson@stjohnsvilla.net; Web: stjohnsvilla.net. Timothy Everline, Pres. Residential facility for persons with developmental disabilities.

St. John's Villa Bed Capacity 55; Faculty 108; Residents 49; Tot Asst. Annually 49; Total Staff 108; Adult Day Services/Vocational Habilitation 40; Non-Medical Transportation 40.

[H] MONASTERIES AND RESIDENCES OF PRIESTS AND BROTHERS

STEUBENVILLE. *Diocesan Brotherhood of Immaculate Heart of Mary*, Villa Maria Motherhouse, 609 N. Seventh St., 43952. Tel: 740-283-2462; Email: dcarroll@diosteub.org. Bro. Dominic Carroll, I.H.M., Supr.

Brothers of the Immaculate Heart of Mary Professed Brothers 3.

Holy Spirit Friary, 1235 University Blvd., 43952. Tel: 740-283-6403; Fax: 740-283-6348; Email: friary@franciscan.edu; Web: www.franciscan.edu. Revs. Seraphim Beshoner, T.O.R.; Brian Cavanaugh, T.O.R.; Donald S. Frinsko, T.O.R.; Timothy Harris, T.O.R.; Nathan Malavolti, T.O.R.; Richard Martignetti, O.F.M.; Daniel Pattee, T.O.R; Gregory Plow, T.O.R.; Shawn Roberson, T.O.R.; Matthew Russick, T.O.R.; Dominic Scotto, T.O.R.; John Shanahan, T.O.R.; Sean Sheridan, T.O.R.; Joseph Yelenc, T.O.R.; Bro. John Paul McMahon, T.O.R. Brothers 1; Priests 13.

BLOOMINGDALE. *Holy Family Hermitage*, 1501 Fairplay Rd., Bloomingdale, 43910-7971. Tel: 740-765-4511; Fax: 740-765-4511; Email: dcook@diosteub.org; Web: www.camaldolese.org. Revs. Basil Corriere, E.C., Prior; Nicolas Luna, E.C., (Recluse); Stephen Hwang, E.C.; Paul Vankeirsbilck, E.C.; Bros. Anthony Rumpf, First Prof.; Solanus Balleza, E.C., (Novice). Hermits 7.

CARROLLTON. *Opus Angelorum, Inc.*, 164 Apollo Rd., S.E., Carrollton, 44615. Tel: 330-969-9900; Email: frludwig@opusangelorum.org. Revs. Ludwig M. Oppl, O.R.C., Pres.; Matthew Hincks, O.R.C., Treas.; Wolfgang Seitz, O.R.C., Sec.

Order of the Holy Cross, Inc., 164 Apollo Rd., S.E., Carrollton, 44615. Tel: 330-313-1331; Email: frludwig@opusangelorum.org. Revs. Ludwig M. Oppl, O.R.C., Supr.; John Eudes Brohl; Matthew Hincks, O.R.C.; Wolfgang Seitz, O.R.C.; William Wagner, O.R.C.; Bros. Raphael Gotschol; Isaac Yagley, O.R.C.

[I] CONVENTS AND RESIDENCES FOR SISTERS

CARROLLTON. *Sisters of Our Lady of Charity of the Good Shepherd-Carrollton, Inc.*, 620 Roswell Rd., N.W., P.O. Box 340, Carrollton, 44615. Tel: 330-627-7647; Fax: 330-627-4415; Email: peacedovegl@hotmail.com. Sr. Cruz Celia Gomez, R.G.S., Supr.; Rev. Msgr. Gene W. Mullett, Chap. Sisters 22; Professed Sisters 22.

Sisters of the Holy Cross OA, Inc. Pontifical Right Institute 164 Apollo Rd. S.E., Carrollton, 44615. Tel: 330-476-7020; Email: localsuperior.usa@avecrux.org; Email: oasrsoffice@gmail.com; Web: www.avecrux.org. Sr. Maria Benigna Fischer, Supr. Sisters 7.

[J] ASSOCIATIONS OF THE FAITHFUL

BLOOMINGDALE. *Mount Carmel Hermitage of Ohio, Inc*, 1619 Township Rd. 204, Bloomingdale, 43910. Tel: 740-765-5409; Email: dcook@diosteub.org. Sr. Barbara Wright, O.C.D. Sisters 1.

HOPEDALE. *The Order of the Sacred and Immaculate Hearts of Jesus and Mary*, 48765 Annapolis Rd., Hopedale, 43976. Tel: 740-946-9000; Email: twohearts1@mac.com. Rev. Francis Dankoski, Contact Person. Sisters 2.

TORONTO. *Franciscan Sisters Third Order Regular of Penance of the Sorrowful Mother*, 369 Little Church Rd., Toronto, 43964. Tel: 740-544-5542; Fax: 740-544-5543; Email: franciscans@torsisters.org; Web: www.franciscansisterstor.org. Mother Mary Ann Kessler, T.O.R., Rel. Order Leader. Novices 4; Postulants 2; Sisters 33.

[K] SHRINES

FRANKLIN FURNACE. *Our Lady of Fatima Shrine*, 603 County Rd. 1A, Franklin Furnace, Ironton, 45638-0499. P.O. Box 499, Ironton, 45638-0499. Tel: 740-532-0712; Email: dhuffman@diosteub.org. Rev. David L. Huffman, Tel: 740-532-0712; Fax: 740-534-0557.

[L] NEWMAN CENTERS

ATHENS. *Christ the King University Parish - Ohio University*, 75 Stewart St., Athens, 45701. Tel: 740-592-2711; Fax: 740-593-8908; Email: mmoore@diosteub.org; Web: www.athenscatholic.org. Revs. Thomas A. Nelson, Parochial Vicar; Mark A. Moore.

NELSONVILLE. *Hocking Technical College*, 110 E. Washington St., Nelsonville, 45764. 31 Republic Ave., Glouster, 45732. Tel: 740-767-3068; Email: dhorak@diosteub.org. Rev. Msgr. Donald E. Horak, Dir., (Retired).

Campus Ministry / Newman Center, Res.: Holy Cross Church, 31 Republic Ave., Glouster, 45732. Tel: 740-767-3068; Email: dhorak@diosteub.org. Rev. Msgr. Donald E. Horak; Contact Person, (Retired).

RIO GRANDE. *Rio Grande University*, 85 State St., Gallipolis, 45631. Tel: 740-446-0669; Email: stlouis85@att.net. Rev. Thomas F. Hamm Jr., Contact Person.

ST. CLAIRSVILLE. *Ohio University - Eastern*, c/o St. Mary's Church, 212 W. Main St., St. Clairsville, 43950. Tel: 740-695-9993; Fax: 740-695-6503; Email: office@stmaryschurchstc.com. Very Rev. Thomas A. Chillog, M.Div., Contact Person.

[M] MISCELLANEOUS LISTINGS

STEUBENVILLE. *Boy Scouts*, 7457 State Hwy. 152, Richmond, 43944. Tel: 740-765-4142; Email: jmccoy@diosteub.org. Rev. John J. McCoy Jr., Dir. Total Staff 2.

Campaign for Human Development, Office of Family & Social Concerns, 422 Washington St., P.O. Box 969, 43952. Tel: 740-282-3631; Fax: 740-282-3327; Email: msantin@diosteub.org; Web: www.diosteub.org. Michele Santin, Dir.

**Catholics United for the Faith, Inc.*, 85882 Water Works Rd., Hopedale, 43976-8600. Tel: 740-283-2484; Email: administrativeassistant@cuf.org; Web: www.cuf.org. Philip Gray, Pres.

**Dietrich von Hildebrand Legacy Project*, 1235 University Blvd., 43952. Tel: 740-263-3002; Fax: 740-263-3002; Email: info@hildebrandproject.org; Web: www.hildebrandproject.org. John Henry Crosby, Pres.

**Dirty Vagabond Ministries, Inc.*, 1819 Plum St., P.O. Box 4284, 43952. Tel: 720-635-0857; Email: Karen@dirtyvagabond.com; Web: www.dirtyvagabond.com. Robert Lesnefsky, Founder; Karen Reynolds, Pres.

**Fraternity of Priests, Inc.*, P.O. Box 442, 43952. Tel: 740-283-4400; Email: contact@fraternityofpriests.org; Web: www.fraternityofpriests.org. Rev. Robert Franco, Apostolic Admin.

Lay Employees Pension Plan, 422 Washington St., P.O. Box 969, 43952. Tel: 740-282-3631; Fax: 740-282-1409; Email: shughes@diosteub.org; Web: diosteub.org. Shannon Minch-Hughes, Dir.

Mt. Calvary Cemetery Association, 94 Mt. Calvary Ln., 43952. Tel: 740-264-1331; Fax: 740-264-9203; Email: mtcalvarycemetery@att.net. Richard Pizzoferrato, Supt.

**Pastoral Solutions Institute*, 234 St. Joseph Dr., 43952. Tel: 740-266-6461; Email: gpopcak@CatholicCounselors.com; Web: www.catholiccounselors.com. Gregory K. Popcak, Pres.

**St. Paul Center for Biblical Theology*, 1468 Parkview Cir., 43952. Tel: 740-264-9535; Fax: 740-283-4011; Email: scotthahn@stpaulcenter.com; Web: www.stpaulcenter.com. Dr. Scott Hahn, Pres. The St. Paul Center is also the parent organization for Emmaus Road Publishing, Emmaus Academic, and the international theological journal Nova et Vetera.

Twelve Rivers Foundation, 221 Aten Rd., Munsonville, NH 03457. P.O. Box 4857, 43952. Tel: 740-314-0007; Email: office@lciaustria.org; Web: www.lciaustria.org. Jennifer Healy, Pres. We do business as The Language and Catechetical Institute (LCI).

BLOOMINGDALE. *Apostolate for Family Consecration* aka Catholic Familyland/John Paul II Holy Family Center, 3375 County Rd. 36, Bloomingdale, 43910-7903. Tel: 740-765-5500; Fax: 740-765-5561; Email: info@afc.org; Web: www.afc.org. Theresa Schmitz, Pres.

CARROLLTON. *Our Lady of Charity Center Caritas House, Inc.*, 620 Roswell Rd., N.W., P.O. Box 340, Carrollton, 44615. Tel: 330-627-1641; Email: cs.provincial@gssweb.org. Sr. Francisca Aguillon, Member.

GALLIPOLIS. *RCIA*, 85 State St., Gallipolis, 45631. Tel: 740-446-0669; Email: thamm@diosteub.org. Rev. Thomas F. Hamm Jr., Dir.

GLOUSTER. *Marriage Encounter*, 422 Washington St., 43952. Tel: 740-282-3631; Email: tchillog@diosteub.org. Very Rev. Thomas A. Chillog, M.Div., Dir.

RELIGIOUS INSTITUTES OF MEN REPRESENTED IN THE DIOCESE

For further details refer to the corresponding bracketed number in the Religious Institutes of Men or Women section.

[0680]—*Brothers of the Immaculate Heart of Mary*—I.H.M.

[0230]—*Camaldolese Hermits of the Congregation of Monte Corona*—ER. CAM.

[0740]—*Marians of the Immaculate Conception (B.V.M. Mother of Mercy Province)*—M.I.C.

[0400]—*The Order of Canons Regular of The Holy Cross*—O.S.C.

[]—*The Order of the Sacred & Immaculate Hearts of Jesus & Mary.*

[0560]—*Third Order of Saint Francis. (Sacred Heart Prov.)*—T.O.R.

RELIGIOUS INSTITUTES OF WOMEN REPRESENTED IN THE DIOCESE

[0370]—*Carmelite Sisters of the Most Sacred Heart of Los Angeles*—O.C.D.

[]—*Daughters of Holy Mary of The Heart of Jesus* (Spain).

[1115]—*Dominican Sisters of Peace* (Columbus, OH)—O.P.

[1230]—*Franciscan Sisters of Christian Charity, Manitowac, WI*—O.S.F.

[1830]—*Our Lady of Charity of the Good Shepherd - Carrollton, Inc.*—R.G.S.

[2970]—*School Sisters of Notre Dame*—S.S.N.D.

[0500]—*Sisters of Charity of Nazareth*—S.C.N.

[]—*Sisters of St. Francis of Perpetual Adoration*—O.S.F.

[1600]—*Sisters of St. Francis of the Martyr St. George*—F.S.G.M.

[]—*Sisters of the Holy Cross* (Carrollton)—O.A.

An asterisk (*) denotes an organization that has established tax-exempt status directly with the IRS and is not covered by the USCCB Group Ruling.

Diocese of Stockton

(Dioecesis Stocktoniensis)

Most Reverend

MYRON J. COTTA

Bishop of Stockton; ordained September 12, 1987; appointed Titular Bishop of Muteci and Auxiliary Bishop of Sacramento January 24, 2014; installed March 25, 2014; appointed Bishop of Stockton January 23, 2018; installed March 15, 2018. *Chancery Office, 212 N. San Joaquin St., Stockton, CA 95202.*

Most Reverend

STEPHEN E. BLAIRE, D.D.

Retired Bishop of Stockton; ordained April 29, 1967; appointed Titular Bishop of Lamzella on March 20, 1990; ordained Auxiliary Bishop of Los Angeles May 31, 1990; appointed Bishop of Stockton January 19, 1999; installed March 16, 1999; retired January 23, 2018. *Office: 212 N. San Joaquin St., Stockton, CA 95202.* Tel: 209-466-0636.

Chancery Office: 212 N. San Joaquin St., Stockton, CA 95202. Tel: 209-466-0636; Fax: 209-941-9722.

ESTABLISHED JANUARY 13, 1962

Square Miles 9,938.

Comprises six Counties in the State of California-viz., Alpine, Calaveras, Mono, San Joaquin, Stanislaus and Tuolumne.

Legal Title: The Roman Catholic Bishop of Stockton, a Corporation Sole.
For legal titles of parishes and diocesan institutions, consult the Chancery Office.

STATISTICAL OVERVIEW

Personnel	
Bishop	1
Retired Bishops	1
Priests: Diocesan Active in Diocese	42
Priests: Diocesan Active Outside Diocese	5
Priests: Retired, Sick or Absent	19
Number of Diocesan Priests	66
Religious Priests in Diocese	17
Total Priests in Diocese	83
Extern Priests in Diocese	21
Ordinations:	
Transitional Deacons	2
Permanent Deacons in Diocese	57
Total Brothers	1
Total Sisters	46
Parishes	
Parishes	35
With Resident Pastor:	
Resident Diocesan Priests	32
Resident Religious Priests	3
Missions	14
Pastoral Centers	1
Professional Ministry Personnel:	
Sisters	46
Welfare	
Catholic Hospitals	1
Total Assisted	177,431
Health Care Centers	1
Total Assisted	11,139
Special Centers for Social Services	1
Total Assisted	81,108
Educational	
Students from This Diocese	3
Diocesan Students in Other Seminaries	3
Total Seminarians	6
High Schools, Diocesan and Parish	2
Total Students	1,166
Elementary Schools, Diocesan and Parish	11
Total Students	2,782
Catechesis/Religious Education:	
High School Students	3,389
Elementary Students	14,123
Total Students under Catholic Instruction	21,466
Teachers in the Diocese:	
Priests	4
Brothers	3
Sisters	4
Lay Teachers	185
Vital Statistics	
Receptions into the Church:	
Infant Baptism Totals	5,229
Minor Baptism Totals	360
Adult Baptism Totals	174
Received into Full Communion	246
First Communions	5,597
Confirmations	4,400
Marriages:	
Catholic	763
Interfaith	84
Total Marriages	847
Deaths	1,483
Total Catholic Population	237,165
Total Population	1,407,409

Former Bishops—Most Revs. HUGH A. DONOHOE, D.D., Ph.D., ord. June 14, 1930; appt. Titular Bishop of Taium and Auxiliary of San Francisco Aug. 2, 1947; cons. Oct. 7, 1947; appt. to Stockton Feb. 21, 1962; installed April 24, 1962; transferred to Fresno Aug. 27, 1969; died Oct. 26, 1987; MERLIN J. GUILFOYLE, D.D., J.C.D., ord. June 10, 1933; appt. Titular Bishop of Bulla and Auxiliary of San Francisco Aug. 15, 1950; cons. Sept. 21, 1950; translated to Bishop of Stockton Nov. 19, 1969; installed Jan. 13, 1970; retired Feb. 26, 1980; died Nov. 20, 1981; ROGER M. MAHONY, D.D., ord. May 1, 1962; appt. Titular Bishop of Tamascani and Auxiliary of Fresno, Jan. 7, 1975; cons. March 19, 1975; translated Bishop of Stockton Feb. 26, 1980; installed April 17, 1980; elevated to Archbishop of Los Angeles July 16, 1985; elevated to Cardinal, June 28, 1991; DONALD W. MONTROSE, D.D., ord. May 7, 1949; appt. Titular Bishop of Vescovio and Auxiliary of Los Angeles March 25, 1983; cons. May 12, 1983; translated Bishop of Stockton Dec. 19, 1985; installed Feb. 20, 1986; retired Jan. 19, 1999; died May 7, 2008.; STEPHEN E. BLAIRE, D.D., ord. April 29, 1967; appt. Titular Bishop of Lamzella on March 20, 1990; ord. Auxiliary Bishop of Los Angeles May 31, 1990; appt. Bishop of Stockton Jan. 19, 1999; installed March 16, 1999; retired Jan. 23, 2018.

Chancery Office—212 N. San Joaquin St., Stockton, 95202. Tel: 209-466-0636; Fax: 209-941-9722; Web: www.stocktondiocese.org.

Vicar General—Rev. Msgr. RICHARD J. RYAN, J.C.D., V.G.

Chancellor—MS. DYAN HOLLENHORST, Email: chancellor@stocktondiocese.org.

Executive Assistant—MS. ALICIA ALCANTARA, Email: aalcantara@stocktondiocese.org.

Vicar for Priests—Rev. Msgr. JOHN ARMISTEAD, S.T.L.

Chief Financial Officer—MR. DOUG ADEL.

Director of Human Resources—MS. LINDA DILLON.

Director of Human Resources—MR. THOMAS BUTLER.

Social Action Consultor—Deacon MICHAEL WOFFORD.

Diocesan Tribunal—212 N. San Joaquin St., Stockton, 95202. Tel: 209-466-0636; Fax: 209-464-2617; Web: stocktondiocese.org.

Judicial Vicar—Rev. LUIS GERARDO NAVARRO, J.C.L.

Vice-Officialis—Rev. Msgr. RICHARD J. RYAN, J.C.D., V.G.

Judges—MS. MARLA PRUNEDA, J.C.L.; Rev. DENNIS GRABRIAN, J.C.L.; MS. LYNETTE TAIT, J.C.L.; MRS. DEBORAH A. BARTON, J.C.L.; MS. CHERRY CLARK, J.C.L.

Moderator—Rev. LUIS GERARDO NAVARRO, J.C.L.

Tribunal Personnel—Notaries: PAT CUMPIAN; REBECCA MORENO.

Defenders of the Bond—Rev. KENNETH HARDER, J.C.L.; MR. RAPHAEL S. FRACKIEWICZ, J.C.D.; MS. ELISA UGARTE, J.C.L.; MR. CARLOS J. SACASA, J.C.L.

Presbyteral Council—Members: Rev. Msgr. JOHN M. ARMISTEAD, S.T.L.; Revs. RAMON BEJARANO; MISAEL AVILA; WILLIAM KRAFT; BRANDON M. WARE; MARK WAGNER, S.T.L.; SAMUEL G. WEST; CHAD WAHL; JOHN PETER PRAGASAM; JOSEPH MAGHINAY. Recording Secretary: Rev. ERNESTO MADRIGAL. Ex Officio: Rev. Msgr. RICHARD J. RYAN, J.C.D., V.G. Observer: MS. DYAN HOLLENHORST.

College of Consultors—Members: Rev. Msgr. JOHN ARMISTEAD, S.T.L.; Revs. RAMON BEJARANO; MISAEL AVILA; WILLIAM KRAFT; BRANDON M. WARE; MARK WAGNER, S.T.L.; SAMUEL G. WEST; CHAD WAHL; JOHN PETER PRAGASAM; JOSEPH MAGHINAY. Recording Secretary: Rev. ERNESTO MADRIGAL. Ex Officio: Rev. Msgr. RICHARD RYAN, J.C.D., V.G.

Deans—Revs. JOHN PETER PRAGASAM, Deanery 1; ALVARO H. DELGADO, Deanery 2; Deacon SAMUEL WOODS, Deanery 3; Revs. DAVID DUTRA, Deanery 4; RICHARD E. MORSE, O.S.F.S., Deanery 5; MANUEL F. SOUSA, Deanery 6; MARK WAGNER, S.T.L., Deanery 7; JOHN E. FITZGERALD, V.F., Deanery 8.

The Roman Catholic Welfare Corporation of Stockton—212 N. San Joaquin St., Stockton, 95202. Tel: 209-466-0636; Fax: 209-941-9722.

Diocesan Building Committee—Rev. Msgr. RICHARD J. RYAN, J.C.D., V.G., Chm.; MR. DOUG ADEL; Deacons GREG YEAGER; ALAN MOZNETT; MR. RAYMOND TUNKEL.

Diocesan Finance Council—MR. PAUL SCHAEFER, Chm.; MR. JOSEPH ARIAS; MR. DOUG ADEL, Staff; MR. KEVIN DOUGHERTY; MR. TOM DRISCOLL; MR.

RALPH JUAREZ; Rev. BRANDON M. WARE; MRS. TERESA LOCKE; MR. FRED LEE; MRS. MARIA STOKMAN; Rev. Msgr. RICHARD J. RYAN, J.C.D., V.G., Staff & Consultant; MR. PETER MORELLI; MR. BILL TREZZA.

Personnel Board—Rev. Msgrs. JOHN ARMISTEAD, S.T.L., Ex Officio; RICHARD J. RYAN, J.C.D., V.G., Ex Officio; ROBERT J. SILVA; Revs. JOHN PETER PRAGASAM; BRANDON M. WARE; CESAR MARTINEZ; CHAD WAHL; DAVID DUTRA.

Diocesan Offices and Directors

Apostleship of the Sea—MR. WILLIAM NAHORN, Tel: 209-466-0636.

Catholic Charities—MS. ELVIRA RAMIREZ, Tel: 209-444-5900; Fax: 209-444-5933.

Catholic Youth Organization—212 N. San Joaquin St., Stockton, 95202. Tel: 209-466-0636. MS. GINA RATTO, Dir.

Cemeteries—MR. AL VIGIL, Dir. Cemeteries, Mailing Address: P.O. Box 1137, Stockton, 95201.

Censor Librorum—Rev. JOSE JUAN SERNA, S.T.L.

Apostolado Hispano—MRS. DIGNA RAMIREZ-LOPEZ, Dir., 212 N. San Joaquin St., Stockton, 95202. Tel: 209-466-0636.

Development—MR. VICTOR MITRE JR., Dir.

Continuing Education of Clergy—Rev. Msgr. JOHN ARMISTEAD, S.T.L., 212 N. San Joaquin St., Stockton, 95202. Tel: 209-466-0636; Fax: 209-941-9722.

Communications Office—JOSEPH DONDERO.

Cursillo Movement-English and Spanish—MR. JESUS GONZALES, Dir.

Ecumenism—Office of the Bishop.

Office of Religious Education—212 N. San Joaquin St., Stockton, 95202. Tel: 209-466-0636. MRS. GRACIELA GARZA-AYALA, Dir. Contact this office for various CCD Centers.

Office for Deacon Formation—Sr. WANDA BILLION, M.S.C.

Office for Seminarians—Sr. WANDA BILLION, M.S.C.

Engaged Encounter—MR. MICHAEL BABOWAL; CRYSTAL BABOWAL, Tel: 209-645-0267.

School of Ministry—212 N. San Joaquin St., Stockton, 95202. Tel: 209-466-0636. MR. DOMINADOR BOMBONGAN JR.

Episcopal Liaison of Catholic Charismatic Renewal—English: Deacon WILLIAM BRENNAN, Ph.D., 13 Pardee Ln., Stockton, 95207. Tel: 209-474-0571. Spanish: Rev. JOSE DOMINGO RUIZ, Tel: 209-465-0416.

Liturgical Commission—

Executive Committee—Most Rev. MYRON J. COTTA, D.D., Pres., Ex Officio; Deacon JOSE REYES, Chm.; MR. MICHAEL SCHMITZ, Ex Officio.

Members-At-Large—MS. CAROLYN CANO; MS. JASON JEFFERY; Rev. JOSE SALVADOR LEDESMA; MRS. MARGARITA REYES; MR. GERARD SCHEUERMANN; Deacon DAVID SPRINGER; MR. DENNIS TARICCO; MRS. EILEEN YEAGER.

Newman Apostolate—The Newman House at University of the Pacific MS. LISANDRO PENA, Dir.; Rev. MATTHEW O'DONNELL, Cal. State Stanislaus, 1 University Cir., Turlock, 95382. Tel: 209-667-3122.

Filipino Pastoral Ministry—Rev. JOSEPH MAGHINAY, Tel: 209-472-2150.

Office of Catechumenate—212 N. San Joaquin St., Stockton, 95202. Tel: 209-466-0636. MR. MICHAEL SCHMITZ.

Permanent Diaconate Program—Mailing Address: P.O. Box 232, Lockeford, 95237. Tel: 209-727-3912. Deacon GREGORY YEAGER, Dir.

Diaconate Formation—Sr. WANDA BILLION, M.S.C.

Pontifical Association of Holy Childhood—MRS. DIGNA RAMIREZ-LOPEZ, 212 N. San Joaquin St., Stockton, 95202.

Propagation of the Faith212 N. San Joaquin St., Stockton, 95202. Tel: 209-466-0636. MS. ALICIA ALCANTARA.

Life and Dignity Office—MRS. KIM FUENTES, Dir., 212 N. San Joaquin St., Stockton, 95202. Tel: 209-466-0636.

Vicar for Religious Women—Sr. WANDA BILLION, M.S.C., 212 N. San Joaquin St., Stockton, 95202. Tel: 209-466-0636.

Catholic Schools Office—MRS. MARIAN DEGROOT GRAHAM, Dir. Schools; MRS. JUDEE SANI, Curriculum & Instruction Coord.; MS. KELLIE O'CONNOR, Curriculum & Instruction Coord.

Vocations—212 N. San Joaquin St., Stockton, 95202. Tel: 209-466-0636. Revs. CESAR MARTINEZ MARTINEZ SOTO; ERNESTO MADRIGAL; SAMUEL G. WEST; TOM ORLANDO.

Office for Worship—MR. MICHAEL SCHMITZ, Dir.

Office of Youth Ministry—VACANT, English Coord.; JOSE LOPEZ CEJA, Spanish Coord., 212 N. San Joaquin St., Stockton, 95202. Tel: 209-466-0636.

Catholic Committee on Scouting—VACANT, Tel: 209-814-0499.

Migrant Ministry Team—MR. JOSE LOPEZ-CEJA, Leader; Sisters ALICIA LOPEZ; LOURDES GONZALES, M.G.Sp.S.

Victim Assistance Coordinator—MS. CONNIE JACOB, Email: cjacob@stocktondiocese.org.

CLERGY, PARISHES, MISSIONS AND PAROCHIAL SCHOOLS

CITY OF STOCKTON

(SAN JOAQUIN COUNTY)

1—CATHEDRAL OF THE ANNUNCIATION (PASTOR OF) (1944)
425 W. Magnolia St., 95203-2412. Tel: 209-463-1305; Email: info@annunciationstockton.org; Web: www.annunciationstockton.org. Rev. Msgr. John M. Armistead, S.T.L.; Revs. John Hieu Ngo, Parochial Vicar; Cesar Martinez Martinez Soto; Deacons Greg Yeager, Pastoral Assoc.; Michael Wofford; Martin Baeza. In Res., Rev. Luis Gerardo Navarro, J.C.L.
School—Cathedral of the Annunciation School, (Grades K-8), 1110 N. Lincoln St., 95203. Tel: 209-444-4000; Fax: 209-444-4013; Email: jloewen@annunciationsaints.org; Web: www.annunciation-school.org. Beverly Fondacabe, Prin. Lay Teachers 14; Students 263.
Catechesis Religious Program—Email: lbobadilla@annunciationstockton.org. Liliana Bobadilla, D.R.E. Students 460.

2—ST. BERNADETTE CHURCH (PASTOR OF) (1955)
2544 Plymouth Rd., 95204. Tel: 209-465-3081; Email: stbernstockton@gmail.com; Email: gcasillas.stbern@gmail.com; Web: www.saintbernadettes.com. Rev. John Peter Pragasam, Admin.
Catechesis Religious Program—Email: mdelgadobraun@yahoo.com. Students 209.

3—ST. EDWARD CHURCH (PASTOR OF) (1967) (Hispanic)
731 S. Cardinal Ave., 95215. Tel: 209-466-3020; Fax: 209-466-0719; Email: Stedwardsoffice@aol.com; Email: Stedwardccd@aol.com. Rev. Alvaro H. Delgado.
Catechesis Religious Program—Students 523.

4—ST. GEORGE CHURCH (PASTOR OF) (1951)
120 W. Fifth St., 95206-2695. Tel: 209-463-3413; Fax: 209-463-0167; Email: george_parish52@yahoo.com. Revs. Martin Garcia Marin; Dante U. Dammay, (Philippines); Deacon Kevin Amen; Marie Lou Paulino, Business Mgr.; Linda Reyes, D.R.E.
School—St. George School, (Grades K-8), 144 W. Fifth St., 95206. Tel: 209-463-1540; Fax: 209-463-2707; Email: principal@stgeorgeschoolstockton.org; Web: stgeorgeschoolstockton.org. Ms. Deborah Fox, Prin. Lay Teachers 4; Students 72.
Endowment—St. George REALMS Foundation.
Catechesis Religious Program—Linda Reyes, D.R.E.; Marie Lou Paulino, Business Mgr. Students 571.
Mission—Good Shepherd, P.O. Box 354, French Camp, San Joaquin Co. 95231. Tel: 209-982-0578; Fax: 209-858-4836. Deacon Matthew Joseph.

5—ST. GERTRUDE CHURCH (PASTOR OF) (1913) [CEM] (Mexican-American)
1655 E. Main St, 95205. Tel: 209-466-0278; Email: gertrudeschurch@sbcglobal.net; Web: www.stgertrudestockton.com. Rev. Jose Reyes-Cedillo, O.R.C., (Mexico); J. Santos Licea Anguiano; Deacon Louis Juarez.
Res.: 1663 E. Main St., 95205.
Catechesis Religious Program—Tel: 209-969-5345. Ms. Vicky Rand, D.R.E. Students 393.

6—ST. LINUS CHURCH (PASTOR OF) (1956) (Hispanic—Asian)
2620 S. B St., 95206. Tel: 209-465-1430; Fax: 209-475-8535; Email: linusparish@gmail.com. Rev. Benjamin Puente, (Mexico); Deacon Joe Orzal.
Catechesis Religious Program—Students 577.

7—ST. LUKE CHURCH OF STOCKTON (PASTOR OF) (1951)
3847 N. Sutter St., 95204. Tel: 209-948-3450; Email: khall@stlukestockton.us; Web: stlukestockton.us. Revs. Ramon Zarate, S.D.B., (Philippines); Paul Hung Tran, S.D.B., (Vietnam); Marc Rougeau; Ms. Victoria Kimball, Parish Admin.; Deacons Haet Tansaeng, (Laos); Glenn Sell.
School—St. Luke School, (Grades K-8), 4005 N. Sutter St., 95204. Tel: 209-464-0801; Fax: 209-466-1150; Email: jrieschick@stlukestockton.com; Email: dcurtis@stlukestockton.com; Web: stlukestockton.com. Mr. John Rieschick, Prin. Religious Teachers 1; Lay Teachers 12; Students 226.
Catechesis Religious Program—Tel: 209-462-0410; Tel: 209-981-0837; Email: srodetta@aol.com; Email: irmamsc@yahoo.com. Sr. Odetta Bonini, D.R.E.; Irma Cruz, D.R.E. Students 430.
Convent—230 E. Atlee St., 95204.

8—ST. MARY OF THE ASSUMPTION CHURCH (PASTOR OF) (1851)
203 E. Washington St., 95202. Tel: 209-948-0661; Email: OurLady1851@gmail.com. Revs. Edwin Musico, (Philippines); Camilo Garcia, (Mexico) Admin.; Deacons Jorge Torres; Mel R. Tahod. In Res., Revs. Christian Ezeh; George Okoro.
Catechesis Religious Program—Ms. Martha Hernandez, D.R.E. Students 205.

9—ST. MICHAEL CHURCH OF STOCKTON (PASTOR OF) (1921) (Italian)
Mailing Address: 5882 N. Ashley Ln., 95215-9307. Tel: 209-931-0639; Email: stmike5882@sbcglobal.net; Web: www.stmichaelparish.net. Rev. Msgr. Agustin Gialogo; Deacons Allen Moznett; Ed Formosa. In Res., Rev. Msgr. Richard J. Ryan, J.C.D., V.G.
Catechesis Religious Program—Tel: 209-931-2696; Email: stmichaelcatmin@sbcglobal.net. Students 331.

10—PRESENTATION CHURCH (PASTOR OF) (1952)
6715 Leesburg Pl., 95207. Tel: 209-472-2150; Fax: 209-472-0541; Email: frontdesk@presentationchurch.net; Web: www.presentationchurch.net. 1515 W. Benjamin Holt Dr., 95207. Rev. Msgr. Robert J. Silva; Rev. Joseph Son Nguyen, Parochial Vicar; Jose Maghinay; Deacons Benjamin Joe; William Brennan, Ph.D.; Scott Johnson; Mike Navarec.
School—Presentation School, (Grades K-8), 1635 W. Benjamin Holt Dr., 95207. Tel: 209-472-2140; Fax: 209-320-1515; Email: office@presentationschool.org; Web: www.presentationschool.org. Maria Amen, Prin. Lay Teachers 12; Students 279.
Catechesis Religious Program—1626 McClellan Ave., 95207. Tel: 209-472-2150; Email: religioused@presentationchurch.net. Nancy Gomez, Headmaster. Students 698.

OUTSIDE CITY OF STOCKTON

ANGELS CAMP, CALAVERAS CO., ST. PATRICK CHURCH OF ANGELS CAMP (PASTOR OF) (1856) [CEM] [JC]
820 S. Main St., P.O. Box 576, Angels Camp, 95222. Tel: 209-736-4575; Email: stpatrick's_acamp@sbcglobal.net. Revs. Rolando C. Petronio, (Philippines); Suresh Babu Ery, Parochial Vicar.
Catechesis Religious Program—Tel: 209-736-9180. Students 70.
Missions—St. Patrick—621 Sheep Ranch Rd., Murphys, Murphys Co. 95247. Tel: 209-728-2854.
Our Lady of the Sierra, 1301 Linebaugh Rd., Arnold, Arnold Co. 95223. Tel: 209-795-7625.
St. Ignatius Mission, Poker Flat Community Center, Copperopolis, 95228.

CERES, STANISLAUS CO., ST. JUDE CHURCH (PASTOR OF) (1962) (Hispanic)
3824 Mitchell Rd., Ceres, 95307-9422. Tel: 209-537-0516; Email: stjudeparish@att.net. Revs. Gustavo Quintero V; Ray Abella, O.S.F.S.; Ernesto Madrigal.
Catechesis Religious Program—3824 Mitchell Road, Ceres, 95307. Tel: 209-537-7439 (English Prog.); Tel: 209-538-8136 (Spanish Prog.); Email: sylviaochoastjude@gmail.com. Students 1,624.
Mission—Ntra. Senora de Guadalupe, 425 Broadway Ave., Modesto, Stanislaus Co. 95351. Tel: 209-606-6246.

HUGHSON, STANISLAUS CO., ST. ANTHONY CHURCH OF HUGHSON (PASTOR OF) (1921) [CEM] (Hispanic)
7820 Fox Rd., Hughson, 95326-9309. Email: tom.hollcraft@stanthony-hughson.org. Revs. Armando Vergara; Kondayya Mocherla.
Res.: 2020 Euclid Rd., Hughson, 95326.
Catechesis Religious Program—Tel: 209-883-0694; Email: nikki.sandoval@stanthony-hughson.org; Email: godisgoodallthetme@yahoo.com. Rebeca Beltran, D.R.E.; Nikki Sandoval, D.R.E. Students 559.
Mission—St. Louis, [CEM] 31201 Floto St., La Grange, Stanislaus Co. 95329. Tel: 209-852-0144; Fax: 209-852-0818. Doris Quinones, Contact Person.

LATHROP, SAN JOAQUIN CO., OUR LADY OF GUADALUPE CHURCH (PASTOR OF) (2002)
16200 Cambridge Dr., Lathrop, 95330. Tel: 209-858-4466; Fax: 209-858-4978; Email: guadalupechurchlathrop@gmail.com. Rev. Jose Salvador Ledesma, Admin.; Ms. Maria Pintos.
Catechesis Religious Program—Tel: 209-858-9391. Luz Juarez, DRE. Students 475.

LINDEN, SAN JOAQUIN CO., HOLY CROSS CHURCH (PASTOR OF) (1963) (Italian—Hispanic)
18633 E. Front St., P.O. Box 52, Linden, 95236.

Tel: 209-887-3341; Email: holycrosscatholicchurch@comcast.net; Web: www.holycrosslinden.org. Rev. William Kraft.
Catechesis Religious Program—Tel: 209-887-4063. Students 193.

LOCKEFORD, SAN JOAQUIN CO., ST. JOACHIM CHURCH OF LOCKEFORD (PASTOR OF) (1882) [CEM] (Hispanic)
13392 Lockeford Ranch Rd, P.O. Box 232, Lockeford, 95237. Tel: 209-727-3912; Fax: 209-727-0403; Email: parish@st-joachim.org; Web: www.stjoachimlockeford.com. Rev. Samuel A. Woods.
Catechesis Religious Program—Tel: 209-727-0406; Email: jmccormack@st-joachim.org. Joanna McCormack, D.R.E. Students 208.

LODI, SAN JOAQUIN CO., ST. ANNE CHURCH (PASTOR OF) (1904) [CEM]
Mailing Address: P.O. Box 480, Lodi, 95241.
Tel: 209-369-1907; Fax: 209-369-1971; Email: bware@stanneslodi.org; Email: bharo@stanneslodi.org; Web: www.stanneslodi.org. 215 W. Walnut St., Lodi, 95240. Revs. Brandon M. Ware; Balaswamy Dande; Hung Joseph Nguyen, (Vietnam); Deacons Thomas Driscoll, Ordinary; Porfirio Cisneros; Karl Welsbacher.
Res.: 150 S. Pleasant St., Lodi, 95240.
School—St. Anne's School, (Grades K-8), 200 S. Pleasant St., Lodi, 95240. Tel: 209-333-7580; Email: general@stanneslodi.org. Elizabeth Mar, Prin. Lay Teachers 14; Students 203.
Catechesis Religious Program—Email: parishoffice@stanneslodi.org. Sisters Isabel de la Eucaristia Abril, E.F.M.S., D.R.E.; Azucena Espinoza, E.F.M.S., D.R.E. Students 1,057.
Mission—Mater Ecclesiae, 26500 Sacramento Blvd., Thornton, San Joaquin Co. 95686.

MAMMOTH LAKES, MONO CO., ST. JOSEPH CHURCH OF MAMMOTH LAKES (1939)
58 Ranch Rd., P.O. Box 372, Mammoth Lakes, 93546. Tel: 760-934-6276; Email: info@mammothcatholicchurch.org; Email: vero.st.josephmammothlakes@gmail.com. Rev. Jorge A. Roman.
Missions—Infant of Prague Mission, Bridgeport—
Our Savior of the Mountains Mission, Lee Vining.
Catechesis Religious Program—Veronica Saray, D.R.E. Students 94.

MANTECA, SAN JOAQUIN CO., ST. ANTHONY CHURCH OF MANTECA (PASTOR OF) (1917)
505 E. North St., Manteca, 95336. Tel: 209-823-7197; Email: mary@st-anthonys.org; Web: st-anthonys.org. Revs. Chad Wahl; Gilberto Arango, Parochial Vicar; Christhudasan Varghese, H.G.N., Parochial Vicar; Deacons Jeff Vierra; Ha Nguyen.
Res.: 525 E. North St., Manteca, 95336.
School—St. Anthony School, (Grades PreSchool-8), 323 N. Fremont, Manteca, 95336. Tel: 209-823-4513; Fax: 209-825-7447; Email: susie.dickert@sasmanteca.org; Web: sasmanteca.org. Susan Dickert, Prin. Lay Teachers 11; Students 223.
Catechesis Religious Program—
Tel: 209-823-7197, Ext. 231; Email: laura@st-anthonys.org. Mrs. Laura Perez, D.R.E. Students 597.
St. Vincent de Paul Society—Tel: 209-823-8099.
Endowment—St. Anthony School Educational Foundation, Tel: 209-239-4513.

MODESTO, STANISLAUS CO.

1—HOLY FAMILY CHURCH (PASTOR OF) (2006)
4212 Dale Rd., Modesto, 95356. Tel: 209-545-3553; Fax: 209-545-3332; Email: frontdesk@holyfamilymodesto.org; Email: assistant@holyfamilymodesto.org; Web: holyfamilymodesto.org. Revs. Juan Serna, S.T.L.; Tom Orlando, Parochial Vicar; Deacon Felipe Vallejo.
Catechesis Religious Program—Students 460.
Mission—Our Lady of San Juan de los Lagos, 4643 Flint Ave., Salida, Stanislaus Co. 95368.

2—ST. JOSEPH CHURCH OF MODESTO (PASTOR OF) (1967)
1813 Oakdale Rd., Modesto, 95355.
Tel: 209-551-4973; Email: tmenezes@stjmod.com; Web: www.stjmod.com. Revs. Mark Wagner, S.T.L.; Chandrasekar Cellian Paulraj; Leonardo Di DelCarmen; Deacon Kenneth Ochinero. In Res., Rev. Michael Brady.
Catechesis Religious Program—Students 915.

3—OUR LADY OF FATIMA CHURCH (PASTOR OF) (1951)
505 W. Granger Ave., Modesto, 95350.
Tel: 209-524-7421; Email: dspringer@olfmodesto.org. Most Rev. Stephen E. Blaire, D.D.; Revs. Khoi Pham; Ronnie Manango, Parochial Vicar; Madhu Appanapalle, Parochial Vicar; Editho Mascardo, Chap.; Deacons James Johnson; Juan Vargas.
School—Our Lady of Fatima School, (Grades K-8), 501 W. Granger Ave., Modesto, 95350.
Tel: 209-524-4170; Email: dspringer@olfmodesto.org. Melissa Neder, Prin. Lay Teachers 14; Students 182; Extended Day Care 45.
Catechesis Religious Program—Email: jteixeira@olfmodesto.org. Joyce Teixeira, D.R.E. Students 421.
Endowment—The Monsignor William P. Kennedy Education Foundation, 501 W. Granger Ave., Modesto, 95350. John Resso, Chm.

4—ST. STANISLAUS CHURCH (PASTOR OF) (1881) [CEM]
709 J St., Modesto, 95354. Tel: 209-524-4381; Email: info@ststanscc.org; Web: www.ststanscc.org. Revs. Ramon Bejarano; Yesobu Banka, Parochial Vicar; Marian Korzeniowski, Parochial Vicar; Deacons Jose Reyes; Jim Kottinger; Oscar Cervantes.
School—St. Stanislaus School, (Grades PreSchool-8), 1416 Maze Blvd., Modesto, 95351. Tel: 209-524-9036; Fax: 209-524-4344; Email: principal@ststanscc.org; Web: www.ststanscs.org. Mercedes Hollcraft, Prin. Lay Teachers 14; Students 209.
Catechesis Religious Program—Tel: 209-522-6534; Fax: 209-523-9128; Email: ezamora@ststanscc.org; Email: rjacobo@ststanscc.org. Ermelinda Zamora, Pastoral Min.; Raquel Jacobo, Pastoral Min. 1080 1,080.

NEWMAN, STANISLAUS CO., ST. JOACHIM CHURCH OF NEWMAN (PASTOR OF) (1909) (Spanish—English)
1121 Main St., Newman, 95360. Tel: 209-862-3528; Fax: 209-862-3512; Email: office@stjoachimnewman.org; Web: www.stjoachimnewman.org. Rev. Jorge W. Arboleda, Admin.; Deacon Lance Valez.
Catechesis Religious Program—Tel: 209-862-2878; Email: julievelez1125@msn.com. Students 525.

OAKDALE, STANISLAUS CO., ST. MARY OF THE ANNUNCIATION CHURCH (PASTOR OF) (1902)
1225 Olive St., Oakdale, 95361. Tel: 209-847-2715; Email: stmaryoakdale@gmail.com. Rev. Richard E. Morse, O.S.F.S.; Jesus Montoya, Parochial Vicar.
Catechesis Religious Program—Tel: 209-404-4874; Tel: 209-581-3822; Email: abcorissetto@gmail.com; Email: ftinamarie3@aol.com. Tina Lucas, D.R.E.; Corinne Rissetto, D.R.E. Students 404.

PATTERSON, STANISLAUS CO., SACRED HEART CHURCH OF PATTERSON (PASTOR OF) (1925)
529 I St., Patterson, 95363. Tel: 209-892-9321; Email: sheartpatterson@gmail.com; Web: www.sacredheartpatterson.org. Revs. Richard Rex Hays, C.M.; Nhan Tran.
School—Sacred Heart School, (Grades K-8), 505 M St., Patterson, 95363. Tel: 209-892-3544;
Fax: 209-892-3214; Email: principal@shcs-patterson.org; Web: www.shcs-patterson.org. Heidi Kuliga, Prin. Lay Teachers 18; Students 198.
Catechesis Religious Program—503 M St., Patterson, 95363. Students 728.
Mission—Immaculate Heart of Mary, 22031 H St., Crows Landing, Stanislaus Co. 95313.

RIPON, SAN JOAQUIN CO., ST. PATRICK CHURCH OF RIPON (PASTOR OF) (1878)
19399 E St., Rte. 120 Hwy., Ripon, 95366.
Tel: 209-838-2133; Email: office@stpatricksripon.com. Rev. Raju Gudimala, Parochial Vicar; Deacon Thomas Ciccarelli, Parish Life Coord.
Catechesis Religious Program—19399 East Highway 120, Ripon, 95366. Tel: 209-838-3101; Email: faithformation@stpatricksripon.com. Maria T. Carrillo, D.R.E. Students 358.

RIVERBANK, STANISLAUS CO., ST. FRANCES OF ROME CHURCH (PASTOR OF) (1953)
2827 Topeka St., Riverbank, 95367.
Tel: 209-869-2996; Fax: 209-863-1004; Email: lupe.zamora@sfrriverbank.com; Web: www.stfrancesofrome.org. Rev. Misael Avila; Rev. Msgr. Bonifacio Baldonado; Deacons Richard Williamsen; Librado Ulloa.
Catechesis Religious Program—Mrs. Guadalupe Zamora, D.R.E.; Mrs. Betty Huffman, Coord. Rel. Educ. Students 484.

SAN ANDREAS, CALAVERAS CO., ST. ANDREW CHURCH OF SAN ANDREAS (PASTOR OF) (1963) [CEM]
162 Church Hill Rd., San Andreas, 95249. Rev. Lonachan W. Arouje, (India); Deacon Mark Caruso.
Res.: 261 Sunset, P.O. Box 550, San Andreas, 95249.
Catechesis Religious Program—Web: www.standrewcatholicparish.org. Kate Leiga, D.R.E. Students 37.
Missions—St. Thomas Aquinas—8398 Lafayette St., Mokelumne Hill, Calaveras Co. 95245.
Our Lady of Fatima, 22581 Hwy. 26, West Point, Calaveras Co. 95255.

SONORA, TUOLUMNE CO., ST. PATRICK CHURCH OF SONORA (PASTOR OF) (1851) [CEM 5] [JC]
116 Bradford St., Sonora, 95370. Tel: 209-532-7139; Email: stpats@stpatssonora.org; Web: www.stpatssonora.org. Revs. Samuel G. West; Joseph Thottukadavil; Deacon Michael Kubasek.
Catechesis Religious Program—Email: kathy@stpatssonora.org. Kathy Casas, D.R.E. Students 117.
Missions—Our Lady of Mt. Carmel—Cemetery Rd., Big Oak Flat, Tuolumne Co. 95305.
St. Anne, 22518 Church Ln., Columbia, Tuolumne Co. 95310.

TRACY, SAN JOAQUIN CO., ST. BERNARD CHURCH (PASTOR OF) (1908)
163 W. Eaton Ave., Tracy, 95376. Tel: 209-835-4560; Email: mwhite@st-bernards.org; Web: www.st-bernards.org. Revs. David Dutra; Delfin Tumaca; Carlos Humberto Fierro; Sleevaraj Pasala; Deacon Peter Ryza, Email: pryza@st-bernards.org.
School—St. Bernard's School, (Grades K-8), 165 W. Eaton Ave., Tracy, 95376. Tel: 209-835-8018;
Fax: 209-835-2496; Web: www.st-bernardschool.org. Patricia Paredes, Prin. Lay Teachers 12; Students 194.
Child Care—St. Bernard's Catholic Pre-School and Daycare, 160 W. Beverly Pl., Tracy, 95376.
Tel: 209-835-4560, Ext. 301 & 304; Email: kabellar@st-bernardschool.org. Students 83; Teachers 7.
Catechesis Religious Program—Email: eorozco@st-bernards.org. Elvira Orozco, D.R.E. Students 1,038.

TURLOCK, STANISLAUS CO.

1—OUR LADY OF THE ASSUMPTION OF THE PORTUGUESE CHURCH (1973) (Portuguese)
Mailing Address: P.O. Box 2030, Turlock, 95381.
Tel: 209-634-2222; Fax: 209-634-2366; Email: ahendrex@olassumption.net; Web: www.olassumption.net. 2602 S Walnut RD, Turlock, 95380. Rev. Manuel F. Sousa; Deacon Edwin Santiago
Legal Name: Our Lady of the Assumption of the Portuguese Church (Pastor of)
Res.: 1343 W. Greenway, Turlock, 95380.
Catechesis Religious Program—Ashley Hendrex, C.R.E. Students 315.

2—PASTOR OF ALL SAINTS UNIVERSITY CHURCH
4040 McKenna Dr., Turlock, 95382.
Tel: 209-669-0473; Email: ryegor@allsaintscsus.org; Web: www.allsaintscsus.org. Rev. William McDonald, Admin.
Catechesis Religious Program—Sandra Ortega-Ramos, D.R.E. Students 153.

3—SACRED HEART CHURCH OF TURLOCK (PASTOR OF) (1910)
1301 Cooper Ave., Turlock, 95380. Tel: 209-634-8578; Email: leticia.sacredheart@gmail.com; Email: sralls@shsturlock.org; Web: shparish.net. 1200 Lyons Ave., Turlock, 95380. Revs. J. Patrick Walker, V.F.; Luis Cordeiro; Marcelino Marquino Malana; Kishor Yerpula.
Res.: 650 Rose St., Turlock, 95380.
School—Sacred Heart School, (Grades PreSchool-8), 1225 Cooper Ave., Turlock, 95380. Tel: 209-634-7787; Fax: 209-634-0156. Linda Murphy-Lopes, Prin. Lay Teachers 30; Students 286.
Child Care—Preschool, Tel: 209-667-5512;
Fax: 209-669-9647. Debra Cannella, Prin. Lay Teachers 17; Students 120.
Catechesis Religious Program—Sacred Heart Religious Education, 1201 Cooper Ave. #1, Turlock, 95380. Tel: 209-634-5111; Email: godisgoodallthatme@yahoo.com. Mr. Feliciano Tapia, Dir.

TWAIN HARTE, TUOLUMNE CO., ALL SAINTS CHURCH (PASTOR OF) (1962) [JC]
18674 Cherokee Dr., P.O. Box 642, Twain Harte, 95383. Tel: 209-586-3161; Fax: 209-586-3161; Email: office@omnsanct.org; Web: www.omnsanct.org. Rev. Jeff Wilson; Deacon Joseph Gomes.
Catechesis Religious Program—Noli Farwell, DRE. Students 21.
Mission—St. Joseph, Gardner St., Tuolumne, Tuolumne Co. 95379.

Chaplains of Public Institutions

STOCKTON. *NA Chaderjian Youth Correction Facility*. Vacant.
O.H. Close School, 7650 Newcastle Rd., P.O. Box 213002, 95213-9001. Tel: 209-944-6364;
Tel: 209-944-6516. Deacon Fidel Carrillo Jr., Chap.

FRENCH CAMP. *San Joaquin County Jail*, 999 W. Matthews Rd., French Camp, 95231.
Tel: 209-468-4562. Rev. Alvaro M. Lopez, (Colombia).
San Joaquin General Hospital, 500 W. Hospital Rd., French Camp, 95231. Tel: 209-468-6000. Rev. Alvaro M. Lopez, (Colombia)St. George Church.

JAMESTOWN. *Sierra Conservation Center*, P.O. Box 497, Jamestown, 95327-1213. Tel: 209-984-5291. Deacon Karl Welsbacher, Chap.

TRACY. *Deuel Vocational Institution*, 23500 Kasson Rd., Tracy, 95376. P.O. Box 400, Tracy, 95378-0600. Tel: 209-835-4141, Ext. 5076. Deacon Edwin Santiago, Chap.

On Duty Outside the Diocese:
Rev. Msgr.—
Foster, John J.M., J.C.D.
Revs.—
Campechano, Javier
Illo, Joseph
McDonald, William
Roldan, Jovito, J.C.L.

Absent on Leave:
Revs.—
Garcia, Louis
Gutierrez, Jose Luis
Kelly, Michael.

Retired:
Rev. Msgrs.—
McGovern, Lawrence, S.T.L., (Retired)
Moore, William C., (Retired)
Rocha, Ivo D., (Portugal) (Retired)
Revs.—
Araque, Alvaro U., (Colombia) (Retired)
Curran, Patrick, (Retired)
Guerrero, Lawrence M., (Retired)
Miani, Titian A., (Retired)
Pacheco, Alexandre, (Retired)
Pereira, Robert J., (Retired), P.O. Box 78072, 95267
Pintacura, Michael, (Retired)
Ryan, William, (Retired)
Trainer, Eugene, (Retired)
Wang, John, (Retired)
Zavala, Octavio "Antonio", (Retired).

Permanent Deacons:
Aguilar, Jesus, St. George, St. Edwards Stockton
Amen, Kevin, St. George, Stockton
Baeza, Martin, Cathedral of the Annunciation, Stockton
Brennan, William, Ph.D., Church of the Presentation, Stockton
Broderick, Thomas, (Retired), School of Ministry, Stockton
Canton, Leo, St. George, Stockton
Carrillo, Fidel Jr., St. Patrick, Ripon
Caruso, Mark, St. Andrew, San Andreas
Cervantes, Oscar, St. Stanislaus, Modesto
Ciccarelli, Ernest, St. Joseph, Modesto
Ciccarelli, Thomas, St. Patrick, Ripon
Cisneros, Porfirio, St. Anne, Lodi
Driscoll, Tom Jr., St. Anne, Lodi
Estupinan, Juan, St. Patrick, Ripon
Evans, Garry, Holy Cross, Linden
Flanders, Raymond, (Retired), St. Anthony, Hughson
Formosa, Ed, St. Michael's
Gomes, Joe, All Saints, Twain Harte
Hoblitzell, Ross, (Retired), St. Stanislaus
Houghland, Eric, All Saints University Parish, Turlock
Hungerford, Jared, St. Patrick, Angels Camp
Janukites, James, (Retired), St. George, Stockton
Joe, Benjamin, Church of the Presentation, BVM
Johnson, James, Our Lady of Fatima, Modesto
Johnson, Scott, Church of the Presentation, Stockton
Joseph, Matthew, Good Shepherd Mission, French Camp
Juarez, Louis, St. Gertrude's, Stockton
Kottinger, Jim, (Retired), Our Lady of Guadalupe, Lathrop
Kubasek, Michael, St. Patrick's, Sonora
Magdaleno, Roberto, (Retired), (Retired), St. Mary, Oakdale
Mendez, Juan, (Retired)
Menezes, Lane, All Saints University Parish, Turlock
Moznett, Al, (Retired), St. Michael, Stockton
Navarec, Mike, Church of the Presentation, Stockton
Nguyen, Ha, St. Anthony de Padua, Manteca
Ochinero, Kenneth, (Retired), St. Jude's, Ceres
Orzal, Joe, (Retired), St. George, Stockton
Parolari, Harvey, (Retired), St. Anthony, Manteca
Reyes, Jose, St. Stanislaus, Modesto
Rodgers, Donald, (Retired), Good Shepherd, French Camp
Ryan, John G., (Retired), St. Bernard, Tracy
Ryza, Peter, St. Bernard's, Tracy
Santiago, Edwin, Our Lady of the Assumption, Turlock
Sell, William (Glenn), (Retired), St. Luke's, Stockton
Tahod, Mel R., (Retired), St. Mary's Assumption, Stockton
Tansaeng, Haet, St. Luke, Stockton
Torres, Jorge, St. Mary's, Stockton
Ulloa, Librado, St. Frances of Rome, Riverbank
Vallejo, Felipe, Holy Family, Modesto
Vargas, Juan, Our Lady of Fatima, Modesto
Velez, Lance, St. Joachim, Newman
Vierra, Jeffrey, Our Lady of Guadalupe, Lathrop; St. Anthony of Padua, Manteca
Warren, William E., (Retired), St. Joachim, Lockeford
Welsbacher, Karl, (Retired), St. Anne, Lodi
Whitlock, Ray, (Retired), St. Bernard, Tracy
Williamsen, Richard, St. Francis of Rome, Riverbank
Wofford, Michael, Cathedral of Annunciation, Stockton
Ybarra, Fred, St. Patrick, Copperopolis
Yeager, Gregory, Cathedral of the Annunciation, Stockton.

INSTITUTIONS LOCATED IN DIOCESE

[A] HIGH SCHOOLS, DIOCESAN

STOCKTON. *St. Mary's High School* (1876) 5648 N. El Dorado St., P.O. Box 7247, 95267-0247. Tel: 209-957-3340; Fax: 209-957-0861; Email: jbrusa@saintmaryshighshool.org; Web: www.saintmaryshighschool.org. James Brusa, Pres.; Ms. Kathy Smith, Prin.; Rev. Matthew Kurry Issac, O.S.F.S., Sacramental Min. Non-resident students. Religious Teachers 1; Lay Teachers 51; Priests 1; Students 796.

St. Mary's High School Foundation, 5648 N. El Dorado, 95207. P.O. Box 7247, 95267-0247. Tel: 209-957-3340; Email: jbrusa@saintmaryshighschool.org. James Brusa, Pres.

MODESTO. *Central Catholic High School* (1966) 200 S. Carpenter Rd., Modesto, 95351. Tel: 209-524-9611; Fax: 209-524-4913; Email: sawicki@cchsca.org; Web: www.cchsca.org. Mr. Jim Pecchenino, Pres., Email: pecchenino@cchsca.org; Mr. Bruce Sawyer, Prin.; Mrs. Theresa Hubert, Librarian, Email: thubert@cchsca.org. Non-resident students. Administrators 6; Religious Teachers 1; Lay Teachers 26; Students 370.

Central Catholic High School Foundation, 200 S. Carpenter Rd., Modesto, 95351. Tel: 209-524-6822; Fax: 209-524-5646; Email: hart@cchsca.org. Mr. Jim Pecchenino, Pres.

[B] CATHOLIC CHARITIES

STOCKTON. *Catholic Charities of the Diocese of Stockton* (1980) 1106 N. El Dorado St., 95202. Tel: 209-444-5900; Fax: 209-444-5933; Email: eramirez@ccstockton.org; Web: www.ccstockton.org. Ms. Elvira Ramirez, Exec. Dir.; Rev. Msgr. John M. Armistead, S.T.L., Chm. Tot Asst. Annually 22,382; Total Staff 100.

Catholic Charities Services for Seniors & Caregivers, 1106 N. El Dorado St., 95202. Tel: 209-444-5923; Fax: 209-444-5929; Email: ddimas@ccstockton.org. Diane Dimas, Prog. Mgr. Homemaker (Housekeeping), Personal Care, Respite Care Program, Caregiver Respite & Caregiver Chore. Tot Asst. Annually 1,442; Total Staff 11.

Multipurpose Senior Service Program (MSSP) Care Management, Respite In-Home, Emergency Call Device, Minor Home Repair, Home Safety Evaluations, Transportation. 1106 N. El Dorado St., 95202. Tel: 209-444-5928; Fax: 209-444-5929; Email: rdarcy@ccstockton.org. Arletha Mark, Supvr. Tot Asst. Annually 160; Total Staff 5.

Immigration Legal Services, 1106 N. El Dorado St., 95202. Tel: 209-444-5910; Fax: 209-460-1624; Email: agonzalez@ccstockton.org. Alexandra Gonzalez, Prog. Mgr. Naturalization/Citizenship, Green Card Renewal/Replacement, Special Case Waivers, Adjustment of Status, Family Immigration, Family Petitions, TPS, Affidavit of Support. Deferred Action for Childhood Arrivals (DACA) Tot Asst. Annually 3,452; Total Staff 7.

Catholic Charities ESL/Citizenship Education Program Offers English as a Second Language (ESL)/Citizenship classes to help prepare Legal Permanent Residents (LPRs) for Citizenship and advance their integration in the United States. 1106 N. El Dorado St., 95202. Tel: 209-444-5910; Fax: 209-460-1624; Email: agonzalez@ccstockton.org. Alexandra Gonzalez, Prog. Mgr. Tot Asst. Annually 789; Total Staff 7.

Food Bank, 1106 N. El Dorado St., 95202. Tel: 209-444-5900; Email: aguzman@ccstockton.org. Ana Guzman, Nutrition Assistance Prog. Mgr. Tot Asst. Annually 5,793; Total Staff 2.

Environmental Justice Program (EJ), 1106 N. El Dorado St., 95202. Tel: 209-396-6921; Email: ypark@ccstockton.org; Web: ejstockton.org. Yolanda Park, Prog. Mgr. Serves to educate and motivate Catholics in the Stockton Diocese to a deeper reverence and respect for God's creation and to engage local parishes in activities to resolve environmental problems, particularly as they affect the poor. Tot Asst. Annually 1,880; Total Staff 3.

Stanislaus County Senior Services, 2351 Tenaya Dr., Ste. D, Modesto, 95354. P.O. Box 576488, Modesto, 95357. Tel: 209-529-3784; Fax: 209-529-6083; Email: srios@ccstockton.org. Simona Rios, Prog. Mgr. Homemaker Program, Long-term Care, Ombudsman Program, Senior Transportation, Social Security Representative Payee Program, Stanislaus Elder Abuse Prevention Alliance. Tot Asst. Annually 3,831; Total Staff 10.

Mother Lode Senior Services, 88 Bradford St., Sonora, 95370. Tel: 209-532-7632; Fax: 209-532-8448; Email: cdriver@ccstockton.org. Catherine Driver, Prog. Dir. Ombudsman Program, Legal Advocacy for Seniors Program, Elder Abuse Prevention Program, Older Adult Outreach and Engagement Program, Rural Health Alliance Project. Health care access, basic needs assistance (GRACE). Tot Asst. Annually 1,041; Total Staff 5.

Health Care Access, 1106 N. El Dorado St., 95202. Tel: 209-444-5940; Fax: 209-943-2587; Email: jgalindo@ccstockton.org. Joanna Galindo, Prog. Mgr. Services: Assist adults & children with enrollment for health insurance and utilization of health care benefits. Assists children to access dental care. Tot Asst. Annually 2,240; Total Staff 3.

Nutritional Assistance Services Program (Calfresh), 1106 N. El Dorado St., 95202. Tel: 209-444-5944; Fax: 209-943-2587; Email: aguzman@ccstockton.org. Ana Guzman, Prog. Mgr. This program is an outreach and eligibility screening campaign designed to increase education and access by eligible individuals and families in San Joaquin and Stanislaus counties to the Supplemental Nutrition Assistance Program (SNAP). Tot Asst. Annually 1,834; Total Staff 4.5.

St. Anne's Place Drop-in center for homeless women and children. 531 W. Lockeford St., Lodi, 95240. Tel: 209-224-8506; Email: jgalindo@ccstockton.org. Jessica Gonzalez, Prog. Coord. Tot Asst. Annually 209; Total Staff 1.

Family Counseling Services The Family Counseling Services Program provides low-cost, short-term counseling services as well as community education workshops and mental health resources and referrals in Stanislaus and San Joaquin Counties and Mother Lode. 2351 Tenaya Dr., Ste. D, Modesto, 95354. P.O. Box 576488, Modesto, 95357. Tel: 209-593-6113; Fax: 209-529-6083; Email: jjimenez@ccstockton.org. Manuel Jimenez, Program Mgr. Tot Asst. Annually 1,096; Total Staff 3.5.

Parenting Education Parenting education classes to assist families through parishes. 1106 N. El Dorado St., 95202. Tel: 209-444-5915; Email: mperez@ccstockton.org. Maria Perez, Prog. Coord. Total Staff 2.5.

[C] GENERAL HOSPITALS

STOCKTON. *St. Joseph's Behavioral Health Center* (1993) 2510 N. California St., 95204. Tel: 209-461-2000; Fax: 209-464-2270; Email: Robert.Sahagian@DignityHealth.org; Web: www.stjosephscanhelp.org. Paul Rains, Pres. Sponsored by the Dominican Sisters of San Rafael, California. Bed Capacity 35; Tot Asst. Annually 11,193; Total Staff 157.

St. Joseph's Medical Center of Stockton (1899) 1800 N. California St., 95204-9008. Tel: 209-943-2000; Fax: 209-461-3299; Email: Robert.Sahagian@DignityHealth.org; Web: www.stjosephscares.org. Donald J. Wiley, Pres. Sponsored by the Dominican Sisters of San Rafael, California. Bed Capacity 335; Sisters 3; Tot Asst. Annually 177,431; Total Staff 2,539.

[D] HOMES FOR AGED

STOCKTON. *Casa Manana Inn*, 3700 N. Sutter St., 95204. Tel: 209-466-4046; Fax: 209-466-3450. Melissa Appling, Admin. Total in Residence 162; Total Staff 4.

[E] CONVENTS AND RESIDENCES FOR SISTERS

STOCKTON. *Dominican Sisters of San Rafael Convent*, 5042 Gadwall Cir., 95207. Tel: 209-956-6953; Email: maureen.mcinerney@sanrafaelop.org; Web: sanrafaelop.org. Sr. Maureen McInerney, Prioress. Sisters 2.

Eucharistic Franciscan Missionary Sisters, 1630 N. Hunter St., 95204. Tel: 209-462-3906; Cell: 209-762-0860; Email: srisabelabril0306@gmail.com. P.O. Box 480, Lodi, 95241. Sr. Isabel de la Eucaristia Abril, E.F.M.S., Supr. Sisters 3.

Missionaries Guadalupanas of the Holy Spirit, 3119 Cass Ln., 95206. Tel: 213-300-1067; Email: alopez@guadalupeusa.org. Sisters Alicia Lopez, Supr.; Maria Malvais, Vocations Dir.; Rosa Hernandez Casillas, Sec.; Lourdes Gonzalez, Ministry. Sisters 4.

Sacro Costato Missionary Sisters (1908) St. Luke's

Convent, 230 E. Atlee St., 95204.
Tel: 209-462-6533; Fax: 209-464-5342; Email: mscstockton@comcast.net. Sr. Rina Odetta Bonini, Supr. Sisters 5.

MODESTO. *Sisters of the Cross of the Sacred Heart of Jesus* (1897) Cloistered Convent. 1320 Maze Blvd., Modesto, 95351. Tel: 209-526-3525;
Fax: 209-426-9757; Email: sistersofthecross@sbcglobal.net; Email: rcmodesto7@hotmail.com; Web: www.religiosasdelacruz.org.mx. Sr. Maria Guerra, Supr. Sisters 9.

PATTERSON. *Daughters of the Holy Spirit* (1706) Sacred Heart Convent. Daughters of the Holy Spirit, 624 N. 64th St., Patterson, 95363. Tel: 209-892-3410; Email: lucilledhs@gmail.com. Sr. Lucille Carreau, D.H.S., Assoc. Advisor. Sisters 1.

TRACY. *The Daughters of the Cross of Liege* (1833) St. Bernard Convent, 165 W. Eaton Ave., Tracy, 95376. Tel: 209-835-7391; Fax: 209-830-6137; Email: fc1833@sbcglobal.net. Sr. Ann Venita Britto, F.C., Supr. Sisters 3.

[F] RETREAT CENTERS

COPPEROPOLIS. *Madonna of Peace Renewal Center* (1982) (Youth Facility) 2010 Hunt Rd., P.O. Box 71, Copperopolis, 95228. Tel: 209-785-2157 (Office) . Mr. John Powell, Pres. Total in Residence 2; Total Staff 2.

[G] MISCELLANEOUS

STOCKTON. *Bishop Ministry Appeal Trust* (2014) 212 N. San Joaquin St., 95202. Tel: 209-466-0636; Email: aalcantara@stocktondiocese.org. Rev. Brandon M. Ware.

The Bishop's Educational Foundation, Diocese of Stockton, 212 N. San Joaquin St., 95202-2409.
Tel: 209-466-0636; Fax: 209-941-9722; Email: aalcantara@stocktondiocese.org. Rev. Msgr. Richard Ryan, J.C.D., V.G., Vicar Gen.

Catholic Professional and Business Club, 212 N. San Joaquin St., 95202-2409. Tel: 209-466-0636;
Fax: 209-941-9722; Email: aalcantara@stocktondiocese.org; Email: cpbcmodesto@gmail.com. Lori Pecchenino, Member; Cathy Pietanza, Member.

Church for Tomorrow Fund, 212 N. San Joaquin St., 95202. Tel: 209-466-0636; Email: aalcantara@stocktondiocese.org. Mr. Rupert Hall, Trustee.

Instituto Fe y Vida (1994) 1737 W. Benjamin Holt Dr., 95207. Tel: 209-951-3483; Fax: 209-478-5357; Email: jmatty@feyvida.org; Email: amdewhirst@feyvida.org; Web: www.bibliaparajovenes.org; Web: www.FeyVida.org. Carmen Cervantes, Exec. Dir. Total Staff 7.

St. John Vianney House of Formation, 4101 N. Manchester, 95207. Tel: 209-463-1305; Email: cmartinez@annunciationstockton.org. Rev. Cesar Martinez Martinez Soto, Contact Person.

St. Joseph's Foundation of San Joaquin, 1800 N. California St., 95204. Tel: 209-467-6347;
Fax: 209-461-6893; Email: abby.newton@dignityhealth.org; Web: www.supportstjosephshospital.org. Drew Gagner, Exec. Dir.

St. Mary's High School Foundation (1982) 5648 N. El Dorado St., P.O. Box 7247, 95267-0247.
Tel: 209-957-3340; Email: jbrusa@saintmaryshighschool.org; Web: www.saintmaryshighschool.org. James Brusa, Pres.

San Lorenzo Ruiz De Manila (1988) 1658 Sicily St., 95206. Natie R. Banasihan, Pres. & Founder.

SEEDS (Assistance for Catholic Education within the Roman Catholic Diocese of Stockton) (2004) 212 N. San Joaquin St., 95202. Tel: 209-466-0636;
Fax: 209-463-5937; Email: rmoreno@stocktondiocese.org; Email: mgraham@stocktondiocese.org. Jeanette Gerlomes, Pres.; Ms. Carla Donaldson, Vice Pres.; Christie Banuelos, Treas.; Sarah Brooks, Sec.; Marian Graham, Member.

LODI. *St. Anne's Endowment* (1986) 215 W. Walnut St., Lodi, 95240. P.O. Box 480, Lodi, 95241.
Tel: 209-369-1907; Fax: 209-369-1971; Email: t.driscoll@sbcglobal.net; Email: bware@stanneslodi.org. Rev. Brandon M. Ware, Pres.

MODESTO. *The Catholic Social Service Guild* (1975) 2524 Peppermint Dr., Modesto, 95355.
Tel: 209-577-5191; Email: marialbaker@sbcglobal.net. Maria Baker, Pres. Tot Asst. Annually 36,000.

Central Catholic High School Foundation, 200 Carpenter Rd., Modesto, 95351. Tel: 209-524-6822; Fax: 209-524-5646; Web: www.cchsca.org. Ms. Joan Hart, Dir. Volunteer Board Members 25.

Father John C. Silva Education Foundation, P.O. Box 4304, Modesto, 95352. Tel: 209-524-4381;
Fax: 209-524-1910; Email: CBanuelos@aol.com. Rev. Ramon Bejarano.

**Mary Mother of God Mission Society*, 1700 Mchenry Ave. Ste. 80, Modesto, 95350. 1736 Milestone Cir., Modesto, 95357. Tel: 209-408-0728;
Fax: 209-408-0728; Email: usoffice@vladmission.org; Web: www.vladmission.org. Very Rev. Myron Effing, C.J.D., Supr.; Rev. Daniel Maurer, Assoc. Pastor; Vicky Trevillyan, Dir. 501(c)3 nonprofit organization providing spiritual and financial support for the work of the Roman Catholic missionary work in Eastern Russia.

The Monsignor William P. Kennedy Education Foundation, 501 W. Granger Ave., Modesto, 95350.
Tel: 209-524-4170; Fax: 209-524-7713; Email: dpringer@olfmodesto.org. John Resso, Chm.; Deacon David Springer, Sec.

TURLOCK. *The Father McElligott Sacred Heart School Foundation*, P.O. Box 1254, Turlock, 95381.
Tel: 209-669-5336; Email: shs.development@yahoo.com. Jackie Cotta, Exec. Dir.; Mr. Al Vigil, Dir. Cemetery Oper.; Jennifer Prieto, Asst. Dir. Oper. Total Staff 2.

RELIGIOUS INSTITUTES OF MEN REPRESENTED IN THE DIOCESE

For further details refer to the corresponding bracketed number in the Religious Institutes of Men or Women section.

[0220]—*Congregation of the Blessed Sacrament*—S.S.S.
[]—*Congregation of the Mission* (Vincentians)—C.M.
[0260]—*Discalced Carmelite Friars*—O.C.D.
[0920]—*Oblates of St. Francis De Sales* (Toledo-Detroit Prov.)—O.S.F.S.
[]—*Operarios del Reino de Christo*—O.R.C.
[1190]—*Salesians of St. John Bosco*—S.D.B.
[]—*Society of St. Sulpice (Sulpicians)*—S.S.

RELIGIOUS INSTITUTES OF WOMEN REPRESENTED IN THE DIOCESE

[]—*Daughters of Mary Immaculate Conception*.
[0780]—*Daughters of the Cross of Liege*—F.C.
[0820]—*Daughters of the Holy Spirit* (Putnam, CT)—D.H.S.
[1150]—*Eucharistic Franciscan Missionary Sisters*—E.F.M.S.
[1845]—*Guadalupan Missionaries of the Holy Spirit*—M.G.Sp.S.
[2575]—*Sisters of Mercy of the Americas*—R.S.M.
[1630]—*Sisters of St. Frances of Penance & Christian Charity*—O.S.F.
[]—*Sisters of the Cross of the Sacred Heart of Jesus* (Mexico City, Mexico)—R.C.S.C.J.
[1960]—*Sisters of the Holy Family* (San Francisco)—S.H.F.
[]—*Verbum Dei Missionaries*.

DIOCESAN CEMETERIES AND MAUSOLEUMS

STOCKTON. *San Joaquin Cemetery and Mausoleum*, 719 E. Harding Way, 95204. Tel: 209-466-6202; Email: avigil@sjcemeteries.com. P.O. Box 1137, 95201. Mr. Al Vigil, Dir. Cemetery Oper.

ESCALON. *St. John Cemetery*, 17871 S. Carrolton Rd., Escalon, 95320. Tel: 209-838-7134; Email: avigil@sjcemeteries.com. P.O. Box 1137, 95201. Mr. Al Vigil, Dir. Cemetery Oper.

MODESTO. *St. Stanislaus Cemetery and Chapel Crypts*, 1141 Scenic Dr., Modesto, 95350.
Tel: 209-529-3905; Email: stanislaussaint@gmail.com. P.O. Box 3073, Modesto, 95353. Mr. Al Vigil, Dir. Cemetery Oper.; Nina Gordan, Office Mgr.

NECROLOGY

† O'Neill, Robert, (Retired), Died Apr. 9, 2018
† Rajanayagam, Thomas M., (Retired), Died Nov. 5, 2018
† White, Nathan Reeves, (Retired), Died Sep. 10, 2018

An asterisk (*) denotes an organization that has established tax-exempt status directly with the IRS and is not covered by the USCCB Group Ruling.

Diocese of Superior

(Dioecesis Superiorensis)

Most Reverend

JAMES P. POWERS

Bishop of Superior; ordained May 20, 1990; appointed Bishop of Superior December 15, 2015; ordained February 18, 2016. *Chancery Office: 1201 Hughitt Ave., P.O. Box 969, Superior, WI 54880.*

DEDUC ME, DOMINE, LUCE TUA

Chancery Office: 1201 Hughitt Ave., Box 969, Superior, WI 54880. Tel: 715-392-2937; Fax: 715-395-3149.

ESTABLISHED MAY 3, 1905

Square Miles 15,715.

Comprises the Counties of Ashland, Barron, Bayfield, Burnett, Douglas, Iron, Lincoln, Oneida, Polk, Price, Rusk, Sawyer, St. Croix, Taylor, Vilas and Washburn in the State of Wisconsin.

Incorporated under the laws of the State of Wisconsin as the Diocese of Superior.

For legal titles of parishes and diocesan institutions, consult the Chancery.

STATISTICAL OVERVIEW

Personnel	
Bishop	1
Priests: Diocesan Active in Diocese	27
Priests: Retired, Sick or Absent	28
Number of Diocesan Priests	55
Religious Priests in Diocese	40
Total Priests in Diocese	95
Extern Priests in Diocese	11
Ordinations:	
Permanent Deacons	1
Permanent Deacons in Diocese	68
Total Sisters	62
Parishes	
Parishes	103
With Resident Pastor:	
Resident Diocesan Priests	25
Resident Religious Priests	5
Without Resident Pastor:	
Administered by Priests	48
Administered by Deacons	19
Administered by Lay People	6
Missions	2
Professional Ministry Personnel:	
Sisters	3
Lay Ministers	86
Welfare	
Catholic Hospitals	6
Total Assisted	185,156
Health Care Centers	2
Homes for the Aged	15
Day Care Centers	1
Residential Care of Disabled	26
Other Institutions	2
Educational	
Diocesan Students in Other Seminaries	3
Total Seminarians	3
Elementary Schools, Diocesan and Parish	14
Total Students	1,846
Catechesis/Religious Education:	
High School Students	1,428
Elementary Students	3,355
Total Students under Catholic Instruction	6,632
Teachers in the Diocese:	
Sisters	5
Lay Teachers	190
Vital Statistics	
Receptions into the Church:	
Infant Baptism Totals	590
Minor Baptism Totals	34
Adult Baptism Totals	25
Received into Full Communion	63
First Communions	700
Confirmations	541
Marriages:	
Catholic	99
Interfaith	67
Total Marriages	166
Deaths	979
Total Catholic Population	63,016
Total Population	437,084

Former Bishops—Rt. Revs. AUGUSTIN FRANCIS SCHINNER, D.D., ord. March 7, 1886; cons. July 25, 1905; resigned Jan. 15, 1913; appt. Bishop of Spokane, WA, March 18, 1914; died Feb. 7, 1937; JOSEPH M. KOUDELKA, D.D., ord. Oct. 8, 1875; cons. Auxiliary Bishop of Cleveland and Titular Bishop of Germanicopolis, Feb. 25, 1908; transferred to Milwaukee as Auxiliary Bishop, Sept. 4, 1911; appt. to the See of Superior, Aug. 6, 1913; died June 24, 1921; JOSEPH G. PINTEN, D.D., ord. Nov. 1, 1890; elected Dec. 3, 1921; cons. May 3, 1922; transferred to the See of Grand Rapids, June 25, 1926; retired Nov. 1, 1940; died Nov. 6, 1945; Most Revs. THEODORE H. REVERMAN, D.D., ord. July 26, 1901; cons. Nov. 30, 1926; died July 18, 1941; WILLIAM PATRICK O'CONNOR, D.D., Ph.D., ord. March 10, 1912; cons. March 7, 1942; transferred to the See of Madison, Jan. 15, 1946; His Eminence ALBERT GREGORY MEYER, S.S.L., D.D., ord. July 11, 1926; appt. Feb. 18, 1946; cons. April 11, 1946; promoted to Archbishop of Milwaukee, July 21, 1953; transferred to Archbishop of Chicago, Sept. 19, 1958; created Cardinal, Dec. 14, 1959; died April 9, 1965; Most Revs. JOSEPH JOHN ANNABRING, D.D., ord. May 3, 1927; appt. Jan. 27, 1954; cons. March 25, 1954; died Aug. 27, 1959; GEORGE A. HAMMES, D.D., Bishop Emeritus of Superior; appt. March 28, 1960; cons. May 24, 1960; retired June 27, 1985; died April 11, 1993; RAPHAEL M. FLISS, ord. May 26, 1956; appt. Coadjutor Bishop of Superior with right of succession Nov. 6, 1979; ord. Dec. 20, 1979; succeeded to See, June 27, 1985; retired June 28, 2007; died Sept. 21, 2015.; PETER F. CHRISTENSEN, M.A.S., ord. May 25, 1985; appt. Bishop of Superior June 28, 2007; cons. Sept. 14, 2007; installed Sept. 23, 2007; appt. Bishop of Boise Nov. 4, 2014.

Chancery—1201 Hughitt Ave., Box 969, Superior, 54880. Tel: 715-392-2937; Fax: 715-395-3149.

Vicar General—Very Rev. JAMES F. TOBOLSKI, J.C.L., V.G., Mailing Address: Office: P.O. Box 969, Superior, 54880. Tel: 715-394-0209; Fax: 715-395-3149.

Administrative Services Director—Tel: 715-394-0211. MR. DANIEL BLANK.

Chancellor—MRS. DEBRA J. LIEBERG, Tel: 715-394-0205; Fax: 715-395-3149.

Secretary to Bishop—Tel: 715-394-0205. MRS. DEBRA J. LIEBERG.

Office of Ecclesial Ministries & Diocesan Consultation—CHRISTINE NEWKIRK, Dir., Tel: 715-394-0204.

Episcopal Vicar for Clergy—Very Rev. KEVIN M. GORDON, Mailing Address: P.O. Box 969, Superior, 54880. Tel: 715-779-5501.

Diocesan Tribunal—

Judicial Vicar—Very Rev. JAMES F. TOBOLSKI, J.C.L., V.G.

Promoter of Justice—Appointed by case.

Defender of the Bond—Rev. THOMAS E. THOMPSON.

Procurator and Advocate—MS. PATTI J. HOLT.

Vicar for Canonical Affairs—Very Rev. JAMES F. TOBOLSKI, J.C.L., V.G.

Diocesan Pastoral Council—South Central Deanery: FLORENCE RUNNHEIM; KATHY MAI. Eastern Deanery: TED WADZINSKI; PAM CIRA. Northwest Deanery: MARGE MCCARDLE; SANDY GUNSKI. North Central Deanery: DEBBIE PALECEK; DEBRA SWARTZ. Southwest Deanery: KEVIN EFFERTZ; JAMES BEISTLE; RON ZIGNEGO; Deacon LAWRENCE E. AMELL, Bishop's Appointee. Ex Officio Members: Most Rev. JAMES P. POWERS, J.C.L.; Sisters PATRICIA E. CORMACK, S.C.S.C.; THERESA SANDOK, O.S.M.; Very Rev. JAMES F. TOBOLSKI, J.C.L., V.G.

Deaneries and Deans—Northwest Deanery: Very Rev. JAMES F. TOBOLSKI, J.C.L., V.G. Southwest Deanery: Very Rev. JOHN R. GERRITTS. North Central Deanery: Very Rev. FRANK KORDEK, O.F.M. South Central Deanery: Very Rev. PHILIP J. JUZA. East Deanery: Very Rev. CHRISTOPHER J. KEMP.

Pastoral Consultors—Very Rev. PHILIP J. JUZA; Revs. JAMES J. KINNEY; RONALD OLSON, O.F.M.Conv.; MICHAEL J. TUPA.

Presbyteral Council & Diocesan Consultors—Rev. RONALD SERRAO, Treas.; Very Revs. JAMES F. TOBOLSKI, J.C.L., V.G., Sec.; CHRISTOPHER J. KEMP, Vice Chm.; KEVIN M. GORDON; FRANK KORDEK, O.F.M.; Revs. GERALD P. HARRIS, Chm.; EDWIN C. ANDERSON; JEROME D'SOUZA, C.M.F.; THOMAS E. THOMPSON; GREGORY J. HOPEFL; ANDREW P. RICCI.

Personnel Placement Board—Very Rev. KEVIN M. GORDON; Rev. THOMAS E. THOMPSON; Very Revs. PHILIP J. JUZA; JAMES F. TOBOLSKI, J.C.L., V.G.; JOHN R. GERRITTS; CHRISTOPHER J. KEMP; FRANK KORDEK, O.F.M.

Diocesan Offices and Directors

Bureau of Information—1201 Hughitt Ave., P.O. Box 969, Superior, 54880. Tel: 715-394-0211. MR. DANIEL BLANK, Dir.

Catholic Charities Bureau—ALAN ROCK, Exec. Dir., Office, 1416 Cumming Ave., Superior, 54880. Tel: 715-394-6617; Fax: 715-394-5951.

Catholic Boy and Girl Scout Chaplain—Tel: 715-392-2937; Fax: 715-395-3149.

Catholic Mutual Group—PAUL ALTMANN, Claims/Risk Mgr., 1201 Hughitt Ave., P.O. Box 969, Superior, 54880. Tel: 715-394-0222.

Catholic Women, Council of—KAREN FIRNSTAHL, Pres.

Moderator—Rev. GERARD I. WILLGER, Mailing Address: St. Joseph's Church, P.O. Box 877, Hayward, 54843.

Charismatic Renewal Liaison—Tel: 715-798-3430. Very Rev. DEAN T. BUTTRICK.

The Bishop George A. Hammes Center—PEGGY SCHOENFUSS, Dir. Faith Formation, 315 W. Fifth St., P.O. Box 280, Haugen, 54841. Tel: 715-234-5044; Fax: 715-234-5241.

Catholic Formation, Department of—PEGGY SCHOENFUSS, Dir., Tel: 715-234-5044, Ext. 4405; CHRIS HURTUBISE, Assoc. Dir., Office: Bishop

George A. Hammes Ctr., 315 W. Fifth St., P.O. Box 280, Haugen, 54841. Tel: 715-234-5044, Ext. 4403.

Diocesan Coordinator of Health Affairs—Very Rev. KEVIN M. GORDON, 1201 Hughitt Ave., P.O. Box 969, Superior, 54880. Tel: 715-394-0229.

Diocesan Sisters Council—Sr. PHYLLIS WILHELM, O.S.F., Pres. & Vicar for Rel., 1023 Chapple Ave., Ashland, 54806. Tel: 715-209-6825.

Ecumenical Commission—Very Rev. JAMES F. TOBOLSKI, J.C.L., V.G., Mailing Address: P.O. Box 969, Superior, 54880. Tel: 715-394-0207.

Finance, Department of—1201 Hughitt Ave., P.O. Box 969, Superior, 54880. Tel: 715-394-0221. LAWRENCE FRENCH, Dir.

Holy Childhood Association—Rev. GREGORY J. HOPEFL, Dir., 13891 W. Mission Rd, Reserve, 54876. Tel: 715-865-3669.

Insurance/Employee Benefits and Payroll, Office of—CINDY GRONSKI, Dir., 1201 Hughitt Ave., P.O. Box 969, Superior, 54880. Tel: 715-394-0230; Fax: 715-395-3758.

Newman Apostolate—Superior: Newman Catholic Campus Ministry, University of WisconsinAdvisor: BRETT JONES. Student Contact: ZACK MAZUREK, Email: superiornewmancenter@gmail.com. St. Thomas More Newman Center: Rev. GERALD P. HARRIS, Coord., Newman Ministry, 423 E. Cascade Ave., River Falls, 54022. Tel: 715-425-7234; Fax: 715-425-6959; Email: pastor@stbparish.com.

Catholic Herald, Superior Edition—Editor/Reporter: ANITA DRAPER, 1201 Hughitt Ave., P.O. Box 969, Superior, 54880. Tel: 715-394-0214; Email: adraper@catholicdos.org.

Parish Accounting, Office of—CINDY GRONSKI, Contact, 1201 Hughitt Ave., P.O. Box 969, Superior, 54880. Tel: 715-394-0230.

Permanent Diaconate and Lay Ministry—CHRISTINE NEWKIRK, Dir., Mailing Address: 1201 Hughitt Ave., P.O. Box 969, Superior, 54880. Tel: 715-394-0204.

Director of Diaconal Life—Deacon JOHN E. GREK, Tel: 715-394-0235.

Assistant Director of Lay Ministry Outreach Program—BLUETTE PUCHNER, Tel: 715-866-4492.

Respect Life Office—Mailing Address: P.O. Box 969, Superior, 54880. BONITA THOM.

Propagation of the FaithRev. GREGORY J. HOPEFL, 13891 W. Mission Rd., Reserve, 54876. Tel: 715-865-3669.

Radio and Television—1201 Hughitt Ave., P.O. Box 969, Superior, 54880. Tel: 715-394-0211. MR. DANIEL BLANK, Dir.

St. Pius Priest Fund—Board of Directors: Revs. GERALD A. HAGEN; ANDREW P. RICCI, Vice Pres. & Vice Chm.; JAMES J. BRINKMAN, (Retired); MICHAEL J. TUPA; DAVID P. OBERTS, (Retired); EDWIN C. ANDERSON; EUGENE A. MURPHY; Very Rev. JOHN R. GERRITTS; Revs. JOHN C. ANDERSON; DAVID L. NEUSCHWANDER.

Stewardship and Development, Department of—MR. STEVEN P. TARNOWSKI, Dir., 1201 Hughitt Ave., P.O. Box 969, Superior, 54880. Tel: 715-394-0223; Fax: 715-395-3149.

Superintendent of Schools—PEGGY SCHOENFUSS, Office: Bishop George A. Hammes Center, 315 W. Fifth St., P.O. Box 280, Haugen, 54841. Tel: 715-234-5044, Ext. 4405; Fax: 715-234-5241.

Diocesan Coordinators of Assistance—Mailing Address: P.O. Box 969, Superior, 54880. KATHY DRINKWINE, Tel: 715-718-1110.

Vocations, Office of—Revs. THOMAS E. THOMPSON, Dir.; PATRICK J. A. MCCONNELL, Asst. Dir., 1201 Hughitt Ave., P.O. Box 969, Superior, 54880. Tel: 715-394-0234.

Office of Worship—PAUL J. BIRCH, 1201 Hughitt Ave., P.O. Box 969, Superior, 54880. Tel: 715-394-0233.

CLERGY, PARISHES, MISSIONS AND PAROCHIAL SCHOOLS

CITY OF SUPERIOR

(DOUGLAS COUNTY)

1—CATHEDRAL OF CHRIST THE KING (1886) [CEM] Also serves St. Anthony, Superior; Holy Assumption, Superior; St. William, Foxboro; St. Anthony, Lake Nebagamon.

Mailing Address: 1410 Baxter Ave., 54880.

Tel: 715-392-8511; Email: info@superiorcathedral.org; Web: www.superiorcathedral.org. Revs. Andrew P. Ricci, Rector; David L. Neuschwander; Deacons Arthur Gil de Lamadrid; Kevin Feind; Robert J. Chammings.

Church: 1111 Belknap Ave., 54880. Email: colleen@superiorcathedral.org; Email: margie@superiorcathedral.org.

School—Cathedral School, (Grades PreK-8), 1419 Baxter Ave., 54880. Tel: 715-392-2976; Fax: 715-392-2977; Email: principal@superiorcathedralschool.org. Mr. Gerald Carr, Prin. Lay Teachers 21; Students 206.

Catechesis Religious Program—Email: susan@superiorcathedral.org. Susan Collins, C.R.E.

2—ST. ANTHONY (1870) Also serves St. Anthony, Lake Nebagamon; Cathedral of Christ the King, Superior; Holy Assumption, Superior; St. William, Foxboro.

Mailing Address: 4315 E. Third St., 54880.

Tel: 715-398-3261; Fax: 715-398-3257; Email: sassecretary1@gmail.com. Revs. Andrew P. Ricci; David L. Neuschwander; Deacons Kevin Feind; Arthur Gil de Lamadrid; Robert J. Chammings.

Catechesis Religious Program—Tel: 218-590-0757; Email: tbrowncre@gmail.com. Tammy Brown, D.R.E. Students 16.

3—SS. CYRIL AND METHODIUS, (Slovak), Closed. For inquiries for sacramental records contact Cathedral of Christ the King.

4—ST. FRANCIS XAVIER (1854) [CEM]

2316 E. 4th St., 54880. Tel: 715-398-7174; Email: mary@stfrancisxavier.us. Very Rev. James F. Tobolski, J.C.L., V.G.

Catechesis Religious Program—Email: sfx4reled@gmail.com. Ernest Swartz, D.R.E. Students 121.

5—HOLY ASSUMPTION (1891) Also serves St. William, Foxboro; Cathedral of Christ the King, Superior; St. Anthony, Superior; St. Anthony, Lake Nebagamon.

Mailing Address: 5601 Tower Ave., 54880.

Tel: 715-394-7919; Fax: 715-394-4883; Email: secretaryhasw@centurylink.net. Revs. Andrew P. Ricci; David L. Neuschwander; Deacons Robert J. Chammings; Arthur Gil de Lamadrid; Kevin Feind.

Catechesis Religious Program—Email: Kberry48@centurytel.net. Kathy Berry, C.R.E., Email: kberry48@centurytel.net.

6—ST. LOUIS, Closed. For inquiries for sacramental records contact Cathedral of Christ the King.

7—ST. PATRICK, Closed. For inquiries for sacramental records contact Cathedral of Christ the King.

8—ST. STANISLAUS, (Polish), Closed. For inquiries for sacramental records contact Cathedral of Christ the King.

9—ST. WILLIAM (1908) [CEM] Also serves Holy Assumption, Superior; Cathedral of Christ the King, Superior; St. Anthony, Superior; St. Anthony, Lake Nebagamon.

Mailing Address: 5601 Tower Ave., 54880.

Tel: 715-394-7919; Email: secretaryhasw@centurylink.net. 3095 E. County Rd. B, Foxboro, 54836. Revs. Andrew P. Ricci; David L. Neuschwander; Deacons Robert J. Chammings; Arthur Gil de Lamadrid; Kevin Feind.

Catechesis Religious Program—Students 10.

OUTSIDE THE CITY OF SUPERIOR

ALMENA, BARRON CO., SACRED HEART OF JESUS CHURCH (1890) [CEM] Also serves St. Anthony Abbot, Cumberland & St. Ann, Turtle Lake.

Mailing Address: 900 St. Anthony St., Cumberland, 54829. Tel: 715-822-2948; Fax: 715-822-3588; Email: stanthony@actinfaith.net; Web: www.actinfaith.net. Very Rev. John R. Gerritts; Rev. Thomas E. Thompson, Sacramental Min.; Deacons Steven G. Linton, Parish Life Coord.; Gregory J. Ricci.

Church: 114 Soo Ave., Almena, 54805.

Catechesis Religious Program—Mary DeNoyer, C.R.E. Students 17.

AMERY, POLK CO., ST. JOSEPH (1890) [CEM]

1050 Keller Ave. N., Amery, 54001.

Tel: 715-268-7717; Email: office@stjosephamery.org. Rev. Eugene A. Murphy; Deacon Lawrence E. Amell. Also serves Our Lady of the Lakes, Balsam Lake.

Catechesis Religious Program—Email: stjoejessicad@amerytel.net. Jessica D'Ambrosio, D.R.E. Students 129.

ASHLAND, ASHLAND CO.

1—HOLY FAMILY, (Polish), Closed. For inquiries for sacramental records contact Our Lady of the Lake Catholic Community, Ashland.

2—OUR LADY OF THE LAKE CATHOLIC COMMUNITY (1872) [CEM] Also serves St. Mary, Odanah, St. Peter, Dauby, St. Florian, Ino & SS. Peter & Paul, Moquah.

Mailing Address: 106 N. 2nd Ave. E., Ashland, 54806. Tel: 715-682-7620; Email: ollcatholicchurch@ourladycc.org; Web: www.ourladycc.org. Revs. Ducahn Pham, O.F.M., Admin.; Joseph Kumar Mayakuntla, Sacramental Min.; Deacons William J. Holzhaeuser; Owen T. Gorman; Clarence L. Campbell; John E. Grek.

Church: 201 Lake Shore Dr. E., Ashland, 54806.

School—Our Lady of the Lake Catholic Community School, (Grades PreK-8), 215 Lake Shore Dr. E., Ashland, 54806. Tel: 715-682-7622; Email: ollschool@ourladycc.org. Betty Swiston, Prin. Clergy 2; Lay Teachers 9; Students 127.

Catechesis Religious Program—Email: relform@ourladycc.org. Anna Richardson, D.R.E. Students 109.

BALSAM LAKE, POLK CO., OUR LADY OF THE LAKES (1875) [CEM 2] Also serves St. Joseph, Amery.

507 W. Main, P.O. Box 399, Balsam Lake, 54810.

Tel: 715-405-2253; Fax: 715-405-2743; Email: ourlady@lakeland.ws; Web: www.ourladyofthelakes.ws. Rev. Eugene A. Murphy; Deacon Lawrence E. Amell.

Catechesis Religious Program—Sally Christiansen, C.R.E. Students 65.

BARRON, BARRON CO., ST. JOSEPH (1907) Also serves St. Peter, Cameron, St. Boniface, Chetek, and Assumption of the Blessed Virgin Mary, Strickland.

827 E. LaSalle Ave., Barron, 54812.

Tel: 715-637-3255; Fax: 715-637-3252; Email: stjosephchurch@chibardun.net; Email: pgerber4127@charter.net. Very Rev. John R. Gerritts, Supervising Pastor; Rev. Balaraju Policetty, Sacramental Min.; Deacon Daniel E. Ford; Patricia Gerber, Parish Dir.

Catechesis Religious Program—Tel: 715-637-3252; Email: astephens@chibardun.net. Anne Stephens, D.R.E.

BAYFIELD, BAYFIELD CO., HOLY FAMILY (1878) [CEM] Also serves St. Ann, Cornucopia, St. Joseph (mission), La Pointe, St. Louis, Washburn, St. Francis, Red Cliff.

232 N. 1st St., P.O. Box 1290, Bayfield, 54814.

Tel: 715-779-3316; Fax: 715-779-9804; Email: hfchurch@ncis.net. Very Rev. Frank Kordek, O.F.M.; Deacons Roger L. Cadotte, Dir. Pastoral Svcs.; Kenneth D. Kasinski.

Catechesis Religious Program—Email: gpbduffy@centurylink.net. Barb Duffy, C.R.E.

BIRCHWOOD, WASHBURN CO., ST. JOHN EVANGELIST (1908) Also serves St. Joseph, Rice Lake, Our Lady of Lourdes, Dobie & Holy Trinity, Haugen.

Mailing Address: 111 W. Marshall St., Rice Lake, 54868. Tel: 715-234-2032; Email: stjoseph@chibardun.net. 107 W. Balsam Ave., Birchwood, 54817. Revs. Edwin C. Anderson; Samuel Schneider; Deacon Dennis C. Geisler.

Church: 408 S. Main, Birchwood, 54817.

Catechesis Religious Program—Rose Schullo, D.R.E.; Kristine Deering, C.R.E. (K-5). Combined with other parishes in cluster.

BLOOMVILLE, LINCOLN CO., ST. JOHN THE BAPTIST (1908) [CEM] Also serves St. Francis Xavier, Merrill.

Mailing Address: 1708 E. 10th St., Merrill, 54452.

Tel: 715-536-2803; Email: kleggett@stfrancismerrill.org. N4887 Hwy. 17, Gleason, 54435. Very Rev. Christopher J. Kemp, Parochial Admin.; Deacon James A. Arndt.

Catechesis Religious Program—Joseph Velie, D.R.E. Combined with St. Francis Xavier, Merrill.

BOULDER JUNCTION, VILAS CO., ST. ANNE (1938) [CEM] Also serves St. Mary, Sayner, and St. Rita, Presque Isle.

10315 Main St., P.O. Box 110, Boulder Junction, 54512. Tel: 715-385-2390; Email: stannechurch@centurytel.net; Web: www.ncc.weconnect.com. Rev. Showri Jojappa Pasala, Parochial Admin.

BRUCE, RUSK CO., ST. MARY (1893) [CEM 2] Also serves Our Lady of Sorrows, Ladysmith, St. Francis of Assisi, Flambeau, St. Mary, Hawkins, St. Anthony de Padua, Tony & SS. Peter and Paul, Weyerhaeuser.

Mailing Address: 611 1st St. S., Ladysmith, 54848.

Tel: 715-532-3051; Fax: 715-609-1059; Email: jp2officedesk@gmail.com; Web: www.ruskcountycatholiccommunity.org. 721 N. 2nd St., Bruce, 54819. Very Rev. Philip J. Juza, Supervising Pastor; Revs. Inna Reddy Pothireddy, Sacramental Min.; David P. Oberts, Weekend Help Out, (Retired); Deacons Craig J. Voldberg, Parish Life Coord.; Thomas E. Fuhrmann; Douglas L. Sorenson, (Retired).

Church: 727 N. 2nd St., Bruce, 54819.

BUTTERNUT, ASHLAND CO., IMMACULATE CONCEPTION (1880) [CEM] Also serves St. Francis of Assisi, Fifield & St. Anthony of Padua, Park Falls.

410 Michigan St., P.O. Box 6, Butternut, 54514.

Tel: 715-762-4494; Email: icchurchbutternut@plbb.us. Rev. Shaji Joseph Pazhukkathara, Admin.; Deacons Chester E. Ball Jr.; Robert L. Schienebeck.

Catechesis Religious Program—Tel: 715-769-3913; Email: bhirtreiter@centurytel.net. Bette Hirtreiter, D.R.E. Students 31.

CABLE, BAYFIELD CO., ST. ANN (1902)

13645 County Hwy. M, P.O. Box 37, Cable, 54821-0037. Tel: 715-798-3855; Fax: 715-798-3850; Email: stanns1902@cheqnet.net. Rev. Gerard I. Willger; Deacons Brian McCaffery; Michael Ryan; David B. DiSera.

Catechesis Religious Program—Email: religious1@centurytel.net. Teri Radcliffe, D.R.E.

CAMERON, BARRON CO., ST. PETER (1908) Also serves St. Joseph, Barron, St. Boniface, Chetek, & Assumption of the Blessed Virgin Mary, Strickland.
Mailing Address: 827 E. LaSalle Ave., Barron, 54812. Tel: 715-637-3255; Email: pgerber4127@charter.net. Creamery Rd. & Hwy. 8, Cameron, 54812. Very Rev. John R. Gerritts, Supervising Pastor; Rev. Balaraju Policetty, Sacramental Min.; Patricia Gerber, Parish Dir.
Catechesis Religious Program—Tel: 715-637-3252; Email: astephens@chibardun.net. Anne Stephens, D.R.E. Students 119.

CATAWBA, PRICE CO., ST. PAUL THE APOSTLE (1907) [CEM] Also serves St. Therese of Lisieux, Phillips & St. John the Baptist, Prentice.
Mailing Address: 655 S. Lake Ave., Phillips, 54555. Tel: 715-339-2222; Email: oln@pctcnet.net. W0485 Hwy. 8, Catawba, 54515. Rev. Gerald A. Hagen.
Church: W9485 Hwy. 8, Catawba, 54515.
Catechesis Religious Program—
Fax: snoylag9@gmail.com. Gloria Lyons, C.R.E.

CENTURIA, POLK CO., ST. PATRICK (1856) Closed. For inquiries for sacramental records, please contact Our Lady of the Lakes, Balsam Lake.

CHELSEA, TAYLOR CO., ASSUMPTION OF THE BLESSED VIRGIN MARY (1887) Closed. For inquiries for sacramental records please contact Good Shepherd, Rib Lake.

CHETEK, BARRON CO., ST. BONIFACE (1880) [CEM] Also serves St. Joseph, Barron, St. Peter, Cameron & Assumption of the Blessed Virgin Mary, Strickland.
Mailing Address: 827 E. LaSalle Ave., Barron, 54812. Tel: 715-924-3514; Email: stjosephchurch@chibardun.net. 425 S. 3rd St., Chetek, 54728. Very Rev. John R. Gerritts, Supervising Pastor; Rev. Balaraju Policetty, Sacramental Min.; Patricia Gerber, Dir.
Catechesis Religious Program—Patricia Gerber, D.R.E. & Parish Dir.; Anne Stephens, Faith Formation. Combined with other parishes in cluster.

CLAM LAKE, ASHLAND CO., ST. GEORGE (1948) Summer Chapel for Worship
Grant and 2nd St., Clam Lake, 54517.
Tel: 715-274-3701; Email: mostholyrosary@centurytel.net. P.O. Box 17, Mellen, 54546. Rev. Papi Yeruva, Admin.
Church: W. Hwy. 77, Clam Lake, 54517.
Tel: 715-264-3471; Fax: 715-264-3472.

CLEAR LAKE, POLK CO., ST. JOHN (1890) Also serves St. John the Baptist, Glenwood City & St. Bridget, Wilson.
Mailing Address: 761 1st St., Glenwood City, 54013. Tel: 715-265-7133; Email: stjohnbaptist@cltcomm.net; Web: www.jbjsaints.com. 811 4th St., Clear Lake, 54005. Rev. John R. Long; Deacon Wesley G. Tuttle.
Catechesis Religious Program—Tel: 715-977-2031; Email: menjmjm7@yahoo.com. Julie Novak, C.R.E. Students 33.

CORNUCOPIA, BAYFIELD CO., ST. ANN (1914) [CEM] Also serves Holy Family, Bayfield, St. Joseph, LaPointe, St. Francis, Red Cliff & St. Louis, Washburn.
Mailing Address: 232 N. 1st St., P.O. Box 311, Cornucopia, 54827. Tel: 715-779-3316;
Fax: 715-779-9804; Email: hfchurch@ncis.net. Very Rev. Frank Kordek, O.F.M.; Deacons Kenneth D. Kasinski; Roger L. Cadotte.
Church: Superior Ave. & Ash St., Cornucopia, 54827.
Catechesis Religious Program—

CRESCENT LAKE, BURNETT CO., SACRED HEARTS OF JESUS AND MARY (1857) [CEM] Also serves St. John the Baptist, Webster & Our Lady of Perpetual Help, Danbury.
P.O. Box 7, Webster, 54893. Tel: 715-866-7321;
Fax: 715-866-7305; Email: sjoffice@centurytel.net. 24680 County Hwy. H, Crescent Lake, 54830. Rev. Randall Knauf, O.F.M.Cap., Admin.
Church: County Rd. A & H, Crescent Lake, 54830.
Catechesis Religious Program—Gwen Nies, D.R.E. Students 4.

CUMBERLAND, BARRON CO., ST. ANTHONY ABBOT (1883) [CEM 2] Also serves Sacred Heart of Jesus, Almena and St. Ann, Turtle Lake.
900 St. Anthony St., Cumberland, 54829.
Tel: 715-822-2948; Cell: 715-822-8831;
Fax: 715-822-3588; Email: stanthony@actinfaith.net; Web: www.actinfaith.net. Very Rev. John R. Gerritts, Supervising Pastor; Rev. Thomas E. Thompson, Sacramental Min.; Deacons Steven G. Linton, Parish Life Coord.; Gregory J. Ricci; Mrs. Michele Scribner, Sec.
Catechesis Religious Program—Tel: 715-822-3588; Email: ericci@actinfaith.net. Mrs. Elaine Ricci, D.R.E.; Mrs. Angela Schug, Religious Education Coord. Students 93.

DANBURY, BURNETT CO., OUR LADY OF PERPETUAL HELP (1920) Also serves St. John the Baptist, Webster & Sacred Heart of Jesus & Mary, Crescent Lake.
P.O. Box 7, Webster, 54893. Tel: 715-866-7321;
Fax: 715-866-7305; Email: sjoffice@centurytel.net. 7586 Main St., Danbury, 54830. Rev. Randall Knauf, O.F.M.Cap., Admin.
Catechesis Religious Program—Gwen Nies, D.R.E. Students 6.

DAUBY, BAYFIELD CO., ST. PETER (1918) [CEM] Also serves Our Lady of the Lake, Ashland, St. Florian, Ino, SS. Peter & Paul, Moquah & St. Mary, Odanah.
Mailing Address: 106 N. 2nd Ave. E., Ashland, 54806. Tel: 715-682-7620; Email: ricjohnson@ourladycc.org. 23505 County Rd. G, Moquah, 55806. Revs. Joseph Kumar Mayakuntla, Sacramental Min.; Ducahn Pham, O.F.M., Admin.; Deacons William J. Holzhaeuser; Owen T. Gorman; Clarence L. Campbell; John E. Grek.
Church: 65515 County Hwy. F, Dauby, 54847.
Catechesis Religious Program—Combined with other parishes in cluster.

DOBIE, BARRON CO., OUR LADY OF LOURDES (1875) [CEM] Also serves Holy Trinity, Haugen, St. John the Evangelist, Birchwood & St. Joseph, Rice Lake.
111 W. Marshall St., Rice Lake, 54868.
Tel: 715-234-2032; Email: stjoseph@chibardun.net. 2411 23rd St., Rice Lake, 54868. Revs. Edwin C. Anderson; Samuel Schneider; Deacon Dennis C. Geisler.
Catechesis Religious Program—Email: lynnpottingerprice@gmail.com. Lynn Price, D.R.E. Students 32.

EAGLE RIVER, VILAS CO., ST. PETER THE FISHERMAN (1890) [CEM]
5001 County Rd. G, Eagle River, 54521.
Tel: 715-479-8704; Email: info@stpeterseagleriver.org; Web: www.stpeterseagleriver.org. Rev. Patrick J. A. McConnell; Deacon Richard M. Miech, Pastoral Assoc.
Catechesis Religious Program—Email: adele@stpeterseagleriver.org. Adele Svetnicka, C.R.E. & Youth Min. Students 71.

ERIN, ST. CROIX CO., ST. PATRICK (1857) [CEM 2] Also serves Immaculate Conception, New Richmond.
Mailing Address: 151 S. Washington Ave., New Richmond, 54017. Tel: 715-246-5596; Email: icchurch@frontiernet.net; Web: stpatrickserin.tripod.com. 1880 County Rd. G, New Richmond, 54017. Rev. John C. Anderson; Deacons Michael J. Germain, RCIA Coord.; Mel (Carmelo) Riel; Cathy Hilby, Business Mgr.; JoAnn Germain, Contact Person.
Catechesis Religious Program—Tel: 715-248-7205; Email: threshingtablefarm@frontiernet.net. Jody Lenz, D.R.E.; Kim Palmer, D.R.E. Students 34.

FARMINGTON, POLK CO., ASSUMPTION OF THE BLESSED VIRGIN MARY (1869) [CEM] Also serves St. Anne, Somerset & St. Joseph, Osceola.
P.O. Box 9, Somerset, 54025. Tel: 715-247-3310;
Fax: 715-247-3174; Email: rtpete452@gmail.com. 265 State Hwy. 35, Osceola, 54020. Very Rev. John R. Gerritts, Supervising Pastor; Rev. Barg G. Anderson, Parochial Vicar; Deacons Richard T. Peterson, Parish Life Coord.; Thomas P. Rausch; Edward C. Colosky.
Church: 255 State Hwy. 35, Farmington, 54020.
Catechesis Religious Program—Email: rachelm_stanne@somtel.net. Rachel McGurran, D.R.E.; Sara Measner, D.R.E. Students 111.

FIFIELD, PRICE CO., ST. FRANCIS OF ASSISI (1888) Also serves St. Anthony of Padua, Park Falls & Immaculate Conception, Butternut.
Mailing Address: 276 S. 5th Ave., Park Falls, 54552. Tel: 715-762-4494, Ext. 113; Email: stanthony75@hotmail.com. W7231 Balsam St., Fifield, 54524. Rev. Shaji Joseph Pazhukkathara, Parochial Admin.; Deacons Chester E. Ball Jr.; Robert L. Schienebeck.
Catechesis Religious Program—Patricia Hoffman, C.R.E. (Confirmation). Combined with other parishes in cluster.

FLAMBEAU, RUSK CO., ST. FRANCIS OF ASSISI (1866) [CEM] Also serves Our Lady of Sorrows, Ladysmith, St. Mary, Bruce, St. Mary of Czestochowa, Hawkins, St. Anthony de Padua, Tony & SS. Peter & Paul, Weyerhaeuser.
Mailing Address: 611 1st St. S., Ladysmith, 54848. Tel: 715-532-3051; Fax: 715-609-1059; Email: jp2officedesk@gmail.com; Web: www.ruskcountycatholiccommunity.org. W10193 Lehmen Rd., Holcombe, 54745. Very Rev. Philip J. Juza, Pastor; Revs. Inna Reddy Pothireddy, Sacramental Min.; David P. Oberts, Weekend Help Out, (Retired); Deacons Craig J. Voldberg, Parish Life Coord.; Thomas E. Fuhrmann; Douglas L. Sorenson, (Retired).

FREDERIC, POLK CO., ST. DOMINIC (1904) [CEM] (Also serves Immaculate Conception, Grantsburg).
103 W. Birch St., P.O. Box 606, Frederic, 54837.
Tel: 715-327-8119; Fax: 715-327-4174; Email: stdomfrederic@lakeland.ws. Very Rev. John R. Gerritts, Supervising Pastor; Rev. Joseph Madanu, Sacramental Min.; Deacon Stanley J. Marczak, Parish Life Coord.
Rectory & Parish Office: 107 W. Birch St., Frederic, 54837.
Catechesis Religious Program—Tel: 715-825-2208; Email: stdom.ic.dre@gmail.com. Stephanie Weyenberg, D.R.E. Students 36.

GEORGETOWN, POLK CO., OUR LADY OF THE HOLY ROSARY, Closed. For inquiries for sacramental records contact Our Lady of the Lakes Balsam Lake.

GILMAN, TAYLOR CO., SS. PETER AND PAUL (1910) [CEM] (Also serves St. Michael, Jump River; St. John the Apostle, Sheldon and St. Stanislaus, Lublin).
315 E. Davlin St., Gilman, 54433. Tel: 715-447-8510; Email: fivesaintscatholic@gmail.com. Rev. Lourduraju Madanu, Admin.
Catechesis Religious Program—Tel: 715-452-5851; Email: mableidinger@fspa.org. Sr. Marianna Ableidinger, F.S.P.A., D.R.E. Students 75.

GLENWOOD CITY, ST. CROIX CO., ST. JOHN THE BAPTIST (1886) [CEM] Also serves St. John, Clear Lake & St. Bridget, Wilson.
Mailing Address: 761 1st St., Glenwood City, 54013. Tel: 715-265-7133; Email: stjohnbaptist@cltcomm.net; Web: www.jbjsaints.com. 757 1st St., Glenwood City, 54013. Rev. John R. Long; Deacon Wesley G. Tuttle.
Catechesis Religious Program—Tel: 715-265-7331; Email: ffpnewsgc@gmail.com. Jan Caress-Hanson, P.C.L. Students 80.

GLIDDEN, ASHLAND CO., MOST PRECIOUS BLOOD (1884) [CEM] Also serves Most Holy Rosary, Mellen, St. Anthony, Highbridge, St. Anne, Sanborn & St. George, Clam Lake.
246 Grant St., P.O. Box 182, Glidden, 54527.
Tel: 715-274-3701; Fax: 715-274-3703; Email: mpbchurchglidden@yahoo.com. Rev. Papi Yeruva, Admin.
Catechesis Religious Program—Larry Bay, D.R.E.; Mr. Richard Pankratz, D.R.E. Students 11.

GORDON, DOUGLAS CO., ST. ANTHONY OF PADUA (1878) Also serves St. Pius X, Solon Springs & St. Mary, Minong.
P.O. Box 303, Solon Springs, 54873.
Tel: 715-378-4431; Email: stpiusx@centurytel.net. 9718 E. County Rd. Y, Gordon, 54838. Rev. James J. Kinney.
Catechesis Religious Program—Mary Brand, C.R.E. Combined with other parishes in cluster.

GRANTSBURG, BURNETT CO., IMMACULATE CONCEPTION (1909) Also serves Immaculate Conception, Frederic.
103 W. Birch St., P.O. Box 606, Frederic, 54837.
Tel: 715-327-8119; Fax: 715-327-4174; Email: stdomfrederic@lakeland.ws. Very Rev. John R. Gerritts, Supervising Pastor; Rev. Joseph Madanu, Sacramental Min.; Deacon Stanley J. Marczak, Parish Life Coord.
Church: 411 State Rd. 70, Grantsburg, 54840.
Catechesis Religious Program—Email: stdom.ic.dre@gmail.com. Marie Ohnstad, D.R.E. Students 44.

HAMMOND, ST. CROIX CO., IMMACULATE CONCEPTION (1877) [CEM] Also serves St. Bridget, River Falls.
1295 Ridgeway St., P.O. Box 18, Hammond, 54015-0018. Tel: 715-796-2244; Email: toddedelman@smicparish.org. Revs. Gerald P. Harris; Richard Rhinehart.
Church: 1265 Ridgeway St., Hammond, 54015. Web: stmaryshammond.org.
Catechesis Religious Program—Email: jackieaune@smicparish.org. Jackie Aune, D.R.E. Students 283.

HARRISON, LINCOLN CO., ST. AUGUSTINE (1905) [CEM] Also serves St. Mary, Tomahawk & St. Francis of Assisi, Pier Willow.
Mailing Address: N10090 Cty. B, Tomahawk, 54487. Tel: 715-453-2561; Fax: 715-453-4813; Email: sasjb@hughes.net. Hwy. B & D, Harrison, 54487. Rev. Louis Reddy Maram Reddy, Parochial Admin.; Deacons Clarence D. Towle; David C. Bablick; Clifford Eggett.
Catechesis Religious Program—Lynne Dalka, C.R.E. Students 17.

HAUGEN, BARRON CO., HOLY TRINITY (1896) [CEM] Also serves St. Joseph, Rice Lake, Our Lady of Lourdes, Dobie & St. John the Evangelist, Birchwood.
Mailing Address: 111 W. Marshall St., Rice Lake, 54868. Tel: 715-234-2032; Email: stjoseph@chibardun.net. 317 5th St., Haugen, 54841. Revs. Edwin C. Anderson; Samuel Schneider; Deacon Dennis C. Geisler.
Catechesis Religious Program—Kris Deering, C.R.E. (K-5); Rose Schullo, D.R.E. Students 29.

HAWKINS, RUSK CO., ST. MARY OF CZESTOCHOWA (1913) [CEM] Also serves Our Lady of Sorrows, Ladysmith, St. Mary, Bruce, St. Francis of Assisi, Flambeau, St. Anthony de Padua, Tony & SS. Peter & Paul, Weyerhaeuser.
Mailing Address: 611 1st St. S., Ladysmith, 54848. Tel: 715-532-3051; Fax: 715-609-1059; Email: jp2officedesk@gmail.com; Web: www.ruskcountycatholiccommunity.org. N7386 Cty. Hwy.

M, Hawkins, 54530. Very Rev. Philip J. Juza, Supervising Pastor; Revs. Inna Reddy Pothireddy, Sacramental Min.; David P. Oberts, Weekend Help Out, (Retired); Deacons Craig J. Voldberg, Parish Life Coord.; Thomas E. Fuhrmann; Douglas L. Sorenson, (Retired).

HAYWARD, SAWYER CO., ST. JOSEPH (1882) Also serves St. Ann, Cable.
10586 N. Dakota Ave., P.O. Box 877, Hayward, 54843. Tel: 715-634-2867; Email: haystjoe@centurytel.net; Web: www.stjoseph-hayward.org. Rev. Gerard I. Willger; Deacons David B. DiSera; Michael Ryan; Brian McCaffery.
Catechesis Religious Program—Email: religious1@centurytel.net. Teri Radcliffe, D.R.E. Students 99.

HIGHBRIDGE, ASHLAND CO., ST. ANTHONY (1880) Also serves Most Holy Rosary, Mellen, Most Precious Blood, Glidden, St. Anne, Sanborn & St. George, Clam Lake.
P.O. Box 17, Mellen, 54546. Tel: 715-274-3701; Email: mostholyrosary@centurytel.net. 39221 State Hwy. 13, Highbridge, 54846. Rev. Papi Yeruva, Admin.

HUDSON, ST. CROIX CO., ST. PATRICK (1840) [CEM]
1500 Vine St., Hudson, 54016. Tel: 715-381-5120; Email: church@stpatrickofhudson.org; Web: www.stpatrickofhudson.org. Very Rev. John R. Gerritts; Deacons Gregg J. Miller; Howard Cameron; Thomas Kroll.
School—St. Patrick School, (Grades PreK-8), 403 St. Croix St., Hudson, 54016. Tel: 715-386-3941; Email: dbell@stpatrickeducenter.org. Mr. Dan Bell, Prin. Clergy 2; Lay Teachers 27; Students 218.
Catechesis Religious Program—Email: kpreston@spatrickeducenter.org. Katie Preston, D.R.E.

HURLEY, IRON CO., ST. MARY OF THE SEVEN DOLORS (1885) [CEM] Also serves St. Ann, Saxon.
Mailing Address: 404 Iron St., Hurley, 54534.
Tel: 715-561-2606; Email: stmary7@charter.net. Very Rev. Frank Kordek, O.F.M.
Church: Iron St. & 5th Ave., Hurley, 54534.
Catechesis Religious Program—Email: stmaryshurley@gmail.com. Leone Sobrack, C.R.E. Students 70.

INO, BAYFIELD CO., ST. FLORIAN (1913) [CEM] Also serves Our Lady of the Lake, Ashland; St. Peter, Dauby; St. Mary, Odanah & SS. Peter & Paul, Moquah.
Mailing Address: 106 N. 2nd Ave. E., Ashland, 54806. Tel: 715-682-7620; Email: ricjohnson@ourladycc.org. 19315 Keystone Rd., Mason, 54856. Revs. Ducahn Pham, O.F.M., Admin.; Joseph Kumar Mayakuntla, Sacramental Min.; Deacons Clarence L. Campbell; Owen T. Gorman; William J. Holzhaeuser; John E. Grek.
Catechesis Religious Program—Combined with other parishes in cluster.

IRON RIVER, BAYFIELD CO., ST. MICHAEL (1893) [CEM]
68105 S. George St., P.O. Box 97, Iron River, 54847. Tel: 715-372-4756; Email: stmichael@cheqnet.net. Rev. Michael L. Crisp; Deacon John E. Grek.
Catechesis Religious Program—Email: cathyberube@cheqnet.net. Cathy Berube, C.R.E. Students 13.

JUMP RIVER, TAYLOR CO., ST. MICHAEL (1915) Also serves SS. Peter & Paul, Gilman, St. Stanislaus, Lublin & St. John the Apostle, Sheldon.
Mailing Address: 315 E. Davlin St., Gilman, 54433. Tel: 715-447-8510; Fax: 715-447-5742; Email: fivesaintscatholic@gmail.com. Hwy. 73, Jump River, 54434. Rev. Lourduraju Madanu, Admin.
Catechesis Religious Program—Sr. Marianna Ableidinger, F.S.P.A., D.R.E. Combined with other parishes in cluster.

LA POINTE, BAYFIELD CO., ST. JOSEPH (1669) [CEM] (Summer mission only)
P.O. Box 1290, Bayfield, 54814. Tel: 715-547-3358; Email: hfchurch@ncis.net. 266 Airport Rd., La Pointe, 54850. Deacons Roger L. Cadotte, Dir.; Kenneth D. Kasinski, Deacon; Very Rev. Frank Kordek, O.F.M., Supervising Pastor.

LAC DU FLAMBEAU, VILAS CO., ST. ANTHONY OF PADUA (1862) Also serves Our Lady Queen of Peace, Manitowish Waters, and St. Isaac Jogues & Companions, Mercer.
650 Old Abe Rd., P.O. Box 38, Lac du Flambeau, 54538. Tel: 715-588-3148; Email: stanthony@frontier.com. Rev. Ronald Serrao, Parochial Admin.; Deacon John J. Bardos.
Catechesis Religious Program—Email: soulierndv1@frontier.com. Debra Ramsey, D.R.E. Students 11.

LADYSMITH, RUSK CO., OUR LADY OF SORROWS (1906) Also serves St. Mary, Hawkins, and St. Anthony de Padua, Tony; St. Mary, Bruce; St. Francis of Assisi, Flambeau; SS Peter & Paul, Weyerhaeuser.
611 1st St. S., Ladysmith, 54848. Tel: 715-532-3051; Fax: 715-609-1059; Email: jp2officedesk@gmail.com; Web: www.ruskcountycatholiccommunity.org. Very Rev. Philip J. Juza, Supervising Pastor; Revs. Inna Reddy Pothireddy, Sacramental Min.; David P. Oberts, (Retired); Deacons Craig J. Voldberg, Parish Life Coord.; Thomas E. Fuhrmann; Douglas L. Sorenson.
School—Our Lady of Sorrows School, (Grades PreK-8), 105 E. Washington Ave., Ladysmith, 54848. Tel: 715-532-3232; Email: olsschool@centurytel.net. Megan Dieckman, Prin. Clergy 2; Lay Teachers 12; Students 86.

LAKE NEBAGAMON, DOUGLAS CO., ST. ANTHONY CATHOLIC CHURCH (1899) [CEM] Also serves St. Anthony, Superior; Cathedral of Christ the King, Superior; Holy Assumption, Superior; St. William, Foxboro.
Mailing Address: 11648 E. County Rd. B, P.O. Box 397, Lake Nebagamon, 54849. Tel: 715-374-3570; Email: stanthonyln@gmail.com. Revs. Andrew P. Ricci; David L. Neuschwander; Deacons Kevin L. Feind; Robert J. Chammings; Arthur Gil de Lamadrid.
Catechesis Religious Program—Email: tbrowncre@gmail.com. Tammy Brown, D.R.E. Students 18.

LAKE TOMAHAWK, ONEIDA CO., ST. JOHN VIANNEY (1859) Closed. For inquiries for sacramental records please contact Holy Family, Woodruff.

LAND-O'-LAKES, VILAS CO., ST. ALBERT (1948) Also serves St. Mary, Phelps.
4351 County Rd. B, P.O. Box 237, Land O'Lakes, 54540. Tel: 715-547-3558; Email: stalbertstmary@gmail.com; Web: saintsalbertandmary.org. Very Rev. Christopher J. Kemp; Rev. Patrick J. A. McConnell, Sacramental Min.; Deacon Norman J. Mesun Jr.; Michele Rein, Admin.
Church: 4351 Hwy. B, Land O'Lakes, 54540.
Catechesis Religious Program—

LUBLIN, TAYLOR CO., ST. STANISLAUS (1907) [CEM] (Polish) Also serves SS. Peter & Paul, Gilman, St. Michael, Jump River & St. John the Apostle, Sheldon.
Mailing Address: 315 E. Davlin St., Gilman, 54433. Tel: 715-447-8510; Email: fivesaintscatholic@gmail.com. W 13381 S. St., Lublin, 5447. Rev. Lourduraju Madanu, Parochial Admin.
Catechesis Religious Program—Sr. Marianna Ableidinger, F.S.P.A., D.R.E. Combined with other parishes in cluster.

MANITOWISH WATERS, VILAS CO., OUR LADY QUEEN OF PEACE (1958) Also serves St. Anthony of Padua, Lac Du Flambeau & St. Isaac Jogues & Companions, Mercer.
5610 S. Hwy. 51, P.O. Box 325, Manitowish Waters, 54545. Tel: 715-543-8428; Email: queenofpeace@centurytel.net. Rev. Ronald Serrao.
Catechesis Religious Program—Tel: 715-543-2274; Email: nanc54545@yahoo.com. Nancy Benson, D.R.E. Students 21.

MEDFORD, TAYLOR CO.
1—OUR LADY OF PERPETUAL HELP (1891) [CEM] Also serves Our Lady of the Rosary, Medford.
W5409 Whittlesey Ave., P.O. Box 503, Medford, 54451. Tel: 715-748-3366; Fax: 715-748-6643; Email: rspanbauer@holyrosarymedford.org. Very Rev. Philip J. Juza.
Catechesis Religious Program—Email: wendyhartl@yahoo.com. Wendy Hartl, D.R.E. Students 55.
2—OUR LADY OF THE HOLY ROSARY (1870) [CEM] Also serves Our Lady of Perpetual Help, Whittlesey.
215 S. Washington Ave., P.O. Box 503, Medford, 54451. Tel: 715-748-3336; Fax: 715-748-6643; Email: rspanbauer@hrmedford.org. Very Rev. Philip J. Juza.
School—Our Lady of the Holy Rosary School, (Grades PreK-6), Tel: 715-748-3336, Ext. 221; Fax: 715-748-4185; Email: principal@hrmedford.org. Debbie Johnston, Prin. Clergy 3; Lay Teachers 12; Students 91.
Catechesis Religious Program—Email: mbub@hrmedfor.org. Mike Bub, D.R.E.

MELLEN, ASHLAND CO., MOST HOLY ROSARY (1886) Also serves St. Anthony, Highbridge; St. Anne, Sanborn; Most Precious Blood, Glidden; St. George, Clam Lake.
203 N. Main St., P.O. Box 17, Mellen, 54546. Tel: 715-274-3701; Email: mostholyrosary@centurytel.net. Rev. Papi Yeruva, Admin.
Catechesis Religious Program—Email: penmtkennels@yahoo.com. Vicky Ellias, Co-C.R.E.; Sara Schultz, Co-C.R.E. Students 36.

MERCER, IRON CO., ST. ISAAC JOGUES AND COMPANIONS (1912)
Mailing Address: 5214 N. Lakeview Ave., Mercer, 54547. Tel: 715-476-2697; Email: stisaacjogues@centurytel.net. Rev. Ronald Serrao, Parochial Admin.
Church: 2611 W. Garnet St., Mercer, 54547.
Fax: 715-476-2103.
Catechesis Religious Program—Email: soulierndv1@frontier.com. Debra Ramsey, C.R.E.

MERRILL, LINCOLN CO.
1—ST. FRANCIS XAVIER (1875) [CEM] Also serves St. John the Baptist, Bloomville.
1708 E. 10th St., Merrill, 54452. Tel: 715-536-2803; Email: kleggett@stfrancismerrill.org. Very Rev. Christopher J. Kemp; Deacon James E. Arndt.
School—St. Francis School, (Grades PreK-8), Tel: 715-536-6083; Email: sdoughty@stfrancismerrill.org; Web: www.stfrancismerrill.org. Sonja Doughty, Prin. Clergy 2; Lay Teachers 16; Students 108.
Catechesis Religious Program—Email: jvelie@stfrancismerrill.org. Joseph Velie, D.R.E.
2—ST. ROBERT BELLARMINE (1886) Closed. For inquiries for sacramental records contact St. Francis Xavier, Merrill.

MINOCQUA, ONEIDA CO., ST. PATRICK (1894) [CEM] Closed. For inquiries for sacramental records, contact Holy Family, Woodruff.

MINONG, WASHBURN CO., ST. MARY (1904) Also serves St. Pius X, Solon Springs & St. Anthony of Padua, Gordon.
P.O. Box 303, Solon Springs, 54873.
Tel: 715-378-4431; Email: pomp1o2000@yahoo.com. 506 Main St., Minong, 54859. Rev. James J. Kinney. Office & Rectory: 11651 Business 53, Solon Springs, 54873.
Catechesis Religious Program—Email: kathy.stpius@gmail.com. Kathleen Birtzer, C.R.E. & Adult Formation. Students 6.

MONTREAL, IRON CO., SACRED HEART OF JESUS (1904) Closed. For inquiries for parish records please see St. Mary of the Seven Dolors, Hurley.

MOQUAH, BAYFIELD CO., SS. PETER AND PAUL (1912) [CEM 2] Also serves Our Lady of the Lake, Ashland; St. Mary, Odanah; St. Peter, Dauby; St. Florian, Ino.
106 N. 2nd Ave. E, Ashland, 54806.
Tel: 715-682-7620; Email: ollcatholicchurch@ourladycc.org. 23505 CR. G, Moquah, 54806. Revs. Ducahn Pham, O.F.M., Admin.; Joseph Kumar Mayakuntla, Sacramental Min.; Deacons Clarence L. Campbell; Owen T. Gorman; William J. Holzhaeuser.
Catechesis Religious Program—Kathy Huybrecht, C.R.E. Students 7.

NEW POST, SAWYER CO., ST. IGNATIUS (1884) Also serves St. Francis Solanus, Reserve & St. Philip, Stone Lake.
Mailing Address: 13891 W. Mission Rd., Stone Lake, 54876. Tel: 715-865-3669; Email: ghopefl@charter.net; Web: www.stignatiusnewpost.com. Indian Rd., New Post, 54828. Rev. Gregory J. Hopefl.
Catechesis Religious Program—Sr. Felissa Zander, S.S.S.F., D.R.E. Students 2.

NEW RICHMOND, ST. CROIX CO., IMMACULATE CONCEPTION (1883) [CEM] Also serves St. Patrick, Erin.
151 S. Washington Ave., New Richmond, 54017-1523. Tel: 715-246-4652; Email: icchurch@frontiernet.net; Web: www.ic-church.com. Rev. John C. Anderson; Deacons Michael J. Germain; Mel (Carmelo) Riel; Cathy Hilby, Business Mgr.
School—Immaculate Conception School dba St. Mary School, (Grades PreK-8), 257 S. Washington Ave., New Richmond, 54017. Tel: 715-246-2469; Fax: 715-246-6195; Email: principal@st-marysschool.com; Email: saintmry@st-marysschool.com; Web: st-marysschool.com. Laura Jarchow, Prin. Religious Teachers 3; Lay Teachers 13; Students 179.
Catechesis Religious Program—Email: k.palmer@frontiernet.net. Kim Palmer, D.R.E.; Kristan Dittman, C.R.E.; Kendra Mitchell, Youth Min. Students 203.

ODANAH, ASHLAND CO., ST. MARY (1855) Also serves Our Lady of the Lake, Ashland, St. Peter, Dauby, St. Florian, Ino & SS. Peter & Paul, Maquah.
Mailing Address: 106 N. Second Ave. E., Ashland, 54806. Tel: 715-682-7620; Fax: 715-682-7626; Email: spw803@charter.net. 300 Old Hwy. 2, Odanah, 54861. Revs. Joseph Kumar Mayakuntla, Sacramental Min.; Ducahn Pham, O.F.M., Admin.; Deacons Clarence L. Campbell; Owen T. Gorman; William J. Holzhaeuser; John E. Grek.
Catechesis Religious Program—Tel: 715-292-6082; Email: spw803@charter.net. Sr. Phyllis Wilhelm, O.S.F., Pastoral Assoc.

OSCEOLA, POLK CO., ST. JOSEPH (1915) Also serves St. Anne, Somerset & Assumption of the Blessed Virgin Mary, Farmington.
255 10th Ave., P.O. Box 399, Osceola, 54020-0399. Tel: 715-294-2243; Email: stjosephchurch@live.com. Very Rev. John R. Gerritts, Supervising Pastor; Rev. Barg G. Anderson, Parochial Vicar; Deacons Richard T. Peterson, Parish Life Coord.; Thomas P. Rausch; Edward C. Colosky.
Catechesis Religious Program—Rose Klugow, C.R.E. (K-10). Students 106.

PARK FALLS, PRICE CO., ST. ANTHONY OF PADUA (1904) Also serves Immaculate Conception, Butternut; St.

Francis of Assisi, Fifield.
276 S. 5th Ave., Park Falls, 54552.
Tel: 715-762-4494, Ext. 113; Email: stanthony75@hotmail.com; Web: www.stanthonysparkfalls.com. Rev. Shaji Joseph Pazhukkathara, Parochial Admin.; Deacons Chester E. Ball Jr.; Robert L. Schienebeck.
Catechesis Religious Program—Email: sapreligion@gmail.com. Kathy Rominske, D.R.E. Students 79.

PELICAN LAKE, ONEIDA CO., ST. JOHN (1905) [CEM] Also serves Nativity of Our Lord, Rhinelander.
Mailing Address: 105 S. Pelham St., Rhinelander, 54501. Tel: 715-362-3169; Email: mtpriest4dos@gmail.com. Appleton St. & Cty. Hwy. B, Pelican Lake, 54463. Rev. Michael J. Tupa; Deacons Ronald J. Bosi; Richard J. Meier.
Catechesis Religious Program—Students 13.

PENCE, IRON CO., HOLY REDEEMER (1908) Closed. For inquiries for parish records please see St. Mary of the Seven Dolors, Hurley.

PHELPS, VILAS CO., ST. MARY (1908)
P.O. Box 237, Land O'Lakes, 54540.
Tel: 715-547-3358; Email: stalbertstmary@gmail.com; Web: saintsalbertandmary.org. 4494 Town Hall Rd., Phelps, 54554. Very Rev. Christopher J. Kemp, Supervising Pastor; Rev. Patrick J. A. McConnell, Sacramental Min.; Deacon Norman J. Mesun Jr.; Michele Rein, Parish Dir.
Catechesis Religious Program—Students 14.

PHILLIPS, PRICE CO., ST. THERESE OF LISIEUX (1876) [CEM] Also serves St. Paul the Apostle, Catawba; St. John the Baptist, Prentice.
655 S. Lake Ave., Phillips, 54555. Tel: 715-339-2222; Email: oln@pctcnet.net. Rev. Gerald A. Hagen.
Catechesis Religious Program—Email: sttheresere@gmail.com. Sherrie Kandutsch, D.R.E.

PIER-WILLOW, ONEIDA CO., ST. FRANCIS OF ASSISI (1966) [CEM] Also serves St. Mary, Tomahawk & St. Augustine, Harrison.
Mailing Address: 320 E. Washington Ave., Tomahawk, 54487. Tel: 715-453-2878; Email: pastor@smctomahawk.com. 5209 N. Willow Rd., Tripoli, 54564. Rev. Louis Reddy Maram Reddy, Parochial Admin.; Deacons David C. Bablick; Clifford Eggett; C. Dan Towle.
Catechesis Religious Program—Combined with other parishes in cluster.

PRENTICE, PRICE CO., ST. JOHN THE BAPTIST (1886) Also serves St. Therese of Lisieux, Phillips & St. Paul the Apostle, Catawba.
Mailing Address: 655 S. Lake Ave., Phillips, 54555.
Tel: 715-339-2222; Email: oln@pctcnet.net. 935 Town St., Prentice, 54556. Rev. Gerald A. Hagen.
Catechesis Religious Program—Tel: 715-339-4885; Email: snoylag9@gmail.com. Gloria Lyons, C.R.E. Students 21.

PRESQUE ISLE, VILAS CO., ST. RITA (1950) Also serves St. Anne, Boulder Junction & St. Mary, Sayner.
Mailing Address: P.O. Box 110, Boulder Junction, 54512. Tel: 715-385-2390; Email: northwoodscath@yahoo.com. Rev. Showri Jojappa Pasala, Admin.
Church: 11568 Lake St., Presque Isle, 54557.
Catechesis Religious Program—Joan Meeder, C.R.E.

RADISSON, SAWYER CO., SACRED HEART (1919) Also serves St. Peter, Winter.
P.O. Box 216, Winter, 54896. Tel: 715-266-3441; Fax: 715-266-3440; Email: northcentralcluster@hotmail.com. Hwy. 27/70 Marian St., Radisson, 54867. Rev. Jerome D'Souza, C.M.F., Temporary Admin.
Church: Hwy. 27 & Martin St., Radisson, 54867.
Catechesis Religious Program—Email: cboisvert@centurytel.net. Celine Boisvert, D.R.E.

RED CLIFF, BAYFIELD CO., ST. FRANCIS (1861) [CEM] Also serves Holy Family, Bayfield, St. Ann, Cornucopia, St. Joseph, LaPointe & St. Louis, Washburn.
P.O. Box 1290, Bayfield, 54814. Tel: 715-779-3316; Email: hfchurch@ncis.net. Church Rd., Red Cliff, 54814. Very Rev. Frank Kordek, O.F.M., Supervising Pastor; Deacons Roger L. Cadotte, Dir. Pastoral Svcs.; Kenneth D. Kasinski; Sr. Kathy Salewski, O.S.F., Pastoral Min./Coord.
Catechesis Religious Program—Email: bandpduffy26@gmail.com. Barb Duffy, D.R.E.

RESERVE, SAWYER CO., ST. FRANCIS OF SOLANUS (1885) [CEM] (Indian) Also serves St. Ignatius, New Post; St. Philip, Stone Lake.
13891 W. Mission Rd., Stone Lake, 54876.
Tel: 715-865-3669; Email: ghopefl@charter.net; Web: www.stfrancismission.org. Rev. Gregory J. Hopefl.
School—St. Francis Solanus, (Grades PreK-8), 13885 W. Mission Rd., Stone Lake, 54876.
Tel: 715-865-3662; Fax: 715-865-4055; Email: schsis@cheqnet.net. Sr. Felissa Zander, S.S.S.F., Prin. & D.R.E. Clergy 1; Sisters of St. Francis 2; Students 20.
Catechesis Religious Program—Combined with other parishes in cluster.

RHINELANDER, ONEIDA CO.
1—IMMACULATE CONCEPTION (1883) [CEM] Closed. For inquiries for sacramental records please contact Nativity of Our Lord, Rhinelander.
2—ST. JOSEPH'S (1909) [CEM] Closed. For inquiries for sacramental records contact Nativity of Our Lord, Rhinelander.
3—NATIVITY OF OUR LORD (2005) Also serves St. John, Pelican Lake.
Mailing Address: 105 S. Pelham St., Rhinelander, 54501. Tel: 715-362-3169; Fax: 715-362-1811; Email: nativityparish@nativity.me. Rev. Michael J. Tupa; Deacons Ronald J. Bosi; Richard J. Meier.
Worship Site: Nativity of Our Lord, 125 E. King St., Rhinelander, 54501.
School—Nativity of Our Lord School, (Grades PreK-8), 103 E King St., Rhinelander, 54501.
Tel: 715-362-3366; Email: mnycz@nativity.me; Web: nativityofourlord.weconnect.com/school. Melanie Nycz, Prin.; Rev. Randall Knauf, O.F.M.Cap., Parochial Admin.; Joanne Siedschlag, Librarian. Clergy 2; Lay Teachers 18; Students 226.
Catechesis Religious Program—Email: jwagner@nativity.me. Joyce Wagner, D.R.E. Students 89.

RIB LAKE, TAYLOR CO.
1—GOOD SHEPHERD (2005)
Mailing Address: P.O. Box 295, Rib Lake, 54470.
Tel: 715-427-5259; Fax: 715-427-0381; Email: goodshepherd@newnorth.net; Web: www.goodshepherdriblake.org. Rev. Otto N. Bucher, O.F.-M.Cap.
Church: 513 State Rd., Rib Lake, 54470.
Catechesis Religious Program—Mary Kauer, C.R.E. Students 66.
2—ST. JOHN THE BAPTIST (1896) Closed. For inquiries for sacramental records, contact Good Shepherd, Rib Lake.

RICE LAKE, BARRON CO., ST. JOSEPH (1878) [CEM] Also serves Holy Trinity, Haugen, Our Lady of Lourdes, Dobie & St. John the Evangelist, Birchwood.
111 W. Marshall St., Rice Lake, 54868.
Tel: 715-234-2032; Email: stjoseph@chibardun.net. Revs. Edwin C. Anderson; Samuel Schneider; Deacon Dennis C. Geisler.
School—St. Joseph School, (Grades PreK-8), 128 W. Humbird St., Rice Lake, 54868. Tel: 715-234-7721; Fax: 715-234-5062; Email: j.mazourek@sjsricelake.org; Web: stjoesricelake.com. Jerome Van Dyke, Prin. Clergy 3; Lay Teachers 13; Sisters 1; Students 190.
Catechesis Religious Program—Email: lynnpottingerprice@gmail.com. Lynn Price, D.R.E. Students 217.

RIVER FALLS, ST. CROIX CO., ST. BRIDGET (1854) [CEM] Also serves Immaculate Conception, Hammond.
Mailing Address: 211 E. Division St., P.O. Box 86, River Falls, 54022. Tel: 715-425-1870;
Fax: 715-425-1871; Email: recept@stbparish.com. Revs. Gerald P. Harris; Richard Rhinehart.
School—St. Bridget School, (Grades PreK-8), 135 E. Division St., River Falls, 54022. Tel: 715-425-1872; Fax: 715-425-1873; Email: principal@stbparish.com; Web: www.saintbridgets.org/school/. Jeanne McCoy, Prin. Clergy 1; Lay Teachers 18; Students 188.
Catechesis Religious Program—Tel: 715-425-1879; Email: childrensff@stbparish.com. Diane Wengelski, C.R.E. (Pre-K-5); Tessa Schuermann, Youth Min. (6-11). Students 358.

SANBORN, ASHLAND CO., ST. ANNE (1895) Also serves Most Holy Rosary, Mellen, Most Precious Blood, Glidden, St. Anthony, Highbridge & St. George, Clam Lake.
P.O. Box 17, Mellen, 54546. Tel: 715-274-3701; Fax: 715-274-3703; Email: mostholyrosary@centurytel.net. 42070 County Hwy. E, Sanborn, 54806. Rev. Papi Yeruva, Admin.

SARONA, WASHBURN CO., ST. CATHERINE (1917) Also serves St. Francis de Sales, Spooner & St. Joseph, Shell Lake.
Mailing Address: 409 Summit St., Spooner, 54801.
Tel: 715-635-3105; Email: balamadanu26@gmail.com. W5262 Cty. Hwy. D, Sarona, 54870. Rev. Madanu Bala Showry, Parochial Admin.; Deacons Joseph J. Wesley; James R. Stroede.
Catechesis Religious Program—Combined with other parishes in cluster.

SAXON, IRON CO., ST. ANN (1886) Also serves St. Mary of the Seven Dolors, Hurley.
14233 N. Church St., P.O. Box 100, Saxon, 54559.
Tel: 715-893-2236; Email: stmary7@charter.net. Very Rev. Frank Kordek, O.F.M., Parochial Admin.
Catechesis Religious Program—

SAYNER, VILAS CO., ST. MARY (1912) Also serves St. Anne, Boulder Junction & St. Rita, Presque Isle.
P.O. Box 110, Boulder Junction, 54512-0110.
Tel: 715-385-2390; Email: stannechurch@centurytel.net. 8705 Cty. Hwy. N, Sayner, 54560. Rev. Showri Jojappa Pasala, Admin.
Catechesis Religious Program—Email: stannechurch@centurytel.net. Joan Meeder, C.R.E. Students 17.

SHELDON, RUSK CO., ST. JOHN THE APOSTLE (1955) Also serves SS. Peter & Paul, Gilman, St. Michael, Jump River & St. Stanislaus, Lublin.
Mailing Address: 315 E. Davlin St., Gilman, 54433.
Tel: 715-452-5851; Email: fivesaintscatholic@gmail.com. N657 County Rd. V V, Sheldon, 54766. Rev. Lourduraju Madanu, Parochial Admin.
Catechesis Religious Program—Email: mableidinger@fspa.org. Sr. Marianna Ableidinger, F.S.P.A., D.R.E. Students 17.

SHELL LAKE, WASHBURN CO., ST. JOSEPH (1880) [CEM] Also serves St. Francis de Sales, Spooner & St. Catherine, Sarona.
Mailing Address: 409 Summit St., Spooner, 54801.
Tel: 715-635-3105; Email: balamadanu26@gmail.com. 502 N. 2nd St., Shell Lake, 54801. Rev. Madanu Bala Showry, Parochial Admin.; Deacons Joseph J. Wesley; James R. Stroede.
Catechesis Religious Program— Combined with other parishes in cluster.

SOLON SPRINGS, DOUGLAS CO., ST. PIUS X (1878) [CEM] Also serves St. Anthony of Padua, Gordon; St. Mary, Minong.
11651 S. Business 53, P.O. Box 303, Solon Springs, 54873. Tel: 715-378-4431; Email: pomp1o2000@yahoo.com. Rev. James J. Kinney.
Catechesis Religious Program—Email: jodi.stpius@gmail.com. Jody Cosgrove, D.R.E. Students 19.

SOMERSET, ST. CROIX CO., ST. ANNE (1851) [CEM] Also serves Assumption of the Blessed Virgin Mary, Farmington & St. Joseph, Osceola.
141 Church Hill Rd., P.O. Box 9, Somerset, 54025.
Tel: 715-247-3310; Fax: 715-247-3174; Email: stanne@somtel.net. Very Rev. John R. Gerritts, Supervising Pastor; Rev. Barg G. Anderson, Parochial Vicar; Deacons Richard T. Peterson, Parish Life Coord.; Thomas P. Rausch; Edward C. Colosky.
School—St. Anne School, (Grades PreK-8), 140 Church Hill Rd., Somerset, 54025. Tel: 715-247-3762 ; Fax: 715-247-4335; Email: rstanke@stanne-somerset.org. Randall Stanke, Prin. Clergy 2; Lay Teachers 12; Students 114.
Catechesis Religious Program—Email: rachelm_stanne@somtel.net. Rachel McGurran, D.R.E.

SPOONER, WASHBURN CO., ST. FRANCIS DE SALES (1886) [CEM 2] Also serves St. Joseph, Shell Lake; St. Catherine, Sarona.
409 Summit St., Spooner, 54801. Tel: 715-635-3105; Email: balamadanu26@gmail.com. Rev. Madanu Bala Showry, Parochial Admin.; Deacons Joseph J. Wesley; James R. Stroede.
School—St. Francis De Sales School, (Grades PreK-8), 300 Oak St., Spooner, 54801. Tel: 715-635-2774; Email: sfds@centurytel.net. Kathy Kurkiewicz, Prin. Clergy 1; Lay Teachers 12; Students 117.
Catechesis Religious Program—Email: schmidtabbie@gmail.com. Abbie Schmidt, D.R.E. Students 88.

STANTON, ST. CROIX CO., ST. BRIDGET (1875) Closed. For inquiries for parish records please see St. Joseph, Amery.

STETSONVILLE, TAYLOR CO., SACRED HEART OF JESUS (1884) [CEM]
322 W. Cty. Hwy. A, Stetsonville, 54480.
Tel: 715-678-2395; Email: sacredheartchurchstetsonville@gmail.com. Rev. Michael T. Hayden; Deacon Joseph F. Roe.
Catechesis Religious Program—Email: karleensper@gmail.com. Karleen Sperl, C.R.E. Students 40.

STONE LAKE, SAWYER CO., ST. PHILIP (1905) Also serves St. Francis Solanus, Reserve & St. Ignatius, New Post.
Mailing Address: 13891 W. Mission Rd., Stone Lake, 54876. Tel: 715-865-3669; Email: ghopefl@charter.net. 5750 N Frost Ave., Stone Lake, 54876. Rev. Gregory J. Hopefl
St. Philip Catholic Congregation
Catechesis Religious Program—Sr. Felissa Zander, S.S.S.F., D.R.E. Combined with other parishes in cluster.

STRICKLAND, RUSK CO., ASSUMPTION OF THE BLESSED VIRGIN MARY (1897) [CEM] Also serves St. Joseph, Barron, St. Boniface, Chetek & St. Peter, Cameron.
Mailing Address: 827 E. LaSalle Ave., Barron, 54812. Tel: 715-637-3255; Fax: 715-637-3252; Email: stjosephchurch@chibardun.net; Email: pgerber4127@charter.net. W16431 Old 14, Rice Lake, 54868. Very Rev. John R. Gerritts, Supervising Pastor; Rev. Balaraju Policetty, Sacramental Min.; Patricia Gerber, Parish Dir.

SUGAR CAMP, ONEIDA CO., ST. KUNEGUNDA OF POLAND (1892) [CEM] Also serves St. Theresa, Three Lakes.
P.O. Box 8, Three Lakes, 54562-0008.
Tel: 715-272-1191; Email: sttheresa@frontier.com. 6895 Hwy. 17 N., Sugar Camp, 54501. Revs. Patrick

J. A. McConnell; Bala Reddy Allam, Sacramental Min.; Deacon John McCaughn.
Catechesis Religious Program—Email: sttheresa@frontier.com. Jen Metzger, C.R.E. Students 45.

THREE LAKES, ONEIDA CO., ST. THERESA (1892) Also serves St. Kunegunda of Poland, Sugar Camp.
6990 Forest St., P.O. Box 8, Three Lakes, 54562.
Tel: 715-546-2159; Email: sttheresa@frontier.com. Revs. Patrick J. A. McConnell; Bala Reddy Allam, Sacramental Min.; Deacon John McCaughn.
Catechesis Religious Program—Email: ccdsttstk@gmail.com. Jen Metzger, D.R.E. Students 10.

TOMAHAWK, LINCOLN CO., ST. MARY (1887) [CEM] Also serves St. Francis of Assisi, Pier-Willow & St. Augustine, Harrison.
320 E. Washington Ave., Tomahawk, 54487.
Tel: 715-453-2878; Email: pastor@smctomahawk.com. Rev. Louis Reddy Maram Reddy, Parochial Admin.; Deacons David C. Bablick; Clifford Eggett; Clarence D. Towle.
School—St. Mary School, (Grades PreK-5), 221 E. Washington Ave., Tomahawk, 54487.
Tel: 715-453-3542; Email: smsprincipal@stmarystudents.com; Web: www.stmarysschooltomahawk.com/home.html. Rita Lee, Prin. Clergy 1; Lay Teachers 7; Students 72.
Catechesis Religious Program—Email: dreyouth@smctomahawk.com. Kay Berg, D.R.E. & Youth Min. Students 128.

TONY, RUSK CO., ST. ANTHONY DE PADUA (1901) [CEM] Also serves St. Mary, Bruce, St. Francis of Assisi, Flambeau, St. Mary of Czestochowa, Hawkins, Our Lady of Lourdes, Ladysmith & SS. Peter & Paul, Weyerhaeuser.
Mailing Address: 611 1st St. S., Ladysmith, 54848.
Tel: 715-532-3051; Fax: 715-609-1059; Email: jp2officedesk@gmail.com; Web: www.ruskcountycatholiccommunity.org. N5333 Maple St., Tony, 54563. Very Rev. Philip J. Juza, Supervising Pastor; Revs. Inna Reddy Pothireddy, Sacramental Min.; David P. Oberts, Weekend Help Out, (Retired); Deacons Craig J. Voldberg, Parish Life Coord.; Thomas E. Fuhrmann; Douglas L. Sorenson, (Retired).
Church: N5323 Maple St., Tony, 54563.

TURTLE LAKE, BARRON CO., ST. ANN (1882) [CEM 4] Also serves St. Anthony, Cumberland & Sacred Heart of Jesus, Almena.
Mailing Address: 900 St. Anthony St., Cumberland, 54829. Tel: 715-822-2948; Fax: 715-822-3588; Email: stanthony@actinfaith.net; Web: www.actinfaith.net. Very Rev. John R. Gerritts, Supervising Pastor; Rev. Thomas E. Thompson, Sacramental Min.; Deacons Steven G. Linton, Parish Life Coord.; Gregory J. Ricci.
Church: 300 Pine St. S., Turtle Lake, 54889.
Catechesis Religious Program—Mary DeNoyer, C.R.E. Students 24.

WASHBURN, BAYFIELD CO., ST. LOUIS (1882) [CEM] Also serves Holy Family, Bayfield, St. Ann, Cornucopia, St. Francis, Red Cliff & St. Joseph, LaPointe.
217 W. 7th St., P.O. Box 70, Washburn, 54891.
Tel: 715-373-2676; Fax: 715-373-0365; Email: parishoffice@stlouiswashburn.com. Very Rev. Frank Kordek, O.F.M., Supervising Pastor; Deacons Roger L. Cadotte, Dir.; Kenneth D. Kasinski; Caroline Nelson, Sec.; Suzette Psyhogios, Sec.
Catechesis Religious Program—Leah Goodness, D.R.E. Students 29.

WEBSTER, BURNETT CO., ST. JOHN THE BAPTIST (1880) [CEM] Also serves Sacred Hearts of Jesus and Mary, Crescent Lake; Our Lady of Perpetual Help, Danbury.
26455 S. Muskey Ave., P.O. Box 7, Webster, 54893.
Tel: 715-866-7321; Email: sjoffice@centurytel.net. Rev. Randall Knauf, O.F.M.Cap., Admin.; Gwen Nies, Pastoral Assoc.
Catechesis Religious Program—Email: sjff@centurytel.net. Gwen Nies, D.R.E. Students 20.

WESTBORO, TAYLOR CO., ST. THERESA (1904) Closed. For inquiries for sacramental records please contact Good Shepherd, Rib Lake.

WEYERHAEUSER, RUSK CO., SS. PETER AND PAUL (1897) [CEM] Also serves Our Lady of Sorrows, Ladysmith, St. Mary, Bruce, St. Francis of Assisi, Flambeau, St. Mary of Czestochowa, Hawkins & St. Anthony de Padua, Tony.
Mailing Address: 611 1st St. S., Ladysmith, 54848.
Tel: 715-532-3051; Fax: 715-609-1059; Email: jp2officedesk@gmail.com; Web: www.ruskcountycatholiccommunity.org. N3729 1st St., Weyerhaeuser, 54895. Very Rev. Philip J. Juza, Supervising Pastor; Revs. Inna Reddy Pothireddy, Sacramental Min.; David P. Oberts, Weekend Help Out, (Retired); Deacons Craig J. Voldberg, Parish Life Coord.; Thomas E. Fuhrmann; Douglas L. Sorenson, (Retired).

WILSON, ST. CROIX CO., ST. BRIDGET (1886) [CEM] Also serves St. John the Baptist, Glenwood City & St. John, Clear Lake.
Mailing Address: 761 First St., Glenwood City, 54013. Tel: 715-265-7133; Email: stjohnbaptist@cltcomm.net; Web: www.jbjsaints.com. 120 Depot St., Wilson, 54027. Rev. John R. Long; Deacon Wesley G. Tuttle.
Catechesis Religious Program—Jan Caress-Hanson, P.C.L. Combined with other parishes in cluster.

WINTER, SAWYER CO., ST. PETER (1908) [CEM] Also serves Sacred Heart, Radisson.
N 5106 Main St., P.O. Box 216, Winter, 54896.
Tel: 715-266-3441; Fax: 715-266-3442; Email: northcentralcluster@hotmail.com. Rev. Jerome D'Souza, C.M.F., Parochial Admin.
Catechesis Religious Program—Tel: 715-307-7481; Email: cboisvert@centurytel.net. Celine Boisvert, D.R.E. Students 11.

WOODRUFF, ONEIDA CO.
1—HOLY FAMILY (2004)
8950 County Hwy. J., Woodruff, 54568.
Tel: 715-356-6284; Fax: 715-356-2940; Email: nancymccabe@holyfamilywoodruff.org; Email: fraaron@holyfamilywoodruff.org. Rev. Aaron Devett.
Catechesis Religious Program—Email: jamie.klappa@holyfamilywoodruff.org. Jamie Klappa, D.R.E. Students 127.
2—OUR LADY QUEEN OF THE UNIVERSE (1955) [CEM] Closed. For inquiries for sacramental records please contact Holy Family, Woodruff.

Chaplains of Public Institutions.

On Special or Other Diocesan Assignment:
Very Rev.—
Gordon, Kevin M., Episcopal Vicar for Clergy, Chancery Box 969, 54880.

Retired:
Rev. Msgr.—
Heslin, Philip J., (Retired), New Perspective Senior Living, 1915 N. 34th St., 54880. Tel: 218-730-7029; Tel: 715-399-3347
Very Rev.—
Drummy, John A., (Retired), P.O. Box 874, Osceola, 54020. Tel: 715-755-4508
Revs.—
Bartelme, James P., (Retired), 3627 N. 6th St., #205, Wausau, 54403
Brenna, William D., (Retired), 310 12th Ave. N., South Saint Paul, MN 55075. Tel: 715-494-0665
Brinkman, James J., (Retired), 811 4th St., Clear Lake, 54005. Tel: 715-690-5040
Briody, Hugh J., (Retired), Knightsbridge Ct., Longwood Rd., Trim, Co. Meath Ireland. Tel: 011-090-964-4439
Brost, Frederick, (Retired), 615 E. Allman St., Medford, 54451. Tel: 715-748-2141
Buttrick, Dean T., (Retired), 46050 West Tahkodah Lake Rd., Cable, 54821. Tel: 715-798-3430
Byrne, Bernard M., (Retired), 17555 Emmet St., #200, Omaha, NE 68116. Tel: 402-917-2095
Cary, William J., (Retired), 1802 Dublin Tr., Apt. 36, Neenah, 54956. Tel: 920-486-7911
Dahlberg, Daniel J., (Retired), St. Ann's Residence, Rm. 318, 330 E. 3rd St., Duluth, MN 55805. Tel: 218-391-7058
Green, William H., (Retired), 1912 E. 2nd St., Apt. A, 54880. Tel: 715-392-2399
Hardy, J. Patrick, (Retired), c/o Barbara Cox, 7860 S. Clement Ave., Oak Creek, 53154
Heinen, Virgil O., (Retired), 1336 A Carriage Dr., Hudson, 54016. Tel: 715-381-9778
Hoffman, James A., (Retired), 1291 Donald Dr., Arbor Vitae, 54568. Tel: 715-358-2936
Horath, James R., (Retired), 1926 Seville Rd., Mosinee, 54455. Tel: 715-203-2288
Hornung, Eugene H., (Retired), WI Veterans Home, 2175 E. Park Ave., Chippewa Falls, 54729. Tel: 715-443-0006
Kleinheinz, Joseph L., (Retired), 408 East St., Merrill, 54452
Koszarek, Robert J., (Retired), 6600 Szczygiel Rd., Iron River, 54847. Tel: 715-372-5483
Levra, Ronald W., (Retired), Lake Side Villa, 804 N. Lake Ave., Phillips, 54555. Tel: 715-663-0073; Tel: 715-663-0299
Lusson, David R., (Retired), 545 Charlemagne Blvd., Naples, FL 34112. Cell: 715-671-3971
Meulemans, Dennis T., (Retired), 718 Holden Rd., Rib Lake, 54470. Tel: 715-427-3803
Mullen, Dennis M., (Retired), 111 W. Marshall St., Rice Lake, 54868. Tel: 715-566-1781
Murphy, William J., (Retired), 13221 W. Melita Trl., Rathdrum, ID 83858. Tel: 715-977-0322
Oberts, David P., (Retired), 2411 23rd St., Rice Lake, 54868. Tel: 715-234-2492
Trinka, Joseph C., (Retired), Amery Memory Care, 215 Birch St. W., Apt. B124, Amery, 54001.

Permanent Deacons:
Amell, Lawrence E., St. Joseph, Amery; Our Lady of the Lakes, Balsam Lake
Arndt, James E., St. Francis Xavier, Merrill; St. John the Baptist, Bloomville
Bablick, David C., St. Mary, Tomahawk; St. Francis of Assisi, Pier Willow; St. Augustine, Harrison
Ball, Chester E. Jr., St. Anthony of Padua, Park Falls; Immaculate Conception, Butternut; St. Francis of Assisi, Fifield
Bardos, John J., St. Anthony of Padua, Lac Du Flambeau; Our Lady Queen of Peace, Manitowish Waters; St. Isaac Jogues & Companions, Mercer
Bosi, Ronald J., Nativity of Our Lord, Rhinelander; St. John, Pelican Lake
Braam, Peter R., (Retired)
Brossmer, Norbert G., (Retired)
Byrnes, Timothy J., (Living Outside of Diocese)
Cabak, Russell E., (Living Outside of Diocese)
Cadotte, Roger L., Holy Family, Bayfield, St. Ann, Cornucopia; St. Joseph, La Ponte; St. Francis, Red Cliff; St. Louis, Washburn
Cameron, Howard, St. Patrick, Hudson
Campbell, Clarence L., Our Lady of the Lake, Ashland; St. Mary, Odanah; St. Peter, Dauby; St. Florian, Ino; Sts. Peter & Paul, Moquah
Celba, James J., (Retired)
Chammings, Robert J., Holy Assumption, Superior; St. Williams, Superior; Cathedral of Christ the King, Superior; St. Anthony, Superior; St. Anthony, Lake Nebagamon
Colosky, Edward C., St. Anne, Somerset; Assumption of the Blessed Virgin Mary, Farmington; St. Joseph, Osceola
Cullen, Michael D., (Retired)
Dennis, James M., (Retired)
Derrington, J. Patrick, (Living Outside the Diocese)
DiSera, David B., St. Joseph, Hayward
Drahos, Jerome J., (Retired)
Drost, Harvey G., (Retired)
Eggett, Clifford, St. Mary, Tomahawk; St. Francis of Assisi, Pier Willow; St. Augustine, Harrison
Feind, Kevin L., St. Anthony, Superior; St. Anthony, Lake Nebagamon, Cathedral of Christ the King, Superior; Holy Assumption, Superior; St. William, Foxboro
Frederick, James E., Sacred Heart, Radisson; St. Peter, Winter
Fuhrmann, Thomas E., Ss. Peter & Paul, Weyerhaeuser; Our Lady of Sorrows, Ladysmith; St. Mary, Bruce; St. Anthony de Padua, Tony; St. Francis of Assisi, Flambeau; St. Mary, Hawkins
Geisler, Dennis C., St. Joseph, Rice Lake; Our Lady of Lourdes, Dobie; Holy Trinity, Haugen; St. John the Evangelist, Birchwood
Germain, Michael J., Immaculate Conception, New Richmond; St. Patrick, Erin Prairie
Gil de Lamadrid, Arthur, Cathedral of Christ the King, Superior; St. Anthony, Superior; St. Anthony, Lake Nebagamon; Holy Assumption, Superior; St. William, Foxboro
Goodrich, Albert A., (Retired)
Gorman, Owen T., Our Lady of the Lake, Ashland; St. Mary, Odanah; St. Peter, Dauby; St. Florian, Ino; Sts. Peter & Paul, Moquah
Grek, John E., St. Peter & St. Paul, Moquah; St. Michael, Iron River; Our Lady of the Lake, Ashland; St. Mary, Odanah; St. Peter, Dauby; St. Florian, Ino
Harvey, Michael O., (Retired)
Hennemann, Lawrence P., St. Bridget, River Falls; Immaculate Conception, Hammond
Holzhaeuser, William J., Our Lady of the Lake, Ashland; St. Mary, Odanah; St. Peter, Dauby; St. Florian, Ino; Sts. Peter & Paul, Moquah
Jetto, Robert T., (Retired)
Johnson, Fred E., (Retired)
Kasinski, Kenneth D., St. Louis, Washburn; Holy Family, Bayfield; St. Ann, Cornucopia; St. Joseph, La Pointe; St. Francis, Red Cliff
Kuehn, Timothy J.
Linton, Steven G., St. Anthony Abbot, Cumberland; Sacred Heart of Jesus, Almena; St. Ann, Turtle Lake
Lyngdal, Bernard J., (Retired)
Marczak, Stanley J., St. Dominic, Frederic; Immaculate Conception, Grantsburg
McCaffery, Brian, St. Joseph, Hayward; St. Ann, Cable
McCaughn, John, St. Theresa, Three Lakes; St. Kunegunda of Poland, Sugar Camp
Meier, Richard J., (Retired)
Mercier, Stanley J., (Retired)
Mesun, Norman J. Jr., St. Albert, Land O'Lakes; St. Mary, Phelps
Miech, Richard M., St. Peter the Fisherman, Eagle River
Miller, Gregg J., St. Patrick, Hudson
Miller, William D., (Living outside of Diocese)
Paron, Joseph F., (Retired)
Peterson, Richard T., St. Anne, Somerset;

Assumption of the Blessed Virgin Mary, Farmington; St. Joseph, Osceola
Priniski, Mark E., (Living Outside of Diocese)
Rausch, Thomas P., St. Joseph, Osceola; St. Anne, Somerset; Assumption of the Blessed Virgin Mary, Farmington
Ricci, Gregory J., St. Anthony Abbott, Cumberland; Sacred Heart of Jesus, Almena; St. Ann, Turtle Lake
Riel, Mel (Carmelo) A., Immaculate Conception, New Richmond; St. Patrick, Erin Prairie
Roe, Joseph F., Sacred Heart of Jesus, Stetsonville
Ryan, Michael, St. Joseph, Hayward; St. Ann, Cable
Schienebeck, Robert L., St. Anthony of Padua, Park Falls; St. Francis of Assisi, Fifield; Immaculate Conception, Butternut
Smerz, Darrell P., (Retired)
Sorenson, Douglas L., Our Lady of Sorrows, Ladysmith; St. Mary, Bruce; St. Francis of Assisi, Flambeau; St. Mary of Czestochowa, Hawkins; St. Anthony de Padua, Tony; Sts. Peter & Paul, Weyerhaeuser
Stefancin, Joseph, (Living Outside of Diocese)
Stroede, James R., St. Francis de Sales, Spooner; St. Joseph, Shell Lake; St. Catherine, Sarona
Towle, C. Dan, St. Augustine, Harrison; St. Mary, Tomahawk; St. Francis of Assisi, Pier Willow
Tuttle, Wesley G., St. John the Baptist, Glenwood City; St. John, Clear Lake; St. Bridget, Wilson
Voldberg, Craig J., Our Lady of Sorrows, Ladysmith; St. Mary, Bruce; St. Francis of Assisi, Flambeau; St. Mary of Czestochowa, Hawkins; St. Anthony de Padua, Tony; Sts. Peter & Paul, Weyerhaeuser
Weiss, Thomas J., (Retired)
Wesley, Joseph J., St. Frances de Sales, Spooner; St. Joseph, Shell Lake; St. Catherine, Sarona.

INSTITUTIONS LOCATED IN DIOCESE

[A] GENERAL HOSPITALS

SUPERIOR. *St. Mary's Hospital of Superior*, 3500 Tower Ave., 54880. Tel: 715-817-7014; Fax: 715-392-8395; Email: terrance.jacobson@essentiahealth.org; Web: www.essentialhealth.org/stmaryshospitalsuperior/ . Mr. Terry R. Jacobson, Admin.; MaryAnne Korsch, Chap. Bed Capacity 25; Patients Asst Anual. 158,809; Tot Asst. Annually 158,809; Total Staff 300.

EAGLE RIVER. **Ascension Eagle River Hospital, Inc.* Sponsored by Ascension Health Ministries (Ascension Sponsor), a public juridic person. 201 Hospital Rd., Eagle River, 54521.
Tel: 715-356-8000; Fax: 715-356-6097; Email: karla.ashenhurst@ascension.org; Web: https://healthcare.ascension.org. Antonina Olszewski, Dir. Spiritual Care; Debra Standridge, Pres.; Mr. Timothy Waldoch, Chief Mission Integration Officer. f/k/a Eagle River Memorial Hospital, Incorporated Bed Capacity 25; Tot Asst. Annually 3,052; Total Staff 55.

MERRILL. *Ascension Good Samaritan Hospital, Inc.* Sponsored by Ascension Health Ministries (Ascension Sponsor), a public juridic person 601 S. Center Ave., Merrill, 54452. Tel: 715-536-5511; Fax: 715-539-2170; Email: timothy.waldoch@ascension.org; Web: https://healthcare.ascension.org. Debra Standridge, Pres.; Mr. Timothy Waldoch, Chief Mission Integration Officer; Antonina Olszewski, Dir. Spiritual Care
f/k/a Good Samaritan Health Center of Merrill, Wisconsin, Inc. Bed Capacity 25; Tot Asst. Annually 5,369; Total Staff 61.

RHINELANDER. *Ascension Sacred Heart-St. Mary's Hospitals, Inc.* Sponsored by Ascension Health Ministries (Ascension Sponsor), a public juridic person 2251 N. Shore Dr., Rhinelander, 54501.
Tel: 715-361-2000; Fax: 715-361-4877; Email: timothy.waldoch@ascension.org; Web: https://healthcare.ascension.org. Debra Standridge, Pres.; Mr. Timothy Waldoch, Chief Mission Integration Officer; Antonina Olszewski, Dir. Spiritual Care. f/k/a Sacred Heart-Saint Mary's Hospitals, Inc. Bed Capacity 59; Tot Asst. Annually 9,070; Total Staff 333.

TOMAHAWK. *Ascension Sacred Heart-St. Mary's Hospitals, Inc.* Sponsored by Ascension Health Ministries (Ascension Sponsor), a public juridic person. 401 W. Mohawk Dr., Tomahawk, 54487.
Tel: 715-453-7700; Fax: 715-453-7716; Email: timothy.waldoch@ascension.org; Web: https://healthcare.ascension.org. Debra Standridge, Pres.; Mr. Timothy Waldoch, Chief Mission Integration Officer; Antonina Olszewski, Dir. Spiritual Care. f/k/a Sacred Heart-Saint Mary's Hospitals, Inc.Main sponsor: Ascension Health Ministries (Ascension Sponsor) Bed Capacity 18; Tot Asst. Annually 2,204; Total Staff 50.

WOODRUFF. **The Howard Young Medical Center, Inc.* Sponsored by Ascension Health Ministries (Ascension Sponsor), a public juridic person. 240 Maple St., Woodruff, 54568. Tel: 715-356-8000; Fax: 715-356-6097; Email: timothy.waldoch@ascension.org; Web: https://healthcare.ascension.org. Debra Standridge, Pres.; Mr. Timothy Waldoch, Chief Mission Integration Officer; Antonina Olszewski, Dir. Spiritual Care. Bed Capacity 99; Tot Asst. Annually 5,510; Total Staff 200.

[B] HOMES FOR AGED

SUPERIOR. *St. Francis Home, Inc.*, 1416 Cumming Ave., 54880. Tel: 715-394-6617; Fax: 715-394-5951; Email: arock@ccbsuperior.org. Alan Rock, Acting CEO.

MERRILL. *Bell Tower Residence, Inc.*, 1500 O'Day St., Merrill, 54452. Tel: 715-536-5575;
Fax: 715-536-1765; Email: secretary@belltowerresidence.org; Web: www.belltowerresidence.org. Kristine McGarigle, Admin. Assisted Living residence for the elderly. Bed Capacity 90; Tot Asst. Annually 107; Total in Residence 85; Total Staff 90.

WOODRUFF. **Dr. Kate Newcomb Convalescent Center, Inc.*, P.O. Box 470, Woodruff, 54568-0470.
Tel: 715-356-8000; Fax: 715-356-6097; Email: timothy.waldoch@ascension.org. Debra Standridge, Pres.; Mr. Timothy Waldoch, Chief Mission Integration Officer; Antonina Olszewski, Dir. Spiritual Care. Assisted living & low income housing apartments; Sponsored by Ascension Health Ministries (Ascension Sponsor), a public juridic person. Bed Capacity 15; Total Staff 13.

[C] CONVENTS AND RESIDENCES FOR SISTERS

HUDSON. *Carmel of the Sacred Heart*, 430 Laurel Ave., Hudson, 54016. Tel: 715-386-2156; Email: carmelit@pressenter.com; Web: www.pressenter.com/~carmelit/. Sr. Lucia LaMontagne, O.Carm., Prioress. Sisters 5.

LADYSMITH. *Servants of Mary*, 1000 College Ave. W., P.O. Box 389, Ladysmith, 54848-0389.
Tel: 715-532-6153; Email: info@servitesisters.org; Web: www.servitesisters.org. Sr. Theresa Sandok, O.S.M., Pres.
Mary Bradley Corporation; Pooled Investment Trust of the Servants of Mary, Inc.; Servants of Mary Continuing Care Charitable Trust Sisters 35.

MERRILL. *Sisters of Mercy of the Holy Cross*, 1400 O'Day St., Merrill, 54452-3417. Tel: 715-539-1460; Fax: 715-539-1456; Email: provincialoffices@holycrosssisters.org; Web: www.holycrosssisters.org. Sr. Patricia E. Cormack, S.C.S.C., Prov. Sisters 24.

[D] CATHOLIC CHARITIES BUREAU

SUPERIOR. *Catholic Charities Bureau, Inc.*, 1416 Cummings Ave., 54880. Tel: 715-394-6617;
Fax: 715-394-5951; Email: ccbrecep@ccbsuperior.org; Web: www.ccbsuperior.org. Alan Rock, Exec. Dir. Tot Asst. Annually 332,786; Total Staff 694.

Catholic Community Services, Inc., 1416 Cumming Ave., 54880. Tel: 715-394-6617; Fax: 715-394-5951 ; Email: cthursby@ccbsuperior.org. Alan Rock, Exec. Dir.

Challenge Center, Inc., 39 N. 25th St. E., 54880.
Tel: 715-394-2771; Fax: 715-394-2100; Email: bwright@challenge-center.org. Benjamin Wright, Dir.

Challenge Center A, Inc. dba Deer Haven Group Home, 3105 Cumming Ave., 54880.
Tel: 715-394-2771; Fax: 715-394-2100; Email: bwright@challenge-center.org. Benjamin Wright, Dir.

Cypress Group Home, 1415 Cypress, 54880.
Tel: 715-394-2771; Fax: 715-394-2100; Email: bwright@challenge-center.org. Benjamin Wright, Dir.

The Dove, Inc., 1416 Cumming Ave., 54880.
Tel: 715-392-3133; Fax: 715-392-3190; Email: gleiviska@thedovesuperior.com; Web: thedovesuperior.com. Greg Leiviska, Admin.

The Dove Agency, Inc., 1416 Cumming Ave., 54880.
Tel: 715-392-3133; Fax: 715-392-3190; Email: gleiviska@thedovesuperior.com; Web: thedovesuperior.com. Greg Leiviska, Admin.

Foster Grandparent Program (NW WI, NE MN), 1416 Cumming Ave., 54880. Tel: 715-394-5384;
Fax: 715-394-5951; Email: kjacobson@ccbsuperior.org. Ms. Kate Jacobson, Dir.

Harborview Group Home, 910 E. 5th St., 54880.
Tel: 715-394-2771; Fax: 715-394-2100; Email: bwright@challenge-center.org. Benjamin Wright, Dir.

McKenzie Manor, 3317 N. 21st St., 54880.
Tel: 715-394-2771; Fax: 715-394-2100; Email: bwright@challenge-center.org. 39 N 25th St. E, 54880. Benjamin Wright, Dir.

Missouri Gardens Adult Family Home, 2347 Missouri Ave., 54880. Tel: 715-394-2771;
Fax: 715-394-2100; Email: bwright@challenge-center.org. Benjamin Wright, Dir.

Mountain View Group Home, 3319 N. 16th St., 54880. Tel: 715-394-2771; Fax: 715-394-2100; Email: bwright@challenge-center.org. Benjamin Wright, Dir.

Phoenix Villa, Inc., 1100 Weeks Ave., 54880.
Tel: 715-394-2012; Fax: 715-394-5518; Email: acooksey@ccbsuperior.org. Amanda Cooksey, Mgr.

Phoenix Villa, Inc. dba Elmwood Apartments, 1020 Weeks Ave., 54880. Tel: 715-394-2012;
Fax: 715-394-5518; Email: acooksey@ccbsuperior.org. Amanda Cooksey, Mgr.

Phoenix Villa of Superior, Inc. dba Oakwood Apartments, 1112 John Ave., 54880.
Tel: 715-394-2012; Fax: 715-394-5518; Email: acooksey@ccbsuperior.org. Amanda Cooksey, Mgr.

Retired Senior Volunteer Program, 1416 Cumming Ave., 54880. Tel: 715-394-4425; Fax: 715-394-5951 ; Email: kjacobson@ccbsuperior.org. Ms. Kate Jacobson, Dir.

Westbay, Inc., 1104 John Ave., 54880.
Tel: 715-394-2012; Fax: 715-394-5518; Email: acooksey@ccbsuperior.org. Amanda Cooksey, Mgr.

Woodview Family Home, 6001 E. Third St., 54880.
Tel: 715-394-2771; Fax: 715-394-2100; Email: bwright@challenge-center.org. Benjamin Wright, Dir.

AMERY. *Apple River, Inc.*, 401 Minneapolis Ave. S., Amery, 54001. Tel: 715-925-2015;
Fax: 715-925-2014; Email: ctuminaro@ccbsuperior.org; Web: ccbhousing.org. Mailing Address: 1416 Cumming Ave., 54880. Gary Valley, Dir.; Ms. Catherine Tuminaro, Regl. Mgr.

BARRON. *Barron County Developmental Services, Inc.* (2014) 175 N. Lake St., Barron, 54812.
Tel: 715-537-5341; Fax: 715-537-5608; Email: jwacek@ccsuperior.org; Web: ww.barroncountydsi.org. 1416 Cumming Ave., 54880. Joe Wacek, Dir.

CHETEK. *Phoenix Villa, Inc.* dba Evergreen Apartments, 707 Tainter St., Chetek, 54728.
Tel: 715-925-2015; Fax: 715-925-2014; Email: gvalley@ccbsuperior.org. Mailing Address: 1416 Cumming Ave., 54880. Gary Valley, Dir.; Ms. Catherine Tuminaro, Regl. Mgr.

CRANDON. *Phoenix Villa, Inc.* dba Acorn Apartments, 508 W. Washington, Crandon, 54520.
Tel: 715-369-2550; Fax: 715-369-5857; Email: akrouze@ccbsuperior.org. Mailing Address: 1416 Cumming Ave., 54880. Amber Krouze, Mgr.

DULUTH. *Northfield Apartments, Inc.*, 2713 W. Superior St., Duluth, MN 55806. Tel: 715-394-2012 ; Fax: 715-394-5518; Email: acooksey@ccbsuperior.org. Mailing Address: 1416 Cumming Ave., 54880. Amanda Cooksey, Regl. Mgr.

HAYWARD. *Phoenix Villa, Inc.* dba Phoenix Villa of Hayward, 15869 Muriel St., Hayward, 54843.
Tel: 715-236-2366; Fax: 715-236-3161; Email: madamak@ccbsuperior.org. Mailing Address: 1416 Cumming Ave., 54880. Mark Adamak, Mgr.

HUDSON. *United Day Care, Inc.* dba Hudson Community Children's Center, 824 Fourth St., Hudson, 54016. Tel: 715-386-5912;
Fax: 715-386-1467; Email: carmelofthesacredheart@gmail.com; Web: community.pressenter.net/~carmelit/. Mailing Address: 1416 Cumming Ave., 54880. Judy Brekke, Dir.

IRON RIVER. *Phoenix Villa, Inc.* dba Phoenix Villa of Iron River, 62155 County Rd. H, Iron River, 54847.
Tel: 715-394-2012; Fax: 715-394-5518; Email: acooksey@ccbsuperior.org. Mailing Address: 1416 Cumming Ave., 54880. Amanda Cooksey, Mgr.

LAKE NEBAGAMON. *Phoenix Villa, Inc.* dba Phoenix Villa of Lake Nebagamon, 6250 S. Fitch Ave., Lake Nebagamon, 54849. Tel: 715-394-2012;
Fax: 715-394-5518; Email: acooksey@ccbsuperior.org. Mailing Address: 1416 Cumming Ave., 54880. Amanda Cooksey, Mgr.

MEDFORD. *Black River Industries, Inc.*, 650 Jensen Dr., Medford, 54451. Tel: 715-748-2950;
Fax: 715-748-6363; Email: afallos@ccbsuperior.org; Web: www.blackriverindustries.org. Mailing Address: 1416 Cumming Ave., 54880. Amber Fallos, Dir.

Eastwood Apartments, Inc., 741-755 Del Rae Ct., Medford, 54451. Tel: 715-748-6962;
Fax: 715-748-2159; Email: bbrunner@ccbsuperior.org. Mailing Address: 1416 Cumming Ave., 54880. Bonnie Brunner, Regl. Mgr.

Phoenix Villa, Inc. dba Maywood Apartments, 521 Lemke Ave., Medford, 54451. Tel: 715-369-6962;
Fax: 715-748-2159; Email: bbrunner@ccbsuperior.

org. Mailing Address: 1416 Cumming Ave., 54880. Bonnie Brunner, Mgr.

MINONG. *Phoenix Villa, Inc.* dba Acorn Apartments, 405 2nd St., Minong, 54859. Tel: 715-236-2366; Fax: 715-236-3161; Email: madamak@ccbsuperior.org. Mailing Address: 1416 Cumming Ave., 54880. Mark Adamak, Mgr.

PLOVER. *Phoenix Villa, Inc.* dba Maywood Apartments, 2601 Madison Ave., Plover, 54467. Tel: 715-341-7616; Fax: 715-712-0387; Email: tobermeier@ccbsuperior.org. Mailing Address: 1416 Cumming Ave., 54880. Teri Obermeier, Mgr.

RHINELANDER. *Headwaters. Inc.*, 1441 E. Timber Dr., P.O. Box 618, Rhinelander, 54501. Tel: 715-369-1337; Fax: 715-369-1793; Email: jfelty@headwatersinc.org; Web: www.headwatersinc.org. Mailing Address: 1416 Cumming Ave., 54880. Jenny Felty, Dir.

Phoenix Villa, Inc. dba Phoenix Villa of Rhinelander, 1011 Mason St., Rhinelander, 54501. Tel: 715-369-2550; Fax: 715-369-5857; Email: akrouze@ccbsuperior.org. Mailing Address: 1416 Cumming Ave., 54880. Amber Krouze, Mgr.

Phoenix Villa, Inc. aka Evergreen Apartments/ Timberlane, 880 E. Timber Dr., Rhinelander, 54501. Tel: 715-369-2550; Fax: 715-369-5857; Email: akrouze@ccbsuperior.org. Mailing Address: 1416 Cumming Ave., 54880. Amber Krouze, Regl. Mgr.

Retired Senior Volunteer Program, 1835 N. Stevens St., Ste. 22, Rhinelander, 54501. Tel: 715-362-1919 ; Email: lbushong@ccbsuperior.org. Mailing Address: 1416 Cumming Ave., 54880. Lori Bushong, Dir.

Sumac Trail Apartments, Inc., 1313 Phillip St., Rhinelander, 54501. Tel: 715-369-2550; Fax: 715-369-5857; Email: akrouze@ccbsuperior.org. Mailing Address: 1416 Cumming Ave., 54880. Amber Krouze, Mgr.

RICE LAKE. *Blue Valley, Inc.*, 1310 N. Wisconsin Ave., Rice Lake, 54868. Tel: 715-236-2366; Fax: 715-236-3161; Email: madamak@ccbsuperior.org. Mailing Address: 1416 Cumming Ave., 54880. Mark Adamak, Regl. Mgr.

Phoenix Villa, Inc. dba Phoenix Villa North, 1305 N. Wisconsin St., Rice Lake, 54868. Tel: 715-236-2366 ; Fax: 715-236-3161; Email: madamak@ccbsuperior.org. Mailing Address: 1416 Cumming Ave., 54880. Mark Adamak, Mgr.

SHELL LAKE. *Phoenix Villa, Inc.* dba Evergreen Apartments, 797 N. Lake Dr., Shell Lake, 54871. Tel: 715-236-2366; Fax: 715-236-3161; Email: madamak@ccbsuperior.org. Mailing Address: 1416 Cumming Ave., 54880. Mark Adamak, Mgr.

SIREN. *Diversified Services Center, Inc.*, 7649 Tower Rd., P.O. Box 501, Siren, 54872. Tel: 715-349-5724; Fax: 715-349-5505; Email: jwacek@ccbsuperior.org; Web: www.dsisiren.com. Mailing Address: 1416 Cumming Ave., 54880. Joe Wacek, Dir.

Lilac Grove Apartments, Inc., 24145 1st Ave., Siren, 54872. Tel: 715-925-2015; Fax: 715-925-2014; Email: gvalley@ccbsuperior.org. Mailing Address: 1416 Cumming Ave., 54880. Gary Valley, Dir.; Ms. Catherine Tuminaro, Regl. Mgr.

Phoenix Villa, Inc. dba Evergreen Apartments/ Lakewood, 24121 Fourth St., Siren, 54872. Tel: 715-925-2015; Fax: 715-925-2014; Email: gvalley@ccbsuperior.org. Mailing Address: 1416 Cumming Ave., 54880. Gary Valley, Dir.; Ms. Catherine Tuminaro, Regl. Housing Mgr.

WINTER. *Winterhaven Apartments, Inc.*, 5038 N. Ellen St., Winter, 54896. Tel: 715-236-2366; Fax: 715-236-3161; Email: madamak@ccbsuperior.org. Mailing Address: 1416 Cumming Ave., 54880. Mark Adamak, Mgr.

WISCONSIN RAPIDS. *Phoenix Villa, Inc.* dba Acorn Apartments, 2721 Tenth St. S., Wisconsin Rapids, 54494. Tel: 715-421-0080; Fax: 715-712-0387; Email: tobermeier@ccbsuperior.org. Mailing Address: 1416 Cumming Ave., 54880. Teri Obermeier, Regl. Mgr.

[E] RETREAT HOUSES

ARBOR VITAE. *Marywood Franciscan Spirituality Center (FSPA)*, 3560 Hwy. 51 N., Arbor Vitae, 54568-9538. Tel: 715-385-3750; Email: marywood.center@gmail.com; Web: www.marywoodsc.org. Sr. Elizabeth Amman, O.P., Dir.

[F] NEWMAN CENTERS

SUPERIOR. *Newman Catholic Campus Ministry*, 801 N. 28th St., 54880. Tel: 715-392-8511; Email: superiornewmancenter@gmail.com. Brett Jones, Advisor; Zach Mazurek, Student Contact. Newman Center Ministry to Young Adults.

RIVER FALLS. *St. Thomas More Newman Center*, 423 E. Cascade, River Falls, 54022. Tel: 715-425-7234; Fax: 715-425-6959; Email: thomas.j.weiss@uwrf.edu; Web: uwrfnewman.org. Deacon Thomas J. Weiss, Dir.; Rev. Richard Rhinehart.

[G] ASSOCIATION OF THE FAITHFUL

LUCK. HERMITS OF MT. CARMEL, 2514 92nd St., Luck, 54853. Tel: 715-472-2570; Email: mountcarmelhermitage@gmail.com. Sr. Kristine Haugen, O.C.D.H., Coord.

[H] MISCELLANEOUS

SUPERIOR. *St. Augustine Seminarian Foundation, Inc.*, 1201 Hughitt Ave., P.O. Box 969, 54880. Tel: 715-392-2937; Email: dblank@catholicdos.org. Mr. Daniel Blank, Admin.

Challenge Center Foundation Inc., 1416 Cumming Ave., 54880. Tel: 715-394-6617; Email: arock@ccbsuperior.org. Alan Rock, Exec.

Society of St. Vincent de Paul Sacred Heart of Jesus Conference of Superior, WI, 1416 Cumming Ave, 54880. Tel: 715-398-4039. Anita Johnson, Pres.

Superior Retired Priest Health Care Foundation, Inc., 1201 Hughitt Ave., P.O. Box 969, 54880. Tel: 715-392-2937; Email: dblank@catholicdos.org. Mr. Daniel Blank, Admin.

LADYSMITH. *Mary Bradley Corporation*, 1000 College Ave. W., P.O. Box 389, Ladysmith, 54848-0389. Tel: 715-532-6153, Ext. 306; Email: info@servitesisters.org. Sr. Theresa Sandok, O.S.M., Pres.

Pooled Investment Trust of the Servants of Mary, Inc., 1000 College Ave. W., P.O. Box 389, Ladysmith, 54848-0389. Tel: 715-532-6153; Email: info@servitesisters.org. Sr. Theresa Sandok, O.S.M., Trustee.

Servants of Mary Continuing Care Charitable Trust, 1000 College Ave. W., P.O. Box 389, Ladysmith, 54848-0389. Tel: 750-535-6153, Ext. 306; Email: info@servitesisters.org. Sr. Theresa Sandok, O.S.M., Trustee.

LUCK. *Mount Carmel Hermitage*, 2514 92nd St., Luck, 54853. Tel: 715-472-2570; Email: mountcarmelhermitage@gmail.com. Sr. Kristine Haugen, O.C.D.H., Coord.

MERRILL. *Good Samaritan Health Center Foundation of Merrill, Wisconsin, Inc.* Sponsored by Ascension Health Ministries (Ascension Sponsor), a public juridic person. 601 S. Center Ave., Merrill, 54452. Tel: 715-536-5511; Fax: 715-539-5040; Email: timothy.waldoch@ascension.org; Web: https://healthcare.ascension.org/donate. Jane Bentz, Dir.; Mr. Timothy Waldoch, Chief Mission Integration Officer; Ms. Lisa Froemming, Vice Pres. for Philanthropy.

Sisters of Mercy of the Holy Cross Community Support Charitable Trust, 1400 O'Day St., Merrill, 54452-3417. Tel: 715-539-1460; Fax: 715-539-1458; Email: dniemann@holycrosssisters.org. Sisters Dorothy Niemann, S.C.S.C., Trustee; Rose Jochmann, O.S.F., Trustee; Craig Nienow, Trustee; John Tortolani, Trustee; William Wulf, Trustee.

RHINELANDER. *Headwaters Foundation*, 1441 E. Timber Dr., P.O. Box 618, Rhinelander, 54501. Tel: 715-394-6617; Email: arock@ccbsuperior.org. Alan Rock, Exec.

**Ascension Medical Group - Northern Wisconsin, Inc.* Sponsored by Ascension Health Ministries (Ascension Sponsor), a public juridic person. 2251 N. Shore Dr., Rhinelander, 54501. Tel: 715-361-4779; Fax: 715-361-4877; Email: timothy.waldoch@ascension.org; Web: https://healthcare.ascension.org. Mary Beth McDonald, Pres.; Mr. Timothy Waldoch, Chief Mission Integration Officer; Antonina Olszewski, Dir. Spiritual Care. f/k/a Ministry Medical Group, Inc.

Ministry Weight Management, Inc., 2251 N. Shore Dr., Rhinelander, 54501. Tel: 715-361-2000; Fax: 715-361-2011; Email: timothy.waldoch@ascension.org; Web: https://healthcare.ascension.org. Debra Standridge, Pres.; Mr. Timothy Waldoch, Chief Mission Integration Officer; Antonina Olszewski, Dir. Spiritual Care.

WEBSTER. *Thomas More Center for Preaching and Prayer, Inc.*, 27781 Leef Rd., Webster, 54893. Tel: 715-866-7436; Email: achamplinm@gmail.com; Web: www.thomasmorecenter.org. Revs. Michael A. Champlin, O.P., Pres., Email: achamplinm@gmail.com; Nicholas W. Punch, O.P., Treas.; Sr. Joan Bukrey, O.S.F., Vice Pres. and Sec.

WINTER. *Camp WeHaKee* (Girls) 8104 N. Barker Lake Rd., Winter, 54896. Tel: 715-266-3263; Tel: 800-582-2267; Fax: 608-787-8257; Email: info@wehakeecampforgirls.com; Email: bob@wehakeecampforgirls.com; Email: maggie@wehakeecampforgirls.com; Web: www.wehakeecampforgirls.com. 715 28th ST S, La Crosse, 54601. Bob Braun, Co-Dir.; Maggie Braun, Co-Dir. Students 300.

WOODRUFF. **Howard Young Health Care, Inc.* Sponsored by Ascension Health Ministries (Ascension Sponsor), a public juridic person. 240 Maple St., Woodruff, 54568. Tel: 715-356-8000; Fax: 715-356-6097; Email: timothy.waldoch@ascension.org; Web: https://healthcare.ascension.org. Debra Standridge, Pres.; Mr. Timothy Waldoch, Chief Mission Integration Officer; Antonina Olszewski, Dir. Spiritual Care. Total Staff 5.

RELIGIOUS INSTITUTES OF MEN REPRESENTED IN THE DIOCESE

For further details refer to the corresponding bracketed number in the Religious Institutes of Men or Women section.

[0470]—*Capuchin Franciscan Friars*—O.F.M.Cap.

[0480]—*Conventual Franciscans* (Arroyo Grande, CA)—O.F.M.Conv.

[0520]—*Franciscan Friars* (St. Louis, MO)—O.F.M.

[0430]—*Order of Preachers, Dominican Province of St. Albert the Great* (Dominican Central Province)—O.P.

[1060]—*Society of the Precious Blood* (Cincinnati Province)—C.P.P.S.

RELIGIOUS INSTITUTES OF WOMEN REPRESENTED IN THE DIOCESE

[0320]—*Carmelite Nuns of the Ancient Observance*—O.Carm.

[1780]—*Congregation of the Sisters of the Third Order of St. Francis of Perpetual Adoration (Franciscan Sisters of Perpetual Adoration)*—F.S.P.A.

[1710]—*Congregation of the Third Order of St. Francis of Mary Immaculate* (Joliet, IL)—O.S.F.

[1070-40]—*Dominican Sisters of Grand Rapids*—O.P.

[2970]—*School Sisters of Notre Dame* (Central Pacific Province)—S.S.N.D.

[1680]—*School Sisters of St. Francis*—S.S.S.F.

[3590]—*Servants of Mary (Servite Sisters)*—O.S.M.

[2630]—*Sisters of Mercy of the Holy Cross*—S.C.S.C.

[1705]—*Sisters of St. Francis of Penance and Charity*—O.S.F.

[3930]—*Sisters of St. Joseph of the Third Order of St. Francis* (Prov. of Immaculate Conception; St. Joseph Prov.)—S.S.J.-T.O.S.F.

NECROLOGY

† Meulemans, Edward G., (Retired), Died Dec. 24, 2018
† Fraher, Leonard W., (Retired), Died Apr. 9, 2018
† Kelchak, Joseph M., (Retired), Died Nov. 9, 2018

An asterisk (*) denotes an organization that has established tax-exempt status directly with the IRS and is not covered by the USCCB Group Ruling.

Diocese of Syracuse

(Dioecesis Syracusensis)

Most Reverend

ROBERT JOSEPH CUNNINGHAM

Bishop of Syracuse; ordained May 24, 1969; appointed Bishop of Ogdensburg March 9, 2004; ordained and installed May 18, 2004; appointed Bishop of Syracuse April 21, 2009; installed as Tenth Bishop of Syracuse May 26, 2009. *Office: 240 E. Onondaga St., Syracuse, NY 13202.*

Chancery Office: 240 E. Onondaga St., Syracuse, NY 13202. Tel: 315-422-7203; Fax: 315-478-4619.

Web: www.syracusediocese.org

ESTABLISHED NOVEMBER 26, 1886

Square Miles 5,749.

Corporate Title: The Roman Catholic Diocese of Syracuse NY.

Comprises the Counties of Broome, Chenango, Cortland, Madison, Oneida, Onondaga and Oswego.

For legal titles of parishes and diocesan institutions, consult the Chancery Office.

STATISTICAL OVERVIEW

Personnel	
Bishop	1
Priests: Diocesan Active in Diocese	97
Priests: Diocesan Active Outside Diocese	5
Priests: Retired, Sick or Absent	76
Number of Diocesan Priests	178
Religious Priests in Diocese	30
Total Priests in Diocese	208
Extern Priests in Diocese	13
Ordinations:	
Diocesan Priests	1
Transitional Deacons	1
Permanent Deacons	10
Permanent Deacons in Diocese	97
Total Brothers	5
Total Sisters	203
Parishes	
Parishes	121
With Resident Pastor:	
Resident Diocesan Priests	79
Resident Religious Priests	1
Without Resident Pastor:	
Administered by Priests	28
Administered by Deacons	3
Missions	8
Closed Parishes	1
Professional Ministry Personnel:	
Sisters	17
Lay Ministers	11
Welfare	
Catholic Hospitals	3
Health Care Centers	1
Homes for the Aged	53
Day Care Centers	18
Specialized Homes	2
Special Centers for Social Services	2
Residential Care of Disabled	14
Educational	
Diocesan Students in Other Seminaries	12
Seminaries, Religious	1
Students Religious	16
Total Seminarians	28
Colleges and Universities	1
Total Students	3,500
High Schools, Diocesan and Parish	4
Total Students	1,270
High Schools, Private	2
Total Students	843
Elementary Schools, Diocesan and Parish	18
Total Students	3,156
Elementary Schools, Private	1
Total Students	67
Catechesis/Religious Education:	
High School Students	3,480
Elementary Students	10,322
Total Students under Catholic Instruction	22,666
Teachers in the Diocese:	
Priests	1
Sisters	4
Lay Teachers	411
Vital Statistics	
Receptions into the Church:	
Infant Baptism Totals	2,226
Minor Baptism Totals	84
Adult Baptism Totals	98
Received into Full Communion	187
First Communions	2,053
Confirmations	2,116
Marriages:	
Catholic	526
Interfaith	198
Total Marriages	724
Deaths	3,387
Total Catholic Population	227,431
Total Population	1,192,000

Former Bishops—Rt. Revs. PATRICK ANTHONY LUDDEN, D.D., ord. June 21, 1864; cons. May 1, 1887; died Aug. 6, 1912; JOHN GRIMES, D.D., ord. Feb. 19, 1882; cons. May 16, 1909; Coadjutor Bishop, 1909-1912; succeeded to the See, Aug. 6, 1912; died July 26, 1922; Most Revs. DANIEL JOSEPH CURLEY, D.D., ord. May 19, 1894; cons. May 1, 1923; died Aug. 3, 1932; JOHN ALOYSIUS DUFFY, D.D., ord. June 13, 1908; cons. June 29, 1933; installed July 11, 1933; appt. Bishop of Buffalo, Jan. 9, 1937; installed in See of Buffalo, April 14, 1937; died Sept. 27, 1944; WALTER A. FOERY, D.D., Ph.D., ord. June 10, 1916; appt. May 26, 1937; cons. Aug. 18, 1937; appt. assistant at the Pontifical Throne, Dec. 11, 1961; retired and named Titular Bishop of Miseno-Cape, Aug. 4, 1970; died May 10, 1978; DAVID F. CUNNINGHAM, D.D., ord. June 12, 1926; appt. Titular Bishop of Lampsacus and Auxiliary Bishop of Syracuse, April 5, 1950; cons. June 8, 1950; appt. Coadjutor Bishop "Cum jure successiones," June 19, 1967; succeeded to the See, Aug. 4, 1970; died Feb. 22, 1979; FRANK J. HARRISON, D.D., ord. June 4, 1937; appt. Titular Bishop of Aquae and Auxiliary Bishop of Syracuse, March 1, 1971; cons. April 22, 1971; appt. Bishop of Syracuse, Nov. 16, 1976; retired June 16, 1987; died May 1, 2004; JOSEPH T. O'KEEFE, D.D., ord. April 17, 1948; appt. Titular Bishop of Tre Taverne and Auxiliary Bishop of New York, July 3, 1982; cons. Sept. 8, 1982; appt. Bishop of Syracuse, June 16, 1987; installed in See of Syracuse, Aug. 3, 1987; retired April 4, 1995; died Sept. 2, 1997; JAMES M. MOYNIHAN, ord. Dec. 15, 1957; appt. Bishop of Syracuse April 4, 1995; cons. and installed in See of Syracuse May 29, 1995; retired April 21, 2009; died March 6, 2017.

Vicar General—Very Rev. Msgr. TIMOTHY S. ELMER, J.C.L., V.G., 240 E. Onondaga St., Syracuse, 13202.

Vicars Forane—Northern Area Vicar: Rev. GAETANO T. BACCARO, St. Paul, 50 E. Mohawk St., Oswego, 13126. Southern Area Vicar: Rev. Msgr. JOHN P. PUTANO, 157 Clark St., Vestal, 13850. Eastern Area Vicars: Revs. RAYMOND P. MATHIS, 22 Church St., Camden, 13316; MARK P. KAMINSKI, Ph.D., D.Min., 422 Tilden Ave., P.O. Box 4156, Utica, 13501-4156. Western Area Vicars: Rev. JOHN D. MANNO, 4845 S. Salina St., Syracuse, 13205-2704; Rev. Msgr. JAMES T. O'BRIEN, (Retired), St. John's, 8290 Soule Rd., Liverpool, 13090-1399.

Chancery Office—Mailing Address: 240 E. Onondaga St., Syracuse, 13202. Tel: 315-422-7203; Fax: 315-478-4619. Office Hours: Mon.-Fri. 8:30-4:30Send official mail, including marriage dispensations, to Chancery.

Chancellor—MRS. DANIELLE CUMMINGS, 240 E. Onondaga St., Syracuse, 13202.

Secretary to the Bishop—Rev. JOSEPH O'CONNOR, 240 E. Onondaga St., Syracuse, 13202.

Board of Diocesan Consultors—Revs. RAYMOND P. MATHIS; JOHN D. MANNO; Rev. Msgr. JAMES P. LANG; Rev. GAETANO T. BACCARO; Rev. Msgr. JAMES T. O'BRIEN, (Retired); Rev. MARK P. KAMINSKI, Ph.D., D.Min.; Rev. Msgr. JOHN P. PUTANO; Very Rev. Msgr. TIMOTHY S. ELMER, J.C.L., V.G.

Administration Team—Most Rev. ROBERT J. CUNNINGHAM, J.C.L., D.D.; Rev. Msgr. JAMES P. LANG; Very Rev. Msgr. TIMOTHY S. ELMER, J.C.L., V.G.; Rev. Msgr. RICHARD M. KOPP; MR. WILLIAM CRIST; Rev. JOSEPH O'CONNOR; MR. STEPHEN BREEN; MRS. DANIELLE CUMMINGS.

Pastoral Council—Most Rev. ROBERT J. CUNNINGHAM, J.C.L., D.D., Pres.; MS. KATHLEEN M. DYER, Exec. Sec., Res.: 101 Ridge Rd., Fulton, 13069. Tel: 315-592-5566.

Presbyteral Council—Most Rev. ROBERT J. CUNNINGHAM, J.C.L., D.D., Pres.; Revs. GAETANO T. BACCARO; JOHN D. MANNO; JOHN A. BUEHLER; RALPH A. BOVE; Rev. Msgr. RONALD C. BILL, (Retired); Revs. LAURENCE J. LORD, (Retired); DONALD H. KARLEN, (Retired); Very Rev. Msgr. TIMOTHY S. ELMER, J.C.L., V.G.; Rev. Msgrs. JAMES P. LANG; JAMES T. O'BRIEN, (Retired); Rev. GEORGE V. COYNE, S.J.; Rev. Msgr. JOHN P. PUTANO; Revs. MARK P. KAMINSKI, Ph.D., D.Min.; LOUIS F. AIELLO; PAUL F. ANGELICCHIO; CHRISTOPHER CELENTANO; FREDERICK D. DALEY; MARK A. PASIK; PAUL R. MATHIS; JOHN J. KURGAN.

Diocesan Pastoral Examiners—Revs. ANDREW E. BARANSKI; KEVIN CORCORAN; JOHN J. KURGAN; E. PETER REDDICK, (Retired); THOMAS J. RYAN.

Diocesan Tribunal—

Judicial Vicar—Very Rev. Msgr. TIMOTHY S. ELMER, J.C.L., V.G., Tel: 315-470-1435; Fax: 315-474-6893.

Adjutant Judicial Vicar—Rev. JOHN P. DONOVAN, J.C.L.

Associate Judges—Revs. ROBERT P. HYDE JR., J.C.L.; JAMES SALAMY, J.C.L.

Defender of the Bond—Rev. CLIFFORD H. AUTH, J.C.L.

Promoter of Justice—VACANT.

Assistant to the Judicial Vicar—Rev. JAMES SALAMY, J.C.L.

Notary of the Tribunal—BARBARA REITER.

Case Coordinator / Staff—BARBARA REITER.

Vicar for Administration—Very Rev. Msgr. TIMOTHY S.

ELMER, J.C.L., V.G., 240 E. Onondaga St., Syracuse, 13202. Tel: 315-470-1435.

Director for Community Services—240 E. Onondaga St., Syracuse, 13202. Tel: 315-470-1415. MR. MICHAEL F. MELARA.

Vicar for Parishes—Rev. Msgr. JAMES P. LANG, 240 E. Onondaga St., Syracuse, 13202. Tel: 315-470-1437.

Vicar for Priests—Rev. Msgr. RICHARD M. KOPP, 240 E. Onondaga St., Syracuse, 13202. Tel: 315-470-1460.

Vicar for Religious—240 E. Onondaga St., Syracuse, 13202. Tel: 315-470-1005.

Diocesan Offices

Accounting—CAROL PIEKLIK, Mailing Address: 240 E. Onondaga St., Syracuse, 13202. Tel: 315-422-9045; Fax: 315-422-9139.

Administration—Mailing Address: 240 E. Onondaga St., Syracuse, 13202. Tel: 315-422-7203. Very Rev. Msgr. TIMOTHY S. ELMER, J.C.L., V.G.; MR. STEPHEN BREEN, CFO.

Archives—MS. MICKEY BRUCE, Archivist, Mailing Address: 240 E. Onondaga St., Syracuse, 13202. Tel: 315-470-1493; Email: syrarchivesed@aol.com.

Asian Apostolate—Rev. JOHN BAPTIST NGUYEN; YIN LEE, 527 N. Salina St., Syracuse, 13208. Tel: 315-289-7695.

Benefits—MS. ROSEMARY SMITH, Admin., Mailing Address: 240 E. Onondaga St., Syracuse, 13202. Tel: 315-422-9091.

Boy Scouts/Girl Scouts—Rev. Msgr. JAMES P. LANG, Chap., 240 E. Onondaga St., Syracuse, 13202. Tel: 315-470-1437.

Building Commission—Most Rev. ROBERT J. CUNNINGHAM, J.C.L., D.D.; Very Rev. Msgr. TIMOTHY S. ELMER, J.C.L., V.G.; Rev. JOSEPH E. SCARDELLA; MR. EDWARD T. KING; WILLIAM DORAN; Rev. Msgrs. RICHARD M. KOPP; JAMES P. LANG; MR. STEPHEN BREEN.

Catholic Cemeteries—2315 South Ave., Syracuse, 13207. Tel: 315-475-4639; Fax: 315-422-0363. MARK BARLOW, Dir.

Catholic Charities—Mailing Address: 240 E. Onondaga St., Syracuse, 13202. Tel: 315-470-1416; Fax: 315-459-7159. MR. MICHAEL F. MELARA.

Onondaga County Director—MR. MICHAEL F. MELARA, 1654 W. Onondaga St., Syracuse, 13204. Tel: 315-424-1800.

Broome County Director—LORI ACCARDI, Dir., 232 Main St., Binghamton, 13905. Tel: 607-729-9166.

Chenango County Director—MRS. ROBIN (BECKWITH) COTTER, Dir., 3 O'Hara Dr., Norwich, 13815. Tel: 607-334-8244.

Cortland County Director—MARIE WALSH, 33-35 Central Ave., Cortland, 13045. Tel: 607-756-5992.

Oneida and Madison Counties Director—DENISE L. CAVANAUGH, 1404 Genesee St., Utica, 13502. Tel: 315-724-2158.

Oswego County Director—MARY MARGARET PEZZELLA-PEKOW, 365 First St., Fulton, 13069. Tel: 315-598-3980.

Catholic Deaf Community—MICHELE MURPHY, 240 E. Onondaga St., Syracuse, 13202. Tel: 315-470-1463.

Catholic Relief Services—Mailing Address: 240 E. Onondaga St., Syracuse, 13202. Tel: 315-470-1416. MR. MICHAEL F. MELARA.

Catholic Schools—Mailing Address: 240 E. Onondaga, Syracuse, 13202. Tel: 315-470-1450;
Fax: 315-470-1470. MR. WILLIAM CRIST, Supt.; BARBARA MESSINA, Internal Dir., Leadership Devel. & Mission Effectiveness. Assistant Superintendents: LEONARD CARULLI; MR. PETER CIARELLI, Dir. Educational Technology; MS. NICOLE DAVIS, Human Resources.

Southern Region—Broome County Catholic School Office, 17 Adams St., P.O. Box 90, Binghamton, 13905. Tel: 607-723-1547; Fax: 607-723-5697.

Catholic School Endowment Fund of the Roman Catholic Diocese of Syracuse—(established to provide tuition assistance for students in diocesan Catholic schools) Most Rev. ROBERT J. CUNNINGHAM, J.C.L., D.D., Pres., 240 E. Onondaga St., Syracuse, 13202.

The Catholic Sun—240 E. Onondaga St., Syracuse, 13202. Tel: 315-422-8153; Tel: 800-333-0571; Fax: 315-422-7549; Email: catholicsun@yahoo.com; Web: www.sydio.org. KATHERINE LONG, Editor-in-Chief & Gen. Mgr.

Catholic Television—MR. RICK MOSSOTTI, Production Coord., 240 E. Onondaga St., Syracuse, 13202. Tel: 315-472-3584; Fax: 315-472-8409.

Christopher Community—MR. DOUGLAS REICHER, Exec. Dir., 990 James St., Syracuse, 13203. Tel: 315-414-1821.

Clerical Fund Society of the Roman Catholic Diocese of Syracuse—Most Rev. ROBERT J. CUNNINGHAM, J.C.L., D.D., Pres.; Rev. Msgr. J. ROBERT YEAZEL, Vice Pres., (Retired); Very Rev. Msgr. TIMOTHY S. ELMER, J.C.L., V.G., Sec. & Treas.

Office of Communications—MRS. DANIELLE CUMMINGS, Dir., Mailing Address: 240 E. Onondaga St., Syracuse, 13202. Tel: 315-470-1476; Fax: 315-478-4619; Email: dcummings@syracusediocese.org.

Stewardship & Development Office—240 E. Onondaga St., Syracuse, 13202. Tel: 315-472-0203;
Tel: 315-472-7902; Fax: 315-472-8409. MR. TIMOTHY MAHAR.

Ecumenical Commission—Rev. JON K. WERNER, Dir., 37 Fayette St., Binghamton, 13901.

Family Life/Respect Life Office—LISA HALL, Dir., 240 E. Onondaga St., Syracuse, 13202. Tel: 315-470-1418.

Finance Committee—Most Rev. ROBERT J. CUNNINGHAM, J.C.L., D.D.; Rev. Msgr. RICHARD M. KOPP; MRS. DANIELLE CUMMINGS; Very Rev. Msgr. TIMOTHY S. ELMER, J.C.L., V.G.; MR. STEPHEN BREEN, CFO; Rev. JOHN D. MANNO; JOHN MIRABITO; MR. JAMES TUOZZOLO; MR. THOMAS FISCOE; MR. MATTHEW SCHIRO; MR. WILLIAM CRIST; MRS. KIMBERLY TOWNSEND; MR. TIMOTHY ROSBROOK; MR. FRANK CALIVA.

Formation for Ministry—240 E. Onondaga St., Syracuse, 13202. Tel: 315-470-1420;
Fax: 315-579-3564. EILEEN ZIOBROWSKI, Assoc. Dir.

Liturgy and RCIA—Rev. JOSEPH E. SCARDELLA, 240 E. Onondaga St., Syracuse, 13202. Tel: 315-470-1420; Fax: 315-579-3564.

Health Care—Holy Cross Church, 4112 E. Genesee St., DeWitt, 13214-2104. Tel: 315-446-0473. Deacon DARE DUTTER, Dir.

Heritage Campaign—c/o Development Office, 240 E. Onondaga St., Syracuse, 13202. Tel: 315-472-0203.

HOPE Appeal—240 E. Onondaga St., Syracuse, 13202. Tel: 315-472-0203; Fax: 315-472-8409. MR. TIMOTHY MAHAR; DANIELLE MENSING.

Ruth Ministry—Syracuse Diocese Response to Domestic Violence LISA HALL, Dir., Mailing Address: 240 E. Onondaga St., Syracuse, 13202. Tel: 315-470-1418; Fax: 315-478-4619.

Parish Services—Mailing Address: 240 E. Onondaga St., Syracuse, 13202. Tel: 315-422-9089. MR. THOMAS O'CONNOR, Dir.; MR. NICK CROSBY, Internal Auditor.

Permanent Diaconate—240 E. Onondaga St., Syracuse, 13202. Tel: 315-470-1466. Deacons GREGORY T. CROSS, Dir.; DR. ROBERT FANGIO, Asst. Dir.

Priest Personnel—Rev. Msgr. RICHARD M. KOPP, 240 E. Onondaga St., Syracuse, 13202. Tel: 315-470-1460; Fax: 315-478-4619.

Priests' Personnel Committee—Most Rev. ROBERT J. CUNNINGHAM, J.C.L., D.D.; Revs. LOUIS F. AIELLO; JOHN A. BUEHLER; Rev. Msgr. RICHARD M. KOPP; Very Rev. Msgr. TIMOTHY S. ELMER, J.C.L., V.G., Ex Officio; Rev. JOHN F. HOGAN JR.; Rev. Msgr. JAMES T. O'BRIEN, (Retired); Rev. JASON HAGE; Rev. Msgr. JAMES P. LANG, Ex Officio; Revs. ROBERT L. KELLY; JON K. WERNER; JOHN F. ROSE, (Retired); HENRY J. PEDZICH; Rev. Msgr. MICHAEL T. MEAGHER.

Project Rachel—Post Abortion Healing LISA HALL, Dir., 240 E. Onondaga St., Syracuse, 13202. Tel: 315-424-3737.

Personal Resource Center—Rev. Msgr. NEAL E. QUARTIER, Dir., 215 N. State St., Syracuse, 13217-6482. Tel: 315-470-1462.

Pontifical Mission Societies240 E. Onondaga St., Syracuse, 13202. Tel: 315-472-3442. Deacon GREGORY T. CROSS, Dir.

Public Policy—240 E. Onondaga St., Syracuse, 13202. Rev. JAMES SALAMY, J.C.L.

Religious Education—(Office of Faith Formation) *Mailing Address: 240 E. Onondaga St., Syracuse, 13202.* Tel: 315-470-1431; Fax: 315-478-4619. VACANT, Dir.

Eastern Region—ANDREA SLAVEN, Assoc. Dir., One Sherman St., New Hartford, 13413. Tel: 315-797-4030; Fax: 315-797-4031.

Southern Region—ANDREA SCHAFFER, Assoc. Dir., 705 W. Main St., Endicott, 13760. Tel: 607-348-0746; Fax: 607-786-9650.

Western Region—240 E. Onondaga St., Syracuse, 13202. Tel: 315-472-6753; Fax: 315-472-8409. THERESA WHITE, Assoc. Dir.; MARGARET BABCOCK, Catechetical & Digital Media Asst., Tel: 315-472-6752.

Religious Retirement Fund—Retirement Plan for The Roman Catholic Diocese of Syracuse, NY. Est. January 1, 1988.Contact: MRS. DANIELLE CUMMINGS, Mailing Address: 240 E. Onondaga St., Syracuse, 13202. Tel: 315-422-9045; Fax: 315-422-9139.

Laymen & Laywomen Retreats—Christ the King Retreat House, 500 Brookford Rd., Syracuse, 13224. Tel: 315-446-2680. VACANT.

Spanish Apostolate—Rev. ROBERT D. CHRYST, Dir., 170 Seymour St., Syracuse, 13204. Tel: 315-442-9390.

Syracuse Catholic Press Association, Inc.—The Catholic Sun KATHERINE LONG, Editor-in-Chief & Gen. Mgr.; Most Rev. ROBERT J. CUNNINGHAM, J.C.L., D.D., Pres., 240 E. Onondaga St., Syracuse, 13202. Tel: 315-422-8153; Tel: 800-333-0571; Fax: 315-422-7549.

Victim Assistance Coordinator—JACQUELINE BRESSETTE, 240 E. Onondaga St., Syracuse, 13202. Tel: 315-470-1465; Fax: 315-478-4619.

Vocation Formation—Mailing Address: 240 E. Onondaga St., Syracuse, 13202. Tel: 315-470-1452; Fax: 315-478-4619. Rev. JOHN D. MANNO, Dir.

Vocation Promotion—Rev. JOSEPH O'CONNOR, Dir., 240 E. Onondaga St., Syracuse, 13202. Tel: 315-470-1468; Fax: 315-478-4619.

Youth & Young Adult Ministry—Mailing Address: 240 E. Onondaga St., Syracuse, 13202.
Tel: 315-470-1402; Fax: 315-478-4619. MR. ROBERT WALTERS, Dir., Tel: 315-470-1419; Fax: 315-478-4619.

CLERGY, PARISHES, MISSIONS AND PAROCHIAL SCHOOLS

CITY OF SYRACUSE

(ONONDAGA COUNTY)
SYRACUSE

1—THE CATHEDRAL OF THE IMMACULATE CONCEPTION (1841) 259 E. Onondaga St., 13202.
Tel: 315-422-4177; Email: bpronesti@syrdio.org. Rev. Msgr. Neal E. Quartier, Rector; Most Rev. Robert J. Cunningham, J.C.L., D.D.; Revs. John C. Schopfer, (Retired); William R. Jones, Parochial Vicar, (Retired); Deacons Paul Biermann, RCIA Coord.; Robert T. Burke; Sharon Secor, Pastoral Assoc.
Consolidated with Our Lady of Pompei School, Syracuse.
Catechesis Religious Program—Students 62.
Stations—Central Park—
Tel: 315-478-1641.
McCarthy Manor
Tel: 315-475-6390.

2—ALL SAINTS, Rev. Frederick D. Daley.
Res.: 1342 Lancaster Ave., 13210. Tel: 315-472-9934; Email: parish@allsaintssyracuse.org.
Catechesis Religious Program—Students 80.

3—ST. ANDREW THE APOSTLE (1953) Closed. For inquiries for parish records contact St. Lucy Church.

4—ST. ANN (1955) Merged with St. Charles Borromeo to form St. Charles - St. Ann, Syracuse.

5—ST. ANTHONY OF PADUA (1901) 1515 Midland Ave., 13205. Tel: 315-475-4114; Email: st. anthony1@verizon.net. Rev. Robert D. Chryst.
Catechesis Religious Program—

6—ASSUMPTION B.V.M. (1844) [CEM] (German) Franciscan Church of the Assumption Friars Richard Ricciolі, O.F.M.Conv.; Robert Amrhein, O.F.M.Conv.; James Smycha, O.F.M.Conv., Chap.; Nevin Hammon, O.F.M.Conv.; Gerald Waterman, O, F,M.Conv., Campus Min.; Edward Falsey, O.F.M.Conv., Guardian; James Amrhein, O.F.M.Conv., Dir. Assumption Food Pantry & Soup Kitchen; Brennan-Joseph Farleo, O.F.M.Conv.; Adam Keltos, O.F.M.Conv.; Nader Ata; Deacon Philip Slominski; Sisters Dolores Bush, Dir. Franciscan Northside Ministries; James Peter Ridgeo, Dir. Poverello Health Center; Mr. Alexander LaPoint, Dir.; Mr. Charles Rus, Music Min. In Res., Friar Richard Ricciolі, O.F.M.Conv.
St. Francis Friary: 812 N. Salina St., 13208.
Tel: 315-422-4833; Email: jennifer@assumptionsyr. org; Email: edfal@gmail.com; Web: www. assumptionsyr.org.
ASSUMPTION CEMETERY CORPORATION
2401 Court St., 13208. Tel: 315-454-3841;
Fax: 315-454-4931; Email: assump812@aol.com.

7—BASILICA OF THE SACRED HEART (1892) [CEM 2] (Polish) 927 Park Ave., 13204. Tel: 315-422-2343; Email: shbasilica@syrdio.org. Rev. Andrew E. Baranski, Rector; Deacons Frank Timson; Richard Galloway.
Catechesis Religious Program—
Tel: 315-422-4086. Sr. Melanie Jaworski, D.R.E. Students 38.

8—BLESSED SACRAMENT (1921) 3127 James St., 13206. Tel: 315-437-3394; Email: blschurch@syrdio. org. Very Rev. Msgr. Timothy S. Elmer, J.C.L., V.G., Admin.; Deacons Michael Colabufo; Daniel Stevens.
School—Blessed Sacrament School, (Grades PreK-6),

3129 James St., 13206. Tel: 315-463-1261; Fax: 315-463-1628; Email: apolcaro@syrdiocese.org; Web: www.blessedsacramentschool.org. Mrs. Andrea Polcaro, Prin. Parish school with nursery. Lay Teachers 18; Students 250.
Catechesis Religious Program—Students 162.
9—ST. BRIGID AND ST. JOSEPH (1926 and 1869) Merged with St. Patrick's on October 1, 2017. All of their records are stored at St. Patrick's, Syracuse.
10—ST. CHARLES - ST. ANN (2012) 4461 Onondaga Blvd., 13219. Tel: 315-468-1803; Email: stcharles.stanns@gmail.com; Web: stcharles-stanns.com. Rev. Kevin Maloney; Deacon Anthony J. Paratore; Ellen Flynn, Business Mgr.
Catechesis Religious Program—
Email: tcondon@syrdio.org. Teresa Condon, Youth Min. Students 166.
11—ST. CHARLES BORROMEO (1929) Merged with St. Ann to form St. Charles - St. Ann, Syracuse.
12—ST. DANIEL (1932) 3004 Court St., 13208. Tel: 315-454-4946; Fax: 315-454-0978; Email: stdaniels@syrdio.org; Web: www.stdaniel.com. Rev. Msgr. Eugene M. Yennock; Deacon Joseph Celentano.
Catechesis Religious Program—Students 84.
13—HOLY TRINITY (1891) (German), Merged with St. John the Baptist to form St. John the Baptist/Holy Trinity, Syracuse.
14—ST. JAMES (1925) Merged with Our Lady of Lourdes, Syracuse to form Our Lady of Hope, Syracuse.
15—ST. JOHN THE BAPTIST (1827) Merged with Holy Trinity to form St. John the Baptist/Holy Trinity, Syracuse. Rev. Daniel M. Caruso.
16—ST. JOHN THE BAPTIST/HOLY TRINITY (2012) 406 Court St., 13208. Tel: 315-478-0916; Email: nbergeson@syrdio.org. Rev. Daniel M. Caruso.
Catechesis Religious Program—
Email: olopsyracuse@syrdio.org. Mary Beth Meade, D.R.E. Students 21.
17—ST. JOHN THE EVANGELIST (1851) Merged For inquiries for parish records contact the Cathedral.
18—ST. LUCY (1872) 432 Gifford St., 13204.
Tel: 315-475-7273; Email: bulletin@saintlucys.org. Rev. James D. Mathews.
Catechesis Religious Program—Students 34.
19—MOST HOLY ROSARY (1913) 111 Roberts Ave., 13207-1397. Tel: 315-478-5749; Fax: 315-478-8629; Email: mhrsyracuse@syrdio.org; Web: mhrsyracuse.org. Rev. Frederick R. Mannara.
School—Most Holy Rosary School, (Grades PreK-6), 1031 Bellevue Ave., 13207. Tel: 315-476-6035; Fax: 315-476-0219; Email: ckompf@syrdiocese.org; Email: jpetosa@syrdiocese.org; Web: www.mhrsyr.org. Jennifer Toman Petosa, Prin.; Sr. Joan Ottman, I.H.M., Librarian; Sue Limpert, Librarian. Clergy 1; Lay Teachers 16; Sisters 1; Students 135.
Catechesis Religious Program—Students 240.
20—OUR LADY OF HOPE, 4845 S. Salina St., 13205.
Tel: 315-469-7789; Email: info@ourladyofhopesyr.org; Web: ourladyofhopesyr.org. Rev. Christopher J. Ballard.
Station—Onondaga Valley.
21—OUR LADY OF LOURDES (1947) Merged For inquiries for parish records contact Our Lady of Hope, Syracuse.
22—OUR LADY OF POMPEI (1924) (Italian), Merged with St. Peter, Syracuse to form Our Lady of Pompei-St. Peter, Syracuse.
23—OUR LADY OF POMPEI/ST. PETER (1924) (Italian) 301 Ash St., 13208. Tel: 315-422-7163; Email: olopsyracuse@syrdio.org. Revs. Daniel M. Caruso; Tuoi (John) V. Nguyen, Chap. In Res., Rev. Frederick A. Pompei.
School—Our Lady of Pompei/St. Peter School, (Grades PreK-6),
915-917 N. McBride St., 13208. Tel: 315-422-8548; Fax: 315-472-0754; Email: hacharlebois@syrdiocese.org. Sr. Helen Ann Charlebois, I.H.M., Prin. Lay Teachers 12; Students 87.
Catechesis Religious Program—
Tel: 315-472-2260. Mary Beth Meade, D.R.E. Students 129.
24—OUR LADY OF SOLACE (1926) Merged with St. Therese the Little Flower of Jesus, Syracuse to form All Saints, Syracuse.
25—ST. PATRICK (1870) 216 N. Lowell Ave., 13204.
Tel: 315-475-2185; Email: stpats@stpatrickssyr.org. Rev. Kevin Maloney.
Catechesis Religious Program—Judith Piedmonte, D.R.E. Students 106.
26—ST. PETER (1890) (Italian), Merged with Our Lady of Pompeii, Syracuse to form Our Lady of Pompeii-St. Peter, Syracuse.
27—ST. STEPHEN (1915) (Slovak), Merged with the Basilica of the Sacred Heart. For inquiries for parish records please contact Sacred Heart, Syracuse.
28—ST. THERESE THE LITTLE FLOWER OF JESUS (1926) Merged with Our Lady of Solace, Syracuse to form All Saints, Syracuse.
29—TRANSFIGURATION (1911) (Polish) 740 Teall Ave., 13206. Tel: 315-479-6129; Email: transfigurationsyr@syrdio.org. Rev. Thomas P. Kobuszewski.
30—ST. VINCENT DE PAUL (1893) 342 Vine St., 13203. Tel: 315-479-6689; Email: stvincentsyr@syrdio.org; Email: vdepaul@twcny.rr.com. Rev. John F. Rose, Admin., (Retired).
Catechesis Religious Program—Students 80.

OUTSIDE THE CITY OF SYRACUSE

ALTMAR, OSWEGO CO., ST. MARY'S MISSION, Closed. For inquiries for records please see Christ of Light, Pulaski.
BAINBRIDGE, CHENANGO CO., ST. JOHN THE EVANGELIST (1914)
34 S. Main St., Bainbridge, 13733. Tel: 607-967-4481 ; Email: stjohnbain@syrdio.org. Rev. Darr F. Schoenhofen, Admin.
Catechesis Religious Program—Students 10.
Mission—St. Agnes, 18 Spring St., Afton, 13730.
BALDWINSVILLE, ONONDAGA CO.
1—ST. AUGUSTINE (1966)
7333 O'Brien Rd., Baldwinsville, 13027.
Tel: 315-638-0585; Email: kraddell@staugustinesparish.org; Web: www.staugustinesparish.org. Rev. Clifford H. Auth, J.C.L.
Catechesis Religious Program—Tel: 315-638-0864; Email: kskinner@staugustinesparish.org. Kristine Skinner, D.R.E. Students 120.
2—ST. ELIZABETH ANN SETON (1985)
3494 NY State Rte. 31, Baldwinsville, 13027.
Tel: 315-652-4300; Email: mainoffice@stelizabethbville.org; Web: stelizabethbville.org. Rev. Joseph O'Connor, Admin.; Deacon William A. Dotterer.
Catechesis Religious Program—Tel: 315-652-3900; Fax: 315-622-1761. Students 860.
3—ST. MARY OF THE ASSUMPTION (1852) [CEM]
47 Syracuse St., Baldwinsville, 13027.
Tel: 315-635-5762; Fax: 315-635-8137; Email: stmarysbville@syrdio.org; Web: www.stmarysassumption.org. Rev. Clifford H. Auth, J.C.L.; Deacons Robert J. Talomie; Joseph Casper.
School—St. Mary's Academy, (Grades PreK-6), 49 Syracuse St., Baldwinsville, 13027.
Tel: 315-635-3977; Email: rehenderson@syrdiocese.org; Web: www.stmarysbaldwinsville.com. Mrs. Renae Henderson, Admin.; Ms. Iveliz Lopez, Librarian. Clergy 1; Lay Teachers 11; Students 105.
Catechesis Religious Program—Email: faithformation@stmarysassumption.org. Catherine Mackey, D.R.E. Students 180.
BINGHAMTON, BROOME CO.
1—ST. ANDREW (1955) Merged with St. John the Evangelist, Binghamton to form Saints John & Andrew, Binghamton.
2—ST. ANN (1925) (Slovak), Merged with St. Joseph, Binghamton and St. Stanislaus Kostka, Binghamton to form Holy Trinity, Binghamton.
3—ST. CATHERINE OF SIENA (1929) Merged with St. Christopher, Binghamton to form St. Francis of Assisi, Binghamton.
4—ST. CHRISTOPHER (1940) Merged with St. Catherine of Siena, Binghamton to form St. Francis of Assisi, Binghamton.
5—SS. CYRIL AND METHOD (1904) (Slovak)
148 Clinton St., Binghamton, 13905.
Tel: 607-724-1372; Email: stcyrilmethodius@syrdio.org; Web: www.sscyrilandmethod.org. Rev. Msgr. John P. Putano, Admin.; Revs. Charles Opondo-Owora, (Africa) Mod.; Fredrick Mwangi Kooro, (Africa) Pastoral Care; Barbara Hill, Pastoral Assoc.
Catechesis Religious Program—Email: acarey@syrdio.org. Andrea Carey, D.R.E. Students 18.
6—ST. FRANCIS OF ASSISI
1031 Chenango St., Binghamton, 13901-1746.
Tel: 607-722-4388; Email: jcarpenter@syrdio.org. Rev. Timothy J. Taugher; Deacon Steve Blabac; Mr. Joseph Carpenter, Admin.; Mr. David Bollinger, Pastoral Assoc.
Catechesis Religious Program—Email: mkirk@syrdio.org. Maria Kirk, D.R.E. Students 170.
7—HOLY TRINITY (2003)
346 Prospect St., Binghamton, 13905.
Tel: 607-797-1856; Tel: 607-724-1372; Email: holytrinitybing@syrdio.org; Web: holytrinitybinghamton.org. Revs. Charles Opondo-Owora, (Africa) Moderator; Alfred J. Bebel, (Retired); Barbara Hill, Pastoral Assoc.
Catechesis Religious Program—Email: acarey@syrdio.org. Andrea Carey, D.R.E. Students 17.
8—SAINTS JOHN & ANDREW
1263 Vestal Ave., Binghamton, 13903.
Tel: 607-722-0493; Email: stsjohnandrew@syrdio.org; Web: www.saintsjohnandandrew.com. Saints John and Andrew - Parish Office: 7 Livingston St., Binghamton, 13903. Rev. Msgr. Michael T. Meagher. In Res., Revs. Krzysztof Boretto; Robert J. Sullivan, (Retired); Christopher Seibt.
Catechesis Religious Program—7 Livingston St., Binghamton, 13903. Email: mhurchla@syrdio.org. Madonna Hurchla, D.R.E. Students 189.
9—ST. JOHN THE EVANGELIST (1907) Merged with St. Andrew, Binghamton to form Saints John & Andrew, Binghamton.
10—ST. JOSEPH (1914) (Lithuanian), Merged with St. Ann, Binghamton and St. Stanislaus Kostka, Binghamton to form Holy Trinity, Binghamton.
11—ST. MARY OF THE ASSUMPTION (1887; 1913)
37 Fayette St., Binghamton, 13901-2501.
Tel: 607-723-5383; Email: stsmary.paul@gmail.com. 15 Doubleday St., Binghamton, 13901. Rev. Jon Werner. In Res., Rev. Francis W. Kocik.
12—ST. PATRICK (1838) (Irish)
9 Leroy St., Binghamton, 13905. Tel: 607-722-1060; Email: stpatrick@sta-sp.org; Web: sta-sp.org. Rev. Msgr. John P. Putano; Rev. Fredrick Mwangi Kooro, (Africa) Parochial Vicar; Deacon Leslie Distin, (Retired).
Catechesis Religious Program—Tel: 607-797-3304; Email: jeanne@sta-sp.org. Jeanne Higgins, D.R.E. Students 139.
Convent—Sisters of St. Joseph of Carondelet, 46 Oak St., Binghamton, 13905.
13—ST. PAUL (1896)
15 Doubleday St., Binghamton, 13901-2501.
Tel: 607-722-6492; Email: stsmary.paul@gmail.com. Revs. Jon Werner; Francis W. Kocik; Sr. Lucia Mugambi, Sacramental Min.
Catechesis Religious Program—Tel: 607-724-5449; Fax: 607-724-3377. Students 35.
14—ST. STANISLAUS KOSTKA (1914) (Polish), Merged with St. Ann, Binghamton and St. Joseph, Binghamton to form Holy Trinity, Binghamton.
15—ST. THOMAS AQUINAS (1927)
One Aquinas St., Binghamton, 13905.
Tel: 607-797-4015; Email: stthomas@sta-sp.org; Web: www.sta-sp.org. Rev. Paul Machira, (Africa) Admin.; Rev. Msgr. John P. Putano; Rev. Fredrick Mwangi Kooro, (Africa).
Catechesis Religious Program—9 Leroy St., Binghamton, 13905. Tel: 607-797-3304; Email: jeanne@sta-sp.org. Jeanne Higgins, D.R.E. Students 143.
BOONVILLE, ONEIDA CO.
1—CHRIST OUR HOPE PARISH (1875) [CEM]
112 Charles St., Boonville, 13309. Tel: 315-942-4618; Fax: 315-942-3686; Email: christourhope108@aol.com; Web: christourhoperc.org. 108 Charles St., Boonville, 13309. Rev. Thomas I. Ward.
Res.: 110 Charles St., Boonville, 13309.
Missions—St. Patrick—11996 River Rd., Forestport, 13338. Email: christourhoperc@syrdio.org.
St. Mary of the Snows, 14040-NY 28, Forestport, 13338. (Summers Only).
2—ST. JOSEPH, Merged with St. Patrick, Forestport to form Christ Our Hope Parish, Boonville.
BREWERTON, ONONDAGA CO., ST. AGNES ORATORY (1958) Merged with St. Michael, Central Square to become Divine Mercy Parish. Property sold in 2016. There is no longer any Oratory. Records are kept at Divine Mercy, Central Square.
BRIDGEPORT, ONONDAGA CO., ST. FRANCIS OF ASSISI (1951)
7820 Bridgeport-Minoa Rd., Bridgeport, 13030.
Tel: 315-437-8318; Email: stfrancisbridge@syrdio.org. Mailing Address: 229 W. Yates St., East Syracuse, 13057. Rev. Shawn P. O'Brien.
Parish Center—7820 Rte. 298, Bridgeport, 13030.
Catechesis Religious Program—Tel: 315-633-5661. Students 47.
CAMDEN, ONEIDA CO., ST. JOHN THE EVANGELIST (1852) [CEM]
18 Church St., Camden, 13316. Tel: 315-245-1603; Email: stjohncamden@syrdio.org. Mailing Address: 35 Third St., Camden, 13316. Rev. R. Paul Mathis; Mrs. Nancy Choquette, Pastoral Assoc. & D.R.E.; Glynis Smith, Office Mgr.
Catechesis Religious Program—Students 51.
CAMILLUS, ONONDAGA CO., ST. JOSEPH (1852)
5600 W. Genesee St., Camillus, 13031.
Tel: 315-488-8490; Email: businessmanager@stjosephscamillus.org. Rev. Peter Worn.
Catechesis Religious Program—Students 607.
CANASTOTA, MADISON CO., ST. AGATHA (1883) [CEM]
329 N. Peterboro St., Canastota, 13032.
Tel: 315-697-7104; Email: revwirkes@yahoo.com. Rev. Stephen P. Wirkes; Deacon Adolph J. Uryniak.
Catechesis Religious Program—Tel: 315-697-7827. Students 110.
Mission—St. Mary, Verona Beach, 13162.
Tel: 315-761-4016.
ST. JOHN, North Bay, 13123.
CAZENOVIA, MADISON CO., ST. JAMES (1847) [CEM]
6 Green St., Cazenovia, 13035. Tel: 315-655-3441; Email: stjamesc@stjamescaz.com; Web: www.stjamescaz.org. Rev. Kevin J. Corcoran; Deacon John Addante.
Catechesis Religious Program—Email:

faithformation@stjamescaz.com. Lisa Matto, D.R.E. Students 279.

CENTRAL SQUARE, OSWEGO CO.

1—DIVINE MERCY (1928)
592 S. Main St., Central Square, 13036.
Tel: 315-676-2898; Email: divinemercy@syrdio.org; Web: www.divinemercycny.org. Rev. Christopher Celentano; Deacons Donald Mula; Mark Berube
Legal Title: St. Michael Catholic Church.
Res.: 589 S. Main St., Central Square, 13036.
Catechesis Religious Program—Tel: 315-676-4210. Students 126.
Mission—St. Bernadette, 1667 State Rte. 49, Constantia, 13044.

2—ST. MICHAEL, Merged with St. Agnes, Brewerton to become Divine Mercy, Central Square.

CHADWICKS, ONEIDA CO., ST. PATRICK-ST. ANTHONY (1907) St. Anthony, Chadwicks merged with St. Patrick, Clayville.
3364 Oneida St., P.O. Box 429, Chadwicks, 13319.
Tel: 315-316-0506; Email: stanthchadwicks@syrdio.org. Rev. Arthur Krawczenko.
Catechesis Religious Program—Students 141.

CHENANGO FORKS, BROOME CO., ST. RITA (1946) Closed. with St. Catherine of Siena, now St. Francis, Binghamton.

CHITTENANGO, MADISON CO., ST. PATRICK (1853) [CEM]
1341 Murray Dr., Chittenango, 13037.
Tel: 315-687-6105; Fax: 315-687-0046; Email: stpatschitt@syrdio.org; Web: www.stpatrickschittenango.com. Rev. Kevin J. Corcoran.
Catechesis Religious Program—Tel: 315-687-6561. Students 160.

CICERO, ONONDAGA CO., SACRED HEART (1888)
8229 Brewerton Rd., Cicero, 13039.
Tel: 315-699-2752; Email: sheart@syrdio.org; Web: www.sacredheartofcicero.com. Rev. Richard P. Prior Jr.; Deacon Kenneth N. Money.
Catechesis Religious Program—Tel: 315-699-7678. Students 818.

CLARK MILLS, ONEIDA CO., CHURCH OF THE ANNUNCIATION (1908)
Mailing Address: 7616 E. South St., Clinton, 13323. Rev. Kevin J. Bunger.
Catechesis Religious Program—Parish Center, Clarey Ave., Clark Mills, 13321. Email: erinlynn1308@yahoo.com. Erin Robinson, D.R.E. Students 93.

CLAYVILLE, ONEIDA CO., ST. PATRICK (1864) [CEM] Closed. For inquiries for parish records contact St. Patrick-St. Anthony, Chadwicks.

CLEVELAND, OSWEGO CO., ST. MARY OF THE ASSUMPTION ORATORY (1854) [CEM]
148 State Rte. 49, Cleveland, 13042.
Tel: 315-676-2898; Email: divinemercy@syrdio.org. 592 S. Main St., Central Square, 13036. Rev. Christopher Celentano, Admin. Made an Oratory - November 2015.
Res.: 598 S. Main St., Central Square, 13036.

CLINTON, ONEIDA CO., ST. MARY (1850) [CEM]
13 Marvin St., Clinton, 13323. Tel: 315-853-2935; Email: parishoffice@stmarys-clinton.com. Rev. John P. Croghan.
Catechesis Religious Program—Tel: 315-853-6196; Fax: 315-853-1440. Students 280.

CORTLAND, CORTLAND CO.

1—ST. ANTHONY OF PADUA (1917) (Italian)
50 Pomeroy St., Cortland, 13045. Tel: 607-756-9967; Email: staoffice@centralny.twcbc.com. Mailing Address: 59 N. Main St., Cortland, 13045. Revs. Joseph Zareski; Kenneth R. Kirkman, Parochial Vicar; Deacon Joseph During, Business Mgr.
Rectory—44 N. Main St., Cortland, 13045.
Catechesis Religious Program—Robert Densmore, C.R.E.; Stephanie Passeriu-Densmore, C.R.E. Students 66.

2—ST. MARY (1855)
46 N. Main St., Cortland, 13045. Tel: 607-756-9967; Email: stmoffice@centralny.twcbc.com. Mailing Address: 59 N. Main St., Cortland, 13045. Rev. Joseph Zareski; Deacons Joseph During; Stephen Smith.
School—St. Mary School, (Grades PreK-6), 61 N. Main St., Cortland, 13045. Tel: 607-756-5614; Fax: 607-756-5626; Email: dhall@syrdiocese.org. Mrs. Denise Hall, Prin. Clergy 1; Lay Teachers 12; Students 151.
Catechesis Religious Program—Email: religiousedk8@gmail.com. Jennifer Fischer, C.R.E. Students 155.

DEPOSIT, BROOME CO., ST. JOSEPH (1851) [CEM]
98 Second St., Deposit, 13754. Tel: 607-775-0086; Email: sebroomecatholics@syrdio.org. Mailing Address: 975 NY Rte. 11, Kirkwood, 13795. Barbara Kane, Parish Life Coord.
Catechesis Religious Program—Students 25.

DEWITT, ONONDAGA CO., HOLY CROSS (1943)
4112 E. Genesee St., DeWitt, 13214.
Tel: 315-446-0473; Email: info@holycrossdewitt.org; Web: www.holycrossdewitt.org. Revs. John J. Kurgan; Matthew Rawson, Parochial Vicar; Deacon Dare Dutter.
School—Holy Cross School, (Grades PreK-6), 4200 E. Genesee St., DeWitt, 13214. Tel: 315-446-4890; Fax: 315-446-4799; Email: moleary@syrdiocese.org. Martha O'Leary, Prin. Lay Teachers 13; Students 149.
Catechesis Religious Program—Email: julie@holycrossdewitt.org. Julie Sheridan, D.R.E.; Stephen Nepil, D.R.E. Students 410.

DURHAMVILLE, ONEIDA CO., ST. FRANCIS (1860) [CEM] (German), Closed. For inquiries for parish records contact St. Joseph, Oneida.

EAST SYRACUSE, ONONDAGA CO., ST. MATTHEW (1880)
229 W. Yates St., East Syracuse, 13057.
Tel: 315-437-8318; Email: stmatthews@syrdio.org. Revs. Sean O'Brien; Severine Yagaza.
Catechesis Religious Program—Students 118.

ENDICOTT, BROOME CO.

1—ST. AMBROSE (1908)
203 Washington Ave., Endicott, 13760.
Tel: 607-754-2330; Email: stambrose@syrdio.org. Rev. Michael Galuppi.
Catechesis Religious Program—Students 65.

2—ST. ANTHONY OF PADUA (1917) (Italian)
306 Odell Ave., Endicott, 13760. Tel: 607-754-4333; Fax: 607-239-4886; Email: stanthendicott@syrdio.org; Web: stanthonyendicott.org. 906 Jenkins St., Endicott, 13760. Rev. James P. Serowik; Deacons Frank Longo; William Matts.
Child Care—St. Anthony's Learning Center, Tel: 607-748-5184; Fax: 607-786-3965; Email: stanthonytlc@stny.rr.com. (Pre-School).
Catechesis Religious Program—Email: dhurd@syrdio.org. Danea Hurd, D.R.E. Students 155.
Convent—Little Sisters of St. Francis, 304 Oak Hill Ave., Endicott, 13760. Tel: 607-786-5006.

3—ST. CASIMIR (1928) (Polish), Merged with St. Joseph, Endicott. For inquiries for parish records contact St. Joseph Church, Endicott.

4—ST. JOSEPH (1923) (Slovak)
207 Hayes Ave., Endicott, 13760. Tel: 607-748-0442; Email: stjoesendicott@syrdio.org. Rev. James P. Serowik; Deacon William Matts.
Catechesis Religious Program—Email: sherceg@syrdio.org. Sally Herceg, D.R.E. Students 95.

5—OUR LADY OF GOOD COUNSEL (1941)
701 W. Main St., Endicott, 13760. Tel: 607-748-7417; Email: tharley-olgc@stny.rr.com; Web: olgcendicott.org. Rev. Michael Galuppi; Deacon Thomas M. Harley, Pastoral Min./Coord.
Catechesis Religious Program—Email: bcargill-olgc@stny.rr.com. Bob Cargil, D.R.E. Students 230.

ENDWELL, BROOME CO.

1—CHRIST THE KING (1949) Merged with Our Lady of Angels, Endwell to become Holy Family Church. For inquiries for parish records contact Holy Family Church, Endwell.

2—CHURCH OF THE HOLY FAMILY (2008)
3600 Phyllis St., Endwell, 13760. Tel: 607-754-1266; Email: churchoftheholyfamily@gmail.com; Web: holyfamilyendwell.com. Rev. Clarence F. Rumble; Deacon George Phillips Jr.
Res.: 3011 Phyllis St., Endwell, 13760.
Catechesis Religious Program—Tel: 607-785-4581. Students 312.

3—OUR LADY OF ANGELS (1964) Merged with Christ the King, Endwell to become Holy Family Church, Endwell.

FABIUS, ONONDAGA CO., ST. PAUL, Closed. Former mission of Immaculate Conception, Pompey.

FAIRMOUNT, ONONDAGA CO., HOLY FAMILY (1935)
127 Chapel Dr., 13219. Tel: 315-488-3139; Email: holyfamily@holyfamilysyr.org; Web: www.holyfamilysyr.org. Revs. John D. Manno; Matthew Lyons; Rev. Msgr. J. Robert Yeazel, Sacramental Min., (Retired); Deacons Robert Fangio, Pastoral Assoc.; Scott Harris, Pastoral Assoc.
School—Holy Family School, (Grades PreK-6), 130 Chapel Dr., 13219. Tel: 315-487-8515; Email: cluczynski@syrdiocese.org; Web: www.holyfamilyschoolsyr.org. Sr. Christina Marie Luczynski, Prin. Clergy 1; Lay Teachers 18; Students 260.
Catechesis Religious Program—Denise Pedercini, D.R.E. Students 571.

FAYETTEVILLE, ONONDAGA CO., IMMACULATE CONCEPTION (1869) [CEM]
400 Salt Springs St., Fayetteville, 13066.
Tel: 315-637-9846; Fax: 315-637-9846; Email: icfayetteville@syrdio.org. Rev. Thomas J. Ryan. In Res., Rev. Msgr. Ronald C. Bill, (Retired).
School—Immaculate Conception School, (Grades PreK-6), Tel: 315-637-3961; Email: dmills@syrdiocese.org; Email: efaigle@syrdiocese.org. Mr. Donald Mills, Prin. Clergy 2; Lay Teachers 24; Students 196.
Catechesis Religious Program—Tel: 315-637-9840; Email: avoutsinas@syrdio.org. Anne Marie Voutsinas, D.R.E. Students 150.

FLORENCE, ONEIDA CO., ST. MARY ORATORY (1845) [CEM] For inquiries for parish records contact St. John the Evangelist Church, Camden.
148 State Rte. 49, Cleveland, 13042.
Tel: 315-676-2898; Email: divinemercy@syrdio.org. Divine Mercy Parish: 592 S. Main St., Central Square, 13036. Rev. Christopher Celentano, Admin.

FORESTPORT, ONEIDA CO., ST. PATRICK (1848) [CEM] Merged with St. Joseph, Boonville to become Christ Our Hope Parish.

FULTON, OSWEGO CO.

1—CHURCH OF THE HOLY TRINITY
309 Buffalo St., Fulton, 13069. Tel: 315-598-2118; Email: smarc@windstream.net. Revs. John Canorro; James A. Schultz, Parochial Vicar; Deacon David Sweenie.
Rectory—57 S. 3rd St., Fulton, 13069.
Catechesis Religious Program—Students 110.

2—HOLY FAMILY-ST. MICHAEL'S (1930) Merged with Immaculate Conception, Fulton to form Church of the Holy Trinity, Fulton.

3—IMMACULATE CONCEPTION (1854) [CEM] Merged with Holy Family-St. Michael's, Fulton to form Church of the Holy Trinity, Fulton.

4—ST. MICHAEL (1924) (Polish), Merged into Holy Trinity, Fulton.

GLENMORE, ONEIDA CO., ST. PATRICK, Closed. Former mission of St. Patrick, Taberg.

GREENE, CHENANGO CO., IMMACULATE CONCEPTION (1889)
1180 NY Hwy. 206, Greene, 13778-1193.
Tel: 607-656-9546; Fax: 607-656-7667; Email: immcongreene@syrdio.org; Web: iccgreene.wordpress.com. Rev. Msgr. John P. Putano, Admin.; Rev. Paul Machira, (Africa); Mary Wentlent, Pastoral Assoc.
Catechesis Religious Program—Students 47.

HAMILTON, MADISON CO., ST. MARY (1869) [CEM]
16 Wylie St., Hamilton, 13346. Tel: 315-824-2164; Email: stmaryshamilton@syrdio.org; Web: stmarysandstjoans.org. Rev. Jason Hage, Admin.; Deacons Paul Lehmann, Hospital Chap.; Mark Shiner, Campus Min.
Catechesis Religious Program—Tel: 315-824-3027; Email: peggyrhyde@yahoo.com. Margaret Rhyde, D.R.E. Twinned with St. Joan, Morrisville. Students 102.
Mission—St. Joan of Arc (1931) 6 Brookside Dr., P.O. Box 1087, Morrisville, 13408.

HANNIBAL, OSWEGO CO., OUR LADY OF THE ROSARY (1954) Mission of St. Mary's, Oswego.
931 Cayuga St., Hannibal, 13074. Tel: 315-343-3953; Email: olotrhannibal@syrdio.org. Mailing Address: 103 W. 7th St., Oswego, 13126. Rev. John F. Hogan Jr., Admin.
Mission—St. Joseph, Southwest Oswego, Oswego Co.. (Closed).

HINCKLEY, ONEIDA CO., ST. ANN (1895) [CEM] Merged with St. Leo, Holland Patent to form St. Leo & St. Ann. For parish records contact St. Leo & St. Ann, Holland Patent.

HOLLAND PATENT, ONEIDA CO., ST. LEO & ST. ANN (1882)
7937 Elm St., P.O. Box 185, Holland Patent, 13354.
Tel: 315-865-5371; Email: stleos@syrdio.org. Rev. Vincent P. Long.
Catechesis Religious Program—Students 214.

HOMER, CORTLAND CO., ST. MARGARET (1908)
14 Copeland Ave., Homer, 13077. Tel: 607-749-2542; Email: stmarghomer@syrdio.org. Rev. Paul J. Alciati.
Catechesis Religious Program—Email: christine.williams@stmargaret-homer.org. Christine Williams, D.R.E. Students 85.

JAMESVILLE, ONONDAGA CO., ST. MARY, Closed. Mission of Holy Cross, DeWitt.

JOHNSON CITY, BROOME CO.

1—BLESSED SACRAMENT (1945) Merged with St. Vincent, Vestal to form St. Vincent-Blessed Sacrament, Vestal.

2—ST. JAMES (1900)
147 Main St., Johnson City, 13790.
Tel: 607-729-6147; Email: sjjcoffice@yahoo.com. Rev. Charles Opondo-Owora, (Africa); Deacons Edward Blaine, Pastoral Assoc.; William Fitzpatrick, Asst. Pastoral Assoc.; Carol Hall, Asst. Pastoral Assoc. In Res., Rev. Laurence J. Lord, (Retired).
Catechesis Religious Program—Students 297.

JORDAN, ONONDAGA CO., ST. PATRICK (1858) [CEM]
28 N. Main St., P.O. Box 567, Jordan, 13080-0567.
Tel: 315-689-6240; Email: stpatsjordan@syrdio.org. Rev. John R. DeLorenzo.
Catechesis Religious Program—Mary E. Badger, Dir. Faith Formation. Students 60.

KIRKWOOD, BROOME CO., ST. MARY (1888)
975 NY Rte. 11, Kirkwood, 13795. Tel: 607-775-0086; Email: sebroomecatholics@syrdio.org. Barbara Kane, Parish Life Coord.
Catechesis Religious Program—Students 60.

LACONA, OSWEGO CO., ST. FRANCES XAVIER CABRINI (1946) Merged with St. John, Pulaski to form Christ

Our Light. For inquiries for parish records contact Christ Our Light, Pulaski.

LAFAYETTE, ONONDAGA CO., ST. JOSEPH (1866)
6104 Cherry Valley Rd., Box 169, Lafayette, 13084. Tel: 315-677-3439; Email: parish@stjosephslafayette.org. Rev. James H. Carey, Admin.
Catechesis Religious Program—Tel: 315-677-7735; Fax: 315-677-3858. Students 63.

LAKELAND, ONONDAGA CO., OUR LADY OF PEACE (1935)
203 Halcomb St., 13209. Tel: 315-488-3221; Email: stcecelias@syrdio.org; Web: olpsyracuse.org. Mailing Address: 105 Stanton Ave., Solvay, 13209. Rev. Joseph J. Clemente; Deacon John Bowden.
Catechesis Religious Program—Students 42.

LEE CENTER, ONEIDA CO., ST. JOSEPH (1923)
5748 Stokes Lee Center Rd., Lee Center, 13363. Tel: 315-533-6655; Email: st.josephs.leecenter@syrdio.org. Rev. Robert L. Kelly.
Parish Center—Tel: 315-336-2661; Fax: 315-336-8418.
Catechesis Religious Program—Students 49.

LEONARDSVILLE, CHENANGO CO., OUR LADY OF THE VALLEY, Merged with St. Theresa, New Berlin. Former mission of St. Theresa of the Infant Jesus, New Berlin.

LIVERPOOL, ONONDAGA CO.

1—CHRIST THE KING (1964)
21 Cherry Tree Cir., Liverpool, 13090. Tel: 315-652-9266; Tel: 315-652-5782; Email: christtheking@syrdio.org; Web: www.ctkcny.com. Rev. Zachary K. Miller, Admin.; Deacons Thomas Cuskey, Pastoral Assoc.; Thomas Hachey; Michael Ruf.
Catechesis Religious Program—Tel: 315-652-5782; Email: ctkfaithformation@syrdio.org. Anthony Maio, D.R.E. Students 88.

2—IMMACULATE HEART OF MARY (1950)
425 Beechwood Ave., Liverpool, 13088. Tel: 315-451-5070; Email: info@ihmsjw.org; Web: www.ihmsjw.org. Rev. Daniel J. O'Hara; Deacon Stephen Manzene, Pastoral Assoc., Visitation; Sr. Rose Marie Caravaglio, C.S.J., Music Min. In Res., Rev. Msgr. James P. Lang.
Catechesis Religious Program—Email: faithformation@ihmsjw.org. Amy Wojcikowski, D.R.E. Students 197.

3—ST. JOSEPH THE WORKER (1890)
1001 Tulip St., Liverpool, 13088. Tel: 315-457-6060; Email: jeggert@ihmsjw.org; Email: info@ihmsjw.org; Web: www.ihmsjw.org. Rev. Daniel J. O'Hara; Deacon Stephen Manzene, Pastoral Assoc., Visitation.
Res.: 425 Beechwood Ave., Liverpool, 13088.
Catechesis Religious Program—Tel: 315-451-5070; Email: faithformation@ihmsjw.org. Amy Wojcikowski, D.R.E. Students 175.

4—POPE JOHN XXIII RC CHURCH (1971)
8290 Soule Rd., Liverpool, 13090. Tel: 315-652-6591; Fax: 315-652-6631; Email: johnxxiii@syrdio.org; Web: popejohnchurch.org. Rev. Msgr. James T. O'Brien, (Retired); Elizabeth Fallon, Pastoral Assoc.
Catechesis Religious Program—Tel: 315-652-1094; Email: faithformation@verizon.net. Elizabeth Fallon, D.R.E. Students 274.

MAINE, BROOME CO., MOST HOLY ROSARY (1944)
2596 Main St., P.O. Box 248, Maine, 13802. Tel: 607-862-3216. Rev. Clarence F. Rumble, Admin.; Deacon Gary DiLallo, Pastoral Assoc.
Catechesis Religious Program—Jim Tokos, D.R.E. Students 90.

MANLIUS, ONONDAGA CO., ST. ANN (1920)
St. Ann's Church, 104 Academy St., Manlius, 13104. Tel: 315-682-5181; Email: parishoffice@saintannschurch.com. Rev. Brian E. Lang.
Catechesis Religious Program—Tel: 315-682-9443. Students 473.

MARATHON, CORTLAND CO., ST. STEPHEN (1870) Merged with St. Patrick, Whitney Point to form The Catholic Community of St. Stephen-St. Patrick.
16 Academy St., Marathon, 13803. Tel: 607-849-3480; Email: ststephenstpat@syrdio.org. Rev. Douglas D. Cunningham, Admin.
Mailing Address: P.O. Box 711, Whitney Point, 13862.
Res.: 12 Academy St., Marathon, 13803-0475.
Catechesis Religious Program—Students 31.
Mission—Our Lady of Perpetual Help, 2708 Lower Cincinnatus Rd., P.O. Box 310, Cincinnatus, 13040.

MARCELLUS, ONONDAGA CO., ST. FRANCIS XAVIER (1873) [CEM]
1 W. Main St., P.O. Box 177, Marcellus, 13108. Tel: 315-673-2531; Email: jfalge@syrdio.org. Rev. Daniel C. Muscalino; Deacon John Falge.
Catechesis Religious Program—53 North St., Marcellus, 13108. Students 207.

MATTYDALE, ONONDAGA CO., ST. MARGARET (1926)
203 Roxboro Rd., Mattydale, 13211. Tel: 315-455-5534; Email: stmargmattydale@syrdio.org. Rev. Robert P. Hyde Jr., J.C.L.; Deacons Donald R. Whiting; David G. Losito.
School—St. Margaret School, (Grades PreK-6), 200 Roxboro Rd., 13211. Tel: 315-455-5791, Ext. 3. Mailing Address: 201 Roxboro Rd., Mattydale, 13211. Michael McAuliff, Prin. Lay Teachers 13; Students 128.
Catechesis Religious Program—200 Roxboro Rd., Mattydale, 13211. Students 212.

MEXICO, OSWEGO CO., ST. ANNE, MOTHER OF MARY (1914) Linked with Christ Our Light, Pulaski.
3352 Main St., P.O. Box 487, Mexico, 13114-0487. Tel: 315-963-7182; Fax: 315-292-2701; Email: stannemexico@syrdio.org; Web: www.stannemotherofmary.com. Rev. James A. Schultz, Admin.; Deacon Daniel Caughey.
Catechesis Religious Program—88 N. Jefferson St., P.O. Box 613, Mexico, 13114-0613. Email: lbuckley@syrdio.org. Linda A. Buckley, D.R.E. Students 78.

MINETTO, OSWEGO CO., OUR LADY OF PERPETUAL HELP (1932)
West River Rd., P.O. Box 236, Minetto, 13115. Tel: 315-343-7922; Email: gbaccaro@syrdio.org. Rev. Guy Baccaro. Created a mission of St. Paul, Oswego.

MINOA, ONONDAGA CO., ST. MARY (1834) [CEM]
401 N. Main St., Minoa, 13116. Tel: 315-437-8318; Fax: 315-463-6399. Mailing Address: 229 W. Yates St., East Syracuse, 13057. Revs. Sean O'Brien; Craig David; Deacon Dean Brainard.
Catechesis Religious Program—Tel: 315-656-4220; Email: cvieau1@gmail.com. Students 124.

MUNNSVILLE, MADISON CO., ST. THERESE OF THE INFANT JESUS (1926) Closed. For inquiries for parish records contact St. Patrick, Oneida.

NEW BERLIN, CHENANGO CO., ST. THERESA OF THE INFANT JESUS (1955)
24 N. Main St., P.O. Box 780, New Berlin, 13411-0780. Tel: 607-847-6851; Email: cphoughton@frontiernet.net. Rev. Darr F. Schoenhofen; Patricia Houghton, Pastoral Coord.
Catechesis Religious Program—386 Co. Rte. 17, New Berlin, 13411. Tel: 607-847-8590; Email: snogaret64@gmail.com. Sue Nogaret, D.R.E. Students 27.

NEW HARTFORD, ONEIDA CO.

1—ST. JOHN THE EVANGELIST (1883)
66 Oxford Rd., New Hartford, 13413. Tel: 315-732-8521; Fax: 315-735-1569; Web: www.stjohnsnh.com. Rev. Kevin J. Bunger; Deacon Edward W. Kernan. In Res., Rev. Arthur R. Hapanowicz, (Retired).
Catechesis Religious Program—One Sherman St., New Hartford, 13413. Cheryl Smith, D.R.E. Students 473.

2—OUR LADY OF THE ROSARY (1949)
1736 Burrstone Rd., New Hartford, 13413. Tel: 315-724-0402; Email: Parishoffice@olrosarynh.org. Rev. Joseph A. Salerno.
Catechesis Religious Program—Students 318.

3—ST. THOMAS (1957)
150 Clinton Rd., New Hartford, 13413. Tel: 315-735-8381; Email: dsears@syrdio.org. Rev. G. David Sears, M.S., C.S.W.

NEW LONDON, ONEIDA CO., HOLY CROSS (1968) Merged with St. Frances of Assisi, Durhamville. For inquiries for parish records please see St. Francis, Durhamville.

NEW YORK MILLS, ONEIDA CO., CHURCH OF SACRED HEART AND ST. MARY (1909) [CEM] (Sacred Heart Church, Utica merged with St. Mary, New York Mills to become Church of Sacred Heart & St. Mary Our Lady of Czestochowa.) Rev. Artur Krawczenko, (Poland).
Res.: 201 Main St., New York Mills, 13417. Tel: 315-316-0506; Email: akrawczenko@yahoo.com; Web: www.sacredheart-stmary.org.
Catechesis Religious Program—Tel: 315-527-8399; Email: lspringer@syrdio.org. Lynn Springer, D.R.E. Students 148.

NORTH BAY, ONEIDA CO., ST. JOHN (1843) [CEM] (Oratory of St. Agatha, Canastota)
2191 Rte. 49, P.O. Box 289, North Bay, 13123. P.O. Box 240, Verona Beach, 13162. Rev. Stephen Wirkes.
Catechesis Religious Program—Students 50.

NORTH BROOKFIELD, MADISON CO., ST. MARY, Closed. Former mission of St. Bernard, Waterville.

NORTH SYRACUSE, ONONDAGA CO., ST. ROSE OF LIMA (1926)
409 S. Main St., North Syracuse, 13212. Tel: 315-458-0283; Email: strose12@yahoo.com. Rev. John Canorro; Rev. Msgr. Francis A.C. Nyarko, (Ghana) Parochial Vicar; Rev. Daniel W. Heintz, In Res., (Retired).
Res.: 407 S. Main St., North Syracuse, 13212.
Child Care—Preschool, Students 160.
School—St. Rose of Lima School, (Grades PreK-6), 411 S. Main St., North Syracuse, 13212. Tel: 315-458-6036; Fax: 315-458-6038; Email: mcrysler@syrdiocese.org. Mrs. Mary Crysler, Prin. Lay Teachers 18; Preschool 160; Sisters of the Third Franciscan Order (Syracuse, NY) 1; Students 120.
Catechesis Religious Program—Tel: 315-458-6592. Patricia Decker, D.R.E.; Douglas Pyke, Music Dir. Students 400.

NORWICH, CHENANGO CO.

1—ST. BARTHOLOMEW THE APOSTLE (1919) (Italian)
73 E. Main St., Norwich, 13815. Tel: 607-336-2222; Tel: 607-336-2215; Fax: 607-337-2218; Email: stbarts@syrdio.org; Web: www.stbartsnorwichny.com. Mailing Address: 30 Pleasant St., Norwich, 13815. Rev. Ralph A. Bove.
Catechesis Religious Program—Tel: 607-337-2200; Email: stpaulsnorwich@syrdio.org. Sr. M. Bartholomew Biviano, C.S.J., D.R.E. Students 82.

2—ST. PAUL, [CEM]
30 Pleasant St., Norwich, 13815. Tel: 607-337-2222; Fax: 607-334-6521; Email: stpaulsnorwich@syrdio.org. Rev. Ralph A. Bove; Deacon David Kirsch.
School—Holy Family School, (Grades PreK-6), 17 Prospect St., Norwich, 13815. Tel: 607-337-2207; Fax: 607-337-2210; Email: ntestani@syrdiocese.org. Lydia Brenner, Prin. Lay Teachers 12; Students 149.
Catechesis Religious Program—Tel: 607-337-2200. Sr. M. Bartholomew Biviano, C.S.J., D.R.E. Students 56.
Convent—79 E. Main St., Norwich, 13815.

ONEIDA, MADISON CO.

1—ST. JOSEPH (1893)
121 St. Joseph Pl., Oneida, 13421. Tel: 315-363-3280; Email: stjoesoneida@syrdio.org. Rev. Richard J. Kapral.
Parish Center—111 St. Joseph Pl., Oneida, 13421.
Catechesis Religious Program—Students 81.

2—ST. PATRICK (1843) [CEM]
347 Main St., Oneida, 13421. Tel: 315-363-7570; Email: stpatsoneida@syrdio.org. Rev. Richard J. Kapral.
School—St. Patrick School, (Grades PreK-6), 354 Elizabeth St., Oneida, 13421. Tel: 315-363-3620; Fax: 315-363-5075; Email: khealt@syrdiocese.org. Kristin Healt, Prin.; Jackie Carll, Librarian. Lay Teachers 9; Students 128.
Catechesis Religious Program—Lisa Spooner, D.R.E. Students 76.

ONONDAGA HILL, ONONDAGA CO., ST. MICHAEL & ST. PETER (1874)
4782 W. Seneca Tpke., 13215. Tel: 315-469-6995; Email: stmichaelstpeter@syrdio.org. Rev. Henry J. Pedzich; Deacon Gregory T. Cross, Pastoral Assoc.
Catechesis Religious Program—Students 260.

ORISKANY FALLS, ONEIDA CO., ST. JOSEPH (1870) [CEM]
229 Main St., Oriskany Falls, 13425. Tel: 315-841-4481; Email: stjoesofalls@syrdio.org. Rev. Lukasz Kozlowski.
Res.: 199 Stafford Ave., Waterville, 13480.
Catechesis Religious Program—Students 27.

ORISKANY, ONEIDA CO., ST. STEPHEN, PROTOMARTYR (1929) Merged with St. Paul, Whitesboro. For inquiries for Parish records contact St. Paul, Whitesboro.

OSWEGO, OSWEGO CO.

1—ST. JOHN THE EVANGELIST (1869) Merged with St. Mary, Oswego. For inquiries for parish records please see St. Mary, Oswego.

2—ST. JOSEPH (1915) (Italian)
240 W. First St., Oswego, 13126. Tel: 315-343-2160; Email: stjosephoswego@gmail.com; Web: stjosephoswego.com. Mailing Address: 178 W. Second St., Oswego, 13126. Deacon Nick A. Alvaro, Admin.
Catechesis Religious Program—Tel: 315-342-3967; Email: patbdre.teachers@gmail.com. Patricia Barnett, D.R.E. Students 78.

3—ST. LOUIS (1870) (French), Merged with St. Peter, Oswego. For inquiries for parish records, please contact St. Peter, Oswego.

4—ST. MARY OF THE ASSUMPTION (1848)
103 W. Seventh St., Oswego, 13126. Tel: 315-343-3953; Email: stmarysoswego@syrdio.org; Web: stmarysoswego.org. Rev. John F. Hogan Jr. For further information please see Trinity Catholic School under Consolidated Schools located in the Institution section.

5—ST. PAUL (1840) (Irish)
50 E. Mohawk St., Oswego, 13126. Tel: 315-343-2333; Fax: 315-343-2334; Email: stpaulsoswego@syrdio.org. Rev. Gaetano T. Baccaro; Deacon F. Phillip Kehoe, Pastoral Min./Coord.
Church: 134 E. Fifth St., Oswego, 13126.
For further information see Trinity Catholic School under Consolidated Schools in the Institution section.
Catechesis Religious Program—Tel: 315-342-4382; Email: dzeller@syrdio.org. Diane Zeller, D.R.E. Students 71.
Mission—Our Lady of Perpetual Help, W. River Rd., Minetto, 13115.

6—ST. PETER (1862) (German)
83 E. Albany St., Oswego, 13126. Tel: 315-343-1352; Email: stpetersoswego@syrdio.org. Rev. George E. Wurz, Admin.

Catechesis Religious Program—Tel: 315-342-5075. Rosemary Place, D.R.E. Students 14.
Mission—Sacred Heart, 3472 County Rte. 176, Oswego, 13126.
7—ST. STEPHEN THE KING (1908) (Polish)
138 Niagara St., Oswego, 13126. Tel: 315-343-2160; Email: stjosephoswego@gmail.com. Mailing Address: 178 W. Second St., Oswego, 13126. Rev. Richard P. Morisette, In Res., (Retired); Deacon Nick A. Alvaro.
Catechesis Religious Program—Students 41.
OXFORD, CHENANGO CO., ST. JOSEPH (1849) [CEM]
3 Scott St., P.O. Box 352, Oxford, 13830.
Tel: 607-843-7021; Email: stjoesoxford@syrdio.org. Rev. Msgr. John P. Putano, Admin.
Catechesis Religious Program—Gwen Hornbeck, D.R.E. Students 26.
Station—New York State Veterans' Home, Oxford, 13830.
PARISH, OSWEGO CO., ST. ANNE (1950) [CEM] Closed. Merged with St. Mary, Star of the Sea, Mexico to form St. Anne, Mother of Mary, Mexico.
PHOENIX, OSWEGO CO., ST. STEPHEN (1880)
469 Main St., Phoenix, 13135. Tel: 315-695-4531; Email: ststephenphoenix@syrdio.org; Web: www.ststephensphoenix.com. Rev. Joseph E. Scardella; Deacon Jeffrey Dean.
Catechesis Religious Program—Tel: 315-695-4608; Email: ststephensfaithformation@syrdio.org. Margaret Ostaszewski, D.R.E. Students 67.
POMPEY, ONONDAGA CO., IMMACULATE CONCEPTION (1850) [CEM]
7386 Academy St., P.O. Box 102, Pompey, 13138.
Tel: 315-677-3061; Email: icpompey@yahoo.com. Rev. James H. Carey, Admin.
Catechesis Religious Program—Tel: 315-415-9733; Email: jeanettelkb@gmail.com. Jeanette Burghardt, D.R.E. Students 101.
PULASKI, OSWEGO CO.
1—CHRIST OUR LIGHT (2003) Linked with St. Anne, Mother of Mary, Mexico.
23 Niagara St., Pulaski, 13142-4425.
Tel: 315-298-5350; Tel: 315-298-3863 (Res.); Email: christourlight@syrdio.org; Web: colcom.org. Rev. James A. Schultz, Admin.
Catechesis Religious Program—Tel: 315-963-7182; Email: lbuckley@syrdio.org. Linda A. Buckley, D.R.E. Students 65.
2—ST. JOHN THE EVANGELIST, Merged with St. Frances Xavier Cabrini, Lacona to form Christ Our Light, Pulaski.
ROME, ONEIDA CO.
1—ST. JOHN THE BAPTIST (1909) [CEM] (Italian)
210 E. Dominick St., Rome, 13440. Tel: 315-337-0990 ; Email: stjhnpub@twcny.rr.com; Web: www.stjohnbaptist.info. Rev. Paul F. Angelicchio; Deacon Michael Gudaitis.
Catechesis Religious Program—Tel: 315-886-6597; Tel: 315-272-9319; Email: amhunzinger@yahoo.com; Email: stjohnslifeteen10@gmail.com. Ann Marie Hunzinger, D.R.E.; Robin Calandra, Youth Min. Students 171.
2—ST. MARY OF THE ASSUMPTION (1848) [CEM] Merged with St. Peter, Rome to form St. Mary's-St. Peter's, Rome.
3—ST. MARY'S-ST. PETER'S
105 E. Liberty St., P.O. Box 627, Rome, 13440.
Tel: 315-336-5072; Fax: 315-336-0855. Rev. Philip A. Hearn; Deacon Nicholas A. Rosher.
Catechesis Religious Program—Students 338.
4—ST. PAUL (1954)
1807 Bedford St., Rome, 13440-2199.
Tel: 315-336-3082; Email: stpaulsrome@syrdio.org; Web: stpaulsrome.com. Rev. Robert L. Kelly; Deacon Edgar Doyle Jr.
Catechesis Religious Program—Tel: 315-334-9570; Email: jstokes@syrdiocese.org. Julianne Stokes, D.R.E. Students 135.
5—ST. PETER (1837) [CEM] Merged with St. Mary of the Assumption, Rome to form St. Mary's-St. Peter's, Rome.
6—TRANSFIGURATION (1909) (Polish)
Mailing Address: 210 E. Dominick St., Rome, 13440. Rev. Paul F. Angelicchio.
Church: 111 Ridge St., Rome, 13440.
Tel: 315-337-0990; Email: transfiguration@twcny.rr.com.
Catechesis Religious Program—
SANITARIA SPRINGS, BROOME CO., ST. JOSEPH (1914)
659 NY Rte. 7-B, Sanitaria Springs, 13833.
Tel: 607-775-0086; Email: sebroomecatholics@syrdio.org. Mailing Address: 975 NY Rte. 11, Kirkwood, 13795. Barbara Kane, Parish Life Coord.
Catechesis Religious Program—Students 14.
SHERBURNE, CHENANGO CO., ST. MALACHY (1858) [CEM]
Mailing Address: 29 E. State St., P.O. Box 722, Sherburne, 13460-0722. Tel: 607-674-9625; Fax: 607-674-2792; Email: stmalachysherburne@gmail.com; Web: stmalachysherburne.com. Rev. Darr F. Schoenhofen; Patricia Mulligan, Contact Person.

Catechesis Religious Program—Students 52.
SHERRILL, ONEIDA CO., ST. HELENA (1917)
210 Primo Ave., Sherrill, 13461. Tel: 315-363-3882; Email: sthelenas@syrdio.org; Web: sthelenas-holyfamily.org. Rev. William A. Mesmer.
Catechesis Religious Program—Tel: 315-361-1566. Mary LaForest, D.R.E. Students 92.
SKANEATELES, ONONDAGA CO., ST. MARY OF THE LAKE (1855) [CEM]
81 Jordan St., Skaneateles, 13152. Tel: 315-685-5083 ; Email: generalmail@stmarysskaneateles.com; Web: www.stmarysskaneateles.com. Mailing Address: 10 W. Austin St., Skaneateles, 13152. Rev. Richard B. Dunn.
Catechesis Religious Program—Tel: 315-685-6377. Students 310.
SOLVAY, ONONDAGA CO., ST. CECILIA (1903) (Italian)
1001 Woods Rd., Solvay, 13209. Tel: 315-488-3221; Email: stcecilias@syrdio.org. Mailing Address: 105 Stanton Ave., Solvay, 13209. Rev. Joseph J. Clemente.
Catechesis Religious Program—Tel: 315-243-6244. Students 40.
SOUTH ONONDAGA, ONONDAGA CO., CORPUS CHRISTI (1938) Closed. For inquiries for parish record contact St. Leo, Tully.
SOUTHWEST OSWEGO, OSWEGO CO., ST. JOSEPH, Closed. Former mission of Our Lady of the Rosary, Hannibal.
SPLIT ROCK, ONONDAGA CO., ST. PETER, Merged with St. Michael, Onondaga Hill to form St. Michael-St. Peter, Onondaga Hill.
TABERG, ONEIDA CO., ST. PATRICK (1876) [CEM]
9168 Main St., Taberg, 13471. Tel: 315-336-4079; Email: stpatstaberg@syrdio.org. Rev. Francis A. Wapen.
Catechesis Religious Program—Students 33.
TRUXTON, CORTLAND CO., ST. PATRICK (1854) [CEM]
3656 Rte. 13, Box 15, Truxton, 13158.
Tel: 607-842-6326; Email: jhp4461@yahoo.com. Rev. Joseph H. Phillips, (Retired); Deacon Laurence Brickner.
Catechesis Religious Program—Students 65.
Mission—St. Lawrence, 1672 Cortland St., De Ruyter, 13052. Tel: 315-852-6446.
TULLY, ONONDAGA CO., ST. LEO (1891)
10 Onondaga St., P.O. Box 574, Tully, 13159.
Tel: 315-696-5092; Email: parish@stleostully.org; Web: www.stleostully.org. Rev. James H. Carey.
Res.: 6104 US Rte. 20, P.O. Box 169, La Fayette, 13084.
Catechesis Religious Program—Students 90.
UTICA, ONEIDA CO.
1—ST. AGNES (1887) Merged with St. Anthony of Padua, Utica to become St. Anthony and St. Agnes Church, Utica.
2—ST. ANTHONY AND ST. AGNES CHURCH
422 Tilden Ave., Utica, 13501. Tel: 315-732-1177; Email: stanthutica@syrdio.org. Rev. Mark P. Kaminski, Ph.D., D.Min.; Deacon William Dischiavo; Sr. Lisa Cirillo, C.S.J., Pastoral Assoc., Faith Formation.
Catechesis Religious Program—Students 95.
3—BLESSED SACRAMENT (1924) Merged with St. Mary of Mt. Carmel, Utica to form St. Mary of Mt. Carmel/ Blessed Sacrament.
4—ST. FRANCIS DE SALES (1876) Closed. Merged with St. John's, Utica. Parish records available at St. John's, Utica.
5—ST. GEORGE (1911) [CEM] (Lithuanian), Merged For inquiries for parish records contact St. Joseph and St. Patrick, Utica.
6—HISTORIC OLD ST. JOHN'S CHURCH aka The St. John's Catholic Society of the City of Utica (1819)
240 Bleecker St., Utica, 13501. Tel: 315-724-6159; Fax: 315-798-9731; Email: stjohnsutica@syrdio.org; Email: historicstjohns@roadrunner.com; Web: www.historicoldstjohnschurch.com. Revs. John A. Buehler; Luis Olguin, Spanish Apostolate, Tel: 315-724-0389; Tuoi (John) V. Nguyen, Asian Min.; Sisters Elizabeth Greim, Pastoral Assoc.; Paula Mayer, D.C., Pastoral Assoc. & Outreach Dir.; Deacon William R. Dischiavo.
Parish Center—520 John St., Utica, 13501.
Tel: 315-732-2417.
Catechesis Religious Program—Email: agape@syrdio.org. Annette Gape, Dir. Faith Formation, Grades 1-10. Students 100.
7—HOLY TRINITY (1896) [CEM] (Polish)
1206 Lincoln Ave., Utica, 13502. Tel: 315-724-7238; Email: holytrinitychurch@roadrunner.com. Rev. Canon John E. Mikalajunas; Rev. Joseph E. Moskal, (Retired).
Catechesis Religious Program—Students 52.
Convent—1218 Lincoln Ave., Utica, 13502.
8—ST. JOSEPH AND ST. PATRICK (1841 and 1849) [CEM]
702 Columbia St., Utica, 13502. Tel: 315-735-4429; Email: sjsputica@syrdio.org. Rev. Richard E. Dellos. In Res., Rev. Anthony LaFache, (Retired).
Catechesis Religious Program—Tel: 315-507-2661; Email: cstaley@syrdio.org. Cheryl Staley, D.R.E. Students 21.

9—ST. MARK (1963)
440 Keyes Rd., Utica, 13502. Tel: 315-724-1645; Email: stmarks@syrdio.org; Web: stmarkschurchutica.weebly.com. Rev. Mark A. Pasik; Deacon Richard Prusko.
Catechesis Religious Program—Teale LaBarbera, D.R.E. Students 100.
10—ST. MARY (1870) (German), Closed. For inquiries for parish records contact St. John, Utica.
11—ST. MARY OF MT. CARMEL/BLESSED SACRAMENT (1896)
648 Jay St., Utica, 13501. Tel: 315-735-1482; Fax: 315-735-9806; Email: stmaryutica@syrdio.org; Web: www.mountcarmelblessedsacrament.com. Rev. James M. Cesta; Patrick Zasa, Dir. Maintenance; Mary Beth La Neve, Business Admin.; Peter Elacqua, Music Dir. In Res., Rev. Luis Olguin.
Catechesis Religious Program—Tel: 315-724-3950; Email: tpanuccio@syrdio.org; Email: aelacqua@syrdio.org. Terese Panuccio, Dir. Faith Formation, K-6; Anne Elacqua, Dir. Faith Formation, 7-10. Students 147.
12—OUR LADY OF LOURDES (1919)
2222 Genesee St., Utica, 13502. Tel: 315-724-3155; Email: mmorosco@gmail.com; Web: www.ourladyoflourdesutica@dreamscape.com. Mailing Address: 2 Barton Ave., Utica, 13502. Rev. Joseph A. Salerno; Deacon John Kopec; Sr. Lois Mary Paciello, C.S.J.
See Notre Dame Elementary School under Consolidated Schools located in the Institution section.
Catechesis Religious Program—Tel: 315-404-2495; Email: kim327@roadrunner.com. Kimberly Smith, Faith Formation; William Smith, Faith Formation. Students 284.
13—ST. PETER (1872) [CEM]
422 Coventry Ave., Utica, 13502. Tel: 315-724-6310; Email: stpetersutica@syrdio.org. Rev. David J. Orzel.
Catechesis Religious Program—Tel: 315-735-7077. Students 22.
14—SACRED HEART (1926) Merged with St. Mary, New York Mills to form Sacred Heart & St. Mary, New York Mills. For inquiries for parish records contact St. Mary, New York Mills.
15—ST. STANISLAUS (1911) [CEM] (Polish), Closed. and merged with Holy Trinity, Utica. For inquiries for parish records, contact Holy Trinity, Utica.
VERNON, ONEIDA CO., HOLY FAMILY (1926; 1976)
4352 Peterboro St., P.O. Box 988, Vernon, 13476.
Tel: 315-829-3295; Email: holyfamilyvernon@syrdio.org; Web: sthelenas-holyfamily.org. Rev. William A. Mesmer.
Res.: St. Helena Rectory, 210 Primo Ave., Sherrill, 13461.
Catechesis Religious Program—4343 Peterboro St., P.O. Box 988, Vernon, 13476. Tel: 315-829-9895. Mary LaForests, D.R.E. Students 82.
VERONA, ONEIDA CO., OUR LADY OF GOOD COUNSEL (1913)
5652 E. Main St., P.O. Box 135, Verona, 13478.
Tel: 315-363-7696; Email: frcastronovo@gmail.com. Rev. Edmund A. Castronovo.
Res.: 5259 Beacon Light Rd., Verona, 13478.
Catechesis Religious Program—Students 96.
VESTAL, BROOME CO.
1—OUR LADY OF SORROWS (1941)
801 Main St., Vestal, 13851. Tel: 607-748-8287; Email: office@olsvestal.org; Web: www.olsvestal.org. P.O. Box 326, Vestal, 13851. Rev. John P. Donovan, J.C.L.; Deacon Dale Crotsley.
Catechesis Religious Program—Tel: 607-748-4766. Students 305.
2—ST. VINCENT DE PAUL-BLESSED SACRAMENT (1965)
165 Clifton Blvd., Vestal, 13850. Tel: 607-722-3988; Web: www.stvbs.org. Rev. Corey S. Van Kuren; Deacons Anthony Miller; Thomas N. Picciano.
Catechesis Religious Program—465 Clubhouse Rd., Vestal, 13850. Students 120.
WARNERS, ONONDAGA CO., OUR LADY OF GOOD COUNSEL (1913) Merged with St. Joseph, Camillus.
WATERVILLE, ONEIDA CO., ST. BERNARD (1850) [CEM]
199 Stafford Ave., Waterville, 13480.
Tel: 315-841-4481; Email: stbernards@syrdio.org. Rev. Lukasz Kozlowski.
Catechesis Religious Program—Students 87.
WHITESBORO, ONEIDA CO.
1—ST. ANNE (1965) Merged with St. Paul, Whitesboro. Records are being maintained at St. Paul's Whitesboro.
2—ST. PAUL (1883)
16 Park Ave., Whitesboro, 13492. Tel: 315-736-1124; Email: stpauls@stpaulswhitesboro.org. Rev. Thomas P. Durant.
Catechesis Religious Program—Students 243.
WHITNEY POINT, BROOME CO., THE CATHOLIC COMMUNITY OF ST. STEPHEN-ST. PATRICK (1869) [CEM]
59 Keibel Rd., P.O. Box 711, Whitney Point, 13862.
Tel: 607-692-3911; Email: ststephenstpat@syrdio.org. Rev. Douglas D. Cunningham.

Catechesis Religious Program—Students 62.
Mission—Our Lady of Perpetual Help, P.O. Box 310, Cincinnatus, 13040.

WILLIAMSTOWN, OSWEGO CO., ST. PATRICK'S MISSION, Merged with St. John, Camden. For inquiries for parish records please see St. John, Camden.

WINDSOR, BROOME CO., OUR LADY OF LOURDES (1947) 594 Kent St., Windsor, 13865. Tel: 607-775-0086. Mailing Address: 975 NY Rt. 11, Kirkwood, 13795. Barbara Kane, Parish Life Coord.
Catechesis Religious Program—Jennifer Barton, D.R.E. Students 25.

Chaplains of Public Institutions

Hospitals

SYRACUSE.
St. Camillus Health & Rehab Center, 813 Fay Rd., 13219. Tel: 315-703-0686. Revs. Louis F. Aiello, Chap., Candance Lawrence, Chap., Deacon Anthony J. Paratore, Chap.
Crouse Irving Memorial Hospital, 736 Irving Ave., 13210. Tel: 315-470-7615. Rev. Kate Day, Managing Chap., Tom Anderson, Chap.
James Square Nursing Home, Tel: 315-474-1561. Attended from Blessed Sacrament Parish.
St. Joseph's Hospital Health Center, 301 Prospect Ave., 13203. Tel: 315-448-5116. Rev. Severine Yagaza, Joshua Czyz, Coord., Bridget Dunn, Sr. Adelbert Durant, O.S.F., Joy Magee, Chap., Sr. Christine Wald, Chap., Deborah Welch, Vice Pres., People, Sr. Baptiste Westbrook, Chaplain.
Loretto Geriatric Center, 700 E. Brighton Ave., 13205. Tel: 315-469-5570, Ext. 3295. Deacon John Bowden, Chap.
University Hospital at Community Campus Hospital, 4900 Broad Rd., 13215. Tel: 315-492-5740. Rev. Joseph Smyth, Min., Deacon Glenn Nappa, Sr. Mary Bernard Sabel, O.S.F., Patricia Williams.
Upstate University Hospital, 750 E. Adams St., 13210. Tel: 315-464-5540. Revs. Terry Ruth Culbertson, Dir., Innocent Onyenagubo, (Nigeria) Chap., Deacon Dare Dutter, Sr. Mary Emebo.
Van Duyn Home & Hospital, 5060 W. Seneca Tpke., 13215. Tel: 315-449-6000, Ext. 6169. Deacon Michael Letizia.
Veterans Administration Hospital, Res: 800 Irving Ave., 13210. Tel: 315-476-7461. Rev. Craig David, Chap.

BINGHAMTON.
Binghamton General Hospital, Binghamton. Tel: 607-762-2200. Rev. Corey S. Van Kuren, Chap. & Dir., UHS, Don Burgin, Barbara Eggleston, Chap., UHS, John Koopman, Chap.
Our Lady of Lourdes Memorial Hospital, 179 Riverside Dr., Binghamton, 13905. Tel: 607-798-5111. Revs. Krzysztof Boretto, Chap., Greg Johnson, Baptist Chap., David Seaver, Baptist Chap., Bro. James Bagans, Lynda Crane, Lay Min., Br. Daniel Galluci, Mary Alice Westerlund, Dir.
The Greater Binghamton Health Center, Tel: 607-724-1391, Ext. 4254. Rev. Wilfredo Baez, United Methodist-Vestal, Deacon Thomas N. Picciano, Don Burgin.

JOHNSON CITY.
Wilson Memorial Hospital, 33 Harrison St., Johnson City, 13790. Tel: 607-763-6000. Rev. Corey S. Van Kuren, Chap., Don Burgin, Barbara Eggleston, Chap.

UTICA.
St. Elizabeth Hospital, 2209 Genesee St., Utica, 13501. Tel: 315-801-8102. Deacon Paul Lehmann, Dir., Bro. Andrew Siuta.
Faxton St. Luke's Health Care, 1656 Chaplin Ave., New Hartford, 13413. Tel: 315-624-6218 Spiritual Care Office. 1676 Sunset Ave., Utica, 13502. Deacon Paul Lehmann, Dir., Pastoral Care, Sr. Sharon Ann Boyd, I.H.M., Chap., Bonnie Waldron, Chap.

VESTAL.
Binghamton Nursing Homes, Our Lady of Sorrows, 157 Clark St., Vestal, 13850. Tel: 607-748-8287. Deacon Dale Crotsley.

Psychiatric Facilities

MARCY.
Central New York Psychiatric Center, Old River Rd., Box 330, Marcy, 13403. Tel: 315-765-3101. Rev. Richard V. O'Neill, Chap., (Retired).

UTICA.
Mohawk Valley Psychiatric Center, 1400 Noyes at York, Utica, 13502. Tel: 315-738-3800.

Jails

SYRACUSE.
Elmcrest Children's Center, 960 Salt Springs Rd., 13224. Tel: 315-446-6250. Hassan Yamini.
Hillbrook Detention Center, 4949 Velasko Rd., 13215.
Jail Ministry Office, 208 Slocum Ave., 13204. Tel: 315-440-6407. Keith Cieplicki, Coord., Bill Cuddy, Spiritual Min., Victoria Moore, Bail Coord., Tel: 315-383-3644.
Justice Center, 259 E. Onondaga St., 13202. Rev. John C. Schopfer, (Retired), Keith Ciedlicki, Jail Ministry.

BINGHAMTON.
Broome County Jail. Rev. Stanley J. Gerlock, (Retired).

CORTLAND.
Cortland County Jail. Vacant.

JAMESVILLE.
Jamesville Penitentiary, P.O. Box 143, Jamesville, 13078. Tel: 315-469-5581. Sr. Maura Rhode.

MARCY.
Marcy Correctional Facility, 900 Old River Rd., P.O. Box 5000, Marcy, 13403-5000. Tel: 315-768-1400. Rev. Vincent P. Long.
Mid-State Correctional Facility, 210 W. Liberty St., Marcy, 13403. Tel: 315-768-8581. Deacon Daniel Hurley.

NORWICH.
Chenango County Jail.

ONEIDA.
Mohawk Correctional Facility, 578 Main St., P.O. Box 8450, Oneida, 13421. Rev. Vincent P. Long.

ORISKANY.
Oneida County Jail, 120 Dexter Ave., Oriskany, 13424. Tel: 315-736-9033. Vacant.

OSWEGO.
Oswego County Jail, 178 W. Second St., Oswego, 13126. Tel: 315-349-3300. Rev. George E. Wurz.

ROME.
Walsh Regional Medical Unit, Rome. Tel: 315-339-5232. Rev. Luis Olguin.

Special Assignment:
Most Rev.—
Cunningham, Robert J., J.C.L., D.D.
Very Rev. Msgr.—
Elmer, Timothy S., J.C.L., V.G.
Rev. Msgrs.—
Kopp, Richard M.
Lang, James P.
Quartier, Neal E.
Revs.—
Aiello, Louis F.
Cunningham, Douglas D.
Drobin, Paul J., (Retired)
Fukes, Gary M., 2247 Towering Oak Cir., Seffner, FL 33584
James, David J.
Olguin, Luis
Pompei, Frederick A.
Schopfer, John C., (Retired)
Weber, Robert C.

On Duty Outside the Diocese:
Rev. Msgr.—
Rossetti, Stephen, 126 E. St., S.E., Washington, DC 20003
Revs.—
Bassano, Michael, M.M., Mary Knoll (Incardinated)
Guida, Amedeo G., Ave Maria Univ., 5050 Ave Maria Blvd., Ave Maria, FL 34142
Nichols, Louis J.
Seibt, Christopher, Theological College, 400 Michigan Ave., NE, Washington, DC 20017.

Absent on Leave:
Revs.—
Harer, Eric K.
Krul, Valentine C.
Madej, Paul D.

Retired:
Rev. Msgrs.—
Bill, Ronald C., (Retired), 400 Salt Springs St., Fayetteville, 13060
Elkin, Frederic F., (Retired)
Fahey, Charles J., (Retired)
Flanagan, John P., (Retired)
Heagerty, John J., (Retired)
Kennedy, James M., (Retired)
Lutz, James M., (Retired)
McGraw, John T., (Retired)
O'Brien, James T., (Retired)
Sheehan, George F., (Retired)
Yeazel, J. Robert, (Retired)
Revs.—
Ahern, John V., (Retired)
Aho, Charles A., (Retired)
Bebel, Alfred J., (Retired), Binghamton, NY
Bourgeois, Donald E., (Retired)
Brockmyre, Philip C., (Retired)
Brown, Matthew F., (Retired)
Buckley, Gerald J., (Retired)
Cahill, William C., (Retired)
Carey, Paul V., (Retired)
Carmola, Michael J., (Retired)
Cerwonka, Clarence J., (Retired)
DeLorme, R. Daniel, (Retired)
Donovan, J. Michael, (Retired)
Drobin, Paul J., (Retired)
Dudkiewicz, Stanley, (Poland) (Retired)
Dwyer, Robert D., (Retired)
Esper, Abraham L., (Retired)
Fetcho, John E., (Retired)
Finnegan, John S., (Retired)
Fitzpatrick, Thomas P., (Retired)
Florczyk, Walter, (Retired)
Fritzen, James C., (Retired)
Gerlock, Stanley J., (Retired)
Hapanowicz, Arthur R., (Retired)
Hayes, Dennis J., (Retired)
Heintz, Daniel W., (Retired)
Hobbes, Thomas F., (Retired)
Jones, William R., (Retired)
Karlen, Donald H., (Retired)
Katz, Jerome A., (Retired)
Keeffe, Anthony J., (Retired)
Kehoe, Joseph F., (Retired)
Kelly, Vincent J., (Retired)
LaFache, Anthony, (Retired)
Larkin, Joseph M., (Retired)
Lord, Laurence J., (Retired)
Lupa, Gerard, (Retired)
McGrath, Thomas J., (Retired)
Morbito, Angelo L., (Retired)
Morisette, Richard P., (Retired)
Moskal, Joseph E., (Retired)
O'Neill, Richard V., (Retired)
Phillips, Joseph H., (Retired)
Pilla, P. Carl, (Retired)
Queen, James T., (Retired)
Quinn, John M., (Retired)
Reddick, E. Peter, (Retired)
Reimer, Edward J., (Retired)
Roock, John D., (Retired)
Rose, John F., (Retired)
Rudnik, Tadeusz, (Poland) (Retired)
Sambor, David R., (Retired)
Schopfer, John C., (Retired)
Smegelsky, John J., (Retired)
Smith, Lester E., (Retired)
Stirpe, Carlo C., (Retired)
Sullivan, Robert J., (Retired)
Tormey, James D., (Retired)
Tucker, Richard, (Retired)
Vavonese, Charles S., (Retired)
Votraw, Wilbur J., (Retired)
Wagner, John P., (Retired)
Wood, Raymond B., (Retired)
Young, Francis P., (Retired)
Zandy, Edward J., (Retired).

Permanent Deacons:
Addante, John, Cazenovia
Alvaro, Nick A., Syracuse
Berube, Mark, Pennellville
Biermann, Paul, Liverpool
Blabac, Stephen Jr., Port Crane
Blaine, Edward, Endicott
Borchert, Robert, (On Leave)
Bowden, John, Syracuse
Brainard, Dean, East Syracuse
Brickner, Laurence, Marathon
Burke, Robert T., Liverpool
Camaione, Richard Jr., Syracuse
Casper, Joseph, Baldwinsville
Caughey, Daniel, Pulaski
Celentano, Joseph Sr., Syracuse
Chappell, James M., Oneida
Cholette, Frederick, (Retired), Greensboro, NC
Colabufo, Michael, Syracuse
Collins, John H., (Retired), Pennellville
Connelly, Robert, Syracuse
Crosby, James P., (Retired), Brevard, NC
Cross, Gregory T., Syracuse
Crossett, Thomas F., (Retired), Johnson City
Crotsley, Dale, Vestal
Crowley, James, (Retired), Vestal
Cuskey, Thomas, Liverpool
Dean, Jeffrey, Pennellville
DiLallo, Gary, Maine, NY
Dischiavo, William R., Utica
Distin, Leslie, (Retired), Johnson City
Dotterer, William A., Liverpool
Doyle, Edgar A. Jr., Rome, NY
During, Joseph, Cortland
Dutter, Dare, DeWitt
Dwyer, Richard J., (Retired), Fort Pierce, FL
Engle, Christopher Sr., Oriskany
Falge, John, Marcellus
Dr. Fangio, Robert, Syracuse
Ferguson, William, Lafayette
Fitzpatrick, William, Newark Valley
Forish, Frank M., (Retired), Baldwinsville
Galloway, Richard, Syracuse
Grigson, Thomas, Syracuse
Gudaitis, Michael, Rome
Gunn, Nathan, DeWitt
Hachey, Thomas, North Syracuse

Harley, Thomas, Endicott
Harris, Scott
Hart, Guy W. Sr., (Retired)
Heizman, Bernard, (Retired), Zephyr Hills, FL
Jahnige, Ralph B., Fayetteville
Kearney, Garrett, Clay (On Leave)
Kehoe, F. Phillip, Oswego
Kernan, Edward W., Clinton
Kirsch, David, Norwich
Kopec, John, Marcy
Lalande, John II, Oswego
Lauri, Brian, Clay
Lehmann, Paul, Hamilton
Letizia, Michael, Camillus
Longo, Frank, Holiday, FL (On Leave); Endicott
Losito, David G., Cicero
Manzene, Stephen, Liverpool
Matts, William, Endicott
Maynard, George E., (Retired), Fulton
McCabe, Donald, (Retired), Jamesville
McGrath, Michael B., Syracuse
McNerney, Timothy, Guilford
Miller, Anthony, Binghamton
Money, Kenneth N., Syracuse
Mula, Donald, (On Leave), Brewerton
Mullin, Paul, (Retired), Bradenton, FL
Mulvey, John, (Retired), N. Fort Myers, FL
Murray, John, (Retired), Clayton
Nadeau, Gilbert, Clark Mills
Nappa, Glenn, Liverpool
Niles, Elbert, Oneida
Paparella, Anthony, Whitesboro
Paratore, Anthony J., Syracuse
Pedrotti, John, Baldwinsville
Phillips, George Jr., Endwell
Picciano, Thomas N., Endwell
Prusko, Richard, Utica
Rosher, Nicholas A., Rome
Ruf, Michael, Liverpool
Schiltz, David, Minoa
Shiner, Mark, Hamilton
Slominski, Philip, Liverpool
Smith, Stephen, Cortland
Stella, John, Binghamton
Stevens, Daniel, Syracuse
Street, Robert, Manlius
Sweenie, David, (Retired)
Talomie, Robert J., Baldwinsville
Timson, Frank, Syracuse
Uryniak, Adolph J., Canastota
Warren, Frank, (Retired), Oswego, NY
Whiting, Donald R., (Retired), Cicero
Wilber, Richard, Cheshire, CT, (On Leave)
Wilson, William, Camillus
Woloszyn, John, Liverpool
Young, Steven, New Baltimore (On Leave).

INSTITUTIONS LOCATED IN DIOCESE

[A] SEMINARIES, RELIGIOUS, OR SCHOLASTICATES

SYRACUSE. *Saint Andrew Hall*, 420 Demong Dr., 13214-1499. Tel: 315-445-3500; Fax: 315-446-9472; Email: standrewhallnovitiate@yahoo.com. Revs. Joseph C. Sands, S.J., Dir.; Richard J. Zanoni, S.J., Min.; Stephen Surovick, Socius. Novitiate of the Maryland and U.S.A. Northeast Provinces of the Society of Jesus. Novices 10; Priests 3.

[B] COLLEGES AND UNIVERSITIES

SYRACUSE. *Le Moyne College*, 1419 Salt Springs Rd., 13214-1302. Tel: 315-445-4100; Fax: 315-445-4691; Email: officeofthepresident@lemoyne.edu; Web: www.lemoyne.edu. timothy Lee, Vice Pres. Enrollment Mgmt.; Dr. Linda M. LeMura, Pres.; Dr. Margaret Wells, Interim Dean, Purcell School of Professional Studies; Dr. James Hannan, Dean, Learning Assessment; Ms. Inga Barnello, Interim Dir. Library; Revs. Donald J. Kirby, S.J., Acting Rector; David C. McCallum, S.J., Vice Pres. Mission Integration & Devel.; Joseph G. Marina, S.J., Provost & Vice Pres. Academic Affairs; Dr. Deborah M. Cady Melzer, Vice Pres. Student Devel.; Mr. Roger W. Stackpoole, Senior Vice Pres. Fin., Enrollment, & Admin., & Treas.; Mr. William H. Brower, Vice Pres. Communications & Advancement; Ms. Cynthia A. Alibrandi, Senior Dir. Enrollment Mgmt. & Registrar; Dr. Kathleen Costello-Sullivan, Dean, Arts & Sciences; Mr. James E. Joseph, Dean, Madden School of Bus. & Spec. Asst. to the Pres. for Strategic Initiatives; Ms. Anne E. Kearney, Dean, Student Devel.; Mr. Shaun C. Black, Senior Dir. I.T. A private four-year comprehensive college founded in 1946 enrolling approximately 3,500 students in a program of liberal arts, sciences, business and pre-professional studies. Le Moyne offers 33 academic majors leading to BA and BS degrees and also offers graduate programs in business administration, education, nursing and physician assistant studies. Clergy 7; Lay Teachers 158; Sisters 1; Students 3,431; Total Enrollment 3,431; Clergy / Religious Teachers 7; Jesuits 7.

[C] HIGH SCHOOLS, DIOCESAN

SYRACUSE. *Bishop Ludden Junior / Senior High School*, (Grades 7-12), 815 Fay Rd., 13219. Tel: 315-468-2591; Fax: 315-468-0097; Email: lcosgrove@syrdiocese.org; Email: srounds@syrdiocese.org; Web: www.syrdio.org. Leo Cosgrove, Prin.; W. Michael Morgan, Asst. Prin.; Rev. Daniel C. Muscalino, Pastoral Min./Coord.; Sr. Beth Ann Dollin, Campus Min. Lay Teachers 28; Priests 1; Students 310.

BINGHAMTON. *Seton Catholic Central of Broome County*, 70 Seminary Ave., Binghamton, 13905. Tel: 607-723-5307; Fax: 607-723-4811; Email: mmartinkovic@syrdio.org. Matthew Martinkovic, Prin.; Patrick Monachino, Asst. Prin.; Ms. Kathryn Frech, Librarian. Lay Teachers 26; Sisters 2; Students 366.

EAST SYRACUSE. *Bishop Grimes Jr. / Sr. High School*, (Grades 7-12), 6653 Kirkville Rd., East Syracuse, 13057. Tel: 315-437-0356; Fax: 315-437-0358; Email: bnolan@syrdiocese.org; Email: pkinne@syrdiocese.org; Web: www.bishopgrimes.org. Mr. Brian Nolan, Prin.; Patrick Kinne, Prin.; Sue Collins, Dir.; Ashlea Schad, Dir.; Mrs. Cathleen Hendrick, Librarian. Lay Teachers 33; Sisters 1; Students 357.

UTICA. *Notre Dame Jr. / Sr. High School*, (Grades 7-12), 2 Notre Dame Ln., Utica, 13502. Tel: 315-724-5118 ; Fax: 315-724-9460; Email: rspadafora@syrdiocese.org. Mr. Roy Kane, Prin.; Mr. Ronald Spadafora, Prin. Lay Teachers 37; Sisters 1; Students 310.

[D] HIGH SCHOOLS, PRIVATE

SYRACUSE. *Christian Brothers Academy*, (Grades 7-12), 6245 Randall Rd., 13214. Tel: 315-446-5960; Fax: 315-446-3393; Web: www.cbasyracuse.org. Bro. Joseph Jozwiak, F.S.C., Pres.; Matthew Keough, Prin.; Karen Shull, Librarian. Brothers of the Christian Schools 2; Lay Teachers 56; Sisters of Third Order of St. Francis 2; Students 780.

[E] CONSOLIDATED SCHOOLS

BINGHAMTON. *St. John the Evangelist*, (Grades PreK-6), 9 Livingston St., Binghamton, 13903. Tel: 607-723-0703; Fax: 607-772-6210; Email: krosen@syrdiocese.org. James Fountaine, Prin. Lay Teachers 20; Students 201.

ENDICOTT. *All Saints Catholic School*, (Grades PreK-6), 1112 Broad St., Endicott, 13760. Tel: 607-748-7423 ; Fax: 607-484-9576; Email: atierno@syrdiocese.org. Angela Tierno-Sherwood, Prin. Lay Teachers 22; Preschool 85; Students 135.

JOHNSON CITY. *St. James School*, (Grades PreK-6), 143 Main St., Johnson City, 13790. Tel: 607-797-5444; Fax: 607-797-6794; Email: skitchen@syrdiocese.org. Susan Kitchen, Prin. Lay Teachers 21; Students 186.

OSWEGO. *Trinity Catholic School*, (Grades PreK-6), 115 E. 5th St., Oswego, 13126. Tel: 315-343-6700; Fax: 315-342-9471; Email: bsugar@syrdiocese.org. Ms. Barbara Sugar, Prin. Lay Teachers 22; Students 185.

ROME. *Rome Catholic School*, (Grades PreK-6), 400 Floyd Ave., Rome, 13440. Tel: 315-336-6190; Fax: 315-336-6194; Email: pbliss@syrdiocese.org. Ms. Patricia Bliss, Prin. Lay Teachers 8; Students 95.

UTICA. *Notre Dame Elementary School*, (Grades PreK-6), 11 Barton Ave., Utica, 13502. Tel: 315-732-4374 ; Fax: 315-738-9720; Email: mrossi@syrdiocese.org; Web: notredameelem.org. Mrs. Mary Rossi, Prin. Lay Teachers 25; Students 365.

[F] CATHOLIC CHARITIES OF SYRACUSE

SYRACUSE. *Catholic Charities of the Roman Catholic Diocese of Syracuse*, 1654 W. Onondaga St., 13204. Tel: 315-424-1800; Fax: 315-424-8262; Email: mmelara@syrdio.org; Web: www.ccsyrdio.org. Mr. Michael F. Melara, Dir.

Jail Ministry, Slocum House, 208 Slocum Ave., 13204. Tel: 315-234-9262. Keith Ciedlicki, Coord.

BINGHAMTON. *Associated Catholic Charities for Community Development in Broome County*, 232 Main St., Binghamton, 13905. Tel: 607-729-9166; Fax: 607-729-2062; Web: www.catholiccharitiesbc.org. Lori Accardi, Exec.

Catholic Charities of Broome County, 232 Main St., Binghamton, 13905. Tel: 607-729-9166; Fax: 607-729-2062; Email: laccardi@ccbc.net; Web: www.catholiccharitiesbc.org. Sandra Ohlsen, Dir.; Grazia Tonelli, L.C.S.W.-R., Supvr. of Clinical Svcs.; Shelly Kaminsky, L.C.S.W.-R., Supvr. Pregnancy, Parenting & Adopting Program.

CORTLAND. *Catholic Charities of Cortland County*, 33-35 Central Ave., Cortland, 13045. Tel: 607-756-5992; Fax: 607-756-5999; Email: info@ccocc.org; Web: www.ccocc.org. Marie Walsh, Exec. Tot Asst. Annually 2,500; Total Staff 65.

Case Management Services, Tel: 607-756-5992; Fax: 607-756-5999; Email: info@ccocc.org.

Residential Services, Tel: 607-756-5992; Fax: 607-756-5999. Mike Pisa, Dir. Residential Svcs. Residential services for adult mental health and substance abuse recovery.

Emergency Assistance, Tel: 607-756-5992; Fax: 607-756-5999; Email: info@ccocc.org; Web: www.ccocc.org. Ann Marie Phelps, Assoc. Dir. Emergency & Basic Needs Assistance (Food Pantry, Medication, Advocacy Referral & Support).; Summer Lunch Program for Children.

Catholic Charities-STEPS, 33-35 Central Ave., Cortland, 13045. Tel: 607-756-5992; Fax: 607-756-5999; Email: info@ccocc.org. (Supportive Teen Education-Parents Services); Case Management; Adolescent Group Activities.

NORWICH. *Chenango House*, 49 Fair St., Norwich, 13815. Tel: 607-336-8939; Fax: 607-336-4359. Supervised by Community Residence Program.

Apartment Treatment Program 49 Fair St., Norwich, 13815. Tel: 607-336-8939; Fax: 607-336-4359.

Supported Housing Program 34-36 Berry St., Norwich, 13815. Tel: 607-336-4492.

Community Residence Program, 3 O'Hara Dr., Norwich, 13815. Tel: 607-334-8244. Provides housing for mentally ill and intellectually disabled adults.

Catholic Charities of Chenango County, 3 O'Hara Dr., Norwich, 13815. Tel: 607-334-8244; Fax: 607-336-5779; Email: jchesbro@ccofcc.com; Email: mcasella@ccofcc.com. Mr. Jeff Chesebro, Dir.; Mrs. Robin (Beckwith) Cotter, Exec. Tot Asst. Annually 4,000; Total Staff 100.

The Counseling Program, 3 O'Hara Dr., Norwich, 13815. Tel: 607-334-8244; Email: dsitts@ccofcc.com; Web: www.ccofcc.com. Mr. Jeff Chesebro, Dir.; Mrs. Robin Cotter, Exec. Provides comprehensive counseling for children and adults, also specialized counseling for abused children and individuals with developmental disabilities.

Catholic Charities of Chenango County, 3 O'Hara Dr., Norwich, 13815. Tel: 607-334-8244; Fax: 607-336-5779; Web: www.ccofcc.com. Mrs. Robin (Beckwith) Cotter, Dir.

ONEIDA. *Catholic Charities of Oneida - Madison Counties*, 248 Main St., Oneida, 13421. Tel: 315-363-5274; Web: www.catholiccharitiesom.org. Denise L. Cavanaugh, Dir.

Madison County Catholic Charities, 248 Main St., Box 10, Oneida, 13421. Tel: 315-363-5274; Fax: 315-363-4925. Denise L. Cavanaugh, Dir.

ONONDAGA. *Catholic Charities of Onondaga County*, 1654 W. Onondaga St., 13204. Tel: 315-424-1800; Fax: 315-424-8262; Email: cwillson@ccoc.us. Mr. Michael F. Melara, Exec. Tot Asst. Annually 20,000; Total Staff 350.

Crisis, Stabilization & Capacity Building Services, 1654 W. Onondaga St., 13204. Tel: 315-424-1800; Fax: 315-424-8262; Email: cwillson@ccoc.us; Web: www.ccoc.us. Mr. Michael F. Melara, Exec. Crisis Services: emergency services including financial, pantries & relocation services; shelter services for men, women and women with children; Stabilization Services: refugee resettlement; stability services including supportive housing, health care management & elderly services; Capacity Building Services: child development services including UPK, after-school & Medicaid case management; parent education services including counseling; social venture including culinary arts & property maintenance Tot Asst. Annually 20,000; Total Staff 350.

UTICA. *Catholic Charities Family & Community Support Services*, 1408 Genesee St., Utica, 13502. Tel: 315-724-2158; Fax: 315-724-5318; Email: bpotter@cchari tyom.org. Brad Potter, Dir.; Denise L. Cavanaugh, Dir.

Catholic Charities of Oneida - Madison Counties, 1408 Genesee St., Utica, 13502. Tel: 315-724-2158; Fax: 315-724-5318; Email: vpaolozzi@ccharityom.org; Web: www.catholiccharitiesom.org. Denise L. Cavanaugh, Dir.; Jan Stasaitis, Dir.; Anthony J. Conestabile, Dir.; Jack Callaghan, Dir.; Brad Potter, Dir. Tot Asst. Annually 12,500; Total Staff 130.

[G] OFFICES OF HUMAN DEVELOPMENT

BINGHAMTON. *Catholic Charities Office of Social Concerns - Broome County*, 232 Main St., Binghamton, 13905. Tel: 607-729-9166; Fax: 607-729-2062; Web: www.catholiccharitiesbc.org. Lori Accardi, Contact Person. Staff 450.

[H] CATHOLIC CHARITIES OF OSWEGO COUNTY

FULTON. *Catholic Charities Thrift Shop*, 365 W. First St., Fulton, 13069. Tel: 315-598-3980; Fax: 315-593-8440; Email: hhoefer@ccoswego.com.

[I] CATHOLIC YOUTH ORGANIZATIONS

SYRACUSE. *Bishop Foery Foundation*, 100 Edmund Ave., 13205. Tel: 315-424-1800; Fax: 315-424-8262; Email: cormsby@ccoc.us. Christopher Curry, Chief Prog. Officer.

Catholic Charities of Onondaga County, 1654 W. Onondaga St., 13204. Tel: 315-424-1800; Fax: 315-424-8262; Email: cwillson@ccoc.us. Mr. Michael F. Melara, Exec.; Scott Kelso, Business Mgr.; Tia Sales, Dir. Tot Asst. Annually 20,000; Total Staff 350.

Hawley Youth Organization, 716 Hawley Ave., 13203. Tel: 315-424-1800; Fax: 315-424-8262.

Northside CYO, 527 N. Salina St., 13208. Tel: 315-424-1800; Fax: 315-424-8262.

Toomey Residential and Community Services Corp., 1654 W. Onondaga St., 13204. Tel: 315-424-1845; Fax: 315-424-7567; Email: jdamore@ccoc.us. Judith D'Amore, Exec. Dir.

Vincent House, 514 Seymour St., 13204. Tel: 315-424-1800; Fax: 315-424-8262.

BINGHAMTON. *Broome County CYO*, 86-88 Walnut St., Binghamton, 13905. Tel: 607-584-7800; Fax: 607-584-7801; Email: cyo@ccbc.net. Sandra Ohlsen, Dir.

FULTON. *Catholic Charities of Oswego Co.*, 808 W. Broadway, Fulton, 13069. Tel: 315-598-3980; Email: mmpekow@ccoswego.com; Web: www.ccoswego.com. Staff 84.

[J] CHILDREN'S INSTITUTIONS AND DAY CARE CENTERS

SYRACUSE. *Gingerbread House Preschool & Childcare Center*, 3020 Court St., 13208. Tel: 315-471-4198; Fax: 315-471-4198; Email: dave@gingerbreadsyracuse.com. David Cole, Dir.

[K] DIOCESAN SUMMER CAMPS

SYRACUSE. *Lourdes Camp*, Office: 1654 W. Onondaga St., 13204. Tel: 315-424-1812; Tel: 315-673-2888 (Summer); Email: info@lourdescamp.com; Web: www.lourdescamp.com. Summer: 1150 Ten Mile Point Rd., Skaneateles, 13152. Michael Preston, Dir. Students 1,700.

UTICA. *Camp Nazareth*, 1408 Genesee St., Utica, 13502. Tel: 315-724-2158.

112 Long Lake Rd., Woodgate, 13494. Tel: 315-392-3791; Fax: 315-392-6545. Brad Potter, Dir. Family & Community Support Svcs.

[L] FAMILY LIFE BUREAUS

SYRACUSE. *Office of Family / Respect Life Ministry*, 240 E. Onondaga St., 13202. Tel: 315-472-6754; Fax: 315-295-1415; Email: familyrespectlife@syrdio.org; Web: www.syrdio.org. Lisa Hall, Dir.; Tracey Swienton, Prog. Coord.; Debra Oliva, Project Rachel Prog. Coord.; Bethany Ryan, Social Media Programmer; Dean Brainard, Coord., Separated/Divorced; Sharon Flanagan, Chastity/Theology of the Body Educator; Mary Kortright, Prog. Coord.; Sue & Ronald Kielar, Marriage Preparation, Eastern Region; Kathy Colligan, Marriage Preparation, Southern Region; Stephanie Stewart, Third Option Marriage Prog.; Mary Puthawala, Marriage Preparation, Southern Region; Morgan Durfee, NFP/Fertility Educ. Prog. Coord.; Elizabeth Giordano, NFP/Fertility Educ. Prog. Coord.

EAST SYRACUSE. *Office of Faith Formation - West*, c/o 240 E. Onondaga St., 13202. Tel: 315-472-6753; Email: twhite@syrdio.org. Theresa White, Assoc. Faith Formation.

ENDWELL. *Southern Region Family / Respect Life Ministry*, 400 Corey Ave., Endwell, 13760. Tel: 607-748-4743. Kathleen Colligan, Dir.

[M] GENERAL HOSPITALS

SYRACUSE. *St. Joseph's Hospital Health Center*, 301 Prospect Ave., 13203. Tel: 315-448-5111; Fax: 315-448-6161; Email: marcomm@sjhsyr.org; Web: www.sjhsyr.org. College for Nurses. Bed Capacity 431; Trinity Health 20; Students 300; Tot Asst. Annually 26,000; Total Staff 3,600.

BINGHAMTON. *Our Lady of Lourdes Memorial Hospital, Inc.*, 169 Riverside Dr., Binghamton, 13905. Tel: 607-798-5111; Fax: 607-798-7681; Email: kathryn.connerton@ascension.org; Web: lourdes.com. Kathryn Connerton, Pres. Bed Capacity 242; Tot Asst. Annually 13,335; Total Staff 2,522.

UTICA. *St. Elizabeth Medical Center*, 2209 Genesee St., Utica, 13501. Tel: 315-801-8100; Fax: 315-801-8598; Email: sperra@mvhealthsystem.org; Web: www.mvhealth.org. Scott H. Perra, Pres. College of Nursing. Bed Capacity 202; Sisters of the Third Franciscan Order 12; Students 222; Tot Asst. Annually 434,277; Total Staff 1,862.

[N] FACILITIES FOR THE AGED

SYRACUSE. *Bernardine Apartments, Inc.*, 417 Churchill Ave., 13205. Tel: 315-469-7786. Rick Mills, Admin.

St. Camillus Health & Rehabilitation Center, 813 Fay Rd., 13219. Tel: 315-488-2951; Fax: 315-703-0640; Email: aileen.balitz@st-camillus.org; Web: www.st-camillus.org. Mrs. Aileen M. Balitz, Pres. Bed Capacity 284; Total Staff 650; Total Assisted 3,700.

Loretto Geriatric Community Residences, Inc., 5018 S. Salina St., 13205. Tel: 315-492-0896.

4810 S. Salina St., 13205. Tel: 315-469-8562.

50 Syracuse St., Baldwinsville, 13027. Tel: 315-635-1647.

Loretto Rest Realty Corp., 700 E. Brighton Ave., 13205. Tel: 315-413-3733; Fax: 315-413-3555. Mr. Jack Pease, Admin.

Loretto Health & Rehabilitation Center Bed Capacity 583; Staff 800; Total Assisted 2,000.

Loretto Rest, Inc., 700 E. Brighton Ave., 13205. Tel: 315-413-3206; Fax: 315-498-9073. Mr. John Murray, Corp. Controller; Sr. Cathleen Moore, S.S.V., Chap. Adult Home.

Loretto and Loretto Apartments Housing Development Fund Co., Inc., c/o Loretto, 700 E. Brighton Ave., 13205. Tel: 315-469-5570; Fax: 315-498-9073.

OSWEGO. *Saint Luke's Health Care Services*, 299 E. River Rd., Oswego, 13126. Tel: 315-342-3166; Fax: 315-343-6531; Email: tgorman@stlukehs.com; Web: www.stlukehs.com. Mr. Terrence Gorman, Admin. Bed Capacity 200; Tot Asst. Annually 69,000; Total Staff 350.

UTICA. *St. Joseph Nursing Home*, 2535 Genesee St., Utica, 13501. Tel: 315-797-1230; Fax: 315-797-5171; Email: fdeck@stjosephnh.org; Web: www.stjosephnh.org. Frederick Deck, Admin. Bed Capacity 120; Tot Asst. Annually 200; Total Staff 185.

[O] SPECIALTY HOUSING

SYRACUSE. *Bartell Road Housing Development Co., Inc.*, 990 James St., 13203. Tel: 315-424-1821; Fax: 315-424-6048. (Brewerton); Housing for well elderly.

Christopher Community, Inc., 990 James St., 13203. Tel: 315-424-1821; Fax: 315-424-6048; Email: kbesaw@christopher-community.org. Mr. Douglas Reicher, Exec. Professional management and consultants of housing programs for the elderly, families and special populations. Total Staff 35.

Churchill Manor, Inc., 750 E. Brighton Ave., 13205. Tel: 315-492-1329; Fax: 315-492-6076; Email: cahika@lorettosystem.org. Mary Koenig, Admin. A nonprofit corporation founded to provide housing for low and moderate income families and individuals. Bed Capacity 80.

Harbor View Housing Development Fund Co., Inc., 12541 Harbor View Dr., Henderson, 13650. Tel: 315-424-1821; Fax: 315-424-6048; Email: kbesaw@christopher-community.org. 990 James St., 13203. Mr. Douglas Reicher, Pres.

Hawley Winton Housing Development Fund, Inc., Walter Ludovico Apts., 340 Winton St., 13203. Tel: 315-422-0475; Fax: 315-471-1554; Email: kbesaw@christopher-community.org. 990 James St., 13203. Mr. Douglas Reicher, Pres. 32 one-bedroom units occupied. Christopher Community Inc., (Managing Agent).

Ludden Housing Development Fund Company, Inc., 817 Fay Rd., 13219. Tel: 315-424-1821; Fax: 315-424-6048; Email: kbesaw@christopher-community.org. 990 James St., 13203. Mr. Douglas Reicher, Pres. Fifty one-bedroom apartments for the elderly and handicapped. Christopher Community Inc., (Managing Agent).

Marcellus Apartments Housing Development Fund Company, Inc., 990 James St., 13203. Tel: 315-424-1821; Fax: 315-424-6048; Email: kbesaw@christopher-community.org. Mr. Douglas Reicher, Pres. Christopher Community, Inc., (Managing Agent).

Mount St. James Corporation, 338 Jamesville Ave., 13210. Tel: 315-424-1821; Fax: 315-424-6048; Email: kbesaw@christopher-community.org. 990 James St., 13203. Mr. Douglas Reicher, Pres. Engaged in the operation of a nonprofit housing facility known as Mount St. James Apartments, at 338 Jamesville Ave., for persons of low to moderate income. Christopher Community, Inc., (Managing Agents).

St. Peter's Italian Church Housing Development Fund Co., Inc. Villa Scalabrini Apts., 825 E. Willow St., 13203. Tel: 315-424-1821; Email: kbesaw@christopher-community.org. 990 James St., 13203. Mr. Douglas Reicher, Pres. Operation of a nonprofit housing facility for aged, well persons of low income at the 800 block of E. Willow St. in Syracuse. 120 units, one-bedroom apartments. Christopher Community, Inc., (Managing Agent).

Pompei Housing Development Fund Company, Inc., 143 Mary St., 13208. Tel: 315-424-1821, Ext. 636; Email: kbesaw@christopher-community.org. 990 James St., 13203. Mr. Douglas Reicher, Pres. 50 one-bedroom apartments for the elderly and handicapped. Christopher Community, Inc., (Managing Agent).

c/o Christopher Community, Inc., 143 Mary St., 13208. Tel: 315-424-1821; Fax: 315-424-6048; Email: pompeinorth@christopher-community.org. 990 James St., 13203. Mr. Douglas Reicher, Pres. Tot Asst. Annually 20; Total Staff 2.

Pond St. Housing Development Fund Co., Inc., Bishop Harrison Apartments, 300 Pond St., 13208. Tel: 315-476-8630; Fax: 315-474-0806; Email: kbesaw@christopher-community.org. 990 James St., 13203. Mr. Douglas Reicher, Pres. Operation of 47 units, one bedroom apartments for the elderly and handicapped. Christopher Community Inc., (Managing Agent). Emergency Maintenance Services 24; Staff 2.

Providence House Apartments, 1700 W. Onondaga St., 13204. Tel: 315-471-8427; Fax: 315-474-1224; Email: mquirk@christopher-community.org. 990 James St., 13203. Mr. Douglas Reicher, Pres. Senior citizen housing, 100 units. Christopher Community Inc., (Managing Agent).

Legal Name: Onondaga Apartments HDFC, Inc. Staff 3.

Stoneleigh Housing Development Fund Co., Inc., Stoneleigh Apartments, 400 Lamb Ave., Canastota, 13032. Fax: 315-697-9097; Fax: 315-697-2847; Email: kbesaw@christopher-community.org. 990 James St., 13203. Mr. Douglas Reicher, Pres. Engaged in the construction and operation of a nonprofit housing facility for elderly and handicapped persons of low income. 100 units, one bedroom apartments. Christopher Community, Inc., (Managing Agent). Staff 2.

Tyson Place Housing Development Fund Company, Inc., 900 Tyson Pl., 13206. Tel: 315-424-1821; Fax: 315-424-6048; Email: kbesaw@christopher-community.org. 990 James St., 13203. Mr. Douglas Reicher, Pres. Christopher Community, Inc., (Managing Agent).; (40 apartments for the elderly).

AUBURN. *Mercy Housing Development Fund Co., Inc.*, 1 Thornton Ave., Auburn, 13021. Tel: 315-424-1821; Fax: 315-424-6048; Email: kbesaw@christopher-community.org. 990 James St., 13203. Mr. Douglas Reicher, Pres. 40 one-bedroom units for the elderly and handicapped. Christopher Community, Inc., (Managing Agent).

BALDWINSVILLE. *Smokey Hollow Housing Development Fund Company, Inc.*, 100 LaMadre Way, Baldwinsville, 13027. Tel: 315-424-1821; Fax: 315-424-6048; Email: kbesaw@christopher-community.org. 990 James St., 13203. Mr. Douglas Reicher, Pres. Christopher Community, Inc., (Managing Agent).

BREWERTON. *Bartell Road Housing Development Fund Co., Inc.* dba Long Manor Apts., 5500 Miller Rd., Brewerton, 13029. Tel: 315-668-9871 (Tues./Thurs. 8am-4pm; Fri. 12pm-4pm); Fax: 315-668-0048; Email: longmanor@christophercommunity.org; Email: kbesaw@christopher-community.org. 990 James St., 13203. Mr. Douglas Reicher, Contact Person. 20 units, one bedroom apartments. Christopher Community, Inc., (Managing Agent).

CICERO. *Cicero Housing Development Fund Company Inc.*, 8365 Factory St., Cicero, 13039. Tel: 315-424-1821; Fax: 315-424-6048; Email: kbesaw@christopher-community.org. 990 James St., 13203. Mr. Douglas Reicher, Pres.

Sacred Heart Apartments, 990 James St., 13203. Tel: 315-424-1821, Ext. 658. Mr. Douglas Reicher, Pres. Christopher Community, Inc., (Managing Agent).

FAYETTEVILLE. *Redfield South Housing Development Fund Co., Inc.*, Redfield Village Apartments, 380 Salt Springs Rd., Fayetteville, 13066. Tel: 315-637-8280; Fax: 315-637-2376; Email: lgrosso@christopher-community.org; Email: kbesaw@christopher-community.org. 990 James St., 13203. Mr. Douglas Reicher, Pres. 50 one-bedroom units. Christopher Community, Inc., (Managing Agent). Total Staff 2; Units 1; Total Assisted 50.

NORTH SYRACUSE. *Pitcher Hill-Christopher Housing Development Fund Co., Inc.*, 114 Elbow Rd., 13212. Tel: 315-424-1821; Fax: 315-424-6048; Email: pitcherhill@christophercommunity.org; Email: kbesaw@christopher-community.org. 990 James St., 13203. Mr. Douglas Reicher, Pres. Engaged in the construction and operation of nonprofit housing facilities for elderly and handicapped persons of low income. 100 units, one bedroom apartments.

Christopher Community, Inc., (Managing Agent). Total Staff 4; Total Assisted 98.

OSWEGO. *St. Luke's Housing Development Fund Co., Inc.*, St. Luke's Apartments, W. First St., Oswego, 13126. Tel: 315-343-0821; Fax: 315-343-0619; Email: kbesaw@christopher-community.org. 990 James St., 13203. Mr. Douglas Reicher, Pres. Engaged in the construction and operation of a nonprofit housing facility for elderly and handicapped persons of low income. 100 units, one bedroom apartments. Christopher Community, Inc., (Managing Agent).

ROME. *Rome Mall Housing Development Fund Company, Inc.*, 146 W. Dominick St., Rome, 13440. Tel: 315-424-1821; Fax: 315-424-6048; Email: kbesaw@christopher-community.org. 990 James St., 13203. Mr. Douglas Reicher, Pres. 45 one-bedroom units for the elderly. Christopher Community, Inc., (Managing Agent).

Rome Mall Apts., 201 E. Laurel St., Rome, 13440. Tel: 315-492-6308; Fax: 315-492-3407; Email: sacredhc@verizon.net; Web: www.sacredheartapostolate.com. Thomas Mueller, Chm.; Anna Costa, Pres.

TOWN OF GATES. *Steger Housing Development Fund Co., Inc.*, 4100 Lyell Rd., Town of Gates, 14606. Tel: 315-424-1821; Email: kbesaw@christopher-community.org. 990 James St., 13203. Mr. Douglas Reicher, Pres. 56 apartments for well elderly.

1654 W. Onondaga St., 13204. Tel: 315-424-1821; Fax: 315-424-6048.

UTICA. *Catherine St. Housing Development Fund Company, Inc.*, 659 Catherine St., Utica, 13501. Tel: 315-424-1821; Fax: 315-424-6048; Email: kbesaw@christopher-community.org. 990 James St., 13203. Mr. Douglas Reicher, Pres. Christopher Community, Inc., (Managing Agent).

[P] PROGRAMS FOR THE HANDICAPPED

SYRACUSE. *L'Arche of Syracuse, Inc.*, 920 Spencer St., 13204. Tel: 315-479-8088; Fax: 315-479-8118; Email: larche@larchesyracuse.org; Web: www.larchesyracuse.org. Peggy Harper, Community Leader. A Christian Community concerned with life sharing between persons with a developmental disability and persons who assist them; Homes at 310 Galster Ave, 4550 Cleveland Rd., 211 Croyden Rd., 140 Highland Ave., Syracuse. Bed Capacity 16; Tot Asst. Annually 16; Staff 40.

UTICA. *St. John and St. Joseph Home, Inc.*, 1408 Genesee St., Utica, 13502. Tel: 315-724-2158; Fax: 315-724-5318. Anthony J. Conestabile, Contact Person.

[Q] MONASTERIES AND RESIDENCES OF PRIESTS AND BROTHERS

SYRACUSE. *Jesuits at LeMoyne, Inc.*, 1419 Salt Springs Rd., Jesuit Residence, 13214. Tel: 315-445-4604; Fax: 315-445-4722; Email: jesuitres@lemoyne.edu; Web: www.lemoyne.edu/Values/Heritage-and-Commitment/Jesuit-Community/Meet-the-Jesuit-Community. Mr. Matthew Cortese, Prof.; Rev. Msgr. Charles J. Fahey, Pastor, (Retired); Revs. William J. Bosch, S.J., Archivist; David J. Casey, S.J., Treas.; George V. Coyne, S.J., Prof.; James H. Dahlinger, S.J., Prof.; William S. Dolan, S.J., Prof.; Vincent W. Hevern, S.J., Prof.; Donald J. Kirby, S.J., Rector; David C. McCallum, S.J., Prof.; Daniel J. Mulhauser, S.J., Pastor; Paul S. Naumann, S.J., In Res.; Robert E. Scully, S.J., Prof.; Joseph G. Marina, S.J., Vice Pres.; Louis P. Sogliuzzo, S.J., Pastoral Min./Coord.; Gerard R. McKeon, S.J., Chap.; Francis J. Nash, S.J., Chap.; Michael Guzik, Prof. Priests 16; Scholastics 1.

BINGHAMTON. *McDevitt Residence for Retired Priests*, 68 Seminary Ave., Binghamton, 13905. Tel: 607-771-6207. Revs. Thomas F. Hobbes, (Retired); Gerald J. Buckley, (Retired); Stanley J. Gerlock, (Retired).

MAINE. *Mount St. Francis Hermitage, Inc.*, 120 Edson Rd., Endicott, 13760. Tel: 607-754-0001; Fax: 607-754-0001; Email: ffimaine@gmail.com; Email: mountsaintfrancis@gmail.com; Web: www.mtstfrancis.com. P.O. Box 236, Maine, 13802. Rev. John Joseph Mary Cook, F.I., Supr.; Bros. Cyprian Costello, Sec.; Didacus Cortes, F.I., Vicar. Brothers 3; Priests 2; Religious 5.

[R] CONVENTS AND RESIDENCES FOR SISTERS

SYRACUSE. *Dominican Monastery of the Perpetual Rosary*, 802 Court St., 13208-1766. Tel: 315-471-6762; Email: violetbop2@verizon.net; Web: www.dominicanmonastery.net. Sr. Bernadette Marie, O.P., Prioress. Sisters 8.

Sisters of St. Francis of the Neumann Communities (1860) 960 James St., 2nd Fl., 13203. Tel: 315-634-7000; Tel: 315-422-8652; Fax: 315-634-7023; Fax: 315-634-7031; Email: sisters@sosf.org; Web: www.sosf.org. Sisters Barbara Jean Donovan, O.S.F., Gen. Min.; Pam Conte, O.S.F., Gen. Councilor; Patricia Larkin, O.S.F., Gen. Councilor; Louise Alff, O.S.F., Asst. Gen. Min.; Jeanne Weisbeck, O.S.F., Gen. Councilor & Sec.; Donna Zwigart, O.S.F., Gen. Councilor & Treas. Sisters 116; Associates in the Region 69; Total in Community 351.

BINGHAMTON. *Little Sisters of Saint Francis of Assisi Mission*, 4 Aquinas St., Binghamton, 13905. Tel: 607-821-1821; Fax: 607-821-1821; Email: lsosfmission12@gmail.com.

WINDSOR. *Transfiguration Monastery*, 701 NY Rte. 79, Windsor, 13865-2700. Tel: 607-655-2366; Fax: 607-655-4024; Email: transfigurationmonastery@gmail.com. Sr. Sheila Long, O.S.B.Cam., Prioress. Camaldolese Benedictine Nuns Sisters 4.

[S] RETREAT HOUSES

SYRACUSE. *Christ the King Retreat House*, 500 Brookford Rd., 13224. Tel: 315-446-2680; Fax: 315-446-2689; Email: TKretreat@syrdio.org. Rev. John F. Rose, Dir., (Retired); Marianne Carbone, Sec. General retreat house for priests, nuns, laity and youth of upstate New York. Priests 1.

MAINE. *Mount St. Francis Hermitage, Inc.*, 120 Edson Rd., Endicott, 13760. Tel: 607-754-0001; Fax: 607-754-0001; Email: ffimaine@gmail.com; Email: mountsaintfrancis@gmail.com; Web: www.mtstfrancis.com. P.O. Box 236, Maine, 13802. Rev. John Joseph Mary Cook, F.I., Supr.

UTICA. *The Good News Foundation of Central New York*, 10475 Cosby Manor Rd., Utica, 13502. Tel: 315-735-6210; Fax: 315-735-7090; Email: info@thegoodnewscenter.org; Web: www.thegoodnewscenter.org. Ms. Judith Hauck, Exec.; Michelle Holliday, Accounting & Opers. Mgr.

[T] NEWMAN CENTERS

SYRACUSE. *LeMoyne College Campus Ministry*, 1419 Salt Springs Rd., 13214. Tel: 315-445-4110; Fax: 315-445-4797; Email: andinotm@lemoyne.edu. Revs. John P. Bucki, S.J., Rector; William S. Dolan, S.J.

Syracuse University Catholic Center & St. Thomas More Foundation, Inc., Catholic Center at Syracuse University, 110 Walnut Pl., 13210. Tel: 315-443-2600; Fax: 315-443-4465; Email: fwaterma@syr.edu; Email: jedeep@syr.edu; Email: gmstooke@syr.edu; Web: www.sucatholic.org. Friar Gerald Waterman, O,F,M.Conv., Chap.

CAZENOVIA. *Cazenovia College Newman Center*, 10 Seminary St., Cazenovia, 13035. Tel: 315-655-7375 ; Fax: 315-655-7536; Email: stjyouth@stjamescaz.com. 22 Sullivan St., Cazenovia, 13035. Rev. Kevin Corcoran, Chap.

CLINTON. *Hamilton College Newman Center*, 198 College Hill Rd., Clinton, 13323. Tel: 315-859-4129 ; Fax: 315-859-4041; Email: jcroghan@hamilton.edu. Rev. John P. Croghan, Chap.

CORTLAND. *Newman Foundation of Cortland, Inc. at the State University College of New York*, 8 Calvert St., Cortland, 13045. Tel: 607-753-6737; Web: www.cortland.edu/ministry/catholic.html.

MORRISVILLE. *Newman Association at SUNY Morrisville*, Mathasis Health Bldg., Morrisville, 13408. Tel: 315-684-6201; Web: www.morrisville.edu/pages/newman. Chaplain's Office, P.O. Box 901, Morrisville, 13408.

St. Joan of Arc Newman Association at the State University of New York (SUNY) Morrisville Agricultural and Technical College.

OSWEGO. *Newman Foundation of Oswego, Inc.*, 36 New St., P.O. Box 207, Oswego, 13126. Tel: 315-312-7222; Fax: 315-216-6593; Email: newctr@oswego.edu; Web: www.hallnewmancenter.org. Michael Huynh, Dir.

UTICA. *Newman Center at SUNY Poly Tech Institute*, Newman Community, P.O. Box 8087, Utica, 13505-8087. Tel: 315-792-3284; Fax: 315-792-4401; Email: pdrobin@utica.edu. Rev. Paul J. Drobin, Chap., (Retired)

State University of New York (SUNY) Poly Tech Institute Newman Center.

Utica College Newman Center, SUNY Poly Tech and Utica College, P.O. Box 8087, Utica, 13505-8087. Tel: 315-792-3284; Fax: 315-792-4401; Email: pdrobin@utica.edu. Rev. Paul J. Drobin, Chap., (Retired).

Campus Ministry/Newman Center, Newman Community, P.O. Box 8087, Utica, 13505-8087. Tel: 315-792-3284; Email: pdrobin@utica.edu. Rev. Paul J. Drobin, Dir., (Retired).

VESTAL. *Binghamton University Newman Center*, 400 Murray Hill Rd., Vestal, 13850. Tel: 607-798-7202; Email: rcasaleno@binghamton.edu. Sr. Rose Casaleno, Campus Min.

[U] MISCELLANEOUS LISTINGS

SYRACUSE. **Brady Faith Center, Inc.*, 404 South Ave., 13204. Tel: 315-472-9077; Fax: 315-472-9077; Email: trevoratbfc@gmail.com; Web: www.bradyfaithcenter.org. Rev. John C. Schopfer, Pastoral Dir., (Retired); Kevin Frank, Exec. Dir.

Father Champlin's Guardian Angel Society, 420 Montgomery St., 13202. Tel: 315-422-7218; Fax: 315-422-2471; Email: kfedrizzi@GuardianAngelSoc.org; Web: GuardianAngelSoc.org. 259 E. Onondaga St., 13202. Kathy Fedrizzi, Exec. Dir.

The Foundation of the Roman Catholic Diocese of Syracuse, 240 E. Onondaga St., 13202. Tel: 315-422-7023. Mr. Timothy Mahar, Contact Person.

Grimes Foundation, 240 E. Onondaga St., 13202. Tel: 315-422-7203; Fax: 315-478-4619. Most Rev. Robert J. Cunningham, J.C.L., D.D., Pres.; Very Rev. Msgr. Timothy S. Elmer, J.C.L., V.G., Treas.; Rev. John J. Kurgan. Corporation created to establish and maintain charitable, religious and educational facilities within the Roman Catholic Diocese of Syracuse, New York.; (Incorporated by special act of the New York State Legislature, May 1, 1916).

Lasalle Syracuse, Inc., 6245 Randall Rd., 13214. Tel: 315-446-5960; Fax: 315-446-3393; Web: www.cbasyracuse.org.

Loretto Apartments Housing Development Fund Co., Inc., 700 E. Brighton Ave., 13205. Tel: 315-413-3206; Fax: 315-498-9073; Email: jmurray@lorettosystem.org.

Onondaga County Catholic School Foundation (Western Region Catholic School Foundation), 240 E. Onondaga St., 13202. Tel: 315-470-1450; Fax: 315-470-1470.

**Our Lady of Lourdes Hospitality - North American Volunteers, Ltd.*, P.O. Box 3820, 13220. Tel: 315-476-0026; Fax: 419-730-4540. Public Association of the Christian Faithful founded in 2002 sharing authentic Marian devotion through the Message of Lourdes with "Virtual Pilgrimage" and bringing sick, handicapped and volunteers to Lourdes, France.

Partners in Franciscan Ministries Inc., 960 James St., 13203. Tel: 315-634-7086; Fax: 315-634-7087; Email: scrossett@pinfm.org; Web: www.sosf.org. Susan M. Crossett, Pres. & CEO. Sponsored by the Sisters of St. Francis of the Neumann Communities.

The Saint Thomas Aquinas Fund Inc., 240 E. Onondaga St., 13202.

Spiritual Renewal Center, 1342 Lancaster Ave., 13210. Tel: 315-472-6546; Email: mail@spiritualrenewalcenter.com; Web: www.spiritualrenewalcenter.com. James Krisher, Dir.

The Robert L. McDevitt, K.S.G., K.C.H.S. and Catherine H. McDevitt, L.C.H.S. Foundation, Inc., 240 E. Onondaga St., 13202. Tel: 315-422-7023. Very Rev. Msgr. Timothy S. Elmer, J.C.L., V.G., Vicar General.

The Syracuse Diocesan Investment Fund, Inc., 240 E. Onondaga St., 13202. Tel: 315-422-7023. Very Rev. Msgr. Timothy S. Elmer, J.C.L., V.G.

BINGHAMTON. *Ladies of Charity*, 100 Main St., Binghamton, 13905. Tel: 607-723-0194.

Samaritan House, 11 Fayette St., Binghamton, 13901. Tel: 607-724-3969; Fax: 607-771-0356.

The Robert L. McDevitt, K.S.G., K.C.H.S. and Catherine H. McDevitt, L.C.H.S. Fund of St. Patrick's Catholic Church of Binghamton, N.Y., 9 Leroy St., Binghamton, 13905. Tel: 607-722-1060; Email: stpatrick@sta-sp.org. Rev. Msgr. John P. Putano.

The Robert L. McDevitt, K.S.G., K.C.H.S. and Catherine H. McDevitt, L.C.H.S. Fund of St. Thomas Aquinas Church, 1 Aquinas St., Binghamton, 13905. Tel: 607-797-4015; Email: stthomas@sta-sp.org. Rev. Msgr. John P. Putano.

CANASTOTA. *Catholic Diocese of Nakuru Mission Office, Inc.*, 406 Spencer St., Canastota, 13032. Tel: 315-697-8795; Fax: 315-697-8959; Email: cdnmission@yahoo.com; Web: Cdnmission.org. Rev. Fredrick Mwangi Kooro, (Africa) Dir.

DEWITT. *Joseph & Elaine Scuderi Foundation*, 5786 Widewaters Pkwy., P.O. Box 3, DeWitt, 13214.

Rev. Msgr. J. Robert Yeazel Catholic Education/Vocation Scholarship, c/o Holy Cross Church, 4112 E. Genesee St., DeWitt, 13214.

ENDICOTT. *Roman Catholic Diocese - Bishop Harrison Education Trust* (1994) 240 E. Onondaga St., 13202.

JOHNSON CITY. *The Robert L. McDevitt, K.S.G., K.C.H.S. and Catherine H. McDevitt, L.C.H.S. Fund of St. James Church of Lestershire, N.Y.*, 147 Main St., Johnson City, 13790. Tel: 607-729-6147. Rev. Charles Opondo-Owora, (Africa).

RICHLAND. *Rural & Migrant Ministry of Oswego Co. Inc.*, 15 Stewart St., P.O. Box 192, Richland, 13144-0192. Tel: 315-298-1154; Email: rmmoc@yahoo.com. Shawn Doyle, Pres., Bd. Directors.

UTICA. *Christ Child Society of Utica*, 140 Hawthorne

Ave., Utica, 13502. Tel: 315-797-0748; Email: ckelly140@roadrunner.com. Cindy Kelly, Pres.

RELIGIOUS INSTITUTES OF MEN REPRESENTED IN THE DIOCESE

For further details refer to the corresponding bracketed number in the Religious Institutes of Men or Women section.

[0330]—*Brothers of the Christian Schools* (New York Prov.)—F.S.C.

[0480]—*Conventual Franciscans*—O.F.M.Conv.

[0533]—*Franciscan Friars of the Immaculate* (Griswold, CT)—F.F.I.

[0690]—*Jesuit Fathers and Brothers* (New York Prov.)—S.J.

RELIGIOUS INSTITUTES OF WOMEN REPRESENTED IN THE DIOCESE

[0230]—*Benedictine Sisters of Pontifical Jurisdiction* (Erie, PA)—O.S.B.

[0235]—*Camaldolese Benedictine Sisters*—O.S.B.Cam.

[0760]—*Daughters of Charity of St. Vincent de Paul*—D.C.

[]—*Daughters of Divine Love Community.*

[0940]—*Daughters of St. Mary of Providence*—D.S.M.P.

[1050]—*Dominican Contemplative Nuns*—O.P.

[1170]—*Felician Sisters*—C.S.S.F.

[1180]—*Franciscan Sisters of Allegany, New York*—O.S.F.

[]—*Little Sisters of St. Francis*—L.S.O.S.F.

[1360]—*Missionary Franciscan Sisters of the Immaculate Conception*—O.S.F.

[1800]—*Sisters of St. Francis of the Neumann Communities*—O.S.F.

[3840]—*Sisters of St. Joseph of Carondelet*—C.S.J.

[1970]—*Sisters of the Holy Family of Nazareth*—C.S.F.N.

[]—*Sisters of the Immaculate Heart of Mary, Mother of Christ* (Africa)—I.H.M.

[2160]—*Sisters, Servants of the Immaculate Heart of Mary*—I.H.M.

DIOCESAN CEMETERIES

SYRACUSE. *St. Mary-St. Agnes*, 2315 South Ave., 13207. Tel: 315-475-4639; Email: catholiccemeteries@syrdio.org; Web: syracusecatholiccemeteries.org. Danielle Rafte, Family Svc. Mgr.; Tina Smith, Family Svc. Counselor

Catholic Cemeteries of the Roman Catholic Diocese of Syracuse, Inc.

BALDWINSVILLE. *Our Lady of Peace Cemetery*, 8668 Oswego Rd., Rte. 57, Baldwinsville, 13027. Tel: 315-303-4901; Email: catholiccemeteries@syrdio.org; Web: syracusecatholiccemeteries.org. Danielle Rafte, Family Svc. Mgr.; Scott Bivens, Supvr.

Catholic Cemeteries of the Roman Catholic Diocese of Syracuse, Inc.

CORTLAND. *St. Mary's Cemetery*, 4101 West Rd., Cortland, 13045. Tel: 607-756-8838; Fax: 607-756-8838; Email: catholiccemeteries@syrdio.org; Web: syracusecatholiccemeteries.org. Randy Ramey, Opers. Mgr.; Danielle Rafte, Family Svc. Mgr.; Wayne Moore, Supvr.; Colin Ramey, Family Svc. Counselor

Catholic Cemeteries of the Roman Catholic Diocese of Syracuse, Inc.

JOHNSON CITY. *Calvary-St. Patrick*, 501 Fairview St., Johnson City, 13790. Tel: 607-797-2906; Email: catholiccemeteries@syrdio.org; Web: syracusecatholiccemeteries.org. Randy Ramey, Opers. Mgr.; Danielle Rafte, Family Svc. Mgr.; Colin Ramey, Family Svc. Counselor

Catholic Cemeteries of the Roman Catholic Diocese of Syracuse, Inc.

OSWEGO. *St. Peter & St. Paul*, 379 E. River Rd., Oswego, 13126. Tel: 315-343-5002; Email: catholiccemeteries@syrdio.org; Web: syracusecatholiccemeteries.org. Danielle Rafte, Family Svc. Mgr.; Dunsmoor Jason, Supvr.

Catholic Cemeteries of the Roman Catholic Diocese of Syracuse, Inc.

UTICA. *Calvary Cemetery*, 2407 Oneida St., Utica, 13501. Tel: 315-735-2727; Email: catholiccemeteries@syrdio.org; Web: syracusecatholiccemeteries.org. Timothy Moynihan, Opers. Mgr.; Danielle Rafte, Family Svc. Mgr.; Mary Kernan, Family Svc. Counselor; Bethany Rogers, Family Svc. Counselor

Catholic Cemeteries of the Roman Catholic Diocese of Syracuse, Inc.

Holy Trinity Cemetery, 1500 Champlin Ave., Utica, 13502. Tel: 315-724-0616; Email: catholiccemeteries@syrdio.org; Web: syracusecatholiccemeteries.org. 2407 Oneida St., Utica, 13502. Timothy Moynihan, Opers. Mgr.; Danielle Rafte, Family Svc. Mgr.; Mary Kernan, Family Svc. Counselor

Catholic Cemeteries of the Roman Catholic Diocese of Syracuse, Inc.

St. Mary's Cemetery, 2515 Church Rd., Clayville, 13322. Tel: 315-735-2727; Email: catholiccemeteries@syrdio.org; Web: syracusecatholiccemeteries.org. 2407 Oneida St., Utica, 13501. Timothy Moynihan, Opers. Mgr.; Danielle Rafte, Family Svc. Mgr.; Mary Kernan, Family Svc. Counselor

Catholic Cemeteries of the Roman Catholic Diocese of Syracuse, Inc.

WHITESBORO. *Mount Olivet Cemetery*, 70 Wood Rd., Whitesboro, 13492. Tel: 315-736-4446; Email: catholiccemeteries@syrdio.org; Web: syracusecatholiccemeteries.org. 2407 Oneida St., Utica, 13501. Timothy Moynihan, Opers. Mgr.; Danielle Rafte, Family Svc. Mgr.; Mary Kernan, Family Svc. Counselor

Catholic Cemeteries of the Roman Catholic Diocese of Syracuse, Inc.

NECROLOGY

† Costello, Thomas J., Retired Auxiliary Bishop of Syracuse, Died Feb. 15, 2019

† Fuchs, Moritz A., (Retired), Died Jun. 19, 2018

† Jones, Robert S., (Retired), Died Jul. 22, 2018

† Keebler, Paul J., (Retired), Died Apr. 26, 2018

† Kennedy, Laurence W., (Retired), Died Mar. 11, 2018

† Major, Charles M., (Retired), Died Sep. 5, 2018

† Roark, John L., (Retired), Died Feb. 24, 2018

† Wallace, Harry C., (Retired), Died Jan. 16, 2018

An asterisk (*) denotes an organization that has established tax-exempt status directly with the IRS and is not covered by the USCCB Group Ruling.

Diocese of Toledo

(Dioecesis Toletana in America)

DOMINUS MEUS ET DEUS MEUS

Most Reverend

DANIEL E. THOMAS

Bishop of Toledo; ordained May 18, 1985; appointed Titular Bishop of Bardstown and Auxiliary Bishop of Philadelphia June 8, 2006; consecrated July 26, 2006; appointed Bishop of Toledo August 26, 2014; installed October 22, 2014. *Chancery: 1933 Spielbusch Ave., Toledo, OH 43604-5360.*

Chancery: 1933 Spielbusch Ave., Toledo, OH 43604-5360. Tel: 419-244-6711; Fax: 419-244-4791.

Web: www.toledodiocese.org

Email: bishopsoffice@toledodiocese.org

ESTABLISHED APRIL 15, 1910.

Square Miles 8,222.

Comprises the following Counties of northwest Ohio: Williams, Fulton, Lucas, Ottawa, Defiance, Henry, Wood, Sandusky, Erie, Paulding, Putnam, Hancock, Seneca, Huron, Van Wert, Allen, Wyandot, Crawford and Richland.

For legal titles of parishes and diocesan institutions, consult the Chancery.

STATISTICAL OVERVIEW

Personnel	
Bishop	1
Priests: Diocesan Active in Diocese	86
Priests: Diocesan Active Outside Diocese	5
Priests: Retired, Sick or Absent	60
Number of Diocesan Priests	151
Religious Priests in Diocese	43
Total Priests in Diocese	194
Extern Priests in Diocese	4
Ordinations:	
Diocesan Priests	3
Permanent Deacons in Diocese	182
Total Brothers	10
Total Sisters	413
Parishes	
Parishes	122
With Resident Pastor:	
Resident Diocesan Priests	71
Resident Religious Priests	11
Without Resident Pastor:	
Administered by Priests	35
Administered by Deacons	1
Administered by Religious Women	4
Closed Parishes	1
Professional Ministry Personnel:	
Sisters	10
Lay Ministers	100
Welfare	
Catholic Hospitals	7
Total Assisted	960,595
Homes for the Aged	12
Total Assisted	1,110
Day Care Centers	1
Total Assisted	1,455
Special Centers for Social Services	5
Total Assisted	131,565
Residential Care of Disabled	2
Total Assisted	170
Other Institutions	1
Total Assisted	3,165
Educational	
Diocesan Students in Other Seminaries	18
Total Seminarians	18
Colleges and Universities	2
Total Students	2,770
High Schools, Diocesan and Parish	9
Total Students	1,988
High Schools, Private	4
Total Students	2,083
Elementary Schools, Diocesan and Parish	55
Total Students	9,893
Elementary Schools, Private	5
Total Students	640
Catechesis/Religious Education:	
High School Students	2,402
Elementary Students	11,738
Total Students under Catholic Instruction	31,532
Teachers in the Diocese:	
Priests	9
Scholastics	0
Brothers	3
Sisters	15
Lay Teachers	1,181
Vital Statistics	
Receptions into the Church:	
Infant Baptism Totals	1,849
Minor Baptism Totals	486
Adult Baptism Totals	339
Received into Full Communion	495
Confirmations	2,834
Marriages:	
Catholic	545
Interfaith	911
Total Marriages	1,456
Deaths	2,924
Total Catholic Population	246,584
Total Population	1,443,094

Former Bishops—Most Rev. JOSEPH SCHREMBS, D.D., appt. Auxiliary Bishop of Grand Rapids, MI Jan. 8, 1911; cons. Feb. 22, 1911; transferred to Toledo, Aug. 11, 1911; transferred to Cleveland, OH, May 11, 1921; died Nov. 2, 1945; His Eminence SAMUEL CARDINAL STRITCH, D.D., cons. Bishop of Toledo, Nov. 30, 1921; appt. Archbishop of Milwaukee, Aug. 30, 1930; appt. Archbishop of Chicago, Dec. 27, 1939; created Cardinal, Feb. 18, 1946; named Pro-Prefect of the Sacred Congregation of the Propagation of the Faith, March 1, 1958; died in Rome, May 27, 1958; Most Revs. KARL J. ALTER, D.D., LL.D., appt. Bishop of Toledo, April 17, 1931; cons. June 17, 1931; appt. Archbishop of Cincinnati, June 21, 1950; retired July 23, 1969; died Aug. 23, 1977; GEORGE REHRING, D.D., cons. Oct. 7, 1937; appt. Auxiliary Bishop of Cincinnati, Oct. 7, 1937; appt. Bishop of Toledo, July 18, 1950; retired Feb. 25, 1967; died Feb. 29, 1976; JOHN A. DONOVAN, D.D., ord. Dec. 8, 1935; Titular Bishop of Rhasus and Auxiliary of Detroit, Michigan Sept. 6, 1954; ord. Bishop of Detroit, Michigan Oct. 26, 1954; appt. to Toledo, Feb. 25, 1967; retired July 29, 1980; died Sept. 18, 1991; JAMES R. HOFFMAN, D.D., J.C.L., ord. July 28, 1957; appt. Titular Bishop of Italica and Auxiliary Bishop of Toledo April 18, 1978; ord. June 23, 1978; appt. Bishop of Toledo Feb. 17, 1981; died Feb. 8, 2003; LEONARD P. BLAIR, ord. June 26, 1976; appt. Titular Bishop of Voncariana and Auxiliary Bishop of Detroit July 9, 1999; cons. Aug. 24, 1999; appt. Bishop of Toledo Oct. 7, 2003; installed Dec. 4, 2003; appt. Archbishop of Hartford Oct. 29, 2013.

Office of the Bishop

Vicar General/Moderator of the Curia—Rev. Msgr. WILLIAM J. KUBACKI, V.G., Pastoral Center, 1933 Spielbusch Ave., Toledo, 43604. Tel: 419-244-6711; Fax: 419-244-4791; Email: wkubacki@toledodiocese.org.

Tribunal—Rev. Msgr. CHRISTOPHER P. VASKO, J.V., V.F., J.C.D., Pastoral Center, 1933 Spielbusch Ave., Toledo, 43604. Tel: 419-244-6711; Fax: 419-244-4791; Email: cvasko@toledodiocese.org.

Chancellor—1933 Spielbusch Ave., Toledo, 43604. Tel: 419-244-6711; Fax: 419-244-4791. Sr. MARY NIKA SCHAUMBER, R.S.M., (Interim), Email: mnschaumber@toledodiocese.org.

Catholic Education Department

Senior Director—Pastoral Center: 1933 Spielbusch Ave., Toledo, 43604. Tel: 419-244-6711; Fax: 419-255-8269. MR. MATTHEW DANIELS, Email: mdaniels@toledodiocese.org.

Catholic Schools Office—MS. KATHRYN SLIWINSKI, Assoc. Dir. Finance & Planning, Email: ksliwinski@toledodiocese.org; MR. TIMOTHY MAHONEY, Curriculum Consultant, Email: tmahoney@toledodiocese.org; MR. JUSTIN COMBS, Technology Coord., Email: jcombs@toledodiocese.org; MRS. VICKI FITTS, Licensure/Certification, Email: vfitts@toledodiocese.org; MRS. PEGGY RIEHL, Coord. for Instruction, Email: priehl@toledodiocese.org; MR. ANTHONY J. MASS, Govt. Programs Dir./High School Consultant, Email: amass@toledodiocese.org; MRS. KATHY CONROY, Inclusion Consultant, Email: kconroy@toledodiocese.org; MS. JENNIFER MICHAELS, Federal Title Funds Consultant & Grant Writer, Email: jmichaels@toledodiocese.org.

Central City Ministry of Toledo (CCMT)—1933 Spielbusch Ave., Toledo, 43604. Tel: 419-244-6711; Fax: 419-255-8269. MR. MATTHEW DANIELS, Sr. Dir. Catholic Educ., Email: mdaniels@toledodiocese.org.

Catechetical Formation—MR. DAVID MCCUTCHEN, Dir., Pastoral Center, 1933 Spielbusch Ave., Toledo, 43604. Tel: 419-244-6711; Fax: 419-255-8269; Email: dmccutchen@toledodiocese.org.

Homeschool—Pastoral Center: 1933 Spielbusch Ave., Toledo, 43604. Tel: 419-244-6711; Fax: 419-255-8269. MR. MATTHEW DANIELS, Sr. Dir. Catholic Educ., Email: mdaniels@toledodiocese.org.

Catholic Social Services Department

Senior Director—MR. RODNEY O. SCHUSTER, Pastoral Center, 1933 Spielbusch Ave., Toledo, 43604. Tel: 419-244-6711; Fax: 419-244-4860; Email: rschuster@toledodiocese.org.

Catholic Charities—MR. RODNEY O. SCHUSTER, Exec. Dir., Toledo Office: Pastoral Center, 1933 Spielbusch Ave., Toledo, 43604-5360. Tel: 419-244-6711; Fax: 419-244-4860; Email: rschuster@toledodiocese.org. Mansfield Office: 2 Smith Ave., Mansfield, 44905. Tel: 419-524-0733; Fax: 567-247-5459; Email: rowens@toledodiocese.org. Norwalk Office: 48 Executive Dr., Unit B, Norwalk, 44857. Tel: 419-668-3073; Fax: 419-663-5070; Email: cwheeler@toledodiocese.org. Sandusky Office: 428 Tiffin Ave., Sandusky,

44870. Tel: 419-502-0043; MR. RICH HOOVER, Oper. Dir., Email: rhoover@toledodiocese.org.

Family Support and Guidance—MR. BRIAN ROME, Coord., Tel: 419-214-4939; Email: brome@toledodiocese.org.

Crisis Navigation—Lucas County - Toledo Office: MS. LINDA KRAFT, Tel: 419-214-4905; Email: lkraft@toledodiocese.org. Richland County - Mansfield Office: MS. DIANE BEMILLER, Tel: 419-524-0733; Email: dbemiller@toledodiocese.org. Erie County - Sandusky Office: VACANT.

Adult Advocacy Services—(Erie, Richland & Huron Counties) MS. CAROL WHEELER, Tel: 419-668-3073; Email: cwheeler@toledodiocese.org.

Helping Hands of St. Louis—443 Sixth St., Toledo, 43605. Tel: 419-691-0613; Email: sshrewsbery@toledodiocese.org. MS. SUE SHREWSBERY, Dir.

H.O.P.E. Food Pantry—523 Park Ave. E., Mansfield, 44905. Tel: 419-524-0733. MS. SUSAN DYSON, Email: sdyson@toledodiocese.org.

La Posada Family Emergency Shelter—MS. JEANELLE ADDIE, Coord., 435 Eastern Ave., Toledo, 43609. Tel: 419-244-5931; Fax: 419-244-4993; Email: jaddie@toledodiocese.org.

Permanent Supportive Housing—MS. JEN VOIGT, Coord., Tel: 419-214-4955; Email: jvoigt@toledodiocese.org.

Miriam House Huron County Transitional Housing—249 W. Main St., Norwalk, 44857. Tel: 419-663-6341. MRS. VICKIE A. SMITH, Coord., Email: vsmith@toledodiocese.org.

Office for Life and Justice—

Respect Life Ministry—MR. PETER RANGE, Coord., Tel: 419-214-4933; Email: prange@toledodiocese.org.

Project Rachel—MS. CLARISSA LAPINSKI, Coord., Tel: 419-583-6817; Email: clapinski@toledodiocese.org.

Jail and Prison Ministry—Deacon ED IRELAN, Coord., Tel: 419-214-4958; Email: eirelan@toledodiocese.org.

Disaster Relief—MS. REBECCA OWENS, Tel: 419-524-0733; Email: rowens@toledodiocese.org.

Rural Life Ministry—MR. RODNEY O. SCHUSTER, Tel: 419-214-4943; Email: rschuster@toledodiocese.org.

Human Trafficking—MR. PETER RANGE, Tel: 419-214-4933; Email: prange@toledodiocese.org.

Care for God's Creation—MR. RODNEY O. SCHUSTER, Tel: 419-214-4943; Email: rschuster@toledodiocese.org.

Immigration—MR. RODNEY O. SCHUSTER, Tel: 419-214-4943; Email: rschuster@toledodiocese.org.

Catholic Campaign for Human Development—MR. PETER RANGE, Tel: 419-214-4933; Email: prange@toledodiocese.org.

Catholic Club Educational Child Care and Family Center—MR. PAUL SZYMANSKI, Dir., 1601 Jefferson Ave., Toledo, 43604. Tel: 419-243-7255; Fax: 419-243-6337; Email: paul@catholicclub.org.

Clergy, Consecrated Life, and Vocations Department

Senior Director/Vicar for Clergy—Rev. Msgr. MARVIN G. BORGER, J.C.L., Pastoral Center, 1933 Spielbusch Ave., Toledo, 43604. Tel: 419-244-6711; Fax: 419-244-4791; Email: mborger@toledodiocese.org.

Office for Diocesan Priestly Vocations—Pastoral Center: 1933 Spielbusch Ave., Toledo, 43604. Tel: 419-244-6711; Fax: 419-244-4791; Email: psmith@toledodiocese.org. Rev. PHILIP A. SMITH, S.T.L., Dir.

Delegate for Permanent Deacons—1933 Spielbusch Ave., Toledo, 43604. Tel: 419-244-6711; Fax: 419-244-4791. Deacon HAROLD WELCH, Email: hwelch@toledodiocese.org.

Delegate for Consecrated Life—Pastoral Center: 1933 Spielbusch Ave., Toledo, 43604. Tel: 419-244-6711; Fax: 419-244-4791. Sr. MARIA LIN PACOLD, R.S.M., Email: mpacold@toledodiocese.org.

Mission Appeals and Awareness—Pastoral Center: 1933 Spielbusch Ave., Toledo, 43604. Tel: 419-244-6711; Fax: 419-244-4791. Sr. MARIA LIN PACOLD, R.S.M., Dir., Email: mpacold@toledodiocese.org.

Ecumenical and Interfaith Relations—Rev. KENT R. KAUFMAN, Dir., St. Charles Borromeo Parish, 2200 W. Elm St., Lima, 45805. Tel: 419-228-7635; Email: kkaufman@st-charles.org.

Communication Department

Senior Director—Pastoral Center: 1933 Spielbusch Ave., Toledo, 43604. Tel: 419-244-6711; Fax: 419-244-0468. MS. KELLY DONAGHY, Email: kdonaghy@toledodiocese.org.

Creative Services—1933 Spielbusch Ave., Toledo, 43604. Tel: 419-244-6711; Fax: 419-244-0468. MR. KEITH TARJANYI, Mgr., Email: ktarjanyi@toledodiocese.org.

Marketing—1933 Spielbusch Ave., Toledo, 43604. Tel: 419-244-6711; Fax: 419-244-0468. MS. NANCY COOKE, Communications & Mktg. Specialist, Email: ncooke@toledodiocese.org.

Social Media—1933 Spielbusch Ave., Toledo, 43604. Tel: 419-244-6711; Fax: 419-244-0468. MRS. ANNIE LUST, Communications & Social Media Specialist, Email: alust@toledodiocese.org.

Diocesan Pastoral Services Department

Archives—Sr. MARY NADINE MATHIAS, S.N.D., Pastoral Center, 1933 Spielbusch Ave., Toledo, 43604. Tel: 419-244-6711; Fax: 419-244-4791; Email: nmathias1@toledodiocese.org.

Office of Conciliation and Arbitration—Pastoral Center: 1933 Spielbusch Ave., Toledo, 43604. Tel: 419-244-6711; Fax: 419-244-4791. MR. THOMAS ANTONINI, Email: tantonini@toledodiocese.org.

Office of Divine Worship—Pastoral Center: 1933 Spielbusch Ave., Toledo, 43604. Tel: 419-244-6711; Fax: 419-244-4791. Rev. DAVID J. CIRATA, V.F., Dir., Email: dcirata@toledodiocese; MR. DANIEL J. DEMSKI, Liturgy Coord., Email: ddemski@toledodiocese.org; MR. PAUL J. MONACHINO, Dir. Liturgical Music, Email: pmonachino@toledodiocese.org.

Child and Youth Protection and Victim Assistance—MR. FRANK DILALLO, Victim Assistance Coord., Pastoral Center, 1933 Spielbusch Ave., Toledo, 43604. Tel: 419-244-6711; Fax: 419-244-4791; Email: fdilallo@toledodiocese.org. Diocesan Safe Environment Compliance Officer: *Pastoral Center: 1933 Spielbusch Ave., Toledo, 43604.* Tel: 419-244-6711; Fax: 419-244-4791. MRS. JACQUELINE MAUME, Email: jmaume@toledodiocese.org.

Management Corporation

Chief Operations/Financial Officer—Pastoral Center: 1933 Spielbusch Ave., Toledo, 43604. Tel: 419-244-6711; Fax: 419-244-4791. MR. PHILIP RENDA, Email: prenda@toledodiocese.org.

Audits—Pastoral Center: 1933 Spielbusch Ave., Toledo, 43604. Tel: 419-244-6711; Fax: 419-244-4791. MR. DAVID REED, CPA, Dir., Email: dreed@toledodiocese.org; MR. DAVID WILLIAMS, CPA, Mgr., Email: dwilliams@toledodiocese.org; MS. KATHERINE KELLMURRAY, Parish Accounting Assoc., Email: kkellmurray@toledodiocese.org.

Finance—MRS. RENE YUHAS SCHMIDBAUER, Dir., Pastoral Center, 1933 Spielbusch Ave., Toledo, 43604. Tel: 419-244-6711; Fax: 419-244-4791; Email: rschmidbauer@toledodiocese.org.

Office of Risk Management—Pastoral Center: 1933 Spielbusch Ave., Toledo, 43604. Tel: 419-244-6711; Fax: 419-244-4791. MR. THOMAS ANTONINI, Email: tantonini@toledodiocese.org.

Human Resources—Pastoral Center: 1933 Spielbusch Ave., Toledo, 43604. Tel: 419-244-6711; Fax: 419-244-4791. MRS. ROSEMARY MUNOZ, Dir., Email: rmunoz@toledodiocese.org; MRS. MEGHAN REED, Benefits Admin., Email: mreed@toledodiocese.org; MRS. ERIN GOMEZ, Human Resources Generalist, Email: egomez@toledodiocese.org.

Retirement Plan for Lay Employees (RPLE)—MR. MATTHEW HOPEWELL, Plan Admin., Nyhart Company, 8415 Allison Pointe Hwy, Ste. 300, Indianapolis, IN 46250. Tel: 800-205-4864; Email: toledodiocese@nyhart.com.

Tax Deferred Savings Program for Employees (403 (b))—MS. PAMELA HAUGABROOK, Recordkeeper, Nyhart Company, 8415 Allison Pointe Hwy., Ste. 300, Indianapolis, IN 46250. Tel: 800-428-7106; Email: toledodiocese@nyhart.com.

General Counsel—Pastoral Center: 1933 Spielbusch Ave., Toledo, 43604. Tel: 419-244-6711; Fax: 419-244-4791. MR. THOMAS ANTONINI, Email: tantonini@toledodiocese.org.

Stewardship & Development—Pastoral Center: 1933 Spielbusch Ave., Toledo, 43604. Tel: 419-214-4943; Fax: 419-244-4791. MR. RODNEY O. SCHUSTER, Email: rschuster@toledodiocese.org; MR. CHRISTOPHER HOLINSKI, Email: cholinski@toledodiocese.org; MS. HALEIGH LINGOHR, Devel. Database Admin., Email: hlingohr@toledodiocese.org.

Catholic Foundation, Inc.—Pastoral Center: 1933 Spielbusch Ave., Toledo, 43604. Tel: 419-244-6711; Fax: 419-720-0053. MR. CHRISTOPHER HOLINSKI, Email: cholinski@toledodiocese.org.

Information Technology—Pastoral Center: 1933 Spielbusch Ave., Toledo, 43604. Tel: 419-244-6711; Fax: 419-244-4791. MS. SHARON LANDIS, Network Admin., Email: slandis@toledodiocese.org.

Pastoral Center Services—MS. PATRICIA L. STEIN, Facilities Mgr., Pastoral Center, 1933 Spielbusch Ave., Toledo, 43604. Tel: 419-244-6711; Fax: 419-244-4791; Email: pstein@toledodiocese.org.

Catholic Cemeteries—5725 Hill Ave., Toledo, 43615. Tel: 419-531-5747; Fax: 419-531-0946. MS. NATASHA BAILEY, Dir., Email: nbailey@cfcmission.org.

Cemeteries—Calvary Cemetery, 2224 Dorr St., Toledo, 43607. Tel: 419-536-3751. *Mount Carmel Cemetery, 15 E. Manhattan Blvd., Toledo, 43608.* Tel: 419-536-3751. *Resurrection Cemetery, 5725 Hill Ave., Toledo, 43615.* Tel: 419-531-5747.

Discipleship and Family Life Department

Senior Director—Deacon JOSEPH MALENFANT, 1933 Spielbusch Ave., Toledo, 43604. Tel: 419-244-6711; Fax: 419-244-4791; Email: jmalenfant@toledodiocese.org.

Ministry Assistant—MRS. ALICE JACOBS, Email: ajacobs@toledodiocese.org.

Marriage and Family Life—Pastoral Center: 1933 Spielbusch Ave., Toledo, 43604. Tel: 419-244-6711; Fax: 419-244-4791. MR. NICHOLAS DE LA TORRE, Coord., Email: ndelatorre@toledodiocese.org.

Evangelization and Pastoral Care of Parishes—MR. BRET HUNTEBRINKER, Email: bhuntebrinker@toledodiocese.org.

Toledo Diocesan Council of Catholic Women (TDCCW)—Pastoral Center: 1933 Spielbusch Ave., Toledo, 43604. Tel: 419-244-6711; Fax: 419-244-4791. MS. DEBBI LUMAN, Pres., Email: dluman@frontier.com.

Catholic Men's Ministry—Pastoral Center: 1933 Spielbusch Ave., Toledo, 43604. Tel: 419-244-6711; Fax: 419-244-4791. MR. BRET HUNTEBRINKER, Coord., Email: bhuntebrinker@toledodiocese.org.

Ministry to Catholic Charismatic Renewal (MCCR)—MR. STEVEN TOTH, Dir., 300 Warner St., Walbridge, 43465. Tel: 419-691-6686; Email: mccrholyspirit@gmail.com.

Youth, Young Adult and Campus Ministry—MR. RICHARD MAUME, Coord., Pastoral Center, 1933 Spielbusch Ave., Toledo, 43604. Tel: 419-244-6711; Fax: 419-244-4791; Email: rmaume@toledodiocese.org.

Teens Encounter Christ (TEC)—MR. RICHARD MAUME, Coord., Pastoral Center, 1933 Spielbusch Ave., Toledo, 43604. Tel: 419-244-6711; Fax: 419-244-4791; Email: rmaume@toledodiocese.org.

Intercultural Ministries—Pastoral Center: 1933 Spielbusch Ave., Toledo, 43604. Tel: 419-244-6711; Fax: 419-244-4791. MS. ANDREA DE LA ROCA, Coord., Email: adelaroca@toledodiocese.org.

Hispanic Ministries—MS. ANDREA DE LA ROCA, Coord., Email: adelaroca@toledodiocese.org.

Black Catholic Ministries—MRS. ELLEN JONES, Coord., Email: blackcatholicministry@toledodiocese.org.

Ministries with Persons with Disabilities—MRS. MARSHA RIVAS, Coord., Email: mrivas@toledodiocese.org.

Catholic Youth Organization—Pastoral Center: 1933 Spielbusch Ave., Toledo, 43604. Tel: 419-244-6711; Fax: 419-255-8269. MS. JULIE DUBIELAK, Dir., Email: jdubielak@toledodiocese.org; MR. JACK JORDAN, Asst. Dir., Email: jjordan@toledodiocese.org.

Advisory Bodies

College of Consultors—Rev. Msgrs. KENNETH G. MORMAN, V.F., S.S.L., Chm.; WILLIAM J. KUBACKI, V.G.; CHRISTOPHER P. VASKO, J.V., V.F., J.C.D.; Very Revs. DENNIS G. WALSH, V.F.; MICHAEL J. ZACHARIAS, V.F.; TODD M. DOMINIQUE, V.F.; Rev. ADAM L. HERTZFELD; Very Revs. GREGORY R. HITE, S.T.L., V.F.; JOSEPH T. POGGEMEYER, V.F., S.T.D.

Presbyteral Council—Pastoral Center, 1933 Spielbusch Ave., Toledo, 43604. Tel: 419-244-6711; Fax: 419-244-4791. Ex Officio Members: Most Rev. DANIEL E. THOMAS, Pres.; Rev. Msgrs. WILLIAM J. KUBACKI, V.G.; MARVIN G. BORGER, J.C.L. Deans of the Diocese of Toledo: Revs. JOHN R. BLASER, (Retired); ADAM L. HERTZFELD; GILBERT MASCARENHAS, S.A.C.; CHARLES OBINWA; JAMES SZOBONYA, C.Ss.R.; JEFFERY WALKER; Very Revs. NATHAN BOCKRATH, V.F.; DANIEL E. BORGELT, V.F.; MICHAEL G. DANDURAND; MARK E. DAVIS; TODD M. DOMINIQUE, V.F.; THOMAS J. EXTEJT, V.F.; GREGORY R. HITE, S.T.L., V.F.; CHRISTOPHER KARDZIS, V.F.; JEFFREY R. MCBETH, V.F.; Rev. Msgr. KENNETH G. MORMAN, V.F., S.S.L.; Very Revs. JOSEPH T. POGGEMEYER, V.F., S.T.D.; WILLIAM J. ROSE, V.F.; JEROME A. SCHETTER, V.F.; ERIC P. SCHILD, V.F.; DENNIS G. WALSH, V.F.

Deans—Saint Teresa of Calcutta Deanery: Very Rev. THOMAS J. EXTEJT, V.F. Our Lady of the Lake Deanery: Very Rev. JEFFREY R. MCBETH, V.F. Our Lady, Queen of Peace Deanery: Very Rev. DANIEL E. BORGELT, V.F. Precious Blood of Jesus Deanery: Very Rev. NATHAN BOCKRATH, V.F. St. Agnes Deanery: Very Rev. WILLIAM J. ROSE, V.F. St. George Deanery: Very Rev. JEROME A. SCHETTER, V.F. St. John Neumann Deanery: Rev. Msgr. KENNETH G. MORMAN, V.F., S.S.L. St. Juan

Diego Deanery: Very Rev. GREGORY R. HITE, S.T.L., V.F. Saint Junipero Serra Deanery: Very Rev. DENNIS G. WALSH, V.F. Saint Kateri Tekakwitha Deanery: Very Rev. ERIC P. SCHILD, V.F. St. Maximilian Kolbe Deanery: Very Rev. JOSEPH T. POGGEMEYER, V.F., S.T.D. St. Luke Deanery: Very Rev. MICHAEL M. DANDURAND. Saint Katherine Drexel Deanery: Very Rev. MARK E. DAVIS. Saint Francis of Assisi Deanery: Very Rev. TODD M. DOMINIQUE, V.F. Saint Philomena Deanery: Very Rev. CHRISTOPHER KARDZIS, V.F.

Priest Personnel Board—Rev. Msgr. MARVIN G. BORGER, J.C.L., Chm., Pastoral Center, 1933 Spielbusch Ave., Toledo, 43604. Tel: 419-244-6711; Fax: 419-244-4791; Email: mborger@toledodiocese.org.

Deacon Personnel Board—Rev. Msgr. MARVIN G. BORGER, J.C.L., Chm., Pastoral Center, 1933 Spielbusch Ave., Toledo, 43604. Tel: 419-244-6711; Tel: 419-244-6711; Fax: 419-244-4791; Email: mborger@toledodiocese.org.

Pastoral Advisory Council—Pastoral Center, 1933 Spielbusch Ave., Toledo, 43604. Tel: 419-244-6711; Fax: 419-244-4791.

Diocesan Finance Council—Pastoral Center: 1933 Spielbusch Ave., Toledo, 43604. Tel: 419-244-6711; Fax: 419-244-4791. MR. PHILIP RENDA, Email: prenda@toledodiocese.org.

Diocesan Education Council—Pastoral Center: 1933 Spielbusch Ave., Toledo, 43604. Tel: 419-244-6711; Fax: 419-244-4791. DR. VINCENT DE PAUL SCHMIDT, Email: vschmidt@toledodiocese.org.

Diocesan Building Commission—MR. DAVID REED, CPA, Pastoral Center, 1933 Spielbusch Ave., Toledo, 43604. Tel: 419-244-6711; Fax: 419-244-4791.

CLERGY, PARISHES, MISSIONS AND PAROCHIAL SCHOOLS

CITY OF TOLEDO

(LUCAS COUNTY)

1—ST. ADALBERT (1907) [JC] (Polish), Closed. For inquiries for parish records contact the chancery.

2—SS. ADALBERT & HEDWIG (2010)
3233 Lagrange St., 43608-1898. Tel: 419-241-4179; Fax: 419-241-1136; Email: stadalbert2014@gmail.com; Web: ssadalberthedwig.org. Rev. Monte J. Hoyles, J.C.L., Parochial Admin.; Deacon Gerald Ignatowski.

3—ST. AGNES (1910) Closed. For inquiries for parish records contact the chancery.

4—ST. ANN, Consolidated with St. Teresa to form St. Martin de Porres. See separate listing.

5—ST. ANTHONY (1882) (Polish), Closed. For inquiries for parish records contact the chancery.

6—ST. CATHERINE OF SIENA (1930) [JC]
Mailing Address: 4555 N. Haven Ave., 43612-2350. Tel: 419-478-9558; Fax: 419-478-9434; Email: pneary@stcatherinetoledo.com. Rev. Francis Speier; Deacon Michael R. Learned Sr.
School—St. Catherine of Siena School, 1155 Corbin Rd., 43612-2366. Tel: 419-478-9900; Email: ckummer@stcatherineearlyed.org. Mrs. Chris Kummer, Dir. Students 82.
Catechesis Religious Program—Theresa Paredes, D.R.E.

7—ST. CHARLES BORROMEO (1903) [JC] Rev. Gregory L. Peatee, V.F.; Deacon Michael W. Pence.
Church: 1842 Airport Hwy., 43609-2069.
Tel: 419-535-7077; Fax: 419-535-1813; Email: stcharlessthyacinthtoledo@gmail.com; Web: www.stcharlessthyacinthtoledo.org.
Catechesis Religious Program—

8—CHRIST THE KING (1953) [JC3]
4100 Harvest Ln., 43623-4399. Tel: 419-475-4348; Fax: 419-475-4050; Email: mail@cktoledo.org; Web: www.cktoledo.org. Very Rev. William J. Rose, V.F.; Rev. Joseph Panakkal Joseph, S.A.C., Parochial Vicar; Deacon Robert Beisser.
School—Christ the King School, (Grades PreK-8), Tel: 419-475-0909; Fax: 419-475-4050; Email: school@cktoledo.org; Web: www.ckschool.org. Mr. Joseph Carroll, Prin. Lay Teachers 23; Students 386; Pre K Enrollment 51.
Catechesis Religious Program—Email: strabbic@cktoledo.org. Mrs. Sandra L. Trabbic, D.R.E. Students 163.

9—ST. CLEMENT (1947) [JC] Rev. Francis Speier; Deacon Ronald J. Plenzler.
Church: 3030 Tremainsville Rd., 43613-1901.
Tel: 419-472-2111; Email: st.clement08@yahoo.com; Web: stclementtoledo.com.
Catechesis Religious Program—Tel: 419-472-1259.

10—COMMUNITY OF THE RISEN CHRIST (1972) Closed. For inquiries for parish records contact the chancery.

11—CORPUS CHRISTI (UNIVERSITY OF TOLEDO) (1970) [JC] Very Rev. Msgr. Michael R. Billian, V.F.; Rev. Jeremy P. Miller, Parochial Vicar; Deacon Justin S. Moor, Pastoral Assoc.
Church: 2955 Dorr St., 43607-3023.
Tel: 419-531-4992; Email: kwilliams@ccup.org; Web: www.ccup.org.

12—EPIPHANY OF THE LORD PARISH (2013)
729 White St., 43605. Very Rev. Michael A. Geiger, V.F.; Rev. Vicente Antonio Vera, Parochial Vicar; Deacon Jose Garcia.
Saint Thomas Aquinas Campus—
Saint Stephen Campus, 1878 Genesee St., 43605.
Sacred Heart of Jesus Campus, 509 Oswald St., 43605.
See The Kateri Catholic School System, Oregon under Consolidated Elementary Schools located in the Institution Section.

13—ST. FRANCIS DE SALES (1841) Closed. For inquiries for parish records contact the chancery. Chapel remains open.

14—GESU (1920) [JC] Rev. Martin C. Lukas, O.S.F.S.; Larry Kruez, Business Mgr.; Dianna Walsh, Sec.
Church: 2049 Parkside Blvd., 43607-1597.
Tel: 419-531-1421; Email: gesubiz@bex.net; Email: mlosfs@aol.com; Web: www.gesutoledo.org.
School—Gesu School, (Grades K-8), 2045 Parkside Blvd., 43607-1555. Tel: 419-536-5634; Fax: 419-531-8932; Email: gonzales@gesutoledo.com; Web: gesutoledo.com. Mr. Manuel Gonzales, Prin. Lay Teachers 23; Students 275.
Catechesis Religious Program—Email: skowronski@gesutoledo.com. Laurie Skowronski, D.R.E. Students 47.

15—GOOD SHEPHERD (1873) [JC] Closed. For inquiries for parish records contact the chancery.

16—ST. HEDWIG (1875) [JC] (Polish), Closed. For inquiries for parish records contact the chancery.

17—HISTORIC CHURCH OF SAINT PATRICK (1863) [JC] (Irish) Rev. Msgr. Christopher P. Vasko, J.V., V.F., J.C.D.; Deacons Thomas S. Carone; David E. Smith.
Church: 130 Avondale Ave., 43604.
Tel: 419-243-6452; Email: parish@stpatshistoric.org; Web: www.stpatshistoric.org.

18—HOLY ROSARY (1906) (Slovak), Closed. For inquiries for parish records contact the chancery.

19—ST. HYACINTH (1927) [JC] (Polish) Rev. Gregory L. Peatee, V.F.; Deacon Michael W. Pence.
Office: 719 Evesham Ave., 43607-3806.
Tel: 419-535-7077; Fax: 419-535-1813; Email: stcharlessthyacinthtoledo@gmail.com; Web: www.stcharlessthyacinthtoledo.org.
Church: Parkside Blvd. at Victory Ave., 43607.
Catechesis Religious Program—

20—IMMACULATE CONCEPTION (1868) [JC] Rev. Msgr. Christopher P. Vasko, J.V., V.F., J.C.D.; Rev. Rudi O. Schwarzkopf, O.S.F.S., Pastoral Associate; Deacons Thomas S. Carone; David E. Smith.
Church: 434 Western Ave., 43609-2886.
Tel: 419-243-1829; Fax: 419-241-9642; Email: toldarbyicc@sbcglobal.net; Web: iccatdarby.org.

21—ST. JAMES (1913) Closed. For inquiries for parish records contact the chancery.

22—ST. JOAN OF ARC (1978) [JC]
Mailing Address: 5856 Heatherdowns Blvd., 43614-4570. Tel: 419-866-6181; Fax: 419-866-6142; Email: kasmus@joanofarc.org; Web: www.joanofarc.org. Revs. Adam L. Hertzfeld; Manoj Mammen; Sr. Valerie Schneider, S.N.D., Pastoral Assoc.; Deacons Russell Shoemaker; Richard Nelson; Edward Maher.
School—St. Joan of Arc School, (Grades PreSchool-8), 5950 Heatherdowns Blvd., 43614-4500.
Tel: 419-866-6177; Fax: 419-866-4107; Email: jguzman@school.joanofarc.org; Email: swelker@school.joanofarc.org; Email: kwitker@school.joanofarc.org; Web: joanofarc.org/school. Ms. Jennifer Guzman, Prin. Clergy 16; Lay Teachers 29; Students 459.
Catechesis Religious Program—Terri LaFollette, D.R.E.; Sr. Elaine Marie Clement, S.N.D., Adult Educ. Students 30.

23—ST. JOHN THE BAPTIST (1918) [JC] Rev. David J. Cirata, V.F.
Church: 5153 Summit St., 43611-2786.
Tel: 419-726-2034; Email: stjohnptplace@buckeye-express.com.
Catechesis Religious Program—Email: sjweber@bex.net. Faith Weber, D.R.E. Students 70.

24—ST. JOSEPH (1854) [JC]
Mailing Address: 3233 Lagrange St., 43608.
Tel: 419-261-3928; Fax: 419-241-1136; Email: stjodowntown@gmail.com. 628 Locust St., 43604. Rev. Matthew R. Rader, Parochial Admin.

25—ST. JUDE (1955) [JC] Closed. For inquiries for parish records contact the chancery.

26—LITTLE FLOWER OF JESUS (1928) [JC] Rev. David W. Nuss; Deacon Douglas Bullimore.
Church: 5522 Dorr St., 43615-3612.
Tel: 419-537-6655; Email: parishcenter@littleflowertoledo.org; Web: www.littleflowertoledo.org.
See St. Benedict School under Consolidated Elementary Schools in the Institution Section.
Catechesis Religious Program—

27—ST. LOUIS (1872) (French), Closed. For inquiries for parish records contact the chancery.

28—ST. MARTIN DE PORRES (1990) [JC]
1119 W. Bancroft St., 43606. Tel: 419-241-4544; Email: stmartindeporrestoledo@gmail.com. Sr. Virginia Welsh, O.S.F., Pastoral Leader; Rev. Raphael Karekatt, M.S.F.S., Presbyteral Moderator.
Catechesis Religious Program—

29—ST. MARY OF THE ASSUMPTION (1854) Closed. For inquiries for parish records contact the chancery.

30—ST. MICHAEL THE ARCHANGEL (1900) [JC]
420 Sandusky St., 43611-3535. Tel: 419-726-1947; Email: stmike@bex.net. Rev. David J. Cirata, V.F.; Ms. Suzanne Stapleton, Parish Mgr., Email: sstapleton@bex.net.

31—MOST BLESSED SACRAMENT (1924) [JC] Very Rev. Michael A. Geiger, V.F.; Deacons Harold Welch; Robert Fedynich.
Office: 2240 Castlewood Dr., 43613.
Tel: 419-472-2288; Email: mbillian@mbsptoledo.org; Web: www.blessedsacramenttoledo.com.
School—Most Blessed Sacrament Parish School, (Grades K-8), (Consolidated) 4255 Bellevue Rd., 43613. Tel: 419-472-1121; Fax: 419-472-1679; Email: gsattler@mbsptoledo.org; Web: www.mbsptoledo.org. Gregory Sattler, Prin. Lay Teachers 17; Students 230.
Catechesis Religious Program—Tel: 419-473-1161; Email: dklein62@sbcglobal.net. Joan Klein, D.R.E.

32—OUR LADY OF LOURDES (1926) [JC] Rev. David R. Bruning; Deacon Gary Thrun.
Church: 6149 Hill Ave., 43615-5699.
Tel: 419-865-2345; Email: lpierson@olltoledo.com; Web: www.olltoledo.com.
See St. Benedict School under Consolidated Elementary Schools in the Institution Section.
Catechesis Religious Program—*P.R.E.P.*

33—OUR LADY OF PERPETUAL HELP (1918) [JC] Very Rev. David L. Ritchie, V.F.; Deacon Daniel R. Waters.
Church: 2255 Central Grove, 43614-4321.
Tel: 419-382-5511; Email: lpierson@olltoledo.com; Web: www.olphtoledo.org.
School—Our Lady of Perpetual Help School, (Grades PreK-8), Tel: 419-382-5696; Email: kbonnell@olphtoledo.org. Mrs. Kari Bonnell, Prin. Students 199.
Catechesis Religious Program—

34—OUR LADY QUEEN OF THE MOST HOLY ROSARY CATHEDRAL (1915) [JC] Rev. Msgr. William J. Kubacki, V.G., Rector; Deacons Brendan Gillen; Michael J. Sarra; James D. Caruso, J.D. In Res., Rev. Msgrs. Marvin G. Borger, J.C.L.; Charles E. Singler, D.Min.; Rev. Monte J. Hoyles, J.C.L.
Office & Church: 2535 Collingwood Blvd., 43610.
Tel: 419-244-9575; Email: roscath@totalink.net; Web: www.rosarycathedral.org.
Res.: 2544 Parkwood Ave., 43610-1317.
Tel: 419-255-1890.
See Rosary Cathedral Campus under Consolidated Elementary Schools located in the Institution Section.
Catechesis Religious Program—

35—ST. PATRICK OF HEATHERDOWNS (1956) [JC] Revs. Anthony A. Borgia; James R. Sanford, Parochial Vicar, (Retired); Deacons Joel F. Junga; David J. Karpanty; Dennis T. Rife; Joseph H. Kest Jr.
Church: 4201 Heatherdowns Blvd., 43614-3099.
Tel: 419-381-1540; Email: mary.miller@toledostpats.org; Web: toledostpats.org.
School—St. Patrick of Heatherdowns School, (Grades PreK-8), Tel: 419-381-1775; Email: tina.abel@toledostpats.org. Mrs. Tina Abel, Prin. Students 452.
Catechesis Religious Program—Email: rebecca.reamer@toledostpats.org. Rebecca Reamer, D.R.E. Students 205.

36—SS. PETER AND PAUL (1866) [JC] (Hispanic) Rev. Juan Francisco Molina; Deacon Salvador Sanchez.
Office: 738 S. St. Clair St., 43609-2432.
Tel: 419-241-5822; Email: sspeterpaul@sbcglobal.net.
Church: 736 S. St. Clair St., 43609.
Catechesis Religious Program—Tel: 419-283-0884.

37—ST. PIUS X (1953) [JC]
Mailing Address: 3011 Carskaddon Ave., 43606-1662. Tel: 419-535-7672; Fax: 419-535-7810; Email: stpius@buckeye-express.com. Revs. David M. Whalen, O.S.F.S.; John Lehner, O.S.F.S., In Res.
Church: 2950 Ilger Ave., 43606.
School—St. Pius X School, (Grades PreK-8), Tel: 419-535-7688; Email: stpiusx_richardson@nwoca.net. Ms. Susan Richardson, Prin. Students 199.

38—REGINA COELI (1954) [JC] Rev. John A. Miller; Deacon James Dudley.
Church: 530 Regina Pkwy., 43612-3398.
Tel: 419-476-0922; Email: rc3office@gmail.com; Web: www.reginacoelitoledo.org.
School—Regina Coeli School, (Grades K-8), 600 Regina Pkwy., 43612-3399. Tel: 419-476-0920; Fax: 419-476-6792; Email: dbloomquist@regina-coeli.org. Corrine Sharrit, Prin. Lay Teachers 13; Students 236.
Catechesis Religious Program—
39—SACRED HEART OF JESUS (1883) [JC] (German), Closed. For inquiries for parish records contact the chancery.
40—ST. STANISLAUS (1908) (Polish), Closed. For inquiries for parish records contact the chancery.
41—ST. STEPHEN (1898) [JC] (Hungarian), Closed. For inquiries for parish records contact the chancery.
42—ST. TERESA, Consolidated with St. Ann to form St. Martin de Porres. See separate listing.
43—ST. THOMAS AQUINAS (1915) [JC] Closed. For inquiries for parish records contact the chancery.
44—ST. VINCENT DE PAUL (1928) Closed. For inquiries for parish records contact the chancery.

OUTSIDE THE CITY OF TOLEDO

ALVADA, SENECA CO., ST. PETER (1854) [CEM] Closed. For inquiries for parish records contact the chancery.
ANTWERP, PAULDING CO., ST. MARY (1868) [JC] Closed. For inquiries for parish records contact the chancery.
ARCHBOLD, FULTON CO., ST. PETER (1846) [CEM] Rev. Stephen L. Stanberry.
Church: 614 N. Defiance St., Archbold, 43502-1105.
Tel: 419-446-2150; Email: stpeter@rtecexpress.net; Web: www.parishesonline.com/find/st-peter-church-43502.
Catechesis Religious Program—Tel: 419-212-1357; Email: tkunesh66@gmail.com. Ms. Tami Kunesh, D.R.E. Students 67.
ATTICA, SENECA CO.
1—OUR LADY OF HOPE (2005) Very Rev. Jacob A. Gordon, V.F.
Church: 320 Stump Pike Rd., Attica, 44807-9465.
Tel: 419-426-3043; Email: ourladyofhopeattica@frontier.com.
Catechesis Religious Program—
2—SS. PETER AND PAUL (1882) [CEM] Closed. For inquiries for parish records contact the chancery.
BASCOM, SENECA CO., SS. PATRICK & ANDREW (1864) [CEM]
6230 W. Tiffin, P.O. Box 226, Bascom, 44809-0226.
Tel: 419-937-2715; Fax: 419-937-2751; Email: patrick2@bright.net. Rev. Timothy M. Kummerer; Deacon John F. Walter.
Worship Sites—
Church: 3761 N. State Rte. 635, Fostoria, 44830.
Catechesis Religious Program—Carol Brickner, D.R.E. Students 111.
BELLEVUE, HURON CO.
1—ST. GASPAR DEL BUFALO (2005) (Seneca County.)
16209 E. County Rd. 46, Bellevue, 44811-4661.
Tel: 419-483-3231; Fax: 419-483-4661; Email: stgaspar@htmcltd.net. Very Rev. Jacob A. Gordon, V.F.
Catechesis Religious Program—
2—IMMACULATE CONCEPTION (1859) [CEM] Rev. Jonathan C. Wight.
Church: 231 E. Center St., Bellevue, 44811-1404.
Tel: 419-483-3417; Email: parish@icbell.org; Web: www.icbell.org.
School—Immaculate Conception School, (Grades PreK-8), 304 E. Main St., Bellevue, 44811-1404.
Tel: 419-483-6066; Fax: 888-836-9549; Email: pgreibel@icbell.org. Mrs. Pamela Griebel, Prin. Lay Teachers 13; Students 165.
Catechesis Religious Program—
BISMARK, HURON CO., ST. SEBASTIAN (1846) [CEM] (German), Closed. For inquiries for parish records contact the chancery.
BLAKESLEE, WILLIAMS CO., ST. JOSEPH (1865) [CEM] (German), Closed. Church transferred to a chapel of Saint Mary, Edgerton.
BLUFFTON, ALLEN CO., ST. MARY (1865)
160 N. Spring, Bluffton, 45817. Tel: 419-358-8631; Email: cinkrott@embarqmail.com. Rev. John F. Stites, Chap., (Retired); Sr. Carol Inkrott, O.S.F., Pastoral Leader; Deacon Michael R. Marcum II.
Catechesis Religious Program—Email: khski7@aol.com. Kelly Honse, D.R.E. Students 93.
BOWLING GREEN, WOOD CO.
1—ST. ALOYSIUS (1862)
150 S. Enterprise St., Bowling Green, 43402-0485.
Tel: 419-352-4195; Email: parishoffice@stalbg.org; Web: www.stalbg.org. Very Rev. Mark E. Davis; Deacons James Cavera; Phillip Avina.
School—St. Aloysius School, (Grades PreK-8), 148 S. Enterprise, Bowling Green, 43402-4738.
Tel: 419-352-8614; Fax: 419-352-4738; Email: principal@stalschoolbg.org. Andrea Puhl, Prin. Lay Teachers 17; Students 237.
Catechesis Religious Program—Email: religioused@stalbg.org. Jean Bargiel, D.R.E. Students 230.
2—ST. THOMAS MORE UNIVERSITY PARISH (1967) Rev. Jason J. Kahle.
Church: 425 Thurstin Ave., Bowling Green, 43402-1901. Tel: 419-352-7555; Fax: 419-352-7557; Email: info@sttoms.com; Email: receptionist@sttoms.com; Web: www.sttoms.com.
Catechesis Religious Program—
BRYAN, WILLIAMS CO., ST. PATRICK (1857) Rev. James E. Halleron; Deacons Steve St. John, Sacramental Min.; Dennis F. Jackson; Thomas F. Dominique.
Church: 610 S. Portland St., Bryan, 43506-2059.
Tel: 419-636-1044; Email: jhalleron@cityofbryan.net; Web: www.stpatbryan.org.
School—St. Patrick School, (Grades PreK-8),
Tel: 419-636-3592; Email: cniese@saintpatrickschoolbryan.org. Ms. Connie Niese, Prin. Students 133.
Catechesis Religious Program—Tel: 616-633-0994; Email: philipdezern@gmail.com. Philip Dezern, D.R.E. Students 38.
BUCYRUS, CRAWFORD CO., HOLY TRINITY (1865) [CEM] (German)
760 Tiffin St., Bucyrus, 44820-1551.
Tel: 419-562-1346; Email: htcbucyrus@gmail.com; Web: holytrinitybucyrus.org. Rev. Paul A. Fahrbach, V.F.; Deacon Jerome A. Gubernath.
Catechesis Religious Program—Email: llabdite@hotmail.com. Mrs. Elizabeth Wurm, D.R.E. Students 86.
CAREY, WYANDOT CO., OUR LADY OF CONSOLATION (1867) [CEM] Basilica and National Shrine of Our Lady of Consolation, Parish & Shrine
315 Clay St., Carey, 43316-1498. Tel: 419-396-1523; Fax: 419-396-3355; Email: parishoffice@olcshrine.com. Revs. Thomas Merrill, O.F.M.Conv.; John Bamman, O.F.M.Conv.; Deacon James F. Kitzler.
School—Our Lady of Consolation, Basilica-National Shrine School, (Grades PreK-8), 401 Clay St., Carey, 43316-1496. Tel: 419-396-6166; Email: cfletcher@olcschoolonline.org. Mr. Brian Gerber, Prin. Lay Teachers 12; Students 187.
Catechesis Religious Program—Email: PRE@olcshrine.com. Bro. Ian Bremar, D.R.E. Students 85.
CECIL, PAULDING CO., IMMACULATE CONCEPTION (1879) Closed. For inquiries for parish records contact the chancery.
CLOVERDALE, PUTNAM CO., ST. BARBARA (1898) [CEM] (German) Very Rev. Jerome A. Schetter, V.F.
Church: 160 Main St., P.O. Box 8, Cloverdale, 45827.
Tel: 419-488-2391; Email: stbarbaras@bright.net.
Catechesis Religious Program—
CLYDE, SANDUSKY CO., ST. MARY (1890) [CEM] Sr. Regina Fisher, S.N.D., Pastoral Leader; Rev. Edward J. Schleter, V.F., Presbyteral Moderator & Chap., (Retired).
Church: 609 Vine St., Clyde, 43410-1537.
Tel: 419-547-9687; Email: clydestmary@gmail.com; Web: clydestmary.org.
Catechesis Religious Program—
COLUMBUS GROVE, PUTNAM CO., ST. ANTHONY OF PADUA (1912) [CEM] (German) Very Rev. Thomas J. Extejt, V.F.
Church: 512 W. Sycamore St., Columbus Grove, 45830-1020. Tel: 419-659-2263; Email: siefkem@sa.noacsc.org.
School—St. Anthony of Padua School, (Grades K-8), 520 W. Sycamore St., Columbus Grove, 45830-1020.
Tel: 419-659-2103; Fax: 419-659-4194; Email: giesigl@sa.noacsc.org. Mr. Scott Hummel, Prin. Lay Teachers 10; Students 111.
Catechesis Religious Program—Email: judyfhc@yahoo.com. Judy Schroeder, C.R.E. Students 106.
CONTINENTAL, PUTNAM CO., ST. JOHN THE BAPTIST (1907) [JC] Revs. Mark Hoying, C.PP.S.; Richard Friebel, C.PP.S.
Church: 4893 St. Rte. 634, N, Continental, 45831.
Tel: 419-596-4319; Fax: 419-596-4318; Email: hoyingmark@yahoo.co.nz; Email: wjmatthews1@gmail.com.
Catechesis Religious Program—
CRESTLINE, CRAWFORD CO., ST. JOSEPH (1861) [JC] (German)
331 N. Thoman St., Crestline, 44827.
Tel: 419-683-2015; Email: jpalm@stjosephcrestline.org; Web: stjosephcrestline.org. Rev. Christopher Bohnsack.
School—St. Joseph School, (Grades PreSchool-8), 333 N. Thoman St., Crestline, 44827-1445.
Tel: 419-683-1284; Fax: 419-683-8957; Email: dsalvati@stjosephcrestline.org. Daniel Salvati, Prin. Lay Teachers 8; Students 45.
Catechesis Religious Program—
CUBA, PUTNAM CO., ST. ISIDORE (1917) Closed. For inquiries for parish records contact the chancery.
CUSTAR, WOOD CO., ST. LOUIS (1864) [CEM] [JC]
22792 Defiance Pike, P.O. Box 125, Custar, 43511-9716. Tel: 419-669-1864; Email: stlouischurch@midohio.twcbc.com. Rev. Walter E. Tuscano, S.A.C.
School—St. Louis School, (Grades PreSchool-6), 22776 Defiance Pike, P.O. Box 125, Custar, 43511-9716. Tel: 419-669-1875; Fax: 419-669-2878; Email: stlouis@midohio.twcbc.com. Rev. Walter E. Tuscano, S.A.C., Supt.; Mrs. Ellie Panning, Admin. Clergy 5; Lay Teachers 6; Students 65.
CYGNET, WOOD CO., SACRED HEART (1890) Closed. For inquiries for parish records contact the chancery.
DEFIANCE, DEFIANCE CO.
1—IMMACULATE CONCEPTION (1873) [CEM] Closed. For inquiries for parish records contact the chancery.
2—ST. ISIDORE (2005) (Twinned with St. Michael, St. Michael's Ridge.)
Mailing Address: 05480 Moser Rd., Defiance, 43512-9150. Tel: 419-497-2161; Fax: 419-497-2058; Email: kb8biq@centurylink.net; Web: www.saintisidoreparish.org. Rev. Robert J. Kill; Deacon Scott D. Graham.
Church: 06324 State Rte. 15 at Glenburg Rd., Defiance, 43512.
Catechesis Religious Program—Email: nachoalisongarcia@gmail.com. Alison Garcia, D.R.E. Students 81.
3—ST. JOHN THE EVANGELIST (1850) [CEM]
510 Jackson Ave., Defiance, 43512-2189.
Tel: 419-782-7121; Email: stjohn@stjohndefiance.org; Web: www.stjohndefiance.org. Rev. Eric L. Mueller; Deacons Dominick J. Varano; Mark A. Homier.
See Holy Cross Catholic School of Defiance under Consolidated Elementary Schools located in the Institution section.
Catechesis Religious Program—Tel: 419-782-2776; Email: jessicawest@metalink.net. Jessica West, D.R.E.
4—ST. MARY (1873) Rev. Randy P. Giesige; Deacon Jeff M. Mayer.
Church: 715 Jefferson Ave., Defiance, 43512.
Tel: 419-782-2776; Email: st-marys@defnet.com.
See Defiance Holy Cross Catholic School of Defiance under Consolidated Elementary Schools located in the Institution section.
Catechesis Religious Program—Students 140.
5—ST. MICHAEL (1861) [CEM] Rev. Robert J. Kill; Deacon Scott D. Graham.
Tel: 419-497-2161; Email: kb8biq@centurylink.net; Web: www.saintmichaelridge.org.
Catechesis Religious Program—Tel: 419-497-3122; Email: fabaronitwo@yahoo.com. Ronda Fabiano, D.R.E. Students 118.
DELPHOS, ALLEN CO.
1—ST. JOHN THE BAPTIST (1866) [CEM]
14755 Landeck Rd., Delphos, 45833-9438.
Tel: 419-692-0636; Email: schurch1@woh.rr.com. Very Rev. Dennis G. Walsh, V.F.; Revs. Douglas D. Taylor, Parochial Vicar; Daniel Parackkukizhakkethil, Parochial Vicar; Immcolata Scarogni, Contact Person.
Catechesis Religious Program—Email: sccjoy@yahoo.com. Sr. Immaculata Scarogni, S.C.C., D.R.E. Students 69.
2—ST. JOHN THE EVANGELIST (1844) [CEM] (German)
210 N. Pierce St., Delphos, 45833. Tel: 419-695-4050; Fax: 419-695-4060; Email: hanf@delphosstjohns.org; Email: dwalsh@delphosstjohns.org; Web: delphosstjohnparish.org. Very Rev. Dennis G. Walsh, V.F.; Revs. Douglas D. Taylor; Scott Perry; Stephen J. Blum, In Res., (Retired); Deacons David J. Ricker; John P. Sheeran.
Church: 331 E. Second St., Delphos, 45833.
School—St. John the Evangelist School, (Grades PreK-6), 110 N. Pierce St., Delphos, 45833.
Tel: 419-692-8561; Email: stant@delphosstjohns.org; Web: delphosstjohns.org. Mr. Nathan Stant, Prin. Religious Teachers 2; Lay Teachers 25; Sisters of Notre Dame 2; Students 318.
High School—St. John the Evangelist High School, 515 E. Second St., Delphos, 45833. Tel: 419-692-5371 ; Email: lee@delphosstjohns.org. Mr. Adam Lee, Prin. Religious Teachers 1; Lay Teachers 20; Students 272.
Catechesis Religious Program—Tel: 419-692-1286.
DESHLER, HENRY CO., IMMACULATE CONCEPTION (1871) Rev. Arthur J. Niewiadomski.
Church: 230 Allendale Ave., P.O. Box 23, Deshler, 43516-1103. Tel: 419-278-3686; Email: deshler_icc@yahoo.com.
Catechesis Religious Program—
EDGERTON, WILLIAMS CO., ST. MARY (1865) [CEM] (German)
Mailing Address: 317 S. Locust St., P.O. Box 355, Edgerton, 43517. Very Rev. Daniel E. Borgelt, V.F.; Deacons Joseph Timbrook; Rod Conkle.
Church: 300 S. Michigan Ave., Edgerton, 43517.
Tel: 419-298-2540; Email: stmarycatholic@frontier.com; Web: www.stmaryedgerton.net.
School—St. Mary School, (Grades PreSchool-6), 314 S. Locust St., Edgerton, 43517. Tel: 419-298-2531; Email: jtaylor@stmaryedgerton.org; Web: www.

stmaryedgerton.org. Mrs. Juliana M. Taylor, Prin. Lay Teachers 9; Students 74.
Catechesis Religious Program—Mrs. Karrie Kimpel, D.R.E. Students 106.

FAYETTE, FULTON CO., OUR LADY OF MERCY (1943)
409 E. Main St., P.O. Box 429, Fayette, 43521-0429. Tel: 419-237-2441; Email: ourladyofmercy@frontier.com; Web: www.ourladyofmercyfayette.parishesonline.com. Rev. Stephen L. Stanberry.
Catechesis Religious Program—

FINDLAY, HANCOCK CO., ST. MICHAEL THE ARCHANGEL (1834) [CEM]
750 Bright Rd., Findlay, 45840-2448. Tel: 419-422-2646; Email: dcampbell@findlaystmichael.org. Very Rev. Michael J. Zacharias, V.F.; Rev. Kyle Gase; Deacons David Sadler; Michael Eier; Armando Gonzalez; Keith J. Talbert.
Church (Downtown): 617 W. Main Cross, Findlay, 45840.
School—St. Michael the Archangel School, (Grades PreSchool-8), 723 Sutton Pl., Findlay, 45840-6965. Tel: 419-423-2738; Fax: 419-423-2720; Email: parish@findlaystmichael.org; Web: www.findlaystmichaelschool.org. Amy Holzwart, Prin. Lay Teachers 28; Students 515.
Catechesis Religious Program—

FORT JENNINGS, PUTNAM CO., ST. JOSEPH (1848) [CEM] (German) Rev. Charles Obinwa; Deacon Lawrence Schimmoeller.
Church: 135 N. Water St., P.O. Box 68, Fort Jennings, 45844. Tel: 419-286-2132; Email: stjoeparishofc@bright.net; Web: www.stjosephfortjennings.org.
Catechesis Religious Program—Tel: 419-286-2019; Email: stjoereled@bright.net. Rhonda Liebrecht, D.R.E. Students 257.

FOSTORIA, SENECA CO., ST. WENDELIN (1850) [CEM] Very Rev. Todd M. Dominique, V.F.; Deacon David L. Schiefer.
Church: 323 N. Wood St., Fostoria, 44830. Tel: 419-435-6692; Email: parish@stwendelin.org; Web: stwendelin.org.
School—St. Wendelin School, (Grades K-12), 533 N. Countryline St., Fostoria, 44830-2246. Tel: 419-435-8144; Email: teresa.kitchen@stwendelin.org. Teresa Kitchen, Prin. Lay Teachers 13; Students 95.
Catechesis Religious Program—Fax: 419-435-6692; Email: shellie.gabel@stwendelin.org. Mrs. Shellie Gabel, D.R.E. Students 103.

FREMONT, SANDUSKY CO.
1—ST. ANN (1843) [JC] Rev. Michael P. Roemmele; Very Rev. Nathan Bockrath, V.F., Parochial Vicar; Deacon James Heyman.
Church: 1021 W. State St., Fremont, 43420-2103. Tel: 419-332-7472; Fax: 419-332-3556; Email: stann_church@outlook.com.
Catechesis Religious Program—
2—ST. CASIMIR (1915) (Polish), Closed. For inquiries for parish records contact the chancery.
3—ST. JOSEPH (1857) [CEM] [JC] (German) Rev. Michael P. Roemmele; Very Rev. Nathan Bockrath, V.F., Parochial Vicar; Deacon Melvin J. Shell.
Church: 709 Croghan St., Fremont, 43420-2482. Tel: 419-334-2638; Email: stjoefrem@sbcglobal.net.
See Bishop Hoffman Catholic School under Consolidated Elementary Schools located in the Institution Section.
Catechesis Religious Program— Clustered with St. Ann, Fremont.
4—SACRED HEART (1956) [JC] Rev. Krzysztof Kardzis; Deacon Alfredo Diaz.
Church: 550 Smith Rd., Fremont, 43420-9567. Tel: 419-332-7339; Email: office@sacredheart-fremont.org; Web: www.sacredheart-fremont.org.
See Bishop Hoffman Catholic School under Consolidated Elementary Schools located in the Institution Section.
Catechesis Religious Program—

FRENCHTOWN, SENECA CO., ST. NICHOLAS (1856) [CEM] (German—French), Closed. For inquiries for parish records contact the chancery.

GALION, CRAWFORD CO., ST. JOSEPH (1853) [CEM]
135 N. Liberty St., Galion, 44833-2017. Tel: 419-468-2884; Email: baker.brittany@sjsaints.org. Rev. Paul A. Fahrbach, V.F.; Deacons Alfred Sisson; Gregory Kirk.
School—St. Joseph School, (Grades PreK-8), 138 N. Liberty St., Galion, 44833-2016. Tel: 419-468-5436; Email: principal@sjsaints.org. Tammy Haus, Prin. Lay Teachers 6; Students 98.
Catechesis Religious Program—Anissa Tuttle, D.R.E. Students 28.

GENOA, OTTAWA CO., OUR LADY OF LOURDES (1856)
204 Main St., Genoa, 43430-1609. Tel: 419-855-8501; Email: secretary@ourladygenoa.org; Web: www.ourladygenoa.org. Rev. Timothy F. Ferris; Deacon Frank A. Tello.
Catechesis Religious Program—Tel: 419-559-4001.

GIBSONBURG, SANDUSKY CO., ST. MICHAEL THE ARCHANGEL CHURCH (1892) [CEM]
317 E. Madison St., Gibsonburg, 43431-1498. Tel: 419-637-2255; Fax: 419-637-2255; Email: gburgstmichael@woh.rr.com. Rev. Stanislaw Tabor, Admin.
Catechesis Religious Program—Tel: 419-637-9929.

GLANDORF, PUTNAM CO., ST. JOHN THE BAPTIST (1834) [CEM] [JC] (German) Revs. Anthony Fortman, C.PP.S.; Richard Friebel, C.PP.S.; Deacon Donald W. Inkrott.
Church: 109 N. Main St., Box 48, Glandorf, 45848-0048. Tel: 419-538-6928; Email: stjohns@bright.net; Web: stjohnglandorf.org.
Catechesis Religious Program—

GRAND RAPIDS, WOOD CO., ST. PATRICK (1842) [CEM] (Irish) Rev. Walter E. Tuscano, S.A.C.
Church: 14010 S. River Rd., Grand Rapids, 43522-9678. Tel: 419-832-5215; Email: spgr@frontier.com; Web: www.stpatrickgrandrapids.parishesonline.com.
Catechesis Religious Program—

HAMLER, HENRY CO., ST. PAUL (1886) Closed. For inquiries for parish records contact the chancery. Chapel remains open.

HELENA, SANDUSKY CO., ST. MARY (1859) [CEM] Rev. Christopher G. Bazar.
Church: 865 State Rte. 635, Helena, 43435-9792. Tel: 419-638-3042; Email: msmparishoffice@cros.net.
Catechesis Religious Program—Students 49.

HICKSVILLE, DEFIANCE CO., ST. MICHAEL (1878)
100 Antwerp Dr., Hicksville, 43526. Tel: 419-542-8202; Tel: 419-542-8714; Fax: 419-542-9513; Email: saintmichaelhicksville@gmail.com; Web: saintmichaelhicksville.org. Very Rev. Daniel E. Borgelt, V.F.; Deacons Rod Conkle; Joseph Timbrook.
Catechesis Religious Program—Email: stmikeCCD@gmail.com. Dean Smalley II, D.R.E. Students 98.

HOLGATE, HENRY CO., ST. MARY (1886) [CEM]
316 Chicago Ave., P.O. Box 487, Holgate, 43527-0487. Tel: 419-264-3321; Email: smchurch@embarqmail.com. Rev. Nicholas J. Cunningham.
Catechesis Religious Program—Tel: 419-264-6596.

HURON, ERIE CO., ST. PETER (1888) [JC] Very Rev. Jeffrey R. McBeth, V.F.
Church: 430 Main St., Huron, 44839-1678. Tel: 419-433-5725; Email: pastor@stpetershuron.org; Email: offmgr@stpetershuron.org; Web: www.stpetershuron.org.
School—St. Peter School, (Grades PreK-8), 429 Huron St., Huron, 44839-1753. Tel: 419-433-4640; Fax: 419-433-2118; Email: principal@huronstpeterschool.org. Ms. Anne Asher, Prin. Lay Teachers 13; Students 169.
Catechesis Religious Program—

JUNCTION, PAULDING CO., ST. MARY (1846) Closed. For inquiries for parish records contact the chancery.

KALIDA, PUTNAM CO., ST. MICHAEL (1878) [CEM] Revs. Mark Hoying, C.PP.S.; Richard Friebel, C.PP.S.; Deacon Robert Klausing.
Church: 312 N. Broad St., P.O. Box 387, Kalida, 45853-0387. Tel: 419-532-3474; Email: stmich@bright.net; Web: stmichaelskalida.org.
Catechesis Religious Program—Tel: 419-532-3494.

KANSAS, SENECA CO., ST. JAMES (1890) Closed. For inquiries for parish records contact the chancery.

KELLEY'S ISLAND, ERIE CO., ST. MICHAEL (1861)
Chappel St., P.O. Box 490, Put-In-Bay, 43456. Tel: 419-285-2741; Email: deaconmike@live.com. Mr. Jimmy McCoy, Pastoral Leader; Very Rev. Nathan Bockrath, V.F., Presbyteral Mod.
Catechesis Religious Program—

KIRBY, WYANDOT CO., ST. MARY (1861) [CEM] Closed. For inquiries for parish records contact the chancery.

LEIPSIC, PUTNAM CO., ST. MARY (1873) [CEM] Rev. William A. Pifher; Deacons Thomas B. Niese; Benjamin R. Valdez.
Church: 318 State St., Leipsic, 45856-1332. Tel: 419-943-2952; Email: parishoffice@metalink.net; Web: leipsicstmaryparish.org.
School—St. Mary School, (Grades K-8), 129 St. Mary St., Leipsic, 45856-1328. Tel: 419-943-2801; Fax: 419-943-3555; Email: nschroeder@ls.noacsc.org. Sr. Carol Ann Mary Smith, S.N.D., Prin. Lay Teachers 8; Sisters of Notre Dame 1; Students 85.
Catechesis Religious Program—

LEXINGTON, RICHLAND CO., RESURRECTION (1969) Rev. Nelson G. Beaver, V.F.; Deacon Thomas R. Dubois.
Church: 2600 Lexington Ave., Lexington, 44904-1426. Tel: 419-884-0060; Email: resparishadm@gmail.com; Web: resurrectionlexington.org.
Catechesis Religious Program—

LIBERTY, SENECA CO., ST. ANDREW (1834) [CEM] Merged with St. Patrick, Bascom to form SS. Patrick & Andrew.

LIMA, ALLEN CO.
1—ST. CHARLES BORROMEO (1953) [JC]
2200 W. Elm, Lima, 45805-2697. Tel: 419-228-7635; Email: burgesse@stcharleslima.org; Web: www.stcharleslima.org. Rev. Kent R. Kaufman; Deacons Fred Wuebker; James S. Bronder.
School—St. Charles Borromeo School, (Grades PreK-8), 2175 W. Elm St., Lima, 45805-2673. Tel: 419-222-2536; Email: scheidm@sccslima.org; Web: sccslima.org. Megan Scheid, Prin. Lay Teachers 28; Students 408.
2—ST. GERARD (1916)
240 W. Robb Ave., Lima, 45801-2899. Tel: 419-224-3080; Email: cheryln@sgslima.org; Web: www.stgerardchurch.org. Revs. James Szobonya, C.Ss.R.; Michael Houston, C.Ss.R.; Michael Sergi, C.Ss.R.; Mrs. Marta Truex, Business Mgr.
School—St. Gerard School, (Grades PreSchool-8), 1311 N. Main St., Lima, 45801-2818. Tel: 419-222-0431; Fax: 419-224-6580; Email: mtruex@sgslima.org; Web: www.sgslima.org. Mrs. Natalie Schoonover, Prin. Clergy 3; Lay Teachers 16; Students 180.
Catechesis Religious Program—Tel: 419-224-3080, Ext. 230; Email: sparker@sgslima.org. Mrs. Shanda Parker, D.R.E. Students 188.
3—ST. JOHN THE EVANGELIST (1901) [JC]
Mailing Address: 222 S. West St., Lima, 45801-4842. Tel: 419-222-5521; Fax: 419-228-8439; Email: jmstombaugh@wcoil.com; Web: stroselimaohio.org. Very Rev. David M. Ross, V.F., S.T.L., J.C.D.; Deacon Theodore J. Kaser Jr.
Church: 777 S. Main St., Lima, 45804.
Catechesis Religious Program—Tel: 567-242-3089; Email: amick@wcoil.com. Amanda Mick, D.R.E.
4—ST. ROSE OF LIMA (1856) [JC]
Mailing Address: 222 S. West St., Lima, 45801-4842. Tel: 419-222-5521; Fax: 419-228-8439; Email: jmstambaugh@wcoil.com; Web: www.stroselimaohio.org. Very Rev. David M. Ross, V.F., S.T.L., J.C.D.; Deacon Theodore J. Kaser Jr.
Church: McKibben St. & N. West St., Lima, 45801-4294.
School—St. Rose of Lima School, (Grades PreK-8), 523 N. West St., Lima, 45801-4237. Tel: 419-223-6361; Fax: 419-222-2032; Email: judyd@srslima.org. Ms. Donna Judy, Prin. Lay Teachers 9; Sisters 1; Students 128.
Catechesis Religious Program—Tel: 419-222-2087.

LYONS, FULTON CO., OUR LADY OF FATIMA (1946) Closed. For inquiries for parish records contact the chancery.

MANSFIELD, RICHLAND CO.
1—ST. MARY OF THE SNOWS (1949) [JC]
1630 Ashland, Mansfield, 44905-1896. Tel: 419-589-2114; Email: rennpage.mary@mansfieldstmarys.org; Web: www.mansfieldstmarys.org. Rev. Nelson G. Beaver, V.F.; Deacon Allan D. Kopp.
School—St. Mary of the Snows School, (Grades PreK-8), Email: sanders.sue@mansfieldstmarymail.org. Mrs. Susan Sanders, Prin. Students 102.
Catechesis Religious Program—Email: jewingii@gmail.com; Email: mtrmancha@gmail.com; Email: ejh59@hotmail.com. Jenny Ewing, D.R.E.; Mary Mancha, D.R.E.; Judy Hess Pompei, D.R.E.
2—ST. PETER (1844) [CEM]
60 S. Mulberry St., Mansfield, 44902. Tel: 419-524-2572; Email: reindl.kristi@myspartans.org; Web: www.mansfieldstpeters.org. Mailing Address: 104 W. 1st St., Mansfield, 44902-2199. Very Rev. Gregory R. Hite, S.T.L., V.F.; Rev. Austin A. Ammanniti; Deacon John P. Reef.
Church: 54 S. Mulberry St., Mansfield, 44902.
Schools—St. Peter School—(Grades PreK-6), 63 S. Mulberry St., Mansfield, 44902-1909. Tel: 419-524-3351; Fax: 419-524-3366; Email: bauer.madalyn@myspartans.org. Mrs. Madalyn Bauer, Prin. Lay Teachers 25; Students 296.
St. Peter School, (Grades 7-12), Tel: 419-524-0979; Fax: 419-524-3336; Email: haus.tammy@myspartans.org. Michael Wisiniak, Prin. Lay Teachers 27; Students 248.

MARBLEHEAD, OTTAWA CO., ST. JOSEPH (1867) [CEM] [JC] (Slovak)
Mailing Address: 113 James St., Marblehead, 43440-2118. Tel: 419-798-4177; Fax: 419-798-4260; Email: stjoseph@cros.net; Web: stjosephmarblehead.org. 822 Barclay St., Marblehead, 43440. Rev. James E. Brown.
Catechesis Religious Program—Email: carolann@cros.net. Ms. Carol Arntz, D.R.E. Students 64.

MARTIN, OTTAWA CO., OUR LADY OF MT. CARMEL (1917) Rev. Mark J. Herzog, V.F.
Church: 1105 Elliston Rd., Martin, 43445-9601. Tel: 419-836-7681; Email: olmc30@aol.com; Web: olmcbono.parishesonline.com.
Catechesis Religious Program—

MARYGROVE, LUCAS CO., IMMACULATE CONCEPTION (1840) Merged with Saint Elizabeth of Hungary, Richfield Center, and St. Mary of Assumption, Assumption to form Holy Trinity Catholic Parish, Assumption.

MARYWOOD, SENECA CO., ST. MICHAEL'S (1839) [CEM] (German), Closed. For inquiries for parish records contact the chancery.

MAUMEE, LUCAS CO., ST. JOSEPH (1841) [CEM]
104 W. Broadway, Maumee, 43537-2137.
Tel: 419-893-4848; Email: jennifer.drouillard@stjosephmaumee.org. Rev. Keith A. Stripe; Deacons Edgar E. Irelan; Dennis Scherger; Joseph Malenfant; Stephen J. Delisle.
School—St. Joseph School, (Grades PreSchool-8), 112 W. Broadway St., Maumee, 43537-2137.
Tel: 419-893-3304; Fax: 419-891-6969; Email: dianna.johnson@stjosephmaumee.org; Web: stjosephmaumee.org. Mr. David Nichols, Prin. Lay Teachers 20; Students 209.

MILAN, ERIE CO., ST. ANTHONY (1862) [CEM] Rev. Gilbert Mascarenhas, S.A.C.; Deacon David F. Rospert.
Church: 145 Center St., P.O. Box 1200, Milan, 44846-9757. Tel: 419-499-4274; Email: stanthony@neohio.twcbc.com; Web: www.milanstanthony.org.
Catechesis Religious Program—130 S. Main St., Milan, 44846. Tel: 419-499-4300.

MILLER CITY, PUTNAM CO., ST. NICHOLAS (1888) [CEM] Rev. Msgr. Charles E. Singler, D.Min.; Deacon Doyle J. Erford.
Church: 201 E. Main Cross, P.O. Box 40, Miller City, 45864-0040. Tel: 419-876-3481; Email: snhf@fairpoint.net; Web: stnicholasholyfamily.org.
Catechesis Religious Program—Email: dwehri@fairpoint.net. Deborah Wehri, D.R.E. Students 441.

MONROEVILLE, HURON CO., ST. JOSEPH (1861) [CEM]
66 Chapel St., Monroeville, 44847. Tel: 419-465-4142; Email: st.alphonsus.st.joseph.office@gmail.com; Web: stalphonsus-stjoseph.org. Rev. Ronald A. Schock; Deacon Michael L. Wasiniak.
School—St. Joseph School, (Grades PreK-8), 79 Chapel St., Monroeville, 44847. Tel: 419-465-2625; Fax: 419-465-2170; Email: sjs@msjcs.org; Web: www.msjcs.org. Mr. David McDowell, Prin.; Rev. Ronald A. Schock, Admin. Clergy 5; Lay Teachers 8; Students 89.
Catechesis Religious Program—Tel: 419-512-1713; Email: nurse21853@aol.com. Mrs. Diane Wasiniak, D.R.E.

MONTPELIER, WILLIAMS CO., SACRED HEART (1911)
Mailing Address: 220 S. East Ave., Montpelier, 43543-1504. Tel: 419-485-5914; Email: michelea@frontier.com. Rev. James E. Halleron.
Catechesis Religious Program—Tel: 419-272-3181; Email: lahf@frontier.com. Lucinda Held-Faulhaber, D.R.E.

NAPOLEON, HENRY CO., ST. AUGUSTINE (1856) [CEM]
210 E. Clinton St., Napoleon, 43545-1602.
Tel: 419-592-7656; Email: saintaugustineoffice@gmail.com. Rev. J. Douglas Garand; Deacon Jon A. Gottron.
School—St. Augustine School, (Grades PreK-8), 722 Monroe St., Napoleon, 43545-1631.
Tel: 419-592-3641; Email: jim.george@augustinenapoleon.com; Web: staugie@henry-net.com. Jim George, Prin. Lay Teachers 11; Students 58.
Catechesis Religious Program—

NEW BAVARIA, HENRY CO., SACRED HEART OF JESUS (1893) [CEM] (German)
13779 County Rd. Y, New Bavaria, 43548-9738.
Tel: 419-653-4157; Email: shchurch@metalink.net. Rev. Nicholas J. Cunningham.
Catechesis Religious Program—Tel: 419-635-4121.

NEW CLEVELAND, PUTNAM CO., HOLY FAMILY (1862) [CEM]
201 E. Main Cross St., P.O. Box 40, Miller City, 45864. Tel: 419-876-3481; Email: snhf@fairpoint.net. Rev. Msgr. Charles E. Singler, D.Min.; Deacon Doyle J. Erford.
Church: 7359 St. Rte. 109, New Cleveland, 45875.
Catechesis Religious Program—

NEW LONDON, HURON CO., OUR LADY OF LOURDES (1853) [CEM] Rev. Douglas D. Taylor.
Church: 18 Park Ave., New London, 44851-1163.
Tel: 419-929-4401; Email: frkishore.olol@gmail.com; Web: www.ourladyoflourdesnewlondon.webley.com.
Catechesis Religious Program—

NEW RIEGEL, SENECA CO.
1—ALL SAINTS (2005) Rev. Timothy M. Kummerer; Deacon John F. Walter.
Church: 41 N. Perry St., P.O. Box 89, New Riegel, 44853. Tel: 419-595-2567; Email: officeallsaintsparish@midohio.twcbc.com.
Catechesis Religious Program—
Chapels—St. Peter Chapel—11125 W. Twp. Rd. 96, Alvada, 44802.
St. Nicholas Chapel, 8981 W. County Rd. 6, Carey, 43316.
2—ST. BONIFACE (1834) [CEM] Closed. For inquiries for parish records contact the chancery.

NEW WASHINGTON, CRAWFORD CO., ST. BERNARD (1844) [CEM]
412 W. Mansfield, New Washington, 44854.
Tel: 419-492-2295; Email: stbernard@woh.rr.com; Web: www.stbernardnwo.com. 422 W. Mansfield, New Washington, 44854. Rev. George W. Mahas III.
School—St. Bernard School, (Grades K-8), 320 W. Mansfield St., New Washington, 44854.
Tel: 419-492-2693; Fax: 419-492-2604; Email: rking@nwstbernard.k12.oh.us; Email: mobringer@nwstbernard.k12.oh.us; Web: www.nwstbernard.org. Mary Obringer, Prin. Religious Teachers 1; Lay Teachers 5; Students 38.
Catechesis Religious Program—Email: tweithman@nwstbernard.k12.oh.us. Tami Weithman, C.R.E. Students 50.

NORTH AUBURN, CRAWFORD CO., MOTHER OF SORROWS (1879) Closed. For inquiries for parish records contact the chancery. Chapel remains open.

NORTH BALTIMORE, WOOD CO.
1—HOLY FAMILY (2001) Rev. Arthur J. Niewiadomski.
Church: 115 E. Cherry St., North Baltimore, 45872-1134. Tel: 419-257-2319; Email: hfcc@midohio.twcbc.com.
2—OUR LADY OF THE MIRACULOUS MEDAL (1891) Consolidated with Sacred Heart, Cygnet to form Holy Family, North Baltimore.

NORTH CREEK, PUTNAM CO., ST. JOSEPH (1887) (German), Closed. For inquiries for parish records contact the chancery.

NORWALK, HURON CO.
1—ST. ALPHONSUS LIGUORI (1828) [CEM] (Other)
Mailing Address: 66 Chapel St., Monroeville, 44847.
Tel: 419-465-4142; Email: st.alphonsus.st.joseph.office@gmail.com; Web: www.stalphonsus-stjoseph.org. Rev. Ronald A. Schock; Deacon Michael L. Wasiniak.
Church: 1322 Settlement Rd., Norwalk, CA 44857.
Catechesis Religious Program—Email: nurse21853@aol.com. Mrs. Diane Wasiniak, D.R.E.
2—ST. MARY, MOTHER OF THE REDEEMER (1860) [CEM] (Irish) Rev. Gilbert Mascarenhas, S.A.C.; Deacons David F. Rospect; Jack Bleile.
Church: 38 W. League St., Norwalk, 44857-1397.
Tel: 419-668-2005; Email: saintmarys@neohio.twcbc.com; Web: www.stmarynorwalk.org.
Catechesis Religious Program—
3—ST. PAUL (1876) [CEM] (German)
91 E. Main St., Norwalk, 44857-1798.
Tel: 419-668-6044; Fax: 419-663-5770; Email: admin@stpaulchurch.org; Email: katem@stpaulchurch.org; Web: www.stpaulchurch.org. Rev. Msgr. Kenneth G. Morman, V.F., S.S.L.; Rev. Paul A. Schreiner, Parochial Vicar; Deacon James A. Reichert; Mrs. Patricia Krause, Pastoral Assoc.
School—Norwalk Catholic Schools - St. Paul Campus, (Grades PreK-12), 93 E. Main St., Norwalk, 44857-1341. Tel: 419-668-3005; Fax: 419-668-6417; Email: ddoughty@ncsmail.org. Mr. Dennis J. Doughty, Pres.; Mr. James Tokarsky, Prin. (7-12); Mrs. Valerie French, Prin. (Elementary Grades). Lay Teachers 42; Students 734.
Catechesis Religious Program—Email: patk@stpaulchurch.org; Email: kellye@stpaulchurch.org. Kelly Ericsson, D.R.E.; Mrs. Patricia Krause, D.R.E.

OAK HARBOR, OTTAWA CO., ST. BONIFACE (1866)
215 N. Church St., Oak Harbor, 43449-1216.
Tel: 419-898-1389; Email: secretary@sb-oh.org; Web: www.sb-oh.org. Rev. Timothy F. Ferris; Deacon Frank A. Tello.
School—St. Boniface School, (Grades PreSchool-8), 215 Oak St., Oak Harbor, 43449-1227.
Tel: 419-898-1340; Email: school@sb-oh.org; Email: mgreggila@sb-oh.org. Millie Greggila, Prin. Lay Teachers 7; Students 70.
Catechesis Religious Program—Email: dreyouth@gmail.com. Michael Dazley, D.R.E. Students 65.

OREGON, LUCAS CO., ST. IGNATIUS (1883) [CEM] (Territorial) Rev. Mark J. Herzog, V.F.
Church: 212 N. Stadium Rd., Oregon, 43616-1536.
Tel: 419-693-1150; Email: church@stiggys.org; Web: www.stiggys.org.
Catechesis Religious Program—Email: jmittendorf@stiggys.org. Julie Mittendorf, D.R.E.

OTTAWA, PUTNAM CO., SS. PETER AND PAUL (1868) [CEM] Revs. Matthew Jozefiak, C.PP.S.; Richard Friebel, C.PP.S.; Deacon James A. Rump.
Church: 307 N. Locust St., Ottawa, 45875-1495.
Tel: 419-523-5216; Email: jellerbrock@spps.noacsc.org.
School—SS. Peter and Paul School, (Grades K-8), 320 N. Locust St., Ottawa, 45875-1496.
Tel: 419-523-3697; Email: nlanwehr@sppsknights.org. William Wisher, Prin. Lay Teachers 17; Students 260.
Catechesis Religious Program—Students 310.

OTTOVILLE, PUTNAM CO., IMMACULATE CONCEPTION (1848) [CEM]
189 Church St., P.O. Box 296, Ottoville, 45876-0296.
Tel: 419-453-3513; Fax: 419-453-2513. Very Rev. Jerome A. Schetter, V.F.

PAULDING, PAULDING CO.
1—DIVINE MERCY PARISH
417 N. Main St., Paulding, 45879-1291.
Tel: 419-399-2576; Fax: 419-399-2577; Email: finance@divinemercycatholic.com; Web: divinemercycatholic.com. Very Rev. Joseph T. Poggemeyer, V.F., S.T.D.; Deacons David Jordan; David Laker; Rosalio M. Martinez; Robert Lee Nighswander.
Church: 315 N. Main St., Paulding, 45879.
Church: Antwerp Campus, 303 Monroe St., Antwerp, 45813.
Church: Payne Campus, 203 W. Townline St., Payne, 45880.
School—Divine Mercy Parish School, (Grades 1-6), 120 Arturus St., P.O. Box 98, Payne, 45880.
Tel: 419-263-2114; Email: principle@dmcschool.com. Joseph Linder, Prin. Clergy 1; Lay Teachers 5; Students 73.
Catechesis Religious Program—Email: DRE@divinemercycatholic.com. Students 221.
2—ST. JOSEPH (1894) Closed.

PAYNE, PAULDING CO., ST. JOHN THE BAPTIST (1892) [CEM] Closed. Church transferred to a chapel of Divine Mercy, Paulding.

PERRYSBURG, WOOD CO.
1—SAINT JOHN XXIII (2005) Very Rev. Herbert F. Weber, V.F.; Deacon Thomas Headley.
Church: 24250 Dixie Hwy., Perrysburg, 43551.
Tel: 419-874-6502; Email: hweber@stjohn23.org; Web: www.stjohn23.org.
2—ST. ROSE (1861) [CEM] Revs. George E. Wenzinger, V.F.; David Kidd, Parochial Vicar; Deacons Charles W. McDaniel; Victor DeFilippis; Thomas K. Wray; Mr. Robert Hohler, Business Mgr.
Church: 215 E. Front St., Perrysburg, 43551-2193.
Tel: 419-874-4559; Fax: 419-874-4375; Email: parish@saintroseonline.org; Web: www.saintroseonline.org.
School—St. Rose School, (Grades PreK-8), 217 E. Front St., Perrysburg, 43551-2192.
Tel: 419-874-5631; Email: borgelt@saintroseonline.org; Web: saintroseonline.org/school. Dr. Bryon Borgelt, Prin.; Mr. Robert Hohler, Business Mgr. Lay Teachers 27; Students 345.
Catechesis Religious Program—

PLYMOUTH, HURON CO., ST. JOSEPH (1864) Rev. Christopher M. Mileski; Deacon Frederick E. Stockmaster.
Church: 117 Sandusky St., Plymouth, 44865-1132.
Tel: 419-687-4611; Email: stjoeplymouth@gmail.com.
Catechesis Religious Program—

PORT CLINTON, OTTAWA CO., IMMACULATE CONCEPTION (1861) Rev. John C. Missler, V.F.; Deacon Maury A. Hall.
Church: 414 Madison St., Port Clinton, 43452-1922.
Tel: 419-734-4004; Email: icchurchpc@frontier.com; Web: immaculateconceptionpc.com.
School—Immaculate Conception School, (Grades PreK-5), 109 W. Fourth St., Port Clinton, 43452-1816. Tel: 419-734-3315; Fax: 419-734-6172; Email: csnyder@portclintonics.net; Web: www.portclintonics.net. Mrs. Constance Snyder, Prin. Clergy 1; Lay Teachers 8; Students 109.

PUT-IN-BAY, OTTAWA CO., MOTHER OF SORROWS (1866)
Mailing Address: 620 Catawba Ave., P.O. Box 179, Put-In-Bay, 43456-0179. Tel: 419-285-2741; Email: deaconmike@live.com. Very Rev. Nathan Bockrath, V.F., Chap.; Mr. Jimmy McCoy.
Catechesis Religious Program—

REED, SENECA CO., ASSUMPTION (1867) [CEM] (German), Closed. For inquiries for parish records contact the chancery.

REPUBLIC, SENECA CO., ST. ALOYSIUS (1879) [CEM] Closed. For inquiries for parish records contact the chancery.

RICHFIELD CENTER, LUCAS CO., ST. ELIZABETH OF HUNGARY (1914) Merged with Immaculate Conception, Marygrove and St. Mary of Assumption, Assumption to form Holy Trinity Catholic Parish, Assumption. Sacramental records at the Chancery.

ROSSFORD, WOOD CO., ALL SAINTS (1990) Rev. Anthony L. Recker; Deacon Gerald E. Galernik.
Church: 628 Lime City Rd., Rossford, 43460.
Tel: 419-666-1393; Fax: 419-666-5734; Email: parishoffice@allsaintsrossford.com; Web: www.allsaintsrossford.org.
School—All Saints School, (Grades PreSchool-8), 630 Lime City Rd., Rossford, 43460. Tel: 419-661-2070; Fax: 419-661-2077; Email: tfischer@allsaintscatholic.org; Web: www.allsaintscatholic.org. Mrs. Teri Fischer, Prin. Clergy 1; Lay Teachers 18; Students 205.
Catechesis Religious Program—Email: svanhersett@allsaintsrossford.com. Mrs. Susan Van Hersett, D.R.E. Students 51.

ST. STEPHEN, SENECA CO., ST. STEPHEN (1844) [CEM] Closed. For inquiries for parish records contact the chancery.

SALEM TWP., WYANDOT CO., ST. JOSEPH (1849) [CEM]

(English), Closed. For inquiries for parish records contact the chancery.

SANDUSKY, ERIE CO.

1—HOLY ANGELS (1839) [JC]
428 Tiffin Ave., Sandusky, 44870. Tel: 419-625-3698; Email: mhoyles@sanduskycatholic.org; Web: holyangelssandusky.org. Revs. Monte J. Hoyles, J.C.L.; Matthew C. Frisbee; Jeffery Walker.
See Sandusky Central Catholic School, Sandusky under Consolidated Elementary Schools located in the Institution section.

2—ST. MARY'S (1855) [CEM] [JC3] (German)
429 Central Ave., Sandusky, 44870.
Tel: 419-625-7465; Fax: 419-626-2834; Email: office@stmarysandusky.org. Revs. Monte J. Hoyles, J.C.L.; Jeffery Walker; Matthew C. Frisbee; Deacons William G. Burch; Jeff Claar; Philip J. Dinovo.
See Sandusky Central Catholic School, Sandusky under Consolidated Elementary Schools located in the Institution section.

3—SS. PETER AND PAUL (1866) [CEM] [JC]
510 Columbus Ave., Sandusky, 44870.
Tel: 419-625-6655; Tel: 419-625-7500;
Fax: 419-625-6576; Email: office@stspeterpaul.com; Web: peterpaulsandusky.org. Revs. Monte J. Hoyles, J.C.L.; Matthew C. Frisbee; Jeffrey Walker; Deacons William G. Burch; Jeff Claar; Philip J. Dinovo.
See Sandusky Central Catholic School, Sandusky under Consolidated Elementary Schools located in the Institution section.

SHELBY, RICHLAND CO.

1—MOST PURE HEART OF MARY (1866) [CEM] (German) Rev. Christopher M. Mileski.
Church: 29 West St., Shelby, 44875-1155.
Tel: 419-347-2381; Email: parishoffice@stmaryshelby.org; Web: omphm.org.
School—Most Pure Heart of Mary School, (Grades PreK-6), 26 West St., Shelby, 44875-1148.
Tel: 419-342-2626; Fax: 419-347-2763; Email: kstover@stmaryshelby.org; Web: www.stmaryshelby.org. Mrs. Kimberly Stover, Prin. Clergy 2; Lay Teachers 9; Students 106.

2—SACRED HEART OF JESUS (1833) [CEM] (German)
5742 State Rte. 61 S., Shelby, 44875-9080.
Tel: 419-342-2256; Tel: 419-683-1697; Email: jpalm@stjosephcrestline.org; Web: sacredheartbethlehem.org. Rev. Christopher Bohnsack.
School—Sacred Heart of Jesus School, (Grades PreK-8), 5754 State Rte. 61 S., Shelby, 44875-9802.
Tel: 419-683-1697; Fax: 419-342-2797; Email: lmyers@shelbysacredheart.org; Web: sacredheartbethlehem.org. Lisa Myers, Prin. Lay Teachers 8; Students 114.

SPENCERVILLE, ALLEN CO., ST. PATRICK (1858) [JC]
500 S. Canal St., P.O. Box 63, Spencerville, 45887.
Tel: 419-647-6202; Email: stpats45887@gmail.com. Very Rev. Dennis G. Walsh, V.F.; Revs. Douglas D. Taylor, Parochial Vicar; Scott Perry, Parochial Vicar; Immcolata Scarogni, Contact Person.
Catechesis Religious Program—Sr. Immaculata Scarogni, S.C.C., Contact Person.

STRYKER, WILLIAM CO., ST. JOHN THE EVANGELIST (1861) [JC] Closed. For inquiries for parish records contact the chancery.

SWANTON, FULTON CO.

1—HOLY TRINITY (2003) [CEM 4] (German—Irish) Very Rev. Michael G. Dandurand; Deacon Robert Gillen.
Church: 2649 U.S. Hwy. 20, Swanton, 43558-9558.
Tel: 419-644-4014; Email: cgurica@htassumption.org; Web: holytrinityswanton.com.
School—Holy Trinity School, (Grades PreK-8), 2639 U.S. Hwy. 20, Swanton, 43558-9558.
Tel: 419-644-3971; Fax: 419-644-9372; Email: bkulka@htassumption.org; Web: www.holytrinityschool.com. Mr. Brandon Kulka, Prin. Clergy 1; Lay Teachers 16; Students 135.
Catechesis Religious Program—Email: sroof@htassumption.org. Sarah Roof, D.R.E. Students 73.

2—ST. MARY OF ASSUMPTION (1877) (German—Irish), Merged with Immaculate Conception, Marygrove and Saint Elizabeth of Hungary, Richfield Center to form Holy Trinity Catholic Parish, Swanton.

3—ST. RICHARD (1893) [CEM] Revs. Adam L. Hertzfeld, Presbyteral Mod.; Francis Maridas, Parochial Vicar.
Church: 333 Brookside Dr., Swanton, 43558-1097.
Tel: 419-826-2791; Email: parishsec@saintrichard.org; Web: www.saintrichard.org.
School—St. Richard School, (Grades PreK-8),
Tel: 419-826-5041; Email: principal@saintrichard.org. Sr. Jean Marie Walczak, S.N.D., Prin. Students 75.
Catechesis Religious Program—

SYCAMORE, WYANDOT CO., ST. PIUS X (1951)
Mailing Address: 85 S. Sandusky St., Tiffin, 44883.
Tel: 419-447-2087; Fax: 419-447-9940; Email: dscherger@stmarychurch.com. Revs. Gary R. Walters; Anthony J. Coci; Deacon John Daniel.
Church: Saffel St., Sycamore, 44882.
Catechesis Religious Program—Email: torlex@syctelco.com. Kelli Smith, D.R.E.

SYLVANIA, LUCAS CO., ST. JOSEPH (1873) [CEM]
5411 Main St., Sylvania, 43560-2177.
Tel: 419-885-5791; Email: parish@stjoesylvania.org; Web: www.stjoesylvania.org. Very Rev. Msgr. Michael R. Billian, V.F.; Rev. Christopher Hudgin, O.S.F.S.; Deacons Paul J. White; Anthony J. Pistilli.
School—St. Joseph School, (Grades PreK-8),
Tel: 419-882-6670; Fax: 419-885-1990; Email: redwards@stjoesylvania.org. Mr. Robert Edwards, Prin. Lay Teachers 30; Sisters 2; Students 559.
Catechesis Religious Program—Tel: 419-885-2181; Fax: 419-885-8251; Email: rhunyor@stjoesylvania.org. Mrs. Rachael Hunyor, D.R.E. Students 552.

THE BEND, DEFIANCE CO., ST. STEPHEN (1855) [CEM] Closed. For inquiries for parish records contact the chancery.

TIFFIN, SENECA CO.

1—ST. JOSEPH (1845) [CEM]
36 Melmore St., Tiffin, 44883-3098.
Tel: 419-447-5848; Email: stjoetif@tiffinstjoseph.org; Web: tiffinstjoseph.org. Rev. Joseph P. Szybka, V.F.; Deacon David Mileski, Pastoral Assoc.; Mrs. Linda Bowers, Business Mgr.
See Tiffin Calvert Schools under Consolidated Elementary Schools located in the Institution Section.

2—ST. MARY (1831) [CEM] Revs. Gary R. Walters; Anthony J. Coci.
Church: 85 S. Sandusky St., Tiffin, 44883-2140.
Tel: 419-447-2087; Email: tfry@stmarychurch.com; Web: www.stmarychurch.com.
See Tiffin Calvert Schools under Consolidated Elementary Schools located in the Institution Section.
Catechesis Religious Program—Email: rgaietto@stmarychurch.com. Rose Ann Gaietto, D.R.E.

UPPER SANDUSKY, WYANDOT CO.

1—ST. PETER (1857) [CEM] [JC] Closed. For inquiries for parish records contact the chancery.

2—TRANSFIGURATION OF THE LORD (2005) Rev. Antony V. Vattaparambil, O.F.M.Conv.; Deacon Kevin Wintersteller.
Church: 225 N. Eighth St., Upper Sandusky, 43351-1299. Tel: 419-294-1268; Email: ilenemz51@gmail.com.
School—St. Peter Catholic School, (Grades PreK-6), 310 N. 8th St., Upper Sandusky, 43351-1144.
Tel: 419-294-1395; Fax: 419-209-0295; Email: panderson@stpetersupper.com. Ms. Patricia Anderson, Prin. Lay Teachers 10; Students 136.
Chapel—St. Mary Chapel, Main St. at State Rte. 639, Upper Sandusky, 43351.

VAN WERT, VAN WERT CO., ST. MARY OF THE ASSUMPTION (1876) Rev. Stanley S. Szybka; Deacon Andrew McMahon.
Church: 601 Jennings Rd., Van Wert, 45891-9702.
Tel: 419-238-3979; Email: info@stmarysvanwert.com; Web: www.stmarysvanwert.com.
School—St. Mary of the Assumption School, (Grades K-6), 611 Jennings Rd., Van Wert, 45891-9701.
Tel: 419-238-5186; Fax: 419-238-5842; Email: dmetzger@stmarysvanwert.com. Daniel Metzger, Prin. Lay Teachers 8; Students 77.
Catechesis Religious Program—Tel: 419-238-3079.

VERMILION, ERIE CO., ST. MARY (1851) [JC] Rev. Ronald J. Brickner.
Tel: 440-967-8711; Email: parish@stmaryvermilion.org; Web: www.stmaryvermilion.org.
School—St. Mary School, (Grades K-6), 5450 E. Ohio St., Vermilion, 44089-1340. Tel: 440-967-7911;
Fax: 440-967-8287; Email: bbialko@stmaryvermilion.org. Barbara Bialko, Prin. Students 132.

WAKEMAN, HURON CO., ST. MARY (1852) [CEM]
46 E. Main St., P.O. Box 576, Wakeman, 44889.
Tel: 440-839-2023; Email: cschem39@gmail.com. Rev. Kishore Kottana, Chap.; Sr. Carroll Schemenauer, S.N.D., Pastoral Min./Coord.
Catechesis Religious Program—

WALBRIDGE, WOOD CO., ST. JEROME (1962) Very Rev. Eric P. Schild, V.F.; Deacon Paul D. Nungester Sr.
Church: 300 Warner St., Walbridge, 43465-1142.
Tel: 419-666-2857; Email: office@stjeromewalbridge.org; Web: www.stjeromewalbridge.org.
See The Kateri Catholic School System, Oregon under Consolidated Elementary Schools located in the Institution Section.

WAUSEON, FULTON CO., ST. CASPAR (1850) [CEM] [JC]
1205 N. Shoop Ave., Wauseon, 43567-1828.
Tel: 419-337-2322; Email: stcaspar@centurylink.net; Web: www.stcaspar.org. Rev. Stanislaw Tabor.
Catechesis Religious Program—Email: stcasparb@centurylink.net. Ms. Barbara M. Bonfert, C.R.E. Students 197.

WILLARD, HURON CO., ST. FRANCIS XAVIER (1875) [CEM]
Mailing Address: 25 W. Perry St., Willard, 44890-1694. Tel: 419-935-1149; Email: sfxparishoffice@willard-oh.com. Revs. George W. Mahas III, Parochial Admin.; Michael Diemer, M.J., In Res.; Deacon Vincent Foos.
Church: 21 W. Perry St., Willard, 44890-1694. Email: parishangelj@willard-oh.com.
School—St. Francis Xavier School, (Grades K-6),
Tel: 419-935-4744; Email: mcdowell.donna@sfxwillard.org; Web: www.sfxwillard.net. Mrs. Donna McDowell, Prin. Clergy 1; Lay Teachers 8; Students 118.
Catechesis Religious Program—Students 108.

On Duty Outside the Diocese:
Revs.—
Cardone, Joseph P., Sr. Vice Pres. Mission & Values Integration, Mercy Health, Cincinnati
McQuillen, Thomas J., 6616 Beechmont Ave., Cincinnati, 45230
Oxley, Walter R., Congregation for the Doctrine of the Faith, Vatican City State, 00120.

Military Chaplains:
Rev.—
Kirk, David R., Chap. U.S. Army.

Retired:
Rev. Msgr.—
Metzger, Dennis M., V.F., (Retired)
Very Rev.—
Ritter, Charles F., V.F., P.O. Box 341568, 43635
Revs.—
Auth, James E., J.C.L., (Retired), 3030 Tremainsville,, 43613
Bacik, James J., (Retired)
Blaser, John R., (Retired)
Blum, Stephen J., (Retired), 201. N. Pierce St., Delphos, 45833
Brown, Michael O., (Retired)
Caballero, Francisco, (Retired)
Ceranowski, Albert B., (Retired), 26324 Edgewater Dr., Perrysburg, 43551
Ceranowski, Gerald L., V.F., (Retired), 26324 Edgewater Dr., Perrysburg, 43551
Chmiel, Gerald J., (Retired)
Denny, Charles J., (Retired)
DeSloover, A. Robert, (Retired)
Donnelly, P. Martin, (Retired), 2255 Eastbrook Dr., 43613
Duschl, Frederick J., (Retired)
Eckart, Frank K., (Retired), 5600 Cresthaven Ln. #33, 43614
Ensman, Raymond E., (Retired)
Feltman, Philip S., (Retired), 2020 Sanford, Sandusky, 44870
Fisher, Raymond A., (Retired)
Fleck, John W., (Retired)
Gallagher, Anthony, (Retired)
Gorman, Thomas J., (Retired)
Holden, Robert A., (Retired)
Holmer, James J., (Retired)
Howe, J. Norbert, (Retired)
Kehres, Franklin P., (Retired)
Laudick, John R., (Retired)
Lautermilch, David J., (Retired)
LeJeune, Ronald J., (Retired)
Leyland, Thomas J., (Retired)
Lill, Kenneth J., V.F., (Retired)
Littelmann, Edward J., (Retired)
Malanyaon, Joven V., (Retired)
Murd, Francis A., (Retired), 192 St. Francis Ave., Villa 26, Tiffin, 44883
Nassr, Martin B., (Retired)
Nietfeld, Fred J., (Retired), 2860 U.S. 127, Apt. 306, Celina, 45822
Notter, Richard E., (Retired), 5713 Bernath Ct., 43615
Nowakowski, Jerome F., (Retired)
Odey, Thomas E., (Retired)
Peiffer, James E., (Retired)
Reinhart, Robert J., (Retired)
Ring, Daniel J., (Retired), 4649 Allen Cove Rd., Luna Pier, MI 48157
Risacher, James E., (Retired)
Rodrigues, Tommy, (Retired)
Rohen, Patrick J., (Retired)
Sanford, James R., (Retired)
Say, James K., (Retired)
Scherger, Herman F., (Retired)
Schill, Frederick J., (Retired)
Schleter, Edward J., V.F., (Retired)
Schroeder, Stephen L., (Retired), 6607 U.S. State Rte. 224, Ottawa, 45875
Sheperd, Raymond C., (Retired)
Sikorski, Jeffery P., (Retired)
Steinle, James, (Retired)
Stites, John F., (Retired), 10680 Water St., Defiance, 43512
Weibl, Nicholas, (Retired), 760 Tiffin St., Bucyrus, 44820

Weigman, Joseph A., (Retired)
Wilhelm, Robert J., (Retired)
Wurzel, Richard T., S.T.D., (Retired)
Zak, Daniel, (Retired), 1855 Albon Rd., Holland, 43528.

Permanent Deacons:
Ackerman, Thomas
Avina, Phillip, St. Aloysius, Bowling Green
Beisser, Robert A., Christ the King, Toledo
Billmaier, Robert C.
Bistak, Leo T.
Bleile, Jack, St. Mary, Norwalk; St. Anthony, Milan
Bost, Robert
Brahier, Daniel J., St. Thomas More, Bowling Green
Bronder, James S., St. Charles Borromeo, Lima
Bullimore, Douglas, Little Flower of Jesus, Toledo
Burch, William G., St. Mary, Sandusky; Holy Angels, Sandusky; Sts. Peter & Paul, Sandusky
Burkhart, Joseph L.
Busam, John, St. Peter, Huron
Calvillo, Pedro
Campbell, John E.
Carnahan, Richard
Carone, Thomas, Historic Church of St. Patrick & Immaculate Conception, Toledo
Caruso, James D., J.D., Our Lady, Queen of the Most Holy Rosary, Toledo
Cavera, James J.
Claar, Jeff, St. Mary, Sandusky; Holy Angels, Sandusky; Sts. Peter & Paul, Sandusky
Compton, Jeffrey W., Ss. Peter & Paul, Ottawa
Conkle, Rodney C., St. Mary, Edgerton; St. Michael, Hicksville
Coughlin, Donald J.
Daniel, John
DeFilippis, Victor A., St. Rose, Perrysburg
DeLisle, Steven, St. Joseph, Maumee
Derr, Floyd
Diaz, Alfredo, Sacred Heart, Fremont
Dickey, Kenneth G.
Dinovo, Philip J., Holy Angels; St. Mary; Ss. Peter & Paul, Sandusky
Dominique, Thomas, St. Patrick, Bryan
Downey, John F.
Dubois, Thomas R., Resurrection, Lexington
Dudley, James M., Regina Coeli, Toledo
Dunn, James E.
Eier, Michael, St. Michael, Findlay
Erford, Doyle J., Holy Family, New Cleveland; St. Nicholas, Miller City
Fedynich, Robert, Blessed Sacrament, Toledo
Fernandez, Trevor
Flores, Jose
Foos, Vincent
Fritz, Julius J., Holy Trinity, Bucyrus
Galernik, Gerald E., All Saints, Rossford
Garcia, Jose, Epiphany of the Lord, Toledo
Garza, Ignacio
Giaetto, Richard A., St. Mary, Tiffin
Gillen, Brendan, Our Lady, Queen of the Most Holy Rosary, Toledo
Gillen, Robert
Gonzalez, Armando, St. Michael the Archangel, Findlay
Gonzalez, Rene S.
Gottron, Jon A., St. Augustine, Napoleon
Graham, Scott D., St. Isidore, Marysdale
Gubernath, Jerome A., Holy Trinity, Bucyrus
Hall, Maury A., Immaculate Conception, Port Clinton
Hammer, James E.
Hartings, Leo J.
Headley, Thomas, St. John XXIII, Perrysburg
Heban, Richard D.
Heeter, Joseph M.
Heyman, James, St. Ann, Fremont
Hohman, Floyd J.
Holmer, Leon M., Epiphany of the Lord, Toledo
Homier, Mark A., St. John the Evangelist, Defiance
Horning, William L.
Hostutler, James E.
Houghton, Leroy H.
Huffman, David A., Immaculate Conception, Port Clinton
Hulderman, Joseph
Ignatowski, Gerald
Inkrott, Donald W., St. John the Baptist, Glandorf
Irelan, Edgar E., St. Joseph, Maumee
Jackson, Dennis F., St. Patrick, Bryan
Jones, Paul R.
Jordan, David
Junga, Joel F., St. Patrick of Heatherdowns, Toledo
Karpanty, David J., St. Patrick of Heatherdowns, Toledo
Kaser, Theodore J. Jr., St. Rose of Lima
Keller, Stephen
Kern, Mark, St. Michael the Archangel, Findlay
Kest, Joseph Jr., St. Patrick of Heatherdowns, Toledo
Kirk, Gregory, St. Joseph, Galion
Kitzler, James F., Our Lady of Consolation, Carey
Klausing, Robert R., St. Michael, Kalida
Kopp, Allan D., St. Mary, Mansfield
Kromer, John T., St. Wendelin, Fostoria
Lackney, Robert
Laker, David C., Divine Mercy, Paulding
Leahy, Michael D., Mother of Sorrows, Put-in-Bay; St Michael, Kelleys Island
Learned, Michael R. Sr.
Lederman, Paul B., Little Flower of Jesus, Toledo
Lesinski, Robert J., Our Lady of Perpetual Help, Toledo
Lisk, Frederick
Llanas, Ramon
Lochotzki, William
Lottier, Larry F.
Maher, Edward R., St. Joan of Arc, Toledo
Malenfant, Joseph, St. Joseph, Maumee
Marcum, Michael R. II, St. Mary, Bluffton
Martinez, Rosalio M.
Mayer, Jeffrey L., St. Mary, Defiance
McCabe, Patrick
McCoy, Jimmie
McDaniel, Charles W., St. Rose of Lima, Perrysburg
McMahon, Andrew P., St. Mary, Van Wert
Meyer, Donald
Mileski, David, St. Joseph, Tiffin
Miller, George
Moncher, James
Moor, Justin S., Corpus Christi, Toledo
Nelson, Richard, St. Joan of Arc, Toledo
Newton, George E.
Niese, Thomas B., St. Mary, Leipsic
Nighswander, Robert Lee
Nungester, Paul D. Sr., St. Jerome, Walbridge
Nye, Harold
Ovalle, Eduardo
Peeps, Ronald G.
Pence, Michael W.
Perez, Diego E.A.
Petersen, Laurence
Phillips, Eugene D.
Pina, Elias, (Retired)
Pistilli, Anthony J., St. Joseph, Sylvania
Plenzler, Ronald J.
Pluciniak, Edward R.
Przybylek, Stanley
Quinn, Daniel P.
Reef, John P., St. Peter, Mansfield
Reichert, James A., St. Paul, Norwalk
Reinhart, Lewis E.
Ricker, David J., St. John, Delphos
Rife, Dennis T., St. Patrick of Heatherdowns, Toledo
Romo, Bernabe
Romo, Jose
Rospert, David F., St. Anthony, Milan; St. Mary, Norwalk
Rump, James A., Saints Peter and Paul, Ottawa
Sadler, David L., St. Michael the Archangel, Findlay
Sanchez, Salvador
Sarra, Michael J., Queen of the Most Holy Rosary Cathedral, Toledo
Schaupp, Lawrence
Schiefer, David L., St. Wendelin, Fostoria
Schimmoeller, Lawrence, St. Joseph, Fort Jennings
Selmek, Zenon J.
Sheehan, Thomas K., St. Martin de Porres, Toledo
Sheeran, John P., St. John the Evangelist, Delphos
Shell, Melvin J., St. Joseph, Fremont
Shoemaker, Russell M., St. Joan of Arc, Toledo
Siefker, Donald L., St. Anthony of Padua, Columbus Grove
Sisson, Alfred N., St. Joseph, Galion
Smith, David E., St. Patrick Historia, Toledo
St. John, Steven L., St. Patrick, Bryan
Striker, Dennis D.
Talbert, Keith J., St. Michael the Archangel, Findlay
Tello, Frank A., Our Lady of Lourdes, Genoa; St. Boniface, Oak Harbor
Thrun, Gary, Our Lady of Lourdes, Toledo
Tiefenbach, Lawrence
Timbrook, Joseph, St. Michael, Hicksville
Ulmer, William A.
Valdez, Benjamin R., St. Mary, Leipsic
Varano, Dominick J., St. John the Evangelist, Defiance
Vogt, Steven R., Sacred Heart of Jesus, Bethlehem
Vrooman, David
Walter, John F., Saints Patrick & Andrew, Bascom
Warren, Richard
Wasiniak, Michael L., St. Joseph, Monroeville; St. Alphonsus, Peru
Waters, Daniel R., Our Lady of Perpetual Help, Toledo
Weber, John C.
Welch, Harold, Blessed Sacrament, Toledo
Westrick, Eugene
Wethington, Norbert A.
White, Paul J., St. Joseph, Sylvania
Wilson, Larry J., (Serving in Diocese of Columbus)
Wintersteller, Kevin, Transfiguration of the Lord, Upper Sandusky
Wray, Thomas K., St. Rose of Lima, Perrysburg
Wuebker, Frederick J.
Yakir, Michael, serving in the Archdiocese for the Military Services
Zachrich, Lawrence, St. Peter, Archbold
Ziemkiewicz, Jerry, (Serving in the Diocese of Nashville).

INSTITUTIONS LOCATED IN DIOCESE

[A] COLLEGES AND UNIVERSITIES

TOLEDO. *Mercy College of Ohio* (1994) (Grades Associate-Bachelors), 2221 Madison Ave., 43604. Tel: 415-251-1313; Email: susan.wajert@mercycollege.edu; Web: www.mercycollege.edu. Susan C. Wajert, Ph.D., Pres.; Mark Adkins, Vice Pres., Student Affairs; Lori Edgeworth, Vice Pres. Strategic Planning & Enrollment Mgmt.; Trevor Bates, Vice Pres.; Deborah Johnson, Librarian. Sisters of Mercy of the Americas, Mercy Sisters; Sister of Charity of Montreal, Grey Nuns. Clergy 1; Students 1,512; Total Staff 150; Sisters of Notre Dame 1; Clergy/Religious Teachers 1.

SYLVANIA. *Lourdes University*, (Grades Associate-Masters), 6832 Convent Blvd., Sylvania, 43560. Tel: 419-885-3211; Fax: 419-882-3987; Email: tholup@lourdes.edu; Web: www.lourdes.edu. Dr. Mary Ann Gawelek, Pres.; Dr. Geoffrey Grubb, Provost; Mary Arquette, Vice Pres. Inst. Advancement; Sr. Ann Carmen Barone, O.S.F., Vice Pres. Mission & Ministry; Dr. Robert Rood, Vice Pres. Finance & Admin.; Rachel Duff-Anderson, Dean of Student Life; Michelle Rable, Dean; Sr. Sandra Rutkowski, O.S.F., Librarian. Sisters of St. Francis of the Congregation of Our Lady of Lourdes, (O.S.F.). Clergy 6; Sisters 10; Students 1,356; Total Enrollment 1,356; Lay Faculty 60.

Franciscan Theatre and Conference Center of Lourdes University, 6832 Convent Blvd., Sylvania, 43560. Tel: 419-517-8950; Email: mbuehrer@lourdes.edu; Web: www.franciscancenter.org. Michelle Buehrer, Operations Coord.

[B] HIGH SCHOOLS, DIOCESAN

TOLEDO. *Central Catholic High School*, 2550 Cherry St., 43608. Tel: 419-255-2280; Fax: 419-259-2848; Email: info@centralcatholic.org; Web: www.centralcatholic.org. Lori Langenderfer, Asst. Prin.; Kristine Malik, Asst. Prin.- Curriculum & Instruction; Mr. Gregory Dempsy, Asst. Prin.- Athletics; Rev. Matthew R. Rader, Chap. Conducted by Diocesan Priests, Sisters and Laity. Lay Teachers 38; Priests 1; Students 600; Teaching Sisters 1.

LIMA. *Central Catholic High School* (1955) 720 S. Cable Rd., Lima, 45805. Tel: 419-222-4276; Fax: 419-222-6933; Email: swilliams@apps.lcchs.edu; Web: www.lcchs.edu. Mrs. Stephanie Williams, Prin.; Jennifer Patterson, Campus Min. Lay Teachers 21; Students 290.

TIFFIN. *Calvert High School*, 152 Madison St., Tiffin, 44883-0836. Tel: 419-447-3844; Fax: 419-447-2922; Email: mkaucher@calvertcatholic.org; Web: www.calvertcatholic.org. Mr. Michael J. Kaucher, Pres. Lay Teachers 16; Priests 1; Students 205.

[C] HIGH SCHOOLS, PRIVATE

TOLEDO. *St. Francis de Sales High School*, 2323 W. Bancroft St., 43607-1399. Tel: 419-531-1618; Fax: 419-531-9740; Email: esmola@sfstoledo.org; Web: www.sfsknights.org. Rev. Geoffrey N. Rose, O.S.F.S., Pres.; Mr. Eric Smola, Prin. Oblates of St. Francis de Sales.School for boys. Lay Teachers 46; Priests 7; Students 607.

St. John's Jesuit High School and Academy, (Grades 6-12), 5901 Airport Hwy., 43615-7344. Tel: 419-865-5743; Fax: 419-861-5002; Email: pskeldon@sjjtitans.org; Email: lhoyt@sjjtitans.org; Web: www.sjjtitans.org. Mr. Michael Savona, Pres.; Mr. Christopher Knight, Vice Pres.; Spencer Root, Admin.; Philip Skeldon, Admin.; Revs. Brian Lehane, Theology Teacher; Bernie Owens, In Res. USA Midwest Province.School for boys. Lay Teachers 60; Students 670; Clergy/Religious Teachers 2.

Notre Dame Academy, (Grades 7-12), 3535 W. Sylvania Ave., 43623-4479. Tel: 419-475-9359; Fax: 419-724-2640; Email: scullum@nda.org; Web:

www.nda.org. Mrs. Kim Grilliot, Pres.; Mrs. Sarah Cullum, Prin. Sisters of Notre Dame.All-girls college preparatory school, grades 7-12. Lay Teachers 49; Sisters 2; Students 624.

St. Ursula Academy (1854) (School for girls- grades 6-12) 4025 Indian Rd., 43606. Tel: 419-531-1693; Fax: 419-534-5777; Email: mjoseph@toledosua.org; Web: www.toledosua.org. Mrs. Mary Werner, Pres.; Mrs. Nichole Flores, Prin. Sponsored by Ursuline Sisters of the Sacred Heart. Lay Teachers 46; Sisters 1; Students 524.

[D] CONSOLIDATED ELEMENTARY SCHOOLS

TOLEDO. *St. Benedict School*, (Grades PreK-8), 5522 Dorr St., 43615. Tel: 419-536-1194; Fax: 419-531-5140; Email: mhartman@stbenedicttoledo.org; Web: www.stbenedicttoledo.com. Mrs. Martha Hartman, Prin. Little Flower of Jesus & Our Lady of Lourdes schools consolidated to form St. Benedict School. Lay Teachers 15; Students 234.

Central City Ministry of Toledo Schools (CCMT), (Grades K-8), 1933 Spielbusch Ave., 43604-5360. Tel: 419-244-6711; Fax: 419-255-8269; Email: mkravetsky@toledodiocese.org. Mrs. Michelle Kravetsky, Devel. A consortium of two Catholic schools joined together: Rosary Cathedral and Queen of Apostles.

Queen of Apostles Campus, (Grades K-8), 235 Courtland Ave., 43609-2699. Tel: 419-241-7829; Fax: 419-241-4180; Email: jweeman@ccmtschool.org. Sr. Joselyn Weeman, S.N.D., Prin. Clergy 2; Lay Teachers 15; Sisters 3; Students 190.

Rosary Cathedral Campus, (Grades K-8), 2535 Collingwood Blvd., 43610-1400. Tel: 419-243-4396; Fax: 419-243-6049; Email: lsnyder@ccmtschool.org; Web: www.rosarycathedralschool.org. Sr. M. Lynda Snyder, S.N.D., Prin. Lay Teachers 15; Students 220.

DEFIANCE. *Holy Cross Catholic School of Defiance*, (Grades PreK-8), 1745 S. Clinton St., Defiance, 43512. Tel: 419-784-2021; Fax: 419-784-2073; Email: principal@defianceholycross.org; Web: www.defianceholycross.org. Mrs. Rose Reinhart. Holy Cross Catholic School (PreK-8) Lay Teachers 13; Students 137.

FREMONT. *Bishop Hoffman Catholic School*, (Grades K-12), 702 Croghan St., Fremont, 43420. Tel: 419-332-9947; Email: dperin@bishop-hoffman.net. Mr. Tim Cullen, Supt. Students 425.

Sacred Heart Campus, (Grades PreK-5), 500 Smith Rd., Fremont, 43420. Tel: 419-332-7102; Fax: 419-332-1542; Email: awhitfield@bishop-hoffman.net. Teresa Kitchen, Prin. Lay Teachers 9; Students 235.

Saint Joseph Campus, (Grades 6-12), 702 Croghan St., Fremont, 43420. Tel: 419-332-9947; Email: dperin@bishop-hoffman.net. Teresa Kitchen, Prin. Lay Teachers 9; Students 190.

OREGON. *St. Kateri Catholic Schools*, (Grades PreK-12), 3225 Pickle Rd., Oregon, 43616. Tel: 419-693-0465; Fax: 419-697-2816; Email: gskibinski@cardinalstritch.org; Web: www.cardinalstritch.org. Very Rev. Eric P. Schild, V.F., Pres.; Mr. Kevin Parkins, Prin.; Mrs. Melissa Empie, Asst. Prin., Academic Dean. Clergy 1; Lay Teachers 30; Students 530.

SANDUSKY. *Sandusky Central Catholic School*, (Grades PreK-12), 410 W. Jefferson St., Sandusky, 44870-2427. Tel: 419-626-1892; Fax: 419-621-2252; Email: gpalmer@sanduskycc.org; Web: www.sanduskycentralcatholicschool.com/. Mr. Geoff Palmer, Pres. Lay Teachers 55; Students 604.

Sandusky Central Catholic School Elementary, (Grades PreK-5), 410 W. Jefferson St., Sandusky, 44870. Tel: 419-626-1892; Email: gpalmer@sanduskycc.org; Web: www.sanduskycentralcatholicschool.com. Mr. Geoff Palmer, Pres. Students 342.

Sandusky Central Catholic School, MS/HS, (Grades 7-12), SCCS Middle School: Grades 6-8. St. Mary's High School: Grades 9-12 410 W. Jefferson St., Sandusky, 44870-2427. Tel: 419-626-1892; Fax: 419-621-2252; Email: gpalmer@sanduskycc.org. Mr. Geoff Palmer, Pres. SMCC Junior High 102; SMCC High School 160.

TIFFIN. *Calvert Elementary School*, (Grades K-8), 357 S. Washington St., Tiffin, 44883-2879. Tel: 419-447-5790; Email: mkaucher@calvertcatholic.org; Web: www.calvertcatholic.org. Mr. Michael J. Kaucher, Pres. Clergy 1; Lay Teachers 10; Students 345.

[E] ELEMENTARY SCHOOLS, PRIVATE

WHITEHOUSE. *Lial Catholic School* (1972) (Grades PreK-8), 5700 Davis Rd., Whitehouse, 43571-9669. Tel: 419-877-5167; Fax: 419-877-9385; Email: pmcclain@lialschool.org; Web: www.lialschool.org. Sr. Patricia M. McClain, S.N.D., Prin. Sisters of Notre Dame. Clergy 3; Lay Teachers 19; Sisters 3; Students 231.

[F] GENERAL HOSPITALS

TOLEDO. *Mercy Health - St. Anne Hospital, LLC* (2002) 3404 W. Sylvania Ave., 43623. Tel: 419-407-2663; Fax: 419-407-3888; Email: Dorothy_thum@mercy.com; Web: www.mercyweb.org. Mr. Brad Bertke, CEO. Bed Capacity 128; Tot Asst. Annually 129,960; Total Staff 682.

Mercy Health - St. Vincent Medical Center, LLC, 2213 Cherry St., 43608-2691. Tel: 419-251-3232; Fax: 419-251-3810; Email: Dorothy_thum@mercy.com; Web: www.mercyweb.org. Mr. Jeffrey Dempsey, Pres. Grey Nuns and Sisters of Mercy.Affiliated with Mercy Health Partners. Bed Capacity 568; Sisters 1; Tot Asst. Annually 215,638; Total Staff 2,575.

Mercy Health - St. Vincent Medical Center, LLC dba Mercy Children's Hospital, 2222 Cherry St., 43608-2801. Tel: 419-251-3232; Tel: 800-860-6652; Fax: 419-251-3878; Email: Dorothy_thum@mercy.com; Web: www.mercyweb.org. Barbara Diawda-Martin; Mr. Jeffrey Dempsey, Pres.

DEFIANCE. *Mercy Health - Defiance Hospital LLC*, 1404 E Second St., Defiance, 43513. Tel: 419-782-8444; Email: julie_landoll@mercy.com. Deacon Jeffrey L. Mayer, Chap. Bed Capacity 23; Tot Asst. Annually 12,204; Staff 228.

LIMA. *Mercy Health St. Rita's Medical Center* (1918) 730 W. Market St., Lima, 45801-4602. Tel: 419-227-3361; Tel: 800-467-0308; Fax: 419-226-9750; Email: admarcum@mercy.com; Web: www.stritas.org. Mr. Robert Baxter, CEO; Mr. Timothy Rieger, Vice Pres. Finance; Mrs. Amy D. Marcum, Vice Pres. Mission Svcs.; Mr. Matthew Etzkorn, Dir. Spiritual Care; Rev. Charles Obinwa, Chap. Bed Capacity 425; Tot Asst. Annually 431,576; Total Staff 3,141.

OREGON. *Mercy Health - St. Charles Hospital, LLC* (1953) 2600 Navarre Ave., Oregon, 43616. Tel: 419-696-7200; Fax: 419-696-7328; Email: Dorothy_thum@mercy.com; Web: www.mercyweb.org. Craig Albers, Pres. Mercy Health Partners. Bed Capacity 410; Sisters 1; Tot Asst. Annually 132,146; Total Staff 1,057.

TIFFIN. *Mercy Health - Tiffin Hospital, LLC*, 45 St. Lawrence Dr., Tiffin, 44883. Tel: 419-455-7000; Fax: 419-455-7059; Email: julie_landoll@mhsnr.org; Web: www.mercyweb.org. Ms. Lynn Detterman, Pres. & CEO; Ms. Julie Landoll, Dir. Mission & Values Integration and Pastoral Care. Sisters of Mercy of the Americas - Catholic Healthcare Partners. Bed Capacity 120; Patients Asst Anual. 120,000; Tot Asst. Annually 84,679; Total Staff 377.

WILLARD. *Mercy Health - Willard Hospital, LLC*, 1100 Neal Zick Rd., Willard, 44890. Tel: 419-964-5000; Email: Julie_landoll@mercy.com; Web: www.mercyweb.org. Ms. Lynn Detterman, Pres.; Ms. Julie Landoll, Dir. Mission Pastoral Care; Sr. Diane Hay, O.S.F., Chap. Sisters of Mercy of the Americas. Bed Capacity 25; Tot Asst. Annually 39,534; Total Staff 163.

[G] HOMES FOR AGED

TOLEDO. *Franciscan Care Center*, 4111 Holland Sylvania Rd., 43623-2503. Tel: 419-882-6582; Fax: 419-885-1422; Email: jmelia@chilivingcomm.org; Web: www.homeishere.org. Sr. Jordan Schaefer, O.S.F., Chap.; Mr. James Melia, Admin. CHI Living Communities, a subsidiary of Catholic Health Initiatives. Skilled Nursing Beds 109; Staff 125.

Oblate Residences (1980) 1225 Flaire Dr., 43615. 2043 Parkside Blvd., 43607-1597. Tel: 419-724-9851; Email: ertle@oblates.us. Very Rev. Kenneth N. McKenna, O.S.F.S., Prov. Apartments 100.

OREGON. *Sacred Heart Home*, 930 S. Wynn Rd., Oregon, 43616. Tel: 419-698-4331; Fax: 419-698-1109; Email: msoregon@littlesistersofthepoor.org. Sr. Alice Marie Jones, L.S.P., Supr./Pres.; Rev. Joseph A. Weigman, Chap., (Retired). Little Sisters of the Poor. Aged Residents 74; Sisters 10; Tot Asst. Annually 90; Total Staff 102; Independent Living Apartments 18.

SANDUSKY. **The Commons of Providence*, 5000 Providence Dr., Sandusky, 44870. Tel: 419-624-1171; Fax: 419-624-1175; Email: slehmkuhl@chilivingcomm.org; Web: www.homeishere.org. Staci Lehmkuhl, Exec. Dir.; Ms. Rebecca Hilton, Spiritual Adviser / Care Svcs. CHI Living Communities, a subsidiary of Catholic Health Initiatives.; Independent, Assisted Living and Memory Care for Seniors Memory Care 50; Assisted Living 56; Staff 90; Total Assisted 106.

Providence Care Center, 2025 Hayes Ave., Sandusky, 44870. Tel: 419-627-2273; Fax: 419-627-5588; Email: slehmkuhl@chilivingcomm.org; Web: www.homeishere.org. Staci Lehmkul, Exec.; Cheryl Royster, Admin.; Ms. Rebecca Hilton, Spiritual Adviser / Care Svcs. CHI Living Communities, a subsidiary of Catholic Health Initiatives. Skilled Nursing Beds 138; Staff 145.

**Providence Residential Community Corp Apartment and Villa Home Independent Living*, 5055 Providence Dr., Sandusky, 44870. Tel: 419-624-1171; Fax: 419-624-1175; Email: slehmkuhl@chilivingcomm.org; Web: www.homeishere.org. Staci Lehmkuhl, Exec.; Ms. Rebecca Hilton, Spiritual Adviser / Care Svcs. CHI Living Communities, a subsidiary of Catholic Health Initiatives. Residents 87.

[H] MONASTERIES AND RESIDENCES OF PRIESTS AND BROTHERS

TOLEDO. *Oblates of St. Francis de Sales*, 2043 Parkside Blvd., 43607. Tel: 419-724-9851; Email: ertle@oblates.us; Web: www.oblates.us. Revs. Geoffrey N. Rose, O.S.F.S., Pres.; Joseph Newman, O.S.F.S., Vice Pres.; Ronald W. E. Olszewski, O.S.F.S., Chm.; Very Rev. Kenneth N. McKenna, O.S.F.S., Prov.; Revs. Martin C. Lukas, O.S.F.S.; David F. Whalen, O.S.F.S.; Robert F. Schramm, O.S.F.S., Chap.; James F. Cryan, O.S.F.S., Senior Religious, (Retired); Thomas A. Landgraff, O.S.F.S., Senior Religious, (Retired); Bros. Alfred D. Durant, O.S.F.S., Senior Religious; James Petrait, Senior Religious; James Dorazio, In Res.; Revs. Roland Calvert, Editor; John Lehner, O.S.F.S., Instructor, Asst. Pastor; Rudi O. Schwarzkopf, O.S.F.S., Instructor; Alan D. Zobler, O.S.F.S., Instructor; Mr. Craig Irwin, Instructor; Mr. Joseph Katarsky, Instructor. *Provincial Offices*, 2043 Parkside Blvd., 43607-1597. Tel: 419-724-9851; Email: ertle@oblates.us. Very Rev. Kenneth N. McKenna, O.S.F.S., Prov. *Gesu Parish*, 2049 Parkside Blvd., 43607. Tel: 419-531-1421; Fax: 419-531-0270; Email: gesutoledo@gesutoledo.org; Web: gesutoledo.org. Revs. Robert F. Schramm, O.S.F.S., Chap., I.H.M. Motherhouse, Monroe, MI; Martin C. Lukas, O.S.F.S.; James F. Cryan, O.S.F.S., (Retired). *St. Francis de Sales School Faculty House*, 2323 W. Bancroft, 43607. Tel: 419-531-1619; Fax: 419-531-9740; Email: mckenna@oblates.us. Revs. Geoffrey N. Rose, O.S.F.S., Pres.; Joseph Newman, O.S.F.S., Dir.; Christopher Hudgin, O.S.F.S., Instructor; Rudi O. Schwarzkopf, O.S.F.S., Instructor; Alan D. Zobler, O.S.F.S., Instructor; William F. Fisher, O.S.F.S.; Thomas A. Landgraff, O.S.F.S., (Retired); Ronald W. E. Olszewski, O.S.F.S.; Bro. Alfred D. Durant, O.S.F.S. *St. Pius X*, 3011 Carskaddon, 43606. Tel: 419-535-7672; Fax: 419-535-7810; Email: mckenna@oblates.us. Revs. David M. Whalen, O.S.F.S., Instructor & Pastor, St. Pius X; John Lehner, O.S.F.S. *St. Francis de Sales High School Foundation, Inc.* Rev. Ronald W. E. Olszewski, O.S.F.S., Pres. Brothers 2; Priests 13.

BELLEVUE. **Mary Lay Center*, 4500 State Rte. 269, Bellevue, 44811-8921. Tel: 419-483-7381; Fax: 419-483-6400; Email: sorrowfulmother@yahoo.com. Rev. Scott Kramer, C.PP.S., Dir. Total in Residence 5.

Residence for Staff of Sorrowful Mother Shrine. Revs. Yuri (George) J. Kuzara, C.PP.S.; Harold C. Brown, C.PP.S.; Scott Kramer, C.PP.S., Rector; Gene Wilson, C.PP.S.; Bro. Terrence Nufer, C.PP.S.

HOLLAND. *St. John's Jesuit High School Jesuit Community*, 604 Scenic Cir., Holland, 43528. Tel: 313-231-0915; Email: blehane@jesuits.org. Rev. Brian Lehane, Supr.

[I] CONVENTS AND RESIDENCES FOR SISTERS

TOLEDO. *Monastery of the Visitation* (1915) (Contemplative) 1745 Parkside Blvd., 43607-1599. Tel: 419-536-1343; Fax: 419-536-6025; Email: vhm-superior@toast2.net; Web: www.toledovisitation.org. Sr. Marie de Sales Kasper, Supr. Contemplative Order of the Sisters of the Visitation of Toledo, Ohio.

The Contemplative Order of the Visitation of Toledo, Ohio Sisters 19; In Formation 5; Perpetual Vows 14.

Notre Dame Academy Convent, 3535 W. Sylvania Ave., 43623. Tel: 419-913-9712; Email: jrecker@ndec.org. Sr. Joan Marie Recker, S.N.D. Sisters of Notre Dame. Sisters 21.

Sisters of Notre Dame Province Offices (1924) 3912 Sunforest Ct., Ste. B, 43623. Tel: 419-474-5485; Fax: 419-474-1336; Email: awillman@toledosnd.org; Web: www.toledosnd.org. Sr. Mary Delores Gatliff, S.N.D., Prov. Supr. Notre Dame Academy; Double ARC; Maria Early Learning Center; Lial Catholic School, Convent and Renewal Center; Holy Trinity Mission, Papua New Guinea. Perpetually Professed 174.

Ursuline Convent of the Sacred Heart (1854) Congregational Offices, 4045 Indian Rd., 43606. Tel: 419-536-9587; Fax: 419-536-0019; Email: ursulines@toledoursulines.org; Web: www.

toledoursulines.org. Sr. Sandra Sherman, O.S.U., Pres. Associates 137; Professed Sisters 33.

FREMONT. *St. Bernardine Home* (1970) 1220 Tiffin St., Fremont, 43420. Tel: 419-332-8208; Fax: 419-332-4423; Email: jking@mercysc.org. Sr. Joanne Mary Boellner, R.S.M., Community Life Coord.; Joanne Kosta, Dir., Nursing; Rev. Edward J. Schleter, V.F., Chap., (Retired); James M. King, Admin. Sisters of Mercy of the Americas, South Central Community. Sisters 35.

SYLVANIA. *Sisters of St. Francis of the Congregation of Our Lady of Lourdes*, 6832 Convent Blvd., Sylvania, 43560-2897. Tel: 419-882-2016; Fax: 419-824-3626; Email: lstout@sistersosf.org; Web: www.sistersosf.org. Sr. Mary Jon Wagner, O.S.F., CEO. Sponsored ministries include Lourdes University, Sylvania Franciscan Ministries and Sisters of St. Francis Foundation

Sisters of St. Francis of Sylvania, Ohio Sisters 134.

TIFFIN. *St. Francis Convent*, 200 St. Francis Ave., Tiffin, 44883-3458. Tel: 419-447-0435; Fax: 419-447-1612; Email: osftiffin@tiffinfranciscans.org; Web: www.tiffinfranciscans.org. Sr. Sara Aldridge, O.S.F., Community Min.; Rev. Francis A. Murd, Chap., (Retired). Motherhouse and Novitiate, Sisters of St. Francis of Tiffin. Sisters 85; Associates 85.

WHITEHOUSE. *Lial Residence, Sisters of Notre Dame*, 5908 Davis Rd., Whitehouse, 43571. Tel: 419-877-0431; Email: smhmissler@yahoo.com. Sr. Susan M. Missler, S.N.D., Coord. Sisters 5.

[J] RETREAT HOUSES AND CENTERS OF SPIRITUALITY

BELLEVUE. *Sorrowful Mother Shrine* (1850) 4106 State Rte. 269, Bellevue, 44811-9793. Tel: 419-483-3435; Fax: 419-483-6400; Email: sorrowfulmother@yahoo.com; Web: www.sorrowfulmothershrine.org. Revs. Scott Kramer, C.PP.S., Rector; Harold C. Brown, C.PP.S.; Bro. Terrence Nufer, C.PP.S.

CAREY. *Our Lady of Consolation Retreat House*, 321 Clay St., Carey, 43316. Tel: 419-396-7970; Fax: 419-396-3355; Email: retreats@olcshrine.com; Web: www.olcshrine.com. Bro. Tom Hercegovics, O.F.M.Conv., Mgr. Auspices of Shrine of Our Lady of Consolation, Carey, OH.

FREMONT. *Our Lady of the Pines Retreat Center* (1962) 1250 Tiffin St., Fremont, 43420-3562. Tel: 419-332-6522; Fax: 419-333-0238; Email: olprc@pinesretreat.org; Email: saramccoy@pinesretreat.org; Web: www.pinesretreat.org. Sara McCoy, Dir. Sisters of Mercy Total Staff 18.

SYLVANIA. *Sophia Center, Inc.*, 6832 Convent Blvd., Sylvania, 43560. Tel: 419-882-4529; Fax: 419-885-7612; Email: bduffey@sophia.center; Web: www.thesophiacenter.org. Sr. Rachel Marie Nijakowski, O.S.F.S., Dir.; Barbara M. Duffey, C.P.A., Business Mgr.; Sr. Sharon Pollnow, C.S.A., Counselor. Sophia Center provides counseling and psychological testing services to children, families, and adults with a focus on the under-served.

TIFFIN. *St. Francis Spirituality Center*, 200 St. Francis Ave., Tiffin, 44883-3491. Tel: 419-443-1485; Fax: 419-447-1612; Email: peace@franciscanretreats.org; Web: www.franciscanretreats.org. Sr. Edna Michel, O.S.F., Dir. Sisters of St. Francis, Tiffin.

[K] CAMPUS MINISTRY

BLUFFTON. *Bluffton University Campus Ministry*, 160 N. Spring St., Bluffton, 45817. Tel: 419-358-8631; Fax: 419-358-0647; Email: cinkrott@embarqmail.com. Sr. Carol Inkrott, O.S.F., Campus Min.

BOWLING GREEN. *Bowling Green State University Campus Ministry* Attended by St. Thomas More University Parish. 425 Thurstin Ave., Bowling Green, 43402. Tel: 419-352-7555; Fax: 419-352-7557; Email: info@sttoms.com; Web: www.sttoms.com. Rev. Jason J. Kahle; Alicia Schmiesing, Campus Min. Total in Residence 1; Total Staff 14.

DEFIANCE. *Defiance College Catholics on Campus*, 701 N. Clinton, Defiance, 43512. Tel: 419-783-2352; Email: baveresch@defiance.edu. Brenda Averesch, Advisor.

FINDLAY. *University of Findlay Newman Campus Ministry*, 750 Bright Rd., Findlay, 45840. Tel: 419-422-2646; Fax: 419-422-2602; Email: abrown@findlaystmichael.org. Janice Blum, Campus Min.

TIFFIN. *Heidelberg University Newman Campus Ministry*, 310 E. Market St., Campus Center 301, Tiffin, 44883. Tel: 419-448-2066; Fax: 419-448-2209; Email: pstark@heidelberg.edu; Web: www.heidelberg.edu/offices/student/affairs/religion.html. Sr. Barbara Jean Miller, O.S.F., Campus Min.; Paul Stark, Faculty Adviser.

[L] NATIONAL SHRINE

CAREY. *Basilica and National Shrine of Our Lady of Consolation*, 315 Clay St., Carey, 43316. Tel: 419-396-7107; Fax: 419-396-3355; Email: shrineoffice@olcshrine.com; Web: olcshrine.com. Revs. Thomas Merrill, O.F.M.Conv., Rector; John Bamman, O.F.M.Conv.; Bro. Tom Hercegovics, O.F.M.Conv., Pilgrimage/Retreat House Dir.; Rev. Conrad Sutter, O.F.M.Conv., In Res.

[M] MISCELLANEOUS LISTINGS

TOLEDO. *Catholic Charitable Ministries Fund*, 1933 Spielbusch Ave., 43604. Tel: 419-244-6711; Fax: 419-720-0053; Email: wnevolis@toledodiocese.org. Mr. Walter J. Nevolis, CPA, CIA, Sec. Finance & Admin.

**Catholic Charities - Diocese of Toledo, Inc.*, 1933 Spielbusch Ave., 43604. Tel: 419-244-6711; Fax: 419-244-4860; Email: rschuster@toledodiocese.org; Web: www.catholiccharitiesnwo.org. Mr. Rodney O. Schuster, Exec. Dir.

Catholic Club, The (1942) 1601 Jefferson Ave., 43604. Tel: 419-243-7255; Fax: 419-243-6337; Email: info@catholicclub.org; Web: www.catholicclub.org. Mr. Paul Szymanski, Dir.

Catholic Foundation of the Diocese of Toledo, 1933 Spielbusch Ave., 43604. Tel: 419-244-6711; Fax: 419-720-0053; Email: mkravetsky@toledodiocese.org; Web: www.toledodiocese.org. Mrs. Michelle Kravetsky, Contact Person.

Christ Child Society of Toledo, P.O. Box 352254, 43635. Tel: 419-882-1532; Fax: 419-882-1532; Web: christchildsocietytoledo.org. Ms. Jane Larsen, Pres.; Mrs. Anne Marie Blank, Treas.; Ms. Karen Smith, Sec.; Ms. Cecile Bennett, Parliamentarian.

Farley Health Care Corporation, 2200 Jefferson Ave., 43604. Tel: 419-251-2889; Email: barry_hudgin@mhsnr.org. Barry Hudgin, Legal Counsel.

St. Francis de Sales High School Foundation, Inc., 2323 W. Bancroft St., 43607. Tel: 419-531-1618; Fax: 419-531-9740; Email: rolszewski@sfstoledo.org; Web: sfstoledo.org. Rev. Ronald W. E. Olszewski, O.S.F.S., Dir.

Hope Manor, 4702 Violet Rd., 43623. Tel: 419-246-4733; Fax: 419-246-4734; Email: akott@vmc.org. Ms. Cindy Kasprzak, Mgr. Units 100.

Saint John's Jesuit High School and Academy Foundation, 5901 Airport Hwy., 43615. Tel: 419-865-5743; Fax: 419-861-5002; Email: lhoyt@sjjtitans.org; Web: www.sjjtitans.org. Mr. Michael Savona, Pres.

LifeStar Ambulance, Inc. Ambulance & medical transport company. 1402 Lagrange St., 43608. Tel: 419-245-6220; Email: Dorothy_Thum@mercy.com; Web: www.mercyweb.org. Sr. Dorothy Thum, R.S.M., Contact.

Madonna Homes, Inc., 722 Huron St., 43604. P.O. Box 4719, 43620. Tel: 419-244-3758; Fax: 419-246-4738; Email: akott@vmc.org. Ms. Troydean Alexander, Mgr. Units 171.

Mareda, Inc., 1931 Scottwood Ave., Ste. 700, P.O. Box 4719, 43620. Tel: 419-242-2300; Fax: 419-246-4703; Email: akott@vmc.org. Andy Kott, Exec. Dir., Cell: 419-205-1930. Housing Agency of the Diocese of Toledo.

Mercy Foundation, 2213 Cherry St., 43608. Tel: 419-251-2117; Email: Dorothy_thum@mercy.com. Mr. Timothy Koder, Pres.

Mercy Health North, LLC, 2409 Cherry St., MOBI, Ste. 400, 42608. Tel: 419-251-0715; Fax: 419-251-0722; Email: dorothy_thum@mercy.com; Web: www.mercyweb.org. Mr. Robert Baxter, Pres. Total Staff 7,386.

Michaelmas Manor, Inc., 3260 Schneider Rd., 46314. Tel: 419-389-4615; Fax: 419-389-4620; Email: akott@vmc.org. P.O. Box 4719, 43620. Ms. Michelle Smith, Mgr. A corporation organized and operated for the purpose of providing housing facilities and services to elderly persons and handicapped persons. Units for the Elderly 70; Units for the Physically Handicapped 24.

Moody Manor, LLC, 2293 1/2 Kent St., 43620. P.O. Box 4719, 43620. Tel: 419-246-4737; Email: akott@vmc.org. Ms. Gwen Jones, Mgr. Family & Elderly Units 119.

Notre Dame Academy Foundation, 3535 Sylvania Ave., 43623.

Plaza Apartments, 2520 Monroe St., 43620. Tel: 419-244-1881; Fax: 419-246-4710; Email: akott@vmc.org. P.O. Box 4719, 43620. Ms. Angela Shaw, Project Mgr.

Regina Manor, LLC, 3731 N. Erie St., 43611. P.O. Box 4719, 43620. Tel: 419-726-6186; Fax: 419-726-6343; Email: akott@vmc.org. Ms. Kiesha McDuffy, Mgr. Family & Elderly Units 180.

Sylvania Franciscan Health (1984) 3231 Central Park W., Ste. 106, 43617. Tel: 419-882-8373; Fax: 419-882-7360; Email: mwagner@sistersosf.org; Web: www.sylvaniafranciscanhealth.org. Mr. Robert Tracz, C.F.O. An Affiliate of Catholic Health Initiatives.

Sylvania Franciscan Health Foundation, 3231 Central Park W., Ste. 106, 43617. Tel: 419-882-8373; Fax: 419-882-7360; Email: mwagner@sistersosf.org. Sr. Mary Jon Wagner, O.S.F., Supr. An Affiliate of Catholic Health Initiatives.

U.T. Newman Foundation for Student Education and Development, 2955 Dorr St., 43607-3023. Tel: 419-531-4992; Fax: 419-531-1775; Email: kwilliams@ccup.org. Very Rev. Msgr. Michael R. Billian, V.F.

St. Ursula Academy Foundation, Inc., 4025 Indian Rd., 43606. Tel: 419-531-1693; Fax: 419-534-5777; Email: mjoseph@toledosua.org. Mrs. Mary Werner, Pres.

Ursuline Center of Toledo, 4035 Indian Rd., 43606.

Ursuline Convent of the Sacred Heart Foundation, Inc., 4045 Indian Rd., 43606.

CAREY. *Franciscan Mission Association*, 322 West St., Carey, 43316. Tel: 419-396-6455; Email: rmallett1@hotmail.com. Rev. Raymond Mallett, O.F.M.Conv., Dir.

DELPHOS. *St. John Parish Foundation, Inc.*, 201 N. Pierce St., Delphos, 45833. Tel: 419-695-4050; Fax: 419-695-4060; Email: parishfoundation@delphosstjohns.org. Very Rev. Dennis G. Walsh, V.F., Trustee.

FINDLAY. *St. Michael School Educational Foundation*, 750 Bright Rd., Findlay, 45840. Tel: 419-422-2646; Fax: 419-422-2602; Email: dcampbell@findlaystmichael.org. Mr. Dave Seman, Pres.

St. Michael the Archangel School Foundation, St. Michael the Archangel Parish Foundation & St. Michael the Archangel Capital Fund.

FREMONT. *Delaware Acres, Inc.* (1972) 725 Buchanan St., Fremont, 43420. P.O. Box 4719, 43620. Tel: 419-334-9558; Fax: 419-334-9555; Email: akott@vmc.org. Ms. Marcella Miller, Mgr. Family Units 68.

LIMA. *Lima Central Catholic Educational Foundation* (1955) 720 S. Cable Rd., Lima, 45805. Tel: 419-222-4276; Fax: 419-222-6933; Email: kroberts@apps.lcchs.edu. Karen Roberts, Dir.

Magnificat of Lima, Ohio, 8825 Bice Rd., Spencerville, 45887. Tel: 419-647-4888; Email: sharreeb64@gmail.com. Ms. Sharree Reehling, Dir.

S.R.H.C. Foundation, 730 W. Market St., Lima, 45801-4667. Tel: 419-226-9775; Fax: 419-226-9750; Email: JLDaley-Perrin@mercy.com. Jacqueline Daley-Perrin, Pres.; Mr. Timothy Rieger, Chief Fin. Officer.

MONROEVILLE. *Our Lady of the Lake Magnificat Inc.*, 155 Sandusky St., P.O. Box 482, Monroeville, 44847. Tel: 419-465-2691; Email: beddinger155@aol.com; Web: huronmagnificat.weebly.com. Brandy Eddinger, Coord.

PERRYSBURG. **St. Clare Commons*, 12469 Five Point Rd., Perrysburg, 43551. Tel: 419-931-0059; Email: jcuhran@chilivingcomm.org; Web: www.homeishere.org. Mr. James Cuhran, Admin.; Sisters Diana Lynn Eckel, O.S.F., Dir. Mission Integration; Joy Barker, O.S.F., Chap. CHI Living Communities, a subsidiary of Catholic Health Initiatives. Aged Residents 80; Skilled Nursing Beds 60.

SANDUSKY. *Sandusky Central Catholic Educational Foundation, Inc.*, 410 W. Jefferson St., Sandusky, 44870. Tel: 419-626-1892; Email: gpalmer@sanduskycc.org. Rev. Joseph R. Steinbauer, Admin.

SWANTON. *St. Richard's School Endowment Foundation* (1987) 333 Brookside Dr., Swanton, 43558-1097. Tel: 419-826-2791; Fax: 419-826-7256; Email: ahertzfeld@joanofarc.org; Web: saintrichard.org. Deacon Jerry Ziemkiewicz.

SYLVANIA. *Double ARC*, 5800 Monroe St., Bldg. F-5, Sylvania, 43560. Tel: 419-724-1370; Fax: 419-724-1372; Email: info@doublearc.org; Web: doublearc.org. Ms. Janet Bosserman.

**Franciscan Living Communities*, 5942 Renaissance Pl., Ste. A, 43623. Tel: 567-455-0414; Fax: 567-455-0417; Email: aiffland@chilivingcomm.org; Web: www.homeishere.org. Rick Ryan, Pres.

Franciscan Properties, Inc. (1987) 6832 Convent Blvd., Sylvania, 43560. Tel: 419-882-2016; Fax: 419-824-3626; Email: lstout@sistersosf.org. Sr. Mary Jon Wagner, O.S.F., Pres.

Franciscan Shelters-Bethany House, 6832 Convent Blvd., Sylvania, 43560. Tel: 419-727-4948; Fax: 419-729-2053; Email: execdirector@bethanyhousetoledo.org; Web: www.BethanyHouseToledo.org. Ms. Deidre Lashley, Exec. Dir.

Rosary Care Center (1975) 6832 Convent Blvd., Sylvania, 43560. Tel: 419-824-3600;

Fax: 419-824-3626; Email: jphillips@rosarycare.org. Mr. Jason Phillips, Admin. Skilled Nursing Beds 76.

Sisters of St. Francis Foundation, 6832 Convent Blvd., Sylvania, 43560. Tel: 419-882-2016; Fax: 419-824-3626; Email: lstout@sistersosf.org. Sr. Mary Jon Wagner, O.S.F., Pres.

Sylvania Franciscan Ministries, 6832 Convent Blvd., Sylvania, 43560. Tel: 419-882-2016; Fax: 419-824-3626; Email: lstout@sistersosf.org. Sr. Mary Jon Wagner, O.S.F., Pres. Sponsored ministries include Franciscan Properties, Franciscan Shelters, Rosary Care Center and Sophia Center.

TIFFIN. *CSJI-Tiffin, Inc.*, 182 St. Francis Ave., Tiffin, 44883-3491.

St. Francis Home Inc., 182 St. Francis Ave., Tiffin, 44883. Tel: 419-447-2723; Fax: 419-448-1337; Email: sean.riley@stfrancishome.org; Web: www.stfrancistiffin.org. Sean Riley, Exec.; Tyler Webb, Chm. Bed Capacity 121; Residents 146; Tot Asst. Annually 332; Total Staff 218.

St. Francis Senior Ministries Day Care, Inc., 182 St. Francis Ave., Tiffin, 44883. Tel: 419-447-2723; Fax: 419-448-1337; Email: sean.riley@stfrancishome.org; Web: stfrancistiffin.org. Sean Riley, Exec.; Tyler Webb, Chm.

St. Francis Senior Ministries Memorial Foundation, Inc., 182 St. Francis Ave., Tiffin, 44883. Tel: 419-447-2723; Fax: 419-448-1337; Email: Sean.Riley@stfrancishome.org; Web: www.stfrancistiffin.org. Sean Riley, Exec.

Saint Francis Senior Ministries, Inc., 182 St. Francis Ave., Tiffin, 44883. Tel: 419-447-2723; Fax: 419-448-1337; Email: Elizabeth.Westphal@stfrancishome.org; Web: www.stfrancistiffin.org. Sean Riley, Exec.

St. Francis Villas, Inc., 182 St. Francis Ave., Tiffin, 44883. Tel: 419-447-2723; Fax: 419-448-1337; Email: sean.riley@stfrancishome.org; Web: www.stfrancistiffin.org. Sean Riley, Exec.; Tyler Webb, Chm.

**Franciscan Earth Literacy Center*, 194 St. Francis Ave., Tiffin, 44883.

Friedman Village at Saint Francis, LLC, 175 Saint Francis Ave., Tiffin, 44883. Tel: 419-443-1445; Fax: 419-443-1508; Email: sean.riley@stfrancishome.org; Email: carrie.boes@stfrancishome.org. Sean Riley, Exec.; Carrie Boes, Admin.

Tiffin Calvert Foundation (1974) 152 Madison St., Tiffin, 44883-0836. Tel: 419-447-3844; Email: eric@engleshook.com. Mr. Michael J. Kaucher, Pres.; Rev. Anthony J. Coci, Chap.

VERMILION. *St. Mary's Church Education Endowment Foundation*, 731 Exchange St., Vermilion, 44089-1330. Tel: 440-967-8711; Fax: 440-967-8712; Email: parish@stmaryvermilion.org; Web: www.stmaryvermilion.org. Rev. Ronald J. Brickner.

WILLARD. *Mercy Willard Foundation*, 1100 Neal Zick Rd., Willard, 44890. Tel: 419-964-5107; Fax: 419-245-6073; Email: dorothy_thum@mercy.com; Web: mercyweb.org.

RELIGIOUS INSTITUTES OF MEN REPRESENTED IN THE DIOCESE

For further details refer to the corresponding bracketed number in the Religious Institutes of Men or Women section.

[]—*Congregation of the Holy Ghost of the Immaculate Heart of Mary (Holy Ghost Fathers)* (Nigeria).

[0480]—*Conventual Franciscans* (Our Lady of Consolation Prov.)—O.F.M.Conv.

[0690]—*Jesuit Fathers and Brothers*—S.J.

[]—*Missionaries of St. Francis de Sales* (USA Vice Province)—M.S.F.S.

[0910]—*Oblates of St. Francis de Sales*—O.S.F.S.

[1070]—*Redemptorist Fathers* (Baltimore Prov.)—C.SS.R.

[0990]—*Society of the Catholic Apostolate (Pallottines)*—S.A.C.

[1060]—*Society of the Precious Blood* (Cincinnati Prov.)—C.PP.S.

RELIGIOUS INSTITUTES OF WOMEN REPRESENTED IN THE DIOCESE

[3710]—*Congregation of the Sisters of Saint Agnes*—C.S.A.

[4190]—*The Contemplative Order of the Sisters of the Visitation of Toledo, Ohio*—V.H.M.

[1430]—*Franciscan Sisters of Our Lady of Perpetual Help*—O.S.F.

[2575]—*Institute of the Sisters of Mercy of the Americas* (Cincinnati, OH)—R.S.M.

[2340]—*Little Sisters of the Poor* (Baltimore Prov.)—L.S.P.

[2519]—*Religious Sisters of Mercy of Alma, Michigan*—R.S.M.

[0440]—*Sisters of Charity of Cincinnati, Ohio*—S.C.

[0660]—*Sisters of Christian Charity* (Mendham, NJ)—S.C.C.

[2990]—*Sisters of Notre Dame*—S.N.D.

[1530]—*Sisters of St. Francis of the Congregation of Our Lady of Lourdes, Sylvania, Ohio*—O.S.F.

[3930]—*Sisters of St. Joseph of the Third Order of St. Francis*—S.S.J.-T.O.S.F.

[3260]—*Sisters of the Precious Blood* (Dayton, OH)—C.PP.S.

[1760]—*Sisters of the Third Order of St. Francis of Penance and Charity*—O.S.F.

[4120-06]—*Ursuline Nuns of the Congregation of Paris*—O.S.U.

DIOCESAN CEMETERIES

TOLEDO. *Calvary*, 2224 Dorr St., 43607. Tel: 419-536-3751; Email: info@cathcemtoledo.org; Web: www.cathcemtoledo.org. Mr. Bob Shenefield, Dir.

Mount Carmel, 15 E. Manhattan Blvd., 43608. Tel: 419-536-3751; Fax: 419-531-0946; Email: info@cathcemtoledo.org. Mailing Address: 5725 Hill Ave., 43615. Mr. Robert Shenefield, Dir.

Resurrection, 5725 Hill Ave., 43615. Tel: 419-531-5747; Fax: 419-531-0946; Email: info@cathcemtoledo.org; Web: www.cathcemtoledo.org. Mr. Bob Shenefield, Dir.

FREMONT. *St. Joseph*, Tel: 419-332-8756

LIMA. *Gethsemane*

SANDUSKY. *Catholic Cemeteries of Sandusky*, 2020 Sanford St., Sandusky, 44870. Tel: 419-625-2673; Fax: 419-502-3011; Email: Catholiccemeteries@bex.net. Deacon Jeff Claar, Dir.

NECROLOGY

† Knueven, Gerald E., (Retired), Died Nov. 23, 2018
† Parker, William C., (Retired), Died Dec. 6, 2017
† Ricker, John Michael, (Retired), Died Sep. 6, 2017
† Schroeder, Dennis A., (Retired), Died Jan. 27, 2018

An asterisk (*) denotes an organization that has established tax-exempt status directly with the IRS and is not covered by the USCCB Group Ruling.

Diocese of Trenton

(Dioecesis Trentonensis)

Most Reverend

DAVID M. O'CONNELL, C.M., J.C.D., D.D.

Bishop of Trenton; ordained May 29, 1982; appointed Coadjutor Bishop of Trenton June 4, 2010; consecrated July 30, 2010; appointed Tenth Bishop of Trenton December 1, 2010. *Office: Chancery/Pastoral Center, 701 Lawrenceville Rd., Trenton, NJ 08648.*

MINISTRARE NON MINISTRARI

Chancery/Pastoral Center: 701 Lawrenceville Rd., Trenton, NJ 08648. Tel: 609-406-7400; Fax: 609-406-7412.

ESTABLISHED AUGUST 11, 1881.

Square Miles 2,156.

Legal Corporate Title: "The Diocese of Trenton."

Comprises four Counties in the State of New Jersey: Burlington, Mercer, Monmouth and Ocean.

For legal titles of parishes and diocesan institutions, consult the Chancery Office.

STATISTICAL OVERVIEW

Personnel	
Bishop	1
Priests: Diocesan Active in Diocese	147
Priests: Diocesan Active Outside Diocese	6
Priests: Retired, Sick or Absent	59
Number of Diocesan Priests	212
Religious Priests in Diocese	23
Total Priests in Diocese	235
Extern Priests in Diocese	6
Ordinations:	
Diocesan Priests	4
Transitional Deacons	1
Permanent Deacons in Diocese	233
Total Brothers	48
Total Sisters	207
Parishes	
Parishes	99
With Resident Pastor:	
Resident Diocesan Priests	85
Resident Religious Priests	8
Without Resident Pastor:	
Administered by Priests	6
New Parishes Created	7
Closed Parishes	14
Professional Ministry Personnel:	
Brothers	10
Sisters	15
Lay Ministers	49
Welfare	
Catholic Hospitals	2
Total Assisted	135,000
Health Care Centers	1
Total Assisted	3,010
Homes for the Aged	2
Total Assisted	100
Day Care Centers	11
Total Assisted	1,988
Specialized Homes	7
Total Assisted	389
Special Centers for Social Services	79
Total Assisted	194,962
Residential Care of Disabled	10
Total Assisted	72
Other Institutions	231
Total Assisted	13,693
Educational	
Diocesan Students in Other Seminaries	16
Total Seminarians	16
Colleges and Universities	1
Total Students	2,300
High Schools, Diocesan and Parish	6
Total Students	4,085
High Schools, Private	5
Total Students	730
Elementary Schools, Diocesan and Parish	31
Total Students	8,922
Elementary Schools, Private	3
Total Students	420
Catechesis/Religious Education:	
High School Students	150
Elementary Students	44,242
Total Students under Catholic Instruction	60,865
Teachers in the Diocese:	
Priests	4
Brothers	4
Sisters	17
Lay Teachers	1,229
Vital Statistics	
Receptions into the Church:	
Infant Baptism Totals	6,076
Minor Baptism Totals	432
Adult Baptism Totals	188
Received into Full Communion	87
First Communions	7,045
Confirmations	7,476
Marriages:	
Catholic	975
Interfaith	241
Total Marriages	1,216
Deaths	5,771
Total Catholic Population	733,000
Total Population	2,047,623

Former Bishops—Rt. Revs. MICHAEL J. O'FARRELL, D.D., cons. Nov. 1, 1881; died April 2, 1894; JAMES A. MCFAUL, D.D., LL.D., cons. Oct. 18, 1894; died June 16, 1917; Most Revs. THOMAS J. WALSH, S.T.D., J.C.D., cons. July 25, 1918; transferred to Newark, NJ, March 2, 1928; JOHN J. MCMAHON, D.D., cons. April 26, 1928; died Dec. 31, 1932; MOSES E. KILEY, S.T.D., cons. March 17, 1934; appt. Archbishop of Milwaukee, Jan. 1, 1940; WILLIAM A. GRIFFIN, D.D., appt. Bishop of Trenton, May 22, 1940; cons. May 1, 1938; died Jan. 1, 1950; GEORGE W. AHR, S.T.D., appt. Bishop of Trenton, Jan. 28, 1950; cons. March 20, 1950; retired June 23, 1979; died May 5, 1993; JOHN C. REISS, D.D., J.C.D., ord. May 31, 1947; appt. Titular Bishop of Simidicca and Auxiliary of Trenton Oct. 21, 1967; cons. Dec. 12, 1967; appt. Bishop of Trenton March 4, 1980; installed April 22, 1980; resigned July 1, 1997; died March 4, 2012.; JOHN M. SMITH, J.C.D., D.D., ord. May 27, 1961; appt. Titular Bishop of Tre Taverne and Auxiliary Bishop of Newark Dec. 1, 1987; cons. Jan. 25, 1988; appt. Bishop of Pensacola-Tallahassee June 25, 1991; installed July 31, 1991; appt. Coadjutor Bishop of Trenton Nov. 21, 1995; appt. Bishop of Trenton July 1, 1997; retired Dec. 1, 2010; died Jan. 22, 2019.

Chancery/Pastoral Center—701 Lawrenceville Rd., Trenton, 08648. Tel: 609-406-7400; Fax: 609-406-7412.

Vicar General and Moderator of the Curia—Rev. Msgr. THOMAS N. GERVASIO, 701 Lawrenceville Rd., Trenton, 08648.

Chancellor—701 Lawrenceville Rd., Trenton, 08648. MRS. TERRY GINTHER.

Episcopal Vicars—Ocean County: Very Rev. STANLEY P. LUKASZEWSKI, E.V. Burlington County: Very Rev. PHILLIP C. PFLEGER, E.V. Mercer County: Rev. Msgr. MICHAEL J. WALSH. Monmouth County: Rev. Msgr. EDWARD J. ARNISTER, J.C.L.

Vice Chancellors—Rev. Msgr. JAMES G. INNOCENZI; Rev. MICHAEL T. MCCLANE, J.C.L.

Episcopal Master of Ceremonies—Rev. CARLO CALISIN.

Executive Administrative Assistant to the Bishop—MRS. GRACE MAGEE.

Records Analyst and Archivist—Sr. NANCY HERRON, R.S.M.

Office of Canonical Services and the Tribunal—Chancery/Pastoral Center, 701 Lawrenceville Rd., P.O. Box 5147, Trenton, 08638-0147. Tel: 609-406-7411; Fax: 609-406-7424.

Judicial Vicar—Rev. Msgr. JAMES G. INNOCENZI.

Adjutant Judicial Vicars—Rev. MICHAEL T. MCCLANE, J.C.L.; Very Rev. OSCAR B. SUMANGA, J.C.D.

Defenders of the Bond—Revs. PETER J. ALINDOGAN, J.C.L.; MICHAEL T. MCCLANE, J.C.L.; Deacon JOSEPH A. HANNAWACKER, J.C.L.

Promoter of Justice—Rev. PETER J. ALINDOGAN, J.C.L.

Tribunal Judges—Revs. FELIKS M. KOSAT, S.V.D., J.C.L.; MICHAEL M. NGUYEN, C.M., J.C.L.; JAVIER A. DIAZ, J.C.L.; Rev. Msgrs. EDWARD J. ARNISTER, J.C.L.; JOHN K. DERMOND, J.C.L., (Retired); WALTER E. NOLAN, (Retired); EUGENE M. REBECK, (Retired); RALPH W. STANSLEY, (Retired); Revs. JOHN J. SCULLY, (Retired); CHARLES B. WEISER, (Retired).

Secretary of the Tribunal and Notary—MS. EVELYN AGUIAR; MS. ROSEIMELDA MOORE.

College of Consultors—Rev. Msgrs. EDWARD J. ARNISTER, J.C.L.; THOMAS N. GERVASIO; THOMAS J. MULLELLY, J.D., LL.M.; LEONARD F. TROIANO, (Retired); Very Revs. ROBERT S. GRODNICKI, V.F.; DAMIAN J. MCELROY, V.F.; PHILLIP C. PFLEGER, E.V.; Rev. JACEK W. LABINSKI, S.T.D.

Episcopal Council—Rev. Msgrs. EDWARD J. ARNISTER, J.C.L.; THOMAS N. GERVASIO; THOMAS J. MULLELLY, J.D., LL.M.; MICHAEL J. WALSH; LEONARD F. TROIANO, (Retired); Very Revs. JEFFREY E. LEE; STANLEY P. LUKASZEWSKI, E.V.; PHILLIP C. PFLEGER, E.V.; DANIEL F. SWIFT.

Vicars Forane (Deans)—Rev. Msgr. SAM A. SIRIANNI, V.F.; Very Revs. DENNIS A. APOLDITE, V.F.; JOHN P. BAMBRICK, V.F.; TIMOTHY J. CAPEWELL, V.F.; ROBERT S. GRODNICKI, V.F.; DANIEL HESKO, V.F.; ROBERT HOLTZ, V.F.; DAMIAN J. MCELROY, V.F.; MICHAEL MANNING, V.F.

Council of Deacons and Vicariate Representatives—Burlington Co.: Deacon GARY L. SCHMITT. Mercer Co.: Deacon RICHARD ARCARI. Monmouth Co.: Deacon STEPHEN A. SANSEVERE. Ocean Co.: Deacon STEVEN A. WAGNER.

Diocesan Finance Council—Most Rev. DAVID M. O'CONNELL, C.M., Pres.; Rev. Msgr. THOMAS N. GERVASIO; MR. A. KEVIN CIMEI, CFO; MR. HARRY R. HILL, Esq.; MR. ROBERT J. DUNNE III, Chm.; MR. MICHAEL J. CASTELLANO; MR. WILLIAM N. DOOLEY; MR. ANTHONY J. MINGARINO; MR. ROBERT D. FINAN; MR. WILLIAM S. HAINES JR.; Deacon JAMES J. KNIPPER; MR. THOMAS P. MULLOOLY; MR. EDWARD J. SMITH.

Censores Librorum—Revs. JOHN P. CZAHUR; PABLO T. GADENZ, S.T.D., S.S.L.; MICHAEL J. HALL; Very Rev. DAMIAN J. MCELROY, V.F.; Revs. GEORGE A. MEDINA; DAVID S. SWANTEK, M.A., M.Div.; JOEL R. WILSON.

Office of Fiscal Administration

CFO—Mr. A. Kevin Cimei.

Department of Finance—Chancery/Pastoral Center: 701 Lawrenceville Rd., Trenton, 08648. Tel: 609-403-7120; Fax: 609-406-7414. Mrs. Carolynn Thompson, Dir.

Department of Development—Chancery/Pastoral Center: 701 Lawrenceville Rd., Trenton, 08648. Tel: 609-403-7128; Fax: 609-406-7443. Mr. Stephen J. Nicholl, Dir.; Ms. Mariann Gilbride, Assoc. Dir. Devel.

Department of Computer Services—Chancery/Pastoral Center, 701 Lawrenceville Rd., Trenton, 08648. Tel: 609-403-7166; Fax: 609-406-7442. Mr. Anthony DeLorenzo, Dir.

Department of Property and Construction—Chancery/Pastoral Center: 701 Lawrenceville Rd., Trenton, 08648. Tel: 609-403-7195; Fax: 609-406-7412. Mr. Scot Pirozzi, Dir. Associate Directors: Mr. Kenneth J. Nowak, Facilities Mgmt.; Deacon Neil Pirozzi, Property.

Department of Cemeteries—Chancery: 701 Lawrenceville Rd., Trenton, 08648. Tel: 609-403-7120; Fax: 609-406-7414. Deacon David O'Connor, Dir.

St. Mary Cemetery & Mausoleum, Hamilton—1200 Cedar Ln., Hamilton, 08610. Tel: 609-394-2017; Fax: 609-393-1293. Mrs. Erin Gallway-Blatt, Office Mgr.

Jesus, Bread of Life Cemetery—3055 Fostertown Rd., Mount Laurel, 08054. Tel: 856-317-6400. Ms. Maria Guzman-Paczkowski, Office Mgr.

Construction & Real Estate Commission—Mr. Scot Pirozzi, Chm., Tel: 609-403-7195; Fax: 609-406-7412.

Office of Temporal Administration

CAO—Chancery: 701 Lawrenceville Rd., Trenton, 08648. Tel: 609-403-7208; Fax: 609-406-7450. Mr. Joseph Bianchi, SPHR, SHRM-SCP.

Department of Risk Management—Chancery: 701 Lawrenceville Rd., Trenton, 08648. Tel: 609-403-7189; Fax: 609-403-7215. Mr. Joseph Cahill, Dir.

Department of Human Resources—Chancery: 701 Lawrenceville Rd., Trenton, 08648. Ms. Angela Gitto, Dir., Tel: 609-403-7164; Fax: 609-406-7450; Mrs. Erica Armitage, Assoc. Dir. Benefits, Tel: 609-403-7219; Fax: 609-406-7450.

Office of Worship

Office of Worship—Rev. Michael J. Hall, Dir., Tel: 609-403-7160; Ms. Carolyn Norbut, Administrative Asst., Tel: 609-403-7171.

Office of Child and Youth Protection

Office of Child & Youth Protection—Mr. Joseph Bianchi, SPHR, SHRM-SCP, Exec. Dir., Tel: 609-403-7208; Fax: 609-406-7450; Mrs. Margaret Dziminski, Assoc. Dir., Fax: 609-406-7441; Mrs. Maureen Fitzsimmons, L.P.C., Victim Assistance Coord., Tel: 609-403-7129.

Office of Diocesan Planning

Vicar for Diocesan Planning—Rev. Msgr. Leonard F. Troiano, Vicar, (Retired), Tel: 609-403-7159.

Vocations

Director of Vocations—Rev. Michael W. Wallack, Tel: 609-403-7152; Very Rev. Daniel F. Swift, Assoc. Dir., Tel: 609-654-8208; Rev. Garry Koch, Assoc. Dir., Tel: 732-264-4712.

Office of Catholic Education

Vicar for Catholic Education—Rev. Gabriel Zeis, T.O.R., B.A., M.Div., Th.M., Ed.M., Tel: 609-406-9396; Fax: 609-406-7429.

Department of Catholic Schools—Mrs. JoAnn Tier, Supt., Tel: 609-403-7145; Fax: 609-406-7429; Dr. Margaret Boland, Assoc. Supt., Tel: 609-403-7147; Mr. Daniel O'Connell, Assoc. Dir. Curriculum & Instruction, Tel: 609-403-7173; Mrs. Judith Nicastro, Assoc. Dir. School Boards, Mktg. & Government Programs, Tel: 609-403-7127; Fax: 609-406-7416.

Department of Catechesis (Catechetics, Sacraments of Initiation, & RCIA)—Mrs. Denise Contino, Dir., Tel: 609-406-7179; Fax: 609-406-7418; Mr. Brian Jefferes, Assoc. Dir., Tel: 609-403-7133.

Holy Innocents Society—Mrs. Patricia Hertz, Pres., 170 Cranberry Rd., Toms River, 08753. Tel: 732-255-6216.

Office of Communications and Media

Office of Communications and Media—Email: dotcom@dioceseoftrenton.org.

Executive Director—Ms. Rayanne Bennett, Chancery/Pastoral Center, 701 Lawrenceville Rd., Trenton, 08648. Tel: 609-403-7188; Email: rbenne@dioceseoftrenton.org.

Associate Director and Coordinator of Spanish Language, Communications and Media—Mr. Matthew Greeley, Tel: 609-403-7212; Email: mgreel@dioceseoftrenton.org.

Coordinator of Digital and Social Media—Tel: 609-403-7137. Ms. Brittany Wilson; Ms. Katie Cerni, Email: kcerni@dioceseoftrenton.org.

The Monitor—Chancery/Pastoral Center: 701 Lawrenceville Rd., Trenton, 609-403-7188. Tel: 609-403-7199. Ms. Rayanne Bennett, Assoc. Publisher, Tel: 609-403-7188; Email: rbenne@dioceseoftrenton.org; Ms. Jennifer Mauro, Mng. Editor, Tel: 609-403-7135; Email: jmauro@dioceseoftrenton.org; Ms. Mary Stadnyk, Assoc. Editor, Tel: 609-403-7172; Email: mstadn@dioceseoftrenton.org; Ms. Ann Pilato, Business Office, Tel: 609-403-7131; Email: apilat@dioceseoftrenton.org.

Department of Multimedia Productions—Chancery/Pastoral Center, 701 Lawrenceville Rd., Trenton, 08648. Web: www.realfaithtv.com. Ms. Marianne Hartman, Dir., Tel: 609-406-7402; Fax: mhartm@dioceseoftrenton.org; Ms. Rosemary Kimball, Assoc. Dir., Tel: 609-406-7405; Email: rkimba@dioceseoftrenton.org.

Office of Pastoral Life & Mission

Executive Director—Mrs. Terry Ginther, Tel: 609-403-7143; Fax: 609-406-7456.

Department of Pastoral Care—Mrs. Deanna V. Sass, M.A., Dir., 701 Lawrenceville Rd., Trenton, 08648. Tel: 609-403-7157; Fax: 609-406-7458.

Department of Evangelization & Family Life—Mr. Josue Arriola, Dir., Tel: 609-403-7155; Fax: 609-406-7403.

Department of Youth & Young Adult Ministries—Tel: 609-403-7140; Fax: 609-406-7403. Mr. Daniel Waddington, Dir.

Department of Pastoral Planning—Mrs. Terry Ginther, Dir., Tel: 609-403-7143; Fax: 609-406-7456.

Campus Ministries—Mrs. Terry Ginther.

Bede House—College of New Jersey, 492 Ewingsville Rd., Trenton, 08638. Tel: 609-771-0543. Rev. Erin Brown, Chap. & Catholic Campus Min.

Rider University Catholic Campus Ministry—(see St. Ann Parish, Lawrenceville): 1253 Lawrence Rd., Lawrenceville, 08648. Tel: 609-882-8077. Rev. Leandro B. Dela Cruz, Admin.

Aquinas Institute—Princeton Univ., 24 Charlton St., Princeton, 08540. Tel: 609-924-1820. Rev. Gabriel Zeis, T.O.R., B.A., M.Div., Th.M., Ed.M., Chap. & Catholic Campus Min.

Catholic Center—Monmouth Univ., 16 Beechwood Ave., West Long Branch, 07764. Tel: 732-229-9300. Mrs. Cristina D'Averso Collins, Catholic Campus Min.

Catholic Scouting—Rev. Michael A. Santangelo, Chap., Church of the Epiphany, 615 Thiele Rd., Brick, 08724. Tel: 732-458-0220.

Ecclesial Movements

Charismatic Renewal—Rev. Jeffrey J. Kegley, St. Mary Parish, 19 Cherry Tree Farm Rd., Middletown, 07748. Tel: 732-671-0071; Fax: 732-671-6125.

Cursillo—Rev. Edward H. Blanchett, Visitation Parish, 730 Lynwood Ave., Brick, 08723. Tel: 732-477-0028; Fax: 732-477-1274.

Legion of Mary—Rev. Marian F. Kokorzycki, Chap., St. Mary of the Lake, 43 Madison Ave., Lakewood, 08701.

Retreat Centers

Francis House of Prayer—Sr. Marcella Springer, S.S.J., Dir., Mailing Address: P.O. Box 392, Rancocas, 08073. Tel: 609-877-0509; Fax: 609-877-5810; Email: fhop@verizon.net; Web: www.fhop.org.

Upper Room—Co-Directors: Sisters Maureen Christensen, R.S.M.; Maureen Conroy, R.S.M.; Trudy Ahern, S.S.J., 3455 W. Bangs Ave., Bldg. 2, Neptune, 07754. Tel: 732-922-0550; Fax: 732-922-3904; Email: office@theupper-room.org; Web: www.theupper-room.org.

Office of Clergy and Consecrated Life

Vicar for Clergy & Consecrated Life, Director of Seminarians—Rev. Msgr. Thomas J. Mullelly, J.D., LL.M., Tel: 609-403-7181; Fax: 609-406-7453.

Ministry of Clergy Personnel—Rev. Msgr. Thomas J. Mullelly, J.D., LL.M., Dir., Tel: 609-403-7181; Fax: 609-406-7453; Deacon Michael J. Riley, Assoc. Dir., Tel: 609-403-7134; Fax: 609-406-7453.

Ministry of Consecrated Life—Sr. Rose McDermott, S.S.J., Delegate for Rel. & Institutes of Consecrated Life, Tel: 609-406-7430; Fax: 609-406-7413.

Office of Catholic Social Services

Executive Director—Chancery: 701 Lawrenceville Rd., Trenton, 08648. Tel: 609-403-7180; Fax: 609-406-7412. Ms. Brenda L. Rascher, M.S.W., J.D.

Parish Counseling Services—Mrs. Maureen Fitzsimmons, L.P.C., Chancery: 701 Lawrenceville Rd., Trenton, 08648. Tel: 609-403-7129; Fax: 609-406-7412.

Collier Youth Services—Sr. Deborah M. Drago, L.C.S.W., Exec. Dir., 160 Conover Rd., P.O. Box 300, Wickatunk, 07765. Tel: 732-946-4771; Fax: 732-332-1240; Web: www.collieryouthservices.org.

**Mercy Center Corporation*—Sr. Carol Ann Henry, R.S.M., M.S.W., Dir., 1106 Main St., Asbury Park, 07712. Tel: 732-774-9397; Fax: 732-988-8709; Web: www.mercycenternj.org.

**Project Paul*—Mr. Sal Cortale, Exec. Dir., 211 Carr Ave., Keansburg, 07734. Tel: 732-787-4887; Fax: 732-495-7072; Email: propaul@aol.com; Web: www.propaul.org.

**Long Beach Island Community Center Inc.—4700 Long Beach Blvd., Long Beach Township, 08008.* Tel: 609-494-8861; Fax: 609-494-3956; Web: www.stfranciscenterlbi.org. Ms. Wendy Saunders, L.C.S.W., Exec. Dir.

**Visitation Home, Inc.*—Ms. Denise Reil, Exec. Dir., Mailing Address: P.O. Box 11242, Hamilton, 08620. Tel: 609-838-1187; Email: visitationhome@gmail.com.

Catholic Charities—Ms. Marlene Lao'-Collins, Exec. Dir., 383 W. State St., P.O. Box 1423, Trenton, 08607-1423. Tel: 609-394-5181; Fax: 609-695-6978; Web: www.catholiccharitiestrenton.org.

Catholic Campaign for Human Development—Rev. John C. Garrett, Dir., 260 Conrow Rd., Delran, 08075. Tel: 856-461-6555.

Catholic Relief Services—223 E. Union St., Burlington, 08016. Tel: 609-386-0152. Rev. Michael Kennedy, Dir.

Mount Carmel Guild—73 N. Clinton Ave., Trenton, 08609. Tel: 609-392-5159; Fax: 609-392-5903; Email: information@mtcarmelguild.org; Web: www.mtcarmelguild.org. Ms. Mary Inkrot, Exec. Dir.

Mercer County CYO—Mr. Thomas G. Mladenetz, Exec. Dir., 920 S. Broad St., Trenton, 08611. Tel: 609-396-8383; Email: tom@cyomercer.org; Web: www.cyomercer.org.

**Center for FaithJustice*—Ms. Stephanie J. Peddicord, Exec. Dir., 24 Rossa Ave., Lawrenceville, 08648. Tel: 609-498-6216; Fax: 609-498-6216; Email: speddicord@faithjustice.org; Web: www.faithjustice.org.

CLERGY, PARISHES, MISSIONS AND PAROCHIAL SCHOOLS

CITY OF TRENTON

(Mercer County)

1—St. Mary Cathedral (1868)
151 N. Warren St., 08608. Tel: 609-396-8447; Email: smc.office@smc-trenton.org; Web: saintmaryscathedral-trenton.org. 149 N. Warren St., 08608. Rev. Msgr. Joseph L. Roldan, Rector; Rev. Neiser Cardenas, Vicar; Deacons Emiliano Vazquez; Jose Beauchamps; Luis Ramos.
Catechesis Religious Program—211 N. Warren St., 08608. Email: jalvarez@smc-trenton.org. Julio Alvarez, D.R.E. Students 228.

2—St. Anthony (1921) Closed. Sacramental records maintained at Our Lady of Sorrows-St. Anthony Parish, Hamilton.
High School—McCorristin High School, Closed. Records maintained at Trenton Catholic Academy, Hamilton.

3—Blessed Sacrament (1912) Closed. Sacramental records maintained at Blessed Sacrament-Our Lady of the Divine Shepherd Parish, Trenton.

4—Blessed Sacrament-Our Lady of the Divine Shepherd (2005) Merged with Sacred Heart, Trenton to form Parish of the Sacred Heart, Trenton.

5—The Church of the Incarnation-St. James (2006)
1545 Pennington Rd., 08618. Tel: 609-882-2860; Fax: 609-637-0460; Email: isjparishoffice@gmail.com; Web: www.incarnationstjames.org. Revs. Thomas Morris, O.SS.T.; Kenneth G. Borgesen, O.SS.T., In Res.; Charles J. Flood, O.SS.T., In Res.; Deacons Thomas H. Rivella; Joseph A. Hannawacker, J.C.L.; James A. Alessi; Ronald Kraemer Sr., Business Mgr.
Catechesis Religious Program—Email: isjfaithformation@gmail.com. Sr. Lucy Ptak, L.S.I.C., D.R.E. Students 64.

6—DIVINE MERCY PARISH (2005) Merged with Sacred Heart, Trenton. Sacramental records at Parish of the Sacred Heart, Trenton.

7—ST. FRANCIS OF ASSISIUM (1844) [CEM 2] Closed. Sacramental records maintained at Sacred Heart Church, Trenton.

8—ST. HEDWIG (1904) [CEM 2] (Polish)
872 Brunswick Ave., 08638. Tel: 609-396-9068; Email: sthedwig@comcast.net. Rev. Jacek W. Labinski, S.T.D.; Deacons Thomas H. Watkins Jr.; Barry Zadworny.
Catechesis Religious Program—Dorothy Zadworny, C.R.E. Students 282.

9—HOLY ANGELS (1921) Closed. Sacramental records maintained at St. Raphael-Holy Angels Parish, Hamilton.

10—HOLY CROSS (1891) [CEM] Closed. Sacramental records maintained at Divine Mercy Parish, Trenton.

11—IMMACULATE CONCEPTION (1874) Closed. Sacramental records maintained at Our Lady of the Angels Parish, Trenton.

12—INCARNATION (1947) Closed. For inquiries for parish records, see Incarnation-St. James Parish, Trenton.

13—ST. JAMES (1919) Closed. For inquiries for parish records, see Incarnation-St. James Parish, Trenton.

14—ST. JOACHIM (1901) Closed. Sacramental records maintained at Our Lady of Angels Parish, Trenton.

15—ST. JOSEPH (1891) (Spanish)
540 N. Olden Ave., 08638. Tel: 609-394-5757; Email: elena@sjctrenton.com. Rev. Msgr. Joseph L. Roldan.
Catechesis Religious Program—37 Sherman Ave., 08638. Tel: 609-218-6834; Email: erickaro2010@gmail.com. Miss Ericka Rodriguez, D.R.E. Students 158.

16—ST. MICHAEL (1921) Closed. Sacramental records maintained at Church of St. Ann, Lawrenceville.

17—OUR LADY OF GOOD COUNSEL (1942)
137 W. Upper Ferry Rd., West Trenton, 08628. Tel: 609-882-3277; Email: parishrectory@olgcc.net. Rev. Michael J. Hall; Deacons John Bonner; Steven K. Szmutko.
Catechesis Religious Program—Tel: 609-883-9005. Brenda O'Callaghan, Dir. Students 115.

18—OUR LADY OF MOUNT CARMEL, Closed. For Sacramental records please contact St. Mary Cathedral, Trenton.

19—OUR LADY OF SORROWS (1939) Closed. Sacramental records maintained at Our Lady of Sorrows-St. Anthony Parish, Hamilton.

20—OUR LADY OF THE ANGELS PARISH (2005)
19 Bayard St., 08611. Tel: 609-695-6089; Email: olaparish@olanj.org. Rev. Cesar A. Rubiano, Admin.; Deacons Guido Mattozzi; Benito Torres; Sisters Carolyn Houck, M.P.F., Pastoral Assoc.; Domenica Troina, M.P.F., Asst. Pastoral Assoc.; Greys Lopez, Admin. Asst.
Office: 21-23 Bayard St., 08611.
Catechesis Religious Program—Students 200.

21—OUR LADY OF THE DIVINE SHEPHERD (1941) Closed. Sacramental records maintained at Blessed Sacrament-Our Lady of the Divine Shepherd Parish, Trenton.

22—SACRED HEART, Merged with Blessed Sacrament-Our Lady of the Divine Shepherd, Trenton to form Parish of the Sacred Heart, Trenton.

23—PARISH OF THE SACRED HEART (1814) [CEM]
343 S. Broad St., 08608. Tel: 609-393-2801; Email: secretary@trentonsacredheart.org. Very Rev. Dennis A. Apoldite, V.F.; Revs. Thomas Kunnath, Parochial Vicar; Edward Kwoka, Parochial Vicar; Charles Muorah, Parochial Vicar
Legal Name: Parish of the Sacred Heart, Trenton, N.J.
Catechesis Religious Program—Email: reled@trentonsacredheart.org. Mary Tovar, D.R.E. Students 154.

24—SS. PETER AND PAUL (1899) [CEM] Closed. Sacramental records maintained at Divine Mercy Parish, Trenton.

25—ST. RAPHAEL (1943) Closed. Sacramental records maintained at St. Raphael-Holy Angels Parish, Hamilton.

26—ST. STANISLAUS (1890) [CEM] Closed. Sacramental records maintained at Divine Mercy Parish, Trenton.

27—ST. STEPHEN (1903) [CEM] Closed. Sacramental records maintained at Our Lady of the Angels Parish, Trenton.

28—ST. VINCENT DE PAUL (1954)
555 Yardville Allentown Rd., 08620. Tel: 609-585-6470; Email: rectory@svdpnj.org. Revs. Stanley Krzyston; Rogatus Mpeka; Adam Midor, Parochial Vicar.
Catechesis Religious Program—Tel: 609-585-5484. Johanna Kraemer, D.R.E. Students 117.

OUTSIDE THE CITY OF TRENTON

ALLENTOWN, MONMOUTH CO., ST. JOHN (1878) [CEM]
1282 Yardville-Allentown Rd., Allentown, 08501-1830. Tel: 609-259-3391; Email: stjohnallentown@optonline.net; Web: www.stjohnromancatholic.org. Rev. Brian P. Woodrow; Deacon Joseph Hepp.
Catechesis Religious Program—Tel: 609-259-3586; Email: sjbreled@optimum.net. Mrs. Lauren Walters, C.R.E. Students 425.

ASBURY PARK, MONMOUTH CO.

1—THE CHURCH OF MOTHER OF MERCY, ASBURY PARK, N.J. (2014) [CEM]
1212 First Ave., Asbury Park, 07712. Tel: 732-775-1056; Email: cshafto@momapnj.org; Web: www.momapnj.org. Revs. Miguel Virella, S.V.D.; George Koottappillil, S.V.D.; Paul Janvier, S, V.D.; Messan Tettekpoe, S.V.D.
Res.: 805 Pine St., Asbury Park, 07712.
School—Our Lady of Mt. Carmel School, (Grades K-8), First Ave. & Pine St., Asbury Park, 07712. Tel: 732-775-8989; Fax: 732-775-0108; Email: judeboyce@hotmail.com. Sr. Jude Catherine Boyce, S.S.J., Prin. Clergy 1; Lay Teachers 14; Sisters 1; Students 210.
Catechesis Religious Program—Tel: 732-776-7164; Email: bchiriboga@momapnj.org. Blanca Chiriboga, D.R.E. Students 405.

2—HOLY SPIRIT (1879) [CEM] Merged with Our Lady of Mt. Carmel, Asbury Park to form The Church of Mother of Mercy, Asbury Park. Sacramental records at The Church of Mother of Mercy.

3—OUR LADY OF MT. CARMEL (1905) Merged with Holy Spirit, Asbury Park to form The Church of Mother of Mercy, Asbury Park.

4—ST. PETER CLAVER (1943) (African American), Closed. Sacramental records maintained at Our Lady of Mount Carmel Parish, Asbury Park.

ATLANTIC HIGHLANDS, MONMOUTH CO., THE CHURCH OF OUR LADY OF PERPETUAL HELP-SAINT AGNES, ATLANTIC HIGHLANDS, N.J. (1890)
103 Center Ave., Atlantic Highlands, 07716. Tel: 732-291-0272; Email: kpost@olph-sta.org. Rev. Fernando A. Lopez; Deacon Robert J. Johnson.
Catechesis Religious Program—Tel: 732-291-2035. Mr. Kevin Conolly, D.R.E. Students 396.

AVON-BY-THE-SEA, MONMOUTH CO., ST. ELIZABETH (1907) Merged with Ascension, Bradley Beach to form Parish of St. Teresa of Calcutta, Bradley Beach.

BARNEGAT, OCEAN CO., ST. MARY (1942) [CEM]
747 W. Bay Ave., P.O. Box 609, Barnegat, 08005-0609. Tel: 609-698-5531; Email: stmarys19@comcast.net; Web: www.stmarybarnegat.com. Rev. Msgr. Kenard J. Tuzeneu; Revs. Nestor Chavenia; Walter Andre Quiceno, Parochial Vicar; Deacons Patrick Martin; Philip Fiore; Ronald Haunss; Joseph A. Vivona; Frank Campione; Steven A. Wagner; James Petrauskas; Joseph A. Fiorillo; John Hoey.
Parish Center: 100 Bishop Ln., Manahawkin, 08050.
Catechesis Religious Program—Tel: 609-597-7600; Email: cindy@stmarybarnegat.com. Cynthia Craft, C.R.E. Students 1,110.
Mission—St. Mary of the Pines.

BAY HEAD, OCEAN CO., SACRED HEART (1913)
751 Main Ave., Bay Head, 08742. Tel: 732-899-1398, Ext. 1; Email: shrcbh@comcast.net; Web: www.sacredheartbyhead.com. Rev. Douglas Freer.
Catechesis Religious Program—John Paglione, D.R.E. Students 134.

BAYVILLE, OCEAN CO., ST. BARNABAS (1966)
33 Woodland Rd., P.O. Box I, Bayville, 08721-0320. Tel: 732-269-2208; Email: parishoffice@stbarnabasbayville.com; Web: www.stbarnabasbayville.com. Very Rev. Stanley P. Lukaszewski, E.V.; Rev. Carlos A. Florez, Parochial Vicar; Deacons Robert Gay; Stanley D. Kendrick; George J. Swanson.
Catechesis Religious Program—Email: mbritanak@stbarnabasbayville.com. Mary P. Britanak, C.R.E. Students 1,072.

BELMAR, MONMOUTH CO., ST. ROSE (1888)
603 Seventh Ave., Belmar, 07719. Tel: 732-681-0512; Email: carol@strosebelmar.com; Web: strosebelmar.com. Rev. Msgr. Edward J. Arnister, J.C.L.; Rev. Christopher Dayton; Deacons Eugene G. Malhame Jr.; Richard J. Weber; Eugene Genovese; Robert Folinus.
School—St. Rose School, (Grades K-8), 605 Sixth Ave., Belmar, 07719. Tel: 732-681-5555; Fax: 732-681-5890; Email: wroberts@srgs.org. Gregory Guito, Prin. Lay Teachers 23; Students 337.
Catechesis Religious Program—
Tel: 732-681-0512, Ext. 419; Email: srdonna@strosebelmar.com. Sr. Donna D'Alia, D.R.E. Students 290.
Convent—610 Eighth Ave., Belmar, 07719.

BEVERLY, BURLINGTON CO., ST. JOSEPH (1864) Merged with St. Peter's, Riverside to form The Church of Jesus, the Good Shepherd, Riverside, N.J.

BORDENTOWN, BURLINGTON CO.

1—ST. MARY, Merged with Parish of Saints Francis and Clare, Florence Township to form Parish of Mary, Mother of the Church, Bordentown.

2—PARISH OF MARY, MOTHER OF THE CHURCH (1837) [CEM]
45 Crosswicks St., Bordentown, 08505. Tel: 609-298-0261; Email: calphonse@mmotcp.org; Web: www.stmarysbordentown.org. Revs. Joseph G. Hlubik; Felix F. Venza, In Res., (Retired); Deacons Gary T. Richardson; Thomas F. Shea; Ronald F. Zalegowski; Lawrence W. Finn Sr.
Legal Name: Parish of Mary, Mother of the Church, Bordentown, N.J.
Catechesis Religious Program—Tel: 609-291-8281; Email: office@stmarysre.org. Margaret Zola, C.R.E. Students 482.

BRADLEY BEACH, MONMOUTH CO.

1—ASCENSION, Merged with St. Elizabeth Church, Avon-by-the-Sea to form Parish of St. Teresa of Calcutta, Bradley Beach.

2—PARISH OF ST. TERESA OF CALCUTTA (1907)
501 Brinley Ave., Bradley Beach, 07720. Tel: 732-774-0456; Email: saintteresa@stocp.org. Very Rev. Jerome M. Nolan, V.F., (Retired); Deacons John Kopcak; Richard D. Coscarelli
Legal Name: Parish of St. Teresa of Calcutta, Bradley Beach, N.J.
Catechesis Religious Program—Karen Kopcak, Dir. Students 99.

BRANT BEACH, OCEAN CO., ST. FRANCIS OF ASSISI (1971)
4700 Long Beach Blvd., Long Beach Township, 08008-3926. Tel: 609-494-8813; Email: jscullion@dioceseoftrenton.org; Email: mhuber@stfrancislbi.org; Web: www.stfrancisparishlbi.org. Revs. James Scullion, O.F.M.; John Frambes; Scott Brookbank; Deacon Robert Cunningham; Michelle Beck, Dir. Music Ministry; Jo Anne Reeder, Dir. Worship Ministry.
Catechesis Religious Program—Theresa Cassata, O.F.S., Family Faith Formation Coord.; Brian Ott, Youth Min.; Ellen Halvorsen, Elementary Coord.; Marion Pierri, Conformation Coord. Students 320.
Missions—St. Thomas Aquinas—2nd & Atlantic, Beach Haven, 08008.
St. Clare, 56th & Long Beach Blvd., Loveladies, 08008.
St. Thomas of Villanova, 13th & Long Beach Blvd., Surf City, 08008.

BRICK TOWN, OCEAN CO.

1—ST. DOMINIC (1962)
250 Old Squan Rd., Brick, 08724. Tel: 732-840-1410; Email: bwoodrow@dioceseoftrenton.org. Rev. Msgr. James J. Brady, V.F., (Retired); Revs. Joseph Gnarackatt, (Retired); Michael Gentile; Deacons Damian Ayers; Edward Buecker; Ms. Brigid Hughes, Pastoral Ministry.
School—St. Dominic School, Tel: 732-840-1412; Email: cbathmann@stdomschool.org; Web: www.stdomschool.org. Carol Bathmann, Prin. Lay Teachers 35; Students 485.
Catechesis Religious Program—Mrs. Marge Moran, D.R.E. Students 596.

2—EPIPHANY (1973)
615 Thiele Rd., Brick, 08724. Tel: 732-458-0220; Email: carol@churchofepiphany.org. Rev. Michael A. Santangelo; Deacons Ron Nowak; Michael Mullarkey; Louis Commisso.
Res.: 641 Thiele Rd., Brick Town, 08724.
Epiphany Parish Hall—621 Herbertsville Rd., Brick, 08724.
Catechesis Religious Program—Tel: 732-785-0872; Fax: 732-458-0855. Students 316.

3—VISITATION (1942); (Established as parish 1948)
755 Mantoloking Rd., Brick, 08723. Tel: 732-477-0028; Email: info@visitationRCchurch.org; Web: www.visitationRCchurch.org. 730 Lynnwood Ave., Brick, 08723-5397. Revs. Edward H. Blanchett; Joseph A. Jakub, Parochial Vicar; Deacons Edward Fischer III, (Retired); Salvatore Vicari; Nicola Stranieri.
Catechesis Religious Program—Tel: 732-477-5217; Email: ngrodberg@visitationrcchurch.org. Ms. Nancy Grodberg, C.R.E. Students 396.

BROWNS MILLS, BURLINGTON CO., ST. ANN (1906)
22 Trenton Rd., Browns Mills, 08015-3236. Tel: 609-893-3246; Email: stannschurch22@hotmail.com; Web: www.stannschurch.org. Revs. Krzysztof Pipa, Admin.; Pierre Lunimbu, Parochial Vicar; Deacons Michael J. O'Brien; Charles D. Raylman.
Catechesis Religious Program—Students 154.
Stations—Burlington Co. Minimum Security Jail—Pemberton Township.
Burlington Co. Juvenile Detention Center, Pemberton.
Deborah Heart & Lung Center, Browns Mills. Tel: 609-893-6611.
Aspen Hills, Tel: 609-726-7000.

BURLINGTON, BURLINGTON CO.

1—ALL SAINTS (1910) (Polish), Closed. For inquiries for parish records please see St. Katharine Drexel Parish, Burlington.

2—THE PARISH OF ST. KATHARINE DREXEL (2008) [CEM 3]
223 E. Union St., Burlington, 08016.
Tel: 609-386-0163; Tel: 609-386-0152;

Fax: 609-386-0085; Email: parish@stkatharinedrexel-nj.org; Web: www.stkatharinedrexel-nj.org. Revs. Christopher P. Picollo; Michael Kennedy, Parochial Vicar; Deacons Alexander A. Punchello Sr., RCIA Coord.; Alfred Pennise; Walter J. Karpecik Jr.
Legal Name: The Parish of St. Katharine Drexel, Burlington, N.J.
School—St. Paul School, (Grades PreK-8), 250 James St., Burlington, 08016. Tel: 609-386-1645; Fax: 609-386-1345; Email: info@stpaulbrl.org; Web: stpaulbrl.org. Kimberly Cioci, Prin. Lay Teachers 20; Students 163.
Catechesis Religious Program—Email: kdelprato@stkatharinedrexel-nj.org; Email: alexpunchello@comcast.net. Kathleen Del Prato, C.R.E. Students 460.

CINNAMINSON, BURLINGTON CO., ST. CHARLES BORROMEO (1961)
2226 Riverton Rd., P.O. Box 2220, Cinnaminson, 08077. Tel: 856-829-3322; Email: dkirk@pcscb.com. Rev. Daniel E. Kirk; Deacons William S. Sepich; Carl Sondeen; Gerald Doughty; John Hvizdos; Romeo B. Modelo Jr.
School—St. Charles Borromeo School, (Grades PreK-8), 2500 Branch Pike, Cinnaminson, 08077.
Tel: 856-829-2778; Fax: 856-829-3411; Email: mglass@scbpschool.com. Mrs. Kathryn Chesnut, Prin. Clergy 1; Lay Teachers 24; Students 265.
Catechesis Religious Program—Tel: 856-829-9119; Email: phafner@pcscb.com. Mrs. Patricia Hafner, C.R.E. Students 598.

COLTS NECK, MONMOUTH CO., ST. MARY'S (1887)
1 Phalanx Rd., Colts Neck, 07722. Tel: 732-780-2666; Fax: 732-780-0394; Email: parishoffice@stmaryscoltsneck.org; Web: www.stmaryscoltsneck.org. Very Rev. Jeffrey E. Lee; Deacon John Wedemeyer; Mr. Edwin Sevillano, Business Mgr.; Andrew J. Macirowski, Pastoral Min./Coord.; Dr. James J. Bridges, Pastoral Min./Coord.
Legal Title: St. Mary's Catholic Church
Res.: 4 Williamsburg South, Colts Neck, 07722.
Catechesis Religious Program—
Tel: 732-780-2666, Ext. 305; Email: religioused@stmaryscoltsneck.org. Dr. James J. Bridges, D.R.E.; Deacon Vincent L. Rinaldi, Pastoral Assoc. Students 507.

DEAL, MONMOUTH CO., ST. MARY OF THE ASSUMPTION (1901) Merged with St. Jerome Church, West Long Branch to form Parish of Our Lady of Hope, West Long Branch.

DELRAN, BURLINGTON CO.
1—CHURCH OF THE HOLY NAME (1972) Merged with St. Casimir, Riverside to form The Church of the Resurrection, Delran Township, N.J.
2—THE CHURCH OF THE RESURRECTION (2008)
260 Conrow Rd., P.O. Box 1099, Delran, 08075.
Tel: 856-461-6555; Email: resurrection2@comcast.net; Web: www.resurrection2.org. Rev. John C. Garrett; Deacons William E. Briggs; Daniel J. Meehan; James F. Cattanea
Legal Name: The Church of the Resurrection, Delran Township, N.J.
Res.: 502 New Jersey Ave., Riverside, 08075.
Catechesis Religious Program—Email: rich@resurrection2.org. Rich Scanlon, D.R.E. Students 150.

EATONTOWN, MONMOUTH CO.
1—ST. DOROTHEA (1905)
240 Broad St., Eatontown, 07724. Tel: 732-542-0148; Email: fathchuck@aol.com; Email: karin@strdorothea.org; Web: stdorothea.org. Revs. Charles M. Schwartz; Silvano B. Amora; Deacons John A. Notaro; Edward R. Herr, (Retired); Nick Donofrio; Ilsoo P. Barng; Mary Escueta, Music Min.
Catechesis Religious Program—Tel: 732-542-4095; Email: john@stdorothea.org. Students 224.
2—IMMACULATE CONCEPTION (1984) (Korean)
64 Broad St., Eatontown, 07724. Tel: 732-389-3830; Email: eatoncatholic@eatoncatholic.org. Rev. Cha Yong (Paul) Lee, Admin.
Catechesis Religious Program—Gabriel Park, Dir. Students 59.

ENGLISHTOWN, MONMOUTH CO., OUR LADY OF MERCY (1948) [CEM] Merged with St. Thomas More, Manalapan.

EVESHAM TOWNSHIP, BURLINGTON CO., ST. ISAAC JOGUES (1996)
3 Lord Pl., Marlton, 08053. Tel: 856-797-0999; Fax: 856-797-0463; Email: saintisaacs@stisaacjogues.org. Very Rev. Phillip C. Pfleger, E.V.; Revs. Christopher Colavito, Parochial Vicar; Michael G. Dunn, Parochial Vicar; Deacons David O'Connor; Joseph DeRosa.
Catechesis Religious Program—Tel: 856-797-1811; Web: www.rc.net/trenton/st.isaac/. Sr. Clare Sabini, D.R.E. Students 475.

FAIR HAVEN, MONMOUTH CO., CHURCH OF THE NATIVITY (1954)
180 Ridge Rd., Fair Haven, 07704. Tel: 732-741-1714; Email: carolynm@nativitychurchnj.org; Email: frjim@nativitychurchnj.org. Rev. James J. Grogan Sr.; Deacons James Kelly; Paul Lang; Sean P. Murphy; Anthony Scalzo.
Catechesis Religious Program—Email: sueh@nativitychurchnj.org. Sue Hodgkiss, D.R.E. Students 1,000.

FARMINGDALE, MONMOUTH CO., ST. CATHERINE OF SIENA (1912)
31 Asbury Rd., Farmingdale, 07727-3531.
Tel: 732-938-5375; Email: frontoffice@sienachurch.org; Web: www.sienachurch.org. Rev. Angelito Anarcon; Deacon Daniel C. Sakowski.
Catechesis Religious Program—Tel: 732-938-6229; Email: dre@sienachurch.org. Kyle Galante, D.R.E. Students 350.

FLORENCE, BURLINGTON CO.
1—ST. CLARE (1874) [CEM] (Irish—Italian), Closed. For inquiries for parish records contact the chancery.
2—PARISH OF SAINTS FRANCIS AND CLARE (1913) Merged with St. Mary, Bordentown to form Parish of Mary, Mother of the Church, Bordentown.

FORKED RIVER, OCEAN CO., ST. PIUS X (1961)
300 Lacey Rd., Forked River, 08731-3598.
Tel: 732-693-5107; Email: fkopack@churchofstpius.org; Web: www.churchofstpius.org. Rev. Richard Basznianin; Deacons Anthony Martucci; Earl Lombardo; Philip T. Craft; Joseph F. Gilli; Tony Repice.
Catechesis Religious Program—Tel: 609-693-0368. Mrs. Patricia Colando, C.R.E. Students 1,120.

FREEHOLD, MONMOUTH CO.
1—CO-CATHEDRAL OF ST. ROBERT BELLARMINE (1971)
61 Georgia Rd., Freehold, 07728. Tel: 732-462-7429; Fax: 732-409-3496; Email: receptionist@strobert.cc; Web: www.strobert.cc. Rev. Msgr. Sam A. Sirianni, V.F., Rector; Rev. Arian Wharff, Parochial Vicar; Deacons Francis J. Weber Jr.; Rolf B. Friedmann; Henry J. Cugini; Andy Smith; Vincent L. Rinaldi; Jen Schlameuss-Perry, Pastorial Assoc.
Catechesis Religious Program—
Tel: 732-462-7429, Ext. 122; Email: lclarke@strobert.cc. Lisa Clarke, D.R.E. Students 1,162.
2—ST. ROSE OF LIMA (1864) [CEM]
16 McLean St., Freehold, 07728. Tel: 732-462-0859; Email: parish@stroseoflimachurch.org; Web: www.stroseoflima.com. Revs. James Conover; Francisco J. Saenz-Lozada, O.P., Parochial Vicar; Michael Brizio, I.M.C., Parochial Vicar; Deacons Andrew Luhman; R. Michael McKenna; Rodolfo A. Santos.
School—St. Rose of Lima School, 51 Lincoln Pl., Freehold, 07728. Tel: 732-462-2646;
Fax: 732-462-0331; Email: srpatriciadoyle@stroseoflima.com; Web: www.stroseoflimafreehld.com. Sr. Patricia Doyle, Prin. Clergy 3; Lay Teachers 19; Sisters 3; Students 282.
Catechesis Religious Program—Tel: 732-308-0215; Email: reled@stroseoflimachurch.org. Dr. Steven Olson, D.R.E. Students 1,063.
Convent—81 Randolph St., Freehold, 07728.
Tel: 732-462-0599.

HAINESPORT, BURLINGTON CO., OUR LADY QUEEN OF PEACE (1944)
1603 Marne Hwy., Hainesport, 08036.
Tel: 609-267-0230; Email: carol@olqponline.org; Web: ourladyqop.org. Rev. Joselito M. Noche; Deacon Lee Zito, Pastoral Assoc.
Catechesis Religious Program—Email: ginny@olqponline.org. Mrs. Ginny Fama, C.R.E. Students 206.

HAMILTON, MERCER CO.
1—OUR LADY OF SORROWS-ST. ANTHONY PARISH (2005)
3816 E. State St. Ext., Hamilton, 08619.
Tel: 609-587-4372; Email: info@ols-sa.org; Web: ols-sa.org. Rev. Msgr. Thomas N. Gervasio; Rev. Jean Felicien; Deacons James J. Challender; Jeffrey Pierfy; Kevin J. O'Boyle; Joseph Jaruszewski; Luders Desire.
School—Our Lady of Sorrows-St. Anthony Parish School, (Grades PreK-8), 3800 E. State St. Ext., Hamilton, 08619. Tel: 609-587-4140;
Fax: 609-584-8853; Email: mtuohy@olsschool.us; Web: olsschool.us. Mr. Donald Costantino, Prin. Lay Teachers 20; Students 218.
Catechesis Religious Program—Email: mfrancis@ols-sa.org. Mariyam Iqbal Francis, D.R.E. Students 341.
Station—Hamilton Grove, Hamilton.
2—ST. RAPHAEL-HOLY ANGELS PARISH (2005)
3500 S. Broad St., Hamilton, 08610.
Tel: 609-585-7049; Email: parishoffice@srhap.org; Web: www.straphaell-holyangels.com. Revs. Gene P. Daguplo; Edward M. Jawidzik; Deacons Richard Arcari; Thomas Lavelle; Salvatore Marcello; Robert Tharp; William R. Palmisano; David C. Colter; Gregory J. Costa; Sr. Sandra Kulick, S.S.J., Pastoral Assoc.; Dennis M. Heffernan, Business Mgr.; Lori Hoos, Dir. Music.
School—St. Raphael School, (Grades PreK-8), 151 Gropp Ave., Hamilton, 08610. Tel: 609-585-7733;
Fax: 609-581-8436; Email: ann.cwirko@srsnj.org; Web: www.srsnj.org. Ms. Ann M. Cwirko, Prin. Lay Teachers 21; Students 235.
Catechesis Religious Program—Tel: 609-585-0542; Email: wpalmisano@srhap.org. Students 480.
Worship Sites—
Holy Angels Church—1733 S. Broad St., Hamilton, 08610.
St. Raphael Church.
Stations—Robert Wood Johnson University Hospital at Hamilton—One Hamilton Health Pl., Hamilton, 08690.
Care One Assisted Living at Hamilton, 1660 Whitehorse-Hamilton Sq. Rd., Hamilton, 08690.
Brookdale Hamilton, 1645 Whitehorse-Mercerville Rd., Hamilton, 08619.
B Well Post Acute Care of Hamilton, 3 Hamilton Health Pl., Hamilton, 08690.

HAMILTON SQUARE, MERCER, ST. GREGORY THE GREAT (1953)
4620 Nottingham Way, Hamilton Square, 08690.
Tel: 609-587-4877; Email: webmaster@stgregorythegreatchurch.org; Web: www.stgregorythegreatchurch.org. Revs. Michael T. McClane, J.C.L.; Augusto L. Gamalo, Parochial Vicar; Leandro B. Dela Cruz, Parochial Vicar; Deacons Charles M. Moscarello; William A. Wilson; Andrew A. Sabados Sr.; Joseph E. Latini; Joseph J. Moore Jr.; John A. DiLissio; John R. Isaac; Neil Pirozzi
Legal Name: Church of St. Gregory the Great.
Res.: 5 Mario Dr., Hamilton Square, 08690.
School—St. Gregory the Great Academy, (Grades PreSchool-8), 4680 Nottingham Way, Hamilton Square, 08690. Tel: 609-587-1131; Fax: 609-587-0322; Email: jbriggs@stgregorythegreat.org; Email: mrivera@stgregorythegreat.org; Email: sfurman@stgregorythegreat.org; Web: www.stgregorythegreatacademy.org. Dr. Jason C. Briggs, Prin. Clergy 2; Lay Teachers 35; Sisters 2; Students 524.
Catechesis Religious Program—Email: chouck@stgregorythegreat.org. Sr. Carolyn Houck, M.P.F., D.R.E. Students 1,185.
Convent—13 Stanley Dr., Robbinsville, 08691.

HIGHLANDS, MONMOUTH CO., OUR LADY OF PERPETUAL HELP (1883) Closed. Sacramental records maintained at Our Lady of Perpetual Help-St. Agnes Parish, Atlantic Highlands.

HIGHTSTOWN, MERCER CO., ST. ANTHONY OF PADUA (1885)
251 Franklin St., Hightstown, 08520-3223.
Tel: 609-448-0141; Email: info@stanthonychurch.org; Web: www.stanthony-hightstown.net. 156 Maxwell Ave., Hightstown, 08520. Revs. Patrick J. McDonnell; Juan Rojas, Parochial Vicar; Deacon Thomas Garvey.
Catechesis Religious Program—
Tel: 609-448-0141, Ext. 21; Email: michelle@stanthonychurch.org. Michelle Angelo, D.R.E. Students 658.

HOLMDEL, MONMOUTH CO.
1—ST. BENEDICT (1959)
165 Bethany Rd., Holmdel, 07733-1699.
Tel: 732-264-4712, Ext. 17; Email: parishoffice@stbenedictnj.org; Email: finance@stbenedictnj.org. Revs. Garry Koch; John Michael Patilla; Deacons Raymond R. Pelkowski; Richard L. Morris; Stephen G. Scott; John L. Clymore; Fran DeMuria, Business & Finance Mgr.
School—St. Benedict School, (Grades PreK-8),
Tel: 732-264-5578; Email: kdonahue@stbenedictnj.org. Kevin Donahue, Prin. Lay Teachers 32; Students 405.
Catechesis Religious Program—
Tel: 732-264-4712, Ext. 26; Email: cesario@stbenedictnj.org; Email: mdayton@stbenedictnj.org. Melissa Dayton, D.R.E.; Matthew Santucci, Youth Min. Students 530.
2—CHURCH OF SAINT CATHARINE (1879)
108 Middletown Rd., P.O. Box 655, Holmdel, 07733.
Tel: 732-842-3963; Email: parishoffice@stcatharine.net; Web: www.stcatharine.net. Rev. Msgr. Gregory D. Vaughan; Deacons John P. Flanagan; Christopher L. Hansen; Thomas J. DiCanio; Michael Lonie; Kathleen McBurnie, Pastoral Assoc.
Catechesis Religious Program—Tel: 732-758-8568; Email: dvullo@stcatharine.net. Mrs. Dominica Vullo, C.R.E. Students 1,085.

HOPEWELL, MERCER CO., ST. ALPHONSUS (1877) [CEM]
54 E. Prospect St., Hopewell, 08525.
Tel: 609-466-0332; Email: parishoffice@stalphonsushopewell.org; Web: stalphonsushopewell.org. Rev. Msgr. Michael J. Walsh.
Catechesis Religious Program—Tel: 609-466-2694. Mrs. Donna Millar, C.R.E. Students 116.

HOWELL TOWNSHIP, MONMOUTH CO.
1—ST. VERONICA (1962)
4215 Hwy. 9 N., Howell, 07731. Tel: 732-363-4200; Email: info@stveronica.com; Web: stveronica.com. Revs. Vincent Euk; Vicente Magdaraog, (Philippines) Parochial Vicar; Deacons Tomasz Cechulski; Charles Daye Jr.; John J. Franey; Louis (Gino) S. Esposito.

School—St. Veronica School, (Grades K-8), 4219 Hwy. 9 N., Howell, 07731. Tel: 732-364-4130; Fax: 732-363-4932; Email: srcheree@stveronica.com. Sr. Cherree Ann Power, Prin. Clergy 1; Lay Teachers 13; Sisters 3; Students 200.
Catechesis Religious Program—Tel: 732-364-4137; Email: sr.ann@stveronica.com. Sr. Ann Elizabeth, C.R., D.R.E. Students 155.
Convent—4217 Hwy. 9 N., Howell, 07731.
2—ST. WILLIAM THE ABBOT (1985)
2740 Lakewood-Allenwood Rd., Howell, 07731.
Tel: 732-840-3535; Email: stwilliam@optonline.net; Web: www.stwilliamtheabbot.com. Rev. Thomas F. Maher; Deacons Michael Abatemarco; Kevin Smith; George A. Prevosti Jr.
Res.: 2400 Allenwood-Lakewood Rd., Brick, 08724.
Catechesis Religious Program—Mrs. Dawn Cappetto, Admin. Students 523.
Station—Geraldine Thompson Nursing Home, 2350 Hospital Rd., Allenwood, 08720.
JACKSON, OCEAN CO.
1—ST. ALOYSIUS (1964)
935 Bennetts Mills Rd., Jackson, 08527.
Tel: 732-370-0500; Email: frbambrick@saintaloysiusonline.org; Web: www.saintaloysiusonline.org. Very Rev. John P. Bambrick, V.F.; Revs. Sheldon Amasa; James R. Smith; Deacons Rene Perez; Uku Mannikus.
School—Saint Aloysius Grammar School, (Grades PreK-8), Tel: 732-370-1515; Email: principaloconnor@staloysiusschool.com; Web: www.staloysiusschool.com. Lay Teachers 20; Students 245.
Catechesis Religious Program—Email: jpetrillo@saintaloysiusonline.org. Jennifer Petrillo, C.R.E. Students 1,290.
2—CHURCH OF ST. MONICA (1953)
679 W. Veteran's Hwy., Jackson, 08527.
Tel: 732-928-0279; Fax: 732-928-1853; Email: stmonicanj@yahoo.com; Web: www.saintmonica.com. Rev. Alexander Enriquez, Parish Admin.; Deacons Christian Knoebel; Gene F. Moir Sr.
Catechesis Religious Program—Tel: 732-928-4038; Email: stmonicaccd@yahoo.com. Karen Badach, C.R.E. Students 250.
JOBSTOWN, BURLINGTON CO., ST. ANDREW'S CHURCH (1880) Merged with Church of the Assumption, New Egypt to form Parish of St. Isidore the Farmer, New Egypt.
KEANSBURG, MONMOUTH CO., ST. ANN (1924)
311 Carr Ave., Keansburg, 07734. Tel: 732-787-0315; Email: stannkeansburg@gmail.com. Rev. Daniel G. Cahill, (Retired).
Child Care—St. Ann Child Care Center, 121 Main St., Keansburg, 07734. Students 65.
Catechesis Religious Program—Tel: 732-787-5744. Theresa Kelley, D.R.E. Students 275.
BAYSHORE SENIOR HEALTH, EDUCATION & RECREATION CENTER, 100 Main St., Keansburg, 07734. Tel: 732-495-2454; Fax: 732-495-7897. Sisters 1; Seniors Served 1,350.
**Project Paul*—211 Carr Ave., Keansburg, 07734.
KEYPORT, MONMOUTH CO.
1—JESUS, THE LORD CHURCH, Merged with St. Joseph, Keyport to form Parish of Our Lady of Fatima, Keyport.
2—ST. JOSEPH, Merged with Jesus the Lord, Keyport to form Parish of Our Lady of Fatima, Keyport.
3—PARISH OF OUR LADY OF FATIMA
376 Maple Pl., Keyport, 07735. Tel: 732-264-0322; Email: jcano@fatimakeyport.org. Rev. Kenneth W. Ekdahl, (Retired); Deacon John Clymore
Legal Name: Parish of Our Lady of Fatima, Keyport, N.J.
Catechesis Religious Program—Tel: 732-264-0304. Students 275.
LAKEHURST, OCEAN CO., ST. JOHN (1969)
619 Chestnut St., Lakehurst, 08733.
Tel: 732-657-6347; Email: churchofstjohn@comcast.net. Rev. James O'Neill, Admin.; Deacons Edward Holowienka; Richard T. Glogoza; James Gonzalez; Larry D'Amico.
Catechesis Religious Program—Tel: 732-657-2348; Fax: 732-657-8105. Mrs. Mary Ann Dempkowski, D.R.E. Students 360.
LAKEWOOD, OCEAN CO.
1—ST. ANTHONY CLARET (1977) (Hispanic Parish for Ocean Co.)
780 Ocean Ave., Lakewood, 08701-3644.
Tel: 732-367-8486; Email: svdclaret@aol.com. Revs. Pedro L. Bou, S.V.D.; Pelagio Calambia Pateno, S.V.D.; Guilherme A. Andrino, S.V.D.
Catechesis Religious Program—David Roman, D.R.E. Students 534.
2—ST. MARY OF THE LAKE (1889) [CEM]
43 Madison Ave., Lakewood, 08701.
Tel: 732-363-0139; Email: smloffice@smlparish.net; Web: SMLparish.net. Revs. Michael D. Sullivan; Marian F. Kokorzycki; Deacons William Malone; Silverius Galvan; James G. McGrath; John Cullinane.
Catechesis Religious Program—Tel: 732-363-3043. Maria Kozlowska, Admin. Students 380.
Mission—Holy Family Church, 1139 E. County Line Rd., Lakewood, 08701.
LAVALLETTE, OCEAN CO., THE CHURCH OF ST. PIO OF PIETRELCINA (1921)
103 Washington Ave., Lavallette, 08735.
Tel: 732-793-7291; Email: office@stpioparish.com. Rev. Douglas Freer
Legal Name: The Church of St. Pio of Pietrelcina, Lavallette, N.J.
Catechesis Religious Program—Tel: 732-793-3020. Ms. Nancy Grodberg, Faith Formation Coord. Students 30.
LAWRENCEVILLE, MERCER CO.
1—ST. ANN (1937)
1253 Lawrenceville Rd., Lawrenceville, 08648.
Tel: 609-882-6491; Fax: 609-882-0327; Email: ldelacruz@churchofsaintann.net; Web: churchofsaintann.net. Rev. Leandro B. Dela Cruz, Admin.; Deacon James Scott; Sr. Pat McGinley, S.S.J., Pastoral Assoc.; Mr. Gary Maccaroni, Pastoral Assoc.
School—St. Ann School, (Grades PreK-8), 34 Rossa Ave., Lawrenceville, 08648. Tel: 609-882-8077; Email: dschramke@churchofsaintann.net. Mr. John McKenna, Prin.; Mr. Donald Schramke, Business Mgr. Lay Teachers 30; Students 264.
Catechesis Religious Program—Tel: 609-882-1212. Mrs. Kelly Wolf, C.R.E. Students 701.
2—THE CHURCH OF THE KOREAN MARTYRS (1994) (Korean)
Mailing Address: 1130 Brunswick Ave., 08638.
Tel: 609-695-6300; Email: baegepa@gmail.com. Rev. Si Young Kim, (South Korea) Admin.
Catechesis Religious Program—Students 49.
LINCROFT, MONMOUTH CO., ST. LEO THE GREAT (1958)
50 Hurley's Ln., Lincroft, 07738. Tel: 732-747-5466; Email: parish@stleothegreat.com; Web: stleothegreat.com. Rev. John T. Folchetti; Deacons Edward H. Wilson; Richard W. Tucker; Sr. Jeanne Belli, S.S.J., Pastoral Assoc.; Mr. Joseph Manzi, Admin.; Mark Russoniello, Pastoral Assoc.
School—St. Leo the Great School, (Grades K-8), 550 Newman-Springs Rd., Lincroft, 07738.
Tel: 732-741-3133; Fax: 732-741-2241; Email: joemanzi@stleothegreat.com; Web: saintleothegreatschool.com. Mr. Joseph Manzi, Admin.; Cornelius Begley, Prin. Clergy 2; Lay Teachers 40; Students 618.
Catechesis Religious Program—Tel: 732-530-0717; Email: faithformation@stleothegreat.com. Mark Russoniello, Pastoral Assoc. Students 1,000.
LONG BRANCH, MONMOUTH CO.
1—THE CHURCH OF CHRIST THE KING, LONG BRANCH, N.J. (2009) [CEM]
380 Division St., Long Branch, 07740.
Tel: 732-222-3216; Email: mary@cklb.org. Rev. Javier A. Diaz, J.C.L.
Catechesis Religious Program—375 Exchange Pl., Long Branch, 07740. Email: christthekingparish@comcast.net. Mrs. Amelia Flego, C.R.E. Students 313.
2—HOLY TRINITY (1906) Closed. For inquiries for parish records contact the chancery. Rev. Msgr. Sam A. Sirianni, V.F.
3—ST. JOHN THE BAPTIST (1984) Closed. For inquiries for parish records contact the chancery.
4—ST. MICHAEL (1885)
800 Ocean Ave., West End, 07740. Tel: 732-222-8080 ; Email: mvalan@stmichaelnj.com; Web: www.stmichaelnj.com. Revs. John Butler; Mark Nillo, Parochial Vicar.
Catechesis Religious Program—6 W. End Ct., Long Branch, 07740. Tel: 732-483-0360; Email: pchavez@stmichaelnj.com. Patricia Chavez, D.R.E. Students 343.
MANALAPAN, MONMOUTH CO., ST. THOMAS MORE (1970)
186 Gordons Corner Rd., Manalapan, 07726.
Tel: 732-446-6661; Email: ENZI04@aol.com; Web: moremercy.org. Rev. Mark W. Crane; Rev. Msgr. Peter Kochery, (In Res.); Rev. John Large, Parochial Vicar; Deacons Keith J. Casey; James Davis; John J. Zebrowski; Matthew P. Nicosia; Michael Lee Foster; Mrs. Vincenza Magliano, Admin.; Colton Martin, Music Min.
Catechesis Religious Program—Tel: 732-456-3232; Email: bill.staub@moremercy.org. Mr. William Staub, C.R.E. Students 1,500.
MANASQUAN, MONMOUTH CO., ST. DENIS (1909)
90 Union Ave., Manasquan, 08736.
Tel: 732-223-0287; Email: st.denis@verizon.net; Web: www.churchofstdenis.org. Rev. William J. P. Lago; Deacons George R. Kelder Jr.; Gary J. Pstrak.
Catechesis Religious Program—119 Virginia Ave., Manasquan, 08736. Tel: 732-223-1161; Email: stdenisdre@verizon.net. Ms. Barbara Evans, D.R.E. Students 540.
Chapel—Our Lady Star of the Sea Chapel, 544 E. Main St., Manasquan, 08736.
MAPLE SHADE, BURLINGTON CO., OUR LADY OF PERPETUAL HELP (1920)
236 E. Main St., Maple Shade, 08052.
Tel: 856-667-8850; Email: frwilson@olphparish.com. Revs. Richard C. Vila; Cesar Tolentino; Deacons Joseph A. Card, (Retired); Michael P. Boehm, (Retired); Ronald S. Meyers; Fernando Linka; James A. Manaloris; Sean McMahon.
School—Our Lady of Perpetual Help School, (Grades PreSchool-8), Tel: 856-667-8850, Ext. 210; Email: tmccloskey@olphparish.com; Web: olphparish.com. Carl Jankowski, Prin. Clergy 1; Lay Teachers 17; Students 225.
Catechesis Religious Program—Tel: 856-779-7529; Email: shunkins@olphparish.com. Sherri Hunkins, C.R.E. Students 250.
MARLBORO, MONMOUTH CO., ST. GABRIEL (1885) [CEM]
100 N. Main St., Marlboro, 07746. Tel: 732-946-4487; Email: info@stgabrielsparish.org. Revs. Eugene J. Roberts; Joy T. Chacko, Parochial Vicar; Deacons Stephen Sansevere, Pastoral Admin.; Lester Owens; Richard Scotti; Richard G. Roenbeck.
Catechesis Religious Program—Email: mmykityshyn@stgabrielsparish.org. Mary Mykityshyn, M.D., D.R.E. Students 878.
MARLTON, BURLINGTON CO., ST. JOAN OF ARC (1961)
100 Willow Bend Rd., Marlton, 08053.
Tel: 856-983-0077, Ext. 311; Email: Theresa.segin@stjoans.org; Web: www.stjoans.org. Rev. Msgr. Richard D. LaVerghetta; Revs. Michael DeSaye; Jorge Bedoya; Deacons Barry Tarzy; Thomas W. Murphy, Pastoral Assoc.; Jeffrey DeFrehn; William R. Mueller; Sr. Peg Boyle, S.S.J., Pastoral Assoc.
School—St. Joan of Arc School, (Grades K-8), 101 Evans Rd., Marlton, 08053. Tel: 856-983-0774; Fax: 856-983-3278; Email: p.pycik@stjoansk-8.org; Web: stjoansk-8.org. Sr. Patricia Pycik, S.S.J., Prin. Lay Teachers 24; Sisters of St. Joseph 1; Students 402.
Catechesis Religious Program—Tel: 856-983-7575; Fax: 856-983-3479; Email: linda.mueller@stjoans.org. Mrs. Linda Mueller, D.R.E. Students 1,079.
Convent—99 Evans Rd., Marlton, 08053.
MATAWAN, MONMOUTH CO., ST. CLEMENT (1965)
172 Freneau Ave., Matawan, 07747.
Tel: 732-566-3616; Email: admin@stclementmatawan.org; Web: www.stclementmatawan.org. Revs. Thomas M. Vala; Gregg Abadilla; Deacon Tom Wadolowski.
Catechesis Religious Program—Email: stclementprep@optonline.net. Ms. Patricia Thein, C.R.E. Students 629.
MEDFORD, BURLINGTON CO., ST. MARY OF THE LAKES (1943)
40 Jackson Rd., Medford, 08055.
Tel: 609-654-8208, Ext. 110; Fax: 609-975-0137; Email: email@smlparish.org; Web: www.smlparish.org. Very Rev. Daniel F. Swift; Rev. Roy Ballacillo, Parochial Vicar; Deacon Joseph Tedeschi.
School—St. Mary of the Lakes School, (Grades PreK-8), 196 Rte. 70, Medford, 08055. Tel: 609-654-2546; Fax: 609-654-8125; Email: arash@smlschool.org; Web: www.smlschool.org. Amy Rash, Prin. Lay Teachers 27; Students 278.
Catechesis Religious Program—
Tel: 609-654-2546, Ext. 310; Email: mscordato@smlparish.org. Mary Pat Scordato, D.R.E. Students 800.
Convent—Sisters of St. Joseph, 31 S. Poplar Ave., Maple Shade, 08052. Email: rmccalla@smlparish.org.
St. Vincent DePaul Society-Medford—1 Jones Rd., Medford, 08055. Tel: 609-953-0021. Dr. James (Jim) Dwyer, Pres.; Joel Martin, Treas.
MIDDLETOWN, MONMOUTH CO.
1—ST. CATHERINE (1948)
130 Bray Ave., Middletown, 07748.
Tel: 732-787-1318; Email: stcathek1@aol.com; Web: stcathek.org. Very Rev. Daniel Hesko, V.F.; Deacons John C. Orlando; John G. McGrath; Julia Fehlhaber, Business Mgr.
Catechesis Religious Program—20 Shore Acres Ave., Middletown, 07748. Tel: 732-495-7779; Email: churchlady000000@aol.com. Mrs. Lillian Jacqueline Callahan, D.R.E. Students 346.
2—ST. MARY (1878)
19 Cherry Tree Farm Rd., Middletown, 07748.
Tel: 732-671-0071; Email: edonohue@stmarychurchnj.org. Revs. Jeffrey J. Kegley; Jordan McConway; Richard Osborn; Deacons Carlo Squicciarini; Martin K. McMahon.
School—St. Mary School, (Grades PreSchool-8), 538 Church St., Middletown, 07748. Tel: 732-671-0129; Fax: 732-671-2653; Email: cpalmer@stmaryes.org; Web: stmaryes.org. Craig Palmer, Prin.; Dennis Poracky, Asst. Prin. Lay Teachers 40; Students 534.
Catechesis Religious Program—Email: pegodun@gmail.com. Mrs. Margaret Dunne, C.R.E. Students 1,211.
MONMOUTH BEACH, MONMOUTH CO., CHURCH OF THE PRECIOUS BLOOD (1891)
72 Riverdale Ave., Monmouth Beach, 07750.

Tel: 732-222-4756; Email: rfkap@aol.com; Email: churchofthepreciousblood@comcast.net; Web: www.churchofthepreciousblood.org. Rev. Robert F. Kaeding.
Catechesis Religious Program—Tel: 732-963-9982; Email: eileen@relilgiouseducation.comcastbiz.net. Eileen Lang, C.R.E. Students 420.

MOORESTOWN, BURLINGTON CO., OUR LADY OF GOOD COUNSEL (1879) [CEM] Very Rev. Damian J. McElroy, V.F.; Rev. John A. Bogacz, Parochial Vicar; Deacons David F. Papuga, Business Mgr.; Edward A. Heffernan; Thomas F. Kolon; John F. Bertagnolli; Dr. Linda M. Dix, D.Min., Dir. & D.R.E.; Stephen J. Lucasi, Dir. of Sacred Music.
Res.: 42 W. Main St., Moorestown, 08057.
Tel: 856-235-0181; Email: parish@olgcnj.org; Email: papugad@olgcnj.org.
School—Our Lady of Good Counsel School, (Grades PreK-8), 23 W. Prospect St., Moorestown, 08057.
Tel: 856-235-7885; Fax: 856-235-2570; Email: school@olgc.me; Web: www.olgc.me. Dr. Carla Chiarelli, Prin. Lay Teachers 28; Students 405.
Catechesis Religious Program—122 W. Main St., Moorestown, 08057. Tel: 856-235-7136; Email: dixl@olgcnj.org. Students 1,029.

MOUNT HOLLY, BURLINGTON CO.
1—CHRIST THE REDEEMER (1976) (Hispanic)
426 Pine St., Mount Holly, 08060. Tel: 609-261-0181; Email: mhollyparish@yahoo.com. 113 South Ave., Mount Holly, 08060. Revs. John Czahur, Admin.; Roberto Padilla Lopez, Parochial Vicar; Deacons Michael Adorno; Brando Duarte.
Catechesis Religious Program—Students 55.
2—SACRED HEART (1848) [CEM]
260 High St., Mount Holly, 08060-1404.
Tel: 609-267-0209; Email: secretary@parishofsacredheart.org; Web: parishofsacredheart.org. Rev. John P. Czahur; Deacons John F. Hoefling, Ordinary; James Casa; William Rowley; Stanley Orkis.
School—Sacred Heart School, 250 High St., Mount Holly, 08060. Tel: 609-267-1728; Fax: 609-267-4476; Email: schooloffice@sacred-heart-school.org; Web: www.sacred-heart-school.org. Ms. Kathryn Besheer, Prin. Find us on Facebook, Instagram, and Twitter! Lay Teachers 19; Students 185.
Catechesis Religious Program—Email: jdonohue@parishofsacredheart.org. Jessica Donohue, D.R.E. Students 680.
Stations—County Jail—Tel: 609-267-3300.
Burlington County Hospital Extended Care Center, Tel: 609-367-0700.

MOUNT LAUREL, BURLINGTON CO., ST. JOHN NEUMANN (1978)
560 Walton Ave., Mount Laurel, 08054.
Tel: 856-235-1330; Email: stjohnneumannmtl@comcast.net. Very Rev. Phillip C. Pfleger, E.V.; Revs. Christopher Colavito; Michael G. Dunn; Deacons Joseph Barbara; Thomas J. Knowles.
Catechesis Religious Program—Tel: 856-235-6555; Email: stjohnneumannmtlre@comcast.net; Web: www.sjrmtl.org. Mrs. Helen Graziano, D.R.E. Students 350.

NEPTUNE, MONMOUTH CO.
1—HOLY INNOCENTS (1959)
3455 W. Bangs Ave., Neptune, 07753. Mailing Address: P.O. Box 806, Neptune, 07753.
Tel: 732-922-4242; Email: brenda@holyinnocentschurch.net; Email: toddcarterpriest@gmail.com; Web: holyinnocentschurch.net. Revs. H. Todd Carter; Evarist Kabagambe; Deacons James Walsh; John Klincewicz; Robert L. Cerefice.
School—Holy Innocents School, (Grades PreK-8), Tel: 732-922-3141, Ext. 12; Fax: 732-922-6531; Email: creimer@holyinnocents.net. Cynthia Reimer, Prin. Lay Teachers 15; Students 150.
Catechesis Religious Program—
Tel: 732-922-4242, Ext. 20; Fax: 732-922-3752. Sr. Bernadette Schuler, O.S.F., D.R.E. Students 480.
Stations—Convacenter Nursing Home—
Tel: 732-774-3500.
Imperial Nursing Home, Neptune. Tel: 732-922-3400.
Heritage Hall Nursing Home, Neptune, 07754.
Tel: 732-922-9330.
Medicenter Nursing Home, Neptune, 07754.
Tel: 732-774-8300.
The Lodge, Kings Manor, Tel: 732-922-1900.
2—OUR LADY OF PROVIDENCE (1981) (Spanish), Closed. Sacramental records maintained at Our Lady of Mount Carmel parish, Asbury Park.

NEW EGYPT, OCEAN CO.
1—THE CHURCH OF THE ASSUMPTION, Merged with St. Andrew, Jobstown to form Parish of St. Isidore the Farmer, New Egypt.
2—PARISH OF ST. ISIDORE THE FARMER (1853) [CEM]
28 Monmouth Rd., Wrightstown, 08562.
Tel: 609-758-2153; Email: Information@SaintIsidoreParish.Church; Web: SaintIsidoreParish.Church. 76 Evergreen Rd., Parish Office, New Egypt, 08533. Rev. Joseph J. Farrell; Mr. Mark Hoeler, Music Min.; Mary Steen, Business Mgr.
Legal Name: Parish of St. Isidore the Farmer, New Egypt, N.J.
Catechesis Religious Program—Tel: 609-758-3535; Email: brookey@assumption.church. Barbara Rookey, D.R.E. Students 320.

NORMANDY BEACH, OCEAN CO., OUR LADY OF PEACE (1979) Closed. For inquiries for parish records contact the chancery.

PENNINGTON, MERCER CO., ST. JAMES (1897)
115 E. Delaware Ave., Pennington, 08534.
Tel: 609-737-0122; Email: parishoffice@stjamespennington.org; Web: www.stjamespennington.org. Rev. Msgr. Michael J. Walsh; Rev. Jarlath Quinn; Rev. Msgr. Thomas J. Mullelly, J.D., LL.M., In Res.; Deacons Richard J. Hobson; Richard Currie; William Moore Hank; Patrick R. Brannigan.
Catechesis Religious Program—Email: stjamesedu@gmail.com. Nancy Lucash, D.R.E. Students 480.

PERRINEVILLE, MONMOUTH CO., ST. JOSEPH (1879) [CEM]
91 Stillhouse Rd., Millstone Township, 08510.
Tel: 732-792-2270; Fax: 732-792-2271; Email: frmikestjoseph@optonline.net; Web: www.stjosephmillstone.org. Rev. Michael P. Lang; Deacon Chris Chandonnet; Carmen Santos, Pastoral Assoc.
Catechesis Religious Program—Mrs. Genevieve Semanchick, D.R.E. Students 770.

POINT PLEASANT BEACH, OCEAN CO., ST. PETER'S (1882)
406 Forman Ave., Point Pleasant Beach, 08742.
Tel: 732-892-0049; Email: pdeoliveira@dioceseoftrenton.org. Revs. Robert Benko, O.F.M.Conv.; Michael Lorentsen, O.F.M.-Conv., Parochial Vicar; Richard Rossell, O.F.M.-Conv., (Retired).
School—St. Peter's School, (Grades K-8), 415 Atlantic Ave., Point Pleasant Beach, 08742.
Tel: 732-892-1260; Fax: 732-892-3488; Email: info@stpschool.org; Web: www.stpschool.org. Mrs. Tracey Korbin, Prin. Lay Teachers 16; Students 210.
Catechesis Religious Program—Tel: 732-899-4839; Fax: 732-899-6841; Email: religioused@saintpetersonline.org. Mrs. Merrie Brambilla, D.R.E. Students 325.
Convent—401 Atlantic Ave., Point Pleasant Beach, 08742.

POINT PLEASANT, OCEAN CO., ST. MARTHA (1972)
3800 Herbertsville Rd., Point Pleasant, 08742.
Tel: 732-295-3630; Fax: 732-295-9315; Email: business@saintmartha.net; Email: admin@saintmartha.net; Web: www.saintmartha.net. Rev. David S. Swantek, M.A., M.Div.; Deacon Francis Groff; Nancy A. Dormanski, Business Mgr. & Accountant.
Res. & Mailing Address: 512 Church Rd., Point Pleasant, 08742.
Catechesis Religious Program—Email: dre@saintmartha.net. Mrs. Georgina Kotz, D.R.E. Students 500.

PRINCETON, MERCER CO., ST. PAUL (1850) [CEM]
216 Nassau St., Princeton, 08542. Tel: 609-924-1743; Fax: 609-924-7510; Email: mheucke@stpaulsofprinceton.org; Web: www.stpaulsofprinceton.org. Rev. Msgr. Joseph N. Rosie, S.T.L.; Revs. Miguel Valle; Carlo Calisin; Deacons Jim Knipper; Frank Crivello.
Res.: 214 Nassau St., Princeton, 08542.
School—St. Paul School of Princeton, 218 Nassau St., Princeton, 08542. Tel: 609-921-7587;
Fax: 609-921-0264; Email: rkilleen@spsprinceton.org; Web: www.spsprinceton.org. Ryan Killeen, Ed. D., Prin. Clergy 3; Lay Teachers 34; Students 335.
Catechesis Religious Program—Tel: 609-524-0509; Email: jmcguire@stpaulsofprinceton.org. Mr. John Michael McGuire, Pastoral Assoc. for Faith Formation. Students 677.

RED BANK, MONMOUTH CO.
1—ST. ANTHONY CHURCH (1920) (Italian)
121 Bridge Ave., Red Bank, 07701. Tel: 732-747-0813; Fax: 732-224-0059; Email: officemgr@stanthonysofredbank.net; Web: stanthonysofredbank.net. Revs. Alberto W. Tamayo; Nicholas Dolan, Parochial Vivcar; Bros. Daniel Bower; Donald J. Ronning Jr. The Parish of St. Anthony of Padua is served by the priests and brothers of the Red Bank Oratory of St. Philip Neri (Community-in-Formation).
2—ST. JAMES (1864) [CEM]
94 Broad St., Red Bank, 07701. Tel: 732-741-0500; Email: saintjamesredbank@stjames-redbank.com; Web: www.stjames-redbank.com. Rev. Msgr. Philip A. Lowery; Revs. Daison Areepparampil, Parochial Vicar; Ariel Robles; Vincente Magdaraog; Deacon Bryan P. Davis.
Child Care—Preschool, Tel: 732-933-1041. Lay Teachers 3; Students 48.
School—St. James Grammar School, (Grades PreK-8), 30 Peters Pl., Red Bank, 07701. Tel: 732-741-3363; Fax: 732-933-4960; Email: office@mysaintjames.com; Web: mysaintjames.com. Mrs. Joann Giordano, Prin.; Catherine Golden, Vice Prin. Lay Teachers 28; Students 365.
High School—Red Bank Catholic High School, 112 Broad St., Red Bank, 07701. Tel: 732-747-1774;
Fax: 732-747-1936; Email: alabat@redbankcatholic.com. Robert Abatemarco, Prin. Lay Teachers 106; Sisters 5; Students 1,069.
Catechesis Religious Program—Tel: 732-747-6006; Email: religioused@stjames-redbank.com. Mrs. Fillie Duchaine, C.R.E. Students 1,142.
Convent—Sisters of Mercy, 25 Drummond Pl., Red Bank, 07701.
Station—Riverview Hospital, Red Bank.

RIVERSIDE, BURLINGTON CO.
1—ST. CASIMIR (1913) (Polish), Merged with Church of the Holy Name, Delran to form The Church of the Resurrection, Delran Township, N.J.
2—THE CHURCH OF JESUS, THE GOOD SHEPHERD (2008)
805 Warren St., Beverly, 08010. Tel: 856-461-0100; Email: info@jesusthegoodshepherd.org; Web: www.jesusthegoodshepherd.org. Rev. Selvam J. Asirvatham; Deacons Herman J. Mosteller; Eduardo Trani; Gary L. Schmitt; Richard K. Benner; Verna Zelaney, Music Min.
Res.: 524 Warren St., Beverly, 08010.
Catechesis Religious Program—Tel: 856-461-9343; Email: m.gimello@jesusthegoodshepherd.org. Mrs. Maria B. Gimello, D.R.E. Students 253.
Worship Sites—
St. Peter Church—101 Middleton St., Riverside, 08075.
St. Joseph Church.
3—ST. PETER (1878) [CEM] Merged with St. Joseph, Beverly to form The Church of Jesus, the Good Shepherd, Riverside, N.J.

RIVERTON, BURLINGTON CO., SACRED HEART (1878)
103 Fourth St., Riverton, 08077. Tel: 856-829-0090; Email: sacredheartriverton@comcast.net; Web: www.shcriverton.org. Very Rev. Robert Holtz, V.F.; Rev. Roberto Ignacio; Deacons Joseph M. Donadieu; Michael J. Stinsman; Kenneth W. Heilig; Robert J. Bednarek; Susan Barnett, Music Min.
Catechesis Religious Program—102 Fourth St., Riverton, 08077. Tel: 856-829-1848. Mrs. Patricia Hutchinson, D.R.E. Students 645.

RUMSON, MONMOUTH CO., HOLY CROSS (1884)
30 Ward Ave., Rumson, 07760. Tel: 732-842-0348;
Fax: 732-842-3226; Email: webmaster@holycrossrumson.org; Web: www.holycrossrumson.org. Very Rev. Michael Manning, V.F.; Eugenia Kelly, Pastoral Assoc.; Jim Trainor, Business Admin.; Lori La Plante, Pastoral Assoc.
School—Holy Cross School, (Grades PreK-8), 40 Rumson Rd., Rumson, 07760. Fax: 732-741-3134; Email: schooloffice@holycrossrumson.org; Web: www.holycrossschoolrumson.org. Mark DeMareo, Prin. Lay Teachers 30; Students 305.
Catechesis Religious Program—Sally Kabash, C.R.E.; Michael Feerst, Youth Min. Students 400.

SEA GIRT, MONMOUTH CO., ST. MARK (1953)
215 Crescent Pkwy., Sea Girt, 08750.
Tel: 732-449-6364; Email: rectory@stmarkseagirt.com; Web: www.stmarkseagirt.com. Rev. Msgr. Sean P. Flynn; Rev. Jose Fernandez-Bangueses, (Spain).
Catechesis Religious Program—
Tel: 732-449-6364, Ext. 105. Ms. Diana Zuna, C.R.E. Students 497.

SEASIDE HEIGHTS, OCEAN CO., OUR LADY OF PERPETUAL HELP (1942) Merged with St. Catharine of Siena Church, Seaside Park to form the Parish of St. Junipero Serra, Seaside Park.

SEASIDE PARK, OCEAN CO.
1—ST. CATHARINE OF SIENA, Merged with Our Lady of Perpetual Help Church, Seaside Heights to form Parish of St. Junipero Serra, Seaside Park.
2—PARISH OF ST. JUNIPERO SERRA (1906)
50 E. St., Box A, Seaside Park, 08752.
Tel: 732-793-0041; Fax: 732-793-6252; Email: stjuniperoserra@optonline.net; Web: www.stjuniperoserra.org. Rev. Michael Lorentsen, O.F.M. Conv.; Friar Thomas Bahn, O.F.M. Conv., Parochial Vicar; Rev. Antone Kandrac, O.F.M.Conv., In Res.; Bros. Stephen Merrigan, O.F.M. Conv., In Res.; James Moore, O.F.M. Conv., In Res.; Vincent Vivian, O.F.M. Conv., In Res.
Legal Name: Parish of St. Junipero Serra, Seaside Park
Catechesis Religious Program—Renee Casadonte, C.R.E. Students 232.

SPRING LAKE, MONMOUTH CO., ST. CATHARINE-ST. MARGARET (1901) [CEM 2]
215 Essex Ave., Spring Lake, 07762.
Tel: 732-449-5765; Fax: 732-449-0916; Email: contactus@stcatharine-stmargaret.org; Web: www.stcatharine-stmargaret.org. Revs. Harold F. Cullen, Ph.D.; William M. Dunlap; Charles B. Weiser, (In

Res.), (Retired); Deacons Edward Jennings; John L. Little.

School—St. Catharine-St. Margaret School, (Grades PreK-8), 301 2nd Ave., Spring Lake, 07762. Tel: 732-449-4424; Fax: 732-449-7876; Email: rdougherty@stcatharineschool.net; Email: jprofita@stcatharineschool.net; Email: kciak@stcatharineschool.net; Web: www.stcatharineschool.net. Robert Dougherty, Prin. Religious Teachers 1; Lay Teachers 26; Sisters 1; Students (K-8) 369; Pre-K 51.

Catechesis Religious Program—Tel: 732-449-4424, Ext. 305; Email: tsablom@stcatharine-stmargaret.org. Mrs. Tamara Sablom, C.R.E. Students 422.

Convent—211 Essex Ave., Spring Lake, 07762.

Mission—St. Margaret Church, 302 Ludlow Ave., Spring Lake, 07762.

TABERNACLE, BURLINGTON CO., HOLY EUCHARIST (1982) 520 Medford Lakes Rd., Tabernacle, 08088. Tel: 609-268-8383; Email: hec@holyeucharist.org; Web: www.holyeucharist.org. Rev. Andrew Jamieson; Deacons Joseph DeLuca; Kenneth S. Domzalski; Regan Peiffer, Music Dir.

Catechesis Religious Program—Tel: 609-268-7742; Email: dremaley@holyeucharist.org. Donna Remaley, Faith Formation Coord. Students 376.

Stations—New Lisbon Developmental Center—New Lisbon.

Leisuretown Senior Citizen Community, Southampton.

TOMS RIVER, OCEAN CO.

1—ST. JOSEPH (Dover Township) (1883) [CEM] Mailing Address: 685 Hooper Ave., Toms River, 08753. Tel: 732-349-0018; Fax: 732-286-7064; Email: parish@stjosephtomsriver.org; Web: www.stjosephtomsriver.org. Revs. G. Scott Shaffer, V.F.; Carlos Aguirre; Jerome Guld; Selvam J. Asirvatham, Parochial Vicar; Deacons Francis J. Babuschak; Frank J. McKenna, (Retired); Romeo D. Aquino, (Retired); Robert M. Barnes; Gerard Luongo; Patrick J. Stesner Sr.; Michael A. Taylor; Thomas Genovese; Gina Corrao, Music Min.; Thomas McMahon, Business Admin.

School—St. Joseph School, (Grades K-8), 711 Hooper Ave., Toms River, 08753. Tel: 732-349-2355; Fax: 732-349-1064; Email: mwilliams@sjgs.nj.k12us.com; Web: sjgs.nj.k12us.com. Madeline Kinloch, Prin. Clergy 4; Lay Teachers 35; Students 628.

Catechesis Religious Program—Tel: 732-349-0018, Ext. 2224. Celine Fowler, Dir. Pastoral Care; Marge Halloran, Dir. Faith Formation; Catherine Werner, Youth Min. Students 991.

Mission—St. Gertrude, Ocean & Central Aves., Island Heights, 08732. (June-Sept.).

2—ST. JUSTIN (Dover Township) (1972) 975 Fischer Blvd., Toms River, 08753. Tel: 732-270-3980; Email: mkreder@dioceseoftrenton.org. Revs. Mark Kreder; John A. Bogacz; Deacons Richard Hauenstein; Frederick C. Ebenau Sr.; James L. Campbell; James Gillespie.

Catechesis Religious Program—Tel: 732-270-3797. Ellen Noble, C.R.E. Students 653.

3—ST. LUKE (Dover Township) (1982) 1674 Old Freehold Rd., Toms River, 08755. Tel: 732-286-2222; Email: kmuzzio@stlukestomsriver.org; Web: www.stlukestomsriver.org. Very Rev. Robert S. Grodnicki, V.F.; Deacons Joseph DeMaria; Robert B. Pladek; Kathleen Muzzio, Business Mgr.; Thomas Hinz, Dir. Music & Liturgy.

Res.: 1241 Church Rd., Toms River, 08755.

Catechesis Religious Program—Tel: 732-505-0108. Teresa Frassetto, C.R.E. Students 586.

4—ST. MAXIMILIAN KOLBE (Berkeley Township) (1985) 130 St. Maximilian Ln., P.O. Box 4144, Toms River, 08757. Tel: 732-914-0300; Email: stmaximiliankolbechurch@gmail.com; Web: www.saintmaximiliankolbe.org. Revs. Stephen M. Piga; Carlos Castilla, Parochial Vicar; Vince Coppola, Parochial Vicar; Deacon Stanley Kwiatek.

TUCKERTON, OCEAN CO., ST. THERESA (1944) 450 Radio Rd., Little Egg Harbor Twp., 08087. Tel: 609-296-2504; Email: info@sttheresa450.org; Web: sttheresa-littleeggharbor.com. Revs. K. Michael Lambeth; Arian Wharff; Cathy Mazanek, Business Mgr.

Catechesis Religious Program—Tel: 609-296-2504, Ext. 224. Donna Ann Powers, C.R.E. Students 310.

UNION BEACH, MONMOUTH CO., HOLY FAMILY (1942) 727 Hwy. 36 W., P.O. Box 56, Keyport, 07735. Tel: 732-264-1484; Email: hfrccubnj@aol.com. Revs. Matthew J. Pfleger; Francis Cheruparambil, V.C.; Deacon James J. Neubauer; Grace Fagan, Business Mgr.

Catechesis Religious Program—Tel: 732-264-7043; Email: hreligioused@verizon.net. Students 320.

WASHINGTON CROSSING, MERCER CO., ST. GEORGE (1924) 1370 River Rd., P.O. Box 324, Titusville, 08560. Tel: 609-737-2015; Email: parishoffice@stgeorgetitusville.org. Rev. Msgr. Michael J. Walsh; Deacons Lawrence E. Gallagher; Michael J. Riley.

Catechesis Religious Program—Tel: 609-730-1703. Mrs. Margaret Dziminski, C.R.E. Students 66.

Station—Mercer County Correction Center, Tel: 609-989-6901.

WAYSIDE, MONMOUTH CO., ST. ANSELM (1972) 1028 Wayside Rd., Wayside, 07712. Tel: 732-493-4411; Email: StAnselm2@gmail.com. Rev. Eugene B. Vavrick.

Catechesis Religious Program—Students 440.

WEST LONG BRANCH, MONMOUTH CO.

1—ST. JEROME, Merged with St. Mary of the Assumption, Deal to form Parish of Our Lady of Hope, West Long Branch.

2—PARISH OF OUR LADY OF HOPE (1956) 254 Wall St., West Long Branch, 07764. Tel: 732-222-1424; Email: office@ladyofhopeparish.org. Rev. Peter James R. Alindogan; Deacon Louis E. Jakub. St. Jerome and St. Mary of the Assumption, Deal merged into parish named Parish of Our Lady of Hope, W. Long Branch

Legal Name: Parish of Our Lady of Hope, West Long Branch, N.J.

School—St. Jerome School, 250 Wall St., West Long Branch, 07764. Tel: 732-222-8686; Fax: 732-263-0343; Email: apelliccia@saintjeromeschool.org. Sr. Angelina Pelliccia, Prin. Lay Teachers 16; Sisters 2; Students 210.

Catechesis Religious Program—Email: etoft@saintjeromeschool.org. Sr. Elizabeth Toft, M.P.F., D.R.E. Students 150.

Convent—250A Wall St., West Long Branch, 07764.

WEST WINDSOR, MERCER CO., CHURCH OF ST. DAVID THE KING (1988) Mailing Address: 1 New Village Rd., Princeton Jct., 08550. Tel: 609-275-7111; Email: Parishoffice@stdavidtheking.com; Web: www.stdavidtheking.com. Very Rev. Timothy J. Capewell, V.F.; Deacons Thomas Baker; Roger Dinella; Carol Sullivan, Dir. Music; Ms. Nanci Bachman, Dir.

Res.: 517 Village Rd. W., Princeton Jct., 08550.

Catechesis Religious Program—Fax: 609-799-1984; Email: dre@stdavidtheking.com. Sr. Catherine Morgan, O.P., D.R.E. Students 400.

WHITING, OCEAN CO., ST. ELIZABETH ANN SETON (1976) 30 Schoolhouse Rd., Whiting, 08759. Tel: 732-350-5001; Email: pastor@easeton.org. Revs. Pasquale A. Papalia; Mark T. Devlin, (Retired); Deacons Kyran J. Purcell; Joseph Rider; Christopher O'Brien, (Retired); Peter F. Downing; Robert F. Scharen; Ms. Linda Quinn, Business Mgr.

Catechesis Religious Program—Tel: 732-350-7391; Email: ccd@easeton.org. Deborah Milecki, C.R.E. Students 132.

WILLINGBORO, BURLINGTON CO., CORPUS CHRISTI (1959) 63 Sylvan Ln., Willingboro, 08046. Tel: 609-877-5322 ; Email: CCNJ@mycorpuschristichurch.com. Rev. John J. Testa; Deacons James E. Ayrer; Michael J. Hagan.

Catechesis Religious Program—11 S. Sunset Rd., Willingboro, 08046. Students 41.

Convent—71 Sylvan Ln., Willingboro, 08046.

Chaplains of Public Institutions

TRENTON. *Capital Health System: Mercer Campus & Fuld Campus*. Revs. Thomas Kunnath, Chap., Edward Kwoka, Chap., Adam Midor, Chap.

St. Francis Medical Center. Rev. Carmen Carlone, Chap.

New Jersey State Prison, CN 861, 08629. Sr. Elizabeth Gnam, Chap.

BURLINGTON. *Virtua Memorial Hospital*. Attended from Sacred Heart Church.

260 High St., Mount Holly, 08060. Tel: 609-702-1848. Marge McGinley, Chap.

Burlington County Jail. Attended from Sacred Heart Church

260 High St., Mount Holly, 08060. Tel: 609-702-1848.

FREEHOLD. *Monmouth County Jail*, Tel: 732-462-7429. Rev. Francisco J. Saenz-Lozada, O.P., Chap. Attended from St. Rose of Lima Church, Freehold, NJ.

HAMILTON. *Robert Wood Johnson University Hospital*. Rev. Charles J. Flood, O.SS.T., Chap.

LAWRENCEVILLE. *St. Lawrence/Morris Hall*. Rev. Angelo Amaral, Chap.

LONG BRANCH. *Monmouth Medical Center*, c/o Christ the King Parish, 390 Division St., Long Branch, 07740. Rev. Andres Alberto Serna.

MARLTON. *Virtua West Jersey Hospital*. Sr. Peg Boyle, S.S.J., Chap.

NEPTUNE. *Jersey Shore Medical Center*.

NEW LISBON. *New Jersey State Colony*. Attended from Holy Eucharist Church, Tabernacle, NJ 08088, Tel: 609-726-1000.

TOMS RIVER. *Ocean County Jail*, Tel: 732-349-0018. Attended from St. Joseph, Toms River.

YARDVILLE. *Garden State Correctional Center*, P.O. Box 11401, Yardville, 08620. Rev. Longinus Vewvegbeiem, Chap.

WILLINGBORO. *Lourdes Medical Center of Burlington*. Sr. Rose Colanzi, Chap.

Military Installations

COLTS NECK. *Naval Weapons Station Earle*. Served by chaplains assigned by the Archdiocese for the Military Service.

JOINT BASE MCGUIRE-DIX-LAKEHURST. Served by chaplains assigned by the Archdiocese for the Military Service.

On Duty Outside the Diocese:

Revs.—

Felicien, Jean, Catholic University, Washington, DC

Gadenz, Pablo T., S.T.D., S.S.L., South Orange, 07079

Kimtis, Kevin J., Rome, Italy

Krisak, Anthony F., S.S., 934 Kearny St., N.E., Washington, DC 20017-3516

Lankford, Michael G., Veterans Administration

McPartland, Patrick, Chap., U.S. Navy

Peirano, Juan Daniel, Gregorian University, Rome.

Leave of Absence:

Revs.—

Butch, Brian T.

Griffiths, Charles L.

Polczyk, Stanislaus

Ricciardelli, Albert.

Retired:

Rev. Msgrs.—

Bacovin, Ronald J., (Retired), 2301 Lawrenceville Rd., Lawrenceville, 08648

Brady, James J., V.F., (Retired)

Brietske, Richard C., (Retired), P.O. Box 771, Barnegat Light, 08006

Dermond, John K., J.C.L., (Retired), 2301 Lawrence Rd., Lawrenceville, 08648

Dubell, James H., (Retired)

Flood, Peter J., Chap. Col., (Retired), 102 Halle Blvd., Ste. 263, San Antonio, TX 78243

Gartland, R. Vincent, (Retired), 2301 Lawrence Rd., Lawrenceville, 08648

Gibbons, John, (Retired), 610 Bedford Ln., Manchester, 08759

Ladzinski, Casimir H., (Retired), 2301 Lawrenceville Rd., Lawrenceville, 08648

McGovern, James J., (Retired), 3225 Brunswick Ln., Sarasota, FL 34239

Nolan, Walter E., (Retired)

Punderson, Joseph R., (Retired)

Rebeck, Eugene M., (Retired)

Ronan, Hugh F., (Retired), 2301 Lawrenceville Rd., Lawrenceville, 08648

Stansley, Ralph W., (Retired), 2301 Lawrenceville Rd., Lawrenceville, 08648

Troiano, Leonard F., (Retired), 22 White Cap, Brick, 08723

Valentino, Frederick A., (Retired), 509 Woodland Ave., Brielle, 08730

Very Revs.—

Nolan, Jerome M., V.F., (Retired), 2A Pines St., Toms River, 08757

Schecker, Robert J.W., V.F., (Retired), Lions Head South, 29 Tennis Ct., Brick Town, 08723

Revs.—

Bausch, William J., (Retired), Box 1068, Point Pleasant Beach, 08742

Bowden, John V., (Retired), 2301 Lawrenceville Rd., Lawrenceville, 08648

Burns, Michael J., (Retired), 2301 Lawrenceville Rd., Lawrenceville, 08648

Cahill, Daniel G., (Retired), 2301 Lawrenceville Rd., Lawrenceville, 08648

Carotenuto, Anthony M., (Retired)

Castles, Patrick J., (Retired)

Cioffi, Ronald J., (Retired), 16 Brookwood, Freehold, 07728

Cuomo, Rocco A., (Retired), 26D Holly St., Toms River, 08757
DeSandre, John G., (Retired), P.O. Box 483, Pine Beach, 08741
Deutsch, George E., (Retired), 1967 E. Lakeview Dr., Sebastian, FL 32958
Devlin, Mark T., (Retired), 2301 Lawrenceville Rd., Lawrenceville, 08648
Ekdahl, Kenneth W., (Retired)
Gallagher, Richard, (Retired), Villa Vianney, 2301 Lawrenceville Rd., Lawrenceville, 08648
Gnarackatt, Joseph, (Retired), St. Dominic Church, 250 Old Squan Rd., Brick, 07824
Griswold, Edward J., (Retired), 5400 Roland, Baltimore, MD 21210
Gronifillo, Alejandro, (Retired), 2301 Lawrenceville Rd., Lawrenceville, 08648
Hughes, Raymond E., (Retired), 2301 Lawrenceville Rd., Lawrenceville, 08648
Jackiewicz, Frederick W., (Retired), 19 Pettit Ave., South River, 08882
Kearns, Adam, (Retired), 1 Bishop Dr., Lawrenceville, 08648
Keigher, Bernard J., (Retired)
Magee, Patrick F., (Retired)
Mathias, Edwin J., (Retired), 2301 Lawrenceville Rd., Lawrenceville, 08648
McCormick, Brian J., (Retired), 2301 Lawrenceville Rd., Lawrenceville, 08648
Miele, Joseph J., (Retired), 388 Cherry Quay Rd., Brick, 08723-6308
Milewski, Casimir, (Retired), U1.M. Karlowicza 22 33-100, Tarnow, Poland
Milewski, Richard R., (Retired), 2301 Lawrenceville Rd., Lawrenceville, 08648
O'Connor, Michael J., (Retired), 2301 Lawrenceville Rd., Lawrenceville, 08648
Pearson, Robert A., (Retired), 73 Rolling Meadows Blvd. S., Ocean, 07712
Poovakulam, Antony P., (Retired), India
Radomski, Joseph A., (Retired), 2381 Lawrenceville Rd., 08648
Ruggiero, Philip, (Retired)
Sauchelli, James J., (Retired), 152A Gramercy Ct., Lakewood, 08701
Schabowski, Henry F., (Retired), 3 Jed Ct., Hamilton, 08609
Schneider, William T., (Retired), 209 Laurel Rd. #209, Voorhees, 08043
Scully, John J., (Retired), 2301 Lawrence Rd., Lawrenceville, 08648
Sloyan, Gerard S., (Retired), Byron House, 9210 Kentsdale Dr. #102, Potomac, MD 20854
Sweeny, Richard R., (Retired), 2381 Lawrenceville Rd., Lawrenceville, 08648
Thelly, Matthew, (Retired), India
Triggs, Thomas J., (Retired), 71 Hillside, Sayreville, 08872
Venza, Felix F., (Retired), 605A Arena Dr., Hamilton, 08610
Vona, Michael S., (Retired), 5 Doral Way, Neptune, 07753
Wake, John F., (Retired), 2301 Lawrenceville Rd., Lawrenceville, 08648
Weiser, Charles B., (Retired)
Williams, H. Brendan, (Retired), 2301 Lawrenceville Rd., Lawrenceville, 08648
Zec, John, (Retired), 713 Colgate Ave., Perth Amboy, 08861.

Permanent Deacons:

Acosta, Amado F., (On Duty Outside the Diocese, SC)
Adorno, Miguel, Christ the Redeemer, Mt. Holly
Alessi, James A., Incarnation - St. James, Trenton
Andre, Edner
Andrews, Stephen W., (On Duty Outside the Diocese, Raleigh, NC)
Aquino, Romeo D., (Retired), St. Joseph's, Toms River
Arcari, Richard A., St. Raphael-Holy Angels, Hamilton
Armstrong, Robert B., St. Teresa of Calcutta, Bradley Beach
Auleta, Michael A., (Retired), Outside the Diocese
Ayers, Damian, St. Dominic, Brick
Ayrer, James E., (Retired), Corpus Christi, Willingboro
Babuschak, Francis J., (Retired), St. Joseph, Toms River
Baeza, Adolfo, St. Joseph, Trenton
Baker, Thomas, St. David the King, Princeton Junction
Barbara, Joseph F., St. John Neumann, Mt. Laurel
Barnes, Robert M., St. Joseph, Toms River
Barng, Ilsoo P., St. Dorothea, Eatontown
Beauchamps, Jose, (Retired), St. Mary Cathedral, Trenton
Bednarek, Robert J., Sacred Heart, Riverton
Begley, Thomas D. III, Our Lady of Good Counsel, Moorestown
Benner, Richard K., (On Duty Outside the Diocese)
Bertagnolli, John F., Our Lady of Good Counsel, Moorestown
Bittner, Robert W., (On Leave)
Blackwell, M. Darrell, (On Duty Outside the Diocese, ME)
Boehm, Michael P., Our Lady of Perpetual Help, Maple Shade
Bonner, John J., (Retired)
Brannigan, Patrick R., (Retired), St. James, Pennington
Briggs, William E., Church of the Resurrection, Delran
Buecker, Edward J., St. Dominic, Brick
Byrne, Kevin M., (On Duty Outside the Diocese, Washington, DC)
Campbell, James L., St. Justin, Toms River
Caponigro, Alfred E., (On Duty Outside the Diocese, AZ)
Card, Joseph A., (Retired), Our Lady of Perpetual Help, Maple Shade
Cartnick, Louis C., (Retired), St. Luke, Toms River
Casa, James L., Sacred Heart, Mount Holly
Casey, Keith J., St. Thomas More, Manalapan
Cattanea, James F., Resurrection, Delran
Cechulski, Thomasz J., St. Veronica, Howell
Cerefice, Robert L., (Retired), Holy Innocents, Neptune
Challender, James J., (Retired), Our Lady of Sorrows-St. Anthony, Hamilton
Chandonnet, Christopher H., St. Joseph, Millstone Township
Chase, Daniel A., (Retired), St. Isidore the Farmer, New Egypt
Cheu, Richard A., (Retired)
Clausen, Peter M., (Retired), St. Barnabas, Bayville
Clymore, John L., (Retired), St. Benedict, Holmdel
Coccia, Christopher A., (On Duty Outside the Diocese, New York)
Collins, Michael B., St. Joseph, Trenton
Colter, David C., St. Raphael-Holy Angels, Hamilton
Commisso, Louis V., (Retired), Epiphany, Brick
Cordasco, Ralph, (Retired), St. Elizabeth Ann Seton, Whiting
Coscarelli, Richard D., St. Teresa of Calcutta, Bradley Beach
Costa, Gregory J., St. Raphael-Holy Angels, Hamilton
Craft, Philip T., St. Pius X, Forked River
Cugini, Henry J., CoCathedral of St. Robert Bellarmine, Freehold
Cullinane, John, (Retired), (On Duty Outside the Diocese, NY)
Cummings, James H., (Retired), St. Barnabas, Bayville
Cunningham, Robert, St. Francis of Assisi, Brant Beach
Currie, Richard J., St. James, Pennington
D'Angelo, V. Richard, (Retired), (On Duty Outside the Diocese, Charleston, SC)
Davis, Bryan P., St. James, Red Bank
Davis, James R., St. Thomas More, Manalapan
Daye, Charles Jr., St. Veronica, Howell
DeFrehn, Jeffrey, St. Joan of Arc, Marlton
DelGuidice, John V., (On Duty Outside the Diocese, Orlando, FL)
DeLuca, Joseph W., (Retired), Holy Eucharist, Tabernacle
Desire, Luders, O.L. Sorrows - St. Anthony, Hamilton
DiCanio, Thomas J., St. Catharine, Holmdel
DiCesare, Anthony N., (Retired), Our Lady of Hope, West Long Branch
DiLissio, John A., St. Gregory the Great, Hamilton
Dinella, Roger P., (Retired), St. David the King, Princeton Junction
Domzalski, Kenneth S., Holy Eucharist, Tabernacle
Donadieu, Joseph M., (Retired), Sacred Heart, Riverton
Donofrio, Nicholas, (Retired), St. Dorothea, Eatontown
Doughty, Gerald A., (Retired), St. Charles Borromeo, Cinnaminson
Downing, Peter F., St. Elizabeth Ann Seton, Whiting
Ebenau, Frederick C. Sr., St. Justin, Toms River
Ernst, Henry J., (Retired)
Esposito, Louis (Gino) S., St. Veronica, Howell
Fanelle, John D., (On Duty Outside the Diocese, San Diego, CA)
Fatovic, Andrew J., (On Duty Outside the Diocese, SC)
Finn, Lawrence W. Sr., (Retired), Mary, Mother of the Church, Bordentown
Fiorillo, Joseph A., St. Mary, Barnegat
Fischer, Edward III, (Retired), (Retired), Visitation, Brick
Flanagan, John P., (Retired), St. Catharine, Holmdel
Folinus, Robert, St. Rose, Belmar
Foster, Michael Lee, St. Thomas More, Manalapan
Franey, John J., St. Veronica, Howell
Franklin, Paul H., (On Duty Outside the Diocese, Atlanta, GA)
Friedmann, Rolf B., CoCathedral of St. Robert Bellarmine, Freehold
Fullen, Michael P. Sr., (On Leave)
Fung, Matthew V., St. David the King, Princeton Junction
Gallagher, James V., (On Duty Outside the Diocese, NY)
Gallagher, Lawrence E., St. George, Titusville
Gallagher, Paul A., (On Leave)
Gallagher, William J., Jail & Prison Ministry
Galvan, Silverius F., St. Mary of the Lake, Lakewood
Garvey, Thomas J., (Retired), St. Anthony of Padua, Hightstown
Gay, Robert, St. Barnabas, Bayville
Genovese, Eugene, St. Rose, Belmar
Genovese, Thomas, (Retired), St. Joseph, Toms River
Gettlefinger, Robert J., (On Duty Outside the Diocese, NC)
Gillespie, James, St. Justin, Toms River
Gilli, Joseph F., (On Leave)
Golazeski, Frances G., St. Ann, Lawrenceville
Gomez, Victor L., St. Anthony Claret, Lakewood
Gregory, Gabriel, (Retired), (On Duty Outside the Diocese, MN)
Gregory, Thomas J., (Retired), Arizona
Groff, Francis W., (Retired), St. Martha, Point Pleasant
Grussler, John R., (Retired), Sacred Heart, Trenton
Gwiazda, Edward J., (On Duty Outside the Diocese, FL)
Hagan, Michael J., Corpus Christi, Willingboro
Hambleton, Richard N., (Retired), (On Duty Outside the Diocese, Charleston, SC)
Hank, William Moore, St. James, Pennington
Hanna, John H., (Retired), St. Pio of Pietrelcina, Lavallette
Hannawacker, Joseph A., J.C.L., Incarnation-St. James, Trenton
Hansen, Christopher L., St. Catharine, Holmdel
Hauenstein, Richard A., (Retired), St. Justin, Toms River
Haunss, Ronald J., (Retired), St. Mary, Barnegat
Heffernan, Edward A., Our Lady of Good Counsel, Moorestown
Heilig, Kenneth W., (Retired), Sacred Heart, Riverton
Heller, James T., (Retired), St. Pius X, Forked River
Hepp, Joseph L., (Retired), St. John the Baptist, Allentown
Hoag, Edward A., St. Ann, Lawrenceville
Hobson, Richard J., St. James, Pennington
Hoefling, John F., Sacred Heart, Mt. Haely
Hughes, John P., (Retired), St. John Neumann, Mount Laurel
Hvizdos, John F., St. Charles Borromeo, Cinnaminson
Iadanza, John M., (On Duty Outside the Diocese, FL)
Isaac, John R., St. Gregory the Great, Hamilton
Jackson, Frank W., (Retired), Epiphany, Brick
Jakub, Louis E., Our Lady of Hope, West Long Branch
Jaruszewski, Joseph, Our Lady of Sorrows-St. Anthony, Hamilton
Jennings, Edward F., (Retired), St. Catharine, Spring Lake
Jimenez, Jose J., Corpus Christ, Willingboro
Johnson, James G., (On Duty Outside the Diocese, Washington, DC)
Johnson, Robert J., Our Lady of Perpetual Help-St. Agnes Parish, Atlantic Highlands
Johnston, George A., (On Duty Outside the Diocese, Charleston, SC)
Karpecik, Walter J. Jr., St. Katherine Drexel, Burlington
Kelder, George R. Jr., St. Denis, Manasquan
Kelly, James A., (Retired), Nativity, Fair Haven
Kendrick, Stanley D., St. Barnabas, Bayville
Kennedy, Patrick W., (Retired), (On Duty Outside the Diocese, GA)
Kerr, Ronald J. Sr., (Retired), St. John, Lakehurst
Klein, Robert, (Retired), St. Mary, Barnegat
Klincewicz, John G., Holy Innocents, Neptune
Knipper, James J., St. Paul, Princeton
Knoebel, Christian, St. Monica, Jackson
Knowles, Thomas J., St. John Neumann, Mount Laurel
Kohut, David S., (On Duty Outside the Diocese, VA)
Kolon, Thomas F., Our Lady of Good Counsel, Moorestown
Kopcak, John, St. Teresa of Calcutta, Bradley Beach
Korbelak, George M., St. Peter, Pt. Pleasant Beach

Krupa, Bradford A., On Duty Outside the Diocese (Atlanta, GA)
Lafond, Robert H., (On Leave)
Lancieri, Salvatore, (Retired)
Lang, Paul, Church of Nativity, Fair Haven
Latini, Joseph E., St. Gregory the Great, Hamilton
Laurita, Daniel J., J.C.L., (On Duty Outside the Diocese, AL)
Lavelle, Thomas J. Jr., St. Raphael-Holy Angels, Hamilton
Linka, Fernando, Our Lady Perpetual Help, Maple Shade
Little, John L., St. Catharine, Spring Lake
Littlefield, James J., On Leave
Lombardo, Earl H., (Retired), St. Pius X, Forked River
Lonie, Michael, St. Catharine, Holmdel
Loughran, Thomas, (Retired)
Lovejoy, C. Doug Jr., (On Duty Outside of Diocese, Baltimore, MD)
Luhman, Andrew G. Jr., St. Rose of Lima, Freehold
Luongo, Gerard, St. Joseph, Toms River
Malhame, Eugene G. Jr., St. Rose, Belmar
Mammoliti, Anthony, (On Duty Outside the Diocese, Brooklyn, NY)
Manaloris, James A., (Retired), Our Lady Perpetual Help, Maple Shade
Mannikus, Uku R., St. Aloysius, Jackson
Marcello, Salvatore, St. Raphael-Holy Angels, Hamilton
Marino, Charles J., On Leave
Martin, Patrick J., (Retired), St. Mary, Barnegat
Martucci, Anthony R., (Retired), St. Pius X, Forked River
Mattozzi, Guido J., Our Lady of the Angels, Trenton
McGrath, James G., (Retired), St. Mary of The Lakes, Lakewood
McGrath, John G., (Retired), St. Catherine, Middletown
McKenna, Francis A., (Retired), St. Joseph, Toms River
McKenna, Robert M., St. Rose of Lima, Freehold
McMahon, Martin K., St. Mary, Middletown
McMahon, Sean, Our Lady of Perpetual Help, Maple Shade
Meehan, Daniel J., (Retired), Resurrection, Delran
Mendonca, Glen L., Our Lady of Fatima, Keyport
Meyer, Richard G., (On Duty Outside the Diocese, FL)
Meyers, Ronald S., Our Lady of Perpetual Help, Maple Shade
Miller, Daniel S. Sr., (On Duty Outside the Diocese, Orlando, FL)
Miller, Donald C., (Retired), St. Elizabeth Ann Seton, Whiting
Modelo, Romeo B. Jr., St. Charles Borromeo, Cinnaminson
Moir, Gene F. Sr., (Retired), St. Monica, Jackson
Moore, Joseph J. Jr., St. Gregory the Great, Hamilton
Morris, Richard L., St. Benedict, Holmdel
Morton, James E., (On Duty Outside the Diocese, FL)
Moscarello, Charles M., St. Gregory The Great, Hamilton
Mosteller, Herman J., (Retired), Jesus the Good Shepherd, Beverly
Motylinski, Kenneth E., St. Mary of The Lakes, Medford
Mueller, William R., St. Joan of Arc, Marlton
Mullarkey, Michael F., Epiphany, Brick
Murphy, Christopher J., (On Duty Outside the Diocese, VA)
Murphy, Sean P., Church of Nativity, Fair Haven
Murphy, Thomas W., St. Joan of Arc, Marlton
Napolitano, Richard J., On Leave
Neubauer, James J., Holy Family, Keyport
Nicosia, Matthew P., (Retired), St. Thomas More, Manalapan
Nimon, Robert R., (Retired), On Duty Outside the Diocese, FL
Nnajiofor, Christian M., Sacred Heart, Trenton
Notaro, John A., St. Dorothea, Eatontown
Nowak, Ronald, Epiphany, Bricktown
O'Boyle, Kevin J., Our Lady of Sorrows-St. Anthony, Hamilton
O'Brien, Christopher D., (Retired), St. Elizabeth Ann Seton, Whiting
O'Brien, Michael J., St. Ann, Browns Mills
O'Connor, David, St. Isaac Jogues, Marlton
O'Donnell, John J., (Retired), Our Lady Queen of Peace, Hainesport
Orkis, Stanley, (Retired), Sacred Heart, Mt. Holly
Orlando, John C., St. Catherine, Middletown
Owens, Lester J., (Retired), St. Gabriel's, Marlboro
Pacitti, Albert, (Retired), St. Maximilian Kolbe, Toms River
Palmisano, William R., St. Raphael-Holy Angels, Hamilton
Papuga, David F., Our Lady of Good Counsel, Moorestown
Paul, Joseph A., (Retired), Our Lady of Good Counsel, Moorestown
Pelkowski, Raymond R., (Retired), St. Benedict, Holmdel
Pennise, Alfred, (Retired), St. Katherine Drexel, Burlington
Perez, Rene P., St. Aloysius, Jackson
Perusi, Donald L., (On Duty Outside the Diocese, Arlington, VA)
Petrauskas, James J., (Retired), St. Mary, Barnegat
Pierfy, Jeffrey, (Retired), Our Lady of Sorrows-St. Anthony, Hamilton
Pirozzi, Neil, (Retired), St. Gregory the Great, Hamilton
Pitt, John R., (On Leave)
Pladek, Robert B., St. Luke, Toms River
Policastro, Donald M., Our Lady of Fatima, Keyport
Porter, Thomas P., On Duty Outside the Diocese (Raleigh, NC)
Prevosti, George A. Jr., St. William the Abbot, Howell
Price, Walter L., (On Duty Outside the Diocese, Orlando, FL)
Prihoda, Frank J., (On Leave)
Pstrak, Gary J., St. Denis, Manasquan
Punchello, Alexander A. Sr., (Retired), St. Katherine Drexel, Burlington
Purcell, Kyran J., (Retired), St. Elizabeth Ann Seton, Whiting
Ramos, Alfonso, St. Joseph, Trenton
Ramos, Luis A., St. Mary's Cathedral, Trenton
Rasmussen, Guy C., (On Duty Outside the Diocese, FL)
Raylman, Charles D., St. Ann, Browns Mills
Repice, Anthony, (Retired), St. Pius X, Forked River
Ricciardi, Vincent P. Sr., Our Lady of Fatima, Keyport
Richardson, Gary T., Mary, Mother of the Church, Bordentown
Richichi, Joseph, Christ the King, Long Branch
Rider, Joseph H., St. Elizabeth Ann Seton, Whiting
Riley, Michael J., St. George, Titusville
Rinaldi, Vincent L., CoCathedral of St. Robert Bellarmine, Freehold
Rivella, Thomas H., (Retired), Incarnation-St. James, Trenton
Rodriguez, Feliz, (On Duty Outside the Diocese, PR)
Rodriguez, Jose G., On Duty Outside the Diocese, FL
Roenbeck, Richard G., St. Gabriel, Marlboro
Rowley, William R., (Retired), Sacred Heart, Mt. Holly
Russo, James C., (On Duty Outside the Diocese, Allentown, PA)
Sabados, Andrew A. Sr., (Retired), St. Gregory the Great, Hamilton
Sakowski, Daniel C., St. Catherine of Siena, Farmingdale
Sansevere, Stephen A., St. Gabriel, Marlboro
Santos, Rodolfo A., St. Rose of Lima, Freehold
Scanlon, John J., (On Leave)
Scannella, Michael V., Our Lady of the Angels, Trenton
Scharen, Robert F., St. Elizabeth Ann Seton, Whiting
Schmitt, Gary L., Jesus the Good Shepherd, Beverly
Schwoebel, Ronald V., Mary, Mother of the Church, Bordentown
Sciarrotta, Samuel P., (Retired), Outside the Diocese, FL
Scott, James M. III, St. Ann, Lawrenceville
Scott, Stephen G., St. Benedict, Holmdel
Scotti, Richard, St. Gabriel, Marlboro
Sepich, William S., (Retired), St. Charles Borromeo, Cinnaminson
Shapiro, David L., (On Leave)
Shea, Thomas F., Mary, Mother of the Church, Bordentown
Slavin, Dennis E., (Retired), Our Lady of Permanent Sorrows, St. Anthony, Hamilton
Slee, Louis F., (Retired), Outside the Diocese
Smigelski, Michael A., (On Duty Outside the Diocese, Charleston, SC)
Smith, Andrew M., CoCathedral of St. Robert Bellarmine, Freehold
Smith, Charles J., (Retired), St. Mary, Middletown
Smith, Kevin M., St. William The Abbot, Howell
Somma, Eugene A., (On Leave)
Sondeen, Carl R., (Retired), St. Charles Borromeo, Cinnaminson
Sorrentino, Fernando A., (Retired), Outside the Diocese
Squicciarini, Carlo, St. Mary, Middletown
Staub, Raymond W., (Retired), St. Isidore the Farmer, New Egypt
Stesner, Patrick J. Sr., St. Joseph, Toms River
Stinsman, Michael J., Sacred Heart, Riverton
Stranieri, Nicola, (On Leave)
Swanson, George J., St. Barnabas, Bayville
Szmutko, Steven K., Our Lady of Good Counsel, W. Trenton
Tarzy, Barry R., (Retired), St. Joan of Arc, Marlton
Taylor, Michael A., (Retired), St. Joseph, Toms River
Tedeschi, Joseph R., (Retired), St. Mary of the Lakes, Medford
Tharp, Robert, (Retired), St. Raphael-Holy Angels, Hamilton
Titmas, Richard C., (Retired), Outside the Diocese, FL
Toca, Frederick M., (On Duty Outside the Diocese, Atlanta, GA)
Toolan, James W., (On Duty Outside the Diocese, Allentown, PA)
Torres, Benito, St. Mary Cathedral, Trenton
Trani, Eduardo, (Retired), Jesus the Good Shepherd, Riverside
Tucker, Richard W., St. Leo the Great, Lincroft
Valentin, Juan E., (On Duty Outside the Diocese, PA)
Vassallo, John F. Jr., (On Duty Outside the Diocese, VA)
Vazquez, Emiliano, St. Mary Cathedral, Trenton
Vicari, Salvatore J. Jr., Visitation, Brick Town
Vignolini, Robert J., Christ the King, Long Branch
Vivona, Joseph A., (Retired), St. Mary, Barnegat
Vogel, Anthony D., (Retired), Outside the Diocese, PA
Wadolowski, Thomas P., St. Clement, Matawan
Wagner, Steven A., St. Mary, Barnegat
Walsh, James P., Holy Innocents, Neptune
Wanat, John A., St. Aloysius, Jackson
Watkins, Thomas H. Jr., St. Hedwig, Trenton
Weber, Francis J. Jr., CoCathedral of St. Robert Bellarmine, Freehold
Weber, Richard J., St. Rose, Belmar
Wilson, Edward H., St. Leo The Great, Lincroft
Wilson, William A., (Retired), St. Gregory the Great, Hamilton Square
Young, Donald A., (On Duty Outside the Diocese, Arlington, VA)
Zadworny, Barry J., St. Hedwig, Trenton
Zalegowski, Ronald F., (Retired), Mary, Mother of the Church, Bordentown
Zapcic, William J. Jr., St. Anselm, Wayside
Zebrowski, John J., (Retired), St. Thomas More, Manalapan
Zito, Lee, Our Lady Queen of Peace, Hainesport.

INSTITUTIONS LOCATED IN DIOCESE

[A] COLLEGES AND UNIVERSITIES

LAKEWOOD. *Georgian Court University*, 900 Lakewood Ave., Lakewood, 08701-2697. Tel: 732-987-2200; Fax: 732-987-2018; Email: president@georgian.edu; Web: www.georgian.edu. Joseph R. Marbach, Ph.D., Pres.; Rev. Anthony DiPalma, Chap.; Janice Warner, Interim Provost. Lay Teachers 127; Priests 1; Sisters 4; Students 2,019; Clergy/Religious Teachers 5.

[B] HIGH SCHOOLS, DIOCESAN AND PARISH

TRENTON. *Notre Dame High School*, 601 Lawrence Rd., Lawrenceville, 08648. Tel: 609-882-7900; Fax: 609-882-5723; Email: duff@ndnj.org; Web: www.ndnj.org. Ms. Mary E. Ivins, Pres.; Mrs. Joanna Barlow, Prin.; Mrs. Lisa Lenihan, Vice Prin.; Mrs. Eleanor MacIsaac, Vice Prin.; Rev. Jason M. Parzynski, Chap. Lay Teachers 71; Students 1,024; Clergy/Religious Teachers 1.

BELMAR. *Saint Rose High School*, 607 Seventh Ave., Belmar, 07719. Tel: 732-681-2858; Fax: 732-280-2745; Email: knace@strose.k12.nj.us; Web: www.strose.k12.nj.us. Sr. Kathleen Nace, S.S.J., Prin. Lay Teachers 39; Sisters 4; Students 489.

HAMILTON. *Trenton Catholic Academy (Upper School)*, 175 Leonard Ave., Hamilton, 08610. Tel: 609-586-3705; Fax: 609-586-6584; Email: dpayne@trentoncatholic.org; Email: ckroekel@trentoncatholic.org. Sr. Dorothy Payne, S.S.J., Pres.; Charles Kroekel, Prin.; Mr. Michael Knowles, Project Lead the Way Dir. Lay Teachers 20; Sisters 1; Students 208.

HOLMDEL. *St. John Vianney High School*, 540 A Line Rd., Holmdel, 07733-1697. Tel: 732-739-0800; Fax: 732-739-0824; Email: dimezza@sjvhs.com; Web: www.sjvhs.com. Mr. Joseph F. Deroba, Pres.; Steven DiMezza, Prin. Lay Teachers 65; Sisters 1; Students 1,000.

RED BANK. *Red Bank Catholic High School*, 112 Broad St., Red Bank, 07701. Tel: 732-747-1774; Fax: 732-747-1936; Email: alabat@redbankcatholic.com; Web: www.redbankcatholic.org. Robert Abatemarco, Prin. Lay Teachers 100; Sisters 2; Students 831.

TOMS RIVER. *Donovan Catholic*, 711 Hooper Ave., Toms River, 08753. Tel: 732-349-8801; Fax: 732-349-8956 (Main); Tel: 732-355-2474 (Admissions); Tel: 732-914-2474 (Athletics); Tel: 732-349-8441 (Guidance); Email: egere@donovancatholic.org; Web: www.donovancatholic.org. Dr. Edward G. Gere, Ed.D., Prin. Lay Teachers 64; Priests 4; Students 716; Clergy/Religious Teachers 5.

[C] HIGH SCHOOLS, PRIVATE

TRENTON. *Villa Victoria Academy*, 376 W. Upper Ferry Rd., 08628. Tel: 609-882-1700; Fax: 609-882-8421; Email: srlesley@villavictoria.org; Email: srlillian@villavictoria.org; Web: www.villavictoria.org. Sisters Lillian Harrington, Pres.; Lesley Draper, M.P.F., Prin. Grades 6-12 (Girls) Lay Teachers 19; Students 110; Clergy/Religious Teachers 6.

DELRAN. *Holy Cross Preparatory Academy*, 5035 Rte. 130 S., Delran, 08075. Tel: 856-461-5400; Fax: 856-764-0806; Email: bstonis@gmail.com. William Stonis, Prin. Lay Teachers 20; Priests 1; Students 300.

LINCROFT. *Christian Brothers Academy*, 850 Newman Springs Rd., Lincroft, 07738. Tel: 732-747-1959; Fax: 732-747-1643; Email: President@cbalincroftnj.org; Web: www.cbalincroftnj.org. Bros. Ralph Montedoro, F.S.C., Vice Pres.; Frank Byrne, F.S.C., Pres.; R. Ross Fales, Prin.; Matthew Meehan, Admin.; Sean Nunan, Admin.; Maureen Szablewski, Admin.; Sylvia McInerney, Librarian. Brothers 7; Lay Teachers 75; Priests 1; Students 896; Clergy/Religious Teachers 5.

MIDDLETOWN. *Mater Dei Prep*, 19 Cherry Tree Farm Rd., Middletown, 07748. Tel: 732-671-9100; Fax: 732-671-9214; Email: jhauenstein@materdeiprep.org; Web: www.materdeiprep.org. James Hauenstein, Pres. & Prin.; Elana Maloney, Librarian. Lay Teachers 28; Priests 1; Students 350.

[D] REGIONAL SCHOOLS

WILLINGBORO. *Pope John Paul II Regional School*, (Grades PreK-8), 11 S. Sunset Rd., Willingboro, 08046. Tel: 609-877-2144; Fax: 609-877-3153; Email: pjp2business@gmail.com; Email: pjp2rs-principal@comcast.net; Web: www.pjpiirs.com. Catherine Zagola, Prin.; Kimberly Sheaffer, Sec. Lay Teachers 15; Students 147.

[E] INTER-PARISH ELEMENTARY SCHOOLS

HAMILTON. *Trenton Catholic Academy (Lower School)*, (Grades PreK-8), 177 Leonard Ave., Hamilton, 08610. Tel: 609-586-5888; Fax: 609-631-9295; Email: dpayne@trentoncatholic.org; Web: www.trentoncatholic.org. Anne Reap, Prin.; Sr. Dorothy Payne, S.S.J., Prin.; Candace Andrako, Librarian. Lay Teachers 20; Students 325; Clergy/Religious Teachers 1.

MANAHAWKIN. *All Saints Regional Catholic School*, (Grades PreSchool-8), 400 Doc Cramer Blvd., Manahawkin, 08050. Tel: 609-597-3800; Fax: 609-597-2223; Email: asrc@asrcs.org; Web: asrcs.org. Kathleen Blazewicz, Prin. Lay Teachers 19; Students 192; Total Enrollment 192; Clergy/Religious Teachers 5.

[F] ELEMENTARY SCHOOLS, PRIVATE

PRINCETON. *Princeton Academy of the Sacred Heart*, (Grades K-8), 1128 Great Rd., Princeton, 08540. Tel: 609-921-6499; Fax: 609-921-9198; Email: adugan@princetonacademy.org; Web: www.princetonacademy.org. Alfred Dugan III, Headmaster; Ellen Dowling, Librarian. Private elementary and middle school for boys. Lay Teachers 26; Students 188.

Stuart Country Day School of the Sacred Heart, (Grades PreK-12), 1200 Stuart Rd., Princeton, 08540. Tel: 609-921-2330; Fax: 609-497-0784; Email: admissions@stuartschool.org; Email: pfagin@stuartschool.org; Web: stuartschool.org. Dr. Patty L. Fagin, Headmaster. Lay Teachers 80; Students 435.

[G] CATHOLIC CHARITIES, DIOCESE OF TRENTON

TRENTON. *Catholic Charities*, 383 W. State St., P.O. Box 1423, 08607-1423. Tel: 609-394-5181; Fax: 609-695-6978; Email: mlaocollins@cctrenton.org; Web: catholiccharitiestrenton.org. Ms. Marlene Lao'-Collins, Exec. Dir.; Adriana Torres-O'Connor, Exec.; George Bontcue, Assoc. Exec. Dir., Fiscal Affairs; Susan Loughery, Dir. Operations; Nancy B. Tompkins, Devel. Dir. Tot Asst. Annually 100,000; Total Staff 650.

Behavioral Health Services Burlington County, 25 Ikea Dr., Westampton, 08060. Tel: 609-267-9339; Fax: 609-267-6655; Email: atorresoconnor@cctrenton.org. Adriana Torres-O'Connor, Dir. Total Staff 650.

Behavioral Health Services Mercer County, 10 Southard St., 08609. Tel: 609-396-4557; Fax: 609-394-1412; Email: atorres-oconnor@cctrenton.org. Adriana Torres-O'Connor, Dir. Total Staff 650.

Children & Family Services Monmouth/Ocean Counties, 145 Maple Ave., Red Bank, 07701. Tel: 732-747-9660; Fax: 732-747-7590; Email: rgering@cctrenton.org. Ronald C. Gering, L.P.C., C.C.M.H.C., Svc. Area Dir. Tot Asst. Annually 774; Total Staff 8.

Community Services, 801 Burlington Ave., Delanco, 08075. Tel: 856-764-6945; Fax: 856-764-6948; Email: AValentin@cctrenton.org. Arnold Valentin Jr., Dir. Total Staff 650.

Community Services (Mercer), 132 N. Warren St., 08608. Tel: 609-394-8847; Email: avalentin@cctrenton.org. Arnold Valentin Jr., Dir. Total Staff 650.

Community Services (Ocean), 200 Monmouth Ave., Lakewood, 08701. Tel: 732-363-5322; Fax: 732-363-3203; Email: AValentin@cctrenton.org. Arnold Valentin Jr., Dir. Total Staff 650.

Children & Family Services Mercer County, 55 N. Clinton Ave., 08609. Tel: 609-394-7680; Fax: 609-278-1836; Email: rgering@cctrenton.org. Ronald C. Gering, L.P.C., C.C.M.H.C., Svc. Area Dir. Services for victims and perpetuators of family violence. Tot Asst. Annually 588; Total Staff 10.

Providence House Domestic Violence Services, 595 Rancocas Rd., Westampton, 08060. Tel: 856-824-0599; Fax: 856-824-9340; Email: mpettrow@cctrenton.org. Mary Pettrow, C.S.W., Assoc. Dir. Services to women and children in danger of physical abuse. Total Staff 650.

Providence House Domestic Violence Services (Ocean), 88 Schoolhouse Rd., Ste. 1, Whiting, 08759. Tel: 732-350-2120; Fax: 732-350-2725; Email: mpettrow@cctrenton.org; Web: www.catholiccharitiestrenton.org. Mary Pettrow, C.S.W., Dir. Tot Asst. Annually 4,500; Total Staff 65.

[H] DAY CARE CENTERS

BRANT BEACH. *St. Francis of Assisi Day Care Center*, 4700 Long Beach Blvd., Long Beach Township, 08008. Tel: 609-494-8861; Fax: 609-494-0489; Email: wsaunders@stfrancislbi.org; Web: stfranciscenterlbi.org. Katie Opauski, Contact Person. Students 152.

KEANSBURG. *St. Ann Day Care*, 121 Main St., Keansburg, 07734-1728. Tel: 732-787-7220; Fax: 732-787-2136; Email: jma.stann@yahoo.com. Jane M. Abrahamsen, Dir. Students 80; Full-time Teachers 4; Full-time Assistant Teachers & Caregivers 24; Cook 1; Assistant Kitchen Help 2.

[I] GENERAL HOSPITALS

TRENTON. *St. Francis Medical Center*, 601 Hamilton Ave., 08629. Tel: 609-599-5000; Fax: 609-695-2744; Email: rhansel@stfrancismedical.org; Web: www.stfrancismedical.com. Mr. Russ Hansell, Vice Pres. Mission & Ministry. Affiliate of Catholic Health East. Bed Capacity 238; Sisters of St. Francis of Philadelphia 7; Tot Asst. Annually 128,953; Total Staff 1,117.

Schools for Nurses, Tel: 609-599-5785; Fax: 609-599-6463. Bonny Ross, Dir. School of Nursing; Russ Hansel, Vice Pres., Mission & Ministry. Student Nurses 63.

WILLINGBORO. *Lourdes Medical Center of Burlington County, Inc.* (Parent Corporation: Our Lady of Lourdes Health Care Services, Inc.) 218A Sunset Rd., Willingboro, 08046. Tel: 609-835-2900; Fax: 609-835-3061; Email: info@lourdesnet.org; Web: www.lourdesnet.org. *Lourdes Medical Center of Burlington County.*

[J] SKILLED NURSING AND REHABILITATION

LAWRENCEVILLE. *Morris Hall/Saint Lawrence, Inc.*, St. Lawrence Rehabilitation Center, 2381 Lawrenceville Rd., Lawrenceville, 08648. Tel: 609-896-9500; Fax: 609-895-0242; Email: dhanley@slrc.org; Web: www.slrc.org. Darlene Hanley, CEO; Rev. Angelo Amarel, Chap. St. Lawrence Rehabilitation Center. Bed Capacity 116; Tot Asst. Annually 2,415; Total Staff 459.

Morris Hall/Saint Lawrence, Inc. St. Joseph's Nursing Center 1 Bishops' Dr., Lawrenceville, 08648-2050. Tel: 609-896-0006; Fax: 609-896-8037; Fax: 609-895-0466; Email: epetroski@morrishall.org; Web: www.morrishall.org. Ellen Petroski, M.S.W., L.S.W., L.N.H.A., Admin. & COO; Juvy Gonzales, R.N., Dir. of Nursing. Skilled Nursing Care Facility for the Chronically Ill. Bed Capacity 180; Tot Asst. Annually 173; Total Staff 100.

MorrisHall/Saint Lawrence Inc. - MorrisHall Meadows, Tel: 609-896-9500; Fax: 609-895-0242; Email: dhanley@slrc.org; Web: www.slrc.org. Darlene Hanley, CEO.

Rosecliff Living-Inc., 2381 Lawrenceville Rd., Lawrenceville, 08648. Tel: 609-896-9500; Fax: 609-895-0242; Email: lconte@slrc.org. Darlene Hanley, CEO. Inactive. Purpose is to provide housing, healthcare and social facilities and services to older adults.

[K] SPECIALIZED YOUTH AGENCIES

RED BANK. *Collier Group Home*, 180 Spring St., Red Bank, 07701. Tel: 732-842-8337; Fax: 732-530-7096; Email: mkale@collieryouthservices.org; Web: www.collieryouthservices.org. Maureen Kale, Dir. Sanctuary Certified, Trauma Informed Care provided to females ages 14-18. Sponsored by the Sisters of the Good Shepherd. Bed Capacity 10; Tot Asst. Annually 16; Total Staff 8.

Collier House, 386 Maple Pl., Keyport, 07735. Tel: 732-264-3222; Fax: 732-264-3277; Email: mkale@collieryouthservices.org; Web: www.collieryouthservices.org. Maureen Kale, Dir. Transitional Aging-Out Program. Sanctuary Certified, Trauma Informed Care provided to females ages 16-21 years old. Sponsored by the Sisters of the Good Shepherd. Bed Capacity 5; Tot Asst. Annually 7; Total Staff 6.

WICKATUNK. *Collier Youth Services, Collier School*, Collier School, 160 Conover Rd., Wickatunk, 07765. Tel: 732-946-4771; Fax: 732-946-3519; Email: info@collieryouthservices.org; Web: www.collieryouthservices.org. Sr. Deborah M. Drago, L.C.S.W., Exec. Dir. Collier School serves boys and girls in grades 5-12, providing strong academic and therapeutic support in a nurturing environment. Bed Capacity 10; Tot Asst. Annually 250; Total Staff 145.

Kateri Day Camp, 160 Conover Rd., Wickatunk, 07765. Tel: 732-946-9694; Fax: 732-946-9785; Email: kstackhouse@collieryouthservices.org; Web: www.collieryouthservices.org. Karen Stackhouse, Dir. Kateri Day Camp serves children 5-12 years old Tot Asst. Annually 200; Staff 50.

[L] ASSISTED LIVING FOR THE AGED

LAWRENCEVILLE. *Morris Hall-Saint Lawrence, Inc., St. Mary's Residence & Assisted Living*, 1 Bishops' Dr., Lawrenceville, 08648-2050. Tel: 609-896-0006; Fax: 609-896-8037; Fax: 609-895-0466; Email: epetroski@morrishall.org; Web: www.morrishall.org. Darlene Hanley, CEO; Ellen Petroski, M.S.W., L.S.W., L.N.H.A., COO; Rev. Angelo Amarel. Morris Hall - St. Mary's Residence & Assisted Living. Bed Capacity 98; Residents 71; Tot Asst. Annually 86; Total Staff 45.

[M] MONASTERIES AND RESIDENCES FOR PRIESTS AND BROTHERS

TRENTON. *Villa Vianney*, 2301 Lawrenceville Rd., 08648. Tel: 609-219-0177; Fax: 609-896-8037; Email: tboyle@slrc.org. Mr. Thomas E. Boyle, Contact Person

Legal Title: Morris Hall/St. Lawrence, Inc.

BORDENTOWN. *Society of the Divine Word*, 101 Park St., Bordentown, 08505. Tel: 609-298-0549; Fax: 609-298-6013; Email: jefferson.pool@verizon.net. Revs. Jefferson Pool, S.V.D., Supr.; Leo Dusheck, S.V.D., Member, (Retired); Feliks M. Kosat, S.V.D., J.C.L., Member; Florencio Lagura, S.V.D., Member; Raymond T. Lennon, S.V.D., Member, (Retired); James Liebner, S.V.D., Member; Robert Mirsel, S.V.D., Member; Martin Padovani, S.V.D., Member, (Retired); Steven Schuler, S.V.D., Member; Vinh The Trinh, S.V.D., Member; Charles Kennedy, (Retired).

EATONTOWN. *Christian Brothers of Frederick*, 444A Rte. 35 S., Eatontown, 07724-2200. Tel: 732-380-7926; Fax: 732-380-7937; Email: juliano@fscdena.org. Bros. Timothy Froehlich, F.S.C., Treas.; Joseph Juliano, F.S.C., Sec.

La Salle Provincialate Inc., 444A Rte. 35 S., Eatontown, 07724-2200. Tel: 732-380-7926; Fax: 732-380-7937; Email: froehlich@fscdena.org; Email: juliano@fscdena.org. Bros. Timothy Froehlich, F.S.C., Treas.; Joseph Juliano, F.S.C., Sec. Brothers of the Christian Schools.

LINCROFT. *Christian Brothers, St. La Salle Auxiliary*, 850 Newman Springs Rd., P.O. Box 238, Lincroft, 07738-1698. Tel: 732-842-4359; Email: cards@dlsaux.org; Web: dlsaux.org. Bro. William Martin, F.S.C., Dir. *LaSalle Lincroft, Inc.*, 800 Newman Springs Rd., Lincroft, 07738-0238. Tel: 732-380-7926; Fax: 732-380-7937; Email: juliano@fscdena.org; Web: www.fscdena.org. Bro. Joseph Juliano, F.S.C., Dir.

De La Salle Hall, 810 Newman Springs Rd., Lincroft, 07738. Tel: 732-530-9470; Fax: 732-842-6436; Email: jok3fsc@yahoo.com. Bro. Jules Knight, F.S.C., Dir. Brothers Licensed Nursing Home. Brothers 3; Patients 32.

[N] CONVENTS AND RESIDENCES FOR SISTERS

TRENTON. *Morning Star House of Prayer*, 312 Upper Ferry Rd., 08628. Tel: 609-882-2766; Fax: 609-882-2766; Email: morningstarh@comcast.net; Web: www.morningstarprayerhouse.org. Sr. Josephine Aparo, M.P.F., Dir. Religious Sisters Filippini. Sisters 1.

Notre Dame Diocesan Convent, 681 Lawrence Rd., 08648. Tel: 609-406-7437; Fax: 609-406-7412; Email: dpayne@trentoncatholic.org; Web: dioceseoftrenton.org. Sr. Dorothy Payne, S.S.J., House Mother. Lawrenceville; Intercongregational Living. Sisters 9.

Villa Victoria Academy Convent, 376 W. Upper Ferry Rd., 08628. Tel: 609-883-0064; Fax: 609-882-8421; Email: srlillian@villavictoria.org; Web: www.villavictoria.org. Sr. Lillian Harrington, Supr. Religious Teachers Filippini. Sisters 6.

ASBURY PARK. *Missionaries of Charity*, 144 Ridge Ave., Asbury Park, 07712. Tel: 732-775-1101. Sr. Rose Terese Joseph, Supr. Sisters 4.

CHESTERFIELD. *Monastery of Saint Clare*, 150 White Pine Rd., Chesterfield, 08515. Tel: 609-324-2638; Fax: 609-324-2938; Email: mvarleyosc@verizon.net; Web: www.poorclaresofnewjersey.com. Sr. Miriam Varley, O.S.C., Abbess. Sisters 13.

HARVEY CEDARS. *Maris Stella Retreat and Conference Center*, 7201 Long Beach Blvd., Box 3135, Harvey Cedars, 08008. Tel: 609-494-1152; Fax: 609-494-1182; Email: mmorleysc@gmail.com. Sisters Mary Morley, S.C., Admin.; Patricia Dotzauer, S.C., Asst. Admin. Sisters of Charity of St. Elizabeth, Convent Station. Sisters 2.

OCEAN GROVE. *Emmaus House*, 21 Main Ave., Ocean Grove, 07756. Tel: 732-776-5458; Fax: 732-776-7065; Email: bernateh@aol.com; Web: www.emmaushouse.com. Sr. Patricia Mary Walsh, O.P., Admin. Sisters 14.

Memorare, 20 Pitman Ave., Ocean Grove, 07756. Tel: 732-776-5458; Fax: 732-776-7065; Email: Bernateh@aol.com; Web: www.emmaushouse.com. Sr. Patricia Mary Walsh, O.P., Admin.

WICKATUNK. *Convent of the Sisters of Good Shepherd*, 160 Conover Rd., P.O. Box 300, Wickatunk, 07765. Tel: 732-946-7877; Fax: 732-332-1240; Email: rosalyn.menard@nygoodshepherd.org. Rosalyn Menard, Coord. Sisters of Good Shepherd, Province of New York / Toronto. Sisters of Good Shepherd, Province of New York. Sisters 3.

[O] CHAPELS

LAWRENCEVILLE. *Our Lady of the Rosary Chapel*, 1 Bishops' Dr., Lawrenceville, 08648-2050. Tel: 609-896-0006; Fax: 609-895-0466; Email: info@morrishall.org; Web: www.morrishall.org. Rev. Angelo Amaral, Chap. Located in Morris Hall.

[P] HOUSES OF PRAYER

TRENTON. *Morning Star House of Prayer*, 312 W. Upper Ferry Rd., 08628. Tel: 609-882-2766; Fax: 609-882-2766; Email: sisterjo@morningstarprayerhouse.org; Web: morningstarprayerhouse.org. Sr. Josephine Aparo, M.P.F. Religious Teachers Filippini 2.

MOUNT HOLLY. *Francis House of Prayer*, 39 Springside Rd., Westampton, 08060. Email: FHOP@verizon.net; Web: www.FHOP.org. Mailing Address: P.O. Box 392, Rancocas, 08073-0392. Tel: 609-877-0509. Sr. Marcella Springer, S.S.J., Dir.

NEPTUNE. *The Upper Room Spiritual Center*, 3455 W. Bangs Ave. - Bldg. 2, Neptune, 07753. Tel: 732-922-0550; Fax: 732-922-3904; Email: office@theupper-room.org; Web: www.theupper-room.org. Sisters Maureen Christensen, R.S.M., Co-Dir.; Maureen Conroy, R.S.M., Co-Dir.; Trudy Ahern, S.S.J., Co-Dir.

[Q] RETREAT HOUSES

LONG BRANCH. *San Alfonso Retreat House*, 755 Ocean Ave., P.O. Box 3098, Long Branch, 07740. Tel: 732-222-2731; Fax: 732-870-8892; Email: info@sanalfonsoretreats.org; Web: www.sanalfonsoretreats.org. Revs. James A. Wallace, C.Ss.R., Rector/Dir.; Dennis Foley, C.Ss.R.; John McGowan, C.Ss.R.; Kevin J. O'Neil, C.Ss.R.; Bro. Bernard Colleran, C.Ss.R. Brothers 1; Priests 4. In Res. Revs. John Collins, C.Ss.R.; William Gaffney, C.Ss.R.; Michael Hopkins, C.Ss.R.

SOUTH MANTOLOKING. *St. Joseph by the Sea Retreat House*, 400 Rte. 35 N., South Mantoloking, 08738. Tel: 732-892-8494; Email: sjbsea@comcast.net; Web: www.sjbsea.org. Sisters Brunilda Ramos, M.P.F., Dir. & Supr.; Dolores Bianchi, M.P.F., Admin. Asst. Sec. Sisters 2.

[R] PERSONAL PRELATURES

PRINCETON. *Opus Dei* Prelature of the Holy Cross and Opus Dei Mercer House, 34 Mercer St., Princeton, 08540. Tel: 609-497-9448; Fax: 609-497-0906; Email: mercerhouse34@aol.com; Web: www.opusdei.org. Rev. Joseph Thomas, Chap.

[S] NEWMAN CENTERS

PRINCETON. *Aquinas Institute: Catholic Campus Ministry at Princeton University*, 24 Charlton St., Princeton, 08540-5221. Tel: 609-924-1820; Email: aquinas@princeton.edu; Email: tuchez@princeton.edu; Web: princetoncatholic.org. Rev. Gabriel Zeis, T.O.R., B.A., M.Div., Th.M., Ed.M., Chap.; Stephany A. Tuchez, Business Mgr. / Campus Min.

Emmaus House, Rider University, 2116 Lawrenceville Rd., 08648. Tel: 609-896-0394; Fax: 609-219-9203; Email: daverso@rider.edu. Cristina D'Averso-Collins, Campus Min.; Carlo Calisin, Chap.

Bede House, College of New Jersey, 492 Ewingville Rd., 08638. Tel: 609-771-0543; Email: ejb81333@gmail.com. Rev. Erin Brown, Chap. Clergy 1.

Georgian Court University, 900 Lakewood Ave., Lakewood, 08701. Tel: 732-364-2200, Ext. 600; Fax: 732-901-7151; Email: ksmith@georgian.edu. Jeffrey Shaffer, Dir. Campus Ministry.

Catholic Center at Monmouth University, 16 Beechwood Ave., West Long Branch, 07764. Tel: 732-229-9300; Fax: 732-229-1050; Email: cdaverso@monmouth.edu; Web: mucatholic.com. Cristina D'Averso-Collins, Campus Min.; Rev. Mark Nillo, Chap.

[T] MISCELLANEOUS LISTINGS

TRENTON. *Diocese of Trenton Charitable Trust for Aged, Infirm and Disabled Priests*, 701 Lawrenceville Rd., 08648. Tel: 609-406-7440; Fax: 609-406-7445; Email: kcimei@dioceseoftrenton.org. Mr. A. Kevin Cimei, Admin.

Diocese of Trenton Endowment Trust - Catholic Social Services, 701 Lawrenceville Rd., 08648. Tel: 609-406-7440; Email: kcimei@dioceseoftrenton.org. Mr. A. Kevin Cimei, Admin.

Diocese of Trenton Endowment Trust - Diocesan Assistance for Parishes, 701 Lawrenceville Rd., 08648. Tel: 609-406-7440; Email: kcimei@dioceseoftrenton.org. Mr. A. Kevin Cimei, Admin.

Diocese of Trenton Endowment Trust for Catholic Charities, 701 Lawrenceville Rd., 08648. Tel: 609-406-7440; Fax: 609-406-7445; Email: kcimei@dioceseoftrenton.org. Mr. A. Kevin Cimei, Admin.

Diocese of Trenton Endowment Trust for Catholic Education and Religious Formation, 701 Lawrenceville Rd., 08648. Tel: 609-406-7440; Fax: 609-406-7445; Email: kcimei@dioceseoftrenton.org. Mr. A. Kevin Cimei, Admin.

Diocese of Trenton Endowment Trust for Seminary and Diaconate Formation, 701 Lawrence Rd., 08648. Tel: 609-406-7440; Fax: 609-406-7445; Email: kcimei@dioceseoftrenton.org. Mr. A. Kevin Cimei, Admin.

**Foundation for Student Achievement, Inc.*, 701 Lawrenceville Rd., 08648. Tel: 609-403-7128; Fax: 609-406-7443; Email: snicho@dioceseoftrenton.org. Mr. Stephen J. Nicholl, Admin.

New Jersey Catholic Conference, 149 N. Warren St., 08608. Tel: 609-989-1120; Fax: 609-989-1152; Email: info@njcatholic.org; Web: www.njcatholic.org. Most Rev. John J. Myers, D.D., J.C.D., Pres.; Deacon Patrick R. Brannigan, Exec. Dir.

Trenton Diocesan Union of Holy Name Societies, 701 Lawrenceville Rd., P.O. Box 5147, 08638-0147. Tel: 609-406-7400; Web: dioceseoftrenton.org.

ASBURY PARK. *Mercy Center, Inc.*, 1106 Main St., Asbury Park, 07712. Tel: 732-774-9397; Fax: 732-988-8709; Email: sistercarol@mercycenternj.org; Web: mercycenternj.org. Sr. Carol Ann Henry, R.S.M., M.S.W., Dir.

DELRAN. *Lancer Fund*, c/o Holy Cross Preparatory Academy, 5035 Rte. 130 S., Delran, 08075. Tel: 609-970-3121; Email: sciortips@verizon.net. Peter Sciortino, Contact Person.

EATONTOWN. *Brothers of the Christian Schools District of Eastern North America, Inc.* aka FSC DENA, 444A Rte. 35 S., Eatontown, 07724-2200. Tel: 732-380-7926; Fax: 732-380-7937; Email: juliano@fscdena.org; Web: www.fscdena.org. Bros. Timothy Froehlich, F.S.C., Treas.; Joseph Juliano, F.S.C., Dir. Admin.; Dennis Lee, F.S.C., Provincial; Richard Galvin, Provincial Asst.; Thomas Casey, Provincial Asst.; Mrs. Janice Shea, Sec.; Mr. Alan Weyland, Exec. Dir., Office for Mission & Ministry; Bro. Robert Wickman, Provincial Delegate for Ministry Governing Bds.

Christian Brothers Retirement and Continuing Care Trust, 444A Rte. 35 S., Eatontown, 07724-2200. Tel: 732-380-7926; Fax: 732-380-7937; Email: froehlich@fscdena.org. Bro. Timothy Froehlich, F.S.C., Treas.

District of Eastern North America Ministry Corporation, 444A Rte. 35 S., Eatontown, 07724-2200. Tel: 732-380-7926; Fax: 732-380-7937; Email: froehlich@fscdena.org; Email: juliano@fscdena.org. Bros. Robert Wickman, Chm.; Dennis Lee, F.S.C., Pres.; Timothy Froehlich, F.S.C., Trustee; Joseph Juliano, F.S.C., Trustee; Mr. Alan Weyland, Trustee.

FSC DENA Endowment Trust, 444A Rte. 35 S., Eatontown, 07724-2200. Tel: 732-380-7926; Fax: 732-380-7937; Email: froehlich@fscdena.org. Bro. Timothy Froehlich, F.S.C., Treas.

FSC DENA Real Estate Holding Corporation, 444A Rte. 35 S., Eatontown, 07724-2200. Tel: 732-380-7926; Fax: 732-380-7937; Email: froehlich@fscdena.org; Email: juliano@fscdena.org. Bros. Timothy Froehlich, F.S.C., Treas.; Joseph Juliano, F.S.C., Sec.

FSC DENA Real Estate Trust, 444A Rte. 35 S., Eatontown, 07724-2200. Tel: 732-380-7926; Fax: 732-380-7937; Email: froehlich@fscdena.org; Email: juliano@fscdena.org. Bro. Timothy Froehlich, F.S.C., Treas.

HAMILTON. **Visitation Home, Inc.*, P.O. Box 11242, Hamilton, 08620. Tel: 609-585-2151; Email: denise817@optonline.net. Ms. Denise Reil, Dir.

LAWRENCEVILLE. **Center for Faith Justice*, 24 Rossa Ave., Lawrenceville, 08648. Tel: 609-498-6216; Fax: 609-498-6216; Email: speddicord@faithjustice.org; Web: faithjustice.org. Ms. Stephanie J. Peddicord, Pres.

The Foundation of Morris Hall/St. Lawrence, Inc., 2381 Lawrenceville Rd., Lawrenceville, 08648. Tel: 609-896-9500, Ext. 2215; Fax: 609-895-1602; Email: jmillner@slrc.org; Web: www.slrc.org. Mr. Thomas E. Boyle, CFO & Contact Person.

Morris Hall/St. Lawrence, Inc., 1 Bishops' Dr., Lawrenceville, 08648-2050. Tel: 609-896-0006; Fax: 609-896-8037; Email: epetroski@morrishall.org; Web: www.morrishall.org. Ellen Petroski, M.S.W., L.S.W., L.N.H.A., Admin. Bed Capacity 180; Bed Licensure 180.

Morris Hall, 1 Bishops Dr., Lawrenceville, 08648. Tel: 609-896-0006; Fax: 609-896-8037; Email: epetroski@morrishall.org; Web: www.morrishall.org. Darlene Hanley, CEO; Ellen Petroski, M.S.W., L.S.W., L.N.H.A., COO. Priests 1; Total Staff 145; Total Assisted 300.

LINCROFT. *Christian Brothers of Lincroft, NJ, Inc.*, 854 Newman Springs Rd., Lincroft, 07738-1698. Tel: 732-842-6712; Fax: 732-758-8310; Email: rmontedoro@cbalincroftnj.org. Bro. Ralph Montedoro, F.S.C., Dir.

TOMS RIVER. *Holy Redeemer Visiting Nurse Agency, Inc.*, (Ocean County Office), 1228 Rte. 37 W., Toms River, 08755. Tel: 732-240-2449; Fax: 732-288-2669; Email: pobrien@holyredeemer.com; Web: www.holyredeemer.com. Ms. Patricia O'Brien, Pres.

RELIGIOUS INSTITUTES OF MEN REPRESENTED IN THE DIOCESE

For further details refer to the corresponding bracketed number in the Religious Institutes of Men or Women section.

[0330]—*Brothers of the Christian Schools*—F.S.C.
[0480]—*Conventual Franciscans*.
[0520]—*Franciscan Friars* (Prov. of the Most Holy Name of Jesus)—O.F.M.
[1310]—*Order of the Holy Trinity*—O.SS.T.
[1070]—*Redemptorist Fathers & Brothers* (Baltimore & Denver Prov.)—C.Ss.R.
[0420]—*Society of the Divine Word*—S.V.D.
[0560]—*Third Order Regular of St. Francis*—T.O.R.
[1330]—*Vincentian Congregation*—C.M.

RELIGIOUS INSTITUTES OF WOMEN REPRESENTED IN THE DIOCESE

[1810]—*Bernardine Sisters of Third Order of St. Francis*—O.S.F.
[2410]—*Congregation of the Marianites of Holy Cross*—M.S.C.
[0850]—*Daughters of Mary Help of Christians*—F.M.A.
[1070-05]—*Dominican Sisters* (Amityville, NY)—O.P.
[1070-11]—*Dominican Sisters* (Sparkill, NY)—O.P.
[1070-15]—*Dominican Sisters* (Blauvelt, NY)—O.P.
[1070-18]—*Dominican Sisters* (Caldwell, NJ)—O.P.
[1105]—*Dominican Sisters of Hope* (Ossining, NY)—O.P.
[1180]—*Franciscan Sisters of Allegany, NY*—O.S.F.
[2300]—*Little Servant Sisters of the Immaculate Conception*—L.S.I.C.
[2710]—*Missionaries of Charity*—M.C.
[3760]—*Order of St. Clare*—O.S.C.
[3430]—*Religious Teachers Filippini*—M.P.F.
[1690]—*School Sisters of St. Francis* (Pittsburgh, PA).
[]—*Sisters for Christian Community*—S.F.C.C.
[0590]—*Sisters of Charity of Saint Elizabeth, Convent Station*—S.C.
[2575]—*Sisters of Mercy of the Americas*—R.S.M.

[1630]—*Sisters of St. Francis of Penance and Christian Charity*—O.S.F.
[1650]—*The Sisters of St. Francis of Philadelphia*—O.S.F.
[3893]—*Sisters of St. Joseph of Chestnut Hill, Philadelphia*—S.S.J.
[3890]—*Sisters of St. Joseph of Peace*—C.S.J.P.
[1830]—*The Sisters of the Good Shepherd*—R.G.S.
[3480]—*Sisters of the Resurrection*—C.R.
[2150]—*Sisters, Servants of the Immaculate Heart of Mary* (Monroe, MI)—I.H.M.
[0810]—*Society of the Daughters of the Heart of Mary*—D.H.M.
[3330]—*Union of Sisters of the Presentation of the Blessed Virgin Mary*—P.B.V.M.

NECROLOGY

† Smith, John M., Bishop Emeritus of Trenton, Died Jan. 22, 2019
† Buni, Leon Salvador A., Neptune, NJ, Holy Innocents, Died Jan. 24, 2019
† Cervenak, Andrew, (Retired), Died Jan. 30, 2018
† Halpin, Joseph A., (Retired), Died Jun. 27, 2018
† Inverso, Leon J., (Retired), Died Jan. 6, 2019
† Modino, Roman A., (Retired), Died Feb. 28, 2018

An asterisk (*) denotes an organization that has established tax-exempt status directly with the IRS and is not covered by the USCCB Group Ruling.

Diocese of Tucson

(Dioecesis Tucsonensis)

Most Reverend

EDWARD J. WEISENBURGER

Bishop of Tucson; ordained December 19, 1987; appointed Bishop of Salina February 6, 2012; consecrated and installed Bishop of Salina at Sacred Heart Cathedral May 1, 2012; appointed Bishop of Tucson October 3, 2017; installed as Seventh Bishop of Tucson November 29, 2017. *Pastoral Center, 64 E. Broadway Blvd., Tucson, AZ 85702.*

Most Reverend

GERALD F. KICANAS, D.D.

Bishop Emeritus of Tucson; ordained April 27, 1967; appointed Titular Bishop of Bela and Auxiliary Bishop of Chicago January 24, 1995; consecrated March 20, 1995; appointed Coadjutor Bishop of Tucson October 30, 2001; installed January 15, 2002; succeeded to See of Tucson March 7, 2003; retired August 18, 2016. *Mailing Address: P.O. Box 31, Tucson, AZ 85702.* Tel: 520-838-2500; Fax: 520-838-2590.

Chancery Office: 192 S. Stone Ave., Tucson, AZ 85701. Mailing Address: P.O. Box 31, Tucson, AZ 85702. Tel: 520-838-2500

Web: www.diocesetucson.org

Email: diocese@diocesetucson.org

ESTABLISHED A VICARIATE-APOSTOLIC 1868.

Square Miles 42,707.

Erected by His Holiness Pope Leo XIII, May 8, 1897.

Comprises the Counties of Cochise, Gila, Greenlee, Graham, La Paz, Pima, Pinal, Santa Cruz and Yuma in the State of Arizona.

For legal titles of parishes and diocesan institutions, consult the Chancery Office.

STATISTICAL OVERVIEW

Personnel	
Bishop	1
Retired Bishops	1
Priests: Diocesan Active in Diocese	71
Priests: Retired, Sick or Absent	20
Number of Diocesan Priests	91
Religious Priests in Diocese	65
Total Priests in Diocese	156
Extern Priests in Diocese	30
Ordinations:	
Diocesan Priests	2
Transitional Deacons	2
Permanent Deacons in Diocese	181
Total Brothers	31
Total Sisters	121
Parishes	
Parishes	78
With Resident Pastor:	
Resident Diocesan Priests	51
Resident Religious Priests	12
Without Resident Pastor:	
Administered by Priests	13
Missions	34
Professional Ministry Personnel:	
Brothers	6
Sisters	42
Lay Ministers	206
Welfare	
Catholic Hospitals	3
Total Assisted	150,000
Health Care Centers	2
Total Assisted	30,000
Homes for the Aged	1
Total Assisted	130
Day Care Centers	1
Total Assisted	365
Specialized Homes	5
Total Assisted	1,522
Special Centers for Social Services	6
Total Assisted	344,472
Other Institutions	3
Total Assisted	54,000
Educational	
Diocesan Students in Other Seminaries	13
Total Seminarians	13
High Schools, Diocesan and Parish	1
Total Students	282
High Schools, Private	5
Total Students	6,541
Elementary Schools, Diocesan and Parish	19
Total Students	4,583
Elementary Schools, Private	2
Total Students	454
Catechesis/Religious Education:	
High School Students	2,014
Elementary Students	9,963
Total Students under Catholic Instruction	23,850
Teachers in the Diocese:	
Priests	2
Brothers	3
Sisters	19
Lay Teachers	493
Vital Statistics	
Receptions into the Church:	
Infant Baptism Totals	3,553
Minor Baptism Totals	482
Adult Baptism Totals	278
Received into Full Communion	1,039
First Communions	4,196
Confirmations	2,894
Marriages:	
Catholic	581
Interfaith	84
Total Marriages	665
Deaths	2,109
Total Catholic Population	440,979
Total Population	2,004,451

Former Bishops—Most Revs. JOHN BAPTIST SALPOINTE, D.D., ord. Dec. 21, 1851; appt. Vicar Apostolic of Arizona and Titular Bishop of Doryla Sept. 25, 1868; ord. June 20, 1869; appt. Coadjutor Archbishop of Santa Fe with right of succession April 12, 1884 and Titular Archbishop of Anazarba Oct. 3, 1884; succeeded to the See of Santa Fe July 18, 1885; resigned; appt. Titular Archbishop of Tomi Jan. 27, 1894; died Tucson, July 15, 1898; PETER BOURGADE, D.D., ord. Nov. 30, 1869; appt. Vicar Apostolic of Arizona Jan. 23, 1885 and Titular Bishop of Thaumacum Feb. 7, 1885 and ord. May 1, 1885; appt. first Bishop of Tucson May 10, 1897; appt. fourth Archbishop of Santa Fe Jan. 7, 1899; died Chicago, May 17, 1908; HENRY REGIS GRANJON, D.D., ord. Dec. 17, 1887; appt. second Bishop of Tucson April 19, 1900; ord. June 17, 1900; died Brignais, France, Nov. 9, 1922; DANIEL JAMES GERCKE, D.D., ord. June 1, 1901; appt. third Bishop of Tucson June 21, 1923; ord. Nov. 6, 1923; resigned; appt. Titular Archbishop of Cotyaeum Oct. 26, 1960; died Tucson, March 19, 1964; FRANCIS JOSEPH GREEN, D.D., ord. May 15, 1932; appt. Titular Bishop of Serra in Proconsulari and Auxiliary Bishop of Tucson May 29, 1953; cons. Sept. 17, 1953; appt. Coadjutor "cum jure successionis" May 11, 1960; succeeded to See to become fourth Bishop of Tucson Oct. 26, 1960; retired July 28, 1981; died May 11, 1995; MANUEL D. MORENO, D.D., ord. April 25, 1961; appt. Titular Bishop of Tanagra and Auxiliary of Los Angeles Dec. 20, 1976; cons. Feb. 19, 1977; appt. Bishop of Tucson Jan. 12, 1982; retired March 7, 2003; died Nov. 17, 2006; GERALD F. KICANAS, ord. April 27, 1967; appt. Titular Bishop of Bela and Auxiliary Bishop of Chicago Jan. 24, 1995; cons. March 20, 1995; appt. Coadjutor Bishop of Tucson Oct. 30, 2001; installed Jan. 15, 2002; succeeded to See of Tucson March 7, 2003; retired Oct. 3, 2017; appt. Apostolic Administrator for the Diocese of Las Cruces Sept. 28, 2018.

Diocesan Officials

Bishop—Most Rev. EDWARD J. WEISENBURGER.

Vicars General—Rev. Msgr. JEREMIAH J. MCCARTHY, M.C., V.G.

Episcopal Vicar for Hispanic Affairs—Rev. Msgr. RAUL P. TREVIZO, E.V.

Vicar General & Moderator of the Curia—Rev. Msgr. JEREMIAH MCCARTHY, M.C., V.G., Email: jmccarthy@diocesetucson.org.

Chancellor—ANNE TERRY MORALES, Email: amorales@diocesetucson.org.

Judicial Vicar—Rev. MANUEL VIERA, O.F.M., J.C.L., Email: mviera@diocesetucson.org.

Vicar for International Priests—Rev. MARTIN B. ATANGA, Email: mbatanga@diocesetucson.org.

Vicar for Religious—Sr. JEANNE BARTHOLOMEAUX, S.C., Email: jbartholomeaux@diocesetucson.org.

Director for Deacons—Deacon RICHARD VALENCIA, Email: valencia@diocesetucson.org.

Chief Financial Officer—Deacon GREGORY HENDERSON, Email: ghenderson@diocesetucson.org.

Vicars Forane—Revs. MICHAEL R. BUCCIARELLI, V.F., Cochise Vicariate; PATRICK M. CRINO, V.F., Pima-Central Vicariate; CHRISTOPHER M. ORNDORFF II,

V.F., Pima-East Vicariate; VILIULFO VALDERRAMA, V.F., Pima-South Vicariate; JOHN P. LYONS, J.C.L., J.D., V.F., Pima-North Vicariate; SERAPHIM MOLINA, O.F.M., V.F., Pima West Vicariate; ARIEL G. LUSTAN, J.C.L., V.F., Pinal-West Vicariate; JAY R. LUCZAK, V.F., Santa Cruz Vicariate; MANUEL FRAGOSO-CARRANZA, V.F., Yuma-La Paz Vicariate; ARNOLD AURILLO, V.F., Gila/Pinal East/Graham/Greenlee Vicariate.

Diocesan Consultative Bodies

College of Consultors—Rev. PATRICK M. CRINO, V.F.; Rev. Msgr. JEREMIAH MCCARTHY, M.C., V.G.; Revs. CHRISTOPHER M. ORNDORFF II, V.F.; DOMENICO C. PINTI; Rev. Msgrs. ALBERT I. SCHIFANO, (Retired); RAUL P. TREVIZO, E.V.; Rev. GONZALO J. VILLEGAS.

Presbyteral Council—Most Rev. EDWARD J. WEISENBURGER; Revs. CHRISTOPHER M. ORNDORFF II, V.F.; JOHN P. LYONS, J.C.L., J.D., V.F.; PATRICK M. CRINO, V.F.; MARTIN B. ATANGA, V.F., Vicar Intl. Priests; MANUEL FRAGOSO-CARRANZA, V.F.; Rev. Msgr. ALBERT I. SCHIFANO, Dir. Vocations, (Retired); Rev. MICHAEL R. BUCCIARELLI, V.F.; Rev. Msgrs. RAUL P. TREVIZO, E.V., Vicar Hispanic Affairs; JEREMIAH MCCARTHY, M.C., V.G.; Revs. ARIEL G. LUSTAN, J.C.L., V.F.; ARNOLD AURILLO, V.F.; JAY R. LUCZAK, V.F.; JORGE FARIAS SAUCEDO, Dir. Vocations; SERAPHIM MOLINA, O.F.M., V.F.; VILIULFO VALDERRAMA, V.F.; MANUEL VIERA, O.F.M., J.C.L.

Finance Council—Ex Officio: Most Rev. EDWARD J. WEISENBURGER, Bishop; Rev. Msgr. JEREMIAH MCCARTHY, M.C., V.G., Moderator of the Curia. D.F.C. Members: NANCY STEPHAN, Chair; LAWRENCE MCDONOUGH; Rev. PATRICK M. CRINO, V.F.; TONY MARTIN; DON ROMANO; ROBERTO RUIZ; OMAR MIRELES; JIM TRESS; Rev. Msgr. ALBERT I. SCHIFANO.

School Board—Ex Officio Members: Most Rev. EDWARD J. WEISENBURGER; MS. SHERI DAHL, Supt.; MS. BARBARA MONSEGUR, Ph.D., Asst. Supt.; LUPITA SANDOVAL, Exec. Asst. Members: DYNSE CRUNKLETON, Pres.; AIDA M. SAMUEL, Vice Pres.; FRANK SCERBO; KARA HALSTEAD; Rev. CHRISTOPHER M. ORNDORFF II, V.F.; YVETTE BRAUN-CALIXTRO; JOSEPH CASEY; ROSE BRITT; DAVE KELLER.

Building Committee—Most Rev. EDWARD J. WEISENBURGER, Honorary Chair & Ex Officio; Rev. Msgr. JEREMIAH MCCARTHY, M.C., V.G., Moderator of the Curia & Ex Officio; OFFICER: JAMES RONSTADT, Chair; BRIAN MCCARTHY, Vice Chm.; Rev. PATRICK M. CRINO, V.F.; MIKE MARUM; DANIEL RORBACH; ERNIE DUARTE; PAT WELCHERT; HECTOR MARTINEZ; Sr. LOIS J. PAHA, O.P., D.Min.; Rev. Msgr. ALBERT I. SCHIFANO. Staff: LIZ AGUALLO, Property & Insurance Admin.; JOHN C. SHAHEEN, A.I.A., Dir. Property & Insurance.

Sexual Misconduct Review Board—DR. ROSEMARY CELAYA ALSTON, M.A., Ed.D., Consultant, Tel: 520-838-2513.

Diocesan Tribunal

Judicial Vicar—Rev. MANUEL VIERA, O.F.M., J.C.L.

Adjunct Judicial Vicars—Revs. JOHN P. ARNOLD, J.C.L., J.D.; ARTHUR J. ESPELAGE, O.F.M., J.C.D.

Promoter of Justice - Penal Cases—Rev. PATRICK R. LAGGES, J.C.D.

Judges—Revs. MANUEL VIERA, O.F.M., J.C.L.; JOHN P. ARNOLD, J.C.L., J.D.; ARTHUR J. ESPELAGE, O.F.M., J.C.D.

Defenders of the Bond—Revs. MICHAEL R. BUCCIARELLI, V.F.; ARIEL G. LUSTAN, J.C.L., V.F.; MS. ZABRINA DECKER, J.C.L.; MS. CHRISTINA HIP-FLORES, J.C.L.; Rev. JOHN P. LYONS, J.C.L., J.D., V.F.

Assessors—MR. KEVIN ARNOLD; MR. RICHARD COSGROVE; MR. LUIS KAMEI; MR. MICHAEL BRESCIA; MR. PEDRO NAJERA; MRS. EMMIE SLOCUM; MR. DENNIS M. FITZGIBBONS; MR. DAVID A. FITZGIBBONS III.

Auditors, Notaries, Case Directors—Mailing Address: P.O. Box 31, Tucson, 85702. Tel: 520-838-2500. VERONICA GARCIA; DIANE COLEMAN; Deacons CHARLES A. GALLEGOS; THOMAS WILLIS.

Professional Consultant—DR. HECTOR BARILLAS, Ph. D., P.C.

Office of Due Process—Mailing Address: Chancery Office, P.O. Box 31, Tucson, 85702. Tel: 520-838-2500.

Diocesan Administrative Offices and Directors

Archives and Library—ANA-ELISA RIVERA ARREDONDO, Archivist, 300 S. Tucson Blvd., Tucson, 85716. Tel: 520-886-5201; Email: archives@diocesetucson.org.

Office of the Bishop—

Executive Assistant to Bishop of Tucson—MS. CLARA I. HESLINGA, Tel: 520-838-2523; Fax: 520-838-2590; Email: cheslinga@diocesetucson.org.

Executive Assistant to Bishop Emeritus—Sr. CHARLOTTE ANNE SWIFT, O.P., Tel: 520-838-2510; Fax: 520-838-2590; Email: cswift@diocesetucson.org.

Chancery—192 S. Stone Ave., Tucson, 85701. Tel: 520-838-2500; Fax: 520-838-2590. *Mailing Address: P.O. Box 31, Tucson, 85702.*

Executive Assistant to Chancellor—KRISTIE L. ROCHE, Tel: 520-838-2511; Email: kroche@diocesetucson.org.

Office of Child, Adolescent & Adult Protection—Mailing Address: P.O. Box 31, Tucson, 85702. DR. ROSEMARY CELAYA-ALSTON, M.A., Ed.D., Dir., Tel: 520-838-2500; RACHEL GUZMAN, Prog. Mgr., Tel: 520-838-2533; Email: rguzman@diocesetucson.org.

Victim Assistance Coordinator—Tel: 520-838-2500. Contact Office of Child, Adolescent, and Adult Protection.

Communications—STEFF KOENEMAN, Dir., Mailing Address: P.O. Box 31, Tucson, 85702. Tel: 520-838-2561; Email: skoeneman@diocesetucson.org.

Newspaper—The Outlook *Mailing Address: P.O. Box 31, Tucson, 85702.* Tel: 520-838-2562; Fax: 520-838-2599. MICHAEL BROWN, Mng. Editor.

Fiscal and Administrative Services—Mailing Address: P.O. Box 31, Tucson, 85702. Tel: 520-838-2500. Deacon GREGORY HENDERSON, CFO, Email: ghenderson@diocesetucson.org; MARGARET YONKOVICH, Controller, Email: myonkovich@diocesetucson.org.

Human Resources—RICHARD M. SERRANO, Dir.; ALICIA CORTI, Asst. Dir.; CAROLINA GRIMALDO, Benefits Admin., 64 E. Broadway Blvd., P.O. Box 31, Tucson, 85702. Tel: 520-838-2500; Fax: 520-838-2583.

Information and Technology Department—DAVID KNIGHT, Network Admin., Email: dknight@diocesetucson.org.

Moderator of the Curia—Rev. Msgr. JEREMIAH MCCARTHY, M.C., V.G.

Office of Corporate Matters—ANDREA BALDENEGRO, Exec. Asst., Email: corpmatters@diocesetucson.org.

Property and Insurance Services—Office: 64 E. Broadway Blvd., Tucson, 85701. Tel: 520-838-2500; Fax: 520-838-2581. JOHN C. SHAHEEN, A.I.A., Dir., Email: jshaheen@diocesetucson.org.

Diocesan Pastoral Offices and Directors

Human Life and Dignity—Sr. LEONETTE KOCHAN, O.S.F., Dir., P.O. Box 31, Tucson, 85702. Tel: 520-838-2560; Fax: 520-838-2583; Email: lkochan@diocesetucson.org. Includes following National Ministries: Catholic Campaign for Human Development; Catholic Relief Services.

Liturgical Coordinators—Rev. REMIGIO "MIGUEL" MARIANO; Sr. LOIS J. PAHA, O.P., D.Min., 64 E. Broadway Blvd., P.O. Box 31, Tucson, 85702. Tel: 520-838-2530; Email: lpaha@diocesetucson.org.

Catechesis for Children, Youth and Families—J. MICHAEL BERGER, Dir., 64 E. Broadway Blvd., P.O. Box 31, Tucson, 85702-0031. Tel: 520-838-2500; Fax: 520-838-2584; Email: mberger@diocesetucson.org.

Catholic Schools Department—MS. SHERI DAHL, Supt., Tel: 520-838-2500; Email: sdahl@diocesetucson.org.

Office of Evangelization and Hispanic Ministry—Sr. GLADYS ECHENIQUE, O.P., Dir., Interim Mailing Address: 64 E. Broadway Blvd., P.O. Box 31, Tucson, 85702-0031. Tel: 520-838-2500; Email: gechenique@diocesetucson.org.

Formation—Sr. LOIS J. PAHA, O.P., D.Min., Dir., 64 E. Broadway Blvd., P.O. Box 31, Tucson, 85702-0031. Tel: 520-838-2500; Fax: 520-838-2584; Email: lpaha@diocesetucson.org; MR. JOSEPH PERDREAUVILLE, Asst. Dir., Email: jperdreauville@diocesetucson.org; MRS. OFELIA JAMES, Exec. Asst., Email: ojames@diocesetucson.org; MRS. ISABEL MADRID, Administrative Asst., Email: imadrid@diocesetucson.org; VACANT, Coord. Lay Ecclesial Ministry Formation.

Permanent Diaconate—Deacon RICHARD VALENCIA, Dir., P.O. Box 31, Tucson, 85702. Tel: 520-838-2500; Fax: 520-838-2583; Email: valencia@diocesetucson.org.

Associate Vicars—Deacons PAT ABILES; JOSEPH KUSHNER III; KENNETH MORELAND; OSCAR F. CHAVEZ.

Propagation of the FaithSr. LOIS J. PAHA, O.P., D.Min., P.O. Box 31, Tucson, 85702. Tel: 520-838-2500.

Priestly Vocations—64 E. Broadway Blvd., P.O. Box 31, Tucson, 85702. Tel: 520-838-2531; Fax: 520-838-2593; Email: vocations@diocesetucson.org. Rev. JORGE FARIAS SAUCEDO, Vocations Dir. - Recruitment; Rev. Msgr. ALBERT I. SCHIFANO, Vocations Dir. - Seminarians, (Retired), Tel: 520-838-2500; MS. CLARA I. HESLINGA, Exec. Asst.

Religious Vocations—Sr. JEANNE BARTHOLOMEAUX, S.C., Mailing Address: P.O. Box 31, Tucson, 85702. Tel: 520-838-2500.

Worship Office—Rev. REMIGIO "MIGUEL" MARIANO, Dir., 64 E. Broadway Blvd., P.O. Box 31, Tucson, 85702-0031. Tel: 520-838-2500; Fax: 520-838-2584; Email: mmariano@diocesetucson.org.

Affiliated Organizations

Catholic Foundation—64 E. Broadway Blvd., P.O. Box 31, Tucson, 85702. Tel: 520-838-2509; Web: www.cathfnd.org. SALVATORE POLIZZOTTO, Exec. Dir.

Priests' Assurance Corporation—Most Rev. EDWARD J. WEISENBURGER, Pres., Ex Officio. Directors: Revs. JOSEPH A. LOMBARDO, (Retired); PATRICK M. CRINO, V.F., Chair; DOMENICO C. PINTI, Sec.; JOHN P. ARNOLD, J.C.L., J.D. DOT Advisory Staff: RICHARD M. SERRANO, Dir. Human Resources; KATHERINE R. RHINEHART, Chancellor.

Catholic Cemeteries, Inc.—MR. THOMAS HANLON, Exec. Dir., Mailing Address: Holy Hope Cemetery, 3555 N. Oracle Rd., P.O. Box 5158, Tucson, 85705. Tel: 520-888-0860; Fax: 520-887-7360.

All Faiths Cemeteries—Our Lady of the Desert Cemetery, 2151 W. Avenida Los Reyes, Tucson, 85748. Tel: 520-885-9173; Fax: 520-733-4186. *Desert Vista Cemetery, 2151 S. Avenida Los Reyes, Tucson, 85748.* Tel: 520-885-9173.

Catholic Tuition Support Organization—GRACIE QUIROZ MARUM, Exec. Dir., Interim Address: 192 S. Stone Ave., Tucson, 85701. Tel: 520-838-2500; Email: gquiroz@diocesetucson.org. Mailing Address: P.O. Box 31, Tucson, 85702.

Other Councils, Programs, and Organizations

Council of Women Religious, Leadership Team & Office for Religious—Sr. JEANNE BARTHOLOMEAUX, S.C., 64 E. Broadway Blvd., P.O. Box 31, Tucson, 85702. Tel: 520-838-2500; Fax: 520-838-2583; Email: jbartholomeaux@diocesetucson.org.

Cursillo Movement—NIVAS BELTRAN, Lay Dir., Mailing Address: 3044 47th Ave., Yuma, 85364. Tel: 928-210-5477; Email: monicanivas@gmail.com; Web: www.tucsoncursillo.org; JUAN LOMELI, Spanish Lay Dir., 3788 W. Pluto St., Somerton, 85350. Tel: 928-446-1410; Email: lomelijuanf@aol.com.

Detention Ministry—Deacon MICHAEL S. GUTIERREZ, Coord., Kolbe Society, 140 W. Speedway Blvd., Ste. 230, Tucson, 85705. Tel: 520-623-0344, Ext. 7046; Email: mikeg@ccs-soaz.org; Rev. RICHARD LANDRY, M.S., Restorative Justice Ministry, Email: richardl@diocesetucson.org.

Ecumenical Commission—64 E. Broadway Blvd., P.O. Box 31, Tucson, 85702-0031. Tel: 520-838-2500; Fax: 520-838-2584. Rev. REMIGIO "MIGUEL" MARIANO, Ecumenical Officer for the Diocese, Email: mmariano@diocesetucson.org.

Renovacion Carismatica Catolica—Deacon MARIO AGUIRRE; MANUELITA AGUIRRE, 4632 E. Timrod St., Tucson, 85711. Tel: 520-795-1036.

Other Canonical Entities

Oratory—Mailing Address: St. Gianna Oratory (Latin Rite), P.O. Box 87350, Tucson, 85754-7350. Tel: 520-883-4360; Email: saintgiannaoratory@gmail.com. Rev. Canon WILLIAM AVIS, I.C.R.S.S.

Quasi-Parish—Our Lady, Star of the Sea Roman Catholic Parish - Tucson (Korean), 3820 N. Sabino Canyon Rd., Tucson, 85750. Mailing Address: 9331 E. Speedway Blvd., Tucson, 85710. Rev. JAMYON (VINCENT) YUN, (South Korea) Tel: 520-505-1278.

CLERGY, PARISHES, MISSIONS AND PAROCHIAL SCHOOLS

CITY OF TUCSON

(PIMA COUNTY)

1—SAINT AUGUSTINE CATHEDRAL (1863)

192 S. Stone Ave., 85701. Tel: 520-623-6351; Email: office@staugustine.tuccoxmail.com; Web: cathedral-staugustine.org. Revs. Gilbert Malu Musumbu; Dennis Bosse, O.F.M.; Deacons Salvador Carmona; Ricardo M. Pinzon; Michael S. Gutierrez; Leon Viviano

Legal Name: Saint Augustine Cathedral Roman Catholic Parish - Tucson

SAN COSME, 460 W. Simpson, 85701.

Catechesis Religious Program—Students 27.

2—SAINT AMBROSE ROMAN CATHOLIC PARISH - TUCSON (1946)

300 S. Tucson Blvd., 85716. Tel: 520-622-6749; Fax: 520-882-3057; Email: stambrose@stambrosetucson.org; Web: www.

stambrosetucson.org. Rev. Mark J. Long; Deacon Thomas Willis
Legal Name: Saint Ambrose Roman Catholic Parish - Tucson
School—St. Ambrose Roman Catholic Parish - Tucson School, (Grades PreK-8), Tel: 520-882-8678; Email: officemanager@stambrosetucson.org. Religious Teachers 1; Lay Teachers 13; Students 221.
Catechesis Religious Program—Email: mgonsowskie@stambrosetucson.org. Marjorie Gonsowskie, D.R.E. Students 23.

3—CORPUS CHRISTI ROMAN CATHOLIC PARISH - TUCSON (1999)
300 N. Tanque Verde Loop Rd., 85748.
Tel: 520-751-4235; Email: kmontano@cccctucson.org; Web: www.cccctucson.org. Rev. Christopher M. Orndorff II, V.F.; Deacon Mark Cesnik
Legal Name: Corpus Christi Roman Catholic Parish
Catechesis Religious Program—Email: sbeste@cccctucson.org. Suzanne Hensel, Coord. Children's Ministry; Stacey Beste, Coord. Youth Min. Students 165.

4—SAINT CYRIL OF ALEXANDRIA (1948)
1750 N. Swan Rd., 85712. Tel: 520-795-1633; Fax: 520-795-1639; Email: pastor@stcyril.com; Web: www.stcyrilchurch-tucson.org. Revs. Ronald A. Oakham, O.Carm., V.F.; Edgar Lopez, O.Carm., Parochial Vicar; Deacons Niyibizi Shukurani; Felix Mario Aguirre. Monthly masses with African and Polish communities.
Legal Name: Saint Cyril of Alexandria Roman Catholic Parish - Tucson
School—St. Cyril of Alexandria School, (Grades 1-8), 4725 E. Pima St., 85712. Tel: 520-881-4240; Email: azeches@diocesetucson.org. Lay Teachers 25; Students 378.
Catechesis Religious Program—Email: bjenkins@stcyril.com. Becki Jenkins, D.R.E. Students 136.

5—SAINT ELIZABETH ANN SETON (1980)
8650 N. Shannon Rd., 85742. Tel: 520-297-7357; Fax: 520-797-8886; Email: church@seastucson.org; Web: www.seastucson.org. Revs. Edward F. Lucero, V.F.; Martin Bosco Ormin, V.C., (Nigeria) Parochial Vicar; Deacons Francis C. Sherlock; Jacinto Trevino Jr.; Leopoldo "Leo" Longoria; Robert P. Carlin; Mario J. Rodriguez; Christian Kimminau; Richard Kiser
Legal Name: Roman Catholic Church of Saint Elizabeth Ann Seton - Tucson
School—St. Elizabeth Ann Seton School, (Grades PreK-8), Tel: 520-219-7650; Email: tdolandixon@school.seastucson.org; Email: lchambers@school.seastucson.org; Web: school.seastucson.org. Theresa Dolan-Dixon, Prin.; Lissett Chambers, Registrar. Clergy 1; Lay Teachers 20; Students 360.

6—SAINT FRANCES CABRINI (1961)
3201 E. Presidio Rd., 85716. Tel: 520-326-7670; Email: cabrini1962@aol.com; Web: www.cabrinitucson.org. Rev. Jens-Peter "Jay" Jensen Jr.; Deacon Charles A. Gallegos
Legal Name: Saint Frances Cabrini Roman Catholic Parish - Tucson
Catechesis Religious Program—Tel: 520-318-9198; Email: cathy_kent@aol.com. Cathy Kent, D.R.E. Students 60.

7—SAINT FRANCIS DE SALES (1971)
1375 S. Camino Seco, 85710. Tel: 520-885-5908; Fax: 520-885-3109; Email: officemgr@saintfrancisdesalestucson.org; Web: www.saintfrancisdesalestucson.org. Rev. Robert G. Tamminga; Deacons Dennis Scalpone; Thai V. Tran; C. Andy Corder; John R. Martin; Andrew Thomas Greeley; Russell Kingery; Daniel Flannagan
Legal Name: Saint Francis de Sales Roman Catholic Parish - Tucson
Catechesis Religious Program—3201 E. Presidio Rd., 85716. Email: ffdfmilly@aol.com. Maureen Kingery, D.R.E. Students 218.

8—HOLY FAMILY ROMAN CATHOLIC PARISH - TUCSON (1915)
338 W. University Blvd., 85705. Tel: 520-623-6773; Email: holyfamilyparishtucson@gmail.com; Web: www.holyfamilychurchtucson.org. Rev. Jonathon Fehrenbacher, Admin
Legal Name: Holy Family Roman Catholic Parish - Tucson
Catechesis Religious Program—Email: sylvia@hfc.phxcoxmail.com. Sylvia Cordova, D.R.E. Students 55.

9—SAINT JOHN THE EVANGELIST (1934)
602 W. Ajo Way, 85713. Tel: 520-624-7409, Ext. 100; Email: stjohnsoffice@netzero.com; Web: www.stjohnevangelisttucson.org. Rev. Msgr. Raul P. Trevizo, E.V.; Rev. Robert A. Gonzales, Ph.D., Parochial Vicar; Deacon Jose Duarte
Legal Name: Saint John the Evangelist Roman Catholic Parish - Tucson
Casa San Juan Migrant Center—Tel: 520-798-0834; Fax: 520-740-1145; Email: casasanjuan@comcast.net; Web: www.casasanjuan.org. Patricia Arteaga, Dir.
School—St. John the Evangelist School, (Grades PreSchool-8), 600 W. Ajo Way, 85713. Tel: 520-624-3865; Fax: 520-622-3193; Email: msolorzano@stjohntucson.org; Web: www.stjohntucson.org. Minh Solorzano, Prin. Lay Teachers 17; Students 426.
Catechesis Religious Program—Tel: 520-300-6760; Email: llopez@diocesetucson.org. Mrs. Lydia Lopez, D.R.E. Students 491.

10—SAINT JOSEPH ROMAN CATHOLIC PARISH - TUCSON (1953)
215 S. Craycroft Rd., 85711. Tel: 520-747-3100; Email: parish@stjosephtucson.org; Web: www.stjosephchurchtucson.org. Rev. Mario (Ricky) V. Ordonez; Deacons Leon Mazza, Business Mgr.; Teodoro Perez; Clifford R. Rambaran
Legal Name: Saint Joseph Roman Catholic Parish - Tucson
School—St. Joseph Roman Catholic Parish - Tucson School, (Grades K-8), Tel: 520-747-3060; Email: kvanloan@stjosephtucson.org. Kathy VanLoan, Prin. Lay Teachers 9; Students 219.
Catechesis Religious Program—Wade Manuel, D.R.E. Students 265.

11—SAINT KATERI TEKAKWITHA (1984) (Native American)
507 W. 29th St., 85713. Tel: 520-622-5363; Email: bl_kateri_tekakwitha@yahoo.com; Web: stkateriparish.net. Revs. Seraphim Molina, S.T.; Abram E. Dono, S.T., Parochial Vicar; Dieudoune Nsom Kindong, Parochial Vicar
Legal Name: Saint Kateri Tekakwitha Roman Catholic Missions Parish - Tucson
Res. & Rectory: 101 W. 31st St., 85713-3336.
Catechesis Religious Program—Rosa Galaz, D.R.E. Students 345.
Saint Kateri Tekakwitha Parish Center—
San Juan Diego Center—7465 S. Camino Benem, 85757.
Missions—San Martin—418 W. 39th St., Pima Co. 85713.
Santa Rosa, 2015 N. Calle Central, Pima Co. 85705.
Cristo Rey, 7500 S. Camino Benem, Pima Co. 85747.
El Senor de los Milagros, 3410 S. 16th Ave., Pima Co. 85713.
San Ignacio de Loyola, 785 W. Sahuaro, Pima Co. 85705.

12—SAINT MARGARET MARY ALACOQUE (1951) [CEM]
801 N. Grande Ave., 85745. Tel: 520-622-0168; Email: parishstmargaret@gmail.com; Web: www.stmargaretmarytucson.com. Revs. Richard T. Awange, C.S.Sp., (Nigeria) Admin.; Jorge Farias Saucedo, In Res.; Deacons Federico T. Valdenegro; Miguel Lopez
Legal Name: Saint Margaret Mary Alacoque Roman Catholic Parish - Tucson
Catechesis Religious Program—Email: religiousedstmargaret@hotmail.com. Rosemary Mungia, D.R.E.; Connie De La Ossa, Youth Min.; Maria Castro, RCIA Coord. Students 251.

13—SAINT MARK ROMAN CATHOLIC PARISH - TUCSON (1999)
2727 W. Tangerine Rd., Oro Valley, 85742.
Tel: 520-469-7835; Fax: 520-219-6003; Email: office@stmarkov.com; Web: www.stmarkov.com. Mailing Address: P.O. Box 68650, 85737. Rev. John P. Arnold, J.C.L., J.D.; Deacons Jose Cuestas III; Andrew Guarriello
Legal Name: Saint Mark Roman Catholic Parish - Tucson
Catechesis Religious Program—Steffanie Rambaran, D.R.E. Students 308.

14—SAINT MONICA ROMAN CATHOLIC PARISH - TUCSON (1964)
212 W. Medina Rd., 85756. Tel: 520-294-2694; Email: santamonicatucson@yahoo.com; Web: www.stmonicatucson.org. Revs. Raul Valencia Garcia; Jesus Acuna Delgado, Parochial Vicar; Deacons Nicolas De La Torre; David Vernon Barfuss; Enrique F. Mendoza; Ignacio Arvizu, RCIA Coord.
Legal Name: Saint Monica Roman Catholic Parish - Tucson
Catechesis Religious Program—Tel: 520-889-1994; Email: jgonzalez@diocesetucson.org. Jannet Gonzalez, D.R.E. Students 516.

15—MOST HOLY TRINITY ROMAN CATHOLIC PARISH - TUCSON (1975)
1300 N. Greasewood Rd., 85745. Tel: 520-884-9021; Email: info@mhtparish.org; Web: mostholytrinityparish.org. Rev. Thomas Tureman, S.D.S.; Deacons John Terry; Kenneth Moreland
Most Holy Trinity Roman Catholic Parish - Tucson
Catechesis Religious Program—Diana Akroush, D.R.E. Students 224.

16—SAINT ODILIA ROMAN CATHOLIC COMMUNITY - TUCSON (1965)
Tel: 520-297-7271; Email: mmariano@diocesetucson.org; Web: www.stodiliaparish.org. Revs. Remigio Miguel Mariano; Frank G. Cady, Parochial Vicar; John Ikponko; Deacons George Scherf; Rodney J. Kulpa; Angel Gonzales
Legal Name: Saint Odilia Roman Catholic Community - Tucson
Catechesis Religious Program—Tel: 520-297-7272; Email: susie78@comcast.net. Suzanna Chapman, D.R.E. Students 156.

17—OUR LADY OF FATIMA ROMAN CATHOLIC PARISH - TUCSON (1972)
1950 W. Irvington Pl., 85746. Tel: 520-883-1717; Email: fatimaintucson@aol.com; Email: crisnegrette@dioceseoftucson.org; Web: www.fatimaintucson.com. Revs. Viliulfo Valderrama, V.F.; Edson Elizarraras, Parochial Vicar; Deacons Anthony Geonnotti; Robert Negrette
Our Lady of Fatima Roman Catholic Church - Tucson
Res.: 5576 S. Monroe St., 85746.
Catechesis Religious Program—Tel: 520-578-1717. Irma Anaya, D.R.E. Students 207.
Mission—St. Mary of the Desert.

18—OUR LADY OF LAVANG ROMAN CATHOLIC PARISH - TUCSON (1999) (Vietnamese)
Mailing Address: 800 S. Tucson Blvd., 85716.
Tel: 520-882-3891; Fax: 520-303-1881; Email: francisdientran@gmail.com. Rev. Francis Tran
Legal Name: Our Lady of La Vang Roman Catholic Parish - Tucson
Res.: 624 S. Tucson Blvd., 85716.
Catechesis Religious Program—Email: joehungle@gmail.com. Students 85.

19—OUR LADY QUEEN OF ALL SAINTS (1987) (Hispanic)
2915 E. 36th St., 85713-4041. Tel: 520-622-8602; Fax: 520-622-4581; Email: olqoas2915@yahoo.com; Web: ourladyqueenofallsaints.com. Rev. Alan Valencia; Deacon Armando L. Valenzuela
Legal Name: Our Lady Queen of All Saints Roman Catholic Parish - Tucson
Catechesis Religious Program—Ms. Carmen Bonillas, C.R.E. (English). Students 182.

20—OUR LADY STAR OF THE SEA
3820 Sabino Canyon Rd., 85710. Cell: 520-490-228; Email: olss@tucsonkcc.org; Web: www.tucsonkcc.org. Mailing Address: 9331 E. Speedway Blvd., 85710. Rev. Jamyon (Vincent) Yun, (South Korea)
Legal Name: Our Lady Star of the Sea Roman Catholic Parish - Tucson
Catechesis Religious Program—Sung Khong, D.R.E. Students 2.

21—OUR MOTHER OF SORROWS (1958)
1800 S. Kolb Rd., 85710. Tel: 520-747-1321; Fax: 520-790-3308; Email: omosparish@omosparish.org; Web: www.omosparish.org. Rev. Msgr. Thomas Cahalane, V.F.; Revs. Thomas Quirk; Liam Leahy, In Res., (Retired); Jorge Farias Saucedo, In Res.; Deacons George Rodriguez; Scott Thrall; Chuck Chajewski; Jose Francisco Zamora Arroyo; Gregory Henderson; Eric Maugans; Joseph Perotti
Legal Name: Our Mother of Sorrows Roman Catholic Parish - Tucson
School—Our Mother of Sorrows School, (Grades PreSchool-8), Tel: 520-747-1027; Fax: 520-747-0797; Email: info@omosschool.com; Web: www.omosschool.com. Mrs. Erin Vu, Prin. Lay Teachers 22; Students 390.
Catechesis Religious Program—Email: lstehle@omosparish.org. Laura Stehle, D.R.E. Students 410.

22—SAINTS PETER AND PAUL ROMAN (1930)
1946 E. Lee St., 85719-4337. Tel: 520-327-6015; Fax: 520-318-3918; Email: info@sspp-parish.org; Web: www.sspp-parish.org. Revs. Patrick M. Crino, V.F.; Bala S. Kommathoti, Parochial Vicar; Albert Miranda, Parochial Vicar; Deacons Thomas Campbell; Paul N. Duckro, Ph.D.; John K. Ackerley
Legal Name: Saints Peter and Paul Roman Catholic Parish - Tucson
School—Sts. Peter and Paul Roman School, (Grades K-8), 1436 N. Campbell Ave., 85719.
Tel: 520-325-2431; Fax: 520-881-4690; Email: Info@sspptucson.org; Web: www.sspptucson.org. Charlene Roll, Prin.; Debbie Nielsen, Librarian. Lay Teachers 24; Students 391.
Catechesis Religious Program—Tel: 520-887-8346. Pat Deitering, D.R.E. Students 141.
Convent—1947 E. Adams St., 85719.

23—SAINT PIUS X ROMAN CATHOLIC PARISH - TUCSON (1969)
1800 N. Camino Pio Decimo, 85715.
Tel: 520-885-3573; Fax: 520-885-0945; Email: general@stpiusxtucson.org; Web: www.stpiusxtucson.org. Rev. Harry Ledwith; Deacon Dennis Ranke
Legal Name: Saint Pius X Roman Catholic Parish - Tucson
Catechesis Religious Program—Email: dlialios@diocesetucson.org. Deanne Lialios, D.R.E. Students 289.

24—SACRED HEART ROMAN CATHOLIC PARISH - TUCSON (1942)
601 E. Ft. Lowell Rd., 85705. Tel: 520-888-1227; Fax: 520-888-1530; Email: sacredhearttucson@gmail.com; Web: www.sacredhearttucson.weconnect.com. 3200 N. Los Altos

Ave., 85705. Rev. Gonzalo J. Villegas; Deacon Eugene Fernandez.
Catechesis Religious Program—Sr. Jerry Brady, S.C., D.R.E. Students 257.

25—SAN XAVIER MISSION ROMAN CATHOLIC PARISH - TUCSON aka San Xavier del Bac Mission (1692) (Native American)
1950 W. San Xavier Rd., 85746. Tel: 520-294-2624; Fax: 520-294-3438; Email: sxmstephen@gmail.com; Web: www.sanxaviermission.org. Rev. Stephen Barnufsky, O.F.M. In Res., Revs. Clifford Herle, O.F.M.; Manuel Viera, O.F.M., J.C.L.; Friar Maximilian Hottle, O.F.M.; Revs. Arthur J. Espelage, O.F.M., J.C.D.; Dennis Bosse, O.F.M.; Friar Edward Fronske, O.F.M.
School—San Xavier Mission Roman Catholic Parish - Tucson School, (Grades K-8), 1980 W. San Xavier Rd., 85746. Tel: 520-294-0628; Fax: 520-294-3465; Email: office@sxmschool.org. William Rosenberg, Prin. Religious Teachers 1; Lay Teachers 13; Students 140.
Catechesis Religious Program—Tel: 520-294-4639; Email: scriach@yahoo.com. Sisters Rachel Sena, O.P., D.R.E.; Carla Riach, O.S.F., RCIA Coord. Students 136.
Convent— aka Franciscan Sisters of Christian Charity1996 W. San Xavier Rd., 85746. Tel: 520-746-4779. Sisters 5.

26—SANTA CATALINA ROMAN CATHOLIC PARISH - TUCSON (1981)
14380 N. Oracle Rd., 85739. Tel: 520-825-9611; Email: office@santacatalinaparish.org; Email: spincus@santacatalinaparish.org; Web: www.santacatalinaparish.org. Rev. Lawrence E. Sanders; Deacons William Krueger; Alfonso De La Riva; Flavio Sanchez; Joseph La Fleur.
Catechesis Religious Program—Email: religiouseducation@santacatalinaparish.org; Email: youthministry@santacatalinaparish.org. Carol Padilla, D.R.E.; Lupita Parra, Youth Min. Students 50.

27—SANTA CRUZ ROMAN CATHOLIC PARISH - TUCSON (1919)
1220 S. 6th Ave., 85713. Tel: 520-623-3833; Email: avemariasc@hotmail.com. Revs. Stephen Watson; Godfrey Chandya-Lega, Parochial Vicar
Legal Name: Santa Cruz Roman Catholic Parish
School—Santa Cruz Roman Catholic Parish - Tucson School, (Grades K-8), 29 W. 22nd St., 85713. Tel: 520-624-2093; Fax: 520-624-2833; Email: aschmidt@santacruzschool.org; Web: www.santacruzschool.org. Angelina Schmidt, Prin. Clergy 2; Lay Teachers 17; Students 234.
Catechesis Religious Program—Tel: 520-882-9687. Anita Romero, D.R.E. Students 199.
Mission—Capilla Guadalupe, 401 E. 31st St., Pima Co. 85713.

28—SAINT THOMAS MORE (1926)
1615 E. 2nd St., 85719. Tel: 520-327-4665, Ext. 113; Email: manny@uacatholic.org; Web: www.uacatholic.org. Revs. John Paul Forte, O.P.; Emmanuel Taylor, O.P., Parochial Vicar
*Legal Name: Saint Thomas More Roman Catholic Newman Parish - Tucson*In Res., Revs. Thomas DeMan, O.P.; Robert Castle.
Catechesis Religious Program—Tel: 520-327-4665; Email: boscoema@earthlink.net. Jane Piaggi-Furet, D.R.E. Students 114.

29—SAINT THOMAS THE APOSTLE (1984)
5150 N. Valley View Rd., 85718-6121. Tel: 520-577-8780; Email: sttomapostle@yahoo.com; Web: statucson.org. Rev. John P. Lyons, J.C.L., J.D., V.F.; Rev. Msgrs. Todd O'Leary, Pastor Emeritus, (Retired); Albert I. Schifano, In Res., (Retired); Deacons Edward P. Sheffer; Philip Garcia; Joe G. Cruz Jr.; Rev. John Gonzales; Deacon Robert Brotherton
Legal Name: Saint Thomas the Apostle Roman Catholic Parish - Tucson
School—St. Thomas the Apostle School, (Grades Toddler-K), Tel: 520-577-0503; Email: sthomaspreschool@gmail.com. Ms. Michelle Garmon, Prin. Lay Teachers 16; Students 90.
Catechesis Religious Program—Tel: 520-577-8782; Email: stareligiousedu@gmail.com. Margaret Brokaw, D.R.E. Students 311.

OUTSIDE THE CITY OF TUCSON

AJO, PIMA CO., IMMACULATE CONCEPTION ROMAN CATHOLIC CHURCH - AJO (1916)
101 W. Rocalla Ave., P.O. Box 550, Ajo, 85321. Tel: 520-387-7049; Fax: 520-413-5567; Email: iccajo@hughes.net; Web: www.iccajo.net. Rev. Peter C. Nwachukwu
Legal Name: Immaculate Conception Roman Catholic Parish - Ajo
Catechesis Religious Program—Tel: 520-709-6123. Bertha Castro, D.R.E. Students 28.

APACHE JUNCTION, PINAL CO., SAINT GEORGE (1968)
300 E. 16th Ave., Apache Junction, 85119. Tel: 480-982-2929; Email: office@stgeorgeaj.com; Web: stgeorgeaj.com. Revs. Domenico C. Pinti; Stanley J. Nadolny, Parochial Vicar; Deacon Bill Jones
Legal Name: Saint George Roman Catholic Parish - Apache Junction
Catechesis Religious Program—Email: collive@stgeorgeaj.com. Christine Ollive, D.R.E. Students 285.

BENSON, COCHISE CO., OUR LADY OF LOURDES (1895)
Mailing Address: 386 E. 5th St., P.O. Box 2198, Benson, 85602. Tel: 520-586-3394; Email: olol@ololparish.org; Web: www.ololparish.org. Rev. Martin B. Atanga; Deacon Richard Valencia
Legal Name: The Roman Catholic Parish of Our Lady of Lourdes - Benson
Office: 244 S. Gila, Benson, 85602.
Res.: 210 E. 8th St., Benson, 85602.
Catechesis Religious Program—P.O. Box 1517, Benson, 85602. Email: maggie@ololparish.org. Dolores Cameron, D.R.E. Students 30.

BISBEE, COCHISE CO., SAINT PATRICK ROMAN CATHOLIC PARISH - BISBEE (1902)
Mailing Address: 100 Quality Hill Rd., P.O. Box 164, Bisbee, 85603. Tel: 520-432-5753; Email: StPatricks@cableone.net; Email: bsaenz@diocesetucson.org; Web: www.stpatsbisbee.com. Revs. Michael R. Bucciarelli, V.F., Canonical Pastor; Matthew Thayil, M.S.F.S., Sacramental Min.; Deacons Tony Underwood, Pastoral Admin.; Guillermo Lugo; Joseph L. Delgado; Jose C. Valle
Legal Name: Saint Patrick Roman Catholic Parish - Bisbee
Catechesis Religious Program—Tel: 520-236-9659; Email: wleikem@diocesetucson.org. Wanda Leikem, D.R.E. Students 28.
Mission—St. Michael, 2090 W. Martinez, Naco, Cochise Co. 85620.

CASA GRANDE, PINAL CO., SAINT ANTHONY OF PADUA (1932)
201 N. Picacho St., Casa Grande, 85122. Rev. Ariel G. Lustan, J.C.L., V.F.; Deacons Patrick L. Dugan; Francisco Solano; Steven R. Dimuzio; Robert Penzenstadler; Dan Hannig
Legal Name: Saint Anthony of Padua Roman Catholic Parish - Casa Grande
Res.: 309 Paseo de Paula, Casa Grande, 85122.
School—St. Anthony of Padua School, (Grades PreK-8), 501 E. 2nd St., Casa Grande, 85122. Tel: 520-836-7247; Fax: 520-836-7289; Email: cseidl@diocesetucson.org; Web: www.stanthonypaduaschool.org. Sr. Carol Seidl, Prin. Religious Teachers 2; Lay Teachers 11; Students 190.
Catechesis Religious Program—Email: religiouseducation@stanthonycg.org. Elizabeth Soza, D.R.E. Students 346.

CLIFTON, GREENLEE CO., SACRED HEART ROMAN CATHOLIC CHURCH AND ST. MARY'S MISSION (1899)
329 Chase Creek Rd., P.O. Box 938, Clifton, 85533. Tel: 928-865-2285; Email: sacheart@vtc.net. Rev. Nathaniel Mma, Admin.
Legal Name: Sacred Heart Roman Catholic Church and St. Mary's Mission - Clifton
Res.: 355 Chase Creek Rd., Clifton, 85533.
Catechesis Religious Program—550 Coronado Blvd., Clifton, 85533. Tel: 928-865-3497. Carol Vozza, D.R.E. Students 18.
Mission—St. Mary, Third St., P.O. Box 938, Clifton, Greenlee Co. 85533.

COOLIDGE, PINAL CO., SAINT JAMES THE APOSTLE ROMAN CATHOLIC PARISH - COOLIDGE (1947) (Caucasian—Hispanic)
401 W. Wilson Ave., Coolidge, 85128. Tel: 520-723-3063; Email: secretary@stjamescoolidge.org. Rev. Adolfo Martinez-Escobar; Deacons Manuel Reyes G. Murrieta; Joseph Lyncha
Legal Name: Saint James Roman Catholic Parish - Coolidge
Catechesis Religious Program—Email: andreafierro@stjamescoolidge.org. Andrea Fierro, D.R.E. Students 167.

DOUGLAS, COCHISE CO.

1—IMMACULATE CONCEPTION (1905)
928 C Ave., P.O. Box 1176, Douglas, 85608. Tel: 520-364-8494; Fax: 520-364-8495; Email: icchurch@hotmail.com. Revs. Virgilio "Jojo" Tabo Jr.; Luis Armando Espinoza, (Argentina) Parochial Vicar; Deacons Mario Castillo; Joaquin Carrasco; Gabriel Espino
Legal Name: Immaculate Conception Roman Catholic Parish - Douglas
Catechesis Religious Program—Tel: 520-368-8197; Email: bpaespino@yahoo.com. Sr. Rosemary Sampon, M.M.S., D.R.E. Students 223.

2—SAINT LUKE ROMAN CATHOLIC CHURCH - DOUGLAS (1950)
1211 15th St., Douglas, 85607. Tel: 520-364-4411; Email: st.luke51@yahoo.com. Revs. Virgilio "Jojo" Tabo Jr.; Luis Armando Espinoza, (Argentina) Parochial Vicar; Deacons Armando Moulinet; Guadalupe Yanez; Ed Gomez; Luciano Gonzales Jr.; Raul Cantua; Gabriel Espino; Gabriel Saspe
Legal Name: Saint Luke Roman Catholic Church - Douglas
School—Loretto Central Catholic, (Grades K-8), 1200 14th St., Douglas, 85607. Tel: 520-364-5754; Fax: 888-364-5869; Email: lorprincipal@lorettoschool.org. Sr. Mary Aloysius Marques, O.C.D., Prin. Clergy 5; Lay Teachers 12; Sisters 4; Students 230.
Catechesis Religious Program—Tel: 520-364-4852; Email: isandoval@diocesetucson.org. Sr. Ines Sandoval, O.C.D., D.R.E. Students 240.
Convent—Carmelite Sisters of the Most Sacred Heart of Los Angeles, Loretto Convent, Douglas.

ELOY, PINAL CO., SAINT HELEN OF THE CROSS (1952)
205 W. 8th St., Eloy, 85131. Tel: 520-466-7258; Email: office@sthelenchurch.com; Web: www.sthelenchurch.com. Rev. Alonzo M. Garcia; Deacon Pasqual Abiles Jr.
Legal Name: Saint Helen of the Cross Roman Catholic Church - Eloy
Catechesis Religious Program—Tel: 520-466-9422; Email: margieruiz6@gmail.com; Email: akers6@cox.net. Mrs. Margie Ruiz, D.R.E.; Mary Akers, RCIA Coord. Students 78.

FLORENCE, PINAL CO., ASSUMPTION OF THE BLESSED VIRGIN MARY (1870)
Mailing Address: 221 E. 8th St., P.O. Box 2550, Florence, 85132. Tel: 520-868-5940; Fax: 520-868-0413; Email: assumptionbvmflorence@yahoo.com; Web: www.assumptionofmary.org. Rev. Jose Maria A. Corvera; Deacon Ernie Trujillo
Legal Name: Assumption of the Blessed Virgin Mary Roman Catholic Parish - Florence
Res.: 177 E. 8th St., P.O. Box 2550, Florence, 85132.
Catechesis Religious Program—P.O. Box 487, Florence, 85132. Email: assumptionre@gmail.com. Linda Pintar, D.R.E. Students 47.
Convent—Chapel of the Gila, (Historical Site) 255 E. 8th St., P.O. Box 2550, Florence, 85132-0550.

GLOBE, GILA CO., HOLY ANGELS ROMAN CATHOLIC CHURCH - GLOBE (1905)
201 S. Broad St., Globe, 85501. Tel: 928-425-3137; Fax: 928-425-3136; Email: haadminasst@cableone.net; Web: https://www.holyangelscatholicchurchglobe.org. Rev. Arnold Aurillo, V.F.; Deacon Frank Castillo
Legal Name: Holy Angels Roman Catholic Church - Tucson
Catechesis Religious Program—Tel: 928-701-1418; Email: gkmarin@hotmail.com. Karie Marin, D.R.E.; Gregg Marin, D.R.E. Students 39.

GREEN VALLEY, PIMA CO., OUR LADY OF THE VALLEY (1970)
505 N. La Canada Dr., Green Valley, 85614. Tel: 520-625-4536; Email: olvgv@diocesetucson.org; Web: www.olvgv.org. Rev. Francisco Maldonado, V.F., (c/o Douglas Lozier); Deacon Joseph Roinick, Pastoral Assoc.
Legal Name: Our Lady of the Valley Roman Catholic Parish - Green Valley
Res.: 354 E. Calle Trona, Green Valley, 85614.
Catechesis Religious Program—Email: mcotsonas@diocesetucson.org. Madeline Cotsonas, D.R.E. Students 196.

HAYDEN, GILA CO., SAINT JOSEPH ROMAN CATHOLIC PARISH - HAYDEN (1913)
Mailing Address: 300 Mountain View Dr., P.O. Box C, Hayden, 85135-1007. Tel: 520-356-7223; Email: stjoseph.haden@yahoo.com. Rev. Alexander Tigga, M.S.F.S., (India)
Legal Name: Saint Joseph Roman Catholic Parish - Hayden
Catechesis Religious Program—Email: ednaDRE@gmail.com. Edna Ortega, D.R.E. Students 53.

KEARNY, PINAL CO., INFANT JESUS OF PRAGUE (1961)
Mailing Address: 501 Victoria Cir., P.O. Box 459, Kearny, 85137. Tel: 520-363-7205; Fax: 520-363-7179; Email: ijp.kearny@yahoo.com. Rev. George Kunnel, M.S.F.S., (India)
Legal Name: Infant Jesus of Prague Roman Catholic Parish - Kearny
Catechesis Religious Program—Angela Lopez, D.R.E. Students 32.

MAMMOTH, PINAL CO., BLESSED SACRAMENT ROMAN CATHOLIC PARISH - MAMMOTH (1970) (Hispanic)
Mailing Address: 122 W. Church Dr., P.O. Box 220, Mammoth, 85618-0220. Tel: 520-487-2451; Email: bscmammoth@hotmail.com. Revs. Bardo Fabian Antunez-Olea, Admin.; Walter Balduck, O.F.M.Cap.
Legal Name: Blessed Sacrament Roman Catholic Parish - Mammoth
Catechesis Religious Program—Tel: 520-487-2182. Helen Ramirez, D.R.E. Students 77.

MARANA, PIMA CO., SAINT CHRISTOPHER ROMAN CATHOLIC PARISH - MARANA (1954)
12101 W. Moore Rd., Marana, 85653. Tel: 520-682-3035; Email: info@stchristophermarana.org; Web: www.stchristophermarana.org. Rev. Callistus Iyorember; Deacon Jorge Munoz
Legal Name: Saint Christopher Roman Catholic Parish - Marana
Catechesis Religious Program—Email:

lllquiroz@comcast.net. Lucy Quiroz, D.R.E. Students 70.

MARICOPA, PINAL CO., OUR LADY OF GRACE ROMAN CATHOLIC PARISH - MARICOPA (2007)
18700 N. St. Gabriel Way, Maricopa, 85138-3228.
Tel: 520-568-4605; Fax: 520-568-0861; Email: information@maricopacatholic.org; Web: www.ourladygracechurch.org. Revs. Marcos Velasquez, V.F.; Showri Raju Narra; Deacons Mario Ortega; Gullermo Castro
Our Lady of Grace Roman Catholic Parish - Maricopa
Catechesis Religious Program—Email: religioused@maricopacatholic.org. Ann Maidman, D.R.E.; Edward Talsness, Business Mgr. Students 314.

MIAMI, GILA CO., OUR LADY OF THE BLESSED SACRAMENT (1915)
844 W. Sullivan St., Miami, 85539.
Tel: 928-473-3568; Email: ourladyromancatholic@yahoo.com; Web: www.ourladymiami.com. Rev. Madhu George
Legal Name: Our Lady of the Blessed Sacrament Roman Catholic Church - Miami
Catechesis Religious Program—Paul Licano, D.R.E. Students 60.
Missions—St. Joseph Chapel—5678 Pineway St., Claypool, Gila Co. 85532.
St. Theresa Chapel, Roosevelt, Gila Co.

MORENCI, GREENLEE CO., HOLY CROSS ROMAN CATHOLIC CHURCH - MORENCI (1913)
205 Fairbanks Rd., Morenci, 85540.
Tel: 928-865-3183; Fax: 928-865-1228; Email: holycross@vtc.net. Rev. Nathaniel Mma
Legal Name: Holy Cross Roman Catholic Church - Morenci
Catechesis Religious Program—Diane Berube, D.R.E. Students 135.

NOGALES, SANTA CRUZ CO.
1—SACRED HEART OF JESUS (1897)
Mailing Address: 272 N. Rodriguez St., Nogales, 85621. Tel: 520-287-9221; Email: shjpoffice@gmail.com. Revs. Jay R. Luczak, V.F.; Marco Carrasco, Parochial Vicar; Deacon David A. Rojas
Legal Name: Sacred Heart of Jesus Roman Catholic Parish - Nogales
School—Sacred Heart of Jesus School, (Grades PreK-8), 207 W. Oak St., Nogales, 85621.
Tel: 520-287-2223; Fax: 520-287-3373; Email: mrothstein@diocesetucson.org; Web: sacredheartnogales.org. Mrs. Vanessa Rothstein, Prin. Clergy 1; Lay Teachers 13; Students 168; Faculty 13; Staff 6.
Catechesis Religious Program—Margarita Treto, D.R.E. Students 214.
2—SAN FELIPE DE JESUS (1987)
1901 N. Jose Gallego Dr., Nogales, 85621.
Tel: 520-761-3100; Email: sanfelipedejesusparish@gmail.com. Mailing Address: P.O. Box 6600, Nogales, 85628. Rev. Jose Manuel Padilla
Legal Name: San Felipe de Jesus Roman Catholic Parish - Nogales
Catechesis Religious Program—Email: ofelia_d@hotmail.com. Ofelia Davila, D.R.E. Students 336.

ORACLE, PINA CO., SAINT HELEN ROMAN CATHOLIC PARISH - ORACLE (1927)
66 E. Maplewood St., Oracle, 85623-6148.
Tel: 520-896-2708; Email: sthelensmission@msn.com; Web: www.sthelenparishoracle.org. Rev. Msgr. Ambrose O. Nwohu
Legal Name: Saint Helen Roman Catholic Parish - Oracle
Catechesis Religious Program—Maria Tellez, D.R.E. Students 28.

PARKER, LA PAZ CO., SACRED HEART ROMAN CATHOLIC PARISH - PARKER (1950)
1101 Joshua Ave., Parker, 85344. Tel: 928-669-2502; Email: shpp@npgcable.com. Rev. Richard T. Kusugh; Deacon Leonel Bejarano
Legal Name: Sacred Heart Roman Catholic Parish - Parker
Catechesis Religious Program—Email: lbejarano@diocesetucson.org. Students 47.
Missions—Saint Kateri Tekakwitha Indian Mission—Poston.
St. John the Baptist, Wenden.
Queen of Peace, Quartzsite.

PATAGONIA, SANTA CRUZ CO., SAINT THERESE OF LISIEUX (1955)
Mailing Address: 222 Third Ave., P.O. Box 435, Patagonia, 85624. Tel: 520-394-2954; Email: sttheresa@dakotacom.net; Web: stccpatagonia.com. Rev. George Holley, Admin.
Legal Name: Saint Therese of Lisieux Roman Catholic Parish - Patagonia
Catechesis Religious Program—Elvia Miranda, D.R.E. Students 17.
Mission—Our Lady of Angels, 22 Los Encinos Dr., Sonoita, Santa Cruz Co. 85637.

PAYSON, GILA CO., SAINT PHILIP THE APOSTLE (1957)
511 S. St. Philip St., Payson, 85541-5144.
Tel: 928-474-2392; Email: rordonez@diocesetucson.org; Web: catholicpayson.com. Rev. Mario "Ricky" Ordonez; Deacons John Scott; Willard Capistrant; William Trudell
Legal Name: Saint Philip the Apostle Roman Catholic Church - Payson
Catechesis Religious Program—Tel: 928-474-1269; Email: ctrudell@diocesetucson.org. Catherine Trudell, D.R.E. Students 73.

PEARCE-SUNSITES, COCHISE CO., SAINT JUDE THADDEUS (1983) [JC]
Mailing Address: 970 N. Hwy. 191, Mile Post 51, P.O. Box 328, Pearce, 85625. Tel: 520-826-3869; Email: mbathineni@diocesetucson.org. Rev. Mohana Bathineni
Legal Name: Saint Jude Thaddeus Roman Catholic Parish - Pearce Sunsites
Catechesis Religious Program—Email: cruegg@diocesetucson.org. Carol Ruegg, D.R.E. Students 30.
Mission—St. Francis of Assisi, 4110 W. Jefferson Rd., Elfrida, 85610.

PIRTLEVILLE, COCHISE CO., SAINT BERNARD ROMAN CATHOLIC CHURCH - PIRTLEVILLE (1914)
2308 N. McKinley St., P.O. Box 3101, Pirtleville, 85626. Rev. Virgilio "Jojo" Tabo Jr.; Deacons Luciano Gonzales Jr.; Guadalupe Yanez
Legal Name: Saint Bernard Roman Catholic Church - Pirtleville
Catechesis Religious Program—340 Grace Ave., Pirtleville, 85626. Tel: 520-364-4411. Ana Morales, D.R.E. Students 30.
Chapels—Double Adobe, Our Lady of La Salette—3879 W. Mission Ln., Double Adobe, 85617.
Douglas, Sacred Heart of Jesus Chapel, 300 17th St., Douglas, 85607.

RIO RICO, SANTA CRUZ CO., MOST HOLY NATIVITY OF OUR LORD JESUS CHRIST (1987)
Mailing Address: 395 Avenida Coatimundi, P.O. Box 4024, Rio Rico, 85648. Tel: 520-281-7414; Fax: 520-281-1713; Email: mostholynativity@qwestoffice.net; Web: www.mhnparish.org. Rev. Francisco Maldonado, V.F., Canonical Pastor; Deacons Javier Fierro; Francisco Padilla
Legal Name: Most Holy Nativity of Our Lord Jesus Christ Roman Catholic Parish - Rio Rico
1123 Plexes Ln. #1, Rio Rico, 85648. Office: 384 Cancun Ct., Rio Rico, 85648.
Catechesis Religious Program—Maria Bustamante, D.R.E. Students 114.

SAFFORD, GRAHAM CO., SAINT ROSE OF LIMA ROMAN CATHOLIC PARISH - SAFFORD (1937)
311 S. Central Ave., Safford, 85546-2655.
Tel: 928-428-4920; Fax: 928-428-4922; Email: stroselima@gmail.com; Web: www.SaintRoseLima-Safford.com. Rev. Nicodemus Shaghel, Admin.; Deacon Carlos Vessels
Legal Name: Saint Rose of Lima Roman Catholic Parish - Safford
Catechesis Religious Program—Tel: 928-348-4785. Students 254.
Missions—St. Martin de Porres Mission—50 S. Main, Pima, Graham Co. 85543.
Newman Center, 3592 W. 4th St., Thatcher, Graham Co. 85552.

SAHUARITA, PIMA CO., SAN MARTIN DE PORRES (2002)
Mailing Address: 15440 S. Santa Rita Rd., P.O. Box 65, Sahuarita, 85629. Tel: 520-625-1154; Fax: 520-399-4480; Email: admin@sanmartinsahuarita.org; Web: www.sanmartinsahuarita.org. Rev. Juan Carlos Aguirre-Borchardt
Legal Name: Roman Catholic Parish of San Martin De Porres - Sahuarita
Catechesis Religious Program—Josh Mangles, D.R.E. Students 184.

SAN CARLOS, GILA CO., SAN CARLOS APACHE COMMUNITY (1918) (Native American)
Mailing Address: 460 San Carlos Ave., P.O. Box 28, San Carlos, 85550. Tel: 928-475-2210; Email: aaurillo@diocesetucson.org. Revs. Arnold Aurillo, V.F.; John Paul Shea
Legal Name: San Carlos Apache Roman Catholic Community - San Carlos
School—San Carlos Apache Community School, (Grades K-7), P.O. Box 339, San Carlos, 85550.
Tel: 928-475-2449; Fax: 928-475-2050; Email: isalter@diocesetucson.org; Web: stcharles@facebook.com. Ina Salter, Prin. Lay Teachers 8; Students 126.
Catechesis Religious Program—Email: jshea@diocesetucson.org. Sr. Ruth Barbara Holthauser, C.S.C., D.R.E. Students 29.
Convent—St. Charles, P.O. Box 338, San Carlos, 85550. Tel: 928-475-2460.
Mission—Saint Kateri Tekakwitha, Bylas, 85530.

SAN LUIS, YUMA CO., SAINT JUDE THADDEUS (1982)
984 N. Main St., P.O. Box 2888, San Luis, 85349.
Tel: 928-627-8011; Email: sjtparish-sla@hotmail.com. Rev. Abraham Guerrero-Quinonez, (Ecuador)
Legal Name: Saint Jude Thaddeus Roman Catholic Parish - San Luis
Catechesis Religious Program—Students 471.

SAN MANUEL, PINAL CO., SAINT BARTHOLOMEW (1954)
609 Park Pl., P.O. Box 607, San Manuel, 85631.
Tel: 520-385-4156; Email: mlsanchez@diocesetucson.org; Email: rrosales@diocesetucson.org. Rev. Raul "Rudy" H. Rosales
Legal Name: Saint Bartholomew Roman Catholic Parish - San Manuel
Catechesis Religious Program—Email: gloriat527@hotmail.com. Gloria Trazas, D.R.E. Students 68.

SAN TAN VALLEY, PINAL CO., SAINT MICHAEL THE ARCHANGEL (2011)
Mailing Address: 25394 N. Poseidon Rd., Florence, 85132. Tel: 520-723-6570; Email: pastor@stmichaels77.org; Email: secretary@stmichaels77.org; Web: www.stmichaels77.org. Rev. Dale A. Branson
Legal Name: Saint Michael the Archangel Roman Catholic Parish - San Tan Valley
Catechesis Religious Program—Email: ccd@stmichaels77.org. Reajean Porter, D.R.E. Students 97.

SIERRA VISTA, COCHISE CO.
1—SAINT ANDREW THE APOSTLE (1958)
800 Taylor Dr., N.W., Sierra Vista, 85635.
Tel: 520-458-2925; Fax: 520-452-0235; Email: bulletin@standrewsv.org; Web: www.standrewsv.org. Revs. Gregory P. Adolf; Marco Basulto-Pitol, Parochial Vicar; Robert Neske, Parochial Vicar; Deacons Joseph Kushner III; John Joseph Klein; Lauro A. Teran
Legal Name: Saint Andrew the Apostle Roman Catholic Parish - Sierra Vista
Catechesis Religious Program—Sr. Joellen Kohlmann, D.R.E. Students 256.
Mission—Good Shepherd, Whetstone, Cochise Co.
2—OUR LADY OF THE MOUNTAINS (1991) [CEM]
1425 Yaqui St., Sierra Vista, 85650.
Tel: 520-378-2720; Fax: 520-378-6825; Email: office@olmaz.org; Email: dparsons@diocesetucson.org; Web: www.olmaz.org. Revs. Michael R. Bucciarelli, V.F.; Rudolf Ofori; Deacons Gene Tackett; Reynaldo Romo; Jose G. Huerta-Nunez
Legal Name: Our Lady of the Mountains Roman Catholic Parish - Sierra Vista
School—All Saints Catholic School, (Grades PreK-6), Tel: 520-378-7012; Email: Schooloffice@ascsaz.org. Carmen Rosado, Prin. Lay Teachers 15; Students 120.
Catechesis Religious Program—Email: k.shilson@olmaz.org. Kathleen Shilson, D.R.E. Students 48.

SOLOMON, GRAHAM CO., OUR LADY OF GUADALUPE (1891) [CEM]
Mailing Address: 2257 S. 1st Ave, P.O. Box 147, Solomon, 85551. Tel: 928-428-0149; Email: OLGSolomon@gmail.com. Rev. Robert A. Rodriguez; Deacon Carl Vessels
Legal Name: Our Lady of Guadalupe Roman Catholic Parish - Solomon
Res.: 311 Central Ave., Safford, 85546.
Catechesis Religious Program—Tel: 520-730-8965; Email: sjurado@saffordusd.com. Sandra Jurado, D.R.E. Students 27.
Mission—San Jose, 1670 S. Church St., San Jose, Graham Co. 85546.

SOMERTON, YUMA CO., IMMACULATE HEART OF MARY (1954)
310 W. Spring St., P.O. Box 597, Somerton, 85350.
Tel: 928-627-2918; Fax: 928-722-5962; Email: parishihm@hotmail.com. Rev. German Bartolome Vazquez Johnston; Deacons Ernesto Jaramillo; Jeff Trujillo; Fernando Mezquita
Legal Name: Immaculate Heart of Mary Roman Catholic Parish - Somerton
Res.: 144 N. Union Ave., P.O. Box 597, Somerton, 85350.
Catechesis Religious Program—Tel: 928-627-0320; Email: olijara@hotmail.com. Olivia Jaramillo, D.R.E. Students 358.

SUPERIOR, PINAL CO., SAINT FRANCIS OF ASSISI (1930)
11 S. Church Ave., Superior, 85173.
Tel: 520-689-2250; Email: info@stfrancissuperior.org; Web: www.stfrancissuperior.org. Rev. Samuel Jandeh, V.C.
Legal Name: Saint Francis of Assisi Roman Catholic Parish - Superior
Catechesis Religious Program—St. Mary's Center, 100 Sunset Dr., Superior, 85173. Kathy Zavala, D.R.E. Students 62.

TOMBSTONE, COCHISE CO., SACRED HEART OF JESUS (1880)
592 E. Safford St., P.O. Box 547, Tombstone, 85638.
Cell: 520-457-3364; Email: sacredheartchurch@powerc.net; Web: www.tombstonescatholicchurch.org. Rev. Matthias Crehan
Legal Name: Sacred Heart of Jesus Roman Catholic Parish - Tombstone
Res.: 596 E. Safford St., P.O. Box 547, Tombstone, 85638.

Catechesis Religious Program—Karrie Marine, D.R.E. Students 9.

TOPAWA, PIMA CO., SAN SOLANO MISSIONS ROMAN CATHOLIC PARISH - TOPAWA (1908) (Native American) (For office and sacramental records pertaining to Tohono O'odham Nation and mission churches on the reservation, please refer to San Solano Missions, Topawa).
Mailing Address: Rte. 19 & Topawa Rd., P.O. Box 210, Topawa, 85639. Tel: 520-383-2350;
Fax: 520-383-3063; Email: ssmissions@mail.com. Revs. Alfonso Ponchie Vasquez, O.F.M.; William J. Minkel, O.F.M., Parochial Vicar; Deacon Alfred M. Gonzales; Friars Peter Boegel, O.F.M., Vicar of San Francisco Solano Friary; David Paz, O.F.M., Guardian of San Francisco Solano Friary.
Catechesis Religious Program—Students 92.

TUBAC, SANTA CRUZ CO., SAINT ANN'S (1987)
2231 E Frontage Rd., Tubac, 85646.
Tel: 520-398-2646; Email: stannsparish3@gmail.com; Web: stannsparishtubacaz.org. Mailing Address: P.O. Box 2911, Tubac, 85629-2911. Rev. Joseph Esson
Legal Name: Saint Ann's Roman Catholic Parish and Missions - Tubac
Catechesis Religious Program—Email: jgrotheer56ccd@gmail.com. Julie Grotheer, D.R.E. Students 14.
Missions—Assumption Chapel—Amado, Santa Cruz Co.
St. Ferdinand, Arivaca, Pima Co. 85646.

VAIL, PIMA CO., SAINT RITA IN THE DESERT (1935)
Mailing Address: 13260 E. Colossal Cave Rd., Vail, 85641. Tel: 520-762-9688; Email: secretary@stritainthedesert.org; Web: www.stritainthedesert.org. Rev. Martin S. Martinez; Deacons Daniel Gullotta; Ronald J. Desmarais
Legal Name: Saint Rita in the Desert Roman Catholic Parish - Vail
Catechesis Religious Program—Email: vreyna@dioceseutucson.org. Veronica Reyna, D.R.E. Students 264.

WELLTON, YUMA CO., SAINT JOSEPH THE WORKER (2005)
8674 S. Ave. 36E, Wellton, 85356. Tel: 928-785-4275; Fax: 928-785-8706; Email: stjoseph157@hotmail.com. Rev. Gregory Okafor; Deacons Wayne L. Preston; Benito Rodriguez
Legal Name: Saint Joseph the Worker Roman Catholic Parish - Wellton
Catechesis Religious Program—Hilda Juarez, D.R.E. Students 64.

WILLCOX, COCHISE CO., SACRED HEART OF JESUS (1936)
215 W. Maley St., Willcox, 85643. Tel: 520-384-3432. Rev. Mark J. Stein
Legal Name: Sacred Heart of Jesus Roman Catholic Church - Willcox
Catechesis Religious Program—Students 69.
Missions—Our Lady of Perpetual Help—San Simon, 85605.
Our Lady of Guadalupe, Bowie, 85605.

YUMA, YUMA CO.

1—SAINT FRANCIS OF ASSISI (1948)
1815 S. 8th Ave., Yuma, 85364. Tel: 928-782-1875; Email: evillegas@diocesetucson.org; Web: www.stfrancisyuma.com. Rev. Emilio Landeros Chapa; Rev. Msgr. Carlos Romero, Parochial Vicar; Rev. Rajeev Bobba, Parochial Vicar; Deacons Paul Muthart; Gary Pasquinelli; Rick Hernandez; Rafael Vidal; Jose Valadez; Lawrence S. Maude; Douglas Nicholls; Arturo E. Sanchez; Mark Nixon; George Fishbach
Legal Name: Saint Francis of Assisi Roman Catholic Parish - Yuma
School—St. Francis of Assisi School, (Grades PreK-8), 700 18th St., Yuma, 85364. Tel: 928-782-1539; Fax: 928-782-0430; Email: vlopez@diocesetucson.org. Rev. Emilio Landeros Chapa. Lay Teachers 15; Students 241.
Catechesis Religious Program—Email: admin@stfrancisyuma.com. Jesus Navarrete, Diocesan D.R.E. Students 256.

2—IMMACULATE CONCEPTION ROMAN CATHOLIC PARISH & GUADALUPE MISSION (1866) [JC]
505 S. Ave. B, Yuma, 85364. Tel: 928-782-7516; Fax: 928-343-0172; Email: mumbower@diocesetucson.org; Email: icchurch@icyuma.com; Web: www.icyuma.com. Revs. Manuel Fragoso Carranza; Martin Moreno, Parochial Vicar; Deacons David Sampson; Oscar F. Chavez; Antonio Gomez; Arnulfo Carbajal; Nieves Hernandez; David Clark; Jorge Gonzalez; Carlos P. Hernandez
Legal Name: Immaculate Conception & Guadalupe Missions Roman Catholic Parish & Guadalupe Mission - Yuma
Res.: 509 S. Ave. B, Yuma, 85364.
School—Immaculate Conception Roman Catholic Parish & Guadalupe Mission School, (Grades PreK-8), 501 S. Ave. B, Yuma, 85364. Tel: 928-783-5225; Email: icschool@icyuma.com. Lydia A. Mendoza, Prin.; Mr. Gustavo Trujillo, Vice Pres. Lay Teachers 15; Franciscan Sisters of Christian Charity 3; Students 225.
Catechesis Religious Program— English and Spanish program. Tel: 928-783-1323; Email: icenglishccd@yahoo.com. Miriam Palencia, D.R.E. (Spanish). Students 237.
Mission—Our Lady of Guadalupe, 417 15th Ave., Yuma, Yuma Co. 85364.
Convent—500 24th Ave., Yuma, 85364. Franciscan Sisters of Christian Charity 4.

3—SAINT JOHN NEUMANN ROMAN CATHOLIC CHURCH - YUMA (1986)
11545 E. 40th St., Yuma, 85367. Tel: 928-342-3544; Email: admin@sjnyuma.com; Web: www.sjnyuma.com. Revs. John F. Friel; Martins Edoka, Parochial Vicar; Deacons Rick Douglas; Giuseppe Tollis; Jerry A. Conrad; William G. Justice
Saint John Neumann Roman Catholic Church - Yuma
Catechesis Religious Program—Tracy Waters, D.R.E. Students 190.

Chaplains of Public Institutions

TUCSON. *Arizona State Prison*, 10000 S. Wilmot Rd., 85777. Vacant
Detention Ministry, P.O. Box 31, 85702.
Tel: 520-481-9149. Deacon Michael S. Gutierrez, Dir.
Arizona Western College, 11750 S. Mesa Dr., Yuma, 85367. Attended from St. John Neumann Parish, Yuma.
Christ the King Chapel, 355 WG/HC, Davis Monthan Air Force Base, 85707. Tel: 520-228-5411;
Tel: 520-228-6581; Email: patricia.poleski.ctr@us.af.mil. Rev. John F. Allt, Assisting Priest, (Retired), Ms. Pat Poleski, Contact Person.
St. Joseph's Hospital, 350 N. Wilmot Rd., 85732.
Tel: 520-873-3000; Email: phess@carondelet.org. Rev. Isaac A. Fynn, Chap., Sr. Marge Foppe, C.S.J, Chap.Bed Capacity 486.
St. Mary's Hospital, 1601 W. St. Mary's Rd., 85745.
Tel: 520-622-5883; Email: Rosa.Vasquez@carondelet.org. Rev. Joseph Saba, Chap. Bed Capacity 400.
Metropolitan Correctional Complex, 8901 S. Wilmot Rd., 85706. Tel: 520-741-3118.
Detention Ministry, P.O. Box 31, 85702.
Tel: 520-481-9149. Deacon Michael S. Gutierrez, Dir.
Northwest Hospital, 6200 N. La Cholla, 85741.
Tel: 520-742-9000. Attended by St. Odilia Parish.
Tucson Medical Center, 5301 E. Grant Rd., 85712. Deacon C. Andy Corder, Chap.Pastoral Care; Attended by St. Cyril Parish, Tucson.
U.S. Veterans Hospital, S. Sixth Ave., 85713.
Tel: 520-792-1450.
University of Arizona Medical Center - South Campus, 2800 E. Ajo Way, 85713.
Tel: 520-694-6826 Pastoral Care. Attended by Our Mother of Sorrows Parish.
University of Arizona Medical Center - University Campus, 1501 N. Campbell, 85724.
Tel: 520-694-6826 Pastoral Care. Attended by Saints Peter & Paul Parish.
Villa Maria Chapel, 4310 E. Grant Rd., 85712.
Tel: 520-323-9351; Email: dmterranova@gmail.com. Donna-Marie Terranova I, Dir.

FORT HUACHUCA. *Fort Huachuca Army Post*, Holy Family Community: 2383 Smith Ave., Fort Huachuca, 85613. Tel: 520-533-4748; Email: chetuya@hotmail.com. Rev. Christopher Adunchezor, Chap.

SAFFORD. *Arizona State Prison*, Safford, 85546.
Tel: 928-428-4698.
Federal Correction Institute, Safford, 85546.
Tel: 602-428-6600. Attended by: St. Rose of Lima Parish, Safford.

YUMA. *MCAS Chapel*, Marine Corps Proving Grounds, P.O. Box 99130, Yuma, 85369. Tel: 928-269-2371; Email: jfriel@diocesetucson.org. Marine Corps Air Station, P.O. Box 99130, Yuma, 85369. Rev. Martins Edoka, Chap.Served by St. John Neumann Parish, Yuma.
Yuma Regional Medical Center,
Tel: 928-328-9297 (Chaplain). Attended from St. Francis of Assisi and Immaculate Conception.

Special Assignment:
Rev. Msgrs.—
McCarthy, Jeremiah, M.C., V.G., Vicar Gen. Mod. of the Curia
Trevizo, Raul P., E.V., Episcopal Vicar Hispanic Affairs, P.O. Box 31, 85702. Tel: 520-838-2500
Revs.—
Arnold, John P., J.C.L., J.D., Adjutant Judicial Vicar
Atanga, Martin B., Vicar, Intl. Priests
Lyons, John P., J.C.L., J.D., V.F., Adjutant Judicial Vicar.

On Duty Outside the Diocese:
Revs.—
Celestial, Ramonito
Martinez, Michael.

Administrative Leave of Absence:
Revs.—
Bradley, Michael
Kohler, William
Martinez, Felipe Antonio
Perez, Javier H., V.F.
Tadeo, Abran R.
Taylor, Daniel.

Leave of Absence:
Revs.—
Ancharski, John J.
Thuerauf, Jeffrey P.

Retired - Administrative Leave:
Rev. Msgr.—
Coleman, James G., (Retired).

Retired:
Most Rev.—
Kicanas, Gerald F., D.D., (Retired)
Rev. Msgrs.—
Millane, Thomas J., (Retired)
O'Keeffe, Richard W., E.V., (Retired)
O'Leary, Todd, (Retired)
Schifano, Albert I., (Retired)
Revs.—
Allt, John F., (Retired)
Brazaskas, Robert, (Retired)
Bryerton, Robert R., (Retired)
Carney, Robert E. Jr., (Retired)
Gagnon, Ronald P., (Retired)
Gameros, Ignacio L., (Retired)
Hyman, Robert A., (Retired)
Kingsley, Richard M., (Retired)
Knapp, Charles, (Retired)
Leahy, Liam, (Retired)
Lobo, Theodore, (Retired)
Lombardo, Joseph A., (Retired)
Mills, Alexander, (Retired)
Modeen, James, (Retired)
Noriega, Arnoldo, (Retired)
Ruiz, Antonio A., (Retired).

Permanent Deacons:
Abiles, Pasqual Jr., St. Helen, Eloy
Ackerley, John K., St. Ss. Peter and Paul, Tucson
Adams, Thomas L., (Retired)
Aguirre, Felix Mario, St. Cyril, Tucson
Andrade, Adalberto, (Serves in Archdiocese of Morelia, Mexico)
Arvizu, Ignacio, St. Monica, Tucson
Barfuss, David Vernon, St. Monica, Tucson
Bejarano, Leonel, Sacred Heart, Parker
Bogushefsky, Joseph, (Retired)
Brotherton, Robert, St. Thomas the Apostle, Tucson (Diocese of Pueblo)
Burke, James, (Lives in Diocese of Dallas)
Callie, Albert, (Retired)
Campbell, Thomas, St. Peter & Paul, Tucson
Cantua, Raul, St. Luke, Douglas
Caponigro, Alfred E., (Diocese of Trenton)
Carbajal, Arnulfo, Immaculate Conception, Yuma
Carlin, Robert P., St. Elizabeth Ann Seton, Tucson
Carmona, Salvador, St. Augustine Cathedral, Tucson
Carrasco, Joaquin, Immaculate Conception, Douglas
Castillo, Frank R., Holy Angels, Globe
Castillo, Jesus, (Inactive)
Castillo, V. Mario, Immaculate Conception, Douglas
Cesnik, Mark, Corpus Christi, Tucson
Chajewski, Charles, Our Mother of Sorrows, Tucson
Chavez, Oscar F., Immaculate Conception, Yuma
Clark, David, Immaculate Conception, Yuma
Collura, Frank J., (Retired)
Conrad, Jerry A., St. John Neumann, Yuma
Corder, C. Andy, St. Francis de Sales, Tucson
Coronado, Javier Domingo, St. Jude, San Luis
Crockette, Alvin, (Inactive)
Cruz, Joe G. Jr., St. Elizabeth Ann Seton, Tucson
Cuestas, Jose III, St. Mark, Tucson
De La Riva, Alfonso, Santa Catalina, Tucson
De La Torre, Nicolas, St. Monica, Tucson
Delgado, Joseph, St. Patrick, Bisbee
Desmarais, Ronald J., (Retired)
Dimuzio, Steven R., St. Anthony of Padua, Casa Grande
Douglas, Rick, St. John Neumann, Yuma
Duarte, Carlos V., (Retired), (Outside the Diocese)
Duarte, Jose, St. John the Evangelist, Tucson

Duckro, Paul N., Ph.D., Saints Peter and Paul, Tucson
Dugan, Patrick, St. Anthony of Padua, Casa Grande
Espino, Gabriel, Immaculate Conception, Yuma
Fernandez, Eugene, Sacred Heart, Tucson
Fierro, Javier, Most Holy Nativity of Our Lord Jesus Christ, Rio Rico
Fischbach, George, (Inactive)
Fisher, Donald, (Inactive)
Flam, Richard, (Retired), (Archdiocese of San Antonio)
Flanagan, Daniel F., St. Francis de Sales, Tucson
Fox, Tom, (Retired), (Diocese of Denver)
Gallegos, Charles A., St. Augustine Cathedral, Tucson
Gamboa, Henry W., (Leave of Absence)
Garcia, John A., (Retired)
Garcia, Marcario, (Retired)
Garcia, Philip, St. Thomas the Apostle, Tucson
Gaun, George, (Retired)
Geonnotti, Anthony Jr., Our Lady of Fatima, Tucson
Giovannini, Louis J., (Serves in the Diocese of Ft. Wayne-South Bend)
Glowdowski, Robert, (Retired), (Diocese of Salt Lake City)
Gomez, Antonio, Immaculate Conception, Yuma
Gomez, Edward, St. Luke, Douglas
Gonzales, Alfred M., San Solano Missions, Sells
Gonzales, Angel, St. Odilia Community, Tucson
Gonzales, Ernie, (Serves in the Diocese of Phoenix)
Gonzales, Jorge, Immaculate Conception, Yuma
Gonzales, Luciano Jr., St. Luke, Douglas
Gonzales, Robert J., (Retired)
Greeley, Andrew Thomas, St. Francis de Sales, Tucson
Grijalva, Richard, (Retired)
Guarriello, Andrew, St. Mark, Tucson
Gullotta, Daniel, St. Rita, Vail (Diocese of San Diego)
Gutierrez, Michael, St. Augustine Cathedral, Tucson
Henderson, Gregory, Fiscal Office, Tucson (Archdiocese of Santa Fe)
Hernandez, Carlos P., Immaculate Conception, Yuma
Hernandez, Nieves J., Immaculate Conception, Yuma
Hernandez, Richard R., St. Francis of Assisi, Yuma
Hill, James, (Retired)
Hilliard, Kenneth, (Serves in the Diocese of Belleville)
Hoerr, Michael Danny, (Inactive)
Huerta-Nunez, Jose G., Our Lady of the Mountains, Sierra Vista
Jaramillo, Ernesto, Immaculate Heart of Mary, Somerton
Jones, William, St. George, Apache Junction
Justice, William G., St. John Neumann, Yuma
Kimminau, Christian, St. Elizabeth Ann Seton, Tucson
Kingery, Russell, St. Francis de Sales, Tucson
Kinney, William J., (Retired), (Diocese of Jefferson City)
Kiser, Richard, St. Elizabeth Ann Seton, Tucson
Klein, John Joseph, St. Andrew the Apostle, Sierra Vista
Kornovich, William, (Retired)
Krieski, Timothy, (Retired)
Krueger, William, Santa Catalina, Tucson; (Archdiocese of Chicago)
Kulpa, Rodney J., St. Odilia, Tucson
Kushner, Joseph III, St. Andrew the Apostle, Sierra Vista
LaFleur, Clyde, Santa Catalina, Tucson; (Archdiocese of Chicago)
LaSalle, James F., (Retired)
Leinfelder, Carl, (Retired)
LeMieux, Richard, (Retired)
Leon, Victor, (Serves in Diocese of Phoenix)
Leon, Viviano
Longoria, Leopoldo "Leo", (Retired)
Lopez, Jose, St. Jude Thaddeus, San Luis
Lopez, Miguel, St. Margaret Mary, Tucson
Lugo, Guillermo A. (Bill), St. Patrick's, Bisbee
Lundgren, Frank S. Jr., (Retired)
Lyncha, Joseph, St. James, Coolidge (Diocese of Erie)
Martin, John R., St. Francis de Sales, Tucson
Maude, Lawrence S., St. Francis of Assisi, Yuma
Maugans, Eric, Our Mother of Sorrow, Tucson
Mazza, Leon S., St. Joseph, Tucson
McNealy, Kenneth J., Redemptorist Renewal Center, Tucson; (Diocese of Rockford)
Medrano, Efren, St. Rita, Vail
Mendoza, Enrique F., St. Monica, Tucson
Mezquita, Fernando, Immaculate Heart of Mary, Somerton
Milazzo, Mike, (Retired)
Miller, Rodger, Our Lady of the Mountains, Sierra Vista
Morales, Tomas, (Retired)
Moreland, Kenneth, Most Holy Trinity, Tucson
Moreno, Francisco Jr., (Retired)
Moulinet, Armando A., St. Luke, Douglas
Munoz, Jorge, St. Christopher, Marana
Murrieta, Manuel Reyes G., St. James, Coolidge
Muthart, Paul, St. Francis of Assisi, Yuma
Negrette, Robert, Our Lady of Fatima, Tucson
Nehmer, David, (Leave of Absence)
Nevins, Robert, (Retired)
Nicholls, Douglas, St. Francis of Assisi, Yuma
Nickel, Clayton, Communications Office, (Archdiocese of Washington, DC)
Nixen, Mark, St. Francis of Assisi, Yuma
Ojeda, Jose, (Retired)
Ortega, Mario, Our Lady of Grace, Maricopa
Padilla, Francisco, Most Holy Nativity of Jesus, Rio Rico
Pasquinelli, Gary, St. Francis of Assisi, Yuma
Penzenstadler, Robert, St. Anthony of Padua, Casa Grande
Perez, Teodoro, St. Joseph Parish, Tucson
Peroti, Joseph, Our Mother of Sorrows, Tucson
Pickett, John Scott, (Services in the Archdiocese of Seattle)
Pinzon, Ricardo M., St. Augustine Cathedral, Tucson
Preston, Wayne L., St. Joseph the Worker, Wellton
Rambaran, Clifford R., St. Joseph, Tucson
Ranke, Dennis, St. Pius X, Tucson (Diocese of Chicago)
Rodriguez, Benito, St. Joseph the Worker, Wellton
Rodriguez, George M., Our Mother of Sorrows, Tucson
Rodriguez, Mario J., St. Elizabeth Ann Seton, Tucson
Roinick, Joseph, Our Lady of the Valley, Green Valley; (Diocese of Scranton)
Rojas, David A., Sacred Heart, Nogales
Romero, William L., Blessed Sacrament, Mammoth
Romo, Reynaldo, Our Lady of the Mountains, Sierra Vista
Rupno, Robert, (Retired), (Archdiocese of Seattle)
Sadorf, Robert G., (Retired)
Sampson, David, Immaculate Conception, Yuma
Sanchez, Arturo E., St. Francis of Assisi, Yuma
Sanchez, Flavio, Santa Catalina, Tucson
Santiago, Nick, (Inactive)
Saspe, Gabriel, (Retired)
Scalpone, Dennis R., St. Francis de Sales, Tucson
Schaff, James, Our Lady of the Mountains, Sierra Vista
Scherf, George, St. Odilia, Tucson
Scott, John, St. Philip the Apostle, Payson (Diocese of Pensacola-Tallahassee)
Sheffer, Edward P., St. Thomas the Apostle, Tucson
Sherlock, Francis C., St. Elizabeth Ann Seton, Tucson
Shukurani, Niyibizi, St. Cyril of Alexander
Solano, Francisco, St. Anthony of Padua, Casa Grande; (Archdiocese of Los Angeles)
Soto, Jesse R., (Leave of Absence)
Stotler, Jim, (Retired)
Tackett, Gene, Our Lady of the Mountains, Sierra Vista
Tarango, Florentino, (Leave of Absence)
Teran, Lauro A., St. Andrew the Apostle, Sierra Vista
Terry, John, Most Holy Trinity, Tucson
Thrall, Scott, Our Mother of Sorrows, Tucson
Tollis, Giuseppe, St. John Neumann, Yuma; (Archdiocese of Miami)
Tran, Thai V., St. Francis de Sales, Tucson
Trevino, Jacinto Jr., St. Elizabeth Ann Seton, Tucson
Trudell, William, St. Phillip, Payson (Archdiocese of Salt Lake City)
Trujillo, Ernie, Assumption of the Blessed Virgin Mary, Florence
Trujillo, Jeff, Immaculate Heart of Mary, Somerton
Underwood, Anthony E., St. Patrick, Bisbee
Valadez, Jose, St. Francis of Assisi, Yuma
Valdenegro, Federico T.
Valencia, Richard, Vicar for Deacons, Our Lady of Lourdes, Benson
Valenzuela, Armando L., Our Lady Queen All Saints, Tucson
Valle, Jose C., St. Patrick, Bisbee
Vessels, Carlos, St. Rose of Lima, Safford
Vidal, Rafael, St. Francis of Assisi, Yuma
Vigil, William, (Leave of Absence)
Whalen, Charles, Our Mother of Sorrows, Tucson; (Diocese of Palm Beach)
Willis, Thomas, St. Ambrose, Tucson
Yanez, Guadalupe, St. Luke, Douglas
Yanez, Jesus L. "Chuy", (Retired)
Zamora Arroyo, Jose Francisco, Our Mother of Sorrows, Tucson.

INSTITUTIONS LOCATED IN DIOCESE

[A] HIGH SCHOOLS, DIOCESAN AND PRIVATE

TUCSON. *St. Augustine Catholic High School*, 8800 E. 22nd St., 85710. Tel: 520-751-8300; Fax: 520-751-8304; Email: info@staugustinehigh.com; Web: www.staugustinehigh.com. Dave Keller, Pres.; Mrs. Lynn Cuffari, Prin. Lay Teachers 35; Students 280.

Immaculate Heart High School (1930) 625 E. Magee Rd., 85704. Tel: 520-297-2851; Fax: 520-797-7374; Email: sisteralicemartinez@gmail.com; Web: www.ihschool.com. Sr. Alice M. Martinez, Prin. Lay Teachers 15; Sisters of the Immaculate Heart of Mary 1; Students 59; Clergy/Religious Teachers 3.

Salpointe Catholic High School (1950) 1545 E. Copper St., 85719. Tel: 520-547-5878; Fax: 520-327-8477; Email: ksullivan@salpointe.org; Web: www.salpointe.org. Mrs. Kay Sullivan, Pres.; Sr. Helen Timothy, I.B.V.M., Prin.; Jennifer Harris, Dir.; Rev. Emanuel Franco-Gomez, Campus Min. Carmelite Order Lay Teachers 85; Priests 2; Sisters 1; Students 1,215; Clergy/Religious Teachers 2. In Res. Revs. Thomas Butler, O.Carm., (Retired); Vernon Malley, O.Carm., (Retired); Ivan C. Marsh, O.Carm., (Retired); Paul Henson, O.-Carm.; Bro. Tom Conlon, O.Carm., (Retired).

San Miguel of Tucson Corporation - San Miguel Catholic High School, 6601 S. San Fernando Rd., 85756. Tel: 520-294-6403; Fax: 520-294-6417; Email: masond@sanmiguelhigh.org; Web: www.sanmiguelcristorey.org. Dave Mason, Pres.; Armando Valenzuela III, Prin.; Christine Miranda, Registrar. Administrators 7; Brothers 3; Lay Teachers 26; Students 346; Clergy/Religious Teachers 1; Staff 18.

YUMA. *Yuma Catholic High School* (2000) 2100 W. 28th St., Yuma, 85364. Tel: 928-317-7900; Fax: 928-317-8558; Email: ycinfo@yumacatholic.org; Web: yumacatholic.org. Rhett Stallworth, Prin.; Louis Pisano, Vice Prin. Lay Teachers 27; Sisters 1; Students 377; Clergy/Religious Teachers 1.

[B] SCHOOLS, PRIVATE

TUCSON. *Immaculate Heart Academy* (1930) (Grades PreK-8), 410 E. Magee Rd., 85704. Tel: 520-297-6672; Fax: 520-297-9152; Email: academyoffice@ihschool.org; Web: ihschool.org. Sr. Veronica Loya, Prin. Lay Teachers 20; Sisters of the Immaculate Heart of Mary 4; Students 198; Clergy/Religious Teachers 1.

NOGALES. *Lourdes Catholic School*, (Grades PreK-12), 555 E. Patagonia Hwy., P.O. Box 1865, Nogales, 85628. Tel: 520-287-5659; Fax: 520-287-2910; Email: highschoolprincipal@lcsnogales.org; Email: elementaryprincipal@lcsnogales.org; Web: www.lcsnogales.org. Sr. Rosa Maria Ruiz, C.F.M.M., Pres.; Sandra Contreras, Prin. (High School); Rosalinda Perez, Prin. (Elementary). Lay Teachers 20; Minim Daughters of Mary Immaculate (C.F.M.M.) 5; Students 330.

[C] CATHOLIC COMMUNITY SERVICES

TUCSON. *Catholic Community Services of Southern Arizona, Inc.* (1933) 140 W. Speedway, Ste. 230, 85705. Tel: 520-623-0344; Fax: 520-770-8514; Email: ccsinfo@ccs-soaz.org; Web: www.ccs-soaz.org. Marguerite Harmon, M.S., CEO; Pat Torrington, Pres. Tot Asst. Annually 100,000; Total Staff 450; Services for Incarcerated 4,576.

Social Service Agencies: Pima County (Including City of Tucson) 140 W. Speedway, Ste. 230, 85705. Tel: 520-623-0344; Fax: 520-770-8514; Email: ccsinfo@ccs-soaz.org; Web: ccs-soaz.org. Marguerite Harmon, M.S., Exec. Tot Asst. Annually 100,000; Total Staff 450.

Catholic Community Services of Southern Arizona, Inc. Marguerite Harmon, M.S., CEO of CCS; Linda Shmyr, Ph.D., Exec. Dir., Catholic Social Svcs.

Catholic Community Services - Tucson, 140 W. Speedway, Ste. 130, 85705. Tel: 520-623-0344; Fax: 520-770-8578; Email: lindah@ccs-soaz.org; Web: www.ccs-soaz.org. Linda Hollis, Exec. Dir. Tot Asst. Annually 163; Total Staff 6.

Catholic Community Services - Sierra Vista, 6049 E. Hwy. 90, Sierra Vista, 85635. Tel: 520-458-4203; Fax: 520-459-1285; Email: michaelv@ccs-soaz.org. Michael Vetter, M.A., Exec. Dir. Tot Asst. Annually 2,000; Total Staff 40.

Sierra Vista Shelter, P.O. Box 1961, Sierra Vista, 85636. Tel: 520-458-9096; Email: michaelv@ccs-soaz.org. Michael Vetter, M.A., Exec. Dir.

Douglas Shelter, P.O. Box 121, Douglas, 85608.

Tel: 520-364-2465; Email: michaelv@ccs-soaz.org. Michael Vetter, M.A., Prog. Dir. Tot Asst. Annually 200; Total Staff 10.

Migration and Refugee Services, 140 W. Speedway, Ste. 130, 85705. Tel: 520-623-0344; Fax: 520-770-8556; Email: margaretp@ccs-soaz.org. Margaret Palmer, Prog. Dir. Tot Asst. Annually 280; Total Staff 12.

Senior Nutrition Services, 5009 E. 29th St., 85711. Tel: 520-624-1562; Fax: 520-519-1303; Email: lindar@ccs-soaz.org. Ms. Linda Rumsey, M.S.R.D., Prog. Dir. Tot Asst. Annually 2,001; Total Staff 12.

Merilac Lodge, 140 W. Speedway, Ste. 130, 85705. Tel: 520-623-0344; Fax: 520-770-8578; Email: marier@ccs-soaz.org; Web: www.ccs-soaz.org. Marie Reyna, Dir. Tot Asst. Annually 15; Total Staff 6.

Immigration Counseling Service, 140 W. Speedway, Ste. 130, 85705. Tel: 520-623-0344; Fax: 520-770-8578; Email: meredithl@ccs-soaz.org. Meredith Lynch, Dir. Tot Asst. Annually 541; Total Staff 6.

Field Offices:.

Gila County Case Management, Center in Globe, P.O. Box 1172, Globe, 85502. Tel: 520-425-5130; Fax: 520-425-2888; Email: ccsinfo@ccs-soaz.org. Linda Hollis. Tot Asst. Annually 192; Total Staff 2.

Catholic Community Services - Yuma, 690 E. 32nd St., Yuma, 85365. Tel: 928-341-9400; Fax: 928-341-8428; Email: emendez@ccs-westaz.org. Eva Mendez-Counts, M.A. Tot Asst. Annually 1,811; Total Staff 70.

St. Jeanne Jugan Ministry with Elders, 140 W. Speedway, Ste. 230, 85705. Tel: 520-623-0344; Fax: 520-770-8514; Email: mannyg@ccs-soaz.org. Manuel Guzman, Dir.; Rev. Raymond Ratzenberger. Tot Asst. Annually 1,750; Total Staff 2.

Community Outreach Program for the Deaf, 268 W. Adams St., 85705. Tel: 520-792-1906; Fax: 520-770-8544; Email: annel@copdaz.org. Anne Levy, M.A., Exec. Dir. Tot Asst. Annually 3,759; Total Staff 41.

Community Living Program, 268 W. Adams, 85705. Tel: 520-792-1906; Fax: 520-770-8544; Email: suehm@clpaz.org. Sue Henning-Mitchell, B.A., Deputy Dir. Tot Asst. Annually 43; Total Staff 120.

Detention Ministry/Kolbe Society, 140 W. Speedway, Ste. 230, 85705. Tel: 520-623-0344; Fax: 520-770-8514. Deacon Michael S. Gutierrez, Prog. Dir.; Rev. Richard Landry, M.S., Restorative Justice Min.

Pio Decimo Neighborhood Center, 848 S. 7th Ave., 85701. Tel: 520-622-2801; Fax: 520-622-4704; Email: marciaz@ccs-pio.org. Marcia Zerler, Exec. Tot Asst. Annually 9,803; Total Staff 45.

Valley Center for the Deaf, 5025 E. Washington St., Ste. 114, Phoenix, 85034. Tel: 602-267-1921; Fax: 602-273-1872; Email: cindyw@vcdaz.org. Cindy Walsh, Agency Dir. Tot Asst. Annually 1,500; Total Staff 15.

[D] GENERAL HOSPITALS

TUCSON. *St. Elizabeth's Health Center, Inc.*, 140 W. Speedway Blvd., Ste. 100, 85705. Tel: 520-628-7871; Fax: 520-205-8461; Email: mauricettem@saintehc.org; Web: www.saintehc.org. Mauricette Montredon, CEO. Tot Asst. Annually 30,000; Staff 56.

[E] MONASTERIES AND RESIDENCES OF PRIESTS AND BROTHERS

TUCSON. *Carmelite Priory* aka Our Lady Of Mt. Carmel Priory (1953) 1540 E. Glenn St., 85719. Tel: 520-325-1537; Email: phenson@carmelnet.org. Rev. Paul Henson, O.Carm., Prior; Bros. Michael Joyce, Teacher; Kevin Keller, Teacher; Revs. Emanuel Franco-Gomez, Campus Min.; Thomas Butler, O.Carm., (Retired); Vernon Malley, O.Carm., (Retired); Ivan C. Marsh, O.Carm., (Retired); Bro. Thomas Conlon, O.Carm., (Retired). Fathers and Brothers at Our Lady of Mt. Carmel Priory. Brothers 3; Priests 5.

Carmelites at St. Thomas Priory, 5010 N. Valley View Rd., 85718. Email: charlie.ocarm@gmail.com. Revs. Angelo Mastria, O.Carm., (Retired); Cyprian Hibner, O.Carm., (Retired); Bro. Charles Kwiatkowski, O.Carm., Prior (Retired), Tel: 630-750-3644. Brothers 1; Clergy 2.

Jesuit Community of the Vatican Observatory, 2017 E. Lee St., 85719. Tel: 520-795-9866; Email: ccorbally@as.arizona.edu. Revs. Paul R. Mueller, S.J., Supr.; Christopher Corbally, S.J., Vice Supr.; Pavel Gabor, S.J., Vice Dir.; Richard P. Boyle, S.J.; Jean-B Kikwaya Eluo, S.J.; Christoforus Bayu Risanto, S.J.; Bros. Guy Consolmagno, S.J., Dir.; Thomas R. Williams, S.J., Treas. Jesuit Residence. Brothers 2; Clergy 6. **Vatican Observatory Foundation*, 2017 E. Lee St., 85719. Tel: 520-795-1694; Email: corbally@as.arizona.edu. Rev. Christopher Corbally, S.J., Contact Person. Brothers 1; Priests 4. *Vatican Observatory Research Group*, Steward Observatory, The University of Arizona, 933 N. Cherry Ave., 85721-0065. Tel: 520-621-6043; Fax: 520-621-1532; Email: vaticanobservatoryrg@gmail.com. Rev. Pavel Gabor, S.J., Dir.

Redemptorist Society of Arizona Desert House of Prayer Residence, 7350 W. Picture Rocks Rd., 85743. P.O. Box 570, Cortaro, 85652. Tel: 520-744-3825; Fax: 520-744-0774; Email: deserthop@live.com; Web: deserthouseofprayer.org. Rev. Thomas D. Picton, C.Ss.R., Dir.; Bro. William Cloughley, C.Ss.R., Member. Priests 1.

San Xavier Mission Friary, 1950 W. San Xavier Rd., 85746. Tel: 520-294-3015; Fax: 520-294-3438; Email: sxmstephen@gmail.com. Rev. Stephen Barnufsky, O.F.M.; Bro. Robert Brady, O.F.M., Supr.; Revs. Clifford Herle, O.F.M., In Res.; Manuel Viera, O.F.M., J.C.L., In Res.; Arthur J. Espelage, O.F.M., J.C.D., In Res.; Friars Maximilian Hottle, O.F.M., In Res.; Edward Fronske, O.F.M., In Res.; Rev. Dennis Bosse, O.F.M., In Res. Brothers 1; Priests 6. *Filial House Retirement*, Atria, 1550 E. River Rd., 85718. Franciscan Friars Filial Retirement House, 1950 W. San Xavier Rd., 85746. Tel: 520-299-1941; Email: sxmstephen@gmail.com. Revs. Elias Galvez, O.F.M., (Retired); Leo Sprietsma, O.F.M., (Retired); Peter Verheggen, O.F.M., (Retired); Joseph Zermeño, O.F.M., (Retired). Clergy 4.

TOPAWA. *San Francisco Solano Friary*, San Francisco Solano Friary, P.O. Box 210, Topawa, 85639. Tel: 520-383-2350; Fax: 520-383-3063; Email: ssmissions@mail.com. Revs. Alfonso Ponchie Vasquez, O.F.M., Pastor; William J. Minkel, O.F.M., Parochial Vicar; Friars Peter Boegel, O.F.M., Vicar; David Paz, O.F.M., Guardian. Brothers 2; Clergy 2. *Filial Houses*, St. Francis Friary, 4110 Jefferson St., P.O. Box 54, Elfrida, 85610. Tel: 520-361-2419; Cell: 314-803-6735; Email: buerofm@gmail.com. Rev. Luis Runde, O.F.M.; Bro. David Buer, O.F.M., Contact Person. Brothers 2; Priests 1.

[F] CONVENTS AND RESIDENCES FOR SISTERS

TUCSON. *St. Ann Convent*, 3820 N. Sabino Canyon Rd., 85750-6534. Tel: 520-298-0064; Fax: 520-886-4273; Email: stanns@q.com. Sr. Luisa Sanchez, I.H.M., Supr. Sisters of the Immaculate Heart of Mary 9.

Immaculate Heart Lodge Convent, 410 E. Magee Rd., 85704. Tel: 520-742-5896; Email: sisteralicemartinez@gmail.com. Sr. Alice M. Martinez, Prov. Supr. Sisters of the Immaculate Heart of Mary 5.

Immaculate Heart Novitiate, 3820 N. Sabino Canyon Rd., 85750-6534. Tel: 520-298-0064; Fax: 520-886-4273; Email: stanns@q.com. Sr. Luisa Sanchez, I.H.M., Supr.

Immaculate Heart of Mary Delegate House Community, 3820 N. Sabino Canyon Rd., 85750-6534. Fax: 520-886-4273; Email: stanns@q.com. Sr. Luisa Sanchez, I.H.M., Supr.

La Paz de Jose Community, 3458 E. Third St., 85716. Tel: 520-795-1974; Email: jbartholomeaux@diocesetucson.org. Sr. Jeanne Bartholomeaux, S.C., Contact Person. Sisters 3.

Maria Community, 7818 N. Blue Brick Dr., 85743. Tel: 520-444-8052; Email: irmao@netzero.net. Sr. Irma Odabashian, C.S.J., Contact Person. Sisters 2.

Saints Peter and Paul Convent (1933) 1947 E. Adams St., 85719. Tel: 520-325-2234; Email: jbartholomeaux@diocesetucson.org. Sr. Consuelo Pacheco, Contact Person. Sisters of Charity of Seton Hill. Sisters 3.

San Xavier Mission Convent aka Franciscan Sisters of Christian Charity (1962) Franciscan Sisters of Christian Charity, 1996 W. San Xavier Rd., 85746. Tel: 520-746-4779; Email: criach@diocesetucson.org. Sr. Carla Riach, O.S.F., Supr. Sisters 5; Solemnly Professed 5.

DOUGLAS. *Loretto Convent*, 1200 14th St., Douglas, 85607. Tel: 520-364-7571; Cell: 520-249-2588; Email: sr.timothymariekennedy@outlook.com; Email: sistertm@lorettoschool.org. Sr. Timothy Marie Kennedy, Contact Person. Sisters 5.

NOGALES. *St. Joseph Convent*, Minim Daughters of Mary Immaculate, 405 N. Carondelet Dr., Nogales, 85621-2454. Tel: 520-287-7139; Email: clmrponce@yahoo.com. Sr. Celia Ma. Ponce, C.F.M.M., Supr. Minim Daughters of Mary Immaculate (C.F.M.M.) 7.

Our Lady of Lourdes Convent, 555 E. Patagonia Hwy., P.O. Box 1865, Nogales, 85628-1865. Tel: 520-287-3377; Fax: 520-287-2910; Email: rruiz@diocesetucson.org. Sr. Rosa Maria Ruiz, C.F.M.M., Supr. Minim Daughters of Mary Immaculate (C.F.M.M.) 6.

SAN CARLOS. *Saint Charles Convent*, Mohave Ave., P.O. Box 338, San Carlos, 85550. Tel: 928-475-2460; Fax: 928-475-2050; Email: sbrennan@cscsisters.org. Sr. Ruth Holtshouser, Contact Person. Sisters of the Holy Cross. Sisters 1.

SONOITA. *Santa Rita Abbey* (1972) 14200 E. Fish Canyon Rd., Sonoita, 85637-6545. Tel: 520-455-5595; Fax: 520-455-5770; Email: sracommty@gmail.com; Web: www.santaritaabbey.org. Mother Victoria Murray, O.C.S.O., Prioress. Cistercian Nuns of the Strict Observance, O.C.S.O. Sisters 9.

YUMA. *Immaculate Conception Convent*, 500 S. 24th Ave., Yuma, 85364. Tel: 928-783-5224; Email: smbkor@hotmail.com. Mary Beth Kornely, O.S.F., Dir. Sisters 7.

[G] RETREAT HOUSES

TUCSON. *Desert House of Prayer Retreat House*, 7350 W. Picture Rocks Rd., 85743. Tel: 520-744-3825; Fax: 520-744-0774; Email: deserthop@live.com; Web: deserthouseofprayer.org. P.O. Box 570, Cortaro, 85652. Rev. Thomas D. Picton, C.Ss.R., Dir.; Bro. William Cloughley, C.Ss.R., Staff.

Redemptorist Society of Arizona Redemptorist Renewal Center, 7101 W. Picture Rocks Rd., 85743. Tel: 520-744-3400; Fax: 520-744-8021; Email: office@desertrenewal.org; Web: www.desertrenewal.org. Revs. Paul Coury, C.Ss.R., Supr. & Dir.; Peter Connolly, C.Ss.R.; Charles Wehrley, C.Ss.R.; Gregory Wiest, C.Ss.R.; Lawrence E. Sanders. Priests 5.

SIERRA VISTA. *La Purisima Retreat Center, Inc.* (2001) 10301 E. Stone Ridge Ave., Hereford, 85615. 800 Taylor Dr., N.W., Sierra Vista, 85635. Tel: 520-458-2925; Tel: 520-559-0649; Fax: 520-452-0235; Email: LPRetreatCenter@gmail.com; Web: lpretreat.org. Tom Felix, Vice Pres.; Rev. Gregory P. Adolf, Sec.; Ann S. Dickson, Treas.

[H] NEWMAN CENTERS

TUCSON. *University of Arizona Newman Center* St. Thomas More Newman Center 1615 E. 2nd St., 85719. Tel: 520-327-4665; Fax: 520-273-3963; Email: newman@uacatholic.org; Web: www.uacatholic.org. Revs. John Paul Forte, O.P.; Emmanuel Taylor, O.P. In Res. Revs. Robert A. Burns, O.P.; Thomas DeMan, O.P.; Nathan Castle.

THATCHER. *Eastern Arizona College - Newman Center*, 3592 W. 4th St., Thatcher, 85552. Mailing Address: 311 S. Central Ave., Safford, 85546. Tel: 928-428-4920; Fax: 928-428-4922; Email: stroselima@gmail.com; Web: SaintRoseLima-Safford.com. Rev. Nicodemus Shaghel, Admin.

St. Rose of Lima, 311 S. Central Ave., Safford, 85546. Tel: 928-428-4920; Fax: 928-428-4922; Email: stroselima@gmail.com; Web: SaintRoseLima-Safford.com. Rev. Robert A. Rodriguez.

[I] MISCELLANEOUS LISTINGS

TUCSON. *Arizona's Catholic Tuition Support Organization (CTSO)*, 192 S. Stone Ave., 85701. Tel: 520-838-2571; Fax: 520-838-2578; Email: gquiroz@diocesetucson.org; Web: www.ctso-tucson.org. P.O. Box 31, 85702. Gracie Quiroz Marum, CEO; Mrs. Amy Euler, Pres.

Ascension Arizona, 2202 N. Forbes Blvd., Exec. Ste., 85745-2682. Mr. Joseph Impicciche, Exec. Carondelet Foundation, Inc.

Carondelet Foundation Inc., 2202 N. Forbes Blvd., Exec. Ste., 85745-2682. Tel: 314-733-8000; Web: www.ascension.org. James Beckmann, Chm.

Casa Maria (1981) 401 E. 26th St., 85713. Tel: 520-624-0312; Email: casamariatucson@yahoo.com; Web: casamariatucson.org. Mr. Brian Flagg, Coord. Tot Asst. Annually 182,000.

Catholic Community Services Foundation, 140 W. Speedway Blvd., Ste. 230, 85705. Tel: 520-670-0809; Fax: 520-770-8514; Email: lizm@ccs-soaz.org. Liz McMahon, Devel. Dir.

Catholic Foundation for the Diocese of Tucson Stewardship and Charitable Giving, 64 E. Broadway Blvd., 85701. Tel: 520-838-2505; Fax: 520-838-2585; Email: khutchinson@diocesetucson.org; Email: skiser@diocesetucson.org; Web: www.cathfnd.org. P.O. Box 31, 85702. Most Rev. Edward J. Weisenburger, Corporate Sole; Deacon Gregory Henderson, CEO; Salvatore Polizotto, Exec. Dir.; John Tellmann, Chm.; Robert Sullivan, Treas.; Alex Miramontez, Sec.; Patricia Kambourian, Past Chair; Steve Borden, Member; Sergio Cardona, Member; Donal Drayne, Member; Mary Anne Fay, Member; Mr. Dennis M. Fitzgibbons, Member; Jeanne Gale, Member; Marilou Lopez, Member; John Meurant, Member; Les Orchekowsky, Member; Luis Parra, Member; Caitlin Sklar, Member.

Ex Officio Members: Rev. Msgr. Jeremiah McCarthy, M.C., V.G.; Tom Arnold, CFO.

Members: Luis Parra; Mary Anne Fay; Lee M. Oser;

Robert Sullivan, Treas.; Steve Bordon; Marilou Lopez; Rick Moisio; Les Orchekowsky; Edward Steinhoff.

Board Members: Donal Drayne; Rev. Viliulfo Valderrama, V.F.

Christ Child Society of Tucson, P.O. Box 36212, 85740. Angela Schneider, Pres.

Diocese of Tucson Catholic Cemeteries (Sole Corporation) 3555 N. Oracle Rd., 85705. Tel: 520-888-0860; Fax: 520-887-7360; Email: info@dotcc.org; Web: www.dotcc.org. Mr. Thomas Hanlon, Exec. Dir.

Diocese of Tucson Catholic Committee on Scouting, Attn: Virginia Robilard, P.O. Box 14256, 85732. Tel: 520-297-5245; Email: varobillard@msn.com. Ms. Virginia Robillard, Chm.; Rev. Robert A. Rodriguez, Chap.

Jordan Ministry Team, Inc., 48 N. Tucson Blvd., #104, 85716. Tel: 520-623-2563; Fax: 520-623-2585 ; Email: jmt@jordanministry.org; Web: www.jordanministry.org. Sr. Jane Eschweiler, S.D.S., Interim CEO / Pres.

Knights of Columbus- Arizona State Council, 14175 W. Indian School, Ste. B4-626, Goodyear, 85395. Tel: 623-535-7653; Email: statedeputy@kofc-az.org; Web: www.kofc-az.org. Thomas Kalisz, Contact Person.

Padre Kino Vocations Ministry for the Diocese of Tucson (2015) 64 E. Broadway Blvd., 85701. Tel: 520-825-9556; Email: johnmhalligan@gmail.com. P.O. Box 31, 85702. John M. Halligan, Pres.

Parish Pooled Investment Trust, 64 E. Broadway Blvd., 85701. P.O. Box 31, 85702. Tel: 520-838-2553; Email: cbarrios@diocesetucson.org; Web: www.diocesetucson.org. Deacon Gregory Henderson, Exec.

**Reachout, Inc.* dba Reachout Women's Center, 2648 N. Campbell Ave., 85719. Tel: 520-321-4300; Fax: 520-321-4519; Email: info@reachoutwomenscenter.com; Web: www.FriendsofRWC.life. RJ Saavedra, Dir.; Sr. Leonette Kochan, O.S.F., Pres.

Retorno (Marriage Retorno), 4321 N. Ventana Dr., 85750. Tel: 520-722-2931; Email: stogskk@mindspring.com; Web: www.marriageretornocpr.org. Rev. Robert Brazaskas, Coordinating Priest, (Retired), Tel: 520-308-4945; Kathie & Kevin Stogsdill, Contact Person, Tel: 520-722-2931. Prayer Retreat for Couples or Marriage Retorno (Couple Prayer Retreat).

The Roman Catholic Diocese of Tucson Our Faith, Our Hope, Our Future, 64 E. Broadway Blvd., P.O. Box 31, 85702-0031. Tel: 520-838-2505; Fax: 520-838-2585; Email: ghenderson@diocesetucson.org; Web: www.diocesetucson.org. Most Rev. Edward J. Weisenburger, Pres.; Rev. Msgr. Jeremiah McCarthy, M.C., V.G.; Deacon Gregory Henderson, Sec.

**Salpointe Catholic Education Foundation*, 1545 E. Copper St., 85719. Tel: 520-547-5878; Fax: 520-327-8477; Email: ksullivan@salpointe.org. Jennifer Harris, Dir.

San Miguel Corporate Internship, 6601 S. San Fernando Rd., 85756. Tel: 520-294-6403; Fax: 520-294-6417; Email: morandon@sanmiguelhigh.org; Web: www.sanmiguelcristorey.org. Dave Mason, Pres.; Natalie Morando, Vice Pres. Lay Staff 4; Students 351.

**Society of St. Vincent de Paul*, 829 S. 6th Ave., 85701. Tel: 520-628-7837; Fax: 520-624-9102; Email: inbox@svdptucson.org; Web: www.svdptucson.org. Ms. Stephany Brown, Pres.

Southwest Medical Aid, 525 W. Plata St., Ste. 400, 85705. Tel: 520-622-2938; Fax: 520-882-3675; Email: sma@southwestmedicalaid.org; Web: www.southwestmedicalaid.org. Mr. Michael Johnson, Dir.

Sr. Jose Women's Center, 1050 S. Park Ave., 85719. P.O. Box 1028, 85702. Tel: 520-909-3905; Tel: 520-954-3373; Email: execdirector@sisterjose.org; Web: sisterjose.org. Jean Fedigan, Contact Person, Exec. Dir. Bed Capacity 35; Tot Asst. Annually 12,775.

The St. Thomas More Society of Southern Arizona, 455 W. Paseo Redondo, 85701. Tel: 520-620-6222; Email: vinzlaw@aol.com. Mr. Vincent Lacsamana, Contact Person.

HEREFORD. *Our Lady of the Sierras Foundation* (1993) 10310 S. Twin Oaks Rd., P.O. Box 269, Hereford, 85615. Tel: 520-378-2950; Email: ourladysierrashrine@msn.com; Web: www.ourladyofthesierras.org. Mr. Gerald A. Chouinard, Pres.

Rachel's Vineyard Retreat Ministries Tucson and Southern Arizona, Inc., 3107 E. Serritos Ranch Rd., P.O. Box 1085, Hereford, 85615. Tel: 520-743-6777; Email: rachelsvineyardtucson@cox.net; Web: www.rachelsvineyardtucson.org. Rev. Msgr. John J. Cusack, Member; Revs. Emilio Landeros Chapa, Member; Robert A. Rodriguez, Member.

NOGALES. *Kino Border Initiative* (2008) 81 N. Terrace Ave., Nogales, 85621. Tel: 520-287-2370; Fax: 520-287-2375; Email: jfierro@diocesetucson.org; Web: www.kinoborderinitiative.org. Mailing Address: P.O. Box 159, Nogales, 85628-0159. Revs. Sean Carroll, S.J., Exec. Dir.; Peter Neeley, S.J., Asst. Dir. Education; Samuel Lozano de los Santos, S.J., Dir. Programs in Mexico; Joanna Williams, Dir. Ed. & Advocacy; Deacon Javier Fierro, Assoc. Dir. Lay Employee 4; Tot Asst. Annually 43,000.

PAYSON. **RIM Catholic Evangelization Association*, 1303 Red Baron Rd., Payson, 85541. Tel: 928-474-2129; Email: TMDJFOX@msn.com. P.O. Box 1635, Payson, 85547. Deacon Tom Fox.

VAIL. *Magnificat - Tucson Chapter*, 702 E. Blue Mesa Pl., Vail, 85641. Tel: 520-237-7060; Email: tucsonmagnificat@gmail.com. Mrs. Elizabeth Celenza, Coord. A ministry to Catholic women.; Pima East Vicariate Chapter.

YUMA. *St. John Neumann Roman Catholic Church Regional Columbarium - Yuma*, 11545 E. 40th St., Yuma, 85367. Tel: 520-888-0860; Email: info@dotcc.org. Mr. Thomas Hanlon, Dir.

[J] DIOCESAN CEMETERIES

TUCSON. *Holy Hope Cemetery and Mausoleum*, Office: 3555 N. Oracle Rd., 85705. Tel: 520-888-0860; Fax: 520-887-7360; Email: info@dotcc.org; Web: www.dotcc.org. Mr. Thomas Hanlon, Dir.

Our Lady of the Desert Cemetery and Mausoleum, Office: 2151 S. Avenida Los Reyes, 85748. Tel: 520-885-9173; Fax: 520-733-4186; Email: info@dotcc.org; Web: www.dotcc.org. Mr. Thomas Hanlon, Dir.

[K] CLOSED INSTITUTIONS

TUCSON. *Diocese of Tucson Archives*, 300 S. Tucson Blvd., 85716. Tel: 520-886-5201; Tel: 520-838-2500 ; Email: archives@diocesetucson.org; Web: www.diocesetucson.org/archives. Ana Elisa Arredondo, Archivist. The following parish, school or orphanage records may be found at the above address unless otherwise indicated. Notations to Sacramental Registers of closed parishes/missions on those listed below should be directed to the Archival Center and should specify the name of the parish. The location of records periodically changes. Inquiries for records of parishes, schools or institutions not on this list should be directed to the above address.

All Saints Parish (Tucson).
Blessed Martin de Porres (Tucson).
Sacred Heart Parish (Bisbee).
St. Anthony Parish (Tiger).
St. Bernard Mission Records located at: Our Lady, Queen of All Saints Parish, 2915 E. 36th St., Tucson, AZ 85713 Tel: 520-622-8602 Fax: 520-622-4581.
St. Helen Parish (Sonora).
All Saints Parochial School (Tucson).
Lestonnac PreK-Kindergarten School (Douglas).
Loretto Academy (Bisbee).
Regina Cleri Seminary (Tucson).
Sacred Heart Parochial School (Tucson).
St. Augustine Parochial School (Tucson).
St. Joseph Academy for Girls (Tucson).
St. Joseph Orphanage (Tucson).
St. Patrick Parochial School (Bisbee).

RELIGIOUS INSTITUTES OF MEN REPRESENTED IN THE DIOCESE

For further details refer to the corresponding bracketed number in the Religious Institutes of Men or Women section.

[0200]—*Benedictine Monks*—O.S.B.
[]—*Benedictine Monks of Erlac*—O.S.B.
[0330]—*Brothers of the Christian Schools*—F.S.C.
[0470]—*Capuchin Friars* (Prov. of St. Joseph)—O.F.M.Cap.
[0270]—*Carmelite Fathers and Brothers* (Prov. of Most Pure Heart of Mary)—O.Carm.
[]—*Congregation of the Holy Spirit Fathers*—C.S.Sp.
[0260]—*Discalced Carmelites*—O.C.D.
[0520]—*Franciscan Friars* (Province of St. Barbara)—O.F.M.
[0520]—*Franciscan Friars* (Province of St. John the Baptist)—O.F.M.
[0690]—*Jesuit Fathers and Brothers* (California Province)—S.J.
[]—*Jesuits of the Vatican Observatory*—S.J.
[0720]—*Missionaries of Our Lady La Salette* (Immaculate Heart of Mary Prov.)—M.S.
[0485]—*Missionaries of St. Francis de Sales*—M.S.F.S.
[0840]—*Missionary Servants of the Most Holy Trinity*—S.T.
[0430]—*Order of Preachers (Dominicans)*—O.P.
[1070]—*Redemptorist Fathers* (Denver Prov.)—C.Ss.R.
[1200]—*Society of the Divine Savior*—S.D.S.
[]—*Via Christi Society*—V.C.
[]—*Vietnamese Redemptorist*—C.Ss.R.

RELIGIOUS INSTITUTES OF WOMEN REPRESENTED IN THE DIOCESE

[1070-13]—*Adrian Dominican Sisters*—O.P.
[0370]—*Carmelite Sisters of the Most Sacred Heart of Los Angeles*—O.C.D.
[0670]—*Cistercian Nuns of the Strict Observance*—O.C.S.O.
[3710]—*Congregation of the Sisters of St. Agnes*—C.S.A.
[]—*Daughters of the Heart of Mary*—D.H.M.
[]—*Dominican Sisters of Mission San Jose*—O.P.
[1070-30]—*Dominican Sisters of Oakford*—O.P.
[1115]—*Dominican Sisters of Peace*—O.P.
[]—*Franciscan Missionaries of Jesus Crucified of Albany, NY*—F.M.J.C.
[]—*Franciscan Missionaries of Mary Sisters*—F.M.M.S.
[1230]—*Franciscan Sisters of Christian Charity*—O.S.F.
[1310]—*Franciscan Sisters of Little Falls, Minnesota*—O.S.F.
[1425]—*Franciscan Sisters of Peace*—F.S.P.
[2370]—*Institute of the Blessed Virgin Mary*—I.B.V.M.
[2490]—*Medical Mission Sisters*—M.M.S.
[2675]—*Minim Daughters of Mary Immaculate*—C.F.M.M.
[2720]—*Mission Helpers of the Sacred Heart*—M.H.S.H.
[]—*Missionary of Eucharistic Love* (Mexico)—M.E.L.
[]—*Order of Benedict*—O.S.B.
[2970]—*School Sisters of Notre Dame*—S.S.N.D.
[]—*Sisters for Christian Community*—S.F.C.C.
[0570]—*Sisters of Charity of Seton Hill, Greensburg, Pennsylvania*—S.C.
[]—*Sisters of Charity of St. Elizabeth, Convent Station, N.J.*
[1930]—*Sisters of Holy Cross*—C.S.C.
[1705]—*The Sisters of St. Francis of Assisi*—O.S.F.
[1710]—*Sisters of St. Francis of Mary Immaculate*—O.S.F.
[3840]—*Sisters of St. Joseph of Carondelet*—C.S.J.
[0260]—*The Sisters of the Blessed Sacrament for Indians and Colored People*—S.B.S.
[1030]—*Sisters of the Divine Savior*—S.D.S.
[1990]—*Sisters of the Holy Names of Jesus and Mary*—S.N.J.M.
[2180]—*Sisters of the Immaculate Heart of Mary*—I.H.M.
[3320]—*Sisters of the Presentation of the Blessed Virgin Mary*—P.B.V.M.
[4070]—*Society of the Sacred Heart*—R.S.C.J.
[]—*Wheaton Franciscans*—O.S.F.

An asterisk (*) denotes an organization that has established tax-exempt status directly with the IRS and is not covered by the USCCB Group Ruling.

Diocese of Tulsa

(Dioecesis Tulsensis)

Most Reverend

DAVID A. KONDERLA

Bishop of Tulsa; ordained June 3, 1995; appointed Bishop of Tulsa May 13, 2016; installed June 29, 2016. *Office: 12300 E. 91st St. S., Broken Arrow, OK 74012.*

Most Reverend

EDWARD J. SLATTERY

Retired Bishop of Tulsa; ordained April 26, 1966; appointed Bishop of Tulsa November 11, 1993; ordained January 6, 1994 in Rome; installed January 12, 1994; retired May 13, 2016.

Chancery Office: 12300 E. 91st St. S., Broken Arrow, OK 74012. Mailing Address: P.O. Box 690240, Tulsa, OK 74169-0240. Tel: 918-294-1904; Fax: 918-294-0920.

Web: www.dioceseoftulsa.org

Email: bishop.office@dioceseoftulsa.org

ESTABLISHED FEBRUARY 7, 1973.

Square Miles 26,417.

The Diocese of Tulsa comprises the following 31 Counties: Adair, Atoka, Bryan, Cherokee, Choctaw, Coal, Craig, Creek, Delaware, Haskell, Hughes, Latimer, LeFlore, McCurtain, McIntosh, Mayes, Muskogee, Nowata, Okfuskee, Okmulgee, Osage, Ottawa, Pawnee, Payne, Pittsburg, Pushmataha, Rogers, Sequoyah, Tulsa, Wagoner and Washington.

For legal titles of parishes and institutions, consult the Chancery Office.

STATISTICAL OVERVIEW

Personnel	
Bishop	1
Retired Bishops	1
Abbots	1
Priests: Diocesan Active in Diocese	51
Priests: Diocesan Active Outside Diocese	7
Priests: Retired, Sick or Absent	18
Number of Diocesan Priests	76
Religious Priests in Diocese	37
Total Priests in Diocese	113
Extern Priests in Diocese	19
Ordinations:	
Diocesan Priests	2
Transitional Deacons	2
Permanent Deacons in Diocese	84
Total Brothers	31
Total Sisters	51
Parishes	
Parishes	77
With Resident Pastor:	
Resident Diocesan Priests	50
Resident Religious Priests	1
Without Resident Pastor:	
Administered by Priests	26
Missions	2
Pastoral Centers	4
Professional Ministry Personnel:	
Brothers	30
Sisters	46
Lay Ministers	114
Welfare	
Catholic Hospitals	7
Total Assisted	1,132,582
Health Care Centers	1
Total Assisted	222
Homes for the Aged	1
Total Assisted	41
Specialized Homes	1
Total Assisted	32
Special Centers for Social Services	7
Total Assisted	60,000
Other Institutions	1
Total Assisted	55
Educational	
Diocesan Students in Other Seminaries	18
Total Seminarians	18
High Schools, Diocesan and Parish	1
Total Students	947
High Schools, Private	1
Total Students	554
Elementary Schools, Diocesan and Parish	9
Total Students	2,303
Elementary Schools, Private	2
Total Students	809
Catechesis/Religious Education:	
High School Students	1,359
Elementary Students	5,516
Total Students under Catholic Instruction	11,506
Teachers in the Diocese:	
Priests	3
Brothers	2
Sisters	5
Lay Teachers	404
Vital Statistics	
Receptions into the Church:	
Infant Baptism Totals	1,335
Minor Baptism Totals	136
Adult Baptism Totals	160
Received into Full Communion	250
First Communions	1,216
Confirmations	1,132
Marriages:	
Catholic	221
Interfaith	96
Total Marriages	317
Deaths	440
Total Catholic Population	61,504
Total Population	1,731,786

Former Bishops—Most Revs. BERNARD J. GANTER, D.D., ord. May 22, 1952; appt. Bishop of Tulsa, Dec. 19, 1972; ord. Feb. 7, 1973; transferred to Beaumont, Oct. 18, 1977; installed Dec. 13, 1977; died Oct. 9, 1993.; EUSEBIUS J. BELTRAN, ord. May 14, 1960; appt. Bishop of Tulsa, Feb. 28, 1978; ord. April 20, 1978; transferred to Archdiocese of Oklahoma City, Nov. 24, 1992; installed Jan. 22, 1993; retired Dec. 16, 2010.; EDWARD J. SLATTERY, (Retired), ord. April 26, 1966; appt. Bishop of Tulsa Nov. 11, 1993; ord. Jan. 6, 1994 in Rome; installed Jan. 12, 1994; retired May 13, 2016.

Vicar General—Rev. ELKIN GONZALEZ, V.G.

Chancery Office—12300 E. 91st St. S., Broken Arrow, 74012. Mailing Address: P.O. Box 690240, Tulsa, 74169. Tel: 918-294-1904; Fax: 918-294-0920. Office Hours: Mon.-Fri. 9-5.

Chancellor—MR. HARRISON GARLICK.

Finance Office—MR. PHILIP J. CREIDER, Assets Mgr.; MR. THOMAS SCHADLE, CFO, Mailing Address: P.O. Box 690240, Tulsa, 74169-0240. Tel: 918-294-1904, Ext. 4926.

Diocesan Consultors—Most Rev. DAVID A. KONDERLA; Revs. MICHAEL PRATT; GARY KASTL; BRIAN D. O'BRIEN; JOE C. TOWNSEND; SEAN T. DONOVAN; JACK GLEASON; LEONARD AHANATU, (Nigeria); BRYAN BROOKS.

Ex Officio—Rev. ELKIN GONZALEZ, V.G.

Diocesan Marriage Tribunal—

Judicial Vicar—Rev. MICHAEL J. KNIPE, J.C.L.

Adjutant Judicial Vicars—Revs. KENNETH J. HARDER, J.C.L.; SAMUEL PEREZ, J.C.L.

Defender of the Bond—Rev. TAM NGUYEN, J.C.L.

Judges—Revs. MICHAEL J. KNIPE, J.C.L.; KENNETH J. HARDER, J.C.L.; SAMUEL PEREZ, J.C.L.; KHIET T. NGUYEN, J.C.L.

Auditor—Deacon DAN PICKETT.

Assessor—Deacon KENNETH LONGBRAKE.

Promoter of Justice—Rev. SAMUEL PEREZ, J.C.L.

Seminary Board—Revs. ELKIN GONZALEZ, V.G.; JACK GLEASON; BRIAN D. O'BRIEN; MICHAEL PRATT; GARY KASTL; JUAN GRAJEDA; MS. ANDREA HYATT; MR. BRANDON WATSON.

Diocesan Offices

Archivist—JOEY SPENCER, Mailing Address: P.O. Box 690240, Tulsa, 74169-0240. Tel: 918-307-4956.

Campus Ministry—Rev. BRYAN KETTERER, Chap.; MEGAN MEUSSNER, Dir. Devel., 440 S. Florence, Tulsa, 74104. Tel: 918-599-0204; Fax: 918-587-0115; Email: tu-newman@utulsa.edu.

Catholic Charities of the Diocese of Tulsa—Deacon KEVIN SARTORIOUS, Exec. Dir., 2450 N. Harvard, Tulsa, 74115. Tel: 918-949-4673; Fax: 918-582-2123. P.O. Box 580460, Tulsa, 74158. Web: www.cctulsa.org; Rev. VAN NGUYEN, Chap.

Pregnancy and Adoption Services—2450 N. Harvard, P.O. Box 580460, Tulsa, 74158. Tel: 918-508-7142.

Emergency Services—2450 N. Harvard, Tulsa, 74115. Tel: 918-508-7186. *Mailing Address: P.O. Box 580460, Tulsa, 74158.*

Madonna House—2450 N. Harvard, Tulsa, 74115. Tel: 918-508-7148. *Mailing Address: P.O. Box 580460, Tulsa, 74158.*

Immigration Office—2450 N. Harvard, Tulsa, 74115. Tel: 918-508-7185; Fax: 918-582-2123. *Mailing Address: P.O. Box 580460, Tulsa, 74158.*

Sallisaw Helping Center—409 N. Adam St., Sallisaw. Tel: 918-775-6111.

Mary Martha Outreach, Bartlesville—1845 W. 4th St., Bartlesville, 74003. Tel: 918-337-3703.

St. Jude Helping Center—217 N. "A" St., McAlester, 74501. Tel: 918-423-7707.

Ministry of Compassion, Broken Arrow—301 S. 9th, Broken Arrow, 74012. Tel: 918-258-5269.

Helping Center, Muskogee—1220 W. Broadway St., Muskogee, 74401. Tel: 918-681-6115.
Immaculate Conception Helping Center—410 N. Bagwell St., Poteau, 74953. Tel: 918-647-2220.
St. Elizabeth Lodge—Tulsa. Tel: 918-949-4673.
Blessed Mother Teresa Dental Center—2450 N. Harvard, Tulsa, 74115. Tel: 918-949-4673. *Mailing Address: P.O. Box 580460, Tulsa, 74158.*

Calvary Cemetery—9101 S. Harvard, Tulsa, 74137. Tel: 918-299-7348; Fax: 918-299-7558. Deacon JOHN J. JOHNSON, CEO.

Clergy Education—Mailing Address: P.O. Box 690240, Tulsa, 74169. Tel: 918-294-1904, Ext. 4900. Rev. BRYAN BROOKS.

Diocesan Catholic Committee on Scouting—MR. DENNIS ZVACEK, Tel: 918-250-8787; Email: dzvacek@cox.net.

Council of Catholic Women—PAT FIKE, Tel: 918-967-7336.

Ecumenism—Rev. Msgr. PATRICK J. GAALAAS, Dir., 4001 E. 101st St., S., Tulsa, 74137. Tel: 918-299-9406.

Education—MR. HARRISON GARLICK, Chancellor & Relg. Educ., Tel: 918-307-4918.

Faith and Works—Mailing Address: P.O. Box 690240, Tulsa, 74169. Tel: 918-307-4942; Fax: 918-294-0920. DEREK LYSSY, Dir., Email: derek.lyssy@dioceseoftulsa.org.

Alcuin Institute for Catholic Culture—Mailing Address: P.O. Box 690240, Tulsa, 74169. RICHARD MELOCHA, Ph.D., Tutor/Pres., Tel: 918-307-4950; Email: richard.meloche@dioceseof tulsa.org; MARCEL BROWN, Ph.D., Tutor/Dean, Tel: 918-307-4906; Email: marcel.brown@dioceseoftulsa.org.

Family Life Office—Mailing Address: P.O. Box 690240, Tulsa, 74169. Tel: 918-307-4914.

Parochial Schools—Mailing Address: P.O. Box 690240, Tulsa, 74169. Tel: 918-294-1904; Email: catholicschools.office@dioceseoftulsa.org; Fax: 918-294-0920. JAMES J. POHLMAN, Supt. Catholic Schools.

Prison and Social Ministry—Deacon KENNETH LONGBRAKE, Dir., P.O. Box 690240, Tulsa, 74169. Email: dcn.kenneth.longbrake@dioceseoftulsa.org.

Hispanic Ministry—Mailing Address: P.O. Box 690240, Tulsa, 74169. Tel: 918-294-1904; Fax: 918-294-0920. Revs. ERNESTO CALVILLO, Coord.; ROBERT M. DYE, Coord. Hispanic Ministries for Heavener & McAlester; CARLOS LOAIZA, Coord. Hispanic Youth Ministry & Family Life; JUAN ANTONIO HERNANDEZ, Coord. Hispanic Ministry for Grove & Stilwel.

Office of Divine Worship—Rev. JOHN L. GRANT, Dir., Tel: 918-446-8124.

Magazine "Eastern Oklahoma Catholic"—DAVE CRENSHAW, Mng. Editor; MASON BEECROFT, Assoc. Editor, Mailing Address: P.O. Box 690240, Tulsa, 74169. Tel: 918-307-4946.

Office of Permanent Diaconate—Mailing Address: P.O. Box 690240, Tulsa, 74169. Tel: 918-307-4921. Deacon LAMAR YARBROUGH.

Propagation of the FaithRev. MATTHEW J. GERLACH, Coord., 301 S. 9th St., Broken Arrow, 74012. Tel: 918-251-4000.

Victim Assistance Coordinator—MR. QUENTIN HENLEY, Tel: 918-508-7135.

Vocations—Rev. MICHAEL PRATT, Dir. Assistant Directors: Revs. GARY KASTL; BRIAN D. O'BRIEN; JUAN GRAJEDA; MRS. THERESA WITCHER, Seminarians, Mailing Address: P.O. Box 690240, Tulsa, 74169. Tel: 918-307-4936.

Young Adult Ministry—Mailing Address: P.O. Box 690240, Tulsa, 74169-0240. Tel: 918-307-4939. SARAH JAMESON, Dir.; CAITLYN GONYA, Asst. Dir.

Youth Ministry—Mailing Address: P.O. Box 690240, Tulsa, 74169-0240. Tel: 918-307-4939. SARAH JAMESON, Dir.; CAITLYN BENEDICT, Asst. Dir.

Webmaster—ROD TREAT, Tel: 918-307-4929.

CLERGY, PARISHES, MISSIONS AND PAROCHIAL SCHOOLS

CITY OF TULSA

(TULSA COUNTY)

1—HOLY FAMILY CATHEDRAL (1899)
122 W. 8th St., 74119. Tel: 918-582-6247; Email: office@holyfamilycathedralparish.com. Rev. Jovita Okonkwo, (Nigeria) Rector; Rev. Msgr. Gregory A. Gier, Pastor Emeritus, (Retired); Deacons Jerry Mattox, (Retired); Thomas Gorman; Kevin Tulipana; Greg Stice.
School—Holy Family Cathedral School, (Grades PreK-8), 820 S. Boulder St., 74119.
Tel: 918-582-0422; Fax: 918-582-9705; Email: hfcs.news@myhfcs.org; Web: www.holyfamilycathedralschool.com. Leslie Southerland, Prin. Lay Teachers 19; Students 175.
Catechesis Religious Program—Students 38.

2—ST. AUGUSTINE'S (1955) (African American)
1728 E. Apache, 74110. Tel: 918-428-3280; Email: saintaugustinetulsa3@yahoo.com; Web: www.staugustine-tulsa.org. Rev. Celestine Obidiegwu; Deacon Steve Litwack.
Catechesis Religious Program—Students 6.

3—ST. BERNARD OF CLAIRVAUX (1978) [CEM]
4001 E. 101st St., 74137. Tel: 918-299-9406; Fax: 918-299-7796; Email: meellingson@stbernardstulsa.org. Rev. Msgr. Patrick J. Gaalaas; Deacons Timothy Sullivan; Richard Campbell; Alan Mikell; Robert Martin; David Johnson; Mike Ellingson, Business Mgr.
Child Care—Preschool, Students 48; Teachers 8.
Catechesis Religious Program—Sharon Lechtenberg, D.R.E. Students 468.

4—ST. CATHERINE (1925)
4532 S. 25th West Ave., 74107. Tel: 918-446-8124; Email: fr.john.grant@dioceseoftulsa.org; Web: www.saintcatherinechurch.org. Rev. John L. Grant; Deacon Craig Victor.
School—St. Catherine School, (Grades PreSchool-8), 2515 W. 46th St., 74107. Tel: 918-446-9756; Email: school@saint-catherine.org; Web: www.saintcatherineschool.org. Michelle Anthamatten, Prin. Lay Teachers 10; Sisters of St. Francis of the Martyr St. George 3; Students 144; Religious Teachers 9.
Catechesis Religious Program—Students 12.
Mission—St. Joseph, P.O. Box 603, Bristow, Creek Co. 74010. Deacon David C. Hamel.
Catechesis Religious Program—Students 6.

5—CHRIST THE KING (1917)
1520 S. Rockford Ave., 74120. Tel: 918-584-4788; Tel: 918-584-4789; Fax: 918-584-0055; Email: ctkparish@christthekingcatholic.church; Web: www.christthekingcatholic.church. Revs. Elkin Gonzalez, V.G.; David Webb; Bryan Ketterer, In Res.; Deacons John L. Sommer, Business Mgr.; Loren F. Luschen, (Retired); John M. Johnson; Dean Wersal, RCIA Coord.; Michael Loeffler; Kevin Malarkey.
Schools—Marquette School—(Grades K-8), 1519 S. Quincy, 74120. Tel: 918-584-4631; Fax: 918-584-4847 . Jay Luetkemeyer, Prin.; Crissy Donatucci, Librarian. Lay Teachers 35; Students 456.
Marquette Early Childhood Development Center (ECDC), (6 mo. - 8th Grade) 1528 S. Quincy Ave., 74120. Tel: 918-583-3334; Fax: 918-583-2140; Email: tracey.robinson@marquetteschool.org; Web: www.marquetteschool.org. Pepper McGough, Dir. Lay Teachers 14; Students 98.
Catechesis Religious Program—Students 543.

6—CHURCH OF ST. MARY (1954)
1347 E. 49th Pl., 74105. Tel: 918-749-1423; Fax: 918-747-9532; Email: church@churchofsaintmary.com; Web: www.churchofsaintmary.com. Rev. Jack Gleason; Rev. Msgr. Dennis C. Dorney, Pastor Emeritus; Rev. Duy Nguyen; Deacons Richard Bender; Gary Gamino; Stephen Craig; Kevin Maloney.
School—School of St. Mary, (Grades PreK-8), 1365 E. 49th Pl., 74105. Tel: 918-749-9361; Fax: 918-712-9604; Email: stmary@schoolofsaintmary.com; Web: www.schoolofsaintmary.com. Maureen Clements, Prin.; Peggy Padalino, Librarian. Lay Teachers 29; Students 325.
Catechesis Religious Program—
Tel: 918-749-1423, Ext. 108. Valerie Howard, Dir. Children's Min. Students 325.

7—CHURCH OF THE MADALENE (1946)
3188 E. 22nd St., 74114. Tel: 918-744-1123; Web: www.madalenetulsa.org. Rev. Desmond Okpogba, (Nigeria); Deacons Joseph Fritsch; Robert DeWeese, (Retired); Larry E. McFadden; Nelson M. Sousa.
Catechesis Religious Program—
Tel: 918-744-0023, Ext. 15. Becky Holder, D.R.E. Students 125.

8—ST. FRANCIS XAVIER CHURCH AND DIOCESAN MARIAN SHRINE & EXPIATORY TEMPLE OF OUR LADY OF GUADALUPE (1926) (Hispanic)
2434 E. Admiral Blvd., 74110. Tel: 918-592-6770; Fax: 918-592-2208; Email: st.francisxavier.church@hotmail.com. Revs. David Medina; Carlos Loaiza.
Res.: 2510 E. 1st St., 74104.
Child Care—Instituto Bilingue Guadalupano,
Tel: 918-592-9179. Maria Alcaraz, Dir. Students 22; Teachers 4.
Catechesis Religious Program—Alfredo Marcelo, D.R.E. Students 550.

9—IMMACULATE CONCEPTION (1923) Closed. For inquiries for parish records contact the chancery.

10—ST. JOSEPH CHURCH (1977) (Vietnamese)
14905 E. 21st St., 74134. Tel: 918-438-1380; Email: fr_dovann@yahoo.com. Rev. Dovan Nguyen.
Catechesis Religious Program—Tel: 918-438-6325. Students 195.

11—ST. MONICA'S (1926) (African American)
633 Marshall Pl., 74106. Tel: 918-587-2965; Fax: 918-582-0699; Email: stmonicachurch@aol.com; Web: www.stmonica-tulsa.org. Rev. Celestine Obidiegwu.
Catechesis Religious Program—Students 10.

12—MOST PRECIOUS BLOOD PARISH (1996)
3029 S. 57th W. Ave., 74107. Tel: 918-615-8404; Email: secretary@mpbptulsa.com; Web: www.mpbptulsa.com. Rev. William Define, F.S.S.P.
Catechesis Religious Program—

13—OUR LADY OF GUADALUPE, Closed. For inquiries for sacramental records contact St. Francis Xavier, Tulsa.

14—SS. PETER AND PAUL (1950)
1419 N. 67th E. Ave., 74115. Tel: 918-836-2596; Tel: 918-836-2165; Fax: 918-836-2597; Email: alejandra.olmosgarcia@yahoo.com. Revs. Michael J. Knipe, J.C.L.; Elmer Rodriguez; Juan Antonio Hernandez, In Res.
Res.: 1436 N. 67th E. Ave., 74115.
School—SS. Peter and Paul School, (Grades PreSchool-8), 1428 N. 67th E. Ave., 74115.
Tel: 918-836-2165; Email: stspeterandpaul@gmail.com; Web: peterandpaultulsa.org. Patrick Martin, Prin. Lay Teachers 14; Students 205.
Catechesis Religious Program—Karen Campbell, D.R.E. Students 266.

15—ST. PIUS X (1955)
1727 S. 75 E. Ave., 74112. Tel: 918-622-4488; Fax: 918-622-1239; Email: parish@spxtulsa.org. Revs. Richard Bradley; Leonardo Medina; Deacons Ernesto Fernandez; Craig Gunter; Isidro Saenz.
Res.: 7628 E. 17th St., 74112.
School—St. Pius X School, (Grades PreK-8), 1717 S. 75 E. Ave., 74112. Tel: 918-627-5367; Fax: 918-627-6179; Email: bkrukowski@spxtulsa.org; Web: spxtulsa.org. Lisa Bell, Prin.; Therese Iten, Librarian. Lay Teachers 28; Students 388.
Catechesis Religious Program—Email: ahausher@spxtulsa.org. Arlene Hausher, D.R.E. Students 95.

16—RESURRECTION (1968)
4804 S. Fulton, 74135. Tel: 918-663-1907; Fax: 918-663-2533; Email: debbis@cotrtulsa.org. Rev. Daniel Campos; Deacons James Scarpitti; Peter Byrne.
Res.: 4338 S. Braden Pl., 74135.
Catechesis Religious Program—Susan Wheeler, D.R.E. Students 118.

17—ST. THOMAS MORE (1972)
2720 S. 129 E. Ave., 74134-2411. Tel: 918-437-0168; Fax: 918-437-0681; Email: alexarevalo22@gmail.com; Web: stthomasmoretulsa.com. Revs. Jose Maria Briones, (Mexico); Ismael Comayagua; Lewandowski Donald, Prior; Deacon Kevin Sartorius.
Catechesis Religious Program—Email: sallygonzalez06@hotmail.com. Alex Arevalo, Hispanic D.R.E.; Sally Gonzalez, English D.R.E. Students 985.

OUTSIDE CITY OF TULSA

ANTLERS, PUSHMATAHA CO., ST. AGNES (1897)
503 E. Main, P.O. Box 206, Antlers, 74523.
Tel: 580-326-7300; Email: jvchirayath@sbcglobal.net. Rev. Joseph Chirayath.
Res.: P.O. Box 99, Hugo, 74743.
Catechesis Religious Program—316 N.W. 3rd St., Antlers, 74523. Tel: 580-298-5138. Dixie Ranallo, D.R.E. Students 14.
Station—McLeod Correctional Center, Farris.
Tel: 405-889-6651; Fax: 405-889-2264.

BARTLESVILLE, WASHINGTON CO.

1—ST. JAMES (1965)
5500 Douglas Ln., Bartlesville, 74006.
Tel: 918-335-0844; Fax: 918-335-0856; Email: office_stjms@sbcglobal.net. Rev. Archelito Fernandez, (Philippines); Deacon Gerard Rutherford.
Res.: 5510 Douglas Ln., Bartlesville, 74006.
Catechesis Religious Program—Email: crebartlesville@gmail.com. Programs are combined with St. John Before the Latin Gate. Students 133.

2—ST. JOHN'S (1906) [CEM]
715 S. Johnstone Ave., Bartlesville, 74003.
Tel: 918-336-4353; Fax: 918-336-4354; Web: www.stjohn-bartlesville.org. Revs. John O'Neill; Juan Grajeda; Deacons Dan Pickett; Charlie Moomaw.
Res.: 701 S. Johnstone Ave., Bartlesville, 74003.
School—St. John's School, (Grades PreK-8), 816 S. Keeler Ave., Bartlesville, 74003. Tel: 918-336-0603; Fax: 918-336-0624; Email: mckee@sjcs-ok.org; Web: sjcs-ok.org. Traci McKee, Prin.; Ashley Hopkins, Librarian. Lay Teachers 16; Students 156.
Catechesis Religious Program—Dorlene Martin, D.R.E. Students 100.

BIXBY, TULSA CO., ST. CLEMENT OF ROME (1957)
15501 S. Memorial Dr., Bixby, 74008.

Tel: 918-366-3166; Email: ereyes@stcbixby.org; Web: www.stcbixby.org. Rev. Jeffrey S. Polasek; Deacons Jose Guzman; Neal Harton; Mrs. Enilda Reyes de Velazquez, Admin.; Cheryl Bruner, D.R.E.; Mrs. Maria Flores, Youth Min.

BROKEN ARROW, TULSA CO.

1—ST. ANNE (1937) [JC]
301 S. 9th St., 74012. Tel: 918-251-4000; Fax: 918-251-8719; Email: parishsec@stanneba.org; Web: www.stanneba.org. Revs. Matthew J. Gerlach; Sean O'Brien; Deacons Thomas Moyes; Steve Creed.
Catechesis Religious Program—Brianna Noonan, Faith Formation Coord. Students 195.

2—ST. BENEDICT (1980)
2200 W. Ithica St., 74012. Tel: 918-455-4451; Email: saintben@tulsacoxmail.com; Web: www.saintben.com. Rev. Bryan Brooks; Deacons Rick Stookey; Gary Beam; Daniel Brennan; Richard Berberet.
Res.: 3105 S. Beech Ave., 74012.
Child Care—Preschool, Students 59; Teachers 12.
Catechesis Religious Program—Carol Bryan, C.R.E.; Peggy Donnelly, RCIA Dir.; Deb Malcom, Dir. Youth Min. Students 430.

CLAREMORE, ROGER CO., ST. CECILIA (1911)
1304 N. Dorothy, Claremore, 74017.
Tel: 918-341-2343; Fax: 918-341-2893; Email: st.cecilia@tulsacoxmail.com; Web: www.stceciliachurch-claremore.com. Rev. Sylvanus Amaobi, (Nigeria).
Catechesis Religious Program—Tel: 918-341-4238. Students 175.

CLEVELAND, OSAGE, ST. JOSEPH (1905) (Native American), See separate listing. Now a mission of Sacred Heart, Fairfax.

COALGATE, COAL CO., BLESSED SACRAMENT ORATORY (1889) [CEM] Closed. For inquiries for parish records contact the chancery.

COLLINSVILLE, TULSA CO., ST. THERESE CHURCH AND DIOCESAN EUCHARISTIC SHRINE OF SAINT THERESE (1908) [CEM]
1007 N. 19th St., Collinsville, 74021.
Tel: 918-371-2704; Fax: 918-371-3895; Email: office@stthereseok.org; Web: www.stthereseok.org. Rev. Jose Calvillo; Deacon Peter McLane; Mrs. Enilda Reyes de Velazquez, Admin.; Amanda Brillhart, D.R.E.; Mrs. Paola Ferrell, Pastoral Min./Coord.; Mrs. Alicia Evicks, Youth Min.; Mr. Jake Brillhart, Editor.

COWETA, WAGONER CO., ST. VINCENT DE PAUL (1981)
15842 S. 297th E. Ave., Coweta, 74429.
Tel: 918-486-4757; Email: svdp1@tulsacoxmail.com; Web: stvincentdepaul-coweta.org. Mailing Address: P.O. Box 597, Coweta, 74014-0597. Rev. Leonard U. Ahanotu.
Catechesis Religious Program—Students 8.

CUSHING, PAYNE CO., SS. PETER AND PAUL (1894) [CEM]
401 E. Oak St., P.O. Box 828, Cushing, 74023.
Tel: 918-225-0644; Fax: 918-225-0646; Email: cushingcatholicchurch@yahoo.com. Rev. Emmanuel-Lugard Nduka, (Nigeria); Deacons Kenneth Longbrake; David C. Hamel.
Res.: 214 N. Steele Ave., Cushing, 74023.
Catechesis Religious Program—Alice Patterson, C.R.E. Students 41.
Mission—St. Mary, 321 S. Cimarron, Drumright, Creek Co. 74030.

DEWEY, WASHINGTON CO., OUR LADY OF GUADALUPE (1954)
400 W. 9th St., Dewey, 74029. Tel: 918-534-3420; Fax: 918-534-3013; Email: ourladyguadalupe@sbcglobal.net. Rev. Jose K. Thottathil, (India); Ms. Mindy Freeman, Admin.; Mrs. Kim Roecker, D.R.E.
Mission—St. Catherine, 217 W. Modoc, Nowata, Nowata Co. 74048.
Catechesis Religious Program—Students 5.

DURANT, BRYAN CO., ST. WILLIAM (1912)
802 University Blvd., Durant, 74701.
Tel: 580-924-1989; Fax: 580-931-3044; Email: churchwilliam@sbcglobal.net; Web: www.stwilliamdurant.com. Rev. Valerian Gonsalves.
Catechesis Religious Program—Ms. Amy Ramos, D.R.E. Students 78.
Mission—St. Patrick Church, Hwy. 69 S., Atoka, Atoka Co. 74701. Tel: 580-889-2846.

FAIRFAX, OSAGE CO., SACRED HEART (1925) (Osage Indian)
333 S. 8th St., Fairfax, 74637. Tel: 918-642-5053. Rev. Desmond Ibeneme.
Catechesis Religious Program—
Missions— aka Saint Joseph, Cleveland (1929) 421 S. Petit, Hominy, Osage Co. 74035. Tel: 918-358-2333.
St. Joseph, Osage & C Ave., Cleveland, Pawnee Co. 74020.

GROVE, DELAWARE CO., ST. ELIZABETH (1949)
1653 113th St., N.W., Grove, 74344.
Tel: 918-786-9312; Email: stelizabethcatholic@yahoo.com; Web: stelizabeth-grove.org. Rev. Tam Nguyen, J.C.L.

Catechesis Religious Program—Students 59.

HARTSHORNE, PITTSBURG CO., HOLY ROSARY (1895) [CEM]
912 Cherokee, P.O. Box 389, Hartshorne, 74547.
Tel: 918-297-2453; Email: fr.bruce.brosnahan@dioceseoftulsa.org. Rev. Bruce Brosnahan.

HENRYETTA, OKMULGEE CO., ST. MICHAEL (1912) [JC]
1004 W. Gentry St., P.O. Box 148, Henryetta, 74437. Tel: 918-652-3445; Fax: 918-652-3445; Email: fr.chi.phung@dioceseoftulsa.org. Rev. Chi Peter Phung.
Catechesis Religious Program—Students 6.
Mission—St. Teresa (1927) 8th and Broadway, Okemah, Okfuskee Co. 74859.
Catechesis Religious Program—

HOLDENVILLE, HUGHES CO., ST. STEPHEN'S (1905)
515 E. Hwy., Holdenville, 74848. Tel: 405-379-2512; Email: fr.hung.le@dioceseoftulsa.org. Rev. Hung Viet Le.
Catechesis Religious Program—

HOMINY, OSAGE CO., ST. JOSEPH (1929) Now a mission under Sacred Heart, Fairfax.

HUGO, CHOCTAW CO., IMMACULATE CONCEPTION (1903)
196 Bearden Springs Rd., P.O Box 99, Hugo, 74743.
Tel: 580-326-7300; Tel: 580-326-3602; Email: jvchirayath@sbcglobal.net. Rev. Joseph Chirayath.
Catechesis Religious Program—Tel: 903-732-3729; Email: dkreilich@msn.com. Dean Kreilich, D.R.E. Students 5.
Mission—St. Jude, 511 11th St., Boswell, Choctaw Co. 74727.

IDABEL, MCCURTAIN CO., ST. FRANCIS DE SALES (1945)
13 S.E. Jefferson St., Idabel, 74745.
Tel: 580-286-3275; Email: fr.stephen.austin@dioceseoftulsa.org; Web: www.stfrancisidabel.org. Rev. Stephen E. Austin.

KREBS, PITTSBURG CO., ST. JOSEPH'S (1886) [CEM]
290 N.W. Church St., P.O. Box 621, Krebs, 74554.
Tel: 918-423-6695; Fax: 918-426-4255; Email: stjosephchurch.krebs@yahoo.com; Web: www.stjoseph-krebs.org. Rev. Kingsley George-Obilonu; Deacon Bill Anderson.
Catechesis Religious Program—Tel: 918-423-7130. Bonnie DeGiacomo, D.R.E. Students 60.
Mission—St. Paul's, [CEM] 502 S. 6th St., P.O. Box 943, Eufaula, 74432. Tel: 918-689-7345; Email: fr.kingsley.georgeobilonu@dioceseoftulsa.org.
Catechesis Religious Program—

LANGLEY, MAYES CO., ST. FRANCES OF ROME (1950)
13286 Hwy. 28, Langley, 74350-0267.
Tel: 918-782-2248; Email: stfrances267@gmail.com. P.O. Box 267, Langley, 74350. Rev. Valentine Ndebilie.
Catechesis Religious Program—Students 19.

MCALESTER, PITTSBURG CO., ST. JOHN (1895) [CEM]
300 E. Washington Ave., P.O. Box 220, McAlester, 74502. Tel: 918-423-0810; Fax: 918-423-0825; Email: stjohnmcalester@yahoo.com. Rev. Leonard H. Higgins.
Catechesis Religious Program—Students 123.
Station—Oklahoma State Penitentiary, McAlester. Tel: 918-423-4700; Fax: 918-423-3862.

MIAMI, OTTAWA CO., SACRED HEART (1900)
2515 N. Main, Miami, 74354. Tel: 918-542-5281; Email: sacredheartmiami@cableone.net; Web: sacredheartmiami.org. Rev. Carl Kerkemeyer; Mrs. Ludivina Morales, Sec.

MUSKOGEE, MUSKOGEE CO.

1—ASSUMPTION, Closed. For inquiries for sacramental records contact Saint Joseph Church, Muskogee.

2—SAINT JOSEPH CHURCH (1992) [CEM]
301 N. Virginia St., Muskogee, 74403.
Tel: 918-687-1351; Email: lferguson@stjosephok.com. Rev. Richard F. Cristler; Deacons Edwin Falleur; John Hale; Carlos Moreno; Ray Wallace.
Church: 321 N. Virginia, Muskogee, 74402.
School—Saint Joseph Church School, (Grades PreK-8), 323 N. Virginia, Muskogee, 74403.
Tel: 918-683-1291; Fax: 918-682-5374; Email: chutchens@stjoseph74403.com; Web: www.stjoseph74403.com. Joanne Myers, Prin.; Julie Rowland, Librarian. Lay Teachers 10; Students 95.
Catechesis Religious Program—Students 120.

3—SACRED HEART, Closed. For inquiries for sacramental records contact Saint Joseph Church, Muskogee.

OKMULGEE, OKMULGEE CO., ST. ANTHONY'S (1910)
515 S. Morton Ave., P.O. Box 698, Okmulgee, 74447.
Tel: 918-756-4385; Email: saumchurches@gmail.com. Rev. Joshua E. Litwack.
Mission—Uganda Martyrs, 808 E. 3rd, Okmulgee, Okmulgee Co. 74447.

OWASSO, TULSA CO., ST. HENRY (1957)
8500 N. Owasso Expwy., Owasso, 74055-0181.
Tel: 918-272-3710; Fax: 918-272-1966; Email: office@sthenryowasso.org; Web: www.sthenryowasso.org. P.O. Box 181, Owasso, 74055. Rev. Matthew G. LaChance; Deacons Vernon Foltz, (Retired); Donald LeMieux, (Retired); Edmundo Martinez; Larry Schneider.
Res.: 903 N. Elm St. E., Owasso, 74055.

Catechesis Religious Program—Tel: 918-272-3740. Kelley Tucker, Dir. Faith Formation. Students 329.

PAWHUSKA, OSAGE CO., IMMACULATE CONCEPTION (1887) (Osage Indian)
1314 N. Lynn Ave., Pawhuska, 74056.
Tel: 918-827-1414; Email: fr.sean.donovan@dioceseoftulsa.org. Rev. Sean T. Donovan.
Catechesis Religious Program—Students 64.
Missions—St. Mary—3rd and Chestnut, Barnsdall, 74002.
St. Ann, Gypsy St. & Taylor St., Shidler, Osage Co. 74652.

PAWNEE, PAWNEE CO., ST. JOHN (1907)
333 S. 8th St., Pawnee, 74058. Tel: 918-225-0644; Email: fr.emmanuel.nduka@dioceseoftulsa.org. Mailing Address: P.O. Box 828, Cushing, 74023. Rev. Emmanuel-Lugard Nduka, (Nigeria).

PLUNKETVILLE, MCCURTAIN CO., ST. HENRY, Closed. For inquiries for parish records see St. Francis De Sales, Idabel.

POTEAU, LEFLORE CO., IMMACULATE CONCEPTION (1903)
502 N. Bagwell, P.O. Box 237, Poteau, 74953.
Tel: 918-647-3475; Email: imcchurch03@yahoo.com; Web: www.occok.org. Rev. James A. Caldwell Jr. Church: 410 Bagwell St., P.O. Box 237, Poteau, 74953.
Catechesis Religious Program—David Jones, D.R.E. Students 74.
Missions—St. Joseph—1204 N.W. 7th St., Stigler, Haskell Co. 74462.
St. Elizabeth Seton, 16526 U.S. Hwy. 271, Spiro, Leflore Co. 74959.

PRYOR, MAYES CO., ST. MARK'S (1942)
1507 S. Vann, Pryor, 74361. Tel: 918-825-4186; Email: admin@stmarkspryor.org. Mailing Address: P.O. Box 576, Pryor, 74362. Rev. Valentine Ndebilie.
Catechesis Religious Program—Katrina Ballou, D.R.E. Students 40.

SALLISAW, SEQUOYAH CO., ST. FRANCIS XAVIER (1952)
2110 N. Dogwood, Sallisaw, 74955.
Tel: 918-775-6217; Email: saintfx@sbcglobal.net. Rev. Lawrence Nwachukwu.
Catechesis Religious Program—Students 48.
Missions—St. John the Evangelist—Hwy. 82, Sallisaw, 74955. P.O. Box 4, Cookson, Cherokee Co. 74427.
St. Joseph, 103 Smith St., P.O. Box 53, Webbers Falls, Muskogee Co. 74470.
Blessed Kateri Tekakwitha, 110840 S. 4760 Rd, Muldrow, 74948. P.O. Box 17, Roland, Sequoyah Co. 74954.

SAND SPRINGS, TULSA CO., ST. PATRICK'S (1919)
204 E. Fourth St., Sand Springs, 74063.
Tel: 918-245-5840; Email: stpatrickcatholicchurch@tulsacoxmail.com. Rev. Todd J. Nance.
Catechesis Religious Program—Tel: 918-245-5840. April Slezak, D.R.E. Students 11.
Mission—Our Lady of the Lake, 450 Cimarron Dr., Mannford, Creek Co. 74044.

SAPULPA, CREEK CO., SACRED HEART (1907)
1777 E. Grayson Ave., Sapulpa, 74066.
Tel: 918-224-0944; Email: sacredheart@tulsacoxmail.com; Web: www.sacredheartsapulpa.com. Rev. Louis C. Obirieze, (Nigeria); Deacons Mark Pittman; Vincent Greuel.
Catechesis Religious Program—Students 27.

SKIATOOK, OSAGE CO., SACRED HEART (1921) (Formerly St. William).
109 W. 5th St., P.O. Box 878, Skiatook, 74070.
Tel: 918-396-1179; Email: shc4luv@yahoo.com. Rev. Kenneth Iheanacho, (Nigeria).
Catechesis Religious Program—Students 18.

STILLWATER, PAYNE CO.

1—ST. FRANCIS XAVIER (1895)
711 N. Country Club Rd., Stillwater, 74075.
Tel: 405-372-6886; Email: leah@sfxstillwater.org; Web: www.sfxstillwater.org. Rev. Brian D. O'Brien; Deacons Paul Govek; Bart Brashears; Glenn Collum; Tom Cabeen.
Catechesis Religious Program—Email: sfx@sfxstillwater.org. Students 266.

2—ST. JOHN THE EVANGELIST PARISH AND CATHOLIC STUDENT CENTER (1965)
201 N. Knoblock, Stillwater, 74075.
Tel: 405-372-6408; Email: catholicpokes@gmail.com. Rev. Kerry J. Wakulich; Deacon Tom Haan.
Catechesis Religious Program—Tel: 405-372-7987.

TAHLEQUAH, CHEROKEE CO., ST. BRIGID aka Catholic Church (1966)
807 Crafton St., Tahlequah, 74464.
Tel: 918-456-8388; Email: stbrigid2@yahoo.com; Web: stbrigidtahlequah.com. Rev. Stuart Crevcoure; Deacons Joseph Faulds; Mark Keeley.
Catechesis Religious Program—Tel: 918-207-1737. Patsy Clifford, D.R.E. Students 145.
Mission—San Juan Mission, 23 W. Division St., Stilwell, Adair Co. 74960.

VINITA, CRAIG CO., HOLY GHOST (1892)
120 W. Sequoyah Ave., Vinita, 74301.
Tel: 918-256-2281; Email: holyghostvinita@gmail.

com. Rev. Michael E. Cashen; Deacon Anthony Hicks.
Catechesis Religious Program—Stephen Miller, C.R.E. Students 20.
Mission—St. Ann, P.O. Box 25, Welch, Craig Co. 74369.
Catechesis Religious Program—Students 13.
Station—Northeastern Correctional Facility, Vinita.

VALIANT, MCCURTAIN CO., GOOD SHEPHERD, Closed. For inquiries for parish records see St. Francis De Sales, Idabel.

WAGONER, WAGONER CO., HOLY CROSS (1895)
708 SW 15th St., Wagoner, 74467. Tel: 918-201-5225; Email: fr.leonard.ahanotu@dioceseoftulsa.org. Mailing Address: P.O. Box 710, Wagoner, 74477-0710. Rev. Leonard U. Ahanotu, C.S.Sp.; Deacon Jim Ruyle.

WILBURTON, LATIMER CO., SACRED HEART (1908) [CEM]
102 Center Point Rd., Wilburton, Latimer Co. 74578. Tel: 918-465-3996; Email: fr.khiet.nguyen@dioceseoftulsa.org. Rev. Khiet T. Nguyen, J.C.L.; Deacon Clement Bradley.
Catechesis Religious Program—
Mission—St. Catherine of Siena, 501 2nd St., Talihina, Leflore Co. 74571. Tel: 918-567-2587.
Catechesis Religious Program—
Mission—Holy Trinity, P.O. Box 747, Clayton, Pushmataha Co. 74536.

Chaplains of Public Institutions.

Special Assignment:
Rev. Msgr.—
Brankin, Patrick M., Deliverance Ministry, Chancery Office
Revs.—
Choorackunnel, John V., C.M.I., (India) Chap., Saint Francis Hospital, Tulsa
Coleman, Gerald J., Chap., St. John Medical Center, Tulsa
Dye, Robert M., Hispanic Ministry
Helbing, Brendan, O.S.B., Chap., St. John Medical Ctr., Tulsa
Hernandez, Juan Antonio, Hispanic Ministry
Ketterer, Bryan, Chap., St. Philip Neri Newman Center, Tulsa, OK
Kim, Robert C., (Myanmar) Pastor, Immaculate Heart of Mary Parish
Nguyen, J. Van, Chap., Catholic Charities
Pham, Dominic C., I.C.M., St. Francis Hospital, 6161 S. Yale, 74136
Pratt, Michael, Vocations Dir.

Graduate Studies:
Revs.—
Duck, Robert, Pontifical North American College, Via del Gianicolo 14, Vatican City State, 00165
Fernandez, Vincent, Pontifical North American College, Via del Gianicolo 14, Vatican City State, 00165.

On Duty Outside the Diocese:
Revs.—
Amaliri, Paul Obi, Military Chap., U.S. Air Force
Cain, Robert K.C.
Minh, Vu Duc, Holy Martyrs, Colorado Springs, CO.

Retired:
Rev. Msgr.—
Gier, Gregory A., (Retired), Holy Family Cathedral, 122 W. 8th St., 74119
Revs.—
Courtright, Lawrence P., (Retired), 1921 S. Xanthus Ave., 74104
Daigle, Christopher P., (Retired), P.O. Box 444, Shidler, 74652
Eastman, Patrick W., (Retired), 30 N. Wall, Cricklade, Wiltshire, England SN66DE
Eichhoff, Paul E., (Retired), 1515 S. Rockford, 74120
Elliott, W. Gregg, (Retired), 2407 Holcomb Blvd., Fort Sam Houston, TX 77021
Le, Hoang Viet, (Retired), 2403 S. 141st East Ave., 74134
Lundberg, John W., (Retired), 43 California Ave., Middletown, NY 10940
McGlinchey, James J., (Retired), 6800 S. Granite Ave., V101, 74136
Morgan, Martin J., (Retired), Montereau, 6800 S. Granite Ave. Apt. V109, 74136
Swett, Charles J., (Retired), 2009 Xanthus, 74104
Vima, Benjamin A., (India) (Retired), 6800 Granite Ave., Apt. 249, 74136
Wade, John J., (Retired), 17110 E. 51st. St., Apt. 4, 74012
White, James D., (Retired), 8177 S. Harvard, Box 520, 74137.

Permanent Deacons:
Anderson, Bill, St. Joseph, Krebs
Axsom, Robert, Immaculate Conception, Pawhuska
Beam, Gary, St. Benedict, Broken Arrow
Bell, Erick, Catholic Charities, Tulsa
Bender, Richard F., Church of St. Mary, Tulsa
Berberet, Richard, St. Benedict, Broken Arrow
Bradley, Clement W., Sacred Heart, Wilburton
Brashears, Bart, St. Francis Xavier, Stillwater
Breazille, James E., (Retired)
Brennan, Daniel, St. Benedict, Broken Arrow
Burns, John, St. Elizabeth Ann Seaton, Spiro
Byrne, Peter, Church of the Resurrection, Tulsa
Campbell, Richard, St. Bernard, Tulsa
Collum, Glenn, St. Francis Xavier, Stillwater
Conro, Jonathan, Holy Family Cathedral, Tulsa
Craig, Stephen, Church of St. Mary, Tulsa
Creed, Steve, St. Anne, Broken Arrow
DeWeese, Robert, (Retired)
Falleur, Edwin E., St. Joseph, Muskogee
Faulds, Joseph M., St. Brigid, Tahlequah
Fernandez, Ernesto, St. Pius X, Tulsa
Foltz, Vernon, (Retired)
Fritsch, Joseph, Church of the Madalene, Tulsa
Gamino, Gary, Church of St. Mary, Tulsa
Garrett, James R., St. Patrick, Sand Springs
Gorman, Tom, Holy Family Cathedral, Tulsa
Govek, Paul, St. Francis Xavier, Stillwater
Greuel, Vincent, Sacred Heart Parish, Sapulpa
Gunter, Craig, St. Pius X, Tulsa
Guzman, Jose, St. Clement, Bixby
Haan, Tom, (Retired)
Hale, John, St. Joseph, Muskogee
Hamel, David C., St. Joseph, Bristow
Harton, Neal, St. Clement, Bixby
Hicks, Anthony, Holy Ghost Parish, Vinita
Hopper, Michael, Chap.
Johnson, Dave, St. Bernard, Tulsa
Johnson, John M., Christ the King, Tulsa
Keeley, Mark, St. Brigid, Tahlequah
LeMieux, Donald J., (Retired)
Litwack, Stephen J., St. Augustine, Tulsa & St. Monica, Tulsa
Loeffler, Michael, Christ the King Parish, Tulsa
Loney, Tom, St. Joseph, Bristow
Longbrake, Kenneth, Sts. Peter and Paul, Cushing
Luschen, Loren F., Christ the King, Tulsa
Malarkey, Kevin, Christ the King, Tulsa
Maloney, Kevin, Church of St. Mary, Tulsa
Martin, Robert, St. Bernard of Clairvaux, Tulsa
Martinez, Edmundo S., St. Henry, Owasso
Mattox, Jerry, (Retired)
McFadden, Larry E., Church of the Madalene, Tulsa
McLane, Peter, St. Therese, Collinsville
Mikell, Alan G., St. Bernard, Tulsa
Mitchell, Kelly, St. William, Durant
Moomaw, Charlie, St. John Before the Latin Gate, Bartlesville
Moreno, Carlos, St. Joseph Parish, Muskogee
Moyes, Thomas, St. Anne, Broken Arrow
Mrasek, Vincent J., (Retired)
Perez, Jose, (Retired)
Pickett, Dan, St. John, Bartlesville
Pittman, Mark, Sacred Heart, Sapulpa
Richard, Joseph N., (Retired)
Rutherford, Gerard, St. James, Bartlesville
Ruyle, Jim, Holy Cross, Wagoner
Saenz, Isidro, St. Pius X, Tulsa
Sartorius, Kevin, Catholic Charities, Tulsa
Scarpitti, James, Church of the Resurrection, Tulsa
Schneider, Larry, St. Therese, Collinsville
Sommer, John L., Christ the King, Tulsa
Sousa, Nelson M., Church of the Madalene, Tulsa
Starr, Sid, Unassigned
Stice, Greg, Holy Family Cathedral, Tulsa
Stookey, Rick, St. Benedict, Broken Arrow, OK
Sullivan, Timothy, St. Bernard of Clairvaux, Tulsa
Toppins, Charles A., (Retired)
Tulipana, Kevin, Holy Family Cathedral, Tulsa
Victor, Craig, St. Catherine, Tulsa
Wallace, Ray, St. Joseph, Muskogee
Wersal, Dean, Christ the King, Tulsa
Yarbrough, Lamar, Deacon Formation Program
Young, Thomas, (Retired).

INSTITUTIONS LOCATED IN DIOCESE

[A] HIGH SCHOOLS, DIOCESAN

TULSA. *Bishop Kelley High School* (1960) 3905 S. Hudson, 74135-5699. Tel: 918-627-3390; Fax: 918-664-2134; Email: frkastl@bishopkelley.org; Web: www.bishopkelley.org. Jerri Berna, Dir. & Campus Min.; Rev. Gary D. Kastl, Pres.; Mr. Jim Franz, Prin.; Mr. Rick Musto, Bus. Mgr.; Mr. Doug Thomas, Admin.
Bishop Kelley High School, Inc. Religious Teachers 4; Lay Teachers 105; Priests 3; Students 946.

[B] HIGH SCHOOLS, PRIVATE

TULSA. *Cascia Hall Preparatory School*, (Grades 6-12), 2520 S. Yorktown Ave., 74114. Tel: 918-746-2600; Fax: 918-746-2636; Email: info@casciahall.com; Web: www.casciahall.com. 2520 S. Yorktown Ave., 74114. Revs. Philip C. Cook, O.S.A., Headmaster; Roland F. Follmann, O.S.A., Counselor; John H. Gaffney, O.S.A.; William A. Hamill, O.S.A.; Bro. Nicholas Mullarkey, O.S.A.; Shawn Gammill, Prin.; Joan O'Brien Hubble, Librarian; Rev. Don Lewandowski, Prior; Bro. Stephen Isley, O.S.A., Chap.; Deacon Michael Loeffler, Campus Min. Augustinians (Order of St. Augustine).Coed College Preparatory School. Brothers 1; Religious Teachers 6; Lay Teachers 55; Priests 3; Students 552.

[C] ELEMENTARY SCHOOLS, DIOCESAN

BROKEN ARROW. *All Saints School*, (Grades PreK-8), 299 S. 9th St., 74012. Tel: 918-251-3000; Fax: 918-258-9879; Email: swilliams@allsaintsba.com. Mrs. Suzette Williams, Prin.; Debbie Lunt, Librarian. Lay Teachers 31; Students 412.

[D] ELEMENTARY SCHOOLS, PRIVATE

TULSA. *Monte Cassino School*, (Grades PreK-8), 2206 S. Lewis, 74114. Tel: 918-742-3364; Fax: 918-742-5206; Email: ksmith@montecassino.org; Web: www.montecassino.org. Marci Jubelirer, Prin.; Kevin Smith, Headmaster; Janou Farrell, Middle School Prin.; Vicky Adams, Elementary School Prin.; Carmen Applegate, Librarian; Aubrey Pettyjohn, Librarian. Religious Teachers 1; Lay Teachers 77; Sisters 4; Students 745.
**San Miguel School of Tulsa, Inc.* (2004) (Grades 6-8), 2444 E. Admiral Blvd., 74110. Tel: 918-728-7337; Fax: 918-551-7606; Email: rogercarter@sanmigueltulsa.org. Mr. Roger Carter, Admin. Lay Teachers 7; Students 68.

[E] GENERAL HOSPITALS

TULSA. *Saint Francis Hospital*, 6161 S. Yale Ave., 74136. Tel: 918-494-2200; Fax: 918-494-8448; Web: www.saintfrancis.com. Douglas Williams, CEO; Mr. Jake Henry Jr., Pres. & CEO; Rev. John V. Choorackunnel, C.M.I., (India) Chap. Bassinets 40; Bed Capacity 1,088; Tot Asst. Annually 444,608; Total Staff 6,426.
Saint Francis Hospital South, LLC, 10501 E. 91st St. S., 74133. Tel: 918-307-6000; Fax: 918-307-6001; Email: tlgrade@saintfrancis.com. David Weil, Admin. Bassinets 12; Bed Capacity 96; Tot Asst. Annually 78,337; Total Staff 621.
**Jane Phillips Memorial Medical Center*, 3500 E. Frank Phillips Blvd., Bartlesville, 74006. Tel: 918-331-1550; Email: Mike.moore@ascension.org; Web: www.jpmc.org. Michael Moore, Pres. Bed Capacity 111; Tot Asst. Annually 125,000; Total Staff 475.
St. John Health System, Inc. (1982) 1923 S. Utica, 74104. Tel: 918-744-2180; Email: debbie.peterson@ascension.org; Web: www.stjohnhealthsystem.com. Michael Mullins, Pres. Bed Capacity 760; Tot Asst. Annually 1,000,000; Total Staff 5,008.
St. John Medical Center, Inc. (1926) 1923 S. Utica Ave., 74104. Tel: 918-744-3606; Fax: 918-744-2357; Email: jeff.nowlin@ascension.org; Email: melodee.ruiz@ascension.org; Web: www.sjmc.org. Jeff Nowlin, Pres.; Revs. Gerald J. Coleman, Chap.; Brendan Helbing, O.S.B., Chap. Bed Capacity 523; Patients Asst Anual. 300,000; Sisters 8; Total Staff 4,000.

BROKEN ARROW. *St. John Broken Arrow, Inc.*, 1000 W. Boise Cir., 74102. Tel: 918-994-8100. David Phillips, Pres. Bed Capacity 44; Patients Asst Anual. 100,000.

OWASSO. *Owasso Medical Facility, Inc.* dba St. John Owasso, 12451 E. 100th St. N., Owasso, 74055. Tel: 918-274-5100; Email: david.l.phillips@ascension.org. David Phillips, Pres. Bed Capacity 36; Tot Asst. Annually 70,000; Total Staff 250.

[F] HOMES FOR THE AGED

TULSA. *St. Teresa of Avila Villa, Inc.*, Mailing Address: 1923 S. Utica, 74104. Tel: 918-371-7771; Email: ron.hoffman@ascension.org. Ron Hoffman, Pres. To assist in accommodating the elderly and disabled with housing facilities and services. Bed Capacity 41; Residents 41.

[G] MONASTERIES FOR MEN

HULBERT. *Our Lady of the Annunciation of Clear Creek Abbey* (1999) Clear Creek Abbey, 5804 W. Monastery Rd., Hulbert, 74441-5698.

Tel: 918-772-2454; Fax: 918-772-1044; Email: abbey@clearcreekmonks.org; Web: www.clearcreekmonks.org. Rt. Rev. Philip Anderson, O.S.B., Abbot; Revs. Christopher Andrews, O.S.B.; Mark Bachmann, O.S.B.; Francis Bales, O.S.B.; Francis Bethel, O.S.B., Prior; Francis Xavier Brown, O.S.B.; Lawrence Brown, O.S.B.; Partrick Carter, O.S.B.; Christian Felkner, O.S.B.; Mary David Howells, O.C.S.O.; Joseph Hudson, O.S.B.; Vincent Hulot, O.S.B.; Jose Maria Lagos, O.S.B.; Philippe Le Bouteiller des Haries, O.S.B.; Peter Miller, O.S.B.; Joshua Morey, O.S.B., Subprior; Robert Nesbit, O.S.B.; Andrew Norton, O.S.B.; Joseph O'Hara, O.S.B.; Matthew Shapiro, O.S.B.; Ulrich Maria Theuerer, O.S.B.; James Ullmer, O.S.B.; Joseph Willett, O.S.B.; Marcin Kordel. Brothers 28; Priests 24.

[H] CONVENTS AND RESIDENCES FOR SISTERS

TULSA. *St. Joseph Monastery* (1879) 2200 S. Lewis, 74114-3100. Tel: 918-742-4989; Fax: 918-744-1374; Email: sisters@stjosephmonastery.org; Web: www.stjosephmonastery.org. Sr. Christine Ereiser, O.S.B., Prioress. Congregation of Benedictine Sisters of Sacred Hearts, Inc. Sisters in Community 17.

Sisters of Saint Joseph, 3942 S. Trenton, 74105. Tel: 918-749-8954; Email: paula.coyne@dioceseoftulsa.org. Sr. Eileen Ward, Contact Person. Sisters in Community 2.

HULBERT. *Foundation for the Benedictine Sisters of Clear Creek*, Queen of Angels Priory, 5813 W. St. Martha's Ln., Hulbert, 74441. Tel: 918-772-2170; Web: www.clearcreeksisters.org; Email: clearcreeksisters@gmail.com. Mother Annuntiata, O.S.B., Prioress. Sisters 2.

[I] NEWMAN CENTERS

TULSA. *St. Philip Neri Newman Center at The University of Tulsa*, 440 S. Florence, 74104. Tel: 918-599-0204; Fax: 918-587-0115; Email: tu-newman@utulsa.edu; Web: www.tu-newman.org. Rev. Bryan Ketterer, Chap.; Megan Meussner, Devel. Dir.

STILLWATER. *St. John's University Parish and Catholic Student Center*, 201 N. Knoblock, Stillwater, 74075. Tel: 405-372-6408; Fax: 405-372-6409; Email: catholicpokes@gmail.com; Web: www.stjohn-stillwater.org. Rev. Kerry J. Wakulich; Cathy Perry, Campus Min.

TAHLEQUAH. *Northeastern State University Catholic Student Organization*, 807 Crafton St., Tahlequah, 74464. Tel: 918-456-8388; Email: fr.stuart.crevcoure@dioceseoftulsa.org. Rev. Stuart Crevcoure.

[J] MISCELLANEOUS

TULSA. *Bishop Kelley High School Endowment Trust*, 3905 S. Hudson Ave., 74135. Tel: 918-627-3390; Fax: 918-664-2134; Email: fr.gary.kastl@dioceseoftulsa.org; Web: www.bishopkelley.org. Rev. Gary Kastl, Pres.

Catholic Foundation of Eastern Oklahoma, Inc., P.O. Box 690240, 74169. Tel: 918-294-1904; Email: philip.creider@dioceseoftulsa.org. Mr. Philip J. Creider, Treas.

**Saint Francis Health System, Inc.*, 6161 S. Yale Ave., 74136. Tel: 918-494-8452; Fax: 918-494-8435; Email: tlgrade@saintfrancis.com. Mr. Jake Henry Jr., Pres. & CEO.

Saint Francis of Assisi Tuition Assistance Trust, Diocese of Tulsa, P.O. Box 690240, 74169-0240. Tel: 918-294-1904; Email: paula.coyne@dioceseoftulsa.org. Rev. Elkin Gonzalez, V.G., Vicar.

St. John Auxiliary, Inc., 1923 S. Utica Ave., 74104. Tel: 918-744-2198; Email: rebecca.brungardt@ascension.org. Rebecca Brungardt, Dir. of Volunteer Svcs.

St. John Health System Foundation, Inc. (1981) 1923 S. Utica, 74104. Tel: 918-744-2186; Fax: 918-744-2716; Email: lucky.lamons@ascension.org. Rev. Richard F. Cristler, Contact Person.

Saint John Vianney Seminary Trust, Diocese of Tulsa, P.O. Box 690240, 74169-0240. Tel: 918-294-1904; Email: info@dioceseoftulsa.org. Rev. Michael Pratt, Contact Person.

Laureate Psychiatric Clinic and Hospital, Inc., 6655 S. Yale, 74136. Tel: 918-481-4000; Fax: 918-481-4063; Email: tlgrade@saintfrancis.com. Michele Keeling, Admin. Bed Capacity 90; Tot Asst. Annually 14,641; Total Staff 458.

Porta Caeli House Corporation, 2440 N. Harvard, P.O. Box 580460, 74158-0460. Tel: 918-935-2600; Fax: 918-935-2625; Email: ghighberger@portacaeli.org. Deacon Kevin Sartorius, Exec. Dir. Capacity 12; Family Members of Guests 922; Volunteers 55; Total Assisted 220.

Priest Retirement Trust of the Roman Catholic Diocese of Tulsa, c/o Diocese of Tulsa, P.O. Box 690240, 74169-0240. Tel: 918-294-1904; Fax: 918-294-0920; Email: paula.coyne@dioceseoftulsa.org. Rev. Elkin Gonzalez, V.G.

BROKEN ARROW. *Te Deum Institute of Sacred Liturgy*, P.O. Box 690240, 74169. Tel: 918-294-1904; Email: joey.spencer@dioceseoftulsa.org. Joey Spencer, Prog. Dir.

COWETA. *Apostolate for the Most Holy Rosary and the Brown Scapular Association*, P.O. Box 1041, Coweta, 74429. Tel: 918-279-9158; Email: highlandhaven@windstream.net. Very Laity Mr. Larry Baker, Dir.

HULBERT. *Foundation for the Annunciation Monastery of Clear Creek* (1999) 5804 W. Monastery Rd., Hulbert, 74441-5698. Tel: 918-772-2454; Fax: 918-772-1044; Email: abbey@clearcreekmonks.org; Web: www.clearcreekmonks.org. Rt. Rev. Philip Anderson, O.S.B., Abbot.

MUSKOGEE. *St. Joseph School Endowment Trust*, 301 N. Virginia, Muskogee, 74403. Tel: 918-687-1351; Email: jmyers@stjosephok.com. Rev. Richard F. Cristler, Contact Person.

RELIGIOUS INSTITUTES OF MEN REPRESENTED IN THE DIOCESE

For further details refer to the corresponding bracketed number in the Religious Institutes of Men or Women section.

[0140]—*The Augustinians (Province of Our Mother of Good Counsel)*—O.S.A.

[0200]—*Benedictine Monks (Solesmes Congregation)*—O.S.B.

[0330]—*Brothers of the Christian Schools* (Midwest Province, Burr Ridge, IL)—F.S.C.

[]—*Incarnatio Consecratio Missio* (Vietnam).

[1065]—*Priestly Order of St. Peter*—F.S.S.P.

RELIGIOUS INSTITUTES OF WOMEN REPRESENTED IN THE DIOCESE

[]—*Benedictine Sisters of Clear Creek*—O.S.B.

[0230]—*Congregation of the Benedictine Sisters of the Sacred Hearts*—O.S.B.

[]—*Congregation of the Lovers of the Holy Cross Thu Duc.*

[]—*Daughters of the Divine Savior, El Salvador.*

[]—*Dominican Sisters of Rosa Lima, Vietnam*—O.P.

[]—*Medical Sisters of St. Joseph, India.*

[2519]—*Religious Sisters of Mercy*—R.S.M.

[1640]—*Sisters of St. Francis of the Martyr of St. George.*

[3830]—*Sisters of St. Joseph*—S.S.J.

[1937]—*Sisters of the Immaculate Heart of Mary, Mother of Christ.*

[4100]—*Sisters of the Sorrowful Mother (Third Order of St. Francis)*—S.S.M.

CEMETERIES

TULSA. *Calvary*, 9101 S. Harvard, 74136. Tel: 918-299-7348; Fax: 918-299-7558. Deacon John J. Johnson, CEO

An asterisk (*) denotes an organization that has established tax-exempt status directly with the IRS and is not covered by the USCCB Group Ruling.

Diocese of Tyler

(Dioecesis Tylerensis)

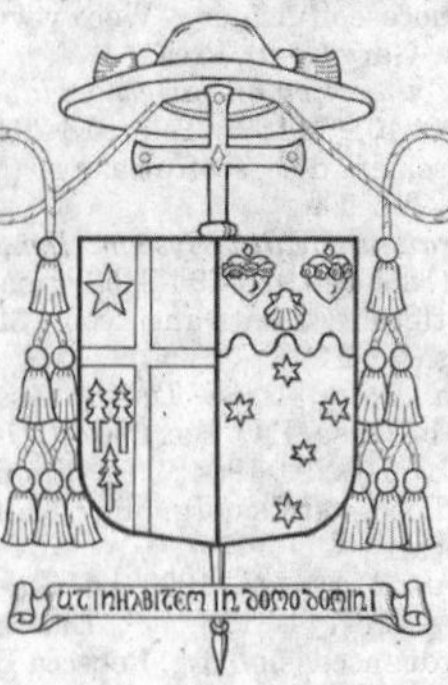

Most Reverend

JOSEPH E. STRICKLAND

Bishop of Tyler; ordained June 1, 1985; appointed Bishop of Tyler September 29, 2012; ordained November 28, 2012. *Chancery: 1015 E.S.E. Loop 323, Tyler, TX 75701-9663.*

Chancery: 1015 E.S.E. Loop 323, Tyler, TX 75701-9663. Tel: 903-534-1077; Fax: 903-534-1370.

ESTABLISHED DECEMBER 12, 1986.

Square Miles 23,443.

Comprises the following Counties in the State of Texas: Anderson, Angelina, Bowie, Camp, Cass, Cherokee, Delta, Franklin, Freestone, Gregg, Harrison, Henderson, Hopkins, Houston, Lamar, Leon, Madison, Marion, Morris, Nacogdoches, Panola, Rains, Red River, Rusk, Sabine, San Augustine, Shelby, Smith, Titus, Trinity, Upshur, Van Zandt, and Wood.

For legal titles of parishes and diocesan institutions, consult the Chancery Office.

STATISTICAL OVERVIEW

Personnel	
Bishop	1
Priests: Diocesan Active in Diocese	66
Priests: Diocesan Active Outside Diocese	7
Priests: Diocesan in Foreign Missions	1
Priests: Retired, Sick or Absent	12
Number of Diocesan Priests	86
Religious Priests in Diocese	5
Total Priests in Diocese	91
Extern Priests in Diocese	7
Ordinations:	
Diocesan Priests	2
Transitional Deacons	1
Permanent Deacons in Diocese	102
Total Sisters	57
Parishes	
Parishes	52
With Resident Pastor:	
Resident Diocesan Priests	38
Resident Religious Priests	2
Without Resident Pastor:	
Administered by Priests	12
Missions	14
Pastoral Centers	2
New Parishes Created	1
Professional Ministry Personnel:	
Sisters	8
Welfare	
Catholic Hospitals	5
Special Centers for Social Services	1
Educational	
Diocesan Students in Other Seminaries	14
Total Seminarians	14
High Schools, Diocesan and Parish	2
Total Students	247
Elementary Schools, Diocesan and Parish	3
Total Students	525
Catechesis/Religious Education:	
High School Students	880
Elementary Students	4,900
Total Students under Catholic Instruction	6,566
Teachers in the Diocese:	
Priests	1
Lay Teachers	82
Vital Statistics	
Receptions into the Church:	
Infant Baptism Totals	1,650
Minor Baptism Totals	146
Adult Baptism Totals	97
Received into Full Communion	181
First Communions	1,580
Confirmations	1,773
Marriages:	
Catholic	317
Interfaith	33
Total Marriages	350
Deaths	347
Total Catholic Population	130,124
Total Population	1,521,923

Former Bishops—Most Revs. CHARLES E. HERZIG, D.D., First Bishop of Tyler; ord. May 31, 1955; appt. Bishop of Tyler Dec. 12, 1986; cons. Feb. 24, 1987; died Sept. 7, 1991; EDMOND CARMODY, D.D., Second Bishop of Tyler; ord. June 8, 1957; appt. Auxiliary Bishop of San Antonio, Nov. 8, 1988; cons. Dec. 15, 1988; appt. Bishop of Tyler, March 24, 1992; installed May 25, 1992; transferred to Diocese of Corpus Christi, March 17, 2000; ALVARO CORRADA DEL RIO, S.J., ord. July 6, 1974; appt. Auxiliary Bishop of Washington DC May 30, 1985; cons. Aug. 4, 1985; on assignment, as Apostolic Administrator, Diocese of Caguas; appt. third Bishop of Tyler Dec. 5, 2000; installed Jan. 30, 2001; appt. Bishop of Mayaguez, Puerto Rico July 6, 2011.

Bishop—Most Rev. JOSEPH E. STRICKLAND, D.D., J.C.L., 1015 ESE Loop 323, Tyler, 75701-9663. Tel: 903-534-1077; Fax: 903-534-1370.

Vicar General—Very Rev. JOHN GOMEZ, J.C.L.

Moderator of Clergy—Very Rev. JOHN GOMEZ, J.C.L.

Moderator of the Curia—Very Rev. JOHN GOMEZ, J.C.L.

Chancellor—MR. PEYTON LOW.

College of Consultors—Rev. Msgr. ZACHARIAS S. KUNNAKKATTUTHARA, (India); Very Revs. GUILLERMO GABRIEL-MASONET; JOHN GOMEZ, J.C.L.; ROBERT H. (HANK) LANIK; Revs. VICTOR HERNANDEZ, (Colombia); JAMES ROWLAND.

Presbyteral Council—Rev. Msgr. ZACHARIAS S. KUNNAKKATTUTHARA, (India); Very Revs. GUILLERMO GABRIEL-MASONET; JOHN GOMEZ, J.C.L.; ROBERT H. (HANK) LANIK; LAWRENCE RASAIAN, J.C.D.; Revs. ARIEL CORTES; GEORGE T. ELLIOTT; VICTOR HERNANDEZ, (Colombia); LAWRENCE L. LOVE; NOLAN LOWRY, S.T.L.; NELSON D. MUNOZ; JOSHUA M. NEU; JAMES ROWLAND; SELVERAJ SINNAPAN.

Deans—Rev. Msgr. ZACHARIAS S. KUNNAKKATTUTHARA, (India) (East Central); Very Revs. MARK KUSMIREK, V.F., (Southwest); GUILLERMO GABRIEL-MASONET, (Southeast); FRANCIS O'DOWD, (Northeast); MATTHEW STEHLING, (West Central); DENZIL J. VITHANAGE, (Northwest).

Diocesan Tribunal

Judicial Vicar—Very Rev. LAWRENCE RASAIAN, J.C.D.

Judges—Very Revs. JOHN GOMEZ, J.C.L.; LAWRENCE RASAIAN, J.C.D.; Rev. JAMES ROWLAND; MR. CRISTIAN CASADO CARMONA.

Defender of the Bond—Rev. GAVIN N. VAVEREK, J.C.L.

Promoter of Justice—Very Rev. JOHN GOMEZ, J.C.L.

Administrator—MRS. MARGARET OPPENHEIMER.

Assistants—MS. TERESA TISCARENO, Tribunal; MRS. MARIA FLORES, Ethics & Integrity.

Diocesan Staff

Bishop's Office—MRS. TERRI BOLTON, Exec. Asst.; MRS. ADELA HERNANDEZ, Administrative Asst.

Catholic Schools—DR. JAMES KLASSEN, Supt. Catholic Schools; MRS. CYNTHIA CUNNINGHAM, Sec.

Secretariat for Administration—MR. PEYTON LOW, Sec.; MRS. ARISELI LARA; MR. FRANK DROBIL; MS. HELEN FOX.

Secretariat for Business and Finance—MR. MARK HENRY, Interim Sec.; MRS. KAREN OSTEEN; MS. CECILIA ALLIGOOD; MRS. JUANITA FAIL.

Secretariat for Stewardship and Development—MR. MARK HENRY, Sec.; MS. ALLYSON GRUBBS; MR. RUSSELL STAGER; MR. DANNY ELZNER.

Permanent Deacons—Deacon FRED ARRAMBIDEZ, Moderator.

Vocations—Rev. JOSHUA M. NEU, Dir.

Pastoral Services

St. Philip Institute for Catechesis and Evangelization—DR. STACY TRASANCOS, Exec. Dir.; MRS. DEANNA JOHNSTON, Dir. Marriage & Family; Rev. JOSHUA M. NEU, Dir. Faith Formation; MR. LUKE HEINTSCHEL, Dir. Media; MR. NICHOLAS WILLEY, Media; MRS. MIKKI SCIBA, Sac. Prep.

Sanctity of Life—Rev. NOLAN LOWRY, S.T.L., Dir.

Prison Ministry—Rev. GARY P. ROTTMAN, Dir.

Other Boards, Offices and Agencies

Catholic East Texas Magazine—MRS. AMANDA MARTINEZ-BECK, Editor; MR. LUKE HEINTSCHEL, Dir. Media; Very Rev. MATTHEW STEHLING, Chap.

Diocesan Council of Catholic Women—MRS. SHEILA COTE, Pres.; Rev. GAVIN N. VAVEREK, J.C.L., Moderator.

Diocesan Finance Council—Very Rev. JOHN GOMEZ, J.C.L.; MR. NEAL SLATEN, Chair; MRS. DIANE FONTAINE; MR. JACK GABRIEL; MR. ROBERT MONAGHAN; MR. PEYTON LOW; MR. DANIEL CRAWFORD; MR. MARC SALITORE; MRS. DEBBIE KAVANAUGH.

Permanent Deacon Council—Deacon RUFINO CORTEZ; ROSA CORTEZ; Deacon STEVEN CURRY; ANITA CURRY; Deacon SHAUN BLACK; CAROL BLACK; Deacon JUAN HUERTA; PAULA HUERTA; Deacon LARRY BATE; MRS. LAURA BATE; Deacon MARCELINO ESPINOSA; GUADALUPE ESPINOSA; Deacon FRED ARRAMBIDEZ; MARY ARRAMBIDEZ.

Priest Pension Board—Very Revs. JOHN GOMEZ, J.C.L.; HANK LANIK; Revs. LAWRENCE L. LOVE; NELSON D. MUNOZ; GARY ROTTMAN; STEVE PARADIS.

Priest Personnel Board—Rev. Msgrs. ZACHARIAS S. KUNNAKKATTUTHARA, (India); XAVIER PAPPU; Very Rev. JOHN GOMEZ, J.C.L.; Deacon GUILLERMO GABRIEL-MAISONET; Very Revs. MARK KUSMIREK, V.F.; FRANCIS O'DOWD; MATTHEW STEHLING; DENZIL J. VITHANAGE; Revs. JOSHUA M. NEU; JAMES ROWLAND.

Tyler Catholic Committee on Scouting—MR. TIMOTHY RUSSELL, Co Chair; MR. MARSHALL BESCH, Co Chair; Very Rev. FRANCIS O'DOWD, Chap.

Society for the Propagation of the Faith—Very Rev. JOHN GOMEZ, J.C.L.

CLERGY, PARISHES, MISSIONS AND PAROCHIAL SCHOOLS

CITY OF TYLER

(SMITH COUNTY)

1—CATHEDRAL OF THE IMMACULATE CONCEPTION (1987)
423 S. Broadway, 75702. Tel: 903-592-1617; Email: agonzalez@thecathedral.info; Email: pcunningham@thecathedral.info. Very Rev. Robert H. (Hank) Lanik, Rector; Revs. Jose Luis Vidarte, Parochial Vicar; Devaraj Arulappa, (India) In Res.; Deacons Bill Necessary; Steven Curry; Fred Arrambidez; Rufino Cortez; Remigio Alfaro; Hal Williams.
SOCIAL SERVICES:.
Res.: 114 W. Front St., 75702.
School—St. Gregory Cathedral School, (Grades PreK-5), 500 S. College Ave., 75702.
Tel: 903-595-4109; Fax: 903-592-8626. Robin Perry, Prin. Lay Teachers 19; Students 210.
Catechesis Religious Program—Lay Teachers 86; Students 284.
Society of St. Vincent de Paul—Mary Thrasher, Dir.; Mrs. Kelly Jackman, Pres.
Chapel—Sts. Peter & Paul Chapel, 1435 ESE Loop 323, 75701.

2—ST. JOSEPH THE WORKER CATHOLIC CHURCH (2003) (Latin Mass only)
5075 FM 14, 75706. Tel: 903-593-5055; Email: latinmasstyler@gmx.com; Web: latinmasstyler.org. P.O. Box 4995, 75712. Rev. Joseph Valentine, F.S.S.P.

3—OUR LADY OF GUADALUPE (1999) (Hispanic)
922 Old Omen Rd., 75701-3709. Tel: 903-593-2006; Fax: 903-593-6033; Email: olgtyler922@gmail.com; Web: olgtyler.org. Rev. Jesus Rodrigo Arroyave.
Catechesis Religious Program—Students 281.

4—ST. PETER CLAVER (1936) [CEM] [JC]
615 W. Cochran St., 75702. Tel: 903-595-2612; Fax: 903-596-9659; Email: st.peterclaver@att.net; Web: stpeterclavertyler.com. Rev. Luis Eduardo Larrea, M.F.E.; Bro. Simon L. Nila, M.F.E.
Catechesis Religious Program—Sr. Maria Elena Gutierrez, R.M., D.R.E. Students 371.

OUTSIDE THE CITY OF TYLER

ATHENS, HENDERSON CO., ST. EDWARD CHURCH (1947) [JC]
800 E. Tyler, Athens, 75751-2140. Tel: 903-675-2509; Tel: 903-292-5222; Email: pastor@stedwardsparish.org; Email: secretarysteward@gmail.com; Web: stedwardsparish.org. Rev. Nolan Lowry, S.T.L.
Catechesis Religious Program—Email: ccddrestedward@gmail.com. Zoila Hunt, D.R.E., Tel: 903-677-1922. Students 350.

ATLANTA, CASS CO., ST. CATHERINE OF SIENA CHURCH (1965) [JC]
Tel: 903-796-4494; Cell: 903-556-3744;
Fax: 903-796-9990; Email: scatlanta1962@gmail.com. Rev. Stephen J. Duyka, Admin.
Catechesis Religious Program—Norma Olvera, D.R.E. Students 57.

BUFFALO, LEON CO., ST. KATERI TEKAKWITHA CHURCH (1979)
208 N. Merrill, P.O. Box 878, Buffalo, 75831.
Tel: 903-322-3705; Email: StKateriTekakwithaBuffaloTX@gmail.com. Rev. Luis Alphonse Roncancio, (Colombia) Admin.
Catechesis Religious Program—Students 90.

CANTON, VAN ZANDT CO., ST. THERESE (1980)
885 1st Monday Ln., Canton, 75103-3676.
Tel: 903-567-4286; Fax: 903-567-0586; Email: sttheresecanton@gmail.com; Web: www.sttheresecanton.org. Rev. Selvaraj Sinnappan; Deacons Alan Stehsel; Jonathan Fadely; James Burkel; Larry Edwards.
Catechesis Religious Program—Students 100.

CARTHAGE, PANOLA CO., ST. WILLIAM OF VERCELLI (1948)
4088 N.W. Loop, Carthage, 75633-3346.
Tel: 903-693-3766; Fax: 903-693-3759; Email: stwilliamofvercelli@hotmail.com; Web: www.stwilliamofvercelli.org. Rev. Steve Paradis; Deacon Lawrence Bate.
Catechesis Religious Program—Debbie Scholl, D.R.E. Students 68.

CENTER, SHELBY CO., ST. THERESE OF LISIEUX (1951)
717 FM 2974, Center, 75935-6006. Tel: 936-598-8458; Email: st.therese.centertx@gmail.com; Email: fathernelson.munoz@yahoo.com. Rev. Nelson D. Munoz, Admin.; Deacon Rafael Landeros.
Catechesis Religious Program—Students 250.
Mission—Epiphany, 3072 U.S. Hwy. 59 S., Timpson, Shelby Co. 75975-9350.

CENTERVILLE, LEON CO., ST. LEO THE GREAT (2013)
549 S. Commerce St., P.O. Box 356, Centerville, 75833-0356. Tel: 903-536-5012; Fax: 903-536-1549; Email: info@stleocenterville.org. Rev. Joseph Lourdusamy.
Catechesis Religious Program—P.O. Box 369, Buffalo, 75831. Tel: 281-844-3945; Email: coachfreeman@yahoo.com. Andrea Freeman, D.R.E. Students 40.
Mission—St. Thomas More Mission, 1 Ranch Rd., P. O. Box 1745, Hilltop Lakes, Leon Co. 77871.
Tel: 936-855-2963; Email: ruth@himecpa.com. Mrs. Ruth Hime, Contact Person.

CHANDLER, ST. BONIFACE
318 S. Broad St., Chandler, 75758. Tel: 903-849-3234; Fax: 903-849-5634; Email: frkey2007@yahoo.com. Rev. Paul R. Key, S.T.L., M.Div.

CLARKSVILLE, RED RIVER CO., ST. JOSEPH (1870) [CEM]
406 E. Broadway St., Clarksville, 75426-3110.
Tel: 903-427-5044; Fax: 903-427-5044; Email: stjosephclarksville@gmail.com. Rev. Ambrose Chinnappa.
Catechesis Religious Program—Students 9.

CROCKETT, HOUSTON CO., ST. FRANCIS OF THE TEJAS (1931)
609 N. 4th St., Crockett, 75835-4001.
Tel: 936-544-5338; Fax: 866-591-9583; Email: stfranciscrockett@windstream.net; Web: stfranciscrockett.com. Rev. Joby Cheradai Thomas, M.S., Admin.
Catechesis Religious Program—Mrs. Nani Wood, D.R.E. Students 75.
St. Francis of the Tejas Ladies Guild—
St. Francis of the Tejas Men's Club—
St. Francis of the Tejas Loaves & Fishes (Food Pantry)—

DAINGERFIELD, MORRIS CO., OUR LADY OF FATIMA (1951) [CEM]
1305 Bert St., Daingerfield, 75638-9704.
Tel: 903-645-5637; Email: fatima51@windstream.net. Very Rev. Francis O'Dowd.
Catechesis Religious Program—Students 62.

DIBOLL, ANGELINA CO., OUR LADY OF GUADALUPE (1971) [CEM]
100 Maynard St., P.O. Box 310, Diboll, 75941-0310.
Tel: 936-829-3659; Fax: 936-829-3659; Email: olg_diboll@hotmail.com. Rev. Luis Fernando Arroyave, (Colombia) Admin.
Res.: 804 Booker St., Diboll, 75941.
Tel: 936-829-2690; Email: fape42@yahoo.com.mx.
Catechesis Religious Program—Tel: 936-366-2829; Email: yvttdlcrz@yahoo.com. Yvette De La Cruz, D.R.E. Students 200.

EMORY, RAINS, CO., ST. JOHN THE EVANGELIST (2013)
551 E. FM 2795, Emory, 75440. Tel: 903-473-5116; Email: st.johns3@verizon.net; Web: stjohnemory.org. Rev. Victor Hernandez, (Colombia); Deacons Federico Aguilar; Marcelino Espinosa.
Mission—St. Celestine, 870 Stadium Dr., Grand Saline, Van Zandt Co. 75140. Tel: 903-962-6350; Email: stcelestine@gmail.com; Web: stcelestine.org. Deacon William Flores.

FAIRFIELD, FREESTONE CO., ST. BERNARD OF CLAIRVAUX (1986)
630 W. Main St., Fairfield, 75840-1418.
Tel: 903-389-4616. Revs. Jonathon Frels, Admin.; Kevin Young, Parochial Vicar.
Catechesis Religious Program—Tel: 903-879-1829; Email: crisypoo1@hotmail.com. Chrissy Moore, D.R.E. Students 52.
Mission—St. Mary, 609 Cedar, Teague, Freestone Co. 75860-1617. Tel: 903-390-4194; Email: Fjoseluis79@yahoo.com.

FLINT, SMITH CO., ST. MARY MAGDALENE CHURCH (2006)
18221 FM 2493, Flint, 75762.
Tel: 903-894-7647, Ext. 13; Web: www.stmarymagdaleneflint.org. Rev. James Rowland; Deacons Larry Gottschalk; Dennis King.

FRANKSTON, ANDERSON CO., ST. CHARLES BORROMEO CATHOLIC CHURCH (Mission 1997) (Established as Parish 2012)
1379 N. Frankston Hwy., Frankston, 75763-2112.
Tel: 903-876-3309; Email: stcharles1379@gmail.com; Web: www.stcharlesfrankston.com. Very Rev. John Gomez, J.C.L.; Deacon Jim Boland.
Catechesis Religious Program—Tel: 903-876-5876; Email: gserc@juno.com. Mrs. Ramona Chance, D.R.E. Students 23.

GILMER, UPSHUR CO., ST. FRANCIS OF ASSISI (1994)
2514 FM 852, Gilmer, 75644-0704. Tel: 903-797-3303; Email: stfrancisgilmer@gmail.com. Revs. Mark Dunne; Cristians Zelaya, Parochial Vicar; Deacons Guylan Blasingame; Gonzalo Rojas.
Catechesis Religious Program—Students 64.

GLADEWATER, UPSHUR CO., ST. THERESA OF THE INFANT JESUS (1945) [JC]
10138 Union Grove Rd., Gladewater, 75647-0967.
Tel: 903-845-2306; Fax: 903-845-7126; Email: office@sttheresagladewater.org; Email: pastor@sttheresagladewater.org; Web: www.sttheresagladewater.org. Rev. Mark Dunne.
Catechesis Religious Program—Students 36.

GUN BARREL CITY, HENDERSON CO., ST. JUDE (1975)
172 Luther Ln., Gun Barrel City, 75156. Email: StJudeGBC@gmail.com. Rev. John-Mary Sayf Bowlin; Deacons Richard Sykora; Juan Cazares.

HEMPHILL, SABINE CO., ST. PIUS I (1939) [CEM]
309 Starr St., P.O. Box 1925, Hemphill, 75948-1925.
Tel: 409-787-4189 (Res.); Email: sp5566@windstream.net; Web: www.stpiuscatholicchurch.org. Rev. Maria Susai J. Avula; Deacon Kenneth Horn.
Catechesis Religious Program—Students 7.
Mission—St. Augustine, P.O. Box 524, San Augustine, 75972-0524.

HENDERSON, RUSK CO., ST. JUDE (1934)
200 Morningside Ave., Henderson, 75652.
Tel: 903-657-4398; Email: stjudeshenderson@gmail.com. Rev. Jose J. Kannampuzha; Deacon Lino Huerta.
Res.: 110 Millville Dr., Henderson, 75652.
Catechesis Religious Program—Students 229.

HOLLY LAKE RANCH, SULPHUR CO., HOLY SPIRIT
1612 S. FM 2869, Holly Lake Ranch, Sulphur Co. 75765-7339. Tel: 903-769-3235; Fax: 903-769-1611; Email: holy.spirit2@yahoo.com; Web: www.holyspirithollylake.com. Rev. Michael T. Snider; Deacon Sam Mullen.
Catechesis Religious Program—Wanda Stephens, D.R.E. Students 19.

JACKSONVILLE, CHEROKEE CO., OUR LADY OF SORROWS (1954)
1023 Corinth Rd., Jacksonville, 75766-3267.
Tel: 903-586-4538; Fax: 903-586-4996; Email: secretary@oloschurch.com. Revs. Patrick Hartnett; Jorge Dinguis; Deacon Juventino Torres.
Catechesis Religious Program—Ana Decious, D.R.E. Students 516.
Missions—Sacred Heart—P.O. Box 947, Rusk, Cherokee Co. 75785. Rev. Juan Carlos Rivera; Deacon Ignacio Panuco.
Our Lady of Guadalupe, 304 FM 235 E., Jacksonville, Cherokee Co. 75766. Rev. Jose Marin. In Res., Rev. Elpidio Lopez.
Venerable Antonio Margil-Alto, Rev. Juan Carlos Rivera.

JEFFERSON, MARION CO., IMMACULATE CONCEPTION (1863) [CEM] [JC]
209 W. Lafayette St., Jefferson, 75657.
Tel: 903-665-2869; Email: icccjefferson@sbcglobal.net. Rev. Msgr. Zach Kunnakkattathava, Admin.; Revs. Roselio Fuentes, Parochial Vicar; Daniel Oghenerukevwe, Parochial Vicar.
Res. & Rectory: 201 N. Vale St., Jefferson, 75657-2143.
Catechesis Religious Program—
Tel: 903-472-9281 (Connie Woods). Students 23.
Mission—St. Lawrence Brindisi, 1465 W. Texas Ave., Waskom, Harrison Co. 75692.
Endowment—Immaculate Conception Catholic Church, Jefferson, TX Foundation, 124 W. Lafayette, Jefferson, 75657-2143.

KILGORE, GREGG CO., CHRIST THE KING (1936) [JC]
1407 Broadway Blvd., Kilgore, 75662-3209.
Tel: 903-483-2500; Fax: 903-483-2501; Email: ctkoffice@ctkkilgore.org; Email: frjhenao@ctkkilgore.org; Web: www.ctkkilgore.org. Mailing Address: 1508 Broadway Blvd., Kilgore, 75662. Rev. John Henao-Lopez, S.T.L., Admin.; Deacons Alejandro Cisneros; Isidro Sanchez; Petra Mojica, Sec.; Mary Gaddy, Sec.; Marcus Arreguin, Music Min.
Res.: 711 Crim Ave., Kilgore, 75662-3209.
Catechesis Religious Program—Sr. Catherine Marie Diaz, E.F.M.S., D.R.E. Students 178.
Mission—Our Lady Queen of Angels, 707 Bradford St., P.O. Box 322, Overton, Rusk Co. 75684.
Tel: 903-483-2400; Tel: 983-834-0251; Email: olqa.overton@gmail.com. Rev. John Thason, Admin.; Lee Hamons, Dir.; Grace Green, D.R.E.; Patricia Harris, Sec.

LINDALE, SMITH CO., HOLY FAMILY (1994)
16314 FM 849, Lindale, 75771-1071.
Tel: 903-882-4079; Fax: 903-882-8382; Email: info@holyfamilylindale.org; Email: secretary@holyfamilylindale.org; Web: www.holyfamilylindale.org. Very Rev. Matthew Stehling.
Catechesis Religious Program—Students 52.

LONGVIEW, GREGG CO.
1—ST. ANTHONY (1880)
508 N. Sixth St., Longview, 75601. Mailing Address: 500 N. Sixth St., Longview, 75601. Tel: 903-758-0116; Fax: 903-758-9550; Web: www.stanthonylongview.org. Revs. Jayaseelanraj Lucas; Robinson Thason, Parochial Vicar; Deacons Joseph Pipak; Manuel Villalobos; Gregorio Sanchez; Gonzalo Rojas; Stephen Ondrick.
Res.: 908 E. Olive, Longview, 75601.
Catechesis Religious Program—406 N. Sixth St., Longview, 75601. Students 250.

2—ST. MARY (1982)
2108 Ridgewood Dr., Longview, 75605-5121.
Tel: 903-757-5855; Fax: 903-758-5074; Email: parish@stmaryslgv.org; Web: www.stmaryslgv.org. Very Rev. Daniel P. Dower, S.T.L., E.V.; Deacons Trevor Wells; Vincent James Wilson; James Petkovsek.

School—St. Mary School, (Grades PreK-12), 405 Hollybrook Dr., Longview, 75605-2464.
Tel: 903-753-1657; Fax: 903-758-7347; Email: admin@stmaryslgv.org. Dr. Darbie Safford, Ed.D., Prin.; Melinda Dunn, Admin. Lay Teachers 30; Students 175; Clergy / Religious Teachers 1.
Mission—Our Lady of Grace, 415 Cypress St., Hallsville, Harrison Co. 75650. Tel: 903-668-5279; Email: parish@ourladyofgrace.net; Web: www.ourladyofgrace.net. Rev. Ralph Eugene Tillekeratne, Admin.; Deacons Juan Gonzalez; William Rhodes.

3—ST. MATTHEW CATHOLIC CHURCH (1999)
2800 Pine Tree Rd., Longview, 75604. 100 Dellbrook Dr., Longview, 75604. Tel: 903-295-3890;
Fax: 903-295-7559; Email: churchoffice@stmattlgv.com. Rev. Msgr. Xavier Pappu; Deacons Joel Gonzalez; Francisco Lopez; Luis Hernandez; Joseph Bianca; John D'Antoni.
Res.: 2900 Pinetree Rd., Longview, 75604.
Catechesis Religious Program—Email: dff@stmattlgv.com. Students 613.

LUFKIN, ANGELINA CO.

1—ST. ANDREW (1998)
1611 Feagin Dr., Lufkin, 75904. Tel: 936-632-9100;
Tel: 936-633-2303; Email: secretary@standrewlufkin.org. Very Rev. Guillermo Gabriel-Masonet; Deacons Gary Trevino; Jesus Reyes.
Catechesis Religious Program—Students 141.

2—ST. PATRICK (1928)
2118 Lowry St., Lufkin, 75901-1316.
Tel: 936-634-6833; Fax: 936-634-6891; Email: stpatrickchurchlufkin@yahoo.com; Web: www.stpatrickslufkin.com. Very Rev. Guillermo Gabriel-Masonet; Rev. Raymundo Garcia, Parochial Vicar; Deacons Martin Aguilar; Abelino Cordero; Juan Mijares; Manuel Ramos; Ray Vann; John Shaffer.
School—St. Patrick School, (Grades PreK-8), 2116 Lowry St., Lufkin, 75901. Tel: 936-634-6719;
Fax: 936-639-2776; Email: admin@stpatricklufkin.com; Web: www.stpatricklufkin.com. Lay Teachers 9; Students 88.
Catechesis Religious Program—
Tel: 936-634-6833, Ext. 225; Email: myorojas@gmail.com. Oralia Aguilar, D.R.E. Students 140.

MADISONVILLE, MADISON CO., ST. ELIZABETH ANN SETON (1978) [JC]
100 S. Tammye Ln., Madisonville, 77864.
Tel: 936-348-6368; Fax: 936-348-5377; Email: pastor.stelizabeth@sbcglobal.net; Web: www.seascc.net.weconnect.com. Very Rev. Mark Kusmirek, V.F.; Deacons Burke J. Landry, (Retired); Steven M. Summers, Hispanic Ministry.
Catechesis Religious Program—Students 95.

MALAKOFF, HENDERSON CO., MARY, QUEEN OF HEAVEN CHURCH (1996)
2269 CR 1730, P.O. Box 508, Malakoff, 75148-0508.
Tel: 903-489-2366; Email: mqhchurch@embarqmail.com. Rev. Nolan Lowry, S.T.L., Admin.
Catechesis Religious Program—Students 60.

MARSHALL, HARRISON CO., ST. JOSEPH (1874) [CEM]
410 N. Alamo Blvd., Marshall, 75670-3450.
Tel: 903-935-2536; Fax: 903-938-1591; Email: saintjosephmarshall@yahoo.com; Web: stjosephmarshall.org. Rev. Msgr. Zach Kunnakkattathava; Revs. Roselio Fuentes, Parochial Vicar; Daniel Oghenerukevwe, Parochial Vicar; Deacons Santiago Suarez; Felipe Pena; Magdaleno Aguirre; John Sargent.
Catechesis Religious Program—Tel: 903-935-5502. Students 352.
Convent—2305 S. Garrett, Marshall, 75670.
Mission—San Pedro the Fisherman, 1835 Chaparrall, Hwy. 43, P.O. Box 430, Tatum, Panola Co. 75691-0430. Rev. Elpidio Lopez-Rodriguez, Admin.; Deacon Jose Mireles.

MINEOLA, WOOD CO., ST. PETER THE APOSTLE (1937) [JC]
203 Meadowbrook Dr., P.O. Box 1022, Mineola, 75773. Tel: 903-569-3665; Fax: 903-569-3665; Email: stpeter75773@gmail.com. Rev. Lawrence L. Love; Deacons Aubrey Fisk; William Faber.
Rectory—1520 N. Newsom, Mineola, 75773-1129.
Catechesis Religious Program—Email: juanabarriga@yahoo.com. Juana Barriga, D.R.E. Students 125.

MOUNT PLEASANT, TITUS CO., ST. MICHAEL (1917)
Mailing Address: 1403 E. 1st St., Mount Pleasant, 75455-4715. Tel: 903-572-5227; Fax: 903-572-9659; Email: office@stmichaelmp.org; Web: www.stmichaelmp.org. Revs. Ariel Cortes; Patrick Fenton; Deacons Joe Moreno; Lorenzo Martinez; Len Sanchez.
Res.: 108 Denman Dr., Mount Pleasant, 75455-4157.
Catechesis Religious Program—Eduardo Mendoza, Dir. Faith Formation. Students 750.

MOUNT VERNON, FRANKLIN CO., SACRED HEART (1986)
406 Texas Hwy. 37 S., P.O. Box 918, Mount Vernon, 75457. Tel: 903-537-2174; Email: mvtxsacredheart@gmail.com. Rev. Freddy Celano.
Church: 406 S. SH-37, Mount Vernon, 75457.
Catechesis Religious Program—Tel: 903-572-3390. Students 114.

NACOGDOCHES, NACOGDOCHES CO., SACRED HEART (1716) [CEM] [JC2]
2508 Appleby Sand Rd., Nacogdoches, 75965-3632.
Tel: 936-564-7807; Email: office@sacredheartnac.org; Web: www.sacredheartnac.org. Revs. George T. Elliott; Hector Arvizu, Parochial Vicar; Luis Pena, Parochial Vicar; Deacons Luis Baca; David Darby; Pedro Gonzalez; Mariano Ibanez; Tony Weatherford.
Missions—Our Lady of Lourdes—P.O. Box 241, Chireno, Nacogdoches Co. 75937. Rev. Joseph Lourdusamy.
Immaculate Conception - Moral, [CEM] [JC3] 1422 Co. Rd. 724, Nacogdoches, Nacogdoches Co. 75964. Rev. Joseph Lourdusamy.
Our Lady of Guadalupe, 4401 Old Lufkin Rd., Nacogdoches, Nacogdoches Co. 75964. Rev. Luis Alphonse Roncancio, (Colombia); Deacon Pedro Gonzalez.
Chapel—Nacogdoches, St. Mary's Chapel, Stephen F. Austin State University, 211 E. College, Nacogdoches, 75961.

NEW BOSTON, BOWIE CO., ST. MARY OF THE CENACLE (1918)
Mailing Address: 216 W. Magnolia St., New Boston, 75570-0914. Tel: 903-628-2323 Hall;
Fax: 903-628-4161; Email: stmarycenacle@yahoo.com. Rev. Msgr. Ronald L. Diegel.
Res.: 214 W. Magnolia St., New Boston, 75570.
Catechesis Religious Program—Students 22.

PALESTINE, ANDERSON CO., SACRED HEART (1893) [CEM]
503 N. Queen St., Palestine, 75801-2718.
Tel: 903-729-2463; Fax: 903-723-9799; Email: shpalestine1893@gmail.com; Web: www.shpalestine.org. Revs. Jonathon Frels; Victor Hamon, (Colombia) Parochial Vicar; Kevin Young, Parochial Vicar; Deacons Juan Huerta; Martin Flynn; Martin Garcia; Daniel Rose.
Catechesis Religious Program—Loiette Dixon, D.R.E.; Dr. Martin Flynn, Youth Min. Students 30.

PARIS, LAMAR CO., OUR LADY OF VICTORY (1880) [JC]
3300 Clarksville St., Paris, 75460. Tel: 903-784-1000; Email: olv@olvparis.org; Web: olvparis.org. Rev. Denzil J. Vithanage; Deacon Luis Garza.
Catechesis Religious Program—
Tel: 903-784-1000, Ext. 17; Email: srgisela@olvparis.org. Nellie Denman, D.R.E.; Sr. Gisela Rodriguez, D.R.E. Students 230.

PITTSBURG, CAMP CO., HOLY CROSS (1987) [JC]
416 Hill Ave., Pittsburg, 75686-1808.
Tel: 903-708-7533; Email: holycrossccpittsburgtx@gmail.com. Rev. Juan Carlos Rivera.
Catechesis Religious Program—Students 130.

SULPHUR SPRINGS, HOPKINS CO., ST. JAMES (1880)
297 Texas St., Sulphur Springs, 75482.
Tel: 903-885-1222; Fax: 903-885-5855; Email: st.james.sulspg@verizon.net. Very Rev. Juan Carlos Sardinas; Deacon Gerald Besze.
Res.: 303 Texas St., Sulphur Springs, 75482.
Catechesis Religious Program—Students 163.

TEXARKANA, BOWIE CO., SACRED HEART (1874) [CEM 2]
4505 Elizabeth St., Texarkana, 75503-2998.
Tel: 903-794-4444; Fax: 903-792-1529; Email: churchoffice@sacredhearttex.com; Web: www.sacredhearttex.com. Revs. Michael J. Adams; Justin Braun, Parochial Vicar; Deacons Larry Benzmiller; Craig Lashford.
Catechesis Religious Program—Email: shpre4505@aol.com. Nancy Hemard, D.R.E. Students 30.

TRINITY, TRINITY CO., MOST HOLY TRINITY (1972)
401 Prospect Dr., Trinity, 75862-9801.
Tel: 936-594-6664; Fax: 936-594-5244; Email: mhtc@valornet.com. Rev. Carlos Rangel
Legal Title: Most Holy Trinity Catholic Church.
Catechesis Religious Program—Students 70.

WHITEHOUSE, SMITH CO., PRINCE OF PEACE CATHOLIC CHURCH (1995)
903 E. Main St., Whitehouse, 75791.
Tel: 903-871-3230; Web: www.princeofpeacewhitehouse.org. Rev. Augustine Tharappel, M.S.F.S., (India); Deacons Ruben Natera; Clarence Blalock; Sr. Gabriela Delgado, R.M., D.R.E.

WILLS POINT, VAN ZANDT CO., ST. LUKE
312 W. O'Neal St., Wills Point, 75169.
Tel: 903-873-3862; Email: stlukeoffice75169@gmail.com. Rev. Gavin Vaverek, J.C.L.; Deacon Edilberto Reyes.
Catechesis Religious Program—Natalie Morales, D.R.E. Students 61.

WINNSBORO, WOOD CO., ST. ANN CATHOLIC CHURCH (1984)
1010 W. Coke Rd. 515, P.O. Box 733, Winnsboro, 75494. Tel: 903-629-7884; Email: stannwinnsboro@gmail.com. Rev. Mani T. Mathai, (India).
Catechesis Religious Program—Mrs. Olinda Mize, D.R.E. Students 32.

On Duty Outside the Diocese:
Very Rev.—
Stoeppel, Anthony, S.T.D.
Revs.—
Dobosz, Jerzy George
Duran, Said
Gonzalez, Daniel
Kelly, Timothy J., (Ireland) S.T.L.
McLaughlin, Anthony K. W.
Palmer, William E.
Thomas, Jesudoss.

Retired:
Rev. Msgrs.—
Brennan, John A., (Retired)
Flynn, John, (Retired)
Priest, Gerald A., (Retired)
Young, James E., (Retired)
Very Rev.—
Ruggles, Christopher V., J.C.L., V.F., (Retired)
Revs.—
Barone, Michael J., (Retired)
Daugherty, Daniel L., (Retired)
Figueroa, Ruben, (Retired)
McGrath, Peter, (Retired)
Rodriguez, Matias, (Retired)
Savarimuthu, Pancras, (Retired)
Suarez, Octavio, (Retired)
Walsh, Richard (Denis) L., (Retired)
Rt. Rev.—
Flynn, John, (Retired).

Permanent Deacons:
Aguilar, Federico, St. John the Evangelist, Emory
Aguilar, Martin, St. Patrick, Lufkin
Aguirre, Magdaleno, St. Joseph, Marshall
Alfaro, Remigio, Our Lady of Guadalupe, Tyler
Arrambidez, Fred, Cathedral of the Immaculate Conception, Tyler
Baca, Luis, Sacred Heart, Nacogdoches
Bate, Lawrence, St. William of Vercelli, Carthage
Benzmiller, Lawrence, Sacred Heart, Texarkana
Besze, Gerald, St. James, Sulphur Springs
Bianca, Joseph, St. Matthew, Longview
Black, Shaun, St. Peter Claver, Tyler
Blalock, Clarence, Prince of Peace, Whitehouse
Blasingame, Guylan, St. Francis of Assisi, Gilmer
Boland, James, St. Charles Borromeo, Frankston
Burkel, James, St. Therese, Canton
Cazares, Juan, St. Jude, Gun Barrel City
Cisneros, Alejandro, Christ the King, Kilgore
Cordero, Abelino, St. Patrick, Lufkin
Cortez, Rufino, Cathedral of the Immaculate Conception, Tyler
Curry, Steven, Cathedral of the Immaculate Conception, Tyler
D'Antoni, John, St. Matthew, Longview
Daniel, Scott B. J., St. Anthony, Longview
Darby, David, St. Mary Catholic Campus Ministry, Nacogdoches
Edwards, Larry, St. Therese, Canton
Espinosa, Marcelino, St. John the Evangelist, Emory
Faber, William, St. Peter the Apostle, Mineola
Fadely, Jonathan, St. Therese, Canton
Fisk, Aubrey, St. Peter the Apostle, Mineola
Flores, William, St. Celestine, Grand Saline
Flynn, Martin, Sacred Heart, Palestine
Garcia, Martin, Sacred Heart, Palestine
Garza, Luis, Our Lady of Victory, Paris
Gleason, Kemper, St. Edwards, Athens
Gonzales, Pedro, Our Lady of Guadalupe, Nacogdoches
Gonzalez, Joel, St. Matthew, Longview
Gonzalez, Juan, Our Lady of Grace, Hallsville
Gonzalez, Ramon, St. Peter Claver, Tyler
Gottschalk, Larry, St. Mary Magdalene, Flint
Hernandez, Luis, St. Matthew, Longview
Horn, Kenneth, St. Pius I, Hemphill
Huerta, Juan, Sacred Heart, Palestine
Huerta, Lino, St. Jude, Henderson
Ibanez, Mariano, Our Lady of Guadalupe, Nacogdoches
King, Dennis, St. Mary Magdalene, Flint
Landeros, Rafael, St. Therese of Lisieux, Center
Lashford, Craig, Sacred Heart, Texarkana
LeFors, Ronald, Sacred Heart, Texarkana
Lopez, Francisco, St. Matthew, Longview
Martinez, Lorenzo, St. Michael, Mt. Pleasant
Martinez, Ramiro, Cathedral of the Immaculate Conception, Tyler
Mijares, Juan, St. Patrick, Lufkin
Mireles, Jose, San Pedro the Fisherman, Tatum
Moreno, Joe, St. Michael, Mt. Pleasant
Mullen, Sam, Holy Spirit, Holly Lake Ranch
Natera, Ruben, Prince of Peace, Whitehouse
Necessary, Bill, Cathedral of the Immaculate Conception, Tyler
O'Brien, William, St. James, Sulphur Springs

Ondrick, Stephen, St. Anthony, Longview
Panuco, Ignacio, Sacred Heart, Rusk
Pena, Felipe, St. Joseph, Marshall
Petkovsek, James, St. Mary, Longview
Pipak, Joseph, St. Anthony, Longview
Prendergast, Allen, St. Ann, Winnsboro
Ragland, John, Our Lady of Lourdes, Chireno
Ramos, Manuel, St. Patrick, Lufkin
Reyes, Edilberto, St. Luke, Willspoint
Reyes, Jesus, St. Andrew the Apostle, Lufkin
Rhodes, William, Our Lady of Grace, Hallsville
Rojas, Gonzalo, St. Anthony, Longview
Rose, Daniel, Sacred Heart, Palestine
Sanchez, Gregorio, St. Anthony, Longview
Sanchez, Isidro, Christ the King, Kilgore
Sanchez, Len, St. Michael, Mt. Pleasant
Sargent, John, St. Joseph, Marshall
Seely, Loren, St. James, Sulphur Springs
Shaffer, John, St. Patrick, Lufkin
Sosa, Librado, Sacred Heart, Nacogdoches
Stehsel, Alan, St. Therese, Canton
Suarez, Santiago, St. Joseph, Marshall
Summers, Stephen, St. Elizabeth Ann Seton, Madisonville
Tapia, Ezequiel, Our Lady of Guadalupe, Nacogdoches
Tiscareno, Jose, Our Lady of Guadalupe, Tyler
Torres, Juventino, Our Lady of Sorrows, Jacksonville
Trevino, Gary, St. Andrew the Apostle, Lufkin
Vann, Raymond, St. Patrick, Lufkin
Villalobos, Manuel, St. Anthony, Longview
Weatherford, Tony, Sacred Heart, Nacogdoches
Wells, Trevor, St. Mary, Longview
Williams, Hal, Cathedral of the Immaculate Conception, Tyler
Wilson, Vincent James, St. Mary, Longview.

INSTITUTIONS LOCATED IN DIOCESE

[A] REGIONAL SCHOOLS

TYLER. *Bishop T. K. Gorman Regional School*, (Grades 6-12), 1405 E.S.E. Loop 323, 75701.
Tel: 903-561-2424; Fax: 903-561-2645; Email: rperry@bishopgorman.net; Web: bishopgorman.net. Rev. Anthony J. Stoeppel, Pres.; Robin Perry, Prin.; Rev. Charles Vreeland, Chap., Email: fvreeland@bishopgorman.net; Elizabeth Alexander, Librarian. Religious Teachers 4; Faculty 41; Lay Teachers 38; Students 357.

[B] GENERAL HOSPITALS

TYLER. *CHRISTUS Trinity Mother Frances Health System* (1937) 800 E. Dawson St., 75701.
Tel: 903-593-8441; Email: andy.navarro@tmfhc.org; Web: www.tmfhs.org. Chris Glenney, CEO; Rev. Luka U. Kalarickal, M.S.F.S., Chap. & Assoc. Dir. Pastoral Care. Bed Capacity 472; Sisters of the Holy Family of Nazareth 6; Tot Asst. Annually 471,187; Total Staff 4,109.

LUFKIN. **Memorial Health System of East Texas* dba CHI St. Lukes Health Memorial, 1201 W. Frank Ave., Lufkin, 75904.

**Memorial Specialty Hospital* dba CHI St. Lukes Health Memorial Specialty Hospital, 1201 W. Frank Ave., Lufkin, 75904.

MADISONVILLE. *Madison St. Joseph Health Center*, P.O. Box 698, Madisonville, 77864. Tel: 936-348-2631; Fax: 936-348-3404. Rick Napper, Pres. & CEO; Marybeth Murphy, Admin. An Affiliate of Catholic Health Initiatives. Bed Capacity 25; Tot Asst. Annually 19,276; Total Staff 93.

SAN AUGUSTINE. **Memorial Medical Center - San Augustine*, 511 E. Hospital St., San Augustine, 75972.

TEXARKANA. *CHRISTUS Health Ark-La-Tex* dba CHRISTUS St. Michael Health System, 2600 St. Michael Dr, Texarkana, 75503. Tel: 903-614-1000; Fax: 903-614-2030; Email: lawrence.chellaian@christushealth.org; Web: www.christusstmichael.org. Mr. Jason Rounds, Pres.; Rev. Lawrence Chellaian, (India) Chap. Rehabilitation Hospital. Christus St. Michael Hospital - Atlanta.Operated by Christus Health, Irving, TX. Bed Capacity 311; Tot Asst. Annually 193,669; Total Staff 1,520.

CHRISTUS St. Michael Rehabilitation Hospital, 2400 St. Michael Dr., Texarkana, 75503.
Tel: 903-614-4000; Fax: 903-614-4064; Web: www.christusstmichael.org. Patrick Flannery, Admin.; Rev. Lawrence Chellaian, (India) Chap. Operated by Christus Health Ark-La-Tex. Bed Capacity 50; Tot Asst. Annually 51,742; Total Staff 218.

[C] MONASTERIES AND RESIDENCES OF PRIESTS

PALESTINE. *Hermitage* (1968) 10020 An. Co. Rd. 404, Palestine, 75803. Tel: 903-549-2950. Rev. Denis Walsh. Total in Residence 1; Total Staff 1; Other Institutions: Houses of Religious Men 1.

Prayer Mountain Hermitage (1985) 10089 An. Co. Rd. 404, Palestine, 75803. Sr. Mary Vogel, H.S.S.R.

[D] CONVENTS AND RESIDENCES FOR SISTERS

TYLER. *Daughters of Divine Hope*, 1910 E.S.E. Loop 323, PMB 240, 75701. Tel: 936-554-6120; Email: info@daughtersofdivinehope.org. Sr. Susan Catherine Kennedy, Supr. Sisters 1.

Instituto Santa Mariana de Jesus, 2706 Shady Ln., 75702. Tel: 903-593-8933; Email: gadelmar85@aol.com; Web: www.marianitas.org. Sr. Maria Gutierrez Sanchez, Supr. Sisters 2.

LUFKIN. *Monastery of the Infant Jesus*, 1501 Lotus Ln., Lufkin, 75904-2699. Tel: 936-634-4233; Fax: 936-634-2156; Email: srmariaguadalupe@gmail.com; Email: lufkinnuns@gmail.com. Rev. Marcos Ramos, O.P., Chap.; Sr. Maria Guadalupe, O.P., Prioress. Cloistered Dominican Nuns. Sisters 23.

PALESTINE. *Dominican Sisters of Our Lady of the Rosary of Fatima*, 419 E. Neches St., Palestine, 75801. Tel: 903-724-3548; Email: dominicanasdefatima.tylertx@gmail.com. Sr. Maria Santiago, Supr. Sisters 3.

[E] CAMPUS MINISTRY

TYLER. *John Paul the Great Catholic Campus Ministry*, 2603 Old Omen Rd., 75701. Tel: 903-266-9110; Email: stjohnpaulgreatccm@gmail.com. Rev. Charles Vreeland, Chap. Diocese of Tyler.

NACOGDOCHES. *St. Mary's Catholic Campus Ministry* (1959) Stephen F. Austin State Univ., 214 Wettermark St., Nacogdoches, 75965.
Tel: 936-564-0661; Email: stmarysccm@gmail.com; Web: www.sfacatholic.net. Rev. George T. Elliott, Chap. Other Institutions: St. Mary's Chapel Total in Residence 1; Total Staff 11.

[F] MISCELLANEOUS

TYLER. *Catholic Charities - Diocese of Tyler*, 202 W. Front St., 75702. Tel: 903-258-9492, Ext. 105; Fax: 903-258-6012; Email: kharry@cctyler.org; Web: www.cctyler.org. P.O. Box 2016, 75710-2016. Very Rev. John Gomez, J.C.L., Pres.; Mrs. Kathy Shieldes Harry, Exec. Dir. Tot Asst. Annually 80,000; Total Staff 7.

**East Texas Catholic Foundation Inc.*, 1015 E.S.E. Loop 323, 75701. Tel: 903-534-1077; Email: mhenry@dioceseoftyler.org. Mr. Mark Henry, Pres.

Catholic Parish and Mission Assistance Program, 1015 E.S.E. Loop 323, 75701. Tel: 903-534-1077; Email: mhenry@dioceseoftyler.org. Mr. Mark Henry, Pres.; Very Rev. Robert H. (Hank) Lanik, Chm.

St. Philip Institute of Catechesis and Evangelization, 1015 E. Southeast Loop 323, 75701.
Tel: 903-303-2487; Email: strasancos@stphilipinstitute.org. Dr. Stacy Trasancos, Dir.

Society of St. Vincent de Paul, Immaculate Conception Conference, 410 S. College Ave., 75702. Tel: 903-592-0027; Email: svdpicc@aol.com. Mary Thrasher, Dir.; Bernie Tures, Sec.

**Tyler Catholic School Foundation*, P.O. Box 131175, 75713. Tel: 903-526-5988; Fax: 903-526-0750; Email: demery@tcsf.net; Web: www.tcsf.net. Don V. Emery, Exec. Dir.

BIG SANDY. **The Pines Education Group* dba The Pines Catholic Camp, 300 White Pine Rd., Big Sandy, 75755. Tel: 214-522-6533; Tel: 903-845-5834; Email: registrar@thepines.org. 14833 Midway Rd., Ste. 210, Addison, 75001. Mr. John Egan, Dir.; Rick Villarreal, Dir.

LONGVIEW. **Longview Catholic School Endowment Fund*, 405 Hollybrook Dr., Longview, 75605.
Tel: 903-753-1657; Fax: 903-758-7347; Web: www.stmaryslgv.org.

LUFKIN. **St. Patrick School Foundation* (1983) 2116 Lowry St., Lufkin, 75901. Tel: 936-634-6719;
Fax: 936-639-2776; Email: admin@stpatricklufkin.com; Web: www.stpatricklufkin.com. Very Rev. Robert H. (Hank) Lanik, Pastor.

SULPHUR SPRINGS. *CHRISTUS Hopkins Health Alliance*, 115 Airport Rd., Sulphur Springs, 75482.

TEXARKANA. *CHRISTUS St. Michael Foundation* (2014) 2600 St. Michael Dr., Texarkana, 75503.
Tel: 903-614-2448; Fax: 903-614-6972; Email: susan.landreaux@christushealth.org; Web: www.christusstmichaelfoundation.org. Sr. Jeanne Connell, Member.

RELIGIOUS INSTITUTES OF MEN REPRESENTED IN THE DIOCESE

For further details refer to the corresponding bracketed number in the Religious Institutes of Men or Women section.

[0220]—*Congregation of the Blessed Sacrament*—S.S.S.
[]—*Missionaries of St. Francis de Sales*—M.S.F.S.
[]—*Order of Preachers*—O.P.
[1065]—*Priestly Fraternity of St. Peter*—F.S.S.P.

RELIGIOUS INSTITUTES OF WOMEN REPRESENTED IN THE DIOCESE

[0280]—*The Brigittine Sisters*—O.SS.S.
[]—*Congregation of the Mother of Carmel*—C.M.S.
[0470]—*Congregation of the Sisters of Charity of the Incarnate Word. Houston, Texas* (San Antonio, TX)—C.C.V.I.
[]—*Daughters of Divine Hope*—D.D.H.
[1050]—*Dominican Contemplative Nuns* (Cloistered)—O.P.
[1070-19]—*Dominican Sisters of Houston, Texas (Congregation of the Sacred Heart)*—O.P.
[]—*Dominican Sisters of Our Lady of the Rosary of Fatima*—H.D.N.S.R.F.
[]—*Hermit Sisters of St. Romuald*—H.S.S.R.
[]—*Instituto Santa Mariana de Jesus* (Marianitas)—R.M.
[]—*Misioneras Guadalupanas de Santa Anna*—M.G.S.A.
[]—*Religious Sisters of the Sacred Heart*—R.S.C.J.
[1970]—*Sisters of the Holy Family of Nazareth*—C.S.F.N.

NECROLOGY

† Anthony, Alphonse, (Retired), Died Apr. 12, 2018

An asterisk (*) denotes an organization that has established tax-exempt status directly with the IRS and is not covered by the USCCB Group Ruling.

Diocese of Venice

(Dioecesis Venetiae in Florida)

Most Reverend

FRANK J. DEWANE

Bishop of Venice; ordained July 16, 1988; appointed Coadjutor Bishop of Venice April 25, 2006; Episcopal ordination July 25, 2006; appointed Second Bishop of Venice January 19, 2007. *Res.: 1000 Pinebrook Rd., Venice, FL 34285.*

Catholic Center: 1000 Pinebrook Rd., Venice, FL 34285. Tel: 941-484-9543; Fax: 941-484-1121.

Web: dioceseofvenice.org

Email: info@dioceseofvenice.org

ESTABLISHED OCTOBER 25, 1984.

Square Miles 9,035.

Comprises the Counties of Charlotte, Collier, DeSoto, Glades, Hardee, Hendry, Highlands, Lee, Manatee and Sarasota in the State of Florida.

For legal titles of parishes and diocesan institutions, consult the Chancellor.

STATISTICAL OVERVIEW

Personnel	
Bishop	1
Priests: Diocesan Active in Diocese	76
Priests: Diocesan Active Outside Diocese	6
Priests: Diocesan in Foreign Missions	1
Priests: Retired, Sick or Absent	30
Number of Diocesan Priests	113
Religious Priests in Diocese	48
Total Priests in Diocese	161
Extern Priests in Diocese	58
Ordinations:	
Diocesan Priests	1
Transitional Deacons	2
Permanent Deacons in Diocese	28
Total Brothers	6
Total Sisters	53
Parishes	
Parishes	61
With Resident Pastor:	
Resident Diocesan Priests	47
Resident Religious Priests	14
Missions	10
Pastoral Centers	2
Professional Ministry Personnel:	
Brothers	1
Sisters	4
Lay Ministers	106
Welfare	
Homes for the Aged	9
Total Assisted	599
Day Care Centers	2
Total Assisted	58
Specialized Homes	4
Total Assisted	47
Special Centers for Social Services	13
Total Assisted	31,304
Other Institutions	17
Total Assisted	807
Educational	
Diocesan Students in Other Seminaries	17
Total Seminarians	17
Colleges and Universities	1
Total Students	1,123
High Schools, Diocesan and Parish	4
Total Students	1,529
Elementary Schools, Diocesan and Parish	11
Total Students	2,752
Elementary Schools, Private	1
Total Students	252
Non-residential Schools for the Disabled	1
Total Students	70
Catechesis/Religious Education:	
High School Students	3,367
Elementary Students	9,071
Total Students under Catholic Instruction	18,181
Teachers in the Diocese:	
Sisters	6
Lay Teachers	455
Vital Statistics	
Receptions into the Church:	
Infant Baptism Totals	2,112
Minor Baptism Totals	1,401
Adult Baptism Totals	182
Received into Full Communion	294
First Communions	3,114
Confirmations	2,031
Marriages:	
Catholic	380
Interfaith	99
Total Marriages	479
Deaths	2,589
Total Catholic Population	239,708
Total Population	2,320,084

Former Bishop—Most Rev. JOHN J. NEVINS, D.D., ord. June 6, 1959; appt. Titular Bishop of Rusticiana and Auxiliary of Miami Feb. 6, 1979; cons. March 24, 1979; appt. First Bishop of Venice July 17, 1984; installed Oct. 25, 1984; retired Jan. 19, 2007; died Aug. 26, 2014.

Catholic Center—1000 Pinebrook Rd., Venice, 34285. Tel: 941-484-9543; Fax: 941-484-1121.

Office of the Bishop—MRS. SHEILA HAASE, Exec. Sec.; MRS. MARIANNE MARZIANO, Receptionist & Sec.

Vicar General—Rev. Msgr. STEPHEN E. MCNAMARA, V.G., V.F.

Chancellor—DR. VOLODYMYR SMERYK, M.A., M.B.A., J.C.D., J.D.

Administrative Assistant to the Chancellor—MRS. LYNN SLOCKBOWER.

College of Consultors—Rev. Msgr. STEPHEN E. MCNAMARA, V.G., V.F.; Very Rev. JOSE GONZALES, V.F.; Rev. JIOBANI BATISTA; Very Rev. JOHN COSTELLO; Revs. ROBERT T. DZIEDZIAK, J.C.L.; HUGH MCGUIGAN, O.S.F.S.; GEORGE RATZMANN; MICHAEL VANNICOLA, O.S.F.S.; TOMASZ ZALEWSKI; Very Rev. FAUSTO STAMPIGLIA, S.A.C., V.F.

Deans—Very Rev. JOSE ANTONIO GONZALEZ, V.F., Eastern Deanery; Rev. Msgr. STEPHEN E. MCNAMARA, V.G., V.F., Central Deanery; Very Revs. ROBERT KANTOR, V.F., Southern Deanery; FAUSTO STAMPIGLIA, S.A.C., V.F., Northern Deanery.

Presbyteral Council—Rev. Msgr. STEPHEN E. MCNAMARA, V.G., V.F.; Very Revs. FAUSTO STAMPIGLIA, S.A.C., V.F.; JOSE ANTONIO GONZALEZ, V.F.; ROBERT KANTOR, V.F.; Rev. ROBERT T. DZIEDZIAK; Rev. Msgr. JOSEPH E. STEARNS, (Retired); Revs. MICHAEL VANNICOLA, O.S.F.S.; JANUSZ JAY JANCARZ, S.T.L.; STEVEN CLEMENTE; ERIC SCANLAN; VINCENT L. CLEMENTE; EDUARDO COLL; MARK L. HEUBERGER; CASEY JONES; JEAN WOADY LOUIS; SEAN MORRIS, O.M.V.; DUONG NGUYEN; LUIS HURTADO PACHECO; GORDON ZANETTI.

Theologian to the Bishop—Very Rev. FAUSTO STAMPIGLIA, S.A.C., V.F.

Vicar for Priests—VACANT.

Director for Deacons—Deacon DAVID REARDON.

Director for Religious—VACANT.

Continuing Education of Clergy—Very Rev. GEORGE RATZMANN, V.F.

Child Protection and Safe Environment Issues—DR. VOLODYMYR SMERYK, M.A., M.B.A., J.C.D., J.D., Chancellor.

Victim Assistance Coordinator—Tel: 941-416-6114. MS. SUSAN BENTON.

Official Archivist—DR. VOLODYMYR SMERYK, M.A., M.B.A., J.C.D., J.D., Chancellor.

Historical Archivist—MRS. CARA SMITH.

Diocesan Tribunal—All Pastoral Center searches for information prior to October 25, 1984 should be directed to the Diocese of St. Petersburg for Manatee, Hardee, Sarasota, DeSoto, Glades, Charlotte and Lee Counties; to the Diocese of Orlando for Highlands Co. and to the Archdiocese of Miami for Hendry and Collier Counties

Judicial Vicar—Very Rev. JOSEPH L. WATERS, J.C.L.

Auditor—Very Rev. FAUSTO STAMPIGLIA, S.A.C., V.F.

Defender of the Bond—Rev. ANTHONY HEWITT, J.C.L.

Promoter of Justice—Rev. ANTHONY HEWITT, J.C.L.

Judges—Very Rev. JOSEPH L. WATERS, J.C.L.; Rev. ROBERT T. DZIEDZIAK, J.C.L.; DR. VOLODYMYR SMERYK, M.A., M.B.A., J.C.D., J.D.; Revs. PHILLIP SCHWEDA, J.C.L.; JAROSLAW (JAREK) SNIOSEK, J.C.L.

Ecclesiastical Notary/Case Assessor—MS. LILY MENDEZ.

Diocesan Offices

Building Department—MR. BOHDAN NEPIP, Dir.; MS. JANE GAIA, Project Mgr.

Catholic Campaign for Human Development—MR. SEAN MYERS.

Catholic Charities of the Diocese of Venice, Inc.—MS. PHILOMENA A. PEREIRA, CEO.

Catholic Relief Services/Operation Rice Bowl—MR. SEAN MYERS.

Communications Department—MRS. SUSAN LAIELLE, Dir.

The Florida Catholic, Venice Edition—Most Rev. FRANK J. DEWANE, Publisher; MR. ROBERT REDDY, Editor, Venice Edition, Tel: 941-486-4701; Fax: 941-486-4763.

Stewardship and Development Department—MS. CARLA REPOLLET, Dir.

Diaconate—Very Rev. FAUSTO STAMPIGLIA, S.A.C., V.F.

Ecumenical and Interreligious Office—Deacon PATRICK C. MACAULAY.

Education—DR. BEN MOORE, Dir. Educ.

Finance Department—MR. PETER MCPARTLAND, CPA, C.D.F.M., Dir.; MRS. DEBORAH HOAGLAND, Controller; DONNA FOTI, Risk Mgmt. Coord.

Human Resources—MRS. ELLEN STINE, Dir.; LISA HOUDE, Employee Rels./Benefits Coord.; MRS. MELISSA PRECOURT, Payroll Specialist; MS. TARA PETERS, Payroll Coord.; MS. AMELIA VILLADA.

Information Technology—MR. ROGER NAVARRO, Dir.; MR. SCOTT PHAYRE, Technical Asst.; MR. ANDREI KROT, System Admin.

Internal Financial Services—MRS. LORRAINE VANLEDE-BROWN, Dir.

Legal—DiVito and Higham, P.A., Gen. Counsel.

Hispanic, Migrant and Spanish Speaking Apostolate—Rev. CLAUDIO STEWART, I.V.E., Dir.

Juventud Hispana (Hispanic Youth Outreach)—Very Rev. JOSE ANTONIO GONZALEZ, V.F., Dir.

Haitian Ministry—Rev. JEAN-MARIE FRITZ LIGONDE.
Lee and Charlotte Counties—Rev. TONY CHERMEIL.
Collier County—Rev. BENJAMIN CASIMIR, C.S.
Manatee County—Rev. JEAN WOADY LOUIS.
Hardee County—Rev. ANTONIO JEAN, M.A.

Outreach to People with HIV/AIDS—MS. COLLEEN MCMENAMIN, Sarasota and Manatee Counties.

Office of Worship—MR. SEAN MYERS.

Department of Evangelization—MR. JOSHUA MAZRIN, Dir.
Charismatic Renewal—Revs. CLAUDIO STEWART, I.V.E., Spiritual Moderator; ANTONY LUKKA; MS. RENEE MARAZON, Asst. Lay Dir.
Spanish—Revs. CLAUDIO STEWART, I.V.E.; ELBANO MUNOZ, Spiritual Dir.; MR. JOSE SOTO, Asst. Lay Dir.
Prison Ministry—MR. JOSHUA MAZRIN, Dir.; ROBERT HINIKER.
Family Life Office—MR. JOSHUA MAZRIN, Dir.; MRS. KIM ELSMORE, Coord.; MS. JANET THORNE, Admin. Asst.
Divorced and Separated Ministry—MR. JOSHUA MAZRIN; MRS. KIM ELSMORE.
Youth & Young Adult Outreach—MS. NINA KOZIUK.
Scouting—MS. NINA KOZIUK, Coord.
Peace and Social Justice Department—MR. SEAN MYERS.
Respect Life Department—Rev. DENNIS J. COONEY, Moderator; MRS. JEANNE BERDEAUX, Dir.
Project Rachel—Tel: 877-908-1212 (Toll Free). MS. SYLVIA JIMENEZ, Coord.

Real Estate Department—DR. VOLODYMYR SMERYK, M.A., M.B.A., J.C.D., J.D., Dir.; SHANNON BARROWS, Coord. Real Estate.

Vocations/Seminarian Formation—Rev. ERIC SCANLAN, Dir.; MRS. SUSANNE THOMPSON.

Other Office

Propagation of the Faith/Mission Cooperative ProgramVery Rev. ROBERT JOSEPH KANTOR, Dir.

Organizations

Cursillo Movement—
Secretariado Hispano de Cursillos—Rev. JOSE DEL OLMO; BERNABE SORTO, Lay Dir.

Courage—Rev. EDUARDO COLL, Diocesan Coord.

Emmaus Retreat—Spiritual Directors: Revs. LUIS ALBARRACIN; JIOBANI BATISTA; LUIS HURTADO PACHECO.

Marriage, Dialogue and Follow-up—Rev. PABLO RUANI, I.V.E., Spiritual Dir. Diocesan Coordinators: MR. JORGE REZA; MRS. IRENE REZA.

Order of Malta—MR. PETER D. BEWLEY, KM.

Padres Madres Orando Por Sus Hijos (PMO)—Rev. JOSE DEL OLMO, Spiritual Dir. Diocesan Coordinators: MR. CARLOS SENA; MRS. ADRIANA SENA.

Equestrian Order of the Holy Sepulchre of Jerusalem—MR. JOHN DESTEFANO, Diocesan Representative.

International Order of Alhambra, Diego Caravan 255—MR. MARVIN A. PESCHEL, Supreme Dir.

Knights of Columbus—MR. JAMES CLARK, Public Rels.; MR. DONALD KAHRER, State Deputy.

Legion of Mary—Rev. MARK RUCKPAUL, Spiritual Dir.

Venice Diocesan Council of Catholic Women—Rev. JOSEPH CONNOLLY, T.O.R., Spiritual Dir.; MRS. BRENDA DOLAN, Pres.

Advisory Groups to the Bishop

Audit Committee—MR. ERNEST SKINNER, Chm.

Finance and Investment Committee—MR. ERNEST SKINNER, Chm.; DR. VOLODYMYR SMERYK, M.A., M.B.A., J.C.D., J.D.; Rev. Msgr. STEPHEN E. MCNAMARA, V.G., V.F.; MR. PETER MCPARTLAND, CPA, C.D.F.M.; MR. JOE STEPHAN; MR. PAUL J. VON MERVELDT; MR. STEPHEN W. BUCKLEY; DAVID RYAN; MR. KENNETH BOEHL.

Diocese of Venice Pension Plan Board of Trustees—Revs. JEROME A. CAROSELLA; ROBERT T. DZIEDZIAK, J.C.L.; MR. PETER MCPARTLAND, CPA, C.D.F.M.; DR. VOLODYMYR SMERYK, M.A., M.B.A., J.C.D., J.D.

Investment Advisory Committee—MR. BERNIE WALSH, Chm.; MR. CHARLES AGLES; MR. BRAD CAMPBELL; MR. JOE STEPHAN; MR. PAUL MOSTEK.

Liturgical Commission—Very Rev. FAUSTO STAMPIGLIA, S.A.C., V.F.; Rev. JEROME A. CAROSELLA; Deacon CHARLES PATRICK MACAULAY; DR. VOLODYMYR SMERYK, M.A., M.B.A., J.C.D., J.D.; MR. SEAN MYERS.

Planning and Development Committee—Very Rev. ROBERT KANTOR, V.F., Chm.; Rev. Msgr. STEPHEN E. MCNAMARA, V.G., V.F.; DR. VOLODYMYR SMERYK, M.A., M.B.A., J.C.D., J.D.; MR. PETER MCPARTLAND, CPA, C.D.F.M.; MR. BO NEPIP; MR. STEVE ANDERSON; Rev. PHILIP SCHEFF; MR. NORBERT WALZ.

Priest Personnel Board—Rev. Msgr. STEPHEN E. MCNAMARA, V.G., V.F., Chm.; Rev. ROBERT T. DZIEDZIAK, J.C.L.; Very Rev. ROBERT KANTOR, V.F.; Rev. JEAN-MARIE FRITZ LIGONDE.

Real Estate Advisory Board—DR. VOLODYMYR SMERYK, M.A., M.B.A., J.C.D., J.D., Chm.; MR. STEPHEN W. BUCKLEY; Rev. Msgr. STEPHEN E. MCNAMARA, V.G., V.F.

Review Board—MRS. EVELYN L. MOYA, Chm.; Rev. STEVEN CLEMENTE; MR. JAMES PRIBE; Deacon DAVID REARDON; MR. JOSEPH P. D'ALESSANDRO, Esq.; Rev. MICHAEL A. SCHEIP; MRS. KAREN WELLS; MR. EDDY REGNIER, Ph.D.; MS. STEPHANY DOBOSZ.

CLERGY, PARISHES, MISSIONS AND PAROCHIAL SCHOOLS

CITY OF VENICE

(SARASOTA COUNTY)

1—EPIPHANY CATHEDRAL (1955) [CEM]
310 Sarasota St., 34285. Tel: 941-484-3505; Fax: 941-488-9333. Rev. John F. Costello, Rector; Rev Charles Ruoff, Parochial Vicar; Revs. Ricky Varner, Parochial Vicar; James M. Shea, (Retired); Deacons James Hanks; Epimaco Roca Jr.; Scott Little
Legal Title: Epiphany Cathedral Catholic Parish in Venice, Inc.
School—Epiphany Cathedral School, (Grades PreK-8), 316 Sarasota St., 34285. Tel: 941-488-2215; Fax: 941-480-1565; Email: ecs@ecstigers.com; Web: www.ecstigers.com. Mary Heffner, Prin. Clergy 1; Lay Teachers 18; Students 146.
Catechesis Religious Program—Sr. Frances Lalor, R.S.M., D.R.E. Students 376.

2—OUR LADY OF LOURDES (1986)
1301 Center Rd., 34292. Tel: 941-497-2931; Fax: 941-497-5849; Email: slockbower@diocesseofvenice.org. Revs. Janusz Jay Jancarz, S.T.L., Admin.; Marcin Koziola, Parochial Vicar; Deacons Lindley Pennypacker; Dennis McDonald; David Mulvaney; William E. Bauer; Joseph Mercurio, (Retired)
*Legal Title: Our Lady of Lourdes Parish in Venice, Inc.*In Res., Rev. Vincent J. Sheehy, (Retired).
Catechesis Religious Program—Email: Elisa.Dacey@ollvenice.org. Elisa Dacey, D.R.E.

OUTSIDE THE CITY OF VENICE

ARCADIA, DE SOTO CO., ST. PAUL (1885)
1208 E. Oak St., Arcadia, 34266. Tel: 863-494-2611; Email: slockbower@diocesseofvenice.org. Revs. Pablo Ruani, I.V.E., Admin.; Luis Albarracin; Deacon Sam Puleo
Legal Title: St. Paul Parish in Arcadia, Inc.
Catechesis Religious Program—Students 425.
Mission—St. Juan Diego Mission, 5241 S.W. Hwy. 17, Nocatee, De Soto Co. 34266. Tel: 863-993-4095.

AVE MARIA, COLLIER CO., AVE MARIA PARISH
5068 Annunciation Cir., Ste. 101, Ave Maria, 34142. Tel: 239-261-5555; Email: craig.k@avemariaparish.org. Revs. Cory A. Mayer; Piotr Paciorek, (Poland) S.T.D., Parochial Vicar; Mark Ruckpaul, Parochial Vicar; Deacons John Jarvis; Gary Ingold
Legal Title: Ave Maria Parish, Inc.
Catechesis Religious Program—Email: arielle.h@avemariaparish.org. Arielle Harms, D.R.E. Students 187.
School—Rhodora J. Donahue Academy of Ave Maria, (Grades PreK-12), 4955 Seton Way, Ave Maria, 34142. Tel: 239-842-3241; Email: susan.nutt@donahueacademy.org; Web: www.donahueacademy.org. Dr. Daniel P. Guernsey, Prin.; Mr. Mark Jahnke, Vice Prin.; Mary Clare Dant, Librarian. Clergy 3; Lay Teachers 22; Students 267.

AVON PARK, HIGHLANDS CO., OUR LADY OF GRACE (1956)
595 E. Main St., Avon Park, 33825. Tel: 863-453-4757; Fax: 863-453-2620; Email: slockbower@diocesseofvenice.org. Rev. Nicholas McLoughlin
Legal Title: Our Lady of Grace Parish in Avon Park, Inc.
Catechesis Religious Program—Tel: 863-453-7537; Email: Angie.HeiringEDU@ologap.org. Angie Heiring, D.R.E. Students 305.

BOCA GRANDE, LEE CO., OUR LADY OF MERCY (1988)
240 Park Ave., P.O. Box 181, Boca Grande, 33921. Tel: 941-964-2254; Fax: 941-964-1124; Email: slockbower@diocesseofvenice.org. Rev. Jerome A. Carosella
Legal Title: Our Lady of Mercy Parish in Boca Grande, Inc.
Catechesis Religious Program—Students 4.

BOKEELIA, LEE CO., OUR LADY OF THE MIRACULOUS MEDAL (1965)
12175 Stringfellow Rd., Bokeelia, 33922. Tel: 239-283-0456; Fax: 239-283-1118; Email: olmmchurch@earthlink.net. Rev. Jacek Mazur; Deacon William Beck
Legal Title: Our Lady of the Miraculous Medal Parish in Bokeelia, Inc.
Catechesis Religious Program—Students 74.

BONITA SPRINGS, LEE CO., ST. LEO THE GREAT (1962)
28290 Beaumont Rd., Bonita Springs, 34134. Tel: 239-992-0901; Email: jmcfarland@stleocatholicchurch.org; Web: www.stleocatholicchurch.org. Revs. Jaroslaw (Jarek) Sniosek, J.C.L.; Kristian Villafana, Parochial Vicar; Fr. Felix Gonzalez, Parochial Vicar
Legal Title: St. Leo Parish in Bonita Springs, Inc.
Catechesis Religious Program—Students 282.

BRADENTON, MANATEE CO.

1—ST. JOSEPH (1927)
2704 33rd Ave. W., Bradenton, 34205. Tel: 941-756-3732; Fax: 941-758-1244; Email: info@sjcfl.org; Web: www.sjcfl.org. 3100 26th St. W., Bradenton, 34205. Revs. Rafal Ligenza, Admin.; Lawton Lang, Parochial Vicar; Shawn Roser, Parochial Vicar
Legal Title: St. Joseph Parish in Bradenton, Inc.
Res.: 2708 33rd Ave. W., Bradenton, 34205.
School—St. Joseph School, (Grades PreK-8), 2990 26th St. W., Bradenton, 34205. Tel: 941-755-2611; Fax: 941-753-6339; Email: dsuddarth@sjsfl.org; Web: sjsfl.org. Deborah Suddarth, Prin. Lay Teachers 25; Students 253.
Catechesis Religious Program—Michael John, D.R.E. Students 159.

2—SS. PETER AND PAUL THE APOSTLES (1987)
2850 75th St. W., Bradenton, 34209. Tel: 941-795-1228; Fax: 941-794-0127; Email: parishoffice@sspeterandpaul.org; Web: sss.sspeterandpaul.org. Revs. Mark L. Heuberger; Michal Szyszka
Legal Title: St. Peter and Paul the Apostles Parish in Bradenton, Inc.
Catechesis Religious Program—Tel: 941-798-9705; Fax: 941-794-3012. Students 125.

3—SACRED HEART (1969)
Mailing Address: 1220 15th St. W., Bradenton, 34205. Tel: 941-748-2221; Fax: 941-748-1744; Email: slockbower@diocesseofvenice.org. Revs. Sack Juan, I.V.E., Admin.; Jean Woady Louis, Haitian Ministry
Legal Title: Sacred Heart Parish in Bradenton, Inc.
Catechesis Religious Program—
Tel: 941-748-2221, Ext. 118. Students 230.

CAPE CORAL, LEE CO.

1—ST. ANDREW (1964)
2628 Del Prado Blvd. S., Cape Coral, 33904. Tel: 239-574-4545; Fax: 239-574-2450; Email: slockbower@diocesseofvenice.org. Revs. Gordon Zanetti, Admin.; Eduardo Coll, Parochial Vicar; Jan Antonik, Parochial Vicar; Paul Nguyen; Deacons Edison Gibbons; Peter Fullen
Legal Title: St. Andrew Parish in Cape Coral, Inc.
School—St. Andrew School, (Grades PreK-5), 1509 S.E. 27th St., Cape Coral, 33904. Tel: 239-772-3922; Fax: 239-772-7182; Email: kbutler@standrewcs.org; Web: www.standrewcs.org. Dr. Judi Hughes, Prin. Lay Teachers 23; Students 280.
Catechesis Religious Program—Tel: 239-574-2411; Email: jharrington@standrewrcc.org. Jerry Harrington, D.R.E. Students 97.

2—SAINT KATHARINE DREXEL (1990)
1922 S.W. 20th Ave., Cape Coral, 33991. Tel: 239-283-9501; Fax: 239-283-9502; Email: slockbower@diocesseofvenice.org. Revs. Piotr W. Zugaj; Mark Ruckpaul, Parochial Vicar; Deacon Richard Spiro
Legal Title: St. Katharine Drexel Parish in Cape Coral, Inc.
Catechesis Religious Program—Tel: 239-283-0525; Email: teri@drexelcc.org. Theresa Idler, D.R.E.

CLEWISTON, HENDRY CO., ST. MARGARET (1932) (Hispanic)
318 E. Osceola Ave., Clewiston, 33440. Tel: 863-983-8585; Fax: 863-983-9673; Email: stmargaretoffice@stmargaretcc.org. 208 N. Deane Duff Ave., Clewiston, 33440. Rev. Jiobani Batista
Legal Title: St. Margaret Parish in Clewiston, Inc.
Res.: 312 N. Deane Duff Ave., Clewiston, 33440.
Catechesis Religious Program—Sr. Minerva Nicholson, M.H.M.L., D.R.E. Students 120.
Chapel—St. Margaret, Clewiston, Hendry Co.

Mission—Santa Rosa de Lima Mission, 845 Mayoral St., Clewiston, Hendry Co. 33440. Tel: 863-983-8585; Fax: 863-983-9673.

ENGLEWOOD, SARASOTA CO., ST. RAPHAEL (1957)
770 Kilbourne Ave., Englewood, 34223.
Tel: 941-474-9595; Fax: 941-475-5697; Email: office@strapheng.org; Web: www.strapheng.org. Rev. Mark Schaffner, O.Carm.
Legal Title: St. Raphael Parish in Englewood, Inc.

FORT MYERS BEACH, LEE CO., ASCENSION (1962)
6025 Estero Blvd., Fort Myers Beach, 33931.
Tel: 239-463-6754; Email: ascensionfmb@yahoo.com. Revs. William Adams; Grzegorz Klich, Parochial Vicar
Legal Title: Ascension Parish in Fort Myers Beach, Inc.

FORT MYERS, LEE CO.

1—ST. CECILIA (1965) [CEM]
5632 Sunrise Dr., Fort Myers, 33919-1798.
Tel: 239-936-3635, Ext. 10; Email: elong@saintcecilias.net. Revs. Stanley J. Dombrowski, O.S.F.S.; Francis Hanlon, O.S.F.S.
Legal Title: St. Cecilia Parish in Fort Myers, Inc.
Catechesis Religious Program—Students 111.

2—CHURCH OF THE RESURRECTION OF OUR LORD (1974)
8121 Cypress Lake Dr., Fort Myers, 33919.
Tel: 239-481-7171; Fax: 239-481-8007; Email: parishoffice@resurrectionch.org; Web: resurrectionch.org. Rev. Msgr. Stephen E. McNamara, V.G., V.F.; Revs. Oliver Toner, Parochial Vicar; Edward Martin, Parochial Vicar; Deacons Michael Esper; David Reardon
Legal Title: Church of the Resurrection of Our Lord Catholic Parish in Fort Myers, Inc.
Church: 8051 Cypress Lake Dr., Fort Myers, 33919.
Catechesis Religious Program—Tel: 239-482-6883; Email: deanna@resurrectionch.org. Deanna Latell, D.R.E. Students 261.

3—ST. COLUMBKILLE (1993) [CEM]
12171 Iona Rd., Fort Myers, 33908.
Tel: 239-489-3973; Email: office@stcolumbkille.com. Revs. Lorenzo Gonzalez; Jean-Marie Fritz Ligonde
Legal Title: St. Columbkille Parish in Fort Myers, Inc.
Catechesis Religious Program—Students 83.

4—ST. FRANCIS XAVIER (1910)
2133 Heitman St., P.O. Box 912, Fort Myers, 33901.
Tel: 239-334-2161; Email: slockbower@diocesseofvenice.org. Revs. Anthony Hewitt, J.C.L.; Jean-Marie Fritz Ligonde; Paul Nguyen; Grzegorz Klich
Legal Title: St. Francis Xavier Parish in Fort Myers, Inc.
School—St. Francis Xavier School, (Grades PreK-8), 2055 Heitman St., Fort Myers, 33901.
Tel: 239-334-7707; Fax: 239-334-8605; Email: admin@stfrancisfortmyers.org; Web: www.stfrancisfortmyers.org. John Gulley, Prin. Lay Teachers 30; Students 480.
Catechesis Religious Program—2050 Heitman St., Fort Myers, 33901.

5—JESUS THE WORKER (JESUS OBRERO) (1973) (Hispanic)
P.O. Box 50909, Fort Myers, 33994.
Tel: 239-693-5333; Fax: 239-693-5626; Email: oficina@jesustheworker.org; Web: www.jesustheworker.org. 881 Nuna Ave., Fort Meyers, 33905. Revs. Patrick T. O'Connor, O.S.F.S.; Jose Del Olmo, Parochial Vicar; Mr. Jose Soto, Business Mgr.
Legal Title: Jesus the Worker Parish in Fort Myers, Inc.
Catechesis Religious Program—Sisters Rosemary Le, D.R.E.; Angelica Flores, D.R.E. Students 351.
Mission—San Jose Mission (1968) 10750 Gladiolus Dr., Fort Myers, 33908. Tel: 239-481-1134.
Catechesis Religious Program—Students 81.

6—ST. JOHN XXIII (2002)
13060 Palomino Ln., Fort Myers, 33912.
Tel: 239-561-2245; Email: info@johnxxiii.net. Revs. Robert D. Tabbert; Saji Ellickal Joseph, Parochial Vicar; Lawrence Nguyen, Parochial Vicar; Deacons Richard Klish; Nick Jurasevitch
Legal Title: St. John XXIII Catholic Parish in Fort Myers, Inc.
Catechesis Religious Program—Students 420.

7—OUR LADY OF LIGHT (1990) [CEM]
19680 Cypress View Dr., Fort Myers, 33967.
Tel: 239-267-7088; Fax: 239-267-5481; Email: parishinfo@ourladyoflight.com. Revs. Hugh J. McGuigan, O.S.F.S.; Anthony Gilborges, O.S.F.S., Parochial Vicar; Deacons Francis J. Camacho; Ralph Catanese
Legal Title: Our Lady of Light Parish in Fort Myers, Inc.
Res.: 9404 Windlake Dr., Fort Myers, 33967.
Tel: 239-432-9095.
Catechesis Religious Program—Email: lori@ourladyoflight.com. Lori Crawford, D.R.E. Students 47.

8—ST. THERESE (2003)
20115 N. Tamiami Tr., North Fort Myers, Lee Co. 33903. Tel: 239-567-2315; Fax: 239-567-2316; Email: sttheresech@embarqm.co. Rev. Thomas Heck
Legal Title: St. Therese Parish in North Fort Myers, Inc.
Catechesis Religious Program—Nelson Perez, D.R.E. Students 5.

9—ST. VINCENT DE PAUL (1986)
13031 Palm Beach Blvd., Fort Myers, 33905.
Tel: 239-693-0818; Email: slockbower@diocesseofvenice.org. Rev. Murchadh O'Madagain, Admin.
Legal Title: St. Vincent de Paul Parish in Fort Myers, Inc.
Catechesis Religious Program—Students 43.

GROVE CITY, CHARLOTTE CO., ST. FRANCIS OF ASSISI (1978)
5265 Placida Rd., Englewood, 34224.
Tel: 941-697-4899; Email: slockbower@diocesseofvenice.org. Rev. Richard York; Deacon Robert Godlewsky
Legal Title: St. Francis of Assisi Parish in Grove City, Inc.
Catechesis Religious Program—Students 62.

HOLMES BEACH, MANATEE CO., ST. BERNARD (1956)
248 S. Harbor Dr., Bradenton Beach, 34217.
Tel: 941-778-4769; Email: stbernardcc@hotmail.com. Rev. Michael Mullen, (Retired)
Legal Title: St. Bernard Parish in Holmes Beach, Inc.
Catechesis Religious Program—Students 27.

IMMOKALEE, COLLIER CO., OUR LADY OF GUADALUPE (1957)
207 S. 9th St., Immokalee, 34142. Tel: 239-657-2666; Fax: 239-657-3431; Email: slockbower@diocesseofvenice.org. Revs. Carlos Reyes, C.S.; Wilner Durosler, Parochial Vicar; Onorio Benacchio, C.S., Priest in Residence, (Retired)
Legal Title: Our Lady of Guadalupe Parish in Immokalee, Inc.
Catechesis Religious Program—Email: Cynthia.Garcia@olguadalupeparish.org. Mrs. Cynthia Garcia, D.R.E.

LABELLE, HENDRY CO., OUR LADY QUEEN OF HEAVEN (1975)
355 S. Bridge St., P.O. Box 357, LaBelle, 33935.
Tel: 863-675-0030; Fax: 863-675-0756; Email: slockbower@diocesseofvenice.org. David Vidal, Admin.; Rev. Juan Lorenzo, Parochial Vicar
Legal Title: Our Lady Queen of Heaven Parish in LaBelle, Inc.
Catechesis Religious Program—Estellar Aguilar, D.R.E. Students 400.
Mission—Holy Martyrs Mission, 4290 Crescent Ave., S.W., Labelle, Hendry Co. 33935.

LAKE PLACID, HIGHLAND CO.

1—COMMUNIDAD CATOLICA HISPANA SANTIAGO APOSTOL (1991) [JC] (Hispanic), See separate listing. Mission of St. James Catholic Parish in Lake Placid, Inc.
685 C.R. 621 E., Lake Placid, 33852-5351.
Tel: 863-465-2470; Cell: 863-633-0922; Email: lorie.raimondi@stjameschurchlp.org. 3380 Placid View Dr., Lake Placid, 33852-5351.

2—ST. JAMES (1962) [JC]
3380 Placid View Dr., Lake Placid, 33852.
Tel: 863-465-3215; Fax: 863-465-0649; Email: lorie.raimondi@stjameschurchlp.org; Web: www.stjameschurchlp.org. Revs. Vincent Clemente; Victor Caviedes
Legal Title: St. James Catholic Parish in Lake Placid, Inc.
Mission—Communidad Catolica Hispana Santiago Apostol Mission, [JC] 685 CR. 621 E., Lake Placid, Highland Co. 33852. Tel: 863-633-0922;
Fax: 863-465-2470; Email: loriestjameschurch@embarqmail.com.
Legal Name: Mission of St. James Catholic Parish in Lake Placid, Inc. Elementary School Students 54.
Catechesis Religious Program—Connie Rollins, D.R.E. Students 54.

LAKEWOOD RANCH, MANATEE CO., OUR LADY OF THE ANGELS (1999) [CEM]
12905 SR 70 E., Lakewood Ranch, 34202.
Tel: 941-752-6770; Fax: 941-752-6821; Email: parishinfo@olangelscc.org; Web: www.olangelscc.org. Revs. Michael A. Scheip, Admin.; John Nghia Hoang, C.M.C., Parochial Vicar
Legal Title: Our Lady of the Angels Parish in Lakewood Ranch, Inc.
Catechesis Religious Program—Students 476.

LEHIGH ACRES, LEE CO., ST. RAPHAEL (1962)
2514 Lee Blvd., Lehigh Acres, 33971.
Tel: 239-369-1831; Fax: 239-369-1039; Email: parishoffice@saintraphaelccla.org. Rev. Dennis J. Cooney; Deacons Joseph Allison; Edward Gwiazda
Legal Title: St. Raphael Parish in Lehigh, Inc.
Catechesis Religious Program—Tel: 239-369-6424; Email: joseph.allison@saintraphaelccla.org.

LONGBOAT KEY, MANATEE CO., ST. MARY STAR OF THE SEA (1973)
4280 Gulf of Mexico Dr., Longboat Key, 34228.
Tel: 941-383-1255; Email: slockbower@diocesseofvenice.org. Rev. Msgr. Gerard Finegan; Rev. Phillip Schweda, J.C.L.
Legal Title: St. Mary Star of the Sea Parish in Longboat Key, Inc.
Catechesis Religious Program—

MARCO ISLAND, COLLIER CO., SAN MARCO (1971)
851 San Marco Rd., Marco Island, 34145.
Tel: 239-394-5181; Fax: 239-394-1385; Email: slockbower@diocesseofvenice.org. Revs. Timothy M. Navin; Duong Nguyen, Parochial Vicar; Deacons John Minicozzi; Mark Leonard
Legal Title: San Marco Parish in Marco Island, Inc.
Catechesis Religious Program—Kim Adamson, D.R.E. Students 130.
Mission—Holy Family Mission, Everglades City, Collier Co.

MOORE HAVEN, GLADES CO., ST. JOSEPH THE WORKER (1960) [JC] (Spanish)
24065 U.S. Hwy. 27, P.O. Box 1109, Moore Haven, 33471. Tel: 863-946-0696; Fax: 863-946-3444; Email: office@stjosephtheworkerfl.org. Rev. Marcial I. Garcia
Legal Title: St. Joseph the Worker Parish in Moore Haven, Inc.
Mission—St. Theresa of the Child Jesus Mission, 1027 Chobee Loop, Okeechobee, Okeechobee Co. 34974.

NAPLES, COLLIER CO.

1—ST. AGNES
7775 Vanderbilt Beach Rd., Naples, 34120-1641.
Tel: 239-592-1949. Very Rev. Robert Kantor, V.F.; Revs. Krzysztof Piotrowski, Parochial Vicar; Michael Orsi, Parochial Vicar; Deacons Henry de Mena; Roberto Landron; Hugh Mueller
Legal Title: St. Agnes Parish in Naples, Inc.
Catechesis Religious Program—Email: Ivy@Stagnesnaples.org. Ivy O'Malley, D.R.E. Students 668.

2—ST. ANN (1955)
475 Ninth Ave. S., Naples, 34102. Tel: 239-262-4256; Fax: 239-262-4296; Email: secretary@naplesstann.com. Revs. Michael Vannicola, O.S.F.S.; William Davis, Parochial Vicar
*Legal Title: St. Ann Catholic Parish in Naples, Inc. a Florida non-profit corporation*In Res., Bernard O'Connor.
School—St. Ann School, (Grades PreK-8), 542 Eighth Ave. S., Naples, 34102. Tel: 239-262-4110; Fax: 239-262-3991; Email: ggroch@stann.net; Web: www.stann.net. Gina Groch, Prin.; Becky Meinert, Vice Prin. Religious Teachers 1; Lay Teachers 24; Sisters 1; Students 265.
Catechesis Religious Program—Email: faithformation@naplesstann.com. Sybil Jean Steuart, D.R.E.

3—ST. ELIZABETH SETON (1975)
5260 28th Ave., S.W., Naples, 34116.
Tel: 239-455-3900; Email: slockbower@diocesseofvenice.org. Revs. Casey Jones, Admin.; Luis Pacheco; Deacon Roberto Landron
Legal Title: St. Elizabeth Seton Parish in Naples, Inc.
School—St. Elizabeth Seton Catholic School, (Grades PreK-8), 2730 53rd Ter. S.W., Naples, 34116.
Tel: 239-455-2262, Ext. 305; Email: niebuhr@seseton.org; Web: www.saintelizabethseton.com. Maria Niebuhr, Prin. Lay Teachers 25; Students 190.
Catechesis Religious Program—Students 120.

4—ST. FINBARR CATHOLIC CHURCH
13520 Tamiami Tr. E., Naples, Collier Co. 34114-8703. Tel: 239-417-2084; Email: office@stfinbarr.org; Web: stfinbarr.org. Rev. Leo Smith, Admin.; Deacon Alfred J. Mauriello
Legal Title: St. Finbarr Parish in Naples, Inc.
Catechesis Religious Program—

5—ST. JOHN THE EVANGELIST (1988)
625 111th Ave. N., Naples, 34108. Tel: 239-566-8740; Email: info@sjecc.com; Web: sjecc.com. Revs. Tomasz Zalewski; Paul R. D'Angelo; Robert Murphy; Deacon Harold Brenner
Legal Title: St. John the Evangelist Parish in Naples, Inc.
Catechesis Religious Program—Web: sjecc.com/education. Mrs. Natalie Campbell, D.R.E. Students 410.

6—ST. PETER THE APOSTLE (1974)
5130 Rattlesnake Hammock Rd., Naples, 34113.
Tel: 239-774-3337; Email: business@stpeternaples.com; Web: www.stpeternaples.org. Revs. Gerard F. Critch; Chuck Ruoff; Elbano Munoz; Benjamin Casimir, C.S.; Deacons David Nolan; Peter Pavlyshin
Legal Title: St. Peter the Apostle Parish in Naples, Inc.
Catechesis Religious Program—5025 Rattlesnake Hammock Rd., Naples, 34113.

7—ST. WILLIAM (1973)
750 Seagate Dr., Naples, 34103-2886.
Tel: 239-261-4883; Fax: 239-261-8729; Email: slockbower@diocesseofvenice.org. Revs. George Ratzmann; Steven Clemente, Parochial Vicar; Antony Lukka, Parochial Vicar; Deacons Robert Chalhoub; Ed O'Connell
St. William Parish in Naples, Inc.
Catechesis Religious Program—Tel: 239-263-5429;

Fax: 239-403-4435. Mary Jane Spirk, D.R.E. Students 216.

NORTH PORT, SARASOTA CO., SAN PEDRO (1964)
14380 Tamiami Tr., North Port, 34287.
Tel: 941-426-2500; Tel: 941-426-6810;
Fax: 941-423-8710; Email: bookkeeper@sanpedrocc.org. Revs. Patrick C. Organ; Leszek Trojanowski, Parochial Vicar; Deacon Richard Frohmiller
Legal Title: San Pedro Parish in North Port, Inc.
Catechesis Religious Program—Tel: 941-426-2893; Fax: 941-429-8785; Email: faithformation@sanpedrocc.org. Anne Rohde, D.R.E.

OSPREY, SARASOTA CO., OUR LADY OF MOUNT CARMEL (2000)
425 S. Tamiami Tr., P.O. Box 1097, Osprey, 34229.
Tel: 941-966-0807; Fax: 941-966-3909; Email: ftillotson@olmc-osprey.org; Web: www.olmc-osprey.org. Revs. Frederick Tillotson, O.Carm.; Richard Supple, O.Carm., Parochial Vicar; Deacon Thomas Grant
Legal Title: Our Lady of Mount Carmel Parish in Osprey, Inc.
Res.: 554 Pine Ranch E. Rd., Osprey, 34229.
Tel: 941-918-2032.
Catechesis Religious Program—Email: rsupple@olmc-osprey.org. Students 13.

PALMETTO, MANATEE CO., HOLY CROSS (1956)
505-26th St. W., Palmetto, 34221. Tel: 941-729-3891; Fax: 941-721-9402; Email: slockbower@diocesseofvenice.org. Rev. Bernard P. Evanofski
Legal Title: Holy Cross Parish in Palmetto, Inc.
Catechesis Religious Program—Tel: 941-729-4338. Students 383.

PARRISH, MANATEE CO., SAINT FRANCES XAVIER CABRINI (1992)
12001 69th St. E., Parrish, 34219. Tel: 941-776-9097; Fax: 941-776-1307; Email: secsfxc@verizon.net. Rev. James Cogan
Legal Title: St. Frances Xavier Cabrini Parish in Parrish, Inc.
Catechesis Religious Program—Students 250.

PORT CHARLOTTE, CHARLOTTE CO.

1—ST. CHARLES BORROMEO (1959)
2500 Easy St, Port Charlotte, 33952. Revs. John Fitch, Admin.; Zenon Kurzyna; Philip J. Scheff; Deacon Thomas Caliguire
Legal Title: St. Charles Borromeo Parish in Port Charlotte, Inc.
School—St. Charles Borromeo School, (Grades PreK-8), Tel: 941-625-5533; Email: info@stcbs.org; Web: www.stcbs.org. Ms. Tonya Peters, Prin. Lay Teachers 16; Students 264.
Catechesis Religious Program—

2—ST. MAXIMILIAN KOLBE (1988)
1441 Spear St., Port Charlotte, 33948.
Tel: 941-743-6877; Email: parishoffice@stmaxcatholic.org. Revs. Teofilo Useche; Anthonio Jean, Parochial Vicar; Deacon Joe Plummer
Legal Title: St. Maximilian Kolbe Parish in Port Charlotte, Inc.
Res.: 1538 Castlerock Ln., Port Charlotte, 33948.
Catechesis Religious Program—Cindy Kuykendall, D.R.E. Students 109.

3—SAN ANTONIO (1993)
24445 Rampart Blvd., Port Charlotte, 33980.
Tel: 941-624-3799; Fax: 941-624-6184; Email: frstuart@sanantoniorcc.org; Web: sanantoniorcc.org. Rev. Stuart Gullan-Steel, Admin.
Legal Title: San Antonio Parish in Port Charlotte, Inc.
Catechesis Religious Program—Tel: 941-624-5156. Students 39.

PUNTA GORDA, CHARLOTTE CO., SACRED HEART (1954)
211 W. Charlotte Ave., Punta Gorda, 33950-5546.
Tel: 941-639-3957; Fax: 941-639-2061; Email: info@sacredheartfl.org. Revs. Jerome P. Kaywell; Mario Kono, Parochial Vicar; Deacon George Riegger
Legal Title: Sacred Heart Parish in Punta Gorda, Inc.
Catechesis Religious Program—Tel: 941-639-9545. Sr. Josine Perez, D.R.E. Students 125.

SANIBEL, LEE CO., ST. ISABEL (1973)
3559 Sanibel Captiva Rd., Sanibel, 33957.
Tel: 293-472-2763; Email: parishoffice@saintisabel.org; Web: www.saintisabel.org. Kim Scott, Sec.; Rev. Joseph Gates, Parochial Vicar; Raymond Myslakowski, Music Min.; Ms. Debi Almeida, Music Asst.; Mr. Arthur Warner, Maintenance
Legal Title: St. Isabel Parish in Sanibel, Inc.
Catechesis Religious Program—Khristy Scheer, D.R.E. / Business Mgr. Students 41.

SARASOTA, MANATEE CO., OUR LADY QUEEN OF MARTYRS (1959)
833 Magellan Dr., Sarasota, 34243.
Tel: 941-755-1826; Fax: 941-753-1654; Email: queenofmartyrs@olqm.net; Web: www.olqm.net. Rev. Joseph F. Connolly, T.O.R.; Friar Timothy Harris
Legal Title: Our Lady Queen of Martyrs Parish in Sarasota, Inc.
Catechesis Religious Program—6600 Pennsylvania Ave., Sarasota, 34243. Tel: 941-755-3497; Email: faithformation@olqm.net. Maryellen Wilson-Smith, D.R.E.; Kathleen Tortdiano, D.R.E. Students 65.

SARASOTA, SARASOTA CO.

1—CHRIST THE KING PARISH IN SARASOTA, INC.
1900 Meadowood St., Sarasota, 34231.
Tel: 941-924-2777; Email: office@christthekingsarasota.org; Web: www.christthekingsarasota.org. Revs. Stephane Dupre, F.S.S.P.; Gregory Bartholomew, F.S.S.P.

2—INCARNATION (1958)
2929 Bee Ridge Rd., Sarasota, 34239.
Tel: 941-921-6631; Fax: 941-927-2521; Email: dgordon@incarnationchurch.org; Email: bduncan@incarnationschool.edu; Web: www.incarnationchurch.org. 2901 Bee Ridge Rd., Sarasota, 34239. Revs. Eric Scanlan, Admin.; Ronnie Sison, Parochial Vicar; Deacons John Crescitelli; Stephen Beck; Patrick Palumbo; Kevin McKenny; Kim Cohen
*Legal Title: Incarnation Parish in Sarasota, Inc.*In Res.
School—Incarnation School, (Grades PreK-8), 2911 Bee Ridge Rd., Sarasota, 34239. Tel: 941-924-8588; Fax: 941-925-1248; Email: bduncan@incarnationschool.edu. Mrs. Coleen Curlett, Prin. Lay Teachers 17; Students 127.
Catechesis Religious Program—Tel: 941-924-9566; Email: cmaida@incarnationchurch.org. Rochelle Maida, D.R.E. Students 20.

3—ST. JUDE (2006)
3930 17th St., Sarasota, 34235. Tel: 941-955-3934; Fax: 941-365-4760; Email: frcelestino@st-judeparish.org; Web: www.stjudehispamerctr.com. Revs. Celestino Gutierrez; Robert Tatman; Oscar Mendoza; Deacons Leonardo Pastore; Humberto R. Alvia
Legal Title: St. Jude Parish in Sarasota, Inc.
Catechesis Religious Program—Students 259.

4—ST. MARTHA (1913)
200 N. Orange Ave., Sarasota, 34236.
Tel: 941-366-4210, Ext. 3234; Fax: 941-954-8434; Email: sbrinn@stmartha.org; Web: www.stmartha.org. Very Rev. Fausto Stampiglia, S.A.C., V.F.; Revs. Wojciech Stachura, S.A.C., Parochial Vicar; John Vu Tien Cao, C.M.C.; Jan Rykala; R. Wilson; Deacons R. Patrick Macaulay; William Ladroga; John Robert Gaitens
Legal Title: St. Martha Parish in Sarasota, Inc.
School—St. Martha School, (Grades PreK-8), 4380 Fruitville Rd., Sarasota, 34232. Tel: 941-953-4181; Fax: 941-366-5580; Email: syoung@stmarthaschool.net; Web: www.stmarthaschool.net. Siobhan Young, Prin. Clergy 1; Lay Teachers 30; Religious 1; Students 446.
Catechesis Religious Program—Mrs. Patricia Sileo, D.R.E. Students 253.
Mission—The Vietnam Catholic Community of Our Lady of Lavang Mission.

5—ST. MICHAEL THE ARCHANGEL (1958)
5394 Midnight Pass Rd., Sarasota, 34242.
Tel: 941-349-4174; Fax: 941-349-6388; Email: parishoffice@stmichaelssiesta.com; Web: www.stmichaelssiesta.com. Rev. Michael J. Cannon
Legal Title: St. Michael the Archangel Parish in Sarasota, Inc.
Res.: 1014 Glebe Ln., Sarasota, 34242.
Catechesis Religious Program—Students 25.

6—ST. PATRICK (1988)
7900 Bee Ridge Rd., Sarasota, 34241.
Tel: 941-378-1703; Email: slockbower@diocesseofvenice.org. Revs. Robert T. Dziedziak, J.C.L.; Russell Wright, S.T.L.; Deacons Raymond Lyons; Harry Antrim
Legal Title: St. Patrick Catholic Parish in Sarasota, Inc.
Catechesis Religious Program—Students 208.

7—ST. THOMAS MORE (1979)
2506 Gulf Gate Dr., Sarasota, 34231.
Tel: 941-923-1691; Fax: 941-923-1692; Email: info@stthomasmoresrq.org; Web: stthomasmore.org. Revs. Joseph G. Clifford; James G. Simko, Parochial Vicar; Deacons John Robert Gaitens; David Wagner
Legal Title: St. Thomas More Parish in Sarasota, Inc.
Catechesis Religious Program—Sr. Judy Baldino, S.S.J., D.R.E. Students 225.

SEBRING, HIGHLANDS CO., ST. CATHERINE (1929) [JC]
Mailing Address: 882 Bay St., Sebring, 33870.
Tel: 863-385-0049; Fax: 863-385-5169; Email: office@stcathe.com; Web: www.stcathe.com. 820 Hickory St., Sebring, 33870. Very Rev. Jose Antonio Gonzalez, V.F.; Rev. Pawel Kawalec; Deacon Max Severe
Legal Title: St. Catherine Parish in Sebring, Inc.
Res.: 862 Bay St., Sebring, 33870.
School—St. Catherine School (2008) (Grades PreK-7), 2835 Kenilworth Blvd., Sebring, 33870.
Tel: 863-385-7300; Fax: 863-385-7310; Email: school@stcathe.com; Web: www.stcatheschool.org. Lay Teachers 24; Students 198.
Catechesis Religious Program—872 Hickory St., Sebring, 33870. Email: rlazo@stcathe.com. Rebecca Lazo, D.R.E. Students 200.

WAUCHULA, HARDEE CO., ST. MICHAEL (1969) (Spanish—Creole)
408 Heard Bridge Rd., Wauchula, 33873.
Tel: 863-773-4089, Ext. 1; Email: michaelwauc@gmail.com. Rev. Timothy Van Zee
Legal Title: St. Michael Parish in Wauchula, Inc.
Catechesis Religious Program—Students 581.
Missions—Holy Child Mission—4315 Chester Ave., Bowling Green, Hardee Co. 33834.
San Alfonso Mission, 3027 Schoolhouse Rd., Zolfo Springs, Hardee Co. 33890.

Military Chaplains:
Very Rev.—
Cannon, Col. Robert R., J.C.L., Chancellor, Archdiocese of the Military
Revs.—
Kelly, Thomas N.
Sikorski, Leszek, Chap., U.S. Navy.

On Administrative Leave:
Revs.—
Senk, Christopher
Ssekiranda, Remigious.

On Leave:
Very Rev.—
Ludden, John J.
Revs.—
Grady, Matthew
Martin, Vincent
Menzies, Scott
Ortez, Sofonias
Ruggerio, Russell.

Retired:
Rev. Msgrs.—
La Femina, Anthony A., S.T.L., J.C.D., (Retired)
Mouch, Frank M., (Retired)
Stearns, Joseph E., (Retired)
Revs.—
Arle, David, (Retired)
Brubaker, Claude, (Retired)
Ellis, John H.R., (Retired)
Feliz, Normando, (Retired)
Flemming, James K., (Retired)
Gioeli, Leonard, (Retired)
Glackin, Thomas J., (Retired)
Grogan, Gerald P., (Retired)
Henry, Donald H., (Retired)
Lobato, Nicanor, (Retired)
Malarz, Andrew, (Retired)
Mattingly, Robert B., (Retired)
McCarthy, Eugene, (Retired)
McLaughlin, Paul F., (Retired)
Mullen, Michael, (Retired)
Murphy, Timothy, (Retired)
O'Connell, William, (Retired)
Pick, Edward, V.F., (Retired)
Rourke, John, (Retired)
Ryan, Eugene, (Retired)
Sheehy, Vincent J., (Retired)
Sullivan, Kevin, (Retired)
Zebrowski, Arnold, (Retired).

Permanent Deacons:
Allison, Joseph
Arnold, Maurice, (Retired)
Beck, Stephen
Brenner, Harold
Caliguire, Thomas
Camacho, Francis, (Retired)
Cassidy, William
Esper, Michael
Fullen, Peter
Gaitens, John Robert
Gibbons, Edison
Godlewsky, Robert
Grant, Thomas
Hanks, James
Healy, M. Donald
Ladroga, William, Dir., Diaconate Formation
Landron, Roberto
Lundy, Edward, (Retired)
Lyons, Raymond
Macaulay, Patrick C., (Retired)
McKenney, Kevin
Mueller, Martin, (Leave of Absence)
Mulvaney, David
Nolan, David W.
Pastore, Leonardo
Readon, David, Dir., Diaconate Personnel
Roca, Epimaco Jr.
Spiro, Richard.

INSTITUTIONS LOCATED IN DIOCESE

[A] COLLEGES AND UNIVERSITIES

AVE MARIA. *Ave Maria University*, Ave Maria University, 5050 Ave Maria Blvd., Ave Maria, 34142-9505. Tel: 239-280-2511; Tel: 877-283-8648; Fax: 239-352-2392; Email: webmail@avemaria.edu; Web: www.avemaria.edu. H. James Towey, Pres. Catholic University. Clergy 19; Students 1,100.

[B] HIGH SCHOOLS

FORT MYERS. *Bishop Verot Catholic High School* (1962) 5598 Sunrise Dr., Fort Myers, 33919.
Tel: 239-274-6700; Fax: 239-274-6798; Email: information@bvhs.org; Web: www.bvhs.org. Dr. Denny Denison, Prin.; Rev. Casey Jones, Chap. Lay Teachers 55; Students 685; Total Staff 80; Clergy/Religious Teachers 1.

NAPLES. **St. John Neumann Catholic High School, Inc.* (1985) 3000 53rd St., S.W., Naples, 34116.
Tel: 239-455-3044; Fax: 239-455-2966; Email: proche@sjnceltics.org; Web: www.sjnceltics.org. Sr. Patricia Roche, F.M.A, Prin.; Jam Stryffeler, Admin.; Mrs. Stephanie Sweeney, Admin.; Rev. Michael Orsi, Chap. Lay Teachers 30; Religious 3; Students 241; Total Staff 43.

SARASOTA. *Cardinal Mooney Catholic High School, Inc.*, 4171 Fruitville Rd., Sarasota, 34232.
Tel: 941-371-4917; Fax: 941-371-6924; Email: toneill@cmhs-sarasota.org; Web: www.cmhs-sarasota.org. Mr. Ben Hopper, Prin.; Rev. Eric Scanlan, Chap. Lay Teachers 32; Priests 1; Students 490; Total Staff 58; Clergy/Religious Teachers 4.

[C] PRIVATE SCHOOLS

NAPLES. **Royal Palm Academy* (2008) 16100 Livingston Rd., Naples, 34110. Tel: 239-594-9888; Fax: 239-594-9893; Email: sbaier@royalpalmacademy.com; Web: www.royalpalmacademy.com. Mr. Scott Baier, Prin. Lay Teachers 31; Students 268; Total Staff 46.

[D] SCHOOLS FOR SPECIAL NEEDS

SARASOTA. *St. Mary Academy*, (Grades PreK-8), Sarasota Campus, 4380 Fruitville Rd., Sarasota, 34232-1623. Tel: 941-366-4010; Fax: 941-366-3819; Email: rreynolds@stmarysarasota.org; Web: www.stmarysarasota.org. Rebecca Reynolds, Prin.; Sandra Julian, Librarian. Lay Teachers 9; Students 65.

[E] SCHOOLS FOR THEOLOGICAL, SPIRITUAL, PASTORAL AND PERSONAL FORMATION

ARCADIA. *Institute for Catholic Studies and Formation, Inc.* (1995) 10299 S.W. Peace River St., Arcadia, 34269-4068. Tel: 941-766-7334; Fax: 941-629-8555; Email: institute@institute-dov.org; Web: institute-dov.org. Dr. David Glasow, Dir.; Mrs. Kathryn DeNinno, Registrar/IT Admin.; Mrs. Cindy Crane, Business Mgr. Lay Teachers 2; Students 20; Total Staff 4.

[F] RESIDENCES FOR THE AGED

VENICE. *St. John II Housing, Inc.*, 1000 Pinebrook Rd., 34285. Tel: 941-488-5581; Email: rombalski@dioceseofvenice.org; Email: pereira@dioceseofvenice.org. Ms. Philomena A. Pereira, CEO.

St. Mark's Housing of Venice, Inc. dba Villa San Marco, 1030 Albee Farm Rd., 34285.
Tel: 941-483-1960; Fax: 941-483-3934; Email: Yajairad@spm.net. Very Rev. John Costello, Pres. Total in Residence 80; Total Staff 5.

FORT MYERS. *St. John XXIII Housing, Inc.*, 13251 Apaloosa Ln., Fort Myers, 33912.
Tel: 239-561-3535; Fax: 239-561-3536; Email: yajairad@spm.net. Rev. Robert D. Tabbert, Pres. Total in Residence 68; Total Staff 3.

Villa Francisco (1984) 2140 Cottage St., Fort Myers, 33901. Tel: 239-332-3229; Fax: 239-332-3229; Email: Anthony.Hewitt@stfrancisfm.org. Rev. Anthony Hewitt, J.C.L., Pres. Total in Residence 58; Total Staff 1.

St. Vincent de Paul Housing, Inc. aka Villa Vincente, 13071 Palm Beach Blvd., Fort Myers, 33905.
Tel: 239-693-1333; Fax: 239-693-1329; Email: Yajairad@spm.net. Dr. Volodymyr Smeryk, M.A., M.B.A., J.C.D., J.D., Pres. Total in Residence 65; Total Staff 3.

PALMETTO. *Holy Cross Manor, Inc.*, 510 26th St. W., Palmetto, 34221-5426. Tel: 941-729-2063;
Fax: 941-729-2386; Email: rhondas@spm.net. Rev. Bernard P. Evanofski, Pres. Total in Residence 68; Total Staff 4.

Holy Cross Manor II, Inc., 540 26th St. W., Palmetto, 34221-5425. Tel: 941-729-2111; Fax: 941-722-3803; Email: rhondas@spm.net. Rev. Bernard P. Evanofski, Pres. Total in Residence 70; Total Staff 4.

PORT CHARLOTTE. *St. Charles Housing I, Inc.* aka Villa San Carlos, 2550 Easy St., Port Charlotte, 33952.
Tel: 941-624-2266; Fax: 941-624-2283; Email: marlenes@spm.net. Rev. John Fitch, Pres. Total in Residence 50; Total Staff 4.

St. Charles Housing II, Inc. dba Villa San Carlos II, 22250 Vick St., Port Charlotte, 33980-2026.
Tel: 941-624-4404; Fax: 941-624-5556; Email: marlenes@spm.net. Rev. John Fitch, Pres. Residents 53; Total Staff 4.

SARASOTA. *St. Martha's Housing II, Inc.* (Casa Santa Marta II) 800 N. Lemon Ave., Sarasota, 34236.
Tel: 941-365-7913; Fax: 941-365-8887; Email: rhondas@spm.net. Very Rev. Fausto Stampiglia, S.A.C., V.F., Pres. Total in Residence 52; Total Staff 3.

St. Martha's Housing, Inc. (Casa Santa Marta) 1576 8th St., Sarasota, 34236. Tel: 941-366-4448;
Fax: 941-366-2544; Email: rhondas@spm.net. Very Rev. Fausto Stampiglia, S.A.C., V.F., Pres. Total in Residence 78; Total Staff 5.

[G] MONASTERIES AND RESIDENCES OF PRIESTS AND BROTHERS

VENICE. *Xaverian Brothers*, 609 Cornwell on the Gulf, 34285. Tel: 941-484-9641; Email: smeryk@dioceseofvenice.org; Web: www.xaverianbrothers.org. Dr. Volodymyr Smeryk, M.A., M.B.A., J.C.D., J.D., Chancellor. Brothers of St. Francis Xavier Brothers 2.

NOKOMIS. *Carmel at Mission Valley*, 955 Laurel Rd. E., Nokomis, 34275-4507. Tel: 941-412-0678;
Fax: 941-485-5716; Email: mdube@carmelnet.org. Rev. Marcel Dube, O.Carm., Prior. Order of Carmelites Inc. Priests 8.

SARASOTA. *Congregation of the Holy Spirit*, 459 Beach Rd., Sarasota, 34242. Tel: 412-292-0807; Email: smeryk@dioceseofvenice.org. Dr. Volodymyr Smeryk, M.A., M.B.A., J.C.D., J.D., Chancellor.

Holy Cross Florida Regional Center (1973) 1635 4th St., Sarasota, 34236-5007. Email: lskitzki@sbcglobal.net. Dr. Volodymyr Smeryk, M.A., M.B.A., J.C.D., J.D., Chm. Holy Cross Brothers Residence. Total in Residence 1.

[H] CONVENTS AND RESIDENCES FOR SISTERS

FORT MYERS BEACH. *San Damiano Monastery of St. Clare.* (Solemn Vows, Papal Enclosure) 6029 Estero Blvd., Fort Myers Beach, 33931-4325.
Tel: 239-463-5599; Fax: 239-463-4993; Email: saintclare@comcast.net; Web: www.fmbpoorclare.com. Sr. Mary Frances Fortin, O.S.C., Abbess. Poor Clares. Sisters 7; Cloistered Sisters 6.

NAPLES. *Daughters of Mary Help of Christians* (2011) St. Mary Mazzarello Convent, 3000 53rd St., S.W., Naples, 34116. Tel: 239-348-2911; Email: secnaplesmm19@gmail.com; Web: www.salesiansisters.org. Sr. Carmen Pena, F.M.A., Supr. Sisters 3.

[I] RETREAT CENTERS

VENICE. *Our Lady of Perpetual Help Retreat and Spirituality Center, Inc* (1996) 3989 S. Moon Dr., 34292. Tel: 941-486-0233; Fax: 941-486-1524; Email: riley@olph-retreat.org; Web: www.olph-retreat.org. Rev. Sean Morris, O.M.V., Dir.

LAKE PLACID. *Campo San Jose* (1996) 170 S. Sun 'n' Lake Blvd., Lake Placid, 33852. Tel: 863-385-6762; Fax: 863-385-5169; Email: frjose@stcathe.com; Web: www.camposanjose.com. 882 Bay St., Sebring, 33870. Very Rev. Jose Antonio Gonzalez, V.F., Dir.

[J] CATHOLIC CHARITIES

VENICE. *Catholic Charities, Diocese of Venice, Inc.*, 1000 Pinebrook Rd., 34285. Tel: 941-488-5581;
Fax: 941-441-1150; Email: rombalski@dioceseofvenice.org; Email: pereira@dioceseofvenice.org; Web: www.catholiccharitiesdov.org. Ms. Philomena A. Pereira, CEO; Mrs. Sharon Aragona, Exec. Tot Asst. Annually 40,000; Total Staff 116.

Catholic Charities, District I (Sarasota & Manatee Counties) 5055 N. Tamiami Tr., Sarasota, 34234.
Tel: 941-355-4680; Fax: 941-359-8374; Email: jpierse@ccdis1.org; Email: rombalski@dioceseofvenice.org. Joan Pierse, Contact Person; Ms. Philomena A. Pereira, CEO. Tot Asst. Annually 10,000; Total Staff 5.

Catholic Charities, District II (Lee, Henry & Glades Counties) 4235 Michigan Ave. Link, Fort Myers, 33916. Tel: 239-337-4193; Tel: 239-334-4007;
Fax: 239-332-2799; Email: canderson@ccslee.org. Chuck Anderson, Dir.; Ms. Philomena A. Pereira, CEO. Tot Asst. Annually 16,000; Total Staff 25.

African Caribbean American Catholic Center, 3861 Michigan Ave., Fort Myers, 33916.
Tel: 239-461-0233; Tel: 781-484-9543;
Fax: 239-461-0236; Email: aragona@dioceseofvenice.org; Email: rombalski@dioceseofvenice.org. Mrs. Sharon Aragona, Contact Person; Ms. Philomena A. Pereira, CEO. Tot Asst. Annually 175; Total Staff 6.

Catholic Charities, District III (Collier County) 2210 Santa Barbara Blvd., Naples, 34116.
Tel: 239-455-2655; Fax: 239-455-7235; Email: maryshaughnessy@catholiccharitiescc.org; Email: rombalski@dioceseofvenice.org. Mary Shaughnessy, Dir.; Ms. Philomena A. Pereira, CEO. Tot Asst. Annually 20,000; Total Staff 19.

Catholic Charities, Rural Services (Charlotte, De Soto, Hardee & Highland Counties) 1210 E. Oak St., Arcadia, 34266. Tel: 863-494-1068;
Tel: 941-488-5581; Fax: 863-494-1671; Email: charity2@embarqmail.com; Email: ctownsend@embarqmail.com; Email: rombalski@dioceseofvenice.org. Andy Herigodt, Dir. Tot Asst. Annually 5,000; Total Staff 4.

Catholic Charities Housing, Diocese of Venice, Inc., 1000 Pinebrook Rd., 34285. Tel: 941-488-5581;
Fax: 941-484-1150; Email: aragona@dioceseofvenice.org; Email: rombalski@dioceseofvenice.org. Mrs. Sharon Aragona, Dir.; Ms. Philomena A. Pereira, CEO. Tot Asst. Annually 200; Total Staff 2.

Casa San Jose, 3900 17th St., Sarasota, 34235.
Tel: 941-366-1886; Fax: 941-362-9733; Email: cmcmenamin@ccdis1.org; Email: rombalski@dioceseofvenice.org. Ms. Colleen McMenamin, Dir.; Ms. Philomena A. Pereira, CEO. Tot Asst. Annually 44; Total Staff 4.

Casa San Juan Bosco, Inc., 2358 S.E. Arnold Andrews Ave., Arcadia, 34266. Tel: 863-884-2134;
Tel: 863-884-2123; Fax: 863-884-2114; Email: casa@ndcassetmanagement.com; Email: casaleasing@ndcassetmanagement.com; Email: rombalski@dioceseofvenice.org. Mrs. Sharon Aragona, Contact Person; Ms. Philomena A. Pereira, CEO. Tot Asst. Annually 55; Total Staff 3.

Casa San Juan Bosco II, Inc., 2358 S.E. Arnold Andrews Ave., Arcadia, 34266. Tel: 941-488-5581; Tel: 863-884-2123; Tel: 863-884-2134;
Fax: 941-441-1150; Fax: 863-884-2114; Email: casaleasing@ndcassetmanagement.com; Email: casa@ndcassetmanagement.com; Email: rombalski@dioceseofvenice.org. Mrs. Sharon Aragona, Dir.; Ms. Philomena A. Pereira, CEO. Tot Asst. Annually 43; Staff 3.

Marian Manor, Inc., 4200 Lister St., Port Charlotte, 33980. Tel: 941-391-5669; Email: marionmanor@ndcassetmanagement.com; Email: rombalski@dioceseofvenice.org. Barbara Breault, Contact Person; Ms. Philomena A. Pereira, CEO. Tot Asst. Annually 31; Total Staff 3.

Catholic Charities Refugee Programs, 5900 Pan American Blvd., Ste. 202, North Port, 34287.
Tel: 941-564-8738; Fax: 941-876-3913; Email: yk@catholiccharitiesrs.org; Email: rombalski@dioceseofvenice.org. Yuri Kaplun, Dir.; Ms. Philomena A. Pereira, CEO. Tot Asst. Annually 100; Total Staff 3.

Catholic Charities Immigration Programs, 5900 Pan American Blvd., Ste. 203, North Port, 34287.
Tel: 941-876-3164; Fax: 941-876-3913; Email: lacken@ccslee.org; Email: rombalski@dioceseofvenice.org. Lucille Acken, Dir.; Ms. Philomena A. Pereira, CEO. Tot Asst. Annually 1,154; Total Staff 6.

New Paradigm of Catholic Charities, Inc., 2800 Placida Rd., Unit 111, Englewood, 34224.
Tel: 941-681-2194; Fax: 941-828-1460; Email: kathleen@thenpf.org; Email: rombalski@dioceseofvenice.org. Kathleen Nelson, Dir.; Ms. Philomena A. Pereira, CEO. Tot Asst. Annually 12; Total Staff 2.

SARASOTA. *Bethesda House - HIV/AIDS Ministries*, 1670 4th St., Sarasota, 34236. Tel: 941-366-1886;
Fax: 941-362-9733; Email: cmcmenamin@ccdis1.org; Email: rombalski@dioceseofvenice.org; Email: pereira@dioceseofvenice.org. Ms. Colleen McMenamin, Dir. (AIDS Ministry) Tot Asst. Annually 11; Total Staff 4.

Catholic Charities Housing Sarasota, Inc., 1000 Pinebrook Rd., 34285. Tel: 941-488-5581; Email: rombalski@dioceseofvenice.org; Email: pereira@dioceseofvenice.org. Ms. Philomena A. Pereira, Dir.; Mrs. Sharon Aragona, Exec. Tot Asst. Annually 44; Total Staff 3.

St. Monica Residence, 1575 Dr. Martin Luther King Way, Sarasota, 34234. Tel: 941-391-5669;
Tel: 941-488-5581; Fax: 941-391-5679; Email: marianmanor@ndcassetmanagement.com; Email: rombalski@dioceseofvenice.org. Barbara Breault, Contact Person; Ms. Philomena A. Pereira, CEO. Tot Asst. Annually 31; Total Staff 3.

St. Dominic Manor, 1023 Putnam Dr., Sarasota, 34232. Tel: 941-391-5669; Tel: 942-488-5581;
Fax: 941-391-5679; Email:

marianmanor@ndcassetmanagement.com; Email: rombalski@dioceseofvenice.org. Barbara Breault, Dir.; Ms. Philomena A. Pereira, CEO. Tot Asst. Annually 12; Total Staff 3.

[K] FOUNDATIONS

VENICE. *Catholic Community Foundation of Southwest Florida, Inc.*, 1000 Pinebrook Rd., 34285. Tel: 941-441-1124; Fax: 941-484-1121; Email: ccf@dioceseofvenice.org; Web: ccfdioceseofvenice.org/. Michael Morse, Exec.

Catholic Charities Foundation of the Diocese of Venice, Inc., 1000 Pinebrook Rd., 34285. Tel: 941-488-5581; Fax: 941-441-1150; Email: pereira@dioceseofvenice.org; Email: rombalski@dioceseofvenice.org. Ms. Philomena A. Pereira.

SARASOTA. *Cardinal Mooney High School Foundation*, 4171 Fruitville Rd., Sarasota, 34232. Tel: 941-371-4917; Fax: 941-371-6924; Email: slockbower@dioceseofvenice.org; Web: www.cmhs-sarasota.org. Dr. Volodymyr Smeryk, M.A., M.B.A., J.C.D., J.D., Chancellor.

Incarnation School Foundation, 2911 Bee Ridge Rd., Sarasota, 34239. Tel: 941-924-8588; Fax: 941-925-1248; Email: ccurlett@incarnationschool.edu; Web: www.incarnationschool.edu. Mrs. Coleen Curlett, Prin.

St. Martha School Foundation, 4380 Fruitville Rd., Sarasota, 34232. Tel: 941-954-8434; Email: kmarshall@stmarthaschool.net; Web: www.stmarthaschool.net. Very Rev. Fausto Stampiglia, S.A.C., V.F., Pastor.

[L] MISCELLANEOUS LISTINGS

VENICE. *All Saints Catholic Cemetery Inc.*, 1000 Pinebrook Rd., 34285. Tel: 941-484-9543; Email: finance@dioceseofvenice.org. Mr. Peter McPartland, CPA, C.D.F.M., Treas.

Diocese of Venice in Florida, Inc., 1000 Pinebrook Rd., 34284. Tel: 941-484-9543; Email: slockbower@dioceseofvenice.org. Dr. Volodymyr Smeryk, M.A., M.B.A., J.C.D., J.D., Contact Person.

Diocese of Venice Savings and Loan Trust Fund, 1000 Pinebrook Rd., 34285. Tel: 941-484-9543; Email: slockbower@dioceseofvenice.org. Dr. Volodymyr Smeryk, M.A., M.B.A., J.C.D., J.D., Contact Person.

Trinity Enterprise Holdings, Inc., 1000 Pinebrook Rd., 34284. Tel: 941-484-9543; Email: smeryk@dioceseofvenice.org. Dr. Volodymyr Smeryk, M.A., M.B.A., J.C.D., J.D., Contact Person.

Trinity Trust, 1000 Pinebrook Rd., 34284. Tel: 941-484-9543; Email: slockbower@dioceseofvenice.org. Dr. Volodymyr Smeryk, M.A., M.B.A., J.C.D., J.D., Contact Person.

FORT MYERS. *Magnificat-Ft. Myers, FL-Mother of Mercy Chapter of the Diocese of Venice*, 5549 Boynton Ln., Fort Myers, 33919. Tel: 239-333-0437 ; Fax: 239-933-0437; Email: margaretrose205@comcast.net. Margaret R. Adams, Contact Person & Coord.

NAPLES. *Hope for Haiti, Inc.*, 1021 5th Ave. N., Naples, 34102. Tel: 239-434-7183; Email: info@hopeforhaiti.com; Web: www.hopeforhaiti.com. JoAnne Kuehner, Founder & Chair.

SARASOTA. *Christ Child Society of Sarasota, Inc.*, 8859 Bloomfield Blvd., Sarasota, 34238. Tel: 941-484-9543; Email: jdeangelostyle@aol.com; Web: www.nationalchristchildsoc.org. Rosann Yanis, Pres. Local affiliate of national non-profit organization whose member-volunteers serve needy children.

RELIGIOUS INSTITUTES OF MEN REPRESENTED IN THE DIOCESE

For further details refer to the corresponding bracketed number in the Religious Institutes of Men or Women section.

[1350]—*Brothers of St. Francis Xavier*—C.F.X.
[]—*Brothers of the Catholic Apostolate*—S.A.C.
[0600]—*Brothers of the Congregation of Holy Cross*—C.S.C.
[0470]—*Capuchin Friars*—O.F.M.Cap.
[0270]—*Carmelite Fathers*—O.Carm.
[]—*Congregation of the Mother of the Redeemer*—C.R.M.
[]—*Congregation of the Oratory of St. Philip Neri*—C.O.
[]—*Congregation of the Resurrection*—C.R.
[]—*Institute of the Incarnate Word*—I.V.E.
[]—*Missionaries of Compassion*—M.O.C.
[1210]—*Missionaries of St. Charles Scalabrians*—C.S.
[0920]—*Oblates of St. Francis de Sales*—O.S.F.S.
[0940]—*Oblates of the Virgin Mary*—O.M.V.
[1065]—*Priestly Fraternity of St. Peter*—F.S.S.P.
[0990]—*Society of the Catholic Apostolate*—S.A.C.
[0560]—*Third Order Regular of St. Francis*—T.O.R.

RELIGIOUS INSTITUTES OF WOMEN REPRESENTED IN THE DIOCESE

[1070-15]—*Congregation of St. Dominic (Sisters of St. Dominic of Blauvelt, NY)*—O.P.
[3832]—*Congregation of the Sisters of St. Joseph*—C.S.J.
[1105]—*Dominican Sisters of Hope*—O.P.
[]—*Franciscan Sisters of Mary Immaculate*—F.M.I.
[]—*Maryknoll Missionaries of St. Dominic*—M.M.
[]—*Missionaries Daughters of Our Blessed Lady of the Light, Yucatan, Mexico*—M.H.M.L.
[2800]—*Missionary Sisters of the Most Sacred Heart of Jesus of Hilltrup*—M.S.C.
[3760]—*Order of St. Clare*—O.S.C.
[3465]—*Religious of the Sacred Heart of Mary* (Eastern North American Province)—R.S.H.M.
[]—*Salesian Sisters*—F.M.A.
[2970]—*School Sisters of Notre Dame* (St. Louis Prov. & Baltimore Prov.)—S.S.N.D.
[]—*Servants of the Lord and the Virgin of Matara*—S.S.V.M.
[0590]—*Sisters of Charity of St. Elizabeth, Convent Station*—S.C.
[0430]—*Sisters of Charity of the Blessed Virgin Mary*—B.V.M.
[]—*Sisters for Christian Community*—S.F.C.C.
[2575]—*Sisters of Mercy of the Americas* (New Jersey Prov.)—R.S.M.
[2549]—*Sisters of Mercy, Co. Sligo, Ireland*—R.S.M.
[3360]—*Sisters of Providence of St. Mary-of-the-Woods, IN*—S.P.
[]—*Sisters of St. Joseph of Chestnut Hill, Philadelphia*—S.S.J.
[1990]—*Sisters of the Holy Name of Jesus and Mary*—S.N.J.M.

NECROLOGY

† Baier, Donald, (Retired), Died Sep. 27, 2018
† Soy, Esteban, (Retired), Died Jul. 10, 2018

Diocese of Victoria in Texas

(Dioecesis Victoriensis in Texia)

Most Reverend

BRENDAN J. CAHILL, S.T.D.

Bishop of Victoria; ordained May 19, 1990; appointed Third Bishop of Victoria in Texas April 23, 2015; consecrated and installed June 29, 2015. *Mailing Address: P.O. Box 4070, Victoria, TX 77903.*

Chancery Office: P.O. Box 4070, Victoria, TX 77903. Tel: 361-573-0828; Fax: 361-573-5725.

Most Reverend

DAVID E. FELLHAUER, PH.D., J.C.D.

Retired Bishop of Victoria; ordained May 29, 1965; appointed Second Bishop of Victoria in Texas April 7, 1990; consecrated and installed May 28, 1990; retired April 23, 2015. *Mailing Address: P.O. Box 4070, Victoria, TX 77903.*

ESTABLISHED AND CREATED A DIOCESE, MAY 29, 1982.

Square Miles 9,609.

Comprises the Counties of Calhoun, DeWitt, Goliad, Jackson, Lavaca, Matagorda, Victoria, Wharton and Colorado; also Fayette County west of the Colorado River in the State of Texas.

Legal Title: Diocese of Victoria in Texas.
For legal titles of parishes and diocesan institutions, consult the Chancery Office.

STATISTICAL OVERVIEW

Personnel	
Bishop	1
Retired Bishops	1
Priests: Diocesan Active in Diocese	42
Priests: Retired, Sick or Absent	8
Number of Diocesan Priests	50
Religious Priests in Diocese	1
Total Priests in Diocese	51
Extern Priests in Diocese	9
Permanent Deacons in Diocese	35
Total Sisters	63
Parishes	
Parishes	50
With Resident Pastor:	
Resident Diocesan Priests	33
Without Resident Pastor:	
Administered by Priests	12
Missions	17
Professional Ministry Personnel:	
Lay Ministers	29
Educational	
Diocesan Students in Other Seminaries	14
Total Seminarians	14
High Schools, Diocesan and Parish	2
Total Students	181
High Schools, Private	1
Total Students	307
Elementary Schools, Diocesan and Parish	11
Total Students	1,970
Elementary Schools, Private	1
Total Students	322
Catechesis/Religious Education:	
High School Students	2,393
Elementary Students	5,023
Total Students under Catholic Instruction	10,210
Teachers in the Diocese:	
Sisters	11
Lay Teachers	283
Vital Statistics	
Receptions into the Church:	
Infant Baptism Totals	1,044
Minor Baptism Totals	126
Adult Baptism Totals	73
Received into Full Communion	66
First Communions	1,108
Confirmations	866
Marriages:	
Catholic	256
Interfaith	56
Total Marriages	312
Deaths	994
Total Catholic Population	73,249
Total Population	293,729

Former Bishops—Most Revs. CHARLES V. GRAHMANN, D.D., ord. March 17, 1956; appt. Titular Bishop of Equilio and Auxiliary of San Antonio, June 30, 1981; cons. Aug. 29, 1981; appt. First Bishop of Victoria, April 14, 1982; installed May 29, 1982; appt. Coadjutor of Dallas, Dec. 18, 1989; succeeded to See, July 14, 1990; retired March 6, 2007; died Aug. 14, 2018.; DAVID E. FELLHAUER, J.C.D., ord. May 29, 1965; appt. Second Bishop of Victoria in Texas April 7, 1990; cons. and installed May 28, 1990; retired April 23, 2015.

Chancery Office—1505 E. Mesquite Ln., Victoria, 77901. Mailing Address: P.O. Box 4070, Victoria, 77903. Tel: 361-573-0828; Fax: 361-573-5725. Office Hours: Mon.-Fri. 8:30-4:30.

Office of Vicars General—1505 E. Mesquite Ln., Victoria, 77901. Tel: 361-573-0828; Fax: 361-827-7176. *Mailing Address: P.O. Box 4070, Victoria, 77903.* Very Rev. GARY W. JANAK, J.C.L., M.Ed., L.P.C.; Rev. Msgr. JOHN C. PETERS, V.G., Vicar for Clergy.

Office of the Chancellor—Very Rev. GARY W. JANAK, J.C.L., M.Ed., L.P.C., Mailing Address: P.O. Box 4070, Victoria, 77903. 1505 E. Mesquite Ln., Victoria, 77901. Tel: 361-573-0828, Ext. 14; Fax: 361-827-7176; Email: chancellor@victoriadiocese.org.

Office of Vicar for Religious—Sr. M. STEPHANA MARBACH, I.W.B.S., Mailing Address: Incarnate Word and Blessed Sacrament Sisters, 1101 N.E. Water St., Victoria, 77901. Tel: 361-575-2266; Email: srstephana@yahoo.com.

Diocesan Consultors—Rev. Msgr. JOHN C. PETERS, V.G.; Very Revs. GARY W. JANAK, J.C.L., M.Ed., L.P.C., Vicar Gen./Chancellor; SAMUEL APPIASI, V.F.; CHARLES E. OTSIWAH, V.F.; MICHAEL ROTHER, V.F.; GREGORY E. KORENEK, V.F.; MATTHEW H. HUEHLEFELD, J.C.L., V.F.; TIMOTHY KOSLER, V.F.

Consultors for Pastors—Very Revs. SAMUEL APPIASI, V.F.; GREGORY E. KORENEK, V.F.; Revs. EDWARD J. WINKLER; CLEMENT QUAINOO; WAYNE N. FLAGG; KIRBY HLAVATY.

Vicars Forane—Victoria Deanery: Very Rev. SAMUEL APPIASI, V.F., St. Patrick Catholic Church, P.O. Box 2122, Bloomington, 779951. Tel: 361-897-1155; Fax: 361-897-1064; Email: saintpatricks@tisd.net; Web: www.saintpatrickschurch.net. Cuero Deanery: Very Rev. CHARLES E. OTSIWAH, V.F., Immaculate Conception Catholic Church, 238 N. Commercial St., Goliad, 77963. Tel: 361-645-3095; Fax: 361-645-3097; Email: pastor@goliadcatholic.org; Web: www.goliadcatholic.org. Edna Deanery: Very Rev. GREG KORENEK, V.F., Holy Cross Catholic Church, 2001 Katy Ave., Bay City, 77414. Tel: 979-245-6379; Fax: 979-244-5481; Email: hc3_office@holycrossbaycity.org; Web: www.holycrossbaycity.org. El Campo Deanery: Very Rev. MICHAEL ROTHER, V.F., St. Philip the Apostle Catholic Church, 304 W. Church St., El Campo, 77437-3317. Tel: 979-543-3770; Fax: 979-578-8831; Email: pastor@stphilipapostle.org; Web: stphilipapostle.org. Hallettsville Deanery: Very Rev. MATTHEW H. HUEHLEFELD, J.C.L., V.F., St. Joseph Catholic Church, 210 Schrimscher St., P.O. Box 734, Yoakum, 77995. Tel: 361-293-3518; Fax: 361-293-5355; Email: pastor@stjcatholicchurch.com; Web: www.stjcatholicchurch.com. Schulenburg Deanery: Very Rev. TIMOTHY KOSLER, V.F., St. Rose of Lima Catholic Church, 1010 Lyons Ave., P.O. Box 310, Schulenburg, 78956. Tel: 979-743-3117; Fax: 979-743-4712; Email: strosecc@verizon.net.

Presbyteral Council—Rev. Msgr. JOHN C. PETERS, V.G., Consultor; Very Revs. GARY W. JANAK, J.C.L., M.Ed., L.P.C., Vicar Gen./Chancellor & Consultor; GREGORY E. KORENEK, V.F., Consultor Dean; MATTHEW H. HUEHLEFELD, J.C.L., V.F., Consultor Dean; SAMUEL APPIASI, V.F., Consultor Dean; CHARLES E. OTSIWAH, V.F., Consultor Dean; TIMOTHY KOSLER, V.F., Consultor Dean; MICHAEL ROTHER, V.F., Consultor Dean; Revs. SCOTT J. HILL, Edna Deanery Rep.; JASPER LIGGIO, Cuero Deanery Rep.; ROBERT E. KNIPPENBERG, El Campo Deanery Rep.; MICHAEL LYONS, Schulenburg Deanery Rep.; BRYAN HEYER, Hallettsville Deanery Rep.; GABRIEL BENTIL, Victoria Deanery Rep.; GABRIEL D. ESPINOSA, Bishop Appointee; TOMMY CHEN, Bishop Appointee.

Diocesan Tribunal—Very Rev. MATTHEW H. HUEHLEFELD, J.C.L., V.F., 1505 E. Mesquite Ln., Victoria, 77901. Tel: 361-573-0760; Fax: 361-827-7176; Email: judicialvicar@victoriadiocese.org. P.O. Box 4070, Victoria, 77903.

Judicial Vicar—Very Rev. MATTHEW H. HUEHLEFELD, J.C.L., V.F.

Judges—Very Revs. GARY W. JANAK, J.C.L., M.Ed., L.P.C., Vicar Gen./Chancellor; GREGORY E. KORENEK, V.F.

Promoter of Justice—Rev. GABRIEL MAISON, J.C.D.

Procurator Advocate—Very Revs. SAMUEL APPIASI, V.F.; MICHAEL ROTHER, V.F.

Defenders of the Bond—Very Rev. TIMOTHY KOSLER, V.F.; Rev. ROBERT E. KNIPPENBERG.

Auditors—Revs. SCOTT J. HILL; PHILIP BRUNE.

Notaries—MRS. SHERRY KAINER; Sr. ROSARIO RESENDEZ.

Priests' Personnel Board—Very Rev. GARY W. JANAK, J.C.L., M.Ed., L.P.C., Vicar Gen./Chancellor; Rev.

Msgr. JOHN C. PETERS, V.G.; Very Revs. CHARLES E. OTSIWAH, V.F.; SAMUEL APPIASI, V.F.; GREGORY E. KORENEK, V.F.; TIMOTHY KOSLER, V.F.; MATTHEW H. HUEHLEFELD, J.C.L., V.F.; MICHAEL ROTHER, V.F.

Priests' Pension Board—Very Rev. GREGORY E. KORENEK, V.F.; Revs. ROGER HAWES; KIRBY HLAVATY; MICHAEL PETERING; EDWARD J. WINKLER.

Lay Pension Board—MR. JOHN MCQUILLEN, Chm.; MR. BILLY MACHA; MR. KENNY FRENCH; MR. HARDY MCCULLOUGH; MR. ROBERT COFFEY.

Building Board—Most Rev. BRENDAN J. CAHILL; MR. TONY MARTINEZ; MR. JOHN GEHRKE; MR. ED MARTINKA, Chair; MR. JAMES MIORI; MR. BRAD KOCUREK; MR. BILL JOHNSTON.

School Board - Diocesan School Advisory Council (DSAC)—DR. JOHN QUARY, Supt. Schools.

Members—DEBRA ROEDER; ALISON KORELL; JULIA BOEHME; MRS. MELISSA SALINAS; SARITA VILLAFRANCA RICHMOND; MRS. THERESA DENT; Most Rev. BRENDAN J. CAHILL; MR. TONY MARTINEZ; DAVID SCHMIDT; ROSHANDA THOMAS; CORINNE COPELAND; Rev. Msgr. JOHN C. PETERS, V.G.; Sr. EVELYN KORENEK, I.W.B.S.; Rev. GABRIEL ODURO TAWIAH; MR. THOMAS MAJ.

Office of Business and Finance—MR. TONY MARTINEZ, CFO, Tel: 361-573-0828, Ext. 2268; Email: tmartinez@victoriadiocese.org; MR. RENE GARCIA, Tel: 361-573-0828, Ext. 2220; Email: rgarcia@victoriadiocese.org; MRS. ZOILA SHOEMAKE, Tel: 361-573-0828, Ext. 2229; Email: zshoemake@victoriadiocese.org; MRS. JERI JOSEPH, Mailing Address: P.O. Box 4070, Victoria, 77903. Tel: 361-573-0828, Ext. 2219; Email: jjoseph@victoriadiocese.org.

Office of Human Resources—MRS. MELISSA SALINAS, Dir., Mailing Address: P.O. Box 4070, Victoria, 77903. Tel: 361-573-0828, Ext. 2252; Tel: 361-827-7177 (Direct Line); Email: msalinas@victoriadiocese.org; MRS. ANGELA MARTINEZ, Front Desk Receptionist, Email: amartinez@victoriadiocese.org; MRS. BRENDA MORALES, Chancery Administrative Asst., Email: bmorales@victoriadiocese.org.

Campaign for Human Development and Catholic Relief Services—MRS. DEBBIE VANELLI, Dir., Holy Family JMJ Catholic Church, 704 Mallette Dr., Victoria, 77904. Tel: 361-573-5304; Fax: 361-573-6053; Email: dkvanelli@gmail.com; Web: www.hfccvic.org.

Office of Catholic Youth and Young Adult Ministry—Mailing Address: P.O. Box 4070, Victoria, 77903. MS. WENDY EGGERT, Dir., Tel: 361-573-0828, Ext. 2232; Email: weggert@victoriadiocese.org; MRS. SHANNON THOMAS, Assoc. Dir., Tel: 361-573-0828, Ext. 2250; Email: sthomas@victoriadiocese.org.

Catholic Outreach Prison Ministry—Catholic Community of Cuero, 309 E. Church St., Cuero, 77954. Tel: 361-275-3554; Fax: 361-277-3924; Email: stmchurch@sbcglobal.net.

Council of Catholic Women (DCCW)—Rev. MICHAEL PETERING, Mod., St. Agnes Church, 506 N. Allen, Edna, 77957. Tel: 361-782-6171; Fax: 361-782-8827; Email: stagnesedna@sbcglobal.net; MRS. JANICE OHRT, Chm., 2221 FM 237, Victoria, 77905. Tel: 361-575-2056.

Diocesan Cemeteries—GARY RANGNOW, Dir., P.O. Box 4070, Victoria, 77903. Tel: 361-573-0828, Ext. 2233; Fax: 361-573-5725; Email: cemeteries@victoriadiocese.org; Web: www.vccms.org. Administrative Assistant: MRS. ALICE CAPELO, Mailing Address: P.O. Box 4070, Victoria, 77903. Tel: 361-573-0828, Ext. 2233; Email: cemeteries@victoriadiocese.org; Web: www.vccms.org.

Diocesan Finance Board—Mailing Address: P.O. Box 4070, Victoria, 77903. Most Rev. BRENDAN J. CAHILL; MR. TONY MARTINEZ, CFO, Tel: 361-573-0828, Ext. 2268; Email: tmartinez@victoriadiocese.org; MRS. BEATRIZ GONZALEZ; MR. JOHN HALL; Very Rev. GARY W. JANAK, J.C.L., M.Ed., L.P.C., Vicar Gen./Chancellor; Deacon DENNIS KUTACH; MR. HARDY MCCULLOUGH; Rev. Msgr. JOHN C. PETERS, V.G.; MR. ROMAN SHIMEK; MR. JOHN STEVENSON; MR. GLENN VILLAFRANCA; MR. MARK WESTERMAN; MR. JOHN ZACEK.

Diocesan Services Appeal—MR. RENE GARCIA, DSA Capital Campaign, Lay & Priest Pension, 1505 E. Mesquite Ln., P.O. Box 4070, Victoria, 77901. Tel: 361-573-0828, Ext. 2220.

Spiritual Renewal Center - Retreat Center—718 Gussie Schmidt Rd., Victoria, 77905-4303. Tel: 361-572-0836, Ext. 3221; Fax: 361-572-0816; Email: renewalcenter@victoriadiocese.org. Deacon JOSE (JOE) DUPLAN, Tel: 361-572-0836, Ext. 3221; Email: jduplan@victoriadiocese.org; MS. JULIA AMADOR, Asst. Mgr. & Exec. Cook, 718 Gussie Schmidt Rd., Victoria, 77905-4303. Tel: 361-827-7155, Ext. 3223; Tel: 361-827-7154 (Kitchen); Email: jamador@victoriadiocese.org.

Ecumenical Commission—VACANT.

The Emmaus Center - Counseling in the Catholic Tradition—Mailing Address: 1508 E. Airline, La Victoria, 77901. Tel: 361-212-0830. Very Rev. GARY W. JANAK, J.C.L., M.Ed., L.P.C., Exec. Dir.; MRS. ANNIE COFFEY, M.Ed., L.P.C.-S., Dir. Clinical Svcs., Email: acoffey@victoriadiocese.org.

Presidio La Bahia—(located one mile South of Goliad). A National Historic Landmark, the only Spanish fort remaining in possession of the Catholic Church in North America. The Presidio houses a museum and a visitor center and offers a tour program available to groups. MR. SCOTT MCMAHON, Dir., Mailing Address: P.O. Box 57, Goliad, 77963. Tel: 361-645-3752; Fax: 361-645-1706; Email: smcmahon.presidiolabahia@gmail.com; Web: www.presidiolabahia.org.

Liturgical Commission—MRS. CYNTHIA GOERIG, Tel: 979-543-5706.

Office of Catholic Schools—DR. JOHN QUARY, Supt., Tel: 361-573-0828, Ext. 2221; Email: jquary@victoriadiocese.org; MRS. JANIE CARRALES, Administrative Asst., Mailing Address: P.O. Box 4070, Victoria, 77903. Tel: 361-573-0828, Ext. 2213; Email: jcarrales@victoriadiocese.org.

Permanent Diaconate Formation—Deacon CHARLES J. GLYNN, Dir., 2668 Zimmerscheidt Rd., Alleyton, 78935. Tel: 979-253-9616; Email: cglynn@victoriadiocese.org.

Diaconate Ministry and Life—Deacons DENNIS KUTACH, Dir., Tel: 361-741-2657; Email: deacon@stjcatholicchurch.com; LEO SHARRON, Pres., Deacon's Council, Tel: 361-648-1634; Email: dcnsharron@victoriadiocese.org.

Missionary Childhood AssociationVery Rev. GARY W. JANAK, J.C.L., M.Ed., L.P.C., Vicar Gen./ Chancellor.

Mission Cooperative Plan—Very Rev. GARY W. JANAK, J.C.L., M.Ed., L.P.C., Vicar Gen./ Chancellor, Mailing Address: Diocese of Victoria, P.O. Box 4070, Victoria, 77903. Office of the Chancellor, 1505 E. Mesquite Ln., Victoria, 77901. Tel: 361-573-0828, Ext. 2214.

Office of Catechetical Ministry—MRS. CHRISTELLA ALVAREZ, Dir., Tel: 361-573-0828, Ext. 2225; Tel: 361-827-7171 (Direct Line); Fax: 361-573-5725; Email: calvarez@victoriadiocese.org; MS. BRUNILDA ORTIZ, Administrative Asst., Tel: 361-573-0828, Ext. 2224; Email: catecheticalsec@victoriadiocese.org; Email: pisecretary@victoriadiocese.org.

Respect Life-Pro Life—Rev. JASPER LIGGIO, St. Michael Catholic Church, 309 E. Church, Cuero, 77954-2906. Email: stmchurch@sbcglobal.net.

Scouting—MR. DAVE KOUBA, Eagle Court, Catholic Committee on Scouting - District Advancement, Recording & Recognition Chm., Tel: 361-575-6693; Email: dkouba@suddenlink.net.

Office of Communications/"The Catholic Lighthouse"—MS. SARITA VILLAFRANCA RICHMOND, Editor, Tel: 361-573-0828, Ext. 2231; Email: srichmond@victoriadiocese.org; MRS. REGINA MATUS JANAK, Production & Advertising Asst., 1505 E. Mesquite Ln., Victoria, 77901. Tel: 361-573-0828, Ext. 2230; Email: janakr@victoriadiocese.org. Mailing Address: P.O. Box 4070, Victoria, 77903. Email: lighthouse@victoriadiocese.org.

Office of Safe Environment—1505 E. Mesquite Ln., Victoria, 77903. MRS. MELISSA PERALES, Dir., Tel: 361-573-0828, Ext. 2249; Email: mperales@victoriadiocese.org; MRS. VICKI PYATT, L.M.S.W., Assoc. Dir., Tel: 361-573-0828, Ext. 2222; Email: vpyatt@victoriadiocese.org; MRS. PAULINE CASTANEDA, Safe Environment Prog. Asst., Tel: 361-573-0828, Ext. 2243; Email: pcastaneda@victoriadiocese.org; MS. RUBY RUIZ, Safe Environment Prog. Asst., Tel: 361-573-0828, Ext. 2270; Email: rruiz@victoriadiocese.org.

Vietnamese Apostolate—Rev. DOMINIC TRUNG NGUYEN, St. Anthony Church, P.O. Box 900, Palacios, 77465. Tel: 361-972-2446; Fax: 361-972-2606; Email: dtnguyenscr@yahoo.com.

Office of Vocations—Revs. TOMMY CHEN, Dir., Tel: 361-552-6140; Email: tchen@victoriadiocese.org; Web: www.victoriavocations.org; KRISTOPHER L. FUCHS, Assoc. Dir., Tel: 361-575-4741; Email: frkristopher@olvcathedral.org; Deacon CHARLES J. GLYNN, Assoc. Dir., Tel: 979-253-9616; Email: cglynn@victoriadiocese.org.

Director of Seminarians—Rev. TOMMY CHEN, Mailing Address: Our Lady of the Gulf Catholic Church, 415 W. Austin St., Port Lavaca, 77979. Tel: 361-552-6140; Email: tchen@victoriadiocese.org; Web: www.victoriavocations.org.

Pastoral Care and Outreach—Mailing Address: P.O. Box 4070, Victoria, 77903. Tel: 361-827-7186; Email: pastoralcare@victoriadiocese.org. *1505 E. Mesquite Ln., Victoria, 77901.* MRS. VICKI PYATT, L.M.S.W., Coord.

CLERGY, PARISHES, MISSIONS AND PAROCHIAL SCHOOLS

CITY OF VICTORIA

(VICTORIA COUNTY)

1—THE CATHEDRAL OF OUR LADY OF VICTORY (1957)
Mailing Address: 1309 E. Mesquite Ln., 77901.
Tel: 361-575-4741; Fax: 361-573-5555; Email: pbena@olvcathedral.org; Web: www.olvcathedral.org. Very Rev. Gary W. Janak, J.C.L., M.Ed., L.P.C.; Rev. Kristopher L. Fuchs, Parochial Vicar; Glenn Hunter, Music Min.; Jennifer Vincent, Pastoral Assoc.
School—Our Lady of Victory Cathedral School, (Grades PreK-8), Tel: 361-575-5391; Email: srlaura@ourladyvictory.org; Web: www.ourladyvictory.org. Sr. Laura Toman, I.W.B.S., Prin. Clergy 2; Lay Teachers 31; Students 457.
Catechesis Religious Program—Tel: 361-575-8132; Email: ourladyofvictory.ccd@gmail.com. Betty Mitchell, D.R.E.; Sr. Donna Bonorden, RCIA Coord. Students 593.

2—HOLY FAMILY OF JOSEPH, MARY & JESUS (1981) [JC]
704 Mallette Dr., 77904. Tel: 361-573-5304;
Fax: 361-573-6053; Email: parish@hfccvic.org; Web: www.hfccvic.org. Revs. Gabriel Bentil; Patrick S. Knippenberg, Parochial Vicar; Deacon Edward Huse, Parish Life Coord.; Jeff Williams, Business Mgr.; Mrs. Debbie Vanelli, Pastoral Assoc.
Catechesis Religious Program—Tel: 361-573-5445; Email: hkallus@hfccvic.org. Heather Kallus, D.R.E. Students 471.

3—ST. MARY'S, [JC]
Mailing Address: 402 S. Main, P.O. Box 2448, 77902. Tel: 361-573-4328; Fax: 361-573-4308; Email: sec@stmvictoria.org; Web: stmvictoria.org. Rev. Stephen Vacek, Admin.; Deacon Jim Koenig.
Catechesis Religious Program—Tel: 361-578-7724; Email: ccd@stmvictoria.org. Mrs. Diana Starnes, D.R.E. Students 94.

4—OUR LADY OF LOURDES (1875)
105 N. William, 77901. Tel: 361-575-3813; Email: janet@lourdesvictoria.org; Email: ollvic@lourdesvictoria.org; Web: lourdesvictoria.org. Rev. Albert Yankey, Parochial Admin.
Catechesis Religious Program—Email: marthan60@hotmail.com. Martha Nichols, D.R.E.; Tammy Fikac, D.R.E. Students 69.

5—OUR LADY OF SORROWS (1913) [JC]
Mailing Address: 208 W. River St., 77901.
Tel: 361-575-2293; Fax: 361-582-0405; Email: abeltran@ourladysorrows.org. Revs. Jacob A. Koether; Eliecer Patino, Parochial Vicar; Deacons Edward Molina; Jesus Perez; Jose (Joe) Duplan.
Catechesis Religious Program—Tel: 361-570-7854. Students 370.
Mission—Holy Trinity, 2901 Pleasant Green Dr., Victoria Co. 77901.

OUTSIDE THE CITY OF VICTORIA

AMMANNSVILLE, FAYETTE CO., ST. JOHN THE BAPTIST, [CEM]
Mailing Address: 7745 Mensik Rd., Schulenburg, 78956. Tel: 979-743-3117; Email: strosecc@verizon.net. Very Rev. Timothy Kosler, V.F.; Rev. Ty J. Bazar, Parochial Vicar.
Mission—St. Wenceslaus, [CEM] FM Road 155, Holman, Fayette Co. 78945. Program is combined with St. Rose - Schulenburg.

BAY CITY, MATAGORDA CO.

1—HOLY CROSS (1909) [CEM 2] [JC]
Mailing Address: 2001 Katy Ave., Bay City, 77414. Email: hc3_office@holycrossbaycity.org; Web: www.holycrossbaycity.org. Very Rev. Gregory E. Korenek, V.F.; Deacons Guadalupe Rodriguez; Larry Koether.
School—Holy Cross School, (Grades PreK-5), Tel: 979-245-5632; Fax: 979-245-6120; Email: ikucera@bcholycrossschool.org; Web: bcholycrossschool.org. Mrs. Inez Kucera, Prin. Lay Teachers 12; Students 69.
Catechesis Religious Program—Mrs. Terri Busha, D.R.E. Students 141.
Mission—Sacred Heart, 13594 State Hwy. 60 S., Wadsworth, Matagorda Co. 77483.

2—OUR LADY OF GUADALUPE
Mailing Address: 1412 12th St., Bay City, 77414.
Tel: 979-245-2010; Fax: 979-245-1038; Email:

olg2003@sbcglobal.net. Rev. Gabriel D. Espinosa; Deacons Luan Van Tran; Joe Ramos.
Catechesis Religious Program—Mrs. Amanda Carlin, D.R.E. Students 507.

BLESSING, MATAGORDA CO., ST. PETER'S (1930) [CEM] [JC]
Mailing Address: 206 Hickory St., Box 395, Blessing, 77419. Tel: 361-588-6241; Tel: 361-588-1156;
Fax: 361-588-1421; Email: stpeterblessing@tisd.net; Web: www.stpeterblessing.org. Rev. Gabriel J. Mensah, Parochial Admin., (Retired).
Catechesis Religious Program—Cynthia Nemec, D.R.E. Students 76.
Mission—St. Robert, FM Rd. 1468, Markham, Matagorda Co. 77456.

BLOOMINGTON, VICTORIA CO., ST. PATRICK'S (1959) Very Rev. Samuel Appiasi, V.F.; Deacon Fred Soto.
Res. & Church: 13316 State Hwy. 185, P.O. Box 2122, Bloomington, 77951. Tel: 361-897-1155;
Fax: 361-897-1064; Email: St.Patrick@C3J.net.
Catechesis Religious Program—Ramona Torres, D.R.E. Students 101.

CISTERN, FAYETTE CO., SS. CYRIL AND METHODIUS (1877) [CEM 2] [JC2]
Mailing Address: P.O. Box 186, Flatonia, 78941.
Tel: 361-865-3568; Email: sacredheart186@sbcglobal.net; Web: shsscm.org. 113 Manchester, Flatonia, 78941. Rev. Edward J. Winkler.
Catechesis Religious Program—Students 6.

COLUMBUS, COLORADO CO., ST. ANTHONY'S (1930) [CEM]
1602 Bowie, P.O. Box 669, Columbus, 78934.
Tel: 979-732-2562; Email: tracey@stanthonycolumbustx.net; Email: fraugustine@stanthonycolumbustx.net; Email: frnelson@stanthonycolumbustx.net; Web: stanthonycolumbustx.net. Revs. Augustine N. Asante; Nelson Gonzalez Nieto, Parochial Vicar; Deacons Bennie Holesovsky; Charlie Novosad.
School—St. Anthony's School, (Grades PreK-8), 635 Bonham St., Columbus, 78934. Tel: 979-732-5505;
Fax: 979-732-9758; Email: pri@stanthonycolumbus.net; Web: stanthonycolumbus.net. John O'Leary, Prin. Lay Teachers 18; Students 207.
Catechesis Religious Program—Tel: 979-732-6336; Email: lorrainenovosad@gmail.com. Lorraine Novosad, D.R.E. Students 139.

CUERO, DEWITT CO.
1—ST. MICHAEL (1875)
309 E. Church St., Cuero, 77954-2906.
Tel: 361-275-3554; Fax: 361-277-3924; Email: stmchurch@sbcglobal.net. Revs. Jasper Liggio; Jacob Mendoza, Parochial Vicar; Deacon Leo Sharron.
School—St. Michael School, (Grades PreK-5), 208 N. McLeod, Cuero, 77954. Tel: 361-277-3854;
Tel: 361-275-3554, Ext. 0; Fax: 361-275-3618; Email: jsaenz@stmschoolcuero.org; Web: www.stmschoolcuero.org. Jennifer Saenz, Prin. Lay Teachers 11; Students 89.
Catechesis Religious Program— Combined with Our Lady of Guadalupe Catholic Church, Cuero. Email: jrodriguez@catholiccuero.org. Jon Eric Rodriguez, D.R.E. Students 97.
2—OUR LADY OF GUADALUPE (1923)
705 W. Broadway, P.O. Box 547, Cuero, 77954.
Tel: 361-275-3554; Email: stmchurch@sbcglobal.net. Mailing Address: 309 E. Church St., Cuero, 77954. Revs. Jasper Liggio; Jacob Mendoza, Parochial Vicar.

EAGLE LAKE, COLORADO CO., PARISH OF THE NATIVITY (1995)
308 Stevenson St., Eagle Lake, 77434.
Tel: 979-234-2842; Fax: 979-234-5828; Email: nativity1@sbcglobal.net; Web: parishofthenativity.org. P.O. Box 307, Eagle Lake, 77434. Rev. Robert F. Guerra.
Catechesis Religious Program—309 Stevenson St., Eagle Lake, 77434. Elida Salazar, P.C.L. Students 179.

EAST BERNARD, WHARTON CO., HOLY CROSS (1901) [CEM]
Mailing Address: 839 Church St., P.O. Box 1325, East Bernard, 77435-1325. Tel: 979-335-7551;
Fax: 979-335-7038; Email: ebholycross@gmail.com; Web: www.eastbernardholycross.com. Revs. Donald R. Ruppert; Matthew Kesssler, Parochial Vicar.
Catechesis Religious Program—Tel: 979-335-4071; Email: holycross.pcl@hotmail.com. Patricia Krenek, D.R.E. Students 304.
Cemetery Office—839 Church St., East Bernard, 77435-1325. Tel: 979-335-7551; Email: hccemetery@hotmail.com.

EDNA, JACKSON CO., ST. AGNES (1880) Rev. Michael Petering.
Res.: 506 N. Allen, Edna, 77957. Tel: 361-782-3588;
Fax: 361-782-8827; Email: stagnesedna@sbcglobal.net.
Catechesis Religious Program—Tel: 361-782-6171; Email: stagnesccd@att.net. Mrs. Patricia Kromka, D.R.E. Students 179.

EL CAMPO, WHARTON CO.
1—ST. PHILIP THE APOSTLE, [CEM]
304 W. Church St., El Campo, 77437.
Tel: 979-543-3770; Fax: 979-578-8831; Email: apostle@stphilipapostle.org. Very Rev. Michael Rother, V.F.; Rev. Peter Oscar Kofi-Amo, Parochial Vicar; Deacons Jarrel Nohavitza; Jerome Grahmann; Lawrence Hoelscher.
School—St. Philip the Apostle School, (Grades PreK-8), Tel: 979-543-2901; Email: gwene@stphilipschool.org. Mrs. Gwen Edwards, Prin. Lay Teachers 31; Students 300.
Catechesis Religious Program—Tel: 979-541-9457; Email: cce@stphilipapostle.org. Nancy Fenner, D.R.E. Students 207.
2—ST. ROBERT BELLARMINE (1928) Rev. Philip Brune; Deacon Margarito Cervantez Jr.
Res.: 512 Tegner St., El Campo, 77437.
Tel: 979-543-4298; Fax: 979-541-5399; Email: sanroberto@sbcglobal.net; Web: sanrobertochurch.org.
Catechesis Religious Program—Tel: 281-793-9918; Email: kinderamigo@yahoo.com. Mrs. Maria Aldana, D.R.E. Students 376.

FLATONIA, FAYETTE CO., SACRED HEART (1912) [CEM] [JC]
P.O. Box 186, Flatonia, 78941. Tel: 361-865-3568;
Fax: 361-865-2518; Email: sacredheart186@sbcglobal.net; Web: shsscm.org. 516 South Faires, Flatonia, 78941. Rev. Edward J. Winkler.
Catechesis Religious Program—Students 130.

FRELSBURG, COLORADO CO., SS. PETER AND PAUL (1836) [CEM]
1031 Church Ln., New Ulm, 78950.
Tel: 979-732-3430; Email: frmichael@saintrochparish.org. Rev. Michael Lyons; Deacons Charles J. Glynn; Douglas B. Tromblee.
Catechesis Religious Program—Email: andreakrenek@yahoo.com. Andrea Krenek, D.R.E. Students 41.

GANADO, JACKSON CO., ASSUMPTION OF THE B.V.M. (1914) [CEM]
Mailing Address: P.O. Box 369, Ganado, 77962.
Tel: 361-771-3425; Fax: 361-771-3526; Email: abvmchurch@ykc.com; Web: www.abvmganado.org. Rev. Kirby Hlavaty; Deacon Anthony Hensley.
Res.: 109 S. Sixth St., Ganado, 77962.
Catechesis Religious Program—Tel: 361-771-3200; Email: ymabvmchurch@ykc.com. Heather Supak, Youth Min. Students 234.

GOLIAD, GOLIAD CO., IMMACULATE CONCEPTION, [CEM 2]
238 N. Commercial St., Goliad, 77963.
Tel: 361-645-3095; Fax: 361-645-3097; Email: office@goliadcatholic.org; Web: www.goliadcatholic.org. Very Rev. Charles E. Otsiwah, V.F.
Shrine—Our Lady of Loreto (Old Franciscan Mission), 217 US HWY. 183, Goliad, 77963.
Catechesis Religious Program—225 N. Commercial, Goliad, 77963. Tel: 361-648-2289; Email: glorymoral51@gmail.com. Gloria Morales, D.R.E. Students 123.

HALLETTSVILLE, LAVACA CO.
1—ST. MARY (1840) [CEM 4] Rev. Msgr. John C. Peters, V.G.; Rev. Max A. Landman, Parochial Vicar.
Church: 1648 FM 340, P.O. Drawer H, Hallettsville, 77964. Tel: 361-798-5888; Tel: 361-798-2128;
Fax: 361-798-4970; Email: rectory@shcatholicchurch.org.
Catechesis Religious Program—Email: rother.carol@gmail.com. Carol Rother, D.R.E. Students 86.
2—SACRED HEART (1882) [CEM]
Mailing Address: 400 E. Fifth St., P.O. Box H, Hallettsville, 77964. Tel: 361-798-5888;
Fax: 361-798-4970; Email: rectory@shcatholicchurch.org; Web: www.shcatholicchurch.org. Rev. Msgr. John C. Peters, V.G.; Rev. Max A. Landman, Parochial Vicar; Deacons Michael Tankersley; Joey Targac; Linard Harper.
School—Sacred Heart School, (Grades PreK-8), Tel: 361-798-4251; Email: Kevin.Haas@shschool.org; Web: www.shschool.org. Kathy Haas, Sec. Religious Teachers 2; Lay Teachers 18; Students 180.
High School—Sacred Heart High School, (Grades 9-12), 313 S. Texana, Hallettsville, 77964.
Tel: 361-798-4251; Email: Kevin.Haas@shschool.org; Web: www.shschool.org. Kathy Haas, Sec. Religious Teachers 2; Lay Teachers 16; Students 84.
Catechesis Religious Program—Tel: 361-798-3124; Email: AngelaMcconnell@shcatholicchurch.org. Angela McConnell, D.R.E. Students 258.

HIGH HILL, FAYETTE CO., NATIVITY OF THE BLESSED VIRGIN MARY, [CEM]
Mailing Address: 2833 FM 2672, Schulenburg, 78956-5603. Tel: 979-561-8455; Email: strosecc@verizon.net. Very Rev. Timothy Kosler, V.F.; Rev. Ty J. Bazar, Parochial Vicar.

HILLJE, WHARTON CO., ST. ANDREW (1909) [CEM]
Mailing Address: 270 St. Andrew St., El Campo, 77437. Tel: 979-648-2864; Fax: 979-648-2024; Email: standrew@ykc.com. Rev. Clement Quainoo; Deacon Edward Wendel.
Catechesis Religious Program—Tel: 979-541-6413; Email: steph_michell@hotmail.com. Stephanie Garrett, D.R.E. Students 120.
Mission—St. Procopius (1944) [CEM] 814 Elm St., Louise, Wharton Co. 77455.

HOSTYN, FAYETTE CO., QUEEN OF THE HOLY ROSARY (1856) [CEM]
936 FM 2436, La Grange, 78945. Tel: 979-247-4441;
Fax: 979-247-5008; Email: hostynch@cvctx.com; Web: www.HostynPlumCatholic.org. Rev. Daniel P. Kahlich; Deacon John McCourt.
Catechesis Religious Program—Mrs. Gina Kozelsky, C.R.E. Students 31.

HUNGERFORD, WHARTON CO., ST. JOHN THE BAPTIST (1917) [CEM]
Mailing Address: 101 Church St., P.O. Box 121, Hungerford, 77448. Tel: 979-532-4747;
Fax: 979-532-4748; Email: stjohnhungerford@gmail.com. Rev. Charles O. Dwomoh.
Catechesis Religious Program—Tel: 979-532-5648. Mrs. Janet Bubela, D.R.E. Students 67.

INEZ, VICTORIA CO., ST. JOSEPH CATHOLIC CHURCH (1873) [CEM] [JC5] Rev. Barnabas Kyeah, Parochial Admin.; Deacon Steve Borowicz.
Church: 17 Church St., P.O. Box 337, Inez, 77968.
Tel: 361-782-3181; Tel: 361-781-0459 (Rectory); Email: stjosephchurch@tisd.net; Web: stjosephinez.org.
Catechesis Religious Program—Email: stjccd@tisd.net. Stephanie Charbula, P.C.L. Students 158.

KOERTH, LAVACA CO., ST. JOHN THE BAPTIST 1887 [CEM] [JC]
Mailing Address: 13202 FM 531, P.O. Box 201, Sweet Home, 77987. Tel: 361-741-3206; Email: pastor@qpcatholicchurch.com; Web: qpcatholicchurch.com. Rev. Dominic Antwi-Boasiako.

MENTZ, COLORADO CO., ST. ROCH (1850) [CEM]
Mailing Address: 1600 Frelsburg Rd., Alleyton, 78935. Tel: 979-732-3460; Fax: 979-733-0908; Email: bethany@saintrochparish.org; Web: www.saintrochparish.org. Rev. Michael Lyons; Deacons Douglas B. Tromblee; Charles J. Glynn.

MEYERSVILLE, DEWITT CO., SS. PETER & PAUL (1858) [CEM]
Mailing Address: 11220 FM 237, Meyersville, 77974.
Tel: 361-275-3868; Email: stspp@gvec.net; Web: www.catholiccommunityofcuero.org. Revs. Jasper Liggio; Jacob Mendoza, Parochial Vicar.
Catechesis Religious Program—Tel: 361-575-2056; Email: janiceohrt@yahoo.com. Mrs. Janice Ohrt, D.R.E. Students 35.
Mission—St. Aloysius, 19 Catholic Church Ln., Westhoff, 77994.

MOULTON, LAVACA CO., ST. JOSEPH'S (1888) [CEM]
Mailing Address: 601 N. Pecan St., P.O. Box 399, Moulton, 77975. Tel: 361-596-4674;
Fax: 361-596-4826; Email: st_joe@sbcglobal.net; Web: www.stjosephsmoulton.org. Rev. Gabriel Maison, J.C.D.; Deacons Milburn Kram; Kenneth Fishbeck.
Catechesis Religious Program—Tel: 361-596-7559. Donna Perez, D.R.E. Students 94.

NADA, COLORADO CO., NATIVITY OF THE BLESSED VIRGIN MARY (1897) [CEM] Rev. Peter Yeboah-Amanfo; Deacon Edward Wendel.
Res. & Church: 1261 Old Nada Rd., P.O. Box 97, Nada, 77460. Tel: 979-758-3218; Email: stmarynadaparish@gmail.com.
Catechesis Religious Program—Students 86.

NEW TAITON, WHARTON CO., ST. JOHN NEPOMUCENE (1912) [CEM]
Mailing Address: 1843 CR 469, El Campo, 77437.
Tel: 979-543-6985; Fax: 979-543-3434; Email: saintjohnchurch@outlook.com. Rev. Gabriel Oduro Tawiah; Deacons Patrick Kubala; Edward Wendel.
Catechesis Religious Program—Diann Srubar, D.R.E. Students 63.

PALACIOS, MATAGORDA CO., ST. ANTHONY'S (1912, Mission); (1954, Parish)
Mailing Address: 1004 Magnusson, Box 900, Palacios, 77465. Tel: 361-972-2446;
Fax: 361-972-2606; Email: pasaop@yahoo.com. Revs. Dominic Trung Nguyen; Francis Tam Nguyen III, Parochial Vicar; Deacon Michael Vieira.
Catechesis Religious Program—Email: brandigwest@gmail.com. Brandi West, D.R.E. Students 300.
Vietnamese Apostolate—100 Vietnam, Palacios, 77465.

PLUM, FAYETTE CO., SS. PETER AND PAUL (1897) [CEM 2]
126 Plum Church Rd., La Grange, 78945.
Tel: 979-247-4441; Fax: 979-247-5008; Email: hostynch@cvctx.com; Web: www.HostynPlumCatholic.org. Mailing Address: 936 FM 2436, La Grange, 78945. Rev. Daniel P. Kahlich; Deacon John McCourt.

Catechesis Religious Program—Mrs. Gina Kozelsky, C.R.E. Students 18.

PORT LAVACA, CALHOUN CO., OUR LADY OF THE GULF (1865)
415 W. Austin St., Port Lavaca, 77979.
Tel: 361-552-6140; Fax: 361-552-4300; Email: olg@olgulf.org; Web: www.olgulf.org. Revs. Tommy Chen; Scott J. Hill, Parochial Vicar; Tim Dent, Business Mgr.
Child Care—Preschool/Day Care,
Tel: 361-552-6140, Ext. 556. 412 W. Austin St., Port Lavaca, 77979. Mrs. Rosie Padron, Dir. Lay Teachers 8; Students 89.
School—Our Lady of the Gulf School, (Grades PreK-8), 301 S. San Antonio St., Port Lavaca, 77979.
Tel: 361-552-6140; Email: olgmariners@olgulf.org; Web: www.olgmariners.org. Mrs. Theresa Dent, Prin. Religious Teachers 2; Lay Teachers 22; Students 122.
Catechesis Religious Program—
Tel: 361-552-6140, Ext. 100. Mrs. Linda Beard, D.R.E.; Mrs. Mary Reyes, RCIA Coord. Students 380.
Missions—St. Ann—709 Lamar, Point Comfort, Calhoun Co. 77978.
St. Joseph, 101 Washington St., Port O'Connor, Calhoun Co. 77982.
St. Patrick, 306 W. Cleveland, Seadrift, Calhoun Co. 77983.

PRAHA, FAYETTE CO., ASSUMPTION OF THE BLESSED VIRGIN MARY CATHOLIC CHURCH (1855) [CEM]
821 FM 1295, Flatonia, 78941. Tel: 361-596-4674; Fax: 361-596-4826; Email: st_joe@sbcglobal.net; Web: www.stmaryspraha.org. Rev. Gabriel Maison, J.C.D., Admin.
Catechesis Religious Program—

ST. JOHN, FAYETTE CO., ST. JOHN THE BAPTIST (1888) [CEM]
7026 FM 957, Schulenburg, 78956.
Tel: 361-798-5888; Fax: 361-798-4970; Email: rectory@shcatholicchurch.org; Web: www.shcatholicchurch.org. Mailing Address: P.O. Box H, Hallettsville, 77964. Rev. Msgr. John C. Peters, V.G.; Rev. Max A. Landman, Parochial Vicar.
Catechesis Religious Program—Tel: 713-822-3019; Email: danadau@cvctx.com. Mrs. Dana Daughtry, D.R.E. Students 20.
Mission—Ascension of Our Lord (1913) [CEM] 11134 FM 957 (Moravia), P.O. Box H, Hallettsville, Lavaca Co. 77964.

SCHULENBURG, FAYETTE CO., ST. ROSE OF LIMA (1889) [CEM]
Mailing Address: 1010 Lyons Ave., Box 310, Schulenburg, 78956. Tel: 979-743-3117;
Fax: 979-743-4712; Email: strosecc@verizon.net. Very Rev. Timothy Kosler, V.F.; Rev. Ty J. Bazar, Parochial Vicar.
School—St. Rose of Lima School, (Grades PreK-8), 405 Black, Schulenburg, 78956. Tel: 979-743-3080; Fax: 979-743-4228; Email: r.gallia@strosecardinals.org. Mrs. Rosanne Gallia, Prin. Lay Teachers 18; Students 160.
Catechesis Religious Program—Tel: 979-743-4428; Email: strosecc@verizon.net. Nicole Michalke, (Grades 1-8); Lynne Machac, (Grades 9-11). Students 180.

SHINER, LAVACA CO., SS. CYRIL AND METHODIUS, [CEM]
Mailing Address: 306 S. Ave. F, Shiner, 77984.
Tel: 361-594-3836; Fax: 361-594-2850; Email: rectory@sscmshiner.org; Email: frbryan@sscmshiner.org; Email: aduke@sscmshiner.org; Web: www.sscmshiner.org. Rev. Bryan Heyer; Deacon Joseph Machacek.
School—St. Ludmila Elementary School, (Grades PreK-8), P.O. Box 725, Shiner, 77984.
Tel: 361-594-3843; Fax: 361-594-8599; Email: nyackel@shinercatholicschool.org; Web: www.shinercatholicschool.org. Neely Yackel, Prin.; Laura Sprinkle, Librarian. Lay Teachers 19; Sisters 1; Students 191.
High School—St. Paul High School,
Tel: 361-594-2313; Email: ssiegel@shinercatholicschool.org. Lay Teachers 13; Sisters 1; Students 97.
Catechesis Religious Program—Tel: 361-594-3234; Email: kulcak@sscmshiner.org. Kim Ulcak, Youth Min. Students 207.

SWEET HOME, LAVACA CO., QUEEN OF PEACE, [CEM] [JC]
Mailing Address: 7372 FM 531, P.O. Box 201, Sweet Home, 77987. Tel: 361-741-3206; Email: secretary@qpcatholicchurch.com; Web: qpcatholicchurch.com. Rev. Dominic Antwi-Boasiako.
Catechesis Religious Program—Email: faithformation@qpcatholicchurch.com. Skye Anderle, D.R.E. Students 96.

VANDERBILT, JACKSON CO., ST. JOHN BOSCO (1947) Rev. Johnson Owusu-Boateng.
Office: 232 Main St., P.O. Box 337, Vanderbilt, 77991-0337. Tel: 361-284-3361; Fax: 361-284-3391; Email: sjbchurch@tisd.net.
Res.: 121 Garcitas St., P.O. Box 337, Vanderbilt, 77991. Tel: 361-284-3737.
Catechesis Religious Program—Email: mzb_63@yahoo.com. Emilia Benavides, D.R.E. Students 65.
Mission—St. Theresa, [CEM] 4612 CR 325, La Salle, Jackson Co. 77969.

WEIMAR, COLORADO CO., ST. MICHAEL (1883) [CEM]
Rev. Wayne N. Flagg.
Res. & Church: 410 N. Center, Box 36, Weimar, 78962. Tel: 979-725-6714; Fax: 979-725-8146; Email: stmichaelwei@yahoo.com; Web: www.stmichaelweimar.org.
School—St. Michael School, (Grades PreK-8),
Tel: 979-725-8461; Email: cmcafee@stmichaelswords. Mrs. Carolanne McAfee, Prin. Lay Teachers 13; Students 91.
Catechesis Religious Program—Tel: 979-820-7263; Email: irmarerich@gmail.com. Irma Reich, D.R.E. Students 130.
Mission—SS. Cyril and Methodius, FM Rd. 1383, Dubina, Fayette Co. 78962.

WHARTON, WHARTON CO.
1—HOLY FAMILY, [JC]
2011 Briar Ln., Wharton, 77488-4470.
Tel: 979-532-3593; Email: office@hfwharton.org; Web: www.hfwharton.org. Revs. Robert E. Knippenberg; Felix Twumasi, Parochial Vicar; Deacons Alvin Matthys; David Valdez.
Catechesis Religious Program—Vicki Elaine Simper, D.R.E. Students 100.
Mission—St. Joseph, 106 Lalla Rookh, Boling, Wharton Co. 77420. Email: pastor@hfwharton.org.
2—OUR LADY OF MT. CARMEL (1948) [JC]
Mailing Address: 506 S. East Ave., Wharton, 77488.
Tel: 979-532-3492; Fax: 979-532-2321; Email: office@olmcwharton.org. Rev. Antonio Perez, Parochial Admin.
Catechesis Religious Program—Email: religiouseducation@olmcwharton.org. Olayita Compian, D.R.E. Students 185.

YOAKUM, LAVACA CO., ST. JOSEPH (1869) [CEM]
Mailing Address: Box 734, Yoakum, 77995.
Tel: 361-293-3518; Tel: 361-293-7572;
Fax: 361-293-5355; Email: secretary@stjcatholicchurch.com; Web: www.stjcatholicchurch.com. 401 Orth St., Yoakum, 77995. Very Rev. Matthew H. Huehlefeld, J.C.L., V.F.; Deacon Dennis Kutach.
School—St. Joseph School, (Grades PreK-8),
Tel: 361-293-9000; Email: smooney@stjcatholicschool.com; Web: www.stjcatholicschool.com. Sean Mooney, Prin. Clergy 1; Lay Teachers 12; Students 104.
Catechesis Religious Program—401 Orth St., Yoakum, 77995. Email: faithformation@stjcatholicchurch.com. Jana Guajardo, D.R.E. Students 281.
Mission—St. Ann, [CEM] 4162 State Hwy. 111 W., Hochheim, DeWitt Co. 77967.

YORKTOWN, DEWITT CO., HOLY CROSS (1866) [CEM 2]
Mailing Address: 1214 Zorn Rd., Yorktown, 78164-1907. Tel: 361-564-2893; Fax: 361-564-9315; Email: holycross1214@sbcglobal.net; Email: frroger@sbcglobal.net; Web: holycrossyorktown.net. Rev. Roger Hawes.
Catechesis Religious Program—Students 79.
Missions—San Luis—502 E. Second, 1214 Zorn Rd., Yorktown, DeWitt Co. 78164.
St. Ann's, Hwy. 72 W., Nordheim, DeWitt Co. 78141.

Retired:
Rev. Msgrs.—
Anders, Arnold, (Retired)
Bily, John C., (Retired)
Cernoch, Gerard, (Retired)
Hybner, Joseph, (Retired)
Jarzombek, Casimir, (Retired)
Revs.—
Henninger, George, (Retired)
Lenz, Frank, (Retired)
Mensah, Gabriel J., Military Chap., U.S. Navy, (Retired).

Permanent Deacons:
Borowicz, Stephen James Michael
Cervantez, Margarito Candelario Jr.
Duplan, Jose (Joe)
Fishbeck, Kenneth
Glynn, Charles J.
Grahmann, Jerome J.
Harper, Linard
Hensley, Anthony
Hoelscher, Lawrence
Holesovsky, Bennie
Huse, Eddie
Key, Billy, (Retired)
Koenig, James Nicholas
Koether, Larry
Kubala, Patrick
Kutach, Dennis
Machacek, Joseph
Matthys, Alvin
McCourt, John
Molina, Edwardo Pina
Nohavitza, Jarrel Joseph
Novosad, Charlie
Perez, Jesus Castillo
Ramos, Joseph
Rodriguez, Guadalupe
Sharron, Leo
Soto, Fred
Tankersley, Michael
Targac, Joseph
Tran, Luan Van
Tromblee, Douglas B.
Valdez, David
Vieira, Michael
Warzecha, Anthony, (Retired)
Wendel, Edward.

INSTITUTIONS LOCATED IN DIOCESE

[A] HIGH SCHOOLS, PRIVATE

VICTORIA. *St. Joseph High School*, 110 E. Red River, 77901. Tel: 361-573-2446; Fax: 361-573-4221; Email: tmaj@stjflyers.com; Web: www.stjvictoria.com. Mr. Thomas Maj, Pres. & Prin.; Victoria Stawik-Raven, Librarian. Religious Teachers 1; Lay Teachers 20; Students 307.

[B] ELEMENTARY SCHOOLS, PRIVATE

VICTORIA. *Nazareth Academy Catholic School* (1867) (Grades PreK-8), 206 W. Convent, 77901.
Tel: 361-573-6651; Fax: 361-573-1829; Email: srevelyn@nazarethacademy.org; Web: www.nazarethacademy.org. Sisters Evelyn Korenek, I.W.B.S., Prin.; Ann Meletio, I.W.B.S., Business Mgr.; Bernarda Bludau, I.W.B.S., Admin. Attended from St. Mary's, Our Lady of Lourdes, Our Lady of Victory, Holy Family and Our Lady of Sorrows Churches. Lay Teachers 25; Students 322; Sisters of the Incarnate Word and Blessed Sacrament 7.

[C] PERSONAL PRELATURES

SCHULENBURG. *Opus Dei*, Featherock Conference Center, 934 Holub Rd., Schulenburg, 78956-5324. Tel: 979-743-4642; Email: men@featherock.net. Rev. Paul Kais, Vicar.

[D] CONVENTS AND RESIDENCES FOR SISTERS

VICTORIA. *Incarnate Word Convent*, Incarnate Word Convent, 1101 N.E. Water St., 77901-9233.
Tel: 361-575-2266; Fax: 361-575-2165; Email: skgoike@gmail.com; Web: www.iwbsvictoria.org. Sisters Kathleen Goike, I.W.B.S., Supr.; Geraldine Pavlik, Local Supr. Sisters 34.
Missionary Catechists of the Sacred Hearts of Jesus and Mary, 203 E. Sabine St., 77901.
Tel: 361-570-3332; Fax: 361-570-3377; Email: wumidory@hotmail.com. Sr. Midory Wu, M.C.S.H., Prov. Supr.
Immaculate Heart of Mary Province Religious 11; Sisters 10.

PORT LAVACA. *Vietnamese Community*, 319 S. Nueces St., Port Lavaca, 77979. Tel: 361-552-6140; Email: olg@olgulf.org. 415 W Austin St., Port Lavaca, 77979. Sr. Hang Ta, Supr. Sisters 3.

[E] MISCELLANEOUS

VICTORIA. *Amor Meus Spirituality Center*, 1101 N.E. Water St., 77901. Tel: 361-575-7111;
Fax: 361-575-2165; Email: amormeus@yahoo.com. Sr. Emilie Eilers, I.W.B.S., Dir.
Endowment Fund for the Catholic Diocese of Victoria in Texas, 1505 E. Mesquite Ln., 77901.
Tel: 361-573-0828; Fax: 361-573-5725; Email: tmartinez@victoriadiocese.org; Web: www.victoriadiocese.org. P.O. Box 4070, 77903. Mr. Tony Martinez, Business Mgr.
Jeanne Chezard De Matel Fund, Jeanne Chezard de Matel Fund, 1101 N.E. Water St., 77901-9233.
Tel: 361-575-2266; Fax: 361-575-2165; Email: skgoike@gmail.com; Web: www.iwbsvictoria.org. Sr. Kathleen Goike, I.W.B.S., Supr.
Nazareth Academy, Inc., 1101 N.E. Water St., 77901.
Tel: 361-572-9321; Fax: 361-575-2165; Email: iwbsbusofc@yahoo.com. Sr. Evelyn Korenek, I.W.B.S., Pres.
Sisters of the Incarnate Word and Blessed Sacrament of Victoria, Texas, Medical and Retirement Trust, Sisters of the Incarnate Word and Blessed

Sacrament of Victoria, Texas, Medical and Retirement Trust, 1101 N.E. Water St., 77901-9233. Tel: 361-572-9321; Fax: 361-575-2165; Email: iwbsbusofc@yahoo.com. Sr. Kathleen Goike, I.W.B.S., Supr.

Sisters of the Incarnate Word and Blessed Sacrament, Victoria, Texas, Inc., Sisters of the Incarnate Word and Blessed Sacrament, Victoria, Texas, Inc., Attn: Sr. Stephana Marbach, I.W.B.S., 1101 N.E. Water St., 77901-9233. Tel: 361-575-2266; Fax: 361-575-2165; Email: skgoike@gmail.com; Web: www.iwbsvictoria.org. Sr. Kathleen Goike, I.W.B.S., Supr. Scholastics 1; Perpetually Professed 56.

RELIGIOUS INSTITUTES OF WOMEN REPRESENTED IN THE DIOCESE

For further details refer to the corresponding bracketed number in the Religious Institutes of Men or Women section.

[2200]—*Congregation of the Incarnate Word and Blessed Sacrament*—I.W.B.S.

[2700]—*Missionary Catechists of the Sacred Hearts of Jesus and Mary*—M.C.SS.CC.

[0460]—*Sisters of Charity of Incarnate Word*—C.C.V.I.

[]—*Sisters of the Incarnate Word and Blessed Sacrament of Victoria, Texas.*

[]—*Vietnamese Dominican Sisters*—O.P.

NECROLOGY

† Franks, Gabriel, (Retired), Died Mar. 19, 2018

An asterisk (*) denotes an organization that has established tax-exempt status directly with the IRS and is not covered by the USCCB Group Ruling.

Archdiocese of Washington

(Archidioecesis Washingtonensis)

His Eminence

DONALD CARDINAL WUERL, S.T.D.

Retired Archbishop of Washington; ordained December 17, 1966; appointed Titular Bishop of Rosemarkie and Auxiliary Bishop of Seattle December 3, 1985; consecrated January 6, 1986; appointed and canonically installed Bishop of Pittsburgh February 12, 1988; liturgically installed March 25, 1988; appointed Archbishop of Washington May 16, 2006; installed June 22, 2006; created Cardinal priest of Saint Peter in Chains November 20, 2010; installed May 8, 2011; retired October 12, 2018; appointed Apostolic Administrator of Washington October 12, 2018; ceased May 21, 2019. *Office: Archdiocesan Pastoral Center, 5001 Eastern Ave., Hyattsville, MD 20782-3447.* Tel: 301-853-4500; Fax: 301-853-5359. *Mailing Address: P.O. Box 29260, Washington, DC 20017-0260.*

Most Reverend

FRANCISCO GONZALEZ, S.F., D.D., V.G.

Retired Auxiliary Bishop of Washington; ordained May 1, 1964; appointed Auxiliary Bishop of Washington and Titular Bishop of Lamfua December 28, 2001; Episcopal ordination February 11, 2002; retired May 27, 2014. *Mailing Address: 401 Randolph Rd., Silver Spring, MD 20914.*

Most Reverend

MARIO E. DORSONVILLE, D.D., V.G.

Auxiliary Bishop of Washington; ordained November 23, 1985; appointed Auxiliary Bishop of Washington and Titular Bishop of Kearney March 20, 2015; ordained April 20, 2015. *Office: Archdiocesan Pastoral Center, 5001 Eastern Ave., Hyattsville, MD 20782.*

Most Reverend

WILTON D. GREGORY

Archbishop of Washington; ordained May 9, 1973; appointed Auxiliary Bishop of Chicago and Titular Bishop of Oliva October 31, 1983; consecrated December 13, 1983; appointed Bishop of Belleville December 29, 1993; installed February 10, 1994; appointed Archbishop of Atlanta December 9, 2004; installed January 17, 2005; appointed Archbishop of Washington April 4, 2019; installed May 21, 2019. *Archdiocesan Pastoral Center, 5001 Eastern Ave., Hyattsville, MD 20782-3447.* Tel: 301-853-4500; Fax: 301-853-5346. *Mailing Address: P.O. Box 29260, Washington, DC 20017-0260.*

Archdiocesan Pastoral Center: 5001 Eastern Ave., Hyattsville, MD 20782. Mailing Address: P.O. Box 29260, Washington, DC 20017. Tel: 301-853-4500; Fax: 301-853-5346.

Email: chancery@adw.org

Most Reverend

ROY E. CAMPBELL

Auxiliary Bishop of Washington; ordained May 26, 2007; appointed Titular Bishop of Ucres and Auxiliary Bishop of Washington March 8, 2017; installed April 21, 2017. *Office: 5001 Eastern Ave., Hyattsville, MD 20782.*

Most Reverend

MICHAEL W. FISHER

Auxiliary Bishop of Washington; ordained June 23, 1990; appointed Titular Bishop of Truentum and Auxiliary Bishop of Washington June 8, 2018; installed June 29, 2018. *Office: 5001 Eastern Ave., Hyattsville, MD 20782.*

THEODORE E. MCCARRICK, PH.D., D.D.

ordained May 31, 1958; appointed Auxiliary Bishop of New York May 24, 1977; Episcopal ordination June 29, 1977; appointed First Bishop of Metuchen November 19, 1981; installed January 31, 1982; appointed Archbishop of Newark May 30, 1986; installed July 25, 1986; appointed Archbishop of Washington November 21, 2000; installed January 3, 2001; created Cardinal priest February 21, 2001; retired May 16, 2006; resigned from College of Cardinals July 27, 2018; dismissed from the clerical state February 15, 2019.

Square Miles 2,104.

Established Archdiocese July 22, 1939; Separated from Baltimore November 15, 1947; Became a Metropolitan See October 12, 1965.

Comprises the District of Columbia and Montgomery, Prince George's, St. Mary's, Calvert and Charles Counties in Maryland.

The Province of Washington has as a Suffragan, the Diocese of St. Thomas in the Virgin Islands.

For legal titles of parishes and archdiocesan institutions, consult the Chancery Office.

STATISTICAL OVERVIEW

Personnel	
Retired Cardinals	1
Archbishops	1
Auxiliary Bishops	3
Retired Bishops	1
Abbots	1
Priests: Diocesan Active in Diocese	182
Priests: Diocesan Active Outside Diocese	9
Priests: Diocesan in Foreign Missions	7
Priests: Retired, Sick or Absent	75
Number of Diocesan Priests	273
Religious Priests in Diocese	448
Total Priests in Diocese	721
Extern Priests in Diocese	133
Ordinations:	
Diocesan Priests	3
Religious Priests	10
Transitional Deacons	12
Permanent Deacons in Diocese	265
Total Brothers	181
Total Sisters	458
Parishes	
Parishes	139
With Resident Pastor:	
Resident Diocesan Priests	113
Resident Religious Priests	13
Without Resident Pastor:	
Administered by Priests	13
Missions	9
Pastoral Centers	1
Professional Ministry Personnel:	
Brothers	5
Sisters	31
Welfare	
Catholic Hospitals	4
Total Assisted	434,780
Health Care Centers	81
Total Assisted	1,120,187
Homes for the Aged	31
Total Assisted	3,276
Day Care Centers	12
Total Assisted	434
Specialized Homes	24
Total Assisted	17,558
Special Centers for Social Services	61
Total Assisted	351,118
Residential Care of Disabled	6
Total Assisted	18
Other Institutions	6
Total Assisted	1,658
Educational	
Seminaries, Diocesan	3
Students from This Diocese	67
Students from Other Diocese	94
Diocesan Students in Other Seminaries	20
Seminaries, Religious	11
Students Religious	132
Total Seminarians	219
Colleges and Universities	3
Total Students	26,925
High Schools, Diocesan and Parish	2
Total Students	740
High Schools, Private	16
Total Students	9,272
Elementary Schools, Diocesan and Parish	61
Total Students	14,195
Elementary Schools, Private	12
Total Students	1,924
Non-residential Schools for the Disabled	1
Total Students	40
Catechesis/Religious Education:	
High School Students	2,059
Elementary Students	21,510
Total Students under Catholic Instruction	76,884
Teachers in the Diocese:	
Brothers	27
Sisters	13
Lay Teachers	2,656
Vital Statistics	
Receptions into the Church:	
Infant Baptism Totals	5,919
Minor Baptism Totals	905
Adult Baptism Totals	577
Received into Full Communion	806
First Communions	5,293
Confirmations	4,931
Marriages:	
Catholic	1,038
Interfaith	378
Total Marriages	1,416
Deaths	2,627
Total Catholic Population	666,470
Total Population	3,027,407

Former Archbishops—Most Rev. MICHAEL J. CURLEY, cons. Bishop of St. Augustine, June 30, 1914; promoted to the See of Baltimore, Aug. 10, 1921; named Archbishop of Baltimore and Washington, July 22, 1939; died May 16, 1947; His Eminence PATRICK CARDINAL O'BOYLE, cons. Jan. 14, 1948; created Cardinal June 26, 1967; retired March 3, 1973; died Aug. 10, 1987; WILLIAM CARDINAL BAUM, S.T.D., installed May 8, 1973; appt. Prefect, Congregation for Catholic Education in the Vatican, Jan. 15, 1980; Major Penitentiary; appt. April 6, 1990; retired Nov. 22, 2001; died July 23, 2015; JAMES CARDINAL HICKEY, S.T.D., J.C.D., ord. Auxiliary Bishop of Saginaw April 14, 1967; appt. Bishop of Cleveland June 5, 1974; appt. Archbishop of Washington June 17, 1980; installed Aug. 5, 1980; created Cardinal June 28, 1988; retired Nov. 21, 2000; died Oct. 24, 2004; THEODORE E. MCCARRICK, Ph.D., D.D., ord. May 31, 1958; appt. Auxiliary Bishop of New York May 24, 1977; Episcopal ord. June 29, 1977; appt. First Bishop of Metuchen Nov. 19, 1981; installed Jan. 31, 1982; appt. Archbishop of Newark May 30, 1986; installed July 25, 1986; appt. Archbishop of Washington Nov. 21, 2000; installed Jan. 3, 2001; created Cardinal priest Feb. 21, 2001; retired May 16, 2006; resigned from College of Cardinals July 27, 2018; dismissed from the clerical state Feb. 15, 2019.; His Eminence DONALD CARDINAL WUERL, ord. Dec. 17, 1966; appt. Titular Bishop of Rosemarkie and Auxiliary Bishop of Seattle Dec. 3, 1985; cons. Jan. 6, 1986; appt. and canonically installed Bishop of Pittsburgh Feb. 12, 1988;

liturgically installed March 25, 1988; appt. Archbishop of Washington May 16, 2006; installed June 22, 2006; created Cardinal priest of Saint Peter in Chains Nov. 20, 2010; installed May 8, 2011; retired Oct. 12, 2018; appt. Apostolic Administrator of Washington Oct. 12, 2018.

Unless otherwise indicated, all Archdiocesan Offices, including the Chancery and the Tribunal, are located in the Archdiocesan Pastoral Center, 5001 Eastern Ave., Hyattsville, MD 20782. Mailing Address: P.O. Box 29260, Washington, 20017. Tel: 301-853-4500; Fax: 301-853-5346Office Hours: Mon.-Fri. 8:30-5.

Vicars General—Most Revs. ROY E. CAMPBELL, D.D., V.G.; MARIO E. DORSONVILLE, D.D., V.G.; MICHAEL W. FISHER, V.G.

Moderator of the Curia—Rev. Msgr. CHARLES V. ANTONICELLI, J.D., J.C.L.; MR. TERENCE J. FARRELL, Exec. Sec. of Curia.

Chancellor and General Counsel—KIM VITI FIORENTINO, Esq.

Vice Chancellor—Rev. GEORGE E. STUART, J.C.D.

Office of Child Protection and Safe Envrionment—COURTNEY CHASE, Exec. Dir., Tel: 301-853-5302; Fax: 301-853-7675; Email: cchase@adw.org.

Archivist—DR. STEPHANIE JACOBE, Tel: 301-853-5316.

Secretary to the Archbishop—Rev. DANIELE REBEGGIANI, Tel: 301-853-5350; Fax: 301-853-5359.

Secretariats—(See separate sections for each Secretariat below) Most Rev. MICHAEL W. FISHER, V.G., Vicar for Clergy & Sec. Ministerial Leadership; MS. JEANNINE MARINO, J.C.L., Sec. Pastoral Ministry & Social Concerns; MR. EDWARD MCFADDEN, Sec. Communications.

Office of Canonical Services—

Episcopal Vicar for Canonical Services—Rev. Msgr. CHARLES V. ANTONICELLI, J.D., J.C.L., Admin., Office of Administrative Procedures, Tel: 301-853-5325; Fax: 301-853-7674.

Administrative Support—NANETTE LOWE, Human Resources; WILLIAM POTTER, Information Technology.

The Tribunal

Tribunal—Tel: 301-853-4543; Fax: 301-853-7674; Email: tribunal@adw.org.

The Office of the Tribunal is an ecclesiastical court primarily dealing with marriage nullity cases and assists with canonical questions that arise in parishes or agencies of the archdiocese. The Tribunal is the court of first instance for the Archdiocese of Washington and the Diocese of St. Thomas in the Virgin Islands, as well the Appellate court for the Archdiocese of Cincinnati.

Judicial Vicar—Rev. Msgr. KEVIN T. HART, J.C.D., Tel: 301-853-4536.

Adjutant Judicial Vicars—Rev. Msgrs. CHARLES V. ANTONICELLI, J.D., J.C.L.; GODFREY T. MOSLEY, J.C.D.; Rev. MARK E. TUCKER, J.C.L., Tel: 301-853-5322.

Moderator of the Tribunal Chancery—SOFIA SEGUEL, S.T.L., J.C.L., Tel: 301-853-5326; Email: seguels@adw.org.

Judges—Rev. Msgr. JOSEPH F. SADUSKY, J.C.D., (Retired); SOFIA SEGUEL, S.T.L., J.C.L.

Promoter of Justice—Rev. GEORGE E. STUART, J.C.D., Tel: 301-853-5327.

Defenders of the Bond—Rev. GEORGE E. STUART, J.C.D., Tel: 301-853-5327; DR. JACLYN MCEACHERN, J.C.D.; Deacon JAMES QUINN, J.C.L.

Advocates—Rev. Msgr. GEORGE E. DOBES, J.C.L.; Deacon GARY L. BOCKWEG; LINDA BUDNEY, J.C.L.; Revs. WILLIAM H. GURNEE III, J.C.L.; MARCO FEDERICO SCHAD, J.D.; DAVID G. WELLS; JUSTIN A. HUBER.

Auditors—CRISTINA HIP-FLORES, J.C.D.; PATRICIA A. PERKINSON, Tel: 301-853-4544.

Office of Canonical Affairs

The Office of Canonical Services grants marriage dispensations, approves files to be sent to other dioceses and assists with canonical questions that arise in parishes or agencies of the archdiocese.

Canonical Affairs—Rev. GEORGE E. STUART, J.C.D., Vice Chancellor, Tel: 301-853-5327; MELISSA HUNSIKER, Administrative Asst., Tel: 301-853-5325; Email: hunsikerm@adw.org.

Consultative Groups

Archdiocesan College of Consultors—Most Revs. MARIO E. DORSONVILLE, D.D., V.G.; MICHAEL W. FISHER, V.G.; ROY E. CAMPBELL, D.D., V.G.; Rev. Msgrs. DONALD S. ESSEX, (Retired); CHARLES V. ANTONICELLI, J.D., J.C.L.; PETER J. VAGHI, J.D., V.F.; JAMES D. WATKINS; Revs. SCOTT R. HAHN, V.F.; DAVID M. FITZ-PATRICK; MARK D. KNESTOUT; WILLIAM E. FOLEY, V.F.

Secretariat for Ministerial Leadership and Vicar for Clergy

Secretariat for Ministerial Leadership and Vicar for Clergy—Most Rev. MICHAEL W. FISHER, V.G., Tel: 301-853-4550; Fax: 301-853-7668.

Pastoral Care of Priests—Rev. Msgr. JOSEPH A. RANIERI, Coord., (Retired), Tel: 301-853-5361; Fax: 301-853-7668.

Vocations for Men—Revs. MARK R. IVANY, Dir., Tel: 202-561-4178; SCOTT WOODS, Asst. Dir., Tel: 301-862-4200; MARIO A. MAJANO, Asst. Dir., Tel: 301-891-3500.

Continuing Education for Clergy—Rev. Msgr. ROBERT PANKE, Tel: 202-636-9020.

St. John Vianney House—Kensington, MD Tel: 301-942-1191.

Director, Permanent Diaconate—Deacon DONALD R. LONGANO, Tel: 301-853-4583; Fax: 301-853-7669.

Coordinator of Pastoral Care—Deacon JOSEPH F. CURTIS JR., Tel: 301-853-4586; Fax: 301-853-7669.

Director of Formation, Permanent Diaconate—Deacon CHARLES P. HUBER, Fax: 301-853-7669.

Priests Retirement Board—Rev. Msgr. V. JAMES LOCKMAN, V.F., (Retired), (Term Expires Aug. 31, 2020), Res.: 2130 Ganton Green, #403, Woodstock, 21163. Tel: 301-651-3374; Email: lockmanj@adw.org; Revs. MARK F. HUGHES, (Term Expires June 30, 2021), Holy Redeemer, 9705 Summit Ave., Kensington, 20895. Tel: 301-942-2333; Email: hughesm@adw.org; FREDERICK J. CLOSE, (Term Expires: June 30, 2021), St. Anthony of Padua, 1029 Monroe St., N.E., Washington, 20017. Tel: 202-250-8208; Email: closef@adw.org; SAVERIO T. VITTURINO, (Retired), (Term expires Aug. 31, 2020), 6050 California Cir., #108, Rockville, 20852. Tel: 240-242-3771; Email: vitturinos@adw.org; FRANCISCO E. AGUIRRE, (Term expires June 30, 2019), Res.: St. Catherine Laboure, 11801 Claridge Rd., Wheaton, 20902. Tel: 301-946-3636; Email: aguirref@adw.org; DAVID G. WELLS, (Term Expires June 30, 2020), Res.: St. Martin of Tours, 201 S. Frederick Ave., Gaithersburg, 20877. Tel: 301-990-3203; Email: wellsd@adw.org. Ex Officio Members: Rev. Msgr. CHARLES V. ANTONICELLI, J.D., J.C.L., Moderator of the Curia; Most Rev. MICHAEL W. FISHER, V.G., Sec. Ministerial Leadership; KIM VITI FIORENTINO, Esq., Chancellor; Rev. Msgr. JOSEPH RANIERI, Coord. Pastoral Care of Priests; Rev. C. GREGORY BUTTA, Chap., Cardinal O'Boyle Res. for Priests.

Cardinal O'Boyle Residence for Priests—Rev. C. GREGORY BUTTA, Mailing Address: P.O. Box 29206, Washington, 20017. Tel: 202-269-7818.

Saint John Paul II Seminary—Rev. Msgr. ROBERT J. PANKE, Rector & Dir. Clergy Formation, Tel: 301-853-4580; Fax: 301-853-7668; Revs. MARK R. IVANY, Dir. Spiritual Formation; CARTER H. GRIFFIN, Vice Rector, Dean of Students, Tel: 301-853-5378; Fax: 301-853-7668; KEVIN J. REGAN, Adjunct Spiritual Dir.; MARK L. SMITH, Dir. Pastoral Formation.

Deans—Revs. SCOTT R. HAHN, V.F., Middle Prince George's County; JOHN H. KENNEALY, V.F., Upper Prince George's County; THOMAS G. LAHOOD, Lower Prince George's County; LEROY J. FANGMEYER, V.F., Upper-West Montgomery County; Rev. Msgrs. ROBERT G. AMEY, V.F., Upper-East Montgomery County; PETER J. VAGHI, J.D., V.F., Middle Montgomery County; EDDIE E. TOLENTINO, V.F., Lower Montgomery County; CHARLES E. POPE, V.F., Northeast, D.C.; Rev. KEVIN C. KENNEDY, V.F., Northwest East, D.C.; Rev. Msgr. W. RONALD JAMESON, Northwest West, D.C.; Rev. RAYMOND H. MOORE, V.F., Southeast, D.C.; Rev. Msgr. MICHAEL WILSON, V.F., Calvert County; Revs. RORY T. CONLEY, Charles County; DAVID W. BEAUBIEN, V.F., St. Mary's County.

Secretariat For Education

Secretary for Catholic Education—DR. JEM SULLIVAN, Tel: 301-853-5331; Fax: 301-853-7691.

Catholic Schools Office—

Superintendent for Catholic Schools—WILLIAM H. RYAN, Tel: 301-853-4508; Fax: 301-853-7670; Email: ryanw@adw.org.

Associate Superintendent for Academics and Leadership—MRS. WENDY ANDERSON, Tel: 301-853-4588; Fax: 301-853-7670; Email: andersonw@adw.org.

Associate Superintendent for Strategic Planning and Operations—MS. KELLY A. BRANAMAN, Tel: 301-853-4553; Fax: 301-853-7670; Email: branamank@adw.org.

Assistant Superintendent for Catholic Identity and Accreditation—MRS. LAURA ROLAND, Tel: 301-853-4590; Fax: 301-853-7670; Email: rolandl@adw.org.

Pre-Kindergarten Specialist—MS. CYNTHIA BRASSEUX, Tel: 301-853-4590; Email: brasseuxc@adw.org.

Director for Government and Grant Programs—MR. BRIAN RADZIWILL, Tel: 301-853-5357; Fax: 301-853-7670; Email: radziwillb@adw.org.

Director for Educational Technology—MRS. SHANNON NORRIS, Tel: 301-853-4549; Fax: 301-853-7670; Email: norriss@adw.org.

Director of Special Education—MRS. ANNE DILLON, Tel: 301-853-4569; Fax: 301-853-7670; Email: dillona@adw.org.

Assistant Superintendent for School Operations and Student Services—MR. CHRISTIAN BUCHLEITNER, Tel: 301-853-5353; Fax: 301-853-7670; Email: buchleitnerc@adw.org.

Counseling Services Coordinator—Tel: 301-853-5354.

Assistant Superintendent for Advancement and Enrollment Management—MRS. WENDI M. WILLIAMS, Tel: 301-853-4531; Fax: 301-853-7670; Email: williamsw@adw.org.

Manager for Funding and Enrollment—MR. SEAN BROWN, Tel: 301-853-5356; Fax: 301-853-7670; Email: browns@adw.org.

Director for Curriculum and Instruction—MRS. VICKY MCCANN, Tel: 301-853-4548; Fax: 301-853-7670; Email: mccannv@adw.org.

Director for Assessment and Research—MR. JEREMY MCDONALD, Tel: 301-853-4598; Fax: 301-853-7670; Email: mcdonaldj@adw.org.

Data Coordinator—MRS. UCHE OWELLE, Tel: 301-853-5303; Fax: 301-853-7670; Email: owelleu@adw.org.

Hispanic Outreach Coordinator—MS. MIRYAN CABRERA, Tel: 301-853-4551; Fax: 301-853-7670; Email: cabreram@adw.org.

Consortium of Catholic Academies of the Archdiocese of Washington, Inc.—MRS. ROSIO GONZALEZ, Pres., Tel: 301-853-5340; Email: rosio.gonzalez@catholicacademies.org.

Board of Education—MRS. PATRICIA REIMER, Pres.

Office for Catechesis—

Director of Catechesis—MS. SARA BLAUVELT, Tel: 301-853-5368; Email: blauvelts@adw.org.

Coordinator of Adult Formation and Hispanic Catechesis—MS. KATELY JAVIER, Tel: 301-853-5384; Email: javierk@adw.org.

Coordinator of Children's Catechesis and Curriculum—MR. DOUGLAS LAWRENCE, Tel: 301-853-5385; Email: lawrenced@adw.org.

Secretariat for Pastoral Ministry and Social Concerns

Secretary for Pastoral Ministry and Social Concerns—MS. JEANNINE MARINO, J.C.L., Tel: 301-853-4596; Fax: 301-853-7671; Email: marinoj@adw.org.

Assistant Secretary for Pastoral Ministry and Social Concerns/CCHD Diocesan Director/Catholic Relief Services Liaison—MS. DEBORAH MCDONALD, Tel: 301-853-4466; Fax: 301-853-7671; Email: mcdonald@adw.org.

Assistant Secretary for Pastoral Ministry and Social Concerns—MR. JONATHAN LEWIS, Tel: 301-853-4559; Fax: 301-853-7671; Email: lewisj@adw.org; MR. ANTHONY ESSER, Coord. Parish Evangelization, Tel: 301-853-5347; Fax: 301-853-7671; Email: essera@adw.org; MRS. MEGAN PHILIP, Coord., Campus & Young Adult Ministry, Tel: 301-853-5308; Email: philipm@adw.org.

Office for Family Life—MRS. CARLA FERRANDO-BOWLING, Dir., Tel: 301-853-4499; Fax: 301-853-7671; Email: ferrando-bowlingc@adw.org.

Office for Ecumenical and Interreligious Affairs—Rev. CHARLES A. CORTINOVIS, Dir., St. Ambrose, 3107 63rd Ave., Cheverly, 20785. Tel: 301-773-9300.

Catholic Charismatic Renewal—Rev. FREDERICK J. CLOSE, St. Anthony of Padua, 1029 Monroe St., NE, Washington, 20017. Tel: 202-526-8822.

Catholic Spanish Charismatic Renewal—Rev. ROBERTO J. CORTES, St. Mark the Evangelist, 7501 Adelphi Rd., Hyattsville, 20783. Tel: 301-422-8300.

Department of Special Needs Ministries—Pope Francis Center, 7202 Buchanan St., Landover Hills, 20784. MRS. MARY O'MEARA, Exec. Dir., Tel: 301-853-4431 (Voice); Tel: 240-667-7715 (Video Phone); Email: omearam@adw.org; MRS. RACHEL CHUNG, Coord. Office for Persons with Disabilities, Tel: 301-853-4435 (Voice); Email: chungr@adw.org; MS. LAUREEN LYNCH-RYAN, Coord. Office of Deaf Ministry, Tel: 301-200-5430 (Video Phone); Email: lynch-ryanl@adw.org; MS. CHRISTINA DI SALVO, Coord., Interpreter Svcs., Tel: 301-853-4432 (Voice); Tel: 301-841-8210 (Video Phone); Email: disalvoc@adw.org.

Office of Worship—Rev. CONRAD MURPHY, Dir., Tel: 301-853-4595; Fax: 301-853-7684; Email: murphyc@adw.org.

Commission on Sacred Art and Architecture—Rev.

Msgr. W. RONALD JAMESON, Chm., Cathedral of St. Matthew the Apostle, 1725 Rhode Island Ave., NW, Washington, 20036. Tel: 202-347-3215; Fax: 202-347-7184.

Office of Missions—Sr. ANNAI D'SOUZA, S.S.V.M., MCA Mission Educ. Coord. & Missionary Cooperative Plan Coord., Tel: 301-853-5388; Fax: 301-853-7685; Email: dsouzaa@adw.org.

Department of Life Issues—MS. MARY FORR, Dir., Tel: 301-853-5318; Fax: 301-853-7671; Email: forrm@adw.org; MR. DAVID DRY, Prog. Coord., Tel: 301-853-4555; Fax: 301-853-7671; Email: dryd@adw.org.

Project Rachel Ministry—Catholic Charities Center, 12247 Georgia Ave., Silver Spring, 20902. MS. JULIA SHELAVA, Dir., Tel: 301-853-4451; Email: shelavaj@adw.org; MRS. MARIA TIRADO, Participant & Outreach Coord., Tel: 301-853-4454; Email: tiradom@adw.org; Sr. PRISCILLA DE GUZMAN, S.P.C., Participant & Outreach Coord., Tel: 301-853-4453; Email: deguzmanp@adw.org.

Office of Cultural Diversity and Outreach—MS. SANDRA COLES-BELL, Prog. Dir., Tel: 301-853-4469; Fax: 301-853-7671; Email: colesbells@adw.org; MRS. CLAUDIA BARTOLINI, Coord. Resource Devel., Tel: 301-853-5335; Fax: 301-853-7671; Email: bartolinic@adw.org.

Catholic Youth Organization of Washington DC and the Greater Metropolitan Area—Pope Francis Center, 7202 Buchanan St., Landover Hills, 20784. MR. KEVIN DONOGHUE, Pres./CEO, Tel: 301-853-4463; Fax: 301-853-7660; Email: donoghuek@adw.org; MR. TEX PHELPS, Dir., Youth Ministry, Tel: 301-853-4467; Fax: 301-853-7660; Email: phelpst@adw.org; MR. JUAN AZNARAN, Regl. Coord., Tel: 301-853-4461; Fax: 301-853-7660; Email: aznaranj@adw.org; MRS. MARY FAVA, OYM/CYO Prog. Coord., Tel: 301-853-4465; Fax: 301-853-7660; Email: favam@adw.org.

Boy Scouts / Girl Scouts / Camp Fire Boys & Girls—MR. RICHARD STEVICK, Coord. Archdiocesan Catholic Committee on Scouting/Camp Fire, Tel: 301-490-7855; Email: dstevick@verizon.net.

Girl Scout Chair, Catholic Committee for Girl Scouts—VACANT.

Boy Scout Chair, Catholic Committee for Boy Scouts—MR. CHRIS MURRAY, Tel: 301-251-0359; Email: chris.murray3@yahoo.com.

Camp Fire Lay Coordinator—MS. ROSEMARY PEZUTTO, Tel: 301-262-1631; Email: copier22@aol.com.

Archdiocesan Chaplain - Catholic Committee on Boy Scouts—Rev. SCOTT WOODS, Tel: 301-862-4600.

Archdiocesan Chaplain - Catholic Committee on Girl Scouts—Rev. RONALD A. POTTS, Tel: 301-262-0704.

Archdiocesan Finance Council—His Eminence DONALD CARDINAL WUERL, S.T.D.; W. SHEPHERDSON ABELL, Esq.; CAROL G. BATES; GEORGE P. CLANCY JR.; JOAN CONLEY; RAUL FERNANDEZ; Sr. CAROL KEEHAN, D.C.; J. MICHAEL KELLY; J. PAUL MCNAMARA; WILLIAM J. SHAW; DR. ENRIQUE SEGURA. Staff: Rev. Msgrs. CHARLES V. ANTONICELLI, J.D., J.C.L., Moderator of the Curia; JOHN J. ENZLER, E.V., Pres. & CEO Catholic Charities; KIM VITI FIORENTINO, Esq., Chancellor & Gen. Counsel; ERIC SIMONTIS, CFO; JENNIFER CASE, Controller.

Secretariat for Finance and Management

Finance and Management—ERIC SIMONTIS, CFO, Tel: 301-853-5365.

Office of Finance—JENNIFER CASE, Controller, Tel: 301-853-4504.

Parish and School Financial Operations—MS. ADRIENNE WILLICH, Dir., Tel: 301-853-5373; Fax: 301-853-7664.

Facilities Management—MS. MICHELLE SHELTON, Exec. Dir. Real Estate & Facilities Mgmt. Office, Tel: 301-853-4522; Fax: 301-853-7665; ROBERT R. MESSER JR., Facilities Mgr., Tel: 301-853-4477; Fax: 301-853-7665; PHILIP DUCK, Asst. Dir. Bldg. Facilities Mgmt., Tel: 301-853-4530; Fax: 301-853-7673.

Personnel and Benefits—NANETTE LOWE, Exec. Dir. Human Resources, Tel: 301-853-5366; Fax: 301-853-7680.

Secretariat for Development

Development Office—Coordinates all Archdiocesan development and fundraising and stewardship efforts and oversees the Cardinal's Appeal, parish resource development, planned giving, major donors, grant writing, Forward in Faith Campaign, Retired Priests Collection and the Archdiocesan Tuition Assistance Fund. Tel: 301-853-5375; Fax: 301-853-7678; Fax: 301-853-7692; Email: gillmerj@adw.org.

Vicar of Development—VACANT, Tel: 202-772-4300; Fax: 301-853-7692.

Annual Appeal—Tel: 301-853-4574; Fax: 301-853-7678 . MS. ELIZABETH SHAUGHNEY, Dir., Email: shaughneye@adw.org.

Planned Giving—VACANT.

Forward in Faith—MR. JOSEPH GILLMER, Dir., Tel: 301-853-5375; Fax: 301-853-7678.

Retired Priests Collection—VACANT.

Archdiocesan Tuition Assistance Fund—MR. JOSEPH GILLMER, Tel: 301-853-5375; Fax: 301-853-7678.

Stewardship—Tel: 301-853-5374; Fax: 301-853-7678. MR. ROBERT BART III, Dir.

Archdiocesan Building Commission—Rev. Msgr. JOSEPH A. RANIERI, Chm., (Retired).

Archdiocesan Sacred Arts Committee—Rev. Msgr. W. RONALD JAMESON, 1725 Rhode Island Ave. N.W., Washington, 20036. Tel: 202-347-3215; Fax: 202-347-7184.

Catholic Education Foundation of the Archdiocese of Washington, Inc.—MR. ROBERT LANE, Chm., Mailing Address: P.O. Box 29260, Washington, 20017. Tel: 301-853-5312.

Priest Retirement Benefit Trust of the Archdiocese of Washington—Rev. Msgr. DONALD S. ESSEX, Chm., (Retired), Email: dessex@adwparish.org.

Secretariat for Communications

Secretary for Communications—MR. EDWARD MCFADDEN, Tel: 301-853-4516.

Office of Media and Public Relations—MS. CHIEKO NOGUCHI, Dir., Tel: 301-853-4516.

Office of Digital Media—MS. DAPHNE STUBBOLO, Tel: 301-853-4484.

Office of Multimedia Production—MR. CHRISTOPHER BAKER, Dir., Tel: 301-853-4519.

TV Mass Producer—MR. JOHN CAPOBIANCO, Tel: 301-853-4516.

Carroll Media Company—His Eminence DONALD CARDINAL WUERL, S.T.D., Publisher.

Newspaper "The Catholic Standard"—MR. MARK ZIMMERMANN, Editor, Tel: 202-281-2412; Fax: 202-281-2408; Email: mark@cathstan.org.

Newspaper "El Pregonero"—MR. RAFAEL RONCAL, Editor, Tel: 202-281-2442; Fax: 202-281-2408; Email: rafael@elpreg.org.

CLERGY, PARISHES, MISSIONS AND PAROCHIAL SCHOOLS

DISTRICT OF COLUMBIA

1—ST. MATTHEW CATHEDRAL (1840)
1725 Rhode Island Ave., N.W., 20036.
Tel: 202-347-3215; Fax: 202-347-7184; Email: cathstmatt@stmatthewscathedral.org; Web: www.stmatthewscathedral.org. Rev. Msgr. W. Ronald Jameson; Rev. Agustin Lopez; Deacons Bartholomew J. Merella, (Retired); Juan Cayrampoma; Pamela Erwin, Business Mgr. In Res., Revs. John Hurley, (Retired); Conrad Murphy.
Catechesis Religious Program—Students 112.

2—ST. ALOYSIUS (1859) Merged with Holy Redeemer, Washington, DC.

3—ST. ANN (1869)
4001 Yuma St., 20016. Tel: 202-966-6288;
Fax: 202-966-7722; Email: stann@stanndc.org; Web: www.stanndc.org. Rev. Msgr. Godfrey T. Mosley, J.C.D.
Catechesis Religious Program—
Tel: 202-363-9524; Email: dre@stanndc.org. Students 48.
Mission—
4133 Yuma St., NW, 20016. Tel: 202-244-2617.

4—ANNUNCIATION (1948)
3125 39th St., N.W., 20016-5409. Tel: 202-362-3323; Email: parish@annunciationdc.org; Web: annunciationdc.org. Rev. Msgr. Michael J. Mellone, V.F.; Rev. Andrew Wakefield, Parochial Vicar; Rev. Msgr. Charles V. Antonicelli, J.D., J.C.L., In Res.; Deacon William T. Maksymiec.
School—Annunciation School
3825 Klingle Pl., N.W., 20016-5434.
Tel: 202-362-1408; Fax: 202-363-4057; Email: info@annunciationschool.net; Web: www.annunciationschool.net. Nathaniel Juarez, Prin. Lay Teachers 16; Students 121.
Catechesis Religious Program—Ms. Patrice Morace, D.R.E. Students 131.

5—ST. ANTHONY OF PADUA (1892)
1029 Monroe St., N.E., 20017. Tel: 202-250-8208;
Fax: 202-250-6223; Email: stanthony.dc@adwparish.org. Revs. Frederick J. Close; Joseph D. Kirkconnell, In Res.; Andrew S. LaFramboise, In Res.; Bruno Maurel, (France) In Res.
School—St. Anthony School
3400 Lawrence St., N.E., 20017. Tel: 202-526-4657;
Fax: 202-832-5567; Web: www.stanthonyschooldc.org. Mr. Michael R. Thomasian, Prin. Lay Teachers 19; Students 219.
Catechesis Religious Program—
Email: alinder@verizon.net. Arthur Linder, D.R.E. Students 65.

6—CHURCH OF THE ASSUMPTION OF THE BLESSED VIRGIN MARY (1916)
3411 Martin Luther King Jr. Ave., S.E., 20032-1597.
Tel: 202-561-4178; Fax: 202-561-0336; Email: info@assumptiondc.org. Rev. Gregory William Shaffer.
Catechesis Religious Program—Shelah Gray, D.R.E. Students 18.

7—ST. AUGUSTINE (1858) (African American)
1419 V St., N.W., 20009. Tel: 202-265-1470. Revs. Patrick A. Smith; Paul John T. Camiring, Parochial Vicar.
Res.: 1425 V St., N.W., 20009.
School—St. Augustine School
1421 V St., N.W., 20009. Tel: 202-667-2608. Donna Edwards, Prin. Lay Teachers 18; Students 173.
Catechesis Religious Program—Students 155.

8—BASILICA OF THE NATIONAL SHRINE OF THE IMMACULATE CONCEPTION (1920)
Mailing Address: 400 Michigan Ave., N.E., 20017-1566. Tel: 202-526-8300; Fax: 202-526-8313; Email: info@nationalshrine.com; Web: www.nationalshrine.com.

9—ST. BENEDICT THE MOOR (1946)
320 21st St., N.E., 20002. Tel: 202-397-3895;
Fax: 202-398-3415; Email: rectory@stbenedictofdc.org; Web: www.stbenedictofdc.org. Rev. Andrew B. Gonzalo.
Catechesis Religious Program—Students 17.

10—ST. BLAISE (1984) (Croatian) (Croatian Pastoral Mission)
Our Lady of Victory, 4835 Macarthur Blvd., N.W., 20007. Tel: 202-255-0856; Fax: 202-338-4759; Email: hrkmisija.svblaz@gmail.com. Rev. Maurus Dolcic, T.O.R.
Catechesis Religious Program—Students 10.

11—BLESSED SACRAMENT, SHRINE OF THE MOST (1911)
Mailing Address: 3630 Quesada St., N.W., 20015-2538. Rev. Ronald A. Potts; Rev. Msgr. Maurice V. O'Connell, (Retired); Revs. Percival L. D'Silva, (Retired); Alexander B. Scott; Deacons Donald Mays; Kenneth Angell.
Res.: 6001 Western Ave., N.W., 20015-2423.
Tel: 202-966-6575; Fax: 202-966-9255; Web: www.blessedsacramentdc.org.
School—Blessed Sacrament School, Shrine of the Most
5841 Chevy Chase Pkwy., N.W., 20015-2599.
Tel: 202-966-6682; Fax: 202-966-4938; Web: www.bsstoday.org. Mr. Christopher Kelly, Prin. Lay Teachers 45; Students 515.
Catechesis Religious Program—
Tel: 202-449-3989; Email: mbalch@blessedsacramentdc.org. Michelle Balch, D.R.E., Email: mbalch@blessedsacramentdc.org. Students 374.

12—CHURCH OF ST. LOUIS (1972) (French) (Paroisse St. Louis de France-French-speaking Parish of Washington)
4125 Garrison St., N.W., 20016. Tel: 202-537-0709;
Fax: frenchparish@saintlouisdefrance.us; Web: www.saintlouisdefrance.us. Rev. Pierre Henri Montagne.
Catechesis Religious Program—Students 151.

13—ST. DOMINIC CHURCH & PRIORY (1852)
630 E St., S.W., 20024. Tel: 202-554-7863;
Fax: 202-554-0231; Email: pastor@stdominicchurch.org; Web: www.stdominicchurch.org. Revs. George P. Schommer, O.P., M.Div.; Jacob Restrick, O.P., Prior; Hyacinth Cordell, O.P., Parochial Vicar. In Res., Revs. George Christian, O.P.; Luke Clark, O.P.; Thomas Davenport, O.P.; Cyril Dettling, O.P.; Henry Thomas Donoghue, O.P.; Ambrose Eckinger, O.P.; Peter Fegan, O.P.; Luke Hoyt, O.P.; Theodore John Baptist Ku, O.P., S.T.L.; Gerard Lessard, O.P.; Carl Louis Mason, O.P., B.A.; Edmund McCullough, O.P.; J. Andrew Nicolicchia, O.P.; Matthew Rzeczkowski, O.P.; Gregory R. Salomone, O.P.; Bede Shipps, O.P.; Raymond Vandegrift, O.P.; Bruce Williams, O.P.; Bros. Patrick Foley, O.P.; Ignatius Perkins, O.P.; Deacons Aquinas Beale, O.P.; Leo Camurati, O.P.; Timothy Danaher, O.P.; Peter Gautsch, O.P.; Humbert Kilanowski, O.P.; Mannes Matous, O.P.; Isaac Morales, O.P.; Henry Stephan, WDC. Brothers 6.

14—EPIPHANY (1923)
2712 Dumbarton St., N.W., 20007. Tel: 202-965-1610 ; Fax: 202-337-8377; Email: epiphanygeorgetown@gmail.com; Web: www.georgetownepiphany.org. Rev. Msgr. Godfrey T. Mosley, J.C.D.
Catechesis Religious Program—Sr. Martina Koh, L.S.H.F., D.R.E.

15—ST. FRANCIS DE SALES (1722)
2021 Rhode Island Ave., N.E., 20018.
Tel: 202-529-7451; Email: bsanderfoot@adwparish.

org; Web: www.stfrancisdesaleswdc.org. Rev. Brian P. Sanderfoot, J.C.L. In Res., Rev. Henry Slevin.
Catechesis Religious Program—Students 12.

16—St. Francis Xavier (1924)
2800 Pennsylvania Ave., S.E., 20020.
Tel: 202-582-5021; Fax: 202-581-7224; Email: sfxdcparish@gmail.com. Rev. Mark A. Cusick, Admin.

17—St. Gabriel (1919)
26 Grant Cir., N.W., 20011. Tel: 202-726-9092; Fax: 202-291-0334. Rev. Avelino A. Gonzalez; Deacon Roberto Salgado. In Res., Rev. Tesfamarian Baraki.
Catechesis Religious Program—
Tel: 202-726-9212. Students 196.

18—Holy Comforter - St. Cyprian (1893) (African American)
1357 E. Capitol St., S.E., 20003. Tel: 202-546-1885; Fax: 202-544-1385; Email: hcscstaff@hcscchurch.org; Web: www.hcscchurch.org. Rev. Msgr. Charles E. Pope, V.F.; Revs. F. Michael Bryant, In Res.; Araia Ghiday Ghebray, In Res.; D.B. Thompson, In Res.; Thomas Valayathil, In Res.; Deacons Kevin Butler; Ralph Cyrus.
Catechesis Religious Program—Shirley Austin, Min. of Rel. Educ. Students 41.

19—Holy Name (1891)
920 11th St., N.E., 20002. Tel: 202-397-2525; Fax: 202-397-6639. Rev. Michael W. Briese. In Res., Rev. Francis M. Walsh.
Catechesis Religious Program—Students 18.

20—Holy Redeemer (1919) (African American)
206 New York Ave., N.W., 20001. Tel: 202-347-7510; Tel: 202-347-9268; Fax: 202-638-4831; Email: holyredeemer.dc@adwparish.org. Rev. David Bava.
St. Aloysius Church Annex Office: 19 Eye St., N.W., 20001. Tel: 202-336-7211.
Catechesis Religious Program—Students 50.

21—Holy Rosary (1913) (Italian)
595 Third St., N.W., 20001-2703. Tel: 202-638-0165; Fax: 202-638-0793; Email: casaitaldc@gmail.com; Web: www.holyrosarychurchdc.org. Rev. Ezio Marchetto, C.S.
Catechesis Religious Program—Students 12.

22—Holy Trinity (1787)
3513 N St., N.W., 20007. Tel: 202-337-2840; Email: communications@trinity.org; Email: kgillespie@trinity.org; Web: www.trinity.org. Revs. C. Kevin Gillespie, S.J.; Paul Brian Campbell, S.J.; William J. Kelley, S.J.
School—Holy Trinity School, (Grades PreK-8), 1325 36th St. N.W., 20007-2604. Mr. Kevin McShane, Prin. Lay Teachers 47; Students 342.
Catechesis Religious Program—Students 700.

23—Immaculate Conception (1864) (African American)
1315 8th St., N.W., 20001. Tel: 202-332-8888; Fax: 202-332-0173; Web: www.immaculateconceptionchurchdc.org. Rev. Adam Y. Park.
Catechesis Religious Program—Students 30.

24—Incarnation (1934) (African American)
880 Eastern Ave., N.E., 20019. Tel: 202-396-0942; Fax: 202-396-6064. Rev. John A. Carroll, S.S.J.; Deacon Joseph E. Bell.
Catechesis Religious Program—Students 123.

25—St. Joseph's on Capitol Hill (1868)
313 Second St., N.E., 20002. Tel: 202-547-1223; Fax: 202-547-4189; Email: stjosephsdc@st-josephs.org; Web: www.st-josephs.org. Revs. William H. Gurnee III, J.C.L.; Christopher T. Begg, Ph.D., Ph.B., S.T.D., Prof.; Eugene Hemrick, (In Res.); Deacon Gary L. Bockweg.
Catechesis Religious Program—
Email: catholic@st-josephs.org. Students 30.

26—Kidane-Mehret Ge'ez Rite Catholic Church (1984) (Ethiopian—Eritrean)
1001 Lawrence St., N.E., P.O. Box 29616, 20017. Tel: 202-756-2756; Fax: 202-756-2755; Email: kmgeezrite@aol.com; Web: www.kidane.mehret.org. Rev. Araia Ghiday Ghebray.
Rectory—
1357 E. Capitol St., S.E., 20003. Tel: 202-546-1885.
Catechesis Religious Program— CCD held at St. Vincent de Paul Parish Students 127.

27—St. Luke (1957) (African American)
4925 E. Capitol St., S.E., 20019-5202.
Tel: 202-584-8322; Fax: 202-584-3421; Email: stluke.dc@adwparish.org. Rev. Cornelius K. Ejiogu. In Res., Rev. Denis Mandamuna.
Catechesis Religious Program—Students 45.

28—St. Martin of Tours (1901) (African American)
1908 N. Capitol St., 20002. Tel: 202-232-1144; Fax: 202-832-6772; Email: mjkelley@verizon.net; Web: www.stmartinsdc.org. Rev. Michael J. Kelley.
Catechesis Religious Program—Students 46.

29—St. Mary, Mother of God (1845) [CEM]
727 Fifth St., N.W., 20001. Tel: 202-289-7771; Fax: 202-408-1989; Email: stmarys20001@gmail.com. Rev. Alfred J. Harris. In Res., Revs. Joel R. Wilson; Kevin Augustyn.
Catechesis Religious Program—
Tel: 202-289-7770.

30—Nativity (1901) (African American)
6000 Georgia Ave., N.W., 20011. Tel: 202-726-6262; Fax: 202-722-7170; Email: nativityccdc2010@aol.com; Web: www.nativitychurch.net. Rev. Blake Evans-Campos. In Res., Revs. Mark E. Tucker, J.C.L.; William L. Montgomery, (Retired).
Catechesis Religious Program—Students 76.

31—Nigerian Catholic Community (1994) (Nigerian), Closed. For inquiries for parish records contact the chancery.

32—Our Lady of Fatima Parish (1999) (Portuguese)
5700 St. Bernard's Dr., Riverdale, 20737.
Tel: 301-277-1000; Fax: 301-277-3464; Email: bernard.fatimachurch@gmail.com. Revs. Jefferson Bariviera, C.S.; Lino Garcia, C.S.
Catechesis Religious Program—
Email: teresadluna@gmail.com. Mrs. Teresa Luna, D.R.E. Students 75.

33—Our Lady of Perpetual Help (1920) (African American)
1600 Morris Rd., S.E., 20020-6312.
Tel: 202-678-4999; Fax: 202-610-3189; Email: info@olphsedc.com; Web: www.olphsedc.com. Very Rev. Thomas R. Frank, S.S.J.; Rev. Kingsley Ogbuji, Parochial Vicar; Deacons Thomas Jones; Timothy E. Tilghman.
Catechesis Religious Program—Cynthia Battle, D.R.E. Students 18.

34—Our Lady of Victory (1909)
4835 MacArthur Blvd., N.W., 20007.
Tel: 202-337-4835; Tel: 202-337-4836;
Fax: 202-338-4759. Rev. David M. Fitz-Patrick; Deacon Leo Flynn. In Res., Revs. Daniel B. Carson; Leo D. Lefebure, Matteo Ricci Chair, Georgetown University; Prof. of Theology.
School—Our Lady of Victory School
4755 Whitehaven Pkwy., N.W., 20007.
Tel: 202-337-1421; Fax: 202-337-2068; Web: olvschooldc.org. Mrs. Sheila Martinez, Prin. Lay Teachers 27; Students 223.
Catechesis Religious Program—
Tel: 202-337-4835, Ext. 14; Fax: 202-338-4759; Email: dre@olvparish.org. Students 67.

35—Our Lady Queen of Peace (1948) (African American)
3800 Ely Pl., S.E., 20019. Tel: 202-582-8600; Fax: 202-575-3317. Rev. Pawel Sass; Deacon Alfred Miller.
Catechesis Religious Program—
Tel: 202-581-4986. Students 47.
Convent—
3740 Ely Pl., S.E., 20019. Tel: 202-581-4963; Fax: 202-584-1922.

36—Our Lady Queen of the Americas (1986) (Hispanic)
2200 California St., N.W., 20008. Tel: 202-332-8838; Fax: 202-332-2967. Rev. Evelio Menjivar-Ayala; Deacon Jorge W. Vargas.
Catechesis Religious Program—Lilian Cifuentes, C.R.E. Students 190.

37—St. Patrick (1794)
619 Tenth St., N.W., 20001-4587. Tel: 202-347-2713; Fax: 202-347-1401; Email: office@saintpatrickdc.org; Web: saintpatrickdc.org. Rev. Msgr. Salvatore A. Criscuolo; Ronald Stolk, Music Dir. In Res., Revs. Frederick H. MacIntyre, (Retired); Roderick D. McKee, (Retired); Fabrizio Meroni, P.I.M.E.
Catechesis Religious Program—Robert Quinlan, D.R.E. (Adult).

38—St. Peter (1821)
313 Second St., S.E., 20003. Tel: 202-547-1430; Fax: 202-547-5732; Email: rectory@saintpetersdc.org; Web: saintpetersdc.org. Rev. Gary R. Studniewski. In Res., Rev. Msgr. Joseph F. Sadusky, J.C.D., (Retired).
School—St. Peter School, (Grades PreK-8), 422 Third St., S.E., 20003. Tel: 202-544-1618; Fax: 202-547-5101; Email: info@stpeterschooldc.org; Web: stpeterschooldc.org. Karen Clay, Prin. Lay Teachers 26; Daughters of St. Anne 2; Students 234.
Catechesis Religious Program—Students 103.

39—Shrine of the Sacred Heart (1899)
3211 Pine St., 20010. Tel: 202-234-8000;
Tel: 202-234-8002; Fax: 202-234-9159. Revs. Moises Villalta, O.F.M.Cap.; Kevin Thompson, O.F.M.Cap.; Pierre Mike Pettit-Houne; Francis Nguyen, (Vietnamese Apostolate); Deacon Nehemias J. Molina. In Res., Revs. James P. Froehlich, O.F.M.Cap., M.A., M.S., Ph.D.; John Pavlik, O.F.M.Cap.
School—Shrine of the Sacred Heart School
1625 Park Rd., N.W., 20010. Tel: 202-265-4828; Fax: 202-265-0595; Email: beverly.bonilla@catholicacademies.org. Elise Heil, Prin. Lay Teachers 22; Students 214.
Catechesis Religious Program—
Tel: 202-667-2446. Students 625.

40—St. Stephen Martyr (1867)
2436 Pennsylvania Ave., N.W., 20037.
Tel: 202-785-0982; Fax: 202-785-1574; Email: saintstephenmartyrdc@gmail.com; Web: www.ststephenmartyrdc.org. Rev. Msgr. Paul Dudziak; Rev. Klaus J. Sirianni.

41—St. Teresa of Avila (1879) (African American)
1401 V St., S.E., 20020-5692. Tel: 202-678-3709; Fax: 202-678-3325. Rev. Msgr. Raymond G. East; Deacon William J. Hawkins.
Res.: 1430 Minnesota Ave., S.E., 20020-5692.
Tel: 202-678-3037; Fax: 202-678-3325; Web: stachurch.org.
Church: 1244 V. St. S.E., 20020.
Catechesis Religious Program—Students 64.

42—St. Thomas Apostle (1913)
2665 Woodley Rd., N.W., 20008. Tel: 202-234-1488; Fax: 202-234-1480. Rev. Richard A. Mullins; Deacon William C. Boesman.
Catechesis Religious Program—Students 14.

43—St. Thomas More (1952) (African American)
4275 4th St., S.E., 20032. Tel: 202-562-0431; Fax: 202-563-7347; Email: stmchurch@comcast.net. Rev. Raymond H. Moore, V.F.
School—St. Thomas More, (Grades PreK-8), Tel: 202-561-1189; Fax: 202-562-2336. Gearld Smith, Prin. Lay Teachers 22; Students 158.
Catechesis Religious Program—Students 75.

44—St. Vincent De Paul (1903) (African American)
14 M St., S.E., 20003-3511. Tel: 202-488-1354; Fax: 202-488-7899. Rev. Andrew B. Gonzalo. In Res.
Catechesis Religious Program—Students 75.

CHURCHES IN MARYLAND

Avenue, St. Mary's Co., Holy Angels (1906) [JC]
21340 Colton Point Rd., Avenue, 20609-2422.
Tel: 301-769-3332; Fax: 301-769-2541; Email: holy01angels@aol.com; Web: www.parishes.org/holyangels.html. Rev. Anthony E. Lickteig; Deacon Joseph W. Lloyd Jr.
Catechesis Religious Program—Students 37.

Baden, Prince Georges Co., St. Michael's (1957)
17510 Horsehead Rd., Brandywine, 20613.
Tel: 240-681-3551; Fax: 301-579-0019; Email: stmichaels.baden@comcast.net; Web: stmichaelsbaden.weconnect.com. Rev. Martin E. Flum, Admin.; Deacon Tyrone Johnson.
Catechesis Religious Program—Tel: 301-888-1498; Fax: 301-579-0019. Students 10.
Mission—St. Dominic's, [CEM] 22400 Aquasco Rd., Aquasco, Prince Georges Co. 20608.

Barnesville, Montgomery Co., St. Mary Church and Shrine of Our Lady of Fatima (1807) [CEM]
18230 Barnesville Rd., P.O. Box 67, Barnesville, 20838. Tel: 301-972-8660; Fax: 301-349-0916; Email: stmarysb@yahoo.com; Web: stmaryonline.com. Rev. Kevin P. O'Reilly; Deacon David Cahoon.
Catechesis Religious Program—Tel: 301-972-8576. Liz Smith, D.R.E. Students 102.

Beltsville, Prince Georges Co., St. Joseph (1963)
11007 Montgomery Rd., Beltsville, 20705.
Tel: 301-937-7183; Fax: 301-937-7780; Web: www.stjos.org. Rev. Msgr. Karl A. Chimiak, V.F.; Deacon Chris Schwartz. In Res., Rev. Joseph F. Wimmer, O.S.A.
School—St. Joseph School, 11011 Montgomery Rd., Beltsville, 20705. Tel: 301-937-7154;
Fax: 301-937-1467; Email: schooloffice@stjos.org. Lay Teachers 18; Students 174.
Catechesis Religious Program—Email: reled@stjos.org. Students 52.

Benedict, Charles Co., St. Francis de Sales (1903)
7185 Benedict Ave., P.O. Box 306, Benedict, 20612-0306. Tel: 301-274-3416; Tel: 301-870-4991;
Fax: 301-274-0689; Email: francisben@comcast.net. Rev. Kevin M. Cusick.
Catechesis Religious Program—7209 Benedict Ave., P.O. Box 306, Benedict, 20612. Tel: 301-274-0904; Email: religiousedd@stfrancisdesalescc.org. Students 30.

Bethesda, Montgomery Co.

1—St. Bartholomew (1960)
6902 River Rd., Bethesda, 20817. Tel: 301-229-7933; Fax: 301-229-7998; Email: stbartsrectory@gmail.com. Revs. Mark D. Knestout; Timothy G. Daniel; Rev. Msgr. John J. Enzler, E.V., In Res.
School—St. Bartholomew School, 6900 River Rd., Bethesda, 20817. Tel: 301-229-5586;
Fax: 301-229-8654; Email: admissions@stbartholomew.org; Web: www.school.stbartholomew.org. Frank English, Prin. Lay Teachers 24; Students 144.
Catechesis Religious Program—Tel: 301-229-3431. Students 181.

2—St. Jane Frances de Chantal (1950)
9601 Old Georgetown Rd., Bethesda, 20814.
Tel: 301-530-1550; Fax: 301-493-8953; Email: parish.office@stjanedechantal.org; Web: www.stjanedechantal.org. Mailing Address: 9701 Old Georgetown Rd., Bethesda, 20814-1795. Revs. Samuel C. Giese; Keith T. Burney; Deacon Chester G. Chen.
School—St. Jane Frances de Chantal School, 9525 Old Georgetown Rd., Bethesda, 20814.

Tel: 301-530-1221; Fax: 301-530-1688; Email: ehamilton@dechantal.org; Web: www.dechantal.org. Mrs. Betsy Hamilton, Prin. Lay Teachers 30; Students 414.
Catechesis Religious Program—9625 Old Georgetown Rd., Bethesda, 20814. Tel: 301-530-1640 ; Email: seton.center@stjanedechantal.org. Sally Daniel, D.R.E. Students 243.

3—LITTLE FLOWER (1948)
5607 Massachusetts Ave., Bethesda, 20816.
Tel: 301-320-4538; Fax: 240-743-4614; Email: pwhitty@lfparish.org; Web: www.lfparish.org. Rev. Msgr. Peter J. Vaghi, J.D., V.F.; Revs. Patrick S. Lewis; Stephen Giulietti, In Res.; George E. Stuart, J.C.D., In Res.
School—Little Flower School, 5601 Massachusetts Ave., Bethesda, 20816. Tel: 301-320-3273;
Fax: 301-320-2867; Email: rrynn@lfschool.org; Web: lfschool.org. Lay Teachers 27; Sisters of the Immaculate Heart of Mary 5; Students 269.
Catechesis Religious Program—Tel: 301-320-5833; Email: thompsonr@lfschool.org. Sr. Roberta Thompson, S.N.J.M., D.R.E. Students 482.

4—OUR LADY OF LOURDES (1926) (Spanish)
7500 Pearl St., Bethesda, 20814. Tel: 301-654-1287; Fax: 301-986-8716; Email: office@lourdesbethesda.net; Web: www.lourdesbethesda.net. Rev. Msgr. Edward J. Filardi; Rev. Rafael Barbieri.
School—Our Lady of Lourdes School,
Tel: 301-654-5376; Fax: 301-654-2568; Web: www.bethesda-lourdes.org. Patricia K. McGann, Prin. Lay Teachers 26; Students 220.
Catechesis Religious Program—Tel: 301-654-5954. Students 312.

BOWIE, PRINCE GEORGES CO.

1—ASCENSION (1893) [CEM]
Mailing Address: 12700 Lanham-Severn Rd., Bowie, 20720. Tel: 301-262-2227; Fax: 301-805-5053; Email: ascensionbow@aol.com. Rev. Lawrence A. Young. In Res., Rev. William F. Goode, (Retired).
Catechesis Religious Program—Gregory Rozanski, D.R.E. Students 64.

2—ST. EDWARD (1972)
1940 Mitchellville Rd., Bowie, 20716.
Tel: 301-249-9199. Rev. John M. Barry; Deacon David Barnes.
Res.: 16304 Pond Meadow Ln., Bowie, 20716.
Catechesis Religious Program—Tel: 301-249-9599; Fax: 301-249-1303. Students 120.

3—ST. PIUS X (1962)
14720 Annapolis Rd., Bowie, 20715.
Tel: 301-262-2141; Fax: 301-262-2632; Email: office@spxbowie.org; Web: spxbowie.org. Mailing Address: 3300 Moreland Pl., Bowie, 20715. Rev. Michael T. Jones.
School—St. Pius X Regional School, 14710 Annapolis Rd., Bowie, 20715. Tel: 301-262-0203;
Fax: 301-805-8875. Lay Teachers 55; Students 550.
Catechesis Religious Program—Tel: 301-262-3644. Anne Brennan, D.R.E., Child Min. and Sacramental Prep. Coord. Brothers 4; Students 159.

4—SACRED HEART (1729) [CEM]
16501 Annapolis Rd., Bowie, 20715.
Tel: 301-262-0704; Fax: 301-805-4686; Email: parishoffice@sacredheartbowie.org; Web: www.sacredheartbowie.org. Rev. Msgr. Charles J. Parry, V.F.; Rev. Scott S. Holmer, Parochial Vicar; Deacon Dan D. Abeyta.
Catechesis Religious Program—Tel: 301-805-4686; Email: ccdsacredheart@gmail.com. Mrs. Mary Hager, C.R.E.; Mr. Stephen McGinley, Youth Min. & Adult Educ. Coord. Students 195.

BRYANTOWN, CHARLES CO., ST. MARY (1793) [CEM]
13715 Notre Dame Pl., Bryantown, 20617-2224.
Tel: 301-870-2220; Tel: 301-274-3187;
Fax: 301-274-0253. Rev. Rory T. Conley; Deacons Eugene Burroughs; Henry Middleton; Daniel E. Ford.
School—St. Mary School, 13735 Notre Dame Pl., Bryantown, 20617. Tel: 301-932-6883;
Fax: 301-274-0626. Lay Teachers 17; Students 235.
Catechesis Religious Program—Tel: 301-274-3800. Students 90.

BURTONSVILLE, MONTGOMERY CO., RESURRECTION PARISH (1981)
3315 Greencastle Rd., Burtonsville, 20866.
Tel: 301-236-5200; Fax: 301-236-5204; Web: www.resurrectionadw.org. Rev. Jeffrey M. Defayette. In Res., Rev. Msgr. Francis G. Kazista, (Retired); Rev. William M. Brailsford.
Catechesis Religious Program—Tel: 301-288-4664. Students 305.

BUSHWOOD, ST. MARY'S CO., SACRED HEART (1755) [JC]
23080 Maddox Rd., P.O. Box 37, Bushwood, 20618.
Tel: 301-769-3100; Fax: 301-769-3200. Rev. Anthony E. Lickteig.
Catechesis Religious Program—Students 40.

CAMP SPRINGS, PRINCE GEORGES CO., ST. PHILIP THE APOSTLE (1957)
5416 Henderson Way, Camp Springs, 20746.
Tel: 301-423-4244; Fax: 301-423-1226; Email: st.philipparish@comcast.net. Rev. Edward Anthony Hegnauer.
School—St. Philip the Apostle School, 5414 Henderson Way, Camp Springs, 20746.
Tel: 301-423-4740; Fax: 301-423-4716; Email: principal@stphiliptheapostlemd.org; Email: OfficeManager@stphiliptheapostlemd.org; Web: http://www.stphiliptheapostlemd.org/. Mr. Stephen Lamont, Prin. Clergy 1; Lay Teachers 23; Students 200.
Catechesis Religious Program—Students 50.

CHAPEL POINT, CHARLES CO., ST. IGNATIUS (1641) [CEM]
8855 Chapel Point Rd., Port Tobacco, 20677.
Tel: 301-934-8245; Email: CliffordT@adw.org; Web: www.chapelpoint.org. Rev. Thomas F. Clifford, S.J. In Res., Revs. Thomas Gavin; William Noe, S.J.; Paul J. McCarren, S.J.
Catechesis Religious Program—Email: ignatiusreligion@yahoo.com. Shannon Whitmore, D.R.E. Students 133.

CHAPTICO, ST. MARY'S CO., OUR LADY OF THE WAYSIDE (1938)
37575 Chaptico Rd., P.O. Box 97, Chaptico, 20621-0097. Tel: 301-884-3165; Fax: 301-884-3165. Rev. Charles M. Gallagher.
School—Mother Catherine Spalding Tri Parish School, Lay Teachers 20; Students 122.
Catechesis Religious Program—Students 56.

CHEVERLY, PRINCE GEORGES CO., ST. AMBROSE (1886)
3107 63rd Ave., Cheverly, 20785. Tel: 301-773-9300; Email: ambroserectory@gmail.com; Web: sacheverly.org. Rev. Charles A. Cortinovis.
School—St. Ambrose School, 6310 Jason St., Cheverly, 20785. Rev. Charles A. Cortinovis, Prin. Lay Teachers 20; Students 241.

CHILLUM, PRINCE GEORGES CO., ST. JOHN BAPTIST DE LA SALLE (1951)
5706 Sargent Rd., Chillum, 20782. Tel: 301-559-3636 ; Fax: 301-559-3062. Rev. Diego Ruiz, I.V.E.
Catechesis Religious Program—Tel: 301-559-3637. Students 200.

CLINTON, PRINCE GEORGES CO., CHURCH OF ST. JOHN THE EVANGELIST (1875) [CEM]
8908 Old Branch Ave., Clinton, 20735.
Tel: 301-868-1070; Fax: 301-868-7915; Email: st.johnchurch01@gmail.com. Rev. Jaime B. Hernandez. Church: 8910 Old Branch Ave., Clinton, 20735.
School—Church of St. John the Evangelist School, (Grades PreK-8), 8912 Old Branch Ave., Clinton, 20735. Tel: 301-868-2010; Fax: 301-856-8941; Email: principal@saintjohnsschool.org; Web: saintjohnsschool.org. Lay Teachers 21; Students 208.
Catechesis Religious Program—Tel: 301-868-3026. Students 165.

COLLEGE PARK, PRINCE GEORGES CO., HOLY REDEEMER (1912)
4902 Berwyn Rd., College Park, 20740.
Tel: 301-474-3920; Fax: 301-441-4954; Email: parish@holy-redeemer.org. Revs. Mark Leo Smith; Andrew Clyne.
School—Holy Redeemer School, (Grades PreK-8),
Tel: 301-474-3993; Email: school@holy-redeemer.org; Web: www.holy-redeemer.org. Maria Bovich, Prin. Lay Teachers 19; Students 250.
Catechesis Religious Program—Email: beth.berard@holy-redeemer.org. Rev. Jonathan A. Berard, D.R.E. Students 81.

DAMASCUS, MONTGOMERY CO., ST. PAUL (1957)
9240 Damascus Rd., Damascus, 20872.
Tel: 301-253-2027; Fax: 301-391-6755. Rev. Joseph B. Pierce; Deacons John Finerty; David Terrar; Maury Huguley Jr.
Catechesis Religious Program—Tel: 301-253-5941. Students 770.

DARNESTOWN, MONTGOMERY CO., OUR LADY OF THE VISITATION (1991) [CEM]
14135 Seneca Rd., Darnestown, 20874-3337. Revs. Raymond L. Fecteau; Mathew Punchayil, (India); Deacons Robert Fischer; Thaddeus A. Dmuchowski.
Res.: 14200 Darnestown Rd., Darnestown, 20874-3008.
Church: 14139 Seneca Rd., Darnestown, 20874.
Tel: 301-948-5536; Email: parishoffice@olvp.org; Web: www.olvp.org.
Catechesis Religious Program—Students 179.

DERWOOD, MONTGOMERY CO., ST. FRANCIS OF ASSISI (1972)
6701 Muncaster Mill Rd., Derwood, 20855.
Tel: 301-840-1407; Fax: 301-258-5080; Email: dzezzo@sfadw.org; Web: www.sfadw.org. Revs. John J. Dillon, V.F., S.T.B., Ph.D.; Jonathan A. Berard, Parochial Vicar; Deacons James J. Datovech; Daniel F. Finn VI; James McCann. In Res.
Catechesis Religious Program—Tel: 301-258-9193; Email: sanderson@sfadw.org. Susan Anderson, D.R.E. Students 374.

FORESTVILLE, PRINCE GEORGE CO.

1—CHURCH OF THE HOLY SPIRIT (1966)
1717 Ritchie Rd., Forestville, 20747.
Tel: 301-336-3707; Fax: 301-324-1649. Revs. Everett Pearson, Admin.; Mathai Mannoorvadakkethil, Priest In Charge. In Res., Rev. Jeffrey F. Samaha.
Catechesis Religious Program—Combined with Mt. Calvary School, Forestville.

2—MT. CALVARY (1942) [CEM]
6700 Marlboro Pike, Forestville, 20747.
Tel: 301-735-5532; Fax: 301-735-2005; Email: mtcalvary.md@adw.org; Web: mountcalvarycatholicchurch.org. Rev. Everett Pearson; Deacon Lawrence Miles.
Catechesis Religious Program—
Tel: 301-735-5262, Ext. 17; Email: caziegler7@yahoo.com. Cathy Ziegler, D.R.E. Students 47.

FORT WASHINGTON, PRINCE GEORGES CO., ST. IGNATIUS (1849) [CEM]
2315 Brinkley Rd., Fort Washington, 20744.
Tel: 301-567-4740; Fax: 301-567-0046; Web: www.saint-ig.org. Rev. G. Paul Herbert, J.C.L.
Catechesis Religious Program—St. Columba, 7800 Livingston Rd., Oxon Hill, 20745. Tel: 301-567-6546. Students 21.

GAITHERSBURG, MONTGOMERY CO.

1—ST. JOHN NEUMANN (1978) [CEM]
Mailing Address: 8900 Lochaven Dr., Gaithersburg, 20882-4460. Email: info@saintjohnneumann.org; Web: www.saintjohnneumann.org. Rev. Joseph E. Rogers, V.F.; Deacons Eugene Cummins; Carlo Caraballo; Michael W. Davy.
Church: 9000 Warfield Rd., Gaithersburg, 20882.
Tel: 301-977-5492; Fax: 301-977-3559.
Catechesis Religious Program—Tel: 301-977-7990; Fax: 301-330-3235. Students 303.

2—ST. MARTIN OF TOURS (1920)
201 S. Frederick Ave., Gaithersburg, 20877.
Tel: 301-990-3203; Fax: 301-990-7538; Email: parish@stmartinsweb.org; Email: communications@stmartinsweb.org; Web: www.stmartinsweb.org. Revs. David G. Wells, Admin.; Tony A. D'Souza, Parochial Vicar; Jonathan Santiago Vanegas Calderon, Parochial Vicar; Deacons Lawrence Bell; William A. Vita Jr.; Mauricio O. Rivas.
School—St Martin of Tours School, (Grades PreK-8), 115 S. Frederick Ave., Gaithersburg, 20877.
Tel: 301-990-2441; Fax: 301-990-2688; Email: office@smsmd.org; Web: www.smsmd.org. Mr. Stephen Lamont, Prin. Lay Teachers 21; Students 223.
Catechesis Religious Program—Tel: 301-990-2556; Fax: 301-990-2622; Email: faithformation@stmartinsweb.org. Mr. Josh Moldiz, D.R.E. Sisters 3; Students 980.

3—ST. ROSE OF LIMA (1972) [CEM]
11701 Clopper Rd., Gaithersburg, 20878-1024.
Tel: 301-948-7545; Fax: 301-869-2170; Email: strose@strose.com; Web: www.strose-parish.org. Revs. Agustin Mateo-Ayala; Justin A. Huber, Parochial Vicar; Oscar A. Astigarraga, Parochial Vicar; Deacons Mario F. Moreno; Albert L. Opdenaker; Leo F. Schneider.
Catechesis Religious Program—Susan Joseph, D.R.E. (K-5, English), Tel: 301-948-7545, Ext. 245; Ivonne Salazar, D.R.E. (K-6, Spanish); Molly Gradowski, D.R.E. (6-12, English), Tel: 301-948-7545, Ext. 225; Christine Jeffrey, Adult Faith Formation & Dir. Liturgy. Students 717.

GARRETT PARK, MONTGOMERY CO., HOLY CROSS (1960)
4900 Strathmore Ave., P.O. Box 249, Garrett Park, 20896. Tel: 301-942-1020; Fax: 301-949-3543; Email: parishsecretary@hcrosschurch.org; Web: www.hcrosschurch.org. Revs. Robert P. Buchmeier; Joseph F. Perkins, In Res.; Deacons Robert Hubbard, (Retired); Robert W. Stout III.
School—Holy Cross School, (Grades PreK-8),
Tel: 301-949-0053; Fax: 301-949-5074; Email: office@hcross.org; Web: www.hcross.org. Lisa Maio Kane, Prin. Lay Teachers 29; Students 211.
Catechesis Religious Program—Tel: 301-942-8790; Email: ilagan@hcrosschurch.org. Michelle Ilagan, D.R.E. Students 108.

GERMANTOWN, MONTGOMERY CO., MOTHER SETON PARISH (1974) [CEM]
19951 Father Hurley Blvd., Germantown, 20874.
Tel: 301-924-3838; Fax: 301-428-4951; Email: motherannseton@gmail.com; Web: mothersetonparish.org. Revs. LeRoy J. Fangmeyer, V.F.; Louis J. Faust, Senior Priest, (Retired); Santiago Martin Sedano, Parochial Vicar; Deacons Stephen M. Maselko; Francis W. Bendel; Fidencio Gonzalez.
Catechesis Religious Program—Tel: 301-444-3496; Tel: 301-444-3495. Students 591.

GREAT MILLS, ST. MARY'S CO., HOLY FACE (1879) [CEM]
20408 Point Lookout Rd., Great Mills, 20634.
Tel: 301-994-0525; Fax: 301-994-1547. Rev. Jaroslaw S. Gamrot; Deacon Paul A. Bielewicz, Pastoral Assoc.
School—Little Flower, 20410 Point Lookout Rd., Great Mills, 20634. Tel: 301-994-0404;
Fax: 301-994-2055. Lay Teachers 16; Students 140.
Catechesis Religious Program—Laura Lang, D.R.E. Students 120.

GREENBELT, PRINCE GEORGES CO., SAINT HUGH OF

GRENOBLE (1947)
135 Crescent Rd., Greenbelt, 20770.
Tel: 301-474-4322; Fax: 301-474-9263; Email: sthughoffice@gmail.com; Web: www.sthughs.com. Rev. Walter J. Tappe, V.F.
Catechesis Religious Program—Email: shreligioused4@gmail.com.

HILLCREST HEIGHTS, PRINCE GEORGES CO., HOLY FAMILY (1952) (African American)
2210 Callaway St., Hillcrest Heights, 20748.
Tel: 301-894-2222; Fax: 301-894-2938. Rev. Kevin J. Regan.
School—Holy Family School, 2200 Callaway St., Hillcrest Heights, 20748. Tel: 301-894-2323.
Catechesis Religious Program—Students 246.

HILLTOP, CHARLES CO., ST. IGNATIUS LOYOLA (1851) [CEM]
6455 Port Tobacco Rd., P.O. Box 278, Port Tobacco, 20677. Tel: 301-934-9630; Fax: 301-934-8320; Web: www.stignatiusmd.org. Rev. Kenneth J. Gill.

HOLLYWOOD, ST. MARY'S CO., ST. JOHN FRANCIS REGIS (1690) [CEM]
43950 St. John's Rd., Hollywood, 20636.
Tel: 301-373-2281; Fax: 301-373-8984; Email: haydenp@sjchollywood.org. Rev. Raymond F. Schmidt; Deacon Ammon S. Ripple. In Res., Rev. Eamon Dignan, (Retired).
School—St. John Francis Regis School,
Tel: 301-373-2142; Email: office@sjshollywood.org; Web: www.sjshollywood.org. Susan McDonough, Prin. Lay Teachers 25; Students 216.
Catechesis Religious Program—Email: rolon@sjchollywood.org. Richard Olon, D.R.E. Students 317.

HUNTINGTOWN, CALVERT CO., JESUS THE DIVINE WORD PARISH (1994)
885 Cox Rd., Huntingtown, 20639. Tel: 410-414-8304 ; Fax: 410-535-9057; Email: office@jesusdivineword.org; Web: www.jesusdivineword.org. Rev. John T. Dakes, S.T.L.; Deacon Ronald J. Burns; Tracey Smith, Dir. Youth Min.
Catechesis Religious Program—Fax: 410-535-5097; Email: religioused@jesusdivineword.org. Karen Burns, D.R.E. Students 304.

HYATTSVILLE, PRINCE GEORGES CO.
1—ST. JEROME (1886)
5205 43rd Ave., 20781. Tel: 301-927-6684; Email: Ajstjerome@hotmail.com. Rev. Scott R. Hahn, V.F.; Deacon Neal T. Conway. In Res., Revs. Isadore Dixon; Charles Edeh, Chap., Nigerian Catholic Community.
School—St. Jerome School, 5207 42nd Pl., 20781.
Tel: 301-277-4568; Fax: 301-779-2428; Email: dflynn@stjeromes.org. Daniel Flynn, Prin. Lay Teachers 20; Students 330.
Convent—5300 43rd Ave., 20781. Tel: 301-864-2016.
Child Care—Child Center, 20781. Tel: 301-699-1314. Students 60; Clergy / Religious Teachers 15.
Catechesis Religious Program—Email: religioused@stjeromes.org. Students 33.
2—ST. MARK (1958)
7501 Adelphi Rd., 20783. Tel: 301-422-8300;
Fax: 301-422-2313; Email: rectory@stmarkhyattsville.org; Web: www.stmarkhyattsville.org. Revs. Roberto J. Cortes; Paul Sullins, Parochial Vicar; Gustavo Perez, Parochial Vicar; Deacons Jose Renato Molina; Curtis Turner. In Res., Most Rev. Michael W. Fisher, V.G.
Catechesis Religious Program—Tel: 301-422-7822; Email: religioused@stmarkhyattsville.org. Steward Benalcazar, D.R.E. Students 434.

INDIAN HEAD, CHARLES CO., ST. MARY STAR OF THE SEA (1909) [CEM]
30 Mattingly Ave., Indian Head, 20640.
Tel: 301-753-9177; Tel: 301-743-5770;
Fax: 301-743-6670; Email: parish@staroftheseaindianhead.org; Web: www.staroftheseaindianhead.org. Rev. Brian Alick Coelho, Admin.
Catechesis Religious Program—Students 38.

ISSUE, CHARLES CO., HOLY GHOST (1880) [CEM]
15848 Rock Point Rd., Newburg, 20664.
Tel: 301-259-2515; Fax: 301-259-2289; Email: holyghostchurch@verizon.net; Web: parishesonline.com/holyghostissue. Rev. Gregory S. Coan; Deacon Walter G. Rourke.
Catechesis Religious Program—Students 71.
Mission—St. Francis de Sales, Newburg. 13675 Furbush Rd., Rock Point, Charles Co. 20682.

KENSINGTON, MONTGOMERY CO., HOLY REDEEMER (1948)
9705 Summit Ave., Kensington, 20895.
Tel: 301-942-2333; Fax: 301-942-1041; Email: parish@hrs-ken.org; Web: www.hrkensington.org. Revs. Mark F. Hughes; Ryan I. Pineda, Parochial Vicar; Mark E. Tucker, J.C.L., Adjutant Judicial Vicar.
School—Holy Redeemer School, 9715 Summit Ave., Kensington, 20895. Tel: 301-942-3701;
Fax: 301-942-4981; Web: hrs-ken.org. Colleen Ryan, Prin. Lay Teachers 29; Students 460.
Catechesis Religious Program—
Tel: 301-942-2333, Ext. 200. Marylou McDonald, C.R.E. Students 251.

LA PLATA, CHARLES CO., SACRED HEART (1901) [CEM]
201 St. Mary's Ave., P.O. Box 1390, La Plata, 20646.
Tel: 301-934-2261; Fax: 301-934-5435; Email: shclp@verizon.net; Web: www.sacredheartlaplata.org. Revs. Lawrence C. Swink; Martin E. Flum; Deacons Anthony Barrasso, (Retired); Albert E. Graham Jr., (Retired); Walter G. Rourke, Minister to homebound, hospitals & nursing homes.
School—Archbishop Neale School, (Grades PreK-8), 104 Port Tobacco Rd., La Plata, 20646.
Tel: 301-934-9595; Fax: 301-934-8610; Email: office@archbishopnealeschool.org; Web: www.archbishopnealeschool.org. Ms. Linda Bourne, Prin. Lay Teachers 30; Students 332.
Catechesis Religious Program—Tel: 301-934-3386. Students 160.

LANDOVER HILLS, PRINCE GEORGE'S CO.
1—ST. MARY'S CATHOLIC CHURCH (1948)
7401 Buchanan St., Landover Hills, 20784-2323.
Tel: 301-577-8844; Fax: 301-306-5543; Email: secretary@saintmarylandoverhills.org; Web: www.saintmarylandoverhills.org. Rev. Richard K. Gancayco; Deacon Stephen M. Robinson.
School—St. Mary's Catholic Church School, 7207 Annapolis Rd., Landover Hills, 20784.
Tel: 301-577-0031; Fax: 301-577-5485; Email: admin.stmarys@comcast.net; Web: stmaryslh.org. Mr. Christian Buchleitner, Prin. Lay Teachers 23; Students 240.
Catechesis Religious Program—Students 380.
2—SYRO-MALANKARA MISSION (1985) (Indian)
7401 Buchanan St., Landover Hills, 20784-9998.
Tel: 301-577-8844; Fax: 301-306-5543; Email: matmvy@gmail.com. Rev. Mathai Mannoorvadakkethil.
Catechesis Religious Program—Students 25.

LANHAM, PRINCE GEORGES CO., ST. MATTHIAS APOSTLE (1960)
9475 Annapolis Rd., Lanham, 20706-3020.
Tel: 301-459-4814; Fax: 301-306-4582; Email: pford@stmatthias.org; Email: tereme@stmatthias.org; Web: www.stmatthias.org. Rev. John H. Kenealy, V.F.; Deacon Alton Davis. In Res., Rev. Canice Enyiaka.
Res.: 9471 Annapolis Rd., Lanham, 20706-3020.
Tel: 301-459-8078.
School—St. Matthias Apostle School, 9473 Annapolis Rd., Lanham, 20706-3020. Tel: 301-577-9412;
Fax: 301-577-2060; Web: www.stmatthias.org. Mrs. Patricia Schratz, Prin. Lay Teachers 19; Students 122.
Catechesis Religious Program—
Tel: 301-459-4814, Ext. 205. Students 99.

LARGO, PRINCE GEORGES CO., ST. JOSEPH (1922)
2020 St. Joseph Dr., Largo, 20774. Tel: 301-773-4838 ; Fax: 301-773-6832. Rev. Roy Edward Campbell, V.F.; Deacon Alton Davis.
Catechesis Religious Program—Tel: 301-773-2480. Students 14.

LAUREL, PRINCE GEORGES CO.
1—ST. MARY (1843) [CEM]
114 St. Mary's Pl., Laurel, 20707. Tel: 301-725-3080;
Fax: 301-725-2409; Web: www.stmaryslaurel.org. Rev. Msgr. Michael J. Mellone, V.F., Tel: 301-853-4550; Rev. Phillip Ilg, Parochial Vicar, Youth Min.; Deacons Brandon B. Justice; Perfecto Santiago; Robert L. Gignilliat; Gina Iampieri, Music & Liturgy Dir.
School—St. Mary School, 106 St. Mary's Pl., Laurel, 20707. Tel: 301-498-1433; Fax: 301-498-1170; Web: www.stmaryofthemill.org. Mrs. Alisha Jordan, Prin. Lay Teachers 28; Students 340.
Catechesis Religious Program—Tel: 301-490-8770. Mrs. Gretchen Magno, Child Protection Coord.; Jennifer Juzwiak, D.R.E. (Adults, Teens, Children). Students 435.
2—ST. NICHOLAS (1967)
8603 Contee Rd., Laurel, 20708. Tel: 301-490-5516;
Fax: 301-490-1527; Email: st.nicholaschurch@verizon.net. Rev. Mel Ayala; Deacon Perry Iannaconi.
Catechesis Religious Program—
Tel: 301-490-5116, Ext. 109. Students 71.

LEONARDTOWN, ST. MARY'S CO., ST. ALOYSIUS (1710) [CEM]
22800 Washington St., P.O. Box 310, Leonardtown, 20650. Tel: 301-475-8064; Fax: 301-475-8762; Web: www.saintaloysiuschurch.org. Rev. David W. Beaubien.
School—Father Andrew White, S.J., 22850 Washington St., P.O. Box 1756, Leonardtown, 20650.
Tel: 301-475-9795; Fax: 301-475-3537; Email: fradwh@verizon.net; Web: www.fatherandrewwhite.org. Ms. Heather Francisco, Prin. Clergy 8; Lay Teachers 20; Students 257.
Catechesis Religious Program—Email: lwathen@saintaloysiuschurch.org. Students 232.

LEXINGTON PARK, ST. MARY'S CO., IMMACULATE HEART OF MARY (1947) [CEM]
22375 Three Notch Rd., Lexington Park, 20653-0166.
Tel: 301-863-8144; Fax: 301-863-8180; Email: office@ihmrcc.org; Web: www.ihmrcc.org. Revs. Marco Federico Schad, J.D.; Jose Rodriguez Blandon, Parochial Vicar; Deacons Michael J. Crowe; Juan C. Ortiz; Ms. Jacinta Thompson, Business Mgr.
Catechesis Religious Program—Tel: 301-863-8793; Email: dre@ihmrcc.org; Web: ihmcff.weebly.com. Janet Harmon, D.R.E. Students 130.

MCCONCHIE, CHARLES CO., ST. CATHERINE OF ALEXANDRIA (1911) [CEM]
7865 Port Tobacco Rd., P.O. Box 278, Port Tobacco, 20677. Tel: 301-934-9630; Fax: 301-934-8320; Email: admin.stcatherine-alexandria.md@adw.org; Web: www.stcatherinemd.org. Rev. Kenneth J. Gill.

MECHANICSVILLE, ST. MARY'S CO., IMMACULATE CONCEPTION (1876)
28297 Old Village Rd., P.O. Box 166, Mechanicsville, 20659. Tel: 301-884-3123; Fax: 301-884-7437; Email: immaculateconception.md@adw.org; Web: icchurchmd.org. Rev. Michael E. Tietjen; Deacon William L. Kyte.
Catechesis Religious Program—Tel: 240-230-3167; Email: deacon.kyte@gmail.com. Students 230.

MEDLEY'S NECK, ST. MARY'S CO., OUR LADY'S (1767) [CEM]
41348 Medley's Neck Rd., Leonardtown, 20650.
Tel: 301-475-8403; Fax: 301-475-6632. Rev. Thomas G. LaHood; Deacon Thomas C. Spalding Sr.
Catechesis Religious Program—Students 71.

MITCHELLVILLE, PRINCE GEORGES CO., HOLY FAMILY (1890) [CEM]
Mailing Address: 12010 Woodmore Rd., Mitchellville, 20721. Tel: 301-249-2266;
Fax: 301-249-2524; Email: holyfamilyadmin@msn.com; Web: holyfamilywoodmore.com. Rev. Joseph A. Jenkins.
Catechesis Religious Program—Tel: 301-249-1167. Students 115.

MORGANZA, ST. MARY'S CO., ST. JOSEPH (1700) [CEM 2] [JC]
29119 Point Lookout Rd., P.O. Box 175, Morganza, 20660. Tel: 301-475-3293; Fax: 301-475-0491; Email: sjcmorganza@gmail.com; Web: www.stjosephmorganza.org. Rev. Andrew Francis Royals; Deacon James A. Somerville, (Retired).
Catechesis Religious Program—Students 105.

MOUNT RAINIER, PRINCE GEORGES CO., ST. JAMES (1905)
3628 Rhode Island Ave., Mount Rainier, 20712.
Tel: 301-927-0567; Fax: 301-927-5289; Email: st.jamescatholicchurch@gmail.com. Revs. Pablo Bonello, I.V.E.; Nathaniel Dreyer, I.V.E. In Res., Rev. Javier Ibarra, I.V.E.
Catechesis Religious Program—Sr. Maria de San Juan de los Lagos Vargas, S.S.V.M., D.R.E. Students 725.

NEWPORT, CHARLES CO., ST. MARY (1674) [CEM]
11555 St. Mary's Church Rd., Charlotte Hall, 20622.
Tel: 301-934-8825; Fax: 301-934-0245. Rev. Michael W. Briese.
Catechesis Religious Program—Mary Ellen Heinze, D.R.E. Students 67.

NEWTOWNE, ST. MARY'S CO., ST. FRANCIS XAVIER (1640) [CEM]
21370 Newtowne Neck Rd., Leonardtown, 20650.
Tel: 301-475-9885; Fax: 301-745-5662; Email: gertiethomas@outlook.com; Web: stfrancisxavierchurch.org. Rev. Robert G. Maro; Deacon William J. Nickerson.
Catechesis Religious Program—Paula McLeod, D.R.E. Students 68.

NORTH BEACH, CALVERT CO., ST. ANTHONY'S (1905)
8900 Bay Ave., P.O. Box 660, North Beach, 20714.
Tel: 443-646-5721; Tel: 443-646-5722; Email: office@stanthonycal.us; Web: www.stanthonycal.us. Rev. James M. Stack; Deacons Eric B. Mueller; Francis E. Baker Jr.
Catechesis Religious Program—Tel: 443-646-5724. Deborah Wheeler, D.R.E. & Youth Min. Students 199.

OLNEY, MONTGOMERY CO.
1—ST. ANDREW KIM (1974) (Korean)
17615 Old Baltimore Rd., Olney, 20832.
Tel: 301-260-1981; Fax: 301-260-1983.
Catechesis Religious Program—Tel: 301-275-3734. Students 210.
2—ST. PETER (1953)
2900 Olney-Sandy Spring Rd., Olney, 20832.
Tel: 301-924-3774; Fax: 301-774-5259; Email: info@stpetersolney.org; Web: www.stpetersolney.org. Revs. Thomas M. Kalita; Andrew M. Morkunas; Aaron M. Qureshi, Parochial Vicar; Deacons Thomas Cioffi; Rory P. Crawford; Chang Choi; Vincent J. Wolfinger; Mrs. Elizabeth Harper, Business Mgr.
School—St. Peter School, Tel: 301-774-9112;
Fax: 301-924-6698; Email: school@stpetersolney.org. Mrs. Mary Elizabeth Whelan, Prin. Lay Teachers 42; Students 384.
Catechesis Religious Program—Tel: 301-570-4952. Cindy Dixon, D.R.E. (Grades K-8). Students 557.

OWINGS, CALVERT CO., JESUS THE GOOD SHEPHERD (1985) [CEM]
1601 W. Mt. Harmony Rd., Owings, 20736.
Tel: 410-257-3810; Email: community@ccjgs.org; Web: ccjgs.org. Rev. Michael J. King, J.C.D., V.F.; Deacon Paul Fagan.
Res.: 1555 W. Mt. Harmony Rd., Owings, 20736.
Tel: 410-257-3810, Ext. 20.
School—Cardinal Hickey Academy, (Grades PreK-8), 1601 W. Mt. Harmony Rd., Owings, 20736.
Tel: 410-286-0404; Fax: 410-286-6334; Email: office@cardinalhickeyacademy.org; Web: www.cardinalhickeyacademy.org. Mrs. Jennifer Griffith, Prin. (Regional) Lay Teachers 16; Students 193.
Catechesis Religious Program—
Tel: 410-257-3810, Ext. 18; Fax: 410-257-6334; Email: religioused@ccjgs.org. Mrs. Cynthia Wagenhofer, D.R.E. Students 437.

OXON HILL, PRINCE GEORGES CO., ST. COLUMBA (1960)
7804 Livingston Rd., Oxon Hill, 20745.
Tel: 301-567-5506; Fax: 301-567-6546; Email: stcolumbachurch@verizon.net. Rev. Gary T. Villanueva; Deacons Robert C. Villanueva; Leandro Y. Espinosa.
School—St. Columba School, (Grades PreK-8), 7800 Livingston Rd., Oxon Hill, 20745. Tel: 301-567-6212; Fax: 301-567-6907; Email: schooloffice@stccatholic.org; Web: www.stccatholic.org. Mrs. Katrina Fernandez, Prin. Lay Teachers 18; Students 171.
Catechesis Religious Program—Tel: 301-567-6113. Sr. Luzviminda, M.C.S.T., D.R.E. Students 159.

PISCATAWAY, PRINCE GEORGES CO., ST. MARY'S CHURCH OF PISCATAWAY (1640) [CEM]
13401 Piscataway Rd., Clinton, 20735-4564.
Tel: 301-292-0527; Fax: 301-292-8786; Email: parish@stmaryspiscataway.org; Web: www.saintmaryspiscataway.net. Rev. Timothy K. Baer; Deacons George Ames, (Retired); Stephen McKimmie.
School—St. Mary's Church of Piscataway School, 13407 Piscataway Rd., Clinton, 20735.
Tel: 301-292-2522; Fax: 301-292-2534; Email: school@stmaryspiscataway.org; Web: www.stmaryspiscataway.org. Lay Teachers 15; Students 140.
Catechesis Religious Program—
Tel: 301-292-0527, Ext. 104; Email: aholk@stmaryspiscataway.org. Students 70.

POMFRET, CHARLES CO., ST. JOSEPH (1763) [CEM]
4590 St. Joseph Way, Pomfret, 20675.
Tel: 301-539-3903; Fax: 301-539-3912; Web: www.stjoepomfret.weconnect.com. Rev. Harry J. Stokes; Deacons John R. Barnes; James M. Tittinger.
Catechesis Religious Program—Email: stjoeformation@comcast.net. Students 117.

POOLESVILLE, MONTGOMERY CO., OUR LADY OF THE PRESENTATION (1992)
17220 Tom Fox Ave., P.O. Box 428, Poolesville, 20837. Tel: 301-349-2045; Tel: 301-349-2788;
Fax: 301-349-5423; Email: olpresentation@verizon.net; Web: www.ol-presentation-md.org. Rev. Vincent J. Rigdon, J.C.L., V.F.; Deacon William H. Stevens.
Catechesis Religious Program—Email: joss.fmbell@gmail.com. Jocelyn Bell, D.R.E. Students 89.

POTOMAC, MONTGOMERY CO.
1—NATIVITY OF THE BLESSED VIRGIN (GERMAN MISSION) (1992) (German)
6330 Linway Ter., McLean, VA 22101-4150.
Tel: 703-356-4473. Rev. Christian Bock.
2—OUR LADY OF MERCY (1959) [CEM]
9200 Kentsdale Dr., Potomac, 20854.
Tel: 301-365-1415; Fax: 301-365-3104; Email: church@olom.org; Web: www.olom.org. Revs. William D. Byrne; Stephen P. Wyble, Parochial Vicar; Deacon Charles P. Huber. In Res.
School—Our Lady of Mercy School, 9222 Kentsdale Dr., Potomac, 20854. Tel: 301-365-4477; Email: schooloffice@olom.org; Web: www.schoololom.org. Mrs. Deborah Thomas, Prin. Lay Teachers 35; Students 219; Clergy / Religious Teachers 11.
Catechesis Religious Program—Tel: 301-365-1318; Email: awalker@olom.org; Email: alanave@olom.org. Anne Walker, Children's Faith Formation; Anna LaNave, Adult Faith Formation. Students 511.

PRINCE FREDERICK, CALVERT CO., ST. JOHN VIANNEY (1965) [CEM]
105 Vianney Ln., Prince Frederick, 20678-4123.
Tel: 410-535-0223; Fax: 410-535-4422; Email: secretary@sjvchurch.net; Web: www.sjvchurch.net. Rev. Peter J. Daly, V.F., (Retired).
Catechesis Religious Program—Tel: 410-535-4395. Kimberly Stack, D.R.E. Students 295.

RIDGE, ST. MARY'S CO., ST. MICHAEL (1824) [CEM]
16566 Three Notch Rd., P.O. Box 429, Ridge, 20680.
Tel: 301-872-4321; Email: church.stmichaels@md.metrocast.net; Web: saintmichaelscatholicchurch.org. Rev. Peter M. Giovanoni.
School—St. Michael School, 16560 Three Notch Rd., P.O. Box 259, Ridge, 20680. Tel: 301-872-5454; Email: principal@saint-michaels-school.org. Mrs. Lila Ridgell Hofmeister, Prin. Lay Teachers 16; Students 190.
Catechesis Religious Program—Students 40.

RIVERDALE PARK, PRINCE GEORGES CO., ST. BERNARD (1950)
5700 St. Bernard Dr., Riverdale Park, 20737-2102.
Tel: 301-277-1000; Fax: 301-277-3464; Email: bernard.fatimachurch@gmail.com. Revs. Jefferson Bariviera, C.S.; Lino Garcia, C.S., Parochial Vicar; Deacon Desmond Yorke.
Catechesis Religious Program—Email: teresadluna@gmail.com. Mrs. Teresa Luna, D.R.E. Students 618.

ROCKVILLE, MONTGOMERY CO.
1—ST. ELIZABETH (1964)
917 Montrose Rd., Rockville, 20852.
Tel: 301-881-1380; Fax: 301-881-3068; Email: office@stelizabethchurchmd.org. Rev. Msgr. John F. Macfarlane, (Retired); Rev. Jacob C. George.
School—St. Elizabeth School, (Grades PreK-8),
Tel: 301-881-1824; Fax: 301-881-6035. Lay Teachers 47; Students 584.
Catechesis Religious Program—Students 434.
2—ST. MARY (1813) [CEM]
520 Veirs Mill Rd., Rockville, 20852.
Tel: 301-424-5550; Fax: 301-424-5579; Email: stmaryrockville@yahoo.com; Web: www.stmarysrockville.org. Rev. Msgr. Robert G. Amey, V.F.; Rev. Kevin Fields, Parochial Vicar; Deacons Louis J. Brune III; Daniel Kostka. In Res., Rev. M. Valentine Keveny.
School—St. Mary School, (Grades PreK-8), 600 Veirs Mill Rd., Rockville, 20852. Tel: 301-762-4179;
Fax: 301-762-9550. Debra Eisel, Prin. Lay Teachers 20; Students 204.
Catechesis Religious Program—Tel: 301-762-8750; Email: smrockville@gmail.com. Thomas Patchan, D.R.E. Students 241.
3—OUR LADY OF CHINA PASTORAL MISSION
1001 Grandin Ave., Rockville, 20851.
4—ST. PATRICK (1966)
4101 Norbeck Rd., Rockville, 20853.
Tel: 301-924-2284; Fax: 301-929-3017; Email: parishoffice@stpatrickadw.org; Web: www.stpatricksmd.org. Rev. Msgr. Charles J. Parry, V.F.; Rev. Martino I. Choi, Parochial Vicar; Deacons James T. Nalls; David J. Suley.
Catechesis Religious Program—Tel: 301-929-9314; Email: saintpatrickreled@gmail.com. Mrs. Jane Baily, D.R.E. Students 976.
5—ST. RAPHAEL (1966)
1592 Kimblewick Rd., Rockville, 20854.
Tel: 301-762-2143; Fax: 301-762-0719; Email: salahm@adw.org; Web: www.straphaels.org. Mailing Address: 1513 Duntster Rd., Rockville, 20854. Revs. Michael A. Salah, V.F.; Daniel T. Gallaugher, Parochial Vicar; Thomas G. Morrow, In Res., (Retired); Deacons Richard Mattocks, (Retired); Frank Salatto, (Retired); Jose R. Carbonell; Jorge Gatica.
Catechesis Religious Program—
Tel: 301-762-2143, Ext. 124; Email: mbeaudoin@straphaels.org. Mary Beaudoin, D.R.E. Students 619.
6—SHRINE OF ST. JUDE (1956) [CEM]
12701 Veirs Mill Rd., Rockville, 20853.
Tel: 301-946-8200; Fax: 301-946-4527; Web: www.shrinestjude.org. Revs. Paul D. Lee, S.T.D.; John Tung Nguyen; Kenneth J. Gill; Daniele Rebeggiani; Deacons Nicholas E. Scholz; Donald Mays.
School—Shrine of St. Jude School, 4820 Walbridge St., Rockville, 20853. Tel: 301-946-7888;
Fax: 301-929-8927; Email: stjudemain@yahoo.com; Web: www.stjudesschool.org. Lay Teachers 24; Students 196.
Catechesis Religious Program—Tel: 301-949-2336; Web: shrinestjude.org/organizations. Students 366.

ST. INIGOES, ST. MARY'S CO., ST. PETER CLAVER (1903) [CEM] (African American)
16922 St. Peter Claver Church Rd., P.O. Box 240, St. Inigoes, 20684. Tel: 301-872-5460; Fax: 301-872-5672. Rev. Scott Woods.
Catechesis Religious Program—Students 30.

ST. MARY'S CITY, ST. MARY'S CO., ST. CECILIA (1974) [CEM]
47950 Mattapany Rd., P.O. Box 429, St. Mary's City, 20686. Tel: 301-862-4600. Rev. Scott Woods.
Catechesis Religious Program—Clustered with St. Michael's, Ridge. Students 3.

SEAT PLEASANT, PRINCE GEORGES CO., ST. MARGARET (1908) (African American)
408 Addison Rd. S., Seat Pleasant, 20743.
Tel: 301-336-3345; Fax: 301-336-5501. Revs. David Reid, SS.CC.; Fintan Sheeran, SS.CC.; Deacon Samuel Miror.
Catechesis Religious Program—Tel: 301-336-3344. Students 108.

SILVER SPRING, MONTGOMERY CO.
1—ST. ANDREW APOSTLE (1959)
11600 Kemp Mill Rd., Silver Spring, 20902.
Tel: 301-649-3700; Fax: 301-681-3527; Email: saabulletins@yahoo.com. Revs. Daniel P. Leary; Mario A. Majano, Parochial Vicar; Rev. Msgr. Kevin T. Hart, J.C.D., V.F., In Res.; Deacons Michael Bond; Steven R. Reeves; Stephen D. O'Neill.
School—St. Andrew Apostle School,
Tel: 301-649-3555; Fax: 301-649-2352; Email: standrew20902@yahoo.com. Susan M. Sheehan, Prin. Lay Teachers 30; Students 326.
Catechesis Religious Program—Julie Benjamin, D.R.E. Students 125.
Mission San Andres—12247 Georgia Ave., Silver Spring, 20902. Tel: 301-202-9496; Fax: 301-789-6274; Email: sacerdote@misionsanandres.org.
2—ST. BERNADETTE (Four Corners) (1948)
70 University Blvd., E., Silver Spring, 20901.
Tel: 301-593-0357; Fax: 301-593-3088; Email: parish@stbernadetteschurch.org. Rev. Msgr. K. Bartholomew Smith; Rev. Emanuel Magro, Parochial Vicar; Deacon Thomas E. Roszkowski.
School—St. Bernadette School, 80 University Blvd., E., Silver Spring, 20901. Tel: 301-593-5611;
Fax: 301-593-9042; Web: www.saintbernadetteschool.org. Cheri Wood, Prin. Lay Teachers 29; Students 322.
Catechesis Religious Program—Email: reled@stbernadetteschurch.org. Mr. Neil Sloan, D.R.E. Students 181.
3—ST. CAMILLUS (1951)
1600 St. Camillus Dr., Silver Spring, 20903.
Tel: 301-434-8400; Fax: 301-434-8041; Web: stcamilluschurch.org. Revs. Chris Posch, O.F.M.; Jean-Marie Kabango, O.F.M.; Jacek Orzechowski, O.F.M.; Erick Lopez, O.F.M.; Edgardo Java, O.F.M.; Deacons Peter Barbernitz; Francisco J. Cartagena.
School—St. Francis International School, (Grades K-8), 1500 St. Camillus Dr., Silver Spring, 20903.
Tel: 301-434-2344; Fax: 301-434-7726; Email: tharkleroad@sfismd.org; Web: www.saintfrancisinternational.org. Tobias A. Harkleroad, Prin. Lay Teachers 43; Students 409.
Catechesis Religious Program—Tel: 301-434-2111; Email: faithformation@stcamilluschurch.org. William Pineda, Dir., Faith Formation & Family Catechesis. Students 669.
Mission—Catholic Community of Langley Park, 1408 Merrimac Dr., Langley Park, Prince George's Co. 20787. Tel: 301-328-5105;
Fax: 301-328-5105 (Call first).
4—ST. CATHERINE LABOURE (Wheaton) (1951)
11801 Claridge Rd., Wheaton, 20902.
Tel: 301-946-3636; Fax: 301-946-5064. Revs. Francisco E. Aguirre; Alberto Biondi, Parochial Vicar; Deacons Raymond L. Chaput; G. Stephane Philogene; Rafael G. Pagan, Email: rafael_pagan@msn.com; Bartolo Serafini.
Catechesis Religious Program—
Tel: 301-946-3010 (English);
Tel: 301-946-1606 (Hispanic Religious Education); Email: sclredirector@gmail.com. Students 590.
5—CHRIST THE KING (Wheaton) (1961)
2300 East West Hwy., Silver Spring, 20910.
Tel: 301-495-2306; Fax: 301-576-5264. Rev. Rodolfo A. Salinas, Admin.; Deacon Stephen Mitchell. In Res.
Catechesis Religious Program—Tel: 301-495-2306; Fax: 301-576-5264. Students 130.
6—ST. JOHN THE BAPTIST (Spring Brook) (1960)
12319 New Hampshire Ave., Silver Spring, 20904.
Tel: 301-622-1122; Fax: 301-625-9266; Email: secretary@sjbssparish.org; Web: www.sjbssparish.org. Revs. Y. David Brault; Cezary T. Kozubek; Deacons James J. Gorman; Edward J. McCormack.
School—St. John the Baptist School, (Grades PreK-8), Tel: 301-622-3076; Email: brian.blomquist@sjbsilverspring.org; Web: www.sjbsilverspring.org/school. Brian Blomquist, Prin. Lay Teachers 28; Students 238.
Catechesis Religious Program—Email: adultdre@sjbssparish.org. Louis J. Milone, Dir. Faith Formation. Students 170.
7—ST. JOHN THE EVANGELIST (1774) [CEM]
10103 Georgia Ave., Silver Spring, 20902.
Tel: 301-681-7663; Fax: 301-681-8793; Email: office@sjeparish.org. Revs. Joseph A. Calis; Mark A. Cusick, Parochial Vicar; Deacon Alan Jeeves.
School—St. John the Evangelist School, 10201 Woodland Dr., Silver Spring, 20902.
Tel: 301-681-7656; Fax: 301-681-0754; Email: office@sjte.org; Web: www.sjte.org. Mrs. Margaret Durney, Prin. Clergy 3; Lay Teachers 19; Religious 1; Students 200.
Catechesis Religious Program—Tel: 301-681-7634; Email: hardingr@sjeparish.org. Sr. Roberta Harding, I.H.M., D.R.E. Students 190.
8—ST. MICHAEL (1930)
824 Pershing Dr., Silver Spring, 20910.
Tel: 301-589-1155; Fax: 301-589-3470; Web: www.stmichaelsilverspring.parishesonline.com. Rev. Msgr. Eddie E. Tolentino, V.F.; Revs. Saulo S. Vicente; Alberto Biondi, Parochial Vicar; Deacons Ronald Ealey, Life Dir.; Stephen B. Frye; Carlos E. Hernandez.
Catechesis Religious Program—Tel: 301-587-2395;

Fax: 301-589-3470; Email: stmichaelreled@yahoo.com. Students 379.

9—OUR LADY OF GRACE (Leisure World) (1983)
15661 Norbeck Blvd., Silver Spring, 20906.
Tel: 301-924-0067; Tel: 301-924-4927;
Fax: 301-924-6809; Email: ourladyofgrace@comcast.net; Web: ourladyofgracelw.weebly.com. Rev. James D. Boccabella; Deacon William J. Heineman. In Res., Rev. Michael Murray.

10—OUR LADY OF VIETNAM (1990) (Vietnamese)
11812 New Hampshire Ave., Silver Spring, 20904.
Tel: 301-622-4895; Fax: 301-625-9384; Email: info@olvn-dc.org; Web: www.olvn-dc.org. Rev. Paul Tam X. Tran; Deacons John Huong Nguyen, (Retired); Nguyen T. Nguyen.
Catechesis Religious Program—Students 495.

11—OUR LADY QUEEN OF POLAND AND SAINT MAXIMILIAN KOLBE (Leisure World) (1983) (Polish)
9700 Rosensteel Ave., Silver Spring, 20910.
Tel: 301-589-1857; Fax: 301-589-4401. Rev. Jan Fiedurek, T.Chr.
Catechesis Religious Program—Students 80.

SOLOMONS, CALVERT CO., OUR LADY STAR OF THE SEA (1888) [CEM]
50 Alexander Ln., P.O. Box 560, Solomons, 20688.
Tel: 410-326-3535; Fax: 410-326-3679; Email: olstarsea.md@adw.org. Rev. Msgr. Michael Wilson, V.F.; Deacons Anton J. Geisz; Chad Martin.
School—Our Lady Star of the Sea School,
Tel: 410-326-3171; Email: olssschool@comcast.net. Mary Bartsch, Prin. Clergy 1; Lay Teachers 10; Students 100.
Catechesis Religious Program—Email: youthministry@olss.org. Joanne Pensenstadler, D.R.E. Sisters 1; Students 160.

SUITLAND, PRINCE GEORGE'S CO., ST. BERNARDINE OF SIENA (1966)
2400 Brooks Dr., Suitland, 20746-1101.
Tel: 301-736-0707; Fax: 301-736-2984; Email: st.bernardine@verizon.net. In Res., Rev. Jose Raul DeLeon.
Catechesis Religious Program—Students 206.

TAKOMA PARK, PRINCE GEORGES CO., OUR LADY OF SORROWS (1932)
1006 Larch Ave., Takoma Park, 20912.
Tel: 301-891-3500; Fax: 301-891-1523. Revs. Raymond J. Wadas, (Retired); Mario A. Majano; Deacons Trinidad Soc; Patrick L. Brown.
Catechesis Religious Program—Tel: 301-891-2033. Students 345.

UPPER MARLBORO, PRINCE GEORGES CO.

1—MOST HOLY ROSARY (1966) [CEM]
11704 Duley Station Rd., Upper Marlboro, 20772.
Tel: 301-856-3880; Fax: 301-856-3944; Email: mostholyrosary@outlook.com; Web: www.mostholyrosarychurch.org. Rev. Roger A. Soley.
Catechesis Religious Program—Twinned with St. Mary of the Assumption, Upper Marlboro.

2—SAINT MARY OF THE ASSUMPTION (1848) [CEM]
14908 Main St., Upper Marlboro, 20772.
Tel: 301-627-3255; Fax: 301-627-5533; Email: parish@stmaryum.org; Web: www.stmaryum.org. Rev. Thomas G. LaHood; Deacons Frank Klco; Thomas J. Molineaux.
School—Saint Mary of the Assumption School, (Grades PreK-8), 4610 Largo Rd., Upper Marlboro, 20772. Tel: 301-627-4170; Fax: 301-627-6383; Email: tcampbell@stmaryum.org. Dr. Steven Showalter, Prin. Lay Teachers 14; Students 242.
Catechesis Religious Program—Mrs. Regina Piazza, Coord. R.C.I.A.; Mrs. Shirley Byrd, C.R.E. Students 30.

VALLEY LEE, ST. MARY'S CO., ST. GEORGE (1851) [CEM]
19199 St. George Church Rd., Valley Lee, 20692.
Tel: 301-994-0607; Fax: 301-994-1793; Email: secretary@stgeorgercc.org; Web: www.stgeorgercc.org. Rev. Paul Dean Nguyen; Deacon Joel P. Carpenter.
Catechesis Religious Program—Tel: 301-994-0737; Email: kim.browne@stgeorgercc.org. Kimberley Browne, D.R.E. Students 110.
Chapel—St. George's Island, St. Francis Xavier.

WALDORF, CHARLES CO.

1—OUR LADY HELP OF CHRISTIANS (1980)
100 Village St., Waldorf, 20602-2183.
Tel: 301-645-7112; Fax: 301-645-3635; Email: olhc@verizon.net; Web: www.olhoc.org. Deacon Reginald A. Thomas.
Res.: 930 Barrington Dr., Waldorf, 20602-2183.
Tel: 301-843-8823; Fax: 301-645-3635.
Catechesis Religious Program—Mrs. Kathleen White, D.R.E. Students 308.

2—ST. PETER (1700) [CEM]
3320 St. Peter's Dr., Waldorf, 20601.
Tel: 301-843-8916; Fax: 301-632-6272; Email: parishsecretary@stpeterswaldorf.org; Web: stpeterswaldorf.org. Rev. Keith Woods; Rev. Msgr. Oliver W. McGready, Parochial Vicar, (Retired); Rev. Jorge E. Ubau, Parochial Vicar; Deacon Robert L. Martin.
School—St. Peter School, 3310 St. Peter's Dr., Waldorf, 20601. Tel: 301-843-1955;
Fax: 301-632-6272. J.R. West, Prin. Lay Teachers 16; Students 274.
Catechesis Religious Program—Alice Culbreth, Dir. Christian Formation. Students 200.

Chaplains of Public Institutions

WASHINGTON. *Children's National Medical Center*, 111 Michigan Ave., NW, 20010. Tel: 202-476-3321. Revs. Francis Nhi Nguyen, Chap., Raymond Nwabueze, O.P., Chap.
St. Elizabeths Hospital (Government Operated), 1100 Alabama Ave., SE, 20032. Tel: 202-299-5400; Email: ghebraya@adw.org. Revs. Araia Ghiday Ghebray, Chap., Henry G. Heffernan, S.J., Chap.
MedStar National Rehabilitation Hospital, 102 Irving St., NW, 20010. Tel: 202-877-6691. Rev. Fidelis Umukoro, O.P., Chap.
MedStar Washington Hospital Center, 110 Irving St. NW, 20010. Tel: 202-877-6691. Revs. Denis Mandamuna, Chap., Fidelis Umukoro, O.P., Chap.
Armed Forces Retirement Home, 3700 N. Capitol St., NW, 20011. Tel: 202-541-7617. Rev. Carlos Roman Toro, Chap.
Washington, DC VA Medical Center, 50 Irving St., NW, 20422. Tel: 202-745-8140. Rev. Romeo Jose Axalan, WDC, Chap.
The Washington Home & Community Hospices. Served by priests of St. Ann Parish. Tel: 202-966-6288.

BETHESDA, MD. *National Institutes of Health, Clinical Center*, 9000 Rockville Pike, Bethesda, 20892. Tel: 301-496-3407. Chorbishop Dominic Ashkar.
Walter Reed National Military Medical Center, 4494 N. Palmer Rd., Bethesda, 20889. Tel: 301-295-1510 . Rev. Grant Gaskin, Chap.

Cheverly, MD
University of Maryland Prince George's Hospital Center. Served by priests of St. Ambrose Parish, Cheverly. Tel. 301-773-9300 Cheverly, 20785.

La Plata
University of Maryland Charles Regional Medical Center, La Plata, 20646. Served by priests of Sacred Heart Parish, La Plata. Tel: 301-934-2261.

LANHAM, MD. *Doctors Community Hospital*, Lanham, 20706. Tel: 301-459-4814. Served by the priests of St. Matthias Parish.

Laurel, MD
University of Maryland Laurel Regional Hospital, Laurel, 20707. Served by priests of St. Mary of the Mills Parish. Tel: 301-725-3080.

Leonardtown, MD
MedStar St. Mary's Hospital, Leonardtown, 20650. Served by the parishes of St. Mary's County. St. Aloysius Parish. Tel: 301-475-8064.

Olney, MD
MedStar Montgomery Medical Center, Olney, 20832. Served by priests of St. Peter Parish, Olney. Tel: 301-924-3774.

Prince Frederick, MD
CalvertHealth Medical Center, Prince Frederick, 20678. Served by priests of St. John Vianney Parish. Tel: 410-535-0223.

Special Ministries:
Rev. Msgrs.—
Criscuolo, Salvatore A., Chap., Police and Fire Dept.
Enzler, John J., E.V., Pres. & CEO, Catholic Charities
Murray, Michael J., Priest Dir., Catholic Cemeteries
Revs.—
Adams, John E., Dir., S.O.M.E.
Begg, Christopher T., Ph.D., Ph.B., S.T.D., Catholic University of America
Bryant, F. Michael, Chap., District of Columbia Jail
Butta, Gregory C., Dir., Cardinal O'Boyle Residence; Chap., Carroll Manor
Conley, Rory T., Archdiocesan Historian
Gallagher, Charles M., George Washington University Newman Center
Kemp, Raymond B., Fellow, (Retired), Woodstock Theological Center, Georgetown University
O'Brien, Raymond C., J.D., Asst. Dean, Catholic University
Pertiné, Ivan, American University
Walsh, Robert E., Newman Center, University of Maryland
Wright, Frank A., S.M.A., Chap., Center for the Deaf & Gallaudet University.

Pastoral Center Special Ministries:
Most Rev.—
Fisher, Michael W., V.G., Vicar for Clergy, Sec. Ministerial Leadership
Rev. Msgrs.—
Antonicelli, Charles V., J.D., J.C.L., V. Vicar Canonical Svcs. & Mod. Curia
Dempsey, Patrick E., Archdiocesan Records Mgr., Archdiocesan Archives; Notary, Archdiocesan Office of Canonical Svcs.
Panke, Robert J., Rector
Ranieri, Joseph A., Coord. of Pastoral Care of Priests, (Retired)
Revs.—
Griffin, Carter H., Vice Rector
Ivany, Mark R., Dir. of Spiritual Formation
Murphy, Conrad, Dir. Office of Worship
Rebeggiani, Daniele, Sec. to Archbishop Wuerl
Santaballa, Francisco Javier, Vice Rector, Redemptoris Mater Seminary
Stuart, George E., J.C.D., Tribunal, Vice Chancellor
Tucker, Mark E., J.C.L., Tribunal
Vicente, Saulo S., Dir., Spiritual Formation, Redemptoris Mater Seminary.

Hospital & Nursing Home Ministries:
Revs.—
Baraki, Tesfamarian, Howard University Hospital
Butta, Gregory C., Cardinal O'Boyle Residence, Carroll Manor
Coan, Gregory S., Adventist HealthCare Washington Adventist Hospital
Ghebray, Araia Ghiday, United Medical Center
Keveny, M. Valentine, Adventist HealthCare Shady Grove Medical Center
Salinas, Rodolfo A., Sibley Memorial Hospital
Samaha, Jeffrey F., MedStar Southern Maryland Hospital Center
Simo, Philip, O.S.B., Little Sisters of the Poor, Jeanne Jugan Residence
Sirianni, Klaus J., George Washington University Hospital
Venditti, J. Michael, Suburban Hospital.

On Duty Outside the Archdiocese:
Revs.—
Ailer, Gellert Jozsef, Szechenyi, Hungary
Benitez, Carlos A., Philadelphia, PA
Culkin, Michael, Lancaster, PA
DeNigris, Emanuele, Miami, FL
DiNoia, Joseph Augustine, O.P., Ph.D., Sub-Secretary for the Congregation of the Doctrine of the Faith, Rome
Esposito-Garcia, Juan, J.C.D., Rome, Italy
Gonzalez, Avelino A., Rome, Italy
Izac, Andre C., North Carolina
Kuebler, A.M. Seamus, Maine
Kurzawinski, Zygmunt, Capetown, South Africa
Malaver, Daniel, Valinda, CA
Oberle, James P., S.S., University of Dallas, Irving, TX
Park, Adam, Rome, Italy
Ryan, William A., Togo, West Africa
Sanz, Jose, D.L.P., California
Slevin, Henry, Vietnam
Walsh, Francis M.

Graduate Studies:
Rev.—
Seith, Christopher J., The Catholic University of America, Washington, DC.

Military Chaplains:
Revs.—
Garrett, Benton Lee
Gaskin, Grantley DaCosta
Reutemann, John F. III, U.S.A.F.
Riffle, Patrick J.

Absent On Leave:
Revs.—
Bozek, Robert
Defayette, Jeffrey M.
Paris, Michael S.
Rogers, Joseph E., V.F.
Woods, Thomas Matthew.

Retired:
Most Rev.—
Gonzalez, Francisco, S.F., D.D., V.G., (Retired), 401 Randolph Rd., Silver Spring, 20904
Rev. Msgrs.—
Bazan, Joaquin, (Retired), Jeanne Jugan Residence, 4200 Harewood Rd., NE, 20017
Brady, John B., (Retired), 7201 Pyle Rd., Bethesda, 20817
Cassin, Andrew J., (Retired), St. Peter, 3200 St. Peter's Dr., Waldorf, 20601
English, William J., (Retired), 613 Spinnaker Way, Havre De Grace, 21078
Essex, Donald S., (Retired), 15211 Elkridge Way, Apt. 1J, Silver Spring, 20906
Hill, R. Cary, (Retired), 3456 Cleary Ave. #305, Metairie, LA 70002
Kane, Thomas A., (Retired), Cardinal O'Boyle Residence, P.O. Box 29206, 20017
Kazista, Francis G., (Retired), Grace House, 3214 Norbeck Rd., Silver Spring, 20906

Laczko, T. Ansgar, (Retired), 290 Devonshire Rd., Hedgesville, WV 25427
Langsfeld, Paul J., S.T.D., (Retired), Jeanne Jugan Residence, 4200 Harewood Rd., NE, 20017
Lockman, James V., (Retired), 2130 Ganton Green, Woodstock, 21163
Macfarlane, John F., (Retired), Holy Cross, 490 Strathmore Ave., P.O. Box 249, Garrett Park, 20896
McGready, Oliver W., (Retired), St. Peter's, 3320 St. Peter's Dr., Waldorf, 20601
Myslinski, John F., (Retired), 196 Holmes Rd., Pittsfield, MA 01201
O'Connell, Maurice V., (Retired), Shrine of the Most Blessed Sacrament, 3630 Quesada St., NW, 20015-2443
Otero, Henry, (Retired), 613 Old Stage Rd., S.W., Glen Burnie, 21061
Ranieri, Joseph A., (Retired), Jeanne Jugan Residence, 4200 Harewood Rd., NE, 20017
Sadusky, Joseph F., J.C.D., (Retired), St. Peter, 313 Second St., SE, 20017

Revs.—
Alliata, Peter R., (Retired), 105 Vianney Ln., Prince Frederick, 20678
Alvarez-Garcia, Julio, (Retired), 211 Phoenetia Ave., Coral Gables, FL 33134
Brice, Donald, (Retired), Cardinal O'Boyle Residence, P.O. Box 29206, 20017
D'Silva, Percival L., (Retired), Shrine of the Most Blessed Sacrament, 3630 Quesada St., NW, 20015-2443
Daly, Peter J., V.F., (Retired), P.O. Box 15723, 20003
DeRamos, Fidel, (Retired), P.O. Box 60, Lucena City, Philippines 4301
Dignan, Eamon, (Retired), St. John, 43950 St. John's Rd., Hollywood, 20636
Dixon, J. Isidore, (Retired), 6335 Bumpy Oak Rd., La Plata, 20646
Dolan, Michael F., (Retired), 7901 S.W. Pkwy, Austin, TX 78735
Downs, L. James, (Retired), 22783 Dogwood Dr., Lewes, DE 19958
Duggan, Robert D., (Retired), 24536 Fossen Rd., Damascus, 20872. Washington, DC
Early, Francis J., (Retired), 3707 Dulwick Dr., Silver Spring, 20906
Faust, Louis J., (Retired), Mother Seton, 19951 Father Hurley Blvd., Germantown, 20874
Finamore, Robert A., (Retired), P.O. Box 5146, Palm Springs, CA 92263
Gardiner, Richard E., (Retired), 5345 Cypress Links Blvd., Elkton, FL 32033
Goode, William F., (Retired), Ascension, 12700 Lanham-Severn Rd., Bowie, 20719
Green, Charles C., (Retired), Jeanne Jugan Residence, 4200 harewood Rd., NE, 20017
Gude, Thomas A., (Retired), Sacred Heart Nursing Home, 5805 Queens Chapel Rd., 20782
Guillen, Robert, (Retired), Bartholomew House, 6904 River Rd., Bethesda, 20817
Hill, W. Paul, (Retired), 13901 Belle Chase Blvd., #313, Laurel, 20707
Holloway, James P., (Retired), 300 Ocean Blvd., #6, St. Simons Island, GA 31522
Holt, Paul-Stephen, (Retired), St. Francis Nursing Home, 4 Ridgewood Pkwy, Hampton, VA 23602
Hurley, John, (Retired), Cathedral of St. Matthew, 1725 Rhode Island Ave., NW, 20036
Ihrie, Bernard R. Jr., (Retired), 3736 Bay Dr., Edgewater, 21037
Izac, C. Andre, (Retired), 1124 Savery St., North Port, FL 34287
Januszkiewicz, Henry, (Retired), 9910 Rookery Cir., Estero, FL 33928
Jordan, Milton E., (Retired), 14106 School Ln., Upper Marlboro, 20772
Keffer, Robert F., (Retired), 132 Big Red Oak Rd., Harpers Ferry, WV 25425
Kemp, Raymond B., (Retired), 4000 Cathedral Ave., NW, 20016
Kennedy, Joseph P., (Retired), 5 Brush Island Ct., Berlin, 21811
MacIntyre, Frederick H., (Retired), St. Patrick, 619 Tenth St., NW, 20001
McCann, Charles, (Retired), St. John the Evangelist, 8908 Old Branch Ave., Clinton, 20735
McKay, John F., (Retired), 6222 Rockhurst Rd., Bethesda, 20817
McKee, Roderick D., (Retired), St. Patrick, 619 Tenth St., NW, 20001
McManus, Eamon, (Retired), Ave Maria Univ., 1025 Commons Cir., Naples, FL 34119
Meyers, James P., (Retired), Cardinal O'Boyle Residence, P.O. Box 29206, 20017
Montgomery, William L., (Retired), St. Thomas More Rectory, 65 E. 89th St., New York, NY 10208
Morrow, Thomas G., (Retired), St. Raphael, 1513 Dunster Rd., Rockville, 20854
Mudd, John, (Retired), 2236 Washington Ave., Silver Spring, 20910
Muzzey, Charles H., (Retired), 4016 Decatur Ave., Kensington, 20895
Reynierse, Peter, (Retired), 212 Creekside Dr., Locust Grove, VA 22508
Richardson, Robert C., (Retired), Unit 301, 3850 Washington St., Hillcrest Bldg. 27, Hollywood, FL 33021
Russell, David P., (Retired), 505 Howard Ave., Tracys Landing, 20779
Salcedo, Luis G., (Retired), 5G Castle Hills Rd., Agawam, MA 01001
Sileo, Joseph R., (Retired), 729 Watford Ct., Sterling, VA 20164
Sweeney, Peter T., (Retired), St. John Neumann, 8900 Lochaven Dr., Gaithersburg, 20882
Tou, Louis A., (Retired), Cardinal O'Boyle Residence, P.O. Box 29206, 20017
Ulshafer, Thomas, P.S.S., (Retired), 93 Sabbe St., Magnolia, DE 19962
Vitturino, Saverio T., (Retired), 6050 California Cir., #108, Rockville, 20852
Wadas, Raymond J., (Retired), Redemptoris Mater Seminary, 4900 La Salle Rd., 20782
Wilkinson, George A. Jr., (Retired), 39335 Burch Rd., Avenue, 20609
Wintermyer, John S., (Retired), 15316 Pine Orchard Dr., 2K, Silver Spring, 20906.

Permanent Deacons:
Abeyta, Dan D., Sacred Heart, Bowie, MD
Allen, Robert F., (Retired), Diocese of Richmond
Alvarez, Sergio, Diocese of Arlington
Ames, George B. Jr., (Retired)
Angell, Kenneth, Shrine of the Most Blessed Sacrament, D.C.
Baker, Francis E. Jr., St. Anthony, North Beach, MD
Barbernitz, Peter M., St. Camillus, Silver Spring, MD
Barnes, David, St. Edwards the Confessor, Bowie
Barnes, John R., (Retired)
Barrasso, Anthony T., (Retired)
Barrett, Kenneth, (Retired)
Barrett, Raymond J., Diocese of Venice, FL
Barros, Alfred M., Delaware
Bell, Joseph, Incarnation, Washington, DC
Bell, Lawrence G., St. Martin, Gaithersburg, MD
Bendel, Francis W., Mother Seton, Gaithersburg, MD
Bieberich, Charles J., Resurrection, Burtonsville, MO
Bielewicz, Paul A., Holy Face, Great Mills, MD
Birkel, Richard, (On Leave of Absence)
Blanco-Eccleston, Julio, (Retired)
Bobbitt, John W., (Retired)
Bockweg, Gary L., St. Joseph's on Capitol Hill, Washington, DC
Boesman, William C., (Retired)
Bond, Stuart Michael, St. Andrew the Apostle, Silver Spring, MD
Briscoe, John A., (Retired)
Brown, Patrick L., Our Lady of Sorrows, Takoma, MD
Brune, Louis J. III, St. Mary, Rockville, MD
Burns, Ronald J., Jesus the Divine Word, Huntingtown, MD
Burroughs, Eugene, (Retired)
Butkiewicz, Jerome, (Leave of Absence)
Byrne, Kevin, St. Elizabeth, Rockville
Cadigan, James, Diocese of Wilmington
Cahoon, David L. Jr., St. Mary, Barnesville, MD
Cain, Leonard F., (Retired)
Caldwell, James L., St. John Vianney, Prince Frederick, MI
Calvo, Raul R., Mother Seton, Germantown, MD
Caraballo, Carlo, St. John Neumann, Gaithersburg, MD
Carbonell, Jose R., St. Raphael, Rockville, MD
Carpenter, Joel P., St. George, Valley Lee, MD
Carroll, Donald T., (Retired), (Wilmington)
Cartagena, Francisco J., St. Camillus, Silver Spring, MD
Carter, William N., Sacred Heart, La Plata, MD
Cayrampoma, Juan, Cathedral of St. Matthew, Washington, DC
Chaput, Raymond L., (Retired)
Chase, Ira E., Basilica of the National Shrine of the Immaculate Conception, Washington, DC
Chen, Chester G., (Retired)
Choi, Chang Sup, St. Peter, Olney, MD
Chrzanowski, Edmund A. Jr., St. John Vianney, Prince Frederick, MD
Cioffi, Thomas, St. Peter, Olney, MD
Class, John S., St. Bartholomew, Bethesda, MD
Close, Edward G., St. Paul, Damascus, MD
Coates, Vincent J. Jr., (Retired), Fall River
Collins, Gerald A., Holy Family, Hillcrest Heights, MD
Connor, John E., (Retired)
Contreras, Carlos E., (Retired), VA
Conway, Neal T., St. Jerome, Hyattsville, MD
Cooper, Philip J., Charlotte
Cordova-Ferrer, Nathaniel, (Retired)
Crawford, Rory P., St. Peter, Olney
Crowe, Michael J., Immaculate Heart of Mary, Lexington Park, MD
Crowley, Ronald C., (Leave of Absence)
Cruz, George C., St. Bartholomew, Bethesda, MD
Cummins, Don E., Seattle
Curtis, Joseph F. Jr., (Retired), Basilica of the National Shrine of Immaculate Conception, Washington, DC
Cyrus, Ralph W., Holy Comforter-St. Cyprian, Washington, DC
Daniels, Willis, Holy Redeemer, Washington DC
Danko, Edward, Wilmington
Datovech, James J., St. Francis of Assisi, Derwood
Davis, Alton Jr., (Retired), St. Joseph, Largo, MD
Davis, Harry, (Retired)
Davis, William E., (Retired), Las Vegas
Davy, Michael W., St. John Neumann, Gaithersburg
Devaney, Thomas J., St. Ann, Washington DC
DeVillier, Moise, Archdiocese of Baltimore
Ditewig, William, St. Petersburg, FL
Divins, David L., (NH)
Dmuchowski, Thaddeus A., Our Lady of the Visitation, Darrestown, MD
Dominic, James, St. Michael, Ridge
Doyle, James, St. Pius X, Bowie, MD
Dubicki, Richard F., Our Lady Help of Christians, Waldorf, MD
Duggin, David, Harrisburg
Dwyer, Thomas F., Florida
Ealey, Ronald R., (Retired)
Elliott, Thomas B., Richmond
Enright, Timothy D., Wilmington
Espinosa, Leandro Y., (Retired)
Fagan, Paul, Jesus the Good Shepherd, Dunkirk, MD
Feeley, John, St. Anthony of Padua, Washington, DC
Fernandez, Elmer, Archdiocese of San Antonio
Finerty, John F., (Retired)
Finn, Daniel F. VI, St. Francis of Assisi, Derwood, MD
Fischer, Robert A., Our Lady of the Visitation, Darnestown
Flores, Francisco, Diocese of Arlington
Flynn, Leo, Shrine of the Most Blessed Sacrament, Washington, DC
Ford, Daniel E., Leave of Absence
Gallerizzo, William, Fall River
Garcia, David F., Santa Fe
Garcia, James A., Cathedral of St. Matthew the Apostle, Washington, DC
Gatica-Delgado, Jorge, St. Raphael, Rockville
Geisz, Anton J., Our Lady, Star of the Sea, Solomons, MD
Genis, Thomas P., Immaculate Conception, Washington, DC
Gignilliat, Robert L., St. Mary of the Mills, Laurel
Glenn, Clark, (Retired)
Gonzalez, Fidencio, Mother Seton, Germantown, MD
Gorman, James J., (Retired)
Gorospe, Santiago B., (Retired), Los Angeles, CA
Graham, Albert E. Jr., (Retired)
Greenfield, William Mike, Incarnation, Washington, DC
Hawkins, William J., St. Teresa of Avila, Washington, DC
Heineman, William J., Our Lady of Grace, S.S., MD
Hernandez, Carlos E., Leave of Absence
Hernandez-Viera, Ivan, Palm Beach, FL
Hidalgo, Alfredo, (Retired)
Holson, Edward, Wilmington
Hong, Pascal, (Retired)
Hopson, Frank, (Retired)
Houle, Matthew P., Our Lady of Victory, Washington, DC
Hubbard, Robert, (Retired)
Huber, Charles P., Our Lady of Mercy, Potomac, MD
Huete, Stephen, Harrisburg, PA
Huguley, Maury Jr., St. Paul, Damascus, MD
Hume, W. Michael, Nashville
Iannaconi, Perry F., (Retired)
Jackson, Harold I., Charleston
Jeeves, Alan K., St. John the Evangelist, Silver Spring, MD
Jensen, Christopher, Florida
Johnson, Alfred, Leave of Absence
Jones, Thomas R., Our Lady of Perpetual Help, Washington, DC
Justice, Brandon B., Leave of Absence
Keller, Grafton T., St. Augustine, FL
Kelly, Richard F., (VA) Diocese of Arlington
Klco, Frank, St. Mary of the Assumption, Upper Marlboro, MD

Koeniger, Ludwig, (Retired), (FL)
Koester, Paul P., St. John the Evangelist, Clinton, MD
Kostka, Daniel S., St. Mary, Rockville, MD
Kraemer, Francis W. Sr., (Retired)
Kyte, William L., Immaculate Conception, Mechanicsville, MD
Lee, Kenneth, St. Anthony of Padua, Washington, DC
Lemon, John G., Wilmington
Levy, Barry A., St. John Neumann, Gaithersburg, MD
Levy, Richard A. Jr., (Leave of Absence)
Liu, John C., St. Stephen Martyr, D.C.
Lloyd, Joseph W. Jr., Holy Angels, Avenue, MD and Sacred Heart, Bushwood, MD
Locke, John W., (Retired)
Longano, Donald R., Church of the Little Flower, Bethesda, MD
Luetjen, Palmer, (Retired)
Lynch, John F., (Retired)
Lyons, Robert A., Arlington, VA
Lyons, Robert R., New York
Maksymiec, William T., Church of the Annunciation, D.C.
Martin, E. Chad, Our Lady of the Sea, Solomons, MD
Martin, Robert L., St. Peter, Waldorf, MD
Maselko, Stephen M., Mother Seton, Germantown, MD
Mastrangelo, Eugene K., (Retired)
Mattocks, Richard E., (Retired)
Mays, Donald, St. Paul, Damascus, MD
McCann, James C., St. Francis of Assisi, Derwood, MD
McCarthy, Michael, (Leave of Absence)
McCormack, Edward J., St. John the Baptist, Silver Spring, MD
McGinness, John J., (Retired)
McKimmie, Stephen, St. Mary, Piscataway, MD
Merella, Bartholomew J., (Retired)
Meyer, Ronald J., (South Carolina)
Middleton, Henry D. III, (Retired)
Miles, Lawrence A., (Retired)
Miller, Alfred A. Jr., (Retired)
Miller, Lawrence L., Military Service
Mills, Joseph F., St. John Vianney, Prince Frederick, MD
Mitchell, Stephen, Holy Redeemer, Kensington, MD
Molina, Jose Renato, St. Mark the Evangelist, Hyattsville, MD
Molina, Nehemias J., Christ the King, Silver Spring, MD
Molineaux, Thomas J., St. Mary of the Assumption, Upper Marlboro, MD
Montgomery, John E., (Retired), Holy Rosary, Rosaryville, MD
Moreno, Mario F., St. Rose of Lima, Gaithersburg
Mueller, Eric B., St. Anthony, North Beach, MD
Mukri, Kevin, Florida
Munno, James, St. Mary of the Mills, Laurel, MD
Murati, George, St. Augustine
Nalls, James T., St. Patrick, Rockville, MD
Nash, Steven A., St. Joseph, Largo
Nguyen, John H., (Retired)
Nguyen, Nguyen T., Our Lady of Vietnam, Silver Spring, MD
Nickel, Clayton A., Tucson, AZ
Nickerson, William J., (Retired)
Nosacek, Andrew J., (Retired)
O'Neill, Stephen D., St. Andrew the Apostle, Silver Spring, MD
Oettinger, Frank F., Las Vegas
Oguledo, Valentine, North Carolina
Om, Michael, (Retired)
Opdenaker, Albert L., St. Rose of Lima, Gaithersburg, MD
Ortiz, Juan C., Immaculate Heart of Mary, Lexington, Park, MD
Pagan, Rafael G., St. Catherine Laboure, Wheaton, MD
Payne, Brian M., Holy Family, Mitchellville, MD
Perkins, Gary, Austin, TX
Philogene, G. Stephane, St. Catherine Laboure, Wheaton, MD
Picard, Adrien D., (Retired)
Pineda, Roberto L., Miami
Price, Robert, Raleigh
Reeves, Steven R., St. Andrew Apostles, S.S., MD
Reilly, Matthew B., (Retired), Charlotte
Ricker, Philip W., Wilmington
Ripple, Ammon S., St. John, Hollywood, MD
Rivas, Mauricio O., St. Martin of Tours, Gaithersburg, MD
Robinson, John E. Jr., Holy Redeemer, Washington, DC
Robinson, Stephen M., St. Mary, Landover Hills, MD
Rodney, Curtis C., St. Michael the Archangel, S.S., MD
Roszkowski, Thomas E., St. Bernadette, Silver Spring, MD
Rourke, Walter G., (Retired)
Ruffo, Paul, New York
Salatto, Frank J. Jr., (Retired)
Salgado, Roberto, (Retired)
Santiago, Perfecto, (Retired)
Schmitt, Paul E., Shrine of St. Jude, Rockville, MD
Schneider, Leo F., St. Rose of Lima, Gaithersburg, MD
Schneider, Ronald W., (Retired), Milwaukee
Scholz, Nicholas E., Shrine of St. Jude, Rockville, MD
Schwartz, Patrick C., St. Joseph, Beltsville, MD
Scott, William T., Our Lady Help of the Christians, Waldorf, MD
Seith, Robert P., Sacred Heart, Bowie, MD
Serafini, Bartolo, (Retired)
Sferrella, Joseph J., (Retired)
Shanahan, James R., Church of the Little Flower, Bethesda, MD
Shewmaker, John B., (Retired)
Sinchak, J. Douglas, Archdiocese of Mobile
Smith, McBurnett J., Diocese of Pensacola-Tallahassee
Soc, Trinidad, Our Lady of Sorrows, Takoma Park, MD
Somerville, James, (Retired)
Somerville, John, (Retired)
Somerville, Keith J., St. Margaret of Scotland, Seat Pleasant, MD
Soto, Alfredo, Galveston-Houston
Spalding, Thomas C. Sr., (Retired)
Springer, James R., El Paso (Leave of Absence)
Stackpole, Terrell U., (Retired)
Stevens, William H., Our Lady of the Presentation, Poolesville, MD
Stout, Robert W. III, Holy Cross, Garrett Park, MD
Suley, David J., St. Patrick, Rockville
Sweeney, Anthony J. III, (Retired)
Terrar, David B., St. Paul, Damascus, MD
Testudine, Joseph, (Retired)
Tilghman, Timothy E., Our Lady of Perpetual Help, Washington, DC
Tittinger, James M., St. Joseph, Pomfret, MD
Turner, Al Douglas, Georgia
Turner, B. Curtis, St. Mark the Evangelist, Hyattsville, MD
Vargas, Jorge W., Our Lady Queen of the Americas, Washington, DC
Vavrus, Joseph R., St. Aloysius, Leonardtown, MD
Vikor, Desider L., North Carolina
Villanueva, Robert C., St. Columba, Oxon Hill, MD
Vince, Robert J., St. Jane Frances de Chantal, Bethesda, MD
Vita, William A. Jr., St. Martin of Tours, Gaithersburg, MD
Wakefield, Walter W. III, Lexington
Walker, Richard Jr., St. Luke, Washington, DC
Welch, Joseph, (Retired)
Weschler, Charles A., Wilmington
Whitaker, Robert W., (Retired)
White, Robert C. Sr., St. Martin of Tours, Washington, DC
Wolfe, Willis R., NY
Wolfinger, Vincent J., St. Peter, Onley, MD
Wolfkill, Timothy J., St. Ignatius, Fort Washington, MD
Work, Boyd Jr., (Retired), Cathedral of St. Matthew, Washington, DC
Yorke, Desmond, St. Bernard, Riverdale Park, MD.

INSTITUTIONS LOCATED IN DIOCESE

[A] SEMINARIES, ARCHDIOCESAN

WASHINGTON. *Saint John Paul II Seminary* (2011) 145 Taylor St., N.E., 20017. Tel: 202-636-9020; Fax: 202-636-9025; Email: jp2seminary@adw.org; Web: www.dcpriest.org. Rev. Msgr. Robert J. Panke, Rector; Revs. Carter H. Griffin, Vice-Rector; Mark R. Ivany, Spiritual Dir. Seminarians 49.

Theological College of the Catholic University of America, 401 Michigan Ave., N.E., 20017. Tel: 202-756-4900; Fax: 202-756-4909; Web: www.theologicalcollege.org. Sulpician Fathers.

Theological College, Inc. Deacons 1; Priests 7; Students 89; Lay Faculty 1.

Faculty: Revs. Gerald D. McBrearity, P.S.S., M.A., S.T.B., D.Min., Rector; David D. Thayer, P.S.S., S.T.L., Ph.D., Faculty Advisor; Hy Khac Nguyen, P.S.S., Vice Rector; James P. Froehlich, O.F.M.Cap., M.A., M.S., Ph.D., Faculty Advisor; Rob Cro, Faculty Advisor; Dominic G. Ciriaco, Faculty Advisor, 1801 N. Broom St., Wilmington, DE 19802; Melvin C. Blanchette, P.S.S., M.A., Ph. D., Formation Faculty; Deacon Edward J. McCormack, Faculty Advisor; Mrs. Kathi Kramer, M.Div., Dir. Pastoral Formation Program.

HYATTSVILLE, MD. *Redemptoris Mater Archdiocesan Missionary Seminary* (2002) 4900 Lasalle Rd., 20782. Tel: 301-277-4960; Fax: 301-277-5295; Email: seminary@rmwashington.org; Web: www.rmwashington.org. Revs. José Matías Díaz, Rector; Francisco Javier Santaballa, Vice Rector; Saulo S. Vicente, Spiritual Dir. Clergy 5; Religious Teachers 3; Priests 3; Students 28.

[B] SEMINARIES, RELIGIOUS OR SCHOLASTICATES

WASHINGTON. *Atonement Seminary-Franciscan Friars of the Atonement*, 5207 Colorado Ave., N.W., 20011. Tel: 202-722-0461; Fax: 202-722-1716. Revs. Dennis Polanco, S.A., Vocation Dir. & Dir. Atonement Seminary; C. Donald Howard, S.A., (Retired). Priests 2.

Deshairs Community-Oblates of St. Francis de Sales Residence, 1621 Otis St., N.E., 20018-2321. Tel: 202-529-1926. Revs. John W. Crossin, O.S.F.S.; Richard DeLillio, O.S.F.S.

Diocesan Laborer Priests, House of Studies (1966) 3706 15th St., N.E., 20017. Tel: 202-832-4217; Fax: 202-526-5692; Email: info@solinstitutedc.com; Web: www.solinstitutedc.com. Revs. Ovidio Pecharroman, US Delegate & Dir.; Victor Salomon. Priests 3; Total Enrollment 3.

Discalced Carmelite Friars (1918) 2131 Lincoln Rd., N.E., 20002-1199. Tel: 202-832-6622; Fax: 202-832-5711; Email: brpaquette@aol.com; Email: salocd@aol.com. Revs. Michael Berry, Dir.; Salvatore Sciurba, O.C.D., Prior; Marc Foley, O.C.D.; Emmanuel Betasso, O.C.D.; Regis Jordan, O.C.D.; Kieran Kavanaugh, O.C.D.; Francis Miller, O.C.D., (Retired); Bros. Edward O'Donnell, O.C.D.; Bryan Paquette, O.C.D.; Michael Stoeghauer; Robert Sentman; Rev. John Sullivan, O.C.D.

Discalced Carmelite Friars, Inc. Brothers 4; Clergy 7; Priests 7; Students 3.

Dominican House of Studies, 487 Michigan Ave., N.E., 20017. Tel: 202-529-5300; Fax: 202-636-4460; Email: prior@dhs.edu; Web: www.dhspriory.org. Very Rev. John Albert Langlois, O.P., S.T.D., Pres., Pontifical Faculty of the Immaculate Conception; Revs. Jacob Thomas Petri, O.P., Vice Pres. & Academic Dean Pontifical Faculty of the Immaculate Conception; Jeremy Aquinas Gilbeau, O.P., Prior; Guy Albert Trudel, O.P., Registrar; John Martin Ruiz, O.P., Dominican Theological Librarian; Theodore John Baptist Ku, O.P., S.T.L., Prof.; John Chrysostom Kozlowski, O.P., Prof.; Gregory Pine, O.P., Prof.; Nicholas E. Lombardo, O.P., Prof.; Timothy Bellamah, O.P., S.T.L.; James Brent, O.P.; Brian Chrzastek, O.P., Asst. Student Master, Students; Basil Burr Cole, O.P.; John Dominic Corbett, O.P.; Dominic Langevin, O.P., S.T.B., Asst. Student Master, Students; David Dominic Legge, O.P.; Michael J. McCormack, O.P., M.Div., M.A.; Stephen Desmond Ryan, O.P.; Jordan Joseph Schmidt, O.P.; Michael O'Connor, Doctoral Student; Gregory Schnakenberg, Doctoral Student. (Pontifical Faculty & Dominican Friars, Priory of the Immaculate Conception) Religious Teachers 19; Students 102. In Res. Revs. John Mark Igboalisi, O.P.; Colm Mannion, O.P.; Lawrence Lew, O.P.

St. Francis Friary-Capuchin College, 4121 Harewood Rd., N.E., 20017-1593. Tel: 202-529-2188; Fax: 202-526-6664; Email: joekusnir@capuchin.com. Revs. Paul Dressler, O.F.M.Cap., Guardian - Dir. Formation; William Gillum, O.F.M.Cap., Asst. Dir.; Robert L. McCreary, O.F.M.Cap., Confessor; Matthew Palkowski, Preaching and Evangelization; Emett Schuler, O.F.M.Cap., Nursing Home Chap.; Thomas Weinandy, O.F.M.Cap., Writing; Bros. Matthew Hindelang, O.F.M.Cap., Fraternity Service; Robert Herrick, O.F.M.Cap., Formation Work & Music Ministry; Michael Meza, Asst. Directory, Liturgy; Revs. Joseph Mindling, O.F.M.-Cap., Provincial Library Liaison; J. Daniel Mindling, O.F.M.Cap., Librarian, Mt. St. Mary, Emittsburgh, MD; Anil Gonsalves, O.F.M.Cap.; Brian Newman, O.F.M.Cap.; Francis X. Russo, O.-F.M.Cap.; Wolfgang Pisa, O.F.M.Cap. Brothers 3; Priests 12; Scholastics 16; Total Enrollment 36.

St. Joseph's Seminary (1888) 1200 Varnum St. N.E., 20017. Tel: 202-526-4231; Tel: 202-526-4229 (Student); Fax: 202-526-7811. Most Rev. John Ricard, Rector; Revs. Goodwin Akpan, S.S.J., Vice Rector; Joseph Doyle, S.S.J., Dir. Novices. St. Joseph's Society of the Sacred Heart-Josephite Fathers & Brothers. Priests 4; Seminarians 6; Franciscan Sisters of St. Joseph 5. In Res. Revs. Frederick Nnebue; Albert Shuyaka; Joseph Ssemakula; Leo Udeagu, S.S.J.

Josephite Pastoral Center, 1200 Varnum St., N.E., 20017. Tel: 202-526-9270; Tel: 202-526-9271; Fax: 202-526-7811; Email: ssjpastrcntr@aol.com. Rev. James E. McLinden, S.S.J., Dir.; Maria M.

Lannon, Admin. Brothers 1; Deacons 1; Priests 1; Lay Women 3.

Marian Fathers Scholasticate (1673) 3885 Harewood Rd., N.E., 20017. Tel: 202-526-8884; Email: marian.scholasticate.office@gmail.com; Web: www.marian.org. Revs. James McCormack, M.I.C., Supr.; Thaddaeus Lancton, Treas.; Bro. Leonard Konopka, M.I.C., Asst. Treas.; Revs. Piotr Lach, Confessor and Spiritual Dir.; Casimir Krzyzanowski, M.I.C.; David Gunter. Brothers 1; Religious Teachers 5; Novices 6; Priests 5; Seminarians 8; Students 13.

Marist College, Provincialate of the Marist Society in the USA (1892) Society of Mary (Marists) (S.M.) 815 Varnum St., N.E., 20017-2144.
Tel: 202-529-2821; Fax: 202-635-4627; Email: randyh@maristsociety.org; Web: www.societyofmaryusa.org. Very Rev. Paul Frechette, S.M., Provincial; Rev. Timothy G. Keating, S.M., Rector; Bro. Randy T. Hoover, S.M., Admin.; Niklas Rodewald, Student. Clergy 2; Religious Teachers 2; Students 1.

Maryknoll Fathers and Brothers, 1233 10th St. N.W., 20001. Tel: 202-450-3756; Web: www.maryknoll.org. Bro. Wm. Timothy Raible, M.M., Dir. Maryknoll House; Rev. David J. Schwinghamer, M.M., Africa Desk, Maryknoll Office of Global Concerns.

Maryknoll Office of Global Concerns, 200 New York Ave NW, 20001. Tel: 202-832-1780; Email: ogc@maryknoll.org. Gerry Lee, Dir.

Oblates of St. Francis de Sales, 1409 Kearney St., N.E., 20017. Tel: 202-269-2014; Email: jlosfs@yahoo.com; Web: www.oblates.org. Rev. John W. Crossin, O.S.F.S., Spiritual Advisor/Care Services; James Cummins, Pastoral Min./Coord.; Rev. John J. Loughran, O.S.F.S., Dir.; Harold McGovern. Priests 3; Temporary Professed 1.

Brisson Hall Residence: Rev. John J. Loughran, O.S.F.S., Supr. & Dir. Formation.

Paulist Washington Community, 1200 Varnum St. N.E., 20017-1102. Tel: 202-832-6262;
Fax: 202-269-2507; Email: paulistsdc@gmail.com. Revs. Francis P. DeSiano, C.S.P., D.Min., Supr. & Dir., Formation & Assoc. Dir.; Richard J. Colgan, C.S.P., M.A., Dir., Novices; Kenneth G. Boyack, C.S.P., D.Min.; John E. Lynch, C.S.P., Ph.D., (Retired); Ronald G. Roberson, C.S.P., S.E.O.D.; Ms. Denise Eggers, Coord. Paulist Fathers. Clergy 6; Religious Teachers 5; Novices 3; Priests 5; Students 6.

Queen of Pious Schools, Inc., 1339 Monroe St., N.E., 20017-2510. Tel: 202-529-7734;
Fax: 202-529-7734 (Call first); Email: Queenofpiousschools@gmail.com. Rev. Andrew C. Buechele, Sch.P., Ph.D., Rector, Librarian, Treas.; Very Rev. Fernando Negro, Provincial, Piarist Fathers, USA-Puerto Rico Province. Priests 2.

Whitefriars Hall, 1600 Webster St., N.E., 20017.
Tel: 202-526-1221; Fax: 202-526-9217; Email: qconners@carmelnet.org. Revs. Quinn Conners, O.Carm., Prior; David Blanchard, O.Carm.; Irtikandik Darmawanto, O.Carm.; Craig Morrison, O.Carm.; Will Thompson; Dimas Pele Alu. Clergy 7; Religious Teachers 7; Priests 7; Students 10; Friars in Solemn Profession 7; Friars in First Profession 8.

The Carmelitana Library, Tel: 202-526-1221;
Fax: 202-526-9217. Patricia O'Callagan, Librarian.

BELTSVILLE, MD. *The Saint LaSalle Auxiliary* (1918) 6001 Ammendale Rd., Beltsville, 20705-1202.
Tel: 301-210-7443; Fax: 301-210-7466; Email: martinfsc104@gmail.com. Br. Martin Zewe, F.S.C, Dir. The Saint La Salle Auxiliary Inc. is the Development Office for the Christian Brothers of the Baltimore Province.

SILVER SPRING, MD. *St. Bonaventure Friary*, 10400 Lorain Ave., Silver Spring, 20901.
Tel: 301-593-3018; Email: schlomy@alumni.nd.edu. Friars Paul Schloemer, Guardian, Formation Dir.; Nicholas Rokitka, Vicar; John Burkhard, O.F.M.Conv. Brothers 1; Religious Teachers 2; Priests 3; Students 8.

Holy Family Seminary (Retreat House) 401 Randolph Rd., P.O. Box 4138, Silver Spring, 20904-4138. Tel: 301-622-1184; Fax: 301-622-2959; Email: holyfamilyseminary@gmail.com; Web: www.holyfamilyseminary.com. Very Rev. Luis Picazo, S.F., Delegate Supr.; Rev. Ronald Carrillo, S.F. Sons of the Holy Family Priests 3. In Residence: Most Rev. Francisco Gonzalez, S.F., D.D., V.G., Auxiliary Bishop Emeritus of Washington, (Retired).

Holy Name College (Residence) 1650 St. Camillus Dr., Silver Spring, 20903. Tel: 301-434-3400;
Tel: 646-473-0265; Fax: 301-434-4624; Email: kathy.ennis.hnc@gmail.com; Email: wliss@hnpfriar.org; Email: dwilson@hnp.org. Rev. Vincent de Paul Cushing, O.F.M., Chap.; Bro. Ed Demyanovich, Chap.; Rev. Jacek Orzechowski, O.F.M., Chap.; Bros. David W. Schlatter, O.F.M., Chap.; John Gutierrez, Dir.; Walter Liss, Dir.; Rev. Charles Miller, Dir.; Juan Perez, Dir. Postulancy for the Order of Friars Minor. Brothers 4; Clergy 3; Religious Teachers 4; Priests 3; Students 12.

Salvatorian Community (1888) 1700 Briggs Chaney Rd., Silver Spring, 20905-5527.
Tel: 301-370-2471 (Rev. Willis' Cell); Email: glenwillis@verizon.net; Web: www.sds.org. Revs. Glen Willis, S.D.S., Area Coord.; Richard Maloney, S.D.S.; Eliot Nitz, S.D.S., First Consultor; Roman Stadtmueller, S.D.S., (Retired); Julian Guzman, S.D.S.; Bros. Roger Nelson, S.D.S., M.A., Vicar Coord.; Sean McLaughlin, S.D.S. Society of the Divine Savior/Salvatorians.Camp St. Charles Brothers 2; Priests 5; Lay Members 20.

WEST HYATTSVILLE, MD. *Pallottine Seminary at Green Hill* (1961) 2009 Van Buren St., P.O. Box 5399, West Hyattsville, 20782-1761. Tel: 301-422-3777; Fax: 301-422-4070; Email: frfrank@sacapostles.org. Revs. Frank S. Donio, S.A.C., Rector; Louis F. Micca, S.A.C., M.A., Dir. Postulancy; Vyacheslav Grynevych, Student; Joseph Kuchar. Society of the Catholic Apostolate. Priests 4.

[C] COLLEGES AND UNIVERSITIES

WASHINGTON. **Catholic University of America, The* (1887) Nugent Hall/Executive Offices, 620 Michigan Ave., N.E., 20064. Tel: 202-319-5000; Fax: 202-319-4441; Email: webmaster@cua.edu; Web: www.catholic.edu. His Eminence Donald Cardinal Wuerl, S.T.D., Chancellor; John H. Garvey, J.D., Pres.; Andrew Abela, Ph.D., Provost; Robert M. Specter, Vice Pres. Finance & Treas.; John C. McCarthy, Ph.D., Dean, School of Philosophy; Aaron Dominguez, Ph.D., Dean, School of Arts & Sciences; Daniel F. Attridge, J.D., Dean, Columbus School of Law; Patricia McMullen, Ph.D., J.D., Dean, School of Nursing; Grayson Wagstaff, Ph.D., Dean, Benjamin T. Rome School of Music; William C. Rainford, Ph.D., Dean, Natl. Catholic School of Social Svc.; Randall Ott, M.Arch., Dean, School of Architecture & Planning; Vincent Kiernan, Ph.D., Dean, Metropolitan School of Professional Studies; Rev. Gerald D. McBrearity, P.S.S., M.A., S.T.B., D.Min., Rector, Theological College; Lynn Mayar, Ph.D., Vice Provost & Dean Undergraduate Studies; J. Steven Brown, Ph.D., Vice Provost & Dean, Graduate Studies; Matthew McNally, B.S., CIO; Ralph Albano, M.B.A., Assoc. Provost for Sponsored Research; Rev. Jude DeAngelo, O.F.M.Conv., Univ. Chap. & Dir. Campus Ministry; Julie Isha, M.A., Registrar; Trevor C. Lipscombe, Ph.D., Dir., CUA Press; Christopher P. Lydon, Vice Pres. Enrollment Mgmt. & Mktg.; Lawrence J. Morris, J.D., Gen. Counsel; Maureen C. Brookbank, B.S., B.A., M.B.A., Assoc. Vice Pres. & Chief Human Resources Officer; William Bowman, Dean, School of Business & Economics; Michael S. Allen, Ph.D., Vice Pres. for Student Affairs; Very Rev. Mark Morozowich, S.E.O.D., Dean, School of Theology & Rel. Studies; Rev. Msgr. Ronny E. Jenkins, S.T.L., J.L.D., Dean; John Judge, Dean. Clergy 22; Priests 22; Sisters 2; Students 6,023; Lay Faculty 375.

Priests Associated with the University Full-Time: Rev. Msgrs. Michael G. Clay, (Raleigh); Kevin W. Irwin; Ronny E. Jenkins, S.T.L., J.L.D.; Robert S. Sokolowski; John Wippel, Ph.D., S.T.L., M.A.; Revs. Regis Armstrong, O.F.M.Cap., M.Div., Th.M., M.S.Ed., Ph.D.; John P. Beal, J.C.D.; Christopher T. Begg, Ph.D., Ph.B., S.T.D.; John T. Ford, C.S.C., M.A., S.T.D.; John P. Galvin, D.Th.; James Froehlich, O.F.M.Cap., B.A., M.A., Ph.D.; John P. Heil, S.S.D.; Joseph Jensen, O.S.B., S.S.L., S.T.D., Lecturer; Nicholas E. Lombardo, O.P.; Emmanuel Magro, M.S.L.S., M.A., Ph.D.; Gerald D. McBrearity, P.S.S., M.A., S.T.B., D.Min.; Mark Morozowich, S.E.O.D., Dean, Theology; Raymond C. O'Brien, J.D.; Dominic F. Serra, S.T.D.; Raymond Studzinski, O.S.B., Ph.D.; Paul Sullins; David D. Thayer, P.S.S., S.T.L., Ph.D.; Michael G. Witczak, M.Div., S.L.D.; James Brent, O.P.; Rev. Msgr. Stephen J. Rossetti, Ph.D., D.Min.; Revs. Ignacio de Ribera Martin, D.C.J.M.; Stefanos Alexopoulos, (Church of Greece).

Clerical Members, Board of Trustees: His Eminence Daniel N. DiNardo, S.T.L.; Timothy Cardinal Dolan, Ph.D.; Sean Cardinal O'Malley, O.F.M.Cap., Ph.D., Bd. Chm.; Donald Cardinal Wuerl, S.T.D., Chancellor; Most Revs. Samuel J. Aquila, S.T.L.; Robert J. Banks, D.D., Trustee Emeritus; Michael J. Bransfield, Trustee Emeritus; Michael F. Burbidge, D.D., Ed.D., V.G.; Charles J. Chaput, O.F.M.Cap., D.D.; Octavio Cisneros; Edward P. Cullen, D.D., Trustee Emeritus; Daniel E. Flores, S.T.D.; Jose H. Gomez, S.T.D.; Wilton D. Gregory, S.L.D.; Joseph E. Kurtz, M.Div., M.S.W.; William E. Lori; Paul S. Loverde, D.D., S.T.L., J.C.L., Tel: 703-841-2511; Gregory J. Mansour, S.T.L.; Robert J. McManus, S.T.D.; William Francis Murphy, S.T.D., L.H.D., Trustee Emeritus; John J. Myers, J.C.D., D.D., Trustee Emeritus; Thomas J. Olmsted, J.C.D.; Joseph A. Pepe, D.D., J.C.D.; Thomas J. Tobin; Thomas G. Wenski, M.Div., M.A.; Rev. Msgrs. Paul A. Lenz, P.A., Trustee Emeritus; Walter R. Rossi, J.C.L.; Peter J. Vaghi, J.D., V.F.

**Georgetown University* (1789) 37th and O Sts., N.W., 20057. Tel: 202-687-0100; Email: gucomm@georgetown.edu; Web: www.georgetown.edu. John J. DeGioia, Ph.D., Pres.; Robert M. Groves, Ph.D., Provost & Exec. Vice Pres. of the Main Campus; William M. Treanor, Ph.D., J.D., Exec. Vice Pres., Dean of the Law Center & Prof. of Law; Spiros Dimolitsas, Ph.D., Senior Vice Pres., Research & CTO; David Rubenstein, Vice Pres. of Fin. & University Treas.; Todd A. Olson, Ph.D., Vice Pres. Student Affairs & Dean of Students; Erik Simulson, Vice Pres. Public Affairs & Senior Adviser to the Pres.; Judd Nicholson, Interim Chief Information Officer; Lisa Brown, J.D., Vice Pres. & Gen. Counsel; Robin A. Morey, Vice Pres., Planning & Facilities Mgmt.; Rev. Joseph E. Lingan, S.J., Rector, Georgetown Jesuit Community; Paul Almeida, Dean; Michael A. Bailey, Dean; Rev. Mark Bosco, Vice Pres. for Mission and Ministry; Christopher Celenza, Dean; Patricia Cloonan, Ph. D., R.N., Dean; Ahmad S. Dallal, Dean; Norberto M. Grzywacz, Dean; Edward B. Healton, Exec. Vice Pres. for Health Sciences and Exec. Dean of the School of Medicine; Joel Hellman, Ph.D., Dean; Marie Mattson; Deacon Stephen Mitchell, Dean; Kelly J. Otter, Ph.D., Dean. Clergy 47; Lay Teachers 2,573; Sisters 3; Sisters 18,148; Total Enrollment 18,148; Jesuits 44.

The following are the Schools and Colleges which compose the University:

Undergraduate Admissions.

Georgetown College (1789) Chester Gillis, Dean.

Graduate School of Arts & Sciences (1820) Norberto M. Graywacz, Dean.

School of Medicine (1851) 3900 Reservoir Rd., N.W., 20007. Edward B. Healton, Exec Vice Pres., Health Sciences & Exec. Dean, School of Medicine.

Law Center (1870) 600 New Jersey Ave., N.W., 20001. William M. Treanor, Ph.D., J.D., Vice Pres., Dean of the Law Center & Prof. of Law.

School of Nursing & Health Studies (1903) 3700 Reservoir Rd., N.W., 20007. Patricia Cloonan, Ph. D., R.N., Dean.

Edmund A. Walsh School of Foreign Service (1919) Joel Hellman, Ph.D., Dean.

Robert Emmett McDonough School of Business (1957) Rohan Williamson, Ph.D., Interim Dean McDonough School of Business.

McCourt School of Public Policy (1990) 37th St. & O St., N.W., 20057. Edward Montgomery, Ph.D., Dean & Prof.

School of Continuing Studies (1974) Kelly J. Otter, Ph.D., Dean.

Joseph Mark Lauinger Library Artemis G. Kirk, M.A., Univ. Librarian.

Office of the University Registrar Anna Marie Bianco, Ph.D., Assoc. Vice Pres. and University Registrar.

Office of Advancement, 2115 Wisconsin Ave., N.W., Ste. 500, 20057. Tel: 202-687-4111.

Office of Institutional Diversity, Equity & Affirmative Action, 37th St. & O St., N.W., 20057.
Tel: 202-687-4798; Fax: 202-687-7778. Rosemary Kilkenny, J.D., Vice Pres. for Inst. Diversity & Equity. Priests Associated with the University: Revs. Joseph E. Lingan, S.J.; Matthew E. Carnes, S.J.; Drew Christiansen, S.J., Ph.D.; David J. Collins, S.J.; Christopher J. Duffy, S.J.; James F. Duffy, S.J.; Stephen M. Fields, S.J.; Kevin T. FitzGerald, S.J.; David Hollenbach, S.J., Ph.D.; John P. Langan, S.J., Ph.D.; Daniel A. Madigan, S.J., (Australia) Ph.D.; William C. McFadden, S.J., Ph.D.; Dennis L. McNamara, S.J., Ph.D.; G. Ronald Murphy, S.J., Ph.D.; John W. O'Malley, S.J., Ph.D.; Ladislas Orsy, S.J., Ph.D.; Paul K. Rourke, S.J., J.D.; Christopher W. Steck, S.J., Ph.D.

Trinity College, 125 Michigan Ave., N.E., 20017.
Tel: 202-884-9000; Fax: 202-884-9229; Email: pauleya@Trinitydc.edu; Web: www.trinitydc.edu. Patricia A. McGuire, Pres.; Sr. Mary Johnson, S.N.D., Community Representative; Dr. Robert Preston, Vice Pres. Academic Affairs. Sisters of Notre Dame de Namur. Priests 1; Sisters 5; Students 1,600; Lay Professors 54.

[D] HIGH SCHOOLS, ARCHDIOCESAN

WASHINGTON. *Archbishop Carroll High School*, 4300 Harewood Rd, N.E., 20017. Tel: 202-529-0900;
Fax: 202-526-8879; Email: ipuryear@achsdc.org; Web: www.achsdc.org. Mr. Larry Savoy, Pres.; Ms. Elana Gilmore, Vice Prin. Student Affairs; Revs. Jordan Kelly, O.S.P.; John Mudd, (Retired). (Coed) Religious Teachers 1; Deacons 1; Lay Teachers 42; Priests 2; Sisters 1; Students 340; Staff 25.

Don Bosco Cristo Rey High School of the Archdiocese of Washington, Mailing Address: P.O. Box 56481, 20040-6481. Tel: 301-891-4750; Fax: 301-270-1459;

Email: conwaym@dbcr.org; Web: www.dbcr.org. Rev. Michael Conway, S.D.B., Pres.; Mr. Elias Blanco, Prin. Brothers 1; Religious Teachers 4; Lay Teachers 58; Priests 3; Students 405.

[E] HIGH SCHOOLS, PRIVATE

WASHINGTON. *St. Anselm's Abbey School, Inc,* (Grades 6-12), 4501 South Dakota Ave., N.E., 20017-2795. Tel: 202-269-2350; Fax: 202-269-2373; Email: mainoffice@saintanselms.org; Web: www.saintanselms.org. Rev. Dom Peter Weigand, O.S.B., Pres.; William Crittenberger, Headmaster; Very Rev. Dom Michael Hall, O.S.B., Chap. Separate subsidiary corporation of The Benedictine Foundation at Washington, DC (St. Anselm's Abbey).Seven-year college preparatory course. Brothers 1; Priests 3; Students 256; Lay Faculty and Staff 60.

Georgetown Visitation Preparatory School, Inc., 1524 35th St., N.W., 20007. Tel: 202-337-3350; Email: dan.kerns@visi.org; Web: www.visi.org. Mr. Dan Kerns, Head at School; Mary Kate Blaine, Prin.; Elizabeth Burke, Librarian. Religious Teachers 1; Lay Teachers 55; Students 500.

Gonzaga College High School, 19 Eye St., N.W., 20001. Tel: 202-336-7100; Fax: 202-336-7172; Email: info@ganzaga.org; Web: www.gonzaga.org. Rev. Stephen W. Planning, S.J., Pres.; Thomas K. Every II, Headmaster. Society of Jesus, Maryland Province. Lay Teachers 75; Priests 3; Sisters 1; Students 960. In Res. Revs. Gasper F. LoBiondo, S.J.; Gerald V. O'Connor, S.J.

St. John's College High School (1851) (Coed Grades 9-12) 2607 Military Rd., N.W., 20015. Tel: 202-363-2316; Fax: 202-686-5162; Email: stjohnschs@stjohnschs.org; Web: stjohnschs.org. Mr. Christopher Themistos, Prin.; Mr. Jeffrey Mancabelli, Pres. Brothers of the Christian Schools.College Preparatory, Elective Army Junior ROTC.

St. John's College High School Brothers 3; Religious Teachers 4; Lay Teachers 96; Sisters 1; Students 1,140.

**San Miguel School*, 7705 Georgia Ave., NW, 20012. Tel: 202-232-8345; Fax: 202-232-3987. Martha W. Kendall, Exec. Dir.; Bro. Francis Eells, F.S.C., Prin.

BETHESDA, MD. *Mater Dei School, Inc.*, 9600 Seven Locks Rd., Bethesda, 20817. Tel: 301-365-2700; Tel: 301-365-2701; Fax: 301-365-2710. Mr. Edward N. Williams, Headmaster; Mr. Christopher S. Abell, Pres. Students 225.

Stone Ridge School of the Sacred Heart, 9101 Rockville Pike, Bethesda, 20814. Tel: 301-657-4322 ; Fax: 301-657-4393; Email: ckarrels@stoneridgeschool.org; Web: www.stoneridgeschool.org. Mrs. Catherine Ronan Karrels, Head of School; Carla Bosco, Librarian. Religious of the Sacred Heart. Lay Teachers 93; Students 684.

BLADENSBURG, MD. *Elizabeth Seton High School* (1959) 5715 Emerson St., Bladensburg, 20710-1844. Tel: 301-864-4532; Fax: 301-864-8946; Email: ehagar@setonhs.org; Email: mlucian@setonhs.org; Web: www.setonhs.org. Sr. Ellen Marie Hagar, D.C., Pres.; Nancy Hernick, Dean, Operations; Mrs. Kim Tremble, Librarian. Girls 600; Lay Staff 36; Lay Teachers 54; Students 600; Daughters of Charity of St. Vincent de Paul 6; Administration & Staff 24; Facilities & Cafeteria 7.

FORESTVILLE, MD. *Bishop McNamara High School* (Coed) 6800 Marlboro Pike, Forestville, 20747. Tel: 301-735-8401; Fax: 301-735-0934; Email: marco.clark@bmhs.org; Web: www.bmhs.org. Dr. Marco Clark, Pres. & CEO; Nigel Traylor, Prin. Congregation of Holy Cross. Lay Teachers 84; Students 885.

HYATTSVILLE, MD. *DeMatha Catholic High School*, 4313 Madison St., 20781. Tel: 240-764-2200; Fax: 240-764-2275; Email: tpaolucci@dematha.org; Email: mkerley@dematha.org; Web: www.dematha.org. Rev. James R. Day, O.SS.T., Pres.; Dr. Daniel J. McMahon, Ph.D., Prin. Conducted by the Order of the Most Holy Trinity, Province of the Immaculate Heart of Mary.Boys, 9-12. Brothers 1; Lay Teachers 80; Priests 2; Students 853.

KENSINGTON, MD. *The Academy of the Holy Cross, Inc.* (1868) 4920 Strathmore Ave., Kensington, 20895. Tel: 301-942-2100; Fax: 301-929-6440; Email: schooloffice@academyoftheholycross.org; Web: academyoftheholycross.org. Kathleen Ryan Prebble, Pres.; Melissa Huey-Burns, Prin.; John Sullivan, Asst. Prin.; Katherine Miner, Chief Financial Officer; Jean Cotter, Librarian

The Academy of the Holy Cross, Inc. Lay Teachers 50; Students 480.

LAUREL, MD. *St. Vincent Pallotti High School* (1921) 113 St. Mary's Pl., Laurel, 20707. Tel: 301-725-3228; Fax: 301-776-4343; Email: admissions@pallottihs.org; Web: www.pallottihs.org. Jeffrey A. Palumbo, Pres. & Prin. Pallottine Missionary Sisters of the Catholic Apostolate. Deacons 1; Lay Teachers 35; Priests 1; Sisters 1; Students 500.

LEONARDTOWN, MD. *St. Mary's Ryken High School* (1885) 22600 Camp Calvert Rd., Leonardtown, 20650. Tel: 301-475-2814; Fax: 301-373-4195; Email: hurlburtmj@smrhs.org; Web: www.smrhs.org. Mrs. Mary Joy Hurlburt, Pres.; Rick Wood, Prin. Sponsored by the Xaverian Brothers. Lay Teachers 60; Students 674.

NORTH BETHESDA, MD. *Georgetown Preparatory School*, 10900 Rockville Pike, North Bethesda, 20852. Tel: 301-493-5000; Fax: 301-530-9531; Web: www.gprep.org. Rev. Scott R. Pilarz, S.J., Pres.; Mr. John Glennon, Headmaster; Rev. David A. Sauter, S.J., Supr. Jesuit Community; Society of Jesus. Lay Teachers 58; Priests 2; Students 488.

OLNEY, MD. *Our Lady of Good Counsel High School*, 17301 Old Vic Blvd., Olney, 20832. Tel: 240-283-3200; Fax: 240-283-3250; Email: pbarker@olgchs.org; Web: olgchs.org. Dr. Paul Barker, Pres.; Thomas Campbell, Prin.; Rev. Thomas Lavin, O.F.M.; Amelia Davis, Librarian. Xaverian Brothers. Lay Teachers 118; Priests 1; Students 1,253.

POTOMAC, MD. *Connelly School of the Holy Child*, (Grades 6-12), 9029 Bradley Blvd., Potomac, 20854. Tel: 301-365-0955; Fax: 301-365-0981; Web: www.holychild.org. Shannon Gomez, Ed.D., Head of School; Julie Burke, Dean of Students; Claire Drummond, Librarian, Information Literacy, Tech. Sisters of the Holy Child Jesus.College Preparatory for Girls. Lay Teachers 48; Students 295.

[F] ELEMENTARY SCHOOLS, ARCHDIOCESAN

DARNESTOWN, MD. *Mary of Nazareth Roman Catholic Elementary School* (1994) (Grades PreK-8), 14131 Seneca Rd., Darnestown, 20874. Tel: 301-869-0940 ; Fax: 301-869-0942; Email: mfriel@maryofnazareth.org; Email: mwray@maryofnazareth.org; Web: www.maryofnazareth.org. Mr. Michael J. Friel, Prin.; Rev. Raymond L. Fecteau, Canonical Admin. Lay Teachers 33; Students 459.

[G] ELEMENTARY SCHOOLS, PRIVATE

BETHESDA, MD. *The Woods Academy*, 6801 Greentree Rd., Bethesda, 20817. Tel: 301-365-3080; Fax: 301-469-6439; Email: jpowers@woodsacademy.org; Web: www.woodsacademy.org. Joseph E. Powers, Head of School; Katya Pilong, Media Curriculum Specialist. Lay Teachers 39; Students 317.

GAITHERSBURG, MD. *Emmanuel, Inc.* dba Mother of God School (1987) (Grades PreK-8), 20501 Goshen Rd., Gaithersburg, 20879. Tel: 301-990-2088; Fax: 301-947-0574; Email: mog@mogschool.com; Web: www.mogschool.com. William Hall Miller, Prin. Lay Teachers 23; Students 199; Total Staff 39.

POTOMAC, MD. *The Heights School*, 10400 Seven Locks Rd., Potomac, 20854. Tel: 301-365-4300; Fax: 301-365-4303; Email: adevicente@heights.edu; Web: www.heights.edu. Mr. Alvaro de Vicente, Headmaster; Rev. Diego Daza, Chap.; Mr. Michael Moynihan, Upper School Head; Mr. Andrew Reed, Middle School Head; Colin Gleason, Lower School Head; Mr. Joseph Cardenas, Dean Advisory; Mr. Thomas Royals, Asst. Headmaster; James Nelson, Librarian. Private, Independent, Spiritual Formation and Religious Education provided by the Prelature of Opus Dei. Lay Teachers 70; Priests 2.

[H] SPECIAL SCHOOLS

WASHINGTON. *Lt. Joseph P. Kennedy, Jr., Institute*, 801 Buchanan St., N.E., 20017. Deacon Richard C. Birkel, Ph.D., Pres. & CEO. The Lt. Joseph P. Kennedy, Jr., Institute of the Archdiocese of Washington is a private, nonprofit organization providing education, training and employment, therapeutic and residential services to children and adults with developmental disabilities.

Nonprofit Organizations Serving Children and Adults With Developmental Disabilities:

Adult Learning & Employment Services, Tel: 202-529-0500; Fax: 202-529-8211. Participants 364.

Family & Personal Support Services, Tel: 301-251-2860; Fax: 301-251-8559. Participants 102; Staff 25.

Kennedy Education, Tel: 202-529-7600; Fax: 202-529-2028. (Includes Kennedy School, Outreach Program to Catholic Schools and Inclusion 2000) Students 140; Staff 52.

*Community Living Partnership*Families 50; Total Staff 3.

[I] CATHOLIC CHARITIES OF THE ARCHDIOCESE

WASHINGTON. *Catholic Charities of the Archdiocese of Washington, Inc.*, 924 G St., N.W., 20001. Tel: 202-772-4300; Fax: 202-772-4308; Email: john.enzler@cc-dc.org; Web: catholiccharitiesdc.org. Rev. Msgr. John Enzler, V.E., Pres. Tot Asst. Annually 142,000; Total Staff 798.

Anchor Mental Health Association/Division of Adult and Family Clinical Services, 1001 Lawrence St., N.E., P.O. Box 29058, 20017. Tel: 202-635-5940; Fax: 202-481-1431; Email: denise.capaci@cc-dc.org; Web: https://www.catholiccharitiesdc.org. Denise Capaci. Tot Asst. Annually 19,983.

CCS Housing, Inc., 924 G St., N.W., 20001. Tel: 202-772-4300; Email: john.enzler@cc-dc.org. Rev. Msgr. John Enzler, V.E.

The Catholic Charities Foundation of the Archdiocese of Washington, 924 G St., N.W., 20001. Rev. Msgr. John Enzler, V.E., Pres., Tel: 202-772-4373; Fax: 202-772-4411; Tara Arras, CDO.

Division of Catholic Charities Enterprises, Employment and Education, 1001 Lawrence Street NE, 20017. Tel: 202-635-5970; Email: scott.lewis@cc-dc.org. Scott Lewis, Contact Person. Tot Asst. Annually 49,086.

Division of Housing and Support Service, 1001 Lawrence St. NE, 20017. Tel: 202-481-1435; Email: amanda.chesney@cc-dc.org; Web: www.catholiccharitiesdc.org. Amanda Chesney, Dir. Tot Asst. Annually 12,287.

Montgomery County Family Center, 12247 Georgia Ave., Silver Spring, 20902. Tel: 301-933-3164; Fax: 301-949-1371; Email: faye.frempong@cc-dc.org. Faye Frempong, Contact Person.

Division of Children's Services, 924 G St. N.W., 20001. Tel: 202-772-4300, Ext. 003; Email: Lovannia.Dofat-Avent@cc-dc.org; Web: www.catholiccharitiesdc.org. Lovannia Dofat-Avent, Contact Person.

Southeast Family Center, 220 Highview Pl., S.E., 20032. Tel: 202-574-3442; Fax: 202-574-3474; Email: peggy.lawrence@cc-dc.org. Peggy Lawrence, Contact Person. Total Staff 850; Total Assisted 102,895.

LANDOVER, MD. *SHARE Food Network*, 3222 Hubbard Rd., Landover, 20785-2005. Tel: 301-864-3115; Email: jaynee.acevedo@cc-dc.org. Jaynee Acevedo, Dir. Tot Asst. Annually 34,670; Total Staff 7.

[J] ARCHDIOCESAN VOLUNTEER ORGANIZATIONS

WASHINGTON. *Archdiocesan Association of Ladies of Charity*, P.O. Box 10038, 20018. Tel: 301-292-9315. Mrs. Viola Johnson-Robinson, Pres. Purpose: Individual charity work, usually of emergency nature and supports various other agencies, food banks, child care centers and pregnancy aid centers.

Christ Child Society, Inc., 5101 Wisconsin Ave., N.W., Ste. 304, 20016. Tel: 202-966-9250; Fax: 202-966-2880; Email: kcurtin@christchilddc.org. Ms. Kathleen Curtin, Exec. Dir.

Serra Club of Downtown Washington, 4409 Westover Pl., N.W., 20016. Tel: 202-362-2477; Tel: 703-821-0449; Email: cathcap@aol.com. Mr. Gerrald Giblin, Chap.; Alice Middleton, Pres.

The Washington Cursillo Movement, 6312 2nd St. N.W., 20011. Tel: 202-330-7227. Jacquelyn DeMesme-Gray, Dir.; Rev. William E. Foley, V.F., Spiritual Dir., Tel: 301-627-3255.

BERLIN, MD. *Holy Name Society*, 141 Nottingham Ln., Berlin, 21811-1663. Tel: 443-614-5411; Email: joelatchford@gmail.com. Mr. Joseph Latchford, Vice Pres., Region XIV.

BETHESDA, MD. *Ladies of Charity*, 5403 Linden Ct., Bethesda, 20814. Tel: 301-564-5793. Ms. Maryanne Rooney, Pres.

CHARLOTTE HALL, MD. *Serra Club of Southern Maryland*, 10548 Wicomoco Ridge Rd., Charlotte Hall, 20622. Mrs. Walter Rourke, Pres.

GAITHERSBURG, MD. *Serra Club of Washington, D.C.*, 422 Sanders Ln., Gaithersburg, 20877. Tel: 301-670-1069. Cindy Selby, Pres.

SILVER SPRING, MD. *Archdiocesan Council of Washington*, 12447 Georgia Ave., Silver Spring, 20902. Tel: 202-362-0403; Email: SVDPADCCWASH@gmail.com. Ms. Tommye Grant, Pres.; Ms. Ann Barbagallo, Vice Pres.

**Society of St. Vincent de Paul*, Cardinal McCarrick Center, 12447 Georgia Ave., Silver Spring, 20902. Tel: 301-942-1110.

Office of Archdiocesan Council.

St. Vincent de Paul Society.

[K] ORPHANAGES AND INFANT HOMES

HYATTSVILLE, MD. *St. Ann's Center for Children, Youth and Families*, 4901 Eastern Ave., 20782. Tel: 301-559-5500; Fax: 301-853-6985; Email: donations@stanns.org; Web: www.stanns.org. Sr. Mary Bader, D.C., CEO & Local Supr. Daughters of Charity. Clergy 1; Day Care 70; Sisters 2; Students 7; Children in Transitional Housing 31;

Mothers in Teen Mother-Baby Program 14; Mothers in Transitional Housing 29.

Faith House, 4903 Eastern Ave., 20782.
Tel: 301-559-5500; Fax: 301-853-6985; Email: peggy.gatewood@stanns.org. Sr. Mary Bader, D.C., CEO. Children 8; Mothers 8.

[L] GENERAL HOSPITALS

WASHINGTON. *De Paul Foundation, Inc.*, 1150 Varnum St., N.E., 20017. Tel: 202-854-7153;
Fax: 202-854-7687; Email: phfdn@provhosp.org. Mr. Philip Mazzara, Pres. De Paul Foundation, Inc. was Organized to Provide Fund Development, Financial and Other Assistance to Provide Hospital and Other Subsidiaries of De Paul Foundation for the Health Care, Medical, Educational and Human Needs of the District of Columbia and Vicinity, by Functioning as a Charitable Nonprofit, Nonstock Corporation.

Providence Health Foundation, 1150 Varnum St., N.E., 20017. Tel: 202-269-7776; Fax: 202-269-7687 ; Email: phfdn@provhosp.org; Email: philip.mazzara@ascension.org; Web: www.providencehealthfoundation.org. Mr. Philip Mazzara, Pres. Providence Health Foundation, Inc. (PHF), a District of Columbia Charitable Nonprofit Corporation, was Organized to Support the Mission of Providence Hospital by Conducting Fundraising and Development Activities, by Receiving and Managing Donations, by Making Grants and by Promoting Educational Activities and Scientific Research.

Medstar Georgetown University Hospital, 3800 Reservoir Rd., N.W., 20007. Tel: 202-444-3030;
Fax: 202-444-3095; Email: thomas.j.devaney@gunet.georgetown.edu; Web: www.georgetownuniversityhospital.org. Michael C. Sachtleben, M.H.A., Pres.; Deacon Thomas J. Devaney, Dir. Mission & Pastoral Care; Revs. John O. Ekeocha, Chap.; Albert Shuyaka, Position Chap. Bed Capacity 609; Priests 2; Total Staff 5,127.

Providence Health Services, Inc., 1150 Varnum St., N.E., 20017. Tel: 202-854-4805; Tel: 202-854-7807; Email: darmita.wilson@ascension.org; Email: mejebi.mayor@ascension.org. Dr. Mejibi Mayor, Admin.; Mrs. Darmita Wilson, Admin. Ambulatory-Outpatient Care, Promote Wellness and Carry Out Educational Activities and Scientific Research. Tot Asst. Annually 147,937; Total Staff 253.

Providence Hospital, 1150 Varnum St., N.E., 20017.
Tel: 202-854-7000; Fax: 202-854-7160; Email: keith.vanderkolk@ascension.org; Email: ellen.reilly@ascension.org; Web: www.provhosp.org. Keith Vander Kolk, Pres.; Revs. Maurus Dolcic, T.O.R., Chap.; Kenneth Chukwu, Chap. Daughters of Charity of St. Vincent de Paul. Bed Capacity 408; Sisters 5; Tot Asst. Annually 165,000; Total Staff 1,307.

SILVER SPRING, MD. **Holy Cross Health, Inc.*, 1500 Forest Glen Rd., Silver Spring, 20910.
Tel: 301-754-7000; Tel: 301-754-7858;
Fax: 301-754-7012; Email: thomps@holycrosshealth.org; Web: www.holycrosshealth.org. Norvell Coots, Pres.; Steven Fowler, Exec.; Rev. Casmir Onyegwara. A member of Trinity Health which is sponsored by Catholic Health Ministries. Bed Capacity 475; Sisters of the Holy Cross 7; Tot Asst. Annually 294,118; Total Staff 4,137.

[M] HOUSING

WASHINGTON. *Cardinal O'Boyle Residence for Priests*, 1150 Varnum St., N.E., P.O. Box 29206, 20017-0206. Tel: 202-359-1593;
Tel: 202-269-7810 (Rector); Email: c.butta0181@yahoo.com. Rev. C. Gregory Butta, Dir. Residents 9; Total Staff 3; Suites 12. In Res. Revs. Louis A. Tou, (Retired); Donald Brice, (Retired); Thomas A. Kane; Gerard A. Trancone, (Retired), (Retired); C. Gregory Butta, Dir. Pastoral Care, Carroll Manor & Rector O'Boyle Residence for Retired Priests.

Little Sisters of the Poor of Washington, D.C., Inc. (1871) 4200 Harewood Rd., N.E., 20017-1554.
Tel: 202-269-1831; Fax: 202-269-1134; Email: washington@littlesistersofthepoor.org; Web: www.littlesistersofthepoorwashingtondc.org. Sr. Mary Michael Nickles, L.S.P., Supr. Little Sisters of the Poor. Residents 85; Sisters 10; Total Staff 100; Apartments 24.

HYATTSVILLE, MD. *Sacred Heart Home Inc.*, 5805 Queens Chapel Rd., 20782. Tel: 301-277-6500;
Fax: 301-277-3181; Email: sistervacha@sacredhearthome.org; Web: www.sacredhearthome.org. Sr. Waclawa Kludziak; Rev. Emett Schuler, O.F.M.Cap. Sisters, Servants of Mary Immaculate. Residents 102; Sisters 6.

ROCKVILLE, MD. *Palmer Park Seniors Housing, Inc.* (2001) c/o Victory Housing, Inc., 11400 Rockville Pike, Ste. 505, Rockville, 20852. Tel: 301-493-6000; Fax: 301-493-9788; Email: info@victoryhousing.org; Web: www.victoryhousing.org. Leila Finucane, Pres. Apartment Units 69.

Rosaria Communities in Colesville, Inc., 15400 Calhoun Dr., Ste. 125, Rockville, 20855.
Tel: 301-279-2020; Email: tom@jrwinc.com. Thomas Welch Jr., Pres.

Rosaria Communities in Gaithersburg, Inc., 15400 Calhoun Dr., Ste. 125, Rockville, 20855.
Tel: 301-279-2020; Email: tom@jrwinc.com. Thomas Welch Jr., Pres.

Rosaria Communities in Montgomery County, Inc., 15400 Calhoun Dr., Ste. 125, Rockville, 20855.

Rosaria Communities in Olney, Inc., 15400 Calhoun Dr., Ste. 125, Rockville, 20855. Tel: 301-279-2020; Email: tom@jrwinc.com. Thomas Welch Jr., Pres.

Rosaria Communities in Silver Spring, Inc., 15400 Calhoun Dr., Ste. 125, Rockville, 20855.
Tel: 301-279-2020; Email: tom@jrwinc.com. Thomas Welch Jr., Pres.

Rollingcrest Commons, Inc., 11400 Rockville Pike, Rockville, 20852. Tel: 301-493-6000; Email: info@victoryhousing.org. Leila Finucane, Pres. Tot Asst. Annually 60.

Takoma Tower, Inc. (2001) c/o Victory Housing, Inc., 11400 Rockville Pike, Ste. 505, Rockville, 20852.
Tel: 301-493-6000; Fax: 301-493-9788; Email: info@victoryhousing.org; Web: www.victoryhousing.org. Leila Finucane, Pres. Apartment Units 187.

Victory Housing, Inc., 11400 Rockville Pike, Ste. 505, Rockville, 20852. Tel: 301-493-6000;
Fax: 301-493-9788; Email: jspencer@victoryhousing.org. Leila Finucane, Pres. Total Apartments 2,079; Tot Asst. Annually 2,500; Total Staff 190; Units (Assisted Living) 201.

Andrew Kim House, Inc., 2100 Olney Sandy-Spring Rd., Olney, 20832. Tel: 301-260-2500;
Fax: 301-260-2720; Email: manager435@habitatamerica.com; Web: http://www.victoryhousing.org/ilkim.html. Yasmin Ghani, Community Mgr.

Avondale Park Apartments, Inc., 4915 Eastern Ave., 20782. Tel: 301-853-7787; Fax: 301-853-3988; Email: manager418@habitatamerica.com. Ms. Barbara Miller, Property Mgr.

Bartholomew House, Inc., 6904 River Rd., Bethesda, 20817. Tel: 301-320-6151; Fax: 301-320-4420; Email: bartholomew@victoryhousing.org; Web: http://www.victoryhousing.org/albartholomew.html. Joseph Hanle, Dir.

Byron House, Inc., 9210 Kentsdale Dr., Potomac, 20854. Tel: 301-469-9400; Fax: 301-765-8112; Email: byron@victoryhousing.org; Web: http://www.victoryhousing.org/albyron.html. Pearl Botchway, Dir.

Cambridge Apartments, Inc., 676 Houston Ave., Takoma Park, 20912. Tel: 301-585-3750;
Fax: 301-585-4072; Email: manager413@habitatamerica.com; Web: http://www.victoryhousing.org/wfcambridge.html. Sandra Robinson, Property Mgr.

Cheval Court, Inc., 2611 Luana Dr., Forestville, 20747. Tel: 301-736-0685; Fax: 301-736-0705; Email: manager419@habitatamerica.com; Web: http://www.victoryhousing.org/ilcheval.html. Ms. Arlita Matthews, Property Mgr.

Grace House, Inc., Victory Housing, Inc., 11400 Rockville Pike, Ste. 505, Rockville, 20852.
Tel: 301-493-6000; Fax: 301-493-9788; Email: info@victoryhousing.org. Leila Finucane, Pres.

Malta House, Inc., 4916-18 LaSalle Rd., 20782-3302. Tel: 301-699-8600; Fax: 301-699-1696; Email: malta@victoryhousing.org; Web: http://www.victoryhousing.org/almalta.html. Ms. Elisabeth Orchard, Dir.

Manor Apartments, Inc., 4907 Eastern Ave., 20782.
Tel: 301-853-2900; Fax: 301-853-3418; Email: manager417@habitatamerica.com; Web: http://www.victoryhousing.org/ilmanor.html. Ms. Barbara Miller, Property Mgr.

Marian Assisted Living, Inc., 19109 Georgia Ave., Brookeville, 20833. Tel: 301-570-3190;
Fax: 301-570-3638; Email: marian@victoryhousing.org; Web: http://www.victoryhousing.org/almarian.html. Marcy Hunter, Dir.

Palmer Park Seniors Housing, Inc., 7801 Barlowe Rd., Palmer Park, 20785. Tel: 301-341-4995;
Fax: 301-341-4997; Email: manager405@habitatamerica.com; Web: http://www.victoryhousing.org/ilpalmer.html. Ms. Brenda Wines, Property Mgr.

Parkfair Associates, LLC, Parkfair Apartments, 1611 Park Rd., N.W., 20010. Tel: 202-986-1600; Email: manager319@habitatamerica.com; Web: http://www.victoryhousing.org/wfparkfair.html. Ms. Marcia Urquiza, Property Mgr.

Raphael, Inc., 1515 Dunster Rd., Rockville, 20854.
Tel: 301-217-9116; Fax: 301-217-9119; Email: raphael@victoryhousing.org; Web: http://www.victoryhousing.org/alraphael.html. Nellia Kaiyo, Dir.

Takoma Tower, Inc., 7051 Carroll Ave., Takoma Park, 20912. Tel: 301-270-1858; Fax: 301-270-4715 ; Email: manager412@habitatamerica.com. Ms. Jannice Bray, Property Mgr.

Trinity Terrace, Inc., 6001 Fisher Rd., Temple Hills, 20748. Tel: 301-630-7717; Fax: 301-630-1798; Email: manager402@habitatamerica.com; Web: http://www.victoryhousing.org/iltrinity.html. Ms. Arlita Matthews, Property Mgr.

Victory Crest, Inc., 6100 Sargent Rd., 20782.
Tel: 301-559-3891; Fax: 301-559-3868; Email: egibson@hrehllc.com; Web: http://www.victoryhousing.org/ilvcrest.html. Eva Gibson, Property Mgmt.

Victory Forest, L.P., 10000 Brunswick Ave., Silver Spring, 20910. Tel: 301-589-4030;
Fax: 301-589-7349; Email: manager406@habitatamerica.com; Web: http://www.victoryhousing.org/ilvforest.html. Karen Smith, Property Mgr.

Victory Heights, Inc., 1369 Irving St., N.W., 20010.
Tel: 202-939-1431; Fax: 202-939-1433; Email: manager320@habitatamerica.com; Web: http://www.victoryhousing.org/ilvheights.html. Tamara Shaw, Property Mgr.

Victory Terrace, Inc., 9440 Newbridge Dr., Potomac, 20854. Tel: 301-983-9600; Fax: 301-983-9606; Email: manager401@habitatamerica.com. Travia Mitchell, Property Mgr.

Winslow House, Inc., 666 Houston Ave., Takoma Park, 20912. Tel: 301-585-3750; Fax: 301-585-4072 ; Email: manager413@habitatamerica.com; Web: http://www.victoryhousing.org/wfwinslow.html. Sandra Robinson, Property Mgr.

Winslow House, Inc. (2002) c/o Victory Housing, Inc., 11400 Rockville Pike, Ste. 505, Rockville, 20852.
Tel: 301-493-6000; Fax: 301-493-9788; Email: info@victoryhousing.org; Web: www.victoryhousing.org. Leila Finucane, Pres. Apartment Units 46.

[N] MISSIONARIES OF CHARITY

WASHINGTON. *Gift of Peace House*, 2800 Otis St., N.E., 20018. Tel: 202-269-3313. Sr. Clovis, Supr.

Queen of Peace House, 3310 Wheeler Rd., S.E., 20032. Sr. Maria Bernadette, M.C., Supr.

[O] MONASTERIES AND RESIDENCES OF PRIESTS AND BROTHERS

WASHINGTON. *St. Anselm's Abbey* (1923) 4501 S. Dakota Ave., N.E., 20017. Tel: 202-269-2300;
Fax: 202-269-2312; Email: jwiseman@saintanselms.org; Web: www.stanselms.org. Rt. Revs. Aidan Shea, O.S.B.; James A. Wiseman, O.S.B., M.A., S.T.D., Abbot; Revs. Michael Hall, O.S.B., M.A., Ph.D., Prior; Joseph Jensen, O.S.B., S.S.L., S.T.D.; Gabriel Myers, O.S.B.; Philip Simo, O.S.B.; Boniface von Nell, O.S.B.; Peter Weigand, O.S.B.; Christopher Wyvill, O.S.B.; Bros. Ignacio Gonzalez, O.S.B.; Matthew Nylund, O.S.B.; Dunstan Robidoux, O.S.B.; Samuel Springuel, O.S.B. Benedictine Foundation at Washington, DC, Order of St. Benedict. Brothers 4; Priests 9.

Center for Assisted Living (1993) Dominican Fathers and Brothers. 630 E St., S.W., 20024-2503.
Tel: 202-488-4188; Fax: 202-554-5735. Rev. Carl Louis Mason, O.P., B.A., Dir. *Franciscan Monastery USA Inc.*, 1400 Quincy St. N.E., 20017.
Tel: 202-526-6800; Fax: 202-529-9889; Email: secretariatusa@myfranciscan.com; Web: www.myfranciscan.com. Very Rev. Larry C. Dunham, O.F.M., Guardian; Friar Thomas Courtney, O.F.M.; Friar-Deacon John-Sebastian Laird-Hammond, O.F.M., Secretariat to Franciscan Monastery; Revs. Garrett Edmunds, O.F.M., Vice Commissary; Edward Flanagan, O.F.M.; Romuald Green, O.F.M.; Friars Simon McKay, O.F.M.; Roger Petras, O.F.M.; Revs. Kevin Treston, O.F.M.; David Wathen, O.F.M., Dir. Holy Land Tours; Friar Maximilian Wojciechowski, O.F.M., Gift Shop Mgr.; Rev. Manuel Ybarra, O.F.M., Finance Office; Friars Christopher Coppock, O.F.M.; Gregory Giannoni, O.F.M.; Revs. Gregory F. Friedman, O.F.M., Special Projects; James Gardiner, S.A., Communications. Brothers 6; Deacons 1; Priests 8; Solemnly Professed 15.

The Jesuit Community at Georgetown University, 37th and O Sts., N.W., 20057-1200.
Tel: 202-687-4000; Fax: 202-687-7679; Email: gk491@georgetown.edu. Revs. Joseph E. Lingan, S.J., Rector; Ronald J. Anton, S.J.; Thomas J. Buckley, S.J.; Matthew E. Carnes, S.J.; David J. Collins, S.J.; Charles L. Currie, S.J.; Andrew J. Christiansen, S.J.; Christopher J. Duffy, S.J.; James F. Duffy, S.J.; Stephen M. Fields, S.J.; Kevin T. FitzGerald, S.J.; Gerald P. Fogarty, S.J.; Thomas P. Gaunt, S.J.; Charles G. Gonzalez, S.J.; Howard J. Gray, S.J.; Otto H. Hentz, S.J.; J. Leon

Hooper, S.J.; Salvador R. Jordan, S.J.; Gustaaf M. Keppens, S.J., (Retired); Robert J. Kaslyn, S.J.; John P. Langan, S.J., Ph.D.; Daniel A. Madigan, S.J., (Australia) Ph.D.; Brian O. McDermott, S.J.; William C. McFadden, S.J., Ph.D.; Dennis L. McNamara, S.J., Ph.D.; Thomas F. Michel, S.J., (Indonesia); G. Ronald Murphy, S.J., Ph.D.; Charles M. Gallagher; Jerome T. Hayes, S.J.; David Hollenbach, S.J., Ph.D.; Gregory N. P. Konz, S.J., Admin.; Richard J. Ryscavage, S.J.; Gregory A. Schenden, S.J.; John W. O'Malley, S.J., Ph.D.; Ladislas Orsy, S.J., Ph.D.; Lawrence C. Smith, S.J.; Patrick D. Rogers, S.J.; Paul K. Rourke, S.J., J.D.; Francis Schemel, S.J.; Christopher W. Steck, S.J., Ph.D.

The Jesuit Community of St. Aloysius Gonzaga, 19 I St., N.W., 20001. Tel: 202-336-7186; Fax: 202-336-7217; Email: globiondo@gonzaga.org. Very Rev. Timothy Kesicki, S.J., Pres.; Revs. Michael J. Sheeran, S.J., Pres.; Gasper F. LoBiondo, S.J., Supr.; Patrick J. Conroy, S.J., Chap., U.S. House of Representatives; Stephen W. Planning, S.J., Pres., High School; Sean D. Michaelson, S.J., Prov. Asst.; Bro. Lawrence Lundin, S.J., Business Mgr.; Revs. William H. Muller, S.J., Admin.; Edward Penton, Admin.; Paul Holland, Admin.; Henry G. Heffernan, S.J.; Joseph A. Sobierajski, S.J.; Gerald V. O'Connor, S.J.; Philip Ganir; Ruben Orbeta; Thomas J. Reese, S.J.
Jesuit Community of St. Aloysius Gonzaga Total in Community 18.

Leonard Neale House, 1726 New Hampshire Ave., N.W., 20009. Very Rev. Timothy Kesicki, S.J., Pres., Jesuit Conference; Bro. Michael E. Breault, S.J., Dir. National Vocation Promotion of the Jesuit Conference; Revs. Sean D. Michaelson, S.J., Exec. Sec. & Treas. Jesuit Conference; David A. Godleski, S.J., Delegate, Formation & Jesuit Life, Jesuit Conference; Joseph A. Koczera, S.J., Graduate Student, Catholic Univ.; William H. Muller, S.J., Exec. Dir., Jesuit Schools Network; Thomas J. Reese, S.J., Senior Analyst, National Catholic Reporter; Michael J. Sheeran, S.J., Pres., Assn. of Jesuit Colleges & Universities. Brothers 1; Priests 7; Total Staff 8.

St. Louis Friary, 831 Varnum St., N.E., 20017-2144. Tel: 202-529-0171; Fax: 202-832-8513. Benedict Jurchak, T.O.R., Rel. Supr. & Dir., Formation; Revs. Jordan Hite, T.O.R.; Maurus Dolcic, T.O.R.; Dominic T. Foster, T.O.R.; Ambrose K. Phillips, T.O.R. House of Post-Novitiate Formation for Franciscan Friars, T.O.R., Province of the Most Sacred Heart of Jesus. Priests 4; Total in Residence 16; Friars in Post-Novitiate Formation 8; First Vows (Students) 8.

Marist Center (1900) Society of Mary (Marist) (S.M.) 4408 8th St., N.E., 20017-2298. Tel: 202-529-4800; Fax: 202-526-2295; Email: randyh@maristsociety.org. Revs. Joseph Fenton, S.M., Chap. Admin., The Claremont Colleges; Peter R. Blanchard, S.M., (Retired); Robert Champagne, S.M., (Retired); Richard K. Colbert, S.M., (Retired); Faustino Cruz, S.M., Theology Prof.; Rev. Colonel Joseph M. Fleury, S.M., Army Chap.; Revs. Philip S. Gage, S.M., (Retired); Donald S. Gagne, S.M., (Retired); Walter L. Gaudreau, S.M., (Retired); Andre L. Gosselin, S.M., Chap.; Robert Graham, S.M., (Retired); James B. McCafferty, S.M., (Retired); Joseph M. Pusateri, S.M., (Retired); Howard C. Smith, S.M., (Retired); Gerard Timmerman, S.M.; Rev Paul Morrissey, S.M.; Rev. Paul Hachey, S.M.; Bro. Richard McKenna, S.M., Vice-Supr.; Revs. Paul Cabrita, Sabbatical; Kevin Duggan, Sabbatical; Very Rev. Paul Frechette, S.M., Prov.; Revs. John H. Harhager, S.M., Rel Order Leader; Souvenir Jean-Paul, Chap.; Normand Martin; John Ulrich, Chap.; John F. Beckley, S.M., Asst. to Prov. for Senior Care; James LaCrosse, Senior Religious. The Marist Finance Center of the Atlanta Province of the Society of Mary, Marist Fathers and Brothers.

Missionaries of La Salette (1968) 1243 Monroe St., N.E., 20017. Tel: 202-526-8070; Fax: 202-269-0775; Email: mlsadmin@aol.com; Web: www.lasalette.org. Revs. Brian Schloth, M.S., Dir., Novices; Ronald A. Beauchemin, M.S., Asst. Dir.
Missionaries of La Salette Corporation.

Missionary Oblates of Mary Immaculate (1816) 391 Michigan Ave., N.E., 20017-1516.
Tel: 202-529-4505; Fax: 202-529-4572; Email: province@omiusa.org; Web: www.omiusa.org. Revs. Richard Hall, O.M.I., Supr.; James Brobst, O.M.I., Vicar Prov., Mission&Ministry; Councilor; Arthur Flores, O.M.I., Vicar Prov., Personnel; Councilor; Seamus P. Finn, O.M.I., Dir., JPIC; James Chambers, O.M.I., Treas.; Tuan N. Pham, O.M.I., Vocation Dir., Oblate Vocation Officer; J. William Morell, Dir. OMSI; Very Rev. Louis Studer, O.M.I., Prov.; Revs. Jose Antonio Ponce Diaz, O.M.I., Prov. Council; Raymond Cook, O.M.I., Prov. Councilor; Francis Santucci, O.M.I., Prov. Councilor; James Taggart, O.M.I., Prov. Councilor; Edgar Garcia, Asst. to the Asst. Treas.; Rocky Grimard, O.M.I., Asst. Treas.; Roger Hallee, O.M.I., Assoc. Pastor; Daniel LeBlanc, O.M.I., Pastor; Raymond Lebrun, O.M.I., Assoc. Pastor; Thomas Coughlin, O.M.I., Exec. Admin.; Leopoldo Perez, Dir., Pontifical Mission Societies; Andrew Small, O.M.I., Dir., Pontifical Mission Societies; David Uribe, Dir., OMSI; Rufus Whitley, O.M.I., Legal Admin.; Karl Davis, Prof.; Bevil Bramwell, O.M.I., Prof.; Warren Brown, O.M.I.; Harold M. Fisher, O.M.I.; George Knab, O.M.I.; Bro. Jason Rossignol; Revs. Arthur Craig; Charles Hurkes, O.M.I.; George Kirwin, O.M.I.; Louis Villarreal.
Provincial Offices of the United States Province of the Missionary Oblates of Mary Immaculate (1999) 391 Michigan Ave., N.E., 20017-1516.
Tel: 202-529-4505; Fax: 202-529-4572. Very Rev. Louis Studer, O.M.I., Prov.; Revs. Jose Antonio Ponce Diaz, O.M.I., Dir. Justice & Peace; Councilor; Seamus P. Finn, O.M.I., Consultant, JPIC/FCI Investing; Richard Hall, O.M.I., Vocation Dir., Oblate Vocation Office, San Antonio, TX; Tuan N. Pham, O.M.I., Vocation Dir., Vocation Office, Lowell, MA; James Chambers, O.M.I., Treas.; J. William Morell, O.M.I., Dir., Fundraising; Warren Brown, O.M.I., Gen. Councilor; James Taggart, O.M.I., Councilor; James Brobst, O.M.I., Vicar Prov., Mission & Ministry; Councilor; Arthur Flores, O.M.I., Vicar Prov., Personnel; Councilor; George Knab, O.M.I., Preacher; Thomas Coughlin, O.M.I., Asst. to Admin. Team; Raymond Cook, O.M.I., Councilor; Francis Santucci, O.M.I., Councilor; Harold M. Fisher, O.M.I., Vocation Dir., Oblate Vocation Office, Belleville, IL.
Legal Titles and Holdings:. *The United States Province of the Missionary Oblates of Mary Immaculate, Inc.* (1999) Tel: 202-529-4505; Fax: 202-529-4572. *Oblate Service Corporation* (1999) Tel: 202-529-4505; Fax: 202-529-4572. *Oblate Shrines and Renewal Centers, Inc.* (1999) Tel: 202-529-4505; Fax: 202-529-4572. *Oblate Title Holding Corporation* (1999) Tel: 202-529-4505; Fax: 202-529-4572. *Oblate Continuing Care Trust* (1999) Tel: 202-529-4505; Fax: 202-529-4572. *Oblate Education and Formation Trust* (1999) Tel: 202-529-4505; Fax: 202-529-4572. *Oblate Annuity Trust* (1999) Tel: 202-529-4505; Fax: 202-529-4572. *Oblate Endowment Trust* (1999) Tel: 202-529-4505; Fax: 202-529-4572. *Oblate Patrimony Trust* (1999) Tel: 202-529-4505; Fax: 202-529-4572. *Oblate Service Trust* (1999) Tel: 202-529-4505; Fax: 202-529-4572. *Oblate Real Estate Trust* (1999) Tel: 202-529-4505; Fax: 202-529-4572.

Oblate Community, 391 Michigan Ave., N.E., 20017-1516. Tel: 202-529-4505; Fax: 202-529-4572; Email: province@omiusa.org; Web: www.omiusa.org. Very Rev. Louis Studer, O.M.I., Prov.; Revs. Jose Antonio Ponce Diaz, O.M.I., Dir. Justice & Peace; Seamus P. Finn, O.M.I., Consultant, JPIC/FCI Investing; Charles Hurkes, O.M.I., Newsletter Editor; Raymond A. Lebrun, O.M.I., Spiritual Dir. Natl. Shrine of the Immaculate Conception; Andrew Small, O.M.I., Dir., Pontifical Mission Societies in U.S.; J. William Morell, O.M.I., Dir., Fundraising; Daniel LeBlanc, O.M.I., Assoc. Justice & Peace Ministry; Bevil Bramwell, O.M.I., Prof.; Rufus Whitley, O.M.I., Dir., Oblate Investment Pool; George Kirwin, O.M.I., (In Res.); Thomas Coughlin, O.M.I., Asst. to Admin. Team; Rocky Grimard, O.M.I., Asst. Treas.; James Brobst, O.M.I., Vicar Prov., Mission & Ministry; James Chambers, O.M.I., Treas.; Arthur Flores, O.M.I., Vicar Prov., Personnel; Bro. Jason Rossignol, Dir. Justice & Peace. Priests 16.

Piarist Fathers, Province of the U.S.A. and Puerto Rico, 1339 Monroe St., N.E., 20017.
Tel: 202-529-7734; Fax: 954-776-8060; Email: piaristfl@bellsouth.net; Web: www.piarist.info. Revs. Francisco Aisa, Provincial Asst.; John Callan, Provincial Asst.; Nelson Henao, Provincial Asst.; Very Rev. Fernando Negro, Provincial; Rev. Emilio Sotomayor, Provincial Asst. Deacons 1; Novices 1; Priests 34; Professed 15.

Society of Missionaries of Africa (1868) 1624 21st St., N.W., 20009-1003. Tel: 202-232-5154; Email: usasuperior@mafrdc.org; Web: www.missionariesofafrica.org. Revs. David J. Goergen, M.Afr., Treas.; Barthelemy Bazemo, M.Afr., AFJN/Delegate Supr.; Robert C. McGovern, M.Afr., (Retired); Thomas W. Reilly, M.Afr., (Retired); Bro. James M. Heintz, M.Afr., Bursar; Revs. Julien Cormier, M.Afr., Guestmaster; Komi Sedomo (Antonio) Koffi, Student. U.S.A. Sector Brothers 1; Priests 6; Total Staff 7.

Society of the Divine Word/Divine Word House, 832 Varnum St., N.E., 20017. Tel: 202-635-7810; Fax: 202-635-7813. Revs. Dominikus Boak, S.V.D.; Georges Kintiba, S.V.D.; Binh Thanh Nguyen, S.V.D.; Bro. Brian McLauchlin, S.V.D. S.V.D. Priests 5.

ADELPHI, MD. *Father Judge Missionary Cenacle*, 1733 Metzerott Rd., Adelphi, 20783. Tel: 301-439-3171; Fax: 301-434-0848; Email: fjcenacle@aol.com. Bros. Loughlan Sofield, S.T., Dir.; William Coombs, S.T., Asst. Dir.; Revs. Joel Bladt, S.T.; Rudy Breunig, S.T.; Victor Seidel, S.T.; Anselm Deehr, S.T.; Edwin Dill, S.T., M.A.; Stephen T. Ernst, S.T.; Daniel McLaughlin, S.T.; Louis Murphy, S.T.; James O'Bryan, S.T.; Walter O'Donnell, S.T.; Bros. Jordan Baxter, S.T.; Richard McCann, S.T.; Rev. Joseph Keenan. Senior Ministry Residence.

BELTSVILLE, MD. *Ammendale Normal Institute of Prince George's County-La Salle Hall* (1880) 6001 Ammendale Rd., Beltsville, 20705.
Tel: 301-210-7443; Email: juliano@fscdena.org. Br. Martin Zewe, F.S.C, Dir. Brothers of the Christian Schools.Residence for Retired and Convalescent Brothers. Brothers 25; Total Staff 4.

BETHESDA, MD. *Priestly Fraternity of the Missionaries of St. Charles Borromeo, Inc.*, 7600 Carter Ct., Bethesda, 20817. Tel: 301-983-4624;
Tel: 617-290-9127; Email: a.lopez@sancarlo.org; Web: http://sancarlo.org/. Revs. Antonio Lopez, F.S.C.B.; Roberto Amoruso, F.S.C.B.; Ettore Ferrario, F.S.C.B.; Pietro Rossotti, F.S.C.B.; Paolo Prosperi, F.S.C.B.; Jose Medina, F.S.C.B.

BROOKEVILLE, MD. *Divine Mercy Chapel, Brookeville* Affiliated with Marian Fathers Scholasticate, Washington DC 19109 Georgia Ave., Brookeville, 20833-2699. Tel: 202-526-8884; Email: marian.scholasticate.office@gmail.com; Web: www.marian.org. Rev. James McCormack, M.I.C. Marian Residence & Marian Assisted Living
Congregation of Marian Fathers of the Immaculate Conception of the Blessed Virgin Mary, Inc. Priests 1.

CHILLUM, MD. *Institute of the Incarnate Word*, 5706 Sargent Rd., Chillum, 20782. Tel: 301-853-2789; Cell: 347-491-8123; Fax: 301-559-1713; Email: prov.immaculate.conception@ive.org; Web: iveamerica.org. Revs. Alberto Barattero, Prov.; Pablo Bonello, I.V.E., Prov. Asst. Bro. 3; Clergy 56; Tot in Congregation 823.

MOUNT RAINIER, MD. *Dominican Province of Saint Joseph the Worker: Nigeria and Ghana, Inc.*, 4504 21st St., Mount Rainier, 20712.

POTOMAC, MD. *Legionaries of Christ*, 10211 Norton Rd., Potomac, 20854. Tel: 301-299-0806; Email: mpschneider@legionaries.org. Revs. Jacob Munoz, L.C., Supr.; Stephen Howe, L.C., Family Pastor; Juan Pablo Duran, L.C., Family Pastoral; Robert Presutti, L.C., Academic Vice Dir.; Matthew Schneider, L.C., Student; Charles Sikorsky, L.C., Pres., IPS; Bro. Luke Rawicki, L.C., Youth Min. Asst.; Deacon Andrew Gronotte, L.C., Youth Dir.; Revs. Stephen Costello, Chap.; Stephen Ellis, Chap.; Bro. Andrew Torrey, Youth Min.

RIVERDALE, MD. *Holy Spirit Missionary Cenacle* (1996) 5809 Riverdale Rd., Riverdale, 20737.
Tel: 301-277-7442; Email: hfpiller@gmail.com. Bro. Howard F. Piller, S.T., Local Supr. In Res. Revs. Sidney H. Griffith, S.T.; Stephen Giorno, S.T.; J. Roberto Mena, S.T.; Gary M. Banks, S.T.; Bro. David Sommer, S.T.

SILVER SPRING, MD. *Missionary Servants of the Most Holy Trinity* dba Trinity Missions, Generalate, 9001 New Hampshire Ave., Ste. 300, Silver Spring, 20903-3626. Tel: 301-434-0092; Fax: 301-434-0255; Email: secgen@trinitymissions.org; Web: www.trinitymissions.org. Very Rev. Michael K. Barth, S.T., Rel. Order Leader; Bro. Steven Vesely, S.T., Sec. Gen.

TAKOMA PARK, MD. *Society of African Missions (S.M.A.)*, Tel: 301-891-2037; Email: takomahouse@smafathers.org; Web: www.smafathers.org. Revs. Nelson Adjei-Bediako, S.M.A., Local Supr.; Austin Charles Ochu, S.M.A.; Daniel Lynch, S.M.A. *House of Studies*, 209 Lincoln Ave., Takoma Park, 20912-5738.
Tel: 301-270-2008; Fax: 301-270-0132; Email: smausa-o@smafathers.org; Web: www.smafathers.org. Rev. Austin Charles Ochu, S.M.A. *Takoma House*, 256 N. Manor Cir., Takoma Park, 20912-4551. Tel: 301-891-2037; Email: takomahouse@smafathers.org; Web: www.smafathers.org. Revs. Nelson Adjei-Bediako, S.M.A., Dir.; Daniel Lynch, S.M.A.

[P] MINISTRY TO PRIESTS

KENSINGTON, MD. *St. John Vianney House*, 4214 Saul Rd., Kensington, 20895. Tel: 301-942-1191; Fax: 301-942-1191; Email: yaom@adw.org. Mrs. Mary Yao, Admin.

[Q] CONVENTS AND RESIDENCES FOR SISTERS

WASHINGTON. *Carmelite Sisters of Charity, Vedruna*, North American Delegation, 1222 Monroe St., N.E., 20017. Tel: 202-832-2114; Email:

maureenfoltz@hotmail.com. Sisters Maureen Foltz, C.C.V., North American Regl. Supr.; Maria Dolores Mairlot, C.C.V., Sec.; Ms. Delfina Castro, Treas. Sisters 12.

St. Cecilia Congregation, St. Anthony Convent, 721 Lawrence St., N.E., 20017. Tel: 202-525-2223. Sr. Mary Juliana Cox, O.P., Convent Supr. Sisters 4.

Religious of Jesus and Mary, Inc. (1818) 821 Varnum St., N.E., 20017-2144. Sisters Margaret Perron, R.J.M., Prov.; Anne Magner. Sisters 71; Total Staff 2; Administrative Team 4.

Other Residences:*Religious of Jesus and Mary* (1818) 6709 41st Ave., University Park, 20782. Tel: 301-779-0662; Email: amagner@rjmusa.org. Sr. Anne Magner. Sisters 1. *Religious of Jesus and Mary*, 4602 Clemson Rd., College Park, 20740. Tel: 301-699-3931; Email: amagner@rjmusa.org. Sr. Anne Magner. Sisters 2. *Religious of Jesus and Mary*, 3521 13th St., N.W., 20010. Tel: 202-265-8812; Email: amagner@rjmusa.org. Sr. Anne Magner. Sisters 3.

Franciscan Sisters of Atonement, 4000 Harewood Rd., N.E., 20017. Tel: 202-529-1111; Fax: 202-529-2102; Email: washretreat@juno.com; Web: www.graymoor.org. Sr. Josephine Dullaghan, Dir. Sisters 6; Total Staff 12.

Georgetown Visitation Monastery (1799) 1500 35th St., N.W., 20007. Tel: 202-337-3350, Ext. 2313; Fax: 202-558-7976; Email: mary.siegel@visi.org; Web: www.gvmonastery.org. Sr. Mary Berchmans Hannan, V.H.M., Supr. Professed Sisters 16.

Institute of Our Lady of Mount Carmel (1854) Scrilli Day Care Center, 4415 8th St., N.E., 20017. Tel: 202-526-5106. Total Staff 8; Total Assisted 65.

Missionaries of Charity, 3310 Wheeler Rd., S.E., 20032. Tel: 202-562-6890. Sr. Mary Clovis, M.C., Supr. Sisters 7; Total Assisted 16,181.

Missionaries of Charity, Gift of Peace Convent (1986) 2800 Otis St., N.E., 20018. Tel: 202-269-3313. Sr. M. Lisseria, M.C., Supr. Total in Residence 38; Total Assisted 75.

North American Delegation, Carmelites of Charity, Vedruna, 1222 Monroe St., N.E., 20017. Tel: 301-277-2963; Tel: 202-832-2114.

Oblates Sisters of the Most Holy Eucharist, 2907 Ellicott Ter., N.W., 20008. Tel: 202-244-7714; Email: oblatesdc@hotmail.com. Sr. Margarita Jaime, O.S.S.E., Supr. Sisters 7.

Poor Clares of Perpetual Adoration (1954) 1150 Varnum Street, NE, 20017-2699. Tel: 202-526-6808; Fax: 202-526-0678; Email: ourprayer4u@poorclareswdc.org; Web: www.poorclareswdc.org. Cloistered Monastery of Perpetual Adoration. Cloistered Nuns 5.

Religious of the Sacred Heart Oakview Community. 1215 Perry St., N.E., 20017. Tel: 202-832-0071. Sr. Fleisa Garcia, Contact Person.

Rosary House of Studies-Dominican Sisters of The Presentation, 1201 Monroe St., N.E., 20017. Tel: 202-529-1768; Fax: 202-529-1768; Email: rosaryhouseop@gmail.com. Sisters 3.

**Servants of the Lord and Virgin of Matara, Inc.*, 28 15th St., S.E., 20003. Tel: 202-543-2064; Email: m.immaculate@servidoras.org; Web: www.ssvmusa.org. Mother Mary of the Immaculate Conception, Prov. Supr.

Sisters of the Holy Child Jesus, 1033 Newton St., N.E., 20017. Tel: 202-526-6832; Web: www.shcj.org. Novitiate Community. Sisters 3.

Sisters of St. Francis of the Neumann Communities NIA Place 3916 Queensbury Rd., 20782. Tel: 240-603-9933; Email: jebert@sosf.org; Web: www.sosf.org. Sr. Marie Joette Ebert, O.S.F., Contact Person & Treas. Sisters 1.

ANACOSTIA, WASHINGTON. *Missionaries of Charity (Contemplatives)*, 1244 V St., S.E., Anacostia, Washington, 20020-7016. Tel: 202-889-6100. Sr. M. Dorothy Bly, M.C., Supr.

CLINTON, MD. *The Missionary Catechists of St. Therese of the Infant Jesus, Inc.*, 8914 Old Branch Ave., Clinton, 20735. Tel: 301-839-7751; Email: mcstusa@yahoo.com. Sr. Helen B. Sumander, M.C.S.T., Pres. Sisters 6.

Religious Sisters of Mercy of Alma, MI (1973) St. Andrew Home of Mercy 6100 Wolverton Lane, Clinton, 20735. Tel: 301-297-5617; Fax: 301-297-5618; Email: saintandrews@rsmofalma.org; Web: www.rsmofalma.org. Sr. Mary Christine Cremin, R.S.M., Local Supr. & Contact Person. Sisters 7.

KENSINGTON, MD. *Congregation of the Sisters of the Holy Cross*, St. Angela Hall, 4910 Strathmore Ave., Kensington, 20895. Tel: 301-946-7750; Fax: 301-946-7751; Email: sbrennan@cscsisters.org. Sr. Suzanne Brennan, Treas. Independent Living House for the Sisters of the Holy Cross. *Sisters of the Holy Cross, Inc.*

LA PLATA, MD. *Discalced Carmelites of Maryland, Inc.* (1790) Carmel of Port Tobacco, 5678 Mt. Carmel Rd., La Plata, 20646-3625. Mother Virginia O'Connor, Prioress; Sr. Marie Penland, Treas. Novices 2; Professed 8; Sisters 10.

LAUREL, MD. *Pallotti Convent*, 404 Eighth St., Laurel, 20707. Tel: 301-725-1717. Sisters M. Karen Lester, S.A.C., Sponsorship Dir.; Bernadette Peterson, S.A.C., Local Supr. Total Staff 2; Professed Sisters 4.

POTOMAC, MD. *Little Sisters of the Holy Family*, 13529 Magruder Farm Ct., Potomac, 20854. Tel: 301-947-1955; Fax: 240-631-1786. Sr. Domina Son, L.S.H.F., Supr.

RIVERDALE, MD. *Carmelite Sister of Christ - Vedruna*, 5410 56th Pl., #101, Riverdale, 20737. Tel: 301-277-2963.

SILVER SPRING, MD. *Sisters of Charity of St. Charles Borromeo*, St. Elizabeth Convent, 11320 Classical Ln., Silver Spring, 20901. Tel: 301-681-9665; Fax: 301-681-0693.

Sisters of Mercy of the Americas - Institute Administrative Offices (1831) 8380 Colesville Rd., Ste. 300, Silver Spring, 20910. Tel: 301-587-0423; Fax: 301-587-0533; Web: www.sistersofmercy.org. Legal Holdings: Mercy Action, Inc.; Mercy Volunteer Corps, Inc.; Sisters of Mercy of the Americas, Inc. Sisters 2,747.

Institute Leadership Team: Sisters Patricia McDermott, R.S.M., Pres.; Eileen Campbell, R.S.M., Vice Pres.; Anne Curtis, R.S.M., Councilor; Mary Patricia Garvin, R.S.M., Councilor; Deborah Troillett, R.S.M., Councilor.

Sisters of the Good Shepherd, 504 Hexton Hill Rd., Silver Spring, 20904-3300. Tel: 301-384-1169; Fax: 301-384-1025; Email: caridadtamayo@aol.com; Web: www.sistersofthegoodshepherd.com. Sr. Caridad Tamayo, Contact Person. Sisters 2.

Sisters of the Holy Names (S.N.J.M.), 9603 Flower Ave., Silver Spring, 20901. Tel: 301-587-1717; Email: kksnjm@gmail.com; Web: www.snjmusontario.org. Sisters 3.

Other Convents:*Sisters of the Holy Names (S.N.J.M.)*, 519 Varnum St., N.W., 20011. Tel: 202-829-8671. Sisters 3.

Sisters of the Holy Names (S.N.J.M.), 9212 Glenville Rd., Silver Spring, 20901. Tel: 301-445-0309. Sisters 2.

Sisters of the Holy Names (S.N.J.M.), Church of the Annunciation, 3200 39th St. N.W., 20016. Tel: 202-362-1464. Sisters 2.

Sisters of the Holy Names (S.N.J.M.), 12007 Bernard Dr., Silver Spring, 20902. Tel: 301-942-0701. Sisters 2.

[R] RETREAT HOUSES

WASHINGTON. *Washington Retreat House, Inc.* (1930) 4000 Harewood Rd., N.E., 20017. Tel: 202-529-1111; Fax: 202-259-2102; Email: washretreat@juno.com; Web: www.graymoor.org. Sisters Josephine Dullaghan, Dir.; Sara Dwyer, Contact Person. Franciscan Sisters of the Atonement. Sisters 7; Total in Residence 6; Total Staff 12.

FAULKNER, MD. *Loyola Retreat House*, 9270 Loyola Retreat Rd., P.O. Box 9, Faulkner, 20632. Tel: 301-392-0800; Fax: 301-392-0808; Email: director@loyolaretreat.org; Email: reservations@loyolaretreat.org; Web: www.loyolaonthepotomac.com. Mr. Jim Palmer, Dir. Total Staff 21.

Staff: Revs. John Thomas Kelly, S.J.; Richard C. Schmidt, S.J.; Sr. Patricia McDermott, I.H.M., Dir.; Rev. Gerald J. Fitzpatrick, S.J.

UPPER MARLBORO, MD. *Our Lady of Mattaponi Youth Retreat and Conference Center* (1987) 11000 Mattaponi Rd., Upper Marlboro, 20772. Tel: 301-952-9074; Fax: 301-952-0609; Email: mattaponi@adw.org. Total Staff 2.

[S] NATIONAL SHRINES

WASHINGTON. **John Paul II Shrine & Institute, Inc.*, 3900 Harewood Rd., N.E., 20017. Tel: 202-635-5400; Email: VisitorServices@jp2shrine.org; Web: www.jp2shrine.org. Mr. Patrick Kelly, Exec.; Mr. Maxime Nogier, Dir.

Basilica of the National Shrine of the Immaculate Conception, 400 Michigan Ave., N.E., 20017-1566. Tel: 202-526-8300; Fax: 202-526-8313; Email: info@nationalshrine.com; Web: www.nationalshrine.com. Rev. Msgr. Walter R. Rossi, Rector; Revs. Raymond A. Lebrun, O.M.I., Spiritual Dir.; Michael D. Weston, Dir. Liturgy; Rev. Msgr. Vito A. Buonanno, Dir. Pilgrimages.

[T] HOUSES OF PRAYER

WASHINGTON. *Catholic Information Center*, 1501 K St., N.W., Ste. 175, 20005-1401. Tel: 202-783-2062; Fax: 202-783-6667; Email: director@cicdc.org; Web: www.cicdc.org. Rev. Charles Trullols, Dir. Total Staff 7.

Madonna House, 220 C St., N.E., 20002. Tel: 202-547-0177; Email: madonnahousedc@gmail.com; Web: www.madonnahouse.org. Ms. Elizabeth Holmes, Staff Worker; Ms. Echo Lewis, Staff Worker. Total Staff 2.

[U] OFFICES OF CAMPUS MINISTRY

WASHINGTON. *Archdiocesan Campus Ministry*

American University Catholic Community, Kay Spiritual Life Center, 4400 Massachusetts Ave., N.W., 20016-8010. Tel: 202-885-3327; Fax: 202-885-3317; Email: priest@american.edu. Rev. Carlos B. Quijano, O.P., Chap.; Dr. Karin Thornton, Assoc. Campus Min., Tel: 202-885-3326; Ms. Grace Hegarty, Campus Min.

Gallaudet University Catholic Community, 800 Florida Ave., N.E., 20002. Tel: 202-651-5102. Revs. Gerard A. Trancone, Chap., (Retired); Joseph J. Bruce, S.J., Chap.

7202 Buchanan St., Landover Hills, 20784. Tel: 301-459-7467; Tel: 301-459-7464; Fax: 301-459-8186.

George Washington Univ. Newman Center, 2210 F St., N.W., 20037. Tel: 202-676-6855; Fax: 202-676-6859. Rev. Gregory W. Shaffer, Chap.

Howard Univ. Newman Center, 818 Newman Center, 20059. Tel: 202-238-2687; Fax: 202-806-4641. Deacon Joseph Bell, Campus Min.

University of Maryland Catholic Student Center, 4141 Guilford Dr., College Park, 20740. Tel: 301-864-6223; Tel: 301-864-6224; Fax: 301-864-8411; Email: catholicterps@catholicterps.org; Web: www.catholicterps.org. Rev. Robert E. Walsh, Chap.; Ann Gradowski, Admin. & Devel.; Matthew Aujero, Campus Min.; Lisa Lytwyn, Campus Min.

St. Mary's College Campus Ministry, 47950 Mattapany Rd., P.O. Box 429, St. Mary's City, 20686. Tel: 301-862-4600; Tel: 913-426-4074; Email: peter@ihmrcc.org. Rev. Scott Woods, Chap.

[V] PERSONAL PRELATURES

WASHINGTON. *Prelature of the Holy Cross and Opus Dei*, 2301 Wyoming Ave., N.W., 20008. Tel: 202-234-1567; Fax: 202-238-0621; Email: alvarojdevicente@gmail.com; Web: www.opusdei.org. Revs. Salvador S. Vahi, Chap.; Joe Landauer, Chap.; Charles Trullols, Chap.

Other Centers:

Tenley Study Center, 4300 Garrison St., N.W., 20016. Tel: 202-362-2419; Fax: 202-362-0318. Revs. Diego Daza; Javier Bujalance.

[W] SECULAR INSTITUTES

WASHINGTON. *Caritas Christi* (1937) 5410 Connecticut Ave., N.W. #506, 20015-2821. Tel: 202-363-2839. Therese Druart, Gen. Councilor. A Secular Institute of Pontifical Right.

Community of Christ, 1003 Kearney St., N.E., 20017. Tel: 202-832-9710; Tel: 202-797-8806; Fax: 202-265-3849; Email: frjohn@some.org. Rev. John E. Adams, Moderator. A Private Association Community of Archdiocesan Right for Priests, Lay Men and Lay Women. The Community of Christ Purpose is Simple Lifestyle, Poverty Ministry, Spiritual Growth and Prayer of Community Members.

Washington Province Discalced Carmelite Secular Order, Inc., 2131 Lincoln Rd., N.E., 20002-1101. Tel: 202-269-3792; Email: ocdsmainoffice@gmail.com; Web: ocdswashprov.org. Rev. Salvatore Sciurba, O.C.D., Pres.; Mary Harrington, O.C.D.S., Admin.

BETHESDA, MD. *Missionaries of the Kingship of Christ* A Franciscan Secular Institute of Pontifical Right. 5223 River Rd. #5030, Bethesda, 20816. Tel: 917-327-0255; Email: susanlark2@aol.com; Web: www.simkc.org. Rev. Dominic Monn, O.F.M., Ecclesiastical Asst., Tel: 617-542-6440; Email: dmonti@sbu.edu.

[X] MISCELLANEOUS

WASHINGTON. **Africa Faith & Justice Network*, 3025 4th St., N.E., Ste. 122, 20017. Tel: 202-817-3670; Fax: 202-817-3671; Email: afjndevelopment@gmail.com; Email: director@afjn.org; Email: afjnpolicyanalyst@gmail.com; Web: www.afjn.org. Rev. Aniedi Okure, O.P., Exec. Dir. Priests 2; Total Staff 5.

The Americas (1944) Catholic University of America, Gibbons Hall, Room B 17, 20064. Tel: 202-319-5890; Fax: 202-319-5569; Email: americas@cua.edu; Web: www.theamericasjournal.org.

St. Anselm's Abbey School Donor Trust, 4501 S. Dakota Ave., N.E., 20017-2795. Tel: 202-281-1645; Fax: 202-281-1648; Email: mcommins@saintanselms.org. Mark Commins, Admin.

Asian and Pacific Catholic Network, 913 Hamilton St., N.E., 20011.

Association of Catholic Colleges and Universities (1899) One Dupont Cir. N.W., Ste. 650, 20036. Tel: 202-457-0650; Fax: 202-728-0977; Email: accu@accunet.org; Web: www.accunet.org. Michael Galligan-Stierle, Pres. & CEO. Total Staff 12.

Association of Jesuit Colleges and Universities, One Dupont Cir., N.W., Ste. 405, 20036. Tel: 202-862-9893; Fax: 202-862-8523; Web: www.ajcunet.edu. Rev. Michael J. Sheeran, S.J., Pres. Established in 1970, The Association of Jesuit Colleges and Universities (AJCU) is a national voluntary organization whose mission is to serve its member institutions, the 28 Jesuit colleges and universities in the United States, and its associate members. Though each institution is separately chartered and is legally autonomous under its own board of trustees, the institutions are bonded together by a common heritage, vision and purpose. They engage in a number of collaborative projects in the United States and around the world.

Bethlehem House, 1401 Lawrence St., N.E., 20017. Tel: 202-526-3222; Fax: 202-635-2434.

Black Leadership and Christ's Kingdom Society, P.O. Box 410, Waldorf, 20604-0410. Tel: 301-888-2566; Email: bodyofchristfarm@yahoo.com. Rev. Robert S. Pittman, S.S.S., Pres. Total Staff 2.

CARA, Center for Applied Research in the Apostolate (1964) 2300 Wisconsin Ave., N.W., Ste. 400, 20007. Tel: 202-687-8080; Fax: 202-687-8083; Email: cara@georgetown.edu; Web: cara.georgetown.edu. Rev. Thomas P. Gaunt, S.J., Exec. Dir.

Carmelite Institute of North America (1993) 1600 Webster St., N.E., 20017. Tel: 202-526-1221; Fax: 202-526-9217; Web: www.carmelstream.org. Rev. Patrick McMahon, O.Carm., Ph.D., Pres.

Carroll Manor Nursing & Rehabilitation Center, 1150 Varnum St., N.E., 20017-2180. Tel: 202-854-7100; Fax: 202-854-7816; Email: lakesha.mcallister@ascension.org; Tel: ybouchel@ascension.org; Email: crystal.scott@ascension.org. Revs. C. Gregory Butta, Chap.; Kenneth Chukwu, Chap. Bed Capacity 240; Total Staff 294.

Catholic Biblical Association of America (1936) Catholic University of America, 433 Caldwell Hall, 620 Michigan Ave., NE, 20064. Tel: 202-319-5519; Fax: 202-319-4799; Email: cba-office@cua.edu; Web: http://catholicbiblical.org. Dr. Joseph C. Atkinson, B.A., B.Ed., B.Th., M.Div., S.T.L., S.T.D., Exec. Dir.

Catholic Climate Covenant, 415 Michigan Ave., N.E., Ste. 260, 20017.

Catholic Daughters of the Americas Court #2344 - Our Lady of the Americas, 5715-9th St. N.W., 20011. Tel: 202-882-5553. Patricia A. Walker, Regent.

Catholic Mobilizing Network, 415 Michigan Ave., N.E., Ste. 210, 20017. Tel: 202-541-5290; Email: caitlin@catholicsmobilizing.org; Email: info@catholicsmobilizing.org; Web: www.catholicsmobilizing.org. Krisanne Vaillancourt Murphy, Exec.

Center of Concern (1971) 1627 K Street, N.W., 11th Fl., 20006-1710. Tel: 202-635-2757; Email: coc@coc.org; Web: www.coc.org. Lester A. Myers, Ph.D., J.D., CPA, CFF, CGMA, Pres.

Centro Maria (1996) 650 Jackson St., N.E., 20017-1424. Tel: 202-635-1697; Fax: 202-526-1708; Email: rmi@centromariadc.org; Web: www.religiosasmariainmaculada.org. Sr. Antonia Sanchez, Local Supr. Residence for young students and working women (18-30). Bed Capacity 40; Religious 5; Tot Asst. Annually 134.

Christ Child Society of Washington, DC, Inc. (1887) 5101 Wisconsin Ave., N.W., Ste. 102, 20016. Tel: 202-966-9250; Fax: 202-966-2880; Email: info@christchilddc.org; Web: www.charityadvantage.com/christchilddc. Ms. Kathleen Curtin, Exec. Dir. A nonprofit, volunteer organization of approximately 600 persons serving the emotional and material needs of children, through layette distribution, school counseling, camp scholarships, uniform assistance, and community outreach. Total Staff 21; Total Assisted 6,000.

Christ Our Hope Foundation, Inc., P.O. Box 29260, 20017.

Christian Brothers Conference, 415 Michigan Ave., Ste. 300, 20017-4501. Tel: 202-529-0047; Fax: 202-529-0775; Email: jlindsay@cbconf.org; Web: www.lasallian.info. Bro. Timothy Coldwell, F.S.C., Gen. Councilor; Mr. James G. Lindsay, Dir. Administration. Institutions owned and/or sponsored: Bethlehem University of the Holy Land; Sangre de Cristo Center, Santa Fe, NM; Christian Brothers Services, Romeoville, IL.Organizations and programs served by this office: Regional Conference of Christian Brothers; Huether Lasallian Conference; Buttimer Institute of Lasallian Studies; Bro. John Johnston Institute of Contemporary LaSallian Practice; Lasallian Education Council.

Christian Brothers Major Superiors, Inc.

Christian Life Communities, Washington Area Promoters: 5040 Nebraska Ave., N.W., 20008-2938. Tel: 202-363-4593. Ms. Margaret Fox.
201 E. Wayne Ave., Silver Spring, 20901-3808. Tel: 301-495-2969; Fax: 301-495-7318. Fred Leone; Betty Leone.

Commissariat of the Holy Land, Franciscan Monastery - Mount St. Sepulchre, 1400 Quincy St., N.E., 20017. Tel: 202-526-6800, Ext. 887; Fax: 202-529-9889; Email: commissarywdcusa@myfranciscan.com; Email: secretariatusa@myfranciscan.com; Web: www.myfranciscan.com. Very Rev. Larry C. Dunham, O.F.M., Commissary; Rev. Garrett Edmunds, O.F.M., Vice Commissary; Friar-Deacon John-Sebastian Laird-Hammond, O.F.M., Secretariat. Priests 8; Solemnly Professed 16; Friars 16.

Communio: International Catholic Review, P.O. Box 4557, 20017. Tel: 202-526-0251; Fax: 202-526-1934 ; Email: communio@aol.com; Web: www.communio-icr.com. David L. Schindler, Editor.

Council for Research in Values and Philosophy (1983) Gibbons Hall B-20, The Catholic University of America, 20064. Tel: 202-319-6089; Email: cua-rvp@cua.edu; Web: www.crvp.org. William Barbieri Jr., Chm.

Diocesan Laborer Priests, 3706 15th St., N.E., 20017. Tel: 202-832-4217; Fax: 202-526-5692.

DISC Diocesan Information Systems Conference, 1250 Connecticut Ave., N.W., Ste. 200, 20036. Tel: 419-214-4908; Email: president@discinfo.org; Web: discinfo.org. Sharon Landis, Pres.

District of Columbia Detention Facility, Office of Chaplain, 1357 E. Capitol St. S.E., 20003. Tel: 202-547-1715 (Office); Fax: 202-544-1385; Email: mbryantabc@msn.com. Rev. F. Michael Bryant, Chap. Total in Residence 1,100; Total Staff 4.

Don Bosco Cristo Rey Work-Study of the Archdiocese of Washington, Mailing Address: P.O. Box 56481, 20040-6481. Tel: 301-891-4750; Fax: 301-270-1459; Email: conwaym@dbcr.org; Web: www.dbcr.org. 1010 Larch Ave., Takoma Park, 20912. Rev. Michael Conway, S.D.B., Pres.; Ms. Ana Chapa, Exec. Dir.

Engaged Encounter, 6514 7th Pl., N.W., 20012. Tel: 202-320-3254; Email: registration@dcengagedencounter.org. Adam Hughes, Registration Coord.; Mary Kate Hughes, Registration Coord.

Equestrian Order of the Holy Sepulchre of Jerusalem - Middle Atlantic Lieutenancy U.S.A., Franciscan Monastery of the Holy Land, 1400 Quincy St., N.E., 20017. Tel: 202-526-4217; Fax: 202-526-4218; Email: Secretary@midatlanticeohs.com; Web: http://www.midatlanticeohs.com/. H.E. Valencia Yvonne Camp LGCHS, Lieutenant.

Father McKenna Center, 19 Eye St., N.W., 20001. Tel: 202-842-1112; Fax: 202-842-7401; Email: kcox@fathermckennacenter.org; Web: www.fathermckennacenter.org. Kimberly Cox, Pres. Volunteers 600; Total Assisted 3,500.

Fellowship of Catholic Scholars, John Paul II Institute, 620 Michigan Ave., N.E., 20064. Tel: 718-817-3291; Fax: 718-817-3300; Email: koterski@fordham.edu; Web: www.catholicscholars.org. Dr. William Saunders, Pres.

Foundation for the Nativity & Miguel Schools, 900 Varnum St., N.E., 20017. Tel: 202-832-3667; Fax: 202-832-8098; Email: jjordan@nativitymiguel.org; Web: www.nativitymiguelschools.org. Rev. Msgr. John W. Jordan, Exec. Dir.

Sts. Francis and Alphonsus Corporation, 4036 Alabama Ave. SE, 20020. Tel: 202-678-5898; Email: asimplehouse@gmail.com. Clark Massey, Dir.

Franciscan Custody of the Holy Land USA, 1400 Quincy St., N.E., 20017.

Franciscan Mission Service of North America, 415 Michigan Ave., N.E., Ste. 104, 20017. Tel: 202-832-1762; Fax: 202-449-1323; Email: info@franciscanmissionservice.org; Web: franciscanmissionservice.org. Liz Hughes, Dir. Lay Staff 4; Volunteers 3.

Friends of Lasallian Volunteers, Inc., c/o Christian Brothers Conference, 415 Michigan Ave., N.E., Ste. 300, 20017. Tel: 202-529-0047; Fax: 202-529-0775; Email: kswain@cbconf.org; Web: lasallianvolunteers.org. Kathleen Swain, Dir.

Friends of the Benedictines in the Holy Land, Inc., 2715 Jenifer St., N.W., 20015. Email: jsheridany@gmail.com.

The Friends of the Ethiopian Catholic University of St. Thomas Aquinas, c/o Holy Rosary Church, 595 Third St., N.W., 20001.

Friends of the Pontifical Irish College, Rome, Inc. (2000) c/o Roha & Flaherty, 1725 I St., N.W., Ste. 300, 20006. Tel: 202-833-0033; Email: tom@princebush.com. Thomas Prince, Pres.

Gregorian University Foundation, 1055 Thomas Jefferson St. N.W., Ste 302, 20007-5243. Tel: 202-333-1551; Fax: 202-333-1553; Email: president@gregorianfoundation.org; Email: info@gregorianfoundation.org; Web: www.gregorianfoundation.org. Revs. Alan J. Fogarty, S.J., Pres.; William L. George, Senior Advisor.

Holy Family Hospital of Bethlehem Foundation, 2000 P St. N.W., Ste. 310, 20036. Tel: 202-785-0801; Email: michele.bowe@icloud.com; Web: www.birthplaceofhope.org.

Imago Dei, Inc., 4393 Embassy Park Dr., NW, 20016. Tel: 301-905-8700; Email: stsash@aol.com; Web: imagodei-tob.org. Suzanne Shaffer, Chm.

Institute of Carmelite Studies and ICS Publications (1973) 2131 Lincoln Rd., N.E., 20002-1199. Tel: 800-832-8489; Fax: 202-832-8967; Email: brpaquette@aol.com; Email: publisher@icspublications.org; Web: www.icspublications.org. Rev. Marc Foley, O.C.D., Dir.; Bro. Bryan Paquette, O.C.D., Exec.

Discalced Carmelite Friars, Inc. Religious 6.

Jesuit Conference, Inc., 1016 16th St. N.W., Ste. 400, 20036. Tel: 202-462-0400; Fax: 202-328-9212; Email: skrudys@jesuits.org; Web: www.jesuits.org. Very Rev. Timothy P. Kesicki, S.J., Pres.; Rev. Sean D. Michaelson, S.J., Socius.

Jesuit Health Trust, 1016 16th St., N.W., Ste. 400, 20036. Tel: 202-462-0400; Email: JCUTreasurer@jesuits.org.

Jesuit Missions, Inc., 1016 16th St., N.W., Ste. 400, 20036. Rev. Sean D. Michaelson, S.J., Exec. Dir.

Jesuit Refugee Service (1984) 1016 16th St. N.W., Ste. 500, 20036. Tel: 202-462-5200; Fax: 202-462-7008; Email: gmcpherson@jesuits.org; Web: www.jrsusa.org. Giulia McPherson, Dir.

Jesuit Schools Network, 1016 16th St. N.W., Ste. 200, 20036. Tel: 202-667-3888; Email: JCUseced@jesuits.org; Web: jesuitschoolsnetwork.org. Rev. William H. Muller, S.J., Exec. Dir.; Jeffrey M. Howard, M.A., Dir., Ignatian Mission Formation; Timothy G. Sassen, Ph.D., Dir., Global Partnerships and Communications; Iliana M. Brown, Exec. Asst.; Julia Andrette, Administrative Assoc.; Kristin Cully, Dir. of Research and Global Initiatives. Total Staff 6.

Jesuit Social and International Ministries-National Office, 1016 16th St. N.W., Ste. 400, 20036. Tel: 202-462-0400; Fax: 202-328-9212; Email: outreach@jesuits.org; Email: jcusimsec@jesuits.org; Web: www.jesuits.org. Rev. Jean Dennis Saint Felix.

The John Carroll Society, P.O. Box 454, Glen Echo, 20812. Tel: 301-654-4399; Email: johncarrollsociety1951@gmail.com; Web: www.johncarrollsociety.org. Thomas Loughney, M.D., Pres.; Rev. Msgr. Peter J. Vaghi, J.D., V.F.

John Paul II Fellowship, CT Corp System, 1015 15th St., N.W., Ste. 1000, 20005. Tel: 202-384-8182

St. Joseph Trust, 1326 Quincy St., N.E., 20017. Tel: 202-543-1179; Email: economia.usa@servidoras.org. Mother Mary of the Immaculate Conception Ambrogio, Pres.

Kidane-Mehret Ge'ez Rite Ethiopian Catholic Church, 415 Michigan Ave., N.E., Ste. 65, P.O. Box 29616, 20017. Tel: 202-756-2756; Email: kmgeezrite@aol.com; Web: www.catholic-forum.com/churches/kidanemehret. Rev. Abayneh Gebremichael, Dir.

Knights of St. Jerome Bobby Gant, Pres.

The Leonine Forum, Inc., 1501 K St., N.W., Ste. 175, 20005. Tel: 202-783-2062; Email: mitch.boersma@leonineforum.org. Mike Boersma, Contact Person.

Morley Publishing Group, Inc., 2100 M St. N.W., #170-339, 20037. Tel: 202-861-7790; Fax: 202-403-3362; Email: mail@insidecatholic.com; Web: www.insidecatholic.com.

Mount Carmel House, 471 G Pl., N.W., 20001. Tel: 202-289-6315; Fax: 202-289-1710. Mary Bridget Klinkenbergh, Senior Program Mgr. Transitional Housing for Women with 20 beds.

NAC Humility Street Foundation, c/o Pontifical North American College, 3211 Fourth St., N.E., 20017. Tel: 202-541-5411; Email: pnacdc@pnac.org.

NAC Janiculum Hill Foundation, Director of Finance - 19th Fl., Archdiocese of New York - 1011 First Ave., New York, NY 10022-4112. Tel: 215-327-7788; Email: jmcrowley@msn.com. Most Revs. James F. Checchio, Pres.; William Francis Murphy, S.T.D., L.H.D., Treas.; Paul S. Loverde, Sec.

National Black Sisters' Conference, 1200 Varnum St., N.E., 20017-2740. Tel: 202-529-9250; Fax: 202-529-9370; Email: tthenationalblacksistersconfer@verizon.net; Web:

www.nbsc68.com. Sr. Roberta Fulton, S.S.M.N., Pres. Total Staff 1.

National Catholic Conference for Interracial Justice, 1200 Varnum St., N.E., 20017-2796.
Tel: 202-529-6480; Fax: 202-526-1262. Deacon Joseph M. Conrad Jr., Exec. Dir.

National Institute for the Family (1979) 1200 Varnum St., N.E., Ste. 54, 20017-2796.
Tel: 202-302-1339; Tel: 202-557-4468 (alternate); Fax: 202-526-7811; Email: dconroy@comcast.net. Rev. Donald B. Conroy, S.T.L., Ph.D., Pres.; Dr. John Przypysz, Exec. Team Members; Lauri Przypysz, Exec. Team Members. Research Program: Parish Renewal, Intergenerational Ministry and Lay Leadership Formation in cooperation with the Christian Family Movement. Administrators 1.

Oblate Missionary Society, Inc., 391 Michigan Ave., N.E., 20017. Tel: 202-529-4505; Tel: 202-529-4572; Email: province@omiusa.org. Very Rev. Louis Studer, O.M.I., Prov.

Order of Malta Lourdes Endowment Trust, c/o SMOM-Federal Assn., 1730 M St., N.W., Ste. 403, 20036. Email: info@orderofmalta-federal.org. Deacon Michael J. Stankewicz, Dir.

Paulist Evangelization Ministries (1977) 1200 Varnum St. N.E., 20017-1102. Tel: 202-832-5022; Fax: 202-269-0209; Email: admin@pemdc.org; Email: lwilliams@pemdc.org; Web: www.pemdc.org. Revs. Francis P. DeSiano, C.S.P., D.Min., Pres.; Kenneth G. Boyack, C.S.P., D.Min., Vice Pres.

Pax Romana / Catholic Movement for Intellectual and Cultural Affairs-USA (1927) 1025 Connecticut Ave., NW, Ste. 1000, 20036. Tel: 202-657-4613; Fax: 888-453-1237; Email: pax-romana-cmica-usa@comcast.net; Web: www.pax-romana-cmica-usa.org. Edward Joe Holland, Ph.D., Pres.

Pope John Paul II Cultural Foundation, Inc., 3900 Harewood Rd., N.E., 20017. Tel: 202-635-5407; Fax: 202-635-5411.

**Prison Outreach Ministry* (1982) P.O. Box 51583, 20091. Tel: 202-347-3218; Fax: 202-347-9217; Email: pomsvb@yahoo.com. Rev. F. Michael Bryant, Chap.

RJM Endowment and Continuing Care Trust, 821 Varnum St., N.E., 20017. Tel: 202-526-3203; Email: amagner@rjmusa.org. Sisters Anne Magner, Trustee; Margaret Perron, R.J.M., Trustee.

RJM Ministry Corporation, 821 Varnum St., N.E., 20017. Tel: 202-526-3203; Email: amagner@rjmusa.org. Sisters Anne Magner; Margaret Perron, R.J.M., Pres.

RJM Real Estate Trust, 821 Varnum St., N.E., 20017. Tel: 202-526-3203; Email: amagner@rjmusa.org. Sisters Anne Magner, Trustee; Margaret Perron, R.J.M., Trustee.

Rosary Shrine of St. Jude Dominican Fathers and Brothers. St. Dominic's Church, 630 East St., S.W., 20024-2598. Tel: 212-595-3664; Email: df@dominicanfriars.org. 141 East 65th St., New York, NY 10065. Rev. Gabriel Gillen, O.P., M.A., Dir.

Roundtable Association of Catholic Diocesan Social Action Directors, P.O. Box 96503 #81001, 20090. Tel: 202-854-8806; Email: coordinator@catholicroundtable.org; Web: www.catholicroundtable.org. Jean Hill, Chm.; Catherine Orr, Contact Person.

S.N.D.B.C. Charitable Trust, 125 Michigan Ave. N.E., 20017. Tel: 202-884-9750; Email: gailsnd@aol.com. Sisters Gail Grimes, S.N.D.de.N., Trustee; Patricia O'Malley, S.N.D.de.N., Trustee; Virginia West, S.N.D.de.N., Trustee.

Sisters of Notre Dame de Namur Base Communities, Inc. (1989) 125 Michigan Ave. N.E., 20017-1004.
Tel: 202-884-9750; Email: sndbcunit@aol.com; Web: www.SNDdeN.org. Sr. Virginia West, S.N.D.de.N., Canonical Liaison. Sisters 7.

Sisters of the Visitation of Georgetown Continuing Care Trust, 1500 35th St., N.W., 20007.

Sovereign Military Order of Malta-Federal Association, 1730 M St., N.W., Ste. 403, 20036.
Tel: 202-331-2494; Email: info@orderofmalta-federal.org; Web: www.orderofmalta-federal.org. Deacon Michael J. Stankewicz, Exec. Dir.

Spanish Catholic Center, Administrative Office: P.O. Box 11450, 20008-0650. Tel: 202-939-2437; Fax: 202-234-7323; Email: infoscc@yahoo.com; Web: www.centrocatolicohispano.org. Rev. Donald F. Lippert, O.F.M.Cap.

Mt. Pleasant Branch, 1618 Monroe St., N.W., 20010. Tel: 202-939-2437; Fax: 202-234-7323.

Medical Clinic, Tel: 202-939-2400; Fax: 202-232-1970.

Dental Clinic, Tel: 202-939-2423; Fax: 202-234-7349.

Social Services, Tel: 202-939-2414; Fax: 202-232-1970.

Immigration Services, Tel: 202-939-2420; Fax: 202-234-7349.

Langley Park Office, 1015 University Blvd. E., Silver Spring, 20903. Tel: 301-431-3773; Fax: 301-431-0886.

Adult Clinic, Tel: 301-434-8381; Fax: 301-434-8067.

Pediatric Clinic, Tel: 301-434-3999; Fax: 301-434-5160.

Social, Employment & Immigration Services, Tel: 301-587-0582; Fax: 301-587-8209.

Medical Clinic, Tel: 301-929-0207; Fax: 301-929-0594.

Piney Branch Office, 8545 Piney Branch Rd., Silver Spring, 20901.

Gaithersburg Branch, 117 N. Frederick Ave., Gaithersburg, 20877. Tel: 301-417-9113; Fax: 301-417-9895.

Social, Employment & Immigration Services, Tel: 301-417-9113; Fax: 301-417-9895.

Spiritual Life (1954) 2131 Lincoln Rd., N.E., 20002-1199. Tel: 888-616-1713; Fax: 202-832-6622; Email: edodonnell@aol.com; Web: www.spiritual-life.org. Bros. Edward O'Donnell, O.C.D., Editor; Bryan Paquette, O.C.D., Business & Promotion Mgr. A Quarterly of Contemporary Spirituality. Priests 1; Total Staff 3.

Support Our Aging Religious, Inc. (SOAR!) aka SOAR! (1986) (Support Our Aging Religious) 3025 4th St., N.E. - Ste. 14, 20017. Tel: 202-529-7627; Fax: 202-529-7633; Email: info@soar-usa.org; Web: www.soar-usa.org. Sr. Kathleen Lunsmann, I.H.M., Pres.; Elizabeth Goral-Makowski, Dir. Devel. Total Staff 7.

**The Foundation for the Sacred Arts*, 1413 K St., N.W., Ste. 1000, 20005.

**The Paulus Institute*, 308 S. Green St., Berkeley Springs, WV 25411. Cell: 304-350-0680; Email: pn308king@gmail.com; Web: www.thepaulusinstitute.org. P.O. Box 201, Great Cacapon, WV 25422.

US Province of the Religious of Jesus and Mary, Inc., 821 Varnum St., N.E., 20017. Tel: 202-526-3203; Email: amagner@rjmusa.org. Sisters Anne Magner; Margaret Perron, R.J.M., Prov.

Victory Youth Center, 4265 4th St., S.E., 20032. Tel: 202-562-7590; Email: fosterd@adw.org. Mr. Darren Foster, Mgr.

Victory Youth Centers, Inc., c/o ADW, P.O. Box 29260, 20017. Tel: 301-908-1072; Fax: 301-469-8677; Email: jdonatellia@verizon.net. Julie Donatelli, Exec. Dir.

Washington Catholic Charismatic Service Committee, 1029 Monroe St., N.E., 20017.
Tel: 301-249-9199; Fax: 301-249-1303; Email: oremus2005@earthlink.net. Rev. Frederick J. Close, Dir.

**Washington Jesuit Academy*, 900 Varnum St., N.E., 20017. Tel: 202-832-7679; Email: wwhitaker@wjacademy.org; Web: www.wjacademy.org. William B. Whitaker, Pres.

**The Washington School for Girls*, 1901 Mississippi Ave. SE, 20020. Tel: 202-678-1113; Fax: 202-678-1114; Email: breaves@wsgdc.org; Email: lnelson@wsgdc.org; Web: www.washingtonschoolforgirls.org. Dr. Beth Reaves, Pres.

Women's Retreat League, 4000 Harewood Rd., N.E., 20017-1507. Tel: 202-529-1111; Fax: 202-529-2102. Mrs. Cynthia Perry, Pres.

**Workers of St. Joseph*, 5542 Friendship Station, 21770. Tel: 301-399-2480; Email: tony_s1@verizon.net. 415 Michigan Ave. N.E., Ste. 110, 20017. Fr. Brian Newman, Spiritual Advisor/Care Services.

ALEXANDRIA, VA. *Catholic War Veterans of the United States*, 411 N. Lee St., Alexandria, VA 22314.
Tel: 703-549-3622; Fax: 703-684-5196. Fred Schwally, Natl. Commander; Lupita Martinez, Pres.

**Culture of Life Foundation*, P.O. Box 320637, Alexandria, VA 22320. Tel: 202-289-2500; Email: info@cultureoflife.org; Web: www.cultureoflife.org.

BELTSVILLE, MD. *The Bethlehem University Foundation, Inc.*, 6002 Ammendale Rd., Ste. 200, Beltsville, 20705. Tel: 240-241-4381; Fax: 240-553-7691; Email: Info@bufusa.org; Web: www.bufusa.org. P.O. Box 355, Beltsville, 20704-0355. Sr. Irene O'Neill, Chair; Most Rev. Denis Madden, Vice Chm.; Mr. Benjamin Monastero, Treas.; Mr. Ghassan Salahem, Sec.; John L. Schlageter Esq., Exec. Dir.; Margaret McCarty, D.Min., Dir. Devel.

BETHESDA, MD. **Alliance for Communities in Action, Inc.*, 5403 Waneta Rd., Bethesda, 20816-2131.
Tel: 301-229-0351; Email: richard@allact.org. Deacon Richard Schopfer, Pres., Tel: 561-624-3375; Juan Claudio Devincenti, Vice Pres.

Alpha Omega, Inc. Programming includes Spiritual Exercises retreats, marriage preparation program and marriage enrichment retreats and workshops. Our Lady of Bethesda Retreat Center, 7007 Bradley Blvd., Bethesda, 20817. Tel: 301-365-0612; Email: info@ourladyofbethesda.org; Web: www.ourladyofbethesda.org. Rev. Juan Pablo Duran, Pres.

Lay Women's Association / Secular Institute of the Missionaries of the Kingship of Christ, 5223 River Rd. #5030, Bethesda, 20816. Tel: 917-327-0255; Email: suslark2@aol.com; Web: www.simkc.org. National Headquarters of the LWA.

Mission Network Young Men's Program USA, Inc., 7007 Bradley Blvd., Bethesda, 20817.
Tel: 301-365-7614; Fax: 301-299-0809; Email: fformolo@legionaries.org. Rev. Frank Formolo.

Woodmont Educational Foundation, Inc., 7007 Bradley Blvd., Bethesda, 20817. Tel: 770-828-4950; Email: fformolo@legionaries.org. Rev. Frank Formolo, Contact Person.

BOWIE, MD. *Sodality Union*, 3300 Moreland Pl., Bowie, 20715. Tel: 301-262-2141; Fax: 301-262-2632. Rev. Lawrence C. Swink, Spiritual Dir. & Mod.; Cindy Perry, Pres.

COTTAGE CITY, MD. *Marriage Encounter-Worldwide*, 4011 Parkwood St., Cottage City, 20722.
Tel: 301-395-5369; Email: don.wink68@gmail.com; Web: welovematrimony.org. Don Flanders, Contact Person; Wink Flanders, Contact Person.

FORT WASHINGTON, MD. *Birhen Ng Antipolo, USA, Inc.* (1997) 8504 Oxon Hill Road, Fort Washington, 20744. Tel: 301-567-4914; Fax: 301-567-4914; Web: www.antipolo.us. Eddie D. Caparas, Pres. & Chm.

GAITHERSBURG, MD. *Knights of Columbus*, 16584 Sioux Ln., Gaithersburg, 20878. Tel: 301-921-4035; Fax: 301-921-4035 (Call First); Email: tryzub1@verizon.net. Lawrence Sosnowich, Immediate Past State Deputy.

GLEN ECHO, MD. *John Carroll Society*, P.O. Box 454, Glen Echo, 20812. Tel: 301-654-4399; Email: johncarrollsociety1951@gmail.com; Web: www.johncarrollsociety.com. Carol G. Bates, Pres.; Rev. Msgr. Peter J. Vaghi, J.D., V.F., Chap.; Colleen Mudlaff, Exec. Dir.

HYATTSVILLE, MD. *St. Ann's Donor Trust*, 4901 Eastern Ave., 20782. Tel: 301-559-5500; Email: srmaryb@stanns.org. Sr. Mary Bader, D.C., CEO.

KENSINGTON, MD. *Inter Mirifica*, 2812 Jutland Rd., Kensington, 20895. Tel: 301-949-4840; Email: jdhoconnell@comcast.net. John O'Connell, Contact Person. Religious publications.

LANDOVER HILLS, MD. *Archdiocese of Washington, Department of Special Needs Ministries*, 7202 Buchanan, Landover Hills, 20784.
Tel: 301-459-7464 (TTY/Voice); Fax: 301-459-8186; Email: specialneedsministry@adw.org. Rev. Frank A. Wright, S.M.A., Chap. Total Staff 5.

LAUREL, MD. *Pallotti Early Learning Center at St. Mary of the Mills*, 800 Main St., Laurel, 20707.
Tel: 301-776-6471; Tel: 410-724-0097; Fax: 301-776-0019; Email: kdavenport@stmaryofthemills.org; Web: pallottiearlylearningcenter.net. Sr. Karen Lester, S.A.C., Rel. Teacher (part-time); Mrs. Alisha Jordan, Dir.; Kelli Davenport, Admin. Day Care 92; Lay Teachers 15; Sisters (Part Time) 1; After School 30.

McLEAN, VA. *German Speaking Catholic Mission, Washington DC*, 6330 Linway Ter., McLean, VA 22101-4150. Tel: 703-356-4473; Email: kontakt@kathde.org; Web: www.kathde.org. Rev. Christian Bock.

MOUNT RAINIER, MD. *Dominican Fathers & Brothers Inc. Province of Nigeria*, Development and Mission Office, 4504 21st St., Mount Rainier, 20712.
Tel: 301-927-0387; Fax: 301-927-0388; Email: rayezeop@yahoo.com; Web: www.dominicans.org.ng/. Rev. Raymond Nwabueze, O.P., Mission Dir. Priests 126; Total Assisted 206.

IVE Real Estate Trust, 3706 Rhode Island Ave., Mount Rainier, 20712. Tel: 347-491-8123; Email: prov.immaculate.conception@ive.org. Rev. Alberto Barattero, Pres.

MT. VICTORIA, MD. *Sacred Military Constantinian Order of St. George, American Delegation*, P.O. Box 7, Mount Victoria, 20661. Tel: 301-870-1033; Fax: 301-870-0993; Email: mtvictoriafarm@gmail.com; Web: constantinianorderofstgeorge.org. Michael J. Sullivan, Delegate & Contact Person.

POTOMAC, MD. *Potomac Pastoral Center Inc.*, 10211 Norton Rd., Potomac, 20854. Tel: 301-299-0806; Fax: 301-299-0809; Email: fformolo@legionaries.org. Rev. Frank Formolo.

ROCKVILLE, MD. *Archdiocesan Council of Catholic Women*, 520 Veirs Mill Rd., Rockville, 20852.
Tel: 301-424-5550; Fax: 301-424-5579. Rev. Msgr. Robert G. Amey, V.F., Moderator & Spiritual Dir.; Ellen-Jane Pairo, Pres.

Avondale Park Apartments, Inc. (1997) c/o Victory Housing, 11400 Rockville Pike, Ste. 505, Rockville, 20852. Tel: 301-493-6000; Fax: 301-493-9788; Email: info@victoryhousing.org; Web: www.victoryhousing.org. Leila Finucane, Pres.

National Christ Child Society, Inc. (1887) 6110 Executive Blvd., Ste. 504, Rockville, 20852.
Tel: 301-881-2490; Fax: 301-881-2493; Email:

office@nationalchristchild.org; Email: cpumphrey@nationalchristchild.org; Web: www.nationalchristchild.org. Mrs. Carolyn Pumphrey, Exec. Dir. A national nonprofit organization with 44 affiliate chapters consisting of nearly 6,000 member volunteers serving under-resourced children across the United States through educational and clothing programs.

Rosaria Communities Foundation, Inc., 15400 Calhoun Dr., Ste. 125, Rockville, 20855. Tel: 301-279-2020.

Victory Court, Inc., 11400 Rockville Pike, Ste. 505, Rockville, 20852. Tel: 301-493-6000; Fax: 301-493-9788; Email: info@victoryhousing.org. Leila Finucane, Pres.

Victory Crest, Inc., c/o Victory Housing, Inc., 11400 Rockville Pike, Ste. 505, Rockville, 20852. Tel: 301-493-6000; Fax: 301-493-9788; Email: info@victoryhousing.org; Web: www.victoryhousing.org. Leila Finucane, Pres.

Victory Lakeside, Inc., 11400 Rockville Pike, Ste. 505, Rockville, 20852. Tel: 301-493-6000; Fax: 301-493-9788; Email: info@victoryhousing.org. Leila Finucane, Pres.

Victory Oaks, Inc., 11400 Rockville Pike, Ste. 505, Rockville, 20852. Tel: 301-493-6000; Fax: 301-493-9788; Email: info@victoryhousing.org. Leila Finucane, Pres.

SILVER SPRING, MD. *The Blue Army, Archdiocese of Washington Division* World Apostolate of Fatima P.O. Box 4934, Silver Spring, 20914. Tel: 301-589-7829. Mrs. Jane Baily, Pres.; Rev. Msgr. Charles E. Pope, V.F., Spiritual Dir.

Camp St. Charles, Inc. (1952) Summer Camp Address: Camp St. Charles, 15375 Stella Maris Dr., Rock Point, 20664. Rev. Glen Willis, S.D.S., Exec. Dir.; Ms. Laura Hall, Dir. Brothers 1; Lay Staff 40; Priests 1; Children Served 550.

Conference for Mercy Higher Education (2002) 8380 Colesville Rd., Ste. 300, Silver Spring, 20910. Tel: 301-273-9736; Tel: 301-587-0423, Ext. 2237; Email: mkdittmeier@gmail.com; Web: www.mercyhighered.org. Moya K. Dittmeier, Ed.D., Exec. Dir. The Conference for Mercy Higher Education is separately incorporated for the preservation and development of the Catholic identity and mission of Mercy higher education in accord with the spirit, mission, and heritage of the Sisters of Mercy of the Americas. Each of the 15 active member institutions of the Conference is separately chartered and is legally incorporated with its own board of trustees.

The Daughters of Mary Immaculate, Inc., 13004 Marlow Farm Dr., Silver Spring, 20904. Tel: 301-288-7663; Email: thuyliendmi@gmail.com. Thuy-Lien Doan, Pres.

**Friends in Solidarity, Inc.*, 8808 Cameron St., Silver Spring, 20910. Tel: 734-731-3726; Email: info@solidarityfriends.org; Web: https://www.solidarityfriends.org. Sr. Joan Mumaw, Pres.

Friends of John Paul II Foundation (1985) 3885 Harewood Rd., N.E., 20017. Bro. Leonard Konopka, M.I.C., Chap.; Raymond Glembocki, Treas.

Irish Apostolate USA, Inc. (1997) 9900 Blundon Dr., #202, Silver Spring, 20902. Tel: 617-470-1172; Email: coordinator@usairish.org; Web: www.usairish.org. Revs. Brendan McBride, Pres.; Daniel Finn, Sec. & Treas.; Sr. Marie Prefontaine Snoden, Coord. & Contact Person.

Leadership Conference of Women Religious in the U.S.A., 8737 Colesville Rd., Ste. 610, Silver Spring, 20910. Tel: 301-588-4955; Fax: 301-587-4575; Email: director@lcwr.org; Web: www.lcwr.org. Sisters Mary Pellegrino, C.S.J., B.A., M.A., M.S., Pres.; Teresa Maya, C.C.V.I., B.A., M.A., Ph.D., Pres. Elect; Mary Beth Gianoli, O.S.F., M.A., Sec.; Kate Katoski, Treas.; Carole Shinnick, S.S.N.D., Exec.; Sharlet Ann Wagner, C.S.C., B.J., J.D., Pres.

Mercy Education System of the Americas, 8380 Coleville Rd., Ste. 560, Silver Spring, 20910.

Missionary Cenacle Family, 9001 New Hampshire Ave., Ste. 300, Silver Spring, 20903-3626.

**St. Luke Institute Foundation*, 8901 New Hampshire Ave., Silver Spring, 20903. Tel: 301-445-7970; Fax: 301-422-5400; Email: getinfo@sli.org. Rev. David Songy, O.F.M.Cap., S.T.D., Psy.D., Pres.

Saint Luke Institute, Inc., 8901 New Hampshire Ave., Silver Spring, 20903. Tel: 301-445-7970; Fax: 301-422-5400; Email: getinfo@sli.org; Web: www.sli.org. Rev. David Songy, O.F.M.Cap., S.T.D., Psy.D., Pres.; Taryn Millar, Psy.D., COO. The Institute provides education and research and is an accredited treatment center for clergy and religious. Bed Capacity 54; Tot Asst. Annually 594; Total Staff 77.

Lumen Catechetical Consultants, Inc. (1982) P.O. Box 1761, Silver Spring, 20915. Tel: 301-593-1066; Tel: 800-473-7980; Email: lumen@lifeaftersunday.com; Web: lifeaftersunday.com. Mr. John M. Capobianco, Pres. Provides Consulting & Production Services to Catholic Organizations; Assist in Development and Production of Catechetical Materials in Various Media. Publishes "Life After Sunday.".

MIA-USA Fundraising Inc., 8380 Colesville Rd., Ste. 300, Silver Spring, 20910-6264. Tel: 301-587-0423; Email: pmcdermott@sistersofmercy.org; Web: https://www.sistersofmercy.org. Sr. Patricia McDermott, R.S.M., Pres.

Sisters of Mercy of the Americas CCASA Community, Inc., 8380 Colesville Rd., Ste. 300, Silver Spring, 20910. Tel: 301-587-0423; Fax: 301-587-0533; Email: pmcdermott@sistersofmercy.org; Web: www.sistersofmercy. Sr. Julie Matthews, R.S.M., Pres.

U.S. Good Shepherd Conference, a Corporation National Advocacy Center of the Sisters of the Good Shepherd. 504 Hexton Hill Rd., Silver Spring, 20904. Tel: 301-622-6838; Fax: 301-384-1025; Email: info@gsadvocacy.org; Web: www.gsadvocacy.org. Lawrence Couch, Dir.

SPRINGFIELD, VA. *St. Francis de Sales Association*, 8002 Gosport Ln., Springfield, VA 22151-2007. Tel: 703-321-7856; Fax: 703-321-3032. Brenda Soares, Directress of the Washington Group, 8002 Gosport Ln., Springfield, VA 22151-2007. Tel: 703-321-7856; Email: bmsoares@verizon.net.

WEST HYATTSVILLE, MD. *Catholic Apostolate Center, Inc.*, 2009 Van Buren St., West Hyattsville, 20782. Tel: 301-448-1880; Fax: 301-422-4070; Email: director@catholicapostolatecenter.org. Rev. Frank S. Donio, S.A.C., Dir.

RELIGIOUS INSTITUTES OF MEN REPRESENTED IN THE ARCHDIOCESE

For further details refer to the corresponding bracketed number in the Religious Institutes of Men or Women section.

[0140]—*The Augustinians*—O.S.A.
[0200]—*Benedictine Monks*—O.S.B.
[]—*Brothers of Charity*—F.C.
[1350]—*Brothers of St. Francis Xavier*—C.F.X.
[0330]—*Brothers of the Christian Schools* (Baltimore Prov.)—F.S.C.
[0600]—*Brothers of the Congregation of Holy Cross*—C.S.C.
[0470]—*The Capuchin Friars* (Prov. of St. Augustine)—O.F.M.Cap.
[0270]—*Carmelite Fathers & Brothers*—O.Carm.
[]—*Congregation of the Sacred Hearts of Jesus and Mary*—SS.CC.
[0480]—*Conventual Franciscans*—O.F.M.Conv.
[0260]—*Discalced Carmelite Fathers (Prov. of the Immaculate Heart of Mary)*—O.C.D.
[0520]—*Franciscan Friars (Commissariat of the Holy Land)*—O.F.M.
[0530]—*Franciscan Friars of the Atonement*—S.A.
[0685]—*Institute of the Incarnate Word*—IVE.
[0690]—*Jesuit Fathers and Brothers (Prov. of Maryland)*—S.J.
[0730]—*Legionaries of Christ*—L.C.
[0740]—*Marian Fathers*—M.I.C.
[0780]—*Marist Fathers and Brothers*—S.M.
[0800]—*Maryknoll*—M.M.
[0850]—*Missionaries of Africa*—M.Afr.
[0720]—*The Missionaries of Our Lady of La Salette*—M.S.
[1210]—*Missionaries of St. Charles (Scalabrinians)*—C.S.
[0590]—*Missionaries of the Holy Apostle*—M.S.A.
[]—*Missionary Servants of Christ*—M.S.C.
[0840]—*Missionary Servants of the Most Holy Trinity*—S.T.
[0910]—*Oblates of Mary Immaculate (Eastern Prov.)*—O.M.I.
[0920]—*Oblates of St. Francis de Sales*—O.S.F.S.
[]—*Order of Preachers (Dominican)* (Prov. of Nigeria)—O.P.
[0430]—*Order of Preachers (Dominican)* (Prov. of St. Joseph)—O.P.
[1310]—*Order of the Holy Trinity (American Prov.)*—O.SS.T.
[1030]—*Paulist Fathers*—C.S.P.
[1040]—*Piarist Fathers*—Sch.P.
[1205]—*Priestly Fraternity of the Missionaries of St. Charles Borromeo*—F.S.C.B.
[1070]—*Redemptorist Fathers* (Baltimore Prov.)—C.SS.R.
[1190]—*Salesians of Don Bosco*—S.D.B.
[0110]—*Society of African Missions*—S.M.A.
[1260]—*Society of Christ*—S.Ch.
[0990]—*Society of the Catholic Apostolate (Immaculate Conception Prov.)*—S.A.C.
[1200]—*Society of the Divine Savior* (Milwaukee, WI)—S.D.S.
[0420]—*Society of the Divine Word*—S.V.D.
[0640]—*Sons of the Holy Family*—S.F.
[0700]—*St. Joseph Society of the Sacred Heart*—S.S.J.
[0560]—*Third Order Regular of Saint Francis (Prov. of the Immaculate Conception)*—T.O.R.

RELIGIOUS INSTITUTES OF WOMEN REPRESENTED IN THE ARCHDIOCESE

[0100]—*Adorers of the Blood of Christ*—A.S.C.
[0340]—*Carmelite Sisters of Charity*—C.C.V.
[]—*Congregation of Our Lady of Mercy*—O.L.M.
[]—*Congregation of the Daughters of Mary Immaculate*—D.M.I.
[3832]—*Congregation of the Sisters of St. Joseph* (Baden, PA)—C.S.J.
[1920]—*Congregation of the Sisters of the Holy Cross*—C.S.C.
[0760]—*Daughters of Charity of St. Vincent de Paul*—D.C.
[0793]—*Daughters of Divine Love*—D.D.L.
[0916]—*Daughters of Mary* (India)—D.M.
[]—*Daughters of St. Anne*—F.S.A.
[0420]—*Discalced Carmelite Nuns*—O.C.D.
[1070-03]—*Dominican Sisters* (Sinsinawa, WI)—O.P.
[1100]—*Dominican Sisters of Charity of the Presentation of the Blessed Virgin*—O.P.
[0677]—*Dominican Sisters of Mary, Mother of the Eucharist*—O.P.
[]—*Dominican Sisters of Our Lady of the Rosary of Fatima*—O.P.
[1190]—*Franciscan Sisters of the Atonement*—S.A.
[0793]—*Handmaids of the Holy Child Jesus*—H.H.C.J.
[0410]—*Institute of the Sisters of Our Lady of Mt. Carmel*—O.Carm.
[]—*Institute Servants of the Lord and the Virgin of Matara*—S.S.V.M.
[2340]—*Little Sisters of the Poor*—L.S.P.
[2345]—*Little Workers of the Sacred Hearts of Jesus and Mary*—P.O.S.C.
[2490]—*Medical Mission Sisters*—M.M.S.
[2720]—*Mission Helpers of the Sacred Heart*—M.H.S.H.
[2710]—*Missionaries of Charity*—M.C.
[1475]—*Missionary Catechists of St. Therese*—M.C.S.T.
[2820]—*Missionary Sisters of Our Lady of Africa*—M.S.O.L.A.
[2900]—*Missionary Sisters of St. Charles Borromeo*—M.S.C.S.
[]—*Oblate Sisters of the Most Holy Eucharist*—O.S.S.E.
[3210]—*Poor Clares of Perpetual Adoration*—P.C.P.A.
[3450]—*Religious of Jesus and Mary*—R.J.M.
[3460]—*Religious of Mary Immaculate*—R.M.I.
[2519]—*Religious Sisters of Mercy* (Alma, MI)—R.S.M.
[2970]—*School Sisters of Notre Dame*—S.S.N.D.
[3620]—*Sister Servants of Mary Immaculate*—S.S.M.I.
[]—*Sisters of Charity of St. Charles Borromeo*—S.C.B.
[0430]—*Sisters of Charity of the Blessed Virgin Mary*—B.V.M.
[1000]—*Sisters of Divine Providence* (Melbourne, KY)—C.D.P.
[2265]—*Sisters of Life*—S.V.
[]—*Sisters of Loretto*—S.L.
[2575]—*Sisters of Mercy of the Americas*—R.S.M.
[2630]—*Sisters of Mercy of the Holy Cross*—S.C.S.C.
[2990]—*Sisters of Notre Dame*—S.N.D.
[3000]—*Sisters of Notre Dame de Namur* (Maryland, Chesapeake & Base Communities, Prov.; Boston and Connecticut)—S.N.D.deN.
[3360]—*Sisters of Providence of St. Mary-of-the-Woods, IN*—S.P.
[3893]—*Sisters of Saint Joseph of Chestnut Hill, Philadelphia*—S.S.J.
[1070-07]—*Sisters of St. Dominic of St. Cecilia* (Nashville, TN)—O.P.
[1650]—*Sisters of St. Francis of Philadelphia*—O.S.F.
[3850]—*Sisters of St. Joseph, Carondelet*—C.S.J.
[3980]—*Sisters of St. Paul de Chartres*—S.P.C.
[3150]—*Sisters of the Catholic Apostolate (Pallotines)*—S.A.C.
[1830]—*Sisters of the Good Shepherd*—R.G.S.
[1990]—*Sisters of the Holy Names of Jesus and Mary*—S.N.J.M.
[3320]—*Sisters of the Presentation of the Blessed Virgin Mary*—P.B.V.M.
[4100]—*Sisters of the Sorrowful Mother*—S.S.M.
[1490]—*Sisters of the Third Franciscan Order* (Syracuse, NY)—O.S.F.
[1720]—*Sisters of the Third Order Regular of St. Francis of the Congregation of Our Lady of Lourdes*—O.S.F.
[2160]—*Sisters, Servants of the Immaculate Heart of Mary*—I.H.M.
[4060]—*Society of the Holy Child Jesus*—S.H.C.J.
[4070]—*Society of the Sacred Heart*—R.S.C.J.
[4120-06]—*Ursuline Nuns of the Congregation of Paris* (Toledo, OH)—O.S.U.
[]—*Vietnamese Dominican Sisters*—O.P.
[4190]—*Visitation Nuns*—V.H.M.

ARCHDIOCESAN CEMETERIES

WASHINGTON. *The Catholic Cemeteries of the Archdiocese of Washington, Inc.*, 13801 Georgia Ave., Silver Spring, 20906. Tel: 301-871-1300 (All offices 9-4:30 P.M.); Email: mrm@ccaw.org; Web: www.ccaw.org. Michael R. Mazzuca, Pres.

Mount Olivet Cemetery & St. Mary's Cemetery, 1300 Bladensburg Rd., N.E., 20002. Tel: 202-399-3000; Email: mto@ccaw.org; Web: www.ccaw.org. Cheryl Tyiska, Business Mgr.

GERMANTOWN, MD. *All Souls Cemetery*, 11401 Brink Rd., Germantown, 20876. Tel: 301-428-1995; Email: asc@ccaw.org; Web: www.ccaw.org. Ms. Melissa Baughman, Business Mgr.

MECHANICSVILLE, MD. *St. Mary's Queen of Peace Cemetery*, 38888 Dr. Johnson Rd., P.O. Box 497, Mechanicsville, 20659. Tel: 301-475-5005; Email: qop@ccaw.org; Web: www.ccaw.org. Juli A. Tolson, Business Mgr.

SILVER SPRING, MD. *Gate of Heaven Cemetery*, 13801 Georgia Ave., Silver Spring, 20906. Tel: 301-871-6500; Email: goh@ccaw.org; Web: www.ccaw.org. Ms. Carmen Salazar, Business Mgr.

Resurrection Cemetery, 8000 Woodyard Rd., P.O. Box 151, Clinton, 20735. Mrs. Autumn Buck, Business Mgr.

NECROLOGY

† Beattie, James T., (Retired), Died Apr. 13, 2018
† Duffy, Thomas M., (Retired), Died Oct. 15, 2018
† Brainerd, Winthrop J., (Retired), Died Jul. 31, 2018
† Debicki, John, Potomac, MD The Heights School; Washington DC, Prelature of the Holy Cross and Opus Dei., Died Feb. 1, 2019
† DePorter, Arnold W., (Retired), Died Jun. 10, 2018
† Kleinstuber, Joseph J., (Retired), Died Nov. 6, 2018
† Tran-Khac-Hy, Hilarius, (Retired), Died Jul. 14, 2018

An asterisk (*) denotes an organization that has established tax-exempt status directly with the IRS and is not covered by the USCCB Group Ruling.

Diocese of Wheeling-Charleston

(Dioecesis Vhelingensis Carolopolitanus)

Most Reverend

WILLIAM E. LORI, S.T.D.

Apostolic Administrator of Wheeling-Charleston and Archbishop of Baltimore; ordained May 14, 1977; appointed Titular Bishop of Bulla and Auxiliary Bishop of Washington April 20, 1995; appointed Bishop of Bridgeport January 23, 2001; installed March 19, 2001; appointed Archbishop of Baltimore March 20, 2012; installed May 16, 2012; appointed Apostolic Administrator of Wheeling-Charleston September 13, 2018.

(VACANT SEE)

Chancery Office: 1311 Byron St., P.O. Box 230, Wheeling, WV 26003. Tel: 304-233-0880; Fax: 304-233-0890.

Web: www.dwc.org

Email: ccarter@dwc.org

Most Reverend

MICHAEL J. BRANSFIELD

Retired Bishop of Wheeling-Charleston; ordained May 15, 1971; appointed Bishop of Wheeling-Charleston December 9, 2004; ordained February 22, 2005; retired September 13, 2018. *1311 Byron St., Wheeling, WV 26003.* Tel: 304-233-0880.

Square Miles 24,282.

Established as Diocese of Wheeling July 19, 1850; Redesignated Diocese of Wheeling-Charleston October 4, 1974.

Comprises the entire State of West Virginia.

For legal titles of parishes and diocesan institutions, consult the Chancery Office.

STATISTICAL OVERVIEW

Personnel	
Retired Bishops	1
Priests: Diocesan Active in Diocese	51
Priests: Retired, Sick or Absent	34
Number of Diocesan Priests	85
Religious Priests in Diocese	41
Total Priests in Diocese	126
Extern Priests in Diocese	26
Ordinations:	
Diocesan Priests	1
Transitional Deacons	1
Permanent Deacons in Diocese	53
Total Brothers	5
Total Sisters	98
Parishes	
Parishes	91
With Resident Pastor:	
Resident Diocesan Priests	61
Resident Religious Priests	11
Without Resident Pastor:	
Administered by Priests	19
Missions	20
Closed Parishes	3
Professional Ministry Personnel:	
Brothers	1
Sisters	13
Welfare	
Catholic Hospitals	1
Total Assisted	689,711
Health Care Centers	1
Total Assisted	764
Homes for the Aged	2
Total Assisted	717
Day Care Centers	1
Total Assisted	103
Specialized Homes	1
Total Assisted	19
Special Centers for Social Services	22
Total Assisted	9,658
Educational	
Diocesan Students in Other Seminaries	10
Total Seminarians	10
Colleges and Universities	1
Total Students	1,116
High Schools, Diocesan and Parish	6
Total Students	1,303
Elementary Schools, Diocesan and Parish	19
Total Students	3,749
Catechesis/Religious Education:	
High School Students	839
Elementary Students	3,805
Total Students under Catholic Instruction	10,822
Teachers in the Diocese:	
Lay Teachers	503
Vital Statistics	
Receptions into the Church:	
Infant Baptism Totals	616
Minor Baptism Totals	82
Adult Baptism Totals	128
Received into Full Communion	199
First Communions	820
Confirmations	833
Marriages:	
Catholic	119
Interfaith	110
Total Marriages	229
Deaths	1,003
Total Catholic Population	72,235
Total Population	1,805,832

Former Bishops—Rt. Revs. RICHARD VINCENT WHELAN, D.D., cons. March 21, 1841; Bishop of Richmond; transferred to Wheeling in 1850; died July 7, 1874; JOHN JOSEPH KAIN, D.D., cons. May 23, 1875; transferred June 15, 1893, to the Titular Archiepiscopal See of Oxyrynchia; appt. July 6, 1893; Coadjutor "cum jure successionis" to the Most Rev. Archbishop of St. Louis, MO; created Archbishop of St. Louis, May 21, 1895; died Oct. 13, 1903; PATRICK JAMES DONAHUE, D.D., cons. April 8, 1894; died Oct. 4, 1922; Most Revs. JOHN J. SWINT, D.D., LL.D., appt. Auxiliary Bishop of Wheeling Feb. 22, 1922; cons. May 11, 1922; appt. Bishop of Wheeling Dec. 11, 1922; promoted to rank of Archbishop "ad personam," March 12, 1954; died Nov. 23, 1962; THOMAS J. MCDONNELL, D.D., LL.D., cons. Sept. 15, 1947; appt. Auxiliary Bishop of New York, June 21, 1947; appt. Coadjutor of Wheeling, "cum jure successionis," March 7, 1951; died Feb. 25, 1961; JOSEPH H. HODGES, D.D., ord. Dec. 8, 1935; appt. Titular Bishop of Rusadus and Auxiliary of Richmond Aug. 8, 1952; cons. Oct. 15, 1952; transferred to Wheeling See as Coadjutor, "cum jure successionis", May 24, 1961; succeeded to the See Nov. 23, 1962; died Jan. 27, 1985; FRANCIS B. SCHULTE, D.D., ord. May 10, 1952; appt. Titular Bishop of Afufenia and Auxiliary Bishop of Philadelphia June 27, 1981; cons. Bishop Aug. 12, 1981; transferred to Wheeling July 31, 1985; transferred to Archdiocese of New Orleans Feb. 14, 1989; retired Jan. 3, 2002; died Jan. 17, 2016.; BERNARD W. SCHMITT, D.D., ord. May 28, 1955; appt. Titular Bishop of Walla Walla and Auxiliary Bishop of Wheeling-Charleston May 31, 1988; ord. to the Episcopacy Aug. 1, 1988; app. Seventh Bishop of Wheeling-Charleston March 30, 1989; installed May 17, 1989; retired Dec. 9, 2004; died Aug. 16, 2011.; MICHAEL J. BRANSFIELD, ord. May 15, 1971; appt. Bishop of Wheeling-Charleston Dec. 9, 2004; ord. to the Episcopacy Feb. 22, 2005; retired Sept. 13, 2018.

Delegate of Administrative Affairs—Mailing Address: P.O. Box 230, Wheeling, 26003. Tel: 304-233-0880; Fax: 304-233-0890. MR. BRYAN E. MINOR.

Vicar General and Moderator of the Curia—Mailing Address: P.O. Box 230, Wheeling, 26003. Tel: 304-233-0880; Fax: 304-230-2231. VACANT.

Chancery Office—Mailing Address: P.O. Box 230, Wheeling, 26003. Tel: 304-233-0880; Fax: 304-233-0890. Office Hours: Mon.-Fri. 8:30-4:30.

Chancellor—MR. CHAD R. CARTER, M.B.A., B.A., Mailing Address: P.O. Box 230, Wheeling, 26003. Tel: 304-233-0880; Fax: 304-233-0890.

Assistant to the Bishop—Rev. Msgr. KEVIN MICHAEL QUIRK, J.C.D., J.V.

Diocesan Tribunal—All Rogatory Commissions should be addressed to the office of the Diocesan Tribunal, *Mailing Address: P.O. Box 230, Wheeling, 26003.* Tel: 304-233-0880.

Judicial Vicar—Rev. Msgr. KEVIN MICHAEL QUIRK, J.C.D., J.V.

Promoter of Justice—Rev. JAMES R. DEVIESE JR., J.C.L.

Defenders of Bond—Deacon DENNIS W. NESSER, J.C.L.; Rev. JOSEPH M. AUGUSTINE, H.G.N., J.C.L.

Judges—Rev. Msgr. EUGENE S. OSTROWSKI, V.F., (Retired); Very Rev. JOHN S. LEDFORD, V.F.; Deacon DENNIS W. NESSER, J.C.L.

Diocesan Consultors—Rev. Msgrs. ANTHONY CINCINNATI, S.T.D., V.E.; EUGENE S. OSTROWSKI, V.F., (Retired); PAUL A. HUDOCK; JOSEPH L. PETERSON, V.F.; KEVIN MICHAEL QUIRK, J.C.D., J.V.; Very Revs. CARLOS L. MELOCOTON JR., V.F.; PAUL J. WHARTON, V.F.; Rev. JAMES R. DEVIESE JR., J.C.L.

Delegate for Consecrated Life—Sr. ELLEN F. DUNN, O.P., Mailing Address: P.O. Box 230, Wheeling, 26003-0010. Tel: 304-233-0880; Fax: 304-233-8551.

Episcopal Vicar for Clergy—Rev. Msgr. ANTHONY CINCINNATI, S.T.D., V.E., Mailing Address: P.O. Box 230, Wheeling, 26003-0010. Tel: 304-233-0880; Fax: 304-230-1583.

Vicars Forane—Rev. Msgr. JOSEPH L. PETERSON, V.F., Wheeling Vicariate; Very Revs. PAUL J. WHARTON, V.F., Beckley Vicariate; CASEY B. MAHONE, V.F., Clarksburg Vicariate; Very Rev. Msgr. DEAN G. BORGMEYER, V.F., Charleston Vicariate; Very Revs. CARLOS L. MELOCOTON JR., V.F., Martinsburg Vicariate; J. STEPHEN VALLELONGA, V.F., Parkersburg Vicariate; DONALD X. HIGGS, V.F., Assoc., Charleston Vicariate.

Finance Council—Mailing Address: P.O. Box 230, Wheeling, 26003.

Chief Financial Officer—MR. WILLIAM G. FISHER, CPA, Mailing Address: P.O. Box 230, Wheeling, 26003. Tel: 304-233-0880.

Diocesan Offices and Directors

Apostleship of Prayer—Rev. Msgr. KEVIN MICHAEL QUIRK, J.C.D., J.V., Mailing Address: P.O. Box 230, Wheeling, 26003.

Archivists—MR. JON-ERIK GILOT, M.L.I.S.; MR. CHAD R. CARTER, M.B.A., B.A., Chancellor, Mailing Address: P.O. Box 230, Wheeling, 26003. Tel: 304-233-0880; Fax: 304-233-0890.

Behavioral Counseling and Ministry—Rev. ROBERT G.

PARK, Dir., Mailing Address: P.O. Box 230, Wheeling, 26003. Tel: 304-233-0880.

Diocesan School Board—Mailing Address: P.O. Box 230, Wheeling, 26003. Tel: 304-233-0880. MR. BRANN ALTMEYER, Chm.

Buildings and Properties—MR. JOHN REARDON, Dir., Mailing Address: P.O. Box 230, Wheeling, 26003. Tel: 304-233-0880.

(CCWVa) Catholic Charities West Virginia—Mailing Address: 2000 Main St., Wheeling, 26003. Tel: 304-905-9860; Fax: 304-905-9861. *Northern Regl. Office: 2000 Main St., Ste. #200, Wheeling, 26003.* Tel: 304-905-9860. *Western Regl. Office: 1116 Kanawha Blvd., E., Charleston, 25301.* Tel: 304-380-0162. *Mailing Address: Southern Regl. Office: P.O. Box 386, Princeton, 24740.* Tel: 304-425-4306. *Eastern Regl. Office: 224 S. Queen St., Martinsburg, 25401.* Tel: 304-267-8837. MRS. BETH ZARATE, CEO, Email: bethzarate@ccwva.org.

(CCWVa) Advancement Office—MS. PATRICIA PHILLIPS-BEST, Dir., 2000 Main St., Wheeling, 26003. Tel: 304-905-9860.

(CCWVa) Child and Adult Care Food Program—MRS. JANE ROSE, State Dir., 2000 Main St., Wheeling, 26003. Tel: 304-230-1280.

(CCWVa) Child Care Resource Center—965 Hartman Run Rd., Morgantown, 26505. Tel: 304-292-7357. MRS. BRITTANY LUCCI.

(CCWVa) Home Care Services—MRS. BARBARA HIGGINBOTHAM, Dir., 1116 Kanawha Blvd. E., Charleston, 25312. Tel: 304-345-2103.

(CCWVa) WV Birth to Three Region One—MS. WENDY MILLER, Dir., 2000 Main St., Wheeling, 26003. Tel: 304-214-5775.

Diocesan Newspaper: "The Catholic Spirit"—MRS. COLLEEN ROWAN, Exec. Editor, Mailing Address: P.O. Box 230, Wheeling, 26003-0030. Tel: 304-233-0880.

Diocesan Spokesperson—Mailing Address: P.O. Box 230, Wheeling, 26003-0030. Tel: 304-233-0880; Fax: 304-230-2029. MR. TIM BISHOP.

Catholic University of America, Friends of the—Mailing Address: P.O. Box 230, Wheeling, 26003. Tel: 304-233-0880. VACANT.

Cemeteries—Deacon DOUG BREIDING, Mailing Address: 1685 National Rd., Wheeling, 26003. Tel: 304-242-0460.

Censor Librorum—Rev. Msgr. KEVIN MICHAEL QUIRK, J.C.D., J.V.

Computer Information Systems—MR. RICHARD A. HARROLD, Dir. Technological Svcs.; MRS. KAREN KOVACS, Technology Support Svcs.; MR. ROBERT WICKHAM, Sr. Internet Technologies Engineer; MR. NICHOLAS GULISEK, Website Developer.

Stewardship and Development, Office of—MRS. KRISTEN BENSON, Dir.; MRS. HEIDI SFORZA, Asst. Dir.

Diaconate Executive Committee—Deacon ANTHONY F. MACIOROWSKI, Chm., 1759 Terrapin Neck Rd., Shepherdstown, 25443.

Finance Office—MR. WILLIAM G. FISHER, CPA, CFO; MR. MICHAEL DEEMER, CPA, Dir. Finance Oper.; MR. ALEX J. NAGEM, CPA, Dir. Finance for Risk Mgmt., Parishes & Schools; MR. FRANK BONACCI, Comptroller; MR. JUSTIN PASTORIUS, CPA, Mgr. Parish & School Finance; MR. SCOTT M. MILLARD, Purchasing Agent, Mailing Address: P.O. Box 230, Wheeling, 26003-0010. Tel: 304-233-0880; Fax: 304-232-7364.

Holy Childhood Association—Tel: 304-233-0880. VACANT.

Diocesan and Foreign Missions, Office of—Mailing Address: P.O. Box 230, Wheeling, 26003. VACANT, Coord.

Diocesan (Home) Missions—Mailing Address: P.O. Box 230, Wheeling, 26003. VACANT.

Propagation of the Faith, Pontifical Society for—Mailing Address: P.O. Box 230, Wheeling, 26003. VACANT.

Human Resources, Office of—Mailing Address: P.O. Box 230, Wheeling, 26003. Tel: 304-233-0880. MR. BRYAN E. MINOR, Dir.

Priests' Health and Retirement Association—Rev. Msgr. ANTHONY CINCINNATI, S.T.D., V.E., Vice Pres. & Mod.; MR. CHAD R. CARTER, M.B.A., B.A., Sec., Mailing Address: P.O. Box 230, Wheeling, 26003. Tel: 304-233-0880.

Justice and Life, Office of—Rev. BRIAN P. O'DONNELL, S.J., Ph.D., Interim Dir., 1116 Kanawha Blvd. E., Charleston, 25301. Tel: 304-380-0155.

Migration and Refugee Services - Charleston, Office of—1116 Kanawha Blvd. E., Charleston, 25301. Tel: 304-343-1036. MRS. ELIZABETH RAMSEY, Immigration & Refugee Spec.

Migration and Refugee Services - Martinsburg, Office of—224 S. Queen St., Martinsburg, 25401. CHRISTINE L. GLOVER, Immigration Attorney.

Formation and Mission, Dept. of—Mailing Address: 1322 Eoff St., 4th Fl., P.O. Box 230, Wheeling, 26003. Tel: 304-233-0880. MR. NICHOLAS S. MAYRAND, Dir.; MR. CHRISTOPHER BAYARDI, Formation Assoc., Marriage & Family Life.

Youth, Young Adult Ministry and Campus Ministry—MR. ROBERT PERRON, Dir., Mailing Address: P.O. Box 230, Wheeling, 26003. Tel: 304-233-0880.

Permanent Diaconate Formation—Rev. Msgr. ANTHONY CINCINNATI, S.T.D., V.E., Dir.; Deacon LOUIS J. BELLDINA, M.S., Prog. Assoc., P.O. Box 230, Wheeling, 26003. Tel: 304-233-0880.

Presbyteral Council—Rev. JAMES R. DEVIESE JR., J.C.L., Pres.

Prison Ministry, Office of—

Federal Facilities—Deacon JOHN W. SARRAGA, Dir., Mailing Address: P.O. Box 36, Buckhannon, 26201. Tel: 304-472-1217.

State Facilities—Deacon RUE C. THOMPSON JR., Dir., P.O. Box 36, Buckhannon, 26201. Tel: 304-472-1217.

Ecumenism, Office of—St. James XXIII Pastoral Center, 100 Hodges Rd., Charleston, 25314. Tel: 304-342-0507. MR. ERIC MILAM.

Safe Environment, Office of—MRS. SHARON K. GOUDY, Coord., Mailing Address: P.O. Box 230, Wheeling, 26003. Tel: 304-233-0880.

Catholic Committee on Scouting—MR. RICHARD E. FAUSS, Chm.; Rev. DENNIS R. SCHUELKENS JR., Chap.

Victim Assistance Coordinator—DR. PATRICIA M. BAILEY, Ph.D., 4 Poplar Ave. #5, Wheeling, 26003. Contacts to Report: Rev. Msgr. ANTHONY CINCINNATI, S.T.D., V.E., Episcopal Vicar for Clergy, Tel: 304-233-0880; Email: acincinnati@dwc.org; Sr. ELLEN F. DUNN, O.P., Email: edunn@dwc.org; MR. BRYAN E. MINOR, Email: bminor@dwc.org.

Vocations and Seminarians, Office of—Revs. DENNIS R. SCHUELKENS JR., Dir.; BRIAN J. CRENWELGE, Asst. Dir.; MR. RICHARD M. TEACHOUT, Office Mgr., Vocations.

Catholic Conference of West Virginia—Mailing Address: 1116 Kanawha Blvd. E., Charleston, 25301. Rev. BRIAN P. O'DONNELL, S.J., Ph.D., Exec. Dir.

Catholic Charismatic Renewal—Tel: 304-229-5014. Deacon BEN BRIAN CRIM, Liaison.

Office of Worship and Sacraments—MS. BERNADETTE MCMASTERS-KIME, D.Min., Dir., Mailing Address: P.O. Box 230, Wheeling, 26003-0030. Tel: 304-233-0880.

Diocesan Liturgical Commission—MS. BERNADETTE MCMASTERS-KIME, D.Min., Mailing Address: P.O. Box 230, Wheeling, 26003. Tel: 304-233-0880.

Department of Catholic Schools—

Schools, Superintendent of—Mailing Address: P.O. Box 230, Wheeling, 26003-0030. Tel: 304-233-0880. MRS. MARY ANN DESCHAINE, Ed.S., Supt.

Associate Superintendent for Accreditation and Technology—MS. JENNIFER L. HORNYAK.

Curriculum and Instruction—MRS. THERESA DIPIERO, Dir.

CLERGY, PARISHES, MISSIONS AND PAROCHIAL SCHOOLS

CITY OF WHEELING

(OHIO COUNTY)

1—CATHEDRAL OF ST. JOSEPH (1828) Including former parishes: Blessed Trinity, St. Joan of Arc, and Sacred Heart.
1218 Eoff St., 26003. Tel: 304-233-4121. 13th & Eoff Sts., 26003-0051. Email: cathedralofstjosephwheeling@dwc.org. Rev. Msgr. Kevin Michael Quirk, J.C.D., J.V., Rector. In Res., Rev. Robert G. Park.
Res.: 14 13th St., 26003-0051. Students 6.

2—ST. ALPHONSUS (1856) Including former parishes St. Mary and St. Ladislaus.
2111 Market St., 26003-3827. Tel: 304-232-4353; Fax: 304-905-8470; Email: saintalphonsuswheeling@gmail.com. Rev. Arui Anthony; Deacon George Smoulder.
Res.: 2103 Market St., 26003-3827.
Catechesis Religious Program—Sr. Ann Marie Cole, D.R.E. Students 21.

3—BLESSED TRINITY (1931) Closed. Merged with St. Joseph's Cathedral.

4—CORPUS CHRISTI (1916)
Mailing Address: 1518 Warwood Ave., 26003-7197. Tel: 304-277-2911; Fax: 304-277-1287; Email: office@corpuschrisitwheeling.org. Rev. Msgr. Eugene S. Ostrowski, V.F., (Retired); Deacon Douglas W. Breiding.
Res.: 1516 Warwood Ave., 26003-7197.
School—Corpus Christi School, 1512 Warwood Ave., 26003. Tel: 304-277-1220; Fax: 304-277-2823; Email: dtaylor26003@yahoo.com. Mr. Dick Taylor, Prin. Lay Teachers 13; Students 119.
Catechesis Religious Program—Students 35.

5—IMMACULATE CONCEPTION (ST. MARY) (1873) Closed. Merged with St. Alphonsus.

6—ST. JOAN OF ARC (1923) Closed. Merged with St. Joseph's Cathedral.

7—ST. LADISLAUS (1902) Closed. Merged with St. Alphonsus.

8—ST. MICHAEL (1897) [CEM]
1225 National Rd., 26003-5791. Tel: 304-242-1560; Fax: 304-243-5710; Email: stmikes@stmikesparish.org. Rev. Msgr. Joseph L. Peterson, V.F.; Revs. William K. Matheny Jr., V.F.; Martin Smay.
School—St. Michael School, 1221 National Rd., 26003. Tel: 304-242-3966; Fax: 304-214-6578; Email: mrskovalski@smpswv.org. Mrs. Jamie Kovalski, Prin. Lay Teachers 25; Students 316.
Catechesis Religious Program—Students 71.

9—OUR LADY OF PEACE (Mt. Olivet) (1962)
690 Mt. Olivet Rd., 26003. Tel: 304-242-6579; Email: parish@olpw.org. Rev. Joseph M. Augustine, H.G.N., J.C.L.
Res.: 26 Allendale Rd., Mt. Olivet, 26003-4602.
School—Our Lady of Peace School, Tel: 304-242-1383; Email: mkerr@olpschool.org. Maureen Kerr, Prin.
Catechesis Religious Program—Students 32.

10—SACRED HEART (1903) Closed. Merged with St. Joseph's Cathedral.

11—ST. VINCENT DE PAUL (1895) [CEM]
2244 Marshall Ave., 26003-7440. Tel: 304-242-0406; Fax: 304-243-0837; Email: info@saintvincentparish.org. Rev. Msgr. Paul A. Hudock.
School—St. Vincent de Paul School, 127 Key Ave., 26003. Tel: 304-242-5844; Fax: 304-243-1624; Email: lrossell@stvincentschool.org. Mrs. Laurajenn Rossell, Prin. Lay Teachers 17; Students 135; Religious Teacher 1.
Catechesis Religious Program—Sr. Rosella Uding, C.D.P., D.R.E. Students 50.
Mission—Our Lady of Seven Dolors, [CEM] Tel: 304-547-5342.

CITY OF CHARLESTON

(KANAWHA COUNTY)

1—ST. AGNES (1923)
4807 Staunton Ave., S.E., Charleston, 25304. Tel: 304-925-2836; Email: stagneschurch@suddenlink.net. 49th St. and Staunton Ave., S.E., Charleston, 25304. Rev. Jose Manuel Escalante.
School—St. Agnes School, 4801 Staunton Ave., S.E., Charleston, 25304. Tel: 304-925-4341; Fax: 304-925-4423; Email: cbulger@stagneswv.org; Web: www.stagneswv.org. Mr. Christopher Bulger, Prin. Lay Teachers 15; Students 130.
Catechesis Religious Program—Students 20.

2—ST. ANTHONY (1905)
1000 Sixth St., Charleston, 25302. Tel: 304-342-2716 ; Email: secretary@stanthonywv.com; Web: www.stanthonywv.com. Revs. Tijo George, Admin.; Charles Anemelu, In Res.; Deacon David Wuletich.
Catechesis Religious Program—Email: mwuletich.lpc@gmail.com. Mary Wuletich, D.R.E. Students 8.

3—BASILICA OF THE CO-CATHEDRAL OF THE SACRED HEART (1866) [CEM]
1114 Virginia St. E., Charleston, 25301-2407. Tel: 304-342-8175; Fax: 304-344-3907; Email: sacredheart@shccwv.us. 1032 Virginia St. E, Charleston, 25301. Very Rev. Donald X. Higgs, V.F., Rector; Revs. Binu Emmanuel, Rector; Brian P. O'Donnell, S.J., Ph.D., In Res.
School—Basilica of the Co-Cathedral of the Sacred Heart School, 1035 Quarrier St. E., Charleston, 25301. Tel: 304-346-5491; Fax: 304-342-0870; Web: shgs.us. Susan Malinoski, Prin. Lay Teachers 33; Students 344.
Catechesis Religious Program—Alyce Penniman, D.R.E. Students 83.

OUTSIDE THE CITIES OF WHEELING AND CHARLESTON

ALDERSON, GREENBRIER CO., ST. MARY (1978) Closed. See St. Patrick, Hinton.

BANCROFT, PUTNAM CO., ST. PATRICK MISSION (1892) Holy Trinity Parish, P.O. Box 339, Nitro, 25143. Tel: 304-586-3485; Email: nitrocatholic@aol.com. 207

Jefferson St., Bancroft, 25011. Rev. Prakash Sebastian, H.G.N., Admin.
Catechesis Religious Program—Lisa Bailey, D.R.E. Students 18.

BARRACKVILLE, MARION CO., ALL SAINTS, Merged with St. Joseph, Fairmont; St. Anthony, Grant Town, and Our Lady of the Assumption, Rivesville to form St. Peter the Fisherman, Fairmont.

BARTOW, POCAHONTAS CO., ST. MARK THE EVANGELIST MISSION (1977) [CEM] See St. John Neumann, Marlinton
Tel: 304-799-6778. Rev. Arthur Bufogle.
Catechesis Religious Program—Students 3.

BECKLEY, RALEIGH CO., ST. FRANCIS DE SALES (1907) [CEM]
614 S. Oakwood Ave., Beckley, 25801.
Tel: 304-253-3695 (Rectory);
Tel: 304-256-3594 (Parish); Fax: 304-253-3694; Email: church@stfrancis-wv.org; Web: st-francis-wv.org. Very Rev. Paul J. Wharton, V.F.; Deacons W. Donald Wise; John F. Ziolkowski; Harry K. Evans.
School—St. Francis de Sales School, (Grades K-8), 622 S. Oakwood Ave., Beckley, 25801.
Tel: 304-252-4087; Fax: 304-252-4087; Email: sfschool@suddenlinkmail.com. Mrs. Karen Wynne, Prin. Lay Teachers 15; Students 194.
Catechesis Religious Program—626 S. Oakwood Ave., Beckley, 25801. Tel: 304-255-4694; Email: osfjanice@stfrancis-wv.org. Students 87.

BELLE, KANAWHA CO., ST. JOHN (1951) Closed. For inquiries for parish records contact the chancery.

BENWOOD, MARSHALL CO., ST. JOHN (1875)
Mailing Address: c/o St. Alphonsus Parish 2111 Market St., 26003. Tel: 304-232-6455. 622 Main St., Benwood, 26031. Rev. Arui Anthony, Admin.
Res.: 2103 Market St., 26003.
Catechesis Religious Program—Mrs. Mary Rose Robbins, D.R.E. Students 10.

BERKELEY SPRINGS, MORGAN CO., ST. VINCENT DE PAUL (1931) [CEM]
67 Liberty St., P.O Box 634, Berkeley Springs, 25411-0634. Rev. Leonard A. Smith.
Catechesis Religious Program—Students 47.

BLUEFIELD, MERCER CO., SACRED HEART (1895)
Mailing Address: P.O. Box 608, Bluefield, 24701-0608. Tel: 304-327-5623; Fax: 304-327-7769; Email: khickman@sacredheartblfd.org; Email: dianeott@sacredheartblfd.org. 1003 Wyoming St., Bluefield, 24701. Rev. Sebastian Embrayil Devasya; Deacon Donald Hammond.
Res.: 1019 Wyoming St., Bluefield, 24701-0608.
Catechesis Religious Program—Students 50.

BOOMER, FAYETTE CO., ST. ANTHONY'S SHRINE (1954) See Immaculate Conception, Montgomery
Immaculate Conception Parish, P.O. Box 65, Montgomery, 25136-0065. Rev. Dominikus Baok, S.V.D., Admin.

BRIDGEPORT, HARRISON CO., ALL SAINTS (1946)
317 E. Main St., Bridgeport, 26330-1750.
Tel: 304-842-2283; Fax: 304-842-2299; Email: allsaintswv@gmail.com. Rev. Benedict E. Kapa.
School—Harrison Co. Catholic School System.
Catechesis Religious Program—Students 171.

BUCKHANNON, UPSHUR CO., HOLY ROSARY (1921)
35 Franklin St., P.O. Box 848, Buckhannon, 26201-0848. Tel: 304-472-3414; Email: hrp2306buc@dwc.org. Rev. Joseph J. McLaughlin, S.M.; Bro. Roy Madigan, S.M.; Deacon Rue Thompson Jr.
Rectory—9 Lincoln Heights Dr., Buckhannon, 26021.
Catechesis Religious Program—Students 50.
Mission—Sacred Heart (1902) [CEM] Pickens, Randolph Co. 26230.

CAIRO, RITCHIE CO., ST. WILLIAM CHURCH, Closed. See Christ Our Hope, Harrisville.

CAMDEN, LEWIS CO., ST. BONIFACE (Leading Creek) (1875) [CEM]
9140 U.S. Hwy. 33 W., Camden, 26338-8256.
Tel: 304-269-1767; Email: saintbonifacechurch@yahoo.com. Rev. James R. DeViese Jr., J.C.L.
Chapel—St. Clare, St. Clare, [CEM] .
Catechesis Religious Program—Students 13.

CAMERON, MARSHALL CO., ST. MARTIN OF TOURS CHAPEL (1871) [CEM]
1 Fitzgerald Ave., Cameron, 26033. Mailing Address: c/o St. Francis Xavier Church, 912 7th St., Moundsville, 26041. Tel: 304-845-1593; Email: sfxmoundsville@comcast.net. Rev. That Son Ngoc Nguyen.
Catechesis Religious Program—Mary Helen Marling, D.R.E. Students 2.

CAROLINA, MARION CO., ST. MARY, Closed. Consolidated with St. Peter's Church, Farmington.

CENTURY, UPSHUR CO., OUR LADY OF SORROWS, Closed. See Holy Rosary, Buckhannon. Suppressed as a mission 12/20/96.

CHAPMANVILLE, LOGAN CO., ST. BARBARA (1979) See St. Francis, Logan
Tel: 304-855-7962; Email: nbuchlein@dwc.org. Rev. Neil R. Buchlein.
Catechesis Religious Program—
Mission—St. Barbara Catholic Community Church, 33 Saw Mill Rd., Chapmanville, 25508.
Tel: 304-855-7962.

CHARLES TOWN, JEFFERSON CO., ST. JAMES (1889) [CEM] Includes St. Peter, Harper's Ferry.
Mailing Address: 49 Crosswinds Dr., Charles Town, 25414-3933. Tel: 304-725-5558; Fax: 304-728-9039; Email: parsec@stjameswv.org. Very Rev. John S. Ledford, V.F.; Rev. Jose Manuel Escalante; Deacons James T. Munuhe; Luis A. Pagano; David E. Galvin; Mr. Gary Penkala, Liturgy & Music.
Res.: 311 S. George St., Charles Town, 25414-1633.
Tel: 304-725-6801.
Catechesis Religious Program—Students 350.
Chapel—St. Peter.

CHEAT LAKE, MONONGALIA CO., ST. LUKE THE EVANGELIST (1980)
19 Jo Glen Dr., Morgantown, 26508-4434.
Tel: 304-594-2353; Fax: 304-594-2359; Email: st.luke.secretary@comcast.net. Rev. Biju T. Devassy.
School—St. Francis Central Catholic School, 41 Guthrie Ln., Morgantown, 26508. Tel: 304-291-5070; Fax: 304-291-5104; Email: ammore@stfrancismorgantown.com. Mr. Arthur Moore, Prin. Students 380.
Catechesis Religious Program—Students 85.

CHESTER, HANCOCK CO., SACRED HEART (1902)
418 4th St., Chester, 26034-0313. Tel: 304-387-0198; Email: shp2226ches@dwc.org; Web: sacredheart1925.dudaone.com. 424 4th St., Chester, 26034-0313. Rev. Jeeson Venattu Stephan, Admin.
Catechesis Religious Program—Web: sacredheart1925@comcast.net. Mr. Robert Glass, D.R.E. Students 68.

CLARKSBURG, HARRISON CO.
1—HOLY ROSARY, Merged See Immaculate Conception, Clarksburg.
2—HOLY TRINITY, Closed. See Immaculate Conception, Clarksburg.
3—IMMACULATE CONCEPTION (1864) [CEM]
126 E. Pike St., Clarksburg. Mailing Address: 150 S. Maple Ave., Clarksburg, 26301. Tel: 304-622-8243; Email: icchurchclarksburg@gmail.com. Very Rev. Casey B. Mahone, V.F.
Catechesis Religious Program—Students 140.
4—ST. JAMES THE APOSTLE (1924)
2107 Pride Ave., Clarksburg, 26301-1819.
Tel: 304-622-1668; Fax: 304-622-4618; Email: stjamesparishclarksburg@gmail.com. Pride Ave. & N. 21st St., Clarksburg, 26301. Rev. Akila Gayan Rodrigo, T.O.R.
School—Harrison County Catholic School System, Tel: 304-623-1026; Tel: 304-622-9831;
Fax: 304-623-1026. See Immaculate Conception.
Catechesis Religious Program—Tel: 304-624-5811. Students 41.
5—ST. JOHN THE BAPTIST, Closed. See Immaculate Conception, Clarksburg.

CLENDENIN, KANAWHA CO., ST. ANNE, Closed. See Our Lady of the Hills, Elkview.

COALBURG, KANAWHA CO., GOOD SHEPHERD MISSION (1866) Closed. Suppressed to a chapel.

COALTON, RANDOLPH CO., ST. PATRICK CHURCH (1918) [CEM 4]
200 Church St., Coalton, 26257. Mailing Address: P.O. Box 99, Coalton, 26257-0099. Tel: 304-636-0546; Email: joconnor@dwc.org. Rev. James O'Connor, Pastor.
Catechesis Religious Program—Students 9.

DAVIS, TUCKER CO., ST. VERONICA (1897) Closed. For inquiries for parish records, please see St. Thomas Aquinas Church, Thomas.

DUNBAR, KANAWHA CO., CHRIST THE KING (1942)
Holy Trinity Parish, P.O. Box 339, Nitro, 25143-0339. Tel: 304-755-0791; Fax: 304-755-3473; Email: nitrocatholic@aol.com. 1504 Grosscup Ave., Dunbar, 25064. Rev. Prakash Sebastian, H.G.N.
Catechesis Religious Program—Students 21.

ELIZABETH, WIRT CO., ST. ELIZABETH OF HUNGARY (1977) See Holy Redeemer, Spencer.
24 Butternut St., Elizabeth, 26143.
Tel: 304-275-4226; Email: rprechtl@dwc.org. Rev. Ronald G. Prechtl, Pastor.

ELKINS, RANDOLPH CO., ST. BRENDAN (1897) [CEM]
Mailing Address: 181 Street Brendan Way, Elkins, 26241. Tel: 304-636-0546; Email: stbrendanchurch.elkinswv@gmail.com. Rev. James O'Connor; Deacons John W. Sarraga; Raymond Godwin.
Res.: R.R. 4, Box 515, Elkins, 26241.
Catechesis Religious Program—Students 63.
Chapel—St. John Bosco (1948) Rte. 1, Box 9D, Huttonsville, 26273-9737.
Station—Huttonsville Correctional Center, Huttonsville. Tel: 304-338-6323.

ELKVIEW, KANAWHA CO., OUR LADY OF THE HILLS (1977)
100 Jackson Dr., Elkview, 25071. St. Anthony Catholic Church, 1000 6th St., Charleston, 25302. Rev. Tijo George, Admin.
Catechesis Religious Program—Tel: 304-343-0631; Email: mu_wvit@msn.com. Tina Stodola, D.R.E. Students 14.

FAIRMONT, MARION CO.
1—ST. ANTHONY (1964)
1660 Mary Lou Retton Dr., Fairmont, 26554.
Tel: 304-363-1328; Email: parishoffice@sahswv.org. Rev. Vincent Ezhanikatt Joseph, (India).
School—Fairmont Catholic Grade School, 416 Madison St., Fairmont, 26554. Tel: 304-363-5313; Email: sspadafore@fairmontcatholic.com. Stacey Spadafore, Prin. Clergy 6; Lay Teachers 13; Students 144.
Catechesis Religious Program—Students 43.
2—IMMACULATE CONCEPTION (1960)
Mailing Address: 406 Alta Vista Ave., Fairmont, 26554. Tel: 304-363-5796; Fax: 304-366-4937; Email: church@icfairmont.com. 329 Maryland Ave., Fairmont, 26554. Rev. Walter M. Jagela; Sr. Stella Cronauer, C.S.J., Pastoral Assoc.
School—Fairmont Catholic Grade School, 416 Madison St., Fairmont, 26554. Tel: 304-363-5313; Email: sspadafore@fairmontcatholic.com. Stacey Spadafore, Prin. Faculty 15; Students 138.
Catechesis Religious Program—Students 65.
3—ST. JOSEPH'S (1909) Merged with St. Peter's, Fairmont to form The New St. Peter the Fisherman, Fairmont.
4—ST. PETER THE FISHERMAN CATHOLIC CHURCH (1873) [CEM 2]
407 Jackson St., Fairmont, 26554-2941.
Tel: 304-363-7434; Fax: 304-363-2660; Email: churchoffice@thefisherman.org; Web: www.thefisherman.org. Rev. Joseph Konikattil, Admin.; Deacon David P. Lester.
School—Fairmont Catholic Grade School, 416 Madison St., Fairmont, 26554. Tel: 304-363-5313;
Fax: 304-363-7701; Email: sspadafore@fairmontcatholic.com. Stacey Spadafore, Prin. Faculty 15; Students 201.
Catechesis Religious Program—Students 15.

FARMINGTON, MARION CO., ST. PETER'S (1921)
Mailing Address: 204 Furbee Ave., Mannington, 26582-1399. Tel: 304-986-2321; Email: stpatstpete@comcast.net. 1304 Mill St., Farmington, 26571. Rev. Vincy Sebastian Illickal, T.O.R., Admin.
Catechesis Religious Program—Missy Latocha, D.R.E. Students 9.

FOLLANSBEE, BROOKE CO., ST. ANTHONY (1906)
1017 Jefferson St., Follansbee, 26037-1334.
Tel: 304-527-2286; Fax: 304-527-2548; Email: stanthonychurch@comcast.net. Rev. Cody C. Ford, Admin.
Catechesis Religious Program—Students 93.

FORT ASHBY, MINERAL CO., ANNUNCIATION OF OUR LORD (1981)
Mailing Address: 8819 Frankfort Hwy., P.O. Box 1560, Fort Ashby, 26719-1560. Tel: 304-298-3392;
Fax: 304-298-3419; Email: annunciationchurch@atlanticbbn.net. Rev. J. Michael O. Lecias.
Res.: 8871 Frankfort Hwy., Fort Ashby, 26719-1560.
Catechesis Religious Program—Students 15.

FRANKLIN, PENDLETON CO., ST. ELIZABETH ANN SETON (1975)
167 Walnut St., P.O. Box 890, Franklin, 26807.
Tel: 304-358-7012; Tel: 304-668-9517; Email: seton9@sksrt.net. Rev. Mario R. Claro, (Retired); Deacon John E. Windett.
Rectory—141 Walnut St., Franklin, 26807.
Catechesis Religious Program—Students 22.

GARY, MCDOWELL CO., OUR LADY OF VICTORY CHAPEL (1904) [CEM]
81 Miracle Mountain Rd., Gary, 24836.
Tel: 304-436-2014; Email: llascon@dwc.org. Mailing Address: c/o 111 Virginia Ave., Welch, 24801. Rev. Luis A. Lacson.
Church: 38 Church St., Gary, 24836.
Tel: 304-448-2749.
Catechesis Religious Program—Students 2.

GASSAWAY, BRAXTON CO., ST. THOMAS (1973)
624 Kanawha St., Gassaway, 26624-1208.
Tel: 304-364-5895; Email: stthomasgassaway@gmail.com. Rev. Thien Duc Nguyen, S.V.D., Admin.
Catechesis Religious Program—

GLEN DALE, MARSHALL CO., ST. JUDE (1968)
710 Jefferson Ave., P.O. Box 147, Glen Dale, 26038-0147. Tel: 304-845-2646; Fax: 304-845-3015; Email: office@stjudewv.com. Very Rev. John S. Ledford, V.F.
Catechesis Religious Program—Students 20.

GLENVILLE, GILMER CO., GOOD SHEPHERD (1958)
701 Mineral Rd., Glenville, 26351-1310.
Tel: 304-462-7130; Email: goodshepherdglenville@gmail.com. Rev. James R. DeViese Jr., J.C.L., Pastor.
Catechesis Religious Program—Students 5.

GRAFTON, TAYLOR CO., ST. AUGUSTINE (1852) [CEM 2] (Irish)
17 W. Washington St., Grafton, 26354-1398.
Tel: 304-265-1848; Tel: 304-265-3861;
Fax: 304-265-2810; Email:

staugustinegrafton@comcast.net. Rev. Binu Sebastian, Admin.
Catechesis Religious Program—Students 12.
GRANT TOWN, MARION CO., ST. ANTHONY'S (1907) Merged with St. Joseph, Fairmont; Our Lady of the Assumption, Rivesville and All Saints, Barrackville to form St. Peter the Fisherman, Fairmont.
GRANTSVILLE, CALHOUN CO., JESUS CHRIST, PRINCE OF PEACE (1977) Closed. See Holy Redeemer, Spencer. Suppressed as a mission 12/1/08.
HAMLIN, LINCOLN CO., CHRIST IN THE HILLS, Closed. See St. Stephen, Ona or St. Mary, Madison.
HARPERS FERRY, JEFFERSON CO., ST. PETER (1830) Closed. Merged with St. James, Charles Town.
HARRISVILLE, RITCHIE CO., CHRIST OUR HOPE MISSION (1980) [CEM]
117 Plum Alley, Harrisville, 26362-7357.
Tel: 304-643-4261; Email: prcatholicwv@gmail.com. St. John Parish, 310 Washington St., St. Marys, 26170. Rev. Ronald G. Prechtl.
Catechesis Religious Program—Students 6.
HEDGESVILLE, BERKELEY CO., ST. BERNADETTE MISSION (1982) See St. Joseph, Martinsburg
113 W. Main St., P.O. Box 11, Hedgesville, 25427.
Tel: 304-754-7830; Fax: 304-754-7830; Email: office@stbernadettewv.org. Rev. Thomas R. Gallagher, Pastor; Mrs. Shannon Winkelman, Sec.; Rev. George Pucciarelli.
Catechesis Religious Program—Students 39.
HINTON, SUMMERS CO., ST. PATRICK (1874) [CEM 2] (Irish)
309-2nd Ave., Hinton, 25951-0008. Tel: 304-466-3966 ; Email: StPatHintonWV@yahoo.com; Web: www.StPatrickHintonWV.org. Rev. William K. Matheny Jr., V.F., Admin.; Deacons Robert A. Holliday, Pastoral Assoc.; Peter F. Minogue, Pastoral Assoc.
Chapel—St. Colman (1882) (Irish Mountain, WV).
Catechesis Religious Program—Email: psychedinwv@yahoo.com. Cam Pulliam, D.R.E. Students 14.
HOLDEN, LOGAN CO., ST. MARY'S (1961) Consolidated with Our Lady of Mount Carmel, Logan, to form St. Francis of Assisi, Logan.
HUNTINGTON, CABELL CO.
1—ST. JOSEPH CATHOLIC CHURCH (1872) [CEM]
1304 Sixth Ave., P.O. Box 369, Huntington, 25708.
Tel: 304-525-5202; Fax: 304-525-0903; Email: dborgmeyer@dwc.org; Web: www.stjoeshuntington.org. Very Rev. Msgr. Dean G. Borgmeyer, V.F.
Schools—St. Joseph Catholic School—(Grades PreK-8), 1326 Sixth Ave., Huntington, 25701.
Tel: 304-522-2644; Fax: 304-522-2512; Email: ctempleton@stjosephgs.org; Web: www.stjosephgs.org. Mrs. Carol Templeton, Prin. Lay Teachers 49; Students 400.
St. Joseph Central Catholic High School, 600 13th St., Huntington, 25701. Tel: 304-525-5096;
Fax: 304-525-0781; Email: bill.archer@stjosephs.org; Web: www.stjosephhs.org. Mr. William Archer, Prin. Lay Teachers 14; Students 161.
Catechesis Religious Program—Matthew Nadalin, D.R.E. Students 30.
2—OUR LADY OF FATIMA (1952)
545 Norway Ave., Huntington, 25705.
Tel: 304-525-0866; Email: church@olofatima.org. Rev. Paul Yuenger.
School—Our Lady of Fatima School, 535 Norway Ave., Huntington, 25705. Tel: 304-523-2861;
Fax: 304-525-0390; Email: jnaswadi@olofatima.org. Ms. Jena Saseen, Prin. Lay Teachers 20; Students 178.
Catechesis Religious Program—Students 45.
3—ST. PETER CLAVER (1937) (African American)
P.O. Box 326, Huntington, 25708. Tel: 304-523-7311; Email: spchwv@gmail.com. 828-15th St., Huntington, 25701. Rev. Douglas A. Ondeck.
Catechesis Religious Program—Students 14.
4—SACRED HEART (1934)
2015 Adams Ave., Huntington, 25704-1419.
Tel: 304-429-4318; Fax: 304-429-4319; Email: shcchwv@gmail.com. Rev. Douglas A. Ondeck; Sr. Mary Terence Wall, S.A.C., Pastoral Assoc.
Catechesis Religious Program—Students 33.
HURRICANE, PUTNAM CO., CATHOLIC CHURCH OF THE ASCENSION (1980)
905 Hickory Mill Rd., Hurricane, 25526.
Tel: 304-562-5816; Email: ascensionwv@hotmail.com. Rev. Leon F. Alexander, Admin., (Retired).
Catechesis Religious Program—Students 142.
INWOOD, BERKELEY CO., ST. LEO (1982)
2109 Sulphur Springs Rd., P.O. Box 93, Inwood, 25428-0093. Tel: 304-229-8945; Fax: 304-229-6609; Email: aobiudu@dwc.org. Rev. Alfred U. Obiudu, (Nigeria).
Catechesis Religious Program—Students 250.
KEYSER, MINERAL CO., ASSUMPTION (1874) [CEM]
34 James St., Keyser, 26726-2721. Tel: 304-788-2488 ; Fax: 304-788-0647; Email: acckwv@gmail.com. Revs. Thomas Sebastian, Admin.; Binoy Thomas.
Catechesis Religious Program—Students 85.
KINGWOOD, PRESTON CO., ST. SEBASTIAN (1914) [CEM 2]
322 E. Main St., Kingwood, 26537-1237.
Tel: 304-329-1519; Fax: 304-329-2546; Email: prestoncountycatholic@yahoo.com. 324 E. Main St., Kingwood, 26537. Rev. Andrew M. Switzer.
Catechesis Religious Program—Students 50.
Mission—St. Edward, 1204 E. State Ave., Terra Alta, Preston Co. 26764.
LEWISBURG, GREENBRIER CO., ST. LOUIS, KING OF FRANCE, Closed. See St. Catherine, Ronceverte.
LITTLETON, WETZEL CO., ASSUMPTION OF THE BLESSED VIRGIN MARY, Closed. For inquiries for parish records contact the chancery.
LOGAN, LOGAN CO., ST. FRANCIS OF ASSISI (1996)
561 Main St., Logan, 25601-3899. Tel: 304-752-3017; Email: stfap1916log@dwc.org. Rev. Yesu Golla, H.G.N.; Mrs. Connie Bazzilla, Pastoral Assoc.
Catechesis Religious Program—Students 9.
Mission—St. Barbara Catholic Community, HC-74 Box 25508, Chapmanville, 25508. Tel: 304-855-7962; Web: chapmanvillewvcatholicweb.com.
LOVEBERRY, LEWIS CO., ST. BERNARD, Suppressed as a mission. See St. Patrick, Weston.
Snowshoe Dr., Snowshoe, 26209. Tel: 304-799-6778; Email: abufogle@dwc.org. Rev. Arthur Bufogle, Pastor.
LUBECK, WOOD CO., ST. MONICA MISSION (1976) [CEM]
1942 Harris Hwy., Lubeck, 26181. Mailing Address: c/o St. Francis Xavier, 609 Market St., Parkersburg, 26101-5144. Tel: 304-422-6768; Email: jrice@dwc.org. Rev. John Rice.
Catechesis Religious Program—Students 3.
MADISON, BOONE CO., ST. MARY, QUEEN OF HEAVEN (1957)
P.O. Box 467, Madison, 25130. Tel: 304-369-4538. Rev. Neil R. Buchlein.
Church: 51 Madison Ave., Madison, 25130.
Catechesis Religious Program—
Mission—St. Joseph the Worker, State Route 3, Whitesville, 25209. Tel: 304-854-2997; Email: nbuchlein@dwc.org.
MAN, LOGAN CO., ST. EDMUND (1961)
106 N. Bridge St., Man, 25635. Tel: 304-583-2476; Fax: 304-239-3131; Email: ygolla@dwc.org. Rev. Yesu Golla, H.G.N.
Catechesis Religious Program—Karen Arons, D.R.E.
MANNINGTON, MARION CO., ST. PATRICK'S (1897) (Irish)
204 Furbee Ave., Mannington, 26582-1399.
Tel: 304-986-2321; Email: stpatstpete@comcast.net. Rev. Vincy Sebastian Illickal, T.O.R.
Catechesis Religious Program—April Powell, D.R.E. Students 13.
Mission—Assumption of the Blessed Virgin Mary (1859) [CEM 2] (Suppressed Sept. 1, 2001).
MARLINTON, POCAHONTAS CO., ST. JOHN NEUMANN (1977)
Mailing Address: 714 10th Ave., Marlinton, 24954-1314. Tel: 304-799-6778; Email: pastor@pocahontascatholic.org. Rev. Arthur Bufogle. Res.: 718 10th Ave., Marlinton, 24954-1314.
Mission—St. Mark the Evangelist (1977) Catholic Church Rd., Bartow, Pocahontas Co. 24920.
Chapel—St. Bernard, Snowshoe, 10 Snowshoe Dr., Snowshoe, 26209.
Catechesis Religious Program—Students 2.
MARTINSBURG, BERKELEY CO., ST. JOSEPH'S (1803) [CEM 2]
Mailing Address: 336 S. Queen St., Martinsburg, 25401. Tel: 304-267-4893; Fax: 304-263-7357; Email: office@stjosephwv.org. 225 S. Queen St., Martinsburg, 25401. Rev. Thomas R. Gallagher. Res.: 219 S. Queen St., Martinsburg, 25401-3213.
School—St. Joseph's School, 110 E. Stephen St., Martinsburg, 25401. Tel: 304-267-6447;
Fax: 304-267-6573; Email: info@sjswv.org; Web: www.sjswv.org. Lay Teachers 25; Students 295.
Catechesis Religious Program—Students 140.
Mission—St. Bernadette, Office: 113 W. Main St., P.O. Box 11, Hedgesville, Berkeley Co. 25427.
Tel: 304-754-7830; Fax: 304-754-7830; Email: stbernadette@frontier.com.
MASONTOWN, PRESTON CO., ST. ZITA MISSION (1962) [CEM]
33 Maple St., Masontown, 26542. Tel: 304-329-1519; Email: prestoncountycatholic@yahoo.com. Mailing Address: c/o St. Sebastian Church, 322 E. Main St., Kingwood, 26537-1237. Rev. Andrew M. Switzer.
Rectory—St. Zita Rectory, 152 Roosevelt Ave., Masontown, 26542. Tel: 304-329-1519; Email: stzitamasontown@dwc.org.
Catechesis Religious Program—Students 8.
MAYSEL, CLAY CO., RISEN LORD MISSION (1972)
Mailing Address: 67 Wallback Rd., Maysel, 25133.
Tel: 304-587-4740; Email: risenlordchurch@gmail.com. Rev. Thien Duc Nguyen, S.V.D., Admin.
Catechesis Religious Program—Students 2.
MCMECHEN, MARSHALL CO., ST. JAMES (1900)
Mailing Address: c/o St. Alphonsus Parish 2111 Market St., 26003. Tel: 304-232-1227; Email: offices@saintjamesandjohn.org. 328 Logan St., McMechen, 26040. Rev. Arui Anthony.
Catechesis Religious Program—Students 10.
MIDDLEBOURNE, TYLER CO., ST. LAWRENCE, Closed. Suppressed as a Mission Oct. 1, 2014.
MONONGAH, MARION CO., HOLY SPIRIT (1975) [CEM] (Polish—Italian)
687 Maple Ter., Monongah, 26554-1116.
Tel: 304-534-3020; Email: parishoffice@sahswv.org. Rev. Vincent Ezhanikatt Joseph, (India).
Catechesis Religious Program—Students 38.
MONTGOMERY, FAYETTE CO., IMMACULATE CONCEPTION (1888)
708 First Ave., P.O. Box 65, Montgomery, 25136-0065. Tel: 304-442-2101; Email: IC_SA@frontier.com. Rev. Dominikus Baok, S.V.D., Admin.; Deacon John Divita.
Catechesis Religious Program—Students 15.
Mission—St. Anthony Shrine (1928) 2764 Midland Trail, Rte. 60, Boomer, Fayette Co. 25031.
Tel: 304-779-5561.
MOOREFIELD, HARDY CO., EPIPHANY OF THE LORD (1980) [CEM] [JC]
2029 State Rd. 55, Moorefield, 26836.
Tel: 304-434-2547; Email: ephiphanyrc@hardynet.com. Rev. Joshua R. Stevens.
Catechesis Religious Program—Students 12.
MORGANTOWN, MONONGALIA CO.
1—ST. FRANCIS DE SALES CATHOLIC CHURCH (2003) (Formerly The New St. Theresa & St. Elizabeth Ann Seton)
One Guthrie Ln., Morgantown, 26508-4837.
Tel: 304-296-5353; Email: stfrancissecretary@gmail.com; Web: www.stfrancisdesalesparish.com. Rev. Msgr. Anthony Cincinnati, S.T.D., V.E.; Deacon John Yaquinta; Sr. Nancy White, C.S.J., Pastoral Assoc.
School—St. Francis Central Catholic School, 41 Guthrie Ln., Morgantown, 26508. Tel: 304-291-5070; Email: amoore@stfrancismorgantown.com. Mr. Arthur Moore, Prin.
Catechesis Religious Program—Students 90.
2—ST. JOHN UNIVERSITY PARISH, NEWMAN HALL (1966)
1481 University Ave., Morgantown, 26505-5598.
Tel: 304-296-8231; Fax: 304-296-4650; Email: stjohnmorgantown@comcast.net; Web: www.mountaineercatholic.com. Rev. Walter M. Jagela; Deacon Joseph Prentiss.
School—St. Francis Central Catholic School, 41 Guthrie Ln., Morgantown, 26508. Tel: 304-291-5070; Fax: 304-291-5104; Email: amoore@stfrancismorgantown.com. Mr. Arthur Moore, Prin.
Catechesis Religious Program—Students 70.
MOUNDSVILLE, MARSHALL CO., ST. FRANCIS XAVIER'S (1857)
912 - 7th St., Moundsville, 26041-2106.
Tel: 304-845-1593; Fax: 304-845-2006; Email: sfxmoundsville@comcast.net. 7th & Jefferson Ave., Moundsville, 26041. Rev. That Son Ngoc Nguyen. Church: 610 Jefferson Ave., Moundsville, 26041-2106.
Catechesis Religious Program—Students 12.
Station—Northern Regional Jail and Correctional Facility, Moundsville. Tel: 304-843-4067.
MULLENS, WYOMING CO., ST. JOHN THE EVANGELIST (1923) Merged with St. Peter, Welch.
NEW CUMBERLAND, HANCOCK CO., IMMACULATE CONCEPTION (1904)
1016 Ridge Ave., New Cumberland, 26047-0666.
Tel: 304-564-5068; Email: iccparish@comcast.net. Rev. Jeeson Venattu Stephan, Admin.
Catechesis Religious Program—Tel: 304-564-3457. Lori Kaczmarek, D.R.E. Students 8.
NEW MARTINSVILLE, WETZEL CO., ST. VINCENT DE PAUL (1901)
21 Rosary Rd., New Martinsville, 26155-1602.
Tel: 304-455-4615; Fax: 304-455-4617; Email: office@svdpnm.org. Rev. Symeon Galazka, O.S.B., Admin.
Catechesis Religious Program—Students 33.
NITRO, KANAWHA CO., HOLY TRINITY (1962)
2219 - 22nd St., P.O. Box 339, Nitro, 25143-0339.
Tel: 304-755-0791; Fax: 304-755-3473; Email: nitrocatholic@aol.com. Rev. Thomas Kalapurackal.
Catechesis Religious Program—Students 30.
Mission—St. Patrick, 207 Jefferson St., P.O. Box 339, Nitro, Putnam Co. 25143. Tel: 304-586-3485.
OAK HILL, FAYETTE CO., SS. PETER AND PAUL (1906) [CEM]
129 Elmore St., Oak Hill, 25901-2628.
Tel: 304-465-5445; Email: ssppp1216oh@dwc.org. Rev. Soosai Arpudam Arokiadass, H.G.N., (India). Res.: 122 Elmore St., Oak Hill, 25901-2628.
School—SS. Peter and Paul School, 123 Elmore St., Oak Hill, 25901-2628. Tel: 304-465-5045;
Fax: 304-465-8726; Email: principal@ssppcatholic.org. Mr. Ricky White, Prin. Lay Teachers 8; Students 96.
Catechesis Religious Program—Students 71.
ONA, CABELL CO., ST. STEPHEN CATHOLIC CHURCH (1980)
2491 James River Tpke., Ona, 25545.
Tel: 304-743-3234; Email:

ststephens@suddenlinkmail.com. Rev. Thomas Kalapurackal.
Catechesis Religious Program—Students 16.

PADEN CITY, TYLER AND WETZEL COS., MATER DOLOROSA (1921)
302 E. Main St., Paden City, 26159-1736.
Tel: 304-337-9837; Email: mdp2136pc@dwc.org. Rev. Brian J. Crenwelge, Admin.; Deacon N. Rollin Fagert.
Catechesis Religious Program—Students 2.

PARKERSBURG, WOOD CO.
1—ST. FRANCIS XAVIER (1853) [CEM 3]
Mailing Address: 609 Market St., Parkersburg, 26101. Tel: 304-422-6786; Email: stxoffice@stxpburg.org. 532 Market St., Parkersburg, 26101. Rev. John Rice; Deacon Douglas A. Deem.
Catechesis Religious Program—Students 43.
2—ST. MARGARET MARY (1923)
2500 Dudley Ave., Parkersburg, 26101-2695.
Tel: 304-428-1262; Fax: 304-442-4905; Email: jvallelonga@dwc.org. Very Rev. J. Stephen Vallelonga, V.F.; Deacons George B. Showalter; John Maher; Stephen E. Wharton.
Catechesis Religious Program—Tel: 304-865-1470; Email: stmmpsr@suddenlinkmail.com. Students 107.

PARSONS, TUCKER CO., OUR LADY OF MERCY MISSION (1959) See St. Thomas, Thomas
P.O. Box 300, Thomas, 26292-0300.
Tel: 304-463-4488; Email: father@sttsite.com. 221 Water St., Parsons, 26287. Rev. Timothy J. Grassi.
Catechesis Religious Program—Students 17.

PENNSBORO, RITCHIE CO., ST. JOSEPH CHAPEL, Closed. For inquiries for parish record please see Christ Our Hope, Harrisville.

PETERSBURG, GRANT CO., ST. MARY'S (1971) [JC]
5 Pierpont St., Petersburg, 26847-1633.
Tel: 304-257-1057; Email: smcc@frontier.net. 4 Grant St., Petersburg, 26847. Rev. Joshua R. Stevens.
Church: 18 Pierpont St., Petersburg, 26847-1633.
Fax: 304-257-9442.
Catechesis Religious Program—Students 13.

PHILIPPI, BARBOUR CO., ST. ELIZABETH PARISH (1953)
104 Canter St., Philippi, 26416-8383. College Hill, Philippi, 26416. Rev. James O'Connor.
Catechesis Religious Program—Philippi. Sam Santilli, D.R.E. Students 7.

PICKENS, RANDOLPH CO., SACRED HEART CHAPEL (1963) See Holy Rosary, Buckhannon. Now a chapel.
P.O. Box 848, Buckhannon, 26201-0848. Email: jmclaughlin@dwc.org. 35 Franklin St., Pickens, 26230. Rev. Joseph J. McLaughlin, S.M.
Catechesis Religious Program—Doris Sandreth, D.R.E.

PINEVILLE, WYOMING CO., HOLY CROSS CHAPEL (1963) Suppressed.
c/o 111 Virginia Ave., Welch, 24801. 595 Appalachian Hwy., Pineville, 24874. Tel: 304-732-6199; Email: llacson@dwc.org. Rev. Luis A. Lacson.
Catechesis Religious Program—

POINT PLEASANT, MASON CO., SACRED HEART MISSION (1948)
St. Matthew Parish, 600 Crooks Ave., Ravenswood, 26164. Rev. Penumaka Manikyalarao, H.G.N., Pastor.
Res.: 2222 Jackson Ave., Point Pleasant, 25550-2004.
Tel: 304-675-4602; Email: sacredheartpointpleasant@dwc.org.
Catechesis Religious Program—Students 20.
Mission—St. Joseph (1856) [CEM] 580 Pomeroy St., Mason, Mason Co. 25260.

POWHATAN, MCDOWELL CO., SACRED HEART (1895)
Rte. 52, 35508 Coal Heritage Rd., Powhatan, 24868.
Tel: 304-436-2014; Email: llacson@dwc.org. Rev. Luis A. Lacson.
Catechesis Religious Program—Students 6.

PRINCETON, MERCER CO., SACRED HEART (1915)
507 Harrison St., Princeton, 24740-3198.
Tel: 304-425-3664; Fax: 304-425-3676; Email: church@sacredheartprinceton.org; Web: www.sacredheartprinceton.org. P.O. Box 1310, Princeton, 24740-1310. Rev. Sebastian Embrayil Devasya.
Res.: 1003 Wyoming St., Bluefield, 24701.
Catechesis Religious Program—Students 35.
Campus Ministry, Concord College—Athens, 24712. Tel: 304-384-9502.

RAINELLE, GREENBRIER CO., SACRED HEART (1951) [CEM 2]
St. Patrick Parish, 309 2nd Ave., Hinton, 25951. 109-13th St., Rainelle, 25962. Rev. William K. Matheny Jr., V.F., Admin.; Deacons Robert A. Holliday; Peter F. Minogue. Now a mission of St. Patrick, Hinton.
Chapel—SpringDale, Sacred Heart, [CEM] (1876).
Catechesis Religious Program—Tel: 304-466-3966; Email: psychedinwv@yahoo.com. Cam Pulliam, D.R.E. Students 5.

RAVENSWOOD, JACKSON CO., ST. MATTHEW (1957)
400 Kaiser Ave., Ravenswood, 26164. Mailing Address: 600 Crooks Ave., Ravenswood, 26164-1312. Tel: 304-273-2175; Email: stmatthewravens@gmail.com. Rev. Penumaka Manikyalarao, H.G.N.
Catechesis Religious Program—Students 25.
Mission—St. Elizabeth of Hungary, 24 Butternut St., Elizabeth, 26143. Tel: 304-275-4226; Email: mcnulty.jeanne@gmail.com. Sr. Jeanne McNulty, Pastoral Assoc.

RICHWOOD, NICHOLAS CO., HOLY FAMILY (1902) [CEM]
4 Maple St., Richwood, 26261-1318.
Tel: 304-846-2873; Fax: 304-846-2873; Email: hfp124rich@dwc.org. Rev. Quy Dang.
Catechesis Religious Program—Students 2.

RIDGELEY, MINERAL CO., ST. ANTHONY (1916)
P.O. Box 1560, Fort Ashby, 26719-1560.
Tel: 304-298-3392; Fax: 304-298-3419; Email: annunciationchurch@atlanticbbn.net. 121 Main St., Ridgeley, 26753. Rev. J. Michael O. Lecias.
Res.: 8871 Frankfort Hwy., Fort Ashby, 26719.
Catechesis Religious Program—Students 10.

RIVESVILLE, MARION CO., OUR LADY OF THE ASSUMPTION, Merged with St. Joseph, Fairmont; St. Anthony, Grant Town; Our Lady of the Assumption, Rivesville, and All Saints, Barrackville to form St. Peter the Fisherman, Fairmont. See St. Anthony, Grant Town.

ROANOKE, LEWIS CO., ST. BRIDGET CHAPEL, Suppressed as a mission. See St. Patrick, Weston
210 Center Ave., Weston, 26452-2029.
Tel: 304-269-3048. Rev. James R. DeViese Jr., J.C.L., Admin.

ROMNEY, HAMPSHIRE CO., OUR LADY OF GRACE (1951) [CEM]
299 School St., Romney, 26757. Tel: 304-822-5561; Email: ourladyofgrace@alanticcbn.net. Revs. Thomas Sebastian, Admin.; Binoy Thomas; Deacon Lawrence Hammel.
Catechesis Religious Program—Students 9.

RONCEVERTE, GREENBRIER CO., ST. CATHERINE OF SIENA (1892)
40798 Midland Trail, White Sulphur Springs, 24986.
Tel: 304-536-1813; Email: stborromeo@frontier.com. 407 Walnut St., Ronceverte, 24970. Revs. John P. McDonough; James C. Conyers; Deacons William B. Strange Jr.; Thomas J. Soper.
Res. & Mailing Address: 325 W. Main St., White Sulphur Springs, 24986-2413.
Catechesis Religious Program—Tom Soper, D.R.E. Students 30.
Chapel—The Immaculate Conception of the Blessed Virgin Mary, [CEM] .
Chaplaincy—WV School of Osteopathic Medicine, Lewisburg, 24901.
Chapel—St. Louis, King of France.

ST. ALBANS, KANAWHA CO., ST. FRANCIS OF ASSISI (1947) [CEM]
1023 Sixth Ave., St. Albans, 25177.
Tel: 304-727-3033; Email: parish@stfranciswv.org; Web: www.stfranciswv.org. Rev. Patrick M. McDonough.
School—St. Francis of Assisi School, (Grades PreK-5), 525 Holley St., Saint Albans, 25177.
Tel: 304-727-5690; Email: sfswv@yahoo.com; Web: sfswv.com. Lay Teachers 9; Students 148.
Catechesis Religious Program—Students 37.

ST. CLARA, DODDRIDGE CO., ST. CLARE, Closed. See St. Boniface, Camden.

ST. JOSEPH SETTLEMENT, MARSHALL CO., ST. JOSEPH (1853) [CEM] (German)
64 Frohnapfel Ln., Proctor, 26055. Rev. Symeon Galazka, O.S.B., Admin.
Res. & Mailing Address: 21 Rosary Rd., New Martinsville, 26155. Tel: 304-447-3999; Email: office@scdpnm.org.
Catechesis Religious Program—Cindy Fox, D.R.E. Students 2.

ST. MARYS, PLEASANTS CO., ST. JOHN (1913)
310 Washington St., P.O. Box 338, St. Marys, 26170-1313. Tel: 304-684-7669; Email: stjohnsm@suddenlinkmail.com. Rev. Charles E. McGinnis Jr.
Catechesis Religious Program—Students 6.
Chapel—St. Joseph.

SALEM, HARRISON CO., SACRED HEART MISSION (1915) [CEM]
53 Sacred Heart Ln., Salem, 26426. Mailing Address: c/o St. James the Apostle, 2107 Pride Ave., Clarksburg, 26301-1819. Tel: 304-782-2277; Email: arodrigo@dwc.org. Revs. Akila Gayan Rodrigo, T.O.R., Admin.; L.J. Asantha Perera, Assoc. Pastor.
Res.: 75 Sacred Heart Ln., Salem, 26426.
Catechesis Religious Program—Students 16.

SHEPHERDSTOWN, JEFFERSON CO., ST. AGNES (1794) [CEM]
Mailing Address: P.O. Box 1603, Shepherdstown, 25443-1603. Tel: 304-876-6436; Email: office@stagnesshepherdstown.org. 200 S. Duke St., Shepherdstown, 25443. Rev. T. Mathew Rowgh; Deacon Anthony F. Maciorowski.
Res.: 216 S. Duke St., Shepherdstown, 25443-1603.
Catechesis Religious Program—Students 136.

SHINNSTON, HARRISON CO., ST. ANN CATHOLIC CHURCH (1923)
43 Mahlon St., Shinnston, 26431-1451.
Tel: 304-592-2733; Email: stannshinnston@aol.com. 610 Pike St., Shinnston, 26431. Rev. Akila Gayan Rodrigo, T.O.R.
Catechesis Religious Program—Gina Tate, D.R.E. Students 40.

SISTERSVILLE, TYLER CO., HOLY ROSARY MISSION (1898)
Email: mdp2136pc@dwc.org. Rev. Brian J. Crenwelge, Admin.; Deacon N. Rollin Fagert.
Church: 519 Main St., Sistersville, 26175-1405.
Tel: 304-652-6381; Email: holyrosarysistersville@dwc.org.
Catechesis Religious Program—Students 5.

SOUTH CHARLESTON, KANAWHA CO., BLESSED SACRAMENT (1941) [CEM]
305 E St., South Charleston, 25303-1597.
Tel: 304-744-5523; Fax: 304-744-5669; Email: blessedsac@suddenlinkmail.com; Web: www.blessedsacramentwv.org. Rev. John H. Finnell; Deacon John J. Hanna.
Catechesis Religious Program—Jeanne Haas, D.R.E. Students 78.

SPELTER, HARRISON CO., HOLY FAMILY, Suppressed as a mission. See St. Ann's, Shinnston.

SPENCER, ROANE CO., HOLY REDEEMER (1957)
602 Parkersburg Rd., Spencer, 25276-1024.
Tel: 304-927-2013; Email: hrp2141spen@dwc.org. Rev. Ronald G. Prechtl.
Catechesis Religious Program—Pat Williams, D.R.E. Students 8.

STAR CITY, MONONGALIA CO., ST. MARY (1953) [CEM]
3334B University Ave., P.O. Box 4204, Star City, 26504. Tel: 304-599-3747; Fax: 304-599-3769. Rev. John V. DiBacco Jr.
School—St. Francis Central Catholic School, 41 Guthrie Ln., Morgantown, 26508. Tel: 304-598-0133; Fax: 304-598-2690; Email: amoore@stfrancismorgantown.com. Mr. Arthur Moore, Prin.
Catechesis Religious Program—Tel: 304-225-1163; Email: kkerzak@comcast.net. Students 151.

STONEWOOD, HARRISON CO., OUR LADY OF PERPETUAL HELP (1955)
8092 3rd St., Stonewood, 26301-4854.
Tel: 304-623-2334; Fax: 304-622-9021; Email: info@olphwv.com. Rev. D. Kent Durig.
Catechesis Religious Program—
Tel: 304-623-2334, Ext. 11. Students 62.

SUMMERSVILLE, NICHOLAS CO., ST. JOHN THE EVANGELIST (1849) [CEM]
1704 Webster Rd., Summersville, 26651-1096.
Tel: 304-872-2554; Email: stjohnsummersville@gmail.com. Rev. Rene Gerona, S.V.D.
Catechesis Religious Program—Students 50.

SWEET SPRINGS, MONROE CO., ST. JOHN, Closed. See St. Charles, White Sulphur Springs.

TERRA ALTA, PRESTON CO., ST. EDWARD THE CONFESSOR MISSION (1975) [CEM] See St. Sebastian, Kingwood
Mailing Address: 322 E. Main St., Kingwood, 26537-1237. Tel: 304-329-1519; Email: stetcm1640terra@dwc.org. 1204 E. State Ave., Terra Alta, 26764. Rev. Andrew M. Switzer.
Catechesis Religious Program—See St. Sebastian.

THOMAS, TUCKER CO., ST. THOMAS AQUINAS (1897) [CEM]
316 Brown St., P.O. Box 300, Thomas, 26292-0300.
Tel: 304-463-4488; Email: father@sttsite.com; Web: sttsite.com. Rev. Timothy J. Grassi.
Church: 308 Brown St., Thomas, 26292.
Catechesis Religious Program—Students 15.
Mission—Our Lady of Mercy (1960) 221 Water St., Parsons, Tucker Co. 26287.

TRIADELPHIA, OHIO CO., OUR LADY OF SEVEN DOLORS MISSION (1869) [CEM] For inquiries for parish records, please see St. Vincent de Paul, Wheeling.
Tel: 304-547-5342; Fax: 304-243-0837; Email: phudock@dwc.org. Rev. Msgr. Paul A. Hudock.

UNION, MONROE CO., ST. ANDREW, Closed. See St. Catherine of Siena, Ronceverte.

VIENNA, WOOD CO., ST. MICHAEL (1956) [JC]
213 55th St., Vienna, 26105-2007. Tel: 304-295-6109; Email: stmoffice@frontier.com. 55th Grand Central Ave., Vienna, 26105. Rev. John R. Gallagher.
Catechesis Religious Program—Students 19.

WAR, MCDOWELL CO., CHRIST THE KING, WAR (1942) (Chapel)
13896 Rocket Boys Dr., Rte. 16 S., War, 24892. Rev. Luis A. Lacson.
Office: 111 Virginia Ave., Welch, 24801-2424.
Tel: 304-436-2014; Email: christthekingwar@dwc.org.
Catechesis Religious Program—Students 2.

WAYNE, WAYNE CO., NATIVITY OF OUR LORD (1980) Merged with St. Joseph, Huntington.

WEBSTER SPRINGS, WEBSTER CO., ST. ANNE (1920)
160 McGraw, Webster Springs, 26288-1134.
Tel: 304-847-5512; Fax: 304-847-5512; Email: stannechurch@frontier.net. Rev. Quy Ngoc Dong, S.V.D., Admin.; Deacon Raymond Godwin, Pastoral Assoc.; Rev. Romeo Bacalso, In Res.

Catechesis Religious Program—Students 3.

WEIRTON, BROOKE CO., ST. PAUL (1910) [CEM]
140 Walnut St., Weirton, 26062-4521.
Tel: 304-748-6710; Fax: 304-748-4118; Email: stpaulschurch@comcast.net. Rev. Babu Joseph Elamturuthil.
School—St. Paul School, Tel: 304-748-5225; Email: dtomshack@weirtonstpaul.org. Deena Tomshack, Prin.
Catechesis Religious Program—Students 26.

WEIRTON, HANCOCK CO.

1—ST. JOSEPH THE WORKER (1957)
229 California Ave., Weirton, 26062-3790.
Tel: 304-723-2054; Fax: 304-723-3961; Email: stjosephtheworker229@yahoo.com. Rev. Dennis R. Schuelkens Jr.
School—St. Joseph the Worker Grade School, 151 Michael Ave., Weirton, 26062. Tel: 304-723-1970; Email: r.fuscardo@weirtonstjoseph.net. Mr. Alfred Boniti, Prin. Lay Teachers 13; Students 188.
Catechesis Religious Program—Students 78.

2—SACRED HEART OF MARY (1911) (Polish)
200 Preston Ave., P.O. Box 2247, Weirton, 26062-1447. Tel: 304-723-7175; Email: shmparish@frontier.com. Revs. Dennis R. Schuelkens Jr.; Anthony Thurston, Pastoral Assoc.; Deacon Vincent P. Olenick.
Catechesis Religious Program—Students 14.

WELCH, MCDOWELL CO., ST. PETER (1923)
111 Virginia Ave., Welch, 24801-2424.
Tel: 304-436-2014; Fax: 304-436-2332; Email: spcc@citilink.net. Rev. Luis A. Lacson.
Catechesis Religious Program—Students 8.

WELLSBURG, BROOKE CO., ST. JOHN THE EVANGELIST (1857) [CEM]
1300 Charles St., Wellsburg, 26070-1408.
Tel: 304-737-0429; Email: stjohn1300@comcast.net. Rev. Joseph Daniel Pisano.
Catechesis Religious Program—Students 39.

WESTON, LEWIS CO., ST. PATRICK'S (1845)
210 Center Ave., Weston, 26452-2029.
Tel: 304-269-3048; Email: secretary@spchurchweston.net; Web: www.spchurchweston.net. Rev. James R. DeViese Jr., J.C.L.
Res.: 222 Center Ave., Weston, 26452-2029.
School—St. Patrick's School, 224 Center Ave., Weston, 26452. Tel: 304-269-5547; Email: st.pats@stpatswv.org. Mrs. Maureen Gildein, Prin. Clergy 1; Lay Teachers 10; Students 134.
Catechesis Religious Program—Students 55.
Chapels—Loveberry, St. Bernard—[CEM] .
Roanoke, St. Bridget, [CEM] .
Chaplaincy—Weston State Hospital.

WESTOVER, MONOGALIA CO., ST. ELIZABETH ANN SETON (1977) Merged with St. Theresa, Morgantown, to form The New St. Theresa & St. Elizabeth Ann Seton, Morgantown.

WHITE SULPHUR SPRINGS, GREENBRIER CO., ST. CHARLES BORROMEO (1903) [CEM] [JC]
40798 Midland Trail, White Sulphur Springs, 24986.
Tel: 304-536-1813; Email: stborromeo@frontier.com. Revs. John P. McDonough; James C. Conyers; Deacons William B. Strange Jr.; Thomas J. Soper.
Catechesis Religious Program—St. Louis Catholic Center, Lewisburg, 24901. Students 40.
Chapel—Sweet Springs, St. John (1859) [CEM 2] .

WHITESVILLE, BOONE CO., ST. JOSEPH THE WORKER (1958) Closed. See St. Mary Queen of Heaven, Madison.

WILLIAMSON, MINGO CO., SACRED HEART (1911)
110 W. Fourth Ave., Williamson, 25661.
Tel: 304-235-3027; Email: administration@sacredheartwilliamson.com. Rev. Tom Chacko.
Catechesis Religious Program—Students 11.

WINDSOR HEIGHTS, BROOKE CO., ST. THERESE, Closed. For inquiries for parish records, please see St. John, Wellsburg.

Absent on Leave:
Revs.—
Dagle, Thomas W.
Hall, Eric
Kranyc, Andrew G.
Kuchinsky, William J.
Mulcahy, John P.
Sobus, James M.
Stichweh, Ryan L.
Utietiang, Bekeh Ukelina.

Retired:
Rev. Msgrs.—
Fryer, Patrick L., (Retired), P.O. Boc 710, Gerrardstown, 25420
Luciana, Lawrence J., (Retired), 101 13th St., Rm. 105, Huntington, 25708
McSweeney, Jeremiah F., (Retired), Welty Apts. 408, 1276 National Rd., 26003
Ostrowski, Eugene S., V.F., (Retired), 94 MacCallan Ln., #11, Triadelphia, 26059
Sacus, Samuel S., V.F., (Retired), 689 Alexander Ct., River Vale, NJ 07675
Sadie, P. Edward, P.A., V.F., S.T.L., (Retired), 5012 Virginia Ave., S.E., Charleston, 25304
Revs.—
Alexander, Leon F., (Retired), 100 Hodges Rd., Charleston, 25314
Anderson, William A., (Retired), P.O. Box 108, Salem, 26426
Cann, Hilarion V., (Retired), 174 Ridgeway Dr., Bridgeport, 26330
Claro, Mario R., (Retired), Pendelton Manor, Unit 15, 43 St. Luke Dr., Franklin, 26807
Cramer, Harry N., (Retired), 27 Gable Dr., Milton, 25541
Cullinane, Jeremiah J., (Retired), 1702 S. 18th St., Manitowoc, WI 54220
Dorsch, Larry W., (Retired), P.O. Box 2825, Weirton, 26062
Duhaime, John N., (Retired), P.O. Box 116, Rainelle, 25962
Getsinger, Ronald A., (Retired), P.O. Box 2843, Weirton, 26062
Iaquinta, Patsy J., (Retired), 2372 Buckhanon River Rd., Volga, 26238
LeVasseur, Giles, (Retired), 7120 Jersey Mountain Rd., Romney, 26757
Manjadi, George, (Retired), Malappuram Dist., Kerala India 679332
McGinnity, John C., (Retired), Welty Home #316, 21 Washington Ave., 26003
Perriello, Robert A., V.F., (Retired), Clara Welty Apts. #402, 1276 National Rd., 26003
Petro, William, (Retired), P.O. Box 338, Dunbar, 25064
Reich, John C., (Retired), P.O. Box 735, Little River, SC 29566
Schmitt, David J., (Retired), 409 Mossack Dr. #2, Kettering, OH 45429
Sutton, Douglas B., (Retired), 10 Woodstream Ct., #11, Owings Mills, MD 21117
Wash, Pat J., (Retired), 182 N. 22nd St., Clarksburg, 26301
Wrenn, Lawrence, (Retired), 54 Willowmere Dr., Thurles, Co. Tipperary Ireland.

Permanent Deacons:
Belldina, Louis J., M.S., St. Anthony Parish, Fairmont; Holy Spirit, Monogah
Bittner, Robert W., (Retired)
Breiding, Douglas W., Director of Cemeteries, Diocese of Wheeling-Charleston; Cathedral of St. Joseph Parish, Wheeling
Ceslovnik, John F., St. John the Evangelist, Summersville & Holy Family, Richwood
Crim, Ben Brian, St. Leo, Inwood
Deem, Douglas A., (Retired)
Divita, John, Immaculate Conception, Montgomery
Doerr, George J., (On Leave Outside the Diocese); (Leave of Absence)
Evans, Harry K., St. Francis de Sales, Beckley
Fagert, Rollin N., Mater Dolorosa, Paden City
Galvin, David E., St. James, Charles Town
Garland, Todd E., (On Leave)
Godwin, Raymond G., St. Brendan, Elkins; St. Patrick, Coalton; St. Anne, Webster Springs
Goetemann, Gerald B., (Retired)
Grant, Russell J., (On Leave Outside the Diocese)
Hammel, Lawrence, Our Lady of Grace, Romney
Hammond, Don M., Campus Ministry, Beckley Vicariate & Sacred Heart, Bluefield
Hanna, John J., Blessed Sacrament, South Charleston
Holliday, Robert A., Sacred Heart, Rainelle; St. Patrick, Hinton
Iafrate, Albert L., (Retired)
Kelly, James R., (Retired)
Lester, David P., Pastoral Assoc., St. Peter the Fisherman, Fairmont
Lilly, Robert B., (Retired)
Lipscomb, Truman A., (Retired)
Lynch, John J., (Retired)
Maciorowski, Anthony F., St. Agnes, Shepherdstown
Maher, John F., St. Margaret Mary Parish, Parkersburg
Minogue, Peter F., St. Patrick, Hinton; Sacred Heart, Rainelle
Munuhe, James T., St. James, Charleston
Nelson, Helgi P., St. Vincent de Paul, Berkeley Springs
Nesser, Dennis W., J.C.L., Tribunal Dir., Christ the King, Dunbar
Olenchock, Stephen A., (On Leave Outside of the Diocese)
Olenick, Vincent P., St. Joseph the Worker, Weirton; Sacred Heart of Mary, Weirton
Pagano, Luis A., St. James, Charles Town; St. Joseph, Martinsburg
Prentiss, Joseph J., St. John University, Morgantown
Pressi, Marcus C., St. Joseph, Martinsburg; St. Bernadette Mission, Hedgesville
Prestera, Michael R. Jr., (On Leave Outside of the Diocese)
Quigley, Charles C., (Retired)
Sarraga, John W., Office of Prison Ministry (Federal Prison) & St. Brendan, Elkins
Shaw, A. Ray III, (Retired)
Showalter, George B., St. Margaret Mary, Parkersburg
Smith, Paul J., (Retired)
Smoulder, George, (On Leave Outside the Diocese)
Soper, Thomas J., St. Catherine of Siena, Ronceverte; St. Louis, King of France Catholic Center, Lewisburg; St. Charles Borromeo, White Sulphur Springs
Strange, William B. Jr., St. Charles Borromeo, White Sulphur Springs
Thompson, Rue C. Jr., Office of Prison Ministry (State Prisons and Regional Jails) & Holy Rosary, Buckhannon
Trunzo, Thomas, (On Leave Outside the Diocese)
Wharton, Stephen E., St. Margaret Mary, Parkersburg
Windett, John E., Pastoral Svcs. (Home Health Care) & St. Elizabeth Ann Seton, Franklin
Wise, W. Donald, St. Francis De Sales, Beckley
Wuletich, David E., St. Anthony, Charleston
Yaquinta, John W., St. Francis de Sales, Morgantown
Ziolkowski, John F., St. Francis De Sales, Beckley.

INSTITUTIONS LOCATED IN DIOCESE

[A] COLLEGES AND UNIVERSITIES

WHEELING. *Wheeling Jesuit University*, 316 Washington Ave., 26003-6243. Tel: 304-243-2000; Fax: 304-243-2120; Web: www.wju.edu. Dr. Michael Mihalya Jr., Pres.; Revs. Ignatius H. Sasmita, S.J., Campus Min.; William George, S.J., Gov't Relations Officer; Very Rev. James R. Conroy, S.J., Rector, Jesuit Community; Revs. Luis A. Tampe, S.J., Prof.; James J. Fleming, S.J.; William C. Rickle, S.J.; Donald M. Serva, S.J.; Michael F. Steltenkamp, S.J.; Michael J. Woods, S.J. Jesuit Fathers. Lay Teachers 79; Priests 9; Students 1,304.

CHARLES TOWN. *Catholic Distance University* Archbishop Timothy Broglio, Chancellor; Dr. Marianne Evans Mount, President; email mmount@cdu.edu; Dr. Peter Brown, Dean, email pbrown@cdu.edu; Admissions: email admissions@cdu.edu. Web: www.cdu.edu. Lay Faculty 27; Clergy 5; Students 1,000. 115 W. Congress St., Charles Town, 25414.
Tel: 304-724-5000; Email: cdu@cdu.edu; Web: www.cdu.edu. Archbishop Timothy Broglio, Chancellor; Dr. Marianne Mount, Pres.; Dr. Peter Brown, Dean. Religious Teachers 5; Students 1,000.

[B] HIGH SCHOOLS, CENTRAL

WHEELING. *Central Catholic High School*, 75-14th St., 26003. Tel: 304-233-1660; Fax: 304-233-3187; Email: wheelingcentral@cchsknights.org; Web: www.cchsknights.org. Mr. Lawrence Bandi, Pres.; Mrs. Becky Sancomb, Prin. Lay Teachers 26; Students 258.

CHARLESTON. *Charleston Catholic High School* (1923) (Grades 6-12), 1033 Virginia St. E., Charleston, 25301. Tel: 304-342-8415; Fax: 304-342-1259; Email: admin@charlestoncatholic-crw.org; Web: www.charlestoncatholic-crw.org. Colleen Hoyer, Prin. Lay Teachers 35; Students 424.

CLARKSBURG. *Notre Dame High School* (1924) (Grades 7-12), 127 E. Pike St., Clarksburg, 26301.
Tel: 304-623-1026; Fax: 304-624-5654; Email: shardman@notredamewv.org. Dr. Carroll Kelly Morrison, Prin. Faculty 20; Lay Teachers 20; Students 216.

HUNTINGTON. *St. Joseph Central Catholic High School*, 600 13th St., Huntington, 25701.
Tel: 304-525-5096; Fax: 304-525-0781; Email: bill.archer@stjosephhs.org; Web: www.stjosephhs.org. Mr. William Archer, Prin. Faculty 15; Students 161.

PARKERSBURG. *Parkersburg Catholic Junior-Senior High School*, (Grades 7-12), 3201 Fairview Ave., Parkersburg, 26104. Tel: 304-485-6341;
Fax: 304-485-4697; Email: pchs@pchs1.com; Web:

pchs1.com. Mr. Gregory Zecca, Pres.; John Golebiewski, Prin. Clergy 16; Students 152.

WEIRTON. *Madonna High School*, 150 Michael Way, Weirton, 26062. Tel: 304-723-0545; Fax: 304-723-0564; Email: jlesho@weirtonmadonna.org; Web: www.weirtonmadonna.org. James Lesho, Prin. Faculty 22; Students 171.

[C] ELEMENTARY SCHOOLS, CENTRAL

CLARKSBURG. *St. Mary's Central Grade School* (1914) (Grades PreSchool-6), 107 E. Pike St., Clarksburg, 26301. Tel: 304-622-9831; Fax: 304-622-9831; Email: stmaryswv@gmail.com. Nicole A. Folio, Prin. Consolidation of the following parishes: All Saints, Bridgeport; Immaculate Conception, Clarksburg; St. James, Clarksburg; Our Lady of Perpetual Help, Stonewood; St. Ann, Shinnston; Sacred Heart, Salem. Total Faculty 20; Lay Teachers 20; Students 173.

FAIRMONT. *Fairmont Catholic Grade School* (1928) (Grades K-8), Consolidation of the following parishes: St. Peter; Immaculate Conception; St. Anthony. 416 Madison St., Fairmont, 26554. Tel: 304-363-5313; Fax: 304-363-7701; Email: sspadafore@fairmontcatholic.com. Stacey Spadafore, Prin. Lay Teachers 13; Students 138.

MORGANTOWN. *St. Francis de Sales Central Catholic School*, (Grades PreK-8), 41 Guthrie Ln., Morgantown, 26508. Tel: 304-291-5070; Fax: 304-291-5104; Email: amoore@stfrancismorgantown.com; Web: www.stfrancismorgantown.com. Mr. Arthur Moore, Prin. Lay Teachers 31; Students 406.

PARKERSBURG. *Parkersburg Catholic Elementary School*, (Grades PreK-6), 810 Juliana St., Parkersburg, 26101. Tel: 304-422-6694; Fax: 304-422-2469; Email: pces@pchs1.com; Web: pceswv.org. Mr. Kevin Simonton, Prin. Lay Teachers 12; Students 128; Staff 21.

[D] PASTORAL CENTERS

CHARLESTON. *Saint John XXIII Pastoral Center* (1985) 100 Hodges Rd., Charleston, 25314. Tel: 304-342-0507; Fax: 304-342-4786; Email: johnxxiii@dwc.org; Web: johnxxiiipc.org. Mr. Eric Millam, Dir. Capacity 200.

HUTTONSVILLE. *Mary Help of Christians Pastoral Center* (1977) 39 Catholic Conference Center, Huttonsville, 26273. Tel: 304-335-2165; Fax: 304-335-2165; Email: office@bishophodges.org; Web: www.bishophodges.org. Mr. Shawn Madden, Dir. Capacity 352.

KEARNEYSVILLE. *Priest Field Pastoral Center*, 4030 Middleway Pike, Kearneysville, 25430. Tel: 304-725-1435; Fax: 304-725-1437; Email: info@priestfield.org; Web: www.priestfield.org. Ms. Susan Kersey, Dir. Capacity 90.

[E] ASSOCIATED SPIRITUAL AND PASTORAL LIFE CENTERS

WHEELING. *St. Joseph Center*, 137 Mount St. Joseph Rd., 26003-1799. Tel: 304-232-8160; Fax: 304-232-0506; Email: atroiani@csjoseph.org; Email: pwarbritton@csjoseph.org; Web: www.csjoseph.org. Ms. Anna Marie Troiani, Dir. Congregation of St. Joseph Overnight Capacity 10; Daytime Capacity 25.

[F] GENERAL HOSPITALS

WHEELING. *Bishop Joseph H. Hodges Continuous Care Center*, 236 Bransfield Pl., P.O. Box 6316, 26003. Tel: 304-243-3800; Fax: 304-243-3398; Email: crtarr@wheelinghospital.org; Web: www.wheelinghospital.org. Mr. Ronald L. Violi, CEO; Christy Tarr, Admin. Skilled and Intermediate Care. Bed Capacity 144; Tot Asst. Annually 764; Total Staff 157.

Wheeling Hospital (1850) 1 Medical Park, 26003. Tel: 304-243-3000; Fax: 304-243-5045; Email: jmurdy@wheelinghospital.org; Web: www.wheelinghospital.com. Mr. Ronald L. Violi, CEO; Sr. Mary Ann Rosenbaum, C.S.J., Dir. of Pastoral Care Dept.; Rev. Cyprian Osuegbu, Chap. (Licensed) 223; Sisters of St. Joseph 3; Tot Asst. Annually 689,711; Total Staff 2,570.

[G] NURSING HOMES

WHEELING. *Good Shepherd Nursing Home LC*, 159 Edgington Ln., 26003. Tel: 304-242-1093; Fax: 304-242-1121; Email: good.shepherd@comcast.net. Mr. Donald R. Kirsch, Admin.; Rev. John Beckley, S.M., Chap. Bed Capacity 192; Sisters 2; Tot Asst. Annually 267; Total Staff 240.

[H] HOMES FOR AGED

WHEELING. *Welty Home for the Aged, Inc.*, 159 Edgington Ln., 26003-6261. Tel: 304-242-1093. Bed Capacity 244; Total Apartments 126; Tot Asst. Annually 450; Total Staff 315.

Welty Home LC, 21 Washington Ave., 26003-6261. Tel: 304-242-5233; Fax: 304-230-1132. Mr. Randy Forzano, Admin.

Welty Trust, Inc., 83 Edgington Ln., 26003. Tel: 304-242-2300; Fax: 304-243-0890.

Trustees: Most Rev. Michael J. Bransfield, Pres.; Rev. Msgr. Anthony Cincinnati, S.T.D., V.E.; Mr. William Yaeger, Treas.; Mr. Lawrence Bandi.

Welty Retirement Apartments LC, 1276 National Rd., 26003. Tel: 304-242-5820; Fax: 304-230-5600. Mrs. Betty Toland, Mgr.

[I] HEALTH SERVICES

HUNTINGTON. *Pallottine Health Services, Inc.* (1988) 2900 First Ave., Huntington, 25702. Tel: 304-526-1028; Fax: 304-526-1538; Email: sister.diane@st-marys.org; Web: www.st-marys.org. Sr. M. Diane Bushee, S.A.C., Contact Person. Sponsored by the Pallottine Missionary Sisters. Bed Capacity 393; Students 332; Tot Asst. Annually 526,987; Total Staff 2,572.

Parent Corp. for:.

St. Mary's Medical Center, Inc. (1924) 2900 First Ave., Huntington, 25702. Tel: 304-526-1234; Fax: 304-526-1538; Web: www.st-marys.org. Bed Capacity 315; Students 299; Total Staff 2,567; Total Assisted 517,031.

[J] SOCIAL SERVICE INSTITUTIONS

WHEELING. *Catholic Charities Neighborhood Center*, 125-18th St., 26003-0713. Tel: 304-232-7157; Fax: 304-238-7133; Email: gcoleman@ccwva.org. Mr. Grant Coleman, Neighborhood Center Interim Coord.

HUTTONSVILLE. *Camp Bosco*, 223 Catholic Conference Center, Huttonsville, 26273. Tel: 304-335-2130 (In Season); Tel: 304-233-0880 (Out of Season); Fax: 304-230-0508; Email: rperron@dwc.org. 39 Catholic Conference Center, Huttonsville, 26273. Mr. Shawn Madden, Dir.; Mr. Robert Perron, Admin. Diocesan Children's Camp.

KERMIT. *A.B.L.E. Families, Inc.* (1994) 100 Lincoln St., P.O. Box 1249, Kermit, 25674. Tel: 304-393-4987; Fax: 304-393-2600; Email: mspaulding@ablefamilies.org; Web: www.ablefamilies.org. Marlene Spaulding, Exec. Dir. Tot Asst. Annually 425; Total Staff 11.

SALEM. *Nazareth Farm, Inc.* (1979) 665 Nazareth Farm Rd., Salem, 26426. Tel: 304-782-2742; Fax: 304-782-4358; Email: nazarethfarm@gmail.com; Web: www.nazarethfarm.org. Mr. Brian Suehs-Vassel, Dir. Tot Asst. Annually 700; Total Staff 6.

[K] HOMES FOR DEPENDENT CHILDREN

WHEELING. *St. John's Home for Children* (1856) 141 Key Ave., 26003-7412. Tel: 304-242-5633; Fax: 304-243-4911; Email: terry@stjohnshome.net; Web: www.stjohnshomeforchildren.org. Terence A. McCormick, Exec. Dir. Children 12; Total Assisted 21.

[L] CONVENTS AND RESIDENCES FOR SISTERS

WHEELING. *Sisters of Our Lady of Charity of the Good Shepherd Central South U.S. Province* (1900) 141 Edgington Ln., 26003. Tel: 304-242-7070; Fax: 304-242-0042; Email: carol.pregno@gssweb.org. Sr. Carol Pregno, Supr.

Sisters of Our Lady of Charity of the Good Shepherd - Wheeling, Inc. Sisters 3.

Wheeling Center, Congregation of St. Joseph, 137 Mount St. Joseph Rd., 26003-1799. Tel: 304-232-8160; Fax: 304-232-0506; Email: pwarbritton@csjoseph.org; Web: www.csjoseph.org. Ruthann Scherer, Contact Person. Wheeling Center-Congregation of St. Joseph.Attended by Wheeling Jesuit University. Sisters 54.

[M] FOUNDATIONS

WHEELING. *Central Catholic High School Educational Foundation, Inc.*, 75-14th St., 26003. Tel: 304-233-1660; Fax: 304-233-3187; Email: wheelingcentral@cchsknights.org.

**Clarence L. Christ Trust*, Office of the Vicar General: Diocese of Wheeling-Charleston, P.O. Box 230, 26003. Tel: 304-233-0880; Email: ccarter@dwc.org. 1311 Byron St., 26003. Mr. Chad R. Carter, M.B.A., B.A., Chancellor.

John S. Thoner Family Charitable Trust (1995) P.O. Box 230, 26003. Tel: 304-233-0880; Fax: 304-233-0890; Email: ccarter@dwc.org. Mr. Chad R. Carter, M.B.A., B.A., Chancellor.

Medical Park Foundation (1995) One Medical Park, 26003. Tel: 304-243-2969; Email: jmurdy@wheelinghospital.org. Mr. Ronald L. Violi, CEO.

**Michael Christ Trust*, Office of the Vicar General: Diocese of Wheeling-Charleston, P.O. Box 230, 26003. Tel: 304-233-0880; Email: ccarter@dwc.org. Mr. Chad R. Carter, M.B.A., B.A., Chancellor.

The Sisters of St. Joseph Health & Wellness Foundation, 137 Mount St. Joseph Rd., 26003-1799. Tel: 304-233-4500; Fax: 304-232-1404; Email: ssjhwf@aol.com; Email: helenssj@aol.com; Web: www.ssjhealthandwellnessfoundation.org. Sr. Helen Skormisley, C.S.J., Co-Exec. Dir.; Clara Crinkey, Contact Person.

Sisters of St. Joseph of Wheeling Foundation, Inc. (1974) 137 Mount St. Joseph Rd., 26003-1799. Tel: 304-232-8160; Fax: 304-232-1401; Email: pwarbritton@csjoseph.org; Web: www.csjoseph.org. Sr. Patricia Warbritton, Treas.

West Virginia Catholic Foundation, 1311 Byron St., P.O. Box 230, 26003. Tel: 304-233-0880; Fax: 304-233-0890; Email: bminor@dwc.org; Web: wvcf.dwc.org. Mr. Bryan E. Minor, Exec. Dir.

PARKERSBURG. *Parkersburg Catholic Schools Foundation, Inc.*, 3201 Fairview Ave., Parkersburg, 26104-2111. Tel: 304-428-7528; Fax: 304-428-8159; Email: pcsf@pchs1.com; Web: pchs1.com.

Sisters Health Foundation (1997) 4420 Rosemar Center., Ste. 204, P.O. Box 4440, Parkersburg, 26104-4440. Tel: 304-424-6080; Fax: 304-424-6081; Email: rsteffen@sistershealthfdn.org; Web: www.sistershealthfdn.org. Renee L. Steffen, CEO; Sr. Molly Bauer, C.S.J., Admin.; Sheiron Sanchez, Admin.

[N] NEWMAN CENTERS

CHARLESTON. *St. John Paul II Catholic Campus Ministry Center*, 310-26th St., Charleston, 25304. Tel: 304-342-9940.

ATHENS. *Concord University Newman Center*, 3001 Vermillion St., P.O. Box 447, Athens, 24712. Tel: 304-320-6037; Email: deacondon@sacredheartblfd.org. Deacon Don M. Hammond. See Sacred Heart, Princeton.

BETHANY. *St. John Fisher Chapel*, 201 Richardson St., Bethany, 26032. Tel: 304-829-4622; Email: jpisano@dwc.org. P.O. Box 6689, 26003. Rev. Joseph Daniel Pisano, Chap.; Mrs. Shirley Carter, Campus Ministry.

BUCKHANNON. *West Virginia Wesleyan College Newman Center*, 35 Franklin St., Box 848, Buckhannon, 26201-0848. Tel: 304-472-3414; Email: frronsm@comcast.net. Rev. Joseph J. McLaughlin, S.M., Chap.; Bro. Roy Madigan, S.M.

FAIRMONT. *Fairmont State University Newman Center*, 1200 College Park, Fairmont, 26554. Tel: 304-363-2300; Email: gparks@dwc.org. Very Rev. Robert Perriello, V.F., Chap.; Mr. Graham Parks, Campus Min.

HUNTINGTON. *Marshall Catholic Newman Center*, 1609 Fifth Ave., Huntington, 25703. Tel: 304-525-4618; Fax: 304-522-4115; Email: tferguson@dwc.org; Web: www.marshallcatholic.com. Traci Ann Ferguson, Dir. Campus Min.

PHILIPPI. *Alderson-Broaddus College Newman Center*, Newman Center, College Hill, 104 Canter St., Philippi, 26416. Tel: 304-457-2641; Email: kstillion@dwc.org. Rev. James O'Connor.

SHEPHERDSTOWN. *Good Shepherd Catholic Campus Ministry Center*, 101 W. High St., P.O. Box 1163, Shepherdstown, 25443. Tel: 304-876-0231. Rev. Jose Manuel Escalante, Chap.; Kate Didden, Campus Min.

WEST LIBERTY. *West Liberty State College, St. Thomas Aquinas Campus Ministry*, P.O. Box 6689, West Liberty, 26074. Tel: 304-336-7751; Email: scarter@dwc.org. Rev. Cody C. Ford, Chap.; Mrs. Shirley Carter, Campus Min.

[O] CHILD CARE CENTERS

WHEELING. *Holy Family Child Care & Development Center, Inc.*, 161 Edgington Ln., 26003. Tel: 304-242-5222; Fax: 304-242-5379; Email: director@holyfamilychildcarecenter.com; Web: www.holyfamilychildcarecenter.com. Michele Forsythe, Exec. Dir. Students 97; Total Staff 18; Total Assisted 103.

[P] MISCELLANEOUS

WHEELING. *St. Joseph Health Initiative, Inc.*, 137 Mount St. Joseph Rd., 26003-1799. Tel: 304-232-8160; Fax: 304-232-0506; Email: pwarbritton@csjoseph.org. Sr. Marguerite O'Brien, C.S.J., Pres.

Retirement Trust Agreement of the Priests' Health and Retirement Association (1997) P.O. Box 230, 26003. Tel: 304-233-0880; Fax: 304-233-0890; Email: ccarter@dwc.org. Mr. Chad R. Carter, M.B.A., B.A., Chancellor.

CLAYTON. *Bethlehem Farm, Inc.*, 572 Bethlehem Farm Ln., Alderson, 24910. P.O. Box 415, Talcott, 24981. Tel: 304-445-7143; Fax: 304-445-2936; Email: caretakers@bethlehemfarm.net; Email: eric.fitts@bethlehemfarm.net; Web: www.bethlehemfarm.net. Mr. Eric Fitts, Dir.

MADISON. *St. Mary Queen of Heaven*, 51 Madison Ave., P.O. Box 467, Madison, 25130-0467.
Tel: 304-369-4538; Email: nbuchlein@dwc.org. Rev. Neil R. Buchlein.
St. Joseph the Worker.

MORGANTOWN. *Morgantown Magnificat Chapter of the Diocese of Wheeling-Charleston*, 24 Millan St., Morgantown, 26501. Tel: 304-296-8950; Email: phiggi87@comcast.net. Mrs. Barbara Higginbotham, Contact Person; Rev. Jim O'Connor, Spiritual Advisor / Care Svcs.

RELIGIOUS INSTITUTES OF MEN REPRESENTED IN THE DIOCESE

For further details refer to the corresponding bracketed number in the Religious Institutes of Men or Women section.

[]—*Canons Regular of the New Jerusalem*—C.R.N.J.
[]—*Congregation of Our Lady of Monte Oliveto*—O.S.B. Oliv.
[]—*Franciscan Friars Third Order Regular* (Province of Our Lady of Lanka, Sri Lanka)—T.O.R.
[0585]—*Heralds of Good News*—H.G.N.
[0690]—*Jesuit Fathers and Brothers*—S.J.
[]—*Little Flower Congregation* (C.S.T. Fathers - St. Thomas Province, Kerala, India)—C.S.T.
[0770]—*Marist Brothers*—F.M.S.
[0780]—*Marist Fathers*—S.M.
[]—*Missionary Congregation of the Blessed Sacrament* (Kerala, India)—M.C.B.S.
[0840]—*Missionary Servants of the Most Holy Trinity*—S.T.
[0975]—*Society of Our Lady of the Most Holy Trinity*—S.O.L.T.
[0420]—*Society of the Divine Word*—S.V.D.
[0590]—*Society of the Missionaries of the Holy Apostles*—M.S.A.
[]—*Third Order Regular of St. Francis of Assisi (St. Francis Province)* (Ranchi, India)—T.O.R.

RELIGIOUS INSTITUTES OF WOMEN REPRESENTED IN THE DIOCESE

[0130]—*Apostles of the Sacred Heart of Jesus*—A.S.C.J.
[3110]—*Congregation of Our Lady of the Retreat in the Cenacle* (North American Prov.)—R.C.
[3832]—*Congregation of the Sisters of St. Joseph* (Wheeling Center)—C.S.J.
[1105]—*Dominican Sisters of Hope* (Ossining, NY)—O.P.
[1115]—*Dominican Sisters of Peace*—O.P.
[]—*Eudist Servants of the Eleventh Hour*—E.S.E.H.
[1450]—*Franciscan Sisters of the Sacred Heart*—O.S.F.
[]—*Missionary Sisters Servants of the Word*—H.M.S.P.
[3150]—*Pallottine Missionary Sisters*—S.A.C.
[]—*Sisters for Christian Community*—S.F.C.C.
[0570]—*Sisters of Charity of Seton Hill, Greensburg, PA*—S.C.
[0990]—*Sisters of Divine Providence (Marie de la Roche Prov.)*—C.D.P.
[2575]—*Sisters of Mercy of the Americas*—R.S.M.
[3000]—*Sisters of Notre Dame de Namur* (U.S. E.-W. Province - Mid Atlantic Region)—S.N.D.DeN.
[1830]—*Sisters of Our Lady of Charity of the Good Shepherd* (Central South U.S. Province)—R.G.S.
[1630]—*Sisters of St. Francis of Penance and Christian Charity*—O.S.F.
[3893]—*Sisters of St. Joseph of Chestnut Hill* (Philadelphia)—S.S.J.
[3830-13]—*Sisters of St. Joseph of Pittsburgh* (Baden)—C.S.J.
[3830-05]—*Sisters of St. Joseph of Rockville Centre* (Brentwood)—C.S.J.
[]—*Sisters of the Child Jesus* Zimbabwe—S.J.I.
[2110]—*Sisters of the Humility of Mary*—H.M.

DIOCESAN CEMETERIES

WHEELING. *Mount Calvary* (1872) 1685 National Rd., 26003-5599. Tel: 304-242-0460; Fax: 304-242-9506; Email: dbreiding@dwc.org. Deacon Doug Breiding, Dir.

NECROLOGY

† Cupp, Edwin F., (Retired), Died Jan. 24, 2018
† Lydon, Leo B., (Retired), Died May. 27, 2018
† Shoda, Richard W., J.C.L., V.F., (Retired), Died Aug. 9, 2018

An asterisk (*) denotes an organization that has established tax-exempt status directly with the IRS and is not covered by the USCCB Group Ruling.

Diocese of Wichita

(Dioecesis Wichitensis)

Most Reverend

CARL ALAN KEMME

Bishop of Wichita; ordained May 10, 1986; appointed Bishop of Wichita February 20, 2014; installed May 1, 2014. *Chancery: 424 N. Broadway, Wichita, KS 67202.*

The Chancery: 424 N. Broadway, Wichita, KS 67202. Tel: 316-269-3900; Fax: 316-269-3902.

Web: www.CatholicDioceseOfWichita.org

ESTABLISHED AUGUST 2, 1887.

Square Miles 20,021.

New boundaries established by Apostolic Letters dated May 19, 1951. Bounded on the west by the west lines of Rice, Reno, Kingman and Harper counties, south by Oklahoma, east by Missouri, and north by the north lines of Bourbon, Allen, Woodson, Greenwood, Morris, Marion, McPherson and Rice Counties in Kansas.

For legal titles of parishes and diocesan institutions, consult the Chancery Office.

STATISTICAL OVERVIEW

Personnel	
Bishop	1
Priests: Diocesan Active in Diocese	100
Priests: Diocesan Active Outside Diocese	8
Priests: Retired, Sick or Absent	19
Number of Diocesan Priests	127
Religious Priests in Diocese	1
Total Priests in Diocese	128
Extern Priests in Diocese	12
Ordinations:	
Diocesan Priests	10
Transitional Deacons	3
Permanent Deacons in Diocese	3
Total Sisters	203
Parishes	
Parishes	90
With Resident Pastor:	
Resident Diocesan Priests	65
Without Resident Pastor:	
Administered by Priests	25
Pastoral Centers	37
Professional Ministry Personnel:	
Sisters	14
Lay Ministers	94
Welfare	
Catholic Hospitals	6
Total Assisted	370,758
Homes for the Aged	9
Total Assisted	1,960
Day Care Centers	1
Total Assisted	70
Specialized Homes	1
Total Assisted	40
Special Centers for Social Services	1
Total Assisted	625
Residential Care of Disabled	1
Total Assisted	529
Other Institutions	1
Total Assisted	1,050
Educational	
Seminaries, Diocesan	1
Students from This Diocese	16
Diocesan Students in Other Seminaries	22
Total Seminarians	38
Colleges and Universities	1
Total Students	3,373
High Schools, Diocesan and Parish	4
Total Students	2,549
Elementary Schools, Diocesan and Parish	35
Total Students	7,960
Catechesis/Religious Education:	
High School Students	1,650
Elementary Students	5,020
Total Students under Catholic Instruction	20,590
Teachers in the Diocese:	
Priests	7
Scholastics	1
Sisters	17
Lay Teachers	163
Vital Statistics	
Receptions into the Church:	
Infant Baptism Totals	1,282
Minor Baptism Totals	567
Adult Baptism Totals	269
Received into Full Communion	279
First Communions	2,214
Confirmations	2,067
Marriages:	
Catholic	398
Interfaith	180
Total Marriages	578
Deaths	979
Total Catholic Population	120,905
Total Population	986,525

Former Bishops—Most Revs. JAMES O'REILLY, D.D., Bishop-Elect; died July 26, 1887; JOHN JOSEPH HENNESSY, D.D., cons. Nov. 30, 1888; died July 13, 1920; AUGUSTUS JOHN SCHWERTNER, D.D., ord. June 12, 1897; cons. June 8, 1921; installed June 22, 1921; died Oct. 2, 1939; CHRISTIAN HERMAN WINKELMANN, S.T.D., ord. June 11, 1907; cons. Auxiliary Bishop of St. Louis, Nov. 30, 1933; installed March 5, 1940; died Nov. 18, 1946; MARK K. CARROLL, S.T.D., ord. June 10, 1922; appt. Feb. 15, 1947; cons. April 23, 1947; installed May 6, 1947; resigned Sept. 27, 1967; died Jan. 12, 1985; LEO C. BYRNE, D.D., ord. June 10, 1933; appt. Titular Bishop of Sabidia and Auxiliary of St. Louis, May 21, 1954; cons. June 29, 1954; transferred to Wichita, "cum jure successionis" 1961; appt. Apostolic Administrator, Feb. 25, 1963; transferred to St. Paul and Minneapolis, Sept. 27, 1967; died Oct. 21, 1974; DAVID M. MALONEY, S.S., S.T.L., J.C.D., former Bishop of Wichita; ord. Dec. 8, 1936; appt. Titular Bishop of Ruspae Auxiliary of Denver, Nov. 9, 1960; cons. Jan. 4, 1961; transferred to Wichita, Dec. 6, 1967; resigned July 16, 1982; died Feb. 15, 1995; EUGENE J. GERBER, D.D., Bishop of Wichita; ord. May 19, 1959; appt. Bishop of Dodge City Oct. 16, 1976; ord. Dec. 14, 1976; installed Dec. 15, 1976; appt. Bishop of Wichita Nov. 23, 1982; installed Feb. 9, 1983; resigned Oct. 4, 2001; died Sept. 29, 2018.; THOMAS J. OLMSTED, J.C.D., ord. July 2, 1973; appt. Coadjutor Bishop of Wichita Feb. 16, 1999; Episcopal ord. April 20, 1999; appt. Bishop of Wichita Oct. 4, 2001; appt. Bishop of Phoenix Dec. 20, 2003; MICHAEL OWEN JACKELS, ord. May 30, 1981; appt. Bishop of Wichita Jan. 28, 2005; ord. April 4, 2005; appt. Archbishop of Dubuque April 8, 2013.

Chancery Office—424 N. Broadway, Wichita, 67202. Tel: 316-269-3900; Fax: 316-269-3902; Web: www.catholicdioceseofwichita.org.

Vicar General—Rev. DAVID J. LIES.

Moderator of the Diocesan Curia—Rev. DAVID J. LIES, 424 N. Broadway, Wichita, 67202.

Vicar for Clergy—Rev. PATRICK G. YORK.

Chancellor—Rev. MICHAEL M. SIMONE, S.T.L.

Vice Chancellor—MRS. THERESE SEILER.

College of Consultors—Revs. CHAD J. ARNOLD; JOHN V. HOTZE, J.C.L.; ADAM J. KEITER; Very Rev. JOHN P. LANZRATH, S.T.L.; Revs. DAVID J. LIES; MICHAEL M. SIMONE, S.T.L.

Presbyteral Council—Revs. CHAD J. ARNOLD; DARYL W. BELFORT; JAMES J. BILLINGER; JUAN G. GARZA; BERNARD X. GORGES; ADAM J. KEITER; DAVID J. LIES; DANIEL S. LORIMER; JAMES S. MAINZER; BENJAMIN N. NGUYEN; WAYNE L. SCHMID, (Retired); MICHAEL M. SIMONE, S.T.L.; BRIAN D. NELSON; PATRICK G. YORK.

Tribunal—424 N. Broadway, Wichita, 67202. Tel: 316-269-3960; Email: martinc@catholicdioceseofwichita.org.

Judicial Vicar—Rev. BRIAN D. NELSON.

Adjutant Judicial Vicar—Rev. MICHAEL E. NOLAN, J.C.L.

Promoter of Justice—Rev. STUART M. SMELTZER, J.C.L.

Judges—Revs. DOUGLAS L. CAMPBELL, J.C.L., (Retired); JOHN V. HOTZE, J.C.L.; Very Rev. JOHN F. JIRAK, J.C.L.; Rev. MICHAEL E. NOLAN, J.C.L.

Defender of the Bond—Rev. STUART M. SMELTZER, J.C.L.

Notaries—MRS. CHERYL MARTIN; MRS. TRACY WINSLOW.

Ongoing Formation of the Clergy Committee—Very Rev. JOHN F. JIRAK, J.C.L.; Revs. BENJAMIN S. SAWYER, Prog. Dir.; PATRICK G. YORK; ANDREW J. WALSH; ANDREW K. HOFFMAN; MR. DUSTY GATES.

Diocesan Offices and Directors

Unless otherwise indicated, all Diocesan Offices and Ministries addresses and telephone numbers: 424 N. Broadway, Wichita, KS 67202; Tel: 316-269-3900; Web: www.catholicdioceseofwichita.org.

Catholic Diocese of Wichita—Most Rev. CARL A. KEMME, D.D.

Catholic Charities—437 N. Topeka St., Wichita, 67202. Tel: 316-264-8344; Email: wglick@catholiccharitieswichita.org. MRS. WENDY GLICK, Exec. Dir.

Cemeteries—MR. JIM SHELDON, 1640 N. Maize Rd., Wichita, 67212. Tel: 316-722-1971; Email: catholiccem@sbcglobal.net.

Communications Office—MR. MATT VAINER, Dir., Tel: 316-269-3921; Email: vainerm@catholicdioceseofwichita.org.

Cursillo (Spanish language)—Rev. JEROME A. BEAT, Spiritual Dir., (Retired), 6900 E. 45th St. N., Wichita, 67226. Tel: 316-518-4683; Email: frjabeat@gmail.com.

Cursillo (English language)—VACANT.

Building Commission—MR. BRYAN R. COULTER, CPA; Rev. KENT A. HEMBERGER; MR. MICHAEL W. WESCOTT; MR. LARRY MCLAIN; Rev. DAVID J. LIES, Chm.; Sr. LORETTA BECKIUS; MR. BRENT WOOTEN.

Stewardship Office—Rev. KENNETH S. VAN HAVERBEKE, Vicar for Stewardship and Parish Life, Email: vanhaverbekek@catholicdioceseofwichita.org;

MRS. AUDREY RONNFELDT, Coord., Email: ronnfeldta@catholicdioceseofwichita.org.

Father Kapaun Guild—Attn: Rev. John Hotze Email: hotzej@catholicdioceseofwichita.org. MR. SCOTT CARTER, Prog. Coord., Email: carters@catholicdioceseofwichita.org; Web: www.fatherkapaun.org.

Office of Faith Formation—MR. ANTHONY KEISER, Dir., Tel: 316-269-3940; Email: keisera@catholicdioceseofwichita.org; VACANT, Prog. Coord., Youth & Young Adult and College Outreach; MR. CHRIS BARNARD, Prog. Coord. Rel. Educ., Email: barnardc@catholicdioceseofwichita.org; MS. VERONICA HILL, Prog. Coord. Totus Tuus, Email: hillv@catholicdioceseofwichita.org.

Mission Formator—MS. JANICE AZIZ, Prog. Coord., Email: azizj@catholicdioceseofwichita.org.

Finance and Administrative Services Office—MR. BRYAN R. COULTER, CPA, Dir. Finance, Email: bryan.coulter@catholicdioceseofwichita.org; MR. WES ETHEREDGE, Controller, Email: etheredgew@catholicdioceseofwichita.org.

Finance Council—Most Rev. CARL A. KEMME, D.D.; Rev. DAVID J. LIES; MR. BRYAN R. COULTER, CPA; Rev. MICHAEL M. SIMONE, S.T.L.; MS. JOYE HANEBERG; MR. MARK KUHN; MR. BRADLEY SPICER; MR. VERN STRECKER; MRS. MICHELLE BECKER; MR. GEORGE DINKEL.

Health Affairs - Diocesan Liaison—Rev. MICHAEL M. SIMONE, S.T.L., Email: simonem@catholicdioceseofwichita.org.

Lord's Diner—520 N. Broadway, Wichita, 67214. Tel: 316-266-4966; Fax: 316-265-6646. Attn: Jan Haberly; Email: janh@thelordsdiner.org; Web: www.thelordsdiner.org.

Ministry with Persons with Disabilities Office—MRS. MYRA JACOBS, Dir., Email: jacobs@catholicdioceseofwichita.org.

Catholic School Office—MRS. JANET EATON, Supt., Tel: 316-269-3950; Email: supt@catholicdioceseofwichita.org.

Wichita Catholic Secondary Schools—424 N. Broadway, Wichita, 67202. Tel: 316-269-3950; Email: supt@catholicdioceseofwichita.org.

Legion of Mary—Rev. JAMES S. MAINZER, St. Jude Church, 3130 Amidon, Wichita, 67204. Tel: 316-838-1963; Email: frmainzer@stjudewichita.org.

Office of Marriage and Family Life—MR. JAKE SAMOUR, Dir., 437 N. Topeka St., Wichita, 67202. Tel: 316-685-5240; Email: samourj@catholicdioceseofwichita.org; MRS. BECKY KNAPP, Prog. Coord. Natural Family Planning, Email: knappb@catholicdioceseofwichita.org; SHARON WITZELL, Ministry to Seniors, Prog. Coord., Email: witzells@catholicdioceseofwichita.org.

Marriage Encounter—6900 E. 45th St., N., Wichita, 67226. Tel: 316-440-3087. Rev. PAUL J. OBORNY, (Retired).

Engaged Encounter—Rev. ANDREW E. HEIMAN, Contact Person, Email: frheiman@yahoo.com.

Newspaper: "The Catholic Advance"—MR. CHRISTOPHER M. RIGGS, Editor, Tel: 316-269-3921; Email: riggsc@catholicdioceseofwichita.org; MR. BRYAN R. COULTER, CPA, Business Mgr., Email: bryan.coulter@catholicdioceseofwichita.org.

Development and Planned Giving Office—MR. MICHAEL W. WESCOTT, Dir., Email: westcottm@catholicdioceseofwichita.org; MR. TRAVIS PEARSON, Planned Giving Coord., Tel: 316-269-3917; Email: pearsont@catholicdioceseofwichita.org.

Worship Office—Sr. JOHN PATRICK BECKIUS, Dir., Email: beckiusj@catholicdioceseofwichita.org; Rev. MICHAEL E. NOLAN, J.C.L., Moderator, Email: fathermike@holyspiritwichita.com.

Respect Life and Social Justice Office—MRS. BONNIE TOOMBS, Dir., Email: toombsb@catholicdioceseofwichita.org.

St. Dismas Ministry to the Incarcerated—7100 E. 45th St. N., Wichita, 67226. Tel: 316-744-0167; Email: bugnerj@catholicdioceseofwichita.org. MRS. JENNIFER BUGNER, Prog. Coord.; Rev. ROBERT K. SPENCER, Part-time Chap.

Retreats—Rev. KENNETH S. VAN HAVERBEKE, Dir., Spiritual Life Center, 7100 E. 45th St. N., Wichita, 67226. Tel: 316-744-0167; Email: vanhaverbekek@catholicdioceseofwichita.org.

Rural Life Ministry—MRS. BONNIE TOOMBS, Email: toombsb@catholicdioceseofwichita.org.

Victim Assistance Coordinator—MRS. THERESE SEILER, Tel: 316-269-3945; Email: seilert@catholicdioceseofwichita.org.

Safe Environment Program—MRS. KATHY ROBBEN, Prog. Coord., Email: robbenk@catholicdioceseofwichita.org.

Spiritual Life Center—Rev. KENNETH S. VAN HAVERBEKE, Dir., Email: vanhaverbekek@catholicdioceseofwichita.org.

Vocations—Rev. CHAD J. ARNOLD, Dir., Email: wichitavocations@gmail.com.

Hispanic Ministry Office—MRS. DANNY KRUG, Dir., 437 N. Topeka St., Wichita, 67202. Tel: 316-269-3919; Email: krugd@catholicdioceseofwichita.org.

Human Resource Office—MRS. THERESE SEILER, Dir., Email: seilert@catholicdioceseofwichita.org; MR. RANDY PHELPS, Personnel/Benefits Coord., Email: phelpsr@catholicdioceseofwichita.org.

CLERGY, PARISHES, MISSIONS AND PAROCHIAL SCHOOLS

CITY OF WICHITA

(SEDGWICK COUNTY)

1—CATHEDRAL OF THE IMMACULATE CONCEPTION (1887) 430 N. Broadway St., 67202. Tel: 316-263-6574; Fax: 316-201-1306; Email: parish@wichitacathedral.com. Revs. Adam J. Keiter, Rector; Andrew K. Hoffman, Parochial Vicar; Garett Burns, Parochial Vicar. Res.: 440 N. Topeka St., 67202.

Catechesis Religious Program—Ms. Maribel Benedict, D.R.E. Students 306.

2—ALL SAINTS (1946) [JC3] 3205 E. Grand St., 67218. Tel: 316-682-1415; Fax: 316-682-1096; Email: info@allsaintswichita.com; Web: www.allsaintswichita.com. Rev. Hien Paul Nguyen.

School—All Saints School, (Grades PreK-8), 3313 E. Grand, 67218. Tel: 316-682-6021; Fax: 316-682-8734; Email: schoolinfo@allsaintswichita.com; Web: www.allsaintswichita.com/school. Mrs. Joyce Frederiksen, Prin. Lay Teachers 13; Students 199.

Catechesis Religious Program—Email: lisenegger@allsaintswichita.com. Mrs. Sandra Nettleton, D.R.E. Students 164.

3—ST. ANNE (1955) 2801 S. Seneca, 67217-2399. Tel: 316-522-2383; Fax: 316-524-2370; Email: church@stannewichita.org; Web: www.stannewichita.org. Revs. David Marstall; John Betzen, Parochial Vicar.

School—St. Anne School, (Grades PreK-8), Tel: 316-522-6131; Fax: 316-469-0096; Email: school@stannewichita.org. Rev. John Betzen, Vice Chancellor; Pam Stead, Prin. / Librarian. Lay Teachers 13; Students 205.

Catechesis Religious Program—Email: smartinez@stannewichita.org. Andrea Zuniga. Students 133.

4—ST. ANTHONY (1887) (German) 1214 E. 2nd St. N., 67214. Tel: 316-269-4101; Email: Fr.BenNguyen@gmail.com; Web: www.stanthonywichita.com. Rev. Benjamin N. Nguyen.

Catechesis Religious Program—Khoa Tran. Students 144.

5—ST. CATHERINE OF SIENA (2008) 3642 N. Ridge Rd., 67205. Tel: 316-425-0595; Fax: 316-425-0685; Email: jrump@saintcatherinewichita.com; Web: www.saintcatherinewichita.com. Revs. Daniel J. Spexarth; Nicholaus Jurgensmeyer, Parochial Vicar.

School—St. Catherine of Sienna Catholic School, (Grades PreK-8), 3660 N. Ridge Rd., 67205. Tel: 316-719-2917; Fax: 316-719-2930; Email: school@saintcatherinewichita.com; Web: saintcatherinewichita.com/school. Jeremy Barr, Prin.; Andrea Iseman, Librarian. Lay Teachers 12; Students 246.

Catechesis Religious Program—Email: StCatherinePSR@gmail.com. Jill Rump, D.R.E. Students 224.

6—CHRIST THE KING (1950) 4411 Maple Ave., 67209. Tel: 316-943-4353; Fax: 316-943-8196; Email: cdutton@ctkwichita.org. Revs. Benjamin S. Sawyer; Edmund Herzog, Parochial Vicar.

School—Christ the King School, (Grades PreK-8), 4501 Maple Ave., 67209. Tel: 316-943-0111; Fax: 361-943-0147; Email: school@ctkwichita.org; Web: ctkwichita.org. Mrs. Cindy Chrisman, Prin. / Librarian. Lay Teachers 11; Sisters, Adorers of the Blood of Christ 1; Students 130.

Catechesis Religious Program—Tel: 316-204-0701; Email: rwinter@ctkwichita.org. Robyn Winter, D.R.E. Students 140.

7—CHURCH OF BLESSED SACRAMENT (1927) [JC] 124 N. Roosevelt, 67208. Tel: 316-682-4557; Fax: 316-682-4558; Email: mfoley@blessedsacramentwichita.com. Revs. Andrew E. Heiman; Andrew Bergkamp, Parochial Vicar; Adam Grelinger, Parochial Vicar; Curtis D.L. Hecker, In Res.

Rectory—401 S. Roosevelt Ave., 67218. Email: parish@blessedsacramentwichita.com.

School—Blessed Sacrament School, (Grades PreK-8), 125 N. Quentin, 67208. Tel: 316-684-3752; Fax: 316-687-1082; Email: school@blessedsacramentwichita.com. Mr. Dan Dester, Prin.; Pam Loyle, Librarian. Religious Teachers 1; Lay Teachers 28; Students 461.

Catechesis Religious Program—Vanessa O'Brien, PSR Coord. Students 66.

8—CHURCH OF THE MAGDALEN (1950) 12626 E. 21st St. N., 67206. Tel: 316-634-2315; Fax: 316-634-3948; Email: info@magdalenwichita.com. Very Rev. John F. Jirak, J.C.L.; Revs. Matt Davied, Parochial Vicar; Chris Martin, Parochial Vicar; Sr. Connie Beiriger, C.S.J., Pastoral Assoc.; Deacon Jeff Jacobs.

School—Magdalen School, (Grades PreK-8), 2221 N. 127th St. E, 67226. Tel: 316-634-1572; Fax: 316-634-6957; Email: wprue@magdalenwichita.com; Email: kschmitz@magdalenwichita.com; Web: www.magdalenwichita.com/school. Mrs. Kristin Schmitz, Prin. / Librarian. Lay Teachers 32; Students 504.

Catechesis Religious Program—Erin Nowicki, P.C.L.; Steve Nowicki, P.C.L. Students 137.

9—CHURCH OF THE RESURRECTION (1965) 4910 N. Woodlawn, 67220. Tel: 316-744-2776; Fax: 316-744-3027; Email: church@resurrectionwichita.com; Web: www.resurrectionwichita.org. Rev. Michael Schemm.

School—Resurrection School, (Grades PreK-8), 4900 N. Woodlawn, 67220. Tel: 316-744-3576; Email: school@resurrectionwichita.com; Web: resurrectionwichita.com/school. Kori Heiman, Prin. / Librarian. Lay Teachers 18; Students 264.

Catechesis Religious Program—Email: mweiss@resurrectionwichita.com. Molly Weiss, D.R.E. Students 77.

10—ST. ELIZABETH ANN SETON (1982) 645 N. 119th St. W., 67235. Tel: 316-721-1686; Fax: 316-721-1723; Email: church@seaswichita.com. Revs. Sherman A. Orr; Kyle Dugan, Parochial Vicar; James Schibi, Parochial Vicar.

School—St. Elizabeth Ann Seton School, (Grades PreK-8), Tel: 316-721-5693; Email: school@seaswichita.com; Web: www.seaswichita.com/school. Mr. David Charles, Prin.; Mrs. Vicki Munsinger, Librarian. Lay Teachers 37; Students 564.

Catechesis Religious Program—Email: kshorter@seaswichita.com. Karen Shorter. Students 144.

11—ST. FRANCIS OF ASSISI (1959) 861 N. Socora, 67212. Tel: 316-722-4404; Email: sfac@stfranciswichita.com; Web: www.stfranciswichita.com. Revs. C. Jarrod Lies; Andrew Labenz, Parochial Vicar; Isaac Coulter, Parochial Vicar. In Res., Rev. Samuel R. Brand.

School—St. Francis of Assisi School, (Grades PreK-8), 853 N. Socora, 67212. Tel: 316-722-5171; Fax: 316-722-0492; Email: school@stfranciswichita.com. Mary Carter, Prin.; Ashley Wescott, Library Specialist. Lay Teachers 41; Sisters 1; Students 674.

Catechesis Religious Program—Tel: 316-729-1350. Joan Hampton, D.R.E. Students 221.

12—HOLY SAVIOR (1948) (African American) 1425 N. Chautauqua, 67214. Tel: 316-682-8712; Fax: 316-682-4797; Email: holysavior@holy-savior.org. Rev. James J. Billinger.

School—Holy Savior School, (Grades PreK-8), 4640 E. 15th St., 67208. Tel: 316-684-2141; Fax: 316-684-4318; Email: school@holy-savior.org. Dr. Delia Shropshire, Prin. / Librarian. Lay Teachers 15; Students 143.

Catechesis Religious Program—Andrea Penelton. Students 62.

13—ST. JOSEPH (1886) [JC] 132 S. Millwood Ave., 67213. Tel: 316-261-5812; Fax: 316-261-5806; Email: saintjosephwichita@gmail.com; Web: stjosephwichita.com. Rev. Patrick G. York.

School—St. Joseph School, (Grades PreK-8), 139 S. Millwood Ave., 67213. Tel: 316-261-5801; Email: jcooke@stjosephwichita.com; Web: www.stjosephwichita.com/school. Ms. Ellen Albert, Prin. / Librarian. Lay Teachers 12; Students 120.

Catechesis Religious Program—Tel: 316-838-1963. Mike McDaneld, D.R.E. Students 7.

14—ST. JUDE (1958) 3030 Amidon Ave., 67204. Tel: 316-838-1963; Email: sjoffice@stjudewichita.org; Web: stjudewichita.org. Rev. James S. Mainzer.

Res.: 3130 Amidon Ave., 67204.

School—St. Jude School, (Grades PreK-8), Tel: 316-838-0800; Email: school@stjudewichita.org; Web: stjudewichita.org/school. Mrs. Danelle Urban, Prin. / Librarian. Lay Teachers 15; Students 185.

Catechesis Religious Program—Nicole Donohue, D.R.E. Students 133.

15—ST. MARGARET MARY (1954)

2701 S. Pattie St., 67216. Tel: 316-262-1821; Tel: 316-267-4911; Fax: 316-262-4057; Fax: 316-267-1707; Email: school@smmwichita.com; Email: parish@smmwichita.com; Web: smmwichita.com. Revs. Ned Blick; Michael Brungardt, Parochial Vicar.
School—St. Margaret Mary School, (Grades PreK-8), 2635 S. Pattie St., 67216. Web: smmwichita.com/school. Mrs. Theresa Lam, Prin.; Lisa Hinson, Librarian, Email: lhinson@smmwichita.com. Religious Teachers 1; Lay Teachers 15; Students 204.
Catechesis Religious Program—Tel: 316-522-4104. Mr. Cruz Narvarrete, C.R.E.; Mrs. Laura Diaz, C.R.E. Students 139.

16—OUR LADY OF GUADALUPE, Closed. For sacramental records contact St. Margaret Mary, Wichita.

17—OUR LADY OF PERPETUAL HELP (1927) [JC]
2351 N. Market St., 67219. Tel: 316-838-8373; Fax: 316-821-9250; Email: olphwichita@gmail.com. Rev. Jose Machado.
Res.: 2354 N. Market St., 67219. Tel: 316-838-3190; Email: olphwichitaks@gmail.com.
Catechesis Religious Program—Maria Lopez, D.R.E. Students 179.
Parish Center—2409 N. Market St., 67219. Tel: 316-838-5750.

18—ST. PATRICK (1910) [JC]
2007 Arkansas Ave., 67203. Tel: 316-262-4683; Fax: 316-262-0791; Email: stpatrickchurch@stpatswichita.org; Web: stpatswichita.org. Revs. James Weldon; Jacob Carlin, Parochial Vicar.
School—St. Patrick School, (Grades PreK-8), 2023 Arkansas Ave., 67203. Tel: 316-262-4071; Fax: 316-262-6217; Web: stpatswichita.org/school. Mr. Brandon Relph, Prin.; Cathy Hardesty, Librarian & Lead Teacher. Lay Teachers 15; Students 191.
Catechesis Religious Program—Students 290.
Convent—2045 Arkansas Ave., 67203. Tel: 316-267-0021. Sr. Silvia Dominquez, Prov. Sisters 4.

19—ST. PAUL PARISH (1970)
1810 N. Roosevelt, 67208. Tel: 316-684-6896; Email: stpaul@stpauluniversityparish.com; Web: www.stpauluniversityparish.com. Revs. David Michael Htun; Zachary G.B. Pinaire, Parochial Vicar.

20—ST. THOMAS AQUINAS (1957)
1321 Stratford Ln., 67206. Tel: 316-683-6569; Fax: 316-683-6672; Email: church@stthomaswichita.com; Web: www.stthomaswichita.com. Revs. Matthew C. McGinness; Joshua R. Evans, Parochial Vicar; Derek Thome, Parochial Vicar.
School—St. Thomas Aquinas School, (Grades PreK-8), 1215 Stratford Ln., 67206. Tel: 316-684-9201; Email: school@stthomaswichita.com; Web: stthomaswichita.com/school. Miss Mary Sweet, Prin.; Jane Kriwiel, Librarian. Lay Teachers 37; Students 580.
Catechesis Religious Program—1321 N. Stratford Ln., 67206. Laura Gouvion, D.R.E. Students 56.

21—ST. VINCENT DE PAUL (1955)
123 N. Andover, Andover, 67002. Tel: 316-733-1423; Fax: 316-733-1687; Email: kathleen@svdpks.org; Web: svdpks.org. Rev. Kent A. Hemberger.
Catechesis Religious Program—Email: susie@svdpks.org. Teresa Marshall-Patterson, Dir. of RCIA & Liturgical Min. Students 115.

OUTSIDE THE CITY OF WICHITA

ALEPPO, SEDGWICK CO., IMMACULATE CONCEPTION dba St. Mary, Aleppo (1890) [CEM] (German)
25741 W 13th N, P.O. Box 275, Garden Plain, 67050. Tel: 316-531-2662; Email: office@stanthonygardenplain.com. Rev. H Jay Setter. In Res., Rev. Thomas M. Hoisington, S.T.L.

ANDALE, SEDGWICK CO., ST. JOSEPH (1890) [CEM] (German)
Mailing Address: 318 Rush Ave., Box 8, Andale, 67001. Tel: 316-444-2196; Email: office@stjosephandale.com; Web: www.stjosephandale.com. Rev. Daryl Befort.
Res.: 314 Rush Ave., Andale, 67001. Email: fr.befort@stjosephandale.com.
Catechesis Religious Program—Mary Jo Hieger, D.R.E. Students 261.

ANTHONY, HARPER CO., SACRED HEART (1934) Closed. For inquiries for parish records contact St. Joan of Arc, 1023 W. Main St., Box 218, Harper, KS 67058. Merged with Immaculate Conception, Danville & St. Patrick, Harper to form Joan of Arc, Harper.

ARKANSAS CITY, COWLEY CO., SACRED HEART (1886)
Mailing Address: 302 S. B St., Arkansas City, 67005. Tel: 620-442-0566; Fax: 620-441-0935; Email: parish@sacredheartarkcity.org; Web: www.sacredheartac.com. Rev. Patrick R. Reilley.
Res.: 308 S. B St., Arkansas City, 67005.
School—Sacred Heart School, (Grades PreK-5), 312 S. B St., Arkansas City, 67005. Tel: 620-442-6550; Email: jlarson@sacredheartarkcity.org. Eva Harmon, Prin. / Librarian; Jamie Larson, Sec. Lay Teachers 5; Students 89.
Catechesis Religious Program—Email: dre@sacredheartarkcity.org. Theresa Kuffler, D.R.E., (Grades 1-12). Students 92.

ARMA, CRAWFORD CO., ST. JOSEPH (1934)
310 W. South St., P.O. Box 948, Arma, 66712. Tel: 620-347-4525; Email: stjoseph@ckt.net. Rev. Floyd E. McKinney.
Catechesis Religious Program—

AUGUSTA, BUTLER CO., ST. JAMES THE GREATER (1879) [CEM]
1012 Belmont Ave., Augusta, 67010. Tel: 316-775-2155; Tel: 316-775-5127; Email: frjohn@saintjamesaugusta.com. Rev. John N. Hay.
School—St. James School, (Grades PreK-7), Tel: 316-775-5721; Email: stjames_sec@hotmail.com. Richard Guy, Prin. / Librarian. Lay Teachers 7; Students 125.
Catechesis Religious Program—Tel: 316-775-6312; Email: kmartinez@saintjamesaugusta.com. Kathi Martinez, D.R.E. Students 130.

BAXTER SPRINGS, CHEROKEE CO., ST. JOSEPH (1917) [JC]
115 W. Walnut, Columbus, 66725. Tel: 620-429-2639; Email: ckcocatholics@live.com; Web: www.ckcocatholics.org. 324 E. 12th St., Baxter Springs, 66713. Rev. Jeremy S. Huser.
Catechesis Religious Program—

BURNS, MARION CO., IMMACULATE CONCEPTION, Closed. For sacramental records contact Holy Family, Marion.

BUSHTON, RICE CO., HOLY NAME OF JESUS (1878) [CEM] (German)
296 3rd Rd., Bushton, 67427. Tel: 620-257-3503; Email: parishoffice@stpaulslyons.com. 415 Saint Francis St., Lyons, 67554. Rev. Patrick S. Kotrba.
Catechesis Religious Program—Tel: 620-562-3662. Jennifer Short, D.R.E.

CALDWELL, SUMNER CO., ST. MARTIN OF TOURS (1888) [JC]
428 N. Main, P.O. Box 289, Caldwell, 67022. Tel: 620-845-6763; Email: stmartinscaldwell@gmail.com. Rev. Hung Quoc Pham. Mission of St. Anthony/St. Rose Parish, Wellington.

CANEY, MONTGOMERY CO., SACRED HEART (1910)
301 N. Hooker, Caney, 67333. Rev. Robert K. Spencer.
Catechesis Religious Program—Tel: 620-879-2883; Email: communications@catholicdioceseofwichita.org. Janette Buster, D.R.E. Students 5.

CAPALDO, CRAWFORD CO., ST. ALICE, Closed. For sacramental records contact Sacred Heart, Frontenac.

CASTLETON, RENO CO., ST. AGNES (1872) Closed. For inquiries for sacramental records contact St. Teresa, Hutchinson.

CEDAR VALE, CHAUTAUQUA CO., ST. JOSEPH, Closed. For inquiries for parish records contact the chancery.

CHANUTE, NEOSHO CO., ST. PATRICK (1873) [CEM 2]
424 S. Central, Chanute, 66720. Tel: 620-431-3165; Fax: 620-431-6587; Email: frlinnebur@gmail.com. Rev. Michael J. Linnebur.
School—St. Patrick School, (Grades PreK-6), 409 S. Malcolm, Chanute, 66720. Tel: 620-431-4020; Email: mdurand@stpatrickchanute.org; Web: stpatrickchanute.org/school. Mary Durand, Prin. / Librarian. Lay Teachers 7; Students 99.
Catechesis Religious Program—Tel: (620-431-9263; Email: 92atonpeters@gmail.com. Dennis Peters, D.R.E. Students 95.

CHASE, RICE CO., ST. MARY (1888) (German), Closed. For inquiries for sacramental records contact St. Paul, Lyons.

CHEROKEE, CRAWFORD CO., ST. ANASTASIA, Closed. For sacramental records contact Our Lady of Lourdes, Pittsburg.

CHERRYVALE, MONTGOMERY CO., ST. FRANCIS XAVIER (1871) [CEM] (German)
202 S. Liberty St., Cherryvale, 67335. Tel: 620-331-1789; Email: standrewindp@sbcglobal.net. Rev. Marco A. de Loera.
Catechesis Religious Program—Students 6.

CHETOPA, LABETTE CO., SACRED HEART (1873) [CEM] Closed. For sacramental records contact Mother of God Parish, Oswego.

CHICOPEE, CRAWFORD CO., ST. BARBARA, Closed. For sacramental records contact Our Lady of Lourdes, Pittsburg.

COFFEYVILLE, MONTGOMERY CO., HOLY NAME (1869) [CEM 2] (Irish—German)
408 Willow St., Coffeyville, 67337. Tel: 620-251-0475; Email: d.howard878@gmail.com. Rev. Daniel S. Lorimer.
School—Holy Name School, (Grades PreK-6), 406 Willow St., Coffeyville, 67337. Tel: 620-251-0480; Fax: 620-251-1651; Email: schooloffice@holyname.kscoxmail.com. Lisa Payne, Prin. / Librarian. Lay Teachers 8; Students 82.
Catechesis Religious Program—Email: jabrittain@csjoseph.org. Sr. Janelle Brittain, D.R.E. Students 90.

COLUMBUS, CHEROKEE CO., ST. ROSE (1887) [JC]
115 W. Walnut St., Columbus, 66725. Tel: 620-429-2639; Email: ckcocatholics@live.com; Web: www.ckcocatholics.org. Rev. Jeremy S. Huser.
Catechesis Religious Program—Tel: 620-429-2938; Email: jabrittain@csjoseph.org. Regina Jameson, Contact. Students 35.

COLWICH, SEDGWICK CO.

1—ST. MARK (1876) [CEM] (German)
19230 W. 29th St. N., Colwich, 67030. Tel: 316-796-1604; Fax: 316-796-0511; Email: secretary@stmarkks.org; Web: stmarkks.org. Rev. Brian D. Nelson, J.C.L.
Catechesis Religious Program—Email: mollym@stmarksks.org. Molly Milana, D.R.E. Students 171.

2—SACRED HEART (1901) [CEM]
311 S. Fifth St., P.O. Box 578, Colwich, 67030. Tel: 316-796-1224; Email: office@sacredheartcolwich.org; Web: www.sacredheartcolwich.org. Rev. Eric M. Weldon; Mrs. Julie Bardon, Sec.; Mrs. Kathy Seltenreich, Bookkeeper.
Res.: 231 S. Fifth St., Colwich, 67030. Tel: 316-796-0759.
Catechesis Religious Program—Tel: 316-796-1604; Email: croth@sacredheartcolwich.org. Christopher Roth. Students 98.

CONWAY SPRINGS, SUMNER CO., ST. JOSEPH (1886) [CEM] (German)
217 N. Sixth St., Conway Springs, 67031. Tel: 316-456-2276; Fax: 316-456-3317; Email: sjcs@juno.com. Rev. Stuart M. Smeltzer, J.C.L.
School—St. Joseph School, (Grades PreK-6), 218 N. 5th St., Conway Springs, 67031. Tel: 316-456-2270; Fax: 316-456-2272; Email: kbaalmann@stjoecs.org; Web: stjoecs.org/school. Joel Arnold, Prin. / Librarian. Lay Teachers 7; Students 97.
Catechesis Religious Program—Students 122.

COUNCIL GROVE, MORRIS CO., ST. ROSE OF LIMA (1883) [CEM] [JC2]
300 Spencer St., Council Grove, 66846. Tel: 620-767-6412; Fax: 620-767-5370; Email: rosalima@cgtelco.net. Rev. Theodore Khin.
Catechesis Religious Program—Tel: 620-528-3797; Email: julieg@satelephone.com. Julie Galloway, C.R.E., Tel: 620-528-3797. Students 65.

CUNNINGHAM, KINGMAN CO., SACRED HEART (1908) [CEM] (German)
8035 S.W. 160th Ave., Cunningham, 67112. Tel: 620-246-5370; Email: judicis20@yahoo.com. 404 E. First St., Cunningham, 67035. Rev. Roger S. Lumbre.
Catechesis Religious Program—Renee D. Adelhardt, D.R.E. Students 52.

DANVILLE, HARPER CO., IMMACULATE CONCEPTION (1883) Closed. For inquiries for parish records contact St. Joan of Arc, 1023 W. Main St., Box 218, Harper, KS 67058. Merged with St. Patrick, Harper & Sacred Heart, Anthony to form Joan of Arc, Harper.

DERBY, SEDGWICK CO., ST. MARY CATHOLIC CHURCH (1954)
2300 E. Meadowlark Rd., Derby, 67037. Tel: 316-788-5525; Fax: 316-788-1577; Email: questions@stmarysderby.com; Web: stmarysderby.com. Rev. Joseph A. Eckberg.
School—St. Mary Catholic School, (Grades PreK-8), 2306 E. Meadowlark Rd., Derby, 67037. Tel: 316-788-3151; Fax: 316-788-6895; Email: alesley@stmarysderby.com. Mr. Richard Montgomery, Prin.; Jean Schif, Librarian. Lay Teachers 25; Students 365.
Catechesis Religious Program—Tel: 316-776-0831; Email: religioused@stmarysderby.com. Catherine Wilson, Dir. Students 47.

EL DORADO, BUTLER CO., ST. JOHN THE EVANGELIST (1915)
302 N. Denver Ave., El Dorado, 67042. Tel: 316-321-4796; Fax: 316-321-1831; Email: mail@stjohneldorado.com. Very Rev. John P. Lanzrath, S.T.L.
Catechesis Religious Program—Tel: 316-321-4933. Lynca Cope, D.R.E. Students 19.

ERIE, NEOSHO CO., ST. AMBROSE (1915)
519 N. Main, Erie, 66733. Tel: 620-449-2224; Email: saintfrancis66771@gmail.com. Rev. Samuel J. Pinkerton.
Res: P.O. Box 216, St. Paul, 66771.
Catechesis Religious Program—Email: stfrancis@rlrnews.com. Suzie Diskin, D.R.E. Students 116.

EUREKA, GREENWOOD CO., SACRED HEART (1881) [JC] (German)
514 N. Elm St., Eureka, 67045. Tel: 620-583-7100; Email: gronert1@yahoo.com. Rev. Stephen F. Gronert.
Catechesis Religious Program—Students 23.

FLORENCE, MARION CO., ST. PATRICK, Closed. Merged with St. Mark, Marion; St. John Nepomucene, Pilsen and Holy Redeemer, Tampa to form Holy Family, Marion.

FORT SCOTT, BOURBON CO., MARY QUEEN OF ANGELS (1860) [CEM]
716 S. Eddy St., Fort Scott, 66701-2506.
Tel: 620-223-4340; Fax: 620-223-6060; Email: mqa@mqaftscott.com. Rev. Robert B. Wachter.
School—Mary Queen of Angels School, (Grades PreK-5), 702 S. Eddy St., Fort Scott, 66701-2506. Email: sms@smsftscott.com; Web: smsftscott.com. Krista Gorman, Prin.; Jill Gorman, Librarian. Lay Teachers 5; Students 64.
Catechesis Religious Program—705 S. Holbrook St, Fort Scott, 66701. Email: michaudjennifer@gmail.com. Jennifer Michaud, D.R.E. Students 54.

FREDONIA, WILSON CO., SACRED HEART (1906) [CEM]
1223 Madison, P.O. Box 537, Fredonia, 66736.
Tel: 620-378-3658; Email: sacredheart.fkb@gmail.com. Rev. Daniel L. Vacca.
Catechesis Religious Program—Mrs. Sandy Borror, D.R.E. Students 33.

FRONTENAC, CRAWFORD CO., SACRED HEART (1891) [CEM] (Italian)
100 S. Cherokee St., Frontenac, 66763.
Tel: 620-231-7747; Email: sacredheart@kscoxmail.com. Rev. Philip John (P.J.) Voegeli Jr.
Catechesis Religious Program—Email: monawachter46@gmail.com. Mona Wachter, P.C.L. (Parish Catechetical Leader). Students 109.

FULTON, BOURBON CO., ST. PATRICK, Closed. For sacramental records contact Mary Queen of Angels, Fort Scott.

GALENA, CHEROKEE CO., ST. PATRICK (1879) [JC]
115 W. Walnut, Columbus, 66725. Tel: 620-429-2639; Email: ckcocatholics@live.com; Web: www.ckcocatholics.org. 307 Galena Ave., Galena, 66739. Rev. Jeremy S. Huser.
Catechesis Religious Program—Students 7.

GARDEN PLAIN, SEDGWICK CO., ST. ANTHONY (1901) [CEM] (German)
607 N. Main, Garden Plain, 67050.
Tel: 316-531-2252; Email: office@stanthonygardenplain.com. 616 Biermann St., P.O. Box 275, Garden Plain, 67050. Rev. H Jay Setter.
Res.: 615 N. Main, Garden Plain, 67050. Email: admin@stanthony.kscoxmail.com.
Catechesis Religious Program—Email: jpuetz@sta.kscoxmail.com. Julie Puetz, D.R.E. Students 304.

GIRARD, CRAWFORD CO., ST. MICHAEL (1925) (Irish—German)
106 N. Western St., Girard, 66743. Tel: 620-724-8717 ; Email: padreflojo007@live.com. Rev. Floyd E. McKinney.
Catechesis Religious Program—Email: stjoseph@ckt.net. Michelle Puckett, D.R.E. (6-12th Grade); Barb Duling, D.R.E. (Grade School). Students 85.

GODDARD, SEDGWICK CO., CHURCH OF THE HOLY SPIRIT (1998)
18218 W. Hwy. 54, Goddard, 67052.
Tel: 316-794-3496; Fax: 316-794-3795; Email: parish@holyspiritwichita.com; Web: www.holyspiritwichita.com. Rev. Matthew D. Marney.
Res.: 1206 Harvest Ln., Goddard, 67052. Email: fmarney@holyspiritwichita.com.
School—Holy Spirit School, (Grades PreSchool-8), Tel: 316-794-8139; Email: kbright@holyspiritwichita.com; Web: www.holyspiritwichita.com/school. Rev. Michael E. Nolan, J.C.L., Contact Person; Kelly Bright, Prin. / Librarian. Lay Teachers 13; Students 174.
Catechesis Religious Program—Email: rkerschen@holyspiritwichita.com. Rita Kerschen, D.R.E. Students 173.

GREENBUSH, CRAWFORD CO., ST. ALOYSIUS, Closed. For sacramental records contact St. Michael, Girard.

HALSTEAD, HARVEY CO., SACRED HEART PARISH (1874) [JC]
419 Poplar, Halstead, 67056.
Tel: 316-830-2818 (Office); Email: shcsecretary@hotmail.com; Web: www.SacredHeartHalstead.com. Rev. Jeffery A. Fasching.
Catechesis Religious Program—Tel: 316-830-2764. Carolyn Armendariz, D.R.E. Students 50.

HAMILTON, GREENWOOD CO., ST. JOHN (1888) (German)
514 N. Elm St., Eureka, 67045. Tel: 620-583-7100; Email: gronert1@yahoo.com. Rev. Stephen F. Gronert.
Catechesis Religious Program—Students 19.

HARPER, HARPER CO.
1—ST. JOAN OF ARC (1997) (Irish—German) Consolidation of St. Patrick, Harper; Immaculate Conception, Danville & Sacred Heart, Anthony. Merged in 1997.
1023 W. Main, P.O. Box 218, Harper, 67058.
Tel: 620-896-7886; Fax: 620-896-2249; Email: stjoan@cyberlodge.com. Rev. Babu Pinninti.
Immaculate Conception—102 Ashman St., Danville, 67036.
St. Patrick, 1023 W. Main St., Harper, 67058.
Sacred Heart, Anthony, 121 S. Madison Ave., Anthony, 67003.
Catechesis Religious Program—Students 39.
2—ST. PATRICK (1882) Closed. For inquiries for parish records contact St. Joan of Arc, 1023 W. Main St., Box 218, Harper, KS 67058. Merged with Immaculate Conception, Danville & Sacred Heart, Anthony to form Joan of Arc, Harper.

HAYSVILLE, SEDGWICK CO., ST. CECILIA (1959)
1900 W. Grand, Haysville, 67060. Tel: 316-524-7801; Fax: 316-524-6183; Email: fr.yanceyburgess@stceciliahaysville.org. Rev. Yancey Q. Burgess.
School—St. Cecilia School, (Grades PreK-8), 1912 W. Grand, Haysville, 67060. Tel: 316-522-0461; Email: mbowmaker@stceciliahaysville.org. Mr. Gerry Hamilton, Prin.; Jane Betzen, Librarian. Lay Teachers 9; Students 89.
Catechesis Religious Program—Email: mamiller2006@swbell.net. Marcia Miller, D.R.E. Students 60.

HUMBOLDT, ALLEN CO., ST. JOSEPH (1867) [CEM]
Mailing Address: St. Patrick Catholic Church, 424 S. Central Ave., Chanute, 66720.
Tel: 620-431-3165 (Chanute - St. Patrick Office); Fax: 620-431-6587; Email: frlinnebur@gmail.com. 514 Central, Humboldt, 66748. Rev. Michael J. Linnebur.
Catechesis Religious Program—Students 23.

HUTCHINSON, RENO CO.
1—CHURCH OF THE HOLY CROSS (1957) [CEM 3] [JC]
2631 Independence Rd., Hutchinson, 67502.
Tel: 620-665-5163; Fax: 620-662-5085; Email: rectory@holycross-hutch.com. Revs. Aaron Spexarth; Michael Kerschen; Deacon Hap Ramsey.
School—Holy Cross School, (Grades PreK-6), 2633 Independence Rd., Hutchinson, 67502.
Tel: 620-665-6168; Email: doohl@holycross-hutch.com; Web: holycross-hutch.com/school. Mrs. Amy Wagoner, Prin. / Librarian. Religious Teachers 1; Lay Teachers 20; Students 291.
Catechesis Religious Program—Kim Griffith, D.R.E. Students 119.
2—OUR LADY OF GUADALUPE (1927) (Hispanic)
612 S. Maple, South Hutchinson, 67505-2099.
Tel: 620-662-6443; Fax: 620-662-6443; Email: olgnewton@gmail.com. Revs. Juan G. Garza; Todd Shepherd, Parochial Vicar.
Catechesis Religious Program—Email: office@olghutch.com. Jim Hoover, D.R.E. Students 101.
3—ST. TERESA (1897) [CEM]
211 E. Fifth Ave., Hutchinson, 67501.
Tel: 620-662-7812; Fax: 620-259-6921; Email: stteresahutchinson@gmail.com. Rev. Michael J. Maybrier.
Catechesis Religious Program—Tel: 620-662-5234; Email: Stevedechant@cox.net. Steve Dechant, Contact. Students 18.

INDEPENDENCE, MONTGOMERY CO., ST. ANDREW (1869) [CEM 2] (German—Mexican)
210 N. Fourth St., Independence, 67301.
Tel: 620-331-1789; Fax: 620-331-6496; Email: standrewindp@sbcglobal.net. Rev. Marco A. de Loera.
School—St. Andrew School, (Grades PreK-8), 215 N. Park Blvd., Independence, 67310. Tel: 620-331-2870; Email: school@standrewindependence.com; Web: standrewindependence.com/school. Becky Brown, Prin. / Librarian. Lay Teachers 10; Students 136.
Catechesis Religious Program—Tel: 316-253-5989. Students 22.

IOLA, ALLEN CO., ST. JOHN (1897) [CEM] [JC]
310 S. Jefferson Ave., Iola, 66749. Tel: 620-365-2277; Email: cessnan17255@gmail.com. Rev. John P. Miller; Deacon Theodore Stahl.
Res.: 314 S. Jefferson Ave., Iola, 66749.
Tel: 620-365-3454; Email: faithformation@stjohnsclonmel.org.
Catechesis Religious Program—Tel: 316-365-8488. Cassi Fitzgerard. Students 17.
ST. MARTIN, 1368 Xylan Rd. KS 66761, Piqua, 66761.

KINGMAN, KINGMAN CO., ST. PATRICK (1885) [JC] (Irish)
638 Ave. D W., Kingman, 67068. Tel: 316-532-5440; Email: office@stpatskingman.org; Web: www.stpatskingman.org. Rev. Andrew J. Walsh.
School—St. Patrick School, (Grades PreK-8), 630 Ave. D W., Kingman, 67068. Tel: 620-532-2791; Email: eharmon@stpatskingman.org; Web: stpatskingman.org/school. Eva Harmon, Prin.; Mary Meng, Librarian. Lay Teachers 14; Students 157.
Catechesis Religious Program—Students 39.

LIBERTY, MONTGOMERY CO., ALL SAINTS, Closed. For inquiries for parish records contact the chancery.

LINDSBORG, MCPHERSON CO., ST. BRIDGET OF SWEDEN (1985)
Mailing Address: 520 E Northview, McPherson, 67460. Tel: 620-241-0821; Fax: 620-245-9677; Email: office@stjosephmcpherson.com. 206 W Swennson, Lindsborg, 67456. Rev. Benjamin D. Shockey.
Res.: 1524 Sonora Dr., McPherson, 67460.
Catechesis Religious Program—Laurie Rutherford. Students 28.

LITTLE RIVER, RICE CO., HOLY TRINITY (1885) [JC]
Mailing Address: 455 Harrison St., Little River, 67457. Tel: 620-665-5163; Email: rectory@holycross-hutch.com. Revs. Aaron Spexarth; Michael Kerschen. Office & Res.: 2631 Independence Rd., Hutchinson, 67502.
Catechesis Religious Program—Tel: 620-897-7740; Email: grasser@lrmutual.com. Mrs. Shayla Grasser, D.R.E. Students 40.

LYONS, RICE CO., ST. PAUL (1927) [JC]
415 Saint Francis St., Lyons, 67554.
Tel: 620-257-3503; Fax: 620-257-3021; Email: parishoffice@stpaulslyons.com; Web: stpaulslyons.com. 1205 S. Douglas, Lyons, 67554. Rev. Patrick S. Kotrba.
Catechesis Religious Program—Tel: 620-680-0441; Email: only1damama@yahoo.com. Donetta Birzer, D.R.E. Students 95.

MADISON, GREENWOOD CO., ST. TERESA OF AVILA (1954) [JC] (German)
514 N. Elm St., Eureka, 67045. Tel: 620-583-7100; Email: stteresahutchinson@gmail.com. Rev. Stephen F. Gronert.
Catechesis Religious Program—

MARION, MARION CO., HOLY FAMILY (1992) [CEM] [JC2] Parish formed from merger of St. Mark, Marion; St. John Nepomucene, Pilsen; St. Patrick, Florence; Holy Redeemer, Tampa and Immaculate Conception, Burns.
415 N. Cedar St., Marion, 66861. Tel: 620-382-3369; Email: hfpmarion@yahoo.com; Web: hfpmc.org. Rev. Brian D. Bebak.
St. Patrick—201 W. 8th, Florence, 66851.
St. Mark, 415 N. Cedar, Marion, 66861.
St. John Nepomucene, 2744 Remington, Pilsen, 66861.
Catechesis Religious Program—Heather Schlehuber; Theresa Cady. Students 99.
HOLY REDEEMER CHURCH, 426 Main, Tampa, 67483.

MCPHERSON, MCPHERSON CO., ST. JOSEPH (1880)
520 E. Northview, McPherson, 67460.
Tel: 620-241-0821; Fax: 620-245-9677; Email: lharger@stjosephmcpherson.com. Rev. Benjamin D. Shockey.
Res.: 1524 Sonora Dr., McPherson, 67460. Email: office@stjosephmcpherson.com.
School—St. Joseph School, (Grades PreK-6), Tel: 620-241-3913; Email: school@stjosephmcpherson.com; Web: stjosephmcpherson.com/school. Peggy Bahr, Prin. / Librarian. Lay Teachers 11; Students 129.
Catechesis Religious Program—Linda Harger, D.R.E. Students 102.

MOLINE, ELK CO., ST. MARY'S (1899) [CEM]
320 N. Main, Box 276, Moline, 67353-0276.
Tel: 620-647-3577; Email: bailadores33@yahoo.com. Rev. Robert K. Spencer.
Catechesis Religious Program—Students 15.

MOUNT VERNON, KINGMAN CO., ST. ROSE (1911) [CEM] (German—Irish)
13015 E. Maple Grove Rd., Mount Hope, 67030.
Tel: 316-444-2210; Email: frdanieljduling@gmail.com. 4813 N.E. 150 Ave., Cheney, 67025. Rev. Daniel J. Duling.
Catechesis Religious Program—Tel: 316-542-3990; Email: tammiehopper@gmail.com. Tammie Hopper, D.R.E. Students 6.

MULBERRY, CRAWFORD CO., ST. GABRIEL, Closed. For sacramental records contact Sacred Heart, Frontenac.

MULVANE, SUMNER CO., ST. MICHAEL THE ARCHANGEL (1948)
525 E. Main St., Mulvane, 67110. Tel: 316-777-4221; Email: stmichaelmulvane@sbcglobal.net. Rev. John V. Hotze, J.C.L.
Res.: 545 E. Main St., Mulvane, 67110.
Tel: 316-777-4749.
Catechesis Religious Program—Email: dre@stmichaelmulvane.org. Mrs. Joanne Nesmith, D.R.E. Students 175.

NEODESHA, WILSON CO., ST. IGNATIUS (1876) [CEM]
801 N 8th, P.O. Box 186, Neodesha, 66757.
Tel: 620-325-5215; Email: stignatiusneodesha@gmail.com. Rev. Daniel L. Vacca.
Catechesis Religious Program—816 Grant St., Neodesha, 66757. Jodi Stover, D.R.E. Students 29.

NEWTON, HARVEY CO.
1—ST. MARY (1872) [CEM]
106 E. Eighth St., Newton, 67114. Tel: 316-282-0459; Email: parish@stmarynewton.org; Web: www.stmarynewton.org. Rev. Nicholas A. Voelker.
School—St. Mary School, (Grades PreK-8), 101 E. 9th St., Newton, 67114. Tel: 316-282-1974; Email: mkellogg@smcsnewton.org; Web: smcsnewton.org/school. Philip Stutey, Prin. / Librarian. Lay Teachers 10; Students 208.
Catechesis Religious Program—Tel: 620-960-5602;

Email: rtierney@stmarynewton.org. Rob Tierney, Coord. Parish Ministries. Students 53.
2—OUR LADY OF GUADALUPE (1919) [JC] (Hispanic)
421 S. Ash St., Newton, 67114. Tel: 316-283-3499; Fax: 316-283-6813; Email: olgnewton@gmail.com. Rev. Devin T. Burns.
Catechesis Religious Program—Brenda Thompson, D.R.E. Students 69.
OST, RENO CO., ST. JOSEPH (1880) [CEM] (German)
13015 E. Maple Grove Rd., Mount Hope, 67108. Tel: 316-444-2210; Email: frdanieljduling@gmail.com. Rev. Daniel J. Duling.
School—St. Joseph Catholic School - Ost, (Grades PreK-8), 12917 E. Maple Grove Rd., Mount Hope, 67108. Tel: 316-444-2548; Fax: 316-444-2448; Email: ehohl@stjoeost.com. Erin Hohl, Prin.; J. Simon, Librarian. Lay Teachers 12; Students 170.
Catechesis Religious Program—Email: eastbeast2001@hotmail.com. Deanna Helten, D.R.E. Students 15.
OSWEGO, LABETTE CO., MOTHER OF GOD (1878) [JC]
1105 4th St., Oswego, 67356. Tel: 620-795-2262; Email: mogoswego@gmail.com. Rev. Larry Parker, Parochial Admin., (Retired).
Catechesis Religious Program—Email: lparker64@cox.net. Pam Overman, D.R.E. Students 47.
OXFORD, SUMNER CO., ST. MARY'S
608 N. Sumner, Oxford, 67119. Tel: 620-455-9955; Email: gwalker@holynamewinfield.org. Rev. Kenneth J. Schuckman.
PARSONS, LABETTE CO.
1—MARY QUEEN OF PEACE (1909) Closed. For inquiries for parish records contact St. Patrick, Parsons.
2—ST. PATRICK (1872) [CEM 2]
1807 Stevens Ave., Parsons, 67357. Tel: 620-421-6762; Email: rectory@stpatricksparsons.org; Web: stpatricksparsons.org. Rev. Curtis L. Robertson.
School—St. Patrick School, (Grades PreSchool-8), 1831 Stevens Ave., Parsons, 67357. Tel: 620-421-0710; Fax: 620-421-2429; Email: school@stpatricksparsons.org; Web: stpatricksparsons.org/school. Emilio Aita, Prin. / Librarian. Lay Teachers 11; Students 126.
Catechesis Religious Program—Jane Alexander, Catechetical Leader. Students 90.
PILSEN, MARION CO., ST. JOHN NEPOMUCENE, Closed. Merged with St. Mark, Marion; St. Patrick, Florence and Holy Redeemer, Tampa to form Holy Family, Marion.
PIQUA, WOODSON CO., ST. MARTIN (1884) (German), Closed. For inquiries for sacramental records contact St. John, Iola.
PITTSBURG, CRAWFORD CO., OUR LADY OF LOURDES (1881) [CEM]
Mailing Address: 109 E. 9th St., P.O. Box 214, Pittsburg, 66762. Tel: 620-231-2135; Fax: 620-231-4804; Email: ourladyoflourdes@ollsmc.com. Revs. Jerome J. Spexarth; Clay Kimbro, Parochial Vicar; Jorge Lopez, Parochial Vicar; David M. Voss, In Res.
Res.: 916 N. Locust, Pittsburg, 66762.
Schools—St. Mary's Elementary School—(Grades PreK-8), (Elementary) 301 E. 9th St., Pittsburg, 66762. Tel: 620-231-6941; Fax: 620-235-7442; Email: smeschool@ollsmc.com. Nancy Hicks, Prin., (Pre-K-6); Terri Tener, Librarian. Religious Teachers 1; Lay Teachers 20; Students 303.
St. Mary's Colgan Junior High, (Grades 7-8), 212 E. 9th St., Pittsburg, 66762. Tel: 620-231-4690; Fax: 620-231-0690; Web: www.ollsmc.com. David Stephenson, Prin.; Beverly Mitchelson, Librarian. Lay Teachers 6; Students 73.
High School—St. Mary's Colgan High School, Tel: 620-231-4690; Fax: 620-231-0690; Email: smcjhhs@ollsmc.com. David Stephenson, Prin.; Beverly Mitchelson, Librarian. Religious Teachers 4; Lay Teachers 17; Students 156.
Catechesis Religious Program—Fax: 620-231-0690. Students 22.
ST. LEO, KINGMAN CO., ST. LEO THE GREAT (1906) [CEM] (German)
8035 S.W. 160 Ave., Nashville, 67112. Tel: 620-246-5370; Email: judicis20@yahoo.com. Rev. Roger S. Lumbre.
Catechesis Religious Program—Tel: 620-298-2601.
ST. PAUL, NEOSHO CO., ST. FRANCIS (1847) [CEM 2]
208 Washington St., P.O. Box 216, St. Paul, 66771-0216. Tel: 620-449-2224; Email: saintfrancis66771@gmail.com. Rev. Samuel J. Pinkerton.
Catechesis Religious Program—Tel: 620-449-2672; Email: suzdiskin@yahoo.com. Suzie Diskin, D.R.E. Students 113.
SCAMMON, CHEROKEE CO., ST. BRIDGET'S (1868) [CEM]
115 W. Walnut, Columbus, 66725. Tel: 620-479-2601; Fax: 620-429-2639; Email: ckcocatholics@live.com; Web: www.ckcocatholics.org. 406 N Keith, Scammon, 66773. Rev. Jeremy S. Huser.
Catechesis Religious Program—Tel: 620-479-2236. Students 33.
SCHULTE, SEDGWICK CO., ST. PETER THE APOSTLE (1905) [CEM]
11000 S.W. Blvd., 67215. Tel: 316-524-4259; Fax: 316-524-0932; Email: psecretary@stpeterschulte.com; Web: www.stpeterschulte.com. Rev. Bernard X. Gorges.
Res.: 10980 S.W. Blvd., 67215. Tel: 316-522-4728; Email: ckcocatholics@live.com.
School—St. Peter the Apostle School, (Grades PreK-8), 11010 S.W. Blvd., 67215. Tel: 316-524-6585; Fax: 316-524-1656; Email: school@stpeterschulte.com; Web: stpeterschulte.com/school. Brenda Hickok, Prin. / Librarian. Religious Teachers 1; Lay Teachers 24; Preschool 49; Sisters 1; Students 301.
Catechesis Religious Program—Tel: 620-762-1626. Madeline Lubbers, Youth Min. Students 40.
SEDAN, CHAUTAUQUA CO., ST. ROBERT BELLARMINE (1962)
320 N. Main, P.O. Box 276, Moline, 67353-0276. Tel: 620-647-3577; Email: bailadores33@yahoo.com. 407 S. Montgomery, Sedan, 67361. Rev. Robert K. Spencer.
Catechesis Religious Program—Tel: 620-725-3812. Students 10.
STRONG CITY, CHASE CO., ST. ANTHONY OF PADUA (1880) [CEM] [JC]
300 Spencer, Council Grove, 66846. Tel: 620-767-6412; Fax: 620-767-5370; Email: rosalima@cgtelco.net. Rev. Theodore Khin.
Catechesis Religious Program—Tel: 620-273-8617. Frances Unruh, C.R.E. Students 31.
VIOLA, SEDGWICK CO., ST. JOHN (1878) [CEM]
18630 W. 71st St., Viola, 67149. Tel: 620-545-7171; Tel: 620-545-7211 (Parish Hall); Email: parish@stjohnsclonmel.org; Web: www.stjohnsclonmel.org. Rev. Joseph C. Tatro.
Parish Center—
Catechesis Religious Program—Email: dtamburro@stjohnsclonmel.org; Email: faithformation@stjohnsclonmel.org; Email: frjtatro@stjohnsclonmel.org. Cassi FitzGerald, D.R.E. Students 138.
WALNUT, CRAWFORD CO., ST. PATRICK, Closed. For sacramental records contact St. Francis Church, St. Paul.
WATERLOO, KINGMAN CO., ST. LOUIS (1881) [CEM] [JC] (German—Irish)
13015 E. Maple Grove Rd., Mount Hope, 67108. Tel: 316-444-2210; Email: frdanieljduling@gmail.com. 9800 N.E. 20th St., Murdock, 67111. Rev. Daniel J. Duling.
Catechesis Religious Program—Email: omwsecretary@gmail.com. Tammie Hopper, Contact Person. Students 93.
WEIR, CHEROKEE CO., SACRED HEART, Closed. For sacramental records contact St. Rose of Lima, Columbus.
WELLINGTON, SUMNER CO.
1—ST. ANTHONY (1884) Merged with St. Rose of Lima, Wellington to form St. Anthony/St. Rose, Wellington. For inquiries for parish records contact St. Anthony/St. Rose.
2—ST. ANTHONY/ST. ROSE (1907)
217 N. C. St., Wellington, 67152. Tel: 620-326-2522; Email: revpham@gmail.com. Revs. Hung Quoc Pham; Maximilian Blitz, In Res.
Catechesis Religious Program—Tel: 620-326-3480. Pam Robinett, D.R.E. Students 107.
3—ST. ROSE OF LIMA (1949) (Hispanic), Merged with St. Anthony, Wellington to form St. Anthony/St. Rose, Wellington. For inquiries for parish records, contact St. Anthony/St. Rose, Wellington.
WEST MINERAL, CHEROKEE CO., IMMACULATE CONCEPTION, Closed. For sacramental records contact St. Rose of Lima, Columbus.
WILLOWDALE, KINGMAN CO., ST. PETER (1884) [CEM] (German)
8035 S.W. 160th Ave., Nashville, 67112. Tel: 620-246-5370; Email: judicis20@yahoo.com. 10044 SW 90 St., Spivey, 67142. Rev. Roger S. Lumbre.
Catechesis Religious Program—
WINFIELD, COWLEY CO., HOLY NAME (1878) [JC]
412 E. Eighth St., Winfield, 67156. Tel: 620-221-3610 ; Fax: 316-221-3528; Email: gwalker@holynamewinfield.org. Rev. Kenneth J. Schuckman.
School—Holy Name School, (Grades PreK-6), 700 Fuller, Winfield, 67156. Tel: 620-221-0230; Email: school@holynamewinfield.org. Kim Porter, Prin. / Librarian. Lay Teachers 9; Students 69.
Catechesis Religious Program—Sr. Charlotte Brungardt, D.R.E. Students 54.
YATES CENTER, WOODSON CO., ST. JOSEPH (1957) [JC]
310 S. Jefferson, Iola, 66749. Tel: 620-365-2277; Email: cessnan17255@gmail.com. 105 E. Bell, Yates Center, 66783. Rev. John P. Miller; Deacon Theodore Stahl.
Catechesis Religious Program—Tel: 620-625-2806. Leon Weber, D.R.E.; Mary Weber, D.R.E. Students 18.
ZENDA, KINGMAN CO., ST. JOHN (1908) [CEM] (German)
8035 S.W. 160th Ave., Nashville, 67112. Tel: 620-246-5370; Email: judicis20@yahoo.com. 109 N. Ada, Zenda, 67159. Rev. Roger S. Lumbre.
Catechesis Religious Program—Renee D. Adelhardt, D.R.E. Students 2.

Chaplains of Public Institutions

WICHITA. *El Dorado Correctional Facility*. Very Rev. John P. Lanzrath, S.T.L.
Sedgwick County Adult Local Detention Facility. Rev. John P. Sherlock, (Retired).
Veterans Administration Hospital. Rev. H. Patrick Malone, (Retired).
HUTCHINSON. *Kansas State Industrial Reformatory*. Rev. Juan G. Garza.

On Duty Outside the Diocese:
Revs.—
Borkenhagen, Jason W.
Carney, Lawrence D. III
Klag, Michael A.
Kline, Edmond G.
Nguyen, Scott C.
Ortiz-Montelongo, Ruben
Seiwert, Charles F., J.C.L.

Temporary Leave of Absence:
Rev.—
Leland, Thomas H.

Retired:
Rev. Msgr.—
Carr, William, (Retired), 6700 E. 45th St. N., Bel Aire, 67226
Revs.—
Beat, Jerome A., (Retired), 6900 E. 45th St. N., Bel Aire, 67226
Birket, Dwight J., (Retired), 13015 E. Maple Grove, Mount Hope, 67108
Boor, Colin J., (Retired), 10603 W. Douglas Ave., 67209
Campbell, Douglas L., J.C.L., (Retired), 515 S. Main, Apt. 309, 67202
Eck, Ivan C., (Retired), 26906 S. Paul and Mary Ct., Cheney, 67025
Joyce, Raymond, (Retired), 115 S. Rutan #4D, 67218
Kerschen, Leon J., (Retired), 6900 E. 45th St. N, Bel Aire, 67226
Larkin, Patrick, (Retired), 6900 E. 45th St. N., Bel Aire, 67226
Malone, H. Patrick, (Retired), 7077 E. Central, 67206
Mannion, J. Patrick, (Retired), 6900 E. 45th St., Bel Aire, 67226
Maung, Chrysostom Ah, (Retired), 1372 Xylan Rd., Piqua, 66761
McElwee, Robert W., (Retired), 4084 Mt. Carmel Rd., Frontenac, 66763
Oborny, Paul J., (Retired), 6900 E. 45th St. N., Bel Aire, 67226
Parker, Larry J., (Retired), 1105 4th St., Oswego, 67356
Scheier, Steven, (Retired), 6900 E. 45th St. N., Bel Aire, 67226
Schmid, Wayne L., (Retired), 1408 S. Gasaway Dr., Derby, 67037
Sherlock, John P., (Retired), 136 S. Hillside Dr., 67230
Stroot, Thomas J., (Retired), 100 S. Cherokee, Frontenac, 66763
Thapwa, Stephen M., (Retired), 31667 Chelsea Way, Temecula, CA 92592.

INSTITUTIONS LOCATED IN DIOCESE

[A] COLLEGES AND UNIVERSITIES

WICHITA. *Newman University*, 3100 McCormick St., 67213-2008. Tel: 316-942-4291; Fax: 316-942-4483; Email: mcgareyt@newmanu.edu; Web: www.newmanu.edu. Dr. Noreen M. Carrocci, Ph.D., Pres.; Revs. Joseph M. Gile, S.T.D., Dean of Graduate Studies, Assoc. Prof.; John P. Fogliasso, Chap.; Mrs. Jennifer Gantz, VPFA; Mr. J. V. Johnston, VP University Advancement; Mr. Norm Jones, VP Enrollment Management; Kimberly McDonald Long, Ph.D., Provost/VPAA; Mr. Victor Trilli, M.S. Ed., VP Student Affairs/Dir. of Athletics; Mr. Jason

Pool, Dir. of Human Resources; Ms. Lori Gibbon, Registrar; Ms. Tracy McGarey, Exec. Asst. and Sec. of the Corporation; Mr. Clark Schafer, Dir. of Univ. Relations; Mr. Steve Hamersky, Librarian. Coeducation liberal arts college, founded in 1933 by the Sisters of Adorers of the Blood of Christ. (Accredited by the Higher Learning Commission). Clergy 2; Religious Teachers 10; Faculty 94; Lay Teachers 89; Priests 2; Sisters 2; Students 3,373; Total Staff 147.

[B] HIGH SCHOOLS, DIOCESAN

WICHITA. *Bishop Carroll Catholic High School* (1964) 8101 W. Central, 67212. Tel: 316-722-2390; Fax: 316-722-6670; Email: nielsenleticia@bcchs.org; Web: www.bcchs.org. Mrs. Leticia C. Nielsen, Pres.; Mrs. Vanessa Harshberger, Prin.; Rev. Samuel R. Brand, Chap.; Mrs. Taylor Dugan, Media Specialist; Rev. Edmund Herzog, Chap. Religious Teachers 6; Lay Teachers 67; Priests 2; Sisters 4; Students 1,171; Total Staff 73.

Kapaun Mt. Carmel Catholic High School, 8506 E. Central, 67206. Tel: 316-634-0315; Fax: 316-636-2437; Email: rknapp@kapaun.org; Web: www.kapaun.org. Mr. Robert Knapp, Pres.; Mr. Christopher Bloomer, Prin.; Jodi Gerken, Librarian; Revs. Curtis D.L. Hecker, Chap.; Gabriel Greer, Chap. Religious Teachers 4; Lay Teachers 63; Priests 2; Sisters 2; Students 894; Total Staff 81.

HUTCHINSON. *Trinity Catholic High School* (1966) (Grades 7-12), 1400 E. 17th, Hutchinson, 67502. Tel: 620-662-5800; Fax: 320-662-1233; Email: jhammersmith@trinity-hutch.com; Web: www.trinity-hutch.com. Mr. Joe Hammersmith, Prin.; Rev. Todd Shepherd, Chap.; Nancy McElgunn, Librarian. Religious Teachers 4; Lay Teachers 14; Priests 1; Sisters 3; Students 235; Total Staff 18.

[C] GENERAL HOSPITALS

WICHITA. *Ascension Via Christi Health, Inc.* (1995) 8200 E. Thorn Dr., 67226. Tel: 316-858-4944; Email: michael.mullins@ascension.org; Web: www.viachristi.org. Michael L. Mullins, FACHE, CEO & Kansas Ministry Market Leader. Subsidiary of Ascension Health and sponsored by the sponsoring congregations of Ascension Health. Owned Hospital organizations include: five acute care facilities, one rehabilitation hospital, and one behavioral health hospital.

Ascension Via Christi Health Partners, Inc. (1982) 8200 E. Thorn Dr., 67226. Tel: 316-858-4900; Email: todd.conklin@ascension.org; Web: www.viachristi.org. Todd Conklin, Exec.

Ascension Via Christi Hospital St. Teresa, Inc., 14800 W. St. Teresa, 67235. Tel: 316-796-7000; Fax: 316-796-7809; Email: robyn.chadwick@ascension.org; Web: www.viachristi.org. Robyn Chadwick, Vice Pres.; Brenda Larson, Chief Nursing Officer. Bed Capacity 72; Tot Asst. Annually 15,263; Total Staff 158.

Ascension Via Christi Hospitals Wichita, Inc., 929 N. St. Francis, 67214. Tel: 316-268-5000; Fax: 316-291-7999; Email: kevin.strecker@ascension.org; Web: www.viachristi.org. Kevin Strecker, Pres. Bed Capacity 1,433; Tot Asst. Annually 102,014; Total Staff 2,863.

Via Christi Hospital St. Francis, 929 N. St. Francis, 67214. Tel: 316-268-5000; Fax: 316-291-7999; Email: Sherry.Hausmann@ascension.org; Web: www.viachristi.org. Mrs. Sherry Hausmann, Pres.; Rev. Benjamin F. Green, Chap. Bed Capacity 857; Tot Asst. Annually 70,007; Total Staff 2,216.

Via Christi Hospital St. Joseph, 3600 E. Harry, 67218. Tel: 316-689-5312; Fax: 316-691-6706; Email: Laurie.Labarca@ascension.org; Web: www.viachristi.org. Ms. Laurie Labarca, Pres.; Rev. Dominic (Sekhar) Potnuru, Chap. Bed Capacity 226; Tot Asst. Annually 32,007; Total Staff 655.

**Ascension Via Christi Property Services, Inc.* (1998) 1100 N. St. Francis, Ste. 240, 67214. Tel: 316-858-4906; Fax: 316-291-4785; Email: todd.conklin@ascension.org; Web: www.viachristi.org. 8200 E. Thorn Dr., 67226. Todd Conklin, Exec. Total Staff 3.

Ascension Via Christi Rehabilitation Hospital, Inc. (1995) 1151 N. Rock Rd., 67206. Tel: 316-634-3400; Fax: 316-634-1141; Email: kevin.strecker@ascension.org; Email: cynthia.hagerty@ascension.org; Email: cammy.runa@ascension.org; Email: joelle.dreiling@ascension.org; Web: www.viachristi.org. Kevin Strecker, Pres.; Cynthia Hagerty, Vice Pres. Bed Capacity 60; Tot Asst. Annually 52,016; Total Staff 154.

COLUMBUS. *Mercy Hospital Columbus*, 220 N. Pennsylvania Ave., Columbus, 66725. Tel: 620-429-2545; Fax: 620-429-1984; Email: Marynell.Ploch@Mercy.Net. Susan Hannasch, Reg. Gen. Counsel.

FORT SCOTT. *Mercy Hospital* dba Mercy Kansas Communities, Inc., 401 Woodland Hills Blvd., Fort Scott, 66701. Tel: 620-223-7057; Fax: 620-223-5327; Email: maryjane.young@mercy.net. Mrs. Reta Baker, Pres. Bassinets 6; Bed Capacity 46; Lay Staff 249; Tot Asst. Annually 84,135; Total Staff 303; Pastoral Care Director 1; Home Health Visits 7,424.

PITTSBURG. *Ascension Via Christi Hospital Pittsburg, Inc.* (1903) 1 Mt. Carmel Way, Pittsburg, 66762. Tel: 620-231-6100; Fax: 620-232-0493; Email: Randy.Cason@ascension.org; Web: www.viachristi.org. Mr. Randy Cason, Hospital Pres. Pittsburg. Bed Capacity 89; Tot Asst. Annually 15,316; Total Staff 544.

[D] HOMES FOR AGED

WICHITA. *Caritas Center, Inc.*, 1165 Southwest Blvd., 67213. Tel: 316-942-2201; Fax: 877-942-0859; Email: lohkampg@adorers.org; Web: www.adorers.org. Greg Lohkamp, Admin. Total Staff 50; Skilled Nursing (Beds) 22.

Catholic Care Center, Inc., 6700 E. 45th St. N., 67226. Tel: 316-744-2020; Fax: 316-744-2182; Email: cindy.lafleur@ascension.org. Mrs. Cindy LaFleur, Exec. Dir.; Revs. Andrew H. Kuykendall, Chap.; Andrew J. Seiler, Chap. Operated by Catholic Diocese of Wichita & Via Christi Villages, a Subsidiary of Ascension Health Senior Care. Bed Capacity 350; Sisters 7; Total Staff 340; Skilled Nursing (Beds) 176; Assisted Living (Beds) 80; Memory Care (Beds) 40; Independent Living 76.

*Shepherd's Crossing*Tot Asst. Annually 50; Independent Living Units 54; Staff 1.

Cornerstone Assisted Living, Inc. (2001) 3636 N. Ridge Rd. #400, 67205. Tel: 316-636-5101; Fax: 316-636-2841; Email: jennifer.stastny@ascension.org; Email: Larry.Nanny@ascension.org; Web: www.viachristi.org/villages. Mr. Larry Nanny Jr., CEO. Tot Asst. Annually 46; Total Assisted Living Beds 37.

Siena Ridge Plaza, 3636 N. Ridge Rd., #400, 67205. Tel: 316-462-3636; Fax: 316-462-3676; Email: larry.nanny@ascension.org; Web: www.viachristi.org/villages. Mr. Larry Nanny Jr., CEO. Tot Asst. Annually 204; Total Staff 164; Long Term Care Beds 80; Total Assisted Living Beds 60.

Sheridan Village, Inc., 1051 S. Bluffview, 67218. Tel: 316-681-1172; Fax: 316-681-0979; Email: sheridanvillage@keymgmtsites.com; Web: www.keymgmt.com/properties/1051-s-bluffview-wichita-ks. Ms. Denise Gannon, CEO. (HUD Low Income Senior Housing) Tot Asst. Annually 73; Total Staff 3; Apartments 66.

Via Christi Healthcare Outreach Program for Elders, Inc. (HOPE) (2002) 2622 W. Central, Ste. 101, 67203. Tel: 316-858-1111; Fax: 316-946-5106; Email: jennifer.campbell1@ascension.org; Email: melissa.mcpherson@ascension.org; Email: Malissa.Newberry@ascension.org; Web: www.viachristi.org/HOPE. Melissa McPherson, Exec. Bed Capacity 300; Tot Asst. Annually 282; Total Staff 120.

Via Christi Village Georgetown, Inc. (1985) 1655 S. Georgetown, 67218. Tel: 316-685-0400; Fax: 316-685-0174; Email: malayia.reece@ascesnion.org; Web: www.ascensionliving.org. Mr. Larry Nanny Jr. Assisted Living 68; Independent Living 130; Condominiums 17; Personnel 118; Staff 92.

Via Christi Village McLean, Inc., 777 N. McLean Blvd., 67203. Tel: 316-942-7000; Fax: 316-946-5727; Email: bethany.leland@ascension.org; Web: www.viachristi.org/villages. Ms. Caitlin Hendrix, Pastoral Min./Coord. Tot Asst. Annually 222; Total Staff 109; Total Beds 137; Total Nursing Beds 36; Total Independent Beds 42; Assisted Living Apartments 59.

Via Christi Villages, Inc. (1985) 2622 W. Central, Ste. 100, 67203. Tel: 316-946-5200; Fax: 316-946-5299; Email: hildee.jones@ascension.org; Web: www.viachristi.org/villages. Hildee Jones, Business Mgr. Total Staff 79.

MULVANE. *Villa Maria, Inc.* (1950) 116 S. Central, Mulvane, 67110. Tel: 316-777-1129; Fax: 316-777-4406; Email: susan.billinger@villamariainc.com. Ms. Susan Billinger, Admin. Bed Capacity 64; Guests 98; Total Staff 95; Total Assisted 34.

Maria Court Assisted Living, 633 E. Main, Mulvane, 67110. Tel: 316-777-9917; Email: pam.darnell@villamariainc.com. Ms. Pam Darnall, Dir. Residents 34.

PITTSBURG. *Via Christi Village Pittsburg, Inc.* (2003) 1502 E. Centennial, Pittsburg, 66762. Tel: 620-235-0020; Fax: 620-235-0520; Email: daniel.busby@ascension.org; Web: www.ascensionliving.org. Mr. Daniel Busby Jr., Admin. Skilled Nursing Beds 96; Tot Asst. Annually 232; Total Staff 170; Total Assisted Living Beds 32.

[E] MONASTERIES AND RESIDENCES FOR PRIESTS AND BROTHERS

BEL AIRE. *Priests Retirement Center*, 6900 E. 45th St. N., Bel Aire, 67226. Tel: 316-744-2020; Fax: 316-744-2182; Email: bryan.coulter@catholicdioceseofwichita.org. Mrs. Cindy LaFleur. Residents 12.

[F] CONVENTS AND RESIDENCES FOR SISTERS

WICHITA. *Adorers of the Blood of Christ U.S. Region*, Wichita Center, 1165 Southwest Blvd., 67213. Tel: 316-942-2201; Fax: 877-942-0859; Email: schumerf@adorers.org; Email: rawlingsd@adorers.org; Web: www.adorers.org. Sisters Fran Schumer, Dir.; Diana Rawlings, Dir.; Rev. Thomas Welk, C.PP.S., Chap. Sisters 52; Total Membership of the U.S. Region 183.

Dominican Sisters of Peace (1933) 201 S. Millwood, 67213. Tel: 316-267-4551; Email: winslowt@catholicdioceseofwichita.org. Sr. Kathy Goetz, Rel. Order Leader. Residents 4; Sisters 4.

Medical Sisters of St. Joseph-United States Foundation (1985) 3435 E. Funston, 67218. Tel: 316-686-4746; Email: josmy61@yahoo.com.au. Sr. Laly Josmy George, Supr. Sisters 3; Professed Sisters 3.

Sisters of the Immaculate Heart of Mary of Wichita, Inc. (I.H.M.) (1979) 3550 N. 167th St. W., Colwich, 67030. Tel: 316-722-9316; Tel: 316-722-9778; Email: ihmmail@sistersihmofwichita.org; Web: www.sistersihmofwichita.org. Mother Mary Magdalene O'Halloran, I.H.M., Gen. Supr. Novices 1; Sisters 26; Professed Sisters 25.

Wichita Center, Congregation of the Sisters of St. Joseph, 3700 E. Lincoln, 67218-2099. Tel: 316-686-7171; Fax: 316-689-4056; Email: mnugent@csjoseph.org; Email: pwabritton@csjoseph.org; Web: www.csjoseph.org. Rev. Joseph M. Gile, S.T.D., Chap.; Sr. Margaret Nugent, C.S.J., Contact Person. Sisters 82; Professed Sisters 82.

VALLEY CENTER. *Discalced Carmelite Monastery of Divine Mercy and Our Lady of Guadalupe*, 7445 N. Woodlawn, P.O. Box 278, Valley Center, 67147. Tel: 316-744-2652; Fax: 316-744-2652; Email: winslowt@catholicdioceseofwichita.org. Mother Ann Hernandez, Rel. Order Leader. Sisters 7; Total in Community 7.

[G] COMMUNITY CENTERS

WICHITA. **Center of Hope, Inc.*, 400 N. Emporia, 67202-2514. Tel: 316-267-3999; Fax: 316-267-7778; Email: george@centerofhopeinc.org; Web: www.centerofhopeinc.org. Mr. George Dinkel, Exec. Dir., Tel: 316-267-0222; Fax: 316-267-7778. Sponsored by Adorers of the Blood of Christ. Tot Asst. Annually 12,121; Total Staff 4.

Sisters of St. Joseph "Dear Neighbor" Ministries, Inc., 1329 S. Bluffview, 67218-3031. Tel: 316-684-5120; Fax: 316-684-3983; Email: klambertz@dearneighbor.org; Web: www.dearneighbor.org. Ms. Katherine J. Lambertz, L.M.S.W., Exec. Dir. Congregation of St. Joseph. Tot Asst. Annually 6,083; Total Staff 8.

**StepStone, Inc.*, 1329 S. Bluffview, 67218-3031. Tel: 316-265-1611; Fax: 316-265-0738; Email: klambertz@stepstoneks.org; Web: www.stepstoneks.org. Ms. Katherine J. Lambertz, L.M.S.W., Exec. Dir. Total Staff 17.

[H] NEWMAN CENTERS

WICHITA. *St. Paul Catholic Student Center* (1970) 1810 N. Roosevelt, 67208. Tel: 316-684-6896; Fax: 316-684-2679; Email: frdavid@stpauluniversityparish.com; Web: www.stpauluniversityparish.com. Revs. David Michael Htun, Pastor; Zachary G.B. Pinaire, Parochial Vicar.

PITTSBURG. *St. Pius X Catholic Student Center (Pittsburg State University)*, 301A E. Cleveland, Pittsburg, 66762. Tel: 620-235-1138; Email: vossd@catholicgorillas.org; Email: spx@catholicgorillas.org; Web: catholicgorillas.org. Rev. David M. Voss, Chap.

[I] CATHOLIC CHARITIES

WICHITA. *Catholic Charities, Inc. - Diocese of Wichita* (1943) 437 N. Topeka St., 67202-2413. Tel: 316-264-8344; Fax: 316-264-4442; Email: comms@catholiccharitieswichita.org; Web: catholiccharitieswichita.org. Mrs. Wendy Glick, Exec. Dir. Tot Asst. Annually 15,000; Total Staff 155; Total Agency Staff 155; Total Individuals Assisted 15,000.

Adult Day Services (1975) 5920 W. Central, 7011 W. Central, Ste. 205, 67212. Tel: 316-942-2008; Fax: 316-942-2260; Email: hwelch@CatholicCharitiesWichita.org. Mrs. Wendy Glick, CEO. Tot Asst. Annually 97; Total Staff 22.

Cana Counseling, 437 N. Topeka St., 67202. Tel: 316-263-6941; Fax: 316-263-5259; Email: hwelch@catholiccharitieswichita.org. Mrs. Wendy Glick, Dir. Tot Asst. Annually 817; Total Staff 7; Individuals Served 817.

Foster Grandparent Program (1981) 437 N. Topeka St., 67202-2413. Tel: 316-264-8344; Fax: 316-262-5356; Email: hwelch@catholiccharitieswichita.org. Mrs. Wendy Glick, CEO. Provides 102,917 hours of service. Tot Asst. Annually 121; Total Staff 2; Hours of Service to Children 102,917; Total Foster Grandparents 121.

Harbor House (1992) P.O. Box 3759, 67201. Tel: 316-263-6000; Fax: 316-263-8347; Email: hwelch@catholiccharitieswichita.org. Mrs. Wendy Glick, CEO. Tot Asst. Annually 859; Total Staff 27; Women & Children Assisted and Victim's Advocate Program 859.

Immigration Services, 437 N. Topeka St., 67202. Tel: 316-264-0282; Fax: 316-262-5356; Email: hwelch@catholiccharitieswichita.org. Mrs. Wendy Glick, CEO. Tot Asst. Annually 1,040; Total Staff 4.

Our Daily Bread Food Pantry, 2825 S. Hillside, 67216. Tel: 316-264-8344, Ext. 1504; Fax: 316-262-5356; Email: hwelch@catholiccharities.org. Mrs. Wendy Glick, CEO. Total Staff 1; Total Assisted 56,877.

St. Anthony Family Shelter (1988) 256 N. Ohio, 67214. Tel: 316-264-7233; Fax: 316-267-3774; Email: hwelch@catholiccharitieswichita.org. Mrs. Wendy Glick, CEO. Tot Asst. Annually 16; Total Staff 16; Individuals Assisted In Shelter 919.

Southeast Kansas Services - Pittsburg, 411 E. 12th St., Pittsburg, 66762. Tel: 620-235-0633; Fax: 620-235-0633; Email: hwelch@catholiccharitieswichita.org. Mrs. Wendy Glick, CEO. Clients Served 542; Staff 2.

[J] MISCELLANEOUS

WICHITA. **Casting Net Ministries, Inc.*, 1117 Hazelwood, 67212. Tel: 800-217-5710; Email: info@CastingNetsMinistries.com; Web: www.CastingNetsMinistries.com. Hector Molina, CEO; Mr. Chris Stewart, COO; Mr. Tony Brandt, Pres.

Guadalupe Clinic, Inc. (1985) 940 S. St. Francis, 67211. Tel: 316-264-8974; Fax: 316-262-4938; Email: dgear@guadalupeclinic.com; Web: www.guadalupeclinic.com. Mr. David Gear, Exec. Dir. Safety-Net Clinic. Tot Asst. Annually 9,121; Total Staff 22.

Guadalupe Clinic, Inc., 841 N. Broadway, 67214. Tel: 316-264-8974; Email: Guadalupe@GuadalupeClinic.com. Mr. David Gear, Dir.

Guadalupe Health Foundation, 940 S. St. Francis, 67211. Tel: 316-264-8974; Fax: 316-262-4938; Email: Guadalupe@GuadalupeClinic.com. Mr. David Gear, Dir. Purpose: to support, assist and promote the interests and welfare of the programs and activities of the Diocese of Wichita which provide health care services and health education to poor, distressed and underprivileged individuals.

Holy Family Special Needs Foundation, 424 N. Broadway, 67202. Tel: 316-269-3900; Fax: 316-269-3902; Email: jacobsm@catholicdioceseofwichita.org. Mrs. Myra Jacobs, Staff to Bd. Dirs.

Leaven International Corporation, 4233 Sulphur Ave., St. Louis, MO 63109. Tel: 314-351-6294; Fax: 314-351-6789; Email: renzj@adorers.org; Web: www.adorers.org. Sr. Jan E. Renz, A.S.C., Treas. A charitable organization of the Adorers of the Blood of Christ.

MDM Hearts & Hands, Inc., 1165 Southwest Blvd., 67213. Tel: 316-942-2201; Fax: 877-942-0859; Email: welsbys@adorers.org; Web: www.adorers.org. Sr. Susan Welsby, A.S.C., Admin. Total Staff 3.

Mount St. Mary, Inc., 3700 E. Lincoln, 67218. Tel: 316-686-7171; Email: pwarbritton@csjoseph.org. Ms. Denise Gannon, CEO.

Priests' Retirement and Education Fund of Wichita (2001) 424 N. Broadway, 67202. Tel: 316-269-3900; Fax: 316-269-3902; Email: bryan.coulter@catholicdioceseofwichita.org. Rev. Dwight J. Birket, Pres., (Retired).

**Support for Catholic Schools, Inc*, 424 N. Broadway, 67202. Tel: 316-269-3900; Email: wescottm@catholicdioceseofwichita.org. Mike Wescott, Dir., Dir.

RELIGIOUS INSTITUTES OF MEN REPRESENTED IN THE DIOCESE

For further details refer to the corresponding bracketed number in the Religious Institutes of Men or Women section.

[1060]—*Society of the Precious Blood* (Kansas City Prov.)—C.PP.S.

RELIGIOUS INSTITUTES OF WOMEN REPRESENTED IN THE DIOCESE

[0100]—*Adorers of the Blood of Christ*—A.S.C.

[]—*Carmelite Sisters of St. Teresa*—C.S.S.T.

[]—*Congregation of the Holy Spirit.*

[3832]—*Congregation of the Sisters of St. Joseph*—C.S.J.

[]—*Discalced Carmelite Sisters of Divine Mercy and Our Lady of Guadalupe*—O.C.D.

[1115]—*Dominican Sisters of Peace*—O.P.

[2500]—*Medical Sisters of St. Joseph*—M.S.J.

[]—*Missionary Catechists of the Poor*—M.C.P.

[]—*Servants of the Trinity.*

[]—*School Sisters of Notre Dame.*

[]—*Sisters of Mercy South Central Regional Community*—R.S.M.

[2185]—*Sisters of the Immaculate Heart of Mary of Wichita*—I.H.M.

NECROLOGY

† Gerber, Eugene J., Bishop Emeritus of Wichita, Died Sep. 29, 2018

† Hemberger, Robert E., (Retired), Died Nov. 8, 2018

† Scaletty, Thomas F., (Retired), Died Feb. 7, 2018

† Spexarth, James L., (Retired), Died Jan. 8, 2018

An asterisk (*) denotes an organization that has established tax-exempt status directly with the IRS and is not covered by the USCCB Group Ruling.

Diocese of Wilmington

(Dioecesis Wilmingtoniensis)

Most Reverend

WILLIAM FRANCIS MALOOLY, D.D.

Bishop of Wilmington; ordained May 9, 1970; appointed Titular Bishop of Flumenzer and Auxiliary Bishop of Baltimore December 12, 2000; Episcopal ordination March 1, 2001; appointed Bishop of Wilmington July 7, 2008; installed September 8, 2008. *Chancery: 1925 Delaware Ave., P.O. Box 2030, Wilmington, DE 19899.* Tel: 302-573-3100; Fax: 302-573-6817; Email: pbossi-smedley@cdow.org.

Chancery Office: P.O. Box 2030, Wilmington, DE 19899-2030. Tel: 302-573-3100; Fax: 302-573-6836.

Web: www.cdow.org

Email: chancery@cdow.org

ESTABLISHED MARCH 3, 1868.

Square Miles Delaware 1,932; Maryland 3,375; Total 5,307.

Comprises the State of Delaware and the Counties of Caroline, Cecil, Dorchester, Kent, Queen Anne's, Somerset, Talbot, Wicomico and Worcester in Maryland.

For legal titles of parishes and diocesan institutions, consult the Chancery Office.

STATISTICAL OVERVIEW

Personnel	
Bishop	1
Priests: Diocesan Active in Diocese	62
Priests: Diocesan Active Outside Diocese	2
Priests: Retired, Sick or Absent	46
Number of Diocesan Priests	110
Religious Priests in Diocese	59
Total Priests in Diocese	169
Extern Priests in Diocese	17
Permanent Deacons in Diocese	109
Total Brothers	7
Total Sisters	158
Parishes	
Parishes	56
With Resident Pastor:	
Resident Diocesan Priests	41
Resident Religious Priests	6
Without Resident Pastor:	
Administered by Priests	9
Missions	18
Professional Ministry Personnel:	
Sisters	4
Lay Ministers	65
Welfare	
Catholic Hospitals	1
Total Assisted	50,823
Health Care Centers	1
Total Assisted	1,909
Homes for the Aged	6
Total Assisted	667
Day Care Centers	3
Total Assisted	88
Specialized Homes	3
Total Assisted	159
Special Centers for Social Services	16
Total Assisted	200,922
Residential Care of Disabled	1
Total Assisted	162
Other Institutions	3
Total Assisted	6,638
Educational	
Diocesan Students in Other Seminaries	11
Total Seminarians	11
High Schools, Diocesan and Parish	5
Total Students	1,842
High Schools, Private	4
Total Students	1,726
Elementary Schools, Diocesan and Parish	17
Total Students	5,185
Elementary Schools, Private	6
Total Students	846
Catechesis/Religious Education:	
High School Students	636
Elementary Students	8,624
Total Students under Catholic Instruction	18,870
Teachers in the Diocese:	
Priests	4
Brothers	3
Sisters	16
Lay Teachers	1,030
Vital Statistics	
Receptions into the Church:	
Infant Baptism Totals	1,277
Minor Baptism Totals	627
Adult Baptism Totals	280
Received into Full Communion	215
First Communions	2,421
Confirmations	2,142
Marriages:	
Catholic	327
Interfaith	138
Total Marriages	465
Deaths	1,640
Total Catholic Population	246,218
Total Population	1,489,002

Former Bishops—Rt. Revs. THOMAS A. BECKER, D.D., ord. June 18, 1859; cons. Aug. 16, 1868; transferred to Savannah, 1886; died July 29, 1899; ALFRED A. CURTIS, D.D., ord. Dec. 19, 1874; cons. Nov. 14, 1886; resigned 1896; named Titular Bishop of Echinus; died July 11, 1908; Most Revs. JOHN J. MONAGHAN, D.D., ord. Dec. 19, 1880; cons. May 9, 1897; resigned and named Titular Bishop of Lydda, July 10, 1925; died Jan. 7, 1935; EDMOND JOHN FITZMAURICE, D.D., ord. May 1904; cons. Nov. 30, 1925; resigned March 2, 1960 and named Titular Archbishop of Tomi; died July 25, 1962; HUBERT J. CARTWRIGHT, D.D., ord. June 11, 1927; cons. Coadjutor "with right of succession," Oct. 24, 1956; Titular Bishop of Neve; died March 6, 1958; MICHAEL W. HYLE, D.D., ord. March 12, 1927; cons. Sept. 24, 1958 as Titular Bishop of Christopolis and Coadjutor with right of succession; succeeded to See, March 2, 1960; died Dec. 26, 1967; THOMAS J. MARDAGA, D.D., ord. May 14, 1940; cons. Jan. 25, 1967; named Titular Bishop of Mutugenna; appt. Bishop of Wilmington, March 13, 1968; installed April 6, 1968; died May 28, 1984; JAMES C. BURKE, O.P., ord. June 18, 1956; cons. May 25, 1967; named Titular Bishop of Lamiggiga; Vicar Apostolic of Chimbote, Peru, 1962-1978; Served in Diocese of Wilmington, 1978-1994; died May 28, 1994; ROBERT E. MULVEE, D.D., J.C.D., ord. June 30, 1957; Auxiliary Bishop of Manchester and Titular Bishop of Summa, Feb. 15, 1977; cons. April 14, 1977; appt. Bishop of Wilmington, Feb. 19, 1985; installed April 11, 1985; appt. to Diocese of Providence as Coadjutor Bishop of Providence, Feb. 7, 1995; installed March 27, 1995; succeeded to See, June 11, 1997; retired March 31, 2005; died Dec. 28, 2018.; MICHAEL A. SALTARELLI, D.D., ord. May 28, 1960; appt. Titular Bishop of Mesarfelta and Auxiliary Bishop of Newark, June 12, 1990; Episcopal ord. July 30, 1990; appt. Eighth Bishop of Wilmington Nov. 21, 1995; installed Jan. 23, 1996 retired July 7, 2008; died Oct. 8, 2009.

Office of the Bishop—Mailing Address: P.O. Box 2030, Wilmington, 19899. PATRICIA BOSSI-SMEDLEY, Sec. to Bishop & Notary for the Curia, Tel: 302-573-3100; Fax: 302-573-6817; Email: pbossi-smedley@cdow.org.

Vicar General and Moderator of the Curia—Rev. Msgr. STEVEN P. HURLEY, V.G., S.T.L., 1925 Delaware Ave., P.O. Box 2030, Wilmington, 19899. Tel: 302-573-3118; Fax: 302-573-6947.

Associate Moderator of the Curia—1925 Delaware Ave., P.O. Box 2030, Wilmington, 19899. Very Rev. GLENN M. EVERS.

Chancellor—1925 Delaware Ave., P.O. Box 2030, Wilmington, 19899. Tel: 302-573-3100; Fax: 302-573-6836. Very Rev. JOSEPH W. MCQUAIDE IV.

Vicar for Clergy—Rev. Msgr. DAVID F. KELLEY, V.C., 1925 Delaware Ave., P.O. Box 2030, Wilmington, 19899. Tel: 302-573-3144; Fax: 302-573-6947.

Offices and Departments

Chancery Department

Chancery Office—Mailing Address: P.O. Box 2030, Wilmington, 19899. Office: 1925 Delaware Ave., Wilmington, 19806. Tel: 302-573-3100; Fax: 302-573-6836; Email: chancery@cdow.org; Web: www.cdow.org. Very Rev. JOSEPH W. MCQUAIDE IV, Chancellor. Office Hours: Mon.-Fri. 8:30-4:30. Send all marriage dispensation requests and marriage envelopes to the Chancery Office.

Archives—MRS. SUSAN KIRK RYAN, Archivist, 8 Old Church Rd., Greenville, 19807. Tel: 302-655-0597; Email: skirkryan@cdow.org.

Censor of Books—Very Rev. JAMES S. LENTINI, V.F., Church of the Holy Cross, 631 S. State St., Dover, 19901.

Mission OfficePropagation of the Faith and Holy Childhood Association, 1626 N. Union St., P.O. Box 2030, Wilmington, 19899. Tel: 302-573-3104; Fax: 302-573-6944. Rev. CHRISTOPHER R. COFFIEY, Dir.

Office of Worship—1626 N. Union St., Wilmington, 19899. Tel: 302-573-3137; Fax: 302-573-6944. Very Rev. JAMES T. KIRK JR., V.F., Dir.

Catholic Charities Department

Catholic Charities—MS. RICHELLE A. VIBLE, M.B.A., Exec. Dir., Fourth St. & Greenhill Ave., P.O. Box 2610, Wilmington, 19805. Tel: 302-655-9624; Fax: 302-655-9753. (Refer to separate listings in the Institutions for detailed information on Catholic Charities and related organizations).

Catholic Education Department

Secretary—DR. LOUIS DEANGELO, Ed.D.

Catholic Schools Office—DR. LOUIS DEANGELO, Ed.D., Supt.; MS. CAROL RIPKEN, Assoc. Supt.; Sr. WILLIAM ADELE, S.S.J., Asst. Supt., 1626 N. Union St., Wilmington, 19806. Tel: 302-573-3133; Fax: 302-573-6945.

Religious Education—MS. COLLEEN L. LINDSEY, Dir.,

1626 N. Union St., Wilmington, 19806. Tel: 302-573-3130; Fax: 302-573-6944.

Education Ministry for Persons With Special Needs—1626 N. Union St., Wilmington, 19806. DEBBIE CIAFRE, Coord. Spec. Rel. Educ. Hearing Impaired: Please call Religious Education Office: 302-573-3130.

Office for Marriage and Family Life—Mailing Address: P.O. Box 2030, Wilmington, 19899. Tel: 302-295-0684. MS. COLLEEN L. LINDSEY, Dir.; ALISON DIPAOLA, Coord. Pre-Cana.

Office for Catholic Youth and Young Adult Ministry—1626 N. Union St., Wilmington, 19806. Tel: 302-658-3800; Fax: 302-658-7617; Web: www.cdow.org. PAMELA URBANSKI, Assoc. Dir.; MATTHEW CARUCCI, Coord., CYM Sports.

Catholic Scouting Program—Rev. MICHAEL J. CARRIER, Chap., Girl Scouts, Church of the Holy Child, 2500 Naamans Rd., Wilmington, 19810. Tel: 302-475-6486; Deacon THOMAS E. WATTS SR., Chap., Boy Scouts, 1626 N. Union St., Wilmington, 19806. Tel: 302-658-3800; Fax: 302-658-7617.

Catholic Campus Ministry—Rev. EDWARD F. OGDEN, O.S.F.S.; KIM ZITZNER, Campus Min., Univ. of Delaware, 45 Lovett Ave., Newark, 19711. Tel: 302-368-4728; Fax: 302-368-2548.

Communications Department

Secretary—MR. ROBERT G. KREBS.

Office of Public Relations and Media—MR. ROBERT G. KREBS, Dir., 1925 Delaware Ave., Wilmington, 19899. Tel: 302-573-3116; Fax: 302-573-6836.

Catholic Press Inc., "The Dialog"—Mailing Address: P.O. Box 2208, Wilmington, 19899. 1925 Delaware Ave., Wilmington, 19806. Tel: 302-573-3109 (Newsroom); Tel: 302-573-3112 (Advertising); Fax: 302-573-6948; Email: news@thedialog.org; Web: www.thedialog.org. Most Rev. W. FRANCIS MALOOLY, D.D., Publisher; JOSEPH P. OWENS, Editor & Gen. Mgr.

Finance Department

Chief Financial Officer and Secretary—MR. JOSEPH P. CORSINI, Mailing Address: P.O. Box 2030, Wilmington, 19899. 1925 Delaware Ave., Wilmington, 19806. Tel: 302-573-3105; Fax: 302-573-6869.

Development Department

Secretary and Diocesan Development Director—MRS. DEBORAH A. FOLS, Mailing Address: P.O. Box 2030, Wilmington, 19899. Tel: 302-573-3121; Fax: 302-573-6947.

Annual Catholic Appeal—MRS. DEBORAH A. FOLS, Dir., Mailing Address: P.O. Box 2030, Wilmington, 19899. Tel: 302-573-3100; Fax: 302-573-6947.

Human Resources Department

Secretary and Director—Mailing Address: P.O. Box 2030, Wilmington, 19899. Tel: 302-573-3126; Fax: 302-573-6944. MRS. KELLY ANNE DONAHUE, SPHR, SHRM-SCP.

Diocesan Tribunal

Mailing Address: P.O. Box 2030, Wilmington, 19899. 1925 Delaware Ave., Wilmington, 19806. Tel: 302-573-3107; Fax: 302-573-6947.

Judicial Vicar—Very Rev. MARK S. MEALEY, O.S.F.S., J.C.D., J.V.

Judges—Very Rev. MARK S. MEALEY, O.S.F.S., J.C.D., J.V.; Rev. Msgrs. JOSEPH F. REBMAN, V.G., S.T.L., J.C.L., C.C.C.E., V.G.; GEORGE J. BRUBAKER, J.C.L.; Revs. MICHAEL CONNOLLY, J.C.L.; DENNIS G. VOLMI, J.C.D., (Retired); MR. JOSEPH F. NELAN, J.C.D.

Defenders of the Bond—MR. JACK D. ANDERSON, J.C.D.; Sr. PATRICIA SMITH, O.S.F., J.C.D.

Secretary/Notary—MRS. GAIL ESPOSITO.

Offices Reporting to Vicar General/Moderator of the Curia

Catholic Cemeteries—Rev. Msgr. JOSEPH F. REBMAN, V.G., S.T.L., J.C.L., C.C.C.E., V.G., Dir.; MR. MARK A. CHRISTIAN, C.C.C.E., Exec. Dir., Mailing Address: 2400 Lancaster Ave., Wilmington, 19805. Tel: 302-656-3323; Fax: 302-656-1069.

Catholic Ministry to the Elderly—Rev. Msgr. STEVEN P. HURLEY, V.G., S.T.L., Sec., Mailing Address: P.O. Box 2030, Wilmington, 19806. Tel: 302-573-3118; Fax: 302-573-6947.

Delegate for Religious—Sr. ANN DAVID STROHMINGER, O.S.F., Delegate, 1626 N. Union St., P.O. Box 2030, Wilmington, 19899. Tel: 302-573-3124; Fax: 302-573-6944.

Diocesan Planning—Rev. Msgr. STEVEN P. HURLEY, V.G., S.T.L., Mailing Address: P.O. Box 2030, Wilmington, 19899. Tel: 302-573-3118; Fax: 302-573-6947.

Diocesan Real Estate Committee—Rev. Msgr. STEVEN P. HURLEY, V.G., S.T.L., Chm., Mailing Address: P.O. Box 2030, Wilmington, 19899. Tel: 302-573-3118; Fax: 302-573-6947.

Information Technology—MRS. NANCY MOORE, Dir., Mailing Address: P.O. Box 2030, Wilmington, 19899. 1925 Delaware Ave., Wilmington, 19806. Tel: 302-573-3122; Fax: 302-573-6947.

Office for Cultural Ministries—Mailing Address: 1925 Delaware Ave., Wilmington, 19806. Tel: 302-295-0667; Fax: 302-573-6836. Very Rev. GLENN M. EVERS, Dir.

Hispanic Ministry—1626 N. Union St., Wilmington, 19806. Tel: 302-295-0667. Rev. CARLOS OCHOA, Coord.

Korean Catholics—Rev. TAE-GEUN (PETER) KIM; MR. JEESANG ANDREW JUNG, Korean Catholic Community Parish Coord., 2710 Duncan Rd., Wilmington, 19808. Tel: 302-998-7609.

Ministry of Black Catholics—Rev. PAUL M. WILLIAMS, O.F.M., Dir., 1012 N. French St., Wilmington, 19801. Tel: 302-658-4535; Fax: 302-658-2006.

Native American Community—MS. SHARON WARD, Coord., St. Elizabeth Ann Seton Church, 345 Bear Christiana Rd., Bear, 19701-1048. Tel: 302-322-6430.

Office of Safe Environments—1626 N. Union St., Wilmington, 19806. Tel: 302-295-0668; Fax: 302-573-6944. MR. MICHAEL D. CONNELLY, Dir.

Office for Pro Life Activities—Very Rev. LEONARD R. KLEIN, Dir., Mailing Address: P.O. Box 2030, Wilmington, 19899. Tel: 302-295-0626.

Offices Reporting to Vicar for Clergy

Coordinator of Institutional Chaplains—Rev. Msgr. DAVID F. KELLEY, V.C., Mailing Address: P.O. Box 2030, Wilmington, 19899-2030. Tel: 302-573-3144; Fax: 302-573-6947.

Office of Priestly and Religious Vocations and Seminarians and Newly Ordained—Very Rev. NORMAN P. CARROLL, V.F., Dir., 1626 N. Union St., P.O. Box 2030, Wilmington, 19899. Tel: 302-573-3113; Fax: 302-573-6944.

Office for Deacons—1626 N. Union St., P.O. Box 2030, Wilmington, 19899. Tel: 302-573-2390; Fax: 302-573-6944. Rev. JOHN A. GRASING, Dir.

Priest Personnel Committee—Rev. Msgr. DAVID F. KELLEY, V.C., Mailing Address: P.O. Box 2030, Wilmington, 19899-2030. Tel: 302-573-3144.

Other Ministries

Liaison for Non-Christian Religions—Rev. LEONARD J. KEMPSKI, Liaison, (Retired), 3200 Philadelphia Pike, Claymont, 19703. Tel: 302-798-2904.

Liaison for Evangelization—Rev. WILLIAM J. LAWLER, Liaison, (Retired), Mailing Address: P.O. Box 218, Cambridge, MD 21613. Tel: 410-228-4770.

Ecumenical Liaison—Rev. Msgr. JOSEPH F. REBMAN, V.G., S.T.L., J.C.L., C.C.C.E., V.G., Dir., Mailing Address: P.O. Box 2030, Wilmington, 19899. Tel: 302-573-3100.

Marian Devotions—Rev. BRIAN S. LEWIS, Dir.

Principal Advisory Groups to the Bishop

College of Consultors—Rev. Msgrs. STEVEN P. HURLEY, V.G., S.T.L.; DAVID F. KELLEY, V.C.; Very Rev. NORMAN P. CARROLL, V.F.; Revs. ROGER F. DIBUO; JOHN J. MINK; JAMES NASH; TIMOTHY M. NOLAN.

Priests' Council—Mailing Address: P.O. Box 2030, Wilmington, 19899. Tel: 302-573-3118. Very Rev. JOSEPH W. MCQUAIDE IV, Sec.

Deans—Rev. Msgr. JOHN P. HOPKINS, V.F.; Very Revs. NORMAN P. CARROLL, V.F.; JOHN B. GABAGE, V.F.; PAUL F. JENNINGS JR., V.F.; JAMES T. KIRK JR., V.F.; JAMES S. LENTINI, V.F.; JOSEPH J. PIEKARSKI, V.F.

Finance Council—MR. JOSEPH P. CORSINI, Sec., Mailing Address: P.O. Box 2030, Wilmington, 19899. Tel: 302-573-3105.

Priests' Personnel Committee—Rev. Msgr. DAVID F. KELLEY, V.C., Mailing Address: P.O. Box 2030, Wilmington, 19899.

Other Advisory Groups

Priests' Continuing Formation Committee—Rev. JAMES NASH, Chm., Ss. Peter and Paul Church, 7906 Ocean Gateway, Easton, MD 21601. Tel: 410-822-2344; Fax: 410-770-5080.

Diocesan School Board—DR. LOUIS DEANGELO, Ed.D., Sec., Mailing Address: P.O. Box 2030, Wilmington, 19899. Tel: 302-573-3133.

Diocesan Religious Education Board—MS. COLLEEN L. LINDSEY, Sec., Mailing Address: 1626 N. Union St., Wilmington, 19806. Tel: 302-573-3130; Fax: 302-573-6944.

Diocesan Building Committee—ROMEO AQUINO, Chm.; Rev. Msgr. STEVEN P. HURLEY, V.G., S.T.L., Bishop's Rep., Mailing Address: P.O. Box 2030, Wilmington, 19899. Tel: 302-573-3118; Fax: 302-573-6947.

Pastoral Council—Mailing Address: P.O. Box 2030, Wilmington, 19899. Tel: 302-573-3100; Fax: 302-573-6836. VACANT, Exec. Officer.

Public Policy Committee—Rev. Msgr. STEVEN P. HURLEY, V.G., S.T.L., Mailing Address: P.O. Box 2030, Wilmington, 19899. Tel: 302-573-3118; Fax: 302-573-6947.

Due Process Commission—Contact: Very Rev. MARK S. MEALEY, O.S.F.S., J.C.D., J.V., Mailing Address: P.O. Box 2030, Wilmington, 19899. Tel: 302-573-3107; Fax: 302-573-6947.

Diocesan Corporations

Catholic Cemeteries, Inc.—Rev. Msgr. JOSEPH F. REBMAN, V.G., S.T.L., J.C.L., C.C.C.E., V.G., Vice Pres.; MR. MARK A. CHRISTIAN, C.C.C.E., Sec., Mailing Address: 2400 Lancaster Ave., Wilmington, 19805. Tel: 302-656-3323.

Catholic Diocese of Wilmington, Inc.—A corporation sole under the laws of the State of Delaware. Rev. Msgr. STEVEN P. HURLEY, V.G., S.T.L., Vice Pres., Mailing Address: P.O. Box 2030, Wilmington, 19899. Tel: 302-573-3118. Office, 1925 Delaware Ave., Wilmington, 19899.

Catholic Diocese Foundation—MR. JOSEPH P. CORSINI, Exec. Dir., Mailing Address: P.O. Box 2030, Wilmington, 19899. Tel: 302-573-3105.

Catholic Ministry to the Elderly, Inc.—Rev. Msgr. STEVEN P. HURLEY, V.G., S.T.L., Treas., Mailing Address: P.O. Box 2030, Wilmington, 19899. Tel: 302-573-3118.

Catholic Press of Wilmington, Inc.—Rev. Msgr. STEVEN P. HURLEY, V.G., S.T.L., Vice Pres. & Sec., Mailing Address: P.O. Box 2208, Wilmington, 19899. Tel: 302-573-3118.

Catholic Charities, Inc.—Rev. Msgr. STEVEN P. HURLEY, V.G., S.T.L., Contact Person, Fourth St. & Greenhill Ave., P.O. Box 2610, Wilmington, 19806. Tel: 302-655-9624.

Catholic Youth Organization, Inc.—Rev. Msgr. STEVEN P. HURLEY, V.G., S.T.L., Vice Pres., Mailing Address: P.O. Box 2030, Wilmington, 19899. Tel: 302-573-3118.

Children's Home, Inc.—Rev. Msgr. STEVEN P. HURLEY, V.G., S.T.L., Contact Person, 4th St. & Greenhill Ave., P.O. Box 2610, Wilmington, 19806. Tel: 302-655-9624.

Diocese of Wilmington Schools, Inc.—Rev. Msgr. STEVEN P. HURLEY, V.G., S.T.L., 1925 Delaware Ave., Wilmington, 19805. Tel: 302-573-3118.

Seton Villa, Inc.—Rev. Msgr. STEVEN P. HURLEY, V.G., S.T.L., Contact Person, 4th St. & Greenhill Ave., P.O. Box 2610, Wilmington, 19806. Tel: 302-655-9624.

Siena Hall, Inc.—Rev. Msgr. STEVEN P. HURLEY, V.G., S.T.L., Contact Person, 4th St. & Greenhill Ave., P.O. Box 2610, Wilmington, 19806. Tel: 302-655-9624.

Activities

Apostleship of Prayer—VACANT.

Catholic Campaign for Human Development—4th St. & Greenhill Ave., P.O. Box 2610, Wilmington, 19806. Tel: 302-655-9624.

Catholic Charismatic Renewal—Rev. THOMAS A. FLOWERS, Chap., St. Jude the Apostle Church, 152 Tulip Dr., Lewes, 19958. Tel: 302-644-7300.

Catholic Relief Services, Inc.—Rev. Msgr. GEORGE J. BRUBAKER, J.C.L., Diocesan Dir., 801 N. DuPont Hwy., Wilmington Manor, New Castle, 19720. Tel: 302-328-3431.

Black & Native American Missions—Mailing Address: P.O. Box 2030, Wilmington, 19899. Tel: 302-573-3118; Fax: 302-573-6836. Very Rev. GLENN M. EVERS.

Cursillo Movement—Deacon JOSE RODRIQUEZ-TREJO, Spiritual Dir., St. Michael the Archangel Church, Georgetown, 19947. Tel: 302-856-6451; MS. ANA SCHMITT, Lay Dir., St. Paul Parish, 1010 W. 4th St., Wilmington, 19805. Tel: 302-655-6596.

Delmarva Catholic Network, Inc.—MR. ROBERT G. KREBS, Contact Person, Mailing Address: P.O. Box 2030, Wilmington, 19899. Tel: 302-573-3116.

KAIROS Ministries, Inc.—Rev. GREGORY M. CORRIGAN, Contact Person, (Retired).

Korean Catholic Community, Inc.—Rev. TAE-GEUN (PETER) KIM; MR. LAWRENCE CHI YOUNG KIM, Community Council, 2712 Duncan Rd., Wilmington, 19808. Tel: 302-998-7730.

St. Thomas More Society—Very Rev. LEONARD R. KLEIN, Chap., St. Mary of the Immaculate Conception, 1414 King St., Wilmington, 19801. Tel: 302-652-0743.

Diocese of Wilmington - Diocesan Vocations Guild—(formerly The Serra Club) Mailing Address: P.O. Box 2030, Wilmington, 19899. Tel: 302-573-3113. LINDA MONDZELEWSKI, Pres.; Very Rev. NORMAN P. CARROLL, V.F., Chap.

Organizations With Which Diocese Has Liaison

**Birthright of Delaware, Inc.—1311 N. Scott St., Wilmington, 19806.* Tel: 302-656-7080. TINISHA BROWN, Dir.

**Delaware Right To Life—Mailing Address: P.O. Box 1222, Wilmington, 19899.* Email: email@derighttolife.org. MOIRA SHERIDAN.

Delawareans United for Education—Rev. Msgr. STEVEN P. HURLEY, V.G., S.T.L., Mailing Address: P.O. Box 2030, Wilmington, 19899. Tel: 302-573-3118.

Maryland Catholic Conference—(An agency of the Archdioceses of Baltimore, Washington and the Diocese of Wilmington) *10 Francis St., Annapolis, MD 21401.* Tel: 410-269-1155; Fax: 410-269-1790. *Mailing Address: P.O. Box 2030, Wilmington, 19899.* Tel: 302-573-3118. JENNIFER BRIEMAN, Exec. Dir.

National Conference for Community and Justice—Rev. CLEMENS D. MANISTA JR., Our Mother of Sorrows Church, 303 Chesterfield Ave., Centreville, MD 21617. Tel: 410-758-0143.

Regina Coeli Society—Very Rev. LEONARD R. KLEIN, 1414 King St., Wilmington, 19801. Tel: 302-652-0743.

Survivors Assistance Coordinator—PEGGY MCLAUGHLIN, Tel: 302-468-4507; Email: mmclaughlin@ccwilm.org.

World Wide Marriage Encounter—Contact Persons: BARNEY BELLARD; KATHY BELLARD, St. John the Beloved Parish. Tel: 302-239-2571; Email: ktbellard@verizon.net.

CLERGY, PARISHES, MISSIONS AND PAROCHIAL SCHOOLS

DELAWARE, CITY OF WILMINGTON

(NEW CASTLE COUNTY)

1—CATHEDRAL OF ST. PETER (1796)
500 N. West St., 19801. Tel: 302-654-5920; Fax: 302-654-3197; Email: cathedralstp@comcast.net; Web: www.cathedralofstpeter.org. Very Rev. Leonard R. Klein, Rector; Rev. John C. McVoy III.
School—St. Peter's Cathedral School, (Grades PreK-8), Clergy 1; Lay Teachers 13; Daughters of Charity of St. Vincent de Paul 3; Students 145.

2—ST. ANN (1887)
2013 Gilpin Ave., 19806. Tel: 302-654-5519; Email: stannschurch@stannwilmington.com. Rev. John J. Mink; Richard Jasper.
School—St. Ann School, (Grades 1-8), Tel: 302-652-6567; Email: ssolomon@thesaintannschool.org. Lay Teachers 13; Students 250.
Catechesis Religious Program—Patricia Walker, D.R.E.

3—ST. ANTHONY OF PADUA (1924) (Italian)
901 N. DuPont St., 19805. Tel: 302-421-3700; Fax: 302-421-3705; Email: parish@stanthonynet.org; Web: www.sapde.org. Rev. Mark J. Wrightson, O.S.F.S. In Res., Very Rev. Mark S. Mealey, O.S.F.S., J.C.D., J.V.; Revs. Brian D. Zumbrum, O.S.F.S.; Francis Rinaldi, O.S.F.S.
School—St. Anthony of Padua School, (Grades PreK-8), 9th & Scott Sts., 19805. Tel: 302-421-3743; Fax: 302-421-3796; Email: office@stanthonynet.org; Web: www.sapgs.org. Mrs. Judith Jakotowicz White, Prin. Lay Teachers 24; Students 223.
High School—Padua Academy, 905 N. Broom St., 19806. Tel: 302-421-3739; Fax: 302-421-3748; Email: info@paduaacademy.org; Web: www.paduaacademy.org. Cindy Hayes Mann, Prin. Lay Teachers 61; Students 624.
Catechesis Religious Program—Students 42.
Endowment—St. Anthony's Education Fund, Inc., 901 N. DuPont St., 19805. Mr. Ray Ianni, Dir.

4—CHRIST OUR KING (1926-2016) Closed. Formerly at 28th & Madison Streets in Wilmington. Sacramental records at Diocesan Archives.

5—ST. ELIZABETH (1908)
809 S. Broom St., 19805-4296. Tel: 301-652-3626; Email: office@steparish.org. Very Rev. Norman P. Carroll, V.F.; Deacon Kenneth Pulliam Sr.
School—St. Elizabeth School, (Grades 1-12), 1500 Cedar St., 19805-4249. Tel: 302-656-3369; Fax: 302-655-5457; Email: cpapili@viking.pvt.k12.de.us; Web: www.steschools.org. Mrs. Tina Wecht, Lower School Prin.; Mrs. Shirley Bounds, Prin. Aides 4; Clergy 6; Lay Teachers 47; Students 530; Staff 22.
High School—St. Elizabeth High School, Tel: 302-656-3369; Email: contact@steschools.org. Joseph Papili, Pres.
Catechesis Religious Program—

6—ST. HEDWIG (1890) (Polish)
408 S. Harrison St., 19805. Tel: 302-594-1400, Ext. 0; Email: sthedwigchurch@comcast.net; Web: sthedwigde.org. Rev. Andrew Molewski; Marek Szczur; Deacon Raymond R. Zolandz Jr.
Catechesis Religious Program—Roweena Rego, D.R.E.

7—ST. JOSEPH'S R.C. CHURCH OF WILMINGTON, INC. (1889)
1012 N. French St., 19801. Tel: 302-658-4535; Fax: 302-658-2006; Email: parishsecretary@stjosephfrenchst.org; Web: www.stjosephfrenchst.org. Rev. Paul M. Williams, O.F.M.; Deacon Robert J. Cousar Jr.
Res.: 1010 W. 4th St., 19805.

8—ST. MARY OF THE IMMACULATE CONCEPTION (1858)
1414 King St., 19801. Tel: 302-652-0743; Email: shirley_mckeown@verizon.net. Very Rev. Leonard R. Klein, Admin.; Rev. John C. McVoy.
Church: 6th & Pine Sts., 19801.

9—ST. PATRICK (1880)
1414 King St., 19801. Tel: 302-652-0743; Email: shirley_mckeown@verizon.net. Very Rev. Leonard R. Klein; Rev. John C. McVoy.
Catechesis Religious Program—Students 5.

10—ST. PAUL'S (1869)
1010 W. 4th St., 19805. Tel: 302-655-6596; Email: saintpaulrectory@gmail.com. Revs. Rodolfo Ramon; Paul J. Breslin, O.F.M. In Res., Rev. Paul M. Williams, O.F.M.
Catechesis Religious Program—Students 200.

11—SACRED HEART (1874) Reopened as Sacred Heart Oratory, Inc. (1998) A Center for Evangelization. Sacramental records 1874-1948 at Diocesan Archives. Sacramental records 1949-1996 at Cathedral of St. Peter.
917 N. Madison St., 19801. Tel: 302-428-3658; Email: srjyothsna@ministryofcaring.org. Rev. Ronald Giannone, O.F.M.Cap.
Catechesis Religious Program—Students 3.

12—ST. STANISLAUS KOSTKA (1912) (Polish), Closed. Sacramental records at Diocesan Archives.

13—ST. THOMAS THE APOSTLE (1903)
301 N. Bancroft Pkwy., 19805. Tel: 302-658-5131; Fax: 302-652-6222; Email: rectory@sainttom.org; Web: www.sainttom.org. Rev. Msgr. Steven P. Hurley, V.G., S.T.L.; Deacon Francis A. Quinlan.

DELAWARE OUTSIDE THE CITY OF WILMINGTON

BEAR, NEW CASTLE CO., ST. ELIZABETH ANN SETON (1978) 345 Bear-Christiana Rd., Bear, 19701-1048. Tel: 302-322-6430; Email: office@setonparish.net. Rev. Roger F. DiBuo; Deacons William Kibler; Cruz Rodriguez.
Catechesis Religious Program—Students 405.

BELLEFONTE, NEW CASTLE CO., ST. HELENA (Wilmington P.O.) (1936) 602 Philadelphia Pike, 19809. Tel: 302-764-0325; Email: ecuthbertson@sainthelenas.org. Rev. Msgr. Stanley J. Russell, V.F. In Res., Rev. Edward J. Fahey.
Catechesis Religious Program—
210 Bellefonte Ave., 19809. Helen Pennell, D.R.E. Students 110.
Convent—
610 Philadelphia Pike, 19809.

BELVEDERE, NEWPORT CO., OUR MOTHER OF MERCY (1927) Closed. 1971. Sacramental records 1927-1971 at Diocesan Archives.

BETHANY BEACH, SUSSEX CO., ST. ANN (1955) 691 Garfield Ave., Bethany Beach, 19930. Tel: 302-539-6449; Email: office@stannsbethany.org. Revs. John P. Klevence; Ralph T. Castelow; Deacons Edward Danko, (Retired); Dennis Hayden; John Freebery; Michael J. Malecki.
Catechesis Religious Program—Students 179.
Mission—Our Lady of Guadalupe
35318 Church Rd., Frankford, Sussex Co. 19945.

BRANDYWOOD, NEW CASTLE CO., CHURCH OF THE HOLY CHILD (Wilmington P.O.) (1969) 2500 Naamans Rd., 19810. Tel: 302-475-6486; Email: mcarrier@chcparish.org; Web: chcparish.org. Rev. Michael J. Carrier; Sr. Ann Hughes, S.S.J., Pastoral Assoc.; Deacons Joseph Cilia Jr.; William J. Johnston Jr.; Kevin Mucchetti, Music Min.
Catechesis Religious Program—Margie Fiorella, D.R.E.

CLAYMONT, NEW CASTLE CO., HOLY ROSARY (1921) 3200 Philadelphia Pike, Claymont, 19703. Tel: 302-798-2904; Email: office@hrparish.com. Rev. John J. Gayton; Deacons Richard J. Maichle; Jose Perez. In Res., Rev. Leonard J. Kempski, (Retired).
Catechesis Religious Program—Students 130.

DELAWARE CITY, NEW CASTLE CO., ST. PAUL (1852) 209 Washington St, P.O. Box 544, Delaware City, 19706-0544. Tel: 302-834-4321; Fax: 302-834-7517; Email: stpaulsdecity@verizon.net; Web: www.stpaulsrcchurch.org. Rev. Msgr. George J. Brubaker, J.V.; Rev. David F. Murphy; Deacon Charles Schauber Sr.
Catechesis Religious Program—Ms. Linda Michel, D.R.E. Students 29.

DOVER, KENT CO., HOLY CROSS (1870) [CEM] 631 S. State St., Dover, 19901. Tel: 302-674-5787; Email: secretary@holycrossdover.org. Very Rev. James S. Lentini, V.F.; Revs. Idongesit A. Etim; Timothy J. Brady, O.de.M.; Mano Salla; Deacons Robert McMullen; Philip Belt; Vincent Pisano; John Harvey; H. Scott Peterson. In Res., Rev. Msgr. Daniel J. McGlynn, (Retired).
School—Holy Cross School, (Grades PreK-8), Tel: 302-674-5787, Ext. 111; Email: school@holycrossdover.org; Web: holycrossdover.org/school. Very Rev. James S. Lentini, V.F. Lay Teachers 32; Students 453.
High School—Saint Thomas More Academy
133 Thomas More Dr, Magnolia, 19962. Tel: 302-697-8100; Email: office@saintmore.org; Web: www.saintmore.org. Lay Teachers 15; Students 74.
Catechesis Religious Program—Students 340.

ELSMERE, NEW CASTLE CO., CORPUS CHRISTI (Wilmington P.O.) (1948) 905 New Rd., Elsmere, 19805. Tel: 302-994-2922; Email: corpuschristichurch@comcast.net; Web: www.ccparishwilmington.org. Rev. Michael P. Darcy; Deacon David M. DeGhetto.
Catechesis Religious Program—Students 275.
Convent—
912 New Rd., Elsmere, 19805.

FAIRFAX, NEW CASTLE CO., ST. MARY MAGDALEN (Wilmington P.O.) (1951) 7 Sharpley Rd., 19803. Tel: 302-652-6800; Email: lisa.borgia@smmchurch.org; Web: SMMchurch.org. Very Rev. James T. Kirk Jr., V.F. In Res., Very Rev. Joseph W. McQuaide IV.
School—St. Mary Magdalen School, (Grades K-8), 9 Sharpley Rd., 19803. Tel: 302-656-2745; Fax: 302-656-7889; Email: kotoole@smmschoolde.com; Web: smmschoolde.com. Mrs. Kathy O'Toole, Prin. Lay Teachers 29; Students 553.
Catechesis Religious Program—Students 253.

GARFIELD PARK, NEW CASTLE CO., HOLY SPIRIT (New Castle P.O.) (1954) 521 Harmony St, New Castle, 19720. Tel: 302-658-1069; Email: hscathchurch@aol.com. Rev. Timothy M. Nolan; Deacons Patrick Johnston; P. Michael Olliver; Christopher M. Moran.
Res.: 12 Winder Rd., Garfield Park, New Castle, 19720.
Catechesis Religious Program—Students 97.

GEORGETOWN, SUSSEX CO., ST. MICHAEL THE ARCHANGEL (1956) 202 Edward St., Georgetown, 19947. Tel: 302-856-6451; Fax: 302-856-2353; Email: info@smammop.com; Web: smammop.com. Revs. Robert E. Coine; John E. Olson; Deacons Barry Taylor; Kenneth J. Hall; Rev. Idelmo Mego Diaz, In Res.
Catechesis Religious Program—Natalie Blakely, D.R.E.
Mission—Mary Mother of Peace
30839 Mt. Joy Rd. at Rte. 24, Millsboro, Sussex Co. 19966.

GLASGOW, NEW CASTLE CO., ST. MARGARET OF SCOTLAND (1999) 2431 Frazer Rd., Newark, 19702. Tel: 302-834-0225; Email: parishoffice@margaretofscotland.org; Web: margaretofscotland.org. Rev. Msgr. John P. Hopkins, V.F.; Deacons Thomas E. Watts; Austin A. Lobo.
Catechesis Religious Program—Students 411.

GREENVILLE, NEW CASTLE CO., ST. JOSEPH ON THE BRANDYWINE (1841) [CEM 2] 10 Old Church Rd., 19807. Tel: 302-658-7017; Email: f.harkins@verizon.net. Rev. Msgr. Joseph F. Rebman, V.G., S.T.L., J.C.L., C.C.C.E., V.G.; Rev. Brian S. Lewis; Deacon Michael J. Stankewicz.
Catechesis Religious Program—Ms. Eva Marie Lyons, D.R.E. Students 160.

HOCKESSIN, NEW CASTLE CO., ST. MARY OF THE ASSUMPTION (1772) [CEM] 7200 Lancaster Pike, Hockessin, 19707. Tel: 302-239-7100; Email: office@stmaryoftheassumption.org. Rev. Charles C. Dillingham; Very Rev. Glenn M. Evers, Pastoral Assoc.; Deacons Larry Brecht, Contact Person; John Giacci; Joseph W. Jackson Sr.; Larry Morris.
Catechesis Religious Program—Mary Body, D.R.E. Students 626.

LEWES, SUSSEX CO., ST. JUDE THE APOSTLE (2002) 152 Tulip Dr., Lewes, 19958. Tel: 302-644-7300; Tel: 302-644-7413; Fax: 302-644-7415; Email: office@stjudelewes.org; Web: www.stjudelewes.org. Revs. Thomas A. Flowers; Jones Kukatla; Deacons Donald E. Lydick; William McGann; Martin J. Barrett; Howard C. League; Alfred Manuel Barros.
Catechesis Religious Program—Mary Body, D.R.E. Students 200.

LIFTWOOD, NEW CASTLE CO., IMMACULATE HEART OF MARY (Wilmington P.O.) (1955) 4701 Weldin Rd., Liftwood, 19803. Tel: 302-764-0357; Email: parishoffice@ihm.org. Rev. Robert A. Wozniak; Theresa G. DeFonzo, Pastoral Assoc., Evangelization; Deacon Francis C. Conway.
School—Immaculate Heart of Mary School, (Grades PreK-8),

1000 Shipley Rd., Liftwood, 19803. Tel: 302-764-0977 ; Fax: 302-764-0375; Email: office@ihm.org; Web: ihm.org/IHM_School. John Mitchell, Prin.; Terry Delorbe, Vice Pres. Clergy 2; Lay Teachers 31; Students 494.
Catechesis Religious Program—Students 215.
MIDDLETOWN, NEW CASTLE CO., ST. JOSEPH (1883) [CEM 2] Sacramental records 1790-1964 at Diocesan Archives. 371 E. Main St., Middletown, 19709.
Tel: 302-378-5800; Email: office@stjosephmiddletown.com; Web: www.stjosephmiddletown.com/. Rev. Msgr. David F. Kelley, V.C.; Rev. Christopher Hanley; Deacons Timothy D. Enright; David Feaster II; Michael A. Boyd Sr.
Mission—St. Rose of Lima
Lock St., Chesapeake City, Cecil Co. MD 21915.
Shrine—St. Francis Xavier-Old Bohemia
1604 Church Rd, Warwick, MD 21912.
MILFORD, KENT AND SUSSEX COS., ST. JOHN THE APOSTLE (1910) 506 Seabury Ave., Milford, 19963-2217. Tel: 302-422-5123; Fax: 302-422-5720; Email: stjohn@stjohnsmilford.com; Email: admin@stjohnsmilford.org; Web: www.stjohnsmilford.com. Revs. Anthony Giamello; Johnny Laura Lazo; Deacons James D. Malloy, (Retired); Robert C. Herzog; John Yaeger; R. Paul Woofter, (Retired); John G. Molitor; Scott J. Landis.
Res.: 504 Seabury Ave., Milford, 19963-2217.
Catechesis Religious Program—Judy Purcell, D.R.E. Students 190.
Mission—St. Bernadette
109 Dixon, Harrington, Kent Co. 19952.
Tel: 302-398-8269; Fax: 302-398-0253.
NEW CASTLE, NEW CASTLE CO., ST. PETER THE APOSTLE (1845) [CEM] 521 Harmony St., New Castle, 19720. Tel: 302-328-2335; Email: parish@stpeternewcastle.org. Rev. Timothy M. Nolan; Deacons Thomas G. Halko; Christopher M. Moran.
School—St. Peter the Apostle School, (Grades PreK-8),
515 Harmony St., New Castle, 19720.
Tel: 302-328-1191; Fax: 302-328-8049; Email: info@saintpeternewcastle.org; Web: www.stpeternewcastle.org. Mark Zitz, Prin. Clergy 1; Lay Teachers 12; Students 158.
Catechesis Religious Program—Students 20.
NEWARK, NEW CASTLE CO.
1—ST. JOHN THE BAPTIST-HOLY ANGELS (1891) [CEM] 82 Possum Park Rd., Newark, 19711.
Tel: 302-731-2200; Email: aahar@holyangels.net; Web: www.stjohn-holyangels.com. Revs. James M. Jackson; Carlos Ochoa.
School—Holy Angels School, (Grades PreK-8),
Tel: 302-731-2210; Email: bsnively@holyangelsschool.org; Web: www.holyangelsschool.org. Mrs. Barbara Snively, Prin. Lay Teachers 33; Students 416.
Catechesis Religious Program—Mary Alberici, D.R.E. Students 573.
2—PARISH OF THE RESURRECTION (1969) 3000 Videre Dr., Skyline Ridge, 19808. Tel: 302-368-0146; Email: office@resurrectionde.org; Web: www.resurrectionde.org. Revs. William F. Graney; Gregory Corrigan, (Retired); Deacon John J. Falkowski.
Catechesis Religious Program—Elaine Little, D.R.E. Students 103.
3—ST. THOMAS MORE ORATORY (1975) (Personal Parish for Students & Faculty of University of Delaware). 45 Lovett Ave., Newark, 19711.
Tel: 302-368-4728; Fax: 302-368-2548; Email: udcatholic@gmail.com; Web: www.udcatholic.org. Rev. Edward F. Ogden, O.S.F.S.; Kim Zitzner, Pastoral Assoc. & Campus Min.
Catechesis Religious Program—Students 43.
OGLETOWN, NEW CASTLE CO., HOLY FAMILY (Newark P.O.) (1979) 15 Gender Rd., Newark, 19713.
Tel: 302-368-4665; Fax: 302-368-4667; Email: parish@holyfamilynewark.org; Web: www.holyfamilynewark.org. Very Rev. Mark A. Kelleher; Deacons Joseph F. Certesio Sr.; Darrell J. LaShomb; Joseph P. Roach. In Res., Rev. Theophilius Okpara.
Catechesis Religious Program—Mare Draper, D.R.E. Students 188.
PRICES CORNER, NEW CASTLE CO.; ST. CATHERINE OF SIENA (Wilmington P.O.) (1960) 2503 Centerville Rd., 19808. Tel: 302-633-4900; Email: stcathwilm@comcast.net; Web: scswilmde.org. Rev. John M. Hynes; Deacon Gianni Chicco. In Res., Rev. Thomas J. Peterman, (Retired).
Catechesis Religious Program—Students 455.
REHOBOTH BEACH, SUSSEX CO., ST. EDMOND (1952) 402 King Charles St., P.O. Box 646, Rehoboth Beach, 19971. Tel: 302-227-4550; Email: serbde@comcast.net. Revs. William T. Cocco; Christopher Hanley; Deacons James M. Walls; Dana J. Ackerson; Weston Pete Nellius; Robert J. Leonzio; James J. Cadigan.
Catechesis Religious Program—Marie Kopf, D.R.E.
SEAFORD, SUSSEX CO., OUR LADY OF LOURDES (1945) [CEM] 528 Stein Hwy., P.O. Box 719, Seaford, 19973-0719. Tel: 302-629-3591; Email: ollseaf@comcast.net; Web: www.ollseaford.org. Revs. Clement J. Vadakkedath, C.Ss.R.; Paul M. Kuzhimannil; Deacons Axel Blanco; James M. Mueller
Our Lady of Lourdes Church, Inc.
Catechesis Religious Program—Students 220.
SHERWOOD PARK, NEW CASTLE CO., ST. JOHN THE BELOVED (1955) 907 Milltown Rd., Vianney House, 19808. Tel: 302-999-0211; Email: parish@sjbde.org; Email: sohanlon@sjbde.org; Web: www.sjbde.org. Very Rev. Joseph J. Piekarski, V.F.; Revs. Christopher R. Coffiey; Lance S. Martin; Deacons Mark A. Fontana; Dennis Wuebbels; Thomas A. Bailey.
School—St. John the Beloved School, (Grades PreK-8),
905 Milltown Rd., 19808. Tel: 302-998-5525;
Fax: 302-998-1923; Email: sjtbschooloffice@sjbdel.org; Web: www.sjbdel.org. Richard D. Hart, Prin. Lay Teachers 31; Sisters of St. Francis of Philadelphia 1; Students 531; Students in Early Learning 4-yr-old program 70.
Catechesis Religious Program—Dolores Ballintyn, D.R.E. Students 296.
SMYRNA, KENT CO., ST. POLYCARP (1883) 55 Ransom Ln., Smyrna, 19977. Tel: 302-653-8279; Email: office@saintpolycarp.org; Web: www.saintpolycarp.org. Rev. James D. Hreha; Deacon Charles Robinson.
Catechesis Religious Program—Patricia Freedman, D.R.E. Students 167.
WILMINGTON MANOR, NEW CASTLE CO., OUR LADY OF FATIMA (New Castle P.O.) (1948) 801 Dupont Blvd., New Castle, 19720. Tel: 302-328-3431; Email: rectory@olfnewcastle.com. Rev. Msgr. George J. Brubaker, J.V.; Rev. David F. Murphy; Deacon Eliezer Soto.
Catechesis Religious Program—Mary Lou May, Interim C.R.E. Students 270.
WOODCREST, NEW CASTLE CO., ST. MATTHEW (1941) 1013 E. Newport Pike, 19805. Tel: 302-633-5850; Email: pastor@stmatthewsde.com. 901 E. Newport Pike, 19804. Rev. Michael P. Darcy; Deacons Michael T. Wilber; William A. Kaper; Sean Sudler. In Res., Rev. William M. Hazzard, (Retired).
Catechesis Religious Program—
1 Fallon Ave., 19804.

MARYLAND

BERLIN, WORCESTER CO., ST. JOHN NEUMANN ROMAN CATHOLIC CHURCH (2007)
11211 Beauchamp Rd., Berlin, MD 21811.
Tel: 410-208-2956; Fax: 410-208-4584; Email: parishoffice@stjnrcc.com; Web: www.stjohnneumannrcc.com. Rev. Joseph M.P.R. Cocucci; Deacons Charles A. Weschler; David Kolesky.
Catechesis Religious Program—Nancy F. Groves, D.R.E.
CAMBRIDGE, DORCHESTER CO., ST. MARY REFUGE OF SINNERS (1885) [CEM]
1515 Glasgow St., P.O. Box 218, Cambridge, MD 21613. Tel: 410-228-4770; Email: stmarys@comcast.net; Web: www.stmaryscambridge.org. Rev. Stephen C. Lonek.
Catechesis Religious Program—Rosemary Robbins, D.R.E. Students 80.
Mission—St. Mary, Star of the Sea, [CEM] Church Creek, Dorchester Co. MD 21622.
CENTREVILLE, QUEEN ANNE CO., OUR MOTHER OF SORROWS (1892) [CEM]
303 Chesterfield Ave., Centreville, MD 21617.
Tel: 410-758-0143; Email: mosparish@verizon.net. Rev. Clemens D. Manista Jr.
Catechesis Religious Program—Students 180.
Mission—St. Peter, 5319 Ocean Gateway, Queenstown, Queen Anne Co. MD 21658.
Tel: 410-827-8404.
CHESTER, KENT ISLAND QUEEN ANNE CO., ST. CHRISTOPHER (1954)
1861 Harbor Dr., Chester, MD 21619. Email: ParishOffices@stchristopherski.org; Web: www.StChristophersKI.org. Rev. Paul J. Campbell; Deacons John E. Robinson Jr.; Robert A. Wilson.
Catechesis Religious Program—Katherine Sukley, D.R.E.
CHESTERTOWN, KENT CO., SACRED HEART (1876) [CEM]
508 High St., Chestertown, MD 21620.
Tel: 410-778-3160; Fax: 410-810-0427; Email: sacredparish@gmail.com. Rev. John A. Grasing.
Catechesis Religious Program—Email: barbara.kelly.dre@gmail.com. Students 60.
Mission—St. John, W. Main St., Rock Hall, Kent Co. MD 21661. Tel: 410-778-3160; Fax: 410-810-0427.
EASTON, TALBOT CO., SS. PETER AND PAUL (1868) [CEM]
1210 S. Washington St., Easton, MD 21601. Revs. James Nash; Michael A. Angeloni.
Res.: 7906 Ocean Gateway, Easton, MD 21601.
School—SS. Peter and Paul School, (Grades 1-12), 900 High St., Easton, MD 21601. Tel: 410-822-2251;
Fax: 410-820-0136; Email: lhaas@ssppeaston.org; Web: www.ssppeaston.org. Mr. James Nemeth, Prin.; Dr. Faye Schilling, Prin. Lay Teachers 54; Students 559.
High School—SS. Peter and Paul High School,
Tel: 410-822-2275; Email: jnemeth@ssppeaston.org. Mr. James Nemeth, Prin.
Catechesis Religious Program—Students 195.
Missions—St. Joseph—13209 Church Ln., Cordova, Talbot Co. MD 21625.
St. Michael, 109 Lincoln Ave., St. Michaels, Talbot Co. MD 21663.
ELKTON, CECIL CO., IMMACULATE CONCEPTION (1849) [CEM 2]
455 Bow St., Elkton, MD 21921. Tel: 410-398-1100;
Fax: 410-398-1175; Email: office@iccparish.org; Web: iccparish.weconnect.com. Revs. James R. Yeakel, O.S.F.S.; Gerald Dunne, O.S.F.S.; Deacon Michael Truman. In Res., Rev. Francis J. Blood, O.S.F.S.
Res.: 300 Maryland Ave., Elkton, MD 21922.
School—Immaculate Conception School, 452 Bow St., Elkton, MD 21921. Tel: 410-398-2636;
Fax: 410-398-1190; Email: info@icschoolweb.org; Web: www.icschoolweb.org. Mrs. Jeanne Dinkle, Prin. Lay Teachers 19; Felician Sister 1; Students 144.
Catechesis Religious Program—Sr. Grace Andrews, D.R.E. Students 221.
Mission—St. Jude, 928 Turkey Point, North East, Cecil Co. MD 21901.
GALENA, KENT CO., ST. DENNIS (1855) [CEM]
153 N. Main St., P.O. Box 249, Galena, MD 21635.
Tel: 410-648-5145; Fax: 410-648-5767; Email: stdennischurch@aol.com; Web: stdennischurch.org. Rev. James D. Hreha.
Catechesis Religious Program—Jennifer Hinton, D.R.E. Students 92.
MARYDEL, CAROLINE CO., IMMACULATE CONCEPTION (1916)
522 Main St., P.O. Box 399, Marydel, MD 21649.
Tel: 410-482-7687; Tel: 410-482-8939 DRE;
Fax: 410-482-7253; Email: dre@iccmarydel.org; Web: www.iccmarydel.org. Very Rev. James S. Lentini, V.F.; Rev. Idongesit A. Etim; Deacons James M. Tormey; Sherman Mitchell III.
Catechesis Religious Program—Alicia Poppiti, D.R.E. Students 182.
OCEAN CITY, WORCESTER CO.
1—ST. LUKE-ST. ANDREW (1985)
14401 Sinepuxent Ave., Ocean City, MD 21842.
Tel: 410-250-0300; Fax: 410-250-0417; Email: stluke@stlukeoc.com; Web: www.stlukeoc.com. Very Rev. Paul F. Jennings Jr., V.F.; Revs. Steven B. Giuliano; John A. Lunness; Deacons Edward Holson; Joseph Carraro; Robert J. McNulty Jr. In Res., Rev. William J. Lawler, (Retired).
Catechesis Religious Program—Students 51.
Mission—St. Andrew.
2—ST. MARY, STAR OF THE SEA (1877)
1705 Philadelphia Ave., Ocean City, MD 21842.
Tel: 410-289-0652; Email: office@stmarystaroftheseaocmd.com. 200 Baltimore Ave., Ocean City, MD 21842-4106. Rev. Stanislao Esposito; Deacon David S. McDowell.
Catechesis Religious Program—Students 150.
Mission—Holy Savior.
PERRYVILLE, CECIL CO., CHURCH OF THE GOOD SHEPHERD (1949)
810 Aiken Ave., Perryville, MD 21903.
Tel: 410-642-6534, Ext. 10; Email: gsparish@goodshephrd.org; Web: www.goodshepherdcecilmd.org. Rev. Jay R. McKee; Deacon Luke E. Yackley.
School—Good Shepherd Catholic School, 800 Aiken Ave., Perryville, MD 21903. Tel: 410-642-6265;
Fax: 410-642-6522; Email: info@goodshepherdschool.net; Web: www.goodshepherdschool.net. Mrs. Sharon Hodges, Prin. Lay Teachers 15; Students 91.
Catechesis Religious Program—Mrs. Jean Marie Sepka, D.R.E. Students 131.
Missions—St. Teresa—162 N. Main St., Port Deposit, Cecil Co. MD 21904.
St. Patrick, (Inactive) 287 Pleasant Grove Rd., Conowingo, Cecil Co. MD 21918.
St. Agnes, 150 S. Queen St., Rising Sun, Cecil Co. MD 21911.
POCOMOKE CITY, WORCESTER CO., HOLY NAME OF JESUS (1943)
1913 Old Virginia Rd., P.O. Box 179, Pocomoke City, MD 21851. Tel: 410-957-1215; Email: hnj7@hotmail.com. Rev. William J. Porter; Deacon Thomas S. Cimino, (Retired).
Catechesis Religious Program—Students 160.
Mission—St. Elizabeth, 8734 Old Westover Rd., Westover, Somerset Co. MD 21871.
RIDGELY, CAROLINE CO., ST. BENEDICT (1896) [CEM 2]
408 Central Ave., P.O. Box 459, Ridgely, MD 21660.
Tel: 410-634-2253; Email: parishoffice@beparish.com. Very Rev. John B. Gabage, V.F.; Deacons Harold D. Jopp Jr.; William G. Nickum.
Catechesis Religious Program—Maureen Duggan-Cassidy, D.R.E. Students 123.
Mission—St. Elizabeth of Hungary, [CEM] 106 S. First St., Denton, Caroline Co. MD 21629.
SALISBURY, WICOMICO CO., ST. FRANCIS DE SALES (1910)

514 Camden Ave., Salisbury, MD 21801.
Tel: 410-742-6443; Email: parish@visitstfrancis.org. Revs. Christopher W. LaBarge, V.F.; Daniel Staniskis; Deacons Bruce Abresch; William M. Folger; Don Q. Geaga. In Res., Rev. Edward M. Aigner Jr., (Retired).
School—St. Francis De Sales School, (Grades 4-8), 500 Camden Ave., Salisbury, MD 21801.
Tel: 410-749-9907; Fax: 410-749-9507; Email: dtraum@sfdscs.org; Web: stfrancisdesales.net. Debra Traum, Prin. Clergy 9; Lay Teachers 16; Students 193.
Catechesis Religious Program—Pat Burbage, D.R.E.
Mission—Holy Redeemer, Bi-State Blvd. & Chestnut St., Delmar, Wicomico Co. MD 21875.
SECRETARY, DORCHESTER CO., OUR LADY OF GOOD COUNSEL (1891) [CEM]
109 Willow St., P.O. Box 279, Secretary, MD 21664.
Tel: 410-943-4300; Email: olgc25@yahoo.com. Rev. Stephen C. Lonek.
Catechesis Religious Program—Students 37.

Chaplains of Public Institutions.

National Guard

WILMINGTON. *Delaware Air National Guard*.
801 DuPont Blvd., New Castle, 19720.
Tel: 302-328-3431. Revs. Anthony Giamello, John J. Mink, Chap., David F. Murphy, Chap.

Health Care

WILMINGTON. *St. Francis Hospital*, 7th St. & Clayton St., 19805. Tel: 302-421-4577; Email: LMancini@che-east.org. Vacant.
DELAWARE CITY. *Governor Bacon Health Center*. Rev. Msgr. George J. Brubaker, J.V., Tel: 302-834-4321.
ELSMERE. *Veteran's Hospital*, 1601 Kirkwood Hwy., Elsmere, 19805. Tel: 302-994-2511. Rev. Peter Igwilo.
NEW CASTLE. *Delaware Psychiatric Hospital*.
NEWARK. *Christiana Care Health Services, Inc.*, 4755 Ogletown-Stanton Rds., Newark, 19726.
Tel: 302-733-1900; Tel: 302-733-1280; Email: chancery@cdow.org. Janice Nevin, CEO
Wilmington Hospital, 14th & Washington Streets, 19805. Tel: 302-733-1280. Revs. Volodymyr Klanichka, John C. McVoy III, Chap.
PERRY POINT, MD. *Veterans Admin.*. Rev. Jonathan Morse.
SMYRNA, MD. *Delaware Home & Hospital for the Chronically Ill*. Rev. James D. Hreha, Chap., Tel: 302-653-8279.

Correctional Facilities Deacon Michael Truman, Coord. Prison Ministry
WILMINGTON. *Ferris School*. Vacant.
Howard R. Young Correctional Institution. Deacon Gianni Chicco.
NEW CASTLE. *Delores J. Baylor Women's Correctional Institution*. Rev. Paul M. William, O.F.M.
SMYRNA, MD. *Delaware State Correctional Center*.
WESTOVER, MD. *Eastern Correctional Institution*. Rev. Edward M. Aigner Jr., Chap., (Retired), Tel: 410-742-6443.

Campus Ministry

CHESTERTOWN, MD. *Washington College*, Sacred Heart, 508 High St., Chestertown, MD 21620.
Tel: 410-778-3160.
DOVER. *Wesley College*, Holy Cross Parish, 631 S. State St., Dover, 19901. Tel: 302-674-5787;
Fax: 302-674-5783.
NEWARK. *University of Delaware*, St. Thomas More Oratory, 45 Lovett Ave., Newark, 19711.
Tel: 302-368-4728. Rev. Edward F. Ogden, O.S.F.S., Chap., Kim Zitzner, Pastoral Assoc. & Campus Min.

Nursing Homes:
Rev.—
Fahey, Edward J., NCC Health Care Facilities, 602 Philadelphia Pike, 19809. Tel: 302-764-0325.

Unassigned or Leave of Absence:
Revs.—
Breslin, Cornelius J., P.O. Box 2030, 19899
Grimm, John S., P.O. Box 2030, 19899
Lee, J.M. Gregory, P.O. Box 2030, 19899
Magana, Salvador, P.O. Box 2030, 19899
Protack, Thomas J., S.T.L., P.O. Box 2030, 19899
Wisniewski, Joseph F., P.O. Box 2030, 19899.

On Duty Outside the Diocese:
Rev.—
Cardone, Anthony F., 600 Newbridge Rd., East Meadow, NY 11554.

Military Chaplains:
Rev.—
Kopec, Christopher A., c/o Archdiocese for the Military Service, P.O. Box 4469, Washington, DC 20017-0469.

Retired:
Rev. Msgrs.—
Brown, Charles L. III, V.F., (Retired), 516 Stonebridge Blvd., New Castle, 19720
Cini, J. Thomas, V.G., (Retired), Annecy Hall, 1120 Blue Ball Rd., Childs, MD 21916
Koper, Francis B., (Retired), Gladwin, MI
Lemon, Clement P., (Retired), 185 Salem Church Rd., Newark, 19713-2997
Martin, Ralph L., (Retired), 185 Salem Church Rd., Newark, 19713-2997
McGlynn, Daniel J., (Retired), 631 S. State St., Dover, 19901
McMahon, Kevin T., S.T.B., S.T.L., S.T.D., (Retired), Sea Isle City, NJ
Revs.—
Aigner, Edward M. Jr., (Retired), 514 Camden Ave., Salisbury, MD 21801
Blakely, Leonard J., (Retired), 32011 Oak Orchard Rd., Millsboro, 19966
Byrolly, Bruce, (Retired), 2 Bay View Ave., P.O. Box 43, Cambridge, MD 21613
Casari, Michael T., (Retired), P.O. Box 146, Secretary, MD 21664
Cook, Michael J., (Retired), c/o Holy Family Church, 15 Gender Rd., Newark, 19713
Coppinger, Edmund, (Retired), 225 28th St., Richmond, CA 94804
Corrigan, Gregory M., (Retired), P.O. Box 2030, 19899
Drobinski, Joseph J., (Retired), 23 Standiford Cr., Hershey Run, 19804
Fiore, Arthur B., V.F., (Retired), 150 Loomis Ave., Coatesville, PA 19320
Forester, Raymond L., (Retired), 255 Possum Park Rd., Rm. 1102, Newark, 19711
Gallagher, Michael J., (Retired), 3125 13th St. N.W., Unit 402, Washington, DC 20005
Gerres, Daniel W., (Retired), 726 Loveville Rd., Hockessin, 19707
Gomolski, Joseph T., (Retired), 921 Begonia Rd., Apt. 201, Celebration, FL 34747
Hanley, Thomas E., (Retired), 899 Little Creek Rd., Dover, 19901
Hazzard, William M., (Retired), 1403 Shallcross Ave. #301, 19806
Kaczorowski, Edward J., (Retired), 1 Grosvenor Ct., 19804
Kavanaugh, John J., (Retired), P.O. Box 264, Charlestown, MD 21914
Kempski, Leonard J., (Retired), 3200 Philadelphia Pike, Claymont, 19703
Kochan, Frederick A., (Retired), 2201-A Baltimore Ave., Lavellette, NJ 08735
Lawler, William J., (Retired), 14401 Sinepuxent Ave., Ocean City, MD 21842
Mast, Paul, (Retired), P.O. Box 1104, Clayton, 19938
Mathesius, William P., (Retired), 103 Atlantic Ave., Washington Hgts., Rehoboth Beach, 19971
McMahon, Joseph R., (Retired), P.O. Box 4239, 19807
Melnick, William D., (Retired), P.O. Box 2030, 19899
Peterman, Thomas J., (Retired), 2505 Centerville Rd., 19808
Pollard, Roy F., (Retired), 255 Possum Park Rd., Apt. 2212, Newark, 19711
Roark, Michael B., V.F., (Retired), 282 Country Village Dr., Apt. JJ276, Smyrna, TN 37167
Rodgers, Hilary R., (Retired), 185 Salem Church Rd., Newark, 19713-2997
Sheekey, Philip P., (Retired), 1403 Shallcross Ave. #106, 19806
Smith, James B., (Retired), 4765 Weatherhill Dr., 19808
Turley, Sean F., (Retired), Staffordshire, England
Volmi, Dennis G., J.C.D., (Retired), 10 E. Green Ln., Milford, 19963
Weisman, Raymond F., (Retired), 514 Camden Ave., Salisbury, MD 21801.

Permanent Deacons:
Abresch, Bruce, St. Francis de Sales, Salisbury, MD
Ackerson, Dana J., St. Edmond, Rehoboth Beach, DE
Bailey, Thomas A., St. John the Beloved Parish, Wilmington, DE
Barrett, Martin J., St. Jude, Lewes, DE
Barros, Alfred Manuel, St. Jude the Apostle, Lewes, DE
Belt, Philip, Holy Cross, Dover, DE
Blanco, Axel, Our Lady of Lourdes, Seaford, DE
Boyd, Michael A. Sr., Holy Cross, Dover, DE
Cadigan, James J., St. Edmond, Rehoboth Beach, DE
Carraro, Joseph, St. Luke & St. Andrew, Ocean City, MD
Carroll, Donald T., (Retired)
Certesio, Joseph F. Sr., Holy Family Parish, Newark, DE
Chalfant, Harold F., (Retired)
Chicco, Gianni, St. Catherine of Siena and Howard Young Correctional Institution, Wilmington, DE
Cilia, Joseph A. Jr., Asst. Chap., Next Step Group, Church of the Holy Child, Wilmington, DE
Cimino, Thomas S., (Retired), (Retired)
Conway, Francis C., Immaculate Heart of Mary, Wilmington, DE
Cousar, Robert J. Jr., St. Joseph Parish, Wilmington, DE
Danko, Edward, (Retired), (Retired)
Davis, John, Sacred Heart, Chestertown, MD
Dean, James E., (Retired)
DeGhetto, David M., Corpus Christi, Wilmington, DE
Enright, Timothy D., St. Joseph, Middletown, DE
Falkowski, John J., Resurrection Parish, Wilmington, DE
Feaster, David II, St. Joseph, Middletown, DE
Folger, William M., St. Francis de Sales Parish, Salisbury, MD
Fontana, Mark A., St. John the Beloved, Wilmington, DE
Freebery, John W. Jr., St. Ann, Bethany Beach, DE
Gardner, Edward Sr., (Retired)
Geaga, Don Q., St. Francis de Sales Church, Salisbury, MD
Giacci, John, (Retired)
Halko, Thomas G., St. Peter the Apostle Parish, New Castle, DE
Hall, Kenneth, St. Michael the Archangel, Georgetown
Handlir, James, (Retired)
Harvey, John, Church of the Holy Cross, Dover, DE
Hayden, Dennis L., St. Ann, Bethany Beach, DE (Sabbatical)
Herzog, Robert C., St. John the Apostle, Milford, DE
Holson, Edward G., St. Luke/St. Andrew, Ocean City, MD
Huhn, Francis J., (Retired)
Jackson, Joseph W. Sr., St. Mary of the Assumption Parish, Hockessin, DE
Johnston, Patrick K., Holy Spirit Parish, New Castle, DE
Johnston, William J., Church of the Holy Child, Wilmington, DE
Jopp, Harold D. Jr., St. Benedict's, Ridgely, MD
Juliano, Richard, St. Ann, Bethany Beach, DE
Kaper, William A., St. Matthew Parish, Wilmington, DE
Kibler, William III, St. Elizabeth Ann Seton, Bear, DE
Kledzik, James I., Our Lady of Fatima, New Castle, DE
Kolesky, David, St. John Neumann, Berlin, MD
Lafferty, James J. Jr., (Retired)
Landis, Scott J., St. John the Apostle, Milton, DE
LaShomb, Darrell J., Holy Family, Newark, DE
League, Howard C., St. Jude the Apostle, Lewes, DE
Lemon, John G., (Retired)
Lobo, Austin A., St. Margaret of Scotland Church, Newark, DE
Lydick, Donald E., St. Jude the Apostle, Lewes, DE
Lynch, Edmund F., (Retired)
Maichle, Richard J., Holy Rosary, Claymont, DE
Malecki, Michael J., St. Ann's, Bethany Beach, DE
Malloy, James D., (Retired), (Retired)
Masino, Thomas R., (Retired)
McDowell, David S., St. Mary Star of the Sea, Ocean City, MD
McGann, William, St. Jude the Apostle, Lewes, DE
McMullen, Robert E., Holy Cross Parish, Dover, DE
McNulty, Robert J., St. Luke, Ocean City, MD
Mitchell, Sherman III, Immaculate Conception, Marydel, MD
Molitor, John G., St. John the Apostle, Milford, DE
Moran, Christopher M., St. Peter the Apostle, New Castle, DE
Morris, Larry, St. Mary of the Assumption, Hockessin, DE
Mueller, James M., Our Lady of Lourdes Parish, Seaford, DE
Murrian, William J., (Retired)
Nellius, Weston E., St. Edmond, Rehoboth, DE
Nickum, William G., St. Benedict Parish, Ridgely, MD
Olliver, P. Michael, Holy Spirit Parish, New Castle, DE
Paolucci, Robert, (Retired)
Parisi, John G., (Retired)
Perez, Jose, Holy Rosary, Claymont, DE
Peterson, H. Scott, Church of the Holy Cross, Dover, DE

Pisano, Vincent, Holy Cross, Dover, DE
Pulliam, Kenneth Sr., St. Elizabeth, Wilmington, DE
Quinlan, Francis A., St. Thomas the Apostle, Wilmington, DE
Ricker, Philip W., St. Edmond, Rehoboth Beach, DE
Rivera, Angel, St. Paul, Wilmington, DE
Roach, Joseph P., Holy Family, DE
Robinson, Charles, St. Polycarp, Smyrna, DE
Robinson, John R. Jr., St. Christopher, Chester, MD
Rodriguez, Cruz, St. Elizabeth Ann Seton, Bear, DE
Rodriguez-Trejo, Jose N., (Retired)
Sanchez, Jose A., St. Elizabeth Ann Seton, Bear, DE
Schauber, Charles Sr., St. Paul, Delaware City, DE
Siers, Ronald, (Retired)
Snow, Austin M. Jr., (Retired)
Soto, Eliezer, Our Lady of Fatima, New Castle, DE
Stam, Bernardus C., Resurrection, Wilmington, DE
Stankewicz, Michael J., St. Joseph on the Brandywine, Greenville, DE
Sudler, Sean, St. Matthew, Wilmington, DE
Taylor, Barry, St. Michael the Archangel, Georgetown, DE
Taylor, Bradley D., SS. Peter & Paul, Easton, MD
Tormey, James M., (Retired)
Truman, Michael, Immaculate Conception, Elkton, MD
Walls, James M., St. Edmond, Rehoboth, DE
Watts, Thomas E. Sr., St. Margaret of Scotland, Newark, DE
Wendt, Fred, (Retired)
Weschler, Charles A., St. John Neumann, Berlin, MD
Wilber, Michael T., St. Matthew Parish, Wilmington, DE
Wilson, Robert A., St. Christopher, Chester, MD
Wolf, Allen S., (Retired)
Woofter, R. Paul, (Retired)
Wuebbels, Dennis, St. John the Beloved, Wilmington, DE
Yackley, Luke E., Church of the Good Shepherd, Perryville, MD
Yaeger, John A., St. John the Apostle, Milford, DE
Zolandz, Raymond R. Jr., St. Hedwig, Wilmington.

INSTITUTIONS LOCATED IN DIOCESE

[A] HIGH SCHOOLS, DIOCESAN

WILMINGTON. *St. Mark's High School*, 2501 Pike Creek Rd., 19808. Tel: 302-738-3300; Fax: 302-738-5132; Email: bmoore@stmarkshs.net; Web: www.stmarkshs.net. Mr. Guy Townsend, Prin.; Richard A. Bayhan, Prin.; Mr. Francis Corrigan, Asst. Prin. for Mission & Academics; Mr. Peter Curcio, Dir.; Sr. Sandra Grieco, I.H.M., Pastoral Assoc.; Mrs. Misty Boyle, Librarian; Mrs. Alissa McGrisken, Dir. Lay Teachers 42; Sisters 1; Students 509.

MAGNOLIA. *St. Thomas More Academy* (1999) 133 Thomas More Dr., Magnolia, 19962.
Tel: 302-697-8100; Fax: 302-697-8122; Email: office@saintmore.org; Web: www.saintmore.org. Ms. Rachel Casey, Prin. Lay Teachers 19; Students 167.

[B] HIGH SCHOOLS, PRIVATE

WILMINGTON. *Salesianum School*, 1801 N. Broom St., 19802. Tel: 302-654-2495; Fax: 302-654-7767; Email: principal@salesianum.org; Web: www.salesianum.org. Revs. J. Christian Beretta, O.S.F.S., Prin.; Joseph G. Morrissey, School Admin.; John A. Kolodziej, O.S.F.S., Supr.; Brian D. Zumbrum, O.S.F.S., School Chap.; Francis J. Pileggi, O.S.F.S.; Michael C. Connolly, O.S.F.S.; Joseph P. Jocco, O.S.F.S.; Sean P. Connery, O.S.F.S.; William J. Keech, O.S.F.S.; Thomas J. McGee, O.S.F.S.; John M. Mokluk, O.S.F.S. Boys 1,000; Religious Teachers 3; Lay Teachers 74; Priests 8; Students 1,000. In Res. Revs. Sean P. Connery, O.S.F.S.; William J. Hultberg, O.S.F.S.; William J. Keech, O.S.F.S.; Thomas J. McGee, O.S.F.S.; Joseph J. McKenna, O.S.F.S.; John M. Mokluk, O.S.F.S.; Edward J. Roszko, O.S.F.S.

Ursuline Academy of Wilmington, DE, Inc., 1106 Pennsylvania Ave., 19806. Tel: 302-658-7158;
Fax: 302-658-4297; Email: info@ursuline.org; Web: ursuline.org. Trisha Medeiros, Pres.; Laura Fodge, Prin.; Ann Phillips, Prin. (Coed Grades Early Childhood-5, All Girls Grades 6-12) Students 405; Ursuline Nuns 1; Lay Faculty 76.

CLAYMONT. *Archmere Academy* (1932) 3600 Philadelphia Pike, Claymont, 19703.
Tel: 302-798-6632; Fax: 302-798-7290; Email: generale-mailbox@archmereacademy.com; Web: www.archmereacademy.com. Michael Marinelli, Headmaster; Mr. John J. Jordan III, Prin.; Rev. Joseph P. McLaughlin, O.Praem., Chap.; Ms. Rosemary Conway-Bauer, Librarian. High School (Private Preparatory). Lay Teachers 46; Priests 2; Students 508.

[C] INTERPAROCHIAL SCHOOLS

WILMINGTON. *All Saints Catholic School*, (Grades PreK-8), 907 New Road, 19805. Tel: 302-995-2231; Fax: 302-993-0767; Email: allsaints@ascsde.org; Web: www.ascsde.org. Mary Elizabeth Muir, Prin. Lay Teachers 17; Students 205; Total Staff 30.

BEAR. **Aquinas Academy*, (Grades K-12), 2370 Red Lion Rd., Bear, 19701. Tel: 302-838-9601; Email: jack.moore@aquinasacademy.net; Web: www.aquinasacademy.net. Mr. John J. Moore. Faculty 10; Lay Teachers 10; Students 100.

BERLIN, MD. *Most Blessed Sacrament Catholic School*, 11242 Racetrack Rd., Berlin, MD 21811.
Tel: 410-208-1600; Fax: 410-208-4957; Email: mostblessedss@yahoo.com; Web: mostblessedsacramentschool.com. Mr. Mark J. Record, Prin. Lay Teachers 22; Students 220; Total Staff 32.

NEWARK. *Christ the Teacher Catholic School*, (Grades PreK-8), 2451 Frazer Rd., Newark, 19702.
Tel: 302-838-8850; Fax: 302-838-8854; Email: slking@christtheteacher.org; Web: cttcs.org. Sr. La Verne King, R.S.M., Prin. Religious Teachers 2; Lay Teachers 29; Sisters 2; Students 606; Total Staff 55.

[D] ELEMENTARY SCHOOLS, PRIVATE

WILMINGTON. *Saint Edmond's Academy*, (Grades K-8), 2120 Veale Rd., 19810. Tel: 302-475-5370; Fax: 302-475-2256; Email: brubio@stedmondsacademy.org; Web: stedmondsacademy.org. Brian Ray, Headmaster; Tricia G. Scott, Ed.D., Prin.; Bill D'Amato, Asst. Headmaster; Tammy Hayes-Hartman, Librarian. Boys 247; Religious Teachers 1; Lay Teachers 25; Students 247.

Nativity Preparatory School, 1515 Linden St., 19805. Tel: 302-777-1015; Fax: 302-777-1225; Email: info@nativitywilmington.org; Web: nativitywilmington.org. Dr. Eric Ruoss, Pres.; Paul Webster, Prin.; Andrea Rotsch, Dir. of Institutional Advancement. Lay Teachers 7; Students 48.

CHILDS, MD. *Mount Aviat Academy*, (Grades PreK-8), 399 Childs Rd., Childs, MD 21916.
Tel: 410-398-2206; Fax: 877-398-8063; Email: school@mountaviat.org; Email: principal@mountaviat.org; Web: www.mountaviat.org. Sisters John Elizabeth Callaghan, O.S.F.S., Prin.; Anne Elizabeth Eder, O.S.F.S., Business Mgr.; Tricia Few, Librarian. Oblate Sisters of St. Francis de Sales. Lay Teachers 15; Sisters 5; Students 223.

[E] DIOCESAN CATHOLIC CHARITIES PROGRAM

WILMINGTON. *Catholic Charities, Inc.*, 2601 W. 4th St., 19805-0610. Tel: 302-655-9624; Fax: 302-655-9753; Email: chancery@cdow.org; Web: www.ccwilm.org. Ms. Richelle A. Vible, M.B.A., Exec. Dir; Mr. Frederick Jones, M.S., Dir. Prog. Opers. Tot Asst. Annually 15,000; Total Staff 97; Individuals Served 100,000; Fuel Program 14,696.

Delaware Energy Assistance Program,
Tel: 302-654-9295; Email: energy@ccwilm.org. Ms. Richelle A. Vible, M.B.A., Dir. Total Staff 3.

New Castle County Office, 2601 W. 4th St., 19805.
Tel: 302-654-9295; Fax: 302-654-9757; Email: energy@ccwilm.org.

Sussex County Office, 406 S. Bedford St., Ste. 9, Georgetown, 19947. Tel: 302-856-6310;
Fax: 302-856-6332; Email: energy@ccwilm.org. Catholic Charities, 2601 W. 4th St., 19805.

Kent County Office DE Energy Assistance Program, Dover Office 2099 S. DuPont Hwy., Dover, 19901.
Tel: 302-674-1782; Fax: 302-531-0849; Email: energy@ccwilm.org. Catholic Charities, 2601 W. 4th St., 19805. Ms. Richelle A. Vible, M.B.A., Dir. Tot Asst. Annually 7,290; Total Staff 15.

Behavioral Health Services

New Castle County Office, 2601 W. 4th St., 19805.
Tel: 302-655-9624; Fax: 302-654-6432; Email: counseling@ccwilm.org.

Kent County Office Behavioral Services, Dover Office 2099 S. DuPont Hwy., Dover, 19901.
Tel: 302-674-1600; Fax: 302-674-1005; Email: counseling@ccwilm.org. Catholic Charities, 2601 W. 4th St., 19805. Ms. Richelle A. Vible, M.B.A., Dir. Tot Asst. Annually 700; Total Staff 3.

Sussex County Office, 406 S. Bedford St., Ste. 9, Georgetown, 19947. Tel: 302-856-9578;
Fax: 302-856-6297; Email: counseling@ccwilm.org. Catholic Charities, Inc., 2604 W. 4th St., 19805.

Eastern Shore Office Behavioral Health Services 30632 Hampden Ave., P.O. Box 401, Princess Anne, MD 21853. Tel: 410-651-9608;
Fax: 410-651-1437; Email: counseling@ccwilm.org. Catholic Charities, 2601 W. 4th St., 19805. Ms. Richelle A. Vible, M.B.A., Dir. Tot Asst. Annually 110; Total Staff 3.

HIV Services

New Castle County Office, 2601 W. 4th St., 19805.
Tel: 302-655-9624; Fax: 302-654-9721; Email: HIVServices@ccwilm.org. Paula Savini, Contact Person.

Basic Needs Program

New Castle County Office, 2601 W. 4th St., 19805.
Tel: 302-655-9624; Fax: 302-654-6432; Email: BasicNeeds@ccwilm.org.

Kent County Office Basic Needs, Dover Office 2099 S. DuPont Hwy., Dover, 19901. Tel: 302-674-4016; Fax: 302-674-4018; Email: basicneeds@ccwilm.org. Catholic Charities, 2601 W. 4th St., 19805. Ms. Richelle A. Vible, M.B.A., Dir. Tot Asst. Annually 700; Total Staff 3.

Sussex County Office, 406 S. Bedford St., Ste. 9, Georgetown, 19947. Tel: 302-856-9578;
Fax: 302-856-6332; Email: basicneeds@ccwilm.org. Catholic Charities, 2601 W. 4th St., 19805.

Eastern Shore Office Basic Needs Program 30632 Hampden Ave., P.O. Box 401, Princess Anne, MD 21853. Tel: 410-651-9608; Fax: 410-651-1437; Email: basicneeds@ccwilm.org. Catholic Charities, 2601 W. 4th St., 19805. Ms. Richelle A. Vible, M.B.A., Exec. Tot Asst. Annually 547; Total Staff 2.

Immigration & Refugee Services

New Castle County Office, 2601 W. 4th St., 19805-0610. Tel: 302-655-9624; Fax: 302-654-9757; Email: immigration@ccwilm.org.

Kent County Office Immigration & Refugee Services 2099 S. DuPont Hwy., Dover, 19901.
Tel: 302-674-1600; Email: immigration@ccwilm.org. Catholic Charities, 2601 W. 4th St., 19805. Ms. Richelle A. Vible, M.B.A., Dir. Tot Asst. Annually 124; Total Staff 3.

Sussex County Office, 406 S. Bedford St., Ste. 9, Georgetown, 19947. Tel: 302-856-9578;
Fax: 302-856-6297; Email: immigration@ccwilm.org. Catholic Charities, Inc., 2604 W. 4th St., 19805.

Eastern Shore Office Immigration and Refugee Services 30632 Hampden Ave., P.O. Box 401, Princess Anne, MD 21853. Tel: 410-651-9608;
Fax: 410-651-1437; Email: immigration@ccwilm.org. Catholic Charities, 2601 W. 4th St., 19805. Ms. Richelle A. Vible, M.B.A., Dir. Tot Asst. Annually 90; Total Staff 2.

Catholic Charities Thrift Center, 1320 E. 23rd St., 19802. 2601 W. 4th St., 19805. Tel: 302-764-2717;
Fax: 302-764-2743; Email: thriftcenter@ccwilm.org; Email: chancery@cdow.org. Ms. Richelle A. Vible, M.B.A., Exec. Tot Asst. Annually 9,971; Total Staff 5.

CACFP (Child & Adult Care Food Program)

New Castle County Office, 2604 W. 4th St., 19805.
Tel: 302-655-9624; Fax: 302-654-9753; Email: cacfp@ccwilm.org.

Kent County Office Child & Adult Care Food Program 2099 S. DuPont Hwy., Dover, 19901.
Tel: 302-674-1600; Fax: 302-674-4018; Email: cacfp@ccwilm.org. Catholic Charities, 2601 W. 4th St., 19805. Ms. Richelle A. Vible, M.B.A., Dir. Tot Asst. Annually 1,089; Total Staff 3.

Sussex County Office, 406 S. Bedford St., Ste. 9, Georgetown, 19947. Tel: 302-856-9578;
Fax: 302-856-6332; Email: cacfp@ccwilm.org. Catholic Charities, Inc., 2604 W. 4th St., 19804.

Addiction and Substance Abuse Counseling

New Castle County Office, 2601 W. 4th St., 19805.
Tel: 302-655-9624; Fax: 302-654-6432; Email: substanceabuse@ccwilm.org.

Kent County Office, 2099 S. DuPont Hwy., Dover, 19901. Tel: 302-674-1600; Fax: 302-674-4018; Email: substanceabuse@ccwilm.org. Catholic Charities, 2601 W. 4th St., 19805. Ms. Richelle A. Vible, M.B.A., Dir. Addiction & Substance Abuse Counseling, Kent County Office Tot Asst. Annually 99; Total Staff 5.

Sussex County Office, 406 S. Bedford St., Ste. 9, Georgetown, 19947. Catholic Charities, 2601 W. 4th Street, 19805. Tel: 302-856-9578;
Fax: 302-856-6297; Email: substanceabuse@ccwilm.org.

Residential Services

Bayard House, Maternity Services, Pregnancy Counseling, 300 Bayard Ave., 19805.
Tel: 302-654-1184; Fax: 302-654-8570; Email: bayardhouse@ccwilm.org. Catholic Charities, 2601 W. 4th St., 19805. Ms. Richelle A. Vible, M.B.A., Exec. Tot Asst. Annually 250; Total Staff 7.

Casa San Francisco, 127 Broad St., P.O. Box 38, Milton, 19968. Tel: 302-684-8694;
Fax: 302-684-2808; Email: casa@ccwilm.org; Email: chancery@cdow.org. Catholic Charities,

2601 W. 4th St., 19805. Alan Southard, Prog. Mgr. Tot Asst. Annually 112; Total Staff 7.

Seton Center, 30632 Hampden Ave., P.O. Box 401, Princess Anne, MD 21853. Tel: 410-651-9608; Fax: 410-651-1437; Email: setoncenter@ccwilm.org.

[F] CHILDREN'S SERVICES

WILMINGTON. *Seton Villa, Inc.* (Catholic Charities) 4th St. & Greenhill Ave., 19805. Tel: 302-655-9624; Email: CommunityRelations@ccwilm.org; Web: www.cdow.org. Ms. Richelle A. Vible, M.B.A., Dir.

[G] OTHER WELFARE AGENCIES (Not under jurisdiction of Department of Social Concerns)

WILMINGTON.

Family Counseling Center of St. Paul's, Inc., 1010 W. 4th St., 19805-3602. Tel: 302-576-4121; Fax: 302-655-7684; Email: saintpaulrectory@gmail.com; Web: www.stpaulscounseling.org. Rev. Rodolfo Ramon.

Ministry of Caring, Inc. (1977) 115 E. 14th St., 19801-3209. Anna Halverson, Contact Person.

Ministry of Caring, 115 East 14th St., 19801. Tel: 302-652-5523; Fax: 302-652-1919; Email: ahalverson@ministryofcaring.org; Web: ministryofcaring.org. Gregory Varallo Esq., Pres.; Rev. Ronald Giannone, O.F.M.Cap., Exec. Dir.; William Hayes Sr., CFO; Deborah Philips, Chief of Staff; Anthea Piscarick, Senior Grant Writer; John Bates, Dir.; Chaz Emerio, Dir.; Marie Keefer, Human Resources Dir.; Rebecca Klug, Dir.; Priscilla Rakestraw, Devel. Dir.; Annie Halverson, Paralegal/Exec. Asst. Total Staff 24.

Nazareth Long Term Housing, 207 S. Van Buren St., 19805. Tel: 302-652-5523; Fax: 302-652-1919; Email: jbates@ministryofcaring.org. John Bates, Dir. Transitional residence for families.

Nazareth Long Term Housing, 109-1/2 & 111 N. Jackson St., 19805. Ministry Caring Inc., 115 E. 14th St., 19801. Tel: 302-652-5523; Fax: 302-652-1919; Email: mail@ministryofcaring.org. John Bates, Dir. Transitional residence for families.

Benedictine Park, 731 W. 9th St., 19801. 115 E. 14th St., 19801-3209. Tel: 302-652-5523; Fax: 302-652-1919; Email: ahalverson@ministryofcaring.org. Bro. Ronald Giannone, O.F.M.Cap., Dir.

Andrisani Building (1996) 1803 W. 6th St., 19805. 115 E. 14th St., 19801-3209. Tel: 302-428-3702; Fax: 302-428-3705; Email: dcornish@ministryofcaring.org. Shannon Ayres, Mental Health Counselor; Durand Cornish, Drug & Alcohol Counselor. Tot Asst. Annually 100; Total Staff 2.

Child Care Center (1992) 221 N. Jackson St., 19805-3649. Tel: 302-652-8992; Fax: 302-594-9442; Email: pannane@ministryofcaring.org. Paulette Annane, Prog. Dir. Child care for homeless children, from infancy to 4 years old. Students 34.

Guardian Angel Child Care (1998) 1000 Wilson St., 19801-3432. Tel: 302-428-3620; Fax: 302-428-3622; Email: jchandler@ministryofcaring.org. Janet Chandler, Site Mgr. Students 34.

Il Bambino (2002) 903 N. Madison St., 19801. Tel: 302-594-9449; Fax: 302-594-9450; Email: pannane@ministryofcaring.org. Paulette Annane, Prog. Dir. Infant day care program. Bed Capacity 24; Capacity 24; Total Staff 10.

St. Clare Medical Outreach (1992) 7th & Clayton Sts., 19805-3156. Tel: 302-575-8218; Email: ebrown@che-east.org. Ebony Brown, Mgr. Mobile medical van which provides health services for the poor. Tot Asst. Annually 780; Total Staff 4.

Mary Mother of Hope House Permanent Housing, 818-820 Jefferson St., 19801-1432. Tel: 302-594-9448; Fax: 302-594-9434; Email: amountain@ministryofcaring.org. Ministry of Caring, Inc., 115 E. 14th St., 19801. Annie Mountain, Prog. Dir. Transitional residence for single women. Bed Capacity 9; Capacity 9; Total Staff 2.

House of Joseph II, 9 W. 18th St., 19802-4833. Tel: 302-594-9473; Fax: 302-594-9494; Email: srchrista@ministryofcaring.org. Sr. Christa Rowe, O.S.C., Prog. Dir. Hospice for people with AIDS. Bed Capacity 16; Capacity 16; Total Staff 16.

Maria Lorenza Longo House (2003) 822 Jefferson St., 19801. Tel: 302-420-7781; Email: amountain@ministryofcaring.org. Annie Mountain, Prog. Dir. Transitional Residence for Families. Bed Capacity 6; Capacity 6; Total Staff 2.

Pierre Toussaint Dental Office (1995) 830 Spruce St., 19801-4205. Tel: 302-652-8947; Fax: 302-652-8994; Email: jbates@ministryofcaring.org. John Bates, Dir. Dental office for the homeless. Total Staff 4.

Angela Merici House (1993) 1105 W. 8th St., 19806-4605. Tel: 302-655-4817. Sr. Bernadette McGoldrick, O.S.F., Admin. Residence for Sisters of St. Francis. Religious Sisters 3.

St. Francis Transitional Residence (1995) 103-107 N. Jackson St., 19805-3648. Email: jspencer@ministryofcaring.org. Kim Boulden, Prog. Dir. Transitional living for women and children. Tot Asst. Annually 5,898; Total Staff 1.

House of Joseph Transitional Residence (1998) 704 West St., 19801-1523. Tel: 302-652-0904; Fax: 302-594-9472; Email: krobinson@ministryofcaring.org. Khadija Robinson, Dir. Transitional residence for employable, formerly homeless persons. Bed Capacity 13; Total Staff 2.

Samaritan Outreach (1995) 1410 N. Claymont St., 19802-5227. Tel: 302-594-9476; Fax: 303-594-9478; Email: gfoster@ministryofcaring.org. Georgette Foster, Dir. Social outreach for the homeless. Tot Asst. Annually 388; Total Staff 1.

Mary Mother of Hope House I (1977) 1103 W. 8th St., 19806. Tel: 302-652-8532; Fax: 302-594-9434; Email: amountain@ministryofcaring.org. Annie Mountain, Prog. Dir. Emergency shelter for homeless women. Bed Capacity 21; Capacity 21; Total Staff 9.

Mary Mother of Hope House II (1983) 121 N. Jackson St., 19805-3670. Tel: 302-652-1935; Fax: 302-594-9475; Email: kboulden@ministryofcaring.org. Kim Boulden, Prog. Dir. Emergency shelter for women with children. Bed Capacity 30; Capacity 30; Total Staff 11.

Mary Mother of Hope House III (1988) 515 N. Broom St., 19805-3114. Tel: 302-652-0970; Fax: 302-594-9496; Email: kboulden@ministryofcaring.org. Kim Boulden, Prog. Dir. & Case Mgr. Emergency shelter for women with children. Bed Capacity 20; Capacity 20; Total Staff 6.

Job Placement Center (1985) 1100 Lancaster Ave., 19805-4009. Tel: 302-652-5522; Fax: 302-652-0917; Email: gfoster@ministryofcaring.org. Georgette Foster, Dir. Employment agency to assist the poor.

House of Joseph I (1985) 1328 W. 3rd St., 19805. Tel: 302-652-0904; Fax: 302-594-9472; Email: krobinson@ministryofcaring.org. Khadija Robinson, Dir. Shelter for homeless employable men who are seeking employment. Bed Capacity 12; Capacity 12; Total Staff 10.

Emmanuel Dining Room, West (1979) 121 N. Jackson St., 19805-3670. Tel: 302-652-3228; Fax: 302-652-2576; Email: mlafate@ministryofcaring.org. Ms. Maureen LaFate, Dir. Total Staff 8.

Emmanuel Dining Room, East, 226 N. Walnut St., 19801-3934. Tel: 302-652-2577; Fax: 302-652-2576; Email: dsmith@ministryofcaring.org. Mr. DeWitt Smith, Site Mgr. Total Staff 5.

Emmanuel Dining Room, South, 500 Rogers Rd., New Castle, 19720. Tel: 302-622-4555; Fax: 302-652-2576; Email: srkodonnell@ministryofcaring.org. Sr. Kathleen O'Donnell, O.S.F., Site Mgr. Total Staff 3.

Ministry of Caring Distribution Center, 1410 N. Claymont St., 19802-5227. Ministry of Caring, Inc., 115 E. 14th St., 19801. Tel: 302-652-0969; Fax: 302-594-9478; Email: rradcliff@ministryofcaring.org. Mr. Robert Radcliff, Dir. Maintenance & Safety. Total Staff 6.

Ministry of Caring Guild (1990) 506 N. Church St., 19801-4812. Ministry of Caring, Inc., 115 E. 14th St., 19801. Tel: 302-427-9447; Fax: 302-778-5286; Email: mail@ministryofcaring.org. Jimmy Horty, Pres.

Nazareth House I (1998) 106 N. Broom St., 19805-4241. Ministry of Caring, 115 E. 14th St., 19801. Tel: 302-652-0790; Fax: 302-594-9496; Email: mail@ministryofcaring.org. Kim Boulden, Prog. Dir. Bed Capacity 3; Capacity (Families) 3.

Bethany House (1999) 601 N. Jackson St., 19805-3241. Tel: 302-656-8391; Email: amountain@ministryofcaring.org. Annie Mountain, Prog. Dir. Permanent housing for women with special needs. Bed Capacity 8; Capacity 8; Tot Asst. Annually 2,168; Total Staff 1.

Bethany House II, 615 N. Jackson St., 19805. Tel: 302-652-1266; Email: amountain@ministryofcaring.org. Annie Mountain, Prog. Dir. Bed Capacity 6; Total Staff 1.

Margaret Nusbaum House, 207 S. Van Buren St., 19805. Tel: 302-275-6380; Email: amountain@ministryofcaring.org. Annie Mountain, Prog. Dir. Bed Capacity 2; Total Staff 1.

Sacred Heart Permanent Housing, 917 N. Madison St., 19801. Tel: 302-275-6380; Email: amountain@ministryofcaring.org. Annie Mountain, Prog. Dir. Bed Capacity 12; Total Staff 1.

Nazareth House II (1998) 898 Linden St., 19805-4423. Tel: 302-275-9379; Email: kboulden@ministryofcaring.org. Kim Boulden, Prog. Dir. Transitional residence for families. Bed Capacity 13; Capacity 4; Total Staff 1.

Nazareth Long Term Housing (1998) 203 N. Jackson St., 19805-3649. Tel: 302-652-5523; Fax: 302-652-1919; Email: jbates@ministryofcaring.org. John Bates, Dir. Long term housing.

Nazareth Long Term Housing (1998) 807 W. 6th St., 19805. Tel: 302-652-5523; Fax: 302-652-1919; Email: jbates@ministryofcaring.org. John Bates, Dir. Long term housing. Capacity 1; Families 1.

Francis X. Norton Center (2002) 917 N. Madison St., 19801. Tel: 302-594-9455; Fax: 302-428-3655; Email: bbradley@ministryofcaring.org. Ms. Linda Richardson, Prog. Dir.; William Bradley, Exec. Chef/Banquet Manager. Multigenerational community center. Total Staff 6.

Padre Pio House, 213 N. Jackson St., 19805. Ministry of Caring, Inc., 115 E. 14th St., 19801. Tel: 302-652-0904; Email: krobinson@ministryofcaring.org. Torris Portis, Mgr. Permanent housing for men with special needs. Bed Capacity 5; Capacity 5; Total Staff 2.

Sacred Heart Convent, 700 W. 9th St., 19801. Tel: 302-652-5523; Email: rg@ministryofcaring.org. Bro. Ronald Giannone, O.F.M.Cap., Exec. Residence for the Sisters of the Sacred Heart of Jesus. Capacity 3.

St. John Paul II Convent, 111 N. Jackson St., 19805. Tel: 302-354-5550; Email: sragnes@ministryofcaring.org. Sr. Dolly Kaniyamkandathil, Supr. Residence for Sisters of Christ the Light.

Josephine Bakhita Convent, 401 Washington St., 19801. Tel: 302-691-3010; Email: srchrista@ministryofcaring.org. Sr. Christa Rowe, O.S.C., Supr. Residence for Sisters of the Order of St. Clare.

**Mother Teresa House, Inc.*, 829 N. Church St., 19801. Ministry of Caring, Inc., 115 E. 14th St., 19801. Tel: 302-540-6544; Email: rmosley@ministryofcaring.org. Renee Mosley, Dir.

NEWARK.

Our Lady of Grace Home, Inc., 487 E. Chestnut Hill Rd., Newark, 19713-2682. Tel: 773-463-3806; Fax: 773-463-2059; Email: chancery@cdow.org.

RIDGELY, MD.

St. Martin's Ministries, Inc. (1983) 14374 Benedictine Ln., P.O. Box 996, Ridgely, MD 21660. Tel: 410-634-2537; Fax: 410-634-1507; Email: execdir@stmartinsministries.org; Web: www.stmartinsministries.org. Jean F. Austin, CEO; Sr. Patricia Gamgort, O.S.B., Exec. Dir., Emerita. Sisters of St. Benedict. Total Staff 2.

St. Martin's Barn, 14374 Benedictine Ln., P.O. Box 996, Ridgely, MD 21660. Tel: 410-634-1140; Fax: 410-634-1507; Email: execdir@stmartinsministries.org; Web: stmartinsministries.org. Sue McLernon, Dir., Fin. Tot Asst. Annually 500; Total Staff 6; Volunteers 50.

St. Martin's House, 14374 Benedictine Ln., P.O. Box 996, Ridgely, MD 21660. Tel: 410-634-2537; Fax: 410-634-1293; Email: execdir@stmartinsministries.org. Deborah H. Vornbrock, Dir., Devel. Tot Asst. Annually 250; Total Staff 19; Volunteers 12; Staff 7; Total Assisted 31.

[H] HOMES FOR AGED

WILMINGTON. *The Antonian*, 1701 W. 10th St., 19805. Tel: 302-421-3758; Fax: 302-421-3759; Email: antonian@stanthonycenter.org. Tori Daniello, Mgr. Congregate Housing for the Elderly. Residents 143; Total Staff 6; Apartments 136.

**Sacred Heart Village II, Inc.*, 625 E. 10th St., 19801. Tel: 302-300-3771; Fax: 302-652-1919; Email: srmgraney@sacredheartvillage2.org. 115 East 14th St., 19801. Bro. Ronald Giannone, O.F.M.Cap., Exec. Dir.; Sr. Margaret Graney, Dir.

NEWARK. *Jeanne Jugan Residence* (1978) 185 Salem Church Rd., Newark, 19713. Tel: 302-368-5886; Fax: 302-738-5610; Email: msnewark@littlesistersofthepoor.org. Margaret Regina Halloran, L.S.P., Supr.; Rev. Anthony M. Pileggi, Chap. Conducted by the Little Sisters of the Poor. Residents 77; Sisters 10.

Marydale Retirement Village, 135 Jeandell Dr., Newark, 19713. Tel: 302-368-2784; Fax: 302-731-0584; Email: marydale@ccwilm.org. Scott Josephson, Admin.; Sr. Mary Rita Smith, Pastoral Care Coord. Apartments for elderly. Residents 118; Apartments 108.

[I] GENERAL HOSPITALS

WILMINGTON. *Saint Francis Hospital, Inc.*, 701 N. Clayton St., 19805-0500. Tel: 302-575-8305; Fax: 302-575-8307; Email: lbranco@che-east.org; Web: www.stfrancishealthcare.org. Brian Dietz, Pres. & CEO; Linda Branco, Dir. Spiritual Care; Revs. John Connery, O.S.F.S.; Joseph J. McKenna, O.S.F.S.; Mrs. Catherine P. Weaver. Bed Capacity 395; Tot Asst. Annually 52,875; Total Staff 850.

LIFE at St. Francis Healthcare, Inc., 1072 Justison St., 19801. Tel: 302-660-3351; Fax: 302-575-8236; Email: info@stfrancismedical.org. Amy L. Milligan, Exec. Dir. Tot Asst. Annually 175; Total Staff 56.

[J] MONASTERIES AND RESIDENCES OF PRIESTS AND BROTHERS

WILMINGTON. *Brothers of Holy Cross, Saint Edmond's Academy*, 2120 Veale Rd., 19810.
Tel: 302-475-5370; Fax: 302-475-2256; Email: advancement@stedmondsacademy.org. Bros. Michael A. Smith, C.S.C., Headmaster; Joseph W. Ash, C.S.C., Dir. Rel.; Thomas Meany, C.S.C., Trans. Coord. Brothers 3.

Capuchin Franciscan Friars, St. Francis of Assisi Friary, 1901 Prior Rd., 19809. Tel: 302-798-1454; Fax: 302-798-3360; Email: chancery@cdow.org. Revs. Cyprian Rosen, O.F.M.Cap., S.T.L., Vicar; Francis Sariego, O.F.M.Cap., Guardian; William Arlia, O.F.M.Cap.; Vincent Fortunato, O.F.M.Cap.; Robert W. Williams, O.F.M.Cap.

St. Felix Friary, 119 N. Jackson St., 19805-3670.
Tel: 302-652-5523; Fax: 302-652-8943; Email: mail@ministryofcaring.org. Rev. Ronald Giannone, O.F.M.Cap., Guardian. Priests 1.

Wilmington-Philadelphia Province of the Oblates of St. Francis de Sales, 2200 Kentmere Pkwy., 19806.
Tel: 302-656-8529; Fax: 302-658-8052; Email: ghoffman@oblates.org; Web: www.oblates.org. Revs. Lewis Fiorelli, Prov.; Michael S. Murray, O.S.F.S., Prov. Asst.; Barry R. Strong, O.S.F.S., Supr.; John W. Lyle, O.S.F.S.; Marc Gherardi, O.S.F.S.; William R. Gore, O.S.F.S.; William T. McCandless, O.S.F.S. Priests 7.
Rev. Oblates Attached to the Provincial Residence: Revs. Marc Gherardi, O.S.F.S.; William R. Gore, O.S.F.S.; William T. McCandless, O.S.F.S.

CHILDS, MD. *Oblates of St. Francis De Sales* (1907) 1120 Blue Ball Rd., Childs, MD 21916-0043.
Tel: 410-398-3040; Fax: 410-620-6131; Email: nmyron@oblates.org; Web: www.oblates.org. Rev. Michael A. Vogt, O.S.F.S., Supr. *Retirement and Assisted Care Facility*, 1120 Blue Ball Rd., Childs, MD 21916-0043. Tel: 410-398-3040;
Fax: 410-620-6131; Email: nmyron@oblates.org; Web: www.oblates.org. Rev. Michael A. Vogt, O.S.F.S., Rel. Supr. Brothers 7; Priests 18. In Res. Revs. Robert D. Ashenbrenner, O.S.F.S., (Retired); John W. Brennan, O.S.F.S., (Retired); James P. Byrne, O.S.F.S.; John J. Dennis, O.S.F.S., (Retired); Hugh E. Duffy, O.S.F.S., (Retired); John A. Finn, O.S.F.S., (Retired); Peter J. Harvey, O.S.F.S., (Retired); Very Rev. Mark A. Hushen, O.S.F.S.; Revs. Eugene L. Kelly, O.S.F.S., (Retired); John F. Kenny, O.S.F.S., (Retired); Anthony J. Larry, O.S.F.S., (Retired); Thomas F. Malloy, O.S.F.S.; R. Douglas Smith, O.S.F.S., (Retired); Thomas J. Tucker, O.S.F.S., (Retired); Bros. Thomas P. Brophy, O.S.F.S., (Retired); John M. Carroll, O.S.F.S., (Retired); Robert M. Carter, O.S.F.S., (Retired); John J. Dochkus, O.S.F.S.; Joseph H. Hayden, O.S.F.S.; Gerald M. Sweeney, O.S.F.S., (Retired); Revs. Joseph E. Tustin, O.S.F.S., (Retired); Albert J. Gondek, O.S.F.S, (Retired); Gerard J. Mahoney, O.S.F.S.; John P. Spellman, O.S.F.S.; Bro. Harry F. McGovern, O.S.F.S.

MIDDLETOWN. *Immaculate Conception Priory of the Canons Regular of Premontre* (1997) 1269 Bayview Rd., Middletown, 19709. Tel: 302-449-1840, Ext. 31 ; Fax: 302-449-1217; Email: chancery@cdow.org. Rev. James B. Herring, Prior; Very Rev. Brian Zielinski, O.Praem.; Rev. James D. Bagnato, O.-Praem. Priests 5.

Norbertine Fathers of Delaware, Inc. (1997) 1269 Bayview Rd., Middletown, 19709.
Tel: 302-449-1840; Fax: 302-449-1217; Email: chancery@cdow.org. Very Revs. Brian Zielinski, O.-Praem., Supr.; James D. Bagnato, O.Praem.

[K] CONVENTS AND RESIDENCES FOR SISTERS

WILMINGTON. *St. Benedict*, 113 Canterbury Dr., 19803.
Tel: 302-478-3754; Fax: 302-478-9305; Email: margosb@aol.com. Sr. Mary DeMeglio, Contact Person. Sisters of St. Benedict 3.

Monastery of St. Veronica Giuliani (Strict Enclosure) 816 Jefferson St., 19801. Tel: 302-654-8727;
Fax: 302-652-3929; Email: capuchinpoorc@comcast.net. Mother Maria de La Luz Solorio, O.S.C.Cap., Abbess; Rev. Ronald Giannone, O.F.M.Cap., Chap. Capuchin Poor Clare Nuns of Delaware. Sisters 12.

Ursuline Academy, Inc., The (1893) 1106 Pennsylvania Ave., 19806. Tel: 914-712-0060;
Fax: 914-712-3134; Email: ursruepr@aol.com. Sr. Brenda Buckley, Pres.

CHILDS, MD. *Oblate Sisters of St. Francis de Sales, Inc.*, 399 Childs Rd., Childs, MD 21916.
Tel: 410-398-3699; Fax: 877-398-8063; Email: oblatesisters@mountaviat.org; Web: www.oblatesisters.org. Sisters Anne Elizabeth Eder, O.S.F.S., Supr.; John Elizabeth Callaghan, O.S.F.S., Asst. Supr. Oblate Sisters of St. Francis de Sales. Sisters 10.

Aviat Foundation Endowment Trust, 399 Childs Rd., Childs, MD 21916.
Tel: 410-398-2206, Ext. 211; Email: principal@mountaviat.org; Email: oblatesisters@mountaviat.org. Sisters Anne Elizabeth Eder, O.S.F.S., Pres.; John Elizabeth Callaghan, O.S.F.S., Prin.

Villa Aviat, Inc., 399 Childs Rd., Childs, MD 21916.
Tel: 410-398-3699; Fax: 877-398-8063; Email: oblatesisters@mountaviat.org. Sr. Anne Elizabeth Eder, O.S.F.S., Supr.

NEW CASTLE. *Caterina Benincasa Dominican Monastery, Inc.*, 6 Church Dr., New Castle, 19720. Tel: 302-654-1206; Email: chancery@cdow.org. Rev. Timothy M. Nolan. Sisters 3.

NEWARK. *St. Gertrude's Monastery, Motherhouse and Novitiate of the Sisters of St. Benedict* (1857) 25 Gender Rd., Newark, 19713. Tel: 302-414-8076; Email: bantry65@yahoo.com; Web: www.ridgelybenedictines.org. Sr. Catherine Godfrey, Prioress. Benedictine Sisters of Saint Gertrude Sisters 14.

PRINCESS ANNE, MD. *St. Joseph Novitiate*, 10572 Anderson Rd., Princess Anne, MD 21853.
Tel: 410-651-5309; Fax: 410-742-3390; Email: lsjm@comcast.net; Web: thejosephhouse.org. Sr. Marilyn Bouchard, L.S.J.M., Vicar. Novices 1; Sisters 4.

Sisters of Charity (1983) (Convent Station) 30255 Mt. Vernon Rd., Princess Anne, MD 21853.
Tel: 410-651-9672; Fax: 410-651-1437; Email: setoncenter@ccwilm.org. Cecilia McManus, Contact Person. Sisters 4; Assisted 8,200.

SALISBURY, MD. *Joseph House, Little Sisters of Jesus & Mary*, P.O. Box 1755, Salisbury, MD 21802.
Tel: 410-543-1645; Fax: 410-742-3390; Email: lsjm@comcast.net; Web: www.thejosephhouse.org. Sr. Constance R. Ladd, L.S.J.M., Supr. Gen. Sisters 3.

[L] SECULAR INSTITUTES

WILMINGTON. *De Sales Secular Institute*, 406 Delaware Ave., Talleyville, 19803. Tel: 302-478-9438; Email: chancery@cdow.org; Web: www.secularinstitutes.org/sfs.htm. Madeline Rice, Directress, Assoc.

Secular Franciscan Order (San Damiano Fraternity) 2508 Oakfield Ln., 19810. Tel: 302-478-6593; Email: carisio@yahoo.com. Teresa Carisio, Min.; Sr. Elise Betz, O.S.F., Spiritual Asst.

Secular Franciscan Order (St. Patrick's Fraternity) 1901 Prior Rd., 19809. Tel: 302-798-1454; Email: StPatrick@skdregion.org. John Oscar, O.F.S., Local Min.; Rev. William Arlia, O.F.M.Cap., Spiritual Asst.

BEAR, MD. *Secular Order of Discalced Carmelites*, 769 Fox Chase Cir., Bear, 19701. Tel: 302-836-3843; Email: blizzard.2000@yahoo.com. Mary An Love, Pres.; Bro. Bryan Paquette, O.C.D., Spiritual Asst. (Annunciation Community).

SALISBURY, MD. *Secular Order of Discalced Carmelites* (Community of Mary) 3 Hudson Pl., Berlin, MD 21811. Tel: 301-717-6271; Email: formation@carmelife.com; Web: www.carmelife.net. Mrs. Cindy Ostrowski, Pres.; Mrs. Marianne Chapin, Councilor; Bro. Bryan Paquette, O.C.D., Spiritual Asst. Professed 13.

[M] RETREAT HOUSES, GENERAL

WILMINGTON. *De Sales Spirituality Services*, 2200 Kentmere Pkwy., 19806. Tel: 302-383-3585;
Fax: 302-658-8052; Email: mmurray@oblates.org; Web: www.oblates.org/dss. Rev. Michael S. Murray, O.S.F.S., Dir.

St. Francis of Assisi Friary, 1901 Prior Rd., 19809. Tel: 302-798-1454; Fax: 302-798-3360. Revs. Cyprian Rosen, O.F.M.Cap., S.T.L., Vicar; Francis Sariego, O.F.M.Cap., Guardian; Robert W. Williams, O.F.M.Cap., Dir. of Formation; William Arlia, O.F.-M.Cap.; Vincent Fortunato, O.F.M.Cap. Priests 5.

**Jesus House*, 2501 Milltown Rd., 19808.
Tel: 302-995-6859; Fax: 302-995-6833; Email: info@jesushousecenter.org; Web: www.jesushousecenter.org. Angela Malmgren, Pres.

[N] RETREAT HOUSES, WOMEN

CHILDS, MD. *Oblate Sisters of St. Francis de Sales*, 13828 Duck Hollow Rd., Galena, MD 21635.
Tel: 410-398-3699; Fax: 877-398-8063; Email: oblatesisters@mountaviat.org; Web: www.oblatesisters.org. 399 Childs Rd., Childs, MD 21916. Sisters Anne Elizabeth Eder, O.S.F.S., Supr.; John Elizabeth Callaghan, O.S.F.S., Asst. Supr.

[O] NEWMAN CENTERS

NEWARK. *Catholic Campus Ministry, Univ. of Delaware*, St. Thomas More Oratory, 45 Lovett Ave., Newark, 19711. Tel: 302-368-4728;
Fax: 302-368-2548; Email: kimztmo@udel.edu; Web: www.udcatholic.org. Rev. Edward F. Ogden, O.S.F.S.

Delmar Organization of Catholic Students - DOCS, Tel: 302-368-4728; Fax: 302-368-2548. Kimberly S. Zitzner, B.A.

Salisbury University, 211 W. College Ave., Salisbury, MD 21801. Tel: 410-219-3376; Email: campusministry@hotmail.com.

University of Maryland Eastern Shore, 211 W. College Ave., Salisbury, MD 21801.
Tel: 410-219-3376; Fax: 410-219-3376; Email: campusministry@hotmail.com.

Wesley College Newman Center, Tel: 302-368-4728; Fax: 302-368-2548.

Washington College, 45 Lovett Ave., Newark, 19711. Tel: 302-368-4728; Fax: 302-368-2548; Email: campusministry@hotmail.com.

Wesley College Catholic Campus Ministry, St. Thomas More Oratory, 45 Lovett Ave., Newark, 19711. Tel: 302-368-4728; Fax: 302-368-2548; Email: udcatholic@gmail.com. Rev. Edward Ogden, Campus Min.

[P] MISCELLANEOUS

WILMINGTON. *Brisson Fund* (1989) 2200 Kentmere Pkwy., 19806. Tel: 302-656-8529; Email: ghoffman@oblates.org. Rev. Lewis Fiorelli, Pres.

Nativity Preparatory School of Wilmington Trust, 2200 Kentmere Pkwy., 19806. Tel: 302-654-2495; Email: jmorrissey@salesianum.org. Very Rev. Joseph G. Morrissey, O.S.F.S., Treas.

Oblate Development Fund, 2200 Kentmere Pkwy., 19806. Tel: 302-656-8529; Email: ghoffman@oblates.org. Rev. Michael S. Murray, O.S.F.S., Dir.

OSFS Wilmington-Philadelphia Province, Inc., 2200 Kentmere Pkwy., 19806. Tel: 302-656-8529; Email: ghoffman@oblates.org. Rev. Lewis Fiorelli, Dir.

OSFS Endowment Trust, 2200 Kentmere Pkwy., 19806. Tel: 302-656-8529; Email: ghoffman@oblates.org. Rev. Michael S. Murray, O.S.F.S., Trustee.

OSFS Real Estate Holding Corporation, 2200 Kentmere Pkwy., 19806. Tel: 302-656-8529; Email: ghoffman@oblates.org. Rev. Lewis Fiorelli, Dir.

OSFS Real Estate Trust, 2200 Kentmere Pkwy., 19806. Tel: 302-656-8529; Email: ghoffman@oblates.org. Rev. Michael S. Murray, O.S.F.S., Treas.

OSFS Service Corporation, 2200 Kentmere Pkwy., 19806. Tel: 302-656-8529; Email: ghoffman@oblates.org. Rev. Lewis Fiorelli, Dir.

Salesianum School Endowment Trust I, 2200 Kentmere Pkwy., 19806. Tel: 302-654-2495; Email: mdrake@salesianum.org. Very Rev. Joseph G. Morrissey, O.S.F.S., Treas.

Salesianum School Endowment Trust II, 2200 Kentmere Pkwy., 19806. Tel: 302-654-2495; Email: mdrake@salesianum.org. Rev. Joseph G. Morrissey, Treas.

CLAYMONT. *The Archmere Fund*, 3600 Philadelphia Pike, Claymont, 19703.
Tel: 302-798-6632, Ext. 702; Fax: 302-792-2997; Email: lcarney@archmereacademy.com. John F. Cirillo III, Treas.

**Saint Pio Foundation, Inc.*, 270 N. Ave., Ste. 808, New Rochelle, NY 10801. Tel: 203-416-1471; Email: info@saintpiofoundation.org; Web: www.saintpiofoundation.org. Luciano Lamonarca, Pres.

RELIGIOUS INSTITUTES OF MEN REPRESENTED IN THE DIOCESE

For further details refer to the corresponding bracketed number in the Religious Institutes of Men or Women section.

[0900]—*Canons Regular of Premontre*—O.Praem.
[0470]—*The Capuchin Friars* (Prov. of the Stigmata)—O.F.M.Cap.
[0520]—*Franciscan Friars* (Holy Name Province)—O.F.M.
[0920]—*Oblates of St. Francis de Sales*—O.S.F.S.
[0970]—*Order of Our Lady of Mercy*—O.deM.
[1070]—*Redemptorist Fathers* (Baltimore, MD)—C.SS.R.
[1200]—*Society of the Divine Savior*—S.D.S.
[1290]—*Society of the Priests of St. Sulpice*—P.S.S.
[0560]—*Third Order Regular of Saint Francis*—T.O.R.

RELIGIOUS INSTITUTES OF WOMEN REPRESENTED IN THE DIOCESE

[0100]—*Adorers of the Blood of Christ*—A.S.C.
[0230]—*Benedictine Sisters of Pontifical Jurisdiction*—O.S.B.
[3765]—*Capuchin Poor Clare Sisters*—O.S.C.Cap.
[]—*Congregation of the Sisters of St. Clare, Inc.* (Delaware)—O.S.C.
[0760]—*Daughters of the Charity of St. Vincent de Paul*—D.C.
[1050]—*Dominican Contemplative Nuns*—O.P.
[1070-11]—*Dominican Sisters*—O.P.
[1170]—*Felician Sisters*—C.S.S.F.

[2331]—*Little Sisters of Jesus and Mary*—L.S.J.M.
[2340]—*Little Sisters of the Poor*—L.S.P.
[2790]—*Missionary Servants of the Most Blessed Trinity*—M.S.B.T.
[3060]—*Oblates Sisters of St. Francis de Sales*—O.S.F.S.
[2575]—*Religious Sisters of Mercy Mid-Atlantic Community* (Baltimore, MD; Merion, PA)—R.S.M.
[2575]—*Religious Sisters of Mercy South Central Community*—R.S.M.
[2970]—*School Sisters of Notre Dame*—S.S.N.D.
[]—*Sisters for Christian Community*—S.F.C.C.
[0590]—*Sisters of Charity of Saint Elizabeth, Convent Station* (Southern, Western Provs.)—S.C.
[]—*Sisters of Christ the Light, Inc.*—C.J.S.
[3000]—*Sisters of Notre Dame* (Base Communities Prov.; Maryland Prov.)—S.N.D.deN.
[]—*Sisters of Notre Dame de Namur, Ohio Province*—S.N.D.deN.
[1650]—*Sisters of St. Francis of Philadelphia*—O.S.F.
[3893]—*Sisters of St. Joseph of Chestnut Hill, Philadelphia*—S.S.J.
[2160]—*Sisters, Servants of Immaculate Heart of Mary* Scranton, PA—I.H.M.
[2150]—*Sisters, Servants of Immaculate Heart of Mary* Monroe, MI—I.H.M.
[4110]—*Ursuline Nuns (Roman Union)* (Eastern Prov.)—O.S.U.

DIOCESAN CEMETERIES

WILMINGTON. *All Saints Cemetery*, 6001 Kirkwood Hwy., 19808. Tel: 302-737-2524; Fax: 302-737-4091; Email: tkane@cathcemde.com. Thomas J. Kane, Supt.; Mr. Mark A. Christian, C.C.C.E., Exec. Dir.

Cathedral Cemetery, 2400 Lancaster Ave., 19805. Tel: 302-656-3323; Fax: 302-656-1069; Email: shudson@cathcemde.org; Web: www.cathcemde.com/cemeteries. Mr. Mark A. Christian, C.C.C.E., Exec. Dir.; Scott Hudson, Supt.

DAGSBORO. *Gate of Heaven Cemetery*, 32112 Vines Creek Rd., Dagsboro, 19939. Tel: 302-732-3690; Fax: 302-732-3692; Email: nhoopes@cathcemde.org; Web: www.cdow.org/cemeteries. Mr. Mark A. Christian, C.C.C.E., Exec. Dir.; Nicholas Hoopes, Supt.

An asterisk (*) denotes an organization that has established tax-exempt status directly with the IRS and is not covered by the USCCB Group Ruling.

Diocese of Winona-Rochester

(Dioecesis Vinonaensis-Roffensis)

Most Reverend

JOHN M. QUINN, M.DIV.

Bishop of Winona-Rochester; ordained March 17, 1972; appointed Auxiliary Bishop of the Archdiocese of Detroit and Titular See of Ressiana August 12, 2003; appointed Coadjutor Bishop of Winona October 15, 2008; Mass of Welcome December 11, 2008; Succeeded to See May 7, 2009. *Pastoral Center: 55 W. Sanborn St., P.O. Box 588, Winona, MN 55987.*

Most Reverend

BERNARD J. HARRINGTON, D.D.

Retired Bishop of Winona; ordained June 6, 1959; appointed Auxiliary Bishop of the Archdiocese of Detroit and Titular Bishop of Uzali November 23, 1993; ordained January 6, 1994; appointed Bishop of Winona November 5, 1998; installed January 6, 1999; retired May 7, 2009.

ESTABLISHED NOVEMBER 26, 1889. RENAMED DIOCESE OF WINONA-ROCHESTER JANUARY 23, 2018.

Square Miles 12,282.

Comprises the Counties of Winona, Wabasha, Olmsted, Dodge, Steele, Waseca, Blue Earth, Watonwan, Cottonwood, Murray, Pipestone, Rock, Nobles, Jackson, Faribault, Martin, Freeborn, Mower, Fillmore and Houston in the State of Minnesota.

For legal titles of parishes and diocesan institutions, consult the Pastoral Center.

Pastoral Center: 55 W. Sanborn St., P.O. Box 588, Winona, MN 55987. Tel: 507-454-4643; Fax: 507-454-8106.

Web: www.dowr.org

Email: diocese@dowr.org

STATISTICAL OVERVIEW

Personnel	
Bishop	1
Retired Bishops	1
Priests: Diocesan Active in Diocese	47
Priests: Diocesan Active Outside Diocese	1
Priests: Retired, Sick or Absent	40
Number of Diocesan Priests	88
Religious Priests in Diocese	5
Total Priests in Diocese	93
Extern Priests in Diocese	14
Ordinations:	
Diocesan Priests	2
Transitional Deacons	1
Permanent Deacons in Diocese	26
Total Brothers	13
Total Sisters	342
Parishes	
Parishes	106
With Resident Pastor:	
Resident Diocesan Priests	42
Resident Religious Priests	2
Without Resident Pastor:	
Administered by Priests	62
Closed Parishes	1
Professional Ministry Personnel:	
Sisters	1
Lay Ministers	113
Welfare	
Catholic Hospitals	1
Total Assisted	39,081
Homes for the Aged	6
Total Assisted	1,017
Day Care Centers	1
Total Assisted	31
Special Centers for Social Services	7
Total Assisted	6,412
Educational	
Seminaries, Diocesan	1
Students from This Diocese	7
Students from Other Diocese	44
Diocesan Students in Other Seminaries	7
Seminaries, Religious	1
Students Religious	21
Total Seminarians	35
Colleges and Universities	1
Total Students	1,087
High Schools, Diocesan and Parish	4
Total Students	987
Elementary Schools, Diocesan and Parish	19
Total Students	3,548
Catechesis/Religious Education:	
High School Students	3,313
Elementary Students	5,240
Total Students under Catholic Instruction	14,210
Teachers in the Diocese:	
Priests	4
Brothers	2
Sisters	1
Lay Teachers	479
Vital Statistics	
Receptions into the Church:	
Infant Baptism Totals	1,411
Minor Baptism Totals	65
Adult Baptism Totals	75
Received into Full Communion	130
First Communions	1,224
Confirmations	1,177
Marriages:	
Catholic	256
Interfaith	90
Total Marriages	346
Deaths	1,074
Total Catholic Population	133,442
Total Population	595,193

Former Bishops—Rt. Revs. JOSEPH B. COTTER, D.D., ord. May 3, 1871; cons. Dec. 27, 1889; died June 28, 1909; PATRICK R. HEFFRON, D.D., ord. Dec. 22, 1884; cons. May 19, 1910; died Nov. 23, 1927; Most Revs. FRANCIS M. KELLY, D.D., ord. Nov. 1, 1912; cons. June 9, 1926; transferred to Diocese of Winona, Feb. 10, 1928; transferred to Titular See of Nasal, Oct. 17, 1949; died June 24, 1950; EDWARD A. FITZGERALD, D.D., ord. July 25, 1916; cons. Sept. 12, 1946; appt. Titular Bishop of Cantanus and Auxiliary Bishop of Dubuque; transferred to Winona, Oct. 20, 1949; retired and transferred to the Titular See of Zerta, Jan. 8, 1969; died March 30, 1972; LORAS J. WATTERS, D.D., ord. June 7, 1941; appt. Titular Bishop of Fidoloma and Auxiliary Bishop of Dubuque, June 23, 1965; cons. Aug. 26, 1965; transferred to Winona, Jan. 8, 1969; retired Oct. 14, 1986; appt. Apostolic Administrator, Oct. 14, 1986; died March 30, 2009; JOHN G. VLAZNY, D.D., ord. Dec. 20, 1961; appt. Auxiliary Bishop of Chicago and Titular Bishop of Stagno, Oct. 31, 1983; cons. Dec. 13, 1983; appt. Bishop of Winona, May 19, 1987; installed July 29, 1987; appt. Archbishop of Portland, Oct. 28, 1997; retired Jan. 29, 2013; BERNARD J. HARRINGTON, D.D., ord. June 6, 1959; appt. Auxiliary Bishop of Archdiocese of Detroit and Titular Bishop of Uzali Nov. 23, 1993; ord. Jan. 6, 1994; appt. Bishop of Winona Nov. 5, 1998; installed Jan. 6, 1999; retired May 7, 2009.

Vicar General—Rev. Msgr. THOMAS P. MELVIN, Tel: 507-858-1267; Email: tmelvin@dowr.org.

Moderator of the Curia—Rev. Msgr. THOMAS P. MELVIN, Tel: 507-858-1267; Email: tmelvin@dowr.org.

Chancellor—Very Rev. GLENN K. FRERICHS, J.C.L., Tel: 507-858-1261; Email: gfrerichs@dowr.org.

Vicar for Clergy—Very Rev. MARK C. MCNEA, Tel: 507-858-1267; Email: mmcnea@dowr.org.

Assistant Vicar for Clergy—Rev. PETER L. SCHUSTER, Tel: 507-858-1267; Email: frpschuster@yahoo.com.

Deans—Rev. Msgr. GERALD C. KOSSE, Worthington; Very Revs. PETER J. KLEIN, Mankato; MARK C. MCNEA, Winona; MARREDDY POTHIREDDY, Austin-Albert Lea; THOMAS A. LOOMIS, Rochester.

Diocesan Consultors—Rev. Msgr. THOMAS P. MELVIN; Very Revs. MARK C. MCNEA; GLENN K. FRERICHS, J.C.L.; JAMES D. RUSSELL, (Retired); Revs. ANDREW J. BEERMAN, S.T.L.; JAMES C. BERNING; MICHAEL J. CRONIN, J.C.L.; TIMOTHY T. REKER, S.T.L.; RUSSELL G. SCEPANIAK; PETER L. SCHUSTER; MR. ANDREW D. BRANNON, CPA.

Finance Council—Most Rev. JOHN M. QUINN; Rev. Msgr. THOMAS P. MELVIN; Revs. RUSSELL G. SCEPANIAK; WILLIAM D. THOMPSON; MR. ANDREW D. BRANNON, CPA; Sr. JEAN KENIRY, O.S.F.; MR. JAMES ANDERSON, CPA; MS. MARGARET V. MICHALETZ; MR. ROBERT WOODEN; Bro. LOUIS DE THOMASIS, F.S.C., Ph.D.; MR. MICHAEL BRINKMAN; MR. PAUL TIESKOETTER.

Diocesan Board of Administration—(Civil Corporation): Most Rev. JOHN M. QUINN, Pres.; Rev. Msgr. THOMAS P. MELVIN, Vice Pres.; Very Rev. GLENN K. FRERICHS, J.C.L., Sec.; MR. ANDREW D. BRANNON, CPA, Treas.; MR. TIM MCMANIMON.

Tribunal—(First Instance) Please direct all inquiries concerning marriage nullity, dispensations and permissions, and pre-marriage documentation to this office: *Tribunal: 55 W. Sanborn St., P.O. Box 588, Winona, 55987-0588.* Tel: 507-454-4643; Fax: 507-454-8106.

Judicial Vicar—Very Rev. GLENN K. FRERICHS, J.C.L.
Censor of Books and Periodicals—Rev. TIMOTHY J. HALL, S.T.L.
Associate Judges—Rev. Msgr. R. PAUL HEITING, J.C.L.; Rev. DAVID WECHTER, O.C.S.O., J.C.L.; MS. JENNA M. COOPER, J.C.L.
Defenders of the Bond—Very Rev. TIMOTHY FERGUSON, J.C.L.; Rev. JOHN GRIFFITHS, J.C.D.; Sr. VICTORIA VONDENBERGER, R.S.M., J.C.L.; MS. THERESA WYBURN, J.C.L. Experts: Sr. MARA LESTER, R.S.M., M.D.; DR. MICHAEL ZACCARIELLO, Ph.D., L.P.
Advocates—DR. RAPHAEL FRACKIEWICZ, J.C.D.; MR. ALDEAN HENDRICKSON, J.C.L.; MR. ANTHONY ST. LOUIS-SANCHEZ, J.C.L.; MR. JAY CONZEMIUS, J.C.L.; MR. PAUL MATENAER, J.C.L.; MR. JOHN BALK; MR. RICHARD VERVER; MR. JOSEPH JOHNSON; MR. TIMOTHY OLSON, J.C.L.; MR. DANIEL SHAKAL, J.C.L.; MR. JAMES ZAHLEN, J.C.L.
Second Instance Court—Metropolitan Tribunal of the Archdiocese of St. Paul/Minneapolis.
Promoters of Justice—Sr. VICTORIA VONDENBERGER, R.S.M., J.C.L.; Very Rev. TIMOTHY FERGUSON, J.C.L.
Ecclesiastical Notaries—MS. CYBIL KALLEVIG; MRS. JULIE WRIGHT.

Diocesan Offices and Directors

All Diocesan Offices and Directors are located at the Pastoral Center (unless otherwise indicated), 55 W. Sanborn St., P.O. Box 588, Winona, 55987. Tel: 507-454-4643; Fax: 507-454-8106; Web: www.dowr.org.

Curia—
Vicar General—Rev. Msgr. THOMAS P. MELVIN, Tel: 507-858-1267; Email: tmelvin@dowr.org.
Chancellor—Very Rev. GLENN K. FRERICHS, J.C.L., Tel: 507-858-1261; Email: gfrerichs@dowr.org.
Vicar for Clergy—Tel: 507-858-1267. Very Rev. MARK C. MCNEA, Email: mmcnea@dowr.org; Rev. PETER L. SCHUSTER, Asst. Vicar for Clergy, Email: frpschuster@yahoo.com.
Vice Chancellor—VACANT.
Finance & Administration—MR. ANDREW D. BRANNON, CPA, CFO & Administrative Officer, Tel: 507-858-1248; Email: abrannon@dowr.org.
Catholic Charities—MR. ROBERT TEREBA, Exec. Dir., 111 Market St., P.O. Box 379, Winona, 55987. Tel: 507-454-2270; Fax: 507-454-4024; Email: rtereba@ccsomn.org.
Catholic Foundation of Southern Minnesota—MRS. MONICA HERMAN, Exec. Dir., Tel: 507-858-1276; Email: mherman@catholicfsmn.org.
Divine Worship—Very Rev. PATRICK O. ARENS, Dir., Tel: 507-858-1259; Email: parens@dowr.org.
Human Resources—MR. DAVID FRICKE, Dir., Tel: 507-858-1250; Email: dfricke@dowr.org.
Lay Formation and RCIA—MR. TODD GRAFF, Dir., Tel: 507-858-1270; Email: tgraff@dowr.org.
Catholic Schools—MRS. MARSHA STENZEL, Supt., Tel: 507-858-1269; Email: mstenzel@dowr.org.
Vocations—Rev. JASON L. KERN, Dir., Tel: 507-858-1266; Email: jkern@dowr.org.
Vicar for Hispanic Ministry—Very Rev. RAUL I. SILVA, Queen of Angels Parish, 1001 E. Oakland Ave., Austin, 55912. Tel: 507-433-1888; Email: rsilva@dowr.org.
Life—Family; Marriage; Natural Family Planning. MR. PETER MARTIN, S.T.L., Dir., Tel: 507-858-1273; Email: pmartin@dowr.org.
Youth and Young Adults and Communications—MR. AARON LOFY, Tel: 507-858-1258; Email: bfrost@dowr.org.
Additional Ministries—
Permanent Deacons—Tel: 507-858-1266. Rev. Msgr. THOMAS P. MELVIN, Dir., Email: tmelvin@dowr.org; Deacon ROBERT YERHOT, Asst. Dir., Email: byerhot@dowr.org.
Co Vicars for Senior Priests—Very Revs. JAMES D. RUSSELL, (Retired), 202 Alpine Ridge, Unit B, Wabasha, 55981. Tel: 651-564-1089; Email: jrussell1@hbci.com; DONALD J. SCHMITZ, (Retired), 203 Alpine Ridge, Wabasha, 55981. Tel: 507-281-8323; Email: don.schmitz6508@gmail.com.
Ecumenism—Rev. WILLIAM D. THOMPSON, 4135 N.W. 18th Ave., Rochester, 55901. Tel: 507-282-8741; Email: wthompson@paxchristichurch.org.
Propagation of the Faith—Rev. TIMOTHY E. BIREN, Tel: 507-858-1244; Email: mhamann@dowr.org.
Coordinator of Diocesan Health Ministry—Rev. JOHN L. EVANS, Diocesan Dir. of Hospitals, 200 First St., S.W., Rochester, 55905. Tel: 507-255-5780; Email: evans.john@mayo.edu.
Advisory Bodies—
Presbyteral Council—
Ex Officio—Rev. Msgr. THOMAS P. MELVIN; Very Rev. MARK C. MCNEA; Rev. PETER L. SCHUSTER.
Elected Senior Member—Very Rev. JAMES D. RUSSELL, (Retired).
Appointed Members—Very Rev. RAUL I. SILVA; Revs. PETER L. SCHUSTER; RUSSELL G. SCEPANIAK; WILLIAM D. THOMPSON.
Elected At-Large Representatives—Revs. JAMES P. STEFFES; MICHAEL J. CRONIN, J.C.L.
Elected Deanery Representatives—Rev. Msgr. RICHARD M. COLLETTI; Very Rev. GLENN K. FRERICHS, J.C.L.; Revs. ANDREW J. BEERMAN, S.T.L.; TIMOTHY E. BIREN; THOMAS M. NIEHAUS, J.C.L.
Clergy Personnel Committee—Rev. Msgrs. THOMAS P. MELVIN; GERALD C. KOSSE; Very Revs. MARK C. MCNEA; PETER J. KLEIN; THOMAS A. LOOMIS; MARREDDY POTHIREDDY; RAUL I. SILVA; Revs. JASON L. KERN; MARTIN T. SCHAEFER; PETER L. SCHUSTER.
Priests' Pension Board—Most Rev. JOHN M. QUINN; Rev. Msgr. THOMAS P. MELVIN; Very Revs. MARK C. MCNEA; DONALD J. SCHMITZ, (Retired); Revs. EDWARD F. MCGRATH; ANDREW P. VOGEL; MR. ANDREW D. BRANNON, CPA; MR. THOMAS CROWLEY; MR. DANIEL KUTZKE; MR. TIM SCANLON.
Commission on Sacred Liturgy—Very Rev. PATRICK O. ARENS; Rev. TIMOTHY J. HALL, S.T.L.; MR. DAVID U'REN; MR. SEBASTIAN MODARELLI.
Diocese of Winona-Rochester Incardination Board—Very Revs. PATRICK O. ARENS; GLENN K. FRERICHS, J.C.L.; MARK C. MCNEA; Revs. JOHN M. SAUER, S.T.L.; PETER L. SCHUSTER; Deacons JOHN KLUCZNY; THOMAS DERIENZO.

Winona-Rochester Diocesan Organizations-Agencies-Programs

Archives—Very Rev. GLENN K. FRERICHS, J.C.L., Tel: 507-858-1261; Email: gfrerichs@dowr.org.
Scouting—Rev. ANDREW P. VOGEL, Tel: 507-524-3127; Email: frapvogel@gmail.com.
Catholic Charities—MR. ROBERT TEREBA, Exec. Dir., Administrative and Winona Regional Office, 111 Market St., P.O. Box 379, Winona, 55987. Tel: 507-454-2270; Fax: 507-454-4024; Email: rtereba@ccsomn.org; Web: www.ccsomn.org.
Catholic Charities Board—MR. SCOT BERKLEY, Chm., Email: scot.berkley@gmail.com; Web: www.ccsomn.org.
Regional Offices—*Mankato: 201 N. Broad St., Ste. 100, Mankato, 56001.* Tel: 507-387-5586; Fax: 507-387-5587. *Rochester: 903 W. Center St., Ste. 220, Rochester, 55902.* Tel: 507-287-2047; Fax: 507-287-2050. *Worthington: 1234 Oxford St., Worthington, 56187.* Tel: 507-376-9757; Fax: 507-376-9758. *Winona: 111 Market St., P.O. Box 379, Winona, 55987.* Tel: 507-454-2270; Fax: 507-457-3027. *Albert Lea: 308 E. Fountain, Albert Lea, 56007.* Tel: 507-377-3664. *Owatonna: 577 State Ave., Owatonna, 55060.* Tel: 507-455-2008. *Austin: 430 10th St., N.E., Ste. 3, P.O. Box 366, Austin, 55912.* Tel: 507-433-3062.
Parish Social Ministry—MR. THOMAS PARLIN, Prog. Dir., 111 Market St., Ste. 2, Winona, 55987. Tel: 507-454-2270; Fax: 507-457-4024; Email: tparlin@ccsomn.org. Coordination of: Parish Social Ministry, Catholic Campaign for Human Devel., Catholic Relief Svcs., Disaster Relief Svcs.
Refugee Resettlement—MS. KRISTINA HAMMELL, Dir., 903 W. Center St., Ste. 220, Rochester, 55902. Tel: 507-287-2047; Fax: 507-287-2050; Email: khammell@ccsomn.org.
Family and Individual Counseling—ANNETTE KRUTSCH, Dir. & Licensed Psychologist, 111 Market St., Ste. 2, Winona, 55987. Tel: 507-454-2270; Fax: 507-457-3027; Email: akrutsch@ccsomn.org.
Pregnancy, Parenting & Adoption Program—MS. SARAH VETTER, L.S.W., Dir., 903 W. Center St., Ste. 220, Rochester, 55902. Tel: 507-287-2047, Ext. 32; Fax: 507-289-3860; Email: svetter@ccsomn.org.
Active Aging Programs—MRS. JENNIFER HALBERG, Dir., 111 Market St., P.O. Box 379, Winona, 55987. Tel: 507-454-2270; Fax: 507-457-3027; Email: jhalberg@ccsomn.org.
Guardian/Conservator Program—111 Market St., P.O. Box 379, Winona, 55987. Tel: 507-454-2270; Fax: 507-457-3027. PAMELA BOYD, Dir., Email: pboyd@ccsomn.org.
Cemeteries—MR. LAWRENCE J. DOSE, Pastoral Center, 55 W. Sanborn St., P.O. Box 588, Winona, 55987. Tel: 507-858-1265; Fax: 507-454-8106; Email: ldose@dowr.org.
Council of Catholic Women—MS. JEANETTE FORTIER, Pres., 1915 3rd Ave., S.W., Rochester, 55902. Tel: 507-358-7144; Email: fortierjeanette@gmail.com; Rev. Msgr. THOMAS J. HARGESHEIMER, Diocesan Moderator, (Retired), 65460 142nd Ave., Wabasha, 55981. Tel: 507-458-0738; Email: frtom60@wabasha.net.
Diocesan Self-Insurance Plan—MR. RYAN CHRISTENSON, Catholic Mutual Group, 1160 W. 7th St., Winona, 55987. Tel: 507-454-6452; Tel: 800-494-6452; Fax: 800-335-8141; Fax: 507-454-8141; Email: rchristenson@catholicmutual.org.
Catholic Foundation of Southern Minnesota—MRS. MONICA HERMAN, Exec. Dir., Tel: 507-858-1276; Email: mherman@catholicfsmn.org; Web: www.catholicfsmn.org.
Hospital Chaplains—200 First St., S.W., Rochester, 55905. Tel: 507-255-5780; Fax: 507-266-7882. Revs. JOHN L. EVANS, Email: evans.john@mayo.edu; JOSE L. MORALES, Email: jloralesr2008@yahoo.es.
Catholic Medical Association—DR. JOHN I. LANE, M.D., 200 First St., S.W., Rochester, 55905. Tel: 507-266-3412; Fax: 507-266-1657; Email: lane.john@mayo.edu.
Marriage Preparation/Enrichment—MR. PETER MARTIN, S.T.L., Dir., Tel: 507-858-1273; Fax: 507-454-8106; Email: pmartin@dowr.org.
Pathways TEC (Teens Encounter Christ)—MR. AARON LOFY, Dir., Tel: 507-858-1258; Fax: 507-454-8106; Email: alofy@dowr.org.
Misconduct Issues—Very Rev. MARK C. MCNEA, Tel: 507-858-1267; Email: mmcnea@dowr.org; MRS. MARY HAMANN, Tel: 507-858-1244; Fax: 507-454-8106; Email: mhamann@dowr.org.
Ministerial Standards Board—Very Revs. GLENN K. FRERICHS, J.C.L.; ROBERT S. HORIHAN; MS. TAMMY SHEFELBINE, Chair; MRS. NELLE MORIARTY; MR. KENNETH REED; MR. ROBERT TEREBA; MR. JOHN ANDERSON; MR. THOMAS BRAUN; MR. DON CARLSON; MRS. MARY HAMANN.
Retrouvaille—MR. PETER MARTIN, S.T.L., Tel: 507-858-1273; Email: pmartin@dowr.org.
Victim Assistance—55 W. Sanborn St., P.O. Box 588, Winona, 55987. Tel: 507-454-2270, Ext. 255.

CLERGY, PARISHES, MISSIONS AND PAROCHIAL SCHOOLS

CITY OF WINONA

(WINONA COUNTY)

1—CATHEDRAL OF THE SACRED HEART (1950) [JC]
360 Main St., 55987-3299. Tel: 507-452-4770; Fax: 507-454-1974; Email: info@cathedralwinona.org. Very Rev. Mark C. McNea, Rector; Rev. Brian Mulligan, Parochial Vicar; Deacon James Welch; Del Kahlstorf, Liturgy Dir.; Mrs. Anna Therneau, D.R.E.; Mrs. Sandra Smith, Sec. In Res., Rev. Msgr. Thomas P. Melvin.

2—BASILICA OF ST. STANISLAUS (1871)
625 E. Fourth St., 55987-4297. Tel: 507-452-5430; Fax: 507-452-3355; Email: ststans@hbci.com. Rev. Patrick Arens, Rector; Deacon Justin Green.
See St. Stanislaus Middle School, Winona under Centralized Catholic Schools located in the Institution section.

3—ST. CASIMIR (1906) [JC] Attended by
626 W. Broadway, 55987-2721. Tel: 507-452-4770; Email: info@cathedralwinona.org. 360 Main St., 55987. Very Rev. Mark C. McNea; Rev. Brian Mulligan, Parochial Vicar; Deacon James Welch.

4—ST. JOHN NEPOMUCENE (1888) Attended by
625 E. Fourth St., 55987-4297. Tel: 507-452-5430; Fax: 507-452-3355; Email: ststans@hbci.com; Web: www.ssk-sjn.weconnect.com. 558 E. Broadway, 55987. Rev. Patrick Arens; Deacon Justin Green.

5—ST. MARY'S (1911) [JC]
1303 W. Broadway, 55987-2395. Tel: 507-452-5656; Fax: 507-452-5477; Email: stmarys@wacs1.org. Rev. Jason L. Kern, Parochial Admin.
See St. Mary's Primary School, Winona under Centralized Catholic Schools located in the Institution section.

CITY OF ROCHESTER

(OLMSTED COUNTY)

1—CO-CATHEDRAL OF ST. JOHN THE EVANGELIST (1863) [JC]
11 4th Ave., S.W., Rochester, 55902-3098. Tel: 507-288-7372; Fax: 507-288-7373; Email: stjohn@sj.org; Web: www.sj.org. Rev. Msgr. Gerald A. Mahon, Rector; Deacon Gerald Freetly; Mr. Mike Gehring, Facility Mgr.; Mrs. Margaret Kelsey,

Admin.; Mr. Sebastian Modarelli, Dir. Liturgy & Music; Mrs. Cindy Paz, Admin. Asst.; Mrs. Debbie Thompson, Bookkeeper; Mrs. Mary Vlazny, Dir. Social Action.
See St. John School, Rochester under Centralized Catholic Schools located in the Institution section.
Catechesis Religious Program—Megan Rodriguez, PreK, Baptism, Confirmation; Neal Abbott, Grades 1-8, Youth Min.; Philip Lomneth, RCIA, Adult, Homebound. Students 200.

2—ST. FRANCIS OF ASSISI (1937) [JC]
1114 3rd St., S.E., Rochester, 55904-7293.
Tel: 507-288-7313; Email: parishadmin@stfrancis-church.org; Web: www.stfrancis-church.org. Revs. James C. Berning; Luis Vargas, Parochial Vicar.
See St. Francis of Assisi School, Rochester under Centralized Catholic Schools located in the Institution section.

3—HOLY SPIRIT (1990) [JC]
5455 50th Ave., N.W., Rochester, 55901.
Tel: 507-280-0638; Email: hspirit@holyspiritrochester.org. Very Rev. Thomas A. Loomis; Deacon Joseph Weigel.
See Holy Spirit School, Rochester under Centralized Catholic Schools located in the Institution section.

4—PAX CHRISTI (1973) [JC]
4135 18th Ave., N.W., Rochester, 55901-0460.
Tel: 507-282-8542; Email: bvelez@paxchristichurch.org. Revs. William D. Thompson; The Hoang, Parochial Vicar; Deacon Christopher Orlowski.

5—ST. PIUS X (1954) [JC]
1315 12th Ave., N.W., Rochester, 55901-1744.
Tel: 507-288-8238; Fax: 507-286-8769; Email: church@piusx.org; Web: www.piusx.org. Rev. Russell G. Scepaniak.
See St. Pius X School, Rochester under Centralized Catholic Schools located in the Institution section.

6—RESURRECTION (1967) [JC]
1600-11th Ave., S.E., Rochester, 55904-5499.
Tel: 507-288-5528; Email: pastor@rescathroch.org; Email: officemgr@rescathroch.org; Web: www.rescathroch.org. Revs. Peter L. Schuster; Shawn J. Haremza, Parochial Vicar; Ms. Erica Stiller, Admin.

OUTSIDE THE CITIES OF WINONA AND ROCHESTER

ADAMS, MOWER CO., SACRED HEART (1886) [CEM]
412 W. Main St., P.O. Box 352, Adams, 55909.
Tel: 507-582-3321; Fax: 507-582-1033; Email: office@sacredheartadams.org. Rev. Swaminatha R. Pothireddy.
School—Sacred Heart School, (Grades K-8), 11 5th St. S.W., P.O. Box 249, Adams, 55909.
Tel: 507-582-3120; Web: sacredheartadams.org. Darlene Boe, Prin. Lay Teachers 9; Students 115.

ADRIAN, NOBLES CO., ST. ADRIAN (1877) [CEM]
512 Maine Ave., P.O. Box 475, Adrian, 56110-0475.
Tel: 507-483-2317; Email: stadriancluster@hotmail.com. Rev. Msgr. Richard M. Colletti.

ALBERT LEA, FREEBORN CO., ST. THEODORE (1882) [CEM]
Mailing Address: 308 E. Fountain St., Albert Lea, 56007-2456. Tel: 507-373-0603; Fax: 507-373-0604; Email: office@sttheo.org; Web: www.sttheo.org. Rev. Kurt P. Farrell.

ALTURA, WINONA CO., ST. ANTHONY'S (1919) [JC]
180 S. Fremont, Lewiston, 55952. Tel: 507-796-6271; Tel: 507-523-2428 (Rectory); Email: strose@hbci.com; Web: www.st-rose.org. 123 1st St., N.E., Altura, 55910. Very Rev. Glenn K. Frerichs, J.C.L.

AUSTIN, MOWER CO.

1—ST. AUGUSTINE'S (1857) [JC]
405 Fourth St. N.W., Austin, 55912-1599. Rev. James P. Steffes; Deacons John Kluczny; Richard Aho.
See Austin Catholic Elementary School, under Centralized Catholic Schools located in the Institution section.

2—ST. EDWARD'S (1960) [JC]
405 N.W. Fourth St., Austin, 55912-3091.
Tel: 507-433-1841; Email: fathersteffes.ae@gmail.com; Web: www.staugustinestedward.org. 2000 Oakland Ave. W., Austin, 55912-1599. Rev. James P. Steffes; Deacons John Kluczny; Richard Aho.
See Austin Catholic Elementary School, under Centralized Catholic Schools located in the Institution section.

3—QUEEN OF ANGELS (1936) [JC]
1001 Oakland Ave. E., Austin, 55912-3896.
Tel: 507-433-1888; Tel: 507-433-8474; Email: fatherraul@queenofangels.church; Web: www.queenofangelsaustinmn.net. Very Rev. Raul I. Silva.
See Austin Catholic Elementary School, under Centralized Catholic Schools located in the Institution section.

BLOOMING PRAIRIE, STEELE CO., ST. COLUMBANUS (1878) [CEM]
114 E. Main St., Blooming Prairie, 55917-1427.
Tel: 507-583-2784; Email: columbanusbp@gmail.com. Rev. Thomas M. Niehaus, J.C.L.

BLUE EARTH, FARIBAULT CO., SS. PETER AND PAUL'S (1866) [CEM]
214 S. Holland, Blue Earth, 56013-1331.
Tel: 507-526-5626; Email: patsspp@bevcomm.net. Very Rev. Peter J. Klein.
Catechesis Religious Program—Email: angieyouthministry@bevcomm.net. Angie Nagel, D.R.E. Students 97.

BREWSTER, NOBLES CO., SACRED HEART (1901) [CEM]
516 10th St., P.O. Box 187, Brewster, 56119.
Tel: 507-842-5545; Email: sacreds@centurytel.net. Rev. Pratap Reddy Salibindla, O.F.M., (India).

BROWNSVILLE, HOUSTON CO., ST. PATRICK'S (1871) [CEM] [JC2] Attended by
423 S Second St., La Crescent, 55947. 604 Adams St., Brownsville, 55919. Rev. Gregory G. Havel; Deacon Robert Yerhot.

BYRON, OLMSTED CO., CHRIST THE KING (1965)
202 Fourth St., N.W., P.O. Box 1000, Byron, 55920-1000. Tel: 507-775-6455; Email: pastoralassistantckhf@gmail.com. Rev. John Lugala Lasuba.

CALEDONIA, HOUSTON CO., ST. MARY (1975) [CEM]
Mailing Address: 453 S. Pine St., P.O. Box 406, Caledonia, 55921-0406. Tel: 507-725-3804; Email: stmaryschurch@acegroup.cc; Web: www.churchofstmary.net. Rev. Stephen Abaukaka.
School—St. Mary School, (Grades PreK-8), 308 E. South St., Caledonia, 55921. Tel: 507-725-3355; Email: rswedberg@stmaryschoolcal.org; Email: stmarysschool@acegroup.cc; Web: www.stmaryschoolcal.org. Rebecca Swedberg, Prin. / Contact Person. Lay Teachers 14; Students 128.

CANTON, FILLMORE CO., THE ASSUMPTION (1891) [CEM] [JC]
207 N. May, Canton, 55939. Rev. Edward F. McGrath.

CHATFIELD, FILLMORE CO., ST. MARY'S (1866) [CEM 2]
405 Bench St., S.W., Chatfield, 55923.
Tel: 507-867-3922; Email: parishcenter@holyfamilyfillmoreco.org; Web: holyfamilyfillmoreco.org. 323 Twiford St., S.W., Chatfield, 55923. Rev. Edward F. McGrath.

CURRIE, MURRAY CO., IMMACULATE HEART OF MARY (1881) [CEM]
Mailing Address: 501 Mill St., Currie, 56123. Rev. Msgr. R. Paul Heiting, J.C.L.

DAKOTA, WINONA CO., HOLY CROSS (1890) Clustered with Crucifixion Parish in La Crescent.
423 S. 2nd St., La Crescent, 55947.
Tel: 507-895-4720; Fax: 507-895-6880; Email: cruxch@acegroup.cc; Email: cruxacc@acegroup.cc. 180 Washington St., Dakota, 55925. Rev. Gregory G. Havel; Deacons Gerald Trocinski; Robert Yerhot.

DODGE CENTER, DODGE CO., ST. JOHN BAPTIST DE LA SALLE (1945)
20 Second St. N.E., P.O. Box 310, Dodge Center, 55927. Tel: 507-374-6830; Email: office@dodgecatholic.org. Rev. Thomas M. Niehaus, J.C.L.

EAST CHAIN, MARTIN CO., HOLY FAMILY (1897) [CEM] [JC]
901 S. Prairie Ave., Fairmont, 56031.
Tel: 507-235-5535; Fax: 507-235-5536; Email: sjvchurch@midconetwork.com; Web: www.sjvhf.org. 2481 50th St., Fairmont, 56031. Rev. Andrew J. Beerman, S.T.L.

EASTON, FARIBAULT CO., OUR LADY OF MOUNT CARMEL (1866) [CEM]
27 Main St., P.O. Box 8, Easton, 56025. Rev. Matthew J. Fasnacht; Deacon Eugene Paul.

ELBA, WINONA CO., ST. ALOYSIUS (1877) [CEM] Clustered with St. Charles Borromeo in St. Charles.
1900 E. 6th St., St. Charles, 55972.
Tel: 507-932-3294; Email: borromeo@hbcsc.net; Web: www.borromeochurch.org. 150 N. Main St., Elba, 55910. Rev. Timothy E. Biren; Deacon Placido Zavala.

ELLSWORTH, NOBLES CO., ST. MARY'S (1885) [CEM] Merged with St. Catherine, Luverne.

EYOTA, OLMSTED CO., HOLY REDEEMER (1891)
Mailing Address: 1900 E. 6th St., St. Charles, 55972-1426. Tel: 507-932-3294; Email: borromeo@hbcsc.net; Web: www.borromeochurch.org. 22 E. 2nd St., Eyota, 55934. Rev. Timothy E. Biren; Deacon Placido Zavala.

FAIRMONT, MARTIN CO., ST. JOHN VIANNEY (1952) [CEM]
901 S. Prairie Ave., Fairmont, 56031-3023.
Tel: 507-235-5535; Fax: 507-235-5536; Email: sjvchurch@midconetwork.com; Web: www.sjvhf.org. Rev. Andrew J. Beerman, S.T.L.
School—St. John Vianney School, (Grades PreK-6), 911 S. Prairie Ave., Fairmont, 56031.
Tel: 507-235-5304; Fax: 507-235-9099; Email: sstriemer@sjvschool.net; Web: sjvschool.net. Sarah Striemer, Prin. Lay Teachers 10; Students 103.

FULDA, MURRAY CO., ST. GABRIEL'S (1882) [CEM]
309 Lake Ave. W., Fulda, 56131-9402.
Tel: 507-425-2369; Email: stgab2369@gmail.com; Web: www.triparishcfw.org. Rev. Msgr. R. Paul Heiting, J.C.L.

GOOD THUNDER, BLUE EARTH CO., ST. JOSEPH (1879) [CEM]
Mailing Address: P.O. Box 305, Mapleton, 56065.
Tel: 507-524-3127; Email: sjsmst@hickorytech.net. 130 N. Ewing, Good Thunder, 56037. Rev. Andrew P. Vogel.

GRAND MEADOW, MOWER CO., ST. FINBARR'S (1878) [CEM]
504 1st St. S.W., P.O. Box 374, Grand Meadow, 55936. Tel: 507-346-7565; Email: triparishsecretary@gmail.com; Web: tri-parish.net. Rev. Marreddy Pothireddy.

HARMONY, FILLMORE CO., THE NATIVITY OF THE BLESSED VIRGIN (1906)
640 First Ave., S.W., Harmony, 55939-0596.
Tel: 507-886-2393; Email: nativity@harmonytel.net. Rev. Edward F. McGrath.

HAYFIELD, DODGE CO., SACRED HEART (1935) Attended by
150 2nd St. N.E., P.O. Box 27, Hayfield, 55940.
Tel: 507-477-2256; Email: sacredhearthayfield@gofast.am. Rev. Thomas M. Niehaus, J.C.L.

HERON LAKE, JACKSON CO., SACRED HEART (1884) [CEM] Attended by
321 9th St., P.O. Box 377, Heron Lake, 56137.
Tel: 507-793-2357; Email: sacredhearthl@gmail.com; Web: sacredheartheronlake.org. Rev. Pratap Reddy Salibindla, O.F.M., (India).

HOKAH, HOUSTON CO., ST. PETER'S (1860) [CEM] [JC2]
Mailing Address: 34 Main St., P.O. Box 355, Hokah, 55941. Tel: 507-894-4944; Email: stpetersparish@acegroup.cc; Web: www.rootrivercatholics.com. Rev. Gregory G. Havel, Parochial Admin.; Deacon Adam McMillan, Sacramental Min.
School—St. Peter's School, (Grades PreK-8), P.O. Box 357, Hokah, 55941. Tel: 507-894-4375; Email: stpeter@acegroup.cc; Web: www.st-peters-school.net. Mr. Doug Harpenau, Prin. / Contact Person. Lay Teachers 7; Students 57.
Catechesis Religious Program—Email: kochie307@gmail.com. Mr. Joe Kochie, D.R.E. Students 57.

HOUSTON, HOUSTON CO., ST. MARY'S (1873) [CEM]
Mailing Address: 103 N. Mill St., P.O. Box 577, Rushford, 55971. Tel: 507-894-4944; Email: stpetersparish@acegroup.cc; Web: www.rootrivercatholics.com. 202 S. Sheridan St., Houston, 55943. Revs. Gregory G. Havel, Parochial Admin.; Adam J. McMillan, Sacramental Min.
Catechesis Religious Program—Tel: 507-896-4809; Email: deichhouston@acegroup.cc. Dennis Eich, D.R.E. Students 26.

IONA, MURRAY CO., ST. COLUMBA'S (1891) [CEM]
2747 29th St., Slayton, 56172. Tel: 507-836-8030; Email: stabusiness@frontiernet.net; Web: www.acmcatholic.org. 451 McDonnell Ave., Iona, 56141. Rev. Thien Van Nguyen.

JACKSON, JACKSON CO., GOOD SHEPHERD (1891) [CEM]
311 N. Sverdrup Ave., P.O. Box 65, Jackson, 56143-1329. Tel: 507-847-2504; Email: goodshepherd@triparishcommunity.org. Rev. Jonathan Joseph Fasnacht.

JANESVILLE, WASECA CO., ST. ANN (1876) [CEM]
313 W. 2nd St., P.O. Box 218, Janesville, 56048-0218. Tel: 507-234-6244; Fax: 507-234-6237; Email: stannjan@hickorytech.net; Web: stannjan.com. Rev. Michael J. Cronin, J.C.L.

JASPER, PIPESTONE CO., ST. JOSEPH (1918) [CEM] Clustered with St. Leo in Pipestone.
415 S Hiawatha Ave., P.O. Box 36, Pipestone, 56164-0036. Tel: 507-825-3152; Fax: 507-825-4492; Email: om@triparishmn.org; Web: www.triparishmn.org. Rev. Msgr. Gerald C. Kosse.
Catechesis Religious Program—Email: dff@triparishmn.org. Trish Johnson, Faith Formation. Students 18.

JOHNSBURG, MOWER CO., ST. JOHN'S (1859) [CEM]
412 W Main St., P.O. Box 352, Adams, 55909.
Tel: 507-582-3321; Fax: 507-582-1033; Email: office@sacredheartadams.org. 10343 640th Ave., Adams, 55909. Rev. Swaminatha R. Pothireddy.

KASSON, DODGE CO., HOLY FAMILY (1976) [CEM] Attended by
1904 N. Mantorville Ave., P.O. Box 171, Kasson, 55944. Tel: 507-634-7520; Email: pastoralassistantckhf@gmail.com; Web: www.ChristKingHolyFamily.org. Rev. John Lugala Lasuba.

KELLOGG, WABASHA CO.

1—ST. AGNES (1900) [CEM] Attended by
117 3rd St. W., Wabasha, 55981-1201.
Tel: 651-565-3931; Email: office@felixagnes.org; Web: www.wabashakelloggparishes.org. 135 W. Glasgow Ave., Kellogg, 55945. Rev. Gregory W. Parrott; Deacon John Hust.

2—IMMACULATE CONCEPTION (1881) Attended by
St. Joachim Church, 900 W. Broadway, Plainview, 55964. Tel: 507-534-3321; Fax: 507-534-3687; Email: stjoachimchurch@hotmail.com; Web: immconception-

church.org. 22032 County Rd. 18, Kellogg, 55945. Rev. William M. Becker, S.T.D.; Deacon John DeStazio.

LA CRESCENT, HOUSTON CO., THE CHURCH OF THE CRUCIFIXION (1856) [CEM 2]
423 S. Second St., La Crescent, 55947.
Tel: 507-895-4720; Fax: 507-895-6880; Email: cruxch@acegroup.cc; Email: cruxacc@acegroup.cc; Web: cruxcifixionchurch.org. 415 S Second St., La Crescent, 55947. Rev. Gregory G. Havel; Deacon Robert Yerhot.
School—The Church of the Crucifixion School, (Grades PreK-6), 420 S. 2nd St., La Crescent, 55947. Tel: 507-895-4402; Email: dharpenau@crucifixionschool.org; Web: www.crucifixionschool.org. Mr. Doug Harpenau, Prin. Lay Teachers 8; Students 137.

LAKE CITY, WABASHA CO., ST. MARY'S OF THE LAKE (1877) [CEM]
419 Lyon Ave., Lake City, 55041-1649.
Tel: 651-345-4134; Email: stmaryslakecity@gmail.com. Rev. John P. Wilmot; Deacon David Dose.

LAKE CRYSTAL, BLUE EARTH CO., HOLY FAMILY (1900) [CEM] Attended by
Mailing Address: 423 W. 7th St., Mankato, 56001.
Tel: 507-388-3766; Email: office@sjwhf.org; Web: sjwhf.org. 211 N. Hunt St., Lake Crystal, 56055. Rev. Timothy T. Reker, S.T.L.; Deacon John Rudd, Pastoral Assoc.

LAKE WILSON, MURRAY CO., ST. MARY (1916) [JC]
2747 29th St., Slayton, 56172. Tel: 507-836-8030; Email: stabusiness@frontiernet.net; Web: www.acmcatholic.org. 320 Paul Ave., Lake Wilson, 56151. Rev. Thien Van Nguyen.

LAKEFIELD, JACKSON CO., ST. JOSEPH (1897) [CEM]
410 Broadway Ave., P.O. Box 517, Lakefield, 56150.
Tel: 507-847-2504; Fax: 507-847-3734; Email: sjcc@triparishcommunity.com; Email: goodshepherd@triparishcommunity.com. Rev. Jonathan Joseph Fasnacht.

LANESBORO, FILLMORE CO., ST. PATRICK (1871) [JC]
Clustered with St. Mary in Chatfield.
Mailing Address: 405 Bench St., S.W., Chatfield, 55923. Tel: 507-867-3922; Email: parishcenter@holyfamilyfillmoreco.org; Web: holyfamilyfillmoreco.org. 200 Ridgeview Ln., Lanesboro, 55949. Rev. Edward F. McGrath.

LE ROY, MOWER CO., ST. PATRICK'S (1878) [CEM]
436 W. Main St., Le Roy, 55951-0310.
Tel: 507-346-7565; Fax: 507-346-7725; Email: triparishsecretary@gmail.com; Web: tri-parish.net. Rev. Marreddy Pothireddy.

LEWISTON, WINONA CO., ST. ROSE OF LIMA (1876) [CEM]
180 S. Fremont St., Lewiston, 55952.
Tel: 507-523-2428; Email: strose@hbci.org; Web: www.st-rose.org. Very Rev. Glenn K. Frerichs, J.C.L.
Catechesis Religious Program— Included with St. Anthony, Altura, MN.; Immaculate Conception, Wilson, MN. Tel: 507-523-3548; Email: srcff@hbci.com. Ashley Gossen, D.R.E. Students 145.

LISMORE, NOBLES CO., ST. ANTHONY'S (1903) [CEM 2]
P.O. Box 475, Adrian, 56110. Tel: 507-483-2317; Email: stadriancluster@hotmail.com; Web: www.stadriancluster.org. 310 3rd Ave., Lismore, 56155. Rev. Msgr. Richard M. Colletti.

LITOMYSL, STEELE CO., HOLY TRINITY (1877) [CEM]
9946 S.E. 24th Ave., Owatonna, 55060. Rev. John M. Sauer, S.T.L.; Monica Anderson, Pastoral Assoc.

LUVERNE, ROCK CO., ST. CATHERINE'S (1881) [CEM]
203 E. Brown St., Luverne, 56156-1599.
Tel: 507-283-8502; Email: stcatherine@iw.net; Web: www.stcatherineluverne.org. Rev. Msgr. Gerald C. Kosse.
Catechesis Religious Program—Tel: 507-283-8071; Fax: 507-449-3638; Email: kbaustian@iw.net. Mrs. Katie Baustian, D.R.E. Students 196.

LYLE, MOWER CO., QUEEN OF PEACE (1946) (German)
Mailing Address: 412 Main St., P.O. Box 352, Adams, 55909-0352. Tel: 507-582-3321;
Fax: 507-582-1033; Email: office@sacredheartadams.org. 301-399 3rd St., Lyle, 55953. Rev. Swaminatha R. Pothireddy.

MABEL, FILLMORE CO., ST. OLAF (1954) [JC]
114 N. Locust, P.O. Box 8, Mabel, 55954.
Tel: 507-493-5268; Email: stolafcatholic@gmail.com. Rev. Stephen Abaukaka.
Catechesis Religious Program—640 1st Ave., S.W., Harmony, 55939. Tel: 507-886-4433; Email: nativity@harmonytel.net. Maureen Gervais, D.R.E. Combined Rel. Educ. Prog. with Nativity, Harmony & Assumption, Canton. Students attend at Assumption, Canton. Students 21.

MADELIA, WATONWAN CO., ST. MARY (1872) [CEM]
Served by St. James, St. James, MN.
212 First St., N.E., Madelia, 56062-1702.
Tel: 507-642-8305; Fax: 507-642-8310; Email: msandmeyer@outlook.com. Rev. Timothy J. Hall, S.T.L.
School—St. Mary School, (Grades PreK-6), 223 First St. N.E., Madelia, 56062. Tel: 507-642-3324; Fax: 507-642-3899; Email: stmarysdt@ccinternet.net. Jennifer Slater, Prin. Lay Teachers 6; Priests 1; Students 47.

MADISON LAKE, BLUE EARTH CO., ALL SAINTS (1894) [CEM]
605 4th St., P.O. Box 217, Madison Lake, 56063-0217. Tel: 507-243-3319; Fax: 507-243-4308; Email: asoffice@hickorytech.net; Web: as-ic.org. Rev. Robert J. Schneider.
Endowment—Parish Endowment Fund, Inc. of All Saints Church.

MANKATO, BLUE EARTH CO.
1—ST. JOHN THE BAPTIST (1884) [JC]
632 S. Broad St., Mankato, 56001-3890.
Tel: 507-625-3131; Email: stjohnch@stjohnsmankato.net. Rev. John M. Kunz.
2—ST. JOSEPH THE WORKER (1957) [JC]
423 W. 7th St., Mankato, 56001-2131.
Tel: 507-388-3766; Email: office@sjwhf.org; Web: sjwhf.org. Rev. Timothy T. Reker, S.T.L.; Deacon John Rudd, Pastoral Assoc.
3—SS. PETER AND PAUL CATHOLIC CHURCH (1854)
105 N. Fifth St., Mankato, 56001-4442.
Tel: 507-388-2995; Fax: 507-388-7661; Email: sspp@hickorytech.net. Revs. Javier Ibarra; Willian Valle Pacheco, I.V.E., Parochial Vicar; Deacon Andy Kmetz.
4—ST. THOMAS MORE CATHOLIC NEWMAN CENTER PARISH OF MANKATO, MINNESOTA
Minnestoa State University, 1502 Warren St., Mankato, 56001. Tel: 507-387-4154; Email: frapvogel@gmail.com; Web: catholicmavs.org. Rev. Andrew P. Vogel.

MAPLETON, BLUE EARTH CO., ST. TERESA CHURCH (1876) [CEM]
104 Silver St., W., P.O. Box 305, Mapleton, 56065-0305. Tel: 507-524-3127; Email: sjsmst@hickorytech.net; Web: sjsmst.org. 102 Central Ave. N., Mapleton, 56065-0305. Rev. Andrew P. Vogel.

MAZEPPA, WABASHA CO., SS. PETER AND PAUL (1860)
222 First Ave. S., P.O. Box 224, Mazeppa, 55956.
Tel: 507-843-3885; Email: bookkeeper@sspnp.com; Email: secretary@sspnp.com; Web: sspeterandpaulmazeppa.org. Revs. William D. Thompson; The Hoang, Parochial Vicar; Deacon Christopher Orlowski.

MEDFORD, STEELE CO., CHRIST THE KING (1943)
205 N.W. Second Ave., P.O. Box 120, Medford, 55049-0120. Tel: 507-451-6353; Email: christthekingcc@q.com. Rev. James Starasinich; Deacon Patrick Fagan.

MINNEISKA, WABASHA CO., ST. MARY'S (1867)
83 Main St., Rollingstone, 55969. Tel: 507-689-2351; Email: office@htpm.us. 424 Bennett Ave., Minneiska, 55910. Rev. Chinnappa Pothireddy.

MINNESOTA CITY, WINONA CO., ST. PAUL'S (1924) [CEM]
83 Main St., Rollingstone, 55969-9759.
Tel: 507-689-2351; Email: parish@htpm.us. 132 Anderson St., Minnesota City, 55959. Rev. Chinnappa Pothireddy.

MINNESOTA LAKE, FARIBAULT CO., ST. JOHN THE BAPTIST (1865) [CEM]
100 Park St. N, P.O. Box 158, Minnesota Lake, 56068. Rev. Matthew J. Fasnacht; Deacon Eugene Paul.

NEW RICHLAND, WASECA CO., ALL SAINTS (1879) [CEM]
Mailing Address: 313 W. 2nd St., P.O. Box 218, Janesville, 56048. 307 1st St., S.W., New Richland, 56072. Tel: 507-234-6244; Fax: 507-234-6237; Email: stannjan@hickorytech.net; Web: www.stannjan.com. Rev. Michael J. Cronin, J.C.L.

OWATONNA, STEELE CO.
1—ST. JOSEPH (1891)
512 S. Elm Ave., Owatonna, 55060-3399.
Tel: 507-451-4845; Fax: 507-451-4651; Email: parishoffice@stjosephowatonna.org. Rev. James Starasinich; Deacon Patrick Fagan.
2—SACRED HEART (1866) [JC]
810 S. Cedar Ave., Owatonna, 55060-3297.
Tel: 507-451-1588; Fax: 507-446-9979; Email: office@sacredheartowatonna.org; Web: www.sacredheartowatonna.org. Rev. John M. Sauer, S.T.L.
Catechesis Religious Program—730 S. Cedar Ave., Owatonna, 55060. Tel: 507-446-2302; Email: danrbauer@hotmail.com; Web: rep-cyo.org. Dan Bauer, D.R.E. Students 395.

PIPESTONE, PIPESTONE CO., ST. LEO (1887) [CEM]
Mailing Address: 415 S Hiawatha Ave., P.O. Box 36, Pipestone, 56164-0036. Tel: 507-825-3152;
Fax: 507-825-4492; Email: om@triparishmn.org; Web: www.triparishmn.org. Rev. Msgr. Gerald C. Kosse.
Child Care—Noah's Ark Preschool, Email: pt@triparishmn.org. Amy Vandenbosch, Dir. Lay Teachers 2; Students 15.
Catechesis Religious Program—Email: dff@triparishmn.org. Trish Johnson, Faith Formation. Students 202.

PLAINVIEW, WABASHA CO., ST. JOACHIM'S (1858) [CEM]
900 W. Broadway, Plainview, 55964-1039.
Tel: 507-534-3321; Fax: 507-534-3687; Email: stjoachimchurch@hotmail.com. Rev. William M. Becker, S.T.D.; Deacon John DeStazio.

PRESTON, FILLMORE CO., ST. COLUMBAN (1869) [CEM 2] [JC]
408 Preston St. N.W., Preston, 55965.
Tel: 507-867-3922; Email: parishcenter@holyfamilyfillmoreco.org. Tri-Parish, 405 Bench St. S.W., Chatfield, 55923. Rev. Edward F. McGrath.

ROLLINGSTONE, WINONA CO., HOLY TRINITY (1862) [CEM]
83 Main St., Rollingstone, 55969-9759.
Tel: 507-689-2351; Email: office@htpm.us. Rev. Chinnappa Pothireddy.
Catechesis Religious Program—Tina Lehnertz, Faith Formation; Tom Speltz, Sec. Students 35.

ROSE CREEK, MOWER CO., ST. PETER'S (1885) [CEM]
Mailing Address: 412 W Main St., P.O. Box 352, Adams, 55909. Tel: 507-582-3321; Fax: 507-582-1033; Email: office@sacredheartadams.org. 300 Maple St., S.W., Rose Creek, 55970. Rev. Swaminatha R. Pothireddy.

RUSHFORD, FILLMORE CO., ST. JOSEPH (1868) [CEM]
101 Rushford Ave. W., Rushford, 55971.
Tel: 507-894-4944; Email: stpetersparish@acegroup.cc; Web: www.rootrivercatholics.com. Rev. Gregory G. Havel, Parochial Admin.; Deacon Adam McMillan, Sacramental Min.

ST. CHARLES, WINONA CO., ST. CHARLES BORROMEO (1867) [CEM]
Mailing Address: 1900 E. 6th St., St. Charles, 55972-1426. Tel: 507-932-3294; Email: borromeo@hbcsc.net; Web: www.borromeochurch.org. Rev. Timothy E. Biren; Deacon Placido Zavala.

ST. CLAIR, BLUE EARTH CO., IMMACULATE CONCEPTION (1874) [CEM] Attended by
101 Church St., P.O. Box 100, St. Clair, 56080.
Tel: 507-245-3447; Email: icoffice@hickorytech.net; Web: as-ic.org. Rev. Robert J. Schneider.

ST. JAMES, WATONWAN CO., ST. JAMES (1876) [CEM]
707 4th St. S., St. James, 56081-1808.
Tel: 507-375-3542; Fax: 507-375-4170; Email: msandmeyer@outlook.com. Rev. Timothy J. Hall, S.T.L.

SHERBURN, MARTIN CO., ST. LUKE'S (1888) [CEM]
Mailing Address: 303 S. Lake St., P.O. Box 669, Sherburn, 56171. Tel: 507-764-7831; Email: stlukes_ff@hotmail.com. Rev. Jonathan Joseph Fasnacht.

SIMPSON, OLMSTED CO, ST. BRIDGET'S (1857) [CEM]
116 4th Ave., S.E., Stewartville, 55976.
Tel: 507-533-8257; Email: stbernard116@aol.com; Web: www.sbsbparishes.org. 2123 County Rd. 16 S.E., Rochester, 55904. Very Revs. Thomas A. Loomis, Parochial Admin.; Kevin Connolly, Sacramental Min.

SLAYTON, MURRAY CO., ST. ANN'S (1897) [CEM]
2747 29th St., Slayton, 56172-1485.
Tel: 507-836-8030; Email: stabusiness@frontiernet.net; Web: www.acmcatholic.org. Rev. Thien Van Nguyen.

SPRING VALLEY, FILLMORE CO., ST. IGNATIUS (1878) [CEM]
213 W. Franklin St., Spring Valley, 55975-1312.
Tel: 507-346-7565; Email: triparishsecretary@gmail.com; Web: tri-parish.net. Rev. Marreddy Pothireddy.

STEWARTVILLE, OLMSTED CO., ST. BERNARD'S (1894) [CEM]
Mailing Address: 116 Fourth Ave., S.E., Stewartville, 55976. Tel: 507-533-8257; Email: stbernard116@aol.com; Web: sbsbparishes.org. Very Revs. Thomas A. Loomis, Parochial Admin.; Kevin Connolly, Sacramental Min.

TWIN LAKES, FREEBORN CO., ST. JAMES (1876)
Mailing Address: 308 E. Fountain St., Albert Lea, 56007. Tel: 507-373-0603; Fax: 507-373-0604. Rev. Kurt P. Farrell.

VERNON CENTER, BLUE EARTH CO., ST. MATTHEW (1911) [CEM]
P.O. Box 305, Mapleton, 56065-0305.
Tel: 507-524-3127; Email: sjsmst@hickorytech.net; Web: sjsmst.org. 200 Kendall St., Vernon Center, 56090. Rev. Andrew P. Vogel.

WABASHA, WABASHA CO., ST. FELIX (1858) [CEM]
117 W. Third St., Wabasha, 55981-1201.
Tel: 651-565-3931; Email: office@felixagnes.org. Rev. Gregory W. Parrott; Deacon John Hust.
School—St. Felix School, (Grades PreK-6), 130 E. 3rd St., Wabasha, 55981. Tel: 651-565-4446; Email: esonnek@stfelixschool.org; Web: www.stfelixschool.org. Eric Sonnek, Prin. Lay Teachers 11; Students 85.

WALDORF, WASECA CO., ST. JOSEPH (1878) [CEM]
Mailing Address: P.O. Box 218, Janesville, 56048-0218. Tel: 507-234-6244; Fax: 507-234-6237; Email: stannjan@hickorytech.net; Web: stannjan.com. 225 3rd Ave. N, Waldorf, 56091. Rev. Michael J. Cronin, J.C.L.

WASECA, WASECA CO., SACRED HEART (1869) [JC2]

111 Fourth St., N.W., Waseca, 56093-2413.
Tel: 507-835-1222; Fax: 507-833-1498; Email: sacredheart@hickorytech.net. Rev. Gregory P. Leif; Deacon Preston Doyle.
School—Sacred Heart School, (Grades K-4), 308 W. Elm Ave., Waseca, 56093. Tel: 507-835-2780; Email: dahle@sacredheartschoolwaseca.com. LeAnn Dahle, Prin. Lay Teachers 12; Priests 1; Students 97.
Child Care—Sacred Heart Montessori, Jennifer Connors, Dir. Students 50.
Catechesis Religious Program—Tel: 507-835-1500; Email: shfaithformation@hickorytech.net. Kayla Greiner, D.R.E. Students 157.

WELLS, FARIBAULT CO., ST. CASIMIR'S (1880) [CEM]
320 Second Ave., S.W., Wells, 56097-1399.
Tel: 507-553-5391; Email: scasimir@bevcomm.net. Rev. Matthew J. Fasnacht; Deacon Eugene Paul.
School—St. Casimir's School, (Grades PreK-6), 300 2nd Ave., S.W., Wells, 56097. Tel: 507-553-5822; Email: casimir@bevcomm.net; Web: www.stcasimirsschool.net. Rev. Jason L. Kern, Admin.; Mr. Shawn Kennedy, Prin.; Sarah Oldham, Contact Person. Lay Teachers 5; Students 37.

WEST ALBANY, WABASHA CO., ST. PATRICK OF WEST ALBANY (1865) [CEM] Attended by
419 W. Lyon Ave., Lake City, 55041.
Tel: 651-345-4134; Tel: 651-345-2439;
Fax: 651-345-6134; Email: mariaschultzsmsp@gmail.com; Email: dddose49@gmail.com; Web: stpatrickswestalbany.org. 30932 Hwy. 60, Millville, 55957. Rev. John P. Wilmot; Deacon David Dose.

WESTBROOK, COTTONWOOD CO., ST. ANTHONY'S (1909) [CEM]
1153 1st Ave., P.O. Box 278, Westbrook, 56183.
Tel: 507-425-2369 (St. Gabriel);
Tel: 507-274-5946 (St. Anthony); Email: stanthonys@centurytel.net; Web: www.triparishcfw.org. Rev. Msgr. R. Paul Heiting, J.C.L.

WILMONT, NOBLES CO., OUR LADY OF GOOD COUNSEL (1903) [CEM]
605 4th Ave., P.O. Box 475, Wilmont, 56185.
Tel: 507-483-2317; Email: stadriancluster@hotmail.com; Web: www.stadriancluster.org. Rev. Msgr. Richard M. Colletti.

WILSON, WINONA CO., IMMACULATE CONCEPTION (1874)
25729 MN-43, 55987. Mailing Address: 180 S. Fremont St., Lewiston, 55952-0727.
Tel: 507-523-2428; Fax: 507-523-2645; Email: strose@hbci.com; Web: www.st-rose.org. Very Rev. Glenn K. Frerichs, J.C.L.

WINDOM, COTTONWOOD CO., ST. FRANCIS XAVIER CHURCH (1898)
548 17th St., P.O. Box 39, Windom, 56101.
Tel: 507-831-1985; Email: stfxavier@windomnet.com; Web: www.sfxwindom.org. Rev. Pratap Reddy Salibindla, O.F.M., (India).

WINNEBAGO, FARIBAULT CO., ST. MARY'S (1893) [CEM]
Mailing Address: 214 S. Holland, Blue Earth, 56013.
Tel: 507-526-5626; Email: patsspp@bevcomm.net. 40 1st St., N.E., Winnebago, 56098. Very Rev. Peter J. Klein.
Catechesis Religious Program—Tel: 507-236-2195. Pat Salic, D.R.E. Students 27.

WOODSTOCK, PIPESTONE CO., ST. MARTIN (1883) [CEM]
Clustered with St. Leo in Pipestone.
Mailing Address: 415 S. Hiawatha Ave., P.O. Box 36, Pipestone, 56164-0036. Tel: 507-825-3152;
Fax: 507-825-4492; Email: om@triparishmn.org; Web: www.triparishmn.org. Rev. Msgr. Gerald C. Kosse.
Catechesis Religious Program—Trish Johnson, Faith Formation. Students 17.

WORTHINGTON, NOBLES CO., ST. MARY'S (1886) [CEM]
1215 Seventh Ave., Worthington, 56187-2297.
Tel: 507-376-6005; Fax: 507-376-9167; Email: stmaryschurch@vastbb.net. Revs. James F. Callahan; Miguel E. Proanos, Parochial Vicar; Deacon Vernon Behrends, RCIA Coord.
School—St. Mary's School, (Grades K-6), 1206 8th Ave., Worthington, 56187. Tel: 507-376-5236;
Fax: 507-376-6159; Email: Jackie.probst@smswgtn.org; Web: smswgtn.org. Jackie Probst, Prin.; Barb Stirn, Librarian. Clergy 2; Lay Teachers 8; Students 68.

Chaplains of Public Institutions.

On Duty Outside the Diocese:
Rev. Msgr.—
Cook, Thomas E., Villa Stritch, Via della Nocetta, 63, 00164 Roma, Italy.

Absent on Leave:
Very Rev.—
Seitz, James J.
Revs.—
Klein, Eugene M.
Sutton, Brian F.

Retired:
Rev. Msgrs.—
Galles, Francis A., (Retired), Traditions of Preston, 608 Winona St., Preston, 55965
Hargesheimer, Thomas J., (Retired), 65460 142nd Ave., Wabasha, 55981
McCauley, James A., (Retired), P.O. Box 203, Brownsville, 55919
Meyer, Robert G., (Retired)
Very Revs.—
Russell, James D., (Retired), 202 B Alpine Ridge, Wabasha, 55981
Schmitz, Donald J., (Retired), 203 Alpine Ridge, Wabasha, 55981
Revs.—
Arnoldt, David L., (Retired), 6 Branford Pl., Augusta, GA 30904
Brandenhoff, Peter B., (Retired), 8859 Spring Ln., Woodbury, 55125
Breza, Paul J., (Retired), 102 Liberty St., 55987. Tel: 507-454-3431
Buryska, James F., (Retired), 2260 Riverside Ln. NE, Rochester, 55906
Collins, Charles I., (Retired), St. Patrick Church, 436 W. Main St., Le Roy, 55951-0310
Conway, Gerald W., (Retired), 7090 E. Mescal St., Apt. 233, Scottsdale, AZ 85254-6124
Dernek, Richard J., (Retired), 566 E. Third St., 55987
Fogal, Joseph B., (Retired), 1361 Adams St., Mankato, 56001
Haberman, Clayton J., (Retired), 5545 232nd St. W., Faribault, 55021
Hennessy, James W., (Retired), c/o Stan Hennessy, 36 Hodur Ct., Pleasant Hill, CA 94523
Herman, Robert D., (Retired), 1361 S. River Rd., Buffalo City, WI 54622
Jennings, Thomas J., (Retired), 707 N. Hokah St., Caledonia, 55921
Jewison, Harry P., (Retired), 1880 3rd Ave. NW, #317, Rochester, 55901
Kulas, William J., (Retired), 20582 W. Gale Ave., Galesville, WI 54630
Kunz, James H., (Retired), 1427 9th Ave. SE, Rochester, 55904
Loomis, Richard P., (Retired), c/o Laurie Bursiek, 19740 750th Ave., Grand Meadow, 55936
Lovas, Donald J., (Retired), 807 W. Mark St., 55987
Maher, Robert G., (Retired), 9505 Salem Hills Court, Las Vegas, NV 89134-4600
Mountain, Edward C., (Retired), 420 11th St., S.E., Owatonna, 55060-4008
Olsem, Andrew D., (Retired), 610 Reed St., Mankato, 56001
Pete, Joseph P., (Retired), 1302 NW 25th Ave., Faribault, 55021
Peterson, Steven J., (Retired), 6772 S Black Hills Way, Chandler, AZ 85249
Schaefer, Edgar J., (Retired), 9659 111th Ave. N, Sun City, AZ 85351
Schiltz, Roger J., (Retired), 1532 Glenrosa Dr., North Las Vegas, NV 89031-5548
Stamschror, Robert P., (Retired), 2480 Goodview Rd., 55987
Stenzel, Eugene F., (Retired), 60659 200th St., Wells, 56097
Surprenant, Paul W., (Retired), 701 Freedom Pl., Unit 1, Hartford, SD 57033
Traufler, John F., (Retired), 200 18th St. N.W., Austin, 55912
Trocinski, LaVern F., (Retired), 4916 Wildgrass Ln. NW, Rochester, 55901
Tupper, Dale E., (Retired), St. Augustine Church, 405 4th St. NW, Austin, 55912.

Permanent Deacons:
Aho, Richard, St. Edward, Austin; St. Augustine Austin
Behrends, Vernon, St. Mary, Worthington
DeRienzo, Thomas, (Retired), Diocese of Winona-Rochester
DeStazio, John, St. Joachim, Plainview; Immaculate Conception, Kellogg
Dose, David, St. Mary, Lake City; St. Patrick, West Albany
Doyle, Preston, Sacred Heart, Waseca
Ellis, Michael, Diocese of Winona-Rochester
Fagan, Patrick, St. Joseph, Owatonna
Fortini, Eduardo, Diocese of Winona-Rochester
Freetly, Gerald, St. John the Evangelist, Rochester
Fuller, Leonard L., (Retired), Diocese of Winona-Rochester
Green, Justin, Basilica of St. Stanislaus, Winona; St. John Nepomucene, Winona
Hust, John, St. Felix, Wabasha; St. Agnes, Kellogg
Kluczny, John, St. Edward, Austin; St. Augustine, Austin
Orlowski, Christopher, Pax Christi, Rochester; Ss. Peter & Paul, Mazeppa
Paul, Eugene, St. Casimir, Wells; Our Lady of Mt. Carmel, Easton; St. John the Baptist, Minnesota Lake
Quinn, Richard, (Retired), Diocese of Winona-Rochester
Trocinski, Gerald, (Retired), Diocese of Winona-Rochester
Walchuk, Christopher, St. Teresa, Mapleton; St. Joseph, Good Thunder; St. Matthew, Vernon Center
Weigel, Joseph, Holy Spirit, Rochester
Welch, James, Cathedral of the Sacred Heart, Winona; St. Casimir, Winona
Yerhot, Robert, Crucifixion, La Crescent; Holy Cross, Dakota
Zavala, Placido, St. Charles Borromeo, St. Charles; St. Aloysius, Elba; Holy Redeemer, Eyota.

INSTITUTIONS LOCATED IN DIOCESE

[A] SEMINARIES

WINONA. *Immaculate Heart of Mary Seminary*, 750 Terrace Hts., 55987-1320. Tel: 507-205-9237;
Fax: 507-474-7085; Email: info@ihmseminary.org; Web: www.ihmseminary.org. Very Rev. Robert S. Horihan, S.T.D. (Cand.), Rector; Revs. Martin T. Schaefer, Vice Rector & Dean Formation; Jeffrey L. Dobbs, Dir. Spiritual Life; Jason L. Kern, Vocations Dir. Affiliated with Saint Mary's University of MN. Religious Teachers 4; Lay Staff 1; Priests 4; Students 51.

MANKATO. *IVE Formation Program, Inc.*, 512 E. Mulberry St., Mankato, 56001. Tel: 507-387-2565; Email: javieribarra@ive.org; Web: iveminorseminary.com. Revs. Javier Ibarra, Rector; William Valle Pacheco, I.V.E., Dean of Studies. Seminarians 21.

[B] COLLEGES AND UNIVERSITIES

WINONA. *Saint Mary's University of Minnesota* (Coed) 700 Terrace Hts., 55987-1399. Tel: 507-457-1700;
Fax: 507-457-1722; Email: admission@smumn.edu; Web: www.smumn.edu. Rev. James Burns, Pres.; Ann Merchlewitz, Exec. Vice Pres. & Gen. Counsel; Bro. Robert Smith, Sen. Vice Pres Presidential Initiatives & Special Adviser to the President; James Bedtke, Vice Pres. Facilities; Audrey Kintzi, Vice Pres. Advancement & Communication; Benjamin Murray, Sen. Vice Pres. Finance & Operations; Tim Gossen, Vice Pres. Student Affairs & Student Life; Laura Oanes, Dir. Library. DeLaSalle Christian Brothers. Brothers 6; Religious Teachers 5; Priests 5; Sisters 1; Students 1,087; Lay Faculty 100.

[C] CENTRALIZED CATHOLIC SCHOOLS

WINONA. *Cotter High School & Junior High School*, (Grades 7-12), 1115 W. Broadway, 55987.
Tel: 507-453-5000; Fax: 507-453-5006; Email: info@cotterschools.org; Web: www.cotterschools.org. Sr. Judith Schaefer, O.P., Ph.D., Pres.; Mary Eileen Fitch, Prin.; David Forney, Prin.; Marisa Corcoran, Campus Min.; Pam Kimber, Business Mgr.; Mrs. Annmarie DeMarais, Office of Mission Advancement; Marie Barrientos, Dir. Res. Life; Mandi Olson, Intl. Admissions; Seth Haun, Athletic Dir. Lay Teachers 29; Students 344.
Winona Area Catholic Schools, (Grades PreK-6), 602 E. 5th St., 55987. Tel: 507-452-3766;
Fax: 507-454-1473; Email: pbowlin@wacs1.org; Web: www.wacs1.org. Patrick Bowlin, Prin. Religious Teachers 1; Lay Teachers 28; Students 472.
W.A.C.S. - St. Mary Educare, 1315 W. Broadway Ave., 55987. Tel: 507-452-2890; Fax: 507-452-2898; Email: cnichols@wacs1.org; Web: www.wacs1.org. Patrick Bowlin, Prin.; Christine Nichols, Prog. Dir. (Educare at 16 months) Lay Teachers 8; Students 129.

ROCHESTER. *Rochester Catholic Schools*, (Grades PreK-12), 2800 19th St. N.W., Rochester, 55901.
Tel: 507-218-3028; Tel: 507-289-1702; Email: jbarnick@rcsmn.org; Web: rcsmn.org. Haidee Todora, Dir. of Schools. Religious Teachers 1; Lay Teachers 119; Students 1,439.
St. Francis of Assisi School, (Grades PreK-8), 318 11th Ave. S.E., Rochester, 55904.
Tel: 507-288-4816; Fax: 507-288-4815; Email: stfinfo@rcsmn.org; Web: www.rcsmn.org. Mrs. Barb Plenge, Prin. Lay Teachers 21; Students 388.
St. John the Evangelist, (Grades 5-8), 424 W. Center St., Rochester, 55902. Tel: 507-282-5248;
Fax: 507-282-1343; Email: mlangsdale@rcsmn.org;

Web: www.rcsmn.org. Matt Langsdale, Prin. Lay Teachers 12; Students 162.

St. Pius X School, (Grades PreK-4), 1205 12th Ave. N.W., Rochester, 55901. Tel: 507-282-5161; Fax: 507-282-5107; Email: mlangsdale@rcsmn.org; Web: www.rcsmn.org. Matt Langsdale, Prin. Lay Teachers 27; Students 168.

Lourdes High School, (Grades 9-12), 2800 19th St. N.W., Rochester, 55901. Tel: 507-289-3991; Fax: 507-289-3991; Email: kjuliano@rcsmn.org. Karen Juliano, Prin.; Rita Hendrickson, Campus Min. Religious Teachers 1; Lay Teachers 42; Students 430.

Holy Spirit School, (Grades PreK-8), 5455 50th Ave., N.W., Rochester, 55901. Tel: 507-288-8818; Fax: 507-288-5155; Email: csmith@rcsmn.org; Web: www.rcsmn.org. Christopher Smith, Prin. Lay Teachers 17; Students 294.

ALBERT LEA. *St. Theodore School*, (Grades PreK-5), 323 E. Clark St., Albert Lea, 56007. Tel: 507-373-9657; Fax: 507-473-9653; Email: samundson@sttheoschool.org; Web: www.sttheo.org. Mrs. Susan Amundson, Prin.; Rev. Kurt P. Farrell, Apostolic Admin.
Legal Title: St. Theodore Elementary School Lay Teachers 7; Students 56.

AUSTIN. *Pacelli Catholic Schools*, (Grades PreK-12), 311 4th St. N.W., Austin, 55912. Tel: 507-437-3278 ; Email: admin@pacellischools.org; Web: www.pacellischools.org. Jean McDermott, Pres./Prin.; Laura Marreel, Dean of Students. Lay Teachers 17; Students 292.

MANKATO. *Loyola Catholic School* aka Mankato Area Catholic School, (Grades PreK-12), 145 Good Counsel Dr., Mankato, 56001-3146.
Tel: 507-388-0600; Fax: 507-388-3081; Email: abemmels@loyolacatholicschool.org; Web: loyolacatholicschool.org. Adam Bemmels, Prin.; Kevin Elton, Vice Prin. Lay Teachers 46; Sisters 1; Students 438.

OWATONNA. *St. Mary's School*, (Grades PreK-8), 730 South Cedar Ave., Owatonna, 55060.
Tel: 507-446-2300; Fax: 507-446-2304; Email: jswanson@stmarys-owatonna.org; Web: www.stmarys-owatonna.org. Jen Swanson, Prin.; Stacey Ginskey, Dean, Students; Sharleen Berg, Librarian. Lay Teachers 24; Students 371.

[D] GENERAL HOSPITALS

WABASHA. *Saint Elizabeth's Medical Center*, 1200 Grant Blvd., W., Wabasha, 55981.
Tel: 651-565-4531; Fax: 651-565-2482; Email: carmen.tiffany@ascension.org; Web: www.StElizabethsWabasha.org. Mr. Thomas Crowley, Pres.; John Wolfe, Business Mgr.
Ascension Wisconsin. Bed Capacity 25; Tot Asst. Annually 39,081; Total Staff 250.

[E] HOMES FOR AGED

WINONA. *Saint Anne of Winona*, 1347 W. Broadway, 55987. Tel: 507-454-3621; Fax: 507-452-2556; Email: jodi.barton@bhshealth.org; Web: saintanneofwinona.org. Jodi Barton, CEO & Admin. Subsidiary of Benedictine Health Systems, sponsored by the Sisters of St. Scholastica Monastery.

St. Anne of Winona Callista Court, 1455 W. Broadway, 55987. Tel: 507-457-0280;
Fax: 507-494-5117; Email: jodi.barton@bhshealth.org. Jodi Barton, Admin. Subsidiary of Benedictine Health Systems, sponsored by the Sisters of St. Scholastica Monastery.Assisted living for seniors. Residents 106; Total Staff 85; Resident Days 36,426; Units 105.

St. Anne of Winona Benedictine Adult Day Center, 1455 W. Broadway, 55987. Tel: 507-454-3621; Email: tammy.ross@bhshealth.org. Tammy Ross, Dir.; Jodi Barton, Admin. Guest Days 8,011.

St. Anne of Winona Extended Health Care, 1347 W. Broadway, 55987. Tel: 507-454-3621;
Fax: 507-452-2556; Email: jodi.barton@bhshealth.org. Jodi Barton, CEO & Admin.; Cheryl Nash, Dir. Nursing Svcs. Nursing care for the aged, chronically ill or rehab. Bed Capacity 109; Residents 89; Total Staff 184; Resident Days 32,072.

St. Anne of Winona Training Center, 902 E. Second St., 55987. Tel: 507-474-4980; Fax: 507-474-4981; Email: jodi.barton@bhshealth.org. Jodi Barton, Admin.; Kimberly Nahrgang, Contact Person.

ROCHESTER. *Madonna Meadows of Rochester*, 3035 Salem Meadows Dr., S.W., Rochester, 55902.
Tel: 507-252-5400; Email: christine.bakke@bhshealth.org. Ms. Christine Bakke, Admin. Benedictine Health System and Sisters of St. Scholastica Monastery.Assisted living facility. Bed Capacity 78; Guests 76; Total Staff 72.

Madonna Towers of Rochester, Inc., 4001 19th Ave., N.W., Rochester, 55901. Tel: 507-288-3911;
Fax: 507-288-0393; Email: christine.bakke@bhshealth.org. Ms. Christine Bakke, Admin. Independent, assisted and nursing care facility; T. Emil Gauthier Memory Care. Subsidiary of Benedictine Health System. Bed Capacity 62; Tot Asst. Annually 575; Total Staff 375; Apartments 122; Memory Care 16.

Madonna Living Community Foundation of Rochester, 4001 19th Ave., N.W., Rochester, 55901. Tel: 507-288-3911; Fax: 507-288-0393; Email: christine.bakke@bhshealth.org. Ms. Christine Bakke, Admin.

AUSTIN. *Sacred Heart Care Center, Inc.*, 1200 Twelfth St., S.W., Austin, 55912. Tel: 507-433-1808;
Fax: 507-434-9572; Email: rthalver@yahoo.com. Rebecca Mathews Halverson, Admin. Bed Capacity 59; Residents 56; Total Staff 153; Assisted Living Apartments (filled) 23; Adult Day Care (Client Days) 2,469; Alzheimer's Day Program (Client Days) 2,627; Home Health Care (Clients) 75.

WABASHA. *St. Elizabeth's Health Care Center*, 626 Shields Ave., Wabasha, 55981. Tel: 651-565-4581;
Fax: 651-565-3414; Email: carmen.tiffany@ascension.org; Web: www.stelizabethswabasha.org. 1200 Grant Blvd. W., Wabasha, 55981. Mr. Thomas Crowley, Admin. (Conducted in connection with St. Elizabeth's Medical Center.) Tot Asst. Annually 115; Total Staff 130; Skilled Beds 100; Admissions 74.

[F] MONASTERIES AND RESIDENCES OF PRIESTS AND BROTHERS

AUSTIN. *Annunciation Hermitage, Carmelites of St. Joseph*, 1009 Oakland Ave. E., Austin, 55912.
Tel: 507-437-4015; Email: annunciationhermitage@q.com. Rev. Jon H. Moore, O.Carm., Prior. Hermits 3.

[G] CONVENTS AND RESIDENCES FOR SISTERS

WINONA. *Immaculate Heart Convent, Religious Sisters of Mercy*, 700 Terrace Heights #63, 55987.
Tel: 507-474-6939; Email: immaculateheart@rsmofalma.org; Web: www.rsmofalma.org. Sr. Mara Lester, Supr. Sisters 5.

ROCHESTER. *St. Clare's Monastery*, 1001 14th St., N.W., Ste. 200, Rochester, 55901.
Tel: 507-282-7441; Email: hweier1950@outlook.com; Web: www.stclaresrochester.org. Sr. Helen Weier, O.S.C., Abbess. Franciscan Poor Clare Nuns. Sisters 11.

Sisters of St. Francis of the Third Order Regular of the Congregation of Our Lady of Lourdes, Assisi Heights Admin. Ctr., 1001 14th St., N.W., Ste. 100, Rochester, 55901-2511. Tel: 507-282-7441;
Fax: 507-282-7762; Email: elaine.frank@rochesterfranciscan.org; Web: www.rochesterfranciscan.org. Sr. Ramona Miller, O.S.F., Pres.
Academy of Our Lady of Lourdes Sisters 178; Sisters in Motherhouse 105.

HOUSTON. *Hermits of St. Mary of Carmel, (H.S.M.C.)* Carmelite Eremitical Community of Diocesan Right 33005 Stinson Ridge Rd., Houston, 55943-4033. Tel: 507-896-2125; Fax: 507-896-4349; Email: lhubka@dowr.org. Sr. Helen Lee, Prioress; Rev. David Wechter, O.C.S.O., J.C.L., Chap., Tel: 507-896-2125. Sisters 3.

MANKATO. *School Sisters of Notre Dame*, Convent of Our Lady of Good Counsel, 170 Good Counsel Dr., Mankato, 56001-3138. 320 Ripa Ave., St. Louis, MO 63125. Tel: 507-389-4200; Fax: 507-389-4125; Email: mhummert@ssndcp.org; Web: www.ssndmankato.org. Sr. Mary Anne Owens, Prov. Our Lady of Good Counsel Campus Staff 157; Sisters 128; Sisters in DOW-R 136.

[H] NEWMAN CENTERS

WINONA. *St. Thomas Aquinas Newman Center*, 475 Huff St., 55987. Tel: 507-452-2781; Email: newmanwsu@gmail.com; Web: www.winonanewman.org. Mr. Aaron Lofy, Dir.

[I] MISCELLANEOUS LISTINGS

WINONA. *Catholic Foundation of Southern Minnesota*, 750 Terrace Heights, Ste. 105, P.O. Box 30098, 55987. Tel: 507-858-1275; Fax: 507-454-8106; Email: mherman@catholicfsmn.org; Web: www.catholicfsmn.org. Mrs. Monica Herman, Exec. Dir.

Saint Mary's Press, Christian Brothers Publications, 702 Terrace Hts., 55987. Tel: 800-533-8095;
Tel: 507-457-7900; Fax: 800-344-9225; Email: smpress@smp.org; Email: cbittle@smp.org; Web: www.smp.org. Bro. Frank Carr, F.S.C., Dir. Mission; John M. Vitek, Pres. & CEO.

Catholic Schools Foundation of Winona, (Grades PreK-12), 1115 W. Broadway Ave., 55987.
Tel: 507-453-5055; Fax: 507-453-5055; Email: smcglaun@cotterschools.org; Web: www.csfwinona.org. Mike Hanson, Pres. Lay Teachers 56; Students 800.

ROCHESTER. *Diocese of Winona-Rochester Guild of the Catholic Medical Association*, 200 First St., S.W., Rochester, 55905. Tel: 507-266-3412; Fax: 507-266-1657; Email: lane.john@mayo.edu; Email: jaschirger@gmail.com. Dr. John I. Lane, M.D., Pres. A diocesan association of Catholic health care providers affiliated with the the national Catholic Medical Association.

**St. James Coffee*, 4156 18th Ave., N.W., Rochester, 55901. Tel: 507-281-3559; Email: info@stjamescoffee.com; Web: www.stjamescoffee.com. Margaret Mulligan, Contact Person; Zach Rawson, Contact Person; Sarah Gallenberg, Contact Person.

The Roman Catholic Pontifical Lay Association Memores Domini, 6006 Woodridge Ct., N.E., Rochester, 55906. Tel: 507-202-2017; Email: smodarelli@sj.org; Web: www.comunioneliberazione.org. Mr. Sebastian Modarelli, Head of House.

Seeds of Wisdom in South Sudan, 11 Fourth Ave., S.W., Rochester, 55902. Tel: 507-288-7372;
Fax: 507-288-7373; Email: info@sowsouthsudan.org; Web: www.sowsouthsudan.org. Steven Deick, Pres.

ALBERT LEA. *St. Theodore Catholic School Endowment*, 308 E. Fountain St., Albert Lea, 56007-2456.
Tel: 507-373-0603; Fax: 507-373-0604; Email: office@sttheo.org; Web: www.sttheo.org. Rev. Kurt P. Farrell, Contact Person.

RELIGIOUS INSTITUTES OF MEN REPRESENTED IN THE DIOCESE

For further details refer to the corresponding bracketed number in the Religious Institutes of Men or Women section.

[0330]—*Brothers of the Christian Schools*—F.S.C.
[0270]—*Carmelite Fathers and Brothers*—O.Carm.
[0340]—*Cistercian Fathers* (Abbey of Our Lady of New Melleray)—O.S.C.O.
[0685]—*Institute of the Incarnate Word*—I.V.E.
[0690]—*Jesuit Fathers and Brothers* (Wisconsin Province)—S.J.

RELIGIOUS INSTITUTES OF WOMEN REPRESENTED IN THE DIOCESE

[]—*Hermits of St. Mary of Carmel (Contemplative Community)*—H.S.M.C.
[3760]—*Order of St. Clare*—O.S.C.
[2519]—*Religious Sisters of Mercy of Alma, Michigan*—R.S.M.
[2970]—*School Sisters of Notre Dame*—S.S.N.D.
[1680]—*School Sisters of St. Francis*—O.S.F.
[]—*Servants of the Lord and the Virgin of Matara*—S.S.V.M.
[1070-03]—*Sinsinawa Dominican Sisters*—O.P.
[2575]—*Sisters of Mercy of the Americas*—R.S.M.
[1570]—*Sisters of St. Francis of the Holy Family*—O.S.F.
[3320]—*Sisters of the Presentation of the B.V.M.*—P.B.V.M.
[1720]—*Sisters of the Third Order Regular of St. Francis of the Congregation of Our Lady of Lourdes*—O.S.F.

DIOCESAN CEMETERIES

WINONA. *Catholic Cemeteries of Winona*, 55 W. Sanborn St., P.O. Box 588, 55987.
Tel: 507-858-1268; Fax: 507-454-8106; Email: ldose@dowr.org; Web: www.dowr.org/offices/catholic-cemeteries/catholic-cemeteries.html. Mr. Lawrence J. Dose, Dir. Catholic Cemeteries

INTER-PAROCHIAL CATHOLIC CEMETERIES

WINONA. *Saint Mary's Cemetery of Winona, MN*, 1333 Homer Rd., 55987. Tel: 507-452-2769;
Fax: 507-454-0023; Email: office@smcofwinona.org; Web: www.smcofwinona.org. Julie Koehler, Admin.

ROCHESTER. *Calvary Cemetery of Rochester, Minnesota*, 500 11th Ave., N.E., Rochester, 55906. 1700 N. Broadway, Ste. 154, Rochester, 55906. Cell: 507-273-0140; Email: calvarydirector@gmail.com; Web: calvarycemeteryrochester.wordpress.com. Steven Flynn, Dir.

AUSTIN. *Calvary Cemetery*, 1803 4th Ave. S.W., Austin, 55912. Catholic Parishes of Austin, MN, 1001 E. Oakland Ave., Austin, 55912. Tel: 507-433-1707;
Tel: 507-433-1888; Email: bookkeeping@queenofangels.church. Richard Fischer, Chm.; Very Rev. Raul I. Silva, Dir.; Rev. James P. Steffes, Dir.

MANKATO. *Calvary Cemetery Association*, 200 Goodyear Ave., Mankato, 56001. P.O. Box 4143, Mankato, 56002. Tel: 507-995-1010; Email: calvarymankato@gmail.com; Web: calvarymankato.wordpress.com. Rev. Timothy Reker, Canonical Admin.; Terry Miller, Supt.

OWATONNA. *Sacred Heart Cemetery*, 2150 S. Cedar Ave., Owatonna, 55060-3399. c/o St. Joseph Church, 512 S. Elm Ave., Owatonna, 55060-3399. Tel: 507-451-4845; Email: iketen@charter.net. Rev. John M. Sauer, S.T.L.

NECROLOGY

† Mountain, Joseph W., (Retired), Died Mar. 14, 2019

† Schmitz, Donald Peter, (Retired), Died May. 2, 2018
† Engels, Richard Joseph, (Retired), Died Oct. 28, 2018
† LaPlante, Joseph Allen, (Retired), Died Jan. 20, 2019
† Verdick, Jerome Francis, (Retired), Died Jan. 13, 2019

An asterisk (*) denotes an organization that has established tax-exempt status directly with the IRS and is not covered by the USCCB Group Ruling.

Diocese of Worcester

(Dioecesis Wigorniensis)

Most Reverend

ROBERT J. MCMANUS

Bishop of Worcester; ordained May 27, 1978; appointed Auxiliary Bishop of Providence and Titular Bishop of Allegheny December 1, 1998; consecrated February 22, 1999; appointed Bishop of Worcester March 9, 2004; installed May 14, 2004. *Chancery Office: 49 Elm St., Worcester, MA 01609.*

Most Reverend

DANIEL P. REILLY, D.D.

Retired Bishop of Worcester; ordained May 30, 1953; appointed Bishop of Norwich June 17, 1975; consecrated August 6, 1975; appointed Bishop of Worcester October 27, 1994; installed December 8, 1994; retired March 9, 2004. *Res.: St. Paul Cathedral, 38 High St., Worcester, MA 01609.*

CHRISTUS VERITATIS SPLENDOR

ESTABLISHED JANUARY 14, 1950.

Square Miles 1,532.

Comprises the County of Worcester in the State of Massachusetts.

For legal titles of parishes and diocesan institutions, consult the Chancery Office.

Chancery Office: 49 Elm St., Worcester, MA 01609. Tel: 508-791-7171; Fax: 508-754-2768.

Web: www.worcesterdiocese.org

STATISTICAL OVERVIEW

Personnel	
Bishop	1
Retired Bishops	1
Abbots	3
Priests: Diocesan Active in Diocese	119
Priests: Diocesan Active Outside Diocese	5
Priests: Retired, Sick or Absent	51
Number of Diocesan Priests	175
Religious Priests in Diocese	83
Total Priests in Diocese	258
Extern Priests in Diocese	2
Ordinations:	
Diocesan Priests	3
Transitional Deacons	2
Total Brothers	46
Parishes	
Parishes	96
With Resident Pastor:	
Resident Diocesan Priests	88
Resident Religious Priests	2
Without Resident Pastor:	
Administered by Priests	6
Missions	3
Pastoral Centers	2
Professional Ministry Personnel:	
Brothers	1
Sisters	17
Lay Ministers	97
Welfare	
Catholic Hospitals	1
Total Assisted	249,000
Health Care Centers	3
Homes for the Aged	3
Total Assisted	268
Day Care Centers	2
Total Assisted	1,675
Specialized Homes	3
Total Assisted	95
Special Centers for Social Services	6
Total Assisted	59,335
Other Institutions	1
Total Assisted	28
Educational	
Diocesan Students in Other Seminaries	24
Total Seminarians	24
Colleges and Universities	3
Total Students	8,863
High Schools, Diocesan and Parish	4
Total Students	1,137
High Schools, Private	5
Total Students	1,191
Elementary Schools, Diocesan and Parish	15
Total Students	3,145
Elementary Schools, Private	5
Total Students	443
Catechesis/Religious Education:	
High School Students	3,821
Elementary Students	10,985
Total Students under Catholic Instruction	29,609
Teachers in the Diocese:	
Priests	19
Sisters	18
Lay Teachers	1,236
Vital Statistics	
Receptions into the Church:	
Infant Baptism Totals	1,931
Minor Baptism Totals	144
Adult Baptism Totals	121
Received into Full Communion	198
First Communions	2,128
Confirmations	1,974
Marriages:	
Catholic	355
Interfaith	51
Total Marriages	406
Deaths	2,986
Total Catholic Population	279,749
Total Population	809,106

Former Bishops—His Eminence JOHN CARDINAL WRIGHT, D.D., S.T.D., ord. Dec. 8, 1935; appt. Titular Bishop of Aegea and Auxiliary Bishop of Boston, May 10, 1947; cons. June 30, 1947; transferred to new See of Worcester, Jan. 14, 1950; enthroned March 7, 1950; appt. Bishop of Pittsburgh, Jan. 28, 1959; created Cardinal, April 28, 1969; transferred to the Roman Curia Prefect, Sacred Congregation for the Clergy; died Aug. 10, 1979; Most Revs. BERNARD J. FLANAGAN, D.D., J.C.D., retired March 31, 1983; died Jan. 28, 1998; TIMOTHY J. HARRINGTON, D.D., retired Oct. 27, 1994; died March 23, 1997; DANIEL P. REILLY, D.D., ord. May 30, 1953; appt. Bishop of Norwich June 17, 1975; cons. Aug. 6, 1975; appt. Bishop of Worcester Oct. 27, 1994; installed Dec. 8, 1994; retired March 9, 2004.

Vicar General & Moderator of the Curia—Rev. RICHARD F. REIDY, J.C.L., Tel: 508-929-4346; Email: rreidy@worcesterdiocese.org.

Chancery Office—MR. RAYMOND L. DELISLE, Chancellor, 49 Elm St., Worcester, 01609. Tel: 508-929-4313; Email: rdelisle@worcesterdiocese.org.

Diocesan Director of Fiscal Affairs—MR. PAUL G. SCHASEL.

Director of Catholic Relief Services—Rev. RICHARD F. REIDY, J.C.L., 49 Elm St., Worcester, 01609.

Diocesan Expansion Fund—Rev. RICHARD F. REIDY, J.C.L.; MR. PETER J. DAWSON, 49 Elm St., Worcester, 01609.

Diocesan Finance Committee—MR. RICHARD FOURNIER, Chair.

Diocesan Tribunal—Address all communications to, 49 Elm St., Worcester, 01609. Tel: 508-791-7171.

Judicial Vicar and Vicar for Canonical Affairs—Rev. Msgr. F. STEPHEN PEDONE, J.C.L., 49 Elm St., Worcester, 01609.

Associate Judicial Vicar—Rev. PAUL T. O'CONNELL, J.C.D.

Judges—Rev. PAUL T. O'CONNELL, J.C.D.; Rev. Msgr. F. STEPHEN PEDONE, J.C.L.; Rev. DAVID W. MASELLO, J.C.L.

Promoter of Justice—Sr. MARY LOU WALSH, S.N.D., J.C.L.

Psychologist—KATHLEEN KELLEY, Ph.D.

Secretary to the Tribunal—EILEEN CHARBONNEAU.

Defenders of the Bond—Rev. Msgr. ANTHONY S. CZARNECKI, J.C.L.; Revs. RICHARD F. REIDY, J.C.L.; JUAN DAVID ECHAVARRIA.

Advocates—Revs. GEORGE J. RIDICK; MICHAEL A. DIGERONIMO; WILLIAM F. SANDERS; TERENCE T. KILCOYNE, D.Min.

Notary—EILEEN CHARBONNEAU, Address all requests for dispensations to:, Diocesan Tribunal, 49 Elm St., Worcester, 01609.

Diocesan College of Consultors—Rev. Msgr. THOMAS J. SULLIVAN; Revs. H. EDWARD CHALMERS; JOSEPH M. NALLY; RICHARD F. REIDY, J.C.L.; JOSE A. RODRIGUEZ; BRIAN P. O'TOOLE; Rev. Msgrs. F. STEPHEN PEDONE, J.C.L.; FRANCIS J. SCOLLEN.

Deans—Rev. Msgr. FRANCIS J. SCOLLEN, Area I; Rev. STEVEN M. LABAIRE, Area II; Rev. Msgr. THOMAS J. SULLIVAN, Area III; Revs. DAVID E. DOIRON, Area IV; MICHAEL A. DIGERONIMO, Area V; JOHN J. FOLEY, Area VI; WILLIAM F. SANDERS, Area VII; THOMAS LANDRY, Area VIII; JAMES B. CALLAHAN, Area IX; ROBERT D. BRUSO, Area X; EDWIN MONTANA, Area XI; PAUL T. O'CONNELL, J.C.D., Area XII.

Director of Priest Personnel—Rev. WALTER J. RILEY.

Diocesan Offices and Directors

The Adopt-A-Student Endowment Trust—ROBERT PAPE, 49 Elm St., Worcester, 01609. Tel: 508-791-7171.

African Ministry—49 Elm St., Worcester, 01609.

Tel: 508-791-7171. Rev. ENOCH KYEREMATENG, Chap.

Haitian Apostolate—Sr. JUDITH DUPUY, S.S.A., Dir., Tel: 508-929-4328.

Vietnamese Ministry—Our Lady of Vilna, Worcester, 01610. Tel: 508-752-1825. Rev. TAM M. BUI.

Brazilian Ministry—Rev. ADRIANO LESSA NATALINO, C.Ss.R., Office: 41 Hamilton St., Worcester, 01604. Tel: 508-752-6364.

European Ministries—

Lithuanian Churches—St. John, Worcester. VACANT.

Polish Ministry—St. Joseph, Webster, 01570. Tel: 508-943-0467. Rev. Msgr. ANTHONY S. CZARNECKI, J.C.L., Natl. Delegate, St. Joseph Basilica, Webster; Our Lady Czestochowa, Worcester; St. Andrew Bobola, Dudley.

Portuguese Ministry—St. Mary, Milford, 01757. Tel: 508-473-2000. Rev. MATEUS SOUZA.

Hispanic Ministry—Deacon FRANKLIN LIZARDO, Dir.

St. Paul—19 Chatham St., Worcester, 01609. Tel: 508-754-3195. Rev. ANGEL R. MATOS; Sr. MARIA DALLARI, X.M.M.; Deacons ISRAEL FERNANDEZ; FRANCISCO ESCOBAR; Sr. VERONICA PAREDES, X.M.M.

St. Peter—929 Main St., Worcester, 01610. Tel: 508-752-4674. Deacon GEORGE ESTREMERA.

St. Joan of Arc—570 Lincoln St., Worcester, 01605. Tel: 508-852-3232. Rev. NELSON RIVERA; Sr. ANDREA AVELLANEDA, R.O.D.A.

Our Lady of Providence—7 Auburn St., Worcester, 01605. Tel: 508-755-3820. Rev. WILLIAM E. REISER, S.J.; Sr. SUSANA MIRANDA, X.M.M.

St. John—149 Chestnut St., Clinton, 01510. Tel: 978-368-0366. Rev. HENRY RAMIREZ.

St. Joseph—46 Woodland St., Fitchburg, 01420. VACANT.

St. Francis—63 Sheridan St., Fitchburg, 01420. Tel: 978-342-9651. Rev. EMERITO ORTIZ; YESENIA QUINONES.

Annunciation Parish—135 Nichols St., Gardner, 01440. Rev. WILMAR RAMOS.

Holy Trinity—69 Lincoln Terr., Leominster, 01453. Tel: 978-534-5258. Chaplain: Rev. JOSE A. RODRIGUEZ.

St. Mary—27 Pearl St., Milford, 01757. Tel: 508-473-2000. Revs. PETER JOYCE; MATEUS SOUZA.

St. Mary—263 Hamilton St., Southbridge, 01550. Tel: 508-765-0394. Rev. JUAN G. HERRERA; Sr. ROSITA CAMPOS, R.O.D.A.; Deacon TEODORO CAMACHO.

St. Louis—15 Lake St., Webster, 01570. Tel: 508-943-0240. Rev. DARIO ACEVEDO; MS. NOELIA RIVERA.

St. Luke—70 W. Main St., Westborough, 01581. Tel: 508-366-5502. Rev. WILLIAM E. REISER, S.J.; Sr. IRMA GARCIA, R.O.D.A.

Black Catholics: African American—St. Peter, 929 Main St., Worcester, 01610. Tel: 508-752-4674. Rev. Msgr. FRANCIS J. SCOLLEN, Contact Person.

Catholic Charities—10 Hammond St., Worcester, 01609. Tel: 508-798-0191. MR. TIMOTHY MCMAHON, Exec. Dir.

Refugee Apostolate—Urban Missionaries of Our Lady of Hope, 242 Canterbury St., Worcester, 01603. Tel: 508-831-7455. Deacon WALTER F. DOYLE.

Apostleship of Prayer and Eucharistic Crusade—VACANT.

Archivist—MR. RAYMOND L. DELISLE, Chancellor, 49 Elm St., Worcester, 01609. Tel: 508-929-4346.

The Annual Partners in Charity Appeal—MR. MICHAEL GILLESPIE, 49 Elm St., Worcester, 01609. Tel: 508-929-4346.

Diocesan Building Commission Members—Rev. RICHARD F. REIDY, J.C.L.; Rev. Msgr. ROBERT K. JOHNSON; Revs. JOHN FOLEY, Chm.; CHARLES F. MONROE; MR. JORDAN O'CONNOR; MR. JOHN LAURING; MR. RICHARD BREAGY, Staff; MR. ROBERT JOHNSON; MR. KEVIN SEAMAN.

Campus Ministry—VACANT.

Catholic Charities—10 Hammond St., Worcester, 01610-1513. Tel: 508-798-0191. MR. TIMOTHY MCMAHON, Exec. Dir. (Refer to separate listings for detailed information on Catholic Charities and related organizations).

Diocesan Cemeteries Office—260 Cambridge St., Worcester, 01603. Tel: 508-757-7415. MR. ROBERT ACKERMAN, Dir.

Charismatic Renewal, Office of—Sr. CATHERINE MARIE WALSH, R.S.M., Liaison, 72 Birmingham Ct., Milford, 01757. Tel: 508-381-0987; Email: ccmwalsh@yahoo.com.

Clergy Benefit Plan—Revs. H. EDWARD CHALMERS, Pres.; EDWARD D. NICCOLLS, Treas.; LYNNE BRISSETTE, Admin., Tel: 508-832-8623; Email: lynne@clergybenefitplan.org.

Communication Office—MR. RAYMOND L. DELISLE, Dir., 49 Elm St., Worcester, 01609. Tel: 508-929-4313; MR. STEPHEN KAUFMAN, TV Ministry Production Mgr., Tel: 508-791-2039.

Office of Ongoing Priestly Formation—Rev. RONALD FALCO, Dir., 266 Main St., Northborough, 01532. Tel: 508-393-2223.

Cursillo—Rev. ROBERT A. GRATTAROTI, Dir., Mailing Address: P.O. Box 338, Charlton City, 01508. Tel: 508-248-7862.

Stewardship and Development Office—The Annual Partners in Charity Appeal. MR. MICHAEL GILLESPIE, Dir., Tel: 508-929-4368.

Diocesan Expansion Fund—49 Elm St., Worcester, 01609. Rev. RICHARD F. REIDY, J.C.L. Members: Rev. Msgr. JOHN E. DORAN, (Retired); Rev. RICHARD A. JAKUBAUSKAS; MR. TERRENCE SULLIVAN; MR. PAUL G. SCHASEL, Staff; MARTIN CONNORS JR.; JOHN GRAHAM; MR. PETER J. DAWSON, Chm.; WILLIAM JONES.

Diocesan Scouts—Boy Scout Office/Girl Scout Office, 49 Elm St., Worcester, 01609. Tel: 508-791-7171. Deacon WILLIAM WHITE, Liaison.

Ecumenical and Interreligious Affairs, Diocesan Office for—VACANT.

Evangelization, Office of—VACANT, 49 Elm St., Worcester, 01609.

Office of Marriage and Family—ALLISON LEDOUX, Dir., 49 Elm St., Worcester, 01609. Tel: 508-929-4311.

Finance Office—49 Elm St., Worcester, 01609. Tel: 508-791-7171. MR. PAUL G. SCHASEL, Dir.

Haitian Apostolate of the Diocese of Worcester—Sr. JUDITH DUPUY, S.S.A., Dir., 49 Elm St., Worcester, 01609. Tel: 508-929-4328; Fax: 508-753-7180; Email: sjudith41@yahoo.com.

Holy Childhood Association—VACANT.

Holy Name of Jesus House of Studies—51 Illinois St., Worcester, 01610. Rev. JAMES S. MAZZONE, Dir. Vocations.

Newspaper—The Catholic Free Press MRS. MARGARET M. RUSSELL, Exec. Editor, 49 Elm St., Worcester, 01609. Tel: 508-757-6387.

Office for Divine Worship—Rev. Msgr. JAMES P. MORONEY, Interim Dir.; ELIZABETH MARCIL, 19 Chatham St., Worcester, 01609. Tel: 508-798-0417.

Permanent Diaconate—49 Elm St., Worcester, 01609. Tel: 508-929-4332. Deacon WILLIAM A. BILOW JR., Dir.

Presbyteral Council—Most Rev. ROBERT J. MCMANUS, Pres.; Rev. RICHARD F. REIDY, J.C.L., Ex Officio; Rev. Msgrs. F. STEPHEN PEDONE, J.C.L., Ex Officio; THOMAS J. SULLIVAN; FRANCIS J. SCOLLEN; Revs. EDWIN MONTANA; JAMES B. CALLAHAN; WILLIAM F. SANDERS; THOMAS LANDRY; ROBERT D. BRUSO; MICHAEL A. DIGERONIMO; STEVEN M. LABAIRE; PAUL T. O'CONNELL, J.C.D.; JOHN J. FOLEY; DAVID E. DOIRON, 49 Elm St., Worcester, 01609. Tel: 508-791-7171.

Priests' Personnel Board—Rev. WALTER J. RILEY, 353 Grove St., Worcester, 01605.

Ministry to Retired Priests—Sr. MARY ANN BARTELL, C.S.E., 188 Old Worcester Rd., Charlton, 01507. Tel: 508-868-9239.

Respect Life—ALLISON LEDOUX, 49 Elm St., Worcester, 01609. Tel: 508-791-7171.

Propagation of the Faith49 Elm St., Worcester, 01609. Tel: 508-791-7171. Rev. DENNIS J. O'BRIEN.

Religious Education Office—ELIZABETH MARCIL, Dir., 49 Elm St., Worcester, 01609. Tel: 508-929-4303.

St. Paul Catholic Schools Consortium—49 Elm St., Worcester, 01609. Tel: 508-929-4317; Fax: 508-929-4386. MRS. PATRICIA M. HALPIN, Chair.

School Department—DR. DAVID PERDA, Supt.; MR. WILLIAM J. MULFORD, Assoc. Supt.

Diocesan Hispanic Apostolate—Deacon FRANKLIN LIZARDO, 38 High St., Worcester, 01609.

St. Vincent dePaul Society—Central District Council NORMAN CAISSIE, Pres.

Northern Worcester County District Council—PHILIP COLEMAN.

Central Worcester County District Council—NORMAN CAISSIE, Pres.

South Worcester County District Council—MARIE BASTONE, Pres.

Tri-Conference Retirement Fund for Religious—MR. MICHAEL GILLESPIE, Diocesan Coord., 49 Elm St., Worcester, 01609. Tel: 508-791-7171.

Director of Priest Personnel—Rev. WALTER J. RILEY, 353 Grove St., Worcester, 01605.

Episcopal Liaison to Religious—49 Elm St., Worcester, 01609. Sr. PAULA KELLEHER, S.S.J., Interim Liaison.

Vietnamese Apostolate—Rev. TAM M. BUI, 153 Sterling St., Worcester, 01610. Tel: 508-752-1825.

Victim Assistance Coordinator—MRS. JUDITH AUDETTE, Tel: 508-929-4363; Email: jaudette@worcesterdiocese.org.

Vocation Office—Rev. JAMES S. MAZZONE, Dir., 51 Illinois St., Worcester, 01610. Tel: 508-799-2792.

Minister to Priests—Mailing Address: 33 Massasoit Rd., Worcester, 01604. Rev. DENNIS J. O'BRIEN.

Worcester Diocesan Commission for Women—ELAINE FORD.

New Evangelization Worcester for Youth and Young Adults—Tel: 508-929-4360. MR. TIM MESSENGER, Dir.

CLERGY, PARISHES, MISSIONS AND PAROCHIAL SCHOOLS

CITY OF WORCESTER

(WORCESTER COUNTY)

1—ST. PAUL CATHEDRAL (1866)
38 High St., 01609. Tel: 508-799-4193; Fax: 508-752-6308; Email: cathedralofsaintpaul@gmail.com; Web: www.cathedralofsaintpaul.com. 15 Chatham St., 01609. Rev. Msgr. Robert K. Johnson, Rector; Rev. Angel R. Matos; Deacons Francisco Escobar; Franklin Lizardo; Colin Novick; Anthony J. Xatse.
Catechesis Religious Program—19 Chatham St., 01609. Tel: 508-755-1414; Email: rel.edu.stpaulcathedral@gmail.com. Students 272.

2—ST. ANDREW THE APOSTLE (1954) Now a mission of St. Peter, Worcester.
5 Spaulding St., 01603. Tel: 508-752-4647; Email: stpeters_standrewsparishes@verizon.net. 931 Main St., 01610. Rev. Msgr. Francis J. Scollen, Pastor.

3—ASCENSION (1911) Closed. For inquiries for parish records, please see St. John's, Worcester.

4—ST. BERNARD (1916) Closed. Merged with Our Lady of Fatima, Worcester to form Our Lady of Providence, Worcester.

5—BLESSED SACRAMENT (1912)
551 Pleasant St., 01602. Tel: 508-755-5291; Fax: 508-755-6891; Email: blessedsacrament@charter.net. Rev. Richard F. Trainor.
Catechesis Religious Program—Epiphany House, Tel: 508-752-4368. Students 72.

6—ST. CASIMIR (1894) (Lithuanian), Closed. For inquiries for parish records contact St. John, Worcester.

7—ST. CATHERINE OF SWEDEN (1952) Merged with Sacred Heart of Jesus, Worcester to form Sacred Heart of Jesus-St. Catherine of Sweden, Worcester.

8—ST. CHARLES BORROMEO (1954) Closed. For inquiries for parish records please see Blessed Sacrament, Worcester.

9—CHRIST THE KING (1936)
1052 Pleasant St., 01602. Tel: 508-754-5361; Fax: 508-753-0448; Email: tsullivan5@mac.com; Web: ctkworc.org. Rev. Msgr. Thomas J. Sullivan; Deacons Joseph M. Baniukiewicz; Michael Chase. In Res., Rev. Richard F. Reidy, J.C.L.
Catechesis Religious Program—Sr. Ellen Guerin, R.S.M., D.R.E. Students 202.

10—ST. CHRISTOPHER (1956)
950 W. Boylston St., 01606. Tel: 508-853-1492; Fax: 508-853-4338; Email: parish@stchristopherparishworcester.org; Web: www.stchristopherworcester.org. Rev. Stanley F. Krutcik; Deacon John F. LeDoux.
Catechesis Religious Program—Tel: 508-853-3302; Email: religioused@stchristopherparishworcester.org. Diane Dadah, D.R.E. Students 58.

11—ST. GEORGE (1951)
40 Brattle St., 01606. Tel: 508-853-0183; Fax: 508-854-0864; Email: stgeooffice@gmail.com. Revs. Edward D. Niccolls; Charles Omolo; Deacon Paul T. Audette.
Catechesis Religious Program—Tel: 508-852-1784. Sarah Kelly, Rel. Ed. Admin. Students 258.

12—HOLY FAMILY PARISH (2008)
41 Hamilton St., 01604. Tel: 508-754-6722; Email: ndsj@holyfamilyparishworcester.org. 20 Hamilton St., 01604. Revs. Steven M. Labaire; Adriano Lessa Natalino, C.Ss.R.
St. Joseph Church: 35 Hamilton St., 01604.
Catechesis Religious Program—Mary Sanning, D.R.E. Students 100.

13—HOLY NAME OF JESUS (1893) (French), Closed. For inquiries for parish records, please see Holy Family, Worcester.

14—IMMACULATE CONCEPTION (1873)
353 Grove St., 01605. Tel: 508-754-8419; Email: icworc@live.com. Rev. Walter J. Riley.

Catechesis Religious Program—Father Connors Center, Tel: 508-791-5887; Fax: 508-754-8508; Web: www.icworc.com. Students 66.

15—ST. JOAN OF ARC (1950)
570 Lincoln St., 01605. Tel: 508-852-3232; Fax: 508-852-3223; Email: stjoan570@hotmail.com. Revs. Nelson Rivera; Andres A. Araque; Sisters Francisca Candelaria, R.O.D.A., Pastoral Assoc.; Ines Almeida, R.O.D.A., Pastoral Assoc.
Catechesis Religious Program—Sr. Francisca Candelaria, R.O.D.A., C.R.E. Students 111.

16—ST. JOHN'S (1834)
44 Temple St., 01604. Tel: 508-756-7165; Fax: 508-754-5153; Email: stjohnsworc@gmail.com. Rev. John F. Madden; Deacons Paul Dacri; Van X. Nguyen.
Catechesis Religious Program—Mrs. Donna Mastrovito, C.R.E.; Dianne Gustowski, C.R.E. Students 145.

17—ST. MARGARET MARY (1922) Closed. For inquiries for parish records, please see St. Anne, Shrewsbury.

18—NOTRE DAME DES CANADIENS - ST. JOSEPH (1869) [CEM] (French), Closed. For inquiries for parish records please see Holy Family, Worcester.

19—OUR LADY OF CZESTOCHOWA (1903) (Polish)
34 Ward St., 01610. Tel: 508-755-5959; Fax: 508-767-1644; Email: rectory@olcworcester.com; Web: www.olcworcester.com. Revs. Ryszard Polek; Tomasz Gora. In Res., Rev. Edward Michalski.
School—St. Mary's Schools, (Grades PreK-12), 50 Richland St., 01610. Tel: 508-753-1170; Email: acormier@stmaryshigh.org; Web: www.stmarysworcester.org.
Catechesis Religious Program—Students 100.

20—OUR LADY OF FATIMA (1952) (Spanish), Closed. Merged with St. Bernard, Worcester to form Our Lady of Providence, Worcester.

21—OUR LADY OF LORETO (1966)
37 Massasoit Rd., 01604. Tel: 508-753-5001; Fax: 508-754-1537; Email: lisaolmc@gmail.com. Rev. Msgr. F. Stephen Pedone, J.C.L.; Deacons Gerald M. Montiverdi; John Barton.
Res.: 33 Massasoit Rd., 01604.
Catechesis Religious Program—Students 20.

22—OUR LADY OF LOURDES (1949)
1290 Grafton St., 01604. Tel: 508-757-0789; Fax: 508-757-0048; Email: ladyoflourdes1290@gmail.com; Web: ololma.org. Rev. Brian P. O'Toole. In Res., Revs. Francis J. Roach; Robert E. Kelley, (Retired).

23—OUR LADY OF MT. CARMEL AND ST. ANN (1872) (Italian—Irish), Merged with Our Lady of Loreto, Worcester.

24—OUR LADY OF PROVIDENCE PARISH dba St. Bernard's Church
236 Lincoln St., 01605. Tel: 508-755-3820; Email: parish@olpworcester.org; Web: www.olpworcester.org. Rev. Jonathan J. Slavinskas.
St. Bernard Church: 228 Lincoln St., 01605.
Catechesis Religious Program—Email: religioused@olpworcester.org. Sr. Susi Miranda, D.R.E. Students 68.

25—OUR LADY OF THE ANGELS (1916)
1222 Main St., 01603. Tel: 508-791-0951; Fax: 508-753-9531; Email: sallard@ourladyofangels.org; Email: cmonroe@ourladyofangels.org; Email: kbarrowsola@aol.com. Rev. Charles F. Monroe. In Res., Rev. Terrence Dougherty, O.C.D.
School—Our Lady of the Angels School, (Grades PreK-8), 1220 Main St., Rear, 01603. Tel: 508-752-5609; Fax: 508-798-9634; Email: doreen.albert@worcesterdiocesek12.org; Web: www.ourladyoftheangels.us. Doreen J. Albert, Prin. Lay Teachers 15; Students 190.
Catechesis Religious Program—Darleen Farland, D.R.E. Students 140.

26—OUR LADY OF THE ROSARY (1911)
23 Fales St., 01606. Tel: 508-853-1640; Fax: 508-853-2426; Email: olrparish1@gmail.com. Rev. Patrick J. Hawthorne.
Catechesis Religious Program—Father Riley Center, Tel: 508-852-5474; Email: olrparishreled@aol.com. Sr. Irene Moran, M.P.V., C.R.E. Students 152.

27—OUR LADY OF VILNA (1925) (Lithuanian—Vietnamese)
153 Sterling St., Ste. 2, 01610. Tel: 508-752-1825; Email: chatambui@yahoo.com. 151 Sterling St., 01610. Rev. Peter Tam Bui. In Res., Rev. Son Anh Nguyen.
Catechesis Religious Program—Students 180.

28—ST. PETER (1884)
929 Main St., 01610. Tel: 508-752-4674; Fax: 508-767-1511; Email: stpeters_standrewsparishes@verizon.net; Web: stpeters-standrews.com. 931 Main St., 01610. Rev. Msgr. Francis J. Scollen; Deacons Robert F. Dio; Peter Quy Nguyen; George Estremera.
Catechesis Religious Program—Tel: 508-752-0797. Students 165.
Mission—St. Andrew the Apostle Mission, Spaulding St., 01603.

29—SACRED HEART OF JESUS-ST. CATHERINE OF SWEDEN (1880)
596 Cambridge St., 01610. Tel: 508-752-1608; Tel: 508-753-2555; Fax: 508-757-2462; Email: lynn.sacredheart@verizon.net; Web: shscparish.com. Rev. Eric K. Asante, Admin.
Catechesis Religious Program—Judy Keenan, D.R.E. Students 24.

30—ST. STEPHEN'S (1887)
16 Hamilton St., 01604. Tel: 508-755-3165; Fax: 508-755-0937; Email: ststephenchurch2@verizon.net. Rev. Steven M. Labaire; Deacon Bruce Vidito Sr.
School—St. Stephen's School, (Grades PreK-8), 355 Grafton St., 01604. Tel: 508-755-3209; Fax: 508-770-1052; Email: sssoffice@worcesterdiocesek12.org; Web: www.st-stephen.net. Joanne Mallozzi, Prin. Lay Teachers 16; Students 183.
Catechesis Religious Program—Deborah Blicharz, D.R.E., Email: deborahblicharz@gmail.com. Students 9.

OUTSIDE THE CITY OF WORCESTER
(In the County of Worcester)

ASHBURNHAM, ST. DENIS (1951) [CEM] 85 Main St., Ashburnham, 01430. Tel: 978-827-5806; Email: stdenis@comcast.net. Rev. Guillermo J. Ochoa, Admin.; Deacon Richard DesJardins.
Catechesis Religious Program—
Tel: 978-827-4892; Email: StDenisRE@comcast.net. Kim Brown, D.R.E. Students 121.

ATHOL
1—ST. FRANCIS (1912) (Lithuanian) Mailing Address: 192 School St., Athol, 01331. Tel: 978-249-2738. 101 Main St., Athol, 01331. Rev. Edwin Montana; Deacon Scott Colley.
Church: 105 Main St., Athol, 01331.
Catechesis Religious Program— Included in Our Lady Immaculate.
2—OUR LADY IMMACULATE (1882) 192 School St., Athol, 01331-2399. Tel: 978-249-2738; Email: ourladyrectory@hotmail.com. Rev. Edwin Montana; Deacon Bryan A. Lagimoniere.
Catechesis Religious Program—
Tel: 978-249-7690; Fax: 978-249-7639. Sharon Maher, Admin. Students 99.
Mission—Our Lady Queen of Heaven, (Closed) Rte. 68, South Royalston, Worcester Co. 01368. Tel: 978-249-4103.

AUBURN
1—ST. JOSEPH'S (1907) 194 Oxford St. N., Auburn, 01501. Tel: 508-832-2074; Fax: 508-832-8894; Email: stjoes01501@gmail.com. Rev. Paul M. Bomba.
Catechesis Religious Program—
68 Central St., Auburn, 01501. Tel: 508-832-6683; Email: stjoesreledaub@gmail.com. Lisa Wass, D.R.E. Students 155.
2—NORTH AMERICAN MARTYRS (1952) 8 Wyoma Dr., Auburn, 01501. Tel: 508-798-8779; Fax: 508-791-6614; Email: namartyrs01501@gmail.com. Rev. John F. Gee.
Catechesis Religious Program—
Tel: 508-798-0612; Fax: 508-798-0612; Email: namparish@namparish.com. Joan Sundstrom, C.R.E. Students 317.

BALDWINVILLE, ST. VINCENT DE PAUL (1955) 1 Forest St., Baldwinville, 01436. Tel: 978-939-8851; Fax: 978-939-2120; Email: stvinedepaul05@aol.com; Web: saintvincentcatholicchurch.com. 18 Pleasant St., P.O. Box 14, Baldwinville, 01436. Rev. Francis A. Roberge, M.A.; Deacon James A. Connor.
Catechesis Religious Program—
Tel: 978-939-8290. Mrs. Jennifer McNeaney, Coord. Students 49.

BARRE, ST. JOSEPH (1896) [CEM] Merged with St. Thomas-a-Beckett Parish, South Barre to form St. Francis of Assisi Parish, South Barre. For sacramental records contact St. Francis of Assisi, P.O. Box 186, South Barre, MA 01074.

BERLIN, ST. JOSEPH THE GOOD PROVIDER (1973) 52 West St., Box 284, Berlin, 01503-0284.
Tel: 978-838-9922; Fax: 978-838-9933; Email: stjoe9922@charter.net; Web: stjosephberlin.org. Rev. Thomas M. Tokarz.
Catechesis Religious Program—Mrs. Mary Jo Kriz, D.R.E. Students 66.

BLACKSTONE
1—ST. PAUL (1850) [CEM] 48 Saint Paul St., Blackstone, 01504. Tel: 508-883-6726; Fax: 508-883-2079; Email: stpaulblackstone@comcast.net. Rev. Dennis Timothy O'Mara.
Catechesis Religious Program—
Tel: 508-883-2590; Email: religioused@stpaulblackstone.org; Web: www.stpaulblackstone.org. Deb Campano, D.R.E. Students 77.
2—ST. THERESA (1929) (French) 630 Rathbun St., Blackstone, 01504. Tel: 508-883-7206; Fax: 508-883-5250; Email: theresaparish630@gmail.com. Rev. Thien Nguyen.
Catechesis Religious Program—
Tel: 508-883-7527. Students 85.

BOLTON, ST. FRANCIS XAVIER (1954) Merged with St. Theresa's, Harvard to form Holy Trinity, Harvard.

BOYLSTON, ST. MARY OF THE HILLS (1952) 620 Cross St., Boylston, 01505. Tel: 508-869-6771. 630 Cross St., Boylston, 01505. Rev. Manuel A. Clavijo.
Catechesis Religious Program—Anne Dowen, D.R.E. (K-10). Students 170.

BROOKFIELD, ST. MARY'S (1885) Closed. Now a mission of Our Lady of the Sacred Heart, West Brookfield.

CHARLTON CITY, ST. JOSEPH'S (1900) 10 H. Putnam Ext., Box 338, Charlton City, 01508.
Tel: 508-248-7862; Fax: 508-248-5832; Email: stjoecharlton@aol.com. Revs. Robert A. Grattaroti; Donato Infante III; Deacons William Shea; Peter R. Faford; Steve Miller.
Catechesis Religious Program—Sr. Agnes Patricia, D.R.E. Students 394.

CLINTON
1—ST. JOHN THE GUARDIAN OF OUR LADY (1849) [CEM] 149 Chestnut St., Clinton, 01510.
Tel: 978-368-0366; Fax: 978-368-4359; Email: stjohnclintonma@gmail.com; Web: www.stjohnsclinton.org. Revs. Joseph M. Nally; Henry Ramirez; Deacons William Griffin; George O'Connor.
Catechesis Religious Program—
80 Union St., Clinton, 01510. Tel: 978-368-0052. Students 539.
2—OUR LADY OF JASNA GORA (1913) (Polish), Closed. For inquiries for parish records please see St. John the Guardian of Our Lady, Clinton.
3—OUR LADY OF THE ROSARY (1909) Closed. For inquiries for parish records please see St. John the Guardian of Our Lady, Clinton.

DOUGLAS, ST. DENIS (1870) [CEM] 23 Manchaug St., Douglas, 01516. Tel: 508-476-2002; Email: jescudero@saintdenischurch.com; Email: nanorberg@saintdenischurch.com; Email: deaconmike@saintdenischurch.com; Email: karchambault@saintdenischurch.com. Rev. Juan Escudero; Deacon Michael J. Hafferty, RCIA Coord.
Catechesis Religious Program—Students 250.

DUDLEY
1—ST. ANDREW BOBOLA (1963) [JC] (Polish) 54 W. Main St., P.O. Box 98, Dudley, 01571.
Tel: 508-943-5633; Fax: 508-949-6701; Email: rectory@standrewbobola.net. Rev. Krzysztof Korcz.
Catechesis Religious Program—Students 46.
2—ST. ANTHONY (1905) [CEM] 22/24 Dudley Hill Rd., Dudley, 01571. Tel: 508-943-0470; Fax: 508-943-5663; Email: stanthonydudley@charter.net; Web: www.stanthonyofpaduadudley.org. Rev. Daniel E. Moreno; Deacon William White; Valerie Milosh, Sec.
Res.: 22 Dudley Hill Rd., Box 277, Dudley, 01571-0277.
Catechesis Religious Program—
Tel: 508-949-0335; Email: stanthonydudleyreled@gmail.com. Linda Brink, D.R.E. Students 124.

EAST BROOKFIELD, ST. JOHN THE BAPTIST (1952) 121 Blaine Ave., East Brookfield, 01515.
Tel: 508-867-3738; Fax: 508-867-3301; Email: stjohnseb01515@verizon.net; Web: www.stjohnsebma.org. Revs. Richard A. Jakubauskas; Donald C. Ouellette.
Catechesis Religious Program—Mary Gershman, D.R.E. Students 11.

FISKDALE, ST. ANNE AND ST. PATRICK (1883) [CEM] 16 Church St., Fiskdale, 01518. Tel: 508-347-7338; Fax: 508-347-2982; Email: stannestpatoffice@gmail.com; Web: stannestpatrickparish.com. Revs. Alex Castro, A.A.; John Franck, A.A.; Jerome Lively, A.A., Pastoral Assoc.; Bro. Paul Henry, A.A., Pastoral Assoc.; Deacons Keith Caplette; Dominick F. DeMartino; Wesley Stevens.
Catechesis Religious Program—Students 205.

FITCHBURG
1—ST. ANTHONY OF PADUA (1908) (Italian) 84 Salem St., Fitchburg, 01420. Tel: 978-342-4706; Fax: 978-342-8160; Email: church.office@stanthonyfitchburg.net; Web: www.stanthonyfitchburg.org. Rev. Juan Ramirez; Deacon Salvatore Tantillo.
Res.: 2 Beekman St., Fitchburg, 01420.
Tel: 978-342-2216.
Catechesis Religious Program—
Fax: 978-342-5510. Students 31.
2—ST. BERNARD (1847) [CEM] Merged with and located at St. Camilus de Lellis, Fitchburg.
3—ST. BERNARD PARISH AT ST. CAMILLUS DE LELLIS (2010) 333 Mechanic St., Fitchburg, 01420.
Tel: 978-342-7921; Fax: 978-345-2688; Email: stbernardfitch@verizon.net. Rev. Joseph M. Dolan; Deacon Benjamin A. Nogueira.
School—St. Bernard Elementary School, (Grades PreK-8),
254 Summer St., Fitchburg, 01420.
Tel: 978-342-1948; Fax: 978-342-1153; Email: dwright@stbernardselementary.org; Web:

saintbernardselementary.org. Ms. Deborah Wright, Prin. Lay Teachers 16; Sisters 1; Students 240.
Catechesis Religious Program—Susan Saari, D.R.E. Students 82.
4—St. Camillus de Lellis (1953) Merged with St. Bernard, Fitchburg to form St. Bernard Parish at St. Camillus de Lellis, Fitchburg.
5—St. Francis of Assisi (1903) 63 Sheridan, Fitchburg, 01420. Tel: 978-342-9651;
Fax: 978-342-7936; Email: pastor@saintfrancis-fitchburg.com. 81 Sheridan, Fitchburg, 01420. Rev. Emerito Ortiz.
Catechesis Religious Program—
Tel: 978-342-3521. Yesenia Quinones, C.R.E. Students 60.
6—Immaculate Conception (1886) (French), Closed. For inquiries for parish records please see St. Joseph Parish, Fitchburg.
7—St. Joseph's (1890) [CEM] 46 Woodland St., Fitchburg, 01420. Tel: 978-345-7997;
Fax: 978-345-7678; Email: stj2010@verizon.net. Rev. Mark Rainville; Deacon James Couture. In Res., Revs. Laurie L. Leger, M.S.; Theodore R. Laperle, (Retired).
Catechesis Religious Program—
Tel: 978-343-8186. Maureen Beauvais, D.R.E. Students 43.
8—Madonna of the Holy Rosary (1955) Closed. For inquiries for parish records please see St. Joseph, Fitchburg.
9—Sacred Heart of Jesus (1878) (Irish), Closed. For inquiries for parish records please see St. Joseph, Fitchburg.

Gardner
1—Annunciation Parish (1884) [CEM] 135 Nichols St., Gardner, 01440. Tel: 978-632-0253;
Fax: 978-630-1773; Email: office@annunciationgardner.org; Web: www.annunciationgardner.org. Revs. Stephen E. Lundrigan; Wilmar Ramos; Deacon Stanley H. Baczewski.
The Caring Place—
100 Central St., Gardner, 01440. Tel: 978-632-5745; Email: jane@tcpgardner.com; Web: tcpgardner.com. Mrs. Jane Pineo, Dir.
School—Holy Family Academy, (Grades PreK-8),
99 Nichols St., Gardner, 01440. Tel: 978-632-8656;
Fax: 978-630-1433; Email: info@holyfamilyacademyma.org; Web: www.holyfamilyacademyma.org. Andrea Tavaska, Prin. Lay Teachers 16; Students 160.
Catechesis Religious Program—
Email: religiousedv@annunciationgardner.org. Maura L. Sweeney, D.R.E. Students 210.
2—Holy Spirit (1955) Merged with St. Joseph's, Gardner, Our Lady of the Holy Rosary, Gardner & Sacred Heart of Jesus Gardner to form Annunciation Parish, Gardner.
3—St. Joseph's (1908) [CEM] (Polish), Merged with Holy Spirit, Gardner, Our Lady of the Holy Rosary, Gardner & Sacred Heart of Jesus Gardner to form Annunciation Parish, Gardner.
4—Sacred Heart of Jesus (1874) Merged with Holy Spirit, Gardner, St. Joseph's, Gardner & Our Lady of the Holy Rosary, Gardner to form Annunciation Parish, Gardner.

Gilbertville, St. Aloysius (1872) [CEM] 58 Church St., P.O. Box 542, Gilbertville, 01031-0542.
Tel: 413-477-6493; Fax: 413-477-0140; Email: st.aloysius@verizon.net. Rev. Richard Lembo.
Catechesis Religious Program—Lorretta DiPietro, D.R.E. Students 54.
Mission—St. Augustine
98 Church Ln., Wheelwright, Hardwick Co. 01094.

Grafton, St. Philip (1869) [CEM] 12 West St., Grafton, 01519. Tel: 508-839-3325;
Fax: 508-839-1310; Email: stphilipgrafton@gmail.com. Rev. Leo-Paul J. LeBlanc.
Catechesis Religious Program—Students 165.

Harvard
1—Holy Trinity (2009) 15 Still River Rd., P.O. Box 746, Harvard, 01451. Tel: 978-456-3563; Email: htpboltonharvard@aol.com. Rev. Terence T. Kilcoyne, D.Min.
Catechesis Religious Program—
Tel: 978-456-8807. Students 324.
2—St. Theresa's (1950) Merged with St. Francis Xavier, Bolton to form Holy Trinity, Harvard.

Hopedale, Sacred Heart of Jesus (1935) 187 Hopedale St., Hopedale, 01747. Tel: 508-473-1900;
Fax: 508-473-1745; Email: parishoffice@sacredhearthopedale.org; Web: www.sacredhearthopedale.org. Rev. William C. Konicki; Pam Chaplin, Ministry Coord.
Catechesis Religious Program—Students 159.

Jefferson, St. Mary (1884) [CEM] 114 Princeton St., P.O. Box 2200, Jefferson, 01522. Tel: 508-829-4508;
Fax: 508-829-0429; Email: stmaryjeff@stmaryjeff.com. Rev. Timothy M. Brewer; Deacon Timothy Cross.
Catechesis Religious Program—
Tel: 508-829-6758; Email: stmaryreled@charterinternet.com. Students 497.

Lancaster, Immaculate Conception (1915) 28 Packard St., P.O. Box 95, Lancaster, 01523.
Tel: 978-365-6582; Fax: 978-365-3097; Email: iconception@comcast.net. Rev. Thomas H. Hultquist.
Catechesis Religious Program—Students 94.

Leicester
1—St. Aloysius-St. Jude (1904) 491 Pleasant St., Leicester, 01524. Tel: 508-892-8296;
Fax: 508-892-9054; Email: aloysius-jude@charter.net; Web: www.saintaloysiusjude.org. Rev. John M. Lizewski.
Catechesis Religious Program—Mrs. Cynthia Garabedian, A.R.E. Students 75.
2—St. Joseph-St. Pius X Parish (1851) [CEM] 759 Main St., Leicester, 01524. Tel: 508-892-7407;
Fax: 508-892-4753; Email: stjosephstpiusx759@gmail.com. Rev. Robert A. Loftus.
Catechesis Religious Program—
Tel: 508-892-0660. Combined with St. Pius X. Students 150.
3—St. Pius X (1956) Merged with St. Joseph, Leicester to form St. Joseph-St. Pius X Parish, Leicester.

Leominster
1—St. Anna (1937) (Italian) 199 Lancaster St., Leominster, 01453. Tel: 978-537-5293;
Fax: 978-537-2950; Email: stanna9@comcast.net. Rev. Frederick D. Fraini III.
School—St. Anna School, (Grades PreK-8),
Tel: 978-534-4770; Email: bfrench@stannaleom.org; Web: www.stannaschool.org. Clergy 2; Lay Teachers 16; Students 231.
Catechesis Religious Program—Students 95.
2—St. Cecilia (1900) [CEM] (French) 170 Mechanic St., Leominster, 01453. Tel: 978-537-6541;
Fax: 978-840-1965; Email: frbob.stc@verizon.net. Revs. Robert D. Bruso; Miguel Pagan; Deacons Ronald J. Aubuchon, 15 Craven Dr., Leominster, 01453; Robert Connor Jr.
Catechesis Religious Program—
Tel: 978-537-4673. Patricia Secino, D.R.E. Students 127.
3—Holy Family of Nazareth (1963) 750 Union St., Leominster, 01453. Tel: 978-537-3016;
Fax: 978-534-1119; Email: churchonhill@aol.com; Web: holyfamilyofnazareth.org. Rev. Jose A. Rodriguez.
Catechesis Religious Program—
Tel: 978-537-5660. Anne Booth, D.R.E. Students 200.
4—St. Leo (1872) [CEM] 108 Main St., Leominster, 01453. Tel: 978-537-7257; Fax: 978-840-6182; Email: stleoparish@verizon.net; Web: stleosparish.org. Revs. William E. Champlin; Diego Buritica.
School—St. Leo School, (Grades PreK-8),
120 Main St., Leominster, 01453. Tel: 978-537-1007;
Fax: 978-537-7420; Email: nancy.pierce@stleoschool.org; Web: www.stleoschool.org. Mrs. Nancy Pierce, Prin. Clergy 1; Lay Teachers 22; Students 221.
Catechesis Religious Program—
Tel: 978-537-1194; Fax: 978-840-6182; Web: www.stleosparish.org. Students 144.
5—Our Lady of the Lake (1952) 1400 Main St., Leominster, 01453. Tel: 978-342-2978;
Fax: 978-342-8738; Email: information@ourladylake.org. Revs. Michael Broderick; Carlos Ruiz.
Res.: 29 Craven Dr., Leominster, 01453.
Catechesis Religious Program—
Email: lsciacca@ourladylake.org. Lisa Sciacca, D.R.E. Students 68.

Linwood, Good Shepherd (1904) 121 Linwood St., P.O. Box 517, Linwood, 01525. Tel: 508-234-7726;
Fax: 508-234-0964; Email: gshepherd7726@charter.net; Web: www.goodshepherdlinwood.org. Revs. Lawrence J. Esposito; Victor Sierra; Deacon Marc E. Gervais.
Catechesis Religious Program—
Tel: 508-234-5340. Carol A. Zabinski, Music Min. & Rel. Educ. Coord. Students 121.

Lunenburg, St. Boniface (1950) 817 Massachusetts Ave., Lunenburg, 01462. Tel: 978-582-4008;
Fax: 978-582-9355; Email: stbonifaceparish@verizon.net. Rev. Anthony Mpagi.
Catechesis Religious Program—
Tel: 978-582-6650. Loretta DiPietro, D.R.E. Students 120.

Manchaug, St. Anne (1900) Merged with St. Mark, Sutton. For sacramental records please see St. Mark, 356 Boston Rd., Sutton.

Mendon, St. Michael (1952) Merged with Holy Angels, Upton to form St. Gabriel the Archangel, Upton.

Milford
1—St. Mary of the Assumption (1848) [CEM] (Portuguese—Spanish) 17 Winter St., Milford, 01757. Tel: 508-473-2000; Email: pjoyce.smamilford@gmail.com. Revs. Peter Joyce; Mateus Souza; Deacon David F. Vaillancourt.
Catechesis Religious Programs—St. Mary's Parish Center—
Tel: 508-478-7440; Fax: 508-473-6907. Kathy Moran, D.R.E.
Tel: 508-478-7440; Email: kathymoran328@gmail.com; Email: louisasavaria.stmarys@gmail.com. Kathy Moran, D.R.E. Students 632.
2—Sacred Heart of Jesus (1905) [CEM] 5 E. Main St., Milford, 01757. Rev. Richard A. Scioli, C.S.S.; Deacon Pasquale G. Mussulli.
Catechesis Religious Program—
8 Mt. Pleasant St., Milford, 01757. Tel: 508-473-1036; Email: ccdoffice@sacredheartmilford.org. Amy Donahue, C.R.E.; Andrew Tomaski, C.R.E. Students 271.

Millbury
1—Assumption (1884) (French) Mailing Address: c/o St. Brigid Parish, 59 Main St., Millbury, 01527.
Tel: 508-865-6624; Email: secretary@stbrigidparish.org. Rev. Daniel R. Mulcahy Jr.; Deacon Ronald B. Buron.
Res.: 12 Waters St., Millbury, 01527.
Tel: 508-865-2657.
School—Assumption School, (Grades PreK-8),
17 Grove St., Millbury, 01527. Tel: 508-865-5404; Email: john.hoogasian@assumption-cs.org. Dr. John Hoogasian, Ph.D., Prin. Lay Teachers 15; Students 125.
Catechesis Religious Program—Gregory Bernard, Faith Formation. Students 17.
2—St. Brigid (1849) 59 Main St., Millbury, 01527.
Tel: 508-865-6624; Fax: 508-865-3101; Email: secretary@stbrigidparish.org. Rev. Daniel R. Mulcahy Jr.; Deacon Ronald B. Buron.
Res.: 12 Waters St., Millbury, 01527.
Catechesis Religious Program—Gregory Bernard, D.R.E. Students 214.

Millville, St. Augustine (1884) 121 Linwood St., P.O. Box 517, Millville, 01529. Tel: 508-883-6678;
Fax: 508-883-5878; Email: parishoffice@staugustinesmillville.com. Revs. Lawrence J. Esposito, Admin.; Daniel E. Moreno.
Catechesis Religious Program—
15 Lincoln St., Millville, 01529. Tel: 508-883-8794. Students 89.

North Brookfield, St. Joseph (1867) [CEM] 28 Mt. Pleasant St., North Brookfield, 01535.
Tel: 508-867-6811; Fax: 508-867-7756; Email: saintjosephrectory@verizon.net; Web: www.stjosephsnbma.org. Revs. Richard A. Jakubauskas; Donald C. Ouellette.
Church: 296 N. Main St., North Brookfield, 01535.
Catechesis Religious Program—
27 Mt. Pleasant St., North Brookfield, 01535.
Tel: 508-867-9302. Lynne Losurdo, D.R.E. Students 76.

North Grafton, St. Mary (1952) 17 Waterville St., North Grafton, 01536. Tel: 508-839-3993;
Fax: 508-839-1330; Email: fathrleb@gmail.com. Rev. Leo-Paul J. LeBlanc; Deacon Frederick Coggins; Lisa Stewart, Business Mgr.
Catechesis Religious Program—Darleen Farland, D.R.E.; Sr. Yvonne Millman, S.S.A, D.R.E. Students 222.

North Oxford, St. Ann (1906) 652 Main St., P.O. Box 488, North Oxford, 01537. Tel: 508-987-8892;
Fax: 508-987-1598; Email: stannsrectory@hotmail.com; Web: www.stannschurch.us. Rev. Michael N. Lavallee; Deacon James Denning.
Catechesis Religious Program—Students 44.

Northboro
1—St. Bernadette (1959) 266 Main St., Northboro, 01532. Tel: 508-393-2838; Fax: 508-393-2718; Email: office@stb-parish.net; Web: stb-parish.org. Rev. Ronald Falco.
School—St. Bernadette School, (Grades PreK-8),
Tel: 508-351-9905; Fax: 508-351-2941; Email: ofc@stb-school.org; Web: www.stb-school.org. Deborah O'Neil, Prin.; Mary Bardellini, Librarian. Clergy 1; Religious Teachers 1; Lay Teachers 44; Students 421.
Catechesis Religious Program—
Tel: 508-393-7445. Virginia Boland, D.R.E. Students 103.
2—St. Rose of Lima (1883) 244 W. Main St., P.O. Box 685, Northboro, 01532. Tel: 508-393-2413;
Fax: 508-393-4922; Email: saintrose1@verizon.net. Rev. James A. Houston.
Catechesis Religious Program—
P.O. Box 387. Tel: 508-393-6444. Mrs. Susan McGoldrick, D.R.E.; Deacon Riley Duggan. Students 496.

Northbridge, St. Peter (1904) 39 Church Ave., P.O. Box 446, Northbridge, 01534. Tel: 508-234-2156;
Fax: 508-266-0447; Email: parishoffice@stpeterrockdale.org; Web: www.stpeterrockdale.org. Rev. Thomas Landry; Deacon Quat Van Tran.
Catechesis Religious Program—
Tel: 508-234-6355; Email: stplifeteen@charter.net. Students 74.

Otter River, St. Martin Mission (1864) 248 State

Rd., Otter River, 01436. Tel: 978-939-5588; Fax: 978-939-5588; Email: info@saintmartinchurch.org; Web: saintmartinchurch.org. Rev. Patrick Ssekyole.
Catechesis Religious Program—Students 10.

OXFORD, ST. ROCH (1886) [CEM] 334 Main St., Oxford, 01540. Tel: 508-987-8987; Fax: 508-987-8938; Email: strochrectory@gmail.com; Web: www.strochoxford.com. Rev. Michael J. Roy; Deacon Paul R. Connelly.
Catechesis Religious Program—
Tel: 508-987-2382. Terry Ann Renaud, D.R.E. Students 379.

PAXTON, ST. COLUMBA (1951) 10 Richards Ave., Paxton, 01612. Tel: 508-755-0408; Email: stcolumba@charter.net. Rev. David E. Doiron.
Catechesis Religious Program—
Tel: 508-755-0601. Students 193.

PETERSHAM, ST. PETER (1968) 18 North St., Petersham, 01366. Tel: 978-249-2738; Email: ourladyrectory@hotmail.com. Mailing Address: c/o Our Lady Immaculate, 192 School St., Athol, 01331. Rev. Edwin Montana; Deacon Bryan A. Lagimoniere.
Catechesis Religious Program—
Tel: 978-249-7690. High school program combined with Our Lady Immaculate, Athol. Students 24.

PRINCETON, PRINCE OF PEACE (1967) 5 Worcester Rd., P.O. Box 305, Princeton, 01541. Tel: 508-464-2871; Fax: 508-464-0449; Email: princeofpeace@verizon.net; Web: princeofpeacema.org. Rev. H. Edward Chalmers.
Catechesis Religious Program—Mrs. Sharon Bushway, D.R.E. Students 94.

RUTLAND, ST. PATRICK (1938) 290 Main St., Box 939, Rutland, 01543. Tel: 508-886-4309;
Tel: 508-886-4984; Fax: 508-886-2897; Email: arw@stpatricksrutland.org; Web: stpatricksrutland.org. Rev. James Boland, Admin.; Deacons Pierre G.L. Gemme; Brian Stidsen.
Church: 258 Main St., Rutland, 01543.
Tel: 508-886-6131.
Catechesis Religious Program—
9 Pommogusset Rd., Rutland, 01543.
Tel: 508-886-4984; Fax: 508-886-7414. Christine Mulry, D.R.E.; Mrs. Jean Urbanowski, D.R.E. Students 406.

SHREWSBURY
1—ST. ANNE (1950) [CEM] 130 Boston Tpke., Shrewsbury, 01545. Tel: 508-757-5154;
Fax: 508-797-9520; Email: STAREC@aol.com. Revs. John Foley; Paul T. O'Connell, J.C.D., Senior Priest; Eleanor Smith, Pastoral Assoc.; Deacons William A. Bilow Jr.; Peter Ryan.
Catechesis Religious Program—
Tel: 508-752-5040. Mary Courtemanche, D.R.E.; Tracy Flynn, D.R.E. Students 239.
2—ST. MARY'S (1922) Mailing Address: 20 Summer St., Shrewsbury, 01545. Tel: 508-845-6341;
Fax: 508-842-9132; Email: michael.rose@stmarysparish.org; Web: www.stmarysparish.org. 640 Main St., Shrewsbury, 01545. Revs. Michael F. Rose; Javier Julio.
Res.: 11 Summer St., Shrewsbury, 01545.
School—St. Mary's School, (Grades PreK-8),
16 Summer St., Shrewsbury, 01545.
Tel: 508-842-1601; Fax: 508-845-1535; Email: jeannie.macdonough@stmarysparish.org. Jeannie MacDonough, Prin. Lay Teachers 22; Sisters 1; Students 178.
Catechesis Religious Program—
Tel: 508-925-7801; Email: gina.kuruvilla@stmarysparish.org. Gina Kuruvilla, D.R.E. Students 747.

SOUTH ASHBURNHAM, ST. ANNE (1895) Closed. For inquiries for parish records contact St. Denis, Ashburnham.

SOUTH BARRE
1—ST. FRANCIS OF ASSISI PARISH (2013) 398 Vernon Ave., P.O. Box 186, South Barre, 01074-0186.
Tel: 978-355-2228; Email: BarreStFrancisParish@gmail.com; Web: www.saintfrancisofassisiparish.com. Rev. James B. Callahan.
Catechesis Religious Program—Deacon Brian Gadbois, D.R.E. Students 100.
2—ST. THOMAS-A-BECKET (1918) Merged with St Joseph Parish, Barre to form St. Francis of Assisi Parish, South Barre. For sacramental records contact St. Francis of Assisi, P.O. Box 186, South Barre, MA 01074.

SOUTH GRAFTON, ST. JAMES (1887) 89 Main St., South Grafton, 01560. Tel: 508-839-5354;
Fax: 508-839-5430; Email: catstjames@aol.com; Email: ejhanlon3@verizon.net; Web: stjamesgrafton.com. Rev. Edward J. Hanlon.
Catechesis Religious Program—
Tel: 508-839-6800. Students 153.

SOUTHBOROUGH
1—ST. ANNE (1886) 20 Boston Rd., Southborough, 01772. Tel: 508-485-0141; Fax: 508-481-9374; Email: stanne403@stannesouthborough.org. Rev. Albert Irudayasamy.
Catechesis Religious Program—Karla Reuter, C.R.E.; Donna McIntosh, C.R.E. Students 196.
2—ST. MATTHEW (1956) [JC] 105 Southville Rd., Southborough, 01772. Tel: 508-485-2285;
Fax: 508-485-4437; Email: office@stmatthewsb.org. Rev. James B. Flynn, B.A., L.S.T., Ph.D.
Catechesis Religious Program—
Tel: 508-229-2429. Amy Comcowich, D.R.E. Students 434.

SOUTHBRIDGE
1—ST. HEDWIG (1916) [CEM] (Polish), Merged into Saint John Paul II, Southbridge.
2—SAINT JOHN PAUL II (2011) 279 Hamilton St., Southbridge, 01550. Tel: 508-765-3701; Email: MaddieB.stjp2@gmail.com. Revs. Peter Joyce; Juan G. Herrera; Deacons Thomas A. Skonieczny, St. John Paul II, Southbridge; Teodoro Camacho.
Catechesis Religious Program—Religious Education Center
Tel: 508-765-3704. Students 310.
3—ST. MARY (1861) [CEM] Merged into Saint John Paul II, Southbridge.
4—NOTRE DAME (1869) Merged with St. Hedwig, Southbridge and St. Mary Southbridge to form Saint John Paul II, Southbridge.
5—NOTRE DAME OF THE SACRED HEART (1869) Merged with Sacred Heart of Jesus, St. Hedwig & St. Mary to form Saint John Paul II, Southbridge.
6—SACRED HEART OF JESUS (1908) (French), Merged into Saint John Paul II, Southbridge.

SPENCER
1—MARY, QUEEN OF THE ROSARY (1994) [CEM] Merger of St. Mary, Spencer and Our Lady of the Rosary, Spencer. 60 Maple St., Spencer, 01562.
Tel: 508-885-3111; Fax: 508-885-4905; Email: Maryqueen@mqrparish.org; Web: www.maryqueenoftherosary.org. Rev. William Schipper.
Res.: 46 Maple St., Spencer, 01562.
Tel: 508-885-3111, Ext. 108.
Catechesis Religious Program—
Tel: 508-885-3111, Ext. 105. Mrs. Judith Brennan, C.R.E. Students 218.
2—OUR LADY OF THE ROSARY (1854) Merged with St. Mary's, Spencer to form Mary, Queen of the Rosary, Spencer.

STERLING, ST. RICHARD OF CHICHESTER (1953) 4 Bridge St., P.O. Box 657, Sterling, 01564. Tel: 978-422-8881; Tel: 978-422-8921; Fax: 978-422-0291; Email: strichardsterling@comcast.net; Web: strichardsterling.org. Rev. James M. Steuterman; Sr. Anne Marie Wildenhain, S.S.J., Pastoral Assoc.; Kathleen Majikas, Admin.
Catechesis Religious Program—
Email: strichardreled@comcast.net. Susan Gallivan, D.R.E. Students 226.

SUTTON, ST. MARK (1964) [CEM] 356 Boston Rd., Sutton, 01590. Tel: 508-865-3860; Fax: 508-865-5095; Email: St-Mark-Office@verizon.net. Rev. Michael A. DiGeronimo; Deacon Eduardas Meilus, Youth Min.
Catechesis Religious Program—Jennifer DeMora, C.R.E. Students 200.

TEMPLETON, HOLY CROSS (1952) 25 Lake Ave., Templeton, 01468. Tel: 978-632-2121;
Fax: 978-630-3890; Email: hcchurchet@comcast.net. Rev. Patrick Ssekyole; Deacon Richard J. Tatro.
Catechesis Religious Program—
Tel: 978-632-2194. Students 121.
Mission—St. Martin
247 State Rd., Otter River, 01436. Tel: 978-939-5588; Fax: 978-939-2305.
Catechesis Religious Program—

UPTON
1—ST. GABRIEL THE ARCHANGEL (2011) 151 Mendon St., Upton, 01568. Tel: 508-603-1430; Email: info@stgabrielma.org. Rev. Laurence V. Brault.
Catechesis Religious Program—Simone Caron, D.R.E. Students 215.
2—HOLY ANGELS (1900) Merged with St. Michael, Mendon to form St. Gabriel the Archangel, Upton.

UXBRIDGE, ST. MARY'S (1853) [CEM] 77 Mendon St., Uxbridge, 01569. Tel: 508-278-2226;
Fax: 508-278-7949; Email: fathernick@stmaryuxbridge.org; Email: sleighton@stmaryuxbridge.org; Web: www.stmaryuxbridge.org. Rev. Nicholas Desimone; Deacon John Dugan; Rev. Dennis J. O'Brien, In Res.
Catechesis Religious Program—
Tel: 508-278-3777. Annette Gion, D.R.E. Students 136.

WARREN, ST. PAUL (1872) [CEM] 1082 Main St., P.O. Box 1027, Warren, 01083-1027. Tel: 413-436-7327; Email: stpaulstan@yahoo.com. Rev. Daniel J. Becker.
Catechesis Religious Program—Clustered with St. Stanislaus, West Warren. Students 8.

WEBSTER
1—ST. JOSEPH BASILICA (1887) [CEM] (Polish) 53 Whitcomb St., Webster, 01570. Tel: 508-943-0467;
Fax: 508-943-0808; Email: rectory@stjosephwebster.com; Email: rectory@saintjosephbasilica.org; Web: www.saintjosephbasilica.com. Rev. Msgr. Anthony S. Czarnecki, J.C.L.; Rev. Grzegorz Chodkowski.
School—St. Joseph School, (Grades PreK-8),
47 Whitcomb St., Webster, 01570. Tel: 508-943-0378; Fax: 508-949-0581; Email: principal@sjs-webster.com; Web: www.sjs-webster.com. Michael Hackenson, Prin. Clergy 3; Religious Teachers 2; Lay Teachers 15; Felician Sisters 2; Students 230.
Catechesis Religious Program—Elizabeth Sabaj, D.R.E. Students 60.
2—ST. LOUIS (1853) 15 Lake St., Webster, 01570.
Tel: 508-943-0240; Fax: 508-943-0801; Email: father.adam@sacredheartwebster.org. Rev. William F. Sanders.
Catechesis Religious Program—
Tel: 508-943-0817; Fax: 508-943-0817; Email: stlouisreledwebster@gmail.com. Louise Forget, D.R.E. Students 195.
3—SACRED HEART OF JESUS (1870) [CEM] [JC] 18 E. Main St., Webster, 01570. Tel: 508-943-3140;
Fax: 508-461-7023; Email: dan.doyle@sacredheartwebster.org. Rev. Adam R. Reid; Deacon Paul J. Lesieur.
Catechesis Religious Program—Dan Doyle, D.R.E. Students 58.

WEST BOYLSTON, OUR LADY OF GOOD COUNSEL (1869) [CEM] 111 Worcester St., West Boylston, 01583.
Tel: 508-835-3606; Fax: 508-835-5456; Email: terri@goodcounselma.org. Rev. Thirburse F. Millott.
Catechesis Religious Program—
Tel: 508-835-6336. Sr. Elaine Potvin, S.S.A., D.R.E. Students 140.

WEST BROOKFIELD, OUR LADY OF THE SACRED HEART (1950) 10 Milk St., P.O. Box 563, West Brookfield, 01585-0563. Tel: 508-867-6469; Fax: 508-867-3670; Email: rectory@sacredheartwb.com. Rev. Chester J. Misiewicz.
Parish Center—
Tel: 508-867-4460.
Catechesis Religious Program—Students 82.

WEST WARREN
1—ST. STANISLAUS (1913) (Polish) 2270 Main St., P.O. Box 723, West Warren, 01092-0723.
Tel: 413-436-7327; Email: stpaulstan@yahoo.com. Rev. Daniel J. Becker.
Catechesis Religious Program—
2—ST. THOMAS AQUINAS (1893) Closed. For inquiries for parish records contact St. Paul, Warren.

WESTBOROUGH, ST. LUKE THE EVANGELIST (1870) [CEM] 70 W. Main St., Westborough, 01581.
Tel: 508-366-5502; Tel: 508-366-8509;
Fax: 508-366-6049; Email: office@stlukes-parish.org; Web: www.stlukes-parish.org. Rev. Msgr. Michael G. Foley; Rev. Joseph Rice.
Catechesis Religious Program—
One Ruggles St., Westborough, 01581.
Tel: 508-366-8509; Email: religiouseducation@stlukes-parish.org. Dianne Patrick, D.R.E. Students 581.

WESTMINSTER, ST. EDWARD THE CONFESSOR (1951) 10 Church St., Westminster, 01473. Tel: 978-874-2362; Fax: 978-840-1024; Email: office@stedwardconf.org. Rev. Kevin F. Hartford.
Catechesis Religious Program—
Tel: 978-874-1559. Students 226.

WHITINSVILLE, ST. PATRICK (1889) [CEM] 7 East St., P.O. Box 60, Whitinsville, 01588. Tel: 508-234-5656; Fax: 508-234-6845; Email: FrTomasz@MyStPatricks.com. 1 Cross St., Whitinsville, 01588. Rev. Tomasz J. Borkowski.
Catechesis Religious Program—
Tel: 508-234-3511. Christina Pichette, C.R.E. Students 397.

WINCHENDON, IMMACULATE HEART OF MARY (1870) [CEM] 52 Spruce St., Winchendon, 01475.
Tel: 508-297-0280; Fax: 508-297-3577; Email: renee@heartofmary.net; Email: pastor@heartofmary.net; Web: heartofmary.net. Rev. Carlos Ruiz.
Catechesis Religious Program—Mary Laflamme, D.R.E. Students 60.

Chaplains of Public Institutions

WORCESTER. *Memorial Hospital*. Rev. Thomas J. Sheehan, S.J.
University of Mass Medical Center. Rev. Francis J. Roach.
Worcester Belmont House. Serviced by St. Anne Church, Shrewsbury.
BOYLSTON. *Worcester County Jail and House of Correction*.
GARDNER. *North Central Correctional Institution*.
LEOMINSTER. *Health Alliance Hospital*. Cathleen Pimley, Catholic Pastoral Min.

On Administrative Leave of Absence:
Rev.—
Doherty, Paul J.

On Special or Other Diocesan Assignment:
Rev. Msgr.—
Beaulieu, Peter R., Dir., Mission Integration &

Pastoral Care, St. Vincent Hospital, 123 Summer St., 01608

Revs.—

Gemme, Stephen M., St. Vincent Hospital, Worcester

Nguyen, Son Anh, Chap., St. Vincent Hospital.

On Duty Outside the Diocese:

Rev. Msgrs.—

Kelly, Francis D., Canon, Via della Nocetta, 63, Rome, Italy 00164

Mongelluzzo, James A., 158 Berrington Rd., Leominster, 01453

Revs.—

Boucher, Roger R., C.D.R., C.H.C., U.S.N., P.O. Box 148, Gilmanton Iron Works, NH 03837

Damian, Ronald, Chap., Miami, FL 33125

Dunkley, George, San Marcos, CA 92069

Echavarria, Juan David, Special Studies, Pontifical Gregorian Univ., Rome.

Military Chaplains:

Revs.—

Kazarnowicz, Anthony S., Chap., U.S. Army, 44806-2 Washington St., Fort Riley, KS 66442

Nowicki, Marcin, Chap., U.S. Archdiocese for Military Services, P.O. Box 4469, Washington, DC 20017-0469.

Retired:

Rev. Msgrs.—

Collette, Richard, (Retired), 30 Julio Dr., Shrewsbury, 01545

Doran, John E., (Retired)

Revs.—

Armey, Charles R., (Retired)

Bafaro, Michael, (Retired), 30 Julio Dr., Shrewsbury, 01545

Banach, Henry S., (Retired), 64 Oakwood Ln., 01604

Borowski, Charles E.J., (Retired), P.O. Box 236, Webster, 01570

Campbell, Paul F., (Retired), 73 Willow Hill Rd., Cherry Valley, 01611

Carmody, James F., (Retired), 35 Julio Dr. Apt. 416E, Shrewsbury, 01545

Charland, George A., (Retired), 112 Blaine Ave., East Brookfield, 01515

Cormier, William N., (Retired), 31 Captain Bearse Rd., South Yarmouth, 02664

Damian, Rinaldo, (Retired), 165 Providence Rd., Whitinsville, 01588

Dargis, Andre E., (Retired), 9031 E. Corrine Dr., Scottsdale, AZ 85260

Debitetto, Ronald E., (Retired), 66 Stetson St., Hyannis, 02601

Diorio, Ralph A., P.O. Box 344, Auburn, 01501

Donahue, Martin P., (Retired), 101 Wilson Ave., Spencer, 01562

Donoghue, Henry A., (Retired), 29 Saint Elmo Rd., 01602

Dumphy, Charles, (Retired), 30 Julio Dr., Shrewsbury, 01545

Dunkley, George, 1545 Via Brisa del Lago, San Marcos, CA 92078

Dwyer, John A., (Retired), 25 Wayside Ln., Lowell, 01852

Egan, Thomas F., (Retired), One S. Flagg St., 01602

Fleming, Thomas B., (Retired)

Fortin, Richard A., (Retired), 10 Edwards St., Leicester, 01524

Galonek, David B., (Retired), 30 Julio Dr., Apt. 244, Shrewsbury, 01545

Gariepy, Andre M., (Retired), 855 John Fitch Hwy., Unit 27, Fitchburg, 01420

Gariepy, Robert E., (Retired), 35 Julio Dr., Apt. 311, Shrewsbury, 01545

Goodwin, Raymond M. Jr., 149 Chestnut St., Clinton, 01510

Gould, Louis J., (Retired), 875 John Fitch Hwy., #15, Fitchburg, 01420

Grochowski, Bernard J., (Retired), Box 9839, Las Vegas, NV 89191

Horgan, John E., (Retired), 35 Julio Dr., Apt. 328-E, Shrewsbury, 01545

Jurgelonis, Joseph J.

Kelley, Robert E., (Retired), 1290 Grafton St., 01604

Labonte, Richard H., (Retired), 101 Chadwick St., 01605

Lamothe, C. Romeo, (Retired), 35 Julio Dr., Apt. 219E, Shrewsbury, 01545

Laperle, Theodore R., (Retired), 49 Woodland St., Fitchburg, 01420

Lewandowski, Richard P., M.A., (Retired), 59 Belgian Way, Fitchburg, 01420

Mahoney, Thomas E., (Retired), 5 Daniel Dr., North Oxford, 01537

McKiernan, Joseph W., (Retired), 35 Julio Dr., Shrewsbury, 01545

O'Brien, Dennis J., 77 Mendon St., Uxbridge, 01569

O'Leary, Cornelius F., (Retired), 555 Plantation St., 01605

O'Shea, James B., (Retired), 25 Round House Rd., Bourne, 02532

Pecevich, Conrad S., D.M., (Retired)

Remillard, Andre N., (Retired), 12 Brigham Rd., 01609

Ryan, Edward M., (Retired), 8 Presidential Circuit, West Brookfield, 01585

Stachura, Thaddeus X., (Retired), 96 Rockland Rd., Auburn, 01501

Tougas, Paul J., (Retired), 53 Hillside Dr. W., Boylston, 01583

White, Peter H., (Retired), 1001 Sister Barbara Way, Apt. 102, Georgetown, IN 47122.

Permanent Deacons:

Aliskevicz, John J., St. Bernard, Fitchburg

Archibald, Norbert H.

Aubuchon, Ronald J., (Retired)

Audette, Paul T., Our Lady of Mt. Carmel, Worcester, MA

Baczewski, Stanley H., Annunciation Parish, Gardner

Baniukiewicz, Joseph M., Christ the King, Worcester

Barton, John, St. Christopher, Worcester

Bilow, William A. Jr., St. Anne, Shrewsbury & Office of the Diaconate

Bosse, Raymond J., (Retired)

Briggs, Roy F., Blessed Sacrament, Worcester

Buron, Ronald B., St. Brigid, Millbury

Camacho, Teodoro, St. John Paul II, Southbridge

Caplette, Keith, St. Anne / St. Patrick, Sturbridge

Carrier, Mark, St. Anthony of Padua, Fitchburg

Carrier, Paul J., (Retired), (Retired), Annunciation Parish, Gardner

Chase, Michael, Christ The King, Worcester

Clonan, Joseph V., (Retired)

Coggins, Frederick, St. Mary, North Grafton

Colgate, Malcolm, St. Francis of Assisi, South Barre

Colley, Scott, St. Francis of Assisi, Athol

Colon, William B., (On Leave)

Connelly, Paul R., St. Roch, Oxford

Connor, James A., St. Vincent de Paul, Baldwinville

Connor, Michael P., (Retired)

Connor, Robert Jr., St. Cecilia, Leominster

Corby, Michael P., St. Joseph & St. Pius X, Leicester

Cormier, Dennis J., St. Edward the Confessor, Westminster

Couture, James, St. Joseph, Fitchburg

Covino, Paul F.X., Assumption College, Worcester

Cross, Timothy, St. Mary, Jefferson

Croteau, Andre W., (Retired)

Daluga, Richard B., (Retired), Henderson, NV

Deignan, Kevin, Immaculate Conception, Worcester

DeMartino, Dominick F., St. Anne & St. Patrick, Sturbridge

Denning, James, St. Ann, North Oxford

Desjardin, Richard C., St. Denis, Ashburnham

Desmarais, Ernest E., (Retired)

Devine, Philip E., (Retired)

DeVito, Frederick A., (Retired)

Dio, Robert F., St. Peter, Worcester

DiPadua, James F., (Retired), 86 Old East St., Petersham

Doyle, Walter F., (Retired)

Driscoll, Patrick M., St. Richard, Sterling

Dugan, John, St. Mary, Uxbridge

Dunphy, Melvin A., New Port Richey, FL

DuVarney, Joseph T., (Retired)

Escobar, Francisco, St. Paul Cathedral, Worcester

Estremera, George, St. Peter & St. Andrew, Worcester

Faford, Peter R., St. Joseph, Charlton

Fernandez, Israel, St. Paul, Worcester

Ferrarone, William G., (Leave of Absence)

Finan, Christopher R., St. Patrick, Whitinsville

Fiore, Anthony, (Retired)

Franchi, John A., (Retired)

Gadbois, Brian, St. Francis of Assisi, South Barre

Gagliani, Anthony, St. Theresa, Blackstone

Gemme, Pierre G.L., St. Patrick, Rutland

Gendron, Steven P., St. Bernard, Fitchburg

Gervais, Marc E., Good Shepherd, Linwood

Giard, Arthur J. Jr., (Retired)

Graves, James E., St. Anna, Leominster

Green, Amos H. Sr., (Retired)

Griffin, William, St. John, Guardian of our Lady, Clinton

Hafferty, Michael J., St. Denis, East Douglas

Harkins, Frederick A., (Retired)

Hayes, Myles, Our Lady of Providence, Worcester

Hays, William, St. Patrick, Falmouth

Isabelle, David R., Souza-Baranowski Correction Center, Lancaster

King, Loren M., (Retired)

Klug, Dennis J., Prison Ministry

Kohut, Stephen, Our Lady of Czestochowa, Worcester

Lagimoniere, Bryan A., Our Lady Immaculate, Athol

Lajoie, David O., St. Anthony of Padua, Dudley

LeDoux, John F., Our Lady of the Rosary, Worcester

Leger, Robert, (Retired)

Lesieur, Paul J., Sacred Heart of Jesus, Webster

Linderman, James L., (Retired)

Lizardo, Franklin, St. Paul Cathedral, Worcester

Manella, Joseph R., (Retired)

Marshall, Thomas E., (Leave of Absence)

Martino, Richard C., St. Mary of the Hills, Boylston

McCaffrey, Joseph A., (Retired)

Meilus, Eduardas, St. Mark, Sutton

Mello, Paul, (Retired)

Menard, Richard A. III, (Leave of Absence)

Michaud, Roland R., (Retired)

Miller, Gary, (Retired)

Miller, W. Steve, St. Anne / St. Patrick, Sturbridge

Motyka, Peter J., St. Louis, Webster

Mussulli, Pasquale, Sacred Heart of Jesus, Milford

Myska, Frank B. Jr., Immaculate Conception, Worcester

Nguyen, Peter Quy, St. Peter, Worcester

Nguyen, Van X., St. John, Worcester

Nogueira, Benjamin A., (Retired), St. Bernard, Fitchburg

Novick, Colin, Cathedral of St. Paul, Worcester

O'Connor, George, (Retired)

Olson, Richard V., (Retired)

Packard, Lee, (Retired)

Reisinger, Scott R., Blessed Sacrament, New York

Reuter, Paul J., Holy Family & St. Stephen, Worcester

Ryan, Peter, St. Anne, Shrewsbury

Shea, William, St. Joseph, Charlton

Shields, Court J., Holy Trinity, Harvard

Skonieczny, Thomas A.

Stevens, Wesley, St. Ann & St. Patrick, Sturbridge

Stewart, Patrick W., St. Patrick, Whitinsville

Stidsen, Brian, St. Patrick, Rutland

Surozenski, Anthony R., (Retired)

Sweet, Harry M., (Retired)

Tantillo, Salvatore, St. Anthony di Padua, Fitchburg

Tatro, Richard J., Holy Cross, East Templeton

Tran, Vincent Quat, St. Peter, Northbridge

Vaillancourt, David F., St. Mary, Milford

Varney, Thomas J., St. James, South Grafton

Vidito, Bruce R., St. Stephen, Worcester

Wagner, Thomas A., (On Duty Outside the Diocese)

Werner, Robert, (Retired)

White, William, St. Anthony, Dudley; Catholic Scouting

Xatse, Anthony J., Cathedral of St. Paul, Worcester.

INSTITUTIONS LOCATED IN DIOCESE

[A] COLLEGES AND UNIVERSITIES

WORCESTER. *Assumption College* (1904) 500 Salisbury St., 01609. Tel: 508-767-7321; Fax: 508-767-7169; Email: presoffice@assumption.edu; Web: www.assumption.edu. Dr. Francesco C. Cesareo, Pres.; Peter Wells, Exec. Vice Pres.; Louise Carroll Keeley, Exec.; Timothy Stanton, Exec.; Catherine M. Woodbrooks, Exec.; Rev. Richard E. Lamoureux, A.A, Supr.; Robert Mirabile, Exec. A Catholic Liberal Arts College under the auspices of the Augustinians of the Assumption (Assumptionists). Clergy 10; Religious Teachers 4; Lay Teachers 141; Priests 2; Students 2,428.

College of the Holy Cross, Inc. (1843) 01610. Tel: 508-793-2011; Fax: 508-793-3030; Email: lblackwe@holycross.edu; Web: www.holycross.edu. Rev. Philip L. Boroughs, S.J., Pres.; Karen Reilly, Interim Library Dir. A College for Boarders and Day Scholars. Lay Teachers 324; Students 2,937; Jesuit Teachers 8.

PAXTON. *Anna Maria College*, 50 Sunset Ln., Paxton, 01612. Tel: 508-849-3300; Fax: 508-849-3334; Email: toliver@annamaria.edu; Web: www.annamaria.edu. Mary Lou Retelle, Pres.; Barbara Zawalich, Registrar; Tricia Oliver, Dir. College Rel.; Ms. Jan Wilbur, Librarian. Sisters of St. Anne.A Coed Catholic College. Clergy 4; Lay Teachers 230; Priests 1; Sisters 1; Students 1,650.

[B] HIGH SCHOOLS, CENTRAL

WORCESTER. *Holy Name Central Catholic Junior/Senior High School* (1942) (Grades 7-12), 144 Granite St., 01604. Tel: 508-753-6371; Fax: 508-831-1287; Email: ed.reynolds@holyname.

net; Web: www.holyname.net. Mr. Edward M. Reynolds, B.A., M.Ed., Prin., Email: ereynolds@holyname.net; Rev. James B. Flynn, B.A., L.S.T., Ph.D., Senior Counselor. Lay Teachers 45; Priests 1; Students 550.

St. Peter-Marian Central Catholic Junior/Senior High School (1976) (Grades 7-12), 781 Grove St., 01605-3196. Tel: 508-852-5555; Fax: 508-852-7238; Email: spmsroffice@spmguardians.org. Mrs. Denise Allain, B.A., M.A., Prin., High School; Mr. William Driscoll, B.A., M.A., M.Ed., Asst. Prin. for Student Affairs; Michael Clark, Asst. Supt. Lay Teachers 32; Students 376.

FITCHBURG. *St. Bernard's Central Catholic High School* (1926) 45 Harvard St., Fitchburg, 01420. Tel: 978-342-3212; Fax: 978-345-8067; Email: rblanchard@stbernardscchs.org; Web: stbernardscchs.org. Robert Blanchard, M.A., Prin. Lay Teachers 14; Priests 1; Students 160; Total Staff 16.

[C] HIGH SCHOOLS, PAROCHIAL

WORCESTER. *St. Mary's Junior/Senior High School*, (Grades 7-12), 50 Richland St., 01610. Tel: 508-753-1170; Fax: 508-795-0560; Email: acormier@stmaryshigh.org; Web: www.stmarysworcester.org. Adam Cormier, Pres. Our Lady of Czestochowa Parish Lay Teachers 16; Students 90.

[D] HIGH SCHOOLS, PRIVATE

WORCESTER. *Notre Dame Academy*, 425 Salisbury St., 01609. Tel: 508-757-6200; Fax: 508-757-7200; Email: kbarr@nda-worc.org; Web: www.nda-worc.org. Kathryn Barr, Head of School. A Private Day School for Girls. Religious Teachers 1; Girls 200; Lay Teachers 33; Sisters of Notre Dame de Namur 200.

FITCHBURG. *Notre Dame Preparatory School*, 171 South St., Fitchburg, 01420. Tel: 978-343-7635; Fax: 978-343-4379; Email: ndpfa@hotmail.com; Web: www.npdschool.com. Mr. Jeff Hammond, Headmaster. Lay Teachers 3; Students 27.

LANCASTER. *Trivium School* (1979) (Grades 7-12), 471 Langen Rd., Lancaster, 01523. Tel: 978-365-4795; Email: office@triviumschool.com; Web: triviumschool.com. Dr. William M. Schmitt, Headmaster. Lay Teachers 12; Students 85.

SHREWSBURY. *St. John's High School* (1898) 378 Main St., Shrewsbury, 01545. Tel: 508-842-8934; Fax: 508-842-3670; Email: mgranados@stjohnshigh.org; Email: azequeira@stjohnshigh.org; Web: www.stjohnshigh.org. Mr. Alex Zequeira, Headmaster; Mrs. Margaret Granados, Prin.; Stephanie O'Donnell, Librarian; John Ermilio, Admin. Xaverian Brothers Boys 900; Lay Teachers 70; Students 900.

STILL RIVER. *Immaculate Heart of Mary School* (1976) 282 Still River Rd., P.O. Box 1000, Still River, 01467. Tel: 978-456-8877, Ext. 1011; Email: brthomas@saintbenedict.com; Web: www.immaculateheartschool.org. Bro. Thomas Augustine, M.I.C.M., Prin. Brothers 2; Lay Teachers 2; Sisters 8; Students 125; Total Staff 15.

[E] MIDDLE SCHOOLS, PRIVATE

WORCESTER. *Nativity School of Worcester*, (Grades 5-8), 67 Lincoln St., 01605. Tel: 508-799-0100; Fax: 508-799-3951; Email: donate@nativityworcester.org; Web: www.nativityworcester.org. Patrick Maloney, Pres.; Sean Dillon, Prin.; J. Christopher Collins, Chm. Bd. Boys 64; Lay Teachers 20; Priests 1; Students 64.

[F] ELEMENTARY SCHOOLS, CENTRAL

WORCESTER. *St. Peter's Central Catholic Elementary School* (1921) 865 Main St., 01610. Tel: 508-791-6496; Fax: 508-770-0818; Email: meg.kursonis@stpetercc.com; Web: www.stpetercentralcatholic.com. Mrs. Meg Kursonis, Head of School. Lay Teachers 20; Preschool 48; Total Enrollment 344; Elementary School Students 296.

UXBRIDGE. *Our Lady of Valley Regional School* (1964) 75 Mendon St., Uxbridge, 01569. Tel: 508-278-5851; Fax: 508-278-0391. Marilyn F. Willand, Prin. Lay Teachers 11; Students 211; Part-time Teachers 6.

WEBSTER. *All Saints Academy of Webster, Massachussetts, Inc.*, (Grades PreK-8), 12 Day St., Webster, 01570. Tel: 508-943-2735; Email: headofschool@allsaintswebster.org; Web: www.allsaintswebster.org. Mrs. Joan Matys, Prin. Clergy 2; Religious Teachers 1; Lay Teachers 20; Sisters 1; Students 190.

[G] ELEMENTARY SCHOOLS, PAROCHIAL

SOUTHBRIDGE. *Trinity Catholic Academy*, (Grades PreK-8), 11 Pine St., Southbridge, 01550. Tel: 508-765-5991; Fax: 508-765-0017; Email: jcitta@tca11.com; Web: www.trinitycatholicacademy.org. Mrs. Josie Citta, Prin.; Maureen Carra Gher, Librarian. Clergy 1; Lay Teachers 13; Students 153; Total Staff 22.

[H] ELEMENTARY SCHOOLS, PRIVATE

WORCESTER. *Venerini Academy*, (Grades PreK-8), 27 Edward St., 01605. Tel: 508-753-3210; Fax: 508-754-6050; Email: cpolselli@gmail.com; Web: www.veneriniacademy.com. Mrs. Carolyn Polselli, Prin. Religious Teachers 1; Lay Teachers 24; Sisters 3; Students 212.

[I] CATHOLIC CHARITIES

WORCESTER. *Catholic Charities* (1950) 10 Hammond St., 01610-1513. Tel: 508-798-0191; Fax: 508-797-5659; Email: smacmajor@ccworc.org; Web: www.ccworc.org. Laura Becker, CFO; Mr. Timothy McMahon, Dir. Tot Asst. Annually 48,000; Total Staff 265.

North County Area Office, 196 Mechanic St., Leominster, 01453. Tel: 978-840-0696; Fax: 978-345-4161. Maritza Cedeno, Admin.

Homecare Program, 12 Riverbend St., Athol, 01331-2520. Tel: 978-249-4563; Fax: 978-249-2545. Heather MacDonald, Sr. Admin.

Southern Worcester Co. Offices

Southbridge Area Office, 79 Elm St., Southbridge, 01550-2601. Tel: 508-765-5936; Fax: 508-764-4153. Marie Kudron, Admin.

Blackstone Valley/Greater Milford Area Office, 200 Main St., Milford, 01757. Tel: 508-234-3800; Fax: 508-234-2321. Danishka Valdes, Admin.

126 Main St., Rm. 6, Milford, 01757. Tel: 508-478-9632; Fax: 508-478-9632. Noreen Landry, Admin.

Senior Employment Service, 10 Hammond St., 01610-1513. Tel: 508-798-0191; Fax: 508-797-5659. Susan Maedler, Admin.

Family & Community Services, 10 Hammond St., 01610-1513. Tel: 508-798-0191; Fax: 508-797-5659. Marie Kudron, Admin.

Literacy, Citizenship & Immigration, 10 Hammond St., 01610-1513. Tel: 508-798-0191; Fax: 508-797-5659. Madelyn Hennessy, Admin. Tot Asst. Annually 335; Total Staff 4.

Crozier House, 10 Hammond St., 01610-1513. Tel: 508-798-0191; Fax: 508-797-5659. Scott Eaton, Admin. A Half-Way House for Substance Abusing Men.

Mercy Centre (Developmental Disabilities), 25 W. Chester St., 01605-1136. Tel: 508-852-7165; Fax: 508-856-9755. Margaret Buzzell, Admin. Day Program and Employment Training for Adults with Developmental Disabilities. Tot Asst. Annually 122; Total Staff 25.

Youville House Shelter for Homeless Families, 133 Granite St., 01604-4500. Tel: 508-753-3084; Fax: 508-754-0139. Gail Flynn, Admin. Bed Capacity 45; Total Staff 12; Total Assisted 75.

[J] CHILD CARE AGENCIES

WORCESTER. *The Guild of St. Agnes*, 405 Grove St., 01605. Tel: 508-755-2238; Fax: 508-754-2026; Email: swood016@aol.com; Web: www.guildofstagnes.org. Mr. Edward Madaus, Exec. Dir. Centers for Infants, Toddlers, Preschoolers & School-age Children. Children aged 4 weeks-12 years.; Family Day Care Program ages 6 weeks-12 years. Children 1,600; Clergy 225; Total Staff 300.

FITCHBURG. *Guild of St. Agnes*, 62 Dover St., Fitchburg, 01420. Tel: 978-343-3042; Fax: 978-343-2610. Total Staff 7; Total Assisted 75.

LEICESTER. *McAuley Nazareth Home for Boys* (1901) 77 Mulberry St., Leicester, 01524. Tel: 508-892-4886; Fax: 508-892-9736; Email: naz1901@mcauleynazareth.org; Web: www.nazareth-home.org. Kim E. Pare, M.Ed., C.A.G.S., Exec. Dir. Diocese of Worcester. Boys 28; Lay Teachers 2; Sisters 3; Students 15; Special Education School: Boys 15.

[K] SPECIAL HOSPITALS AND SANATORIA

WORCESTER. *Notre Dame Health Care Center, Inc.*, 559 Plantation St., 01605. Tel: 508-852-3011; Fax: 508-852-0397; Email: klemay@notredameltcc.org; Web: www.notredamehealthcare.org. Katherine Lemay, CEO. Bed Capacity 123; Tot Asst. Annually 100; Total Staff 219.

WHITINSVILLE. *St. Camillus Nursing Home Inc.*, 447 Hill St., Whitinsville, 01588. Tel: 508-234-7306. William Graves, Admin.; Bro. Thomas Farrell, O.S. Cam., Dir. Pastoral Care. Bed Capacity 123; Brothers 2; Priests 1.

[L] HEALTH SERVICES

WORCESTER. *Pernet Family Health Service*, 237 Millbury St., 01610. Tel: 508-755-1228; Fax: 508-797-3477; Email: sdooley@pernetfamilyhealth.org; Web: pernetfamilyhealth.org. Sheilah Dooley, Exec. Dir. Mission of the Little Sisters of the Assumption.; Certified Home Health and Social Service Agency. Focus of services toward the parent and young child. Parenting groups, family activities available, Early Childhood Development services also available. Tot Asst. Annually 11,000; Total Staff 28; Little Sisters of the Assumption 1; Total Volunteers 100.

[M] HOMES FOR AGED

WORCESTER. *Notre Dame du Lac*, 555 Plantation St., 01605. Tel: 508-852-5800; Fax: 508-852-1700; Email: klaganelli@notredamehealthcare.org; Web: www.notredamehealthcare.org. Karen Laganelli, Exec. Tot Asst. Annually 158; Total Staff 97; Apartments 108.

LEOMINSTER. *Presentation Health Care Center* (1993) 99 Church St., Leominster, 01453-3147. Tel: 978-537-7856; Fax: 978-840-1564; Email: srmaureenrn@verizon.net. Sr. Patricia Anastasio, P.B.V.M., Pres. Purpose: To operate and maintain a rest home for aged and/or infirmed sisters at Presentation Convent. Bed Capacity 10; Total Staff 25; Total in Residence (Closed Skilled Unit) 10.

SPENCER. *St. Joseph's Abbey Resident Care Facility, Inc.* (2003) 167 N. Spencer Rd., Spencer, 01562-1233. Tel: 508-885-8702; Fax: 508-885-8726; Email: aelredmarrah@yahoo.com; Web: www.spencerabbey.org. Bro. Aelred Marrah, O.C.S.O., Asst. Admin. Bed Capacity 12; Total Staff 12; Total Assisted 18.

[N] MONASTERIES AND RESIDENCES OF PRIESTS AND BROTHERS

WORCESTER. *Assumptionists (Augustinians of the Assumption)* (1845) 50 Old English Rd., 01609. Tel: 508-754-6276; Fax: 508-797-1789; Email: vtgdinh@gmail.com; Web: www.assumption.org. Rev. Eugene LaPlante, A.A., Chap. & Supr.; Bro. Richard Gagnon, A.A., Treas. & College Admissions Officer; Revs. Oliver (Robert) Blanchette, A.A.; Leo Brassard, A.A.; Theodore L. Fortier, A.A.; Aidan M. Furlong, A.A.; Norman Meiklejohn, A.A.; Camillus Thibault, A.A.; Paul Vaudreuil, A.A., A.A.; Dihn Vo Tran Gia, Supr. Brothers 1; Priests 9; Total Staff 2.

Augustinians of the Assumption at Assumption College aka Assumptionists, Emmanuel House, 512 Salisbury St., 01609-1326. Tel: 508-767-7523; Fax: 508-793-9701; Email: relamour@yahoo.com; Web: www.assumption.us. Revs. Richard E. Lamoureux, A.A, Vice Pres.; Roger R. Corriveau, A.A., Treas.; Peter Precourt, A.A., Prov. Dir. of Formation; Ronald Sibugan, A.A., Campus Min., Email: r.sibugan@assumption.edu; Ai Nguyen Chi, Prof.; Donat R. Lamothe, A.A. Priests 6; Total in Residence 6; Total Staff 2.

Jesuits of the Holy Cross, Inc. (1843) 1 College St., 01610. Tel: 508-793-2427; Fax: 508-793-2624; Email: ciampi@holycross.edu; Web: www.holycross.edu/index.html. Revs. Thomas D. McMurray, S.J., Chap./Admissions Nativity School of Worchester; Philip L. Boroughs, S.J.; William F. Campbell, S.J.; William A. Clark, S.J.; Charles J. Dunn, S.J.; Michael F. Ford, S.J.; John F. Gavin, S.J.; Paul F. Harman, S.J.; James M. Hayes, S.J.; Vincent A. Lapomarda, S.J.; Earle L. Markey, S.J.; Janez Percic, S.J.; John P. Reboli, S.J.; William E. Reiser, S.J.; Michael J. Rogers, S.J.; Kevin Spinale, S.J.; William E. Stempsey, S.J.; James R. Stormes, S.J.; Edward J. Vodoklys, S.J.; William Woody. Priests 19.

FITCHBURG. *Missionaries of La Salette (MA), Inc.*, St. Joseph, 46 Woodland St., Fitchburg, 01420. Tel: 978-342-7907; Fax: 978-345-7678. Total in Residence 1.

PETERSHAM. *St. Mary's Monastery*, 271 N. Main St., P.O. Box 345, Petersham, 01366. Tel: 978-724-3350; Email: monks@stmarysmonastery.org; Web: www.stmarysmonastery.org. Rev. Gregory Phillips, O.S.B., Supr. Priest-Monks 2; Monks 4.

SHREWSBURY. *Xaverian Brothers*, 378 Main St., Shrewsbury, 01545. Tel: 508-845-1878; Fax: 508-842-8934; Email: pfeeney@stjohnshigh.org. Bros. Paul Feeney, C.F.X., Dir.; J. Conal Owens, C.F.X.; William Cushing. Brothers 3.

SPENCER. *St. Joseph's Abbey*, Spencer, 01562-1233. Tel: 508-885-8700; Fax: 508-885-8701; Email: monks@spencerabbey.org; Web: www.spencerabbey.org. Rt. Rev. Damian Carr, O.C.S.O.; Revs. Dominic Whedbee, O.C.S.O., Prior; Luke Truhan, O.C.S.O., Dir.; Robert Kevin Anderson, O.C.S.O., (In Service Outside the Community); Gabriel Bertoniere, O.C.S.O.; Patrick Brown, O.C.S.O.; William Dingwall, O.C.S.O.; Matthew Flynn, O.C.S.O.; Kevin Hunt, O.C.S.O.; Aquinas Keane, O.C.S.O.; Isaac Keeley, O.C.S.O.; Eugene

Lacasse, O.C.S.O.; David Lavich, O.C.S.O., (In Service Outside the Community); Simeon Leiva-Merikakis, O.C.S.O.; Aidan (Arthur H.) Logan, O.C.S.O., (On Leave to Military Ordinariate); Emmanuel Morinelli, O.C.S.O.; James Palmigiano, O.C.S.O.; Francis Rodriguez, O.C.S.O.; Peter Schmidt, O.C.S.O.; Timothy Scott, O.C.S.O.; Gerald Sears, O.C.S.O.; Vincent Rogers. Cistercian Order of the Strict Observance (Trappists).

Cistercian Abbey of Spencer, Inc. Novices 2; Solemnly Professed 44; Total Priests in Community 23; Total in Community 53.

STILL RIVER. *Benedictine Monks, St. Benedict Abbey* (Harvard) 252 Still River Rd., P.O. Box 67, Still River, 01467. Tel: 978-456-3221; Fax: 978-456-8181; Email: saintbenedict@abbey.org; Web: www.abbey.org. Rt. Rev. Xavier Connelly, O.S.B., Abbot; Revs. Peter Connelly, O.S.B.; Anthony Kloss, O.S.B.; Marc Crilly, O.S.B.; Very Rev. James Doran, O.S.B., Prior; Rev. Augustine Senz, O.S.B. Brothers 3; Priests 6.

WHITINSVILLE. *St. Camillus Community*, 447 Hill St., Whitinsville, 01588. Tel: 508-234-7306; Fax: 508-234-7597; Email: bgraves@stcamillus.com; Web: www.stcamillus.com.

[O] CONVENTS AND RESIDENCES FOR SISTERS

WORCESTER. *Assumption Residence of the Sisters of the Assumption of the Blessed Virgin*, 316 Lincoln St., 01605. Tel: 508-856-9383; Fax: 978-724-0200; Email: lono9595@aol.com; Web: www.sasv.ca. Sisters 10.

Little Franciscans of Mary (1889) 12 Jones St., Apt. 1, 01604. Tel: 508-755-0878; Fax: 508-755-6822. Sr. Adrienne Lamoureux, P.F.M., Treas. Sisters 5.

Little Sisters of the Assumption, Pernet Family Health Service, Inc., 237 Millbury St., 01610. Tel: 508-755-1228; Fax: 508-797-3477; Email: sdooley@pernetfamilyhealth.org; Web: www.pernetfamilyhealth.org. Mrs. Denise Allain, B.A., M.A., Prov. Family Health Agency. Nursing and Family Development Services-Home Based. Volunteers 100.

Religious Oblates to Divine Love, 50 Moore Ave., 01602-1820. Sr. Rosita Campos, R.O.D.A., Supr. Sisters 2.

Religious Venerini Sisters, 23 Edward St., 01605. Tel: 508-754-1020; Email: trcarchidi1@gmail.com; Web: www.religiousvenerinisisters.org. Sr. Teresa Rose Carchidi, M.P.V., Prov. Sisters 17.

Sisters of St. Joseph, S.S.J., 101 Chadwick St., D22, 01605. Tel: 508-852-1659. Sisters 2.

Sisters of the Assumption of the Blessed Virgin, 316 Lincoln St., 01605. Tel: 508-856-9383; Fax: 508-853-0881; Email: lono9595@aol.com. Sisters Muriel Lemoine, S.A.S.V., Congregational Leader; Lorraine Normand, S.A.S.V., Treas., Tel: 508-856-9450.

Xaverian Missionary Society of Mary, Inc., Headquarters: 242 Salisbury St., 01609-1639. Tel: 508-757-0514; Fax: 508-757-0514; Email: xavsistersusa@yahoo.com.mx. Sr. Rebeca Sanchez Perez, X.M.M., Supr. Sisters 6.

CHARLTON. *Carmelite Sisters of the Eucharist of Worcester, MA*, 188 Old Worcester Rd., Charlton, 01507. Tel: 508-248-2936; Fax: 508-248-3814. Sisters 3.

LEOMINSTER. *The Sisters of the Presentation of the Blessed Virgin Mary, New Windsor, NY*, 99 Church St., Leominster, 01453. Tel: 978-537-7108; Fax: 978-537-3789; Email: pbvmadministration@hvc.rr.com; Web: www.sistersofthepresentation.org. Sisters Patricia Anastasio, P.B.V.M., Pres.; Mary Anne Seliga, P.B.V.M., Admin. Ministries are in the areas of education in parochial elementary schools; pastoral services; health care; social services. Professed Sisters 104.

Sisters of the Presentation of the B.V. Mary, Presentation Convent, 99 Church St., Leominster, 01453. Tel: 978-537-7108. Sisters Patricia Anastasio, P.B.V.M., Pres.; Mary Anne Seliga, P.B.V.M., House Coord.

PETERSHAM. *St. Scholastica Priory* (1980) 271 N. Main St., Petersham, 01366-9503. P.O. Box 606, Petersham, 01366-0606. Tel: 978-724-3213; Email: sspriory@aol.com; Web: www.stscholasticapriory.org. Very Rev. Mother Mary Elizabeth Kloss, O.S.B., Prioress; Sr. Mary Angela Kloss, O.S.B., Subprioress. Benedictine Nuns (Cloistered). Novices 3; Sisters 13; Nuns in Solemn Vows 9; Simple Vows 1.

STILL RIVER. *Sisters of Saint Benedict Center, Slaves of the Immaculate Heart of Mary Inc.* (1949) St. Ann House, 254 Still River Rd., P.O. Box 22, Still River, 01467. Tel: 978-456-8017; Fax: 978-456-8508; Email: micm@verizon.net. Professed Sisters 10.

WEBSTER. *St. Joseph Convent*, 5 Maynard St., Webster, 01570-2425. Tel: 508-943-2228; Email: cssfwebster@feliciansisters.org; Web: www.feliciansistersna.org. Sr. Jeanne Marie Akalski, C.S.S.F., Local Min. Felician Sisters 2.

[P] RETREAT HOUSES AND HOUSE OF PRAYER

SPENCER. *St. Joseph Abbey*, 167 N. Spencer Rd., Spencer, 01562-1233. Tel: 508-885-8710; Fax: 508-885-8701; Email: retreats@spencerabbey.org; Web: www.spencerabbey.org. Rev. Emmanuel Morinelli, O.C.S.O., Guest Master. Guest house and Retreat house.

Mary House, Inc. (1969) 186 N. Spencer Rd. (Rte. 31), P.O. Box 20, Spencer, 01562. Tel: 508-885-5450; Email: maryhousespencer@netzero.com; Web: maryhousespencer.com. Ms. Joyce Thomasmeyer, Pres. House of Prayer and Contemplation.

STILL RIVER. *Benedictine Monks, St. Benedict Abbey* (Harvard) (See separate listing under Monasteries and Residences for Men.) 252 Still River Rd., P.O. Box 67, Still River, 01467. Tel: 978-456-3221; Fax: 978-456-8181; Email: saintbenedict@abbey.org; Web: www.abbey.org. Rt. Rev. Xavier Connelly, O.S.B., Abbot.

[Q] NEWMAN CHAPLAINS AND CENTERS

WORCESTER. *Assumption College*, 500 Salisbury St., 01609. Tel: 508-767-7321; Fax: 508-767-7419; Email: campusministry@assumption.edu. Dr. Francesco C. Cesareo, Pres.; Rev. Ronald Sibugan, A.A., Campus Min.; Deacon Paul F.X. Covino, Dir. Campus Ministry; Stephanie McCaffrey, Asst. Dir. Campus Ministry; Vincent Sullivan-Jaques, Asst. Dir., Campus Ministry; Scott Brill, Inter-varsity Representative; Joseph Kwiatowski, Dir.

Clark University, 930 Main St., 01610. Tel: 508-793-7737. Rev. Msgr. Francis J. Scollen, Chap.

Fitchburg State College (Fitchburg), Newman Center, 333 Mechanic St., Fitchburg, 01420. Tel: 978-342-7921. Rev. Anthony Mpagi, Chap.

Holy Cross College, Campion House, 11 College St., P.O. Box 16A, 01610. Tel: 508-793-2448; Email: mkearns@holycross.edu. Ms. Marybeth Kearns-Barrett, Dir. Sisters 1.

Worcester Polytechnic Institute, Religious Center at WPI, 19 Schussler Rd., 01609. Tel: 508-981-9414; Email: alejitcocano@gmail.com. Rev. Hugo Cano.

Worcester State College, Campus Ministry Center, 17 Candlewood St., 01602. Tel: 508-929-8017. 1052 Pleasant St., Attn: Msgr. Sullivan, 01602. Rev. Msgr. Thomas J. Sullivan, Chap.

PAXTON. *Anna Maria College*, Office of Campus Ministry, 50 Sunset Ln., Paxton, 01612-1198. Tel: 508-849-3205; Email: mclavijo@annamaria.edu; Web: www.annamaria.edu. Rev. Manuel Clavijo; Deacon John Franchi. Total Staff 3.

[R] MISCELLANEOUS

WORCESTER. *Catholic Restoration Apostolate*, 123 Summer St., 01608. Tel: 508-363-5545; Fax: 508-363-5383; Email: peterbeaulieu@verizon.net. Rev. Msgr. Peter R. Beaulieu, Chap.

The Charlton Charitable Corporation, Inc. Diocese of Worcester. 49 Elm St., 01609. Tel: 508-791-7171; Fax: 508-754-2768.

Dismas House of Massachusetts, P.O. Box 30125, 01603. Tel: 508-799-9389; Fax: 508-767-9930; Email: cmdismashouse@aol.com; Web: www.dismashouse.org. David McMahon, Co-Dir.; Colleen Hilferty, Co-Dir. To provide transition for those who are leaving prison.

The Guild of Our Lady of Providence, Chancery Office of the Diocese of Worcester, 49 Elm St., 01609. Tel: 508-791-7171; Fax: 508-753-7180.

Mendon Charitable Corporation, Inc., 49 Elm St., 01609. Tel: 508-791-7171; Fax: 508-754-2768; Email: pschasel@worcesterdiocese.org. Mr. Paul G. Schasel, Mgr., Finance.

Monsignor Thomas Griffin Foundation, 49 Elm St., 01609. Tel: 508-929-4339; Fax: 508-929-4380; Email: pschasel@worcesterdiocese.org. Mr. Paul G. Schasel, Contact Person.

Visitation House, 119 Endicott St., P.O. Box 60115, 01606. Tel: 508-798-0762; Fax: 508-798-8212; Email: evelindquist@visitationhouse.org. Eve Lindquist, Exec. Dir. A transitional home for homeless pregnant women in crisis.

AUBURN. *Kateri Tekakwitha Development, Inc.*, 8 Wyoma Dr., Auburn, 01501. Tel: 508-798-8779; Fax: 508-791-6614; Email: namartyrs01501@gmail.com. Rev. John F. Gee, Contact Person.

Kateri Tekakwitha Housing Corp., 8 Wyoma Dr., Auburn, 01501. Tel: 508-798-8779; Fax: 508-791-6614.

CHARLTON. *Ministry to Retired Priests*, 188 Old Worcester Rd., Charlton, 01507. Tel: 508-868-9239; Fax: 508-248-3814. Sr. Mary Ann Bartell, C.S.E., Dir.

LANCASTER. *Community of St. John*, 465 Langen Rd., Lancaster, 01523. Tel: 978-368-8291; Email: wschmitt@triviumschool.com. Dr. William M. Schmitt, Contact Person. Total in Residence 1.

PETERSHAM. *St. Mary and St. Scholastica Church, Inc.* (1996) 271 N. Main St., P.O. Box 606, Petersham, 01366-0606. Tel: 978-724-3213; Tel: 978-724-3350; Email: srgemmameade@aol.com; Email: vincent@stmarysmonastery.org. Very Rev. Mother Mary Elizabeth Kloss, O.S.B., Pres.; Rev. Gregory Phillips, O.S.B., Vice Pres.

WHITINSVILLE. *St. Camillus Institute, Inc.*, 497 Hill St., Whitinsville, 01588. Tel: 508-266-1045. Order of the Servants of the Sick (St. Camillus).

RELIGIOUS INSTITUTES OF MEN REPRESENTED IN THE DIOCESE

For further details refer to the corresponding bracketed number in the Religious Institutes of Men or Women section.

[]—*Augustinians of the Assumption.*
[1350]—*Congregation of St. Francis Xavier*—C.F.X.
[]—*Congregation of the Sacred Stigmata.*
[0790]—*Maronite Monks of Adoration*—M.M.A.
[0720]—*Missionaries of Our Lady of LaSalette* (Seven Dolors Prov.)—M.S.
[0200]—*Order of St. Benedict* (Petersham; Still River)—O.S.B.
[]—*Society of Jesus*—S.J.
[0350]—*The Cistercians Order of the Strict Observance (Trappists)*—O.C.S.O.

RELIGIOUS INSTITUTES OF WOMEN REPRESENTED IN THE DIOCESE

[0192]—*Carmelite Sisters of the Eucharist, Inc.*—C.S.E.
[]—*Congregation of Sisters of St. Felix of Cantalice*—C.S.S.F.
[3830-01]—*Congregation of St. Joseph* (Boston, Brighton)—C.S.J.
[2575]—*Institute of the Sisters of Mercy of the Americas* (New York, NY)—R.S.M.
[2280]—*Little Franciscans of Mary*—P.F.M.
[2310]—*Little Sisters of the Assumption*—L.S.A.
[]—*Order of St. Benedict* Petersham—O.S.B.
[3390]—*Religious of the Assumption*—R.A.
[4180]—*Religious Venerini Sisters*—M.P.V.
[]—*Sisters Oblates to Divine Love*—R.O.D.A.
[2540]—*Sisters of Mercy* (Institute of Religious Sisters of Mercy of the Americas)—R.S.M.
[3000]—*Sisters of Notre Dame de Namur* (Boston, Ipswich, Japan and Connecticut Provs.)—S.N.D.
[3720]—*Sisters of Saint Anne*—S.S.A.
[3830-16]—*Sisters of St. Joseph* (Springfield)—S.S.J.
[0150]—*Sisters of the Assumption of the Blessed Virgin*—S.A.S.V.
[3320]—*Sisters of the Presentation of the B.V.M.*—P.B.V.M.
[]—*Slaves of the Immaculate Heart of Mary*—M.I.C.M.
[4230]—*Xaverian Missionary Society of Mary, Inc.*—X.M.M.

DIOCESAN CEMETERIES

WORCESTER. *St. John's Cemetery*, 260 Cambridge St., 01603. Tel: 508-757-7415; Fax: 508-753-5244; Email: backerman@stjcemetery.com. Mrs. Michele McCarthy, Office Mgr.

Sacred Heart Cemetery, Worcester Rd., Webster, 01570. 260 Cambridge St., 01603

Sacred Heart Cemetery, W. Main St., West Brookfield, 01585

Saint Brigid Cemetery, West St., Millbury, 01527. 260 Cambridge St., 01603. Tel: 508-757-7415; Email: rackerman@stjcemetery.com

Saint George Cemetery, Paige Hill, Southbridge, 01550. 260 Cambridge St., 01603. Tel: 508-757-7415; Email: rackerman@stjcemetery.com

Saint Mary Cemetery, Main St., Holden, 01520. 260 Cambridge St., 01603. Tel: 508-757-7415; Email: rackerman@stjcemetery.com

Saint Philip Cemetery, Millbury St., Grafton, 01519. 260 Cambridge St., 01603. Tel: 508-757-7415; Email: rackerman@stjcemetery.com

Calvary Cemetery, 191 Vine St., Athol, 01331

Calvary Cemetery, Oxford Ave., Dudley, 01571. 260 Cambridge St., 01603. Tel: 508-757-7415; Email: backerman@stjcemetery.com

Gethsemane Cemetery, Fielding Way, Athol, 01331. 260 Cambridge St., 01603. Email: rackerman@stjcemetery.com. Mr. Robert Ackerman, Admin.

New Notre Dame Cemetery, Woodstock Rd., Southbridge, 01550. 260 Cambridge St., 01603. Tel: 508-757-7415; Email: rackerman@stjcemetery.com

Old Notre Dame Cemetery, Charlton St., Southbridge, 01550. 260 Cambridge St., 01603. Tel: 508-757-7415; Email: rackerman@stjcemetery.com

Saint Anne Cemetery, Arnold Rd., Sturbridge, 01518. 260 Cambridge St., 01603

NECROLOGY

† Rueger, George E., Retired Auxiliary Bishop of Worcester., Died Apr. 6, 2019
† Roy, F. Gilles, (Retired), Died Oct. 20, 2018
† Dutram, Charles J., (Retired), Died Jun. 28, 2018
† Hoey, James F., (Retired), Died Apr. 5, 2018
† Messier, Raymond P., Died Jul. 3, 2018
† Spellman, Robert M., (Retired), Died Sep. 22, 2018

An asterisk (*) denotes an organization that has established tax-exempt status directly with the IRS and is not covered by the USCCB Group Ruling.

Diocese of Yakima

(Dioecesis Yakimensis)

Most Reverend

JOSEPH J. TYSON

Bishop of Yakima; ordained June 10, 1989; appointed Auxiliary Bishop of Seattle and Titular Bishop of Migirpa May 12, 2005; ordained June 6, 2005; appointed Bishop of Yakima April 12, 2011; installed May 31, 2011.

Most Reverend

CARLOS A. SEVILLA, S.J., D.D.

Bishop Emeritus of Yakima; ordained June 3, 1966; appointed Auxiliary Bishop of San Francisco December 6, 1988; Episcopal ordination January 25, 1989; appointed Bishop of Yakima December 31, 1996; installed February 17, 1997; retired April 12, 2011. *Address all correspondence to: 5301-A Tieton Dr., Yakima, WA 98908.*

ESTABLISHED JUNE 23, 1951.

Square Miles 17,787.

Comprises the following Counties in the State of Washington: Benton, Chelan, Douglas, Grant, Kittitas, Klickitat and Yakima.

Legal Title: Corporation of the Catholic Bishop of Yakima.
For legal titles of parishes and diocesan institutions, consult the Pastoral Office.

Pastoral Office (Chancery): 5301-A Tieton Dr., Yakima, WA 98908. Tel: 509-965-7117; Fax: 509-966-8334.

Email: info@yakimadiocese.net

STATISTICAL OVERVIEW

Personnel	
Bishop	1
Retired Bishops	1
Priests: Diocesan Active in Diocese	52
Priests: Diocesan Active Outside Diocese	8
Priests: Retired, Sick or Absent	11
Number of Diocesan Priests	71
Religious Priests in Diocese	2
Total Priests in Diocese	73
Extern Priests in Diocese	1
Ordinations:	
Diocesan Priests	3
Transitional Deacons	1
Permanent Deacons in Diocese	36
Total Brothers	2
Total Sisters	26
Parishes	
Parishes	40
With Resident Pastor:	
Resident Diocesan Priests	31
Resident Religious Priests	2
Without Resident Pastor:	
Administered by Priests	7
Missions	3
Professional Ministry Personnel:	
Brothers	2
Sisters	26
Lay Ministers	15
Welfare	
Health Care Centers	1
Total Assisted	91,500
Day Care Centers	1
Total Assisted	180
Special Centers for Social Services	5
Total Assisted	43,766
Educational	
Diocesan Students in Other Seminaries	11
Total Seminarians	11
High Schools, Private	1
Total Students	222
Elementary Schools, Diocesan and Parish	6
Total Students	1,524
Catechesis/Religious Education:	
High School Students	1,522
Elementary Students	3,546
Total Students under Catholic Instruction	6,825
Teachers in the Diocese:	
Sisters	1
Lay Teachers	138
Vital Statistics	
Receptions into the Church:	
Infant Baptism Totals	2,640
Minor Baptism Totals	263
Adult Baptism Totals	85
Received into Full Communion	357
First Communions	2,693
Confirmations	1,743
Marriages:	
Catholic	352
Interfaith	60
Total Marriages	412
Deaths	470
Total Catholic Population	184,743
Total Population	730,016

Former Bishops—Most Revs. JOSEPH P. DOUGHERTY, D.D., First Bishop of Yakima; ord. June 14, 1930; appt. July 9, 1951; cons. Sept. 26, 1951; resigned Feb. 5, 1969; died July 10, 1970; CORNELIUS M. POWER, D.D., Second Bishop of Yakima; ord. June 3, 1939; appt. Feb. 5, 1969; cons. May 1, 1969; elevated to Metropolitan See of Portland in Oregon, Jan. 24, 1974; died May 22, 1997; NICOLAS E. WALSH, D.D., Third Bishop of Yakima; ord. June 6, 1942; appt. Sept. 5, 1974; cons. Oct. 28, 1974; installed Oct. 30, 1974; transferred to Archdiocese of Seattle as Auxiliary Bishop, Aug. 10, 1976; resigned Sept. 6, 1983; died April 22, 1997; WILLIAM S. SKYLSTAD, D.D., Fourth Bishop of Yakima; ord. May 21, 1960; appt. Feb. 22, 1977; cons. May 12, 1977; transferred to Spokane as Bishop of Spokane, April 17, 1990; FRANCIS E. GEORGE, O.M.I., Ph.D., S.T.D., Fifth Bishop of Yakima; ord. Dec. 21, 1963; appt. July 10, 1990; cons. Sept. 21, 1990; appt. Metropolitan See of Portland in Oregon, April 30, 1996; appt. Metropolitan See of Chicago, April 8, 1997; created Cardinal Priest, Feb. 21, 1998; died April 17, 2015.; CARLOS A. SEVILLA, S.J., ord. June 3, 1966; appt. Auxiliary Bishop of San Francisco Dec. 6, 1988; Episcopal ordination Jan. 25, 1989; appt. Bishop of Yakima Dec. 31, 1996; installed Feb. 17, 1997; retired April 12, 2011.

Pastoral Office (Chancery)—5301-A Tieton Dr., Yakima, 98908. Tel: 509-965-7117; Fax: 509-966-8334.

Vicar General—Very Rev. Msgr. JOHN A. ECKER, 5301-A Tieton Dr., Yakima, 98908-3493.

Vicar for Priests—Very Rev. V. FELIPE PULIDO.

Moderator of the Curia—Rev. Msgr. ROBERT M. SILER.

Chancellor—Rev. Msgr. ROBERT M. SILER.

Vice Chancellor for Personnel & Policies—DIANA E. APARICIO-SOSA.

Office of Canonical Concerns—5301-D Tieton Dr., Yakima, 98908. Tel: 509-965-7123.

Judicial Vicar—Very Rev. MICHAEL J. IBACH, J.C.L.

Adjutant Judicial Vicar—Rev. DAVID J. JIMENEZ ALVAREZ, J.C.L.

Judges—Very Rev. MICHAEL J. IBACH, J.C.L.; Revs. MICHAEL E. BRZEZOWSKI; DAVID J. JIMENEZ ALVAREZ, J.C.L.

Defenders of the Bond—Rev. Msgr. PERRON J. AUVE; Very Rev. THOMAS C. CHAMPOUX; Rev. SALOMON COVARRUBIAS PINA.

Advocates—Clergy and pastoral ministers by appointment.

Notaries—MRS. M. GUADALUPE FLORES; MRS. EILEEN M. WALKER.

Diocesan Consultors—Very Revs. OSMAR R. AGUIRRE; JAIME H. CHACON, M.Div.; MICHAEL J. IBACH, J.C.L.; Very Rev. Msgr. JOHN A. ECKER; Very Revs. ARGEMIRO OROZCO; V. FELIPE PULIDO; LAWRENCE T. REILLY; Rev. Msgrs. ROBERT M. SILER; MARIO A. SALAZAR, (Retired).

Diocesan Offices, Commissions, Committees

Adults with Developmental Disabilities—MICHELE WALL, 12203 Klendon Dr., Yakima, 98908. Tel: 509-965-4642.

Calvary Cemetery—Rev. DARELL J. MITCHELL, Dir., 1405 S. 24th Ave., Yakima, 98902. Tel: 509-457-8462; Fax: 509-457-6267.

CYO—DON ERICKSON, 410 S. 47th Ave., Yakima, 98908. Tel: 509-965-3382.

Campaign for Human Development—5301-A Tieton Dr., Yakima, 98908. MRS. DARLENE DARNELL, M.S.W.

Catholic Charities—5301-C Tieton Dr., Yakima, 98908. Tel: 509-965-7100. MRS. DARLENE DARNELL, M.S.W., Pres. & CEO.

Charismatic Renewal, English—5301-A Tieton Dr., Yakima, 98908. Tel: 509-965-7117.

Charismatic Renewal, Spanish—Very Rev. JAIME H. CHACON, M.Div., St. Aloysius Parish, 213 N. Beech St., Toppenish, 98948.

Cursillo, English—Deacons KERRY TURLEY, Spiritual Dir.; DAN SISK, Lay Dir., 1211 Marshall Ave., Richland, 99354. Tel: 509-946-2264.

Spanish—Deacon FRANK MARTINEZ, Spiritual Dir., 3286 W. Shore Dr., Moses Lake, 98837. Tel: 509-765-9536; TEODORO FLORES, Lay Dir., East Wenatchee, 98802. Tel: 509-885-0630.

Native American—Rev. JOHN M. SHAW, Spiritual Dir., (Retired), 213 N. Beech St., Toppenish, 98948. Tel: 509-865-2400.

Director of Planned Giving—ALMA BENITEZ, 5301-A Tieton Dr., Yakima, 98908. Tel: 509-965-7117.

Development Office/Stewardship—ALMA BENITEZ, Dir., 5301-A Tieton Dr., Yakima, 98908. Tel: 509-367-5299.

Ecumenical Liaison—Very Rev. Msgr. JOHN A. ECKER, 15 S. 12th Ave., Yakima, 98902. Tel: 509-575-3713.

Engaged Encounter—FRANK BECKER; TRACY BECKER, 2080 New Haven Loop, Richland, 99352. Tel: 509-627-1076. Registration Coordinators: PAUL

ACKERMAN; PEGI ACKERMAN, 1503 Queen Ave., Yakima, 98902. Tel: 509-528-4653; Tel: 509-575-4931.

Home Schooling—Deacon DUANE BERGER, Chap.; JONELLA LEADON, 213 S. 62nd Ave., Yakima, 98908.

Marriage Encounter—

English—Coordinators: FRANK BECKER; TRACY BECKER, 2080 New Haven Loop, Richland, 99352. Tel: 509-627-1076.

Registration—Coordinators: PAUL ACKERMAN; PEGI ACKERMAN, 1503 Queen Ave., Yakima, 98902.

Spanish—Rev. JOSE DE JESUS RAMIREZ, Mailing Address: P.O. Box 340, Royal City, 99357-0340. Tel: 509-346-2730; BENJAMIN REYES, 6522 Nelson St., West Richland, 99353. Tel: 509-438-7553; MARIA REYES, Mailing Address: 6522 Nelson St., West Richland, 99353. Tel: 509-438-7553.

Cornerstone Ministry—Deacon MIKHAIL ALNAJJAR, Email: dmikhail925@gmail.com.

Ministry & Education Center—VACANT.

Hispanic Ministries/Hispanic Ministry Formation Director—Very Rev. JAIME H. CHACON, M.Div., Vicar Hispanic Education Ministries.

Deacon Formation—Very Rev. OSMAR R. AGUIRRE, Sacred Heart, 1905 Highland Dr., Prosser, 99350; Deacon ROBERT J. SCHROM, Assoc. Dir., 7240 Rd. 17 S.W., Royal City, 99357. Tel: 509-346-9464.

Religious Education and Hispanic Catechesis—Rev. TOMAS VASQUEZ TELLEZ, 5301-B Tieton Dr., Yakima, 98908. Tel: 509-965-7117.

Youth/Young Adult Director—MARCUS AYERS, 706 N. Sprague, Ellensburg, 98926.

Youth/Young Adult Hispanic Ministry—English: Rev. PETER STEELE, St. Joseph, 212 N. 4th St., Yakima, 98901. Spanish: Very Rev. JOSE M. HERRERA, Blessed Sacrament, 1201 Missouri St., Grandview, 98930.

Deacon Council—Deacon INDALECIO ANDY GONZALEZ; MRS. ELVIA GONZALEZ; Deacon WILLIAM MICH; MARGO MICH; Deacon ROBERT J. SCHROM; TERESA SCHROM.

Permanent Diaconate Liaison with Bishop Joseph Tyson—Deacon ROBERT J. SCHROM, 7240 Rd. 17 S.W., Royal City, 99357. Tel: 509-346-9464.

Press (Central Washington Catholic)—Rev. Msgr. ROBERT M. SILER.

Presbyteral Council Executive Committee—Most Rev. JOSEPH J. TYSON; Rev. Msgr. PERRON J. AUVE; Very Rev. JAIME H. CHACON, M.Div.; Very Rev. Msgr. JOHN A. ECKER, Ex Officio; Very Rev. ARGEMIRO OROZCO; Rev. WILLIAM E. SHAW; Rev. Msgr. ROBERT M. SILER, Ex Officio; Revs. CESAR VEGA; FELIPE PULIDO; Very Revs. MICHAEL J. IBACH, J.C.L.; JOSE M. HERRERA; BROOKS F. BEAULAURIER; Rev. ALEJANDRO TREJO-ESTRADA; Very Rev. JACOB W. DAVIS.

Native American Ministries—Rev. JOHN M. SHAW, (Retired), 213 N. Beech, Toppenish, 98948. Tel: 509-865-4725.

Diocesan Catholic Committee on Scouting—Deacon WILLIAM A. DRONEN, Chap., 306 Railroad Ave., Cashmere, 98815. Tel: 509-782-3976.

St. Joseph Mission at the Ahtanum—17740 Ahtanum Rd., Yakima, 98903. Tel: 509-966-0865; Fax: 509-367-5300. VALERIA FLORES, Administrative Asst., Email: valeria.flores@yakimadiocese.net.

St. Vincent de Paul Society—Very Rev. THOMAS C. CHAMPOUX, Spiritual Dir., 1126 Long Ave., Richland, 99352. Tel: 509-946-1675.

Serra Club—Yakima: TIM WAUZYNSKI, 5302 Richey Rd., Yakima, 98908. Tel: 509-452-6907. Tri Cities: DICK KREMA, 3505 W. Ella St., Pasco, 99301. Tel: 509-547-8538.

Victim Assistance Coordinator—DOROTHY MORALES.

Vocations—Very Rev. V. FELIPE PULIDO, Vicar for Vocations.

CLERGY, PARISHES, MISSIONS AND PAROCHIAL SCHOOLS

CITY OF YAKIMA

(YAKIMA COUNTY)

1—ST. PAUL CATHEDRAL (1914) [CEM]
15 S. 12th Ave., 98902. Tel: 509-575-3713; Fax: 509-453-7497; Email: parish@stpaulyakima.org. Very Rev. Msgr. John A. Ecker; Rev. Jesus Alatorre.
Res.: 1208 W. Chestnut, 98902.
Catholic Young Adult Center—810 S. 16th Ave., 98902. Tel: 314-330-7634.
Catechesis Religious Program—Emma Mendoza, D.R.E. Students 233.

2—HOLY FAMILY (1959)
5315 Tieton Dr., 98908. Tel: 509-966-0830; Fax: 509-965-1742; Email: office@holyfamilyyakima.org. Rev. Cesar Vega Mendoza; Deacons John Cornell; James Kramper. In Res., Very Rev. Michael J. Ibach, J.C.L.
Rectory—302-304 & 306 S. 50th, 98908.
School—Christ the Teacher Catholic School, (Grades PreK-8), 5508 W. Chestnut Ave., 98908. Tel: 509-575-5604; Fax: 509-577-8817; Email: hremillard@stpaulsch.org; Web: ctcsyakima.org. Heather Remillard, Prin. Students 195.
Catechesis Religious Program—5502-04 W. Chestnut Ave, Rm. #11, 98908. Tel: 509-966-0788; Fax: 509-965-0288. Students 427.
Mission—St. Joseph Mission at the Ahtanum, 17740 Ahtanum Rd., Yakima Co. 98908. Tel: 509-966-5649; Fax: 509-966-5649. Sr. Janice Strong, Diocesan Hermit.

3—HOLY REDEEMER (1962) [JC]
1707 S. 3rd Ave., 98902. Tel: 509-248-2241; Fax: 509-457-3312; Email: hroffice1@qwestoffice.net. Rev. Ricardo A. Villarreal; Deacon Duane Berger.
Catechesis Religious Program—

4—ST. JOSEPH PARISH (1847)
212 N. 4th St., 98901-2426. Tel: 509-248-1911; Fax: 509-248-2604; Email: stjosephyakima@yvn.com. Very Rev. V. Felipe Pulido; Rev. Peter Steele; Deacon Nestor Chavez.
School—St. Joseph/Marquette, (Grades PreK-8), 202 N. 4th St., 98901. Tel: 509-575-5557; Fax: 509-457-5621; Email: gpleger@sjmms.org. Gregg Pleger, Prin. Lay Teachers 25; Students 345.
Catechesis Religious Program—Students 283.

OUTSIDE THE CITY OF YAKIMA

BENTON CITY, BENTON CO., ST. FRANCES XAVIER CABRINI (1963)
Mailing Address: 1000 Horne Dr., P.O. Box 179, Benton City, 99320-0179. Tel: 509-588-3636; Email: stfrancisxbc@yakimadiocese.org. Very Rev. Thomas C. Champoux, Admin.; Revs. Daniel O. Steele; John C. Vogl.
Catechesis Religious Program—Students 105.

BRIDGEPORT, DOUGLAS CO., ST. ANNE'S (1964)
Mailing Address: P.O. Box 1089, Chelan, 98816-1089. Tel: 509-682-2433; Fax: 509-682-9147; Email: stfrancischurch@nwi.net. Rev. Rogelio Gutierrez.
Catechesis Religious Program—Students 37.

CASHMERE, CHELAN CO., ST. FRANCIS XAVIER (1915) Merged with Our Lady of the Snows, Leavenworth to form Our Lady of the Assumption in Leavenworth.

CHELAN, CHELAN CO., ST. FRANCIS DE SALES (1904) [CEM]
215 W. Allen Ave., P.O. Box 1089, Chelan, 98816-1089. Tel: 509-682-2433; Fax: 509-682-9147; Email: stfrancischurch@nwi.net. Rev. Rogelio Gutierrez.
Catechesis Religious Program—Students 51.
Mission—St. Mary (1909) Mansfield Blvd. & 2nd, Mansfield, Douglas Co. 98830.

CLE ELUM, UPPER KITTITAS CO., ST. JOHN THE BAPTIST (1914)
303 W. 2nd St., P.O. Box 630, Cle Elum, 98922. Tel: 509-674-2531; Email: fr.higuera@yakimadiocese.org; Web: icsjbparishes.org. Rev. Francisco P. Higuera.
Catechesis Religious Program—Email: faithformation.icsjb@gmail.com. Students 12.

COWICHE, YAKIMA CO., ST. JUAN DIEGO (1959) (Spanish) (Formerly known as St. Peter the Apostle).
15800 Summitview Rd., Cowiche, 98923. Tel: 509-678-4164; Email: stjuandiego@yakimadiocese.org. Rev. Cesar Vega Mendoza.
Catechesis Religious Program—Email: lermamtsi9@hotmail.com.

EAST WENATCHEE, DOUGLAS CO., HOLY APOSTLES (1962)
1315 8th St. N.E., East Wenatchee, 98802. Tel: 509-884-5444; Fax: 509-886-3424; Email: holyapostles@nwi.net. Very Rev. Argemiro Orozco; Rev. Seamus Kerr, (Retired); Deacons Thomas Richtsmeier; Carlos Luna.
Catechesis Religious Program—Students 470.
Mission—St. Joseph Parish, 101 Poplar St., Waterville, 98858. Tel: 509-745-8205; Fax: 509-745-8205; Email: janetchapin@hotmail.com.

ELLENSBURG, KITTITAS CO., ST. ANDREW'S (1884) [CEM]
Mailing Address: 401 S. Willow St., Ellensburg, 98926. Tel: 509-962-9819; Fax: 509-962-9846; Email: standrewparish@yahoo.com; Web: st-andrewsparish.org/. Rev. David J. Jimenez Alvarez, J.C.L.
Res.: 403 S. Willow St., Ellensburg, 98926. Tel: 509-901-3885; Email: padredavid@hotmail.com.
Catechesis Religious Program—Email: standrewparishRE@yahoo.com; Email: standrewparishYM@yahoo.com. Alena Camarata, D.R.E.; Sarah Moore, Youth Min. Students 173.

EPHRATA, GRANT CO., ST. ROSE OF LIMA (1915) [CEM]
Mailing Address: 323 D St., S.W., Ephrata, 98823. Tel: 509-754-3640; Fax: 509-754-4064; Email: strose@nwi.net. Rev. Mauricio Munoz.
Parish Office—560 Nat Washington Way, Ephrata, 98823.
School—St. Rose of Lima School, (Grades PreK-6), 520 Nat Washington Way, Ephrata, 98823. Tel: 509-754-4901; Fax: 509-754-9274; Email: info@saintroseschool.org. Mrs. Stefanie Bafus, Prin.; Stephanie Moore, Librarian. Religious Teachers 7; Lay Teachers 8; Preschool 16; Students 98.
Catechesis Religious Program—Email: strosesecretary@nwi.net. Students 135.

GOLDENDALE, KLICKITAT CO., HOLY TRINITY (1884) [CEM]
210 S. Schuster St., Goldendale, 98620. Tel: 509-773-4516; Email: goldendale.holytrinity@yahoo.com; Web: goldendalechurch.wixsite.com/holytrinity. Rev. William Byron.
Catechesis Religious Program—Rebekah Scarola, D.R.E. Students 31.

GRAND COULEE, GRANT CO., ST. HENRY'S (1955) [JC]
590 Grand Coulee Ave. W., P.O. Box P, Grand Coulee, 99133. Tel: 509-633-1180; Fax: 509-633-6859 ; Email: brooksbeaulaurier@gmail.com. Very Rev. Brooks F. Beaulaurier.
Catechesis Religious Program—
Mission—Holy Angels.

GRANDVIEW, YAKIMA CO., BLESSED SACRAMENT (1954)
1201 Missouri, Grandview, 98930. Tel: 509-882-1657 ; Fax: 509-882-1107; Email: blessedsacrament@yakimadiocese.org. Very Rev. Jose M. Herrera.
Catechesis Religious Program—Students 474.

GRANGER, YAKIMA CO., OUR LADY OF GUADALUPE (1966) [JC] (Hispanic)
608 Granger Ave., P.O. Box 308, Granger, 98932. Tel: 509-854-1181; Email: guadatom@hotmail.com. Rev. Tomas Vidal.
Catechesis Religious Program—Tel: 509-854-2164. Students 126.

HARTLINE, GRANT CO., ST. PATRICK'S (1955) [CEM] Served from St. Henry's, Grand Coulee.
590 W. Grand Coulee Ave., P.O. Box P, Grand Coulee, 99133. Tel: 509-633-1180; Fax: 509-633-6859 ; Email: rhimes@homenetnw.net. Rev. Robert P. Himes, (Retired).
Catechesis Religious Program—

KENNEWICK, BENTON CO.

1—HOLY SPIRIT (1980)
7409 W. Clearwater, Kennewick, 99336. Tel: 509-735-8558; Email: office@holyspiritkennewick.org; Web: www.holyspiritkennewick.org. Rev. Msgr. Perron J. Auve; Deacon Ken Ellis. In Res., Rev. John G. O'Shea, (Retired).
Catechesis Religious Program—Pat Moore, D.R.E. & Youth Min. Students 164.

2—ST. JOSEPH'S (1911)
520 S. Garfield, Kennewick, 99336. Tel: 509-586-3820; Fax: 509-586-3558; Email: parish.office@stjoseph-kennewick.org; Web: stjoseph-kennewick.org/. Rev. Tomas Vazquez; Very Rev. Jacob W. Davis, Parochial Vicar; Deacons William Mich; David Olsen; Very Rev. Lawrence T. Reilly, In Res.
School—St. Joseph's School, (Grades PreSchool-8), 901 W. 4th Ave., Kennewick, 99336. Tel: 509-586-0481; Fax: 509-585-9781; Email: ndodson@stjoseph-kennewick.org; Web: www.sjske.org. Perry Kelly, Prin. Lay Teachers 18; Students 304.
Catechesis Religious Program—Tel: 509-531-7559; Tel: 509-579-0824; Email: hobbsand4@gmail.com. Channa Hobbs, D.R.E.; Amalia Del Pozo, D.R.E. Students 378.

LEAVENWORTH, CHELAN CO.

1—OUR LADY OF THE ASSUMPTION IN LEAVENWORTH
145 Wheeler St., Leavenworth, 98826. Tel: 509-548-5119; Email: olassumption@nwi.net. Very Rev. Miguel Gonzalez.
Catechesis Religious Program—Students 109.

2—OUR LADY OF THE SNOWS (1912) Merged with St. Francis Xavier, Cashmere to form Our Lady of the Assumption in Leavenworth.

MABTON, YAKIMA CO., IMMACULATE CONCEPTION (1910)
Mailing Address: 4th & Adams, P.O. Box 275, Mabton, 98935. Tel: 509-882-1657; Fax: 509-882-1107; Email: guadatom@hotmail.com. Rev. Tomas Vidal; Very Rev. Jose M. Herrera.
Res.: 1201 Missouri, Grandview, 98930.
Catechesis Religious Program—Students 68.

MATTAWA, GRANT CO., OUR LADY OF THE DESERT (1987) [JC]
Mailing Address: 301 8th St., P.O. Box 1185, Mattawa, 99349. Tel: 509-932-5424; Fax: 509-932-4055; Email: ourladyofthedesertparish@gmail.com; Web: ourladyofthedesertparish.org. Rev. Alejandro Trejo-Estrada.
Catechesis Religious Program—Students 495.

MOSES LAKE, GRANT CO., OUR LADY OF FATIMA (1955) [CEM] (Spanish)
200 N. Dale Rd., Moses Lake, 98837.
Tel: 509-765-6729; Fax: 509-765-0114; Email: secretary@olf.church; Web: olf.church. Revs. Dan Dufner; Jorge Granados; Deacons Robert J. Schrom; Agapito Gonzales Jr.
Parish Center—210 N. Dale Rd., Moses Lake, 98837.
Catechesis Religious Program—Carrie Tatum, D.R.E.; Aurea Tapale, D.R.E. (Spanish); Anthony Mejia, Youth Min. Students 492.

MOXEE CITY, YAKIMA CO., HOLY ROSARY (1900) [CEM]
201 N. Iler., P.O. Box 279, Moxee, 98936.
Tel: 509-453-4061; Fax: 509-576-6290; Email: holyrosary29@gmail.com. Rev. John J. Murtagh.
Catechesis Religious Program—Tel: 509-453-6754. Students 192.

NACHES, YAKIMA CO., ST. JOHN (1959)
204 Moxee Ave., P.O. Box 128, Naches, 98937-0128.
Tel: 509-653-2534; Fax: 509-653-2534; Email: stjohnnaches@frontier.com. Rev. Michael Brzezowski.
Catechesis Religious Program—Students 10.

PROSSER, BENTON CO., SACRED HEART (1899)
1905 Highland Dr., Prosser, 99350.
Tel: 509-786-1783; Fax: 509-786-1747; Email: parish@sacredheartprosser.org; Web: www.sacredheartprosser.org. Rev. Francisco Gutierrez.
Catechesis Religious Program—Josefina Lopez, D.R.E. Students 296.

QUINCY, GRANT CO., ST. PIUS X (1955) (Hispanic)
805 N. Central Ave., P.O. Box 308, Quincy, 98848.
Tel: 509-787-2622; Fax: 509-787-6068; Email: saintpius@ifiber.tv. Rev. Msgr. Mario A. Salazar, (Retired).
Catechesis Religious Program—Ana Argueta, D.R.E., (Spanish). Students 207.

RICHLAND, BENTON CO., CHRIST THE KING (1946)
1111 Stevens Dr., Richland, 99354.
Tel: 509-946-1675; Fax: 509-946-9940; Email: bulletin@ckparish.org; Web: www.ckparish.org. Very Rev. Thomas C. Champoux; Revs. Daniel O. Steele; Juan M. Flores; Vandennis Nguyen, In Res., (Retired); Deacons LeRoi Rice, (Retired); Doroteo Collado; Alfredo Jocson; Thomas Huntington; Ross Ronish.
School—Christ the King Catholic School, (Grades PreK-8), 1122 Long Ave., Richland, 99354.
Tel: 509-946-6158; Fax: 509-943-8402; Web: www.CKschoolRichland.org; Email: slasalle@ckschool.net. Sheila LaSalle, Prin. Lay Teachers 28; Students 417.
Catechesis Religious Program—Tel: 509-946-1154; Email: lori@ckparish.org. Lori Wasner, D.R.E. Students 409.

ROSLYN, UPPER KITTITAS CO., IMMACULATE CONCEPTION (1886)
Mailing Address: 303 W. 2nd St., Cle Elum, 98922.
Tel: 509-674-2531; Email: fr.higuera@yakimadiocese.org; Web: imm.stjohns@gmail.com. P.O. Box 630, Cle Elum, 98922-0630. Rev. Francisco P. Higuera.
Res.: 211 N. B St., Roslyn, 98941.
Catechesis Religious Program—Email: faithformation.icsjb@gmail.com. Twinned with St. John the Baptist, Cle Elum. Students 12.

ROYAL CITY, GRANT CO., ST. MICHAEL THE ARCHANGEL (1966) (Hispanic)
145 Daisy St., N.W., P.O. Box 340, Royal City, 99357.
Tel: 509-346-2730; Fax: 509-346-2901; Email: fr.jesusramirez@centurytel.net; Email: stmichaelsroyalcity@gmail.com. Rev. J. Jesus Ramirez; Deacon Francisco Martinez.
Catechesis Religious Program—Tel: 509-346-2236. Students 223.

SELAH, YAKIMA CO., OUR LADY OF LOURDES (1975)
Mailing Address: 1107 W. Fremont Ave., Selah, 98942. Tel: 509-697-4633; Email: ollselah@hotmail.com. Very Rev. Richard D. Sedlacek.
Catechesis Religious Program—Katy Pitzer, D.R.E., Elementary; Kelly Mattson, D.R.E., High School; Paula Mattson, D.R.E., High School. Students 83.

SUNNYSIDE, YAKIMA CO., ST. JOSEPH'S (1936)
907 S. 6th St., Sunnyside, 98944. Tel: 509-837-2243; Fax: 509-837-7063; Email: sjpssecretary@gmail.com; Web: www.saintjosephsunnyside.org. Rev. Thomas J. Bunnell, S.J.; Deacon Kerry Turley.
Res.: 920 S. 6th St., Sunnyside, 98944.
Catechesis Religious Program—Students 502.

TOPPENISH, YAKIMA CO., ST. ALOYSIUS (1908)
Mailing Address: 213 N. Beech St., Toppenish, 98948. Tel: 508-865-4725; Fax: 508-865-7882; Email: st.aloysius47@gmail.com. Very Rev. Jaime H. Chacon, M.Div.; Deacons Berney Alvarado; Peter Fadich.
Religious Education Center—214 N. Beech St., Toppenish, 98948.
Catechesis Religious Program—Students 207.

WAPATO, YAKIMA CO., ST. PETER CLAVER (1906)
509 S. Satus Ave., Wapato, 98951. Tel: 509-877-2813; Fax: 509-479-8662; Email: stpclaver@gmail.com; Web: stpclaver.org. Rev. Roleto B. Amoy; Deacon Genaro Ramos.
Res.: 701 S. Yakima Ave., Wapato, 98951.
Catechesis Religious Program—Email: drestpclaver@gmail.com. Leticia Rios, D.R.E. Students 205.

WARDEN, GRANT CO., QUEEN OF ALL SAINTS (1966) (Spanish)
c/o 200 N. Dale Rd., Moses Lake, 98837.
Tel: 509-765-6729; Fax: 509-765-0114; Email: administrator@olf.church. 1100 Pine St, Warden, 98857. Revs. Dan Dufner; Jorge Granados; Deacons Andres Escamilla; George Legg.
Catechesis Religious Program—Tel: 509-760-1474; Tel: 509-760-9172. Lorena Castillo, D.R.E.; Joe Vela, Youth Min. Students 105.

WATERVILLE, DOUGLAS CO., ST. JOSEPH'S (1892) [CEM] [JC]
103 E. Poplar St., P.O. Box 519, Waterville, 98858.
Tel: 509-745-8205; Email: brooksbeaulaurier@gmail.com. Very Rev. Brooks F. Beaulaurier; Deacon Gregory Haberman.
Catechesis Religious Program—Tel: 509-745-8856; Email: gregstjoes@nwi.net. Students 34.

WENATCHEE, CHELAN CO., ST. JOSEPH'S (1903)
625 S. Elliott St., Wenatchee, 98801.
Tel: 509-662-4569; Fax: 509-663-8437; Email: stjoewen@stjoewen.org; Web: stjosephwen.org. Very Rev. Osmar R. Aguirre; Rev. Teodulo G. Taneo, Parochial Vicar; Deacon Robert Hulligan II, Tel: 509-884-9757.
School—St. Joseph's School, (Grades PreK-5), 600 St. Joseph Pl., Wenatchee, 98801. Tel: 509-663-2644; Fax: 509-663-8474; Email: stjosephschoolwenatchee@yakimadicoese.org; Web: www.saintjosephcatholicschool.org. Sr. Olga Cano, M.D.P.V.M., Prin. Religious Teachers 2; Lay Teachers 12; Preschool 49; Elementary School Students 154.
Catechesis Religious Program—Students 352.

WHITE SALMON, KLICKITAT CO., ST. JOSEPH (1912) (Spanish)
240 N.W. Washington, P.O. Box 2049, White Salmon, 98672. Tel: 509-493-2828; Email: stjosephws@yakimadiocese.org; Web: stjosephwhitesalmon.org. Rev. Salomon Covarrubias-Pina, M.Div.; Deacon Angel Oriz.
Catechesis Religious Program—Email: hshultzy5@yahoo.com. Heidi Shultz, D.R.E. Students 130.

WHITE SWAN, YAKIMA CO., ST. MARY'S (1889) (Native American)
360 Signal Peak Rd., P.O. Box 417, White Swan, 98952-0417. Tel: 509-874-2436; Fax: 509-874-1197; Email: stmarysws@centurylink.net. Rev. William E. Shaw; Deacon Andy Gonzalez; Rev. John M. Shaw, In Res., (Retired).
Catechesis Religious Program—Students 85.

ZILLAH, YAKIMA CO., RESURRECTION (1963)
Mailing Address: 704 Schooley Rd., P.O. Box 567, Zillah, 98953-0567. Tel: 509-829-5433;
Fax: 509-829-5312; Email: office@resurrectionparish.us. Rev. Bill Vogel, S.J.
Catechesis Religious Program—

On Duty Outside the Diocese:
Rev. Msgr.—
Metha, Ronald W., (Retired), Dept. of the Air Force, 56FW/HC, 13968 W. Shooting Star St., Luke Afb, AZ 85309-1624
Revs.—
Hinojosa, Rafael
Izquierdo, Cesar, Studies in Rome
Keolker, Richard F., (Retired), 1 Abbey Dr., St. Benedict, OR 97373
Mariscal, Jesus, Studies in Rome
Milich, Nicholas A., (Retired), 39 Tharp Ave., Watsonville, CA 95076.

Retired:
Rev. Msgrs.—
Metha, Ronald W., (Retired), Luke A.F.B., Glendale, AZ
Salazar, Mario A., (Retired)
Revs.—
Cerezo, Alberto F., (Retired), 11637 100th Ave., N.E., #C2, Kirkland, 98034-6518
DeLoza, Jose, (Retired)
Diez, Alvaro, (Retired), 214 San Bernardo Ave., Laredo, TX 78040
Himes, Robert P., (Retired), P.O. Box P, Grand Coulee, 99133
Inman, Robert D., (Retired)
Kenna, Joseph J., (Retired)
Keolker, Richard F., (Retired), 1 Abbey Dr., St. Benedict, OR 97373
Kerr, Seamus, (Retired)
Milich, Nicholas A., (Retired), 39 Tharp Ave., Watsonville, CA 95076
Nguyen, Vandennis, (Retired), 1111 Stevens Dr., Richland, 99354
O'Shea, John G., (Retired)
Peterson, Maurice F., (Retired), 5301-A Tieton Dr., 98908
Shaw, John M., (Retired)
Surman, Darrell, (Retired), P.O. Box 12523, Thorndon Wellington, New Zealand.

Permanent Deacons:
Alnajjar, Mikhail, 140 Canyon Rd., Richland, 99352. Tel: 509-627-4680
Alvarado, Berney, 15 S. Date St., Toppenish, 98948. Tel: 509-865-1857
Berger, Duane, 1708 Ahtanum, 98903. Tel: 509-961-1591
Chavez, Nestor, 1817 Pleasant Ave., 98903. Cell:
Collado, Doroteo, 108 Patton St., Richland, 99354. Tel: 509-731-6116
Cornell, John, 2504 W. Chestnut, 98902
Cortez, Jose, 4324 W. 15th Ave, Kennewick, 99338. Tel: 509-551-5350
Dronen, William A., 306 Railroad Ave., Cashmere, 98815
Escamilla, Andres, 4765 Rd. V., S.E., Warden, 98857. Tel: 509-349-2450
Escamilla, Armando, 2022 S. Division St., Moses Lake, 98837. Tel: 509-764-0735
Fadich, Peter, 8140 Ashue Rd., Toppenish, 98948. Tel: 509-293-3617
Farrell, Daniel J., 923 Straitview Dr., Port Angeles, 98362
Gonzales, Agapito Jr., P.O. Box 566, Warden, 98857. Tel: 509-349-2607
Gonzalez, Indalecio, 2760 Brownstown Rd., Harrah, 98933. Tel: 509-848-2564
Griek, Don, 8590 SR 410, Naches, 98937. Tel: 509-658-2012
Haberman, Gregory, 290 Road B, S.W., Waterville, 98858. Tel: 509-745-8856
Hudson, William D., 701 Knight Hill Rd., Zillah, 98953. Tel: 509-865-5557
Hulligan, Robert II, 22 French St., East Wenatchee, 98802. Tel: 509-884-9757
Huntington, Thomas, 1008 Fitch St., Richland, 99352. Tel: 509-943-0535
Jada, Simon, 2115 W. Grand Ronde Ave., Kennewick, 99336. Tel: 509-572-9016
Jocson, Alfredo, 1633 Venus Cir., Richland, 99352. Tel: 509-628-2860
Kramper, James, 215 N. 56th Ave., #5, 98908. Tel: 509-945-5432
Legg, George, P.O. Box 572, Warden, 98857. Tel: 509-349-8028
Luna, Carlos, 1947 Easy St., Wenatchee, 98801. Tel: 509-664-0169
Martinez, Frank, 3286 W. Shore Dr., N.E., Moses Lake, 98837. Tel: 509-765-9536
Mich, William, 1550 W. 44th Place, Kennewick, 99337. Tel: 509-735-9057
Miller, Ray, 2412 W. Chestnut, 98902
Muns, James, 917 S. 32nd Ave., 98902
Oriz, Angel, 200 N.W. Simmons Rd., White Salmon, 98672. Tel: 509-493-4620
Parnell, Cary, 513 Cedar Wood Ln., Wenatchee, 98801. Tel: 509-860-5826
Ramos, Genaro, 373 Lombard Loop Rd., Wapato, 98951. Tel: 509-985-6151
Rice, LeRoi, 2552 Orchid Ct., Richland, 99352. Tel: 509-375-4777
Richtsmeier, Thomas, 2901 8th St., S.E., East Wenatchee, 98802. Tel: 509-884-8029
Ronish, Ross, 3187 Willow Pointe Dr., Richland, 99354. Tel: 509-371-0994
Schrom, Robert J., 7240 Rd. 17, S.W., Royal City, 99357. Tel: 509-364-9464
Turley, Kerry, 304 E. Woodin Rd., Sunnyside, 98944. Tel: 509-837-6930.

INSTITUTIONS LOCATED IN DIOCESE

[A] COLLEGES AND UNIVERSITIES

TOPPENISH. **Heritage University* (1982) (Interdenominational University with an Independent Board) 3240 Fort Rd., Toppenish, 98948. Tel: 509-865-8600; Fax: 509-865-7976; Email: ross_k@heritage.edu; Web: www.heritage.edu. Andrew Sund, Pres.; Sr. Kathleen Ross, S.N.J.M., Pres. Emerita & Prof.; Laurie Fathe, Ph.D., Provost and Vice Pres. for Academic Affairs. (Full-time, paid) 130; Lay Teachers 75; Sisters 3; Students 1,200; Religious Teachers 2.

[B] HIGH SCHOOLS

UNION GAP. *La Salle High School of Yakima*, 3000

Lightning Way, Union Gap, 98903.
Tel: 509-225-2900; Fax: 509-225-2994; Email: rsoptich@lasalleyakima.org; Web: www.lasalleyakima.com. Timothy McGree, Pres.; Ted Kanelopoulos, Prin. Lay Teachers 20; Students 218; Staff 10.

[C] HOSPITALS

RICHLAND. *Lourdes Counseling Center*, 1175 Carondelet Dr., Richland, 99354.
Tel: 509-943-9104; Fax: 509-943-7206; Email: leann.norberg@lourdesonline.org; Web: www.lourdeshealth.net. Leann Norberg, Admin. Inpatient 32; Tot Asst. Annually 91,500; Total Staff 217; Crisis Triage 16.

[D] CATHOLIC SOCIAL SERVICE CATHOLIC CHARITIES

YAKIMA. *Carroll Children's Center*, 5301 Tieton Dr., Ste. C, 98908. Tel: 509-965-7104;
Fax: 509-966-9750; Email: ddarnell@catholiccharitiescw.org. Danielle Rasmussen, Prog. Mgr. Capacity 120; Tot Asst. Annually 174; Total Staff 25.

Catholic Charities of the Diocese of Yakima, 5301 Tieton Dr., Ste. C, 98908. Tel: 509-965-7100;
Fax: 509-972-0167; Email: ddarnell@catholiccharitiescw.org; Web: www.catholiccharitiescw.org. Ms. Darlene Darnell, Pres. & CEO. Tot Asst. Annually 43,766; Total Staff 388.

Catholic Charities of the Diocese of Yakima - Moses Lake, 1019 W. Broadway, Moses Lake, 98837.
Tel: 509-765-1875. Mrs. Darlene Darnell, M.S.W., Pres.

Catholic Charities of the Diocese of Yakima - Richland, 2139 Van Giesen, Richland, 99354.
Tel: 509-946-4645; Email: ddarnell@catholiccharitiescw.org. Mrs. Darlene Darnell, M.S.W., Pres.

Catholic Charities of the Diocese of Yakima - Wenatchee, 145 S. Worthen St., Wenatchee, 98801.
Tel: 509-662-6761; Email: ddarnell@catholiccharitiescw.org. Mrs. Darlene Darnell, M.S.W., Pres.

St. Vincent Centers - Kennewick, 731 N. Columbia Ctr. Blvd,, Ste 114, Kennewick, 99336.
Tel: 509-783-7020; Email: ddarnell@catholiccharitiescw.org; Email: ppalmer@catholiccharitiescw.org. Mrs. Darlene Darnell, M.S.W., Pres.; Paul Palmer, Admin.

St. Vincent Centers - Union Gap, 2629 Main St., Union Gap, 98903. Tel: 509-457-5111; Email: ddarnell@catholiccharitiescw.org. Mrs. Darlene Darnell, M.S.W., Pres.; Paul Palmer, Admin.

St. Vincent Centers, 2629 Main St., Union Gap, 98903. Tel: 509-457-5111; Fax: 509-457-3526; Email: ddarnell@catholiccharitiescw.org; Web: www.catholiccharitiescw.org. Mrs. Darlene Darnell, M.S.W., Pres.; Mr. Paul Palmer, Admin.

KENNEWICK. *St. Vincent Centers*, 120 N. Morain, Kennewick, 99336. Tel: 509-783-7020;
Fax: 509-783-7039; Email: ppalmer@catholiccharitiescw.org; Web: www.catholiccharitiescw.org. Mrs. Darlene Darnell, M.S.W., Pres.; Paul Palmer, Admin.

RICHLAND. *Catholic Charities Serving Central Washington*, 2139 Van Giesen, Richland, 99354.
Tel: 509-946-4645; Fax: 509-943-2068; Email: ddarnell@catholiccharitiescw.org; Web: www.catholiccharitiescw.org. Mrs. Darlene Darnell, M.S.W., Pres.

WENATCHEE. *Catholic Charities Serving Central Washington*, 145 S. Worthen St., Wenatchee, 98801. Tel: 509-662-6761; Fax: 509-663-3182; Email: ddarnell@catholiccharitiescw.org; Web: www.catholiccharitiescw.org. Mrs. Darlene Darnell, M.S.W., Pres.

[E] RETIREMENT HOMES

YAKIMA. **The Gamelin Association-Providence House* dba Providence House*, 312 N. 4th St., 98901.
Tel: 509-452-5017; Fax: 509-452-1947; Email: isidro.renteria@providence.org; Web: providence.org/supportive-housing/providence- yakima/. Isidro Renteria, Dir. Providence Ministries: Johnny Cox, Vice Pres., Barbara Savage, Past Pres., Anita Butler, SP, Treas., Barbara Schamber, SP, Sec.Low income housing for elderly & disabled 18 & older. Bed Capacity 48; Tot Asst. Annually 47; Total Staff 1.

[F] VOLUNTEER SERVICES

YAKIMA. *St. Paul's Parish Conference*, 15 S. 12th Ave., 98902. Tel: 509-575-3713; Fax: 509-453-7497; Email: stpaul@wolfenet.com. Greg Vavricka, Pres.; Jeffrey Arkills, Treas.; Patty Schumm, Sec. Tot Asst. Annually 250.

EAST WENATCHEE. *Holy Apostles Parish*, 1315 N.E. 8th St.,, East Wenatchee, 98801. Tel: 509-884-5444; Fax: 509-886-3424; Tel: 509-884-0681;
Tel: 509-886-7624; Email: holyapostles@nwi.net; Web: www.holyapostlesew.net. Lee Gale, Pastoral Council Pres.; Very Rev. Argemiro Orozco.

KENNEWICK. *St. Joseph Parish Conference* St. Vincent de Paul 520 S. Garfield St., Kennewick, 99336.
Tel: 509-586-3820; Fax: 509-586-3558; Email: parish.office@stjoseph-kennewick.org. Rev. Tomas Vazquez.

RICHLAND. *Christ the King Parish Conference* (1955) 1111 Stevens Dr., Richland, 99354.
Tel: 509-946-1675; Fax: 509-946-9940; Email: lori@ckparish.org; Web: www.ckparish.org. Lori Wasner, DRE. Tot Asst. Annually 200; Total Staff 28.

WENATCHEE. *St. Joseph Parish Conference, St. Vincent de Paul*, 625 S. Elliott Ave., Wenatchee, 98801.
Tel: 509-667-7837; Fax: 509-663-8437; Email: svdp.wenatcheeconference@gmail.com. Very Rev. Osmar R. Aguirre, Pastor. Tot Asst. Annually 275.

[G] CAMPUS MINISTRY

ELLENSBURG. *Catholic Campus Ministry at Central Washington University*, 706 N. Sprague St., Ellensburg, 98926. Tel: 509-925-3043; Email: info@cwucatholics.org (Primary); Web: cwucatholics.com. Marcus Ayers, Dir. & Campus Min. Total in Residence 4; Total Staff 1.

[H] MISCELLANEOUS LISTINGS

YAKIMA. **Catholic Charities Housing Services, Diocese of Yakima*, 5301 Tieton Dr., Ste. G, 98908-3479.
Tel: 509-853-2800; Fax: 509-853-2805; Email: bketcham@catholiccharitiescw.org; Web: www.catholiccharitiescw.org. Ms. Darlene Darnell, Pres.; Brian Ketcham, Dir.

**Central Washington Catholic Foundation* (2002) 5301 Tieton Dr., Ste. F, 98908-3479.
Tel: 509-972-3732; Fax: 509-972-2417; Email: info@cwcatholicfoundation.org; Web: www.cwcatholicfoundation.org. Kathleen Wilmes, Exec. Dir.

Diocese of Yakima Capital Revolving Program, 5301-A Tieton Dr., 98908. Tel: 509-965-7117;
Fax: 509-966-8019; Email: sue.schoolcraft@yakimadiocese.net. Susan Schoolcraft, CFO.

Irrevocable Priest Retirement Trust for the Diocese of Yakima, 5301-A Tieton Dr., 98908.
Tel: 509-965-7117; Fax: 509-966-8019; Email: sue.schoolcraft@yakimadiocese.net. Susan Schoolcraft, CFO.

Irrevocable Seminarian Education Trust for the Diocese of Yakima, 5301-A Tieton Dr., 98908.
Tel: 509-965-7117; Fax: 509-966-8019; Email: sue.schoolcraft@yakimadiocese.net. Susan Schoolcraft, CFO.

TOPPENISH. *Association of Catholic Sisters for Educational Opportunities for the Poor*, Kateri House, 109 North E. St., Toppenish, 98948.
Tel: 509-865-3836; Email: ross_k@heritage.edu. Sr. Kathleen Ross, S.N.J.M., Pres.

UNION GAP. *La Salle Foundation of Yakima*, 3000 Lightning Way, Union Gap, 98903.
Tel: 509-225-2990; Fax: 509-225-2994; Email: lpaniagua@lasalleyakima.org; Web: www.lasalleyakima.com. Timothy McGree, Pres.

ZILLAH. *Catholics In Action* (200) P.O. Box 673, Zillah, 98953. Tel: 509-790-7696; Fax: 509-829-9503; Email: yakimacatholicradio@gmail.com. Mr. Richard Sevigny, Pres.

RELIGIOUS INSTITUTES OF MEN REPRESENTED IN THE DIOCESE

For further details refer to the corresponding bracketed number in the Religious Institutes of Men or Women section.

[0200]—*Benedictine Monks (American Cassinese Congregation)*—O.S.B.
[0330]—*Brothers of the Christian Schools* (Prov. of San Francisco)—F.S.C.
[0690]—*Jesuit Fathers and Brothers (Oregon Province)*—S.J.

RELIGIOUS INSTITUTES OF WOMEN REPRESENTED IN THE DIOCESE

[]—*Diocesan Hermit*.
[1070-20]—*Dominican Sisters*—O.P.
[]—*Misioneras Trabajadoras Sociales de la Inglesia*—M.T.S.I.
[]—*Missionary Daughters of the Most Pure Virgin Mary*—M.D.P.V.M.
[3350]—*Sisters of Providence* (Mother Joseph Prov.)—S.P.
[]—*Sisters of St. Francis*—O.S.F.
[3840]—*Sisters of St. Joseph of Carondelet*—C.S.J.
[1990]—*Sisters of the Holy Names of Jesus and Mary*—S.N.J.M.
[2160]—*Sisters, Servants of the Immaculate Heart of Mary*—I.H.M.

NECROLOGY

† Lane, Thomas V., (Retired), Died May. 11, 2018

An asterisk (*) denotes an organization that has established tax-exempt status directly with the IRS and is not covered by the USCCB Group Ruling.

Diocese of Youngstown

(Dioecesis Youngstoniensis)

Most Reverend

GEORGE V. MURRY, S.J.

Bishop of Youngstown; ordained June 9, 1979; appointed Auxiliary Bishop of Chicago and Titular Bishop of Fuerteventura January 24, 1995; appointed Coadjutor Bishop of Saint Thomas in the Virgin Islands May 5, 1998; succeeded June 29, 1999; appointed Bishop of Youngstown January 30, 2007; installed March 28, 2007. *Chancery Office: 144 W. Wood St., Youngstown, OH 44503.* Tel: 330-744-8451; Fax: 330-742-6448.

Chancery Office: 144 W. Wood St., Youngstown, OH 44503. Tel: 330-744-8451; Fax: 330-742-6448; Fax: 330-744-2848.

Web: www.doy.org

Email: chancery@doy.org

Established May 15, 1943.

Square Miles 3,404.

Canonically Erected July 22, 1943.

Comprises six Counties in the northeastern part of the State of Ohio, namely, Ashtabula, Columbiana, Mahoning, Portage, Stark and Trumbull Counties.

For legal titles of parishes and diocesan institutions, consult the Chancery Office.

STATISTICAL OVERVIEW

Personnel	
Bishop	1
Priests: Diocesan Active in Diocese	69
Priests: Diocesan Active Outside Diocese	2
Priests: Retired, Sick or Absent	45
Number of Diocesan Priests	116
Religious Priests in Diocese	14
Total Priests in Diocese	130
Extern Priests in Diocese	4
Ordinations:	
Diocesan Priests	2
Permanent Deacons in Diocese	78
Total Brothers	9
Total Sisters	194
Parishes	
Parishes	87
With Resident Pastor:	
Resident Diocesan Priests	72
Resident Religious Priests	4
Without Resident Pastor:	
Administered by Priests	6
Administered by Deacons	1
Administered by Religious Women	2
Administered by Lay People	2
Missions	1
Professional Ministry Personnel:	
Sisters	28
Lay Ministers	74
Welfare	
Catholic Hospitals	4
Total Assisted	920,632
Health Care Centers	42
Total Assisted	15,000
Homes for the Aged	10
Total Assisted	2,268
Day Care Centers	1
Total Assisted	100
Specialized Homes	6
Total Assisted	440
Special Centers for Social Services	14
Total Assisted	48,881
Educational	
Diocesan Students in Other Seminaries	17
Total Seminarians	17
Colleges and Universities	1
Total Students	2,896
High Schools, Diocesan and Parish	6
Total Students	1,879
Elementary Schools, Diocesan and Parish	22
Total Students	4,626
Catechesis/Religious Education:	
High School Students	1,270
Elementary Students	9,360
Total Students under Catholic Instruction	20,048
Teachers in the Diocese:	
Lay Teachers	571
Vital Statistics	
Receptions into the Church:	
Infant Baptism Totals	1,132
Minor Baptism Totals	83
Adult Baptism Totals	113
Received into Full Communion	170
First Communions	1,323
Confirmations	1,517
Marriages:	
Catholic	323
Interfaith	168
Total Marriages	491
Deaths	2,192
Total Catholic Population	151,826
Total Population	1,182,309

Former Bishops—Most Revs. JAMES A. MCFADDEN, S.T.D., LL.D., appt. Titular Bishop of Bida and Auxiliary of Cleveland, May 13, 1932; cons. Sept. 8, 1932; appt. Bishop of Youngstown, June 2, 1943; died Nov. 16, 1952; EMMET M. WALSH, D.D., ord. Jan. 15, 1916; appt. Bishop of Charleston, June 20, 1927; appt. Titular Bishop of Rhaedestus and Coadjutor, Sept. 8, 1949; succeeded to See, Nov. 16, 1952; died March 16, 1968; JAMES W. MALONE, D.D., ord. May 26, 1945; appt. Titular Bishop of Alabanda and Auxiliary, Jan. 2, 1960; appt. Apostolic Administrator, Jan. 22, 1966; succeeded to See, May 2, 1968; retired Dec. 4, 1995; died April 9, 2000; THOMAS J. TOBIN, D.D., ord. July 21, 1973; appt. Titular Bishop of Novica and Auxiliary Bishop of Pittsburgh, Nov. 3, 1992; appt. Fourth Bishop of Youngstown installed Feb. 2, 1996; appt. Bishop of Providence March 31, 2005.

All Diocesan offices and personnel can be reached at 144 W. Wood St., Youngstown, OH, 44503. Tel: 330-744-8451, Fax: 330-742-6448; 744-2848 unless otherwise indicated.

Chancery Office

Vicar General & Moderator of the Curia—Very Rev. Msgr. ROBERT J. SIFFRIN, V.G.

Chancellor—Rev. Msgr. JOHN A. ZURAW, J.C.L.

"The Catholic Exponent", Diocesan Newspaper—Most Rev. GEORGE V. MURRY, S.J., Publisher, Tel: 330-744-5251.

College of Consultors—Very Rev. Msgr. ROBERT J. SIFFRIN, V.G.; Rev. JOHN JEREK; Very Rev. Msgr. PETER M. POLANDO, J.C.L.; Revs. WILLIAM B. KRAYNAK; BENSON CLARET OKPARA; Very Rev. FRANK L. ZANNI, V.F.; Rev. Msgr. JOHN A. ZURAW, J.C.L.

Presbyteral Council—Very Rev. Msgrs. PETER M. POLANDO, J.C.L.; ROBERT J. SIFFRIN, V.G.; Very Rev. FRANK L. ZANNI, V.F.; Rev. Msgr. JOHN A. ZURAW, J.C.L.; Revs. CHRISTOPHER CICERO; SHAWN CONOBOY; ZACHARY COULTER; DANIEL FINNERTY; JOHN JEREK; JAMES KORDA; WILLIAM B. KRAYNAK; JOHN-MICHAEL LAVELLE, D.Min.; BENSON CLARET OKPARA; JOSEPH RUGGIERI; MELVIN E. RUSNAK, (Retired).

Finance Council—Very Rev. Msgr. ROBERT J. SIFFRIN, V.G., Chm.; Rev. Msgr. FRANK A. CARFAGNA; Very Rev. Msgr. PETER M. POLANDO, J.C.L.; THERESA DELLICK; Sr. ANDRIENE IHNOT, H.M.; ROBERT MARKS; PARKER MCHENRY; MR. PAT KELLY; MR. ROBERT A. HOFFMAN.

Diocesan Pastoral Council—MR. PETER SCHAFER.

Communications—

Catholic Television Network of Youngstown (CTNY)—Rev. JAMES KORDA, Pres.; BOB GAVALIER, Gen. Mgr., Mailing Address: P.O. Box 430, Canfield, 44406-0430. Tel: 330-533-2243.

Public-Media Relations—Rev. Msgr. JOHN A. ZURAW, J.C.L.

Development / Stewardship—MR. PAT PALOMBO, Dir.

Ecumenism—Rev. JOSEPH W. WITMER, Dir., Ecumenical Commission, (Retired), 1515 California Ave., Louisville, 44641. Tel: 330-875-4635.

Office of Evangelization—MR. PETER SCHAFER, Dir.

Office of Propagation of the Faith and Missions—Rev. EDWARD R. BRIENZ, Dir.

Scouting, Diocesan Office—Rev. TERRENCE J. HAZEL.

Department of Canonical Services

Department of Canonical Services—Very Rev. Msgr. PETER M. POLANDO, J.C.L., Exec. Dir., 141 W. Rayen Ave., Youngstown, 44503. Tel: 330-744-8451; Fax: 330-742-6450.

Office of Conciliation—

Matrimonial Dispensations—

Tribunal—

Judicial Vicar—Very Rev. Msgr. PETER M. POLANDO, J.C.L.

Adjutant Judicial Vicar—Rev. MARTIN CELUCH, J.C.L.

Judges—Rev. Msgrs. FRANK A. CARFAGNA; WILLIAM J. CONNELL, J.C.L.; Very Rev. Msgr. MICHAEL J. CARIGLIO JR., J.C.L.; Revs. MARTIN CELUCH, J.C.L.; BERNARD N. GAETA, (Retired); JOHN KEEHNER, J.C.L.; DANIEL J. KULESA, (Retired); THOMAS J. MCCARTHY, (Retired); GARY D. YANUS, J.C.D.; MS. LYNETTE M. TAIT, J.C.L.

Defenders of the Bond—Rev. Msgr. JOHN A. ZURAW, J.C.L.; Revs. TERRENCE J. HAZEL; RAYMOND L. PAUL.

Advocates—PHYLLIS KULICS; MRS. BARBARA ROGICH; VICKI KIDD; LINDA TEDDE; Rev. BERNARD N. GAETA, (Retired).

Promoter of Justice—Rev. Msgr. JOHN A. ZURAW, J.C.L.

Notary—REGINA YAKIMOFF.

Department of Catholic Charities Services

Department of Catholic Charities Services—STEPHEN J. CARATTINI, Dir. Social Concerns.

Catholic Charities Bureau—RACHEL HRBOLICH.

Office of Social Action—STEPHEN J. CARATTINI. Rural Life; Catholic Relief Services; Migration and Refugee Services; Catholic Campaign for Human Development; Parish Social Ministry.

Criminal Justice Ministry—VACANT.

Office of Social Services—STEPHEN J. CARATTINI, Pres., Diocese of Youngstown Catholic Charities Corp.; Dir., Social Svcs. Dept.

Hispanic Ministry—Rev. ERNESTO RODRIGUEZ.

Department of Clergy and Religious Services

Department of Clergy and Religious Services—Rev. JOHN JEREK, Vicar Clergy & Rel. Svcs.

Office of Vocations—Rev. CHRISTOPHER LUONI; Deacon RANDY SMITH; Rev. DANIEL FINNERTY.

Office of Clergy Services—Rev. JOHN JEREK.

Office of Continuing Education and Formation of Priests—Rev. JOHN M. JEREK.

Office of Permanent Diaconate—Rev. Msgr. JOHN A. ZURAW, J.C.L., Dir.

Office of Religious—Sr. JOYCE CANDIDI, O.S.H.J., Dir.

Diocesan Conference of Religious—Sr. JOYCE CANDIDI, O.S.H.J., Dir.

Department of Financial Services

Department of Financial Services—MR. PATRICK A. KELLY, CFO.

Office of Finance—MRS. CHRISTINE JICKESS, Assoc. Dir. Finance.

Office of Information Systems Services—MR. MATTHEW PECCHIA, Dir.

Department of Pastoral and Educational Services

Pastoral and Educational Services—Rev. Msgr. JOHN A. ZURAW, J.C.L.

Office of Catholic Schools—MARY FIALA, Supt.; RANDAL RAIR, Asst. Supt. Human Resources & Govt. Progs.; LORI CROFFORD, Dir. Instructional Technology & Professional Devel.

The Catholic Diocese of Youngstown Educational Fund, Inc.—

Office of Religious Education—BARBARA WALKO, Diocesan Dir., 225 Elm St., Youngstown, 44503. Tel: 330-744-8451. Consultants: CARLA HLAVAC; JOAN LAWSON.

Council for Catechesis—MR. NICHOLAS PERKOSKI, Chm.; KIM MUSILLE, Vice Chair.

Office of Youth and Young Adult Ministry—CINDEE CASE, Dir.

Office of Campus Ministry—MS. CARMEN ROEBKE, Diocesan Dir., 1424 Horning Rd., Kent, 44240. Tel: 330-678-0240.

Hiram College—Rev. STEPHEN ZEIGLER, St. Ambrose Parish, 10692 Freedom St., Garrettsville, 44231. Tel: 330-527-4105.

University Parish Newman Center (Kent State)—Rev. STEVEN J. AGOSTINO, Admin.

Walsh University—MIGUEL CHAVEZ, Dir., 2020 Easton St., N.W., North Canton, 44720. Tel: 330-490-7341.

Youngstown State University—254 Madison Ave., Youngstown, 44504. Tel: 330-747-9202. DR. THOMAS BROZICH, Dir.

Office of Worship—Rev. MICHAEL D. BALASH, Dir.

Office of Lay Ministry Formation—MR. PETER SCHAFER, Dir.

Office of Pro-Life, Marriage & Family Ministry—MR. DAVID R. SCHMIDT, Dir.

Other Ministries

Bishop's Delegate for Retired Priests—Rev. THOMAS C. EISWEIRTH, (Retired), 144 W. Wood St., Youngstown, 44503.

Catholic Women, Diocesan Council of—Rev. JOSEPH W. WITMER, Moderator, (Retired), 1515 California Ave., Louisville, 44641. Tel: 330-875-4635.

Charismatic Prayer Group—Rev. ROBERT R. EDWARDS, Dir., 935 E. State St., Salem, 44460. Tel: 330-332-0336.

Disabled Services—

Physically and Developmentally—Rev. TERRENCE J. HAZEL, Chap., 300 N. Broad St., Canfield, 44406. Tel: 330-533-6839.

Deaf and Hearing Impaired—Rev. TERRENCE J. HAZEL, Chap., 300 N. Broad St., Canfield, 44406. Tel: 330-533-6839.

Victim Assistance Coordinator—DET. SGT. DELPHINE BALDWIN-CASEY, Victim Assistance Coord., Tel: 330-718-1388; Rev. Msgr. JOHN A. ZURAW, J.C.L., Safe Environment Coord., Tel: 330-744-8451.

CLERGY, PARISHES, MISSIONS AND PAROCHIAL SCHOOLS

CITY OF YOUNGSTOWN

(MAHONING COUNTY)

1—CATHEDRAL OF ST. COLUMBA (1847) [JC] Merged with St. Casimir, Youngstown to form St. Columba Parish, Youngstown. Very Rev. Msgr. Peter M. Polando, J.C.L., Rector.

2—ST. ANGELA MERICI PARISH (2011)
397 S. Jackson St., 44506. Tel: 330-747-6080; Fax: 330-747-7003; Email: natalie@stangelayoungstown.org; Web: www.stangelayoungstown.org. Rev. Kevin Peters; Sr. Elisa Bonano, O.S.F., Pastoral Assoc.; Mrs. Patricia Yacucci, Prin.
Rectory—400 Lincoln Park Dr., 44506.
Catechesis Religious Program—Sr. Elisa Bonano, O.S.F., Pastoral Assoc.; Mrs. Patricia Yacucci, C.R.E. Students 55.
Saint Angela Merici Parish, (Worship Site) Tel: 330-747-6090.

3—ST. ANTHONY (1898) (Italian), Merged with Our Lady of Mt. Carmel to form Our Lady of Mount Carmel-St. Anthony of Padua Parish, Youngstown.

4—BASILICA OF OUR LADY OF MOUNT CARMEL - ST. ANTHONY OF PADUA PARISH (1908, elevated 2014)
343 Via Mt. Carmel, 44505. Tel: 330-743-4144; Email: olmc343@aol.com; Web: www.ladymtcarmel.com. Very Rev. Msgr. Michael J. Cariglio Jr., J.C.L.; Deacon Anthony Falasca.
Catechesis Religious Program—Tel: 330-743-3508; Email: OLMCTherese@gmail.com. Therese Ivanisin, D.R.E.; Mr. Joseph Carrabia, C.R.E.; Craig Ziobert, Music Min. Students 103.
St. Anthony—(Worship Site) 1125 Turin Ave., 44510.
Our Lady of Mt. Carmel Basilica - St. Anthony of Padua, (Worship Site).

5—ST. BRENDAN (1923)
2800 Oakwood Ave., 44509. Tel: 330-792-3875; Email: parish103@youngstowndiocese.org. Rev. William J. Loveless.
Catechesis Religious Program—
Tel: 330-792-3875, Ext. 12; Email: dff@stbrendanyo.org. Sisters 1; Students 32.

6—ST. CASIMIR (1906) Merged with Cathedral of St. Columba, Youngstown to form St. Columba Parish, Youngstown.

7—ST. CHRISTINE (1953)
3165 S. Schenley Ave., 44511. Tel: 330-792-3829; Email: parish105@youngstowndiocese.org. Revs. John E. Keehner, J.C.L.; Zachary Coulter, Parochial Vicar; Deacons Robert Cuttica, M.D., Pastoral Min./Coord.; Ronald Layko; Jim Brown; Martin H. Davies.
School—St. Christine School, (Grades K-8), 3125 S. Schenley Ave., 44511. Tel: 330-792-4544; Fax: 330-792-6888; Email: stchristine@youngstowndiocese.org. Lay Teachers 22; Students 390.
Catechesis Religious Program—Email: stchcb@aol.com. Colleen Boyle, Dir. Faith Formation. Students 485.

8—ST. COLUMBA PARISH 1847
159 W. Rayen Ave., 44503. Tel: 330-744-5233; Email: info@stcolumbacathedral.org; Web: www.stcolumbacathedral.org. Very Rev. Msgr. Peter M. Polando, J.C.L., Rector; Dr. Daniel Laginya, Music Min.
Catechesis Religious Program—Email: drestcolumba@yahoo.com. Sr. Martha Reed, D.R.E. Students 74.

9—SS. CYRIL AND METHODIUS (1896) (Slovak), Merged with St. Matthias, Youngstown & Holy Name of Jesus, Youngstown to form Our Lady of Sorrows Parish, Youngstown.

10—ST. DOMINIC (1923)
77 E. Lucius Ave., 44507. Tel: 330-783-1900; Email: parish107@youngstowndiocese.org. Revs. Vincent DeLucia, O.P.; William J. Rock, O.P.
Catechesis Religious Program—Students 50.

11—ST. EDWARD (1917)
240 Tod Ln., 44504. Tel: 330-743-2308; Email: saintedwardparish@saintedwardparish.org. Very Rev. Msgr. Robert J. Siffrin, V.G., Admin.; Deacon James Smith.
Catechesis Religious Program—Email: treerichosu@yahoo.com; Web: www.saintedwardparish.org. Lay Staff 2; Sisters 1; Students 21.

12—ST. ELIZABETH (1922) (Slovak), Closed. For inquiries for parish records contact the chancery.

13—HOLY APOSTLES PARISH (2011) (Croatian)
854 Wilson Ave., 44506. Tel: 330-743-1905; Email: holyapostlesparishyoungstown@gmail.com. Rev. Joseph S. Rudjak.
Catechesis Religious Program—Students 35.
SS. Peter and Paul—(Worship Site) 421 Covington St., 44510.
St. Stephen of Hungary Church, (Worship Site).

14—HOLY NAME OF JESUS (1916) (Slovak), Merged with St. Matthias, Youngstown & SS. Cyril & Methodius, Youngstown to form Our Lady of Sorrows Parish, Youngstown.

15—IMMACULATE CONCEPTION (1882) Closed. Merged with Sacred Heart of Jesus to form St. Angela Merici Parish, Youngstown.

16—ST. JOSEPH (1966)
4545 New Rd., Austintown, 44515. Tel: 330-792-1919 ; Email: austjoseph@zoominternet.net. Very Rev. Gregory F. Fedor, V.F.
Catechesis Religious Program—Mrs. Linda Landers, C.R.E.; Carol Craven, Pastoral Assoc.; Jim Merhaut, Pastoral Assoc. Students 125.

17—ST. MATTHIAS (1914) (Slovak), Merged with Holy Name of Jesus, Youngstown & SS. Cyril & Methodius, Youngstown to form Our Lady of Sorrows Parish, Youngstown.

18—OUR LADY OF MT. CARMEL (1908) (Italian), Merged with St. Anthony, Youngstown to form Our Lady of Mount Carmel-St. Anthony of Padua Parish, Youngstown.

19—OUR LADY OF SORROWS PARISH (2012)
915 Cornell St., 44502. Tel: 330-788-5082; Email: ourlady915@gmail.com; Web: www.ourladyofsorrowsyoungstown.org. Rev. John Jerek.
St. Mattias Church—(Worship Site).
Holy Name of Jesus Church, (Worship Site) 613 N. Lakeview Ave., 44509.
SS. Cyril & Methodius Church, (Worship Site) 252 E. Wood St., 44503.
Catechesis Religious Program— Twinned with Our Lady of Mt. Carmel, Youngstown. Tel: 330-788-5082. Students 8.

20—ST. PATRICK (1911)
1420 Oak Hill Ave., 44507. Tel: 330-743-1109; Email: stpatricks@neo.rr.com; Web: stpatsyoungstown.com. Rev. Edward P. Noga.
Catechesis Religious Program—Tel: 330-743-1109; Email: Marcy-stpatricks@neo.rr.com. Marcy Fessler, D.R.E. Students 52.

21—SS. PETER AND PAUL, Merged with St. Stephen of Hungary, Youngstown to form Holy Apostles Parish, Youngstown.

22—SACRED HEART OF JESUS (1888) Merged with Immaculate Conception, Youngstown to form St. Angela Merici Parish, Youngstown.

23—ST. STANISLAUS KOSTKA (1902) (Polish)
430 Williamson Ave., 44507. Tel: 330-747-8503; Email: parish124@youngstowndiocese.org. Deacon Michael Schlais.
Catechesis Religious Program— Collaborating with St. Columba. Students 8.

24—ST. STEPHEN OF HUNGARY, Merged with SS. Peter and Paul, Youngstown to form Holy Apostles Parish, Youngstown.

OUTSIDE THE CITY OF YOUNGSTOWN

ALLIANCE, STARK CO.

1—ST. JOSEPH (1854) [CEM]
427 E. Broadway, Alliance, 44601. Tel: 330-821-5760 ; Fax: 330-821-5783; Email: stjosephalliance@gmail.com; Web: www.stjoseph-alliance.org. Rev. Maciej Mankowski.
Catechesis Religious Program—Email: mzeni@youngstowndiocese.org. Students 58.

2—REGINA COELI dba Queen of Heaven (1958)
663 Fernwood Blvd., Alliance, 44601-2728. Tel: 330-821-5880; Fax: 330-821-8837; Email: Parish502@YoungstownDiocese.org; Web: reginacoeliparish.com. Rev. Joseph Ruggieri.
School—Regina Coeli School, (Grades PreK-5), 733 Fernwood Blvd., Alliance, 44601-2730. Tel: 330-829-9239; Fax: 330-823-1877; Email: rcelem@youngstowndiocese.org; Web: rcsjalliance.com. Monica Ketler, Librarian. Lay Teachers 9; Students 124; Religious Teachers 1.
Catechesis Religious Program—Parish School of Religion (P.S.R.), Email: ABenedetti@YoungstownDiocese.org. Mrs. Amy Benedetti-Dyke, D.R.E. Students 63.

ANDOVER, ASHTABULA CO., OUR LADY OF VICTORY (1949) [CEM]
481 S. Main St., P.O. Box 669, Andover, 44003-0669. Tel: 440-293-6218; Email: secretary@andoverkinsmanparishes.org. Rev. Michael Mikstay.
Catechesis Religious Program—Students 14.

ASHTABULA, ASHTABULA CO.

1—ST. JOSEPH, Merged with Our Lady of Mt. Carmel, Ashtabula & Mother of Sorrows, Ashtabula to form Our Lady of Peace Parish, Ashtabula.

2—MOTHER OF SORROWS, Merged with St. Joseph, Ashtabula & Our Lady of Mt. Carmel, Ashtabula to form Our Lady of Peace Parish, Ashtabula.

3—OUR LADY OF MT. CARMEL, Merged with St. Joseph, Ashtabula & Mother of Sorrows, Ashtabula to form Our Lady of Peace Parish, Ashtabula.

4—OUR LADY OF PEACE PARISH (2011) [CEM]
Mailing Address: 3312 Lake Ave., Ashtabula, 44004. Tel: 440-992-0330; Email: ourladyofpeace@olopparish.org. Revs. Raymond J.

Thomas; David I. Bridling; Russell Simeone, Business Mgr.; Meagan Howe, D.R.E.; Deacons Richard Johnson; Michael Gardner.
Res.: 1200 E. 21st, Ashtabula, 44004.
Catechesis Religious Program—Students 90.
Mother of Sorrows— (1890) (Worship Site) 1500 W. 6th St., Ashtabula, 44004-3310.
Our Lady of Mt. Carmel (1897) (Worship Site).
St. Joseph Church, (Worship Site) 3400 Lake Ave., Ashtabula, 44004.

AURORA, PORTAGE CO., OUR LADY OF PERPETUAL HELP (1955)
342 S. Chillicothe Rd., Aurora, 44202-7814.
Tel: 330-562-8519; Fax: 330-562-2529; Email: mcorrigan@olphaurora.org; Web: www.olphaurora.org. Rev. James M. Daprile, Ph.D.; Sr. Lu Haidnick, C.D.P., Pastoral Assoc.
Res.: 680-8 Windward Dr., Aurora, 44202.
Catechesis Religious Program—Email: maclapp@olphaurora.org. Margaret A. Clapp, D.R.E. Students 192.

AUSTINTOWN, MAHONING CO., IMMACULATE HEART OF MARY (1954)
4490 Norquest Blvd., Austintown, 44515.
Tel: 330-793-9988; Email: parish113@youngstowndiocese.org. Very Rev. Gregory F. Fedor, V.F.; Mary Ellen Chance.
Catechesis Religious Program—Tel: 330-799-4202; Fax: 330-799-0151. Joan Lawson, Dir. Faith Formation; Jim Merhaut, Dir. Youth Family. Students 175.

BOARDMAN, MAHONING CO.

1—ST. CHARLES BORROMEO (1926)
7345 Westview Dr., Boardman, 44512.
Tel: 330-758-2325; Email: office@stcharlesbdm.org. Revs. Philip E. Rogers; Gerald M. DeLucia, Parochial Vicar; Deacons Paul Lisko, Pastoral Assoc.; Michael A. Kocjancic, Pastoral Assoc.; Nancy Mikos, Dir. Finance & Opers.; Jacek Sobieski, Dir. Music; Karen Stazak, Coord. Ministries; Erica Galvin, Coord. Communications.
School—St. Charles Borromeo School, (Grades K-8), 7325 Westview Dr., Boardman, 44512.
Tel: 330-758-6689; Fax: 330-758-7404; Email: stcharleselem@youngstowndiocese.org. Mary Welsh, Prin.; Jackie Giambattista, Librarian. Lay Teachers 22; Students 330.
Catechesis Religious Program—Tel: 330-758-8063; Email: jdrummond@youngstowndiocese.org. JoAnn Drummond, D.R.E.; Janette Koewacich, C.R.E.; Natalie Wardle, Coord. Youth Min. Students 435.

2—ST. LUKE (1962)
5235 South Ave., Boardman, 44512.
Tel: 330-782-9783; Email: parish115@youngstowndiocese.org. Rev. John Keehner, J.C.L., Canonical Pastor; Sr. Mary Alyce Koval, O.S.U., Parish Leader; Revs. Zachary Coulter, Sacramental Min.; Chidiebere Ogbuagu, Sacramental Min.; Deacons Richard Milanek; Robert T. Redig.
Catechesis Religious Program—Students 59.

BREWSTER, STARK CO., ST. THERESE (1928) [JC] Merged with St. Clement, Navarre to form Holy Family Parish, Navarre.

CAMPBELL, MAHONING CO.

1—CHRIST THE GOOD SHEPHERD PARISH (2012) [CEM]
633 Porter Ave., Campbell, 44405. Tel: 330-755-4141; Email: christthegoodshepherd@aol.com; Web: www.christ-camp.solutiosoftware.com. Very Rev. Msgr. Peter M. Polando, J.C.L.; Deacons John Rentas; Ronald J. Bunofsky.
Catechesis Religious Program—Email: margeomo4@aol.com. Marge O'Malley, D.R.E. Students 86.
St. John the Baptist—(Worship Site) 159 Reed Ave., Campbell, 44405.
St. Joseph the Provider, (Worship Site).
St. Rose of Lima, (Worship Site).
St. Lucy, (Worship Site) 394 Tenney Ave., Campbell, 44405-1695.

2—ST. JOHN THE BAPTIST (1919) [CEM] (Slovak), Merged with St. Joseph the Provider, St. Lucy & St. Rose of Lima to create Christ the Good Shepherd Parish. For inquiries for parish records contact Christ the Good Shepherd Parish, Campbell.

3—ST. JOSEPH THE PROVIDER (1919) (Polish), Merged with St. John The Baptist, St. Lucy & St. Rose of Lima to create Christ the Good Shepherd Parish. For inquiries for parish records contact Christ the Good Shepherd Parish, Campbell.

4—ST. LUCY (1937) (Italian), Merged with St. John The Baptist, St. Joseph the Provider & St. Rose of Lima to create Christ the Good Shepherd Parish. For inquiries for parish records contact Christ the Good Shepherd Parish, Campbell.

5—ST. ROSE OF LIMA (1961) (Hispanic), Merged with St. John The Baptist, St. Joseph the Provider & St. Lucy to create Christ the Good Shepherd Parish. For inquiries for parish records contact Christ the Good Shepherd Parish, Campbell.

CANAL FULTON, STARK CO., SS. PHILIP AND JAMES (1845) [CEM]
412 High St., Canal Fulton, 44614.
Tel: 330-854-2332; Email: sspj@sssnet.com; Web: spjcanalfulton.com. Rev. Kevin McCaffrey.
School—SS. Philip and James School, (Grades PreSchool-8), 532 High St., Canal Fulton, 44614.
Tel: 330-854-2823; Email: sspandjsecretary@youngstowndiocese.org; Web: www.saintsphilipandjames.org. Daniel Mitchell, Prin. Lay Teachers 16; Students 137.
Catechesis Religious Program—Tel: 330-268-3227; Email: bjprosise@sssnet.com. Jackie Prosise, D.R.E. Students 74.

CANFIELD, MAHONING CO., ST. MICHAEL (1962)
300 N. Broad St., Canfield, 44406. Tel: 330-533-6839; Fax: 330-702-0432; Email: info@stmichaelcanfield.org; Web: www.stmichaelcanfield.org. Rev. Terrence J. Hazel; Deacon Tom Soich.
Res.: 281 Glenview Dr., Canfield, 44406.
Catechesis Religious Program—Tel: 330-533-5275. Maureen Hall, Pastoral Min., Youth Liturgy, RCIA. Students 380.

CANTON, STARK CO.

1—ALL SAINTS (1920) (Polish), Closed. Merged with St. Anthony, Canton to form St. Anthony/All Saints Parish, Canton.

2—ST. ANTHONY (1908) (Italian), Merged with All Saints, Canton to form St. Anthony/All Saints Parish, Canton.

3—ST. ANTHONY/ALL SAINTS PARISH (2011)
1530 11th St., S.E., Canton, 44707.
Tel: 330-452-9539; Email: office@stanthonycanton.org. Rev. Thomas P. Kraszewski; Sr. Karen Lindenberger, Hispanic Ministry; Roberta Muoio, Pastoral Assoc.
Catechesis Religious Program—Maggie Connor-Spitale, D.R.E.; Anne Marie Vega, D.R.E.; Sr. Karen Lindenberger, Coord. Hispanic Ministry; Roberta Muoio, Dir. Youth Min. & Evangelization & Adult Educ.; Pattie Condello Konowal, Pastoral Min., Family Life. Students (English & Spanish) 47.

4—BASILICA OF SAINT JOHN THE BAPTIST (1823; Elevated 2012) [CEM]
627 McKinley Ave., N.W., Canton, 44703.
Tel: 330-454-8044; Email: bassillcaofstjohn@gmail.com. Rev. John E. Sheridan, S.T.L., Rector; Deacon Carl Burkhardt.
Catechesis Religious Program—Students 9.

5—ST. BENEDICT (1923) Merged with St. Mary of the Immaculate Conception, Canton to form St. Mary/St. Benedict Parish, Canton.

6—CHRIST THE SERVANT PARISH (2010)
Mailing Address & Res.: 833 39th St., N.W., Canton, 44709. Tel: 330-492-0757; Fax: 330-492-1214; Email: kkraft@christtheservantparish.org; Web: christtheservantparish.org. Rev. Msgr. Lewis F. Gaetano, D.Min., Admin.; Deacon Thomas Mierzwa.
Our Lady of Peace Church (1952) (Worship Site).
School—Our Lady of Peace School, (Grades K-5), 1001 39th St., N.W., Canton, 44709.
Tel: 330-492-0622; Fax: 330-492-0959; Email: olopelem@youngstowndiocese.org. Lenora Krueger, Librarian. Lay Teachers 15; Sisters 4; Students 187; Religious Teachers 2.
Catechesis Religious Program—Email: eschafer@christtheservantparish.org. Elise Schafer, D.R.E.

7—ST. JOAN OF ARC (1944)
4940 Tuscarawas St. W., Canton, 44708-5012.
Tel: 330-477-6796; Email: parish511@youngstowndiocese.org. Rev. G. David Weikart; Deacon David Conversino.
School—St. Joan of Arc School, (Grades PreK-8), 120 Bordner Ave., S.W., Canton, 44710.
Tel: 330-477-2972; Fax: 330-478-2606; Email: stjoaelem@youngstowndiocese.org; Web: www.sjacanton.org. Lay Teachers 21; Students 206.
Catechesis Religious Program—166 Bordner Ave., S.W., Canton, 44710. Tel: 330-477-2972; Email: secretary@sjacanton.com; Email: stjoaelem@youngstowndiocese.org. Chris Pollard, D.R.E.; Terry Sibert, D.R.E.

8—ST. JOSEPH (1902) [CEM]
2427 W. Tuscarawas St., Canton, 44708.
Tel: 330-453-2526; Email: stjosephcanton@catholicweb.com; Web: stjosephcanton.org. Rev. Msgr. Frank A. Carfagna; Deacons Wilbur J. Bagley; Charles E. Ostrout Jr.
Catechesis Religious Program—Tel: 330-454-2144; Email: stjoereled@catholicweb.com. Mrs. Rose Naegeli-Marsi, D.R.E. Students 57.

9—LITTLE FLOWER CATHOLIC CHURCH (1929)
2040 Diamond St., N.E., Canton, 44721. Rev. Leo J. Wehrlin.
Catechesis Religious Program—Web: www.littleflowerparish.com. Students 239.

10—ST. MARY OF THE IMMACULATE CONCEPTION (1899) Merged with St. Benedict, Canton to form St. Mary/St. Benedict Parish, Canton.

11—ST. MARY/ST. BENEDICT PARISH (2011)
1602 Market Ave., S., Canton, 44707.
Tel: 330-453-2110; Email: OfficeStM-StB@sbcglobal.net; Email: BulletinStM-StB@sbcglobal.net. Rev. Benson Claret Okpara, Admin., Email: cocbenson@hotmail.com; Christine Freese; John Metzger, Business Mgr.; Beth Herbst, Music Min.; Judy Cerni, Music Min.; Mr. Shawn Roush, Supt.
Res.: 2207 Third St. S.E., Canton, 44707.
St. Mary of the Immaculate Conception— (1899) (Worship Site).
St. Benedict (1923) (Worship Site) Brenda Jones, Sacramental Min.
Catechesis Religious Program—Sally David, D.R.E. Students 35.

12—ST. MICHAEL THE ARCHANGEL (1952)
3430 St. Michael Blvd., N.W., Canton, 44718.
Tel: 330-492-3119; Fax: 330-492-0339; Email: bruce@stmichaelcanton.org; Web: www.stmichaelcanton.org. Rev. Donald E. King; Deacons Mark J. Fuller; Peter P. Pohl; Mr. Jeff Fricker, Pastoral Assoc.; Mrs. Julie Sutton, Pastoral Assoc.; Justin Huyck, Pastoral Assoc.; Mr. Bruce Gordon, Business Mgr.; Mrs. Ashley Quinn, Youth Min.; Jeanne Ryder; Libby Saxton, Music Min.; Patricia Berring, Liturgy Dir.; Stephanie Bole, Sec.
School—St. Michael the Archangel School, (Grades PreK-8), Tel: 330-492-2657; Fax: 330-492-9618; Email: stmichaelelem@youngstowndiocese.org; Web: www.smscanton.org. Ms. Claire Gatti, Prin. Lay Teachers 25; Students 413.

13—OUR LADY OF PEACE (1952) Merged with St. Paul, Canton to form Christ the Servant Parish, Canton.

14—ST. PAUL (1907) [JC] Merged with Our Lady of Peace, Canton to form Christ the Servant Parish, Canton.

15—ST. PETER (1845) [CEM]
726 Cleveland Ave., N.W., Canton, 44702.
Tel: 330-453-8493; Email: Churchoffice@stpetercanton.org. Rev. John E. Sheridan, S.T.L.
School—St. Peter School, (Grades PreK-5), 702 Cleveland Ave., N.W., Canton, 44702.
Tel: 330-452-0125; Email: office@stpetercanton.org. Sandie Fusillo, Prin. Lay Teachers 7; Students 114.
Catechesis Religious Program—Email: dominic.colucy.dre@gmail.com. Dominic Colucy, D.R.E. Students 402.

CHAMPION, TRUMBULL CO., ST. WILLIAM (1963)
5411 Mahoning Ave., N.W., Warren, 44483.
Tel: 330-847-8677; Email: parishoffice@stwilliamchampion.org; Web: www.stwilliamchampion.org. Rev. Michael D. Balash.
Catechesis Religious Program—Email: ctimko@stwilliamchampion.org. Carol Timko, C.R.E. Students 85.

COLUMBIANA, COLUMBIANA CO., ST. JUDE (1966)
180 Seventh St., Columbiana, 44408.
Tel: 330-482-2351; Fax: 330-532-0027; Email: mburkey.ololstj@gmail.com; Web: www.ololstj.org. Rev. Christopher Cicero.
Res.: 199 Seventh St., Columbiana, 44408.
Catechesis Religious Program—Tel: 330-482-2888. Dr. Thomas Brozich, D.R.E. Students 150.

CONNEAUT, ASHTABULA CO.

1—CORPUS CHRISTI PARISH (2008) [JC]
744 Mill St., Conneaut, 44030. Tel: 440-599-8570; Email: stmsfc@hotmail.com. Rev. Philip Miller.
Church: 480 State St., Conneaut, 44030.
Catechesis Religious Program—Mr. Nicholas Perkoski, D.R.E. Students 76.

2—ST. FRANCES CABRINI (1955) [JC] Merged with St. Mary of the Immaculate Conception, Conneaut to form Corpus Christi, Conneaut.

3—ST. MARY OF THE IMMACULATE CONCEPTION (1888) [CEM] [JC] Merged with St. Frances Cabrini, Conneaut to form Corpus Christi, Conneaut.

CORTLAND, TRUMBULL CO., ST. ROBERT BELLARMINE PARISH (1952)
4659 Niles-Cortland Rd., N.E., Cortland, 44410.
Tel: 330-637-4886; Email: parish602@youngstowndiocese.org. Rev. Carl Kish; Michelle Robbins, Music Min.
Catechesis Religious Program—Email: baileydre@aol.com. Sandy Bailey, D.R.E.

DUNGANNON, COLUMBIANA CO., ST. PHILIP NERI (1817) [CEM]
Mailing Address: 271 W. Chestnut St., Lisbon, 44432. Tel: 330-424-7648; Email: bk307@youngstowndiocese.org; Web: www.stphilipneo.org. 11328 Gavers Rd., Hanoverton, 44423. Rev. Stephen M. Wassie.
Catechesis Religious Program—Combined with St. John, Summitville. Students 1.

EAST LIVERPOOL, COLUMBIANA CO.

1—ST. ALOYSIUS (1838) [CEM] (Irish), Merged with Immaculate Conception, Wellsville to form Holy Trinity Parish, East Liverpool.

2—ST. ANN (1915) Closed. For inquiries for parish records contact the chancery.

3—HOLY TRINITY PARISH (2011) [CEM 2]
512 Monroe St., East Liverpool, 43920.
Tel: 330-385-7131; Email: parish303@youngstowndiocese.org. Rev. Scott Kopp; Kristin McNicol; Kimberly Shaffer, Treas.

Catechesis Religious Program—Email: ccdholytrinity@gmail.com. Mr. Robert Barto, D.R.E. (H.S. Holy Trinity Parish, E. Liv. Ohio 43920) Students 37.

St. Aloysius Church (1838) 235 W. 5th St., East Liverpool, 43920.

EAST PALESTINE, COLUMBIANA CO., OUR LADY OF LOURDES (1880) [CEM]
Mailing Address: 180 Seventh St., Columbiana, 44408. Tel: 330-426-9346; Email: burkeymary@comcast.net. 210 E Main, East Palestine, 44413. Rev. Christopher Cicero.
Catechesis Religious Program—Tel: 330-482-2351; Email: jkoewacich.ololstj@gmail.com. Janette Koewacich, D.R.E. At St. Jude Church, 180 Seventh St., Columbiana, OH 44408.

GARRETTSVILLE, PORTAGE CO., ST. AMBROSE (1944)
10692 Freedom St., Garrettsville, 44231.
Tel: 330-527-4105; Email: parish402@youngstowndiocese.org. Rev. Stephen Zeigler; Deacon Robert Rapp, (Retired).
Catechesis Religious Program—Students 118.

GENEVA, ASHTABULA CO., ASSUMPTION B.V.M. (1915) [JC]
30 Lockwood St, Geneva, 44041. Tel: 440-466-3427; Fax: 440-466-4670; Email: bk208@youngstowndiocese.org; Web: assumptionchurchoh.org. Rev. Daniel Finnerty.
Catechesis Religious Program—(Grades K-8), Students 42.

GIRARD, TRUMBULL CO., ST. ROSE (1892)
48 E. Main St., Girard, 44420. Tel: 330-545-4351; Email: parish603@youngstowndiocese.org. Rev. Msgr. John A. Zuraw, J.C.L.; Deacon Paul Milligan.
School—St. Rose School, (Grades K-8), 61 E. Main St., Girard, 44420. Tel: 330-545-1163; Email: stroseele@youngstowndiocese.org; Web: www.stroseschool.info. Mrs. Linda Borton, Prin. Lay Teachers 20; Students 306; Religious Teachers 1.
Sunny Days Day Care Center—Tel: 330-545-1490; Fax: 330-545-1584; Email: sunnydaysccc@att.net. Michelle Frease, Dir. (Preschool).
Catechesis Religious Program—Sr. Kathleen McCarragher, O.S.U., D.R.E. Students 180.

HUBBARD, TRUMBULL CO., ST. PATRICK (1869) [CEM]
225 N. Main St., Hubbard, 44425. Tel: 330-534-1928; Email: parish406@youngstowndiocese.org. Rev. Michael Swierz; Deacons Robert Friedman, Pastoral Assoc.; John Bartos; Michael Medvec.
Catechesis Religious Program—Tel: 330-534-1928; Email: spreled@aol.com; Web: www.stpatshub.org. Karen Bartos, C.R.E.; Teri Ray, Coord. Youth Min.; Nicole Novotny, Youth Min. Students 333.

JEFFERSON, ASHTABULA CO., ST. JOSEPH CALASANCTIUS (1858)
32 E. Jefferson St., Jefferson, 44047.
Tel: 440-576-3651; Email: schurch10@roadrunner.com; Web: www.stjoseph-standrew.com. Rev. John Ettinger.
Catechesis Religious Program—Tel: 440-576-3339; Email: jppertz@windstream.net. Julianne Pertz, J.D., S.F.O., D.R.E. Students 77.

KENT, PORTAGE CO.
1—ST. PATRICK'S (1864) [JC]
313 N. Depeyster St., Kent, 44240. Tel: 330-673-5849 ; Email: rpentello@youngstowndiocese.org. Rev. Richard J. Pentello; Deacons Timothy DeFrange; Michael W. Stabilla.
School—St. Patrick's School, (Grades K-8), 127 Portage St., Kent, 44240. Tel: 330-673-7232; Fax: 330-678-6612; Email: stpatelemkent@youngstowndiocese.org; Web: www.stpatskent.org. Howard Mancini, Prin. Lay Teachers 21; Students 245.
Catechesis Religious Program—(Grades PreK-8), Tel: 330-677-4453. Students 254.
2—UNIVERSITY PARISH NEWMAN CENTER (1953)
1424 Horning Rd., Kent, 44240. Tel: 330-678-0240; Email: parish415@youngstowndiocese.org. Rev. Steven J. Agostino; Ms. Carmen Roebke, Pastoral Assoc.; Jordan Cinderich, Campus Min.; Dr. John Roebke, Music Min.; Veronica Victoria, Contact Person.
Catechesis Religious Program—Email: croebke@kent.edu; Email: jcinderi@kent.edu.

KINGSVILLE, ASHTABULA CO., ST. ANDREW BOBOLA (1936)
3700 State Rte. 193, Kingsville, 44048.
Tel: 440-224-0987; Email: st.andrew@windstream.net; Web: www.stjoseph-standrew.com. Rev. John Ettinger.
Catechesis Religious Program—Mailing Address: 32 E. Jefferson St., Jefferson, 44047. Julianne Pertz, J.D., S.F.O., D.R.E. Students 37.

KINSMAN, TRUMBULL CO., ST. PATRICK (1957) Attended by Our Lady of Victory, Andover.
6367 State Rte 87, Kinsman, 44428. Rev. Michael Mikstay.
Res.: 481 S. Main St., P.O. Box 669, Andover, 44003-0669.
Catechesis Religious Program—Students 24.

LAKE MILTON, MAHONING CO.
1—ST. CATHERINE (1956) Merged with St. James Parish, North Jackson to form Our Lady of the Lakes Parish, St. Catherine Church, Lake Milton.
2—OUR LADY OF THE LAKES PARISH, ST. CATHERINE CHURCH (2010)
50 Rosemont Rd., North Jackson, 44451.
Tel: 330-538-2602; Fax: 330-538-9580; Email: ourladyofthelakes@att.net; Web: ourladyotl.org. 1254 Grandview Rd., Lake Milton, 44429. Rev. David W. Merzweiler.
Church & Parish Offices: 50 Rosemont Rd., North Jackson, 44451.
Catechesis Religious Program— Combined stats with St. James Church. Students 20.

LEETONIA, COLUMBIANA CO., ST. PATRICK (1861) [CEM]
167 W. Main St., Leetonia, 44431. Tel: 330-427-6577; Email: cyeager@stpaulsalem.org. Rev. Robert R. Edwards, Canonical Admin.; Sr. Joan Franklin, O.P., Pastoral Assoc.; Deacon Lawrence Parks.
Res.: 157 Ohio Ave., Salem, 44460.
Catechesis Religious Program—Tel: 330-337-3019; Email: pfitch@stpaulsalem.org. Peggy Fitch, D.R.E. Students 19.

LISBON, COLUMBIANA CO., ST. GEORGE (1820)
271 W. Chestnut St., Lisbon, 44432.
Tel: 330-424-7648; Email: bk307@youngstowndiocese.org. Rev. Stephen M. Wassie.
Catechesis Religious Program—Tel: 330-424-7500. Students 9.
Mission—St. Agatha, 13523 Washington St. at State Rt. 518, Lisbon, 44432.

LOUISVILLE, STARK CO.
1—ST. LOUIS (1838) [CEM] (French—German)
300 N. Chapel St., Louisville, 44641.
Tel: 330-875-1658; Email: parish520@youngstowndiocese.org. Rev. Robert M. Miller, Admin.
School—St. Louis School, (Grades PreSchool-5), 214 N. Chapel St., Louisville, 44641. Tel: 330-875-1467; Email: stlouiselem@youngstowndiocese.org.
Catechesis Religious Program—(Grades K-8), Email: mcalandros@youngstowndiocese.org. Mr. Mario Calandros, D.R.E.; Sr. Barbara Klodt, S.N.D., D.R.E.; Daniel Kelly, Music Min.
2—SACRED HEART OF MARY (1833) [CEM] Rev. Nicholas Mancini.
Res.: 8277 Nickelplate Ave., N.E., Louisville, 44641.
Tel: 330-875-2827; Fax: 330-875-5511; Email: rsacred@neo.rr.com.
Catechesis Religious Program—Mr. Mario Calandros, D.R.E. Students 28.

LOWELLVILLE, MAHONING CO., OUR LADY OF THE HOLY ROSARY (1867) [CEM]
131 E. Wood St., Lowellville, 44436.
Tel: 330-536-6436; Email: parish132@youngstowndiocese.org. Deacon Frank J. Lellio, Admin.
Catechesis Religious Program—Students 115.

MANTUA, PORTAGE CO., ST. JOSEPH (1923)
11045 St. Joseph Blvd., Mantua, 44255.
Tel: 330-274-2253; Tel: 330-274-2268;
Fax: 330-274-2254; Email: parishoffice@stjosephmantua.com; Web: www.stjosephmantua.com. Rev. Edward Stafford, T.O.R.; Deacon Gerolome P. Scopilliti.
Catechesis Religious Program—Email: phaney@stjosephmantua.com. Mrs. Margaret Haney, D.R.E. Students 100.

MASSILLON, STARK CO.
1—ST. BARBARA (1867) [CEM] (German)
2813 Lincoln Way, N.W., Massillon, 44647.
Tel: 330-833-6898; Email: frcline@saintbarbaraparish.com. Rev. Brian James Cline.
School—St. Barbara School, (Grades PreK-8), 2809 Lincoln Way, N.W., Massillon, 44647.
Tel: 330-833-9510; Fax: 330-833-3297; Email: stbarbaraelem@youngstowndiocese.org. Jacqueline Thomas, Prin. Lay Teachers 10; Students 110.
Catechesis Religious Program—Email: mluginski@youngstowndiocese.org. Mollie Luginski, D.R.E. Students 79.
2—ST. JOSEPH (1863) [CEM]
322 Third St., S.E., Massillon, 44646.
Tel: 330-833-2607; Email: parish504@youngstowndiocese.org. Rev. Raymond L. Paul; Deacons Steven A. Wyles; Donald F. Molinari; Randy Smith.
Catechesis Religious Program—Students 86.
3—SAINT MARY (1839) [CEM]
726 1st St., N.E., Massillon, 44646.
Tel: 330-833-8501; Email: agretchko@youngstowndiocese.org. Rev. A. Edward Gretchko.
Res.: 206 Cherry Rd., N.E., Massillon, 44646.
School—St. Mary School, (Grades PreK-8), 640 First St., N.E., Massillon, 44646. Tel: 330-832-9355; Fax: 330-832-9030; Email: stmaryelem@youngstowndiocese.org; Web: www.stmarymassillon.org. Jennifer Fischer, Prin.; Pamela Bunnenberg, Sec.; Lisa Channel, Librarian; Sr. Kathy Longheier, Archivist. Lay Teachers 11; Sisters 1; Students 200; Religious Teachers 1.
Catechesis Religious Program—Students 96.

MASURY, TRUMBULL CO., ST. BERNADETTE (1940) Merged with St. Vincent de Paul, Vienna to form St. Thomas the Apostle Parish, St. Vincent De Paul Church, Vienna.

MAXIMO, STARK CO., ST. JOSEPH (1850) [CEM]
P.O. Box 219, Maximo, 44650-0219.
Tel: 330-823-7809; Tel: 330-823-5233; Email: Parish524@YoungstownDiocese.org; Web: www.facebook.com/St.Joseph.Maximo. 12055 Easton St NE, Alliance, 44601. Rev. Joseph Ruggieri.
7274 Oak Hill Ave. N.E., Alliance, 44601.
Catechesis Religious Program—Mrs. Theresa Estock, D.R.E. Students 45.

MCDONALD, TRUMBULL CO., OUR LADY OF PERPETUAL HELP (1943)
618 Ohio Ave., McDonald, 44437. Tel: 330-530-1111; Email: olphparish618@aol.com. Rev. Edward R. Brienz, Admin.
Catechesis Religious Program—Heidi Smith, D.R.E.

MINERAL RIDGE, TRUMBULL CO., ST. MARY (1870)
3504 Main St., Mineral Ridge, 44440.
Tel: 330-652-7761; Email: parish608@youngstowndiocese.org. Rev. Richard Murphy, Admin.
Catechesis Religious Program—Tel: 330-565-2449; Email: kdcheryl@aol.com. Cheryl Basista, D.R.E. Students 72.

NAVARRE, STARK CO.
1—ST. CLEMENT (1832) [CEM] Merged with St. Therese, Brewster to form Holy Family Parish, Navarre.
2—HOLY FAMILY PARISH (2011) [CEM]
216 Wooster St., N.E., Navarre, 44662.
Tel: 330-879-5900; Fax: 330-879-5138; Email: holyfamilyparishnavarre@sssnet.com; Web: holyfamilyparishnavarre.org. Pattie Condello, Parish Leader; Rev. G. David Weikart, Canonical Pastor.
Catechesis Religious Program—Email: mrichards@sssnet.com. GeorgeAnn Richards, D.R.E.
St. Clement Church— (1832) (Worship Site)
Tel: 330-879-5900; Fax: 330-879-5138.
St. Therese Church (1928) (Worship Site) 512 Wabash Ave., S., Brewster, 44613. Tel: 330-879-5900

NEW MIDDLETOWN, MAHONING CO., ST. PAUL THE APOSTLE (1952) [JC]
10143 Main St., P.O. Box 515, New Middletown, 44442. Tel: 330-542-3466; Email: parish133@youngstowndiocese.org. Rev. John M. Jerek, Admin.
Catechesis Religious Program—Email: albert.pompeo@gmail.com. Albert Pompeo, D.R.E. Students 168.

NEWTON FALLS, TRUMBULL CO.
1—ST. JOSEPH (1923) [CEM] (Slovak), Merged with St. Mary, Newton Falls to form Saint Mary and Saint Joseph, Newton Falls.
2—ST. MARY (1928) [JC] (Polish), Merged with St. Joseph, Newton Falls to form Saint Mary and Saint Joseph, Newton Falls.
3—ST. MARY AND ST. JOSEPH PARISH (2008) [CEM]
120 Maple Dr., Newton Falls, 44444.
Tel: 330-872-4193; Email: parish609@youngstowndiocese.org. Rev. Shawn Conoboy, Admin.; Ms. Bachelle Barb, Sec.; Mrs. Eileen Petridis, Organist; Ms. Margaret Zeleny, Maintenance.
Church & Rectory: 131 W. Quarry St., Newton Falls, 44444-1560.
Catechesis Religious Program—Students 39.

NILES, TRUMBULL CO.
1—OUR LADY OF MOUNT CARMEL PARISH (1906) (Italian)
381 Robbins Ave., Niles, 44446. Tel: 330-652-5825; Email: parish611@youngstowndiocese.org. Rev. John-Michael Lavelle, D.Min.
Catechesis Religious Program—(Grades K-8), Students 109.
2—ST. STEPHEN (1853) [CEM]
129 W. Park Ave., Niles, 44446. Tel: 330-652-4396; Fax: 330-652-9317; Email: churchofsaintstephen@yahoo.com. Rev. James Korda, Admin.
Catechesis Religious Program—Students 109.

NORTH CANTON, STARK CO., ST. PAUL (1845)
241 S. Main St., North Canton, 44720.
Tel: 330-499-2201; Email: pbrady@stpaulcanton.org. Rev. Msgr. James A. Clarke; Revs. Marian Babjak, (Slovakia); James E. McKarns, Pastor Emeritus, (Retired); Michele Blate, D.R.E., RCIA Coord.; Deacons William Lambert; Ron Reolfi; Edward Laubacher; Peter D. Watry; Dennis Ross.
School—St. Paul School, (Grades PreK-8), 303 S. Main St., North Canton, 44720. Tel: 330-494-0223; Fax: 330-494-3226; Email: stpaulelemncanton@youngstowndiocese.org; Web:

spsnorthcanton.com. Amie Hale, Prin.; Kathy Yackshaw, Librarian. Lay Teachers 28; Students 324.
Catechesis Religious Program—Dustine May, C.R.E. Students 645.

NORTH JACKSON, MAHONING CO.

1—ST. JAMES PARISH (1943) Merged with St. Catherine, Lake Milton to form Our Lady of the Lakes Parish, St. James Church, North Jackson.

2—OUR LADY OF THE LAKES PARISH, ST. JAMES CHURCH (2010)
50 Rosemont Rd., North Jackson, 44451.
Tel: 330-538-2602; Fax: 330-538-9580; Email: ourladyofthelakes@att.net; Web: ourladyotl.org. Rev. David W. Merzweiler.
Res.: 1254 Grandview Rd., Lake Milton, 44429.
Catechesis Religious Program—Students 20.

ORWELL, ASHTABULA CO., ST. MARY (1922) [CEM]
103 N. Maple, Box 217, Orwell, 44076-0217.
Tel: 440-437-6262; Email: parish210@youngstowndiocese.org. Rev. John P. Madden.
Catechesis Religious Program—Tel: 440-437-8216. Mary Jo Parillo-Orsini, D.R.E.

POLAND, MAHONING CO., HOLY FAMILY (1956)
2729 Center Rd., Poland, 44514. Tel: 330-757-1545; Email: holy_family@sbcglobal.net; Web: www.holyfamilypoland.org. Rev. Msgr. William J. Connell, J.C.L.; Deacon Ray Hatala.
School—Holy Family School, (Grades PreK-8), 2731 Center Rd., Poland, 44514. Tel: 330-757-3713; Fax: 330-757-7648; Email: hfelem@youngstowndiocese.org; Web: hfspoland.org. Lay Teachers 20; Students 248.
Catechesis Religious Program—Email: mkelty@youngtowndiocese.org. Students 555.

RANDOLPH TOWNSHIP, PORTAGE CO., ST. JOSEPH (1831) [CEM]
2643 Waterloo Rd., Mogadore, 44260.
Tel: 330-628-9941; Email: parish408@youngstowndiocese.org. Rev. Thomas S. Acker, S.J., Admin.; Deacon Steven Gies.
School—St. Joseph School, (Grades PreK-7), 2617 Waterloo Rd., Mogadore, 44260. Tel: 330-628-9555; Email: stjoeelemmogadore@youngstonwdiocese.org; Web: sjsrandolph.org. Rev. Thomas S. Acker, S.J., Admin. Lay Teachers 15; Students 140.
Catechesis Religious Program—Generations of Faith Students 63.

RAVENNA, PORTAGE CO., IMMACULATE CONCEPTION (1854) [CEM]
409 W. Main St., Ravenna, 44266. Tel: 330-296-9193; Email: parish406@youngstowndiocese.org. Rev. William B. Kraynak; Sr. Yvonne Horning, O.P., Pastoral Assoc.
Catechesis Religious Program—Eileen Edwards, D.R.E. Students 52.

ROCK CREEK, ASHTABULA CO., SACRED HEART (1956) [JC]
3049 SR 45, P.O. Box 310, Rock Creek, 44084.
Tel: 440-563-3010; Email: parish211@youngstowndiocese.org. Rev. John P. Madden.
Catechesis Religious Program—Tel: 440-563-5253; Email: morsini002@gmail.com. Mary Jo Parillo-Orsini, D.R.E.

ROOTSTOWN, PORTAGE CO., ST. PETER OF THE FIELDS (1868) [CEM] (German)
3487 Old Forge Rd., Rootstown, 44272.
Tel: 330-325-7543; Email: st.peterschurch.rootstown@gmail.com. Rev. David M. Misbrener.
Catechesis Religious Program—Students 124.

SALEM, COLUMBIANA CO., ST. PAUL (1881)
935 E. State St., Salem, 44460. Tel: 330-332-0336; Fax: 330-332-7982; Email: cyeager@stpaulsalem.org; Web: stpaulsalem.org. Rev. Robert R. Edwards.
Res.: 157 Ohio Ave., Salem, 44460.
Parish Administration Center—935 E. State St., Salem, 44460.
School—St. Paul School, (Grades PreK-8), 925 E. State St., Salem, 44460. Tel: 330-337-3451; Fax: 330-337-3607; Email: stpaulelemsalem@youngstowndiocese.org; Web: www.stpaul.k12.oh.us. Lay Teachers 12; Students 105.
Catechesis Religious Program—Tel: 330-337-3019; Email: pfitch@stpaulsalem.org. Sr. Mary McFadden, S.N.D., Pastoral Assoc.; Margaret Fitch, D.R.E.

SALINEVILLE, COLUMBIANA CO., ST. PATRICK (1873) [CEM] Closed. For inquiries for parish records contact the chancery.

SEBRING, MAHONING CO., ST. ANN (1908)
323 S. 15th St., Sebring, 44672. Tel: 330-938-2033; Email: stannchurchsebring@gmail.com; Web: stannchurchsebring.org. Rev. Thomas P. Dyer; Deacon Ralph Chase, (Retired).
Catechesis Religious Program—Tel: 330-206-3778; Email: szekelyrebecca@yahoo.com. Rebecca Szekely, D.R.E. Students 23.

STREETSBORO, PORTAGE CO., ST. JOAN OF ARC (1965)
8894 State Rte. 14, Streetsboro, 44241.
Tel: 330-626-3424; Email: parish409@youngstowndiocese.org. Rev. Christopher Luoni.
Catechesis Religious Program—Students 175.

STRUTHERS, MAHONING CO.

1—CHRIST OUR SAVIOR PARISH (2011)
764 5th St., Struthers, 44471. Tel: 330-755-9819; Email: Cosparishstruthers@gmail.com; Web: www.coparish.org. Rev. Martin Celuch, J.C.L.; Deacon John Terranova.
Res.: 250 N. Bridge St., Struthers, 44471.
Parish Office—764 5th St., Struthers, 44471-1704. Tel: 330-755-9819; Email: cosparishstruthers@gmail.com; Web: www.cosparish.org.
School—Saint Nicholas School, (Grades K-8), 762 5th St., Struthers, 44471-1702. Tel: 330-755-2128; Fax: 330-755-2129; Email: Stnickelem@youngstowndiocese.org. Mrs. Pat Fletcher, Librarian. Lay Teachers 15; Students 176.
Catechesis Religious Program—Tel: 330-755-6245; Email: jamie.miller@youngstowndiocese.org. Mrs. Jamie Miller, D.R.E. Students 262.
St. Nicholas Church—(Worship Site).
Holy Trinity Church, (Worship Site).

2—HOLY TRINITY (1907) (Slovak), Merged with St. Nicholas, Struthers to form Christ Our Savior Parish, Struthers.

3—ST. NICHOLAS (1865) Merged with Holy Trinity, Struthers to form Christ Our Savior Parish, Struthers.

SUMMITVILLE, COLUMBIANA CO., ST. JOHN (1839) [CEM]
Mailing Address: 271 W. Chestnut St., Lisbon, 44432. Tel: 330-424-7648; Email: bk307@youngstowndiocese.org. 16017 Smith Rd., Summitville, 43692. Rev. Stephen M. Wassie.
Res.: 16017 Smith Rd., Summitville, 43962.
Catechesis Religious Program—Students 48.

UNIONTOWN, STARK CO., HOLY SPIRIT (1979)
2952 Edison St. N.W., Uniontown, 44685.
Tel: 330-699-5800; Fax: 330-699-9270; Email: parishoffice@holyspiritunoh.org. Rev. John Zapp.
Catechesis Religious Program—Email: cathykasza@holyspiritunoh.org; Email: anneweeks@holyspiritunoh.org; Email: roneill@youngstowndiocese.org. Cathy Kasza, D.R.E.; Anne Weeks, D.R.E. Students 1.

VIENNA, TRUMBULL CO.

1—QUEEN OF THE HOLY ROSARY (1997)
291 Scoville Dr., Vienna, 44473. Tel: 330-856-4201; Email: Parish623@youngstowndiocese.org. Rev. Denis Bouchard, F.S.S.P.
Catechesis Religious Program—Students 49.

2—ST. THOMAS THE APOSTLE PARISH (2016)
4453 Warren-Sharon Rd., P.O. Box 148, Vienna, 44473. Tel: 330-394-2461; Email: theapostlethomas@aol.com; Web: theapostlethomas.com. Very Rev. Frank L. Zanni, V.F.
Catechesis Religious Program—Tel: 330-394-2361. Students 190.

3—ST. VINCENT DE PAUL (1879) Merged with St. Bernadette, Masury to form St. Thomas the Apostle Parish, St. Vincent DePaul Church, Vienna.

WARREN, TRUMBULL CO.

1—BLESSED SACRAMENT (1959)
3020 Reeves Rd., N.E., Warren, 44483.
Tel: 330-372-2215; Email: info@bspcc.org; Web: www.bspcc.org. Revs. Peter Haladej; Thomas C. Eisweirth, Pastor Emeritus, (Retired); Deacon Robert Green.
See John F. Kennedy Catholic School, Lower Campus in the Institution Section under Diocesan Schools.
Catechesis Religious Program—Email: bantenucci@bspcc.org. Brenda Antenucci, D.R.E. Students 459.

2—SS. CYRIL AND METHODIUS (1928) (Slovak), Merged with St. James to form St. Elizabeth Ann Seton Parish, Warren.

3—ST. ELIZABETH ANN SETON PARISH (2012)
2532 Burton St. S.E., Warren, 44484.
Tel: 330-393-9766; Fax: 330-393-0555; Email: parish@seaswarrenohio.org; Web: www.seaswarrenohio.org. Rev. Craig McHenry; Deacons Joseph P. Toth; Robert Simmerly.
SS. Cyril and Methodius Church (1928) 185 Laird Ave., Warren, 44483.
St. James Church—

4—ST. JAMES (1947) Merged with SS. Cyril and Methodius, Warren to form St. Elizabeth Ann Seton Parish, Warren.

5—ST. JOHN PAUL II (2011) [CEM]
1401 Moncrest Dr. N.W., Warren, 44485.
Tel: 330-399-8881, Ext. 711; Email: pastor@saintjohnpauliiparish.org; Web: www.saintjohnpauliiparish.org. Rev. Christopher Henyk.
Res.: 1346 Vernon Ave., N.W., Warren, 44483.
Catechesis Religious Program—Email: rrpetersal@aol.com. Ruby Petersal, D.R.E.
St. Joseph Church (1928) 420 North St., N.W., Warren, 44483. Tel: 330-399-8881; Email: secretary@saintjohnpauliiparish.org; Email: pastor@saintjohnpauliiparish.org; Web: www.saintjohnpauliiparish.org.

6—ST. JOSEPH, Merged with St. Pius X, Warren to form St. John Paul II Parish, Warren.

7—ST. MARY (1835) [CEM]
232 Seneca St., N.E., Warren, 44481.
Tel: 330-393-8721; Email: parish619@youngstowndiocese.org. Rev. Msgr. John A. Zuraw, J.C.L., Chancellor.
Catechesis Religious Program—Ellen Prentice, D.R.E. Students 45.

8—ST. PIUS X, Merged with St. Joseph, Warren to form St. John Paul II Parish, Warren.

WAYNESBURG, STARK CO., ST. JAMES (1928)
400 W. Lisbon St., Waynesburg, 44688.
Tel: 330-866-9449; Email: parish528@youngstowndiocese.org. Rev. Joseph Zamary.
School—St. James School, (Grades PreK-6), Tel: 330-866-9556; Email: stjameselem@youngstowndiocese.org; Web: sjswaynesburg.org. Kathleen Kettler, Prin. Lay Teachers 6.
Catechesis Religious Program—Students 66.

WELLSVILLE, COLUMBIANA CO., IMMACULATE CONCEPTION (1842) [CEM] Merged with St. Aloysius, East Liverpool to form Holy Trinity Parish, East Liverpool.

WINDHAM, PORTAGE CO., ST. MICHAEL (1943)
Mailing Address: 10692 Freedom St., Garrettsville, 44231. Tel: 330-527-4105; Email: st_ambrose44231@yahoo.com. Rev. Stephen Zeigler.
Church: 9736 E. Center St., Windham, 44288.
Catechesis Religious Program—Students 7.

On Duty Outside the Diocese:
Revs.—
Marcelli, Michael
Nuzzi, Ronald.

Sick Leave:
Rev.—
Popovich, Stephen E.

Leave of Absence:
Revs.—
Albright, Matthew
Frient, Lawrence
Lanterman, Robert.

Retired:
Rev. Msgrs.—
Ashton, John P., Ph.D., (Retired)
Kolp, James, (Retired)
Miller, Kenneth E., (Retired)
Reidy, Robert, (Retired)
Rhodes, David W., (Retired)
Torok, Dezso, (Retired)
Revs.—
Balasko, George J., (Retired)
Bantz, William, (Retired)
Beneleit, Edward L., (Retired)
Bishop, Thomas G., (Retired)
Bonnot, Bernard R., (Retired)
Brobst, Richard A., (Retired)
Cavanaugh, James K., (Retired)
Cebula, Thomas W., (Retired)
Deffenbaugh, Joseph T., (Retired)
Eisweirth, Thomas C., (Retired)
Esposito, Anthony, (Retired)
Feicht, Donald L., (Retired)
Franko, George M., (Retired)
Gaeta, Bernard N., (Retired)
Garvey, Michael, (Retired)
Grabowski, Dennis, (Retired)
Hannon, Robert J., (Retired)
Johnson, James, (Retired)
Karas, Stephen, (Retired)
Kaylor, Robert W., (Retired)
Klingler, Ronald, (Retired)
Kulesa, Daniel J., (Retired)
Lang, James Paul, (Retired)
Lehnerd, Frank M., (Retired)
Lody, John, (Retired)
Lukehart, Frederick, (Retired)
Mancini, Nicholas J., (Retired)
McCarthy, Thomas, (Retired)
McKarns, James E., (Retired)
Mulqueen, John D., (Retired)
Neroda, Edward J., (Retired)
O'Neill, Timothy H., (Retired)
Pleban, Leo, (Retired)
Rusnak, Melvin E., (Retired)
Santucci, Louis, (Retired)
Seifert, Michael D., (Retired)
Trimbur, John S., (Retired)
Trucksis, Frederick E., (Retired)
Ungashick, Thomas, (Retired)
Walker, James P., (Retired)
Wieczorek, Edward R., (Retired)

Witmer, Joseph W., (Retired)
Ziegler, Thomas G., (Retired)
Ziemba, Howard, (Retired).

Permanent Deacons:
Arend, David H., Our Lady of Lourdes, Columbiana
Bagley, Wilbur J., St. Joseph, Canton
Bartos, John, St. Patrick, Hubbard
Brechbill, Kenneth W., (Retired)
Brown, James, St. Christine, Youngstown
Bunofsky, Ronald J., Christ the Good Shepherd, Campbell
Burkhardt, Carl R., St. John the Baptist, Canton
Capitena, Michael, Holy Spirit, Uniontown
Chase, Ralph, (Retired)
Conversino, David, St. Joan of Arc, Canton
Cuttica, Robert J., St. Christine, Youngstown
Davies, Martin H., St. Christine, Youngstown
DeFrange, Tim, St. Patrick, Kent
Evans, Christopher, Our Lady of Lourdes, East Palestine
Falasca, Anthony, Our Lady of Mt. Carmel Basilica/ St. Anthony, Youngstown
Friedman, Robert J., St. Patrick, Hubbard
Fuller, Mark J., St. Michael, Canton
Gardner, Michael, St. Joseph, Jefferson; St. Andrew, Kingsville
Germak, Christopher L., Little Flower, Middlebranch
Gies, Steven R., St. Joseph, Mogodore
Green, Robert, Blessed Sacrament, Warren
Hanshaw, Michael, Our Lady of Mt. Carmel, Niles
Hatala, Ray H., Holy Family, Poland
Hawkins, Edward, (Retired)
Heinz, Edward, Our Lady of Victory, Andover and St. Patrick, Kinsman
Ivan, Ellis C., Holy Spirit, Uniontown
Jerzyk, Carl, (On Duty Outside Diocese)
Johnson, Don, (Retired)
Johnson, Richard M., Our Lady of Peace, Ashtabula
Keefer, Gary, Our Lady of Perpetual Help, Aurora
Kenney, Dave, St. James, Waynesburg
Kocjancic, Michael A., St. Charles, Boardman
Krause, Harold R., (Retired)
Lamar, Kevin T., (Retired)
Lambert, William H., St. Paul, North Canton
Laubacher, Edward, St. Paul, North Canton
Layko, Ronald J., St. Christine, Youngstown
Lellio, Frank J., Our Lady of the Holy Rosary, Lowellville
Lisko, Paul, St. Charles, Boardman
Marino, Frank, St. Stephen, Niles
Massacci, James Louis, Immaculate Heart of Mary, Austintown, St. Joseph, Austintown
Medvec, Michael, St. Patrick, Hubbard
Mierzwa, Thomas, Christ the Servant, Canton
Milanek, Richard, St. Luke, Boardman
Milligan, Paul, St. Rose, Girard
Mintus, Robert, (On Leave)
Molinari, Donald F., (Retired)
O'Neill, Russell, Holy Spirit, Uniontown
Ostrout, Charles E. Jr., St. Joseph, Canton
Pallo, John D., (Retired)
Pasko, Lawrence, St. Patrick, Leetonia
Pepoy, Joseph E., Our Lady of Perpetual Help, Aurora
Pfleger, James W., (Retired)
Pohl, Peter P., St. Michael, Canton
Prasek, Alan, (Retired)
Redig, Robert T., St. Luke, Boardman
Rentas, John, Christ the Good Shepherd, Campbell
Reolfi, Ron, St. Paul, North Canton
Ross, Dennis, St. Paul, North Canton
Savo, Gerald L., (Retired)
Schlais, Michael, St. Stanislaus, Youngstown
Scopilliti, Gerolome P., St. Joseph, Mantua
Seaman, Michael T., St. Peter, Canton
Simmerly, Robert, St. James, Warren
Smith, James, St. Edward, Youngstown
Smith, Randy, St. Joseph, Massillon
Soich, Thomas G., St. Michael, Canfield
Stabilla, Michael W., St. Patrick, Kent
Suzelis, Ted, St. Peter of the Fields, Rootstown
Terranova, John, St. Nicholas, Struthers
Toth, Joseph P., St. Elizabeth Ann Seton, Warren
Waldron, Michael K., (Outside Diocese)
Watry, Peter D., St. Paul, North Canton
Wood, Gregory J., St. Peter, Canton
Wyles, Steve, St. Joseph, Massillon.

INSTITUTIONS LOCATED IN DIOCESE

[A] SEMINARIES, RELIGIOUS, OR SCHOLASTICATES

CANFIELD. *Society of St. Paul*, 9531 Akron-Canfield Rd., P.O. Box 595, Canfield, 44406.
Tel: 330-533-5503; Fax: 330-533-1076; Email: provincialoffice@stpauls.us; Web: www.stpauls.us. Rev. Tony Bautista, S.S.P., Prov.; Bro. Dismas Beique, S.S.P.; Kevin Cahill; Bro. Dominic Calabro, S.S.P.; Bienvenido Cana; Bro. Paschal Duesman, S.S.P.; Revs. Edmund Lane, S.S.P.; Sebastian Lee; Jeffrey Mickler, S.S.P.; Bros. Aloysius Milella, S.S.P.; John Naranjo, S.S.P.; Gerard Roche, S.S.P.; Very Rev. Matthew Roehrig, S.S.P., Supr.; Bro. Peter Scalise, S.S.P. Brothers 9; Priests 5; Total Staff 14.

[B] COLLEGES AND UNIVERSITIES

NORTH CANTON. *Walsh University* (Coed) 2020 E. Maple St., North Canton, 44720-3396.
Tel: 330-490-7090; Fax: 330-499-5762; Email: admissions@walsh.edu; Web: www.walsh.edu. Dr. Douglas Palmer, Provost & Vice Pres. Academic Affairs; Richard Jusseaume, Pres.; Michelle Shelly Brown; Teresa Fox, Vice Pres. Mktg.; Mr. Dale Howard, Vice Pres. Athletics; Ms. Amy Malaska, Vice Pres. Student Affairs; Brian Greenwell, Vice Pres. Information Technology; Eric Belden, Vice Pres. of Advancement; Dr. Bradley Beach, Chm., Humanities Division; Miguel Chavez, Vice Pres., Mission Implementation; Laurel Lusk, Vice Pres. Finance; LuAnn Boris, Dir. Library Svcs.; Ben Walther, Dir. Campus Ministry; Derrick Wyman, Assoc. Vice Pres. Strategy & Planning; Rev. Thomas Cebula, Senior Chap.; Stacie Herman, Registrar; Rev. Michael Denk. Brothers of Christian Instruction. Brothers 6; Religious Teachers 12; Lay Teachers 126; Priests 4; Students 2,895; Total Staff 357.

[C] HIGH SCHOOLS, DIOCESAN

YOUNGSTOWN. *Cardinal Mooney High School* (1956) 2545 Erie St., 44507. Tel: 330-788-5007;
Fax: 330-788-4511; Email: moles@youngstowndiocese.org; Email: mooneyhigh@youngstowndiocese.org; Web: www.cardinalmooney.com. Mark Vollmer, Prin.; Mark Oles, Pres. Lay Teachers 34; Students 442.
Ursuline High School (1905) 750 Wick Ave., 44505.
Tel: 330-744-4563; Fax: 330-744-3358; Email: ursulinehigh@youngstowndiocese.org; Web: www.ursuline.com. Rev. Richard Murphy, Pres.; Matthew Sammartino, Prin. Lay Teachers 35; Priests 1; Students 448.

ASHTABULA. *Saint John School* (1953) (Grades PreK-12), St. John School 7911 Depot Rd., Ashtabula, 44004. Tel: 440-997-5531; Fax: 440-998-1661; Web: www.sjheralds.org. Sr. Maureen Burke, S.N.D., Pres.; Mr. Scott Plescia, Prin.; Rebecca Blenman, Prin. Lay Teachers 40; Sisters 2; Students 435.

CANTON. *Central Catholic High School* (1905) 4824 Tuscarawas St. W., Canton, 44708-5118.
Tel: 330-478-2131; Fax: 330-478-6086; Email: doates@youngstowndiocese.org; Web: www.cchsweb.com. Daniel Gravo, Pres.; Mr. David M. Oates, Prin.; Mrs. Noelle Waltenbaugh, Dean of Students; P.J. Chavez, Campus Min. Lay Teachers 28; Students 311; Total Staff 35.

LOUISVILLE. *St. Thomas Aquinas High School & Middle School* (1964) 2121 Reno Dr., N.E., Louisville, 44641. Tel: 330-875-1631;
Fax: 330-875-8469; Email: fritz.schlueter@youngstowndiocese.org; Web: www.stahs.org. Daniel Gravo, Pres.; Rev. Thomas P. Dyer; Mr. Fritz Schlueter, Prin. High School & Middle School; Mrs. Laura Parise, Asst. Prin. High School & Middle School; Mrs. Michelle May, Campus Min. Religious Teachers 1; Lay Teachers 27; Students 248; Total Staff 37.

[D] ELEMENTARY SCHOOLS

BOARDMAN. *Lumen Christi Catholic Schools*, 5225 South Ave., Boardman, 44512. Tel: 330-788-6106; Fax: 330-788-0658. Mr. Wallace Dunne, Interim Pres.; Mr. George Schorsten, Corp. Sec.

CANTON. *Holy Cross Academy*, (Grades K-8), 219 E. Maple St., #203, North Canton, 44720.
Tel: 330-526-8366; Fax: 330-526-8355; Email: jzufall@starkholycrossacademy.com; Web: www.starkholycrossacademy.com. Jackie Zufall, Pres. Students 1,450; Teachers 110.

[E] PRIVATE SCHOOLS

HUBBARD. *Villa Maria Teresa Daycare and Kindergarten*, 50 Warner Rd., Hubbard, 44425.
Tel: 330-759-7383; Fax: 330-759-7290; Email: jcoblate@aol.com. Sr. Kristin Quicker, O.S.H.J., Prin. & Dir. Religious Teachers 9; (Full-time, paid) 4; Lay Teachers 4; Sisters 5; Students 70.

[F] DIOCESAN SCHOOLS

YOUNGSTOWN. *St. Joseph the Provider Catholic School*, (Grades K-8), 1145 Turin St., 44510.
Tel: 330-259-0353; Email: stjoetheproelem@youngstowndiocese.org; Web: stjosephtheprovider.com. Rev. Michael Swierz, Pres.; Mrs. Cheryl Jablonski, Prin.; Sisters Bernadine Janci, S.N.D., Campus Min.; Charlotte Italiano, O.S.U., Dir. Classroom Mgmt. Lay Teachers 17; Sisters 1; Students 170; Religious Teachers 1.

WARREN. *John F. Kennedy Catholic School* (1964) (Grades PreK-12), Upper Campus, 2550 Central Pkwy., S.E., Warren, 44484. Lower Campus, 3000 Reeves Rd., Warren, 44483. Tel: 330-372-2375;
Fax: 330-372-2465; Email: jkenneally@warrenjfk.com; Web: www.warrenjfk.com. Joseph Kenneally, Pres.; Allyse Consiglio, Prin.; Jacquelyn Venzeio, Prin.; Joyce Cahill, Bus. Mgr. Students 577.
Lower Campus, (Grades PreK-5), 3000 Reeves Rd., N.E., Warren, 44483. Tel: 330-372-2375;
Fax: 330-372-2465; Email: jfkelem@youngstowndiocese.org; Web: www.warrenjfk.com. Joseph Kenneally, Pres.; Jackie Venzio, Prin. Lay Teachers 16; Students 267.
Upper Campus, (Grades 6-12), 2550 Central Pkwy., S.E., Warren, 44484. Tel: 330-369-1804;
Fax: 330-369-1125; Email: jkenneally@warrenjfk.com; Web: www.warrenjfk.com. Joseph Kenneally, Pres.; Allyse Consiglio, Prin. Lay Teachers 27; Students 310.

[G] GENERAL HOSPITALS

YOUNGSTOWN. *Mercy Health Youngstown LLC* dba St. Elizabeth Youngstown Hospital (1911) 1044 Belmont Ave., Box 1790, 44501-1790.
Tel: 330-746-7211; Fax: 330-480-7974; Email: marilyn_waddell@mercy.com; Web: www.mercy.com/youngstown. Donald E. Kline, Pres. & CEO, Mercy Health Youngstown; Donald Koenig, EVP & Regional Chief Operating Officer/Pres., St. Elizabeth Youngstown Hospital. Bed Capacity 566; (Includes Austintown Facility) 310,957; Tot Asst. Annually 310,957; Total Staff 2,018.

BOARDMAN. *Mercy Health Youngstown LLC* dba St. Elizabeth Boardman Hospital, 8401 Market St., Boardman, 44512. Tel: 330-729-2929; Email: eugenia_aubel@mercy.com. Donald E. Kline, CEO; Eugenia L. Aubel, Pres. Bed Capacity 294; Tot Asst. Annually 137,420; Total Staff 841; Total Assisted 137,420.

CANTON. **Mercy Medical Center (1908)* (1908) 1320 Mercy Dr., N.W., Canton, 44708. Tel: 330-489-1000 ; Fax: 330-489-1312; Email: mail@cantonmercy.org; Web: www.cantonmercy.org. Paul Hiltz, Interim Pres./CEO. Bassinets 48; Bed Capacity 441; Tot Asst. Annually 629,641; Total Staff 2,660.

WARREN. *Mercy Health Youngstown LLC* dba St. Joseph Warren Hospital (1924) 667 Eastland Ave., S.E., Warren, 44484. Tel: 330-841-4000;
Fax: 330-841-4019; Email: gail_bellan@mercy.com; Web: www.mercy.com. Kathy Cook, Pres. Bassinets 30; Bed Capacity 202; Sisters of the Humility of Mary 1; Tot Asst. Annually 200,378; Total Staff 788.

[H] SPECIAL CARE FACILITIES

GIRARD. *Mercy Health Youngstown LLC*, 979 Tibbetts-Wick Rd., Ste. A, Girard, 44420. Tel: 330-480-3776; Fax: 330-480-4584. Donald E. Kline, CEO; Michael Robinson, Dir. Tot Asst. Annually 10,690; Total Staff 136.

NORTH LIMA. *The Assumption Village, Marian Living Center (Assisted Living Facility)*, 9802 Market St., North Lima, 44452. Tel: 330-549-2434;
Fax: 330-549-0643. Melessa Scattino, L.N.H.A., Me.d, R.D., Exec. Dir.; Kristine Mariotti, Dir. Assisted Living Svcs. & Mktg.; Susan Bangor, L.P.N., Wellness Mgr. Sponsorship: Sisters of the Humility of Mary.Member: Catholic Healthcare Partners Mercy Health; Special Care Unit for residents with Alzheimer's or Dementia; Skilled Nursing Unit with Subacute Care Program; Intermediate Care. Bed Capacity 48; Tot Asst. Annually 155; Total Staff 31.

POLAND. *Hospice of the Valley, Hospice House*, 9803 Sharrott Rd., Poland, 44514. Tel: 330-549-5850;
Fax: 330-549-5859; Email: Liz_McGarry@mercy.com; Web: www.hospiceofthevalley.com. Liz McGarry, Dir. Bed Capacity 16; Tot Asst. Annually 890; Total Staff 140; Staff 50.

[I] HOMES FOR AGED

AUSTINTOWN. *Humility House*, 755 Ohltown Rd., Austintown, 44515. Tel: 330-505-0144;
Fax: 330-544-5694; Email: armiller1@mercy.com. Melessa Scattino, L.N.H.A., Me.d, R.D., Exec.; Kristine Mariotti, Dir.; Mrs. Michele Mazerik, Dir.; Mrs. Amanda Miller, Admin. Capacity 70; Tot Asst. Annually 285; Total Staff 116; Other (Humility House Assisted Living (Same Building) Capacity) 36; Other (Humility House Assisted Living (Same Building) Total Staff) 11; Other (Humil-

ity House Assisted Living (Same Building) Total Assisted Annually) 96.

CANTON. *House of Loreto*, 2812 Harvard Ave., N.W., Canton, 44709. Tel: 330-453-8137; Fax: 330-453-8140; Email: Loreto1955@neohio.twcbc.com; Web: www.sempercaritas.org/ministry-to-the-aged. Sisters Marilee Heuer, C.D.S., Admin.; Janet Harold, C.D.S., Admin.; Michele Beauseigneur, Supr. Administered by the Congregation of the Divine Spirit. Bed Capacity 50; Residents 50; Sisters 21; Tot Asst. Annually 70; Total Staff 56.

HUBBARD. *Villa Maria Teresa* (1894) 50 Warner Rd., Hubbard, 44425. Tel: 330-759-9329 (Villa); Tel: 330-875-4635 (Emmaus House); Fax: 330-759-7290; Email: vmtoblate@aol.com; Web: www.oblatesistersofshj.com. Sr. Joyce Candidi, O.S.H.J., Supr. Retired Priests' Residence. Bed Capacity 17; Tot Asst. Annually 8; Total Staff 5; Villa Residents 2; Emmaus House Residents 6.

LOUISVILLE. *Emmaus House* (1977) 1515 California Ave., Louisville, 44641-8708. Tel: 330-875-4635; Email: joewitmer@juno.com. Rev. Msgr. James Kolp, (Retired); Rev. Joseph W. Witmer, Admin., (Retired). Retired Priests' Residence. Bed Capacity 10; Residents 5; Tot Asst. Annually 5; Total Staff 3.

St. Joseph Care Center, 2308 Reno Dr., Louisville, 44641. Tel: 330-875-5562; Fax: 330-875-8947; Email: sjcc@neo.rr.com; Web: www.saintjosephseniorliving.org. Mrs. Susan Strutner, CEO. Bed Capacity 264; Sisters of St. Joseph of St. Mark 10; Tot Asst. Annually 350; Total Staff 240; Nursing Home 100; Assisted Living 67; Independent Living 66; Adult Day Care 25.

NORTH LIMA. *The Assumption Village, Humility Health Center (Nursing Care)*, 9800 Market St., North Lima, 44452. Tel: 330-549-0740; Fax: 330-549-0701; Email: melessa_scattino@mercy.com. Melessa Scattino, L.N.H.A., Me.d, R.D., Exec. Dir; Lisa Peretti, R.N., Dir. Nursing. Sponsorship: Sisters of the Humility of Mary.Member: Catholic Healthcare Partners and Humility of Mary Health Partners; Skilled Nursing Unit with Subacute Care Program; Special Care Unit for residents with Alzheimer's or cognitive impairment. Nursing Home Beds 150; Tot Asst. Annually 642; Total Staff 191.

[J] MONASTERIES AND RESIDENCES OF PRIESTS AND BROTHERS

YOUNGSTOWN. *Mt. Alverna Friary*, 517 S. Belle Vista Ave., 44509. Tel: 330-799-1888; Fax: 330-799-0723; Email: brvit@hotmail.com. Revs. Jules Wong, O.F.M.; Vit Fiala, O.F.M., Guardian & Dir. Shrine, Rome, Italy; Dennis Arambasick, O.F.M.; Richard Martingetti, O.F.M. Franciscan Friars. Total in Residence 4; Total Staff 4.

[K] CONVENTS AND RESIDENCES FOR SISTERS

CANFIELD. *Motherhouse and Educational Center of the Ursuline Sisters* (1874) 4250 Shields Rd., Canfield, 44406. Tel: 330-792-7636; Fax: 330-792-9553; Email: yoursuline@gmail.com; Web: www.theursulines.org. Sr. Mary McCormick, O.S.U., Gen. Supr. Sisters 40; Total in Residence 26; Total Staff 4; Total in Community 40.

Ursuline Center, 4280 Shields Rd., Canfield, 44406. Tel: 330-799-4941; Fax: 330-799-4988.

Ursuline Sisters Senior Living, 4260 Shields Rd., Canfield, 44406. Tel: 330-792-7636; Fax: 330-792-9553; Email: yoursuline@gmail.com; Web: ursulinesisterssseniorliving.org. Sr. Mary McCormick, O.S.U., Supr. Sisters 40.

CANTON. *Congregation of the Divine Spirit*, 2700 Harvard Ave., N.W., Canton, 44709. Tel: 330-453-8526; Fax: 330-453-8530; Email: adsum409@neohio.twcbc.com; Web: www.sempercaritas.org. Sr. Michele Beauseigneur, Supr. Sisters 22.

Sancta Clara Monastery (1946) 4200 N. Market Ave., Canton, 44714. Tel: 330-492-1171; Email: pcpacanton4200@gmail.com; Web: www.poorclares.org. Mother Gertrude Espenilla, P.C.P.A. Poor Clares of Perpetual Adoration. Cloistered Professed Nuns 10.

HUBBARD. *Oblate Sisters of the Sacred Heart of Jesus Institute, Villa Maria Teresa* (1984) 50 Warner Rd., Hubbard, 44425. Tel: 330-759-9329; Fax: 330-759-7290; Email: vmtoblate@aol.com; Email: jcoblate@aol.com; Web: www.oblatesistersofshj.com. Sr. Joyce Candidi, O.S.H.J., Regl. Supr. & Convent Supr. Novitiate and American Headquarters of Oblate Sisters of the Sacred Heart of Jesus. Novices 1; Sisters 13; Total Staff 4.

VIENNA. *The Missionary Sisters of St. Francis of Assisi*, 333 Scoville Dr., Vienna, 44473. Tel: 330-856-4204; Fax: 330-856-9587; Email: vocations.mssf@gmail.com; Web: www.dominusvobiscum.org. Mother Mary Francis, Gen. Supr.

[L] CATHOLIC CHARITIES SOCIAL SERVICE AGENCIES

YOUNGSTOWN. *Catholic Charities Housing Opportunities Corporation*, 225 Elm St., 44503. Tel: 330-744-8451; Email: nkelley@youngstowndiocese.org; Web: www.ccdoy.org. Rachel Hrbolich, Dir. Purpose: Provides coordination, integration and leadership in the provision of housing services which promote affordable housing in the community. Tot Asst. Annually 200; Total Staff 1; Total Families Assisted 25.

Catholic Charities Regional Agency (1946) 319 W. Rayen Ave., 44502. Tel: 330-744-3320; Fax: 330-744-3677; Email: nvoitus@ccregional.org. Nancy Voitus, Exec. Dir. Social services in the areas of assisting families, homeless, seniors, domestic violence victims, returning citizens and low income in Mahoning, Trumbull and Columbiana Counties. Tot Asst. Annually 18,800; Total Staff 38.

Diocese of Youngstown Catholic Charities Corporation (1999) 144 W. Wood. St., 44503. Tel: 330-744-8451; Email: rhrbolich@youngstowndiocese.org; Web: www.ccdoy.org. Rachel Hrbolich, Contact Person.

ASHTABULA. *Catholic Charities of Ashtabula County* (1944) 4200 Park Ave., 3rd Fl., Ashtabula, 44004. Tel: 440-992-2121; Fax: 440-992-5974; Email: lynnz@doyccac.org; Email: chrise@doyccac.org; Email: info@doyccac.org; Web: www.doyccac.org. Lynn M. Zalewski, Exec. Dir. Total Staff 17; Total Assisted 10,000.

RAVENNA. *Catholic Charities Serving Portage and Stark Counties*, 206 W. Main St., Ravenna, 44266. Tel: 330-297-7745; Fax: 330-297-7763; Email: info@catholiccharitiesps.org. George Garchar, Exec. Dir. Tot Asst. Annually 1,200; Total Staff 20.

[M] HOMES FOR WOMEN

YOUNGSTOWN. *Beatitude House* (1991) 238 Tod Ln., 44504. Tel: 330-744-3147; Fax: 330-744-3991; Email: info@beatitudehouse.com; Email: tboyce@beatitudehouse.com; Email: jdriscoll@beatitudehouse.com; Email: kmoliterno@beatitudehouse.com; Web: www.beatitudehouse.com. Mrs. Teresa Boyce, Dir. Beatitude House has three programs committed to disadvantaged women and children. Permanent supportive and transitional housing with case management for homeless women and children. The Immigrant Outreach program teaches women English and tutors children. Ursuline Sisters Scholars program helps students break the cycle of poverty through post-secondary education. Bed Capacity 128; Tot Asst. Annually 148; Total Staff 26; Total Assisted 302.

[N] RETREAT HOUSES

YOUNGSTOWN. *Our Lady of the Woods Pastoral Center* (1994) 144 W. Wood St., 44503. Tel: 330-744-8451; Fax: 330-744-1702; Email: pkelly@youngstowndiocese.org. 3014 Logan Ave., 44505. Mr. Patrick A. Kelly, Treas.

[O] NEWMAN CENTERS

YOUNGSTOWN. *Newman Center at Youngstown State University* aka YSU Newman Center, 254 Madison Ave., 44504-1627. Tel: 330-747-9202; Email: ysunewmancsa@gmail.com; Web: www.ysunewmancsa.org. Dr. Thomas Brozich, Dir. Total Staff 3.

KENT. *Kent State University Newman Center*, 1424 Horning Rd., Kent, 44240. Tel: 330-678-0240; Fax: 330-678-7780; Email: parish415@youngstowndiocese.org; Web: www.kentnewmancenterparish.org. Rev. Steven J. Agostino; Jordan Cinderich, Campus Min.; Ms. Carmen Roebke, Pastoral Assoc. & Christian Formation; Dr. John Roebke, Music Dir. Total in Residence 1; Total Staff 5.

[P] MISCELLANEOUS LISTINGS

YOUNGSTOWN. *Caritas Communities* Currently inactive 225 Elm St., 44503. Tel: 330-744-8451; Email: rhrbolich@youngstowndiocese.org; Web: www.ccdoy.org. Rachel Hrbolich, Dir. As a member Corporation of Catholic Charities Housing Opportunities and the Humility of Mary Housing Program, Caritas Communities will serve as Property Management Corporation for low income and special needs housing.

The Catholic Exponent, 144 W. Wood St., P.O. Box 6787, 44501-6787. Tel: 330-744-5251; Fax: 330-744-5252; Email: exponent@youngstonwdiocese.org; Web: www.cathexpo.org. Mr. Pete Sheehan, Editor.

Conference of Slovak Clergy, 144 W. Wood St., 44503. Tel: 330-744-8451; Fax: 330-742-6448; Email: rsiffrin@youngstowndiocese.org; Web: www.doy.org. Very Rev. Msgr. Robert J. Siffrin, V.G., Chm.; Revs. Thomas Nasta, Vice Chm.; Martin Celuch, J.C.L., Sec. The Conference was founded April 22, 1985, and incorporated on June 14, 2000. It associates bishops, priests and deacons of Slovak ancestry in the United States for the purposes of mutual pastoral support and financial assistance to those preparing themselves for ordained ministry of the churches in union with Rome, particularly those of Slovak ancestry.

Declaration of Trust of Trumbull, Dept. of Educ., 144 W. Wood St., 44503. Tel: 330-744-8451; Fax: 330-744-5099; Email: mfiala@youngstowndiocese.org. Rev. Msgr. John A. Zuraw, J.C.L., Chancellor. County Catholic School Endowment Fund.

First Friday Club of Greater Youngstown, P.O. Box 11146, 44511. Tel: 330-720-4498; Email: meblegal@aol.com. Rev. Msgr. John A. Zuraw, J.C.L.

Lake to River Telecommunications Corporation, 144 W. Wood St., 44503. Tel: 330-744-8451; Email: pkelly@youngstowndiocese.org. Mr. Patrick A. Kelly, Treas.

Midwest Canon Law Society, 141 W. Rayen Ave., 44503. Tel: 330-744-8451; Fax: 330-742-6450; Email: ppolando@youngstowndiocese.org. Very Rev. Msgr. Peter M. Polando, J.C.L., Rector.

The Roman Catholic Diocese of Youngstown Annual Bishop's Appeal, 144 W. Wood St., 44503. Tel: 330-744-8451; Email: appeal@youngstowndiocese.org; Web: www.doy.org. Rev. John-Michael Lavelle, D.Min., Dir.

Roman Catholic Diocese of Youngstown Foundation, 144 W. Wood St., 44503. Tel: 330-744-8451; Fax: 330-744-2848; Email: pkelly@youngstowndiocese.org. Mr. Patrick A. Kelly, CFO.

Roman Catholic Diocese of Youngstown Property Corporation, 144 W. Wood St., 44503. Tel: 330-744-8451; Fax: 330-744-2848; Email: pkelly@youngstowndiocese.org. Mr. Patrick A. Kelly, CFO.

CANFIELD. *The Ursuline Center* (1993) 4280 Shields Rd., Canfield, 44406. Tel: 330-799-4941; Fax: 330-799-4988; Email: theursulinecenter@theursulinecenter.org; Web: www.theursulinecenter.org. Brigid M. Kennedy, Pres. Resource and outreach services for the poor, including prison ministry, AIDS ministry, retreats, water therapy, adult formation, speech and hearing services, counselling, and tutoring. Sisters 6; Tot Asst. Annually 20,000; Total Staff 18.

Ursuline Ministries, 4280 Shields Rd., Canfield, 44406. Tel: 330-792-7636, Ext. 318; Fax: 330-792-9553; Email: bkennedy@ursulineministries.org. Brigid M. Kennedy, Pres.

Ursuline Sisters Senior Living, 4260 Shields Rd., Canfield, 44406. Tel: 330-792-7636; Fax: 330-792-9553.

CANTON. *Catholic Migrant Farmworker Network, Inc.*, 701 Walnut Ave., N.E., Canton, 44702. Tel: 402-213-6428; Fax: 928-920-1592; Email: zeusariza.1958@gmail.com; Email: teresitakontos@gmail.com. Mr. Ricardo Ariza, Pres.; Mrs. Teresita Kontos, Vice Pres./Coord. Migrant Min.

Early Childhood Resource Center, 1718 Cleveland Ave., N.W., Canton, 44703. Tel: 330-491-3272; Fax: 330-491-0334; Email: shasselman@ecresourcecenter.org; Web: www.sistersofcharityhealth.org. Scott Hasselman, Exec. Dir.

Mercy Development Foundation, 1320 Mercy Dr., N.W., Canton, 44708. Tel: 330-489-1421; Fax: 330-489-1312. Mr. Thomas Turner, Pres.

Sisters of Charity Foundation of Canton (1996) (1996) 400 Market Ave. N., Ste. 300, Canton, 44702-1556. Tel: 330-454-5800; Fax: 330-454-5909; Email: jclose@scfcanton.org; Web: www.scfcanton.org. 5215 East Blvd. NW, Canton, 44718. Joni T. Close, Pres.

LOUISVILLE. *St. Thomas Aquinas High School Endowment Fund* (1964) 2121 Reno Drive, N.E., Louisville, 44641. Tel: 330-875-1631; Fax: 330-875-8469; Email: bmoeglin@youngstowndiocese.org; Web: www.stahs.org. Rev. Thomas P. Dyer, Pres. Emeritus; Bridget Moeglin, Business Mgr.

MASSILLON. *National Shrine of St. Dymphna* (1938) 206 Cherry Rd., N.E., Massillon, 44646. Tel: 330-833-8478; Fax: 330-833-5193; Email: father_gretchko@natlshrinestdymphna.org. P.O. Box 4, Massillon, 44648-0004. Rev. A. Edward Gretchko, Chap.

[Q] DIOCESAN CEMETERIES

YOUNGSTOWN. *Calvary*, 248 S. Belle Vista Ave., 44509. Tel: 330-792-4721; Tel: 330-799-1900; Fax: 330-792-1885; Email: thaffner@youngstowndiocese.org. Donald Goncy,

Supt.; Todd Haffner, Dir.; Mr. Patrick A. Kelly, Exec.
The Catholic Cemeteries of the Diocese of Youngstown, Inc.

Catholic Cemeteries of the Diocese of Youngstown, Inc., 144 W. Wood St., 44503. Tel: 330-744-8451; Fax: 330-744-2848; Email: pkelly@youngstowndiocese.org. Todd Haffner, Dir. Cemetery Opers.

Resurrection, 300 N. Raccoon Rd., 44515. Tel: 330-799-1900; Fax: 330-799-5241; Email: thaffner@youngstowndiocese.org. Todd Haffner, Dir.
The Catholic Cemeteries of the Diocese of Youngstown Inc.

CORTLAND. *All Souls*, 3823 Hoagland Blackstub Rd., Cortland, 44410. Tel: 330-637-2761; Fax: 330-637-9522; Email: cgalterio@youngstowndiocese.org; Email: thaffner@youngstowndiocese.org. Charlotte Galterio, Supt.; Todd Haffner, Dir.
The Catholic Cemeteries of the Diocese of Youngstown Inc.

MASSILLON. *Calvary*, 3469 Lincoln Way E., Massillon, 44646. Tel: 330-832-1866; Fax: 330-832-0059; Email: btully@youngstowndiocese.org; Email: thaffner@youngstowndiocese.org. Becky Tully, Supt.; Todd Haffner, Dir.
The Catholic Cemeteries of the Diocese of Youngstown Inc.

RELIGIOUS INSTITUTES OF MEN REPRESENTED IN THE DIOCESE

For further details refer to the corresponding bracketed number in the Religious Institutes of Men or Women section.

[]—*Apostles of Jesus*—AJ.
[0320]—*Brothers of Christian Instruction*—F.I.C.
[0520]—*Franciscan Friars* (Immaculate Conception Prov. of New York)—O.F.M.
[0430]—*Order of Preachers (Dominicans)* (Prov. of St. Joseph)—O.P.
[1065]—*Priestly Fraternity of St. Peter*—F.S.S.P.
[0690]—*Society of Jesus*—SJ.
[1020]—*Society of St. Paul*—S.S.P.

RELIGIOUS INSTITUTES OF WOMEN REPRESENTED IN THE DIOCESE

[0100]—*Adorers of the Blood of Christ*—A.S.C.
[]—*Antonine Sisters*—A.S.
[]—*Benediction Sisters (Byzantine Sisters)*—O.S.B.
[1040]—*Congregation of the Divine Spirit*—C.D.S.
[1115]—*Dominican Sisters of Peace*—O.P.
[3050]—*Oblate Sisters of the Sacred Heart of Jesus*—O.S.H.J.
[3210]—*Poor Clares of Perpetual Adoration*—P.C.P.A.
[0580]—*Sisters of Charity of St. Augustine*—C.S.A.
[0990]—*Sisters of Divine Providence*—C.D.P.
[2575]—*Sisters of Mercy of the Americas*—R.S.M.
[2990]—*Sisters of Notre Dame*—S.N.D.
[1710]—*Sisters of St. Francis of Mary Immaculate, Joliet, IL*—O.S.F.
[]—*Sisters of St. Francis of the Newman Communities.*
[1660]—*Sisters of St. Francis of the Providence of God*—O.S.F.
[]—*Sisters of St. Francis of Tiffin, OH*—OSF/T.
[3910]—*Sisters of St. Joseph of St. Mark*—S.J.S.M.
[3930]—*Sisters of St. Joseph of the Third Order of St. Francis*—SSJ-TOSF.
[2110]—*Sisters of the Humility of Mary*—H.M.
[3730]—*Sisters of the Order of St. Basil the Great*—O.S.B.M.
[]—*Ursuline Sisters of Cleveland*—O.S.U.
[4120-07]—*Ursuline Sisters of Youngstown*—O.S.U.

NECROLOGY

† Reiss, John E., (Retired), Died Oct. 5, 2018

An asterisk (*) denotes an organization that has established tax-exempt status directly with the IRS and is not covered by the USCCB Group Ruling.

Apostolate to Hungarians

Most Reverend

FERENC CSERHATI, S.T.D.

Titular Bishop of Centuria, Auxiliary to Esztergom-Budapest, especially entrusted with the coordination of the pastoral service of Hungarians abroad; ordained April 18, 1971 in Alba Julia; appointed June 15, 2007; consecrated in Esztergom August 15, 2007. *Res.: MKPK, Kulfoldi Magyar Lelkipasztori Szolgalat, Papnovelde utca 5-7, Budapest, H-1053.* Tel: 36-1-266-4515; Fax: 36-1-266-4515; Email: cserhati@katolikus.hu.

ESTABLISHED MAY 20, 1983.

The Apostolate of the Bishop of Hungarians living outside of Hungary extends territorially to all the Hungarian communities existing outside of Hungary. The main purpose of the Apostolate is to give spiritual assistance to them through and in cooperation with the local ordinary and pastors.

Former Bishops—Most Revs. LADISLAUS A. IRANYI, Sch.P., ord. March 13, 1938; appt. May 20, 1983; cons. July 27, 1983; died March 6, 1987; ATTILA MIKLOSHAZY, S.J., S.T.D., Titular Bishop of Castel Minore and Bishop for the Spiritual Assistance to the Hungarian Emigrant People; ord. June 18, 1961; appt. Aug. 12, 1989; cons. Nov. 4, 1989; resigned April 5, 2006.

Delegate in North America—Rev. BARNABAS G. KISS, O.F.M., Holy Cross Hungarian R.C. Church, 8423 South St., Detroit, MI USA 48209-2709. Tel: 313-842-1133; Fax: 313-842-2773; Email: sztkereszt@comcast.net.

Hungarian Priests' Association in Canada—Revs. BARNABAS G. KISS, O.F.M., Pres., Holy Cross Hungarian R.C. Church, 8423 South St., Detroit, MI USA 48209-2709. Tel: 313-842-1133; Fax: 313-842-2773; Email: sztkereszt@comcast.net; SZABOLCS LICSKO, (Canada) Sec., 90 rue, Guizot Quest, Montreal, QC Canada H2P 1L4. Tel: 514-387-9503; Fax: 514-387-8912; Email: magyarplebania@videotron.ca.

American Hungarian Catholic Priests' Association (USA)—Rev. BARNABAS G. KISS, O.F.M., Holy Cross Hungarian R.C. Church, 8423 South St., Detroit, MI USA 48209-2709. Tel: 313-842-1133; Fax: 313-842-2773; Email: sztkereszt@comcast.net.

Newspapers & Magazines—

Eletunk (Our Life)—MAGYAR KATOLIKUS MISSZIO, Oberforhringer Str. 40, Munchen, Germany D-81925. Tel: 49-89-982-637; Fax: 49-89-985-419; Email: eletuenk@gmx.de.

Tavlatok—(Perspectives), Quarterly on Worldview, Spirituality and Culture, ed. by the Unio Cleri Hungarici. Rev. FERENC SZABO, S.J., Editor, Sodras u. 13., H-1026, Budapest, Hungary. Tel: 36-1-200-8054/112; Fax: 36-1-275-0349; Email: tavlatok@jezsuita.hu.

A Sziv—(Heart, Hungarian Journal), monthly, published by the Hungarian Jesuit Fathers. Rev. JANOS LUKACS, S.J., Editor, Horanszky utca 20, Budapest, Hungary H-1085. Tel: 36-30-486-6531; Email: asziv@jezsuita.hu; Web: www.asziv.hu.

INSTITUTIONS LOCATED IN DIOCESE

STATISTICS

Most personnel and institutions are under the jurisdiction of their local ordinaries.

NECROLOGY

Incorporated in diocesan and archdiocesan listings.

An asterisk (*) denotes an organization that has established tax-exempt status directly with the IRS and is not covered by the USCCB Group Ruling.

Apostolate For Lithuanian Catholics

Living Outside Lithuania

Reverend Monsignor

EDMOND PUTRIMAS, J.C.L.

Delegate of the Lithuanian Bishops Conference; appointed August 19, 2003 to coordinate the pastoral care of Lithuanian Catholics living outside of Lithuania. *Office: 1 Resurrection Rd., Toronto, ON M9A 5G1.* Tel: 416-233-7819; Email: putrimas@sielovada.org.

(VACANT SEE)

Most Reverend

PAUL A. BALTAKIS, O.F.M.

Former Bishop For Lithuanian Catholics; ordained August 24, 1952; appointed Titular Bishop of Egara and Bishop for Spiritual Assistance of Lithuanian Catholics June 1, 1984; cons. Sept. 14, 1984; retired July 12, 2003. *Res.: St. Anthony's Friary, 28 Beach Ave., P.O. Box 980, Kennebunkport, ME 04046.* Tel: 207-967-2011, Ext. 30.

ESTABLISHED JUNE 1, 1984.

The Apostolate for Lithuanian Catholics, extends worldwide to all Lithuanian communities existing outside Lithuania. Seventy-five percent of them in the U.S.A. The purpose of the apostolate is to give spiritual assistance to them in cooperation with the local ordinaries and pastors.

Former Lithuanian Bishops—Most Revs. VINCENTAS BRIZGYS, Ph.D., J.C.D., cons. May 19, 1940; Titular Bishop of Bosana; Auxiliary Bishop of Kaunas, Lithuania (Impeditus); died April 23, 1992; ANTANAS DEKSNYS, Ph.D., cons. Jan. 15, 1969; Titular Bishop of Lavello; died May 5, 1999; PAUL A. BALTAKIS, O.F.M., ord. Aug. 24, 1952; appt. Titular Bishop of Egara and Bishop of Spiritual Assistance of Lithuanian Catholics in diaspora June 1, 1984; cons. Sept. 14, 1984; retired July 12, 2003.

Office of General Counsel—SAULIUS V. KUPRYS, 150 S. Wacker Dr., Ste. 2500, Chicago, IL USA 60606. Tel: 312-346-5275; Email: svkuprys@gmail.com.

Lithuanian R. Catholic Priests' League of Canada—Rev. PAULIUS RUDINSKAS, Pres., Our Lady of Mercy, 58 Dundurn St. N., Hamilton, ON Canada L8R 3E1. Tel: 905-522-5272.

Lithuanian R. Catholic Priests' League of America—Rev. GINTARAS JONIKAS, Pres., 25335 W. Nine Mile Rd., Southfield, MI USA 48033-3937. Tel: 248-354-3429.

Lithuanian Franciscan Province of St. Casimir—Very Rev. JONAS SILEIKA, O.F.M., Delegate, 1 Resurrection Rd., Toronto, ON Canada M9A 5G1. Tel: 1-416-533-0621.

Lithuanian Jesuit Province—Very Rev. ALGIS BANIULIS, S.J., Delegate, Bl. Jurgis Matulaitis R. C. Mission, 14911 W. 127th St., Lemont, IL USA 60439-7417. Tel: 630-257-5613; Fax: 630-257-5695.

Marian Province of Mary Mother of Mercy—Very Rev. KAZIMIERZ CHWALEK, M.I.C., Prov., Stockbridge, MA USA 01262. Tel: 413-298-3691; Fax: 413-298-1211.

Pontifical Lithuanian College of St. Casimir—Very Rev. AUDRIUS ARSTIKAITIS, Teol. Lic., Rector, via Casalmonferrato 20, Rome, Italy 00182. Tel: 06-70-26-774; Fax: 06-70-11-659.

Sisters of the Immaculate Conception of the Blessed Virgin Mary—Sr. IGNE MARIJOSIUTE, Prov., Rte. 21, R.D. 2, Putnam, CT USA 06260. Tel: 860-928-7955; Fax: 860-928-1930.

Poor Sisters of Jesus Crucified and the Sorrowful Mother—261 Thatcher St., Brockton, MA USA 02302. Tel: 508-588-5070. Sr. GERALDINE NEVARAS, Vocation Dir.

Sisters of St. Casimir—Sr. REGINA MARIE DUBICKAS, Gen. Supr., 2601 W. Marquette Rd., Chicago, IL USA 60609. Tel: 773-776-1324.

Sisters of St. Francis—Sr. JOANNE BRAZINSKI, O.S.F., Supr. Gen., Sisters of St. Francis of the Providence of God, 3757 Library Rd., Pittsburgh, PA USA 15234. Tel: 412-882-9911.

**Lithuanian R. Catholic Religious Aid, Inc.—64-25 Perry Ave., Maspeth, NY USA 11378.* Tel: 718-326-5202; Fax: 718-326-5206; Email: lcra@earthlink.net. Very Rev. Msgr. EDMOND PUTRIMAS, J.C.L., Pres.

Lithuanian American R. Catholic Federation—Youth Camp, 15100 Austin Rd., Manchester, MI USA 48158. DANA RUGIENIUS, Pres. Bd. of Dirs.

Lithuanian Roman Catholic Charities, Inc.—4545 W. 63rd St., Chicago, IL USA 60629.

Publications—Draugas (Chicago, IL); Draugas News (Chicago, IL); Teviskes Ziburiai (Toronto, Ontario, Canada); Teviskes Aidai (Adelaide, Australia); Lithuanian Heritage (Chicago, IL); Lithuanian Catholic Press Society.

INSTITUTIONS LOCATED IN DIOCESE

[A] SCHOOLS

THOMPSON. *Marionapolis Prep School*, 26 Chase Rd., Thompson, CT USA 06277. Tel: 860-923-9565; Fax: 860-923-3730. Joseph Hanrahan, Prin.

[B] NURSING HOMES AND HOMES FOR THE AGED

BROCKTON. *St. Joseph Manor Nursing Home*, 215 Thatcher St., Brockton, MA USA 02302.

ELMHURST. *St. Mary's Villa*, 516 St. Mary's Villa Rd., Elmhurst Twp., PA USA 18444.

HOLLAND. *St. Joseph Nursing Home*, 1182 Holland Rd., Holland, PA USA 18966. Tel: 215-357-5511.

LEMONT. *Holy Family Villa*.

PUTNAM. *Matulaitis Nursing Home*, 10 Thurber Rd., Putnam, CT USA 06260. Tel: 860-928-7976.

[C] MISCELLANEOUS

CHICAGO. *Catholic Action Fund*.

Jesuit Lithuanian Center.

**Lithuanian Catholic Press Society*, 4545 W. 63rd St., Chicago, IL USA 60629. Tel: 773-585-9500; Email: administracija@draugas.org. Mr. Vytas Stanevicius, Chm.

Lithuanian Roman Catholic Charities, 4545 W. 63rd St., Chicago, IL USA 60629. Tel: 773-585-9500; Email: administracija@draugas.org. Dr. Linas Sidrys, Pres.

Matulaitis Institute.

MANCHESTER. *Lithuanian American R. Catholic Federation Youth Camp*, 15100 Austin Rd., Manchester, MI USA 48158. Tel: 773-307-9777; Email: danarugienius@gmail.com; Web: dainava.org. 10 Algonquin Rd., Clarendon Hills, IL USA 60514.

PUTNAM. *American Lithuanian Catholic Archives*.

WEST BRATTLEBORO. *Camp Neringa*.

[D] CEMETERIES

CHICAGO. *St. Casimir Lithuanian*, 4401 W. 111th St., Chicago, IL USA 60655

RELIGIOUS INSTITUTES OF MEN REPRESENTED IN THE DIOCESE

For further details refer to the corresponding bracketed number in the Religious Institutes of Men or Women section.

[]—*Congregation of the Marians Province of Mary Mother of Mercy* (Stockbridge, MA).

[]—*Franciscan Fathers of the Lithuanian Province of St. Casimir* (Kennebunkport, ME).

[]—*Jesuit Fathers of Della Strada* (Chicago, IL).

RELIGIOUS INSTITUTES OF WOMEN REPRESENTED IN THE DIOCESE

[3240]—*Poor Sisters of Jesus Crucified and the Sorrowful Mother* (Brockton, MA)—C.J.C.

[2140]—*Sisters of Immaculate Conception of the Blessed Virgin Mary* (Putnam, CT).

[3740]—*Sisters of St. Casimir* (Chicago, IL)—S.S.C.

[1690]—*Sisters of St. Francis* (Pittsburgh, PA)—O.S.F.

STATISTICS

Most personnel and institutions are under the jurisdiction of their local ordinaries.

An asterisk (*) denotes an organization that has established tax-exempt status directly with the IRS and is not covered by the USCCB Group Ruling.

Prelature of the Holy Cross and Opus Dei

(Praelatura Sanctae Crucis et Operis Dei)

Reverend Monsignor

FERNANDO OCARIZ, PH.D., S.T.D.

Prelate of the Prelature of the Holy Cross and Opus Dei; ordained August 15, 1971; appointed January 23, 2017. *Mailing Address: Viale Bruno Buozzi, 73, Rome, 00197.*

PRELATURE OF OPUS DEI

Erected by the Apostolic Constitution, "Ut sit," on November 28, 1982 by Pope John Paul II.

Opus Dei was founded on October 2, 1928 by Saint Josemaria Escriva, to spread in all sectors of society a profound awareness of the universal call to sanctity in ordinary life and, more specifically, in the exercise of one's work.

Former Prelate—Most Rev. JAVIER ECHEVARRIA, ord. Aug. 7, 1955; appt. April 20, 1994; episcopal ord. Jan. 6, 1995; died Dec. 12, 2016.

Curia of the Prelature—Viale Bruno Buozzi 73, Rome, Italy 00197. Tel: 011-39-06-808-961.

Vicar General—Rev. Msgr. MARIANO FAZIO, B.A., Ph. D., Viale Bruno Buozzi 73, Rome, Italy 00197.

Regional Vicar for the United States—Rev. Msgr. THOMAS G. BOHLIN, Ph.D., S.T.D., 139 E. 34th St., New York, NY USA 10016. Tel: 646-742-2700.

Vicar for the Midwest—Rev. JAVIER DEL CASTILLO, B.S., Ph.D., 5800 N. Keating Ave., Chicago, IL USA 60646. Tel: 312-283-5800. Embracing the states of Illinois, Indiana, Missouri and Wisconsin.

Vicar for California—Very Rev. LUKE J. MATA, B.A., Ph.D., 770 S. Windsor Blvd., Los Angeles, CA USA 90005. Tel: 323-930-2844.

Vicar for Texas—Very Rev. PAUL D. KAIS, B.A., M.A., Ph.D., 5505 Chaucer Dr., Houston, TX USA 77005. Tel: 715-523-4351.

Represented in the Archdioceses of Boston, Chicago, Galveston-Houston, Los Angeles, Miami, Milwaukee, Newark, New York, St. Louis, San Antonio, San Francisco, Washington and in the Dioceses of Arlington, Burlington, Dallas, Fort Wayne-South Bend, Gary, Joliet, Oakland, Palm Beach, Peoria, Pittsburgh, Providence, Trenton and Victoria.

Regional Vicar for Puerto Rico—Rev. Msgr. JUSTINIANO GARCIA ARIAS, M.A., J.C.D., Villa Caparra, A35 A St., Guaynabo, PR USA 00966-2211. Tel: 787-781-9123.

Represented in the Archdiocese of San Juan and the Dioceses of Mayaguez and Ponce.

CHAPLAINS FOR THE UNITED STATES.

State of New York

New Rochelle.
99 Overlook Cir., New Rochelle, NY USA 10804. Tel: 914-235-0199. Revs. Bradley K. Arturi, J.C.D., Thomas J. Lamb, Michael J. Manz.

New York.
139 E. 34th St., New York, NY USA 10016. Tel: 646-742-2700. Rev. Msgrs. Thomas G. Bohlin, Ph.D., S.T.D., Reg. Vicar, Javier Garcia de Cardenas, Revs. John C. Agnew, James W. Albrecht, Joseph Keefe, Timothy J. Uhen.
330 Riverside Dr., New York, NY USA 10025. Tel: 212-222-3285. Rev. Malcolm M. Kennedy.

District of Columbia

Washington.
2301 Wyoming Ave., N.W., Washington, DC USA 2008. Tel: 202-234-1567. Revs. John P. Debicki, Joseph Landauer, Charles Trullols, Salvador Vahi.
4300 Garrison St., N.W., Washington, DC USA 20016. Tel: 202-362-2419. Revs. Diego Daza, Joseph P. Ruisanchez.

State of Massachusetts

Cambridge.
25 Follen St., Cambridge, MA USA 02138. Tel: 617-354-3204. Revs. David J. Cavanagh, Jeffrey Langan.

Chestnut Hill.
481 Hammond St., Chestnut Hill, MA USA 02467. Revs. George A. Crafts, John Grieco, Richard W. Rieman, Alvaro Silva.

State of New Jersey

Princeton.
34 Mercer St., Princeton, NJ USA 08540. Tel: 609-497-9448. Rev. Joseph Thomas.

South Orange.
170 Montrose Ave., South Orange, NJ USA 07079. Tel: 973-763-8397. Rev. Robert A. Connor.

State of Pennsylvania

Pittsburgh.
5090 Warwick Ter., Pittsburgh, PA USA 15213. Tel: 412-683-8448. Revs. Martin John Miller, Rene J. Schatteman.

State of Florida

Delray Beach.
4409 Frances Dr., Delray Beach, FL USA 33445. Rev. Victor Cortes.

Miami.
4415 S.W. 88th Ave., Miami, FL USA 33165. Tel: 305-551-7965. Revs. John J. Alvarez, Victor Cortes, Juan R. Velez.

State of Rhode Island

Providence.
224 Bowen St., Providence, RI USA 02906. Tel: 401-272-7834. Rev. George A. Crafts.

State of Illinois

Chicago.
5800 N. Keating Ave., Chicago, IL USA 60646. Tel: 312-283-5800. Revs. Peter V. Armenio, B.S., Ph.D., Javier del Castillo, Vicar for the Midwest, Frank J. Hoffman, Gerald Kolf.
7225 N. Greenview Ave., Chicago, IL USA 60626. Revs. Steven Brock, Deogracias Rosales.
1825 N. Wood St., Chicago, IL USA 60622. Revs. Charles M. Ferrer, Hilary F. Mahaney, John Paul Mitchell, John R. Waiss.

Darien.
7800 Cass Ave., Darien, IL USA 60561. Revs. G. Barry Cole, Derek Esclanda, James Socias.

Urbana.
715 W. Michigan, Urbana, IL USA 61801. Tel: 217-367-6650. Rev. G. Barry Cole.

State of Indiana

South Bend.
1121 N. Notre Dame Ave., South Bend, IN USA 46617. Rev. Oscar Regojo.

State of Missouri

Kirkwood.
100 E. Essex Ave., Kirkwood, MO USA 63122. Revs. Gregory J. Coyne, Michael E. Giesler.

State of Wisconsin

Brookfield.
12900 W. North Ave., Brookfield, WI USA 53005. Tel: 414-784-1523. Revs. Eduardo Castillo, John C. Kubeck.

State of California

Los Angeles.
770 S. Windsor Blvd., Los Angeles, CA USA 90002. Tel: 323-930-2844. Very Rev. Luke J. Mata, B.A., Ph.D., Vicar for California, Rev. John R. Meyer, D.D.S., S.T.D.
655 Levering Ave., Los Angeles, CA USA 90024. Tel: 213-208-0941. Revs. Paul A. Donlan, Mark Mannion.

Menlo Park.
Menlo Park, CA USA 94025. Tel: 415-327-1675. Rev. Msgr. James A. Kelly, Rev. Javier Bujalante.

Berkeley.
1827 Oxford St., Berkeley, CA USA 94709. Revs. Torlach Delargy, Edward G. Maristany.

State of Texas

Houston.
5505 Chaucer Dr., Houston, TX USA 77007. Tel: 770-523-4351. Very Rev. Paul D. Kais, B.A., M.A., Ph.D., Vicar for Texas, Revs. Christopher Schmitt, Francisco Vera.
410 Westcott St., Houston, TX USA 77007. Rev. Pedro Pablo Arriagada.

Irving.
3610 Wingren, Irving, TX USA 75062. Tel: 214-650-0064. Revs. Michael Fagan, Jerome L. Jung.

San Antonio.
1979 Summit Ave., San Antonio, TX USA 78212. Tel: 210-732-3065. Rev. William G. Shaughnessey.

State of Virginia

Reston.
1810 Old Reston Ave., Reston, VA USA 20190. Tel: 703-689-3433. Revs. Lawrence A. Kutz, C. John McCloskey, Martin Joseph Miller.

Puerto Rico

Guaynabo. Rev. Msgr. Justiniano Garcia Arias, M.A., J.C.D., Reg. Vicar
Villa Caparra, A35 A St., Guaynabo, PR USA 00966-2211. Tel: 787-781-9123. Revs. Ramon Alvarez, Patricio Olmos.
Villa Caparra, A48 A St., Guaynabo, PR USA 00966. Tel: 787-783-1987. Revs. Gonzalo Diaz, Andres Eiroa.

San Juan.
808 Baldorioty de Castro St., BDA Blondet, San Juan, PR USA 00925-2434. Tel: 787-759-6193. Revs. Juan Ignacio Ballesteros, Alejandro Zubieta.

Ponce.
Llambias Urb. Alhambra St., Ponce, PR USA 00716-3929. Tel: 787-844-2661. Revs. Jaime Bermudez, Martin Llambias.

Mayaguez.
65 Orquideas St., Ensanche Martinez, Mayaguez, PR USA 00680. Tel: 787-833-6461. Rev. Javier Bernaola.

Holy Protection of Mary Byzantine Catholic Eparchy of Phoenix

Most Reverend

JOHN S. PAZAK, C.SS.R.

Bishop of Eparchy of Phoenix; ordained August 27, 1972; appointed Bishop of Saints Cyril and Methodius of Toronto (Slovakian), Canada; ordained February 14, 2001; appointed Bishop of Holy Protection of Mary Byzantine Catholic Eparchy of Phoenix, USA May 7, 2016. *Office: 8131 N. 16th St., Phoenix, AZ 85020.*

Most Reverend

GERALD N. DINO

Retired Bishop of Eparchy of Phoenix; ordained March 21, 1965; appointed Bishop of Phoenix Byzantine December 6, 2007; consecrated and enthroned March 27, 2008; retired May 7, 2016. *Office: 8105 N. 16th St., Phoenix, AZ 85020.*

Chancery Office: 8131 N. 16th St., Phoenix, AZ 85020. Tel: 602-861-9778; Fax: 602-861-9796.

Web: www.ephx.org

Email: chancellor@ephx.org

Established December 3, 1981.

Established in 1981 as the Byzantine Catholic Eparchy of Van Nuys. The name was changed to Holy Protection of Mary Byzantine Catholic Eparchy of Phoenix on February 10, 2010 by the Holy See.

Embraces all Catholics of the Byzantine-Ruthenian Church in the States of California, Oregon, Washington, Idaho, Nevada, Arizona, Utah, Wyoming, Montana, Colorado, New Mexico, Alaska and Hawaii.

Principal Patron-Holy Protection of the Mother of God (Pokrov).

Legal Titles:
Holy Protection of Mary Byzantine Catholic Bishop of Phoenix, An Arizona Corporation Sole.
Byzantine Catholic, A Corporation Sole.
For Legal Titles of Eparchial and Parish Institutions, please consult the Chancellor.

STATISTICAL OVERVIEW

Personnel	
Bishop	1
Retired Bishops	1
Abbots	1
Retired Abbots	1
Priests: Diocesan Active in Diocese	20
Priests: Diocesan Active Outside Diocese	3
Priests: Retired, Sick or Absent	6
Number of Diocesan Priests	29
Religious Priests in Diocese	1
Total Priests in Diocese	30
Extern Priests in Diocese	1
Ordinations:	
Diocesan Priests	1
Permanent Deacons in Diocese	12
Total Brothers	4
Parishes	
Parishes	19
With Resident Pastor:	
Resident Diocesan Priests	18
Resident Religious Priests	1
Missions	1
Welfare	
Homes for the Aged	1
Total Assisted	26
Educational	
Diocesan Students in Other Seminaries	1
Total Seminarians	1
Elementary Schools, Diocesan and Parish	1
Total Students	90
Catechesis/Religious Education:	
High School Students	110
Elementary Students	390
Total Students under Catholic Instruction	591
Vital Statistics	
Receptions into the Church:	
Infant Baptism Totals	56
Minor Baptism Totals	4
Adult Baptism Totals	19
Received into Full Communion	16
First Communions	64
Confirmations	63
Marriages:	
Catholic	13
Interfaith	1
Total Marriages	14
Deaths	24
Total Catholic Population	2,261

Former Bishops—Most Revs. Thomas V. Dolinay, D.D., ord. May 16, 1948; cons. Nov. 23, 1976; appt. Titular Bishop of Thyatira and Auxiliary of Passaic, Sept. 23, 1976; appt. First Ordinary of the Byzantine Catholic Diocese of Van Nuys, CA; enthroned March 9, 1982; appt. Coadjutor Archbishop of Pittsburgh Byzantine Rite, March 13, 1990; succeeded to June 12, 1991; died April 13, 1993; George M. Kuzma, D.D., ord. May 29, 1955; appt. Auxiliary Bishop of the Byzantine Eparchy of Passaic, Nov. 11, 1986; cons. Feb. 4, 1987; appt. Bishop of Eparchy of Van Nuys Oct. 23, 1990; enthroned as Second Bishop of Van Nuys, Jan. 15, 1991; retired Dec. 5, 2000; died Dec. 7, 2008.; William C. Skurla, ord. May 23, 1987; appt. Bishop of Eparchy of Van Nuys Feb. 19, 2002; cons. April 23, 2002; appt. Bishop of Passaic Dec. 6, 2007; enthroned Jan. 29, 2008; appt. Metropolitan Archbishop of Pittsburgh (Byzantine) on Jan. 19, 2012; enthroned as the 5th Metropolitan Archbishop on April 18, 2012.; Gerald N. Dino, OESL, ord. March 21, 1965; appt. Bishop Eparchy of Van Nuys Dec. 6, 2007; cons. and enthroned March 27, 2008; retired May 7, 2016.

Chancery Office—Byzantine Catholic Eparchy of Phoenix, Pastoral Center, 8131 N. 16th St., Phoenix, 85020. Tel: 602-861-9778; Fax: 602-861-9796; Email: chancellor@ephx.org; Web: www.ephx.org. Office Hours: Mon.-Fri. 8:30 am-4:30 pm.

Protosyncellus (Vicar General)—Most Rev. Gerald N. Dino, OESL, Email: hpmbishop@aol.com.

Chancellor—Very Rev. Diodoro Mendoza.

College of Consultors—Most Rev. Gerald N. Dino, OESL, Protosynellus, (Retired); Very Revs. Mel Rybarczyk, C.R.; Diodoro Mendoza; Brian Escobedo; Marcus Gomori; Michael O'Loughlin; Rt. Revs. Stephen G. Washko; Joseph Stanichar; Very Rev. Robert Rankin.

Finance Officer—Deacon James Danovich, Email: treasurer@ephx.org.

Finance Council—Rt. Rev. Stephen G. Washko; Very Revs. Brian Escobedo; Diodoro Mendoza; Rev. Joseph Hutsko; Deacons James Danovich; John Montalvo III.

Presbyteral Council—All priests having a Pastoral Assignment within the Eparchy.

Secretary for the Presbyteral Council & The College of Consultors—Rev. Stephen Casmus; Very Rev. Marcus Gomori.

Eparchial Tribunal—Office of the Tribunal Eparchy of Phoenix, 8131 N. 16th St., Phoenix, 85020. Tel: 602-861-9778; Fax: 602-861-9796.

Judicial Vicar—Rev. Msgr. Kevin W. McAuliffe, J.C.L.

Adjutant Judicial Vicar—Vacant.

Promoter of Justice—Very Rev. Archpriest Michael Moran, J.C.D., (Retired).

Secretary—Loretta L. Winn.

Defender of the Bond—Very Rev. Archpriest Michael Moran, J.C.D., (Retired).

Judge—Rev. Msgr. Kevin W. McAuliffe, J.C.L.

Auditors/Advocates—Rev. Stephen Casmus; Very Rev. Marcus Gomori.

Notaries—Very Rev. Diodoro Mendoza; Rev. Stephen Casmus; Very Rev. Marcus Gomori.

Eparchial Appeal—Rev. Msgr. Kevin W. McAuliffe, J.C.L.

Building and Sacred Arts Commission—Rt. Rev. Stephen G. Washko; Very Rev. Diodoro Mendoza; Deacon John Montalvo III.

Intereparchial Religious Education Commission—Rev. Anthony Hernandez.

Intereparchial Evangelization Commission—Very Rev. Diodoro Mendoza.

Intereparchial Liturgical Commission—Very Rev. Robert M. Pipta.

Intereparchial Youth Commission—Rev. Artur Bubnevych; Very Rev. Michael O'Loughlin.

Intereparchial Music Commission—Rev. Michael S. Bezruchka.

Safe Environment Coordinator—Email: safeenvironment@ephx.org. Mr. Michael Hanafin, Coord., Email: dcnhanafin@ephx.org; Paul Kilroy, Asst., Email: sbdcnkilroy@ephx.org.

Victim Advocate and Assistance Coordinator—Caroline Bonhom, Email: victimassistancephoenix@gmail.com.

Vocations Office—Rev. Michael Mandelas, Dir.; Very Rev. Michael O'Loughlin, Asst. Dir.

Vocation Review Board—Most Revs. John Pazak, C.Ss.R.; Gerald N. Dino, OESL, (Retired); Very Rev. Michael O'Loughlin; Rev. Michael Mandelas; Deacon James Danovich.

Ecclesiatical Notaries—Rev. Msgr. Kevin W. McAuliffe, J.C.L.; Very Rev. Diodoro Mendoza.

Magazine—Light of the West Most Rev. Gerald N. Dino, OESL, Editor, (Retired); Kathleen Slonka, Dir., Light of the West, Email: lightofthewest@ephx.org.

Social Media—Kathleen Slonka.

Director of Ecumenical Affairs—Rt. Rev. Stephen G. Washko.

Censor—Most Rev. GERALD N. DINO, OESL, Bishop Emeritus, (Retired).
Pro-Life Coordinators—Email: prolife@ephx.org. KENNETH ROBERTS; REBECCA ROBERTS.
Eparchial Website—Deacon BASIL BALKE.
Public Relations Liaison—Email: publicrelations@ephx.org. MR. JOHN SURMAY.
Pension Committee—Most Rev. GERALD N. DINO, OESL; Rev. Msgr. GEORGE N. VIDA; Very Rev. MARCUS GOMORI; Rev. FRANCIS MURIN.
Personnel Board—Most Revs. JOHN PAZAK, C.Ss.R.; GERALD N. DINO, OESL, Bishop Emeritus; Rt. Rev. STEPHEN G. WASHKO; Very Rev. DIODORO MENDOZA.
Financial Stewardship Committee—Rev. Msgr. KEVIN W. MCAULIFFE, J.C.L.; Deacon JAMES DANOVICH; MR. JOHN SURMAY.

CLERGY, PARISHES, MISSIONS AND PAROCHIAL SCHOOLS

STATE OF ARIZONA

PHOENIX, MARICOPA CO., ST. STEPHEN CATHEDRAL (1968) [CEM]
8141 N. 16th St., Frnt., 85020-3999.
Tel: 602-943-5379; Fax: 602-997-4093; Email: rector@ephx.org; Web: www.stsbcc.org. Very Rev. Diodoro Mendoza, Rector; Revs. Joseph Hutsko, Parochial Vicar; Arthur Rojas, Parochial Vicar; Deacons John Montalvo III; James Danovich; Adam Lowe.
Catechesis Religious Program—Email: deaconjm3@gmail.com. Students 38.
Convent—St. Stephen Convent, 8141 N. 16th St., #27, 85020. Tel: 602-944-5121; Fax: 602-997-4093. Sisters 2.

GILBERT, MARICOPA CO., ST. THOMAS THE APOSTLE (1982)
Mailing Address: P.O. Box 667, Gilbert, 85299-0667. Rev. Mykhaylo Sidun; Deacon Michael Sullivan.
Rectory—505 W. Midland Ln., Gilbert, 85233.
Catechesis Religious Program—Students 17.

TUCSON, PIMA CO., ST. MELANY (1974)
1212 N. Sahuara, Tucson, 85712-5018.
Tel: 520-886-4225; Email: frrankin@ephx.org. Very Rev. Robert Rankin.
Catechesis Religious Program—Students 34.

STATE OF ALASKA

ANCHORAGE, ANCHORAGE CO., SAINT NICHOLAS OF MYRA (1958)
2200 Arctic Blvd., Anchorage, AK 99503-1909.
Tel: 907-277-6731; Email: pastorstnick@yahoo.com; Web: www.ak-byz-cath.org. Rev. Joseph Wargacki.
Catechesis Religious Program—Students 22.
Mission—Blessed Theodore Romzha Mission, Sacred Heart Church, 1201 Bogard Rd., Wasilla, AK 99654.

STATE OF CALIFORNIA

ANAHEIM, ORANGE CO., ANNUNCIATION (1969)
995 N. West St., Anaheim, CA 92801-4305.
Tel: 714-533-6292; Email: abcc72069@gmail.com; Web: www.annunciationbyzantine.org. Rt. Rev. Stephen G. Washko.
Rectory—999 N. West St., Anaheim, CA 92801-4305.
Catechesis Religious Program—Email: maryalaureen@hotmail.com. Mrs. Marya Weil, D.R.E. Students 38.

FONTANA, SAN BERNARDINO CO., ST. NICHOLAS (1958)
9112 Oleander Ave., Fontana, CA 92335-5599.
Tel: 909-822-9917; Email: st.nicholas.fontana@gmail.com; Web: stnicholasfontana.org. Rev. Stephen Casmus, Admin.
Catechesis Religious Program—

FRESNO, FRESNO CO., BYZANTINE CATHOLIC COMMUNITY OF FRESNO, CA, Closed. For inquiries for parish records contact the chancery.

LOS GATOS, SANTA CLARA CO., ST. BASIL THE GREAT (1986)
14263 Mulberry Dr., Los Gatos, CA 95032-1208.
Tel: 408-871-0919; Email: FrHernandez@ephx.org; Web: www.stbasil.org. Rev. Anthony Hernandez; Deacon Craig Anderson.
Catechesis Religious Program—Students 4.

PALM SPRINGS, RIVERSIDE CO., BYZANTINE CATHOLIC COMMUNITY OF PALM SPRINGS, CA, Closed. For inquiries for parish records contact the chancery.

SACRAMENTO, SACRAMENTO CO., ST. PHILIP THE APOSTLE (1971)
3866 65th St., Sacramento, CA 95820-2033.
Tel: 916-452-1888; Email: frmurin@ephx.org. Rev. Frantisek Murin.

SAN DIEGO, SAN DIEGO CO., HOLY ANGELS (1958)
2235 Galahad Rd., San Diego, CA 92123-3931.
Tel: 858-277-2511; Fax: 858-277-5792; Email: pastorhasd@yahoo.com; Web: www.holyangelssandiego.com. Very Rev. Brian Escobedo.
Catechesis Religious Program—Students 29.

SAN LUIS OBISPO, SAN LUIS OBISPO CO., SAINT ANNE (1986)
222 E. Foothill Blvd., San Luis Obispo, CA 93405-1540. Tel: 805-543-8883; Fax: 805-543-8832; Email: stannesol@gmail.com. Rev. Michael S. Bezruchka.
Catechesis Religious Program—Email: frbezruchka@ephx.org; Web: www.stanneslo.org. Students 16.

SAN MATEO, SAN MATEO CO., ST. MACRINA, Closed. All records at the Chancery Office.

SHERMAN OAKS, LOS ANGELES CO., ST. MARY PROTO-CATHEDRAL (1956)
5329 Sepulveda Blvd., Sherman Oaks, CA 91411-3441. Tel: 818-905-5511; Email: cath7@sbcglobal.net; Web: protocathedralso.org. Very Rev. Mel Rybarczyk, C.R., Rector.
Catechesis Religious Program—5335 Sepulveda Blvd., Sherman Oaks, CA 91411. Cynthia Bosak, D.R.E. Students 3.

STOCKTON, SAN JOAQUIN CO., BYZANTINE CATHOLIC COMMUNITY OF STOCKTON, Closed. For inquiries for parish records contact the chancery.

STATE OF COLORADO

COLORADO SPRINGS, EL PASO CO., BYZANTINE CATHOLIC MISSION, Closed. For inquiries for parish records contact the chancery.

DENVER, DENVER CO., HOLY PROTECTION OF THE MOTHER OF GOD (1974)
1201 S. Elizabeth St., Denver, CO 80210.
Tel: 303-778-8283; Email: pastor@holyprotection.org; Web: www.holyprotection.org. Mailing Address: 1074 S. Cook St., Denver, CO 80209. Very Rev. Michael O'Loughlin; Rev. Joel Barstad, Vicar; Deacon Basil Ryan Balke.
Catechesis Religious Program—Students 23.

STATE OF NEVADA

LAS VEGAS, CLARK CO.
1—ST. GABRIEL THE ARCHANGEL (1977)
2250 E. Maule Ave., Las Vegas, NV 89119-4607.
Tel: 702-361-2431; Email: MGomori@aol.com; Web: Stgabrielbyzantinecatholicchurch.org. Very Rev. Marcus Gomori.
School—St. Gabriel Littlest Angels Catholic Preschool, Mrs. Teri De La Torre, Dir. Lay Teachers 2; Students 18; Clergy / Religious Teachers 1.
Catechesis Religious Program—Email: frgomori@ephx.org. Students 135.
2—*OUR LADY OF WISDOM ITALO-GREEK (1993)
2120 Lindell Rd., Las Vegas, NV 89146-0387.
Tel: 702-873-5101; Email: olowis@embarqmail.com; Web: www.OurLadyOfWisdom.net. Rev. Milan Kasperek, Admin.
Catechesis Religious Program—Email: vegasmary@outlook.com. Mary Weishaar, D.R.E. Students 14.
Our Lady of Mt. Carmel Outreach—

STATE OF NEW MEXICO

ALBUQUERQUE, BERNALILLO CO., OUR LADY OF PERPETUAL HELP (1974)
1837 Avarado Dr., N.E., Albuquerque, NM 87110.
Tel: 505-256-1539; Tel: 505-268-2877; Email: abbaolph@gmail.com; Web: www.olphnm.org. Rev. Artur Bubnevych. In Res., Rev. Christopher L. Zugger, (Retired), Tel: 505-256-1787.
Catechesis Religious Program—Students 44.

LAS CRUCES, DONA ANA CO., BYZANTINE CATHOLIC MISSION, Closed. Records are located at Albuquerque Parish.

STATE OF OREGON

PORTLAND, MULTNOMAH CO., ST. IRENE BYZANTINE CATHOLIC CHURCH
4630 N. Maryland Ave., Portland, OR 97217.
Tel: 503-543-2188; Email: fknusel@gmail.com. Mailing Address: 34799 N. Honeyman Rd., Scappoose, OR 97056. Rev. Frank Knusel; Paul Warilla, Fin. Admin.

STATE OF UTAH

SALT LAKE CITY, SALT LAKE CO., BYZANTINE CATHOLIC MISSION, Closed. For inquiries for parish records contact the chancery.

STATE OF WASHINGTON

OLYMPIA, THURSTON CO., ST. GEORGE BYZANTINE CATHOLIC CHURCH (1989)
9730 Yelm Hwy., Olympia, WA 98513.
Tel: 360-459-8373; Email: stgeorgechurcholympia@yahoo.com; Web: stgeorgeolympia.org. Rev. Vasyl Mutka; Deacon Daniel Dozier.
Catechesis Religious Program—Students 34.

SEATTLE, KING CO., ST. JOHN CHRYSOSTOM (1981)
1305 S. Lander St., Seattle, WA 98144-5038.
Tel: 206-329-9219; Email: frmandelas@ephx.org; Web: www.stjohnchrysostom.org. Rev. Michael Mandelas; Deacon Benjamin Crow.
Catechesis Religious Program—Students 65.
Whatcom, Skagit & Island Outreach—Location: St. Charles R.C. Church, Burlington, WA. (Div. Liturgy Sunday at 5:30 PM).

SPOKANE VALLEY, SPOKANE CO., SS. CYRIL & METHODIUS (1979)
4315 N. Evergreen Rd., Spokane Valley, WA 99216.
Tel: 509-922-4527; Email: sscm.us@gmail.com. Mailing Address: P.O. Box 15314, Spokane Valley, WA 99215-5314. Rev. William O'Brien.
Res.: 4317 N. Evergreen Rd., Spokane, WA 99216-1298.
Catechesis Religious Program—Students 28.

WALLA WALLA, WALLA WALLA CO., BYZANTINE CATHOLIC MISSION, Closed. For inquiries for parish records contact the Spokane parish.

Special Assignments:
Very Rev.—
Barrand, James R.
Revs.—
Lane, James
Perry, Lee.

Retired:
Rev. Msgr.—
Vida, George, (Retired)
Very Rev.—
Petras, David M., 1670 E. El Camino Dr., 85020-3926. (Parma)
Revs.—
Ackley, Randall Wasyl, (Retired)
Daigle, Robert E., (Retired), 6505 O'Bannon Dr., Las Vegas, NV 89146
Gnall, Julian, (Retired)
Michalenko, Alexei, (Retired)
Zugger, Christopher L., (Retired), 1838 Palomas Dr. N.E., Albuquerque, NM 87110
Very Rev. Archpriest—
Moran, Michael, J.C.D., (Retired), 16701 Algonquin St., #307, Huntington Beach, CA 92649-3126
Rt. Rev.—
Stanichar, Joseph, (Retired).

Permanent Deacons:
Anderson, Craig, Los Gatos, CA
Balke, Basil Ryan, Denver, CO
Bradley, John, San Luis Obispo, CA (Leave of Absence)
Crow, Benjamin, Seattle, WA
Danovich, James, Phoenix, AZ
Hanafin, Michael, Phoenix, AZ; (Leave of Absence)
Lowe, Adam, Phoenix, AZ
Montalvo, John III, Phoenix, AZ
Sullivan, Michael, Gilbert, AZ
Vrabel, Stephen, Anchorage, AK.

INSTITUTIONS LOCATED IN DIOCESE

[A] RETIREMENT HOMES

PHOENIX. *St. Stephen Senior Citizen Apartments*, 8141 N. 16th St. FRNT, 85020. Tel: 602-943-5379; Fax: 602-997-4093; Email: rectorss@ephx.org. Very Rev. Diodoro Mendoza, Rector. Residents 28; Senior Citizens Apartments 26.

[B] MONASTERIES AND RESIDENCES OF PRIESTS AND BROTHERS

CALIMESA. *Byzantine Brothers of St. Francis*, St. Francis Monastery, 9443 Sharondale Rd., Calimesa, CA 92320-2017. Tel: 951-850-9625; Email: brmike_7@msn.com. Bro. John Gray, B.B.S.F., Supr.

[C] MISCELLANEOUS

PHOENIX. *Saint Anne, San Luis Obispo Charitable Trust*, 8131 N. 16th St., 85020. Tel: 602-861-9778; Email: chancellor@ephx.org. Very Rev. Diodoro Mendoza, Chancellor.
Annunciation, Anaheim Charitable Trust, 8131 N. 16th St., 85020. Tel: 602-861-9778; Email: chancellor@ephx.org. Very Rev. Diodoro Mendoza, Chancellor.
Saint Basil, Los Gatos Charitable Trust, 8131 N. 16th St., 85020. Tel: 602-861-9778; Email: chancellor@ephx.org. Very Rev. Diodoro Mendoza, Chancellor.
Saints Cyril and Methodius, Spokane Charitable Trust, 8131 N. 16th St., 85020. Tel: 602-861-9778; Email: chancellor@ephx.org. Very Rev. Diodoro Mendoza, Chancellor.
Saint Gabriel, Las Vegas Charitable Trust, 8131 N.

16th St., 85020. Tel: 602-861-9778; Email: chancellor@ephx.org. Very Rev. Diodoro Mendoza, Chancellor.

Saint George, Olympia Charitable Trust, 8131 N. 16th St., 85020. Tel: 602-861-9778; Email: chancellor@ephx.org. Very Rev. Diodoro Mendoza, Chancellor.

Holy Angels, San Diego Charitable Trust, 8131 N. 16th St., 85020. Tel: 602-861-9778; Email: chancellor@ephx.org. Very Rev. Diodoro Mendoza, Chancellor.

Holy Protection of Mary Byzantine Catholic Bishop of Phoenix, 8131 N. 16th St., 85020. Tel: 602-861-9778; Fax: 602-861-9796; Email: Eparch@ephx.org; Web: ephx.org.

Holy Protection of Mary Byzantine Catholic Eparchy of Phoenix dba Byzantine Catholic Eparchy of Phoenix Tel: 602-861-9778; Fax: 602-861-9796; Email: chancellor@ephx.org; Web: ephx.org. Rev. Msgr. Kevin W. McAuliffe, J.C.L., Human Resources & Employee Benefits.

Holy Protection of Mary Facilities Corporation, 8131 N. 16th St., 85020. Tel: 602-861-9778; Fax: 602-861-9796; Email: chancellor@ephx.org. Rev. Msgr. Kevin W. McAuliffe, J.C.L.

Holy Protection of Mary Foundation, 8131 N. 16th St., 85020. Tel: 602-861-9778; Fax: 602-861-9796; Email: chancellor@ephx.org. Very Rev. Diodoro Mendoza, Chancellor.

Holy Protection, Denver Charitable Trust, 8131 N. 16th St., 85020. Tel: 602-861-9778; Email: chancellor@ephx.org. Very Rev. Diodoro Mendoza, Chancellor.

Saint Irene, Portland Charitable Trust, 8131 N. 16th St., 85020. Tel: 602-861-9778; Email: chancellor@ephx.org. Very Rev. Diodoro Mendoza, Chancellor.

Saint John, Seattle Charitable Trust, 8131 N. 16th St., 85020. Tel: 602-861-9778; Email: chancellor@ephx.org. Very Rev. Diodoro Mendoza, Chancellor.

Saint Mary, Sherman Oaks Charitable Trust, 8131 N. 16th St., 85020. Tel: 602-861-9778; Fax: 602-861-9796; Email: chancellor@ephx.org. Very Rev. Diodoro Mendoza, Chancellor.

Saint Melany, Tucson Charitable Trust, 8131 N. 16th St., 85020. Tel: 602-861-9778; Email: chancellor@ephx.org. Very Rev. Diodoro Mendoza, Chancellor.

Saint Nicholas, Anchorage Charitable Trust, 8131 N. 16th St., 85020. Tel: 602-861-9778; Email: chancellor@ephx.org. Very Rev. Diodoro Mendoza, Chancellor.

Saint Nicholas, Fontana Charitable Trust, 8131 N. 16th St., 85020. Tel: 602-861-9778; Email: chancellor@ephx.org. 9112 Oleander Ave., Fontana, CA 92335-5527. Very Rev. Diodoro Mendoza, Chancellor.

Our Lady of Perpetual Help, Albuquerque Charitable Trust, 8131 N. 16th St., 85020. Tel: 602-861-9778; Email: chancellor@ephx.org. Very Rev. Diodoro Mendoza, Chancellor.

Saint Philip, Sacramento Charitable Trust, 8131 N. 16th St., 85020. Tel: 602-861-9778; Email: chancellor@ephx.org. Very Rev. Diodoro Mendoza, Chancellor.

Saint Stephen, Phoenix Charitable Trust, 8131 N. 16th St., 85020. Tel: 602-943-5379; Email: rectorss@ephx.org. Very Rev. Diodoro Mendoza, Rector.

Saint Thomas, Gilbert Charitable Trust, 8131 N. 16th St., 85020. Tel: 602-861-9778; Email: chancellor@ephx.org. Very Rev. Diodoro Mendoza, Chancellor.

RELIGIOUS INSTITUTES OF MEN REPRESENTED IN THE DIOCESE

For further details refer to the corresponding bracketed number in the Religious Institutes of Men or Women section.

[]—*Byzantine Brothers of St. Francis*—B.B.S.F.

[1080]—*Congregation of the Resurrection*—C.R.

[]—*Duchovny Dom*.

[1070]—*Redemptorist Fathers*.

An asterisk (*) denotes an organization that has established tax-exempt status directly with the IRS and is not covered by the USCCB Group Ruling.

Eparchy of Newton (Melkite-Greek Catholic)

Most Reverend

NICHOLAS JAMES SAMRA, D.D.

Bishop of Newton; ordained May 10, 1970; appointed Auxiliary Bishop of Newton June 29, 1989; appointed fifth Bishop of Newton June 15, 2011; enthroned August 23, 2011. *Mailing Address: 3 VFW Pkwy., West Roxbury, MA 02132.*

Most Reverend

JOHN A. ELYA, B.S.O., D.D.

Retired Eparch of Newton; ordained February 17, 1952; appointed Auxiliary Bishop of Newton April 2, 1986; appointed Eparch of Newton November 25, 1993; installed January 25, 1994; retired August 18, 2004. *Res.: 30 East St., Methuen, MA 01844.* Tel: 978-683-2471; Email: bpjohn31@aol.com.

The Chancery: 3 Veterans of Foreign Wars Pkwy., West Roxbury, MA 02132. Tel: 617-323-9922

Web: melkite.org

Established as an Apostolic Exarchate January 10, 1966.

Elevated to Eparchy, June 28, 1976; Embraces all members of the Melkite Greek Catholic Church in the United States.

For legal titles of parishes and institutions, consult the Chancery Office.

STATISTICAL OVERVIEW

Personnel	
Bishop	1
Retired Bishops	1
Priests: Diocesan Active in Diocese	43
Priests: Diocesan Active Outside Diocese	3
Priests: Retired, Sick or Absent	12
Number of Diocesan Priests	58
Total Priests in Diocese	58
Permanent Deacons in Diocese	61
Parishes	
Parishes	43
With Resident Pastor:	
Resident Diocesan Priests	33
Resident Religious Priests	5
Without Resident Pastor:	
Administered by Priests	5
New Parishes Created	2
Educational	
Diocesan Students in Other Seminaries	3
Total Seminarians	3
Catechesis/Religious Education:	
High School Students	184
Elementary Students	803
Total Students under Catholic Instruction	990
Vital Statistics	
Receptions into the Church:	
Infant Baptism Totals	216
Minor Baptism Totals	10
Adult Baptism Totals	8
Received into Full Communion	25
First Communions	241
Confirmations	248
Marriages:	
Catholic	87
Interfaith	10
Total Marriages	97
Deaths	139
Total Catholic Population	21,691

Former Eparchs—Most Revs. Justin A. Najmy, B.A.O., D.D., born April 23, 1898; ord. Dec. 25, 1926; cons. May 29, 1966; installed June 4, 1966; died June 11, 1968; Joseph E. Tawil, D.D., LL.D., ord. July 20, 1936; cons. Jan. 1, 1960; appt. Apostolic Exarch, Oct. 30, 1969; appt. Eparch, June 28, 1976; became emeritus Dec. 2, 1989; died Feb. 17, 1999; Ignatius Ghattas, B.S.O., D.D., born Dec. 25, 1920; ord. July 7, 1946; appt. Dec. 2, 1989; cons. Feb. 23, 1990; died Oct. 11, 1992; John A. Elya, B.S.O., D.D., ord. Feb. 17, 1952; appt. Auxiliary Bishop of Newton April 2, 1986; appt. Eparch of Newton Nov. 25, 1993; installed Jan. 25, 1994; retired Eparch of Newton Aug. 18, 2004; Cyril Salim Bustros, S.M.S.P., ord. June 29, 1962; appt. Archbishop of Baalbek (Melkite) Lebanon Oct. 25, 1988; ord. Nov. 27, 1988; appt. Eparch of Newton June 22, 2004; enthroned August 18, 2004; selected Archbishop of Beirut and Jbeil June 25, 2010; confirmed June 15, 2011; installed July 22, 2011; retired Nov. 9, 2018.

Diocesan Administration

Chancery Office—3 VFW Pkwy., West Roxbury, 02132. Tel: 617-323-9922. Office Hours: Mon.-Fri. 9-5.

Protosyncellus—Rt. Rev. Archimandrite Philip Raczka.

Chancellor—Rev. Theophan Leonarczyk.

Eparchial Tribunal—The Tribunal, Eparchy of Newton: 42 Lake Ave., Ext. #357, Danbury, CT 06811. Tel: 352-683-7637.

Judicial Vicar—Rt. Rev. Archimandrite Michael K. Skrocki, J.C.D., 181 Clapboard Ridge Rd., Danbury, CT 06811.

Judges—Rt. Rev. Archimandrite Michael K. Skrocki, J.C.D.; Rev. Joseph Koury, J.C.D.; Rev. Msgr. Michael Souckar, J.C.D.

Defender of the Bond and Promoter of Justice—Rt. Rev. Exarch Joseph S. Haggar, J.C.L.

Notaries—Rev. Theophan Leonarczyk; Lucille LaRoche; Janice M. Terris.

Chief Finance Officer—Rev. Deacon Robert Shalhoub, Tel: 973-785-4144; Fax: 973-890-9599.

Protopresbyters—Rt. Rev. Archimandrites Mark E. Melone, New England; Damon Geiger, Southeast; Kenneth Sherman, Mid-Atlantic; Alexei Smith, M.A., M.Div., West; Rev. Michel Cheble, Great Lakes.

Consultative Bodies

College of Eparchial Consultors—Rt. Rev. John Azar; Rev. Antoine Rizk, B.S.O.; Rt. Rev. Exarch Joseph S. Haggar, J.C.L.; Rev. Thomas P. Steinmetz; Rev. Archimandrites Alexei Smith, M.A., M.Div.; Philip Raczka; Michael K. Skrocki, J.C.D.

Presbyteral Council—Revs. Francois Beyrouti; Peter Boutros; Michel Cheble; Theophan Leonarczyk; Bryan McNeil; Rt. Rev. Archimandrites Philip Raczka; Damon Geiger; Alexei Smith, M.A., M.Div.; Eugene Mitchell, B.S.O.; Mark E. Melone.

Diocese of Newton for the Melkites in the USA, Inc., a Massachusetts Corporation—Most Rev. Nicholas J. Samra; Rt. Rev. Archimandrite Philip Raczka; Rev. Theophan Leonarczyk; Rev. Deacon Robert Shalhoub.

Finance Council—Rt. Rev. Exarch Joseph S. Haggar, J.C.L.; Rt. Rev. Archimandrite Philip Raczka; Dr. John Nazarian; Karim Kaspar; Mr. Michael Nahill; Regina Arfuso; Rev. Deacons Robert Shalhoub; Thomas Davis; Rev. Theophan Leonarczyk; Mr. Albert Haddad.

Legal Consultants—Camille F. Sarrouf, 95 Commercial Wharf, Boston, 02110. Tel: 617-227-5800.

Pastoral Offices and Commissions

Continuing Education of Clergy Office—Rev. Christopher Manuele.

National Association of Melkite Youth—Rev. Thomas P. Steinmetz, 140 Mitchell St., Manchester, NH 03102.

MAYA (Melkite Assoc. of Young Adults)—Rev. Musil Shihadeh.

Ambassadors—Rev. Peter Boutros, 3718 E. Greenway Rd., Phoenix, AZ 85032. Tel: 602-787-4787.

National Association of Melkite Women—Rev. Michel Cheble, (Warren, MI).

Liturgical Commission—Rt. Rev. Archimandrite Damon Geiger.

Liturgical Arts—Rt. Rev. Archimandrite Mark E. Melone.

Office of Communications—Rev. Theophan Leonarczyk, Dir., 3 VFW Pkwy., West Roxbury, 02132.

Office of Evangelization & Catechesis—Rev. Hezekias Carnazzo.

Vocations Office—Rt. Rev. John Azar, St. John Chrysostom Church, 1428 Ponce de Leon Ave., N.E., Atlanta, GA 30307.

Sophia (A Journal)—Rt. Rev. Archimandrite James K. Babcock, Editor-in-Chief; Vacant, Production.

Order of St. Nicholas—Mailing Address: 3 VFW Pkwy., West Roxbury, 02132. Tel: 617-323-9922; Fax: 617-323-0692.

Associated Melkite Charities—Very Rev. Philaret Littlefield, 1617 W. State St., Milwaukee, WI 53233. Tel: 414-342-1543.

Sophia Press—Rev. Theophan Leonarczyk, Office: 3 VFW Pkwy., West Roxbury, 02132. Tel: 617-323-9922, Ext. 206; Rt. Rev. Archimandrite Michael K. Skrocki, J.C.D.; Ms. Saideh Dagher, Tel: 617-323-9922.

Victim Assistance Coordinator—Rev. Michael Hull.

CLERGY, PARISHES, MISSIONS AND PAROCHIAL SCHOOLS

STATE OF MASSACHUSETTS

BOSTON, SUFFOLK CO., ANNUNCIATION CATHEDRAL
7 V.F.W. Pkwy., 02132. Tel: 617-323-5242; Email: MelkiteCathedral@gmail.com. Rt. Rev. Archimandrite Philip Raczka, Rector; Rev. Deacons John Moses; Ibrahim Zeinieh; Elias (Richard) Bailey
Legal Name: Annunciation Cathedral Melkite Catholic Church Inc.

LAWRENCE, ESSEX CO., ST. JOSEPH
241 Hampshire St., Lawrence, 01841.
Tel: 978-682-8252; Email: mmpapamarco191@gmail.com. Rt. Rev. Archimandrite Mark E. Melone; Rev. Protodeacon Bryan McNeil; Rev. Deacons John Fleshman; Ziad Layous; Michael Macoul.

WORCESTER, WORCESTER CO., OUR LADY OF PERPETUAL HELP
256 Hamilton St., Worcester, 01604.
Tel: 508-752-4174; Fax: 508-752-8351; Email: olphworc@att.net. Rt. Rev. Paul G. Frechette.

STATE OF ALABAMA

BIRMINGHAM, JEFFERSON CO., ST. GEORGE CHURCH
425 Sixteenth Ave. S., Birmingham, AL 35205.
Tel: 205-252-5788; Email: stgeorge@bham.rr.com. Rev. Dr. Justin Rose; Rt. Rev. Frank J. Milienewicz, Pastor Emeritus, (Retired); Rev. Deacons Seraphim Ritchey; Andrew Baroody.

STATE OF ARIZONA

PHOENIX, MARICOPA CO., ST. JOHN OF THE DESERT MELKITE CATHOLIC CHURCH
3718 E. Greenway Rd., Phoenix, AZ 85032.
Tel: 602-787-4787; Email: frpeter@typicon.com; Web: www.stjohnofthedesert.com. Rev. Peter Boutros; Rev. Deacons Zyad Abyad; Marion Rimmer.
Catechesis Religious Program—Parish Education, Tel: 480-234-9974; Email: Education@stjohnofthedesert.com.

STATE OF CALIFORNIA

ARCADIA, ANNUNCIATION MELKITE MISSION
1307 E. Longden Ave., Arcadia, CA 91006.
Tel: 626-447-6202; Email: parish-4510@la-archdiocese.org. Rev. Eugene Herbert.
Catechesis Religious Program—Tel: 626-446-1625. Arcie Reza, Admin. Students 233.

COVINA, ANNUNCIATION MISSION
381 Center St., Covina, CA 91723. Tel: 630-457-8153; Email: basharazar@gmail.com. Rev. Gabriel Azar.

EL SEGUNDO, LOS ANGELES CO., ST. PAUL
538 Concord St., El Segundo, CA 90245.
Tel: 310-322-1892; Email: frARSmith@la-archdiocese.org. Rt. Rev. Archimandrite Alexei Smith, M.A., M.Div., Admin.

NORTH HOLLYWOOD, LOS ANGELES CO., ST. ANNE MELKITE CO-CATHEDRAL (1905)
Mailing Address: 11211 Moorpark St., North Hollywood, CA 91602. Rt. Rev. Fouad Sayegh; Rev. Musil Shihadieh; Rev. Protodeacon George Sayegh; Rev. Deacons George Karout; Tareq Nasrallah; Thom O'Malley; Estephanos Helo.
Res.: 11245 Rye St., North Hollywood, CA 91602.
Tel: 818-761-2034; Email: office@stannecathedral.org.
Catechesis Religious Program—

PLACENTIA, ORANGE CO., HOLY CROSS
451 W. Madison Ave., Placentia, CA 92870.
Tel: 714-985-1710; Email: office@HolyCrossMelkite.org. Rev. Francois Beyrouti; Rev. Deacon Elias Kashou. Melkite Catholic Parish in Orange County, California.

SACRAMENTO, SACRAMENTO CO., ST. GEORGE MELKITE CHURCH INC.
1620 Bell St., Sacramento, CA 95825.
Tel: 916-920-2900; Web: www.StGeorgeMelkite.org. P.O. Box 660425, Sacramento, CA 95866. Rev. Hezekias Carnazzo.

SAN BERNARDINO, SAN BERNARDINO CO., ST. PHILIP
923 W. Congress St., San Bernardino, CA 92410.
Tel: 909-889-3579; Email: comeandsee@earthlink.net. Rev. Dr. Justin Rose; Rev. Protodeacon Stephen Ghandour, (Retired); Rev. Deacons Jacob Pesta; Michael Mobley.

SAN DIEGO, SAN DIEGO CO., ST. JACOB MISSION, Services at Holy Angels Church, San Diego.
Mailing Address: 2235 Galahad Rd., P.O. Box 231328, San Diego, CA 92123. Tel: 858-987-2864; Email: mail@stjacobmelkite.org; Email: rsamaan1@hotmail.com; Web: stjacobmelkite.org. Rev. Rezkallah Samaan; Rev. Protodeacon Edward Bagdasar; Rev. Deacon Antoine Kabane.

SAN JOSE, SANTA CLARA CO., ST. ELIAS
14263 Mulberry Dr., Los Gatos, CA 95032.
Tel: 408-785-1212; Email: steliasmelkite@gmail.com; Web: steliasmelkite.org. Mailing Address: P.O. Box 26274, San Jose, CA 95159. Rev. Sebastian A. Carnazzo, Admin.

TEMECULA, RIVERSIDE CO., VIRGIN MARY MISSION
42030 Avenida Alvarado - Ste. A, P.O. Box 1679, Temecula, CA 92590. Tel: 909-289-2098; Email: virginmarymgcc@gmail.com; Web: virginmarymgcc.com. Rev. Paul (Adham) Fallouh; Rev. Protodeacon Habib Khasho.

STATE OF CONNECTICUT

DANBURY, FAIRFIELD CO., ST. ANN
181 Clapboard Ridge Rd., Danbury, CT 06811.
Tel: 203-743-5119; Fax: 203-743-2007; Email: info@stanndanbury.org. Rt. Rev. Archimandrite Michael K. Skrocki, J.C.D.; Rev. Deacons Nicholas Bourjaili; Thomas Davis.

WATERFORD, NEW LONDON CO., ST. ANN
41 Cross Rd., Waterford, CT 06385.
Tel: 860-442-2211; Email: denmccarthy@challiance.org. Rev. Deacon Dennis J. McCarthy.

STATE OF FLORIDA

DELRAY BEACH, PALM BEACH CO., ST. NICHOLAS
5715 Lake Ida Rd., Delray Beach, FL 33484.
Tel: 305-856-8666. Rt. Rev. Exarch Gabriel Ghanoum, B.S.O.; Rev. Protodeacon Magdi Negm.

MIAMI, DADE CO., ST. JUDE
126 S.E. 15 Rd., Miami, FL 33129-1207.
Tel: 305-856-1500; Email: Damonosst@aol.com; Web: stjudemiami.org. Rt. Rev. Archimandrite Damon Geiger.

STATE OF GEORGIA

ATLANTA, DEKALB CO., ST. JOHN CHRYSOSTOM
1428 Ponce de Leon Ave., N.E., Atlanta, GA 30307.
Tel: 404-373-9522; Email: stjchrys@bellsouth.net; Web: stjohnmelkite.org. Rt. Rev. John Azar; Rev. Deacons Elie Hanna; Sami Jajeh
Legal Title: St. John Chrysostom Melkite Church, Inc.
Catechesis Religious Program—Church School, Gregory Pharo, D.R.E.

AUGUSTA, RICHMOND CO., ST. IGNATIOS OF ANTIOCH
Mailing Address: P.O. Box 3351, Augusta, GA 30914-3351. Tel: 706-364-9511; Email: rodeorector@hotmail.com. Rev. Michael Hull; Rev. Deacons Michael Willoughby; Kent Plowman.
Church: 1003 Merry St., Augusta, GA 30904.

STATE OF ILLINOIS

NORTHLAKE, COOK CO., ST. JOHN THE BAPTIST
200 E North Ave, Northlake, IL 60164. Rev. Ezzat Bathouche; Rev. Protodeacon Antoine Shehata; Rev. Deacon Fadi Rafidi.
Res.: 318 E. Hirsch Ave., Northlake, IL 60164.
Tel: 708-492-0391; Email: stjohnthebaptistchicago@hotmail.com; Web: www.stjohnmelkite.com.

STATE OF INDIANA

HAMMOND, LAKE CO., ST. MICHAEL THE ARCHANGEL (1978)
606 141st St., Hammond, IN 46327.
Tel: 219-933-1457; Email: AYALASAUCEDO@YAHOO.COM. Rev. Sergio Ayala.

STATE OF MICHIGAN

LANSING, INGHAM CO., ST. JOSEPH
725 W. Mt Hope Ave., East Lansing, MI 48910.
Tel: 517-575-6264; Email: frjamie@earthlink.net; Web: www.facebook.com/MelkiteChurchLansing. Mailing Address: 921 Westover Cir., Lansing, MI 48917. Rev. James K. Graham.

PLYMOUTH, WAYNE CO., ST. MICHAEL
585 N. Mill St., Plymouth, MI 48170.
Tel: 734-589-9394; Email: abouna24elie@gmail.com. Rev. Elie Eid, Admin.

WARREN, MACOMB CO., OUR LADY OF REDEMPTION
30518 Freda Dr., Warren, MI 48093. Rev. Michel Cheble; Rev. Deacons David Herr; Rick Trabulsy.
Res.: 29293 Lorraine, Warren, MI 48093.
Tel: 586-751-6017; Email: info@olormelkite.org.

STATE OF NEW HAMPSHIRE

MANCHESTER, HILLSBOROUGH CO., OUR LADY OF THE CEDARS
140 Mitchell St., Manchester, NH 03103.
Tel: 603-623-8944; Email: oloc.church@comcast.net. Rev. Thomas P. Steinmetz; Rt. Rev. Andre St. Germain, (Retired); Rev. Theophan Leonarczyk.

STATE OF NEW JERSEY

CLIFFSIDE PARK, BERGEN CO., ST. DEMETRIUS
184 Cliff St., Cliffside Park, NJ 07010.
Tel: 201-840-8554. Rt. Rev. Archimandrite Kenneth Sherman; Rev. Choukri Sabbagh.

WEST PATERSON, PASSAIC CO., ST. ANN
802 Rifle Camp Rd., West Paterson, NJ 07424.
Tel: 973-785-4144; Fax: 973-890-9599. Rt. Rev. Archimandrite Kenneth Sherman; Revs. Jean Ghaby, (Retired); Choukri Sabbagh; Rev. Archdeacon Edward Bsarany; Rev. Deacons Roland Basinski; Robert Shalhoub.

STATE OF NEW YORK

BROOKLYN, KINGS CO., CHURCH OF THE VIRGIN MARY
216 Eighth Ave., Brooklyn, NY 11215.
Tel: 718-788-5454; Email: cvm@melkitesofnyc.net; Cell: www.ChurchOfTheVirginMary.net. Rev. Antoine Rizk, B.S.O.; Rev. Deacon Nagi Youssef.

ROCHESTER, MONROE CO., ST. NICHOLAS aka St. Nicholas the Wonderworker
1492 Spencerport Rd., Rochester, NY 14606.
Tel: 585-426-4218; Email: stnicholasrochester@gmail.com. Rev. Michael Copenhagen, Admin.; Rev. Deacons Edmond Elhilow; Elias Sarkis.

UTICA, ONEIDA CO., ST. BASIL
901 Sherman Dr., Utica, NY 13501.
Tel: 315-732-4662; Email: sabashofany@yahoo.com; Email: stbasilsutica@gmail.com; Web: stbasiutica.org. Rev. Saba Shofany.

YONKERS, WESTCHESTER CO., CHRIST THE SAVIOR CHURCH, Rev. Fares Al Khlaifat, B.S.O.; Rev. Protodeacon Saleem Naber.
Church: 491 Palisade Ave., Yonkers, NY 10703.
Tel: 914-963-6680.

STATE OF OHIO

AKRON, SUMMIT CO., ST. JOSEPH
600 W. Exchange St., Akron, OH 44302.
Tel: 330-535-7364; Fax: 330-294-0235; Email: office@stjosephakron.org. Rt. Rev. Archimandrite Eugene Mitchell, B.S.O.; Rev. Deacon Dennis Jebber
Legal Title: St Joseph Melkite Church, Inc.
Catechesis Religious Program—Helen Humphrys, D.R.E. Students 30.

BROOKLYN, CUYAHOGA CO., ST. ELIAS
8023 Memphis Ave., Brooklyn, OH 44144.
Tel: 216-661-1155; Fax: 216-661-3838. Rev. Naim Khalil, B.S.O.

COLUMBUS, FRANKLIN CO., HOLY RESURRECTION
8148 Wildflower Ln., Westerville, OH 43081.
Tel: 614-783-0042; Email: columbus.melkite@gmail.com. Rev. Ignatius Harrington.
Church: 4611 Glen Mawr Ave., Columbus, OH 43224.

STATE OF PENNSYLVANIA

COPLAY, LEHIGH CO., ALLENTOWN MELKITE MISSION
1525 Clearview Rd., Coplay, PA 18037.

SCRANTON, LACKAWANNA CO., ST. JOSEPH CATHOLIC CHURCH, INC. (1897)
130 St. Francis Cabrini Ave., Scranton, PA 18504.
Tel: 570-343-6092; Email: stjosephscranton@gmail.com. Rev. Christopher Manuele.

STATE OF RHODE ISLAND

LINCOLN, PROVIDENCE CO., ST. BASIL THE GREAT
15 Skyview Dr., Lincoln, RI 02865. Tel: 401-722-1345. Mailing Address: 111 Cross St., Central Falls, RI 02863. Rt. Rev. Exarch Joseph S. Haggar, J.C.L.; Rev. Archdeacon George M. Yany; Rev. Deacons Gilbert Altongy; Edmond Raheb.

STATE OF TEXAS

HUMBLE, HARRIS CO., ST. BARBARA THE GREAT-MARTYR MISSION
706 E. Main St., Humble, TX 77338.
Tel: 832-846-5720; Email: houstonmelkite@gmail.com; Email: f_mimass@hotmail.com.

STATE OF VIRGINIA

MCLEAN, FAIRFAX CO., HOLY TRANSFIGURATION
8501 Lewinsville Rd., McLean, VA 22102.
Tel: 703-734-9566; Email: office@holytransfiguration.org. Rt. Rev. Joseph F. Francavilla; Rev. Ephrem Handal; Rev. Protodeacon David Baroody; Rev. Deacon David Black; Deacon Oliver Black; Rev. Deacon Joseph Olt.
Catechesis Religious Program—Georgianna Kostak, D.R.E. Students 99.

STATE OF WASHINGTON

SEATTLE, KING CO., ST. JOSEPH MISSION
12038 31st Ave. N.E. #306, Seattle, WA 98125.
Tel: 206-362-2519; Fax: 206-362-2519; Email: samirabulail@gmail.com. Rev. Samir Abu-Lail.

STATE OF WISCONSIN

MILWAUKEE, MILWAUKEE CO., ST. GEORGE
1617 W. State St., Milwaukee, WI 53233.
Tel: 414-342-1543; Email: info@byzantinemilwaukee.com; Web: byzantinemilwaukee.com. Benjamin Newman, Admin.
Legal Title: St. George's Syrian Congregation.

Military Chaplain:
Rev.—
Brown, Shaun S.

Leave of Absence:
Rev.—

Saato, Fred
Rev. Deacons—
Klockowski, Daniel A.
Spencer, Robert.

Retired:
Revs.—
Alam, Alam, (Retired)
Ghaby, Jean, (Retired)
Golini, Ronald, (Retired)
Kerby, Robert, (Retired)
Leonard, John, (Retired)
Matta, Nassir, (Retired)
Moloney, Patrick W., (Retired)
Rt. Rev.—
Russo, Romanos, (Retired)
Revs.—
Samra, Basil, (Retired)
Wehby, Albert, B.A.O., (Retired)
Rt. Revs.—
Gosselin, Lawrence, (Retired)
Kakaty, Edward, (Retired)
Milienewicz, Frank J., (Retired)
Samaha, Victor, B.C.O., (Retired)
St. Germain, Andre, (Retired)
Rt. Rev. Archimandrite—
Aboody, Charles, (Retired).

Archdeacons:
Rev. Archdeacons—
Bsarany, Edward, Woodland Park, NJ
Yany, George M., Lincoln, RI.

Protodeacons:
Protodeacons—
Baroody, David, McLean, VA
Daratony, Joseph, Plymouth, MI
Ghandour, Stephen, San Bernardino, CA
Khasho, Habib, Northlake, IL
Naber, Saleem, Yonkers, NY
Negm, Magdi, Miami, FL
Sayegh, George, North Hollywood, CA
Shehata, Antoine, Northlake, IL.

Deacons:
Rev. Deacons—
Abyad, Zyad
Altongy, Gilbert
Bailey, Elias (Richard), Boston, MA
Baroody, Andrew, Birmingham, AL
Basinski, Roland, West Paterson, NJ
Black, David, McLean, VA
Bourjaili, Danbury, CT
Burke, Thomas, Boston, MA
Davis, Thomas J. Jr., Danbury, CT
Elhilow, Edmond, Rochester, NY
Faulk, Edward, Lago Vista, TX
Fleshman, John, Lawrence, MA
Hanna, Elie, Atlanta, GA
Helo, Estephanos, Los Angeles, CA
Herr, David, Warren, MI
Jajeh, Sami, Atlanta, GA
Jebber, Dennis, Akron, OH
Kabbane, Antoine, San Diego, CA
Kaiser, Joseph, Maple Valley, WA
Karout, George, North Hollywood, CA
Kashou, Elias, Placentia, CA
Layous, Ziad, Lawrence, MA
MacMillan, John, Lawrence, MA
Macoul, Michael
McCarthy, Dennis, Worcester, MA
McGrath, Stephen, (Retired), Danbury, CT
Mobley, Michael, San Bernardino, CA
Moses, John, Boston, MA
Nasrallah, Tareq, North Hollywood, CA
O'Malley, Thom, N. Hollywood, CA
Olt, Joseph, McLean, VA
Pesta, Jacob, San Bernardino, CA
Plowman, Kent, Augusta, GA
Rafidi, Fadi, Northlake, IL
Raheb, Edmond, Lincoln, RI
Richardson, David W., Charleston, SC
Rimmer, Marion, Phoenix, AZ
Ritchey, Seraphim, Birmingham, AL
Sarkis, Elias, Rochester, NY
Shalhoub, Robert, West Paterson, NJ
Spencer, Robert, Manchester, NH
Trabulsy, Rick, Warren, MI
Versage, Joseph V., (Retired)
Willoughby, Michael, Augusta, GA
Youssef, Nagi, Brooklyn, NY
Zeinieh, Ibrahim, Boston, MA.

Priests Serving Outside the Eparchy:
Revs.—
Anatolios, Khaled
McCarthy, Emmanuel Charles
Parent, Basil R.

Deacons Serving Outside the Eparchy:
Rev. Deacons—
Haddad, Gregory
Hill, James A.
Kaiser, Joseph
Macmillan, John
Nasser, Andre P.

INSTITUTIONS LOCATED IN DIOCESE

[A] SEMINARIES.

STATE OF MASSACHUSETTS

METHUEN. *Monastery of St. Basil the Great*, 30 East St., Methuen, 01844. Tel: 978-683-2471. Rev. Fares Al Khlaifat, B.S.O., Dean. Priests 4.

WEST ROXBURY. *Seminary of St. Gregory the Theologian*, 3 VFW Pkwy., 02132. Priests 1.

[B] MONASTERIES AND RESIDENCES FOR PRIESTS AND BROTHERS.

STATE OF MASSACHUSETTS

METHUEN. *Basilian Salvatorian Order*, 30 East St., Methuen, 01844. Tel: 978-683-2471; Fax: 978-794-3452. Rt. Rev. Archimandrite Martin A. Hyatt, B.S.O.; Revs. Lawrence Tumminelli, B.S.O.; Joseph Thomas, B.S.O.; Clement Youssef, B.S.O.

[C] CONVENTS AND RESIDENCES FOR SISTERS.

STATE OF CONNECTICUT

DANBURY. *Community of The Mother of God of Tenderness*, 79 Golden Hill Rd., Danbury, CT 06811-4631. Tel: 203-794-1486; Email: maryanns333@sbcglobal.net. Sr. Mary Ann Socha, C.M.G.T., Pres. Sisters 2.

[D] MISCELLANEOUS.

STATE OF MASSACHUSETTS

METHUEN. *St. Basil's Salvatorian Center*, 30 East St., Methuen, 01844. Tel: 978-683-2959; Fax: 978-794-3379; Email: stbasilcenter@comcast.net; Web: www.saintbasils.org. Rt. Rev. Archimandrite Martin A. Hyatt, B.S.O., Dir.

STATE OF PENNSYLVANIA

WARREN CENTER. *Our Lady of Solitude Cloister & Retreat*, 550 Lake of Meadows Rd., Little Meadows, PA 18830. Fax: 570-395-0235.

RELIGIOUS INSTITUTES OF MEN REPRESENTED IN THE EPARCHY

For further details refer to the corresponding bracketed number in the Religious Institutes of Men or Women section.

[]—*Basilian Chouerite Order* (St. John Monastery, Khonchara, Lebanon)—B.C.O.

[0190]—*Basilian Salvatorian Order* (Holy Saviour Monastery, Sidon, Lebanon)—B.S.O.

An asterisk (*) denotes an organization that has established tax-exempt status directly with the IRS and is not covered by the USCCB Group Ruling.

Diocese of Our Lady of Deliverance

Eparchia Nostrae Dominae Liberationis Novarcensis Syrorum

Most Reverend

MAR BARNABA YOUSIF HABASH

Second Bishop of Our Lady of Deliverance; ordained priest August 31, 1975; ordained Bishop June 11, 2010; installed Bishop of Our Lady of Deliverance Syriac Catholic Diocese in the United States and Canada July 31, 2010. *Mailing and Residential Address: 21 E. 23rd St., NJ 07002-3737.* Tel: 201-455-8151; Fax: 201-455-8152.

Chancery Office: 21 E. 23rd St., Bayonne, NJ 07002-3737. Tel: 201-455-8151; Fax: 201-455-8152.

Web: www.syriaccatholic.us

Email: marbarnaba@yahoo.com

Email: syriac_chancery@yahoo.com

DIOCESE ESTABLISHED NOVEMBER 16, 1995.

Comprises the United States.

STATISTICAL OVERVIEW

Personnel	
Bishop	1
Priests: Diocesan Active in Diocese	13
Number of Diocesan Priests	13
Religious Priests in Diocese	1
Total Priests in Diocese	14
Extern Priests in Diocese	1
Permanent Deacons in Diocese	3
Parishes	
Parishes	9
With Resident Pastor:	
Resident Diocesan Priests	9
Resident Religious Priests	1
Without Resident Pastor:	
Administered by Priests	1
Missions	3
New Parishes Created	1
Educational	
Diocesan Students in Other Seminaries	2
Total Seminarians	2
Catechesis/Religious Education:	
High School Students	123
Elementary Students	300
Total Students under Catholic Instruction	425
Vital Statistics	
Receptions into the Church:	
Infant Baptism Totals	80
Minor Baptism Totals	5
First Communions	118
Confirmations	85
Marriages:	
Catholic	38
Total Marriages	38
Deaths	14
Total Catholic Population	11,857

Former Bishop—Most Rev. MAR EPHREM JOSEPH YOUNAN, ord. Sept. 12, 1971; ord. Bishop of Our Lady of Deliverance Diocese Jan. 7, 1996; installed Feb. 10, 1996; appt. Patriarch of the Syriac Catholic Church of Antioch, Mar Ignatius Yousif III Younan, Lebanon; confirmed Jan. 22, 2009; installed Feb. 15, 2009.

Chancery—

Chancellor—Rev. LUKE A. EDELEN, O.S.B., Mailing and Residential Address: 21 E. 23rd St., Bayonne, 07002-3737. Tel: 201-978-0316; Fax: 201-455-8152; Email: syriac_chancery@yahoo.com.

Episcopal Vicar—Rev. CAESAR RUSSO, S.T.L., M.A., J.C.L., Vicar Gen., Saint Ephrem Syriac Church, 4650 Kernan Blvd. S., Jacksonville, FL 32224. Tel: 904-240-8527; Email: qaisarrusso@gmail.com.

Officialis—Rev. LUKE A. EDELEN, O.S.B., 21 E. 23rd St., Bayonne, 07002-3737. Tel: 201-978-0316; Fax: 201-455-8152.

CLERGY, PARISHES, MISSIONS AND PAROCHIAL SCHOOLS

STATE OF NEW JERSEY

BAYONNE, HUDSON CO.

1—SAINT JOSEPH SYRIAC CATHOLIC CATHEDRAL (2010) Served by the Chancery.
21 E. 23rd St., 07002-3737. Tel: 201-978-0316; Email: syriac_chancery@yahoo.com. Revs. Luke A. Edelen, O.S.B., Rector; Rabee Habash.

2—OUR LADY OF DELIVERANCE PARISH (1986) Served by chancery.
21 E. 23rd St., 07002-4678. Tel: 201-328-7501; Email: olodeliverance@gmail.com. Rev. Nimatullah Muneam Butrus; Mr. Nabil Cherbaka, Parish Council Chair.
Catechesis Religious Program—Students 18.
Worship Site: St. Michael Byzantine Cathedral Chapel, 415 Lackawanna Ave., Woodland Park, 07424.

STATE OF ARIZONA

PHOENIX, SAINTS BEHNAM AND SARAH MISSION (2000)
11001 N 40th St, Phoenix, AZ 85028.
Tel: 480-745-4693; Email: anwar_zomaya@yahoo.com. Rev. Anwar Zomaya, Admin.; Hanodi Ryiad, Head of Council.
Catechesis Religious Program—Ms. Rashil Moma. Students 20.

STATE OF CALIFORNIA

EL CAJON, SAN DIEGO CO., OUR MOTHER OF PERPETUAL HELP CHURCH (1994)
1101 S. Mollison Ave., El Cajon, CA 92020.
Tel: 619-440-5555; Email: syriaccatholicchurchsd@gmail.com. Rev. Msgr. Emad Hanna Al-Shaikh; Subdeacon Dhela Tozy.
Catechesis Religious Program—Deacon Dheia Tozi, D.R.E.; Ms. Aklas Sheai Yassi, D.R.E. Students 120.

LOS ANGELES, LOS ANGELES CO., JESUS SACRED HEART CHURCH (1993)
10837 Collins St., North Hollywood, CA 91601-2009. Cell: 818-318-5858; Email: raad_muoshe@yahoo.com. Rev. Aphram (Raad) Mushe; Deacons Joseph Yaqoob, (Retired); Hanna Nasi, (Retired); Sammon Simon Bakar, Parish Council Chair; Malcom Badrya, Music Min.; Lydia Kassab, Music Min.
Catechesis Religious Program—George Ibrahim Maida, Youth Min. Students 22.

OCEANSIDE, SAN DIEGO CO., SAINT JOSEPH MISSION (2008)
1101 S. Mollison Ave., El Cajon, CA 92020.
Tel: 619-440-5555; Email: msgrhannashaikh@yahoo.com. Rev. Msgr. Emad Hanna Al-Shaikh.
Worship Site: St. Luis Rey R.C. Church.

STATE OF FLORIDA

JACKSONVILLE, DUVAL CO.

1—SAINT EPHREM SYRIAC CHURCH (1986)
4650 Kernan Blvd., S., Jacksonville, FL 32224.
Tel: 248-567-9699; Email: haddadmuntaser@gmail.com. Revs. Caesar Russo, M.A., J.C.L., S.T.L., Admin., (Retired); Muntaser Haddad, Parochial Vicar; Deacon Joseph Al-Saigh.
Catechesis Religious Program—Mr. Pierre Abdmalak, D.R.E.; Mrs. Raina Gabriel, D.R.E. Students 55.

2—OUR LADY OF PEACE SYRIAC CATHOLIC CHURCH (2012)
5854 University Blvd. W., Jacksonville, FL 32216.
Tel: 904-536-7509; Fax: 904-356-9122; Email: abunatalaat@yahoo.com. Rev. Talat Yazji, Admin.
Legal Name: Our Lady of Peace Syriac Catholic Church Incorporated
Catechesis Religious Program—Habsch Zaidan, D.R.E. Students 88.

STATE OF ILLINOIS

NORTHBROOK, COOK CO., SAINT MARY VIRGIN IMMACULATE MISSION (1999) Metropolitan Chicago area. Served by Chancery personnel.

STATE OF MASSACHUSETTS

NEWTON, MIDDLESEX CO., OUR LADY OF MESOPOTAMIA MISSION (2009) Closed. For inquiries for parish records contact the chancery.

WORCESTER, WORCESTER CO., ST. IGNATIUS OF ANTIOCH SYRIAC CATHOLIC MISSION
Worcester, MA 01601. Tel: 201-455-8151; Email: syriac_chancery@yahoo.com.

STATE OF MICHIGAN

FARMINGTON HILLS, OAKLAND CO., SAINT TOMA CHURCH (1986)
25600 Drake Rd., Farmington Hills, MI 48335.
Tel: 818-913-8156; Email: andrwoshabash@yahoo.com. Rev. Andrwos Habash; Mr. Charles Halabu, Parish Council Chair.
Catechesis Religious Program—Ms. Luna Sequeira, D.R.E. Students 35.

LANSING, INGHAM CO., ST. ISAAC OF NINEVEH SYRIAC CATHOLIC CHURCH
1314 Ballard St., Lansing, MI 48906.
Tel: 818-913-8156; Email: andrwoshabash@yahoo.com. Rev. Andrwos Habash.

TROY, OAKLAND CO., CHRIST THE KING CHURCH (2009)
2300 John R. Rd., Troy, MI 48083. Tel: 248-818-2886; Fax: 248-478-9074; Email: shabash466@gmail.com. Revs. Safaa Habash; Fadi Matlob, Parochial Vicar; Mr. Adwar Bunni, Parish Council Chair.
Catechesis Religious Program—Mrs. Heather Farjo, D.R.E.; Mr. Sadeer Farjo, D.R.E. Students 65.

STATE OF PENNSYLVANIA

ALLENTOWN, LEHIGH CO., OUR LADY OF MERCY PARISH

(2002) Closed. For inquiries for parish records contact the chancery.

STATE OF RHODE ISLAND

RHODE ISLAND, SAINT JAMES BROTHER OF THE LORD MISSION
21 E. 23rd St., 07002-3737. Tel: 201-455-8151; Fax: 201-455-8152. Served by the chancery.

On Leave:
Revs.—
Shoni, Bassim
Taponi, Selwan Sulaiman.

Retired:

Rt. Rev. Chorbishop—
Azizo, Toma B., (Retired).

An asterisk (*) denotes an organization that has established tax-exempt status directly with the IRS and is not covered by the USCCB Group Ruling.

Eparchy of Our Lady of Lebanon of Los Angeles

Most Reverend

A. ELIAS ZAIDAN

Bishop of the Eparchy of Our Lady of Lebanon of Los Angeles; ordained July 20, 1986; appointed Bishop of Our Lady of Lebanon of Los Angeles July 10, 2013; consecrated September 28, 2013.

Pastoral Center: 1021 S. 10th St., St. Louis, MO 63104. Tel: 314-231-1021; Fax: 314-231-1316.

Web: www.eparchy.org

Email: jamileh@eparchy.org

Comprises the States of Ohio, West Virginia, Illinois, Alabama, Michigan, Minnesota, Missouri, Texas, Utah, Arizona, Nevada, Oregon, California, Alaska, Hawaii, Indiana, Kentucky, Tennessee, Mississippi, Wisconsin, Iowa, Arkansas, Louisiana, North Dakota, South Dakota, Kansas, Oklahoma, Nebraska, Montana, Wyoming, Colorado, New Mexico, Idaho and Washington.

STATISTICAL OVERVIEW

Personnel	
Bishop	1
Abbots	1
Priests: Diocesan Active in Diocese	34
Priests: Diocesan Active Outside Diocese	2
Priests: Retired, Sick or Absent	6
Number of Diocesan Priests	42
Religious Priests in Diocese	20
Total Priests in Diocese	62
Ordinations:	
Diocesan Priests	2
Transitional Deacons	2
Permanent Deacons in Diocese	16
Total Brothers	1
Total Sisters	9
Parishes	
Parishes	34
With Resident Pastor:	
Resident Diocesan Priests	23
Resident Religious Priests	9
Missions	8
Professional Ministry Personnel:	
Brothers	1
Sisters	9
Welfare	
Homes for the Aged	1
Total Assisted	100
Educational	
Diocesan Students in Other Seminaries	7
Total Seminarians	7
Catechesis/Religious Education:	
High School Students	195
Elementary Students	946
Total Students under Catholic Instruction	1,148
Vital Statistics	
Receptions into the Church:	
Infant Baptism Totals	253
Minor Baptism Totals	12
Adult Baptism Totals	24
Received into Full Communion	80
First Communions	318
Confirmations	317
Marriages:	
Catholic	105
Interfaith	35
Total Marriages	140
Deaths	197
Total Catholic Population	46,700

Former Bishop—Most Revs. JOHN GEORGE CHEDID, D.D., ord. Dec. 21, 1951; appt. Titular Bishop of Callinicum and Auxiliary Bishop of St. Maron of Brooklyn, Oct. 28, 1980; cons. Jan. 25, 1981; appt. Bishop of Our Lady of Lebanon of Los Angeles, Feb. 19, 1994; retired Dec. 5, 2000; died March 21, 2012.; ROBERT J. SHAHEEN, ord. May 2, 1964; appt. Dec. 5, 2000; cons. Feb. 15, 2001; retired July 10, 2013; died Aug. 9, 2017.

Pastoral Center—Tel: 314-231-1021 (Office); Fax: 314-231-1316. Deacon LOUIS PETERS, Chancellor; MRS. JAMILEH KOURY, Chief Fiscal Officer; Rev. ALBERT CONSTANTINE, Vice Chancellor.

College of Consultors—Chorbishops RICHARD D. SAAD; ANTHONY SPINOSA; Rev. Msgrs. PETER KARAM; DONALD SAWYER; Chorbishop SHARBEL MAROUN; Rev. ELIAS SLEIMAN, M.L.M.

Commission for Lebanon & The Middle East—Rev. TOUFIC M. NASR.

Protosyncellus—Chorbishop RICHARD D. SAAD.

Tribunal—

Defender of the Bond—Rev. JOHN CARONAN, S.T.L., C.F.M.

Judicial Vicar—Chorbishop WILLIAM LESER, S.T.B.

Moderator of the Tribunal—Most Rev. A. ELIAS ZAIDAN.

Procurator/Advocate—Revs. RAMSINE HAGE-MOUSSA, Petitioner; ELIAS SLEIMAN, M.L.M., Respondent.

Promoter of Justice—Rev. JOHN CARONAN, S.T.L., C.F.M.

Assessor—IVETTE JACKSON; Rev. ALBERT CONSTANTINE.

Notaries—IVETTE JACKSON; MRS. JAMILEH KOURY.

Personal Secretary—Rev. MILAD T. YAGHI, M.L.M.

Eparchial Pastoral Council—Chorbishop MICHAEL J. KAIL.

Eparchial Newsletter—The Maronite Voice Chorbishop JOHN FARIS, St. Anthony, 4611 Sadler Rd., Glen Allen, VA 23060. Tel: 804-762-4301; Fax: 804-273-9914; Email: john.jd@gmail.com; Rev. PIERRE BASSIL, Consultor.

Office for Immigration—Chorbishop FAOUZI ELIA.

Office of Communications—Rev. Msgr. ANTOINE BAKH; Rev. RAMSINE HAGE-MOUSSA.

Office of Inter-faith/Ecumenical Affairs—Rev. ANDRE MAHANNA.

Office of Liturgy—Chorbishop MICHAEL J. KAIL.

Office of Ministries—Rev. ROBY ZIBARA.

Office of Priestly Vocations—Rev. GARY GEORGE, C.Ss. R.

Office of Religious Education—Sr. MARTHA MECHLEB.

Office of Youth Ministries—Rev. GARY GEORGE, C.Ss.R.

Master of Ceremonies—Rev. MILAD T. YAGHI, M.L.M.

Office of Evangelization & Outreach—Chorbishop SHARBEL MAROUN.

Office of Young Adult Ministry—Rev. TONY MASSAD.

Presbyteral Council—Chorbishop RICHARD D. SAAD, Ex Officio; Revs. JOHN NAHAL; ELIAS SLEIMAN, M.L.M., Ex Officio; Rev. Msgr. PETER KARAM; Rev. TONY MASSAD; Rev. Msgr. DONALD SAWYER, D.Min.; Rev. TOUFIC M. NASR; Chorbishops SHARBEL MAROUN; ANTHONY SPINOSA; Rev. GEORGE HAJJ; Rev. Msgr. ANTOINE BAKH.

Pro-Life & Family Life Office—MR. ALBERTO TOHME; MS. LYNN TOHME.

Eparchial App and Facebook—Rev. JOHN NAHAL.

Properties Owned—

Father Tobia Retirement Home—North Jackson, OH.

Maronite Catholic Pastoral Center—St. Louis, MO.

Protopresbyters—Chorbishops SHARBEL MAROUN, Mid-America Region; ANTHONY SPINOSA, Midwest Region; Rev. ELIAS SLEIMAN, M.L.M., Southwest Region; Rev. Msgr. DONALD SAWYER, D.Min., Southern Region.

Spiritual Director for the National Apostolate of Maronites—Rev. ALBERT CONSTANTINE.

Order of St. Sharbel—Eparchy of Our Lady of Lebanon, 1021 S. 10th St., St. Louis, 63104. Rev. Msgr. PETER AZAR, Spiritual Dir.; MS. BERNADETTE SHALHOUB, Natl. Pres.; MS. MARY MILTON, Vice Pres.

Victim Assistance Coordinator—MS. LAURA KAHWAJI.

Office of Protection of Minors—Rev. Msgr. PETER KARAM, Dir., 7800 Brookside Rd., Independence, OH 44131. Tel: 216-520-5081; Fax: 216-524-2659; Web: www.eparchy.org.

Personnel Board—Chorbishop ANTHONY SPINOSA; Rev. Msgr. DONALD SAWYER, D.Min.; Chorbishop SHARBEL MAROUN; Rev. Msgr. PETER KARAM; Rev. ELIAS SLEIMAN, M.L.M.

Liturgical Music Commission—Chorbishop ALFRED BADAWI.

Eparchial Newsletter Consulter—Rev. PIERRE BASSIL.

Technology—Rev. JOHN NAHAL.

Office of Building Oversight—Chorbishop FAOUZI ELIA.

Legal Counsel Board—Rev. Msgr. PETER KARAM.

Noursat—Chorbishop SHARBEL MAROUN.

Catholic Schools Assistance Fund Lebanon—Rev. CHARLES H. KHACHAN, M.L.M.

Inter-Eparchial History Committee—Rev. GEORGE HAJJ.

Caritas Lebanon—Rev. JOHN NAHAL, M.L.M.

Office for the Protection of Minors—Rev. Msgr. PETER KARAM.

Project Roots—Rev. CHARLES H. KHACHAN, M.L.M.

Continuing Education for Clergy—Rev. Msgr. PETER KARAM.

Priests' Retirement Fund—Chorbishops FAOUZI ELIA; ANTHONY SPINOSA; Rev. Msgr. JIBRAN BOUMERHI; Rev. ALBERT CONSTANTINE.

Archivist—RANDA HAKIM.

Board of Pastors—Chorbishop WILLIAM LESER, S.T.B.; Rev. Msgr. PETER KARAM; Rev. MILAD T. YAGHI, M.L.M.

Vicar for Clergy—Rev. Msgr. PETER KARAM.

Eparchial Stewardship—MR. JOHN KUREY.

Office of Caregivers—Rev. Msgr. DONALD SAWYER, D.Min.

Office of Our Lady of Lebanon Seminary Alumni—Revs. GEORGE HAJJ; CHRISTOPHER FABRE.

CLERGY, PARISHES, MISSIONS AND PAROCHIAL SCHOOLS

STATE OF CALIFORNIA

CARMICHAEL, SACRAMENTO CO., OUR LADY OF THE ROSARY MISSION (2011)
6811 Fair Oaks Blvd., Carmichael, CA 95608.
Tel: 916-546-8973; Tel: 916-483-6691; Email: ghattaskhoury@sbcglobal.net. Rev. Ghattas Khoury; Christian Rogers, D.R.E.
Mission—St. Sharbel Maronite Catholic Mission, 4981 E Eight Mile Rd, Stockton, San Joaquin Co. CA 95212.

LOS ANGELES, LOS ANGELES CO., OUR LADY OF MT. LEBANON-ST. PETER MARONITE CATHOLIC CATHEDRAL (1923)
333 S. San Vicente Blvd., Los Angeles, CA 90048.
Tel: 310-275-6634; Fax: 310-858-0856; Email: ourladymtlebanon@yahoo.com; Email: olmlcathedral@yahoo.com. Most Rev. Abdallah E. Zaidan; Revs. Elias Sleiman, M.L.M., Rector; Albert Constantine; Deacon Mikael Zaarour.
Catechesis Religious Program—Students 45.

MILLBRAE, SAN MATEO CO., OUR LADY OF LEBANON MARONITE CATHOLIC CHURCH (1979) [JC]
Mailing Address: 600 El Camino Real, Millbrae, CA 94030. Tel: 650-741-6342; Email: ourladyol.sf@gmail.com; Web: www.olol-sf.org. Rev. Gary George, C.Ss.R.; Subdeacon Tony Boukhalil, Liturgy Dir.
Catechesis Religious Program—Tel: 650-741-6342. Subdeacon Fadi Bazouzi, D.R.E. Students 50.

ORANGE, ORANGE CO., ST. JOHN MARON MARONITE CATHOLIC CHURCH (1988)
Mailing Address: 300 S. Flower St., Orange, CA 92868. Tel: 714-940-0009; Fax: 714-594-4036; Email: fr.bakh@johnmaron.org; Web: www.stjohnmaronchurch.org. Rev. Msgr. Antoine Bakh; Subdeacon Charles Doche.
Res.: 601 N. Woods, Fullerton, CA 92832-1027.
Catechesis Religious Program—

RIVERSIDE, RIVERSIDE CO., ST. JOSEPH MARONITE CATHOLIC MISSION
3870 Castleman St., Riverside, CA 92503.
Tel: 951-406-1406; Email: StJosephMCC2017@gmail.com. Rev. Msgr. Antoine Bakh, Admin.

SAN DIEGO, SAN DIEGO CO., ST. EPHREM MARONITE CATHOLIC CHURCH (1989) [CEM]
750 Medford St., El Cajon, CA 92020.
Tel: 619-337-1350; Email: stephrem@sbcglobal.net; Web: www.stephremchurch.com. Rev. Toufic M. Nasr; Deacon Georges Ghosn.
Catechesis Religious Program—Tel: 619-508-5401; Email: ghosn@att.net. Students 22.

SIMI VALLEY, VENTURA CO., SAINTS PETER AND PAUL MARONITE CATHOLIC CHURCH (2002)
1059 Ashland, Simi Valley, CA 93065.
Tel: 805-422-8524; Email: sppmaronite@gmail.com; Web: www.sppmission.org. Rev. Joe Daccache.
Catechesis Religious Program—

WEST COVINA, LOS ANGELES CO., ST. JUDE MARONITE CATHOLIC CHURCH (1999)
1437 W. Badillo St., West Covina, CA 91790.
Tel: 626-962-0222; Email: hramsine@hotmail.com. Rev. Ramsine Hage-Moussa; Subdeacons Pierre El-Khoury; George Haddad.
Catechesis Religious Program—Tel: 310-275-6634. Students 115.

STATE OF ALABAMA

BIRMINGHAM, JEFFERSON CO., ST. ELIAS MARONITE CATHOLIC CHURCH (1910)
836 Eighth St. S., Birmingham, AL 35205-4567.
Tel: 205-251-5057; Email: eliasbham@aol.com; Web: www.stelias.org. Chorbishop Richard D. Saad; Rev. Rami Razzouk.
Catechesis Religious Program—Beverly Kimes, D.R.E.; Dora Bolus, D.R.E.

STATE OF ARIZONA

PHOENIX, MARICOPA CO., ST. JOSEPH MARONITE CATHOLIC CHURCH (1992)
5406 E. Virginia Ave., Phoenix, AZ 85008.
Tel: 602-667-3280; Email: stjosephmaronitechurch@gmail.com; Web: www.stjosephphoenix.org. Rev. Wissam Akiki.
Catechesis Religious Program—Mrs. Manal Akiki, D.R.E. Students 59.
Mission—Maronite Catholic Mission of Tuscan.

STATE OF COLORADO

LAKEWOOD, JEFFERSON CO, ST. RAFKA MARONITE CATHOLIC CHURCH (2007)
2301 Wadsworth Blvd., Lakewood, CO 80214.
Tel: 720-833-0354; Fax: 720-833-0390; Email: infostrafka@gmail.com; Web: StRafkaDenver.org. Rev. Andre Mahanna.
Catechesis Religious Program—

STATE OF ILLINOIS

LOMBARD, DUPAGE CO., OUR LADY OF LEBANON MARONITE CATHOLIC CHURCH (1952)
950 N. Grace St., Lombard, IL 60148.
Tel: 630-932-9640; Web: www.ollchicago.org. Rev. Pierre El Khoury, M.L.M.; Deacon John Sfire; Subdeacon Thomas Podraza.
Catechesis Religious Program—

PEORIA, PEORIA CO., ST. SHARBEL MARONITE CATHOLIC CHURCH (1973)
2920 W. Scenic Dr., Peoria, IL 61615.
Tel: 309-688-5555; Email: stsharbel1@gmail.com. Mailing Address: 2914 W. Scenic Dr., Peoria, IL 61615. Chorbishop Faouzi Elia; Rev. Bechara Awada; Deacons James Siedlecki; George Geagea; Subdeacon George Romanos.
Catechesis Religious Program—

STATE OF KENTUCKY

LOUISVILLE, JEFFERSON CO., MARONITE CATHOLIC COMMUNITY OF LOUISVILLE (1910) Closed.

STATE OF LOUISIANA

1—MARONITE COMMUNITY OF LOUISIANA, Closed. For inquiries for parish records contact the chancery.

BATON ROUGE, EAST BATON ROUGE PARISH, ST. SHARBEL MARONITE CATHOLIC MISSION
4981 E. Eight Mile Rd., Stockton, CA 95212. Cell: 602-680-8749; Email: jamileh@eparchy.org. Rev. Gary George, C.Ss.R., Admin., Tel: 314-363-3300.

LAFAYETTE, CONTRA COSTA PARISH, MARONITE CATHOLIC COMMUNITY, Closed. For inquiries for parish records contact the chancery.

LAKE CHARLES, CALCASIEU PARISH, MARONITE CATHOLIC COMMUNITY, Closed. For inquiries for parish records contact the chancery.

NEW ORLEANS, ORLEANS PARISH, MARONITE CATHOLIC COMMUNITY, Closed. For inquiries for parish records contact the chancery.

STATE OF MICHIGAN

CLINTON TOWNSHIP, MACOMB CO., ST. SHARBEL MARONITE CATHOLIC CHURCH (1987)
43888 Hayes Rd., Clinton Township, MI 48038.
Tel: 586-630-0002; Email: stsharbelmichigan@gmail.com; Web: www.stsharbelmichigan. Chorbishop Alfred Badawi; Subdeacon Michael Magyar.
Catechesis Religious Program—Stacy Saker, Youth Min.; Michael Saba, Youth Min. Students 113.

DETROIT, WAYNE CO., ST. MARON MARONITE CATHOLIC CHURCH (1910) [CEM]
11466 Kercheval, Detroit, MI 48214.
Tel: 313-824-0196; Email: saintmarondetroit@gmail.com. Rev. Roby Zibara.
Catechesis Religious Program—

FLINT, GENESEE CO., OUR LADY OF LEBANON MARONITE CATHOLIC CHURCH (1973)
4133 Calkins Rd., Flint, MI 48532. Tel: 810-733-1259 ; Email: olol-flint@sbcglobal.net. Rev. Pierre Bassil; Deacon Martin J. Rachid; Subdeacons Earl Matte; Joseph Pavlovich.
Catechesis Religious Program—

LIVONIA, MACOMB CO., ST. RAFKA MARONITE CATHOLIC CHURCH (2003)
Mailing Address: 32765 Lyndon Ave., Livonia, MI 48154. Tel: 734-525-2828; Email: st.rafkachurch@gmail.com; Web: www.saintrafkamichigan.com. Rev. Tony Massad.
Catechesis Religious Program—Madlein Kobrossi, D.R.E. Students 40.

STATE OF MINNESOTA

MINNEAPOLIS, HENNEPIN CO.
1—ST. MARON MARONITE CATHOLIC CHURCH (1903) [CEM] [JC]
602 University Ave., N.E., Minneapolis, MN 55413.
Tel: 612-379-2758; Web: www.stmaron.com. Chorbishop Sharbel Maroun.
Catechesis Religious Program—Tel: 651-341-3337. Jaonnie Moses, D.R.E. Students 95.
2—ST. SHARBEL MARONITE CATHOLIC MISSION - MILWAUKEE
4816 7th Ave, Kenosha, WI 53140. Tel: 619-654-1888 ; Email: pmarienabil@gmail.com. Rev. Nabil Mouannes, Admin.

MENDOTA HEIGHTS, DAKOTA CO., HOLY FAMILY MARONITE CATHOLIC CHURCH (1918) [CEM]
1960 Lexington Ave. S., Mendota Heights, MN 55118. Tel: 651-291-1116; Email: emanuelng@hotmail.com. Rev. Emmanuel Makhle-Ghorr.
Rectory—849 Mendakota Ct., Mendota Heights, MN 55120. Tel: 651-452-1931; Fax: 651-222-3033; Email: info@holyfamilymaronitechurch.org; Web: www.holyfamilymaronitechurch.org.
Catechesis Religious Program—

STATE OF MISSOURI

SAINT LOUIS, ST. LOUIS CITY CO., ST. RAYMOND MARONITE CATHOLIC CATHEDRAL (1913)
931 Lebanon Dr., 63104. Tel: 314-621-0056; Email: rector@straymond-mc.org. Rev. John Nahal, M.L.M., Rector; Deacon Louis Peters, Admin.; Subdeacons Anthony Simon; David Wahby.
Catechesis Religious Program—

STATE OF NEVADA

LAS VEGAS, CLARK CO., ST. SHARBEL MARONITE CATHOLIC MISSION (1991)
10325 Rancho Distino Rd., Las Vegas, NV 89183.
Tel: 702-616-6902; Fax: 702-616-4032; Email: stsharbel.lv@gmail.com; Web: www.stsharbellasvegas.org. Rev. Nadim Abou Zeid, M.L.M., Admin.
Catechesis Religious Program—Danelle Marek, D.R.E.

STATE OF OKLAHOMA

NORMAN, CLEVELAND CO., OUR LADY OF LEBANON MARONITE MISSION
Mailing Address: 500 Alameda, Norman, OK 73071.
Tel: 405-321-3097; Email: marwanabinadder@gmail.com. Rev. Marnan Abinader, M.L.M.

TULSA, TULSA CO., ST. THERESE OF THE CHILD JESUS MARONITE CATHOLIC CHURCH (1998)
8315 S. 107th Ave., E., Tulsa, OK 74133.
Tel: 918-872-7400; Email: MARWANABINADDER@GMAIL.COM. Rev. Marnan Abinader, M.L.M.
Rectory—8311 S. 107th Ave., E., Tulsa, OK 74133. Email: bello1975@aol.com; Web: www.sainttherese.org.
Catechesis Religious Program—

STATE OF OHIO

CINCINNATI, HAMILTON CO., ST. ANTHONY OF PADUA MARONITE CATHOLIC CHURCH (1910) [CEM] [JC]
2530 Victory Pkwy., Cincinnati, OH 45206.
Tel: 513-961-0120; Email: saintanthonycincinnati@gmail.com; Web: www.staparish.org. Rev. George Hajj; Subdeacons Tom Simon; Donald George; Mark Floyd; Mrs. Ashley Farris, Sec.
Catechesis Religious Program—Ruda Talamas, D.R.E.

CLEVELAND, CUYAHOGA CO., ST. MARON MARONITE CATHOLIC CHURCH (1915) [JC]
7800 Brookside Rd., Independence, OH 44131.
Tel: 216-520-5081; Email: saintmaroncleveland@gmail.com; Web: www.saintmaron-clev.org. Rev. Msgr. Peter Karam; Rev. Elias Yazbeck; Deacon George M. Khoury; Subdeacons Lattouf Lattouf; Ghazi Faddoul; Georges Faddoul; Bechara Daher.
Church: 1245 Carnegie, Cleveland, OH 44115.
Catechesis Religious Program—Elias Kanaan, D.R.E. Students 208.

DAYTON, MONTGOMERY CO.
1—SAINT IGNATIUS OF ANTIOCH MARONITE CATHOLIC CHURCH (1993) [JC]
5915 Springboro Pike, Dayton, OH 45449.
Tel: 937-428-0372; Email: info@stiparish.org; Web: Stiparish.org. Rev. Alexander Harb, Parochial Vicar.
Catechesis Religious Program—William Thomas, D.R.E.; Laura Thomas, D.R.E.
2—OUR LADY OF LEBANON MARONITE CATHOLIC MISSION (2003)
893 Hamlet, Columbus, OH 43201-3536.
Tel: 818-620-0100. Most Rev. A. Elias Zaidan, Contact Person.

FAIRLAWN, SUMMIT CO., OUR LADY OF THE CEDARS OF MT. LEBANON MARONITE CATHOLIC CHURCH (1937)
507 S. Cleveland-Massillon Rd., Fairlawn, OH 44333-3019. Tel: 330-666-3598; Email: ourladyofthecedarschurch@gmail.com; Web: www.ourladyofthecedarschurch.org. Rev. Msgr. William Bonczewski; Deacons Robert Foster; Tom Maroon.
Catechesis Religious Program—

TOLEDO, LUCAS CO., MARONITE CATHOLIC COMMUNITY (1999) Closed.

YOUNGSTOWN, MAHONING CO., ST. MARON MARONITE CATHOLIC CHURCH (1902)
1555 S. Meridian Rd., Youngstown, OH 44511-1199.
Tel: 330-792-2371; Fax: 330-792-3026; Email: parishoffice@stmaronyoungstown.org; Web: www.stmaronyoungstown.org. Chorbishop Michael J. Kail; Deacon William George; Subdeacons James Essad; Albert Dohar.
Catechesis Religious Program—Tel: 330-538-9822; Email: srjinane@hotmail.com. Sr. Jinane Farah, D.R.E.

STATE OF OREGON

PORTLAND, MULTNOMAH CO., SAINT SHARBEL MARONITE CATHOLIC CHURCH (1970)
1804 S.E. 16th Ave., Portland, OR 97214.
Tel: 503-231-3853; Email: stsharbelpdx@gmail.com. Rev. Christopher Faber, Admin.; Deacons Wadih Kaldawi; Antoine Karam.
Catechesis Religious Program—Email: n.

redmond@comcast.net. Nadia Redmond, D.R.E., Tel: 503-671-0440.

STATE OF TEXAS

AUSTIN, TRAVIS CO., OUR LADY'S MARONITE PARISH (1982)
1320 E. 51st St., Austin, TX 78723.
Tel: 512-458-3693; Fax: 512-451-9554; Email: email@ourladysmaronite.org; Web: www.ourladysmaronite.org. Rev. Msgr. Donald J. Sawyer, D.Mim.; Deacons Michael Cunningham; Guy Helou.
Catechesis Religious Program—

EL PASO, EL PASO CO., ST. SHARBEL MARONITE CATHOLIC MISSION (1997)
851 Thorn Ave., El Paso, TX 79912.
Tel: 330-509-0098; Email: stsharbelelpaso@gmail.com; Web: www.stsharbelelpaso.org. Mailing Address: 3617 Breckenridge Dr., El Paso, TX 79936. Rev. Ronald W. Eid, Admin.

HOUSTON, HARRIS CO., OUR LADY OF THE CEDARS MARONITE CATHOLIC CHURCH (1990) [JC]
11935 Bellfort Village Dr., Houston, TX 77031.
Tel: 281-568-6800; Email: parish@olchouston.org; Web: www.ourladyofthecedars.net. Revs. Milad T. Yaghi, M.L.M.; Edward Hanna, M.L.M.
Catechesis Religious Program—Rev. Nabil Joubran, D.R.E.

LEWISVILLE, DENTON CO., OUR LADY OF LEBANON MARONITE CATHOLIC CHURCH (1990)
719 University Pl., Lewisville, TX 75067.
Tel: 972-436-7617; Email: ladyofl719@gmail.com. Rev. Assaad El Basha, M.L.M.
Catechesis Religious Program—Tel: 817-491-0763; Email: smarincel001@tx.rr.com. Sue Marincel, D.R.E. Students 66.

SAN ANTONIO, BEXAR CO., ST. GEORGE MARONITE CATHOLIC CHURCH (1925) [JC] (Maronite)
6070 Babcock Rd., San Antonio, TX 78240.
Tel: 210-690-9569; Fax: 210-690-5093; Email: stgeorgemaronitechurch@gmail.com. Rev. Charles H. Khachan, M.L.M.
Catechesis Religious Program—

STATE OF UTAH

MURRAY, SALT LAKE CO., SAINT JUDE MARONITE CATHOLIC CHURCH (1975)
4893 Wasatch St., Murray, UT 84107.
Tel: 801-268-2820; Email: saintjudemaronite@gmail.com. Rev. Msgr. Jibran BouMerhi; Subdeacon Athony Allam.
Church: 4900 Wasatch St., Murray, UT 84107.
Catechesis Religious Program—Sherry Twomey, D.R.E.

STATE OF WEST VIRGINIA

WHEELING, OHIO CO., OUR LADY OF LEBANON MARONITE CATHOLIC CHURCH (1906)
2216 Eoff St., Wheeling, WV 26003.
Tel: 304-233-1688; Email: ololwv@comcast.net. Rev. Msgr. Bakhos Chidiac.
Catechesis Religious Program—Lou Khoury, D.R.E. Students 5.

STATE OF WASHINGTON

SEATTLE, KING CO., ST. JOSEPH MARONITE CATHOLIC MISSION (2001)
Pastoral Center, 3870 Castleman St, Riverside, CA 92503. Tel: 951-406-1406; Email: padreakiki@hotmail.com. Rev. Freiha Akiki, Admin.
Catechesis Religious Program—

Special Assignment:
Revs.—
Constantin, Rodrigue, Washington, D.C.
Elkhoury, Armando, Our Lady of Lebanon Seminary, Washington, D.C.
Fisher, David, Studying in Rome/pursuing his S.T.D.; Disability Leave- Philadelphia, PA
Kimes, John Paul, Rome, Italy. Congregation for the Doctrine of the Faith, Vatican City, Rome.
Salim, Anthony, Washington, DC. Tel: 508-586-1428; Fax: 508-587-8139. P.O. Box 2567, Brockton, MA 02305-2567. St. Joseph Church, St. Olean, NY.

Retired:
Rev. Msgrs.—
Kayrouz, Victor, (Retired)
Michael, Kenneth, (Retired)
Very Rev.—
Decker, W. Jonathan, M.M.J.M.J., (Retired).

INSTITUTIONS LOCATED IN DIOCESE

[A] MONASTERIES AND RESIDENCES OF PRIESTS AND BROTHERS

LOS ANGELES. *The Congregation of Maronite Lebanese Missionaries*, 333 S. San Vicente Blvd., Los Angeles, CA 90048. Tel: 310-275-6634;
Fax: 310-858-0856; Email: olmlcathedral@yahoo.com. Rev. Elias Sleiman, M.L.M.

ANN ARBOR. *Maronite Order of the Blessed Virgin Mary*, 4405 Earhart Rd., Ann Arbor, MI 48105.
Tel: 734-662-4822; Fax: 734-662-4822; Email: pilotjohnny@hotmail.com. Revs. John Tayar, Supr.; Roger Chekri, Dir.; Joseph Khalil, O.M.M., Dir.; Nabil Habchi, O.M.M., Treas.; Paul Tarabay, O.M.M., Sec. Total in Residence 3.

HOUSTON. *The Congregation of Maronite Lebanese Missionaries* (1865) Our Lady of the Cedars, 11935 Bellfort Village, Houston, TX 77031.
Tel: 281-568-6800; Fax: 281-564-6961; Email: frmilad@usa.com. Revs. Pierre El Khoury, M.L.M.; Milad T. Yaghi, M.L.M.; Ramsine Hage-Moussa, M.L.M.; Assaad El Basha, M.L.M.; Elias Sleiman, M.L.M., Supr.; Charles H. Khachan, M.L.M.; Nadim Abou Zeid, M.L.M.; Edward Hanna, M.L.M.; Marwan Abi Nader, M.L.M.

PORTLAND. *Sacred Heart Maronite Monastery* Maronite Monks of Jesus, Mary & Joseph. 3880 N.W. 171 Pl., Beaverton, OR 97006. Tel: 503-690-4425;
Fax: 503-533-8524; Email: kasheesho@frontier.com; Web: maronitemonastery.com. Revs. W. Jonathan Decker, M.M.J.M.J., Abbot; Anthony J. Alles, M.M.J.M.J., J.C.L., Subprior; Subdeacon John M. Morgan, M.M.J.M.J., Novice Master; Bros. Daniel Harris, M.M.J.M.J.; Raphael T. Lefvere, M.M.J.M.J.

[B] CONVENTS AND RESIDENCES FOR SISTERS

NORTH JACKSON. *Antonine Maronite Sisters of Youngstown, Inc.*, 2691 N. Lipkey Rd., North Jackson, OH 44451. Tel: 330-538-2567;
Tel: 330-538-9822; Fax: 330-538-9820; Email: anto9srs@aol.com; Web: www.antoninesisters.com. Sr. Jinane Farah, Supr. Sisters 6. *Antonine Sisters Adult Day Care, Inc.*, 2675 N. Lipkey Rd., North Jackson, OH 44451. Tel: 330-538-9822;
Fax: 330-538-9820; Email: anto9srs@aol.com; Web: www.antoninevillage.org. Sr. Jinane Farah, Exec. Total Staff 14; Total Assisted 105.
Antonine Village, 2675 N. Lipkey Rd., North Jackson, OH 44451. Tel: 330-538-9822;
Fax: 330-538-9820; Web: anto9srseantoninevillage.org; Web: www.antoninevillage.org. Sr. Jinane Farah, Exex.

[C] NATIONAL SHRINES

NORTH JACKSON. *Basilica & National Shrine of Our Lady of Lebanon*, 2759 N. Lipkey Rd., North Jackson, OH 44451. Tel: 330-538-3351;
Fax: 330-538-0455; Email: office@ourladyoflebanonshrine.com; Web: www.ourladyoflebanonshrine.com. Chorbishop Anthony Spinosa, Rector.

[D] RELIGIOUS COMMUNITIES OF MEN

PORTLAND. *Oblates of Jesus, Mary & Joseph*, Maronite Monks of Jesus, Mary & Joseph, 3880 N.W. 171 Pl., Beaverton, OR 97006. Tel: 503-690-4425;
Fax: 503-533-8524; Email: kasheesho@frontier.com. Very Rev. W. Jonathan Decker, M.M.J.M.J., Prior, (Retired); Rev. Anthony J. Alles, M.M.J.M.J., J.C.L., Subprior; Subdeacon John M. Morgan, M.-M.J.M.J., Novice Master; Bros. Daniel Harris, M.-M.J.M.J.; Raphael T. Lefvere, M.M.J.M.J.

[E] RESIDENCES FOR CLERGY

NORTH JACKSON. *Father Tobia Retirement Home*, 2759 N. Lipkey Rd., North Jackson, OH 44451.
Tel: 330-538-3351; Fax: 330-538-0455; Email: office@ourladyoflebanonshrine.com; Web: www.ourladyoflebanonshrine.com. Chorbishop Anthony Spinosa, Rector & Protopresbyter.

[F] MISCELLANEOUS

NORTH JACKSON. *Antonine Therapy Center* (2015) 2675 N. Lipkey Rd., North Jackson, OH 44451.
Tel: 330-538-2517; Email: anto9srs@aol.com. Sr. Jinane Farah, Supr.

SAINT LOUIS. *Bishop's Charities*, 1021 S. 10th St., 63104. Tel: 314-231-1021; Fax: 314-231-1316; Email: jamileh@eparchy.org. Most Rev. A. Elias Zaidan, Chm.
Caritas Lebanon, 1021 S. 10th St., 63104.
Tel: 314-231-1021; Fax: 314-231-1316; Email: jamileh@eparchy.org. Rev. John Nahal, M.L.M., Contact Person.
Catholic School Assistance Fund, 1021 S. 10th St., 63104. Tel: 314-231-1021; Fax: 314-231-1316; Email: jamileh@eparchy.org; Web: www.eparchy.org. Most Rev. A. Elias Zaidan.
Eparchial Endowments, 1021 S. 10th St., 63104.
Tel: 314-231-1021; Fax: 314-231-1316; Email: jamileh@eparchy.org. Most Rev. A. Elias Zaidan, Chm.
St. Ephrem Maronite Cath Ch El Cajon Real Estate Trust, 1021 S. 10th St., 63104. Tel: 314-231-1021; Email: jamileh@eparchy.org. Most Rev. A. Elias Zaidan, Trustee.
St. George Maronite Catholic Church-San Antonio Real Estate Trust, 1021 S. 10th St., 63104.
Tel: 314-231-1021; Email: jamileh@eparchy.org. Most Rev. A. Elias Zaidan, Trustee.
Holy Family Maronite Catholic Church-St. Paul, MN Real Estate Trust, 1021 S. 10th St., 63104.
Tel: 314-231-1021; Email: mdenny@usamronite.org. Most Rev. A. Elias Zaidan, Trustee.
St. John Maron Maronite Catholic Church-Orange Real Estate Trust, 1021 S. 10th St., 63104.
Tel: 314-231-1021; Email: jamileh@eparchy.org. Most Rev. A. Elias Zaidan, Trustee.
St. Joseph Maronite Catholic Church-Phoenix Real Estate Trust, 1021 S. 10th St., 63104.
Tel: 314-231-1021; Email: jamileh@eparchy.org. Most Rev. A. Elias Zaidan, Trustee.
St. Jude Maronite Catholic Church-W. Covina Real Estate Trust, 1021 S. 10th St., 63104.
Tel: 314-231-1021; Email: jamileh@eparchy.org. Most Rev. A. Elias Zaidan, Trustee.
LEAF USA, Inc., 1021 S. 10th St., 63104.
Tel: 314-231-1021; Fax: 314-231-1316; Email: jamileh@eparchy.org. Most Rev. A. Elias Zaidan, Contact Person.
St. Maron Maronite Cath Ch- Minneapolis Real Estate Trust, 1021 S. 10th St., 63104.
Tel: 314-231-1021; Email: jamileh@eparchy.org. Most Rev. A. Elias Zaidan, Trustee.
Maronite Heritage Institute, 1021 S. 10th St., 63104.
Tel: 314-231-1021; Fax: 314-231-1316; Email: mdenny@usamaronite.org. Mrs. Jamileh Koury, Business Mgr.
Maronite Outreach, 1021 S. 10th St., 63104.
Tel: 314-231-1021; Fax: 314-231-1316; Email: info@maroniteoutreach.org; Web: www.maroniteoutreach.org. Most Rev. A. Elias Zaidan, Chm.
Our Lady of Lebanon Maronite Catholic Church-Lewisville Real Estate Trust, 1021 S. 10th St., 63104. Tel: 314-231-1021; Email: jamileh@eparchy.org. Most Rev. A. Elias Zaidan, Trustee.
Our Lady of Lebanon Maronite Mission-Norman Real Estate Trust, 1021 S. 10th St., 63104.
Tel: 314-231-1021; Email: jamileh@eparchy.org. Most Rev. A. Elias Zaidan, Trustee.
Our Lady of Mt. Lebanon-St. Peter Maronite Catholic Cathedral-LA Real Estate Trust, 1021 S. 10th St., 63104. Tel: 314-231-1021; Email: jamileh@eparchy.org. Most Rev. A. Elias Zaidan, Trustee.
Our Lady of the Cedar Maronite Catholic Church-Houston Real Estate Trust, 1021 S. 10th St., 63104.
Tel: 314-231-1021; Email: jamileh@eparchy.org. Most Rev. A. Elias Zaidan, Trustee.
Our Lady of the Rosary Maronite Cath Mission-Carmichael Real Estate Trust, 1021 S. 10th St., 63104. Tel: 314-231-1021; Email: jamileh@eparchy.org. Most Rev. A. Elias Zaidan, Trustee.
Our Lady's Maronite Catholic Church-Austin Real Estate Trust, 1021 S. 10th St., 63104.
Tel: 314-231-1021; Email: jamileh@eparchy.org. Most Rev. A. Elias Zaidan, Trustee.
Saint Peter and Paul Maronite Catholic Mission Simi Valley Real Estate Trust, 1021 S. 10th St., 63104. Tel: 314-231-1021; Email: jamileh@eparchy.org. Most Rev. A. Elias Zaidan, Trustee.
Priest's Retirement Fund, 1021 S. 10th St., 63104.
Tel: 314-231-1021; Fax: 314-231-1316; Email: jamileh@eparchy.org; Web: www.eparchy.org. Mrs. Jamileh Koury, Contact Person.
St. Rafka Maronite Cath Ch-Livonia Real Estate Trust, 1021 S. 10th St., 63104. Tel: 314-231-1021; Email: jamileh@eparchy.org. Most Rev. A. Elias Zaidan, Trustee.
St. Rafka Maronite Catholic Church-Lakewood, CO Real Estate Trust, 1021 S. 10th St., 63104.
Tel: 314-231-1021; Email: jamileh@eparchy.org. Most Rev. Abdallah E. Zaidan, Contact Person.
St. Raymond Maronite Catholic Cathedral - Real Estate Trust, 1021 S. 10th St., 63104.
Tel: 314-231-1021; Email: jamileh@eparchy.org. Most Rev. A. Elias Zaidan, Trustee.
St. Sharbel Manonite Catholic Mission - El Paso Real Estate Trust, 1021 S. 10th St., 63104.
Tel: 314-231-1021; Email: jamileh@eparchy.org. Most Rev. A. Elias Zaidan, Trustee.
St. Sharbel Maronite Catholic Church - Michigan Real Estate Trust, 1021 S. 10th St., 63104.

Tel: 314-231-1021; Email: jamileh@eparchy.org. Most Rev. A. Elias Zaidan, Trustee.

St. Sharbel Maronite Catholic Church - Portland Real Estate Trust, 1021 S. 10th St., 63104. Tel: 314-231-1021; Email: jamileh@eparchy.org. Most Rev. A. Elias Zaidan, Trustee.

St. Sharbel Maronite Catholic Mission - Las Vegas Real Estate Trust, 1021 S. 10th St., 63104. Tel: 314-231-1021; Email: jamileh@eparchy.org. Most Rev. A. Elias Zaidan, Trustee.

RELIGIOUS INSTITUTES OF MEN REPRESENTED IN THE DIOCESE

For further details refer to the corresponding bracketed number in the Religious Institutes of Men or Women section.

[0785]—*The Congregation of Maronite Lebanese Missionaries* (Houston, TX)—M.L.M.

[0785]—*Maronite Monks of Jesus, Mary & Joseph* (Portland, OR).

[0782]—*Maronite Order of Blessed Virgin Mary* (Ann Arbor, MI)—O.M.M.

[]—*The Congregation of Maronite Lebanese Missionaries* (Los Angeles, CA)—M.L.M.

RELIGIOUS INSTITUTES OF WOMEN REPRESENTED IN THE DIOCESE

[]—*Congregation of the Maronite Sisters of the Holy Family*.

[]—*Antonine Maronite Sisters*.

An asterisk (*) denotes an organization that has established tax-exempt status directly with the IRS and is not covered by the USCCB Group Ruling.

Armenian Catholic Eparchy of Our Lady of Nareg in the United States of America and Canada

Most Reverend

MIKAEL ANTOINE MOURADIAN, I.C.P.B.

Armenian Catholic Eparch of Our Lady of Nareg; ordained October 24, 1987; appointed Eparch of Our Lady of Nareg May 21, 2011; ordained July 31, 2011; installed October 2, 2011. *Chancery: 1510 E. Mountain St., Glendale, CA 91207-1226.*

Most Reverend

MANUEL BATAKIAN

Eparch Emeritus of Our Lady of Nareg; born November 5, 1929; ordained December 8, 1954; appointed Titular Bishop of Caesarea of Cappadocia January 8, 1995; ordained March 12, 1995; appointed third Apostolic Exarch for Armenian Catholics in United States and Canada November 30, 2000; installed January 20, 2001; nominated as the first Eparch of Our Lady of Nareg September 12, 2005; retired May 21, 2011. *Office: Patriarcat Armenien Catholique, Rue Hopital Orthodoxe, P.O. Box 2400, Geitawi, Beyrouth, 2078-5605.* Tel: 961-1-570555.

Legal Title: Armenian Catholic Eparchy of Our Lady of Nareg in the United States and Canada.

Chancery & Vicar General Office: 1510 E. Mountain St., Glendale, CA 91207-1226. Tel: 818-243-8400; Fax: 818-243-0095.

STATISTICAL OVERVIEW

Personnel	
Bishop	1
Retired Bishops	1
Priests: Diocesan Active in Diocese	4
Number of Diocesan Priests	4
Religious Priests in Diocese	5
Total Priests in Diocese	9
Permanent Deacons in Diocese	2
Total Sisters	7
Parishes	
Parishes	9
With Resident Pastor:	
Resident Diocesan Priests	4
Resident Religious Priests	4
Without Resident Pastor:	
Administered by Priests	1
Missions	3
Professional Ministry Personnel:	
Sisters	7
Educational	
High Schools, Diocesan and Parish	1
Total Students	314
Elementary Schools, Private	4
Total Students	632
Catechesis/Religious Education:	
High School Students	34
Elementary Students	76
Total Students under Catholic Instruction	1,056
Teachers in the Diocese:	
Priests	1
Sisters	2
Lay Teachers	146
Vital Statistics	
Receptions into the Church:	
Infant Baptism Totals	128
Minor Baptism Totals	40
First Communions	94
Confirmations	168
Marriages:	
Catholic	58
Interfaith	23
Total Marriages	81
Deaths	62
Total Catholic Population	51,000

Former Bishops—Most Revs. NERSES MIKAEL SETIAN, ord. April 13, 1941; appt. Titular Bishop of Ancera and Apostolic Exarch for the Armenian Catholics in the U.S.A. and Canada July 3, 1981; ord. Dec. 5, 1981; installed Dec. 27, 1981; retired Sept. 18, 1993; died Sept. 9, 2002; HOVHANNES TERTZAKIAN, O.M.Ven., ord. Sept. 8, 1948; appt. Titular Bishop of Trebisonda and Apostolic Exarch for Armenian Catholics in the United States and Canada Jan. 6, 1995; ord. April 29, 1995; installed May 7, 1995; retired Nov. 30, 2000; died Jan. 28, 2002; MANUEL BATAKIAN, born Nov. 5, 1929; ord. Dec. 8, 1954; appt. Titular Bishop of Caesarea of Cappadocia Jan. 8, 1995; ord. March 12, 1995; appt. third Apostolic Exarch for Armenian Catholics in United States and Canada Nov. 30, 2000; installed Jan. 20, 2001; nominated as the first Eparch of Our Lady of Nareg Sept. 12, 2005; retired May 21, 2011.

Chancery & Vicar General Office—1510 E. Mountain St., Glendale, 91207-1226. Tel: 818-243-8400; Fax: 818-243-0095.

Vicar General—Rev. GEORGES ZABARIAN, Tel: 818-243-8400.

Business Chancellor—Rev. THOMAS GARABEDIAN, Tel: 818-243-8400.

Newspaper Diocesan Bulletin—The Eternal Flame *1510 E. Mountain St., Glendale, 91207-1226.* Tel: 818-243-8400.

Newspaper Diocesan Bulletin "VERELK"—1510 E. Mountain St., Glendale, 91207-1226. Tel: 818-243-8400.

CLERGY, PARISHES, MISSIONS AND PAROCHIAL SCHOOLS

STATE OF CALIFORNIA

GLENDALE, LOS ANGELES CO., ST. GREGORY ARMENIAN CATHOLIC CATHEDRAL (1998) Rev. Antoine Noradounghian.
Res.: 1510 E. Mountain St., 91207-1226.
Tel: 818-243-8400; Fax: 818-243-0095.

LOS ANGELES, LOS ANGELES CO., OUR LADY QUEEN OF MARTYRS (1951) Rev. Armenag Bedrossian.
Res.: 1327 Pleasant Ave., Los Angeles, 90033-2328.
Tel: 323-261-9898; Fax: 323-261-0522.

STATE OF MASSACHUSETTS

BOSTON, MIDDLESEX CO., HOLY CROSS (1940) Rev. Antoine Adamian; Deacon M.J. Connolly.
Res.: 200 Lexington St., Belmont, MA 02478-1241.
Tel: 617-489-2280; Fax: 617-484-0218.

STATE OF MICHIGAN

DETROIT, WAYNE CO., ST. VARTAN'S (1948) (African American) Rev. Michel Bassaleh.
Res.: 34080 Edmonton St., Farmington, MI 48335.
Cell: 248-877-3718; Tel: 508-244-2333 (Church);
Fax: 248-991-3766 (Church).

STATE OF NEW JERSEY

PATERSON, PASSAIC CO., SACRED HEART (1927)
155 Long Hill Rd., Little Falls, NJ 07424-2318.
Tel: 973-890-0447; Email: shacc01@gmail.com. Revs. George Kalousieh; Richard Shackil.

STATE OF NEW YORK

NEW YORK, NEW YORK CO., ST. ANN'S ARMENIAN CATHOLIC CHURCH (1983)
155 Long Hill Rd., Little Falls, NJ 07424-2374.
Tel: 973-890-0447; Email: shacc01@gmail.com. Rev. George Kalousieh.

STATE OF PENNSYLVANIA

PHILADELPHIA, PHILADELPHIA CO., ST. MARK'S ARMENIAN CATHOLIC (1924)
400 Haverford Rd., Wynnewood, PA 19096-2699.
Tel: 610-896-7789; Email: armcathphil@gmail.com. Most Reverend Mikael Antoine Mouradian, I.C.P.B., Admin.

INSTITUTIONS LOCATED IN DIOCESE

[A] SCHOOLS.

STATE OF CALIFORNIA

MONTROSE. *Armenian Sisters of the Immaculate Conception*, 2361 Florencita Dr., Montrose, 91020-1817. Tel: 818-249-8783; Fax: 818-249-9773. Sr. Lucia Al-Haik, Prin.

TUJUNGA. *Mekhitarist School*, 6470 Foothill Blvd., Tujunga, 91042-2729. Tel: 818-353-3003;
Fax: 818-353-0815. Rev. Tavit Ghazarian, Prin.
6507 Alta Gracia Dr., Tujunga, 91042-3403.
Tel: 818-352-3048; Fax: 818-352-2647.

STATE OF MASSACHUSETTS

LEXINGTON. *Armenian Sisters Academy*, 20 Pelham Rd., Lexington, MA 02421-5702. Tel: 781-861-8303 ; Fax: 781-862-8479. Sr. Cecile Keheyan, Prin.

STATE OF PENNSYLVANIA

RADNOR. *Armenian Sisters Academy*, 440 Upper Gulph

Rd., Radnor, PA 19087-4699. Tel: 610-687-4100; Fax: 610-687-2430; Web: ameniansrsacademy.org. Sr. Emma Moussayan, Prin.

[B] RELIGIOUS INSTITUTES AND CONVENTS FOR WOMEN.

STATE OF CALIFORNIA

MONTROSE. *Armenian Sisters of the Immaculate Conception*, 2361 Florencita Dr., Montrose, 91020-1817. Tel: 818-249-7493. Sr. Lucia Al-Haik, Prin.

STATE OF MASSACHUSETTS

LEXINGTON. *Armenian Sisters of the Immaculate Conception*, 6 Eliot Rd., Lexington, MA 02173. Tel: 781-863-5962; Fax: 781-674-0410. Sr. Cecile Keheyan, Prin.

STATE OF PENNSYLVANIA

RADNOR. *Armenian Sisters of the Immaculate Conception*, 440 Upper Gulph Rd., Radnor, PA 19087-4699. Tel: 610-687-4100; Tel: 610-688-9360; Fax: 610-687-2430; Email: sisteremma@asaphila.org; Web: www.asaphila.org. Sr. Emma Moussayan, Supr.

An asterisk (*) denotes an organization that has established tax-exempt status directly with the IRS and is not covered by the USCCB Group Ruling.

Byzantine Catholic Eparchy of Parma

Most Reverend

MILAN LACH, S.J.

Bishop of Parma; ordained July 1, 2001; appointed Auxiliary Bishop of Presov, Slovakia and Titular Bishop of Ostracine April 19, 2013; ordained June 1, 2013; appointed Apostolic Administrator of Parma June 24, 2017; installed July 21, 2017; Succeeded to See June 1, 2018; installed June 30, 2018.

Most Reverend

JOHN M. KUDRICK

Retired Bishop of Parma; ordained May 3, 1975; consecrated and installed July 10, 2002; retired May 7, 2016.

SERVIRE

Chancery Office: 5000 Rockside Rd., Ste. 310, Independence, OH 44131. Tel: 216-741-8773; Fax: 216-741-9356.

Web: www.parma.org

ESTABLISHED FEBRUARY 21, 1969.

Embraces all Byzantine Ruthenian Rite Catholics in the States of Illinois, Indiana, Iowa, Kansas, Michigan, Minnesota, Missouri, Nebraska, North Dakota, South Dakota and Wisconsin. Also the entire State of Ohio excluding the Counties of Ashtabula, Trumbull, Mahoning, Columbiana, Carroll, Harrison, Guernsey, Noble, Morgan, Athens, Meigs, Gallia and Lawrence.

For legal titles of parishes and diocesan institutions, consult the Chancery Office.

STATISTICAL OVERVIEW

Personnel	
Bishop	1
Retired Bishops	1
Priests: Diocesan Active in Diocese	23
Priests: Diocesan Active Outside Diocese	1
Priests: Retired, Sick or Absent	16
Number of Diocesan Priests	40
Religious Priests in Diocese	39
Total Priests in Diocese	79
Permanent Deacons in Diocese	15
Total Sisters	6
Parishes	
Parishes	28
With Resident Pastor:	
Resident Diocesan Priests	20
Without Resident Pastor:	
Administered by Priests	8
Missions	2
Professional Ministry Personnel:	
Sisters	6
Welfare	
Day Care Centers	1
Total Assisted	22
Special Centers for Social Services	1
Total Assisted	6,500
Educational	
Students from This Diocese	3
Total Seminarians	3
Elementary Schools, Diocesan and Parish	1
Total Students	195
Catechesis/Religious Education:	
High School Students	40
Elementary Students	225
Total Students under Catholic Instruction	463
Teachers in the Diocese:	
Lay Teachers	14
Vital Statistics	
Receptions into the Church:	
Infant Baptism Totals	58
Minor Baptism Totals	6
Adult Baptism Totals	1
First Communions	52
Confirmations	54
Marriages:	
Catholic	7
Interfaith	2
Total Marriages	9
Deaths	111
Total Catholic Population	5,015

Former Bishops—Most Revs. EMIL J. MIHALIK, D.D., ord. Sept. 21, 1945; appt. first Bishop of the Ruthenian Eparchy of Parma, March 22, 1969; installed June 12, 1969; died Jan. 27, 1984; ANDREW PATAKI, D.D., appt. Titular Bishop of Tellmisus and Auxiliary of Passaic, NJ, May 30, 1983; installed Aug. 23, 1983; succeeded to See, June 19, 1984; transferred to Parma See, Aug. 16, 1984; transferred to Byzantine Eparchy of Passaic, Nov. 21, 1995; BASIL MYRON SCHOTT, O.F.M., ord. Aug. 29, 1965; cons. and installed as Bishop of Parma July 11, 1996; transferred to Archeparchy of Pittsburgh July 9, 2002; died June 10, 2010.; JOHN M. KUDRICK, ord. May 3, 1975; cons. and installed July 10, 2002; retired May 7, 2016.

Chancery Office—5000 Rockside Rd., Ste. 310, Independence, 44131. Tel: 216-741-8773; Fax: 216-741-9356.

Protosyncellus—Very Rev. Mitred Archpriest MAREK VISNOVSKY.

Chancellor—Rev. GARY YANUS.

Eparchial Finance Council—JERRY C. CIRINO; MARTIN KOPMEYER; JAMES NIEHAUS; Very Rev. Mitred Archpriest MAREK VISNOVSKY; AL VONDRA.

Syncellus for Great Lakes Region—Very Rev. MYCHAIL ROZMARYNOWYCZ.

Syncellus for Midwest Region—Very Rev. THOMAS LOYA, S.T.B., M.A.

Syncellus for Ohio Region—Very Rev. BRUCE RIEBE.

Presbyteral Council—Revs. JAMES J. BATCHA; JAN CIZMAR; CYRIL FARMER; MIRON KERUL-KMEC; MICHAEL LEE; Very Revs. THOMAS LOYA, S.T.B., M.A.; BRUCE RIEBE; MYCHAIL ROZMARYNOWYCZ; Revs. CHARLES STREBLER, J.C.L.; ANDREW SUMMERSON; Very Rev. Mitred Archpriest MAREK VISNOVSKY; Rev. JOSEPH A. WEBER.

Eparchial Pastoral Council—VIRGILDEE DANIEL; Rev. STEVEN KOPLINKA; Very Rev. THOMAS LOYA, S.T.B., M.A.; NICHOLAS NAGRANT; LORETTA NEMETH; KATHRYN SZILAGYE; Very Rev. Mitred Archpriest MAREK VISNOVSKY.

Finance Officer—MARTIN KOPMEYER.

Eparchial Consultors—Rev. MIRON KERUL-KMEC; Very Revs. THOMAS LOYA, S.T.B., M.A.; BRUCE RIEBE; MYCHAIL ROZMARYNOWYCZ; Rev. CHARLES STREBLER, J.C.L.; Very Rev. Mitred Archpriest MAREK VISNOVSKY.

Protopresbyters—Ohio: Very Rev. BRUCE RIEBE. Midwest: Rev. ANDREW SUMMERSON. Great Lakes: Very Rev. MYCHAIL ROZMARYNOWYCZ.

Vicar Judicialis—Rev. CHARLES STREBLER, J.C.L.

Judges—VINCET M. GARDINER, J.C.L.; LYNETTE TAIT, J.C.L.

Defender of the Bond—Revs. WILLIAM M. JERSE, J.C.L.; A. JONATHAN ZINGALES, J.C.L.

Promoter of Justice—Rev. RICHARD BONA, J.C.D.

Notary—MARIE A. GOLIAS.

Eparchial Censor—Very Rev. Archpriest DAVID PETRAS, S.E.O.D., (Retired).

Eparchial Commissions

Sacred Liturgy—Very Rev. Mitred Archpriest MAREK VISNOVSKY; Deacon JOHN PETRUS, M.D.

Building Commission—Deacon WILLIAM FREDRICK; MARK PAPKE; FRANK TOMBAZZI.

Office of Religious Education—JOHN POPP.

Safe Envrionment—Deacon WILLIAM FREDRICK.

Office of Youth Ministry—Very Rev. BRUCE RIEBE, Dir.; Rev. MICHAEL LEE.

Office of Vocations—Very Rev. Mitred Archpriest MAREK VISNOVSKY.

Seminary Education Formation Board—Rev. MIRON KERUL-KMEC; Very Rev. Mitred Archpriest MAREK VISNOVSKY.

Priest's Pension Board—Very Rev. BRYAN R. EYMAN, D.Min., D.Phil.; MARTIN KOPMEYER; JAMES NIEHAUS; Rev. JOSEPH REPKO, M.Div.; Very Rev. BRUCE RIEBE; Rev. GARY YANUS; Very Rev. Mitred Archpriest MAREK VISNOVSKY.

Eparchial Shrine of Our Lady of Mariapoch—(Burton, OH)President: Most Rev. MILAN LACH, S.J., Ordinary of the Parma Eparchy, Tel: 440-834-0700; Deacon WILLIAM FREDRICK, Admin., Tel: 216-469-1425.

Respect Life Office—Very Rev. THOMAS LOYA, S.T.B., M.A.

Pre-Cana Office—Very Rev. THOMAS LOYA, S.T.B., M.A.

Victim Assistance Coordinator—SHARON DILAURO PETRUS, M.D., Tel: 216-741-8773, Ext. 246; Email: dilauropetrus@yahoo.com.

Safe Environment Review Board—MADELINE ZAWORSKI, Chm.; RONDA AMBROZIAK; RITA BASALLA; WILLIAM BOCKANIC; JEAN MCNOSKY. Ex Officio: Rt. Rev. Mitred Archpriest JOHN S. KACHUBA, M.A.; Very Rev. JAMES KUBAJAK, M.Div., (Retired).

Byzantine Catholic Cultural Center—JOHN POPP.

CLERGY, PARISHES, MISSIONS AND PAROCHIAL SCHOOLS

STATE OF OHIO

PARMA, CUYAHOGA CO.

1—SAINT JOHN THE BAPTIST, CATHEDRAL (1898) (Ruthenian)
1900 Carlton Rd., Parma, 44134-3129.
Tel: 216-661-8658; Fax: 216-661-8221; Email: frmvisnovsky@parma.org. Very Rev. Mitred Archpriest Marek Visnovsky, Admin.; Rev. Michal Bucko, Parochial Vicar; Deacon Gregory Loya.
Res.: 1703 Carlton Rd., Parma, 44134.
Catechesis Religious Program—Students 16.

2—HOLY SPIRIT (1969) [CEM 2]
5500 W. 54th St., Parma, 44129-2274.
Tel: 440-884-8452; Fax: 440-884-8453; Email: contactus@holyspiritbyzantine.org; Web: holyspiritbyzantine.org. Very Rev. Mitred Archpriest Marek Visnovsky, Admin.; Rev. Michal Bucko, Parochial Vicar; Deacon Robert Cripps.
Catechesis Religious Program—

AKRON, SUMMIT CO., ST. MICHAEL THE ARCHANGEL (1916) [CEM] Closed. For inquiries for parish records contact the chancery.

BARBERTON, SUMMIT CO., ST. NICHOLAS (1916) [CEM]
1051 E. Robinson St., Barberton, 44203-3852.
Tel: 330-753-2031; Fax: 330-745-5500; Email: stnickbyz@gmail.com; Web: www.stnickbyz.com. Rev. Miron Kerul-Kmec, Admin.; Deacon Eugene Senderak.
Catechesis Religious Program—Students 31.

BEDFORD, CUYAHOGA CO., ST. EUGENE (1963)
264 Warrensville-Center Rd., Bedford, 44146-2741.
Tel: 216-741-8773; Email: chancery@parma.org. Very Rev. Bruce Riebe, Admin.
Catechesis Religious Program—

BRECKSVILLE, CUYAHOGA CO., ST. JOSEPH (1913)
8111 Brecksville, Brecksville, 44141-1204.
Tel: 440-526-1818; Fax: 440-526-6464; Email: stjoebyz@sbcglobal.net; Web: www.stjoebyz.com. Very Rev. Bruce Riebe; Deacons William Fredrick; Robert Kirschner.
Catechesis Religious Program—Students 77.

BRUNSWICK, MEDINA CO., ST. EMILIAN (1975)
1231 Substation Rd., Brunswick, 44212-0843.
Tel: 330-225-9857; Email: jerejjan@gmail.com; Web: www.stemilian.com. Rev. Jan Cizmar, Admin.; Deacon John Petrus, M.D.
Res.: 4705 Hickory Ridge Ave., Brunswick, 44212.
Catechesis Religious Program—Students 12.

CLEVELAND, CUYAHOGA CO.

1—HOLY GHOST (1909) Closed. For inquiries for parish records contact the chancery.

2—ST. MARY (1938)
3518 Stickney Ave., Cleveland, 44109.
Tel: 216-741-7979; Fax: 216-741-6622; Email: marekvisnovsky@yahoo.com; Web: www.stmarybyz.com. Very Rev. Mitred Archpriest Marek Visnovsky; Rev. Michal Bucko, Parochial Vicar; Deacon Joseph Hnat.
Church: 4600 State Rd., Cleveland, 44109.
School—St. Mary School, (Grades K-8),
Tel: 216-749-7980; Email: basalla4@att.net. Rita Basalla, Prin. Lay Teachers 14; Students 192.
Catechesis Religious Program—Students 164.

3—ST. NICHOLAS (1902) (Croatian)
3431 Superior Ave., Cleveland, 44114-4160.
Tel: 440-884-8452; Email: contactus@holyspiritbyzantine.org. Very Rev. Mitred Archpriest Marek Visnovsky, Admin.; Rev. Michal Bucko, Parochial Vicar.
Catechesis Religious Program—

COLUMBUS, FRANKLIN CO., ST. JOHN CHRYSOSTOM (1961)
5858 Cleveland Ave., Columbus, 43231-2862.
Tel: 614-882-7578; Fax: 614-890-6048; Email: stjohnbyz@hotmail.com; Web: www.byzantinecolumbus.com. Rev. Robert Stash; Deacon Jeffrey Martin.
Catechesis Religious Program—Students 4.

DAYTON, MONTGOMERY CO., ST. BARBARA, Closed. For inquiries for parish records contact the chancery.

EUCLID, CUYAHOGA CO., ST. STEPHEN (1955)
532 Lloyd Rd., Euclid, 44132-1721.
Tel: 216-732-7292; Fax: 216-732-9434; Email: ststephenbyz@gmail.com. Very Rev. Bruce Riebe, Admin.; Rev. Robert Jager, Parochial Vicar.
Catechesis Religious Program—Students 18.

FAIRPORT HARBOR, LAKE CO., ST. MICHAEL (1926) Closed. For inquiries for parish records contact the chancery.

FAIRVIEW PARK, CUYAHOGA CO., ST. MARY MAGDALENE (1966)
5390 W. 220th St., Fairview Park, 44126-2968.
Tel: 440-734-4644; Fax: 440-734-4645; Email: stmmbyzantinechurch@gmail.com; Web: www.stmarymagdalenebyzantine.org. Rt. Rev. Mitred Archpriest John S. Kachuba, M.A.; Deacon Daniel Surniak.
Catechesis Religious Program—Students 6.

LAKEWOOD, CUYAHOGA CO., ST. GREGORY THE THEOLOGIAN (1905) Closed. For inquiries for parish records contact the chancery.

LORAIN, LORAIN CO.

1—ST. MICHAEL, Closed. For inquiries for parish records contact the chancery.

2—ST. NICHOLAS (1914)
2711 W. 40th St., Lorain, 44053-2252.
Tel: 440-282-7525; Fax: 440-282-9185; Email: jerejjan@gmail.com; Web: www.stnicks.org. Revs. Jan Cizmar, Admin.; Andrew Nagrant, Pastoral Assoc.
Catechesis Religious Program—Students 6.

MARBLEHEAD, OTTAWA CO., ST. MARY (1897) [CEM]
506 E. Main St., Marblehead, 43440-2232.
Tel: 419-798-4283; Fax: 419-798-4095; Email: frbobkelly@gmail.com. Rev. Robert D. Kelly, (Retired).
Catechesis Religious Program—Students 3.

MENTOR-ON-THE-LAKE, LAKE CO., HOLY TRANSFIGURATION (1974)
5768 Andrews Rd., Mentor-on-the-Lake, 44060-2608.
Tel: 440-257-3620; Fax: 440-257-6524; Email: holytransfiguration@gmail.com. Very Rev. Bruce Riebe, Admin.; Rev. Robert Jager, Parochial Vicar.
Res.: 532 Lloyd Rd., Euclid, 44132.
Catechesis Religious Program—Students 1.

NORTHWOOD, LUCAS CO., ST. MICHAEL THE ARCHANGEL (1915)
2526 Skagway Dr., Northwood, 43619.
Tel: 419-691-5656; Fax: 419-691-7669; Email: jrprussell@gmail.com; Web: www.stmichaelstoledo.org. Rev. John Russell, Admin.; Deacon James Sofalvi.
Church: 4001 Navarre Ave., Oregon, 43616.
Catechesis Religious Program—

SOLON, CUYAHOGA CO., ST. JOHN THE BAPTIST (1892)
36125 Aurora Rd., Solon, 44139-3841.
Tel: 440-218-4096; Email: chancery@parma.org. Very Rev. Bruce Riebe, Admin.
Res.: 264 Warrensville Center Rd., Bedford, 44146.
Catechesis Religious Program—Students 5.

STATE OF ILLINOIS

CHICAGO, COOK CO., ST. MARY, Closed. For inquiries for parish records contact the chancery.

HOMER GLEN, WILL CO., ANNUNCIATION BYZANTINE CATHOLIC CHURCH (1999) [CEM]
14610 S. Will-Cook Rd., Homer Glen, IL 60491-9212.
Tel: 708-645-0241; Fax: 708-645-0243; Email: annuncbyzchurch@aol.com; Web: www.byzantinecatholic.com. Very Rev. Thomas Loya, S.T.B., M.A.; Deacons J. Timothy Tkach; John Evancho.
Catechesis Religious Program—Students 45.

JOLIET, WILL CO., ST. MARY ASSUMPTION, Closed. For inquiries for parish records contact the chancery.

STATE OF INDIANA

EAST CHICAGO, LAKE CO., ST. BASIL'S, Closed. For inquiries for parish records contact the chancery.

INDIANA, HARBOR CO., HOLY GHOST, Closed. For inquiries for parish records contact the chancery.

INDIANAPOLIS, MARION CO., ST. ATHANASIUS CHURCH (1980)
1117 S. Blaine Ave., Indianapolis, IN 46221-1110.
Tel: 317-632-4157; Fax: 317-632-2988; Email: pastor@saindy.com; Web: www.saindy.com. Very Rev. Bryan R. Eyman, D.Min., D.Phil.
Catechesis Religious Program—Students 21.

MERRILLVILLE, LAKE CO., ST. MICHAEL (1911)
557 W. 57th Ave., Merrillville, IN 46410-2540.
Tel: 219-980-0600; Fax: 219-980-0127; Email: frasummerson@parma.org; Web: www.stmichaelbyz.org. Rev. Andrew Summerson, Admin.
Catechesis Religious Program—Students 3.

MUNSTER, LAKE CO., SAINT NICHOLAS (1922) [CEM]
8103 Columbia Ave., Munster, IN 46321-1802.
Tel: 219-838-9380; Email: spkoplinka@att.net. Rev. Steven Koplinka.
Catechesis Religious Program—Students 12.

WHITING, LAKE CO., ASSUMPTION OF THE BLESSED VIRGIN (1899) [CEM]
2011 Clark St., Whiting, IN 46394-2023.
Tel: 219-659-0277; Fax: 219-659-1687; Email: stmarywhiting@aol.com; Web: stmarywhiting.org. Rev. Andrew Summerson, Admin.; Deacon Timothy Woods.
Catechesis Religious Program—

STATE OF MICHIGAN

ALLEN PARK, WAYNE CO., ST. STEPHEN (1941)
4141 Laurence Ave., Allen Park, MI 48101-3049.
Tel: 313-382-5901; Fax: 313-382-5902; Email: jrprussell@gmail.com. Rev. John Russell, Admin.
Catechesis Religious Program—Students 13.

BAY CITY, BAY CO., SAINT GEORGE (1967)
204 N. Van Buren St., Bay City, MI 48706-6519.
Tel: 810-659-4887; Fax: 810-659-8363; Email: stgeorgebyzantine@gmail.com. Rev. James J. Batcha, Admin.
Catechesis Religious Program—Students 10.

CLINTON TOWNSHIP, ST. NICHOLAS (1921)
23300 King Dr., Clinton Township, MI 48035.
Tel: 586-791-1052; Fax: 586-791-1059; Email: frrepko@ameritech.net; Web: www.stnicksdetroit.com. Rev. Joseph Repko, M.Div.
Catechesis Religious Program—Students 25.

DETROIT, WAYNE CO., ST. JOHN THE BAPTIST, Closed. For inquiries for parish records contact the chancery.

FLUSHING, GENESEE CO., ST. MICHAEL (1917)
2333 N. Elms Rd., Flushing, MI 48433-9426.
Tel: 810-659-4887; Fax: 810-659-8363; Email: stmichaelbyz@gmail.com. Rev. James J. Batcha.
Catechesis Religious Program—Students 18.

LIVONIA, WAYNE CO., SACRED HEART (1957)
29125 W. Six-Mile Rd., Livonia, MI 48152-3661.
Tel: 734-522-3166; Fax: 734-261-8562; Email: shbyzantine@sbcglobal.net; Web: www.shbyzantine.com. Rev. Joseph Marquis.
Res.: 16881 Savoie St., Livonia, MI 48154.
Catechesis Religious Program—Students 19.

OMER, ARENAC CO., ST. JOHN (1981) Closed. For inquiries for parish records contact the chancery.

STERLING HEIGHTS, MACOMB CO., ST. BASIL (1962)
4700 Metropolitan Pkwy., Sterling Heights, MI 48310-3905. Tel: 586-268-1082; Fax: 586-268-2548; Email: mrozmar05@aol.com; Web: www.stbasilbyz.com. Very Rev. Mychail Rozmarynowycz, Admin.; Deacon Paul Latcha.
Catechesis Religious Program—Students 6.

TAYLOR, WAYNE CO., CHRIST THE KING, Closed. For inquiries for parish records contact the chancery.

STATE OF MINNESOTA

MINNEAPOLIS, HENNEPIN CO., ST. JOHN THE BAPTIST (1907)
2205 3rd St., N.E., Minneapolis, MN 55418-3422.
Tel: 612-789-6252; Email: stjohnminneapolis@comcast.net; Web: www.stjohnsminneapolis.webs.com. Mailing Address: 2215 3rd St., N.E., Minneapolis, MN 55418. Rev. Cyril Farmer.
Catechesis Religious Program—Students 14.

STATE OF MISSOURI

ST. LOUIS, ST. LOUIS CO., ST. LOUIS MISSION (1981)
320 Ripa Ave., Bldg. G, St. Louis, MO 63125.
Tel: 314-434-4211, Ext. 336; Email: stlbyzcath@att.net; Web: www.stlouis.byzcath.org. P.O. Box 23865, Belleville, IL 62223. Revs. Joseph A. Weber, Admin.; Steven Hawkes-Teeples, S.J., Pastoral Assoc.; Paul Niemann, Pastoral Assoc.
Church: Blessed John XXIII Center, 8300 Morganford Rd., St. Louis, MO 62123. Students 8.

SUGAR CREEK, JACKSON CO., ST. LUKE, BYZANTINE CATHOLIC PARISH (1980)
11411 Chicago Ave., Sugar Creek, MO 64054.
Tel: 816-231-7100; Email: stlukebyz@gmail.com. P.O. Box 520022, MO 64052. Rev. Michael Lee, Admin.; Deacon Nicholas Szilagye, M.D.

STATE OF WISCONSIN

BRISTOL, KENOSHA CO., ST. IRENE, Closed. For information regarding the Byzantine Catholic Community contact the Chancery.

Absent on Leave:
Very Rev.—
Hutsko, Basil
Revs.—
Chelena, Thomas
Muth, Stephen
Plishka, Richard
St. Germain, Brian.

Retired:
Rev. Msgr.—
Korba, Frank, V.F., (Retired), 8103 Columbia Ave., Munster, IN 46321. Tel: 219-838-9380
Very Revs.—
Evanick, Michael, (Retired), 2371 Deerpath Dr., Unit 111, Schererville, IN 46375
Hannes, David A., J.C.L., (Retired), 118 W. Main St., Marblehead, 43440
Kubajak, James, M.Div., (Retired), 10349 W. Rodgers Cir., Sun City, AZ 85351
Rachford, Nicholas, J.C.L., (Retired), 2823 Viki Terr., Cincinnati, 45211
Revs.—
Kelly, Robert D., (Retired), 506 E. Main St., Marblehead, 43440
Kovach, John, (Retired), P.O. Box 20510, Los Angeles, CA 90006
Linowski, Eugene R., (Retired), 2221 Glenmere Rd., Columbus, 43220. Tel: 614-488-0427
Very Rev. Archpriests—

Hayduk, Michael, (Retired), 7002 W. White Dove Ln., #101, Middleburg Heights, 44130
Kachuba, John S., (Retired), 5390 W. 220th, Fairview Park, 44126
Petras, David, S.E.O.D., (Retired), 1670 E. El Camino Dr., Phoenix, AZ 85020-3926

Rev. Archpriest—
Hrubiak, Dennis M., (Retired), 14567 Madison Ave., #411, Lakewood, 44107.

Permanent Deacons:
Cripps, Robert, Holy Spirit, Parma, OH
Evancho, John, Annunciation, Homer Glen, IL
Fredrick, William, St. Joseph, Brecksville, OH
Hendricks, Lawrence, St. Stephen, Allen Park, MI
Hnat, Joseph, St. Mary, Cleveland, OH
Kirschner, Robert, St. Joseph Byzantine Catholic Church, Brecksville, OH
Latcha, Paul, St. Basil, Sterling Heights, MI
Loya, Gregory, Cathedral, Parma, OH
Martin, Jeffrey, St. John Chrysostom, Columbus, OH
Petrus, John, M.D., St. Emilian, Brunswick, OH
Senderak, Eugene, St. Nicholas, Barberton, OH
Surniak, Daniel, St. Mary Magdalene, Fairview Park, OH
Szilagye, Nicholas, M.D., St. Luke, Kansas City, MO
Tkach, J. Timothy, Annunciation, Homer Glen, IL
Woods, Timothy, St. Mary, Whiting, IN.

INSTITUTIONS LOCATED IN DIOCESE

[A] CONVENTS AND RESIDENCES FOR SISTERS

BURTON. *Christ the Bridegroom Monastery*, 17485 Mumford Rd., Burton, 44021. Tel: 440-834-0290; Email: christthebridegroom@gmail.com; Web: www.christthebridegroom.org. Mother Theodora Strohmeyer, Admin. Sisters 6.

NORTH ROYALTON. *Motherhouse and Novitiate*, 6688 Cady Rd., North Royalton, 44133. Tel: 216-741-8773; Email: chancery@parma.org. Sr. Mary Lucille Tepper, B.P.C.N., Supr.

[B] RELIGIOUS SHRINES

BURTON. *Shrine of Mariapoch*, 17486 Mumford Rd., Burton, 44021. Tel: 216-469-1425; Email: wfred8745@sbcglobal.net. 5000 Rockside Rd., Ste. 310, 44131. Deacon William Fredrick, Admin.

[C] MISCELLANEOUS

CLEVELAND. *St. Mary Hospitality House*, 5500 W. 54th St., Parma, 44129. Tel: 440-884-8452; Fax: 440-884-8453; Email: contactus@holyspiritbyzantine.org. Dorothy Papke, Dir.

DAYTON. *St. Barbara Prayer Community* Prayer Center. 1114 Troy St., Dayton, 45404. Tel: 513-434-9205; Email: frbobstash@hotmail.com. Rev. Robert Stash, Admin. Estimated Number of Catholics 20; Number of Registered Parishioner Households 13.

RELIGIOUS INSTITUTES OF WOMEN REPRESENTED IN THE DIOCESE

For further details refer to the corresponding bracketed number in the Religious Institutes of Men or Women section.

[]—*Byzantine Nuns of St. Clare* (Parma Eparchy)—B.P.C.N.

[]—*Christ the Bridegroom Monastery*.

NECROLOGY

† Attak, Cyril, (Retired), Died Apr. 16, 2018
† Radvansky, Joseph R., (Retired), Died Dec. 25, 2018

An asterisk (*) denotes an organization that has established tax-exempt status directly with the IRS and is not covered by the USCCB Group Ruling.

Byzantine Catholic Eparchy of Passaic

Most Reverend

KURT BURNETTE, D.D., J.C.L.

Bishop of Passaic; ordained April 26, 1989; appointed Bishop of Passaic October 29, 2013; ordained and enthroned December 4, 2013. *Office: 445 Lackawanna Ave., Woodland Park, NJ 07424.*

Chancery Office: 445 Lackawanna Ave., Woodland Park, NJ 07424. Tel: 973-890-7777; Fax: 973-890-7175.

Web: www.eparchyofpassaic.com

Email: bishop@eparchyofpassaic.com

ESTABLISHED JULY 31, 1963.

Embraces all Catholics of the Byzantine-Ruthenian Rite in the States of New Jersey, Connecticut, Delaware, District of Columbia, Florida, Georgia, Maine, Maryland, Massachusetts, New Hampshire, New York, North Carolina, Rhode Island, South Carolina, Vermont, Virginia and all Eastern Pennsylvania within the western boundaries of the Counties of Franklin, Juniata, Lycoming, Mifflin, Union and Tioga.

For legal titles of parishes and diocesan institutions, consult the Chancery Office.

STATISTICAL OVERVIEW

Personnel	
Bishop	1
Priests: Diocesan Active in Diocese	40
Priests: Diocesan Active Outside Diocese	2
Priests: Retired, Sick or Absent	22
Number of Diocesan Priests	64
Religious Priests in Diocese	4
Total Priests in Diocese	68
Extern Priests in Diocese	16
Permanent Deacons in Diocese	27
Total Brothers	1
Total Sisters	13
Parishes	
Parishes	85
With Resident Pastor:	
Resident Diocesan Priests	34
Resident Religious Priests	4
Without Resident Pastor:	
Administered by Priests	42
Missions	5
Educational	
Diocesan Students in Other Seminaries	3
Total Seminarians	3
Catechesis/Religious Education:	
High School Students	81
Elementary Students	271
Total Students under Catholic Instruction	355
Vital Statistics	
Receptions into the Church:	
Infant Baptism Totals	109
Minor Baptism Totals	8
Adult Baptism Totals	5
Received into Full Communion	17
First Communions	108
Confirmations	97
Marriages:	
Catholic	28
Interfaith	8
Total Marriages	36
Deaths	344
Total Catholic Population	11,303

Former Bishops—Most Revs. STEPHEN J. KOCISKO, D.D., ord. March 30, 1941; appt. Titular Bishop of Theveste and Auxiliary of Exarchate of Pittsburgh, July 20, 1956; appt. First Eparch of Passaic, July 31, 1963; appt. Eparch of Pittsburgh, Dec. 21, 1967; installed March 5, 1968; elevated to Metropolitan Archbishop of Pittsburgh, Feb. 21, 1969; retired June 12, 1991; died March 7, 1995; MICHAEL J. DUDICK, D.D., ord. Nov. 13, 1945; appt. Bishop of Passaic, Aug. 21, 1968; installed Oct. 24, 1968; retired Nov. 21, 1995; died May 30, 2007.; ANDREW PATAKI, J.C.L., D.D., ord. Feb. 24, 1952; appt. Titular Bishop of Tellmisus and Auxiliary Bishop of Passaic, May 30, 1983; cons. Aug. 23, 1983; appt. Bishop of Parma June 19, 1984; enthroned Aug. 16, 1984; transferred to Passaic Nov. 6, 1995; enthroned Feb. 8, 1996; retired & appt. Apostolic Administrator Dec. 6, 2007; appt. Protosyncellus and Moderator of Eparchial Curia March 1, 2008; died Dec. 8, 2011.; WILLIAM C. SKURLA, ord. May 23, 1987; appt. Bishop of the Eparchy of Van Nuys Feb. 19, 2002; cons. and enthroned April 23, 2002; transferred to the Eparchy of Passaic Dec. 6, 2007; enthroned Jan. 29, 2008; appt. Metropolitan Archbishop of Pittsburgh Jan. 19, 2012.

Syncellates and Protopresbyterates—

Susquehanna Valley Syncellate—

Syncellus—Very Rev. GARY J. MENSINGER, St. Michael, 205 N. Main St., Pittston, PA 18640. Tel: 570-654-4564.

Northern Pennsylvania/Northern New York Protopresbyterate—VACANT.

Wyoming Valley Protopresbyterate—Very Rev. MICHAEL J. SALNICKY, Protopresbyter, Carpathian Village, 802 Snow Hill Rd., Cresco, PA 18326. Tel: 570-595-3265.

Central Pennsylvania Syncellate—

Syncellus—Very Rev. PETER J. HOSAK, M.S., SS. Peter and Paul, 1140 Johnston Dr., Bethlehem, PA 18017. Tel: 610-867-2322.

Mid-Pennsylvania Protopresbyterate—Ss. Peter & Paul Church, 107 S. Fourth St., Minersville, PA 17954. Tel: 570-544-2074. Very Rev. GREGORY J. NOGA, M.A., Protopresbyter.

South Pennsylvania Protopresbyterate—Very Rev. EDWARD J. HIGGINS, Protopresbyter, Holy Ghost Church, 2310 S. 24th St., Philadelphia, PA 19145. Tel: 215-334-5129.

New Jersey Syncellate—

Syncellus—96 First St., Passaic, 07055. Tel: 973-777-2553. Very Rev. JOHN S. CUSTER, S.S.L., S.T.D.

Northern New Jersey Protopresbyterate—Very Rev. JOHN S. CUSTER, S.S.L., S.T.D., 96 First St., Passaic, 07055. Tel: 973-777-2553.

Central New Jersey Protopresbyterate—Very Rev. FRANCIS J. RELLA, Our Lady of Perpetual Help, 1937 Church St., Toms River, 08753.

New York-New England Syncellate—

Syncellus—Very Rev. NICHOLAS A. DADDONA, B.A., M.S., St. Andrew Church, 275 Ellison Ave., Westbury, NY 11590.

New York/New England Protopresbyterate—Very Rev. RONALD J. HATTON, St. Nicholas Church, 13 Pembroke Rd., Danbury, CT 06811.

Middle States Syncellate—

Syncellus—Very Rev. JOHN G. BASARAB, M.A., Epiphany of Our Lord Church, 3410 Woodburn Rd., Annandale, VA 22003. Tel: 703-573-3986.

Middle States Protopresbyterate—Very Rev. CONAN H. TIMONEY, Ph.D., Patronage of Mother of God Church, 1260 Stevens Ave., Baltimore, MD 21227. Tel: 410-247-4936.

Southern States Syncellate—

Syncellus—Very Rev. ROBERT EVANCHO, Syncellus, St. Therese, 4265 13th Ave., N., Saint Petersburg, FL 33713. Tel: 727-323-4022.

Southern States Protopresbyterate—Very Rev. SALVATORE A. PIGNATO, Protopresbyter, St. Nicholas of Myra, 5135 W. Sand Lake Rd., Orlando, FL 32819. Tel: 407-351-0133.

Protosyncellus—Rt. Rev. Mitred Archpriest JAMES HAYER.

Vicar for Clergy—Very Rev. PETER J. HOSAK, M.S.

Chancery Office—Eparchial Center, 445 Lackawanna Ave., Woodland Park, 07424. Tel: 973-890-7777; Fax: 973-890-7175. Office Hours: Mon.-Fri. 9-12 & 1-4.

Chancellor—Very Rev. NICHOLAS A. DADDONA, B.A., M.S.

Vice Chancellor—Very Rev. RONALD BARUSEFSKI, J.C.L.

Eparchial Finance Officer/Controller/CFO—Rev. Deacon ROBERT SHALHOUB.

Eparchial Finance Council—Rt. Rev. Mitred Archpriest JAMES HAYER; Rev. Deacon ROBERT SHALHOUB; MR. STEPHEN KOWALSKI; THOMAS DUCH, Esq.; DANIEL SEAMAN, Esq.

Eparchial College of Consultors—Rt. Rev. Mitred Archpriest JAMES HAYER; Very Revs. MARCEL SZABO; JOHN G. BASARAB, M.A.; PETER J. HOSAK, M.S.; ROBERT J. HOSPODAR, J.C.L.; GARY J. MENSINGER; Rev. MICHAEL G. POPSON; Very Rev. STEVEN GALUSCHIK.

Presbyteral Council—Rt. Rev. Mitred Archpriest JAMES HAYER, Ex Officio; Very Revs. JOHN G. BASARAB, M.A., Ex Officio; ROBERT EVANCHO, Ex Officio; JOHN S. CUSTER, S.S.L., S.T.D., Ex Officio; PETER J. HOSAK, M.S., Ex Officio; ROBERT J. HOSPODAR, J.C.L., Ex Officio; GARY J. MENSINGER, Ex Officio; EDWARD J. HIGGINS; CONAN H. TIMONEY, Ph.D.; SALVATORE A. PIGNATO; MICHAEL J. SALNICKY; Rev. MICHAEL G. POPSON; Very Rev. MICHAEL KERESTES; Rev. VINCENT M. BRADY; Very Revs. EDWARD G. CIMBALA, D.Min.; RONALD J. HATTON; Rev. MYKHAYLO PRODANETS.

Eparchial Tribunal—445 Lackawanna Ave., Woodland Park, 07424. Tel: 973-890-7777.

Judicial Vicar—Rev. Msgr. T. MARK CONDON, J.C.D.

Adjutant Judicial Vicar—Very Revs. RONALD BARUSEFSKI, J.C.L.; EDUARD SHESTAK, J.C.L., S.T.D.

Judges—Rev. Msgr. ROBERT SENETSKY, J.C.D., (Retired).

Defenders of the Bond—Very Revs. ROBERT J. HOSPODAR, J.C.L.; EDUARD SHESTAK, J.C.L., S.T.D.

Advocate—Very Rev. EDUARD SHESTAK, J.C.L., S.T.D.

Promoter of Justice—Very Rev. EDUARD SHESTAK, J.C.L., S.T.D.

Notaries—Very Revs. GARY J. MENSINGER; GREGORY J. NOGA, M.A.; EDUARD SHESTAK, J.C.L., S.T.D.; MRS. MAUREEN FRENCH; MRS. DIANE RABIEJ.

Commissions, Departments and Institutions

Building and Liturgical Arts Commission—Rt. Rev. Mitred Archpriest JAMES HAYER, Chm.; Very Revs. PETER J. HOSAK, M.S.; MICHAEL GEORGE POPSON; VITALIY PUKHAYEV.

Cemeteries Commission—Rt. Rev. Mitred Archpriest JAMES HAYER; Rev. ROBERT W. LOZINSKI, C.S.C.; Very Revs. JOHN S. CUSTER, S.S.L., S.T.D.; MICHAEL J. SALNICKY, Chm.

Clergy Continued Education—Very Rev. JOHN S. CUSTER, S.S.L., S.T.D.

Commission for Ecumenism—Very Rev. EDUARD HIGGINS.

Communications and Telecommunications—Rt. Rev. Mitred Archpriest JAMES HAYER.

Evangelization—Very Rev. JOHN S. CUSTER, S.S.L., S.T.D.; Rev. JOSEPH BERTHA, Ph.D., Chm.; Very

Revs. JOHN G. BASARAB, M.A.; CONAN H. TIMONEY, Ph.D.

Respect Life—Rev. G. SCOTT BOGHOSSIAN, Asst. Dir.; Very Rev. VASYL CHEPELSKYY, (Ukraine) S.T.D.

Family Life—VACANT.

Eparchial Historian—Very Rev. JOHN S. CUSTER, S.S.L., S.T.D.

Eparchial Music Commission—MR. ELIAS ZAREVA, Member & Representative; JOSEPH K. FERENCHICK, Member & Rep.

Eparchial Newspaper—The Eastern Catholic Life Rev. JAMES BADEAUX, Editor; Very Rev. RONALD J. HATTON, Assoc. Editor; Rev. LEWIS RABAYDA, Layout Editor; MRS. DIANE RABIEJ, Copy Editor, Tel: 973-890-7794; MRS. MAUREEN FRENCH, Circulation.

Office for Eastern Christian Formation (formerly: Office of Religious Education)—Very Rev. VASYL CHEPELSKYY, (Ukraine) S.T.D.

Retirement Plan Board—Rt. Rev. Mitred Archpriest JAMES HAYER, Ex Officio; Rev. JOSEPH BERTHA, Ph. D.; Very Revs. EDWARD J. HIGGINS; MICHAEL J. SALNICKY; STEVEN GALUSCHIK; CONAN H. TIMONEY, Ph.D.

Saint Nicholas Shrine - Carpathian Village—Very Rev. MICHAEL J. SALNICKY, Dir., Mailing Address: P.O. Box 616, Canadensis, PA 18325. Tel: 570-595-3265; Fax: 570-595-6177.

Vocations—Very Revs. MICHAEL KERESTES; GARY J. MENSINGER; CONAN H. TIMONEY, Ph.D.; Rev. G. SCOTT BOGHOSSIAN.

Deacons Diaconate Formation Program—Very Rev. NICHOLAS A. DADDONA, B.A., M.S.; Deacon LAWRENCE FORAN.

Eastern Catholic Associates—Publication: "God With Us" *445 Lackawanna Ave., Woodland Park, 07424.*

Safe Environment Program—Rev. DAVID J. BARATELLI, Coord., Email: fr.dave.ewr@juno.com.

Victim Assistance Coordinator—DR. MAUREEN DADDONA, Ph.D., Tel: 516-623-6456. National Child Abuse Hotline:. Tel: 800-442-4453.

Eparchial Cultural Archives Commission—Very Rev. JOHN S. CUSTER, S.S.L., S.T.D., Chm.; Rev. JOSEPH BERTHA, Ph.D.; Rt. Rev. Mitred Archpriest JAMES HAYER; MRS. DIANE RABIEJ.

Bishop Michael J. Dudick Institute—Rev. MICHAEL G. POPSON, Dir.

CLERGY, PARISHES, MISSIONS AND PAROCHIAL SCHOOLS

STATE OF NEW JERSEY

PASSAIC, PASSAIC CO., ST. MICHAEL CATHEDRAL, [CEM]
96 First St., Passaic, 07055. Tel: 973-777-2553; Fax: 973-777-9474; Email: passaiccathedral@gmail.com; Web: stmichaelsarchangel.org. Very Rev. John S. Custer, S.S.L., S.T.D.
Catechesis Religious Program—Eastern Christian Formation, Students 10.
Chapel—St. Michael's Cathedral Chapel, 445 Lackawanna Ave., 07424.

BAYONNE, HUDSON CO., ST. JOHN THE BAPTIST
15 E. 26th St., Bayonne, 07002. Tel: 201-339-1840; Email: passaiccathedral@gmail.com. Very Rev. Marcel Szabo.

CARTERET, MIDDLESEX CO., ST. ELIAS
42 Cooke Ave., Carteret, 07008. Tel: 732-541-5213; Email: vitalgugle@gmail.com. Very Rev. Vitaliy Pukhayev, Admin.; Rev. Edward Semko, Pastor Emeritus.

DUNELLEN, MIDDLESEX CO., ST. NICHOLAS
121 Madison Ave., Dunellen, 08812.
Tel: 732-968-3337; Email: stnicholasdunellen@gmail.com. Rev. James Badeaux.

EAST BRUNSWICK, MIDDLESEX CO., NATIVITY OF OUR LORD
700 Old Bridge Tpke., East Brunswick, 08816. Cell: 570-507-4483; Email: korostil.00@mail.ru. Iaroslav Korostil, (Ukraine).

EDISON, MIDDLESEX CO., ST. NICHOLAS, Closed. For inquiries for parish records, please contact the chancery.

ELIZABETH, UNION CO., SS. PETER AND PAUL, Closed. For inquiries for parish records contact the chancery.

FLANDERS, MORRIS CO., HOLY WISDOM, Administered from St. Michael Cathedral, Passaic, NJ.
96 1st Street, Passaic, 07055. Tel: 973-777-2553; Fax: 973-777-9474; Email: holywisdomnj@gmail.com. 197 Emmans Rd., Flanders, 07836. Very Rev. John S. Custer, S.S.L., S.T.D., Admin.

HILLSBOROUGH TOWNSHIP, SOMERSET CO., ST. MARY'S
1900 Brooks Blvd., Hillsborough Township, 08844.
Tel: 908-725-0615; Fax: 908-725-9615; Email: pastor@stmaryhillsboroughnj.org; Web: www.stmaryhillsboroughnj.org. Rev. James Badeaux.
Catechesis Religious Program—Eastern Christian Formation, Julie Klikus, D.R.E. Students 68.

JERSEY CITY, HUDSON CO., ST. MARY'S, Administered from St. John the Baptist, Bayonne, NJ.
231 Pacific Ave., Jersey City, 07304.
Tel: 201-333-2975; Email: stmarybyzjerseycity@gmail.com. Very Rev. Marcel Szabo, Admin.; Rev. Hryhoriy Lozinskyy, Parochial Vicar.

LINDEN, UNION CO., ST. GEORGE THE GREAT MARTYR
417 McCandless St., Linden, 07036.
Tel: 908-486-6500; Email: stgeorgelinden@gmail.com; Web: stgeorgelinden.com. Rev. Vitaliy Pukayev, (Ukraine).

MAHWAH, BERGEN CO., HOLY SPIRIT, Administered from St. Michael Cathedral, Passaic, NJ
104 Church St., Mahwah, 07430. Tel: 973-777-2553; Fax: 973-777-9474; Email: holyspiritmahwah@gmail.com; Web: holyspiritmahwah.com. Mailing Address: 768 North St., East White Plains, NY 10605. Rev. Igor Vorontsov, Admin.

NEW BRUNSWICK, MIDDLESEX CO., ST. JOSEPH
30 High St., New Brunswick, 08901.
Tel: 732-545-1686; Email: SsPeterPaul1969@gmail.com. Rev. Mykhaylo Kravchuk, (Ukraine) Admin.

NEWARK, ESSEX CO., ST. GEORGE, Administered from St. John the Baptist, Bayonne, NJ.
214 Warwick St., Newark, 07105. Tel: 973-589-7202; Email: fr.dave.ewr@juno.com. Very Rev. Marcel Szabo, Admin.; Rev. David J. Baratelli, Sacramental Min.

PERTH AMBOY, MIDDLESEX CO.
1—ST. MICHAEL, [CEM]
P.O. Box 1297, Perth Amboy, 08862-1297. Rev. Martin Vavrak, (Slovakia).
Catechesis Religious Program—Eastern Christian Formation, Students 23.
Res.: 757 Gornik Dr., Perth Amboy, 08861.
Tel: 732-826-0792; Email: stmichaelspa@gmail.com.
2—ST. NICHOLAS, [CEM] (Administered to by St. Michael, Perth Amboy)
Mailing Address: P.O. Box 1030, Perth Amboy, 088621030. Tel: 732-442-0418; Email: stnicholaspa@gmail.com. 320 Washington St., Perth Amboy, 08861. Rev. Martin Vavrak, (Slovakia) Admin.

PHILLIPSBURG, WARREN CO., SS. PETER AND PAUL
723 S. Main St., Phillipsburg, 08865.
Tel: 610-867-2322; Email: DrPartagas@msn.com. Mailing Address: c/o 1140 Johnston Dr., Bethlehem, PA 18017. Very Rev. Peter J. Hosak, M.S., Admin.

RAHWAY, UNION CO., ST. THOMAS THE APOSTLE
1410 Church St., Rahway, 07065. Tel: 732-382-5300; Email: stthomasbyz@aol.com; Web: StThomasTheApostle.org. Rt. Rev. Mitred Archpriest James Hayer.

ROEBLING, BURLINGTON CO., ST. NICHOLAS, [CEM] Administered from St. Mary's, Trenton, NJ.
Tel: 609-447-0688; Email: yuriyorosit@gmail.com; Web: stnicholasroebling.org. Rev. Yuriy Oros, Admin.

SOMERSET, SOMERSET CO., SS. PETER AND PAUL, Administered by St. Joseph Catholic Church (Byzantine Rite), New Brunswick, NJ
285 Hamilton St., Somerset, 08873.
Tel: 732-545-5500; Email: SsPeterPaul1969@gmail.com. Rev. Mykhaylo Kravchuk, (Ukraine)
Saints Peter and Paul Byzantine Catholic Church.

TOMS RIVER, OCEAN CO., OUR LADY OF PERPETUAL HELP
1937 Church Rd., Toms River, 08753.
Tel: 732-255-6273; Fax: 732-255-9702; Email: ourladytomsriver@comcast.net; Web: www.facebook.com/groups/OLPHTomsRiver/. Very Rev. Francis J. Rella.

TRENTON, MERCER CO.
1—ST. MARY, [CEM]
411 Adeline St., Trenton, 08611. Tel: 609-394-5004; Email: yuriyorosit@gmail.com; Web: www.avmbcc.org/. Rev. Yuriy Oros, Admin.
2—ST. NICHOLAS, Closed. For parish records contact St. Mary of the Assumption, Trenton, NJ.

WOODLAND PARK
ST. MICHAEL'S CATHEDRAL CHAPEL
415 Lackawanna Ave., 07424.

STATE OF CONNECTICUT

BRIDGEPORT, FAIRFIELD CO., HOLY TRINITY, Closed. For inquiries for parish records contact the chancery.

DANBURY, FAIRFIELD CO., SAINT NICHOLAS BYZANTINE CATHOLIC CHURCH
13 Pembroke Rd., Danbury, CT 06811.
Tel: 203-743-1106; Fax: 203-743-5326; Email: stnicholasdanbury@icloud.com; Web: stnicholasdanbury.org. Very Rev. Ronald J. Hatton; Deacon Stephen Russo.
Catechesis Religious Program—Eastern Christian Formation, Ann Devine, D.R.E.

MERIDEN, NEW HAVEN CO., ST. NICHOLAS OF MYRA
89 Summer St., Meriden, CT 06450.
Tel: 860-229-2531; Email: StNicholasMer@earthlink.net. Rev. Lee Perry.

NEW BRITAIN, HARTFORD CO., HOLY TRINITY, [CEM]
121 Beaver St., New Britain, CT 06051.
Tel: 860-229-2531; Fax: 860-827-0564; Email: leperry025@gmail.com. Revs. Lee Perry, Admin.; Anthony P. DeFronzo.

TRUMBULL, FAIRFIELD CO., ST. JOHN THE BAPTIST
100 St. John's Dr., Trumbull, CT 06611.
Tel: 203-377-5967; Email: stjohnbyz@gmail.com. Rev. Joseph Bertha, Ph.D., Admin.

STATE OF FLORIDA

COCONUT CREEK, BROWARD CO., OUR LADY OF THE SIGN
7311 Lyons Rd., Coconut Creek, FL 33073.
Tel: 954-429-0056. Rev. Michael Kane, Ph.D.

FORT PIERCE, PORT ST. LUCIE CO., SS. CYRIL AND METHODIUS
1002 Bahama Ave., Fort Pierce, FL 34982.
Tel: 772-595-1021; Email: cmchurchoffice@gmail.com; Web: www.fortpiercebyzantine.com/. Rev. Frank A. Hanincik.

JACKSONVILLE, DUVAL CO., PROTECTION OF THE MOTHER OF GOD, Closed. For parish records, contact Holy Dormition, Ormond Beach, FL.

LAKE WORTH, DUVAL CO., HOLY APOSTLES, Closed. For parish records contact St. Basil, Miami, FL.

MIAMI, DADE CO., ST. BASIL (1966)
1475 N.E. 199 St., Miami, FL 33179.
Tel: 786-320-5125. Rev. Michael N. Kane, Ph.D.

NEW PORT RICHEY, PASCO CO., ST. ANNE'S
7120 Massachusetts Ave., New Port Richey, FL 34653. Tel: 727-849-1190; Email: olexiynebesnyk@gmail.com; Web: stannebyzantine.org. Rev. Olexiy Nebesnyk, Admin.
Catechesis Religious Program—Eastern Christian Formation, Students 10.

NORTH FORT MYERS, LEE CO., ALL SAINTS BYZANTINE CATHOLIC
10291 Bayshore Rd., North Fort Meyers, FL 33917. Very Rev. Steven Galuschik, Admin. In Res.

ORLANDO, ORANGE CO., ST. NICHOLAS OF MYRA
5135 W. Sand Lake Rd., Orlando, FL 32819.
Tel: 407-351-0133; Email: stnicholascatholicchurch@cfl.rr.com; Web: www.orlandobyzantine.com. Very Rev. Salvatore A. Pignato.

ORMOND BEACH, VOLUSIA CO., HOLY DORMITION, Administered from St. Nicholas of Myra, Orlando, FL.
Mailing Address: 5135 W. Sand Lake Rd., Orlando, FL 32819. Very Rev. Salvatore A. Pignato, Admin. In Res., Rev. Vincent M. Brady.
Church: 17 Buckskin Ln., Ormond Beach, FL 32174.

ST. PETERSBURG, PINELLAS CO., ST. THERESE
4236 13th Ave. N., St. Petersburg, FL 33713. Very Rev. Robert Evancho.
Catechesis Religious Program—Eastern Christian Formation, Students 14.

STATE OF GEORGIA

ROSWELL, FULTON CO., EPIPHANY OF OUR LORD BYZANTINE CATHOLIC CHURCH (1977)
2030 Old Alabama Rd., Roswell, GA 30076.
Tel: 770-993-0973; Email: office@epiphanybyz.org; Web: epiphanybyz.org. Rev. Lewis Rabayda; Deacons James Smith; Michael Tisma.
Catechesis Religious Program—Eastern Christian Formation, Karen Madrigal, D.R.E. Students 34.

STATE OF MARYLAND

BALTIMORE, BALTIMORE CO., PATRONAGE OF THE MOTHER OF GOD, Very Rev. Conan H. Timoney, Ph. D.
Church: 1260 Stevens Ave., Baltimore, MD 21227.
Tel: 410-247-4936; Email: patronage.church@gmail.com; Web: www.patronagechurch.com.
Missions—St. Francis—1450 Abingdon Rd., Abingdon, Harford Co. MD 21009. Tel: 410-734-6973; Email: dfrkotlar@comcast.net. Deacon Anthony Kotlar, Contact Person.
St. Ann's, 1525 Oak Hill Ave., Hagerstown, Washington Co. MD 21742. Tel: 301-797-5847; Web: www.patronagechurch.com/hagerstown-mission/welcome. Joseph Repasi, Contact Person.
Catechesis Religious Program—Eastern Catholic Formation (ECF), Cell: 410-703-5099; Email: lisaguba@sprintmail.com. Lisa Guba, D.R.E. Students 12.

BELTSVILLE, PRINCE GEORGE'S CO., ST. GREGORY OF NYSSA
12420 Old Gunpowder Rd. Spur, Beltsville, MD 20705. Tel: 301-953-9323; Email: info@stgregoryofnyssa.net; Web: stgregoryofnyssa.net. Very Rev. Conan H. Timoney, Ph.D., Admin.; Rev. Sergij Deiak, Parochial Vicar; Deacon William Szewczyk.
Catechesis Religious Program—Eastern Catholic Formation.

STATE OF MASSACHUSETTS

SOUTH HADLEY, HAMPSHIRE CO., ST. MICHAEL'S, Closed. For inquiries for parish records contact the chancery.

STATE OF NEW YORK

AMHERST, ERIE CO., ST. STEPHEN'S, Closed. For inquiries for parish records contact the chancery.

BINGHAMTON, BROOME CO., HOLY SPIRIT, [CEM]
360 Clinton St., Binghamton, NY 13905.
Tel: 607-203-1151; Email: holyspiritbyzchurch@yahoo.com. Rev. Peter Tomas, S.J.P.

BROOKLYN, KINGS CO., ST. ELIAS, Closed. For inquiries for parish records please contact Byzantine Catholic Eparchy of Passaic
Mailing Address: 445 Lackawanna Ave., 07424.
Tel: 973-890-7777; Email: drabiej@eparchyofpassaic.com. Most Rev. Kurt Burnette, D.D., J.C.L.
St. Elias Greek Rite Roman Catholic Church.

ENDICOTT, BROOME CO., SS. PETER AND PAUL'S, [CEM] Administered from Holy Spirit, Binghamton, NY
Mailing Address: c/o 360 Clinton St., Binghamton, NY 13905. Rev. Peter Tomas, Admin.

GRANVILLE, WASHINGTON CO., SS. PETER AND PAUL, [CEM] Administered from St. Mary's, New York, NY
Mailing Address: c/o 246 E. 15th St., New York, NY 10003. Tel: 212-677-0516; Email: pastorsaintmary@gmail.com. Very Rev. Robert J. Hospodar, J.C.L., Admin.
Church: 2 Park Ave., Granville, NY 12832.

NEW YORK, NEW YORK CO.
1—EXALTATION OF HOLY CROSS, Administered from St. Mary's, New York, NY
Mailing Address: 246 E. 15th St., New York, NY 10003. Tel: 212-677-0516; Email: pastorsaintmary@gmail.com. Very Rev. Edward G. Cimbala, D.Min., Admin.
Greek Rite Catholic Church of Exaltation of Holy Cross (and) Exaltation of the Holy Cross Byzantine Catholic Church
Church: 323 E. 82nd St., New York, NY 10028.
2—ST. MARY'S
246 E. 15th St., New York, NY 10003.
Tel: 212-677-0516; Email: fredcimbala@gmail.com. Very Rev. Edward G. Cimbala, D.Min.

OLEAN, CATTARAGUS CO., ST. MARY'S, (Administered to by St. Mary, Scranton, PA)
718 Fountain St., Olean, NY 14760.
Tel: 973-890-7777; Email: ndaddona@epachyofpassaic.com. Very Rev. Nicholas A. Daddona, B.A., M.S., Contact Person.

PEEKSKILL, WESTCHESTER CO., SS. PETER AND PAUL
705 Shenandoah Ave., Peekskill, NY 10566.
Tel: 914-737-8249; Email: robsen@aol.com. Very Rev. Ronald J. Hatton, Admin.; Rev. Msgr. Robert Senetsky, J.C.D., Pastor Emeritus, (Retired).

SMITHTOWN, SUFFOLK CO., RESURRECTION, [CEM]
225 Ellison Ave., Westbury, NY 11590. Cell: 631-759-6083; Email: resurrectionsmithtown@gmail.com. Rev. Tyler A. Strand, Admin.
Church: 38 Mayflower, Smithtown, NY 11787.

WESTBURY, NASSAU CO., ST. ANDREW THE APOSTLE
275 Ellison Ave., P.O. Box 684, Westbury, NY 11590.
Tel: 516-404-1162; Email: deaconnick88@gmail.com. Very Rev. Nicholas A. Daddona, B.A., M.S., Admin.
Catechesis Religious Program—Eastern Christian Formation, Students 4.

WHITE PLAINS, WESTCHESTER CO., ST. NICHOLAS OF MYRA
768 North St., White Plains, NY 10605.
Tel: 914-681-0659; Email: frvorontsov@gmail.com; Web: www.stnicholas.life. Rev. Igor Vorontsov, Admin.

YONKERS, WESTCHESTER CO., ST. NICHOLAS OF MYRA, Closed. For inquiries for parish records please contact St. Nicholas of Myra, White Plains, NY.

STATE OF NORTH CAROLINA

CARY, WAKE CO., SS. CYRIL & METHODIUS BYZANTINE CATHOLIC
2510 Piney Plains Rd., Cary, NC 27511.
Tel: 919-239-4877; Email: rfmark@nc.rr.com. Very Rev. Mark Shuey, Admin.

STATE OF PENNSYLVANIA

ALLENTOWN, LEHIGH CO.
1—ST. ANDREW THE APOSTLE, Closed. For parish records, contact St. Michael, Allentown.
2—ST. MICHAEL
Tel: 610-432-6773; Email: drpartagas@msn.com; Web: byzcath.org/allentown. Very Rev. Peter J. Hosak, M.S., Admin.

BEAVER MEADOWS, CARBON CO., SS. PETER AND PAUL, [CEM]
119 Berwick St., P.O. Box 206, Beaver Meadows, PA 18216. Tel: 570-455-1442; Email: ssppbyz@ptd.net. Rev. James J. Demko.
Catechesis Religious Program—Eastern Christian Formation, Students 24.

BETHLEHEM, NORTHAMPTON CO., SS. PETER AND PAUL
1140 Johnston Dr., Bethlehem, PA 18017.
Tel: 610-867-2322; Email: drpartagas@msn.com. Very Rev. Peter J. Hosak, M.S.

BROCKTON, SCHUYLKILL CO., ST. MARY'S, [CEM] Administered from St. Mary's, Mahanoy City, PA.
Mailing Address: c/o 621 Mahanoy Ave., Mahanoy City, PA 17948. Tel: 570-773-2631; Email: jimc12@ptd.net. Rev. James Carroll, O.F.M., Admin.
Church: Green St., Brockton, PA 17925.

CLARKS SUMMIT, LACKAWANNA CO., TRANSFIGURATION, Closed. For parish records contact St. Mary, Scranton, PA.

COATESVILLE, CHESTER CO., ST. MARY'S, Administered from St. Michael, Mont Clare, PA.
88 Gap Rd., Coatesville, PA 19320. Tel: 610-933-2819 ; Email: pastor@stmichaelbyz.net; Web: www.bvmdormition.org. Very Rev. Edward J. Higgins, Admin.

DUNMORE, LACKAWANNA CO., ST. MICHAEL, [CEM]
Tel: 570-344-2521; Email: rwlcsc18505@aol.com. Rev. Robert W. Lozinski, C.S.C.
Catechesis Religious Program—Eastern Christian Formation, Students 12.

FOREST CITY, SUSQUEHANNA CO., ST. JOHN THE BAPTIST, [CEM] Administered from Holy Ghost, Jessup, PA
Mailing Address: c/o 313 First Ave., Jessup, PA 18434. Tel: 570-489-2353; Fax: 570-489-7049; Email: holyghostjessup@yahoo.com. 306 Susquehanna St., Forest City, PA 18421. Rev. John J. Cigan, J.C.B., Admin.; Deacon Robert Behrens.
Catechesis Religious Program—Eastern Christian Formation, Students 2.

FREELAND, LUZERNE CO., ST. MARY'S, [CEM]
643 Fern St., Freeland, PA 18224. Tel: 570-636-0700; Fax: ; Email: frscottb@gmail.com. Rev. G. Scott Boghossian, Admin.

GLEN LYON, LUZERNE CO., ST. MICHAEL, Closed. For parish records contact St. Mary's, Kingston, PA.

HARRISBURG, DAUPHIN CO., ST. ANN
5408 Locust Ln., Harrisburg, PA 17109.
Tel: 717-652-1415; Email: michaelpopson@aol.com; Web: www.stannbyz.org. Rev. Michael G. Popson.

HAZLETON, LUZERNE CO.
1—ST. JOHN THE BAPTIST CHURCH, [CEM]
5 E. 20th St., Hazleton, PA 18201. Tel: 570-454-1142; Fax: 570-454-6120; Email: stjohnbyz18201@gmail.com. Rev. Jerome Wolbert, O.F.M.; Deacon Lawrence Foran.
Catechesis Religious Program—Eastern Christian Formation, Monica Washko, D.R.E. Students 14.
2—ST. MARY'S
227 E. Beech St., Hazleton, PA 18201.
Tel: 570-455-3232; Email: peter.donish@mygait.com. Rev. Peter M. Donish.

HILLTOWN, BUCKS CO., BYZANTINE CATHOLIC MISSION OF BUCKS COUNTY, PA, Closed. For mission records contact Holy Ghost, Philadelphia, PA.

JESSUP, LACKAWANNA CO., HOLY GHOST, [CEM]
313 First Ave., Jessup, PA 18434. Tel: 570-489-2353; Fax: 570-489-7049; Email: holyghostjessup@yahoo.com; Web: www.holyghostjessup.weebly.com. Rev. John J. Cigan, J.C.B.; Deacon Robert Behrens.
Catechesis Religious Program—Eastern Christian Formation, Joyce Covaleski, D.R.E. Students 15.

KINGSTON, LUZERNE CO., ST. MARY'S, [CEM]
321 Chestnut Ave., Kingston, PA 18704.
Tel: 570-287-0282; Email: SaintMaryKingston@Yahoo.com. Rev. Mykhaylo Prodanets.

LANSFORD, CARBON CO., ST. JOHN THE BAPTIST, [CEM]
116 E. Bertsch St., Lansford, PA 18232.
Tel: 570-645-2640; Email: sjpastor@ptd.net; Web: www.stjohnsbyzantinecatholicchurch.org. Very Rev. Vasyl Chepelskyy, (Ukraine) S.T.D., Admin., (Eparchy of Buchach, Ukraine).

LOPEZ, SULLIVAN CO., SS. PETER AND PAUL, [CEM] Closed. For inquiries for parish records please contact St. Mary's, Scranton, PA.

MAHANOY CITY, SCHUYLKILL CO., ST. MARY'S, [CEM]
621 W. Mahanoy Ave., Mahanoy City, PA 17948.
Tel: 570-773-2631; Email: jimc12@ptd.net. Rev. James Carroll, O.F.M., Admin.
Catechesis Religious Program—Eastern Christian Formation, Students 24.

MCADOO, SCHUYLKILL CO., ST. MICHAEL, [CEM]
17 E. Blaine St., McAdoo, PA 18237.
Tel: 570-929-1062; Email: gcollie@ptd.net. Rev. Gregory Hosler.

MINERSVILLE, SCHUYLKILL CO., SS. PETER AND PAUL, [CEM]
107 S. Fourth St., Minersville, PA 17954.
Tel: 570-544-2074; Fax: 570-544-9441; Email: sspnp1074@gmail.com. Very Rev. Gregory J. Noga, M.A.

MONT CLARE, MONTGOMERY CO., ST. MICHAEL, [CEM]
203 Jacob St., Mont Clare, PA 19453.
Tel: 610-933-2819; Email: parish@stmichaelbyzantine.org; Web: stmichaelbyzantine.org/. Very Rev. Edward J. Higgins, Admin.

NANTICOKE, LUZERNE CO., ST. MARY'S, Closed. (Hanover) For inquiries for parish records contact St. John's, Wilkes-Barre, PA.

NESQUEHONING, CARBON CO., ST. MARY'S, [CEM] Administered from St. John the Baptist, Lansford, PA.
141 W. High St., Nesquehoning, PA 18240.
Tel: 570-645-2640; Email: sjpastor@ptd.net. Very Rev. Vasyl Chepelskyy, (Ukraine) S.T.D., Admin.

NEWTOWN, BUCKS CO., OUR LADY OF PERPETUAL HELP
1773 Woodbourne Rd., Levittown, PA 19057.
Tel: 215-968-8707; Web: frvasylolph@gmail.com. P.O. Box 777, Levittown, PA 19058. Very Rev. Edward J. Higgins, Admin.; Revs. Vasyl Sokolovych, Parochial Vicar; Myron M. Badnerosky, Pastor Emeritus.
Res.: 2 Coral Rock Rd., Levittown, PA 19057.
Tel: 908-872-2928; Email: fredcimbala@gmail.com.

OLD FORGE, LACKAWANNA CO., ST. NICHOLAS, [CEM]
140 Church St., Old Forge, PA 18518.
Tel: 570-457-3042; Email: edshestak@yahoo.com. Very Rev. Eduard Shestak, J.C.L., S.T.D., Admin.

PALMERTON, CARBON CO., SS. PETER AND PAUL, Administered from St. Michael's, Allentown, PA
Mailing Address: c/o 156 Green St., Allentown, PA 18102. Tel: 610-432-6773; Email: stmichaelallentown@ptd.net; Web: byzcath.org/allentown. Very Rev. Peter J. Hosak, M.S., Admin.
Church: 142 Lafayette Ave., Palmerton, PA 18071.

PHILADELPHIA, PHILADELPHIA CO.
1—HOLY GHOST
2310 S. 24th St., Philadelphia, PA 19145.
Tel: 215-334-5129; Fax: 215-334-1797; Email: schnauzerfred@aol.com. Very Rev. Edward J. Higgins.
Catechesis Religious Program—Eastern Christian Formation, Justine Leach, D.R.E. Students 18.
2—HOLY TRINITY, Administered from Holy Ghost, Philadelphia, PA.
6801 N. 10th St., Philadelphia, PA 19126.
Tel: 215-334-5129; Fax: 215-334-1797; Email: schnauzerfred@aol.com. Very Rev. Edward J. Higgins, Admin.

PITTSTON, LUZERNE CO., ST. MICHAEL, [CEM]
205 N. Main St., Pittston, PA 18640.
Tel: 570-654-4564; Email: gfire3363@gmail.com; Web: stmichaelsbyzantine.com. Very Rev. Gary J. Mensinger, Admin.

POCONO SUMMIT, MONROE CO., ST. NICHOLAS
2121 Commerce St., P.O. Box 515, Pocono Summit, PA 18346. Tel: 570-839-8090; Tel: 570-595-3265; Tel: 570-650-3252; Email: stnicpoc@earthlink.net. Very Rev. Michael J. Salnicky.
Catechesis Religious Program—Eastern Christian Formation.

POTTSTOWN, MONTGOMERY CO., ST. JOHN'S GREEK CATHOLIC CHURCH POTTSTOWN PA, [CEM]
301 Cherry St., Pottstown, PA 19464.
Tel: 610-326-1877; Email: stjohnbyzcathchurch@gmail.com. Rev. Nicholas DeProspero.

ST. CLAIR, SCHUYLKILL CO., ST. MARY'S, [CEM] Administered from SS. Peter and Paul, Minersville, PA.
Mailing Address: c/o 107 S. 4th St., Minersville, PA 17954. Tel: 570-544-2074; Email: sspnp@gmail.com. Very Rev. Gregory J. Noga, M.A., Admin.
Church: 131 S. Morris St., St. Clair, PA 17970.

SCRANTON, LACKAWANNA CO.
1—ST. JOHN THE BAPTIST, [CEM] Administered from St. Mary's, Scranton, PA.
Mailing Address: c/o 310 Mifflin Ave., Scranton, PA 18503. Tel: 570-342-8429; Fax: 570-342-6773; Email: revleonardmartinsj@hotmail.com. Rev. Leonard A. Martin, S.J., Admin.
Church: 310 Broadway, Scranton, PA 18505.
2—ST. MARY'S, [CEM]
310 Mifflin Ave., Scranton, PA 18503.
Tel: 570-342-8429; Email: revleonardmartinsj@hotmail.com. Rev. Leonard A. Martin, S.J.

SHEPPTON, SCHUYLKILL CO., ST. MARY'S, [CEM] Administered from SS. Peter and Paul, Beaver Meadows, PA
Mailing Address: c/o P.O. Box 206, Beaver Meadows, PA 18216. Tel: 570-455-1442; Email: ssppbyz@ptd.net. Rev. James J. Demko, Admin.

SWOYERSVILLE, LUZERNE CO., ST. NICHOLAS, [CEM] Administered from St. Michael, Pittston, PA
Mailing Address: c/o 205 N. Main St., Pittston, PA 18640. Tel: 570-654-4564; Email: gfire3363@gmail.com. Very Rev. Gary J. Mensinger, Admin.
Church: 271 Tripp St., Swoyersville, PA 18704.

TAYLOR, LACKAWANNA CO., ST. MARY'S, [CEM] Administered from St. Nicholas, Old Forge, PA
Mailing Address: c/o 140 Church St., Old Forge, PA 18518. Very Rev. Eduard Shestak, J.C.L., S.T.D., Admin.
Church: 700 Oak St., Taylor, PA 18517.
Tel: 570-457-3042; Email: edshestak@yahoo.com.

WILKES-BARRE, LUZERNE CO.
1—ST. JOHN'S, Administered from St. Mary's,

Kingston, PA.
526 Church St., Wilkes-Barre, PA 18702.
Tel: 570-825-4338; Email: SaintMaryKingston@yahoo.com. Rev. Mykhaylo Prodanets, Admin.
2—ST. MARY'S, [CEM]
695 N. Main St., Wilkes-Barre, PA 18705.
Tel: 570-822-6028; Email: secretary@stmarywb.com. Very Rev. Michael Kerestes.
WILLIAMSTOWN, DAUPHIN CO., HOLY SPIRIT, [CEM] Closed. For inquiries for parish records contact SS. Peter and Paul, Minersville, PA.

STATE OF VIRGINIA

ANNANDALE, FAIRFAX CO., EPIPHANY OF OUR LORD
3410 Woodburn Rd., Annandale, VA 22003.
Tel: 703-573-3986; Fax: 703-573-0344; Email: epiphanyva@aol.com; Email: epiphanyofourlord@verizon.net; Web: www.eolbcc.org. Very Rev. John G. Basarab, M.A.
Mission—Mother of God Community School, 20501 Goshen Rd., Gaithersburg, MD 20879.
Catechesis Religious Program—Epiphany Eastern Catholic Formation, Tel: 703-573-1042. Mary Ellen Kepick, D.R.E. Students 56.
WILLIAMSBURG, YORK CO., ASCENSION OF OUR LORD
Mailing Address: P.O. Box 5096, Williamsburg, VA 23188. Tel: 757-220-8098; Email: Pastor@ascensionva.org; Web: AscensionVA.org. 114 Palace Ln., Williamsburg, VA 23185. Rev. Alex Shuter, Archeparchy of Lviv, Ukraine.
Mission—Our Lady of Perpetual Help, 216 S. Parliament Dr., Virginia Beach, Virginia Beach Co. VA 23462.

Special or Other Diocesan Assignment:
Very Rev.—
Barusefski, Ronald, J.C.L.
Rev.—
DeFronzo, Anthony P.

On Duty Outside Diocese:
Rev.—
Fulton, Eugene J., One Pryer Manor Rd., Larchmont, NY 10538. Tel: 914-632-3743.

Leave of Absence:
Revs.—
Drucker, James N.
Kapron, Alan
Krulak, Michael
Mitchko, James
Slesinski, Robert F., Ph.D.
Sopoliga, Michael.

Retired:
Rev. Msgrs.—
Puhak, Nicholas I., (Retired), 643 Fern St., Freeland, PA 18224. Tel: 570-636-0700
Senetsky, Robert, J.C.D., (Retired), 705 Shenandoah Ave., Peekskill, NY 10566
Revs.—
Badnerosky, Myron, (Retired), 1787 Woodbourne Rd., Levittown, PA 19056
Bitsko, Daniel J., (Retired)
Brown, Charles, M.D., (Retired), 7140 Wissahickon Ave., Philadelphia, PA 19119. Tel: 011-22-48-38-78
Bujnak, George A., (Retired), 17 E. Blaine St., McAdoo, PA 18237
Gera, Francis, (Retired)
Kraynak, Nicholas, (Retired), 328 S. Belle Vista Ave., Youngstown, OH 44509
Petruska, Christopher, (Retired), 15544 Bellflower Blvd., Apt. C, Bellflower, CA 90706
Scott, Philip P., Ph.D., (Retired)
Tigyer, Paul, (Retired), 107 Clarkson Ave., Jessup, PA 18434. Tel: 570-383-7573
Untereiner, Harry P., (Retired), 67 Mansfield Dr., Brick, 08724
Yurista, Michael J., (Retired), 121 Madison Ave., Dunellen, 08812
Zeyack, John, S.T.L., (Retired), 53 Blue Ridge Dr., Brick, 08724.

Deacons:
Behrens, Robert
Dozier, Daniel
Foran, Lawrence
Fraser, James IV
Frey, Edward
Guze, John G., (Leave of Absence)
Kotlar, Anthony, (Leave of Absence)
Kubik, Alexander
Laskowski, Charles J.
Obsitnik, Vincent, (Inactive)
Opalka, Michael
Pekarik, Elmer
Quinn, Edward
Russo, Stephen
Senoyuit, Michael III
Shubeck, Thomas
Smith, James
Soroka, Basil
Sotack, Nicholas
Szewczyk, William
Thomas, David, (Retired)
Tisma, Michael
Tizio, William, (Retired)
Tokarcsik, George M., (Leave of Absence)
Turko, Peter
Wolfe, Daniel, (Leave of Absence)
Worlinsky, Lawrence.

INSTITUTIONS LOCATED IN DIOCESE

[A] MONASTERIES

SYBERTSVILLE, PA. *Holy Dormition Friary*, 712 Rte. 93, Sugarloaf, PA 18249. Tel: 570-788-1212;
Fax: 570-788-2431; Email: holydormition@gmail.com; Web: byzfranciscan.org. P.O. Box 270, Sybertsville, PA 18251. Revs. James Carroll, O.F.M.; Jerome Wolbert, O.F.M.; Bro. Augustine Paulik, O.F.M.

[B] CONVENTS AND RESIDENCES FOR SISTERS

SUGARLOAF, PA. *Holy Annunciation Monastery*, 403 W. County Rd., Sugarloaf, PA 18249.
Tel: 570-788-1205; Fax: 570-788-3329; Email: marija@ptd.net; Web: www.byzantinediscalcedcarmelites.com. Mother Marija Shields, Abbess. Discalced Carmelite Nuns of the Byzantine Rite. Sisters 14.
WILKES-BARRE, PA. *Sisters of Saint Basil The Great Saint Mary of the Assumption Convent*, 522 Madison St., Wilkes-Barre, PA 18705.
Tel: 570-824-3973; Email: srreginaosbm@verizon.net. Sr. Regina Adams, Supr. Sisters 2.

[C] SHRINES AND SPIRITUAL RENEWAL CENTERS

CANADENSIS, PA. *Carpathian Village*, 802 Snow Hill Rd., Cresco, PA 18326. Tel: 570-595-3265; Cell: 570-650-3252; Email: carpathianvillage@earthlink.net. Very Rev. Michael J. Salnicky, Dir.

[D] MISCELLANEOUS

DANBURY, CT. *Maria Theresa Foundation, Inc.* (2018) 13 Pembroke Rd., Danbury, CT 06811.
WOODLAND PARK, NJ. *Eastern Catholic Associates*, 445 Lackawanna Ave., 07424. Tel: 973-890-7777;
Fax: 973-890-7175; Email: bishop@eparchyofpassaic.com. Most Rev. Kurt Burnette, D.D., J.C.L., Pres.
God with Us Publications, Tel: 973-890-7777;
Fax: 973-890-7175; Email: ndaddona@eparchyofpassaic.com. Most Revs. John Michael Botean, Pres.; Paul Chomnycky, O.S.B.M.; Bohdan Danylo, Sec.; John M. Kudrick, Treas.; Kurt Burnette, D.D., J.C.L., Trustee.

RELIGIOUS INSTITUTES OF MEN REPRESENTED IN THE DIOCESE
For further details refer to the corresponding bracketed number in the Religious Institutes of Men or Women section.
[0520]—*Franciscan Friars*—O.F.M.
RELIGIOUS INSTITUTES OF WOMEN REPRESENTED IN THE DIOCESE
[0420]—*Discalced Carmelite Nuns (Byzantine Rite)*—O.C.D.
[3730]—*Sisters of the Order of St. Basil the Great*—O.S.B.M.

NECROLOGY

† Ellis, Frank, (Retired), Died Feb. 26, 2018
† Yastishock, Charles, Toms River, NJ Our Lady of Perpetual Help, Died Feb. 19, 2018

An asterisk (*) denotes an organization that has established tax-exempt status directly with the IRS and is not covered by the USCCB Group Ruling.

Metropolitan Archeparchy of Philadelphia Ukrainian

Most Reverend

ANDRIY RABIY

Auxiliary Bishop of Philadelphia Ukrainian; ordained December 19, 2001; appointed Titular Bisho pof Germaniciana and Auxiliary Bishop of Philadelphia Ukrainian August 8, 2017; installed September 24, 2017; appointed Apostolic Administrator of Philadelphia Ukrainian April 16, 2018; ceased June 4, 2019. *Office: 827 N. Franklin St., Philadelphia, PA 19123.*

Most Reverend

STEFAN SOROKA

Archbishop Emeritus of Philadelphia Ukrainian; ordained June 13, 1982; appointed Auxiliary Bishop of Winnipeg (Ukrainian) March 29, 1996; ordained Auxiliary Bishop of Winnipeg (Ukrainian) June 13, 1996; appointed Archbishop of Philadelphia Ukrainian November 29, 2000; installed Archbishop of Philadelphia Ukrainian February 27, 2001; retired April 16, 2018.

Most Reverend

BORYS ANDRIJ GUDZIAK

Archbishop of Philadelphia Ukrainian; ordained November 26, 1998; appointed Titular Bishop of Carcabia and Apostolic Exarch of France (Ukrainian); ordained August 26, 2012; installed Apostolic Exarch of France (Ukrainian) December 2, 2012; appointed Saint Vladimir-Le-Grand de Paris (Ukrainian) January 19, 2013; appointed Philadelphia Ukrainian February 18, 2019; installed June 4, 2019.

Chancery Office: 810 N. Franklin St., Philadelphia, PA 19123-2097. Tel: 215-627-0143; Fax: 215-627-0377.

Email: ukrmet@ukrcap.org

Most Reverend

STEPHEN SULYK

Archbishop Emeritus of Philadelphia Ukrainian; ordained June 14, 1952; appointed Archbishop of Philadelphia Ukrainian December 29, 1980; ordained March 1, 1981; retired November 29, 2000.

Most Reverend

JOHN BURA

Auxiliary Bishop of Philadelphia Ukrainian; ordained February 14, 1971; appointed Auxiliary Bishop of Philadelphia Ukrainian and Titular Bishop of Limisa January 3, 2006; ordained February 21, 2006; appointed Apostolic Administrator of the Eparchy of St. Josaphat in Parma July 29, 2009; resigned Apostolic Administrator August 7, 2014.

ESTABLISHED MAY 28, 1913.

The jurisdiction of the Metropolitan Archdiocese of Philadelphia includes the District of Columbia, the States of Virginia, Maryland, Delaware, New Jersey and eastern Pennsylvania to the eastern boundaries of the following Counties: Potter, Clinton, Center, Mifflin, Huntington and Fulton. With regard to persons, his subjects are all Catholics of the Byzantine Rite: 1. Who immigrated to this country from Galicia, Bucovina and other Ukrainian provinces; 2. Who descend from such persons (can. 755); 3. Women married to men referable to 1. and 2. if they comply with can. 98, n. 4; 4. Who in accordance with can. 98, n. 3 changed their Rite; 5. Converts to the Catholic Church of the Byzantine Rite; 6. And in fact all other Catholics of the Byzantine Rite who are attached to parishes subject to the jurisdiction of the Archbishop.

For legal titles of parishes and archdiocesan institutions, consult the Chancery Office.

STATISTICAL OVERVIEW

Personnel	
Archbishops	1
Retired Archbishops	2
Auxiliary Bishops	2
Abbots	1
Priests: Diocesan Active in Diocese	43
Priests: Diocesan Active Outside Diocese	1
Priests: Retired, Sick or Absent	7
Number of Diocesan Priests	51
Religious Priests in Diocese	3
Total Priests in Diocese	54
Extern Priests in Diocese	2
Permanent Deacons in Diocese	6
Total Sisters	57
Parishes	
Parishes	62
With Resident Pastor:	
Resident Diocesan Priests	40
Resident Religious Priests	1
Without Resident Pastor:	
Administered by Priests	21
Missions	2
Professional Ministry Personnel:	
Sisters	2
Lay Ministers	3
Welfare	
Homes for the Aged	2
Total Assisted	311
Educational	
Seminaries, Diocesan	1
Students from This Diocese	3
Total Seminarians	3
Colleges and Universities	1
Total Students	580
High Schools, Private	1
Total Students	270
Elementary Schools, Diocesan and Parish	3
Total Students	320
Catechesis/Religious Education:	
High School Students	125
Elementary Students	846
Total Students under Catholic Instruction	2,144
Teachers in the Diocese:	
Priests	1
Sisters	6
Lay Teachers	125
Vital Statistics	
Receptions into the Church:	
Infant Baptism Totals	226
Minor Baptism Totals	3
Adult Baptism Totals	10
Received into Full Communion	64
First Communions	178
Confirmations	303
Marriages:	
Catholic	58
Interfaith	16
Total Marriages	74
Deaths	558
Total Catholic Population	13,141

Former Bishops—Most Revs. STEPHEN SOTER ORTYNSKY, O.S.B.M., D.D., First Ukrainian Catholic Bishop of the United States; ord. July 18, 1891; cons. May 12, 1907; died March 24, 1916; CONSTANTINE BOHACHEVSKY, D.D., S.T.D., appt. Bishop in the United States, May 20, 1924; appt. Metropolitan Archbishop of the Philadelphia Archeparchy, Byzantine Rite, Aug. 6, 1958; cons. June 15, 1924; died Jan. 6, 1961; AMBROSE SENYSHYN, O.S.B.M., D.D., appt. Auxiliary Bishop to the Philadelphia Bishop, July 6, 1942; appt. Exarch of Stamford, July 20, 1956; appt. Eparch of Stamford, Nov. 1, 1958; appt. Metropolitan Archbishop of Philadelphia, Aug. 14, 1961; died Sept. 11, 1976; JOSEPH M. SCHMONDIUK, D.D., appt. Titular Bishop of Zeugma and Auxiliary of the Archeparchy of Philadelphia, July 20, 1956; cons. Nov. 8, 1956; transferred to the Diocese of Stamford See, Nov. 9, 1961; appt. Metropolitan Archbishop of Philadelphia, Oct. 1, 1977; died Dec. 25, 1978; His Eminence MYROSLAV CARDINAL LUBACHIVSKY, D.D., appt. Metropolitan Archbishop of Philadelphia, Sept. 21, 1979; appt. Apostolic Administrator of Philadelphia, Oct. 3, 1979; cons. in Rome, Nov. 12, 1979; named Coadjutor Major Archbishop of Lviw, March 24, 1980; transferred to Rome; Assumed position of Major Archbishop of Lviw, Sept. 7, 1984. Created Cardinal, May 25, 1985; died Dec. 14, 2000; Most Revs. STEPHEN SULYK, D.D., (Retired), appt. Archbishop of Philadelphia for Ukrainians and Metropolitan of the Ukrainian Catholic Church in the USA, Dec. 29, 1980; ord. March 1, 1981; retired Nov. 29, 2000; STEFAN SOROKA, ord. June 13, 1982; appt. Auxiliary Bishop of Winnipeg (Ukrainian) March 29, 1996; ord. Auxiliary Bishop of Winnipeg (Ukrainian) June 13, 1996; appt. Archbishop of Philadelphia for Ukrainians and Metropolitan of the Ukrainian Catholic Church in the USA, Nov. 29, 2000; installed Feb. 27, 2001; retired April 16, 2018.

Protosyncellus—Email: vicargeneral@ukrcap.org. VACANT.

Chancellor—Tel: 215-627-0143; Email: chancellor@ukrcap.org. Rev. Msgr. PETER D. WASLO, J.C.L.

Vice Chancellor—Very Rev. Archpriest JOHN M. FIELDS, Email: ibah@ukrcap.org.

Secretary—OLGA KUZEWYCZ.

Chancery Office—810 N. Franklin St., Philadelphia, 19123-2097. Tel: 215-627-0143; Fax: 215-627-0377.

College of Archeparchial Consultors—Most Rev. JOHN BURA; Very Rev. JOHN SENIW, J.C.L.; Rev. MARK FESNIAK; Very Rev. ROBERT J. HITCHENS; Revs. TARAS SVIRCHUK, C.Ss.R.; IVAN TURYK; Rev. Msgr. PETER D. WASLO, J.C.L.

Presbyteral Council—Rev. Msgr. PETER D. WASLO, J.C.L.; Very Revs. IVAN DEMKIV; ROBERT J. HITCHENS; Rev. Archpriest DANIEL TROYAN; Rev. STEPAN BILYK; Very Rev. Archpriest DANIEL GUROVICH; Very Revs. NESTOR IWASIW; ROMAN PITULA; MARK FESNIAK; WASYL KHARUK; JOHN CIURPITA; Very Rev. Archpriest JOHN M. FIELDS.

Archeparchial Corporation—Very Most Rev. ANDRIY RABIY, Pres.; Most Rev. JOHN BURA; JOHN DROZD, Treas.; Very Revs. ROBERT J. HITCHENS, Sec.; JOHN SENIW, J.C.L.

Archdiocesan Tribunal—810 N. Franklin St., Philadelphia, 19123. Tel: 215-627-0143; Email: metropolitantribunal@ukrcap.org.

Judicial Vicar—Rev. Msgr. PETER D. WASLO, J.C.L.

Judge—Rev. MYKOLA IVANOV, J.C.L.

Promoter of Justice—VACANT.

Auditor—VACANT.

Defender of the Bond—Rev. RUSLAN ROMANYUK, J.C.L.

Notary—GLORIA LEINART.

Director of Evangelization—Very Rev. Archpriest JOHN M. FIELDS.

Archeparchial Council for Economic Affairs—Very Most Rev. ANDRIY RABIY; JOHN DROZD; HELEN CHELOC; LEONARD MAZUR; ANDREW FYLYPOWYCH; KEN HUTCHINS; ANNA KERDA.

Financial Officer—JOHN DROZD.

Archeparchial Finance Council—VACANT.

Protopresbyters (Deans)—Rev. Msgr. PETER D. WASLO, J.C.L., Philadelphia; Very Revs. JOHN SENIW, J.C.L., Lehigh-Schuylkill Valley, North Anthracite; NESTOR IWASIW, North Anthracite; TARAS LONCHYNA, New Jersey; Very Rev. Archpriest MICHAEL HUTSKO, South Anthracite; Very Rev. ROBERT J. HITCHENS, Washington.

Diocesan Offices and Directors

Youth Ministry—VACANT, Dir.

Pro-Life and Family Ministry—Very Rev. TARAS LONCHYNA.

Apostolate—JOHN DROZD.

Cemeteries—TARAS HANKEWYCH.

Censor—Rev. Msgr. RONALD P. POPIVCHAK, Ph.D.

Ecumenical Relations—VACANT.

Insurance Commission—JOHN DROZD.

Director of Communications—Very Rev. Archpriest JOHN M. FIELDS, Dir.; Rev. IHOR BLOSHCHYNSKYY, (Ukraine) Asst. Dir., Email: communications@ukrcap.org.

Director of Development—Rev. MARK FESNIAK.

The Way - Online Newspaper—Email: theway@ukrarcheparchy.us; Web: www.ukrarcheparchy.us. TERESA SIWAK, Editor; Very Rev. Archpriest JOHN M. FIELDS, Editor; Rev. D. GEORGE WORSCHAK, Asst. Editor.

Archdiocesan Bulletin—Office: 810 N. Franklin St., Philadelphia, 19123.

Priests Beneficial Fund—Very Most Rev. ANDRIY RABIY, Pres.; Very Rev. Archpriest JOHN M. FIELDS, Sec. & Treas.; Rev. Msgr. PETER D. WASLO, J.C.L.; Very Revs. TARAS LONCHYNA; IVAN DEMKIV; JOHN SENIW, J.C.L. Board Members: Rev. Archpriest MICHAEL HUTSKO; Very Rev. Archpriest JOHN M. FIELDS; Very Rev. JOHN SENIW, J.C.L.; Rev. Msgr. JAMES T. MELNIC; Very Rev. WASYL KHARUK, Alternate Member.

Office of Vocations—Rev. PAUL J. MAKAR, Dir., Tel: 215-627-0143; Email: vocations@ukrcap.org.

Archeparchial Seminary Advisory and Admissions Board—Very Most Rev. ANDRIY RABIY; Very Revs. ROBERT J. HITCHENS; NESTOR IWASIW.

Department of Religious Education—Email: ukrcatecheticaloffice@ukrcap.org. Very Rev. Archpriest JOHN M. FIELDS, Dir.

Byzantine Church Supplies—MRS. MYROSLAVA DEMKIV, Tel: 215-627-0660; Email: byzsupplies@yahoo.com.

Archeparchial Museum—Treasury of Faith. Tel: 215-627-3389; Email: tofmuseum@ukrcap.org. Sisters EVHENIA PRUSNAY, M.S.M.G.; TIMOTHEA KONYU, M.S.M.G.

Victim Assistance Coordinator—KEN HUTCHINS, Tel: 215-873-6162; Email: ukrchildprotection@ukrcap.org.

Deacon Formation—Very Rev. Archpriest JOHN M. FIELDS, Dir.

CLERGY, PARISHES, MISSIONS AND PAROCHIAL SCHOOLS

CITY OF PHILADELPHIA

(PHILADELPHIA COUNTY)

1—IMMACULATE CONCEPTION OF BLESSED VIRGIN MARY, CATHEDRAL, [CEM]
819 N. 8th St., 19123. Tel: 215-922-2845; Email: cathedralonfranklin@comcast.net. 830 N. Franklin St., 19123. Very Rev. Roman Pitula, Rector; Deacon Michael P. Waak.
Chapel—Missionary Sisters of Mother God Convent.

2—ST. ANDREW, Closed. For inquiries for parish records contact the Cathedral of the Immaculate Conception, Philadelphia.

3—ANNUNCIATION OF THE B.V.M. (1962)
1206 Valley Rd., Melrose Park, 19027-3035.
Tel: 215-635-1627; Email: a.b.v.m@verizon.net. Rev. Ihor Bloshchynskyy.
Church: 1204 Valley Rd., Melrose Park, 19027-3035.

4—CHRIST THE KING (1949)
1629 W. Cayuga St., 19140. Tel: 215-455-2416; Email: ctkucc@aol.com. Rev. Yaroslav Kurpel
Legal Title: Christ the King Ukrainian Catholic Church.
Catechesis Religious Program—Maria Kasian, D.R.E.
Mission—St. Nicholas, 871 N. 24th St., 19130.

5—ST. JOSAPHAT'S, Closed. For inquiries for parish records contact the chancery.

6—ST. NICHOLAS (1943)
871 N. 24th St., 19130. Tel: 215-769-3863; Email: snukrcc@aol.com. Rev. Yaroslav Kurpel, Admin.
Legal Title: St. Nicholas Ukrainian Catholic Church
Church: 24th & Poplar St., 19130-1988.

7—PROTECTION OF BLESSED VIRGIN MARY, Closed. For inquiries for parish records please see SS. Peter and Paul, Clifton Heights, PA.

8—SACRED HEART, Closed. For inquiries for parish records contact the chancery.

STATE OF DELAWARE

WILMINGTON, NEW CASTLE CO., ST. NICHOLAS
801 Lea Blvd., Wilmington, DE 19802.
Tel: 302-762-5511; Fax: 302-762-5849; Email: stnicholas2@verizon.net. Rev. Volodymyr Klanichka.

STATE OF MARYLAND

BALTIMORE, BALTIMORE CO., ST. MICHAEL'S (1913) [CEM]
2401 Eastern Ave., Baltimore, MD 21224.
Tel: 410-675-7557; Email: tserkva@yahoo.com; Web: baltoukrainiancathparishes.org. Rev. Vasyl Sivinskyi, Admin.

CHESAPEAKE CITY, CECIL CO., ST. BASIL THE GREAT, Attended by St. Nicholas, Wilmington, DE
Mailing Address: 231 Basil Ave., Chesapeake City, MD 21915. Tel: 302-762-5511; Email: stnicholas2@verizon.net. Rev. Volodymyr Klanichka, Admin.

CURTIS BAY, BALTIMORE CO., SS. PETER AND PAUL (1910) Attended by St. Michael's, Baltimore, MD
1506 Church St., Curtis Bay, MD 21226.
Tel: 410-675-7557; Email: tserkva@yahoo.com; Web: baltoukrainiancathparishes.org. Mailing Address: 2401 Eastern Ave., Baltimore, MD 21224. Rev. Vasyl Sivinskyi, Admin.

SILVER SPRING, MONTGOMERY CO., HOLY TRINITY (1980)
Tel: 301-421-1739; Email: alexanderd715@aol.com. Rev. Alexander Dumenko, (Ukraine).
Catechesis Religious Program—

STATE OF NEW JERSEY

BAYONNE, HUDSON CO., ASSUMPTION B.V.M. (1916) Attended by SS. Peter and Paul, Jersey City, NJ
30 E. 25th St., Bayonne, NJ 07002.
Tel: 201-432-3122; Email: vputera@yahoo.com. Mailing Address: 30 Bentley Ave., Jersey City, NJ 07304. Rev. Vasyl Putera.

CARTERET, MIDDLESEX CO., ST. MARY'S (1949)
719 Roosevelt Ave., Carteret, NJ 07008.
Tel: 732-366-2156; Email: neokozak@msn.com; Web: stmaryscarteret.org. Rev. Vasyl Vladyka.

CHERRY HILL, CAMDEN CO., ST. MICHAEL'S (1923) [CEM]
675 Cooper Landing Rd., Cherry Hill, NJ 08002.
Tel: 856-482-0938; Email: stmichaelscherryhill@gmail.com. Rev. Roman Sverdan.
Catechesis Religious Program—Students 9.
Mission—Wildwood Crest, 5901 Pacific Ave., Wildwood Crest, NJ 08260.

ELIZABETH, UNION CO., ST. VLADIMIR'S (1903)
309 Grier Ave., Elizabeth, NJ 07202-3310.
Tel: 908-352-8823; Email: ourstvladimir@gmail.com; Web: stvladimirnj.com. Rev. Ruslan Romanyuk, J.C.L.
Catechesis Religious Program—

GREAT MEADOWS, WARREN CO., ST. NICHOLAS (1923)
Mailing Address: 335 Rte. 46, P.O. Box 162, Great Meadows, NJ 07838. Tel: 908-799-3386;
Fax: 908-689-2352; Email: stnicholasgm@gmail.com; Web: www.stnicknj.org. Rev. Evhen Moniuk.

HILLSIDE, UNION CO., IMMACULATE CONCEPTION (1957)
Mailing Address: 719 Roosevelt Ave., Carteret, NJ 07008. Tel: 732-366-2156; Email: icukrainiancatholic@yahoo.com; Web: byzcath.org/ImmaculateConception. Rev. Vasyl Vladyka.
Church: Bloy St. and Liberty Ave., Hillside, NJ 07205.
Catechesis Religious Program—Joseph Shatynski, D.R.E. Students 12.

JERSEY CITY, HUDSON CO., SS. PETER AND PAUL (1886)
549 Bergen Ave., Jersey City, NJ 07304.
Tel: 201-432-3122; Email: vputera@yahoo.com. Res.: 30 Bentley Ave., Jersey City, NJ 07304. Rev. Vasyl Putera.
Catechesis Religious Program—

HILLSBOROUGH, SOMERSET CO., ST. MICHAEL'S (1950)
1700 Brooks Blvd., Hillsborough, NJ 08844.
Tel: 908-526-9195; Email: stmichaelucc@yahoo.com; Web: stmichaelucc.org. Rev. Orest Kunderevych.
Res.: 63 N. 18th Ave., Manville, NJ 08835.

MARLBORO, MONMOUTH CO., ST. VOLODYMYR'S, Closed. For inquiries for parish records contact the chancery.

MILLVILLE, CUMBERLAND CO., ST. NICHOLAS, [CEM] Attended from Cathedral of the Immaculate Conceptions (Philadelphia)
801 Carmel Rd., Millville, NJ 08332.
Tel: 856-825-4826; Email: stnicholasmilleville@gmail.com. Rev. Roman Sverdan.
Church: 824 Carmel Rd., Millville, NJ 08332.
Tel: 856-482-0938; Email: stmichaelucc@verizon.net.

NEW BRUNSWICK, MIDDLESEX CO., NATIVITY OF B.V.M. (1951) Attended by St. Michael, Hillsborough, NJ.
80 Livingston Ave., New Brunswick, NJ 08901. Mailing Address: 1700 Brooks Blvd., Hillsborough, NJ 08844. Tel: 732-246-1516; Email: nativitybvmucc@yahoo.com; Web: nbvmchurch.com. Rev. Orest Kunderevych.
Catechesis Religious Program—

NEWARK, ESSEX CO., ST. JOHN THE BAPTIST
Res.: 719 Sanford Ave., Newark, NJ 07106. Revs. Mykola Bychok, C.Ss.R.; Taras Svirchuk, C.Ss.R.
Catechesis Religious Program—

PASSAIC, PASSAIC CO., ST. NICHOLAS (1910)
217 President St., Passaic, NJ 07055.
Tel: 973-471-9727; Email: stnicholasucc@gmail.com; Web: www.st.nicholasucc.org. 60 Holdsworth Ct., Passaic, NJ 07055. Rev. Andriy Dudkevych.
School—St. Nicholas School, (Grades K-8),
Tel: 973-779-0249; Email: snucs.news@gmail.com; Web: www.stnicholaschool.com/. Rev. Andriy Dudkevych, Admin. Clergy 2; Lay Teachers 11; Students 89.
Catechesis Religious Program—Sr. Eliana Ilnitski, S.S.M.I., D.R.E. Students 115.

PERTH AMBOY, MIDDLESEX CO., ASSUMPTION OF B.V.M. (1908)
684 Alta Vista Pl., Perth Amboy, NJ 08861.
Tel: 732-826-0767; Email: assumptionchurch@verizon.net; Web: www.assumptioncatholicchurch.net. Rev. Ivan Turyk; Deacon Paul Makar.
School—Assumption of B.V.M. School, (Grades 1-8), Tel: 732-826-8721; Email: ACSschooloffice@gmail.com; Web: assumptioncatholicschool.net. Lissette Shumny, Prin.; Rev. Ivan Turyk, Admin. Missionary Sisters of Mother of God 3; Lay Teachers 15; Students 135.
Catechesis Religious Program—Tel: 732-826-8721; Email: acsschooloffice@gmail.com. Lissette Shumny, Prin. Students 167.

RAMSEY, BERGEN CO., ST. PAUL 1904
Tel: 201-478-0102; Email: evhenmoniuk@gmail.com. Rev. Evhen Moniuk.
Church: 79 Cherry Ln., Ramsey, NJ 07446.
Catechesis Religious Program—

RUTHERFORD, BERGEN CO., ANNUNCIATION B.V.M., Closed. For inquiries for parish records please see St. Vladimir, Elizabeth.

TOMS RIVER, OCEAN CO., ST. STEPHEN'S
1344 White Oak Bottom Rd., Toms River, NJ 08755.
Tel: 732-505-6053; Fax: 732-505-6053; Email: pastor@ststephenchurch.us; Web: www.ststephenchurch.us. Very Rev. Volodymyr Popyk.

TRENTON, MERCER CO., ST. JOSAPHAT'S (1949)
1195 Deutz Ave., Trenton, NJ 08611-3239.
Tel: 609-695-3771; Fax: 609-815-0232; Email: tarlonch@gmail.com. Very Rev. Taras R. Lonchyna.

WHIPPANY, MORRIS CO., ST. JOHN THE BAPTIST (1920)
60 N. Jefferson Rd., Whippany, NJ 07981.
Tel: 973-887-3616; Email: stjohnukrcc@gmail.com; Web: sjucc.com. Rev. Stepan Bilyk.
Catechesis Religious Program—Students 177.

WILLIAMSTOWN, GLOUCESTER CO., SS. PETER AND PAUL (1920) [CEM] Closed.

WOODBINE, CAPE MAY CO., ST. NICHOLAS, Closed. For inquiries for parish records contact St. Nicholas, Millville, NJ.

STATE OF PENNSYLVANIA

ALDEN STATION, LUZERNE CO., ST. VLADIMIR, Closed. For inquiries for parish records contact St. Nicholas, Glen Lyon, PA.

ALLENTOWN, LEHIGH CO., IMMACULATE CONCEPTION OF B.V.M., Closed. For inquiries for parish records contact St. Josaphat, Bethlehem, PA.

BERWICK, COLUMBIA CO., SS. CYRIL AND METHODIUS (1909) [CEM]
706 N. Warren St., Berwick, 18603.
Tel: 570-752-3172; Fax: 570-752-0378; Email: sscm1@pa.metrocast.net; Web: www.sscyrilandmethodius.net. Rev. Roman Petryshak, (Ukraine).
Catechesis Religious Program—Students 3.

BETHLEHEM, LEHIGH CO., ST. JOSAPHAT'S (1918) [CEM]
1826 Kenmore Ave., Bethlehem, 18018-3305.
Tel: 610-865-2521; Fax: 610-865-4490; Email: stjosaphatbethlehem@gmail.com; Web: www.stjosaphatbethlehem.us. Very Rev. Archpriest Daniel Gurovich.
Catechesis Religious Program—Students 26.

BRIDGEPORT, MONTGOMERY CO., SS. PETER AND PAUL (1924) [CEM]
519 Union Ave., P.O. Box 126, Bridgeport, 19405.
Tel: 610-272-7035; Email: rppopivchak@aol.com. Rev. Msgr. Ronald P. Popivchak, Ph.D.

Catechesis Religious Program—George Maxim, D.R.E. Students 80.

BRISTOL, BUCKS CO., ST. MARY'S (1954)
2026 Bath Rd., Bristol, 19007. Tel: 215-788-7117; Email: stmarychurch2@yahoo.com. Very Rev. Ivan Demkiv.
Catechesis Religious Program—

CENTRALIA, COLUMBIA CO., ASSUMPTION OF B.V.M. (1911) [CEM] Attended by Mt. Carmel.
Mailing Address: 131 N. Beech St., Mount Carmel, 17851. Tel: 570-339-0650; Email: stsppmc@ptd.net. N. Paxton St., Centralia, 17927. Rev. Archpriest Michael Hutsko, Admin.
Church: 538 S. Center St., Aristes, 17920.

CHESTER, DELAWARE CO., HOLY GHOST (1909) Closed.

CLIFTON HEIGHTS, DELAWARE CO., SS. PETER AND PAUL (1911) Closed.

EDWARDSVILLE, LUZERNE CO., ST. VLADIMIR'S (1910) [CEM] Mission of Ss Peter & Paul Ukrainian, Wilkes-Barre, PA.
Mailing Address: 70 Zerby Ave., Edwardsville, 18704. Tel: 570-287-9718; Email: frpaulwol63570@aol.com. Rev. Paul Wolensky.

FRACKVILLE, SCHUYLKILL CO., ST. MICHAEL'S (1921) [CEM]
335 W. Oak St., Frackville, 17931. Tel: 570-874-1101 ; Email: ssjohnmikefrack12@ptd.net. 243 S. Middle St., Frackville, 17931. Rev. Petro Zvarych; Deacon Paul Mark Spotts.

GLEN LYON, LUZERNE CO., ST. NICHOLAS (1894) Attended by Ss Cyril and Methodius, Berwick, PA
Mailing Address: 153 E. Main St., Glen Lyon, 18617. Tel: 570-752-3172; Fax: 570-752-0378; Email: stNicholasGL@gmail.com. Rev. Roman Petryshak, (Ukraine).

HAZLETON, LUZERNE CO., ST. MICHAEL'S (1910) [CEM]
74 N. Laurel St., Hazleton, 18201. Tel: 570-455-0643; Email: usalemko@ukrcap.org. Rev. D. George Worschak.
Catechesis Religious Program—Students 3.

JENKINTOWN, MONTGOMERY CO., ST. MICHAEL THE ARCHANGEL (1976)
1013 Fox Chase Rd., Jenkintown, 19046.
Tel: 215-576-5827; Email: kostyuk123@yahoo.com; Web: www.mykhailivka.org. Rev. Volodymyr Kostyuk, (Ukraine).

LANSDALE, MONTGOMERY CO., PRESENTATION OF OUR LORD (1969) Attended by St. Anne's, Warrington, PA 1564 Allentown Rd., Lansdale, 19446. Email: vbunik@gmail.com; Tel: 215-343-0779; Web: www.presentationukrainiancc.com. Mailing Address: 1545 Easton Rd., Warrington, 18976. Rev. Wasyl Bunik, Admin.
Catechesis Religious Program—

MAHANOY CITY, SCHUYLKILL CO., ST. NICHOLAS, [CEM] Closed. For inquiries for parish records contact the chancery.

MAIZEVILLE, SCHUYLKILL CO., ST. JOHN THE BAPTIST (1908) [CEM] Attended by St. Michael, Frackville.
1408 Main St., Maizeville, 17934. Email: ssjohnmikefrack12@ptd.net. Mailing Address: 243 S. Middle St., Frackville, 17931. Rev. Petro Zvarych, Admin.

MARION HEIGHTS, NORTHUMBERLAND CO., PATRONAGE OF THE MOTHER OF GOD (1911) Attended by Transfiguration, Shamokin.
145 E. Melrose St., Marion Heights, 17832.
Tel: 570-373-3441; Tel: 570-648-5932; Email: transfigurationshamokin@gmail.com. Mailing Address: 303 N. Shamokin St., Shamokin, 17872. Rev. Mykola Ivanov, J.C.L.

MCADOO, SCHUYLKILL CO., ST. MARY'S (1891) [CEM]
210 W. Blaine St., McAdoo, 18237. Tel: 570-455-0643 ; Email: usalemko@ukrcap.org. Rev. D. George Worschak.
Catechesis Religious Program—Students 4.

MIDDLEPORT, SCHUYLKILL CO., NATIVITY OF B.V.M. (1910) [CEM]
Kaska St., Middleport, 17953. Tel: 570-544-4581; Fax: 570-544-9653; Email: NativityBVM.Middleport@gmail.com. Mailing Address: St. Nicholas Rectory, 415 N. Front St., Minersville, 17954. Rev. Paul J. Makar, Admin.; Christine Palko, Trustee.

MINERSVILLE, SCHUYLKILL CO., ST. NICHOLAS (1896) [CEM]
415 N. Front St., Minersville, 17954.
Tel: 570-544-4581; Fax: 570-544-9653; Cell: 215-300-9147; Email: pastoratstnicks@gmail.com; Web: www.facebook.com/StNicksChurchMinersvillePA/. Rev. Paul J. Makar.
School—St. Nicholas School, (Grades PreK-8), 515 N. Front St., Minersville, 17954. Tel: 570-544-2800; Fax: 570-544-6471; Web: www.snsminersville.com. Mr. David Holland, Prin.; Rev. Paul J. Makar, Admin.; Mrs. Mary Ann Batz, Sec. Religious Teachers 2; Lay Teachers 11; Students 109.
Catechesis Religious Program—St. Nicholas Convent, 509 N. Front St., Minersville, 17954. Tel: 570-544-3639; Email: sisternatalya@gmail.com. Sisters Natayla Stoczanyn, S.S.M.I., D.R.E.; Zenovia Chmilar, S.S.M.I., CCD Instructor. Students 21.

MOSCOW, LACKAWANNA CO., HOLY GHOST, Closed. For inquiries for parish records contact St. Vladimir, Scranton, PA.

MOUNT CARMEL, NORTHUMBERLAND CO., SS. PETER AND PAUL (1891) [CEM]
131 N. Beech St., Mount Carmel, 17851.
Tel: 570-339-0650; Email: stsppmc@ptd.net. Rev. Archpriest Michael Hutsko.
Catechesis Religious Program—Christine Bogner, D.R.E. Students 24.

NANTICOKE, LUZERNE CO.
1—ST. NICHOLAS, Closed. For inquiries for parish records contact Transfiguration of Our Lord, 240 Center St., Nanticoke.
240 Center St., Nanticoke, 18634. Tel: 570-735-2262; Email: TransfigurationUCC@comcast.net; Web: transfigurationucc.org/.
2—TRANSFIGURATION OF OUR LORD (1912) [CEM] Rev. Walter Pasicznyk.

NORTHAMPTON, NORTHAMPTON CO., ST. JOHN THE BAPTIST (1900) [CEM]
1343 Newport Ave., Northampton, 18067.
Tel: 610-262-4104; Email: stjohn1900@rcn.com. Rev. Ivan Seniw.
Catechesis Religious Program—Students 30.

OLYPHANT, LACKAWANNA CO., SS. CYRIL AND METHODIUS aka St. Cyril's Church (1888) [CEM]
137 River St., Olyphant, 18447. Tel: 570-291-4451; Fax: 570-489-6918; Email: sscyrilandmethodius@comcast.net; Web: stcyrils.weconnect.com. 135 River St., Olyphant, 18447. Very Rev. Nestor Iwasiw.
Catechesis Religious Program—Sandra Berta, D.R.E. Students 29.

PALMERTON, CARBON CO., ST. VLADIMIR'S
101 Lehigh Ave., Palmerton, 18071.
Tel: 610-826-2359; Email: stvlad@ptd.net. Rev. Volodymyr Baran.

PHOENIXVILLE, CHESTER CO., SS. PETER AND PAUL, [CEM]
301 Fairview St., Phoenixville, 19460.
Tel: 610-933-7801; Email: iroyik@hotmail.com. Mailing Address: 472 Emmett St., Phoenixville, 19460. Rev. Ihor Royik, Admin.

PLYMOUTH, LUZERNE CO., SS. PETER AND PAUL (1898)
Tel: 570-779-3323; Email: sspeterandpaulucc@gmail.com; Web: sspeterandpaulucc.org. Rev. Walter Pasicznyk.
Res.: 240 Center St., Nanticoke, 18634.
Church & Mailing Address: 20 Nottingham St., P.O. Box 60, Plymouth, 18651.

POTTSTOWN, MONTGOMERY CO., ST. MICHAEL'S (1936) [CEM] Served by SS. Peter & Paul Church, Phoenixville, PA.
Res.: 425 W. Walnut St., Pottstown, 19464.
Tel: 610-933-7801; Email: stmichaelthearchangel@outlook.com. Rev. Ihor Royik, Admin.
Catechesis Religious Program—

READING, BERKS CO., NATIVITY OF BLESSED VIRGIN MARY (1906) [CEM]
504 Summit Ave., Reading, 19611. Tel: 610-376-0586 ; Email: nativitybvmchurch@gmail.com; Web: ukrainianchurchreadingpa.com. Mailing: 501 Summit Ave., Reading, 19611. Rev. Mark Fesniak.
Mission—St. Andrew the Apostle, 1834 Lititz Pike, Lancaster, 17601. Tel: 267-303-8041; Email: st_andrew_church@outlook.com.
Catechesis Religious Program—Debbie Marco, D.R.E.

ST. CLAIR, SCHUYLKILL CO.
1—HOLY TRINITY, [CEM] Closed. For inquiries for parish records, contact St. Nicholas, St. Clair, PA.
2—ST. NICHOLAS, [CEM] Attended by St. Michael, Shenandoah.
105 N. Morris St., Saint Clair, 17970.
Tel: 570-462-0809; Fax: 570-462-0517; Email: stnicholassc@verizon.net. Mailing Address: 114 S. Chestnut St., Shenandoah, 17976. Rev. Msgr. Myron Grabowsky, Admin.

SAYRE, BRADFORD CO., ASCENSION OF OUR LORD (1911) [CEM] Attended by Served by Priest from St. Nicholas Ukrainian Catholic Church, Elmira Heights NY.
108 N. Higgins Ave., Sayre, 18840. Tel: 607-734-1221 ; Email: frbob8@msn.com. 410 E. McCanns Blvd., Elmira Heights, NY 14903. Rev. Robert Moreno.

SCRANTON, LACKAWANNA CO., ST. VLADIMIR'S (1908) [CEM]
430 N. Seventh Ave., Scranton, 18503.
Tel: 570-342-7023; Email: myronyukm@yahoo.com. Rev. Myron Myronyuk, (Ukraine).
Catechesis Religious Program—Shirley Nidoh, D.R.E. Students 16.
Mission—SS. Peter & Paul, 47 Rittenhouse St., Simpson, 18407.

SHAMOKIN, NORTHUMBERLAND CO., TRANSFIGURATION OF OUR LORD, [CEM]
303 N. Shamokin St., Shamokin, 17872-5460.
Tel: 570-648-5932; Fax: 570-648-3871; Email: transfigurationshamokin@gmail.com; Web: transfigurationukrainiancatholicchurch.com. Rev. Mykola Ivanov, J.C.L.; Deacon Theodore Spotts.
Catechesis Religious Program—Students 15.

SHENANDOAH, SCHUYLKILL CO., ST. MICHAEL'S (1884) [CEM]
114 S. Chestnut St., Shenandoah, 17976.
Tel: 570-462-0809; Email: stmichaelsukrainian@verizon.net; Web: www.first-ukrainian.com/. Rev. Msgr. Myron Grabowsky.
Catechesis Religious Program—Alice Blacznik, D.R.E. Students 5.

SIMPSON, LACKAWANNA CO., SS. PETER AND PAUL (1904) [CEM] Attended by St. Vladimir Church, Scranton, PA.
430 N. Seventh Ave., Scranton, 18503.
Tel: 570-342-7023; Email: sspeterandpauluce@gmail.com. Rev. Myron Myronyuk, (Ukraine).
Church: 43 Rittenhouse St., Simpson, 18407.

SWARTHMORE, HOLY MYRRH-BEARERS UKRAINIAN CATHOLIC CHURCH (2015)
900 Fairview Rd., Swarthmore, 19081.
Tel: 610-544-1215; Email: hmbchurch@verizon.net. Very Rev. John Ciurpita.
Catechesis Religious Program—Students 14.

WARRINGTON, BUCKS CO., ST. ANNE'S (1963)
1545 Easton Rd., Warrington, 18976.
Tel: 215-343-0779; Email: vbunik@gmail.com. Rev. Wasyl Bunik, Admin.
Catechesis Religious Program—Tel: 215-763-6443; Email: susa.lewyckyj@gmail.com. Susan Lewyckyj, D.R.E. Students 26.

WEST EASTON, NORTHAMPTON CO., HOLY GHOST (1921) [CEM]
315 Fourth St., West Easton, 18042.
Tel: 610-252-4266; Email: holyghostukr@outlook.com; Web: www.holyghost_ukr.org. Rev. Archpriest Daniel Troyan.
Catechesis Religious Program—Christine Mattes, D.R.E. Students 10.

WILKES-BARRE, LUZERNE CO., SS. PETER AND PAUL
635 N. River St., Wilkes-Barre, 18705.
Tel: 570-823-1821; Fax: 570-371-3329; Email: frpaulolwol63570@aol.com. Rev. Paul Wolensky.

STATE OF VIRGINIA

MANASSAS, PRINCE WILLIAM CO., ANNUNCIATION OF THE BLESSED VIRGIN MARY (1925) [CEM]
6719 Token Valley Rd., Manassas, VA 20112.
Tel: 703-791-6635; Email: alexanderd715@aol.com; Web: www.stmarysbyz.com. Rev. Alexander Dumenko, (Ukraine).
Catechesis Religious Program—Helen Troy, D.R.E. Students 8.

RICHMOND, HENRICO CO., ST. JOHN THE BAPTIST (1966) Closed. For inquiries for parish records contact the chancery.

DISTRICT OF COLUMBIA

WASHINGTON, DISTRICT OF COLUMBIA
1—SAINTS JOACHIM AND ANNA UKRAINIAN CATHOLIC CHURCH, Attended by
201 Taylor St., N.E., Washington, DC 20017.
Tel: 202-529-1177, Ext. 115; Email: ssjoachimandannaucc@gmail.com; Web: www.ssjoachimandanna.org. HLI Chapel, 4 Family Life Ln., Front Royal, VA 22630. Very Revs. Robert J. Hitchens, Admin.; Wasyl Kharuk. Holy Family Ukrainian Natholical Catholic Shrine.
2—UKRAINIAN CATHOLIC NATIONAL SHRINE OF THE HOLY FAMILY (1949)
4250 Harewood Rd. N.E., Washington, DC 20017.
Tel: 202-526-3737; Fax: 202-526-1327; Email: ucnsholyfamily@gmail.com; Web: www.ucns-holyfamily.org. Very Revs. Robert J. Hitchens, Admin.; Wasyl Kharuk, Admin.
Catechesis Religious Program—

Special Assignment:
Very Rev. Archpriest—
Fields, John M.

Retired:
Most Revs.—
Soroka, Stefan, D.D., Ph.D., (Retired), 810 N. Franklin St., 19123
Sulyk, Stephen, D.D., (Retired), The Manor at St. Mary's, 220 St. Mary's Dr., Ste. 421, Cherry Hill, NJ 08003
Revs.—
Dubitsky, Roman, (Retired)
Maslak, Gregory, (Retired)
Patrylak, Frank, (Retired), St. Mary's Catholic Home, 210 St. Mary's Dr., Cherry Hill, NJ 08003
Wysochansky, John, (Retired), 118 Second St., Blakely, 18447
Very Rev. Archpriest—
Markewych, Uriy, (Retired), 990 Summerhill Rd., Auburn, 17922.

net; Web: www.stgeorgebyzantinecatholicchurch.org. Deacon Thomas J. Klacik.

AMBRIDGE, BEAVER CO., ST. MARY'S (1940)
624 Park Rd., Ambridge, 15003. Tel: 724-266-2030; Email: stmarybyzantine@verizon.net. Deacon Thomas J. Klacik, Admin.

ARCADIA, INDIANA CO., ASCENSION, [CEM] Closed. For inquiries for parish records contact the chancery.

AVELLA, WASHINGTON CO., ST. JOHN THE BAPTIST (1916) [CEM] Attended by
176 Cross Creek Rd., P.O. Box 565, Avella, 15312. Email: stjohnavella@gmail.com. Rev. Vasyl Symyon, Admin.

BEAVER, BEAVER CO., SAINT NICHOLAS CHAPEL (1995) Attended by St. Mary's Ambridge
5400 Tuscarawas Rd., Beaver, 15009-9513.
Tel: 724-266-2030; Email: rupp.william@gmail.com; Web: www.gcuusa.com/snc.htm. Rev. William J. Rupp, Admin.

BEAVERDALE, CAMBRIA CO., ST. MARY'S (1906) [CEM] Attended by Sts. Peter and Paul, Portage.
513 Cameron Ave., P.O. Box 610, Beaverdale, 15921.
Tel: 814-736-9780; Email: james_armand_spontak@verizon.net. Deacon Daniel F. Perich.

BRADDOCK, ALLEGHENY CO., SS. PETER AND PAUL (1896)
431 George St., Braddock, 15104. Tel: 412-466-3578; Fax: 412-271-1297; Email: stspeterpaulbc@gmail.com. 4200 Homestead-Duquesne Rd., Munhall, 15120. Rev. Vitalii Stashkevych, Admin.

BRADENVILLE, WESTMORELAND CO., ST. MARY'S (1902) [CEM]
112 St. Mary's Way, Bradenville, 15620-1017.
Tel: 724-537-5839; Email: archpitt@aol.com. Rev. Joseph Borodach.

BROWNSVILLE, FAYETTE CO., ST. NICHOLAS (1911) [CEM]
302 Third Ave., Brownsville, 15417.
Tel: 724-785-7573; Email: frchris53@gmail.com. Rev. Christopher R. Burke.

CANONSBURG, WASHINGTON CO., ST. MICHAEL (1912) [CEM]
166 E. College St., Canonsburg, 15317.
Tel: 717-724-7117; Email: frj455@outlook.com. Very Rev. R. Joseph Raptosh; Deacon Lance D. Weakland.

CHARLEROI, WASHINGTON CO., HOLY GHOST (1899)
828 Meadow Ave., Charleroi, 15022.
Tel: 724-379-9751; Email: stmichaelstmary@comcast.net. Rev. Stephen J. Wahal, Admin.

CLAIRTON, ALLEGHENY CO., ASCENSION OF OUR LORD (1907) [CEM]
318 Park Ave., Clairton, 15025. Tel: 412-233-7422; Email: cuccaro701@comcast.net; Web: www.ascensionclairton.com/. Rev. John J. Cuccaro, Admin.

CLARENCE, CENTRE CO., DORMITION OF THE MOTHER OF GOD (1906) [CEM] Attended by Hawk Run, PA. St. John the Baptist Byzantine Catholic Parish.State College, PA. Byzantine Catholic Community.
Mailing Address: c/o St. John the Baptist Church, P.O. Box 2, Hawk Run, 16840. Tel: 814-387-4161; Tel: 814-342-4315; Cell: 724-388-6176; Email: stjohns024@comcast.net; Email: golden15739@gmail.com; Web: www.archpitt.org/place/clarencepa-2; Web: www.byzcath.org/centralpa. 104 Byzantine Ln., P.O. Box 304, Clarence, 16829-0304. Rev. James A. Ragan, Admin.; Deacon John A. Custaney, Contact Person.

CLYMER, INDIANA CO., ST. ANNE (1907)
360 Franklin St., Clymer, 15728. Tel: 814-938-4244; Email: wmash@comcast.net. Rev. Wesley M. Mash, Admin.

COAL RUN, INDIANA CO., HOLY CROSS, Closed. For inquiries for parish records contact the chancery.

CONEMAUGH, CAMBRIA CO., HOLY TRINITY (1908) [CEM]
217 Fourth St., Conemaugh, 15909.
Tel: 814-535-5231; Email: byzbob@aol.com. Rev. Robert F. Oravetz.

DONORA, WASHINGTON CO., ST. MICHAEL (1904) [CEM]
511 Murray Ave., Donora, 15033. Tel: 724-379-9751; Email: stmichaelstmary@comcast.net. Rev. Stephen J. Wahal, Admin.

DU BOIS, CLEARFIELD CO., NATIVITY OF THE MOTHER OF GOD (1907) Attended by Holy Trinity, Sykesville.
200 McCullough St., Du Bois, 15801.
Tel: 814-371-4911; Email: pboboige@yahoo.com. Rev. Vasyl Banyk, Admin.; Deacons Paul M. Boboige; George M. Fatula.
Catechesis Religious Program—All Generations, Tel: 814-371-4276. Students 14.

DUNLO, CAMBRIA CO., SS. PETER AND PAUL (1909) [CEM] Attended by Sts. Peter and Paul, Portage
Mailing Address: P.O. Box 610, Beaverdale, 15921-0610. Tel: 814-736-9780; Email: james_armand_spontak@verizon.net. Roberts St., Dunlo, 15930. Very Rev. James A. Spontak.

DUQUESNE, ALLEGHENY CO.
1—ST. MARY'S (1915) Closed. For inquiries for parish records contact the chancery.
2—SS. PETER AND PAUL (1904) [CEM]
701 Foster Ave., Duquesne, 15110. Tel: 412-466-3578; Email: cuccaro701@comcast.net. Rev. John J. Cuccaro; Deacon Sean Petrisko.

EAST PITTSBURGH, ALLEGHENY CO., ST. MARY (1930) Closed. For inquiries for parish records contact the chancery.

ERIE, ERIE CO., SS. PETER AND PAUL (1912)
3415 Wallace St., Erie, 16504. Tel: 814-825-8140; Email: eriecountybyzantines@verizon.net. Rev. John J. Mihalco, S.E.O.L.
Catechesis Religious Program—Eastern Christian Formation, Tel: 814-282-6401. Andrew Pushchak, D.R.E.

ERNEST, INDIANA CO., ST. JUDE THADDEUS (1949) Attended by SS. Peter and Paul, Punxsutawney.
330 Main St., P.O. Box 130, Ernest, 15739. Email: vasylradar@gmail.com. Rev. Vasyl Kadar, Admin.

GIBSONIA, ALLEGHENY CO., ST. ANDREW THE APOSTLE (1975) Attended by Sts. Peter and Paul, Tarentum, 339 E. 10th Ave., Tarentum, PA 15084.
235 Logan Rd., Gibsonia, 15044. Tel: 724-625-1160; Email: info@standrewtheapostle.com. Rev. Adam Horstman, Admin.

GIRARD, ERIE CO., SS. CYRIL AND METHODIUS (1952) Attended by Sts. Peter and Paul, Erie.
1022 Tilden Ave., Girard, 16417. Tel: 814-774-3281; Email: jjmihalco@gmail.com. Rev. John J. Mihalco, S.E.O.L.

GREENSBURG, WESTMORELAND CO., ST. NICHOLAS OF MYRA (1955)
624 E. Pittsburgh St., Greensburg, 15601.
Tel: 724-837-0295; Email: archpitt@aol.com. Rev. Regis J. Dusecina.

HANNASTOWN, WESTMORELAND CO., ST. MARY'S (1906) Attended by St. Nicholas of Myra, Greensburg.
Pollins Ave., Hannastown, 15635. Tel: 724-837-0295; Email: archpitt@aol.com. 624 E. Pittsburgh St., Greensburg, 15601. Rev. Regis Dusecina, Admin.

HAWK RUN, CLEARFIELD CO.
1—ST. JOHN THE BAPTIST (1904) [CEM]
Mailing Address: 24 Fulton St., P.O. Box 2, Hawk Run, 16840. Tel: 814-342-4315; Cell: 724-388-6176; Email: stjohns024@comcast.net; Email: golden15739@gmail.com; Web: www.archpitt.org/place/hawkrunpa-2/; Web: www.byzcath.org/centralpa. Rev. James A. Ragan, Admin.; Deacons John A. Custaney; Dennis M. Prestash.
Catechesis Religious Program—Email: dprestash3273@comcast.net. Students 18.
2—STATE COLLEGE PA BYZANTINE CATHOLIC COMMUNITY (2005)
P.O. Box 431, State College, 16804-0431.
Tel: 814-861-2005; Tel: 814-342-4315; Cell: 724-388-6176; Email: stjohns024@comcast.net; Email: golden15739@gmail.com; Web: www.archpitt.org/place/state-college-byzantine-catholic-community; Web: www.byzcath.org/centralpa. P.O. Box 2, Hawk Run, 16840. Rev. James A. Ragan, Admin.

HERMINIE, WESTMORELAND CO., ST. MARY'S (1923)
5 Second St., Herminie, 15637. Tel: 724-446-5570; Email: lencorn@earthlink.net. Rev. Leonard Cornelius, O.F.M., Admin.

HERMITAGE, MERCER CO., ST. MICHAEL (1905) [CEM]
2230 Highland Rd., Hermitage, 16148.
Tel: 724-981-6680; Email: kevmarks630@gmail.com. Rev. Kevin E. Marks.
Catechesis Religious Program—ECF, Tel: 724-456-7899; Email: william_dzuricsko@hermitage.k12.pa.us. Mr. William Dzuricsko, D.R.E. Students 10.

HOMER CITY, INDIANA CO., ST. MARY'S HOLY PROTECTION (1919)
279 Yellow Creek St., Homer City, 15748.
Tel: 724-479-2206; Email: wmash@comcast.net. Rev. Wesley M. Mash, Admin.

JEROME, SOMERSET CO., SS. PETER AND PAUL (1913) [CEM] Attended by
139 Phillips St., Jerome, 15937. Tel: 814-467-7309; Email: irusyn21@gmail.com. 803 Somerset Ave., Windber, 15963. Rev. Ivan Rusyn, Admin.

JOHNSTOWN, CAMBRIA CO., ST. MARY'S (1895) [CEM]
411 Power St., Johnstown, 15906. Tel: 814-535-4132; Email: stmarys@atlanticbb.net. Rev. Msgr. Raymond A. Balta.

LATROBE, WESTMORELAND CO., ST. MARY (1894) [CEM]
4480 Rte. 981, Latrobe, 15650. Tel: 724-423-3673; Email: st.marytrauger@gmail.com. Rev. Paul-Alexander Shutt, O.S.B.
Parish Center:Tel: 724-423-8838; Email: st.marytrauger@yahoo.com; Web: www.stmarybyzantinecatholic.org.

LEISENRING, FAYETTE CO., ST. STEPHEN (1892) [CEM] Attended by St. Nicholas, Perryopolis
3120 W. Crawford Ave., Leisenring, 15425.
Tel: 724-628-6611; Email: rplark@hotmail.com. P.O. Box 128, Leisenring, 15455. Rev. Oleh Seremchuk.

LYNDORA, BUTLER CO., ST. JOHN THE BAPTIST (1910) [CEM]
105 Kohler Ave., Lyndora, 16045. Tel: 724-287-5000; Email: radko.blichar@gmail.com; Web: stjohnsbyzantinelyndora.com. Rev. Radko Blichar, Admin.; Deacon Paul Simko.

MCKEES ROCKS, ALLEGHENY CO., HOLY GHOST (1907)
225 Olivia St., McKees Rocks, 15136.
Tel: 412-771-3324; Email: Secretary225@verizon.net; Web: www.holyghost-byzantinecatholic.org. Very Rev. Frank A. Firko, S.T.L.
Catechesis Religious Program—Tel: 412-897-4650; Email: steve@puluka.com. Steven Puluka, D.R.E.

MCKEESPORT, ALLEGHENY CO.
1—ST. NICHOLAS (1901) [CEM]
410 Sixth St., McKeesport, 15132. Tel: 412-664-9131; Email: stnickmck@gmail.com. Rev. Donald J. Voss.
2—TRANSFIGURATION OF OUR LORD (1913) Closed. Parish suppressed. For inquiries for parish records, contact St. Nicholas, McKeesport.

MONESSEN, WESTMORELAND CO., ASSUMPTION OF THE BLESSED VIRGIN (1902) [CEM] Attended by St. Michael, Donora.
125 McKee Ave., Monessen, 15062.
Tel: 724-379-9751; Email: stmichaelstmary@comcast.net. Rev. Stephen J. Wahal, Admin.; Deacon John M. Hanchin.

MONONGAHELA, WASHINGTON CO., ST. MACRINA, Closed. For inquiries for parish records contact the chancery.

MONROEVILLE, ALLEGHENY CO., CHURCH OF THE RESURRECTION (1969)
455 Center Rd., Monroeville, 15146.
Tel: 412-372-8650; Email: COTR455@gmail.com. Rev. Donald McChesney Bolls.

MUNHALL, ALLEGHENY CO.
1—ST. JOHN THE BAPTIST CATHEDRAL (1897) [CEM]
210 Greentree Rd., Munhall, 15120.
Tel: 412-461-0944; Email: stjohnsbyzantinecathedral@gmail.com. Very Rev. Andrew J. Deskevich, Rector.
2—ST. ELIAS (1907) [CEM]
4200 Homestead-Duquesne Rd., Munhall, 15120.
Tel: 412-461-1712; Email: steliasbcc@comcast.net. Rev. Vitalii Stashkevych, Admin.

NANTY-GLO, CAMBRIA CO., ST. NICHOLAS (1919) Attended by Holy Trinity, Conemaugh.
1191 Second St., Nanty-Glo, 15943.
Tel: 814-535-5231; Email: byzbob@aol.com. Rev. Robert F. Oravetz, Admin.

NEW SALEM, FAYETTE CO., ST. MARY'S (1903) [CEM] Attended by St. Nicholas, Brownsville.
Mailing Address: 12 Center St. Ext., P.O. Box 487, New Salem, 15468. Tel: 724-245-7188; Email: frchris53@gmail.com. Rev. Christopher R. Burke, Admin.

NORTH HUNTINGDON, WESTMORELAND CO., ST. STEPHEN'S (1972)
90 Bethel Rd., North Huntingdon, 15642.
Tel: 724-863-6776; Email: ststephennh@outlook.com; Web: www.ststephensbyzcath.org. Very Rev. Archpriest John G. Petro.

NORTHERN CAMBRIA, CAMBRIA CO., ST. JOHN THE BAPTIST aka St. John the Baptist Byzantine Catholic Church (1897) [CEM]
719 Chestnut Ave., Northern Cambria, 15714-1459.
Tel: 814-674-5552; Email: n.cambriabyzcath@gmail.com; Web: www.ncambriabyzcath.org. Very Rev. Vasyl Polyak.

PATTON, CAMBRIA CO., SS. PETER AND PAUL aka SS. Peter & Paul Byzantine Catholic Church (1900) [CEM] Attended by St. John, Northern Cambria.
516 Palmer Ave., Patton, 16668. Tel: 814-674-5552; Email: pattonbyzcath@gmail.com; Web: www.pattonbyzcath.org. Very Rev. Vasyl Polyak; Deacon Raymond J. Zadzilko.

PERRYOPOLIS, FAYETTE CO., ST. NICHOLAS (1911) [CEM]
102 Railroad St., Perryopolis, 15473.
Tel: 724-887-5072; Email: olegseremchuk@gmail.com. Rev. Oleh Seremchuk.

PITTSBURGH, ALLEGHENY CO.
1—HOLY GHOST (1902) Attended by Filial Parish of Holy Ghost, McKees Rocks.
1437 Superior Ave., 15212. Tel: 412-771-3324; Email: Secretary225@verizon.net. Very Rev. Frank A. Firko, S.T.L., Dean.
2—HOLY SPIRIT (1907)
4815 Fifth Ave., 15213. Tel: 412-687-1220; Email: HolySpiritInformation@gmail.com; Web: www.HolySpiritChurchPgh.org. Rev. Msgr. Russell A. Duker, S.E.O.D.
3—ST. JOHN CHRYSOSTOM (1910)
506 Saline St., 15207. Tel: 412-421-9243; Email: stjohnchrysostom@comcast.net. Rev. Thomas Schaefer.
4—ST. JOHN THE BAPTIST (1900) [CEM]
1720 Jane St., 15203. Tel: 412-431-1090; Email: stjohnbaptist@comcast.net. Rev. Thomas Schaefer.
5—NATIVITY OF B.V.M. (1932) Closed. For inquiries for parish records, contact the Cathedral of St. John the Baptist, Munhall.
6—ST. PIUS X (1954)
2336 Brownsville Rd., 15210. Tel: 412-881-8344;

Email: msgrduker@gmail.com. Rev. Msgr. Russell A. Duker, S.E.O.D.
PORTAGE, CAMBRIA CO., SS. PETER AND PAUL (1917) [CEM]
143 Church Rd., Portage, 15946. Tel: 814-736-9780; Email: james_armand_spontak@verizon.net; Web: www.ByzantineCatholic.net. Very Rev. James A. Spontak.
PUNXSUTAWNEY, JEFFERSON CO., SS. PETER AND PAUL (1893) [CEM 2]
714 Sutton St., Punxsutawney, 15767.
Tel: 814-938-6564; Email: peter_and_paul@verizon.net. Rev. Vasyl Kadar, Admin.; Deacon Steven F. White.
RANKIN, ALLEGHENY CO., ST. JOHN'S, Closed. For inquiries for parish records contact the chancery.
SAGAMORE, ARMSTRONG CO., ST. MARY'S, [CEM] Closed. For inquiries for parish records contact the chancery.
SCOTTDALE, WESTMORELAND CO., ST. JOHN THE BAPTIST (1912) [CEM]
525 Porter Ave., Scottdale, 15683. Tel: 724-887-5072; Email: st.johnsbyz@zoominternet.net. Rev. Oleh Seremchuk, Admin.
SHEFFIELD, WARREN CO., ST. MICHAEL (1905) [CEM]
407 School St., P.O. Box 471, Sheffield, 16347.
Tel: 814-968-5478; Email: fatherdavid@westpa.net. Very Rev. David A. Bosnich.
SOUTH FORK, CAMBRIA CO., ST. MICHAEL'S, [CEM] Closed. Nov. 13, 2011. For inquiries for parish records, contact Sts. Peter and Paul, Portage.
SYKESVILLE, JEFFERSON CO., HOLY TRINITY (1907) [CEM]
104 Shaffer St., Sykesville, 15865. Tel: 814-894-5440; Email: holytrinitysykesville@gmail.com. Rev. Vasyl Banyk, Admin.; Deacon Lucas M. Crawford.
TARENTUM, ALLEGHENY CO., STS. PETER AND PAUL (1918)
339 E. 10th Ave., Tarentum, 15084-1003.
Tel: 724-224-3026; Email: adam.horstman@gmail.com. Rev. Adam Horstman, Admin.
UNIONTOWN, FAYETTE CO., ST. JOHN THE BAPTIST (1911) [CEM]
185 E. Main St., Uniontown, 15401.
Tel: 724-438-6027; Email: stjohnthebaptistuniontown@verizon.net. Very Rev. Ronald P. Larko.
UPPER ST. CLAIR, ALLEGHENY CO., ST. GREGORY NAZIANZUS (1971)
2005 Mohawk Rd., Upper St. Clair, 15241.
Tel: 412-835-7800; Email: stgregoryusc@aol.com; Web: stgregoryusc.org. Very Rev. Valerian M. Michlik, J.C.O.L.; Deacons Timothy J. Corbett; Michael E. George.
WALL, ALLEGHENY CO., HOLY TRINITY (1928) Attended by Church of the Resurrection, Monroeville.
472 Wall Ave., Wall, 15148. Tel: 412-372-8650; Email: fatherdonbolls@gmail.com. Rev. Donald McChesney Bolls, Admin.
WINDBER, SOMERSET CO., ST. MARY (DORMITION) CHURCH (1900) [CEM]
803 Somerset St., Windber, 15963. Tel: 814-467-7309; Email: irusyn21@gmail.com. Rev. Ivan Rusyn, Admin.

STATE OF LOUISIANA

NEW ORLEANS, ST. NICHOLAS OF MYRA MISSION (1976)
2435 S. Carrollton Ave., New Orleans, LA 70118.
Tel: 504-861-0806; Fax: 985-872-9123; Email: stnicholasnola@yahoo.com; Web: www.archpitt.org/place/neworleansla-2/. Mailing Address: P.O. Box 1359, Gray, LA 70359-1359. Deacon Gregory A. Haddad, Admin.; Revs. Phillip J. Linden Jr., S.S.J.; Etido Jerome.

STATE OF OHIO

BOARDMAN, MAHONING CO., INFANT JESUS OF PRAGUE (1907)
7754 South Ave., Boardman, OH 44512.
Tel: 330-758-6019; Email: farynec@gmail.com; Web: infantjesusbyz.org. Rev. Mykhaylo Farynets.
CAMPBELL, MAHONING CO., ST. MICHAEL (1922) [CEM] Attended by
463 Robinson Rd., Box 426, Campbell, OH 44405. Email: kevmarks@hotmail.com. Rev. Kevin E. Marks.
MINGO JUNCTION, JEFFERSON CO., ST. JOHN THE BAPTIST (1923) Attended by St. Joseph, Toronto.
207 Standard St., Mingo Junction, OH 43938.
Tel: 740-535-0271; Email: revfrjohn@sbcglobal.net. Rev. John J. Kapitan Jr., O.F.M., Admin.
NEWTON FALLS, TRUMBULL CO., ST. MICHAEL (1924) Closed. For inquiries for parish records contact the chancery.
PLEASANT CITY, GUERNSEY CO., ST. MICHAEL THE ARCHANGEL (1898) [CEM] Attended from St. Mary, Massillon, OH.
408 Walnut St., Pleasant City, OH 43772.
Tel: 330-832-1270; Email: romkat206@yahoo.com. Rev. A. Edward Gretchko.
TORONTO, JEFFERSON CO., ST. JOSEPH (1901)
814 N. Fifth St., Toronto, OH 43964.
Tel: 740-537-1026; Email: revfrjohn@sbcglobal.net. Rev. John J. Kapitan Jr., O.F.M.
WARREN, TRUMBULL CO., SS. PETER AND PAUL'S (1925) [CEM]
180 Belvedere Ave., N.E., Warren, OH 44483.
Tel: 330-372-1875; Email: sppbyzchurch@gmail.com. Rev. Simeon B. Sibenik.
YOUNGSTOWN, MAHONING CO.
1—ASSUMPTION OF THE BLESSED VIRGIN (1899) [CEM]
356 S. Belle Vista, Youngstown, OH 44509.
Tel: 330-799-8163; Email: stmarysyoungstown@att.net. Very Rev. Richard I. Lambert.
2—ST. GEORGE (1914) Attended by Assumption of the Blessed Virgin, Youngstown
1726 Canfield Rd., Youngstown, OH 44511.
Tel: 330-799-8163; Email: stmarysyoungstown@att.net. Rev. Richard Lambert, Admin.
3—ST. JOHN THE BAPTIST, Closed. For inquiries for parish records contact St. Nicholas, 1898 Wilson Ave., Youngstown, OH 44506. Tel: 330-743-0419.
4—ST. NICHOLAS (1912) [CEM] Attended by Infant Jesus of Prague, Boardman.
1898 Wilson Ave., Youngstown, OH 44506.
Tel: 330-743-0419; Email: stnick9000@aol.com. 3801 Shady Run Rd., Youngstown, OH 44502. Rev. Mykhaylo Farynets, Admin.

STATE OF TEXAS

HOUSTON, HARRIS CO., ST. JOHN CHRYSOSTOM (1982)
5402 Acorn St., Houston, TX 77092-4255.
Tel: 713-681-3580; Email: st.john.chrysostom@gmail.com. Very Rev. Elias L. Rafaj; Deacon Andrew F. Veres.
IRVING, DALLAS CO., ST. BASIL THE GREAT (1988)
1118 E. Union Bower Rd., Irving, TX 75061.
Tel: 972-438-5644; Email: fr.christopher.andrews@gmail.com. Rev. Christopher Andrews, Admin.

STATE OF TENNESSEE

KNOXVILLE, KNOX CO., HOLY RESURRECTION MISSION (1999)
6515 Millertown Pike, Knoxville, TN 37924.
Tel: 865-333-5518; Email: tjscripa2@gmail.com. Timothy Scripa, Admin.

STATE OF WEST VIRGINIA

MORGANTOWN, MONONGALIA CO., ST. MARY HOLY PROTECTION (1918) Attended by Chaplain, Mt. St. Macrina, Uniontown, PA
2115 Listravia Ave., Morgantown, WV 26505.
Tel: 304-296-2455; Email: fatherbotsko@gmail.com. Rev. Jerome G. Botsko, Admin.
WEIRTON, HANCOCK CO., ST. MARY'S (1924)
3116 Elm St., Weirton, WV 26062. Tel: 304-748-2780; Email: stmaryweirton@gmail.com. Rev. Vasyl Symyon.

Retired:
Rev. Msgrs.—
Mihalik, Alexis E., (Retired), 4300 Westford Pl., #6-C, Canfield, OH 44406-7010
Tay, Peter P., (Retired), 1200 San Pedro St., 15212
Very Revs.—
Jugan, Joseph, (Retired), 115 Barron Ave., Johnstown, 15906
Mina, John L., Ph.D., (Retired), 10950 Patina Ct., San Diego, CA 92131
Revs.—
Anthony, Julian, (Retired), 22 Arulananda Nagar, 6th Cross, Thanjavur, India 613 007 Tamilnadu
Borsuk, Ronald W., (Retired), 429 Manor Dr., #529, Ebensburg, 15931
Karl, Robert J., (Retired), 235 Logan Rd., Gibsonia, 15044
Pyo, Edward J., (Retired), 272 Farmers Tpke., Lilly, 15938
Schubert, Roy R., (Retired), 520 W. Main St., Uniontown, 15401
Very Rev. Archpriests—
Bogda, Dennis M., (Retired), St. Barnabas Nursing Home, 5827 Meridian Rd., Gibsonia, 15044
Yackanich, Eugene P., (Retired), 6329 Malaluka Rd., North Port, FL 34287. Tel: 941-426-2470.

INSTITUTIONS LOCATED IN DIOCESE

[A] SEMINARIES, ARCHIEPARCHIAL

PITTSBURGH. *Byzantine Catholic Seminary of SS. Cyril and Methodius*, 3605 Perrysville Ave., 15214-2229. Tel: 412-321-8383; Fax: 412-321-9936; Email: rector@bcs.edu; Web: www.bcs.edu. Very Rev. Robert M. Pipta, Rector, Tel: 412-321-7550; Revs. William J. Rupp, Spiritual Advisor; Christiaan Kappes, Ph.L., Academic Dean; Carol Przyborski, Registrar; Sandra A. Collins, Ph.D., Librarian, Tel: 412-321-8383, Ext. 23; Sr. Marion Dobos, O.S.B., Pastoral Min. Administrators 3; Clergy 3; Religious Teachers 12; Lay Teachers 7; Priests 2; Seminarians 15; Students 11; Staff 9.

[B] HOMES FOR AGED

UNIONTOWN. *Mt. Macrina Manor*, 520 W. Main St., Uniontown, 15401-2602. Tel: 724-437-1400; Fax: 724-430-1173; Email: info@mtmacrinamanor.com; Web: www.mtmacrinamanor.com. Richard Leonard NHA, Admin. Bed Capacity 139; Sisters of St. Basil the Great 1.

WARREN. *Infant of Prague Manor*, 169 Kenmore, N.E., Warren, OH 44483. Tel: 330-372-4700; Email: praguemanor@gmail.com. Susan Gresley, Bus. Mgr.; Very Rev. Simeon B. Sibenik, Admin. Independent senior housing. Total in Residence 41; Total Staff 3; Apartments 45.

[C] MONASTERIES AND RESIDENCES OF PRIESTS AND BROTHERS

LYNDORA. *Holy Trinity Monastery*, P.O. Box 990, Butler, 16003-0990. Tel: 724-996-0472; Email: hegumenleo@aol.com. Rt. Rev. Leo R. Schlosser, Abbot/Hegumen; Bro. Michael Zetzer, Procurator. Brothers 1; Priests 1.

[D] CONVENTS AND RESIDENCES FOR SISTERS

ALIQUIPPA. *St. George Convent*, 1000 Clinton St., Aliquippa, 15001. Tel: 724-378-0238; Email: pastor@stgeorgebyzantinecatholicchurch.org. Sr. Mary Virginia Ermany, Admin. Sisters 1.

UNIONTOWN. *Monastery and Novitiate of the Sisters of St. Basil the Great*, 500 W. Main St., P.O. Box 878, Uniontown, 15401. Tel: 724-438-8644; Fax: 724-438-8660; Email: osbmolph@verizon.net; Web: www.sistersofstbasil.org. Sr. Ruth Plante, O.S.B.M., B.A., M.A., Prov. Supr.; Rev. Jerome G. Botsko, Chap. Sisters 38; Professed Sisters 38.

WARREN. *Queen of Heaven Monastery*, 169 Kenmore Ave. N.E., #302, Warren, OH 44483. Tel: 330-856-1813; Fax: 330-856-9528; Email: qohm@byzben.com; Web: www.benedictinebyzantine.org. Sr. Barbara Pavlik, Admin. Benedictine Sisters of the Byzantine Rite 4.

YOUNGSTOWN. *Byzantine Convent*, 3295 Cricket Dr., Youngstown, OH 44511. Tel: 330-757-9186; Email: stmarysyoungstown@att.net. Sr. Bernarda Sevachko, O.S.B.M., Admin. Sisters of St. Basil the Great 2.

[E] MISCELLANEOUS

UNIONTOWN. *Mt. St. Macrina House of Prayer*, 510 W. Main St., P.O. Box 878, Uniontown, 15401-0878. Tel: 724-438-7149; Email: hpmsm@verizon.net; Web: www.sistersofstbasil.org. Sr. Carol Petrasovich, O.S.B.M., Dir.

RELIGIOUS INSTITUTES OF WOMEN REPRESENTED IN THE ARCHDIOCESE

For further details refer to the corresponding bracketed number in the Religious Institutes of Women section.

[0230]—*Benedictine Sisters of the Byzantine Church*—O.S.B.

[3730]—*Sisters of the Order of St. Basil the Great*—O.S.B.M.

Romanian Catholic Diocese of Saint George in Canton

Most Reverend

JOHN MICHAEL BOTEAN, D.D.

Bishop for the Romanian Catholic Diocese of Canton; ordained May 18, 1986; appointed Bishop for the Romanian Catholic Diocese of Canton July 15, 1996; Episcopal Ordination August 24, 1996. *Res.: 1325 Skyway St., N.E., Canton, OH 44721.* Tel: 330-493-9355; Fax: 330-493-9963.

Chancery: 1121 44th St., N.E., Canton, OH 44714-1297. Tel: 330-493-9355; Fax: 330-493-9963.

Web: www.romaniancatholic.org

Email: ovim@rcdcanton.org

Elevated from Apostolic Exarchate for Romanian Byzantine to the Rank of an Eparchy (Diocese) March 26, 1987

The Jurisdiction of the Romanian Catholic Diocese of Canton extends territorially to all of the United States and Canada.

Legal Title: The Romanian Catholic Diocese of Canton.

STATISTICAL OVERVIEW

Personnel	
Bishop	1
Abbots	1
Priests: Diocesan Active in Diocese	11
Priests: Diocesan Active Outside Diocese	1
Priests: Retired, Sick or Absent	8
Number of Diocesan Priests	20
Religious Priests in Diocese	2
Total Priests in Diocese	22
Extern Priests in Diocese	6
Ordinations:	
Diocesan Priests	1
Permanent Deacons in Diocese	6
Total Brothers	8
Total Sisters	5
Parishes	
Parishes	14
With Resident Pastor:	
Resident Diocesan Priests	10
Resident Religious Priests	1
Without Resident Pastor:	
Administered by Priests	2
Administered by Religious Women	1
Missions	5
Professional Ministry Personnel:	
Lay Ministers	5
Educational	
Catechesis/Religious Education:	
High School Students	12
Elementary Students	30
Total Students under Catholic Instruction	42
Vital Statistics	
Receptions into the Church:	
Infant Baptism Totals	24
Minor Baptism Totals	2
Adult Baptism Totals	5
Received into Full Communion	8
First Communions	29
Confirmations	29
Marriages:	
Catholic	10
Interfaith	8
Total Marriages	18
Deaths	16
Total Catholic Population	5,000

Former Bishop—Most Rev. LOUIS PUSCAS, D.D., ord. May 14, 1942; appt. Exarch, Dec. 4, 1982; Episcopal ordination, June 26, 1983; installed Aug. 28, 1983; promoted to first Eparch, April 16, 1987; retired July 15, 1993; died Oct. 3, 2009.

Vicar General (Protosyncellus)—Very Rev. IULIU-VASILE MUNTEAN.

Chancery—1121 44th St., N.E., Canton, 44714.

Chancellor and Moderator of the Curia—Very Rev. OVIDIU IOAN MARGINEAN.

Diocesan Secretary—MISS ANN FOSNAUGHT.

Secretary to the Bishop for IT and Communications—MR. RAUL BOTHA.

Economos—Very Rev. OVIDIU IOAN MARGINEAN.

Assistant to the Economos for Risk Management—Deacon GEORGE WENDT.

College of Consultors—Very Revs. OVIDIU IOAN MARGINEAN; IULIU-VASILE MUNTEAN; Rev. SERGIU CORNEA.

Protopresbyters: Deans & Deaneries in US—

Canton Deanery—Very Rev. OVIDIU IOAN MARGINEAN.

Aurora Deanery—Very Rev. CALIN TAMIIAN.

Trenton Deanery—Very Rev. GEORGE DAVID.

Vicar for Theological Affairs—Sr. THERESA KOERNKE, I.H.M., Ph.D.

Vicar for Clergy—VACANT.

Director of Vocations—Very Rev. IULIU-VASILE MUNTEAN.

Office to Aid the Church in Romania—Very Rev. MICHAEL MOISIN, Coord.

Presbyteral Council—Most Rev. JOHN MICHAEL BOTEAN, D.D.; Very Rev. IULIU-VASILE MUNTEAN; Rt. Rev. Archimandrite NICHOLAS ZACHARIADIS; Very Revs. CALIN TAMIIAN, Dean; GEORGE DAVID, Dean; OVIDIU IOAN MARGINEAN, Dean; MICHAEL MOISIN, Dean; Revs. SERGIU CORNEA; EMIL JUDE.

Finance Council—Most Rev. JOHN MICHAEL BOTEAN, D.D.; Very Revs. IULIU-VASILE MUNTEAN; OVIDIU IOAN MARGINEAN; MICHAEL MOISIN; Rev. RADU N. TITONEA; TERRENCE SEEBERGER, Attorney; MR. DOREL NASUI; MR. MARIUS MARITA; MR. VINICIUS ZETEA.

Child Protection Office Director and Safe Environment Coordinator—MS. JULIE SHOCKSMIDER, 1121 44th St., N.E., Canton, 44714. Tel: 330-493-9355; Email: julies@rcdcanton.org.

Victim Assistance Coordinator—MISS ANN FOSNAUGHT, 1121 44th St., N.E., Canton, 44714. Tel: 330-493-9355; Email: annf@rcdcanton.org.

Communications—MR. RAUL BOTHA.

Tribunal of the Eparchy—The Romanian Catholic Eparchy of St. George in Canton has as its Tribunal the Tribunal of the Eparchy of St. Maron of Brooklyn.

Judicial Vicar—Very Rev. FRANCIS J. MARINI, J.D., J.C.D.

CLERGY, PARISHES, MISSIONS AND PAROCHIAL SCHOOLS

STATE OF OHIO

CANTON, STARK CO., ST. GEORGE CATHEDRAL (1912) 1123 44th St., N.E., 44714-1297. Very Rev. Ovidiu Ioan Marginean, Rector; Deacon George Wendt.
Church & Res.: 1121 44th St., N.E., 44714-1297. Tel: 330-492-8413; Email: ovim@rcdcanton.org; Web: www.stgeorgeoh.org.
Bishop's Residence:—1325 Skyway St., N.E., 44721.
Catechesis Religious Program—Email: annf@rcdcanton.org. Carol Popa, D.R.E. Students 6.

ALLIANCE, STARK CO., ST. THEODORE (1909) Under Diocesan Administration.
Mailing Address: 1121 44th St. N.E., 44714-1297. Tel: 330-493-9355; Fax: 330-493-9963; Email: iulium@rcdcanton.org. Very Rev. Iuliu-Vasile Muntean, Admin.
Church: 820 S. Linden St., Alliance, 44601.

CHESTERLAND, GEAUGA CO., MOST HOLY TRINITY (1912) 8549 Mayfoeld Rd., Chesterland, 44026-2625. Tel: 216-729-7636; Email: ovim@rcdcanton.org. Rev. Charles Works, Admin.
Catechesis Religious Program—

CLEVELAND, CUYAHOGA CO., ST. HELENA (1904) 1367 W. 65th St., Cleveland, 44102-2109. Tel: 216-651-0965; Email: mihaltanu@yahoo.com. Very Rev. Petru Stinea; Alin Adrian Veres, Music Min.
Catechesis Religious Program—Mrs. Cristina Suciu, D.R.E.; Carmen Stinea, D.R.E. Students 10.

YOUNGSTOWN, MAHONING CO., ST. MARY (1906) 1121 44th St NE, 44714. Very Rev. Ovidiu Ioan Marginean, Diocesan Chancellor.
Church & Res.: 7782 Glenwood Ave., Boardman, 44512-5823. Tel: 330-493-9355; Email: ovim@rcdcanton.org.

STATE OF CALIFORNIA

LAGUNA HILLS, ORANGE CO., ST. JOHN THE BAPTIST ROMANIAN CATHOLIC MISSION (2009) St. Jeanne de Lestonnac School Chapel, 16791 E. Main St., Tustin, CA 92780. 821 W. Stevens Ave Apt. 10, Santa Ana, CA 92707. Rev. Chris Terhes, Admin.
Res. & Mailing Address: 290 Duranzo Isle, Irvine, CA 92606. Tel: 714-746-0623; Email: cterhes@gmail.com.

LOS ANGELES, LOS ANGELES CO., PRESENTATION OF MARY ROMANIAN CATHOLIC CHURCH (1974) 5329 Sepulveda Blvd., Sherman Oaks, CA 91411. Mailing Address: 458 N. Doheny Dr., Unit 69A 81, Los Angeles, CA 90069. Rev. Adrian V. Rosca.

OXNARD, VENTURA CO., ST. JOHN THE EVANGELIST ROMANIAN CATHOLIC MISSION (2009) 150 N. F St., Oxnard, CA 93030. Mailing Address: 1951 St. Andrew Ct., Oxnard, CA 93036. Very Rev. Calin Tamiian.
Res. & Mailing Address: 1447 Iguana Cir., Ventura, CA 93003-6337. Tel: 805-671-9936; Email: ctamiian@hotmail.com.

STATE OF ILLINOIS

AURORA, KANE CO.

1—ST. GEORGE (1935) 720 Rural St., Aurora, IL 60505. Tel: 630-851-4002; Email: fpeterson@marmion.org; Web: saintgeorgeaurora.org. Rev. Frederick Peterson, O.S.B.; Deacons George Dzuricsko; Paul Crawford.
Res.: 850 Butterfield Rd., Aurora, IL 60502-8609.
Catechesis Religious Program—Colin York, D.R.E. Students 22.

2—ST. MICHAEL (1906) [CEM] 609 N. Lincoln Ave., Aurora, IL 60505-2112. Tel: 630-897-8115; Email: ctamiian@hotmail.com.

Very Revs. Calin Tamiian; Aurel Pater, Pastor Emeritus, (Retired).

CHICAGO, COOK CO., SS. PETER AND PAUL CHURCH (1994)
1472 Burr Oak Cir., Aurora, IL 60506-1396.
Tel: 630-205-4806; Email: slcornea@aol.com. Rev. Sergiu Cornea.
Church: 3107 W. Fullerton Ave., Chicago, IL 60647-2809.

STATE OF INDIANA

EAST CHICAGO, LAKE CO., ST. NICHOLAS (1913)
4309 Olcott Ave., East Chicago, IN 46312-2649.
Tel: 219-398-3760; Email: alind@rcdcanton.org. Rev. Alin Nadir Dogaru, Admin.

STATE OF MASSACHUSETTS

BOSTON, MIDDLESEX CO., ROMANIAN CATHOLIC MISSION OF BOSTON (2000)
9 Lake St., Brighton, MA 02135. Very Rev. Michael Moisin, Admin.
Res. & Mailing Address: 8 Druce St., Brookline, MA 02445-4213. Tel: 617-216-4980; Email: mmoisin1@aol.com.

STATE OF MICHIGAN

DEARBORN, WAYNE CO., ST. MARY (1925)
823 S. Military, Dearborn, MI 48124-2109.
Tel: 313-451-1143; Email: stmdearborn@gmail.com. Rev. Cristian Laslo, Admin.

DETROIT, WAYNE CO., ST. JOHN THE BAPTIST (1915)
2371 Woodstock Dr., Detroit, MI 48203-1060.
Tel: 313-305-4781; Email: sjbdetroit@gmail.com. Rev. Constantin Hadarag, Pastoral Assoc.; Sr. Theresa Koernke, I.H.M., Ph.D., Pastoral Assoc.
Catechesis Religious Program—

STATE OF NEW JERSEY

ROEBLING, BURLINGTON CO., ST. MARY (1912) [CEM]
Attended by St. Basil, Trenton.
180 Alden Ave., Roebling, NJ 08554-1125.
Tel: 609-695-6093; Email: FrGeorgeDavid46@gmail.com. Very Rev. George David.

TRENTON, MERCER CO., ST. BASIL (1909) [CEM]
238 Adeline St., Trenton, NJ 08611-2420.
Tel: 609-695-6093; Email: FrGeorgeDavid46@gmail.com. Very Rev. George David.

STATE OF NEW YORK

ASTORIA, QUEENS CO., ST. MARY ROMANIAN CATHOLIC MISSION
11814 83rd Ave., Apt. 2E, Kew Gardens, NY 11415-1309.
Holy Cross Church: 31-12 30th St., Long Island City, NY 11106-2802. Tel: 347-935-5378; Email: rtitonea@gmail.com. Rev. Radu N. Titonea.

STATE OF PENNSYLVANIA

MCKEESPORT, ALLEGHENY CO., ST. MARY
318 26th St., McKeesport, PA 15132-7014.
Tel: 412-673-5552; Email: ovim@rcdcanton.org. Very Rev. Iuliu-Vasile Muntean, Vicar.
Catechesis Religious Program—Students 5.

Unassigned:
Revs.—
Didita, Gabriel
Samayoa, Emmanuel.

Ministry Restricted:
Revs.—
Matthews, Andre
Yossa, Kenneth F.

On Loan to Other Diocese (Eparchies):
Rev.—
Kovacevich, Steve
Deacons—
Puscas, Michael
Puscas, Steven
Puscas, Victor.

Retired:
Rev. Msgr.—
Duma, Gregory, (Retired)
Very Rev.—
Pater, Aurel, (Retired)
Revs.—
Gage, George D., (Retired)
Kirila, Michael, (Retired)
Opris, Gheorghe, (Retired).

INSTITUTIONS LOCATED IN DIOCESE

[A] MONASTERIES

OLYMPIA, WA. *Holy Theophany Monastery*, 10220 66th Ave., S.E., Olympia, WA 98513-9207.
Tel: 360-491-8233; Email: htheophany@earthlink.net; Web: www.holytheophanymonastery.org. Mother Anastasia, Abbess.

ST. NAZIANZ, WI. *Holy Resurrection Monastery*, Mailing Address: 300 S. 2nd Ave., St. Nazianz, WI 54232.
Tel: 920-881-4009; Email: monks@hrmonline.org; Web: www.hrmonline.org. P.O. Box 276, St. Nazianz, WI 54232. Rt. Rev. Archimandrite Nicholas Zachariadis, Abbot; Revs. Maximos Davies, Prior; Hilarion Heagy, Hieromonk; Abouna Moses, Deacon. Novices 4; Solemnly Professed 5.

An asterisk (*) denotes an organization that has established tax-exempt status directly with the IRS and is not covered by the USCCB Group Ruling.

Ukrainian Catholic Diocese of St. Josaphat in Parma

Most Reverend

BOHDAN JOHN DANYLO

Bishop of St. Josaphat in Parma; ordained October 1, 1996; appointed Bishop of St. Josaphat in Parma August 7, 2014; ordained and installed November 4, 2014. *Chancery: 5720 State Rd., P.O. Box 347180, Parma, OH 44134-7180.*

Most Reverend

ROBERT M. MOSKAL, D.D.

Retired Bishop of St. Josaphat in Parma; ordained March 25, 1963; appointed Titular Bishop of Agathopolis and Auxiliary Bishop of the Archeparchy of Philadelphia August 3, 1981; consecrated October 13, 1981; appointed First Bishop of St. Josaphat in Parma December 5, 1983; retired July 29, 2009. *Res.: 5720 State Rd., P.O. Box 347180, Parma, OH 44134.*

Chancery: 5720 State Rd., P.O. Box 347180, Parma, OH 44134-7180. Tel: 440-888-1522; Fax: 440-888-3477.

Email: info@stjosaphateparchy.com

ESTABLISHED DECEMBER 3, 1983.

The jurisdiction of the Bishop of St. Josaphat in Parma extends territorially through all the States of Ohio, Mississippi, West Virginia, Kentucky, Tennessee, Alabama, Georgia, North Carolina, South Carolina, Florida and western Pennsylvania. With regards to persons, his subjects are Catholics of the Byzantine Ukrainian Rite: 1. Who immigrated to this country from Galicia, Bucovina and other Ukrainian provinces; 2. Who descend from such persons (Can. 755); 3. Women married to men referable to 1 and 2, if they comply with (Can. 98, n.4); 4. Who in accordance with (Can. 98, n.3) changed their Rite; 5. Converts to the Catholic Church of the Byzantine Ukrainian Rite; 6. And in fact, all other Catholics of the Byzantine Ukrainian Rite who are attached to parishes subject to the jurisdiction of the Bishop of St. Josaphat in Parma.

For legal titles of parishes and diocesan institutions, consult the Chancery.

STATISTICAL OVERVIEW

Personnel

Bishop	1
Retired Bishops	1
Priests: Diocesan Active in Diocese	33
Priests: Diocesan Active Outside Diocese	5
Priests: Retired, Sick or Absent	15
Number of Diocesan Priests	53
Total Priests in Diocese	53
Ordinations:	
Diocesan Priests	1
Permanent Deacons	2
Permanent Deacons in Diocese	17
Total Brothers	2
Total Sisters	2

Parishes

Parishes	38
With Resident Pastor:	
Resident Diocesan Priests	28
Without Resident Pastor:	
Administered by Priests	10
Missions	9
Professional Ministry Personnel:	
Brothers	2
Sisters	2

Welfare

Other Institutions	3
Total Assisted	180

Educational

Catechesis/Religious Education:	
High School Students	108
Elementary Students	310
Total Students under Catholic Instruction	418

Vital Statistics

Receptions into the Church:	
Infant Baptism Totals	102
Minor Baptism Totals	28
Adult Baptism Totals	11
Received into Full Communion	48
First Communions	141
Confirmations	141
Marriages:	
Catholic	39
Interfaith	5
Total Marriages	44
Deaths	146
Total Catholic Population	10,542

Former Bishop—Most Rev. ROBERT M. MOSKAL, ord. March 25, 1963; appt. Titular Bishop of Agathopolis and Auxiliary Bishop of the Archeparchy of Philadelphia Aug. 3, 1981; cons. Oct. 13, 1981; appt. First Bishop of St. Josaphat in Parma Dec. 5, 1983; retired July 29, 2009.

Chancery—5720 State Rd., P.O. Box 347180, Parma, 44134-7180. Tel: 440-888-1522; Fax: 440-888-3477; Email: stjosaphatparma@gmail.com. Office Hours: Mon.-Fri. 9-12 & 1-4.

Chancellor/Financial Officer—Very Rev. Canon STEVEN PALIWODA.

Vicar General—Very Rev. Archpriest MICHAEL POLOSKY.

Consultors—Rev. IHOR HOHOSHA; Very Rev. Canon STEVEN PALIWODA; Very Rev. Archpriest MICHAEL POLOSKY; Very Rev. Canon ANDREW HANOVSKY; Revs. DOUGLAS LORANCE; VOLODYMYR HRYTSYUK.

Eparchial Corporation—Most Rev. BOHDAN JOHN DANYLO, Pres.; Very Rev. Archpriest MICHAEL POLOSKY; Very Rev. Canon STEVEN PALIWODA, Sec. & Treas.

Administrative Council—Most Rev. BOHDAN JOHN DANYLO; Very Rev. Canon ANDREW HANOVSKY; Revs. MARK MOROZOWICH, S.E.O.D.; IHOR KASIYAN; Deacons DONALD BILLY; MARK PROKOPOVICH.

Vicar for Clergy—Rev. VOLODYMYR HRYTSYUK.

Vicar for Religious—Very Rev. Canon STEVEN PALIWODA.

Liturgical Commission—Most Rev. BOHDAN JOHN DANYLO; Revs. IVAN CHIROVSKY; JOSEPH MATLAK; MARK MOROZOWICH, S.E.O.D.

Examiner of Clergy—Very Rev. Archpriest MICHAEL POLOSKY.

Personnel Board—Rev. VOLODYMYR HRYTSYUK, Chm.; Very Rev. Canon STEVEN PALIWODA, Sec.; Very Rev. Archpriest MICHAEL POLOSKY.

St. Josaphat Sacerdotal Society—Most Rev. BOHDAN JOHN DANYLO, Ex Officio; Very Rev. Canons STEVEN PALIWODA, Ex Officio; ANDREW HANOVSKY, Sec.; Rev. IVAN CHIROVSKY. Alternates: Revs. IHOR KASIYAN; GREGORY MADEYA; IHOR HOHOSHA; VSEVOLOD SHEVCHUK.

Religious Education—Sr. ANN LASZOK, O.S.B.M., Dir.

League of Ukrainian Catholics—Rev. GREGORY MADEYA.

Vocations—Rev. VSEVOLOD SHEVCHUK.

Acolyte Confraternity—Deacon DONALD BILLY; MR. JOSEPH LEVY.

Permanent Deacon Program—Very Rev. MARK SHUEY.

Priests' Continuing Education—Most Rev. BOHDAN JOHN DANYLO.

Eparchial Convention—Most Rev. BOHDAN JOHN DANYLO.

Youth Ministries—Rev. LUBOMIR ZHYBAK.

Lay Ministries—Sisters ANN LASZOK, O.S.B.M.; OLGA MARIE FARYNA, O.S.B.M.

Presbyteral Council—Most Rev. BOHDAN JOHN DANYLO; Very Rev. Canon STEVEN PALIWODA; Very Rev. Archpriest MICHAEL POLOSKY; Revs. JASON CHARRON; JOHN FREISHYN-CHIROVSKY; Very Rev. MICHAEL DROZDOVSKY; Very Rev. Canon ANDREW HANOVSKY; Revs. DOUGLAS LORANCE; MATTHEW SCHROEDER; VSEVOLOD SHEVCHUK; Very Rev. MARK SHUEY; Revs. LUBOMIR ZHYBAK; IHOR HOHOSHA.

Arbitration Board—Rev. IVAN CHIROVSKY; Rev. Msgr. Mitred Archpriest JOHN P. STEVENSKY, (Retired).

Protopresbyteries—

Western Protopresbytery—Very Rev. Canon STEVEN PALIWODA, 3038 Charleston Ave., Lorain, 44055-2464. Tel: 440-277-7114. Akron, OH; Austintown, OH; Canton, OH; Cleveland, OH; Lorain, OH; Parma, OH (Cathedral); Parma, OH (St. Andrew); Parma, OH (Pokrova); Rossford, OH; Solon, OH; Youngstown, OH.

Central Protopresbytery—Very Rev. Archpriest MICHAEL POLOSKY, Sts. Peter & Paul, 404 Sixth St., Ambridge, PA 15003. Tel: 724-266-2262. Aliquippa, PA; Ambridge, PA; Arnold, PA (New Kensington); Carnegie, PA; Jeannette, PA; Lyndora, PA; McKees Rocks, PA; McKeesport, PA; Pittsburgh, PA (St. George); Pittsburgh, PA (St. John); Wheeling, WV.

Eastern Protopresbytery—Very Rev. Archpriest MICHAEL POLOSKY, Ford City, PA; Johnstown, PA; Latrobe, PA; New Alexandria, PA; Northern Cambria, PA (Barnesboro); Ramey, PA; Revloc, PA; West Leechburg, PA., Tel: 724-266-2262.

Southern Protopresbytery—Rev. ANDRII ROMANKIV, 434 90th Ave., N., St. Petersburg, FL 33702. Tel: 727-576-1001. Apopka, FL; Conyers, GA; Spring Hill (Brooksville), FL; Miami, FL; North Port, FL; St. Petersburg, FL.

Mid-Atlantic Protopresbytery—Very Rev. MARK SHUEY, 4801 Topstone Rd., Raleigh, NC 27603. Tel: 919-779-7246. Garner, NC (Ss. Volodymyr and Olha); Raleigh, NC (St. Nicholas); Charlotte, NC (St. Basil); Pineville, NC (St. John the Baptist Mission); Knoxville, TN (St. Thomas the Apostle) Carey, NC (St. Nicholas); Columbia, SC (Holy Cross Mission); Greenville, SC (Dormition of the Mother of God Mission); Nashville, TN (St. Nicholas Mission); Martinez, GA (St. John the Theologian Mission).

Presbyters—Very Rev. Archimandrite GEORGE APPLEYARD, (Retired), Mailing Address: St. Lazarus Retirement Community, P.O. Box 264, Clintonville, PA 16372-0264. Cell: 814-908-0987; Email: gappleyard@zoominternet.net; Rev. RICHARD ARMSTRONG, St. Thomas the Apostle, 2044 Farmstead Ln., Powell, TN 37849. Tel: 865-

859-9785; Email: rarmstrong@dioknox.org. St. Nicholas Mission, 1219 Second Ave., S., Nashville, TN 37216; Very Rev. ANTHONY BALISTRERI, (Retired), 1215 Four Leaf Ln., Holidaysburg, PA 16648. Tel: 814-378-7688; Email: abalistreri@comcast.net; Rev. MICHAEL BLISZCZ, (on loan to St. Nicholas Eparchy), 601 Spring Ave., N.E., Apt. 101, Grand Rapids, MI 49503. Tel: 616-742-0874; Rev. Archpriest PHILIP BUMBAR, (Retired), Sts. Peter & Paul, 2001 Main St., Aliquippa, PA 15001-2724. Tel: 412-320-5449; Email: phil.bumbar@comcast.net; Very Rev. Msgr. Archpriest MARTIN A. CANAVAN, S.T.L., J.C.L., (Retired), 2850 N. Palm Aire Dr. #604, Pompano Beach, FL 33069. Tel: 305-450-8003; Email: macan675@gmail.com; Revs. JASON CHARRON, Holy Trinity Ukrainian Catholic Church, 730 Washington Ave., Carnegie, PA 15106. Tel: 412-279-4652; Email: charronjason@gmail.com. Our Lady of Perpetual Help, 4136 Jacob St., Wheeling, WV 26003. Tel: 304-232-2168; JOHN FREISHYN-CHIROVSKY, (Visiting Priest), St. Michael, 434135 Walnut St., Rossford, 43460; IHOR HOHOSHA, St. George, 3455 California Ave., Pittsburgh, PA 15212-2180. Tel: 412-766-8801; Email: saintgeorgepghs@yahoo.com. St. John the Baptist, 204 Olivia St., McKees Rocks, PA 15136; Very Rev. MICHAEL DROZDOVSKY, Pokrova, 6790 Broadview Rd., Parma, 44134. Tel: 216-524-0918 (Residence & Office); Fax: 216-524-0919; Tel: 216-524-6872 (Hall Office); Tel: 216-524-6871 (Hall); Email: m.drozdovsky@gmail.com; Revs. XAVIER ELAMBASSERY, (Retired), 315 W. 2nd Ave., Latrobe, PA 15650; JOHN GRIBIK, St. Demetrius/Ss. Peter and Paul, 1013 Gaskill Ave., Jeannette, PA 15644. Tel: 724-523-9389. Patronage of the Mother of God, 514 Ninth St., Ford City, PA 16226. Tel: 724-763-1203. St. Michael, Main St., West Leechburg, PA 15656; VOLODYMYR HRYTSYUK, Protection BVM, 27275 Aurora Rd., Solon, 44139-1804. Tel: 440-248-4549; Cell: 440-832-1318; Very Rev. Canon ANDREW HANOVSKY, Ss. Peter & Paul, 2280 W. 7th St., Cleveland, 44113. Tel: 216-861-2176; Cell: 216-401-0004; Email: ahanowsky@gmail.com; Revs. JERRY IKALOWYCH, (Retired), (on leave), 2220 White Rd., Conyers, GA 30012. Tel: 770-760-1111; IHOR KASIYAN, St. Andrew, 7700 Hoertz Rd., Parma, 44134-6404. Tel: 440-843-9149; Tel: 440-845-2270 (Residence); Cell: 440-391-8500; Email: pastor@standrewucc.org; Web: www.standrewucc.org; MICHAEL KOUTS, St. Andrew, 8064 Weeping Willow St., Brooksville, FL 34613. Tel: 352-596-2433; SEVERYN KOVALYSHIN, (on leave), Tel: 941-426-7931; Email: severinokov@yahoo.it; ANDREW KRASULSKI, (Retired), Tel: 814-539-1087; Very Rev. MICHAEL KRUPKA, (Retired), Tel: 216-385-5116; Email: krupka@juno.com; Rev. MICHAEL KULICK, 8455 Sunnydale Dr., Brecksville, 44141. St. John the Baptist Mission, Admin., 7702 Pineville Matthews Rd., Pineville, NC 28226. Cell: 330-724-8277; Email: revmikdds@yahoo.com; Very Rev. Canon IGNATIUS KURY, (on leave); Revs. SEAN J. LABAT, 700 N. 2nd St., Apt. 103, Richmond, VA 23219. Tel: 312-799-1875; Email: sjlabat@yahoo.com; DOUGLAS LORANCE, St. Michael, 610 Hansen Ave., Lyndora, PA 16045-1325. Tel: 724-283-6230; Fax: 724-283-0363; GREGORY MADEYA, St. John the Baptist, 1907 Eden Park Blvd., Mc Keesport, PA 15132. Tel: 412-672-0923. 111 Third St., Dravosburg, PA 15034. Tel: 412-896-1668; Cell: 412-805-3451; Email: greggorio2@aol.com. St. Demetrius, 1015 Gaskill Ave., Jeannette, PA 15644. Assumption of the Mother of God, 526 Hillview Ave., Latrobe, PA 15650; ANDREW MARKO, (Retired), 33225 Electric Blvd., Avon Lake, 44012. Tel: 350-933-6934; CLAUDIO MELNICKI, (on leave), Tel: 440-886-2108; MARK MOROZOWICH, S.E.O.D., 3900 B Watson Pl., N.W., Apt. G3A, Washington, DC 20016. Tel: 202-965-1572 (House); Cell: 202-468-5166; Tel: 202-319-6515 (Voice Mail); Fax: 202-319-4967; Email: morozowich@cua.edu; GEORGE MULLONKAL, Ph.D., (On Leave), Email: 2stm@buckeye-express.com; Very Rev. Canon STEVEN PALIWODA, Protopresbyter, Western, St. John the Baptist, 3038 Charleston Ave., Lorain, 44055-2164. Tel: 440-277-7114; Email: stevenpaliwoda@yahoo.com; Rev. VASYL PETRIV, Presentation of the Most Holy Mother of God, 1078 N. Biscayne Blvd., North Port, FL 34291. Email: uccnp@yahoo.com; Very Rev. Archpriest MICHAEL POLOSKY, Ss. Peter & Paul, 404 Sixth St., Ambridge, PA 15003. Tel: 724-266-2262 (Office); Fax: 724-266-2262; Email: sspandpchurch@gmail.com. Ss. Peter and Paul, 2001 Main St., Aliquippa, PA 15001; Rev. Msgr. MICHAEL REWTIUK, (Retired), 3112 Marioncliff Dr., Parma, 44134. Email: 2189mbr@cox.net; Rev. Msgr. Mitred THOMAS A. SAYUK, (Retired); Revs. MATTHEW SCHROEDER, Garner - Ss. Volodymyr & Olha Mission, 8312 White Oak Rd., Garner, NC 27529. Tel: 919-376-8099; Email: frmatthew@live.com; VSEVOLOD SHEVCHUK, Holy Ghost Ukrainian Catholic Church, 1859 Carter Ave., Akron, 44301. Tel: 330-724-8277. St. Nicholas Mission, 812 Gibbs Ave., Canton, 44704; JAROSLAW SHUDRAK, Protection of the Mother of God, ADM 245 Lake McCoy Dr., Apopka, FL 32712. Tel: 407-880-1640; Very Rev. MARK SHUEY, St. Nicholas Mission, 4801 Topstone Rd., Raleigh, NC 27603. Tel: 919-779-7246; Email: rfmark@nc.rr.com. St. Nicholas Mission, 2510 Piney Plains Rd., Carey, NC 27518. St. John the Theologian Mission, 634 Furys Rd., Martinez, GA 30907; Revs. JOHN SMEREKA, (visiting priest), 410 7th Ave., Carnegie, PA 15106; MICHAEL SOPP, (on leave of absence); ANIBAL SOUTUS, (On Loan); Rev. Msgr. Mitred Archpriest JOHN P. STEVENSKY, (Retired), Tel: 727-492-8685; Email: msgrjps@mindspring.com; Rev. Mitred Archpriest WOLODYMYR WOLOSZCZUK, (Retired), 4240 Timberline Blvd., Venice, FL 34293. Tel: 941-493-7299; Rev. Canon WALTER WYSOCHANSKY, (Retired), 404 Sixth St., Ambridge, PA 15003. Tel: 724-266-2262; Revs. LUBOMIR ZHYBAK, Holy Trinity, 526 W. Rayen Ave., Youngstown, 44502-1124. Tel: 440-886-2108; Email: yngholytrinity@att.net. St. Anne, 4310 Kirk Rd., Youngstown, 44511. Tel: 330-314-5714; YAROSLAV KOVAL, St. Vladimir, 1601 Kenneth Ave., Arnold, PA 15068. Tel: 412-770-4915. St. John the Baptist, 109 S. 7th St., Pittsburgh, PA 15203. Nativity of the Mother of God, P.O. Box 35, New Alexandria, PA 15670; VOLODYMYR PETRYTSYA, Protection of the Mother of God, 2880 Hwy. 138 N.E., Conyers, GA 30013. Tel: 770-760-1111; ROMAN BADIAK, Epiphany of Our Lord, 434 90th Ave. N., St. Petersburg, FL 33702-3022. Tel: 727-576-1001; BOHDAN BARYTSKYY, Admin., St. Josaphat Cathedral, 5720 State Rd., Parma, 44134. Tel: 440-886-2108; Email: officestjosaphat@gmail.com; ANDREW CLARKE, (Retired), 204 Golfview Dr., Monaca, PA 15061. Tel: 814-539-1087; Email: valscar@yahoo.com; Email: clarkeae99@yahoo.com. P.O. Box 124, Monaca, PA 15061; ANDRII ROMANKIV, Assumption of the Blessed Virgin Mary, 39 N.W. 57th Ct., Miami, FL 33126. Tel: 786-606-6120. Mailing Address: 11000 S.W. 128th St., Miami, FL 33176; JOSEPH MATLAK, Admin., Dormition of the Mother of God Mission, 1215 SC-14, Greer, SC 29650. Tel: 412-587-1902. Holy Cross Mission, 306 N. Pines Rd., Blythewood, SC 29016; ALEXANDER WROBLICKY, 244 Voss Rd., Bethel Park, PA 15102; ANDRIY KELT, Admin., Immaculate Conception, 3711 Campbell Ave., Northern Cambria, PA 15714. Protection of the Mother of God, P.O. Box 194, Revloc, PA 15948; Deacon JAMES DAVIDSON, Admin., Annunciation of the Mother of God, 22 Bentz St., Ramey, PA 16671. Tel: 814-762-9846. Mailing Address: P.O. Box 205, Ramey, PA 16671. St. John the Baptist, 606 Maple St., Johnstown, PA 15650. Immaculate Conception, 2024 20th St., Altoona, PA 16601.

CLERGY, PARISHES, MISSIONS AND PAROCHIAL SCHOOLS

STATE OF OHIO

PARMA

1—ST. ANDREW (1965)
7700 Hoertz Rd., 44134-6404. Tel: 440-843-9149; Email: pastor@standrewucc.org. Rev. Ihor Kasiyan.
Catechesis Religious Program—Renata Harmatiy, D.R.E. Students 61.

2—ST. JOSAPHAT CATHEDRAL (1959)
5720 State Rd., 44134-2536. Tel: 440-886-2108; Cell: 216-269-6829; Email: pastorstjosaphat@gmail.com; Email: officestjosaphat@gmail.com; Web: www.stjosaphatcathedral.com. Rev. Bohdan Barytskyy, Rector; Archdeacon Jeffrey Smolilo.
Rectory—5710 State Rd., 44134.
Catechesis Religious Program—God With Us,
Tel: 440-503-9684; Email: ipka@sbcglobal.net. Irene Kulick, D.R.E. Students 58.

3—POKROVA UKRAINIAN CATHOLIC PARISH (1973) [CEM]
6790 Broadview Rd., 44134. Tel: 216-524-0918; Email: pokrovachurch@yahoo.com. Very Rev. Mykhaylo Drozdovsky.
Res.: 6810 Broadview Rd., 44134-4804. Email: m.drozdovsky@gmail.com.
Catechesis Religious Program—CCD, Students 91.

AKRON, SUMMIT CO., HOLY GHOST (1915)
1859 Carter Ave., Akron, 44301. Tel: 330-724-8277; Email: pastor@hgucc.org; Web: www.hgucc.org. Rev. Vsevolod Shevchuk, Admin.; Dr. Maria Griffiths, D.R.E.

AUSTINTOWN, MAHONING CO., ST. ANNE (1967) [JC]
4310 Kirk Rd., Austintown, 44511. Tel: 330-744-5820; Email: yngholytrinity@att.net; Web: www.stanneucc.com. Rev. Lubomir Zhybak, Admin.; Deacon Donald Billy.
Catechesis Religious Program—Students 50.

CANTON, STARK CO., ST. NICHOLAS MISSION, Attended by Akron.
1121 44th St. N.E., Canton, 44714.
Tel: 330-724-8277; Email: pastor@hgucc.org. Mailing Address: 1859 Carter Ave., Akron, 44301. Rev. Vsevolod Shevchuk, Admin.

CLEVELAND, CUYAHOGA CO., SS. PETER AND PAUL, [CEM]
2280 W. 7th St., Cleveland, 44113. Tel: 216-861-2176; Email: motherchurch2008@gmail.com. Very Rev. Canon Andrew Hanovsky.

LORAIN, LORAIN CO., ST. JOHN THE BAPTIST (1913)
3038 Charleston Ave., Lorain, 44055-2164.
Tel: 440-277-7114; Email: stevenpaliwoda@yahoo.com. Very Rev. Canon Steven Paliwoda.
Church: 2445 E. 31st St., Lorain, 44055.

ROSSFORD, WOOD CO., ST. MICHAEL (1912)
135 Walnut St., Rossford, 43460-1248.
Tel: 419-666-3770; Email: 2stm@buckeye-exp.com. Mailing Address: 133 Walnut St., Rossford, 43460-1248. Rev. George Mullonkal, Ph.D.

SOLON, CUYAHOGA CO., PROTECTION OF THE BLESSED VIRGIN MARY
27275 Aurora Rd., Solon, 44139-1804.
Tel: 440-248-4549; Email: stmaryukr@gmail.com. Rev. Volodymyr Hrytsyuk.
Catechesis Religious Program—Students 2.

YOUNGSTOWN, MAHONING CO., HOLY TRINITY 1911 Rev. Lubomir Zhybak, Admin.; Deacon Donald Billy.
Res.: 526 W. Rayen Ave., Youngstown, 44502-1124.
Tel: 330-744-5820; Tel: 330-746-9528; Email: yngholytrinity@att.net; Web: www.holytrinityucc.com.
Catechesis Religious Program—Eastern Christian Formation (ECF), Students 32.

STATE OF FLORIDA

APOPKA, ORANGE CO., PROTECTION OF THE MOTHER OF GOD
245 Lake McCoy Dr., Apopka, FL 32712.
Tel: 407-880-1640; Email: yarkoshudrak@gmail.com. Rev. Jaroslaw Shudrak, Admin.; Deacon Richard Wilhelm.
Catechesis Religious Program—

BROOKSVILLE, HERNANDO CO., ST. ANDREW
8064 Weeping Willow St., Brooksville, FL 34613.
Tel: 352-596-2433; Email: zenonkouts@gmail.com. Rev. Michael Kouts.

MIAMI, DADE CO., ASSUMPTION OF THE BLESSED VIRGIN MARY
39 NW 57 Ct., Miami, FL 33126. Mailing Address: 11000 S.W. 128th St., Miami, FL 33176.
Tel: 786-592-1563; Email: ukrainianmiami@gmail.com; Web: ukrainianmiami.org/en. Rev. Andrii Romankiv.
Catechesis Religious Program—Students 10.

NORTH PORT, SARASOTA CO., PRESENTATION OF THE MOST HOLY MOTHER OF GOD (ST. MARY'S)
1078 N. Biscayne Dr., North Port, FL 34291.
Tel: 941-426-7931; Email: petrivv@yahoo.com. Rev. Vasyl Petriv.

ST. PETERSBURG, PINELLAS CO., EPIPHANY OF OUR LORD (1964)
434 90th Ave. N., St. Petersburg, FL 33702.
Tel: 727-576-1001; Email: rbadiak@aol.com. Rev. Roman Badiak, Admin.

STATE OF GEORGIA

CONYERS, ROCKDALE CO., PROTECTION OF THE MOTHER OF GOD
2880 Hwy. 138, N.E., Conyers, GA 30013.
Tel: 770-760-1111; Email: motherofgodch@aol.com; Web: motherofgodatlanta.com. Rev. Volodymyr Petrytsya, Admin.

MARTINEZ, ST. JOHN THE THEOLOGIAN UKRAINIAN CATHOLIC MISSION
634 Furys Ferry Rd., Martinez, GA 30907.
Tel: 919-779-7246; Email: rfmark@nc.rr.com. Very Rev. Mark Shuey, Admin.

STATE OF NORTH CAROLINA

CARY, WAKE CO., ST. NICHOLAS MISSION
2510 Piney Plains Rd.., Cary, NC 27518.
Tel: 919-239-4877; Email: arcenterpirsellc@gmail.com. Very Rev. Mark Shuey, Admin.

CHARLOTTE, MECKLENBURG CO., ST. BASIL THE GREAT MISSION
1400 Suther Rd., Charlotte, NC 28213.
Tel: 980-785-2764; Email: stbasilcharlotte@gmail.com; Web: stbasil.weebly.com. Rev. Joseph Matlak, Admin.; Deacon Matthew Hanes, Archivist.

GARNER, WAKE CO., SS. VOLODYMYR AND OLHA MISSION (2006)
8312 White Oak Rd., Garner, NC 27529.
Tel: 919-376-8099; Email: frmatthew@live.com; Web: www.stvochurch.com. Rev. Matthew Schroeder.

Catechesis Religious Program—Students 5.
PINEVILLE, ST. JOHN THE BAPTIST MISSION
7702 Pineville Matthews Rd., Pineville, NC 28226.
Tel: 440-503-9685; Email: michael1kulick@gmail.com; Email: okhariouk@gmail.com. Mailing Address: 8455 Sunnydale Dr., Brecksville, 44141. Deacon Michael Kulick, Admin.
RALEIGH, WAKE CO., ST. NICHOLAS MISSION
4801 Topstone Rd., Raleigh, NC 27603.
Tel: 919-779-7246; Email: rfmark@nc.rr.com; Web: www.saintnicholasraleigh.org. Very Rev. Mark Shuey.

STATE OF PENNSYLVANIA

ALIQUIPPA, BEAVER CO., SS. PETER AND PAUL (1916)
2001 Main St., Aliquippa, PA 15001.
Tel: 724-266-2262; Email: sspandpchurch@gmail.com. Very Rev. Archpriest Michael Polosky. Served from St. Peter & Paul, Ambridge.In Res., Rev. Canon Philip Bumbar.
ALTOONA, BLAIR CO., IMMACULATE CONCEPTION, [CEM] Served by Johnstown, Pa.
2024 20th St., Altoona, PA 16601. Tel: 814-535-2634; Email: thelittlewaybodyandsoul@gmail.com. Rev. James Davidson, Admin.; Very Rev. Anthony Balistreri, Visiting Priest, (Retired).
AMBRIDGE, BEAVER CO., SS. PETER AND PAUL (1907) [CEM]
404 6th St., Ambridge, PA 15003. Tel: 724-266-2262; Email: sspandpchurch@gmail.com. Very Rev. Archpriest Michael Polosky. In Res., Rev. Canon Walter Wysochansky, (Retired).
Catechesis Religious Program—Nancy Paliani, D.R.E.; Kathy Rudakewich, D.R.E. Students 44.
Convent—542 Melrose Ave., Ambridge, PA 15003. Sisters of St. Basil the Great.
CARNEGIE, ALLEGHENY CO., HOLY TRINITY UKRAINIAN CATHOLIC CHURCH (1951) [CEM]
730 Washington Ave., Carnegie, PA 15106.
Tel: 412-279-4652; Email: holytrinitycarnegie@gmail.com; Web: www.htucc.com. Revs. Jason Charron; John Smereka, (Visiting Priest).
Catechesis Religious Program—Mark Medwig, D.R.E. Students 50.
FORD CITY, ARMSTRONG CO., PATRONAGE OF THE MOTHER OF GOD, [CEM]
514 Ninth St., Ford City, PA 16226.
Tel: 724-763-1203. Rev. John Gribik.
JEANNETTE, WESTMORELAND CO., ST. DEMETRIUS
1015 Gaskill Ave., Jeannette, PA 15644-3307.
Tel: 412-672-0923; Email: greggorio2@aol.com. Rev. Gregory Madeya.
JOHNSTOWN, CAMBRIA CO., ST. JOHN THE BAPTIST, [CEM]
606 Maple Ave., Johnstown, PA 15901.
Tel: 814-535-2634; Email: thelittlewaybodyandsoul@gmail.com; Email: CambriaGrecoCatholics@gmail.com. Rev. James Davidson, Admin.
Catechesis Religious Program—Amanda Bellock, D.R.E. Students 2.
LATROBE, WESTMORELAND CO., ASSUMPTION OF THE BLESSED VIRGIN MARY (1910)
4827 Rt. 982, Latrobe, PA 15650. Tel: 412-672-0923; Email: greggorio2@aol.com. Rev. Gregory Madeya, Admin.
LYNDORA, BUTLER CO., ST. MICHAEL
610 Hansen Ave., Lyndora, PA 16045-1325.
Tel: 724-283-0363; Tel: 724-283-6230; Email: stmikeschurch@zoominternet.net. Rev. Douglas Lorance.
Catechesis Religious Program—Students 3.
MCKEES ROCKS, ALLEGHENY CO., ST. JOHN THE BAPTIST (1941)
204 Olivia St., McKees Rocks, PA 15136.
Tel: 412-331-5605; Email: revingvar@yahoo.com. Rev. Ihor Hohosha.
MCKEESPORT, ALLEGHENY CO., ST. JOHN THE BAPTIST
1907 Eden Park Blvd., McKeesport, PA 15132.
Tel: 412-672-0923; Email: greggorio2@aol.com. Rev. Gregory Madeya.
NEW ALEXANDRIA, WESTMORELAND CO., NATIVITY OF THE MOTHER OF GOD, [CEM] Attended by Assumption of B.V.M., Latrobe
Shersburg Rd., New Alexandria, PA 15670.
Tel: 412-537-6450; Tel: 412-770-4915; Email: yaro1973@libero.it. Rev. Yaroslav Koval, Admin.
NEW KENSINGTON (ARNOLD), WESTMORELAND CO., ST. VLADIMIR (1912)
1601 Kenneth Ave., Arnold, PA 15068.
Tel: 412-770-4915; Email: yaro1973@libero.it. Rev. Yaroslav Koval.
NORTHERN CAMBRIA, CAMBRIA CO., IMMACULATE CONCEPTION aka St. Mary's Ukrainian Catholic Church (1911)
3711 Campbell Ave., Northern Cambria, PA 15714.
Tel: 814-948-9193; Email: ICBVM@yahoo.com. Rev. Andriy Kelt, Admin.
PITTSBURGH, ALLEGHENY CO.
1—ST. GEORGE (1918)
3455 California Ave., Pittsburgh, PA 15212.
Tel: 412-766-8801; Email: saintgeorgepghs@yahoo.com. Rev. Ihor Hohosha.
2—ST. JOHN THE BAPTIST, [CEM]
109 S. Seventh St., Pittsburgh, PA 15203.
Tel: 412-431-2531; Email: stjohnucc@comcast.net. Rev. Yaroslav Koval, Admin.
Catechesis Religious Program—Irene Borodycia, D.R.E. Students 1.
RAMEY, CLEARFIELD CO., ANNUNCIATION OF THE MOTHER OF GOD 1893 [CEM]
22 Bentz St., P.O. Box 205, Ramey, PA 16671.
Tel: 814-378-7688; Email: thelittlewaybodyandsoul@gmail.com. Rev. James Davidson, Admin.
Catechesis Religious Program—Ms. Anne Janocko, D.R.E.
REVLOC, CAMBRIA CO., PROTECTION BLESSED VIRGIN MARY (1926) Attended by
560 Cambria Ave., P.O. Box 194, Revloc, PA 15948.
Tel: 814-948-9193; Email: keltandriy@yahoo.com; Web: protectionofthebvm.org. Rev. Andriy Kelt, Admin. Share priest with Northern Cambria parish.
Catechesis Religious Program—Mrs. Robin Wagner, D.R.E. Students 9.
WEST LEECHBURG, ARMSTRONG CO., ST. MICHAEL, Attended by Mission parish served by Ford City, PA
Main St., West Leechburg, PA 15656.
Tel: 724-763-1203; Email: jdgribik@windstream.net. Mailing Address: 514 9th St., Ford City, PA 15656. Rev. John Gribik.
WILMERDING, ALLEGHENY CO., SS. PETER AND PAUL, Closed. For inquiries for parish records contact the chancery.

STATE OF SOUTH CAROLINA

BLYTHEWOOD, HOLY CROSS MISSION
306 N. Pines Rd., Blythewood, SC 29016.
Tel: 803-814-4692; Email: colabyzantinecatholic@gmail.com; Web: colabyzcatholic.weebly.com. Mailing Address: 1400 Suther Rd., Charlotte, NC 28213. Rev. Joseph Matlak, Admin.
GREER, DORMITION OF THE MOTHER OF GOD MISSION
1215 SC-14, Greer, SC 29650. Tel: 980-785-2764; Email: dormitiongreenville@gmail.com; Web: dormition.weebly.com. Mailing Address: 1400 Suther Rd., Charlotte, NC 28213. Rev. Joseph Matlak, Admin.

STATE OF TENNESSEE

KNOXVILLE, ST. THOMAS THE APOSTLE MISSION
2304 Ault Rd., Knoxville, TN 37914.
Tel: 865-621-8499; Email: rfmark@nc.rr.com. Rev. Richard Armstrong, Admin.
NASHVILLE, ST. NICHOLAS MISSION
1219 Second Ave. S., Nashville, TN 37210.
Tel: 865-621-8499; Email: rarmstrong@dioknox.org. Rev. Richard Armstrong, Admin.

STATE OF WEST VIRGINIA

WHEELING, OHIO CO., OUR LADY OF PERPETUAL HELP, Served by Holy Trinity, Carnegie.
4136 Jacob St., Wheeling, WV 26003.
Tel: 304-232-2168; Email: holytrinitycarnegie@gmail.com. Rev. Jason Charron.

On Assignment Outside the Diocese:
Revs.—
Bliszcz, Michael, 154 Gold Ave., Grand Rapids, MI 49503
Morozowich, Mark, S.E.O.D., 3900 B Watson Pl., N.W., Apt. G3A, Washington, DC 20016.

On Leave:
Revs.—
Ikalowych, Jerry, (Retired), 2220 White Rd., Conyers, GA 30012
Melnicki, Claudio
Mullonkal, George, Ph.D.
Sopp, Michael
Very Rev. Canon—
Kury, Ignatius.

Retired:
Rev. Msgr.—
Rewtiuk, Michael, (Retired), 3112 Marioncliff, 44134
Very Revs.—
Appleyard, George, (Retired), P.O. Box 264, Clintonville, PA 16372-0264
Balistreri, Anthony, (Retired), 1215 Four Leaf Ln., Hollidaysburg, PA 16648
Bumbar, Philip, (Retired), 2001 Main St., Aliquippa, PA 15001-2724
Sayuk, Thomas, (Retired), 12415 Maycrest Ave., Weeki Wachee, FL 34614
Revs.—
Clarke, Andrew, (Retired), 204 Golfview Dr., P.O. Box 124, Monaca, PA 15061
Elambassery, Xavier, (Retired), 315 W. 2nd Ave., Latrobe, PA 15650
Ikalowych, Jerry, (Retired), 2220 White Rd., Conyers, GA 30012
Krasulski, Andrew, (Retired)
Marko, Andrew, (Retired), 33225 Electric Blvd., Avon Lake, 44012
Very Rev. Msgr. Archpriest—
Canavan, Martin A., S.T.L., J.C.L., (Retired), 2850 N. Palm Aire Dr., #604, Pompano Beach, FL 33069
Rev. Canons—
Krupka, Michael, (Retired), 4617 Turney Rd., Apt. 1, Garfield Heights, 44125
Wysochansky, Walter, (Retired), 404 6th St., Ambridge, PA 15003
Rev. Mitred Archpriest—
Woloszczuk, Wolodymyr, (Retired), 4240 Timberline Blvd., Venice, FL 34293
Rev. Msgr. Mitred Archpriest—
Stevensky, John P., (Retired), 12772 Doula Ln., North Royalton, 44133.

Permanent Deacons:
Bellock, Christopher, 623 W. Ogle St., Ebensburg, PA 15931. Cell: 814-472-9396
Billy, Donald, 2515 McCollum Rd., Youngstown, 44509. Tel: 330-792-3166
Bury, Thomas
Dozier, Stephen Gordon, 15 Village By The Lake, Southern Pines, NC 28387. Tel: 910-724-3351
Dragani, Anthony, 115 Diamond Dr., Ebensburg, PA 15931. Cell: 412-309-0120
Fernandes, Trevor, 2648 Latonia Blvd., Toledo, 43606. Tel: 419-206-0751
Galadza, Paul, 39 N.W. 57th Ct., Miami, FL 33126. Tel: 305-724-5216
Gregory, John, 7629 Normandie Blvd., Apt. B28, Middleburg Heights, 44130. (On Leave)
Hanes, Matthew, 1132 Wylam Dilly Ct., Charlotte, NC 28213
Kibbe, Lee, 2411 Chaise Dr., Rocky Mount, NC 27804. Tel: 252-883-6338
Prokopovich, Mark, 38 Anthony Wayne Ter., Baden, PA 15005. Tel: 724-876-0129
Smolilo, Jeffery, 4546 Shelly Dr., Seven Hills, 44131. Tel: 216-328-0743 (Home); Tel: 216-344-8315 (Office)
Spak, Myron, 326 Rockfield Rd., Pittsburgh, PA 15243
Suchan, Stephen, 133 Willow Village Dr., Pittsburgh, PA 15239. Tel: 412-798-0642
Wilhelm, Richard, 2810 Castle Oak Ave., Orlando, FL 32808
Wirag, Joseph, 807 Pine St., Ambridge, PA 15003-1734. Cell: 724-709-9640
Yupanqul, Buenaventura, 3706 Ranbir Dr., Durham, NC 27713
Bezner, Kevin, 1421 Hartford Ave., Charlotte, NC 28209.

INSTITUTIONS LOCATED IN DIOCESE

[A] MONASTERIES AND RESIDENCES FOR PRIESTS AND BROTHERS

BROOKLYN. *Holy Spirit Monastery*, 4150 Rabbit Run, Brooklyn, 44144. Tel: 216-741-3653; Email: brotherdale@catholicweb.com. Bros. Dale Sefcik, B.H.S.; David Robert, B.H.S. Brothers 2.

[B] CONVENTS

AMBRIDGE. *Ss. Peter & Paul Convent*, 542 Melrose Ave., Ambridge, PA 15003. Tel: 724-266-5578; Email: srannl@aol.com. Most Rev. Bohdan John Danylo, Contact Person. Sisters of St. Basil the Great. Sisters 2.

[C] HOMES FOR THE AGED

PARMA. *Shevchenko Manor*, 5620 W. 24th St., 44134-2751. Tel: 216-459-1440; Fax: 216-459-1442; Email: j.joycejr@retireehousing.com. Jean Waschtschenko, Mgr.
PITTSBURGH. *St. George's Close*, 3505 Mexico St. at Chidel St., Pittsburgh, PA 15212.
Tel: 412-766-8802; Email: j.joycejr@retireehousing.com. Amy Rumsky, Mgr.
Sheptytsky Arms, 3503 Mexico St., Pittsburgh, PA 15212. Tel: 412-766-8802; Email: j.joycejr@retireehousing.com. Amy Rumsky, Mgr.

RELIGIOUS INSTITUTES OF MEN REPRESENTED IN THE DIOCESE

For further details refer to the corresponding bracketed number in the Religious Institutes of Men or Women section.

[0645]—*Brothers of the Holy Spirit*—B.H.S.

An asterisk (*) denotes an organization that has established tax-exempt status directly with the IRS and is not covered by the USCCB Group Ruling.

Eparchy of St. Maron of Brooklyn

Most Reverend

GREGORY J. MANSOUR

Bishop of Saint Maron of Brooklyn; ordained September 18, 1982; appointed Bishop of Saint Maron of Brooklyn January 10, 2004; consecrated March 2, 2004; installed April 27, 2004. *Chancery: 109 Remsen St., Brooklyn, NY 11201.*

Chancery Office: 109 Remsen St., Brooklyn, NY 11201. Tel: 718-237-9913; Fax: 718-243-0444.

Email: chancerystmaron@verizon.net

Web: www.stmaron.org

Established as an Apostolic Exarchate January 10, 1966; Elevated to a Diocese November 11, 1971.

The jurisdiction of the Diocese extends to all the Maronite Catholics in New York, New Jersey, Pennsylvania, Florida, Georgia, North Carolina, South Carolina, Delaware, Virginia, District of Columbia, Maine, New Hampshire, Vermont, Massachusetts, Rhode Island, Connecticut and Maryland.

For legal titles of parishes and diocesan institutions, consult the Chancery Office.

STATISTICAL OVERVIEW

Personnel	
Bishop	1
Abbots	1
Priests: Diocesan Active in Diocese	37
Priests: Retired, Sick or Absent	17
Number of Diocesan Priests	54
Religious Priests in Diocese	12
Total Priests in Diocese	66
Extern Priests in Diocese	8
Ordinations:	
Diocesan Priests	1
Religious Priests	1
Transitional Deacons	1
Permanent Deacons	4
Permanent Deacons in Diocese	25
Total Brothers	6
Total Sisters	3
Parishes	
Parishes	36
With Resident Pastor:	
Resident Diocesan Priests	33
Resident Religious Priests	3
Missions	8
Welfare	
Day Care Centers	1
Total Assisted	110
Educational	
Seminaries, Diocesan	1
Students from This Diocese	5
Students from Other Diocese	3
Diocesan Students in Other Seminaries	1
Total Seminarians	6
Catechesis/Religious Education:	
High School Students	368
Elementary Students	1,286
Total Students under Catholic Instruction	1,660
Vital Statistics	
Receptions into the Church:	
Infant Baptism Totals	319
Minor Baptism Totals	16
Adult Baptism Totals	28
Received into Full Communion	41
First Communions	318
Confirmations	366
Marriages:	
Catholic	104
Interfaith	24
Total Marriages	128
Deaths	222
Total Catholic Population	27,064

Former Bishops—Most Revs. FRANCIS M. ZAYEK, D.D., S.T.D., J.C.D., born Oct. 18, 1920; ord. March 17, 1946; appt. Titular Bishop of Callinicum May 30, 1962; cons. Aug. 5, 1962; appt. Apostolic Exarch of the Maronites of the United States Jan. 27, 1966; appt. Bishop of the Diocese of Saint Maron Nov. 11, 1971; enthroned June 4, 1972; elevated to Archbishop Ad Personam Dec. 22, 1982; retired Nov. 11, 1996; died Sept. 14, 2010.; STEPHEN HECTOR DOUEIHI, S.T.D., born June 25, 1927; ord. Aug. 14, 1955; appt. Second Eparchial Bishop of the Eparchy of Saint Maron of Brooklyn Nov. 23, 1996; cons. Jan. 11, 1997; enthroned Feb. 5, 1997; retired Jan. 10, 2004; died Dec. 17, 2014.

Protosyncellus (Vicar General)—Chorbishop MICHAEL G. THOMAS, J.C.D.

Chancellor—Chorbishop MICHAEL G. THOMAS, J.C.D.

The Chancery—109 Remsen St., Brooklyn, 11201. Tel: 718-237-9913; Fax: 718-243-0444; Email: chancerystmaron@verizon.net. Office Hours: Mon.-Fri. 9-4. Closed on holy days of obligation and national holidays.

Tribunal of the Eparchy of Saint Maron of Brooklyn—300 Wyoming Ave., Scranton, PA 18503-1279. Tel: 570-207-2246; Fax: 570-207-2274; Email: maronitetribunal@aol.com.

Tribunal—

Judicial Vicar—Rev. Msgr. FRANCIS J. MARINI, J.D., J.C.O.D.

Judges—Chorbishop MICHAEL G. THOMAS, J.C.D.; Rev. Msgrs. FRANCIS J. MARINI, J.D., J.C.O.D.; PATRICK J. PRATICO, J.C.D.; Chorbishop JOHN D. FARIS, J.C.O.D.; Rev. Msgr. ANDREW L. ANDERSON, J.C.D.; Revs. DOMINIQUE HANNA, J.C.L.; ELIE G. KAIROUZ, J.C.L.; JOHN PAUL KIMES, J.C.O.D.

Promoter of Justice—Very Rev. WILLIAM J. KING, J.C.D.

Defenders of the Bond—Revs. ANTHONY J. GENEROSE, J.C.L.; JAMES J. WALSH, J.C.L.

Advocates—Rev. TANIOS KOZHAYA AKOURY, J.C.O.L.; Rev. Msgr. NEVIN J. KLINGER, J.C.L.; MARGARET POLL CHALMERS, J.D., J.C.D., Ph.D.

Notaries—MRS. JUDITH MYERSKI; MRS. JOSETTE JORDAN.

Diocesan Offices and Directors

Presbyteral Council—Revs. TONY AKOURY; SIMON EL-HAJJ; Rev. Msgr. FRANCIS J. MARINI, J.D., J.C.O.D., Ex Officio; Chorbishop JOHN D. FARIS, J.C.O.D.; Rev. DOMINIQUE HANNA, J.C.L.; Rev. Msgr. JAMES A. ROOT, Ex Officio; Revs. BASSAM M. SAADE, Ex Officio; ELIE SAADE, O.L.M.; Rev. Msgr. GEORGE M. SEBAALI, Ex Officio; Chorbishop MICHAEL G. THOMAS, J.C.D., Ex Officio; Rev. RODOLPH WAKIM, Ex Officio.

Protopresbyters (Deans)—Rev. Msgr. JAMES A. ROOT, New England Region; Revs. BASSAM M. SAADE, Far South Region; RODOLPH WAKIM, Mid-Atlantic West Region; SIMON EL-HAJJ, Mid-Atlantic East Region; Rev. Msgr. GEORGE M. SEBAALI, South Region.

Lebanon Commission—Chorbishop SEELY BEGGIANI, S.T.D., Chm., 3333 University Blvd. W., Unit 608, Kensington, MD 20895. Email: seebeggiani@comcast.net.

National Apostolate of Maronites National Office—202 Lairds Dr., Coppell, TX 75019. Tel: 214-707-6564. SANDY MOSES, Exec. Dir., Email: sandymoses@namnews.org.

Communications—4611 Sadler Rd., Glen Allen, VA 23060. Tel: 804-270-7234; Fax: 804-273-9914; Email: stmaronpublications@gmail.com. Chorbishop JOHN D. FARIS, J.C.O.D.

Diocesan Newspaper - "The Maronite Voice"—4611 Sadler Rd., Glen Allen, VA 23060. Tel: 804-762-4301; Fax: 804-273-9914; Email: stmaronpublications@gmail.com. Chorbishop JOHN D. FARIS, J.C.O.D., Editor.

Finance Council—Chorbishop MICHAEL G. THOMAS, J.C.D.; MR. EDWARD MASSOUD, Eparchial Finance Officer; Chorbishop SEELY BEGGIANI, S.T.D.; MR. RAYMOND ESPINAL, Eparchial Compliance Officer; JUDGE DIANNE YAMIN; Deacon STEVEN MARCUS; MR. ALBERT ASHKOUTI; DR. PETER GABRIEL; MR. THOMAS KARAM.

Ministries (Permanent Deacons and Subdeacons)—Rev. JACK MORRISON, (Retired), 2630 Huntington Rd., Fayetteville, NC 28303. Tel: 508-817-6121; Email: aboonajack@aol.com.

Order of Saint Sharbel—MRS. ROSANNE SOLOMON, Pres., Mailing Address: 165 Metropolitan Ave., #2, Boston, MA 02131; BERNADETTE SHALHOUB, Vice Pres., 8429 W. Lake Dr., Lake Clarke Shores, FL 33406.

Office of Ecumenism and Interreligious Dialogue—Rev. SAMUEL A. NAJJAR, St. Michael the Archangel Church, 806 Arsenal Ave., Fayetteville, NC 28305. Tel: 910-484-1531; Fax: 910-484-5387; Email: stmikemcc@embarqmail.com.

Family and Sanctity of Life—MRS. MARISE FRANGIE, 76 Dehaven Dr., Apt. 4L, Yonkers, 10703. Email: sanctityoflife@olive.com.

Religious Education—Rev. Msgr. GEORGES Y. EL-KHALLI, Ph.D., 61 Rockwood St., Jamaica Plain, MA 02130. Tel: 617-522-0225; Fax: 617-522-0194; Email: pastor@ourladyofthecedars.org.

Child and Youth Protection Coordinator—Mailing Address: 109 Remsen St., Brooklyn, 11201. Tel: 917-825-3777; Email: vivakchildprotection@gmail.com. MRS. VIVIAN AKEL.

Victim Assistance Coordinator—MRS. ROSANNE SOLOMON, Mailing Address: 165 Metropolitan Ave., #2, Boston, MA 02131. Tel: 617-327-1317; Email: rosannesolomon@hotmail.com.

Vocations—Rev. DOMINIQUE HANNA, J.C.L., Our Lady of Lebanon Cathedral, 113 Remsen St., Brooklyn, 11201. Tel: 718-624-7228; Fax: 718-624-8034; Email: cathrectory@verizon.net.

Youth Ministry Office—Sr. THERESE MARIA TOUMA, Maronite Servants of Christ the Light, 856 Tucker Rd., Dartmouth, MA 02747. Tel: 508-965-6945; Email: srtherese2010@gmail.com.

Young Adult Ministry—Sr. THERESE MARIA TOUMA, Maronite Servants of Christ the Light, 856 Tucker Rd., Dartmouth, MA 02747. Tel: 508-965-6945; Email: srtherese2010@gmail.com.

Board of Pastors—Rev. TONY AKOURY; Rev. Msgr. JAMES A. ROOT; Rev. BASSAM M. SAADE.

College of Consultors—Rev. Msgr. PETER FAHED AZAR;

Rev. Dominique Hanna, J.C.L.; Chorbishop John D. Faris, J.C.O.D.; Rev. Msgrs. James A. Root; George M. Sebaali; Chorbishop Michael G. Thomas, J.C.D.

Immigration Office—Chorbishop Michael G. Thomas, J.C.D., Eparchy of Saint Maron, 109 Remsen St., Brooklyn, 11201. Tel: 718-237-9913; Fax: 718-243-0444; Email: chancerystmaron@verizon.net.

CLERGY, PARISHES, MISSIONS AND PAROCHIAL SCHOOLS

STATE OF NEW YORK

Brooklyn, Kings Co., Cathedral of Our Lady of Lebanon (1902) [JC]
113 Remsen St., 11201. Tel: 718-624-7228; Email: cathrectory@verizon.net; Web: www.ololc.org. Rev. Dominique Hanna, J.C.L., Rector; Deacon Butros (Peter) Frangie; Subdeacon Norbert Vogl.
Catechesis Religious Program—Students 60.

Olean, Cattaraugus Co., St. Joseph Maronite Catholic Church (1919) [JC]
1102 Walnut St., Olean, 14760.
Tel: 716-379-8436, Ext. 10; Email: stjosepholean@roadrunner.com; Web: www.stjosepholean.org. Rev. Anthony J. Salim.
Res.: 225 N. 4th St., Olean, 14760.
Catechesis Religious Program—Students 6.

Sleepy Hollow, Westchester, Co., Saint John Paul II (2011)
Immaculate Conception Church, 199 N. Broadway, Sleepy Hollow, 10591. Tel: 914-631-0446;
Fax: 914-631-4157; Email: jpiimc.ny@gmail.com; Web: www.johnpaul2parish.org. Rev. Dany Abi-Akar; Subdeacon Michel Rabbah.
Catechesis Religious Program—Fadia Nassar, D.R.E. Students 18.

Utica, Oneida Co., St. Louis Gonzaga (1910)
520 Rutger St., Utica, 13501. Tel: 315-732-6019;
Fax: 315-732-6018; Email: saintlouisgonzaga@gmail.com; Web: www.saintlouisgonzaga.org. Rev. Tanios Mouanes; Deacons Paul A. Salamy; Peter M. Hobaica.
Catechesis Religious Program—Tel: 315-796-1910; Email: katemillercny@gmail.com. Katelyn Miller, D.R.E. Students 45.

Watervliet, Albany Co., St. Ann (1905)
1919 3rd Ave., Watervliet, 12189. Tel: 518-272-6073; Email: stannmaronitechurch@gmail.com; Web: www.stann1905.com. Rev. Alaa Issa; Subdeacon Richard Thornton Sr.
Catechesis Religious Program—Students 20.

Williamsville, Erie Co., St. John Maron (1903)
2040 Wehrle Dr., Williamsville, 14221-7041.
Tel: 716-634-0669; Email: stjmaron@gmail.com; Web: www.stjohnmaron.org. Rev. Elie G. Kairouz, J.C.L.
Catechesis Religious Program—Students 115.

STATE OF CONNECTICUT

Danbury, Fairfield Co., St. Anthony (1932)
17 Granville Ave., Danbury, CT 06810.
Tel: 203-744-3372; Fax: 203-794-0949; Email: parish@stanthonydanbury.com; Web: www.stanthonydanbury.com. Rev. Naji Kiwan; Subdeacons George Jabbour; Randall Michael.

Torrington, Litchfield Co., St. Maron (1912)
613 Main St., Torrington, CT 06790.
Tel: 860-489-9015; Fax: 860-482-1614; Email: stmaronchurch@yahoo.com; Web: www.stmaronchurch.org. Rev. Antoine Saab, Admin.; Deacons Steven Marcus; David Leard; Subdeacon Paul Comeau.
Catechesis Religious Program—Students 15.

Waterbury, New Haven Co., Our Lady of Lebanon aka Our Lady of Lebanon Catholic Church Maronite Rite (1975)
8 E. Mountain Rd., Waterbury, CT 06706.
Tel: 203-753-6633; Fax: 203-573-8384; Email: ourladywaterbury@gmail.com; Web: www.ourladyoflebanon-ct.org. Rev. Joseph Khoueiry; Deacon Camille Atallah; Subdeacon Dean Tarsi.
Res.: 1544 Hamilton Ave., Waterbury, CT 06706.
Catechesis Religious Program—Students 12.

STATE OF FLORIDA

Fort Lauderdale, Broward Co., Heart of Jesus Catholic Church (2012)
1800 N.E. 6th Ct., Fort Lauderdale, FL 33304.
Tel: 954-522-3939; Fax: 954-522-3949; Email: heartofjesusfll@gmail.com; Web: www.heartofjesus.org. Chorbishop Michael G. Thomas, J.C.D., Admin.; Deacon John Jarvis, Deacon.
Catechesis Religious Program—Elementary School Students 21; High School Students 7.

Jacksonville, Duval Co., St. Maron Maronite (1995) [JC]
7032 Bowden Rd., Jacksonville, FL 32216.
Tel: 904-448-0203; Fax: 904-448-8277; Email: stmaronjax@comcast.net; Web: www.stmaronjax.com. Rev. Bassam M. Saade, Admin.; Deacon Elias Shami, Deacon.
Catechesis Religious Program—Elementary School Students 30; High School Students 10.

Miami, Dade Co., Our Lady of Lebanon (1973)
Mailing Address: 2055 Coral Way, Miami, FL 33145.
Tel: 305-856-7449; Fax: 305-856-5740; Email: ololmiami@bellsouth.net; Web: www.ololmiami.org. Rev. Elie Saade, O.L.M.; Subdeacon Joseph Lahoud.
Res.: 420 Como Ave., Coral Gables, FL 33146.
Catechesis Religious Program—Students 44.

Orlando, Orange Co., St. Jude (2003)
5555 Dr. Phillips Blvd., Orlando, FL 32819.
Tel: 407-363-7405; Fax: 407-340-0717; Email: stjudemaronitecatholicchurch@gmail.com; Web: www.saintjudechurch.org. Rev. Elie Abi Chedid; Deacon John Manhire.
Res.: 7832 Pine Haven Ct., Orlando, FL 32819-7110.
Catechesis Religious Program—Randa Awad, D.R.E. Students 38.

Tampa, Pasco Co., Mission of Sts. Peter & Paul (2000) [JC]
6201 Sheldon Rd., Tampa, FL 33615.
Tel: 813-886-7413; Tel: 813-474-4527;
Fax: 813-886-9790; Email: peterpaultampa@gmail.com; Web: www.peterpaultampa.com. Rev. Fadi Rouhana, Admin.
Catechesis Religious Program—Christine Rathgeber, D.R.E. Elementary School Students 8; High School Students 2.

Tequesta, Palm Beach Co., Mary Mother of the Light Maronite Mission (1990)
46 Willow Rd., Tequesta, FL 33469.
Tel: 561-427-1331; Fax: 561-841-1153; Email: mmolchurch@gmail.com; Web: www.marymotherofthelight.com. Rev. Aaron Sandbothe, Admin.; Subdeacons Dennis Somerville, Subdeacon; Elias Azzi, Subdeacon.
Catechesis Religious Program—Elementary School Students 3; High School Students 1.

STATE OF GEORGIA

Atlanta, Fulton Co., St. Joseph's Maronite Church (1911) [JC]
6025 Glenridge Dr., Sandy Springs, GA 30328.
Tel: 404-525-2504; Email: sjmcc@sjmcc.org; Web: www.sjmcc.org. Rev. Tony Akoury; Deacon Robert Calabrese; Subdeacon David Nasser.
Catechesis Religious Program—Email: kathie_calabrese@bellsouth.net. Kathie Calabrese, D.R.E. Students 25.

STATE OF MAINE

Waterville, Kennebec Co., St. Joseph (1927)
3 Appleton St., Waterville, ME 04901.
Tel: 207-872-8515; Email: stjoesinmaine@yahoo.com; Web: www.sjmaronite.org. Rev. James Doran; Subdeacon Stephen Crate.
Catechesis Religious Program—Students 11.

STATE OF MASSACHUSETTS

Brockton, Plymouth Co., St. Theresa (1932)
343 N. Main St., P.O. Box 2567, Brockton, MA 02305-2567. Fax: 508-586-1428; Fax: 508-587-8139; Email: Saintheresa@comcast.net; Web: www.sttheresabrockton.org. Rev. Joseph Daiif (Macary); Subdeacon Alexander McKinnon.
Catechesis Religious Program—Students 30.

Fall River, Bristol Co., St. Anthony of the Desert (1911)
300 N. Eastern Ave., Fall River, MA 02723.
Tel: 508-672-7653; Fax: 508-678-1474; Email: saotd@verizon.net. Rev. James A. Root; Deacons Donald P. Massoud; Andre Nasser; Brian Dunn.
Catechesis Religious Program—Samia Yamin-Brownell, D.R.E. Students 42.

Jamaica Plain, Suffolk Co., Our Lady of the Cedars of Lebanon (1893)
61 Rockwood St., Jamaica Plain, MA 02130.
Tel: 617-522-0225; Fax: 617-522-0194; Email: pastor@ourldayofthecedars.org; Web: www.ourladyofhecedars.org. Rev. Msgr. Georges Y. El-Khalli, Ph.D.
Catechesis Religious Program—Students 53.

Lawrence, Essex Co., St. Anthony (1903) [CEM]
145 Amesbury St., Lawrence, MA 01841.
Tel: 978-685-7233; Fax: 978-688-4475; Email: rectory@stanthonylawrence.org; Web: www.stanthonylawrence.org. Revs. Elie Mikhael; Jebrael Moussallem, Parochial Vicar; Deacon Nadim Daou; Subdeacon James Demers.
Catechesis Religious Program—Email: ccd@stanthonylawrence.org. Ms. Susan Veilleux, D.R.E. Students 114.

New Bedford, Bristol Co., Our Lady of Purgatory (1917)
11 Franklin St., New Bedford, MA 02740.
Tel: 508-996-8934; Fax: 508-996-2744; Email: ourladyofpurgatory@verizon.net; Web: www.ourladyofpurgatory.org. Rev. Antoun Youssef, Admin.; Deacon Jean E. Mattar; Subdeacon Joseph Abraham.
Catechesis Religious Program—Students 29.

Springfield, Hampden Co., St. Anthony (1905)
375 Island Pond Rd., Springfield, MA 01118-1002.
Tel: 413-732-0589; Fax: 413-732-6320; Email: stanthony419@comcast.net; Web: www.saintanthonyschurch.org. Mailing Address: 419 Island Pond Rd., Springfield, MA 01118-1002. Rev. George Zina; Deacons Enzo DiGiacomo; Norman Hannoush.
Catechesis Religious Program—Students 14.

Worcester, Worcester Co., Our Lady of Mercy (1923)
341 June St., Worcester, MA 01602-2845.
Tel: 508-752-4287; Fax: 508-796-5919; Email: ourladymercymaroniteworcester@gmail.com; Web: www.ourladyofmercymaronite.org. Rev. Alexander Joseph.
Catechesis Religious Program—Students 6.

STATE OF NEW HAMPSHIRE

Dover, Strafford Co., St. George (1949)
15 Chapel St., P.O. Box 2210, Dover, NH 03821-2210. Tel: 603-740-4287; Fax: 603-740-9624; Email: stgeorgedover@outlook.com; Web: www.stgeorgemaronite.org. Revs. Elie Mikhael; Jebrael Moussallem, Parochial Vicar.

STATE OF NEW JERSEY

Pleasantville, Atlantic Co., Our Lady Star of the East (2002)
25 W. Black Horse Pike, Pleasantville, NJ 08232.
Tel: 609-241-8109; Fax: 609-241-8843; Email: olsechurch@gmail.com; Web: www.olsechurch.org. Rev. Kamil Alchouefati; Subdeacon Fahid Nammour.
Catechesis Religious Program—Raben Nammour, D.R.E. Students 43.

Somerset, Somerset Co., St. Sharbel Maronite Church
7 Reeve St., Somerset, NJ 08873. Tel: 732-828-2055; Fax: 732-828-5488; Email: yamarsharbel@gmail.com; Web: www.saintsharbelnj.org. Rev. Simon El-hajj; Deacon Joseph Chebli, D.R.E.
Catechesis Religious Program—Students 75.

STATE OF NORTH CAROLINA

Charlotte, Saint Stephen Maronite Catholic Church
8015 Ballantyne Commons Pkwy., Charlotte, NC 28227. Tel: 704-543-7677, Ext. 1043;
Fax: 704-542-7244; Email: saintstephenmaronitechurch@gmail.com; Web: www.ststephenmaronite.org. P.O. Box 49021, Charlotte, NC 28277. Rev. Elias Khalil.

Raleigh, Wake Co., Saint Sharbel Mission (2000)
600 Mt. Vernon Church Rd., Raleigh, NC 27614. Mailing Address: P.O. Box 33801, Raleigh, NC 27636. Tel: 919-917-7597; Email: ryfarah@aol.com; Email: abouna@saintsharbelchurch.org; Web: www.saintsharbelchurch.org. Rev. Robert Farah, Admin.; Subdeacon Claude Shiver Jr., Subdeacon.
Catechesis Religious Program—Elementary School Students 19; High School Students 6.

Fayetteville, Cumberland Co., St. Michael the Archangel (1973)
Mailing Address: 806 Arsenal Ave., Fayetteville, NC 28305. Tel: 910-484-1531; Fax: 910-484-5387; Email: stmikemcc@embarqmail.com; Web: www.stmichaelsmaronite.net. Rev. Samuel A. Najjar; Subdeacons Ronald Foster; Charles Van Heusen.
Res.: 212 Bradford Ave., Fayetteville, NC 28301.
Catechesis Religious Program—Students 28.

STATE OF PENNSYLVANIA

Carnegie, Allegheny Co., Our Lady of Victory (1902)
1000 Lindsay Rd., Carnegie, PA 15106.
Tel: 412-278-0841; Fax: 412-278-0846; Email: office@olovpittsburgh.org; Web: www.olovpgh.org. Revs. Rodolph Wakim; Hanna Karam, Parochial Vicar; Subdeacon Bahige Alchoufete.
Catechesis Religious Program—Students 30.

Conway, Beaver Co., Saint Teresa of Calcutta Maronite Mission (2012)
1000 3rd Ave., Conway, PA 15027. Tel: 724-732-4064; Email: stteresamaronite@gmail.com; Web: www.stteresamaronite.org. Rev. Antoine Kairouz, Admin.
Catechesis Religious Program—Thomas Michael, D.R.E. Elementary School Students 4.

Easton, Northampton Co., Our Lady of Lebanon (1931)
54 S. Fourth St., Easton, PA 18042.
Tel: 610-252-5275; Email: ololchurch@yahoo.com; Web: www.ololeaston.org. Rev. Youssef Keikati; Deacon Anthony P. Koury.
Catechesis Religious Program—Students 81.

NEW CASTLE, LAWRENCE CO., ST. JOHN THE BAPTIST (1926)
2 W. Reynolds St., New Castle, PA 16101.
Tel: 724-658-0787; Fax: 724-658-2711; Email: stjohnmaronite@hotmail.com; Web: www.stjohnmaronite.org. Rev. Claude W. Franklin Jr.; Deacon Richard E. Stone; Subdeacon Andrew Demko.
Catechesis Religious Program—Students 31.

NEWTOWN SQUARE, DELAWARE CO., ST. SHARBEL (1983)
3679 Providence Rd., Newtown Square, PA 19073.
Tel: 610-353-5952; Email: rectory@stsharbelpa.org; Email: pastor@stsharbelpa.org; Web: www.stsharbelpa.org. Rev. Joseph Abisaad, Admin.
Catechesis Religious Program—Students 6.

PHILADELPHIA, PHILADELPHIA CO., ST. MARON (1862)
1013 Ellsworth St., Philadelphia, PA 19147.
Tel: 215-389-2000; Fax: 215-334-1884; Email: saintmaronphiladelphia@hotmail.com; Web: www.saintmaron.org. Rev. Vincent Farhat.
Catechesis Religious Program—Zeina Topalian, D.R.E. Students 72.

SCRANTON, LACKAWANNA CO., ST. ANN (1903) [JC]
1320 Price St., Scranton, PA 18504-3336.
Tel: 570-344-2129; Email: StAnnScranton@aol.com; Web: www.saintannmaronite.com. Rev. Msgr. Francis J. Marini, J.D., J.C.O.D.; Subdeacons Said J. Douaihy; Robert Rade.
Res.: 208 N. Summer Ave., Scranton, PA 18504.
Catechesis Religious Program—Students 9.

UNIONTOWN, FAYETTE CO., ST. GEORGE (1927)
6 Lebanon Ter., Uniontown, PA 15401-3011.
Tel: 724-437-5589; Fax: 724-437-3819; Email: info@stgeorgeuniotown.org; Web: www.stgeorgeuniontown.org. Rev. Elbadaoui Habib, M.L.M.; Subdeacons Thomas R. George; Mallard George.
Catechesis Religious Program—Students 40.

WILKES-BARRE, LUZERNE CO., ST. ANTHONY + ST. GEORGE (1911)
79 Loomis St., Wilkes-Barre, PA 18702-4610.
Tel: 570-824-3599; Fax: 570-824-1747; Email: stanthonystgeorge@gmail.com; Web: www.stanthonystgeorge.org. Rev. Paul E. Damien; Subdeacon Oliver Crosby Sparks.
Catechesis Religious Program—311 Park Ave., Wilkes-Barre, PA 18702. Diane Walker, D.R.E. Students 32.

STATE OF RHODE ISLAND

CRANSTON, PROVIDENCE CO., ST. GEORGE (1911)
1493 Cranston St., Cranston, RI 02920.
Tel: 401-723-8444; Fax: 401-728-2032; Email: stgeorgemaronitecatholicchurch@gmail.com; Web: www.stgeorgemaronitecatholicchurch.org. Rev. Edward T. Nedder; Subdeacon Farid Zaarour.
Catechesis Religious Program—Students 20.

STATE OF SOUTH CAROLINA

GREER, GREENVILLE CO., ST. RAFKA MARONITE MISSION (2002)
1215 S. Hwy. 14, Greer, SC 29650. Tel: 864-469-9119 ; Email: saintrafkagreenville@gmail.com; Email: secretary@saintrafka.org; Web: www.saintrafka.org. Rev. Bartholomew Leon, Admin.
Res.: 1213 S. Hwy. 14, Greenville, SC 29601.
Catechesis Religious Program—Alexandria Roman, D.R.E. Elementary School Students 18; High School Students 6.

STATE OF VIRGINIA

GLEN ALLEN, HENRICO CO., ST. ANTHONY'S MARONITE CATHOLIC CHURCH (1912) [JC]
4611 Sadler Rd., Glen Allen, VA 23060.
Tel: 804-270-7234; Fax: 804-273-9914; Email: stanthonymaronitechurch@gmail.com; Web: www.stanthonymaronitechurch.org. Chorbishop John D. Faris, J.C.O.D.; Rev. Raymond Khallouf, Parochial Vicar; Subdeacon Michael Maynes.
Catechesis Religious Program—Mrs. Catherine George, D.R.E. Students 122.

ROANOKE, ROANOKE CITY CO., ST. ELIAS (1917)
4730 Cove Rd., N.W., Roanoke, VA 24017.
Tel: 540-562-0012; Fax: 540-562-1300; Email: secretary@steliaschurch.org; Web: www.steliaschurch.org. Rev. Kevin J. Beaton, S.F.O.
Catechesis Religious Program—Mark Portzer, D.R.E. Students 40.

DISTRICT OF COLUMBIA

WASHINGTON, DISTRICT OF COLUMBIA, OUR LADY OF LEBANON CHURCH (1967)
7142 Alaska Ave., N.W., Washington, DC 20012.
Tel: 202-291-5153; Fax: 202-291-5131. Mailing Address: 7237 15th Pl. N.W., Washington, DC 20012. Rev. Msgr. George M. Sebaali; Deacon Michel Touma.
Catechesis Religious Program—Tony Rahi, D.R.E. Students 99.

Retired:
Rev. Msgrs.—
Asmar, Maroun, (Retired)
Awad, Assad, (Retired)
George, David M., (Retired)
Hayek, Sami, (Retired)
Lahoud, Joseph F., (Retired)
Revs.—
Amar, Joseph P., (Retired)
Andary, John S., (Retired)
Bartoul, William, (Retired)
Beggiani, Seely, (Retired)
Boackle, Paul H., (Retired)
Michael, Lawrence, (Retired)
Mooradd, Paul, (Retired)
Morrison, Jack, (Retired)
Mouawad, Paul, (Retired).

Permanent Deacons:
Abi Nader, Simon, (Retired), Bow, NH
Atallah, Camille, Waterbury, CT
Calabrese, Robert, Cummings, GA
Chebli, Joseph, NJ
Daou, Nadim, Lawrence, MA
DiGiacomo, Enzo, Springfield, MA
Dunn, Brian, Fall River, MA
Frangie, Butros (Peter), Brooklyn, NY
Gebron, Charles, (Retired), Springfield, MA
Hannoush, Norman, Springfield, MA
Hobaica, Peter M., Utica, NY
Jarvis, John, Ft. Lauderdale, FL
Koury, Anthony P., Easton, PA
Leard, David, Torrington, CT
Manhire, John, Orlando
Marcus, Steven, Torrington, CT
Massoud, Donald P., Fall River, MA
Mattar, Jean E., New Bedford, MA
Nasser, Andre, Fall River, MA
Ramey, Allan, (Retired), Lawrence, MA
Salamy, Paul A., Utica, NY
Shami, Elias, Jacksonville, FL
Stone, Richard E., New Castle, PA
Touma, Michel, (Washington D.C.)
Thornton, Richard Sr., Watervliet, NY.

INSTITUTIONS LOCATED IN DIOCESE

[A] SEMINARIES, DIOCESAN

WASHINGTON. *Our Lady of Lebanon Maronite Seminary*, 7164 Alaska Ave., N.W., Washington, DC 20012. Tel: 202-723-8831; Email: maroniteseminary@comcast.net; Web: www.maroniteseminary.org. Rev. Msgr. Peter Fahed Azar, Rector; Rev. Armando Elkhourey, Vice Rector. Priests 2; Students 5.

[B] RELIGIOUS COMMUNITIES OF MEN

PETERSHAM. *Maronite Monks of Adoration - Most Holy Trinity Monastery*, 67 Dugway Rd., Petersham, MA 01366-9725. Tel: 978-724-3347; Email: econome@maronitemonks.org; Web: www.maronitemonks.org. Rt. Rev. William J. Driscoll, M.M.A., Abbot; Very Rev. Louis Marie Dauphinais, M.M.A., Prior; Revs. Michael Gilmary Cermak, M.M.A.; Ignatius (Allen) Dec, M.M.A.; Giles R. Goyette, M.M.A.; Elias Havel, M.M.A.; Patrick Kokorian, M.M.A.; Raphael Magee, M.M.A.; Robert Nortz, M.M.A.; Maron Henricks, M.M.A.; Bros. Bernard Choupin, M.M.A.; Paul Hoover, M.M.A.; John Baptist Livingston, M.M.A.; Ephrem Martin, M.M.A.; Subdeacon Bernardo Vargas-Castro; Bros. Estpehen Kairouz, M.M.A., Novice; Matthew Zaloum. Brothers 6; Priests 10.

[C] RELIGIOUS COMMUNITIES OF WOMEN

DARTMOUTH. *Servants of Christ the Light*, 856 Tucker Rd., Dartmouth, MA 02747-3531.
Tel: 508-996-1753; Email: sister@maroniteservants.org; Web: www.maroniteservants.org. Sisters Marla Lucas, Supr.; Therese Maria Touma; Natalie Salameh. Sisters 3.

[D] RESIDENCES FOR CLERGY

BROOKLYN. *Bishop's Residence*, 8070 Harbor View Ter., 11209. Tel: 718-237-9913; Email: chancerystmaron@verizon.net. Chorbishop Michael G. Thomas, J.C.D., Chancellor.

[E] MISCELLANEOUS

BROOKLYN. *Bishops Retirement Trust Fund*, 109 Remsen St., 11201. Tel: 718-237-9913; Email: chancerystmaron@verizon.net. Chorbishop Michael G. Thomas, J.C.D., Chancellor.
Disability Endowment Trust, 109 Remsen St., 11201.
Endowment Fund Trust, 109 Remsen St., 11201.
Order of St. Sharbel Trust Fund, 109 Remsen St., 11201. Tel: 718-237-9913; Email: chancerystmaron@verizon.net. Chorbishop Michael G. Thomas, J.C.D., Chancellor.
Priest Retirement Trust Fund, 109 Remsen St., 11201. Tel: 718-237-9913; Email: chancerystmaron@verizon.net. Chorbishop Michael G. Thomas, J.C.D., Chancellor.
Seminary Endowment Trust, 109 Remsen St., 11201.
Tele Lumiere and Noursat USA, 109 Remsen St., 11201. Tel: 718-237-9913; Email: chancerystmaron@verizon.net. Chorbishop Michael G. Thomas, J.C.D., Chancellor.

An asterisk (*) denotes an organization that has established tax-exempt status directly with the IRS and is not covered by the USCCB Group Ruling.

Diocese of St. Nicholas in Chicago for Ukrainians

Most Reverend

VENEDYKT ALEKSIYCHUK, M.S.U.

Bishop of St. Nicholas in Chicago; ordained March 29, 1992; appointed Bishop of St. Nicholas of Chicago April 20, 2017; installed June 29, 2017. *Office: 2245 W. Rice St., Chicago, IL 60622.*

Chancery Office: 2245 W. Rice St., IL 60622. Tel: 773-276-5080; Fax: 773-276-6799.

Email: contact@esnucc.org

Web: esnucc.org

Comprises all of the United States west of the western borders of Ohio, Kentucky, Tennessee and Mississippi.

For legal titles of parishes and diocesan institutions, consult the Chancery Office.

STATISTICAL OVERVIEW

Personnel	
Bishop	1
Abbots	2
Priests: Diocesan Active in Diocese	40
Priests: Diocesan Active Outside Diocese	1
Priests: Retired, Sick or Absent	10
Number of Diocesan Priests	51
Religious Priests in Diocese	6
Total Priests in Diocese	57
Extern Priests in Diocese	3
Ordinations:	
Transitional Deacons	1
Permanent Deacons in Diocese	12
Total Brothers	6
Total Sisters	3
Parishes	
Parishes	39
With Resident Pastor:	
Resident Diocesan Priests	34
Resident Religious Priests	5
Without Resident Pastor:	
Administered by Deacons	2
Administered by Lay People	1
Missions	7
Professional Ministry Personnel:	
Sisters	3
Educational	
Elementary Schools, Diocesan and Parish	2
Total Students	296
Catechesis/Religious Education:	
High School Students	19
Elementary Students	63
Total Students under Catholic Instruction	378
Teachers in the Diocese:	
Priests	3
Sisters	2
Lay Teachers	36
Vital Statistics	
Receptions into the Church:	
Infant Baptism Totals	163
First Communions	163
Confirmations	163
Marriages:	
Catholic	30
Interfaith	21
Total Marriages	51
Deaths	65
Total Catholic Population	12,500

Former Bishops—Most Revs. JAROSLAV GABRO, D.D., appt. First Bishop of Chicago, July 12, 1961; cons. Oct. 26, 1961; died March 28, 1980; INNOCENT LOTOCKY, O.S.B.M., D.D., Ph.D., ord. Nov. 24, 1940; appt. Second Bishop of Chicago, Jan. 29, 1981; cons. March 1, 1981; installed April 2, 1981; retired Sept. 28, 1993; died July 4, 2013.; MICHAEL WIWCHAR, C.Ss.R., D.D., ord. June 28, 1959; appt. Third Bishop of St. Nicholas July 2, 1993; ord. Sept. 28, 1993; appt. Bishop of Saskatoon (Ukrainian), Nov. 29, 2000; secondary appt. Apostolic Administrator of St. Nicholas in Chicago, Dec. 9, 2000; RICHARD S. SEMINACK, ord. May 25, 1967; appt. Bishop of St. Nicholas in Chicago March 25, 2003; ord. June 4, 2003; died Aug. 16, 2016.

Protosyncellus—VACANT.

Chancellor—Very Rev. Archpriest MYKHAILO KUZMA.

Vice Chancellor—Rev. FRANK AVANT, (Retired).

Chief Financial Officer and Eparchial Finance Director—MR. JAROSLAW HANKEWYCH, Tel: 773-772-6131; Email: hankewych@msn.com.

Chancery Office—2245 W. Rice St., Chicago, 60622. Tel: 773-276-5080; Fax: 773-276-6799; Email: contact@esnucc.org; Web: esnucc.org. Office Hours: Mon.-Fri. 9-4. Closed all major holy days and legal holidays.

Diocesan Consultors—Very Rev. Canon WAYNE J. RUCHGY; Very Revs. VARCILIO BASIL SALKOVSKI, O.S.B.M.; RICHARD JANOWICZ; Very Rev. Canon MICHAEL STELMACH; Very Rev. Archpriest MYKHAILO KUZMA; Very Revs. BOHDAN NALYSNYK; OLEH KRYVOKULSKY; VOLODYMYR PETRIV.

Presbyteral Council—Very Rev. RICHARD JANOWICZ, Eparchial Admin.; Very Rev. Canon WAYNE J. RUCHGY; Very Rev. Archpriest MYKHAILO KUZMA; Rev. HUGO SOUTUS, Chm.; Very Revs. YAROSLAV MENDYUK, Sec.; VOLODYMYR PETRIV.

Personnel Board—Very Rev. RICHARD JANOWICZ, Eparchial Admin.; Very Rev. Canon WAYNE J. RUCHGY, Chm.; Very Rev. Archpriest MYKHAILO KUZMA.

Tribunal—Through Special Permission of the Holy See, Local Latin Rite Tribunals Handle the Cases Within the Diocese.

Protopresbyteries (Deans)—Detroit: Very Rev. VOLODYMYR PETRIV, Protopresbyter. Chicago: Very Rev. BOHDAN NALYSNYK, Protopresbyter. Minneapolis: Very Rev. Canon MICHAEL STELMACH, Protopresbyter. South-West: Very Rev. RICHARD JANOWICZ, Protopresbyter.

Eparchial Censor—Rev. DEMETRIUS WYSOCHANSKY, O.S.B.M.

Eparchial Office of Religious Education & Catechesis—VACANT.

Stewardship and Development Office—Subdeacon PETRO RUDKA, 2245 W. Rice St., Chicago, 60622. Tel: 773-276-9500; Fax: 773-276-6799; Email: stewardship@esnucc.org.

Office for Protection of Children and Youth—Subdeacon PETRO RUDKA, Dir., Tel: 773-276-5080; Email: child-protection@esnucc.org.

Task Force for a Safe Environment—DR. LINDA HRYHORCZUK, Chm.

New Star - Eparchial Newspaper—Rev. JOHN P. LUCAS, English Editor, Tel: 773-291-0168; Subdeacon PETRO RUDKA, Ukrainian Editor, Tel: 773-276-5080.

CLERGY, PARISHES, MISSIONS AND PAROCHIAL SCHOOLS

STATE OF ILLINOIS

CHICAGO, COOK CO.

1—ST. NICHOLAS UKRAINIAN CATHOLIC CATHEDRAL (1906) [CEM] (Ukrainian)
835 North Oakley Blvd., Chicago, 60622-4811.
Tel: 773-276-4537; Email: office@stnicholaschicago.org. Mailing Address: 2238 W. Rice St., Chicago, 60622. Revs. Serhiy Kovalchuk, Rector; Volodymyr Kushnir, Pastoral Assoc.; Deacons Mychajlo Horodysky; Ihor Khomytsky.
School—St. Nicholas Ukrainian Catholic Cathedral School, (Grades PreK-8), 2200 W. Rice St., Chicago, 60622-4811. Tel: 773-384-7243; Email: admin@stnickschicago.org; Web: www.stnicholascathedralschool.org. Ms. Anna Cirilli, Prin. Clergy 2; Lay Teachers 16; Students 165.
Convent—Sisters of St. Basil the Great, 2230 W. Rice St., Chicago, 60622-4811.

2—ST. JOSEPH (N.W. Chicago) (1956) (Ukrainian)
5000 N. Cumberland Ave., Chicago, 60656.
Tel: 773-625-4805; Email: stjosephucc@gmail.com. Rev. Mykola Buryadnyk, Tel: 773-625-4803; Very Rev. Bohdan Nalysnyk; Deacon Mark Krutiak.
Catechesis Religious Program—Students 43.

3—ST. MICHAEL'S (1917) [JC] (Ukrainian)
12211 S. Parnell Ave., Chicago, 60628.
Tel: 773-291-0168; Email: znamiboh@aol.com. In Res., Rev. John Lucas.

4—SS. VOLODYMYR AND OLHA (1968) [JC] (Ukrainian)
739 N. Oakley Blvd., Chicago, 60612.
Tel: 312-829-5209; Email: stsvo@comcast.net. Mailing Address: 2245 W. Superior St., Chicago, 60612. Very Rev. Oleh Kryvokulsky, Tel: 312-829-6805; Rt. Rev. Mitred Arch Ivan Krotec, Pastor Emeritus; Revs. Stepan Kostiuk; Roman Artymovych, Tel: 773-634-0604.

MADISON, MADISON CO., ST. MARY'S, [JC]
1310 Iowa St., Madison, 62060. Tel: 618-452-9118; Email: obohdanp@gmail.com. Mailing Address: 1312 Iowa St., Madison, 62060. Rev. Robert-Bohdan S. Piorkowski, Admin.

PALATINE, COOK CO., IMMACULATE CONCEPTION (1963) (Ukrainian)
755 S. Benton, Palatine, 60067. Tel: 847-991-0820; Email: frmykhailo@att.net. Mailing Address: 745 S. Benton, Palatine, 60067. Very Rev. Archpriest Mykhailo Kuzma; Rev. Yaroslav Mendyuk.
Catechesis Religious Program—Tel: 847-639-9188. Students 30.

PALOS PARK, COOK CO., NATIVITY OF B.V.M. (1911) (Ukrainian)
8530 W. 131 St., Palos Park, 60464.
Tel: 708-361-8876; Tel: 708-361-8857;
Fax: 708-361-8820; Email: nativityukrainian@sbcglobal.net. Rev. Roman Ilnicki, O.B.S.M.

Catechesis Religious Program—Patricia Kuzmak, D.R.E. Students 7.

STATE OF ARIZONA

PHOENIX, MARICOPA CO., DORMITION OF THE MOTHER OF GOD (1959)
3730 W. Maryland Ave., Phoenix, AZ 85019.
Tel: 602-973-3667; Email: dmofgod@cox.net; Web: www.ukrainianchurch.org. Rev. Hugo Soutus.
Church: 3720 W. Maryland Ave., Phoenix, AZ 85019.

TUCSON, PIMA CO., ST. MICHAEL (1978) [JC] (Ukrainian)
715 W. Vanover Rd., Tucson, AZ 85705-4137.
Tel: 520-298-4967; Email: stmichaeltucson@gmail.com; Web: www.stmichaeltucson.org. Mailing Address: 420 E. Deer's Rest Pl., Tucson, AZ 85704-6939. Rt. Rev. Dr. Andriy Chirovsky, S.T.D.
Catechesis Religious Program—Mrs. Halyna Chirovsky, D.R.E. Students 14.

STATE OF CALIFORNIA

CITRUS HEIGHTS, SACRAMENTO CO., HOLY WISDOM (2002)
6520 Van Maren Ln., Citrus Heights, CA 95621.
Tel: 916-486-0632; Email: twroblicky@aol.com; Web: holywisdomsacramento.org. Mailing Address: 1324 La Serra Dr., Sacramento, CA 95864. Rev. Theodore P. Wroblicky, Pastor Emeritus, (Retired).
Catechesis Religious Program—Students 2.

HOLLYWOOD, LOS ANGELES CO., NATIVITY OF B.V.M. (1947) (Ukrainian)
5154 De Longpre Ave., Los Angeles, CA 90027.
Tel: 323-663-6307; Fax: 323-663-0369; Email: ikoshyk@gmail.com; Email: info@ukrainiancatholicla.com; Web: www.ukrainiancatholicla.com. Rev. Ihor Koshyk, Tel: 773-934-3685.

LA MESA, SAN DIEGO CO., ST. JOHN THE BAPTIZER (1960) (Ukrainian)
4400 Palm Ave., P. O. Box 3116, La Mesa, CA 91941.
Tel: 619-697-5085; Email: yuriisas70@gmail.com; Web: www.stjohnthebaptizer.org. Rev. Yurii Sas.

SACRAMENTO, SACRAMENTO CO., ST. ANDREW THE APOSTLE
7001 Florin Rd., Sacramento, CA 95828.
Tel: 916-383-8614; Email: o.petro.kozar@gmail.com; Email: zswochok@yahoo.com; Web: www.standrewugcc.com. Rev. Petro Kozar.
Catechesis Religious Program—Tel: 916-381-2529; Fax: 916-381-2529.

SAN FRANCISCO, SAN FRANCISCO CO., IMMACULATE CONCEPTION CATHOLIC CHURCH (1957) (Ukrainian)
215 Silliman, San Francisco, CA 94134.
Tel: 415-468-2601; Email: petrodyachok1967@gmail.com. Rev. Petro Dyachok, Admin.
Catechesis Religious Program—Students 8.
Mission—St. Volodymyr, 445 Washington St., Santa Clara, CA 95050.

SANTA CLARA, SANTA CLARA CO., ST. VOLODYMYR UKRAINIAN CATHOLIC MISSION (1963) Attended by Immaculate Conception, San Francisco.
445 Washington Ave., Santa Clara, CA 95050.
Tel: 408-248-1462; Email: st_volodymyr_ucc@att.net; Web: stvolodymyrucc.org. Rev. Petro Dyachok, Admin.

UKIAH, UKIAH CO., ST. PETER EASTERN CATHOLIC MISSION (1999) (Ukrainian)
190 Orr St., Ukiah, CA 95482. Tel: 707-468-4348; Email: sebrowder@att.net. Rev. David Anderson, Admin.

STATE OF COLORADO

DENVER, DENVER CO., TRANSFIGURATION OF OUR LORD (1954) [JC] (Ukrainian)
4118 Shoshone St., Denver, CO 80211.
Tel: 303-455-2717; Email: ukrainiandenver@comcast.net. Rev. Vasyl Hnatkivskyy, Admin.

STATE OF INDIANA

MISHAWAKA, ST. JOSEPH CO., ST. MICHAEL (1962)
712 E. Lawrence St., Mishawaka, IN 46544.
Tel: 574-703-7229; Email: stmichaelugccmishawaka@gmail.com. Rev. George Kuzara, C.PP.S.

MUNSTER, LAKE CO., ST. JOSAPHAT (1958) (Ukrainian)
8624 White Oak Ave., Munster, IN 46321.
Tel: 219-923-0984; Email: st.josaphat@comcast.net; Web: www.stjosaphatugcc.org. Rev. Yuriy Sakvuk, Admin.

STATE OF KANSAS

LAWRENCE, DOUGLAS CO., HOLY APOSTLES aka New Martyrs Ukrainian Greek Catholic Mission (2001)
1301 Vermont St., Lawrence, KS 66044.
Tel: 816-516-4351; Email: nikolaibr93@yahoo.com; Web: www.facebook.com/New-Martyrs-Ukrainian-Greek-Catholic-Mission-154485377926087/. Deacon Randolph Brown, Temporary Admin.

STATE OF MICHIGAN

DEARBORN, WAYNE CO., ST. MICHAEL'S (1962)
6340 Chase Rd., Dearborn, MI 48126.
Tel: 313-582-1424; Cell: 313-580-4412; Email: WRuchgy@gmail.com; Web: stmichaelarchangel.org. Very Rev. Canon Wayne J. Ruchgy.

DEARBORN HEIGHTS, WAYNE CO., OUR LADY OF PERPETUAL HELP (1963) (Ukrainian)
26667 Joy Rd., Dearborn Heights, MI 48127.
Tel: 313-278-0470; Email: olphukr@gmail.com. Mailing Address: 26606 Ann Arbor Trail, Dearborn Heights, MI 48127. Very Rev. Volodymyr Petriv; Rev. Thomas Marick.
Catechesis Religious Program—

DETROIT, WAYNE CO., ST. JOHN THE BAPTIST (1907) (Ukrainian)
3877 Clippert St., Detroit, MI 48210.
Tel: 313-897-7300; Email: valeriykandyuk@comcast.net. Rev. Valeriy Kandyuk.

FLINT, GENESEE CO., ST. VLADIMIR'S UKRAINIAN CATHOLIC CHURCH (1950)
3464 W. Pasadena, Flint, MI 48504.
Tel: 810-394-3091; Email: rybbog@yahoo.com. 3850 Dwight Dr., Warren, MI 48092. Rev. Bogdan Rybchuk.

GRAND RAPIDS, KENT CO., ST. MICHAEL'S (1949) [JC] (Ukrainian)
154 Gold Ave., N.E., Grand Rapids, MI 49504.
Tel: 616-742-0874; Cell: 616-450-7832; Email: rybbog@yahoo.com; Web: stmichaelgrandrapids.org. Rev. Bogdan Rybchuk, Admin.

HAMTRAMCK, WAYNE CO., IMMACULATE CONCEPTION OF B.V.M. aka IC Church (1914) (Ukrainian)
11700 McDougall St., Hamtramck, MI 48212.
Tel: 313-893-1710; Email: frdanieltchai@gmail.com. Rev. Daniel Schaicoski, O.S.B.M., Supr. & Pastor.
School—Immaculate Conception Ukrainian Catholic Schools Association, (Grades K-8), 29500 Westbrook, Warren, MI 48093. Tel: 586-574-2480; Fax: 586-574-3497; Email: frdanieltchai@aol.com; Web: icschools.org. Rev. Daniel Schaicoski, O.S.B.M., Admin. Clergy 2; Lay Teachers 26; Priests 1; Students 251.
Catechesis Religious Program—Sisters RoseAnn Bukaczyk, O.S.B.M., D.R.E.; Theodora Lukiw, D.R.E.; Mrs. Anna Credi, D.R.E. Students 200.
Endowment—Immaculate Conception Endowment Fund Inc.

WARREN, MACOMB CO., ST. JOSAPHAT (1961) [CEM] (Ukrainian)
26401 St. Josaphat Dr., Warren, MI 48091.
Tel: 587-755-1740; Fax: 586-755-1399; Email: stjucch@aol.com; Web: www.stjoschurch.com. Revs. Mario Dacechen, O.S.B.M.; Walter Rybicky, O.S.B.M.
Catechesis Religious Program—Email: sranna@icschools.net. Sr. RoseAnn Bukaczyk, O.S.B.M., D.R.E. Students 0.

STATE OF MINNESOTA

MINNEAPOLIS, HENNEPIN CO., ST. CONSTANTINE (1913) [CEM] (Ukrainian)
515 University Ave., N.E., Minneapolis, MN 55413-1944. Tel: 612-379-2394; Email: frstel1970@aol.com. Very Rev. Canon Michael Stelmach; Rev. Roman Voronchak.
Catechesis Religious Program—Students 21.

STATE OF MISSOURI

ST. JOSEPH, BUCHANAN CO., ST. JOSEPH'S (1918) (Ukrainian), Attended by Omaha, NE.
526 Virginia, St. Joseph, MO 64504.
Tel: 402-345-1552; Email: koteky1@hotmail.com. Mailing Address: 1513 Martha St., Omaha, NE 68108. Rev. Bohdan Kudleychuk, Temporary Admin.

ST. LOUIS, ST. LOUIS CO., ASSUMPTION B.V.M. St. Mary's Assumption Ukrainian Catholic Church (1894) (Ukrainian)
11363 Oak Branch Dr., St. Louis, MO 63128.
Tel: 314-487-1786; Email: ewlogu52@yahoo.com. Mailing Address: P.O. Box 4172, Chesterfield, MO 63006. Deacon Eugene Logusch, Temporary Admin. Served by Chicago.

STATE OF NEBRASKA

LINCOLN, LANCASTER CO., ST. GEORGE'S (1950) (Ukrainian)
3330 N. 13th St., Lincoln, NE 68521.
Tel: 402-345-1552; Email: koteky1@hotmail.com. Mailing Address: 1513 Martha St., Omaha, NE 68108. Rev. Bohdan Kudleychuk, Temporary Admin.

OMAHA, DOUGLAS CO., ASSUMPTION OF B.V.M. (1950) (Ukrainian)
1513 Martha St., Omaha, NE 68108.
Tel: 402-345-1552; Email: koteky1@hotmail.com. Rev. Bohdan Kudleychuk, Temporary Admin.
Mission—St. Joseph, 526 Virginia St., Saint Joseph, MO 64504.

STATE OF NORTH DAKOTA

BELFIELD, STARK CO.
1—ST. DEMETRIUS (1905) [CEM 2] (Ukrainian)
2123 Hwy. 85, S.W., Belfield, ND 58622.
Tel: 701-290-3361; Email: lavkord@outlook.com; Web: www.saint-demetrius.com. 12897 20th St., S.W., Belfield, ND 58622. Rev. Ivan Shkumbatyuk; Deacon Leonard Kordonowy, (Retired).
2—ST. JOHN THE BAPTIST (1946) [CEM 2] (Ukrainian)
305 6th St. NE, Belfield, ND 58622.
Tel: 701-575-4281; Email: iv.shkumbatyuk@gmail.com. Mailing Address: 307 6th St. NE, Belfield, ND 58622. Rev. Ivan Shkumbatyuk; Deacon Leonard Kordonowy, (Retired).

WILTON, MCLEAN CO., SS. PETER AND PAUL (1906) [CEM] (Ukrainian)
106 N. 7th St., P.O. Box 275, Wilton, ND 58579.
Tel: 701-734-6464; Email: RYA@MIDCO.NET. Rev. George L. Pruys, Admin.
Catechesis Religious Program—
Mission—St. Michael, 812 N. Main St., Minot, Ward Co. ND 58703.

STATE OF OREGON

SPRINGFIELD, LANE CO., NATIVITY OF THE MOTHER OF GOD (1981) (Ukrainian)
704 Aspen St., Springfield, OR 97477.
Tel: 541-726-7309; Email: rjano@aol.com; Web: www.nativityukr.org. Very Rev. Richard Janowicz.

STATE OF TEXAS

HOUSTON, HARRIS CO., PROTECTION OF THE MOTHER OF GOD (1957) [JC] (Ukrainian)
9102 Meadowshire St., Houston, TX 77037.
Tel: 281-447-2749; Email: frdovzhuk@sbcglobal.net. Rev. Mykola Dovzhuk, Admin.
Catechesis Religious Program—Students 8.

THE COLONY, ST. SOPHIA UKRAINIAN CATHOLIC CHURCH (1999) (Ukrainian)
5600 N. Colony Blvd., The Colony, TX 75056-1927.
Tel: 972-370-4700; Fax: 972-370-4700; Email: frpavlo@stsophiaukrainian.cc; Web: www.stsophiaukrainian.cc. Revs. Pavlo Popov, Admin.; Frank Avant, In Res., (Retired); Deacon John Novocilsky.
Catechesis Religious Program—Students 14.

STATE OF WASHINGTON

SEATTLE, KING CO., OUR LADY OF ZARVANYCIA (1959)
5321 17th Ave., S., Seattle, WA 98108.
Tel: 206-762-1055; Email: olzarv@gmail.com; Web: www.ukrchurch.org. Rev. Abraham Miller.
Catechesis Religious Program—Oresta Rzhyskij, D.R.E. Students 18.

STATE OF WISCONSIN

MILWAUKEE, MILWAUKEE CO., ST. MICHAELS (1950) [JC] (Ukrainian)
1025 S. 11th St., Milwaukee, WI 53204.
Tel: 414-672-5616; Email: info@stmichaelsukr.org; Web: stmichaelsukr.org. Very Rev. Vasyl Savchyn.

Chaplains of Public Institutions.

Hospitals:
Very Rev.—
Mendyuk, Yaroslav
Revs.—
Buryadnyk, Mykola, Resurrection Health Care Center
Morse, Jonathan K., Veterans Administration Maryland Health Care
Very Rev. Archpriest—
Kuzma, Mykhailo, Resurrection Health Care Center, Alexian Brothers.

On Leave:
Very Rt. Rev.—
Homick, Joseph
Revs.—
Mykyta, Myron
Panchuk, Myron
Plishka, Andrew.

Retired:
Revs.—
Avant, Frank, (Retired)
Bucsek, Basil, (Retired), 17648 W. Voltaire St., Surprise, AZ 85388-5057
Dohman, William, (Retired)
Marick, Thomas D., (Retired), 1801 Dallas Ave., Royal Oak, MI 48067
Wroblicky, Theodore P., (Retired)
Zaiats, Volodymyr, (Retired)
Very Rev. Archpriest—
Dobrowolski, Thomas, (Retired)
Rev. Msgr. Canon—
Bilinsky, William M., (Retired), 84031 Pine Dr., Folsom, LA 70437.

Permanent Deacons:
Brown, Randolph, Holy Apostles Mission, Wichita, KS
Chabin, Nicholas, St. Michael, Milwaukee, WI

Cook, Michael, Nativity of the Blessed Virgin Mary
Horodysky, Mychajlo, St. Nicholas Cathedral, Chicago, IL
Kordonowy, Leonard, St. John the Baptist, Belfield, ND; St. Demetrius, Belfield, ND
Logusch, Eugene, St Mary's Assumption, St. Louis, MO.

INSTITUTIONS LOCATED IN DIOCESE

[A] MONASTERIES

EAGLE HARBOR. *Holy Transfiguration Skete* dba Society of Saint John, Inc. (1983) Society of St. John 6559 State Hwy. M26, Eagle Harbor, MI 49950. Tel: 906-289-4484; Fax: 906-289-8468; Email: htskete@gmail.com; Email: skete@societystjohn.com; Web: societystjohn.com; Web: poorrockabbey.com. Deacon Ambrose Nemeth; Rev. Basil Paris, Hegumen. Deacons 1; Priests 1; Professed Monks 5.

REDWOOD VALLEY. *Holy Transfiguration Monastery*, 17001 Tomki Rd., Redwood Valley, CA 95470. Tel: 707-485-8959; Email: fatherd@earthlink.com; Web: www.monksofmttabor.com. P.O. Box 217, Redwood Valley, CA 95470. Rev. Damien Higgins, Admin. Monks of Mount Tabor. Deacons 1; Novices 1; Postulants 2; Priests 2; Professed Monks 5.

[B] MISCELLANEOUS

CHICAGO. **Ukrainian Catholic Education Foundation*, 2247 W. Chicago Ave., Chicago, 60622. Tel: 773-235-8462; Fax: 773-235-8464; Email: jsolimini@ucef.org; Email: ucef@ucef.org; Web: www.ucef.org. Joseph Solimini, COO.

TUCSON. *Metropolitan Andrey Sheptytsky Institute of Eastern Christian Studies* The Sheptytsky Institute is an educational institution and the Foundation is the 501 c 3 that holds its endowments and supports the Institute's work. 420 E. Deer's Rest Pl., Tucson, AZ 85704. Tel: 480-217-8505; Tel: 416-926-7133; Email: sheptytsky@utoronto.ca; Web: www.sheptytskyinstitute.ca. Very Rev. Peter Galadza, Dir.; Rt. Rev. Dr. Andriy Chirovsky, S.T.D., Prof.

Metropolitan Andrey Sheptytsky Institute Foundation.

RELIGIOUS INSTITUTES OF MEN REPRESENTED IN THE DIOCESE

For further details refer to the corresponding bracketed number in the Religious Institutes of Men or Women section.

[]—*Monks of Mt. Tabor*.

[0180]—*Order of St. Basil the Great*—O.S.B.M.

[]—*Skete of Mt. Tabor*.

RELIGIOUS INSTITUTES OF WOMEN REPRESENTED IN THE DIOCESE

[3730]—*Sisters of the Order of St. Basil the Great*—O.S.B.M.

An asterisk (*) denotes an organization that has established tax-exempt status directly with the IRS and is not covered by the USCCB Group Ruling.

Eparchy of St. Peter the Apostle (Chaldean)

Most Reverend

EMANUEL HANA SHALETA

Second Bishop-Eparch of the Eparchy of Saint Peter the Apostle-Chaldean; ordained May 31, 1984; appointed Chaldean Bishop January 15, 2015; consecrated Bishop February 6, 2015 in Detroit, Michigan; appointed second Eparch to the Eparchy of St. Peter the Apostle-Chaldean Catholic Diocese of America August 9, 2017; installed August 29, 2017. *Office: 1627 Jamacha Way, El Cajon, CA 92019.*

Most Reverend

SARHAD Y. JAMMO

Retired Bishop-Eparch of the Eparchy of Saint Peter the Apostle-Chaldean; ordained December 19, 1964; appointed Chaldean Bishop May 4, 2002; consecrated Bishop July 18, 2002 in Detroit, Michigan; installed July 25, 2002 in San Diego, California; appointed First Bishop Eparch to the Eparchy of Saint Peter the Apostle-Chaldean Catholic Diocese of America July 25, 2002; retired May 7, 2016. *Res.: St. Peter Chaldean Diocese, 1627 Jamacha Way, El Cajon, CA 92019.*

Chancery Office: 1627 Jamacha Way, CA 92019. Tel: 619-579-7997; Fax: 619-588-8281.

Email: stpeterdiocese@gmail.com

ESTABLISHED JULY 25, 2002.

The Jurisdiction of the Eparchy extends territorially to all Western States in the United States of America inclusive. With regards to persons, its subjects are all Catholics of the Chaldean or Assyrian Ancestry: (1) Who immigrated to this country from the Middle East, especially from Iraq and Iran; (2) Who descends from such persons (can. 755); (3) Women married to men referable to (1) & (2) if they comply with can. 98, n.4; (4) Who in accordance with can. 98, n. 3, changed their Rite; (5) converts to the Catholic Church of the Chaldean Rite; (6) And in fact, all other Catholics of the Chaldean Rite who are attached to the parishes subject to the jurisdiction of the Eparch. For legal titles of parishes and diocesan institutions, consult the Chancery Office.

Legal Title: The Chaldean Catholic Diocese of St. Peter the Apostle.

STATISTICAL OVERVIEW

Personnel	
Bishop	1
Retired Bishops	1
Priests: Diocesan Active in Diocese	18
Priests: Diocesan Active Outside Diocese	1
Number of Diocesan Priests	19
Religious Priests in Diocese	1
Total Priests in Diocese	20
Ordinations:	
Diocesan Priests	2
Transitional Deacons	2
Permanent Deacons in Diocese	20
Total Brothers	3
Total Sisters	6
Parishes	
Parishes	12
With Resident Pastor:	
Resident Diocesan Priests	11
Resident Religious Priests	1
New Parishes Created	2
Professional Ministry Personnel:	
Brothers	3
Sisters	6
Educational	
Seminaries, Diocesan	1
Students from This Diocese	5
Total Seminarians	5
Total Students under Catholic Instruction	5
Vital Statistics	
Receptions into the Church:	
Infant Baptism Totals	575
First Communions	462
Confirmations	582
Marriages:	
Catholic	200
Interfaith	5
Total Marriages	205
Deaths	167
Total Catholic Population	44,720

Former Bishop-Eparch—Most Rev. SARHAD Y. JAMMO, ord. Dec. 19, 1964; appt. Chaldean Bishop May 4, 2002; cons. Bishop July 18, 2002 in Detroit, Michigan; installed July 25, 2002 in San Diego, California; appt. First Bishop Eparch to the Eparchy of Saint Peter the Apostle-Chaldean Catholic Diocese of America July 25, 2002; retired May 7, 2016.

Chancery Office—1627 Jamacha Way, El Cajon, 92019. Tel: 619-579-7997; Fax: 619-588-8281.

Vicar General—Rev. Msgr. Archdeacon SABRI A. KEJBO, 799 E. Washington Ave., El Cajon, 92021. Tel: 619-444-9911; Fax: 619-444-7989; Email: st.michaels@cox.net.

Office of Diocesan Chancellor—Sr. ANAHYD MARIAM ARABO.

Chancellor—Rev. SIMON ESSHAKI.

Judicial Officer—Rev. ANKIDO SIPO.

Director of Finance—Diocesan Financial Committee.

Diocesan Advisory Council—SAMAD ATTISHA; DR. NOORI BARKA.

Director of Religious Education—Sr. TARBYTHA MARIAM (RNA) RABBAN.

Child Protection Review Board—Rev. SIMON ESSHAKI.

Chaldean Social Services—Ladies of Hope.

CLERGY, PARISHES, MISSIONS AND PAROCHIAL SCHOOLS

STATE OF CALIFORNIA

EL CAJON, SAN DIEGO CO.

1—*ST. PETER CHALDEAN CATHEDRAL (1973) (Chaldean)
1627 Jamacha Way, El Cajon, 92019.
Tel: 619-579-7913; Email: christine1627@hotmail.com. Most Reverend Emanuel Hana Shaleta, Bishop/Eparch; Revs. Michael J. Bazzi; Andrew Younan; Polis Khami; Simon Esshaki; Peter Shaba; Peter Patros; Most Rev. Sarhad Jammo, Bishop Emeritus.
Catechesis Religious Program—Tel: 619-447-8876. Sr. Anahyd Mariam Arabo, D.R.E.; Ms. Kheloud Allos, D.R.E. Students 717.

2—ST. MICHAEL CHALDEAN CATHOLIC CHURCH (1999) (Chaldean)
799 E. Washington Ave., El Cajon, 92020.
Tel: 619-444-9911; Email: st.michaels@cox.net. Rev. Msgr. Archdeacon Sabri A. Kejbo; Rev. David Stephen.
Catechesis Religious Program—Students 510.

CERES, STANISLAUS CO., ST. MATTHEW'S ASSYRIAN-CHALDEAN CATHOLIC CHURCH
3005 6th St., Ceres, 95307. Tel: 209-541-1660; Fax: 209-541-3952; Email: joekachappilly@hotmail.com. Rev. Joseph Kachappilly.
Catechesis Religious Program—Students 35.

NORTH HOLLYWOOD, LOS ANGELES CO., ST. PAUL ASSYRIAN-CHALDEAN CATHOLIC PARISH (1980) [JC] (Chaldean—Assyrian) Rev. Chorbishop Samuel Dinkha; Rev. Tomy Tomikeh.
Res.: 6628 Alcove Ave., North Hollywood, 91605.
Tel: 818-802-2320; Email: sdinkha2003@gmail.com.
Catechesis Religious Program—Students 33.

ORANGEVALE, SACRAMENTO CO., OUR LADY OF PERPETUAL HELP
7625 Hazel Ave., Orangevale, 95662.
Tel: 209-668-4500; Fax: 209-668-2762; Email: mansoor.mikhael@yahoo.com. Rev. Mikhael Khosho
Legal Name: Our Lady of Perpetual Help Chaldean Catholic Church
Catechesis Religious Program—Tom Simon, D.R.E. Students 16.

SAN JOSE, SANTA CLARA CO., ST. MARY ASSYRIAN-CHALDEAN PARISH (1987) Rev. Michael Barota
Assyrian Chaldean Catholic Church California Corporation
Church & Rectory: 109 N. First St., Campbell, 95008.
Tel: 408-318-8303; Email: frbarota@gmail.com.
Catechesis Religious Program—Students 45.

SANTA ANA, ORANGE CO., ST. GEORGE CHALDEAN CATHOLIC CHURCH (2001) [JC] (Chaldean)
4807 W. McFadden, Santa Ana, 92704.
Tel: 619-579-7997; Email: lucianayoub@yahoo.com. Rev. Simon Esshaki, Admin.
Catechesis Religious Program—Students 59.

TURLOCK, STANISLAUS CO., ST. THOMAS ASSYRIAN-CHALDEAN PARISH (1964) [CEM] [JC] (Chaldean)
2901 N. Berkeley Ave., Turlock, 95380.
Tel: 209-535-6555; Email: joekachappilly@hotmail.com. Rev. Joseph Kachappilly, Admin.
Catechesis Religious Program—Students 8.
Convent—Chaldean Sisters, 2937 N. Berkeley Ave., Turlock, 95380.
St. Thomas Retirement Center—Tel: 209-634-7252.

STATE OF ARIZONA

SCOTTSDALE, MARICOPA CO., MAR AURAHA CHALDEAN CATHOLIC PARISH (1992) [JC] (Chaldean)
6816 E. Cactus Rd., Scottsdale, AZ 85254.
Tel: 480-905-1545; Email: macatholicchurch@gmail.com. Revs. Felix Shabi; Royal Hannosh, Parochial Vicar
The Chaldean Catholic Church of Arizona Corporation
Catechesis Religious Program—Students 200.
Missions—Holy Cross Chaldean Mission—19 W. Bruce Ave., Gilbert, Maricopa Co. AZ 85233.

Holy Family Chaldean Catholic Mission, 12225 N. 68th St., Scottsdale, AZ 85254.
Holy Family Mission, 3847 W. Bluefield Ave., Glendale, AZ 85305.
Catechesis Religious Program—Polly Sesi, D.R.E. Students 120.

STATE OF NEVADA

LAS VEGAS, CLARK CO., ST. BARBARA CHALDEAN CATHOLIC CHURCH
4514 Meadows Ln., Las Vegas, NV 89107.
Tel: 702-542-3390; Email: stbarbarachaldeanchurch@gmail.com; Web: www.saintbarbarachurch.com. 1900 N. Torrey Pines Dr. #209, Las Vegas, NV 89108. Ray Sarkees.
Catechesis Religious Program—Rewayda Coda, D.R.E. Students 43.

INSTITUTIONS LOCATED IN THE DIOCESE

[A] SEMINARIES

EL CAJON. *Seminary of Mar Abba the Great*, 1400 Monument Hill Rd., El Cajon, 92020. Email: simon.esshaki@gmail.com; Web: www.marabba.org. Rev. Simon Esshaki, Rector. Clergy 2; Students 5.

[B] RETIREMENT CENTERS

EL CAJON. *Good Samaritan Retirement Center* (Facility #: 374600950) 1515 Jamacha Way, El Cajon, 92019. Tel: 619-590-1515; Fax: 619-590-0052; Email: info@goodsamretirement1.org; Web: www.goodsamretirement.org. Sr. Alexandra Matti, Exec. Dir.

[C] MONASTERIES AND RESIDENCES FOR PRIESTS AND BROTHERS

EL CAJON. *Sons of the Covenant Monastery*, 1111 N. Pepper Dr., El Cajon, 92021. Email: frankidosipo@gmail.com. Rev. Ankido Sipo, Admin. Monks 3.

PERRIS. *St. George Monastery/Retreat Center*, 13985 Descanso Dr., Perris, 92570. Tel: 619-579-7997. 1627 Jamacha Way, El Cajon, 92019. Email: stpeterdiocese@gmail.com. Rev. Simon Esshaki.

[D] CONVENTS AND RESIDENCES FOR SISTERS

EL CAJON. *Chaldean Sisters*, 1591 Jamacha Way, El Cajon, 92019. Tel: 619-447-4842;
Fax: 619-590-0052; Email: info@goodsamretirement1.org. Sr. Alexandra Matti, Dir. Sisters 5.

[E] MISCELLANEOUS

EL CAJON. *Chaldean Media Center*, 1627 Jamacha Way, El Cajon, 92019. Tel: 619-590-9028;
Fax: 619-590-8273; Email: infokaldu@gmail.com; Web: www.kaldu.org; Web: kaldaya.net. Sr. Tarbytha (Rna) Raban, D.R.E.

SAN JOSE. *Assyrian Chaldean Catholic Church California Corporation*, 109 N. First St., Campbell, 95008.

SCOTTSDALE. *The Chaldean Catholic Church of Arizona Corporation*, 6816 E. Cactus Rd., Scottsdale, AZ 85254.

An asterisk (*) denotes an organization that has established tax-exempt status directly with the IRS and is not covered by the USCCB Group Ruling.

Eparchy of Saint Thomas the Apostle (Chaldean)

Most Reverend

FRANCIS Y. KALABAT

Second Bishop-Eparch of the Eparchy of Saint Thomas the Apostle-Chaldean Catholic Diocese of America; ordained July 4, 1995; appointed second Bishop-Eparch to the Eparchy of Saint Thomas the Apostle-Chaldean Catholic Diocese of America May 3, 2014; ordained and installed June 14, 2014 in Southfield, Michigan. *Res.: 25603 Berg Rd., Southfield, MI 48033.*

Most Reverend

IBRAHIM N. IBRAHIM, D.D.

Bishop Emeritus of the Eparchy of St. Thomas the Apostle, Chaldean Catholic Diocese of America; ordained December 30, 1962; appointed Chaldean Apostolic Exarch and Titular Bishop of Anbar January 26, 1982; consecrated Bishop March 7, 1982 in Baghdad, Iraq; installed April 18, 1982 in Southfield, Michigan; appointed First Bishop Eparch to the Eparchy of Saint Thomas the Apostle-Chaldean Catholic Diocese of America September 14, 1985; appointed Apostolic Visitor ad referendum for the Chaldean faithful in Canada January 23, 2006; retired June 14, 2014. *Office: 25603 Berg Rd., Southfield, MI 48033.* Tel: 248-351-0440; Fax: 248-351-0443; Email: chaldeandiocese-detroit@comcast.net.

Chancery Office: 25603 Berg Rd., Southfield, MI 48033. Tel: 248-351-0440; Fax: 248-351-0443.

Email: chaldeandiocese-detroit@comcast.net

Exarchate Erected January 26, 1982. Elevated to the Rank of Eparchy September 14, 1985.

The Jurisdiction of the Eparchy extends territorially to all Eastern States in the United States of America inclusive. With regard to persons, its subjects are all Catholics of the Chaldean or Assyrian Ancestry: (1) Who immigrated to this country from the Middle East, especially from Iraq and Iran; (2) Who descends from such persons (can. 755); (3) Women married to men referable to (1) & (2) if they comply with can. 98, n. 4; (4) Who in accordance with can. 98, n. 3., changed their Rite; (5) Converts to the Catholic Church of the Chaldean Rite; (6) And in fact, all other Catholics of the Chaldean Rite who are attached to the parishes subject to the jurisdiction of the Eparch.

For legal titles of parishes and diocesan institutions, consult the Chancery Office.

STATISTICAL OVERVIEW

Personnel	
Bishop	1
Retired Bishops	1
Priests: Diocesan Active Outside Diocese	19
Priests: Diocesan in Foreign Missions	2
Priests: Retired, Sick or Absent	4
Number of Diocesan Priests	25
Total Priests in Diocese	25
Ordinations:	
Diocesan Priests	2
Transitional Deacons	2
Parishes	
Parishes	12
With Resident Pastor:	
Resident Diocesan Priests	12
Without Resident Pastor:	
Administered by Priests	4
Welfare	
Homes for the Aged	1
Total Assisted	65
Special Centers for Social Services	1
Total Assisted	50
Educational	
Students Religious	9
Total Seminarians	9
Total Students under Catholic Instruction	9
Vital Statistics	
Receptions into the Church:	
Infant Baptism Totals	1,211
Adult Baptism Totals	6
Received into Full Communion	1,224
First Communions	961
Marriages:	
Catholic	585
Interfaith	92
Total Marriages	677
Deaths	282
Total Catholic Population	180,000

Chancery Office—25603 Berg Rd., Southfield, 48033. Tel: 248-351-0440; Fax: 248-351-0443; Email: chaldeandiocese-detroit@comcast.net; Web: www.chaldeandiocese.org. Most Revs. FRANCIS Y. KALABAT; IBRAHIM N. IBRAHIM, D.D., S.T.D., (Retired).

Vicar General—Rev. MANUEL Y. BOJI, 43700 Merrill Rd., Sterling Heights, 48314. Tel: 586-803-3114; Fax: 586-803-3140.

Judicial Vicar—Rev. RUDY ZOMA.

Presbyteral Council—Revs. MANUEL Y. BOJI; BRYAN KASSA; FADI PHILIP; ANTHONY KATHAWA; ANDREW SEBA; FAWAZ KAKO.

Eparchial College of Consultors—Rev. MANUEL Y. BOJI; Rev. Msgr. ZOUHAIR T. KEJBOU; Revs. RUDY ZOMA; SAMEEM BALIUS; FADI PHILIP; FAWAZ KAKO.

Diocesan Corporation-The Chaldean Catholic Church of U.S.A.—Most Rev. FRANCIS Y. KALABAT, Pres.; Revs. MANUEL Y. BOJI, Treas.; FADI (PHILIP) HABIB, Sec.

Eparchial Tribunal—VACANT.

Office of Safety Environment—MRS. JANAN SENAWI, Dir., 25603 Berg Rd., Southfield, 48033. Tel: 248-351-0440; Fax: 248-351-0443.

Department of Family Counseling—MRS. JANAN SENAWI, Dir., 25603 Berg Rd., Southfield, 48033. Tel: 248-351-0440; Fax: 248-351-0443.

Chaldean Manor Housing for Elders—25775 Berg Rd., Southfield, 48034. Tel: 248-355-9491; Fax: 248-356-5405.

Our Lady of the Fields Camp & Retreat Center—1391 Kellogg Rd., Brighton, 48114. Tel: 800-822-2226 (Toll Free); Tel: 810-822-2226.

Chaldean Voice Radio Program—25775 Berg Rd., Apt. #324, Southfield, 48034. Tel: 248-353-1083; Fax: 248-353-1290; Web: www.chaldeanvoice.org.

CLERGY, PARISHES, MISSIONS AND PAROCHIAL SCHOOLS

STATE OF MICHIGAN

FARMINGTON HILLS, OAKLAND CO., HOLY CROSS CHALDEAN CATHOLIC CHURCH
32500 Middlebelt Rd., Farmington Hills, 48334.
Tel: 248-626-0285; Tel: 248-626-5055; Fax: 248-626-5420; Email: holycrosschaldeancc@gmail.com. Rev. Msgr. Zouhair Toma Keijbou.

GRAND BLANC, GENESEE CO., ST. PAUL CALDEAN CATHOLIC CHURCH, Unassigned.
5150 E. Maple Ave., Grand Blanc, 48439.
Tel: 810-820-8450; Fax: 810-820-8673; Email: st.paulccc@comcast.net.

OAK PARK, OAKLAND CO., MAR ADDAI CHALDEAN PARISH (1979) (Chaldean)
24010 Coolidge Hwy., Oak Park, 48237.
Tel: 248-547-4648; Fax: 248-399-9089. Rev. Stephen H. Kallabat, In Res.
Catechesis Religious Program—Students 100.

SHELBY TWP., OAKLAND CO., ST. GEORGE CHALDEAN CATHOLIC CHURCH (2005)
Mailing Address: 45700 Dequinder Rd., Shelby Twp., 48317. Tel: 586-254-7221; Fax: 586-254-2874; Email: saintgeorgechaldeanchurch@gmail.com. Revs. Fawaz Kako; Matthew Zetouna, Parochial Vicar.
Catechesis Religious Program—Students 350.

SOUTHFIELD, OAKLAND CO., OUR LADY OF CHALDEANS CATHEDRAL (1948) (Chaldean)
Mailing Address: 25585 Berg Rd., 48033.
Tel: 248-356-0565; Tel: 248-356-0569;
Tel: 248-356-9809 (Hall); Fax: 248-356-5235; Email: ourladyofthechaldeans@gmail.com. Most Rev. Francis Y. Kalabat; Revs. Sanharib Youkhanna, Rector; Patrick Setto, Parochial Vicar; Wisam Matti, In Res.
Legal Name: Our Lady of Chaldeans Cathedral, Mother of God Chaldean Parish
Catechesis Religious Program—Tel: 248-356-2448. Students 180.

STERLING HEIGHTS, MACOMB CO., HOLY MARTYRS CHALDEAN CATHOLIC CHURCH (2010)
43700 Merrill Rd., Sterling Heights, 48314.
Tel: 586-803-3114; Fax: 586-803-3140; Email: secretary@holymartyrsccc.org. Revs. Manuel Y. Boji; Andrew Seba, Parochial Vicar.

TROY, OAKLAND CO., ST. JOSEPH CHALDEAN PARISH (1981) (Chaldean)
2442 E. Big Beaver Rd., Troy, 48083.
Tel: 248-528-3676; Fax: 248-524-1957; Email: saintjosephccc@gmail.com. Revs. Rudy Zoma; Bryan Kassa, Parochial Vicar; John Jaddou, Parochial Vicar.

WARREN, MACOMB CO.

1—OUR LADY OF PERPETUAL HELP CHALDEAN CATHOLIC CHURCH
11200 E. 12 Mile Rd., Warren, 48093.
Tel: 586-804-2114; Fax: 586-933-2590; Email: olphmission@gmail.com. Revs. Fadi (Philip) Habib; Fadi Gorgies, Parochial Vicar; Salwon Tapponi, In Res.

2—SACRED HEART CHALDEAN PARISH (1973) (Chaldean)
30590 Dequindre Rd., Warren, 48092.
Tel: 586-313-5809; Fax: 586-393-5812; Email: sacredheartchurch310@gmail.com. Rev. Sameem Balius.
Catechesis Religious Program—Tel: 248-548-0066. Students 150.

WEST BLOOMFIELD, OAKLAND CO., ST. THOMAS CHALDEAN CATHOLIC PARISH (1992) (Chaldean)
6900 Maple Rd., West Bloomfield, 48322.
Tel: 248-788-2460; Fax: 248-788-2153; Email:

stthomaschaldeanchurch@gmail.com. Revs. Bashar Sitto, Admin.; Anthony Kathawa, Parochial Vicar; Jirjis Abrahim, In Res., (Retired).

Catechesis Religious Program—Tel: 248-306-6004. Students 370.

STATE OF ILLINOIS

CHICAGO, COOK CO., ST. EPHREM'S CHALDEAN CATHOLIC CHURCH (1904) [JC] (Chaldean-Assyrian) 2537 W. Bryn Mawr Ave., Chicago, IL 60659-4996. Tel: 773-754-7202; Fax: 773-754-8935; Email: st. ephremchaldeancatholicchurch@yahoo.com. Rev. Hermiz Haddad, Admin.

Catechesis Religious Program—Tel: 773-506-9957. Students 50.

NORTHBROOK, COOK CO., MART MARIAM CHALDEAN CATHOLIC CHURCH (1986) [JC] (Chaldean-Assyrian) 2700 Willow Rd., Northbrook, IL 60062. Tel: 630-847-0149; Fax: 647-897-4808; Email: martmariamchurch@gmail.com. Rev. Ayad Hana.

On Duty Outside the Diocese:
Rev.—
Konja, Pierre, Iraq.

Retired:
Most Rev.—
Ibrahim, Ibrahim N., D.D., S.T.D., (Retired)
Revs.—
Abrahim, Jirjis, (Retired)
Kallabat, Stephen, (Retired)
Marano, Zaya, (Retired)
Rayes, Emanuel, (Retired), Tel: 248-788-2460.

INSTITUTIONS LOCATED IN DIOCESE

[A] CONVENTS AND RESIDENCES FOR SISTERS

CHICAGO, COOK CO.. *Daughters of Mary Our Lady of the Immaculate Conception Order*, 2908 W. Morse, Chicago, IL 60645. Tel: 773-338-8832.

FARMINGTON HILLS, OAKLAND CO.. *Daughters of Mary Our Lady of the Immaculate Conception Order*, 24900 Middlebelt Rd., Farmington, 48336. Tel: 248-615-2951; Fax: 248-615-3482.

[B] MISCELLANEOUS

BLOOMFIELD TOWNSHIP, OAKLAND CO.. *St. Ephrem Re-Evangelization Center*, 4875 Maple Rd., Bloomfield Township, 48301. Tel: 248-538-9903; Fax: 248-538-0969.

Martoma Productions, 4875 Maple Rd., Bloomfield Township, 48301. Tel: 248-538-9903; Fax: 248-538-0969.

RELIGIOUS INSTITUTES OF WOMEN IN THE EPARCHY

For further details refer to the corresponding bracketed number in the Religious Institutes of Men or Women section.

[]—*Daughters of Mary Immaculate* (Baghdad, Iraq); (Farmington Hills, MI; Chicago, IL)—D.M.I.

An asterisk (*) denotes an organization that has established tax-exempt status directly with the IRS and is not covered by the USCCB Group Ruling.

St. Thomas Syro-Malabar Catholic Diocese of Chicago

Most Reverend

JACOB ANGADIATH

Bishop of St. Thomas Syro-Malabar Catholic Diocese of Chicago; ordained January 5, 1972; appointed Bishop of St. Thomas Syro-Malabar Catholic Diocese of Chicago March 13, 2001; Episcopal Ordination July 1, 2001. *Office: 372 S. Prairie Ave., Elmhurst, IL 60126-4020.* Tel: 630-279-1386; Tel: 630-279-1383; Fax: 630-279-1479.

Most Reverend

JOY ALAPPATT

Auxiliary Bishop and (Protosyncellus) of St. Thomas Syro-Malabar Catholic Diocese of Chicago; ordained December 31, 1981; appointed Titular Bishop of Bencenna and Auxiliary Bishop of St. Thomas Syro-Malabar Catholic Diocese of Chicago July 24, 2014; ordained September 27, 2014. *Office: 372 S. Prairie Ave., Elmhurst, IL 60126-4020.* Tel: 201-951-1701; Fax: 630-279-1479; Email: joyalappat@gmail.com.

ESTABLISHED MARCH 13, 2001.

Comprises all of the United States.

Diocesan Office: 372 S. Prairie Ave., IL 60126-4020. Tel: 630-279-1386; Tel: 630-279-1383; Fax: 630-279-1479.

Email: curia@syromail.com

STATISTICAL OVERVIEW

Personnel	
Bishop	1
Auxiliary Bishops	1
Priests: Diocesan Active in Diocese	50
Priests: Diocesan Active Outside Diocese	1
Number of Diocesan Priests	51
Religious Priests in Diocese	26
Total Priests in Diocese	77
Ordinations:	
Diocesan Priests	2
Total Sisters	116
Parishes	
Parishes	45
With Resident Pastor:	
Resident Diocesan Priests	35
Resident Religious Priests	10
Missions	44
Welfare	
Day Care Centers	1
Total Assisted	50
Educational	
Diocesan Students in Other Seminaries	12
Total Seminarians	12
Catechesis/Religious Education:	
High School Students	2,181
Elementary Students	6,626
Total Students under Catholic Instruction	8,819
Vital Statistics	
Receptions into the Church:	
Infant Baptism Totals	425
Minor Baptism Totals	7
Adult Baptism Totals	9
Received into Full Communion	35
First Communions	652
Confirmations	487
Marriages:	
Catholic	167
Interfaith	22
Total Marriages	189
Deaths	93
Total Catholic Population	46,534

Diocesan Office—372 S. Prairie Ave., Elmhurst, 60126-4020. Tel: 630-279-1386; Tel: 630-279-1383; Fax: 630-279-1479; Email: curia@syromail.com.

Administration

Vicar Generals (Syncellus)—Revs. AUGUSTINE PALACKAPARAMBIL, Mar Thoma Shleeha Cathedral, 5000 St. Charles Rd., Bellwood, 60104. Tel: 714-800-3648; Email: rev.pjaugustine@gmail.com; THOMAS MULAVANAL, St. Mary's Syro Malabar Knanaya Catholic Church, 7800 W. Lyons St., Morton Grove, 60053. Tel: 310-709-5111; Email: mulavan@hotmail.com.

Finance Officer - Procurator—372 S. Prairie Ave., Elmhurst, 60126-4020. Tel: 630-279-1386; Cell: 813-420-3436; Fax: 630-279-1479. Rev. GEORGE MALIEKAL, Email: diocesanprocurator@syromail.com.

Chancellor & Secretary to Bishop—372 S. Prairie Ave., Elmhurst, 60126-4020. Cell: 916-803-5307; Fax: 630-279-1479. Rev. JOHNYKUTTY GEORGE, Email: chancellor@syromail.com.

Eparchial Consultors—Revs. AUGUSTINE PALACKAPARAMBIL; THOMAS MULAVANAL; JOHNYKUTTY GEORGE; GEORGE MALIEKAL; PAUL CHALISSERY; THADEUS J. ARAVINDATHU; MATHEW ELAYADATHAMADAM VARKEY, M.S.F.S.; KURIAKOSE KUMBAKEEL; VINOD GEORGE MADATIPARAMBIL; GEORGE DANEVELIL.

Cathedral—Mar Thoma Sleeha Cathedral, 5000 St. Charles Rd., Bellwood, 60104. Tel: 708-544-7250; Fax: 708-544-1040.

Victim Assistance Coordinators—Rev. AUGUSTINE PALACKAPARAMBIL, Tel: 714-800-3648; DR. PAUL CHERIAN, Tel: 630-769-9603 (USA); MR. THOMAS MOOLAYIL, Tel: 630-779-0140. Data Processor: LINDA ROMANSIC, Email: compliance@syromail.com.

Youth and Family Apostolate—Rev. PAUL CHALISSERY, Cell: 919-749-7175; Email: pchalis123@gmail.com.

Office for Formation and Vocations—Rev. PAUL CHALISSERY, Cell: 919-749-7175; Email: pchalis123@gmail.com.

Director of Religious Education—Rev. GEORGE DANEVELIL, Cell: 630-286-3767; Email: gdanavelil@gmail.com.

Curia Secretarial Staff—Sisters MARCELLA NOWAKOWSKI, S.S.J.-T.O.S.F., Tel: 630-279-1383; Email: secretary@syromail.com; MERCITTA PARAVARA, S.S.C., Tel: 773-756-6588; Email: mparavara@yahoo.com.

CLERGY, PARISHES, MISSIONS AND PAROCHIAL SCHOOLS

STATE OF ILLINOIS

BELLWOOD, COOK CO., MAR THOMA SLEEHA CATHEDRAL (CHICAGO) (1985) [JC2] (Indian)
5000 St. Charles Rd., Bellwood, 60104.
Tel: 708-544-7250; Cell: 908-235-8449; Fax: 708-688-1040; Email: frkevinm@smchicago.org; Web: www.smchicago.org. Revs. Thomas Kadukapillil; Kevin Mundackal.
Catechesis Religious Program—Sr. Sheena Pouline, C.M.C., D.R.E. Students 659.

MAYWOOD, COOK CO., SACRED HEART SYRO MALABAR KANAYA CATHOLIC CHURCH (2006) [JC] (Indian)
611 Maple St., Maywood, 60153. Tel: 773-412-6254; Fax: 773-286-8579; Email: mutholath2000@gmail.com; Web: www.shkcparish.us. Mailing Address: 5212 W. Agatite Ave., Chicago, 60630. Rev. Abraham Mutholathu Jacob
Legal Name: Sacred Heart Knanaya Catholic Parish, Chicago
Catechesis Religious Program—Teena Neduvampuzha Thomas, D.R.E. Students 205.

MORTON GROVE, COOK CO., ST. MARY'S SYRO MALABAR KNANAYA CATHOLIC PARISH (2010)
7800 W. Lyons St., Morton Grove, 60053.
Tel: 310-709-5111; Email: mulavan@hotmail.com; Web: www.smkcparish.us. Revs. Bins Jose Chethalil; Thomas Mulavanal, Pastor/Vicar
Legal Name: St. Mary's Syro-Malabar Knanaya Catholic Parish (Morton Grove)
Catechesis Religious Program—Saji Pootrukayil, D.R.E. Students 505.

STATE OF ARIZONA

PHOENIX, MARICOPA CO., HOLY FAMILY (2007)
Mailing Address: 3221 N. 24th St., Phoenix, AZ 85016. Tel: 623-328-5784; Fax: 623-328-5784; Email: frnirappeljames@mail.com; Web: www.syromalabaraz.org. Rev. James Nirappel. Services held at: Holy Family Syro-Malabar Catholic Church, Phoenix, AZ.
Legal Name: Holy Family Syro-Malabar Catholic Church (Phoenix)
Catechesis Religious Program—Cell: 480-276-4421; Email: jaiphil@gmail.com. Rinson John, D.R.E. Students 150.

STATE OF CALIFORNIA

LOS ANGELES, LOS ANGELES CO., ST. PIUS X SYRO-MALABAR KNANAYA CATHOLIC CHURCH (2002) (Indian)
124 N. 5th St., Montebello, CA 90640. Cell: 210-630-2295; Email: skmudakodil@gmail.com. Rev. Siju Kuriakos Mudakodil.
Catechesis Religious Program—26377 Delegado Ave., Loma Linda, CA 92354. Tel: 909-268-7939; Email: susan1mathew@msn.com. Susan Mathew, D.R.E. Students 43.

MILPITAS, SANTA CLARA CO., ST. THOMAS SYRO

MALABAR CATHOLIC CHURCH OF SAN FRANCISCO (2009) [JC] (Indian)
Mailing Address: 200 N. Abbott Ave., Milpitas, CA 95035. Tel: 408-385-1123; Email: vicar@syromalabarsf.org. Rev. George Ettuparayil
Legal Name: St. Thomas Syro-Malabar Catholic Church of San Francisco (Indian)
Child Care—St. Thomas Preschool, (2-4 yr. olds) Tel: 408-946-0190; Email: efronlorenztigas@gmail.com. Mr. Tigas Efren, Prin. Students 60.
Catechesis Religious Program—Tel: 469-623-2612; Email: v.jose.g@gmail.com. jose Vettikat George, D.R.E. Students 43.

SACRAMENTO, SACRAMENTO CO.
1—INFANT JESUS SYRO MALABAR CATHOLIC CHURCH (2009)
6200 McMahon Dr., Sacramento, CA 95824.
Tel: 916-758-6170; Email: jobyjoseph755@gmail.com; Web: syromalabarsac.org. Rev. Jobimon Joseph, M.C.B.S.
Legal Name: Infant Jesus Syro Malabar Catholic Church, Sacramento, CA of St. Thomas Syro Malabar Catholic Diocese of Chicago.
2—ST. JOHN PAUL II SYRO MALABAR KNANAYA CATHOLIC MISSION (2011)
1070 N. Texas St., Fairfield, CA 95127. Cell: 630-828-4513; Email: kalari26@gmail.com. Rev. Abraham K. Chacko, Dir.
Legal Name: St. John Paul II Syro-Malabar Knanaya Catholic Mission, Sacramento.

SAN FERNANDO
1—ST. ALPHONSA SYRO-MALABAR CATHOLIC CHURCH (2008) (Asian—Indian) Rev. Kuriakose Kumbakeel
Legal Name: St. Alphonsa Syro-Malabar Catholic Church of Los Angeles
Church & Mailing Address: 215 N. Macneil St., San Fernando, CA 91340. Tel: 818-365-5522; Cell: 754-366-6765; Email: alphonsa.angeles@gmail.com; Email: frkuku@gmail.com; Web: www.syromalabarla.org.
Catechesis Religious Program—Students 114.
2—ST. CHAVARA (2011) [JC]
11342 Laurel Canyon, San Fernando, CA 91340.
Tel: 818-365-5522; Cell: 754-366-6765;
Fax: 818-365-6646; Email: alphonsa.angeles@gmail.com. Rev. Kuriakose Kumbakeel. Services held at: St. John's School, 4500 Buena Vista Rd., Bakersfield, CA 93311
Legal Name: Bl. Chavara Syro-Malabar Catholic Mission (Bakersfield).

SAN JOSE, SANTA CLARA CO., ST. MARY'S SYRO MALABAR KNANAYA CATHOLIC CHURCH (2000) (Indian)
324 Gloria Ave., San Jose, CA 95127. Mailing Address: 3450 E. Hills Dr., San Jose, CA 95127. Rev. Saji Kurian Pinarkayil
Legal Name: St. Mary's Syro-Malabar Knanaya Catholic Church of San Jose
Catechesis Religious Program—Tel: 408-836-5804; Email: jkurian1568@gmail.com. Students 105.

SANTA ANA, ORANGE CO., ST. THOMAS APOSTLE (2001) (Indian)
Tel: 714-530-2900; Email: pastor@stthomassyromalabarca.org; Web: www.stthomassyromalabar.com. Rev. Jathews Kurian Munjanath
Legal Name: St. Thomas Apostle Syro-Malabar Catholic Church (Santa Ana)
Church: 5021 W. 16th St., Santa Ana, CA 92703.
Catechesis Religious Program—Tel: 714-399-6785; Email: nixon.philip@gmail.com. Nixon Philip, D.R.E. Students 166.

STATE OF COLORADO

DENVER, DENVER CO., ST. THOMAS SYRO-MALABAR CATHOLIC MISSION, DENVER, CO, INC. OF ST. THOMAS SYRO-MALABAR CATHOLIC DIOCESE OF CHICAGO (2013) Services held at: Annunciation Catholic Church, 1408 E. 36th Ave., Denver, CO, 80205.
3554 Humbolt St., Denver, CO 80205. Rev. John Kolencherry, O.F.M.Cap., Dir.
Catechesis Religious Program—Rekha Thomas Kodenkandath, D.R.E. Students 25.

STATE OF CONNECTICUT

HARTFORD, HARTFORD CO., ST. THOMAS SYRO-MALABAR CATHOLIC CHURCH, WEST HARTFORD, CT, INC. OF ST. THOMAS SYRO-MALABAR CATHOLIC DIOCESE OF CHICAGO (1998) (Indian)
Mailing Address: 30 Echo Ln., West Hartford, CT 06107. Tel: 860-521-1921; Cell: 203-233-9321; Email: frjpullikattil@gmail.com; Web: syromalabarct.org. Rev. Joseph Pullikattil, Dir. Services held at: St. Helena Catholic Church, West Hartford, CT.
Legal Name: St. Thomas Syro-Malabar Catholic Mission of Hartford
Catechesis Religious Program—Tel: 860-218-4272; Email: bzmathew@gmail.com. Mr. Baby Mathew, D.R.E. Students 61.

NORWALK, FAIRFIELD CO., OUR LADY OF THE ASSUMPTION SYRO-MALABAR CATHOLIC CHURCH NORWALK, CT INC. (2013)
566 Elm St., Stamford, CT 06902. Cell: 203-451-0017; Email: jamesvc88@gmail.com. Rev. James Vattakunnel, V.C., Dir., Mission. Services held at: 25 Cliff St., Norwalk, CT, 06854.
Catechesis Religious Program—Jaya Giby, D.R.E. Students 23.

STATE OF DELAWARE

BEAR, NEW CASTLE CO., HOLY TRINITY SYRO-MALABAR CATHOLIC CHURCH, DELAWARE, INC. OF ST. THOMAS SYRO-MALABAR CATHOLIC DIOCESE OF CHICAGO (2012) [JC]
Mailing Address: 250 S. Rte. 73, Hammonton, NJ 08037. Cell: 609-878-3878; Fax: 215-745-0587; Email: stephenmcbs@gmail.com. Rev. Stephen Kanippallil, Dir., Mission. Services held at: St. Elizabeth Ann Seton Catholic Church, 345 Bear Christiana Rd., Bear, DE, 19701.
Catechesis Religious Program—Suni Johns, D.R.E.; Raji Mathew, D.R.E. Students 35.

STATE OF FLORIDA

BRANDON, HILLSBOROUGH CO., SACRED HEART (2010)
Mailing Address: 3920 S. Kings Ave., Brandon, FL 33511. Tel: 813-315-9838 (Office); Cell: 248-820-1190; Email: tampaknanayamission@gmail.com; Email: frmeledath@yahoo.com. Rev. Regi Jacob Mathew Meladath
Legal Name: Sacred Heart Syro-Malabar Knanaya Catholic Church (Tampa)
Catechesis Religious Program—Students 178.

CORAL SPRINGS, BROWARD CO., OUR LADY OF HEALTH SYRO-MALABAR CATHOLIC CHURCH, CORAL SPRINGS, FL, INC. OF ST. THOMAS SYRO-MALABAR CATHOLIC DIOCESE OF CHICAGO (2002) (Indian)
201 N. University Dr., Coral Springs, FL 33071.
Tel: 954-227-6985; Cell: 908-235-8449;
Fax: 954-227-6985; Email: jthachara@gmail.com; Web: syromalabarflorida.org. Rev. John Thomas Thachara
Legal Name: Our Lady of Health Syro-Malabar Catholic Church (Coral Springs)
Catechesis Religious Program—Tel: 786-382-9501; Fax: 954-434-9332. Jimmy Emanuel, D.R.E. Students 302.

FORT LAUDERDALE, BROWARD CO., ST. JUDE SYRO MALABAR KNANAYA CATHOLIC PARISH (2007)
Mailing Address: 1105 N.W. 6th Ave., Fort Lauderdale, FL 33311. Tel: 954-530-3335; Cell: 708-953-1912; Email: stjudemiamikna@hotmail.com (Parish email); Email: jsauriamakel@gmail.com (Pastor's email); Web: miamikna.com. Rev. Joseph Sauriamakkel
Legal Name: St. Jude Syro-Malabar Knanaya Catholic Parish of South Florida
Catechesis Religious Program—Students 45.

JACKSONVILLE, DUVAL CO., ST. MARY'S SYRO-MALABAR CATHOLIC MISSION, JACKSONVILLE, FL, INC. OF ST. THOMAS SYRO-MALABAR CATHOLIC DIOCESE OF CHICAGO (2015)
2575 Riverside Ave., #1, Jacksonville, FL 32204.
Tel: 904-521-1019; Fax: 904-308-2856; Email: stmarysjax@gmail.com; Web: stmaryssyromalabarjax.org. Rev. Augustine Jacob, Dir., Mission. Services held at St. Ephrem Syriac Catholic Church, 4650 Kernan Blvd. S., Jacksonville, FL 32224.
Catechesis Religious Program—14501 Woodfield Cir. N., Jacksonville, FL 32258. Tel: 904-480-9664; Email: reena7uk1@rediffmail.com. Reena Thomas, D.R.E. Students 24.

MIAMI, BROWARD CO., ST. GEORGE SYRO-MALABAR CATHOLIC MISSION, MIAMI FL
217 N.W. 95th Ter., Coral Springs, FL 33071. Cell: 630-202-2989; Fax: 954-227-6985; Email: jthachara@gmail.com. Rev. Thomas Kadukapillil, Dir.

ORLANDO, ORANGE, CO., ST. MARY'S SYRO-MALABAR CATHOLIC CHURCH (ORLANDO) (2008)
Cell: 916-844-5483; Email: syromalabarchorlando@gmail.com. Rev. Sibi Kurian, V.C.
2581 S. Sanford Ave., Sanford, FL 32773.
Tel: 321-283-2098; Email: syromalabarchorlando@gmail.com; Web: www.stmarysmcc.com.
Catechesis Religious Program—Tel: 407-463-9492; Email: benoymj@yahoo.com. Rev. Benoy Joseph, D.R.E. Students 118.

TAMPA, HILLSBOROUGH CO., ST. JOSEPH SYRO-MALABAR CATHOLIC CHURCH (TAMPA) (2008) Rev. Raphael Ambadan Ouseph.
Church & Mailing Address: 5501 Williams Rd., Seffner, FL 33584. Tel: 813-621-0570 (Office); Email: vicar@stjosephsmcc.com; Email: ambadan9@yahoo.com; Web: www.stjosephsmcc.org.
Catechesis Religious Program—Email: skarijirakattu@yahoo.com. Sr. Christy Kanjirakkattu, D.R.E. Students 173.

STATE OF GEORGIA

ATLANTA, HOLY FAMILY (2009)
3885 Rosebud Rd., Loganville, GA 30052. Rev. Boby Vattampurath
Legal Name: Holy Family Syro-Malabar Knanaya Catholic Church (Atlanta)
Catechesis Religious Program—Tel: 706-207-9043; Email: sabu@bellsouth.net. Ancy Chemmalakuzhy, D.R.E. Students 63.

LOGANVILLE, GWINNETT CO., ST. ALPHONSA SYRO-MALABAR CATHOLIC CHURCH, ATLANTA (2001) (Indian)
Mailing Address: 4561 Rosebud Rd., Loganville, GA 30052. Tel: 404-921-1267 (Office); Cell: 847-217-8613; Email: stalphonsa2012@gmail.com; Web: www.stalphonsacatholicchurch.org. Rev. Mathew Elayadathamadam Varkey, M.S.F.S.
Catechesis Religious Program—Tel: 770-935-0651; Email: nangiyalil@gmail.com. Mr. Francis Nangiyalil, D.R.E. Students 246.

STATE OF KENTUCKY

LOUISVILLE, JEFFERSON CO., DIVINE MERCY SYRO-MALABAR CATHOLIC MISSION (2006)
Mailing Address: 3926 Poplar Level Rd., Louisville, KY 40213. Cell: 502-322-4282; Email: syromalabarlouisville@gmail.com; Web: www.syromalabarlouisville.org. Rev. George Munjanattu, O.F.M.Conv. Services held at: Holy Family Catholic Church, Louisville, KY.
Legal Name: Divine Mercy Syro-Malabar Catholic Mission Louisville, Kentucky.

STATE OF MARYLAND

BALTIMORE, BALTIMORE CO., ST. ALPHONSA SYRO-MALABAR CATHOLIC CHURCH (2004) (Asian—Indian)
Mailing Address: 5709 Oakland Rd., Baltimore, MD 21227. Tel: 410-247-0240; Cell: 832-614-6654;
Fax: 410-247-0240; Email: info@stalphonsachurch.org; Web: www.stalphonsachurch.org. Rev. Wilson Antony
Legal Name: St. Alphonsa Syro-Malabar Catholic Church Baltimore
Catechesis Religious Program—Students 100.

STATE OF MASSACHUSETTS

BOSTON, SUFFOLK CO., ST. THOMAS THE APOSTLE SYRO-MALABAR CATHOLIC CHURCH (2011)
41 Brook St., Framingham, MA 01701.
Tel: 508-532-8620; Cell: 334-427-5921;
Fax: 508-969-2849; Email: syromalabarchurchboston@gmail.com; Email: tonyalusa@yahoo.com; Web: www.malayamchurchboston.com. Rev. Antony Pullukattu Xavier
Legal Name: St. Thomas the Apostle Syro-Malabar Catholic Church (Boston)
Catechesis Religious Program—Students 109.

STATE OF MICHIGAN

BERKLEY, OAKLAND CO., ST. MARY'S (2010)
Church & Mailing Address: 3238 Royal Ave., Berkley, MI 48072. Tel: 630-400-7162; Cell: 619-307-3390; Email: detroitknanayamission@gmail.com. Rev. Joseph Jemy Puthuseril
Legal Name: St. Mary's Syro-Malabar Knanaya Catholic Church of Detroit
Catechesis Religious Program—Biju Thekkilakattil, D.R.E., Tel: 248-497-1966. Students 45.

SOUTHFIELD, OAKLAND CO., ST. THOMAS SYRO-MALABAR CATHOLIC CHURCH, DETROIT (1995) [JC] (Indian)
Church & Mailing Address: 17235 Mt. Vernon St., Southfield, MI 48075. Tel: 248-552-6620; Cell: 630-822-1905; Fax: 248-552-6620; Email: secretary.stmcc@gmail.com; Web: new.syromalabardetroit.org. Rev. Nicholas Thalakkottur, S.D.B.
Catechesis Religious Program—Students 149.

STATE OF MINNESOTA

ST. PAUL, RAMSEY CO.
1—ST. ALPHONSA (1999) (Indian)
Mailing Address: 261 8th St. E., St. Paul, MN 55101.
Tel: 612-388-4649; Email: syromalabarmn@yahoo.com; Email: antonyts@live.in; Web: www.stalphonsamn.org. Rev. Antony Skaria, C.F.I.C., Dir. Services held at: St. Richard Church, Richfield, MN.
Legal Name: St. Alphonsa Syro-Malabar Catholic Church Minnesota
Catechesis Religious Program—17931 Minnetonka Blvd., Deepheaven, MN 55391. Tel: 952-473-4771; Email: srsanctaezhani@gmail.com. Sr. Sancta Ezhani, D.R.E. Students 24.
2—KNANAYA SYRO-MALABAR CATHOLIC MISSION OF MINNESOTA aka St. Paul Knanaya Catholic Mission of Minnesota (2009)
261 8th St. E., St. Paul, MN 55101.
Tel: 773-412-6254; Fax: 773-286-8579; Email: muthalath2000@gmail.com; Web: www.knanayaregion.us/minnesota.html. Mailing Address: Our Lady of Victory, 5212 W. Agatite Ave., Chicago, 60630. Rev. Abraham Mutholathu Jacob.

STATE OF NEVADA

LAS VEGAS, CLARK CO.
1—ST. MOTHER TERESA SYRO-MALABAR CATHOLIC

CHURCH (2006)
Mailing Address: 240 S. Cholla St., Henderson, NV 89015. Cell: 708-400-3565; Email: fralexcssr@gmail.com; Web: motherteresalv.org. Rev. Alex Viruthakulangara, C.S.S.R.
Catechesis Religious Program—Blessy Paul, D.R.E. Students 52.

2—ST. STEPHEN'S SYRO MALABAR KNANAYA CATHOLIC MISSION (2009)
2461 E. Flamingo Rd., Las Vegas, NV 89121. Cell: 210-630-2295; Email: skmudakodil@gmail.com. Mailing Address: 504 N. Roxbury Dr., Beverly Hills, CA 90210. Rev. Siju Kuriakose Mudakodil, Dir., Email: skmudakodil@gmail.com. Services held at: St. Viator Catholic Church, Las Vegas, NV.
Legal Name: St. Stephen's Syro-Malabar Knanaya Catholic Mission, Las Vegas.

STATE OF NEW JERSEY

FRANKLIN, SOMERSET CO., ST. THOMAS SYRO-MALABAR CATHOLIC CHURCH (2006) (Indian)
Mailing Address: 510 Elizabeth Ave., Somerset, NJ 08873. Tel: 848-216-3363; Tel: 732-873-1620; Email: trustee@stthomassyronj.org; Email: kattiakaran@yahoo.com; Web: www.stthomassyronj.org. Rev. Ligory Johnson Philips
Legal Name: St. Thomas Syro-Malabar Catholic Church Inc. (East Millstone)
Church: 508 Elizabeth Ave., Somerset, NJ 08873.
Catechesis Religious Program—Tel: 732-570-9024; Email: rennypolo@yahoo.com. Renny Polo Murickar, D.R.E. Students 316.

HAMMONTON, ATLANTIC CO., ST. JUDE SYRO-MALABAR CATHOLIC CHURCH, SOUTH JERSEY OF ST. THOMAS SYRO-MALABAR CATHOLIC DIOCESE OF CHICAGO, INC. (2011)
Church & Mailing Address: 250 S. Rte. 73, Hammonton, NJ 08037. Cell: 630-880-7051; Email: stephenmcbs@gmail.com. Rev. Stephen Kanippallil.
Catechesis Religious Program—Tel: 856-366-8392; Email: josemonabraham@comcast.net. Josemon Abraham, D.R.E. Students 51.

ISELIN, MIDDLESEX CO., CHRIST THE KING SYRO MALABAR KNANAYA CATHOLIC MISSION NEW JERSEY, NJ (1998)
Mailing Address: 1900 Meadowbrook Rd., Feasterville, PA 19053. Tel: 847-312-7555;
Fax: 914-737-6882; Email: lumonlukose@gmail.com. 67 Fitch St., Carteret, NJ 07008. Rev. Renny Abraham, (India) Dir.
Legal Name: Christ the King Syro-Malabar Knanaya Catholic Mission New Jersey-N.J.

PATERSON, PASSAIC CO., ST. GEORGE SYRO-MALABAR CATHOLIC CHURCH (2004) (Indian)
Mailing Address: 408 Getty Ave., Paterson, NJ 07503. Tel: 973-345-8010; Cell: 630-828-4003; Email: sffmccpaterson@gmail.com; Web: voiceofparish.com/sgsmccnj.html. Thomas Mangattu Mathai, V.C.
St. George Syro Malabar Catholic Church
Catechesis Religious Program—Students 217.

STATE OF NEW YORK

BRONX, WESTCHESTER CO., ST. THOMAS SYRO-MALABAR CATHOLIC CHURCH (BRONX) (2002) [CEM] [JC] (Asian—Indian)
Mailing Address: 810 E. 221 St., Bronx, NY 10467. Tel: 718-944-4747; Fax: 347-920-4296; Email: stsmcc@optonline.net; Web: www.stsmcc.org. Rev. Jos Kandathikudy.
Catechesis Religious Program—Tel: 914-574-1054; Email: george.kokkatt@gmail.com. George Kokkat, D.R.E. Students 170.

FLORAL PARK, NASSAU CO., SYRO-MALABAR KNANAYA CATHOLIC MISSION INC., BROOKLYN-QUEENS-LONG ISLAND, NY (1993) [JC] (Asian—Indian)
Mailing Address: 384 Clinton St., Hempstead, NY 11550. Cell: 847-322-9503; Email: josetharackal@yahoo.com; Web: ststephensknanayaforanechurchnewyork.corg. Rev. Joseph Tharackal
Legal Name: Brooklyn Queens Long Island Knanaya Catholic Mission Inc. (St. Stephen's Knanaya Catholic Forane Church)
Catechesis Religious Program—Tel: 917-853-4759; Email: joseph3112@yahoo.com. Lissy Vattakalam, D.R.E. Students 107.

HAVERSTRAW, ROCKLAND CO., ST. MARY'S KNANAYA CATHOLIC CHURCH (1994) [JC] (Indian)
46 Conklin Ave, Haverstraw, NY 10927.
Tel: 845-786-2610; Cell: 914-673-6956; Email: st.mary's.kccr@gmail.com; Email: joseadoppillil@gmail.com. Rev. Joseph Mathew Adoppillil
Legal Name: St. Mary's Syro-Malabar Knanaya Catholic Church, Rockland, NY
Catechesis Religious Program—Students 73.

MONSEY, ROCKLAND CO., ST. MARY'S SYRO-MALABAR CATHOLIC MISSION, ROCKLAND (2001) (Indian)
Mailing Address: 5 Willow Tree Rd., Wesley Hills, NY 10952. Tel: 845-490-9307; Email: thadeusa@gmail.com; Web: syromalabarrockland.org. Rev. Thadeus J. Aravindathu, Dir. Services held at: St. Boniface Catholic Church, Wesley Hills, NY.
Legal Name: St. Thomas Syro-Malabar Catholic Diocese of Chicago in Rockland, New York, Inc.
Catechesis Religious Program—Tel: 845-267-0353; Email: jameskanacherril@gmail.com. James Kanacherril, D.R.E.

STATEN ISLAND, RICHMOND CO., BLESSED KUNJACHAN (2002) (Indian)
463 Tompkins Ave, Staten Island, NY 10305.
Tel: 718-207-5445; Email: smcmission@gmail.com; Web: www.facebook.com/smcmission. Mailing Address: 981 Castleton Ave., P. O. Box 140171, Staten Island, NY 10314. Rev. Soju Thekkineth, Dir. Services held at: St. Joseph Catholic Church, Staten Island, NY.
Legal Name: Blessed Kunjachan Syro-Malabar Catholic Mission, Staten Island, NY
Catechesis Religious Program—Students 16.

WEST HEMPSTEAD, NASSAU CO., ST. MARY SYRO MALABAR, OLD BETHPAGE, NEW YORK (2004)
Church & Mailing Address: 926 Round Swamp Rd., Old Bethpage, NY 11804. Cell: 215-808-4052; Email: trustees@stmaryssyromalabar.org; Email: johnmelepuram@gmail.com; Web: www.stmaryssyromalabar.org. Rev. John P. Melepuram
Legal Name: St. Mary Syro-Malabar Catholic Church (Old Bethpage, NY)
Catechesis Religious Program—Tel: 516-491-8765; Email: bettymeenattoor@yahoo.com. Betty Meenattoor, D.R.E. Students 265.

WESTCHESTER, WESTCHESTER CO., ST. JOSEPH SYRO-MALABAR KNANAYA CATHOLIC MISSION (1994) [JC] (Indian)
Mailing Address: 670 Yonkers Ave., Yonkers, NY 10704. Cell: 914-673-6956; Cell: 914-673-6956; Email: joseadoppillil@gmail.com. Rev. Joseph Mathew Adoppillil, Dir.
Legal Name: St. Joseph's Syro-Malabar Knanaya Catholic Mission of Westchester, NY
Catechesis Religious Program—

YONKERS, WESTCHESTER CO.

1—ST. JOSEPH SYRO-MALABAR CATHOLIC MISSION HUDSON VALLEY, NEW YORK OF ST. THOMAS SYRO-MALABAR CATHOLIC DIOCESE OF CHICAGO
3094 Albany Post Rd., Buchanan, NY 10703. Cell: 917-345-2610; Email: rmenolickal@gmail.com; Web: www.stjosephsyrohvny.org. 608 Insham St., New York, NY 10034. Rev. Royson Menolickal Antony, O.F.M.Cap., Dir.
Catechesis Religious Program—Tel: 914-645-4134; Email: bvandanath@gmail.com. Bobby John, D.R.E. Students 63.

2—ST. THOMAS SYRO-MALABAR CATHOLIC MISSION WESTCHESTER, NEW YORK OF ST. THOMAS SYRO-MALABAR CATHOLIC DIOCESE OF CHICAGO
608 Insham St., New York, NY 10034. Cell: 917-345-2610; Email: rmenolickal@gmail.com. Rev. Royson Menolickal Antony, O.F.M.Cap., Dir.

STATE OF NORTH CAROLINA

APEX, WAKE CO., LOURDES MATHA SYRO-MALABAR CATHOLIC CHURCH (2011)
Church: 1400 Vision Dr., Apex, NC 27523.
Tel: 919-439-0305; Cell: 919-600-9412; Email: vicar@lourdesmatha.org; Email: trustees@lourdesmatha.org; Web: www.lourdesmatha.org. Mailing Address: 103 Holmhurst Ct, Cary, NC 27519. Rev. Kuriakose Chacko Vadana, M.S.T.
Lourdes Matha Syro-Malabar Catholic Church, Raleigh/Durham, North Carolina of St. Thomas Malabar Catholic Diocese of Chicago
Catechesis Religious Program—Email: catechism@lourdesmatha.org. Thomas Pulickal, D.R.E. Students 147.

CHARLOTTE, MECKLENBURG, ST. MARY'S SYRO-MALABAR CATHOLIC CHURCH CHARLOTTE, NORTH CAROLINA, INC. OF ST. THOMAS SYRO-MALABAR CATHOLIC DIOCESE OF CHICAGO 2015
715 E. Arrowood Rd., Charlotte, NC 28217.
Tel: 630-279-1386; Email: smsmcc.clt@gmail.com. Rev. George Danavelil.
Catechesis Religious Program—Students 51.

STATE OF OHIO

CINCINNATI, HAMILTON CO., ST. CHAVARA SYRO MALABAR CATHOLIC CHURCH (2009)
Mailing Address: St. Bernard's Church, 401 Berry St., Dayton, KY 41074-1139. Tel: 224-343-1518; Email: jibythek7@gmail.com; Web: www.stchavaracincinnati.org. 17 Farragut Rd., Greenhills, OH 45218. Rev. Jiby Antony Thekkenuriyil, M.S.T., Dir. Services are held at Our Lady of the Rosary Catholic Church, Greenhills.
Legal Name: St. Chavara Syro-Malabar Catholic Church - Cincinnati
Catechesis Religious Program—Our Lady of the Rosary Church, 17 Farragut Rd., Greenhills, OH 45218-1499. Shijo Philip, D.R.E. Students 22.
Worship Site: St. Chavara Syro-Malabar Catholic Mission.

CLEVELAND, CUYAHOGA CO., ST. RAPHEL SYRO-MALABAR MISSION CLEVELAND, OH (2009)
Mailing Address: 2323 W. Bancroft St., Toledo, OH 43607. Tel: 419-531-1619; Cell: 419-450-8760; Email: syromalabarcleveland@gmail.com; Email: karekattraphy@yahoo.in; Web: syromalabarccc.org. 126th St., Cleveland, OH 44120. Rev. Raphael Karekatt, M.S.F.S., (India). Services held at: Our Lady of Peace, 126th St., Shaker Blvd.-12503 Buckingham Ave., Cleveland, OH 44120.
Catechesis Religious Program—

COLUMBUS, DELAWARE CO., ST. MARY SYRO-MALABAR CATHOLIC MISSION COLUMBUS, OH (2004)
893 Hamlet St., Columbus, OH 43201.
Tel: 502-718-7109; Email: smchurchinfo@gmail.com; Email: frkanat@gmail.com; Web: www.columbuschurch.org. US 127 N. Highway, Albany, CT 42602. Rev. Johnykutty George, Dir. Services held at: Sacred Heart Church, Columbus, OH.
Catechesis Religious Program—Greena Benny, D.R.E. Students 30.

STATE OF OKLAHOMA

OKLAHOMA CITY, OKLAHOMA CO., HOLY FAMILY SYRO-MALABAR CATHOLIC CHURCH OKLAHOMA (2005)
Mailing Address: 7501 Northwest Expwy., P.O. Box 32180, Oklahoma City, OK 73123. 3916 S. Highland Park Ave., Oklahoma City, OK 73129.
Tel: 405-677-7976; Cell: 918-829-5115; Email: paulkodakarakaran@hotmail.com. Rev. Paul Kodakarakaran, (India).
Catechesis Religious Program—Tel: 405-474-4647; Email: paulkodakarakaran@hotmail.com. Molly Sunny, D.R.E. Students 39.

STATE OF PENNSYLVANIA

HUNTINGTON VALLEY, MONTGOMERY CO., ST. JOHN NEUMANN (1999) (Indian) Malayalam
Mailing Address: 1900 Meadow Brook Rd., Feasterville, PA 19053. Tel: 215-357-1221;
Fax: 215-938-9071; Email: rennykattel@yahoo.com. Rev. Renny Abraham, (India) Dir. Services held at: St. Albert the Great Catholic Church, 212 Welsh Rd., Huntingdon Valley, PA 19006.
Legal Name: St. John Neumann Syro-Malabar Knanaya Catholic Mission of Greater Philadelphia
Catechesis Religious Program—Students 16.

PHILADELPHIA, PHILADELPHIA CO., ST. THOMAS SYRO MALABAR CATHOLIC CHURCH (2005) (Asian—Indian)
608 Welsh Rd., Philadelphia, PA 19115. Rev. Vinod Madathiparambil George
Legal Name: St. Thomas Syro-Malabar Catholic Church (Philadelphia)
Catechesis Religious Program—Tel: 267-312-2634; Email: jakester174@gmail.com. Jacob Chacko, D.R.E. Students 240.

PITTSBURGH, ALLEGHENY CO., ST. MARY SYRO MALABAR CATHOLIC MISSION (2006)
1607 Greentree Rd., Pittsburgh, PA 15220. Cell: 304-780-2110; Email: jstephan@dwc.og; Email: syromalabarpittsburgh@gmail.com (Office); Web: www.syromalabarpittsburgh.org. 418 4th St., Chester, VA 26034. Rev. Shibi Kattikulakattu, M.C.B.S., Dir.
Legal Name: St. Mary Syro-Malabar Catholic Mission Pittsburgh, PA.

STATE OF TENNESSEE

NASHVILLE, DAVIDSON CO., ST. TERESA OF CALCUTTA (2008)
1227 Seventh Ave., Nashville, TN 37208.
Tel: 615-865-1071 (Office); Cell: 916-803-5307; Email: tjpuly@gmail.com; Web: www.syromalabarnashville.com. Mailing Address: 372 S. Prairie, Elmhurst, 60126. Rev. Tomy Joseph Puliyanampattayil, M.S.F.S. Services held at: Assumption Catholic Church, Nashville, TN 37208.
Legal Name: St. Teresa of Calcutta Syro-Malabar Mission, Nashville, TN
Catechesis Religious Program—Students 45.

STATE OF TEXAS

COPPELL, DALLAS CO., ST. ALPHONS SYRO MALABAR CATHOLIC CHURCH (COPPELL) (2010) Rev. Jacob Christy Parambukattil.
Church: 200 S. Heartz Rd., P.O. Box 1862, Coppell, TX 75019. Tel: 972-782-4197; Cell: 281-904-6622; Cell: 214-412-9736; Email: stalfonsa1@gmail.com; Web: www.saintalphonsachurch.org.
Catechesis Religious Program—Students 430.

EDINBURG, HIDALGO CO., DIVINE MERCY SYRO-MALABAR CATHOLIC CHURCH (2007)
Mailing Address: 300 W. Cano St., Edinburg, TX 78539. Tel: 956-380-1363; Cell: 630-317-4837;
Fax: 956-380-1363; Email: divinemercymalabar@gmail.com; Email: sebyjchittilappilly@gmail.com; Web: www.divinemalabarparish.com. 321 West Mahl St., Edinburg, TX 78539. Rev. Seby Chittilappilly Jacob
Legal Name: Divine Mercy Syro-Malabar Catholic Church (Edinburg), Texas
Catechesis Religious Program—Students 88.

FARMERS BRANCH, DALLAS CO., CHRIST THE KING SYRO MALABAR KNANAYA CATHOLIC CHURCH (2009)

13416 Onyx Ln., Farmers Branch, TX 75234. Rev. Joseph Chirappurathu
Legal Name: Christ the King Syro-Malabar Knanaya Catholic Church DFW
Church: 13565 Webb Chapel Rd., Farmers Branch, TX 75234.
Catechesis Religious Program—Joseph Elakodikal, D.R.E. Students 125.

GARLAND, DALLAS CO., ST. THOMAS THE APOSTLE CATHOLIC CHURCH (1992) (Indian)
4922 Rosehill Rd., Garland, TX 75043.
Tel: 972-240-1100; Email: gelambasseril@gmail.com; Email: vicar@syromalabarchurchdallas.org; Email: trustee@syromalabarchurchdallas.org; Email: secretary@syromalabarchurchdallas.org; Web: www.syromalabarchurchdallas.org. Mailing Address: 1118 Dandelion Dr., Garland, TX 75043. Rev. George Elambasseril
Legal Name: St. Thomas the Apostle Syro-Malabar Forane Catholic Church, Dallas
Catechesis Religious Program—Silvy Chamaparampil, D.R.E. Students 302.

HOUSTON, HARRIS CO., ST. MARY'S SYRO MALABAR KNANAYA CATHOLIC CHURCH (2011) [JC] (Indian)
Tel: 281-957-5264; Tel: 708-953-1912; Email: stmaryshouston@outlook.com; Email: hkcmission@gmail.com. Rev. Suni Thomas Padinjarekkara
Legal Name: St. Mary's Syro-Malabar Knanaya Catholic Church of Houston
Church: 6400 W. Fuqua Dr., Missouri City, TX 77489-2826.
Catechesis Religious Program—Students 476.

MANOR, TRAVIS CO., ST. ALPHONSA SYRO-MALABAR CATHOLIC CHURCH, AUSTIN, TEXAS, INC. OF ST. THOMAS SYRO-MALABAR CATHOLIC DIOCESE OF CHICAGO (2008)
8701 Burleson Manor Rd., Manor, TX 78653.
Tel: 732-357-7757; Tel: 512-272-4005; Email: mcaustin@googlegroups.com (Office); Email: perunilamd@gmail.com; Web: stalphonsaaustin.com. P.O. Box 307, Manor, TX 78653. Rev. Tommy Sebastian Perunilam
Legal Name: St. Alphonsa Syro-Malabar Catholic Church Austin, TX
Catechesis Religious Program—Students 110.

MISSOURI CITY, FORT BEND, CO., ST. JOSEPH SYRO-MALABAR CATHOLIC CHURCH (2001)
211 Present St., Missouri City, TX 77489.
Tel: 281-969-7236; Cell: 510-688-7805; Cell: 813-318-2186; Email: frneduveli@gmail.com; Email: rvphilip5@gmail.com; Web: www.stjosephhouston.org. Revs. Rajeev Philip Valiyaveettil; Kurian N. Varghese.
Catechesis Religious Program—Tel: 832-980-7730; Email: CCEPrincipal@stjosephcce.org. John Palackamattam, D.R.E. Students 678.

PEARLAND, BRAZORIA CO., ST. MARY'S SYRO-MALABAR CATHOLIC CHURCH 2016
1610 O'Day Rd., Pearland, TX 77581.
Tel: 281-412-4322; Cell: 267-616-2951; Email: vicar@stmaryspearland.org; Web: www.stmaryspearland.org. Rev. Ruban Thannickal.

SAN ANTONIO, BEXAR CO.
1—ST. THOMAS SYRO-MALABAR CATHOLIC CHURCH (2006)
8333 Braun Rd., San Antonio, TX 78254. Web: syromalabarsa.org. Mailing Address: 15519 Luna Ridge, Helotes, TX 78023. Tel: 210-372-0189; Email: frgeorgecgeorge@gmail.com. Rev. George C. George
Legal Name: St. Thomas Syro-Malabar Catholic Church of San Antonio
Catechesis Religious Program—Sr. Beena Mathew, D.R.E. Students 35.
2—ST. ANTHONY SYRO-MALABAR KNANAYA CATHOLIC CHURCH (2010)
Mailing Address: 9347 Oakland Rd., San Antonio, TX 78240. Tel: 210-843-5372; Email: stanthonyprayforus@gmail.com; Web: www.sakcpwebs.com. Rev. Benoy Kuriakose Naramangalath
Legal Name: St. Anthony Syro-Malabar Knanaya Catholic Church (San Antonio)
Catechesis Religious Program—Students 36.

STATE OF VIRGINIA

CENTREVILLE, FAIRFAX CO., ST. JUDE (2011) Services at: St. Andrews Catholic Church, Clifton, VA.
6720 Union Mill Rd., Clifton, VA 20124. Cell: 703-634-8575; Email: stjudesyromalabarnva@gmail.com; Email: jusput13@gmail.com; Web: stjudenva.org. Rev. Justin Ouseph Puthussery
Legal Name: St. Jude Syro-Malabar Catholic Church, Northern Virginia of St. Thomas Syro-Malabar Catholic Diocese
Catechesis Religious Program—Students 149.

RICHMOND, HENRICO CO., ST. ALPHONSA SYRO-MALABAR CATHOLIC CHURCH, RICHMOND, VA OF ST. THOMAS SYRO-MALABAR CATHOLIC DIOCESE OF CHICAGO (2010)
Mailing Address: 300 N. Sheppard St., Richmond, VA 23221. Tel: 630-828-4000; Email: st.alphonsarichmondva@gmail.com. 12829 River Rd., Richmond, VA 23238-7206. Rev. Sunil Paul Chiriyankandath, SYM. Services held at: St. Benedict Catholic Church, 300 N. Sheppard St., Richmond, VA 23221.
Legal Name: St. Alphonsa Syro-Malabar Catholic Church of Richmond, VA
Catechesis Religious Program—Students 30.

STATE OF WISCONSIN

WEST ALLIS, MILWAUKEE CO., ST. ANTONY SYRO MALABAR CATHOLIC MISSION
9525 W. Bluemountain Rd., Milwaukee, WI 53226.
Tel: 414-326-0408; Email: josemcbs21@gmail.com; Web: www.malayalammass.com. 3320 S. Colony Ave., Union Grove, WI 53182. Rev. Jose Edapparakal, M.C.B.S. Services held at: St. Therese Catholic Church, Milwaukee, WI.
Legal Name: St. Antony Syro-Malabar Catholic Mission (Wisconsin)
Catechesis Religious Program—Sr. Lisa Anjalikkal, S.S.S.F., D.R.E. Students 13.

DISTRICT OF COLUMBIA

DISTRICT OF COLUMBIA, OUR LADY OF PERPETUAL HELP (1980)
St. Peter's Catholic Church, 2900 Olney Sandy Spring Rd., Olney, MD 20832. Tel: 301-924-3774; Cell: 630-880-8520; Email: roymoolechalil@gmail.com; Web: syromalabargw.org. Rev. Roy Varkey Moolachalil. Services held at: Mother of God Community, Gaithersburg, MD.
Legal Name: Our Lady of Perpetual Help Syro-Malabar Catholic Parish of Greater Washington Inc. of St. Thomas Syro Malabar Diocese of Chicago
Catechesis Religious Program—Tel: 305-778-0045; Email: bissac@gmail.com. Biju Issac, SYM, D.R.E. Students 51.

INSTITUTIONS LOCATED IN THE DIOCESE

[A] CONVENTS AND RESIDENCES FOR SISTERS

BERWYN. *Daughters of St. Thomas Congregation* (1969) 2319 Clarence Ave., Berwyn, 60402.
Tel: 708-898-8622; Email: dsttexas2010@gmail.com; Web: dstsisters.org. Sr. Nirmala Joseph, D.S.T., Mother Supr. Sisters 4.

MARGATE. *Sisters of The Adoration Corporation*, St. Thomas Adoration Convent, 3172 N.W. 72nd Ave., Margate, FL 33063. Tel: 954-323-8373; Email: jollymariak@gmail.com. Sr. Jolly Maria, S.A.B.S., Mother Supr. Sisters 4.

MORTON GROVE. *Visitation Convent*, Mailing Address: 7801 W. Maple St., Morton Grove, 60053.
Tel: 847-324-9480; Fax: 224-432-3217; Email: svminchicago@yahoo.com. Sr. Rajamma Thomas, Supr. Sisters 3.

OAK LAWN. *Congregation of the Mother of Carmel*, 9310 S. 55th Ct., Oak Lawn, 60453. Cell: 708-949-2786; Tel: 708-422-0280; Email: cmcusa16@gmail.com. Sr. Jyothi Maria, C.M.C., Regl. Supr.

SAN ANTONIO. *Missionary Sisters of Mary Immaculate*, 8735 Sarasota Woods, San Antonio, TX 78250.
Tel: 210-647-2947; Email: msmi2usa@yahoo.com. Sr. Beena Mathew, Local Supr. Sisters 2.

STAFFORD. *Missionary Sisters of Mary Immaculate*, 630 Easy Jet Dr., Stafford, TX 77477.
Tel: 281-499-0030; Email: msmisisters@hotmail.com. Sr. Emiline Tharappel, M.S.M.I., Supr. Sisters 3.

[B] MISCELLANEOUS

BENSENVILLE. *Vincentian House - St. Joseph Province*, 1027 Twin Oaks St., Bensenville, 60106.
Tel: 630-422-5236; Fax: 630-422-5326; Email: vcsjprovince@gmail.com. Revs. Joseph J. Arackal, V.C., Procurator; Johnus S. Cherunilath, V.C.

GLENVIEW. *Missionary Society of St. Thomas the Apostle, M.S.T.*, 2909 Central Rd., Glenview, 60025-4047. Tel: 847-904-2306; Cell: 630-670-6899; Email: mstinusa2005@gmail.com; Email: shajit91@gmail.com. Rev. Antony Thundathil, Dir.

PLANT CITY. *Vincentian House, Divine Mercy Prayer House*, 2905 S. Frontage Rd., Plant City, FL 33566.
Tel: 813-567-1226; Email: divinefl12@gmail.com; Web: www.divinefl.org. Rev. Antony Thekkanath, V.C., Dir.

WASHINGTON. *Vincentian House & Divine Prayer Center*, 426 Rte. 57 W., Washington, NJ 07882.
Tel: 908-835-9989; Email: dmhcnj@gmail.com. Revs. Johny Manickathan, V.C., Supr., Vincentian House; Thomas Sunil Aenekatt, V.C., Dir., Divine Prayer Center.

RELIGIOUS INSTITUTES OF MEN REPRESENTED IN THE ARCHDIOCESE

For further details refer to the corresponding bracketed number in the Religious Institutes of Men or Women section.

[]—*Missionary Society of St. Thomas the Apostle* (Glenview, IL)—M.S.T.

[]—*Vincentian Congregation* Marymatha Prov. & Bensenville, IL—V.C.

RELIGIOUS INSTITUTES OF WOMEN REPRESENTED IN THE ARCHDIOCESE

[]—*Congregation of Mother of Carmel* (Schererville, IN).

[]—*Daughters of St. Thomas Congregation* (Berwyn, IL).

[]—*Missionary Sisters of Mary Immaculate* (Stafford, TX).

[]—*Sisters of Adoration of Blessed Sacrament* (Margate, FL).

An asterisk (*) denotes an organization that has established tax-exempt status directly with the IRS and is not covered by the USCCB Group Ruling.

Ukrainian Catholic Diocese of Stamford

Most Reverend

PAUL PATRICK CHOMNYCKY, O.S.B.M.

Bishop of Stamford; ordained October 1, 1988; appointed Apostolic Exarch of Great Britain, Faithful of Eastern Rite & Titular Bishop of Buffada April 5, 2002; ordained June 11, 2002; appointed Bishop of Stamford for Ukrainians January 3, 2006; installed February 20, 2006. *Office: 161 Glenbrook Rd., Stamford, CT 06902-3019.*

Most Reverend

BASIL H. LOSTEN, D.D., S.T.L., LL.D. (HON.)

Retired Bishop of Stamford; ordained June 10, 1957; appointed Titular Bishop of Arcadiopolis and Auxiliary of Ukrainian Catholic Archeparchy of Philadelphia March 15, 1971; consecrated May 25, 1971; appointed Apostolic Administrator of Archeparchy of Philadelphia June 8, 1976; Transferred to the Stamford See September 20, 1977; retired January 3, 2006. *Res.: 122 Clovelly Rd., Stamford, CT 06902.*

ESTABLISHED AUGUST 8, 1956.

The jurisdiction of the Bishop of Stamford extends territorially throughout all of New York State and the New England States. With regard to persons, his subjects are all members of the Ukrainian Catholic Church (Byzantine Rite), irrespective of where they received Baptism.

For legal titles of parishes and diocesan institutions, consult the Chancery Office.

Chancery Office: 161 Glenbrook Rd., Stamford, CT 06902-3019. Tel: 203-324-7698; Fax: 203-357-7681.

Email: stamfordeparchy@optonline.net

STATISTICAL OVERVIEW

Personnel	
Bishop	1
Retired Bishops	1
Priests: Diocesan Active in Diocese	55
Priests: Diocesan Active Outside Diocese	4
Priests: Diocesan in Foreign Missions	1
Priests: Retired, Sick or Absent	5
Number of Diocesan Priests	65
Religious Priests in Diocese	10
Total Priests in Diocese	75
Ordinations:	
Transitional Deacons	1
Permanent Deacons in Diocese	9
Total Brothers	1
Total Sisters	38
Parishes	
Parishes	51
With Resident Pastor:	
Resident Diocesan Priests	48
Resident Religious Priests	3
Missions	3
Educational	
Seminaries, Diocesan	1
Students from This Diocese	7
Diocesan Students in Other Seminaries	1
Total Seminarians	8
High Schools, Diocesan and Parish	1
Total Students	127
Catechesis/Religious Education:	
High School Students	259
Elementary Students	946
Total Students under Catholic Instruction	1,340
Vital Statistics	
Receptions into the Church:	
Infant Baptism Totals	303
Adult Baptism Totals	11
Received into Full Communion	13
First Communions	273
Confirmations	314
Marriages:	
Catholic	53
Interfaith	20
Total Marriages	73
Deaths	261
Total Catholic Population	15,420

Former Bishops—Most Revs. AMBROSE SENYSHYN, O.S.B.M., D.D., installed as first Bishop of Stamford, Dec. 15, 1956; transferred to the Archeparchy of Philadelphia, Oct. 26, 1961; died Sept. 11, 1976; JOSEPH M. SCHMONDIUK, D.D., Bishop of Stamford, Nov. 9, 1961; transferred to the Archeparchy of Philadelphia, Sept. 20, 1977; died Dec. 25, 1978; BASIL H. LOSTEN, D.D., S.T.L., LL.D. (Hon.), ord. June 10, 1957; appt. Titular Bishop of Arcadiopolis and Auxiliary of Ukrainian Catholic Archeparchy of Philadelphia March 15, 1971; cons. May 25, 1971; appt. Apostolic Administrator of Archeparchy of Philadelphia June 8, 1976; transferred to the Stamford See Sept. 20, 1977; retired Jan. 3, 2006.

Chancery Office—161 Glenbrook Rd., Stamford, 06902-3019. Tel: 203-324-7698; Fax: 203-357-7681; Email: stamfordeparchy@optonline.net; Web: www.stamforddio.org. Office Hours: Mon.-Fri. 9-12 & 1-5.

Vicar General—Very Rt. Rev. Mitred Archpriest IHOR MIDZAK.

Econome—Very Rev. ZBIGNIEW CANON BRZEZICKI.

Chancellor & Archivist—Very Rev. Archpriest KIRIL ANGELOV.

Vice Chancellor—Rev. TARAS CHAPARIN.

Chancery Secretary—OKSANA DRAGAN.

Notary Public—OKSANA DRAGAN.

Diocesan Consultors—Very Rt. Rev. Mitred Archpriest IHOR MIDZAK; Very Rev. ZBIGNIEW CANON BRZEZICKI; Rev. MIKHAIL MYSHCHUK; Very Rev. VARCILIO BASIL SALKOVSKI, O.S.B.M.; Very Rev. Archpriest KIRIL ANGELOV.

Diocesan Tribunal—161 Glenbrook Rd., Stamford, 06902-3019. Tel: 203-324-7698.

Judicial Vicar—Very Rev. PAUL LUNIW, J.C.L.

Judge—Rev. Msgr. MARTIN CANAVAN, J.C.L.

Defender of the Bond—Ad Hoc Appointment MRS. NATALIYA PISTUN, B.A., S.T.B., J.C.L.

Notary—Very Rev. Archpriest KIRIL ANGELOV.

Diocesan Protopresbyters (Deans)—Eastern New York: Very Rev. Archpriest IVAN KASZCZAK, Ph.D., M.A., B.A. New England: Rev. KIRIL MANOLEV. New York Metropolia: Rev. PETER SHYSHKA. Western New York: Very Rev. ROMAN SYDOROVYCH.

Presbyteral Council—Most Rev. PAUL P. CHOMNYCKY, O.S.B.M.; Very Rt. Rev. Mitred Archpriest IHOR MIDZAK; Very Rev. Archpriest KIRIL ANGELOV; Rev. IVAN MAZURYK; Very Rev. Archpriest IVAN KASZCZAK, Ph.D., M.A., B.A.; Revs. MIKHAIL MYSHCHUK; PETER SHYSHKA; Very Rev. Archpriest ROMAN MALYARCHUK; Rev. VASILE COLOPELNIC; Very Rev. PAUL LUNIW, J.C.L.

Pastoral Planning Council—Members: Most Rev. PAUL P. CHOMNYCKY, O.S.B.M.; Very Rt. Rev. Mitred Archpriest IHOR MIDZAK; Very Rev. Archpriest KIRIL ANGELOV; Very Rev. BOHDAN TYMNCHYSHYN; Very Rev. Archpriest EDWARD CANON YOUNG; Rev. PETER SHYSHKA; Sisters MICHELE YAKYMOVITCH, S.S.M.I.; NATALYA STOCZANYN, S.S.M.I.; LESYA MURASZCZUK, D.D.S.; MRS. NATALIYA PISTUN, B.A., S.T.B., J.C.L.; SOFIA SHCHUR, R.N.; ANDREW BAMBER; MRS. SONYA SOUTUS.

Diocesan Offices and Directors

All offices are located at the following address unless otherwise noted *161 Glenbrook Rd., Stamford, 06902-3019.* Tel: 203-325-2116; Fax: 203-357-7681; Email: chancellor@optonline.net.

Administrative Council—Most Rev. PAUL P. CHOMNYCKY, O.S.B.M.; Very Revs. ZBIGNIEW CANON BRZEZICKI; YAROSLAW KOSTYK; Rev. MIKHAIL MYSHCHUK; Very Rev. Archpriest KIRIL ANGELOV; Very Rt. Rev. Mitred Archpriest IHOR MIDZAK; Very Rev. Mitred PHILIP CANON WEINER.

Personnel Board—Most Rev. PAUL P. CHOMNYCKY, O.S.B.M.; Very Rt. Rev. Mitred Archpriest IHOR MIDZAK; Very Rev. MICHAEL BUNDZ; Rev. MARIAN KOSTYK; Rt. Rev. Mitred Msgr. JOHN SQUILLER, B.A., S.T.L., (Retired); Sr. MICHELLE YAKYMOVITCH, S.S.M.I.

Apostleship of Prayer—Rev. OLVIAN POPOVICI.

Catechetics—Rev. VASILE COLOPELNIC.

Cemeteries—Holy Spirit Ukrainian Catholic Cemetery, 141 Sarah Wells Trail, Campbell Hall, NY 10916. Tel: 845-496-5506. Directors: Most Rev. PAUL P. CHOMNYCKY, O.S.B.M., Pres. & Chm.; Very Rev. YAROSLAW KOSTYK, Exec. Dir.; Very Rev. Archpriest KIRIL ANGELOV; Very Rt. Rev. Mitred Archpriest IHOR MIDZAK; Very Rev. ZBIGNIEW CANON BRZEZICKI; MR. JOHN SENKO; ANDRIJ SZUL, Esq.

Censor—Very Rev. Archpriests EDWARD CANON YOUNG; IVAN KASZCZAK, Ph.D., M.A., B.A.

Communications—Rev. TARAS CHAPARYN.

Development Office—MRS. NATALIYA PISTUN, B.A., S.T.B., J.C.L.

Diaconate, Permanent—Very Rev. CYRIL MANOLEV.

Diocesan Charities and Missions—Most Rev. PAUL P. CHOMNYCKY, O.S.B.M.; MS. MARIAN KOCZANSKI.

Ecumenical Commission—Most Revs. PAUL P. CHOMNYCKY, O.S.B.M.; BASIL H. LOSTEN, D.D., S.T.L., LL.D. (Hon.); Very Rev. Archpriest KIRIL ANGELOV.

Educational Institutions—Most Rev. PAUL P. CHOMNYCKY, O.S.B.M.; Revs. JAMES MORRIS; PETER SHYSHKA, Supt. Schools.

Family Life—MRS. NATALIYA PISTUN, B.A., S.T.B., J.C.L.

Holy Name Societies—Rev. BOHDAN HEDZ.

League of Ukrainian Catholics—Very Rev. MARIJAN PROCYK, Spiritual Dir. (New York).

Liturgical Commission—Very Rev. BOHDAN TYMNCHYSHYN; Very Rev. Archpriest ROMAN MALYARCHUK.

Missionaries, Diocesan—Sr. NATALYA STOCZANYN, S.S.M.I.

Ukrainian Museum and Library of Stamford, Inc.—161 Glenbrook Rd., Stamford, 06902. Museum Library Research Center, 39 Clovelly Rd., Stamford, 06902. Tel: 203-327-7899. MS. LUBOW WOLYNETZ, B.A., M.L.S., Curator, Librarian & Archivist; MRS. ANNA BOYCHUK; Rt. Rev. Mitred Msgr. JOHN TERLECKY, B.A., M.A., M.L.S., Librarian.

Press, Diocesan: "The Sower"—Revs. TARAS CHAPARYN, Editor-in-Chief, Email: thesower@optonline.net; VASYL S. BEHAY, Ukrainian Editor.

Priests' Benevolent Association—Rev. TEODOR CZABALA.

Religious Communities, Vicar—Very Rev. BASIL SALKOVSKI, O.S.B.M.

Religious Education—Rev. VASILE COLOPELNIC.

Sodalities, B.V.M.—Rev. CYRIL ISZEZUCK, O.S.B.M.

Vocations—Very Rev. BOHDAN TYMNCHYSHYN.

Youth Apostolate—Sr. ELIANE ILNYTCKYJ, S.S.M.I.

Youth-For-Christ Association—Rev. EUGENE KHOMYN, O.S.B.M.

Office of Safe Environment—Rev. PETER SHYSHKA; Very Rev. CYRIL MANOLEV.

Director of Religious Education for Ukrainian Heritage Schools—Very Rev. Archpriest ROMAN MALYARCHUK.

Chaplain to the Ukrainian American Youth Association—Very Rt. Rev. Mitred Archpriest IHOR MIDZAK.

Chaplain to the Ukrainian Scouts Plast Organization—Very Rev. Archpriest IVAN KASZCZAK, Ph.D., M.A., B.A.

CLERGY, PARISHES, MISSIONS AND PAROCHIAL SCHOOLS

STATE OF CONNECTICUT

STAMFORD, FAIRFIELD CO., ST. VLADIMIR CATHEDRAL (1916) (Ukrainian)
24 Wenzel Ter., 06902. Tel: 203-324-0242; Email: stvladimircath@optonline.net. Very Rt. Rev. Mitred Archpriest Ihor Midzak, Rector.

ANSONIA, NEW HAVEN CO., SS. PETER AND PAUL (1897) [CEM] (Ukrainian)
105 Clifton Ave., Ansonia, 06401. Tel: 203-734-3895; Email: younge8073@aol.com. Very Rev. Archpriest Edward Canon Young.
Catechesis Religious Program—Tel: 203-734-3055. Alice O'Doy, D.R.E. Students 12.

BRIDGEPORT, FAIRFIELD CO., PROTECTION OF B.V.M. (1950) (Ukrainian)
457 Noble Ave., Bridgeport, 06608.
Tel: 203-367-5054; Email: pokrova@optimum.net; Web: www.pokrovact.com. 255 Barnum Ave., Bridgeport, 06608. Rev. Ivan Mazuryk.

COLCHESTER, NEW LONDON CO., ST. MARY DORMITION (1948) [CEM] (Ukrainian)
178 Linwood Ave., Colchester, 06415.
Tel: 860-537-2069; Email: cyril_manolev@yahoo.com. Rev. Kiril Manolev.

GLASTONBURY, HARTFORD CO., ST. JOHN THE BAPTIST (1925) (Ukrainian), Attended by St. Mary Dormition, Colchester.
26 New London Tpke., Glastonbury, 06033.
Tel: 860-537-2069; Email: cyril_manolev@yahoo.com. Rev. Kiril Manolev.
Res.: 178 Linwood Ave., Colchester, 06415.
Tel: 860-537-0011.

HARTFORD, HARTFORD CO., ST. MICHAEL (1910) [CEM] (Ukrainian)
125 Wethersfield Ave., Hartford, 06114.
Tel: 860-525-7823; Email: st_michael@comcast.net. Very Rev. Pawlo Martyniuk.
Res.: 135 Wethersfield Ave., Hartford, 06114.
School—Saturday Ukrainian School, (Grades K-8).

NEW BRITAIN, HARTFORD CO., ST. JOSAPHAT (1951) (Ukrainian) Rev. Stepan Bereza.
Res.: 303 Eddy Glover Blvd., New Britain, 06053.
Tel: 860-225-7340; Fax: 860-229-5490.
Catechesis Religious Program—Lay Teachers 2; Priests 1; Students 18.

NEW HAVEN, NEW HAVEN CO., ST. MICHAEL (1909) (Ukrainian)
569 George St., New Haven, 06511.
Tel: 203-865-0388; Email: stmichaels@snet.net. Rev. Iura Godenciuc.
School—St. Michaels Ukrainian Heritage School, (Saturdays).

TERRYVILLE, LITCHFIELD CO., ST. MICHAEL (1910) [CEM] (Ukrainian)
35 Allen St., Terryville, 06786. Tel: 860-922-8088; Email: stmichaels@comcast.net. Very Rev. Paul Luniw, J.C.L.
Catechesis Religious Program—Tel: 860-582-1850. Kristine Meinert, D.R.E.; Dan Czuchta, D.R.E. Lay Teachers 4; Priests 1; Students 11.

WILLIMANTIC, WINDHAM CO., PROTECTION OF B.V.M. (1950) (Ukrainian)
70 Oak St., Willimantic, 06226. Tel: 860-423-5031; Email: ivanbilyk7@gmail.com. Rev. Ivan Bilyk.
Res.: 69 Oak St., Willimantic, 06226.

STATE OF MASSACHUSETTS

BOSTON, SUFFOLK CO., CHRIST THE KING (1968) [CEM]
146 Forest Hills St., Jamaica Plain, MA 02130.
Tel: 617-522-9720; Email: yaroslavnalysnyk@aol.com; Web: www.christ-the-king-ucc.org. Rev. Archpriest Yaroslav Nalysnyk.
School—Saturday Ukrainian School, Religious Teachers 1; Lay Teachers 2; Priests 1; Scholastics 5; Students 25.
Catechesis Religious Program—Lay Teachers 2; Priests 1; Students 9.

FALL RIVER, BRISTOL CO., ST. JOHN-THE-BAPTIST (1914) [JC] Attended by Woonsocket, RI.
339 Center St., Fall River, MA 02724.
Tel: 401-762-2733; Email: mdosyak@gmail.com. Rev. Mykhaylo Dosyak.

LUDLOW, HAMPDEN CO., SS. PETER AND PAUL (1912) (1924) (Ukrainian)
45 Newbury St., Ludlow, MA 01056.
Tel: 413-583-2140; Email: 63krip@cua.edu. Rev. Andriy Krip.
Catechesis Religious Program—Priests 1; Students 4.

PITTSFIELD, BERKSHIRE CO., ST. JOHN THE BAPTIST (1921) (Ukrainian), Closed. For inquiries for parish records contact the chancery.

SALEM, ESSEX CO., ST. JOHN THE BAPTIST (1918) (Ukrainian)
124 Bridge St., P.O. Box 206, Salem, MA 01970-0206. Tel: 978-745-3151; Cell: 781-632-5182; Email: ukrcathsalem@comcast.net; Web: www.saintjohnsukr.com. Rev. James Morris, Admin.
Catechesis Religious Program—Tel: 617-599-8138. Students 3.

SOUTH DEERFIELD, FRANKLIN CO., HOLY GHOST (1920) (Ukrainian)
44 Sugarloaf St., South Deerfield, MA 01373.
Tel: 413-583-2140; Email: 63krip@cua.edu. Rev. Andriy Krip.
Catechesis Religious Program—Priests 1; Students 8.

STATE OF NEW HAMPSHIRE

MANCHESTER, HILLSBORO CO., PROTECTION OF B.V.M. (1908) (Ukrainian) Rev. Ihor Papka.
Church: 54 Walnut St., Manchester, NH 03104.
Tel: 603-622-0034; Fax: 603-642-8961.
Catechesis Religious Program—Lay Teachers 2; Priests 1; Students 14.

STATE OF NEW YORK

AMSTERDAM, MONTGOMERY CO., ST. NICHOLAS (1909) [CEM] (Ukrainian)
24 Pulaski St., Amsterdam, NY 12010.
Tel: 518-841-8731; Email: mkos61@hotmail.com. Rev. Marian Kostyk.

AUBURN, CAYUGA CO., SS. PETER AND PAUL (1901) (Ukrainian)
136 Washington St., Auburn, NY 13021.
Tel: 315-252-5573; Email: vasylcolopelnic@yahoo.com. Rev. Vasile Colopelnic.

BEDFORD HILLS, WESTCHESTER CO., HOLY PROTECTION OF THE MOTHER OF GOD (2000)
2 Green St., Mt. Kisco, NY 10549. Tel: 203-324-7698; Email: holyprotectionm@optonline.net; Web: www.pokrovany.com. 161 Glenbrook Rd., 06902. Rev. Taras Chaparin.
Catechesis Religious Program—Elizabeth Gardasz, D.R.E. Students 5.

BRONX, BRONX CO., ST. MARY PROTECTRESS (1943) [JC] (Ukrainian)
1745 Washington Ave., Bronx, NY 10457.
Tel: 917-499-7862; Email: petrush@verizon.net. Rev. Lawrence Lawryniuk, O.S.B.M.
Res.: E. Beach Dr., Glen Cove, NY 11542.

BROOKLYN, KINGS CO.
1—HOLY GHOST (1913) (Ukrainian)
Mailing Address: 161 N. Fifth St., Brooklyn, NY 11211. Rev. Ivan Tykhovytch.
Church: 160 N. 5th St., Brooklyn, NY 11211.
Tel: 718-782-9592; Fax: 718-599-2905.
2—ST. NICHOLAS (1916) (Ukrainian)
256 19th St., Brooklyn, NY 11215. Tel: 718-389-8744; Email: rmalyarchuk@yahoo.com. Very Rev. Archpriest Roman Malyarchuk.

BUFFALO, ERIE CO., ST. NICHOLAS (1894) (Ukrainian)
308 Fillmore Ave., Buffalo, NY 14206.
Tel: 716-852-7566; Email: stnbuffalo@gmail.com; Web: www.stnbuffalo.com. Very Rev. Marijan Procyk.
Catechesis Religious Program—Tel: 716-825-8169; Email: enowadly@roadrunner.com. Elaine P. Nowadly, D.R.E. Priests 2; Students 32.

COHOES, ALBANY CO., SS. PETER AND PAUL (1907) (Ukrainian)
198 Ontario St., Cohoes, NY 12047.
Tel: 518-237-0535; Email: am3168@verizon.net. Very Rev. Canon Vladimir Marusceac.
Catechesis Religious Program—Lay Teachers 1; Priests 1; Students 7.

ELMIRA HEIGHTS, CHEMUNG CO., ST. NICHOLAS (1895) (Ukrainian)
410 E. McCanns Blvd., Elmira Heights, NY 14903.
Tel: 607-734-1221; Email: frbob8@msn.com. Rev. Robert Moreno.
Catechesis Religious Program—Irene Moffe, D.R.E. Lay Teachers 3; Priests 1; Students 10.

FRESH MEADOWS, QUEENS CO., ANNUNCIATION OF THE B.V.M. (1957) (Ukrainian)
48-26 171st St., Fresh Meadows, NY 11365.
Tel: 718-939-4116; Email: bvm@netzero.net. Very Rev. Zbigniew Canon Brzezicki.

GLEN SPEY, SULLIVAN CO., ST. VOLODYMYR (1961) [JC] (Ukrainian), Attended by Campbell Hall, New York
141 Sarah Wells Tr., Campbell Hall, NY 10916.
Tel: 845-496-5506; Email: yaroslav_01@yahoo.com. P.O. Box 108, Glen Spey, NY 12737. Very Rev. Yaroslaw Kostyk.

HAMPTONBURGH (CAMPBELL HALL), ORANGE CO., ST. ANDREW'S (1983) (Ukrainian)
141 Sarah Wells Tr., Campbell Hall, NY 10916.
Tel: 845-496-5506; Tel: 845-496-4156;
Fax: 845-496-5564; Email: yaroslav_01@yahoo.com; Web: www.holyspirit-saintandrew.org. Rev. Yaroslav Kostyk, Admin.
Catechesis Religious Program—Lay Teachers 1; Priests 1; Students 4.

HEMPSTEAD, NASSAU CO., SAINT VLADIMIR UKRAINIAN CATHOLIC CHURCH (1944) (Ukrainian)
709 Front St., Hempstead, NY 11550.
Tel: 516-481-7717; Email: stvladimir@optonline.net. 718 Front St., Hempstead, NY 11550. Rev. Wasyl Hrynkiw.
Parish Center—226 Uniondale Ave., Uniondale, NY 11553.
School—Saturday Ukrainian School, (Grades 1-12).
Catechesis Religious Program—Lay Teachers 9; Priests 1; Students 38.

HUDSON, COLUMBIA CO., ST. NICHOLAS (1923) (Ukrainian)
206-209 Union St., Hudson, NY 12534.
Tel: 518-828-5226; Email: saintnicholas1922@gmail.com. Rev. Janusz Jedrychowski, (Attends St. John the Baptist, Pittsfield, MA).
Catechesis Religious Program—Students 1.

HUNTER, GREENE CO., ST. JOHN THE BAPTIST (1962) (Ukrainian)
Rte. 23A, P.O. Box 284, Hunter, NY 12442.
Tel: 518-263-3862; Email: info@HolyTrinityNY.org; Web: ukrainianmountaintop.org. Very Rev. Archpriest Ivan Kaszczak, Ph.D., M.A., B.A.

JOHNSON CITY, BROOME CO., SACRED HEART UKRAINIAN CATHOLIC CHURCH (1944) [CEM] (Ukrainian)
230 Ukrainian Hill Rd., Johnson City, NY 13790.
Tel: 607-797-6293; Email: shucc@stny.rr.com; Web: www.sacredheartucc.org. Rev. Teodor Czabala.
School—Saturday Ukrainian School.
Catechesis Religious Program—Cathleen Welte, D.R.E. Lay Teachers 1; Students 20.

KENMORE, ERIE CO., ST. JOHN THE BAPTIST (1902) (Ukrainian)
3275 Elmwood Ave., Kenmore, NY 14217.
Tel: 716-873-5011; Email: stjohnparishk@gmail.com. Rev. Mykola Drofych.

KERHONKSON, ULSTER CO., HOLY TRINITY (1965) (Ukrainian)
Mailing Address: 211 Foordmore Rd., Kerhonkson, NY 12446-2914. Tel: 845-626-2864; Email: info@HolyTrinityNY.org; Web: www.HolyTrinityNY.org. Very Rev. Archpriest Ivan Kaszczak, Ph.D., M.A., B.A.
Holy Trinity Ukrainian Catholic Church.

LACKAWANNA, ERIE CO., OUR LADY OF PERPETUAL HELP (1925) (Ukrainian)
1182 Ridge Rd., Lackawanna, NY 14218.
Tel: 716-823-6182; Email: OLPHuchurch@gmail.com; Web: olphukrchurch.org. Rev. Andriy Kasiyan.
Catechesis Religious Program—Maria Slabyk, D.R.E.; Oksana Kasiyan, D.R.E. Lay Teachers 2; Priests 1.

LANCASTER, ERIE CO., ST. BASIL (1921) (Ukrainian)
12 Embry Pl., Lancaster, NY 14086.
Tel: 716-683-0313; Email: Stbasilchurch@gmail.com. 3657 Walden Ave., Lancaster, NY 14086. Rev. Andriy Kasiyan.

Catechesis Religious Program—Michele Forkl, D.R.E. Students 20.

LINDENHURST, SUFFOLK CO., HOLY FAMILY (1924) (Ukrainian)
225 N. 4th St., Lindenhurst, NY 11757.
Tel: 631-225-1168; Email: olvianpopovic@yahoo.com. Rev. Olvian Popovici.
Catechesis Religious Program—Lay Teachers 2; Priests 1; Students 67.

LITTLE FALLS, HERKIMER CO., ST. NICHOLAS (1912) Attended by Amsterdam. Rev. Marian Kostyk.
Res.: 24 Pulaski St., Amsterdam, NY 12010.
Tel: 518-842-8731; Fax: 518-842-1384.

LONG ISLAND CITY, QUEENS CO., HOLY CROSS (1944) (Ukrainian)
31-12 30th St., Long Island City, NY 11106.
Tel: 718-932-4060; Email: hcukicc@yahoo.com. Rev. Cyril Iszezuck, O.S.B.M.; Very Rev. Bernard J. Panczuk, O.S.B.M.

NEW YORK, NEW YORK CO., ST. GEORGE (1905) (Ukrainian)
30 E. 7th St., New York, NY 10003.
Tel: 212-674-1615; Email: osbmnyc@gmail.com. 16 E. 17th St., New York, NY 10003. Revs. Emilian Dorosh, Admin.; Sebastiyan Bondarenko; Illja Bronovskyy; Peter Shyshka.
School—St. George School, (Grades PreK-12), 215 E. Sixth St., New York, NY 10003. Tel: 212-473-3323; Email: stasiw@sga.nyc; Web: saintgeorgeacademy.net. Mr. Andrew Stasiw, Prin. Clergy 1; Lay Teachers 14; Students 100.
High School—St. George High School, Religious Teachers 1; Lay Teachers 9; Students 50.

NIAGARA FALLS, NIAGARA CO., PROTECTION OF B.V.M. (1920) (Ukrainian)
2713 Ferry Ave., Niagara Falls, NY 14301.
Tel: 347-342-2208; Email: protectionnf@gmail.com. Rev. Mykola Drofych.

OZONE PARK, QUEENS CO., ST. MARY PROTECTRESS (1954) (Ukrainian)
97-06 87th St., Ozone Park, NY 11416.
Tel: 718-845-5366; Email: stmarysozpk@aol.com. Very Rev. Vasile Tivadar, Admin.

RIVERHEAD, SUFFOLK CO., ST. JOHN THE BAPTIST (1924) [CEM] (Ukrainian)
820 Pond View Rd., Riverhead, NY 11901.
Tel: 631-727-2766; Email: info@sjbucc.org; Web: www.sjbucc.org. Rev. Bohdan Hedz.
Church: Franklin St., Riverhead, NY 11901.

ROCHESTER, MONROE CO.

1—ST. JOSAPHAT (1909) (Ukrainian)
940 E. Ridge Rd., Rochester, NY 14621.
Tel: 585-467-6457; Email: rstjosap@rochestere.rr.com; Web: www.stjosaphats.org. Rt. Rev. Mitred Archpriest Philip Weiner; Rev. Volodymyr Dmyterko, Parochial Vicar; Deacon Stephen A. Wisnowski.
Catechesis Religious Program—Lay Teachers 9; Students 42.

2—UKRAINIAN CATHOLIC CHURCH OF EPIPHANY (1958) [JC] (Ukrainian)
202 Carter St., Rochester, NY 14621.
Tel: 585-266-4036; Email: ukr.epiphany@yahoo.com. Very Rev. Roman Sydorovych.
Catechesis Religious Program—Students 41; Teachers 8.

ROME, ONEIDA CO., ST. MICHAEL (1914) [CEM] (Ukrainian), Attended by St. Volodymyr, Utica.
296 Genesee St., Utica, NY 13502. Tel: 315-735-5138 ; Email: stvolodymyr@hotmail.com. 133 River St., Rome, NY 13440. Very Rev. Michael Bundz.

SPRING VALLEY, ROCKLAND CO., SS. PETER AND PAUL (1913) (Ukrainian)
43 Collins Ave., Spring Valley, NY 10977.
Tel: 845-356-1634; Email: jmterlecky@aol.com. 39 Collins Ave., Spring Valley, NY 10977. Rt. Rev. Msgr. John Terlecky.
Catechesis Religious Program—Lay Teachers 2; Students 12.

STATEN ISLAND, RICHMOND CO., HOLY TRINITY (1949) (Ukrainian)
288 Vanderbilt Ave., Staten Island, NY 10304.
Tel: 718-442-2555; Email: frvasile@aol.com. Rev. Vasile Godenciuc.
Catechesis Religious Program—L. Niewiadomski, D.R.E. Students 5.

SYRACUSE, ONONDAGA CO., ST. JOHN THE BAPTIST (1900)
207 Tompkins St., Syracuse, NY 13204.
Tel: 315-478-5109; Email: stjbuccsyracuse@gmail.com. Rt. Rev. Mitred Archpriest Mihai Dubovici, B.A., S.T.B.; Rev. Vasyl Kadylo, Parochial Vicar.
Catechesis Religious Program—Lay Teachers 8; Priests 1; Students 65.

TROY, RENSSELAER CO., PROTECTION OF B.V.M. (1952) [JC] (Ukrainian), Attended by St. Nicholas Watervilet.
459 Second St., Troy, NY 12180. Tel: 518-273-6752; Email: office@cerkva.com. Rev. Mikhail Myshchuk.

UTICA, ONEIDA CO., ST. VOLODYMYR THE GREAT (1950) [CEM] (Ukrainian)
296 Genessee St., Utica, NY 13502.
Tel: 315-735-5138; Email: stvolodymyr@hotmail.com. 4 Cottage Pl., Utica, NY 13502. Very Rev. Michael Bundz, (Attends St. Michael's, Rome, NY).

WATERVLIET, ALBANY CO., ST. NICHOLAS UKRAINIAN CATHOLIC CHURCH (1905) [CEM] [JC] (Ukrainian)
2410-4th Ave., Watervliet, NY 12189.
Tel: 518-273-6752; Email: office@cerkva.com. Rev. Mikhail Myshchuk; Deacon Thomas Gutch.
School—Saturday Ukrainian School.
Catechesis Religious Program—Students 29.

YONKERS, WESTCHESTER CO., ST. MICHAEL (1899) (Ukrainian)
21 Shonnard Pl., Yonkers, NY 10703.
Tel: 914-963-0209; Email: stmichaelsukrainian@gmail.com; Web: stmichaelsukrainian.com. Very Rev. Archpriest Kiril Angelov; Rev. Vasyl S. Behay.
Catechesis Religious Program—School of Ukrainian Studies, Elizabeth Gardasz, Catechist; Svetlana Khromokoska, Dir. Lay Teachers 9; Priests 2; Students 123.

STATE OF RHODE ISLAND

WOONSOCKET, PROVIDENCE CO., ST. MICHAEL (1908) [CEM] [JC]
394 Blackstone St., Woonsocket, RI 02895.
Tel: 401-762-2733; Email: st.michaelucc@verizon.net; Web: www.facebook.com/Saint-Michael-the-Archangel-UCC-446230618795539. Rev. Mykhaylo Dosyak.
Church: 396 Blackstone St., Woonsocket, RI 02895.

On Duty Outside the Diocese:
Revs.—
Forlano, Albert, Diocese of Bridgeport, CT
Kornyckyi, Vasyl, Ireland
Kuklich, Stepan, Archdiocese of Buffalo, NY
Rt. Rev. Mitred Archpriest—
Dubovici, Mihai, B.A., S.T.B., Romania.

Retired:
Rev.—
Hirniak, Mark, (Retired), 1015 Maple Lake Dr., Bushkill, PA 18324
Rt. Rev. Mitred Msgrs.—
Mosko, Leon, (Retired), 195 Glenbrook Rd., 06902
Squiller, John, B.A., S.T.L., (Retired).

Permanent Deacons:
Coleman, Paul, SS. Peter & Paul, Auburn, NY
Evans, Michael, SS. Peter & Paul, Auburn, NY
Galvin, Edward, St. John the Baptist, Syracuse, NY
Gutch, Thomas, St. Nicholas, Watervliet, NY
Hobczuk, John, St. Nicholas, Elmira Heights, NY
Roche, Andrew, Ss. Peter and Paul, Auburn, NY
Stadnick, Thomas, Holy Ghost, Brooklyn, NY
Wisnowski, Stephen A., St. Josaphat, Rochester, NY.

INSTITUTIONS LOCATED IN DIOCESE

[A] SEMINARIES, DIOCESAN

STAMFORD. *Ukrainian Catholic Seminary Inc. St. Basil College - Seminary*, 195 Glenbrook Rd., 06902-3099. Tel: 203-324-4578; Fax: 203-357-7681; Email: ukrcathsem@optonline.net; Web: stbasilseminary.com. Most Rev. Paul P. Chomnycky, O.S.B.M., Chm., Bd. Trustees; Rev. Dr. Bohdan Tymchyshyn, Rector; Mr. Vasile Popovici, Procurator; Ms. Lubow Wolynetz, B.A., M.L.S., Librarian. Religious Teachers 2; Seminarians 7; Students 7.

[B] SEMINARIES, RELIGIOUS

GLEN COVE. *Basilian Fathers Novitiate of the Order of St. Basil the Great*, E. Beach Dr., Glen Cove, NY 11542. Tel: 516-671-0545; Fax: 516-676-7465. Rev. Eugene Khomyn, O.S.B.M. Brothers 1; Priests 3.

[C] ADULT FACILITIES

SLOATSBURG. *St. Joseph's Adult Care Home, Inc.*, 125 Sisters Servants Ln., Sloatsburg, NY 10974-0008. Tel: 845-753-2555; Fax: 845-753-6910. Sisters Michele Yakymovitch, S.S.M.I., Admin.; Barbara Stefaniak, S.S.M.I., Admin. Residents 31; Sisters Servants of Mary Immaculate 5; Total Staff 10.

[D] MONASTERIES AND RESIDENCES OF PRIESTS AND BROTHERS

NEW YORK. *Provincialate of Basilian Fathers*, Res.: 29 Peacock Ln., Locust Valley, NY 11560.
Tel: 516-609-3262; Fax: 516-609-3264; Email: salkovskiv@aol.com. Very Rev. Varcilio Basil Salkovski, O.S.B.M., Protohegumen. Brothers 1; Priests 15.

[E] MONASTERIES OF NUNS

MIDDLETOWN. *Nuns of St. Basil the Great - Contemplative*, Sacred Heart Monastery, 209 Keasel Rd., Middletown, NY 10940-6287.
Tel: 845-343-1308; Fax: 845-343-1308. Mother Georgianna Snihur, O.S.B.M., Supr. Sisters 5.

SLOATSBURG. *Sister Servants of Mary Immaculate, Inc.*, 150 Sisters Servants Ln., 9 Emmanuel Dr., P.O. Box 9, Sloatsburg, NY 10974-0009.
Tel: 845-753-2840; Fax: 845-753-1956; Email: ssminy@aol.com. Sr. Kathleen Hutsko, S.S.M.I., Prov. Supr. Sisters Servants of Mary Immaculate Conception Province. Sisters 23.

[F] MISCELLANEOUS

STAMFORD. *Institute of Catechists of the Heart of Jesus*, 161 Glenbrook Rd., 06902. Tel: 203-327-6374.

NEWARK. *Mary Theotokos Center Inc.*, 572 Lake Rd., Newark, VT 05871. Tel: 802-467-3009. P.O. Box 88, West Burke, VT 05871.

SLOATSBURG. *St. Mary's Villa Spiritual, Cultural & Educational Center*, 150 Sisters Servants Ln., P.O. Box 9, Sloatsburg, NY 10974-0009.
Tel: 845-753-5100; Fax: 845-753-1956; Email: srkath25@gmail.com. Sr. Albina Gregory, S.S.M.I., Coord. Bed Capacity 50; Total Staff 4.

RELIGIOUS INSTITUTES OF MEN REPRESENTED IN THE DIOCESE

For further details refer to the corresponding bracketed number in the Religious Institutes of Men or Women section.

[0180]—*Order of St. Basil the Great*—O.S.B.M.
[1070]—*Redemptorists*—C.Ss.R.

RELIGIOUS INSTITUTES OF WOMEN REPRESENTED IN THE DIOCESE

[]—*Institute of Catechists of the Heart of Jesus.*
[3730]—*Sisters of the Order of St. Basil the Great*—O.S.B.M.
[3610]—*Sisters Servants of Mary Immaculate*—S.S.M.I.

An asterisk (*) denotes an organization that has established tax-exempt status directly with the IRS and is not covered by the USCCB Group Ruling.

St. Mary, Queen of Peace, Syro-Malankara Catholic Eparchy in USA and Canada

Most Reverend

PHILIPOS MAR STEPHANOS

Bishop of the Syro-Malankara Catholic Eparchy in USA and Canada; ordained April 27, 1979; consecrated Bishop March 13, 2010; installed Bishop of the Eparchy in USA and Canada October 28, 2017. *Chancery Office & Res.: 1500 DePaul St., Elmont, NY 11003.* Tel: 516-233-1656; Fax: 516-616-0727.

Chancery Office: 1500 De Paul St., Elmont, NY 11003. Tel: 516-233-1656; Fax: 516-616-0727.

ESTABLISHED JULY 14, 2010

The jurisdiction of the Eparchy is all Syro-Malankara Catholics in the United States of America and Canada.

STATISTICAL OVERVIEW

Personnel	
Bishop	1
Priests: Diocesan Active in Diocese	16
Priests: Diocesan Active Outside Diocese	1
Number of Diocesan Priests	17
Religious Priests in Diocese	1
Total Priests in Diocese	18
Total Sisters	31
Parishes	
Parishes	16
With Resident Pastor:	
Resident Diocesan Priests	15
Resident Religious Priests	1
Missions	4
Vital Statistics	
Receptions into the Church:	
Infant Baptism Totals	41
Adult Baptism Totals	3
Received into Full Communion	2
First Communions	43
Confirmations	45
Marriages:	
Catholic	18
Interfaith	3
Total Marriages	21
Deaths	3
Total Catholic Population	11,500

Former Bishop—Most Rev. THOMAS EUSEBIUS NAICKAMPARAMBIL, ord. priest Dec. 29, 1986; appt. Bishop of the Syro-Malankara Catholic Exarchate in USA July 14, 2010; cons. Sept. 21, 2010; installed Bishop of the Exarchate Oct. 3, 2010; appt. Bishop of St. Mary, Queen of Peace Syro-Malankara Catholic Eparchy in USA & Canada Dec. 18, 2015; installed Bishop of the Eparchy Jan. 23, 2016; appt. Bishop of Parassale (Syro-Malankara), India Aug. 5, 2017; installed Sept. 23, 2017.

Diocesan Curia—

Chief Vicar General—Rt. Rev. Msgr. AUGUSTINE MANGALATH ABRAHAM.

Vicar General—Rt. Rev. Msgr. GIGI PHILIP.

Chancellor—Very Rev. SAJI G. MUKKOOT.

Finance Officer—Rt. Rev. Msgr. AUGUSTINE MANGALATH ABRAHAM.

Judicial Vicar—Rev. GEORGE OONNOONY.

Secretary—Rev. THOMAS AYYANETH.

Tribunal—

Office—1500 De Paul St., Elmont, 11003.

Judicial Vicar—Rev. GEORGE OONNOONY.

Defender of the Bond—Very Rev. SAJI G. MUKKOOT.

Promoter of Justice—Rev. MATHAI MANNOORVADAKKETHIL.

Notary—Rev. THOMAS AYYANETH.

Diocesan Apostolates and Directors—

Vocation Promotion Director—Very Rev. SAJI G. MUKKOOT.

Youth Apostolate: Director—Rev. MICHAEL PHILIPOSE EDATHIL.

Family Apostolate Director—Rev. MATHAI MANNOORVADAKKETHIL.

Faith Formation (Catechism) Director—Rev. ABRAHAM LUKOSE.

Seminary Formation Director—Rev. Msgr. PETER KOCHERY.

Bible Apostolate Director—Rev. JOHN S. PUTHENVILAYIL.

Ecumenism and MCA Director—Rev. JOSEPH NEDUMANKUZHIYIL.

Liturgy Director—Rev. ABRAHAM LUKOSE.

Fathers' Forum Director—Rev. JOHN KURIAKOSE.

Mothers' Forum Director—Rev. BABU MADATHILPARAMBIL.

Malankara Catholic Children's League—Rev. ANTONY VAYALIKAROTTU.

Councils—

Presbyteral Council—Most Rev. PHILIPOS MAR STEPHANOS, Pres.; Rt. Rev. Msgr. GIGI PHILIP, Sec.

Ex Officio Members—Rt. Rev. Msgr. AUGUSTINE MANGALATH ABRAHAM, (Chief Vicar Gen. & Finance Officer); Very Rev. SAJI G. MUKKOOT, Chancellor.

Elected Members—Revs. MATHAI MANNOORVADAKKETHIL; JOHN S. PUTHENVILAYIL; BABU MADATHILPARAMBIL; ANTONY VAYALIKAROTTU; PATHROSE PANUVEL; ABRAHAM LUKOSE; KURIAKOSE MAMBRAKATT; BIJU VARGHESE EDAILAKATTU; THOMAS AYYANETH.

Pastoral Council—Most Rev. PHILIPOS MAR STEPHANOS, Pres. Secretaries: Very Rev. SAJI G. MUKKOOT; MR. JOHN P. VARGHESE.

Ex Officio Members—Rt. Rev. Msgrs. AUGUSTINE MANGALATH ABRAHAM, Chief Vicar Gen.; GIGI PHILIP, Vicar Gen.; MR. MOHAN VARGHESE, PRO.

Priests - Heads of Apostolates—Revs. JOHN S. PUTHENVILAYIL; MATHAI MANNOORVADAKKETHIL; BABU MADATHILPARAMBIL; JOSEPH NEDUMANKUZHIYIL; ANTONY VAYALIKAROTTU; PATHROSE PANUVEL; ABRAHAM LUKOSE; JOHN KURIAKOSE; THOMAS AYYANETH; KURIAKOSE MAMBRAKATT.

Elected Members—MR. VARUGHESE T. JOSEPH; MR. GEEVARUGHESE MATHEWS; MR. CIBY DANIEL; MR. JOHN M. ETTIKKALAYIL; MR. ABRAHAM VARGESE; MR. SUJAN MATHEWS; MR. JIM CHERIAN; MR. PRIYAN SIMON ABRAHAM; MRS. GRACY MATHEW; MRS. DAISAMMA MATHEW; MR. GEORGE KAKKANATT; MR. SELICKS CHERIAN; MR. GEORGE FERNANDUS; MR. STEVE MANNICKAROTTU; MR. BENJAMIN THOMAS; MR. DODLY GEORGE; MR. PRAKASH T. MATHEW; MR. JACOB PUNNOOSE; MR. THOMAS JOHN; MR. PHILIP MATHAI; MR. ALEX JOHN; MR. SHAJI SIMON; MR. SHINE D. THOMAS; MR. PHILIPOSE MATHEW; MRS. MOLLY JACOB; MR. MATHEW KULANGARA; MR. MATHEW GEORGE; MR. BABU MAMOOTTIL; MR. RAJESH JACOB; MR. JOHN THOMAS; MR. JACOB THOMAS; MR. SHAAN RAJAN.

Representatives of Religious Orders—Rev. FRANCIS ASSISI, O.I.C.; Sisters ARPITHA, S.I.C.; AGNES, D.M.; ASISH, D.M.

Nominated Members—Rev. JACOB JOHN; MR. PHILIP JOHN; MR. JOHNSON DANIEL; MR. SIMON ZACHARIAH; MR. JOEY ABRAHAM.

Finance Council—Most Rev. PHILIPOS MAR STEPHANOS, Pres.

Members—Rt. Rev. Msgr. AUGUSTINE MANGALATH ABRAHAM, (Finance Officer); MR. ABRAHAM PONMELIL; MR. ABRAHAM PHILIP; MR. VARGHESE ZACHARIAH; MR. SHAJI SIMON; MR. REJI JOSE; MR. SIMON PLAMTHOTTAM; MR. PRAMOD ZACHARIAH.

Council for Planning and Development—Most Rev. PHILIPOS MAR STEPHANOS, Pres.

Members—Rt. Rev. Msgrs. AUGUSTINE MANGALATH ABRAHAM, Chief Vicar Gen.; GIGI PHILIP, Vicar Gen.; Very Rev. SAJI G. MUKKOOT, Chancellor; MR. GEORGE JAMES; MR. ALEX JOHN THANGALATHIL; MR. BABU STEPHEN; MR. BENJAMIN THOMAS; MR. ROY VARGHESE; MR. GEEVARGHESE THANKACHAN; MR. GEORGE SAMUEL; MR. JOHNSON DANIEL; MRS. CHINNAMMA RAJAN; DR. JOCELYN EDATHIL; MR. SEBIN ALEX; MR. JAMES S. THOMAS.

Council for the Promotion of Culture and Heritage—Very Rev. SAJI G. MUKKOOT, Pres.

Members—MR. PHILIP JOHN; MR. THOMAS ABRAHAM; MR. RAJAN KAKKANATTU; MR. WILSON JOSEPH; MR. SAJI KEEKKADAN; MR. PHILIP VANDAKATHIL; MISS NINA DANIEL.

Eparchy Webteam—Most Rev. PHILIPOS MAR STEPHANOS, Pres.; Rt. Rev. Msgr. AUGUSTINE MANGALATH ABRAHAM, Vice Pres. Members: MR. BINU ABRAHAM, Chicago; MR. GIJO GEORGE, Long Island; MR. JOHN THOMAS, New Jersey; MR. SUNIL CHACKO, Queens; MR. VARGHESE SAMUEL, Philadelphia.

Public Relations Office—Rev. THOMAS AYYANETH, Dir.; MR. MOHAN VARUGHESE, PRO.

CLERGY, PARISHES, MISSIONS AND PAROCHIAL SCHOOLS

STATE OF NEW YORK

BLAUVELT, ROCKLAND CO., ST. PETER'S MALANKARA CATHOLIC CHURCH

614 Western Hwy S., Blauvelt, 10913. Tel: 203-444-8542; Email: mangalath@att.net. 41 Alling St., West Haven, CT 06516. Rt. Rev. Msgr. Augustine Mangalath.

ELMONT, NASSAU CO., ST. VINCENT DE PAUL MALANKARA CATHOLIC CATHEDRAL

1500 DePaul St., 11003. Rev. Thomas Ayyaneth.

YONKERS, WESTCHESTER CO., ST. MARY'S MALANKARA CATHOLIC CHURCH

18 Trinity St., Yonkers, 10701. Tel: 914-218-0758; Fax: 516-616-0727; Email: lijuthundy@gmail.com. Rev. Jerry Mathew.

STATE OF FLORIDA

FORT LAUDERDALE, BROWARD CO., ST. MARY'S MALANKARA CATHOLIC CHURCH

2512 Barbara Dr., Fort Lauderdale, FL 33316.

Tel: 516-428-6909; Email: frantonyvayali@gmail.com. Rev. Antony Vayalikarottu.

STATE OF CALIFORNIA

NORTH HOLLYWOOD, LOS ANGELES CO., ST. MARY'S MALANKARA CATHOLIC CHURCH
6153 Cahuenga Blvd., North Hollywood, CA 91606.
Tel: 215-971-0639; Email: edailakattu@yahoo.co.in. Rev. Daniel Edailakatt, Rector.

SAN JOSE, SANTA CLARA CO., Rev. Biju Varghese Edailakattu. ST. JUDE MALANKARA CATHOLIC CHURCH
7183 Brooktree Ct., San Jose, CA 95120.
Tel: 215-971-0639; Email: edailakattu@yahoo.co.in. Rev. Daniel Edailakatt.

STATE OF ILLINOIS

EVANSTON, COOK CO., ST. MARY'S MALANKARA CATHOLIC CHURCH
1208 Ashland Ave., Evanston, IL 60202.
Tel: 773-754-9638; Email: toChacko123@gmail.com. Rev. Babu Madathilparambil.
Res.: 1534 Wilder Ave., Evanston, IL 60202.
Tel: 847-332-1794; Fax: 847-424-0889.

STATE OF MARYLAND

FORESTVILLE, PRINCE GEORGE CO., ST. MARY'S MALANKARA CATHOLIC CHURCH
1717 Ritchie Rd., Forestville, MD 20747.
Tel: 215-558-8741; Email: michael_edathil@yahoo.com. Rev. Michael Philipose Edathil.

STATE OF MICHIGAN

CENTER LINE, MACOMB CO., ST. JOSEPH'S MALANKARA CATHOLIC CHURCH
8075 Ritter Ave., Center Line, MI 48015. Rev. Pathrose Panuvel.
Res.: 17166 Olympia, Redford, MI 48240.
Tel: 917-673-5318; Fax: 586-725-3647.

STATE OF NEW JERSEY

ELIZABETH, UNION CO., ST. THOMAS MALANKARA CATHOLIC CHURCH
11 Delaware St., Elizabeth, NJ 07206. Rt. Rev. Msgr. Peter Kochery.
Res.: 186 Gordons Corner Rd., Manalapan, NJ 07726.

STATE OF PENNSYLVANIA

PHILADELPHIA, PHILADELPHIA CO., ST. JUDE MALANKARA CATHOLIC CHURCH
244 W. Cheltenham Ave., Philadelphia, PA 19126. Very Rev. Saji G. Mukkoot.
Res.: 2050 Walnut Ln., Philadelphia, PA 19138.
Tel: 267-297-9952.

STATE OF TEXAS

MESQUITE, DALLAS CO., ST. MARY'S MALANKARA CATHOLIC CHURCH
2650 E. Scyene Rd., Mesquite, TX 75181.
Tel: 240-640-9720; Fax: 972-494-3653; Email: matmvy@gmail.com. Rev. Mathai Mannoorvadakkethil.

STAFFORD, FORT BEND CO., ST. PETER'S MALANKARA CATHOLIC CHURCH
3135 5th St., Stafford, TX 77477. Tel: 832-654-3172; Email: frjohnSP@gmail.com. Rev. John S. Puthenvilayil.
Res.: 10330 Hillcroft St., Houston, TX 77096.
Tel: 713-333-3511; Fax: 713-729-3294.

MISSIONS

Mission
Albany.
Mission
Atlanta, GA.
Mission
Boston, MA.
Mission
Phoenix, AZ.

On Duty Outside the Diocese:
Rev.—
Mathew, Jerry, Doctoral studies in Rome.

INSTITUTIONS LOCATED IN DIOCESE

[A] CONVENTS AND RESIDENCES FOR SISTERS

LIVONIA. *Daughters of Mary Convent*, 33315 Broadmoor Ct., Livonia, MI 48154. Tel: 248-543-4127; Email: dmdetroit@hotmail.com. Sisters Litty Maria, D.M., Supr.; Nithya, D.M.; Geo, D.M.; Shanti, D.M.; Sevana, D.M.; Thejus, D.M. Sisters 6.

MONROVIA. *Daughters of Mary Convent*, 340 Norumbega Dr., Monrovia, CA 91016. Tel: 626-335-4581; Tel: 626-988-7461; Email: dayatherese@yahoo.com; Email: nirmal.alphonse@gmail.com. Sisters Daya Therese, D.M., Supr.; Nirmal Alphonse, D.M.; Paul Maria, D.M.; Sidhi Maria, D.M. Sisters 4.

MORTON GROVE. *Bethany Convent* Sisters of the Imitation of Christ 7910 Arcadia St., Morton Grove, IL 60053. Tel: 516-225-2709; Email: bethanysisters@chicagomalankara.org. Sisters Mariam, S.I.C., Supr.; Slooso, S.I.C.; Ivan, S.I.C. Sisters 3.

NEW HYDE PARK. *Bethany Convent*, 1653 Highland Ave., New Hyde Park, 11040. Tel: 516-358-4597; Email: usbethany@gmail.com. Sisters Arpitha, S.I.C., Supr.; Kanchana, S.I.C. Sisters 2.

YONKERS. *Daughters of Mary Convent*, 15 Trinity St., Yonkers, 10701. Tel: 718-885-1842; Email: dmcityisland@optimum.net. Sisters Agnes, D.M., Supr.; Linus Maria, D.M.; Savidha, D.M.; Abel, D.M. Sisters 4.

Daughters of Mary Convent, 45 Verona Ave., Yonkers, 10710. Tel: 914-202-9255; Email: dmconventyonkers@yahoo.com. Sisters Anjaly, D.M., Supr.; Jovina, D.M.; Gracelet, D.M.; Asish, D.M. Sisters 4.

An asterisk (*) denotes an organization that has established tax-exempt status directly with the IRS and is not covered by the USCCB Group Ruling.

Archdiocese of Agana

Most Reverend

MICHAEL J. BYRNES

Archbishop of Agana; ordained May 25, 1996; appointed Auxiliary Bishop of Detroit and Titular Bishop of Eguga March 22, 2011; consecrated May 5, 2011; appointed Coadjutor Archbishop of Agana October 31, 2016; installed November 30, 2016; Succeeded to See April 4, 2019. *Chancery Office: 196 Cuesta San Ramon, Ste. B, Hagatna, GU 96910.*

Chancery Office: 196 Cuesta San Ramon, Ste. B, Hagatna, GU 96910. Tel: 671-472-6116; Tel: 671-472-6573; Tel: 671-562-0000; Fax: 671-477-3519.

Erected by Pope Pius X, March 1, 1911 and Committed to the Order of Friars Minor Capuchin. Extended to all the Marianas Islands, July 4, 1946, Wake Island, June 14, 1948. Elevated to a Diocese, October 14, 1965, as a Suffragan of San Francisco. Elevated to Metropolitan Archdiocese, May 20, 1984 with a Suffragan See, Diocese of Caroline-Marshalls and Diocese of Chalan Kanoa (subsequently added January 13, 1985). Member of CEPAC Conference. Member of Federation of Catholic Bishops Conference of Oceania. Observer to NCCB-USCC Conference.

Guam is a Territory of the U.S.A. by Act of the U.S. Congress July 21, 1949.

Legal Title: Archbishop of Agana, a Corporation Sole.

STATISTICAL OVERVIEW

Personnel	
Archbishops	1
Priests: Diocesan Active in Diocese	28
Priests: Diocesan Active Outside Diocese	13
Priests: Diocesan in Foreign Missions	3
Priests: Retired, Sick or Absent	5
Number of Diocesan Priests	49
Religious Priests in Diocese	11
Total Priests in Diocese	60
Extern Priests in Diocese	9
Permanent Deacons in Diocese	25
Total Brothers	5
Total Sisters	64
Parishes	
Parishes	26
With Resident Pastor:	
Resident Diocesan Priests	21
Resident Religious Priests	5
Professional Ministry Personnel:	
Lay Ministers	11
Welfare	
Homes for the Aged	1
Total Assisted	64
Day Care Centers	4
Total Assisted	112
Specialized Homes	1
Total Assisted	60
Special Centers for Social Services	1
Total Assisted	2,202
Educational	
Diocesan Students in Other Seminaries	4
Total Seminarians	4
High Schools, Diocesan and Parish	2
Total Students	809
High Schools, Private	1
Total Students	191
Elementary Schools, Diocesan and Parish	6
Total Students	2,576
Elementary Schools, Private	5
Total Students	1,000
Catechesis/Religious Education:	
High School Students	1,255
Elementary Students	2,249
Total Students under Catholic Instruction	8,084
Teachers in the Diocese:	
Priests	5
Brothers	1
Sisters	17
Lay Teachers	329
Vital Statistics	
Receptions into the Church:	
Infant Baptism Totals	1,323
Minor Baptism Totals	23
Adult Baptism Totals	42
Received into Full Communion	18
First Communions	1,054
Confirmations	827
Marriages:	
Catholic	200
Interfaith	11
Total Marriages	211
Deaths	609
Total Catholic Population	145,000
Total Population	164,229

Former Vicars-Apostolic—Most Revs. FRANCIS X. VILLA Y MATEU, O.F.M.Cap., D.D., cons. Titular Bishop of Adraha, Oct. 1, 1911; died at Agana, Jan. 1, 1913; AUGUSTIN BERNAUS Y SERRA, O.F.M.Cap., D.D., cons. Titular Bishop of Milopotamo, May 9, 1913; transferred to Vicariate-Apostolic of Bluefields, Nicaragua, 1914; died 1930; JOAQUIN FELIPE OLAIZ Y ZABALZA, O.F.M.Cap., D.D., cons. Titular Bishop of Docimeo, Nov. 30, 1914; died at Pamplona, Spain, Dec. 8, 1945; MIGUEL ANGEL OLANO Y URTEAGA, O.F.M.Cap., D.D., cons. Titular Bishop of Lagina, May 5, 1935; resigned and made Asst. at Pontifical Throne Aug. 20, 1945; died at Agana, Guam May 21, 1970.

Former Diocesan Bishops—Most Revs. APOLLINARIS W. BAUMGARTNER, O.F.M.Cap., D.D., cons. Sept. 18, 1945; appt. First Diocesan Bishop of Agana, Oct. 14, 1965; died at Agana, Guam Dec. 18, 1970; FELIXBERTO CAMACHO FLORES, ord. April 30, 1949; appt. Apostolic Admin., Diocese of Agana, May 2, 1969; appt. Titular Bishop of Stonj, March 19, 1970; cons. May 17, 1970; succeeded to See, May 15, 1971; died Oct. 25, 1985.

Former Archdiocesan Archbishop—Most Rev. ANTHONY SABLAN APURON, O.F.M.Cap., D.D., ord. Aug. 26, 1972; appt. Auxiliary Bishop Dec. 8, 1983; ord. Titular Bishop of Muzuca Feb. 19, 1984; appt. Apostolic Admin. to the Archdiocese Oct. 27, 1985; succeeded to Metropolitan See May 11, 1986; removed March 16, 2018.

Chancery Office—196 Cuesta San Ramon, Ste. B, Hagatna, 96910. Tel: 671-472-6116; Tel: 671-472-6573; Tel: 671-562-0000; Fax: 671-477-3519. Office Hours: Mon.-Fri. 8-12 & 1-4.

Special Assistant to the Archbishop & Weekend Associate for St. Anthony & St. Victor, Tamuning—Tel: 671-562-0000. Rev. RONALD S. RICHARDS.

Moderator of the Curia and Vicar General—Rev. JEFFREY C. SAN NICOLAS, Email: vicargeneral@archagana.org.

Special Projects Administrative Assistant to the Vicar General—Tel: 671-562-0075. MONICA TAIMANGLO.

Chancellor—Rev. RONALD S. RICHARDS, Tel: 671-562-0073; Email: chancellor@archagana.org.

Human Resources Director—Rev. JEFFREY C. SAN NICOLAS, Tel: 671-562-0072; Email: vicargeneral@archagana.org.

Safe Environment Office - Coordinator—Tel: 671-562-0029; Email: safeenvironment@archagana.org. TRICIA L.T. TENORIO.

Victim Assistance Coordinator (VAC)—Sr. DOROTHY LETTIERE, R.S.M., Victims Support Group, Tel: 671-685-7305; Tel: 671-562-0039 (Hotline).

Administrative Assistant to the Chancellor—JOHN JOSEPH BAUTISTA, Tel: 671-562-0073; Email: jbautista@archagana.org.

Administrative Assistant for Human Resources—RICCALYN LIZAMA, Tel: 671-562-0027; Email: hradmin@archagana.org.

Administrative Assistant of the Archbishop—ELIZABETH A. WEISENBERGER, Tel: 671-562-0076; Email: lweisenberger@archagana.org.

Finance Officer—JOSEPHINE G. VILLANUEVA, M.B.A., CPA, CGMA, CGFM, CSAF, Tel: 671-562-0064; Email: jvillanueva@archagana.org.

Diocesan Curia Officials—Revs. JEFFREY C. SAN NICOLAS; RONALD S. RICHARDS; MICHAEL CRISOSTOMO; RICHARD MENO KIDD; JOSEPHINE G. VILLANUEVA, M.B.A., CPA, CGMA, CGFM, CSAF; MR. ANTHONY DIAZ; RICHARD Z ALVIA, M.Ed.

Archdiocesan College of Consultors—Rev. MELCHOR T. CAMINA; Rev. Msgrs. BRIGIDO U. ARROYO; JAMES L.G. BENAVENTE; Revs. ROMEO (ROMY) D. CONVOCAR; MICHAEL CRISOSTOMO; RICHARD MENO KIDD; JEFFREY C. SAN NICOLAS.

Archdiocesan Presbyteral Council—Revs. JOEL DE LOS REYES; RICHARD MENO KIDD; MELCHOR T. CAMINA; Rev. Msgr. JAMES L.G. BENAVENTE; Revs. PATRICK CASTRO, O.F.M.Cap.; ROMEO (ROMY) D. CONVOCAR; MICHAEL CRISOSTOMO; THOMAS B. MCGRATH, S.J.; JEFFREY C. SAN NICOLAS.

Archdiocesan Finance Council—ANTOINETTE (TONI) SANFORD; EDUARDO (CHAMP) CALVO; RICARDO (RICK) C. DUENAS; CHRISTOPHER FELIX; ARTEMIO B. ILAGAN; MARY A.Y. OKADA; JOSEPH E. RIVERA; MR. ROBERT J. STEFFY; Rev. Msgr. JAMES L.G. BENAVENTE; Rev. JEFFREY C. SAN NICOLAS; JOSEPHINE G. VILLANUEVA, M.B.A., CPA, CGMA, CGFM, CSAF; JOHN TERLAJE, Attorney; JENI SHIMIZU.

Metropolitan Tribunal—

Judicial Vicar—Rev. CARLOS S. VILA, J.C.L.

Promoter of Justice—Rev. JOSE G. VILLAGOMEZ, O.F.M.Cap.

Defender of the Bond—Rev. JONATHAN ALVAREZ, J.C.L.

Associate Judges—Revs. JULIUS PAUL FACTORA, O.P., J.C.D.; DANILO RAMIRO FLORES, J.U.D.; JOEFFREY B. CATUIRAN, J.C.L.

Ecclesiastical Notary—Rev. FELIXBERTO LEON GUERRERO, O.F.M.Cap.

Advocate/Auditor—Rev. ROMEO (ROMY) D. CONVOCAR.

Adjunct Judge—Rev. FRANCIS DEMERS, O.M.I., J.C.D.

Canonical Records—JUNE P. UNGACTA, Archives & Records, Tel: 671-562-0061; Email: jungacta@archagana.org; CARMELITA MONDIA, Receptionist, Tel: 671-562-0000; Email: cmondia@archagana.org; LUZ OBERIANO, Archives Asst., Email: luz.oberiano@archagana.org.

Catholic Schools Office—RICHARD Z ALVIA, M.Ed., Supt., Tel: 671-562-0051; Email: superintendent@archagana.org; BEATRICE A. REYES, Admin. Asst., Tel: 671-562-0052; Email: breyes@archagana.org; JOAQUIN PANGELINAN, Faith Formation Coord., Tel: 671-562-0023; Email: jpangelinan@archagana.org.

Other Archdiocesan Pastoral Offices and Directors

The Catholic Cemeteries of Guam, Inc.—Tel: 671-477-9329; Email: catholiccemeteries.aoa@gmail.com. OWEN B.P. BOLLINGER, Admin.

Director of Vocations—Rev. RICHARD MENO KIDD, Tel: 671-477-7256; Email: vocations@archagana.org.

Director for the Ministry and Life of Permanent Deacons—Deacon LEONARD JOHN STOHR, Email: deaconlen@hotmail.com.

Associations and Charitable Organizations in the Archdiocese

Association of Diocesan Clergy of the Archdiocese of Agana (ADCAA)—Revs. DANILO (DAN) C. BIEN; MANUEL (JUN) TRENCHERA JR.; ROMEO (ROMY) D. CONVOCAR; Deacons AUGUSTO (GUS) F. CEPEDA; WILLIAM (BILL) HAGEN.

Gentle Refuge Crisis Pregnancy Center/Project Rachael—Cell: 671-777-6014; Cell: 671-777-5433; Email: gentlerefuge@yahoo.com.

St. Anthony's Catholic Church - STOP VAW Project—(Violence Against Women) Project Rev. MICHAEL CRISOSTOMO, Prog. Dir., Tel: 671-646-8044; MS. ROXANNE AGUON, Prog. Coord.

Ministry to the Homeless—Tel: 671-472-4569;

Fax: 671-477-5654; Email: ministrytothehomeless@gmail.com. Rev. MICHAEL CRISOSTOMO, Exec. Dir.

Ministry to the Homeless Thrift Shop—Tel: 671-472-4569; Email: ministrytothehomeless@gmail.com. Rev. MICHAEL CRISOSTOMO, Exec. Dir.

Catholic Charities of the Archdiocese of Agana/ Catholic Social Services—234 U.S. Army Juan C. Fejeran St., Barrigada, 96913-1407. Tel: 671-635-1406; Tel: 671-635-1441; Tel: 671-635-1442; Fax: 671-635-1444; Email: info@cssguam.org; Web: www.catholicsocialserviceguam.org. MRS. DIANA B. CALVO, Exec. Dir.; RONALD B. CARANDANG, Deputy Dir.

Alee Shelter - Family Violence & Child Abuse and Neglect—Tel: 671-648-4673 (Hotline); Tel: 671-648-5888. PAULA PEREZ, Prog. Mgr., Email: paula.perez@catholicsocialserviceguam.org.

Pontifical Holy Childhood Association & Pontifical Society for the Propagation of the Faith—Rev. Msgr. DAVID C. QUITUGUA, J.C.D., Contact Person, 196 Cuesta San Ramon, Ste. B, Hagatna, 96910. Tel: 671-472-6116; Tel: 671-472-6573; Fax: 671-477-3519.

St. Dominic's Senior Care Home—Tel: 671-632-9370; Tel: 671-632-9372; Tel: 671-632-9378; Tel: 671-632-9379; Fax: 671-637-1679; Email: info@stdominicsguam.org. Sr. MARIA TERESITA VELEZ MANALOTO, O.P., Admin.

Groups, Ecclesial Movements and other Organizations in the Archdiocese

Archdiocesan Liturgical Commission—Revs. PAUL A.M. GOFIGAN; DANILO D. FERRANDIZ; MANUEL (JUN) TRENCHERA JR.; MELCHOR T. CAMINA; RICHARD MENO KIDD; JEFFREY C. SAN NICOLAS; CARL VILLA; ANDRE EDUVALA, O.F.M.Cap.; MICHAEL CRISOSTOMO; Deacon LARRY CLAROS; Sr. FRANCINE PEREZ; MS. CYNTHIA AGBULOS; MR. ISMAEL PEREZ; MR. KARL SOTTO; ASUNCION P. GUERRERO.

Catholic Daughters of the Americas—

Our Lady of Camarin Court #2047—Mailing Address: P.O. Box 2826, Hagatna, 96932. MS. PRISCILLA S.N. MUNA, Regent, Tel: 671-477-7929; Sr. MARY STEPHEN TORRES, R.S.M., Vice Regent.

Court Maria Rainan Y Familia #2450—Mailing Address: P.O. Box 12716, Tamuning, 96931. MAYOR LOUISE RIVERA, Regent, Tel: 671-888-1540; Email: weezierivera@hotmail.com; MS. LORRAINE RIVERA, Vice Regent.

Court Santa Barbara #2055—EVANGELINE M. CEPEDA, Regent, Tel: 671-632-2899; Cell: 671-632-5659; NADINE CEPEDA, Vice Regent.

Catholic Educational Radio (KOLG) The Light 90.9—Tel: 671-475-4448; Email: kolg.guam@gmail.com. Rev. MICHAEL CRISOSTOMO, Exec. Dir.

Catholic Pro-Life Committee—Tel: 671-472-4569. MRS. PATRICIA (PAT) PERRY, Co Chair; MR. JONATHAN BORDALLO, Co Chair.

Confraternity of Christian Mothers—196 Cuesta San Ramon, Ste. B, Hagatna, 96910. Tel: 671-472-6116 ; Tel: 671-562-0000; Tel: 671-989-9732; Fax: 671-477-3519; Email: palemike@yahoo.com. Rev. FELIXBERTO LEON GUERRERO, O.F.M.Cap., Spiritual Dir.; LEILA SAN NICOLAS, Island Bd. Pres.; CARMELITA PAET, Vice Pres.; MRS. ROSA C. SANTOS, Sec.; PRISCILLA QUICHOCHO, Treas.

Divine Mercy Apostolate—Mailing Address: P.O. Box 11924, Tamuning. Tel: 671-483-9464; Email: mercydiv@yahoo.com. Rev. JOEL DE LOS REYES, Contact Person.

El Shaddai, DWXI, PPFI, Fellowship Guam, USA, Guam Chapter—Santa Barbara Catholic Church, 330 Iglesia Cir., Dededo, 96929. Rev. DANILO (DAN) C. BIEN, Spiritual Dir.; VIRGINIA GUANLAO, Coord., Tel: 671-632-5659.

Equestrian Order of the Holy Sepulcher of Jerusalem—Tel: 671-472-6201; Tel: 671-477-1842. Rev. Msgr. JAMES L.G. BENAVENTE, Contact Person.

Guam Cursillo Movement—Mailing Address: P.O. Box 315226, Tamuning, 96931. Rev. JOEL DE LOS REYES, Spiritual Dir., Tel: 671-483-9464; Email: dreyes@guam.net; MS. MARIA S.T. PEREZ, Pres., Email: scm.perez@gmail.com.

Knights of Columbus Guam State Council—P.O. Box 20142, Barrigada, 96921. Tel: 617-888-2621. Rev. JOSEPH ENGLISH, O.F.M.Cap., State Chap.; BOBBY O. PELKEY, State Deputy, Email: bobpelkey55@gmail.com.

Latin Mass Community—Rev. ERIC FORBES, O.F.M.Cap., Contact Person, Tel: 671-472-6339.

Legion of Mary, Guam Comitum—Mailing Address: P.O. Box 503, Hagatna, 96932. Rev. DANILO (DAN) C. BIEN, Spiritual Dir.; IMELDA ZIMARA, Guam Conitium, Tel: 671-649-2834; Tel: 671-987-1955; Email: melzimara@yahoo.com.

Malojloj Retreat Center—Tel: 671-828-8454; Fax: 671-828-8454; Email: malojlojretreatcenter@gmail.com. Rev. GERARDO (GERRY) N. HERNANDEZ, Contact Person; JESSE PEREZ, Asst. Oper. Mgr.

Marriage Encounter—Rev. JEFFREY C. SAN NICOLAS, Presenting Pastor. Executive Couple: DAVID DUENAS; LIZA DUENAS, Mailing Address: P.O. Box 4781, Hagatna, 96932. Tel: 671-789-7100; Web: www.wwme.org.

Neo Catechumenal Way—Dulce Nombre de Maria Cathedral-Basilica VACANT. San Vicente Ferrer Parish: VACANT. Saint Anthony Parish: Rev. Msgr. BRIGIDO U. ARROYO, Presbyter, P.O. Box 7707, Tamuning, 96931. Tel: 671-646-8044; Fax: 671-649-1039. Nino Perdido Parish (Asan): Rev. ANTONINO CAMINITI, Presbyter, P.O. Box 45, Agana, 96910. Tel: 671-477-2211.

Nuestra Senora de la Paz y Buen Viaje Parish—Mailing Address: P.O. Box EC, Hagatna, 96932. Tel: 671-734-3723; Fax: 671-734-3722. VACANT.

Our Lady of Guadalupe Parish—Mailing Address: P.O. Box 7355, Agat, 96928. Tel: 671-565-2160; Fax: 671-565-7078.

Our Lady of Lourdes Parish—Mailing Address: P.O. Box 11001, Yigo, 96929. VACANT.

Our Lady of Mt. Carmel Parish—Mailing Address: P.O. Box 8353, Agat, 96928. Tel: 671-565-2136; Fax: 671-565-9678. Rev. JOSE ALBERTO RODRIGUEZ, Presbyter.

San Dimas & Our Lady of the Rosary Parish—Mailing Address: P.O. Box 6099, Merizo, 96916. Tel: 671-828-8056; Fax: 671-828-3100. Rev. JULIUS B. AKINYEMI, Presbyter.

Secular Franciscans (Third Order)—Spiritual Assistants: Revs. JOSE G. VILLAGOMEZ, O.F.M.Cap.; ERIC FORBES, O.F.M.Cap.; TERESITA R. SABLAN, Minister, Tel: 671-472-3338; RUFINA MENDIOLA, 2nd Minister; MAE FERNANDEZ, Sec., Tel: 671-477-3338; MAGGIE F. QUAN, Treas., Email: maggiequan@gmail.com.

St. Padre Pio Fraternity - Secular Franciscans Order—Tel: 671-472-6339; Fax: 671-472-3335. Rev. PATRICK CASTRO, O.F.M.Cap., Spiritual Asst.; VIOLET MANIBUSAN, Min., Email: violet@netpci.com.

Natural Family Planning Program—VACANT.

Couples for Christ—Mailing Address: P.O. Box 2621, Agana, 96932. Tel: 671-487-1298. Rev. PAUL A.M. GOFIGAN, Spiritual Dir. Chapter Head/Evangelization: GREG CALVO, Email: calvogreg49@gmail.com.

CLERGY, PARISHES, MISSIONS AND PAROCHIAL SCHOOLS

CITY OF HAGATNA

ISLAND OF GUAM, DULCE NOMBRE DE MARIA CATHEDRAL - BASILICA (1669)
207 Archbishop Felixberto C. Flores St., Agana, 96910. Tel: 671-472-6201; Tel: 671-477-1842; Email: info@aganacathedral.org. Rev. Romeo (Romy) D. Convocar, Rector; Rev. Msgr. James L.G. Benavente; Most Rev. Michael J. Byrnes; Rev. Val Gabriel Rodriguez, Parochial Vicar; Deacons John Dierking; Augusto (Gus) F. Cepeda; Rev. Thomas B. McGrath, S.J., In Res.
Catechesis Religious Program—Students 35.

OUTSIDE THE CITY OF HAGATNA

AGANA HEIGHTS, OUR LADY OF THE BLESSED SACRAMENT (1948)
135 Chalan Kapuchino, Agana Heights, 96910. Tel: 671-472-6246; Email: olbsaganaheights@gmail.com; Web: olbsaganaheights.com. Rev. Victor Garcia; Deacon Louis T. Agbulos Jr.
Catechesis Religious Program—Sylvia T. Calvo, D.R.E. (Grades 6-Confirmation); Christine M. Chargualaf, D.R.E. (Grades K-5). Students 155.

AGAT, OUR LADY OF MOUNT CARMEL (1957) [CEM]
Mailing Address: P.O. Box 8353, Agat, 96928. Rev. Jose Alberto Rodriguez.
Res.: 157 S. Eugenio St., Agat, 96915.
Tel: 671-565-2136; Fax: 671-565-9678; Email: mountcarmelchurch@gmail.com.
Catechesis Religious Program—Students 53; RCIA 1.
Chapel—Santa Ana Chapel, Lot No. 306-4-2, Agat, 96928.

ASAN, NINO PERDIDO Y SAGRADA FAMILIA (1947)
P.O. Box 45, 96932. Rev. Antonino Caminiti.
Res.: Nino Perdido St., #142, Asan, 96910.
Tel: 671-477-2211; Email: npsfp@yahoo.com.
Catechesis Religious Program—Students 50.

BARRIGADA, SAN VICENTE FERRER AND SAN ROKE (1947)
229 San Roque Dr., Barrigada, 96913.
Tel: 671-734-4573; Email: sanvicentechurch@gmail.com. Revs. Joel de los Reyes, Parochial Admin.; Vincenzo Acampora, Parochial Vicar; Deacon Larry Claros.
Catechesis Religious Program—Students 135.

CHALAN PAGO, NUESTRA SENORA DE LA PAZ Y BUEN VIAJE (1959) [JC]
P.O. Box EC, 96932. Rev. Carlos S. Vila, J.C.L., Parochial Admin.
Res.: 520 S. Chalan Kanton Tasi Rte. 4, Chalan Pago, 96910. Tel: 671-734-3723; Fax: 671-734-3722; Email: olopsj@gmail.com; Web: www.olopsj.org.
Catechesis Religious Program—Tel: 671-734-4223. Students 79.

DEDEDO
1—ST. ANDREW KIM (1977) [JC] (Korean) Under the Jurisdiction of Santa Barbara Parish, Dededo.
Mailing Address: P.O. Box 1555, Agana, 96932.
Tel: 671-637-4148 (Office);
Tel: 671-637-1116 (Rectory); Fax: 671-637-4149; Email: philips97@hanmail.net; Web: www.guam.catb.kr. St. Andrew Kim Rd. Harmon, Dededo, 96929. Rev. Philip Byeon; Deacon Dominic Kim.
Catechesis Religious Program—Tel: 671-483-8200; Email: bimok67@hanmail.net. Students 35.

2—SANTA BARBARA (1947)
330 Iglesia Cir., Dededo, 96929. Tel: 671-632-5659; Email: santabarbaraguam@gmail.com. Revs. Dan Bien; Francis X. Hezel, S.J., Parochial Vicar; Michael Vincent Jucutan, Parochial Vicar; Deacons Herbert Cruz; Angken Rapun; Kerno Sam; Romeo Hernandez; Joe Gumataotao; Rev. Francesco S. Asproni, In Res.
Res.: 372 Gloria Cir., Dededo, 96929.
Tel: 671-633-7253.
Catechesis Religious Program—Frederica Manosa, C.R.E. Students 406.

INARAJAN, ST. JOSEPH (1680) [CEM]
Building #719 Pale Duenas St., Inarajan, 96917. Rev. Joseph Anore, Parochial Admin.
Res.: 1 San Jose Ave., P.O. Box 170022, Inarajan, 96917. Tel: 671-828-8102; Email: stjoseph_guest@outlook.com.
Catechesis Religious Program—Students 78.

MAINA, OUR LADY OF THE PURIFICATION (1949)
196 Cuesta San Ramon, Ste. B, 96910.
Tel: 671-477-7256; Email: mainacatholicchurch@gmail.com. 220 Maria Candelaria Rd., Maina, 96910. Rev. Richard Meno Kidd.
Catechesis Religious Program—Students 10.

MALOJLO, SAN ISIDRO (1973)
131 San Isidro St., HC 1 Box 17083, Inarajan, 96915. Tel: 671-828-8454; Email: sanisidromalojloj@gmail.com. Rev. Gerardo (Gerry) N. Hernandez.
Catechesis Religious Program—Students 82.

MANGILAO, SANTA TERESITA CATHOLIC CHURCH (1951)
192 S. Rte. 10, Barrigada, 96913. 192 Vietnam Veterans Hwy., Mangilao, 96913. Rev. Joseph English, O.F.M.Cap.; Deacon George Quitugua.
Catechesis Religious Program—Email: ninokev@gmail.com. Students 560.

MERIZO, SAN DIMAS AND OUR LADY OF THE ROSARY (1680) [CEM] (Chamorro) Rev. Julius B. Akinyemi.
Res.: P.O. Box 6099, Merizo, 96916.
Tel: 671-828-8056; Fax: 671-828-3100; Email: sandimasmalesso@gmail.com; Web: www.sandimasmalesso.com. 329 Chalan Canton Tasi, Merizo, 96915.
Catechesis Religious Program—Students 177.

MONGMONG, NUESTRA SENORA DE LAS AGUAS (1969)
139 Roy T. Damian St., Mongmong, 96927.
Tel: 671-477-6754; Email: nsdlaguas@guam.net. P.O. Box 163, 96932. Rev. Manuel (Jun) Trenchera Jr.; Deacon Louis J. Rama.
Catechesis Religious Program—Students 38.

ORDOT, SAN JUAN BAUTISTA (1947) (Chamorro) Rev. Richard Meno Kidd, Admin.; Rev. Msgr. David I.A. Quitugua, (Retired).
Res.: P.O. Box 49, 96932. Tel: 671-472-8341; Email: sjbc2015@hotmail.com. 107A Judge Sablan St., Ordot, 96910.
Catechesis Religious Program—Students 117.

PITI, ASSUMPTION OF OUR LADY (1930)
314 Assumption Dr., Piti, 96915. Tel: 671-472-2272; Email: assumptionpitichurch@gmail.com. Rev. Melchor T. Camina.
Res. & Mailing Address: 314 Assumption Dr., Piti, 96915. Tel: 671-472-2272; Fax: 671-477-1955; Email: assumptionpitichurch@gmail.com.
Catechesis Religious Program—Students 72.

SANTA RITA, OUR LADY OF GUADALUPE (1944)
P.O. Box 7355, Agat, 96928. Tel: 671-565-2160; Fax: 671-565-7078; Email: ologsr@gmail.com. 708 Bishop Olano St., Santa Rita, 96915. Rev. Melchor T. Camina; Deacon John Fernandez.
Catechesis Religious Program—Students 190.

SINAJANA, ST. JUDE THADDEUS (1962)
122 Bien Avenida, Sinajana, 96910. Revs. Patrick

Castro, O.F.M.Cap.; Roland Daigle, O.F.M.Cap.; Deacon Stephen Martinez.
Catechesis Religious Program—Cynthia Eclavea, D.R.E. Students 176.

TALOFOFO, SAN MIGUEL (1945) [JC]
138 San Miguel St., Talofofo, 96915-3606.
Tel: 671-789-1069; Fax: 671-789-7665; Email: father@kuentos.guam.net. Rev. Felixberto Leon Guerrero, O.F.M.Cap.
Catechesis Religious Program—Students 140.

TAMUNING, ST. ANTHONY AND ST. VICTOR (1946) Rev. Msgrs. Brigido U. Arroyo; James L.G. Benavente; Revs. Efren Adversario, Parochial Vicar; Rodolfo G. Arejola, (Retired).
Res.: 507 Chalan San Antonio, P.O. Box 7707, Tamuning, 96913. Tel: 671-646-7181;
Tel: 671-646-8044; Email: mail@stanthonyguam.org; Web: stanthonyguam.org.
Catechesis Religious Program—Students 165.

TOTO, IMMACULATE HEART OF MARY (1948)
Mailing Address: 225 Aragon St., Toto, 96910.
Tel: 671-477-9118; Fax: 671-472-2514; Email: ihom@yahoo.com. Rev. Efren Adversario; Deacons Elias Itoy Ruda; Anthony Leon Guerrero; Rene Dela Cruz; Huan Hosei.
Catechesis Religious Program—Students 117.

TUMON BAY, BLESSED DIEGO LUIS DE SAN VITORES CHURCH (1970)
884 Pale' San Vitores Rd., Tumon, 96913-4013.
Tel: 671-646-5649; Email: blsdiego@yahoo.com. Rev. Jose Antonio P. (Lito) Abad; Deacon William (Bill) Hagen.
Catechesis Religious Program—Students 49.

UMATAC, SAN DIONISIO (1680) [CEM] Rev. Julius B. Akinyemi.
Res.: San Dionisio St., P.O. Box 6099, Merizo, 96915.
Tel: 671-828-8056; Fax: 671-828-3100; Email: dionisioumatac@gmail.com; Web: www.sandimasmalesso.com.
Catechesis Religious Program—Students 40.

YIGO, OUR LADY OF LOURDES (1947)
153 Chalan Pale Ramon Lagu, Unit A, Yigo, 96929.
Tel: 671-653-2584; Email: ourlady@teleguam.net. Revs. Jonathan Alvarez, J.C.L., Parochial Admin.; Edwin Bushy, Parochial Vicar; Vito B. San Andres, Parochial Vicar; Deacons Leonard Stohr; David Richards; Greg Calvo.
Catechesis Religious Program—Tel: 671-653-1102. Femelyne Wesolowski, D.R.E.; Veronica Lizama, Coord., Children's Div.; Glenda Luke, Registrar. Students 426; RCIA 23.

YONA, SAN FRANCISCO DE ASIS (1954) [CEM]
135 Chalan Kapuchino, Agana Heights, 96910.
Tel: 671-789-1491; Email: stfrancis@teleguam.net. 1404 N. Canton Tasi, Yona, 96915. Rev. Andre Eduvala, O.F.M.Cap., Admin.
Catechesis Religious Program—Sharon O'Mallan, D.R.E. Students 146.

Chaplains of Public Institutions

HAGATNA. *Guam Memorial Hospital & Guam Regional Medical Center*. Revs. Francesco S. Asproni, Tel: 671-685-7500, Edwin Bushu, Tel: 671-480-4436.

On Duty Outside the Archdiocese:
Rev. Msgr.—
Quitugua, David C., J.C.D.
Revs.—
Camacho, Luis
Cervantes, Miguel
Cristobal, Adrian
Durango, Pedro
Flor-Caravia, Santiago
Granado, Jason
Oliveira, Edivaldo daSilva
San Andres, Vito
Sanchez Malagon, Julio Cesar
Stoia, Aurelius E.
Wadeson, John, Itinerant Catechist, CA.

Retired:
Rev. Msgr.—
Quitugua, David I.A., (Retired)
Revs.—
Arejola, Rodolfo G., (Retired)
Carriveau, Kenneth L., (Retired).

Permanent Deacons:
Calvo, Greg
Cepeda, Augusto (Gus) F.
Claros, Larry
Cruz, Herbert
Dela Cruz, Rene
Dierking, John
Fernandez, John
Gumataotao, Joe
Hagan, William
Hernandez, Romeo
Hosei, Huan
Kaai, Peter L.
Kim, Dominic
Leon Guerrero, Anthony
Martinez, Stephen
Que, Rudolfo
Quitugua, George
Rama, Louis J.
Rapun, Angken
Richards, David
Ruda, Itoi
Sam, Kerno
San Nicolas, Ronald
Stohr, Leonard John
Tenorio, Francisco.

INSTITUTIONS LOCATED IN DIOCESE

[A] SEMINARIES.

[B] HIGH SCHOOLS

AGANA. *Academy of Our Lady of Guam*, 233 W. Archbishop Felixberto C. Flores St., Agana, 96910.
Tel: 671-477-8203; Fax: 671-477-8555; Email: acad@aolg.edu.gu; Web: www.aolg.edu.gu. Sr. Mary Angela Perez, R.S.M., Pres.; Mrs. Mary Meeks, Prin. Sisters of Mercy. Religious Teachers 1; Lay Teachers 29; Sisters 3; Students 376; Staff 18.

MANGILAO. *Father Duenas Memorial School* (1949) P.O. Box FD, 96932. Tel: 671-734-2261;
Tel: 671-734-2263; Fax: 671-734-5738; Email: fdms@fatherduenas.com; Web: www.fatherduenas.com. Rev. Richard Meno Kidd, Chap.; Tony Thompson, Prin.; Dante Perez, Librarian. Lay Teachers 30; Priests 1; Students 433.

TALOFOFO. *Notre Dame High School, Inc.*, 480 S. San Miguel St., Talofofo, 96915-3540.
Tel: 671-789-1676; Tel: 671-789-1745;
Fax: 671-789-4847; Email: info@ndhsguam.com; Web: ndhsguam.com. Sr. Jean Ann Crisostomo, S.S.N:D., Pres.; Mariesha Cruz-San Nicolas, Prin. Lay Teachers 23; Sisters 1; Students 295.

[C] ELEMENTARY AND JUNIOR HIGH SCHOOLS

AGAT. *Our Lady of Mount Carmel Catholic School* (1957) P.O. Box 7830, Agat, 96928.
Tel: 671-565-3822; Tel: 671-565-5128;
Fax: 671-565-3539; Email: office@mcs51.com. Michael F. Phillips, Mount Carmel Alumni & Endowment Foundation Chm.; William Sarmiento, Prin. Clergy 2; Religious Teachers 2; Lay Teachers 27; Students 385.

BARRIGADA. *San Vicente Catholic School*, 196 Bejong St., Barrigada, 96913. Tel: 671-735-4240;
Fax: 671-734-8718; Email: principal.aquino@svcsguam.com; Web: www.svcsguam.com. Nelba Aquino, Prin. Lay Teachers 15; Sisters 2; Students 174.

DEDEDO. *Santa Barbara Catholic School* (1950) (Grades PreK-8), 274 W. Santa Barbara Ave., Ste. A., Dededo, 96929-5378. Tel: 671-632-5578;
Fax: 671-632-1414; Email: info@sbcs.edu.gu; Web: www.sbcs.edu.gu. Sr. Maria Rosario Gaite, R.S.M., Prin. Lay Teachers 34; Sisters 2; Students 415.

SINAJANA. *Bishop Baumgartner Memorial Catholic School*, (Grades K-8), 281 Calle Angel Flores St., Sinajana, 96910. Tel: 671-472-6670;
Tel: 671-477-2677; Fax: 671-477-4028; Email: principal@bbmcs.org; Email: emilinearterorsm@gmail.com; Web: www.bbmcs.org. Mrs. Rita D. Duenas, Pres.; Lila Lujan, Prin. Cathedral Grade School merged with Bishop Baumgartner Middle School to form Bishop Baumgartner Memorial Catholic School. Religious Teachers 1; Lay Teachers 44; Nuns 1; Sisters 1; Students 593.

TAMUNING. *Saint Anthony Catholic School*, 529 Chalan San Antonio, Tamuning, 96913. Tel: 671-647-1140;
Fax: 671-649-7130; Email: lorfelchaco@gmail.com; Web: www.sacsguam.com. Mrs. Lorena Q. Chaco, Prin. Lay Teachers 42; Students 618.

YIGO. *Dominican Catholic School* (1995) 114 Chalan Pale Ramon-Lagu Rte. 1, Yigo, 96929.
Tel: 671-653-3021; Fax: 671-653-3090; Email: admin@dcsguam.com; Web: www.dcsguam.com. Sr. Esperanza H. Seguban, O.P., Directress & Prin. Clergy 6; Religious Teachers 6; Lay Teachers 10; Students 200.

YONA. *St. Francis School*, P.O. Box 22199, Yona, 96921. Tel: 671-789-1270; Tel: 671-789-1351;
Fax: 671-789-3900; Email: sfcsadmin@guam.net; Web: www.sfsguam.com. Lisa Baza-Cruz, Ed.D., Prin. Lay Teachers 21; Students 191.

[D] KINDERGARTEN AND NURSERY SCHOOLS

AGANA HEIGHTS. *Maria Artero Catholic Preschool & Kindergarten*, 161 A Sunset Dr., Agana Heights, 96910-6451. Tel: 671-472-8777; Fax: 671-472-2326; Email: macpksy12@gmail.com. P.O. Box 3487, Hagana, 96932. Sr. Anotia Addy, M.M.B., Prin. Clergy 2; Religious Teachers 2; Students 22.

ORDOT. *Dominican Child Development Center*, P.O. Box 5668, Agana, 96932. Tel: 671-477-7228;
Tel: 671-472-1524; Fax: 671-472-4282; Email: avegamotin@gmail.com. Sr. Eva P. Gamotin, Prin. Lay Teachers 15; Students 153.

PEREZVILLE-TAMUNING. *Mercy Heights Nursery and Kindergarten, Inc.*, 211 Fr. San Vitores St., Tamuning, 96913. Tel: 671-646-1185;
Fax: 671-649-1822; Email: mhcnk211@gmail.com. Mrs. Belen Defant, Prin. Lay Teachers 18; Students 190.

TAI. *Infant of Prague Nursery and Kindergarten, Inc.*, 164 Sabanan Magas Rd., Mangilao, 96913.
Tel: 671-734-2785; Fax: 671-734-1055; Email: sbarbara0310@gmail.com. Sr. Barbara Ungacta, R.S.M., Prin. Institute of the Sisters of the Mercy of the Americas, South Central Community on Guam. Lay Teachers 21; Students 178.

[E] CATHOLIC CHARITIES

BARRIGADA. *Catholic Social Service of Guam*, 234 U.S. Army Juan C. Fejeran St., Barrigada, 96913-1407. Tel: 671-635-1442; Tel: 671-635-1406;
Fax: 671-635-1444; Email: ccs@catholicsocialserviceguam.org; Web: www.catholicsocialserviceguam.org. Mrs. Diana B. Calvo, Exec. Dir.; Paula Perez, Dir. Tot Asst. Annually 7,217; Total Staff 168; Total Elderly Assisted 2,379; Total Adults Assisted 1,829; Total Children Assisted 1,687; Total Families Assisted 1,311.
Elderly Programs:
Guma Serenidad, Tel: 671-635-1441; Email: gumasanjose@catholicsocialserviceguam.org. Ray Aromin, Prog. Mgr.
Shelter Programs:
Alee I Shelter for Abused Spouses & Children, Tel: 671-648-5888; Email: alee@catholicsocialserviceguam.org. Paula Perez, Prog. Mgr.
Alee II Shelter for Abused Children, Tel: 671-648-5888; Email: alee@catholicsocialserviceguam.org. Paula Perez, Prog. Mgr.
Karidat Shelter for Adults, Tel: 671-635-1441; Email: gumasanjose@catholicsocialserviceguam.org. Teressa Cruz-Blas, Prog. Mgr.
Guma San Jose, Tel: 671-633-2955; Email: gumasanjose@catholicsocialserviceguam.org. Terry Mortera, Prog. Mgr.
Transitional Homeless (Liheng), Tel: 671-635-1441; Email: diana.calvo@catholicsocialserviceguam.org. Mrs. Diana B. Calvo, Dir.
Programs for Persons with Disabilities:
Respite Care, Tel: 671-635-1441; Email: diana.calvo@catholicsocialserviceguam.org. Artemio Conducto, Prog. Mgr.
Community Habilitation Program,
Tel: 671-472-8598; Email: communityhabilitation@catholicsocialserviceguam.org. Kenneth Kai, Contact Person.
Support Services Division:
Support Services, Tel: 671-635-1441; Email: diana.calvo@catholicsocialserviceguam.org. Mrs. Diana B. Calvo, Dir.
Federal Grant dba AOA - St. Anthony Church - STOP Violence Against Women - DOJ - 2018, 507 Chalan San Antonio, Tamuning, 96913.
Tel: 671-646-8044; Email: mail@stanthonyguam.org; Web: www.stanthonyguam.org. Rev. Michael Crisostomo, Dir.; Ms. Roxanne Aguon, Contact Person.
Emergency Food Bank, Tel: 671-635-1441; Email: paula.perez@catholicsocialserviceguam.org. Mrs. Diana B. Calvo, Dir.
Msgr. David I.A. Quitugua Foundation,
Tel: 671-635-1441; Email: diana.calvo@catholicsocialserviceguam.org. Mrs. Diana B. Calvo, Dir.
Finger Printing, 234A U.S. Army Juan G. Fejeran St., Barrigada, 96913. Tel: 671-635-1441; Email: diana.calvo@catholicsocialserviceguam.org. Mrs. Diana B. Calvo, Dir.
Monthly Rummage Sale, Tel: 671-635-1441; Email: diana.calvo@catholicsocialserviceguam.org. Mrs. Diana B. Calvo, Dir.
Thrift Shop, Tel: 671-635-1441; Email: diana.calvo@catholicsocialserviceguam.org. Mrs. Diana B. Calvo, Dir.

[F] MONASTERIES AND RESIDENCES OF PRIESTS

AGANA HEIGHTS. *St. Fidelis Friary*, 135 Chalan Kapuchino, Agana Heights, 96910.
Tel: 671-472-6339; Fax: 671-472-3335; Email: capuchin@netpci.com. Revs. Patrick Castro, O.F.M.Cap., Supr.; Andre Eduvala, O.F.M.Cap.; Joseph English, O.F.M.Cap.; Eric Forbes, O.F.M.Cap.; Felixberto Leon Guerrero, O.F.M.Cap.; Agustin Gumataotao, O.F.M.Cap.; Randolph Nowak, O.F.M.Cap.; Michael Tenorio, O.F.M.Cap.; Jose G. Villagomez, O.F.M.Cap.; Bro. Brian Champoux, O.F.M.Cap.; Revs. Roland Daigle, O.F.M.Cap.; Victor Garcia, O.F.M.Cap. Headquarters of Capuchin Friars (Provincial Custody, Star of the Sea).

TAMUNING. *Society of Jesus Micronesia*, 153 Linda Way, Tamuning, 96913. Tel: 671-649-0073; Email: tbm189@aol.com. P.O. Box 315244, Tamuning, 96931. Revs. Kenneth J. Hezel, S.J., Vicar General, Diocese of Chalan Kanoa, Diocese of Chalon Kanoa, P.O. Box 500745, Saipan, MP 96950; Thomas B. McGrath, S.J., Chap.

[G] CONVENTS AND RESIDENCES FOR SISTERS

DEDEDO. *Santa Barbara Convent*, 274 B. W. Santa Barbara Ave., Dededo, 96929. Tel: 671-632-2384; Fax: 671-632-1414; Email: bibamercy70@gmail.com. Sr. Marian Therese Arroyo, R.S.M., Admin. Institute of the Sisters of Mercy of the Americas, South Central Community on Guam. Sisters 2.

HAGATNA. *Cathedral Mercy Convent*, 221 Archbishop F. C. Flores St., 96910-5102. Tel: 671-477-9291; Fax: 671-477-9293; Email: aperez@mercysc.org. Sisters Mary Emiline Artero, R.S.M.; Francis Jerome Cruz, R.S.M.; Mary Angela Perez, R.S.M. Sisters 3.

Mercedarian Missionaries of Berriz, 161 Sunset Dr., Apt. A, 96910-6451. Tel: 671-477-8303;
Fax: 671-472-2326; Email: mmbmicronesiaregion@gmail.com; Web: www.mmberriz.com. Sisters Mercedes Sierra, M.M.B., Regl. Coord.; Regina Doone, M.M.B., Local Coord.; Agatha Umwech, M.M.B., Councillor; Yolanda Delgadillo, M.M.B., Regl. Admin.; Anotia Addy, M.M.B., Prin. and Vicar. Sisters 5.

ORDOT. *Religious Missionaries of St. Dominic*, 350 N. Sabana Dr., Barrigada Heights, Barrigada, 96913. Tel: 671-653-3021; Tel: 671-472-1524;
Tel: 671-632-7104; Tel: 671-632-9370; Email: smtvmop@hotmail.com; Email: sehsop@yahoo.com; Email: sorveronica2012@yahoo.com; Web: www.opmisionerastaiwan.com. Sisters Esperanza H. Seguban, O.P., Prov. Asst.; Veronica Diaz; Victoria Cambronero, O.P.; Leticia Estero; Milagros Emralino; Stephanie David; Julia Patimo; Versamin Calamiong; Eva P. Gamotin; Bernardita Delos Reyes; Milagros Elesterio, O.P.; Ursula Antazo Apacionado, O.P.; Imelda Aquino, O.P.; Matilde Gabieta; Maria Teresita Velez Manaloto, O.P. Religious 15; Sisters 15; Total in Residence 15.

PEREZVILLE-TAMUNING. *MERCY ACTION MARIANAS, Ltd. (MAML)*, 211 Fr. San Vitores St., Tamuning, 96913. Tel: 671-649-7561; Fax: 671-649-1822; Email: marroyo@mercysc.org; Web: sistersofmercyguam.org. Sr. Mary Cabrini Taitano, R.S.M., Pres. Institute of the Sisters of Mercy of the Americas, South Central Community on Guam. Sisters 2.

Mercy Heights Convent, 211 Fr. San Vitores St., Tamuning, 96913. Tel: 671-646-7246;
Fax: 671-649-1822; Email: marroyo@mercysc.org; Web: sistersofmercyguam.org. Sisters Mary Cecilia Camacho, R.S.M., Local Admin.; Marian Therese Arroyo, R.S.M., Guam Mercy Admin.; Maria Rosario Gaite, R.S.M., Asst. Guam Mercy Admin.; Elizabeth Ann Uncangco, R.S.M. Sisters in residence teaching and working in Tamuning, Agana, Sinajana and infirmed; Residence, retirement residence & administrative offices of the Institute of the Sisters of Mercy of the Americas, South Central Community on Guam. Sisters 16.

TAI. *Tai Mercy Convent and Formation House*, 164 Sabanan Magas Rd., Mangilao, 96913.
Tel: 671-734-3312; Fax: 671-734-2260; Email: bibamercy70@gmail.com; Web: sistersofmercyguam.org. P.O. Box 22865 GMF, Barrigada, 96921-2865. Sr. Marian Therese Arroyo, R.S.M., Admin. Institute of the Sisters of Mercy of the Americas, South Central Community on Guam; Professed Sisters in various Apostolates and Sisters in basic formation as well as retired sisters. Sisters 8.

TALOFOFO. *S.S.N.D. Notre Dame Center*, 480 S. San Miguel St., Talofofo, 96915-3540.
Tel: 671-789-0501; Fax: 671-789-0045; Email: francineperez41@gmail.com; Email: sjaquinene@gmail.com. Sisters Mary Joseph Ann Quinene, S.S.N.D., Supr.; Mary Francine Perez, S.S.N.D., Contact Person. Sisters 17.

[H] MISCELLANEOUS LISTINGS

AGANA. *Secular Franciscans*, 135 Chalan Kapuchino, Agana Heights, 96910. Tel: 671-789-1491;
Tel: 671-472-6339; Fax: 671-789-1400; Email: quanmaggie@gmail.com. Rev. Jose G. Villagomez, O.F.M.Cap., Spiritual Dir.; Teresita R. Sablan, Pres.

BARRIGADA. *Saint Dominic's Senior Care Home*, 350 N. Sabana Dr., Barrigada Heights, 96913-1262.
Tel: 671-632-9370; Tel: 671-632-9378;
Fax: 671-637-1679; Tel: 671-632-7104;
Tel: 671-632-9379; Tel: 671-632-9372; Email: stdom@teleguam.net; Email: info@stdominicsguam.org; Email: smtvmop@hotmail.com; Web: www.stdominicsguam.org. Sisters Bernadita Delos Reyes, O.P., Treas.; Ursula Antazo Apacionado, O.P., Prioress; Veronica Diaz, Pastoral Min./Coord.; Maria Teresita Velez Manaloto, O.P., Admin.; Imelda Aquino, O.P.; Milagros Elesterio, O.P. Bed Capacity 60; Tot Asst. Annually 50; Total Staff 75.

RELIGIOUS INSTITUTES OF MEN REPRESENTED IN THE ARCHDIOCESE

For further details refer to the corresponding bracketed number in the Religious Institutes of Men or Women section.

[0470]—*The Capuchin Friars* (Vice Prov. of Mary, Star of the Sea)—O.F.M.Cap.

[0690]—*The Society of Jesus- Jesuit Fathers and Brothers* (N.Y. Prov.)—S.J.

RELIGIOUS INSTITUTES OF WOMEN REPRESENTED IN THE ARCHDIOCESE

[1780]—*Congregation of the Sisters of the Third Order of St. Francis of Perpetual Adoration* (La Crosse, WI)—F.S.P.A.

[2510]—*Mercedarian Missionaries of Berriz*—M.M.B.

[1145]—*Religious Missionaries of St. Dominic*—O.P.

[2970]—*School Sisters of Notre Dame* (Mequon, WI)—S.S.N.D.

[2575]—*Sisters of Mercy of the Americas* (Belmont, NC)—R.S.M.

An asterisk (*) denotes an organization that has established tax-exempt status directly with the IRS and is not covered by the USCCB Group Ruling.

Diocese of Arecibo, Puerto Rico

(Dioecesis Arecibensis)

Most Reverend

DANIEL FERNANDEZ TORRES

Bishop of Arecibo; ordained January 7, 1995; appointed Titular Bishop of Sufes and Auxiliary Bishop of San Juan, PR February 14, 2007; ordained April 21, 2007; appointed Bishop of Arecibo September 24, 2010; installed October 3, 2010.

Most Reverend

INAKI MALLONA TXERTUDI, C.P.

Bishop Emeritus of Arecibo; ordained March 17, 1956; appointed December 14, 1991; consecrated January 6, 1992; installed January 25, 1992; retired September 24, 2010. *Res.: Hogar Irma Fe Pol, #52 Calle Comercio, Lares, PR 00669.*

ESTABLISHED APRIL 30, 1960.

Square Miles 833.

Comprises the mid-northern part of the Island.

The Chancery: 206 Dr. Salas St., P.O. Box 616, Arecibo, PR 00613. Tel: 787-878-3180; Tel: 787-878-3110; Fax: 787-880-2661.

Email: arecibo@diocesisdearecibo.org

STATISTICAL OVERVIEW

Personnel	
Bishop	1
Retired Bishops	1
Priests: Diocesan Active in Diocese	45
Priests: Diocesan Active Outside Diocese	10
Priests: Diocesan in Foreign Missions	10
Priests: Retired, Sick or Absent	12
Number of Diocesan Priests	77
Religious Priests in Diocese	38
Total Priests in Diocese	115
Extern Priests in Diocese	2
Ordinations:	
Diocesan Priests	2
Religious Priests	1
Transitional Deacons	2
Permanent Deacons in Diocese	31
Total Brothers	5
Total Sisters	111
Parishes	
Parishes	58
With Resident Pastor:	
Resident Diocesan Priests	42
Resident Religious Priests	16
Without Resident Pastor:	
Administered by Priests	1
Missions	229
Closed Parishes	1
Professional Ministry Personnel:	
Brothers	5
Sisters	111
Welfare	
Homes for the Aged	2
Total Assisted	56
Residential Care of Children	3
Total Assisted	31
Specialized Homes	1
Total Assisted	7
Special Centers for Social Services	1
Total Assisted	1,440
Other Institutions	1
Total Assisted	1,460
Educational	
Seminaries, Diocesan	1
Students from This Diocese	7
Total Seminarians	7
Colleges and Universities	1
Total Students	968
High Schools, Diocesan and Parish	6
Total Students	590
High Schools, Private	7
Total Students	1,178
Elementary Schools, Diocesan and Parish	6
Total Students	937
Elementary Schools, Private	7
Total Students	2,246
Total Students under Catholic Instruction	5,926
Teachers in the Diocese:	
Brothers	2
Sisters	11
Lay Teachers	359
Vital Statistics	
Receptions into the Church:	
Infant Baptism Totals	1,217
Minor Baptism Totals	105
Adult Baptism Totals	79
First Communions	1,788
Confirmations	1,692
Marriages:	
Catholic	264
Interfaith	21
Total Marriages	285
Deaths	1,783
Total Catholic Population	316,723
Total Population	565,576

Former Bishops—Most Revs. ALFRED F. MENDEZ, C.S.C., ord. 1935; cons. Oct. 28, 1960; retired Jan., 1974; died Jan. 28, 1995; MIGUEL RODRIQUEZ, C.S.S.R., D.D., ord. June 22, 1958; appt. Jan. 21, 1974; cons. March 23, 1974; retired March, 1990; died Aug. 13, 2001; INAKI MALLONA TXERTUDI, C.P., ord. March 17, 1956; appt. Dec. 14, 1991; cons. Jan. 6, 1992; installed Jan. 25, 1992; retired Sept. 24, 2010.

Secretary to the Bishop—MISS SYLVIA HERNANDEZ.

Director of Communications Media—MRS. VIVIAN MALDONADO.

Chancery Office—206 Dr. Salas St., P.O. Box 616, Arecibo, 00613-0616. Tel: 787-878-3180; Tel: 787-878-3110; Fax: 787-880-2661.

Vicar General—Rev. LUIS A. COLON, S.E.M.V., Mailing Address: P.O. Box 616, Arecibo, 00613. Tel: 787-878-3180; Tel: 787-878-3110.

Secretary and Receptionist—MRS. WALESKA CORDERO.

Economic Administrator—Rev. JORGE L. RUIZ.

Economic Administrator Assistant—MISS MARILUNA ROMAN.

Chancellor—Rev. JORGE L. VIRELLA VAZQUEZ, Mailing Address: P.O. Box 616, Arecibo, 00613. Tel: 787-878-3180.

Secretary—MISS SYLVIA VARGAS.

Diocesan Tribunal of Arecibo—Rev. RAMON OLIVENCIA VÉLEZ, Judicial Vicar.

Adjutant Judges—Revs. JORGE L. VIRELLA; JORGE Y. MORALES; LISIMACO HINCAPIE RAMIREZ.

Promoter of Justice—VACANT.

Defenders of the Bond—Revs. ALBERTO DIAZ COLON; ANGEL MARRERO ROSARIO; ANTONIO OFRAY, S.E.M.V.

Advocate—Rev. OSCAR CHACON GONZALEZ, O.SS.T.

Notary—LUZ S. RIVERA VELAZQUEZ, Sec.

Secretary—MRS. LIVIA E. SERRANO.

Vicar of Diocesan Pastoral Affairs—Rev. ADRIAN N. JIMENEZ ORTIZ.

Secretary—MRS. WANDA I. RIVERA.

Diocesan Consultors—Revs. P. JESUS MONREAL PUJANTE, O.Carm.; LUIS A. COLON, S.E.M.V.; VICTOR ROJAS; RAMON OLIVENCIA VÉLEZ; VICTOR SANCHEZ VELEZ; MELQUIADES ROJAS RODRÍGUEZ.

Priest's Senate (Consejo Presbiteral)—Most Rev. DANIEL FERNANDEZ TORRES; Revs. VICTOR SANCHEZ VELEZ; LUIS A. COLON, S.E.M.V.; RAMON OLIVENCIA VÉLEZ; ERIC HERNÁNDEZ FIGUEROA, M.N.M.; JORGE L. VIRELLA VAZQUEZ; JORGE MORALES RIVERA; TOMAS SANTOS; CARMELO URARTE ABERASTURI; HIRAM SANTIAGO RIVERA, S.D.B.; JESUS MONREAL PUJANTE, O.Carm.; VICTOR ROJAS; ADRIAN N. JIMENEZ ORTIZ; ROY MARTÍNEZ MARTÍNEZ NEGRON; DAVID RIVAS RIVERA; LUIS J. RIVERA; MELQUIADES ROJAS RODRÍGUEZ; GABRIEL ALONSO SÁNCHEZ; JORGE PAREDES BELTRAN.

Diocesan Offices and Directors

Ayuda Social Movimiento Juan XXIII—JUAN ROMAN VEGA, Coord., Mailing Address: P.O. Box 193, Sabana Hoyos, 00688. Web: www.ayudasocialjuanxxiii.org; Tel: 787-815-6626; Email: ayudasocialjuan23@yahoo.com.

Cursillos de Cristiandad—Tel: 787-650-6665. MR. NELSON MORALES, Urb. Vista Azul, Calle 18-S-12, Arecibo, 00612.

Director of Youth—Rev. ELMON HERNANDEZ FANA.

Legion of Mary—MRS. LUCY SALVAT, Mailing Address: P.O. Box 2062, Arecibo, 00613. Tel: 787-309-9266.

Movimiento Familiar Cristiano (CFM)—Rev. VICTOR ROJAS RODRIGUEZ.

Prison Services—Rev. ELVIN A. IRIZARRY ROMAN, Mailing Address: P.O. Box 1282, Sabana Hoyos, 00688-1282. Tel: 787-879-8191; Email: icorazon_de_maria@yahoo.com.

Seminario San Jose College Seminary—Mailing

1—LA CANDELARIA (1738) [JC]
Calle Padial #2, Manati, 00674. Tel: 787-854-2013; Email: lacandelariaysanmatias@yahoo.com. Rev. Emile Athas.
School—Colegio De La Inmaculada Concepcion, (Grades PreK-12), Carr. #2 Km. 49.6, Manati, 00674. Tel: 787-854-2079; Fax: 787-854-2202; Email: cicmanati@outlook.com. Sr. Rosalina Santiago, Prin. Lay Teachers 42; Sisters of Charity 1; Students 824.
Catechesis Religious Program—Tel: 787-854-4021. Luz Delia Santos, D.R.E. Students 79.
Chapels—Chapel Nuestra Senora del Perpetuo Socorro—Bo. Pugnado, Manati, 00674.
Chapel La Milagrosa, Villa Amalia, Manati, 00674.
Chapel Sagrado Corazon, Bo. Cortes, Manati, 00674.
Chapel Nuestra Senora de la Monserrate, Sector Polvorín, Manati, 00674.
Chapel Espiritu Santo, Bo. La Ceiba, Manati, 00674.

2—NUESTRA SENORA DEL MAR (1978) [JC]
Carr. 685 Km 5.0, Bo. Boquillas, P.O. Box 1183, Manati, 00674. Tel: 787-854-5388; Email: peregrino59@hotmail.com. Rev. Carlos Granados Penagos; Deacon Jorge Jimenez Sanchez.
Catechesis Religious Program—Tel: 787-854-9252. Jacqueline Maisonet, D.R.E. Students 73.
Chapels—Chapel Santa Rosa de Lima—Tierras Nuevas, Manati, 00674.
Chapel La Milagrosa, Sector Cantito, Manati, 00674.
Chapel Nuestra Senora de Lourdes, Sector Laguna, Manati, 00674.

3—OUR SAVIOR
Urb. San Salvador Calle Ángel Ramos B-32, P.O. Box 465, Manati, 00674. Tel: 787-884-3664; Email: parroquia.elsalvador@yahoo.com. Rev. Melquiades Rojas Rodríguez; Deacons José Morales Hernáiz; Eddie Pérez González.
School—Colegio Marista El Salvador, (Grades PreK-12), P.O. Box 856, Manati, 00764. Tel: 787-854-1075; Tel: 787-854-2485; Fax: 787-854-6733; Email: oficinamaristamanati@live.com. Bro. Manuel Vallejo, Dir. Marist Brothers 2; Lay Teachers 46; Students 726.
Catechesis Religious Program—Lourdes Robles, D.R.E. Students 103.
Chapels—Chapel San Jose—San José, Manati, 00674.
Chapel San Martin de Porres, Bo. Guayaney, Manati, 00674.

4—SAGRADA FAMILIA (1972) [JC]
Villa Evangelina, Carr. 670, P.O. Box 704, Manati, 00674. Tel: 787-854-2858; Email: manaticm@yahoo.com. Revs. Marion Poncette, C.M.; Emmery Mondesir, Parochial Vicar; Deacon Jose Escudero Ginés.
Catechesis Religious Program—Olga Rivera, D.R.E. Students 105.
Chapels—Chapel San Judas Tadeo—Parcelas Las Marques, Manati, 00674.
Chapel La Monserrate, Palo Alto, Manati, 00674.
Chapel La Milagrosa, Polvorín, Manati, 00674.

MOROVIS

1—NUESTRA SENORA DEL CARMEN (1820) [JC]
Calle El Carmen #12, P.O. Box 428, Morovis, 00687. Tel: 787-862-2620; Email: rivera-1025-@hotmail.com. Revs. Jesus Monreal Pujante, O.Carm.; Hector M. Garcia Morales, Parochial Vicar; Jose Olivera Figueroa, Parochial Vicar; Salvador Rodrigo Gil; Deacons Luis Q. Colon Ortiz; Jaime Rivera Estela.
Catechesis Religious Program—Alberto Gutiérrez, D.R.E. Students 655.
Chapels—Chapel Nuestra Senora del Rosario—San Lorenzo, Morovis, 00687.
Chapel Nuestra Senora del Carmen, Pastos, Morovis, 00687.
Chapel Nuestra Senora del Carmen, Perchas, Morovis, 00687.
Chapel La Milagrosa, Rio Grande, Morovis, 00687.
Chapel San Jose, Jobos, Morovis, 00687.
Chapel San Miguel Arcangel, Unibon, Morovis, 00687.
Chapel Sagrada Familia, Patron, Morovis, 00687.
Chapel Segrado Corazon, Cuchillas, Bo. Pimiento, Morovis, 00687.
Chapel Reina de la Paz, Cuchillas, Morovis, 00687.
Chapel Nuestra Senora del Carmen, Buena Vista, Morovis, 00687.
Chapel San Judas Tadeo, Vega I, Morovis, 00687.

2—ST. PAUL APOSTLE (1985) [JC]
Bo. Barahona Carr. 633 Km 4.3, P.O. Box 537, Morovis, 00687. Tel: 787-862-3445; Email: parroquiasanpabloapostol22@gmail.com. Rev. Lisimaco Hincapie Ramirez.
Catechesis Religious Program—Carmen Meléndez, D.R.E. Students 239.
Chapels—Chapel Divino Nino Jesus de Praga—Franquez Centro, Morovis, 00687.
Chapel Nuestra Senora de La Providencia, Fránquez Carretera, Morovis, 00687.
Chapel Senor de los Milagros, Torrecillas, Morovis, 00687.

OROCOVIS

1—OUR LADY OF FATIMA (1975) [JC]
Carr. 566 Km 0.2, Sector Puente Doble, Bo. Saltos, P.O. Box 2118, Orocovis, 00720. Tel: 787-867-3277; Email: fatimaorocovis@hotmail.com. Rev. Osvaldo Pérez Gonzalez, C.S.Sp.
Catechesis Religious Program—Wanda Rodríguez, D.R.E. Students 185.
Chapels—Chapel Santo Cristo de la Salud—Bermejales, Orocovis, 00720.
Chapel Virgen de los Dolores, Bo. Bauta, Orocovis, 00720.
Chapel Nuestra Senora del Perpetuo Socorro, Damián Arriba, Orocovis, 00720.
Chapel Espiritu Santo, Bo. Pellejas, Orocovis, 00720.
Chapel San Martin de Porres, Miraflores, Orocovis, 00720.

2—SAN JUAN BAUTISTA (1838) [JC]
Calle Ramos Antonini #1, P.O. Box 2114, Orocovis, 00720. Tel: 787-867-2210; Email: parroquiaorocovis@yahoo.com. Revs. Jorge Burgos Rivera, S.D.B.; Hiram Santiago Rivera, S.D.B., Parochial Vicar; Jorge González Santiago, S.D.B., Parochial Vicar; Deacon Eugenio Soto Santiago, D.R.E.
School—Colegio San Juan Bautista, (Grades PreK-11), Carr 157 Km. 23.7 Interior Bo. Barros, P.O. Box 1877, Orocovis, 00720. Tel: 787-867-2295; Fax: 787-567-2295; Email: altarceleste24@gmail.com. Sr. Araceli Reyes, Prin. Lay Teachers 16; Salesian Sisters 3; Students 248.
Catechesis Religious Program—Students 793.
Chapels—Chapel Santos Angeles Custodios—Sabana Abajo, Orocovis, 00720.
Chapel Cristo Resucitado, Botijas 1, Orocovis, 00720.
Chapel Santa Clara, Botijas 2, Orocovis, 00720.
Chapel San Pablo Apostol, Puente - Alturas, Orocovis, 00720.
Chapel Sagrado Corazon, Mata de Caña, Orocovis, 00720.
Chapel Espiritu Santo, Damián, Orocovis, 00720.
Chapel Virgen del Carmen, Montebello, Orocovis, 00720.
Chapel Nuestra Senora de Guadalupe, Barros, Orocovis, 00720.
Chapel Nuestra Senora de la Providencia, Bajuras, Orocovis, 00720.
Chapel San Juan Bosco, El Gato, Orocovis, 00720.
Chapel El Divino Nino, Las Marianas, Orocovis, 00720.

QUEBRADILLAS

1—SACRED HEART (1977) [JC]
Carr. 484 Km 0.6, Bo. Cocos, P.O. Box 1569, Quebradillas, 00678. Tel: 787-895-3033; Email: pscjcocos@gmail.com. Rev. Carmelo Urarte Aberasturi.
Catechesis Religious Program—Carr. 484 Km 0.6, Bo. Cocos, Quebradillas, 00678. Félix Rosado, D.R.E. Students 291.
Chapels—Chapel San Miguel Arcangel—Bo. San Antonio, Quebradillas, 00678.
Chapel Nuestra Senora del Perpetuo Socorro, Bo. Yeguada, Quebradillas, 00678.
Chapel Madre Dolorosa, Sector El Verde, Quebradillas, 00678.

2—SAN RAPHAEL (1828) [JC]
Calle San Carlos #110, Box 57, Quebradillas, 00678. Tel: 787-895-3463; Email: sanrafael1828@gmail.com. Revs. Jorge Virella Vázquez; Kenneth D. Moore Irizarry, S.E.M.V., Parochial Vicar; Deacons Efrain Muniz Perez; Wilfredo López Mora.
School—Colegio San Rafael, (Grades K-12), Calle Lamela #213, Quebradillas, 00678. Tel: 787-895-2280; Email: csrque@gmail.com. Mrs. Dahriana Dorta. Lay Teachers 20; Students 216.
Catechesis Religious Program—Tel: 787-306-8268. Luis Nieves, D.R.E. Students 246.
Chapels—Chapel San Jose—Bo. San José, Quebradillas, 00678.
Chapel Nuestra Senora del Carmen, Quebrada, Quebradillas, 00678.
Chapel Santa Cruz, Bo. Cacao, La Chiva, Quebradillas, 00678.
Chapel La Milagrosa, Cacao, Quebradillas, 00678.
Chapel Nuestra Senora de la Monserrate, San Antonio, Quebradillas, 00678.
Chapel San Antonio, San Antonio, Quebradillas, 00678.
Chapel Nuestra Senora del Perpetuo Socorro, Bo. Charcas, Quebradillas, 00678.
Chapel Nuestra Senora de Guadalupe, Bo. Terranova, Sec. Las Talas, Quebradillas, 00678.

UTUADO

1—NUESTRA SENORA DEL MONTE CARMELO (1981) [JC]
Carr. 613 Km 0.2, Bo. Caonillas, HC-01 Box 4179, Utuado, 00641. Tel: 787-234-2722; Tel: 787-204-3554 ; Email: parr.monte.carmelo.utuado@gmail.com. Rev. William Martinez Pastoriza, Admin.; Deacon Pedro A. Collazo.
Catechesis Religious Program—Idhem Heredia Pérez, D.R.E. Students 37.
Chapels—Chapel San Antonio de Padua—Mameyes, Utuado, 00641.
Chapel Sagrado Corazon, Tetuán III, Utuado, 00641.
Chapel San Salvador, Tetuán I y II, Utuado, 00641.
Chapel La Milagrosa, Bo. Don Alonso, Utuado, 00641.

2—OUR LADY OF ANGELS (1967) [JC]
Carr. 111 Ramal 602 Km 1.3, Bo. Angeles, P.O. Box 98, Angeles, 00611. Tel: 787-933-0371; Email: ofiparr12@gmail.com. Rev. Miguel Mercado Rivera; Deacon Ferdinand Reyes Sisco.
Catechesis Religious Program—Magali Vargas Ocasio, D.R.E. Students 34.
Chapels—Chapel San Jose—El Corcho, Angeles, 00611.
Chapel Nuestra Senora de la Monserrate, Santa Isabel, Angeles, 00611.
Chapel Sagrada Familia, Las Vegas, Bo. Angeles, Angeles, 00611.

3—OUR LADY OF SORROWS (1983) [JC]
Carr. 111 Km 8.9, Bo. Caguana, P.O. Box 2525 CMB-73, Utuado, 00641-2525. Tel: 787-933-4746; Email: ofiparr08@gmail.com. Rev. Juan Perez Torres, Admin.
Catechesis Religious Program—Carmen M. Rivera Capetillo, D.R.E. Students 38.
Chapels—Chapel San Martin de Porres—Bo. Roncador, Utuado, 00641-2525.
Chapel Cristo Rey, Sector Cayuco, Utuado, 00641-2525.
Chapel Nuestra Senora de la Monserrate, Bo. Jácanas, Utuado, 00641-2525.

4—SAN MIGUEL (1746) [JC]
8 Barcelo St., P.O. Box 10, Utuado, 00641-0010. Tel: 787-894-2696; Fax: 787-894-3112; Email: sanmiguelutuado@outlook.com. Revs. Ramón López López, Admin.; José Maldonado Rivas; Edward Maldonado Plaza; Deacons Nelson Perez Martinez; Pedro Collazo Cruz.
Catechesis Religious Program—Sr. Juanita Torres, D.R.E. Students 100.
Chapels—Chapel San Fidel—Bo. Puente Blanco, Utuado, 00641.
Chapel San Martin de Porres, Bo. Arenas, Utuado, 00641.
Chapel Nuestra Senora del Perpetuo Socorro, Bo. Sabana Grande, Utuado, 00641.
Chapel San Jose, Rio Abajo, Utuado, 00641.

5—SAN PEDRO Y SAN PABLO (1988) [JC]
Bo. Paso Palmas Carr. 140 Km 15.4, P.O. Box 1878, Utuado, 00641. Tel: 787-567-3184; Email: p.sanpedroysanpabloutuado@gmail.com. Rev. Fredo Lesly Andre.
Catechesis Religious Program—Rosa M. Vázquez Vélez, D.R.E. Students 48.
Chapels—Chapel San Francisco de Asis—Bo. Las Palmas, Utuado, 00641.
Chapel Inmaculada Concepcion, Viví Arriba, Utuado, 00641.
Chapel La Milagrosa, Bo. La Pica, Utuado, 00641.
Chapel San Jose, Bo. Consejo, Utuado, 00641.
Chapel La Providencia, Bo. Viví Abajo, Utuado, 00641.

VEGA-ALTA

1—IMMACULATE CONCEPTION OF BLESSED VIRGIN MARY (1805)
Calle Georgetti #42, P.O. Box 775, Vega-Alta, 00692. Tel: 787-883-4875; Fax: 787-883-4876; Email: parroquialainmaculada@yahoo.com. Rev. Victor Rojas; Deacon Enrique Laureano Molina.
Catechetical Center—Emily Pantojas, D.R.E. Students 173.
Chapels—Chapel Sagrado Corazon de Jesus—Bo. Maricao, Vega-Alta, 00692.
Chapel Nuestra Senora de Lourdes, Bo. Pámpanos, Vega-Alta, 00692.
Chapel Santa Ana, Bo. Bajura, Vega-Alta, 00692.
Chapel Inmaculado Corazon de Maria, Bo. Candelaria, Vega-Alta, 00692.

2—PERPETUO SOCORRO (1975) [JC]
Carr. 690 Km 5.6, Bo. Breñas, P. O. Box 9018 - Sabana Branch, Vega-Baja, 00694-9018. Email: pquiu@yahoo.com; Tel: 787-883-5776. Rev. Luis Vázquez Santos; Deacon Juan Cantre Salgado.
Catechesis Religious Program—Carmen C. Soto, D.R.E. Students 93.
Chapels—Chapel San Vicente de Paul—Bo. Sabana, Vega-Baja, 00694.
Chapel Nuestra Senora del Carmen, Bo. Cerro Gordo, Vega-Baja, 00694.

3—SANTA ANA (1967)
Urb. Santa Ana Calle 3 H-9, P.O. Box 2105, Vega-Alta, 00692. Tel: 787-883-2502; Email: santaanap49@gmail.com. Rev. Angel Diaz Caceres; Deacon Wilbert Dávila Cortés.
Catechesis Religious Program—María Bruno, D.R.E. Students 98.
Chapel—Chapel Nuestra Senora del Carmen, Espinoza, Vega-Alta, 00692. Tel: 787-883-2505.

VEGA-BAJA

1—THE BLESSED TRINITY (1971)
Almirante Sur Carr. 160 Km 8.6, P.O. Box 58, Vega Baja, 00694-0058. Rev. Elmon Hernandez Fana.

Catechesis Religious Program—Evelyn Santiago, D.R.E. Students 84.
Chapels—Chapel Sagrada Familia—Almirante Norte, Vega Baja, 00694.
Chapel Nuestra Senora de la Providencia, Patron II, Vega Baja, 00694.

2—HOLY ROSARY (1794) [JC]
Calle Betances #36, P.O. Box 1388, Vega-Baja, 00694. Tel: 787-858-2969; Email: pnsrosario@hotmail.com. Rev. Jorge Y. Morales.
School—Colegio Nuestra Senora del Rosario, (Grades PreK-12), Carr. 686 Km. 17.2 Zona Industrial, Vega Baja, 00694. Tel: 787-858-2538; Tel: 787-858-4111; Fax: 787-858-6648; Email: miguelinamelendez@hotmail.com. Mrs. Miguelina Melendez, Prin. Lay Teachers 21; Students 318.
Catechesis Religious Program—María Otero Figueroa, D.R.E. Students 84.
Chapels—Chapel San Jose—Bo. Arenales, Vega-Baja, 00694.
Chapel Nuestra Senora de Fatima, Almirante, Vega-Baja, 00694.
Chapel La Milagrosa, Bo. La Trocha, Vega-Baja, 00694.

3—NTRA. SRA. DE LA PROVIDENCIA (1970) [JC]
Ave. Guarico Calle Providencia #1, Urb. Jardines, P.O. Box 4056, Vega Baja, 00694-4056.
Tel: 787-654-8676; Email: pnsprovidencia@gmail.com. Rev. Angel Diaz Marrero.
Catechesis Religious Program—María Adorno, D.R.E. Students 156.
Chapels—Chapel San Jose—Brisas de Tortuguero, Vega Baja, 00694.
Chapel San Pedro Apostol, Vega Baja Lakes, Vega Baja, 00694.

4—OUR LADY OF CARMEN-PLAYA (1976) [JC]
Ave. Jupiter, Barriada Sandin, Carr. 686 Calle Marte #79, P.O. Box 4095, Vega-Baja, 00694-4095.
Tel: 787-855-5226; Email: p_sradelcarmen@yahoo.com. Rev. Jesus Rodriguez Muñíz.
Catechesis Religious Program—María E. Meléndez, D.R.E. Students 79.
Chapels—Chapel San Judas Tadeo—Los Naranjos, Vega-Baja, 00694-4095.
Chapel Divino Nino Jesus, San Demetrio, Vega-Baja, 00694-4095.

5—OUR LADY OF LOURDES (1984) [JC]
Urb. Alturas de Vega Baja, Calle R. Esquina Q., P.O. Box 4414, Vega-Baja, 00694. Tel: 787-855-4942; Email: luisja15@hotmail.com. Rev. Luis J. Rivera Rivera.
Catechesis Religious Program—P. Luis J. Rivera, D.R.E. Students 107.
Convent—Tel: 787-855-0341. Hermanas Terciarias Capuchinas 3.
Chapels—Chapel Santa Rosa de Lima—Bo. Rio Abajo, Vega-Baja, 00694.
Chapel San Juan Bautista, Bo. Quebrada Arenas, Vega-Baja, 00694.
Chapel San Francisco de Asis, Bo. Las Granjas, Vega-Baja, 00694.

6—OUR LADY OF MT. CARMEL (1968) [JC]
Camelia St. #48, Bo. Caiba, Carmelita, Vega Alta, 00692. Tel: 787-654-7891; Email: parroquiacarmelitavg@gmail.com. P.O. Box 1417, Vega Baja, 00692. Rev. Angel Marrero Rosario, Admin.; Deacon Luis Collazo.
Catechesis Religious Program—Virginia Gaetan, D.R.E. Students 95.
Chapels—Chapel La Milagrosa—Bo. Pueblo Nuevo, Vega Alta, 00692.
Chapel San Judas Tadeo, Bo. Sabana Hoyos, Vega Alta, 00692.
Chapel Nuestra Senora de Guadalupe, Bo. Santa Rosa, Vega Alta, 00692.

7—PARROQUIA DE SAN MARTIN DE PORRES (1967) [JC]
Calle Parque A-2 #5, Parcelas Amadeo, P.O. Box 254, Vega Baja, 00694. Tel: 787-654-9501; Email: s_an_martin@yahoo.com. Rev. Luis J. Rivera, Admin.
Catechesis Religious Program—Tel: 787-858-8651. Aida Rodríguez, D.R.E. Students 37.
Chapels—Chapel Sagrado Corazon—Bo. Panaini, Vega Baja, 00694.
Chapel San Jose.
Chapel St. Anthony de Padua, Villa Colombo, Vega Baja, 00694.

On Duty Outside the Diocese:
Revs.—
Irizarry, Alan M., Fayetteville, NC
Lopez, Carlos A., Boston, MA
Lopez, Juan J., Sunrise, FL
Munoz, Jesus M., Military Service
Perez Perez, Ovidio, Ponce, P.R.
Portalatin, Antonio, Germany
Ramos Rodriguez, Rafael, New York
Romero, Cesar Santos, San Juan
Tejada Henriquez, Francisco, New York.

Retired:
Revs.—
Caraballo, Antonio, (Retired), Spain
Fernandez Minguez, Serapio, (Retired), Spain
Garcia, Jose L., (Retired), Sevilla, Spain
Guerrero, Jose Ma., (Retired), Spain
Hernandez, Jimmy, (Retired), Quebradillas, PR
Jimenez, Victorino, (Retired), Spain
Maduro, Gabriel, (Retired), Arecibo, PR
Morales, Salomon J., (Retired)
Perez, Leon, (Retired), Zaragoza, Spain
Rivera Calderon, Miguel A., (Retired), Comerio, P.R.
Soberal, Jose D., V.G., (Retired), Lares, PR.

INSTITUTIONS LOCATED IN DIOCESE

[A] EDUCATIONAL

ARECIBO. *Pontificia Universidad Catolica de Puerto Rico, Recinto de Arecibo*, P.O. Box 144045, 00614-4045. Tel: 787-881-1212; Fax: 787-680-7045; Web: www.pucpr.edu. Rev. Luis A. Mendez, Office Chap.; Yazdel Martinez Colon, D.B.A., Dean of Academic Affairs; Edwin Hernandez Vera, Ph.D., Chancellor; Luz C. Rivera Correa, Librarian. Lay Teachers 75; Priests 4; Students 1,080.
Seminario San Jose, Calle Fermin Tirapu #28, Villava, Navarra Spain 31610. Tel: 34-948-144-023; Email: arecibo@diocesisdearecibo.org; Email: ssjnavarra@gmail.com; Web: ssjnavarra.blogspot.com.es. Priests 2; Students 7; Total Enrollment 2.

[B] HOMES FOR AGED AND ORPHANS

ARECIBO. *Hogar Sta. Maria Eufrasia*, Carr. Est. 651-10, Sector Junco, 00613. Tel: 787-878-5166; Fax: 787-880-2632; Email: eufrasia86@gmail.com; Web: www.hogareufrasia.org. P.O. Box 1909, 00613. Mother Carmen Brenes, Dir. House for pregnant teens. Bed Capacity 10; Good Shepherd Sisters 3; Tot Asst. Annually 9; Total Staff 11; Babies 1; AARP Employees 4.
La Milagrosa Home for Abused Girls, Urb. Zeno Gandía, Ave. Francisco Jimenez Gonzalez #987, 00612-3877. Tel: 787-878-6231; Tel: 787-878-0341; Fax: 787-817-7822; Email: hogarcolegiolamilagrosa@yahoo.com; Web: http://hogarcolegiolamilagrosa.com/. Sr. Claribel Camacho Figueroa, H.C., Admin. Bed Capacity 21; Girls 18; Sisters 5; Tot Asst. Annually 35; Total Staff 18.
San Rafael Geriatric Center, #49 Calle Cervantes, 00612-4558. Tel: 787-878-3813; Fax: 787-879-4592; Email: asilosanrafael@gmail.com. Bed Capacity 30; Guests 30; Sisters of Charity 5; Tot Asst. Annually 34; Total Staff 26.
Centro Geriatrico San Rafael, Calle Cervantes #49, 00612. Tel: 787-878-3813; Fax: 787-879-4592; Email: nydia.montijo@hotmail.com.

LARES. *Hogar Envejecientes Irma Fe Pol Mendez, Inc.*, P.O. Box 1185, Lares, 00669. Tel: 787-897-6090; Email: hogarirmafe@yahoo.com. Bed Capacity 38; Guests 25; Charity Sisters of St. Joseph (Mexico) 4; Tot Asst. Annually 30; Total Staff 29; Congregacion Hnas. Josefinas Mexico 4.

[C] MISCELLANEOUS

ARECIBO. *Hogar Infantil Santa Teresita del Nino Jesus, Inc.*, P.O. Box 140057, 00614-0057. Tel: 787-817-6651; Tel: 787-650-7731; Fax: 787-650-7771; Email: hogarsantateresita@hotmail.com. Mrs. Melva Arbelo Mangual, Dir. Children 15; Hermanas de la Caridad Dominicas de la Presentacion 1.
Oficina para la Promocion y el Desarrollo Humano, Inc., Carr 651 Km 2.1, Bo. Juncos, 00612. Tel: 787-817-6951; Tel: 787-817-6954; Tel: 787-817-6955; Fax: 787-817-7597; Email: opdhinc@gmail.com; Email: aflores.opdh@gmail.com; Web: www.opdh.org. P.O. Box 353, 00613. Sr. Roberta Grzelak, C.D.P., Founder.

CAMUY. *Hogar de Ninas Fray Luis Amigo*, HC-06 Box 65162, Camuy, 00627-9032. Tel: 787-356-2634. Children 10; Sisters 3.

UTUADO. *Fondita Santa Marta*, #1 Calle Betances, P.O. Box 10, Utuado, 00641. Tel: 787-814-0735; Fax: 787-814-0735; Email: fraymanuelaviles@gmail.com. Bro. Fray Manuel Aviles, O.F.M.Cap., Pres. Guests 52.

RELIGIOUS INSTITUTES OF MEN REPRESENTED IN THE DIOCESE

For further details refer to the corresponding bracketed number in the Religious Institutes of Men or Women section.

[0470]—*Capuchin Friars* (Province of Pittsburgh)—O.F.M.Cap.
[0270]—*Carmelite Fathers and Brothers* (Province de Aragon, Valencia, Espana)—O.Carm.
[]—*Comunidad Misionera de Villaregia*—C.M.V.
[1330]—*Congregation of the Mission* (Vice-Province of Puerto Rico)—C.M.
[1000]—*Congregation of the Passion* (Bilbao, Spain)—C.P.
[]—*Esclavos de la Eucaristia y Maria Virgen*—E.E.M.V.
[0650]—*Holy Ghost Fathers* (Eastern Province)—C.S.Sp.
[0770]—*Marist Brothers*—F.M.S.
[]—*Misioneros Natividad de Maria* (Mexico)—M.N.M.
[1310]—*Order of the Holy Trinity* (Viscaya, Spain Province)—O.SS.T.
[1190]—*Salesians of Don Bosco* (Province of Madrid)—S.D.B.

RELIGIOUS INSTITUTES OF WOMEN REPRESENTED IN THE DIOCESE

[]—*Comunidad Misionera de Villaregia*—C.M.V.
[]—*Convento Madre de Dios, Inc.*
[0760]—*Daughters of Charity of St. Vincent de Paul*—H.C.
[]—*Dominican Sisters of Amityville, N.Y.*
[1100]—*Dominican Sisters of Charity of the Presentation of the Blessed Virgin*—O.P.
[]—*Hermanas de San Jose de Corozal* (Corozal).
[]—*Hermanas del Buen Pastor.*
[]—*Hermanas Esclavas del Santisimo y la Inmaculada.*
[]—*Hermanas Josefinas* (Mexico).
[]—*Hnas. de Nazaret* (El Salvador).
[]—*Misioneras de la Sagrada Familia* (Instituto Secular).
[]—*Salesian Sisters* (Roma).
[]—*Siervas de Maria* (Roma).
[0990]—*Sisters of Divine Providence* (Pittsburgh)—C.D.P.
[]—*Terciarias Capuchina Sgda. Familia* (Roma).

An asterisk (*) denotes an organization that has established tax-exempt status directly with the IRS and is not covered by the USCCB Group Ruling.

Diocese of Caguas, Puerto Rico

(Dioecesis Caguana)

Most Reverend

EUSEBIO RAMOS MORALES

Bishop of Caguas; ordained June 3, 1983; appointed Bishop of Fajardo-Humacao March 11, 2008; consecrated May 31, 2008; appointed Bishop of Caguas February 2, 2017; installed February 26, 2017.

Most Reverend

ENRIQUE HERNANDEZ RIVERA, D.D.

Bishop Emeritus of Caguas; ordained June 8, 1968; appointed Titular Bishop of Vanalla, North Africa and Auxiliary Bishop of San Juan June 11, 1979; consecrated August 17, 1979; appointed Bishop of Caguas February 13, 1981; officially installed March 8, 1981; retired July 28, 1998. *Res.: Bishop's House, HC 04 Box 44015, Caguas, PR 00727.* Tel: 787-747-5885; Tel: 787-747-5787; Fax: 787-747-5616; Fax: 787-747-5767.

Established November 1964.

Square Miles 737.

Comprises east and southeast portion of Puerto Rico.

Patroness of the Diocese: Maria, Madre de la Iglesia - November 12, 1988.

Web: www.diocesisdecaguaspr.org

Email: diocesisdecaguas@gmail.com

STATISTICAL OVERVIEW

Personnel	
Bishop	1
Retired Bishops	1
Priests: Diocesan Active in Diocese	46
Priests: Diocesan Active Outside Diocese	3
Priests: Diocesan in Foreign Missions	1
Number of Diocesan Priests	50
Religious Priests in Diocese	22
Total Priests in Diocese	72
Ordinations:	
Transitional Deacons	2
Permanent Deacons in Diocese	109
Total Sisters	72
Parishes	
Parishes	34
With Resident Pastor:	
Resident Diocesan Priests	28
Resident Religious Priests	6
Pastoral Centers	4
Welfare	
Catholic Hospitals	1
Specialized Homes	1
Special Centers for Social Services	4
Educational	
Seminaries, Diocesan	1
Students from This Diocese	13
Diocesan Students in Other Seminaries	7
Total Seminarians	20
High Schools, Diocesan and Parish	1
Total Students	672
High Schools, Private	5
Elementary Schools, Diocesan and Parish	1
Elementary Schools, Private	5
Vital Statistics	
Receptions into the Church:	
Infant Baptism Totals	2,057
Minor Baptism Totals	195
Adult Baptism Totals	63
First Communions	2,314
Confirmations	2,052
Marriages:	
Catholic	353
Interfaith	11
Total Marriages	364
Deaths	1,968
Total Catholic Population	350,000
Total Population	503,000

Former Bishops—Most Revs. RAFAEL GROVAS, D.D., S.T.D., Ph.D., J.C.L., ord. April 7, 1928; appt. Jan. 19, 1965; cons. March 28, 1965; retired Feb. 13, 1981; died Sept. 9, 1991; ENRIQUE HERNANDEZ RIVERA, D.D., (Retired), ord. June 8, 1968; cons. Aug. 17, 1979; appt. Feb. 13, 1981; retired July 28, 1998; RUBEN ANTONIO GONZALEZ MEDINA, C.M.F., ord. Feb. 9, 1975; appt. Bishop of Caguas Dec. 12, 2000; cons. Feb. 4, 2001; appt. Bishop of Ponce Dec. 22, 2015.

Vicar General—Rev. ANTONIO CARTAGENA.

Sec. Chancellor—Rev. ANGEL MOLINA.

Sec. Vice Chancellor—VACANT.

Diocesan Consultors—Revs. JORGE D. CARDONA; FELIX NUNEZ; CARLOS J. VAZQUEZ; ORLANDO DE JESUS; LUIS ADORNO, C.Ss.R.; BALTAZAR NUNEZ.

Diocesan Tribunal of Caguas—HC 04 Buzon 44015, Caguas, PR USA 00727. Tel: 787-286-8595; Fax: 787-286-8620. Revs. FELIX NUNEZ, Judicial Vicar; ORLANDO DE JESUS; CARLOS J. VAZQUEZ.

Board of Diocesan Government—Revs. ANTONIO CARTAGENA; MIGUEL A. DE ANGEL; CARLOS J. VAZQUEZ; FELIX NUNEZ; Sr. CLETA M. LOPEZ; Rev. ANGEL MOLINA.

Priests Senate—Revs. ANTONIO CARTAGENA; ANGEL MOLINA; MELVIN MONTANEZ; FELIX NUNEZ; MIGUEL CLAUDIO; JORGE D. CARDONA; YAMIL A. VELAZQUEZ; JUAN LUIS NEGRON; ANGEL COLON; CARLOS J. VAZQUEZ; RICARDO SANTIN; ISRAEL RAMOS; MIGUEL A. DE ANGEL; ORLANDO DE JESUS; LUIS ADORNO, C.Ss.R.; ENCARNACIÓN NIEVES; BALTAZAR NUNEZ.

Diocesan Offices and Directors

Economic Administrator—Mailing Address: HC 04, Box 44015, Caguas, PR USA 00727. Tel: 787-747-5885; Tel: 787-747-5787, Ext. 227. MR. ABDEL ALVAREZ GONZALEZ; Rev. MIGUEL A. DE ANGEL.

Planning Vicar—VACANT, HC 04, Box 44015, Caguas, PR USA 00727. Tel: 787-747-5885; Tel: 787-747-5787.

Movimientos y Organizaciones Diocesanas—

Cursillos de Cristiandad—FELIPE SANCHEZ RAMOS, Tel: 787-734-7068.

Legion de Maria—MARIA C. COTTO.

Renovacion Carismatica—NOEL MORALES RODRIGUEZ.

Juan XXIII—ARNALDO RODRIGUEZ, Tel: 787-747-3748.

Apostolado de la Cruz—ANA ACEVEDO, Tel: 787-736-5312.

Caballeros de Colon—JOSE SOTO CARMONA, Tel: 787-746-4747.

Equipos Ntra. Sra.—GUILLERMO TORRES; MILAGROS ORTIZ.

Equipo Ntra. Sra.—ISRAEL ROSADO Y JOAN RUIZ, Tel: 787-206-7744.

Hijas Catolicas—GLORIA M. BENITEZ DE SOLA.

Hnos. Cheos—MR. JOSE ORTIZ, Tel: 787-382-8986.

Misioneros Padre Nuestro—RAMON L. RAMOS.

Schoenstatt—JOSE N. BRACERO, Tel: 787-722-3941.

Vicentinos—CARMENCITA COLON, Tel: 787-747-6546.

Talleres de Oracion y Vida—PETRONILA RUIZ, Tel: 787-745-4123.

Sociedad del Santo Nombre—VICTOR COTTO.

La Piedra que Cristo Edifico en Mi—REGINO VAZQUEZ.

Camino Neo Catecumenal—DOMINGO VEGA.

CASSE—Tel: 787-286-3333. VACANT.

Comisiones Diocesanas—

Pastoral Familiar—Deacon CARLOS LUGO.

Pastoral Preadolescentes—Sr. CLETA M. LOPEZ.

Pastoral Social—Deacon ANTONIO ROSARIO.

Espiritualidad Comunitaria—HERMINIA FONSECA, Tel: 787-746-2669.

Misiones—Rev. JORGE D. CARDONA.

Pastoral Penitenciaria—D. ANIBAL GONZALEZ, Tel: 787-263-0976.

Pastoral Nec. Especiales—VACANT.

Formacion Diac. Permanentes—Rev. RICARDO SANTIN.

Catholic Youth—Mailing Address: Diocesis de Caguas, HC 04, Box 44015, Caguas, PR USA 00727. Tel: 787-744-6738, Ext. 229. Rev. KEVIN R. CINTRON.

Catholic Social Action—VACANT, HC 04, P.O. Box 44015, Caguas, PR USA 00727. Tel: 787-747-5885; Tel: 787-747-5787.

Catholic School Consultors—Mailing Address: P.O. Box 8699, Caguas, PR USA 00726. Tel: 787-743-1171. Sr. IRIS RIVERA.

Catechetical Vicar—Sr. CLETA M. LOPEZ.

Building Commission—VACANT, HC 04, Box 44015, Caguas, PR USA 00727. Tel: 787-747-5885; Tel: 787-747-5787.

Liturgical Consultor—Mailing Address: Diocesis de Caguas, HC 04, Box 44015, Caguas, PR USA 00727. Tel: 787-747-5885, Ext. 222. Rev. RICARDO SANTIN.

Communication Office—Mailing Address: Diocesis de Caguas, HC 04, Box 44015, Caguas, PR USA 00727. Tel: 787-747-5885. Rev. JOSE R. FIGUEROA.

Red de Esperanza y Solidaridad (REDES)—Sisters ANGELO GARCIA RIVERA; MARIA JESUS MOMPO, Mailing Address: Diocesis de Caguas, HC 04, Box 44015, Caguas, PR USA 00727. Tel: 787-747-5767.

Vincentian Society—CARMENCITA COLON, Mailing Address: Diocesis de Caguas, HC 04, Box 44015, Caguas, PR USA 00727.

Hospitals—Rev. ENCARNACIÓN NIEVES, Mailing Address: Diocesis de Caguas, HC 04, Box 44015, Caguas, PR USA 00727.

Legion of Mary—MR. ISABELO HUERTAS, Mailing Address: Diocesis de Caguas, HC 04, Box 44015, Caguas, PR USA 00727.

Master of Ceremonies—Mailing Address: Diocesis de Caguas, HC 04, Box 44015, Caguas, PR USA 00727. Tel: 787-747-5885. Rev. RICARDO SANTIN.

Pastoral Vicar—Mailing Address: Diocesis de Caguas, HC 04, Box 44015, Caguas, PR USA 00727. Tel: 787-286-0075, Ext. 245. Rev. JORGE D. CARDONA.

Schools—Mailing Address: P.O. Box 8699, Caguas, PR USA 00726. Tel: 787-743-1171.
School Superintendent—Sr. IRIS RIVERA.

Vocations—Revs. FELIX NUNEZ; YAMIL A. VELAZQUEZ; CARLOS J. VAZQUEZ, Mailing Address: Diocesis de Caguas, HC 04, Box 44015, Caguas, PR USA 00727. Tel: 787-747-5885, Ext. 243; Fax: 787-857-3585.

Catholic Charities—VACANT, HC 04, Box 44015, Caguas, PR USA 00727. Tel: 787-703-0775; Fax: 787-747-5616.

Commission of Permanent Deacons—Deacon CARLOS LUGO.

CLERGY, PARISHES, MISSIONS AND PAROCHIAL SCHOOLS

CITY OF CAGUAS

1—CATEDRAL DULCE NOMBRE DE JESUS (1771)
44 Betances St., Caguas, PR USA 00725.
Tel: 787-743-4311; Tel: 787-743-2927;
Fax: 787-746-5399; Email: catedraldecaguas@yahoo.com; Web: catedraldecaguas.org. P.O. Box 665, Caguas, PR USA 00726. Revs. Ricardo Santin, Rector; Aurelio Adan, (Retired); Juan B. Medina; Deacons Enrique Santiago; Angel Rosario; Clemente Guzman.
Chapels—Ntra. Sra. Perpetuo Socorro— (1929)
24 Aguayo St., Caguas, PR USA 00726.
San Gerardo (1940)
221 B St., B-14, Jardines de Caguas, PR USA 00726.
San Vicente de Paul
221 B St., Brooklyn, NY USA 11209.
La Sagrada Familia (1978)
1004 P St., Bda. Morales, PR USA.

2—DIVINO NINO (1995)
Mailing Address: P.O. Box 9416, Caguas, PR USA 00726. Tel: 787-746-1450; Fax: 787-744-3497; Email: psantuariodivinonino@gmail.com. Rev. Angel Molina; Deacons Moise's Vargas; Rolando Rocafort; Rafael Aviles.
Catechesis Religious Program—Students 120.
Chapel—San Francisco Javier
Tel: 787-286-0440.

3—EL SALVADOR (1970)
HC 03, Buzon 38888, Caguas, PR USA 00725-9723.
Tel: 787-747-0091; Fax: 787-747-0091. Rev. Feliciano Rodriguez; Deacons Pablo Gonzalez; Libardo Rodriguez.
Parcelas Bo. Boringuen
HC 08, Buzon 38888, Caguas, PR USA 00725-9723.
Email: elsalvador@caribe.net.
Catechesis Religious Program—Students 300.
Chapels—Bo. San Salvador, Cristo Rey— (1922) .
Sector Anon, San Alfonso (1929) .
Sector Hato, Ntra. Sra. del Carmen (1911) .

4—INMACULADO CORAZON DE MARIA (1971) [JC]
Mailing Address: HC 05 P.O. Box 56764, Caguas, PR USA 00725-9228. Tel: 787-747-6336;
Fax: 787-258-4910. Rev. Fausto Cruz; Salvador Salgado; Deacon Rafael Pagan.
Catechesis Religious Program—Students 435.
Chapels—Bo. La Barra, Cristo Rey— (1971) .
San Antonio (1950) .
Bo. La Mesa, Ntra. Sra. Providencia (1982) .
Bo. Quebrada Arenas, San Felipe.
Guasabara, Sta. Teresa del Nino Jesus (1995) .

5—MARIA MADRE DE LA IGLESIA (1972)
Calle Juan M. Morales D-23 Urb Valle Tolima, Caguas, PR USA 00725. Tel: 787-258-4481;
Fax: 787-747-5616. Rev. Jaime Silva Gonzalez, Admin.; Deacons Hipolito Montanez; Felix Cotto Velez.
Chapels—Bo. Canabon, Maria Reina—
Las Carolinas, Ntra. Sra. del Carmen.

6—PARROQUIA NUESTRA SENORA DE LA PROVIDENCIA (1966)
Urb. Villa del Carmen, P.O. Box 6318, Caguas, PR USA 00726. Tel: 787-743-8200; Email: providenciasinfronteras@hotmail.com. Rev. Hermenegildo Alayon; Deacon Ruben Villodas.
Stations—Urb. Mariolga—
Caguas, PR USA.
Caserio Publico
Caguas, PR USA.
Los Flamboyanes
Caguas, PR USA.
Rio Verde
Caguas, PR USA.
Villa Carmen
Caguas, PR USA.
Villa del Rey I
Caguas, PR USA.
Residencial San Carlos.
Residencial San Alfonso
Caguas, PR USA.

7—PARROQUIA NUESTRA SENORA DEL PERPETUO SOCORRO (1966)
Calle 2, A-13, Villa Nueva, Caguas, PR USA 00725.
Tel: 787-744-1420; Fax: 787-258-4341; Email: vpsocorro@hotmail.com. Rev. Miguel A. de Angel; Deacons Francisco Santiago; Miguel Laguerre; Mario Cardona; Roberto Santini.
Stations—San Patricio— (1926)
Bo. Canaboncito, PR USA.
San Judas Tadeo (1960)
Villa Esperanza, PR USA.
Sagrado Corazon
Bo. Canaboncito (Las Parcelas), PR USA.
Ntra. Sra. del Carmen (1988)
Urb. Turabo Gardens, PR USA.

8—SAGRADO CORAZON DE JESUS (1963)
HC 04 P.O. Box 45078, Bo. Beatriz, Caguas, PR USA 00726. Tel: 787-747-5170. Rev. Miguel Claudio; Deacons Pablo Carrillo; Jose L. Santiago.
Chapels—Bo. Beatriz, Cristo Rey— (1960) .
San Martin (1994) .

9—SAN JOSE (1960) (Discalced Carmelites from Spain)
Coral St., Villa Blanca, P.O. Box 1749, Caguas, PR USA 00726. Tel: 787-743-5889; Email: sanjose.caguas@gmail.com. Rev. Fernando Sanchez, O.C.D.; Misael Batista; Deacons Rafael Torres; Bruno Dueno.
School—San Jose School
P.O. Box 1101, Caguas, PR USA 00726.
Tel: 787-743-2032; Email: csje-sec@csje-sec.org; Web: www.csje-sec.org. Sr. Nelly O. Rodriguez, C.M., Prin. Lay Teachers 29; Priests 2; Students 596.
High School—San Jose High School
Coral St., Villa Blanca, Caguas, PR USA 00726.
Tel: 787-744-8993; Fax: 787-744-4111; Email: webmaster_csjs@yahoo.com. Mrs. Brenda Figueroa de Soler, Prin. Lay Teachers 21; Priests 1; Students 450.
Chapel—Nuestra Senora del Rosario (1981)
Boi Bairoa La 25, Puerto Rico.
Catechesis Religious Program—Norma Otie, D.R.E.; Helen Nolasco, D.R.E. Students 120.

10—SAN JUAN APOSTOL Y EVANGELISTA (1982)
Apartado 459, Avenida Bairoa, Caguas, PR USA 00726. Tel: 787-744-6359; Fax: 787-747-4301; Email: sjabairoa@gmail.com. Rev. Angel Molina; Deacons Kenny Figueroa; Francisco Gonzalez; Ruben Huertas; Damaso Roche.
Catechesis Religious Program—Students 200.

11—SAN PABLO APOSTOL (1980) (Hispanic)
Kennedy U-32-B Urb. Jose Mercado, Caguas, PR USA 00725. Tel: 787-743-3546; Email: sanpabloapostol.caguas@gmail.com. Rev. Boris Espinosa; Deacons Antonio Rosario; Jose R. Rivera.
Chapels—Bo. Tomas de Castro I, Ntra. Sra. de Guadalupe— (1928) .
Bo. Tomas de Castro II, Santa Rose de Lima.
Sector Ramal, San Martin de Porres (1969) .
Sector Buenos Aires, San Juan Bautista y Santa Ines.
Sector RM5, Ntra. Sra. de la Monserrate.
Catechesis Religious Program—Students 134.

12—SAN PEDRO APOSTOL (1982)
Urb. Bonneville, P.O. Box 8878, Caguas, PR USA 00726. Tel: 787-744-2036; Email: sanpedroap@gmail.com. Rev. Encarnacian Nieves; Deacon Francisco Morales.

13—SANTISIMA TRINIDAD (1986)
P.O. Box 9630, Caguas, PR USA 00726-9630.
Tel: 787-747-6967; Email: pstcaguaspr@yahoo.com. Rev. Hipalito Torres; Deacon Esteban Dominguez.

14—SANTISIMO SACRAMENTO (1967) Blessed Sacrament Fathers.
Calle Caney A-11, Caguax, Caguas, PR USA 00725.
Tel: 787-745-5165; Email: pss.caguax@gmail.com. Revs. Jesus Maria Maiza, S.S.S.; Antonio Odriozola, S.S.S.; Deacon Leonardo Matos; Rev. Jaime Rodriguez Reyes.
Chapels—Urb. Caguas Norte, San Antonio de Padua—
Ntra. Sra. de Guadalupe
5th St., Caguas, PR USA 00725.

OUTSIDE THE CITY OF CAGUAS FROM LAS AMERICAS EXPRESSWAY TOWARD THE WEST

AGUAS BUENAS, AGUAS BUENAS CO.

1—CHURCH OF TRES SANTOS REYES (1838) Redemptorist Fathers.
4 Munoz Rivera St., P.O. Box 1, Aguas Buenas, PR USA 00703. Tel: 787-732-2741; Email: parroquialostressantosreyes@yahoo.com. Revs. Gerardo Hernandez, C.Ss.R.; Luis Adorno, C.Ss.R.; Antonio Hernandez, C.Ss.R.; Jose Checchia, C.Ss.R.; Deacons Angel Rodriguez; Pedro Montanez; Felipe Flores; Julio Resto; Ramon Rosa.
School—Academia San Alfonso, Tel: 787-732-8288; Fax: 787-732-4115; Email: sanalfonso@prtc.net. Ms. Luz Rodriguez, Prin. Lay Teachers 16; Religious 1; Students 172.
Chapels—Bo. Sumidero, Ntra. Sra. del Perpetuo Socorro— (1933) .
Sector Las Corujas del Barrio Sumidero, Buen Pastor (1984) .
Bo. Sonadora, Sagrado Corazon (1937) .
Bo. Jagueyes Abajo, San Jose (1939) .
Bo. Jagueyes Quintas, Santisimo Redentor (1947) .
Bo. Caguitas, Madre del Perpetuo Socorro (1941) .
Bo. Caguitas, Sector La Brusca, Ntra. del Rosario (1996) .
Parcelas Santa Clara, Santa Clara (1974) .

2—ESPIRITU SANTO (1991)
P.O. Box 40, Aguas Buenas, PR USA 00703.
Tel: 787-732-1270; Email: iglesanto1991@gmail.com. Rev. Kevin Cintron Gonzalez; Deacons Juan Lopez; Jose R. Rivera; Domingo Falcon; Jose Nelson Garcia.
Res.: P.O. Box 1250, Aguas Buenas, PR USA 00703.
Chapels—Carr. 156, Santa Teresita— (1929) .
Bo. Mulitas Alvelo, De Todos los Santos (1974) .
Bo. Mulitas Tiza, San Gerardo Mayela (1974) .
Bo. Juan Ascencio, San Alfonso.

AIBONITO, AIBONITO CO., CHURCH OF ST. JOSEPH (1897)
P.O. Box 2038, Aibonito, PR USA 00705.
Tel: 787-735-3741; Email: parrsanjose@yahoo.com. Revs. Angel Colon; Roberto Gomez; Deacons Jose R. Melendez; Ezequiel Collazo; Juan E. Colon; Carlos Lugo; Humberto Martinez.
Catechesis Religious Program—Tel: 787-735-4856. Students 1,900.
Mission—Barrio Algarrobo, Barrio La Plata, Amoldadero, PR USA. Tel: 787-735-5032.
Chapels—Bo. Asomante (Cuadritos), Ntra. Sra. del Carmen (1959)—Tel: 787-735-1811.
Bo. Asomante (Abejas), Inmaculada Concepcion (1965), Tel: 787-735-6455.
Bo. Pasto, Ntra. Sra. de Guadalupe (1970), Tel: 787-735-6977.
Ntra. Sra. de la Providencia (1982), Tel: 787-735-3072.
Bo. Rabanal (Parcelas), Ntra. Sra. de Fatima (1972), Tel: 787-735-0395.
Ext. San Luis, Ntra. Sra. del Carmen (1986), Tel: 787-735-7189.
La Plata, La Milagrosa (1986), Tel: 787-735-4038.
Llanos, Sector El Juicio, Tel: 787-735-1973.
La Sierra, San Judas Tadeo, Tel: 787-735-2835.

BARRANQUITAS, BARRANQUITAS CO.

1—CHURCH OF ST. ANTHONY OF PADUA (1808; 1988)
P.O. Box 1099, Barranquitas, PR USA 00794.
Tel: 787-857-3585; Fax: 787-857-3585; Email: p_barranquitas@hotmail.com. Revs. Roberto Solivan; Jose Betancourt; Deacons Carlos Colon Bernardi; Candido Torres; Jose L. Nunez.
Catechesis Religious Program—Students 1,800.
Chapels—San Francisco de Asis— (1960) .
Bo. Mana, Virgen del Carmen (1963) .
Bo. Canabon, Virgen de la Providencia (1968) .
Bo. Helechal, San Jose Obrero (1968) .
Bo. Quebrada Grande, Nuestra Sra. de la Monserrate (1968) .
Bo. Palo Hincado, Virgen del Perpetuo Socorro (1975) .
Bo. Lajitas, Ntra. Sra. del Pilar (1970) .
Sector La Torre, Santa Cruz (1975) .
Bo. Helechal, San Martin de Porres (1950) .

2—SAN ANDRES APOSTOL (1986)
HC 02 Box 5840, Comerio, PR USA 00782.
Tel: 787-875-5424. Rev. Raul Morales; Deacons Optaciano Rivera Ortiz; Joaquin Ortiz; Florencio Mercado.
Catechesis Religious Program—Students 241.
Chapels—Bo. Palomas, Comerio, San Jose— (1925) .
Bo. Quebradillas, Barranquitas, Corazon de Jesus (1940; 1987) .
Bo. Cedro Arriba, Naranjito, San Antonio de Padua (1864) .
Bo. Quebradillas, Barranquitas, Inmaculada Concepcion y Santa Cruz (1957) .
Bo. Cedro Arriba, Naranjito, Santuario Maria Auxiliadora (1992) .

CAYEY, CAYEY CO.

1—NUESTRA SENORA DE LA ASUNCION (1787)
P.O. Box 372887, Cayey, PR USA 00737-2887.
Tel: 787-738-2763; Fax: 787-738-7610; Email: asuncion.cayey@gmail.com. Rev. Yamil A. Velazquez; Deacons Libardo Rodriguez; Jose R. Negron;

Rafael Diaz; Ismael Gonzalez; Edgardo Rivera; Jose E. Melendez.
Catechesis Religious Program—Students 1,069.
Chapels—*Bo. Jajome, Sagrado Corazon de Jesus*— (1935).
Bo. Pasto Viejo, Ntra. Sra. del Carmen (1937; 1988).
Bo. Toita, Ntra. Sra. de la Merced (1946).
Res. Brisas de Cayey, San Ramon Nonato (1978).
Bo. Maton Arriba, Santa Teresita del Nino Jesus (1987).

2—NUESTRA SENORA DE LA MERCED (1968)
P.O. Box 1840, Cayey, PR USA 00737.
Tel: 787-738-3872; Fax: 787-263-1810; Email: mercedario_montellano@hotmail.com. Revs. Wilfredo Riveros; Fidel Fernandez, O.de.M.
Reparto Montellano, P.O. Box 372798, Cayey, PR USA 00737.
Chapels—*Bo. Vegas, San Ramon Nonato*— (1961).
Bo. Culebras, Ntra. Sra. del Carmen (1973).
Bo. Farallon, San Pedro Nolasco (1980).
San Pedro Armengol (La Plata) (1994).

3—SAN ESTEBAN PROTOMARTIR (1985)
Bo. Guavate, 22601 Sector Nieves, Cayey, PR USA 00736-9522. Tel: 787-747-4555; Fax: 787-286-7062; Email: p.sanesteban@gmail.com. Rev. Juan Luis Negron; Deacons Anibal Gonzalez Vazquez; Felix Montanez Perez; Silvestre Rodriguez Flores.
Chapels—*Bo. Borinquen Pradera, Nuestra Senora del Carmen*— (1910).
Bo. Guavate, San Jose de la Montana (1951; 1990).

CIDRA, CIDRA CO.

1—NUESTRA SENORA DE FATIMA (1963)
P.O. Box 214, Cidra, PR USA 00739.
Tel: 787-739-0633. Rev. Pastor A. Arroyave; Deacons Enrique Gonzalez; Israel Santiago; Samuel Rodriguez.
Catechesis Religious Program—Students 596.
Chapels—*Bo. Toita, Sagrado Corazon de Jesus*— (1960).
Bo. Salto, San Vicente (1965).
Bo. Honduras, Perpetuo Socorro (1970).
Bo. Rabanal, Jesus Salvador (1970).
Bo. Parcelas, La Milagrosa (1978).
Bo. Salto, Nuestra Senora de la Providencia.
Bo. Salto, Santa Teresita (1982).
Santo Cristo de Los Milagros (1987).

2—NUESTRA SENORA DEL CARMEN (1818)
P.O. Box 359, Cidra, PR USA 00739.
Tel: 787-739-2406. Revs. Melvin Montanez; Karlogs Lopez; Efrain Zabala; Deacons Gary Steven Rivera Figueroa; Diego Reyes Vasquez; Hector Orlando Santos Reyes; Jose Antonio Flores Colon; Ramon Hernandez Zayas; Angel Alberto Perez Arroyo; Rafael Santos Cruz.
Chapels—*Bo. Rio Abajo, Madre del Salvador*—
Urb. Treasure Valley, La Milagrosa.
Bo. Bayamon-Centenejas I, La Inmaculada.
Bo. Montellano, Santa Teresa del Nino Jesus.
Bo. Bayamon-Certenejas II, Perpetuo Socorro.
Bo. Bayamon-Juan del Valle, Nuestra Senora del Rosario.
Bo. Arena-Santa Clara, San Joaquin.
Bo. Ceiba-Hevia, Nuestra Senora del Rosario.
Bo. Arenas, Nuestra Senora de la Providencia.
Bo. Ceiba, Cristo Rey.
Bo. Bayamon-San Jose, San Jose.
Bo. Rincon, San Francisco de Asis.
Bo. Sud, La Milagrosa.
Bo. Sud, San Pablo.

COMERIO, COMERIO CO., SANTO CRISTO DE LA SALUD (1832)
Mailing Address: P.O. Box 1139, Comerio, PR USA 00782. Tel: 787-875-4525; Fax: 787-875-3481; Email: stocristo@coqui.net. Revs. Oscar Rivera; David Diaz; Deacon Rafael Santos.
Res.: Calle Santiago R Palmer #12, Comerio, PR USA 00782.
Chapels—*Bo. Sabana, Nuestra Senora del Santisimo Rosario*— (1966).
Bo. Rio Hondo, Nuestra Senora de Fatima (1953).
Bo. Palomas, Santa Cecilia (1954).
Bo. Cedrito, Virgen de la Providencia (1958).
Bo. Rio Hondo-Sector Las Parcelas, San Pablo (1965).
Bo. Pinas Arriba, Nuestra Senora del Carmen (1973).
Bo. Naranjo-Sector Las Parcelas, San Antonio de Padua (1977).
Bo. Vega Redonda, San Francisco de Asis (1977).
Bo. Cejas, Santa Rosa de Lima (1980).
Bo. Dona Elena, San Martin de Porres (1950).
Rio Hondo II, Maria Madre de la Iglesia.

NARANJITO, NARANJITO CO., SAN MIGUEL ARCANGEL (1831)
Centro Parroquial, P.O. Box 68, Naranjito, PR USA 00719. Tel: 787-869-2840; Email: sanmiguel.parroquia@yahoo.com. Revs. Felix Oliveras Villanueva; Jose Ariel Soto Green; Deacons Abigail Matos; Jose Berrios; Gerardo Rodriguez; Menelio Hernandez; Samuel Velazquez.
Chapels—*Bo. Nuevo, Santa Rosa de Lima*— (1953).
Bo. Lomas Centro, Virgen del Carmen (1954).
Bo. Anones, La Milagrosa (1962).
Bo. Lomas Valles, San Judas Tadeo (1963).
Bo. Guadiana, La Monserrate (1967).
Bo. Achiote, Sagrado Corazon (1978).
Bo. Nuevo Parcelas, San Vicente de Paul (1981).
Bo. Cedro Abajo, San Jose (1981).

OUTSIDE THE CITY OF CAGUAS FROM LAS AMERICAS EXPRESSWAY TOWARD THE EAST COAST

GURABO, GURABO CO., SAN JOSE (1822)
7 Santiago Iglesias St., P.O. Box 733, Gurabo, PR USA 00778. Tel: 787-737-2656; Email: parroquiasan@hotmail.com. Rev. Jorge D. Cardona; Deacons Mateo Gomez; Jose Velazquez.
Catechesis Religious Program—Students 240.
Chapels—*Bo. Jagual, Sagrado Corazon de Jesus*— (1951).
Bo. Jaguas Llano, Virgen del Carmen (1967).
Bo. Santa Rita, Santa Rita (1968).
La Milagrosa (1973) Bo. Hato Nuevo, Gurabo, PR USA 00778.
Bo. Celada, Santa Francisca Javier Cabrini (1967).
Bo. Hato Nuevo, La Milagrosa (1982).
Bo. Jaguas Loma, San Miguel (1989).
Bo. Mamey II, Ntra. Sra. del Carmen.

JUNCOS, JUNCOS CO., INMACULADA CONCEPCION (1797)
Calle Almodovar #18, P.O. Box 1728, Juncos, PR USA 00777. Tel: 787-734-2431; Fax: 787-734-0350; Email: parroquiajuncosuno@gmail.com. Revs. Angel L. Cintron; Jose Ariel Soto Green; Deacons Luis Almodovar; Avelino Perez; Cesar Felix; Luis Lopez.
Res.: Munoz Rivera St. #25 B, Juncos, PR USA 00777.
Catechesis Religious Program—Students 200.
Chapels—*Bo. Canta Gallo, Cristo Redentor*— (1975).
Bo. Ceiba Sur, Sagrado Corazon (1976).
Bo. Valenciano Sector Amigo, Espiritu Santo (1976).
Bo. Ceiba Norte, Cristo Rey (1978).
Bo. Valenciano Arriba, San Juan Bautista (1979).
Bo. Ceiba Norte Sector Chinos, Buen Pastor (1979).
Bo. Pinas, Santa Cruz (1981).
Bo. Lirios, San Jose (1978).
Bo. Canta Gallo Secto Reparto Valenciano, Maria Madre de la Iglesia (1993).
Santisima Trinidad, Bo. Placita, PR USA.

LAS PIEDRAS, LAS PIEDRAS CO.

1—INMACULADA CONCEPCION (1801)
P.O. Box 324, Las Piedras, PR USA 00771.
Tel: 787-733-2381; Fax: 787-733-1180; Email: inmaculadaconcepcionpr@gmail.com. Rev. Jose A. de Leon.
Catechesis Religious Program—Tel: 787-733-8325. Hnas Fatima, D.R.E.; Sr. M. Ines Zayas, O.P., C.R.E.; Deacons Victor M. Cruz; Domingo Figueroa; Jose O. Rosario; Jose Lozada. Students 450.
Mission—Salon Usos Multiples-Urb. April Gardens, Las Piedras PR USA.
Chapels—*Bo. Montones I, Perpetuo Socorro*— (1935).
Bo. Tejas Asomante, Nuestra Senora de la Providencia (1955).
Bo. La Fermina, Jesus de Nazaret (1979).
Bo. Montones IV, Santa Teresa del Nino Jesus (1980).
Bo. Montones II, San Juan Bautista (1982).

2—SAN JUAN BAUTISTA (Bo. Pueblito del Rio) (1971)
HC 02 Buzon 4467, Las Piedras, PR USA 00771.
Tel: 787-733-1479. Rev. Pastor A. Arroyave; Deacons Angel Luis Santiago; Efrain Gomez.
Chapels—*Finca Roig, San Juan Bautista*— (1911; 1940).
Bo. Boqueron, La Sagrada Familia (1957).
Bo. Pena Pobre, Sagrado Corazon (1964).
Bo. Rio Blanco, La Milagrosa (1972).
Bo. Mango, San Francisco Javier.
Bo. Pasto Seco, El Buen Pastor, Las Piedras, PR USA 00771.

MAUNABO, MAUNABO CO., SAN ISIDRO LABRADOR (1799)
P.O. Box 248, Maunabo, PR USA 00707.
Tel: 787-861-5526. Rev. Israel Ramos Cintron; Deacons Luis Reyes; Andres Camacho.
Chapels—*Nuestra Senora del Carmen*— (1962).
Bo. Calzada, Nuestra Senora de la Providencia (1971).
Bo. Matuyas, Nuestra Senora de la Candelaria (1974).
Bo. Palo Seco, San Judas Tadeo (1975).
Bo. Emajaguas, San Antonio de Padua (1977).
Missions—Bo. Quebrada Arenas, PR USA.
Bo. Lizas, PR USA.
Chapel—*Ntra. Sra. del Rosario de Fatima*, Bo. Talante, PR USA.
Missions—Bo. Paloseco, PR USA.
Bo. Talante (La Pica), PR USA.
Bo. Calzada, PR USA.

SAN LORENZO, SAN LORENZO CO.

1—NUESTRA SENORA DE LA MERCEDES (1810) (Hispanic)
Munoz Rivera 55, Apartado 1280, San Lorenzo, PR USA 00754. Tel: 787-736-2571; Fax: 787-736-1213; Email: nsdelasmercedes@gmail.com. Revs. Gerardo Hernandez, C.Ss.R.; Jesus Norberto; Juan Ramon Hernandez, C.Ss.R.; Andres Spacht, C.Ss.R.; Rafael Torres, C.SS.R.; Deacons Javier Lebron; Ramon Rojas; Gaspar Laureano.
Chapels—*Bo. Jagual, Nuestra Senora del Carmen*— (1952).
Bo. Quemados, Nuestra Senora del Perpetuo Socorro (1957).
Bo. Cerro Gordo Abajo, Cristo Redentor (1965).
Bo. Quebrada, Jesus Maestro.
Bo. Florida, Santa Monica.
Bda. Roosevelt, Nuestra Senora del Carmen (1968).
Bo. Hato Km. 6, Nuestra Senora del Perpetuo Socorro (1968).
Bo. Cerro Gordo Arriba, Inmaculada Concepcion (1977).
Bo. Lorenzo del Valle, Inmaculado Corazon de Maria (1978).
Bo. Santa Clara, San Gerardo (1986).
Urb. Los Flamboyanes, Bo. Florida, Nuestra Senora de Lourdes (1988).
Catechesis Religious Program—Students 1,115.

2—SAGRADO CORAZON DE JESUS Y 12 APOSTOLES (Bo. Espino) (1986) Revs. Boris Espinosa; Franklin Rodriguez, (Retired); Deacon Efrain del Valle.
Bo. Espino, HC 30, Box 32716, San Lorenzo, PR USA 00754-9726. Tel: 787-715-6947; Fax: 787-715-6947.
Chapels—*San Francisco de Asis*— (1988).
Santa Rosa de Lima (1989).
San Jose (1959).
Ntra. Sra. del Rosario (1994).
Maria Madre de la Iglesia (1990).
San Pedro (1998).
Santa Teresita del Nino Jesus (1950).

YABUCOA, YABUCOA CO., SANTOS ANGELES CUTODIOS (1793)
Degetau St. #2, Box 7, Yabucoa, PR USA 00767.
Tel: 787-893-3347; Email: iglesiastoangelescustodios@gmail.com. Revs. Orlando de Jesus Gomez; Juan Javier Pena Berrios; Deacons Carlos M. Ramos; Bienvenido Abreu; Antonio Diaz; Artemio Penalbert; Ruben Ramos; Juan R. Rodriguez.
Catechesis Religious Program—Students 930.
Chapels—*Bo. Rosa Sanchez, Santa Rosa de Lima*—
Bo. Jacanas Granjas, San Juan Evangelista.
Bo. Jac. Piedra Blanca, Sagrado Corazon (1976).
Bo. Tejas Piedra Azul, Sta. Maria Reina Paz.
Bo. Martorell, Santa Teresita del Nino Jesus.
Bo. Tejas, Ntra. Sra. de la Divina Providencia.
Bo. Playita Cuesta, San Bernardo.
Bo. Playita Arriba, San Antonio de Padua (1947).
Bo. Playita Parcelas, Virgen Milagrosa.
Bo. Quebradillas, Ntra. Sra. del Carmen.
Bo. Guayabota, La Sagrada Familia (1948).
Bo. Calabazas Arriba, San Jose (1942).
Bo. Quebrada Grande, San Benito.
Bo. Playa Guayanes, Ntra. Sra. del Carmen.
Bo. Aguacate, Ntra. Sra. del Perpetuo Socorro (1937).
Bo. Jagueyes, Inmaculada Concepcion (1910).
Bo. Ingenio, Santisima Trinidad.
Bo. Camino Nuevo, San Jeronimo.
Bo. Jacanas Sur, Divino de Jesus y Beato Diego (1999).
Bo Tejas, Valerio, Corpus Christi.
Camino Nuevo, El Guano, San Esteban.
Jacanas, Piedra Blanca, Sagrado Corazon de Jesus.
Limones, Campo Alegre, San Francisco de Asis.

Chaplains of Public Institutions

CAGUAS. *Hospital Interamericano de Medicina Avanzada (HIMA)*. Rev. Encarnación Nieves.
Hospital Menonita. Rev. Encarnación Nieves.

Retired:
Revs.—
Adan, Aurelio, (Retired)
Munoz, Antonio, (Retired)
Ortiz, Victor R., (Retired)
Rodriguez, Franklin, (Retired)
Santos, Raul, (Retired).

INSTITUTIONS LOCATED IN DIOCESE

[A] PAROCHIAL SCHOOLS

CAGUAS. *Academia Cristo de los Milagros* (1982) Box 7618, Caguas, PR USA 00726-7618.
Tel: 787-743-3131; Tel: 787-743-4242; Tel: 787-743-4855; Fax: 787-746-1428; Email: cristo@acmpr.net. Mrs. Leonides Parrilla de

Carrión, Gen. Dir.; Mrs. Myrna L. Carrion, Gen. Dir.; Mrs. Madeline Carrion; Mrs. Yolanda Flores, Prin.; Mrs. Yanira Flores, Prin.; Mrs. Nilda Aponte, Librarian. Deacons 1; Lay Teachers 58; Priests 1; Students 1,013.

Colegio Catolico Notre Dame (1916) (Grades PreK-12), Ave. Troche Esquina Calle Troche, P.O. Box 937, Caguas, PR USA 00726. Tel: 787-743-2385; Tel: 787-743-2524; Tel: 787-743-3693; Fax: 787-743-7567; Fax: 787-744-6464; Fax: 787-258-9648; Email: ccenotredame@gmail.com; Email: joserivera@ccndpr.com; Email: principal@ccndpr.com; Web: www.ccnde.org; Web: www.ccnd.org. Ms. Luz Rodriguez, Prin.; Mr. Jose J. Grillo, Dir.; Mrs. Doris Gonzalez, Registrar; Mrs. Mary Joe Rodriguez, Sec. Aides 17; Lay Teachers 110; Priests 1; Students 1,537.

Colegio Catolico Notre Dame Superior, Box 937, Caguas, PR USA 00726. Tel: 787-743-3693; Tel: 787-743-5501; Tel: 787-653-0834; Fax: 787-258-9648; Email: joserivera@ccndpr.com; Web: www.ccnd.org. Mr. Jose J. Grillo, Prin.; Mr. Jose Rivera, Assoc. Prin.; Mr. Jose Chidana, Assoc. Prin. & Technologia; Mr. Wilfredo Ocasio, Assoc. Prin.; Aurora Vazquez, Librarian. Religious Teachers 1; Lay Teachers 81; Priests 2; Students 1,252.

Colegio San Jose Elemental (1963) P.O. Box 2005, Caguas, PR USA 00726. Tel: 787-743-2032; Tel: 787-743-3205; Fax: 787-258-0683; Email: csje-sec@csje-sec.org; Web: www.csje-sec.org. Margarita Rosales, Prin.; Carmen I. Rodriguez, Librarian. Lay Teachers 32; Students 351.

Colegio San Jose Superior (1977) Y/O 1749, P.O. Box 1101, Caguas, PR USA 00726. Tel: 787-744-8993; Fax: 787-744-4111; Email: colegiosanjosesuperior@hotmail.com. Rev. Fernando Sanchez, O.C.D., Dir.; Mrs. Brenda Figueroa de Soler, Prin.; Aileen Otero, Librarian. Lay Teachers 17; Priests 1; Students 265.

Colegio San Juan Apostol y Evangelista (1992) P.O. Box 459, Caguas, PR USA 00726-0459. Tel: 787-743-8266; Tel: 787-747-4302; Tel: 787-744-6359; Fax: 787-747-4301; Email: sjabairoa@gmail.com. Marie Lozano, Prin. Supr.; Rev. Antonio Cartagena Veguilla, Dir.; Wilma Roman, Admin.; Natalia Hernandez, Librarian; Teresa Cruz Ortiz, Librarian. Lay Teachers 43; Students 658.

AGUAS BUENAS. *Academia San Alfonso*, (Grades PreK-9), Pio Rechani St., P.O. Box 97, Aguas Buenas, PR USA 00703. Tel: 787-732-8288; Fax: 787-732-4115; Email: asaalfonso@gmail.com. Nydia Velazquez, Prin.; Rev. P. Miguel Garcia, C.Ss.R. Lay Teachers 12; Priests 2; Students 89.

CAYEY. *Colegio Nuestra Senora de la Merced*, P.O. Box 372678, Cayey, PR USA 00736. Tel: 787-738-3438; Fax: 787-263-5837; Email: www.lamercedcayey@yahoo.com. Mrs. Nancy Diaz Morales, Dir.; Mrs. Laura Ortiz, Prin.; Maricarmen Lopez, Librarian. (Nuestra Senora de la Asuncion Parish) Lay Teachers 43; Priests 1; Students 755.

NARANJITO. *Academia Santa Teresita*, 19 Sector Santa Teresita, Naranjito, PR USA 00719. Tel: 787-869-7968; Tel: 787-869-6731; Tel: 787-869-8357; Fax: 787-869-8357; Email: admin@academiasantateresita.com. Mr. Luis A. Figueroa, Prin. Lay Teachers 26; Priests 1; Students 341.

[B] RETREAT HOUSES

AGUAS BUENAS. *Casa Cristo Redentor* (1967) P.O. Box 8, Aguas Buenas, PR USA 00703-0008. Tel: 787-732-5161; Fax: 787-732-1115; Email: pdamian@coqui.net. Revs. Terence Damian Wall, C.Ss.R., S.T.D., Supr.; Miguel A. Torres, C.Ss.R., Dir.; Hector Garcia, C.Ss.R.

AIBONITO. *Casa Manresa*, P.O. Box 1319, Aibonito, PR USA 00705. Tel: 787-735-8016; Tel: 787-735-8017; Fax: 787-735-2421; Email: manresa@caribe.net; Web: www.casamanresaaibonito.org. Rev. Yamil A. Velazquez, Dir.

JUNCOS. *Casa Cursillos de Cristiandad of Caguas* (Lay Corp. of Cursillistas) Salida de Juncos Carretera 919, P.O. Box 1762, Juncos, PR USA 00777. Tel: 787-734-7068; Fax: 787-713-9725.

SAN LORENZO. *Casa Charlie Rodriguez*, P.O. Box 1190, San Lorenzo, PR USA 00754. Tel: 787-736-5750; Fax: 787-715-8946; Email: santuariopr@gmail.com; Web: www.santuariopr.org. Rev. Baltazar Nunez, Rector.

[C] MONASTERIES AND RESIDENCES OF PRIESTS

CAGUAS. *Misioneros Hijos del Inmaculado Corazon de Maria (Claretianos)*, Bo. Rio Canas HC-05, Box 57564, Caguas, PR USA 00725-9233. Tel: 787-747-6336; Fax: 787-258-4910; Email: jvicente@coqui.net; Email: jvmsg@hotmail.com.

AIBONITO. *Casa Salesiana de Retiros*, P.O. Box 2019, Aibonito, PR USA 00705. Tel: 787-735-2486; Fax: 787-735-5501; Email: sdbaibon@coqui.net. Rev. Antonio Robles, S.D.B.

[D] CLOISTER SISTERS

CAGUAS. *Hnas. Hijas de Santa Maria de la Ternura*, Calle Naranjito 220 - Barrio Boringuen Parcelas Viejas, P.O. Box 5097, Caguas, PR USA 00726. Tel: 787-653-5813; Fax: 787-653-5813. Sr. Sonia Maria La Luz, H.S.M.T., Prior.

AGUAS BUENAS. *Santa Clara Monastery* Hermanas Clarisas P.O. Box 725, Cidra, PR USA 00739-0725. Tel: 787-732-5771.

[E] SHRINES

SAN LORENZO. *Diocesan Shrine Our Lady of Mount Carmel*, HC 30 Box 36876, San Lorenzo, PR USA 00754. Tel: 787-736-5750; Fax: 787-715-8946; Email: santuariopr@gmail.com; Web: www.santuariopr.org. Rev. Baltazar Nunez, Rector.

[F] MISCELLANEOUS

CAGUAS. *Centro de Acompanamiento Sico Social Espiritual (CASSE)*, P.O. Box 656, Caguas, PR USA 00726. Tel: 747-286-3333; Fax: 787-286-3612.

Diocesan Tribunal of Caguas, P.O. Box 9779, Caguas, PR USA 00726. Tel: 787-286-8595; Fax: 787-286-8620; Email: tribunaldiocesano@hotmail.com. Revs. Felix Nunez, Judicial Vicar; Orlando de Jesus Gomez; Ricardo Santin; Carlos J. Vazquez; Deacon Ramon Rojas.

Instituto Secular de Ntra. Sra. de la Altagracia, Calle 13, L23. Urb. Delgado, Caguas, PR USA 00725. Tel: 787-744-3628; Fax: 787-744-3628. Isabel Vazquez Rivera; Maria Melendez Sanchez; Ramonita Lopez Diaz; Zoraida Santos Santos; Judith Colon Cruz; Olga Rodriguez Berrios; Maria Isabel Colon; Prixda Santos Agosto; Doris Roque Julia; Natividad Ramos Ramos; Evelyn Rosado Rivera; Brenda Y. Abreu Garcia.

Movimiento Juan XXIII, P.O. Box 7229, Caguas, PR USA 00726. Tel: 787-747-3748. Revs. Hipólito Torres; Karlogs Lopez.

NARANJITO. *Seminario Pablo VI - Theological*, P.O. Box 302, Naranjito, PR USA 00719. Tel: 787-869-0861; Email: jcardona@prtc.net. Rev. Carlos J. Vazquez, Rector.

Casa del Apostol San Andres Rev. Carlos J. Vazquez.

RELIGIOUS INSTITUTES OF MEN REPRESENTED IN THE DIOCESE

For further details refer to the corresponding bracketed number in the Religious Institutes of Men or Women section.

[0360]—*Claretian Fathers*—C.M.F.
[0220]—*Congregation of the Blessed Sacrament* (N. Spain Prov.)—S.S.S.
[]—*Mercedarian Fathers* (Spain).
[]—*Order of Carmelites*—O.Carm.
[1070]—*Redemptorist Fathers* (San Juan Prov.)—C.SS.R.
[1190]—*Salesians of Don Bosco* (Antillas)—S.D.B.

RELIGIOUS INSTITUTES OF WOMEN REPRESENTED IN THE DIOCESE

[0420]—*Discalced Carmelite Nuns* (Spain)—O.C.C.
[]—*Dominicas de la Santisima Virgen.*
[]—*Hermanas Clarisas.*
[]—*Hermanas de Notre Dame.*
[]—*Hermanas Dominicas del Rosario de Fatima.*
[]—*Hermanas Hijas de Santa Maria de la Ternura.*
[]—*Hermanas Mercedarias.*
[]—*Hermanas Misioneras de los Sagrados Corazones.*
[]—*Hermanas Misioneras del Buen Pastor.*
[]—*Hermanas Misioneras Dominicas del Santo Rosario.*
[]—*Misioneras del Sagrado Corazon.*
[2790]—*Missionary Servants of the Most Holy Trinity* (Spain)—M.S.B.T.
[]—*Religiosas del Sagrado Corazon.*
[2970]—*School Sisters of Notre Dame* (Wilton, CT)—S.S.N.D.
[]—*Siervas de Maria* (Spain).
[]—*Siervas de Maria.*
[0640]—*Sisters of Charity of St. Vincent de Paul* (Puerto Rico Prov.)—S.C.
[2150]—*Sisters Servants of the Immaculate Heart of Mary*—I.H.M.

An asterisk (*) denotes an organization that has established tax-exempt status directly with the IRS and is not covered by the USCCB Group Ruling.

Diocese of the Caroline Islands

Most Reverend

AMANDO SAMO, D.D.

Bishop of the Caroline Islands; ordained Priest December 10, 1977; appointed Titular Bishop of Libertina and Auxiliary Bishop of the Caroline and Marshalls May 10, 1987; ordained Bishop August 15, 1987; named Coadjutor February 3, 1994; named Bishop of the Diocese March 25, 1995; installed June 6, 1995. *Res.: P.O. Box 939, Chuuk, FM 96942.* Tel: 691-330-2399; Fax: 691-330-4585.

Most Reverend

JULIO ANGKEL

Coadjutor Bishop of Caroline Islands; ordained December 3, 1983; appointed Coadjutor Bishop of Caroline Islands November 18, 2017; installed February 12, 2018. *P.O. Box 939, Weno, Chuuk, FM 96942.*

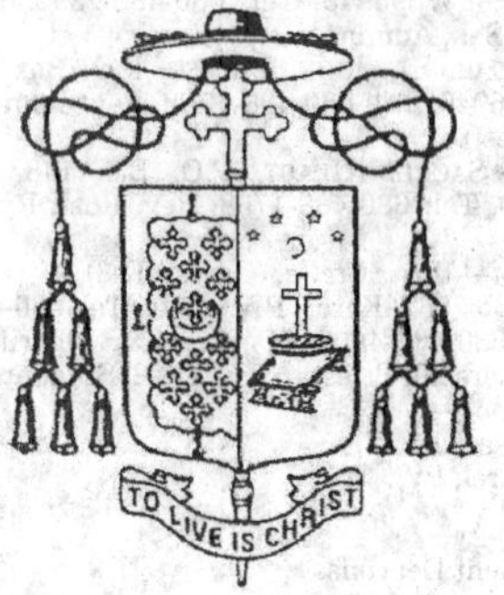

Chancery Office: P.O. Box 939, Weno, Chuuk, FM 96942. Tel: 691-330-2399.

Square Miles Ocean 1,725,000.

Total Population of 135,831.

Vicariate of the Caroline Islands erected December 10, 1905 and committed to the Order of Friars Minor Capuchin, extended to the Mariana Islands March 1, 1911.

Vicariate of the Marianas and Caroline and Marshall Islands erected May 4, 1923 and committed to the Society of Jesus. Marianas Islands separated July 4, 1946. Diocese of the Caroline-Marshalls created February 3, 1980. The Marshalls made a separate Prefecture Apostolic August 15, 1993, and the Diocese renamed "Diocese of the Caroline Islands."

Civilly it includes the four Federated States of Micronesia (Chuuk, Kosrae, Pohnpei and Yap) and the Republic of Palau.

STATISTICAL OVERVIEW

Personnel	
Bishop	2
Priests: Diocesan Active in Diocese	14
Priests: Retired, Sick or Absent	1
Number of Diocesan Priests	15
Religious Priests in Diocese	8
Total Priests in Diocese	23
Permanent Deacons in Diocese	98
Total Sisters	17
Parishes	
Parishes	29
With Resident Pastor:	
Resident Diocesan Priests	12
Resident Religious Priests	3
Without Resident Pastor:	
Administered by Priests	8
Administered by Professed Religious Men	12
Missions	2
Professional Ministry Personnel:	
Brothers	1
Sisters	17
Educational	
Diocesan Students in Other Seminaries	6
Total Seminarians	6
High Schools, Diocesan and Parish	4
Total Students	501
High Schools, Private	1
Total Students	133
Elementary Schools, Diocesan and Parish	4
Total Students	959
Catechesis/Religious Education:	
High School Students	634
Elementary Students	959
Total Students under Catholic Instruction	3,192
Teachers in the Diocese:	
Priests	8
Scholastics	4
Sisters	10
Lay Teachers	107
Vital Statistics	
Receptions into the Church:	
Infant Baptism Totals	1,451
Minor Baptism Totals	105
Adult Baptism Totals	35
First Communions	562
Confirmations	397
Marriages:	
Catholic	140
Interfaith	6
Total Marriages	146
Total Catholic Population	73,824
Total Population	141,968

Former Bishops—Most Revs. SALVADOR WALLAESER, O.F.M.Cap., cons. Vicar Apostolic and Titular Bishop of Tanagra, Aug. 21, 1912; resigned June 23, 1919; died Jan. 1, 1946; SANTIAGO LOPEZ DE REGO, S.J., cons. Vicar Apostolic and Titular Bishop of Dionisiopolis, Aug. 26, 1923; resigned June 2, 1939; died Aug. 5, 1940; THOMAS J. FEENEY, S.J., cons. Vicar Apostolic and Titular Bishop of Agno, Sept. 8, 1951; died Sept. 9, 1955; VINCENT I. KENNALLY, S.J., cons. Vicar Apostolic and Titular Bishop of Sassura, March 25, 1957; resigned Sept. 20, 1971; died April 12, 1977; MARTIN J. NEYLON, S.J., D.D., ord. Bishop, Feb. 2, 1970; succeeded to as Vicar Apostolic, Sept. 20, 1970; named to be Bishop of the new diocese, May 3, 1979; installed as first Bishop of the Diocese of the Carolines-Marshalls, Feb. 3, 1980; retired June 6, 1995; died April 13, 2004.

Chancery Office—Mailing Address: P.O. Box 939, Weno, Chuuk, 96942. Tel: 691-330-2399.

Vicar General—Most Rev. JULIO ANGKEL, D.D., Coadjutor Bishop, Email: dioceseofthecarolineislands@gmail.com.

Chancellor—Rev. ARTHUR LEGER, S.J., Ph.D., Email: artleger@gmail.com.

Diocesan Consultors—Revs. RUSK SABURO, Email: ruskaburo@yahoo.com; KENNETH URUMOLUG, S.J., Email: kenu16@gmail.com; KELLY YALMADAU, Email: dioceseofthecarolineislands@gmail.com; ROSENDO RUDOLF, Email: rosend278@yahoo.com.

Finance Committee—Rev. NICHOLAS P. RAHOY; MR. SANTI ASANUMA, Email: asanumasanty@gmail.com; Deacon BURDENCIOL ANDREAS; MR. AUGUSTINE TAKASHY.

Episcopal Vicars—

Chuuk—Rev. ROSENDO RUDOLF, Mailing Address: P.O. Box 462, Chuuk, 96942. Tel: 691-330-8293; Email: rosend278@yahoo.com.

Palau—Rev. RUSK SABURO, Mailing Address: P.O. Box 128, Koror, PW 96940. Tel: 680-488-6539; Tel: 680-488-2226; Fax: 680-488-1819.

Pohnpei-Kosrae—Rev. KENNETH URUMOLUG, S.J., Mailing Address: P.O. Box 160, Pohnpei, 96941.

Yap—Rev. KELLY YALMADAU, Mailing Address: P.O. Box A, Yap, 96943. Tel: 691-350-2265; Fax: 691-350-2784; Email: dioceseofthecarolineislands@gmail.com.

Diocesan Tribunal—

Judicial Vicar—Mailing Address: P.O. Box 160, Pohnpei, 96941. Tel: 691-350-2265; Fax: 691-350-2784; Email: dioceseofthecarolineislands@gmail.com. Rev. WILLIAM J. RAKOWICZ, S.J.

Defenders of the Bond—Revs. NICHOLAS P. RAHOY, Email: nickprahoy@gmail.com; RUSK SABURO, Email: ruskaburo@yahoo.com.

Notaries—MRS. MIRIAM CHIN; MRS. KARMINA MATHIAS.

Vocations—Most Rev. JULIO ANGKEL, D.D., Coadjutor Bishop.

CLERGY, PARISHES, MISSIONS AND PAROCHIAL SCHOOLS

CHUUK (TRUK) STATE, CAROLINE ISLANDS

Mailing Address for the Vicariate of Chuuk: Rev. Rosendo Rudolf, P.O. Box 250, Chuuk, FM 96942. Tel: 691-330-8293.

FEFAN, SACRED HEART PARISH, P.O. Box 250, 96942. Rev. Fernando Titus; Deacons Anthonio Anthonio; Joe Commor; Tom Edgar; Benisio Joseph; Henry Michael; Gregorio Nedelec.

HALL ISLANDS, HALL ISLANDS PARISH, P.O. Box 939, 96942. Rev. Rosendo Rudolf, Priest-in-Charge; Deacon Kawaichy James, Admin.

MORTLOCK ISLANDS, MORTLOCK PARISH, P.O. Box 939, 96942. Rev. Rosendo Rudolf; Deacon Soichy Buliche.

NEEPWUKOS, HOLY FAMILY PARISH, P.O. Box 120, 96942. Most Rev. Julio Angkel, D.D., Email: angkelj@gmail.com; Deacons Rikarto Fabian; Jimmy Emilio; Sandy Frank; Kandy Koichy; Steve Marcus; Alfred Ray.

PATTIW, PATTIW PARISH, P.O. Box 939, 96942. Deacons Mariano Easu; Julio Naich.

TOL, ASSUMPTION OF THE BLESSED VIRGIN MARY, P.O. Box 939, 96942. Rev. Edmond Ludwick; Deacons Roke Rokop; Gabriel Ykuda; Krispino Raphael; Hauk Paul; Hauk Tonis; Edmond Isac; Faustino Katsuta; Seferino Kuan; John Soichy; Sakuruta Berminar; Kirisos Victus.

TOLOWAS, ST. ANTHONY'S, P.O. Box 250, 96942. Rev. Florentinus Akkin; Deacons Tobias Soram; Rinder Fidel; Basiente Atan; Joseph Kasian Jr.

TUNNUK, IMMACULATE HEART OF MARY CATHEDRAL, P.O. Box 250, 96942. Revs. Kaster Sisam, Rector; Fernando Titus; Deacons Yostaro Noporu; Marselo Ludwig; Redley Noporu; Adarino Pete; Anchelino Rosokow.

School—St. Cecilia School, (Grades K-8), P.O. Box 850. Tel: 691-330-4362. Rev. Fernando Titus, Prin. Lay Teachers 9; Priests 1; Students 141.

UDOT, ST. FRANCIS ASSISI, P.O. Box 939, 96942. Rev. Julio Angkel, Priest-in-Charge; Deacons John Fritz;

Julian Ranu; Kerno Sam; Benry Bernard; Innocent Fred; Rosenino Joseph; Tionisio Moses; Kanda Rousan; Aldon Ruben; Manen Souleng; Diophil Binak Wasan.

UMAN, HOLY CROSS PARISH, P.O. Box 939, 96942. Rev. Dominic Theodor; Deacons Atitor Edmond; Tarsisio Atty; Josuah Hilario; Kapier Kepwe; Terencio Lorenso; Freddy Mailos; Simon Soien Muety; Kantaro Nethon; Yulian Nethon; Henery Nimeisa; Iowan Nimas; Kantino Nimeisa; Peter Ori; Ignacio Stephen; Suchan Stephen; Joseph Suda.

WEITO, WEITO PARISH, P.O. Box 939, 96942. Rev. Florentinus Akkin, Priest-in-Charge; Deacon Christino Afeiluk.

POHNPEI STATE, CAROLINE ISLANDS

Mailing Address for the Vicariate of Pohnpei: Rev. Kenneth Urumolug, P.O. Box 160, Pohnpei, FM 96941. Tel: 691-320-4661.

AWAK, ST. JOSEPH, P.O. Box 671, Kolonia, Pohnpei, 96941. Tel: 691-320-6025; Tel: 691-320-3699. Deacon Henry Donre, Admin.

IPWUTEK, ST. AUGUSTINE, P.O. Box 160, Kolonia, Pohnpei, 96941. Tel: 691-920-7313. Deacons Fred Martin, Admin.; Adelino Lorens.

KOLONIA, OUR LADY OF MERCY, P.O. Box 160, Kolonia, Pohnpei. Tel: 691-320-2557. Deacons Berley Arecely, Admin.; Augustine Damarlane; Burdenciol Andreas; Edgar Martin, (Retired).

School—Pohnpei Catholic School, (Grades K-9), P.O. Box 1650, Kolonia, Pohnpei, 96941. Tel: 691-320-2556. Bernadita Benavente Helstrom, Prin. Lay Teachers 25; Sisters 3; Students 319.

PALIKIR

1—ST. PAUL, P.O. Box 160, Kolonia, Pohnpei, 96941. Tel: 691-320-5822; Tel: 691-320-3615. Rev. Robert Ifamilik; Deacon William Ioanis, Admin.

2—ST. BARNABAS, P.O. Box 160, Kolonia, Pohnpei, 96942. Tel: 691-320-1505. Deacons Innocensio Elias, Admin.; Michael Sardis.

PORRASSAPW, CHRIST THE KING, P.O. Box 2056, Kolonia, Pohnpei, 96941. Tel: 691-320-3744. Deacons Relio Andon, Admin.; Sosua Dungken.

SEINWAR, IMMACULATE HEART OF MARY, P.O. Box 160, Kolonia, Pohnpei, 96941. Tel: 691-320-2244. Deacons Luciano Iowanis, Admin.; Patrick Paul.

SOKEHS, ST. PETER'S, P.O. Box 160, Kolonia, Pohnpei, 96941. Tel: 691-320-4667. Deacons Mikel Dano, Admin.; Bellarmine Ioanis.

TAMOROI, SACRED HEART, P.O. Box 160, Kolonia, Pohnpei, 96941. Tel: 691-320-3200; Tel: 691-320-1957. Deacons Casiano Nennis, Admin.; Ioanis Tihpen.

Missions—St. Ignatius—
Pohnpei.
St. John
Pohnpei.

YAP STATE, CAROLINE ISLANDS

Mailing Address for the Vicariate of Yap: Rev. Kelly Yalmadau, Vicar, P.O. Box "A", Colonia, Yap, FM 96943. Tel: 691-350-2265.

GAGIL-TOMIL, ST. JOSEPH, P.O. Box "A", Colonia, Yap, 96943. Tel: 691-350-2598. Rev. Masco S. Sinaga, S.J.; Deacon Francis Genong.

NEMAR, ST. MARY'S, P.O. Box "A", Colonia, Yap, 96943. Revs. Cuthbert Yiftheg, Parochial Vicar; Moses Tashibelit; Deacon Charles Flanning.

School—St. Mary School
Tel: 691-350-2269. Mr. Rufino Xavier, Prin. Lay Teachers 14; Priests 2; Students 254.

ULITHI AND NEIGHBORING ISLANDS, QUEEN OF HEAVEN, P.O. Box "A", Colonia, Yap, 96943. Rev. Nicholas P. Rahoy.

WOLEAI AND NEIGHBORING ISLANDS, ST. IGNATIUS, P.O. Box "A", Colonia, Yap, 96943. Deacons John Talugmai; Xavier Yarofaliyong.

REPUBLIC OF PALAU, CAROLINE ISLANDS

Mailing Address for the Vicariate of Palau: Rev. Rusk R. Sabaro, Vicar, P.O. Box 128, Koror, Palau PW 96940. Tel: 680-488-1758; Fax: 680-488-1819.

BABELDAOB, ST. THOMAS THE APOSTLE, P.O. Box 128, Koror, PW 96940. Tel: 680-488-2392. Rev. Wayne Tkel, S.J., Admin.

IOUELDOAB, ST. JOHN BAPTIST, P.O. Box 128, Koror, PW 96940. Tel: 680-488-1758. Rev. John Paul Ililau, (In Res.).

KOROR, SACRED HEART, P.O. Box 148, Koror, PW 96940. Tel: 680-488-1758. Rev. Rusk R. Saburo, (In Res.).

School—Maris Stella, (Grades K-8), P.O. Box 787, Koror, PW 96940. Tel: 680-488-2436; Fax: 680-488-4602. Ms. Lorenza Olkeriil, Prin. Lay Teachers 20; Priests 1; Sisters 2; Students 222.

Missions—
Ngcheangl, PW.
Sonsorol, PW.

Permanent Deacons:

Afeiluk, Christino, Nomun Weito, Chuuk
Amor, Tarsisio, Awak, Pohnpei
Andon, Relio, Pohnpei
Andreas, Burdenciol, Pohnpei
Antonio, Antonio
Areceley, Berley, Pohnpei
Atan, Basiente
Atty, Tarsisio
Bernard, Benry
Buliche, Soichy, Satowan, Chuuk
Cholymay, Elliot, Moen, Chuuk
Commor, Joe
Damarlane, Augustine, Pohnpei
Dano, Mikel, Pohnpei
Donre, Henry, Pohnpei
Easu, Mariano, Polowat, Chuuk
Edgar, Martin, Kolonia, Pohnpei
Edgar, Tom
Edmond, Atitor, Uman, Chuuk
Edwin, Bellarmine, Pohnpei
Elias, Innocensio, Pohnpei
Else, Pelsiano, Sapwuahfik, Pohnpei
Emilio, Jimmy
Fabian, Rikarto, Weno, Chuuk
Fidel, Rinder, Toloas, Chuuk
Flanning, Charles, Yap
Frank, Sandy
Fred, Innocent
Fritz, John, Udot, Chuuk
Genong, Francis, Yap
Hauk, Blasito
Hauk, Paul
Hauk, Tonis
Hilario, Josuah
Ioanis, William, Pohnpei
Iowanis, Luciano, Seinwar, Pohnpei
Isac, Edmond
James, Kawaichy, Murilo, Chuuk
Joseph, Benisio
Joseph, Rosenino
Kasian, Joseph Jr.
Katsuta, Faustino
Kepwe, Kapier
Kerno, Sam, Udot, Chuuk
Koichy, Kandy
Kuan, Seferino
Lorens, Adelino, Uh, Pohnpei
Lorenso, Terencio
Ludwig, Marselo
Mailos, Freddy
Marcus, Steve
Meres, Kasto
Michael, Henry
Moses, Tionisio
Muety, Simon Soien
Naich, Julio, Pollap, Chuuk
Nedelec, Gregorio
Nennis, Casiano, Pohnpei
Nethon, Kantaro
Nethon, Yulian
Nimas, Iowan
Nimeisa, Henery
Nimeisa, Kantino
Noporu, Redley
Noporu, Yostaro, Fono, Chuuk
Ori, Peter
Paul, Patrick, Pohnpei
Pete, Adarino
Rano, Julian, Romanum, Chuuk
Raphael, Krispino, Polle, Chuuk
Rapun, Angkel, Tol, Chuuk
Ray, Alfred
Reim, Iownes, Fefan, Chuuk
Rokop, Roke, Tol, Chuuk
Rosokow, Anchelino
Rousan, Kanda
Ruben, Aldon
Ruta, Itol, Tol, Chuuk
Santiago, Valentino, Pohnpei
Sardis, Michael, Pohnpei
Sephin, Ponsiano, Pohnpei
Soichy, John
Soram, Tobias, Tolowas, Chuuk
Sos, Iakim, Uman, Chuuk
Souleng, Manen
Soumwei, Petrus, Kuttu, Chuuk
Stephen, Ignacio
Stephen, Suchan
Suda, Joseph
Sukuruta, Berminar
Susua, Dungken, Pohnpei
Talugmai, John, Yap
Tihpen, Ioanis, Pohnpei
Victus, Kirisos
Wasan, Diophil Binak
Xymoon, Angkel, Fefan, Chuuk
Yarofaliyong, Xavier, Yap
Ykuda, Gabriel, Polle, Chuuk.

INSTITUTIONS LOCATED IN DIOCESE

[A] RESEARCH CENTER

CHUUK. *Micronesian Seminar Library*, 1 Xavier Cir., P.O. Box 220, 96942-0220. Tel: 691-330-4266. Ms. Velpa Veloso, Admin. Lay Assistants 2.

[B] COLLEGE

CHUUK. *Caroline College and Pastoral Institute*, P.O. Box 462, 96942. Tel: 691-330-8293. Rev. Rosendo Rudolf, Pres.; John Martin, Dir. Working in collaboration with Chaminade University of Honolulu through online courses (distance education). Lay Teachers 5; Priests 1; Students 220.

[C] HIGH SCHOOLS

CHUUK. *Saramen Chuuk Academy*, P.O. Box 662, 96942. Tel: 691-330-4442. Mr. Wayne Olap, Prin. Deacons 2; Lay Teachers 9; Sisters 5; Students 183.

Xavier High School, P.O. Box 220, 96942. Tel: 691-330-4266; Fax: 691-330-4753. Rev. Dennis Baker, S.J., Dir.; Mr. Martin K. Carl, Prin. Lay Teachers 15; Priests 1; Scholastics 3; Students 177.

KOROR, PALAU. *Mindszenty High School*, P.O. Box 69, Koror, PW 96940. Tel: 680-488-2437. Rev. Robert Richard McAuliff, S.J., Prin. Lay Teachers 20; Priests 1; Sisters 2; Students 135.

POHNPEI. *Our Lady of Mercy Vocational Training School*, P.O. Box 73, Pohnpei, 96941. Tel: 691-320-2888; Fax: 691-320-3168. Sr. Krista Namio, M.M.B., Prin. Lay Teachers 10; Students 133.

YAP. *Yap Catholic High School*, P.O. Box 950, Yap, 96943. Tel: 691-350-8390. Mr. Michael Wieneck, Prin. Lay Teachers 7; Priests 2; Scholastics 1; Students 87.

[D] RESIDENCES OF PRIESTS AND BROTHERS

KOLONIA, POHNPEI. *Jesuit Community of Pohnpei*, P.O. Box 160, Kolonia, Pohnpei, 96941. Tel: 691-320-2317. Revs. David Andrus, S.J., Pastoral Ministry, (In Res.); Kenneth Urumolug, S.J., Episcopal Vicar, Pohnpei-Kosrae.

Vicariate Residence, P.O. Box 160, Kolonia, Pohnpei, 96941. Tel: 691-320-2557. Rev. Robert Ifamilik, (In Res.).

KOROR, PALAU. *Jesuit Community of Palau, Manresa Jesuit House*, P.O. Box 128, Koror, PW 96940. Tel: 680-488-2226. Revs. Wayne Tkel, S.J., Campus Min. & Teacher, Mindszenty High School; Robert Richard McAuliff, S.J., Prin., Mindszenty High School & Dir., Catholic Schools in Palau; Bro. Juan Ngiraibuuch, S.J., Spiritual Ministries, (In Res.).

Vicariate Residence, P.O. Box 128, Koror, PW 96940. Tel: 680-488-2226. Revs. Rusk R. Saburo; John Paul Ililau.

NEEPWUKOS, CHUUK. *Jesuit Community of Micronesia*, P.O. Box 202, 96942. Tel: 691-330-4266. Revs. Thomas G. Benz, S.J., Supr., (In Res.); Dennis Baker, S.J., Dir., Xavier High School; Dickson D. Tiwelfil, Teacher, Xavier High School; Mr. Naoki Ochi, S.J., Teacher, Xavier High School, (In Res.); Mr. Wylly Fransiskus Asisi Suhendra, S.J., Teacher, Xavier High School, (In Res.).

St. John Vianney Formation House, P.O. Box 939, 96942. Tel: 691-330-3364. Most Rev. Julio Angkel, D.D., Dir.; Rev. David Lewis, (In Res.). Seminarians 13.

TUNNUK, CHUUK. *Vicariate Residence*, P.O. Box 250, Tunnuk, Chuuk, 96942. Tel: 691-330-2313. Revs. Kaster Sisam, (In Res.); Fernando Titus; Rosendo Rudolf.

YAP. *Jesuit Community of Yap*, P.O. Box 1009, Yap, 96943. Tel: 691-350-2148. Revs. John P. Mulreany, S.J., Vice Supr. & Admin., Yap Catholic High School, (In Res.); John S. Hagileiram, S.J., Pastoral Ministry; John J. Mattimore, S.J., Dir. & Teacher, Yap Catholic High School, (In Res.); Masco S. Sinaga, S.J., Pastor, St. Joseph's Church, Yap, (In Res.); Mr. Michael J. Lamanna, S.J., Teacher, Yap Catholic High School, (In Res.).

Vicariate Residence, P.O. Box "A", Yap, 96943. Tel: 691-350-2265. Revs. Kelly Yalmadau, (In Res.); Moses Tashibelit, (In Res.); Cuthbert Yiftheg.

[E] RESIDENCES OF SISTERS

AWAK, POHNPEI. *Sisters of Marie Auxiliatrice*, P.O. Box 1375, Awak, Pohnpei, 96942. Tel: 691-320-2626. Sisters Marie Elerina Umwech, M.A., Coord.; Sophia Marie Robert, M.A., (In Res.); Christina Marie Elias, M.A., (In Res.); Marie Saileen Jack, M.A., (In Res.). Sisters 4.

KOLONIA, POHNPEI. *Mercedarian Missionaries of Berriz*, P.O. Box 73, Kolonia, Pohnpei, 96941.
Tel: 691-320-2558. Sisters Antonina Malsol, M.M.B., Contact Person; Krista Namio, M.M.B., (In Res.); Isabel Seman, M.M.B., (In Res.); Dorothy Nook, M.M.B., (In Res.); Dasko William, M.M.B., (In Res.). Sisters 5.

KOROR, PALAU. *Mercedarian Missionaries of Berriz*, P.O. Box 56, Koror, PW 96940. Tel: 680-488-2272. Sisters Helen Ngirkelau, M.M.B., Coord.; Connie Kinosta, M.M.B., (In Res.); Francisca Main, M.M.B., (In Res.); Brenda Mwarike, M.M.B., (In Res.). Sisters 4.

NEEPWUKOS, CHUUK. *Sisters of the Immaculate Heart of Mary*, P.O. Box 662, Neepwukos, Chuuk, 96942.
Tel: 691-330-4442. Sisters Olivia B. Taynan, S.I.H.M., Contact Person; Erlinda M. Tuliao, S.I.H.M., (In Res.). Sisters 2.

WENO, CHUUK. *Mercedarian Missionaries of Berriz*, P.O. Box 67, Weno, Chuuk, 96942.
Tel: 691-330-4587. Sisters Gloria Billimont, M.M.B., Contact Person; Marlisha Suzumu, M.M.B., (In Res.); Esther Nestor, M.M.B., (In Res.). Sisters 3.

RELIGIOUS INSTITUTES OF MEN REPRESENTED IN THE DIOCESE

For further details refer to the corresponding bracketed number in the Religious Institutes of Men or Women section.

[0690]—*Jesuit Fathers and Brothers* (New York Prov.)—S.J.
[1110]—*Missionaries of the Sacred Heart*—M.S.C.

RELIGIOUS INSTITUTES OF WOMEN REPRESENTED IN THE DIOCESE

[2470]—*Maryknoll Sisters of St. Dominic*—M.M.
[2510]—*Mercedarian Missionaries of Berriz*—M.M.B.
[2970]—*School Sisters of Notre Dame*—S.S.N.D.
[]—*Sisters of Marie Auxiliatrice*—M.A.
[2575]—*Sisters of Mercy of the Americas*—R.S.M.
[]—*Sisters of the Immaculate Heart of Mary*—S.I.H.M.

An asterisk (*) denotes an organization that has established tax-exempt status directly with the IRS and is not covered by the USCCB Group Ruling.

Diocese of Chalan Kanoa

(Dioecesis Vialenbensis)

Most Reverend

RYAN P. JIMENEZ

Bishop of Chalan Kanoa; ordained priest June 8, 2003 by Most Rev. Tomas A. Camacho; appointed Apostolic Administrator December 28, 2010 by his Holiness Pope Benedict XVI; appointed Bishop of Chalan Kanoa June 24, 2016; installed August 14, 2016.

Mailing Address: P.O. Box 500745 CK, Saipan, MP 96950. Tel: 670-234-3000; Fax: 670-234-3002.

Email: bishop@rcdck.org

Web: www.rcdck.org

ESTABLISHED NOVEMBER 8, 1984.

Square Miles 184.

Corporate Title: "Bishop of Chalan Kanoa, a Corporation Sole."

Comprises the Mariana Island chain except for Guam, known legally as the Commonwealth of the Northern Mariana Islands.

For legal titles of parishes and diocesan institutions, consult the Diocesan Curia.

STATISTICAL OVERVIEW

Personnel	
Bishop	1
Priests: Diocesan Active in Diocese	11
Priests: Retired, Sick or Absent	1
Number of Diocesan Priests	12
Religious Priests in Diocese	3
Total Priests in Diocese	15
Permanent Deacons in Diocese	5
Total Sisters	15
Parishes	
Parishes	12
With Resident Pastor:	
Resident Diocesan Priests	11
Resident Religious Priests	3
Missions	1
Pastoral Centers	1
Professional Ministry Personnel:	
Lay Ministers	169
Welfare	
Special Centers for Social Services	2
Total Assisted	153
Educational	
High Schools, Diocesan and Parish	1
Total Students	288
Elementary Schools, Diocesan and Parish	2
Total Students	288
Catechesis/Religious Education:	
High School Students	523
Elementary Students	632
Total Students under Catholic Instruction	1,731
Teachers in the Diocese:	
Sisters	1
Lay Teachers	41
Vital Statistics	
Receptions into the Church:	
Infant Baptism Totals	373
Minor Baptism Totals	33
Adult Baptism Totals	2
First Communions	402
Confirmations	193
Marriages:	
Catholic	49
Interfaith	4
Total Marriages	53
Deaths	142
Total Catholic Population	32,249
Total Population	53,883

Former Bishop—Most Rev. TOMAS A. CAMACHO, (Retired), ord. June 14, 1961; appt. Prelate of Honor by Pope Paul VI in 1974; appt. Bishop of Chalan Kanoa Nov. 8, 1984; cons. and installed Jan. 13, 1985; retired April 6, 2010; died March 5, 2018.

Diocesan Curia—Mailing Address: P.O. Box 500745, Saipan, 96950. Tel: 670-234-3000; Fax: 670-235-3002.

Vicar General—Rev. KENNETH J. HEZEL, S.J.

Chancellor—Rev. JAMES SALAS BALAJADIA.

Diocesan Internal Auditor—MRS. BETTINA LYNETTE G. TERLAJE.

Finance Officer—MR. SHERWIN PASILLOS.

Personnel Officer—VACANT.

Director of Religious Education—Sr. SATURNINA CACCAM, S.J.B.P.

Diocesan Legal Counsel—MR. JESUS C. BORJA.

Superintendent of Catholic Schools—VACANT.

Diocesan Curia Staff

Finance Officer—MR. SHERWIN PASILLOS.

Bishop's Secretary—LOLITA M. BABAUTA.

Assistant Accountant—RUTH TORRECAMPO.

Archivist Librarian—VACANT.

Consultative Bodies

Presbyteral Council—Most Rev. RYAN JIMENEZ; Revs. ISAAC M. AYUYU; KENNETH J. HEZEL, S.J.; CHARLITO A. BORJA; ALLAN A. CABATIAN, O.A.R.; LEO NEIL BULLOS, O.A.R.; HYU WOO (ANDREW) JANG; REY ROSAL; ISIDRO T. OGUMORO; ROMIL APEROCHO; JASON GRANADO; HAROLD FUNA; JAMES SALAS BALAJADIA.

College of Consultors—Revs. KENNETH J. HEZEL, S.J.; ALLAN A. CABATIAN, O.A.R.; JAMES SALAS BALAJADIA; JESSE T. REYES; REY ROSAL.

Diocesan Finance Council—ROSE SOLEDAD; MARTHA CAMACHO; MR. ROSIKY CAMACHO; MICHAEL S. SABLAN; BERNADITA T. SEMAN; GLICERO ARAGO.

Diocesan Tribunal

Judicial Vicar—Rev. CARLOS VILA, J.C.L.

Marriage Tribunal Judge—VACANT.

Defender of the Bond—Rev. JONATHAN ALVAREZ.

Tribunal Auditor—Rev. JAMES S. BAJADIA.

Notary—MRS. LOLITA M. BABAUTA.

Diocesan Commissions

Commission on Worship—Revs. HAROLD FUNA, Coord.; ISAAC M. AYUYU; NEIL BULLOS, O.A.R.; MRS. ANGELICA I. MANGARERO; MRS. ANNIE MARIE BENAVENTE; MRS. CARMEN S. TAIMANAO; JAMES LG. SABLAN; Deacon JEFFREY T. CAMACHO; JOSELITO LENTEJA; LORENZO BARCINAS; MRS. MARGARET C. DELA CRUZ; RITA C. GUERRERO; MALUA PETER; DR. RITA SABLAN.

Diocesan Faith Formation Committee—Rev. KENNETH J. HEZEL, S.J.; Sisters NINA CACCAM, S.J.B.P.; MARYANN HARTMANN, M.M.B.; MRS. ESTHER S. FLEMING; MIKO MORAN; MARTHA CAMACHO; SERAFINA NABORS; Deacon TONY YAROBWEMAL.

Commission on Evangelization—Rev. JAMES SALAS BALAJADIA; Sr. STELLA IFENUK, M.M.B.; GARY ORPIANO; Deacon THOMAS SCHWEIGER; GREGG OMAR; MRS. CARMEN H. ATALIG; DONNA FLORES; ROMOLO ORSINI.

Commission on Marriage and Family Life—Rev. JASON GRANADO, Coord.; MR. GONZALO PANGELINAN; MRS. LINDA PANGELINAN; Deacon STANLEY BENAVENTE; MRS. ANNIE MARIE BENAVENTE; MR. FRANK PEREDO; MRS. OLIVIA PEREDO; MR. TOM THORNBURGH; MRS. ERICA THORNBURGH; NETH ROMERO; MR. SHERWIN PASILLOS; GLORYBEL TAN.

Commission on Vocation Team—Sr. NARCISA PENAREDONDA, S.J.B.P.; MR. JOHN TERLAJE; MRS. BETTY TERLAJE.

Commission on Heritage Cultural of the Church—Most Rev. RYAN JIMENEZ, Chm.

Diocesan Youth Commission—MR. EDWARD S. DELA CRUZ JR., Diocesan Youth Dir.; Sr. EMMA LUSTERIO, S.J.B.P., Asst. Youth Dir.

Mount Carmel Parish—VIRGILIO ABUEME; GERALD DE GUZMAN; JOHN COSTALES; ELIJAH SAN JOSE.

San Vicente Parish—Sr. EMMA LUSTERIO, S.J.B.P., Asst. Dir.; DON TAISACAN; MOLENA MACDUFF.

Kristo Rai Parish—FRANCES SABLAN, Kristo Rai; ELOISE LOPEZ; LORETO ITIBUS.

San Jude Parish—Deacon ANTONIO YAROBWEMAL; SAM SANTOS.

San Roque Parish—OLIVE ANINON; JACE ALLYSON PINEDA.

Santa Remedios Parish—MENAS TITO; VICTORIA CEPEDA.

San Jose Parish—CARLISA VICENTA K. RUBEN; SEPHORA WILLIAMS; VINNIE ORSINI; PETER JEFFREY OLOPAI PIALUR.

Korean Catholic Church—ALEX HWANG.

El Shaddai—CHRISTIAN MERANTE.

San Jose Parish, Tinian—DON KRISTOFFER J. SARMIENTO.

SFDB, Rota Parish—TITO T. HOCOG.

San Isidro Parish, Rota—ROSE LUCERO.

Commission on Social Justice and Outreach—Rev. ALLAN A. CABATIAN, O.A.R.; MRS. LAURIE OGUMORO; MR. GALVIN S. DELEON GUERRERO; CLAIRE SALINGER; TINA SABLAN; Deacon ROSIKY BERNADINO FLORES CAMACHO; MS. JOSEPHINE T. SABLAN.

Commission on Ministerial Development—Rev. KENNETH J. HEZEL, S.J.

Apostolic Works of the Diocese

Diocesan Publications Office—Most Rev. RYAN JIMENEZ, Publisher; Rev. JASON GRANADO, Editor; MIKE TEMPORANTE, Graphic Artist; GLORYBEL TAN, Advertising Mgr.

Electronic Media—Rev. JASON GRANADO; ROMMELL BUENAFLOR.

Hospital Chaplaincy (Saipan)—Rev. LEO NEIL BULLOS, O.A.R.

Mt. Carmel Catholic Cemetery—MR. EDWARD S. TENORIO, Chm.; Rev. ISAAC M. AYUYU; Deacon JEFFREY T. CAMACHO; MRS. DORIS S. NUIQUE.

Prison Chaplaincy—Rev. JESSE T. REYES.

Police and Fire Departments Chaplaincy—Rev. JESSE T. REYES.

Civilly Incorporated Activities of the Diocese

Mount Carmel School, Inc. (Saipan)—Mailing Address: P.O. Box 500006, CK, Saipan, 96950. Tel: 670-235-1251; Tel: 670-234-6184; Fax: 670-234-4751; Email: president.mcs@pticom.com. VICENTE M. BABAUTA JR., Bd. Dir. Chm.; MR. GALVIN S. DELEON GUERRERO, Pres.; MRS. FRANCES T. TAIMANAO, Prin.; HELENE L. MANNING, Vice Prin.; MR. JOHN S. BLANCO, Dir. Inst. Devel.

Eskuelan San Francisco de Borja School, Inc. (Rota)—MR. EDWARD MARATITA, Bd. Dir. Chm.; MRS. CARMEN H. ATALIG, Admin. & Prin.; MRS. LEA D. MARATITA, Business Office in-charge.

Karidat, Inc.—MRS. LAURIE OGUMORO, Exec. Dir.; MS. JOSEPHINE T. SABLAN, Pres. Bd.; MRS. MARCIE M. TOMOKANE, Vice Pres. & Sec.; Sr. STELLA IFENUK, M.M.B., Treas.

Associations of the Faithful

Representatives from Church Organizations & Movements—

Simbang Gabi Group—MRS. MALOU MENDOZA, Pres.

Neocatechumenal Way—MR. FRANK PEREDO; MRS. OLIVIA PEREDO.

Children of God the Father, Inc.—ROXANNE ARANDA ADA, Pres.; Rev. JASON GRANADO, Spiritual Dir.

Confraternity of Christian Mothers—NIEVES L. BABAUTA, Diocesan Bd. Pres.; Rev. JESSE T. REYES, Spiritual Dir.

Couples for Christ—Household Leader: MRS. CECILIA PAGAPULAR.

El Shaddai Movement—Rev. ANTHONY AGUASON, Spiritual Dir.; MR. DANILO BIGALBAL, Leader.

Eucharistic Adoration Society—Most Rev. RYAN JIMENEZ; Rev. ISAAC M. AYUYU; Sr. NARCISA PENAREDONDA, S.J.B.P.

Legion of Mary—Rev. ALLAN A. CABATIAN, O.A.R., Spiritual Dir.

San Roque Parish - Mother of Divine Love Praesidium—ANTONIO LG. CABRERA, Pres.

Legion of Mary at San Antonio Parish/Mother of Perpetual Help Praesidium—MS. CECILIA BOTHEL, Pres.

Legion of Mary at Kristo Rai Parish/Mother Refuge of Sinners, Praesidium—MR. MICHAEL MORAN, Pres.

Light & Salt Catholic Charismatic Community—CELY ZAMORA, Head Servant; Rev. CHARLITO A. BORJA, Spiritual Dir.

Divine Mercy—Rev. JESSE T. REYES, Spiritual Dir.

Marriage Encounter—Section Leaders: MR. GONZALO PANGELINAN; MRS. LINDA PANGELINAN.

CLERGY, PARISHES, MISSIONS AND PAROCHIAL SCHOOLS

ISLAND OF SAIPAN

CHALAN KANOA VILLAGE, CATHEDRAL OF OUR LADY OF MT. CARMEL, Most Rev. Ryan Jimenez; Revs. Isaac M. Ayuyu; Isidro T. Ogumoro; Deacon Jeffrey Melvin Tenorio Camacho; Sr. NarcisA Penarendonda, S.J.B.P., Pastoral Assoc.

Rectory—Mt. Carmel, P.O. Box 500745, 96950. Tel: 670-234-3000; Email: ryansaipan@gmail.com; Email: lalingbabauta@yahoo.com; Web: www.rcdck.org.

Mission—Korean Catholic Church of Saipan, P.O. Box 500541, 96950. Rev. Hyun Woo (Andrew) Jang.

GARAPAN VILLAGE, DISTRICT 11, KRISTO RAI PARISH P.O. Box 500745, 96950. Tel: 670-233-2700; Email: fr.haroldfuna@gmail.com; Web: www.rcdck.org. Beach Road, Garapan, 96950. Rev. Harold Funa, Admin.

MATURANA HOUSE OF PRAYER.

NAVY HILL, COMMONWEALTH HEALTH CENTER CHAPEL.

KAGMAN VILLAGE, SANTA SOLEDAD MISSION PARISH Mailing Address: P.O. Box 500745, 96950. Cell: 670-483-7254; Email: palijessetreyes@gmail.com; Web: www.rcdck.org. Kagman, 96950. Rev. Jesse T. Reyes; Deacon Rosiky Bernadino Flores Camacho.

SAIPAN, SAN JUDE PARISH Chalan Msgr. Martinez Rd., Koblerville, 96950. Deacon Estanislao K. Benavente; Rev. James Salas Balajadia.

Rectory—P.O. Box 500745, 96950. Tel: 670-234-3000, Ext. 114; Email: sansantiagu@gmail.com; Web: www.rcdck.org.

SAN ANTONIO VILLAGE, DISTRICT 6, SAN ANTONIO PARISH San Antonio St., San Antonio, Northern Mariana Islands 96950. Rev. Anthony Aguason, Admin.; Deacon Antonio Yarobwemal.

Rectory—San Antonio, P.O. Box 500745, 96950. Tel: 670-235-4515; Email: aguasonanthony@gmail.com; Web: www.rcdck.org.

SAN JOSE VILLAGE, DISTRICT 7, SAN JOSE PARISH Apengagh Ave., San Jose, 96950. Rev. Charlito A. Borja.

Rectory—P.O. Box 500745, 96950. Tel: 670-234-6981; Email: charlieborja@hotmail.com; Web: www.rcdck.org.

SAN ROQUE VILLAGE, DISTRICT 9, SAN ROQUE PARISH Mamate Loop, San Roque, 96950. Rev. Allan A. Cabatian, O.A.R.

Rectory—P.O. Box 500745, 96950. Tel: 670-322-2404; Email: allanrubett1979@gmail.com.

SAN VICENTE VILLAGE, DISTRICT 10, SAN VICENTE PARISH Isa Dr., San Vicente, 96950. Rev. Jason Granado; Sr. Emma Lusterio, S.J.B.P., Pastoral Assoc.

Rectory—San Vicente, P.O. Box 500745, 96950. Tel: 670-235-8208; Email: frjasongranado@gmail.com; Web: www.rcdck.org.

OUR LADY OF THE MOST HOLY ROSARY, Dandan.

TANAPAG VILLAGE, DISTRICT 8, SANTA REMEDIOS PARISH Santa Remedio Dr., Tanapag, 96950. Rev. Leo Neil Bullos, O.A.R., Admin.; Deacon Thomas Schweiger.

Rectory—P.O. Box 500745, 96950. Tel: 670-322-2404; Email: lnch_1208@yahoo.com.

ISLAND OF ROTA

SONGSONG VILLAGE

1—SAN FRANCISCO DE BORJA PARISH Singsong, Rota, 96951. Rev. Manuel Lim, Admin.

Rectory—San Francisco de Borja, Songsong Village, P.O. Box 542, Rota, 96951. Tel: 670-532-3522; Email: manuellim333@gmail.com; Web: www.rcdck.org.

2—SAN ISIDRO PARISH, (Sinapalo) Sinapalo, Rota, 96951. Rev. Manuel Lim, Admin.

Rectory—Sinapalo Village, P.O. Box 590, Rota, 96951. Tel: 670-532-3522; Email: manuellim333@gmail.com; Web: www.rcdck.org.

ISLAND OF TINIAN

SAN JOSE VILLAGE, SAN JOSE San Jose, Tinian, 96952. Rev. Rey Rosal.

Catholic Rectory, San Jose Village, P.O. Box 131, Tinian, 96952. Tel: 670-433-3000; Email: frreyrosal@yahoo.com; Web: www.rcdck.org.

DIOCESAN MISSIONS

ISLAND OF AGRIHAN, SANTA CRUZ CHAPEL.
ISLAND OF ALAMAGAN, SANTA CRUZ CHAPEL.
ISLAND OF ANATAHAN, SAN JOSE CHAPEL.
ISLAND OF PAGAN, SAN IGNACIO CHAPEL.

Permanent Deacons:
Benavente, Estanislao K.
Flores Camacho, Rosiky Bernadino
Schweiger, Thomas
Tenorio Camacho, Jeffrey Melvin
Yarobwemal, Antonio.

INSTITUTIONS LOCATED IN DIOCESE

[A] RESIDENCES OF SISTERS

SAIPAN. *MMB Maturana Community*, P.O. Box 501178-CK, 96950. Tel: 670-322-9713; Email: mahmmb@yahoo.com; Web: www.mmberriz.com. Sr. Martha Ramarui, M.M.B., Community Coord. Sisters 12.

Pastorelle Sisters Convent (San Antonio Parish), P.O. Box 500745, 96950. Tel: 670-234-1213; Email: narcisasjbp1992@gmail.com. San Antonio, 96950. Sr. Narcisa Penaredonda, S.J.B.P., Local Animator. Sisters 3.

RELIGIOUS INSTITUTES OF MEN REPRESENTED IN THE DIOCESE

For further details refer to the corresponding bracketed number in the Religious Institutes of Men or Women section.

[0690]—*The Society of Jesus*—S.J.

RELIGIOUS INSTITUTES OF WOMEN REPRESENTED IN THE DIOCESE

[2510]—*Mercedarian Missionaries of Berriz*—M.M.B.
[]—*Pastorelle Sisters.*
[1830]—*Sisters of the Good Shepherd*—R.G.S.

An asterisk (*) denotes an organization that has established tax-exempt status directly with the IRS and is not covered by the USCCB Group Ruling.

Diocese of Fajardo-Humacao, Puerto Rico

(Dioecesis Faiardensis-Humacaensi)

ESTABLISHED JUNE 1, 2008

Comprises southeast municipalies of Puerto Rico: Humacao, Naguabo; east municipalies of Puerto Rico: Ceiba, Fajardo, Luquillo, northeast municipalies of Puerto Rico Rio Grande, Loiza, Canovanas and the Islands Municipalies of Culebra and Vieques.

Patroness of the Diocese: Nuestra Senora del Carmen and Santiago Apostol (official).

(VACANT SEE)

Bishop House: Calle 3, Final, K. m 0.7 Urbanizacion Bermudez, Fajardo, PR 00738. Mailing Address: Apartado 888, Fajardo, PR 00738. Tel: 787-801-5700; Tel: 787-801-5800; Fax: 787-801-2600.

Email: cancilleriadfh@gmail.com

STATISTICAL OVERVIEW

Personnel	
Abbots	1
Priests: Diocesan Active in Diocese	16
Priests: Diocesan in Foreign Missions	1
Number of Diocesan Priests	17
Religious Priests in Diocese	13
Total Priests in Diocese	30
Permanent Deacons in Diocese	41
Total Brothers	4
Total Sisters	16
Parishes	
Parishes	22
With Resident Pastor:	
Resident Diocesan Priests	13
Resident Religious Priests	9
Educational	
Colleges and Universities	1
Total Students	27
High Schools, Diocesan and Parish	5
Total Students	927
High Schools, Private	5
Total Students	702
Elementary Schools, Diocesan and Parish	5
Total Students	555
Total Students under Catholic Instruction	2,211
Teachers in the Diocese:	
Sisters	3
Lay Teachers	149
Vital Statistics	
Receptions into the Church:	
Infant Baptism Totals	114
Minor Baptism Totals	104
Adult Baptism Totals	109
Received into Full Communion	34
First Communions	42
Confirmations	295
Marriages:	
Catholic	64
Interfaith	19
Total Marriages	83
Deaths	366
Total Catholic Population	79,187
Total Population	263,958

Former Bishop—Most Rev. EUSEBIO RAMOS MORALES, ord. June 3, 1983; appt. Bishop of Fajardo-Humacao March 11, 2008; cons. May 31, 2008; appt. Bishop of Caguas Feb. 2, 2017; inst. Feb. 26, 2017.

Vicar General—Rev. VICTOR SANTIAGO MATEO, S.T.

Sec. Chancellor—Rev. CANICE CHUKWUEMEKA NJOKU, C.S.Sp.

Judicial & Episcopal Vicar—Rev. LUIS ANTONIO ALICEA RIVERA.

Episcopal Vicar (Mission Loiza)—Rev. JOSE ORLANDO CAMACHO TORRES, C.S.Sp.

Episcopal Vicar (Mission Mision Fajardo)—Rev. PETER FRANCIS OKIH, C.S.Sp.

Diocesan Offices and Directors

Economic Administrator—Deacon HECTOR N. GONZALEZ, CPA, Mailing Address: P.O. Box 888, Fajardo, 00738. Tel: 787-801-5700; Tel: 787-801-5800; Fax: 787-801-2600.

Diocesan Movements y Organizations—VACANT.

Cursillos de Cristiandad—MR. JOHNNY MORALES; MR. JOSE MARRERO.

Legion de Maria—MRS. AIDA JIMENEZ.

Renovacion Carismatica—MRS. LUCY FIGUEROA; NILDA VELAZQUEZ.

Juan XXIII—MR. HECTOR CARINO.

Caballeros de Colon—MR. JUSTINO CRUZ.

Vicentinos—VACANT.

Talleres de Oracion y Vida—VACANT.

Education Vicar—Rev. LUIS ANTONIO ALICEA RIVERA.

Director Caritas (DFH)—Rev. JOSE ORLANDO CAMACHO TORRES, C.S.Sp.

Supervisora de Catequesis Familiar Integral—WILMA Y. GARCIA CARRION.

Spiritual Director Catequesis Familiar Integral—Rev. ORLANDO C. BONILLA, S.T.

Master of Ceremonies—Rev. HECTOR M. RODRIQUEZ VILLANUEVA, Mailing Address: P.O. Box 888, Fajardo, 00738.

Pastoral Vicar—Rev. FLOYD MERCADO VIDRO, Mailing Address: P.O. Box 888, Fajardo, 00738.

Vocations Director—Rev. HECTOR M. RODRIQUEZ VILLANUEVA.

CLERGY, PARISHES, MISSIONS AND PAROCHIAL SCHOOLS

CITY OF FAJARDO

1—CATHEDRAL SANTIAGO APOSTOL (1766)

16 Garrido Morales St., P.O. Box 806, 00738. Tel: 787-863-2365; Email: catedralsantiagodfh@gmail.com. Revs. Hector M. Rodriquez Villanueva, Rector; Donal Sella; Deacons Andres Velazquez; Jorge Moctezuma; Luis A. Cordero.

Catechesis Religious Program—Students 49.

Chapels—Bo. Florencio, Santa Elena— (1962).

Bo. Quebrada Vueltas, Perpetuo Socorro (1965).

La Milagrosa, Santa Isidra (1978).

Madre del Salvador, Bo. Paraiso.

2—SANTISIMO REDENTOR (1993)

Urb. Monte Brisas, Calle C-V-19, 00738. Tel: 787-863-5227; Email: santisimoredentor@mail.com. Rev. Bergson Julien; Deacons Jesus Ramos Torres; Angel F. Ramos Velez.

Catechesis Religious Program—Students 60.

Chapels—Puerto Real, Ntra. Sra. de Carmen—

Sardinera, San Juan Bautista.

Las Croabas, Maria, Madre del Senor.

Fajardo Gardens, Maria, Madre de la Providencia.

CITY OF HUMACAO

1—CONCATHEDRAL DULCE NOMBRE DE JESUS (Pueblo) (1763) [CEM 3] [JC]

5 Font Martelo St., P.O. Box 9087, Humacao, 00791. Tel: 787-852-0868; Email: victor.vrsmst@gmail.com. Revs. Victor Santiago Mateo, S.T., Rector; Luis Manuel Ruiz Lebron; Raymond Calixte; Deacons Hector Velazquez Velazquez; Rafael Medina.

Catechesis Religious Program—Students 380.

Chapels—San Agustin— (1955)

Carr. 927 Km 0 Hm. 6 Parcela 74 Bo. Anton Ruiz, P.O. Box 9087, Humacao, 00792.

Nuestra Senora de la Candelaria (1956)

Carr. 3 Km. 90 Hm. 9 Bo. Candelero Arriba, P.O. Box 9087, Humacao, 00792.

San Jose (1957)

Carr. 198 R 922 Km 1 Hm 1 Bo. Coto Mabu, P.O. Box 9087, Humacao, 00792.

Nuestra Senora de Fatima (1962)

Carr. 3 R 925 Km. 0 Hm. 2 Calle Girasol Esquina Orquidea Bo. Junquito, P.O. Box 9087, Humacao, 00792.

Santa Teresita (1965)

Carr. 3 R 906 Bo. Candelero Abajo 20, P.O. Box 9087, Humacao, 00792.

Nuestra Senora de la Providencia (2000)

Carr. 910 Km. 0.80 Bo. Catano Sector Los Flechas, P.O. Box 9087, Humacao, 00792.

Perpetuo Socorro (1944)

Carr. 3 R 923 Km. 1 9 ML Bo. Buena Vista, P.O. Box 9087, Humacao, 00792.

Inmaculada Concepcion (1996)

Urbanizacion Villa Calle 13 E 1, P.O. Box 9087, Humacao, 00792.

Maria Auxiliadora (1999)

Parcelas Martinez Carr. 3 R 906 Km 8 Hm 0 Interior, P.O. Box 9087, Humacao, 00792.

San Pedro y San Pablo (1989)

Caserio Antonio Roig, P.O. Box 9087, Humacao, 00792.

2—COMUNIDAD CATOLICA LA SAGRADA FAMILIA (CUASIPARROQUIA)

3 Executive Office Dr., Humacao, 00791. Tel: 787-719-5269; Email: lasagradafamiliapdm@hotmail.com; Web: www.facebook.com/ParroquiaSagradaFamiliaPalmasDelMar/. Rev. Floyd Mercado Vidro; Deacon Frankie Lasanta-Gonzalez.

3—MARIA REINA DE LA PAZ (Pueblo) (1989)

Urb. Villa Universitaria, Calle 4 A-20, Humacao, 00791. Cell: 787-850-3081; Email: jortizmrp@gmail.com. Rev. Leonidas de Jesus Abreu Ortiz; Deacons Roberto Garcia Ortiz; Pablo J. Colon Ojeda; Juan Cintron; Rafael L. Ufret Acevedo.
Catechesis Religious Program—Students 210.
Chapels—Sagrado Corazon de Jesus— (1940)
Carr. #3R. 909 K.6 h.3 Int., Bo Mariana III, Humacao.
San Martin de Porres (1962)
Bo. Patagonia Num. 128, Ave. Tejas, Humacao.
Buen Pastor (1970)
Carr. #3 R.908 K. 8. h.7 Int. RO22, Bo. Mariana II, Humacao.
Cristo Rey (1976)
Carr. #189 R.914 K.1, Asturianas RL 26052, Humacao.
Santa Rosa de Lima (1978)
Carr. #3 R909 K3 h.3 Int., Bo. Mariana 1, Humacao.
Casa de Oracion Espiritu Santo
Carr. 908 Bo. Tejas, Humacao.

OUTSIDE THE CITIES OF FAJARDO AND HUMACAO

CANOVANAS

1—NUESTRA SENORA DEL PILAR (1960)
Mailing Address: P.O. Box 10000-PMB 320, Canovanas, 00729. Rev. Eduardo Del Rivero; Deacon Jose A. Bosques.
Res.: Calle Luis Hernaiz #3 Esq. Muñoz Rivera, Canovanas, 00729. Tel: 787-886-3307;
Tel: 787-957-7818; Email: parroquiaelpilar20@gmail.com; Web: www.parroquiansp.org.
School—Nuestra Senora del Pilar School,
Tel: 787-876-3002; Email: tribunaldfh@gmail.com. Mrs. Iris del Valle Jimenez, Dir. Clergy 2; Lay Teachers 50; Students 624.
Catechesis Religious Program—Students 11.
Mission—San Francisco Javier, Bo. Camabalache, Canovanas, 00729.

2—RESURRECCION DEL SEÑOR (1978)
Carr 188, Km 2.0 San Isidro, P.O. Box 896, Canovanas, 00729-0896. Tel: 787-876-9900; Email: theresurrectionpr@hotmail.com. Revs. Canice Chukwuemeka Njoku, C.S.Sp.; Jose Orlando Camacho Torres, C.S.Sp.; Deacons Roberto Ferris Plaza; Pedro Flores Torres.
Catechesis Religious Program—Migdalia Pizarro, D.R.E. Students 128.
Mission—Ntra. Sra. de la Providencia, Villas De Loiza.

3—SAGRADO CORAZON DE JESUS (1991)
PMB 20147, P.O. Box 35000, Canovanas, 00729-0014. Tel: 787-876-1355; Email: pscj_canovanas@yahoo.com; Email: pscj_canovanas@hotmail.com. RR 186 KM 7 HM 6, Bo. Cubuy, Canovanas, 00729. Rev. Vicente Pasqualetto, S.T., Admin.; Deacon Edwin Nieves Jimenez.
Missions—La Milagrosa—Bo. Cuatrocientas, Canovanas, 00729.
San Pedro Apostol, Bo. Lomas, Canovanas, PR.

4—SAN JOSE (1971)
HC-02 Box 6502, Canovanas, 00729-9736.
Teletype: 787-876-7167; Cell: 787-220-0973; Email: psanjosecr@gmail.com. Carr. 185 Km 5.3 Bo. Campo Rico, Canovanas, 00729. Rev. Edvard Jeudy; Deacons Felipe A. Rivera Estremera; Angel J. Rodriguez Otero.
Catechesis Religious Program—Students 25.
Missions—Ntra. Sra. de la Asuncion—Carrt. 957 Km. 6.8, Palma Sola, Canovanas, PR.
Ntra. Sra. del Carmen, Carrt. 185 Km. 5.3, Alturas de Campo Rico, Canovanas, PR.

5—SANTA MARIA MADRE DE DIOS (1971)
Urb. Loiza Valley, Calle Girasol E189, Canovanas, 00729. Tel: 787-876-0827; Email: pstamariamadrededios@gmail.com. Rev. Antonio Marrero Aballe; Deacons Jose L. Casaigne; Jose Alberto Rios.
Catechesis Religious Program—Sr. Gloria Mercedes Gonzalez, M.S.B.T., D.R.E. Students 13.
Missions—Capilla Cristo Salvador—Sector Pueblo Indio, Canovanas, 00729.
Iglesia Santa Maria Madre De Dios, Carr. 8874-Bo. La Central, Canovanas, 00729.

CEIBA, CEIBA CO., SAN ANTONIO DE PADUA (1840)
561 Escolastico Lopez St., P.O. Box 77, Ceiba, 00735. Tel: 787-885-2530; Email: psadp@hotmail.com. Rev. Manuel Ramon Villamor Tarache; Deacon Ruben Borgos Rivera.
Missions—Sagrado Corazon de Jesus—Parcelas Aguas Claras, Ceiba, 00735.
Ntra. Sra. del Perpetuo Socorro, Bo. Rio Abajo, Ceiba, Ceiba Co. 00735.
Chapel—Ntra. Sra. de Fatima (1968) Bo. Daguao, Ceiba, 00735.
Catechesis Religious Program—Students 50.

HUMACAO PLAYA, HUMACAO CO., NUESTRA SENORA DEL CARMEN (Punta Santiago) (1970)
P.O. Box 91, Punta Santiago, 00741.
Tel: 787-656-9202; Email: pcarmen.ps@gmail.com. Calle Marina 33, Punta Santiago, 00741. Rev. Jose Colon Otero; Deacon Angel M. Rodriguez Cedeno.
Catechesis Religious Program—Calle 5, #103 Verde Mar, P.O. Box 91, Punta Santiago, 00741. Students 125.
Chapel—Bo. Pasto Viejo, Sector El Batey, Nuestra Senora del Perpetuo Socorro (1937; 1986)
Tel: 787-852-4421.

LOIZA

1—ESPIRITU SANTO Y SAN PATRICIO (1719)
Box 504, Loiza, 00772-0504. Tel: 787-886-1539. Rev. Rocendo Herrera, Email: stherrera1@hotmail.com; Deacons Pedro D. Recci Dominguez; Marcos Penalosa Lacen.
Res.: Calle Espiritu Santo #10, Loiza, 00772.
Tel: 787-256-2653; Email: parsapatricio@hoymail.com.
Catechesis Religious Program—Ana Matta, D.R.E. Students 79.
Missions—Santa Rosa de Lima—Bo. Pinones, Loiza, 00772.
Ntra. Sra. del Perpetuo Socorro, Bo. La Torre, Loiza, 00772.
Santisima Trinidad, Bo. Mediana Baja, Loiza, 00772.
San Antonio, Bo. Las Cuevas, Loiza, 00772.
Ntra. Sra. de Fatima, Villa Canona, Loiza, 00772.
San Rafael, Villa Alvarez, Loiza, 00772.

2—SANTIAGO APOSTOL, EL MAYOR (1971)
P.O. Box 118, Loiza, 00772-0118. Tel: 939-287-1972; Email: caminantest@gmail.com. Rev. Orlando C. Bonilla, S.T.; Deacon Albert Gutierrez Rosario.
Res.: Carretera 187 Km. 6.1 Bo. Mediana Alta, Loiza, 00772-0118. Tel: 787-256-5785; Email: parroquiasantiagoapostolloiza@gmail.com.
Catechesis Religious Program—Students 15.
Missions—Ntra. Sra. Perpetuo Socorro—Parcelas Suarez, Loiza, 00772.
La Milagrosa, Bo. El Jobos, Loiza, 00772.
La Providencia, Bo. Mini Mine, Loiza, 00772.
Ntra. Sra. De Fatima, Parcelas Vieques, Loiza, 00772.

LUQUILLO

1—MARIA, MADRE DEL REDENTOR (1997)
P.O. Box 591, Luquillo, 00773-0591. Cell: 787-223-1464. Rev. Luis Antonio Alicea Rivera; Deacons Ivan Colon Melendez; Jose M. Lopez Alverio.
Res.: Barrio Pitaya, Sector Casablanca, Carr. 173, Km. 1.5, Luquillo, 00773. Tel: 787-516-8115; Email: martin.cssr@hotmail.com.
Catechesis Religious Program—Students 35.
Missions—Ntra. Sra. del Carmen—Carr. 983 K.2 H.0, Luquillo, 00773.
Ntra. Sra. Milagrosa, Carr. 983 K.6 H.3, Luquillo, 00773.
San Vicente de Paul, Carr. 3H 43 H.9, Luquillo, 00773.
Ntra. Sra. del Perpetuo Socorro, Carr. 984 K.2 H.2, Luquillo, 00773.

2—SAN JOSE (1797)
P.O. Box 493, Luquillo, 00773-0493.
Tel: 787-889-2590; Email: psanjosepr@gmail.com. Rev. P. Peter.
Res.: Calle Soledad No. 15, Luquillo, 00773.
Tel: 787-600-5561; Email: okigubs@yahoo.com.
Missions—San Judas—Bo. Mata de Platano, Luquillo, 00773.
Ntra. Sra. del Cobre, Parcelas Fortuna, Luquillo, 00773.

NAGUABO, NAGUABO CO., NUESTRA SENORA DEL ROSARIO (1794) [CEM 2] [JC] (Hispanic) Rev. Lorenzo Vargas Concepcion; Deacons Jose A. Nevarez Cruz; Emilio Colon Cosme; Ramon Rivera Robles; Rafael Garcia Pizarro.
Res.: Calle Juan R. Garzot n. 12, Box 655, Naguabo, 00718. Tel: 787-874-0150; Email: pvrosario@hotmail.com.
Chapels—Nuestra Senora del Perpetuo Socorro— (1946) .
Nuestra Senora de la Altagracia (1963) Bo. Maizales, Naguabo.
Nuestra Senora de Fatima (1965) Bo. Duque, Naguabo.
Bo. Florida, Nuestra Senora del Perpetuo Socorro (1942) .
Nuestra Senora del Carmen Playa (Hucares) (1920) Bo. Maizales, Naguabo.
Nuestra Senora de la Providencia (1965) Bo. Mariana, Naguabo.
Santa Rosa de Lima (1975) Bo. Sandiago 4 Lima, Naguabo.
Missions—Barrio Rio, Sector Brazo Seco, Naguabo.
Capilla Beato Carlos Manuel Rodriguez, Sector La Fe, Naguabo.

RIO GRANDE

1—CRISTO REY (1970)
Palmer, Rio Gande, P.O. Box 382, Palmer, 00721-0382. Tel: 787-887-3552. Rev. Adrian Alicea Padilla; Deacon Pedro J. Rivera Viera.
Res.: Calle Principal, #50, Palmer, 00721.
Tel: 939-644-1919; Email: sendero137@aol.com.
Missions—La Milagrosa—Palmer. Parcela 69 Hato Rio Grande, Bo. Carola, 00721.
Ntra. Sra. de la Providencia, Bloque S-1 #7, Palmer, 00721.

2—NUESTRA SENORA DEL CARMEN (1840)
Apt. 845, Rio Grande, 00745. Tel: 787-887-2365; Email: delcarmen_9@yahoo.com. Calle del Carmen #9, Rio Grande, 00745. Rev. Jose A. Rivera Maldonado; Deacons Fernando Marrero Coll; Vidal Diaz; Jose M. Carrasquillo.
School—Nuestra Senora del Carmen School, Calle 14 Urb. Alturas de Rio Grande, Apartado 1389, P.O. Box 818, Rio Grande, 00745. Tel: 787-887-4099; Fax: 787-887-0872; Email: cnscrg@yahoo.com. Myrtha Perez, Prin.
Catechesis Religious Program—Students 146.
Missions—Nuestra Senora de Fatima—Bo. El Verde, Rio Grande, 00745.
Ntra. Sra. de Guadalupe, Jardines de Rio Grande, Rio Grande, 00745.
San Pedro, Bo. Bartolo, Rio Grande, 00745.
La Milagrosa, Calle 14, Alturas de Rio Grande, Rio Grande, 00745.
Sagrado Corazon de Jesus, Coco Beach, Rio Grande, 00745.

3—SAN FRANCISCO DE ASIS (1986)
Bo. Malpica, K 2.6, P.O. Box 1449, Rio Grande, 00745-1449. Tel: 787-657-5872; Email: p_sanfcodeasis@hotmail.com; Email: fkabran@hotmail.com. Rev. Frederic Kabran; Deacon Pedro Castro Cuadrado.

OUTSIDE THE MAIN ISLAND OF PUERTO RICO, THE SMALL ISLANDS

CULEBRA, CULEBRA CO., NUESTRA SENORA DEL CARMEN (1889; 1990)
Mailing Address: Calle Ntra. Sra. del Carmen, P.O. Box 236, Culebra, 00775. Tel: 787-742-0637; Email: emeritogomez@yahoo.com. Rev. Emerito Gomez Ortiz, O.F.M.; Deacon Hector N. Gonzalez Rubio.

VIEQUES, VIEQUES CO., SANTIAGO APOSTOL E INMACULADA CONCEPCION (1844) (Hispanic)
442 Lebrum St., Vieques, 00765. Tel: 787-934-9460; Email: . Rev. Jean Augustal Jean Julien; Deacon Roberto Velazquez.
Chapels—Sagrado Corazon de Jesus— (1949) .
Nuestra Senora de Lourdes (1952) .
Nuestra Senora del Perpetuo Socorro (1945) .
Virgen del Carmen (1942) .
Nuestra Senora de Fatima (1950) .
Catechesis Religious Program—Daphene Torres, D.R.E. Students 47.

Permanent Deacons:
Otero Lugo, Jose
Rivera Viera, Pedro J.

INSTITUTIONS LOCATED IN DIOCESE

[A] PAROCHIAL SCHOOLS

FAJARDO. *Colegio Diocesano Santiago Apostol* (1947) (Grades PreK-12), P.O. Box 907, 00738-0907.
Tel: 787-863-0524; Fax: 787-860-6655; Email: santiagoapostolprl@yahoo.com; Web: www.csa-sec.org. Rev. Luis Antonio Alicea Rivera, Dir. Clergy 2; Lay Teachers 21; Students 87.

HUMACAO. *Colegio Nuestra Senora del Perpetuo Socorro de Humacao, Inc.* (1984) (Grades K-12), Carr. 908 KM 2.0 Avenida Tejas, P.O. Box 9107, Humacao, 00792. Tel: 787-852-0845; Fax: 787-852-8706; Email: nuestrasocorro@gmail.com; Web: miperpetuosocorro.com. Michelle Arroyo, Dir.; Isabel Vila, Librarian. Lay Teachers 16; Students 206.
Colegio San Antonio Abad (1950) (Benedictines) P.O. Box 729, Humacao, 00792. Tel: 787-852-1616;
Fax: 787-852-1920; Email: csaa.hermits@gmail.com. Gabriela Resto, Headmistress; Rt. Rev. Oscar Rivera, O.S.B., Dir.; Brunilda Ruiz, Librarian. Brothers 3; Religious Teachers 1; Lay Teachers 31; Priests 3; Students 350.
Colegio San Benito (1963) P.O. Box 728, Humacao, 00792. Tel: 787-852-1365; Fax: 787-285-8137; Web: www.csb.edu.pr. Sisters Mary Ruth Santana, O.S.B., Dir.; Carmen Davila, O.S.B., Admin. Hermanas Benedictinas. Religious Teachers 3; Lay Teachers 34; Sisters 7; Students 435.

CANOVANAS. *College of Our Lady of Pilar*, (Grades PreK-12), Calle Luis Hernaiz #3 Esquina Muñoz Rivera, P.O. Box 1615, Canovanas, 00729.
Tel: 787-876-3002; Fax: 787-256-5767; Email: pilar1615@caribe.net; Email: cnspilar2010@gmail.

com. Mrs. Iris del Valle Jimenez, Dir.; Mr. Alberto Rosario Diaz, Prin. Religious Teachers 4; Lay Teachers 19; Students 531.

RIO GRANDE. *Colegio Nuestra Senora del Carmen*, (Grades PreK-12), Tel: 787-887-4099; Fax: 787-887-0872; Email: perezmyrtha@yahoo.com. Sr. Migdalia Arroyo, Dir. Religious Teachers 2; Lay Teachers 15; Students 130.

[B] MONASTERIES AND RESIDENCES OF PRIESTS

HUMACAO. *San Antonio Abad Abbey of the Order of St. Benedict* Order of St Benedict / Abadia San Anyonio Abad Carretera 908 Km 2.2 Barrio Tejas, P.O. Box 729, Humacao, 00792. Tel: 787-852-1616; Cell: 787-372-7065; Fax: 787-852-1920; Email: oscarmonje1950@yahoo.com. Rt. Rev. Oscar Rivera, O.S.B., Abbot; Revs. Rafael Perez, O.S.B., Prior; Jaime Reyes, O.S.B.; Ignacio Aguirre, O.S.B.; Bros. Aristedes Pacheco Torres, O.S.B., Subprior; Felix Neussendorfer, O.S.B.; Randolph Perkins. Brothers 5; Claustral Oblate 1.

LOIZA. *Siervos Misioneros de la Santisima Trinidad*, Cenacle Rafael Cordero, San Patricio Loiza, P.O. Box 118, Loiza, 00772. Tel: 787-961-0851; Email: victor.vrsmst@gmail.com. Rev. Vicente Pasqualetto, S.T., Regional Coord.

[C] HOMES AND RESIDENCES

CANOVANAS. *Hogar Teresa Toda* (1993) (For Girls) Calle 5-A, R-14, Villa De Loiza, Loiza, 00729. Tel: 787-886-2060; Fax: 787-886-2075; Email: hogaresteresatoda@yahoo.com; Web: www.hogaresteresatoda.org. P.O. Box 868, Canovanas, 00729. Sr. Norma Matar, Dir. Bed Capacity 28; Tot Asst. Annually 60; Total Staff 15.

[D] MISCELLANEOUS

LUQUILLO. *Divine Child Jesus Children's Home of the Hermanas Hijas del Corazon Misericordioso de Maria*, Calle Angel Gutierrez #68, P.O. Box 1413, Luquillo, 00773. Tel: 787-889-6033; Email: convento1973@yahoo.com; Web: hogarinfantildivinoninojesus.org. Sr. Maria Espitia, Dir. Religious Teachers 2; Students 20.

RELIGIOUS INSTITUTES OF WOMEN REPRESENTED IN THE DIOCESE

For further details refer to the corresponding bracketed number in the Religious Institutes of Men or Women section.

[]—*Carmelitas Teresas de San Jose.*
[]—*Cenaculo Misionero Rafael Cordero.*
[]—*Hermanas de Nazareth.*
[]—*Hermanas Dominicas de la Santa Cruz.*
[]—*Hijas de la Caridad de San Vicente de Paul.*
[]—*Hijas del Corazon Misericordioso de Maria.*
[]—*Missioneras de los Sagrados Croazones de Jesus y Maria.*
[]—*Monasterio Santa Escolastica.*

An asterisk (*) denotes an organization that has established tax-exempt status directly with the IRS and is not covered by the USCCB Group Ruling.

Prefecture Apostolic of the Marshall Islands

Reverend Monsignor

ARIEL GALIDO, M.S.C.

Third Prefect Apostolic of the Marshall Islands; ordained June 9, 2004; appointed June 28, 2017. *Res.: Cathedral of the Assumption, Uliga, P.O. Box 8, Majuro, MH 96960.*

Mailing Address: Assumption, Uliga, Majuro, P.O. Box 8, Majuro, MH 96960. Tel: 692-625-6675; Tel: 692-625-8307.

Email: rmi.prefecture93@gmail.com

Reverend Monsignor

JAMES C. GOULD, S.J.

Prefect Emeritus Apostolic of the Marshall Islands; ordained May 4, 1974; appointed First Prefect Apostolic of the Marshall Islands April 23, 1993; resigned December 21, 2007. *Mailing Address: Assumption, Uliga, Majuro, P.O. Box 8, Majuro, MH 96960.*

Reverend Monsignor

RAYMUNDO T. SABIO, M.S.C.

Prefect Emeritus Apostolic of the Marshall Islands; ordained December 20, 1971; appointed Second Prefect Apostolic of the Marshall Islands December 21, 2007; installed January 6, 2008; resigned June 28, 2017. *Mailing Address: P.O., Box 8, Majuro, MH 96960.* Tel: 692-625-6675; Fax: 692-625-5520.

Square Miles 186,000.

Total Population (est.) 53,127

Prefecture Apostolic of the Marshall Islands divided from the Diocese of the Carolines-Marshall Islands and erected on August 15, 1993 and committed to the Society of Jesus, New York Province; and on January 6, 2008 committed to the Missionaries of the Sacred Heart. Area is that of the Republic of the Marshall Islands which is related by Compact of Free Association to the United States.

STATISTICAL OVERVIEW

Personnel	
Priests: Diocesan Active in Diocese	1
Number of Diocesan Priests	1
Religious Priests in Diocese	5
Total Priests in Diocese	6
Permanent Deacons in Diocese	1
Total Sisters	6
Parishes	
Parishes	5
With Resident Pastor:	
Resident Diocesan Priests	1
Resident Religious Priests	4
Missions	8
Pastoral Centers	1
New Parishes Created	1
Professional Ministry Personnel:	
Sisters	7
Lay Ministers	50
Welfare	
Other Institutions	1
Total Assisted	300
Educational	
High Schools, Diocesan and Parish	2
Total Students	98
Elementary Schools, Diocesan and Parish	3
Total Students	527
Catechesis/Religious Education:	
High School Students	120
Elementary Students	584
Total Students under Catholic Instruction	1,329
Teachers in the Diocese:	
Sisters	3
Lay Teachers	10
Vital Statistics	
Receptions into the Church:	
Infant Baptism Totals	85
Minor Baptism Totals	15
Received into Full Communion	14
First Communions	75
Confirmations	43
Marriages:	
Catholic	6
Interfaith	2
Total Marriages	8
Deaths	10
Total Catholic Population	5,234
Total Population	53,190

Former Prefects—Rev. Msgrs. JAMES C. GOULD, S.J., ord. May 4, 1974; appt. First Prefect Apostolic of the Marshall Islands April 23, 1993; installed Aug. 15, 1993; resigned Dec. 21, 2007.; RAYMUNDO T. SABIO, M.S.C., ord. Dec. 20, 1971; appt. Second Prefect Apostolic of the Marshall Islands Dec. 21, 2007; installed Jan. 6, 2008; resigned June 28, 2017.

Prefecture Consultors—Rev. TATIERU EWENTEANG, M.S.C.; Deacon JOHANIS KILMAS, M.S.C.; Rev. ROLANDO CUASITO, M.S.C.; Deacon ALFRED CAPELLE.

Secretary—MRS. VERONICA KILUWE, Assumption, P.O. Box 8, Majuro, 96960.

Religious Formation Ministry Coordinator—Deacon ALFRED CAPELLE.

Catholic Education Ministry Coordinator—Sr. CHRISTEL BECKMANN, M.S.C.

Pastoral and Social Ministry Coordinator—KAIRAMAN TEKITANGA, F.D.N.S.C.

Finance Committee—MR. ALAN FOWLER; MR. DENNIS MOMOTARO; MR. VINCENT MULLER.

Catechists Coordinators—MRS. ROSITA CAPELLE; MRS. DAISY DE BRUM.

Vocations—Rev. ROLANDO CUASITO, M.S.C.

CLERGY, PARISHES, MISSIONS AND PAROCHIAL SCHOOLS

MARSHALL ISLANDS

Mailing Address: Assumption Church, Uliga, P.O. Box 8, Majuro, MH 96960. Tel: (011) 692-625-6675; 692-625-8307; unless otherwise noted.

MAJURO, CATHEDRAL OF THE ASSUMPTION, Tel: 692-625-8307. Rev. Rolando Cuasito, M.S.C.
School—Assumption Elementary School, (Grades K-8), Ms. Biram Stege, Prin.; Mrs. Luisa Kamenio, Asst. Prin; Erica Block, Librarian. Lay Teachers 30; Sisters 2; Students 244.
High School—Assumption High School, Ms. Biram Stege, Prin.; Mrs. Luisa Kamenio, Asst. Prin; Erica Block, Librarian. Lay Teachers 10; Students 80.
Mission—Laura, (St. Francis Xavier) Majuro Atoll.

EBEYE, QUEEN OF PEACE, Mailing Address: P.O. Box 5065, Ebeye, 96970. Tel: 692-329-3828. Rev. Yoseph Rettob, M.S.C.; Deacon Johanis Kilmas, M.S.C.
School—Queen of Peace Elementary School, (Grades K-8), Ms. Jessica Calep, Prin; Mrs. Amenta Jorbwuj, Librarian. Lay Teachers 14; Sisters 1; Students 235.
High School—Fr. Hacker High School, Mr. Nolan deBrum, Prin; Mrs. Brenda Loeak, Librarian. Lay Teachers 6; Students 56.
Missions—Santo—(St. Leonard) Gugeegue, MH.
Guguugue, (St. Thomas).

JALUIT, SACRED HEART OF JESUS, Jabor, Jaluit. Mailing Address: P.O. Box 8, 96960. Rev. Tetoaiti Tokanikai, M.S.C.; Sr. Lumine Beckmann, M.S.C., Pastoral Coord.
School—St. Joseph Elementary School, (Grades K-8), Mr. Sweeter Kalous, Prin. Lay Teachers 9; Sisters 2; Students 87.
Mission—Namdrik, (Our Lady of the Sacred Heart).

KWAJALEIN, BLESSED SACRAMENT, Mailing Address: P.O. Box 1711, USAKA, Kwajalein, MH. Tel: 805-355-2116; Tel: 805-355-4535; Fax: 805-355-8404. Rev. Victor Langhans.

LIKIEP, HOLY ROSARY, Mailing Address: P.O. Box 8, 96960. Rev. Kristianus Fatlolon, M.S.C.
Catechesis Religious Program—Students 22.

OUTER ISLAND, OUTER ISLAND MISSIONS, Rev. Msgr. Ariel A. Galido, M.S.C.
Missions—Arno—(St. Paul).
Wotje, (St. Thomas).
Ailinglaplap: Buoj, (Immaculate Heart of Mary).
Ailinglaplap: Woja, (St. James).

INSTITUTIONS LOCATED IN DIOCESE

[A] MISCELLANEOUS

MAJURO. *Catholic Pastoral Center: Ajeltake*, P.O. Box 8, 96960. Tel: (011) 692-247-7762; Tel: (011) 692-456-2725. Mrs. Marciana Jorju, Contact Person.

An asterisk (*) denotes an organization that has established tax-exempt status directly with the IRS and is not covered by the USCCB Group Ruling.

Diocese of Mayaguez, Puerto Rico

(Dioecesis Maiaguezensis)

Most Reverend

ALVARO CORRADA DEL RIO, S.J.

Bishop of Mayaguez; ordained July 6, 1974; appointed Auxiliary Bishop of Washington DC May 30, 1985; consecrated August 4, 1985; on assignment, as Apostolic Administrator, Diocese of Caguas; appointed Bishop of Tyler December 5, 2000; installed January 30, 2001; appointed Bishop of Mayaguez, Puerto Rico July 6, 2011. *Mailing Address: P.O. Box 2272, Mayaguez, PR 00681.*

Erected by the Bull "Qui arcano Dei" on March 1, 1976, by Pope Paul VI.

Comprises a portion of the southwest of the Island.

STATISTICAL OVERVIEW

Personnel	
Bishop	1
Retired Bishops	1
Priests: Diocesan Active in Diocese	43
Priests: Diocesan Active Outside Diocese	2
Priests: Retired, Sick or Absent	3
Number of Diocesan Priests	48
Religious Priests in Diocese	19
Total Priests in Diocese	67
Extern Priests in Diocese	1
Ordinations:	
Diocesan Priests	3
Transitional Deacons	2
Permanent Deacons in Diocese	59
Total Brothers	1
Total Sisters	81
Parishes	
Parishes	30
With Resident Pastor:	
Resident Diocesan Priests	22
Resident Religious Priests	8
Missions	156
Pastoral Centers	1
Professional Ministry Personnel:	
Brothers	1
Sisters	81
Lay Ministers	757
Welfare	
Catholic Hospitals	1
Total Assisted	8,467
Homes for the Aged	1
Total Assisted	159
Day Care Centers	9
Total Assisted	360
Specialized Homes	2
Total Assisted	160
Special Centers for Social Services	1
Total Assisted	7,500
Educational	
Diocesan Students in Other Seminaries	13
Total Seminarians	13
Colleges and Universities	1
Total Students	1,610
High Schools, Diocesan and Parish	3
Total Students	284
High Schools, Private	6
Total Students	756
Elementary Schools, Diocesan and Parish	4
Total Students	509
Elementary Schools, Private	6
Total Students	1,015
Catechesis/Religious Education:	
High School Students	267
Elementary Students	4,217
Total Students under Catholic Instruction	8,671
Teachers in the Diocese:	
Sisters	5
Lay Teachers	212
Vital Statistics	
Receptions into the Church:	
Infant Baptism Totals	1,653
Minor Baptism Totals	106
Adult Baptism Totals	27
Received into Full Communion	16
First Communions	1,281
Confirmations	1,326
Marriages:	
Catholic	256
Interfaith	18
Total Marriages	274
Deaths	343
Total Catholic Population	391,645
Total Population	489,557

Former Bishop—Most Rev. ULISES AURELIO CASIANO VARGAS, ord. May 30, 1967; appt. Bishop March 4, 1976; ord. April 30, 1976; retired July 6, 2011; died Aug. 5, 2018.

Vicar General—Rev. Msgr. GONZALO DIAZ.

Episcopal Vicars—

Matrimonio y Familia—Rev. Msgr. HUMBERTO LOPEZ BONILLA.

For Pastoral—Rev. Msgr. RAMON E. ALBINO.

For Diocesan Administration—Rev. Msgr. ROGELIO MUR, O.Carm.

Chancery Office—*P.O. Box 2272, Mayaguez, PR USA 00681.* Tel: 787-833-5411. Rev. ERIC IVAN GARCIA-CONCEPCION.

Diocesan Consultors—Rev. Msgr. GONZALO DIAZ HERNANDEZ; Revs. ANGEL LUIS RIOS MATOS; RAMON EMILIO ALBINO GUZMAN; ROGELIO MUR AGUILAR, O.Carm.; JORGE LUIS CARO MORALES; DANIEL HERNANDEZ VELEZ.

Diocesan Board of Administration—Rev. Msgrs. GONZALO DIAZ HERNANDEZ; ROGELIO MUR, O.Carm.; MR. PEDRO J. RIVERA.

Administrator—MR. ALBERTO RODRIGUEZ.

Censor Librorum—Revs. JULIO FERNANDEZ; ISAIAS REVILLA, O.S.A., (Spain).

Parish Priests Consultors—Rev. Msgr. GONZALO DIAZ HERNANDEZ; Rev. ROGELIO MUR AGUILAR, O.Carm.

Diocesan Offices and Directors

Youth Apostolate—Rev. JOSE GUSTAVO TORRES.

Communications Media—Rev. EDGARDO ACOSTA OCASIO.

Cursillos de Cristiandad—Rev. RUBEN FIGUEROA.

Holy Childhood—VACANT.

Legion of Mary—VACANT.

Superintendent of Schools—YOLANDA PAGAN.

Religious Consultor—Rev. JULIO FERNANDEZ.

Catechetics—Sr. MIRIAM NIEVES, O.P.

Religious Coordinator—Rev. JULIO FERNANDEZ.

Development and Planification—Rev. Msgr. ROGELIO MUR, O.Carm.

Vocations—Revs. DELROY THOMAS; DANIEL ENRIQUE HERNANDEZ VELEZ; WILSON MONTES RODRIGUEZ.

Catholic Social Services—Rev. ORLANDO ROSAS MUNIZ, Dir., Carr. 108 Km. 2.8 Int., Calle Obispado Final, Bo. Miradero, Mayaguez, PR USA 00681. Tel: 787-833-3627; Tel: 787-833-3638; Fax: 787-833-3627; Email: sscdmaya@gmail.com.

Seasonal Head Start Program—*Calle Dr. Veve #44, San German, PR USA 00683.* Tel: 787-892-3800; Fax: 787-892-3866. MS. MYRNA CARRERO, Dir.

CLERGY, PARISHES, MISSIONS AND PAROCHIAL SCHOOLS

CITY OF MAYAGUEZ

1—CATHEDRAL OF OUR LADY OF PURIFICATION (1763) Rev. Msgr. Humberto Lopez Bonilla, Rector; Revs. Paulino Mazuelos; Angel Valle Nieves; Deacons Israel Valentin; Eddie O. Perez; Edwin Ramos.
Res.: P.O. Box 220, Mayaguez, PR USA 00681-0220.
Tel: 787-831-2444; Tel: 787-805-5952;
Fax: 787-831-2444.
Schools—*Academy of the Immaculate Conception*—
Tel: 787-834-5400; Tel: 787-834-7824 (High School); Fax: 787-834-5400. Sr. Ileris Velez, Elementary Prin.; Mr. Rene Torres, High School Prin. Lay Teachers 40; Elementary Students 311; High School Students 300.
Colegio La Milagrosa
Tel: 787-834-0350; Fax: 787-834-0350. Sr. Delma Morales, Prin. Lay Teachers 22; Sisters of Charity 1; Elementary Students 114; High School Students 171.
Convent—*Hnas. de Nazaret*
Convento Cristo Rey, 36 Calle Capaira, Ponce de Leon, Mayaguez, PR USA 00681. Tel: 787-833-3481.
Missions—*Maria Socorro de los Cristianos*—
Barrio Leguisamo, Mayaguez, PR USA.
Santa Ana
Quebrada Grande, Mayaguez, PR USA.
Catechesis Religious Program—Students 143.

2—ASCENSION (1968) Deacons Gilberto Martinez; Samuel S. Collazo.
Res.: P.O. Box 279, Mayaguez, PR USA 00681.
Tel: 787-832-0766; Fax: 787-832-0766; Email: laascensiondelsenor@gmail.com; Email: pjrlinares@hotmail.com.
Missions—*St. Teresita*—
Bo. Limon, PR USA.
Our Lady of Perpetual Help
Bo. Las Vegas, PR USA.
Ntra. Sra. de la Providencia (Rep. Masias)
Bo. El Porvenir, PR USA.
Catechesis Religious Program—Students 143.

3—CHURCH DE EL BUEN PASTOR (1986) Revs. Jose Cedeño Diaz, S.J.; Jose Ruiz Andujo, S.J., Vicar.
Res.: Urb. Mayaguez Ter., 5000 Calle San Gerardo, Mayaguez, PR USA 00682-6627. Tel: 787-833-8800; Fax: 787-805-3660; Email: aponte.joser@gmail.com; Email: angelmsj@yahoo.com.
Catechesis Religious Program—Students 74.
Missions—*El Cristo de Los Milagros*—
1116 Calle Perpetuo Socorro, Bo. Algarrobo, Mayaguez, PR USA 00682. Tel: 787-265-5936.
Sta. Teresita
Parcelas Soledad, Mayaguez, PR USA 00682.

4—CHURCH OF THE RESURRECTION (1988) Rev. Orlando Rosas Muniz; Deacon Jose Luis Rodriguez.
Res.: Balboa 285, Mayaguez, PR USA 00680.
Tel: 787-831-6180.

Diocese of Ponce, Puerto Rico

(Dioecesis Poncensis)

Most Reverend

RUBEN ANTONIO GONZALEZ MEDINA, C.M.F.

Bishop of Ponce; ordained February 9, 1975; appointed Bishop of Caguas December 12, 2000; consecrated February 4, 2001; appointed Bishop of Ponce December 22, 2015; installed January 31, 2016. *Mailing Address: Bishop's House, P.O. Box 32205, Ponce, PR 00732-2205.*

Most Reverend

FELIX LAZARO, SCH.P.

Bishop Emeritus of Ponce; ordained April 9, 1961; appointed Coadjutor Bishop of Ponce March 20, 2002; consecrated April 25, 2002; appointed Bishop of Ponce June 11, 2003; retired December 22, 2015. *Res.: Pontifical Catholic Univ. of Puerto Rico, P.O. Box 32183, Ponce, PR 00732.* Tel: 787-987-7461.

ESTABLISHED NOVEMBER 21, 1924.

Square Miles 830.

Comprises the south portion of the Island of Puerto Rico and is in the Ecclesiastical Province of Puerto Rico.

STATISTICAL OVERVIEW

Personnel	
Bishop	1
Retired Bishops	1
Priests: Diocesan Active in Diocese	49
Priests: Diocesan Active Outside Diocese	6
Priests: Retired, Sick or Absent	19
Number of Diocesan Priests	74
Religious Priests in Diocese	28
Total Priests in Diocese	102
Ordinations:	
Diocesan Priests	1
Religious Priests	1
Permanent Deacons in Diocese	94
Total Brothers	3
Total Sisters	163
Parishes	
Parishes	43
With Resident Pastor:	
Resident Diocesan Priests	32
Resident Religious Priests	11
Without Resident Pastor:	
Administered by Priests	3
Missions	249
Pastoral Centers	2
Professional Ministry Personnel:	
Brothers	3
Sisters	163
Lay Ministers	957
Welfare	
Health Care Centers	8
Total Assisted	13,809
Homes for the Aged	2
Total Assisted	158
Residential Care of Children	1
Total Assisted	18
Day Care Centers	2
Total Assisted	52
Specialized Homes	1
Total Assisted	12
Special Centers for Social Services	7
Total Assisted	20,013
Residential Care of Disabled	8
Total Assisted	2,154
Educational	
Seminaries, Diocesan	1
Students from This Diocese	10
Students from Other Diocese	20
Seminaries, Religious	1
Students Religious	6
Total Seminarians	16
Colleges and Universities	1
Total Students	9,824
High Schools, Diocesan and Parish	11
Total Students	1,348
High Schools, Private	5
Total Students	603
Elementary Schools, Diocesan and Parish	13
Total Students	3,329
Elementary Schools, Private	5
Total Students	1,236
Catechesis/Religious Education:	
High School Students	212
Elementary Students	6,638
Total Students under Catholic Instruction	23,206
Teachers in the Diocese:	
Priests	10
Brothers	2
Sisters	10
Lay Teachers	1,142
Vital Statistics	
Receptions into the Church:	
Infant Baptism Totals	2,060
Minor Baptism Totals	166
Adult Baptism Totals	41
Received into Full Communion	41
First Communions	2,143
Confirmations	1,587
Marriages:	
Catholic	305
Interfaith	9
Total Marriages	314
Deaths	1,807
Total Catholic Population	378,792
Total Population	505,520

Former Bishops—Most Revs. EDWIN V. BYRNE, D.D., cons. in Philadelphia, Nov. 30, 1925; transferred to San Juan, PR; promoted to Archbishop of Santa Fe, NM, June 15, 1943; died July 25, 1963; ALOYSIUS J. WILLINGER, C.Ss.R., D.D., ord. July 2, 1911; appt. Bishop of Ponce March 8, 1929; cons. Oct. 28, 1929; appt. Titular Bishop of Bida and Coadjutor of Monterey-Fresno (cum jure successionis), Dec. 12, 1946; installed Bishop of Monterey-Fresno, Jan. 3, 1953; resigned Oct. 25, 1967; died July 25, 1973; JAMES E. MCMANUS, C.Ss.R., D.D., J.C.D., transferred to the Archdiocese of New York, Nov. 18, 1963; died July 1, 1976; His Eminence LUIS CARDINAL APONTE MARTINEZ, D.D., ord. April 10, 1950; appt. Titular Bishop of Lares and Auxiliary of Ponce, July 23, 1960; cons. Oct. 12, 1960; appt. Coadjutor Bishop of Ponce, April 16, 1963; appt. Bishop of Ponce, Nov. 18, 1963; installed Feb. 20, 1964; promoted to Archbishop of San Juan, Nov. 4, 1964; installed Jan. 15, 1965; created Cardinal, March 5, 1973; resigned May 8, 1999; died April 10, 2012.; Most Revs. FREMIOT TORRES OLIVER, D.D., ord. April 10, 1950; appt. Bishop Nov. 4, 1964; cons. Dec. 21, 1964; retired Nov. 10, 2000; died Jan. 26, 2012.; RICARDO SURINACH CARRERAS, D.D., ord. April 13, 1957; appt. Auxiliary Bishop of Ponce May 26, 1975; cons. July 25, 1975; appt. Bishop of Ponce Nov. 10, 2000; installed Nov. 30, 2000; retired June 11, 2003; died Jan. 19, 2005; FELIX LAZARO, Sch.P., ord. April 9, 1961; appt. Coadjutor Bishop of Ponce March 20, 2002; cons. April 25, 2002; appt. Bishop of Ponce June 11, 2003; retired Dec. 22, 2015.

Vicar General—Rev. Msgr. ROBERTO GARCIA BLAY.

Pro-Vicar General—VACANT.

Chancellor—Rev. CHRISTOPHER C. DE HERRERA SANDOVAL, O.S.

Episcopal Vicar for Diocesan Administration—Rev. Msgr. ROBERTO GARCIA BLAY.

Episcopal Vicar for Pastoral Coordination—Rev. Msgr. JUAN RODRIGUEZ ORENGO.

Episcopal Vicar for Family Pastoral—Rev. MANUEL SANTIAGO HERNANDEZ.

Episcopal Vicar for Social Pastoral—Rev. CARLOS A. COLLAZO SANTIAGO.

Episcopal Vicar for Institutes of Consecrated Life and Societies of Apostolic Life—Rev. LUIS OSCAR PADILLA CRUZ, O.F.M. Cap.

Episcopal Vicar for Education—VACANT.

Coordinator of the Sick—Rev. JOSE CARLOS VARGAS OLIVERAS.

Tribunal Diocesano de Puerto Rico—Calle Isabel No. 31, P.O. Box 32229, Ponce, PR USA 00732-2229. Tel: 787-843-4630; Fax: 787-841-7483. First instance for the Diocese of Ponce.

Judicial Vicar—Rev. Msgr. ELIAS S. MORALES RODRIGUEZ.

Associate Judicial Vicars—Rev. MANUEL A. SANTIAGO HERNANDEZ.

Moderator—Most Rev. RUBEN ANTONIO GONZALEZ MEDINA, C.M.F.

Judges—Revs. CARLOS M. GRULLON CAPELLAN; OMAR SOTO TORRES; JOSE I. OLVERA, C.O.R.C.; FELIPE DE JESUS COLON PADILLA.

Diocesan Consultors—Rev. Msgr. ROBERTO GARCIA BLAY; Rev. CHRISTOPHER C. DE HERRERA SANDOVAL, O.S.; Rev. Msgr. ELIAS S. MORALES RODRIGUEZ; Rev. JOSE DIEGO RODRIGUEZ MARTINO; Rev. Msgr. JUAN RODRIGUEZ ORENGO.

Diocesan Board of Administration—LCDA. JEANETTE SOTO VEGA; LCDO. JORGE ALEXIS TORRES MONTES; ING. JAIME BANCHS PIERETTI; Sr. RAFAEL CEPEDA BORRERO, CPA; SRA. LOURDES A. BAEZ QUINTANA; Rev. FERDINAND CRUZ CRUZ.

Parish Priests Consultors—Rev. JOSE DIEGO RODRIGUEZ MARTINO; Rev. Msgr. JUAN RODRIGUEZ ORENGO.

Notary—ALEJANDRA M. RIVERA RIVERA.

Censores Librorum—Rev. ADALIN RIVERA.

Administrator—Rev. Msgr. ROBERTO GARCIA BLAY.

Diocesan Offices and Directors

Centro Diocesano De Pastoral San Juan Diego—

Mailing Address: Diocesis de Ponce, P.O. Box 32205, Ponce, PR USA 00732-2205. Tel: 787-301-0018; Email: cedipa1965@gmail.com. Rev. OVIDIO PEREZ PEREZ, Admin.

Propagation of the Faith—Rev. Msgr. JUAN RODRIGUEZ ORENGO, Diocesan Dir., Mailing Address: Diocese of Ponce, P.O. Box 32205, Ponce, PR USA 00732-2205. Tel: 787-848-5265.

Police Chaplains—Revs. SAMUEL SANTIAGO, Tel: 787-848-3313; SEGISMUNDO CINTRON, Tel: 787-856-3617; JUAN SALIVA, Tel: 787-839-3465.

Master of Ceremonies to the Bishop—Rev. Msgr. JUAN RODRIGUEZ ORENGO, Mailing Address: Diocese of Ponce, P.O. Box 32205, Ponce, PR USA 00732-2205. Tel: 787-848-5265.

Caballeros de Colon (Knights of Columbus)—MR. JOSE DAVILA, Mailing Address: Quintas de Monserrate, 22 Calle 7, Ponce, PR USA 00730.

Camino Neocatacumenal—Lcdo. FELIX NEGRON, 127 Calle Central, Coto Laurel, PR USA 00780-2103. Tel: 787-259-1724; Fax: 787-259-1724; Email: felixnegronlaw@gmail.com.

Centro Diocesano Pro-Vida (Pro-Life Center)—Mailing Address: P.O. Box 32214, Ponce, PR USA 00732-2214. Tel: 787-840-6018; Tel: 787-841-200, Ext. 2583; Email: i.o.f. ponce@gmail.com. VACANT.

Cofradia Diocesana del Sagrado Corazon—ROSIE SANTIAGO, Urb. Jardines del Caribe, 108 Calle 20, Ponce, PR USA 00728-4437. Tel: 787-843-6409; Email: rosie_santiago@hotmail.com.

Comunidades de Oracion y Reflexion Biblica—GILDA CRUZ BATIZ, Urb. Los Caobos, 2353 Calle Pendula, Ponce, PR USA 00716. Tel: 787-843-8207; Email: gcb.corb@gmail.com.

Comunion y Liberacion—WADI ADAMES ROMAN, Urb. Villa Grillasca, 2040 Calle Eduardo Cuevas, Ponce, PR USA 00717-0589. Tel: 787-473-0897; Email: wadar3@gmail.com.

Cursillos de Cristiandad—Mailing Address: P.O. Box 32191, Ponce, PR USA 00732-2191. Tel: 787-432-5228. Rev. GERARDO RAMIREZ TORRES.

Equipo de Nuestra Senora—P. Ntra. Sra. de La Monserrate Rev. LUIS ROSARIO, D.P., 13 Calle Figueras, Jayuya, PR USA 00664. Tel: 787-828-0874; Tel: 787-243-9211; Email: rosariotravel@yahoo.com.

Movimiento Familia de Jesus—JOSE LUCAS RODRIGUEZ, Estancias de Yauco, 12 Calle Turquesa, Yauco, PR USA 00698. Tel: 787-632-1275; Email: joselucasr@gmail.com.

Estudios Peregrinos en la Fe—ANA MONTANEZ, Mailing Address: HC-01, Box 6054, Orocovis, PR USA 00720. Tel: 787-243-5363; Tel: 787-243-8688.

Hijas Catolicas de America (Catholic Daughters of America)—CARMEN NEGRON, Regente, Tel: 787-290-0378.

Hijas de Maria Inmaculada—CELINEL LOYOLA, HC-03 Box 10979, Juana Diaz, PR USA 00795.

Legion de Maria Comitium Ponce (Legion of Mary)—MARICEL RIVERA, Mailing Address: Urb Las Delicias 4333 Calle Gimnasia, Ponce, PR USA 00728. Tel: 787-844-8142.

Movimiento Juan XXIII—RAFAEL LOPEZ, Mailing Address: P.O. Box 801449, Coto Laurel, PR USA 00780-1449. Tel: 787-235-2193; Email: lopezsolivanrafael@yahoo.com.

Orden Ecuestre del Santo Sepulcro—MR. JOSE FRONTERA AGENJO ESQ., Mailing Address: 265 A Nelson Ramirez, Mayaguez, PR USA 00682. Tel: 787-380-8391; Email: jose_frontera@pucpr.edu.

Comunidad Carismatica de la Visitacion y de la Eucaristia—ZOBEIDA NEGRON, Mailing Address: P.O. Box 1726, Coamo, PR USA 00769. Tel: 787-825-0048; Tel: 787-616-6424; Email: cvecoamo. pr@gmail.com.

Renovacion Carismatica Catolica (Catholic Charismatic Renewal)—Rev. ORLANDO LUGO PEREZ, Spiritual Advisor; NOELMA CINTRON, Mailing Address: P.O. Box 941, Villalba, PR USA 00766. Tel: 787-486-4660; Email: rcc.ponce@yahoo. com.

Siervos de Cristo Vivo—MANUEL ACEVEDO, Mailing Address: P.O. Box 2206, Coamo, PR USA 00769. Tel: 787-803-6074; Email: siervoscoamo@hotmail. com.

Sociedad del Santo Nombre (Holy Name Society)—RAMON BERMUDEZ, Urb. La Lula, A10 Calle 1, Ponce, PR USA 00730. Tel: 787-840-6932.

Talleres de Oracion y Vida—DR. LOURDES TORRES RIVERA, Mailing Address: P.O. Box 7371, Ponce, PR USA 00732. Tel: 787-486-7993; Email: drlmatorres@yahoo.com.

Grupo de la Divina Misericordia—NAIDA COSTA, Urb. Constancia, 3362 Calle Riollano, Ponce, PR USA 00717-2238. Tel: 787-259-1752; Email: n. faustina@gmail.com.

Comunidad Jesus Resucitado—MILDRED COLLAZO, Mailing Address: P.O. Box 328, Mercedita, PR USA 00715-0328. Tel: 787-384-2234; Tel: 787-841-6355; Email: mcollazo@mcmedicalpr.com.

Ministerio de Evangelizacion Catolico de la Diocesis de Ponce—Mailing Address: P.O. Box 334151, Ponce, PR USA 00733-4151. Tel: 787-315-0082. MR. CARLOS MELENDEZ.

Ministerio Emaus—Coordinador Hombres: CARLOS IVAN MORENO RIVERA, Mailing Address: HC 03 Box 17346, Coamo, PR USA 00769. Tel: 787-595-0721; Email: pampo1898@gmail.com. Coordinadora Mujeres: TAMMY MARTINEZ CORREA, Mailing Address: HC-3 Box 17352, Coamo, PR USA 00769. Tel: 787-604-0707; Email: tasoly4911@yahoo.es.

Cofradia Virgen Dolorosa—Parroquia Cristo Rey, Urb. La Rambla, Calle Valladolid 2933, Ponce, PR USA 00730-4011. MRS. JUANITA PENA NICOLAO.

Nocturnal Adoration—Rev. JOSE ANTONIO LOPEZ VEGA, Mailing Address: Parroquia Cristo Rey, Urb. La Rambla, 2933 Calle Valladolid, Ponce, PR USA 00730-4011.

Franciscan Third Order (Secular Franciscans Order)—Rev. LUIS OSCAR PADILLA CRUZ, O.F.M. Cap.

Movimiento Schoenstatt—VACANT.

Juventud Mariana Vicentina—Parroquia San Vicente de Paul, 67 Paseo Cantera, Ponce, PR USA 00730-3026. Tel: 787-325-3068; Email: xgarcia1993@outlook.com. MR. XAVIER GARCIA VASQUEZ, Dir.

Boy Scouts of America—MR. ANIBAL DIAZ COLON, Urb. Villa El Encanto, Calle 7 #50, Juana Diaz, PR USA 00795.

Radio Station WEUC - FM Catholic Radio—OMAR PIMENTEL, Dir., 2250 Blvd. Luis A. Ferre, Ste. 529, Ponce, PR USA 00717-9997. Tel: 787-844-8809.

Television Station - Catholic TV - Channel 14—MR. IVAN FALTO, Dir., 2250 Blvd. Luis A. Ferre, Ste. 506, Ponce, PR USA 00717-9997. Tel: 787-841-2000, Ext. 2514 & 2543; Email: cifalto@pucpr.edu.

Pastoral Carcelaria—Rev. GERARDO RAMIREZ, Chap., Parroquia Ntra. Sra. de la Providencia, HC-01 Box 3471, Villalba, PR USA 00766. Tel: 787-867-2052.

Pastoral de la Salud - Hospitales—Rev. JOSE CARLOS VARGAS OLIVERAS.

Catechesis—Mailing Address: P.O. Box 32223, Ponce, PR USA 00732-2223. Tel: 787-842-9178; Fax: 787-840-6206; Email: centrocatequisticoponce@yahoo.com. Sr. CRISTINA MORALES RIVAS, O.P., Mailing Address: P.O. Box 32223, Ponce, PR USA 00732-2223. Tel: 787-842-9178; Fax: 787-840-6206.

Catholic Youth Organization—Rev. ARNALDO ORTIZ.

Children of Mary—Rev. Msgr. JUAN RODRIGUEZ ORENGO.

Committee for Community Planning—Rev. Msgr. ROBERTO GARCIA BLAY.

Communications—Sr. MARIANITA DE JESUS LOPEZ CARRION, O.P., Mailing Address: P.O. Box 330986, Ponce, PR USA 00733-0986. Tel: 787-843-1548; Email: omecosponce@gmail.com.

Ecumenism—Rev. Msgr. JUAN RODRIGUEZ ORENGO, Mailing Address: P.O. Box 32205, Ponce, PR USA 00732-2205.

Liturgical Commission—Rev. OVIDIO PEREZ PEREZ, Coord., Mailing Address: P.O. Box 32210, Ponce, PR USA 00732-2210.

Sacred Music Commission—VACANT.

Interim Superintendent of Schools—Mailing Address: P.O. Box 32158, Ponce, PR USA 00732-2158. Tel: 787-848-4020; Fax: 787-844-5987; Email: superintendencia_ponce@yahoo.com. MRS. LOURDES ZAPATA LOPEZ.

Vigilance for the Faith—Most Rev. RUBEN ANTONIO GONZALEZ MEDINA, C.M.F.

Vocations—Mailing Address: P.O. Box 32110, Ponce, PR USA 00732-2110. Tel: 787-848-4380; Fax: 787-848-4380. Rev. Msgr. ELIAS S. MORALES RODRIGUEZ, Rector; Rev. JUAN CARLOS RIVERA MEDINA, Spiritual Dir.

Institute of Family Orientation—Mailing Address: P.O. Box 32214, Ponce, PR USA 00732-2214. Tel: 787-567-5708; Tel: 787-651-3932. MR. SALVADOR OCASIO; Deacon ARNALDO LOPEZ.

CLERGY, PARISHES, MISSIONS AND PAROCHIAL SCHOOLS

CITY OF PONCE

1—CATEDRAL NUESTRA SENORA DE GUADALUPE (1692)
Box 32210, Ponce, PR USA 00732-2210.
Tel: 787-842-0134; Fax: 787-848-9104; Email: poncecatedral@gmail.com. Plaza las Delicias, Calle Union, Ponce, PR USA 00732. Revs. Arturo Ramos Ramos; Ovidio Perez Perez; Deacon Carlos Rodriguez Sanchez
Catedral Nuestra Senora de Guadalupe
Catechesis Religious Program—
Salon Parroquial, Calle Cristina # 32, Ponce, PR USA 00732. Guether Blanco Borrero, D.R.E. Students 70.
Chapels—Nuestra Senora de la Medalla Milagrosa—
Barrio Tibes, Sector Jacanas, Ponce, PR USA 00731.
Maria Inmaculada.

2—CRISTO REY (1964)
Urb La Rambla, 2933 Calle Valladolid, Ponce, PR USA 00730-4011. Tel: 787-843-3028;
Fax: 787-848-1861; Email: cristoreyponce@hotmail. com. Rev. Jose Antonio Lopez Vega; Deacons Eduardo A. Dosal Lines, Sacramental Min.; Jose Plaud Medina, Sacramental Min.; Manuel Roman Perez, Sacramental Min.; Anibal Rosario, Sacramental Min.
Catechesis Religious Program—Dinorah Diaz Figueroa, D.R.E. Students 286.
Missions—Santa Teresita—
Urb. Santa Teresita, Santa Luisa, Ponce, Ponce Co. PR USA 00730.
Nino Jesus de Praga
Bo. Rio Chiquito, Ponce, Ponce Co. PR USA 00730.
La Dolorosa
Urb. La Rambla, Calle Castellana Final, Ponce, Ponce Co. PR USA 00730-4011. Tel: 787-840-8380.

3—LA RESURRECCION (1967)
PMB-98, P.O. Box 2000, Mercedita, PR USA 00715.
Urb. Glenview Gardens, E-9 Final, Ponce, PR USA 00730. Rev. Jose Carlos Vargas Oliveras; Deacon Jose Rosario Colon, Sacramental Min.
Catechesis Religious Program—Glorimar Santiago, C.R.E. Students 215.
Missions—Immaculate Heart of Mary—
Bo. La Yuca, Ponce, PR USA 00730.
Inmaculado Corazon de Maria.
Our Lady of Monserrate
Bo. El Collado, Ponce, PR USA 00730.
Nuestra Senora de la Monserrate.
San Lucas
Bo. Las Vallas, Ponce, PR USA 00730.
Saint Joseph
Bo. El Paraiso, Ponce, PR USA 00730.
San Jose.
Our Lady of Carmel
Bo. Carmelita, Ponce, PR USA 00730.
Nuestra Senora del Carmen.

4—CORAZON DE JESUS (1969)
P.O. Box 577, Mercedita, PR USA 00715-0577.
Tel: 787-987-8046; Tel: 787-298-4524; Email: corazondejesusponce@gmail.com. Bo. Sabanetas, Ponce, PR USA 00716. Rev. Winston Reinaldo Mendez Silvagnoli; Deacon Rafael Castro Belen
Corazon de Jesus
Catechesis Religious Program—Junita de la Torre, D.R.E. Students 79.

5—SANTISIMO SACRAMENTO (1984)
Mailing Address: P.O. Box 32212, Ponce, PR USA 00732. Tel: 787-843-0245; Email: santisimosacramentoponce@gmail.com. Urb. Vista del Mar, 2238 Calle Marlin, Ponce, PR USA 00716-0834. Rev. Orlando Lugo Perez
Santisimo Sacramento
Catechesis Religious Program—Students 40.

6—EL BUEN PASTOR (1968)
Urb. Jardines del Caribe, Calle 40-NN25, Ponce, PR USA 00728-2675. Tel: 787-843-6202; Email: pastorbonuspr@gmail.com. P.O. Box 7612, Ponce, PR USA 00732-7612. Rev. Pedro J. Guzman Quintana; Deacons Rafael D. Ruiz Irizarry, Sacramental Min.; Edgardo Muniz Rivera, Sacramental Min.
Catechesis Religious Program—Students 128.
Mission—La Milagrosa
Bo. Quebrado del Agua, Calle 5 #69, Ponce, Ponce Co. PR USA 00731.

7—NUESTRA SENORA DE LA MERCED (1928)
P.O. Box 32216, Ponce, PR USA 00732-2216.
Tel: 787-842-0069; Email: parroquialamerced1@gmail.com. 4632 Luna St., Ponce, PR USA 00717-2000. Rev. Juan Jose Saliva Gonzalez; Deacons Emerito López Cosme; Jose D. Ruiz Orengo.
Catechesis Religious Program—Students 6.

8—NUESTRA SENORA DE LA MEDALLA MILAGROSA (1928)
Guadalupe No. 2, Ponce, PR USA 00730-3110.
Tel: 787-842-3188; Email: parmilagrosa@gmail.com. Rev. Socrate Laupe Dorvil, C.M.; Deacons Ramon L. Vazquez, Sacramental Minister; Carlos Juan Ramos Torres, Sacramental Minister; Hector Luis Santiago, Sacramental Min.
School—Colegio La Milagrosa, (Grades K-12), 9 Calle Guadalupe, Ponce, PR USA 00730.

Tel: 787-836-1164; Email: parroquiatallaboa@gmail.com. Rev. Arnaldo Ortiz Dominicci

Sagrado Corazon de Jesus

Catechesis Religious Program—Ruth Montalvo, Coord. Students 95.

Mission—Inmaculado Corazon de Maria, Bo. Tallaboa Poniente, Sector Juncos, Penuelas, PR PR USA 00624.

SALINAS, SALINAS CO., NUESTRA SENORA DE LA MONSERRATE (1854)

Box 1172, Salinas, PR USA 00751. Tel: 787-824-2215 ; Email: parroquia_salinas@yahoo.com. 3 Calle Miguel Ten, Salinas, PR USA 00751. Rev. Carlos Manuel Grullon Capellan; Deacons Jose Luis Rodriguez Collazo, Sacramental Min.; Jose Francisco Martinez Munoz, Sacramental Minister.

Catechesis Religious Program—Lucy Cartagena, C.R.E. Students 262.

Missions—San Jose—Bo. Plena, Salinas, PR USA 00751.

Santa Ana, Bo. Coco, Salinas, PR USA 00751.

Espiritu Santo, Parcelas Vazquez, Salinas, PR USA 00751.

Virgen del Carmen, Bo. Las Palmas, Salinas, Salinas Co. PR USA 00751.

Santa Marta, Bo. Naranjo, Salinas, PR USA 00751.

Inmaculada Concepcion, Bo. Las Ochenta, Salinas, Salinas Co. PR USA 00751.

Virgen Milagrosa, Bo. Playita, Salinas, PR USA 00751.

Virgen del Carmen, Bo. Playa, Salinas, PR USA 00751.

Perpetuo Socorro, Bo. Sabana Llana, Salinas, PR USA 00751.

SANTA ISABEL, SANTA ISABEL CO., PARROQUIA SANTIAGO APOSTOL (1854)

2 Calle Hostos, Box 137, Santa Isabel, PR USA 00757. Tel: 787-845-2450; Email: parroquiasantiagoapostol2017@outlook.com. Revs. Angel M. Sanchez Hernandez; Samuel Santiago De Jesus, Parochial Vicar; Wilson Saldana Sarmiento; Deacon Jose Manuel Rivera Colon, Sacramental Minister.

Catechesis Religious Program—Ms. Karimarie Diaz Rentas, Coord. Students 135.

Missions—San Patricio—Bo. Playita Cortada, Santa Isabel, PR PR USA 00757.

Virgen del Rosario, Bo. Penuelas, Bo. Penuelas Santa Isabel, PR USA 00757.

Virgen del Perpetuo Socorro, Bo. Paso Seco, Santa Isabel, PR PR USA 00757.

Ntra. Sra. del Carmen, Bo. Playa, Santa Isabel, PR USA 00757.

Nuestra Senora de la Monserrate, Bo. Ollas, Santa Isabel, Santa Isabel Co. PR USA 00757.

San Ignacio de Loyola, Bo. Jauca, Santa Isabel, Santa Isabel Co. PR USA 00757.

VILLALBA, VILLALBA CO.

1—NUESTRA SENORA DE LA DIVINA PROVIDENCIA (Mission Noell) (1962)

HC 01 Box 3471, Villalba, PR USA 00766. Bo. Cacao, Carr. 157 Km. 2.2, Orocovis, PR USA 00720. Rev. Gerardo Ramirez Torres

Nuestra Senora de la Divina Providencia

Catechesis Religious Program—Elsa Rivera Rivera, D.R.E. Students 45.

Missions—Nuestra Senora del Carmen—Bo. Alturita Carr 157, Orocovis, Cacao Co. PR USA.

Inmaculada Concepcion, Bo. Cacao Carr 157, Orocovis, Cacao Co. PR USA 00720.

Nino Jesus de Praga, Bo. El Frio, carra 143, Orocovis, PR USA 00720.

Ntra. Sra. del Rosario, Bo. Bauta, Carr 590, Orocovis, PR USA 00720.

Ntra. Sra. del Pilar, Bo. Damian Abajo, Carr 157, Orocovis, PR USA 00720.

Nuestra Senora de la Monserrate, Bo. Pozas, Carr 615, Orocovis, PR USA 00720.

Nuestra Senora del Perpetuo Socorro, Bo. Ala de la Piedra, Carr 149, Orocovis, PR USA 00720.

Sagrado Corazon de Jesus, Bo. Matrullas, Carr 564, Orocovis, PR USA 00720.

San Mateo, Bo. Ortiga, Carr 143, Orocovis, PR USA 00720.

2—NUESTRA SENORA DEL CARMEN (1895)

Box 432, Villalba, PR USA 00766. Tel: 787-847-0695; Email: parroquianscarmenvillalba@gmail.com. Calle Munoz Rivera, Villalba, PR USA 00766. Rev. Jose Rafael Alvarado de Jesus; rEV. Javier Vega Graniela, Parochial Vicar; Deacons Javier Gonzalez Rosado, Sacramental Minister; Jose A. Pagan Rivera, Sacramental Minister; Jaime Luis Rivera Rivera, Sacramental Minister

Nuestra Senora del Carmen

Catechesis Religious Program—Teresita Perez, D.R.E. Students 830.

School—Colegio Nuestra Senora del Carmen, (Grades PreK-9), Walter Mc Jones #1, Villalba, PR USA 00766. Tel: 787-847-2875; Fax: 787-847-6153; Email: colegiodevillalba@gmail.com. Apartado 1033, Villalba, PR USA 00766. Sr. Maria Maldonado Maldonado, Prin. Religious Teachers 1; Lay Teachers 18; Students 203.

Missions—Sagrado Corazon—Bo. Romero, Villalba, PR USA 00766.

Nuestra Senora del Carmen, Bo. Vista Alegre, Carr. 151 Km 3.3, Villalba, Villalba Co. PR USA 00766. Tel: 787-847-0695; Email: parroquianscarmenvillalba@gmail.com.

Santisima Trinidad, Bo. Mogote, Villalba, PR USA 00766.

Espiritu Santo, Bo. Cerro Gordo, Villalba, PR USA 00766.

La Milagrosa, Jagueyes Arriba, Carr. 149 R 513 km 1.7, Villalba, PR PR USA 00766.

San Pedro, Bo. Corillo, Villalba, PR USA 00766.

San Pablo, Bo. Palmarejo, Carr. 149 Km. 46.6, Villalba, Villalba Co. PR USA 00766.

Santisimo Sacramento, Bo. Higuero, Villalba, PR USA 00766.

Jesus Crucificado, Bo. Camarones Arriba, Villalba, PR USA 00766.

Cristo de la Salud, Bo. Sierrita Caonillas, Villalba, PR USA 00766.

Santa Cecilia, Bo. El Semil, Villalba, PR USA 00766.

La Providencia, Barrio Hatillo, Carr. 150 Parc. 33, Barrio Hatillo, PR USA 00766.

San Antonio, Bo. Camarones, Villalba, PR USA 00766.

Vigen Dolorosa, Bo. El Limon, Carr. 151 Km. 8.3, Villalba, PR USA 00766.

Ntra. Sra. del Carmen, Bo. Dajaos, Carr. 151 R 559 Km. 2.0, Villalba, PR USA 00766.

San Francisco de Asis, Bo. La Sierrita de Vacas, Villalba, Villalba PR USA 00766.

La Milagrosa, Bo. El Pino, Villalba, Villalba PR USA 00766.

San Juan Evangelista, Bo. Aceituna Chichon, Villalba, Villalba PR USA 00766.

YAUCO, YAUCO CO.

1—NUESTRA SENORA DEL ROSARIO (1756)

Box 46, Yauco, PR USA 00698. Tel: 787-856-1222; Email: rosariodm014@gmail.com. 11 Calle Comercio, Yauco, PR USA 00698. Revs. Juan Burgos Acevedo, O.P., Admin.; Roberto Arzola Maisonet, Parochial Vicar; Bro. Carlos Rodriguez Villanueva; Deacons Jesus Vazquez Orengo, Sacramental Minister; Luis M. Jusino Cintron, Sacramental Minister; David Fuentes Rivera, Sacramental Minister; Rafael Vargas Roman, Sacramental Minister; Ramon Santiago Ortiz, Sacramental Minister.

School—Colegio Santisimo Rosario, (Grades PreK-12), 10 Calle Dr. A. Gatell, Yauco, PR USA 00698. Tel: 787-856-1001; Fax: 787-267-1238; Email: santisimorosariodeyauco@gmail.com. P.O. Box 26, Yauco, PR USA 00698. Mrs. Elaine Vega, Prin. Religious Teachers 1; Lay Teachers 22; Students 286.

Catechesis Religious Program—Ms. Irene Troche, Coord. Students 179.

Missions—Nuestra Senora del Carmen—Bo. Duey, Yauco, PR USA 00698.

Santiago Apostol, Bo. Barinas, Yauco, PR USA 00698.

Nuestra Senora del Perpetuo Socorro, Bo. Cambalache, Yauco, PR USA 00698.

Nuestra Senora de la Monserrate, Bo. Carrizales, Yauco, PR USA 00698.

Santa Lucia, Bo. Sierra Alta, Yauco, PR USA 00698.

San Antonio, Bo. Naranjo, Yauco, PR USA 00698.

San Antonio de Padua, Bo. Diego Hernandez, Yauco, Yauco Co. PR USA 00698.

Sagrado Corazon de Jesus, Bo. Quebradas, Yauco, PR USA 00698.

La Milagrosa, Bo. Mogotes, Yauco, PR USA 00698.

San Vicente de Paul y San Alvaro de Cordoba, Bo. Jacana, Yauco, PR USA 00698.

2—SAN MARTIN DE PORRES (1969)

Las Palomas, P.O. Box 2005, Yauco, PR USA 00698. Tel: 787-856-7403; Email: parroquia.sanmartin2005@gmail.com. Barrio Las Palomas, 9 Calle 1, Yauco, PR USA 00698. Rev. Edwin Vázquez Vega

San Martin de Porres

Catechesis Religious Program—Ms. Lydia Mercado Martinez, Coord. Students 83.

Missions—Nuestra Senora de la Providencia—Bo. Las Joyas, Yauco, PR USA 00698.

San Francisco de Asis, Bo. Magueyes, Yauco, PR USA 00698.

3—SANTO DOMINGO DE GUZMAN (2001)

Urb. Costa Sur, Calle Padre Alfredo Varina, Yauco, PR USA 00698. Tel: 787-856-8212; Email: psdomingoyauco@gmail.com. P.O. Box 3036, Yauco, PR USA 00698-3036. Rev. Victor Rene Sanchez Muniz; Rev. Deacon Reinaldo Sanchez Caraballo, Sacramental Minister.

Catechesis Religious Program—Ms. Nydia Perez Figueroa, Coord. Students 164.

Missions—Sagrado Corazon—Bo. Collores, Yauco, Yauco PR USA 00698.

Santa Teresita, Bo. Las Vegas, Yauco, Yauco PR USA 00698.

San Jose, Bo. Lluberas, Yauco, Yauco PR USA 00698.

Nuestra Senora de Fatima, Bo. Algarrobos, Yauco, Yauco PR USA 00698.

San Martin de Porres, Bo. Almacigo Bajo, Yauco, Yauco PR USA 00698.

San Juan Macias, Bo. Almacigo Alto, Yauco, Yauco PR USA 00698.

Nuestra Senora de la Monserrate, Bo. Rio Loco, Yauco, Yauco PR USA 00698.

Santa Rosa de Lima, Bo. El Cafetal, Yauco, Yauco PR USA 00698.

On Duty Outside the Diocese:

Revs.—

Harrison, Brian W., O.S., P.O. Box 13230, Saint Louis, MO USA 63157

Kelty, Edward J., O.S., Via Antonio Zanoni, 44, Roma (Castel di Leva), Italy 00134

Malachowski, Christopher, O.S., Nadliwe, Poland 05-281 Urle

Orsini Baez, Jayson, Graduate Studies, Rome

Roman Toro, Carlos

Santiago, Francisco, Graduate Studies, Spain.

Military Service:

Revs.—

Alvarado de Jesus, Jose Rafael

Sanchez Hernandez, Angel M.

Retired:

Rev. Msgrs.—

De Jesus Viera, Herminio, (Retired), Santa Marta Asylum

Espona Jimenez, Juan, (Retired), Madrid, Spain

Pancorbo, Marcos, (Retired), Santa Marta Asylum

Revs.—

Alamo Hernando, Emiliano, (Retired), Spain

Alvarado Flores, Felix Emilio, (Retired)

Berrios Berrios, Angel, (Retired)

Garcia Echevarria, Roberto, (Retired), Bo. Real Anon, Coto Laurel, PR USA 00780

Gusiora, Alphonsus, (Retired), P.O. Box 61, Enugwu-Ukwu (Anambra State), Nigeria

Herrero Mombiela, Jose Maria, (Retired)

Lopez Cruz, Victor Bruno, (Retired)

MacIssac, Charles S., O.S., (Retired), 140 Shepherd Ln., Totowa, NJ USA 07512

Mezquida, Ramon, (Retired), San Jose 4, Alqueria Condesa, Valencia, Spain 46715

Muniz Borrero, Alberto, (Retired)

Munoz Pedros, Rafael, (Retired), P.O. Box 187, Barceloneta, PR USA 00657

Nieves, Carlos, (Retired), HC763, Buzon 4240, Patillas, PR USA 00723

Nischan, James R., (Retired), 1625 Mayo Ave., Owensboro, KY USA 42301

Perez Roigall, Vincente, (Retired), Santa Marta Asylum

Santaella, Esteban, (Retired)

Sirvent, Francisco, (Retired), Capitan Cortes 8-2, Valencia, Spain

Zayas Ortiz, Antonio, (Retired).

Permanent Deacons:

Almodovar Capielo, Jorge

Altori Vargas, Juan

Antonetty Giraud, Rene

Aponte Arroyo, Vicente

Bernard Sierra, Efrain

Burgos Roca, Joseph

Carmona Cruz, Cirilo

Castro Belen, Rafael

Castro, Francisco Carrasquillo

Castro Toro, Alberto

Colon Burgos, William

Colón, Luis Rosario

Cruz Rivera, Wenceslao, (Outside the Diocese)

Diaz, Jaime Ortiz

Dosal Lines, Eduardo

Fabre Torres, Antonio Victor

Figueroa Rivera, Arnaldo

Fuentes Rivera, David

Galarza Mercado, Reinaldo

Garcia Malavet, Pedro

Garcia Rivera, Juan B.

Gelpi Ortiz, Jose E.

Gierbolini Rodriguez, Arnaldo

Gonzalez, Javier

Gonzalez, Luis A.

Gonzalez Plaza, Ildefonso

Jusino Cintron, Luis M.

Lebron Romero, Marcelino

Lopez Cosme, Emerito

Lopez Quirindongo, Arnaldo

Lopez Sanchez, Benjamin

Lugo Santiago, Francisco

Maldonado Plaza, Jose M.

Marcucci, Radames

Martinez, Jaime
Martinez Munoz, Jose Francisco
Martinez Rodriguez, Orlando
Masollet, Joaquin
Mendez Molina, Angel
Mendez Purcell, Jose M.
Morales Colon, Angel R.
Morales, Hector Pagan
Muniz Rivera, Edgardo
Negron Ortiz, Angel
Orama de Jesus, Dalvin
Oramas, Carlos
Pabon Gonzalez, Ruben
Pagan Diaz, Benjamin
Pagan Figueroa, Orlando
Pagan Rivera, Jose E.
Perez Diaz, Glidden
Perez Santos, Jose A.
Plaud Medina, Jose
Portalatin Padua, Edwin
Ramos Rivera, William
Ramos Torres, Carlos Juan
Ramos Torres, David
Rentas, Nestor
Rivera Alicea, Genaro
Rivera Cardona, Alfredo
Rivera Colon, Jose Manuel
Rivera, Esteban
Rivera Garcia, Edgardo
Rivera, Reinaldo
Rivera Rivera, Jaime Luis
Rivera Saez, Jose
Rivera Santana, Juan Esteban
Rivera Velazquez, Esteban
Rodriguez, Casildo
Rodriguez Collazo, Jose Luis
Rodriguez, David
Rodriguez, Feliz
Rodriguez, Jacinto
Rodriguez Mendez, Jose
Rodriguez Rivera, Juan F.
Rodriguez Sanchez, Carlos
Roman Perez, Manuel
Rosario, Anibal
Rosario Colon, Jose A.
Ruiz, Jose D.
Ruiz, Rafael
Sanchez, Reinaldo
Sanchez, Wallis
Santiago, Figueroa William
Santiago, Hector Luis
Santiago Negron, Norberto
Santiago Ortiz, Ramon
Sepulveda, Miguel
Torres Maldonado, Wilfredo
Torres Santiago, Jose
Vargas Roman, Rafael
Vazquez, Carmelo
Vazquez Orengo, Jesus
Vazquez, Ramon
Velez, Jaime.

INSTITUTIONS LOCATED IN DIOCESE

[A] SEMINARIES

PONCE. *Seminario Mayor Regina Cleri* (Major) 32 Calle Cristina, Ponce, PR USA 00732. Tel: 787-812-3024; Email: seminarioreginacleri@gmail.com; Web: www.reginacleri.com. P.O. Box 32110, Ponce, PR USA 00732-2110. Rev. Msgr. Elias S. Morales Rodriguez, Rector; Rev. Juan Carlos Rivera Medina, Spiritual Advisor. Religious Teachers 12; Students 30.

[B] COLLEGES & UNIVERSITIES

PONCE. *The Pontifical Catholic University of Puerto Rico*, 2250 Blvd. Luis A. Ferre, Ponce, PR USA 00717-9997. Tel: 787-841-2000, Ext. 1303; Fax: 787-651-2034; Email: fcortes@pucpr.edu; Web: www.pucpr.edu. Most Rev. Ruben Antonio Gonzalez Medina, C.M.F., Grand Chancellor; Jorge Velez Arocho, Pres.; Dr. Felix Cortes, Vice Pres. Office Devel. Reserach & Planning; Mr. Freddie Martinez, Vice Pres. Student Affairs; Mrs. Maria de los A Muniz, Vice Pres. Assoc. Academic Affairs; Mrs. Irma Rodriguez, Vice Pres. Fin. Affairs; Dr. Edgar Rodriguez, Exec. Dir., Information & Telecommunications; Dr. Leandro Colon-Alicea, Vice Pres-Acad. Officer; Dr. Arvin Baez, Dir., Guidance Center; Mrs. Noelia Padua Flores, Dir., Law Library; Rev. Roberto Martinez Rivera, Dir., Theology & Philosophy Dept.; Mrs. Carmen Torres Hernandez, Dir., Admissions; Mrs. Magda I. Vargas Rodriguez, Dir., Libraries; Dr. Olga Hernandez Patino, Rector; Edwin Hernandez Vera, Rector-Arecibo; Mr. Ivan E. Davila-Ostolaza, Registrar; Ms. Karen Morales, Coord., Continuing Ed.; Rev. Juan Javier Inigo Monreal, C.M., Delegado para la Mision Inst.; Mr. Luis V. Badillo Lozano, Dean, Architecture School; Rev. Juan Luis Negron Delgado, Dean, Arts and Humanities; Mr. Jose Frontera Agenjo Esq., Dean, School of Law; Dr. Alma L. Santiago, Dean, College of Science; Dr. Herman A. Vera-Rodriguez, Dean, College Graduate Studies; Dr. David Zayas Montalvo, Dean, College of Business Admin.; Dr. Myriam Zayas Zengotita, Dean, Education; Rev. Msgr. Herminio De Jesus, Prof.; Rev. Luis A. Rodriguez Vientos, Prof., Theology & Philosophy; Hno. Carlos Rodriguez Villanueva, Prof., History and Fine Arts; Hna. Nancy Arroyo Gonzalez, Prof., Biotechnology; Revs. Edgardo Acosta Ocasio, Prof.-Mayaguez; Geraldo Caraballo Galindo, Prof.-Mayaguez; Segismundo Cintron, Prof.; Ferdinand Cruz Cruz, Prof.; Eladio Diaz Frias, Prof.; Rev. Msgr. Roberto Garcia Blay, Prof.; Jorge Macias De Cespedes, Prof.; Revs. Francisco Medina Santos, Prof.; Floyd Mercado Vidro, Prof.; Carlos Monroig Colon, Prof.-Arecibo; Angel L. Rios Matos, J.C.D., Prof.; Jose Diego Rodriguez Martino, Prof.; Jean Rolex, C.M., Prof.; Julio A. Rolon Torres, Prof.; Omar Soto Torres, Prof.; Luis A. Mendez Acevedo, S.E.M.P., Chap.-Arecibo; Luis Mojica Malave, Prof.; Omar Yanez Cordovas, Prof.; Orlando Lugo Perez, Prof.; Carlos A. Collazo Santiago, Prof.; Arnaldo Ortiz Dominicci, Chap.-Ponce; Adalin Rivera Saez, Prof. The University is composed of the following: College of Arts and Humanities and Graduate Studies in Hispanic Studies; College of Business Administration and Graduate Studies; College of Education and Graduate Studies; College of Science and Graduate Studies; School of Law; College of Graduate Studies in Behavioral Science and Community Affairs; Institute of Social Doctrine of the Church; Student Support Services; Post-Baccalaureate Achievement Program; Upward Bound Program. Brothers 2; Religious Teachers 26; Lay Teachers 648; Sisters 1; Students 9,824.

[C] SCHOOLS - INSTITUTES OF EDUCATION

PONCE. *Academia Cristo Rey Inc.*, Urb. La Rambla, 3011 Calle San Judas, Ponce, PR USA 00730-4091. Tel: 787-843-0766; Fax: 787-843-6443; Email: monarcas@academiacristorey.net; Email: principal@academiacristorey.net. Ave. Tito Castro 609, Ste. 102 PMB 361, Ponce, PR USA 00716-3222. Miss Gicela Bonilla Rodriguez, Prin.; Kim Fausto Ramos, Asst. Prin. Religious Teachers 2; Lay Teachers 44; Students 616.

Centro San Francisco, Bo. Tamarindo, 105 Calle Tamal, Ponce, PR USA 00730. Tel: 787-842-2776; Tel: 787-651-6350; Fax: 787-842-2776. Box 10479, Ponce, PR USA 00732-7440. Email: centrosanfranciscoinc@gmail.com. Sonia Pagan Figueroa, Dir.; Lizabeth Quinones Vargas, Prin.; Carmen Rodriguez Soldevila, Librarian. Sisters of St. Joseph. Lay Teachers 29; Students 182.

Colegio Del Sagrado Corazon De Jesus de Ponce, Inc. (1916) 2511 Calle Obispado, Ponce, PR USA 00716-3836. Tel: 787-843-4718; Tel: 787-842-0339; Fax: 787-843-0250; Email: cscj@sagradoponce.org; Web: www.sagradoponce.org. Mrs. Maria Serrano, Prin.; Miss Lydia Mendez, Librarian. Religious of the Sacred Heart. Lay Teachers 48; Students 747.

Colegio El Ave Maria, Reparto Valle Alegre, 4506 Dr. Bartolomei, Ponce, PR USA 00728-3151. Tel: 787-284-2453; Fax: 787-284-2453; Email: colegioelavemaria@yahoo.com. Sr. Milagros Pizarro, O.D.M., Dir. Operarias del Divino Maestro (Avemarianas). Religious Teachers 3; Lay Teachers 16; Students 205.

Sagrada Familia de Nazaret (1913) 1270 Ave. Hostos, Ponce, PR USA 00717. Tel: 787-842-3208; Fax: 787-844-6773; Email: csfnazaret@gmail.com. Sr. Maribel Gomez, H.C., Dir. Lay Teachers 21; Students 202.

COTO LAUREL. *Colegio Ponceno*, (Grades PreSchool-12), 1900 Carr. 14, Coto Laurel, PR USA 00780-2147. Tel: 787-848-2525; Fax: 787-259-4282; Email: colegio@copin.net; Web: www.copin.net. Rev. Jose A. Basols, Sch.P., Dir.; Juan Sanchez, Prin. (Supr.); Milagros Carmona, Librarian. Piarist Fathers. Religious Teachers 3; Lay Teachers 50; Students 662.

PLAYA PONCE. *Centros Sor Isolina Ferre, Inc.* (1969) Centros Sor Isolina Ferre is a non-profit organization dedicated to community revitalization through education and vocational, technological training programs. We help natural leaders from these communities become its advocates and counselors. Our efforts are aimed at: juvenile delinquency prevention - decreasing youth pregnancy, school dropout rates - special education, vocational & technological training - preparing youngsters & adults for employment - community self-development. We provide the necessary tools to become fully alive & rediscover their abilities. Our emphasis is to promote dignity & self-respect as a preventive measure for high risk groups. Centros Sor Isolina Ferre. P.O. Box 7313, Ponce, PR USA 00732-7313. Dr. Jose Luis Diaz Cotto, Ph.D., CEO & Prin.; Sr. Rosita M. Bauza, M.S.B.T., Historian; Adianis Figueroa, Librarian. Federal state, municipal government and private foundations. Lay Teachers 39; Sisters 4; Students 1,014; Tot Asst. Annually 1,178; Total Staff 364.

[D] HOMES FOR THE AGED

PONCE. *Residencia Santa Marta* Home for Aged and Infirm Calle 4 de Julio Final Serro Betania, Sector Sabanetas, Ponce, PR USA 00715. Tel: 787-840-7575; Fax: 787-651-1080; Email: rsmarta2012@yahoo.com. P.O. Box 242, Mercedita, PR USA 00715-0242. Sr. Gladys Rosario Gomez, Supr. Bed Capacity 200; Tot Asst. Annually 132; Total Staff (Religious) 11.

[E] CONVENTS & RESIDENCES OF SISTERS

PONCE. *Siervas Misioneras de la Santísima Trinidad* (1950) Avenida Padre Noel 30, Ponce, PR USA 00716. Tel: 787-844-1627; Fax: 787-840-5020; Email: smildred@csifpr.org; Web: www.msbt.org. P.O. Box 7282, Ponce, PR USA 00732-7282. Sr. Mildred Vazquez Rivera, M.S.B.T., Custodia Regional. Sisters 6.

Siervas de Maria (1891) Urb. La Rambla, 1703 Calle Siervas de Maria, Ponce, PR USA 00730-4027. Tel: 787-842-2336, Ext. 1; Email: siervasponce@gmail.com. Mother Carmen M. Hernandez Ayala, Supr. Sisters 23.

Religiosas del Apostolado del Sagrado Corazon de Jesus (1891) Bo. Pámpanos, Ramal 2, Ponce, PR USA 00732. P.O. Box 8300, Ponce, PR USA 00732-8300. Sr. Aurea Fuentes Reyes, R.A., Sup. Sisters Apostolate of the Sacred Heart of Jesus 19.

Colegio Perpetuo Socorro, (Grades PreSchool-9), Carr. # 3 km 150.6, Bo. Salinas, PR USA 00751. Tel: 787-853-0041; Fax: 787-853-2531; Email: coquira@yahoo.es; Email: cpscoqui@gmail.com. Bo. Coqui, Aguirre, PR USA 00704. Sr. Aurea E. Fuentes Reyes, R.A.D., Dir.; Wilmar Colon Ortiz, Prin. Lay Teachers 20; Sisters 4; Students 330.

YAUCO. *Hermanas Dominicas de Nuestra Senora del Rosario de Fatima (Casa Generalicia)*, Carretera 326 Km 5.2, Guanica, PR USA 00653. Tel: 787-856-4256; Tel: 787-856-4330; Fax: 787-821-2439; Email: hnasfat@zoho.com. Hermanas Dominicas de Nuestra Senora del Rosario de Fatima, P.O. Box 62, Yauco, PR USA 00698-0062. Sisters Margarita Mangual Colon, O.P., General Prioress; Angeles Pacheco, O.P., Local Prioress; Maria Maldonado Lazu, O.P., General Secy. Sisters 33.

Centro Madre Dominga, Casa Belen (2000) Urb. San Jorge, 3504 Calle Andino Apt. 2, Ponce, PR USA 00717-0777. Tel: 787-290-3627; Fax: 787-844-3240 ; Email: madredominga@gmail.com. Sr. Amarilis Rosario Santos, Dir.

Instituto Especial para el Desarrollo Integral del Individuo, la Familia y la Communidad, Inc., 66 Calle Madre Dominga, Yauco, PR USA 00968. Tel: 787-856-3798; Tel: 787-856-1573; Fax: 787-856-4192; Email: instyco@coqui.net. P.O. Box 1241, Yauco, PR USA 00968-1241. Sr. M. Virgenmina Morell Martell, Dir. Sisters 2; Staff 20; Total Assisted 1,209.

[F] PERSONAL PRELATURES

PONCE. *Prelatura de la Santa Cruz y Opus Dei*, Urb. Alhambra, 1814 calle Alcazar, Ponce, PR USA 00716-3829. Tel: 787-844-2661; Email: pricoinf@coqui.net; Web: opusdei.org.pr. Revs. Martin Llambias Majo, Supr.; Jaime Bermudez Onopa.

[G] MISCELLANEOUS

PONCE. *Fundacion Surinach*, Bo. Canitas, Carretera Estatal 504, Ponce, PR USA 00730. Tel: 787-840-3338; Email: jrorengo@gmail.com. P.O. Box 32205, Ponce, PR USA 00732-2205. Most Rev. Ruben Antonio Gonzalez Medina, C.M.F., Pres.; Mr. Fernando Luis Rosado, Sec.; Rev. Msgr. Juan Rodriguez Orengo, Treas.

Institucion Magdalena Aulina - Operarias Parroquiales (Secular Institute) Urb. Vistas del Mar, 2315 Calle Azabache, Ponce, PR USA 00716. Tel: 939-640-7578; Email: maria007victoria@hotmail.com. Maria Rodriguez Nieve, Contact Person.

Instituto Santa Ana, Carr. 5516, KM 0.2, Sector El Desvio, Adjuntas, PR USA 00601. Tel: 787-829-2504; Fax: 787-829-2121; Email: isahogar@gmail.com; Web: institutosantaana.com.

P.O. Box 554, Adjuntas, PR USA 00601. Sr. Ismaela Castro, Dir. Girls 18.

Jardin Infantil Amor De Dios, (Grades PreK-K), Urb. Constancia, 2456 Calle Eureka, Ponce, PR USA 00717-2218. Tel: 787-842-5079; Fax: 787-984-5544; Email: jardinamordedios@yahoo.com. Sisters Martina Barreira, R.A.D., Dir.; Ana Pujante Rodriguez, Pastoral Coord. Lay Teachers 4; Sisters 3; Students 96.

Memores Domini, Pontificia Universidad Católica de Puerto Rico, 2250 Boulevard Luis A. Ferre, Ponce, PR USA 00717. Tel: 787-515-6464; Email: gzaffaroni@pucpr.edu. P.O. Box 32197, Ponce, PR USA 00732-2197. Mr. Zaffaroni Giuseppe, Supr.

Misioneras de la Caridad (1989) El Tuque, 683 Ramos Antonini, Ponce, PR USA 00728. Tel: 787-841-5443; Email: psjoseobrero@yahoo.com. Mailing Address: P.O. Box 32177, Ponce, PR USA 00732-2177. Sr. Little Gloria Saviour Magdaline, Supr. Misioneras de la Caridad (Madre Teresa de Calcuta) Bed Capacity 42; Sisters 5; Tot Asst. Annually 26; Total Staff 15.

Pastoral de la Salud (1982) Parroquia La Resurreccion, Urb. Glenview Gardens, E-9 Final, Ponce, PR USA 00730. Tel: 787-842-7167; Email: josecvo@hotmail.com. Parroquia La Resurreccion, PMB 98, P.O. Box 2000, Mercedita, PR USA 00715. Rev. Jose Carlos Vargas Oliveras, Coord. Tot Asst. Annually 25,793.

Pontifical Catholic University of Puerto Rico Service Association (PCUSA), 2250 Boulevard Luis A Ferre, Ste. 516, Ponce, PR USA 00717-9997. Tel: 787-841-2000, Ext. 1281; Fax: 787-651-2021; Email: waddy_mercado@pucpr.edu. Dr. Waddy Mercado Maldonado, Interim Dir.

JUANA DIAZ. *Santuario de Schoenstatt*, 14 Calle Padre Kentenich, Juana Diaz, PR USA 00795. Tel: 787-526-6362; Email: santuariojuanadiaz@gmail.com. P.O. Box 800371, Coto Laurel, PR USA 00780-0371. Rev. Antonio Portalatin, Rector.

PENUELAS. *Congregacion Misionera de San Juan Evangelista*, Carretera 385 Km 0.7, Penuelas, PR USA 00624. Tel: 787-836-1512; Email: hermanoscheos@yahoo.com. P.O. Box 118, Penuelas, PR USA 00624. Jose Ortiz Zayas, Pres. Brothers 27.

Oblates of Wisdom (1979) Barrio Canitas, Carretera estatal 504, Ponce, PR USA 00730. Tel: 787-605-1195; Email: p.christopher1997@gmail.com; Web: www.rtforum.org. La Resurreccion Parish, P.O. Box 32205, Ponce, PR USA 00732-2205. Rev. Christopher De Herrera Sandoval, O.S., Chancellor.

RELIGIOUS INSTITUTES OF MEN REPRESENTED IN THE DIOCESE

For further details refer to the corresponding bracketed number in the Religious Institutes of Men or Women section.

[]—*Confraternidad Operarios del Reino de Cristo*—C.O.R.C.

[1330]—*Congregacion de la Mision* (Curia Provincial de Puerto Rico)—C.M.

[0470]—*Frailes Menores Capuchinos* (Vice Provincia de San Juan Bautista, PR)—O.F.M.Cap.

[1070]—*Misioneros Redentoristas* (Provincia de San Juan)—C.Ss.R.

[1310]—*Orden de la Santisima Trinidad* (Provincia de la Inmaculada Concepcion, Vicariato Colombia-Puerto Rico)—O.SS.T.

[0970]—*Orden de Nuestra Senora de la Merced*—O.deM.

[0270]—*Padres Carmelitas Descalzos* (Comisariato "San Jose" Del Caribe)—O.Carm.

[0430]—*Padres Dominicos de Puerto Rico, Inc.* (Vicariato Provincial de la Santa Cruz en Puerto Rico)—O.P.

[1040]—*Piarist Fathers* (Province USA-PR)—Sch.P.

[]—*Society of the Oblates of Wisdom*—O.S.

RELIGIOUS INSTITUTES OF WOMEN REPRESENTED IN THE DIOCESE

[0340]—*Carmelite Sisters of Charity*—C.a.Ch.

[]—*Hermanas Clarisas*—O.S.C.

[]—*Hermanas del Servicio Social.*

[]—*Hermanas de los Ancianos Desamparados.*

[1070-05]—*Hermanas Dominicas de Nuestra Senora del Rosario de Fatima*—O.P.

[]—*Hijas de la Caridad de San Vicente de Paul*—H.C.

[2710]—*Misioneras de la Caridad* (Madre Teresa de Calcuta)—M.C.

[]—*Operarias del Divino Maestro (Avemarianas).*

[]—*Operarias Parroquiales.*

[]—*Religiosas del Amor de Dios.*

[0130]—*Religiosas del Apostolado del Sagrado Corazon de Jesus*—R.A.

[]—*Religiosas Santos Angeles Custodios*—R.A.C.

[]—*School Sisters of Notre Dame*—S.S.N.D.

[3580]—*Siervas de Maria*—S. de M.

[2790]—*Siervas Misioneras de la Santisima Trinidad*—M.S.B.T.

[]—*Sisters of St. Joseph*—S.S.J.

NECROLOGY

† DiMarco, Abel A., (Retired), Died Jun. 17, 2018
† Lozano Guillen, Jose, (Retired), Died Sep. 30, 2018

An asterisk (*) denotes an organization that has established tax-exempt status directly with the IRS and is not covered by the USCCB Group Ruling.

Diocese of St. Thomas in the Virgin Islands

Most Reverend

HERBERT A. BEVARD

Bishop of St. Thomas in the Virgin Islands; ordained May 20, 1972; appointed Bishop of St. Thomas in the Virgin Islands July 7, 2008; ordained and installed September 3, 2008.

Chancery Office: P.O. Box 301825, Charlotte Amalie, VI 00803. Tel: 340-774-3166; Fax: 340-774-5816.

Web: www.catholicvi.com

Email: chancery@islands.vi

ESTABLISHED AS PRELATURE OF VI, JULY 23, 1960.

Established as Diocese of St. Thomas in the Virgin Islands April 20, 1977.

Comprises the Islands of St. Thomas, St. Croix, St. John and Water Island.

STATISTICAL OVERVIEW

Personnel	
Bishop	1
Priests: Diocesan Active in Diocese	10
Priests: Diocesan Active Outside Diocese	4
Priests: Retired, Sick or Absent	1
Number of Diocesan Priests	15
Religious Priests in Diocese	1
Total Priests in Diocese	16
Permanent Deacons in Diocese	28
Total Sisters	17
Parishes	
Parishes	8
With Resident Pastor:	
Resident Diocesan Priests	7
Resident Religious Priests	1
Missions	1
Welfare	
Special Centers for Social Services	5
Total Assisted	75,000
Educational	
Diocesan Students in Other Seminaries	1
Total Seminarians	1
High Schools, Diocesan and Parish	2
Total Students	112
Elementary Schools, Diocesan and Parish	3
Total Students	285
Catechesis/Religious Education:	
High School Students	95
Elementary Students	240
Total Students under Catholic Instruction	733
Teachers in the Diocese:	
Priests	2
Sisters	4
Lay Teachers	50
Vital Statistics	
Receptions into the Church:	
Infant Baptism Totals	88
Minor Baptism Totals	22
Adult Baptism Totals	12
Received into Full Communion	9
First Communions	93
Confirmations	76
Marriages:	
Catholic	19
Interfaith	9
Total Marriages	28
Deaths	125
Total Catholic Population	30,000
Total Population	110,000

Former Bishops—Most Revs. EDWARD J. HARPER, C.Ss. R., D.D., ord. June 18, 1939; appt. July 23, 1960; cons. Oct. 6, 1960; named first residential bishop of Diocese of St. Thomas in the Virgin Islands, April 20, 1977; retired Oct. 15, 1985; died Dec. 2, 1990; SEAN P. O'MALLEY, O.F.M.Cap., ord. Aug. 29, 1970; named coadjutor, May 30, 1984; ord. Bishop, Aug. 2, 1984; installed Oct. 16, 1985; transferred to Fall River Aug. 11, 1992; ELLIOTT G. THOMAS, D.D., ord. June 6, 1986; cons. and installed as Bishop Dec. 12, 1993; retired June 30, 1999; died Feb. 28, 2019.; GEORGE V. MURRY, S.J., ord. June 9, 1979; appt. May 5, 1998; installed June 30, 1999; appt. Bishop of Youngstown Jan. 30, 2007.

Chancery Office—Mailing Address: P.O. Box 301825, Charlotte Amalie, 00803. Tel: 340-774-3166; Fax: 340-774-5816.

Vicar General—Rev. Msgr. JEROME FEUDJIO, Tel: 340-774-0201.

Chancellor—Rev. NEIL SCANTLEBURY, Tel: 340-774-3166; Fax: 340-774-5816.

Vicar for Priest & Religious—Rev. Msgr. JEROME FEUDJIO.

Fiscal Officer—MR. WARREN BUSH.

Diocesan Consultors—Rev. E. PATRICK LYNCH, C.Ss.R.; Rev. Msgrs. JEROME FEUDJIO; MICHAEL F. KOSAK, P.A., (Retired); Revs. NEIL SCANTLEBURY; JOHN K. MARK; EDUARDO ORTIZ-SANTIAGO; ANTHONY ABRAHAM.

Hispanic Ministry—Revs. EDUARDO ORTIZ-SANTIAGO, Mailing Address: P.O. Box 304983, St. Thomas, 00803. Tel: 340-774-0885; Fax: 340-776-9586; JOHN K. MARK, Mailing Address: P.O. Box 2150, St. Croix, 00851. Tel: 340-692-2005; Fax: 340-692-2748.

Catholic Charities of the Virgin Islands, Inc.—MRS. ANDREA SHILLINGFORD, Exec. Dir., Mailing Address: P.O. Box 10736, Charlotte Amalie, 00801. Tel: 340-777-8518; Fax: 340-777-4875.

Catholic Schools Office—Rev. E. PATRICK LYNCH, C.Ss. R., Supt., 416 Custom House St., Frederiksted, 00840. Tel: 340-772-0138; Fax: 340-772-0142.

Vocations—Rev. Msgr. JEROME FEUDJIO, Mailing Address: P.O. Box 301767, St. Thomas, 00803. Tel: 340-774-0201; Fax: 340-776-9586.

Charismatic Movement—MRS. SUSAN EVERSLEY-WELLS, St. Croix, VI; Rev. ANTHONY ABRAHAM, Dir., Mailing Address: P.O. Box 241, St John, 00831-0241. Tel: 340-776-6339; Fax: 340-693-7685.

Caribbean Catholic Network (CCN)—Channel 7, *Mailing Address: P.O. Box 1160, Kingshill, 00851.* Tel: 340-779-3000; Fax: 340-779-3151. Rev. SIMON OBENG, Gen. Mgr.

Catholic Television Network (CTN)—Channel 16, Rev. Msgr. JEROME FEUDJIO, Mailing Address: P.O. Box 301825, Charlotte Amalie, 00803. Tel: 340-774-3166; Fax: 340-774-5816.

Diocesan Newspaper—The Catholic Islander *Mailing Address: P.O. Box 301825, St. Thomas, 00803.* Tel: 340-774-3166; Fax: 340-774-5816. Rev. JOHN FEWEL.

Communications Coordinator—Rev. Msgr. JEROME FEUDJIO, Mailing Address: P.O. Box 301825, St Thomas, 00803; Rev. SIMON OBENG, Mailing Address: P.O. Box 1160, Kingshill, 00851. Tel: 340-778-0484; Fax: 340-779-3151.

Prison Ministry—Rev. Msgr. JEROME FEUDJIO, St. Thomas, Tel: 340-774-3166; Fax: 340-774-5816.

Shelters for the Homeless—MRS. ANDREA SHILLINGFORD, Exec. Dir., Mailing Address: Bethlehem House, P.O. Box 10736, Charlotte Amalie, 00801. Tel: 340-774-4663. St. Croix. Tel: 340-777-8518; Fax: 340-777-4475. Administration.

Vicar for Clergy and Religious—Rev. Msgr. JEROME FEUDJIO, Mailing Address: P.O. Box 301825, St. Thomas, 00803-1825. Tel: 340-774-3166; Fax: 340-774-5816.

CLERGY, PARISHES, MISSIONS AND PAROCHIAL SCHOOLS

ISLAND OF ST. THOMAS

(CATHOLIC POPULATION, 12,500)

1—CATHEDRAL OF SS. PETER AND PAUL (1773) (West Indian)

Mailing Address: P.O. Box 301767, 00803. Rev. Msgr. Jerome Feudjio, Rector; Revs. Yacob Fopa Lonfo; Robert Kensack Ngnintedem; Deacons Jose Vasquez; Wilfredo Acosta; Frank Kearney.

Res.: 22A Kronprindsens Gade (Main St.), 00803.

Tel: 340-774-0201; Tel: 340-776-7384; Email: cathedralvi@gmail.com; Web: www.cathedralvi.com.

School—Sts. Peter and Paul School, (Grades 1-12), 12-17 Kronprindsens Gade, St. Thomas, 00802. Tel: 340-774-5662; Tel: 340-774-2199; Fax: 340-777-5355; Email: sppcs.usvi@gmail.com; Web: sppcsvi.com. Rev. Eduardo Ortiz-Santiago, Prin.; Mrs. Marie Jules-Daniel, Librarian. Clergy 6; Lay Teachers 15; Students 191.

Catechesis Religious Program—Sisters Joan Venyena, D.R.E.; Gisella Kinyuy, D.R.E.; Elizabeth Dzemfe, D.R.E. Students 72.

Convent—Daughters of the Holy Family, 31A Prindcesse Gade, P.O. Box 301767, St Thomas, 00803. Tel: 340-774-9445, Ext. 295; Email: clarisseufiv@gmail.com. Clarisse Yefoue Doungmene, Contact Person.

Mission—Chapel of St. Anne, Altona 42, P.O. Box 306810, Carenage, 00803. Tel: 340-714-5231; Email: ttignoau@gmail.com. Rev. Touchard G. Tignoua, Admin. Sisters 3.

2—HOLY FAMILY PARISH (1969) [JC] (West Indian)

P.O. Box 502218, St. Thomas, 00805. Revs. Neil Scantlebury; Kerly Francois.

Res.: 213 Anna's Retreat, St. Thomas, 00805.

Tel: 340-775-1650; Email: holyfamilyvi@msn.com; Web: www.holyfamilystt.com.

Catechesis Religious Program—Students 55.

3—OUR LADY OF PERPETUAL HELP (1926) [CEM] (West Indian)

Mailing Address: P.O. Box 304983, 00803.

Tel: 340-774-0885; Fax: 340-774-5896; Email: olphmafolie@gmail.com. Estate Elizabeth #8i, 00803. Rev. Eduardo Ortiz-Santiago; Deacon Bernard Gibs; Keya Chonasing Garner, Business Mgr.

Catechesis Religious Program—Students 25.

ISLAND OF ST. JOHN

(CATHOLIC POPULATION 300), OUR LADY OF MT. CARMEL PARISH (1962) Rev. Anthony Abraham; Deacons Cassius Mathurin; Evan Doway; Peter C. Laurencin. Res.: 5AB Cruz Bay, P.O. Box 241, St. John, 00831. Tel: 340-776-6339 (Res. & Office); Fax: 340-693-7685; Email: olmc@hotmail.com; Email: olmcstjohn@gmail.com; Web: olmcvi.org.
Catechesis Religious Program—Maggie Metor, D.R.E. Students 27.

ISLAND OF ST. CROIX

(CATHOLIC POPULATION, APPROX. 17,200)

1—CHURCH OF ST. JOSEPH (1947) [JC]
Mailing Address: P.O. Box 2150, Kingshill, 00851-2150. Tel: 340-692-2005; Fax: 340-692-2748; Email: stjoseph1973@yahoo.com. Rev. John K. Mark; Deacons Conrad Williams; Neville Charles, (Retired); James Verhoff; Guillermo Huertas; Hector Arroyo. In Res., Bro. James Petrait, O.S.F.S.
Res.: Mt. Pleasant #1, Frederiksted, Frederiksted, 00840.
Catechesis Religious Program—Students 35.
Sacred Heart Society—Tel: 340-692-2005; Fax: 340-692-2748. Mrs. Agneta Bailey.

2—CHURCH OF ST. PATRICK (1846) (African-Caribbean)
Mailing Address: 416 Custom House St., Frederiksted, 00840. Tel: 340-772-0138; Fax: 340-772-0142; Email: stpatrickusvi@gmail.com; Web: saintpatrickvi.com. Deacons Ed Cave; Emith Fludd; Rev. Boniface B. Twaibu; Deacon Melford Murray.
School—Church of St. Patrick School, (Grades 1-8), Tel: 340-772-5052; Fax: 340-772-4488; Email: sps1866@yahoo.com. Rev. Boniface B. Twaibu, Prin.; Mrs. Edna Thomas, Prin.; Ms. Anna Doward, Rel. Ed. Dir.; Ms. Devi-Anne Leonce, Office Mgr. Lay Teachers 11; Religious 1; Students 73.
Catechesis Religious Program—Students 15.

3—CHURCH OF THE HOLY CROSS (1755) [CEM 3] [JC] (West Indian) Revs. E. Patrick Lynch, C.Ss.R.; Bruce Anderson; Deacons Ulric Benjamin, (Retired); David Capriola; Vincent Colianni; Benjamin Parrilla; Reynold Modeste.
Res.: 2182 Queen St., Christiansted, 00820.
Tel: 340-773-7564; Email: holycrossstx@gmail.com.
School—St. Mary's, (Grades PreK-8), 2184 Queen St., Christiansted, 00820-4848. Tel: 340-773-0117; Fax: 340-773-1166; Email: office@stmary.gmail.com. Jan Rothwell, Prin. Lay Teachers 12; Students 130.
Catechesis Religious Program—Rev. David Capriola, Coord. Students 17.
Mission—Sacred Heart Chapel, Christiansted, U.S.V.I. 00820.
Convent—Missionaries of Charity, P.O. Box 3058, Christiansted, 00821.

4—CHURCH ST. ANN aka St. Ann's Roman Catholic Congregation, Inc (1823) (Caribbean)
Mailing Address: P.O. Box 1160, Kingshill, 00851-1160. Tel: 340-778-0484; Fax: 340-779-3151; Email: stannbarrenspot@gmail.com; Web: www.catholicvi.com/stann/. 42 Barrenspot Hill, Kingshill, 00850. Revs. Simon Obeng, Admin.; Louis Kemayou, (Retired); Deacons Joseph Mark; Norbert Xavier; Denis Griffith; Rev. Msgr. Michael Kosak, In. Res., (Retired).
Catechesis Religious Program—Patricia Browne, D.R.E. Elementary Enrollment 13; High School Enrollment 10.
Chaplaincy—Herbert Grigg Home for the Aged, Kingshill, 00851.
Shrine—Our Lady of Barrenspot Hill.

On Duty Outside the Diocese:
Revs.—
Corneille, Cecil
Fewel, John
Herrera, Jose
Sanchez, Alejandro.

Permanent Deacons:
Acosta, Wilfredo
Arroyo, Hector
Benjamin, Ulric, (Retired)
Capriola, David
Cave, Edward
Charles, Neville, (Retired)
Colianni, Vincent
Doway, Evan
Fludd, Emith
George, Hyacinthe
Gibs, Bernard
Griffith, Denis
Helenese, Arnold
Heyliger, Lambert, (Retired)
Huertas, Guillermo
Kearney, Frank
Laurencin, Peter C.
Mark, Joseph T.
Mathurin, Cassius
Matthew, James
Modeste, Reynold
Murry, Melford
Parrilla, Benjamin
Summer, William, (Retired)
Thompson, Eugene
Vazquez, Jose
Verhoff, James, (On Leave)
Williams, Conrad
Xavier, Norbert.

INSTITUTIONS LOCATED IN DIOCESE

[A] INTERPAROCHIAL HIGH SCHOOLS

ST. CROIX. *St. Joseph High School* (1964) 3 Mt. Pleasant, Rte. 2, Frederiksted, St. Croix, 00840. Tel: 340-692-2455; Fax: 340-692-2458; Email: sjhs@islands.vi; Email: jktmark@yahoo.com; Web: www.sjhsvi.com. Sandra N. Maynard, Office Mgr. & Dean; Rev. John K. Mark, Prin. Lay Teachers 8; Priests 1; Students 69.

[B] ORGANIZATIONS IN THE DIOCESE

ST. THOMAS. *Miscellaneous Organizations* (For further information contact the Chancery Office) 29A-30A Prindsesse Gade, The Catholic Chancery, 00803-1825. Tel: 340-774-3166; Fax: 340-774-5816; Email: chancery@islands.vi; Email: vichancery@gmail.com. P.O. Box 301825, St. Thomas, 00803-1825. Most Rev. Herbert A. Bevard, CEO; Rev. Msgr. Jerome Feudjio, Vicar.
Catholic Charismatic Renewal, Tel: 340-776-6339; Fax: 340-693-7685. Rev. Anthony Abraham, Dir.; Mrs. Susan Eversley-Wells, Asst. Dir.
Catholic Daughters of the Americas, Tel: 340-775-7846; Fax: 340-775-1750. Ms. Alicia Doute, Regent.
Children of Mary, St. Thomas. Tel: 340-775-2890; Fax: 340-775-1750. Wende Rouse, Pres., Tel: 340-775-1351; Fax: 340-775-1750.
Hispanic Ministry, St. Croix. Tel: 340-692-2005; Fax: 340-692-2748. Rev. John K. Mark.
Knights of Columbus Council 6482, St. Croix.
Knights of Columbus Council 6187, St. Thomas. Tel: 340-775-3537; Fax: 340-776-9586. Alrid Lockhart, Grand Knight.
Legion of Mary (St. John) 5AB Cruz Bay, P.O. Box 241, St. John, 00831. Tel: 340-227-0168; Fax: 340-693-7685; Email: grandmuff1010@gmail.com. Janice Mathurin, Pres.
Legion of Mary, Curia Immaculate Conception, P.O. Box 503302, St Thomas, 00805. Tel: 340-774-0743. Ramona Rivera, Pres.
Legion of Mary, Spanish Community, Presidium Maria, Arca de la Alianza, P.O. Box 8421, St Thomas, 00801. Tel: 340-776-1875. Ramona Rivera, Pres.
Legion of Mary, Holy Family Church, St. Thomas, Presidium Mary, Mystic Rose, St. Thomas. Tel: 340-775-3503; Fax: 340-775-1750. Eubald Rene, Pres.
Legion of Mary, OLPH Morning Star Praesidium, P.O. Box 304983, St Thomas, 00803. Tel: 340-774-0885. Timothy Olive, Pres.
Lumen 2000/Caribbean Region, Tel: 340-778-0484; Fax: 340-779-3151. Rev. Louis Kemayou, (Retired).
Magnificat Ministry For Women, St. Thomas. Tel: 340-774-0201; Fax: 340-776-9586. Carmen Grant, Asst. Chairperson, Tel: 340-775-5369.
Magnificat Ministry For Women - St. John, 5AB Cruz Bay, P.O. Box 241, St. John, 00831. Tel: 340-643-7097; Fax: 340-693-7685; Email: magdalene6054@gmail.com. Maggie Metor, Coord.
Secular Franciscans, Tel: 340-778-5773; Fax: 340-719-3037. Sr. Patricia Alexander, W.I.F., Spiritual Asst.
St. Ann's Stewards of Christ, 42 Barrenspot, Kingshill, 00851. Tel: 340-277-1002; Email: stannbarrenspot@gmail.com. P.O. Box 1160, Kingshill, 00851. Phillip Payne, Pres.
Fraternity Our Lady of the Angels Ms. Fredericka Leonce, S.F.O., Tel: 340-772-9131.
St. Vincent de Paul Society and Young Vincentians, St Thomas, 00805. Tel: 340-775-1650; Fax: 340-775-1750. Alma Wells, Pres., Tel: 340-775-0839; Fax: 340-775-1750.
Catholic Charities of the Virgin Islands, The Catholic Chancery, 29A-30A Prindsesse Gade, 00803-1825. Tel: 340-777-8518; Fax: 340-777-4475 ; Email: ccusvi@outlook.com. P.O. Box 10736, St. Thomas, 00801-0736. Mrs. Andrea Shillingford, Exec. Dir.
St. Joseph Workers, St. Thomas. Tel: 340-775-2890; Tel: 340-775-1351; Fax: 340-775-1750. Orville Rouse, Pres., Tel: 340-775-1351.
Secular Order Discalced Carmelites, St. Croix. Tel: 340-772-1204. Melvina Albert, Dir., Tel: 340-778-8386.
Cursillo Movement, St. Croix. Tel: 340-692-2005; Fax: 340-692-2748. Petra Arroyo, Tel: 340-778-0547.
Hispanic Ministry, P.O. Box 301767, St. Thomas, 00803. Rev. Eduardo Ortiz-Santiago, Chap.
Neocatecumenal Way, St. Croix. Tel: 340-692-2005; Fax: 340-692-2748. Deacon Conrad Williams, Contact Person, S.F.O., Coord.
Sacred Heart Society, St. Patrick Church, 416 Custom House St., Frederiksted, 00840. Tel: 340-772-3042; Fax: 340-772-0142; Email: saintpatrickusvi@gmail.com; Web: www.saintpatrickusvi.org. Mrs. Julia Pankey, Pres.
Shepherds of Christ Associates, Tel: 340-692-2005; Tel: 340-772-1076; Fax: 340-692-2748. Mrs. Merle Seepersad, Dir. St. Croix, VI.
Sacred Heart Society, St. Joseph Church. Tel: 340-692-2005; Fax: 340-692-2748. Mrs. Agneta Bailey, Pres.
Sacred Heart Society, P.O. Box 301767, St Thomas, 00803. Tel: 340-774-0201; Fax: 340-776-9586. Rev. Msgr. Jerome Feudjio, Dir.
Sacred Heart Society, 42 Barrenspot, Kingshill, 00851. Tel: 340-778-0484; Fax: 340-779-3151; Email: stannbarrenspot@gmail.com. St. Ann Church, P.O. Box 1160, Kingshill, 00851. Clara Xavier, Dir.
Bound 4 Life - OLPH, P.O. Box 304983, St Thomas, 00803. Timothy Olive, Pres.
Sons of Mary and Joseph - OLPH, P.O. Box 304983, St Thomas, 00803. Tel: 340-774-0885; Fax: 340-774-5896. Rev. Eduardo Ortiz-Santiago, Spiritual Dir.
Wednesday Prayer Group - OLPH, P.O. Box 304983, St Thomas, 00803. Tel: 340-774-0885.

RELIGIOUS INSTITUTES OF MEN REPRESENTED IN THE DIOCESE

For further details refer to the corresponding bracketed number in the Religious Institutes of Men or Women section.

[1070]—*Redemptorist Fathers*—C.SS.R.

RELIGIOUS INSTITUTES OF WOMEN REPRESENTED IN THE DIOCESE

[]—*Association of West Indian Franciscans*—W.I.F.
[]—*Daughters of the Holy Family*—D.H.F.
[2710]—*Missionaries of Charity*—M.C.
[2750]—*Missionary Sisters of the Immaculate Heart of Mary*—I.C.M.

NECROLOGY

† Thomas, Elliott G., Retired Bishop of St. Thomas in the Virgin Islands., Died Feb. 28, 2019

An asterisk (*) denotes an organization that has established tax-exempt status directly with the IRS and is not covered by the USCCB Group Ruling.

Diocese of Samoa-Pago Pago

Most Reverend

PETER H. BROWN, C.SS.R.

Bishop of Samoa-Pago Pago; ordained December 19, 1981; appointed Bishop of Samoa-Pago Pago May 31, 2013; installed August 22, 2013.

Most Reverend

JOHN QUINN WEITZEL, M.M.

Retired Bishop of Samoa-Pago Pago; ordained June 11, 1955; appointed First Bishop of Samoa-Pago Pago June 9, 1986; ordained October 29, 1986; retired May 31, 2013. *23000 Cristo Rey Dr., Los Altos, CA 94024.*

CREATED A DIOCESE NOVEMBER, 1982.

The Diocese of Samoa-Pago Pago includes the islands of Tutuila; Swains; Manu'a Is., Ofu, Olosega & Ta'u; Aunu'u and Rose Island.

STATISTICAL OVERVIEW

Personnel	
Bishop	1
Retired Bishops	1
Priests: Diocesan Active in Diocese	16
Priests: Diocesan Active Outside Diocese	1
Priests: Retired, Sick or Absent	1
Number of Diocesan Priests	18
Religious Priests in Diocese	2
Total Priests in Diocese	20
Ordinations:	
Diocesan Priests	1
Transitional Deacons	1
Permanent Deacons in Diocese	21
Total Brothers	2
Parishes	
Parishes	18
With Resident Pastor:	
Resident Diocesan Priests	15
Resident Religious Priests	2
Without Resident Pastor:	
Administered by Priests	4
Missions	1
Professional Ministry Personnel:	
Brothers	2
Welfare	
Homes for the Aged	1
Day Care Centers	1
Total Assisted	86
Special Centers for Social Services	1
Total Assisted	110
Educational	
Diocesan Students in Other Seminaries	5
Total Seminarians	5
High Schools, Diocesan and Parish	1
Total Students	291
Elementary Schools, Diocesan and Parish	2
Total Students	325
Catechesis/Religious Education:	
High School Students	650
Elementary Students	1,575
Total Students under Catholic Instruction	2,846
Teachers in the Diocese:	
Brothers	2
Lay Teachers	125
Vital Statistics	
Receptions into the Church:	
Infant Baptism Totals	215
Minor Baptism Totals	86
Adult Baptism Totals	77
Received into Full Communion	302
First Communions	270
Confirmations	303
Marriages:	
Catholic	75
Interfaith	18
Total Marriages	93
Deaths	60
Total Catholic Population	16,500
Total Population	68,250

Former Bishop—Most Rev. JOHN QUINN WEITZEL, M.M., ord. June 11, 1955; appt. First Bishop of Samoa-Pago Pago June 9, 1986; ord. Oct. 29, 1986; retired May 31, 2013.

Vicar General of Diocese—Rev. Msgr. VIANE ETUALE, V.G., M.A., M.Ed.

Chancellor—Rev. KELEMETE L. PUA'AULI.

Diocesan Consultors—Most Rev. PETER HUGH BROWN, C.Ss.R.; Rev. Msgr. VIANE ETUALE, V.G., M.A., M.Ed.; Rev. KELEMETE L. PUA'AULI.

Diocesan Pastoral Council—Most Rev. PETER HUGH BROWN, C.Ss.R., Pres.; Rev. Msgr. VIANE ETUALE, V.G., M.A., M.Ed., Chm.

Fatuoaiga Multipurpose Cultural and Pastoral Center—Rev. Msgr. ETUALE LEALOFI, J.C.D., (Retired). Faculty Members: Rev. Msgr. VIANE ETUALE, V.G., M.A., M.Ed.; Revs. KELEMETE L. PUA'AULI; KOLIO ETUALE, M.Div.; IOSEFO VAITELE TUPUOLA.

St. Anne Society—MRS. KORETI ULBERG, Pres.; MRS. TELEFINA NAUTU, Vice Pres.; MRS. SELESITINA LEILUA, Sec.; MRS. LUSIA SELUSI, Treas.

Sacred Heart Society—MRS. SUNI FELISE, Pres.; MRS. PALU VITALE, Vice Pres.; MRS. EVE LEAUPEPE, Treas./Sec.

Legion of Mary—MRS. AGNES VARGO, Pres.

Children of Mary—MISS MARY AULAUMEA, Pres.; MISS ANTONINA LILOMAIAVA, Vice Pres.; MISS LUPE MAUGAOTEGA, Sec.; MISS ROSE LAFAELE, Treas.

Divine Mercy—MR. GABRIEL MATAMUA, Pres.

Youth—AIGKIN IEREMIA, Pres.

Women's Organization—MRS. MUA SAVUSQ, Pres.; MRS. VALELIA TALO, Vice Pres.; MRS. JOANNE KIMOTO, Treas.; MRS. KALALA KAIO, Sec.

Rosary Society—MRS. KALALA TUITELE, Pres.

Matrimonial Tribunal—

Judicial Vicar—Most Rev. PETER HUGH BROWN, C.Ss.R.

Adjunct Judicial Vicar—Rev. Msgr. ETUALE LEALOFI, J.C.D., (Retired).

Judges—Rev. Msgrs. SCOTT L. MARCZUK, J.C.L.; VIANE ETUALE, V.G., M.A., M.Ed.

Defender of the Bond—VACANT.

Auditors—Revs. SETEFANO T. LUAMANU; KELEMETE L. PUA'AULI; KOLIO ETUALE, M.Div.; HILDRITHO RANOLA, M.A., M.Ed., M.Div.

Tribunal Administrator—VACANT.

Ecclesiastical Notary—MRS. THERESA H. SILAO.

Vicar for Diocesan Youth—Rev. VAIULA IULIO, Dir.

Director of Vocations—Rev. KOLIO ETUALE, M.Div.

Port Chaplain—Deacon AUGUST GABRIEL.

Prison Chaplain—Deacon AUGUST GABRIEL.

Director of Propagation of the FaithRev. IOANE FALANIKO ANITELE'A.

Hospital Chaplain—Rev. PIO GAMIG AFU, Catechist.

CLERGY, PARISHES, MISSIONS AND PAROCHIAL SCHOOLS

SAMOA-PAGO PAGO

1—CATHEDRAL OF THE HOLY FAMILY (1986)
Mailing Address: Fatuoaiga, P.O. Box 3594, Pago Pago, AS USA 96799-3594. Tel: 684-699-1446; Fax: 684-699-1459; Email: iosefovaitele@gmail.com; Email: maurice.lolesio@gmail.com. Most Rev. Peter Hugh Brown, C.Ss.R.; Revs. Iosefo Vaitele Tupuola, Chancellor; Eneliko Auva'a; Rev. Msgr. Etuale Lealofi, J.C.D., (Retired); Rev. Faitau Lemautu; Deacons Malaki Timu; Sauileone Aigofie, F.K.; Chaira Uiagalelei.
Catechesis Religious Program—
Tel: 684-699-2209; Fax: 684-699-1459. Mrs. Patricia Letuli, D.R.E.; Penitito Mika, F.K., Catechist. Students 293.
Mission—Mary, Star of the Sea
Manu'a Island, AS USA.

2—CHRIST THE KING (Amanave)
Mailing Address: P.O. Box 5408, Pago Pago, AS USA 96799. Tel: 684-688-7729; Cell: maurice.lolesio@gmail.com; Email: iosefo.vaitele@gmail.com; Email: maurice.lolesio@gmail.com. Diocese of Samoa Pago, P.O. Box 596, Fatuoaiga, Pago, AS USA 96799. Rev. Setefano T. Luamanu.
Catechesis Religious Program—Meafou Meatuai, F.K., Catechist; Moana Ah-Chee, Catechist. Students 120.

3—CHRIST THE KING (1997)
Mailing Address: P.O. Box 596, Pago Pago, AS USA 96799. Tel: 684-688-2438; Fax: 684-699-1459; Email: jrasalemo@hotmail.com. Diocese of Samoa Pago, P.O. Box 596, Fatuoaiga, Pago, AS USA 96799. Rev. Asalemo Asalemo Jr.; Deacon Filipo Toilolo.
Catechesis Religious Program—Vavatau Maseafa, F.K., F.K., Catechist. Students 53.

4—CHRIST THE KING (Nu'uuli) (1983)
Mailing Address: P.O. Box 596, Pago Pago, AS USA 96799. Tel: 684-699-4465; Fax: 684-699-1459; Email: vaiula_iulio@yahoo.com. Diocese of Samoa Pago, P.O. Box 596, Fatuoaiga, Pago, AS USA 96799. Rev. Vaivla Ivlio; Visesio Tulua, Catechist.
Catechesis Religious Program—Students 78.

5—CHURCH OF ST. PETER AND PAUL (Lauli'i) (1969)
Mailing Address: P.O. Box 985, Pago Pago, AS USA 96799. Tel: 684-644-5581; Email: talofasole@yahoo.com. Diocese of Samoa Pago, P.O. Box 596,

Fatuoaiga Pago, AS USA 96799. Rev. Pale Teofilo Schmidt; Deacon Setefano Lesa.
Catechesis Religious Program—
Tel: 684-644-4697. Tualesolo Talo, F.K., Catechist. Students 50.

6—CHURCH OF THE HOLY CROSS (Leone) (1861)
Mailing Address: Leone, P.O. Box 1206, Pago Pago, AS USA 96799. Tel: 684-688-7663; Cell: 684-733-6323, Ext. 1; Fax: 684-699-1459; Email: nfklp33@yahoo.com. Diocese of Samoa Pago, P.O. Box 596, Fatuoaiga, Pago, AS USA 96799. Rev. Kelemete L. Pua'auli; Deacons Nua Sipiliano; Vaipuna Tia.
Catechesis Religious Program—Tomasi Taavili, F.K., Catechist. Students 151.

7—CHURCH OF THE IMMACULATE CONCEPTION (Lepua) (1867)
Mailing Address: Lepua, P.O. Box 398, Pago Pago, AS USA 96799. Tel: 684-644-5512; Cell: 684-252-3962; Email: iosefo.vaitele@gmail.com. Diocese of Samoa Pagopago, P.O. Box 596, Fatuoaiga, Pago, AS USA 96799. Rev. Falaniko Stowers.
Catechesis Religious Program—
Tel: 684-644-2411. Ameto Lemana, F.K., Catechist, Mission Afono; Tumaai Solimalo, F.K., Catechist, Mission Lepua. Students 106.
Missions—
Afono, AS USA.
Lepua, AS USA.

8—CO-CATHEDRAL OF ST. JOSEPH THE WORKER (Fagatogo) (1974)
Mailing Address: Fagatogo, P.O. Box AA, Pago Pago, AS USA 96799. Tel: 684-633-1483; Email: fatherve@blueskynet.as. Rev. Msgr. Viane Etuale, V.G., M.A., M.Ed.
Catechesis Religious Program—Ierenimo Laupapa, F.K., Catechist. Students 193.
Missions—
Utulei, AS USA.
Faga'alu, AS USA.

9—ST. JOSEPH THE WORKER FUTIGA (2006)
Mailing Address: P.O. Box 596, Pago Pago, AS USA 96799. Tel: 684-688-7765; Cell: 684-731-9987; Email: ketuale@yahoo.com. Rev. Kolio Etuale, M.Div.; Deacon Felise Toilolo, F.K.
Catechesis Religious Program—Students 32.

10—OUR LADY OF FATIMA (2002)
Mailing Address: Aua Parish, P.O. Box 4052, Pago Pago, AS USA 96799. Tel: 684-644-5826;
Fax: 684-699-1459; Email: mar-esa@live.it. Rev. Maresa Kalolo.
Catechesis Religious Program—Aukusitine Paniani, Catechist. Students 110.

11—OUR LADY OF THE ROSARY PARISH
P.O. Box 596, Pago Pago, AS USA 96799.
Tel: 684-688-7729; Cell: 684-770-4516; Email: iosefo.vaitele@gmail.com. Rev. Setefano T. Luamanu.
Catechesis Religious Program—Taumaoe Ioane, Catechist. Students 80.

12—ST. PAUL (Ili'ili) (1974)
Mailing Address: Ili'ili, P.O. Box 2004, Pago Pago, AS USA 96799. Tel: 684-699-7572; Cell: 684-731-9987; Fax: 684-699-1459; Email: ketuale@yahoo.com. Rev. Kolio Etuale, M.Div.; Deacon Iosefo Vitaliano.
Office: Fatuoaiga, P.O. Box 596, Pago Pago, AS USA 96799.
Catechesis Religious Program—Students 226.
Missions—
Faleniu, AS USA.
Pava'ia'i, AS USA.
Aasu/Aoloau, AS USA.

13—STS. PETER & PAUL, (Asili)
Mailing Address: P.O. Box 7286, Pago Pago, AS USA 96799. Tel: 684-688-7236; Cell: 684-733-6323; Email: nfklp33@yahoo.com. Rev. Kelemete L. Pua'auli.
Catechesis Religious Program—Paulo Sagato, F.K., Catechist. Students 22.
Mission—Amaluia.

14—ST. PETER CHANEL PARISH FAGASA
P.O. Box 596, Pago Pago, AS USA 96799.
Tel: 684-644-5512; Cell: 684-258-4349; Email: mar-esa@live.it. Rev. Maresa Kalolo.
Catechesis Religious Program—Students 44.

15—ST. PETER CHANEL-SA'ILELE
Mailing Address: P.O. Box 596, Pago Pago, AS USA 96799. Tel: 684-622-7512; Email: iosefo_vaitele@gmail.com. Rev. Pale Teofilo Schmidt.
Catechesis Religious Program—Faleagafulu Filipo, F.K., Catechist. Students 36.
Missions—
Masefau, AS USA.
Faga'itua, AS USA.

16—SACRED HEART OF JESUS (Alao) (1989)
Mailing Address: Alao, P.O. Box 4175, Pago Pago, AS USA 96799. Tel: 684-622-7029; Cell: 684-254-0375; Fax: 684-699-1459; Email: frpioafu@gmail.com. Rev. Pio Gamig Afu.
Catechesis Religious Program—Moe Sagote, F.K., Catechist. Students 98.
Missions—
Aoa, AS USA.
Amouli, AS USA.

17—SACRED HEART OF JESUS PARISH (2003)
Mailing Address: P.O. Box 596, Pago Pago, AS USA 96799. Tel: 684-688-1965; Cell: 684-770-4000; Email: iosefo.vaitele@gmail.com. Rev. Petelo Siliako Auvaa.
Catechesis Religious Program—Ioane Afoa, Catechist. Students 45.

18—SACRED HEART PARISH-PAGO PAGO (2001) Rev. Tagaloa Tating.
Res.: P.O. Box 596, Pago Pago, AS USA 96799.
Tel: 684-733-0735; Email: samoa_143@yahoo.com.
Catechesis Religious Program—Meaalofa Lotomau, Catechist. Total Enrollment 2.

Permanent Deacons:
Aigofie, Sauileone, F.K.
Augusitino, Iosefo
Auva'a, Lino
Gabriel, August, Chap. Pago-Pago Intl. Airport
Hunkin, Avaletalia
Lafaele, Setefano
Lemana, Penitito
Maugaotega, Tavete
Paselio, Sanele, F.K.
Pereira, Tavita
Puletasi, Andy Niuatoa
Sipiliano, Nua
Tia, Vaipuna
Timu, Malaki, F.K.
Toilolo, Felise, F.K.
Toilolo, Filipo
Toilolo, Iosefo
Toilolo, Moli
Uelese, Alefosio, F.K.
Vitaliano, Iosefo.

INSTITUTIONS LOCATED IN DIOCESE

[A] PRESCHOOLS

PAGO PAGO. *Mary The Mother Montessori Early Education Center*, c/o Diocese of Samoa-Pago Pago, Lepua, P.O. Box 596, Pago Pago, AS USA 96799. Tel: 684-644-1311; Fax: 684-699-1459; Email: fakenese@rocketmail.com. Akenese Felise, Prin. Clergy 1; Lay Teachers 5; Students 40.

[B] ELEMENTARY SCHOOLS, PAROCHIAL

LEONE. *St. Theresa*, (Grades 1-8), Malaeloa, P.O. Box 596, Leone, AS USA 96799-0596. Tel: 684-688-1105; Tel: 684-688-1114 Other; Email: st.theresa1105@gmail.com. Katherine Taleni, Prin. Clergy 1; Lay Teachers 17; Students 145.

LEPUA. *Marist St. Francis*, (Grades 1-8), Fatuoaiga, P.O. Box 429, Lepua, AS USA 96799-0429. Fax: 684-699-1459; Email: alaitupum@gmail.com. Rev. Msgr. Viane Etuale, V.G., M.A., M.Ed., Prin.. Brothers 1; Clergy 3; Priests 1; Students 140; Teachers 10.

[C] HIGH SCHOOLS, PAROCHIAL

LEPUAPUA. *Faasao Marist High School*, P.O. Box 729, Lepuapua, AS USA 96799. Tel: 684-688-7731; Email: kpk684@yahoo.com; Web: fmhs411.weebly.com. Bro. Christopher Poppelwell, Office of Catholic Education Dir.; Kamo Koloi, Prin.; Mrs. Clare Dunstan, Librarian. Brothers 2; Deacons 2; Lay Teachers 22; Priests 1; Students 268; Volunteers 1.

[D] HOMES FOR AGED & SPECIAL CARE FOR CHILDREN

PAGO PAGO. *Hope House*, P.O. Box 596, Pago Pago, AS USA 96799. Tel: 684-699-2101; Fax: 684-699-6051. Aged Residents 15; Clergy 23; Total Staff 48; Special Care Children 5; Montessori Early Education 71; Day Care Center 90.

[E] MISCELLANEOUS

PAGO PAGO. *Catholic Social Services, Inc.*, Fatuoaiga Street, Tafuna, P.O. Box 596, Pago Pago, AS USA 96799. Tel: 684-699-5683; Fax: 684-699-1459; Email: cssfatuoaiga@yahoo.com. Ms. Sulita Schmidt, Dir. Tot Asst. Annually 77; Total Staff 3.

Diocesan Eucharistic League, Diocesan Eucharistic League, P.O. Box 596, Pago Pago, AS USA 96799. Tel: 684-699-1402; Fax: 684-699-1459; Email: ivonamauga@yahoo.com; Email: teri_684@yahoo.com. Mrs. Teuila Love, Pres.; Theresa D. Silao, Sec.

RELIGIOUS INSTITUTES OF MEN REPRESENTED IN THE DIOCESE

For further details refer to the corresponding bracketed number in the Religious Institutes of Men or Women section.

[]—*Missionaries of the Faith*—M.F.

RELIGIOUS INSTITUTES OF WOMEN REPRESENTED IN THE DIOCESE

[]—*Intercessor of the Little Lamb.*

An asterisk (*) denotes an organization that has established tax-exempt status directly with the IRS and is not covered by the USCCB Group Ruling.

Archdiocese of San Juan, Puerto Rico

(Sancti Joannis Portoricensis)

Most Reverend

ROBERTO O. GONZALEZ NIEVES, O.F.M.

Archbishop of San Juan; ordained May 8, 1977; appointed Titular Bishop of Ursona and Auxiliary Bishop of Boston July 19, 1988; consecrated October 3, 1988; appointed Coadjutor Bishop of Corpus Christi May 16, 1995; transferred to Corpus Christi June 26, 1995; succeeded to See April 1, 1997; appointed Archbishop of San Juan March 26, 1999; installed May 8, 1999.

ERECTED AUGUST 8, 1511.

Square Miles 353.

Erected an Archdiocese April 30, 1960.

Comprises the northeast portion of the Island of Puerto Rico, with a Total Population of 1,293,460

Chancery Office: P.O. Box 9021967, San Juan, PR 00902-1967. Tel: 787-727-7373; Fax: 787-726-8280.

STATISTICAL OVERVIEW

Personnel	
Archbishops	1
Retired Bishops	1
Priests: Diocesan Active in Diocese	100
Priests: Diocesan Active Outside Diocese	2
Priests: Retired, Sick or Absent	14
Number of Diocesan Priests	116
Religious Priests in Diocese	133
Total Priests in Diocese	249
Extern Priests in Diocese	4
Ordinations:	
Religious Priests	1
Transitional Deacons	2
Permanent Deacons	17
Permanent Deacons in Diocese	208
Total Brothers	20
Total Sisters	387
Parishes	
Parishes	142
With Resident Pastor:	
Resident Diocesan Priests	56
Resident Religious Priests	47
Without Resident Pastor:	
Administered by Priests	37
Administered by Deacons	1
Administered by Lay People	1
Completely Vacant	1
Missions	143
Professional Ministry Personnel:	
Brothers	20
Sisters	387
Lay Ministers	2,305
Welfare	
Catholic Hospitals	2
Total Assisted	9,500
Health Care Centers	6
Total Assisted	7,200
Homes for the Aged	18
Total Assisted	79,110
Residential Care of Children	8
Total Assisted	10,150
Day Care Centers	7
Total Assisted	15,275
Specialized Homes	21
Total Assisted	12,200
Special Centers for Social Services	10
Total Assisted	23,250
Residential Care of Disabled	1
Total Assisted	2,300
Other Institutions	7
Total Assisted	94,550
Educational	
Seminaries, Diocesan	1
Students from This Diocese	9
Diocesan Students in Other Seminaries	5
Students Religious	3
Total Seminarians	17
Colleges and Universities	2
Total Students	7,300
High Schools, Diocesan and Parish	40
Total Students	5,775
Elementary Schools, Diocesan and Parish	55
Total Students	19,300
Non-residential Schools for the Disabled	1
Total Students	150
Total Students under Catholic Instruction	32,542
Teachers in the Diocese:	
Brothers	20
Sisters	387
Lay Teachers	1,500
Vital Statistics	
Receptions into the Church:	
Infant Baptism Totals	2,100
Minor Baptism Totals	1,350
Adult Baptism Totals	883
Received into Full Communion	6
First Communions	3,554
Confirmations	3,170
Marriages:	
Catholic	1,500
Interfaith	67
Total Marriages	1,567
Total Catholic Population	840,749
Total Population	1,293,460

Former Bishops—Most Revs. ALONSO MANSO, D.D., appt. May 1511; JAMES H. BLENK, S.M.D.D., appt. Bishop of Puerto Rico, June 12, 1899; died April 20, 1917; WILLIAM A. JONES, O.S.A., cons. Feb. 24, 1907; died Jan. 1921; GEORGE J. CARUANA, D.D., appt. Bishop 1921; promoted to the Apostolic Delegation of Mexico, 1925; promoted to Nunciature Apostolic of Cuba, 1927; EDWIN VINCENT BYRNE, D.D., former Bishop of Ponce, Puerto Rico; cons. Nov. 30, 1925; appt. March 1929; promoted to Archdiocese of Santa Fe, June 15, 1943; died July 25, 1963; JAMES PETER DAVIS, (Retired), appt. 1943; cons. Oct. 9, 1943; transferred to Archdiocese of Santa Fe, June, 1963; installed Feb. 25, 1964; retired Oct. 1974; His Eminence LUIS CARDINAL APONTE MARTINEZ, D.D., appt. Auxiliary Bishop of Ponce July 23, 1960; cons. Oct. 12, 1960; appt. Coadjutor Bishop of Ponce April 16, 1963; succeeded to Nov. 18, 1963; installed Feb. 22, 1964; appt. Archbishop of San Juan Nov. 4, 1964; installed Jan. 15, 1965; created Cardinal March 5, 1973; retired March 26, 1999; died April 10, 2012.

Vicars General—Rev. Msgr. LEONARDO J. RODRIGUEZ-JIMENES; Rev. ALBERTO ARTURO FIGUEROA MORALES, O.F.M.Cap.

Episcopal Moderator—

for Administration of Temporalities—Rev. Msgr. LEONARDO J. RODRIGUEZ-JIMENES, Moderator; Rev. ALBERTO ARTURO FIGUEROA MORALES, O.F.M.Cap., Moderator.

for Education—Rev. JUAN SANTA GUZMAN, Web: www.escueloscatolicos-sj.org.

for Pastoral Affairs—Rev. Msgr. ALBERTO LOPEZ FIGUEROA.

for Geographic-Pastoral Zones—San Juan-Santurce: Rev. LUIS MIRANDA, O.Carm. Bayamon: Rev. CARLOS RUBEN ALGARIN LOPEZ, O.S.A. Del Toa y La Plata: Rev. ANGEL PAGAN TORRES. Carolina: Rev. RODNEY ALGARIN ROSADO. Rio Piedras: Rev. TOMAS GONZALEZ GONZALEZ. Guaynabo-Puerto Nuevo: Rev. WALTER S. GOMEZ-BACA.

Chancery Office—Mailing Address: P.O. Box 9021967, San Juan, 00902-1967. Web: www.arqsj.org.

Chancery Affairs—MISS LUCIA GUZMAN ORTA, Chancellor, Email: luciagu@arqsj.org.

Vice Chancellor—Rev. ANIBAL RAFAEL TORRES-ORTIZ.

Metropolitan Curia—

Moderator—Rev. ALBERTO ARTURO FIGUEROA MORALES, O.F.M.Cap.

Secretary to the Archbishop—Rev. ALFONSO GUZMAN-ALFARO, O.F.M., Tel: 787-725-4975; Tel: 787-977-0672.

Executive Assistant to the Archbishop—MR. SAMUEL SOTO-ALONSO, Tel: 787-725-4975; Tel: 787-977-0672.

Judicial Vicar—Rev. RICARDO ROIG LORENZO.

Adjunct Vicars—Revs. LUIS NORBERTO CORREA-GARCIA; PEDRO LUIS REYES LEBRÓN.

Judges—MISS MARIA LUCIA SANCHEZ; MR. ABRAHAM MORALES BERRIOS.

Defender of the Bond—MARIA DEL ROSARIO RINCON-BECERRA.

Instructors—MR. RIGOBERTO HIRALDO RIOS; MILAGROS GONZALEZ; ALTITA DAVILA; MRS. CARMEN J. ACOSTA.

Lawyers—ORLANDO DURAN; MILAGROS GONZALEZ-RODRIQUEZ; XAVIER HIRALDO-SANCHEZ; MARJORIE STEWART; Rev. JORGE SAENZ; JOAN MARIE RODRIGUEZ VEVE.

Diocesan Consultors—Rev. Msgrs. LEONARDO J. RODRIGUEZ-JIMENES; ALBERTO LOPEZ FIGUEROA; JOSE E. CUMMINGS-ESPADA; Revs. RICARDO ROIG LORENZO; ALBERTO ARTURO FIGUEROA-MORALES; Rev. Msgr. EFRAIN RODRIGUEZ-OTERO; Rev. ANGEL PAGAN-TORRES. Censor Librorum: Rev. Msgr. FERNANDO B. FELICES-SANCHEZ

Vicar of Social Communication—VACANT.

Auxiliary Vicar of Social Communication—VACANT.

Vicar of Cultural Affairs—Rev. Msgr. EFRAIN RODRIGUEZ-OTERO.

Vicar of Development—Rev. ALBERTO ARTURO FIGUEROA MORALES, O.F.M.Cap.

Vicar of Economic Affairs—VACANT.

Director of Economic Affairs—MR. SANTIAGO MORALES-ROSARIO; MRS. SANDRA RODRIGUEZ, Asst. to Dir.

Vicar of Ecumenism—Rev. WILLIAM TORRES-PAGAN.

Vicar of Family Affairs—Rev. PHILLIP NUNEZ-CARRION.

Vicar for Pastoral Affairs—Rev. Msgr. ALBERTO LOPEZ FIGUEROA.

Vicar for Education—Rev. JUAN SANTA GUZMAN.

Vicar of Religious—Rev. ALFONSO GUZMAN-ALFARO, O.F.M.

Examinatores Cleri—VACANT.

Vicar for Vocations—Rev. Msgr. IVAN LUIS HUERTAS-COLON.

Pro-Synodal Examiner—VACANT.

Vicar for Priests—Rev. JOAQUIN MAYORGA-FONSECA.

Vicar for Youth—Rev. JOEL ENRIQUE DEL CUETO-SANTIAGO.

Vicar of Sports—Rev. FRANCISCO J. QUINTERO ANGUEIRA.

Archdiocesan Offices and Directors

Boy Scouts—VACANT.

Catechetics—Rev. AGAPITO ANTONIO VARGAS, M.SS.CC.

Catechetics Center—Sr. MERCEDES CADENAS, H.M., Mailing Address: San Juan-Santurce, P.O. Box 9021967, San Juan, 00902-1967. Tel: 787-727-7373. Carolina: Sr. MERCEDES CADENAS, H.M., Valle Arriba Heights, BF-20 Calle Alamo, Carolina, 00983. Bayamon: Sr. LISSETTE AVILES, O.P., Mailing Address: P.O. Box 4152, Bayamon, 00958. Tel: 787-780-1173. Rio Piedras: Sr. ISABEL SOTO, M.SS.S., Mailing Address: P.O. Box 20884, San Juan, 00920. Tel: 787-761-4280. Guaynabo-Pto Nuevo: Sr. ROSE MORALES, M.S.B.T., Mailing Address: P.O. Box 9021967, San Juan, 00902-1967. Tel: 787-731-6100.

Catholic Charities—Rev. ENRIQUE MANUEL CAMACHO-MONSERRATE, Mailing Address: P.O. Box 8812, San Juan, 00910-0812. Tel: 787-727-7373; Fax: 787-728-4100; Email: ssc@arqsj.org.

El Visitante—Weekly Catholic Paper for All Dioceses (Interdiocesan). Published By The P.R., Episcopal Conference. Most Rev. ROBERTO O. GONZÁLEZ-NIEVES, O.F.M., Pres.; Rev. EFRAIN ZABALA, Editor; ENRIQUE LOPEZ, Mailing Address: P.O. Box 41305, Minillas Sta., San Juan, 00940-1305. Tel: 787-728-3710; Fax: 787-268-1748. Offices, Pumarada St. 1704, Santurce, 00914.

Radio Stations—WORO-FM and WKVM-AM 81, MR. ALAN CORALES, Dir., Urb. Baldrich, 415 Calle Ingeniero Carbonell, San Juan, 00918. Mailing Address: P.O. Box 9021967, San Juan, 00902-1967. Tel: 787-731-1380; Tel: 787-751-1018; Fax: 787-758-9967; Email: radiooro@arqsj.org.

Television Station—WPRV-TV CHANNEL 13, Tele Oro, MR. LUIS QUINONEZ MORA, Gen. Mgr., Ave Iturregui Esq. Marginal, Baldorioty De Castro Ave., Carolina, 00982. Tel: 787-276-1300; Fax: 787-276-1307. Mailing Address: P.O. Box 9021967, San Juan, 00902-1967.

Commission for Sacred Liturgy and Popular Piety—Rev. Msgr. LEONARDO J. RODRIGUEZ-JIMENES.

Subcommission for Sacred Art—Urb. Baldrich Calle Rossy #202, San Juan, 00918. Tel: 787-763-9154. Rev. Msgr. LEONARDO J. RODRIGUEZ-JIMENES; HECTOR BALVANERA.

Subcommission for Sacred Music—Rev. MIGUEL TRINIDAD.

Subcommission for Popular Piety—VACANT.

Subcommission for Ministries—Rev. Msgr. LEONARDO J. RODRIGUEZ-JIMENES.

Clergy Social Security (Prevision Social del Clero)—Revs. RICARDO HERNANDEZ, Treas.; ALBERTO DIAZ; ANGEL MENDEZ; Rev. Msgr. MANUEL GARCIA PEREZ; VACANT, Sec., P.O. Box 4682, San Juan, 00940-0682. Tel: 787-728-1650; Fax: 787-728-1654; Rev. JORGE ERNESTO TORRES RIVERA.

ISTEPA—Rev. Msgr. FRANCISCO MEDINA, Ext. Forrest Hills, Calle Caracasy, Valparaiso, Bayamon, 00961. Tel: 787-200-6891; Fax: 787-200-6305; Rev. ANIBAL RAFAEL TORRES-ORTIZ, Vice Rector.

San Juan Bautista Regional Seminary—Rev. Msgr. IVAN L. HUERTAS-COLON, Vice Rector. Spiritual Directors: Revs. JOSE VICENTE MARTINEZ, C.M.F.; EDWIN ALBEIRO LONDONO ZULUAGA, Mailing Address: P.O. Box 11714, San Juan, 00922-1714. Tel: 787-783-0645; Tel: 787-273-8090; Fax: 787-783-0645. Ave. De Diego 930, Urb. La Riviera, Rio Piedras, 00921. Email: seminary@coqui.net.

Serra Club—VACANT.

Vocations Promoter—Rev. EDWIN ALBEIRO LONDONO ZULUAGA, Mailing Address: P.O. Box 11714, San Juan, 00922-1714. Tel: 787-706-9455; Tel: 787-273-8090.

Superintendent of Schools—MRS. ANA CORTES, Supt.; VACANT, Rel. Prog. Dir., Urb. Los Maestros, 789 Calle Jaime Drew, San Juan, 00923. Tel: 787-731-6100; Fax: 787-731-0000; Web: www.esculelascatolicas-sj.org.

Archdiocesan Historical Archive—MRS. ELSE ZAYAS LEON, Calle San Sebastian 5-N, San Juan, 00902. Mailing Address: P.O. Box 9021967, San Juan, 00902-1967. Tel: 787-977-1447.

Youth Ministries—VACANT.

Police Chaplains—Rev. Msgrs. BAUDILIO MERINO MERINO, (Spain) Tel: 787-767-6552; VALERIANO MIGUÉLEZ, (Spain) Tel: 787-754-0570; Rev. ANTONIO GARCIA CASTEJON, Tel: 787-757-4454; Deacon JOSE PENA GONZALEZ, Tel: 787-786-5309.

Society for the Protection of Children—Most Rev. ROBERTO O. GONZÁLEZ-NIEVES, O.F.M., Mailing Address: P.O. Box 9021967, San Juan, 00902-1967. Tel: 787-727-7373.

United Against Hunger (Unidos Contra El Hambre)—Deacon HECTOR CRUZ DECHOUDENS, San Jorge St., No. 201, Santurce, 00914. Mailing Address: P.O. Box 11547, San Juan, 00910-2647. Tel: 787-727-7373, Ext. 240; Fax: 787-727-7938; Email: uch@arqsj.org.

Propagation of the FaithRev. JOSE ORLANDO CAMACHO-TORRES, C.S.Sp., 106 Ruiz Belvis St., P.O. Box 191882, Floral Park, San Juan, 00919.

Pius Union of the Clergy—VACANT, P.O. Box 9021967, San Juan, 00902-1967. Tel: 787-727-7373.

Catholic Charismatic Renewal—Revs. MILTON AGUSTIN RIVERA-VIGO, Dir.; MARIANO MARTINEZ GALVEZ, O.M.I., Tel: 787-765-6240 Arzobispado de San Juan; Tel: 787-727-7373.

Master of Ceremonies to the Archbishop—MR. LUIS DACOSTA-DEJESUS.

Pre Cana Conferences—VACANT, Dir., 1765 Calle Lesbos, San Juan, 00926. Tel: 787-761-6586; MR. MANUEL SANCHEZ, Urb. Country Club, 1031 Calle Genoveva De Lugo, San Juan, 00924. Tel: 787-769-3565.

Caritas of Puerto Rico—Rev. ENRIQUE MANUEL CAMACHO-MONSERRATE, Exec. Dir., Mailing Address: P.O. Box 8812, San Juan, 00910-0812. Tel: 787-727-7373; Fax: 787-728-4100.

Centro Apostolado De La Cruz—MARICARMEN RIVERA, Coord., Urb. Sans Souci, Z 10 Calle 19, Bayamon, 00956. Tel: 787-797-1481; Fax: 787-269-3190.

Cursillos De Cristiandad—Rev. TOMAS GONZALEZ-GONZALEZ.

Immigrant Aid—Mailing Address: Catholic Social Services, P.O. Box 9021967, San Juan, 00902-1967. Tel: 787-727-7373.

Holy Childhood Association—Rev. JOSE ORLANDO CAMACHO-TORRES, C.S.Sp.

Holy Name Society—MR. MIGUEL A. RODRIGUEZ, Archdiocesan Dir., Mailing Address: P.O. Box 31164, San Juan, 00929. Tel: 787-276-2212; Tel: 787-605-9292; MR. FRANCISCO FIGUEROA, Sec., Tel: 787-768-4787.

Renovacion Conyugal (Fundacion Fernando Martinez Calle, Inc.)—Rev. JORGE AMBERT, S.J., Dir., Urb. Ext. Roosevelt, 576 Calle Eddie Gracia, San Juan, 00918. Tel: 787-751-6001; Tel: 787-766-1363; Email: ambertsj@aol.com; Web: www.renovacion.net.

Courage Puerto Rico—Rev. OVIDIO ORTEGA, Encourage: Padres, Familia y Amigos, Tel: 787-941-7311; Email: poncepr@courage-latino.org; Email: sanjuanpr@courage-latino.org.

Equipo De Impacto Matrimonial—Deacon MIGUEL A. MARRERO, Dir., Urb Sabana Gardens, #15 Calle 9 Blq 4, Carolina, 00983. Tel: 787-750-0609; Fax: 787-750-0609.

Grupo Misioneros De Amor Y Fe—JOSE A. MENDEZ, Coord. y Fundador, Urb. Paseo Las Vistas, B31 Calle 1, San Juan, 00926. Tel: 787-397-1612; Email: joseamendez@misionerosdeamoryfe.org; Web: www.misionerosdeamoryfe.org.

La Mujer Por La Familia Catolica En Puerto Rico—TERUCA RULLAN, Pres., Mailing Address: Fernandez Juncos Station, P.O. Box 19241, San Juan, 00910. Tel: 787-723-1620; Fax: 787-725-9455.

Proyecto Reencuentro Familiar—MAXIMINO DIAZ GUZMAN, Dir., 500 Ave Los Filtros, Boulevard del Rio II Apt. 119, Guaynabo, 00971. Tel: 787-797-4500 (Office); Tel: 787-797-4288 (Casa de Retiro).

Legion of Mary—MISS DORIS MARTINEZ, Pres., Mailing Address: PMB 822, Box 7891, Guaynabo, 00970-7891; Rev. ANGEL L. CIAPPI-AZCORRA, Spiritual Dir., Urb. Munoz Rivera, C. Betania #34, Guaynabo, 00969. Tel: 787-360-0508.

Encuentro Catolico de Novios—MRS. ESPERANZA MIRANDA DIAZ, Natl. Coord.; Deacon LUIS ALVAREZ SURIA.

Marriage Encounter—MR. GERARDO SALAZAR; MRS. MILLY SALAZAR, Jardines del Parque, 59 Boulevard Media Luna, Apt. 1803, Carolina, 00987-4935. Tel: 787-757-3432.

Spiritual Director—VACANT.

Catholic Daughters of America—MRS. IRMA BONILLA, c/o Julio Bonilla #50, Isabela, 00662. Tel: 787-872-6831.

Spiritual Director—VACANT.

Knights of Columbus—MR. MIGUEL A. TORRES ORTIZ, RR4, Box 3451, Bayamon, 00956. Tel: 787-782-8250, Ext. 6280; Fax: 787-792-7553.

Nocturnal Adoration—MR. ANGEL PAGAN, Pres., Mailing Address: P.O. Box 190199, San Juan, 00919-0199. Tel: 787-749-0502; MR. ISMAEL SUAREZ, Sec. Guaynabo, Tel: 787-728-0670; MR. RAMON MENDEZ, Santa Maria de Cana, Cell: 787-312-2224.

Spiritual Director—Rev. RICARDO HERNANDEZ MORALES.

Talleres De Oracion y Vida P. Larranaga—MRS. EMILIA DIAZ, Dir., Urb. Montehiedra, 33 Calle Garza, San Juan, 00926-9537. Tel: 787-728-2894; Tel: 787-731-1358.

Tourism and Apostleship of the Sea—

Casamar—VACANT.

UPR Catholic Student Center—Rev. RAFAEL RODRIGUEZ, S.J., Mariana Bracetti 10, Rio Piedras, 00925-2201. Tel: 787-767-3348; Fax: 787-758-4145.

San Juan International Airport Chapel—Ntra. Sra de la Providencia Deacon EDUARDO GONZALEZ, Tel: 789-487-3731.

Carmelite Third Order—Rev. LUIS MIRANDA, O.Carm., Tel: 787-726-2631.

Casa San Clemente—

Psychological and Pastoral Counseling—257 Ponce De Leon, San Juan, 00906. Tel: 787-723-6915.

Pro-Life Center (Human Life International)—VACANT.

Pro-Life Pharmacists International—MISS SANDRA FABREGAS, Dir.

Consejo De Accion Social Arquidiocesano—Mailing Address: P.O. Box 31155, San Juan, 00929-2155. Tel: 787-276-1413. VACANT, Dir.; MRS. IDIS OTERO, Coord.

Servicios Pastorales Paules—Rev. SANTIAGO ARRIBAS, C.M., Dir., 1650, Ave. Fernandez Juncos, San Juan, 00910-0118. Tel: 787-728-0670; Fax: 787-728-0670. Mailing Address: P.O Box 19118, San Juan, 00910-9118.

Franciscan Third Order (Secular Franciscan Order)—VACANT, Spiritual Dir.; MRS. AWILDA VASQUEZ, Natl. Min., Mailing Address: P.O. Box 3915, Carolina, 00984. Tel: 787-752-7363.

Focolares—Deacon JOSE HERNANDEZ, Dir., Urb Fairview, 1937 Calle Melchor Maldonado, San Juan, 00926. Tel: 787-761-4993. Women: MISS DIANA RIVERA, Urb. Fairview, 1911 Francisco Zuniga, San Juan, 00926. Tel: 787-543-3160.

Secretariado Sagrado Corazon—MRS. ANA M. BONET, Pres., Urb. Prado Alto, C6 Calle 4, Guaynabo, 00966. Tel: 787-781-6295.

Grupo Reina De La Paz—MISS IVETTE PACHECO, Pres., PMB 258, Ste. 2, Ave. Esmeralda 405, Guaynabo, 00969. Tel: 787-644-8256; Fax: 787-731-8256; MRS. IVONNE MELENDEZ, Sec., Tel: 787-754-8383; VACANT, Spiritual Dir.

Union Eucaristica Reparadora (UNER)—Rev. VICTORIANO RAMOS, Spiritual Dir., (Retired); MRS. MARIA MERCEDES MAIZ, Dir., Cond. El Paraiso, 7-D Calle Parania 1560, San Juan, 00926. Tel: 787-751-1821; MRS. ESTHER VARGAS, Urb. Ponce de Leon, Calle 23 #250, Guaynabo, 00969. Tel: 787-789-6660; DOLLIE MORALES; MARIZA BELARANA; LUIGUI BENITEZ; SONIA RENIOS.

Consejo Arquidioceseano De Accion Social (CASA)—MR. MIGUEL A. RODRIGUEZ, Coord., Apartado 31164, San Juan, 00929. Tel: 787-605-9292.

Sociedad San Vicente De Paul—MRS. CARMEN E. ARROYO, Calle Rafallar 566, Urb. La Merced, San Juan, 00918.

Maranatha House of Prayer—SILVIA SAAVEDRA DE BADIA, Dir., Urb. La Arboleda, Calle Alameda B #13, Guaynabo, 00966. Tel: 787-759-7734; Email: cmaranatha@prw.net; Web: www.casamaranathapr.org; Rev. BAUDILIO GUZMAN, S.J., Dir. Esp.

Cofradia De Los Santos Angeles De La Guarda—MARIA T. PAGAN, Pres., Urb. Colinas Verdes, A-43 Calle 1, San Juan, 00924.

Cofradia Peregrinos De Tierra Santa—Deacon ANGEL ANTONIO NIEVES COLON, #1214 Paseo Doncella, Toa Baja, 00949. Tel: 787-948-1512.

Grupo Devocion Divina Misericordia—Deacon JULIO SANCHEZ, Oficina Diaconal, Caparra Heights, Calle Encarnacion 1564, San Juan, 00920-4739. Tel: 787-720-5714.

Grupos Para La Juventud—

Consejo Arquidiocesano De Pastoral Juvenil—VACANT.

Grupo Juvenil Damasco—GEORGIE FERNANDEZ, Dir., Mailing Address: P.O. Box 360764, San Juan, 00936. Tel: 787-281-0707 (Office); Tel: 787-706-8906 (Res.); Fax: 787-281-0708.

Grupos De Retiros—

Grupo de Retiros Paz y Bien—Sr. OSVALDO ROMAN, Dir., Urb. Levittown, 1418 Paseo Delfin, Toa Baja, 00949. Tel: 787-784-5579.

Juventud Mariana Vicenciana (JMV)—MISS DAMARIS RIVERA, Dir., Seminario San Vicente De Paul, Ave Ponce de Leon, 1711 Pda. 26, Santurce, San Juan, 00909. Tel: 787-727-3963; Sr. MILAGROS OLIVENCIA, H.C., Archdiocesan Representative, Hospital Auxilio Mutuo.

Asociacion De Profesionales Catolicos—MR. JOSE VARELA, Committee Coord., Tel: 787-738-5189; LELIS RODRIGUEZ, Tel: 787-565-4884; Email: lelis@onelinkpr.net.

Hermandad Ntra. Sra. De La Caridad—Mailing

Address: P.O. Box 32, Guaynabo, 00970-0032. CALLE S. PEDRO MARTIR, Tel: 787-720-2361; Rev. Msgr. MARIO GUIJARRO, Dir. Espiritual; VACANT, Dir., P.O. Box 10151, San Juan, 00922-0151. Tel: 787-783-3522.

Movimiento Juan XXIII—MR. ANGEL L. RIOS, Pres., Villa Contessa, F35 Calle Aragon, Bayamon, 00976. Tel: 787-787-5984; Fax: 787-785-1024.

Movimiento De Schoenstatt—MR. MARIO SANCHEZ; MRS. MARIO SANCHEZ, Urb. Pinero, 12 Calle Alanebra, San Juan, 00917-3128.

World Apostolate of Fatima—Prof. AMERICO LOPEZ-ORTIZ, Intl. Pres.; Rev. Msgr. FERNANDO B. FELICES-SANCHEZ, Spiritual Dir., Mailing Address: P.O. Box 1968, Fernandez Juncos Sta., Mayaguez, 00681-1968. Tel: 787-833-0509; Tel: 787-487-5383; Email: alfatima@coqui.net; Web: www.apostoladomundialdefatima.org.

Neocatecumenal Way—Deacon JULIO ALVAREZ, Dir., Urb. El Conquistador, F-7 Calle 8, Trujillo Alto, 00976. Tel: 787-761-1667.

Our Lady of Providence Association—VACANT.

Perpetual Adoration—MRS. VIRGINIA ALVAREZ, Asst., Mailing Address: Box S-763, San Juan, 00902. Tel: 787-725-7734.

Padre Nuestro—MR. SAMUEL VALENTIN, Pres., Urb. Las Colinas, Calle 6, F. 35, Toa Baja, 00949. Tel: 787-368-3810.

Movimiento De Seglares Claretianos—MRS. CARMEN SANCHEZ, Dir., San Antonio Maria Claret Parish. Tel: 787-797-3337.

Apostolado Del Cenaculo Misionero—Rev. VICENTE PASQUALETTO, S.T., Spiritual Dir.; MRS. ALMA ROBLES, Urb. Los Colobos, Calle Robles #516, Carolina, 00987. Tel: 787-752-9327; Tel: 787-876-0827.

Conferencia Mariana De Puerto Rico—MR. RICARDO HERNANDEZ; MRS. RICARDO HERNANDEZ. Spiritual Directors: Rev. Msgr. FERNANDO B. FELICES-SANCHEZ; Rev. RICARDO HERNANDEZ MORALES.

CLERGY, PARISHES, MISSIONS AND PAROCHIAL SCHOOLS

CITY OF SAN JUAN

1—CATEDRAL DE SAN JUAN BAUTISTA (1522) (Nuestra Sra. de los Remedios).
151 Cristo St., P.O. Box 9022145, 00902-2145.
Tel: 787-722-0861; Email: catedral1521@gmail.com. Revs. Benjamin Antonio Perez Cruz; Ernesto Gonzalez Gonzalez, Pastoral Assoc.; Deacons Louis Marin; Angel Antonio Nieves Colon; Roberto Gonzalez Rosado.
Chapels—Santo Cristo—
San Jose
Tel: 787-725-7501.
Santa Ana.

2—ASUNCION DE LA VIRGEN (1972)
Urb. Antonsanti, Calle Calve No. 1484, Rio Piedras, 00927. Tel: 787-250-6771; Email: 100.asuncion@gmail.com. Rev. Jose Carrion Leyva, Admin.

3—CORPUS CHRISTI (1972)
Calle Jose Abad, 1224 Urb. Club Manor, 00924.
Tel: 787-757-5821; Email: jjffquintero23@gmail.com. Rev. Jose Francisco Quintero-Angueira; Rev. Deacons Luis Aparicio; Juan Minier; Francisco Gierbolini; Jose Perez; Luis Fernando Amador; Luis Ramon Perez-Aviles.
Mission—Santo Domingo de Guzman
Carretera 849 Km. 8.7, Sector Santo Domingo, Penuelas Co.

4—CRISTO REDENTOR (1971)
Urb. El Paraiso, 140 Calle Ganges, 00926-2928.
Tel: 787-946-1999; Email: pangelciappi@me.com. Rev. Angel L. Ciappi-Azcorra.

5—CRISTO REY (1956)
Mailing Address: Urb. Los Maestros, 789 Calle Jaime Drew, 00923. Tel: 787-767-3289; Email: parroquiacristorey2014@outlook.com. Rev. Msgr. Manuel Garcia-Perez; Deacons Victor Reyes; Miguel Roman Del Valle.

6—ESPIRITU SANTO (1941)
Mailing Address: P.O. Box 190259, 00919-0259.
Tel: 787-754-0570; Email: director@colespiritusanto.com. Urb Floral Park, Calle Ruiz Belvis 75, Hato Rey, 00919. Rev. Msgr. Valeriano Miguélez, (Spain).
School—Espiritu Santo School
P.O. Box 191715, 00917. Tel: 787-754-0490;
Tel: 787-754-0555; Fax: 787-754-7154. Mrs. Milagros Zurkowsky, Assoc. Prin. Lay Teachers 35; Priests 1; Students 450.

7—FRANCISCA JAVIERA CABRINI (1968) (Mother Cabrini) Rev. Joaquin Mayorga Fonseca.
Res.: 1564 Encarnacion St., 00920. Tel: 787-783-7447; Fax: 787-706-2073.
Catechesis Religious Program—Students 90.

8—INMACULADO CORAZON DE MARIA (1961)
Urb. Santiago Iglesias, #1740 Calle Rodriguez Vera, 00921-3625. Tel: 787-782-0245; Fax: 787-782-4176; Email: corazondemaria1704@hotmail.com; Web: inmaculadocorazon.tripod.com. Rev. Carlos Dionisio Cruz-Davila; Deacons Benjamin Antonio Ramos Rivera; Israel Suarez; Benjamin Totti Lugo.
Res.: Rodriguez Vera y Ferrer St., Urb. Santiago Iglesias, 00922.
Catechesis Religious Program—Students 112.
Mission—Capilla
San Fernando, San Juan.
Chapel—Ntra. Sra. del Camino, Metropolitan Hospital, [JC].

9—JESUS MAESTRO (1969)
Urb. Rio Piedras Heights, 1725 Segre, 00926-3246.
Tel: 787-763-8291; Email: oficina@parroquiajm.org. Rev. Jean Rolex.
Mission—Jesus Nazareno
Calle Guadiana #1666, Urb. El Cerezal, 00926.

10—JESUS MEDIADOR (1988)
Urb. Country Club, 1000 Calle Demetrio O'Daly, 00924. Tel: 787-752-2410; Email: parroquiajesusmediador@yahoo.com. Rev. Jan Krol, C.S.M.A.; Deacons Candido Martinez; Edwin Rivera; Santiago Roman Ramirez.

11—MARIA AUXILIADORA (1962)
Mailing Address: P.O. Box 14367, 00916-4367.
Tel: 787-727-5346; Email: cancilleria2018@arqsj.org. Cantera, Calle Constitucion Esq Santa Elena, 00915. Revs. Mario Leonardo Hernandez; Carlos Piantini, Pastoral Assoc.; Nicolas Navarro Quintana, S.D.B., In Res.; Bro. Jose Cabo.
Catechesis Religious Program—
Missions—Sagrado Corazon—
Sector Buenavista.
Nra. Sra. del Altagracia
Sector Buenavista.
Ntra. Sra. de Fatima
Sector Ultimo Chance-Cerro.
Santisima Trinidad
Ave. Borinquen Final.

12—MARIA MADRE DE LA IGLESIA (1967)
Urb. Villa Nevarez, 1120 Calle 5, 00927.
Tel: 787-765-0600; Email: parrmmiglesia@yahoo.com; Email: tggonzalez@yahoo.com. Rev. Tomas Gonzalez-Gonzalez.

13—MARIA REINA DEL MUNDO (1971)
Mailing Address: G.P.O. Box 3828, 00936-3828.
Tel: 787-781-0303; Fax: 787-781-0303. Rev. Mariano Martínez Galvez, O.M.I.
Res.: Caserio Nemesio Canales, Roosevelt Ave., 00936.
Catechesis Religious Program—Students 20.

14—NTRA. SRA. DE LA CARIDAD DEL COBRE (1969)
Urb. Buena Vista, Calle 5, No. 124, 00917.
Tel: 787-777-8696; Email: pfeedie@yahoo.com; Email: lbriosotex@yahoo.com. P.O. Box 194649, 00919-4649. Rev. Luis R. Brioso Texidor.
Mission—Sma. Trinidad
Calle Buenos Aires, No. 25, Parada 27, Hato Rey, San Juan Co. 00919.

15—NTRA. SRA. DE FATIMA (1967)
Urb Baldrich, Ave Munoz Rivera 608, P.O. Box 190396, 00919-0396. Tel: 787-753-6334;
Fax: 787-764-3571; Email: pnsdefatima@yahoo.com. Rev. Elias Lorenzana Fernandez, O.de.M., (Spain).
School—La Merced (1949)
P.O. Box 364048, 00936-4048. Tel: 787-765-7342;
Tel: 787-754-1162; Fax: 787-765-3970. Mrs. Rosa M. Figueroa, Prin. Lay Teachers 36; Students 485.
Mission—Egida del Maestro.

16—NTRA. SRA. DE LA MEDALLA MILAGROSA (1957)
Mailing Address: Urb. Perez Moris, 209 Calle Mayaguez, 00917-5147. Tel: 787-751-2335; Email: lamilagrosahatorey@hotmail.com. Rev. Carlos Verdia Nay.

17—NTRA. SRA. DE LA MONSERRATE (1919)
Mailing Address: P.O. Box 13726, 00908-3726.
Tel: 787-722-3134; Fax: 787-723-7838. Rev. Antonio Then De la Cruz, O.S.A.
Res.: 1058 Fernandez Juncos Ave., 00907. Email: wwthen@hotmail.com.
School—Santa Monica School
Tel: 787-723-2573 (Elem.); Tel: 787-723-3845 (H.S.);
Fax: 787-723-3992.
Catechesis Religious Program—Students 14.
Mission—Santa Ana
Santurce, San Juan Co. 00908.

18—NTRA. SRA. DEL PERPETUO SOCORRO (1941) Rev. Msgr. Jose Emilio Cummings-Espada.
Res.: Calle Marti 704, Miramar, Santurce, 00907-3227. Tel: 787-721-1015; Tel: 787-721-1016.
School—Ntra. Sra. del Perpetuo Socorro School
Jose Marti St. 704, 00907. Tel: 787-724-1447;
Tel: 787-721-4540; Fax: 787-725-8104 (Elem.);
Fax: 787-723-4550 (H.S.). Dr. Angel Cintron, Prin. Lay Teachers 126; Priests 1; Students 1,210.

19—NUESTRA SENORA DE BELEN (1960)
Mailing Address: P.O. Box 10845, 00922-0845.
Tel: 787-793-2485; Fax: 787-792-8541. Rev. Reinaldo Sagardia.
Res.: Calle Jacinto Galib Final, Ave. San Patricio, Guaynabo.

20—NUESTRA SENORA DE LA ALTAGRACIA (1958)
Mailing Address: Apartado 29493, 00929-0493.
Tel: 787-451-5927; Tel: 787-590-2022; Email: altagraciapr04@yahoo.com. Urb Villa Prades, Calle Felipe Gutierrez #672, 00924. Rev. Jorge Ernesto Torres-Rivera; Deacons Hector Rivera; Jorge Camacho; Freddie Acevedo Toledo.
Catechesis Religious Program—
Tel: 787-764-0614. Students 376.

21—NUESTRA SENORA DE LA CARIDAD DEL COBRE, Rev. Pedro Luis Zaballa; Deacon Manuel Duprey.
Res.: Urb. La Riviera, Calle 3 S.O. 1027, 00921-2517.
Tel: 787-792-2640; Email: luciagu@arqsj.org.

22—NUESTRA SENORA DE LA ESPERANZA (1962)
Mailing Address: P.O. Box 8532, Fernandez Juncos Sta., 00910-8532. Tel: 787-723-5998; Email: virgenmariadelaesperanza@gmail.com. Urb Hipodromo, Calle Republica 864, 00910. Rev. Miguel Rivera-Borges.
Mission—Ntra. Sra. de la Providencia
Barriada Figueroa.
Chapel—Doctors Hospital
Tel: 787-723-2950; Fax: 787-721-3155.

23—NUESTRA SENORA DE LA MERCED (1940)
Mailing Address: P.O. Box 364133, 00936-4133.
Tel: 787-763-3657; Email: lamercedhr@yahoo.com. Urb Roosevelt, Calle Pedro Espada 430, 00918. Rev. Ramon Conde-Ocampo, O.M., (Spain).
Catechesis Religious Program—Students 50.

24—NUESTRA SENORA DE LA PIEDAD (1956)
Mailing Address: P.O. Box 79520, Carolina, 00984. Email: lapiedad_cp@yahoo.com. 1001 Marginal Baldorioty de Castro, Ext Villamar A B-1, Carolina, 00979. Revs. Aribal Rodriguez Sr.; Manuel Elejalde, C.P.; Jesús Etxeandia Ormaetzea, C.P., Supr.; Florencio Landa, C.P., (Spain).
School—Nuestra Senora de la Piedad School
Tel: 787-727-7585 (H.S.); Tel: 787-727-2460 (Elem.);
Fax: 787-268-0664 (H.S.); Fax: 787-728-0125 (Elem.).
Mrs. Lizette Matos, Prin.; Rev. Florencio Landa, C.P., (Spain) Dir. Priests 1.

25—NUESTRA SENORA DE LA PROVIDENCIA (1959)
Urb. San Gerardo, 1730 Santa Agueda St., Rio Piedras, 00926. Tel: 787-765-6240; Tel: 787-767-6755; Email: academialaprovidencia@gmail.com. Rev. Msgr. Baudilio Merino Merino, (Spain); Deacons Luis Vazquez; Ricardo Martinez.
School—Nuestra Senora de la Providencia School
Carretera #176, Km. 2.7, Calle Santa Agueda 1733, Urb. San Gerardo, Rio Piedras, 00926.
Tel: 787-767-6552; Tel: 787-767-6755. Yolanda I. Martínez, Prin. Lay Teachers 21; Students 247.
Catechesis Religious Program—Students 247.

26—NUESTRA SENORA DE LA PROVIDENCIA (1973) Rev. Olin Pierre-Louis.
Res. & Mailing Address: 219 Aponte St., 00912.
Tel: 787-727-1878.

27—NUESTRA SENORA DE LOURDES (1969)
P.O. Box 14452, Bo. Obrero Sta., 00916-4452.
Tel: 787-726-4643; Email: lourdes.villapalmeras@gmail.com. Villa Palmeras, Esq. Calle Colton 288, Ave Gilberto Monroig, 00915. Deacon Manuel Duprey.

28—NUESTRA SENORA DEL CARMEN (1923)
Ave Borinquen, Esq Calle Tapia 609, Barrio Obrero, P.O. Box 7275, 00916-7275. Tel: 787-727-0737;
Fax: 787-728-4860; Email: pnsdelcarmenbo@gmail.com. Rev. Giovanni Perez Berrios; Deacon Jose Corazon De Jesus.
Missions—Capilla Sagrado Corazon—
Universidad del Sagrado Corazon, 00916.
San Martin de Porres
Calle: Tito Rodriguez #719 Barrio Obrero, Barrio Obrero, 00916.

29—NUESTRA SENORA DEL PILAR (1714)
Plaza de Recreo, Rio Piedras, Box 21134, 00928-1134. Tel: 787-764-5088; Email: elpilarriopiedras@gmail.com. Revs. Carlos Gonzalez Santiago; Oscar Granados Del Valle; Deacon Jose L. Velazquez-González.
Catechesis Religious Program—Sr. Manuela Corona Moncilla, D.R.E.
Mission—Santa Teresita de Nino Jesus
Calle, Tanque #37, Barriada Venezuela, Rio Piedras, San Juan Co. 00925.
Chapel—Hogar Crea
Barriada Venezuela. Tel: 787-751-5640.

30—NTRA. SRA. DE GUADALUPE (1951)
Mailing Address: G.P.O. Box 364125, 00936-4125.
Tel: 787-782-0016; Fax: 787-782-0016. Rev. Neil Macaulay, O.M.I., (Canada). In Res., Rev. Mariano Martínez Galvez, O.M.I.

Res.: Calle 19 N.E. No. 1, Puerto Nuevo, 00920.
School—Ntra. Sra. de Guadalupe School
Tel: 787-782-0330; Fax: 787-782-0454. Mrs. Genevieve Zayas, Prin. Lay Teachers 35; Students 530.
Catechesis Religious Program—Students 73.

31—RESURRECCION DEL SENOR (1968) Revs. Isaac Gonzalez-Saldana, O.F.M.; Esteban Melians-Figueredo, O.F.M., Tel: ; Mariano Errasti, O.F.M.; Alfonso Guzman-Alfaro, O.F.M.; Deacon Jose M. Sanchez.
Res. & Mailing Address: Calle 31, S.O. #797, Urb. Las Lomas, 00921-1205. Tel: 787-792-5939.

32—SAGRADA FAMILIA (1971)
Parcelas Hill Brothers, Calle 7 #112 Ave 65 Inf., P.O. Box 29311, 00929-9311. Tel: 787-767-1723; Email: padrerafaelgarcia@gmail.com. Rev. Rafael Garcia-Molina.
Catechesis Religious Program—Students 2.

33—SAGRADO CORAZON DE JESUS (1971)
Calle Oxford 251, Esq. Howard Urb. University Gardens, 00927. Tel: 787-765-4798; Email: info@psagradocorazon.org. Revs. Jose Santos Nunez, C.M.F., (Spain); Anulfo Del Rosario Sosa, C.M., (Dominican Republic) Pastoral Assoc.
School—Sagrado Corazon de Jesus School
Esq. Iteramericana y Palma Real: Urb. University Gardens, Rio Piedras, 00927-4826. Tel: 787-765-9430 ; Fax: 787-765-5267.
Catechesis Religious Program—Students 37.

34—SAGRADO CORAZON DE JESUS (1909)
Mailing Address: F. Juncos Sta., Box 8312, 00910-8312. Rev. Miguel Rivera-Borges; Deacon Pedro Nel Arevalo Hernandez.
Res.: Ponce de Leon Ave., #1308, Stop 19, Santurce, 00910. Tel: 787-722-0235; Fax: 787-722-4845.

35—SAN AGUSTIN (1889)
Ave. Constitucion 265, Puerto de Tierra, P.O. Box 9024108, 00902-4108. Tel: 787-722-4289; Email: sanagustiniglesia@yahoo.com. Rev. Esteban De la Rosa-Martinez, C.Ss.R.; Deacon Jorge Colon Velez. In Res., Revs. P. Manuel Rodriguez, C.Ss.R.; Damian Wall, C.Ss.R.; Hector Colon, C.Ss.R.
School—Colegio San Agustin
255 Constitution Ave., Box 9024078, 00902-4078. Tel: 787-722-4544; Fax: 787-977-1700. Marie Benitez Alonso, Prin. Lay Teachers 7; Students 53.
Catechesis Religious Program—Students 11.

36—SAN ANTONIO DE PADUA (1908) [JC]
P.O. Box 21350, 00928-1350. Tel: 787-765-0606; Email: sanantoniopr@gmail.com. Calle Arzuaga # 218, 00925. Rev. Ramon J. Casellas Rivera, O.F.M.-Cap.; Friars Carlos Reyes, Pastoral Assoc.; Jose Villaran, Pastoral Assoc.
Res.: Calle Arzuaga #218, Esq. Frailes Capuchinos, Aptdo. 25177, 00928. Tel: 787-765-8247 (Convent); Fax: 787-765-1180; Fax: 787-763-9832 (Convent).
School—San Antonio de Padua School
Tel: 787-764-0090; Fax: 787-763-7592. Sisters 1.
Catechesis Religious Program—Students 863.
Mission—Nuestra Senora del Buen Consejo
Calle De Diego, 00928.

37—SAN FRANCISCO DE ASIS (1858)
301 San Francisco St., Viejo San Juan, Box 9024231, 00902-4231. Tel: 787-724-1131; Email: sanfrancisco.vsj@gmail.com. Friars Luis Gonzalez, O.F.M.Cap.; Roberto Martinez Rivera, Pastoral Assoc.
Catechesis Religious Program—Students 12.
Mission—Capilla San Conrado
Bo. La Perla, 00902.

38—SAN FRANCISCO DE MONTE ALVERNIA (1985)
Calle 10, #15 Ext. San Agustin, 00926.
Tel: 787-765-8824; Email: perezjuansilva@gmail.com. Deacon Juan B. Perez Silva, Admin.

39—SAN FRANCISCO JAVIER (1967)
Urb. Fair View, Calle 19, G46., 00926.
Tel: 787-761-2115; Email: oficina@sanfj.com. Rev. Jose Maria Solano-Uribe, (Colombia); Deacons Jose Hernandez; Fernando M. Padilla Nazario; Raul A. Perez Gonzalez; Edwin R. Torregrosa-Ochoa.
Catechesis Religious Program—Students 150.

40—SAN IGNACIO DE LOYOLA (1956) Revs. Lawrence Searles-Revels, S.J.; Samuel Wilson, S.J.; Deacon Carmelo Rivera.
Res. & Mailing Address: Urb. Santa Maria, 1904 Calle Narciso, 00927-6706. Tel: 787-293-7960; Tel: 787-751-7512; Fax: 787-751-7000; Email: parroquiasanignaciopr@hotmail.com.
School—Academia San Ignacio de Loyola
1908 Calle Narciso, Rio Piedras, 00936.
Tel: 787-765-8190; Fax: 787-765-3635. Glorimar Soegaard, Prin. Students 631.
Chapel—Cond. Jardines de San Francisco.

41—SAN JORGE (1965)
Calle San Jorge 157, Santurce, P.O. Box 6427, Loiza Sta, 00914-6427. Tel: 787-724-7780; Email: sanjorgeparroquiapr@gmail.com. Rev. Pedro L. Reyes-Lebron.

42—SAN JOSE (Villa Caparra) (1948) Rev. Ricardo Hernandez Morales. In Res., Rev. Jose Miguel Cardona Matta.
Res.: Villa Caparra, 215 Carr. #2, Guaynabo, 00966-1915. Tel: 787-781-1155; Email: psanjosevc@yahoo.com.
School—San Jose School
Tel: 787-781-1212; Fax: 787-792-7440 (Elem.). Emma Morales Hernandez, Prin. (Elementary), Dir. Assoc.; Sr. John Christian, Prin. (High School). Lay Teachers 29; Priests 1; Sisters 2; Students 279.

43—SAN JOSE OBRERO (1956)
Mailing Address: Calle Belmonte 470, 00923.
Tel: 787-767-1448; Fax: 787-753-5392; Email: proyjose@coqui.net. Rev. Rogelio Salazar-Valero, (Mexico).
Res.: Urb. San Jose, Calle Belmonte 470, Rio Piedras, 00923.
Catechesis Religious Program—Students 65.
Mission—San Antonio Ma. Claret
Embalse Sector.

44—SAN JUAN BOSCO (1945)
P.O. Box 14125, Barrio Obrero Sta., 00916-4125.
Tel: 787-727-2187; Email: cancilleria2018@arqsj.org. Villa Palmeras, Calle Lutz 368, 00915. Rev. Andres Rivera Vazquez.
Res.: 370 Lutz St., Villa Palmeras, 00915.
Tel: 787-726-7317; Fax: 787-726-1420.
Missions—La Milagrosa—
Villa Palmeras, C. Lutz 300 Final, Santurce, Mayaguez Co. 00915. Tel: 787-728-2175; Fax: 787-726-7313.
Ntra. Sra. del Rosario
Fajardo St., 00915.
San Martin de Porres
Union St. #58, Playita, Yabucoa Co. 00915.

45—SAN JUAN DE LA CRUZ (1990)
PMB 216, Urb La Cumbre, Calle Sierra Morena, 00926-5583. Tel: 787-526-1779; Email: parroquiasanjuandelacruz@life.com. Urb. Borinquen Gardens, Calle Julio Rueda 1925, 00926. Rev. Jose-Juan Cardona Diaz; Deacons Jorge Colon Velez; Luis Francisco Hernandez; Omar Santamarina.

46—SAN JUAN M. VIANNEY (1972) (Santo Cura de Ars)
Urb Garcia Calle, Calle A- 12, 00932.
Tel: 787-980-8515; Email: cancilleria2018@arqsj.org. Rev. Luis Norberto Correa-Garcia; Deacon Manuel Andino.
Res. & Mailing Address: Calle 2, F-14, Urb. Hillside, 00926. Tel: 787-585-3495; Email: ncorrea78@yahoo.com.
Missions—La Milagrosa—
Urb Hillside Calle 2 I 14, San Juan Co. 00926.
Cristo del Perdon
Parcelas Canejas, Bo. Caimito Bajo.
Dulce Nombre de Maria
Bo. Dulce, Caimito Bajo.
Ntra. Sra. del Carmen
Calle Fidalgo, Sector Corea, Bo. Caimito Bajo.

47—SAN LUCAS (1972)
Urb. El Senorial, Calle Pio Baroja 380, 00926.
Tel: 787-761-5476; Email: psanlucas.evangelista@gmail.com. Rev. Ramon Orlando Tirado.
Catechesis Religious Program—Students 72.

48—SAN LUIS GONZAGA (1965)
Urb. Villa Andalucia, Calle Ronda A-17, 00926.
Tel: 787-761-9438; Email: parroquiasanluisgonzaga1965@gmail.com. Rev. Victor Modesto Torres-Cesneros, (Panama).

49—SAN LUIS REY (1968)
Mailing Address: Urb. Reparto Metropolitano, 869 Calle 43 S.E., Ste. #65, 00921. Rev. Marco Antonio Rivera-Perez; Deacon Carlos J. Amador-Hernandez.
Res.: Calle 43 S.E. Final, Urb. Reparto Metropolitano, Rio Piedras, 00921. Tel: 787-767-6235 ; Fax: 787-767-6235; Email: psanluisrey869@gmail.com.

50—SAN MATEO (1773)
Mailing Address: P.O. Box 6081, 00914-6081.
Tel: 787-722-4158. Calle San Mateo, Esq San Jorge, 00912. Rev. Olin Pierre Louis.
Res.: Calle San Mateo, Esq. San Jorge, Stop 25, Santurce, 00912.

51—SAN PABLO (1965) Rev. Msgr. Francisco Medina Santos.
Res.: Duero St., No. 370, Urb. Villa Borinquen, 00920. Tel: 787-755-7788; Email: parrsanpapostolpn@arqsj.org.
Mission—Ntra. Sra. de la Caridad
Del Cobre Borinquen Towers, San Juan Co. 00920.

52—SAN VICENTE DE PAUL (1940) [CEM]
Mailing Address: P.O. Box 19118, 00910-0118.
Tel: 787-727-3963; Fax: 787-726-7986. Rev. Marion Poncette, C.M.
Res.: 1650 Ave Fernandez Juncos, Stop 24, Santurce, 00910. Fax: 787-728-0670.
School—San Vicente de Paul School
709 Bolivar St., Box 8699, 00910. Tel: 787-727-4273; Fax: 787-728-2263. Emilio Roldan, Prin. Lay Teachers 23; Students 380.
Catechesis Religious Program—Students 36.

53—SANTA BERNARDITA SOUBIROUS (1982)
Mailing Address: P.O. Box 29826, 65 Infanteria Sta., 00929-9826. Tel: 787-762-0375; Tel: 787-257-7643; Fax: 787-757-6642; Email: santabernarditapr@yahoo.com; Web: www.parroquiasantabernardita.org. Urb Country Club, Calle Espioncela y Torcaza, 00929. Rev. Msgr. Wilfredo Pena-Moredo; Deacon Ernesto Rivera Negron.

54—SANTA CATALINA LABOURE (1977)
Mailing Address: P.M.B. 507, 267 Calle Sierra Morena, 00926-5583. Tel: 787-720-0303; Fax: 787-731-7166; Email: eusebiocfernandez@yahoo.com. Carr 842 KM 3.6, Barrio Caimito, 00926. Rev. Eusebio C. Fernandez Salazar, (Colombia).
Missions—Medalla Milagrosa—
Barrio Los Romeros, Bo. Caimito 00926-5636.
San Pablo
Carretera 842, Bo. Caimito 00926.

55—SANTA CECILIA (1969)
El Senorial Sta., P.O. Box 415, 00926-0415.
Tel: 787-755-8670; Email: danilo.martinezduarte@gmail.com. Urb Riveras de Cupey, Ave Ceciliana #1, 00926. Rev. Danilo Martinez; Deacon Victor Merced de la Paz.
Catechesis Religious Program—Students 33.
Chapels—Hogar Santa Teresa Jornet—
Tel: 787-761-5805; Fax: 787-755-5575.
Capilla San Agustin
Carretera 844, Cupey Bajo.

56—SANTA LUISA DE MARILLAC (1962)
PMB 17, 267 Calle Sierra Moreno, 00926-5583.
Tel: 787-720-3150; Fax: 787-200-6227; Email: parroquiasantaluisademarillac2@gmail.com. Urb. La Cumbre Ave., Emiliano Pol, 00926. Rev. Alberto Arturo Figueroa-Morales; Deacons Francisco Colon; Eddie Lopez Alonso.

57—SANTA MARIA DE LOS ANGELES (1954)
Mailing Address: Box 10716, 00922-0716.
Tel: 787-792-2640; Fax: 787-792-2640. Rev. Miguel Angel Trinidad-Fonseca; Deacons Rafael Reyes Crespo; George Echautegui-Ramos.
Res.: De Diego Ave., No. 930, Urb. La Rivera, Rio Piedras, 00936.

58—SANTA ROSA DE LIMA (1971)
Urb. Venus Gardens, 1765 Calle Lesbos, 00926-4843.
Tel: 787-761-6586; Email: santarosadelimapr@yahoo.com; Web: santarosadelimapr.blogspot.com. Rev. Carlos Perez Toro; Deacons Pedro Costa; Jose R. Amezaga; Edwin Rodriguez; Jose A. Torres.

59—SANTA TERESA DE JESUS JORNET (1985)
Mailing Address: El Senorial Mail Sta., P.O. Box 415, 00926-0415. Tel: 787-748-2978; Email: pstdj@gmail.com. Carr 176 Km 10.0, Camino Los Gonzalez, Cupey Alto, 00926. Rev. Leonardo Rodriguez-Ochoa; Deacons Vicente Lasanta; Martin Cuevas.
Missions—San Martin de Porres—
Camino El Mudo. Cupey, Alto, 00926.
Ntra. Sra. de la Salud
Camino Guayabos Carr. 176, Km. 9.5, Cupey, Alto, 00926.
Parroquia Santa Teresa de Jesus Jornet, [CEM]
Camino Los Gonzalez, Km. 5.3.

60—SANTA TERESITA DEL NINO JESUS (1930)
Mailing Address: P.O. Box 6065, Loiza Sta., 00914-6065. Revs. Luis M. Miranda Rivera, O.Carm.; Feliz Antonio Rivera Rivera, O.Carm.; Jose Maldonado Vazquez, O.Carm.
Res.: 2059 Loiza St., 00911-1799. Tel: 787-727-0181; Tel: 787-727-0030; Fax: 787-728-0056; Email: tmgf@prmail.net; Web: www.parroquiasantateresita.com.
Mission—Sagrada Familia
Residencial, Luis Llorens Torres, San Juan Co. 00913. Tel: 809-726-0570.

61—SANTISIMO SALVADOR (1966)
Urb. Villa Capri, Niza St., 575, 00924.
Tel: 787-761-3314; Email: parroquiadelsalvador@gmail.com. Revs. Cecilio LaCruz, Sch.P., (Spain); Agustin Lopez, Sch.P., (Spain); Juan L. Cabrerizo, Sch.P., (Spain); Deacons Luis A. Medina; Luis O. del Rio.
School—Calasanz (1968)
Ave. Montecarlo, Esq. Z, Urb. Montecarlo, P.O. Box 29067, 00929-0067. Tel: 787-750-2500; Fax: 787-257-0450. Ana Celia Santos, Prin. (High School); Glenda Laureano, Prin. (Elementary). Lay Teachers 25; Priests 3; Students 341.
Catechesis Religious Program—Students 65.
Missions—Ntra. Sra. Reina de la Paz—
Calle #1 Esq. C-8 Urb. Berwind States, Rio Piedras, San Juan Co. 00924.
San Jose de Calasanz
Calle #23 408, Parc. Hills Brothers, Rio Piedras, San Juan Co. 00924.

62—SANTISMO SACRAMENTO (1967)
Urb. Matienzo Cintron, 500 Jerusalem St., Rio Piedras, 00923. Tel: 787-764-3438; Email: rogersalazarvalero@yahoo.com. Rev. Rogelio Salazar-Valero, (Mexico).
Catechesis Religious Program—Students 40.

63—SANTOS PEDRO Y PABLO LOS APOSTOLES (1980)
Urb Jardines de Berwind, Calle 1 Lote K, P.O. Box

30666, 00929-1666. Tel: 787-226-7616; Email: padrerafaelgarcia@gmail.com. Rev. Rafael Garcia-Molina.
Res.: Urb. Jardines De Berwind, Calle Las Casitas, Lote K, 65 Infanteria, Rio Piedras, 00929.
Tel: 787-768-1424.
64—STELLA MARIS (1965) Rev. Msgr. Antonio Jose Vazquez Colon. In Res., Revs. Ovidio Ortega Lemus, (Cuba); Enrique Manuel Camacho-Monserrate.
Res.: 69 Cervantes St., Condado, San Juan, 00907-1947. Tel: 787-723-2240; Tel: 787-723-2359;
Fax: 787-722-3200.

OUTSIDE THE CITY OF SAN JUAN

BAYAMON
1—ASCENSION DEL SENOR (1984)
Mailing Address: P.O. Box 3367, Bayamon, 00958-3367. Tel: 787-799-6120; Fax: 787-730-7389; Email: trinita@prtc.net. Rev. Pedro Gorena, O.SS.T., (Spain).
Res.: Calle 31, Final, Urb. Rexville, Bayamon, 00957.
Catechesis Religious Program—Tel: 787-380-0626. Estrella Rios, D.R.E. Students 175.
2—CATALINA DE SIENA (1963)
Mailing Address: Urb Hnas Davila, Q-3 Calle 10, Bayamon, 00959. Tel: 787-785-2381; Email: psantacatalina@gmail.com. Rev. Silvestre Gomez-Rueda, O.P.; Deacon Jose Rios.
Catechesis Religious Program—Students 94.
3—CRISTO SALVADOR (1998)
Mailing Address: PMB 464, P.O. Box 7891, Guaynabo, 00970-7891. Rev. Luis Felipe Rodriguez Garnica.
Church: Parroquia Cristo Salvador, Guaynabo, 00970. Tel: 787-720-6596; Tel: 787-309-2448;
Fax: 787-720-6596; Email: cristosalvador08@hotmail.com.
4—ESPIRITU SANTO (2002)
Urb Bella Vista Gardens, Y-300 Calle 24, Bayamon, 00957. Tel: 787-799-8604; Tel: 787-799-6120; Email: espiritusantobayamon@gmail.com. Rev. Johnny Cruz Velazquez, Admin.
5—INVENCION DE LA SANTA CRUZ (1772)
12 Degetau St., Bayamon, 00961. Tel: 787-785-2134; Email: parr.delasantacruz@gmail.com. Rev. Marcos Espinel Arauzo, O.P., (Spain).
6—LA RESURRECCION DEL SENOR (1987)
Urb. Royal Town, F-1 Calle 12, Bayamon, 00956.
Tel: 787-688-8558; Email: resurreccionroyaltown@gmail.com. Rev. Edwin A. Cruz Garcia; Deacons Nicanor Mercado; Jose Rosario Rivera.
Catechesis Religious Program—Students 60.
7—NTRA. SRA. DE LA MONSERRATE (1985)
Mailing Address: P.O. Box 3948, Bayamon, 00958-3948. Tel: 787-797-7340; Email: lamonserrate.bayamonpr@gmail.com. Bo Santa Olaya, Carr 829 KM 6.2, Bayamon, 00956. Revs. Antonio Then De la Cruz, O.S.A.; Domingo Aller, O.S.A., (Spain) Vicar.
Missions—Cristo Rey—Bo. Guaraguao, Sector La Morenita.
Santa Monica, Bo. Guaraguao, Sector Pena, Bayamon, Bayamon Co. 00619.
Ntra. Sra. de la Esperanda, Carr 8829, Km. 1.5, Bo. Dajaos Sector El Chicharo, Bayamon, 00956.
8—NUESTRA SENORA DE LA MILAGROSA (1968)
Carr 864 Interseccion 80, Bo Hato Tejas, P.O. Box 2104, Bayamon, 00960-2104. Tel: 787-785-6620; Email: parroquialamilagrosa@hotmail.com. Rev. Carlos Algarin Lopez, Admin.
Res.: Carr. 864, No. 82, Bo. Hato Tejas, Bayamon, 00960.
9—NUESTRA SENORA DEL PERPETUO SOCORRO (1976)
Comerio St. No. 190, Bayamon, 00956.
Tel: 787-778-2328; Email: frayrafael@dominicospr.com. Friar Rafael Gonzalez Padro; Deacons Ramon L. Ramos; Miguel Velez.
10—NUESTRA SENORA DEL ROSARIO (1971)
Urb. Villa Espana, Calle Zaragoza, Bloque, B No. 34, Esq. Calle Vizcaya, Bayamon, 00961.
Tel: 787-787-0418; Email: parroquiadelrosario.090@gmail.com. Rev. Anibal Rafael Torres-Ortiz; Deacons Luis A. Navedo; Antonio Colon Rivera.
Missions—Minillas—San Jose.
Ntra. Sra. del Carmen, Bella Vista.
Sagrado Corazon de Jesus.
11—NTRA. SRA. DE LOS DOLORES (1976)
Urb. Alturas de Famboyan, Bloque DD 25 Calle 18, Bayamon, 00959-0069. Tel: 787-786-7494; Email: cancilleria2018@arqsj.org. Urb Alturas de Flamboyan, Bloque DD 25 Calle 18, Bayamon, 00957. Rev. Jorge Ramirez Sanchez, Admin.; Deacon Francisco Hernandez.
Catechesis Religious Program—Students 12.
12—NTRA. SRA. DEL ROSARIO (1993)
Carr 816 KM 5.6 Bo Nuevo, P.O. Box 3917, Bayamon, 00958-3917. Tel: 787-730-6000; Email: p.ntrasradelrosariobayamon151@yahoo.com. Rev. Abelardo Mojica Paez; Deacons Hector Rivera; Enrique Resto-Vargas.
Missions—San Juan Bautista—Montellano Co.
Jesus Maestro, Dajaos Co.
La Providencia, Dajaos Co.
13—SAGRADA FAMILIA (1976)
Mailing Address: P.O. Box 8478, Bayamon, 00959-8478. Tel: 787-798-2010; Email: parroquiasagradafamilia.bayamon@gmail.com. Extension Forrest Hills, Calle Valparaiso Esq Calle Caracas, Bayamon, 00959. Rev. Edwin Hernandez-Ralat, P.B.R.O.; Deacons Luis Antonio Colton-Rosa; Higinio Santiago Santos.
Res.: #A-468 Cuba St., Urb. Ext. Forest Hills, Bayamon, 00960.
14—SAN AGUSTIN (1964)
P.O. Box 4263, Bayamon Gardens Sta., Bayamon, 00958-4263. Tel: 787-785-8611; Email: bayamonsanagustin@hotmail.com. Urb Lomas Verdes, Calle Duende Blq 2E # 21, Bayamon, 00956. Revs. Edwin Lorenzo; Mario Gonzalez, O.S.A., (Spain); Deacons Cristobal Rivera; Alberto Irizarry Caro; Juan Rosario Nieves.
School—San Agustin School (1964) Bayamon Gardens Sta., P.O. Box 4263, Bayamon, 00958-4263. Tel: 787-786-8055. Mrs. Mercedes Diaz, Prin. Lay Teachers 25; Students 234.
Missions—San Martin de Porres—Calle 1 Barrio Juan Sanchez, Bayamon, Bayamon Co. 00959.
Ntra. Sra. del Buen Consejo, Villas de San Agustin, Bayamon, Bayamon Co. 00959.
15—SAN ANTONIO MARIA CLARET (1966)
Mailing Address: P.O. Box 3292, Bayamon Gardens Sta., Bayamon, 00958-3292. Tel: 787-797-3337; Email: parroquiaclaretbayamon@gmail.com. Urb Bayamon Gardens, Ave Castiglione D-24, Bayamon, 00957. Rev. Jose Vicente Martinez-Santos Sr.; Deacon Juan Carlos Monroy Morales, C.M.F.
Catechesis Religious Program—Students 250.
16—SAN JOSE (1964) [CEM]
Urb Forest View, Dakar, F-169, Bayamon, 00956.
Tel: 787-785-6675; Email: sanjose_claret@yahoo.com. Rev. Hector Cuadrado, C.M.F.; Coadjutor Tomas Cabello Miguelez; Rev. Jose Nieto, C.M.F.
School—Academia Claret, Tel: 787-787-6685;
Tel: 787-786-7976. Nilda Rivera Miranda, Prin. Lay Teachers 30; Priests 2; Students 315.
17—SAN JUAN BAUTISTA DE LA SALLE (1979)
Estancias de Rio Hondo 1ra. Secc., A-19 Rio Cialitos, Bayamon, 00961. Tel: 787-787-9567; Email: plasallepr@gmail.com. Rev. Antonio Romero Iglesias, MM.SS.CC.; Deacons Francisco Ortiz; Jose Vega.
18—SAN MIGUEL ARCANGEL (1962)
Mailing Address: P.O. Box 361714, 00936-1714.
Tel: 787-787-4459; Fax: 787-787-4459. Rev. Luis Marrero Padilla.
Res.: Urb. Jardines de Caparra, Calle 12A Bloque AB., No. 32, Bayamon, 00959.
Mission—San Miguel, Barriada San Miguel, Guaynabo, Guaynabo Co. 00657.
19—SANTA ELENA (1978)
Mailing Address: P.O. Box 366, Bayamon, 00960-0366. Tel: 787-785-6604; Email: cancilleria2018@arqsj.org. Urb Santa Elena, Calle 6 A-14, Bayamon, 00957. Rev. Jorge Saenz; Deacon Ramon Ramos Rodriguez.
20—SANTA MARIA (1984)
Urb. Cana, Calle 24 #II-1, Bayamon, 00957.
Tel: 787-797-7248; Tel: 787-797-8230; Email: psantamariacmf@gmail.com. Revs. Norberto Padilla Cruz, C.M.F.; Jose Santos Nunez, C.M.F., (Spain); Jose Minaya Silvero, Supr.; Deacons Jose Ramon Cruz; Rafael Araya.
Res.: Calle 24, Esq. 23, Urb. Cana, Bayamon, 00957.
Missions—San Gerardo Mayela—Bo. Buena Vista, Bayamon, Bayamon Co. 00957.
Sagrado Corazon, Bo. Cerro Gordo, Bayamon, Bayamon Co. 00956.
21—SANTA RITA DE CASIA (1967)
Urb. Santa Juanita, NS-8 Ave., Hostos, Bayamon, 00956-5102. Tel: 787-786-3971; Email: santaritapr@hotmail.com. Revs. Carlos Cordero, O.S.A.; Jean Matchado, Vicar; Friars Gonzalo Gonzalez Pereda, Vicar; Saturmino Juan Vega, Vicar; Deacons Ramon L. Rivera; Obed Eliezer Toro; Noel Vasquez.
Missions—San Jose—Carretera 831, Bo. Minillas, Bayamon, Bayamon Co. 00619. Fax: 787-778-3806.
Ntra. Sra. Del Carmen, Calle Reno P-54, Urb. Vista Bella, Bayamon, Bayamon Co. 00619.
Sagrado Corazon De Jesus, Calle Palestina D, Z-10, Bayamon, Bayamon Co. 00619.
22—SANTA ROSA DE LIMA (1976)
Mailing Address: Urb. Santa Rosa, 28-9, Calle 12, Bayamon, 00959. Tel: 787-798-2300;
Tel: 787-787-1676; Fax: 787-780-3680; Email: bayamonsantarosa@gmail.com; Web: asantarosabay.wix.com/academia. Rev. Virgilio Martinez, (Spain).
Res.: Urb. Santa Rosa, Av. Main, Calles 11, 12, 13, Bayamon, 00959.
School—Santa Rosa de Lima School, Urb. Santa Rosa, Ave. Main, Bayamon, 00959. Tel: 787-798-2829; Tel: 787-798-2539; Fax: 787-780-3680;
Fax: 787-288-4996. Lorrie M. Cuevas Torres, Prin. Lay Teachers 33; Students 576.
Catechesis Religious Program—Students 85.
23—SANTA TERESA DE JESUS (1983)
Urb Santa Teresita, F-10 Calle 12, P.O. Box 9204, Bayamon, 00960-9204. Tel: 787-269-6749; Email: parsteresa@gmail.com. Rev. Carlos Santiago Ramirez; Deacon Jimmy Martinez Perez.
Missions—San Martin de Porres—Rio Plantation Urb., Bayamon, 00961. Tel: 787-269-6749;
Fax: 787-269-6749.
Convento Missioneras de La Caridad, Sector Punta Brava. Tel: 787-269-0207.
24—SANTIAGO APOSTOL (1966) [CEM]
Urb. Sierra Bayamon, 23-17 Calle 23, Bayamon, 00961-4418. Tel: 787-786-9179; Tel: 787-288-1966;
Fax: 787-269-3965; Email: p.sanapostol@yahoo.com. Deacon Angel Pabon.
School—Santiago Apostol School, Tel: 787-786-9179; Fax: 787-269-3965. Neyda Perez-Hernandez, Prin. Lay Teachers 21; Priests 2; Students 229.
Catechesis Religious Program—Students 229.
25—SANTO DOMINGO DE GUZMAN (1976)
Ext. La Milagrosa, Calle 2 # 200, Bayamon, 00959.
Tel: 787-636-1062; Email: cancilleria2018@arqsj.org. P.O. Box 4188, Bayamon, 00960-4188. Friar Rafael Gonzalez Padro; Deacons Hèctor Negrón; Rubén González.
Catechesis Religious Program—
26—SANTO DOMINGO DE GUZMAN (1984)
P.O. Box 3342, Bayamon, 00958-3342.
Tel: 787-797-5510; Email: cancilleria2018@arqsj.org. Urb Van Scoy, Calle Principal Esq Calle 3 Oeste, Bayamon, 00957. Rev. Francisco J. Quinones Diaz; Deacons Virgilio Andino; Ramon L. Ramos; Pedro Gonzalez-Rosario.
Catechesis Religious Program—Students 160.
Missions—Santisima Trinidad—Carretera 167 Km. 10, Bo. Ortiz, Corozal Co.
Ntra. Sra. de la Providencia, Urb. Los Dominicos, Bayamon, 00958.
Carlos Manuel Rodriguez, Urb. Los Palacios, Toa Alta, 00954.

CAROLINA
1—CRISTO REY (1971)
Mailing Address: P.O. Box 1215, Carolina, 00986-1215. Tel: 787-752-9939; Email: parroquiacristorey92@gmail.com. Urb Parque Ecuestre, Calle Dulce Sueno U-8, Carolina, 00987. Rev. Rafael DeJesus Gonzalez Ayala.
Missions—San Francisco de Asis—Entre las calles Tinajero y Dulce Sueno, Parque Encuestre.
Maria Auxiliadora, Carrt. 857 Km. 3.6, Bo. Canovanillas.
Divino Nino Jesus, Ubanizaciones: Ciudad Jardin y Colobos Park, Bo. Cambute, Carolina Co.
Cristo Rey, Bo. Carruzos.
2—EPIFANIA DEL SENOR (1982)
Calle Calais 425, Ext. El Comandante, Carolina, 00982. Tel: 787-752-1149; Email: parroquia.epifania@yahoo.com. Rev. Grzegorz Okarma, C.S.M.A.
Catechesis Religious Program—Students 19.
3—INMACULADA CONCEPCION (1966)
Mailing Address: P.O. Box 3562, Carolina, OH 00984-3562. Tel: 787-276-1527; Email: pinmacconc@gmail.com. Urb Valle Arriba Heights, Calle Almendro A-15, Carolina, 00983. Rev. Tomas Felipe Chacon-Mora; Deacon Miguel A. Colon.
Catechesis Religious Program—Students 58.
4—NTRA. SRA. DE FATIMA (1998)
Mailing Address: HC 03 Box 12076, Bo. Cedros, Carolina, 00985. Tel: 787-750-2168; Email: nsdefatima853@yahoo.com. Carr 853 Km 13.6, Bo Cedros, Carolina, 00985. Rev. Victor Manuel Llenas-Urenas; Deacons Orlando Rodriguez; Eduardo Betancourt MederoBetancourt.
Missions—Ntra. Sra. del Carmen—Carr 853, Km. 8.0, Carolina, Barrazas 00987.
Santa Teresa de Jesus, Bo. Carr 853, Km. 5.0, Carolina, Cacao 00987.
5—NTRA. SRA. DEL CARMEN (1984)
P.O. Box 299, Carolina, 00986-0299.
Tel: 787-752-8708; Tel: 787-757-5729; Email: parroquiadelcarmen132@yahoo.com. Urb Lomas de Carolina, Calle Monte Membrillo K-8, Carolina, 00987. Rev. Antonio Garcia, (Spain); Deacons Ernie Diaz; Cesar Avila; Jose Rosa Diaz.
School—Academia del Carmen, Calle Monte Britton, Esq. Monte Membrillo, Lomas de Carolina, Carolina, 00987. Tel: 787-757-4489; Tel: 787-757-4454; Email: academiadelcarmen@gmail.com. Mrs. Aitza Vázquez-Padilla, Sub-Dir. Lay Teachers 18; Priests 1; Students 139.
Catechesis Religious Program—Students 128.
6—NTRA. SRA. REINA DE LA PAZ (1969)
Urb Sabana Gardens, Calle 6 Final, P.O. Box 3688, Carolina, 00984-6388. Tel: 787-750-4538; Email: parroquiareinadelapaz@yahoo.com. Rev. Tomas Felipe Chacon-Mora; Deacons Euripides Lugo; Efigenio Rivera.

Mission—Divino Nino Jesus.
7—NTRA. SRA. REINA DE LOS ANGELES (1960)
Urb. Los Angeles, 29 Calle Lira, Carolina, 00979-1659. Tel: 787-791-2594; Email: reinadelosangeles29@gmail.com. Rev. Carmelo Soto-Tanon; Deacon Vicente Nieves De Leon.
8—NUESTRA SENORA DE LOURDES (1956)
Mailing Address: Urb. El Comandante, 1173 Calle Alejo Cruzado, 00924. Tel: 787-752-3716; Email: parrlourdescomandante@aol.com. Rev. Grzegorz Okarma, C.S.M.A.
9—SAN ANDRES (1982)
Urb. Country Club (4 Ta. Ext.), MF-15 Calle 482, Carolina, 00982. Tel: 787-769-7076; Email: cancilleria2018@arqsj.org. Rev. Rafael Mendez-Hernandez, P.B.R.O.; Deacons Jorge L. Camacho Gerena; Gilberto Mejias.
10—SAN FELIPE APOSTOL (1971)
Urb Villa Carolina 4ta Extension, Calle 419 Blq 165 #3, P.O. Box 1494, Carolina, 00984-1494.
Tel: 787-762-6250; Email: parroquiasanfelipe@yahoo.com. Rev. Rodney Algarin-Rosado; Deacons Manuel Correa Cruz; Jose Jaramillo.
11—SAN FERNANDO (1851)
Calle Ignacio Arzuaga #157, P.O. Box 128, Carolina, 00986-0128. Tel: 787-769-0170; Email: sanfernandoreydelacarolina@gmail.com. Rev. Msgr. Efrain Rodriguez-Otero; Deacons Jose Birriel; Santiago Diaz Rosa; Presbitero Rivera; Richard Rodriguez De Jesus.
12—SAN FRANCISCO DE ASIS (1988)
Calle 22 #0-31 A, Urb. Metropolis, Carolina, 00987. Tel: 787-998-8331; Email: parsanfa@gmail.com. Rev. Frank de la Rosa Peguero, (Dominican Republic); Deacon Joseph Vizcarrondo Perez.
13—SAN JUAN DE DIOS (1971)
Mailing Address: P.O. Box 3179, Carolina, 00984-3179. Tel: 787-757-5060; Email: parroq89@gmail.com. Urb Jardines de Borinquen, Calle Canaria R-9, Carolina, 00985. Rev. Julio Ortiz-Mangual; Deacon Jose Otero Lugo.
Res.: R-19 Canaria St., Jardines de Borinquen, Carolina, 00985.
Catechesis Religious Program—Rosa W. Quiles, D.R.E.
Mission—La Sagrada Familia, C. Progreso A-79A, Villa Esperanza, Carolina Co. 00985.
14—SAN VALENTIN (1971)
Urb Rolling Hills, 128 Calle San Luis, P.O. Box 9382, Carolina, 00988-9382. Tel: 787-750-5277;
Fax: 787-750-5277; Email: parroquiasanvalentin083@gmail.com. Rev. Natividad Acevedo Viscaya; Deacon Jose A. Pappaterra.
Mission—San Antonio, Urb. San Anton, Calle Ortiz Esq. Quercado, Carolina, Carolina Co. 00987.
15—SANTA CLARA DE ASIS (1966)
Urb. Villa Fontana, JL-456 Via 14, Carolina, 00983.
Tel: 787-768-1708; Email: parroquiasantaclara1@yahoo.com. Rev. Luis S. Olmo, O.F.M., (Spain); Deacons Luis Del Rio Pitre; Jose A. Morales, (Retired); Luis Montes.
School—Santa Clara de Asis School (1968)
Tel: 787-768-7110; Fax: 787-757-5044. Mrs. Lillivette Torres, Prin. Lay Teachers 23; Students 355.
Missions—San Francisco de Asis—
Parque Boliviano 5-JL, Villa Fontana Park, Carolina, Carolina Co. 00983.
16—SANTA GEMA GALGANI PARISH SANCTUARY (1971)
Mailing Address: P.O. Box 2789, Carolina, 00984-2789. Tel: 787-769-5663; Fax: 787-750-3090; Email: andyrrpassio@gmail.com. Avenida Galicia Final, Carolina, 00983. Revs. Anibal Rodriguez; Luis Lopez-Galarza.
School—Santa Gema Galgani Parish Sanctuary School, Tel: 787-768-3082; Tel: 787-757-2505;
Fax: 787-750-3090. Sr. Maria Rafaela Ojeda, Dir. Lay Teachers 51; Students 803.
Catechesis Religious Program—Students 865.
17—SANTISIMA TRINIDAD (1982)
Ave. Campo Rico PA-16, 3ra Ext. Urb. Country Club, Carolina, 00982. Tel: 787-769-5665; Email: santismatrinidad.carolina@gmail.com. Rev. William Torres Pagan; Deacons Ibrahim Suarez; Esteban Valle; Bienvenido Domenech; Gaspar Orozco.
Catechesis Religious Program—Students 175.
18—SANTO CRISTO DE LA AGONIA (1971)
P.O. Box 5108, Carolina, 00984-5108.
Tel: 787-768-0374; Email: cancilleria2018@arqsj.org. Urb Eduardo J Saldana, Sector La Ceramica, Calle Roble C-29, Carolina, 00983. Rev. Campo Emilio Ariza Rincon; Deacon Miguel A. Marrero-Nieves.
Catechesis Religious Program—Students 30.
Mission—Ntra. Sra. de la Esperanza, Sabana Abajo, Carolina Co.
19—SANTO CRISTO DE LOS MILAGROS (1971)
P.O. Box 834, Carolina, 00986-0834.
Tel: 787-768-3810; Email: oficina@pscmpr.org. Urb Villa Carolina, 3ra Extension, Ave Sanchez Castano Blq 122 #42-A, Carolina, 00985. Rev. Msgr. Nestor Yulfo-Hoffman; Deacon Jorge Rivera.

CATANO
1—NUESTRA SENORA DEL CARMEN (1893)
Mailing Address: P.O. Box 427, Catano, 00963-0427. Rev. Jaime Rodriguez Ribo; Deacon Angel Oquendo.
Res.: Calle Tren Num. 42, Catano, 00963.
Tel: 787-275-1309; Tel: 787-765-6542.
Catechesis Religious Program—Pedro Crespo, D.R.E. Students 40.
Missions—San Martín de Porres—Urb. Bayview.
San José Obrero.
2—SAN FRANCISCO DE SALES (1969)
Mailing Address: P.O. Box 567, Catano, 00963-8163. Revs. Mario Antonio Leonardo-Hernandez; Jorge L. Gonzalez, S.D.B., Supr.
Res.: Ave. Flor del Valle Bloque BB-No. 108, Urb. Las Vegas, Catano, 00963. Tel: 787-788-5036;
Fax: 787-788-8163.
Missions—Santo Domingo De Guzman—Puente Blanco, Catano Co.
Maria Auxiliadora, Urb. Vistas Del Morro.
San Judas Tadeo (Santuario), Parcelas Bo. Palmas.
Immaculada Concepcion, Sector La Cucharilla.

DORADO
1—NTRA. SRA. DE LA SALUD (1982)
Mailing Address: Bo. Higuillar, P.O. Box 470, Dorado, 00646-0470. Rev. Angel Pagan Torres; Deacons Hilario De Leon; Luis Antonio Alayon-Legrand.
Res.: Parcela 202, Calle Principal 210, Sector San Antonio, Dorado, 00646. Tel: 787-626-4849; Email: pntrasradelasalud@gmail.com.
2—SAN ANTONIO DE PADUA (1848)
Mailing Address: P.O. Box 602, Dorado, 00646-0602.
Tel: 787-278-1416; Fax: 787-278-1154; Email: saintantny@coqui.net. Rev. Jose Angel Rodriguez Reyes; Deacons Benito Lugo Soto; José E. Colon; José C. Diaz.
Res.: 184 Calle Norte, Dorado, 00646.
Mission—San Martin de Porres, Calle Principal Bo Mameyal, Dorado, 00646.
Shrine—Christ of Reconciliation (2001) Urb. Martorell, Paseo Del Cristo Lot #8, Dorado, 00646.

GUAYNABO
1—BUEN PASTOR (1965)
Urb. Apolo QQIA Calle Acropolis, Guaynabo, 00969-5014. Web: www.elbuenpastorguaynabo.net. Rev. Jesus Garcia Rodriguez, (Venezuela).
2—CORAZON DE JESUS (1992)
Mailing Address: HC-4 P.O. Box 5735, Guaynabo, 00971-0225. Tel: 787-789-5421; Email: corazondejesuspr@gmail.com. Rev. Leandro Antonio Blandon Rojas.
Res.: Carr. 834 Km. 4.0, Bo. Sonadora, Guaynabo, 00970.
Missions—San Juan Bosco—Bo. Mamey 1.
Sagrada Familia, Bo. Sonadora, Villa Jalena, Bo. Sonadora.
3—DIVINO NINO JESUS (1992)
Mailing Address: PBM 143, HC-01, P.O. Box 29030, Caguas, 00725. Tel: 787-720-0203;
Fax: 787-720-0203. Rev. Rodolfo Lamas; Deacons Andres Figueroa; Milton Valladares.
Res.: Urb. Lomas Del Sol, Calle Principal, Guaynabo, 00971.
Missions—San Rafael Arcangel—Barrio Camarones, Carr. #20, Guaynabo, Guaynabo Co. 00970.
Jesus Nazareno, Bo. Mamey, Guaynabo, Guaynabo Co. 00970.
El Buen Pastor, Carr. #1, Guaynabo, Guaynabo Co. 00970. Tel: 787-798-9596.
Ntra. Sra. de la Paz, Bo. Quebrada Arenas, Guaynabo, Guaynabo Co. 00971.
4—MARIA MADRE DE LA MISERICORDIA (1995)
Mailing Address: Ave. Santa Ana. #150, Guaynabo, 00969. Rev. Msgr. Leonardo J. Rodriguez-Jimenes; Revs. Joel Enrique del Cueto-Santiago; Ricardo Augusto Roig Lorenzo; Carlos Rafael Santiago-Ramirez; Deacon Ivan Llado-Gonzalez.
Res.: Carretera 833 Km. 13.2, Bo. Santa Rosa 3, Guaynabo, 00969. Tel: 787-789-0090;
Fax: 787-790-7596.
5—MARIA MADRE DE MI SENOR (1988)
Mailing Address: P.O. Box 2150, Guaynabo, 00970-2150. Tel: 787-789-1837; Tel: 787-720-1709. Rev. Phillip Nunez-Carrion; Deacon Luis Alvarez Suria.
Res.: Bo. Tortugos, Carretera 873, #1904, Guaynabo, 00970.
Mission—Ntra. Sra. del Carmen, Bo. Frailes Llanos, Sector Los Baez, Guaynabo, Guaynabo Co. 00657.
6—NUESTRA SENORA DE LA PAZ (1992)
Mailing Address: PMB 774, P.O. Box 7891, Guaynabo, 00970-7891. Tel: 787-287-5714. Rev. Jairo Enrique Granados-Benavides; Deacons Porfirio Franco; Jose M. Castillo; Pablo Manzano Lopez.
Res.: 833 Rd. LM 3.5, Bo. Guaraguao, Guaynabo, 00970.
Missions—Ntra. Sra. de la Divina Providencia— Cantagallo, Guaynabo, Juncos Co. 00971.
Espiritu Santo, Bo. Sta. Rosa I, Guaynabo, 00971.
Tel: 787-287-2335.
Inmaculada Concepcion, Bo. Camarones Centro, Guaynabo, Ciales Co. 00971.
San Jose Obrero, Bo. Sta. Rosa II, Guaynabo, 00971.
7—SAGRADOS CORAZONES (1968) Revs. Victor Hugo Mira Alvarez, SS.CC.; Mateo Mateo, SS.CC.; Luis Alberto Hernandez Pineda; Deacons Ivan E. Dominguez; Ulpiano H. Rivera; Olimpio R. Zambrana Ortega.
Res.: Urb. Ponce de Leon, 208 Ave. Esmeralda, Guaynabo, 00969. Tel: 787-720-6151;
Fax: 787-720-6151.
School—Sagrados Corazones School, Avenue A, Guaynabo, 00969. Tel: 787-720-2585;
Tel: 787-720-6316; Fax: 787-720-6035; Email: ssccgnb@gmail.com.
Catechesis Religious Program—Awilda Rodriguez, D.R.E.; Griselle Coites, D.R.E.
Mission—Virgen de la Paz, Bda. Cruz Melendez, Guaynabo, 00969.
8—SAN JUAN EVANGELISTA (1962)
Mailing Address: P.O. Box 10151, 00922-0151.
Tel: 787-783-3522; Fax: 787-781-0236; Email: info@psje.us. Rev. Walter S. Gomez-Baca; Deacons Miguel De La Sota; Isidro Garcia.
Res.: Calle Church Hill, J-5, Urb. Torrimar, Guaynabo, 00966.
School—San Juan Evangelista School,
Tel: 787-781-5325; Fax: 787-793-8076. Lay Teachers 37; Priests 1; Students 260.
Catechesis Religious Program—Tafty Beuicos, D.R.E.
Mission—San Francisco de Asis, [CEM] Carretera 19, La Marina, Guaynabo Co. 00966.
9—SAN PEDRO MARTIR DE VERONA (1769)
Mailing Address: P.O. Box 32, Guaynabo, 00970-0032. Rev. Msgr. Mario A. Guijarro de Corzo, (Cuba); Deacons Carlos Rivera Martinez; Humberto Reyes Anciano; Angel Loyola Zayas; Gregory A. Guijarro.
Res.: Calle Tapia No. 5, Guaynabo, 00970.
Tel: 787-720-2361; Tel: 787-272-6739;
Tel: 787-287-1791; Fax: 787-287-2833.
School—San Pedro Martir de Verona School, Alpierre St. Final, Urb. Colimar, P.O. Box 2560, Guaynabo, 00970-2560. Tel: 787-720-2219;
Fax: 787-272-8770. Mr. Leonardo L. Cuadros, Prin.; Deacon Gregory A. Guijarro, Prof. & Vice Dir. Lay Teachers 19; Priests 1; Sisters 1; Students 258.
Catechesis Religious Program—Students 267.
10—SANTA ROSA DE LIMA (1973) Rev. Jose Gregorio Guaipo; Deacon William Paz Gonzalez.
Res. & Mailing Address: 16 Parque St., Barrio Amelia, Guaynabo, 00965. Tel: 787-781-5855;
Tel: 787-783-9731; Fax: 787-781-5855;
Fax: 787-783-9731.
Mission—La Milagrosa, Barriada Vietnam.

TOA ALTA
1—NTRA. SRA. DE LA PROVIDENCIA (1968)
Mailing Address: P.O. Box 3836, Bayamon Gardens Sta., Bayamon, 00958-3836. Tel: 787-797-1618. Rev. William Torres-Pagan; Deacons Gregorio Cuevas; Pedro Gonzalez.
Res.: Bo. Pinas, Carretera 861 Km. 5.2, Toa Alta, 00954.
Catechesis Religious Program—Students 160.
Missions—Ntra. Sra. de Fatima—Sector Rincon, Bo. Pinas, Comerio Co.
La Resurreccion, Villa del Rio, Bo. Pinas, Comerio Co.
Ntra. Sra. del Carmen, Sector del 7.
Sagrada Familia, Villa Juventud, Bo. Pinas, Comerio Co.
San Ricardo, Barrios Pinas, Toa Alta, 00954.
2—NUESTRA SENORA DE LA MEDALLA MILAGROSA
Mailing Address: P.O. Box 335, Toa Alta, 00954-0335. Rev. Jose A. Ortiz Garcia; Deacon German Hernandez Pagan.
Res.: Bo. Quebrada Cruz, Carretera 824, Km. 3.8, Toa Alta, 00954. Tel: 787-870-4090;
Fax: 787-870-8125.
Mission—Nuestra Senora del Carmen, Sector El Cuco, Bo. Quebrada Cruz, Toa Alta, Toa Alta Co. 00953.
3—SAN ESTEBAN, PROTOMARTIR (1997) Rev. Hernan Berdugo-Sanjuan; Deacons Jose Ramon Perez-Bracero; Rafael Morales Figueroa; Emerito Ventura Ruiz.
Res. & Mailing Address: P.O. Box 3729, Bayamon, 00958. Tel: 787-799-2925; Email: parroquiasanesteban@prtc.net.
Catechesis Religious Program—Students 171.
Missions—Capilla Cristo Rey—Sector La Cuerda, Barrio Bucarabones, Toa Alta, Toa Alta Co. 00953.
Ntra. Sra. del Rosario.
4—SAN FERNANDO REY (1751) [JC]
Mailing Address: P.O. Box 63, Toa Alta, 00954-0063. Email: sfdo2585@coqui.net. Rev. Eddie Rivera-Marzan; Deacons Jose Narvaez; Felipe Collazo; Pablo Irene.
Res.: Calle Jose de Diego #10, Toa Alta, 00953.
Tel: 787-870-2585.
Catechesis Religious Program—Students 20.
Mission—San Antonio, Rio Lajas, Dorado, Dorado Co. 00646.

5—SAN JOSE (1998)
Mailing Address: P.O. Box 777, Toa Alta, 00954-0777. Rev. Cesar Santos Romero; Deacon Luis R. Nieves Marrero.
Res.: Sector Jazmin, Carretera 823, Rio Lajas, Toa Alta, 00954. Tel: 787-644-0474.
Missions—Ntra. Sra. del Camino—Bo. Espinosa, Carretera #2, Dorado, Dorado Co. 00646.
San Francisco de Asis, Bo. Maguayo, Dorado, Dorado Co. 00646.
Cristo de los Milagros.
Santa Teresita, Bo. Rio Lajas, Toa Alta, Toa Alta Co. 00758.
Sagrada Familia, Sector Marzan, Bo. Rio Lajas, Toa Alta, Toa Alta Co. 00758.
Sagrado Corazon, Sector Los Mudos, Bo. Quebrada Arenas, Toa Alta, Toa Alta Co. 00758.

6—SAN JUDAS TADEO (2002)
Mailing Address: P.O. Box 1006, Toa Alta, 00954-1006. Revs. Pius Wesonga, A.J.; Gerald Nuqotri, A.J.; Deacons Jose Mojica-Torres; Luis Rivera-Albino; Luis Alvira-Rolon.
Res.: Carretera 804 Km. 1.2, Bo. Galateo Centro, Toa Alta, 00954. Tel: 787-870-8016; Fax: 787-870-8018.
Catechesis Religious Program—Students 120.
Missions—San Martin de Porres—Bo. Galateo.
Santa Teresa De Jesus, Bo. Quebrada Cruz, Toa Alta, Toa Alta Co. 00758.

TOA BAJA

1—ESPIRITU SANTO (1965)
Mailing Address: Levittown Sta., P.O. Box 50272, Toa Baja, 00950. Email: parroqespiritusanto072@gmail.com. Rev. Milton Agustin Rivera-Vigo; Deacons Martin Estrada; Miguel A. Torres; Guillermo M. Vaello Perez; Manuel Sanchez; Jose Aguilera.
Res.: Urb. Levittown 1453, Pasco Damisela, Toa Baja, 00949. Tel: 787-784-4805; Fax: 787-795-1248.
School—Espiritu Santo School, 1454 Paseo Damisela, Toa Baja, 00949. Tel: 787-784-0905; Fax: 787-795-5418. Lay Teachers 26; Students 307.
Catechesis Religious Program—Students 140.
Mission—Ntra. Sra. del Carmen, Calle Carmen, Bo. Palo Seco, Toa Baja, 00649.

2—NTRA. SRA. DE LA CANDELARIA (1960)
Mailing Address: P.O. Box 892, Toa Baja, 00951-0892. Rev. Jose Dario Martinez Tobon, (Colombia).
Res.: Carretera No. 863, Km. 0.6, Bo. Pajaros, Toa Baja, 00951. Tel: 787-251-0503.
Missions—Cristo Rey—Calle 10, Bo. Bucarabones, Toa Alta, Toa Alta Co. 00758.
Santa Maria La Mayor, Carretera #2 R.063, Bo. Macun, Bo. Macun, Toa Baja Co. 00759.
Santisima Trinidad, Urb. Las Colinas, Toa Baja, Toa Baja Co. 00759.
Buen Pastor, Urb. Sta. Maria, Toa Baja, Toa Baja Co. 00759.

3—NUESTRA SENORA DE COVADONGA (1984)
Mailing Address: P.O. Box 9076, Bayamon, 00960-9076. Tel: 787-251-6466; Fax: 787-251-6466. Rev. Jairo Salazar Castano; Deacon Efrain Narvaez.
Res.: Calle 13, 2-C-4, Esq. Calle 14, Urb. Covadonga, Toa Baja, 00949.
Missions—Ntra. Sra. de Lourdes—Bo. Candelaria Arenas, Toa Baja, Toa Baja Co. 00759.
San Martin de Porres, Bo. Kennedy, Toa Baja, Toa Baja Co. 00759.
Divino Nino Jesus, Urb. El Plantio, Toa Baja, Toa Baja Co. 00759.

4—SAN JOSE OBRERO (1965)
Mailing Address: Box 173, Sabana Seca, 00952-0173. Tel: 787-784-1400. Revs. Santos Perez Castillo, O.F.M., Supr.; Jit Manuel Castillo, O.F.M.; Deacon Ramon L. Colon-Hernandez.
Res.: Carretera 2-R 866, Km. 3 #6, Sabana Seca, Toa Baja, 00952. Tel: 787-795-3141.
Catechesis Religious Program—Students 103.
Missions—Ntra. Sra. del Carmen—Carr. 2-R 866 K4 H4 Int., Los Bravos, Sabana Seca.
San Martin de Porres, Carr. 816 PAR 1034, Villa Marisol, Sabana Seca.

5—SAN PEDRO APOSTOL (1745)
Mailing Address: P.O. Box 513, Toa Baja, 00951-0513. Rev. Calixto Soto Silvera, (Colombia); Deacon Joaquin Rivera Vazquez.
Res.: 47 Las Flores St., Toa Baja, 00949.
Tel: 787-794-1327; Fax: 787-794-5967.
Catechesis Religious Program—Students 232.
Missions—Santa Teresita—Calle Quintero.
Ntra. Sra. de Guadalupe, Calle Crisantemo, Parcela 137-A.
San Jose, Calle San Jose #303.
San Pablo, Calle Universo, Parcela #9, Toaville.
La Virgen de la Providencia, Bo. Villa Calma.

6—SANTISIMA TRINIDAD (1978)
Mailing Address: Apartado 50378, Levittown, 00950-0378. Tel: 787-784-2889; Fax: 787-261-2911. Rev. Juan M. Beristain, (Spain); Deacons Eusebio Jaca; Gaspar Orozco; Edwin Negron Rivera.
Res.: Ave. Los Dominicos, Esquina Dr. Sanchez Cardona, Levittown, Toa Baja, 00950.

TRUJILLO ALTO

1—EXALTACION DE LA SANTA CRUZ (1801)
Calle J. G Diaz 515, P.O. Box 1808, Trujillo Alto, 00977-1808. Tel: 787-761-0570; Email: santacruzpr@yahoo.com. Rev. Carlos Alberto Contreras Tribaldo; Deacons Domingo Vargas; Cesar Guiven; Alfredo Aponte.
Catechesis Religious Program—Students 51.

2—GRUTA DE LOURDES (1975)
Mailing Address: P.O. Box 1081, Trujillo Alto, 00977-1081. Tel: 787-761-0571; Email: grutadelourdes1925@yahoo.com; Web: lagrutadelourdes.org. Barrio Cuevas Carr 876 Km 1.7, Trujillo Alto, 00976. Rev. Msgr. Fernando Benicio Felices Sanchez; Deacon Pablo Torres.

3—MARIA LLENA DE GRACIA (1997)
Urb Rincon Espanol, Calle 1 Esq 4, P.O. Box 1618, Trujillo Alto, 00977-1618. Tel: 787-945-5289; Email: jmcdno@gmail.com. Rev. Jose Miguel Cedeno Velez.

4—SAN BARTOLOME (1985)
Urb. Ciudad Universitaria, X-1 Calle 16, Trujillo Alto, 00976. Tel: 787-755-0120; Email: parr. sanbartolome@yahoo.com. Rev. Rafael Delgado-Diaz, O.P., Admin.; Deacon Alberto Gomez Maldonado.

5—SAN FRANCISCO DE ASIS (1992)
Mailing Address: P.O. Box 1316, Trujillo Alto, 00977-1316. Tel: 787-755-5661; Email: sanfrancisco092011@yahoo.com. Comunidad Ramon T Colon, Calle 2 # 32 Qda. Negrito, Trujillo Alto, 00976. Rev. Luis Amaury Jose Volques; Deacons Hector Rivera; Alfredo Aponte; William Rios.
Res.: Carr. #181 R-852, Bo. Quelseada Negrito, Quebrada Negrito, Trujillo Alto, 00977.
Tel: 787-305-0660.
Missions—Espiritu Santo—Bo. Kennedy Hills, Carretera 181 Km. 10.
San Jose de la Montana, Carretera #181 R-851, Bo. Sabana.
La Inmaculada Concepcion, Bo. Talanco, Carretera #181 R-852.

6—SAN JUDAS TADEO (1980)
Mailing Address: Apartado 1535, Trujillo Alto, 00977-1535. Tel: 787-755-5993; Email: psanjudastadeopr@gmail.com. Urb El Conquistador, Calle 7 Esq. 8, Trujillo Alto, 00977. Rev. Ivan R. Serrano-Rivera; Deacon Marcos Arcay-Garcia.
Catechesis Religious Program—Students 75.
Missions—Madre del Divino Pastor—Carretera 844 Km. 0.2, Parcelas Carraizo, Trujillo Alto, Trujillo Alto Co. 00760.
Virgen del Carmen, Carretera 175, Bo. Carraizo Alto, Trujillo Alto, Trujillo Alto Co. 00760.

7—SAN PIO X (1971)
Bo. Saint Just, Carr 848 Km 1.4, P.O. Box 631, Trujillo Alto, 00978-0631. Tel: 787-761-5040; Email: sanpio2010@yahoo.com. Rev. Alberto Lopez-Figueroa; Deacons Julio Sanchez; Jose I. Bustillo Formoso; Martin Rosado; Rolando Flores Rivera.
Mission—Ntra. Sra. del Rosario, Calle Lirio, Esq. Orquidea, Urb. Round Hill, Rio Piedras, San Juan Co. 00923.

Chaplains of Public Institutions

SANTURCE. *Ashford Presbyterian Community Hospital*, 1451 Ave. Ashford, Condado, Santurce, 00940. Tel: 787-725-8820; Tel: 787-724-8320; Tel: 787-722-5765. Rev. Msgr. Antonio Jose Vazquez Colon.
Doctors Community Hospital, 1395 Calle San Rafael, Santurce, 00940. Tel: 787-723-2950. Rev. Miguel Garcia Borges, S.D.B.
Hospital Del Nino San Jorge, 255 Calle San Jorge, Santurce, 00940. Tel: 787-727-1000. Rev. Olin Pierre Louis, Tel: 787-722-4158.
Hospital Pavia-Santurce, 1462 Calle Asia, Santurce, 00940. Tel: 787-727-6060. Rev. Marion Poncette, C.M., Tel: 787-727-3963.

Resident Chaplains:
Rev.—
Martinez, Danilo.

On Duty Outside the Archdiocese:
Revs.—
Del Valle, Tomas
Pierino, Vicente, Coleman, FL
Roldan, Juan, Caguas, P.R.
Sutil, Florencio
Torres Graciani, Ivan, Rochester, NY.

Graduate Studies:
Revs.—
Cruz, Jaime Ortiz, Rome, Italy
Samuel, Velazquez Serrano, Rome, Italy.

Military Services:
Revs.—
Gomez-Baca, Walter S., (Air Force)
Perez Vazquez, Juan De La Cruz, (Army)
Tirado, Orlando, C.M., (Air Force).

Retired:
Rev. Msgr.—
Cruz, Remberto, (Retired)
Revs.—
Candela, Rafael, (Retired)
Cruz, Gilbert J., (Spain) (Retired)
Cruz Gonzalez, Gil, (Retired)
De Carlo Mena, Francisco, (Retired)
Diaz, Alvaro, (Retired)
Fuentes Rodriguez, Jose, (Retired)
Gonzalez Chao, Luis, (Retired)
Ramos, Victoriano, (Retired)
Sanz, Florentino, (Spain) (Retired).

Permanent Deacons:
Acevedo-Denis, Angel
Aguilera-Casiano, Jose Rafael
Alayon-Legrand, Luis Antonio
Alicea Rivera, Angel L.
Alvarez Suria, Luis
Alvira-Rolon, Luis
Amador Melendez, Luis F.
Amador-Hernandez, Carlos J.
Amezaga, Jose R.
Andino Cintron, Virgilio
Andino Santos, Manuel
Aparicio Amengual, Luis A.
Aponte Diaz, Alfredo
Aponte-Torres, Norman
Araya Brenes, Rafael F.
Arcay-Garcia, Marcos
Arevalo Hernandez, Pedro Nel
Arroyo Acevedo, Americo
Avila Rodriguez, Cesar
Baez Cotto, Pedro J.
Baez Navarro, Jose
Berrios Berrios, Ildefonso
Birriel Rodriguez, Jose
Bustillo Formoso, Jose I.
Caban, Vicente
Camacho Gerena, Jorge L.
Carmona, Eduardo Figueroa
Caro Ruiz, Humberto Juan
Caro-Ruiz, Humberto Juan
Castillo Lopez, Jose M.
Charriez, Victor Manuel
Collazo Montalvo, Felipe
Colon Colon, Rafael
Colon Hernandez, Ramon L.
Colon Rivera, Francisco
Colon Rivera, Jose E.
Colon Velez, Jorge
Colton-Rosa, Luis Antonio
Cordero Mercado, Luis
Cosme Varela, Nicomedes
Costa, Pedro Tomas
Cruz De Choudens, Hector M.
Cruz, Manuel Correa
Cruz Maysonet, Jim
Cruz Trinidad, Jose Lionel
Cruz Vasquez, Ramon Jose
Cruz-Nives, Jose Ramon
Cuevas Nieves, Gregorio
D'Auria, Ricardo
Davila Casado, Angel L.
Davila Pizarro, Nelson
De Jesus Ramos, Confesor
De Jesus Robles, Filiberty
De La Sota Pumarejo, Miguel
De Leon Sanchez, Hilario
Del Rio Ortiz, Luis Orlando
Del Rio Pitre, Luis
Del Rio Rey, Jose
Del Rio-Rey, Jose
Del Valle Gonzalez, Reinaldo
Diaz Miranda, Ernie P.
Diaz Rivera, Jose
Diaz Rosa, Santiago
Diaz Sifonte, Agapito
Domenech, Bienvenido
Dominguez, Ivan
Duprey Concepcion, Manuel
Echautegui-Ramos, George
Echegaray Martinez, Luis
Estrada Galarza, Martin
Febres Maeso, Jose
Fetro Rodriguez, Tomas
Figueroa Acevedo, Andres
Figueroa Carrasquillo, Fernando
Figueroa Carrasquillo, Raul
Figueroa Sanchez, Juan
Fonseca Soto, Jorge Luis
Franco Torres, Porfirio
Galinarez Llorens, Angel
Garcia-Toro, Isidro
Gierbolini Santiago, Francisco

Gomez Maldonado, Alberto
Gonzalez Gonzalez, Ernesto
Gonzalez Reyes, Ruben
Gonzalez Rodriguez, Eduardo
Gonzalez Rosario, Pablo
Gonzalez Rosario, Pedro
Gonzalez Segarra, George
Guijarro del Corzo, Gregory A.
Guiven Flores, Cesar H.
Guzman Rivera, Ramon Antonio
Henriquez Rodriguez, David A.
Hernandez Adorno, Francisco
Hernandez, Antonio
Hernandez Hernandez, Marino
Hernandez Jorge, Jose A.
Hernandez Pagan, German
Hernandez Velez, Luis F.
Herrera Fuentes, Boanerges
Irene Vargas, Pablo
Irrizary Brignoni, Roberto
Jaca Hernandez, Eusebio
Jaramillo Ocasio, Jose R.
Kerr Matta, Frederick
LaSanta Arroyo, Vicente
Laureano Molina, Enrique
Llado-Gonzalez, Ivan
Longueira, Ricardo
Lopez Negroni, Rafael
Loyola Zayas, Angel A.
Lugo Lugo, Euripides
Lugo Soto, Benito
Manzano Lopez, Pablo
Marin Mingaro, Louis
Marrero Nieves, Miguel A.
Martinez Duran, Ricardo L.
Martinez Perez, Jimmy
Martinez Santiago, Candido
Martinez-Pacini, Francisco
Matos Arroyo, William
Medina Rivera, Luis A.
Mejias Nunez, Gilberto
Mendez Santiago, Miguel
Mercado Vila, Nicanor
Merced De La Paz, Victor M.
Mestre Sonelez, Ibrahim
Minier Cespedes, Juan A.
Miranda Irrizary, Radames Ivan
Miranda Mercado, Anselmo
Mojica-Torres, Jose
Montalvo-Aviles, Javier
Montanez Ortiz, Jorge L.
Montes Quevedo, Luis J.
Morales Figueroa, Rafael
Morales Gonzalez, Jose A.
Morales Rodriguez, Carlos R.
Morales-Rodriguez, Jose E.
Narvaez Hernandez, Jose E.
Narvaez Santiago, Efrain
Navedo Rodriguez, Luis A.
Negron Rivera, Edwin
Negron Santana, Hector
Nel Alvelo, Pedro
Nieves Colon, Angel Antonio
Nieves Marrero, Luis R.
Nieves Vazquez, Santos
Nunez, Quinones Pedro Arcadio
O'Neill Rosario, Luis R.
Oquendo Serrano, Angel
Orozco Carrasquillo, Gaspar
Ortiz Alvarado, Justo
Ortiz Collazo, Francisco
Ortiz Pastrana, Carlos A.
Ortiz Rodriguez, Jacinto
Ortiz Rosado, Perfecto
Otero Lugo, Jose
Otero Torres, Haraldo
Oyola Figueroa, Angel L.
Pabon Hernandez, Angel R.
Pabon Molina, Angel A.
Padilla Nazario, Fernando M.
Pappeterra Arthur, Jose A.
Paz Gonzalez, William
Perez Bracero, Jose R.
Perez Fuentes, Raul
Perez Gonzalez, Ignacio
Perez Gonzalez, Raul A.
Perez Guadalupe, Jose
Perez, Guillermo M. Vaello
Perez Silva, Juan B.
Perez-Aviles, Luis Ramon
Ramirez Abreu, Tomas
Ramon Ramon, Ramon L.
Ramos Rivera, Benjamin Antonio
Ramos Rodriguez, Ramon L.
Ramos-Pesquera, Gilberto
Recio Gomez, Gilberto
Resto-Vargas, Enrique
Reyes Anciano, Humberto
Reyes Crespo, Rafael
Reyes Matos, Manuel
Reyes Torres, Victor M.
Reyes-Vargas, Hector
Rios Aponte, William
Rios Arroyo, Jose M.
Rivera Albino, Luis
Rivera Alequin, Ulpiano H.
Rivera Baez, Eugenio
Rivera, Carmelo
Rivera Collazo, Angel
Rivera Colon, Ramon
Rivera De Jesus, Efigenio
Rivera Diaz, Hector R.
Rivera Fuentes, Jorge L.
Rivera Garcia, Edwin
Rivera Martinez, Carlos
Rivera Mojica, Jose D.
Rivera Negron, Ernesto
Rivera Rios, Cristobal
Rivera Rivera, Ramon L.
Rivera Rodriguez, Presbitero
Rivera Vazquez, Joaquin
Rodriguez Acevedo, Ramon
Rodriguez, Edwin
Rodriguez Gutierrez, Edwin
Rodriguez Melendez, Orlando
Rodriguez Rodriguez, Francisco
Rodriguez Rodriguez, Jose M.
Rodriguez Rodriguez, Wilfredo
Rodriguez Serrano, William
Roman Del Valle, Miguel A.
Roman Maldonado, Jose M.
Roman Maldonado, Miguel A.
Roman Ramirez, Santiago
Rosado Yambo, Martin
Rosario Rivera, Jose
Ruiz-Torres, Ramon L.
Sanabria Lopez, Rafael
Sanchez Acosta, Oscar
Sanchez, Israel
Sanchez Marquez, Jose Manuel
Sanchez Ortiz, Julio
Sanchez Vazquez, Manuel
Santamarina Dorta, Omar
Santiago, Antonio
Santiago, Ramon C.
Santiago Santos, Higinio
Santos Negron, Marcos A.
Sepulreda-Rivera, Juan
Serrano Rivera, Servy A.
Suarez, Ibrahim
Suarez Molina, Israel
Toro, Obed Eliezer
Torregrosa-Ochoa, Edwin R.
Torres Acevedo, Pablo L.
Torres Burgos, Miguel A.
Torres Diaz, Eugenio
Torres Irizarry, Jose
Torres Rodriguez, Dionilo
Torres Torres, Jose A.
Totti Lugo, Benjamin
Trujillo Cardona, Gerardo
Ubarri Mestres, Juan
Vaello-Perez, Guillermo
Valez Maldonado, Jose Antonio
Valladares Almodovar, Milton
Valle Valle, Esteban
Vargas Ramos, Domingo
Vazquez Garcia, Luis A.
Vazquez Rosario, Noel A.
Vega Laureano, Victor
Vega Vega, Jose P.
Veguilla Colon, Victor
Veguilla, Victor
Velazquez Gonzalez, Jose L.
Velazquez Reyes, Rafael
Velez Roman, Miguel
Ventura Ruiz, Emerito
Ventura-Ruiz, Emerito
Villamil Marrero, Fco. E.
Zambrana, Olimpio
Zambrana Ortega, Olimpio R.

INSTITUTIONS LOCATED IN DIOCESE

[A] COLLEGES & UNIVERSITIES

SAN JUAN. *Sacred Heart University*, (Grades Associate-Masters), Calle Rosales esq. San Antonio, Parada 26 1/2, Santurce, 00940. P.O. Box 12383, 00914-0383. Tel: 787-728-1515; Email: jjrivera@sagrado.edu; Web: www.sagrado.edu. The University has the following Departments and Programs: Departments of Communications, Humanities, Business Administration, Education, Natural Sciences and Social Sciences. The Graduate Programs include: Masters of Business Administration in Management of Systems Information, Masters of Arts & Communications, Masters of Art & Education, Masters of Occupational Nursing. Faculty 128; Total Enrollment 6,295.

Governing Board: Mr. Ramon Ruiz Comas, Pres. Bd. of Trustees; Dr. Jose Jaime Rivera, Pres.; Dr. Lydia Espinet, Dean Academic & Student Affairs; Mr. Jose L. Ricci Jr., Dean Admin.; Adlin Rios, Dean Devel.; Dr. Pedro Fraile, Assoc. Dean Student Affairs; Dr. Isabel Yamin, Dir. Humanities; Elmer Gonzalez, Dir. Communications; Migdalia Oquendo, Dir. Educ.; Marta Almeyda, Dir. Business Admin.; Zaida Gracia, Dir. Natural Sciences; Amelissa DeJesus, Dir. Social Sciences; Hylsa Silva Janer Esq., License & Legal Counsel; Ms. Mildred Pineiro, Registrar; Ms. June Andrade, Dir. Student Financial Aid; Juan Jose Rivera, Dir. Campus Ministry.

BAYAMON. *Universidad Central de Bayamon, Inc.*, (Grades Associate-Doctorate), Avenida Zaya Verde, Bo. Hato Tejas, P.O. Box 1725, Bayamon, 00960-1725. Tel: 787-786-3030; Fax: 787-785-1427; Email: lnegron@ucb.edu.pr; Web: ucb.edu.pr. The University has the following colleges: Liberal Arts and Humanities; Sciences and Health Professions; Business Administration and Technology; Education and Behavioral Professions; Graduate Studies; Central Institutes; Continuing Education and Student Service Program. Lay Teachers 169; Total Enrollment 2,221.

Governing Board: Rev. Oscar Morales-Cruz, O.P., Pres. Council of Founders; Encarnita Catalan-Marchand Esq., Pres. Bd. of Trustees.

Administration: Lillian Negron-Colon, Ph.D., Pres.; Mr. Angel Valentin-Roman, Vice Pres.; Dr. Luz C. Valentin-Caban, Dean Academic Affairs; Enid Rivera-Diaz, Interim Dean; Mrs. Niza E. Zayas-Marrero, Dean Student Affairs; Rev. Yamil Samalot, O.P., Dir. Liberal Arts and Humanities; Dr. Caroline Gonzalez-Millian, Dir. Education; Dr. Pedro Robles-Centeno, Prof. & Dir. Sciences and Health; Mr. Pedro Bermudez, Dir. Institutional Devel.; Virtua Rivera-Roman, Dir. Human Resources; Mrs. Kendra M. Ortiz-Kivera, Registrar; Wanda Aponte-Luciano, Dir. Admissions; Edna Ortiz, Dir. Student Financial Aid; Annette Valentin Roman, Dir. Academic Resource Ctr.; Dr. Nidia Colon-Quintana, Prof. Business Admin. and Tech.

Faculty: Revs. Mario Rodriguez-Leon, O.P.; Ismael Fernandez-Torres, O.P.; Alfonso Guzman-Alfaro, O.F.M.; Angel Diaz-Caceres, P.B.R.O.; Edwin Hernandez-Ralat, P.B.R.O.; Roberto Martinez-Rivera, O.F.M.Cap.; Rafael Mendez-Hernandez, P.B.R.O.; Baltazar Nunez-Hernandez, P.B.R.O.; Ricardo Santin-Flores, P.B.R.O.; Yaniel Samalot-Rivera, O.P.

GUAYNABO. *ISTEPA (Instituto Superior de Teologia y Pastoral - Luis Cardenal Aponte Martinez)*, Calle Cuba #464, P.O. Box 9021967, 00902-1967.
Tel: 787-200-6891; Fax: 787-294-6961; Email: mdjr7566@gmail.com. Rev. Msgr. Francisco Medina Santos, Rector; Rev. Anibal Rafael Torres-Ortiz, Vice Rector. (Theology, Biblical and Pastoral courses for lay ministers and Deacons) Deacons 2; Lay Teachers 7; Priests 6; Students 700.

[B] ELEMENTARY & HIGH SCHOOLS

SAN JUAN. *Academia Perpetuo Socorro*, (Grades PreK-12), 704 Calle Jose Martí, 00907-3227.
Tel: 787-721-4540 (H.S.);
Tel: 787-724-1497 (Elem.);
Fax: 787-723-4550 (H.S.);
Fax: 787-725-8104 (Elem.); Email: perpetuo@perpetuo.org. Rev. Juan Santa Guzman, Dir./Prin.; Sarita Vazquez, Sr. Prin., Preschool; Mr. Jose M. Leavitt, Sr. Vice-Prin.; Mr. Ernesto Chiesa, Librarian- High School; Wanda Toro, Librarian- Elementary School; Ms. Jeannette Sanchez, Prin. Elementary School; Mr. Luis Sanchez, Vice Prin. Jr. High School; Ms. Enid Pereira, Vice Prin. High School. Lay Teachers 120; Priests 3; Total Enrollment 1,050; Religious Sisters 2.

Academia San Ignacio de Loyola, Urb. Santa Maria, 1908 Calle Narciso, 00927-6716. Tel: 787-765-8190; Fax: 787-765-3635; Email: academia@asiloyola.org; Web: www.asiloyola.org. Rev. Lawrence P. Searles, S.J., Pastor; Luis O. Pino-Rivera, Dir.; Glorimar Soegaard, Prin.; Adela Sabater, Librarian. Lay Teachers 48; Total Enrollment 504.

Colegio Angeles Custodios, Urb. San Jose #13 Calle Sicilia, 00923. Tel: 787-763-3829;
Fax: 787-764-9496; Email: angelescustodios1954@gmail.com. Maria Aranzazu Labak, Dir.; Sr. Luis Roberto Rivera Cepeda, Prin.; Rev. Rogelio Salazar-Valero, (Mexico); Soamy Velez Perez, Librarian. Students (K-8) 81; Students (9-12) 101.

Colegio Calasanz, Montecarlo Ave., 00929-0067.

Tel: 787-750-2500; Fax: 787-257-0450; Email: calasanzpr@cc-rpi.org. P.O. Box 29067, 00929-0067. Revs. Juan L. Cabrerizo, Sch.P., (Spain); Francisco Javier Lopez, Sch.P., (Spain) Campus Min.; Agustin Lopez, Sch.P., (Spain) Campus Univ.; Maritere del Rio, Counselor; Ana Celia Santos, Prin. (High School); Glenda Laureano, Prin. (Elementary); Ruben Tirado, Librarian. Lay Teachers 25; Priests 3; Total Enrollment 310.

Colegio Corazon De Maria (Archdiocesan School) PMB 266, P.O. Box 78791, Guaynabo, 00970-7891. Tel: 787-783-3275; Fax: 787-774-5682. Maria A. Rodriguez Reyes, M.A.Ed., Prin. Lay Teachers 18; Priests 1; Students 245.

Colegio Espiritu Santo, Pachín Marín Esq. Suiza St., 00917. Tel: 787-754-0490; Fax: 787-754-7154. P.O. Box 191715, 00917-1715. Rev. Msgr. Valeriano Miguélez, (Spain) Dir.; Mrs. Milagros Zurkowsky, Prin.; Mrs. Elena Rivera, Academic Prin.; Mrs. Olga D. Torres, Librarian; Mrs. Maria I. Orta. Lay Teachers 33; Students 420.

Colegio Maria Auxiliadora, 2273 Eduardo Conde, 00915. Tel: 787-726-8288; Fax: 787-727-6497; Email: smmmfma@hotmail.com. Sr. Magna M. Martinez, F.M.A., Prin.; Elba Varela, Librarian. Sisters 8.

Colegio Nuestra Senora de Guadalupe, 19 N.E. St. #1, Puerto Nuevo, 00920. Tel: 787-782-0330; Fax: 787-782-0454. P.O. Box 364125, 00936-4125. P. Neil Macaulay, Dir.; Mrs. Genevieve Zayas, Prin.; Teresita Hernández, Vice Prin.; Jackeline Wys, Librarian. Lay Teachers 35; Students 599.

Colegio Nuestra Senora de Lourdes, (Grades PreK-12), 1050 Demetrio O'Daly, Country Club, 00924. Tel: 787-769-6284; Tel: 787-769-6275; Fax: 787-750-7805; Fax: 787-757-1245. P.O. Box 29193, 65 INF Station, 00929-0193. Janet Hernandez, Dir. & Prin.; Melissa Carrera, Vice Prin. High School; Marisol Quinones, Librarian; Nilsa Menéndes, Librarian. Lay Teachers 30; Students 278.

Colegio Nuestra Senora Del Carmen, R.R. 2, Box 15, 00926-9701. Tel: 787-761-8010; Fax: 787-748-2505; Email: melisea@coqui.net. Sisters Arlyn Medina Vazquez, Dir.; Elizabeth Andino, Prin.; Lissette Torres, Prin.; Liliana Santiago, Prin. Lay Teachers 38; Sisters 8; Students 510.

Colegio Reina De Los Angeles, Urb. Villa Andalucia, M19 Calle Frontera, 00926-2304. Tel: 787-761-7455; Fax: 787-761-7440; Email: colegio1972reina@gmail.com. Ivelisse Vazquez Severino, Dir.; Ana Román, Registrar; Gisela Espada, Prin.; Ileana Fabregat, Librarian. Lay Teachers 15; Sisters 3; Students 172.

Colegio San Ignacio de Loyola, Urb. Santa Maria, 1940 Calle Sauco, 00927-6718. Tel: 787-765-3814; Fax: 787-758-4145. Rev. Flavio I. Bravo, S.J., Dir.; Wildred J. Calvesbert, Pres. & Prin. Priests 2; Students 637.

Colegio San Vicente de Paul, 709 Bolivar St., 00910. Tel: 787-727-4273; Fax: 787-728-6135. P.O. Box 8699, Fernández Juncos Sta., 00910-8699. Rev. Marion Poncette, C.M., Dir.; Emilio Roldan, Prin.; Marina Perez, Librarian; Maria del C. Cordova, Counselor. Operated by: Congregacion de la Misión de San Vincente de Paúl, Inc. (Padres Paúles) Lay Teachers 23; Priests 2; Students 380.

Colegio Santo Domingo Savio, Ave. Gilberto Monroig 2278, 00916. Tel: 787-728-2175; Fax: 787-982-2903. P.O. Box 14125, Bo. Obrero Sta., 00916-4125. P. Miguel A. Rivera Borges, Dir.; P. Lorenzo Ruiz Victoria, Admin. Lay Teachers 1.

Nuestra Senora De Belen (Archdiocesan School) P.O. Box 10845, 00922-0845. Tel: 787-792-3115; Fax: 787-781-4920; Email: colegiobelen11@yahoo.com. Eleonor Marrero, Prin. (Elementary); Eduardo Rodríguez, Prin. (High School); Mayra Mendez Barreto, Dir. Lay Teachers 49; Students 752.

Nuestra Senora de la Altagracia, (Grades PreK-12), (Archdiocesan School) P.O. Box 29493, 00929-0493. Urb Villa Prades, Calle Felipe Gutierrez 672, 00924. Tel: 787-763-7755; Email: altagraciapr04@yahoo.com. Sr. Marta Gonzalez, Prin.; Rev. Jorge Ernesto Torres. Clergy 5; Lay Teachers 18; Students 120.

San Jorge (Archdiocesan School) 1701 Colon St., 00911-2041. Tel: 787-722-3182; Fax: 787-725-4580; Email: sanjorge@iname.com. Mrs. Maritza Rosario, Prin.; Mrs. Vanesa Valdes, Dir. Lay Teachers 70; Students 681.

BAYAMON. *Academia Maria Reina*, Urb. College Park, Glasgow #1879, 00921-4899. Tel: 787-764-0690; Fax: 787-282-7556. Sr. Judith Burchyns, C.S.J., Pres.; Rita Hernández, Prin.; Lucila Aponte, Librarian. Catholic Girls School. Lay Teachers 80; Sisters 2; Students 664.

Academia Santa Maria del Camino, (Grades PreSchool-8), P.O. Box 4228, Bayamón Gardens Station, Bayamon, 00958-1218. Tel: 787-780-5770; Fax: 787-785-7373. Sr. Lucy del Blanco, O.S.R., Dir.; Margarita Montesinos Ortiz, Prin.; Myrna Lee Román Miró, Librarian. Lay Teachers 16; Sisters 1; Students 231.

Colegio Beato Carlos Manuel Rodriguez, 3000 Jazmin, Urb. Lomas Verdes, Bayamon, 00956. Tel: 787-798-5260; Tel: 787-798-1548; Tel: 787-798-2329; Fax: 787-787-2620; Email: pjmartinez@colegiobeato.org; Web: www.cbcmr-bay.org. P.O. Box 4225, Bayamon, 00958. Pedro J. Martinez, School Dir.; Luisa M. Morales, School Prin.; Jaime Solivan, Librarian. Students 300.

Colegio Ntra. Sra. del Rosario, Calle 5, AA-7, Rep. Valencia, Bayamon, 00659. Tel: 787-798-5100; Fax: 787-269-7551. Sr. Ma. Ana Jimenez Maldonado, O.P., Dir.; Elba I. Soto, Prin. Students 300.

Colegio Santa Rosa, P.O. Box 6032, Bayamon, 00960. Tel: 787-785-1195 (H.S.); Tel: 787-785-0381 (Elem.); Fax: 787-740-0115 (H.S.); Fax: 787-785-3791 (Elem.). Neymi A. Aponte, Prin. (High School); Mrs. Nilsa Gonzales, Prin. (Elementary). Lay Teachers 30; Priests 1; Total Enrollment 976.

CAROLINA. *Academia Del Carmen*, Urb. Lomas de Carolina, Calle Monte Britton, Esq. Monte Membrillo, Carolina, 00987. Tel: 787-757-4454; Fax: 787-762-6656; Email: academiadelcarmen@gmail.com; Web: academiadelcarmen.com. P.O. Box 299, Carolina, 00986-0299. Mrs. Aitza Vázquez-Padilla, Subdirector (Elem. & High School); Mrs. Gladymir Montanez, Librarian. Lay Teachers 19; Priests 1; Total Enrollment 20.

Colegio Maria Auxiliadora, Box 7770, Carolina, 00986-7770. Tel: 787-762-0350; Tel: 787-768-6924; Fax: 787-257-3760; Web: auxiliadorapr.org. Rev. Msgr. Nestor Yulfo-Hoffman, Dir.; Rosa Perez, Prin. Lay Teachers 38; Priests 1; Students 570.

Colegio Santa Gema, 100 Galicia Ave., Vistamar, Carolina, 00983. Tel: 787-768-3082; Fax: 787-750-3090. P.O. Box 2789, Carolina, 00984-2789. Mrs. Francine M. Ildefonso, Prin.; Wanda Sánchez, Librarian. Lay Teachers 54; Students 814.

GUAYNABO. *Colegio Marista*, Alturas de Torrimar #6 Calle Marcelino Champagnat, Guaynabo, 00969-3251. Tel: 787-720-2186; Tel: 787-720-2187; Fax: 787-720-7020; Email: secretaria@maristasguaynabo.org. Bro. Balbino Juarez, F.M.S., Pres.; Gloria Garcia-DeJesus, Prin. Marist Brothers. Administrators 12; Brothers 4; Lay Teachers 110; Priests 1; Students 1,298.

Colegio Sagrados Corazones, P.O. Box 3902, Guaynabo, 00970-3902. Tel: 787-720-2585; Fax: 787-720-6035. Ms. Lourdes Rodríguez, Dir. Lay Teachers 38; Students 443.

Colegio San Pedro Martir, Alpierre (Final), Guaynabo, 00969. Tel: 787-720-2219; Fax: 787-272-8770. P.O. Box 2560, Guaynabo, 00970-2560. Rev. Msgr. Mario Guijarro, Dir.; Mr. Leonardo L. Cuadros, Prin. Lay Teachers 28; Sisters 1; Students 357.

Preescolar San Juan Evangelista, Urb. Torrimar, JA-5 Calle Church Hill, Guaynabo, 00966-3109. Tel: 787-781-5325; Fax: 787-793-8076. Ms. Lourdes Rodríguez, Administrative Dir.; Flor María Lugo, Prin. Lay Teachers 33; Students 270.

HATO REY. *Colegio Lourdes*, 87 Mayaguez St., 00917. Tel: 787-767-6106; Tel: 787-756-5436; Fax: 787-765-3388; Email: clourdes@coqui.net; Web: colegiolourdes.net. P.O. Box 190847, 00919-0847. Sisters Maria Milagros Velez, O.P., Dir.; Anabelle Flores, O.P., Prin. (Elementary); Dr. Isamari Cruz, Prin. (High School); Sra. Maria Carmen Gracia, Vice Prin. Lay Teachers 40; Sisters 5; Students 580.

Colegio Nuestra Senora de La Merced, Calle Sargento Luis Medina #374, Hato Rey, 00936. Tel: 787-765-7342; Tel: 787-754-1162; Fax: 787-765-3970. P.O. Box 364048, 00936-4048. William Súarez, Dir.; Mrs. Coville Auoyo, Prin.; Marina Azofra, Librarian. Lay Teachers 35; Students 376.

RIO PIEDRAS. *Colegio Mater Salvatoris*, Carretera 838 Km 4.8 de Rio Piedras Caguas, Rio Piedras, 00926-9690. Tel: 787-765-0130. R.R. 37 Box 3080, 00926-9601. Madre Isabel Fejervary Rappard, C.S. Lay Teachers 79; Sisters 6; Students 726.

Colegio Nuestra Senora De La Providencia (Girls) Ave. San Ignacio #1358, Urb. Altamesa, Rio Piedras, 00921. Tel: 787-781-7506; Tel: 787-782-6344; Fax: 787-792-7888; Email: zegri@coqui.net. Mailing Address: P.O. Box 11610, 00922-1610. Sr. Lourdes Martínez, Prin. Mercedarian Sisters. Lay Teachers 46; Priests 1; Sisters 4; Students 950.

Colegio Sagrado Corazon de Jesus, (Grades PreK-8), University Gardens, 251 Calle Oxford Esq. Howard, 00927-4826. Tel: 787-765-4798; Fax: 787-765-5267; Email: info@psagradocorazon.org. Hna. Mary Andreen Rusin, O.S.F., Prin.; Rev. Anulfo Del Rosario Sosa, C.M., (Dominican Republic) Dir.; Milagros Lugo, Librarian. Lay Teachers 52; Priests 2; Sisters 2; Students 674; Teacher's Assit. 5.

Colegio San Jose, (Grades 7-12), Box 21300, 00928-1300. Tel: 787-751-8177; Fax: 866-955-7644; Email: sanjose@csj-rpi.org; Web: www.csj-rpi.org. Calle Paz Esq. Los Marianistas, Rio Piedras, 00925. Bro. Francisco T. Gonzalez, S.M., M.D., Dir. & Prin. Brothers 2; Lay Teachers 41; Priests 1; Students 489.

SANTURCE. *Academia Sagrado Corazon*, Fernandez Juncos Sta., Box 11368, 00910. Tel: 787-721-3300; Fax: 787-725-1865; Email: asagradocorazon@gmail.com. Rev. Francisco Javier Quinones, Spiritual Dir.; Emely Astacio, Dir.; Isabel Barreto, Librarian. Lay Teachers 24; Priests 1; Students 211.

Colegio de La Inmaculada, (Grades PreK-12), 1711 Ponce de Leon Ave., 00909-1997. Tel: 787-727-6673; Fax: 787-728-7768; Email: inmaculadasanturce@yahoo.com; Web: www.inmaculadasanturce.com. Sr. Maria Dolores Viceues, H.C., Dir.; Ana Matos, Prin.; Maria Acosta Perez, Librarian. Lay Teachers 22; Sisters 3; Students 217.

Colegio Sagrada Familia (Archdiocesan School) Urb. Llorens Torres #2059, Calle Loiza, 00913. Tel: 787-726-1742; Fax: 787-726-0718. Ines Y. Elias, Prin.; Vanessa Valdes, Dir. Lay Teachers 6; Students 164.

Colegio San Juan Bosco, Carpenter Rd., Constitucion Santos Elena, 00915. Tel: 787-726-1995; Fax: 787-268-1869. Mailing Address: P.O. Box 14367, 00916-4367. Rev. Hiriam Santiago, S.B.D., Dir.; Mrs. Lissette M. Ruiz. Lay Teachers 22; Priests 2; Religious 15; Students 301.

TRUJILLO ALTO. *Santa Cruz* (Archdiocesan School) Dr. Fernandez St., #203, Trujillo Alto, 00977. Tel: 787-761-1100; Fax: 787-755-3065. Mailing Address: P.O. Box 1809, Trujillo Alto, 00977-1809. Rev. Carlos Alberto Contreras Tribaldo, Dir.; Mrs. Ana L. Monzon de Matos, Prin. Lay Teachers 25; Sisters 1; Students 371.

[C] SPECIAL SCHOOLS AND SEMINARIES

BAYAMON. *Casa Mision Claret* (Claretians) R.R. 12, Box 10131, Bo. Buena Vista, Bayamon, 00956. Tel: 787-797-8230.

Convento Ntra. Sra. del Rosario (Dominicans) P.O. Box 1968, Bayamon, 00960. Tel: 787-785-6542; Tel: 787-786-4508; Fax: 787-798-2712; Web: dominicospr.com.

Seminario Agustiniano Sto. Tomas De Villanueva, Carretera 830 km 5.1, Camino Los Muleros, Barrio Santaolaya, Bayamon, 00961. P.O. Box 3948, Bayamon, 00958. Tel: 787-797-0708; Fax: 787-797-9953; Email: tomasdevillanuevapr@yahoo.es. Revs. Beniqno Palomo, O.S.A.; Carlos Ruben Alqarin, O.S.A.; Jose Rafael Cepeda, O.S.A. (Augustinians) Brothers 1; Priests 3.

CATANO. *Prenoviciado Salesiano* (Don Bosco Salesians) Ave. Flor Del Valle, Bloque BB #108, Urb. Las Vegas, Catano, 00962. Tel: 787-275-1921; Fax: 787-788-8163; Email: sanfasal@coqui.net. P.O. Box 567, Catano, 00963-8163. Rev. Adan Marrero, S.D.B.

DORADO. *Estudiantado Pasionista* (Passionists) Carretera 695 km. 3.3, Sector Los Puertos, Barrio Higuillar, Dorado, 00646. Tel: 787-278-0517. P.O. Box 593, Dorado, 00646-0593. Rev. Ramon Gurtubay, C.P., (Spain) Supr. Priests 2; Students 6.

RIO PIEDRAS. *Colegio San Antonio*, P.O. Box 21350, 00928-1350. Tel: 787-764-0090; Fax: 787-763-7592; Email: helenperezdiaz@hotmail.com. Sr. Maria Ramon Santiago, Dir.; Nayda Jimenez, Librarian (Intermediate & High School); Annie Rivera, Librarian (Elementary School); Mrs. Marlene Feliu, Prin.; Katherine Gibbs, Prin. Brothers 1; Priests 2; Sisters 2; Full Time Lay Teachers 65; Part Time Lay Teachers 2.

Fraternidad San Antonio (Capuchin Postnovitiate) P.O. Box 25177, 00928. Revs. Jose Angel Torres Rivera, O.F.M.Cap., Guardian; Ramon J. Casellas Rivera, O.F.M.Cap.; Anibal Rosario Mercado, O.F.-M.Cap.; Mario Mastrangelo Tuscano; Bros. Jose David Maldonado Rivas; Roberto Colon Ortiz; Gabriel Juaibe Perez. Brothers 4; Priests 4.

Fraternidad Santa Maria de Los Angeles (Centro Capuchins) Care.877 Km.1 Hm 6, Rio Piedras, 00936. Tel: 787-761-8060; Tel: 787-761-8410; Fax: 787-293-1682. Aptdo. 29882, 00929-0882. Rev. Jose Fernando Irizzary, O.F.M.Cap., Dir.; Bro. Jaime Perez Munoz, O.F.M.Cap.

Seminario Mayor Arquidiocesano (Diocesan) Ave. De Diego No. 930, Urb. La Riviera, 00921. Tel: 787-273-8090; Tel: 787-706-9455; Fax: 787-706-9455; Email: seminario.mayor@yahoo.com; Email: vocacionesarq@yahoo.com. Mailing Address: Apdo. 11714, Rio Piedras,

00922-1714. Rev. Msgr. Ivan L. Huertas-Colon, Rector. Priests 1.

TOA BAJA. *Post-Noviciado San Jose Obrero* (Franciscans) Carretera 866 Km. 3.4, Sabana Seca, Sabana Seca, 00952. Tel: 787-795-3141. P.O. Box 173, Sabana Seca, 00952-0173. Rev. Eddie Caro, O.F.M., Rector.

[D] SPECIAL CENTERS

SAN JUAN. *Renovacion Conyugal* dba Fundacion Fernando Martinez, 573 Calle Alverio, 00918. Tel: 787-751-6001; Fax: 787-766-1363; Email: renovacionpr@yahoo.com; Web: geocities.com/renovacionpr. Rev. Jorge Ambert, S.J., Dir.

Santa Ana Chapel Perpetual Adoration Calle Tetuan 203, P.O. Box 9022145, 00902. Tel: 787-722-0861; Fax: 787-722-0861. Rev. Benjamin Antonio Perez Cruz, Rector.

PUERTO NUEVO. *San Gabriel School For The Deaf,* Prolongacion Calle 19 NE, Puerto Nuevo, 00920. Tel: 787-783-3455; Fax: 787-781-3770. P.O. Box 360347, 00936-0347. Sr. Amparo Blasco, Dir.

RIO PIEDRAS. *Centro Universitario Catolico,* 10 Mariana Bracetti St., 00925-2201. Tel: 787-763-5432; Tel: 787-767-3348; Fax: 787-296-3068; Email: elcuc2003@hotmail.com; Web: www.administracion@centrouniversitariocatolics.org. Rev. Rafael Rodríguez, S.J., Dir.

[E] CLINICS, HEALTH CENTERS

SAN JUAN. *Casa La Providencia, Inc.* Drug Rehabilitation Center P.O. Box 9020614, 00902-0614. Tel: 787-725-5358; Fax: 787-725-0058; Email: casalaprovidencia@hotmail.com; Web: casalaprovidenciapr.org. Sr. Maria Socorro Sandoval, Dir. Bed Capacity 32; Sisters Oblates of the Most Holy Redeemer 4; Tot Asst. Annually 100; Total Staff 20.

Centro Medico de P.R., Calle 10 #1030, Puerto Nuevo, Aptdo. 347, 00920. Tel: 787-763-7272. Rev. Msgr. Antonio Jose Vazquez Colon, Vicario, Tel: 787-777-3535; Tel: 787-723-2240; Cell: 787-562-2065; Revs. Francisco Arana, (Spain) Chap., Hospital Oncologico, Tel: 787-251-6466; Pedro Luis Zaballa, Chap., Hospital Universitario; Marcos Rivera-Perez, Chap. Hospital Municipal, Tel: 787-796-3418; Fabian Rodriguez Rodriguez, S.J., Chap., Hospital Cardiovascular, Tel: 787-740-3425; Francisco J. Marrodan, C.M., (Spain) Hosp. Auxilio Mutuo, Tel: 787-758-2000, Ext. 3070; Rev. Msgr. Valeriano Miguélez, (Spain) Hosp. Pavia, Hato Rey, Tel: 787-754-0570; Rev. Hector Diaz, Hosp. Veteranos, Tel: 787-641-7582, Ext. 3350; Carlos Cruz Davila, Hosp. Metropolitano, Tel: 787-782-4176; Deacons Jose R. Rivera, Hosp. Pediatrico, Tel: 787-475-7849; Andres Figueroa, Hosp. Pediatrico, Tel: 787-505-9973; Rev. Jorge Saenz, Hosp. San Pablo, Tel: 787-785-6874.

VA Medical Center, 10 Calle Casia, 00921-3200. Tel: 787-641-7582; Tel: 787-641-7575; Email: hrd198254@yahoo.com. Rev. Hector Diaz Estrada, Chap. Bed Capacity 535.

BAYAMON. *Hospital Hermanos Melendez,* Oficina de Administracion, P.O. Box 306, Bayamon, 00960-0306. Tel: 787-785-6542.

Hospital Hima San Pablo, Oficina de Administracion, P.O. Box 236, 00959-0236. Bayamon, 00960. Tel: 787-620-4747; Tel: 787-620-4762; Fax: 787-620-9273. Rev. Jorge Saenz, Chap., Tel: 787-785-6874.

Hospital Matilde Brenes, Oficina de Administracion, P.O. Box 2957, Bayamon, 00960-2957. Tel: 787-785-2381.

Hospital Universitario, Oficina de Administracion, Ave. Laurell, Bayamon, 00956. Tel: 787-785-8611. Dr. Ramon Ruiz Arnau, Dir.

CAROLINA. *Hospital de la Universidad de Puerto Rico, Dr. Federico Trilla,* Oficina de Administracion, P.O. Box 6021, Carolina, 00984. Tel: 787-757-1800; Fax: 787-276-2205; Email: dmaldonado@hospitalupr.org; Web: hospitalupr.org. Rev. Frank de la Rosa, Chap.

HATO REY. *Hospital Auxilio Mutuo,* Hato Rey. Tel: 787-758-2000, Ext. 3070; Fax: 787-771-7960; Web: www.auxiliomutuo.com. P.O. Box 1277, 00919. Rev. Francisco J. Marrodan, C.M., (Spain) Chap. Bed Capacity 591; Total Staff 1,230.

Hospital Pavia, Oficina de Administracion, P.O. Box 190828, 00919-0828. Ave. Pone De Leon, Hato Rey, 00917. Tel: 787-754-0570. Rev. Msgr. Valeriano Miguélez, (Spain).

RIO PIEDRAS. *Hospital del Maestro,* Calle Flamboyanes #218, Hyde Park, Rio Piedras, 00929. Tel: 787-763-8383. Rev. Jose Francisco Quintero-Angueira, Tel: 787-723-2240.

Hospital San Francisco, Oficina de Administracion, P.O. Box 29025, 00929-0025. Rio Piedras, 00926. Tel: 787-765-0606.

SANTURCE. *Doctor's Community Hospital,* Oficina de Administracion, P.O. Box 11338, 00910. Santurce, 00909. Tel: 787-999-7620; Fax: 787-725-2124; Email: echevarria@dchpr.com. Rev. Miguel Rivera Borges, S.D.B., Chap.

Hospital Pavia, Oficina de Administracion, P.O. Box 11137, 00910-1137. Santurce, 00912. Tel: 787-727-3963. Vincentian Fathers (Chaplains).

Hospital San Juan Capestrano, Oficina de Administracion, RR2 Box 11, 00926. Rio Piedras, 00926. Tel: 787-625-2900; Fax: 787-760-6875; Email: laura.vargas@uhsinc.com; Web: sjcapestrano.com. Bed Capacity 108; Tot Asst. Annually 5,000; Total Staff 230.

San Jorge's Children Hospital, Oficina de Administracion, P.O. Box 6308, 00914-6308. Santurce, 00912. Tel: 787-727-1000; Fax: 787-268-3610; Email: cruz.vivaldi@sanjorgechildrenshospital.com; Web: www.sanjorgechildrenshospital.com. Rev. Olin Pierre Louis. Bed Capacity 167.

[F] HOMES AND RESIDENCES

SAN JUAN. *Casa de Ninos Manuel Fernandez Juncos* (Orphans and Abused Boys) Calle Villa Verde Esq. Refugio, Pda 11, Miramar, 00902. Tel: 787-724-2904; Tel: 787-725-6328; Fax: 787-724-0980. P.O. Box 9020163, 00902-0163. Revs. Jose Brenes-Chavarria; Pablo Julio Osario Carmona; Bro. Jose Ramon Rodriguez-Abreu. Total Staff 22.

Casa La Providencia (Drug Addicted Women) 200 Calle Norzagaray, 00901-1122. Tel: 787-725-5358; Fax: 787-725-0058; Email: casalaprovidencia@hotmail.com. P.O. Box 9020614, 00902-0614. Sr. Adela Dominguez, Dir. Bed Capacity 24; Patients Asst Anual. 50; Total Staff 18.

Centro De Orientacion Vocacional Nuestra Senora del Consuelo, Floral Park, 20 C. Matienzo Cintron, 00919. Tel: 787-250-6323; Fax: 787-250-6323; Email: oblahchr@prte.net. Tot Asst. Annually 60; Total Staff 8.

BAYAMON. *Hogar Del Nino "El Ave Maria Corp."* (For Abused Children) Carretera 861, km 2.0, Bo. Pajaros Americanos, Bayamon, 00957. Tel: 787-797-2382; Tel: 787-279-3003; Fax: 787-797-2382. Mailing Address: PMB 239-A, P.O. Box 607071, Bayamon, 00960-7071. Sr. Florencia Santos, Dir. Bed Capacity 18; Tot Asst. Annually 35; Total Staff 27.

Hogar Escuela Sor Maria Rafaela (Girls with Problems) Carretera 871, km 1.0, Bo. El Volcan, Hato Tejas, Bayamon, 00961. Tel: 787-785-9517; Tel: 787-785-1125; Fax: 787-787-5324; Email: hogar.sormaria@gmail.com. P.O. Box 3024, Bayamon, PR 00960. Sr. Nelida Gonzalez, Dir. Bed Capacity 50; Tot Asst. Annually 40; Total Staff 30.

Hogar Fatima (Girls) Ave. Santa Juanita Final, Camino Esteban Cruz, Bayamon, 00961. Fax: 787-780-9763; Email: fatima001@prttc.net; Web: www.osrhogarfatimainc.com. P.O. Box 4228, Bayamon Garden Sta., Bayamon, 00958-4228. Tel: 787-787-2580; Fax: 787-780-9763. Sr. Maria Saez, Dir. Bed Capacity 36; Patients Asst Anual. 50; Staff 18.

DORADO. *Santuario del Espiritu Santo-Congregacion del Espiritu Santo,* Box 187, Dorado, 00646-0187. Tel: 787-796-2798; Fax: 787-796-1359; Email: puertoricocssp@espiritanos.com; Web: www.espiritanos.com. Revs. Jonas Rivera-Martinez, C.S.Sp., Rector; Eduardo Caron, C.S.Sp.; Jose Orlando Camacho-Torres, C.S.Sp.; Francis Peter Okib, C.S.Sp.

PUERTA DE TIERRA. *Asylum For The Aged and Infirm* (Hogar de Ntra. Sra. de la Providencia) Stop 5, Edif. 205, Puerta De Tierra, 00906-6571. Tel: 787-722-1331; Tel: 787-723-2419; Tel: 787-724-3574; Fax: 787-725-4308. Sr. Gladys Rosario, Supr.; Rev. Esteban Antonio De La Rosa, Chap. Sisters of the Poor. Patients Asst Anual. 207; Sisters 12.

RIO PIEDRAS. *Centro Santa Luisa* (1972) (Services for the Elderly) Carretera 842, Camino Los Romeros km 1.5, Bo. Caimito, 00926. Tel: 787-720-2764; Fax: 787-731-7795; Email: centrosantaluisa@yahoo.com. Mailing Address: R.R. 6 Box 9492, 00926-9492. Sr. Altagracia Rosario, H.C., Dir. Elderly Assisted Annually 73; Total Staff 8.

Hermanitas de los Ancianos Desamparados Hogar Santa Teresa Jornet de Cupey Inc., Cupey Alto, Ave. Las Cumbres, Km. 14. 3, Rio Piedras, 00926. Tel: 787-761-5805; Fax: 787-755-5575. 181 Calle Teresa Jornet, 00926-7542. Sor Angeles Garrido, Mother Supr. Sisters of the Poor. Bed Capacity 200; Residents 200; Sisters 11; Total Staff 88.

Hogar Carmelitano Julian Bengochea Final (Elderly Retirement Hospice) Calle Julian Bengoechea Final, 00924. Tel: 787-769-6510; Tel: 787-769-3110 ; Fax: 787-768-1240. Sr. Maribelle Mejias Muniz, Admin. Carmelite Sisters (Spain). Bed Capacity 224; Patients Asst Anual. 167; Total Staff 91.

Hogares Rafaela Ibarra (Orphan or Abused Girls) Urb.San Jose 432 Calle Torrelaguna, 00923. Tel: 787-763-1204; Fax: 787-763-6266; Web: www.hogaresrafaelaybarra.com. 432 Calle Torrelaguna, 00923-1773. Sr. Julia Jose, Dir. Patients Asst Anual. 40; Staff 14.

SANTURCE. *Politecnico Amigo* (For School Dropout Boys) Calle Refugio #960, Pda II, Santurce, 00940. Tel: 787-725-2059; Cell: 1-410-254-8941; Fax: 787-722-3436; Email: peosoriocarmona@gmail.com. P.O. Box 13204, 00908.

TOA ALTA. *Hogar Santisima Trinidad* (Drug Addiction Rehabilitation Home) Lote A y Lote B, km 7.0, Bo Mucarabones, Carr. 861, Toa Alta, 00954. Tel: 787-799-6208; Fax: 787-799-1977; Email: hstrinita@gmail.com. PMB 326-A, P.O. Box 607071, Bayamon, 00960-7071. Rev. Pedro Gorena, O.SS.T., (Spain). Patients Asst Anual. 93; Total Staff 14.

TOA BAJA. *Hogar Divino Nino Jesus,* Carretera 854, Km. 3.5, Toa Baja, 00949. Tel: 787-794-0020; Fax: 787-794-3124; Email: divinoninojesus@yahoo.es. P.O. Box 2464, Toa Baja, 00951-2662. Julio Pacheco, Dir. (Detox and Tx Residencial).

[G] PERSONAL PRELATURES

GUAYNABO. *Opus Dei* (Prelature of the Holy Cross and Opus Dei), Region of Puerto Rico of the Prelature Urb. Villa Caparra, #35 Calle A, Guaynabo, 00966-2211. Tel: 787-783-6206; Fax: 787-783-1201; Email: info@opusdei.org.pr; Web: www.opusdei.org.pr. Rev. Msgr. Justiniano Garcia Arias, Regl. Vicar, Puerto Rico; Revs. Gonzalo Diaz; Martin Llambias; Juan Aramendi; Ramon Alvarez Infiesta.

[H] MONASTERIES AND RESIDENCES FOR PRIESTS AND BROTHERS

SAN JUAN. *The Capuchin Formation Trust of Puerto Rico,* c/o P.O. Box 21350, 00928-1350. Tel: 787-764-3090; Fax: 787-764-4070. Rev. Roberto Martinez, O.F.M.Cap. *Capuchin Health and Retirement Trust of Puerto Rico*
Asociacion Frailes Capuchinos, Inc.

Comunidad Jesuita, Colegio San Ignacio, Urb. Santa Maria, 1940 Calle Sauco, 00927-6718. Tel: 787-758-1717, Ext. 1721; Fax: 787-750-8640. Revs. Baudilio Guzmán, S.J., Supr.; Flavio I. Bravo, S.J.

The Custody of Saint John the Baptist, Puerto Rico, of the Order Friars Minor Capuchin (1905) 216 Arzuaga St., P.O. Box 21350, 00928-1350. Tel: 787-764-3090; Fax: 787-764-4070; Email: secretaria.capuchinospr@gmail.com; Web: www.capuchinospr.org. Friars Roberto Martinez, O.F.M.Cap., Custodian; Jose A. Torres, O.F.M.Cap., Second Councillor & Treas.; Luis Gonzalez, O.F.M.Cap., Third Councillor & Sec. Properties owned, staffed & sponsored: Fraternities 2; Parishes 5; Retreat Centers 2; Friaries 5; Development Office 1; School 1.Represented in the Archdiocese of San Juan, PR, the Diocese of Arecibo, PR & the Diocese of Mayaguez, PR and Diocese of Caguas, PR.
Asociacion de Frailes Capuchinos, Inc.; Asociacion Misionera Capuchina, Inc.; Capuchin Formation Trust of Puerto Rico; Capuchin Health and Retirement Trust of Puerto Rico; San Antonio de Rio Piedras, Inc.; Monasterio San Miguel de Utuado, Inc.; Centro Capuchinos, Inc.; Caridades Capuchinas, Inc.; Casa Divina Pastora de Barranquitas, Inc.; Santa Teresita de Ponce, Inc. Postulants 4; Friars 22; Novitiates 3.

TRUJILLO ALTO. *Carmelite Monastery of St. Joseph* (1651) (Monasterio Carmelita De San Jose) Trujillo Alto, 00977-0568. Tel: 787-761-9548; Fax: 787-283-7235; Email: mcsjose@prtc.net. Mailing Address: P.O. Box 568, Trujillo Alto, 00977-0568. Sr. Madre Ines Maria Carmona Ortiz, O.Carm, Prioress.

[I] MISCELLANEOUS

SAN JUAN. *Caritas de Puerto Rico, Inc.,* 201 San Jorge St., 00910-0812. Tel: 787-300-4953, Ext. 1156; Tel: 787-727-7373, Ext. 1153; Tel: 787-300-4953, Ext. 1108; Fax: 787-728-3207; Email: info@caritas.pr; Web: caritas.pr. Mailing Address: P.O. Box 8812, 00910-0812. Rev. Enrique Manuel Camacho-Monserrate.

Casa San Clemente (Spiritual, Personal, Pastoral, and Psychological Counseling) 257 Ave. de la Constitucion, Puerta De Tierra, 00901. Tel: 787-723-6915; Fax: 787-977-8156. P.O. Box 9066315, 00902-3545. Rev. Terence Damian Wall, C.Ss.R., S.T.D., Exec. Dir.; Domingo G. Perez, Exec. Dir.

Centro Sor Isolina Ferre, Box 9511, 00926. Tel: 787-731-5700; Fax: 787-272-3390; Email: lurema@coqui.net; Email: lortiz@csifpr.org. Mrs.

Lourdes M. Ortiz, M.T.S. (Social Improvement of the Poor).

Hogar de Niñas de Cupey, Inc., Carr. 176 Km. 4.2 Bo. Cupey Alto, 00926. Tel: 787-761-2805; Fax: 787-283-1345; Email: info@hogardeninasdecupez.org; Web: hogardeninasdecupez.org. Mailing Address: P.O. Box 20667, 00928-0667. Employees 14.

Hogar Del Buen Pastor (Homeless Shelter) Constitucion #250, Puerta de Tierra, 00901. Tel: 787-721-8579; Fax: 787-921-8709. Mailing Address: P.O. Box 9066547, 00906-6547. Sr. Rosemarie Gonzalez, S.S.N.D.

Hogar Padre Venard, Inc., Calle San Francisco 305, 00901. Tel: 787-724-1131; Fax: 787-727-4616. Mailing Address: P.O. Box 9020274, 00902-0274.

R. R. Siervas de Maria Ministras de los Enfermos, 1 Calle Fortaleza, 00901-1501. Tel: 787-723-4558; Tel: 787-724-2228; Fax: 787-721-0140. Sr. Altagracia Urena, Supr. Sisters 24.

RIO PIEDRAS. *Paulinas Multimedia* (Books, Cassettes and Catholic Publications) Calle Arzuaga #164, 00925-3322. Tel: 787-764-4885; Tel: 787-765-4390; Fax: 787-767-6214; Email: libecria@paulinaspr.com; Web: www.paulinaspr.com.

SANTURCE. *Corporacion La Fondita De Jesus* (Supportive, spiritual and psychosocial services and transitional/permanent housing) Calle Monserrate 704, PDA 16 1/2, Santurce, 00909. Tel: 787-724-4051; Fax: 787-722-0992; Email: cartas@lafonditadejesus.org. P.O. Box 19384, 00910-1384. Tel: 787-725-0660; Fax: 787-722-0992. Socorro Rivera Rosa, Exec. Dir. Personnel 48; Total Assisted 3,100.

Servicios Pastorales Paules (Books, Leaflets and Catholic Publications) P.O. Box 19118, 00910. Tel: 787-728-0670; Email: centrosp@onelinkpr.net. Rev. Santiago Arribas, C.M., Dir.

Res.: 1650 Fernández Juncos, Santurce, 00910-9118. Email: centrosp@onelinkpr.net.

RELIGIOUS INSTITUTES OF MEN REPRESENTED IN THE ARCHDIOCESE

For further details refer to the corresponding bracketed number in the Religious Institutes of Men or Women section.

[0140]—*Augustinian Friars* (Spain)—O.S.A.
[0470]—*The Capuchin Friars* (Vice Prov. of Puerto Rico)—O.F.M.Cap.
[0270]—*Carmelite Fathers & Brothers* (Prov. of Aragon, Valentina, Spain)—O.Carm.
[0360]—*Claretian Missionaries* (Spain)—C.M.F.
[]—*Confraternidad de Operarios del Reino de Cristo*—C.O.R.C.
[0310]—*Congregation of Christian Brothers* (Antilles Prov.)—C.F.C.
[]—*Congregation of St. Michael Arcangel*—C.S.M.A.
[0820]—*Congregation of the Fathers of Mercy* (Madrid, Spain)—C.P.M.
[1330]—*Congregation of the Mission* (Prov. of Puerto Rico)—C.M.
[1000]—*Congregation of the Passion* (Bilbao)—C.P.
[]—*Congregation of the Sacred Heart* (Spain)—C.SS.CC.
[]—*Congregation of the Terciarios Capuchinos Ntra. Sra. de los Dolores* (Spain)—T.C.
[0520]—*Franciscan Friars* (Spain)—O.F.M.
[0650]—*Holy Ghost Fathers* (American Prov.)—C.S.Sp.
[0690]—*Jesuit Fathers and Brothers* (Prov. of Puerto Rico)—S.J.
[0740]—*Marian Fathers*—M.I.C.
[0770]—*The Marist Brothers*—F.M.S.
[]—*Misioneros Contemplativos Ad-Gentes*.
[1120]—*Missionaries of the Sacred Hearts of Jesus and Mary* (Spain)—M.SS.CC.
[0840]—*Missionary Servants of the Most Holy Trinity*—S.T.
[0910]—*Oblates of Mary Immaculate* (Peru Prov.)—O.M.I.
[0430]—*Order of Preachers-Dominicans* (Gen. Vicariate of P.R.)—O.P.
[1310]—*Order of the Holy Trinity* (Spain)—O.SS.T.
[1040]—*Piarist Fathers* (Spain)—Sch.P.
[1070]—*Redemptorist Fathers* (San Juan Prov.)—C.SS.R.
[]—*Regular Canonical Laterans Congregation*—C.R.L.
[1190]—*Salesians of Don Bosco* (Antilles Prov.)—S.D.B.
[0760]—*Society of Mary* (New York Prov.)—S.M.

RELIGIOUS INSTITUTES OF WOMEN REPRESENTED IN THE ARCHDIOCESE

[]—*Custodia Franciscana del Caribe "Santa Maria de la Esperanza"* (Frailes Franciscanos).
[1070-05]—*Dominican Sisters*—O.P.
[1070-06]—*Dominican Sisters*—O.P.
[1070-13]—*Dominican Sisters*—O.P.
[]—*Dominicanas Terciarias del Santisimo Sacramento* (Cadiz, Spain).
[]—*Hermanas Carmelitas de la Caridad* (Rome, Italy)—C.ach.
[]—*Hermanas Carmelitas de Madre Candelaria (Venezuela)*.
[]—*Hermanas Carmelitas Teresas de San Jose (Barcelona, Spain)*.
[]—*Hermanas de la Amistad Misionera en Cristo Obrero* (Amico and Madrid, Spain).
[]—*Hermanas de la B.V. Maria del Monte Carmelo* (Madrid, Spain)—H.Carm.
[]—*Hermanas de la Caridad del Cardenal Sancha* (San Domingo)—H.C.C.S.
[]—*Hermanas de la Caridad Del Sagrado Corazon De Jesus* (Madrid, Spain).
[]—*Hermanas de la Compania del Salvador* (Spain).
[]—*Hermanas De La Divina Providencia* (Rome, Italy)—C.D.P.
[]—*Hermanas de Santos Angeles Custodios* (Bilbao, Spain).
[]—*Hermanas Dominicas de la Presentacion* (Tours, France; Colombia).
[]—*Hermanas Dominicas de Nuestra Senora del Rosario de Fatima* (Yauco).
[]—*Hermanas Franciscanas de Los Sagrados*—HH.FF.SSCC.
[]—*Hermanas Hospitalarias de Jesus Nazareno* (Cordoba, Spain).
[]—*Hermanas Mercedarias de la Caridad* (Madrid, Spain).
[]—*Hermanas Misioneras de la Madre Dolorosa y San Francisco de Asis* (Buga, Colombia).
[]—*Hermanas Pasionistas de San Pablo de la Cruz*—C.P.
[]—*Hermanitas de los Ancianos Desamparados* (Valencia, Spain).
[]—*Hijas de la Pasion de Jesucristo y de Maria Delorosa*—C.P.
[]—*Hijas de Maria Auxiliadora* (Torino, Italy).
[]—*Hijas Del Corazon Misericordioso De Maria* (Bogota, Colombia).
[0950]—*Instituto Misionero Hijas de San Pablo* (Rome, Italy).
[]—*Instituto Santa Mariana de Jesus (Hermanas Marianitas)* (Ecuador)—R.M.
[]—*Lumen Dei* (Madrid, Spain)—U.L.D.
[]—*Madres de Desamparados y San Jose de la Montana* (Valencia, Spain).
[]—*Madres Escolapias* (Rome).
[]—*Misioneras de Cristo Salvador*.
[2710]—*Misioneras De La Caridad* (Calcutta, India)—M.C.
[]—*Misioneras del Buen Pastor* (San Juan).
[]—*Misioneras del Santisimo Sacramento y Maria Inmaculada* (Spain).
[]—*Misioneras Dominicas del Santisimo Rosario* (Madrid, Spain).
[]—*Misioneros Contemplativos Ad-Gentes*.
[2720]—*Mission Helpers of the Sacred Heart*—M.H.S.H.
[2790]—*Missionary Servants of the Most Blessed Trinity* (Philadelphia, PA)—M.S.B.T.
[]—*Monjas de la Orden de la Bienventurada Virgen Maria de Monte Carmelo*—O.Carm.
[]—*Oblatas De La Santisima Trinidad* (Spain).
[]—*Oblatas del Santisimo Redentor* (Madrid, Spain).
[]—*Operarias Del Divino Maestro* (Valenzia, Spain).
[]—*Religiosas del Sagrado Corazon* (Rome, Italy).
[]—*Religiosas Oblatas del Divino Amor*.
[]—*Religiosas Teatinas de la Inmaculada Concepcion* (Rome)—R.T.
[]—*Religiosas Terciarias de San Francisco de Asis y de la Inmaculada Concepcion* (Valencia, Spain).
[2970]—*School Sisters of Notre Dame* (Wilton, CT)—S.S.N.D.
[]—*Siervas De La Verdad* (Bayamon, Puerto Rico).
[3600]—*Siervas de Maria y Ministras de los Enfermos* (Rome, Italy)—S.M.
[2570]—*Sisters of Mercy* (Pittsburgh, PA)—R.S.M.
[]—*Sisters of Nazareth*.
[1620]—*Sisters of Saint Francis of Millvale, Pennsylvania*—O.S.F.
[1650]—*Sisters of St. Francis of Philadelphia*—O.S.F.
[1800]—*Sisters of St. Francis of the Third Order Regular* (Williamsville, New York)—O.S.F.
[3830]—*Sisters of St. Joseph* (Brentwood)—C.S.J.
[3930]—*Sisters of St. Joseph of the Third Order of St. Francis*—S.S.J.-T.O.S.F.
[1970]—*Sisters of the Holy Family of Nazareth*—C.S.F.N.
[1490]—*Sisters of the Third Franciscan Order*—O.S.F.
[2150]—*Sisters, Servants of the Immaculate Heart of Mary*—I.H.M.
[]—*Terciarias Franciscanas de la Purisima* (Murcia, Spain).

NECROLOGY

† Rivera, Hector M., Retired Auxiliary Bishop of San Juan., Died Apr. 9, 2019

An asterisk (*) denotes an organization that has established tax-exempt status directly with the IRS and is not covered by the USCCB Group Ruling.

Index for Religious Institutes of Men

Religious Order Initials for Men

A.A.	Assumptionists	[0130]
B.G.S.	Little Brothers of the Good Shepherd	[0580]
B.H.S.	Brothers of the Holy Spirit-Cleveland	[0645]
B.S.O.	Basilian Salvatorian Fathers	[0190]
C.F.A.	Alexian Brothers	[0120]
C.F.C.	Congregation of Christian Brothers	[0310]
C.F.P.	Brothers of the Poor of St. Francis	[0460]
C.F.R.	Franciscan Friars of the Renewal	[0535]
C.F.X.	Brothers of St. Francis Xavier	[1350]
C.I.C.M.	Missionhurst Congregation of the Immaculate Heart of Mary	[0860]
C.J.	Josephite Fathers	[0710]
C.J.M.	Congregation of Jesus and Mary	[0450]
C.M.	Congregation of the Mission	[1330]
C.M.C.	Congregation of Mother Coredemptrix	[0865]
C.M.F.	Claretian Missionaries	[0360]
C.M.I.	Carmelites of Mary Immaculate	[0275]
C.M.L.M.	The Congregation of Maronite Lebanese Missionaries	[0785]
C.M.M.	Congregation of Mariannhill Missionaries, Mariannhill Fathers & Brothers	[0750]
C.O.	Oratorians	[0950]
C.P.	Congregation of the Passion	[1000]
C.P.M.	Congregation of the Fathers of Mercy	[0820]
C.PP.S.	Society of the Precious Blood	[1060]
C.R.	Congregation of the Resurrection	[1080]
C.R.	Theatine Fathers	[1300]
C.R.L.	Canons Regular of the Lateran	[0250]
C.R.M.	Adorno Fathers	[0100]
C.R.S.	Somascan Fathers	[1250]
C.R.S.P.	Clerics Regular of St. Paul	[0160]
C.S.	Missionaries of St. Charles-Scalabrinians	[1210]
C.S.B.	Basilian Fathers	[0170]
C.S.C.	Brothers of the Congregation of Holy Cross	[0600]
C.S.C.	Priests of the Congregation of Holy Cross	[0610]
C.S.J.	Congregation of St. Joseph	[1150]
C.S.P.	Paulist Fathers	[1030]
C.S.P.X.	Brothers of Saint Pius X	[1180]
C.S.S.	Stigmatine Fathers and Brothers.	[1280]
C.S.Sp.	Congregation of the Holy Spirit	[0650]
C.Ss.R.	Redemptorist Fathers	[1070]
C.S.V.	Clerics of St. Viator	[1320]
Er.Cam.	Camaldolese Hermits of the Congregation of Monte Corona	[0230]
F.C.	Brothers of Charity	[0290]
F.D.P.	Sons of Divine Providence	[0410]
F.F.I.	Franciscan Friars of the Immaculate	[0533]
F.F.S.C.	Franciscan Brothers of the Holy Cross	[0510]
F.I.C.	Brothers of Christian Instruction	[0320]
F.M.M.	Brothers of Mercy	[0810]
F.M.M.	Missionary Fraternity of Mary	[0855]
F.M.S.	The Marist Brothers	[0770]
F.M.S.I.	Sons of Mary Missionary Society	[1270]
F.S.C.	Brothers of the Christian Schools	[0330]
F.S.C.B.	Priestly Fraternity of the Missionaries of St. Charles Borromeo	[1205]
F.S.E.	Brothers of the Holy Eucharist	[0620]
F.S.P.	Brothers of St. Patrick	[1160]
F.S.R.	Brothers of the Congregation of Our Lady of the Holy Rosary	[0960]
F.S.S.P.	Priestly Fraternity of St. Peter	[1065]
G.H.M.	The Glenmary Home Missioners	[0570]
H.G.N.	Heralds of Good News	[0585]
I.C.	Institute of Charity	[0300]
I.C.	Institute of Christ the King - Sovereign Priest	[0305]
I.H.M.	Brothers of the Immaculate Heart of Mary	[0680]
I.M.C.	Consolata Missionaries	[0390]
I.V.E.	Institute of the Incarnate Word	[0685]
L.B.S.F.	Little Brothers of Saint Francis	[1144]
L.C.	Legionaries of Christ	[0730]
M.Afr.	Missionaries of Africa	[0850]
M.C.C.J.	Comboni Missionaries of the Heart of Jesus (Verona)	[0380]
M.H.M.	Mill Hill Missionaries	[0830]
M.I.	Camillian Fathers and Brothers	[0240]
M.I.C.	Congregation of Marians of the Immaculate Conception	[0740]
M.J.	Missionaries of Jesus, Inc.	[0852]
M.M.	Maryknoll	[0800]
M.M.A.	Maronite Monks of Adoration	[0790]
M.S.	The Missionaries of Our Lady of La Salette	[0720]
M.S.A.	Society of the Missionaries of the Holy Apostles	[0590]
M.S.C.	Missionaries of the Sacred Heart	[1110]
M.S.F.	Congregation of the Missionaries of the Holy Family	[0630]
M.S.F.S.	Missionaries of St. Francis de Sales	[0485]
M.S.P.	Missionary Society of St. Paul of Nigeria	[0854]
M.Sp.S.	Missionaries of the Holy Spirit	[0660]
M.S.S.	Missionaries of the Blessed Sacrament	[0825]
M.SS.CC.	Missionaries of the Sacred Hearts of Jesus and Mary	[1120]
O.A.R.	Order of Augustinian Recollects	[0150]
O.Carm.	Carmelite Fathers and Brothers	[0270]
O.Cart.	Order of Carthusians	[0280]
O.C.D.	Discalced Carmelite Friars	[0260]
O.Cist.	Cistercian Abbey	[0340]
O.C.S.O.	The Cistercian Order of the Strict Observance (Trappists)	[0350]
O.de.M.	Order of Our Lady of Mercy	[0970]
O.F.M.	Franciscan Friars	[0520]
O.F.M.Cap.	The Capuchin Franciscan Friars	[0470]
O.F.M.Conv.	Conventual Franciscans	[0480]
O.H.	Hospitaller Brothers of St. John of God	[0670]
O.M.	Minim Fathers	[0835]
O.M.I.	Oblates of Mary Immaculate	[0910]
O.M.M.	Maronite Order of the Blessed Virgin Mary	[0782]
O.M.V.	Oblates of the Virgin Mary	[0940]
O.P.	Order of Preachers (Dominicans)	[0430]
O.Praem.	Canons Regular of Premontre	[0900]
O.S.A.	The Augustinians	[0140]
O.S.B.	Benedictine Monks	[0200]
O S.B.M.	Order of St. Basil the Great	[0180]
O.S.C.	Canons Regular of the Order of the Holy Cross	[0400]
O.S.F.	Congregation of the Religious Brothers of the Third Order Regular of St. Francis	[0490]
O.S.F.	Franciscan Brothers of the Third Order Regular	[0515]
O.S.F.	Franciscan Missionary Brothers of the Sacred Heart of Jesus	[0540]
O.S.F.S.	Oblates of St. Francis de Sales	[0920]
O.S.J.	Oblates of St. Joseph	[0930]
O.S.M.	Servites	[1240]
O.S.P.P.E.	Pauline Fathers	[1010]
O.Ss.S.	Brigittine Monks	[0895]
O.SS.T.	Order of the Most Holy Trinity	[1310]
P.I.M.E.	Pontifical Institute for Foreign Missions	[1050]
P.S.S.	Society of the Priests of Saint Sulpice	[1290]
R.C.J.	Rogationist Fathers	[1090]
S.A.	Franciscan Friars of the Atonement	[0530]
S.A.C.	Society of the Catholic Apostolate	[0990]
S.C.	Brothers of the Sacred Heart	[1100]
S.C.	Servants of Charity	[1220]
S.Ch.	Society of Christ	[1260]
Sch.P.	Piarist Fathers.	[1040]
S.C.J.	Congregation of the Priests of the Sacred Heart	[1130]
S.D.B.	Salesians of Don Bosco	[1190]
S.D.S.	Society of the Divine Savior	[1200]
S.D.V.	Vocationist Fathers	[1340]
S.F.	Sons of the Holy Family	[0640]
S.J.	Jesuit Fathers and Brothers	[0690]
S.M.	Society of Mary (Marianists)	[0760]
S.M.	Marist Fathers	[0780]
S.M.A.	Society of African Missions	[0110]
S.M.M.	Montfort Missionaries	[0870]
S.O.L.T.	Society of Our Lady of the Most Holy Trinity	[0975]
s.P.	Servants of the Paraclete	[1230]
S.P.S.	St. Patrick's Missionary Society	[1170]
S.S.C.	Society of St. Columban	[0370]
SS.CC.	Congregation of the Sacred Hearts of Jesus and Mary	[1140]
S.S.E.	Society of Saint Edmund	[0440]
S.S.J.	St. Joseph's Society of the Sacred Heart	[0700]
S.S.P.	Pauline Fathers and Brothers	[1020]
S.S.S.	Congregation of the Blessed Sacrament	[0220]
S.T.	Missionary Servants of the Most Holy Trinity	[0840]
S.X.	Xaverian Missionary Fathers	[1360]
S.V.D.	Society of the Divine Word	[0420]
V.C.	Vincentian Congregation (India)	[1335]
T.O.R.	Third Order Regular of Saint Francis	[0560]

Religious Institutes of Men

The Conference of Major Superiors of Men of the United States, Inc.—7300 Hanover Dr., Suite 304, Greenbelt, MD 20770. Tel: 301-588-4030; Fax: 240-650-3697. Website: www.cmsm.org. Bro. Larry Schatz, F.S.C., Pres.; Very Rev. Timothy P. Kesicki, S.J., Sec. & Treas.; Very Rev. Mark Padrez. O.P., Exec. Dir. A canonical conference of the major superiors of religious communities and institutes of men for the purpose of promoting the spiritual and apostolic welfare of priests and brothers.

[0100] (C.R.M.)—ADORNO FATHERS

(Clerics Regular Minor)

General Motherhouse: Via Alpi Apuane 1, 00141, Rome, Italy, Very Rev. Raffaele Mandolesi, C.R.M., Supr. Gen.

U.S. Foundation (1936): St. Michael's Seminary, 575 Darlington Ave., Ramsey, NJ 07446. Tel: 201-327-7375; Fax: 201-327-8131. Rev. Liam Reza M. Panganiban, C.R.M., Rector; Rev. Teodoro O. Kalaw, C.R.M., U.S.-Philippines Delegate.

Priests 12; Brothers 5

Represented in the Archdiocese of Newark and in the Diocese of Charleston.

[0110] (S.M.A.)—SOCIETY OF AFRICAN MISSIONS

(Societas Missionum ad Afros)

Founded Dec. 8, 1856 with the approval of Pope Pius IX. A clerical society of apostolic life.

Generalate: Via della Nocetta 111, 00164, Rome, Italy, Rev. Fachtna O'Driscoll, S.M.A., Supr. Gen.; Rev. Antonio Porcellato, S.M.A., Vicar Gen.; Rev. Francis Rozario, S.M.A., Gen. Councillor; Rev. Francois de Paul Houngue, S.M.A., Gen. Councillor.

American Province (1941): 23 Bliss Ave., Tenafly, NJ 07670. Tel: 201-567-0450; Fax: 201-241-1280. Very Rev. Michael P. Moran, S.M.A., Prov. Supr.; Rev. John P. Brennan, S.M.A., Vice Prov.; Rev. James J. McConnell, S.M.A., Councilor.

Legal Title: Society of African Missions, Inc. NJ.

Priests 17; Lay Associates in Temporary Commitment: 4; Lay Associate in Permanent Commitment: 1; Priest Associates: 2

Represented in the Archdioceses of Boston, Newark and Washington.

[0120] (C.F.A.)—ALEXIAN BROTHERS

(Congregatio Fratrum Cellitarum seu Alexianorum)

Generalate: Signal Mountain, TN 37377. Tel: 423-886-2969. Bro. Lawrence Krueger, C.F.A., Supr. Gen.; Bro. Dermot O'Leary, Asst. Supr. Gen.; Bro. Benedikt M. Ende, C.F.A., Gen. Councilor, Germany; Bro. John of God Oblina, C.F.A., Gen. Councilor Davao City, Philippines.

General Motherhouse: Congregation of Alexian Brothers, 198 James Blvd., Signal Mountain, TN 37377. Tel: 423-551-3969; Fax: 423-886-0208.

United States Province: 600 Alexian Way, Elk Grove Village, IL 60007. Tel: 847-264-8701; Fax: 847-264-8679. Email: Daniel.McCormick@Alexian.net. Councilors: Bro. Daniel McCormick, C.F.A., Prov.; Bro. Richard Lowe, C.F.A., Asst. Prov.; Bro. Jeffrey Callander, C.F.A.; Bro. Warren Longo, C.F.A.

Professed Brothers 25; Novice Brothers 4

Properties owned or sponsored: Novitiate 1; Wellness Center (Davao City, Philippines) 1

Represented in the Archdioceses of Chicago, Milwaukee and St. Louis and in the Diocese of Knoxville. Also in Davao City, Philippines and Györ, Hungary.

[0130] (A.A.)—ASSUMPTIONISTS

(Augustinians of the Assumption)

General House: via San Pio V, 55, 00165, Rome, Italy, Very Rev. Benoit Griere, A.A., Supr. Gen.

Province of North America (1946): 330 Market St., Brighton, MA 02135. Tel: 617-783-0400. Rev. Dennis M. Gallagher, A.A., Prov. Supr. Councilors: Rev. Peter Precourt, A.A; Rev. Richard Lamoureux, A.A.; Rev. Alex Castro, A.A., Treas.

Priests 44; Brothers 20; Parishes 3; Shrines: 1; Colleges 1; Formation Centers 3; Novitiates 1; Residences: 11

Represented in the Archdiocese of Boston and in the Diocese of Worcester. Also in Philippines, Kenya, Mexico, Tanzania, Italy and Canada.

[0140] (O.S.A.)—THE AUGUSTINIANS

(Ordo Sancti Augustini)

Founded in 1244, first American foundation 1796.

Generalate: Curia Generalizia Agostiniana, Via Paolo I # 25, 00193, Rome, Italy, Tel: 011-39-06-68-00-61; Fax: 011-39-06-68-00-6299. Most Rev. Alejandro Moral Anton, O.S.A., Prior Gen.; Very Rev. Joseph L. Farrell, O.S.A., Vicar Gen.; Rev. John R. Flynn, O.S.A., Sec. Gen.; Very Rev. Michael F. Di Gregorio, O.S.A., Prior Prov.; Rev. James D. McBurney, O.S.A., Province Sec.; Rev. Francis J. Horn, O.S.A., Province Treas.

Province of St. Thomas of Villanova (1796): Provincial Offices: St. Augustine Friary, 214 Ashwood Rd., P.O. Box 340, Villanova, PA 19085-0340. Tel: 610-527-3330; Fax: 610-520-0618. Counselors: Rev. Francis J. Doyle, O.S.A; Rev. Robert P. Hagan, O.S.A; Rev. John F. Deary, O.S.A; Rev. Craig M. McMahon, O.S.A; Rev. Arthur P. Purcaro, O.S.A; Rev. Raymond F. Dlugos, O.S.A; Paul Ashton, Abuse Prevention & Educ. Coord.; Joanna Bowen, Dir. Augustinian Volunteers; Rev. Joseph Narog, O.S.A., Dir. Vocations; Rev. Bro. Richard Ekmann, O.S.A., Province Archivist; Rev. John E. Deegan, O.S.A., Dir. Justice & Peace.

Legal Title: The Brothers of the Order of Hermits of Saint Augustine (The Brothers of the Order of Hermits of St. Augustine, a corporation in the state of Pennsylvania 1804).

Professed Friars: 153; Ordained Priests 143; Permanent Deacons 1; Non-Ordained Brothers 6; Novices 2; Students of Theology: 6; Pre-Theology Students: 2; Parishes (U.S.): 10; Parishes (Japan): 4; Major Seminaries 1; Pre-Novitiate Houses 1; Colleges 1; Universities: 1; Preparatory Schools 2; Foreign Missions (Japan): 5

Represented in the Archdioceses of Boston, New York and Philadelphia and in the Dioceses of Albany, Camden and Venice. Also in Czech Republic, Italy, Japan, Peru and Rome

Province of Our Mother of Good Counsel (Order of St. Augustine) (1941): Augustinian Province Offices, 5401 S. Cornell Ave., Chicago, IL 60615-5664. Tel: 773-595-4000; Fax: 773-595-4004. Email: secretary@midwestaugustinians.org; Web: www.MidwestAugustinians.org. Very Rev. Bernard C. Scianna, O.S.A., Prior Prov.; Rev. John D. Merkelis, O.S.A., Vicar Prov. & Personnel Dir.; Rev. Richard J. McGrath, O.S.A., Treas.; Rev. Richie P. Mercado, O.S.A., Vocation Dir.; Bro. Thomas P. Taylor, O.S.A., Prov. Sec.

Fathers 62; Bishops 2; Professed Brothers 20; Parishes 6; High Schools 3; Residences: 3

Represented in the Archdioceses of Chicago, Milwaukee, New York and Philadelphia and in the Dioceses of Gary, Joliet and Tulsa. Also in Peru, South America.

The Province of St. Augustine in California: 3180 University Ave., Ste. 255, San Diego, CA 92104-2045. Tel: 619-235-0247. Email: osa-west@sbcglobal.net. Very Rev. Kevin C. Mullins, O.S.A., Prov. Counselors: Rev. Alvin M. Paligutan, O.S.A., Sec.; Rev. Robert W. Gavotto, O.S.A; Rev. Michael McFadden, O.S.A; Rev. Carlos Medina, O.S.A.

Priests 25; Deacons 2; Brothers 10; Parishes 3; High Schools 2; Orphanages: 1

Legal Holdings or Titles: St. Augustine High School, San Diego, CA; Monica House, San Diego, CA; Tierra del Sol, Boulevard, CA; St. Rita House, San Francisco, CA; Villanova Preparatory School, Ojai, CA; Austin House, San Diego, CA.

Represented in the Archdioceses of Chicago, Los Angeles, Milwaukee and Portland in Oregon and in the Diocese of San Diego.

Augustinian Monastery: 611 Cedar Ave., P.O. Box 279, Richland, NJ 08350-0279. Tel: 856-697-2600; Fax: 856-285-7108. Rev. Francis X. Devlin, O.S.A., Prior; Rev. Donald F. Reilly, O.S.A., Pres.; Rev. Patrick B. McStravog, O.S.A., Asst. to Pres. for Mission & Ministry; Rev. Dennis J. Harten, O.S.A.; Rev. Joseph F. Girone, O.S.A., Treas.

Represented in the Archdiocese of Philadelphia and in the Diocese of Camden.

Region U.S.A. (1993): Cristo Rey Church, 767 Ave. A, Beaumont, TX 77701. Tel: 409-835-7788. Rev. Luis Urriza, O.S.A.

Fathers 4

Represented in the Archdiocese of San Antonio and in the Diocese of Beaumont.

[0150] (O.A.R.)—ORDER OF AUGUSTINIAN RECOLLECTS

(Ordo Augustinianorum Recollectorum)

General Motherhouse: Viale dell' Astronomia, 27, asella Postale 10760, 00144, Rome, Italy, Very Rev. Miguel Miro, O.A.R., Prior Gen.

Province of St. Augustine (1943): Augustinian Recollects, 29 Ridgeway Ave., West Orange, NJ 07052-3297. Tel: 973-731-0616; Fax: 973-731-1033. Rev. J. Michael Rafferty, O.A.R., Prior Prov.; Rev. Marlon Beof, O.A.R., 1st Councilor & Vicar; Rev. Fredric Abiera, O.A.R., 2nd Councilor; Rev. Gerard Cosgayon, O.A.R., 3rd Councilor; Rev. Charles Huse, O.A.R., 4th Councilor.

Bishops 1; Priests 32; Brothers 2; Professed Clerics: 1; Permanent Deacons 3.

Represented in the Archdioceses of Los Angeles, Newark and New York and in the Diocese of Orange. Also in Mexico.

Province of St. Nicholas of Tolentine (U.S.A. Delegation): 3021 Frutas Ave., El Paso, TX 79905. Rev. Jesus M. Mena, O.A.R., Prov. Delegate.

Priests 18; Brothers 1

Represented in the Archdiocese of Newark and in the Dioceses of El Paso and Las Cruces.

[0160] (C.R.S.P.)—CLERICS REGULAR OF ST. PAUL

(Barnabite Fathers)

(Ordo Clericorum Regularium Sancti Pauli)

Founded in Milan, Italy in 1533. First foundation in the United States in 1952 in Buffalo, NY.

General Motherhouse: Historical Motherhouse: Church of St. Barnabas, Milan, since 1545. Via Giacomo Medici, 15, Rome, Italy, Most Rev. Francisco M. Silva, C.R.S.P., Supr. Gen.

North American Province: 981 Swann Rd., P.O. Box 167, Youngstown, NY 14174-0167. Tel: 716-754-7489. Very Rev. Peter M. Calabrese, C.R.S.P., Prov. Supr

Legal Title: Order of Barnabite Fathers, Inc.

Priests 10

Fathers staff and serve: Parishes; Marian Shrine; Colleges; Spiritual Centers. Properties Owned or Sponsored: Our Lady of Fatima Shrine and Barnabite Fathers Seminary, Youngstown, NY; Barnabite Spiritual Center, Bethlehem, PA; St. Anthony M. Zaccaria Seminary.

Represented in the Dioceses of Allentown, Buffalo, and San Diego. Also in Hamilton, Ontario, Canada.

[0170] (C.S.B.)—BASILIAN FATHERS

(Congregatio Presbyterorum a St. Basilio)

General Curia: Cardinal Flahiff Basilian Centre, 95 St. Joseph St., M5S 3C2, Toronto, Tel: 416-921-6674; Fax: 416-920-3413. Email: katulski@basilian.org. Very Rev. Kevin J. Storey, C.S.B., Supr. Gen.; Rev. David Katulski, C.S.B., Vicar Gen.; Rev. Jack Hanna, C.S.B., Sec./Treas. Gen.

U.S. Headquarters: Catholic Central High School, 27225 Wixom Rd., Novi, MI 48374. Rev. Dennis Noelke, C.S.B., Gen. Councilor.

[0180] (O.S.B.M.)—ORDER OF ST. BASIL THE GREAT

(Ordo Sancti Basilii Magni)

General Superior "Protoarchimandrita": Via San Giosafat 8, (Aventino), 00153, Rome, Italy, Rev. Genesio Viomar, O.S.B.M.

American Province (1948): 29 Peacock Ln., Locust Valley, NY 11560. Tel: 516-609-3262; Fax: 516-609-3264. Very Rev. Varcilio Basil Salkovski, O.S.B.M., Prov. Superior.

Fathers 16; Brothers 4; Deacons 1; Novices 1; Parishes 6; Community Houses 8; Novitiates 1; Monasteries: 3; Retreat Houses 1; Libraries: 1

Represented in the Archdiocese of Chicago and Diocese of Stamford.

[0190] (B.S.O.)—BASILIAN SALVATORIAN FATHERS

General Motherhouse: Holy Savior Monastery, Saida, Lebanon, Archimandrite Tony Dib, B.S.O., Supr. Gen.

American Headquarters: Basilian Salvatorian Fathers, 30 East St., Methuen, MA 01844. Rev. Fares Al Khlaifat, B.S.O., Local Supr.; Rev. Lawrence Tumminelli, B.S.O; Rt. Rev. Archimandrite John

Jadaa, B.S.O; Rev. Youssef Aziz, B.S.O., Gen. Economos; Rt. Rev. Archimandrite Martin A. Hyatt, B.S.O; Rev. Antoine Rizk, B.S.O., Regl. Supr.
Fathers in American Region: 14
Novitiate and House of Studies: St. Basils Seminary; Methuen, MA.
Parishes Canada 4; U.S.A. 5.
Represented in the Archdioceses of Boston and Miami and in the Dioceses of Cleveland and Newton.

[0200] (O.S.B.)–BENEDICTINE MONKS

(Ordo Sancti Benedicti)

American Cassinese Congregation of the Order of Saint Benedict (Established by Pope Pius IX, August 24, 1855.) 230 Mendham Rd., Morristown, NJ 07960. Tel & Fax: 973-538-3763; Web: www.amcass.org; Email: president@amcass.org. Rt. Rev. Elias R. Lorenzo, O.S.B., Abbot Pres.; Rt. Rev. Mark Cooper, O.S.B., First Councilor, St. Anselm Abbey, Manchester, NH; Rt. Rev. Douglas Nowicki, O.S.B., Second Councilor, St. Vincent Archabbey, LaTrobe, PA; Very Rev. Edward Mazick, O.S.B., Third Councilor, St. Vincent Archabbey, LaTrobe, PA; Rev. James Flint, O.S.B., Fourth Councilor, St. Procopius Abbey, Lisle, IL; Very Rev. Michael Calhoun, O.S.B., Exec. Sec., St. Bede Abbey, Peru, IL; Rev. Geraldo Gonzalez y Lima, O.S.B., Procurator Gen., Sant'Anselmo, Rome, Italy.

St. Mary's Abbey: Delbarton, 230 Mendham Rd., Morristown, NJ 07960. Tel: 973-538-3235; Fax: 973-538-7109; Web: www.osbmonks.org. Rt. Rev. Richard Cronin, O.S.B., Abbot; Very Rev. Edward Seton Fittin, O.S.B., Prior; Rev. John Hesketh, O.S.B., Subprior.
Priests 22; Brothers 4; Deacons 1; Preparatory Schools 1; Retreat Centers 1
Monastery founded in 1857 and raised to an Abbey in 1884.
Represented in the Diocese of Paterson.

St. Procopius Abbey: 5601 College Rd., Lisle, IL 60532. Tel: 320-363-3935; Fax: 320-363-3082. Rt. Rev. Hugh R. Anderson, O.S.B., Abbot & Pres.
The Abbeys and Priories belonging to this Congregation are as follows:

Saint Vincent Archabbey: 300 Fraser Purchase Rd., Latrobe, PA 15650-2690. Tel: 724-532-6600. Rt. Rev. Douglas R. Nowicki, O.S.B., Archabbot; Most Rev. Rembert G. Weakland, O.S.B., Resigned Archbishop of Milwaukee; Rev. Peter Augustine Pierjok, O.S.B.; Rev. David Klecker, O.S.B.; Rev. Joachim Morgan, O.S.B.; Rev. Martinho Chaves, O.S.B.; Rev. Lawrence Machia, O.S.B.
Legal Title: The Benedictine Society of Westmoreland County; Saint Vincent College Corporation; The Wimmer Corporation; The Saint Vincent Cemetery Corporation.
Priests 105; Deacons 3; Solemn Professed Choir-Monks: 33; Junior Professed Monks: 16; Choir Novices 7
Represented in the Archdiocese of Baltimore and in the Dioceses of Altoona-Johnstown, Erie, Greensburg, Harrisburg, Pittsburgh, Richmond, Savannah and Wheeling-Charleston.

American Cassinese Congregations

St. John's Abbey: 2900 Abbey Plaza, P.O. Box 2015, Collegeville, MN 56321-2015. Tel: 320-363-2546; Fax: 320-363-3082. Rt. Rev. John Klassen, O.S.B., Abbot; Very Rev. Bradley Jenniges, O.S.B., Prior; Bro. David-Paul Lange, O.S.B., Subprior.
Fathers 77; Professed Brothers 41; Oblates: 1; Abbeys: 1; Parishes 11; Chaplaincies 4; Schools of Theology: 1; Universities: 1; High Schools 1; Novitiates 1; Publishing Houses 1
Monastery founded in 1856 and raised to an Abbey in 1866.
Legal Holdings: Saint John's Seminary; Saint John's Preparatory School; Saint John's Abbey; Liturgical Press. Sponsored Apostolate: Saint John's University.
Represented in the Archdiocese of St. Paul and Minneapolis and in the Dioceses of St. Cloud and San Bernardino.

St. Benedict's Abbey: 1020 N. Second St., Atchison, KS 66002-1499. Tel: 913-367-7853; Fax: 913-367-6230. Rt. Rev. James R. Albers, O.S.B., Abbot; Rt. Rev. Barnabas Senecal, O.S.B., Retired Abbot; Rt. Rev. Ralph Koehler, O.S.B., Retired Abbot; Very Rev. Jeremy Heppler, O.S.B., Prior; Bro. Leven Harton, O.S.B., Subprior.
Fathers 27; Brothers 12; Abbeys: 1; Parishes 6; Missions: 1; Chaplaincies 3; Colleges 1; High Schools 1
Founded in 1857 and raised to an Abbey in 1876.
Represented in the Archdiocese of Kansas City in Kansas. Also in Brazil.

Newark Abbey: 528 Dr. Martin Luther King, Jr. Blvd., Newark, NJ 07102. Tel: 973-643-4800; Fax: 973-643-6922. Rt. Rev. Melvin J. Valvano, O.S.B., Abbot; Very Rev. Augustine J. Curley, O.S.B., Prior; Bro. Patrick Winbush, O.S.B., Subprior.
Priests 9; Brothers 4; Novices 2; Abbeys: 1; Public Oratory: 1; Preparatory High Schools 1
Priory founded 1857; Abbey in 1884; title transferred from Newark to Morristown, N.J. in 1956; became Abbey again in 1968 and known as Newark Abbey under the patronage of the Immaculate Conception.
Legal Holding: St. Benedict Preparatory School, Newark, NJ.
Represented in the Archdiocese of Newark.

Belmont Abbey: 100 Belmont-Mount Holly Rd., Belmont, NC 28012-1802. Tel: 704-461-6675; Fax: 704-461-6242. Rt. Rev. Placid D. Solari, O.S.B., Abbot; Very Rev. Christopher Kirchgessner, O.S.B., Prior.
Legal Title: Southern Benedictine Society of North Carolina, Incorporated.
Priests 9; Brothers 11
Monastery founded in 1876, raised to an Abbey in 1884 and erected into an Abbey Nullius in 1910; Abbey Nullius suppressed January 1, 1977 and incorporated into Diocese of Charlotte.
Properties owned or sponsored: Belmont Abbey College, Belmont, NC.

St. Bernard Abbey (1891): Cullman, AL 35055. Tel: 256-734-8291; Fax: 256-734-3885. Rt. Rev. Cletus D. Meagher, O.S.B., Abbot; Ven. Bro. Leo Borelli, O.S.B., Prior & Novice Master; Rev. John O'Donnell, O.S.B., Subprior.
Legal Title: Benedictine Society of Alabama, Inc.
Priests 14; Brothers 19
Represented in the Archdiocese of Mobile and in the Diocese of Birmingham.

St. Procopius Abbey: 5601 College Rd., Lisle, IL 60532. Tel: 630-969-6410; Fax: 630-969-6426; Web: www.procopius.org. Rt. Rev. Austin G. Murphy, O.S.B., Abbot; Very Ven. Guy Jelinek, O.S.B., Prior & Business Mgr; Rev. Thomas Chisholm, O.S.B., Subprior; Rev. James Flint, O.S.B., Treas. & Procurator.
Priests 15; Brothers 8
Monastery founded in 1885 and raised to an Abbey in 1894.
Legal Holdings or Titles: Benedictine University, Lisle, IL; Benet Academy, Lisle, IL; Benedictine Chinese Mission, Lisle, IL; Slav Mission, Lisle, IL; St. Procopius Abbey Endowment, Lisle, IL.
Represented in the Diocese of Joliet.

St. Gregory's Abbey: 1900 W. MacArthur St., Shawnee, OK 74804. Tel: 405-878-5491; Fax: 405-878-5189. Rt. Rev. Lawrence Stasyszen, O.S.B., Abbot; Rt. Rev. Adrian Vorderlandwehr, O.S.B., Resigned Abbot & Treas.; Very Rev. Boniface T. Copelin, O.S.B., Prior; Rt. Rev. Martin Lugo, O.S.B, Resigned Abbott; Rev. Joachim Spexarth, O.S.B., Subprior.
Legal Titles: Benedictine Fathers of Sacred Heart Mission, Inc.; Endowment Foundation, Inc., Shawnee, OK; Saint Gregory's Abbey Benefit Trust.
Priests 13; Brothers 8; Military Installations: 3
Monastery founded in 1875 and raised to an Abbey in 1896.
Ministries in 1 Parish; 2 military installations; 1 Catholic hospital.
Represented in the Archdiocese of Oklahoma City.
Properties owned or sponsored: Mabee-Gerrer Museum of Art, Shawnee, OK.

Saint Leo Abbey: 33601 SR 52, P.O. Box 2350, Saint Leo, FL 33574. Tel: 352-588-8624; Fax: 352-588-5217; Email: abbey@saintleo.edu; Web: www.saintleoabbey.org. Rt. Rev. Isaac Camacho, O.S.B., Abbot
Legal Title: Order of St. Benedict of Florida, Inc. Fathers 6; Brothers 10; Internal Oblates: 2 Founded in 1889 and raised to an Abbey in 1902.
Represented in the Diocese of St. Petersburg.

Assumption Abbey: P.O. Box A, Richardton, ND 58652.Tel: 701-974-3315. Rt. Rev. Daniel Maloney, O.S.B., Abbot; Bro. Michael Taffe, O.S.B., Prior; Rev. Jacob Deiss, O.S.B., Subprior.
Priests 22; Brothers 26
Founded in 1893 and raised to an Abbey in 1903.
Represented in the Dioceses of Bismarck, Cheyenne and Fargo. Also in Colombia
Properties owned or sponsored: Abbey; Dependent Priory; Parishes 2; Chaplaincies 5; Indian Mission.

St. Bede Abbey: 24 W. U.S. Hwy. 6, Peru, IL 61354. Tel: 815-223-3140. Rt. Rev. Philip D. Davey, O.S.B., Abbot; Very Rev. Michael Calhoun, O.S.B., Prior; Rev. Dominic M. Garramone, O.S.B., Subprior.
Legal Title: The Benedictine Society of Saint Bede.
Priests 8; Brothers 6
Monastery founded in 1891 and raised to an Abbey in 1910.
Represented in the Diocese of Peoria. Properties owned or sponsored: Parishes 1 & St. Bede Academy.

St. Martin's Abbey: 5000 Abbey Way S.E., Lacey, WA 98503-7500. Rt. Rev. Neal G. Roth, O.S.B; Rt. Rev. Adrian Parcher, O.S.B., Resigned Abbot; Bro. Nicolaus Wilson, O.S.B., Prior; Bro. Ramon Newell, O.S.B., Subprior.
Priests 13; Brothers 9
Monastery founded in 1895 and raised to an Abbey in 1914.
Legal Holdings or Titles: St. Martin's Abbey; St. Martin's University.
Represented in the Archdiocese of Seattle.

Holy Cross Abbey: 2951 E. Hwy. 50, Canon City, CO 81212. Tel: 719-275-8631. Rev. Maurice C. Haefling, O.S.B., Vicar Admin.; Rt. Rev. Kenneth C. Hein, O.S.B., Retired Abbot.
Fathers 2; Oblates: 1
Founded in 1886 and raised to an Abbey in 1925.
Represented in the Archdiocese of Denver and in the Diocese of Pueblo.

St. Anselm Abbey: 100 St. Anselm Dr., Manchester, NH 03102-1310. Tel: 603-641-7652; Fax: 603-641-7267. Rt. Rev. Mark A. Cooper, O.S.B., Abbot; Rt. Rev. Matthew K. Leavy, O.S.B., 4th Abbot; Most Rev. Joseph John Gerry, O.S.B., 3rd Abbot, Tenth Bishop of Portland, ME; Very Rev. Anselm Smedlie, O.S.B., Prior; Rev. Peter J. Guerin, O.S.B., Subprior.
Legal Title: Order of Saint Benedict of New Hampshire.
Bishops 1; Abbots: 2; Fathers 21; Brothers 6.
Monastery founded in 1889 and raised to an Abbey in 1927.
Represented in the Archdiocese of San Francisco and in the Diocese of Manchester.

St. Andrew Abbey: 10510 Buckeye Rd., Cleveland, OH 44104. Tel: 216-721-5300. Rt. Rev. Gary Hoover, O.S.B., Abbot; Rev. Timothy Buyansky, O.S.B., Prior; Ven. Bro. Gabriel Balazovic, O.S.B., Subprior.
Bishops 1; Abbots: 3; Priests 17; Brothers 8; Abbeys: 1; Parishes 1; High Schools 1; Chaplaincies 1
Founded in 1922 and raised to an Abbey in 1934.
Legal Holdings or Titles: Benedictine Order of Cleveland; Benedictine High School.
Represented in the Diocese of Cleveland.

Benedictine Priory: 6502 Seawright Dr., Savannah, GA 31406. Tel: 912-356-3520; Fax: 912-356-3527. Very Rev. Jean-Luc Zadroga, O.S.B., Prior.
Priests 5; Brothers 2; High Schools 1
Founded 1902, dependent priory of St. Vincent Archabbey, Latrobe, PA.
Represented in the Diocese of Savannah.

Woodside Priory: 302 Portola Rd., Portola Valley, CA 94028. Tel: 650-851-8220. Very Rev. Martin J. Mager, O.S.B., Supr.
Legal Title: Benedictine Fathers of the Priory, Inc.
Priests 3; High Schools 1; Middle Schools 1
Founded in 1956, erected as Conventual Priory 1958, became a dependent Priory upon St. Anselm's Abbey, Manchester, NH, 1976.
Represented in the Archdiocese of San Francisco.

Abadia de San Antonio Abad: P.O. Box 729, Humacao, PR 00792. Tel: 787-852-1616; Tel: 787-852-1766; Fax: 787-852-1920. Rt. Rev. Oscar Rivera, O.S.B., Abbot; Rev. Rafael Quiñones, O.S.B., Prior; Bro. Aristedes Pacheco, Subprior.
Priests 4; Brothers 4
Monastery founded in 1947 and became an Abbey in 1984.

Mary Mother of the Church Abbey: 12829 River Rd., Richmond, VA 23238-7206. Tel: 804-784-3508; Fax: 804-708-5064. Rt. Rev. Placid D. Solari, O.S.B., Canonical Admin.
Priests 4; Brothers 5; Abbeys: 1; Chaplaincies 3; High Schools 1 Community founded in 1911 and became an Abbey in 1989.
Legal Holdings: Benedictine High School of Richmond; Mary Mother of the Church Abbey
Represented in the Diocese of Richmond.

Mount Saviour Monastery: 231 Monastery Rd., Pine City, NY 14871-9787. Tel: 607-734-1688; Fax: 607-734-1689; Email: info@msaviour.org. Bro. John Thompson, O.S.B., Prior Admin.; Rev. James Cronen, O.S.B. Professed Monks: 10 Monastery founded in 1950, raised to Independent Priory 1957.
Represented in the Diocese of Rochester.

Swiss-American Congregation

Marmion Abbey: 850 Butterfield Rd., Aurora, IL 60502. Tel: 630-966-7750; Fax: 630-897-0393. Rt. Rev. Vincent Bataille, O.S.B., Abbot & Pres. President's Council: Rev. Justin DuVall, O.S.B., St. Meinrad Archabbey; Very Rev. Patrick Caveglia, O.S.B., Conception Abbey; Rev. Paul Thomas, O.S.B., Mt. Angel Abbey.

Established by Pope Leo XIII, April 5, 1881.

The Abbeys and Priories belonging to this Federation are as follows:

St. Meinrad Archabbey: No. 100 Hill Dr., Saint Meinrad, IN 47577. Tel: 812-357-6611; Fax: 812-357-6551. Rt. Rev. Justin DuVall, O.S.B., Resigned Archabbot; Rt. Rev. Lambert Reilly, O.S.B., Resigned Archabbot; Rt. Rev. Bonaventure Knaebel, O.S.B., Retired Archabbot; Rt. Rev. Kurt Stasiak, Archabbot; Rev. John McMullen, Prior.

Priests 50; Brothers 28; Parishes 4; Schools of Theology: 1; Chaplaincies 2

Founded 1854; raised to an Abbey in 1870.

Represented in the Archdioceses of Indianapolis, San Francisco, and Washington and in the Dioceses of Evansville and Pensacola-Tallahassee.

Conception Abbey: 37174 State Hwy. VV, Conception, MO 64433. Tel: 660-944-3100; Fax: 660-944-2800. Rt. Rev. Benedict Neenan, O.S.B., Abbot; Rev. Daniel Petsche, O.S.B., Prior; Rev. Paul Sheller, O.S.B., Subprior.

Legal Title: Conception Abbey, Inc.

Archbishops 1; Fathers 34; Brothers 17; Parishes 6; Seminary College: 1; Chaplaincies 2

Founded December 8, 1873; Abbey April 5, 1881.

Represented in the Archdioceses of Kansas City in Kansas and Omaha and in the Dioceses of Dodge City, Kansas City-St. Joseph, Madison and Springfield-Cape Girardeau.

Mount Michael Abbey: 22520 Mount Michael Rd., Elkhorn, NE 68022-3400. Tel: 402-289-2541; Fax: 402-289-4539. Rt. Rev. Michael Liebl, O.S.B., Abbot; Rev. Richard Thell, O.S.B., Prior; Bro. Jerome Kmiecik, O.S.B., Subprior.

Fathers 11; Brothers 12

Legal Holdings & Titles: Mount Michael Benedictine Abbey; Mount Michael Benedictine School; Mount Michael Foundation.

Monks serve and staff: Parishes 2.

Represented in the Archdiocese of Omaha and in the Diocese of Pueblo.

Subiaco Abbey: Subiaco, AR 72865. Tel: 479-934-1000; Fax: 479-934-4328. Vocation Director Email: brfrancis@subi.org; Assistant Vocation Director Email: frpatrick@subi.org. Rt. Rev. Leonard Wangler, O.S.B., Prior; Bro. Edward Fischesser, O.S.B., Prior; Bro. Ephrem O'Bryan, O.S.B., Subprior.

Fathers 12; Perpetually Professed Brothers 23; Temporarily Professed Brothers 3

Properties staffed or sponsored: Parishes 5; High School 1.

Represented in the Diocese of Little Rock.

St. Joseph Abbey: Saint Benedict, LA 70457. Tel: 985-892-1800; Fax: 985-867-2270. Vocations Email: frephrem@sjasc.edu. Web: www.sjasc.edu. Rt. Rev. Justin Brown, O.S.B., Abbot; Bro. Brian Harrington, O.S.B., Prior.

Fathers 18; Brothers 9; Parishes 1; Novices 3; Seminary College: 1

Legal Holdings: St. Joseph Seminary College, St. Benedict, LA.

Represented in the Archdiocese of New Orleans.

Mt. Angel Abbey: 1 Abbey Dr., Saint Benedict, OR 97373. Tel: 503-845-3030; Fax: 503-845-3594. Rt. Rev. Jeremy Driscoll, O.S.B., Abbot; Very Rev. Vincent Trujillo, O.S.B., Prior; Rev. Odo Recker, O.S.B., Subprior.

Finally Professed Monks (Priests): 27; Finally Professed Monks (Brothers): 14; Temporarily Professed Monks (Brothers): 9

Founded on Oct. 30, 1882, from Engelberg in Switzerland and raised to an Abbey on March 24, 1904.

Legal Holdings or Titles: Monastery of Our Lady of the Angels, Cuernavaca, Morelos, Mexico.

Marmion Abbey: 850 Butterfield Rd., Aurora, IL 60502. Tel: 630-897-7215. Rt. Rev. John Brahill, O.S.B., Abbot; Rt. Rev. Vincent Bataille, O.S.B., Abbot Emeritus; Very Rev. Paul Weberg, O.S.B., Prior; Bro. André Charron, O.S.B., Subprior.

Priests 20; Brothers 8

Founded as Dependent Priory of St. Meinrad's Abbey, June 20, 1943; Abbey since March 21, 1947.

Represented in the Diocese of Rockford. Also in Quetzaltenango, Guatemala.

Properties staffed or sponsored: Parishes 1; High Schools 2.

St. Benedict's Abbey: 12605 224th Ave., Benet Lake, WI 53102-1000. Tel: 262-396-4311; Fax: 262-396-4365; Email: patrick@conception.edu. Rt. Rev. Edmund J. Boyce, O.S.B., Abbot Resigned and Subprior; Very Rev. Patrick Caveglia, O.S.B., Prior; Rev. Phillip Schoofs, O.S.B.

Legal Titles: Benedictine Monks, Inc.; St Benedict's Home Missionary Society.

Priests 3; Brothers 1

Monastery founded in 1945 and raised to an Abbey in 1952; became dependent priory of Conception Abbey in 2014.

Represented in the Archdiocese of Milwaukee.

Glastonbury Abbey: 16 Hull St., Hingham, MA 02043. Tel: 781-749-2155; Fax: 781-749-6236. Rt. Rev. Thomas O'Connor, Abbot.

Monks in Solemn Vows 9

Represented in the Archdiocese of Boston.

Blue Cloud Abbey: P.O. Box 68, Milbank, SD 57252. Tel: 605-398-9200. Rt. Rev. Denis Quinkert, O.S.B., Abbot.

Legal Title: Blue Cloud Abbey, Inc.; Asociacion Benedictina de Coban.

Priests 3; Brothers 1

Monastery founded June 24, 1950; raised to a Priory August 5, 1952; raised to an Abbey March 21, 1954.

Represented in the Diocese of Sioux Falls. Also in Guatemala.

Prince of Peace Abbey: 650 Benet Hill Rd., Oceanside, CA 92054. Tel: 760-967-4200; Email: princeabby@aol.com. Email: princeabby@aol.com; Web: www.princeofpeaceabbey.org. Very Rt. Rev. Sharbel Ewen, O.S.B., Abbot; Bro. Raphael Meyer, O.S.B., Prior.

Priests 7; Brothers 14

St. Benedict Abbey: 252 Still River Rd., P.O. Box 67, Still River, MA 01467. Tel: 978-456-3221; Fax: 978-456-8181; Email: saintbenedict@abbey.org. Rt. Rev. Xavier Connelly, O.S.B., Abbot; Very Rev. James Doran, O.S.B., Prior.

Priests 6; Brothers 2

Represented in the Diocese of Worcester.

Congregation of St. Ottilien for Foreign Missions

St. Paul's Abbey: 289 U.S. Hwy. 206 S., P.O. Box 7, Newton, NJ 07860-0007. Tel: 973-383-2470; Fax: 973-383-5782. Rt. Rev. Joel P. Macul, O.S.B., Abbot Emeritus; Rt. Rev. Justin E. Dzikowicz, O.S.B., Resigned Abbot; Very Rev. Samuel Kim, O.S.B., Prior.

Solemnly Professed Monks: 10; Priests 4 (Benedictine Missionaries)

Monastery established March 15, 1924; elevated to an Abbey June 9, 1947.

Represented in the Diocese of Paterson.

Christ the King Priory (1985) - Benedictine Mission House (1935): Benedictine Mission House was founded in 1935 and raised to the rank of Priory in 1985. P.O. Box 528, Schuyler, NE 68661. Tel: 402-352-2177; Fax: 402-352-2176. Rt. Rev. Joel Macul, O.S.B., Prior; Rev. Volker Futter, O.S.B; Rev. Thomas Leitner, O.S.B; Rev. Paul L. Kasun, O.S.B; Rev. Adam Patras, O.S.B; Rev. Thomas Hillenbrand, O.S.B.

Fathers 6; Brothers 4

Represented in the Archdiocese of Omaha.

Congregation of the Annunciation

St. Andrew's Abbey: P.O. Box 40, Valyermo, CA 93563. Tel: 661-944-2178. Rev. Damien Toilolo, O.S.B., Abbot; Rev. Joseph Brennan, O.S.B., Prior.

Monks in Solemn Vows 18

Represented in the Archdiocese of Los Angeles.

Camaldolese Benedictine Congregation (Congregatio Camaldulensis Ordinis Sancti Benedicti)

U.S. Foundation (1958): New Camaldoli Hermitage, 62475 Hwy. 1, Big Sur, CA 93920. Tel: 831-667-2456. Email: monks@contemplation.com. Rev. Cyprian Consiglio, O.S.B.Cam., Prior; Rev. Thomas Matus, O.S.B.Cam.; Rev. Isaiah Teichert, O.S.B.Cam.; Rev. Raniero Hoffman, O.S.B.Cam.; Rev. Zacchaeus Naegle, O.S.B.Cam.

Fathers 5; Professed Brothers 5; Professed Monks (including priests): 10

Represented in the Dioceses of Monterey and Oakland.

English Benedictine Congregation

St. Anselm's Abbey: 4501 S. Dakota Ave., N.E., Washington, DC 20017. Tel: 202-269-2300; Fax: 202-269-2312. Rt. Rev. James Wiseman, O.S.B., Abbot.

Legal Title: Benedictine Foundation at Washington DC.

Professed Monks: 14

Abbey of St. Gregory the Great: 285 Cory's Ln., Portsmouth, RI 02871. Tel: 401-683-2000; Fax: 401-682-1750. Rev. Michael Brunner, O.S.B., Prior Admin.

Choir Religious: 11

Abbey of St. Mary and St. Louis: 500 S. Mason Rd., Saint Louis, MO 63141-8500. Tel: 314-434-3690; Fax: 314-434-0795. Rt. Rev. Thomas Frerking, O.S.B., Abbot.

Solemnly Professed Monks: 28; Priests 21; Simply Professed Monks: 4; Oblates: 1

Founded as a dependent Priory 1955, granted independence 1973, raised to status of Abbey 1989.

Sylvestrine Benedictine Congregation (Monachorum Silvestrinorum, O.S.B.)

Foundations in the U.S. (1910): Saint Benedict Priory, 2711 E. Drahner Rd., Oxford, MI 48370. Tel: 248-628-2249. Rev. Damien G. Jonaj, O.S.B., Conventual Prior.

Brothers 3; Priests 5; Regular Oblates: 2

Represented in the Archdiocese of Detroit and in the Diocese of Paterson.

Olivetan Benedictines (Congregatio Sanctae Mariae Montis Oliveti Ordinis Sancti Benedicti)

General Motherhouse: St. Sylvester Monastery, Fabriano, Italy, Very Rev. Michael Kelly, O.S.B., Abbot Gen.

U.S. Foundations: Holy Trinity Monastery, P.O. Box 298, Saint David, AZ 85630. Tel: 520-720-4642; Fax: 520-720-4202. Rev. Henri Capdeville, O.S.B., Prior. Solemnly Professed 4

Represented in the Diocese of Tucson.

Our Lady of Guadalupe Abbey: P.O. Box 1080, Pecos, NM 87552-1080. Tel: 505-757-6415. Rev. Aidan Gore, O.S.B; Bro. James Marron; Rev. Aidan Gov, O.S.B., Abbot.

Priests 3; Brothers 7

Represented in the Archdiocese of Santa Fe.

Benedictine Monastery of Hawaii: 67-290 Farrington Hwy., P.O. Box 490, Waialua, HI 96791. Tel: 808-637-7887; Fax: 808-637-8601; Email: monastery@hawaiibenedictines.org; Web: www.hawaiibenedictines.org. Rev. David Barfknecht, O.S.B., Supr.

Legal Title: Mary, Spouse of the Holy Spirit Monastery.

Priests 2

Subiaco Benedictine Congregation

Monastery of Christ in the Desert (1964): Abiquiu, NM 87510. Tel: 575-613-4233. Rt. Rev. Philip Lawrence, O.S.B., Abbot.

Monks: 100

Independent 1983; Abbey 1996.

Represented in the Archdiocese of Santa Fe. Also in Costa Rica, Mexico, Rome and South Africa.

***Benedictine Monastery of Thien Tam:** 13055 S.E. CR 4271, Kerens, TX 75144. Tel: 903-396-3201. Rev. Dominic Hanh Nguyen, O.S.B., Prior.

Saint Mary's Monastery: P.O. Box 345, Petersham, MA 01366. Tel: 978-724-3350. Rev. Dom Gregory Phillips, O.S.B., Supr.

Monks: 6

Dependent Monastery 1987.

Represented in the Diocese of Worcester.

Subiaco Cassinese Benedictine Congregation

Monastery of the Holy Cross: 3111 S. Aberdeen St., Chicago, IL 60608-6503. Tel: 773-927-7424; Fax: 773-927-5734; Email: fatheredwardglanzmann@gmail.com; Web: www.chicagomonk.org. Rev. Peter Funk, O.S.B., Prior.

Monastery established by Pope Benedict XVI on February 7, 2013 with the incorporation of the Cassinese Congregation of the OSB, established in 1408, into the Subiaco Congregation of the OSB, established by Pope Pius in 1872.

Solesmes Congregation

Benedictine Monks, Solesmes Congregation: Our Lady of Clear Creek Abbey, 5804 W. Monastery Rd., Hulbert, OK 74441. Tel: 918-772-2454; Fax; 918-772-1044; Email: abbey@clearcreekmonks.org; Web: www.clearcreekmonks.org. Rt. Rev. Philip Anderson, O.S.B., Abbot.

Legal Title: Foundation for the Annunciation Monastery of Clear Creek.

Outside the Congregation

Weston Priory (1952): 58 Priory Hill Rd., Weston, VT 05161. Tel: 802-824-5409; Fax: 802-824-3573.

Email: brothers@westonpriory.org. Very Rev. Richard Iaquinto, O.S.B., Prior.
Founded in 1952 and established as a Conventual Priory July 18, 1968 under the jurisdiction of the Abbot Primate.
Legal Title: The Benedictine Foundation of the State of Vermont, Inc.
Monks: 12
Represented in the Diocese of Burlington.

[0220] (S.S.S.)—CONGREGATION OF THE BLESSED SACRAMENT

(Congregatio Sanctissimi Sacramenti)

Generalate: 46 Via Giovanni Battista de Rossi, 00161, Rome, Italy, Very Rev. Eugenio Barbosa Martins, S.S.S., Supr.

Province of St. Ann (1931): 5384 Wilson Mills Rd., Cleveland, OH 44143. Tel: 440-442-6311. Rev. Anthony Schueller, S.S.S., Prov. Supr.; Rev. Robert Stark, S.S.S., Consultor & Prov. Treas.; Rev. Anthony Marshall, S.S.S., Vocation Dir.
Priests 28; Permanent Deacons 1; Brothers 8
Properties staffed or owned: Parishes 6; Community Houses 7; Novitiate 1.
Represented in the Archdioceses of Chicago, Galveston-Houston, New York and San Antonio and in the Dioceses of Cleveland and St. Petersburg.

[0230] (ER. CAM.)—CAMALDOLESE HERMITS OF THE CONGREGATION OF MONTECORONA

(Eremitae Camaldulenses Congregationis Montis Coronae)

General Motherhouse: Sacro Eremo Tuscolano, Via del Tuscolo 45, 00078 Monte Porzio Catone, Rome, Italy, Rt. Rev. Elias Castillo, Er.Cam., Father Major.

U.S. Foundation (1959): Holy Family Hermitage, 1501 Fairplay Rd., Bloomingdale, OH 43910-7971. Tel: 740-765-4511. Email: dcook@diosteub.org. Very Rev. Basil Corriere, Er.Cam., Prior.
Hermit Priests 4; Professed 5
Represented in the Diocese of Steubenville.

[0240] (M.I.)—CAMILLIAN FATHERS AND BROTHERS OR ORDER OF ST. CAMILLUS

(Ministers of the Infirm)
(Ministri degli Infermi)

General Motherhouse: Casa Generalizia, Ministri degli Infermi, Piazza della Maddalena 53, 00186, Rome, Italy, Rev. Leocir Pessini, M.I., Gen. Supr.; Rev. Laurent Zoungrana, M.I., Gen. Vicar; Bro. Jose Ignacio Santaolalla Saez, M.I., Consultor Gen.; Rev. Aris Miranda, M.I., Consultor Gen.; Rev. Gianfranco Lunardon, M.I., Consultor Gen.

U.S.A. Camillian (1923): Delegation of Brazilian Prov., 10101 W. Wisconsin Ave., Wauwatosa, WI 53226. Tel: 414-259-4744. Rev. Pedro Tramontin, M.I., Delegate.
Fathers 12; Professed Brothers 1
Legal Titles: St. Camillus Health Center Inc., Wauwatosa, WI; St. Camillus Health System, Wauwatosa, WI; San Camillo, Inc., Wauwatosa, WI; St. Camillus Ministries Inc., Wauwatosa, WI; St. Camillus Communities Inc., Wauwatosa, WI; Order of St. Camillus Foundation, Wauwatosa, WI.
Represented in the Archdiocese of Milwaukee and in the Dioceses of Savannah and Pittsburgh.

[0250] (C.R.L.)—CANONS REGULAR OF THE LATERAN

(Ordo Canonicorum Regularium S. Augustini Congregations Ss. Salvatoris Lateranensis)

General House: Curia Generalizia dei Canonicio Regolari Lateranensi, Piazza S. Pietro in Vincoli, 4A, 00184, Roma, Italy.

United States: Canons Regular of the Lateran, 130 Beekman Ave., Sleepy Hollow, NY 10591. Tel: 914-631-0720. Rev. Rumando Peralta, C.R.L., Supr.
Priests 5
Represented in the Archdiocese of New York.

[0260] (O.C.D.)—DISCALCED CARMELITE FRIARS

(Ordo Carmelitarum Discalceatorum)

Founded Mt. Carmel, Palestine in the 13th Century.

Generalate: Carmelitani Scalzi, Corso d'Italia, 38, 00198, Rome, Italy, Very Rev. Saverio Cannistra, O.C.D., Supr. Gen.

California-Arizona Province (1983): 926 E. Highland Ave., P.O. Box 8700, Redlands, CA 92375. Tel: 909-793-0424; Fax: 909-335-1304. Rev. Stephen Watson, O.C.D., Prov.
Legal Title: Discalced Carmelite Province of California.
Fathers 34; Brothers 3; Students: 3
Represented in the Archdioceses of Los Angeles, Portland in Oregon and Seattle and in the Dioceses of San Jose, San Bernardino, Santa Rosa and Tucson. Also in Uganda.
Properties owned, staffed or sponsored: Parishes 3; Retreat House; Novitiate; House of Studies; House of Prayer; Institute of Spirituality.

Province of St. Therese of Oklahoma (1935): Provincial House, 906 Kentucky Ave., San Antonio, TX 78201. Tel: 201-735-9127. Rev. Luis J. Castaneda, O.C.D., Prov.
Fathers 18; Brothers 1
Represented in the Archdioceses of Oklahoma City and San Antonio and in the Dioceses of Dallas and Little Rock.
Properties staffed or sponsored: Parishes 3; Community Houses 1; Novitiate 1.

Washington Province of the Immaculate Heart of Mary (1947): Discalced Carmelites-Prov. Office, 1233 S. 45th St., Milwaukee, WI 53214-3693. Tel: 414-672-7212; Fax: 414-672-3138. Very Rev. Jude Peters, O.C.D., Prov.
Fathers 52; Brothers 11; Temporary Professed Brothers 11; Novices 4; Postulants: 7
Represented in the Archdioceses of Boston, Milwaukee and Washington. Also in Kenya & Nairobi.

Washington Province Discalced Carmelite Secular Order, Inc. (2018): OCDS Main Office, 2131 Lincoln Rd., N.E., Washington, DC 20002-1101. Tel: 202-269-3792. Email: ocdsmainoffice@gmail.com. Rev. Salvatore Sciurba, O.C.D., Prov. Delegate; Mary Harrington, O.C.D.S., Admin.
Properties owned or sponsored: Community Houses 7.

Polish Province of the Holy Spirit, Poland (1949): Monastery of Our Lady of Mt. Carmel, 1628 Ridge Rd., Munster, IN 46321. Tel: 219-838-7111; Fax: 219-838-7214; Email: carmelmunster@yahoo.com. Rev. Francisek Czaicki, O.C.D., Prior.
Priests 9; Brothers 2
Represented in the Diocese of Gary.

[0270] (O.CARM.)—CARMELITE FATHERS & BROTHERS

(Ordo Fratrum Beatissimae Virginis Mariae de Monte Carmelo)

General Curia: Via Giovanni Lanza, 138, 00184, Rome, Italy, Fernando Millan Romeral, O.Carm., Prior Gen.

Province of the Most Pure Heart of Mary (1864): Carmelite Provincial Office, 1317 Frontage Rd., Darien, IL 60561. Tel: 630-971-0050; Fax: 630-971-0195. Email: vfabela@carmelnet.org. Very Rev. William J. Harry, O.Carm., Prior Prov.; Very Rev. Carl J. Markelz, O.Carm., Vice Prior Prov.; Rev. Joseph R. Atcher, O.Carm., Treas. Councilors:
Rev. Paul Henson, O.Carm.; Rev. Quinn Conners, O.Carm.; Rev. Emilio Rodriguez, O.Carm.; Bro. Daryl Moresco, O.Carm.; Rev. Robert E. Colaresi, O.Carm., Dir. Little Flower Society; Rev. Joseph O'Brien, O.Carm., Dir.-Carmelite Mission Office; Rev. Peter McGarry, O.Carm., Delegate to Lay Carmelites. Priests 128; Clerics: 3; Pre-Novitiates 18; Novices 6; Brothers 29
Ministries in 35 Parishes.
Properties owned: Spiritual Centers 3; Shopping-center Chapels 1; High Schools 8; Community Houses 48; House of Study 6; Shrine 2.
Represented in the Archdioceses of Chicago, Kansas City in Kansas, Los Angeles, Newark, New York, Philadelphia, San Francisco and Washington and in the Dioceses of Joliet, Oakland, Phoenix, Sacramento, Tucson and Venice. Also in Australia, Canada, El Salvador, Italy, Peru and Mexico.

Province of the Most Pure Heart of Mary: St. Therese Priory, 75 E. Mariposa St., Phoenix, AZ 85012-1631. Rev. Charles Kurgan, O.Carm.; Rev. Valentine Boyle, O.Carm.; Rev. James Mueller, O.Carm.

Province of St. Elias (1931): P.O. Box 3079, Middletown, NY 10940-0890. Tel: 845-344-2223. Email: wward@carmelites.com. Very Rev. Michael Kissane, O.Carm., Prov. Rev. Brent Alexis, O.Carm.; Rev. Nhat Tran, O.Carm.; Rev. Khoa Nguyen, O.Carm.; Rev. Hung Tran, O.Carm.; Rev. Nicholas Dustin Blackwell, O.Carm.; Rev. Tinh Pham, O.Carm.; Rev. Huynh Dinh, O.Carm.
Fathers 57; Deacons 3; Brothers 5; Novices 3; Pre-Novices 10; Professed Students: 12; Members: 90
Legal Holdings or Titles: The Missionary Society of Our Lady of Mt. Carmel of the State of New York; The Carmelite Fathers, Inc. of New York; Carmelite Fathers, Inc. of the Commonwealth of Massachusetts; Mt. Carmel Hermitage; Order of Carmelites of Palm Beach, Inc.; National Shrine of Our Lady of Mount Carmel, Inc.
Represented in the Archdioceses of New York, Newark and Washington and in the Dioceses of Albany, Dodge City, Greensburg, Palm Beach, Rochester, Sioux Falls and Winona-Rochester. Also in Trinidad & Vietnam.
Properties staffed, owned or sponsored: Parishes 6; Priories 16; Houses of Study 1; Novitiate 1; Hermitages 2; Shrines 1.

Pre-Novitiate: St. Eliseus Priory, 324 Jersey St., Harrison, NJ 07029-1704. Tel: 973-485-7233; Fax: 973-485-7244. Very Rev. Mario Esposito, O.Carm, Dir.; Bro. Robert Bathe, O.Carm.
Priests 1; Brothers 1; Pre-Novices 10

Mt. Carmel Hermitage: 244 Baileys Rd., Bolivar, PA 15923. Tel: 724-238-0423; Fax: 724-238-0423. Rev. Bede J.K. Mulligan, O.Carm.; Rev. Simeon D. Marro, O.Carm.; Bro. Robert Ryba, O.Carm.
Fathers 2; Brothers 1
Founded in 1970, became dependent upon St. Elias Province in 1995.
Represented in the Diocese of Greensburg.

Carmelite Hermitage of the Blessed Virgin Mary (O.Carm): 8249 de Montreville Tr. N., Lake Elmo, MN 55042-9545. Tel: 651-779-7351; Fax: 651-779-7351; Email: carmelbvm@gmail.com; Web: www.carmelitehermitage.org. Rev. John M. Burns, O.Carm., Prior; Rev. Peter Peach, O.Carm.
Fathers 3; Brothers 5

[0275] (C.M.I.)—CARMELITES OF MARY IMMACULATE

(Congregatio Fratrum Carmelitarum B.V. Mariae Immaculatae)

Founded by Saint Kuriakose Elias Chavara and Companions at Mannanam, Kerala, India in 1831.

Generalate: CMI Generalate Chavara Hills, P.B. No. 3105, Kakkanad P.O., 682030, Kochi, India, Tel: 91-484-288-1816; Fax: 91-484-288-1811. Rev. Paul Achandy, C.M.I., Prior Gen.

North American Headquarters: 862 Manhattan Ave., Brooklyn, NY 11222. Tel: 718-383-3339; Email: cmiusa@hotmail.com. Rev. Kavungal Davy, C.M.I., Delegate Superior
Legal Title: Carmelites of Mary Immaculate, Inc.
Priests in U.S. & Canada: 110
Ministries in Parishes; Hospitals; Universities; Prisons; Syro-Malabar Catholics.
Represented in the Archdioceses of Boston, Los Angeles, Louisville, Miami, New York and Philadelphia and in the Dioceses of Alexandria, Austin, Baker, Beaumont, Biloxi, Brooklyn, Camden, Charleston, Covington, Gary, Joliet, Knoxville, Lafayette, Lake Charles, Metuchen, Nashville, Orlando, Rockville Center, Sacramento, Sioux Falls, St. Augustine, St. Paul & Minneapolis, Salina, San Angelo, Shreveport and Tulsa. Also in Canada.

[0280] (O.CART.)—ORDER OF CARTHUSIANS

(Ordo Cartusianorum)

Motherhouse: Grande Chartreuse, St. Pierre de Chartreuse (Isere), France, Rev. Francois Marie Velut, O.Cart., Supr. Gen.

U.S. Charterhouse of the Transfiguration (1951): Carthusian Monastery, 1084 Ave Maria Way, Arlington, VT 05250. Tel: 802-362-2550; Fax: 802-362-3584; Email: carthusians_in_america@chartreuse.info; Web: www.chartreux.org; Web: transfiguration.chartreux.org. Rev. Lorenzo Maria T. De La Rosa Jr., O.Cart., Prior.
Total in Community: 15
Legal Titles: Carthusian Foundation in America, Inc.; Carthusian Foundation, Association Fraternelle Romande.
Represented in the Diocese of Burlington.

[0290] (F.C.)—BROTHERS OF CHARITY

(Congregatio Fratrum Caritate)

General Motherhouse (1807): Via G.B. Pagano 35, 00167, Rome, Italy, Bro. Rene Stockman, F.C., Supr. Gen.

American District (1963): Region of Our Lady of Charity, 7720 Doe Ln., Glenside, PA 19038. Bro. John Fitzgerald, F.C., Regl. Supr. for Province of the Americas.
Represented in the Archdioceses of Philadelphia and Washington.

[0300] (I.C.)—INSTITUTE OF CHARITY

(Rosminians Institutum Charitatis)

General Motherhouse: Collegio Rosmini Via Porta, Latina 17, Rome, Italy, Very Rev. Vito Nardin, I.C., Supr. Gen.

U.S. Foundation (1877): 11565 66th Ave. N., Seminole, FL 33772. Email: frickpilger@sairf.com. Rev. Rick Pilger, I.C.

Fathers in the U.S: 8; Parishes 3

Represented in the Dioceses of St. Petersburg.

[0305] (I.C.)—INSTITUTE OF CHRIST THE KING-SOVEREIGN PRIEST

(Institutum Christi Regis Summi Sacerdotis)

General Motherhouse and House of Formation: Villa Martelli, Via di Gricigliano 52, 50065, Sieci, Italy, Rev. Msgr. Gilles Wach, Prior Gen.

U.S. Mailing Address: Institute of Christ the King-Sovereign Priest, 6415 S. Woodlawn Ave., Chicago, IL 60637.

American Headquarters: Shrine of Christ the King Sovereign Priest, 6415 S. Woodlawn Ave., Chicago, IL 60637. Tel: 773-363-7409; Fax: 773-363-7824; Email: info@institute-christ-king.org. Rev. Msgr. R. Michael Schmitz, Vicar Gen.; Rev. Matthew L. Talarico, Prov. Supr.; Rev. Jean-Baptiste Commins, Vice-Rector; Rev. Joel Estrada, Bursar; Rev. Matthew Weaver, Sec.

[0310] (C.F.C.)—EDMUND RICE CHRISTIAN BROTHERS NORTH AMERICA CONGREGATION OF CHRISTIAN BROTHERS

Founded in Ireland in 1802. First foundation in the United States in 1906.

Edmund Rice Christian Brothers North America, a province of the Congregation of Christian Brothers (1916): 260 Wilmot Rd., New Rochelle, NY 10804-1526. Tel: 914-636-6194. Email: seb@cbinstitute.org; cab@cbinstitute.org. Bro. Kevin M. Griffith, C.F.C., Prov. Leader; Bro. Michael L. Colasuonno, Deputy Prov. Leader. Councilors: Bro. Patrick Sean Moffett, C.F.C.; Bro. Raymond Vercruysse, C.F.C.; Bro. Peter E. Zawot, C.F.C.; Bro. Peter O'Loughlin, C.F.C.

Legal Title: The Christian Brothers' Institute; Christian Brothers of Ireland, Inc.; Mount Sion Community, Inc.

Brothers 166

Represented in the Archdioceses of Boston, Chicago, Detroit, Miami, New York, Newark and Seattle in the Dioceses of Brownsville, Charleston, Honolulu, Jackson, Monterey, Providence, Rochester and St. Petersburg. Also in Canada and West Indies.

Ministries: Colleges 1; High Schools 16; Grade Schools 3; Houses of Formation 1; Care Center 1; Parishes 1; Retreat Center 1; Outreach Ministries 8.

Development Office: The Christian Brothers Foundation, dba Edmund Rice Christian Brothers Foundation, 260 Wilmot Rd., New Rochelle, NY 10804. Tel: 914-636-1035. Bro. Kevin Griffith, C.F.C., Pres., Email: kmg@cbinstitute.org; Sara Barber, Treas., Email: seb@cbinstitute.org; Colleen Noonan, Dir., Email: cfn@cbfoundation.org.

[0320] (F.I.C.)—BROTHERS OF CHRISTIAN INSTRUCTION

(La Mennais Brothers)

(Institutum Fratrum Instructionis Christianae)

General Motherhouse: Casa Generalizia, Via della Divina Provvidenza, 44, 00166, Rome, Italy, Tel: (39) 06-66-41-56-18; Fax: (39) 06-45-44-35-92. Bro. Herve Zamor, Supr. Gen.

LaMennais - North American Province American Delegation (2016): P.O. Box 159, Alfred, ME 04002. Tel: 207-324-6612. Bro. Daniel Caron, Prov. Delegate

Brothers 16; Colleges 1; Retreat Centers 1

Represented in the Dioceses of Portland (In Maine) and Youngstown.

[0330] (F.S.C.)—BROTHERS OF THE CHRISTIAN SCHOOLS

(Fratres Scholarum Christianarum)

General Motherhouse: Casa Generalizia, Via Aurelia 476, CP 9099 00100, Rome, Italy, Web: www.lasalle.org. Bro. Robert Schieler, F.S.C., Supr. Gen.; Bro. Jorge Gallardo de Alba, F.S.C., Vicar Gen.

Christian Brothers Conference: 415 Michigan Ave., N.E., Ste. 300, Washington, DC 20017-4501.Tel: 202-529-0047; Fax: 202-529-0775. Bro. Timothy Coldwell, F.S.C., Gen. Councilor; Mr. James G. Lindsay, Dir. of Administration.

Legal Title: Christian Brothers Major Superiors, Inc.

Organizations and programs served by this office: Regional Conference of Christian Brothers; Lasallian Volunteers; Huether Lasallian Conference; Buttimer Institute of Lasallian Studies; Brother John Johnston Institute of Contemporary Lasallian Practice; Lasallian Social Justice Institute; Lasallian Education Council.

Organizations associated with this office: Christian Brothers Major Superiors.

Institutions owned and/or sponsored: Bethlehem University of the Holy Land; Sangre de Cristo Center, Santa Fe, NM; Christian Brothers Services, Romeoville, IL.

Brothers of the Christian Schools (Midwest Province): 7650 S. Country Line Rd., Burr Ridge, IL 60527-7959. Tel: 630-323-3725; Fax: 630-323-3779; Email: info@cbmidwest.org. Bro. Larry Schatz, F.S.C., Visitor; Bro. Michael Kadow, F.S.C., Aux. Visitor & Vocation Ministry; Bro. Bede Baldry, F.S.C., Aux. Visitor; Bro. Joseph Saurbier, F.S.C., Dir. Admin. & Operations; Mr. Anthony Chimera, Dir. Devel. Officer; Dr. Scott Kier, Supt., LaSallian Educ.

Brothers 127

Legal Titles: The Christian Brothers of the Midwest, Inc.; The Christian Brothers of Illinois; Brothers of the Christian Schools of the St. Louis District; The Christian Brothers of Minnesota.

Represented in the Archdioceses of Chicago, Cincinnati, Milwaukee, St. Louis and St. Paul-Minneapolis and the Dioceses of Green Bay, Helena, Joliet, Kansas City-St. Joseph, Memphis, Omaha, Tulsa and Winona-Rochester.

Properties owned, staffed or sponsored: Communities 24; Universities 3; High Schools 13; Middle Schools 4; Elementary Schools 1; Retreat Houses 4; Publishing Houses 1.

Province of San Francisco New Orleans (1868): Brothers of the Christian Schools Provincial Office, P.O. Box 3720, Napa, CA 94558-0372. Tel: 707-252-0222. Bro. Donald Johanson, F.S.C., Prov.

Brothers 117

Represented in the Archdioceses of Denver, Los Angeles, New Orleans, Portland in Oregon, San Francisco and Santa Fe and the Dioceses of El Paso, Lafayette, Oakland, Orange, Sacramento, Santa Rosa, Tucson and Yakima. Also in Ethiopia, Mexico, Rome and Vietnam.

Legal Holdings or Titles: NOSF, Inc.; St. La Salle Auxiliary; Brothers of the Christian Schools of Lafayette Retirement Trust; Christian Brothers Charitable Trust; Magnolia Lafayette, Inc.; Lasallian Education Corporation; Lasallian Christian Brothers Foundation, Inc.; Lasallian Education Fund; De La Salle Institute.

Properties owned, staffed or sponsored: Colleges 1; High Schools 18; Middle and Elementary Schools 3; Community Houses 16; Retreat & Conference Centers 1.

District of Eastern North America: 444A Rte. 35 S., Eatontown, NJ 07724-2200. Tel: 732-380-7926; Fax: 732-380-7937. Email: info@fscdena.org; Web: www.fscdena.org. Bro. Dennis Lee, F.S.C., Visitor/Prov. & Pres.; Bro. Thomas Casey, F.S.C., Auxiliary; Bro. Richard Galvin, F.S.C., Auxiliary; Bro. Joseph Juliano, F.S.C., Dir. Admin. & Sec.; Bro. Timothy J. Froehlich, F.S.C., Dir. Finance & Treas.; Mr. Alan Wickman, F.S.C., Prov. Delegate for Ministry Governing Boards; Mr. Alan Weyland, Exec. Dir. Mission & Ministry; Ms. H. Carroll Bennett, Admin. Asst.; Mr. Philip De Rita, Dir. Communications & Public Rels.; Bro. Francis Eells, F.S.C., Vocations Dir.; Bro. Michael Andrejko, F.S.C., Dir. College Contacts; Mrs. Janice Shea, Personal Asst. to the Brother Visitor; Bro. Patrick Donahue, Dir. Advancement.

Legal Titles: Brothers of the Christian Schools, District of Eastern North America, Inc. (d/b/a: FSC DENA); Brothers of the Christian Schools, Long Island-New England Province; Christian Brothers of Frederick, Inc.; La Salle Provincialate, Inc.; Ammendale Normal Institute of Prince George's County, Inc.

Brothers 262

Represented in the Archdioceses of Baltimore, Detroit, New York, Philadelphia and Washington and in the Dioceses of Albany, Brooklyn, Buffalo, Camden, Palm Beach, Pittsburgh, Providence, Rockville Centre, Syracuse and Trenton.

[0340] (O.CIST.)—CISTERCIAN ABBEY

(Ordo Cisterciensis)

Headquarters: Piazza del Tempio di Diana, 14 I-00153, Rome, Italy, Rt. Rev. Mauro-Giuseppe Lepori, O.Cist., Abbot Gen.

Cistercian Monastery: Our Lady of Dallas, 3550 Cistercian Rd., Irving, TX 75039. Tel: 972-438-2044. Email: knevitt@cistercian.org. Rt. Rev. Peter Verhalen, O.Cist., Abbot; Rev. Paul McCormick, O.Cist., Prior; Rev. Thomas Esposito, O.Cist., Subprior.

Priests 22; Junior Monks: 5

Staff: Universities 1; Preparatory School 1; Novitiate 1.

Properties owned: Abbey and Preparatory School.

Represented in the Dioceses of Dallas.

Cistercian Monastery of Our Lady of Fatima: 564 Walton Ave., Mount Laurel, NJ 08054. Tel: 856-235-1330. Rev. Lino S. Parente, O.Cist., Prior; Rev. Maurizio Nicoletti, O.Cist.; Rev. Awte Weldu, O.Cist.; Rev. Musie Tesfayohannes.

Established in 1961 as a dependent Monastery of the Congregation of Casamari (Italy).

Property owned: Fatima House and the Monastery.

Cistercian Conventual Priory: St. Mary's Priory, 70 Schuylkill Rd., New Ringgold, PA 17960. Tel: 570-943-2645; Fax: 570-943-3035. Very Rev. Luke Anderson, O.Cist., Ph.D., Prior.

Legal Title: The Cistercian Monastery of Pennsylvania.

Monks: 2

Monastery of Chau Son Sacramento: 14080 Leary Rd., P.O. Box 99, Walnut Grove, CA 95690. Tel: 916-776-1356; Fax: 916-776-1921. Rev. Vincent Hau Dinh Nguyen, O.Cist., Prior; Rev. Dominic Hung Tran, O.Cist.; Rev. Nicolas Thanh Quang Le, O.Cist.; Rev. Leo Tiên Van Nguyen, O.Cist.

Established in Sacramento in 2004.

Represented in the Diocese of Sacramento. Also in Vietnam.

[0350] (O.C.S.O.)—THE CISTERCIAN ORDER OF THE STRICT OBSERVANCE

(TRAPPISTS)

(Ordo Cisterciensium Strictioris Observantiae)

Generalate: Casa Generalizia O.C.S.O., 33 Viale Africa, 00144, Rome, Italy, Rt. Rev. Dom Eamon Fitzgerald, O.C.S.O., Abbot Gen.

Abbey of Gethsemani (1848): No. 3642 Monks Rd., Trappist, KY 40051. Tel: 502-549-3117. Rt. Rev. Elias Dietz, O.C.S.O., Abbot.

Priests 10; Brothers 30

Abbey of Our Lady of New Melleray (1849): 6632 Melleray Cir., Peosta, IA 52068. Tel: 563-588-2319. Vocation Director Email: vocationdirector@newmelleray.org. Rt. Rev. Mark A. Scott, O.C.S.O., Abbot; Rev. David Block, O.C.S.O., Prior; Rev. Ephrem Poppish, O.C.S.O., Subprior; Rev. Stephen Verbest, O.C.S.O., Novice Master and Vocation Dir.

Priests 10; Professed Monks: 24

St. Joseph's Abbey (1825): 167 N. Spencer Rd., Spencer, MA 01562-1233. Tel: 508-885-8700; Fax: 508-885-8701. Rt. Rev. Damian Carr, O.C.S.O., Abbot.

Legal Title: Cistercian Abbey of Spencer, Inc.

Total in Community: 55; Priests 23; Solemnly Professed 50; Novices 4

Monastery of the Holy Spirit, Inc. (1944): 2625 Hwy. 212, S.W., Conyers, GA 30094. Tel: 770-483-8705; Fax: 770-760-0989. Rev. Francis Michael Stiteler, O.C.S.O., Abbot.

Priests 13; Professed Monks: 37

Represented in the Archdiocese of Atlanta.

Abbey of Our Lady of Guadalupe (1948): 9200 N.E. Abbey Rd., Carlton, OR 97111-9504. Tel: 503-852-7174; Fax: 503-852-7748. Rt. Rev. Peter McCarthy, O.C.S.O., Abbot; Rev. Dominique-Savio Nelson, O.C.S.O., Prior; Bro. Phillip Wertman, O.C.S.O., Subprior.

Solemnly Professed 27; Priests 13

Abbey of the Genesee (1951): 3258 River Rd., P.O. Box 900, Piffard, NY 14533. Tel: 585-243-0660. Rev. Gerard D'Souza, O.C.S.O., Abbot; Rt. Rev. John Denburger, O.C.S.O., Abbot Emeritus; Rt. Rev. John Eudes Bamberger, O.C.S.O., Abbot Emeritus; Rev. Jerome J. Machar, O.C.S.O; Rev. Isaac Slater, O.C.S.O., Prior; Bro. Anthony Weber, O.C.S.O., Novice Master Retreat House.

Solemnly Professed 28; Professed Priests 11

Mepkin Abbey (1949): 1098 Mepkin Abbey Rd., Moncks Corner, SC 29461. Tel: 843-761-8509; Fax: 843-761-6719. Rev. Kevin V. Walsh, O.C.S.O., Novice Master & Prior; Rt. Rev. Stan Gumula, O.S.C.O., Abbot; Bro. John Corrigan, O.C.S.O., Business Mgr.

Priests 7; Monks in Community: 16

Abbey of Our Lady of the Holy Cross (1950): 901 Cool Spring Ln., Berryville, VA 22611-2700. Tel: 540-955-4536; Fax: 540-955-1356. Email: information@hcava.org. Rt. Rev. Joseph Wittstock, O.C.S.O., Abbot;

Bro. Efrain Sosa, O.C.S.O., Novice Master & Vocation Dir.

Legal Title: Community of Cistercians of the Strict Observance, Inc.

Solemnly Professed 9; Priests 4

Assumption Abbey: Rte. 5, Box 1056, Ava, MO 65608. Tel: 417-683-5110; Fax: 417-683-5658. Rt. Rev. Alberic Maisog, O.C.S.O., Supr.; Rt. Rev. Cyprian Harrison, O.C.S.O., Abbot (Retired).

Priests 2; Professed 1

Abbey of New Clairvaux (1955): Trappist-Cistercian Abbey, Vina, CA 96092. Tel: 530-839-2161. Rt. Rev. Paul Mark Schwan, O.C.S.O., Abbot.

Legal Title: Abbey of New Clairvaux, Inc.

Solemn Vows 15; Simple Vows 1

St. Benedict's Monastery (1956): 1012 Monastery Rd., Snowmass, CO 81654. Tel: 970-279-4400. Rt. Rev. Joseph Boyle, O.C.S.O., Abbot; Rev. Charles Albanese, O.C.S.O., Prior; Bro. Raymond Roberts, O.C.S.O., Subprior.

Professed Monks: 14

[0360] (C.M.F.)—CLARETIAN MISSIONARIES

(Missionary Sons of the Immaculate Heart of Mary)
(Congregatio Missionariorum Filiorum Immaculati Cordis Beatae Mariae Virginis.)

General Headquarters: Via Sacro Cuore di Maria 5, Rome, Italy, Very Rev. Mathew Vattamattam, C.M.F., Supr. Gen.

Claretian Missionaries U.S.A. - Canada Province: Claretian Missionaries Headquarters, 205 W. Monroe St., 7th Fl., Chicago, IL 60606. Tel: 312-236-7782; Fax: 312-236-7230. Very Rev. Rosendo Urrabazo, C.F.M., Prov. Supr.; Rev. Thomas McGann, C.M.F., Treas. & Consultor; Rev. Jose Sanchez, C.M.F., Consultor; Rev. Paul Keller, C.M.F., Consultor; Rev. Fernando Ferrera, C.M.F., Consultor.

Fathers 90 Brothers 9; Students 4

Legal Holdings or Titles: Claret Center, Chicago, IL; Claretian Volunteer Program, Chicago, IL; Claretian Associates, Chicago, IL; Claretians, Inc.; St. Jude League, Inc.; Claretian Missionaries - Western Province, Inc.; Dominguez Seminary, Inc., Compton, CA.

Represented in the Archdioceses of Atlanta, Chicago, Los Angeles and San Antonio and in the Dioceses of Fresno, Metuchen, Phoenix and Springfield-Cape Girardeau. Also in Canada.

[0370] (S.S.C.)—SOCIETY OF ST. COLUMBAN

(Societas Sancti Columbani pro missionibus ad Exteros)

Central Administration (1918): Missionary Society of St. Columban, No 3 and 4 Ma Yau Tong Village, Po Lam Rd., Tseung Kwan O, Kowloon, Hong Kong, Very Rev. Kevin O'Neill, S.S.C., Supr. Gen.

Members: 575

Region in the United States: Society of St. Columban, P.O. Box 10, St. Columbans, NE 68056. Tel: 402-291-1920. Very Rev. Timothy Mulroy, S.S.C., Dir.; Very Rev. John Burger, S.S.C., Vice Dir. Council: Rev. William Morton, S.S.C.; Rev. Robert Mosher, S.S.C.; Rev. John Brannigan, S.S.C.

Fathers 66

Legal Titles: St. Columban's Foreign Mission Society; The Columban Fathers; Missionary Society of St. Columban.

Represented in the Archdioceses of Chicago, Los Angeles, Omaha and Washington and in the Dioceses of Buffalo, El Paso, Orange, Providence and San Bernardino.

[0380] (M.C.C.J.)—COMBONI MISSIONARIES OF THE HEART OF JESUS

(Verona Fathers) Missionarii Comboniani Cordis Jesu)
(A Pontifical World Missionary Congregation Of Priests And Brothers)

Founded by Saint Daniel Comboni in 1867, First foundation in the United States in 1939.

General Motherhouse: Missionari Comboniani, Via Luigi Lilio 80, 00142, Rome, Italy, Very Rev. Tesfaye Tadesse Gebresilasie, M.C.C.J., Supr. Gen.

North American Province (1950): Comboni Mission Center, 1318 Nagel Rd., Cincinnati, OH 45255-3120. Tel: 513-474-4997; Fax: 513-474-0382; Email: info@ComboniMissionaries.org; Web: www.ComboniMissionaries.org. Rev. John M. Converset, M.C.C.J., Prov.; Rev. Ruffino Ezama, M.C.C.J., Mission Office Dir.

Legal Title: Comboni Missionaries of the Heart of Jesus, Inc.

Priests 26; Home Mission Parishes 5; Mission Centers 3

Represented in the Archdioceses of Chicago, Cincinnati, Los Angeles and Newark and Diocese of San Bernardino.

[0390] (I.M.C.)—CONSOLATA MISSIONARIES

(Institutum Missionum a Consolata)

General Motherhouse: Viale delle Mura Aurelie 11, Rome, Italy, Very Rev. Stefano Camerlengo, Supr. Gen.

Headquarters in the U.S.: 2624 Rte. 27, North Brunswick, NJ 08902. Mailing Address: P.O. Box 5550, Somerset, NJ 08875-5550. Tel: 732-297-9191. Email: cimcrao@aol.com. Rev. Paolo Fedrigoni, I.M.C., Supr.

Legal Title: Consolata Society for Foreign Missions.

Priests 8

Properties owned: Mission Community House 1.

Represented in the Dioceses of Metuchen and San Bernardino.

[0400] (O.S.C.)—CANONS REGULAR OF THE ORDER OF THE HOLY CROSS

(Crosier Fathers and Brothers)

Canonici Regulares Ordinis Sanctae Crucis (Cruciferi) Generalate: Generalatus Ordinis S. Crucis, Via del Velabro 19, 00186, Rome, Italy, Very Rev. Laurentius Tarpin, O.S.C., Master Gen.

United States National Headquarters: Conventual Priory of the Holy Cross, 717 E. Southern Ave., Phoenix, AZ 85040-3142. Tel: 602-443-7100; Email: crosier@crosier.org. Rev. Thomas A. Enneking, O.S.C., Conventual Prior; Councilors: Bro. Jeffrey Breer, O.S.C.; Rev. Kermit Holl, O.S.C.; Rev. Glen Lewandowski, O.S.C.

Fathers 30; Brothers 15

Legal Titles: Crosier Fathers and Brothers Province, Inc.; Canons Regular of the Order of the Holy Cross.

Represented in the Dioceses of Phoenix and St. Cloud.

Properties owned, sponsored or staffed: Houses 2; Novitiates 1; Parishes 9.

[0410] (F.D.P.)—SONS OF DIVINE PROVIDENCE

(Filiorum Divinae Providentiae)

General Motherhouse: Via Etruria 6, 00183, Rome, Italy, Very Rev. Flavio Peloso, F.D.P., Supr. Gen. Founded in 1893 by St. Luis Orione.

Missionary Delegation-Our Lady Mother of the Church-U.S. Foundation: 150 Orient Ave., East Boston, MA 02128. Tel: 617-569-8792; Fax: 617-569-8701. Very Rev. Tarcisio Vieira, F.D.P., Supr. Gen.; Rev. Oreste Ferrari, F.D.P.

Priests 5

Properties staffed or owned: Parishes 1; Nursing Homes 1; Shrines 1.

Represented in the Archdiocese of Boston.

[0420] (S.V.D.)—SOCIETY OF THE DIVINE WORD

(Societatis Verbi Divini)

General Motherhouse: Collegio del Verbo Divino, Via dei Verbiti 1, 00154, Rome, Italy, Very Rev. Heinz Kuluke, S.V.D., Supr. Gen.

Founded 1875, in Steyl, Netherlands; First U.S.A. province erected in 1897 with Headquarters at St. Mary's Mission House (Divine Word Seminary) Techny, Illinois; later separating into four provinces. In 1985 the Eastern and Northern Provinces combined.

Chicago Province (1985): Province of Saint Joseph Freinademetz, S.V.D. Province Center, 1985 Waukegan Rd., P.O. Box 6038, Techny, IL 60082-6038. Tel: 847-272-2700; Fax: 847-412-9505. Rev. Thomas J. Ascheman, S.V.D., Prov.; Rev. Adam MacDonald, S.V.D., Vice Prov.; Rev. Dariusz Garbaciak, S.V.D., Treas.

Legal Titles: Society of the Divine Word; Divine Word Funds, Inc.; Divine Word International; Techny Towers Conference and Retreat Center; Blessed Arnold Charitable Trust; DWTCRE Charitable Trust; S.V.D. Funds, Inc.

Priests 174; Brothers 35; Theologians 29; Brothers in Temporary Vows 4. College Minor Seminarians 34; Novices 6.

Properties owned: Theologate; College; 3 Retreat Houses; House of Studies; Conference Center; 3 Retirement Houses.

Represented in the Archdioceses of Boston, Chicago, Dubuque, Indianapolis, Milwaukee, St. Louis and Washington and in the Dioceses of Memphis, Pittsburgh, Trenton and Wheeling-Charleston. Also in Canada, Jamaica, Dutch Caribbean, British Virgin Islands, and the West Indies.

Eastern Province: Amalgamated with Northern Province. See Chicago Province.

Divine Word Missionaries: 1835 Waukegan Rd., P.O. Box 6099, Techny, IL 60082-6099.Tel; 847-272-7600. Email: hebner@svdmissions.org. Bro. Dan Holman, S.V.D., Pres.

Divine Word Missionaries is within the territory of the Chicago Province but assists members of all three United States S.V.D. Provinces serving overseas and reports directly to Rome regarding its international fundraising activities.

Legal Titles: Divine Word Missionaries, Inc.; S.V.D. Catholic Universities.

Southern Province: Southern Province of St. Augustine, 204 Ruella St., Bay Saint Louis, MS 39520. Tel: 228-467-4322; Tel: 228-467-3815; Email: ussprovincial@gmail.com. Rev. Paul Kahan, S.V.D., Prov.; Rev. Mike Somers, S.V.D., Vice Prov.; Rev. George Gormley, S.V.D., Treas.

Fathers 59; Brothers 3; Parishes 34; Mission Stations: 10; Elementary Schools 3

Address applications for Retreats and Missions to: Rev. Joseph Dang, S.V.D.

Represented in the Archdioceses of Galveston-Houston and New Orleans and in the Dioceses of Baton Rouge, Beaumont, Biloxi, Fort Worth, Jackson, Lafayette (LA), Lake Charles, Little Rock and Pensacola-Tallahassee.

Western Province (1964): Province of St. Therese of the Child Jesus, 11316 Cypress Ave, Riverside, CA 92505. Tel: 951-687-7600; Fax: 951-687-3158. Very Rev. Soney Sebastian, S.V.D., Prov.; Rev. Alan Jenkins, S.V.D., Vice Prov.; Rev. Pavol Sochulak, S.V.D., Prov. Treas.

Fathers 63; Brothers 2

Represented in the Archdioceses of Los Angeles and San Francisco and in the Dioceses of Oakland, Orange, San Bernardino and San Diego.

Properties staffed, sponsored or owned: Parishes 18; Hospitals 1; Prisons 1; Retreat Centers 1.

[0430] (O.P.)—ORDER OF PREACHERS

(Dominicans Fratres Sacri Ordinis Praedicatorum)

Generalitia: Convento Santa Sabina, Piazza Pietro d'Illiria, Aventino 00153, Rome, Italy, Most Rev. Bruno Cadore, O.P., 87th Master of the Order; Very Rev. Christopher Eggleton, O.P., Socius for the United States Provs. & Vietnamese Vicariate; Very Rev. Benjamin Earl, O.P., Procurator Gen.

Province of St. Joseph-Eastern Dominican Province (1805): Dominican Provincial Offices, 141 E. 65th St., New York, NY 10065-6618. Tel: 212-737-5757; Fax: 212-861-4216. Very Rev. Kenneth R. Letoile, O.P., Prior Prov.; Very Rev. Darren Michael Pierre, O.P., Socius & Vicar Prov.; Rev. Allen Morgan O.P., Econ. Admin.; Rev. Peter M. Batts, O.P., Archivist; Rev. James Sullivan, O.P., Dir. Continuing Formation; Rev. Jacob Bertrand Janczyk, O.P., Dir., Vocations; Rev. David C. Adilletta, O.P, Mission Sec.; Rev. Francis Belanger, O.P., Promoter of Catholic Social Teaching; Rev. Hugh Vincent Dyer, O.P., Promoter, Holy Name Society; Rev. Charles Shonck, O.P., Promoter, Confraternity of the Most Holy Rosary; Very Rev. Kevin Gabriel Gillen, O.P., Dir. for Advancement; Very Rev. John Albert Langlois, O.P., Pres., Pontifical Faculty of the Immaculate Conception (Washington, D.C.); Rev. James Brent, O.P., Promoter, Angelic Warfare Confraternity.

Professed 302; Solemnly Professed 256; Simply Professed 46; Priests 230; Novices 16; (Arch)Bishops 3; Cooperator Brothers 9

Corporate Title: Dominican Fathers Province of St. Joseph, Inc.

Legal Titles: Retirement Plan and Pension Plan; Dominican Fathers, Province of St. Joseph; Dominican Friars' Guilds, Inc.; Deserving Poor Boys Priesthood Association, Inc.; St. Jude Dominican Missions, Inc.; St. Martin de Porres Guild, Inc.; Dominican Foreign Missions; Handicapped Children's Fund, Peru; Rosary Shrine of St. Jude, (Washington, DC); Rosary Apostolate; Dominican Foundation of Dominican Friars, Province of St. Joseph, Inc.

Represented in the following U.S. dioceses: Baltimore, Boston, Buffalo, Chicago, Cincinnati, Columbus, Denver, Fort Wayne-South Bend, Harrisburg, Hartford, Los Angeles, Louisville, Manchester, Nashville, New York, Newark, Philadelphia, Providence, Richmond, Rockville Centre, San Francisco, Springfield, Syracuse, Washington and Youngstown.

Properties owned, staffed or sponsored: Priories 10; Houses 8; Parishes 16; Campus Ministries 7; Colleges 1; Houses of Study 2; Novitiates 1; Mission Abroad 1; Health Care Ministry 1; Health Care Facility 1.

Province of the Most Holy Name of Jesus-Western Dominican Province (1912): 5877 Birch Ct., Oakland, CA 94618-1626. Tel: 510-658-8722; Fax: 510-658-1061; Email: WDP@opwest.org. Very Rev. Mark Padrez, O.P., Prior Prov.; Very Rev. Christopher Fadok, O.P., Vicar to the Prov. & Socius; Rev. Martin Walsh, O.P., Dir. Mission Foundation; Rev. Bryan Kromholtz, O.P., Regent of Studies; Rev. Michael Augustine Amabisco, O.P., Syndic; Rev. Stephen Maria Lopez, O.P., Dir. Vocations; Rev. Jude Eli, O.P., Dir. Preaching; Very Rev. Reginald Martin, O.P., Prov. Archivist.

Legal Title: Province of the Holy Name, Inc.

Fathers 111; Brothers 5; Professed Clerics: 20; Novices 9; Donatus: 1; Parishes 8; Newman Centers/Personal Parishes 7; Retreat Houses 1; Houses of Study: 1; Novitiates 1

Represented in the Archdioceses of Anchorage, Los Angeles, Portland in Oregon, San Francisco, and Seattle and in the Dioceses of Fall River, Las Vegas, Oakland, Providence, Sacramento, Salt Lake City, San Jose and Tucson. Also in Germany, Guatemala, Israel, Italy, Mexico and Switzerland.

Province of St. Albert the Great-Central Dominican Province (1939): 1910 S. Ashland Ave., Chicago, IL 60608. Tel: 312-243-0011; Fax: 312-829-8471. Email: office@opcentral.org. Rev. James V. Marchionda, O.P., Prov.; Rev. Louis S. Morrone, O.P., Socius, Vicar Prov. & Archivist; Rev. Andrew Carl Wisdom, O.P., Dir., Society Vocational Support & Vicar, Mission Advancement; Rev. Jude McPeak, O.P., Promoter, Vocations; Rev. Jay Harrington, O.P., Regent; Rev. Patrick Tobin, O.P., Dir., Shrine of St. Jude; Rev. Patrick R. Rearden, O.P., Dir. St. Dominic Mission Society.

Fathers 118; Professed Clerics: 13; Novices 2; Brothers 9

Legal Titles: Dominicans, Province of St. Albert the Great, U.S.A.; Shrine of St. Jude Thaddeus, Inc.; Society for Vocational Support, Inc.; St. Dominic Mission Society; Dominican Social Action Fund; Dominican Laity; Dominican Central Productions; The Bolivian Trust of the Dominicans, Office for Mission Advancement.

Represented in the Archdioceses of Chicago, Denver, Detroit, Indianapolis, St. Louis, St. Paul and Minneapolis and Santa Fe and in the Dioceses of Jefferson City, Lafayette in Indiana, Madison, Springfield in Illinois and Superior.

Properties owned, staffed or sponsored: Parishes 9; Convents 6; Houses 6; Houses of Studies 1; Novitiate 1; High Schools 1.

Southern Dominican Province of St. Martin de Porres (1979): 1421 N. Causeway Blvd., Ste. 200, Metairie, LA 70001-4144. Tel: 504-837-2129; Fax: 504-837-6604. Email: provassistant@opsouth.org. Very Rev. Thomas M. Condon, O.P., Prov.; Rev. Victor Laroche, O.P., Socius; Rev. John Dominic Sims, O.P., Syndic; Very Rev. José David Padilla, O.P., Promoter for Permanent Formation; Very Rev. Marcos Ramos, O.P., Regent of Studies; Rev. Francis Orozco, O.P., Dir. of Vocations; Rev. Juan Torres, Dir. of Devel.

Fathers 78; Professed Clerics: 6; Brothers 4; Deacons 2; Novices 2

Legal Holdings or Titles: Southern Dominican Foundation; Retirement and Community Support Plan, Southern Dominican Province, U.S.A.; Shrine of St. Martin de Porres.

Represented in the Archdioceses of Atlanta, Galveston-Houston, Miami, New Orleans, San Antonio and St. Louis and in the Dioceses of Austin, Baton Rouge, Dallas, Fort Worth, Lubbock, Memphis and Tucson.

Properties owned, staffed or sponsored: Parishes 9; Priories 5; Houses 6; Shrines 1; Provincial Offices 1.

[0440] (S.S.E.)—SOCIETY OF SAINT EDMUND

(Societas Sancti Edmundi)

General Motherhouse: Edmundite Generalate, 270 Winooski Park, Colchester, VT 05439. Tel: 802-654-3400; Fax: 802-654-3409. Very Rev. Stephen W. Hornat, S.S.E., Supr. Gen. Councilors: Rev. Stanley Deresienski, S.S.E; Rev. Brian J. Cummings, S.S.E; Rev. David J. Theroux, S.S.E; Rev. David G. Cray, S.S.E.

Legal Title: Society of St. Edmund, Inc.; Fathers of St. Edmund, Southern Missions, Inc.

Fathers 24; Brothers 3

Represented in the Archdiocese of Mobile and in the Dioceses of Burlington and Norwich. Also in Venezuela and France.

Properties owned, staffed or sponsored: Parishes 11; College 1; Shrine; Novitiate; Edmundite Missions.

[0450] (C.J.M.)—CONGREGATION OF JESUS AND MARY

Founded in 1643 by St. John Eudes in Caen, France as a Society of Apostolic Life.

General Motherhouse: Via dei Querceti, 15, 00184, Rome, Italy, Rev. Camilo Bernal Hadad, C.J.M., Supr. Gen. 744 Sonrisa St., Solana Beach, CA 92075. Rev. John H. Howard, C.J.M., Regl. Supr.

Priests 13; Seminarians: 3

Represented in the Archdiocese of Los Angeles and the Dioceses of Buffalo, Phoenix and San Diego.

[0460] (C.F.P.)—BROTHERS OF THE POOR OF ST. FRANCIS

(Congregatio Fratrum Pauperum)

Motherhouse: Aachen, Germany, Bro. Lukas Junemann, C.F.P., Min. Gen.

U.S.A. Community of St. Joseph: P.O. Box 30359, Cincinnati, OH 45230-0359. Tel: 513-924-0111; Fax: 513-321-3777. Bro. Edward Kesler, C.F.P., U.S.A Community Min.

Professed Brothers 14

Brothers serve and staff: High School; Elementary Schools. Brothers' Special Mission: Care and education of youth; elementary & secondary education; pastoral ministry.

Represented in the Archdioceses of Cincinnati and Newark and in the Dioceses of Covington, Davenport, Las Cruces and Little Rock.

[0470] (O.F.M.CAP.)—THE CAPUCHIN FRANCISCAN FRIARS

(Ordo Fratrum Minorum Capuccinorum)

Generalate: Curia Generale dei Cappuccini, Via Piemonte 70, 00187, Rome, Italy, Web: www.ofmcap.org. Bro. Mauro Johri, O.F.M.Cap., Gen. Min.

Province of St. Joseph (1857): Calvary Province, 1820 Mt. Elliott St., Detroit, MI 48207-3485. Tel: 313-579-2100; Fax: 313-579-2275. Rev. Michael Sullivan, O.F.M.Cap., Prov. Min.; Rev. Steven Kropp, O.F.M.Cap., Prov. Vicar; Rev. Daniel Fox, O.F.M.Cap., Councilor; Bro. Jerome Johnson, O.F.M.Cap., Councilor; Rev. David Preuss, O.F.M.Cap., Councilor; Rev. Perry McDonald, O.F.M.Cap., Sec.-Rel. Affairs; Bro. T.L. Michael Auman, O.F.M.Cap., Dir. Communications; Rev. John Celichowski, O.F.M.Cap., Dir., Post-Novitiate Min. & Continuing Educ.; Rev. William Cieslak, O.F.M.Cap., Dir. Office of Preaching & Evangelization; Rev. Lester Bach, O.F.M.Cap., Prov. Asst.-Secular Franciscan Order; Rev. George Kooran, O.F.M. Cap., Dir. Solanus Guild; Ms. Junia Yasenov, Archivist; Rev. Robert Wotypka, O.F.M.Cap., Corp. Responsibility Agent; Ms. Diane Simpkins, Corp. Sec./Treas.; Ms. Debi Piontkowski, Admin. Asst.; Mr. Jeff Parrish, Dir., Prov. Ministries & Dir., Human Resources; Ms. Amy Peterson, Dir., Office of Pastoral Care & Conciliation; Mr. Tim Hinkle, Dir. Public Rels.; Ms. Debra Van Ermen, Dir. Wellness; Rev. Edward Foley, O.F.M.Cap., Vice Postulator Cause of Bl. Solanus Casey.

Legal Title: Province of St. Joseph of the Capuchin Order, Inc.

Priests 112; Perpetually Professed Lay Friars: 29

Parishes, Hospitals, Nursing Homes, Prisons, Retreat Centers, Soup Kitchens; Direct Services to the Poor; Educational Institutions; Home and Foreign Missions.

Represented in the Archdioceses of Chicago, Detroit, Los Angeles and Milwaukee and in the Dioceses of Great Falls-Billings, Green Bay, La Crosse, Marquette Saginaw and Tucson. Also in the Apostolic Vicariate of Northern Arabia and in the Diocese of Panama.

Province of St. Augustine (1873): Provincial Office, 220 37th St., Pittsburgh, PA 15201. Tel: 412-682-6011; Fax: 412-682-0506. Very Rev. Thomas Betz, O.F.M.Cap., Prov. Min. Rev. Michael Joyce, O.F.M.Cap., Vicar Prov.; Rev. Francis Yacobi, O.F.M.Cap., Exec. Sec.; Mr. R. Joseph Kusnir, C.F.O. Definitors: Bro. James Mungovan, O.F.M.Cap.; Rev. Stephen Fernandes, O.F.M.Cap.; Rev. Robert Marva, O.F.M.Cap. Vocations Director: Rev. Rafael Anguiano-Rodriguez, O.F.M.Cap.

Cardinals: 1; Bishops 2; Priests 109; Brothers 37; Professed in Formation: 32; Novices 8; Postulants: 13

Legal Titles: Province of St. Augustine of the Capuchin Order; Headquarters of Capuchin Franciscan Volunteer Corps., Inc.; Augustine Province of the Capuchin Order; National Headquarters of Archcon fraternity of Christian Mothers; Mission Office of Seraphic Mass Association; Secular Franciscan Order of St. Augustine, Province; Capuchin Friars Sick and Elderly Trust Fund; St. Fidelis, Inc.; Capuchin Friars Formation and Education Trust Fund.

Represented in the Archdioceses of Baltimore, Philadelphia and Washington and in the Dioceses of Altoona-Johnstown, Cleveland, Harrisburg and Pittsburgh. Also in Papua New Guinea and Puerto Rico.

Properties owned, staffed or sponsored: Parishes 20; Formation Houses 1; Friaries 18; Postulancy Houses 1; Hospital Chaplains 8; Missions 2.

The Province of St. Mary of the Capuchin Order: St. Conrad Friary, 30 Gedney Park Dr., White Plains, NY 10605-3599. Tel: 914-761-3008; Fax: 914-948-6429. Email: smpcomcap@gmail.com. Very Rev. Michael J. Greco, O.F.M.Cap., Prov. Min.; Very Rev. Robert J. Abbatiello, O.F.M.Cap., Vicar Prov. Min.; Councilors: Bro. Lake A. Herman, O.F.M.Cap.; Bro. James M. Peterson, O.F.M.Cap.; Rev. Salvatore Cordaro, O.F.M.Cap.

Legal Title: The Province of St. Mary of the Capuchin Order.

Bishops 2; Priests 97; Permanent Deacons 1; Professed Lay Brothers 28; Temporary Professed Friars 10.

Represented in the Archdioceses of Agaña, Boston and New York and in the Dioceses of Bridgeport, Brooklyn, Burlington, Manchester, Norwich, Portland (In Maine), Rochester, Rockville Centre and St. Petersburg. Also in Japan.

Properties staffed or sponsored: Parishes 11; Chaplaincies 20; Novitiate 1.

Development Office: Sacred Heart Friary, 110 Shonnard Pl., Yonkers, New York, NY 10703.

Province of the Sacred Stigmata of St. Francis: Our Lady Guadalupe Friary, 319 - 36th St., P.O. Box 809, Union City, NJ 07087. Tel: 201-865-0611; Fax: 201-866-7035. Email: stigmatanj@aol.com. Rev. Remo DiSalvatore, O.F.M.Cap., Prov. Min.; Rev. Robert Williams, O.F.M.Cap., Prov. Vicar. Councilors: Rev. Francisco Arredondo, O.F.M.Cap.; Rev. Ronald Giannone, O.F.M.Cap.; Rev. Robert Perez, O.F.M.Cap.

Priests 20; Brothers 12; Parishes 4; Friaries 4; Retreat Houses 1

Represented in the Archdioceses of Newark and New York and in the Dioceses of Charlotte and Wilmington.

Our Lady of Angels, Western America Province: 1345 Cortez Ave., Burlingame, CA 94010. Email: finance@olacapuchins.org. Very Rev. Harold Snider, O.F.M.Cap., Prov.; Rev. Donal Burke, O.F.M.Cap., Dir.-Devel.; Rev. Miguel Angel Ortiz, O.F.M.Cap., Dir.-Foreign Missions, Sec. Councilors: Rev. Joseph Seraphin Dederick, O.F.M.Cap., Vicar; Rev. Hung Nguyen, O.F.M.Cap; Rev. Antonio (Tony) Marti, O.F.M.Cap; Bro. Tran Vu, O.F.M.Cap.

Priests 29; Brothers 8; Brothers in Formation: 3; Postulants: 2; Novice: 1

Ministries in Parishes, High Schools, Novitiates, Chaplaincies, House of Study, Retreats, Foreign Missions, Campus Ministry, Prison Chaplaincy and Hospital Chaplaincy.

Represented in the Archdioceses of Los Angeles and San Francisco and in the Diocese of Oakland. Also in Mexico.

Province of SS. Stanislaus and Adalbert (1948): St. Stanislaus Friary, 2 Manor Dr., Oak Ridge, NJ 07438. Tel: 973-697-7757. Rev. Andrzej Kiejza, O.F.M.Cap., Prov. Min.; Rev. Zdzislaw Tokarczyk, O.F.M.Cap., Financial Dir.; Rev. Joseph Kubiak, O.F.M.Cap; Deacon Jerzy Krzyskow, Admin.

Fathers 4

Represented in the Dioceses of Metuchen and Paterson.

Custody of Our Lady of Guadalupe: Capuchin Franciscan Friars of Texas, 2911 Lapsley St., Dallas, TX 75212. Tel: 214-377-7643; Fax: 214-637-2454. Fathers 4

Members serve and staff: Parishes 2; Cursillo Centers 1.

Represented in the Dioceses of Dallas and Fort Worth.

Province of Mid-America (1977): 3613 Wyandot St., Denver, CO 80211-2950. Tel: 303-477-5436; Fax: 303- 477-6925; Email: contact@capuchins.org; Web: www.capuchins.org. Rev. Christopher Popravak, O.F.M.Cap., Prov. Min.; Rev. John Cousins, O.F.M.Cap., Prov. Vicar; Rev. David Songy, O.F.M.Cap., Treas.; Rev. Sojan Parappilly,

O.F.M.Cap. (KSF), Second Councilor; Rev. Bill Kraus, O.F.M.Cap., Third Councilor & Corporate Sec.; Rev. John Schmeidler, O.F.M.Cap., Fourth Councilor; Rev. Blaine Burkey, O.F.M.Cap., Archivist & Communications; Rev. Joseph Mary Elder, O.F.M.Cap., Vocations; Bishops 2; Priests 47; Lay Brothers 10; Temporarily Professed Brothers 8; Novices 2; Postulants: 1

Legal Titles: Capuchin Province of Mid-America, Inc.; St. Francis Seminary Endowment Foundation, Inc.

Represented in the Archdioceses of Denver, Kansas City in Kansas and San Antonio and in the Dioceses of Colorado Springs, Kansas City-St. Joseph, Pueblo, and Salina.

Custody of St. John the Baptist (1905): Custody Offices, 216 Arzuaga St., P.O. Box 21350, San Juan, PR 00928-1350. Tel: 787-764-3090; Fax: 866-234-1781; Email: secretaria.capuchinospr@gmail.com; Web: www.capuchinospr.org. Friar Ramón H. Negrón-Cruz, O.F.M.Cap., Custos; Friar José A. Cruz-Collazo, O.F.M.Cap., First Councilor; Friar Luis O. Padilla-Cruz, O.F.M.Cap., Second Councilor; Rev. Ramón J. Casellas-River, O.F.M.Cap., Director of Assoc. Misioner Capuchina, Inc.

Friars: 22; Postulants: 2

Legal Titles: Asociación de Frailes Capuchinos, Inc.; Asociación Misionera Capuchina; Capuchin Formation Trust of Puerto Rico; Capuchin Health and Retirement Trust of Puerto Rico; San Antonio de Rio Piedras, Inc.; Centro Capuchinos, Inc.

Represented in the Archdiocese of San Juan and in the Dioceses of Arecibo, Caguas, Mayagüez and Ponce.

Properties owned, staffed and sponsored: Formation Fraternities 3; Parishes 5; Retreat Centers 1; Friaries 7; Schools 1.

[0480] (O.F.M.CONV.)—CONVENTUAL FRANCISCANS

(Friars Minor Conventual)

(Ordo Fratrum Minorum S. Francisci Conventualium)

General Curia: Piazza SS. Apostoli, 51, 00187, Rome, Italy, Very Rev. Marco Tasca, O.F.M.Conv., Min. Gen.

Our Lady of the Angels Province: Satellite Office, 77 St. Francis Pl., P.O. Box 629, Rensselaer, NY 12144. Tel: 518-472-1000; Fax: 518-472-1013. Email: provsec1@olaprovince.org; Web: www.franciscanseast.org. Very Rev. James McCurry, O.F.M.Conv., Min. Prov.; Rev. Brad A. Milunski, O.F.M.Conv., Vicar Prov.

Legal Titles: Order of Friars Minor Conventual Immaculate Conception; Province Charitable Trust; Franciscorps, Inc., Rensselaer, NY; The Franciscan Center for Spirituality, Inc., Albany, NY; Franciscans in Collaborative Ministry, Inc., Rensselaer, NY.

Represented in the Archdioceses of New York and Washington, DC and in the Dioceses of Albany, Charlotte, Raleigh, Syracuse and Trenton. Also in Canada.

Our Lady of the Angels Province, Inc. (2014): Provincial House, 12300 Folly Quarter Rd., Ellicott City, MD 21042-1419. Tel: 410-531-1400; Fax: 410-531-4881. Email: provsec1@olaprovince.org. Very Rev. James McCurry, O.F.M.Conv., Minister Prov.; Rev. Brad A. Milunski, O.F.M.Conv., Vicar; Rev. Mitchell Sawicki, O.F.M.Conv., Treas.; Rev. Richard Jacob Forcier, O.F.M.Conv., Sec. Definitors: Rev. Donald Grzymski, O.F.M.Conv.; Rev. Michael Heine, O.F.M.Conv.; Rev. Anthony Kall, O.F.M.Conv.; Rev. Jude Surowiec, O.F.M.Conv.; Bro. James Moore, O.F.M.Conv.

Priests 179; Brothers in Solemn Vows 24; Clerics in Temporary Vows 7; Novices 3; Candidates 4; Friaries 25; Filial Houses 8

Legal Titles: St. Francis High School of Athol Springs, NY, Inc.; The Father Justin Rosary Hour, Inc.; Franciscan Fathers Minor Conventuals of Buffalo, NY, Inc.; The Franciscan Center, Inc.; St. Anthony of Padua Province, Franciscan Fathers Minor Conventual, U.S.A., Inc.; Order of Friars Minor Conventual, Inc.; Conventual Franciscan Friars, St. Anthony of Padua Province, Franciscan Mission Association, Inc.; Franciscan Fathers Minor Conventual, St. Anthony of Padua Province U.S.A., MA. Inc.; Franciscan Friars, St. Anthony of Padua Province, Education Fund, Inc.; Franciscan Friars, St. Anthony of Padua Province, Fund for the Aged and Infirm, Inc.; Franciscan Minor Conventuals of Maryland, of Ellicott City, MD, Inc.; The Franciscan Fathers, Minor Conventuals of St. Stanislaus Church of Baltimore City, MD, Inc.; St. Francis of Assisi Community, Inc.; Order of Friars Minor Conventual, St. Anthony of Padua Province, U.S.A., Inc.; St. Stanislaus Cemetery, Inc.; Anthony Corps, Inc.; Fr. Justin Ministry Fund, Inc.; Carrollton Hall Inc.; Order Minor Conventuals, Inc.

Represented in the Archdioceses of Atlanta, Baltimore, Boston, Hartford and Washington, DC and in the Dioceses of Albany, Altoona-Johnstown, Bridgeport, Brooklyn, Buffalo, Charlotte, Fall River, Harrisburg, Norwich, Palm Beach, Paterson, Raleigh, Springfield in Massachusetts, Syracuse and Trenton. Also in Ontario and Canada.

Apostolates owned, staffed or sponsored: Novitiates 1; Houses of Study 1; Parishes 28; Campus Ministries 4; High Schools 2; Youth-Crisis Shelter 1; Sisters' Chaplaincies 1; Hospital-Nursing Home Chaplaincies 3; Apostolates Radio Apostolate; Healing Ministry; Preaching Apostolate; Foreign Missions 3; Youth Ministry; Post-Formation House.

St. Bonaventure Province (1939): 6107 N. Kenmore Ave., Chicago, IL 60660-2797. Tel: 773-274-7681; Fax: 773-274-9751. Definitors: Rev. Michael Zielke, O.F.M.Conv., Min. Prov.; Rev. Paul Schneider, O.F.M.Conv., Vicar; Bro. Joseph Schenk, O.F.M.Conv., Sec.; Rev. James Ciaramitaro, O.F.M.Conv.; Rev. Benedict La Volpe, O.F.M.Conv.; Rev. Paul Langevin, O.F.M.Conv.; Rev. Robert Melnick, O.F.M.Conv., Treas.; Rev. Hans Flondor, O.F.M.Conv., Vocation Dir.

Priests 31; Brothers 16; Seminarians 3

Legal Titles: Conventual Franciscans of St. Bonaventure Province; Franciscan Friars Educational Corp.; Conventual Franciscan Friars of Marytown; Shrine of St. Maximilian Kolbe; St. Hedwig Cemetery and Mausoleum; The Conventual Franciscans of Saint Bonaventure Province Charitable Continuing Care Trust Fund.

Represented in the Archdioceses of Chicago, Detroit and Milwaukee and in the Dioceses of Peoria and Rockford. Also in Australia.

Properties owned or sponsored: Parishes 14; Marian Center; Shrine.

Province of Our Lady of Consolation (1926): 101 Anthony Dr., Mount Saint Francis, IN 47146. Tel: 812-923-8444. Very Rev. James Kent, Min. Prov.; Bro. Nicholas Wolfla, O.F.M.Conv., Sec.

Priests 63; Brothers 16; Permanent Deacons 1; Professed Clerics: 4; Novices 4; Candidates 3; Houses of Formation: 1; Retreat Renewal Centers 4; Missions: 3; Chaplaincies 5

Development Office: 103 St. Francis Blvd., Mount Saint Francis, IN 47146. Tel: 812-923-5250.

Province of St. Joseph of Cupertino (1981): Holy Family Friary, 19697 Redwood Rd., Castro Valley, CA 94546-3456. Phone: 510-582-7314; Fax: 510-582-7455 Rev. John Heinz, O.F.M.Conv., Min. Prov.; Very Rev. Victor P. Abegg, O.F.M.Conv., Vicar Prov.; Bro. James M. Reiter, O.F.M.Conv., Definitor & Sec.; Rev. Jacob Carazo, O.F.M.Conv., Definitor; Rev. Joseph Kim, O.F.M.Conv., Definitor; Bro. George Cherrie, O.F.M.Conv., Treas.

Legal Title: Conventual Franciscans of California, Inc.

Priests 28; Brothers (includes seminarians): 47

Represented in the Archdioceses of Los Angeles and San Francisco and in the Dioceses of Fresno, Monterey, Oakland, Reno and Vietnam.

Properties owned, staffed or sponsored: Parishes 6; Chaplaincies 3; Houses of Formation 4.

[0485] (M.S.F.S.)—MISSIONARIES OF ST. FRANCIS DE SALES

(Missionariorum Sancti Francisci Salesii)

Founded in Annecy, France 1838. Ministering in the United States from 1969 and established as a Vice Province on July 3, 2013.

MSFS - Generalate - Rome: Missionari de S. Francesco di Sales, Via delle Testuggini, 21, I-00143, Roma, Italy.

MSFA Provincial House: 3887 Rosebud Rd., Loganville-Atlanta, GA 30052-4656. Tel: 470-268-4069. Email: viceprovincialusamsfs@gmail.com; Web: www.fransaliansusa.org. Rev. Tomy Joseph Puliyanampattayil, M.S.F.S., Prov.

MSFS House of Formation: Villa Luyet, 3474 Pate Dr., Snellville, GA 30078-5000.

Wellspring: Fransalian Center for Spirituality, P.O. Box 440, Whitehouse, TX 75791.

Legal Title: Missionaries of St. Francis de Sales, Inc

Fathers 19; Fathers from Provinces Outside U.S: 45

Properties Staffed: Religious Houses 3; Parishes 45; Convents 1.

Properties Owned: MSFS Provincial House, Loganville-Atlanta, GA; Villa Luyet, Snellville, GA; "Wellspring", Fransalian Center for Spirituality, Whitehouse, TX.

Represented in the Archdioceses of Atlanta, Detroit, Galveston-Houston, Kansas City in Kansas, New York and St. Louis and in the Dioceses of Alexandria, Allentown, Cleveland, Dodge City, Harrisburg, Houma-Thibodaux, Kalamazoo, Knoxville, Lansing, La Crosse, Nashville, St. Augustine, St. Thomas Syro-Malabar Diocese of Chicago, Toledo, Tucson, Tyler and Wichita.

[0490] (O.S.F.)—CONGREGATION OF THE RELIGIOUS BROTHERS OF THE THIRD ORDER REGULAR OF ST. FRANCIS

(Franciscan Brothers of Brooklyn)

Generalate (1858): St. Francis Monastery, 135 Remsen St., Brooklyn, NY 11201-4212. Tel: 718-858-8217; Fax: 718-858-8306. Bro. Christopher Thurneau, O.S.F., Supr. Gen. Councilors: Bro. Damian Novello, O.S.F; Bro. David Anthony Migliorino, O.S.F; Bro. Joshua DiMauro, O.S.F; Bro. Edward Wesley, O.S.F.

Brothers 64

Legal Titles and Holdings: St. Francis Monastery; Franciscan Brothers' Generalate; Franciscan Brothers, Inc., Brooklyn, NY; Mount Alvernia, Inc.; St. Francis Center, Inc., Rockville Centre, NY.

Ministries in the field of Education at all levels; Pastoral Ministries, Social Services; Spirituality Centers.

Represented in the Dioceses of Brooklyn, Paterson, Rockville Centre and Springfield-Cape Girardeau.

[0510] (F.F.S.C.)—FRANCISCAN BROTHERS OF THE HOLY CROSS

Generalate: St. Josefshaus, 53547 Hausen-Wied, Germany, Bro. Ulrich Schmitz, F.F.S.C., Supr. Gen.

American Region (1924): 2500 St. James Rd., Springfield, IL 62707. Tel: 217-528-4757; Fax: 217-528-4824. Bro. John Francis Tyrrell, F.F.S.C., Pres./Supr.; Bro. Stephen Bissler, F.F.S.C., Treas. & Vicar; Bro. Christian Guertin, F.F.S.C., Vice Pres. & Councilor; Bro. Ulrich Schmitz, F.F.S.C.; Bro. Joel Mark Rousseau, F.F.S.C., Sec.

Brothers 10

Represented in the Archdiocese of St. Louis and in the Diocese of Springfield in Illinois.

Properties owned, staffed or sponsored: Home for Mentally Handicapped; Adult Training Center for Mentally Handicapped; Secretarial; Chaplaincy; Novitiate; Community Living Facility; Pastoral leadership.

[0515] (O.S.F.)—FRANCISCAN BROTHERS OF THE THIRD ORDER REGULAR

Generalate: Franciscan Brothers' Generalate, Mountbellow, Ireland, United States Region: 4522 Gainsborough Ave., Los Angeles, CA 90027. Tel: 323-644-2740. Bro. Hilarion O'Connor, O.S.F., Reg. Supr.

Brothers 5

Ministries in the field of secondary education.

Represented in the Archdiocese of Los Angeles.

[0520] (O.F.M.)—FRANCISCAN FRIARS

(Ordinis Fratrum Minorum)

General Headquarters: Curia Generalizia dei Frati Minori, Via S. Maria Mediatrice, 25, 00165, Rome, Italy, Very Rev. Michael A. Perry, O.F.M., Min. Gen.; Rev. Francis Walter, O.F.M., English-Speaking General Definitor.

Order of Friars Minor: English Speaking Conference, 14 N. Bennet St., Boston, MA 02113. Tel: 617-209-4410. Rev. Thomas Washburn, O.F.M., Exec. Sec.; Very Rev. John Puodziunas, O.F.M., Pres.; Very Rev. Hugh McKenna, O.F.M., Vice Pres.

Includes: Order of Friars Minor Provinces 12; Custodies 1: of the United States, Canada, England, Ireland, Lithuania and Malta.

Province of St. John the Baptist (1844): 1615 Vine St., Cincinnati, OH 45202-6400. Tel: 513-721-4700; Fax: 513-421-9672. Rev. Jeffrey Scheeler, O.F.M., Prov. Min.; Rev. Luis Aponte-Merced, O.F.M., Vocation Dir.; Rev. Manuel Viera, O.F.M., Prov. Canonist. Councillors: Rev. Mark Soehner, O.F.M.; Bro. Vincent Delorenzo, O.F.M.; Rev. Page Polk, O.F.M.; Bro. Alexander Krate, O.F.M., Prov. Sec.; Rev. Kenan Freson, O.F.M., Prov. Liaison to Sponsored Ministries; Rev. Maynard Tetreault, O.F.M., Bldg. Coord.; Rev. Patrick McCloskey, O.F.M., Dir. Continuing Educ./Formation; Bro. Scott Obrecht, O.F.M. Dir. Office of Peace, Justice & Integrity of Creation; Bro. Vincent Delorenzo, O.F.M., Dir. Franciscan Mission Office;

Rev. Daniel J. Anderson, O.F.M., Prov. Sec.; Bro. Juniper Crouch, O.F.M., Prov. Spiritual Asst. for Secular Order; Rev. Frank J. Jasper, O.F.M., Prov. Vicar & Treas.; Mr. David O'Brien, CFO; Rev. John Bok, O.F.M., Co-Dir.-Friar Works/Franciscan Mission & Ministry; Ms. Colleen Cushard, Co-Dir. Friar Works/Franciscan Mission & Ministry; Ms. Toni Cashnelli, Dir.-Office of Communications; Mr. Ronald Cooper, Prov. Archivist.

Priests 90; Temporary Professed 2; Novices 1; Brothers 47

Represented in the Archdioceses of Chicago, Cincinnati, Detroit, Galveston-Houston, Indianapolis, Military Services, Milwaukee, New Orleans, Santa Fe and Washington and in the Dioceses of Allentown, Lafayette, Pittsburgh, Shreveport, Springfield-Cape Girardeau, St. Petersburg, Tucson and Venice.

Province of The Sacred Heart (1858): 3140 Meramec St., Saint Louis, MO 63118. Tel: 314-353-3421. Email: provsec@thefriars.org. Very Rev. Thomas Nairn, O.F.M., Prov. Min.; Very Rev. John Eaton, O.F.M., Prov. Vicar; Rev. James Lause, O.F.M., Sec. of the Province; Rev. Michael Hill, O.F.M., Prov. Treas.; Bro. Joseph Rogenski, Prov. Promoter of the Missions, Commissary of the Holy Land, Secretariat Missionary Evangelization. Councilors: Rev. Gerald Bleem, O.F.M.; Rev. William Burton, O.F.M.; Bro. Doug Collins, O.F.M.; Rev. Duc Pham, O.F.M.; Rev. Dennis Schafer, O.F.M.; Bro. Michael Ward, O.F.M.

Bishops 1; Solemnly Professed Priests 121; Brothers 43; Novices 1

Legal Titles: Franciscan Fathers of the State of Missouri; Franciscan Fathers of the State of Illinois; Franciscan Press; Franciscan Tertiary Province of the Sacred Heart, Incorporated; Mayslake Village; Franciscan Mayslake Village; Cloister Courts; Employees of the Franciscan Orders; St. Germain Friary.

Represented in the Archdioceses of Chicago, Indianapolis, St. Louis and San Antonio and the Dioceses of Belleville, Cleveland, Fairbanks, Fort Worth, Gaylord, Green Bay, Joliet, Shreveport, Springfield in Illinois, Springfield-Cape Girardeau, Superior and Milwaukee, WI.

Properties owned, sponsored or staffed: Friaries 23; Parishes 15; Missions 17; Chaplains 7; Chaplaincies for Religious 6; Formation Houses 2; Novitiates 1; Colleges 1; High Schools 1.

Province of the Assumption of the Blessed Virgin Mary, Inc. (1887): Provincial Office, 9230 W. Highland Park Ave., Franklin, WI 53132. Tel: 414-525-9253; Fax: 414-525-9289; Email: jgannon@Ofm-abvm.org; Web: www.franciscan-friars.org. Rev.James Gannon, O.F.M., Prov. Min.; Rev. Joachim Studwell, O.F.M., Vicar Prov. Provincial Councilors:Rev. John Cella, O.F.M.; Bro. Craig Wilking, O.F.M.; Rev. Edward Tlucek, O.F.M. Prov. Secretary; Rev. John Cella, O.F.M., Prov. Bursar, Dir. of Evangelization; Rev. Jerome J. Wolbert, O.F.M., Prov. Spiritual Asst. of Secular Franciscan Order; Fr. William Stout, O.F.M., Prov. Archivist; Rev. Anthony F. Janik, O.F.M., Dir., Ongoing Formation; Bro. Craig Wilking, O.F.M., Dir. Franciscan Missionary Union.

Priests 69; Professed Brothers 28; Deacons 1

Legal Holdings or Titles: Queen of Peace Friary, Burlington, WI; San Damiano, La Crosse, WI; Our Lady of Lourdes Friary, Cedar Lake, IN; St. Francis of Assisi School, Greenwood, MS; Francis and Clare Friary, Franklin, WI; Franciscan Pilgrimage Programs, Inc., Franklin, WI; Holy Dormition Friary, Sybertsville, PA; Holy Name Friary, Chicago, IL; St. Francis of Assisi Friary, Greenwood, MS; Assumption BVM Friary, Pulaski, WI; Junipero Serra Friary, McAllen, TX.

Properties owned or staffed: Parishes 16; Friaries 12.

Represented in the Archdioceses of Chicago, Milwaukee, Philadelphia and Pittsburgh Byzantine and in the Dioceses of Brownsville, Gary, Green Bay, Jackson, La Crosse, Parma, Passaic, and Scranton.

Province of Our Lady of Guadalupe (1985): The Curia, 1204 Stinson St., S.W., Albuquerque, NM 87121-3440. Tel: 505-831-9199; Fax: 505-831-9577. Email: ofmprovsec@aol.com. Very Rev. Jack Clark Robinson, O.F.M., Min. Prov.; Rev. Carlos Martinez, O.F.M., Vicar Prov. & Sec. Formation; Rev. Ron Walters, O.F.M. Treas.; Rev. Erasmo Romero, O.F.M., Vocation Dir.; Councilors: Rev. Gerald Steinmetz, O.F.M.; Rev. Dale Jamison, O.F.M.; Rev. Patrick Schafer, O.F.M.; Bro. Efren Quintero, O.F.M., Sec., Province Notary.

Priests 29; Brothers 15

Legal Titles: The Province of Our Lady of Guadalupe of the Order of Friars Minor, Inc.

Represented in the Archdioceses of San Antonio and Santa Fe and in the Dioceses of Gallup and Las Cruces.

Franciscan Friars - Holy Name Province (1901): 129 W. 31st. St., 2nd Fl., New York, NY 10001-3403. Tel: 646-473-0265; Fax: 800-420-1078; Email: hnp@hnp.org. Provincial Administration: Very Rev. Kevin J. Mullen, O.F.M., Prov. Minister; Rev. Lawrence J. Hayes, O.F.M., Prov. Vicar; Bro. Michael J. Harlan, O.F.M., Prov. Sec.; Rev. Dennis M. Wilson, O.F.M., Prov. Treas. Provincial Councilors: Rev. William L. Beaudin, O.F.M.; Bro. Brian C. Belanger, O.F.M.; Rev. David Convertino, O.F.M.; Bro. Frederick C. Dilger, O.F.M.; Bro. Robert M. Frazzetta, O.F.M.; Rev. Joseph J. Nangle, O.F.M. Other Administrative Offices: Bro. Basil J. Valente, O.F.M., Dir. Vocations; Rev. Gonzalo de Jesus Torres-Acosta, O.F.M., Assoc. Dir. Vocations; Rev. David I. Convertino, O.F.M, Dir. Office of Devel., St. Anthony's Guild, Natl. Shrines of St. Anthony & St. Jude & Dir. Franciscan Missionary Union; Bro. Paul O'Keeffe, O.F.M., Moderator of Missionary Evangelization; Rev. John J. Coughlin, O.F.M., Canonical Counsel; Rev. Gene B. Pistacchio, O.F.M., Spiritual Asst., Secular Franciscan Order (OFS); Rev. Thomas R. Hartle, O.F.M., Spiritual Asst., Poor Clares; Ms. Jocelyn Thomas, Dir. Office of Communications.

Priests 214; Brothers 53; Temporary Professed Brothers 5; Temporary Professed Clerics: 7; Temporary Professed Novices 4; Permanent Deacons 3

Solemn Profession: Archbishops 1; Priests 214; Brothers 53; Permanent Deacons 3; Temporary Profession: Brothers 5; Clerics 7; Novices 4.

Represented in the Archdioceses of Atlanta, Baltimore, Boston, Hartford, Miami, Military Services, Milwaukee, Newark, New York, Philadelphia, San Juan and Washington and in the Dioceses of Albany, Arlington, Brooklyn, Buffalo, Camden, Charleston, Charlotte, Columbus, Fall River, Gallup, Norwich, Paterson, Phoenix, Providence, Raleigh, San Diego, Savannah, St. Petersburg, Trenton and Wilmington. Also in Archdiocese of Lima, Peru.

Properties owned or sponsored: Province Parishes 23; Missions 1; University 1; Colleges 1; Community Houses-Residences 33; Houses of Formation 1; Shrine Churches 3; Campus Ministry 5.

Province of St. Barbara (1915): The Franciscan Friars of California (1900), 1500 34th Ave., Oakland, CA 94601. Tel: 510-536-3722; Fax: 510-536-3970. Very Rev. David Gaa, O.F.M., Prov. Min.; Rev. Martin Ibarra, O.F.M., Vicar Prov. Definitors: Rev. Joe Schwab, O.F.M.; Rev. Bill Minkel, O.F.M.; Rev. Dan Lackie, O.F.M.; Rev. Anthony Garibaldi, O.F.M.; Rev. Garrett Galvin, O.F.M.; Bro. John Gutierrez, O.F.M.; Rev. Tom West, O.F.M., Prov. Sec.

Priests 89; Solemnly Professed Lay Brothers 54; Simply Professed Brothers 5; Novices 2; Pre-Novitiates 3

Legal Titles: Franciscan Friars of California; Franciscan Friars of Arizona; Franciscan Friars of Oregon.

Represented in the Archdioceses of Los Angeles, Portland in Oregon and San Francisco and in the Dioceses of Gallup, Monterey, Oakland, Orange, Phoenix, Sacramento, San Diego, San Jose, Spokane and Tucson.

Province of the Immaculate Conception (Friars Minor of the Order of St. Francis): 125 Thompson St., New York, NY 10012. Tel: 212-674-4388. Rev. Robert M. Campagna, O.F.M., Minister Prov.; Rev. Patrick D. Boyle, O.F.M. Vicar Prov.; Definitors: Bro. Gabriel Aceto, O.F.M., St. Christopher Friary, Boston, MA; Rev. Rafael Fernandez, O.F.M., Iglesia Inmaculada Concepcion, Ataco, El Salvador, Central America; Rev. Ronald Gliatta, O.F.M., St. Christopher Friary, Boston, MA; Rev. Antonio Riccio, O.F.M., Convento San Francesco, Rome, Italy; Rev. Jimmy Zammit, O.F.M., St. Francis of Assisi Church, Toronto, Ontario; Rev. Pierre John Farraugia, O.F.M., SFO Prov. Spiritual Asst., Dir. of Postulants, St. Francis Centre for Religious Studies, Caledon, Ontario; Rev. Pierre John Farraugia, O.F.M., St. Francis Centre for Religious Studies, Caledon, Ontario; Rev. James Goode, O.F.M., Promoter of the Franciscan Missions; Rev. Robert M. Campagna, O.F.M., Pius League of St. Anthony; Ms. Madeline Bonnici, Exec. Dir. Franciscan Mission Associates 274-280 W. Lincoln Ave., Mount Vernon, NY 10550.

Fathers 86; Bishops 3; Brothers 16; Permanent Deacons 1

Properties owned or staffed: Parishes 17; Residences 16.

Represented in the Archdioceses of Boston, Hartford and New York and in the Dioceses of Albany, Brooklyn, Fall River, Manchester, Pittsburgh, St. Petersburg and Youngstown. Also in Central America, Toronto and Italy.

Commissariat of The Holy Cross (1912): 14246 Main St., P.O. Box 608, Lemont, IL 60439. Tel: 630-257-2494; Fax: 630-257-2359. Rev. Metod Ogorevc, O.F.M., Pres. & Guardian. Councilors: Rev. Bernard Karmanocky, O.F.M.; Rev. Krizolog Cimerman, O.F.M.; Rev. Christian Gostecnik, O.F.M.

Fathers 3; Monasteries: 1; Retreat Houses 1; Mission Centers 1

Legal Titles: The Slovene Franciscan Fathers, Order of Friars Minor, Commissariat of the Holy Cross, Lemont, IL; St. Mary's Retreat House, Lemont, IL. Represented in the Archdioceses of Chicago and New York and in the Diocese of Altoona-Johnstown.

Holy Family Friary: 232 S. Home Ave., Pittsburgh, PA 15202-2899. Tel: 412-761-2550; Fax: 412-202-2559. Rev. David Moczulski, O.F.M., Guardian; Rev. Leonard Cornelius, O.F.M., Vicar; Rev. John Joseph Gonchar, O.F.M.; Bro. Felix Nowakowski, O.F.M.

Franciscan Friars: Mt. Alverna Friary, 517 S. Belle Vista Ave., Youngstown, OH 44509. Tel: 330-799-1888. Rev. Jules Wong, O.F.M.; Rev. Vit Fiala, O.F.M., Dir. & Guardian; Rev. Richard Martignetti, O.F.M.; Rev. Dennis Arambasick, O.F.M.

Represented in the Diocese of Youngstown.

Croatian Franciscan Custody of the Holy Family of U.S. & Canada (1926): 4851 S. Drexel Blvd., Chicago, IL 60615-1703. Tel: 773-536-0552; Fax: 773-536-2094; Email: chicagoofm@gmail.com; Web: crofranciscans.com. Rev. Joe Grbes, O.F.M., Custos. Councilors: Rev. Nikola Pasalic, O.F.M.; Rev. Drazan Boras, O.F.M.; Rev. Miro Grubisic, O.F.M.; Rev. Marko Puljic, O.F.M.

Fathers 23; Friaries 1; Parishes 7; Missions in Canada 6

Represented in the Archdioceses of Chicago, Milwaukee, New York and St. Louis as well as Military Chaplaincy. Also in Canada.

Lithuanian Franciscan Province of St. Casimir: 28 Beach Ave., P.O. Box 980, Kennebunkport, ME 04046-0980. Tel: 207-967-2011; Fax: 207-967-0423; Email: jonasbac@gmail.com; Web: www.framon.net. Rev. John J. Bacevicius, O.F.M., Guardian; Rev. Raimundas Bukauskas, O.F.M., Treas. of Friary, Vicar, Assistant Delegate of Province in North America Delegate of St. Casimir's Prov.; Rev. Andrew R. Bisson, O.F.M.; Rev. Aurelijus Gricius, O.F.M.

Legal Title: Society of the Franciscan Fathers of Greene, Maine.

Fathers 4

Properties owned or sponsored: Friaries 2; Parishes 1; Summer Camps 1; Guest House 1.

Represented in the Dioceses of Portland (In Maine) and St. Petersburg. Also in Toronto, Canada.

U.S. Foundation (1940): Province of the Holy Gospel Roger Bacon College, 2400 Marr St., El Paso, TX 79903. Rev. Flavio Alberto Hernandez, O.F.M.

Priests 2; Lay Brother 1.

Represented in the Diocese of El Paso.

Franciscan Monastery: 1400 Quincy St., N.E., Washington, DC 20017. Tel: 202-526-6800; Fax: 202-529-9889; Email: secretariatU.S.A.@myfrancsican.com; Web: www.myfranciscan.com. Rev. Larry Dunham, O.F.M., Commissary and Guardian; Friar Christopher Coppock, O.F.M.; Friar Thomas Courtney, O.F.M.; Friar Gregory Giannoni, O.F.M.; Friar Michael Raum, O.F.M.; Friar Simon McKay, O.F.M.; Rev. Kevin Treston, O.F.M.; Rèv. David Wathen, O.F.M., Dir. Holy Land Pilgrimage; Friar Maximilian Wojciechowski, O.F.M.; Rev. Manuel Ybarra, O.F.M.; Rev Benjamin Owusu, O.F.M.; Friar-Deacon John Sebastian, O.F.M., Sec. to the Commissary/Guardian, Vicar and Vice Commissary; Rev. Gregory F. Friedman, O.F.M., Editor Holy Land Review; Rev. James Gardiner, S.A.; Rev Charles Smiech, O.F.M.; Rev Michael Cusato, O.F.M.; Rev. Romuald Green, O.F.M.; Friar Jude Lustyk, O.F.M.

Priests 10; Brothers 7; Permanent Deacons 1; Solemnly Professed 18

Represented in the Archdiocese of Washington.

Academy of American Franciscan History: 1712 Euclid Ave., Berkeley, CA 94709. Dr. Jeffrey M. Burns, Dir.

Legal Title: Academy of American Franciscan History.

[0530] (S.A.)—FRANCISCAN FRIARS OF THE ATONEMENT

(Societas Adunationis T.O.R.)

Motherhouse: St. Paul Friary, New York Office of the Minister General PO Box 300, Garrison, NY 10524-0300. Tel: 845-424-2113; Fax: 845-424-2166. Email: csharon@atonementfriars.org.

Priests 44; Professed Brothers 22; Friaries 15; Parishes (U.S. & Canada): 5; Overseas Ministries (England, Italy & Japan): 3; Ecumenical Institute: 1; Pastoral Center: 1; Retreat & Conference Center: 1; Rehabilitation Center for Alcoholics: 1; Shelter for Homeless Men: 1; Correctional Facility Chaplaincies 1

Legal Titles: St. Christopher's Inn; St. James Friary; St. Paul Friary; St. Francis of Assisi Novitiate; Friars of the Atonement, Inc.; Friars of the Atonement (Canada), Inc.; Graymoor Village, Inc.; Union That Nothing Be Lost, Inc.; Paul Wattson Human Resources, Inc.

Represented in the Archdioceses of Boston, New York and Washington and in the Dioceses of Albany, Brooklyn, Charlotte, Ogdensburg and Raleigh.

[0533] (F.F.I.)—FRANCISCAN FRIARS OF THE IMMACULATE

General Motherhouse: Founded 1990. Benevento, Italy.

American Motherhouse: Marian Friary of Our Lady of Guadalupe, 199 Colonel Brown Rd., Griswold, CT 06351. Tel: 860-376-6840. Rev. Jacinto Chapin, F.I., General Delegate.

Legal Title: Marian Friary of Our Lady of Guadalupe.

Represented in the Archdiocese of Indianapolis and in the Dioceses of Fall River, La Crosse, Norwich and Syracuse.

[0535] (C.F.R.)—FRANCISCAN FRIARS OF THE RENEWAL

Central House: Our Lady of the Angels, 427 E. 155th St., Bronx, NY 10455. Tel: 718-402-8255. Email: franciscanfriarsnyc@gmail.com. Rev. John Paul Ouellette, C.F.R., Gen. Servant; Rev. John Anthony Boughton, C.F.R, Gen. Vicar; Councilors: Bro. Shawn O'Conner, C.F.R.; Rev. Solanos Benfatti, C.F.R.; Rev. Agostino Torres, C.F.R.;. Rev. Emmanuel Mansford, C.F.R., Vocations Dir.; Bro. Peter Marie Westall, C.F.R., Gen. Steward; Bro. John Joseph Brice, C.F.R., Gen. Almoner; Bro. Maximilian Mary Stelmachowski, C.F.R., Gen. Sec.

Legal Titles: The Community of the Franciscan Friars of the Renewal

Represented in the Archdioceses of Chicago, Newark, New York and Santa Fe and in the Diocese of Paterson. Also in England, Ireland, Northern Ireland, Nicaragua and Honduras.

St. Crispin Friary: 420 E. 156th St., Bronx, NY 10455. Tel: 718-665-2441; Fax: 718-292-2432. Bro. Peter Westall, C.F.R., Local Servant; Rev. Innocent Montgomery, C.F.R. Local Vicar; Rev. Herald Brock, C.F.R.; Rev. Louis Leonelli, C.F.R.; Bro. Simon Dankoski, C.F.R.; Rev. James Atkins, C.F.R.; Rev. Juniper Adams, O.F.M.; Bro. Juniper Galdo, C.F.R.; Bro. Masseo O'Neil, C.F.R.

Our Lady of the Angels Friary: 427 E. 155th St., Bronx, NY 10455. Tel: 718-933-3405; Fax: 718-992-9997. Rev. Bonaventure Rummell, C.F.R., Local Servant; Rev. Luke Leighton, C.F.R., Local Vicar; Rev. Stan Fortuna, C.F.R.; Rev. Bob Lombardo, C.F.R.; Rev. Fidelis Moscinski, C.F.R.; Rev. John Paul Ouellette, C.F.R.; Bro. Joseph Michael Fino, C.F.R.; Bro. František Chloupek, C.F.R.; Bro. Seraphim Pio Baalbaki, C.F.R.; Bro. Jonah Moreno, C.F.R.

St. Joseph Friary: 523 W. 142nd St., New York, NY 10041. Tel: 212-234-9089; Fax: 212-234-8871. Postulants Vocation Office: 212-281-4355. Rev. Gabriel Mary Bakkar, C.F.R., Local Servant; Bro. John-Mary Johannssen, C.F.R., Local Vicar; Rev. Glenn Sudano, C.F.R.; Rev. Emmanuel Mansford, C.F.R.; Rev. Sebastian Kajko, C.F.R.; Bro. Giles Barrie, C.F.R.; Bro. Benjamin Burwell, C.F.R.; Bro. Pier Giorgio Welch, C.F.R.; Bro. Rosendo Lopez, C.F.R.

St. Leopold Friary: 259 Nepperhan Ave., Yonkers, NY 10701. Tel: 914-965-8143; Fax: 914-709-8986. Rev. Anthony Baetzold, C.F.R., Local Servant; Rev. Luke Mary Fletcher, C.F.R., Local Vicar; Rev. Andrew Apostoli, C.F.R.; Rev. Solanus Benfatti, C.F.R.; Rev. Albert Osewski, C.F.R.; Bro. Justin Alarcón, C.F.R.; Bro. Francesco Gavazzi, C.F.R.; Bro. Tansi Ibisi, C.F.R.; Bro. Roch Greiner, C.F.R.; Bro. Oisín Martin, C.F.R.; Bro. Stephen Dufrene, C.F.R.; Bro. Malachy Napier, C.F.R.; Bro. Gabriel Emmanuel Monahan, C.F.R.; Bro. Pierre Toussaint Guiteau, C.F.R.; Bro. Mark-Mary Ames, C.F.R.; Bro. Angelus Montgomery, C.F.R.

Most Blessed Sacrament Friary: 375 13th Ave., Newark, NJ 07103. Tel: 973-622-6622; Fax: 973-624-8998. Rev. Francis Mary Roaldi, C.F.R., Local Servant; Rev. Xavier Mariae Meiergerd, C.F.R., Local Vicar; Bro. Thomas Joseph McGrinder, C.F.R.; Rev. Pio Maria Hoffman, C.F.R.; Rev. Raphaël Chilou, C.F.R.; Bro. John Joseph Brice, C.F.R.; Bro. André Manders, C.F.R.; Bro. Seamus Laracy, C.F.R.; Bro. Kolbe Blashock, C.F.R.; Bro. Joseph Maria Austin, C.F.R.; Bro. Mario Crowley, C.F.R.; Novices.

St. Michael Friary: 190 Butler St., Paterson, NJ 07524. Tel: 973-345-7082; 973-345-7081. Rev. Mariusz Koch, C.F.R., Local Servant; Rev. Leo Fisher, C.F.R., Local Vicar; Rev. Terry Messer; Bro. Gerard Kanapes, C.F.R.; Rev. Paulus Tautz, C.F.R.; Rev. Agustino Torres, C.F.R.; Bro. Pius Marie Gagne, C.F.R.

St. Juan Diego Friary: 404 San Mateo Blvd., N.E., Albuquerque, NM 87108. Tel: 505-990-3001; Fax: 505-990-0187. Rev. Joseph Mary Deane, C.F.R., Local Servant; Bro. Joachim Bellavance, C.F.R., Local Vicar; Bro. Maximilian Stelmachowski, C.F.R.; Rev. Daniel Williamson, C.F.R.; Bro. Isaiah Hofmann, C.F.R.; Bro. Vittorio Pesce, C.F.R.; Bro. Elijah Perri, C.F.R.

[0540] (O.S.F.)—FRANCISCAN MISSIONARY BROTHERS OF THE SACRED HEART OF JESUS

(Fratres Missionarii sti Francisci de Sso. Corde Jesu)

Motherhouse (1927): Our Lady of Angels Monastery, 265 Saint Joseph Hills Rd., Pacific, MO 63069. Tel: 636-938-5361. Email: shrine1olc@aol.com. Mailing Address: Box 181, Eureka, MO 63025. Bro. John A. Spila, O.S.F., Dir. Gen.

Brothers 5

Legal Holdings or Titles: The Black Madonna Shrine and Grottos (Our Lady of Czestochowa).

Represented in the Archdiocese of St. Louis and in the Diocese of Joliet.

[0560] (T.O.R.)—THIRD ORDER REGULAR OF SAINT FRANCIS

(Tertius Ordo Regularis de Poenitentia)

General Motherhouse: SS. Cosmas and Damian, Via dei Fori Imperiali, 1, Rome, Italy, Very Rev. Nicholas Polichnowski, T.O.R.; Rev. Amando Trujillo Cano, T.O.R., Vicar Gen. Councilors: Rev. Paolo Benanti, T.O.R., 1st Councilor; Rev. Tomeu Pastor Oliver, T.O.R., 2nd Councilor; Rev. Thomas Kochuchira, T.O.R., 3rd Councilor; Rev. Calogero Favata, T.O.R., 4th Councilor.

Province of the Most Sacred Heart of Jesus (1910): Provincial Office, P.O. Box 137, Loretto, PA 15940. Tel: 814-419-8890; Fax: 814-472-8992. Rev. Richard Davis, T.O.R., Min. Prov.; Rev. Malachi Van Tassell, T.O.R., Vicar Prov. Councilors: Rev. Christopher Dobson, T.O.R.; Rev. Joseph Lehman, T.O.R.; Rev. Benedict Jurchak, T.O.R., Dir. Vocations; Rev. Richard Eldredge, T.O.R.

Legal Title: Province of the Most Sacred Heart of Jesus, Third Order Regular of Saint Francis (U.S.A.), Loretto, PA.

Fathers 81; Professed Clerics: 13; Brothers 19

Ministries in Parishes; Universities and Colleges; High Schools; Chaplaincies; Houses of Study 1; Novitiates 1; Laymen's Retreat League.

Represented in the Archdioceses of Baltimore, Philadelphia and Washington and in the Dioceses of Altoona-Johnstown, Arlington, Camden, Fort Worth, Pittsburgh, San Diego, St. Petersburg, Steubenville, Trenton and Venice.

Province of the Immaculate Conception: Office of Minister Provincial, P.O. Box 659, Hollidaysburg, PA 16648-0659. Tel: 814-696-3321; Fax: 814-695-1611. Very Rev. J. Patrick Quinn, T.O.R., Min. Prov. Councilors: Rev. Frank A. Scornaienchi, T.O.R., Vicar Prov.; Rev. Carl E. Vacek, T.O.R.; Rev. Anthony Criscitelli, T.O.R.; Rev. Ambrose K. Phillips, T.O.R.

Legal Title: Third Order Regular of St. Francis, Province of the Immaculate Conception (U.S.A.).

Priests 30; Brothers 2

Represented in the Archdioceses of St. Paul-Minneapolis and Washington and in the Dioceses of Altoona-Johnstown, Arlington, Fort Worth, Orlando and Stuebenville.

U.S.A. Franciscan Vice Province of Our Lady of Guadalupe - T.O.R: 301 Jefferson Ave., Waco, TX 76701. Very Rev. Esteban Jasso, T.O.R.; Very Rev. Angel Infante, T.O.R.; Very Rev. Florencio Rodriguez, T.O.R.; Very Rev. Roman Burgos, T.O.R.

Fathers 8

Represented in the Archdiocese of San Antonio and in the Dioceses of Austin and Fort Worth.

[0570] (G.H.M.)—THE GLENMARY HOME MISSIONERS

(Societas Missionariorum Domesticorum Americas)
(The Home Missioners of America)

General Headquarters: P.O. Box 465618, Cincinnati, OH 45246. Tel: 513-874-8900; Web: www.glenmary.org. Rev. Chet Artysiewicz, G.H.M., Pres.; Rev. Neil Pezzulo, G.H.M., 1st Vice Pres.; Bro. Larry Johnson, G.H.M., 2nd Vice Pres.; Sandra M. Wissel, Treas.; Rev. Dominic R. Duggins, House Dir.; Bro. David Henley, G.H.M., Dir.-Vocation Office; Rev. Don Tranel, Devel. Dir.

House of Formation: Glenmary House of Studies, 12484 E. State Rd 62, St. Meinrad, IN 47577. Tel: 812-357-2090. Rev. Bruce C. Brylinski, G.H.M., Dir. Candidacy; Rev. Tom Kirkendoll, G.H.M., Co-Dir. Novices; Rev. Dan Dorsey, G.H.M., Dir., Formation; Lorraine Vancamp, Dir. Dept. of Pastoral Ministers & Pastoral Svcs.; Joseph Grosek, Dir. Volunteer Programs P.O. Box 69, Rutledge, TN 37861

Fathers 36; Brothers 16; Seminarians: 8; Brothers in Training: 1; Aspirants: 3

Represented in the Archdioceses of Cincinnati and Indianapolis and in the Dioceses of Covington, Jackson, Knoxville, Nashville, Raleigh and Savannah.

Properties owned, sponsored or staffed: Missions & Ministries 40; Houses of Study 1; Volunteer Center.

[0585] (H.G.N.)—HERALDS OF GOOD NEWS

Founded on Oct. 14, 1984 at Eluru, Andhra Pradesh, India. Missionary Society of Apostolic Life of Pontifical Right.

Generalate: Heralds of Good News: R.S. Post, W.G. Dt., 534005, Eluru, India, Tel: 91-88-12-235973; Fax: 91-88-12-230256.

U.S. Address: Heralds of Good News: 76 W. Sycamore St., Williamsburg, KY 40965. Tel: 606-422-5775. Rev. Jesuraj Mariasalethu, H.G.N., Mission Legal Representative.

Legal Title: Heralds of Good News Missionary Society, Inc.

Priests in the U.S.: 98

Represented in the Dioceses of Biloxi, Denver, Fort Worth, Gallup, Great Falls-Billings, Lexington, Mobile, Owensboro, Pensacola-Tallahassee, Portland, Pueblo, Salina, Seattle and Wheeling-Charleston. Also in India.

[0590] (M.S.A.)—SOCIETY OF THE MISSIONARIES OF THE HOLY APOSTLES

General Administration: Society of the Missionaries of the Holy Apostles, 8594 rue Berri, H2P 2G4, Montreal, Canada, Tel: 514-387-2222; Fax: 514-387-0863. Very Rev. Isaac M. Chuquizana, M.S.A., Supr. Gen. Animator.

Society of Missionaries of Holy Apostles: Provincial Administration Headquarters, 22 Prospect Hill Rd., Cromwell, CT 06416. Tel: 860-632-3039; 860-316-5926. Very Rev. Luis Luna-Barrera, M.S.A., Prov. Animator.

Priests 34; Brothers 3

Represented in the Archdioceses of Hartford, Los Angeles, New York and Washington and in the Dioceses of Norwich and Pensacola-Tallahassee.

Properties owned, staffed or sponsored: Holy Apostles College and Seminary; 5 Parishes; Hermitage; Hospital Chaplaincies; Retreat House.

[0600] (C.S.C.)—BROTHERS OF THE CONGREGATION OF HOLY CROSS

(Congregatio A Sancta Cruce)

Generalate: Congregazione di Santa Croce, Via Framura 85, 00168, Rome, Italy, Tel: 011-39-06-612-962-10; Fax: 011-39-06-614-7547. Rev. Robert Epping, C.S.C., Supr. Gen.; Bro. Paul Bednarczyk C.S.C., Vicar & 1st Asst.; Rev. Abraham Kochupurackal, C.S.C., 2nd Asst.; Bro. James Ripon Gomes, C.S.C., 3rd Asst.; Rev. Leopold Temba, C.S.C., 4th Asst.; Bro. Nicholas Arthur, C.S.C., 5th Asst.; Rev. Jerome Joseph Jose, C.S.C., 6th Asst.

Midwest Province of the Brothers of Holy Cross (1841): 54515 State Rd. 933 N., P.O. Box 460, Notre Dame, IN 46556. Tel: 574-631-4000; Fax: 574-631-2999. Email: spalmer@brothersoftheholycross.com. Web: www.brothersofholycross.com. Bro. Chester Freel, C.S.C., Prov. Supr.; Bro. Kenneth Haders,

C.S.C., Asst. Prov. & Vicar; Bro. Roy Smith, C.S.C., Councilor; Bro. Paul Kelly, C.S.C., Steward & Treas.; Bro. Lewis T. Brazil, C.S.C., Councilor; Bro. Robert Lavelle, C.S.C., Councilor & Sec.; Bro. James Van Dyke, C.S.C., Councilor.

Legal Title: Notre Dame, Ind. Brothers of Holy Cross, Inc.

Professed Brothers 136

Properties owned, staffed or sponsored: Community Houses 3; Colleges 1; High Schools 6; Scholasticates 2; Foreign Mission Schools 4.

Represented in the Archdioceses of Chicago, Indianapolis and Portland in Oregon and in the Dioceses of Austin, Cleveland, Colorado Springs, Fort Wayne-South Bend, Phoenix and Venice. Also in West Africa, Bangladesh, Chile, Peru, and Vancouver.

Congregation of Holy Cross, Moreau Province: Brother John Baptist Province Center, 1101 St. Edwards Dr., Austin, TX 78704. Tel: 512-442-7856. Email: moreauprovince@gmail.com. Bro. Thomas Dziekan, C.S.C., Prov. Supr.; Bro. Donald Blauvelt, C.S.C., Asst. Prov.; Bro. Richard Critz, C.S.C., Sec.; Bro. Harold Ehlinger, C.S.C., Steward. Councilors: Bro. James J. Branigan, C.S.C.; Bro. Jonathan Beebe, C.S.C.; Bro. James Branigan, C.S.C.

Legal Title: Congregation of Holy Cross Moreau Province, Inc.

Professed Brothers 116; Temporarily Professed 8

Represented in the Archdioceses of Hartford, Los Angeles, New Orleans, New York, San Antonio and Washington and in the Dioceses of Austin, Oakland, San Jose and Wilmington.

Properties owned, staffed or sponsored: High Schools 9; Middle Schools 1; Schools Foreign Mission Schools 5.

[0610] (C.S.C.)—PRIESTS OF THE CONGREGATION OF HOLY CROSS

(Congregatio a Sancta Cruce)

Generalate: Curia Generalizia di Santa Croce, Via Framura 85, 00168, Rome, Italy, Rev. Robert L. Epping, C.S.C., Supr. Gen.; Bro. Paul Bednarczyk, C.S.C., First Asst. & Vicar; Rev. Abraham Kochupurackal, C.S.C., Second Asst.; Bro. James Ripon Gomes, C.S.C., Third Asst.; Rev. Leopold Temba, C.S.C., Fourth Asst.; Bro. Nicholas Kwaku Arthur, C.S.C., Fifth Asst.; Rev. Jerome Joseph Jose, C.S.C., Sixth Asst. & Sec.; Rev. S. Douglas Smith, C.S.C., Gen. Steward; Rev. Carl F. Ebey, C.S.C., Procurator Gen.; Bro. Paul LeBlanc, C.S.C., Admin. Services; Rev. James T. Connelly, C.S.C., U.S. Archivist.

Congregation of Holy Cross, United States Province: Provincial Admin. Office, 54515 State Rd. 933 N., P.O. Box 1064, Notre Dame, IN 46556-1064. Tel: 574-631-6196.

Res: Provincial House, 1304 E. Jefferson Blvd., South Bend, IN 46617. Rev. William M. Lies, C.S.C., Prov. Supr.; Rev. Peter A. Jarret, C.S.C., First Asst. Prov. & Vicar; Rev. Neil F. Wack, C.S.C., Second Asst. Prov. & Sec.; Bro. Mark B. Thesing, C.S.C., Third Asst. Prov. & Steward; Provincial Councilors: Rev. Austin I. Collins, C.S.C.; Rev. John F. Denning, C.S.C.; Rev. Michael M. DeLaney, C.S.C.; Rev, John J. Doherty, C.S.C.; Rev. John A. Herman, C.S.C.; Rev. Daniel J. Issing, C.S.C.; Rev. James R. Lackenmier, C.S.C.; Rev. Patrick M. Neary, C.S.C.; Rev. Mark L. Poorman, C.S.C.

Legal Title: Congregation of Holy Cross, United States Province, Inc.; Priests of Holy Cross, Indiana Province, Inc.; Congregation of Holy Cross, Eastern Province, Inc.; Congregation of Holy Cross, Southern Province, Inc.; Priests of Holy Cross in Oregon, Inc.

Fathers 312; Professed Clerics: 5; Temporary Professed Clerics: 22; Novices 13; Candidates 8; Professed Brothers 12

Represented in the Archdioceses of Atlanta, Chicago, Hartford, Los Angeles, Military Service, U.S.A., New Orleans, New York, Portland in Oregon, San Antonio, and Washington and in the Dioceses of Albany, Austin, Bridgeport, Brooklyn, Burlington, Cleveland, Colorado Springs, Fall River, Fort Wayne-South Bend, Kalamazoo, Lansing, Oakland, Orlando, Palm Beach, Pensacola-Tallahassee, Peoria, Phoenix, Portland in Maine, Raleigh, St. Petersburg, Scranton and Trenton.

Properties owned, sponsored or staffed: College Seminary; Theological Seminary; Novitiate; André House of Arizona; Holy Cross Family Ministries; Mission Center; Casa Santa Cruz; Christopher Lodge; Provincial House; Postulate; Universities 4; Parishes 13; Chaplaincies 23; Publishing House.

Holy Cross Association: Box 771, Notre Dame, IN 46556. Development Director Email: wbeauchamp@holycrossusa.org. Email info@holycrossusa.org. E. William Beauchamp, Dir.

Represented in the Archdioceses of Chicago, Hartford, Los Angeles, Military Services, U.S.A., New Orleans, New York, Portland in Oregon, San Antonio, and Washington and in the Dioceses of Albany, Austin, Bridgeport, Brooklyn, Burlington, Cleveland, Colorado Springs, Fall River, Fort Wayne-South Bend, Gary, Kalamazoo, Lansing, Las Cruces, Oakland, Orlando, Palm Beach, Paterson, Pensacola-Tallahassee, Peoria, Phoenix, Portland in Maine, Raleigh, San Bernardino, San Diego and Scranton.

[0620] (F.S.E.)—BROTHERS OF THE HOLY EUCHARIST

Founded in the United States 1957.

General Motherhouse and Novitiate: P.O. Box 25, Plaucheville, LA 71362. Tel: 318-922-3630. Bro. Andre M. Lucia, F.S.E., Supr. Gen.

Represented in the Diocese of Alexandria.

[0630] (M.S.F.)—CONGREGATION OF THE MISSIONARIES OF THE HOLY FAMILY

(Congregatio Missionariorum a Sacra Familia)

General Motherhouse: Via Odoardo Beccari, 41, Rome 00154 Italy. Tel: 011-39-0657-250639; Fax: 011-39-0657-55192. Very Rev. Edmund Michalski, M.S.F., Supr. Gen.

MSF Center: Provincialate U.S.A. of the Missionaries of the Holy Family, Office, 3014 Oregon Ave., Saint Louis, MO 63118. Tel: 314-577-6300; Fax: 314-577-6301. Vocations Email: Vocations@MSF-America.org; Provincial Superior Email: MSF@MSF-America.org. Rev. Philip Sosa, M.S.F., Prov. Supr.

Fathers 16; Brothers 1

Ministries in House of Study 1; Parishes 5.

Represented in the Archdioceses of St. Louis and San Antonio and in the Dioceses of Brownsville. Also in Canada.

MSF Provincial Residence: 3582 Pearson Pointe Ct., Saint Louis, MO 63139. Tel: 314-416-0299. Email: psosamsf-america.org.

[0640] (S.F.)—SONS OF THE HOLY FAMILY

(Congregatio Filiorum Sacrae Familiae)

General Motherhouse: Entenza 301, 08029, Barcelona, Spain, Very Rev. Jesus Diaz, S.F., Gen. Supr.

U.S. Foundation Sons of the Holy Family (1920): Holy Family Seminary, 401 Randolph Rd., P.O. Box 4138, Silver Spring, MD 20914-4138. Tel: 301-622-1184. Very Rev. Luis Picazo, S.F., Delegate Supr.

Fathers 12

Represented in the Archdioceses of Santa Fe and Washington.

[0645] (B.H.S.)—BROTHERS OF THE HOLY SPIRIT - CLEVELAND

General Motherhouse: Holy Spirit Monastery, 4150 Rabbit Run Dr., Brooklyn, OH 44144. Tel: 216-741-3653; Email: brotherdale@catholicweb.com. Bro. Dale Sefcik, B.H.S., Supr.; Bro. David Robert, B.H.S., Community Councilor.

Legal Title: Brothers of the Holy Spirit Cleveland.

Represented in the Ukrainian Catholic Diocese of St. Josaphat in Parma.

[0650] (C.S.SP.)—CONGREGATION OF THE HOLY SPIRIT

(Congregation of the Holy Spirit under the protection of the Immaculate Heart of Mary, Spiritans)

(Congregatio Sancti Spiritus sub tutela Immaculati Cordis Beatissimae Virginis Mariae)

Generalate: Clivo di Cinna 195, 00136, Rome, Italy, Very Rev. John Fogarty, C.S.Sp.

Province of the United States (1872): 6230 Brush Run Rd., Bethel Park, PA 15102. Tel: 412-831-0302; Fax: 412-831-0970. Very Rev. Jeffrey T. Duaime, C.S.Sp., Prov. Supr. Councilors: Rev. John A. Sawicki, C.S.Sp., Prov. Treas. & Councilor; Rev. Francis Tandoh, C.S.Sp; Rev. Benoit Mukamba, C.S.Sp; Rev. Timothy J. Hickey, C.S.Sp; Rev. James Okoye, C.S.Sp.

Fathers in the U.S: 65; Professed Brothers 2; Scholastics: 1; Lay Spiritans: 16

Legal Holdings: Archconfraternity of the Holy Ghost; Provincial Residence; Duquesne University, Laval House; Holy Ghost Preparatory School; The Spiritan Center.

Represented in the Archdioceses of Baltimore, Chicago, Cincinnati, Detroit, Galveston-Houston, Miami, New York and Philadelphia and in the Dioceses of Arlington, Baton Rouge, Little Rock, Phoenix, Pittsburgh, Providence, San Bernardino, San Diego and Venice. Also in Puerto Rico and the Dominican Republic.

Properties owned, sponsored or staffed: Parishes 19; Retirement Residences 1; Training Centers 1; Spiritan Residence, Houston; Properties in Mexico.

Holy Ghost Fathers of Ireland (1971): 7031 48th Ave., Woodside, NY 11377. Tel: 718-672-4848; Fax: 718-457-4055. Rev. Joseph Glynn, C.S.Sp., Prov. Delegate U.S.A. Councilors: Very Rev. Thomas Basquel, C.S.Sp; Rev. Diarmuid C. Casey, C.S.Sp; Rev. Noel P. O'Meara, C.S.Sp.

Fathers 17

Represented in the Archdioceses of Boston, Miami, and San Francisco and in the Dioceses of Brooklyn, Palm Beach and St. Augustine.

[0660] (M.SP.S.)—MISSIONARIES OF THE HOLY SPIRIT

General Motherhouse: Av. Universidad 1702 04010, Mexico, D.F., Mexico, Tel: 5-658-74-33; Tel: 5-658-7851. Very Rev. Daniel Rivera, M.Sp.S., Supr. Gen.

Provincial House (Christ the Priest Province): 39085 N.W. Harrington Rd., P.O. Box 130, Banks, OR 97106. Tel: 503-324-2492; Fax: 503-324-2493. Rev. Roberto Saldivar, M.Sp.S., Prov. Supr. Council Members: Rev. Mario Rodriguez, M.Sp.S., Vicar; Rev. Joel Quezada, M.Sp.S.; Rev. Juan J. Gonzalez, M.Sp.S., Prov. Treas.

Priests 28; Professed 7; Parishes 3; Houses of Study: 1; Novitiates 1; Theologates 1

Represented in the Archdioceses of Los Angeles, Portland in Oregon and Seattle.

[0670] (O.H.)—HOSPITALLER BROTHERS OF ST. JOHN OF GOD

Province of the Good Shepherd in North America: Hospitaller Brothers of St. John of God, 114 W. Washington St., P.O. Box 736, Momence, IL 60954. Mission Advancement and Stewardship Office Email: development@sjog-na.org; Finance and Corporate Office Email: Judy@sjog-na.org. Bro. Justin Howson, O.H., Prov.; Bro. David Lynch, O.H., Sec. Gen.; Bro. Richard MacPhee, O.H., Treas. Gen.; Bro. Thomas Osorio, O.H., Councilor.

Villa Mathias: 901 Bro. Mathias Pl., N.W., Albuquerque, NM 87102. Tel: 505-243-4238; Fax: 505-764-9721.

Provincial Curia: 84 Grant St., P.O. Box 1003, Hamilton, ON L8N 2X7 Canada. Tel: 905-521-1841; Fax: 905-521-6481. Email: visern@gsch.ca.

Brothers 24; Solemnly Professed 24; Priest 4

Sponsorships: Properties owned and/or sponsored: temporary shelters for marginalized men and women 14; shelter for battered women & children 6; residence for persons with AIDS 1; palliative care 1; rehabilitation 2; medical clinic 1; special needs education 1.

Legal Holdings and Titles: Caritas Deus, Inc.; Camillus House Inc.; Camillus Health Concern Inc.; Charity Unlimited; BGS Charitable Trust; Brother Mathias Barrett, Inc. of Illinois; Brothers of the Good Shepherd of Florida, Inc.; The Brothers of the Good Shepherd; Good Shepherd Center Inc.; Little Brothers of the Good Shepherd, Inc.; Villa Mathias, Inc.; Brother Keily Place, Inc.; Brownsville Housing Inc.; Brothers of the Good Shepherd Inc. of California; Charity Unlimited of Florida, Inc.; Hospitaller Order of St. John of God; St. John of God Community Services; Hospitaller Order of St. John of God Province of the Good Shepherd in North America, Inc.; Charity Unlimited Foundation, Inc.; Emmaus Place, Inc.; Good Shepherd Villas, Inc.; Labre Place, Inc.; Matt Talbot House, Inc.; Somerville Residence, Inc.; New Camillus House Campus, Inc.

Represented in the Archdioceses Miami and Santa Fe and in the Dioceses of Camden and Joliet.

[0680] I.H.M.—BROTHERS OF THE IMMACULATE HEART OF MARY

General Motherhouse (1948): 609 N. 7th St., Steubenville, OH 43952. Tel: 740-283-2462. Bro. Dominic Carroll, I.H.M., Supr. Gen.; Bro. Patrick Geary, I.H.M., Novice Master & Vocation Dir.

Professed Brothers 3

Ministries in: Novitiate; Bishop's Residence; CCD Center; Pastoral Associates 3.

Represented in the Diocese of Steubenville.

[0685] I.V.E.—INSTITUTE OF THE INCARNATE WORD

General House: Piazza San Pietro 2, 00037, Segni,Italy, Tel: 0039-0697 66068. Via Arnaldo Di Colonia, 9 Acilia (RM) 00126 Italy. Tel: 39-06-591-5896; Fax: 39-06-454-33003

Provincial House: Province of the Immaculate Conception of the Institute of the Incarnate Word, 5706 Sargent Rd., Chillum, MD 20782. Tel: 301-853-2789; Fax: 301-559-1713; Email: prov.immaculate.conception@ive07.org; Web: www.iveamerica.org. Rev. Alberto Barattero, I.V.E., Provincial Supr.

Fathers 57; Brothers 2; Students in Major Seminary: 45; Students in High School Seminary: 20

Represented in the Archdioceses of Chicago, New York, Philadelphia and Washington, DC and in the Dioceses of Bridgeport, Brooklyn, Columbus, Dallas, Fall River, Phoenix, San Jose, Winona-Rochester and Venice. Also in Canada, Guyana and Mexico.

Provincial House: 5706 Sargent Rd., Chillum, MD 20782. Tel: 301-853-2789; Fax: 301-559-1713.

[0690] S.J.—JESUIT FATHERS AND BROTHERS

(Societas Jesu)

Generalate: Borgo S. Spirito 4, 00193, Rome, Italy, Rev. Arturo Sosa, S.J., Gen.; Rev. Antoine Kerhuel, S.J., Sec.; Rev. Douglas W. Marcouiller, S.J., U.S. Asst.

Jesuit Conference: The Society of Jesus in Canada and the United States, 1016 16th St., N.W., Ste. 400, Washington, DC 20036. Tel: 202-462-0400; Fax: 202-328-9212. Very Rev. Timothy P. Kesicki, S.J., Pres.; Rev. Sean D. Michaelson, S.J., Socius & Treas.; Rev. Paul Holland, S.J., Delegate for Formation & Jesuit Life; Michael Jordan Laskey, Sec. Communications; Rev. William H. Muller, S.J., Sec. Secondary & Pre-Secondary Educ.

Maryland Province of the Society of Jesus (1833): 8600 LaSalle Rd., Ste. 620, Towson, MD 21286-2014. Tel: 443-921-1310; Fax: 443-921-1313. Rev. Robert M. Hussey, S.J., Prov.; Rev. Vincent G. Conti, S.J., Socius; Ms. Rose Ann D'Alesandro, Asst. Treas.; Maura Parker, Asst. for Healthcare; Rev. Philip A. Florio, S.J., Vocations Dir.; Rev. John C. Wronski, S.J., Asst. for Formation; Rev. Thomas M. McCoog, S.J., Archivist; Rev. Liborio J. LaMartina, S.J., Resident Archivist; Rev. Joseph C. Sands, S.J., Novice Dir.; Rev. James A. O'Brien, S.J., Promoter, Christian Life Communities; Rev. Richard A. McGowan, S.J., Treas.; Rev. George M. Witt, S.J., Asst. for Spirituality Ministries; Rev. Edward J. Quinnan, S.J., Asst., Pastoral Ministries; Bro. Lawrence J. Lundin, S.J., Revisor, Province Finances; Rev. Joseph P. Parkes, S.J., Asst. Secondary Education; Mr. Nicholas Napolitano, Asst. Social Ministries; Rev. James D. Redington, S.J., Interreligious Dialogue; Rev. James J. Miracky, S.J., Asst., Higher Educ.

Legal Title: Corporation of the Roman Catholic Clergymen, Maryland.

Fathers 223; Scholastics: 25; Brothers 10

Represented in the Archdioceses of Atlanta, Baltimore, Philadelphia and Washington and in the Dioceses of Allentown, Charlotte, Raleigh, Richmond, Scranton and Wheeling-Charleston.

Properties owned, sponsored or staffed: Parishes 9; Universities 5; High Schools 7; Middle and Grammar Schools 3; Houses of Retreats 4; Residences 16.

U.S.A. Northeast Province (1943): 39 E. 83rd St., New York, NY 10028. Tel: 212-774-5500; Fax: 212-794-1036. Rev. John J. Cecero, S.J., Prov.; Rev. John J. Hanwell, S.J., Socius & Exec. Asst. to the Prov.; Rev. Michael C. McFarland, S.J., Prov. Treas.; Rev. Michael G. Boughton, S.J., Asst. for Formation-Maryland & U.S.A. Northeast Provs; Rev. Charles A. Frederico, S.J., Dir. of Vocations, Maryland & U.S.A. Northeast Provs; Rev. James F. Keenan, S.J., Dir., Donor Rels.; Rev. Edward J. Quinnan, S.J., Asst. for Pastoral Ministry, Maryland & U.S.A. Northeast Provs.

Legal Title: The New York Province of the Society of Jesus, New York, NY.

Fathers 567; Scholastics: 59; Brothers 21

Represented in the Archdioceses of Newark and New York and in the Dioceses of Albany, Brooklyn, Buffalo, Paterson, Rochester, Rockville Centre and Syracuse Also in Guam, the Caroline Islands, Chalan Kanoa and the Prefecture Apostolic of Marshall Islands, Philippines, West Africa - Nigeria & Ghana.

Properties owned, sponsored or staffed: Parishes 8; Universities 2; Colleges 2; High Schools 8; Houses for Laymen's Retreats 1; House of Study 1; Novitiates 1; Community Houses 4.

U.S. Central and Southern Province, Society of Jesus: Province Offices, 4511 W. Pine Blvd., Saint Louis, MO 63108-2191. Tel: 314-361-7765; Fax: 314-758-7164. Email: UCSSocius@jesuits.org. Rev. Ronald A. Mercier, S.J., Prov.; Rev. William Huete, S.J., Socius; Rev. J. Daniel Daly, S.J., Treas.; Rev. John F. Armstrong, S.J. Province Sec.; Rev. Michael G. Harter, S.J., Asst. for Formation; Rev. Michael D. Dooley, S.J., Dir. Vocations; Dr. Geoffrey Miller, Asst. for Secondary & Pre-Secondary Education; Dr. David P. Miros, Archivist; Rev. Mark D. McKenzie, S.J., Asst. for Pastoral & Spiritual Ministries; Therese Meyerhoff, Dir., Communications; Rev. Thomas P. Greene, S.J., Delegate, Social & Intl. Ministries; Mr. John Fitzpatrick, Asst. for Advancement; Ana Casey, Asst. for Healthcare.

Fathers 303; Students in Major Seminary: 35; Novices 19; Brothers 21

U.S. Central and Southern Province, Society of Jesus. Ministries in Parishes; Universities; High Schools; Middle Schools; Novitiate; First Studies House; Curia; Retreat Houses.

Represented in the Archdioceses of Denver, Galveston-Houston, Kansas City in Kansas, Miami, Mobile, New Orleans, San Antonio, Santa Fe and St. Louis and in the Dioceses of Baton Rouge, Colorado Springs, Dallas, El Paso, Ft. Worth, Kansas City-St. Joseph, Lafayette and St. Petersburg. Also in Belize and Puerto Rico.

California Province (1909): 300 College Ave., P.O. Box 519, Los Gatos, CA 95031-0519. Tel: 408-884-1600. Very Rev. Michael F. Weiler, S.J., Prov.; Rev. Alfred E. Naucke, S.J., Exec. Asst.; Rev. Michael C. Gilson, S.J., Asst., Secondary Educ.; Rev. Glenn Butterworth, S.J., Asst. for Formation; Rev. Christopher T. Nguyen, S.J., Dir. Vocations; Rev. Stephen A. Privett, S.J., Asst. for Higher Educ. & Social Ministries; Rev. Theodore E. Gabrielli, S.J., Asst. for Intl. Min.; Rev. Dennis R. Parnell, S.J., Prov. Treas.; Ms, Siobhán T. Lawlor, Asst. for Advancement & Communications; Bro. Daniel J. Peterson, S.J., Prov. Archivist; Rev. Gerdenio M. Manuel, S.J., Asst., Planning; Rev. Charles J. Tilley, S.J., Special Projects Mgr; Rev. Christopher S. Weekly, Asst., Parish & Social Ministries.

Legal Title: The California Province of the Society of Jesus.

Fathers 258; Brothers 20; Scholastics: 52; Scholastic Novices 11

Represented in the Archdioceses of Los Angeles and San Francisco and in the Dioceses of Fresno, Oakland, Orange, Phoenix, Sacramento, San Diego, San Jose and Tucson.

Properties owned, sponsored or staffed: Parishes 10; Universities 3; High Schools 7; Novitiates 1; Retreat Center 2.

U.S.A. Northeast Province (1926): Province Office at Weston, P.O. Box 456, Weston, MA 02493. Tel: 617-607-2800; Fax: 617-607-2888. Rev. Michael C. McFarland, S.J., Prov. Treas., Rev. Michael G. Boughton, S.J., Prov. Asst. Formation; Rev. Charles A. Frederico, S.J., Dir. Vocations; Rev. Edward J. Quinnan, S.J., Prov. Asst. for Pastoral Ministries; Mr. Nicholas Napolitano, Prov. Asst. for Social Ministries.

Legal Title: The Society of Jesus of New England.

Fathers 247; Scholastics: 16; Brothers 8; Parishes 1; Universities: 2; Colleges 1; High Schools 3; Houses of Retreat: 2; Seminaries 1

Represented in the Archdioceses of Atlanta, Baltimore, Boston, Chicago, New Orleans, New York, St. Louis, Seattle and Washington and in the Dioceses of Baton Rouge, Bridgeport, Brooklyn, Buffalo, Honolulu, Manchester, Oakland, Portland (In Maine), Rapid City, San Diego, San Jose, Scranton, Spokane, Syracuse and Worcester.

U.S.A. Midwest Province of the Society of Jesus (S.J.) (2011): (Canonical Title) 1010 N. Hooker St., Chicago, IL 60642. Tel: 773-975-6363; Fax: 773-975-0230. Very Rev. Brian G. Paulson, S.J., Prov.; Rev. Albert J. DiUlio, S.J., Prov. Treas.

Legal Titles: U.S.A. Midwest Province of the Society of Jesus; Chicago Province of the Society of Jesus; Detroit Province of the Society of Jesus; U.S.A. Midwest Province of the Society of Jesus Apostolic Works Trust; U.S.A. Midwest Province of the Society of Jesus Aged and Infirmed Trust; U.S.A. Midwest Province of the Society of Jesus Formation Trust; U.S.A. Midwest Province of the Society of Jesus Foundation Trust; U.S.A. Midwest Province of the Society of Jesus St. Ignatius Trust; Jesuit International Missions; Jesuit Seminary Association; Bellarmine Jesuit Retreat House; Colombiere Center, Clarkston, MI; Jesuit Retreat House of Cleveland, Ohio; John Carroll Jesuit Community Corporation; The Jesuit Community Corporation at the University of Detroit; Jesuit Community Corporation, Loyola University Chicago; St. Ignatius College Prep, Chicago.

Priests 406; Brothers 28; Scholastics: 77

Represented in the Archdioceses of Baltimore, Boston, Chicago, Cincinnati, Detroit, Indianapolis, Los Angeles, Louisville, Military Services, Mobile, Milwaukee, New York, Omaha, St. Paul and Minneapolis and Washington and in the Dioceses of Charlotte, Cleveland, Columbus, Covington, Fort Wayne-South Bend, Gaylord, Green Bay, Joliet, Lafayette in Indiana, Lansing and Lexington.

Properties Sponsored: Parishes 12; Universities 6; High Schools 15; Retreat Houses 7.

Oregon Province - Society of Jesus (2017): 3215 S.E. 45th Ave, P.O. Box 86010, Portland, OR 97286-0010. Tel: 503-226-6977. Email: ljordahl@jesuits.org. Rev. Scott Santarosa, S.J., Prov.; Rev. John D. Martin, S.J., Treas.; Rev. Glen Butterworth, S.J., Asst. for Formation; Rev. Michael S. Bayard, S.J., Socius; Rev. Michael C. Gilson, S.J., Asst. for Secondary & Pre-Secondary Education.

Fathers 398; Scholastics: 74; Brothers 22

Legal Titles: Society of Jesus, Oregon Province, Portland, OR; The Pioneer Educational Society, Spokane, WA; Montana Catholic Missions, SJ; The Society of Jesus, Alaska.

Represented in the Archdioceses of Los Angeles, Portland in Oregon, San Francisco and Seattle and in the Dioceses of Baker, Boise, Fairbanks, Fresno, Great Falls-Billings, Helena, Oakland, Orange, Phoenix, Sacramento, San Diego, San Jose, Spokane, Tucson and Yakima.

Properties owned, sponsored or staffed: Parishes 18; Universities 5; High Schools 11; Middle Schools 2; Novitiates 1; Retreat Centers 2.

Wisconsin Province - Society of Jesus (S.J.) (1955): 3400 W. Wisconsin Ave., P.O. Box 080288, Milwaukee, WI 53208-8004. Tel: 414-937-6949; Fax: 414-937-6950. Very Rev. Thomas A. Lawler, S.J., Prov.; Rev. Mark A. Carr, S.J., Asst. Prov.; Rev. Timothy R. Lannon, S.J., Prov. Asst. for Formation; Rev. James A. Stoeger, S.J., Prov. Asst. for Vocations; Rev. Daniel C. McDonald, S.J., Prov. Asst. Higher Educ.

Legal Title: Wisconsin Province of the Society of Jesus.

Fathers 180; Novices 11; Brothers 12; Scholastics: 23

Represented in the Archdioceses of Milwaukee, Omaha and St. Paul - Minneapolis and in the Dioceses of Des Moines, Green Bay, Rapid City and Winona-Rochester.

Properties owned, sponsored or staffed: Parishes 5; Universities 2; High Schools 5; Middle Schools 1; Elementary Schools 3; Community Houses 12; Novitiate; Native American Missions 2; Retreat Houses 4.

U.S. Address: 12725 S.W. 6th St., Miami, FL 33184. Tel: 786-621-4594; Fax: 305-554-0017. Email: agarciasj@belenjesuit.org. Rev. Javier Vidal, S.J., Prov.; Rev. Alberto Garcia, S.J., Miami Reg. Supr.

Fathers 91; Scholastics: 26; Brothers 7

Represented in the Archdiocese of Miami. Also in Santo Domingo.

Properties owned, staffed or sponsored: High Schools Loyola in Dominican Republic, Belen Jesuit Prep in Miami; Novitiate 1; House of Retreat 3 in Santo Domingo; Casa Manresa in Miami; Residences 2

Puerto Rico Province - Society of Jesus (1987): Urb.Santa Maria, 1940 Calle Sauco, San Juan, PR 00927-6718. Tel: 787-294-4301; Fax: 787-294-4302. Rev. Mario A. Torres, S.J., Regl. Supr.; Rev. John F. Talbot, S.J., Exec. Asst., Regl. Supr.; Rev. Alvaro Velez, S.J., Auditor.

Bishop: 1; Fathers 19; Scholastics: 6

Represented in the Archdioceses of Miami, Omaha and San Juan and in the Diocese of Mayaguez.

Properties owned, sponsored or staffed: Parishes 2; High Schools 1; Residences 3; Campus Ministry Centers 1.

[0700] (S.S.J.)—ST. JOSEPH'S SOCIETY OF THE SACRED HEART

(The Josephites)

(Societas Sancti Joseph SSmi Cordis)

Central House Administration: 1097-C West Lake Ave., Baltimore, MD 21210. Tel: 410-727-3386; Fax:

410-727-1006; Email: josephite1@aol.com; Web: www.josephite.org. Very Rev. Michael L. Thompson, S.S.J., Supr. Gen.

Fathers 63; Brothers 3; Seminarians: 3

Legal Titles: St. Joseph's Society of the Sacred Heart, Inc.; St. Joseph Manor Foundation, Inc.; The Josephite Retirement and Disability Benefits Trust; The Josephite Seminarian Education Trust.

Represented in the Archdioceses of Baltimore, Galveston-Houston, Los Angeles, Mobile, New Orleans and Washington and in the Dioceses of Arlington, Baton Rouge, Beaumont, Biloxi, Birmingham, Jackson and Lafayette (LA). Also in Nigeria.

Properties owned, staffed or sponsored: Parishes 35; Elementary Schools 5; High School; House of Study; Major Seminary; Novitiate; Nigerian Formation House.

[0710] (C.J.)—JOSEPHITE FATHERS

(Institutum Josephitarum Gerardimontensium)

General Motherhouse: Geraardsbergen (Ghent), Belgium, Rev. Jacob Beya, C.J., Supr. Gen.

U.S. Foundation: St. Joseph Seminary, Provincialate and Novitiate, 180 Patterson Rd., Santa Maria, CA 93455. Tel: 805-937-5378; Fax: 805-937-5759. Email: tlane11564@aol.com. Rev. Ludo DeClippel, C.J., Prov. Supr.

Fathers 8; Brothers 2

Ministry to: Parishes; Academic Education.

Represented in the Archdiocese of Los Angeles.

[0720] (M.S.)—THE MISSIONARIES OF OUR LADY OF LA SALETTE

(Congregatio Missionariorum Vulgo "De la Salette")

General House: Piazza Madonna Della Salette 3, 00152, Rome, Italy, Very Rev. Silvano Marisa, M.S., Supr. Gen.

American Region was established in 1892; Canonically erected 1934; Divided into other Provinces in 1945, 1958, 1967 and restructured into one Province in 2000.

Province of Mary, Mother of the Americas (2000): 915 Maple Ave., Hartford, CT 06114-2330. Tel: 860-956-8870. Very Rev. René Butler, M.S., Prov. Supr.; Rev.John R. Nuelle, M.S., Prov. Vicar; Rev. Raymond G. Cadran, M.S., Councilor.

Legal Title: Missionaries of LaSalette Corp.; MLS Religious Trust.

Priests 88; Brothers 24; Oblates: 3

Represented in the Archdioceses of Atlanta, Boston, Chicago, Galveston-Houston Hartford, Milwaukee, St. Louis and Washington and in the Dioceses of Albany, Beaumont, Fall River, Lake Charles, Manchester, Norwich, Orlando, Providence, Raleigh, Springfield in Massachusetts, Tucson and Worcester.

[0730] (L.C.)—LEGIONARIES OF CHRIST

Founded in Mexico in 1941, first foundation in United States 1965.

General Headquarters: Via Aurelia 677, Rome, Italy, Tel: 011-39-06-664-991; Fax: 011-39-06-6649-9372. Very Rev. Eduardo Robles Gil, L.C., Gen. Dir.

North American Headquarters: 8815 Fulham Ct., Cumming, GA 30041. Tel: 678-654-8803; Fax: 678-782-8173. Rev. John Connor, L.C., Territorial Dir.; Rev. Edward Hopkins, L.C., Natl. Vocation Dir.; Rev Kevin Meehan, L.C., Rector.

Priests 154; Religious: 85; Novices 21

Represented in the Archdioceses of Atlanta, Chicago, Cincinnati, Detroit, Galveston-Houston, Hartford, Los Angeles, New Orleans, New York, Philadelphia and Washington and in the Dioceses of Dallas, Gary, Madison, Manchester, Providence and San Jose.

Norcross Pastoral Center: 30 Mansell Ct., Ste. 103, Roswell, GA 30076. Tel: 770-828-4950. Very Rev. John Connor, L.C., Territorial Dir.

Priests 145; Religious: 50

Represented in the Archdioceses of Atlanta, Chicago, Denver, Detroit, Galveston-Houston, Los Angeles and St. Louis and in the Dioceses of Dallas, Gary, Madison, Phoenix, Sacramento and San Jose.

[0740] (M.I.C.)—CONGREGATION OF MARIANS OF THE IMMACULATE CONCEPTION

(Congregatio Clericorum Marianorum ab Immaculatae Conceptionis Beatae Mariae Virginis)

General Motherhouse: Via Corsica 1, 00198, Rome, Italy, Tel: 011-39-06-853-7031; Fax: 011-39-06-853-70322. Rev. Andrzej Pakula, M.I.C.; Very Rev. Joseph Roesch, M.I.C.; Rev. Jovanete Vieira, M.I.C.; Rev. Zbigniew Pilat, M.I.C.; Rev. Wojciech Jasinski, M.I.C. Marian Fathers of the Immaculate Conception of the B.V.M., 2 Prospect Hill Rd., Stockbridge, MA 01262.

Blessed Virgin Mary, Mother of Mercy Province: 2 Prospect Hill Rd., Stockbridge, MA 01262-0951. Tel: 413-298-3931; Fax: 413-298-0207; Email: provincial@marian.org; Web: www.marian.org; Web: www.thedivinemercy.org. Very Rev. Kazimierz Chwalek, M.I.C., Prov. Supr. Provincial Councilors: Very Rev. Donald Calloway, M.I.C.; Rev. Andrew Davy, M.I.C.; Rev. James McCormack, M.I.C.; Rev. Kenneth Dos Santos, M.I.C.

Fathers 48; Brothers 9; Seminarians: 18; Novices 6; Postulants: 4

Legal Holdings: Marian Fathers of the Immaculate Conception of the B.V.M., Inc., 2 Prospect Hill Rd., Stockbridge, MA 01262; Congregation of Marians of the Immaculate Conception; Congregation of Marian Fathers of the Immaculate Conception of the Most Blessed Virgin Mary; Association of Marian Helpers; Marian Service Corporation; Marian Helpers Corporation; Eucharistic Apostles of the Divine Mercy (EADM); John Paul II Institute of Divine Mercy; Marian Helpers Center; Marian House of Studies; Marian Scholasticate; Marianapolis Preparatory School; Mother of Mercy Messengers (MOMM); National Shrine of the Divine Mercy; National Shrine of the Divine Mercy Gift Shop.

Represented in the Archdioceses of Chicago, Milwaukee and Washington and in the Dioceses of Joliet, Norwich, Springfield in Massachusetts and Steubenville. Also in Argentina: Archdiocese of Rosario and the Diocese of Avellaneda.

Sponsorships: Properties owned, staffed or sponsored: 7 Religious Houses; 1 Residence; 7 Parishes; 1 Grade School. Within the Argentine Vicariates 2 Religious Houses; 2 Parishes; 2 Grade Schools; 2 High Schools; 1 Residence.

[0750] (C.M.M.)—CONGREGATION OF MARIANNHILL MISSIONARIES, MARIANNHILL FATHERS AND BROTHERS

(Congregatio Missionariorum de Mariannhill)

Generalate: Via S. Giovanni Eudes 91, 00163, Rome, Italy, Very Rev. Thulani Victor Mbuyisa, C.M.M., Supr. Gen. American-Canadian Province (1938): Our Lady of Grace Monastery, 23715 Ann Arbor Tr., Dearborn Heights, MI 48127-1449. Tel: 313-561-7140; Fax: 313-561-9486. Rev. Thomas Szura, C.M.M., American District Supr. & Procurator.

Fathers 7; Brothers 1

Represented in the Archdiocese of Detroit.

[0760] (S.M.)—SOCIETY OF MARY

(Marianists)

(Societas Mariae--Marianistae)

General Motherhouse: Via Latina 22, 00179, Rome, Italy, Very Rev. André Fétis, S.M., Supr. Gen.

The Province of Cincinnati (1849); Province of the Pacific (1948); Province of St. Louis (1908) and the Province of New York (1961) have merged June 30th, 2002 to form the Marianist Province of the United States.

Marianist Province of the United States (Society of Mary) (2002): 4425 W. Pine, Saint Louis, MO 63108-2301. Tel: 314-533-1207; Fax: 314-533-0778. Rev. Oscar Vasquez, S.M., Prov.; Bro. Bernard J. Ploeger, S.M., Asst. Prov. Councilors: Rev. Timothy Kenney S.M.; Bro. Joseph Markel, S.M.; Bro. CJesse O'Neill, S.M.; Bro. Charles Johnson, S.M.; Rev. Charles Stander, S.M.

Fathers 78; Brothers 169; Perpetual Professed 247; Temporarily Professed 6; Novices 1

Legal Titles and Holdings - Properties owned: Marianist Provincial Office, St. Louis, MO; St. Mary's University, San Antonio, TX; Central Catholic Marianist High School, San Antonio, TX; Tecaboca: Marianist Center for Spiritual Renewal, Ingram, TX; Chaminade Preparatory, St. Louis, MO; St. John Vianney High School, St. Louis, MO; Marianist Retreat & Conference Center, Eureka, MO; Marianist Communities, St. Louis; Mount St. John; Bergamo Center; University of Dayton; Chaminade-Julienne High School; Marianist Mission, Dayton OH; Governor's Island, Huntsville, OH; Marianist Communities in: Cincinnati, OH; Dayton, OH; Marianist Community, Baltimore, MD; Marianist Family Center, Cape May Point, NJ; Marianist Community Residences, Hollywood, FL; Chaminade/Madonna High School, Hollywood, FL; Colegio San Jose, Rio Piedras, PR; Chaminade University, Honolulu, HI; St. Louis School, Honolulu, HI; Marianist Center, Honolulu, HI; Marianist Communities, Honolulu, HI; Marianist Residence, Maui, HI; National Archives, San Antonio, TX.

Members serve and staff: Parishes; Universities, High Schools, Middle Schools and Elementary Schools; Retreat Houses; Apostolic Centers; Missions in India & Mexico.

Represented in the Archdioceses of Baltimore, Cincinnati, Hartford, Los Angeles, Miami, Omaha, Philadelphia, St. Louis, San Antonio, San Francisco, San Juan and Washington, DC and in the Dioceses of Baton Rouge, Camden, Cleveland, Columbus, Honolulu, Pittsburgh, Orange, Rockville Centre and San Jose. Also in Ireland.

Province of Meribah (1976): Marianist Provincial Residence, 240 Emory Rd., Mineola, NY 11501. Tel: 516-742-5555 ext 589. Bro. Timothy S. Driscoll, S.M., Prov. & Asst. for Education; Rev. Thomas A. Cardone, S.M., Asst. Prov. & Asst. for Rel. Life; Bro. James W. Conway, S.M., Asst. for Temporalities. Councilors: Bro. Thomas J. Cleary, S.M.; Rev. Garrett J. Long, S.M.

Legal Holdings: Chaminade High School, Mineola, NY; Kellenberg Memorial High School, Uniondale, NY; Marianist Residence, Accord, NY.

[0770] (F.M.S.)—THE MARIST BROTHERS

(Fratres Maristae a Scholis)

Generalate: Rome, Italy, Rev. Bro. Ernesto Sanchez, F.M.S., Supr. Gen.; Rev. Bro. Luis Carlos Guittierez, F.M.S., Vicar Gen.

Province of the United States of America (2003): Provincial Office, 70-20 Juno St., Forest Hills, NY 11375. Tel: 718-480-1306; Fax: 718-881-7888. Email: patmcnam@aol.com. Bro. Hugh Turley, F.M.S., Co-Dir. Devel.; Mrs. Paulette Karas, Co-Dir. Devel.; Mr. Frank Pellegrino, C.F.O.; Bro. Patrick McNamara, F.M.S., Prov.; Bro. Daniel O'Riordan, F.M.S., Asst. Prov.; Bro. Thomas Schady, F.M.S., Dir., Schools.

Brothers 130

Legal Titles: Marist Brothers of the Schools, Inc.; The Marist Brothers.

Represented in the Archdioceses of Boston, Chicago, Miami, Newark, New Orleans and New York and in the Dioceses of Albany, Brooklyn, Brownsville, Laredo, Rockville Centre and Wheeling-Charleston.

Properties owned, staffed or sponsored; High Schools 15; Community Houses 31; Junior High Schools 2.

[0780] (S.M.)—MARIST FATHERS

(Societas Mariae)

General Motherhouse: via Alessandro Poerio 63, 00152, Rome, Italy, Very Rev. John Larsen, S.M., Supr. Gen.; Rev. John Harhager, S.M., Treas. Gen.

The first Marist foundation in the United States was in 1863, St. Michael's in Convent, Louisiana. The first Marist Province in the United States was established in 1889 under the name of American Province. This Province was subdivided in 1924 into the Washington Province and the Boston Province; On January 1, 1962, the San Francisco Province was established. On January 1, 2000 the San Francisco and Washington Provinces merged. On September 8, 2000 the merged entity became officially known as the Atlanta Province. The Boston Province continues as a separate province.

Atlanta Province (2000): P.O. Box 888263, Atlanta, GA 30356. Tel: 770-451-1316. Very Rev. Paul Frechette, S.M., Prov.; Rev. Joseph Hindelang, S.M.; Rev. Timothy G. Keating, S.M., Prov. Treas., Vicar & Prov Council & Promoter of Marist Laity; Rev. Walter Gaudreau, S.M., Mission Promoter; Rev. Francis J. Kissel, S.M., Archivist; Bro. Randy T. Hoover, S.M., Prov. Council; Rev. William Rowland, S.M., Prov. Council.

Fathers 43; Brothers 5

Legal Holdings & Titles: Marist Society, Inc.; Marist College and Marist Center, Washington, DC; Marist Society of GA; Marist School, Atlanta, GA; Marist Society of OH; Marist Society of LA; Marist Society of PA.

Properties owned, sponsored or staffed: Community Houses 10; Parishes 8; Seminaries/Houses of Study 1; High School 1.

Represented in the Archdioceses of Atlanta, Los Angeles, Miami, Military Services, U.S.A., New York, San Francisco, St. Paul-Minneapolis and Washington and in the Dioceses of Brownsville, Savannah, St. Petersburg and Wheeling-Charleston.

Boston Province (Marist Fathers) (1924): Marist Fathers of Boston, 13 Isabella St., Boston, MA 02116-5216; Tel: 617-426-4448. Very Rev. Paul Frechette,

S.M., Provincial; Rev. Albert DiIanni, S.M., Prov. Dir. of Third Order of Mary; Rev. Joseph Hindelang, S.M., Prov. Council; Rev. William Rowland, S.M., Prov. Council; Bro. Randy T. Hoover, S.M., Prov. Council; Rev. Timothy G. Keating, S.M., Vicar, Prov. Council & Prov. Treas; Rev. George Szal, S.M., Dir. Lourdes Center.

Legal Titles: Marist Fathers of Boston; Marist Fathers of Detroit, Inc.; Marist Fathers of New York; Senior Religious Trust of Marist Fathers of Boston.

Fathers: 30; Brothers: 3

Properties owned, sponsored or staffed: Community Houses 3; High Schools 1.

Represented in the Archdioceses of Boston and Detroit, and in the Diocese of Brooklyn, Portland (In Maine).

[0782] (O.M.M.)—MARONITE ORDER OF THE BLESSED VIRGIN MARY

Maronite Order of the Blessed Virgin Mary: 4405 Earhart Rd., Ann Arbor, MI 48105. Tel: 734-662-4822; Fax: 734-662-4822. Email: abounapilot@hotmail.com. Rev. John Tayar, O.M.M., Supr.; Rev. Paul Tarabay, O.M.M.; Rev. Joseph Khalil, O.M.M.

[0785] (C.M.L.M.)—THE CONGREGATION OF MARONITE LEBANESE MISSIONARIES

Founded at the Monastery of Kreim-Ghosta (Mountain of Lebanon), in the year 1865. Established in the United States March of 1991: Agreement between Archbishop Zayek of the Diocese of St. Maron and the Congregation to serve the parishes of San Antonio, Dallas and Houston.

U.S. Headquarters: Our Lady of the Cedars Maronite Church, 11935 Bellfort Village, Houston, TX 77031. Tel: 281-568-6800; Fax: 281-564-6961. Rev. Elias Sleiman, M.L.M., Supr.

Bishops 4; Priests 98; Seminarians: 16; Postulants: 2; Novices 5

Represented in the Dioceses of Our Lady of Lebanon and the Eparchy of St. Maron.

Our Lady of Mt. Lebanon: St. Peter Cathedral, 333 S. San Vicente Blvd., Los Angeles, CA 90048. Tel: 310-275-6634; Fax: 310-858-0856.

[0790] (M.M.A.)—MARONITE MONKS OF ADORATION

Monastery of the Most Holy Trinity: 67 Dugway Rd., Petersham, MA 01366-9725. Tel: 978-724-3347. Web: www.maronitemonks.org. Rt. Rev. William J. Driscoll, M.M.A., Abbot; Very Rev. Louis Marie Dauphinais, M.M.A., Prior.

Priests 10; Brothers 7; Monks in Community: 17

[0800] (M.M.)—MARYKNOLL

(Catholic Foreign Mission Society of America, Inc.)

U.S. Foundation (1911): Maryknoll Society Center & Admin. Offices, P.O. Box 303, Maryknoll, NY 10545-0303. Tel: 914-941-7590; Fax: 914-944-3600. Email: mklcouncil@maryknoll.org. Rev. Joseph M. Everson III, M.M., Vicar Gen. & Vice Pres.; Rev. Raymond J. Finch, M.M., Supr. Gen. & Pres.; Rev. Russell J. Feldmeier, M.M., Asst. Gen.; Rev. Thomas J. O'Brien, M.M., Asst. Gen.

Legal Title: Catholic Foreign Mission Society of America Incorporated, Maryknoll Society Center, Maryknoll, NY 10545.

Houses in Archdioceses and Dioceses:

Buffalo: Maryknoll Fathers and Brothers, 73 Adam St., Tonawanda, NY 14150. Tel: 716-213-0000; Fax: 716-213-0000.

Chicago: Maryknoll Fathers and Brothers, 5128 S. Hyde Park Blvd., Chicago, IL 60615-4217. Tel: 773-288-3143; Tel: 773-493-3367; Fax: 773-493-3427; Email: chicago@maryknoll.org; Web: www.maryknoll.org. Rev. John W. Eybel, M.M., Rector; Rev. William J. Donnelly, M.M.; Rev. Edward J. Davis, M.M.; Rev. Thomas P. Henehan, M.M.; Rev. William F. Mullan, M.M.; Rev. Stephen R. Booth, M.M., Rector; Bro. Mark Gruenke, M.M.; Mr. Gregory J. Darr, Regl. Dir. (MEPD); Mr. Jay Weingarten, Major Gift Officer.

Cleveland: Maryknoll Fathers and Brothers, 10309 Edgewater Dr., Cleveland, OH 44102. Tel: 216-651-2121; Fax: 216-651-8242. Rev. James H. Huvane, M.M.

Galveston-Houston: Maryknoll Fathers and Brothers, 2360 Rice Blvd., Houston, TX 77005. Tel: 713-529-1912; Fax: 713-529-0372; Email: mklhouston@maryknoll.org.

Los Angeles: Maryknoll Fathers and Brothers, 222 S. Hewitt St., #6, Los Angeles, CA 90012-4309. Tel: 213-747-9676; Fax: 213-908-2317.

Maryknoll Fathers and Brothers 10333 Vincent Ave. S., Bloomington, MN 55431. Tel: 952-884-1024; Email: minneapolis@maryknoll.org; Web: www.maryknoll.org.

San Jose: Maryknoll Residence, 23000 Cristo Rey Dr., Los Altos, CA 94024-7425. Tel: 650-386-4342; Fax: 650-386-4377.

Seattle: Maryknoll Fathers and Brothers, 958 16th Ave., E., Seattle, WA 98112. Tel: 206-322-8831; Fax: 206-324-6909. Anna Johnson, House Dir.; Rev. Robert Wynne, M.M., Priest in Res.

[0810] (F.M.M.)—BROTHERS OF MERCY

General Motherhouse: 54292 Trier, Germany, Bro. Peter Berg, F.M.M., Supr. Gen.

American House (Convent): 4540 Ransom Rd., Clarence, NY 14031. Tel: 716-759-7205, ext. 203; Fax: 716-759-7243. Bro. Kenneth Thomas, F.M.M., House Supr.; Assistants: Bro. Edward Lewis, F.M.M.; Bro. Matthias Moeller, F.M.M.

Brothers 9

Legal Holdings or Titles: Brothers of Mercy Nursing Home Co., Inc.; Brothers of Mercy Housing Co., Inc.; Brothers of Mercy Sacred Heart Home, Inc

Represented in the Diocese of Buffalo.

[0820] (C.P.M.)—CONGREGATION OF THE FATHERS OF MERCY

(Congregatio Presbyterorum a Misericordia)

Generalate and Novitiate (1808): 806 Shaker Museum Rd., Auburn, KY 42206. Tel: 270-542-4146; Fax: 270-542-4147. Email frandycpm@gmail.com; Web: www.fathersofmercy.com. Rev. David Wilton, C.P.M., Supr. Gen.; Rev. Wade Menezes, C.P.M., Asst. Gen.; Rev. Joseph Aytona, C.P.M., Consultor; Rev. Anthony M. Stephens, C.P.M., Consultor; Rev. Joel Rogers, C.P.M., Consultor; Rev. Allan A. Cravalho, C.P.M., Sec. Gen.; Rev. Ricardo N. Pineda, C.P.M., Treas. Gen.

Priests 29; Deacons 1; Students: 6; Novices 2

Represented in the Archdioceses of Louisville and in the Dioceses of Cincinnati, Green Bay, Lexington and Owensboro.

[0825] (M.S.S.)—MISSIONARIES OF THE BLESSED SACRAMENT

(Missionary Priests of the Blessed Sacrament)

Regional Headquarters: 2290 Galloway Rd., B7, Bensalem, PA 19020. Tel: 215-244-9211; Fax: 215-244-9211. Rev. Victor P. Warkulwiz, M.S.S., Supr.

Fathers 1

Ministries in Special Apostolate: Promotion of perpetual Eucharistic adoration.

Represented in the Archdiocese of Philadelphia.

[0830] (M.H.M.)—MILL HILL MISSIONARIES

(St. Joseph's Missionary Society of Mill Hill)

International Headquarters: St. Joseph's Missionary Society, P.O. Box 3608, SL6 7UX, Maidenhead, England, Web: millhillmissionaries.com. Very Rev. Michael Cocoran, M.H.M., Gen. Supr.

American Headquarters: Mill Hill Missionaries, 222 W. Hartsdale Ave., Hartsdale, NY 10530-1667. Tel: 914-682-0645; Fax: 914-682-0862; Email: mhmnyoffice@aol.com. Rev. Robert O'Neil, M.H.M., Society Rep.

Legal Title: Mill Hill Fathers, Inc.

Fathers 8

Represented in the Archdiocese of New York and in the Diocese of Phoenix.

[0835] (O.M.)—MINIM FATHERS

General Motherhouse: Piazza San Francesco di Paola, 10 00184, Rome, Italy, Tel: 011-39-6-4882613; Fax: 011-39-6-4882613. Very Rev. Francesco Marinelli, O.M., Supr. Gen.

North American Delegation (1970): 3431 Portola Ave., Los Angeles, CA 90032. Tel: 323-223-1101. Rev. Mario Pisano, O.M., Delegate Gen.

Legal Title: Minim Fathers.

Priests 4

Represented in the Archdiocese of Los Angeles.

[0840] (S.T.)—MISSIONARY SERVANTS OF THE MOST HOLY TRINITY

(Missionarii Servi Sanctissimae Trinitatis)

(Trinity Missions)

Generalate-Missionary Servants of the Most Holy Trinity: 9001 New Hampshire Ave., Ste. 300, Silver Spring, MD 20903-3626. Tel: 301-434-0092; Fax: 301-434-0255. Email: generalate@trinitymissions.org. Very Rev. Michael K. Barth, S.T., Gen. Custodian; Rev. Jesus Ramirez, S.T., Vicar Gen.; Rev. Victor Hugo Machorro, S.T., Gen. Councilor; Rev. Guy Wilson, S.T., Gen. Councilor; Bro. John A. Skrodinsky, S.T., Gen. Councilor; Bro. Steven Vesely, S.T., Sec. Gen.; Bro. Jordan Baxter, S.T., Treas. Gen.

Legal Title: Missionary Servants of the Most Holy Trinity (aka) Trinity Missions; Missionary Servants Charitable Trust; Father Judge Charitable Trust.

Priests 88; Brothers 17; Student Brothers 8; Candidates 17; Deacons 1; Novices 5

Ministry in the following areas: Missionary Cenacles; Parishes; Missions; Stations and Specialized Apostolates; Lay Apostolate Secretariat; Counseling Centers; Hospitals and Rest Home Chaplains; AA Programs; Protective Institutions; Prison Chaplains; Community Centers.

Properties owned and or sponsored: Generalate, Silver Spring, MD; Parish, rectory and school, Holy Trinity, AL; School Buildings, Camden, MS; St. Joseph Shrine, Stirling, NJ; Former minor seminary building, Monroe, VA; Residences: Harpers Ferry, WV and Senior Ministry Residence, Adelphi, MD.

Represented in the Archdioceses of Baltimore, Chicago, Los Angeles, Mobile and Washington and in the Dioceses of Jackson, Knoxville, Paterson, San Bernardino, Savannah and Tucson. Also in Costa Rica, Colombia, Haiti, Honduras, Mexico and Puerto Rico.

[0850] (M.AFR.)—SOCIETY OF MISSIONARIES OF AFRICA

(Societas Missionariorum Africae)

Generalate: 269 via Aurelia, I-00165, Rome, Italy, Rev. Stanley Lubungo, M.Afr., Supr. Gen.

U.S.A. Sector of the Province of the Americas: 1624 21st. St., N.W., Washington, DC 20009-1003. Tel: 202-232-5154. Rev. Richard Archambault, M.Afr.; Rev. George Markwell, M.Afr.; Rev. John Lynch, M.Afr.; Bro. James Heintz, M.Afr.; Rev. Thomas Reilly, M.Afr.; Rev. Jean-Claude Robitaille, M.Afr., Coord.; Rev. Joseph Elmo Hebert, M.Afr.; Rev. Robert C. McGovern, M.Afr.; Rev. Roger Bisson, M.Afr.; Rev. John Joseph Braun, M.Afr.; Bro. Martin Chapper, M.Afr.; Rev. Roger A. LaBonte, M.Afr.; Rev. Barthelemy Bazemo, M.Afr., Delegate Supr. & Coord.; Rev. Pierre Benson, M.Afr.; Rev. David J. Goergen, M.Afr., Treas.; Rev. Julien Cormier, M.Afr.; Rev. Komi Sedomo Koffi (Antonio), M.Afr.

Priests 15; Brothers 2

Represented in the Archdiocese of Washington and in the Diocese of St. Petersburg.

[0852] M.J.—MISSIONARIES OF JESUS, INC.

Founded in Philippines.

Rev. Melanio Viuya Jr., M.J., Treas., Sec. & Mission Dir. 435 S. Occidental Blvd., Los Angeles, CA 90057. Tel: 213-389-8439 ext 15; Fax: 213-389-1951; Email: info@missionariesofjesus.com; Web: www.missionariesofjesus.com. Rev. Joseph Ricardo Guerrero, M.J., Gen. Supr.; Rev. Manuel Gacad, M.J., Gen. Counselor; Rev. Michael Montoya, M.J., Councillor.

Priests 38; Brothers 1; Seminarians: 17

In the United States, work in parish ministry and work with migrants; in Guatemala, Papua New Guinea and in the Philippines, work with tribal minorities and non-Christians.

[0854] (M.S.P.)—MISSIONARY SOCIETY OF ST. PAUL OF NIGERIA

Generalate: P.O. Box 23, Abuja, Nigeria. Very Rev. Victor Chike Onwukeme, M.S.P., Supr. Gen.

U.S. Region: Missionary Society of St. Paul, Inc., 3607 Meriburr Ln., Houston, TX 77021. Mailing Address: P.O. Box 300145, Houston, TX 77230-0145. Tel: 713-842-6090; 713-747-1722; Fax: 713-741-0245; Web: www.mspfathers.org; www.mspfathers.org/americas. Very Rev. George Okeahialam, M.S.P., Regl. Supr.

Legal Title: Missionary Society of St. Paul, Inc., Houston, TX.

Universal Number of Priests 251; Priests in U.S: 49

Ministries in Parishes; Education; Social Justice; Hospitals; Evangelism.

Represented in the Archdioceses of Baltimore, Chicago, Detroit, Galveston-Houston, Mobile, New York and San Antonio and the Dioceses of Austin, Baton Rouge, Beaumont, Birmingham, Charlotte, Corpus Christi, Dodge City, Great Falls-Billings, Rockville Centre and Savannah.

[0860] (C.I.C.M.)—MISSIONHURST CONGREGATION OF THE IMMACULATE HEART OF MARY

(Congregatio Immaculati Cordis Mariae)
Foreign and Home missions.

Generalate: Casa Generalizia C.I.C.M., Via S. Giovanni Eudes, 95, 00163, Rome, Italy, Very Rev. Charles Phukuta Khonde, CICM, Supr. Gen.

U.S. Province (1946): Missionhurst, 4651 N. 25th St., Arlington, VA 22207. Tel: 703-528-3800; Fax: 703-528-5355. Very Rev. Celso Tabalanza, CICM, Prov. Sup.

Legal Title: American I.H.M. Province, Inc.; Immaculate Heart Missions, Inc.; Missionhurst, Inc.

Fathers 32; Students: 5

Ministries in Parishes; Prison Ministry; Poverty Awareness Ministry; Hospital Pastoral Work.

Represented in the Archdiocese of San Antonio and in the Dioceses of Arlington and Raleigh.

[0865] (C.M.C.)—CONGREGATION OF THE MOTHER COREDEMPTRIX

Founded in the United States 1975.

U.S. Assumption Province: Congregation of the Mother Coredemptrix, 1900 Grand Ave., Carthage, MO 64836- 3500. Tel: 417-358-7787; Fax: 417-358-9508; Email: cmc@dongcong.net. Rev. Louis Minh Nhien, C.M.C., Prov. Supr.

Priests 75; Brothers 42

Represented in the Diocese of Springfield-Cape Girardeau.

[0870] (S.M.M.)—MONTFORT MISSIONARIES

(Missionaries of the Company of Mary)
(Societas Mariae Montfortana)

Generalate: Viale Dei Monfortani 65, 00135, Rome, Italy, Very Rev. Santino Brembilla, S.M.M.

United States Province (1948): Montfort Missionaries, 101-18 104th St., Ozone Park, NY 11416. Tel: 718-551-8651. Very Rev. Matthew J. Considine, S.M.M. Counselors: Rev. Francis Pizzarelli, S.M.M.; Rev. William Considine, S.M.M.; Rev. Gerald Fitzsimmons, S.M.M.

Legal Title: Missionaries of the Company of Mary.

Fathers 20; Brothers 2; Parishes 1; Community Houses 5

Represented in the Archdiocese of Hartford and in the Dioceses of Brooklyn and Rockville Centre. Also in Nicaragua.

[0895] (O.SS.S.)—BRIGITTINE MONKS

(The Order of the Most Holy Savior)

Priory of Our Lady of Consolation: 23300 Walker Ln., Amity, OR 97101. Tel: 503-835-8080; Fax: 503-835-9662; Email: monks@brigittine.org; Web: www.rigittine.org. Bro. Bernard Ner Suguitan, O.Ss.S., Prior.

Professed Monks: 6; Novices 1; Aspirants 2

Represented in the Archdiocese of Portland in Oregon.

[0900] (O.PRAEM.)—CANONS REGULAR OF PREMONTRE

(Norbertines, Order of St. Norbert, Premonstratensians)
(Ordo Canonicorum Regularium Praemonstratensium)
Founded in France in the 12th century. First foundation in the United States in 1893.

Most Rev. Thomas A. Handgratinger, O.Praem., Abbot Gen.

Norbertine Generalate: 27 Viale Giotto, 00153, Rome, Italy, Tel: 011-39-06-571-766-1; Tel: 571-766-212; Fax: 011-39-06-57-80906.

United States: St. Norbert Abbey, 1016 N. Broadway, De Pere, WI 54115-2697. Tel: 920-337-4300; Fax: 920-337-4328. Email: prior@norbertines.org. Rt. Rev. Gary J. Neville, O.Praem., Abbot; Rt. Rev. E. Thomas De Wane, O.Praem., Abbot Emeritus; Rt. Rev. Jerome G. Tremel, O.Praem., Abbot Emeritus; Very Rev. James T. Baraniak, O.Praem., Prior & Vocation Coord.; Rev. John P. Kastenholz, O.Praem., Sec. Treas.; Tony Pichler, Dir. Norbertine Center for Spirituality; Rev. David M. Komatz, O.Praem., Dir. of Formation, St. Norbert Abbey.

Legal Title: The Premonstratensian Fathers; NORBERT & CO., a nominee of The Premonstratensian Fathers; Norbertine Fathers; St. Norbert Abbey, Inc.; The Walnut Markets, Inc.; Los Amigos del Peru, Inc.; Norbertine Generalate, Inc.

Fathers 51; Brothers 3; Novices 4

Properties owned, staffed or sponsored: Dependent Priories 1; House of Studies 1; Colleges 1; Parishes 6.

Represented in the Archdiocese of Chicago and in the Dioceses of Green Bay and Jackson.

Daylesford Abbey: Norbertine Fathers and Brothers, 220 S. Valley Rd., Paoli, PA 19301-1900. Tel: 610-647-2530; Fax: 610-651-0219. Rt. Rev. Domenic A. Rossi, O.Praem., Abbot & Vocation Dir. Email: drossi@saylesford.org; Rt. Rev. Richard J. Antonucci, O.Praem., Abbot Emeritus; Rt. Rev. Ronald J. Rossi, O.Praem., Abbot Emeritus; Very Rev. David A. Driesch, O.Praem., Prior, Email: ddriesch@daylesford.org; Rev. Joseph A. Serano, O.Praem., Treas.

Legal Title: Daylesford Abbey; Norbertine Fathers, Inc.

Fathers 25; Brothers 2

Properties Owned, Staffed or Sponsored: Chaplaincies 1; Parishes 2

Represented in the Archdiocese of Philadelphia.

St. Michael's Abbey: 19292 El Toro Rd., Silverado, CA 92676. Tel: 949-858-0222; Fax: 949-858-4583. Rt. Rev. Eugene J. Hayes, O.Praem., Abbot; Very Rev. Hugh C. Barbour, O.Praem., Prior.

Legal Title: The Norbertine Fathers of Orange, Inc.

Priests 50; Brothers 1; Juniors: 20; Postulants: 8; Novices 5

Properties owned: St. Michael's Preparatory School, Silverado, CA; Summer Camp, Silverado, CA; Abbey, Silverado, CA.

Represented in the Archdiocese of Los Angeles and in the Diocese of Orange.

[0910] (O.M.I.)—OBLATES OF MARY IMMACULATE

General Administration: Casa Generalizia OMI, Via Aurelia 290 I, 00165, Roma, Italy, Most Rev. Louis Lougen, O.M.I., Supr. Gen.; Very Rev. Paolo Archiati, O.M.I., Vicar Gen.

United States Province (1999): Missionary Oblates of Mary Immaculate, Provincial Admin. Office, 391 Michigan Ave., N.E., Washington, DC 20017-1516. Tel: 202-529-4505; Fax: 202-529-4572. Rev. Louis Studer, O.M.I., Prov. Councilors: Rev. José Antonio Ponce Diaz, O.M.I.; Rev. James Taggart, O.M.I.; Rev. James Brobst, O.M.I.; Rev. Arthur Flores, O.M.I.; Rev. Francis Santucci, O.M.I.; Rev. Raymond Cook, O.M.I., Superiors: Rev. Jesse Esqueda, O.M.I., Baja, CA Community; Rev. John Staak, O.M.I., Buffalo, NY Community; Rev. Francis Santucci, O.M.I., De Mazenod Residence Community, San Anotonio, TX; Rev. Salvatore DeGeorge, O.M.I., Houston, TX; Rev. John Hanley, O.M.I., IHM Community, Tewksbury, MA (includes St. William Parish and St. Eugene Community); Rev. Mark Dean, O.M.I., Kings House Community, Belleville, IL; Rev. Lon Konold, O.M.I., Minnesota Community; Bro. Pat McGee, O.M.I., Oblate Novitiate Community, Godfrey, IL; Rev. Juan Gaspar, O.M.I., Our Lady of the Snows Shrine Community, Belleville, IL; Rev. James Allen, O.M.I., St. Henry's Community, Belleville, IL; Rev. Richard Hall, O.M.I., St. Mary's Community, San Antonio, TX (includes Benson Residence, Tepeyac Residence, St. Mary's Parish, San Juan de los Lagos Parish, and Immaculate Conception Parish); Rev. Thomas Coughlin, O.M.I., Washington D.C. Community; Rev. Thomas Rush, O.M.I., Alaska Community; Rev. Lawrence Mariassoosai, O.M.I., Eagle Pass Community, Laredo, TX; Rev. Terrence O'Connell, O.M.I. Garin Community, Lowell, MA; Rev. Raul Salas, O.M.I., George Sexton House of Studies Community, San Antonio, TX; Rev. Charles Banks, O.M.I., Madonna Community, San Antonio, TX; Rev. Emmanuel Mulenga, O.M.I., New Orleans Community, LA; Rev. William Mason, O.M.I., Oakland Community, CA; Rev. Michael Amesse, O.M.I., Rio Grande Valley Community; Rev. Juan Ayala, O.M.I., San Fernando Community, CA.

Fathers 226; Brothers 16; Scholastics: 15

Ministries in Retreat Centers, Shrines, Parishes, Chaplaincies, Religious Residences and Houses and Retirement Centers.

Represented in the Archdioceses of Anchorage, Boston, Chicago, Galveston-Houston, Los Angeles, New Orleans, New York, St. Paul and Minneapolis, San Antonio and Washington and in the Dioceses of Belleville, Brownsville, Buffalo, Corpus Christi, Crookston, Duluth, Juneau, Laredo, Norwich, Oakland, Springfield in Illinois, and Springfield-Cape Girardeau. Also in Brazil, Hong Kong, Mexico, Peru, Rome and Zambia.

[0920] (O.S.F.S.)—OBLATES OF ST. FRANCIS DE SALES

(Congregatio Oblatorum Sancti Francisci Salesii)

General Motherhouse: Via Dandolo 49, Rome, Italy, In July 1966, the American Province was renamed the Wilmington/Philadelphia Province, and the Toledo/Detroit Province was canonically established.

Wilmington-Philadelphia Province (1906): 2200 Kentmere Pkwy., Wilmington, DE 19806. Very Rev. Lewis S. Fiorelli, O.S.F.S., Prov.; Very Rev. Michael S. Murray, O.S.F.S., Asst. Prov.; Provincial Councilors: Very Rev. Matthew Hillyard, O.S.F.S.; Very Rev. Michael Vannicola, O.S.F.S.; Very Rev. John Kolodziej, O.S.F.S. Provincial Staff: Rev. Timothy McIntire, O.S.F.S., Dir. Assoc.; Rev. Very Michael S. Murray, O.S.F.S., DeSales Spirituality Svcs.; Rev. Michael S. Murray, O.S.F.S., Dir. Devel. & Communs & Dir. Prov. Admin.; Rev. Michael J. McCue, O.S.F.S., Dir., De Sales Svc. Works; Rev. John E. McGee, O.S.F.S., Coord. Provincial Special Events. Chapter of the Whole; Rev. John J. Loughran, O.S.F.S.

Fathers 120; Brothers 12; Post-Novitiates 2

Properties owned, staffed or sponsored: Parishes 26; Universities 1; Houses of Study 1; Novitiates 1; High Schools 2; Chaplaincies 8; Foreign Missions 1; Middle Schools 1.

Represented in the Archdioceses of Baltimore, Boston, Military Services, Philadelphia and Washington and in the Dioceses of Allentown, Arlington, Camden, Charlotte, Lansing, Raleigh, Toledo, Venice and Wilmington. Also in Monaco.

Toledo-Detroit Province (1966): 2043 Parkside Blvd., Toledo, OH 43607-1597. Tel: 419-724-9851; Tel: 517-414-0784. Very Rev. Kenneth N. McKenna, O.S.F.S., Prov.; Rev. Michael E. Newman, O.S.F.S., Asst. Prov. & Councilor; Rev. Ronald W. E. Olszewski, O.S.F.S., Treas.; Rev. John Kasper, O.S.F.S., Councilor; Rev. Alan D. Zobler, O.S.F.S., Councilor.

Legal Title: Oblates of St. Francis de Sales, Inc.

Priests 41; Brothers 7; Scholastics: 2

Ministries in Parishes; Schools; Chaplaincies; Missionaries; Senior Citizens Residence.

Properties owned, staffed or sponsored: Provincialate, Toledo, OH; St. Francis de Sales High School, Toledo, OH; Oblate Residence, Toledo, OH; Brisson Hall, Washington, DC; Salesian Studios, Buffalo, NY.

Represented in the Archdioceses of Detroit and Miami and in the Dioceses of Allentown, Arlington, Buffalo, Erie, Kalamazoo, Lansing, Oakland, Saginaw, Toledo and Washington, D.C. Also in Mexico.

[0930] (O.S.J.)—OBLATES OF ST. JOSEPH

(Congregatio Oblatorum S. Joseph)

Founded in Italy in 1878. Founder: Saint Joseph Marello (1844-1895). Cause of Beatification introduced May 28, 1948; Beatified 1993; Canonized 2001. First foundation in U.S. in 1929.

Motherhouse: Corso Alfieri 384, Asti, Italy, General House: Via Boccea 364, Rome, Italy, Rev. Michael Piscopo, O.S.J., Supr. Gen.; Very Rev. John Attulli, O.S.J., Vicar Gen.; Very Rev. Giocondo Bronzini, O.S.J., Procurator Gen.

Oblates of St. Joseph USA Province: 544 W. Cliff Dr., Santa Cruz, CA 95060. Tel: 831-457-1868; Fax: 831-457-1617. Very Rev. Paul A. McDonnell, O.S.J., Prov.

Priests 24; Brothers 2; Parishes 5; Shrine 1; Chapel 1; Community Houses 3; Houses of Studies 2; Youth Center 1.

Properties owned: St. Joseph's Oblate Religious House, Pittston, PA; Oblates Provincial Campus, Santa Cruz, CA; Mount St. Joseph, Loomis, CA.

Represented in the Archdiocese of Philadelphia and in the Dioceses of Fresno, Monterey, Sacramento and Scranton.

[0940] (O.M.V.)—OBLATES OF THE VIRGIN MARY

(Congregation of the Oblates of the Virgin Mary)
(Congregatio Oblatorum Beatae Mariae Virginis)

Generalate: Viale XXX Aprile, 00153, Rome, Italy, Very Rev. David Nicgorski, O.M.V., Rector Major.

St. Ignatius Province: 2 Ipswich St., Boston, MA 02215-3607. Tel: 617-536-4141; Web: www.omvusa.org. Email: office@omvusa.org. Very Rev. James Walther, O.M.V., Prov.

Priests in U.S: 33; Brothers 2

Ministries in Parishes; Hospital and Prison Chaplaincies; Retreats & Parish Missions; Novitiate; Community Houses; College Seminary; Shrine Chaplaincies.

Legal Holdings: St. Clement's Eucharistic Shrine, Boston, MA; St. Joseph House, Milton, MA; St. Ignatius Province of the Oblates of the Virgin Mary, Inc., Boston, MA.

Represented in the Archdioceses of Boston, Denver, and Los Angeles and in the Diocese Springfield in Illinois and Venice. Also in Cebu and Antipolo, Philippines.

[0950] (C.O.)—ORATORIANS

(Confederatio Oratorii S. Philippi Nerii)

A Confederation of Autonomous Houses first founded in Rome, 1575.

General Confederation: Via Di Parione, 33, 1-00186, Rome, Italy, Tel: (39) 06-689-25-37. Email: rhoratory@comporium.net. Rev. Mario A. Aviles, C.O., Procurator Gen.; Rev. Felix Selden, C.O., Delegate of the Holy See Landstrasser Hauptstr, 56, Wien, Austria, A-1030.

The Oratory of Rock Hill: P.O. Box 11586, Rock Hill, SC 29731. Tel: 803-327-2097. Very Rev. Fabio Refosco, C.O., Provost.

Fathers 6; Brothers 3

Represented in the Diocese of Charleston.

The Oratorian Community of Monterey: P.O. Box 1688, Monterey, CA 93942. Tel: 831-373-0476. Very Rev. Peter C. Sanders, Provost. & Major Supr.; Rev. Thomas A. Kieffer, Vicar & Sec.

Total in Community: 2

Oratorian Foundation Inc., Arizona, Yarnell, AZ 85362. An outreach of the Oratorian Community in Monterey.

Represented in the Diocese of Monterey.

The Pittsburgh Oratory: Congregation of the Oratory of St. Philip Neri, 4450 Bayard St., Pittsburgh, PA 15213-1506. Tel: 412-681-3181. Email: info@pittsburghoratory.org. Rev. Drew P. Morgan, C.O.; Very Rev. David S. Abernethy, C.O., Provost; Rev. Michael J. Darcy, C.O., Sec.; Rev. Joshua M. Kibler, C.O., Vice-Provost; Rev. Stephen W. Lowery, C.O., Dir. Campus Ministry; Rev. Paul M. Werley, C.O., Chap. to the Secular Oratory; Rev. Peter J. Gruber, C.O., Campus Min.

Fathers 7; Brothers 3

Represented in the Diocese of Pittsburgh.

The Oratory of Pharr: P.O. Box 1698, Pharr, TX 78577-1630. Tel: 956-843-8217; Fax: 956-843-2946. Very Rev. Leo Francis Daniels, C.O., Provost; Rev. Mario Alberto Aviles, C.O., Treas., Procurator Gen. & Sec.; Rev. Jose Encarnacion Losoya, C.O., Vicar; Rev. Jose Juan Ortiz, C.O.

Ministries in Parish work; Services to the poor; promotion of Mexican-American cultural services; Education at all levels; Spanish language communities.

Properties owned: Casa Maria of the Oratory, Pharr, TX; Oratory Academy-Academia Oratoriana, Pharr; TX; Oratory Athenaeum For University Preparation; Pharr Oratory of St. Philip Neri of Pontifical Right.

Represented in the Diocese of Brownsville. Also in Mexico.

Secular Oratory, Lay institute Founded by St. Philip Neri. Principal Work; Federacion Mexicana del Oratorio de San Felipe Neri, American Office, The Oratory, Rte. 4 Box 118, Pharr, TX 78577. The Pharr Oratory is a member of the Mexican Federation of Oratories and at present serves as the American office of all eleven houses.

The Oratory of St. Philip Neri: 109 Willoughby St., Brooklyn, NY 11201. Tel: 718-875-2096; Fax: 718-875-4678. Very Rev. Dennis M. Corrado, C.O., Provost; Rev. Mark J. Lane, C.O; Rev. Joel M. Warden, C.O; Rev. Anthony Andreassi, C.O; Rev. Michael J. Callaghan, C.O; Bro. James Simon, C.O.; Bro. Mark Paul Amatrucola, C.O.

Fathers 5; Brothers 2

The New Brunswick Congregation of the Oratory of St. Philip Neri: 94 Somerset St., New Brunswick, NJ 08901. Tel: 732-545-6820; Fax: 732-545-4069; Email: oratorians@nboratory.org; Web: www.nboratory.org. Very Rev. Peter R. Cebulka, C.O., Provost; Rev. Jeffrey M. Calia, C.O., Vicar; Rev. Thomas A. Odorizzi, C.O., Treas. & Sec.; Rev. Kevin Patrick Kelly, C.O.; Bro. John Fredy Triana Beltran, C.O.; Bro. Steven J. Bolton, C.O.

Priests 4; Seminarians 1; Novices 1

[0960] (F.S.R.)—BROTHERS OF THE CONGREGATION OF OUR LADY OF THE HOLY ROSARY

Founded in the United States in 1957.

General Motherhouse and Novitiate: 232 Sunnyside Dr., Reno, NV 89503-3510. Tel: 775-747-4441. Email: bros-reno@charter.net. Bro. Matthew Cunningham, F.S.R., Supr.; Bro. Philip Napolitano, F.S.R., Asst. Supr.

Brothers 3

Ministries in the field of Education and Pastoral Ministry. Represented in the Diocese of Reno.

[0970] (O.DE.M)—ORDER OF OUR LADY OF MERCY

(Mercedarians Friars)

(Ordo de Beatae Mariae Virginis de Mercede)

Founded in Barcelona, Spain on August 10, 1218.

Generalate: Curia Generalizia dei PP Mercedari, Via Monte Carmelo 3 00166, Rome, Italy, Most Rev. Juan Carlos Saavedra Lucho, O.de.M., Master Gen.

U.S.A. Provincial Headquarters: Vicariate of Mary, Co-Redemptress, 6398 Drexel Rd., Philadelphia, PA 19151. Tel: 215-473-1669. Rev. Michael R. Rock, O.de.M., Vicar Prov.

Priests 20; Brothers 5

Ministries in Parishes, education, hospital and prison chaplaincies, retreats; Newman campus chaplaincies; mission word.

Properties owned: Monastery of Our Lady of Mercy, Philadelphia, PA; Saint Peter Nolasco Residence, St. Petersburg, FL.

Represented in the Archdiocese of Philadelphia and San Juan and in the Dioceses of Buffalo, Cleveland, St. Augustine and St. Petersburg. Also in South India.

[0975] (S.O.L.T.)—SOCIETY OF OUR LADY OF THE MOST HOLY TRINITY

International Headquarters: Our Lady of Corpus Christi, 1200 Lantana St., Corpus Christi, TX 78407. Tel: 361-289-9095; Fax: 361-289-0088. Rev. Peter Marsalek, S.O.L.T., Gen. Priest Servant; Very Rev. Anthony Blount, S.O.L.T., Vicar Servant; Rev. Fausto Rodel C. Malanyaon, S.O.L.T., 2nd Asst.

Regional Headquarters (American Region): Our Lady of Corpus Christi, 1200 Lantana St., Corpus Christi, TX 78007. Tel: 361-387-8090; Fax: 361-387-3818. Rev. Jerome Drolshagan, S.O.L.T., Regl. Supr.; Rev. Dennis Walsh, S.O.L.T., 1st Asst.; Rev. Mark Wendling, S.O.L.T., 2nd Asst., Vocation Dir.

Priests 77; Brothers 5; Permanent Deacons 1; Seminarians: 5

Pastoral Ministries: Parish Work, Migrant Ministries, Native Americans, Marian Shrine, Hospital Chaplaincies, Prison Chaplaincies, Military Chaplaincy, Retreat Houses, Schools, Nursing Homes, Youth Work, Marian Shrines and specialized ministries. Community Houses. Houses of the Sick and Infirm. Houses of Formation: Novitiate and House of Studies.

Represented in the Archdioceses of Atlanta, Detroit, Galveston-Houston, Military Services, Milwaukee, Santa Fe, Seattle and Washington DC and in the Dioceses of Arlington, Corpus Christi, Fargo, Kansas City-St. Joseph, Laredo, Paterson, Phoenix, Portland (In Maine), Pueblo, Rockville Centre and Springfield.

[0990] (S.A.C.)—SOCIETY OF THE CATHOLIC APOSTOLATE

(Pallottines)

Generalate: Pallottines, Piazza S.V. Pallotti 204 00186, Rome, Italy,

Irish Province (1909): Sandyford Rd., Dundrum, Dublin 16, Ireland, Rev. Derry Murphy, S.A.C., Prov.

Province of the Immaculate Conception (Eastern) (1953): 204 Raymond Ave., P.O. Box 979, South Orange, NJ 07079. Tel: 301-422-3777. Email: vocation@sacapostles.org. Very Rev. Frank S. Donio, S.A.C., Prov.; Rev. Peter T. Sticco, S.A.C., Vicar Prov. & Bursar. Consultors: Rev. Bernard P. Carman, S.A.C.; Rev. Frank Amato, S.A.C.; Bro. James Beamesderfer, S.A.C.

Fathers 13; Professed Brothers 2

Properties owned, sponsored or staffed: Parishes 2; Seminary; High School; Novitiate; St. Jude Shrine, Pallottine Center for Apostolic Causes.

Represented in the Archdioceses of Baltimore, Newark and Washington and in the Dioceses of Brooklyn and Camden.

Mother of God Province (1946): Pallottine Fathers and Brothers, Inc., 5424 W. Blue Mound Rd., Milwaukee, WI 53208. Tel: 414-259-0688; Fax: 414-258-9314. Email: pallotti.milw@pallottines.org; Vocations Email: vocationspall@gmail.com. Very Rev. Joseph Koyickal, S.A.C., Prov.; Bro. James Scarpace, S.A.C., Consultor; Rev. John R. Scheer, S.A.C., 1st Consultor.

Fathers 17; Brothers 1

Ministries in Parishes; Retreat House; Hospital Chaplaincies; High School.

Represented in the Archdiocese of Milwaukee.

U.S. Delegature (Irish Province): 3352 4th St., P.O. Box 249, Wyandotte, MI 48192. Rev. Michael Cremin, S.A.C., Prov. Delegate.

Fathers 9; Brothers 1; Parishes 4; Missions 3.

Represented in the Archdioceses of Detroit and San Francisco and in the Dioceses of Fort Worth and Lubbock.

Mother of Divine Love Province (1909): The Pallottine Fathers, Sandyford Rd., Dundrum, Dublin 16, Ireland. Rev. Jeremiah Murphy Sac, Prov.

U.S. Foundation: Our Lady of Mt. Carmel Shrine and Church, 448 E. 116th, New York, NY 10029. Tel: 212-534-0681.

Fathers 7; Parishes 3.

Represented in the Archdiocese of New York and in the Dioceses of Albany and Pensacola-Tallahassee.

Infant Jesus Delegature of Annunciation Province: Mission House and Infant Jesus Shrine, 3452 Niagara Falls Blvd., North Tonawanda, NY 14120-0563. Rev. John Posiewala, S.A.C., Supr. & Prov. Delegate.

Priests 12

Represented in the Archdiocese of New York and in the Dioceses of Brooklyn, Buffalo and Venice.

[1000] (C.P.)—CONGREGATION OF THE PASSION

(Congregatio Passionis Jesu Christi)

Founded in Italy in 1720 by St. Paul of the Cross. First foundation in the United States in 1852.

Generalate: SS. Giovani e Paolo Monastery, Rome 00184, Italy. Most Rev. Joachim Rego, C.P., Supr. Gen.

St. Paul of the Cross Province (Eastern): Passionist Provincial Office, 111 South Ridge St., Ste. 300, Rye Brook, NY 10573. Very Rev. James O'Shea, C.P., Prov.; Very Rev. Salvatore Enzo Del Brocco, C.P., 1st Consultor; Very Rev. James Price, C.P., 2nd Consultor; Very Rev. William Murphy, C.P., 3rd Consultor; Very Rev. Hugo Esparza-Perez, C.P., 4th Consultor.

Legal Title: St. Paul's Benevolent, Educational and Missionary Institute; Passionist Missions, Inc.; Passionist Missionaries, Inc.

Bishops 1; Fathers 89; Brothers 15

Properties owned, sponsored or staffed: Parishes 12; Monasteries 4; Retreat Houses 4; Schools 3; Residence 3; Houses of Study 1.

Represented in the Archdioceses of Atlanta, Chicago, Hartford, New York, San Francisco and Santa Fe and in the Dioceses of Brooklyn, Columbus, Palm Beach, Pittsburgh, Raleigh, St. Louis, Scranton, Springfield in Massachusetts and Venice. Also in Canada, Haiti and Jamaica.

Holy Cross Province (Western): Passionist Provincial Office, 660 Busse Highway, Park Ridge, IL 60068. Tel: 847-518-8844. Rev. Joseph Moons, C.P., Prov. Consultors: Rev. James Strommer, C.P., Prov. Consultor; Rev. David Colhour, C.P., Consultor; Rev. Philip Paxton, C.P., Consultor; Rev. Alexander Steinmiller, C.P., Consultor.

Legal Title: The Congregation of the Passion, Holy Cross Province.

Fathers 40; Brothers 6; Deacons 1

Properties owned or sponsored: Passionist Provincial Office; St. Vincent Strambi Passionist Community, Chicago, IL.

Represented in the Archdioceses of Chicago, Detroit, Galveston-Houston, Los Angeles and Louisville and in the Dioceses of Birmingham and Sacramento.

[1010] (O.S.P.P.E.)—PAULINE FATHERS

(Ordo Sancti Pauli Primi Eremitae)

Founded in Hungary in the 13th Century. First foundation in the United States in 1953.

General Motherhouse: Ojcowie Paulini - Jasna Gora, ul. Kordeckiego 2 42-225, Czestochowa, Poland, Email: osppe@jasnagora.pl. Rev. Arnold Chrapkowski, O.S.P.P.E., Gen. Supr.

American Provincial Motherhouse (1984): Shrine of Our Lady of Czestochowa, Pauline Fathers Monastery, Beacon Hill, P.O. Box 2049, 654 Ferry Rd., Doylestown, PA 18901. Tel: 215-345-0600; Fax: 215-348-2148; Email: info@czestochowa.us; Web: www.czestochowa.us. Rev. Tadeusz Lizinczyk, O.S.P.P.E., Prov.; Rev. Krzysztof Drybka, O.S.P.P.E., Prior; Rev. Edward Raymond Volz, O.S.P.P.E., Shrine Dir.

Priests in U.S: 25; Brothers 5

Represented in the Archdioceses of Chicago, New York and Philadelphia and in the Dioceses of Buffalo, Greensburg, Orlando and Norwich.

[1020] (S.S.P.)—PAULINE FATHERS AND BROTHERS

(Society of St. Paul for the Apostolate of Communications)

Corporate Name: Pious Society of St. Paul

General Motherhouse: Via Alessandro Severo, 58 00145, Rome, Italy, Very Rev. Valdir DeCastro, S.S.P., Supr. Gen.; Very Rev. Vito Fracchiolla, S.S.P., Vicar Gen.

United States Province (1932): Pious Society of St. Paul, 2187 Victory Blvd., Staten Island, NY 10314. Tel: 718-761-0047. Rev. Matthew R. Roehrig, S.S.P., Prov. Supr.; Bro. Peter Lyne, S.S.P., Vicar Prov.; Bro. Augustine Condon, S.S.P., Prov. Sec. & Councillor; Rev. Arcangel Cardenas, S.S.P., Prov. Councillor; Rev. Sebastian Lee, S.S.P., Prov. Bursar; Rev. Tony Bautista, S.S.P., Prov. Councillor.

Legal Title: Pious Society of St. Paul, Inc.

Priests 11; Brothers 20

Represented in the Archdioceses of Chicago and New York and in the Diocese of Youngstown.

Los Angeles Province: 112 S. Herbert Ave., Los Angeles, CA 90063. Tel: 323-269-5010; Fax: 323-268-4583. Rev. Marco Antonio Vences, S.S.P., Supr.; Rev. Francisco M. Rosas Zevada, S.S.P; Rev. Tomas Martinez, S.S.P.

Priests 5

Miami Province: Society of St. Paul, 8455 S.W. 2nd St., Miami, FL 33144. Tel: 305-480-5377; Web: www.sanpablomia.com. Rev. Arnulfo Gomez, S.S.P., Supr.; Bro. Salvador Ramirez, M.S.S.P., Admin.

Priests 3

[1030] (C.S.P.)—PAULIST FATHERS

(Societas Missionaria a S. Paulo Apostolo)

Paulist Fathers Generalate (1858): 415 W. 59th St., New York, NY 10019. Tel: 212-757-8072. Rev. Eric P. Andrews, C.S.P., Pres.

Legal Titles: Missionary Society of St. Paul the Apostle in the State of New York; The Missionary Society of St. Paul the Apostle in the State of California; Missionary Society of St. Paul the Apostle in Massachusetts; Paulist Productions; Paulist Pictures; Paulist Religious Property Trust; Paulist Press; Paulist Mission Trust; Paulist Foundation, Inc.

Fathers 109; Students in Major Seminary: 6; Novices 3

Sponsored Ministries: Paulist Evangelization Ministries; Paulist Reconciliation Ministries; Paulist Ecumenical and Interfaith Relations.

Represented in the Archdioceses of Boston, Chicago, Los Angeles, Newark, New York, San Francisco and Washington and in the Dioceses of Albany, Austin, Brooklyn, Columbus, Grand Rapids, Knoxville, Oakland and Palm Beach. Also in Rome.

[1040] (SCH.P.)—PIARIST FATHERS

(Ordo Clericorum Regularum Pauperum Matris Dei Scholarum Piarum)

General Motherhouse: San Pantaleo, Piazza De Massimi, 00186, 4, Rome, Italy, Very Rev. Pedro Aguado, Sch.P., Supr. Gen.

Province of the United States of America and Puerto Rico (2011): 1339 Monroe St., N.E., Washington, DC 20017-2510. Tel: 202-529-7734; Tel: 787-309-5520; Fax: 954-771-8060; Email: fernema2003@yahoo.co.uk; Web: www.piarist.info. Very Rev. Fernando Negro, Sch.P., Prov. Supr.

Bishops 1; Priests 35; Deacons 1; Professed Seminarians: 15; Novices 5; Pre-Novices 5

Legal Titles and Holdings: Piarist Fathers-U.S.A. Province, Inc., Washington, DC; Piarist Fathers, Inc.; Order of the Pious Schools, Inc., Washington, DC; Piarist Fathers House of Studies, Washington, DC; Piarist Fathers, Queen of Pious Schools, Inc., Washington, D.C.; The Piarist School, Martin, KY; Piarist Fathers Residence, Prestonsburg, KY; Devon Preparatory School, Devon, PA; Calasanzian Fathers, New York, NY; Casa Calasanz, Miami, FL; Colegio Calasanz, San Juan, PR; Santisimo Salvador, San Juan, PR.

Represented in the Archdioceses of Miami, New York, Philadelphia, San Juan and Washington and in the Dioceses of Lexington and Ponce.

New York-Puerto Rico Vice Province: 1900 Road 14, Coto Laurel, PR 00780-2147. Tel: 787-848-1592; Fax: 787-841-5173. Very Rev. Fernando Negro, Sch.P., Prov. Supr.

Bishops 1; Priests 16; Juniors: 8; Pre-Novices 2 Houses 4; House of Formation 2; Parishes 3; High Schools 2; Schools 4.

Represented in the Archdioceses of New York and San Juan and in the Diocese of Ponce. Also Calasanzian Fathers and Padres Escolapios de P.R. California's Vice Province Piarist Fathers Piarist Fathers Inc., 3940 Perry St., Los Angeles, CA 90063-1174. Tel: 323-261-1386; Fax: 323-266-4907. Rev. Hilario Flores.

Priests 19; Pre-Novices 1; Novices 5; Seminarians: 5

Properties owned, staffed or sponsored: Parishes 7; Grammar Schools 2; High School 1; House of Formation 2.

Represented in the Archdiocese of Los Angeles and in the Diocese of San Diego.

[1050] (PIME)—PONTIFICAL INSTITUTE FOR FOREIGN MISSIONS, INC.

General Motherhouse: Via F. D. Guerrazzi 11, 00152, Rome, Italy, Very Rev. Ferruccio Brambillasca, PIME, Supr. Gen.

U.S. Region: 17330 Quincy Ave., Detroit, MI 48221. Tel: 313-342-4066; Fax: 313-342-6816. Email: secretary@pimeusa.org. Very Rev. George Palliparambil, PIME, Reg. Supr. & Pres.

Fathers 13

Legal Titles and Holdings: PIME Missionaries - PIME Mission Center; PIME College Community, Detroit, MI; PIME Missionaries

Formation Communities 1; Mission Houses 1.

Represented in the Archdioceses of Detroit and New York and in the Dioceses of Brooklyn and Columbus.

[1060] (C.PP.S.)—SOCIETY OF THE PRECIOUS BLOOD

(Congregatio Missionariorum Pretiosissimi Sanguinis Domini Nostri Jesu Christi)

General Motherhouse: Viale di Porta Ardeatina 66, 1-00154 Rome, Italy, Very Rev. William Nordenbrock, C.PP.S., Moderator.

Cincinnati Province: 431 E. Second St., Dayton, OH 45402. Tel: 937-228-9263. Email: prodirsec@cpps-preciousblood.org. Very Rev. Larry Hemmelgarn, C.PP.S, Prov. Dir. Provincial Council: Rev. Kenneth Schnipke, C.PP.S.; Rev. Stephen Dos Santos, C.PP.S.; Rev. Antonio Baus, C.PP.S.; Bro. Joseph J. Fisher, C.PP.S.; Rev. Anthony T. Fortman, C.PP.S.; Rev. Thomas Hemm, C.PP.S.

Fathers 113; Brothers 23; Deacons 2; Students in Major Seminaries 5; Students in Preparatory Seminary: 23

Ministries in Parishes; Missions; Chaplaincies; Shrine; Education; Retreat Preaching; Community Houses; Houses of Study; Precious Blood Ministry of Reconciliation.

Represented in the Archdioceses of Chicago, Cincinnati and Los Angeles and in the Dioceses of Cleveland, Columbus, Gary, Lafayette in Indiana, Oakland, Orlando and Toledo.

Kansas City Province: Precious Blood Society Provincial Office, P.O. Box 339, Liberty, MO 64069-0339. Tel: 816-781-4344; Fax: 816-781-3639. Email: communications@preciousbloodkc.org. Rev. Joseph Nassal, C.PP.S., Prov. Dir.; Rev. Richard Bayuk, C.PP.S., Vice Prov. & Prov. Treas.; Rev. Ronald Will, C.PP.S., 3rd Councilor & Prov. Sec.; Rev. Thomas Welk, C.PP.S., 2nd Councilor; Rev. Mark Miller, C.PP.S, 4th Councilor.

Bishops 1; Fathers 42; Brothers 2

Ministries in Parishes; Missions; Houses of Study; Community House; Chaplaincies.

Represented in the Archdioceses of Chicago, Cincinnati, Denver and Los Angeles and in the Dioceses of Davenport, Jefferson City, Joliet in Illinois, Kansas City-St. Joseph, Oakland and Wichita.

Atlantic Province: Society of the Precious Blood, Atlantic Province, 1261 Highland Ave., Rochester, NY 14620. Tel: 585-244-2692.

Provincial House: 13313 Niagara Pkwy., L2G 0P8, Niagara Falls, Canada, Tel: 905-382-1118. Email: rpwiecek@aol.com. Rev. John A. Colacino, C.PP.S., Vice Prov.

Priests in the U.S: 4

Represented in the Archdioceses of Boston and San Francisco and in the Dioceses of Albany, Oakland, Orlando and Rochester. Also in Canada.

[1065] (F.S.S.P.)—PRIESTLY FRATERNITY OF ST. PETER

Founded in Switzerland in 1988. First foundation in United States in 1991.

General Motherhouse: Fraternitas Sacerdotalis Sancti Petri, Maison St. Pierre Canisius, Chemin du Schoenberg 8, CH-1700 Fribourg, Switzerland, Tel: 41-26-488-0037; Fax: 41-26-488-0038. Rev. Andrzej Komorowski, F.S.S.P., Supr. Gen.

International Seminary: Priesterseminar Sankt Petrus, Kirchstrasse 16, D-88145, Opfenbach-Wigratzbad, Germany, Tel: 49-8385 9221 0; Fax: 49-8385 9221 33. Rev. Vincent Ribeton, F.S.S.P., Rector.

U.S. Headquarters: Priestly Fraternity of St. Peter-North American District Headquarters, 450 Venard Rd., South Abington Township, PA 18411. Tel: 570-842-4000; Fax: 570-319-9770. Rev. Michael Stinson, F.S.S.P., Dist. Supr.; Rev. Zachary Akers, F.S.S.P., Dir.-Devel.; Rev. Simon Harkins, F.S.S.P., Dist. Bursar.

House of Formation: Our Lady of Guadalupe Seminary, 7880 W. Denton Rd., P.O. Box 147, Denton, NE 68339. Tel: 402-797-7700; Fax: 402-797-7705; Email: seminary@fsspolgs.org; Web: www.fsspolgs.org. Very Rev. Josef Bisig, F.S.S.P., Rector; Rev. Robert Ferguson, F.S.S.P; Rev. Joseph Lee, F.S.S.P; Rev. William Lawrence, F.S.S.P; Rev. Charles Ryan, F.S.S.P; Rev. Rhone Lillard, F.S.S.P; Rev. Benoit Guichard, F.S.S.P.; Rev. Anthony Uy, F.S.S.P.

Priests 8; Seminarians: 84

Properties owned or sponsored: Houses 41.

Represented in the Archdioceses of Atlanta, Baltimore, Cincinnati, Denver, Galveston-Houston, Indianapolis, Kansas City, Los Angeles, Oklahoma City, Omaha, St. Paul-Minneapolis and Seattle and in the Dioceses of Allentown, Boise, Colorado Springs, Dallas, El Paso, Fort Wayne-South Bend, Fort Worth, Fresno, Harrisburg, Joliet, Lexington, Lincoln, Little Rock, Manchester, Orlando, Paterson, Phoenix, Rapid City, Richmond, Sacramento, San Diego, Scranton, Springfield (IL), Tulsa, Tyler, Venice and Youngstown. Also Canada.

[1070] (C.SS.R.)—REDEMPTORIST FATHERS

(Congregatio Sanctissimi Redemptoris-Redemptorist)

Generalate: Sant' Alfonso, Via Merulana 31. C.P. 2458 I-00100, Rome, Italy, Rev. Michael Brehl, C.Ss.R., Supr. Gen.; Rev. Alberto Eseverri, C.Ss.R., Vicar Gen.; Rev. John C. Vargas, C.Ss.R., Procurator.

Province of Baltimore (1850): Provincial Residence, 7509 Shore Rd., Brooklyn, NY 11209-2807. Tel: 718-833-1900; Fax: 718-630-5666. Email: secprovince@redemptorists.net. Very Rev. Paul J. Borowski, C.Ss.R., Prov. Supr.; Rev. Gerard J. Knapp, C.Ss.R., Prov. Vicar; Rev. Matthew Allman, C.Ss.R.; Rev. Henry Sattler, C.Ss.R., Sec. & Treas.; Rev. Francis Gargani, C.Ss.R., Rector.

Bishop: 1; Priests 133; Brothers 10; Postulants: 1; Students in Vows 7

Properties owned, staffed or sponsored: Parishes 20; Residences 5; Retreat Houses 2; Community Houses 27.

Properties owned, staffed or sponsored: St. Mary's Annapolis, 109 Duke of Gloucester St. Annapolis, MD 21401; Sacred Heart of Jesus, 600 S. Conklin St., Baltimore, MD 21224; St. Martin of Tours, 40 Seaman Ave, Bethpage, NY 11714; Our Lady of Perpetual Help (Mission Church) 1545 Tremont St. Boston, MA 02120; Immaculate Conception, 389 East 150th St. Bronx, NY 10455; Our Lady of Perpetual Help, 526 59th St. Brooklyn, NY 11220; Our Lady of the Hills, 120 Marydale Lane, Columbia, SC 29210; St. James, 137 Manor Avenue SW, Concord, NC 28025; St. Joseph Parish, 108 St. Joseph St. Kannapolis, NC 28083; St. Gerard Parish, 240 W. Robb Avenue, Lima, OH 45801; Sacred Heart Parish, 998 Fr. Donlan Dr. New Smyrna Beach, FL 32168; Most Holy Redeemer/Nativity Church 173 E. 3rd St. New York, NY 10009; Our Lady of Guadalupe, 211 Irwin Dr. Newton Grove, NC 28366; Immaculate Conception Church, 104 E. John St. Clinton, NC 28328; St. Juan, Old Hwy 701, Ingold NC 28446; St. Peter the Apostle/St John Neumann Shrine 1019 North 5th St. Philadelphia, PA 19123; Visitation of the Blessed Virgin Mary, 2625 "B" St., Philadelphia, PA 19125; St. Clement Parish, 231 Lake Ave. Saratoga Springs, NY 12866; Our Lady of Lourdes, 528 Stein Highway, Seaford, DE 19973; Notre Dame Retreat House, 5151 Foster Rd. Canandaigua, NY 14424; San Alfonso Retreat House, 755 Ocean Avenue, Long Branch, NJ 07740.

Represented in the Archdioceses of Baltimore, Boston, New York, Philadelphia and Washington and in the Dioceses of Albany, Brooklyn, Harrisburg, Rochester, Rockville Centre, Toledo, Trenton and Wilmington. Also in the West Indies.

Redemptorist Office for Mission Advancement: 107 Duke of Gloucester St., Annapolis, MD 21401-2526. Tel: 410-990-1680; Tel: 877-876-7662.

Richmond Vice Province (1942): Vice Provincial Hqtrs., 313 Hillman St., P.O. Box 1529, New Smyrna Beach, FL 32170. Tel: 386-427-3094. Email: vpofrichmond@aol.com. Very Rev. Glenn D. Parker, C.Ss.R., Vice Prov.; Rev. Thomas Burke, C.Ss.R., Vicar. Consultors: Deacon Darrell Cevasco, C.Ss.R., Vocation Dir.; Rev. Joseph Dionne, C.Ss.R., Consultor.

Legal Title: Congregation of the Most Holy Redeemer; Redemptorist Fathers of Florida, Inc; Redemptorists Fathers of South Carolina; Redemptorists Fathers of North Carolina, Inc; Redemptorists Fathers of Virginia, Incorporated; Redemptorists Fathers of Georgia, Incorporated.

Priests 15; Deacons 1

Properties owned, staffed or sponsored: Parishes 5; Retirement Home 1; Residences 1; Missions 3.

Represented in the Dioceses of Charleston, Charlotte and Orlando.

The Redemptorists Denver Province (1996): The Redemptorist Provincial Offices, Administrative Headquarters, 1633 N. Cleveland Ave., Chicago, IL 60614. Tel: 312-248-8894; Fax: 312-248-8852. Web: www.redemptoristsdenver.org. Very Rev. Stephen Rehrauer, C.Ss.R., Prov. Supr.; Rev. John Fahey-Guerra, C.Ss.R., Prov. Vicar; Bro. Laurence Lujan, C.Ss.R., Prov. Consultor; Rev. Gregory May, C.Ss.R., Treas.

Legal Titles: The Redemptorists/Denver Province; The Redemptorists of Denver, Colorado; The Redemptorists of Greeley, Colorado, Inc., Denver, CO; Redemptorist Fathers (Boise, ID), Denver, CO; Redemptorists Society of Oregon (Portland, OR), Denver, CO; The Society of the Redemptorists of the City Grand Rapids, Michigan, Denver, CO; The Redemptorists of Nebraska (Omaha, NE), Denver, CO; Redemptorists of Hamtramck, Denver, CO; The Redemptorist Fathers of Hennepin County (St. Paul-Minneapolis, MN), Denver, CO; Redemptorist Fathers (St. Louis, MO), Denver, CO; The Redemptorist Fathers of Kansas City, Missouri, The Redemptorists of Blessed Sacrament - The Redemptorist Fathers of Chicago (Chicago, IL), Denver, CO; Redemptorist Society of Alaska (Anchorage, AK), Denver, CO; The Redemptorist Society of Arizona (Tucson, AZ), Denver, CO; The Redemptorists Society of Washington, Palisades Retreat Association, A School of Christian Living (Seattle, WA), Denver, CO; The Redemptorist Community of Wichita, Kansas, Inc., Society of the Redemptorist Fathers of Wichita, Kansas, Denver, CO; Redemptorist Fathers of St. Alphonsus Parish (Chicago, IL), Denver, CO; Redemptorist Fathers of Iowa; Redemptorists of Berkeley; Redemptorists of Oakland; Redemptorists of Whittier; The Redemptorists (Glenview, IL) Denver, CO; Redemptorist Fathers, d/b/a Liguori Publications; Holy Redeemer Center; Redemptorist Society of California; Redemptorist Theology Residence; Redemptorist Hispanic Ministry, Inc.; Liguori Mission House/Redemptorists: St. Clement Health Care Center; St. John Neumann House; Our Mother of Perpetual Help Retreat House of Oconomowoc, Wisc. Inc., d/b/a/ Redemptorist Retreat Center; Redemptorist Social Services Center, Inc.; Redemptorists of Mattese; Redemptorist Fathers of Bellaire, Texas; The Redemptorists/San Antonio; The Society of Redemptorists; Redemptorist Vice-Provincialate of New Orleans; Redemptorist Fathers of Baton Rouge, Inc.; The Redemptorists of the South Endowment Fund, Inc.; The Redemptorist Education and Formation Foundation, Inc.; Redemptorists of Tennessee; Redemptorist Vietnamese Ministry; Redemptorists of Mississippi.

Properties owned, sponsored or staffed: Parishes 10; Retreat Houses 4; Residences 7; Community Houses 16.

Represented in the Archdioceses of Chicago, Denver, Detroit, Los Angeles, Milwaukee, New Orleans, New York, San Antonio, St. Louis, St. Paul-Minneapolis and Seattle and in the Dioceses of Baton Rouge, Biloxi, Grand Rapids, Kansas City-St. Joseph Oakland and Tucson. Also in Foreign Missions.

Manaus Vice-Province: Redentoristas, Caixa Postal 217, 69011-970 Manaus-AM, Amazonas South America, Brazil, Very Rev. Zenildo Luiz Pereira DaSilva, C.Ss.R., Vice Prov.

Vice Province of Nigeria: Sts. Michael, Raphael & Gabriel Church, P.O. Box 541, Satellite Town, Nigeria, Very Rev. Kingsley Onyekuru, C.Ss.R., Vice Prov.

[1080] (C.R.)—CONGREGATION OF THE RESURRECTION

(Congregatio a Resurrectione Domini Nostri Jesu Christi)

Generalate: Via San Sebastianello 11 00187, Rome, Italy, Very Rev. Bernard Hylla, C.R.

U.S.A. Province: 3601 N. California Ave., Chicago, IL 60618-4602. Tel: 773-463-7506. Very Rev. Eugene Szarek, C.R., Prov. Supr.; Rev. Gary Hogan, C.R., Vicar Prov. Supr. Councilors: Rev. Paul Sims, C.R.; Rev. Steven Bartczyszyn, C.R.; Rev. Jerzy Zieba, C.R.

Fathers 52; Brothers 3

Ministries in Parishes; Missions; High School; Chaplaincies; University.

Represented in the Archdioceses of Chicago, Los Angeles, Mobile and St. Louis and in the Dioceses of Holy Protection of Mary, Joliet, Kalamazoo, Rockford and San Bernardino. Also in Bermuda.

Ontario Kentucky Province U.S. Address: St. Cecila - Villa Pacis House, 515 D S. Shelby St., Louisville, KY 40202. Tel: 502-589-6113; Fax: 502-589-6116. Email: provincialoffice@resurrectioncollege.ca. Rev. John Lesousky, C.R.; Deacon Brian Karley, C.R., Supr.

Members of Province in U.S.A: 5

Properties owned, sponsored or staffed: Community Houses 3; University 1.

Represented in the Archdiocese of Louisville.

Seminary House: 4252 W. Pine Blvd., Saint Louis, MO 63108. Tel: 314-652-8814. Rev. Gary Hogan, C.R., Rector.

[1090] (R.C.J.)—ROGATIONIST FATHERS

(Congregatio Rogationis-a-Corde-Jesu)

Generalate: via Tuscolana 167 00182, Rome, Italy, Very Rev. Bruno Rampazzo, R.C.J., Supr. Gen.

U.S.A. Delegation: 2688 S. Newmark Ave., P.O. Box 37, Sanger, CA 93657. Tel: 559-875-5808; Tel: 559-875-2025; Fax: 559-875-2618. Rev. Antonio Fiorenza, R.C.J., Delegation Supr.

U.S. Foundations: St. Mary's Church, 828 O St., P.O. Box 335, Sanger, CA 93657. Tel: 559-875-2025. Rev. John Bruno, R.C.J; Rev. Rene Panlasigui, R.C.J.; Rev. Edwin Manio, R.C.J.

Legal Title: Congregation of Rogationists, Inc.

Priests 7

Ministries in Parishes; Vocation Center; Formation House; Social Service Center.

Represented in the Archdiocese of Los Angeles and in the Diocese of Fresno.

U.S. Foundations: St. Elisabeth Church, 6635 Tobias Ave., Van Nuys, CA 91405. Tel: 818-779-1756. Rev. Vito Di Marzio, R.C.J; Rev. Denny Joseph, R.C.J; Rev. Antonio Fiorenza, R.C.J.

[1100] (S.C.)—BROTHERS OF THE SACRED HEART

(Societas Fratrum Sacris Cordis)

Founded in Lyon, France in 1821 by Rev. Andre Coindre. First foundation in the United States in Mobile, AL in 1847.

Generalate: Piazza del Sacro Cuore, No. 3, 00151, Rome, Italy, Bro. Mark Hilton, S.C., Supr. Gen.

Provincial Office: 685 Steere Farm Rd., Pascoag, RI 02859-4601. Tel: 401-568-3361; Fax: 401-568-1450. Bro. Mark E. Hilton, S.C., Prov. Supr. Councilors: Bro. Ronald Hingle, S.C., Vocations; Bro. Joseph Holthaus, S.C.; Bro. Ivy LeBlanc, S.C., Treas.; Bro. Barry Landry, S.C.; Bro. Paul J. Hebert, S.C., Mission Procurator.

Legal Title: The Province of the United States of the Brothers of the Sacred Heart, Inc., (a Delaware Corporation); Brothers of the Sacred Heart of New England, Inc.; Father Andre Coindre Charitable Trust; The Charles Lwango Charitable Trust.

Brothers 135; Novices 4; Ordained Brothers 6

Regional Office: 4600 Elysian Fields Ave., New Orleans, LA 70122. Tel: 504-301-4758; Fax: 504-301-4843. Bro. Ronald Hingle, S.C., Prov. Supr. & Vocations; Councilors: Bro. Barry Landry, S.C.; Bro. Ivy LeBlanc, S.C., Treas.; Bro. Clifford King, S.C.; Bro. Donald Sukanek, S.C.; Bro. Paul Montero, S.C.; Bro. Paul J. Hebert, S.C., Mission Procurator.

Legal Title: Brothers of the Sacred Heart of New Orleans, Inc.; Brothers of the Sacred Heart Foundation, Inc.; Brothers of the Sacred Heart of New Jersey/New York, Inc.

Brothers 125; Novices 3; Ordained Brothers 5

Regional Office: 71-06 31st Ave., East Elmhurst, NY 11370. Tel: 718-898-9600, ext. 17.

Regional Office: Brothers of the Sacred Heart of New Jersey/New York, Inc., 4600 Elysian Fields Ave., New Orleans, LA 70122. Tel: 504-301-4758; Fax: 504-301-4843. Bro. Barry Landry, Pres.

Regional Office: Brothers of the Sacred Heart of New Orleans, Inc., 4600 Elysian Fields Ave., New Orleans, LA 70122. Tel: 504-301-4758; Fax: 504-301-4843.

Represented in the Archdioceses of Mobile and New Orleans and in the Dioceses of Baton Rouge, Biloxi, Brooklyn, Gallup, Houma-Thibodaux, Manchester, Metuchen and Providence. Also in England, Mozambique, the Philippines and Zambia.

[1110] (M.S.C.)—MISSIONARIES OF THE SACRED HEART

(Societas Missionarii Sacratissimi Cordis Jesu)

General Motherhouse: Via Asmara 11 00199, Rome, Italy, Very Rev. Mark McDonald, M.S.C., Supr. Gen.

United States Province (1939): 305 S. Lake St., P.O. Box 270, Aurora, IL 60507. Tel: 630-892-8400; Tel: 630-892-2371; Fax: 630-892-3071. Very Rev. Raymond Diesbourg, M.S.C., Prov. Supr. Consultors: Rev. David Foxen, M.S.C.; Rev. Richard Kennedy, M.S.C., Vice Prov.; Very Rev. Luis Alfonso Segura, M.S.C.; Rev. Michael Miller, M.S.C.; Rev. Adrian Budhi, M.S.C.; Rev. Joseph Kanimea, M.S.C.

Legal Title: Society of the Missionaries of the Sacred Heart.

Fathers 42; Brothers 9; Professed Students: 4

Properties owned, staffed or sponsored: Residential Houses 3; Parishes 15; Chaplaincies 1.

Represented in the Archdioceses of Chicago and Philadelphia and in the Dioceses of Allentown, Ogdensburg, Pensacola-Tallahassee, Rockford and San Bernardino. Also in Colombia and Italy.

U.S. Section of the Irish Province for California and Southern States: Sectional Hqtrs, 123 W. Laurel, San Antonio, TX 78212-4667. Tel: 210-226-5514; Fax: 210-226-5725. Sectional Leadership Team Rev. Kevin Shanahan, M.S.C., Supr.; Rev. William Collins, M.S.C.; Rev. Michael Fitzgibbon, M.S.C.

Priests 11

Represented in the Archdiocese of San Antonio and in the Dioceses of Austin and Charleston.

[1120] (M.SS.CC.)—MISSIONARIES OF THE SACRED HEARTS OF JESUS AND MARY

(Missionarii a Sacris Cordibus Jesus et Mariae)

Founded in Italy in 1833.

General Motherhouse: Via dei Falegnami 23, Rome, Italy, Very Rev. Luigi Toscano, M.SS.CC., Supr. Gen.

American Headquarters: 2249 Shore Rd., Linwood, NJ 08221. Tel: 609-927-5600; Fax: 609-927-5262. Email: mssccusa@aol.com. Rev. Frederick Clement, M.SS.CC; Rev. John Perdue, M.SS.CC; Rev. Damian Anumba, M.SS.CC; Rev. Prashanth Lobo, M.SS.CC; Bro. David Graber, M.SS.CC.

Legal Title: Missionaries of the Sacred Heart of Jesus and Mary.

Priests 9; Brothers 2

Represented in the Dioceses of Camden and Harrisburg.

[1130] (S.C.J.)—CONGREGATION OF THE PRIESTS OF THE SACRED HEART

(Priests of the Sacred Heart)

(Congregazione Dei Sacredoti Del a Cuore di Gesu)

General Motherhouse: Curia Generale, S.C.J., Via Casale S. Pio V, 20 00165, Rome, Italy, Very Rev. Carlos Luis Suarez Codorniú, S.C.J., Supr. Gen.

United States Province (1933): Provincialate Offices, P.O. Box 289, Hales Corners, WI 53130-0289. Tel: 414-425-6910. Email: provsec@usprovince.org. Very Rev. Edward Kilianski, S.C.J., Prov. Supr.

Bishops 1; Priests 60; Clerics: 2; Brothers 13; Deacons 2.

Represented in the Archdioceses of Galveston-Houston, Milwaukee and San Antonio and in the Dioceses of Brownsville, Jackson, Rapid City, St. Petersburg and Sioux Falls.

[1140] (SS.CC.)—CONGREGATION OF THE SACRED HEARTS OF JESUS AND MARY

(Congregatio Sacrorum Cordium)

General Motherhouse: Casa Generalizia-Padri Dei Sacri Cuori-Via, Rivarone 85 00166, Rome, Italy, Very Rev. Alberto Toutin Cataldo, SS.CC., Supr. Gen.

Legal Title: Congregation of the Sacred Hearts of Jesus and Mary.

United States Province: Provincial Administration Office, 77 Adams St., Box 111, Fairhaven, MA 02719-0111. Tel: 508-993-2442; Fax: 508-996-5499.

Provincial House: Box 1365, Kaneohe, Oahu, HI 96744. Tel: 808-247-5035; Fax: 808-235-8849. Rev. Herman Gomes, SS.CC., Prov. Supr.; Rev. Richard McNally, SS.CC., Vicar Prov. Councilors: Rev. Stephen Banjare, SS.CC.; Rev. Richard Danyluk, SS.CC.; Rev. Martin T. Gomes, SS.CC.

Priests 40; Brothers 15; Novices 2

Properties owned or staffed: Parishes 12; Community Houses 4; Houses of Formation 2.

Represented in Dioceses of Brownsville, Fall River and Honolulu.

U.S. West Region of the U.S. Province: Congregation of the Sacred Hearts of Jesus and Mary, 2150 Damien Ave., La Verne, CA 91750. Tel: 909-593-5441; Fax: 909-593-3971. Rev. Richard J. Danyluk, SS.CC., Regional Supr.

Priests 17

Ministries in the field of Religious and Academic Education; Parishes; Chaplaincies.

Represented in the Archdiocese of Los Angeles and in the Dioceses of Orange and San Bernardino.

[1150] (C.S.J.)—CONGREGATION OF ST. JOSEPH

(Congregatio Sancti Joseph)

Founded in Turin, Italy in 1873. First foundation in United States in 1951.

General Motherhouse: Via Belvedere Montello 77, 00166, Rome, Italy, Rev. Mario Aldegani, C.S.J., Supr. Gen.

U.S. and Mexico Vice Province: St. Leonard House, 4076 Case Rd., Avon, OH 44011. Tel: 440-934-6270. Rev. Roberto Landa, C.S.J., Prov. Supr.

Priests 21; Brothers 1; Scholastics: 15

Properties owned, staffed or sponsored: Parishes 5; High Schools 1; Youth Retreat Center.

Properties owned: St. Leonard House, Avon, OH.

Represented in the Archdiocese of Los Angeles and in the Diocese of Cleveland. Also in Mexico.

[1160] (F.S.P.)—BROTHERS OF ST. PATRICK

(Patrician Brothers)

Founded in Ireland 1808 by Bishop Daniel Delaney.

U.S. Foundation (1948): St. Patrick's Novitiate, 7820 Bolsa Ave., Midway City, CA 92655. Tel: 714-897-8181. Email: brophilip5@yahoo.com. Bro. Philip Shepler, F.S.P., Pres.

Brothers 5

Represented in the Archdiocese of Los Angeles and in the Diocese of Orange.

[1170] (S.P.S.)—ST. PATRICK'S MISSIONARY SOCIETY

(St. Patrick Fathers)

Founded March 17, 1932 with the approval of Pope Pius XI. A Pontifical Society of secular priests devoted entirely to the missionary needs of the Church.

International Headquarters: St. Patrick's, Kiltegan, Wicklow, Ireland, Rev. Victor Dunne, S.P.S., Society Leader; Rev. John Marren, S.P.S., Asst. Society Leader; Rev. Cathal Moriarty, S.P.S., Society Councillor; Rev. Bosco Kamau, S.P.S., Society Councillor; Rev. Michael Madigan, S.P.S., Society Leader U.S. Total number of Priests 288; Priests in the U.S: 4

U.S. Foundations (1965): St. Patrick Fathers (1968), 8422 W. Windsor Ave., Chicago, IL 60656-4252. Tel: 773-887-4741. Rev. Michael Moore, S.P.S.; Rev. Michael Madigan, S.P.S.

Legal Titles: St. Patrick's Missionary Society; St. Patrick's Fathers, Guilds & Associates.

[1180] (C.S.P.X.)—BROTHERS OF SAINT PIUS X

Founded in the United States in 1952.

Motherhouse: P.O. Box 284, Spring Valley, WI 54767. Tel: 715-778-4999. Bro. Michael Mandernach, Dir. Ministries in the field of Religious and Academic Education; Health Care; Community services and Administration.

Represented in the Diocese of La Crosse.

[1190] (S.D.B.)—SALESIANS OF DON BOSCO

(Societas Sancti Francisci Salesii)

Generalate: Salesiani Don Bosco, via Della Pisana, 1111, C.P. 18333, 00163 Roma-Bravetta, Italy. Very Rev. Angel Fernandez Artime, Rector Major.

Province of St. Philip the Apostle (1902): 148 Main St., New Rochelle, NY 10801. Tel: 914-636-4225. Very Rev. Steve Shafran, S.D.B., Prov.; Very Rev. Timothy Zak, S.D.B., Vice Prov.; Rev. Dennis Donovan, S.D.B., Prov. Economer & Councilor; Rev. John Serio, S.D.B.. Schools Councilor; Rev. Abraham Feliciano, S.D.B., Dir. of Youth Ministry & Councilor; Rev. David Moreno, S.D.B., Prov. Sec.; Rev. Michael Pace, S.D.B., Councilor.

Legal Title: Salesian Society, Province of St. Philip the Apostle, Inc.

Fathers 119; Professed Clerics: 15; Students in Major Seminaries 6; Coadjutor-Brothers 27

Ministries in: Parishes; High Schools; Boys and Girls Clubs; Camps; Shrine; Retreat Center.

Represented in the Archdioceses of Boston, Chicago, Newark, New Orleans, New York and Washington and in the Dioceses of Palm Beach and St. Petersburg. Also in Canada.

San Francisco Province (1926): Salesian Society - San Francisco, 1100 Franklin St., San Francisco, CA 94109. Tel: 415-441-7144; Fax: 415-441-7155. Email: suosec@salesiansf.org. Rev. Ted Montemayor, S.D.B., Prov.; Rev. Thomas Prendiville, S.D.B., Vice. Prov. Councilors: Rev. Tho Bui, S.D.B., Treas.; Bro. Alphonse Vu, S.D.B; Rev. John T. Itzaina, S.D.B; Rev. Nicholas Reina, S.D.B.

Priests 59; Professed Brothers 17; Seminarians: 9

Ministries in Parishes; High Schools; Retreat House; Youth Centers.

Represented in the Archdioceses of Los Angeles and San Francisco and in the Dioceses of Laredo, Monterey, Oakland and Stockton.

House of Formation: De Sales Hall, 13856 Bellflower Blvd., Bellflower, CA 90706. Tel: 562-925-1973.

[1200] (S.D.S.)—SOCIETY OF THE DIVINE SAVIOR

(Salvatorian Fathers and Brothers)

(Salvatorians - Societas Divini Salvatoris)

Very Rev. Milton Zonta, S.D.S., Supr. Gen.

U.S.A. Province (1892): Salvatorian Provincial Offices, 1735 N. Hi-Mount Blvd., Milwaukee, WI 53208-1720. Tel: 414-258-1735; Fax: 414-258-1934. Email: sds@Salvatorians.com. Very Rev. Jeffrey Wocken, S.D.S., Prov.; Rev. Peter Schuessler, S.D.S., Vicar & Dir., Formation. Consultors: Bro. Sean McLaughlin, S.D.S.; Rev. Scott Wallenfelsz, S.D.S., Treas.; Rev. Douglas S. Bailey, S.D.S.; Rev. Paul Portland, S.D.S.

Fathers 54; Brothers 17; Clerics: 5

Legal Titles: Society of the Divine Savior; Society of the Divine Savior Ongoing Community Support Trust; Camp St. Charles, Inc.; Lay Salvatorians Inc.; Salvatorian Institute of Philosophy and Theology Inc.; Fund Raising and Public Relations Center, Salvatorian Center, New Holstein, WI 53061.

Properties owned, staffed or sponsored: Parishes, Hospitals, Schools 13; Houses of Study and Formation 2.

Represented in the Archdioceses of Indianapolis, Milwaukee, New York and Washington, DC and in the Dioceses of Birmingham, Bismarck, Brooklyn, Green Bay, Nashville, Oakland, Orlando, Phoenix, Sacramento, St. Cloud, St. Petersburg, Tucson, Venice and Wilmington.

[1205] F.S.C.B.—PRIESTLY FRATERNITY OF THE MISSIONARIES OF ST. CHARLES BORROMEO

(Sacerdotalis Fraternitas Missionarium a Sancti Carolo Borromeo)

General Motherhouse: Via Boccea 761, 00166, Rome, Italy, Rev. Massimo Camisasca, F.S.C.B., Supr. Gen.; Rev. Paolo Sottopietra, F.S.C.B., Gen. Vicar; Rev. Gianluca Attanasio, F.S.C.B., Gen. Sec.

North American Regional Delegation: Priestly Fraternity of the Missionaries of St. Charles Borromeo, Inc., 71 Warner St., Medford, MA 02155. Tel: 781-864-3427; Web: www.fraternityofsaintcharles.org. Rev. Antonio Lopez, F.S.C.B., Regl. Delegate; Rev. Stefano Colombo, F.S.C.B., Contact Person; Rev. Jose Medina, F.S.C.B; Rev. Luca Brancolini, F.S.C.B; Very Rev. Michael Carvill, F.S.C.B; Rev. Accursio Ciaccio, F.S.C.B; Rev. Gabriele Azzalin, F.S.C.B; Rev. Antonio Lopez, F.S.C.B; Rev. Roberto Amoruso, F.S.C.B; Rev. Franco Soma, F.S.C.B; Rev. Pietro Rossotti, F.S.C.B; Rev. Jose Maria Cortes, F.S.C.B; Rev. Paolo Prosperi, F.S.C.B.

Legal Title: Priestly Fraternity of the Missionaries of St. Charles Borromeo, Inc.

Priests 12

Properties owned: House of Formation 1; Parishes staffed: 2

Represented in the Archdioceses of Boston, Denver and Washington.

[1210] (C.S.)—MISSIONARIES OF ST. CHARLES-SCALABRINIANS

(Congregatio Missionariorum A Sancto Carolo)

General Motherhouse: Via Ulisse Seni 2, 00153, Rome, Italy, Very Rev. Alessandro Gazzola, C.S., Supr. Gen.

Province of St. Charles Borromeo (188): Scalabrinians Provincial Curia, 27 Carmine St., New York, NY 10014-4423. Tel: 212-675-3993; Fax: 646-998-4625; Email: scbprovince@gmail.com. Rev. Moacir Balen, C.S., Pres. & Prov. Supr.; Rev. Jesus E. Salinas Hernandez, C.S., Vice Pres. & Vicar Prov.; Rev. Angelo Plodari, C.S., Bursar; Councilors: Rev. Horecio C. Anklan, C.S.; Rev. Vincenzo Rosato, C.S.

Legal Title: The Pious Society of the Missionaries of St. Charles Borromeo, Inc.

Fathers 91

Properties staffed or owned: Parishes 29; Missions 6; Homes for Aged 3; Seminaries 6; Scalabrini International Migration Network (SIMN); Center for Migration Studies (CMS).

Represented in the Archdioceses of Atlanta, Boston, Miami, New York and Washington and in the Dioceses of Brooklyn, Orlando, Palm Beach, Providence and Venice. Also in Eastern Canada, Colombia, Ecuador, Haiti and Venezuela.

Province of St. John Baptist (1906): Missionaries of St. Charles - Fathers of St. Charles, 546 N. East Ave., Oak Park, IL 60302. Tel: 708-386-4430; Fax: 708-386-4457. Email: SJBProvince@comcast.net. Rev. Miguel Alvarez, C.S., Prov. Supr.

Fathers 72; Brothers 2

Legal Titles: Fathers of Saint Charles; Scalabrinian Community Support Corp.; Scalabrinian Community Formation Corp.

Ministries in 17 Parishes; 1 Homes for the Aged; 3 Missions; 4 Seminaries; 7 Centers for Migrants and Refugees; 2 Diocesan office for Hispanic Ministry.

Represented in the Archdioceses of Chicago, Galveston-Houston, Kansas City in Kansas and Los Angeles and in the Dioceses of Dallas, Kansas City-St. Joseph, Monterey, San Diego and San Jose. Also in Canada, El Salvador, Guatemala and Mexico.

[1220] (SDC)—SERVANTS OF CHARITY

(Guanellians)

(Congregatio Servorum a Charitate)

General Motherhouse: Vicolo Clementi 41, Rome, Italy, Very Rev. Alfonso Crippa, SdC, Supr. Gen.

U.S. Headquarters: Servants of Charity, 118 Taunton Ave., East Providence, RI 02914. Rev. Satheesh Alphonse Caniton, SdC, Prov. Counselor & U.S. Rep.; Rev. Ronald Jesiah, SdC Prov., Divine Providence Province.

Legal Title: Pious Union of St. Joseph.

Priests 11

Publication: Now And At The Hour.

Ministry for the suffering and dying: Residences for persons with Intellectual disabilities 1; Parishes 2; Chaplaincies 2.

Represented in the Archdioceses of Chicago and Philadelphia and in the Dioceses of Lansing and Providence.

[1230] (S.P.)—SERVANTS OF THE PARACLETE

Generalate: P.O. Box 450, Dittmer, MO 63023. Tel: 636-285-0922; Fax: 636-274-1430; Web: www.theservants.org. Very Rev. David T. Fitzgerald, s.P., Servant Gen.; Rev. Philip Taylor, s.P., Vicar Gen.; Rev. Benedict Livingstone, Treas. Gen.; Very Rev. Liam Hoare, s.P., Sec. Gen.; Rev. Peter Lechner, s.P., Asst. for Apostolate.

Legal Titles: Servants of the Paraclete Generalate: A New Mexico Corporation; Servants of the Paraclete: A New Mexico Corporation; Servants of the Paraclete, A Missouri Corporation; Servants of the Paraclete Foundation.

Represented in the Archdioceses of St. Louis and Santa Fe.

U.S. Motherhouse (1952): Servants of the Paraclete, P.O. Box 489, Jemez Springs, NM 87025-0010. Tel: 505-829-3586; Fax: 505-829-3706; Email: servantgeneral@aol.com. Very Rev. David T. Fitzgerald, s.P.

[1240] (O.S.M.)—SERVITES

(Order of Friar Servants of Mary)

(Ordo Fratrum Servorum Beatae Virginis Mariae)

Generalate: Curia Generalizia dei Servi di Maria, Convento San Marcello Piazza San Marcello al Corso, 5, 00187, Rome, Italy,

Servite Friars (1999): United States of America Province Servite Provincial Center, 3121 W. Jackson Blvd., Chicago, IL 60612-2729. Tel: 773-533-0360; Fax: 773-533-8307. Very Rev. John M. Fontana, O.S.M., Prior Prov.; Rev. Gerald M. Horan, O.S.M., Asst. Prov.; Rev. Eugene M. Smith, O.S.M., Prov. Councilor; Rev. Donald M. Siple, O.S.M., Prov. Councilor & Natl. Asst. to the Servite Secular Order, Province Vocation Team; Rev. Lawrence M. Choate, O.S.M., Prov. Councilor, Prov. Treas. & Province Devel. Dir.; Bro. Michael M. Callary, O.S.M., Prov./Corp. Sec. & Province Mission Procurator; Rev. Paul M. Gins, O.S.M., Province Archivist; Rev. Richard M. Boyle, O.S.M., Rector, Sanctuary of Our Sorrowful Mother, Portland, OR; Mr. Eddie Murphy, Province Vocation Team; Rev. Christopher M. Krymski, O.S.M., Dir. Natl. Shrine of St. Peregrine, O.S.M., Chicago, IL; Rev. Vidal M. Martinez, O.S.M., Province Min. to the Servite Diakonia.

Priests 54; Professed Brothers 9; Temporary Professed Students: 6

Legal Titles: The Order of Friar Servants of Mary United States of America Province, Inc., 3121 W. Jackson Blvd., Chicago, IL, Tel: 773-533-0360; Fax: 773-533-8307; Charitable Trust of the Order of Friar Servants of Mary-United States of America Province, Inc., 3121 W. Jackson Blvd., Chicago, IL 60612-2729, Tel: 773-533-0360; Fax: 773-533-8307; Servite High School, Anaheim, CA, A California Corporation, 1952 W. La Palma Ave., Anaheim, CA 92801, Tel: 714-774-7575; Fax: 714-774-1404; Sanctuary of Our Sorrowful Mother, Inc., P.O. Box 20008, Portland, OR 97294-0008, Tel: 503-254-7371; Fax: 503-254-9682.

Properties Owned, Staffed and Sponsored: Parishes 2 owned, 4 staffed; High Schools 2; Shrines 3; Residences 14; Missions 2; Nursing Home Chaplaincies 1.

Represented in the Archdioceses of Chicago, Denver, Hartford, Portland in Oregon and in the Diocese of Orange. Also in Australia, Ireland and South Africa.

[1250] (C.R.S.)—SOMASCAN FATHERS

(Clericorum Regularium Somaschensium)
(Order of St. Jerome Aemilian)

General Motherhouse: Via Casal Morena, 8 00040, Morena - Rome, Italy, Rev. Franco Moscone, C.R.S., Father Gen.

U.S. Foundation: Pine Haven Boys Center, 133 River Rd., P.O. Box 162, Suncook, NH 03275. Tel: 603-485-7141. Email: info@pinehavenboyscenter.org. Rev. Remo Zanatta, C.R.S., Major Supr.

Priests 10

Represented in the Archdiocese of Galveston-Houston and in the Diocese of Manchester.

[1260] (S.CH.)—SOCIETY OF CHRIST

(Societas Christi Pro Emigrantibus Polonis)

General Motherhouse: 60-962 Poznan Ulica Panny Marii 4, Poland, Very Rev. Ryszard Glowacki, S.Ch., Supr. Gen.; Rev. Matthew John Gardzinski, S.Ch., Procurator Gen Via Pier Ruggero Piccio 55/B, Rome, Italy, 00136.

American-Canadian Province: Provincial House, 786 W. Sunset Ave., Lombard, IL 60148. Tel: 630-424-0401; Fax: 630-424-0409. Email: schprov@aol.com. Rev. Pawel Bandurski, S.Ch., Prov.; Rev. Andrzej Totzke, S.Ch., Vice Prov.; Rev. Zygmunt Ostrwoski, S.Ch., Treas.

Priests 55; Seminarians: 4

Represented in the Archdioceses of Atlanta; Baltimore, Boston, Chicago, Denver, Detroit, Galveston - Houston, Los Angeles, Miami, Milwaukee, New York, Portland in Oregon, St. Paul-Minneapolis, St. Louis, San Francisco, Seattle and Washington and in the Dioceses of Dallas, Joliet, Las Vegas, Phoenix, San Diego and San Jose. Also in Canada.

[1270] (F.M.S.I.)—SONS OF MARY MISSIONARY SOCIETY

(Sons of Mary, Health of the Sick)
(Filii Mariae Salutis Infirmorum)

General Headquarters: 567 Salem End Rd., Framingham, MA01702-5599. Tel: 508-879-6711; Email: sonskevin@gmail.com; Web: www.sonsofmary.com.ph. Bro. Kevin Courtney, F.M.S.I., Coord.; Bro. Francisco Tanega, F.M.S.I., Councilor; Rev. Robert Rivard, F.M.S.I., Councilor.

Professed 6

Represented in the Archdiocese of Boston. Also in the Philippines.

[1280] (C.S.S.)—STIGMATINE FATHERS AND BROTHERS

(Congregation of the Sacred Stigmata)

General Motherhouse: Via Mazzarino No. 16, Rome, Italy, Very Rev. Maurizio Baldessari, C.S.S.

North American Province (1940): 554 Lexington St., Waltham, MA 02452. Tel: 781-209-3100; Fax: 781-894-9785. Very Rev. Robert S. White, C.S.S., Prov. Supr.

Legal Title: Stigmatine Fathers & Brothers, Inc.

Priests 14

Properties owned, staffed or sponsored: Parishes 2; Retreat & Conference Center.

Represented in the Archdiocese of Boston and in the Dioceses of Springfield in Massachusetts and Worcester.

[1290] (P.S.S.)—SOCIETY OF THE PRIESTS OF SAINT SULPICE

(Societas Presbyterorum a S. Sulpitio)

General Motherhouse: 6 rue du Regard, Paris 75006, France, Very Rev. Ronald D. Witherup, P.S.S., Supr. Gen.

U.S. Provincial House: 5408 Roland Ave., Baltimore, MD 21210. Tel: 410-323-5070; Fax: 410-433-6524. Rev. John C. Kemper, P.S.S., Prov.; Carleen P. Kramer, Exec. Asst. to Prov.; Rev. Anthony J. Pogorelc, P.S.S., Dir., Initial Formation; Rev. John W. Lothamer, P.S.S., Prov. Treas.; Rev. Richard M. Gula, P.S.S., Dir. Personnel.

Legal Title: The Associated Sulpicians of the United States, Inc.

Fathers 66

Represented in the Archdioceses of Baltimore, San Antonio, San Francisco and Washington and in the Dioceses of Pittsburgh and Wilmington. Also in Paris, France & Rome. Missions: Lusaka, Zambia and Kachebere, Malawi.

[1300] (C.R.)—THEATINE FATHERS

(Congregatio Clericorum Regularium)

General Motherhouse: Sant' Andrea della Valle, Piazza Vidoni, 6 00186, Rome, Italy, Very Rev. Valentin Arteaga, C.R.

U.S. Headquarters: 1050 S. Birch St., Denver, CO 80246. Tel: 303-757-4280. Very Rev. Antonio Flores, C.R.

Fathers 17; Clerics: 5

Parishes 9; House of Formation 1; Provincial House 1.

Represented in the Archdioceses of Denver and New York and in the Diocese of Pueblo.

[1310] (O.SS.T.)—THE ORDER OF THE MOST HOLY TRINITY AND OF THE CAPTIVES

(Holy Trinity Fathers, Inc.)
(Ordo Sanctissimae Trinitatis; The Trinitarians)

Founded in France in 1198 by St. John de Matha for the ransom of Christian slaves. First settlement in the United States in 1911.

General Curia: Via Massimi, 114/C, 00136, Rome, Italy, Most Rev. Jose T. Narlaly, O.SS.T., Min. Gen.; Very Rev. Albert M. Anuszewski, O.SS.T., Gen Councilor, Economer Gen.

U.S.A. Province (1950): Province of the Immaculate Heart of Mary, P.O. Box 5719, Baltimore, MD 21282-5719. Tel: 410-486-5171. Very Rev. William J. Axe, O.SS.T., Min. Prov. Councilors: Very Rev. Juan Molina, O.SS.T., Vicar Prov. & Councilor; Very Rev. Thomas H. Dymowski, O.SS.T., Councilor; Very Rev. Francis H. Whatley, O.SS.T., Councilor; Very Rev. James R. Day, O.SS.T., Councilor; Rev. Kurt J. Klismet, O.SS.T., Prov. Treas.; Rev. Victor J. Scocco, O.SS.T., Prov. Sec.

Trinitarian Communities in the U.S: 10; Fathers 31; Brothers 2

Ministries in 7 parishes; Seminary Facility Positions; High Schools; Prison Chaplaincies; Hospital Chaplaincies; India Foundation; Mission for Persecuted Christians.

Properties owned: DeMatha Catholic High School, Hyattsville, MD; Holy Trinity Monastery, Pikesville, MD; Trinitarian Residence, Ellicott, MD; Trinitarian Residence, Adelphi, MD; Domus Trinitatis, San Antonio, TX.

Represented in the Archdioceses of Baltimore, Miami and San Antonio and in the Dioceses of Las Vegas and Trenton.

[1320] (C.S.V.)—CLERICS OF ST. VIATOR

(Congregatio Clericorum Sancti Viatoris)

General Motherhouse: Centre Louis Querbes, 3, rue Louis-Querbes, 69390, Vourles, France, Very Rev. Robert M. Egan, C.S.V., Supr. Gen.

Province of Chicago (1882): 1212 E. Euclid Ave., Arlington Heights, IL 60004. Tel: 847-398-1354. Rev. Daniel R. Hall, C.S.V., Prov.; Bro. Michael T. Gosch, C.S.V., Asst. Prov.; Rev. Mark R. Francis, C.S.V., Councilor; Rev. Daniel J. Lydon, C.S.V., Councilor; Bro. Rob Robertson, C.S.V., Councilor.

Fathers 50; Brothers 18

Properties owned, staffed or sponsored: Parishes 9; High Schools 3; Formation Houses 2.

Represented in the Archdiocese of Chicago and in the Dioceses of Joliet, Las Vegas, Peoria, Rockford and San Bernardino. Also in Colombia and France.

[1330] (C.M.)—CONGREGATION OF THE MISSION

(Vincentians)
(Congregatio Missionis Sti. Vincentii a Paulo)

Founded in France in 1625. First foundation in the United States in 1818.

General Motherhouse: Curia Generalizia, Via dei Capasso, 30 00164, Roma, Italy, Very Rev. Tomaz Mavric, C.M., Supr. Gen.; Rev. Paul Parackal, C.M., Econome Gen.

Eastern Province of the U.S.A. (1888): St. Vincent's Seminary, 500 E. Chelten Ave., Philadelphia, PA 19144. Tel: 215-713-2400; Fax: 215-844-2085. Very Rev. Stephen M. Grozio, C.M., Prov.; Rev. Thomas F. McKenna, C.M., Asst. Prov.; Rev. Elmer Bauer III, C.M., Prov. Treas.; Mr. Allen Andrews, Exec. Dir. Finance. Consultors: Rev. Gregory P. Cozzubbo, C.M.; Rev. Aidan R. Rooney, C.M.; Rev. Bernard M. Tracey, C.M.

Legal Title: Congregation of the Mission of St. Vincent de Paul in Germantown, Inc.

Priests 101; Brothers 5; College Seminarians: 13

Properties owned, sponsored or staffed: Parishes 9; Missions in Republic of Panama 5; Universities 2; Novitiates 2.

Represented in the Archdioceses of Baltimore, Mobile, New York and Philadelphia and in the Dioceses of Albany, Allentown, Brooklyn, Buffalo, Charlotte and Rockville Centre.

Western Province of the U.S.A. (1888): 13663 Rider Tr. N., Earth City, MO 63045-1512. Tel: 314-344-1184; Fax: 314-344-2989. Very Rev. Raymond Van Dorpe, C.M., Prov.; Rev. Joseph S. Williams, C.M., Asst. Prov.

Legal Title: Congregation of the Mission Western Province (The Vincentians); Congregation of the Mission Western Province, Texas; Congregation of the Mission Western Province, Louisiana; Congregation of the Mission Western Province, California.

Priests 125; Brothers 15; Permanent Deacons 1

Serving in 20 U.S. (Arch)Dioceses; Universities; Foreign Mission Stations; Houses of Apostolic Activity; Parishes; Home Mission Parishes; Seminaries; Retreat/Evangelization Centers.

Represented in the Archdioceses of Anchorage, Chicago, Denver, Kansas City in Kansas, Los Angeles, Milwaukee, New Orleans, Saint Louis and San Antonio and in the Dioceses of Albany, Arlington, Brooklyn, Dallas, Evansville, Gallup, Little Rock, Phoenix, San Jose and Stockton. Also in France, Italy and Kenya.

The New England Province of the Vincentian Fathers (1975): DePaul Vincentian Provincial Residence, 234 Keeney St., Manchester, CT 06040-7048. Tel: 860-643-2828; Fax: 860-533-9462. Very Rev. Gregorz Marek Sadowski, C.M., Prov.

Fathers 20; Brothers 1

Legal Title: New England Province of the Congregation of the Mission, Inc.; Charitable Trust of the New England Province of the Congregation of the Mission.

Represented in the Archdiocese of Hartford and in the Dioceses of Brooklyn and Manchester.

American Italian Branch (Naples, Italy) (1922): Our Lady of Pompei Church, 3600 Claremont St., Baltimore, MD 21224. Tel: 410-675-7790. Rev. Luigi Esposito, Supr.

Represented in the Archdiocese of Baltimore.

[1335] (V.C.)—VINCENTIAN CONGREGATION

(Vincentians)

Founded by Rev. Fr. Varkey Kattarath at Thottakom, Kerala, India in 1904.

Generalate: Vincentian Generalate, P.O. Box No. 2250 - Edappally Kochi 682 024, Kerala, India, Very Rev. Sebastian Thundathikunnel, V.C., Supr. Gen.

St. Joseph Province: Vincentian Provincial House, S.H. Mount P.O. Kottayam 686 006, Kerala, India, Tel: 481-256-3559. Very Rev. Mathew Kakkattupillil, V.C., Prov. Supr.

North American Headquarters: Vincentian House, 1027 Twin Oaks St., Bensenville, IL 60106. Tel: 630-422-5236. Email: vcsjprovince@gmail.com. Rev. Joseph Perumpanani, V.C., Reg. Coord.; Rev. Joseph J. Arackal, V.C., Mission Procurator; Rev. Johnus Cherunilath, V.C., Assoc. Mission Procurator.

Fathers 6

Represented in the Dioceses of St. Cloud and St. Thomas Syro-Malabar Catholic Diocese of Chicago.

[1340] (S.D.V.)—VOCATIONIST FATHERS

(The Society of Divine Vocations)

Generali: Via Cortina D'Ampezzo, 140 00135, Rome, Italy, Tel: 011 39 06 33 12725; Fax: 011 39 06 33 12758. Rev. Antonio Rafael do Nascimento, S.D.V., Supr. Gen.

American Headquarters: 90 Brooklake Rd., Florham Park, NJ 07932. Tel: 973-966-6262; Fax: 973-845-2996. Rev. Louis Caputo, S.D.V., U.S.A. Delegate.

[1350] (C.F.X.)—BROTHERS OF ST. FRANCIS XAVIER

(Congregatio Fratrum Xaverianorum)

Generalate - Xaverian Brothers 4409 Frederick Ave., Baltimore, MD 21229. Tel: 410-644-0034; Fax: 410-644-2762. Email: lharvey@xaverianbrothers.org Bro. Edward Driscoll, C.F.X., Gen. Supr.; Bro. John Hamilton, C.F.X., Vicar; Bro. Paul Murray, C.F.X., Gen. Councilor for the U.S.; Mr. Christopher Irr, Coord. Membership; Bro. Jerimiah O'Leary, C.F.X., Coord. Peace & Justice; Dr. Patrick J. Slattery, Exec. Dir. Xaverian Brothers Sponsored Schools; Mrs. Rhonda Tully, C.F.O.

Brothers 200

Legal Titles: Xaverian Brothers U.S.A. Inc.; Isidore Charitable Trust; Paul van Gerwen Religious & Charitable Trust.

Ministries in the field of: Religious and Academic Education at all levels; Diocesan Offices; Pastoral Ministry; Mission Schools; Communities; Houses and House of Formation.

Represented in the Archdioceses of Baltimore, Boston, Chicago, Louisville and Washington and in the Dioceses of Brooklyn, Charleston, Norwich, Richmond, Springfield, Syracuse, Venice and Worcester. Also in Bolivia, Belgium, Congo, England, Haiti, Kenya and Lithuania.

[1360] (S.X.)—XAVERIAN MISSIONARY FATHERS

(Saint Francis Xavier Foreign Mission Society)

(Pia Societas Sancti Francisci Xaverii pro Exteris Missionibus)

General Motherhouse: Istituto Saveriano Missioni Estere, Viale Vaticano 40 00165, Rome, Italy, Very Rev. Fernando Garcia Rodriquez, S.X., Supr. Gen.

U.S. Province: Xaverian Missionary Fathers, 12 Helene Ct.,Wayne, NJ 07470. Tel: 973-942-2975; Fax: 973-942-5012. Emails: wayne@xaverianmissionaries.org; provincial@xaverianmissionaries.org. Very Rev. Mark Marangone, S.X., Prov.

Fathers 13

Mission House 1; Houses of Formation 2.

Represented in the Archdioceses of Boston and Milwaukee and in the Diocese of Paterson.

Index for Religious Institutes of Women

(The initial D or P indicates Diocesan or Pontifical Jurisdiction.)

Religious Order Initials for Women

A.B.S.	Auxiliaries of the Blessed Sacrament	[]
A.C.J.	Handmaids of the Sacred Heart of Jesus	[1870]
A.D.	Sisters of the Lamb of God	[2260]
A.I.M.	Association of Mary Immaculate	[]
A.N.G.	A New Genesis	[]
A.P.	Nuns of Perpetual Adoration of Blessed Sacrament	[3190]
A.P.B.	Adorers of the Precious Blood	[0110]
A.P.G.	Sisters of Perpetual Adoration	[3195]
A.R.	Handmaids of Reparation of the Sacred Heart of Jesus	[1880]
A.R.	Augustinian Recollects	[]
A.S.C.	Adorers of the Blood of Christ	[0100]
A.S.C.J.	Apostles of the Sacred Heart of Jesus	[0130]
B.C.	Notre Dame du Bon Conseil (Quebec)	[]
Bethl.	Bethlemita, Daughter of the Sacred Heart of Jesus	[0910]
B.V.M.	Sisters of Charity of Blessed Virgin Mary	[0430]
B.V.M.C.	Blessed Virgin Missionaries of Carmel	[]
C.a.Ch.	Carmelite Sisters of Charity	[0340]
Carmel.D.C.J.	Carmelite Sisters of the Divine Heart of Jesus	[0360]
C.B.S.	Congregation of Bon Secours	[0270]
C.C.	Carmel Community	[0310]
C.C.V.I.	Sisters of Charity of Incarnate Word	[0460]
CCVI	Sisters of Charity of Incarnate Word (Houston, TX)	[0470]
C.C.W.	Carmelite Community of the Word	[0315]
C.D.P.	Sisters of Divine Providence	[0990]
C.D.P.	Sisters of Divine Providence of Melbourne, Kentucky	[1000]
C.D.P.	Sisters of Divine Providence of San Antonio, TX	[1010]
C.D.P.	Capuchin Sisters (Spain)	[]
C.D.S.	Congregation of Divine Spirit	[1040]
C.F.M.M.	Minim Daughters of Mary Immaculate	[2675]
C.F.P.	Feminine Congregation of the Passion	[]
C.F.P.	Mexican Passionist Sisters	[]
C.G.S.	Contemplatives of Good Shepherd	[1830]
C.H.F.	Sisters of Holy Faith	[1940]
C.H.M.	Congregation of Humility of Mary	[2100]
C.H.S.	Community of the Holy Spirit	[2020]
C.I.C.	Sisters of Immaculate Conception	[2120]
C.I.J.	Congregation of Infant Jesus	[2230]
C.J.C.	Poor Sisters of Jesus Crucified and Sorrowful Mother	[3240]
C.K.	School Sisters of Christ the King	[]
C.L.H.C.	Congregation of Our Lady Help of the Clergy	[3090]
C.M.C.	Congregation of Mother of Carmel	[]
C.M.R.	Congregation of Mary, Queen	[0397]
C.M.S.	Comboni Missionary Sisters	[0690]
C.M.S.	Cashel Mercy Sisters	[2515]
C.M.S.T.	Missionary Carmelites of St. Teresa	[0390]
C.N.D.	Congregation De Notre Dame	[2980]
C.O.C.	Companions of Christ	[]
C.P.	Religious of the Passion of Jesus Christ	[3170]
C.P.	Sisters of the Cross and Passion	[3180]
C.P.C.	Capuchin Poor Clares	[]
C.P.C.	St. Clare Capuchin Sisters	[]
C.P.P.S.	Sisters of the Precious Blood Dayton, Ohio	[3260]
C.P.P.S.	Sisters of the Most Precious Blood, (O'Fallon, MO)	[3270]
C.P.S.	Missionary Sisters of the Precious Blood	[2850]
C.R.	Sisters of the Resurrection	[3480]
C.S.	Company of the Savior	[0710]
C.S.	The Christian Sisters (Pious Union)	[]
C.S.A.	Sisters of Charity of St. Augustine	[0580]
C.S.A.	Sisters of St. Agnes	[3710]
C.S.A.	Albertine Sisters (Krakow, Poland)	[]
C.S.A.C.	Sisters of the Catholic Apostolate (Pallottine)	[3140]
C.S.B.	Congregation of St. Brigid	[3735]
C.S.C.	Congregation of Sisters of Holy Cross	[1920]
C.S.C.	Sisters of Holy Cross	[1930]
C.S.C.	Sisters of Holy Cross and Seven Dolors	[]
C.S.E.	Carmelite Sisters of the Eucharist	[]
C.S.F.N.	Sisters of Holy Family of Nazareth	[1970]
C.S.J.	Hermanas Carmelitas de San Jose	[1895]
C.S.J.	Sisters of St. Joseph	[3830]
C.S.J.	Sisters of St. Joseph (Boston, Brighton)	[3830-01]
C.S.J.	Sisters of St. Joseph (Orange)	[3830-03]
C.S.J.	Sisters of St. Joseph (Rockville Centre, Brentwood)	[3830-05]
C.S.J.	Sisters of St. Joseph (Pittsburgh, Baden)	[3830-13]
C.S.J.	Sisters of St. Joseph (Salina, Concordia)	[3830-15]
C.S.J.	Sisters of St. Joseph (Wichita)	[3830-18]
C.S.J.	Congregation of the Sisters of St. Joseph	[3832]
C.S.J.	Sisters of St. Joseph of Carondelet	[3840]
C.S.J.	Sisters of St. Joseph of Chambery	[3850]
C.S.J.	Sisters of St. Joseph (Lyons, France)	[3870]
C.S.J.	Sisters of St. Joseph of Medaille	[3880]
C.S.JB.	Sisters of St. John the Baptist	[3820]
C.S.J.P.	Sisters of St. Joseph of Peace	[3890]
C.S.M.	Sisters of St. Martha of Antigonish N.S	[3937]
C.S.N.	Congregation of Sisters of Nazareth	[3242]
C.S.R.	Sisters of Holy Redeemer	[2000]
C.S.S.F.	Felician Sisters	[1170]
C.S.Sp.	Sisters of Holy Spirit	[2030]
C.S.S.T.	Carmelite Sisters of St. Teresa	[]
C.S.T.	Carmelite Sisters of St. Therese of Infant Jesus	[0380]
C.V.D.	Sisters of Bethany	[0250]
C.V.I.	Congregation of Incarnate Word and Blessed Sacrament	[2190]
C.V.I.	Religious of the Incarnate Word	[3449]
D.C.	Daughters of Charity of St. Vincent de Paul	[0760]
D.C.M.	Diocesan Carmelites of Maine	[]
D.C.P.B.	Daughters of Charity of Most Precious Blood	[0740]
D.D.L.	Daughters of Divine Love	[0793]
D.H.M.	Daughters of Heart of Mary	[0810]
D.H.S.	Daughters of the Holy Spirit	[0820]
D.L.F.	Daughters of Our Lady of Fatima	[]
D.L.J.C.	Disciples of the Lord Jesus Christ	[0965]
D.M.	Daughters of Mary of the Immaculate Conception	[0860]
D.M.	Daughters of Our Lady of Mercy	[0890]
D.M.I.	Daughters of Mary Immaculate (Chaldean)	[]
D.M.J.	Daughters of Mary and Joseph	[0880]
D.M.M.M.	Daughters of Mary Mother of Mercy	[0885]
D.O.M.	Daughters of Mercy (Croatian)	[]
D.S.F.	Daughters of St. Francis of Assisi	[0920]
D.S.M.P.	Daughters of St. Mary of Providence	[0940]
D.W.	Daughters of Wisdom	[0960]
E.F.M.S.	Eucharistic Franciscan Missionary Sisters	[1150]
E.I.N.	Servants of the Immaculate Child Mary	[3615]
E.M.S.	Eucharistic Missionary Society	[]
F.A.S.	Franciscan Apostolic Sisters	[]
F.C.	Daughters of the Cross of Liege	[0780]
F.C.J.	Society of Sisters Faithful Companions of Jesus	[4048]
F.C.S.C.J.	Daughters of Charity of the Sacred Heart of Jesus	[0750]
F.D.C.	Daughters of Divine Charity	[0790]
Fd.CC.	Canossian Daughters of Charity	[0730]
F.D.L.P.	Daughters of Providence	[]
F.D.N.S.C.	Daughters of Our Lady of the Sacred Heart	[0900]
F.D.P.	Daughters of Divine Providence	[0800]
F.D.Z.	Daughters of Divine Zeal	[0795]
F.H.I.C.	Franciscan Hospitaller Sisters of the Immaculate Conception	[1270]
F.H.M.	Franciscan Handmaids of the Most Pure Heart of Mary	[1260]
F.H.M.	Franciscan Sisters Daughters of Mercy	[1235]
F.J.	Congregation of the Daughters of Jesus	[0830]
F.L.G.	Franciscan Sisters of Our Lady of Grace	[]
F.M.A.	Daughters of Mary Help of Christians	[0850]
F.M.I.	Congregation of the Daughters of Mary Immaculate (Marianist Sisters)	[0870]
F.M.I.	Franciscan Sisters of Mary Immaculate of the Third Order of St. Francis of Assisi	[1500]
F.M.I.J.	Franciscan Missionaries of the Infant Jesus	[1365]
F.M.M.	The Franciscan Missionaries of Mary	[1370]
F.M.S.A.	Franciscan Missionary Sisters for Africa	[1320]
F.M.S.C.	Franciscan Missionary Sisters of the Sacred Heart	[1400]
F.M.S.J.	Mill Hill Sisters	[1410]
F.M.S.R.	Daughters of Our Lady of Holy Rosary	[0895]
F.N.S.S.C.	Franciscan Sisters of Our Lady of the Sacred Heart	[]
F.S.E.	Franciscan Sisters of the Eucharist, Inc.	[1250]
F.S.G.M.	Sisters of St. Francis of the Martyr St. George	[1600]
F.S.J.	Religious Daughters of St. Joseph	[0930]
F.S.M.	Franciscan Sisters of Mary	[1415]
F.S.O.L.	Franciscan Sisters of Our Lady	[]
F.S.P.	Pious Society Daughters of St. Paul	[0950]
F.S.P.	Franciscan Sisters of Peace	[1425]
F.S.P.A.	Congregation of the Sisters of the Third Order of St. Francis of Perpetual Adoration	[1780]
F.S.R.	Franciscan Sisters of Ringwood	[1420]
F.S.S.C.	Franciscan Sisters of St. Clare (Pious Union)	[]
F.S.S.E.	Franciscan Sisters of St. Elizabeth	[1460]
F.S.S.J.	Franciscan Sisters of St. Joseph	[1470]
F S.S.M.	Franciscan Sisters of the Sorrowful Mother	[]
F.S.Sp.J.	Franciscan Sisters of the Spirit of Jesus	[]
G.H.M.S.	Home Mission Sisters of America (Glenmary)	[2080]
G.N.S.H.	Grey Nuns of the Sacred Heart	[1840]

H.B.S. Hermanas Contemplativas del Buen Pastor []

H.C.G. Hermanas Catequistas Guadalupanas [1900]

H.F.deS.J. Franciscan Sisters of St. Joseph (Mexico City) []

H.F.S.J. Franciscan Sisters of St. Joseph [1480]

H.G.S. Congregation de Hermanas Guadalupanas de la Salle []

H.H.C.J. Congregation of the Handmaids of the Holy Child Jesus [1855]

H.H.S. Society of Helpers [1890]

H.J. Hermanas Josefinas [1910]

H.J.D. Las Hermanas de Juan Diego []

H.M. Sisters of the Humility of Mary [2110]

H.M.C. Hermits of Mount Carmel []

H.M.S.S. Mercedarian Sisters of the Blessed Sacrament [2590]

H.M.S.S. Religious Sisters of the Apostolate of the Blessed Sacrament [3370]

H.O.Carm. Hermits of Our Lady of Mt. Carmel []

H.P.B. Congregation of the Handmaids of the Precious Blood [1860]

H.R.F. Sisters of the Holy Rosary of Fatima (Mexico) []

H.S.H. Handmaids of the Sacred Heart of Pohang []

H.S.M. Hermit Sisters of Mary []

H.Sp.S. Daughters of the Holy Spirit Nazareth of the Good Shepherd []

H.S.S. Hermanas del Servicio Social []

H.S.S.R. Hermit Sisters of Romuald []

H.T. Handmaids of the Most Holy Trinity []

H.V.M. Sisters, Home Visitors of Mary [2090]

I.B.V.M. Institute of the Blessed Virgin Mary (Loretto Sisters) [2370]

I.B.V.M. Institute of the Blessed Virgin Mary (Loretto Sisters) [2380]

I.C. Vietnamese Sisters Incarnational Consecration []

I.C.M. Incarnatio-Consecratio-Missio [2187]

I.C.M. Missionary Sisters of the Immaculate Heart of Mary [2750]

I.H.M.M. Sisters of the Immaculate Heart of Mary at Mirinae [2182]

I.H.M. Sisters of the Immaculate Heart of Mary Mother of Christ [2183]

I.H.M. Sisters Servants of the Immaculate Heart of Mary [2150]

I.H.M. Sisters Servants of the Immaculate Heart of Mary [2160]

I.H.M. Sisters Servants of the Immaculate Heart of Mary [2170]

I.H.M. Sisters Servants of the Immaculate Heart of Mary [2180]

I.H.M. The California Institute of the Sisters of the Most Holy and Immaculate Heart of the Blessed Virgin Mary [2930]

I.H.M. Sisters of the Immaculate Heart of Mary of Wichita [2185]

I.J. Sisters of the Infant Jesus [2240]

I.M. Sisters of Charity of the Infant Mary []

I.S.S.M. Secular Institute of Schoenstatt Sisters of Mary []

I.W.B.S. Sisters of the Incarnate Word and Blessed Sacrament [2200]

I.W.B.S. Congregation of the Incarnate Word and Blessed Sacrament [2205]

J.S.O.P. Dominican Oblates of Jesus (Spain) []

L.B. Ladies of Bethany []

L.C.M. Sisters of the Little Company of Mary [2270]

L.H.C.N.T. Lovers of the Holy Cross Nha Trang [2385]

L.H.C. Lovers of the Holy Cross Sisters [2390]

L.H.C. Lovers of the Holy Cross Sisters [2392]

L.M.S.C. Little Missionary Sisters of Charity [2290]

L.S. Lasallian Sisters (Vietnam) []

L.S.A. Little Sisters of the Assumption [2310]

L.S.G. Little Sisters of the Gospel (France) [2315]

L.S.I.C. Little Servant Sisters of the Immaculate Conception [2300]

L.S.J. Little Sisters of Jesus [2330]

L.S.J.M. Little Sisters of Jesus and Mary [2331]

L.S.P. Little Sisters of the Poor [2340]

M.C. Consolata Missionary Sisters [0720]

M.C. Missionaries of Charity [2710]

M.C. Poor Clare Missionary Sisters [2840]

M.C.D.P. Missionary Catechists of Divine Providence, San Antonio, TX [2690]

M.Ch.R. Missionary Sisters of Christ the King for Polonia [2715]

M.C.M. Cordi Marian Sisters [0725]

M.C.P. Missioneras Catequestas de los Pobres []

M.C.S. Missionary Sisters of the Sacred Side []

M.C.S.J.M. Congregation of Missionary Catechists of the Sacred Heart of Jesus and Mary []

M.D. Mothers of the Helpless [2920]

M.D.P.V.M. Missionary Daughters of the Most Pure Virgin Mary [2717]

M.E. Missionary Ecumenical (Rome) []

M.C.S.H. Missionary Catechists of the Sacred Hearts of Jesus and Mary [2700]

M.E.S.S.T. Eucharistic Missionaries of the Most Holy Trinity []

M.E.S.T. Eucharistic Missionaries of St. Theresa (Mexico) []

M.F.I.C. Missionary Franciscan Sisters of the Immaculate Conception [1360]

M.F.P. Franciscan Missionaries Our Lady of Peace []

M.G.Sp.S. Missionaries Guadalupanas of the Holy Spirit [1845]

M.H.S. Sisters of the Most Holy Sacrament [2940]

M.H.S.H. Mission Helpers of the Sacred Heart [2720]

M.I.C. Missionary Sisters of the Immaculate Conception (Canada) []

M.J. Missionary Sisters of Jesus []

M.J.M.J. Missionaries of Jesus, Mary and Joseph [2770]

M.M. Maryknoll Sisters of St. Dominic [2470]

M.M.B. Mercedarian Missionaries of Berriz [2510]

M.M.D. Servite Missionary Sisters of the Sorrowful Mother []

M.M.M. Medical Missionaries of Mary [2480]

M.M.S. Medical Mission Sisters [2490]

M.O.M. Missionary Sisters of Our Lady of Mercy [2830]

M.P.F. Religious Teachers Filippini [3430]

M.P.H. Missionary Sisters of Our Lady of Perpetual Help []

M.P.S. Misioneras del Perpetual Socorro []

M.P.S. Missionary Sisters of Our Lady of Perpetual Help []

M.P.V. Religious Venerini Sisters [4180]

M.R. Marianist Sisters []

M.S. Marian Sisters of the Diocese of Lincoln [2400]

M.S.B.T. Missionary Servants of the Most Blessed Trinity [2790]

M.S.C. Congregation of the Marianites of the Holy Cross [2410]

M.S.C. Missionary Sisters of the Most Sacred Heart of Jesus of Hiltrup [2800]

M.S.C. Missionary Sisters of the Sacred Heart [2860]

M.S.C.Gpe. Missionaries of the Sacred Heart of Jesus and of Our Lady of Guadalupe [2865]

M.S.C.K. Missionary Sisters of Christ the King [2715]

M.S.E. Missionary Sisters of the Eucharist [2725]

M.S.F. Missionary Sisters of the Holy Family []

M.S.H.F. Missionary Sisters of the Holy Family (Poland) []

M.S.H.R. Missionary Sisters of the Holy Rosary [2730]

M.S.J. Medical Sisters of St. Joseph [2500]

M.S.K.C.P. Missionary Sisters of Christ the King of Polonia []

M.S.M.G. Missionary Sisters of Mother of God [2810]

M.S.O.L.A. Missionary Sisters of Our Lady of Africa [2820]

M.S.S.A. Missionary Servants of St. Anthony [2890]

M.S.C.S. Missionary Sisters of St. Charles Borromeo [2900]

M.S.S.J. Missionary Servants of St. Joseph (Spain) []

M.S.Sp. Mission Sisters of the Holy Spirit [2740]

M.SS.S. Missionary Sisters of the Most Blessed Sacrament [2780]

M.T.G. Adorers of the Holy Cross [4155]

M.V.Z. Sisters of Charity of St. Vincent de Paul of Zagreb [0630

M.X.Y. The Yarumal Foreign Mission Institute (Colombia) []

N.D. Notre Dame Sisters [2960]

N.D.S. Congregation of Notre Dame de Sion [2950]

O.A.R. Augustinian Recollect Sisters []

O.B.T. Sisters Oblates to the Blessed Trinity [3020]

O.C.A. Carmelite Vietnamese of Our Lady of Mt. Carmel []

O.Carm. Calced Carmelites [0300]

O.Carm. Carmelite Nuns of the Ancient Observance [0320]

O.Carm. Carmelite Sisters for Aged and Infirm [0330]

O.Carm. Carmelite Sisters (Corpus Christi) [0350]

O.Carm. Congregation of Our Lady of Mt. Carmel [0400]

O.Carm. Institute of the Sisters of Our Lady of Mt. Carmel [0410]

O.C.D. Carmelite Sisters of the Most Sacred Heart of Los Angeles [0370]

O.C.D. Discalced Carmelite Nuns [0420]

O.C.D. Carmelitas del Sagrado Corazon []

O.Cist. Cistercian Nuns [0680]

O.C.S.O. Cistercian Nuns of the Strict Observance [0670]

O.D.N. Company of Mary [0700]

O.L.C. Sisters of Our Lady of Charity [3071]

O.L.C. Sisters of Our Lady of Charity [3073]

O.L.G. Sisters of Our Lady of the Garden []

O.L.L. Sisters of Our Lady of Lourdes []

O.L.M. Sisters of Charity of Our Lady of Mercy [0510]

O.L.S. Sisters of Our Lady of Sorrows [3120]

O.L.V.M. Our Lady of Victory Missionary Sisters [3130

O.M.M.I. Oblate Missionaries of Mary Immaculate [

O.M.O. Oblates of the Mother of Orphans [3035

O.P. Collaborative Dominican Novitiate Dominican Sisters [1070

O.P. The Congregation of the Dominican Sisters of Our Lady of the Springs of Bridgeport CT [1025

O.P. Dominican Contemplative Nuns (Cloistered) [1050

O.P. Dominican Contemplative Sisters (Cloistered) [1060

O.P. Dominican Sisters (Sinsinawa, WI) [1070-03

O.P. Dominican Sisters (San Rafael, CA) [1070-04

O.P.	Dominican Sisters (Amityville, NY)	[1070-05]
O.P.	Dominican Sisters (Newburgh, NY)	[1070-06]
O.P.	Dominican Sisters (Nashville, TN)	[1070-07]
O.P.	Dominican Sisters (Racine, WI)	[1070-09]
O.P.	Dominican Sisters (Springfield, IL)	[1070-10]
O.P.	Dominican Sisters (Sparkill, NY)	[1070-11]
O.P.	Dominican Sisters (Fremont, CA)	[1070-12]
O.P.	Dominican Sisters (Adrian, MI)	[1070-13]
O.P.	Dominican Sisters (Grand Rapids, MI)	[1070-14]
O.P.	Dominican Sisters (Blauvelt, NY)	[1070-15]
O.P.	Dominican Sisters (Ossining, NY)	[1070-16]
O.P.	Dominican Sisters (Columbus, OH)	[1070-17]
O.P.	Dominican Sisters (Caldwell, NJ)	[1070-18]
O.P.	Dominican Sisters (Houston, TX)	[1070-19]
O.P.	Dominican Sisters (Tacoma, WA)	[1070-20]
O.P.	Dominican Sisters (Edmonds, WA)	[1070-21]
O.P.	Dominican Sisters (Fall River, MA)	[1070-22]
O.P.	Dominican Sisters (Hawthorne, NY)	[1070-23]
O P.	Dominican Sisters (Saratoga, CA)	[1070-25]
O.P.	Dominican Sisters (Justice, IL)	[1070-27]
O.P.	Dominican Sisters (Spokane, WA)	[1070-29]
O.P.	Dominican Sisters of Oakford	[1070-30]
O.P.	Marian Society of Dominican Catechists	[1090]
O.P.	Dominican Sisters of Charity of the Presentation of the Blessed Virgin	[1100]
O.P.	Dominican Sisters of Hope	[1105]
O.P.	Dominican Sisters of Our Lady of the Rosary and of Saint Catherine of Siena, Cabra	[1110]
O.P.	Dominican Sisters of Peace	[1115]
O.P.	Dominican Sisters of the Roman Congregation	[1120]
O.P.	Dominican Rural Missionaries	[1130]
O.P.	Dominican Sisters of Carondelet	[]
O.P.	Religious Missionaries of St. Dominic (Spanish Prov.)	[1145]
O.P.	Dominican Sisters of Mt. Thabor	[]
O.P.	Dominican Sisters of Our Lady of the Most Holy Rosary	[]
O.P.	Dominican Sisters (Vietnam)	[]
O.P.	Dominican Contemplative Sisters	[]
O.P.	Dominican Sisters (Colombia)	[]
O.P.	Dominican Sisters (Ecuador)	[]
O.P.	Hermanas Dominicanas de la Doctrine Cristiana	[]
O.S.A.	Augustinian Nuns of Contemplative Life	[0160]
O.S.A.	Congregation of Augustinian Sisters Servants of Jesus and Mary	[2145]
O.S.A.	Sisters of St. Rita	[4010]
O.S.A.	Sisters of St. Augustine	[]
O.S.A.	Augustinian Sisters of Our Lady of Consolation	[]
O.S.B.	Benedictine Nuns of the Congregation of Solesmes	[0170]
O.S.B.	Benedictine Nuns of the Primitive Observance	[0180]
O.S.B.	Benedictine Nuns	[0190]
O.S.B.	Benedictine Sisters	[0200]
O.S.B.	Missionary Benedictine Sisters	[0210]
O.S.B.	Congregation of the Benedictine Sisters of Perpetual Adoration of Pontifical Jurisdiction	[0220]
O.S.B.	Benedictine Sisters of Pontifical Jurisdiction	[0230]
O.S.B.	Benedictine Nuns	[0233]
O.S.B.	Olivetan Benedictine Sisters	[0240]
O.S.B.	Congregation of Jesus Crucified	[2250]
O.S.B.	Benedictine Congregation of Our Lady of Monte	[]
O.S.B.	Benedictine Sisters of Sacred Heart	[]
O.S.B.	Contemplative Sisters of St. Benedict	[]
O.S.B.	Benedictine Sisters of Liberty	[]
O.S.B.	Congregation of the Benedictine Sisters of the Sacred Heart	[]
O.S.B.Cam.	Camaldolese Benedictine Sisters	[0235]
O.S.B.M.	Sisters of the Order of St. Basil the Great	[3730]
O.S.B.S.	Oblate Sisters of the Blessed Sacrament	[3010]
O.S.C.	Order of St. Clare	[3760]
O.S.C.	Sisters of St. Clare	[3770]
O.S.C.Cap.	Capuchin Poor Clares	[3765]
O.S.F.	Franciscan Sisters of Allegany New York	[1180]
O.S.F.	The Franciscan Sisters of Baltimore	[1200]
O.S.F.	Franciscan Sisters of Chicago	[1210]
O.S.F.	Franciscan Sisters of Christian Charity	[1230]
O.S.F.	Franciscan Sisters, Daughters of the Sacred Hearts of Jesus and Mary	[1240]
O.S.F.	Franciscan Sisters of the Immaculate Conception	[1280]
O.S.F.	Franciscan Sisters of the Immaculate Conception and St. Joseph for the Dying	[1300]
O S.F.	Franciscan Sisters of Little Falls, Minnesota	[1310]
O.S.F.	Franciscan Missionary Sisters of the Immaculate Conception	[1350]
O.S.F.	Franciscan Missionaries of Our Lady	[1380]
O.S.F.	Franciscan Missionary Sisters of Our Lady of Sorrows	[1390]
O.S.F.	Franciscan Sisters of Our Lady of Perpetual Help	[1430]
O.S.F.	Franciscan Sisters of the Sacred Heart	[1450]
O.S.F.	Franciscan Sisters of St. Paul, MN	[1485]
O.S.F.	Sisters of the Third Franciscan Order	[1490]
O.S.F.	St. Francis Mission Community	[1505]
O.S.F.	Sisters of St. Francis	[1510]
O.S.F.	Sisters of St. Francis of the Congregation of Our Lady of Lourdes, Sylvania, Ohio	[1530]
O.S.F.	Sisters of Saint Francis, Clinton, Iowa	[1540]
O.S.F.	Sisters of St. Francis of the Holy Cross	[1550]
O.S.F.	Sisters of St. Francis of the Holy Eucharist	[1560]
O.S.F.	Sisters of St. Francis of the Holy Family	[1570]
O.S.F.	Sisters of St. Francis of the Immaculate Conception	[1580]
O.S.F.	Sisters of St. Francis of the Immaculate Heart of Mary (Hankinson, North Dakota)	[1590]
O.S.F.	Sisters of Saint Francis of Millvale, Pennsylvania	[1620]
O.S.F.	Sisters of St. Francis of Penance and Christian Charity	[1630]
O.S.F.	Sisters of St. Francis of Perpetual Adoration	[1640]
O.S.F.	Sisters of St. Francis of the Neumann Communities	[1805]
O.S.F.	The Sisters of St. Francis of Philadelphia	[1650]
O.S.F.	Sisters of Saint Francis of the Providence of God	[1660]
O.S.F.	Sisters of St. Francis of Savannah, MO	[1670]
O.S.F.	School Sisters of St. Francis	[1680]
O.S.F.	School Sisters of the Third Order of St. Francis (Pittsburgh, PA)	[1690]
O.S.F.	School Sisters of the Third Order of St. Francis (Panhandle, TX)	[1695]
O.S.F.	School Sisters of the Third Order of St. Francis (Bethlehem, PA)	[1700]
O.S F.	The Sisters of St. Francis of Assisi	[1705]
O.S.F.	Congregation of the Third Order of St. Francis of Mary Immaculate (Joliet, IL)	[1710]
O.S.F.	Sisters of the Third Order Regular of St. Francis of the Congregation of Our Lady of Lourdes	[1720]
O.S.F.	Congregation of the Sisters of the Third Order of St. Francis (Oldenburg, IN)	[1730]
O.S.F.	Sisters of the Third Order of St. Francis of Penance and Charity	[1760]
O.S.F.	Sisters of the Third Order of St. Francis (Peoria, IL)	[1770]
O.S.F.	Sisters of St. Francis of the Third Order Regular (Williamsville, New York)	[1800]
O.S.F.	Bernardine Sisters of the Third Order of St. Francis	[1810]
O.S.F.	Hospital Sisters of the Third Order of St. Francis	[1820]
O.S.F.	Servants of the Holy Infancy of Jesus	[1980]
O.S.F.	Consolation Sisters (Highland, CA)	[]
O.S.F.	Franciscan Sisters of Christ the Divine Teacher	[]
O.S.F.	St. Francis Mission Community	[]
O.S.F.S.	Oblate Sisters of St. Francis de Sales	[3060]
O.S.H.J.	Oblate Sisters of the Sacred Heart of Jesus	[3050]
O.S.M.	Mantellate Sisters, Servants of Mary of Blue Island	[3570]
O.S.M.	Mantellate Sisters, Servants of Mary of Plainfield	[3572]
O.S.M.	Servants of Mary	[3580]
O.S.M.	Servants of Mary (Servite Sisters)	[3590]
O.S.M.	Oblates of St. Martha	[]
O.S.P.	Oblate Sisters of Providence	[3040]
O.S.S.	Sacramentine Nuns	[3490]
O.SS.R.	Order of the Most Holy Redeemer	[2010]
O.SS.R.	Oblates of the Most Holy Redeemer	[3030]
O.SS.S.	The Brigittine Sisters	[0280]
O.SS.T.	Sisters of the Most Holy Trinity	[2060]
O.S.U.	Ursuline Nuns (Roman Union)	[4110]
O.S.U.	Ursuline Nuns of the Congregation of Paris (St. Martin, OH)	[4120]
O.S.U.	Ursuline Nuns of the Congregation of Paris (Cincinnati, OH)	[4120-01]
O.S.U.	Ursuline Nuns of the Congregation of Paris (Louisville, KY)	[4120-03]
O.S.U.	Ursuline Nuns of the Congregation of Paris (Cleveland, OH)	[4120-04]
O.S.U.	Ursuline Nuns of the Congregation of Paris (Owensboro, KY)	[4120-05]
O.S.U.	Ursuline Nuns of the Congregation of Paris (Toledo, OH)	[4120-06]
O.S.U.	Ursuline Nuns of the Congregation of Paris (Youngstown, OH)	[4120-07]
O.S.U.	Ursuline Sisters of the Congregation of Tildonk, Belgium	[4130]
O.S.U.	Irish Ursuline Union	[4150]
P.B.V.M.	Presentation of the Blessed Virgin Mary Sisters	[3280]
P.B.V.M.	Sisters of the Presentation of the B.V.M	[3320]
P B.V.M.	Union of the Sisters of the Presentation of the Blessed Virgin Mary	[3330]
P.C.C.	Order of St. Clare	[3760]
P.C.I.	Pax Christi Institute	[]
P.C.J.	Sisters of the Poor Child Jesus	[3220]
P.C.P.A.	Poor Clares of Perpetual Adoration	[3210]
P.D.D.M.	Pious Disciples of the Divine Master	[0980]
P.F.M.	Franciscans of Mary	[2280]
P.H.J.C.	Poor Handmaids of Jesus Christ	[3230]
P.M.	Sisters of the Presentation of Mary	[3310]
P.O.S.C.	Little Workers of the Sacred Heart	[2345]
P.S.S.F.	The Little Sisters of the Holy Family	[2320]
P.S.S.J.	Poor Sisters of St. Joseph	[3250]
P.V.M.I.	The Parish Visitors of Mary Immaculate	[3160]
R.A.	Religious of the Apostolate of the Sacred Heart	[3380]
R.A.	Religious of the Assumption	[3390]
R.A.	Antonine Sisters	[]
R.A.D.	Sisters of the Love of God	[]
R.C.	Congregation of Our Lady of Retreat in the Cenacle	[3110]
R.C.D.	Sisters of Our Lady of Christian Doctrine	[3080]
R.C.E.	Religious of Christian Education	[3410]
R.C.S.C.J.	Sisters of the Cross of the Sacred Heart of Jesus (Mexico)	[]
R.D.C.	Sisters of the Divine Compassion	[0970]
R.F.	Sisters of St. Philip Neri Missionary Teachers	[]

R.F.R.	Sisters of Our Lady of Refuge	[]
R.G.S.-C.G.S	The Sisters of the Good Shepherd	[1830]
R.H.S.J.	Religious Hospitallers of Saint Joseph	[3440]
R.J.M.	Religious of Jesus and Mary	[3450]
R.M.	Marianitas	[]
R.M.I.	Claretian Missionary Sisters	[0685]
R.M.I.	Religious of Mary Immaculate	[3460]
R.M.M.	Mercedarian Sisters	[]
R.O.D.A.	Sisters Oblates to Divine Love	[]
R.O.L.C.	Our Lady of Charity of Refuge	[3072]
R.S.C.	Religious Sisters of Charity	[3400]
R.S.C.J.	Society of the Sacred Heart	[4070]
R.S.H.M.	Religious of the Sacred Heart of Mary	[3465]
R.S.J.	Religious of St. Joseph of Australia	[]
R.S.M.	Religious Sisters of Mercy of Alma, Michigan	[2519]
R.S.M.	Sisters of Mercy	[2520]
R.S.M.	Sisters of Mercy of Ardagh & Clonmacnois	[2523]
R.S.M.	Sisters of Mercy (Galway)	[2535]
R.S.M.	Sisters of Mercy	[2540]
R.S.M.	Sisters of Mercy (Sligo)	[2549]
R.S.M.	Sisters of Mercy	[2550]
R.S.M.	Sisters of Mercy of the Americas	[2575]
R.S.M.	Sisters of Mercy	[2600]
R.S.M.	Sisters of Mercy (Ballyshannon, Ireland)	[]
R.S.M.	Sisters of Mercy (Mayo, Ireland)	[]
R.S.M.	Sisters of Mercy of Mississippi, Inc.	[]
R.S.M.	Diocesan Sisters of Mercy of Portland	[2655]
R.S.M.	Diocesan Sisters of Mercy	[]
R.S.R.	Congregation of Our Lady of the Holy Rosary	[3100]
R.T.	Theatine Sisters of the Immaculate Conception	[]
R.V.M.	Religious of the Blessed Virgin Mary	[]
S.A.	Franciscan Sisters of the Atonement	[1190]
S.A.A.	Sisters Auxillaries of the Apostolate	[0140]
S.A.B.	Sisters of St. Anne Bangalone	[]
S.A.C.	Sisters of the Guardian Angel	[1850]
S.A.C.	Pallottine Missionary Sisters Queen of Apostles Prov	[3150]
S.A.S.V.	Sisters of the Assumption	[0150]
S.B.S.	The Sisters of the Blessed Sacrament for Indians and Colored People	[0260]
S.C.	Sisters of Charity of Cincinnati, Ohio	[0440]
S.C.	Sisters of Charity of Seton Hill, Greensburg, PA	[0570]
S.C.	Sisters of St. Elizabeth, Convent Station	[0590]
S.C.	Sisters of Charity of St. Vincent de Paul, Halifax	[0640]
S.C.	Sisters of Charity of St. Vincent de Paul, New York	[0650]
S.C.C.	Sisters of Christian Charity	[0660]
Sch.P.	Sisters of the Pious Schools	[3200]
S.C.I.C.	Sisters of Charity of the Immaculate Conception of Ivrea	[0450]
S.C.I.M.	Servants of the Immaculate Heart of Mary	[3550]
S.C.K.	Sisters of Christ the King	[]
S.C.L.	Sisters of Charity of Leavenworth, Kansas	[0480]
S.C.M.C.	Sisters of Charity of Our Lady, Mother of the Church	[0530]
S.C.M.M.	Sisters of Charity of Our Lady Mother of Mercy	[0520]
S.C.M.M.	Medical Mission Sisters	[2490]
S.C.N.	Sisters of Charity of Nazareth	[0500]
S.C.O.	Sisters of Charity of Ottawa (Grey Nuns of the Cross)	[0540]
S.C.Q.	Sisters of Charity of Quebec (Grey Nuns)	[0560]
S.C.R.H.	Sisters of Charity of Rolling Hills	[0565]
S.C.S.C.	Sisters of Mercy of the Holy Cross	[2630]
S.C.S.J.A.	Sisters of Charity of St. Joan Antida	[0600]
S.C.S.L.	Sisters of Charity of St. Louis	[0620]
S.C.S.H.	Sisters of Charity of St. Hyacinthe (Grey Nuns)	[0610]
S.C.V.	Sisters of Charity of St. Vincent de Paul of Suwon	[0655]
S.deM.	Sisters Servants of Mary	[3600]
S.deP.	Sister Servants of the Poor	[]
S.D.R.	Sisters of the Divine Redeemer	[1020]
S.D.S.	Sisters of the Divine Saviour	[1030]
S.D.S.H.	Sisters of the Society Devoted to the Sacred Heart	[4050]
S.D.V.	Vocationist Sisters	[4210]
S.E.	Sisters of Emanuel	[]
S.E.C.	Sisters of the Eucharistic Covenant	[]
S.F.C.C.	Sisters for Christian Community	[]
S.F.M.A.	Franciscan Missionary Sisters of Assisi	[1330]
S.F.P.	Franciscan Sisters of the Poor	[1440]
S.G.M.	Sisters of Charity of Montreal (Grey Nuns)	[0490]
S.G.S.	Hermanas del Buen Pastor	[]
S.H.C.J.	Society of the Holy Child Jesus	[4060]
S.H.F.	Sisters of the Holy Family	[1960]
S.H.J.M.	Sisters of the Sacred Hearts of Jesus and Mary	[3680]
S.H.S.	Sisters of the Holy Spirit	[2040]
S.H.Sp.	Sisters of the Holy Spirit and Mary Immaculate	[2050]
S.I.M.	Missionaries of the Kingship of Christ	[]
S.I.W.	Sisters of the Incarnate Word and the Blessed Sacrament	[2210]
S.J.	Servants of Jesus	[3560]
S.J.A.	Sisters of Ste. Jeanne D'Arc	[3815]
S.J.B.	Sisters of St. John Bosco (Taylor, TX)	[]
S.J.C.	Sisters of St. Joseph of Cluny	[3860]
S.J.S.	Servants of the Blessed Sacrament	[3499]
S.J.S.	Sisters of Jesus the Savior	[2245]
S.J.S.M.	Sisters of St. Joseph of St. Mark	[3910]
S.J.W.	Sisters of St. Joseph the Worker	[3920]
S.L.	Sisters of Loretto at the Foot of the Cross	[2360]
S.L.T.	Pious Society of Our Lady of the Most Holy Trinity	[]
S.L.W.	Sisters of the Living Word	[2350]
S.M.	Sisters of Mercy	[2516]
S.M.	Sisters of Mercy	[2518]
S.M.	Sisters of Mercy	[2570]
S.M.	Misericordia Sisters	[2680]
S.M.	Sisters Servants of Mary	[3600]
S.M.	Sisters of Mercy (Loughrea, Ireland)	[]
S.M.	Sisters of Mercy of Tralee	[]
S.M.G.	Poor Servants of the Mother of God	[3640]
S.M.I.	Sisters of Mary Immaculate	[2440]
S.M.I.C.	Missionary Sisters of the Immaculate Conception of the Mother of God	[2760]
S.M.M.G.	Sisters of Mary, Mother of God	[]
S.M.M.I.	Sisters Minor of the Mary Immaculate	[2677]
S.M.M.S.	Society of Mary Missionary Sisters	[]
S.M.P.	Sisters of Mary of the Presentation	[2450]
S.M.P.	Daughters of Our Mother of Peace	[]
S.M.P.	Society of Our Mother of Peace	[]
S.M.R.	Society of Mary Reparatrix	[2460]
S.M.S.H.	Sisters of Saint Marthe (of St. Hyacinthe)	[3940]
S.M.S.M.	Marist Missionary Sisters	[2420]
S.N.D.	Sisters of Notre Dame	[2990]
S.N.D.deN.	Sisters of Notre Dame de Namur	[3000]
S.N.J.M.	Sisters of the Holy Names of Jesus and Mary	[1990]
S.O.L.M.	Sisters of Our Lady of Mercy	[2670]
S.O.L.P.H.	Sisters of Our Lady of Perpetual Help	[]
S.O.L.T.	Sisters of the Society of Our Lady of the Most Holy Trinity	[3105]
S.P.	Sisters of Providence	[3340]
S.P.	Sisters of Providence	[3350]
S.P.	Sisters of Providence of Saint Mary-of-the-Woods, IN	[3360]
S.P.C.	Sisters of St. Paul of Chartres	[3980]
S.R.	Sisters of Reparation of the Sacred Wounds of Jesus	[3475]
S.R.C.M.	Sisters of Reparation of the Congregation of Mary	[3470]
S.S.A.	Sisters of St. Ann	[3718]
S.S.A.	Sisters of St. Anne	[3720]
S.S.C.	Missionary Sisters of St. Columban	[2880]
S.S.C.	Sisters of St. Casimir	[3740]
S.S.C.	Society of the Sisters of the Church	[]
SS.CC.	Congregation of the Sacred Hearts and of Perpetual Adoration	[3690]
S.S.Ch.	Sisters of St. Chretienne	[3750]
S.S.C.J.	Servants of the Most Sacred Heart of Jesus	[3630]
S.S.C.J.	Sisters of the Sacred Heart of Jesus of Saint Jacut	[3670
S.S.C.K.	Congregation of Sister Servants of Christ the King	[3510]
S.S.C.M.	Servants of the Holy Heart of Mary	[3520]
SS.C.M.	Sisters of Saints Cyril and Methodius	[3780]
S.S.D.	Institute of the Sisters of St. Dorothy	[3790]
S.S.E.	Sisters of St. Elizabeth	[3800]
S.S.F.	Congregation of the Sisters of the Holy Family	[1950]
S.S.F.C.R.-O.S.F.	School Sisters of St. Francis of Christ the King	[1520]
S.S.H.	Sisters Servants of the Most Sacred Heart	[]
S.S.H.J.	Sisters of the Sacred Heart of Jesus	[3658]
S.S.H.J.P.	Servants of the Sacred Heart of Jesus and of the Poor	[3660]
S.S.J.	Servants of St. Joseph	[3595]
S.S.J.	Sisters of St. Joseph (Buffalo)	[3830-06]
S.S.J.	Sisters of St. Joseph (Burlington)	[3830-07]
S.S.J.	Sisters of St. Joseph (Erie)	[3830-09]
S.S.J.	Sisters of St. Joseph (Kalamazoo, Nazareth)	[3830-11]
S.S.J.	Sisters of St. Joseph (Ogdensburg)	[3830-12]
S.S.J.	Sisters of St. Joseph (Rochester)	[3830-14]
S.S.J.	Sisters of St. Joseph, (Springfield, MA)	[3830-16]
S.S.J.	Sisters of St. Joseph (Wheeling, Eng)	[3830-17]
S.S.J.	Sisters of Saint Joseph of Chestnut Hill, Philadelphia	[3893
S.S.J.	Sisters of St. Joseph of St. Augustine, Florida	[3900]
S.S.J.C.	Sisters of St. Joseph Benedict Cottolengo	[]
S.S.J.-T.O.S.F.	Sisters of St. Joseph of the Third Order of St. Francis	[3930]
S.S.L.	Congregation of the Sisters of St. Louis, Juilly-Monaghan	[3935]
S.S.LOG.	Seton Sisters of Our Lady of Guadalupe, Tucson	[]
S.S.M.	Sisters of the Sorrowful Mother (Third Order of St. Francis)	[4100
S.S.M.I.	Sisters Servants of Mary Immaculate	[3510
S.S.M.I.	Sisters Servants of Mary Immaculate	[3610
S.S.M.I.	Sisters Servants of Mary Immaculate	[3620
S.S.M.N.	Sisters of Saint Mary of Namur	[3950
S.S.M.O.	Sisters of St. Mary of Oregon	[3960
S.S.N.D.	School Sisters of Notre Dame	[2970
S.S.P.C.	Missionary Sisters of St. Peter Claver	[3990
S.Sp.S.	Missionary Sisters Servants of the Holy Spirit	[3530
S.Sp.S.-deA.P.	Sister Servants of the Holy Spirit of Perpetual Adoration	[3540
S.S.S.	Servants of the Blessed Sacrament	[3500
S.S.S.	Sisters of Social Service of Los Angeles, Inc.	[4080
S.S.S.	Sisters of Social Service of Buffalo, Inc.	[4090
S.S.S.F.	School Sisters of St. Francis	[1680
S.S.T.V.	Congregation of Sisters of St. Thomas of Villanova	[4030

S.S.V.M Servants of the Lord and Virgin of Matara, Inc. .... [3625]
S.T.J. Society of St. Teresa of Jesus .... [4020]
S.U. Society of St. Ursula .... [4040]
S.U.S.C. Sisters of the Holy Union .... [2070]
S.V. Sisters of Life .... [2265]
S.V.M. Sisters of the Visitation of the Congregation of the Immaculate Heart of Mary .... [4200]
V.D.C. Verbum Dei Community .... []
V.D.M.F. Verbum Dei Missionary Fraternity .... [4140]
V.H.M. Visitation Nuns .... [4190]
V.S. Vestiarski Sisters .... []
V.S.C. Vincentian Sisters of Charity .... [4160]
V.S.C. Vincentian Sisters of Charity .... [4170]
X.M.M. Xaverian Missionary Society of Mary, Inc. .... [4230]
X.S. Catholic Mission Sisters of St. Francis Xavier .... [3810]

Religious Institutes of Women

Leadership of Women Religious in the United States of America—National Office: 8737 Colesville Rd., Suite 610, Silver Spring, MD 20910. Tel: 301-588-4955; Fax: 301-587-4575; Website: www.lcwr.org. Sr. Sharlet Wagner, C.S.C., Pres.; Sr. Teresa Maya, C.C.V.I., Past Pres..; Sr. Jayne Helmlinger, C.S.J., Pres.-Elect; Sr. Theresa Sandok, O.S.M., Sec.; Sr. Kate Katoski, O.S.F., Treas.; Sr. Carol Zinn, S.S.J., Exec. Dir. Council of Major Superiors of Women Religious in the United States of America—415 Michigan Ave., N.E., P.O. Box 4467, Washington, DC 20017-0467. Tel: 202-832-2575; Fax: 202-832-6325; Website: cmswr.org. Mother Mary McGreevy, R.S.M., Chairperson; Sr. Marie Bernadette Mertens, I.H.M., Sec.; Sr. Judith Ann Duvall, O.S.F., Treas.

(The initial (D) or (P) indicates Diocesan or Pontifical Jurisdiction.)

[0100] (A.S.C.)—ADORERS OF THE BLOOD OF CHRIST (P)

Founded in Acuto, Italy, in 1834. First foundation in the United States in 1870.

General Motherhouse: Via Beata Maria De Mattias 10, Rome, Italy, 00183. Sr. Mariamma Kunnackle, A.S.C., Supr. Gen.

Regional Offices - United States Region: Adorers of the Blood of Christ, 4233 Sulphur Ave., Saint Louis, MO 63109. Tel: 314-351-6294; Fax: 314-351-6789. Sr. Barbara Hudock, A.S.C., Regl. Leader.

Professed Sisters: 238.

Properties owned and/or sponsored: Villa Maria, Mulvane, KS; Newman University, Wichita, KS; St. Joseph Villa, David City, NE; St. Anne's Retirement Community, Inc.; De Matias Residence; St. Anne's Independent Living Retirement Village, Columbia PA.

Legal Title: Adorers of the Blood of Christ.

Sisters serve and staff: Colleges; Secondary & Elementary Schools; Special & Religious Education; Hospitals; Pastoral Care; Nursing Homes; Domestic Service in Communities & Institutions; Administration in Religious Orders & Parishes; Prayer Ministry; Retreat Ministry; Social Service; Pastoral & Chaplaincy Ministry; Prison & Minority Ministries; Ministry to the Homeless; Diocesan Offices; Homes for the Aged & Home Nursing; Foreign Missions.

Represented in the Archdioceses of Kansas City in Kansas, Oklahoma City, St. Louis, San Antonio, San Francisco and Washington and in the Dioceses of Belleville, Dodge City, El Paso, Harrisburg, Jefferson City, Kansas City-St. Joseph, Lincoln, Oakland, Salina, San Diego, Springfield-Cape Girardeau, Springfield in Illinois, Wilmington, Wichita and Youngstown. Also in Bolivia, Guatemala, Korea and Rome.

Ruma Center (1876): 2 Pioneer Ln., Red Bud, IL 62278. Tel: 618-282-3848.

Wichita Center (1929): 1165 Southwest Blvd., Wichita, KS 67213-1394. Tel: 316-942-2201.

Columbia Center (1925): 3954 Columbia Ave., Columbia, PA 17512-9714. Tel: 717-285-4536.

[0110] (A.P.B.)—THE SISTERS ADORERS OF THE PRECIOUS BLOOD (P) (Cloistered Contemplative Order)

American Federation: Consisting of Four Autonomous Monasteries: 400 Pratt St., Watertown, NY 13601-4238. Tel: 315-788-1669. Sr. Joan Milot, A.P.B., Pres. American Federation.

Professed Sisters: 44; Novices: 2; Postulants: 1.

Represented in the Dioceses of Brooklyn, Manchester, Ogdensburg and Portland (In Maine).

New York: 5400 Ft. Hamilton Pkwy., Brooklyn, NY 11219. Tel: 718-438-6371.

New Hampshire: 700 Bridge St., Manchester, NH 03104. Tel: 603-623-4264.

New York: 400 Pratt St., Watertown, NY 13601. Tel: 718-788-1669. Professed Sisters: 6.

Maine: 166 State St., Portland, ME 04101. Tel: 207-774-0861.

[0130] (A.S.C.J.)—APOSTLES OF THE SACRED HEART OF JESUS (P)

Founded in Italy in 1894. First Foundation in United States 1902.

General Motherhouse: Apostole del Sacro Cuore di Gesu, Via Germano Sommeiller 38, Rome, Italy, 00185. Mother Miriam Sobrinha Cunha, A.S.C.J., Supr. Gen.; Sr. Maria Josefina Suzin, Sec.

U.S. Provincial Motherhouse: Mt. Sacred Heart, 295 Benham St., Hamden, CT 06514. Tel: 203-248-4225; Fax: 203-230-8341.

Professed Sisters: 116.

Properties owned and/or sponsored: Mount Sacred Heart College for Sisters; Sacred Heart Academy; Sacred Heart Manor; Sacred Heart Manor Nursery and Kindergarten; Clelian Adult Day Center, Hamden, CT; Cor Jesu Academy, St. Louis, MO; Sacred Heart Villa Nursery, St. Louis, MO; Clelian Heights School for Exceptional Children, Greensburg, PA; Sacred Heart Private School, Bronx, NY; Mary, Mother of the Church Convent, Hamden, CT; Mount Sacred Heart Provincialate Convent, Hamden, CT; Sr. Antonine Signorelli Formation House, Hamden, CT; Sacred Heart Academy Convent, Hamden, CT; Sacred Heart Manor Convent, Hamden, CT; Immaculate Heart of Mary Convent, Guilford, CT.

Legal Title: Corporation Name: Apostles of the Sacred Heart of Jesus, Incorporated.

Ministry in the fields of Education, Health Care, Parishes, Adult Day Care and Immigrant Services.

Represented in the Archdioceses of Hartford, New York and St. Louis and in the Dioceses of Bridgeport, Greensburg, Norwich and Pensacola-Tallahassee. Also in Rome and Taiwan.

Clelian House Convent: 5324 Wilson Ave., St. Louis, MO 63110.

Cor Jesu Academy Convent: 10230 Gravois Rd., St. Louis, MO 63123.

Sacred Heart Villa Convent: 2108 Macklind Ave., St. Louis, MO 63110.

Our Lady Queen of Apostles Convent: 800 Montebello Camp Rd., Imperial, MO 63052.

[0150] (S.A.S.V.)—SISTERS OF THE ASSUMPTION (P)

Founded in Saint-Gregoire, P.Q., Canada in 1853. First foundation in the United States in 1891.

General Motherhouse: Nicolet, Canada Sr. Muriel Lemoine, S.A.S.V., Congregational Leader.

United States Region: 316 Lincoln St., Worcester, MA 01605. Tel: 508-856-9383. Sr. Lorraine Normand, S.A.S.V., Regl. Treas.

Total in Region and Professed: 48.

Ministry in all levels of education.

Missions in Japan, Brazil and Ecuador.

Represented in the Archdiocese of Boston and in the Dioceses of Fall River, Portland (In Maine), Providence, Springfield in Massachusetts and Worcester.

[0160] (O.S.A.)—AUGUSTINIAN NUNS OF CONTEMPLATIVE LIFE (P)

Augustinian Contemplative Nuns: Mother of Good Counsel Convent, 440 N. Marley Rd., New Lenox, IL 60451. Sr. Mary Grace Kuppe, O.S.A., Prioress.

Total in Community: 4.

Legal Title: Augustinian Cloistered Nuns, Inc.

Represented in the Diocese of Joliet.

[0170] (O.S.B.)—BENEDICTINE NUNS OF THE CONGREGATION OF SOLESMES (P)

Order originated in Italy, c.529. Congregation of Solesmes formed in France in 1837.

U.S. Establishment (1981): Monastery of the Immaculate Heart of Mary, 4103 VT Rte. 100, P.O. Box 110, Westfield, VT 05874. Tel: 802-744-6525; Fax: 802-744-6236. Email: monastery@ihmwestfield.com. Rev. Mother Maria Magdalen Grumm, O.S.B., Prioress.

Total in Congregation : 816; Total in Community: 16.

Represented in the Diocese of Burlington.

[0180] (O.S.B.)—BENEDICTINE NUNS OF THE PRIMITIVE OBSERVANCE (P)

First founded in Italy in about c.529. First United States establishment in 1948.

Abbey of Regina Laudis: 273 Flanders Rd., Bethlehem, CT 06751. Tel: 203-266-7727; Fax: 203-266-5915. Rt. Rev. Mother Lucia Kuppens, Abbess.

Professed Nuns: 28; Sisters in First Vows: 3; Novices: 5.

[0190] (O.S.B.)—BENEDICTINE NUNS (P)

First founded in Italy in c.529. Founded in the United States in 1931 from St. Walburg Abbey, Eichstatt, Bavaria, Germany.

The Sisters of St. Benedict of Westmoreland County: St. Emma Monastery, 1001 Harvey Ave., Greensburg, PA 15601-1491. Tel: 724-834-3060; Fax: 724-834-5772; Email: benedictinenuns@stemma.org. Mother Mary Anne Noll, O.S.B., Prioress.

Professed Nuns: 9.

Ministry in Monastic Life; Benedictine hospitality extended through adjacent St. Emma Retreat House; Monastic Guest House.

Represented in the Diocese of Greensburg.

Benedictine Nuns: Abbey of St. Walburga, 1029 Benedictine Way, Virginia Dale, CO 80536. Tel: 970-472-0612; Fax: 970-484-4342; Email: abbey@walburga.org. Mother Maria Michael Newe, O.S.B., Abbess; Mother Maria-Thomas Beil, O.S.B., Retired Abbess.

Sisters: 22; Novices: 2; Postulants: 1; Claustral Oblates: 1.

Represented in the Archdiocese of Denver.

[0210] (O.S.B.)—MISSIONARY BENEDICTINE SISTERS (P)

The Congregation of Missionary Benedictine Sisters is of Pontifical Jurisdiction. Its Constitutions were approved by Rome on June 25, 1934; Revised approval June 29, 1983.

Generalate: Rome, Italy

Priory House and Novitiate: Immaculata Monastery (1923), 300 N. 18th St., Norfolk, NE 68701-3622. Tel: 402-371-3438; Fax: 402-371-0127. Sr. Roseann Ocken, O.S.B., Prioress.

Professed Sisters: 37.

Legal Holdings or Titles: Missionary Benedictine Sisters, Inc., Norfolk, NE; Hildegard House, Creighton, NE.

Ministry in the fields of Retreat; Education; Health; Outreach Services with Hispanics and Elderly.

Represented in the Archdiocese of Omaha.

[0220] (O.S.B.)—CONGREGATION OF THE BENEDICTINE SISTERS OF PERPETUAL ADORATION OF PONTIFICAL JURISDICTION (P)

Founded from Maria Rickenbach, Switzerland in 1874 with first monastery at Clyde, MO. Congregation erected by decree of the Holy See on June 16, 1936.

General Motherhouse: Benedictine Convent of Perpetual Adoration, 31970 State Hwy. P, Clyde, MO 64432. Tel: 660-944-2221; Fax: 660-944-2202; Email sister@benedictinesisters.org; Web: benedictinesisters.org. Sr. Dawn Mills, Prioress Gen.

Total in Congregation: 54.

Interdependent Monasteries: 800 N. Country Club Rd., Tucson, AZ 85716.

Ministry in Monastic/Contemplative/Eucharistic Apostolate of Prayer; Liturgy of the Hours four times daily in Choir; Contemplative Prayer and Monastic Atmosphere Shared with Others; Prayer Days and Retreats for Sisters; Editing and Publishing Bimonthly Magazine: Spirit & Life; Production and Distribution of Altar Breads; Liturgical Vestments; Correspondence.

Represented in the Dioceses of Kansas City-St. Joseph and Tucson.

[0230] (O.S.B.)—BENEDICTINE SISTERS OF PONTIFICAL JURISDICTION (P)

(I) The Federation of St. Scholastica

Erected by Decree of the Holy See, February 25, 1922, with final approbation by Decree of June 10, 1930. Eighteen Monasteries in the United States and two in Mexico. Total number in the Federation 646. Sr. Lynn Marie McKenzie, O.S.B., Federation Pres., residing at: Sacred Heart Monastery, 916 Convent Rd., N.E., Cullman, AL 35055. Tel: 256-615-6115.

Benedictine Sisters of Baltimore, Inc: Emmanuel Monastery, 2229 W. Joppa Rd., Lutherville Timonium, MD 21093. Tel: 410-821-5792; Fax: 410-296-9560; Email: bensrs@emmanuelosb.org; Web: www.emmanuelosb.org.

Total in Community: 15.

Ministry in the field of Education; Pastoral Ministry; Retreats and Spiritual Direction; Justice Ministry; Social Services; Hospital Service Ministry.

Represented in the Archdioceses of Baltimore and Newark.

Benedictine Sisters of the Byzantine Rite (1969): Queen of Heaven Monastery, 169 Kenmore Ave.,

N.E., #302, Warren, OH 44483. Tel: 330-856-1813. Sr. Barbara Pavlik, O.S.B., Admin.
Professed Sisters: 4.
Ministry in Religious Education; Pastoral Ministry; Administration.
Represented in the Archdiocese of Pittsburgh Byzantine Rite.

Mount St. Scholastica Inc. (1863): Motherhouse of the Sisters of St. Benedict, 801 S. Eighth St., Atchison, KS 66002-2778. Tel: 913-360-6200; Fax: 913-360-6190. Vocation Director Email: vocation@mountosb.org. Web: www.mountosb.org. Sr. Esther Fangman, O.S.B., Prioress.
Professed Sisters: 116; Novices: 1.
Legal Holdings: Dooley Center, Inc.; Mount St. Scholastica, Inc., Atchison, KS.
Ministry in the field of Academic Education at all levels; Counseling; Retreats; Spirituality Center; Spiritual Direction; Social Services; Hospitality; Pastoral Ministry; Ministry to women of all ages; Missionary Work in Brazil.
Represented in the Archdiocese of Kansas City in Kansas and in the Diocese of Kansas City-St. Joseph. Also in Brazil.

Benedictine Sisters of Erie (1856): Mount St. Benedict Monastery, 6101 East Lake Rd., Erie, PA 16511. Tel: 814-899-0614; Fax: 814-898-4004. Sr. Anne Wambach, O.S.B., Prioress.
Total in Congregation : 90; Final Profession: 86; First Profession: 3; Novices: 1.
Properties owned and/or sponsored: Mount Saint Benedict Monastery; Glinodo Center; St. Benedict Education Center; Benet Center; 6 Community Houses; St. Benedict Community Center.
Sisters serve and staff: Elementary Schools; Colleges; Day Care Centers; Residence for Elderly and Handicapped; Nat'l Mission Office; Social Services; Diocesan Offices; Pastoral Ministry; Religious Education.
Represented in the Dioceses of Cleveland and Erie.

Benedictine Sisters of Chicago O.S.B. (1861): St. Scholastica Monastery, 7430 N. Ridge Blvd., Chicago, IL 60645. Tel: 773-764-2413; Email: prioress@osbchicago.org. Sr. Judith Murphy, O.S.B., Prioress; Sr. Virginia Jung Community Archivist.
Professed Sisters: 36.
Properties owned and/or sponsored: St. Scholastica Monastery, Chicago, IL.
Sisters serve and staff: Parish Ministry; Religious Education; Spiritual Direction; Shelter Ministry; Community Center Work; Social Service & Pastoral Counseling; Massage Therapy; Group Facilitation; Immigrant Support; Interfaith Ministry; University Chaplaincy, Pre-School.
Represented in the Archdioceses of Chicago and New Orleans and in the Diocese of Pueblo.

Benedictine Sisters of the Sacred Heart O.S.B. (1895): Sacred Heart Monastery, 1910 Maple Ave., Lisle, IL 60532-2164. Tel: 630-725-6000. Sr. Mary Bratrsovsky, O.S.B., Prioress.
Professed Sisters: 27.
Legal Title: Benedictine Sisters of the Sacred Heart Charitable Trust.
Sisters serve and staff: Villa St. Benedict; Religious Education; Pastoral Ministry; Independent Positions involving Secretarial, Counseling and Liturgical Works.
Represented in the Diocese of Joliet.

Benedictine Sisters of Elizabeth, NJ O.S.B. (1868): St. Walburga Monastery, 851 N. Broad St., Elizabeth, NJ 07208. Tel: 908-352-4278. Sr. Mary Feehan, O.S.B., Prioress; Sr. Ursula Butler, O.S.B., Sub Prioress.
Professed Sisters: 29.
Legal Holdings and Titles: Benedictine Academy, Elizabeth, NJ; Benedictine Preschool, Elizabeth, NJ.
Represented in the Archdioceses of New York and Newark.

Benedictine Sisters of Pittsburgh, PA O.S.B. (1870): St. Benedict Monastery, 3526 Bakerstown Rd., Bakerstown, PA 15007-9705. Tel: 724-502-2600; Fax: 724502-2601; Email: osbpgh@osbpgh.org; Web: www.osbpgh.org. Sr. Karen R. Brink, O.S.B., Prioress.
Professed Sisters: 47.
Ministry in the field of Education at all levels; Religious; Pastoral Ministry; Social Service; Art Education; Outreach with Poor.
Represented in the Dioceses of Erie, Greensburg and Pittsburgh.

Benedictine Sisters O.S.B. (1879): St. Joseph Monastery, 2200 S. Lewis, Tulsa, OK 74114-3100. Tel: 918-742-4989; Fax: 918-744-1374; Email: srchristine@montecassino.org. Sr. Christine Ereiser, O.S.B., Prioress.
Professed Sisters: 18.
Legal Holdings and Titles: Congregation of the Benedictine Sisters of the Sacred Hearts; Monte Cassino School.
Ministry in the field of Academic Education; Catechetics; Evangelization; Social Work; Pastoral Ministry; Counseling & Spiritual Direction; Religious Education & Religious Formation.
Represented in the Diocese of Tulsa.

Benedictine Sisters of Pontifical Jurisdiction O.S.B. (1857): St. Gertrude Monastery, 14259 Benedictine Ln., Ridgely, MD 21660-1434. Tel: 410-634-2497. Sr. Jacquelyn Ernster, O.S.B., Admin.
Professed Sisters: 15.
Legal Holdings & Titles: St. Benedict, Wilmington, DE.
Ministry in Special Schools; Ministry to the poor and homeless.
Represented in the Diocese of Wilmington.

St. Walburg Monastery of Benedictine Sisters of Covington, KY O.S.B. (1859): St. Walburg Monastery, 2500 Amsterdam Rd., Villa Hills, KY 41017-5316. Tel: 859-331-6324; Fax: 859-331-2136. Sr. Aileen Bankemper, O.S.B., Prioress; Sr. Deborah Harmeling, O.S.B., Community Archivist.
Professed Sisters: 38.
Legal Titles and Holdings: Villa Madonna Montessori School; Villa Madonna Academy.
Sisters serve and staff: Diocesan Offices; Pastoral and Social Ministry; Elementary Schools.
Represented in the Dioceses of Covington and Pueblo.

Benedictine Sisters (1902): Sacred Heart Monastery, 916 Convent Rd., Cullman, AL 35055. Tel: 256-734-2199; Fax: 256-255-0048. Sr. Tonette Sperando, O.S.B., Prioress; Sr. Mary Ruth Coffman, O.S.B., Community Archivist.
Professed Sisters: 38.
Properties owned and/or sponsored: Benedictine Sisters Retreat Center; Benedictine Manor Retirement Home; Sacred Heart Monastery of Cullman, AL Foundation.
Sisters serve and staff: all levels of Academic Education; Pastoral Ministry; Diocesan Offices; Retirement Homes; Conference Centers; Rural Health Center (Doctor); Nurses; Lawyer.
Represented in the Diocese of Birmingham.

Benedictine Sisters of Virginia O.S.B. (1868): St. Benedict Monastery, 9535 Linton Hall Rd., Bristow, VA 20136-1217. Tel: 703-361-0106. Sr. Cecilia Dwyer, O.S.B., Prioress.
Total Professed Sisters: 29.
Legal Holdings and Titles: Benedictine Sisters of Virginia, Inc.; St. Gertrude High School, Richmond, VA; Linton Hall School; Benedictine Pastoral Center; Benedictine Counseling Services, Bristow, VA; B.E.A.C.O.N., Bristow, VA.
Represented in the Dioceses of Arlington and Richmond.

Benedictine Sisters (1911): (Congregation of Benedictine Sisters), 216 W. Highland Dr., Boerne, TX 78006. Tel: 830-816-8504; Fax: 830-249-1365. Sr. Frances Briseño, O.S.B., Prioress.
Total in Community: 15.
Properties owned and/or sponsored: St. Scholastica Monastery; Benedictine Sisters Charitable Trust Fund; Benedictine Sisters Charitable Trust Two.
Represented in the Archdiocese of San Antonio and in the Diocese of Laredo.

Benedictine Sisters of St. Lucy's Priory Inc. O.S.B. (1956): St. Lucy's Priory, 19045 E. Sierra Madre Ave., Glendora, CA 91741. Tel: 626-335-1682. Sr. Elizabeth Brown, O.S.B., Prioress.
Professed Sisters: 9.
Legal Holdings: St. Lucy's Priory High School.
Sisters serve and staff: all levels of Academic Education; Pastoral Ministry.
Represented in the Archdiocese of Los Angeles and in the Diocese of San Bernardino.

Benedictine Sisters of Florida (1889): Holy Name Monastery, P.O. Box 2450, St. Leo, FL 33574-2450. Tel: 352-588-8320; Fax: 352-588-8319. Sr. Roberta Bailey, O.S.B., Prioress; Sr. Roberta Bailey, O.S.B., Archivist.
Professed Sisters: 14.
Represented in the Diocese of St. Petersburg.

Sisters of St. Benedict (1963): Benet Hill Monastery-Motherhouse, 3190 Benet Ln., Colorado Springs, CO 80921-1509. Tel: 719-633-0655; Fax: 719-471-0403. Sr. Clare Carr, O.S.B., Prioress; Sr. S. Margaret Meaney, O.S.B., Community Archivist.
Total in Community: 30.
Properties owned and/or sponsored: Benet Hill Monastery and Ministry Center.
Represented in the Archdioceses of Denver and Santa Fe and in the Diocese of Colorado Springs.

Benedictine Sisters O.S.B. (1989): Queen of Angels Monastery, 23615 N.E. 100th St., Liberty, MO 64068. Tel: 816-750-4618; Fax: 816-750-4620; Web: www.libertybenedictinesisters.org. Sr. Agnes Helgenberger, O.S.B., Prioress.
Professed Sisters: 6.
Ministry in Companioning; food for the hungry; prison ministry; thrift stores; Religious education and retreats; Nursing.
Represented in the Diocese of Kansas City-St. Joseph.
Erected by Decree of the Apostolic See on April 14, 1937, with final approbation by Decree of April 4, 1950.

(II) The Federation of St. Gertrude:

Federation Office: Sacred Heart Monastery (1880), 1005 W. 8th St., Yankton, SD 57078-3389. Tel: 605-668-6000; Fax: 605-668-6153. Sr. Jeanne Weber, O.S.B., Federation Pres.
Total in Federation: 512.

Thirteen member monasteries from this Federation as follows:

Benedictine Sisters O.S.B: Mailing Address: Our Lady of Peace Monastery, 1005 W. 8th St., Yankton, SD 57078. Tel: 605-668-6008; Fax: 605-668-6153. Sr. Jeanne Weber, O.S.B., Admin.
Professed Sisters: 1.
Ministry in Home Health Care.

Monastery of St. Gertrude (1882): 465 Keuterville Rd., Cottonwood, ID 83522-5183. Tel: 208-962-3224; Fax: 208-962-7212. Sr. Mary Forman, O.S.B., Prioress; Rev. Meinrad Schallberger, O.S.B., Chap.
Professed Sisters: 37.
Legal Title: Idaho Corporation of Benedictine Sisters.
Sisters serve in Parish Ministry; Health Care; Retreat Ministry; Social Work; Counseling; St. Gertrude's Museum, Spirit Center Retreat House.
Represented in the Archdioceses of Los Angeles and Seattle and in the Dioceses of Boise and Spokane.

Sisters of St. Benedict of Crookston O.S.B: Mount St. Benedict Monastery (1919): 620 E. Summit Ave., Crookston, MN 56716-2713. Tel: 218-281-3441; Fax: 218-281-6966. Email: crxbenedictines@gmail.com. Sr. Shawn Carruth, O.S.B., Prioress.
Professed Sisters: 43.
Sisters serve and staff: Child Care; Nursery School.
Represented in the Dioceses of Brownsville and Crookston.

Benedictine Sisters O.S.B. (1867): Monastery Immaculate Conception, 802 E. 10th St., Ferdinand, IN 47532-9239. Tel: 812-367-1411; Fax: 812-367-2313. Sr. Barbara Lynn Schmitz, O.S.B., Prioress.
Perpetually Professed Sisters: 127; Exclaustration: 3; Peru: 5. Total: 138.
Legal Title: Sisters of St. Benedict of Ferdinand, Indiana, Inc.
Sponsorships: Benet Hall.
Sisters serve and staff: on all levels of Academic Education; Religious Education; Parish Ministry; Hospitals; Public Health-Social Service Agencies; Diocesan Offices; Foreign Missions; Hispanic Ministries; Retreat House; Community Ministry; Psychology and Counseling Agencies.
Represented in the Archdioceses of Indianapolis and Louisville and in the Dioceses of Evansville and Owensboro. Also in Peru.

Benedictine Sisters, O.S.B. of St. Scholastica Monastery (1879): St. Scholastica Monastery, P.O. Box 3849, Fort Smith, AR 72913-3489. Tel: 479-783-4147; Fax: 479-782-4352.; Email: email@stscho.org. Sr. Maria Goretti DeAngeli, O.S.B., Prioress.
Professed Sisters: 32.
Ministry: House of Prayer; Teaching, Counseling; Spiritual Direction; University/Marketing and sponsor education for orphans in Guatemala.

Benedictine Sisters of Mt. Angel, Oregon (1882): Queen of Angels Monastery, 840 S. Main St., Mount Angel, OR 97362-9527. Tel: 503-845-6141; Fax: 503845-6585; Email: info@benedictine-srs.org; Web: www.benedictine-srs.org. Sr. Jane Hibbard, SNJM, Pastoral Admin.
Professed Sisters: 24.
Ministries: Shalom at the Monastery, Mt. Angel, OR.
Sisters serve: Seminary; Parish Ministry; Retreat and Prayer Ministry; Spiritual Direction; Ministry to Poor and Hispanics.
Represented in the Archdiocese of Portland in Oregon.

Benedictine Convent of St. Martin (1889): St. Martin Monastery, 1851 City Spring Rd., Rapid City,

SD 57702-9613. Tel: 605-343-8011; Fax: 605-399-2723. Sr. Mary Wegher, Prioress.
Professed Sisters: 16; Temporary Professed Sisters: 1.
Ministry in the fields of Religious Education; Parish Ministry; Retreat and Spiritual Direction.
Represented in the Diocese of Rapid City.

Sisters of St. Benedict of Beech Grove, Ind., Inc. (1956): Our Lady of Grace Monastery, 1402 Southern Ave., Beech Grove, IN 46107-1197. Tel: 317-787-3287; Fax: 317-780-2368. Email: prioress@benedictine.com. Sr. Jennifer Mechtild Horner, O.S.B., Prioress.
Professed Sisters: 53.
Legal Titles: Sisters of St. Benedict of Beech Grove, Ind., Inc.; Charitable Trust of the Monastery of Our Lady of Grace, Sisters of the Order of St. Benedict.
Ministry in Education; Retirement Home; Retreat Center; Religious Education; Hospitals.
Represented in the Archdioceses of Cincinnati, Indianapolis and Louisville.
Properties owned and sponsored: Our Lady of Grace Monastery; Benedict Inn Retreat and Conference Center; St. Paul Hermitage; Regina Retreat.

Benedictine Sisters of Richardton, O.S.B. (1916): Sacred Heart Monastery (1916), P.O. Box 364, Richardton, ND 58652-0364. Tel: 701-974-2121; Fax: 701-974-2124. Sr. Paula Larson, O.S.B., Prioress.
Professed Sisters: 17.
Legal Titles or Holdings: Benedictine Sponsorship Board, Inc.; Subiaco Manor Inc.; Sacred Heart Benedictine Foundation; Pia Tegler Foundation.
Ministry in the fields of Academic Education; Hospital Chaplaincy; Native American Ministry; Health Care.
Represented in the Diocese of Bismarck.

The Benedictine Sisters of Mother of God Monastery O.S.B: Mother of God Monastery (1961): 110 28th Ave., S.E., Watertown, SD 57201-8418. Tel: 605-882-6600; Fax: 605-882-6658. Email: prioress@watertownbenedictines.org. Sr. Theresa Hoffman, Prioress.
Perpetual Vows: 47; Temporary Professed: 1
Legal Titles: The Benedictine Sisters of Mother of God Monastery, Watertown, SD; St. Ann's Corporation (includes Benet Place), Watertown, SD; Retirement Trust, Watertown, SD; Benedictine Sisters Foundation of Watertown, SD. Sisters serve and staff: in Elementary Education; Religious Education Centers; Parish Ministry; Prison Ministry; Native American Ministries; Hispanic Ministries; Libraries & Archives; and Congregate Housing for Elderly.
Represented in the Archdiocese of St. Paul-Minneapolis and in the Diocese of Sioux Falls.

St. Benedict's Monastery (1912): 225 Masters Ave., Winnipeg, Canada, R4A 2A1. Tel: 204-338-4601; Fax: 204-339-8775. Email: stbensmon@gmail.com. Sr. Virginia Evard, O.S.B., Prioress.
Professed Sisters: 15.
Ministry in Retreat & Conference Centre; Education; Health Care; Pastoral Care; St. Benedict's Place, Seniors' Residence.
Represented in Canada.

Benedictine Convent of the Sacred Heart: Sacred Heart Monastery (1880), 1005 W. 8th St., Yankton, SD 57078-3389. Tel: 605-668-6000; Fax: 605-668-6153. Sr. Maribeth Wentzlaff, O.S.B., Prioress.
Professed Sisters: 79.
Sisters serve and staff: in Health Care Institutions; all levels of Academic Education; Social Services; Parish Ministry; Pastoral Care; Counseling, Religious Education & Administration.
Represented in the Archdiocese of Omaha and in the Dioceses of Sioux City & Sioux Falls.

Benedictine Sisters of Nanaimo: House of Bread Monastery (1993), 2329 Arbot Rd., Nanaimo, Canada, V9R 6S8. Tel: 250-753-1763. Email: houseofbread@shaw.ca. Sr. Barbara Rinehart, O.S.B., Prioress.
Professed Sisters: 7.
Sisters serve: Spiritual Direction; Prayer Ministry; Artist.
Represented in Canada.

(III): The Federation of St. Benedict: 104 Chapel Ln., St. Joseph, MN 56374-0220. Tel: 320-363-7004; Fax: 320-363-7130. Sr. Kerry O'Reilly, O.S.B., Pres. Total number of Sisters in Federation: 401c.
Legal Title: Federation of St. Benedict.
Erected by decree of the Holy See March 24, 1947.
Ten monasteries form this Federation; in addition to the seven American monasteries listed, three autonomous monasteries exist: Japan, St. Benedict's Monastery (1985) Muroran, Hokkaido; Taiwan, St. Benedict Monastery (1988) Tanshui, Taipei; Bahamas, Saint Martin Monastery (1994) Nassau.

Sisters of the Order of Saint Benedict-O.S.B. (1857): Monasterio Santa Escolastica, Apartado 8526, Humacao, Puerto Rico Tel: 787-852-4222; Fax: 787-850-5279. Sr. Angela Berrios, O.S.B. Sisters: 10; Novices: 1.
Legal Title: Sisters of the Order of Saint Benedict, Inc.
Ministry in the field of Education at all levels; Parish Ministry.
Represented in the Diocese of Caguas.

Sisters of the Order of Saint Benedict-O.S.B. (1857): St. Benedict's Monastery-Motherhouse and Novitiate, 104 Chapel Ln., St. Joseph, MN 56374-0220. Tel: 320-363-7100. Sr. Susan Rudolph, O.S.B., Prioress; Sr. Mariterese Woida, O.S.B., Archivist.
Total Sisters in Congregation: 198.
Legal Title: Sisters of the Order of Saint Benedict, St. Joseph, MN.
Ministry in the field of Education at all levels; Hospitals; Nursing Homes; Individual Apostolates; Parish Ministry; Social Work; Spirituality and Retreat Counseling; Pastoral Ministry.
Represented in the Archdioceses of St. Paul-Minneapolis and Washington, DC and in the Dioceses of La Crosse, New Ulm, St. Cloud, Salt Lake City and Helena, Montana.

Sisters of St. Benedict - St. Scholastica Monastery O.S.B. (1892): 1001 Kenwood Ave., Duluth, MN 55811. Tel: 218-723-6555. Sr. Beverly Raway, O.S.B., Prioress; Sr. Luce Marie Dionne, O.S.B., Archivist.
Total in Community: 60.
Ministry in the field of Academic Education at all levels; Religious Education; Residence for Elderly; Nursing Homes; Hospitals; Pastoral Care and Parish Ministries; Peace and Justice; Retreat Center.
Properties owned and/or sponsored: Benedictine Sisters Benevolent Association, McCabe Renewal Center, Duluth, MN; The College of St. Scholastica; Benedictine Health System; St. Mary's Medical Center, Duluth, MN; Benedictine Living Communities, Inc., Duluth, MN: Benedictine Living Center of Garrison, Garrison, ND; Benedictine Health System Foundation, Duluth, MN; Benedictine Living Communities, Inc., dba St. Gabriel's Community, Bismarck, ND; Prince of Peace Care Center & Evergreen Place, Ellendale, ND; St. Benedict's Health Center & Benedict's Court, Dickinson, ND; Benedictine Living Community of Wahpeton, Wahpeton, ND; St. Rose Care Center & Rosewood Court, LaMoure, ND; Benedictine Health Center; Polinsky Rehabilitation Center, Duluth, MN; St. Joseph's Medical Center, Brainerd, MN; St. Mary's Regional Health Center, Detroit Lakes, MN; St. Francis Regional Medical Center, Shakopee, MN; St. Mary's Hospital & Clinics, Cottonwood, ID; Madonna Towers of Rochester, Inc., Rochester, MN; St. Gertrude's Health Rehabilitation and Center, Shakopee, MN; The Gardens at St. Gertrude's Shakopee, MN; Benedictine Health Dimensions, Cambridge, MN; St. Mary's Hospital, Superior, WI; St. Anne of Winona Callista Court, Winona, MN; Villa St. Benedict, Lisle, IL; Villa St. Vincent, Crookston, MN, Benedictine Care Centers: Benedictine Health Center at Innsbruck, New Brighton, MN; Benedictine Living Community of St. Peter, St. Peter, MN; Madonna Meadows of Rochester, Rochester, MN; Madonna Towers of Rochester, Inc., Rochester, MN; Living Community of St. Joseph, St. Joseph, MO; Benedictine Senior Living at Steeple Pointe, Osseo, MN; Benedictine Health Center of Minneapolis, Minneapolis, MN; Arrowhead Senior Living Community dba St. Michael's Health and Rehabilitation Center, Virginia, MN; Arrowhead Senior Living Community dba St. Raphael's Health and Rehabilitation Center, Eveleth, MN; Benedictine Senior Living Community of New London dba Grace Living Community of Glen Oaks, New London, MN; Benedictine Senior Living Community of Winsted dba St. Mary's Care Center, Winsted, MN; Holy Trinity Hospital, Graceville, MN; Graceville Health Center Clinic, Graceville, MN; Grace Home, Graceville, MN; Grace Village, Graceville, MN; Catholic Residential Services, Inc.; Benedictine Living Community of Wausau, Wausau, WI; Benedictine Living Community of LaCrosse, LaCrosse, WI; Benedictine Health Dimension, Inc., Cambridge, MN; Bridges Care Center DBA Benedictine Living Community of Ada, Ada, MN; Benedictine Living Communities, Inc.; Benedictine Health Center DBA Benedictine Living Community, Duluth, MN.
Represented in the Archdioceses of Chicago, Milwaukee and St. Paul-Minneapolis, and in the Dioceses of Bismarck, Boise, Crookston, Duluth, Fargo, Joliet, Kansas City-St. Joseph; LaCrosse, New Ulm, Peoria, Phoenix, St. Cloud, Sioux Falls, Superior and Winona-Rochester.

Sisters of St. Benedict O.S.B. (1874): St. Mary Monastery, 2200 88th Ave., W., Rock Island, IL 61201-7649. Tel: 309-283-2100; Fax: 309-283-2200; Email: benedictines@smsisters.org. Sr. Sandra Brunenn, O.S.B., Prioress; Sr. Marilyn Roman, Archivist.
Total in Community: 33.
Ministry in the field of Religious and Academic Education; Pastoral Care; Parish Ministry; Retreat Ministry.
Represented in the Diocese of Peoria.

Benedictine Sisters of the Annunciation, B.M.V. (1947): Annunciation Monastery, 7520 University Dr., Bismarck, ND 58504-9619. Tel: 701-255-1520. Sr. Nicole Kunze, O.S.B., Prioress.
Professed Sisters: 38.
Ministry in Hospitals; Parish Ministry and Catechetical Work; Education, Health Care and Spiritual Direction and Social Services.
Represented in the Diocese of Bismarck.

Sisters of St. Benedict (1948): St. Paul's Monastery, 2675 Benet Rd., St. Paul, MN 55109. Tel: 651-777-8181; Fax: 651-773-5124. Email: info@stpaulsmonastery.org. Sr. Paula Hagen, O.S.B., Prioress.
Professed Sisters: 33; Benedictine Associates 2.
Sisters serve and staff: Schools; Long term care facilities; Administration; Ministries to women and children; Retreat Ministries; Parish Ministry; Social Service and various other apostolic work.
Represented in the Archdiocese of St. Paul-Minneapolis.

Sisters of St. Benedict O.S.B. (1952): St. Placid Priory, 500 College St., NE, Lacey, WA 98516. Tel: 360-438-1771. Sr. Sharon McDonald, O.S.B., Prioress.
Professed Sisters: 11.
Sisters serve in the field of Education; Spirituality and Pastoral Care.
Represented in the Archdioceses of Portland in Oregon and Seattle in Washington.

[0233] (O.S.B.)—BENEDICTINE NUNS (P)
Subiaco Congregation

St. Scholastica Priory, Benedictine Nuns (Cloistered): 271 N. Main St., Box 606, Petersham, MA 01366-0606. Tel: 978-724-3213. Email: sspriory@aol.com. Very Rev. Mother Mary Elizabeth Kloss, O.S.B., Prioress; Sr. Mary Angela Kloss, O.S.B., Sub-Prioress.
Junior Professed: 1; Novices 3.

[0235] (O.S.B.)—BENEDICTINE SISTERS (P)

Camaldolese Benedictines

Transfiguration Monastery: 701 NY Rte. 79, Windsor, NY 13865. Tel: 607-655-2366. Email: transfigurationmonastery@gmail.com. Sr. Sheila Long, O.S.B., Prioress.
Professed Nuns: 3.
Ministry in Monastic life and Benedictine hospitality.
Represented in the Diocese of Syracuse.

[0240] (O.S.B.)—OLIVETAN BENEDICTINE SISTERS (D)

Established in the Diocese of Little Rock in 1887.

Motherhouse and Novitiate (1887): Holy Angels Convent, P.O. Drawer 1209, Jonesboro, AR 72403-1209. Tel: 870-935-5810; Fax: 870-935-4210. Sr. Lillian Marie Reiter, O.S.B., Prioress.
Professed Sisters: 39.
Properties owned and/or sponsored: St. Bernards Healthcare, Inc., Jonesboro, AR; St. Bernards Development Foundation, Inc., Jonesboro, AR.
Sisters serve and staff: Healthcare Ministries; Grammar Schools; Diocesan Ministries; CCD Centers & Parish Services; Hispanic Center.
Represented in the Dioceses of Fort Worth and Little Rock.

[0250] (C.V.D.)—SISTERS OF BETHANY (P)

Founded in El Salvador in 1928.

General Motherhouse: Instituto Bethania, Santa Tecla, El Salvador Madre Adriana Maria Giraldo, Supr. Gen.; Mother Foundress Dolores de Maria Zea.
U.S. Address (1949): Bethany House, 850 N. Hobart Blvd., Los Angeles, CA 90029. Tel: 323-665-6937. Sr. Leticia Gomez, C.V.D., Supr.
Professed Sisters: 10.
Ministry in Parish Work, Residence.
Represented in the Archdiocese of Los Angeles.

[0260] (S.B.S.)—THE SISTERS OF THE BLESSED SACRAMENT FOR INDIANS AND COLORED PEOPLE (P)

Founded in the United States in 1891.

General Motherhouse: 1663 Bristol Pike, Bensalem,

PA 19020-5796. Tel: 215-244-9900. Communications Email: sbscm.wenger@gmail.com; Development Email: sbsdevelop1@verizon.net. Sr. Donna Breslin, S.B.S., Pres.

Professed Sisters: 91.

Sisters serve and staff in the field of Education on all levels; Catechetical Schools; Adult Education and Social Service; House of Prayer; Evangelization Center.

Represented in the Archdioceses of Atlanta, Boston, New Orleans, Philadelphia and Santa Fe and in the Dioceses of Gallup, Memphis, Nashville, Palm Beach, Pensacola-Tallahassee, Richmond, Savannah and Tucson. Also in Haiti and Jamaica.

[0270] (C.B.S.)—CONGREGATION OF BON SECOURS (P)

Founded in France in 1824. First foundation in the United States in 1881.

United States: Provincial House and Novitiate, 1525 Marriottsville Rd., Marriottsville, MD 21104. Tel: 410-442-3113; Fax: 410-442-1394. Provincial Offices Email: cbsoffice@bshsi.org; Vocation Office Email: cbsvocations@bshsi.org. Sr. Rose Marie Jasinski, C.B.S., Leader. Sr. Patricia Eck, C.B.S., Congregation Leader.

Total Sisters in U.S.: 27.

Sisters own and operate: Retreat & Conference Center at Bon Secours. Member of UNANIMA International, Inc.

Represented in the Archdioceses of Baltimore and in the Dioceses of Charleston and Richmond.

[0280] (O.SS.S.)—THE BRIGITTINE SISTERS (P)

Founded in Sweden in the 14th century.

Motherhouse: Rome, Italy

Convent in U.S.A. (1957): Convent of St. Birgitta, 4 Runkenhage Rd., Darien, CT 06820. Tel: 203-655-1068; Fax: 203-655-3496; Email: conventsb@optonline.net. Sr. M. Eunice Kulangarathottiyil, O.SS.S., Supr.

Professed Sisters: 7.

Legal Title: Order of the Most Holy Savior of St. Bridget.

Monastic tradition, Semi cloister.

Represented in the Diocese of Bridgeport.

[0300] (O.CARM.)—CALCED CARMELITES (P)

Carmelite Nuns of the Ancient Observance, Strictly Cloistered, belonging in the Second Order of Carmel.

Founded in Naples, Italy in 1536. First foundation in the United States in 1931.

Carmelite Monastery of St. Therese: Little Flower of Jesus and St. M. Magdalen De Pazzi, St. Therese's Valley, 3551 Lanark Rd., Coopersburg, PA 18036-9324. Web: www.carmelite-nuns.com. Mother Mary Gertrude, O.Carm., Prioress.

Professed Sisters: 6.

Legal Title: The Carmelite Sisters of St. Therese's Valley, Inc.

Represented in the Dioceses of Allentown, Fargo, San Angelo and Superior.

[0315] (C.C.W.)—CARMELITE COMMUNITY OF THE WORD (D)

Motherhouse & Novitiate: Incarnation Center (1971), 394 Bem Rd., Gallitzin, PA 16641. Fax: 814-886-7115. Sr. Marilyn Welch, C.C.W., Admin. Gen.

Total in Community: 13.

Ministries in Diocesan Administration; the field of Religious and Academic Education at all levels; Pastoral Care, Institutionalized, Elderly, Family Life Support Groups and the Poor; Parish Ministry; Mission activity in Appalachia & Haiti.

Represented in the Diocese of Altoona-Johnstown.

[0320] (O.CARM.)—CARMELITE NUNS OF THE ANCIENT OBSERVANCE (P)

Carmelite Nuns of the Ancient Observance

Strictly Cloistered, belonging to the Second Order of Carmel. Founded in Guelder, Holland, in 1453. First foundation in the United States in 1930.

Carmel of Mary (1954): 17765 78th St., S.E., Wahpeton, ND 58075. Tel: 701-642-2360. Email: carmelwahpeton@gmail.com. Mother Madonna of the Assumption, O.Carm., Prioress.

Total in Community: 10.

Represented in the Diocese of Fargo.

Monastery of Our Lady of Grace (1989): 6202 CR 339 Via Maria, Christoval, TX 76935-3023. Tel: 325-853-1722; Web: carmelnet.org/christoval/christoval.htm. Sr. Mary Grace, O.Carm., Vicar Prioress.

Professed Sisters: 4; Postulants: 1.

Represented in the Diocese of San Angelo.

Carmel of the Sacred Heart (1963): 430 Laurel Ave., Hudson, WI 54016. Tel: 715-386-2156. Email: carmelit@pressenter.com. Sr. Lucia LaMontagne, O.Carm., Prioress & Archivist.

Professed Sisters: 4.

Legal Title: Carmelite Nuns of the Diocese of Superior, Inc.

Represented in the Diocese of Superior.

[0330] (O.CARM.)—CARMELITE SISTERS FOR THE AGED AND INFIRM (P)

Founded in 1929 in New York, Foundress: Venerable M. Angeline Teresa, O.Carm.

Motherhouse and Novitiate: St. Teresa's Motherhouse and Novitiate, 600 Woods Rd., Avila on the Hudson, Germantown, NY 12526. Email: smrc@stmhcs.org. Mother M. Mark Louis, O.Carm., Prioress Gen.; Sr. M. Richard Carmel O.Carm., Sec. Gen.

Professed Sisters: 146.

Sponsored Works: Carmelite System Inc., Germantown, NY; Carmel Terrace, Framingham, MA; St. Patrick Home, Bronx, NY; St. Margaret Hall, Cincinnati, OH; Carmel Manor, Fort Thomas, KY; Kahl Home for the Aged, Davenport, IA; St. Patrick's Manor, Framingham, MA; Marian Manor, South Boston, MA; St. Patrick's Residence, Naperville, IL; Lourdes - Noreen McKeen Residence, West Palm Beach, FL; Mother Angeline McCrory Manor, Columbus, OH; Avila Institute of Gerontology Inc, Germantown, NY; Our Lady's Manor, Dublin, Ireland; Mount Carmel Care Center, Lenox, MA.

Represented in the Archdioceses of Boston, Cincinnati and New York and in the Dioceses of Albany, Altoona-Johnstown, Brooklyn, Columbus, Covington, Davenport, Joliet, Palm Beach, Scranton and Springfield in Massachusetts.

[0350] (O.CARM.)—CARMELITE SISTERS (CORPUS CHRISTI) (P)

First foundation in the United States in 1920.

General Motherhouse: Mt. St. Benedict, Tunapuna, Trinidad, West Indies Sr. Petronilla Joseph, O.Carm., Prioress Gen.

U.S. Address: Mount Carmel Home-Keen's Memorial, 412 W. 18th, Kearney, NE 68847. Tel: 308-237-2287; Tel: 308-293-6149. Sr. Mary Florence Blavet, O.Carm., Prioress.

Professed Sisters Worldwide: 65; Professed Sisters in U.S.: 4.

Ministry in Home and foreign missions; Academic and Religious Education; Social Work; Catechetics; Youth Ministry.

Represented in the Dioceses of Grand Island and Providence.

[0360] (CARMEL D.C.J.)—CARMELITE SISTERS OF THE DIVINE HEART OF JESUS (P)

Founded in Germany in 1891. First Convent in the United States in 1912.

General Motherhouse: Sittard, Netherlands Antilles Mother Karla Marija, Supr. Gen.

Northern Province: 1230 Kavanaugh Pl., Milwaukee, WI 53213. Tel: 414-453-4040; Fax: 414-453-6503. Email: carmeldcnorth@gmail.com. Sr. Maria Giuseppe, Prov. Supr.; Sr. M. Immaculata, Wauwatosa Supr.

South Central Province: 10341 Manchester Rd., St. Louis, MO 63122. Tel: 314-965-7616. Sr. M. Benedicta, Prov. Supr.

South Western Province: 4130 S. Alameda, Corpus Christi, TX 78411. Sr. M. Lydia Ann Braun, Provincial Supr.

Professed Sisters Worldwide: 457; Total Sisters in U.S: 66; Novices: 72; Postulants: 36.

Sisters minister to Homes for Children 2; Homes for the Aged 9; Day Nurseries 4; Mission work in Africa, Iceland, Nicaragua, Venezuela and Brazil.

Represented in the Archdioceses of Milwaukee, St. Louis and San Antonio and in the Dioceses of Corpus Christi, Gary, Grand Rapids, Owensboro and San Diego.

[0370] (O.C.D.)—CARMELITE SISTERS OF THE MOST SACRED HEART OF LOS ANGELES (P)

General Motherhouse & Novitiate: Carmelite Sisters of the Most Sacred Heart of Los Angeles, 920 E. Alhambra Rd., Alhambra, CA 91801. Tel: 626-289-1353; Fax: 626-308-1913. Email: contacts@carmelitesistersocd.com. Mother Judith Zuniga, O.C.D., Supr. Gen.

Total in Community: 136.

Legal Titles: Carmelite Sisters of the Most Sacred Heart of Los Angeles; Carmelite Sisters of the Most Sacred Heart of Los Angeles Education, Inc.; Sacred Heart Retreat House, Inc.; Mount Carmel in the Desert; Little Flower Center; dba Little Flower Missionary House; dba Little Flower Educational Child Care; Avila Gardens, Inc.; Santa Teresita, Inc.; Marycrest Manor, Inc.; Mount Carmel Health Ministries, Inc.; Flos Carmeli Formation Centers, Inc.; Carmelite Sisters Foundation, Inc.

The sisters serve and staff: Religious and academic education; healthcare centers; skilled nursing facilities for the care of the aged; child care: pre-school, pre-kinder and kindergarten; retreat houses; ministry to the elderly, sick and convalescents; evangelization centers and ministry to the youth.

Represented in the Archdioceses of Denver, Los Angeles and Miami and in the Dioceses of Tucson and Steubenville.

[0380] (C.S.T.)—CARMELITE SISTERS OF ST. THERESE OF THE INFANT JESUS (D)

Founded in the United States in 1917 at Bentley, OK.

General Motherhouse: 7501 W. Britton Rd., #140, Oklahoma City, OK 73132. Tel: 405-837-7068. Sr. Barbara Joseph Foley, Gen. Supr.

Total in Community: 13.

Legal Title: Carmelite Sisters of St. Therese of the Infant Jesus.

Ministry in the field of Academic Education; Religious Education, Serving the Poor and Parish Ministry.

Represented in the Archdiocese of Oklahoma City.

[0390] (C.M.S.T.)—MISSIONARY CARMELITES OF ST. TERESA (P)

Founded in Mexico City in 1903.

General Motherhouse: Fresno No. 150, Col. Santa Maria la Ribera, 06400, Mexico, D.F., Mexico Sr. Maria Margarita Molina, Supr. Gen.

U.S. Holy Family Province (1983): 9548 Deer Trail Dr., Houston, TX 77038. Tel: 281-445-5520; Fax: 281-445-5748. Sr. Victoria Álvarez, C.M.S.T., Prov. Supr. Professed Sisters: 49.

Ministry in Pastoral; Hispanic Ministry and Retreats.

Represented in the Archdioceses of Galveston-Houston and Oklahoma City and in the Dioceses of Beaumont and Little Rock.

[0397] (C.M.R.)—CONGREGATION OF MARY, QUEEN (P)

Founded in Vietnam in 1670 by Bishop Pierre Lambert de la Motte. First foundation in the United States in 1979 in Springfield, MO.

U.S. Regional: 625 S. Jefferson Ave., Springfield, MO 65806. Tel: 417-869-9842; Fax: 417-832-0852. Sr. Marguerite A. Tran, C.M.R., Regl. Leader.

Professed Sisters: 23.

Legal Title: Congregation of Mary Queen, American Region.

Represented in the Archdiocese of St. Louis and in the Dioceses of Dallas, Kansas City-St. Joseph and Springfield-Cape Girardeau.

[0400] (O.CARM.)—CONGREGATION OF OUR LADY OF MOUNT CARMEL (P)

Founded in France in 1824. First foundation in the United States in 1833.

Generalate: 62284 Fish Hatchery Rd., P.O. Box 476, Lacombe, LA 70445. Tel: 504-524-2398; Tel: 985-882-7577; Fax: 504-524-5011. Sr. Lawrence Habetz, O.Carm., Pres.; Sr. Sheila Undang, O.Carm., Vice Pres. & Sec.; Sr. Therese Gregoire, O.Carm., Treas. & Archivist.

Professed Sisters: 76.

Sponsorships: Carmelite Ministries, Inc./Cub Corner Preschool; Carmelite NGO, New Orleans, LA.

Ministry in the field of Education on all levels; Hospitals; Social Service; Religious Education; Pastoral Ministry and Retreat Work; Prison Education Ministry; Child Care.

Represented in the Archdiocese of New Orleans and in the Dioceses of Houma-Thibodaux, Joliet in Illinois and Lafayette (LA). Also in the Philippines and Timor-Leste.

[0410] (O.CARM.)—INSTITUTE OF THE SISTERS OF OUR LADY OF MOUNT CARMEL (P)

Istituto delle Suore di Nostra Signora del Carmelo Founded in Italy in 1854. First foundation in the United States, 1947.

General Motherhouse: Istituto di Nostra Signora del Carmelo, Via dei Baglioni 10, Rome, Italy U.S. Headquarters: Carmelite Sisters, 5 Wheatland St., Peabody, MA 01960. Tel: 978-531-4733. Sr. Kathleen A. Bettencourt, I.N.S.C., Supr.

Professed Sisters: 16.

Ministry in Holy Childhood Nursery; Kindergarten; Preschools; Daycare Centers

Represented in the Archdioceses of Boston and Washington and in the Diocese of St. Augustine.

[0420] (O.C.D.)—DISCALCED CARMELITE NUNS (P)

Founded in Spain in 1562. First foundation in the United States in 1790 in Charles County, Maryland; later this monastery was moved to Baltimore. The Monasteries listed here are strictly contemplative and belong to the Order of Discalced Carmelites.

Carmelite Monastery (1790): 1318 Dulaney Valley Rd., Baltimore, MD 21286. Tel: 410-823-7415; Email: info@baltimorecarmel.org; Web: www.baltimorecarmel.org. Sr. Judith Long, O.C.D., Prioress.

Professed Sisters: 16.

Legal Title: Carmelite Sisters of Baltimore.

Carmel of St. Joseph (1863): 9150 Clayton Rd., St. Louis, MO 63124. Tel: 314-993-6899; Fax: 314-993-4346; Email: prioress@stlouiscarmel.org; Web: www.stlouiscarmel.com. Mother Marya, O.C.D., Prioress.

Professed Cloistered Nuns: 13; Professed Extern Sisters: 1; Temporary Professed: 1; Novices: 1; Postulants: 1.

Monastery of St. Joseph and St. Teresa (1877): Discalced Carmelite Nuns, 73530 River Rd., Covington, LA 70435-2206. Tel: 985-898-0923; Email: covingtoncarmel@yahoo.com; Web: www.covingtoncarmel.org. Sr. Edith Turpin, O.C.D., Prioress.

Solemnly Professed: 5; First Vows: 4.

Carmelite Monastery of Boston (1890): Cloistered, Discalced Carmelite Nuns - O.C.D.61 Mt. Pleasant Ave., Boston, MA 02119. Tel: 617-442-1411; Fax: 617-442-0203; Email: carmelitesofboston@gmail.com; Web: www.carmelitesofboston.org. Sr. Mary Teresa Wisniewski, O.C.D., Prioress.

Professed: 8; Temporary Professed: 1.

Monastery of the Most Holy Trinity: Discalced Carmelite Nuns, 4525 W. 2nd Ave., Hialeah, FL 33012. Tel: 305-558-7122; Fax: 305-558-1190. Mother Teresa Lucia del Inmaculado Corazon, O.C.D., Prioress.

Total in Community: 11.

Legal Title: Discalced Carmelite Nuns, Inc.

Carmelite Monastery (1902): 66th Ave. and Old York Rd., Oak Ln., Philadelphia, PA 19126. Tel: 215-424-6143; Fax: 215-424-6143; Fax: 215-424-6145. Mother Barbara of the Holy Ghost, O.C.D., Prioress.

Professed Nuns: 7.

Monastery of Our Lady of Mt. Carmel (1907): 361 Highland Blvd., Brooklyn, NY 11207. Tel: 718-235-0035; Fax: 718-235-0542; Email: carmelofbrooklyn@gmail.com. Mother Ana Maria, O.C.D.

Monastery of Our Lady of Mt. Carmel and St. Joseph: 361 Highland Blvd., Brooklyn, NY 11207. Tel: 718-235-0035; Fax: 718-235-0542; Email: carmelofbrooklyn@gmail.com. Mother Ana Maria, O.C.D., Prioress.

Total in Community: 7.

Carmelite Monastery of the Infant Jesus (1908): 1000 Lincoln St., Santa Clara, CA 95050. Tel: 408-296-8412. Sr. Emmanuel of Bethlehem, O.C.D., Prioress.

Sisters Solemn Vows: 12; Novices: 1.

St. Joseph's Carmelite Monastery (1908): 2215 N.E. 147th, Shoreline, WA 98155. Tel: 206-363-7150; Fax: 206-365-7335. Sr. Maria Valla, O.C.D., Prioress.

Professed Sisters: 9; Novices: 2.

Legal Title: Carmelite Monastery of Seattle.

Carmel of the Queen of Heaven (Formerly known as Regina Coeli Monastery) (1911): 17937 250th St., Eldridge, IA 52748-9425. Tel: 563-285-8387; Fax: 563-285-7467. Sr. Lynne Elwinger, O.C.D., Prioress.

Professed Sisters: 8.

Discalced Carmelite Nuns (1930): Monastery of Mary Immaculate and St. Joseph, 3115 Lexington Rd., Louisville, KY 40206. Tel: 502-896-3958; Fax: 502-896-3958. Mother John-Baptist, O.C.D., Prioress; Sr. Katherine, O.C.D., Archivist.

Solemnly Professed Sisters: 8.

Legal Title: Carmelite Monastery of Louisville, Inc.

Order of Discalced Carmelites O.C.D. (1913): Carmel of St. Teresa of Los Angeles, Inc., 215 E. Alhambra Rd., Alhambra, CA 91801. Tel: 626-282-2387; Fax: 626-282-0144; Email: teresacarm1913@gmail.com. Mother Brenda Marie Schroeder, O.C.D., Prioress.

Total in Community: 14.

Discalced Carmelite Nuns (1916): Monastery of Our Lady of Guadalupe, 4300 Mount Carmel Dr. N.E., Ada (Parnell), MI 49301. Tel: 616-691-7764. Email: carmelparnell@mymailstation.com; Web: www.carmelitenuns.org. Mother Mary Angela, O.C.D., Prioress.

Professed Nuns: 7; Novices: 2.

Discalced Carmelite Nuns (2000): Carmelite Monastery, 89 Hiddenbrooke Dr., Beacon, NY 12508-2230. Tel: 845-831-5572; Fax: 845-831-5579; Email: carmelitesbeacon@gmail.com; Web: www.carmelitesbeacon. org. Sr. Marjorie Robinson, O.C.D., Prioress.

Total in Community: 13.

Discalced Carmelite Monastery of St. Therese of the Child Jesus (1920): 75 Carmel Rd., Buffalo, NY 14214. Tel: 716-837-6499. Mother Miriam of Jesus, O.C.D., Prioress.

Cloistered Professed Sisters: 10; Extern Professed Sisters: 2; Novices: 2.

Monastery of Discalced Carmelites (1922): 22143 Main St., P.O. Box 260, Oldenburg, IN 47036-0260. Tel: 812-212-5901. Sr. Jean Alice McGoff, O.C.D., Prioress.

Contemplative Professed Nuns: 5.

Legal Title: Monastery of the Resurrection, Discalced Carmelites, Sisters of Our Lady of Mount Carmel Carmelite Monastery, Carmelites of Indianapolis.

Carmel of the Holy Family (1923): 2541 Arlington Rd., Cleveland Heights, OH 44118. Tel: 216-321-6568; Fax: 216-321-1904; Web: clevelandcarmel.org. Sr. Barbara Losh, O.C.D., Prioress.

Contemplative Professed Nuns: 8.

Discalced Carmelites of the Order of Our Lady of Mount Carmel O.C.D. (1925): Monastery of Our Lady and St. Therese, 27601 Hwy. 1, Carmel, CA 93923. Tel: 831-624-3043; Fax: 831-624-5495; Email: carmelitesofcarmelca@gmail.com; Web: carmelitesistersbythesea.org. Mother Teresita of the Holy Face, O.C.D., Prioress.

Professed Sisters: 11.

Legal Title: Carmelite Monastery of Carmel, California, Inc.

Discalced Carmelites O.C.D. (1926): Monastery of the Most Blessed Virgin Mary of Mount Carmel, 189 Madison Ave., Morristown, NJ 07960. Mother Therese, O.C.D., Prioress.

Professed Sisters: 14; Novices: 4.

Order of Discalced Carmelites O.C.D. (1926): Carmelite Monastery of San Diego, 5158 Hawley Blvd., San Diego, CA 92116-1934. Tel: 619-280-5424. Email: smgcarmel@sbcglobal.net. Sr. Michaela Gresko, O.C.D., Prioress.

Professed Nuns: 14.

Monastery of St. Therese of the Child Jesus (1926): 35750 Moravian Dr., Clinton Township, MI 48035-2138. Tel: 586-790-7255. Mother Mary Therese, O.C.D., Prioress.

Professed Nuns: 8; Sisters in Temporary Vows: 3; Novices: 3; Postulants: 5.

Carmel of St. Therese of Lisieux, Inc. (1927): Discalced Carmelite Nuns, P.O. Box 57, Loretto, PA 15940-0057. Tel: 814-472-8620; Email: lorettocarmel@hotmail.com; Web: www.lorettocarmel. org. Mother John of the Cross, O.C.D., Prioress.

Solemn Professed Nuns: 9; Novices: 1; Postulants: 1; Aspirants: 1.

Discalced Carmelite Nuns O.C.D. (1928): Carmelite Monastery of Cristo Rey, 721 Parker Ave., San Francisco, CA 94118-4227. Tel: 415-387-2640. Email: prioress@cmcrnuns.org.

Total in Community: 13.

Carmelite Nuns of Dallas: Monastery of Discalced Carmelites (1928), 600 Flowers Ave., Dallas, TX 75211. Rev. Mother Juanita Marie, O.C.D., Prioress.

Professed Nuns: 12.

Discalced Carmelite Nuns (1930): Monastery of Our Lady and St. Joseph, 1931 W. Jefferson Rd., Pittsford, NY 14534. Tel: 585-427-7094. Email: ocdrochester@gmail.com; Web: www.carmelitesofrochester.org. Mother Therese Marie of Jesus Crucified, O.C.D., Prioress.

Professed Nuns with Solemn Vows: 13; Aspirants: 2.

Legal Title: Carmelite Monastery of Rochester.

Monastery of Discalced Carmelites O.C.D. (1930): Monastery of Our Lady of Mount Carmel and St. Therese of the Child Jesus, 25 Watson Ave., Barrington, RI 02806. Tel: 401-245-3421. Email: barringtoncarmel@fullchannel.net. Sr. Susan Lumb, O.C.D., Prioress.

Total in Community: 12.

Discalced Carmelite Nuns O.C.D. (1934): Monastery of the Infant Jesus of Prague and Our Lady of Guadalupe, 6301 Culebra Rd., San Antonio, TX 78238-4909. Tel: 210-680-1834. Mother Therese Leonard, O.C.D., Prioress.

Total in Community: 8.

Carmel of the Holy Family and St. Therese (1935): 6981 Teresian Way, P.O. Box 4210, Georgetown, CA 95634. Tel: 530-333-1617; Email: georgetown2004@juno.com; Web: www.carmelitemonastery.org. Mother Mary Bethany, Prioress.

Total in Community: 13.

Discalced Carmelite Nuns O.C.D. (1936): Monastery of Mary, Mother of Grace, 1250 Carmel Dr., Lafayette, LA 70501. Tel: 337-232-4651. Email: lafayettecarmelites@gmail.com. Mother Regina Mullins, O.C.D., Prioress.

Total in Community: 15; Solemn Professed: 11; Junior Professed: 1; Novice: 1; Externs in Perpetual Vows: 1; Extern Junior Professed: 1.

Discalced Carmelite Nuns O.C.D. (1939): Carmel of St. Joseph, 2370 Morgan Rd., N.E., Piedmont, OK 73078. Email: vocation@okcarmel.org. Sr. Donna Ross, O.C.D., Prioress.

Total in Community: 8.

Discalced Carmelite Nuns of Milwaukee O.C.D. (1940): Carmel of the Mother of God, W267 N2517 Carmelite Rd., Pewaukee, WI 53072-4528. Tel: 262-691-0336; Fax: 262-695-0143; Email: pewaukeecarmel@aol.com. Sr. Margaret Hansen, O.C.D., Prioress; Rev. Dennis C. Klemme, J.C.D., Chap. (Retired).

Professed Sisters: 6.

Discalced Carmelite Nuns of Alexandria, South Dakota, Inc. O.C.D: Monastery of Our Mother of Mercy and St. Joseph, 221 5th St. W., P.O. Box 67, Alexandria, SD 57311-0067. Tel: 605-239-4382. Mother Mary Elias of the Immaculate Conception, Prioress.

Total in Community: 6.

Carmelite Monastery (1943): 716 Dauphin Island Pkwy., Mobile, AL 36606. Tel: 251-471-3991; 251-401-1223; Web: www.carmelmobileal.com. Mother M. Cecile, Prioress.

Solemnly Professed Nuns: 9; Perpetually Professed Externs: 2; Aspirant: 1.

Discalced Carmelite Monastery (1945): 49 Mount Carmel Rd., Santa Fe, NM 87505-0352. Tel: 505-983-7232. Mother Mary Louise, O.C.D., Prioress.

Total in Community: 9.

Discalced Carmelite Monastery (1946): 275 Pleasant St., Concord, NH 03301-2590. Tel: 603-225-5791. Sr. Claudette Blais, O.C.D., Prioress.

Solemnly Professed Nuns: 9; Perpetually Professed Sisters: 1.

Sisters of Our Lady of Mount Carmel of Terre Haute: Carmelite Monastery, 59 Allendale, Terre Haute, IN 47802-4751. Tel: 812-299-1410; Fax: 812299-5820; Email: carmelth@heartsawake.org. Mother Anne Brackmann, O.C.D., Prioress.

Professed Nuns: 13; Novices: 5.

Discalced Carmelite Nuns of Colorado, Inc. (1948): Carmel of Holy Spirit, 6138 S. Gallup St., Littleton, CO 80120-2702. Tel: 303-798-4176. Mother Mary of Jesus, D.C., Prioress.

Professed Nuns: 10.

Order of Discalced Carmelites O.C.D. (1949): Carmel of Mary Immaculate and St. Mary Magdalen, 26 Harmony School Rd., Flemington, NJ 08822. Email: friendsofcarmelnj@gmail.com. Mother Anne of Christ, O.C.D., Prioress.

Professed: 11; Total in Community: 12.

Discalced Carmelite Nuns O.C.D. (1950): Monastery of the Infant Jesus of Prague, 3501 Silver Lake Rd., Traverse City, MI 49684-8949. Tel: 231-946-4960; Email: tccarmel@charter.net; Web: carmeloftraversecity.org. Mother Mary of Jesus, O.C.D., Prioress.

Solemnly Professed: 4; Sisters in Formation: 1.

Discalced Carmelite Nuns O.C.D. (1951): Monastery of the Holy Cross, N4028 N. Hwy. U.S. 2, P.O. Box 397, Iron Mountain, MI 49801. Tel: 906-774-0561;

Fax: 906-774-0561. Mother Maria of Jesus, O.C.D., Prioress.
Total in Community: 19.

Discalced Carmelite Nuns O.C.D: Monastery of the Holy Name of Jesus, 6100 Pepper Rd., Denmark, WI 54208. Tel: 920-863-5055; Email: mttabor@holynamecarmel.org. Mother Christine Marie, O.C.D., Prioress.

Discalced Carmelite Nuns O.C.D. (1950): Discalced Carmelite Nuns of Little Rock, 7201 W. 32nd St., Little Rock, AR 72204-4716. Tel: 501-565-5121. Sr. Maria Cruz DeLeon, O.C.D., Prioress.
Professed Sisters: 14.
Legal Title: Discalced Carmelite Nuns of Little Rock.

Discalced Carmelite Nuns O.C.D. (1951): Monastery of Our Lady of Mount Carmel and The Little Flower, 2155 Terry Rd., Jackson, MS 39204. Tel: 601-373-1460. Email: jacksoncarmelites@gmail.com. Sr. Mary Jane Agonoy, O.C.D., Prioress.
Professed Nuns: 6.

Carmel of the Immaculate Heart of Mary (1952): 5714 Holladay Blvd., Salt Lake City, UT 84121-1599. Tel: 801-277-6075. Mother Margaret Mary Miller, O.C.D., Prioress; Sr. Therese Bui, O.C.D., Archivist.
Solemn Vows: 9.

Discalced Carmelite Nuns of St. Paul (1952): Carmel of Our Lady of Divine Providence, 8251 Demontreville Trail N., Lake Elmo, MN 55042-9547. Tel: 651-777-3882. Email: carmelbvm@gmail.com. Mother Marie-Ange of the Eucharistic Heart, O.C.D., Prioress.
Professed Sisters: 12; Novices: 1.

Discalced Carmelite Nuns O.C.D. (1953): 1 Maria Hall Dr., Danville, PA 17821. Tel: 570-275-4682; Fax: 570-275-4684. Sr. Angela Pikus, O.C.D., Prioress.
Professed Sisters: 9.

Sisters of Our Lady of Mount Carmel: 1950 La Fond Dr., Reno, NV 89509-3099. Tel: 775-323-3236; Fax: 775-322-1532; Email: renocarmel@carmelofreno.net; Web: www.carmelofreno.com. Sr. Susan Weber, O.C.D., Prioress.
Professed Nuns: 14.

Carmel of Maria Regina O.C.D. (1957): 87609 Green Hill Rd., Eugene, OR 97402. Tel: 541-345-8649; Fax: 541-345-4857. Sr. Elizabeth Mary, O.C.D., Prioress & Community Archivist.
Total in Community: 7.

Monastery of the Holy Family (1957): 510 E. Gore Rd., Erie, PA 16509. Email: carmelites@eriercd.org.
Solemnly Professed Sisters: 3; Novice: 1.

Discalced Carmelite Nuns (1958): 11 W. Back St., Savannah, GA 31419-3219. Tel: 912-925-8505. Sr. Mary Elizabeth Angaine, Prioress.
Total in Community: 8; Professed Nuns: 5.

Monastery of the Most Holy Trinity (1958): 5801 Mt. Carmel Dr., Arlington, TX 76017. Tel: 817-468-1781. Email: supcarmel@aol.com. Mother Anne Teresa Kulinski, O.C.D., Prioress.
Total in Community: 12.

Discalced Carmelite Nuns O.C.D. (1958): Discalced Carmelite Nuns of New Caney, Texas, 1100 Parthenon Pl., New Caney, TX 77357-3276. Email: carmelnewcaney@gmail.com. Sr. Angel Teresa Sweeney, O.C.D., Prioress; Sr. Mary Ann Harrison, O.C.D., 1st Council Sister.
Total in Community: 8.
Legal Title: Discalced Carmelite Nuns of New Caney, TX.

Monastery of Discalced Carmelites (1959): 949 N. River Rd., Des Plaines, IL 60016. Tel: 847-298-4241; Fax: 847-298-4242. Mother Anne of Jesus, Prioress.
Total in Community: 20.

Order of Discalced Carmelites O.C.D. (1958): Carmel of St. Therese, 15 Mt. Carmel Rd., Danvers, MA 01923-3796. Tel: 978-774-3008. Sr. Michael of Christ the King, O.C.D., Prioress.
Legal Title: Discalced Carmelite Nuns of Danvers.

Discalced Carmelite Nuns O.C.D. (1960): Monastery of The Sacred Heart and St. Joseph, 1106 Swifts Highway, Jefferson City, MO 65109. Tel: 573-636-3430. Mother Marie Therese, O.C.D., Prioress.
Solemnly Professed Nuns: 4.

Carmel of the Assumption (1961): 5206 Center Dr., Latrobe, PA 15650-5204. Tel: 724-539-1056. Email: contact@latrobecarmel.org. Sr. Mary Wild, O.C.D., Prioress.
Professed Sisters: 10.

Discalced Carmelite Nuns, Inc. (1962): Our Lady of the Incarnation Monastery, 2901 S. Cecelia St., Sioux City, IA 51106-3299. Tel: 712-276-1680. Email: siouxcitycarmel@gmail.com. Mother Joseph of Jesus, O.C.D., Prioress.
Total in Community: 8.

Carmelite Monastery of the Mother of God (1965): 530 Blackstone Dr., San Rafael, CA 94903. Tel: 415-479-6872; Fax: 415-491-4964; Email: sram@motherofgodcarmel.org. Sr. Anna Marie Vanni, O.C.D., Prioress.
Total in Community: 6.

Carmel of the Holy Trinity: 6301 Pali Hwy., Kaneohe, HI 96744-5224. Tel: 808-261-6542. Email: carmeltrinityhawaii@outlook.com.
Total in Community: 4.

Discalced Carmelite Nuns of the Byzantine Rite (1980): Holy Annunciation Monastery, 403 W. County Rd., Sugarloaf, PA 18249. Tel: 570-788-1205; Fax: 570-788-3329. Mother Maria of the Holy Spirit, O.C.D., Prioress.
Professed Nuns: 12; Novices: 2.
Represented in the Diocese of Passaic.

Discalced Carmelites of Maryland, Inc: Carmel of Port Tobacco (1976), 5678 Mt. Carmel Rd., La Plata, MD 20646-3625. Email: contact@carmelofporttobacco.com. Mother Virginia Marie, O.C.D., Prioress.
Solemn Professed: 8; Novices: 2.

[0430] (B.V.M.)—SISTERS OF CHARITY OF THE BLESSED VIRGIN MARY (P)

Founded in America in 1833.

BVM Center: Mount Carmel, 1100 Carmel Dr., Dubuque, IA 52003-7991. Tel: 563-588-2351; Fax: 563-588-4832; Web: www.bvmcong.org. Sr. Teri Hadro, B.V.M., Pres.
Total in Congregation : 375.
Sisters serve and staff: in the field of Academic Education on all levels; Health Care Services; Religious Education; Chaplaincies; Pastoral Care and Parish Ministry; Campus Ministry; Diocesan School Offices; Diocesan Services-Administration; Social Work; Social Justice/Advocacies.
Represented in the Archdioceses of Chicago, Denver, Dubuque, Los Angeles, Milwaukee, Portland in Oregon, St. Louis, St. Paul-Minneapolis, San Francisco, Seattle and Washington and in the Dioceses of Davenport, Des Moines, Fort Wayne-South Bend, Helena, Honolulu, Kansas City-St. Joseph, Memphis, Peoria, Phoenix, Rockford, St. Petersburg, San Jose, Santa Rosa, Sioux City, Springfield-Cape Girardeau and Venice. Also in Ecuador and Ghana.

[0440] (S.C.)—SISTERS OF CHARITY OF CINCINNATI, OHIO (P)

Founded by Saint Elizabeth Ann Seton, Emmitsburg, MD, 1809. The Cincinnati Community became independent in 1852, Papal approval in 1939.

General Motherhouse (1852): Mount St. Joseph, 5900 Delhi Rd., Mount Saint Joseph, OH 45051. Tel: 513-347-5300; Fax: 513-347-5228; Web: www.srcharitycinti.org. Sr. Joan Elizabeth Cook, S.C., Pres.
Professed Sisters: 298.
Legal Title: Sisters of Charity, Cincinnati, OH.
Sisters serve and staff: Colleges; Secondary and Elementary Schools; Parishes; Healthcare; Foreign Missions; Home for Profoundly Challenged; Senior Care Services; Social Services; Congregational Services; Retreat Center; Spiritual Direction.
Represented in the Archdioceses of Cincinnati, Denver, Detroit, Dubuque, Indianapolis, New Orleans, New York, San Francisco and Santa Fe and in the Dioceses of Brownsville, Cleveland, Colorado Springs, Columbus, Covington, Fort Wayne-South Bend, Helena, Juneau, Kalamazoo, Lansing, Las Cruces, Pueblo, Saginaw, Toledo and Venice. Also in Guatemala, Anapra and Mexico.

[0450] (S.C.I.C.)—SISTERS OF CHARITY OF THE IMMACULATE CONCEPTION OF IVREA (P)

Founded in Italy in the 18th Century. First foundation in the United States in 1961.

General Motherhouse: Via della Renella 85, Rome, Italy Tel: 011-39-06-581-8145. Sr. Raffaella GiudiciPorro, Supr. Gen.
Total in Congregation : 593.

U.S. Foundation (1961): Immaculate Virgin of Miracles Convent, 268 Prittstown Rd., Mount Pleasant, PA 15666. Tel: 724-887-6753. Sr. Angelina Grimoldi, S.C.I.C., Reg. Supr. Tel: 724-887-6753. Email: office@vernamontessorischool.org.
Professed Sisters in the U.S: 8.
Properties owned and/or sponsored: Verna Montessori Children's House, Elementary School & Middle School; Immaculate Virgin of Miracles Convent, Mt. Pleasant, PA.
Sisters serve and staff: Kindergarten and Elementary Schools and Middle School; Parish Services; Religious Education; Pastoral Ministry.
Represented in the Diocese of Greensburg.

[0460] (C.C.V.I.)—CONGREGATION OF THE SISTERS OF CHARITY OF THE INCARNATE WORD (P)

Founded in 1869 at San Antonio, Texas.

Generalate: 4503 Broadway, San Antonio, TX 78209-6209. Tel: 210-828-2224; Fax: 210-828-9741. Sr. Teresa Maya, C.C.V.I., Congregational Leader.
Universal total in Congregation: 287; U.S. Sisters: 143.
Properties owned and/or sponsored: Universities 1; High Schools 3; Hospitals (co-sponsored) 27; Temporary shelters for homeless women & children 2; Retirement Centers 1.
Ministry in the field of Education at all levels; Hospitals and Health Service Agencies; Nursing Homes; Pastoral Ministries; Diocesan Offices; Social Service Agencies.
Represented in the Archdioceses of Chicago, St. Louis, and San Antonio and in the Dioceses of Corpus Christi, Dallas, El Paso, Fort Worth, Grand Rapids, Jefferson City, Joliet, Springfield-Cape Girardeau and Victoria. Also in Chile, Columbia, Ireland, Mexico, Peru, and Zambia.

[0470] (CCVI)—CONGREGATION OF THE SISTERS OF CHARITY OF THE INCARNATE WORD, HOUSTON, TEXAS (P)

Founded in the United States in 1866, St. Mary's Infirmary Galveston, TX.

Motherhouse: Villa de Matel, 6510 Lawndale St., P.O. Box 230969, Houston, TX 77223-0969. Tel: 713-928-6053; Fax: 713-928-8148. Sr. Kevina Keating, CCVI, Congregational Leader.
Total in Congregation : 137.
Legal Titles: Incarnate Word Religious and Charitable Trust; The Congregation of the Sisters of Charity of the Incarnate Word, Houston, Texas; The Claude Marie Dubuis Religious and Charitable Trust; Sisters of Charity of the Incarnate Word, Houston, Texas (SCH).
Sisters serve and staff: Hospitals; Homes for Aged; Elementary and Secondary Schools; Literacy; Social Services; Retreat Centers.
Represented in the Archdioceses of Galveston-Houston, Los Angeles and St. Louis and in the Dioceses of Alexandria, Austin, Lake Charles, San Bernardino, Shreveport and Tyler. Also in Guatemala, Ireland, Kenya, Mexico and San Salvador.

[0480] (S.C.L.)—SISTERS OF CHARITY OF LEAVENWORTH, KANSAS (P)

Founded in the United States in 1858.

Community Offices and Motherhouse: 4200 S. 4th St., Leavenworth, KS 66048-5054. Tel: 913-758-6501; Fax: 913-364-5401. Sr. Constance Phelps, S.C.L., Community Dir.; Tonya Crawford, Archivist.
Total in Community: 200.
Ministries to AIDS Victims; Care of Creation; Cross-culture; Elderly; Immigrants; Prisoners, Handicapped Adults and Youth; Health Service Agencies; Mental Health; Native Americans; and Social Service Agencies.
Properties owned and sponsored: University of Saint Mary, Leavenworth, KS; Cristo Rey Kansas City High School, KCMO. The Sisters' Health Care ministry is currently carried out and sponsored by Leaven Ministries (Public Juridic Person) for the following - Sisters of Charity of Leavenworth Health System (SCLHS), Broomfield, CO: Residential and Day Treatment Centers for Children, Mount St. Vincent Home, Denver, CO; Saint Joseph Hospital, Denver, CO; St. Mary's Hospital & Medical Center, Grand Junction, CO; St. Vincent Healthcare, Billings, MT; St. James Healthcare, Butte, MT; Holy Rosary Healthcare, Miles City, MT; Marian Clinic, Topeka, KS; Caritas Clinics, Inc., Kansas City, KS; Saint Vincent Clinic, Leavenworth, KS (Div. of Caritas Clinics); Duchesne Clinic, Kansas City, KS (Div. of Caritas Clinics).
Sisters serving in Elementary; Secondary and Higher Education; Nursing Education; Religious Education; Hospitals; Latin American Missions; Diocesan Offices; Parish Administration and Pastoral Ministry;

Liturgy- Music Ministry; Campus Ministry; Spiritual Direction; Communications; Social Justice; Housing; Ecology.
Represented in the Archdioceses of Denver, Kansas City in Kansas, Los Angeles, Milwaukee, New Orleans, New York and St. Louis and in the Dioceses of Charlotte, Cheyenne, Grand Island, Great Falls-Billings, Helena, Jefferson City, Kansas City-St. Joseph, Oakland and Pueblo. Also in Italy and Peru.

[0490] (S.G.M.)—SISTERS OF CHARITY OF MONTREAL (P) (Grey Nuns)

Founded in 1737 by Saint Marguerite d'Youville at Montreal, Canada. First foundation in the United States in 1855.
Generalate: General Administration, 138 Rue Saint-Pierre, Montreal, Canada, H2Y 2L7. Tel: 514-842-9411; Web: www.sgm.qc.ca. Sr. Aurore Larkin, S.G.M., Congregational Leader.
St. Joseph Area U.S.A: Area Administration-SGM,10 Pelham Rd., Ste. 1000, Lexington, MA 02421-8499. Tel: 781-674-7407; Emailo: srjeanneepoor@verizon.net. Sr. Jeanne Poor, S.G.M., Area Coord.
Total in Community: 17.
Legal Title: The Grey Nuns Charities, Inc.
Ministry in retreat ministry, social justice, congregational governance & administration, pastoral care and prayer ministry, ESL tutoring and food preparation for the poor.
Represented in the Archdiocese of Boston.

[0500] (S.C.N.)—SISTERS OF CHARITY OF NAZARETH (P)

Founded in the United States in 1812.
SCN Center: P.O. Box 187, Nazareth, KY 40048. Tel: 502-348-1555; Fax: 502-348-1502. Sr. Susan Gatz, S.C.N., Pres.
Total in Congregation : 570.
Legal Title: Nazareth Literary & Benevolent Institution.
Properties owned or sponsored: Camp Maria, Leonardtown, MD; Nazareth Villages Inc., Nazareth Villages II, Inc., Nazareth, KY; Nazareth Home, Inc., Louisville, KY; Vincentian Academy, Pittsburgh, PA; Vincentian Collaborative System, Pittsburgh, PA; Vincentian Home, Inc., Pittsburgh, PA; Vincentian Regency, Pittsburgh, PA; Vincentian DeMarillac, Pittsburgh, PA; Marian Manor Corp., Pittsburgh, PA; Vincentian Collaborative System Rehabilitation Services, Pittsburgh, PA; Vincentian Child Development Center, Pittsburgh, PA; Vincentian Collaborative System Charitable Foundation, Pittsburgh, PA.
Nazareth Office: P.O. Box 187, Nazareth, KY 40048. Tel: 502-331-4072; Fax: 502-331-4073. Email: info@scnfamily.org. Sr. Mary Elizabeth Miller, SCN, Prov.; Sr. Barbara Flores, SCN; Vice Prov.; Sr. Sharon Gray, SCN, Vince Prov.
Sisters serve and staff: in the field of Academic Education on all levels; Special Education Services; Social Services; Libraries; Parish Ministry; Archdiocesan Offices; Health Care Institutions; Retreat Centers; Literacy & Retirement Centers.
Represented in the Archdioceses of Boston, Indianapolis, Louisville, Mobile and Philadelphia and in the Dioceses of Charleston, Cleveland, Columbus, Covington, Greensburg, Jackson, Knoxville, Little Rock, Lexington, Madison, Memphis, Owensboro, Pittsburgh, Scranton, Steubenville and Venice. Also in Belize, Botswana, India and Nepal.
Louisville Office: 676 Atwood, P.O. Box 17545, Louisville, KY 40217. Tel: 502-636-0411; Fax: 502-636-0412. Sr. Sharon Gray, S.C.N., Vice Prov.
Eastern Province: SCN Provincial House, E. Boring Canal Rd., KSV Raman Ln., GPO Box 219, Patna, Bihar, India, 800 001. Tel: 011-91-612-534-121. Sr. Philomena Kottoor, S.C.N., Prov.; Sr. Amrita Manjaly, S.C.N., Prov.; Sr. Amelia Moras, S.C.N., Vice Prov.; Sr. Beena Chirackal, S.C.N., Vice Prov.

[0510] (O.L.M.)—SISTERS OF CHARITY OF OUR LADY OF MERCY (D)

Founded in Charleston, South Carolina in 1829.
Generalate and Motherhouse: Sisters of Charity of Our Lady of Mercy, 424 Fort Johnson Rd., Charleston, SC 29412. Tel: 843-795-2866; Fax: 843-795-6083.
Mailing Address: P.O. Box 12410, Charleston, SC 29422. Sr. Mary Joseph Ritter, O.L.M., Gen. Supr.
Total in Community: 13.
Properties owned and/or sponsored: Motherhouse, May Forest, Charleston, SC.
Legal Title: Sisters of Charity of Our Lady of Mercy. Sisters serve and staff: Parishes; Social Services.
Represented in the Diocese of Charleston.

[0520] (S.C.M.M.)—SISTERS OF CHARITY OF OUR LADY, MOTHER OF MERCY (P)

Founded in Holland 1832. First foundation in the United States in 1874.
General Motherhouse: Den Bosch, The Netherlands
Universal total in Congregation: 440.
SCMM Provincial Center: 32 Tuttle Pl., East Haven, CT 06512. Tel: 203-469-7872. Sr. Mary Ellen Ryley, S.C.M.M., Prov.
Total in Community: 7.
Represented in the Archdioceses of Chicago and Hartford and in the Diocese of San Diego.

[0530] (S.C.M.C.)—SISTERS OF CHARITY OF OUR LADY, MOTHER OF THE CHURCH (P)

First foundation in the United States in 1970.
General Motherhouse: Baltic, CT 06330. Tel: 860-822-8241; Fax: 860-822-9842. Mother M. Marie Julie Saegaert, S.C.M.C., Supr. Gen.
Professed Sisters: 55.
Properties owned, staffed or sponsored: High Schools 1; Nursing Home 1; Elementary Schools 5; Catechetical Schools 7; Shelters for the Homeless 1; Hispanic Ministry 1; Educational Tutoring Centers 1; Assisted Living, CBRF 1.
Represented in the Dioceses of Madison and Norwich.

[0540] (S.C.O.)—SISTERS OF CHARITY OF OTTAWA (P) (Grey Nuns of the Cross)

Founded in Ottawa, Canada, in 1845. First foundation in the United States in 1857.
General Motherhouse: 27 Bruyere St., Ottawa, Canada, K1N 5C9. Sr. Rachelle Watier, S.C.O., Gen. Supr.
Total number of Sisters in Congregation based in Ottawa: 462.
American Province (1950): St. Joseph, 245 University Ave., Lowell, MA 01854-2426. Tel: 978-458-6632; Fax: 978-454-8304. Sr. Prescille Malo, S.C.O., Prov. Supr.; Sr. Pauline Leblanc, S.C.O., Archivist.
Professed U.S. Sisters: 10.
Properties owned and/or sponsored: D'Youville Senior Care, Inc, Lowell, MA; Bachand Hall, Lowell, MA; St. Joseph Residence, Lowell, MA.
Legal Title: Sisters of Charity of Ottawa.
Sisters staff: Grammar Schools; Health Care and Pastoral Ministries; Apostolate of Aging.
Sisters sponsor: D'Youville Life and Wellness Community, Lowell, MA.
Represented in the Archdiocese of Boston.

[0565] (S.C.R.H.)—SISTERS OF CHARITY OF ROLLING HILLS (D)

Founded in Los Angeles, CA in 1964.
General Motherhouse & U.S. House: 28600 Palos Verdes Dr. E., Rancho Palos Verdes, CA 90275. Tel: 310-831-4104. Sr. Virginia Buchholz, S.C.R.H., Supr.
Sisters: 6.
Legal Title: Sisters of Charity of Rolling Hills. Ministries: Service to those in need, supported through ministry in Catholic institutions according to the talents of each sister.
Represented in the Archdiocese of Los Angeles.

[0570] (S.C.)—SISTERS OF CHARITY OF SETON HILL, U.S. PROVINCE, GREENSBURG, PENNSYLVANIA (P)

Founded in the United States in 1870.
Administrative Offices: DePaul Center, 144 DePaul Center Rd, Greensburg, PA 15601. Tel: 724-836-0406; Fax: 724-836-8280; Email: sjenny@scsh.org; Web: www.scsh.org.
Motherhouse: Caritas Christi, 129 DePaul Center Rd, Greensburg, PA 15601. Tel: 724-853-7948; Fax: 724838-1512. Sr. Catherine Meinert, S.C., Prov. Supr.
Total Sisters in Province: 147.
Generalate: Sisters of Charity of Seton Hill, 7005 Baptist Rd., Bethel Park, PA 15102-3905. Tel: 412-831-1242; Fax: 412-831-2184; Email: cblazina@scsh.org.. Sr. Sung Hae Kim, S.C., Gen. Supr.
Total in Community: 342.
Charity House: 133-A Charity Dr., Greensburg, PA 15601. Tel: 724-771-4519

[0580] (C.S.A.)—SISTERS OF CHARITY OF ST. AUGUSTINE (D)

Founded in Cleveland, Ohio in 1851.
Motherhouse: Mount Augustine, 5232 Broadview Rd., Richfield, OH 44286. Email: sisters@srsofcharity.org. Sr. Judith Ann Karam, C.S.A., Congregational Leader; Sr. Mary Denis Maher, C.S.A., Archivist.
Total in Congregation : 28.
Properties owned and sponsored: CSA Health System Ministries (PJP), Cleveland, OH; Sisters of Charity of St. Augustine Health System Inc., Cleveland OH; Mercy Medical Center, Inc., Canton OH; Regina Health Center, Richfield, OH; Sisters of Charity Foundation of Cleveland; Sisters of Charity Foundation of Canton; Sisters of Charity Foundation of South Carolina; St. Vincent Charity Medical Center; Healthy Learners, Columbia, SC; Early Childhood Resource Center, Canton, OH; Light of Hearts Villa, Bedford, OH.
Represented in the Dioceses of Charleston, Cleveland, Lexington and Youngstown.

[0590] (S.C.)—SISTERS OF CHARITY OF SAINT ELIZABETH, CONVENT STATION (P)

Founded in Newark, New Jersey in 1859.
General Motherhouse: Convent of St. Elizabeth Administration Building, P.O. Box 476, Convent Station, NJ 07961-0476. Tel: 973-290-5000; Tel: 973-290-5450; Fax: 973-290-5335. Sr. Rosemary Moynihan, Gen. Supr.; Sr. Noreen Neary, Archivist; Sr. Miriam Teresa, League of Prayer.
Total Enrollment: 283.
Properties and Legal Titles: Sisters of Charity of Saint Elizabeth Academy of Saint Elizabeth, Convent Station, NJ; Saint Vincent Academy, Newark, NJ; Josephine's Place, Elizabeth, NJ.
Sisters serve and staff: Academies; High Schools; Elementary Schools; Hospitals; C.C.D.; Parish Work; Social Work; Health Services; College of Saint Elizabeth.
Represented in the Archdioceses of Atlanta, Chicago, Hartford, Newark and New York and in the Dioceses of Camden, Charlotte, Fall River, Gallup, Metuchen, Paterson, Palm Beach, Raleigh, Trenton, Tucson, Wheeling-Charleston and Wilmington. Also in Haiti, Central America and San Salvador.

[0600] (S.C.S.J.A.)—SISTERS OF CHARITY OF ST. JOAN ANTIDA (P)

Founded in France in 1799 by Saint Joan Antida Thouret. First foundation in the U.S. 1932.
General Motherhouse: Suore della Carita di Santa Giovanna Antida, Via S. Maria in Cosmedin 5, Rome, Italy, 00153. Sr. Nunzia De Gori, Supr. Gen.
North American Province (1976): Regina Mundi Provincial House, 8560 N. 76th Pl., Milwaukee, WI 53223. Tel: 414-354-9233; Fax: 414-355-6463. Email: sisters@scsja.org. Sr. Theresa Rozga, S.C.S.J.A., Prov.
Total in Congregation : 23.
Ministry in schools; neighborhood services and parishes. Properties owned and sponsored: St. Joan Antida High School, Inc; St. Joan Antida High School Foundation, Ltd.
Represented in the Archdiocese of Milwaukee.

[0610] (S.C.S.H.)—SISTERS OF CHARITY OF ST. HYACINTHE (P) (Grey Nuns)

Founded in 1840 in St. Hyacinthe, P.Q., Canada. First United States foundation in 1878.
General House: 16470 Avenue Bourdages, SUD, St. Hyacinthe, Canada, J2T 4J8. Sr. Diane Beaudoin, S.C.S.H., Supr. Gen.; Sr. Marie-Paule Messier, S.C.S.H., Gen. Sec.
Universal total in Congregation: 129.
Legal Title: The Society of the Sisters of Charity, Portland, ME.
U.S. Regional Administration: Sisters of Charity of St. Hyacinthe, Portland, ME 04103-4257. Tel: 207-773-8607. Sr. Diane Beaudoin, Pres.; Sr. Marie-Paule Messier, S.C.S.H., Sec.
Total number in U.S: 3.
Represented in the Dioceses of Manchester and Portland (In Maine). Also in Canada and Haiti.

[0620] (S.C.S.L.)—SISTERS OF CHARITY OF ST. LOUIS (P)

Founded in France in 1803. First foundation in the United States in 1910.
Generalate: 5169 Avenue MacDonald, Montreal, Canada, H3X 2V9. Sr. Alberte Piche, Supr. Gen.
Universal total in Congregation: 481.
American Sector: 4907 S. Catherine St., Apt. 203, Plattsburgh, NY 12901. Tel: 518-802-0331; Email: srbernadetted@gmail.com. Sr. Bernadette Ducharme, Local Supr.
Total in Community: 3.
Represented in the Diocese of Ogdensburg.

[0640] (S.C.)—SISTERS OF CHARITY OF ST. VINCENT DE PAUL, HALIFAX (P)

Founded by Saint Elizabeth Ann Seton, Emmitsburg, Maryland in 1809. Congregation at Halifax became independent in 1856, Papal approved in 1908.

Sisters of Charity Centre: 215 Seton Rd., Halifax, Canada, B3M 0C9. Tel: 902-406-8077; Fax: 902-457-3506. Sr. Joan O'Keefe, S.C., Congregational Leader.

Total in Congregation : 332.

Legal Title: Sisters of Charity (Halifax).

Commonwealth of Massachusetts: Boston Office, 125 Oakland St., Wellesley Hills, MA 02481-5338. Tel: 781-997-1100; Fax: 781-997-1358. Sr. Maryanne Ruzzo, S.C., Congregational Councillor Tel: 617-645-8165.

Legal Titles: Sisters of Charity (Halifax) Supporting Corporation, 125 Oakland St. Wellesley Hills, MA 02481-5338. Phone: 781-997-1110; Fax: 781-237-8152. Sr. Joan O'Keefe, Congregational Leader; Sisters of Charity (Halifax) Corporate Mission, Inc., 125 Oakland St. Wellesley Hills, MA 02481-5338. Tel: 781-997-1100; Fax: 781-997-1358. Sr. Joan O'Keefe, Congregational Leader.

Mount St. Vincent Retirement Community: 125 Oakland St., Wellesley Hills, MA 02481-5338. Tel: 781-997-1110; Fax: 781-237-8152. Sandra Castelluccio, Community Leadership Team Tel: 781-997-1165; Fax: 781-237-8152.

Legal Titles and Holdings: Marillac Residence, Inc., Wellesley Hills, MA; Elizabeth Seton Residence, Inc., Wellesley Hills, MA.

State of NY: Sisters of Charity (Halifax), New York Office, 85-10 61st Rd., Rego Park, NY 11374. Tel: 718-651-1685; Fax: 718-651-5645; Email: scnyoffice@aol.com. Sr. Mary Katherine Hamm, Congregational Councillor Tel: 516-781-4820; Sr. Roberta Kerins, Congregational Councillor Tel: 516-673-4232.

Ministering in education at all levels; parish ministry; spiritual direction/retreats; social services; pastoral ministry; administration.

Represented in the Archdioceses of Boston and New York and in the Dioceses of Brooklyn and Rockville Centre. Also in Canada, Bermuda and Peru.

[0650] (S.C.)—SISTERS OF CHARITY OF ST. VINCENT DE PAUL OF NEW YORK (D)

Founded in Emmitsburg, Maryland in 1809 by Saint Elizabeth Ann Seton.

General Motherhouse: Sisters of Charity Center, 6301 Riverdale Ave., Bronx, NY 10471-1093. Tel: 718-549-9200; Fax: 718-884-3013. Email: emcgrory@scny.org. Sr. Jane Iannucelli, Pres.

Total in Congregation : 225.

Sisters serve and staff: Colleges; High Schools; Elementary Schools; New York Foundling Hospital; House of Prayer; Supportive Housing for low income Elderly; Residence for Senior and Invalid Sisters; Mental Health Divisions, Rest House for Community use; Housing for Homeless; Parish Pastoral Ministry; Advocacy Programs; Outreach Pastoral Ministry; Spirituality Programs.

Represented in the Archdiocese of New York. Also in Guatemala.

[0655] (S.C.V.)—SISTERS OF CHARITY OF ST. VINCENT DE PAUL OF SUWON

Motherhouse is located in Suwon, Korea.

The sisters provide service to the poor, caring for the sick poor, elderly, mentally disabled, single mothers, dying people, prisoners, and refugees from North Korea. Total Members: 230. Sr. Johana Soh, S.C., Pres.

Motherhouse & Generalate: 93-3 Chi-Dong Paddal-Gu, Suwon City, Kyoung Gi Province, Korea, South Tel: 031-241-2151.

U.S. Address (1996): St. Anna's Home, 13901 E. Quincy Ave., Aurora, CO 80015. Tel: 303-627-2986; Fax: 720-379-6308; Email: stannashome@hotmail.com.

Total Sisters in U.S: 3.

Represented in the Archdiocese of Denver.

[0660] (S.C.C.)—SISTERS OF CHRISTIAN CHARITY (P)

Daughters of the Blessed Virgin Mary of the Immaculate Conception

Founded in Germany in 1849. First foundation in the United States in 1873.

Generalate: Haus Mallinckrodt Mallinckrodt Str. 5 D-33098 Paderborn, Germany Tel: 011-495251-68324-20. Sr. Maria del Rosario Castro, Supr. Gen.

Universal total in Congregation: 402.

North American Eastern Province (1927): Mallinckrodt Convent Div. of North American Province, 350 Bernardsville Rd., Mendham, NJ 07945. Tel: 973-543-6528. Sr. Mary Edward Spohrer, S.C.C., Prov. Supr.; Sr. Mary Perpetua Rehle, S.C.C., Archivist.

Professed Sisters: 161.

Ministry in Academic Education; Retreat House; Catechetical Centers; Religion Coordinators; Health care and Parish Ministry.

Properties owned and/or sponsored: Villa Pauline, Retreat House, Mendham, NJ; Divine Providence Hospital, Williamsport, PA; Muncy Calley Hospital, Muncy, PA; Holy Spirit Hospital, Camp Hill, PA; Mallinckrodt Convent Motherhouse, Mendham, NJ; Holy Family Convent, Home for Aged and Retired Sisters, Danville, PA; Muncy Valley Hospital, Muncy, PA.

Represented in the Archdioceses of Newark, New York and Philadelphia and in the Dioceses of Allentown, Camden, Harrisburg, Metuchen, Paterson, Rapid City and Scranton.

North American Western Region: Sisters of Christian Charity - Daughters of the Blessed Virgin Mary of the Immaculate Conception, 2041 Elmwood Ave., Wilmette, IL 60091-1431. Tel: 847-920-9341; Fax: 847-920-9346. Sr. Janice Boyer, S.C.C., Major Supr.; Sr. Anastasia Sanford, Archivist.

Professed Sisters: 34.

Ministry in Academic & Religious Education; Pastoral Ministry; Ministry to Aged; Prayer Ministry; Ministry to the Poor and Multi-Cultural. Properties owned and sponsored: Maria Immaculata Convent; Sacred Heart Convent, Wilmette, IL; the Josephinum Convent and Academy, Chicago, IL. Represented in the Archdioceses of Chicago, Dubuque and New Orleans.

[0670] (O.C.S.O.)—CISTERCIAN NUNS OF THE STRICT OBSERVANCE (P)

Founded at Citeaux, France, in 1098. First foundation in the United States in 1949.

Generalate: Viale Africa 33, Rome, Italy, 00144. Total Universal Number of Nuns in Order: estimated 1,800. Contemplative and Monastic

U.S. Establishments:

Mount St. Mary's Abbey: 300 Arnold St., Wrentham, MA 02093-1799. Tel: 508-528-1282; Fax: 508-528-5360. Mother Maureen McCabe, O.C.S.O., Abbess.

Total in Community: 40.

Represented in the Archdiocese of Boston.

Our Lady of the Mississippi Abbey: 8400 Abbey Hill Rd., Dubuque, IA 52003. Tel: 563-582-2595; Fax: 563-582-5511. Rev. Mother Rebecca Stramoski, O.C.S.O., Abbess.

Total in Community: 20.

Legal Title: Trappistine Nuns, Inc.; Iowa Cistercians of the Strict Observance.

Represented in the Archdiocese of Dubuque.

Santa Rita Abbey: 14200 E. Fish Canyon Rd., Sonoita, AZ 85637-6545. Tel: 520-455-5595. Mother Victoria Murray, O.C.S.O., Prioress.

Total in Community: 11.

Legal Title: Cistercian Nuns of the Strict Observance. Represented in the Diocese of Tucson.

Our Lady of the Redwoods Abbey: 18104 Briceland Thorn Rd., Whitethorn, CA 95589. Tel: 707-986-7419; Email: vocationdirector@redwoodsabbey.org; Web: www.redwoodsabbey.org. Sr. Kathy DeVico, O.C.S.O., Abbess.

Total in Community: 11.

Represented in the Diocese of Santa Rosa.

Our Lady of the Angels Monastery: 3365 Monastery Dr., Crozet, VA 22932. Tel: 434-823-1452; Fax: 434-823-6379. Email: sisters@olamonastery.org. Mother Kathy Ullrich, O.C.S.O., Prioress.

Legal Title: Cistercian Nuns of the Strict Observance in Virginia, Inc.

Represented in the Diocese of Richmond.

[0680] (O.CIST.)—CISTERCIAN NUNS (P)

Founded in 1098 at Citeaux, France. It is composed of monks and nuns in independent houses.

Generalate: Piazza del Tempio di Diana, 14, Rome, Italy, 00153. Rt. Rev. Mauro-Giuseppe Lepori, O.Cist., Abbot Gen.

U.S. Headquarters: Valley of Our Lady Monastery, E11096 Yanke Dr., Prairie Du Sac, WI 53578-9737. Tel: 608-643-3520. Rev. Mother Anne Marie Joerger, O. Cist., Prioress.

Total in Community: 20.

[0685] (R.M.I.)—CLARETIAN MISSIONARY SISTERS (P)

Religious of Mary Immaculate Claretian Missionary Sisters

Founded in Santiago de Cuba, August 25, 1855. Established in the United States in 1956.

Generalate: Via Calandelli 12, Rome, Italy, 00153. Soledad Galeron, Supr. Gen.

U.S. Delegation: 7080 S.W. 99 Ave., Miami, FL 33173. Sr. Ondina Cortes, R.M.I.

Sisters in the World: 600; Sisters in Florida: 11.

Legal Title: Claretian Missionary Sisters of Florida, Inc.

Ministry in Religious Education; Theological Formation in Pastoral Institutes, Seminaries and Universities; Social Ministries; Parish and Diocesan Ministries.

Represented in the Archdiocese of Miami and in the Dioceses of Palm Beach and St. Augustine.

[0690] (C.M.S.)—COMBONI MISSIONARY SISTERS (P)

Founded in Italy in 1872. An international congregation of 1,350 sisters serving in the mission fields of Africa, America, Europe, the Middle East and Sri Lanka. First United States foundation in 1950.

Generalate: Rome, Italy Sr. Luigia Coccia, C.M.S., Supr. Gen.

American Headquarters: 1307 Lakeside Ave., Henrico, VA 23228-4710. Tel: 804-262-8827; Email: usacomboni.deleg@gmail.com; Web: www.combonimissionarysistersusa.org. Sr. Olga Estela Sanchez Caro, C.M.S., Delegate Supr.

Legal Titles & Holdings: Provincial House, Comboni Missionary Sisters, Inc., Richmond, VA.

Represented in the Archdiocese of Baltimore and in the Diocese of Richmond.

[0700] (O.D.N.)—COMPANY OF MARY, OUR LADY (P)

Founded in Bordeaux, France, April 7, 1607, by St. Jeanne de Lestonnac. First foundation in the United States in 1926, in Douglas, Arizona.

General Motherhouse: Rome, Italy Sr. Maria Rita Calvo, O.D.N., Gen. Supr.

Universal total in Congregation: 1306.

U.S. Regional Office (1926): Company of Mary Regional Offices, 16791 E. Main St., Tustin, CA 92780. Tel: 714-541-3125. Sr. Liliana Franco, O.D.N., Prov. Supr.; Sr. Leticia Salazar, O.D.N., Pres. of Corporation; Sr. Kathy Schneider, O.D.N., Archivist.

Professed: 30.

Properties owned and/or sponsored: St. Jeanne De Lestonnac School, Tustin, CA; St. Jeanne de Lestonnac School, Temecula, CA; St. Joseph Residence for Women, Los Angeles, CA; Vina de Lestonnac Ministry Center Retreat, Temecula, CA; Lestonnac Residence for Women, Tustin, CA; Lestonnac Retreat Center, Tustin, CA.

Sisters serve and staff: Pre-Schools; Kindergartens; Elementary & High Schools; Faith Formation Centers; Residences & Retreat Centers.

Represented in the Archdiocese of Los Angeles and in the Dioceses of Orange and San Bernardino.

[0710] (C.S.)—SISTERS OF THE COMPANY OF THE SAVIOR (D)

Founded in Spain in 1952. First United States foundation in 1962.

General Motherhouse: Tapia de Casariego 19, Madrid, Spain, 28023. Mother Amelia Lora-Tamayo, Supr. Gen.

U.S. Foundation: 820 Clinton Ave., Bridgeport, CT 06604. Tel: 203-368-1875. Email: bridgeport@ciasalvador.org. Sr. Araceli Fernández, Supr.

Apostolate: Education.

Professed Sisters: 56; Juniors: 17; Novices: 14.

Represented in the Diocese of Bridgeport.

[0720] (M.C.)—CONSOLATA MISSIONARY SISTERS (P)

Founded in Italy in 1910. First foundation in the United States in 1954.

Motherhouse: Istituto Suore Missionarie della Consolata, Via Umilta 745, Nepi, VT, Italy, 01036. Mother Simona Brambilla, M.C., Supr. Gen.

Universal total in Congregation: 600.

Represented in the Dioceses of Birmingham, Grand Rapids and Phoenix.

U.S. Headquarters: Consolata Missionary Sisters, 6801 Belmont Rd., P.O. Box 371, Belmont, MI

49306. Tel: 616-361-2072; Fax: 616-361-2072; Email: reusamc@consolatasisters.org. Sr. Riccardina Silvestri, M.C., Contact Person.
Total in Community: 23.
Sisters serve and staff: Catechetical and Pastoral Work; Apostolate among Minorities; Elementary Schools and Pastoral Ministries.

[0725] (M.C-M.)—CORDI-MARIAN MISSIONARY SISTERS CONGREGATION (P)

Founded in Mexico City in 1921. First United States foundation in 1926.
General Motherhouse: Apdo. Postal #1109, Toluca, Mexico, 50091. Sr. Bertha Perez, M.C.M., Supr. Gen.
U.S. Provincial House: 11624 FM 471, Apt. 501, San Antonio, TX 78253. Tel: 210-798-8220, ext. 15 or 17; Fax: 210-798-8225. Sr. Catalina Marquez, Prov. Supr.
Total in Congregation: 94; Total number in U.S. community: 27; Novices: 1.
Properties owned and/or sponsored: Cordi-Marian Villa Retreat Center and Provincial House, San Antonio, TX; East St. Louis Catholic Day Care Center and Convent, East St. Louis, IL; Formation House, San Antonio, TX; 10 other properties in Mexico; 5 schools; 2 houses of formation; 2 elderly residences; 2 bookstores; 2 houses of administration.
Ministry in Catechetical Centers; Pastoral Ministry Programs; Kindergarten and Day Care Centers; Retreat Center; Social Service; Rel. Articles & Book Stores; Ministry to Hispanics; 15-acre Cemetery.
Represented in the Archdiocese of San Antonio and in the Dioceses of Belleville and Springfield-Cape Girardeau. Also in Mexico and Central America.

[0730] (FD.CC.)—CANOSSIAN DAUGHTERS OF CHARITY (P)

Canossian Sisters

Founded in Verona, Italy in 1808.
General Motherhouse: Via della Stazione di Ottavia 70, Rome, Italy, 00135.
U.S. Provincial House: Cristo Rey-Canossian Sisters, 5625 Isleta Blvd., S.W., Albuquerque, NM 87105. Tel: 505-873-2854. Sr. Ellen K. Taylor, F.D.C.C., Prov. Leader.
Sisters in U.S: 31.
Ministry in Evangelization; Spirituality Center; Integral Promotion of the Person; Parish Pastoral Ministry; Pastoral Care of the Sick; Intermediate Care Facility for Developmentally Disabled Children; Lay Volunteer Program; Pastoral Outreach to Incarcerated; Education.
Represented in the Archdioceses of San Francisco and Santa Fe and in the Diocese of Sacramento. Also in Canada and Mexico.

[0740] (D.C.P.B.)—DAUGHTERS OFCHARITY OF THE MOST PRECIOUS BLOOD

Founded in Pagani, Italy in 1872. First foundation in United States in 1908.
Generalate: Via Vigna Fabbri 45, Rome, Italy Sr. Alfonsa Bove, Mother Gen.
U.S. Address: Daughters of Charity of the Most Precious Blood, 1482 North Ave., Bridgeport, CT 06604. Tel: 203-334-7000. Sr. Rosamma Joseph, Supr.
Total in Community: 16; Number of Communities: 3.
Represented in the Dioceses of Albany, Bridgeport and Paterson.

[0750] (F.C.S.C.J.)—DAUGHTERS OF THE CHARITY OF THE SACRED HEART OF JESUS (P)

First founded in France at La Salle de Vihiers in 1823. First founded in the United States at Newport, Vermont in October 1905.
Generalate: Montgeron, France
General Motherhouse: La Salle de Vihiers, France Sr. Elaine Voyer, F.C.S.C.J., Supr. Gen.
Mount Sacred Heart Provincial House: Daughters of the Charity of the Sacred Heart of Jesus (1949), 226 Grove St., Littleton, NH 03561. Tel: 603-444-5346; Fax: 603-444-5348. Sr. Bonita Cote, F.C.S.C.J., Prov.
Total number in Province: 24.
Sisters serve and staff: Spiritual Directors; Pastoral Ministry; Foreign Missions.
Represented in the Archdiocese of Boston and in the Dioceses of Burlington, Fall River, Manchester and Ogdensburg.

[0760] (D.C.)—DAUGHTERS OF CHARITY OF ST. VINCENT DE PAUL (P)

Founded in France in 1633. First foundation in the United States in 1809 by Saint Elizabeth Ann Seton, Emmitsburg, MD.
General Motherhouse: Paris, France Sr. Kathleen Appler, D.C., Supr. Gen.
St. Louise Province (2011): 4330 Olive St., St. Louis, MO 63108-2622. Tel: 314-533-4770; Fax: 314-561-4676; Web: www.daughtersofcharity.org. Sr. Catherine Mary Norris, D.C., Prov.
Total in Community: 415.
Legal Title: Daughters of Charity, Inc.; Daughters of Charity Ministries, Inc.
Sisters serve and staff: Religious and Academic Education at all levels; Medical Clinics; Hospitals; Nursing Homes; Ministries to Persons who are Victims of Human Trafficking; Child Care Centers; Social Service Centers; Catholic Charities; Parish Ministries; Outreach Centers; Hispanic Ministry; Hospice; Home Health; Homes for Children; Psychiatric Clinics; Peace and Justice; (Arch) Diocesan Offices; Emergency Relief Centers; Spiritual Direction; Retreats; Campus Ministry; Prison Ministry; Shelters for the Homeless.
Represented in the Archdioceses of Baltimore, Chicago, Detroit, Mobile, New Orleans, New York, Philadelphia, St. Louis, San Antonio and Washington and in the Dioceses of Albany, Belleville, Brownsville, Buffalo, Charleston, El Paso, Evansville, Jackson, Little Rock, Savannah, Syracuse and Wilmington. Also in Canada.
Province of the West (Los Altos Hills) (1969): Seton Provincialate, 26000 Altamont Rd., Los Altos Hills, CA 94022-4317. Tel: 650-941-4490; Fax: 650-949-8883. Web: www.daughtersofcharity.com. Sr. Julie Kubasak, D.C., Prov.
Total in Community: 104.
Properties owned and/or sponsored: Healthcare: Villa Siena, Mountain View, CA; Education: De Marillac Academy, San Francisco, CA; Mother of Sorrows School, Los Angeles, CA; Our Lady of the Miraculous Medal School, Montebello, CA; Our Lady of the Rosary of Talpa School, Los Angeles, CA; Our Lady of the Visitacion School, San Francisco, CA; Sacred Heart Cathedral Preparatory, San Francisco, CA; St. Elizabeth Seton School, Palo Alto, CA; St. Patrick School, San Jose, CA; St. Vincent de Paul School, Phoenix, CA; St. Vincent School, Los Angeles, CA; Social Ministries: Give Me a Chance, Inc., Ogden, UT; Hotel Dieu, Los Angeles, CA; Life Sharing Center, Inc. dba St. Jude Food Bank, Tuba City, AZ; Maryvale, Rosemead, CA; Mount St. Joseph-St. Elizabeth, San Francisco, CA; Rosalie Rendu, Inc., East Palo Alto, CA; St. Vincent's Institution, Santa Barbara, CA; St. Vincent's Senior Citizen Nutrition Program, Los Angeles, CA; Other: Daughters of Charity Ministry Service Corps, Los Altos Hills, CA; Ministry Services of the Daughters of Charity of St. Vincent de Paul, Los Altos Hills, CA; GRACE, Inc., Pasadena, CA; Villa Siena Foundation, Mountain View, CA; Vincentian Marian Youth, Los Altos Hills, CA; Vincentian Service Corps West, Daly City, CA; St. Louise Resource Services, Los Angeles, CA.
Represented in the Archdioceses of Anchorage, Los Angeles and San Francisco and in the Dioceses of Gallup, Phoenix, Salt Lake City and San Jose.

[0780] (F.C.)—DAUGHTERS OF THE CROSS OF LIEGE (P)

Founded in Liege, Belgium in 1833. First foundation in the United States in 1958.
Principal House: St. Bernard Convent, 165 W. Eaton Ave., Tracy, CA 95376.
Total in Community: 5.
Represented in the Diocese of Stockton.

[0790] (F.D.C.)—DAUGHTERS OF DIVINE CHARITY (P)

Founded in Austria on November 21, 1868 by Mother Franziska Lechner. First founded in the United States on October 8, 1913, in New York City.
General Motherhouse: Vienna, Austria
Generalate: Grottaferrata, Rome, Italy
Holy Family Province (2012): Provincialate: 850 Hylan Blvd., Staten Island, NY 10305-2021. Tel: 718-720-7365; Fax: 718-727-5701; Email: smcoffeltfdc@hotmail.com; Web: www.daughtersofdivinecharity.org. Sr. Mary Coffelt, F.D.C., Prov. Supr.
Professed Sisters: 35.
Properties owned and/or sponsored: St. Mary's Residence, NY; St. Joseph Hill Academy, Staten Island, NY; St. Elizabeth Briarbank Home for the Aged, Bloomfield Hills, MI; Leonora Hall and Francesca Residence, Akron, OH.
Legal Title: Congregation of the Daughters of Divine Charity, Inc.
Ministry in Education; Nursing; Residence for Women; CCD; Youth Ministry; Care of the Elderly; Spiritual Direction; Retreat Work; Pastoral Care.
Represented in the Archdiocese of New York and Detroit and in the Diocese of Cleveland, Fort Wayne-South Bend and San Diego.
St. Elizabeth Briarbank: 39315 Woodward Ave., Bloomfield Hills, MI 48304. Tel: 248-644-8052. Sr. Mary Coffelt, F.D.C., Prov. Supr.
Professed Sisters: 3.
Home for the Aged.

[0793] (D.D.L.)—DAUGHTERS OF DIVINELOVE (P)

Founded in Ukpor, Nigeria in 1969. First United States Foundation in 1990.
General House: Fifth Avenue, P.O. Box 546, Enugu, Nigeria Tel: 042-559071; Tel: 042-551742. Rev. Mother Anastasia Dike, D.D.L., Mother Gen.
Professed Sisters in Congregation: 962.
U.S. Regional House: 133 N. Prater Ave., Northlake, IL 60164. Tel: 708-223-4260; Fax: 708-223-0262; Email: ddloveus@aol.com. Sr. Mary Olivia Agbakoba, D.D.L., Reg. Supr.
Professed Sisters in U.S: 65.
Ministry in the field of Administration; Religious and Academic Education at all levels; Special Education; Health Services; Parish and Diocesan Services; Retreat Work; Social Work.
Represented in the Archdioceses of Chicago, Galveston-Houston, Newark, and Washington and in the Dioceses of Austin, Brooklyn, Brownsville, Lexington, Little Rock, Rockford and Syracuse.

[0795] (F.D.Z.)—DAUGHTERS OF DIVINE ZEAL (P)

Founded in Messina, Italy in 1887 by Saint Hannibal Maria DiFrancia. First foundation in the United States in 1951.
Generalate: Figlie Del Divino Zelo, Circonvallazione Appia 144, Rome, Italy, 00179. Mother M. Teolinda Salemi, F.D.Z., Supr. Gen.
Universal total in Congregation: 1000.
U.S. Headquarters: Hannibal House Spiritual Center, 1526 Hill Rd., Reading, PA 19602. Tel: 610-375-1738; Tel: 610-375-9072; Fax: 610-374-0369; Email: srdivinezeal@hotmail.com. Sr. Marietta Castellano, F.D.Z., Supr.
Total in Community: 3.
Ministry in the field of Religious and Academic Education; Parish and Youth Ministry; Retreat, Vocation, Prayer and Apostolate.
Represented in the Diocese of Allentown.

[0810] (D.H.M.)—DAUGHTERS OF THE HEART OF MARY (P)

Founded in France in 1790. First United States foundation in 1851.
Generalate: 39 rue Notre Dame des Champs, Paris, France, 75006.
Provincialate: 1339 Northampton St., Holyoke, MA 01040-1958. Tel: 413-532-7406; Fax: 413-533-4217. Email: dhmvocations@gmail.com. Sr. Miriam Najimy, D.H.M., Prov.
Professed Sisters U.S.A: 36.
Properties owned or sponsored: Marian Center, Holyoke, MA; Maryhill, St. Paul, MN; Ephpheta Center, Chicago, IL; Nardin Academy, Buffalo, NY; Heart of Mary Center, St. Louis, MO; St. Joseph's School for the Deaf, Bronx, NY.
Represented in the Archdioceses of Chicago, Newark, New York, St. Louis and St. Paul-Minneapolis and in the Diocese of Springfield in Massachusetts.

[0820] (D.H.S.)—DAUGHTERS OF THE HOLY SPIRIT

Founded in France in 1706. First foundation in the U.S. in 1902.
Generalate: Congregation des Filles du Saint Esprit, 15 Boulevard Sebastopol, B.P. 50148, Rennes Cedex 3, France, 35101. Sr. Anne Marie Foucher, F.S.E., Supr. Gen.
General Motherhouse: Maison-mere des Filles du Saint Esprit, 20 rue des Capucins BP 4538, Saint-Brieuc Cedex 2, France, 22045.
Provincial House: Daughters of the Holy Spirit,

Inc.,72 Church St., Putnam, CT 06260. Tel: 860-928-0891. Sr. Gertrude Lanouette, D.H.S., Prov.
Total in Community: 68; Total in the Provincial House: 19.
Ministry in the field of Education; Home Health Care and Hospital Support; Various Social and Pastoral Ministries of Service.
Represented in the Archdioceses of Hartford and in the Dioceses of Burlington, Norwich, Sacramento and Stockton.

[0850] (F.M.A.)—DAUGHTERS OF MARY HELP OF CHRISTIANS (P)

Salesian Sisters of St. John Bosco

Founded in Mornese, Italy, in 1872. First foundation in the U.S. in 1908 at Paterson, NJ.
General Motherhouse: Via Ateneo Salesiano, 81, 00139, Rome, Italy Very Rev. Mother Yvonne Reungoat, F.M.A., Mother Gen.
Universal total in Congregation: 12,286.
Province of St. Joseph: Provincial House, 655 Belmont Ave., Haledon, NJ 07508-2301. Tel: 973-790-7963. Sr. Joanne Holloman, F.M.A., Prov.
Total in Community: 91.
Properties owned and/or sponsored: St. Joseph Provincial Center, Haledon, NJ; Mary Help of Christians Academy, North Haledon, NJ; Sacred Heart Center, Newton, NJ; Villa Madonna School-Salesian Sisters of Tampa, Inc., Villa Madonna School, Tampa, FL; Camp Auxilium Center, Newton, NJ; Sacred Heart Novitiate, Newton, NJ.
Legal Title: Missionary Society of the Salesian Sisters, Inc.; Salesian Sisters of Tampa, Inc.
Ministry in the field of academic and religious education at all levels; Youth Ministry; Retreat and Family Ministry.
Represented in the Archdioceses of Miami, Newark, New Orleans and New York and in the Dioceses of Paterson, St. Petersburg and Venice.
Province of Mary Immaculate: FMA Provincial House, 6019 Buena Vista, San Antonio, TX 78237. Tel: 210-432-0090; Fax: 210-432-4016. Sr. Rosann Ruiz, F.M.A., Prov.
Total in Community: 89.
Properties owned and/or sponsored: FMA Provincial House & St. John Bosco School, San Antonio, TX; Mary Help of Christians School, Laredo, TX; Salesian Sisters School - Salesian Sisters: MHC Youth Center, Inc., Corralitos, CA; Salesian Sisters Convent, Colorado Springs, Co; Formation House, Bellflower, CA.
Legal Title: Institute of the Daughters of Mary Help of Christians - Salesian Sisters of St. John Bosco, San Antonio, TX.
Ministry in Education; Youth Ministry; Religious Education and Outreach to the Poor.
Represented in the Archdioceses of Los Angeles, New Orleans, San Antonio and San Francisco and in the Dioceses of Austin, Colorado Springs, Laredo, Monterey and Baker.

[0860] (D.M.)—DAUGHTERS OF MARY OF THE IMMACULATE CONCEPTION (P)

Founded in New Britain in 1904.
Daughters of Mary General: 314 Osgood Ave., New Britain, CT 06053. Tel: 860-225-9406. Mother Mary Jennifer, Supr. Gen.
Total in Community: 21.
Properties owned and/or sponsored: St. Lucian's Home, New Britain, CT; Monsignor Bojnowski Manor, New Britain, CT; Motherhouse and Novitiate Comples, New Britain, CT; St. Joseph's Home, NY; St. Agnes Residence, NY; Our Lady's Guild House, Boston, MA; Sancta Maria Nursing Facility, Cambridge MA; Marian Heights; Prudence Crandall; Mary Immaculate; Miriam House.
Legal Title: Congregation of the Daughters of Mary of the Immaculate Conception, Inc.
Ministry in the field of Education; Home for the Aged; Homes for Working Girls and Students; Skilled Care.
Represented in the Archdioceses of Boston, Hartford and New York.

[0870] (F.M.I.)—CONGREGATION OF THE DAUGHTERS OF MARY IMMACULATE (P)

Marianist Sisters
Founded in France in 1816.
Motherhouse: Rome, Italy Mother Franca Zonta, Supr. Gen.
U.S. Foundation (1949): Marianist Sisters Residence, 235 W. Ligustrum Dr., San Antonio, TX 78228. Tel: 210-433-5501; Fax: 210-433-0300. Sr. Gretchen Trautman, F.M.I., Prov. Supr.
Total in Community: 14.
Properties owned and/or sponsored: Marianist Sisters Residence, San Antonio, TX; Marianist Sisters Communities, Dayton OH.
Represented in the Archdioceses of Cincinnati and San Antonio.

[0880] (D.M.J.)—DAUGHTERS OF MARY AND JOSEPH (P)

Founded in Belgium in 1817. First U.S. Foundation in 1926.
Generalate: 65 Iona Rd., Glasnevin, Dublin, Ireland, 9. Sr. Helen Lane, Supr. Gen.
Regionalate & Novitiate: 5300 Crest Rd., Rancho Palos Verdes, CA 90275-5004. Tel: 310-377-9968; Fax: 310-541-5967. Sr. Linda Webb, D.M.J., Regl. Admin.; Sr. Teresa Groth, Vocation Dir.; Sr. Karen Derr, Formation Contact.
Professed Sisters: 39.
Legal Title: Daughters of Mary and Joseph, California. Sisters staff: Grammar & High Schools, Parish Ministry; Health Ministry; Retreat Work.
Represented in the Archdioceses of Los Angeles and San Francisco and in the Diocese of San Bernardino.

[0885] (D.M.M.M.)—DAUGHTERS OF MARY MOTHER OF MERCY (P)

Founded in Umuahia, Abia State, Nigeria.
Motherhouse: Umuahia, Nigeria
U.S. Regional House: St. Teresa of Avila Parish Convent, 109-26 130th St., South Ozone Park, NY 11420. Tel: 718-843-1364; Email: dmmmusacanadareg@gmail.com.
Total in U.S: 190; Universal total in Congregation: 1025.
Ministry in the fields of teaching, medical, pastoral, orphanages & motherless babies homes, social.

[0890] (D.M.)—DAUGHTERS OF OUR LADY OF MERCY (P)

Founded in Italy in 1837 by Saint Mary Joseph Rossello. First foundation in the United States in 1919.
Generalate: Via Monte Grappa, No. 7, Savona, Italy Rev. Mother M. Beatriz Lassalle, Supr. Gen.
Provincialate: Villa Rossello, 1009 Main Rd., Newfield, NJ 08344. Tel: 856-697-2983. Sr. M. Ambrogina Aldeni, Prov. Supr.; Sr. Loretta Marie Stevens, D.M., Community Archivist.
Total in Community: 28.
Legal Holdings: Our Lady of Mercy Academy, Newfield, NJ; Misericordia Nursing & Rehabilitation Center.
Ministry in the field of Education; Health Services; Skilled Nursing Center; Pastoral Counseling, C.C.D. and Parish Work. Represented in the Dioceses of Camden, Harrisburg and Scranton. Also in Haiti.

[0895] (F.M.S.R.)—DAUGHTERS OF OUR LADY OF THE HOLY ROSARY (P)

Founded in 1946 in Trung Linh, Bui Chu, North Vietnam by Bishop Dominic Maria Ho Ngoc Can. First foundation in the United States in 1967.
Sr. M. Rose Loan Vu, F.M.S.R.
U.S. Provincial Office: Queen of Peace Province, 1492 Moss St., New Orleans, LA 70119-2904. Email: fmsrusaprovince@yahoo.com. Sr. M. John Vianney Vi Huyen Tran, F.M.S.R., Prov. Supr.
Total in Community: 60.
Properties owned and/or sponsored: Six residences. Ministry in the field of Education; Health Services; Pastoral Ministry.
Represented in the Archdioceses of New Orleans and Oklahoma City and in the Dioceses of Baton Rouge, Houma-Thibodaux, Biloxi and Little Rock.

[0900] (F.D.N.S.C.)—DAUGHTERS OF OUR LADY OF THE SACRED HEART (P)

Founded in France in 1882.
Motherhouse: Via Casale S. Pio V, 37, Rome, Italy Sr. Dain Mary Inglis, F.D.N.S.C., Supr. Gen.
U.S. Foundation (1955): St. Francis de Sales Convent, 424 E. Browning Rd., Bellmawr, NJ 08031. Tel: 856-931-8973; Fax: 856-931-7018.
Professed Sisters in the U.S: 10.
Represented in the Diocese of Camden.

[0910] (BETHL.)—BETHLEMITA, DAUGHTER OF THE SACRED HEART OF JESUS (P)

Founded in Guatemala in 1861. First foundation in the United States in Dallas, TX.
Motherhouse: Bogota, Colombia
U.S. Foundation: St. Joseph Residence, Inc., 330 W. Pembroke Ave., Dallas, TX 75208. Tel: 214-948-3597. Sr. Carolina Sanchez Botero, Admin.
Professed Sisters: 4.
Represented in the Diocese of Dallas.

[0920] (D.S.F.)—CONGREGATION OF THE DAUGHTERS OF ST. FRANCIS OF ASSISI

Founded in Hungary, 1894. First foundation in the United States in 1946.
Motherhouse: American Region: St. Joseph's Convent, 507 N. Prairie St., Lacon, IL 61540. Tel: 309-246-2175. Sr. Loretta Matas, D.S.F., Pres.
Professed Sisters: 12.
Legal Title: Congregation of the Daughters of St. Francis of Assisi.
Represented in the Dioceses of Peoria and Springfield-Cape Girardeau.

[0940] (D.S.M.P.)—DAUGHTERS OF ST. MARY OF PROVIDENCE (P)

Founded in Italy in 1881. First foundation in the United States in 1913.
Generalate: Rome, Italy Mother Elisabetta Serena Ciserani, D.S.M.P., Supr. Gen.
Provincialate: Daughters of St. Mary of Providence Immaculate Conception Province, 4200 N. Austin Ave., Chicago, IL 60634. Tel: 773-205-1313; Tel: 773-545-8300. Sr. Rita Butler, Prov.
Professed Sisters: 68.
Represented in the Archdioceses of Chicago and Philadelphia and in the Dioceses of Lansing, New Ulm, Providence, Sioux Falls and Syracuse.

[0950] (F.S.P.)—PIOUS SOCIETY DAUGHTERS OF ST. PAUL (P)

Missionary Sisters of the Media of Communications
Founded in Alba, Piedmont, Italy, on June 15, 1915. First founded in the United States on June 28, 1932, in New York.
General Motherhouse: Rome, Italy Sr. Anna Maria Parenzan, Supr. Gen.
Universal total in Congregation: 2,155.
Provincial House, Novitiate, Publishing House: 50 St. Paul's Ave., Jamaica Plain, MA 02130. Tel: 617-522-8911. Sr. Patricia Mary Maresca, Local Supr.; Sr. Donna William Giaimo, F.S.P., Prov. Supr.
Total in Community: 133.
Properties owned and/or sponsored: Pauline Book and Media Centers, found in 13 locations throughout the U.S.; Provincialate, Boston, MA; St. Thecla Retreat House, Billerica, MA.
Legal Title: Daughters of St. Paul, Inc.
Represented in the Archdioceses of Boston, Chicago, Los Angeles, Miami, New Orleans, New York, St. Louis, San Antonio and San Francisco and in the Dioceses of Arlington, Charleston and Honolulu. Also in Canada.

[0960] (D.W.)—DAUGHTERS OF WISDOM (P)

Founded in France in 1703. First foundation in the United States in 1904.
General Motherhouse: St. Laurent-sur-Sevre, Vendee, France. Superior General Headquarters located in Paris, France.
U.S. Province (1949): Provincial House, 385 Ocean Ave., Islip, NY 11751-4600. Tel: 631-277-2660; Fax: 631-277-3274. Sr. Catherine Sheehan, D.W., Prov. Leader.
Professed Sisters: 67.
Properties owned and/or sponsored: Wisdom House Center for Spirituality, Litchfield, CT; Our Lady of Perpetual Help Convent (Rest Home for Sisters), Sound Beach, NY; Provincial House, Islip, NY. Ministry in all levels of Education; Retreat House; Hospital & Health Services; Social Work.
Represented in the Archdioceses of Hartford and Washington and in the Dioceses of Brooklyn, Charleston, Omaha, Portland (In Maine), Raleigh, Richmond, Rockville Centre, St. Augustine and St. Petersburg.

[0965] (D.L.J.C.)—DISCIPLES OF THE LORD JESUS CHRIST (P)

Founded in the United States in 1972.
Motherhouse: P.O. Box 64, Prayer Town, TX 79010. Tel: 806-534-2312; Fax: 806-534-2223; Email: sistersdljc@gmail.com; Web: www.dljc.org. Mother Juana Teresa Chung, D.L.J.C., Supr. Gen.
Total in Community: 38.

Legal Holdings and Titles: Prayertown Emmanuel Retreat House, Prayer Town, TX.
Ministry in Retreat Work and Evangelization
Represented in the Archdiocese of Santa Fe and in the Dioceses of Amarillo and Pittsburgh. Also in Mexico.

[0970] (R.D.C.)—SISTERS OF THE DIVINE COMPASSION (D)

Founded in the United States in 1886.

General Motherhouse: Good Counsel Convent, 52 N. Broadway, White Plains, NY 10603. Tel: 914-798-1300; Fax: 914-949-5169. Sr. Laura Donovan, R.D.C., Pres.

Total in Community: 74.

Legal Holdings and Titles: Academy of Our Lady of Good Counsel High School and Elementary School, White Plains, NY; Preston High School, Bronx, NY; Migrant Ministry, Goshen, NY; Residence, Hampton Bays, NY; RDC Center for Counseling and Human Development, White Plains, NY; Preston Center of Compassion, Bronx, NY.

Ministry in Preschool, Elementary, Secondary, College and University Education; Religious Education; Educational Consultation; Adult Education; Special Education; Pastoral Ministry; Retreat Work and Spiritual Direction; Counseling; Social Services; Migrant Ministry; Health Services; Administration and Business Services.

Represented in the Archdiocese of New York.

[0980] (P.D.D.M.)—PIOUS DISCIPLES OF THE DIVINE MASTER (P)

Founded in 1924. First foundation in the United States in 1948.

General Motherhouse: Rome, Italy Sr. M. Regina Cesarato, Supr. Gen.

Universal total in Congregation: 1355.

U.S. Headquarters: 60 Sunset Ave., Staten Island, NY 10314. Tel: 718-494-8597; Fax: 718-494-2123. Sr. M. Josephine Fallon, Reg. Supr.

Total number in Region: 48.

Ministry is a Three Dimensional Mission: Eucharistic, Priestly, Liturgical.

Represented in the Archdioceses of Boston, Los Angeles and New York and in the Diocese of Fresno.

[0990] (C.D.P.)—SISTERS OF DIVINE PROVIDENCE (P)

Founded in Germany in 1851. First foundation in the United States in 1876; incorporation granted September 17, 1881.

Amended and restated articles of incorporation on December 28, 2001.

General Motherhouse: Mother of Providence Convent, 12 Christopher St., Wakefield, RI 02879. Tel: 401-782-1785; Fax: 401-782-6967. Sr. Janet Folkl, Gen. Supr.

Marie de la Roche Province (2001): Providence Heights, 9000 Babcock Blvd., Allison Park, PA 15101. Tel: 412-931-5241; Fax: 412-635-5416. Sr. Michele Bisbey, C.D.P., Prov. Supr.; Sr. Juliana Frisoli, C.D.P., Area Asst.-Kingston, MA; Sr. Mary Michael McCulla, C.D.P., Area Asst.-St. Louis, MO.

Total in Community: 181.

Ministry in the fields of Education; Social Services; Pastoral Ministry; and Health Care Services.

Properties owned and sponsored: La Roche College, Pittsburgh, PA; Providence Heights Alpha School, Allison Park, PA; Kearns Spirituality Center, Allison Park, PA; Providence Connections, Inc.; Providence Family Support Center, Pittsburgh, PA; Sisters of Divine Providence of Allegheny County, Allison Park, PA; Sisters of Divine Providence Charitable Trust, Allison Park, PA; Room at the Inn, Bridgeton, MO; Sacred Heart School System, Kingston, MA; Congregation of the Sisters of Divine Providence, Kingston, MA; Sisters of Divine Providence of Missouri, Bridgeton, MO, La Posada Providencia, San Benito, TX.

Represented in the Archdioceses of Boston, Detroit, St. Louis and San Juan and in the Dioceses of Arecibo, Belleville, Brownsville, Columbus, Erie, Fall River, Nashville, Orlando, Pittsburgh, Providence, Raleigh, Springfield in Illinois, Wheeling-Charleston and Youngstown. Also in the Dominican Republic.

[1000] (C.D.P.)—CONGREGATION OF DIVINE PROVIDENCE, MELBOURNE, KENTUCKY (P)

Founded in France in 1762. First foundation in the United States in 1889.

General Motherhouse: St. Jean de Bassel, Fenetrange, France, 57930. Sr. Susan Baumann, Supr. Gen.

American Provincial House (1889): St. Anne Convent, 5300 St. Anne Dr., Melbourne, KY 41059. Tel: 859-441-0679. Sr. Alice Gerdeman, C.D.P., Prov. Supr.; Sr. Dolores Gohs, C.D.P., Archivist.

Total number in Province: 89.

Ministry in the field of Academic Education at all levels; Home for Working Women; Religious Education & Pastoral Ministry; Health & Social Services.

Represented in the Archdioceses of Cincinnati, New York, Boston and Washington and in the Dioceses of Covington, Duluth and Lexington.

[1010] (C.D.P.)—CONGREGATION OF DIVINE PROVIDENCE, SAN ANTONIO, TEXAS (P)

Founded in France in 1762. First foundation in the United States in 1866.

The Generalate: 515 S.W. 24th St., San Antonio, TX 78207. Tel: 210-434-1866; Fax: 210-568-1050. Sr. Ann Petrus, C.D.P., Supr. Gen.; Sr. Charlotte Kitowski, Archivist; Sr. Patricia Regan, C.D.P., Treas. Councilors: Sr. Anita Brenak, C.D.P.; Sr. Lourdes Leal, C.D.P.; Sr. Mary Bordelon, C.D.P.

Novitiate and Formation: Formation/Vocation Office, 515 S.W. 24th St., San Antonio, TX 78207. Tel: 210-587-1135.

Properties owned and/or sponsored: Our Lady of the Lake Retirement Center, San Antonio, TX; Moye Center, Castroville, TX.

Legal Titles & Holdings: Congregation of Divine Providence, Inc.; Providence Trust, San Antonio, TX.

Ministry in all levels of Education; Catechetical Centers; Diocesan Offices; Retreat Houses; Spiritual Direction-Counseling; Pastoral; Social Work; Chaplaincies in Public Institutions; Administration and Campus Ministry.

Represented in the Archdioceses of Denver, Galveston-Houston, San Antonio, and St. Louis and in the Dioceses of Austin, Fort Worth, Lafayette (LA), San Angelo, Beaumont, San Jose and Springfield-Cape Girardeau. Also in Mexico.

[1020] (S.D.R.)—SISTERS OF THE DIVINE REDEEMER (P)

Founded in 1849 at Niederbronn, France. First foundation in the United States on October 3, 1912 at McKeesport.

Generalate: Suore del Divin Redentore, Via Casale Piombino 14, Rome, Italy, 00135. Tel: 011-39-06-305-2512. Sr. Johanna Vogl, Supr. Gen.

American Region (1912): Divine Redeemer Mother house, 999 Rock Run Rd., Elizabeth, PA 15037-2613. Tel: 412-751-8600; Fax: 412-751-0355. Email: sdrarusa@gmail.com. Web: www.divine-redeemer-sister.org. Sr. M. Monica Kosztolnyik, Archivist & Regl. Vicar; Sr. M. Alojziana Spišáková, S.D.R., Regl. Supr.

Total number in Province: 16.

Legal Titles and Holdings: Sisters of the Divine Redeemer Charitable Trust; Divine Redeemer Health Care Ministries Corp., Elizabeth, PA.

Ministry in the fields of education & music education.

Represented in the Diocese of Pittsburgh.

[1030] (S.D.S.)—SISTERS OF THE DIVINE SAVIOR

Founded in Tivoli, Italy, in 1888. First foundation in the United States in 1895.

General Motherhouse: Viale delle Mura Gianicolensi 67, Rome, Italy Sr. Edith Bramberger, Gen. Supr.

North American Province: Sisters of the Divine Savior, 4311 N. 100th St., Milwaukee, WI 53222-1393. Tel: 414-466-0810; Fax: 414-466-4335. Sr. Beverly Heitke, S.D.S., Prov. Supr.; Sr. Mary Jo Stoffel, S.D.S., Archivist.

Total number in U.S. community: 63.

Ministry in all levels of Education; Pastoral and Social Services; Health Care; and Homes for the Aged.

Properties owned or sponsored: St. Anne's Home for the Elderly; Divine Savior Holy Angels High School, Milwaukee, WI; Divine Savior Healthcare, Inc., Portage, WI.

Represented in the Archdiocese of Milwaukee and in the Dioceses of Birmingham, Green Bay, Madison, Phoenix, Sacramento, Sioux Falls and Tucson.

[1040] (C.D.S.)—CONGREGATION OF THE DIVINE SPIRIT (D)

First foundation in Erie, Pennsylvania in 1956.

Motherhouse: 2700 Harvard Ave., N.W., Canton, OH 44709. Sr. Michele Beauseigneur, Supr. Gen.

Membership: 21.

Sisters serve and staff: Parochial Schools; CCD Activities; Home for Aged.

Represented in the Diocese of Youngstown.

[1050] (O.P.)—DOMINICAN CONTEMPLATIVE NUNS (P)

(The Nuns of the Order of Preachers)

Founded in France in 1206. First foundation in the United States in 1880. Monastic contemplative branch of the Order of Preachers. Papal cloister.

Nuns of the Order of Preachers O.P: Corpus Christi Monastery, 1230 Lafayette Ave., Bronx, NY 10474. Tel: 718-328-6996; Fax: 718-328-1974. Sr. Maria Pia of the Eucharist, O.P., Prioress.

Total in Community: 11.

Monastery of the Blessed Sacrament: Nuns of the Order of Preachers, 29575 Middlebelt Rd., Farmington Hills, MI 48334-2311. Tel: 248-626-8321; Tel: 248-626-8253; Fax: 248-626-8724. Sr. Mary of the Sacred Heart, O.P., Prioress.

Cloistered Sisters: 28; Extern Sisters: 3.

Nuns of the Order of Preachers (Cloistered Dominican Nuns, Perpetual Adoration)

Monastery of the Angels: Cloistered Dominican Nuns, 1977 Carmen Ave., Los Angeles, CA 90068. Tel: 323-466-2186. Email: laopnuns@monasteryoftheangels.org; Web: www.monasteryoftheangels.org. Sr. Mary St. Pius, O.P., Prioress.

Sisters: 17.

Legal Title: The Monastery of the Angels.

Monastery of the Angels: Karachi, Pakistan Sr. Mary Martin, O.P., Prioress.

Sisters: 12.

Queen of Angels Monastery: Bocaue, Bulacan, Philippines Sr. Mary Lourdes, O.P., Prioress.

Sisters: 14.

Corpus Christi Monastery: 215 Oak Grove Ave., Menlo Park, CA 94025-3272. Tel: 650-322-1801; Fax: 650-322-6816. Sr. Maria Christine, O.P., Prioress.

Cloistered Total Number in Community: 12.

Dominican Nuns O.P: Monastery of the Mother of God, 1430 Riverdale St., West Springfield, MA 01089-4698. Tel: 413-736-3639; Fax: 413-736-0850. Sr. Mary of the Immaculate Heart, O.P., Prioress.

Total in Community: 11.

Dominican Contemplative Nuns O.P.: Monastery of Our Lady of the Rosary, 335 Doat St., Buffalo, NY 14211-2149. Tel: 716-892-0066; Fax: 716-897-1566. Email: bufprioress@opnuns.org. Sr. Mary Dominic, O.P., Prioress.

Solemnly Professed: 16; Perpetually Professed (Externs): 2; Sisters in Formation: 2.

Legal Title: Dominican Nuns of the Perpetual Rosary.

Monastery of Our Lady of Grace: 11 Race Hill Rd., Guilford, CT 06437-1099. Tel: 203-457-0599. Sr. Claire, O.P., Prioress.

Total in Community: 25.

Legal Title: Dominican Nuns of North Guilford, CT Inc.

Monastery of the Infant Jesus: Dominican Contemplative Nuns, 1501 Lotus Ln., Lufkin, TX 75904. Tel: 936-634-4233; Fax: 936-634-2156. Sr. Maria Guadalupe, O.P., Prioress.

Professed: 21.

Monastery of Our Lady of the Rosary (Rosary Shrine): 543 Springfield Ave., Summit, NJ 07901. Tel: 908-273-1228. Email: info@summitdominicans.org. Sr. Mary Martin, O.P., Prioress.

Solemnly Professed: 13; Temporary Professed: 2; Novices: 1; Postulants: 1.

St. Dominic's Monastery (Contemplative): 2636 Monastery Rd., Linden, VA 22642. Email: monastery@lindenopnuns.org. Sr. Mary Fidelis, O.P., Prioress.

Nuns : 11.

The Dominican Nuns of the Perpetual Rosary (Cloistered-Contemplative): Monastery of the Immaculate Heart of Mary, 1834 Lititz Pike, Lancaster, PA 17601-6585. Tel: 717-569-2104; Fax: 717-569-1598; Email: monlanc@aol.com. Sr. Mary Veronica, O.P., Prioress.

Solemnly Professed: 7.

Dominican Monastery of the Perpetual Rosary: 802 Court St., Syracuse, NY 13208. Tel: 315-471-6762. Sr. Bernadette Marie, O.P., Prioress.

Total in Community: 11.

Dominican Monastery of St. Jude: 143 County Rd. 20 E., P.O. Box 170, Marbury, AL 36051-0170. Tel: 205-755-1322; Fax: 205-755-1322; Email: stjudemonastery@aol.com; Web: www.

marburydominicannuns.org. Mother Mary of the Precious Blood, O.P., Prioress.

Professed Nuns: 6; Temporary Professed Novices: 1; Postulants: 1.

[1060] (O.P.)—DOMINICAN CONTEMPLATIVE SISTERS (D)

Cloistered Contemplative

Founded in Calais, France in 1880.

Monastery of the Dominican Sisters of the Perpetual Rosary (Cloistered): 3980 W. Kimberly Ave., Greenfield, WI 53221-4553. Tel: 414-258-0579; Email: mjoannahastings@gmail.com; Web: www.dsopr.org. Mother Joanna Hastings, O.P., Prioress.

Professed Sisters: 5.

[1070] (O.P.)—COLLABORATIVE DOMINICAN NOVITIATE DOMINICAN SISTERS (P)

There are seventeen Congregations of the Dominican Sisters of the Third Order of St. Dominic in the United States. The list of General Motherhouses follows in the order of seniority. If the Congregation is known under a more familiar name, that name is given under the name of the Congregation.

4928 Washington Blvd., St. Louis, MO 63108-1621. Tel: 314-454-0664.

[1070-03]—SINSINAWA DOMINICAN CONGREGATION OF THE MOST HOLY ROSARY (P)

Generalate: Sinsinawa Dominican Congregation of the Most Holy Rosary, 585 County Rd. Z, Sinsinawa, WI 53824-9701. Tel: 608-748-4411. Communication Office Email: communication@sinsinawa.org. Sr. Antoinette Harris, O.P., Prioress of the Congregation; Sr. Lois Hoh, O.P., Archivist.

Total in Community: 400.

Ministry in a variety of cultures in Preaching & Evangelization; Elementary, Secondary and Higher Education; Medical, Legal and Social Services; Adult and Religious Education; Diocesan and Parish Administration, Spiritual Direction and Counseling; Rural, Migrant Services; Writing Research.

Properties owned or Institutions sponsored: Sinsinawa Dominicans, Inc., Dominican University, River Forest, IL; Sinsinawa Housing, Inc., (Academy Apartments), Sinsinawa, WI; Bethlehem Academy, Faribault, MN; Dominican High School, Whitefish Bay, WI; Trinity High School, River Forest, IL; Sinsinawa Nursing, Inc., (St. Dominic Villa), Sinsinawa, WI; Dominican Motherhouse, Sinsinawa, WI; Camp We-Ha-Kee, Winter, WI; Edgewood Campus School; Edgewood High School; Edgewood College, Madison, WI.

Represented in the Archdioceses of Atlanta, Chicago, Denver, Dubuque, Los Angeles, Miami, Milwaukee, Mobile, Omaha, St. Louis, St. Paul-Minneapolis, San Francisco, Seattle and Washington and in the Dioceses of Austin, Cheyenne, Dallas, Great Falls-Billings, Green Bay, Helena, Joliet, La Crosse, Madison, Oakland, Orlando, Palm Beach, Pensacola-Tallahassee, Rockford, San Jose, St. Augustine, St. Petersburg, Spokane, and Winona-Rochester. Also in Bolivia and Trinidad.

[1070-04]—CONGREGATION OF THE MOST HOLY NAME (P)

Generalate: Dominican Sisters of San Rafael, 1520 Grand Ave., San Rafael, CA 94901. Tel: 415-453-8303; Fax: 415-453-8367. Email: info@sanrafaelop.org. Sr. Maureen McInerney, O.P.

Total in Community: 69.

Legal Holdings and Titles: San Domenico School, San Anselmo, CA; Santa Sabina Retreat Center, San Rafael, CA; St. Rose Corporation, San Francisco, CA; St. Joseph's Regional Health System; Sisters of St. Dominic, Congregation of the Most Holy Name, San Rafael, CA; Mission Holding Corporation, San Rafael, CA.

Represented in the Archdiocese of San Francisco and Chicago and Seattle in the Dioceses of Monterey, Oakland, Santa Rosa and Stockton. Also in Mexico.

[1070-05]—CONGREGATION OF THE HOLY CROSS (D)

General Motherhouse: Queen of the Rosary Mother house, Albany Ave., Amityville, NY 11701. Tel: 631-842-6000; Fax: 631-842-0240. Email: sistersop@amityop.org. Sr. Mary Patricia Neylon, O.P., Prioress; Sr. Margaret Kavanagh, O.P., Archivist.

Total in Community: 390.

Legal Title: The Sisters of the Order of Saint Dominic.

Sisters are engaged in the ministry of Education at all levels; Catechetical Schools; Handicapped, Adult and Continuing Education; Hospitals; Homes for the Aged; Residence for Senior Citizens; Spiritual Life Centers; Chaplaincy; Advocacy; Communications; Social Service Institutions; Shelters; Pastoral Services; Prison Ministry; Retreats; Health Services; Ministry to AIDS Victims; Environmental Education Ministry.

Represented in the Archdioceses of Newark and New York and in the Dioceses of Albany, Brooklyn, Providence, Rockville Centre and Trenton. Also in Puerto Rico.

[1070-07]—CONGREGATION OF ST. CECILIA (P)

General Motherhouse: St. Cecilia Convent, 801 Dominican Dr., Nashville, TN 37228-1905. Tel: 615-256-5486; Fax: 615-687-3512. Vocation Office Email: vocation@op-tn.org. Advancement Office Email: direadvance@op-tn.org. Mother Anna Grace Neenan, O.P., Prioress Gen.; Sr. Lucia Marie Siemering, O.P., Archivist and Sec. Gen. Email: slmsiemering@op-tn.org.

Professed Sisters in Community: 294; Novices: 9; Postulants: 7.

Ministry in the field of Academic Education at all levels. Legal Holdings and Titles: Aquinas College, Nashville, TN.

Represented in the Archdioceses of Atlanta, Baltimore, Cincinnati, Denver, Galveston-Houston, Louisville, St. Louis, St. Paul-Minneapolis, Seattle and Washington and in the Dioceses of Arlington, Birmingham, Charleston, Dallas, Joliet in Illinois, Knoxville, Lafayette in Indiana, Memphis, Nashville, Phoenix, Providence and Richmond. Also in Australia, Canada, Ireland, Italy, Scotland, and The Netherlands.

[1070-09]—CONGREGATION OF ST. CATHERINE OF SIENA (P)

General Motherhouse: Convent of St. Catherine, 5635 Erie St., Racine, WI 53402-1900. Tel: 262-639-4100; Fax: 262-639-9702. Sr. Maryann McMahon, O.P., Pres.; Sr. Shirley Kubat, Archivist.

Total in Community: 121.

Legal Holdings and Titles: Sisters of St. Dominic, Racine, WI; St. Catherine's High School of Racine, Inc., Racine, WI; Racine Dominican Ministries, Inc., Racine, WI; HOPES Center of Racine, Inc.; Siena Retreat Center, Inc.; Eco-Justice Center, Inc.; Senior Companion Program, Inc.; Dominicans at Siena on the Lake, Inc.

Properties sponsored: Sisters of St. Dominic, Racine, WI; Catherine Marian Housing, Inc.

Sisters minister in the areas of Higher and Music Cultural Education; Adult Education; Religious Education; Administration; Parish and Pastoral Ministry; Prison Ministry; Social Justice; Social Services, Hospital and Health Services; Writing Research; Hospital Chaplains; Retreats-Prayer Programs; Community Services.

Represented in the Archdioceses of Detroit, Milwaukee, St. Louis and Santa Fe and in the Dioceses of Grand Rapids, Green Bay, Las Vegas, Madison and Yakima.

[1070-10]—DOMINICAN SISTERS OF SPRINGFIELD, ILLINOIS (P)

General Motherhouse: Sacred Heart Convent, 1237 W. Monroe St., Springfield, IL 62704-1680. Tel: 217-787-0481; Fax: 217-787-8169. Sr. Rebecca Ann Gemma, O.P., Prioress Gen.; Sr. Julia Theobald, O.P., Archivist.

Total in Community: 181.

Legal Holdings or Titles: Dominican Sisters of Springfield, Illinois, Inc., Dominican Sisters of Springfield in Illinois Charitable Trust, Springfield, IL; Jubilee Farm, NFP, Springfield, IL; Dominican Literacy Center, Aurora, IL; Dominican Literacy Center, Chicago, IL; Marian Catholic High School, Chicago Heights, IL; Rosary High School, Aurora, IL; Sacred Heart-Griffin High School, Springfield, IL; St. Dominic-Jackson Memorial Hospital, Jackson, MS.

Ministry in Elementary, Secondary Schools and College, Religious & Academic Education; Learning Centers; Hospitals, Nursing Homes, Congregation's Infirmary and Retirement Centers; Retreat & Renewal Center; Administrative Positions in Parishes and Diocesan Offices; Parish Liturgist/Musician & Pastoral Associates; Prison Ministry; Social Services; Foreign Missions.

Represented in the Archdioceses of Chicago and Indianapolis and in the Dioceses of Belleville, Jackson, Jefferson City, Joliet, Peoria, Rapid City, Rockford, and Springfield in Illinois. Also in Peru.

[1070-11]—CONGREGATION OF OUR LADY OF THE ROSARY (D)

General Motherhouse and Novitiate: Dominican Convent of Our Lady of the Rosary, 175 Rte. 340, Sparkill, NY 10976. Tel: 845-359-4199. Sr. Mary Murray, O.P., Pres.

Total in Community: 252.

Legal Title: Dominican Convent of Our Lady of the Rosary.

Ministry in High Schools and Elementary Schools; Adult Education/Literacy; Parishes; Pastoral; Colleges; Housing and Community Centers; Foreign Missions; Substance Abuse Recovery.

Properties sponsored: Aquinas High School, New York, NY; Albertus Magnus High School, Bardonia, NY; One to One Learning Inc., Nyack, NY; Dowling Housing Corp., Sparkill, NY.

Represented in the Archdioceses of Chicago, Newark, New York and St. Louis and in the Dioceses of Brooklyn, Great Falls-Billings, Jefferson City, Rockville Centre, San Diego and Trenton.

[1070-12]—CONGREGATION OF THE QUEEN OF THE HOLY ROSARY (P)

General Motherhouse: Dominican Convent, 43326 Mission Cir., Fremont, CA 94539. Tel: 510-657-2468; Fax: 510-657-1734. Sr. Cecilia Canales, Congregational Prioress; Sr. Pauline Bouton, Congregational Sec.

Professed: 152.

Legal Title: Dominican Sisters of Mission San Jose, a Corporation, Queen of the Holy Rosary College, a Corporation, St. Catherine's Academy, a Corporation, Anaheim, CA; Immaculate Conception Academy, a Corporation, San Francisco, CA; Flintridge Sacred Heart Academy, a Corporation, La Canada-Flintridge, CA; Pia Backes Support Trust, Fremont, CA; Dominican Sisters Vision of Hope.

The Community is engaged in the Preaching Mission of St. Dominic through ministry in education at all levels, campus ministry, pastoral services, social justice, communications, health services, Congregational services, and full time study.

Represented in the Archdioceses of Los Angeles, San Francisco and St. Louis and in the Dioceses of Oakland, Orange, San Bernardino, San Jose and Tucson. Also in Mexico.

[1070-13]—CONGREGATION OF THE MOST HOLY ROSARY (P)

General Motherhouse: 1257 Siena Heights Dr., Adrian, MI 49221. Tel: 517-266-3400; Fax: 517-266-3545. Sr. Patricia Siemen, O.P., Prioress.

Total in Congregation : 587.

Legal Holdings or Titles: Dominican Sisters of Adrian, MI, Inc., Adrian, MI; Camilla Madden Charitable Trust, Adrian, MI; Adrian Dominican Sisters Office of Development, Adrian, MI; Dominican Hospital, Santa Cruz, CA; Dominican Life Center, Adrian, MI; Regina Dominican High School, Wilmette, IL; Rosarian Academy, West Palm Beach, FL; Siena Heights University, Adrian, MI; St. Rose Dominican Hospitals, Henderson, NV; Weber Retreat Center, Adrian, MI.

Sisters minister in the areas of Formal Education - as administrators, teachers and consultants at elementary, secondary, college, state and diocesan levels; Pastoral Ministry - parishes, hospitals and campuses; Religious Education - coordinators and teachers; Social Services - case workers, administrators, counselors, therapists, consultants, care-givers for elderly and staff for retirement centers; Health Services administrators, nurses, therapists, doctors, physician assistants, psychologists, technologists and dietitians; Business Services - directors, accountants, secretaries, administrative assistants, typists, bookkeepers, office managers, office staff, drivers and housekeeping staff; Spiritual Direction - retreat work, formation, congregation leadership and as diocesan vicars for Religious; Social Justice - coordinators, staff and community organizers; other ministries including research, law, science, public relations, art, communications and full-time study.

Represented in the Archdioceses of Atlanta, Chicago, Cincinnati, Detroit, Galveston-Houston, Indianapolis, Los Angeles, Louisville, Miami, New Orleans, New York, Portland in Oregon, St. Paul-Minneapolis, St. Louis, San Francisco, Santa Fe and Seattle and the Dioceses of Arlington, Burlington, Charleston, Cleveland, El Paso, Gaylord, Green Bay, Joliet,

Kalamazoo, Las Vegas, Lansing, Lexington, Marquette, Milwaukee, Monterey, Oakland, Orange, Orlando, Palm Beach, Phoenix, Providence, Rockford, Saginaw, San Diego, Tucson and Venice. Also in Dominican Republic, Mexico, Norway and Philippines.

Mission Chapters (1982):

Florida Mission Chapter: 810 N. Olive Ave., West Palm Beach, FL 33401. Tel: 561-832-6521. Sr. Mary Ann Caulfield, O.P., Chapter Prioress.

Adrian Crossroads Mission Chapter: 1257 Siena Heights Dr., Adrian, MI 49221. Tel: 517-266-4242. Sr. Mary Jane Lubinski, O.P., Chapter Prioress.

Dominican Midwest Mission Chapter: 10024 S. Central Park Ave., Chicago, IL 60655. Tel: 773-253-3827. Sr. Kathleen Klingen, O.P., Chapter Prioress.

Holy Rosary Mission Chapter: 1257 Siena Heights Dr., Adrian, MI 49221. Tel: 517-266-4105. Sr. Joanne Peters, O.P., Co-Chapter Prioress; Sr. Patricia Ann Dulka, O.P., Co-Chapter Prioress.

Great Lakes Dominican Mission Chapter: 29000 W. 11 Mile Rd., Farmington Hills, MI 48336. Tel: 248-478-4284. Sr. Carol Jean Kesterke, O.P., Chapter Prioress.

Dominican West Mission Chapter: 1216 N.E. 65th St., Seattle, WA 98115. Tel: 206-523-6293. Sr. Lorene Heck, O.P., Chapter Prioress.

[1070-14]—CONGREGATION OF OUR LADY OF THE SACRED HEART (P)

General Motherhouse: Marywood, 2025 E. Fulton St., Grand Rapids, MI 49503. Tel: 616-459-2910; Fax: 616-454-6105. Sr. Sandra Delgado, O.P., Prioress; Sr. Mary Navarre, O.P., Archivist.

Total in Community: 178.

Legal Holdings or Titles: Sisters of the Order of St. Dominic of Grand Rapids; Marywood Academy; Sisters of St. Dominic of the Congregation of Our Lady of the Sacred Heart Charitable Trust.

Sisters are involved in Academic and Religious Education at all levels; Liturgy; Pastoral Ministry and Administration; Diocesan Offices; Food Service; Health Care; Congregational Services; Social Work; Sabbatical Volunteer; Public Education and Study; Foreign Missions; Justice Advocacy.

Represented in the Archdioceses of Chicago, Detroit, St. Louis and Santa Fe and in the Dioceses of Colorado Springs, Fort Wayne-South Bend, Gaylord, Grand Rapids, Helena, Kalamazoo, Lansing, Rapid City, Saginaw and Superior. Also in Peru and Washington, DC.

[1070-15]—CONGREGATION OF SAINT DOMINIC (D)

General Motherhouse: Sisters of Saint Dominic of Blauvelt, 496 Western Hwy., Blauvelt, NY 10913-2097. Tel: 845-359-5600; Fax: 845-359-5773. Sr. Michaela Connolly, O.P., Prioress.

Total in Community: 103.

Sisters serve and staff: Elementary; Secondary; Higher Education; Special Education; Hospital Care; Pastoral Care; Parish Ministry; Retreat Work; Child Care; Neighborhood Services; Services to Migrants; Services to Chemically Dependent.

Represented in the Archdioceses of Newark and New York and in the Dioceses of Orlando, Portland, Providence, Trenton and Venice.

[1070-17]—DOMINICAN CONGREGATION OF ST. CATHERINE DE' RICCI (P)

General Motherhouse: 2320 Airport Dr., Columbus, OH 43219. Tel: 614-416-1900. Sr. Patricia Twohill, O.P., Pres.

Professed Sisters: 523.

Properties owned and/or sponsored: St. Dominic Hall, Elkins Park, PA; St. Catherine Hall, Elkins Park, PA.

Represented in the Archdiocese of Philadelphia.

[1070-18]—SISTERS OF ST. DOMINIC OF THE AMERICAN CONGREGATION OF THE SACRED HEART OF JESUS (D)

Dominican Motherhouse: 1 Ryerson Ave., Caldwell, NJ 07006. Tel: 973-403-3331; Fax: 973-228-9611. Sr. Patrice Werner, O.P., Prioress; Sr. Elaine Keenan, O.P., Archivist.

Total in Community: 119.

Properties owned and/or sponsored: Caldwell College, Caldwell, NJ; Mount Saint Dominic Academy, Caldwell, NJ; St. Dominic Academy, Jersey City, NJ; Lacordaire Academy, Upper Montclair, NJ.

Legal Title: Sisters of St. Dominic of Caldwell, NJ, Inc.

Ministry in Education at all levels; Pastoral Ministry; Health and Human Services.

Represented in the Archdioceses of Newark and Portland in Oregon and in the Dioceses of Metuchen, Paterson and Trenton.

[1070-19]—DOMINICAN SISTERS OF HOUSTON, TEXAS (CONGREGATION OF THE SACRED HEART) (P)

General Motherhouse & Novitiate: Dominican Sisters, 6501 Almeda Rd., Houston, TX 77021. Tel: 713-747-3310; Fax: 713-747-4707. Sr. Donna M. Pollard, O.P., Prioress.

Total in Community: 61.

Legal Title: Dominican Sisters of Houston, Texas, Inc. (aka Sacred Heart Convent of Houston).

Ministry in the field of Academic Education at all levels and parish Ministry.

Properties owned and sponsored: St. Agnes Academy, St. Agnes Academy Foundation, St. Pius X High School, St. Pius X High School Foundation, Inc., The Sacred Heart Convent Retirement Trust.

Represented in the Archdioceses of Galveston-Houston, Indianapolis, Los Angeles and San Antonio and in the Dioceses of Austin, Beaumont, Dallas, Houma-Thibodaux, San Bernardino and Tyler. Also in Guatemala.

[1070-20]—CONGREGATION OF ST. THOMAS AQUINAS (P)

Motherhouse: Tacoma Dominican Center, 935 Fawcett Ave. S., Tacoma, WA 98402-5605. Tel: 253-272-9688; Fax: 253-272-8790. Sr. Sharon Casey, O.P.

Total in Community: 49.

Legal Holdings and Titles: Sisters of St. Dominic, Tacoma Dominican Center; Sisters of St. Dominic Tacoma Charitable Trust.

Ministry in a variety of missions.

Represented in the Archdiocese of Seattle and in the Dioceses of Fresno, San Diego and Yakima.

[1070-23]—DOMINICAN SISTERS, CONGREGATION OF ST. ROSE OF LIMA (P)

General Motherhouse: Rosary Hill Home, 600 Linda Ave., Hawthorne, NY 10532. Tel: 914-769-0114. Vocation Email: vocationdirector@hawthorne-dominicans.org. Mother Mary Francis, O.P., Supr. Gen.

Total in Community: 46.

The work of these sisters is confined entirely to the incurable cancerous poor.

Represented in the Archdioceses of Atlanta, New York and Philadelphia.

[1070-25]—DOMINICAN SISTERS OF ST. CATHERINE OF SIENA (P)

General Motherhouse & Novitiate: 14735 Aloha Ave., Saratoga, CA 95070. Tel: 408-805-0055. Sr. Susan Anne Snyder, O.P., Prioress.

Total in Community: 8.

Properties owned and/or sponsored: Our Lady of Fatima Villa, Saratoga, CA; Mercy Medical Center, Merced, CA.

Legal Title: Dominican Sisters of St. Catherine of Siena, Inc.

Represented in the Dioceses of Fresno and San Jose.

[1070-27]—DOMINICAN SISTERS, IMMACULATE CONCEPTION PROVINCE (D)

Provincial House: 9000 W. 81st St., Justice, IL 60458. Tel: 708-458-3040. Mother M. Natalie, O.P., Vicar Prov.; Mother Helena Cempa, O.P., Prov.

Total in Community: 31.

Represented in the Archdioceses of Chicago and Milwaukee and in the Dioceses of Columbus and Little Rock. Also in Canada.

[1070-30]—DOMINICAN SISTERS OF OAKFORD (P)

U.S. Regional Center: Dominican Sisters of Oakford, 980 Woodland Ave., San Leandro, CA 94577. Tel: 510-638-2822; Fax: 510-633-9734. Sr. Mary de Crus Nolan, O.P., Reg. Prioress.

Total in Community: 15.

Properties owned and/or sponsored: 3 residences in California; Our Lady of Oakford Regional Center, San Leandro, CA.

Ministries in Teaching, Spiritual Direction; Massage Therapy; Counseling; Parish Work; Adult Education; Community Outreach; Social Work, Chaplaincy and Nursing.

Represented in the Dioceses of Oakland and Tucson.

[1100] (O.P.)—DOMINICAN SISTERS OF CHARITY OF THE PRESENTATION OF THE BLESSED VIRGIN (P)

Founded in France in 1696. First foundation in the United States in 1906.

Motherhouse: 15 Quai Portillon, Tours Cedex 2, France, 37081.

Universal total in Congregation: 1986.

Provincial House: 3012 Elm St., Dighton, MA 02715. Tel: 508-669-5425; Tel: 508-669-5433; Tel: 508-669-5023; Fax: 508-669-6521. Email: domsrs@presentation-op-usa.org. Sr. Marta Ines Toro, O.P., Major Supr.

Total number in Province: 30.

Ministry in Hospitals; Homes for the Aged; Residence for Working Women and Students; Dispensaries; Education; Pastoral Ministry.

Represented in the Archdiocese of Washington and in the Dioceses of Brownsville and Fall River. Also in Bolivia, Colombia, Haiti, Honduras, India, Korea, Mexico and Peru.

[1105] (O.P.)—DOMINICAN SISTERS OF HOPE INC. (P)

Founded July 20, 1995, as a merging of three former Congregations: Dominican Sisters of the Congregation of the Most Holy Rosary of Newburgh, NY; Dominican Sisters of the Sick Poor of Ossining, NY and Congregation of Catherine of Siena of Fall River, MA.

General Administrative Offices: Dominican Sisters of Hope, 299 N. Highland Ave., Ossining, NY 10562. Tel: 914-941-4420; Fax: 914-941-1125. Sr. Lorelle Elcock, O.P., Prioress.

Total in Community: 143.

Legal Titles and Holdings: Sisters of St. Dominic Charitable Trust; Dominicare, Inc., Ossining, NY. Ministry in Religious & Academic Education at all levels; health, social, community and pastoral services; Parish service, counseling, retreats and spiritual direction.

Represented in the Archdioceses of Cincinnati, Denver, Hartford, Newark, New York, Oklahoma City and San Juan and in the Dioceses of Albany, Bridgeport, Camden, Fall River, Manchester, Metuchen, Ogdensburg, Orlando, Paterson, Providence, Richmond, Trenton, Venice and Wheeling-Charleston.

[1110] (O.P.)—DOMINICAN SISTERS OF OUR LADY OF THE ROSARY AND OF SAINT CATHERINE OF SIENA, CABRA (P)

Founded in Ireland in 1644.

General Motherhouse: Cabra, Dublin 7, Ireland Region of Louisiana established in 1978.

Regional House: Dominican Sisters, Cabra: 3524 DeSaix Blvd., New Orleans, LA 70119. Tel: 504-267-7867.

Total number in local community: 3.

Ministry in Academic and Religious Education; Parish Ministry; Neighborhood Social Service Agency; Prison Ministry; Adult Education.

Represented in the Archdiocese of New Orleans.

[1115] (O.P.)—DOMINICAN SISTERS OF PEACE (P)

Generalate: 2320 Airport Dr., Columbus, OH 43219-2098. Tel: 614-416-1900; Fax: 614-252-7435. Email: info@oppeace.org. Sr. Patricia Twohill, O.P., Prioress.

Total in Community: 467.

Legal Title: Dominican Sisters of Peace, Inc.

Properties Owned and/or Sponsored: Albertus Magnus College, New Haven, CT; Cedar Park Place, Great Bend, KS; Clausen Manor, Waterford, MI; Crown Point Ecology Center, Bath, OH; Crystal Spring Center for Ecology, Spirituality & Education, Plainville, MA; Dominican Academy, New York, NY; Fox Manor, Waterford, MI; Heartland Center for Spirituality, Great Bend, KS; Heartland Farm, Pawnee Rock, KS; Lourdes Nursing Home & Rehabilitation Center, Waterford, MI; Martin de Porres Center, Columbus, OH Mendelson Assisted Living Home, Waterford, MI; Mohun Health Care Center, Columbus, OH; Ohio Dominican University, Columbus, OH; Our Lady of the Elms School, Akron, OH; Rosaryville Spirit Life Center, Ponchatoula, LA; Peace Center, New Orleans, LA; St. Agnes Academy-St. Dominic School, Memphis, TN; St. Catharine Farm, St. Catharine, KY; St. Mary's Retreat House, Oxford, MI; St. Mary's Dominican High School, New Orleans, LA; St. Rose Spirituality House, Waterford, MI; Sansbury Care Center, St. Catharine, KY Shepherd's Corner, Blacklick, OH;

Dominican Learning Center, Columbus, OH; Siena Learning Center, New Britain, CT; Springs Learning Center, New Haven, CT; Dominican Retreat and Conference Center, Schenectady, NY.

Ministry in Diocesan Offices; the field of Academic Education at all levels; Religious Education; Adult Education Programs; Congregational Infirmary; Art and Ecological/Environment; Hospitals; Care of the Elderly; Parish Ministry; Pastoral Care; Justice and Peace Ministry; Retreat Centers and Spiritual Programs; Foreign Missions; Counseling and Canon Law Ministry; Campus Ministry; Social Work; Health Care Ministries; Ministry to Minorities; Housing.

Represented in the Archdioceses of Boston, Chicago, Cincinnati, Denver, Detroit, Galveston-Houston, Hartford, Louisville, New Orleans, New York, Philadelphia, San Antonio, Santa Fe and St. Louis and in the Dioceses of Albany, Baton Rouge, Brooklyn, Cleveland, Columbus, Dodge City, Fort Wayne-South Bend, Green Bay, Great Falls-Billings, Jefferson City, Lansing, Memphis, Orlando, Pittsburgh, Providence, Pueblo, Sacramento, Steubenville, Tucson, Wichita and Youngstown. Also in Peru and Nigeria.

[1120] (O.P.)—DOMINICAN SISTERS OF THE ROMAN CONGREGATION

Founded in France in 1621. First United States foundation in 1904.

General Motherhouse: Rome, Italy Sr. Ysabel Barroso, Prioress Gen. Universal total in Congregation: 375.

U.S. Vicarial Office: 61 Lisbon Rd., Sabattus, ME 04280-4209. Tel: 207-782-3535; Fax: 207-375-2694. Sr. Monique Belanger, O.P., Vicarial Prioress.

Total in Community: 11.

Properties owned and/or sponsored: Retreat House; Residences 2.

Ministry in the field of Religious & Academic Education; Adult Education; Indian Reservation; Pastoral Ministry; Health Care; Social Work; Ministry to the poor through the Loaves and Fishes Program.

Represented in the Archdioceses of Chicago and New York and in the Dioceses of Gallup and Portland (In Maine).

[1125] (O.P.)—DOMINICAN SISTERS OF OUR LADY OF THE SPRINGS OF BRIDGEPORT (D)

Founded April 2, 2009 in Bridgeport CT.

Motherhouse: Dominican House, 124 Bugg Hill Rd., Monroe, CT 06468. Tel: 203-880-4455. Sr. Mary Elizabeth Donohue, O.P., Prioress.

Total in Congregation: 19.

Legal Title: Dominican Sisters of Our Lady of the Springs of Bridgeport, Inc.

[1145] (O.P.)—RELIGIOUS MISSIONARIES OF ST. DOMINIC, INC. (P)

General Motherhouse: Via di Val Cannuta 138, Rome, Italy, 00166. Tel: 39-06-66-37-521; Email: dominicas.roma@libero.it. Sr. Elvira Diez, O.P., Prioress Gen.

U.S. Delegation Office: 2237 Waldron Rd., Corpus Christi, TX 78418. Tel: 361-937-5978; Fax: 361-939-0890. Sr. Esperanza H. Seguban, O.P., Delegate of the Gen.

Total in Congregation : 667; Sisters in the U.S: 20.

Represented in the Archdiocese of Los Angeles and in the Diocese of Corpus Christi.

[1150] (E.F.M.S.)—EUCHARISTIC FRANCISCAN MISSIONARY SISTERS (D)

Founded in Mexico in 1943. Mother Maria Gemma de Jesus Aranda, Foundress.

Motherhouse: Our Lady's Convent, 943 S. Soto St., Los Angeles, CA 90023. Tel: 323-264-6556.

1421 Cota Ave., Torrance, CA 90501. Tel: 310-328-6725. Mother Rose Seraphim, E.F.M.S., Supr. Gen.; Sr. Miriam Joseph, E.F.M.S., Gen. Sec.

Total in Community: 25.

Legal Title: Eucharistic Franciscan Missionary Sisters of Los Angeles.

Sisters serve and staff: The field of Education; Missionary Activities; Catechetics; Social Work; Diocesan and Administration offices.

Represented in the Archdiocese of Los Angeles and in the Dioceses of Stockton and Tyler.

[1170] (C.S.S.F.)—FELICIAN SISTERS (P) (Congregation of Sisters of St. Felix of Cantalice, of the III Order of St. Francis)

Founded in Poland in 1855. First foundation in the United States in Polonia, Wisconsin in 1874.

Total in North America, Our Lady of Hope Province: 509.

General Motherhouse: Via del Casaletto 540, Rome, Italy, 00151. Sr. Mary Celestine Giertych, C.S.S.F., Min. Gen.

Presentation of the B.V.M. Convent (1874): 36800 Schoolcraft Rd., Livonia, MI 48150-1172. Tel: 734-591-1730; Fax: 734-591-1710; Web: www.feliciansistersna.org. Sr. Mary Christopher Moore, C.S.S.F., Prov. Min.

Professed Sisters: 71.

Properties owned and/or sponsored: Madonna University; Ladywood High School; Montessori Center of Our Lady, Livonia, MI; St. Mary Mercy Hospital, Livonia, MI; The Felician Sisters Child Care Centers, Inc., Livonia, MI; Maryville Center, Holly, MI; Angela Hospice Home Care and Inpatient Facility, Marian Professional Building, Livonia, MI; Marywood Nursing Care Center; Inpatient Facility, Marian Professional Bldg.; Marybrook Manor Assisted Living.

Ministry in the field of Academic Education at all levels; CCD Programs; Pastoral Ministry Programs; DRE Offices; Hospital; Health Care Nursing Homes; Assisted Living; Hospice Inpatient and Home Care Program; Day Care Centers; Retreat Centers; Senior Clergy Residence; Child Care Centers.

Represented in the Archdiocese of Detroit and in the Dioceses of Fort Wayne-South Bend and Lansing.

Immaculate Heart of Mary Convent (1900): 600 Doat St., Buffalo, NY 14211. Tel: 716-892-4141; Fax: 716-892-4177; Web: www.feliciansistersna.org. Sr. Mary Christopher Moore, C.S.S.F., Prov. Min.; Sr. Mary Kenneth Mondrala, C.S.S.F., Community Archivist.

Professed Sisters: 100.

Properties owned and/or sponsored: Villa Maria College of Buffalo.

Ministry in Education on all levels; Religious Education Programs; Outreach Centers; Parish Ministries; Social Services; Prison Ministries; Campus Ministries; Diocesan Office.

Represented in the Archdioceses of Los Angeles and New York and in the Dioceses of Buffalo, Charleston and Syracuse. Also in Italy.

Mother of Good Counsel Convent (1910): 3800 W. Peterson Ave., Chicago, IL 60659. Tel: 773-463-3020; Web: www.feliciansistersna.org. Sr. Mary Christopher Moore, C.S.S.F., Prov. Min.

Professed Sisters: 98.

Ministry in the field of Academic and Religious Education at all levels; Homes for Aged; Independent Living for the Elderly; Assisted Living for the Elderly; Pastoral Ministry; Social Workers; Family Therapists; Day Care Centers; Hospitals; Infirmary for Sisters. Represented in the Archdioceses of Chicago and Milwaukee and in the Dioceses of Belleville, Green Bay and La Crosse.

Immaculate Conception Convent (1913): 260 S Main St., Lodi, NJ 07644-2196. Tel: 973-473-7447; Fax: 973-473-7126; Web: www.feliciansistersna.org. Sr. Mary Christopher Moore, C.S.S.F., Prov. Min.; Sr. Mary Virginia Tomasiak, C.S.S.F., Community Archivist; Sr. Rose Marie Smiglewski, Community Archivist; Sr. Mary Jolene Jasinski, C.S.S.F., Treas.

Professed Sisters: 87.

Properties sponsored: Immaculate Conception High School; Felician University; Felician University Day Care Center; Felician School for Exceptional Children, Lodi, NJ; St. Ignatius Nursing & Rehab Center.

Sisters serve and staff: Colleges; High Schools; Elementary Schools; Home for Aged; Infirmary for Sisters; Day Care Center; School for Exceptional Children; Religious Education; Parish Ministries.

Represented in the Archdioceses of Newark and Philadelphia and in the Dioceses of Metuchen and Wilmington.

Our Lady of the Sacred Heart Convent (1921): 1500 Woodcrest Ave., Coraopolis, PA 15108. Tel: 412-264-2890; Fax: 412-264-7047; Web: www.feliciansistersna.org. Sr. Mary Christopher Moore, C.S.S.F., Prov. Min.

Professed Sisters: 43.

Legal Holdings and Titles: Felician Sisters of Pennsylvania; Our Lady of the Sacred Heart High School.

Ministry in the field of Academic Education at all levels; Religious Education; CCD Centers; Youth and Pastoral Ministry; Home for Mentally Challenged Children & Adults; Infirmary and Home for Aged.

Represented in the Dioceses of Charleston, Greensburg and Pittsburgh.

Our Lady of the Angels Convent (1932): 1315 Enfield St., Enfield, CT 06082-4929. Tel: 860-745-7791; Fax: 860-741-0819; Web: www.feliciansistersna.org. Sr. Mary Christopher Moore, C.S.S.F., Prov. Min.

Professed Sisters: 45.

Ministry in the field of Religious and Academic Education; Pastoral Ministry; Social Services; Healthcare. Properties owned and sponsored: Enfield Montessori School; Felician Adult Day Center, Enfield, CT; St. Francis Residence, Enfield, CT.

Represented in the Archdiocese of Hartford and in the Dioceses of Manchester, Portland (In Maine), Providence, Springfield in Massachusetts and Worcester.

Assumption of the B.V.M. Convent (1953): 4210 Meadowlark Ln., S.E., Rio Rancho, NM 87124-1021. Web: www.feliciansistersna.org. Sr. Mary Christopher Moore, C.S.S.F., Prov. Min.

Professed Sisters: 19.

Legal Titles and Holdings: Felician Sisters of the Southwest, Inc.; St. Felix Pantry Inc. Sisters serve and staff: High Schools; Elementary Schools; Religious Education Centers & Classes; Health Care; Pastoral Care; Food & Clothing Pantry; Youth Ministry; Adult Education; Social Work.

Represented in the Archdioceses of Los Angeles, San Antonio and Santa Fe and in the Diocese of Laredo.

[1180] (O.S.F.)—FRANCISCAN SISTERS OF ALLEGANY, NEW YORK (P)

Founded in the United States in 1859.

General Motherhouse (1859): St. Elizabeth Motherhouse, 115 E. Main St., Allegany, NY 14706. Tel: 716-373-0200; Fax: 716-372-5774. Sr. Margaret Mary Kimmins, O.S.F., Congregational Min.; Laura Whitford, Mission Society Pres.

Total in Community: 215.

Legal Titles and Holdings: Franciscan Sisters of Allegany, NY, Inc.; Canticle Farm, Inc., Allegany, NY; St. Elizabeth Mission Society, Inc., Allegany, NY; Dr. Lyle F. Renodin Foundation, Inc., Allegany, NY; Franciscan Center of Tampa, FL, Inc., Tampa, FL; The Dwelling Place of NY Inc., NY.

Ministry to Evangelization at all levels of Education; Health Care; Social Services; Pastoral; Spiritual Ministries and Social Advocacy.

Represented in the Archdioceses of Boston, Miami, New York and Philadelphia and in the Dioceses of Buffalo, Camden, Metuchen, Palm Beach, St. Petersburg, Springfield in Massachusetts, Syracuse and Trenton. Also in Bolivia, Brazil and Jamaica.

Jamaica: Immaculate Conception Convent, 152 Constant Spring Rd., Box 1654, Kingston, Jamaica Tel: 876-925-6888. Sr. Teresita DeSouza, O.S.F., Local Min.

Brazil Region: Convento Mae Admiravel, C.P. 322, 75001-970 Anapolis, Goias, Brazil Tel: 011-55-62-33333803. Sr. Marinez Arantes da Silva, O.S.F., Regl. Min.

Publication: Zeal.

[1190] (S.A.)—FRANCISCAN SISTERS OF THE ATONEMENT (P)

Founded in the United States in 1898.

Motherhouse: St. Francis Convent-Graymoor, 41 Old Highland Tpke., Garrison, NY 10524. Tel: 845-424-3625; Fax: 845-424-3298. Web: www.graymoor.org. Sr. Mary Patricia Galvin, S.A., Min. Gen.; Sr. Denise Robillard, S.A., Sec. Gen. Email: secretarygeneral@graymoor.org; Tel: 845-230-8235.

Total in Community: 98.

Properties owned and/or sponsored: St. Francis Convent-Complex, Garrison, NY; Mother Lurana House, Garrison, NY; Washington Retreat House, Washington, D.C.

Represented in the Archdioceses of New York and Washington, D.C. and in the Dioceses of Albany, Burlington, Fresno, Lansing, Monterey, Ogdensburg and Reno. Also in Canada, Brazil, Italy, Japan and the Philippines.

[1210] (O.S.F.)—FRANCISCAN SISTERS OF CHICAGO (P)

Founded in Chicago, Illinois in 1894 by Mother Mary Theresa (Josephine Dudzik) Venerable Servant of God.

General Motherhouse: Our Lady of Victory Convent, 11400 Theresa Dr., Lemont, IL 60439-2728. Tel: 630-243-3600; Fax: 630-243-3601; Email: bbajuscik@chicagofranciscans.com; jduckett@chicagofranciscans.com. Sr. M. Bernadette Bajuscik, O.S.F., Gen. Min.

Total in Community: 23.

Properties owned and/or sponsored: Addolorata Villa,

Wheeling, IL; St. Anthony Village, Inc., Crown Point, IN; St. Joseph Village of Chicago, Inc., Chicago, IL; Marian Village, Homer Glen, IL; Mount Alverna Village, Parma, OH; Franciscan Village, Lemont, IL; St. Francis House of Prayer, Lemont, IL; Our Lady of Victory Convent, Lemont, IL; Franciscan Community Services, Crown Point, IN; Franciscan Senior Estates, Louisville, KY; St. James Senior Estates, Crete, IL; St. Jude House, Crown Point, IN; The Village at Victory Lakes, Lindenhurst, IL; University Place, West Lafayette, IN; St. James Senior Estates II, Crete, IL; St. Joseph Senior Housing; *Franciscan Sisters of Chicago Service Corp. DBA/Franciscan Ministries Sponsored by Franciscan Sisters of Chicago, Lemont, IL.

Represented in the Archdioceses of Chicago and Louisville and in the Dioceses of Cleveland, Gary, Joliet and Lafayette.

[1230] (O.S.F.)—FRANCISCAN SISTERS OF CHRISTIAN CHARITY (P)

Founded in the United States in 1869.

Motherhouse: Holy Family Convent, 2409 S. Alverno Rd., Manitowoc, WI 54220. Tel: 920-682-7728; Fax: 920-682-4195. Sr. Natalie Binversie, Community Dir.; Sr. Caritas Strodthoff, Community Archivist.

Total in Community: 222.

Properties owned or sponsored: Holy Family Convent, Manitowoc, WI; Holy Family Convent of Franciscan Sisters of Christian Charity, Inc., Manitowoc, WI; Holy Family Memorial, Inc., Manitowoc, WI; The Retirement Trust of the Franciscan Sisters of Christian Charity, Manitowoc, WI; St. Paul Home and St. Paul Villa (St. Paul Elder Services, Inc.) Kaukauna, WI; Silver Lake College of the Holy Family, Manitowoc, WI; Franciscan Sisters of Christian Charity Sponsored Ministries Inc., Manitowoc, WI; Holy Family Conservatory of Music, Manitowoc, WI; Chiara Convent, Manitowoc, WI; St. Francis Convent, Manitowoc, WI; St. Francis Memorial Hospital & St. Joseph Retirement Community (Franciscan Care Services, Inc.), West Point, NE; Genesis HealthCare System, Zanesville, OH; Genesis Hospital, Zanesville, OH.

Represented in the Archdiocese of Omaha and St. Louis and in the Dioceses of Columbus, Green Bay, Jackson, Marquette, Phoenix, Steubenville, Lincoln and Tucson.

[1235] (F.H.M.)—FRANCISCAN SISTERS DAUGHTERS OF MERCY (P)

Franciscanas Hijas de la Misericordia

Founded in Pina, Mallorca, Spain in 1856. First U.S. establishment in 1962.

General Motherhouse: Calle El Nectar, 18, Madrid, Spain, 28022. Sr. Alicia Garcia Lazaro, Supr. Gen.

Universal total in Congregation: 262.

U.S. Regional and House of Formation: 1207 Montopolis Dr., Austin, TX 78741. Sr. Rose Moreno, F.H.M., Reg. Delegate.

Professed Sisters: 6.

Ministry in Catechetical work; Pastoral work; Kindergarten.

Represented in the Diocese of Austin.

St. Francis Convent: 612 N. 3rd St., Waco, TX 76701.

[1240] (O.S.F.)—FRANCISCAN SISTERS, DAUGHTERS OF THE SACRED HEARTS OF JESUS AND MARY (P)

Founded in Germany in 1860. First foundation in the United States in 1872.

Generalate: Via di S. Alessio 24, Rome, Italy, 00153. Sr. Magdalena Schmitz, Gen. Dir.

Universal total in Congregation: 550.

St. Clara's Province (1877): Convent of Our Lady of the Angels, Motherhouse and Novitiate, P.O. Box 667, Wheaton, IL 60187. Tel: 630-909-6600. Sr. Melanie Paradis, O.S.F., Prov. Dir.

Total number in Province: 43.

Legal Holdings and Titles: Franciscan Health and Education Corporation, Inc., Wheaton, IL; Wheaton Franciscan Services, Inc., Wheaton, IL; Wheaton Franciscan Sisters Religious Charitable Trust, Wheaton, IL; Wheaton Franciscan Sisters Corporation, Wheaton, IL.

Sisters serve, sponsor and staff: Parish Ministry; Spirituality Center; Corporate Offices; Wellness; Spiritual Direction.

Represented in the Archdiocese of Milwaukee and in the Dioceses of Joliet and Springfield-Cape Girardeau. Also in Italy.

[1250] (F.S.E.)—FRANCISCAN SISTERS OF THE EUCHARIST, INC.

Founded December 2, 1973.

Motherhouse: 405 Allen Ave., Meriden, CT 06451. Tel: 203-237-0841. Team Members: Mother Miriam Seiferman, Mother Gen.; Mother Barbara Johnson, F.S.E., Vicar Gen.; Mother Suzanne Gross, F.S.E.; Mother Mary Richards, F.S.E.; Mother Raffaella Petrini, F.S.E.; Mother Clare Hunter, F.S.E. Total in Community: 81.

Legal Title: Franciscan Sisters of the Eucharist, Inc. Schools and programs operated under: Franciscan Life Center Network, Incorporated and Franciscan Family Care Center, Incorporated.

Represented in the Archdioceses of Hartford and Portland in Oregon and in the Dioceses of Arlington, Boise, Burlington, Grand Rapids and Palm Beach. Also in Canada, Israel, Italy and Latin Patriarchate of Jerusalem.

Generalate: Meriden, CT 06451. Tel: 203-237-0841.

[1260] (F.H.M.)—FRANCISCAN HANDMAIDS OF THE MOST PURE HEART OF MARY (D)

Founded in the United States in 1916.

General Motherhouse: 15 W. 124th St., New York, NY 10027. Tel: 212-289-5655. Email: info@franciscanhandmaids.com; Web: www.Franciscanhandmaids.com.

Discernment House: 63 Bayside Ln., Staten Island, NY 10309. Tel: 718-227-5575. Sr. Gertrude Lilly, F.H.M., Congregation Min.; Sr. Loretta Theresa, Dir. Formation; Sr. Jacqueline, Community Archivist.

Vocation/Formation House: 34 Convent Ave., Yonkers, NY 10703. Tel: 914-613-8904. Email: vocation@franciscanhandmaids.com; pfsocialjustice@yahoo.com.

Social Justice/Human Dignity Minstry: Most Pure Heart of Mary Convent, 63 Bayside Ln., Staten Island, NY 10309. Tel: 718-227-5575. Email: socialjustice@franciscanhandmaids.com.

Altar Bread Distribution: 63 Bayside Ln., Staten Island, NY 10309. Tel: 347-852-2306.

Franciscan Handmaids/St. Edward Food Pantry, 6581 Hylan Blvd., Staten Island, NY 10309. Tel: 718-984-1625. Email: st.edwardfoodpantry@gmail.com.

St. Benedict Day Nursery, 21 West 124 St., New York, NY 10027. Tel: 212-423-5715; Fax: 212-423-5917. Email: St.benedictdaynursery@verizon.net.

Total in Community: 17.

Properties owned and/or sponsored: St. Benedict Day Nursery; St. Edward Food Pantry; Franciscan Handmaids of Mary Novitiate; Franciscan Handmaids of Mary Motherhouse.

Ministry in the field of Education, Social Work, Social Svcs., Social Justice and Pastoral Care.

Represented in the Archdiocese of New York. Also in Nigeria.

[1270] (F.H.I.C.)—FRANCISCAN HOSPITALLER SISTERS OF THE IMMACULATE CONCEPTION (P)

Founded in Portugal in 1871.

General Motherhouse: Linda-a-Pastora, Portugal Sr. Maria da Conceição Galvão Ribeiro, Supr. Gen.

U.S. Foundation (1960): St. Joseph Novitiate, 300 S. 17th St., San Jose, CA 95112-2245. Tel: 408-998-2896; Fax: 408-998-3407. Sr. Mary Augustine, F.H.I.C., Regl. Supr.

Total in Community: 16.

Sisters serve and staff: Parishes; Residential care and Skilled Nursing; Social Work.

Represented in the Dioceses of Fresno and San Jose.

[1300] (O.S.F.)—FRANCISCAN SISTERS OF THE IMMACULATE CONCEPTION AND ST. JOSEPH FOR THE DYING (D)

Founded in the United States in December, 1919 at San Carlos Parish, Monterey, California.

General Motherhouse: Ave Maria Convent, 1249 Josselyn Canyon Rd, Monterey, CA 93940. Tel: 831-373-1216.

Legal Holding: Ave Maria Convalescent Hospital, Monterey, CA.

Represented in the Diocese of Monterey.

[1310] (O.S.F.)—FRANCISCAN SISTERS OF LITTLE FALLS, MINNESOTA (P)

Founded in the United States in 1891.

General Motherhouse: St. Francis Convent, Little Falls, MN 56345. Tel: 320-632-2981. Email: info@fslf.org. Sr. Carol Schmit, O.S.F., Community Min./Pres.

Total in Community: 110.

Ministry in Home Health Care; Pastoral and Retreat Ministries; Outreach to Refugees and Migrants; Ecology; Education; Social Services; Counseling; Spiritual Direction; Consulting; Hispanic Ministry; Social Justice and Nonviolent Activities; Education, Lay Leadership Training.

Properties owned or sponsored: St. Francis Music Center; Franciscan Life Center; Franciscan Community Volunteers (FCV).

Represented in the Archdioceses of Milwaukee, St. Paul-Minneapolis, and San Francisco and in the Dioceses of Brownsville, Jackson, Oakland and St. Cloud. Also in Mexico.

[1320] (F.M.S.A.)—FRANCISCAN MISSIONARY SISTERS FOR AFRICA (P)

Generalate: Franciscan Missionary Sisters for Africa, 34a Gilford Rd., Sandymount, Dublin 4, DO4 FN79 Ireland. Tel: 011-353-1-2838376; Fax: 011-353-1-2602049.

American Headquarters: 172 Foster St., Brighton, MA 02135. Tel: 617-254-4343. Sr. Mary Fisher, FMSA Country Rep.

Total in Community: 5.

Represented in the Archdiocese of Boston.

[1330] (S.F.M.A.)—FRANCISCAN MISSIONARY SISTERS OF ASSISI (P)

General Motherhouse: Via San Francesco, 13, Assisi, Italy, 06081. Sr. Juliana Malama, Mother Gen.

U.S. Vice Province (1961): St. Francis Convent/Vice Provincial House and Formation House, 1039 Northampton St., Holyoke, MA 01040. Tel: 413-532-8156; Fax: 413-534-7741. Sr. Regina Mulenga, S.F.M.A., Vice Prov. Supr.

Total in Community: 14.

Represented in the Archdiocese of New York and in the Diocese of Springfield in Massachusetts.

[1350] (O.S.F.)—FRANCISCAN SISTERS OF THE IMMACULATE CONCEPTION (P)

Founded in Mexico in 1874. First foundation in the United States in 1926.

Provincial House: 13367 Borden Ave., Unit A, Sylmar, CA 91342-2804. Tel: 818-364-5557; Tel: 818-364-5558; Fax: 818-362-7536; Email: provstclare@outlook.com. Sr. Catalina Avila, O.S.F., Prov. Supr.; Sr. Yolanda Yanez, O.S.F., Community Archivist.

Total in Community: 91.

Legal Holdings and Titles: Franciscan Missionary Sisters of the Immaculate Conception, Inc.; Poverello of Assisi Retreat House, San Fernando, CA; St. Francis Home, Santa Ana, CA; Mother Gertrude Balcazar Home, San Fernando, CA; Provincialate, Sylmar, CA; St. Clare Convent, Sylmar, CA; Proverello of Assisi Preschool, Sylmar, CA; Novitiate, Sheerwood Forest, CA.

Ministry in the field of Education and Religious Education to Children and Adults; Health Care in Hospitals and Residential Care Facilities for Elderly.

Represented in the Archdiocese of Los Angeles and in the Dioceses of Gallup and Orange in California. Also in Mexico.

House of Formation: 11306 Laurel Canyon Blvd., San Fernando, CA 91340.

Novitiate: 8619 Louise Ave., Sherwood Forest, CA 91325-3417. Tel: 818-709-7523.

[1360] (M.F.I.C.)—MISSIONARY FRANCISCAN SISTERS OF THE IMMACULATE CONCEPTION (P)

Founded in the United States in 1873 in Belle Prairie, Minnesota.

General Motherhouse: Rome, Italy Sr. Pauline Robinson, M.F.I.C., Gen. Min.

Provincialate: Immaculate Conception Province, 790 Centre St., Newton, MA 02458-2530. Tel: 617-527-1004; Fax: 617-527-2528. Sr. Donna Driscoll, M.F.I.C., Prov.

Total number in Province: 100.

Represented in the Archdioceses of Boston, Newark and New York and in the Dioceses of Brooklyn, Providence, Savannah and Syracuse. Also in Bolivia and Peru.

[1365] (F.M.I.J.)—FRANCISCAN MISSIONARY SISTERS OF THE INFANT JESUS (P)

Founded in Aquila, Italy in 1879 by Sr. Maria Giuseppa Micarelli. First foundation in the United States in 1961.

Generalate: Piazza Nicoloso da Recco 13, Rome, Italy,

00154. Tel: 6-575-8358. Mother Teresa Ferrante, F.M.I.J., Supr. Gen.

U.S. Delegation and Novitiate: 1215 Kresson Rd., Cherry Hill, NJ 08003. Tel: 856-428-8834; Fax: 856-428-5599; Email: fmijusdel@yahoo.com. Sr. Gloria Louise Levari, F.M.I.J., Delegate Supr.

Professed Sisters: 13.

Ministries of Evangelization; Education; Social Pastoral Services; Retreat Ministry.

Represented in the Dioceses of Camden and Trenton.

[1370] (F.M.M.)—THE FRANCISCAN MISSIONARIES OF MARY (P)

Founded in India in 1877. First foundation in the United States in 1903.

General Motherhouse: 12 via Giusti, Rome, Italy Sr. Francoise Massy, F.M.M., Supr. Gen.

Franciscan Missionaries of Mary-U.S. Province (1920): 3305 Wallace Ave., Bronx, NY 10467-6599. Tel: 718-547-4693; Fax: 718-325-5102; Email: nmfmm@aol.com; Web: www.fmmusa.org. Sr. Noreen Murray, F.M.M., Prov.

Total in Province: 77.

Ministry in Educational Projects among Minority Group of Immigrants; Cardiac and General Hospital; General Pediatric Hospital with Rehabilitation Specialty; Chaplaincy; Retreat Work; Catechetics; Mission Animation & Formation; Home Visiting & Community Development.

Represented in the Archdioceses of Boston, Chicago and New York and in the Dioceses of El Paso, Las Cruces, Providence and Rockville Centre.

[1380] (O.S.F.)—FRANCISCAN MISSIONARIES OF OUR LADY (P)

Founded in Calais, France in 1854. First U.S. foundation in Monroe, LA, 1911.

Generalate: Paris, France

Provincial and Novitiate House: Maryville Convent, 4200 Essen Ln., Baton Rouge, LA 70809. Tel: 225-922-7443; Fax: 225-922-7497; Email: barbara.arceneaux@fmolhs.org.

Total in Community: 13.

Properties owned and sponsored: Our Lady of the Lake Regional Medical Center, Baton Rouge, LA; Ollie Steele Burden Manor, Inc., Baton Rouge, LA; Our Lady of Lourdes Regional Medical Center, Lafayette, LA; St. Francis Medical Center, Monroe, LA; FMOL Health System, Inc., Baton Rouge, LA; Haiti Mission, Inc., Baton Rouge, LA; St. Elizabeth Hospital, Gonzales, LA., Franciscan Health & Wellness; Our Lady of the Angels Hospital, Bogalusa, LA.

Represented in the Dioceses of Baton Rouge, Lafayette (LA) and Shreveport.

[1390] (O.S.F.)—FRANCISCAN MISSIONARY SISTERS OF OUR LADY OF SORROWS (D)

Founded in Hunan China in 1939. First United States foundation in 1950.

Community Headquarters: Our Lady of Peace Retreat House, 3600 S.W. 170th Ave., Beaverton, OR 97003-4467. Tel: 503-649-7127; Fax: 503-259-9507. Sr. Anne Marie Warren, O.S.F., Supr. Gen.

Total in Community: 41.

Legal Titles and Holdings: Our Lady of Peace Retreat, Beaverton, OR; St. Clare Retreat House, Soquel, CA.

Ministry in religious and academic education; retreat houses, group homes and foreign missions.

Represented in the Archdiocese of Portland in Oregon and in the Diocese of Monterey.

[1400] (F.M.S.C.)—FRANCISCAN MISSIONARY SISTERS OF THE SACRED HEART (P)

Founded in Italy in 1861. First foundation in the U.S. in New York City (1865).

General Motherhouse: Rome, Italy Sr. Paola Dotto, F.M.S.C., Supr. Gen.

St. Francis Province (1869): Mt. St. Francis, 250 South St., Peekskill, NY 10566. Tel: 914-737-5409; Fax: 914-736-9614. Vocations email: sajfmsc@mail.com. Sr. Laura Morgan, F.M.S.C., Prov. Supr.

Universal total in Congregation: 660; Total in United States Province: 25.

Legal Title: Missionary Sisters of the Third Order of St. Francis.

Ministry in Religious and Academic Education; Health Care for Retired Sisters; Pastoral Ministry; Hospital Ministry.

Represented in the Archdioceses of Newark and New York and in Diocese of Paterson, NJ.

[1410] (F.M.S.J.)—MILL HILL SISTERS (P)

Franciscan Missionaries of St. Joseph

Founded in 1883. First United States foundation in 1952.

Generalate: St. Joseph's Convent, 150 Greenleach Ln., Worsley, Manchester, England, M28 2TS. Sr. Maureen Murphy, F.M.S.J., Community Leader.

American Headquarters: Franciscan House, 703 Derzee Ct., Delmar, NY 12054. Tel: 518-512-4362. Sr. Judith Dever, F.M.S.J., Admin.

Total in Community: 2.

Legal Title: Mill Hill Sisters - New York Charitable Trust.

Represented in the Diocese of Albany.

[1415] (F.S.M.)—FRANCISCAN SISTERS OF MARY (P)

Founded in the United States in 1872.

Administrative Offices & Novitiate: Franciscan Sisters of Mary, 3221 McKelvey Rd., Ste. 107, Bridgeton, MO 63044-2551. Tel: 314-768-1824; Fax: 314-768-1880. Email: info@fsmonline.org. Sr. Susan Scholl, F.S.M., Pres.

Total in Community: 62.

[1425] (F.S.P.)—FRANCISCAN SISTERS OF PEACE (D)

Sisters of St. Francis of Peace: Congregation Center, 20 Ridge St., Haverstraw, NY 10927-1115. Tel: 845-942-2527; Fax: 845-429-8141. Sr. Helen Wacker, F.S.P., Congregation Min.

Total in Community: 46.

Legal Titles and Holdings: Cortlandt Manor, NY; Congregation Center, Haverstraw, NY.

Ministry in Youth; Ministry in Administration & Administrative Services; Education; Catechetical; Social Work; Evangelization; Social Services.

Represented in the Archdioceses of Newark, New York and San Francisco and in the Dioceses of Metuchen, Paterson and Tucson.

[1430] (O.S.F.)—FRANCISCAN SISTERS OF OUR LADY OF PERPETUAL HELP (P)

Founded in the United States in 1901.

Motherhouse and Novitiate: Franciscan Sisters of Our Lady of Perpetual Help, 335 S. Kirkwood Rd., St. Louis, MO 63122. Tel: 314-965-3700; Fax: 314-965-3710. Email: info@fsolph.org. Sr. Renita Brummer, O.S.F., Supr. Gen.

Total in Community: 80.

Legal Holdings and Titles: Tau Center, Kirkwood, MO; Perpetual Help Retirement Corporation, St. Louis, MO. Ministry in Education; Faith Formation; Parish Ministries; Retreat and Program Directors; Not for Profit Administration; Hospital Ministry.

Represented in the Archdioceses of Chicago, Cincinnati, Omaha, St. Louis, and Washington, DC and in the Dioceses of Austin, Belleville, Fort Wayne, Kansas City, Las Cruces, Pueblo, Rockford, St. Petersburg, Shreveport, Springfield (IL) and Toledo.

[1440] (S.F.P.)—FRANCISCAN SISTERS OF THE POOR (P)

Founded in Aachen, Germany in 1845. First foundation in the United States in 1858.

Congregational Office: 708 3rd Ave., Ste. 1920, New York, NY 10017. Tel: 718-643-1945; Fax: 212-808-0096. Sr. Licia Mazzia, S.F.P., Congregational Min.

Total in Community: 116.

U.S. Area: 60 Compton Rd., Cincinnati, OH 45215. Tel: 513-761-9040; Fax: 513-761-6703; Email: office@franciscansistersofthepoor.org; Web: www.franciscansistersofthepoor.org; Sr. Marilyn Trowbridge, S.F.P., Congregational Councilor & Contact Person; Sr. Ann Cecile Albers, S.F.P., Community Min.

Sisters in Archdiocese: 37.

Congregation sponsors: Franciscan Sisters of the Poor Foundation, Inc., New York, NY; Franciscan Ministries, Inc., Cincinnati, OH.

Represented in the Archdioceses of Cincinnati and New York and in the Diocese of Brooklyn. Also in Brazil, Italy, Philippines and Senegal.

[1450] (O.S.F.)—FRANCISCAN SISTERS OF THE SACRED HEART (P)

Congregation of the Franciscan Sisters of the Sacred Heart. Founded in Germany 1866. Established in the United States in 1876.

Motherhouse, Novitiate, Postulancy & Portiuncula Center for Prayer: St. Francis Woods, 9201 W. St. Francis Rd., Frankfort, IL 60423-8330. Tel: 815-469-4895; Fax: 815-464-3809. Sr. Joyce Shanabarger, O.S.F., Gen. Supr.

Total in Community: 61.

Legal Title: An Association of Franciscan Sisters of the Sacred Heart; Legal Titles for Health Care entities; St. Anne's Maternity Home; Franciscan Foundation.

Sisters sponsor: St. Anne's Maternity Home, Los Angeles, CA; Franciscan Foundation, Frankfort, IL.

Sisters serve and staff: Academic Institutions; Religious Education Centers; Neighborhood Health Care Centers; Foreign Mission Centers; Diocesan Offices; Retreat Centers; Home Health Agencies, Hospitals, Nursing and Retirement Homes; Home for Unwed Mothers; Parish & Youth Ministry; Liturgical Ministry; Social Work.

Represented in the Archdioceses of Chicago and Los Angeles and in the Dioceses of Fort Wayne-South Bend, Joliet, Rockford and Wheeling-Charleston. Also in Brazil.

[1460] (F.S.S.E.)—FRANCISCAN SISTERS OF ST. ELIZABETH (P)

(Suore Franciscane Elisabettine)

First founded in Naples, Italy, 1865. Founded in the United States in Newark, New Jersey in 1919.

General Motherhouse: Via Marsico Nuovo 35, Rome, Italy Mother Clara Capaso, Supr. Gen.

Delegate House: 499 Park Rd., Parsippany, NJ 07054. Tel: 973-539-3797. Mother Lilly Perapadan, Delegate Gen.

Total number in the U.S: 52; Total in Community: 300.

Ministry in Day Nurseries; Mission Houses; Elementary Schools and Montessori Schools.

Sister Serve Christ in the person of the poor in Schools & Day Nursery Schools; Catechetical Instruction; Hospitals; Homes for the Poor, Aged and Disabled.

Represented in the Archdiocese of Newark and in the Dioceses of Paterson and St. Petersburg. Also in India, Indonesia, Italy, Panama, Philippines and Africa.

[1470] (F.S.S.J.)—FRANCISCAN SISTERS OF ST. JOSEPH OF HAMBURG, NY (P)

Founded in the United States in 1897.

Congretional office: Franciscan Sisters of St. Joseph, Immaculate Conception Convent, 5229 S. Park Ave., Hamburg, NY 14075. Tel: 716-649-1205; Fax: 716-202-4940. Sr. Marcia Ann Fiutko, F.S.S.J., Gen. Min.

Total in Community: 50.

Properties owned and/or sponsored: Immaculata Academy, Hamburg, NY.

Ministry in Education; Health Care; Parish Ministries; Social Services.

Represented in the Archdioceses of Baltimore and in the Dioceses of Allentown, Buffalo and Springfield in Massachusetts.

[1485] (O.S.F.)—FRANCISCAN SISTERS OF ST. PAUL, MN (P)

Franciscan Sisters of the Blessed Virgin Mary of the Holy Angels (Beatae Mariae Virginis Angelorum)

Founded in Germany in 1863. First foundation in the United States in St. Paul in 1923.

General Motherhouse (1863): St. Marienhaus, Waldbreitbach, bei Neuwied, Rhine, Germany Sr. Basina Kloos, O.S.F., Supr. Gen.

Universal total in Congregation: 333.

U.S. Foundation: 225 Frank St. #144, St. Paul, MN 55106. Tel: 654-495-1922. Sr. Mary Lucy Scheffler, O.S.F.

Total in Community: 5.

Represented in the Archdiocese of St. Paul-Minneapolis.

[1500] (F.M.I.)—FRANCISCAN SISTERS OF MARY IMMACULATE OF THE THIRD ORDER OF ST. FRANCIS OF ASSISI (P)

Founded in Switzerland in the 16th Century. First founded in the United States on Aug. 15, 1932 at Amarillo, Texas.

General House: Carrera 81 C No. 24B-20, Barrio Modelia, Bogota, Colombia Sr. Nilka Judith Cerezo Rodríguez, F.M.I., Supr. Gen.

Universal total in Congregation: 508.

St. Francis Convent and Novitiate (1964): St. Francis Convent (1932), 4301 N.E. 18th Ave., Amarillo, TX 79107-7220. Tel: 806-383-5769; Fax: 806-383-6545. Sr. Valentine A. Curry, F.M.I., Local Vicar

Total in Community: 20.

Represented in the Archdiocese of Los Angeles and in the Dioceses of Amarillo, Kansas City-St. Joseph and Venice. Also in Central America.

[1505] (O.S.F.)—ST. FRANCIS MISSION COMMUNITY (P)

Established in 1981 in the United States of America in Amarillo, Texas, as an autonomous province of the Franciscan Sisters of Mary Immaculate.

General Motherhouse: Our Lady of the Angels Convent, 8202 CR 7700, Wolfforth, TX 79382. Tel: 806-863-4904. Sr. Mary Jane Alaniz, O.S.F., Prov. Min.

Professed Sisters: 18.

Ministry in the field of Religious and Academic Education at all levels; Parish Work; Pastoral Care in Hospitals.

Properties owned: St. Francis Convent, Lubbock, TX; 43 acres of real estate.

Represented in the Dioceses of Lubbock and San Angelo.

[1520] (S.S.F.C.R.-O.S.F.)—SCHOOL SISTERS OF ST. FRANCIS OF CHRIST THE KING (D)

Founded in Maribor, Slovenia in 1869 by Sr. Margareta Pucher. First house in the United States at Kansas City, Kansas, in 1909. U.S. Province established in 1922.

Generalate: Grottaferrata, Italy Sr. M. Klara Šimunović, Supr. Gen.

Universal total in Congregation: 955.

North American Provincial House: 13900 Main St., Lemont, IL 60439. Tel: 630-257-7495. Email: lemont.province@ssfcr.org. Sr. Patricia Kolenda, SSFCR, Prov. Supr. U.S.A.

Total in Community: 32.

Ministry in Education, Care for Seniors, Parish Ministry; Retreat Ministry.

Properties owned and sponsored: Mount Assisi Convent, Lemont, IL; Mount Assisi [Academy building] Center; Alvernia Manor, Lemont, IL; Our Lady of Angels House of Prayer, Lemont, IL.

Represented in the Archdiocese of Chicago and in the Diocese of Joliet.

[1530] (O.S.F.)—SISTERS OF ST. FRANCIS OF THE CONGREGATION OF OUR LADY OF LOURDES, SYLVANIA, OHIO (P)

Founded in the United States in 1916 at Sylvania, Ohio. Foundation from Rochester, Minnesota.

General Motherhouse: Convent, 6832 Convent Blvd., Sylvania, OH 43560-2897. Tel: 419-824-3618; Fax: 419-824-3700; Email: lstout@sistersosf.org; Web: www.sistersosf.org. Sr. Mary Jon Wagner, O.S.F., Congregational Min.

Total number in the Congregation: 134.

Ministry in the field of Religious and Academic Education at all levels; Healthcare; Communications; Media Producing; Counseling; Parish Ministries; Retreat Center; Social Services; Administration.

Properties sponsored and owned: Lourdes University, Sylvania, OH.

Sponsored Ministries: Sisters of St. Francis Foundation, Sylvania, OH; Sylvania Franciscan Ministries, Sylvania, OH, including: Rosary Care Center, Sylvania, OH; Franciscan Properties, Sylvania, OH; Franciscan Shelters DBA Bethany House, Toledo, OH; Sophia Center, Sylvania, OH.

Represented in the Archdioceses of Cincinnati, Detroit and St. Paul-Minneapolis and in the Dioceses of Austin, Biloxi, Cleveland, Fort Wayne-South Bend, Nashville, St. Cloud, and Toledo.

[1540] (O.S.F.)—SISTERS OF SAINT FRANCIS, CLINTON, IOWA (P)

Founded in the United States in 1866.

General Motherhouse: Administrative Center, 84313th Ave. N., Clinton, IA 52732-5115. Tel: 563-242-7611; Fax: 563-243-0007; Email: office@clintonfranciscans.com. Sr. Janice Cebula, O.S.F., Pres.

Ministry in the field of Education; Health Care; Pastoral Ministry; Religious Education and Spiritual Direction; Ministry to the Poor; Disabled; Social Justice & Peace.

Properties and Legal Holdings: Sisters of St. Francis, Clinton, IA; Iowa Charitable Trust; The Canticle, Clinton, IA.

Represented in the Archdioceses of Chicago and Dubuque and in the Dioceses of Davenport, Joliet, Portland, Phoenix, Rockford, San Bernardino, San Diego and Sioux City.

[1550] (O.S.F.)—SISTERS OF ST. FRANCIS OF THE HOLY CROSS (P)

Founded in Wisconsin in 1881.

Motherhouse: St. Francis Convent, 3110 Nicolet Dr., Green Bay, WI 54311-7212. Tel: 920-468-1828; Fax: 920-468-1207. Sr. Ann Rehrauer, O.S.F., Pres.

Total in Community: 53.

Legal Title: Sisters of St. Francis of the Holy Cross, Inc.

Ministries in the following areas: Education; Pastoral Ministry and Religious Education; Ministry to the Elderly; Health Care; Hospital Chaplaincy; Retreat Work.

Represented in the Diocese of Green Bay.

[1560] (O.S.F.)—SISTERS OF ST. FRANCIS OF THE HOLY EUCHARIST (D)

Founded in Grimmenstein, Switzerland in 1378. First foundation in the United States in 1892.

Motherhouse, Novitiate and Prayer Center: St. Francis Convent, 2100 N. Noland Rd., Independence, MO 64050. Tel: 816-252-1673; Fax: 816-252-5574. Sr. M. Lucy Lang, O.S.F., Sister Servant Sr. M. Connie Boulch, O.S.F., Vicar.

Total in Community: 13.

Legal Titles: Franciscan Prayer Center, Independence, MO; Sisters of St. Francis of the Holy Eucharist Foundation, Independence, MO.

Ministry in the following areas: Education at all levels; Retreat; Evangelization; Pastoral; Foreign Mission Relief.

Represented in the Diocese of Kansas City-St. Joseph.

[1570] (O.S.F.)—SISTERS OF ST. FRANCIS OF THE HOLY FAMILY (P)

Founded in Germany in 1864. First foundation in the United States in 1875.

Motherhouse and Novitiate: Mount St. Francis, 3390 Windsor Ave., Dubuque, IA 52001-1311. Tel: 563-583-9786; Fax: 563-583-3250. Sr. Cathy Katoski, O.S.F., Pres.; Sr. Maxine Lavell, O.S.F., Community Archivist.

Total in Community: 234.

Ministry in the following areas: Academic and Religious Education at all levels; Spirituality and Parish Ministry; Health-Pastoral Care; Diocesan Offices; Social Service-Social Justice and Peace; Food Service Dietary; Communication Centers; Clerical Work Business; Administration; Campus Ministry; Music Studios; International Missions.

Properties owned and sponsored: Shalom Spirituality Center, Dubuque, IA; Sisters of St. Francis of the Holy Family Charitable Trust, Dubuque, IA.

Represented in the Archdioceses of Chicago, Detroit, Dubuque, St. Paul-Minneapolis and San Antonio and in the Dioceses of Charleston, Davenport, Des Moines, El Paso, Fort Wayne-South Bend, Jackson, Joliet, Madison, Manchester, Phoenix, Reno, Santa Rosa, Sioux City, Superior, Tulsa, Tyler and Winona-Rochester. Also in Canada and Central America.

[1580] (O.S.F.)—SISTERS OF ST. FRANCIS OF THE IMMACULATE CONCEPTION (D)

Founded in the United States in 1891.

Motherhouse: Immaculate Conception Convent, 2408 W. Heading Ave., West Peoria, IL 61604-5096. Tel: 309-674-6168. Sr. Kathleen Ann Mourisse, Pres.; Sr. Mary Louise Hynd, Archivist.

Total in Community: 29.

Properties owned: Immaculate Conception Convent, Peoria, IL; St. Joseph's Home of Springfield in Illinois.

Represented in the Dioceses of Peoria and Springfield in Illinois.

[1590] (O.S.F.)—FRANCISCAN SISTERS OF DILLIGEN, HANKINSON, NORTH DAKOTA (P)

Founded in 1241 in Bavaria. First founded in the United States in 1913 at Collegeville, Minnesota.

General Motherhouse: Dillingen, Germany Sr. Roswitha Heinrich, Supr. Gen.

Province of Hankinson (1928): Franciscan Sisters of Dilligen Provincial House, 102 6th St., S.E., P.O. Box 447, Hankinson, ND 58041-0447. Tel: 701-242-7195. Email: dillingenfranciscansusa@rrt.net; Vocation Director Email: ndfranciscan@yahoo.com. Sr. Donna M. Welder, O.S.F., Prov. Supr.

Professed Sisters: 16.

Legal Holdings or Titles: St. Gerard's Community of Care, Hankinson, ND; St. Anne's Guest Home, Grand Forks, ND.

Ministry in the field of Religious and Academic Education; Health Care in long term care facilities.

Represented in the Diocese of Fargo.

[1600] (F.S.G.M.)—SISTERS OF ST. FRANCIS OF THE MARTYR ST. GEORGE (P)

Founded in Thuine, Germany. First United States foundation in 1923.

General Motherhouse: Thuine, Germany Mother Maria Cordis Reiker, F.S.G.M., Supr. Gen.

Provincial Motherhouse: St. Francis Convent and Novitiate, 1 Franciscan Way, P.O. Box 9020, Alton, IL 62002-9020. Tel: 618-463-2750; Tel: 618-463-2755. Secretary Email: secretariat@altonfranciscans.org. Sr. Mary Maximilia Um, F.S.G.M., Prov. Worldwide.

Total: 1100; Total in American Province: 143.

Properties owned and sponsored: St. Francis Day Care Center, Alton, IL; Mother of Good Counsel Home, St. Louis, MO.

Sisters serve and staff: Hospitals; Skilled Nursing Facility; Foreign Missions; Day Care Center; Retirement Homes for the Aged; Grade & High Schools; University; Retirement Homes for Priests; Archdiocesan & Diocesan Offices.

Represented in the Archdioceses of Kansas City in Kansas and St. Louis and in the Dioceses of La Crosse, Lincoln, Peoria, Springfield in Illinois, Steubenville and Tulsa. Also in Brazil and Cuba.

[1630] (O.S.F.)—SISTERS OF ST. FRANCIS OF PENANCE AND CHRISTIAN CHARITY (P)

Founded in Holland in 1835. First foundation in the United States in 1874.

General Motherhouse: Rome, Italy Sr. Deborah Lockwood, O.S.F., Gen. Min.

Universal total in Congregation: 1256.

Holy Name Province (1928): Sisters of St. Francis, 4421 Lower River Rd., Stella Niagara, NY 14144. Tel: 716-754-4311; Fax: 716-754-7657. Sr. Edith Wyss, O.S.F., Prov. Min.

Total in Community: 104.

Legal Holdings: Stella Niagara Education Park, Stella Niagara, NY; Buffalo Academy of the Sacred Heart, Buffalo, NY; Francis Center, Niagara Falls, NY; Sisters of St. Francis of Holy Name Province, Inc., Stella Niagara, NY; Center of Renewal, Stella Niagara, NY.

Ministry in the field of Academic Education at all levels; Foreign Mission Work; Health and Hospital Care; Social Work; Pastoral Ministry.

Represented in the Archdioceses of Miami and Omaha and in the Dioceses of Buffalo, Columbus, Palm Beach, Trenton, and Wheeling-Charleston.

Sacred Heart Province (1939): 5314 Columbine Rd, Denver, CO 80221. Tel: 303-458-6270; Fax: 303-477-4105; Web: www.franciscanway.org. Sr. Rita Cammack, O.S.F., Prov. Min.

Total in Community: 26.

Legal Title: Sisters of St. Francis, Denver, Colorado

Legal Holdings or Titles: Casa Chiara, Denver, CO; St. Francis Convent and Marian Residence for aged, infirm sisters, Alliance, NE.

Ministry in the following areas: Prayer; Spirituality; Health, human, pastoral services; Education; Advocacy for peace, justice, social concerns; General, administrative support services.

St. Francis Province (1939): 1330 Brewster Ave., P.O. Box 1028, Redwood City, CA 94062-1312. Tel: 650-369-1725; Fax: 650-369-0845. Email: provincialcouncil-SFP@franciscanway.org. Sr. Mary Litell, O.S.F., Prov. Min.

Total in Community: 50.

Legal Title: Sisters of St. Francis - Mount Alverno.

Ministry in the following areas: Diocesan Offices; Parish Ministry; Pastoral Ministry; Service Agencies; Hospitals; CCD Centers; ESL; Advocacy. Represented in the Archdioceses of Los Angeles and San Francisco and in the Dioceses of Oakland and Sacramento.

[1640] (O.S.F.)—SISTERS OF ST. FRANCIS OF PERPETUAL ADORATION (P)

Founded in Germany in 1863. First foundation in the United States in 1875.

Generalate: Olpe, Westfalen, Germany Sr. Magdalena Krol, Supr. Gen. Universal total in Congregation: 369.

Province of the Immaculate Heart of Mary (1875): Provincial House and Novitiate, St. Francis Convent, P.O. Box 766, Mishawaka, IN 46546-0766. Tel: 574-259-5427. Sr. M. Angela Mellady, O.S.F., Prov.

Total in Community: 111.

Ministry in the field of Academic Education at all levels; Health Care in Hospitals; Ecclesial Ministry at parish and diocesan level.

Properties owned: Sisters of St. Francis of Perpetual Adoration, Inc.; St. Francis Convent, Mishawaka, IN; University of Saint Francis, Inc., Fort Wayne, IN; Franciscan Alliance, Inc., Franciscan Alliance Corporate Office, Mishawaka, IN, owns the following:

Franciscan Health Crown Point; Franciscan Health Michigan City; Franciscan Health Crawfordsville; Franciscan Health Lafayette East; Franciscan Health Lafayette Central; Franciscan Health Rensselaer; Franciscan Health Indianapolis; Franciscan Health Mooresville; Franciscan Health Carmel; Franciscan Health Chicago Heights; Franciscan Health Olympia Fields; Franciscan Health Hammond; Franciscan Health Dyer; Franciscan Healthcare Munster; Franciscan Alliance Information Services, Beech Grove, IN.

Represented in the Archdioceses of Chicago and Indianapolis and in the Dioceses of Fort Wayne-South Bend, Gary and Lafayette in Indiana.

Province of St. Joseph (March 19, 1932): Provincial House and Formation House-Mt. St. Francis, 7665 Assisi Heights, Colorado Springs, CO 80919. Tel: 719-598-5486. Sr. Nadine Heimann, O.S.F., Prov.

Professed Sisters: 40.

Ministry in Education; Hospitals; Homes for the Aged; Parish/Pastoral Ministry; Peace & Justice; Social Ministries; Retreat Centers.

Represented in the Archdiocese of Santa Fe and in the Dioceses of Colorado Springs and Pueblo.

[1650] (O.S.F.)—THE SISTERS OF ST. FRANCIS OF PHILADELPHIA (P)

Founded in the United States in 1855.

Congregational Motherhouse: Our Lady of Angels Convent, 609 S. Convent Rd., Aston, PA 19014. Tel: 610-459-4125. Email: archives@osfphila.org. Sr. Mary Kathryn Dougherty, O.S.F., Congregational Min.; Sr. Mary Katherine Farrell, O.S.F., Asst. Congregational Min.; Sr. Marie Colette Gerry, O.S.F., Congregational Sec.; Sr. Helen Jacobson, O.S.F., Archivist.

Total in Community: 416.

Ministry in Health Care; Eldercare; Academic and Religious Education at all Levels; Specialized Education; Parish Ministry; Social Services; Family Centers; Renewal Centers; Diocesan Offices; Retreat Ministry; National Organizations.

Properties owned: Sisters of St. Francis, Sea Isle City, NJ; Bay House, Tacoma, WA; Marion House, Tacoma, WA; St. Ann Convent, Tacoma, WA; Neumann University, Aston, PA; Assisi House, Aston, PA; Portiuncula Convent, Aston, PA; St. Mary Convent, Langhorne, PA; The Catholic High School of Baltimore, Baltimore, MD; Anna Bachmann House, Aston, PA; Sisters of St. Francis, Wilmington, DE; Sisters of St. Francis of Philadelphia, Canticle House, Philadelphia, PA; Sisters of St. Francis of Philadelphia, TAU Convent, Aston, PA; St. Clare Renewal Center, Aston, PA; Sisters of St. Francis of Philadelphia; Convents in Aston, PA: 609 S. Convent Rd., 602A S. Convent Rd., 607 S. Convent Rd., 6 Red Hill Rd.

Represented in the Archdioceses of Baltimore, Boston, Newark, Philadelphia, Portland in Oregon, San Francisco, Seattle, and Washington and in the Dioceses of Allentown, Baker, Camden, Charlotte, Charleston, Cheyenne, Fairbanks, Harrisburg, Jackson, Oakland, Orange, Orlando, Paterson, Pensacola-Tallahassee, Raleigh, San Diego, San Juan, Scranton, Spokane, Trenton, Wilmington and Worcester. Also in Ireland, Kenya and South Sudan.

[1660] (O.S.F.)—SISTERS OF SAINT FRANCIS OF THE PROVIDENCE OF GOD

Founded in Pittsburgh in 1922.

3757 Library Rd., Pittsburgh, PA 15234-2398. Tel: 412-882-9911; Fax: 412-885-7247. Sr. Joanne Brazinski, O.S.F., Gen. Min.

Total Professed: 24.

Ministry in the field of Social Service; Retreat Directors; Ministry in Brazil, Spirituality.

Sponsored Ministry: Franciscan Child Day Care Center.

Represented in the Dioceses of Pittsburgh. Also in Brazil and Bolivia.

[1670] (O.S.F.)—SISTERS OF ST. FRANCIS OF SAVANNAH, MO (P)

Founded in Austria in 1850. Founded in the United States, August 22, 1922.

Provincial House and Novitiate: 908 Franciscan Way, Box 488, Savannah, MO 64485-0488. Tel: 816-324-3179; Fax: 816-324-7264; Web: www.sistersofstfrancis.org. Sr. Christine Martin, O.S.F., Prov. Supr.

Total in Community: 7.

Legal Holdings and Titles: Sisters of St. Francis of Savannah, Inc.; Maintenance and Custodial Care Trust of the Franciscan Sisters of Savannah. Ministry in rural life issues; Peace and Justice; Rural Ministry; Religious Education; Food Pantry.

Represented in the Diocese of Kansas City-St. Joseph.

[1680] (O.S.F.)—SCHOOL SISTERS OF ST. FRANCIS (P)

Founded in the United States in 1874.

General Motherhouse: 1501 S. Layton Blvd., Milwaukee, WI 53215. Tel: 414-808-3779; Fax: 414-944-6060. Sr. Mary Diez, O.S.F., Pres.; Sr. Tresa Abraham Kizhakeparambil, O.S.F., Vice Pres.; Sr. Barbara Kraemer, O.S.F., Vice Pres.; Sr. Lucy Kalapurackel, O.S.F., Vice Pres.; Sr. Catherine M. Ryan, O.S.F., Treas.

Total in Congregation : 671; Total in U.S: 361.

Properties owned and/or sponsored: St. Joseph Convent, Milwaukee, WI; School Sisters of St. Francis, Inc.

U.S. Province: 1515 S. Layton Blvd., Milwaukee, WI 53215. Tel: 414-384-1515. Provincial Team: Sr. Carol Rigali, O.S.F.; Sr. Deborah Fumagalli, O.S.F.; Sr. Marilyn Ketteler, O.S.F.

Properties owned and sponsored: Alverno College, Milwaukee, WI; Clement Manor, Inc., Greenfield, WI; Maryhill Manor, Niagara, WI; Our Lady of the Angels Convent, Greenfield, WI; New Cassel, Omaha, NE; Clare Towers, Milwaukee, WI; St. Clare Management, Inc., Milwaukee, WI; Sacred Heart, Milwaukee, WI; Telos, Inc., Milwaukee, WI; Layton Blvd. West Neighbors, Inc., Milwaukee, WI.

Sisters serve and staff: Universities, Colleges, High Schools, Grade Schools, Adult and Special Education; Diocesan Offices; Hospitals and Nursing Homes; Parish Musicians; Retreat and Spiritual Direction; Social Ministries; Psychotherapy; Health Care Service; Religious Education; Pastoral Ministry; Pastoral Associate; Health Pastoral Care; Retirement Homes; Legal Services; Food Service; Visual Arts; Prison Ministry.

Represented in the Archdioceses of Chicago, Dubuque, Los Angeles, Milwaukee, Omaha and St. Paul-Minneapolis and in the Dioceses of Charlotte, El Paso, Grand Island, Green Bay, Jackson, Joliet, Lincoln, Madison, Nashville, Phoenix, Rockford, San Bernardino, Superior and Tucson.

[1690] (O.S.F.)—SCHOOL SISTERS OF THE THIRD ORDER REGULAR OF ST. FRANCIS UNITED STATES PROVINCE (PITTSBURGH, PA) (P)

Founded in Austria in 1843. First foundation in the U.S. in 1913.

Generalate: Via Nicolo Piccolomini 27, 00165, Rome, Italy Sr. M. Kveta Vinklarkova, O.S.F., Gen. Min.

Novitiate: St. Francis Convent, 395 Bridle Path Rd., Bethlehem, PA 18017. Tel: 610-865-1122.

Motherhouse: Mount Assisi Convent, 934 Forest Ave., Bellevue, Pittsburgh, PA 15202. Tel: 412-761-6004; Fax: 412-761-0290. Sr. Frances Marie Duncan, O.S.F., Prov. Min. Tel: 412-761-2855.

Total in Community: 73.

Legal Title: School Sisters of the Third Order Regular of St. Francis.

Ministry in the following areas: the field of academic education at all levels; Religious Education; Pastoral Ministry; Pastoral Associate; Residence Home for the Elderly; Mission Work; Social Ministry; Evangelization and Catechesis, Retreat Ministry.

Represented in the Archdioceses of San Antonio and in the Dioceses of Allentown, Erie, Metuchen, Paterson, Pittsburgh, San Angelo and Trenton. Also in Italy and South Africa.

[1695] (O.S.F.)—SCHOOL SISTERS OF THE THIRD ORDER OF ST. FRANCIS (PANHANDLE, TEXAS) (P)

Founded in Austria, 1723; The Vienna Foundation in 1845. First founded in the United States in 1931.

General Motherhouse: Vienna, Austria

American Center and Novitiate: 119 Franciscan Way, P.O. Box 906, Panhandle, TX 79068. Tel: 806-537-3182. Sr. Mary Michael Huseman, Regl. Supr.

Total number in U.S: 18.

Ministry in the following areas: Catholic Schools; Faith Formation; Evangelization of youth, young adults and families.

Represented in the Diocese of Amarillo.

[1700] (O.S.F.)—SCHOOL SISTERS OF THE THIRD ORDER REGULAR OF ST. FRANCIS (BETHLEHEM, PA) (P)

Founded in Austria, 1843. First founded in the United States, 1913.

General Motherhouse: Via Nicolo Piccolomini 27, Rome, Italy, 00165. Sr. Mary Xavier Bomberger, O.S.F., Gen. Min.

Bethlehem Novitiate: 395 Bridle Path Rd., Bethlehem, PA 18017-3105. Tel: 610-866-2597; Tel: 610-867-8890; Fax: 610-861-7478. Sr. Elaine Hromulak, O.S.F., Prov. Min. Tel: 412-761-2855.

Sisters: 46.

Properties owned and/or sponsored: St. Francis Center for Renewal, Bethlehem, PA.

[1705] (O.S.F.)—THE SISTERS OF ST. FRANCIS OF ASSISI (P) (Sisters of Penance and Charity)

Founded in the United States in 1849.

General Motherhouse: St. Francis Convent, 3221 S. Lake Dr., Saint Francis, WI 53235-3702. Tel: 414-744-1160; Fax: 414-744-7193; Email: administration @lakeosfs.org; Web: www.lakeosfs.org. Sr. Diana De Bruin, O.S.F., Dir.

Total in Community: 167.

Legal Titles: The Sisters of St. Francis of Assisi, Inc.; The Ongoing Community Support Trust of the Sisters of St. Francis, Inc.; Sisters of St. Francis of Assisi of New Mexico.

Corporate Ministries: St. Elizabeth School, Inc., Baltimore, MD; Franciscan Center, Inc., Baltimore, MD; St. Ann Center for Intergenerational Care, Inc., Milwaukee, WI; St. Francis Convent, Inc., Saint Francis, WI; Cardinal Stritch University, Inc., Milwaukee, WI; St. Coletta of Wisconsin, Inc., Jefferson, WI; St. Coletta of Wisconsin Charitable Foundation, Inc., St. Coletta's of Illinois, Tinley Park, IL; St. Coletta's of Illinois Foundation, Inc., Tinley Park, IL; Cardinal Cushing Centers, Inc., Hanover, MA; Cardinal Cushing Centers, Inc., Braintree St. Coletta School, Braintree, MA. Services to the Elderly: Canticle Court, Inc.; Juniper Court, Inc.; Canticle and Juniper Courts Foundation, Inc., Saint Francis, WI.

Represented in the Archdioceses of Baltimore, Boston, Denver, Dubuque, Milwaukee, San Antonio and Santa Fe and in the Dioceses of Brownsville, Cheyenne, Corpus Christi, Davenport, Ft. Wayne/South Bend, Great Falls; Joliet, Madison, San Diego, Superior and Tucson. Also in Taiwan.

[1710] (O.S.F.)—CONGREGATION OF THE THIRD ORDER OF ST. FRANCIS OF MARY IMMACULATE, JOLIET, IL (P)

Founded in the United States, Joliet, Illinois, in 1865.

Central Administration Offices: 1433 Essington Rd., Joliet, IL 60432-2873. Tel: 815-725-8735. Sr. Dolores Zemont, O.S.F., Pres.

Total in Community: 142.

Legal Titles: Congregation of the Third Order of St. Francis of Mary Immaculate, Joliet, IL; Retirement Plan Trust of the Congregation of the Third Order of St. Francis of Mary Immaculate, Joliet, IL.

Sponsored Institutions: Joliet Catholic Academy, Our Lady of Angels Retirement Home, University of St. Francis.

Ministry in the following areas: School and Adult Education; Retirement Home; House of Prayer. Also engaged in Religious Education; Social Services; Spiritual Direction; Nursing and Health Services; Hospital and Parish Ministry; Prison Ministry; Hispanic Ministry; Senior Housing.

Represented in the Archdioceses of Boston, Chicago, Cincinnati, Denver, Detroit, Milwaukee, New York and in the Dioceses of Cleveland, Colorado Springs, Columbus, Joliet, Peoria, Phoenix, St. Cloud, Springfield in Illinois, Superior, Toledo, Tucson and Youngstown. Also in Brazil.

[1720] (O.S.F.)—SISTERS OF THE THIRD ORDER REGULAR OF ST. FRANCIS OF THE CONGREGATION OF OUR LADY OF LOURDES (P)

Founded in the United States in 1877.

Administration Center: Assisi Heights, 1001 14th St., N.W., Ste 100, Rochester, MN 55901. Tel: 507-282-7441; Fax: 507-282-7762. Sr. Ramona Miller, O.S.F., Congregational Min. & Pres. Tel: 507-529-3533.

Total in Community: 175.

Ministry in the following areas: Education Services; Pastoral Concerns Development; Religious Life Development; Spiritual Life Development; Community Life Development; Social Concerns Development; Business Services; Health Care Services; Support Services.

Properties owned and sponsored: Assisi Heights, Rochester, MN.

Represented in the Archdioceses of Chicago, Denver, St. Paul-Minneapolis, Santa Fe and in the Dioceses of El Paso, Great Falls-Billings, Joliet, La Crosse, New Ulm, Rapid City, St. Cloud, San Bernardino, San Diego, Springfield-Cape Girardeau and Winona-Rochester. Also in Colombia.

[1730] (O.S.F.)—CONGREGATION OF THE SISTERS OF THE THIRD ORDER OF ST. FRANCIS, OLDENBURG, IN (P)

Founded in U.S., Oldenburg, Indiana in 1851.

General Motherhouse and Novitiate: Convent of the Immaculate Conception, Oldenburg, IN 47036. Tel: 812-934-2475. Sr. Christa Franzer, O.S.F., Congregational Min.

Total in Community: 179.

Properties owned and/or sponsored: Marian University, Indianapolis, IN; Oldenburg Academy, Oldenburg, IN.

Sisters serve & staff: Liberal Arts University, Academy, High Schools, Elementary Schools; Navajo, Indian Missions; Religious Education Centers; Hospital & Parish Ministry; Apostolate of Aging; Retreat & Counseling Ministry; Hispanic Ministry; Justice & Peace Offices; Clerical Staff; Social Services.

Represented in the Archdioceses of Cincinnati, Detroit, Indianapolis, St. Louis and Los Angeles and in the Dioceses of Evansville, Gallup, Galveston-Houston, Grand Rapids, Great Falls-Billings, Lexington, and Springfield in Illinois.

[1760] (O.S.F.)—SISTERS OF THE THIRD ORDER OF ST. FRANCIS OF PENANCE AND OF CHARITY (P)

Founded in Tiffin, Ohio in 1869.

General Motherhouse: St. Francis Convent, 200 St. Francis Ave., Tiffin, OH 44883. Tel: 419-447-0435; Fax: 419-447-1612. Sr. Sara Aldridge, O.S.F., Community Min.; Gabe Stoll, Exec. Dir., St. Francis Senior Ministries, Inc.; Tyler Webb, Chm. Bd. Trustees St. Francis Senior Ministries, Inc.

Total in Community: 83.

Legal Title: Sisters of St. Francis of Tiffin, OH. Ministry in the following areas: Ministry to the Aged; Parish Ministry; Retreat and Renewal Centers; Health Care; Health-Pastoral Care; Administration; Childcare; Social Justice Outreach.

Properties owned or sponsored: St. Francis Home, Inc., Tiffin, OH; St. Francis Villas, Inc.; St. Francis Senior Ministries Day Care, Inc.; Friedman Village at St. Francis; St. Francis Spirituality Center (SFSC); St. Francis Senior Ministries (SFSM); Franciscan Earth Literacy Center, 194 St. Francis Ave. Tiffin, 44883.

Represented in the Archdioceses of Detroit and in the Dioceses of Lexington, Owensboro, Toledo, and Youngstown. Also in Mexico.

[1770] (O.S.F.)—THE SISTERS OF THE THIRD ORDER OF ST. FRANCIS (EAST PEORIA, ILLINOIS) (P)

Founded in the United States in 1877.

Motherhouse: 1175 St. Francis Ln., East Peoria, IL 61611-1299. Tel: 309-699-7215. Sr. Judith Ann Duvall, O.S.F., Major Supr.

Total in Community: 22.

Properties owned and sponsored: Saint Francis Medical Center, Peoria, IL; St. Joseph Medical Center, Bloomington, IL; St. Mary Medical Center, Galesburg, IL; St. James-John W. Albrecht Medical Center, Pontiac, IL; Saint Anthony Medical Center, Rockford, IL; St. Francis Hospital, Escanaba, MI; OSF Healthcare System, Peoria, IL; OSF Healthcare Foundation, Peoria, IL; Motherhouse, East Peoria, IL; Holy Family Medical Center, Monmouth, IL; OSF Saint Elizabeth Medical Center, Ottawa, IL; OSF Saint Anthony Health Center, Alton, IL; OSF Saint Luke Medial Center, Kewanee, IL.

Represented in the Dioceses of Marquette, Peoria, Rockford and Springfield.

[1780] (F.S.P.A.)—CONGREGATION OF THE SISTERS OF THIRD ORDER OF ST. FRANCIS OF PERPETUAL ADORATION (P) (Franciscan Sisters of Perpetual Adoration)

Founded in the United States in 1849.

Generalate - Motherhouse and Novitiate: St. Rose Convent, 912 Market St., La Crosse, WI 54601-4782. Tel: 608-782-5610; Fax: 608-782-6301. Email: fspa@fspa.org. Sr. Eileen McKenzie, F.S.P.A., Pres.; Sr. Mary Ann Gschwind, F.S.P.A., Archivist.

Total in Congregation : 192.

Properties owned and sponsored: St. Rose Convent, La Crosse, WI; Villa St. Joseph, La Crosse, WI; Franciscan Spirituality Center, La Crosse; Prairiewoods Franciscan Spirituality Center, Hiawatha, IA; Marywood Franciscan Spirituality Center, Arbor Vitae, WI.

Represented in the Archdioceses of Agana, Chicago, Denver, Dubuque, Philadelphia, Portland in Oregon, Seattle and St. Paul-Minneapolis and in the Dioceses of Colorado Springs, Des Moines, Dodge City, Gallup, Green Bay, Jackson, La Crosse, Phoenix, Savannah, Sioux City, Spokane and Superior. Also in Canada.

[1805] O.S.F.—SISTERS OF ST. FRANCIS OF THE NEUMANN COMMUNITIES (P)

Congregation Offices (1860): 960 James St., 2nd Fl., Syracuse, NY 13203. Tel: 315-634-7000; Fax: 315-634-7023; Email: sisters@sosf.org; Web: www.sosf.org.

Total in Community: 350.

Ministry in academic education at all levels; hospitals; religious education & pastoral ministry; retreat houses; rehabilitation center; home for the dying; child day care; diocesan offices; social services; day nurseries; parishes.

Sponsored ministries: Gingerbread House Day Care & Preschool, Syracuse, NY; St. Elizabeth Medical Center, Utica, NY; Francis House, Syracuse, NY; St. Francis Healthcare System, Honolulu, HI; Saint Francis School, Honolulu, HI; Portiuncula Foundation, Millvale, PA; Mt. Alvernia Day Care & Learning Center, Millvale, PA.

Properties owned: Sisters of St. Francis Centers in Syracuse, Williamsville, Honolulu, HI, Millvale, PA; Alverna Heights Spirituality & Nature Center, Fayetteville, NY.

Represented in the Archdioceses of Newark, New York and Washington and in the Dioceses of Buffalo, Camden, Charleston, El Paso, Greensburg, Honolulu, Joliet, Lubbock, Orlando, Pittsburgh, Scranton, St. Petersburg, Syracuse and Youngstown. Also in Africa & Peru.

[1810] (O.S.F.)—BERNARDINE FRANCISCAN SISTERS (P)

Founded in the United States in 1894.

Congregational Leadership Offices: 450 St. Bernardine St., Reading, PA 19607-1737. Tel: 484-509-4068; Fax: 484-334-6977; Email: Robertaann@bfranciscan.org. Sr. Marilisa Helena da Silva, O.S.F., Congregational Min.

Total in Community: 246.

Total number in the United States: 156.

Ministry in the field of academic education at all levels -preschool to college; religious education of children & adults; hospitals, health & home care; retreat work; social work.

Represented in the Archdioceses of Detroit, Dubuque, Philadelphia, San Antonio and in the Dioceses of Allentown, Bridgeport, Richmond, Saginaw, Scranton and Worcester. Also in Brazil, Dominican Republic, Liberia and Mozambique.

[1820] (O.S.F.)—HOSPITAL SISTERS OF THE THIRD ORDER REGULAR OF ST. FRANCIS (P)

Founded in Germany in 1844. First foundation in the United States in 1875.

General Motherhouse: Muenster, Westphalia, Germany Sr. Sherrey Murphy, O.S.F., Gen. Supr.

American Province (1875): St. Francis Convent, Motherhouse and Novitiate, Box 19431, Springfield, IL 62794. Tel: 217-522-3386. Sr. Maureen O'Connor, O.S.F., Prov. Supr.; Sr. Ann Mathieu, O.S.F., Prov. Sec. & Contact Person.

Total in Community: 64.

Legal Title: Hospital Sisters of St. Francis-USA, Inc.

Properties owned or sponsored: Residences 11; St. Francis Convent, Motherhouse, Novitiate, Springfield, IL; Hospital Sisters Services, Inc., Springfield, IL; Hospital Sisters of St. Francis Foundation, Springfield, IL; Hospital Sisters Health System, Springfield, IL; St. John's Hospital, Springfield, IL; St. John's College of Nursing, Springfield, IL; St. Mary's Hospital, Decatur, IL; St. Anthony Memorial Hospital, Effingham, IL; St. Joseph's Hospital, Highland, IL; St. Francis Hospital, Litchfield, IL; St. Elizabeth's Hospital, Belleville, IL; St. Joseph's Hospital, Breese, IL; St. Mary's Hospital Medical Center, Green Bay, WI; St. Vincent Hospital, Green Bay, WI; Sacred Heart Hospital, Eau Claire, WI; St. Francis Apartments, Eau Claire, WI; St. Nicholas Hospital, Sheboygan, WI; St. Mary's Hospital, Streator, IL; Hospital Sisters Health Care West, Inc., Chippewa Falls, WI; St. Joseph's Hospital, Chippewa Falls, WI; L.E. Phillips Treatment Center for the Chemically Dependent, Chippewa Falls, WI; Hospital Sisters Mission Outreach, Springfield, IL; Chiara Center, Springfield, IL.

Sisters serve and staff: Hospitals; Home Health Services; Catechetical; Care of Chemically Dependent; Social Ministries; Pastoral Ministries.

Represented in the Archdioceses of Chicago and Milwaukee and in the Dioceses of Belleville, Green Bay, La Crosse, and Springfield in Illinois. Also in Germany.

[1830] (R.G.S. - C.G.S.)—THE SISTERS OF THE GOOD SHEPHERD (P)

Congregation of Our Lady of Charity of the Good Shepherd Founded in France in 1835. First foundation in the United States in Louisville, KY, 1842.

Generalate for the Provinces: Suore del Buon Pastore, via Raffaello Sardiello 20, Rome, Italy, 00165. Sr. Ellen Kelly, Supr. Gen.

Province of Mid-North America (2000): Province Center, 7654 Natural Bridge Rd., St. Louis, MO 63121. Tel: 314-381-3400; Fax: 314-381-7102. Sr. Madeleine Munday, R.G.S., Prov.

Professed Apostolic Sisters: 101; Contemplative Sisters: 22.

Legal Title: Sisters of the Good Shepherd Province of Mid-North America; Pelletier Trust, a Charitable Trust of the Sisters of the Good Shepherd; Sisters of the Good Shepherd Province of Mid-North America Foundation.

Properties owned and staffed: Sisters of the Good Shepherd of Detroit aka Vista Maria, Dearborn Heights, MI; CORA Services, Inc., Philadelphia, PA; Good Shepherd Corporation d.b.a. Good Shepherd Neighborhood House, Mediation Program, Philadelphia, PA; House of the Good Shepherd, Baltimore, MD; Good Shepherd Services, Atlanta, GA; Good Shepherd Shelter, Los Angeles, CA; Gracenter, San Francisco, CA; House of the Good Shepherd of Memphis dba DeNeuville Learning Center, Memphis, TN; Immaculate Heart Convent, St. Louis, MO; Good Shepherd Provincialate, St. Louis, MO.

Represented in the Archdioceses of Atlanta, Baltimore, Cincinnati, Detroit, Los Angeles, Louisville, Omaha, Portland in Oregon, Philadelphia, St. Louis, St. Paul-Minneapolis, San Francisco and Washington and in the Dioceses of Chalan Kanoa, Columbus, Covington and Scranton.

Province of New York (1857): Sisters of the Good Shepherd, 25-30 21st. Ave., Astoria, NY 11105. Tel: 718-278-1155; Fax: 718-278-1158. Sr. Maureen McGowan, Prov. Leader.

Professed Apostolic Sisters: 31; Professed Contemplative Sisters: 20.

Legal Title: Sisters of the Good Shepherd, Province of New York.

Legal Holdings or Titles: Good Shepherd Volunteers, Astoria, NY; Madonna Hall, Marlboro, MA; Maria Droste Services (Madonna Hall); Sisters of the Good Shepherd, Marlboro, MA; Collier Youth Services; St. Germaine's Services DBA Maria Droste Counseling Services NYC.

Ministry in Counseling Centers; Social Service Agencies; Special Education Schools; Neighborhood Family Services; Adolescent Residential Programs; Human Services Workshops; Pastoral Ministry; Hospital Chaplaincy.

Programs sponsored: Good Shepherd Services, New York, NY; Maria Droste Counseling Services, New York, NY; Collier Youth Services, Wickatunk, NJ; Good Shepherd Volunteers; Maria Drost Services, Quincy, MA.

Represented in the Archdioceses of Boston, Hartford and New York and in the Dioceses of Albany, Brooklyn, Fall River and Trenton.

Province of Central South US (2014): Sisters of the Good Shepherd, 620 Roswell Rd., N.W., P.O. Box 340, Carrollton, OH 44615. Tel: 330-627-1641; Fax: 330-627-5789. Sr. Francisca Aguillón, R.G.S., Prov.

Professed Apostolic Sisters: 54.

Legal Title: Sisters of Our Lady of Charity of the Good Shepherd - Province Center.

Legal Holdings or Titles: Province Center and Convent Carrollton, OH; Convent, Erie, PA; Nativity Convent, Pittsburgh, PA; Good Shepherd Convent, Wheeling, WV; San Juan Convent, El Paso, TX; Mount St. Michael Convent, Dallas, TX; Convent Green Bay, WI. Sponsored Program: Caritas House, Carrollton, OH.

Ministry in Domestic Abuse, Trafficked, Migrants, Immigration, Pastoral Ministry, Hispanic Ministry.

Represented in the Dioceses of Dallas, El Paso, Erie, Green Bay, Pittsburgh, San Diego, Steubenville and Wheeling-Charleston.

[1840] (G.N.S.H.)—GREY NUNS OF THE SACRED HEART (P)

Generalate, Congregational Offices, Motherhouse: 14500 Bustleton Ave., Philadelphia, PA 19116-1188. Tel: 215-968-4236; Fax: 267-538-3442. Sr. Denise Roche, G.N.S.H., Pres.; Ms. Eileen Dickerson, Dir. Congregational Advancement Office.

Total in Community: 86.

Ministry in Hospital and Hospice Chaplaincy; Pastoral Care; Academic Consultant; Social Services, Social Justice & Peace Activism; Retreat & Spiritual Direction; Addiction Counseling and Eco-Spirituality Advocacy.

Represented in the Archdioceses of Baltimore, New York and Philadelphia and in the Dioceses of Brooklyn, Buffalo and Rochester.

[1845] (M.G.SP.S.)—MISSIONARIES GUADALUPANAS OF THE HOLY SPIRIT (P)

Founded in Morelia, Michoacan, Mexico in 1930 by Rev. Felix de Jesus Rougier, M.Sp.S.

General Motherhouse: Hidalgo #7, Tlalpan 14000, Mexico, D.F., Mexico Mother Ana Maria Pacheco, Supr. Gen.

Provincial House: 5467 W. 8th St., Los Angeles, CA 90036-3811. Tel: 323-424-7208.

Total Sisters in U.S: 44.

Legal Title: Missionary Guadalupanas of the Holy Spirit, Inc. Ministry in Religious Education; Pastoral and Parish Ministries.

Represented in the Archdioceses of Los Angeles and Miami and in the Dioceses of Birmingham, Jackson, Palm Beach, Stockton and Wichita. Also in the Dominican Republic.

U.S. Novitiate: 758 S. Dunsmuir Ave., Los Angeles, CA 90036.

[1850] (S.A.C.)—SISTERS OF THE GUARDIAN ANGEL (P)

Founded in Quillan, France in 1839.

General Motherhouse: Avda, del Valle, 42, Madrid 3, Spain Sr. Sagrario Escudero, S.A.C., Supr. Gen.

U.S. Foundation: 1245 S. Van Ness, Los Angeles, CA 90019. Tel: 213-732-7881.

Represented in the Archdiocese of Los Angeles.

[1855] (H.H.C.J.)—CONGREGATION OF THE HANDMAIDS OF THE HOLY CHILD JESUS (P)

Founded in Calabar, Nigeria in 1931 by Sister Mary Charles Magdalen Walker. Obtained Pontifical Status in 1971; first foundation in United States in 1992.

Generalate and Motherhouse: Handmaids of the Holy Child Jesus - The Generalate, Ifuho, P.O. Box 155, Ikot Ekpene, Nigeria Tel: 080-388-78670. Sr. Leonie Martha O'Karaga, H.H.C.J., Supr. Gen.

U.S.A. Mission: Ancilla Convent, 3614 Englewood Dr., Pearland, TX 77584. Tel: 281-692-0098; Fax: 281-692-0049; Email: usa@hhcj.org; Web: www.hhcj.org. Sr. Germaine Ocansey, H.H.C.J., U.S.A. Mission Supr.; Sr. Betty Kalu, H.H.C.J., Devel. Dir.

Universal Number of Professed Sisters: 802; Professed Sisters in U.S. & Canada: 60.

Ministry in the field of Education at all levels; Pastoral Work; Health Care services; Women Empowerment; Education; Special Education; Youth Ministry; Catechesis; Pastoral Ministry.

Represented in the Archdioceses of Galveston-Houston, Mobile, New York and Washington and in the Dioceses St. Petersburg.

[1860] (H.P.B.)—HANDMAIDS OF THE PRECIOUS BLOOD (P)

Founded in Jemez Springs, New Mexico in 1947.

Motherhouse and Novitiate: Cor Jesu Monastery, 596 Callaway Ridge Rd., New Market, TN 37820. Tel: 423-241-7065. Rev. Mother Marietta, H.P.B., Mother Prioress.

Professed Sisters: 15.

Ministry as Contemplative, Life of Eucharistic Adoration (Perpetual) for the sanctification of priests and for the entire world.

[1870] (A.C.J.)—THE HANDMAIDS OF THE SACRED HEART OF JESUS (P)

Founded in Spain in 1877. First foundation in the United States in 1926.

General Motherhouse: Via Parre, 16, 00188, Rome, Italy Sr. Rosario Fernández Villarán, Supr. Gen. Universal total in Congregation: 980.

Provincial Motherhouse: 616 Coppertown Rd., Haverford, PA 19041-1135. Tel: 610-642-5715; Fax: 610-642-6788; Web: www.acjusa.org. Sr. Belén Escauriaza, A.C.J., Prov.

Total in Community: 29.

Properties owned: St. Raphaela Center, Haverford, PA; Ancillae Assumpta Academy, Wyncote, PA; Handmaids of Sacred Heart of Jesus, Philadelphia, PA; facilities in Georgia and Florida.

Sisters serve and staff: Elementary School; Retreat Center; Mission Center; Parish Ministry; CCD; Hispanic Pastoral Ministry; Social Workers; Pastoral Ministry; Mission work.

Represented in the Archdioceses of Atlanta, Miami and Philadelphia.

[1880] (A.R.)—HANDMAIDS OF REPARATION OF THE SACRED HEART OF JESUS (P)

Founded in Messina, Italy in 1918.

U.S. Foundation (1958): 6300 Capella Ave., Burke, VA 22015. Tel: 703-455-4180. Sr. Donatella Merulla, A.R., Contact Person.

Total number in U.S: 6.

Ministry in Apostolic Work in Religious & Academic Education: Education All Levels; Religious Education; Parish and Diocesan Ministry; CCD Work; Orphanages; Missionary Work in Africa, Brazil and Poland.

Represented in the Dioceses of Arlington and Steubenville. Also in Africa, Brazil, Italy and Poland.

[1890] (H.H.S.)—SOCIETY OF HELPERS (P)

Founded in France in 1856. First foundation in the U.S. in 1892.

Generalate: 16 rue St. J. Baptiste de la Salle, Paris, France, 75006. Sr. Gudrun Bohle, Supr. Gen.

American Provincial Office (1921): 2226 W. Pratt Blvd., Chicago, IL 60645. Tel: 773-405-9884. Leadership Team: Sr. Alicia Gutierrez, S.H.; Tel: 773-209-7597; Email: Cahli23@aol.com; Sr. Jean Kielty, S.H. Tel: 773-405-9884; Email: jeankielty@yahoo.com; Sr. Rayo Cuaya-Castillo, S.H. Tel: 773-301-7128; Email: rayo.javito@hotmail.com.

Total number in U.S. Province: 20.

Legal Title: Society of the Helpers of the Holy Souls; Helpers of the Holy Souls; Province of the Helpers of the Holy Souls in the United States.

Represented in the Archdiocese of Chicago and in the Diocese of Joliet.

[1895] (C.S.J.)—HERMANAS CARMELITASDE SAN JOSE (P)

Founded in El Salvador C.A. in 1916. First foundation in the United States in 2003.

Motherhouse: Final 14 Ave. Norte, Colonia San Antonio Las Palmeras Depto., De La Libertad, El Salvador

Regional House: 141 W. 87th Pl., Los Angeles, CA 90003. Tel: 323-758-6840; Tel: 323-752-2838. Sr. Enedina de Jesus Hernandez, C.S.J., Regl. Supr. U.S. Community.

Total in Congregation: 201; U.S. Community: 4.

Ministry in Pastoral Care: Pastoral assistance in spiritual guidance and counseling; visitation of the sick and elderly; sacramental preparation; religious education for children, youth and/or adults; pastoral visits to the poor; faith formation.

[1900] (H.C.G.)—HERMANAS CATEQUISTAS GUADALUPANAS (P)

Founded in Saltillo, Coahuila, Mexico in 1923. First United States foundation in 1950.

Motherhouse and Novitiate: Saltillo, Coahuila, Mexico

U.S. Address: Hermanas Catequistas Guadalupanas Convent, 4110 S. Flores, San Antonio, TX 78214. Tel: 210-532-9344. Sr. Maria Martha Ruiz, H.C.G., Reg. Delegate.

Total number in the U.S: 11.

Represented in the Archdioceses of San Antonio and in the Diocese of Fort Worth.

[1910] (H.J.)—HERMANAS JOSEFINAS (P)

General Motherhouse: Condor 336, Col. las Aguilas, Delg. Alvaro Obregon, Mexico, 01710. Mother Isabel Vargas Huante, H.J., Gen. & Supr.

U.S. Address: Santa Maria de Guadalupe Casa Delegacion, 2622 W. Summit Ave., San Antonio, TX 78228. Tel: 210-734-0039.

Sisters: 10.

Represented in the Archdioceses of Chicago, Los Angeles and San Antonio and in the Diocese of Joliet in Illinois.

[1920] (C.S.C.)—CONGREGATION OF THE SISTERS OF THE HOLY CROSS (P)

Founded at Le Mans, France in 1841. First foundation in the U.S. in 1843.

General Administration: Sisters of the Holy Cross Generalate, 301 Bertrand Hall-Saint Mary's, Notre Dame, IN 46556-5000. Tel: 574-284-5550; Fax: 574-284-5779. Communications Email: communications@cscsisters.org. Sr. M. Veronique Wiedower, C.S.C., Pres.; Sr. Brenda Cousins, C.S.C., Gen. Sec.

Professed Members: 336; Temporarily Professed: 35; Novices: 28; Candidates: 16.

Legal Title: Sisters of the Holy Cross, Inc.; The Academy of the Holy Cross, Inc., MD; The Corporation of Saint Mary's College, Notre Dame, IN; Holy Cross Ministries of Utah; Society of the Congregation of the Sisters of the Holy Cross, Bangladesh.

Areas and Coordinators:

Area of Africa - Ghana and Uganda Tel: 233-20-8112425. Sr. Esther Adjoa Entsiwah, C.S.C., Coord. Area of Asia-Bangladesh and India. Tel: 88-02-9119393. Sr. Pushpa Teresa Gomes, C.S.C., Coord.

Area of North America - USA & Mexico, Notre Dame, IN, Tel: 574-284-5646. Sr. Joy O'Grady, C.S.C., Coord.

Area of South America - Brazil and Peru. Tel: 011-99953-5865. Sr. Michael Mary Nolan, C.S.C., Coord.

Sisters serve and staff: Colleges; High Schools; Grade Schools; Adult Education Centers; Social Service Centers; Prayer Centers; Counseling Centers; Human Rights Centers; Women's Development Center; Hospitals and other Health Ministries, including Health Systems, Primary Health Care and Long Term Health Care; Parish Ministry; Diocesan Catechetical Services; Other Parish and Diocesan Ministries; Retirement Homes; Senior Citizen Residences; Pastoral Ministry with the Deaf; Correctional Institution.

Represented in the Archdioceses of Baltimore, Chicago, Indianapolis, Los Angeles and Washington and in the Dioceses of Arlington, Austin, Boise, Columbus, Fort Wayne-South Bend, Fresno, Knoxville, Lafayette in Indiana, Lexington, Palm Beach, Raleigh, Richmond, Sacramento, Salt Lake City and Tucson. Also in Bangladesh, Brazil, Ghana, India, Peru, Mexico and Uganda.

[1930] (C.S.C.)—SISTERS OF HOLY CROSS (P)

Founded in Le Mans, France in 1841. First foundation in Canada in 1847.

General Administration: 905 rue Basile-Moreau, St-Laurent, Montreal, Canada, H4L 4A1. Sr. Raymonde Maisonneuve, C.S.C., Congregational Leader.

Universal total in Congregation: 397.

North American Region/U.S. Sector Office: Sisters of Holy Cross, 365 Island Pond Rd., Manchester, NH 03109-4811. Tel: 603-622-9504; Fax: 603-622-9782. Sr. Diane Dupere, C.S.C., Sector Leader. Email: dydupere@srsofholycross.com. Sr. Jacqueline Brodeur, C.S.C., Development. Email: jbdev@srsofholycross.com.

Total number in Region: 85.

Ministry in the field of Academic Education; Social and Family Services; Parish Ministry; Hospital Chaplaincy; Administrative/Diocesan Services; Elderly Assistance; Spiritual Direction; Holy Cross Family Learning Center assisting immigrants and refugees.

Properties owned: Holy Cross Early Childhood Center, Manchester, NH; St. George Manor, Manchester, NH; 136 Lynwood Ln., Manchester, NH 03109; 113 Wedgewood Ln., Manchester, NH 03109; Fairview Rd., R.R. 1, Box 191, Pittsfield, NH 03263; Four units at Crosswoods Path Condos, Merrimack, NH.

Represented in the Dioceses of Bridgeport, Manchester and St. Petersburg. Also in Burkina Faso, Chile, Haiti, Mali, Peru and Italy.

[1940] (C.H.F.)—CONGREGATION OF THE SISTERS OF THE HOLY FAITH (P)

Founded in Ireland in 1856. First foundation in U.S. in 1953. St. John of God School, 13817 Pioneer Blvd., Norwalk, California, 90650.

Motherhouse: Glasnevin, Dublin II, Ireland

U.S. Region: 12322 S. Paramount Blvd., Downey, CA 90242. Tel: 562-869-6092; Fax: 562-869-4609. Sr. Dolores Madden, C.H.F., Regl. Leader.
Total in Community: 28.
Represented in the Archdioceses of Los Angeles, New Orleans and San Francisco and in the Diocese of Sacramento.

[1950] (S.S.F.)—CONGREGATION OF THE SISTERS OF THE HOLY FAMILY (P)

Founded in New Orleans, Louisiana, in 1842.
Motherhouse: 6901 Chef Menteur Hwy., New Orleans, LA 70126. Tel: 504-241-3088. Sr. Greta Jupiter, S.S.F., Congregational Leader.
Total in Community: 84.
Ministry in Secondary and Elementary Schools; Day Care Centers; Pastoral and Social Services; Nursing Home and Apartments for the Elderly, Disabled and Handicapped.
Represented in the Archdiocese of New Orleans and in the Dioceses of Alexandria, Lafayette (LA) and Mobile.

[1960] (S.H.F.)—SISTERS OF THE HOLY FAMILY (P)

Founded in San Francisco, California, in 1872.
General Motherhouse: P.O. Box 3248, Fremont, CA 94539. Tel: 510-624-4596; Fax: 510-933-7395. Email: congsecy@holyfamilysisters.org. Sr. Caritas Foster, S.H.F., Congregational Pres.
Total in Community: 55.
Ministry in the following areas: Pastoral Care; Parish Administration and Ministries; Social Justice Ministry; Ministry to Immigrants.
Represented in the Archdiocese of San Francisco and in the Dioceses of Honolulu, Monterey, Oakland, Reno and Stockton.

[1970] (C.S.F.N.)—SISTERS OF THE HOLY FAMILY OF NAZARETH (P)

Founded in Italy in 1875. First foundation in the United States in 1885.
General Motherhouse: Rome, Italy Mother Jana Zawieja, C.S.F.N., Supr. Gen.
Holy Family Province (1885): 310 N. River Rd., Des Plaines, IL 60016-1211. Tel: 847-298-6760; Fax: 847803-1941. Email: info@nazarethesfn.org. Sr. Kathleen Maciej, C.S.F.N., Prov. Supr.; Sr. Rebecca Sullivan, C.S.F.N., Archivist.
Total number in United States: 225.
Ministry in Academic Education; Hospitals and Health Care; Social Work; Retreat Work; Religious Education; Child Care; Parish Ministry.
Co-Sponsors: CHRISTUS Health.
Represented in the Archdiocese of Chicago.

[1980] (O.S.F.)—CONGREGATION OF THE SERVANTS OF THE HOLY CHILD JESUS OF THE THIRD ORDER REGULAR OF SAINT FRANCIS (P)

Founded in Germany in 1855. First founded in the United States on April 9, 1929, at Staten Island, New York.
General Motherhouse: Kloster Oberzell, Wuerzburg, Germany Mother Katharina Ganz, Supr. Gen.
Regional House: Servants of the Holy Child Jesus Regional House Epiphany Convent, 99 Harrison Ave., North Plainfield, NJ 07060-3606. Tel: 908-370-3616; Fax: 908-756-3933. Sr. M. Antonia Cooper, Reg. Min.
Total in American Region: 9.
Ministry in Social Work.
Represented in the Dioceses of Metuchen and Trenton.

[1990] (S.N.J.M.)—SISTERS OF THE HOLY NAMES OF JESUS AND MARY (P)

Founded by Blessed Marie Rose Durocher, in Longueuil, Quebec, Canada in 1843. First foundation in the U.S. in 1859.
Generalate: 80, rue Saint-Charles Est, Longueuil, Canada, J4H 1A9. Tel: 450-651-8104. Sr. Linda Haydock, Supr.
An international congregation of 710 religious women with missions in Lesotho, Nicaragua, Peru and Brazil. Congregational sponsored works include colleges; adult centers; secondary, elementary and preschools; continuing care retirement community and health clinics.
U.S.-Ontario Province: Provincial Administration, Box 398, Marylhurst, OR 97036. Tel: 503-675-7100; Fax: 503-697-3264; Email: info@snjmnson.org; Web: www.snjmusontario.org. Sr. Maureen Delaney, S.N.J.M., Prov.
Total in Province: 392.
Properties owned and/or sponsored: Academy of the Holy Names, Albany, NY; Academy of the Holy Names, Tampa, FL; Convent, Marylhurst, OR; St. Mary's Academy, Portland, OR; Mary's Woods at Marylhurst, Inc., Marylhurst, OR; Holy Names University, Oakland, CA; Holy Names High School, Oakland, CA; Ramona Convent Secondary School, Alhambra, CA; Villa Maria del Mar, Santa Cruz, CA; Next Step Learning Center, Oakland, CA; Holy Names Academy, Seattle, WA.
Sisters ministering in works sponsored by other institutions/agencies include Formal Education in Universities, Secondary, Elementary and Preschools; Adult Basic Education/Literacy; Administration in Diocesan Offices; Campus Ministry; Pastoral Ministry; Religious Education, Health Care and Social Services.
Represented in the Archdioceses of Los Angeles, Portland, Oregon, San Francisco, Seattle and Washington and in the Dioceses of Albany, Baker, Jackson, Monterey, Oakland, Orlando, St. Petersburg, Spokane, Venice and Yakima.

[2000] (C.S.R.)—SISTERS OF THE REDEEMER (P)

First foundation in the United States on March 19, 1924 in Baltimore, Maryland.
American Province of the Immaculate Conception: 1600 Huntingdon Pike, Meadowbrook, PA 19046. Tel: 215-914-4100; Fax: 215-914-4171. Sr. Anne Marie Haas, C.S.R., Province Leader. Email: amhaas@holyredeemer.com
Legal Holdings and Titles: Holy Redeemer Ministries; Holy Redeemer Health System; Holy Redeemer Hospital; Holy Redeemer St. Joseph Manor; Holy Redeemer Lafayette; Holy Redeemer Transitional Care Unit; Holy Redeemer Home Health and Hospice Services; Redeemer Village & Redeemer Village II; Drueding Center; HRH Management Corporation; Holy Redeemer Multi-Care, Inc.; Convents—Epiphany Community; St. Teresa of Avila Community Convent; Redeemer Community; Annunciation-Formation Community.
Represented in the Archdioceses of Newark and Philadelphia and in the Dioceses of Camden, Metuchen and Trenton.

[2010] (O.SS.R.)—ORDER OF THE MOST HOLY REDEEMER (P) (Redemptoristine Nuns)

Founded 1731 by St. Alphonsus de Liguori and Blessed Maria Celeste. (Contemplative). Rule approved 1750 by Pope Benedict XIV. First United States Monastery (1957) Esopus, New York.
Monastery of St. Alphonsus (1960): 200 Liguori Dr., Liguori, MO 63057. Tel: 636-464-1093; Fax: 636-464-1073. Email: rednuns@gmail.com. Sr. Margaret Eleanor Wilkinson O.Ss.R., Prioress.
Total in Community: 12.
Properties owned and/or sponsored: Order of the Most Holy Redeemer, Monastery of the Most Holy Redeemer, Thailand.
Represented in the Archdioceses of New York and St. Louis.
Redemptoristine Nuns: 89 Hiddenbrooke Dr., Beacon, NY 12508-2230. Tel: 845-831-3132; Fax: 845-831-5579; Email: rednunsny@gmail.com; Web: www.rednunsny.org. Sr. Moira K. Quinn, O.SS.R., Prioress.
Total in Community: 5; Solemnly Professed Nuns: 5. Solemn Vows, Papal Enclosure.

[2030] (C.S.SP.)—SISTERS OF THE HOLY SPIRIT (D)

Founded in the United States 1919; Decree of Establishment 1932.
Motherhouse and Novitiate: 10102 Granger Rd., Cleveland, OH 44125. Sr. Patricia Raelene Peters, C.S.Sp., Supr. Gen.
Total in Community: 2.
Represented in the Diocese of Cleveland.

[2040] (S.H.S.)—SISTERS OF THE HOLY SPIRIT (D)

Founded in the United States in 1913 at Donora, Pennsylvania.
5246 Clarwin Ave., Ross Township, Pittsburgh, PA 15229-2208. Tel: 412-931-1917; Fax: 412-931-3711; Email: srshs@verizon.net; Web: www.sistersoftheholyspirit.com. Sr. Grace Fabich, S.H.S., Gen. Supr.
Total in Community: 27.
Facilities owned and staffed: Martina Spiritual Renewal Center Inc.
Sisters serve and staff: Elementary Schools; Religious Education; Health and Social Services; Retreat Services; Pastoral Ministry.
Represented in the Dioceses of Greensburg and Pittsburgh.

[2050] (S.H.SP.)—SISTERS OF THE HOLY SPIRIT AND MARY IMMACULATE (P)

Founded in America in 1893. Papal Approbation 1930; final Approbation, 1938.
General Motherhouse: Convent of the Holy Spirit and Mary Immaculate, 300 Yucca St., San Antonio, TX 78203. Tel: 210-533-5149. Sr. Geraldine Klein, S.H.Sp., Gen. Supr.
Professed Sisters: 77.
Legal Holdings: Holy Spirit Trust; Holy Spirit Motherhouse; Healy Murphy Center, Inc., San Antonio, TX.
Ministry in the following areas: Education; Health Care; Pastoral Ministry; Catechetical Ministry; Social Service; Retreats.
Represented in the Archdiocese of San Antonio and in the Dioceses of Brownsville, Dallas, Fort Worth, Houma-Thibodaux, Jackson, Lafayette (LA) and Shreveport. Also in Mexico and Zambia.

[2060] (O.SS.T.)—SISTERS OF THE MOST HOLY TRINITY (P)

Founded in Rome in 1198. First foundation in the United States in 1920.
General Motherhouse: Rome, Italy
Provincial House: Immaculate Conception Province, 21281 Chardon Rd., Euclid, OH 44117. Tel: 216-481-8232; Fax: 216-481-6577. Sr. M. Rochelle Guertal, O.SS.T., Reg. Delegate.
Total in Community: 23.
Properties owned and/or sponsored: Our Lady of Lourdes Shrine, Euclid, OH.
Represented in the Archdiocese of Philadelphia and in the Diocese of Cleveland.

[2070] (S.U.S.C.)—HOLY UNION SISTERS (P)

Founded in France in 1826. First foundation in the United States in 1886.
Generalate: Rome, Italy Sr. Paula Coelho, S.U.S.C., Supr. Gen.
United States Province: 444 Centre St., P.O. Box 410, Milton, MA 02186-0006. Tel: 617-696-8765; Fax: 617-696-8571. Email: kathleen.corrigan@husmilton.org. Province Leadership Team: Sr. Kathleen Corrigan, S.U.S.C.; Sr. Joan Guertin, S.U.S.C.; Sr. Carol Regan, S.U.S.C.
Total in Community: 70.
Legal Title: Holy Union Sisters, Inc.
Ministry in the field of Religious and Academic Education; Social Services; Pastoral Care; Pastoral Ministry; Spiritual Renewal; Day Care; Ministry Education; Family Ministry; Nursing; Peace & Justice; Spanish Apostolate; Ministry to the Handicapped; Ministry to Immigrants and Refugees; Clerical & Secretarial services; Diocesan Administrative services.
Represented in the Archdioceses of Baltimore, Boston and New York and in the Dioceses of Brooklyn, Fall River, Harrisburg, Lexington, Providence and Rockville Centre.

[2080] (G.H.M.S.)—HOME MISSION SISTERS OF AMERICA (D) (Glenmary Sisters)

Founded July 16, 1952.
Motherhouse: Glenmary Sisters - Glenmary Center, P.O. Box 22264, Owensboro, KY 42304-2264. Tel: 270-686-8401. Sr. Sharon Miller, Pres.
Total in Community: 10.
Service to Home Missions.
Represented in the Dioceses of Lexington, Owensboro and Springfield Cape-Girardeau.

[2090] (H.V.M.)—SISTERS HOME VISITORS OF MARY (D)

Founded in Detroit, Michigan in 1949.
Motherhouse: 121 E. Boston Blvd., Detroit, MI 48202. Tel: 313-869-2160; Email: homevisitors@att.net. Total in Community: 29.
Ministry in Urban Parishes; Senior Citizen; Schools and Preschools; Religious Education, RCIA; Clinic; Community Org.
Represented in the Archdiocese of Detroit. Also in Nigeria.

[2100] (C.H.M.)—CONGREGATION OF THE HUMILITY OF MARY (P)

Founded in France in 1854. First United States foundation in 1864.

Motherhouse: Humility of Mary Center, Davenport, IA 52804. Email: sisters@chmiowa.org. Sr. Mary Ann Vogel, C.H.M., Pres.

Total in Community: 74.

Legal Titles: Congregation of the Humility of Mary; Congregation of the Humility of Mary Charitable Trust.

Ministry in Schools and Colleges; Migrant Programs; Pastoral Ministry; Social Services; Inner City Programs; Health Services; Ministry to the Elderly; and Retreat Center.

Represented in the Archdiocese of Denver and in the Dioceses of Arlington, Davenport, Des Moines, Great Falls-Billings, Jackson, Peoria, Rockford and Syracuse. Also in Mexico.

[2110] (H.M.)—SISTERS OF THE HUMILITY OF MARY, INC. (P)

Founded in France in 1854. First foundation in the United States in 1864 at Villa Maria, Lawrence County, Pennsylvania, 16155.

Motherhouse: Villa Maria Community Center, P.O. Box 914, Villa Maria, PA 16155-0914. Tel: 724-964-8861; Fax: 724-964-8082. Email: cbender@humilityofmary.org; scunningham@humilityofmary.org. Sr. Jean Tobin Lardie, H.M., Pastoral Leader & Major Supr.; Sr. Joanne Gardner, H.M., Community Archivist.

Total in Community: 125.

Ministry in the field of Academic and Religious Education; Hospitals and Nursing Home, Assisted Living; Parish and Pastoral Ministries; Legal Services; Social Services; Ministry to persons who are Native Americans, Migrants, Hispanics, Haitians and Rural Poor; Housing Ministry to Single Parents, Independent Elderly; Retreat Ministry; Spirituality and Counseling; Advocacy for Eco-justice.

Legal Holdings and Titles: Sisters of the Humility of Mary (Motherhouse), Villa Maria, PA; Sisters of the Humility of Mary Charitable Trust, Villa Maria, PA; Magnificat High School, Rocky River, OH; Villa Maria Education and Spirituality Center, Villa Maria, PA; Humility of Mary Housing, Inc., Akron, OH; HM Housing Development Corporation, Akron, OH; HM Life Opportunity Services, Akron, OH; Villa Maria Residential Services, Villa Maria, PA.

Represented in the Dioceses of Cleveland, Erie, Grand Island, Palm Beach, Pittsburgh, Wheeling-Charleston and Youngstown.

[2140]—SISTERS OF THE IMMACULATE CONCEPTION OF THE BLESSED VIRGIN MARY (LITHUANIAN) (P)

Founded in Marijampole, Lithuania in 1918. First foundation in the United States in 1936.

American Headquarters: Immaculate Conception Convent, 600 Liberty Hwy., Putnam, CT 06260-2503. Tel: 860-928-7955; Fax: 860-928-1930. Sr. Igne Marijosius, Supr.

Total in Community: 9.

Legal Titles & Holdings: Immaculate Conception Convent; Matulaitis Nursing Home, Putnam, CT; Camp Neringa, Marlboro, VT.

Ministry in Nursing Homes; Retreat House; Catechetical Work in Parishes; Summer Camp for Children and Young Adults.

Represented in the Archdiocese of Chicago and in the Dioceses of Burlington and Norwich. Also in Canada.

[2145] (O.S.A.)—CONGREGATION OF AUGUSTINIAN SISTERS SERVANTS OF JESUS AND MARY (P)

Generalate: via Nomentana 514, Rome, Italy Mother Tessie Bezzina, Gen.

Malta Province: 208 Fleur-de-Lys, B'Kara, Malta Mother Atanasia Buhagiar, Prov.

U.S. Foundation: St. John Convent, 531 E. Broadway, Brandenburg, KY 40108. Sr. Lydia Falzon, Supr.

Total in Community: 4.

Represented in the Archdiocese of Louisville.

[2150] (I.H.M.)—SISTERS, SERVANTS OF THE IMMACULATE HEART OF MARY (P)

Founded in the United States in 1845.

SSIHM Leadership Council: 610 W. Elm Ave., Monroe, MI 48162-7909. Tel: 734-240-9700; Fax: 734-240-9784. Sr. Mary Jane Herb, I.H.M., Pres.

Total in Congregation : 378.

Legal Titles: Marian High School for Young Women, Bloomfield Hills, MI; Visitation North Spirituality Center.

Ministry in Academic and Religious Education at all levels; Pastoral Ministry (parish, healthcare, campus and prison settings); Diocesan and Parish Administration; Peace and Justice; Social Service and Counseling; Spiritual Growth and Development; Overseas Ministries; Ministry in Health Care.

Represented in the Archdioceses of Atlanta, Boston, Chicago, Detroit, Galveston-Houston, Louisville, Miami, Milwaukee, Mobile, Oklahoma City, Philadelphia, St. Paul-Minneapolis, San Antonio, San Juan, Santa Fe and Washington and in the Dioceses of Austin, Cleveland, El Paso, Fort Wayne-South Bend, Joliet, Kansas City-St. Joseph, Lansing, Marquette, Oakland, Orange, Orlando, Palm Beach, Phoenix, Portland, Raleigh, Richmond, San Diego, Saginaw, St. Augustine, Toledo and Wilmington. Also in Canada, Mexico and South Africa.

River House - IHM Spirituality Center: 805 W. Elm Ave., Monroe, MI 48162. Tel: 734-240-5494; Email: riverhouse@ihmsisters.org; Web: www.ihmsisters.org.

Sisters: 3.

Sponsorship of I.H.M. Congregation.

Visitation North Spirituality Center: 7227 Lahser Rd., Bloomfield Hills, MI 48301. Tel: 248-433-0950; Fax: 248-433-0952; Email: visitationnorth@ihmsisters.org; Web: www.visitationnorth.org.

Sisters: 4.

Sponsorship of I.H.M. Congregation.

[2160] (I.H.M.)—SISTERS, SERVANTS OF THE IMMACULATE HEART OF MARY (P)

Founded in 1845. Established in Scranton, Pennsylvania in 1871.

General Motherhouse: Immaculate Heart of Mary Center, 2300 Adams Ave., Scranton, PA 18509. Tel: 570-342-6850; Fax: 570-346-5439. Email: communications@sistersofihm.org. Sr. Ellen Maroney, I.H.M., Pres.

Total in Community: 325.

Properties owned and/or sponsored: IHM Center; Pascucci Family Our Lady of Peace Residence; Our Lady of Grace Center; Manhasset, NY. Ministry in the field of Academic Education; Health Care; Retreat Ministries; Directors of Religious Education; Pastoral Ministries; Social Services; Campus Ministry; Volunteer Services; Family Ministry; Drug and Alcohol Counseling; Ministry to Hispanics; Diocesan Offices.

Represented in the Archdioceses of Baltimore, Boston, Detroit, New York, Philadelphia, Santa Fe, San Antonio and Washington and in the Dioceses of Albany, Brooklyn, Camden, Harrisburg, Paterson, Pittsburgh, Raleigh, Rochester, Rockville Centre, St. Augustine, St. Petersburg, Scranton, Syracuse and Wilmington. Also in Mexico and Peru.

[2170] (I.H.M.)—SISTERS, SERVANTS OF THE IMMACULATE HEART OF MARY (P)

Founded in 1845. Established in West Chester, Pennsylvania in 1872.

General Motherhouse: Villa Maria House of Studies, 1140 King Rd., Immaculata, PA 19345. Tel: 610-647-2160; Fax: 610-889-4874. Email: ihmsisters1845@gmail.com. Sr. Lorraine McGrew, I.H.M., Gen. Supr.

Total in Congregation : 714.

Ministry in the field of Academic Education at all levels in the U.S. and Peru; Pastoral Ministry; Literacy Centers; Infirmary Work.

Represented in the Archdioceses of Chicago, Miami and Philadelphia and in the Dioceses of Allentown, Arlington, Camden, Harrisburg, Manchester, Metuchen, Raleigh, Richmond, Savannah and Trenton.

[2180] (I.H.M.)—SISTERS OF THE IMMACULATE HEART OF MARY (P)

Founded in Spain in 1848. First foundation in the United States in 1871.

General Motherhouse: Girona, Spain

U.S. Province: 3820 N. Sabino Canyon Rd., Tucson, AZ 85750-6534. Tel: 520-886-4273. Sr. Alice M. Martinez, Prov. Supr.; Sr. Veronica Loya, Sec. & Community Archivist.

Total in Community: 17.

Ministry in the field of Academic and Religious Education.

Represented in the Diocese of Tucson.

[2182] (I.H.M.M.)—SISTERS OF THE IMMACULATE HEART OF MARY OF MIRINAE (P)

Founded in 1976 by Rev. Francis Haengman Tiyeng, Mirinae, Diocese of Suwon, Korea, under the motto, Through the Immaculate Heart of Mary to the Most Holy Trinity.

Motherhouse: Surichigol, Korea, South

U.S. Foundation: Immaculate Heart of Mary Pre School, 423 South Commonwealth Ave., Los Angeles, CA 90020. Sr. Cyrilla Kim, I.H.M.M., Sec.

Properties owned and/or sponsored: Sisters of the Immaculate Heart of Mary of Mirinae, Los Angeles, CA.

Ministry in retreat work, school, youth and care for the aged.

Represented in the Archdiocese of Los Angeles.

[2183] (I.H.M.)—SISTERS OF THE IMMACULATE HEART OF MARY MOTHER OF CHRIST, NIGERIA (P)

Founded in Nigeria, West Africa in 1937. Classified with the Pontifical Institute Right in 1973.

Motherhouse-Immaculate Heart Generalate: P.O. Box 1551, Odoakpu-Onitsha Anambra State, Nigeria Tel: 234-706-385-0098; Fax: 234-813-569-4827. Mother Mary Claude Oguh, Mother Gen.

Total in Congregation : 983.

U.S.A. Regional House: Immaculate Heart Convent, 1209A South Walnut Ave., Freeport, IL 61032. Tel: 815-297-8287. Email: guadaluperegion@gmail.com. Sr. Marilyn Umunnakwe, Regl. Supr.

Total number of Sisters in the U.S: 44.

Legal Title: The Congregation of the Sisters of the Immaculate Heart of Mary Mother of Christ - Nigeria.

Ministry in Education; Hospital/Clinic, Pastoral/Social Services; Care of the Aged; Diocesan House Care.

Represented in the Archdioceses of Milwaukee, St. Paul-Minneapolis and Santa Fe and in the Dioceses of Belleville, Des Moines, Gallup, Oklahoma, Phoenix, Rockford and Syracuse.

[2185] (I.H.M.)—SISTERS OF THE IMMACULATE HEART OF MARY OF WICHITA (D)

Founded in Olot, Spain, in 1848. First foundation in United States in 1871. Wichita foundation in 1979. Canonically established as a religious institute of Diocesan right in 2007.

Motherhouse: 3550 N. 167th St. W., Colwich, KS 67030. Tel: 316-722-9316. Mother Mary Magdalene O'Halloran, I.H.M., Gen. Supr.

Total in Community: 28.

Apostolate: Contemplation of the Word and the spread of His Message of salvation through the various works and levels of education and retreat work.

Represented in the Diocese of Wichita.

[2187] (I.C.M.)—INCARNATIO-CONSECRATIO MISSIO (P)

Founded in Vietnam in 1969. First foundation in the United States in 1975.

Motherhouse: 403 Tan Ha, Xa Loc Tien, Huyen Bao Loc, Tinh Lam Dong, Vietnam Tel: 011-84-02633-743-666; Email: tuhoiicm@yahoo.com.

U.S. Regional House: Incarnatio-Consecratio-Missio, Inc., 5185 Jetsail Dr., Orlando, FL 32812. Tel: 407-658-4124; Fax: 407-658-4124; Email: icmorlando@yahoo.com. Sr. Marie Nguyen, I.C.M., Contact Person.

Universal Membership: 149; Aspirants: 12.

Ministry in the areas of Education; Healthcare; Missionary Outreach; Parish Ministries, Social Services and Pastoral Care.

Represented in the Dioceses of Baton Rouge and Orlando. Also in Vietnam.

[2190] (C.V.I.)—CONGREGATION OF THE INCARNATE WORD AND BLESSED SACRAMENT (P)

Founded in France in 1625. First foundation in the United States in 1853.

Motherhouse and Novitiate: Incarnate Word Convent, 3400 Bradford Pl., Houston, TX 77025-1398. Tel: 713-668-0423. Sr. Lauren Beck, C.V.I., Gen. Supr.; Sr. Dympna Lyons, Archivist.

Total in Community: 30.

Ministry in the field of Academic Education; Administration; Pastoral Care; Nursing.

Represented in the Archdiocese of Galveston-Houston.

[2200] (I.W.B.S.)—CONGREGATION OF THE INCARNATE WORD AND BLESSED SACRAMENT (P)

Founded in France in 1625. First founded in the United States in 1853.

Motherhouse and Novitiate: Incarnate Word Convent, 1101 N.E. Water St., Victoria, TX 77901-9233. Tel: 361-575-2266; Fax: 361-575-2165. Sr. M. Stephana Marbach, I.W.B.S., Supr. Gen.; Sr. M. Amata Hollas, I.W.B.S., Community Archivist.

Perpetually Professed: 63; Annually Professed: 1.

Legal Titles: Sisters of the Incarnate Word and Blessed Sacrament, Victoria, Texas; Sisters of the Incarnate Word and Blessed Sacrament of Victoria, Texas Medical and Retirement Trust, Victoria, TX.

Ministry in the field of Education; CCD Centers; Hospitals; Pastoral Ministry.

Properties owned or sponsored: Nazareth Academy, Victoria, TX; Blessed Sacrament Academy, San Antonio, TX; Amor Meus Spirituality Center.

Represented in the Archdiocese of San Antonio and in the Diocese of Victoria. Also in Africa.

[2205] (I.W.B.S.)—SISTERS OF THE INCARNATE WORD AND BLESSED SACRAMENT (P)

Founded in France in 1625. First founded in the United States in 1853.

Motherhouse and Novitiate: Incarnate Word Convent, 5201 Lipes Blvd., Corpus Christi, TX 78413. Tel: 361-882-5413; Fax: 361-880-4152. Sr. Annette Wagner, I.W.B.S., Supr. Gen.

Sisters: 47.

Legal Titles: Convent Academy of the Incarnate Word; Incarnate Word Academy Foundation; Fannie Bluntzer Nason Renewal Center, Inc., Corpus Christi, TX.

Sisters serve and staff: Private High Schools; Private Kindergartens; Montessori; Private Middle Schools; Parochial and Private Elementary Schools; Other ministries include Religious Education; Hospital Ministry; Vocation Ministry; Prison Ministry; Social Service; Diocesan Offices; Adult Education; General Administration; Retreat Ministry; Parish Ministry.

Represented in the Dioceses of Beaumont, Brownsville and Corpus Christi.

[2210] (S.I.W.)—SISTERS OF THE INCARNATE WORD AND BLESSED SACRAMENT (P)

Founded in France in 1625. First foundation in the United States in 1853.

Motherhouse and Novitiate: 6618 Pearl Rd., Parma Heights, OH 44130-3808. Tel: 440-886-6440. Sr. Margaret Taylor, S.I.W., Congregational Leader.

Total in Community: 19.

Ministry includes Evangelization; Elementary and Religious Education; Spiritual Ministry (Retreat and Spiritual Direction); Pastoral Ministry in Parishes, Hospitals and Nursing Homes.

Represented in the Diocese of Cleveland.

[2230] (C.I.J.)—CONGREGATION OF THE INFANT JESUS (D)

Founded in France in 1835. First foundation in the United States in 1905.

General Motherhouse: 984 North Village Ave., Rockville Centre, NY 11570. Tel: 516-823-3800; Tel: 516-823-3808; Fax: 516-594-0412. Sr. Mary Louise Kelly, C.I.J., Pres.

Total in Community: 35.

Corporate Title: Nursing Sisters of the Sick Poor Inc. Ministry in the fields of Nursing; Social Work; Physical Therapy; Pastoral Care; Chaplains; Retreat Work; Parish Ministry; and other works related to Health Services.

Represented in the Dioceses of Brooklyn and Rockville Centre.

[2250] (O.S.B.)—CONGREGATION OF BENEDICTINES OF JESUS CRUCIFIED (P)

Founded in France in 1930. First foundation in the United States in Devon, PA in 1955. Second foundation in Newport, RI in 1962. Both foundations merged in Branford, CT in 2001 at the Monastery of the Glorious Cross.

General Motherhouse: Brou-sur-Chantereine, France Sr. Anne Sophie Robitaillie, Prioress Gen.

U.S. Foundations: Monastery of the Glorious Cross, 61 Burban Dr., Branford, CT 06405-4003. Tel: 203-315-9964; Tel: 203-315-0106; Fax: 203-488-0352; Email: mzwenker_osb@hotmail.com; Web: benedictinesjc.org. Sr. Marie-Zita Wenker, O.S.B., Prioress.

Total number in the U.S: 9.

Represented in the Archdiocese of Hartford.

[2265] (S.V.)—SISTERS OF LIFE

Founded 1991.

Annunciation (Motherhouse): 38 Montebello Rd., Suffern, NY 10901. Tel: 845-357-3547; Fax: 845-357-5040. Email: sistersoflife@sistersoflife.org. Mother Agnes Mary Donovan, S.V., Supr. Gen.

Legal Title: Sisters of Life, Inc. Ministry: to advance a sense of the sacredness of human life in all of society by way of prayer and missions 1) serving vulnerable, pregnant women; 2) providing programs of retreats and intercessory prayer 3) spiritual accompaniment and retreats for women suffering after abortion; 4) evangelization on university and college campuses; 5) bringing the message of the sacredness of human life and the sanctity of human love to all; 6) service to the Church through staffing of the Respect Life Office of the Archdiocese of New York.

Represented in the Archdioceses of Denver, New York, Philadelphia and Washington DC and in the Diocese of Bridgeport. Also in Canada.

[2270] (L.C.M.)—LITTLE COMPANY OF MARY SISTERS - USA (P)

Founded in England in 1877. First foundation in the United States in 1893.

Generalate: Little Company of Mary Generalate, 28 Trinity Crescent, Tooting Bec London, England, SW17 7AE.

Universal total in Congregation: 205; Final Professed Sisters: 197; Temporary Professed Sisters: 5; Novices: 1; Candidates: 2.

Provincial Office: Region of the Immaculate Conception, The Little Company of Mary, 9350 S. California Ave., Evergreen Park, IL 60805. Tel: 708-229-5490. Sr. Carol Pacini, L.C.M., Region Leader.

Total in Community: 13.

Ministry in Hospitals and Health Care; Pastoral/Parish areas.

Properties owned: Little Company of Mary Hospital and Health Care Centers, Evergreen Park, IL; Memorial Hospital and Health Care Center, Jasper, IN; Little Company of Mary Health Services (Little Company of Mary Hospital, Torrance, CA and San Pedro Peninsula Hospital, San Pedro, CA)

Represented in the Archdioceses of Chicago and Los Angeles and in the Diocese of Evansville.

[2280] (P.F.M.)—LITTLE FRANCISCANS OF MARY (U.S.)

Founded in the United States in 1889.

General Motherhouse: Baie St. Paul (Charlevoix), Canada Sr. Francoise Duchesne, P.F.M., Supr. Gen.

American Region: 12 Jones St., Apt. 1, Worcester, MA 01604. Tel: 508-755-0878. Sr. Jacquelyn Alix, Treas. Total number in Congregation including Canada and the United States: 160.

Represented in the Dioceses of Portland (In Maine) and Worcester.

[2300] (L.S.I.C.)—LITTLE SERVANT SISTERS OF THE IMMACULATE CONCEPTION (P)

(Congregatio Sororum Servularum Beatae Mariae Virginis Immaculatae Conceptae)

Founded by Blessed Edmund Bojanowski in Poland on May 3, 1850. First foundation in the United States on December 8, 1926.

General Motherhouse: Stara Wies 460, 36-200 Brzozow, skr. poczt. 66, woj. Podkarpackie, Poland Mother Beata Chwistek, L.S.I.C., Supr. Gen.

Total in Congregation : 1240.

Holy Trinity Province: Little Servants Sisters of the Immaculate Conception Provincialate-Novitiate, 1000 Cropwell Rd., Cherry Hill, NJ 08003. Tel: 856-424-1962; Fax: 856-424-5333; Email: lsic.prov@verizon.net; Web: www.littleservantsisters.com. Mother Dorota Baranowska, L.S.I.C., Supr. Prov.; Sr. Bozena Tyborowska, L.S.I.C., Vocation Dir.

Professed Sisters: 68; Novices: 1.

Legal Titles: Congregation of the Little Servant Sisters of the Blessed Virgin Mary of the Immaculate Conception (Congregatio Sororum Servularum Beatae Mariae Virginis Immaculatae Conceptae), (Properties owned) Immaculate Conception Convent: Provincialate-Novitiate, Cherry Hill, NJ; Blessed Edmund Early Childhood Education Center, Cherry Hill, NJ; Marian Residence, Cherry Hill, NJ; St. John's Retreat House, Atlantic City, NJ; St. Joseph's Convent, Woodbridge, NJ; St. Joseph's Senior Home (Assisted Living and Nursing Center), Woodbridge, NJ.

Ministry: all levels of Religious Education, Pre-school and Academic Education; Parish Work; Social Work, Hospital Pastoral Care; Visiting Home Nursing Service; Senior Residential Homes; Assisted Living; Skilled Nursing Homes; Retreat House; Prayer Groups & Youth Ministry.

Represented in the Archdiocese of Newark and in the Dioceses of Camden, Metuchen and Palm Beach. Also in the Philippines.

[2310] (L.S.A.)—LITTLE SISTERS OF THE ASSUMPTION (P)

Founded in France in 1865. First foundation in the United States in 1891.

General Motherhouse: 57 rue Violet, Paris, France, 75015. Sr. Marie Francoise Phelippeau, Supr. Gen.

United States Territory: Little Sisters of the Assumption, 475 E. 115th St., 1st Fl., New York, NY 10029. Tel: 212-289-4014; Web: www.littlesisters.org. Sr. Annette Allain, L.S.A., Prov.

Total in Community: 14.

Ministry in Home Health; Community Development Supportive Family Services Located in Poverty Areas; Services are predominantly provided in the Home Setting and Center-Based.

Represented in the Archdioceses of Boston and New York and in the Diocese of Worcester.

[2330] (L.S.J.)—LITTLE SISTERS OF JESUS (P)

Founded in the Sahara in 1939. First foundation in the United States in 1952.

General Motherhouse: Rome, Italy Sr. Maria Ferrari, Prioress Gen.

Universal total in Congregation: 1235.

U.S. Regional House: 400 N. Streeper St., Baltimore, MD 21224-1230. Tel: 410-327-7823. Sr. Rita Farina, L.S.J., Reg. Dir.

Total number in U.S: 25.

Represented in the Archdioceses of Anchorage, Baltimore and Washington and in the Dioceses of Altoona-Johnstown and Paterson.

[2331] (L.S.J.M.)—LITTLE SISTERS OF JESUS AND MARY (D)

Founded in the United States in 1974. Sr. Mary Elizabeth Gintling, Foundress.

Joseph House: P.O. Box 1755, Salisbury, MD 21802. Tel: 410-543-1645; Fax: 410-742-3390. Sr. Constance R. Ladd, L.S.J.M., Supr. Gen.

Total in Community: 7.

Represented in the Diocese of Wilmington.

[2340] (L.S.P.)—LITTLE SISTERS OF THE POOR (P)

Founded in France in 1839. First foundation in the United States in 1868.

General Motherhouse: 3 La Tour St. Joseph, 35190, St. Pern, France Mother Maria del Monte Auxiliadora, Supr. Gen.

Province of Brooklyn (1868): Queen of Peace Residence, 110-30 221st St., Queens Village, NY 11429. Mother Alice Marie Jones, L.S.P., Prov.

Total number in Province: 101.

Ministry in Homes for the Aged.

Represented in the Archdioceses of Boston, Hartford, Philadelphia and New York and in the Dioceses of Brooklyn, Metuchen, Paterson, Providence and Scranton.

Province of Baltimore: Little Sisters of the Poor, 601 Maiden Choice Ln., Catonsville, MD 21228-3698. Tel: 410-744-9367; Fax: 410-747-0601. Sr. Loraine Marie Maguire, L.S.P., Prov.

Total number in Province: 101.

Ministry in Homes for the Aged.

Represented in the Archdioceses of Baltimore, Cincinnati, Indianapolis, Mobile and Washington and in the Dioceses of Pittsburgh, Richmond, Toledo and Wilmington.

Province of Chicago: Little Sisters of the Poor, Chicago Province, Inc., 80 W. Northwest Hwy., Palatine, IL 60067-3582. Tel: 847-358-5700; Fax: 847-934-6852. Sr. Maria Christine Lynch, L.S.P., Prov.

Total number in Province: 106.

Ministry in Homes for the Aged.

Represented in the Archdioceses of Chicago, Denver, Los Angeles, Louisville, St. Louis, St. Paul-Minneapolis and San Francisco and in the Dioceses of Gallup and Kansas City-St. Joseph.

[2345] (P.O.S.C.)—LITTLE WORKERS OF THE SACRED HEARTS (P)

Founded in Italy in 1892. First foundation in the U.S. in 1948.

General House: Via dei Pamphili 3, Rome, Italy, 00152. Motherhouse and Novitiate: Our Lady of Grace Convent, 635 Glenbrook Rd., Stamford, CT 06906-1409. Tel: 203-348-5531. Sr. Gesuina Gencarelli, P.O.S.C., U.S. Delegate & Supr.

Ministry in Day Care; Catechetics; Preschool.

Represented in the Archdioceses of Philadelphia and Washington and in the Diocese of Bridgeport.

[2350] (S.L.W.)—SISTERS OF THE LIVING WORD (D)

Founded in the United States in 1975.

General Motherhouse: The Living Word Center, 800 N. Fernandez Ave. B, Arlington Heights, IL 60004-5336. Tel: 847-577-5972; Fax: 847-577-5980; Web: www.slw.org. Congregational Leadership: Sr. Sharon Glumb, S.L.W.; Sr. Carrie Miller, S.L.W.; Sr. Kristine Vorenkamp, S.L.W.

Total in Community: 55.

Ministry in the field of Academic and Religious Education; Health Care; Parish Ministry and Social Services.

Represented in the Archdioceses of Chicago, New Orleans, St. Louis and St. Paul-Minneapolis and in the Dioceses of Alexandria and Tampa.

[2360] (S.L.)—SISTERS OF LORETTO AT THE FOOT OF THE CROSS (P)

Founded in America in 1812.

General Motherhouse & Novitiate: Loretto Motherhouse and Novitiate, Nerinx, KY 40049. Tel: 270-865-5811.

Administrative Office: 4000 S. Wadsworth Blvd, Littleton, CO 80123-1308. Tel: 303-783-0450; Fax: 303-783-0611. Sr. Pearl McGivney, S.L., Pres.

Legal Title: Loretto Literary and Benevolent Institution.

Ministry in the field of Academic and Religious Education at all levels; Specialized Education; Health Care-Aging; Community Administration; Pastoral Ministry; Social Justice-Social Service; Administration; Medicine and Nursing; Prayer Retreats; Clerical Offices; Consultants; Spirituality Center.

Represented in the Archdioceses of Denver, Galveston-Houston Indianapolis, Louisville, St. Louis, San Francisco, Santa Fe and Washington and in the Dioceses of El Paso, Kansas City-St. Joseph, Knoxville, Lexington and Rockford.

[2370] (I.B.V.M.)—INSTITUTE OF THE BLESSED VIRGIN MARY (LORETTO SISTERS) (P)

Founded in St. Omer, Belgium, 1609. First foundation in Canada in 1847; in the United States in 1880.

Generalate: Casa Loreto, Via Massaua 3, Rome, Italy, 00162. Sr. Noelle Corscadden, I.B.V.M., Institute Leader.

Total in Congregation : 713.

Province Office United States: P.O. Box 508, Wheaton, IL 60187. Tel: 630-665-3814; Fax: 630-868-2924. Development Office Email: development@ibvm.org. Sr. Judy Illig, I.B.V.M., Prov. Leader. Total in Community: 53.

Ministries: Province Offices; Loretto Development Office; High School; Grade School; Mary Ward Center; Pastoral Ministry; English as a Second Language; Social Work; Spiritual Direction, Art and Spirituality, Vocation Ministry.

Properties owned: Houses in California, Arizona and Illinois.

Represented in the Archdiocese of Chicago and Milwaukee and in the Dioceses of Joliet, Marquette, Phoenix, Sacramento and Tucson.

[2385] (L.H.C.N.T.)—LOVERS OF THE HOLY CROSS OF NHA TRANG (D)

Founded in Vietnam in 1950. First Foundation in the United States in 2003.

Motherhouse: HT25 Cam Hoa Cam Ranh, Khanh Hoa, Nha Trang, Vietnam

Regional House: 12323 Alondra Blvd., Norwalk, CA 90650. Tel: 562-809-1570; 562-567-1502. Sr. Mary Marian Pham, L.H.C.N.T., Rel. Supr.

Total in Congregation: 502; U.S. Community: 9.

Ministry in Pastoral Care: religious education for youth and/or adults, faith formation.

[2390] (L.H.C.)—LOVERS OF THE HOLY CROSS SISTERS (D)

Founded in 1670 in Vietnam by Bishop Pierre Lambert de la Motte. First foundation in the United States in 1976. Established as an autonomous institute of Consecrated Life of Diocesan Right in 1992.

General Motherhouse: Holy Cross Convent, 14700 South Van Ness Ave., Gardena, CA 90249. Tel: 310-768-1906; Tel: 310-516-0271. Sr. Thanh Hao Nguyen, L.H.C., Supr. Gen.

Sisters: 65; Novices: 3; Postulants: 3; Aspirants: 16; Oblates: 1.

Legal Title: Lovers of the Holy Cross Sisters, Inc.

Represented in the Archdiocese of Los Angeles and in the Dioceses of Orange and San Bernardino.

[2392] (L.H.C.)—LOVERS OF THE HOLY CROSS SISTERS (P) (Sisters, Lovers of the Holy Cross)

Founded in Vietnam in 1670 by Bishop Pierre Lambert de la Motte. First foundation in the United States in 1975.

U.S. Foundation: St. Theresa Convent, 43 Crown Ln., Westbury, NY 11590. Tel: 516-333-9464. Sr. Theresa Nguyen, L.H.C., Supr.

Legal Title: Sisters, Lovers of the Holy Cross, Inc.

Represented in the Diocese of Rockville Centre.

[2400] (M.S.)—MARIAN SISTERS OF THE DIOCESE OF LINCOLN (D)

Marycrest Motherhouse: 6765 N. 112th, Waverly, NE 68462. Tel: 402-786-2750; Fax: 402-786-7256; Email: sr.annmarie-zierke@cdolinc.net. Sr. Ann Marie Zierke, M.S., Major Supr.

Total in Community: 36.

Ministry in the field of Education; Special Education; Health Care; Catechetics; Social Work.

Represented in the Diocese of Lincoln.

[2410] (M.S.C.)—CONGREGATION OF THE MARIANITES OF HOLY CROSS (P)

Founded in France in 1841. First foundation in the United States in 1843.

Congregational Administration Headquarters: 21388 Smith Rd., Covington, LA 70435. Tel: 985-893-5201; Web: www.marianites.org. Sr. Ann Lacour, M.S.C., Congregational Leader.

Total Number in North America: 93.

Ministry in Diocesan Administration and Parishes; Social & Health Services; and the field of Education.

Legal Holdings or Titles: University of Holy Cross; Prompt Succor Nursing Home, Opelousas, LA; C'est la Vie (Senior Citizen Independent Living Units), Opelousas, LA.

Represented in the Archdiocese of New Orleans and in the Dioceses of Alexandria, Baton Rouge, Houma-Thibodaux, Lafayette (LA) and Trenton. Also in Burkina-Faso, Canada, France and Ireland.

[2420] (S.M.S.M.)—MARIST MISSIONARY SISTERS (MISSIONARY SISTERS OF THE SOCIETY OF MARY) INC. (P)

Founded in France in 1845 for the mission in the South Pacific. First foundation in the United States in Boston, MA in 1922.

Motherhouse: Via Cassia, 1243, Rome, Italy, 00189.

North American Regional Office: 349 Grove St., Waltham, MA 02453. Tel: 781-893-0149; Fax: 781-899-6838; Email: admin@maristsmsm.org. Sr. Mary Jane Kenney, S.M.S.M., Regl. Leader, Region of the Americas.

Universal Total in Congregation: 397; Total in Region of Americas: 95.

Legal Title: Missionary Sisters of the Society of Mary

Ministries include: catechetical, medical, educational and social services; pastoral ministry; formation of laity for leadership and a great concern for the poorest and most neglected. Working by preference among people of different cultures and languages, to bring about greater understanding, dignity and mutual respect. Formation is international with the novitiate in Belmont, MA.

Represented in 25 countries around the world including the Archdiocese of Boston and in the Dioceses of Oakland, San Bernardino and San Diego. Also in Jamaica and Peru.

[2440] (S.M.I.)—CATECHIST SISTERS OF MARY IMMACULATE HELP OF CHRISTIANS, INC. (P)

Catechist Sisters of Mary Immaculate, Help of Christians Founded in India in 1948 by the late Bishop Louis LaRavoire Morrow, Bishop of Krishnagar, India.

General Motherhouse: Krishnagar, Nadia Dist., West Bengal, India, 741 101. Sr. Dina Vellamaruthunkal, S.M.I., Supr. Gen.

Universal total in Congregation: 665.

U.S. Foundation (1981): Sisters of Mary Immaculate, 118 Park Rd., Leechburg, PA 15656. Tel: 724-845-2828; Email: lbgsmi@gmail.com. Sr. Jessy George, S.M.I., Delegation Supr.

Total in Community:5.

Legal Holdings and Titles: Bishop Morrow Personal Care Home, Leechburg, PA

[2450] (S.M.P.)—SISTERS OF MARY OF THE PRESENTATION (P)

Founded in France. First foundation in the United States in 1903.

General Motherhouse: 27 Rue de la Barriere, B.P. 31, 22250 Broons, France.

U.S. Provincial House & Novitiate at Maryvale: 3150 116A Ave. SE, Valley City, ND 58072-9620. Tel: 701-845-2864. Email: maryvaleSMP@gmail.com. Sr. Suzanne Stahl, Regl. Supr.

Total in Community: 18.

Ministry in the field of Religious and Academic Education; Retreat Centers; Parish Ministry; Hospitals, Nursing Homes and Home Health Agency.

Properties Sponsored: St. Margaret's Health, Spring Valley, IL; Prairieland Home Health Agency, Spring Valley, IL; St. Andrew Health Center, Bottineau, ND; Presentation Medical Center, Rolla, ND; St. Aloisius Medical Center, Harvey, ND; Ave Maria Village, Jamestown, ND; Maryhill Manor, Enderlin, ND; Rosewood on Broadway, Fargo, ND; Villa Maria, Fargo, ND; Sheyenne Care Center, Valley City, ND

Represented in the Dioceses of Bismarck, Fargo and Peoria.

[2460] (S.M.R.)—SOCIETY OF MARY REPARATRIX (P)

Founded in France in 1857. First foundation in the United States in 1908.

Generalate: Society Di Maria Riparatrice, Via dei Lucchesi 3, Rome, Italy, 00187. Sr. Aurora Torres Hernandez, Supr. Gen.

Total International Membership: 550.

U.S. Region: 10065 Northway Ave., Allen Park, MI 48101. Tel: 313-383-3312. Region Team Sr. Veronica Blake, S.M.R.; Sr. Judy Frasinetti; Sr. Ann Kasparek, S.M.R.

Total in Community: 14.

Represented in the Archdioceses of Detroit and New York and in the Diocese of Brooklyn.

[2470] (M.M.)—MARYKNOLL SISTERS OF ST. DOMINIC (P)

Founded in New York 1912.

Orientation Program: Maryknoll Sisters, Sr. Shu Chen Wu, M.M., Dir.

Center: Maryknoll Sisters Center, Maryknoll, NY 10545-0311. Tel: 914-941-7575. Sr. Antoinette Gutzler, M.M., Community Pres.; Sr. Numeriana Mojado, M.M., Vice Pres.; Sr. Anastasia Lott, M.M., Gen. Sec.; Sr. Teruko Ito, M.M., Team Member. Center Coordinators: Sr. Connie Krautkremer, M.M.; Sr. Mary Ellen Kempken, M.M.; Sr. Janet Hockman, M.M.; Sr. Genie Natividad, M.M.

Total in Congregation : 372.

Legal Titles and Holdings: Maryknoll Sisters of St. Dominic, Inc.; Maryknoll Mission Institute.

Represented in the Archdioceses of Baltimore, Boston, Chicago, Cincinnati, Detroit, Galveston-Houston, Hartford, Los Angeles, New York, Portland in Oregon, San Antonio and Washington and in the Dioceses of Baker, Brownsville, Charlotte, Gallup, Harrisburg, Honolulu, Kansas City-St. Joseph, Madison, Oakland, Palm Beach, Phoenix, Providence and San Jose.

[2480] (M.M.M.)—MEDICAL MISSIONARIES OF MARY (P)

Founded in Nigeria in 1937. First United States Foundation in 1950.

Congregation Centre: Rosemount, Booterstown Ave., Blackrock. County Dublin, Ireland Sr. Siobhan Corkery, M.M.M., Congregational Leader. Medical Missionaries of Mary: 3410 W. 60th Pl., Chicago, IL 60629-3602. Tel: 773-737-3458. Email: mmmchi2015@gmail.com; Web: www.mmmworldwide.org. Sr. Joanne Bierl, M.M.M., Area Leader, Area of the Americas.

Total in Congregation : 320.

Represented in the Archdioceses of Boston, Chicago and in the Dioceses of Richmond and San Diego.

[2490] (M.M.S.)—MEDICAL MISSION SISTERS (P)

Generalate: London, England Sr. Irene Fernandez, M.M.S., Society Coord.

Universal total in Congregation: 500.

North American Headquarters (1925): 8400 Pine Rd., Philadelphia, PA 19111. Tel: 215-742-6100; North America Coordinating Team: Sr. Frances Vaughan, M.M.S., Sr. Margaret Moran, M.M.S.; Sr. Mary Kirkhoff, M.M.S.; Sr. Katherine Baltazar, M.M.S.; Sr. Sue Sopczynski, M.M.S.

Total number in North America: 89.

Legal Titles: Society of Catholic Medical Missionaries, Inc.; Society of Catholic Medical Missionaries Generalate, Inc.

Represented in the Archdioceses of Boston, Hartford, Philadelphia and Santa Fe and in the Dioceses of Camden, Harrisburg, Palm Beach, Richmond and Tucson.

[2500] (M.S.J.)—MEDICAL SISTERS OF ST. JOSEPH (P)

Founded in Kerala, South India, 1946.

General Motherhouse: Dharmagiri, P.O. Kothamangalam, Kerala, India, 686691. Mother Pia, M.S.J., Supr. Gen.

U.S. Foundation (1985): Medical Sisters of Joseph, 3435 E. Funston, Wichita, KS 67218. Tel: 316-686-4746. Sr. Laly Josmy George, M.S.J., Supr.

Total in Congregation : 900.

Ministry as Health Care Apostolates.

Represented in the Diocese of Wichita.

[2510] (M.M.B.)—MERCEDARIAN MISSIONARIES OF BERRIZ (P)

Order originated in Berriz, Spain 1548. Transformed into a missionary institute in 1930 in Spain. First foundation in U.S. in 1946 in Kansas City, MO.

Total Number of Sisters in the Institute: 383.

Generalate: Mercedarie Missionarie di Berriz, Via Iberia 8, Rome, Italy, 00183. Tel: 39-068-41-3441. Sr. Lourdes Garostola, M.M.B., Gen. Coord.

U.S. Regional House: Mercedarian Missionaries of Berriz, 2115 Maturanna Dr., #101B, Liberty, MO 64068-7985. Tel: 816-781-8202; Fax: 816-781-8205; Email: mmbus@sbcglobal.net; Web: mmberriz.org. Sr. Sandra Thibodeaux, M.M.B., Reg. Coord.

Total number in Region: 10; Total number in Institute: 383.

Ministries in Health, Pastoral Care and Religious Education.

Property sponsored: Our Lady of Mercy Country Home. Liberty, MO.

Represented in the Diocese of Kansas City-St. Joseph. Also in Africa, Japan, Taiwan, Philippines, Guam, Federated States of Micronesia, Republic of Palau, Commonwealth of the Northern Marianas, Peru, Ecuador, Guatemala, Mexico, Democratic Republic of Congo, Zambia, Spain and Rome, Italy.

[2519] (R.S.M.)—RELIGIOUS SISTERS OF MERCY OF ALMA, MICHIGAN (P)

The Religious Sisters of Mercy of Alma was officially founded on September 1, 1973; Accepted for a foundation in Saginaw Diocese on January 25, 1974; Official pontifical status and approval of Constitutions on June 18, 1982. Final approval of Constitutions May 31, 1991.

Motherhouse and Novitiate: Religious Sisters of Mercy, 1965 Michigan Ave., Alma, MI 48801. Tel: 989-463-6035. Email: religious.sisters.of.mercy@rsmofalma.org. Mother Mary McGreevy, R.S.M., Supr.

Total in Community: 94.

Represented in the Archdioceses of Denver, Philadelphia, Seattle, St. Louis and Washington and in the Dioceses of Knoxville, Lake Charles, Lansing, Phoenix, Saginaw, Toledo, Tulsa and Winona-Rochester. Also in Australia, Germany, Italy and Scotland.

[2549] (R.S.M.)—SISTERS OF MERCY (P)

Founded in Ireland in 1831. First foundation in the United States in 1956.

General Motherhouse: Congregation of the Sisters of Mercy, 13/14 Moyle Park, Clondalkin, Dublin 22, Ireland Tel: 01-467-3737. Sr. Margaret Casey, Congregational Leader.

Total in Congregation : 2200.

U.S. Provincial House: Sisters of Mercy, 1075 Bermuda Dr., Redlands, CA 92374. Tel: 909-798-4747; Fax: 909-798-5300. Sr. Rosaline O'Connor, R.S.M., Prov. Leader.

Professed Sisters in U.S. Province: 52.

Legal Title: Congregation of the Sisters of Mercy-San Bernardino.

Ministry in the field of Religious Education; Parishes; Social Services; Diocesan Offices

Represented in the Archdioceses of Chicago, Miami and in the Dioceses of Memphis, Mobile, Monterey, Oakland, Orlando, Palm Beach, Providence, Sacramento, St. Augustine, San Diego, San Jose, Santa Rosa, San Bernardino and Venice.

U.S. Foundation: St. Joan of Arc, 500 S.W. 4th Ave., Boca Raton, FL 33432. Tel: 561-368-6655. Sr. Rosaline O'Connor, R.S.M., Prov. Leader.

Professed Sisters: 2.

Represented in the Diocese of Palm Beach.

[2575] (R.S.M.)—SISTERS OF MERCY OF THE AMERICAS (P)

Catherine McAuley founded the Sisters of Mercy in Dublin, Ireland, in 1831. Ten years later, she received confirmation of the Rule by Pope Gregory XVI. In 1843 the Sisters of Mercy established their first U.S.A. foundation in Pittsburgh, followed by various amalgamations.

In 1991 the members of the nine provinces of the Union and of 16 other Mercy congregations founded the Sisters of Mercy of the Americas consisting of 25 regional communities.

In 2009, the Sisters of Mercy of the Americas completed a restructuring of the 25 Regional Communities into six communities within the Institute: Caribbean, Central America, South America Community; Mid-Atlantic Community; Northeast Community; New York, Pennsylvania, Pacific West Community; West Midwest Community and South Central Community. The Sisters of Mercy of the Americas are represented in: Argentina, the Bahamas, Belize, Bolivia, Canada, Chile, Guam, Guatemala, Guyana, Haiti, Honduras, Ireland, Jamaica, Panama, Peru, the Philippines, Puerto Rico, South Africa, the United States of America, and West Africa.

Institute Administrative Offices: Mercy Education System of the Americas, 8380 Colesville Rd., #300, Silver Spring, MD 20910-6264. Tel: 301-587-0423; Fax: 301-587-0533.

Total in Congregation : 2901.

Legal Title: Sisters of Mercy of the Americas, Inc.

Mercy Volunteer Corps, Inc. is separately incorporated to conduct a volunteer lay ministry program to further the works of mercy.

Conference for Mercy High Education, Inc., is separately incorporated for the purpose of support, coordination and facilitation of the ministry and educational mission of the institutions of higher education recognized by the Sisters of Mercy of the Americas. Institute Leadership Team: Sr. Patricia McDermott, R.S.M., Pres.; Sr. Eileen Campbell, R.S.M., Vice Pres.; Sr. Anne Curtis, R.S.M.; Sr. Mary Patricia Garvin, R.S.M.; Sr. Deborah Troillett, R.S.M.

Sisters of Mercy of the Americas, CCASA (Caribbean, Central America, South America) Community: 8380 Colesville Rd., #300, Silver Spring, MD 20910-6264. Tel: 301-587-0423; Fax: 301-587-0533. Community Leadership Team: Sr. Julie Matthews, R.S.M., Pres.; Sr. Lillian Silva, R.S.M.; Sr. Angelina Caballero Mitre, R.S.M.

Total in Community: 65.

Legal Title: Sisters of Mercy of the Americas, CCASA Community, Inc.

Sisters of Mercy of the Americas, Northeast Community, Inc: 15 Highland View Rd., Cumberland, RI 02864-1124. Tel: 401-333-6333; Fax: 401-333-6450. Community Leadership Team: Sr. Maureen Mitchell, R.S.M., Pres.; Sr. Peg Sullivan, R.S.M., Vice Pres.; Sr. Ruth Kelly, R.S.M.; Sr. Patricia Moriarty, R.S.M.; Daniel Justynski, Dir. Real Estate Portfolio; Sr. Mary Alice Synkewecz, R.S.M., Dir. Justice & Chair; Mary Lauzon, Dir. Ministry; Sr. Kathleen Sisson, R.S.M., Incorporation Minister; Lisa Driscoll, Dir. Human Resources; Jill Gemma, CFO & COO; Jennifer Giuffrida, Dir. Long Term Care & Retirement Strategy; Beth Watson, Dir. Develop.

Vowed Members: 493; Assoc. Members: 425.

Legal Title: Sisters of Mercy of the Americas-Northeast Community, Inc.

Ministry in the field of spirituality & retreat work; diocesan & pastoral services; peace & justice initiatives; parish ministry; religious & academic education at all levels; hospital; literacy centers; social services; counseling services; transitional houses & foreign missionary work.

Sponsored Ministries: Colleges & Universities: Maria College, Albany, NY; St. Joseph's College, Standish, ME; University of St. Joseph, West Hartford, CT; Salve Regina University, Newport, RI.

Secondary Education: Lauralton Hall, Milford, CT; St. Mary Academy, Bay View, PreK-12, Riverside, RI.

Elementary Education: Mater Christi School, Burlington, VT; Mercymount Country Day School, Cumberland, RI; Mount Saint Mary Academy, Manchester, NH.

Hospitals & Health Care Services: Northern Light Health/Mercy Hospital, Portland, ME; McAuley Residence, Portland, ME; Gary's House, Portland, ME.

Social Services: Circles of Mercy, Albany, NY; McAuley Corporation, Providence, RI; Mercy Connections, Burlington, VT; Mercy Ecology Inc., Cumberland, RI.

Spirituality Centers & Retreat Houses: Mercy Center at Madison, Madison, CT; Mercy Ecology Center Inc., Cumberland, RI.

Represented in the Archdioceses of Baltimore, Boston, Chicago, Denver, Hartford, Miami, New York, Omaha, Philadelphia, Santa Fe, St. Louis, and Washington and in the Dioceses of Albany, Bridgeport, Brooklyn, Burlington, Fall River, Manchester, Norwich, Orlando, Palm Beach, Pittsburgh, Portland in Maine, Providence and Trenton. Also in Haiti and Honduras.

Institute of the Sisters of Mercy of the Americas, Mid-Atlantic Community, Inc: 273 Willoughy Ave., Brooklyn, NY 11205. Tel: 718-622-5750. Sr. Patricia Vetrano, R.S.M., Pres.

Total in Community: 926.

Properties owned or sponsored: MercyFirst, Angel Guardian Campus; Mercy Home for Children; Mercy First, Syosset Campus; Our Lady of Mercy Academy, Syosset

Sisters serve and staff: Elementary and High Schools; Institutions of Higher Education; Child Care Institutions; Pastoral Ministry Programs and Spirituality and Retreat Programs.

Represented in the Archdioceses of Baltimore and Detroit and in the Dioceses of Brooklyn, Orlando and Rockville Centre.

Sisters of Mercy of the Americas (New York, Pennsylvania, Pacific West Community: 625 Abbott Rd., Buffalo, NY 14220. Tel: 716-826-5051; Fax: 716-826-1518; Email: jcourneen@mercynyppaw.org; Web: www.mercynyppaw.org.

Total in Community: 396; Associates: 399.

Legal Title: Sisters of Mercy of the Americas - New York, Pennsylvania, Pacific West Community, Inc.

Ministry in the fields of spirituality and retreat work, diocesan and pastoral services, peace and justice initiatives, parish ministry; religious and academic education at all levels; hospitals and health care services/facilities, literacy centers, hospitality houses, social services; counseling services; transitional houses and foreign missionary work.

Properties owned sponsored or co-sponsored: Carlow University, Pittsburgh, PA; Mercyhurst College, Erie, PA; Trocaire College, Buffalo, NY; Our Lady of Mercy High School, Rochester, NY; Mercyhurst Preparatory School, Erie, PA; Mt. Mercy Academy, Buffalo, NY; Notre Dame High School, Elmira, NY; The Campus School of Carlow University, Pittsburgh, PA; Mercy Center of the Arts, Erie, PA; Pittsburgh Mercy Health System, Pittsburgh, PA; Holy Cross Hospital, Ft. Lauderdale, FL; Catholic Health System, Buffalo, NY; Mercy Terrace Apartments, Erie, PA; Erie DAWN, Inc., Erie, PA; Mercy Center for Women, Erie, PA; Sisters Place, Pittsburgh, PA dba Mercy Outreach Center; Mercy Hilltop Center, Inc. Erie, PA; Mercy Prayer Center, Rochester, NY; Mercy Outreach Ministries Inc.

Represented in the Archdioceses of Miami, San Juan and Washington and in the Dioceses of Bridgeport, Buffalo, Erie, Fall River, Orlando, Palm Beach, Phoenix, Pittsburgh, Rochester and Youngstown. Also in the Philippines.

Community Leadership Team: Sr. JoAnne Courneen, R.S.M., Pres.; Sr. Patricia Prinzing, R.S.M., Vice Pres.; Sr. Sheila Marie Walsh, R.S.M.; Sr. Natalie Rossi, R.S.M.; Sr. Sheila Stevenson, R.S.M.

Mid-Atlantic Community, Convent of Mercy: Convent of the Sisters of Mercy, 515 Montgomery Ave., Merion Station, PA 19066. Tel: 610-664-6650; Fax: 610-664-3429; Email: info@marcymidatlantic.org.

Vowed Members: 808; Associates: 989.
Legal Title: Sisters of Mercy of the Americas, Mid-Atlantic Community, Inc.
Ministry in the field of religious and academic education at all levels; health care services and facilities; social services; parish and pastoral ministry; spirituality & retreat work; housing; counseling & foreign missionary work.
Sponsored Ministries: Colleges and Universities: Georgian Court University, Lakewood, NJ; Gwynedd Mercy University, Gwynedd Valley, PA: Misericordia University, Dallas, PA; Mt. Aloysius College, Cresson PA.
Secondary Education: Our Lady of Mercy Academy, Syosset, NY; St. Catharine Academy, Bronx, NY; Mount Saint Mary Academy, Watchung, NJ; Gwynedd Mercy Academy, Gwynedd Valley, PA; Merion Mercy Academy, Merion, PA; Mercy Career and Technical School, Philadelphia, PA; Walsingham Academy, Williamsburg, VA.
Elementary Education: Sisters Academy, Asbury Park, NJ; Waldron Mercy Academy, Merion, PA; Gwynedd Mercy Academy, Gwynedd Valley, PA; Walsingham Academy, Williamsburg, VA.
Social Services: Mercy Home, Brooklyn, NY; Mercy First, Syosset, NY; Mercy Consultation Services, Dallas, PA; Project Remain, Wilkes Barre, PA; Catherine McAuley Center, Scranton, PA; Mercy Center, Asbury Park, NJ; Mercy Center Bronx, NY; The Pines at Mercy Center, Dallas, PA; Dorothy Bennett Center, Brooklyn, NY; Mercy Services, Wilkes Barre, PA; Mercy Care for the Adirondacks, Inc., Lake Placid, NY.
Spiritual Centers and Retreat Houses: Mount St. Mary House of Prayer, Watchung, NJ; Cranaleith Spiritual Center, Philadelphia, PA.
Represented in the Archdioceses of Baltimore, Hartford, Indianapolis, New Orleans, Newark, Philadelphia, St. Louis, New York and Washington, DC and in the Dioceses of Allentown, Altoona-Johnstown, Brooklyn, Camden, Detroit, Greensburg, Harrisburg, Little Rock, Metuchen, Oakland, Ogdensburg, Orlando, Paterson, Phoenix, Raleigh, Richmond, Rockville Centre, Savannah, Scranton, Trenton, Wilmington and Worcester. Also in Georgetown, Guyana.
Community Leadership Team: Sr. Patricia Vetrano, R.S.M., Pres.; Sr. Patricia Smith, R.S.M., Vice Pres.; Sr. Kathleen Keenan, R.S.M.; Sr. Alicia Zapata, R.S.M.; Sr. Patricia Lapczynski, R.S.M.; Ellie Albright, COO; Timothy Doyle, CFO; Debbi DellaPorta, Dir. Communications; Sr. Suzanne Gallagher, R.S.M., Justice Coord.; Sr. Margaret Taylor, R.S.M., Assoc. Dir. Sponsorship; Sr. Christine McCann, R.S.M., Assoc. Dir., Sponsorship; Sr. Ivette Diaz, R.S.M., Vocation Min.; Sr. Anne Kappler, R.S.M., Vocation Dir.; Sr. Theresa Saetta, R.S.M., Vocation Min.; Sr. Megan Brown, R.S.M., Incorporation Min.; Maureen Keyes, Archivist.

Sisters of Mercy of the Americas, South Central Community: 101 Mercy Dr., Belmont, NC 28012. Tel: 704-829-5260; Fax: 704-829-5267; Email: info@mercysc.org; Web: www.mercysc.org.
Total in Community: 445.
Legal Title: Sisters of Mercy of the Americas, South Central Community, Inc.
Ministry in the following areas: Education: Daycare and Preschool Centers; Elementary Schools; High Schools; Special Education; Adult Education.
Healthcare: Hospitals; Ambulatory Health Care Center; Long Term Care; Multi-Level Long-Term Care Facility and Health Systems; Urgent Care Centers.
Social Services: Developmental Center for Handicapped Children; Social Work Centers; Care and Counseling; AIDS Ministry.
Retreat/Renewal Centers: Psycho-Spiritual Programs, Conference/Retreat Centers.
Housing: Homes for Aged; Transitional housing for women and children.
Parish Ministry: Pastoral Ministry Programs; Parish ministry; Diocesan ministry.
Properties owned, sponsored or co-sponsored: Alpha Academy, Kingston, Jamaica, WI; Alpha Boys' School, Kingston, Jamaica, WI; Alpha Infant School, Kingston, Jamaica, WI; Alpha Primary School, Kingston, Jamaica, WI; Jessie Ripoll Primary School, Kingston, Jamaica, WI; Mt. St. Joseph Prep School, Manchester, Jamaica, WI; St. John Bosco Children's Home, Manchester, Jamaica, WI; Well of Mercy, Inc. Hamptonville, NC; Holy Angels, Belmont, NC; House of Mercy, Belmont, NC; Catherine's House, Belmont, NC; Sisters of Mercy of NC Foundation, Inc., Belmont, NC; Mercy Urgent Care, Inc., Asheville, NC; Mercy Heights Nursery-K, Tamuning, GU; Our Lady of the Pines Retreat Center, Fremont, OH; Mercy Villa Convent, Inc., Murphy Initiative for Justice and Peace, Baltimore, MD; Mercy Villa; Mercy High School, Baltimore, MD; Marian House, Baltimore, MD; Mount de Sales Academy, Macon, GA; Sisters Academy of Baltimore, Baltimore, MD; The Savannah Institute of the Sisters of Mercy, Inc.; (St. Vincent's Academy), Savannah, GA; Mercy Health Services & (Mercy Medical Center & Stella Maris), Baltimore, MD; St. Joseph's/Candler Health System, Savannah, GA; Mercy Action Marianas, Ltd., Tamuning, GU; Infant of Prague Nursery-K, Mangilao, GU; Academy of Our Lady of Mercy, Inc., Louisville, KY; Assumption High School, Inc.; Louisville, KY; McAuley High School, Inc., Cincinnati, OH; Mother of Mercy High School, Inc., Cincinnati, OH; Mercy Montessori Center, Cincinnati, OH; Mercy Education Collaborative of Cincinnati, Cincinnati, OH; Mercy Neighborhood Ministries, Cincinnati, OH; Sisters of Mercy of Jamaica, West Indies, Kingston, Jamaica, West Indies; McAuley LLC, Louisville, KY; Mercy Conference and Retreat Center, St. Louis, MO; Mount St. Mary Academy, Little Rock, AR; Mercy Crest Housing, Inc., Barling, AR; Mount Saint Mary High School, Oklahoma City, OK; Arise - Support Center, Alamo, TX; Arise - Muniz, Edinburg, TX; Arise - Las Milpas, Pharr, TX; Arise South Tower, Alamo, TX; Mercy Housing, Inc., Denver, CO; Mercy McAuley High School, Cincinnati, OH.
Represented in the Archdioceses of Agana, Atlanta, Baltimore, Boston, Cincinnati, Detroit, Louisville, Mobile, New Orleans, Oklahoma City, Philadelphia, Portland in Oregon, St. Louis and Washington and in the Dioceses of Biloxi, Birmingham, Brownsville, Charlotte, Cleveland, Jackson, Knoxville, Laredo, Little Rock, Lubbock, Memphis, Nashville, Portland in Maine, Providence, Savannah, Springfield-Cape Girardeau, Toledo and Wichita. Also in Jamaica.
Leadership Team: Sr. Jane Hotstream, R.S.M., Pres. Tel: 704-829-5260; Fax: 704-829-5267; Email: jhotstream@mercysc.org. Team Members Sr. Mary Rose Bumpus, R.S.M., Vice Pres.; Sr. Patricia Coward, R.S.M.; Sr. Linda Falquette, R.S.M.; Sr. Deborah Lee Kern, R.S.M.

Sisters of Mercy of the Americas, West Midwest Community: 7262 Mercy Rd., Omaha, NE 68124-2389. Tel: 402-393-8225; Fax: 402-393-8145; Web: www.sistersofmercy.org/west-midwest. Community Leadership Team: Sr. Susan Sanders, R.S.M., Substitute for Pres.; Team Members: Sr. Ana Maria Pineda, R.S.M., Pres. Substitute; Sr. Margaret Mary Hinz, R.S.M.; Sr. Maria Klosowski, R.S.M.; Sr. Margaret Maloney, R.S.M.
Total in Community: 529; Total Number of Associates: 605.
Legal Title: Sisters of Mercy of the Americas West Midwest Community, Inc.
Ministry in the following areas: field of spirituality & retreat work; diocesan & pastoral services; peace & justice initiatives; parish ministry; religious & academic education at all levels; hospitals and healthcare services/facilities; literacy centers and programs; hospitality houses; nursing homes; social services; counseling services; transitional houses; foreign ministry work; prison ministry; long-term care facilities for the aged; housing for families and elderly.
Sponsored Ministries (city listed indicates central administrative location of the ministry. Some ministries may have multiple locations): Colleges and Higher Education: Mount Mercy University, Cedar Rapids, IA; Saint Xavier University, Chicago, IL; University of Detroit Mercy, Detroit, MI (co-sponsor); College of Saint Mary, Omaha, NE (affiliated/historical partner). Secondary Education: Cristo Rey High School, Sacramento, CA (co-sponsor); Mercy High School, Burlingame, CA; Mercy High School, San Francisco, CA; Mercy High School, Farmington Hills, MI; Mercy High School, Omaha, NE; Mother McAuley Liberal Arts High School, Chicago, IL; Mercy Education Project, Detroit, MI.
Hospitals & Healthcare Services (city listed indicates central administrative location of the ministry. Some ministries may have multiple locations): Catholic Health Care Federation/Catholic Health Initiatives, Denver, CO (participating entity); Catholic Health Ministries/Trinity Health, Livonia, MI (participating entity); Dignity Health, San Francisco, CA (co-sponsor); Mercy Hospital, Iowa City, IA; Mercy Medical Center, Cedar Rapids, IA; Presence Health Ministries/Presence Health, Chicago, IL (participating entity); Scripps Mercy Chula Vista Hospital, Chula Vista, CA; Scripps Mercy Hospital, San Diego, CA; Elder Care Alliance, Oakland, CA (co-sponsor); and Mercy Retirement and Care Center, Oakland, CA. Mercy Circle, Chicago, IL; Housing & Shelter: Mercy Housing, Inc., Denver, CO (co-sponsor); Social Services: Catherine McAuley Center, Cedar Rapids, IA; Development: Mercy Foundation Sacramento, Rancho Cordova, CA; and Mercy Foundation North, Redding, CA.
Spirituality/Retreat Centers: Knowles Mercy Spirituality Center, Waterloo, NE; Mercy Center, Auburn, CA; Mercy Center, Burlingame, CA.
Represented in the Archdioceses of Chicago, Denver, Detroit, Dubuque, Hartford, Los Angeles, Louisville, Milwaukee, New Orleans, New York, Omaha, Portland in Oregon, St. Louis, San Francisco and Washington and in the Dioceses of Boise, Brownsville, Colorado Springs, Davenport, Des Moines, El Paso, Fresno, Gaylord, Grand Rapids, Helena, Joliet, Kalamazoo, Kansas City-St. Joseph, Knoxville, Lansing, Memphis, Oakland, Orange, Phoenix, Rockford, Sacramento, Saginaw, San Bernardino, San Diego, San Jose, Springfield-Cape Girardeau, Stockton, Wheeling-Charleston, Winona-Rochester and Youngstown. Also in Ireland, South Africa and Uganda.

[2590] (H.M.S.S.)—MERCEDARIAN SISTERS OF THE BLESSED SACRAMENT (P) (Hermanas Mercedarias del Santísimo Sacramento)

Founded in Mexico City in 1910. First foundation in the United States in 1926.
Mercedarian Sisters of the Blessed Sacrament: 227 Keller St., San Antonio, TX 78204. Tel: 210-223-5013; Fax: 210-444-0779.
General Motherhouse: Fernandez Leal #130, Coyoacan, Mexico, 04330. Sr. Mary Rosario Vega-R., H.M.S.S., Regl. Supr.
Regional House: 1355 W. 70th St., Cleveland, OH 44102. Tel: 216-281-9304.
Professed Sisters in the U.S: 27.
Represented in the Archdiocese of San Antonio and in the Dioceses of Baton Rouge, Cleveland and San Diego and Saint Augustine.

[2600] (R.S.M.)—SISTERS OF MERCY (D)

Founded in the United States in 1960.
General Motherhouse: Congregation of the Sisters of Mercy, Rachamin, 13/14 Moyle Park, Clondalkin, Dublin 22, Ireland Sr. Margaret Casey, Supr. Gen.
U.S. Address: Sacred Heart Convent, 6240 105th St., Jacksonville, FL 32244. Tel: 904-771-3858. Sr. Patricia O'Hea, Contact Person.
Represented in the Diocese of St. Augustine.

[2630] (S.C.S.C.)—SISTERS OF MERCY OF THE HOLY CROSS (P)

Founded in Switzerland in 1856. First foundation in the U.S. in 1912.
General Motherhouse: Ingenbohl, Switzerland Sr. Marija Brizar, S.C.S.C., Supr. Gen.
U.S. Provincial Office: Holy Cross Sisters, 1400 O'Day St., Merrill, WI 54452. Tel: 715-539-1460; Fax: 715539-1456. Sr. Patricia E. Cormack, S.C.S.C., Prov.
Total in Community: 24.
Legal Title: Sisters of Mercy of the Holy Cross of Merrill, WI, Inc.; Sponsored Institution: Bell Tower Residence, Inc.
Ministry in the following areas: Schools; Hospitals; Social Ministries and Parishes; Retirement Homes; Adult Education; Prison Ministry.
Represented in the Dioceses of Green Bay and Superior.

[2655] (R.S.M.)—DIOCESAN SISTERS OF MERCY OF PORTLAND (D)

Motherhouse: Diocesan Sisters of Mercy of Portland, 265 Cottage Rd., South Portland, ME 04106. Tel: 207-767-5804. Sr. Karen Hopkins, R.S.M.

[2675] (C.F.M.M.)—MINIM DAUGHTERS OF MARY IMMACULATE (P)

Founded in Leon, Guanajuato, Mexico 1886. Came to the United States in 1926.
U.S. Regional House: Minim Daughters of Mary Immaculate, 555 Patagonia Hwy., Nogales, AZ 85628. Tel: 520-287-3377; Fax: 520-287-2910. Sr. Rosa Maria Ruiz, C.F.M.M., Reg. Supr.

Total Sisters in U.S: 17.
Properties owned and/or sponsored: Lourdes Catholic School, Nogales, AZ. Ministry in Academic and Religious Education and Health Care.
Represented in the Diocese of Tucson.

[2690] (M.C.D.P.)—MISSIONARY CATECHISTS OF DIVINE PROVIDENCE, SAN ANTONIO, TEXAS (P)

Autonomy with Pontifical status granted Dec. 12, 1989.
Administrative House: St. Andrew's Convent, 2318 Castroville Rd., San Antonio, TX 78237. Tel: 210-432-0113; Fax: 210-432-1709. Email: mainoffice@mcdp.org. Sr. Guadalupe Ramirez, M.C.D.P., Congregational Leader.
Total in Community: 31.
Represented in the Archdioceses of Galveston-Houston and San Antonio and in the Dioceses of Austin, Brownsville, Dallas, Dodge City, Fort Worth, San Angelo and San Jose.

[2700] (M.C.S.H.)—MISSIONARY CATECHISTS OF THE SACRED HEARTS OF JESUS AND MARY (P)

Founded in Mexico City, D.F. in 1918. U.S. foundation in 1943 in Victoria, Texas.
Central House: Mexico City, Mexico Sr. Felisa Nava, Gen. Supr.
Immaculate Heart of Mary Province: 203 E. Sabine St., Victoria, TX 77901. Tel: 361-570-3332; Fax: 361-570-3377. Sr. Midory Wu, M.C.S.H., Prov. Supr.
Total number in U.S. Province: 36.
Ministry in Catechetical family ministry in parishes and missions.
Represented in the Archdiocese of Santa Fe and in the Dioceses of Fort Worth, Lubbock, Metuchen and Victoria.

[2710] (M.C.)—MISSIONARIES OF CHARITY (P)

Founded in India, 1950.
General Motherhouse: 54A AJC Bose Rd., Kolkata, India, 700016. Sr. M. Prema, M.C., Supr. Gen.
U.S. Foundation & Office (1971): Missionaries of Charity, 335 E. 145th St., Bronx, NY 10451. Tel: 718-292-0019. Sr. Maria Agnes, M.C., Regl. Supr.
Professed Sisters in Congregation: 5029.
Legal Title: Missionaries of Charity, Inc. Sisters serve and staff: Soup Kitchens; Emergency Shelters for Women; Homes for Unwed Mothers; Shelters for Unwed Mothers; Shelters for Men; Religious Education Programs; After-School and Summer Camp Programs for Children; Homes for AIDS Patients; Prison Ministry; Nursing Homes; Hospital and Shut-in Ministry; Family Counseling and Ministry; Foreign Missionary Work.
Represented in the Archdioceses of Atlanta, Baltimore, Boston, Chicago, Denver, Detroit, Galveston-Houston, Indianapolis, Los Angeles, Miami, New York, Newark, Philadelphia, San Francisco, St. Louis, St. Paul-Minneapolis and Washington and in the Dioceses of Baton Rouge, Bridgeport, Brooklyn, Charlotte, Dallas, Fall River, Gallup, Gary, Lafayette, Lexington, Little Rock, Memphis, Oakland, Peoria, Phoenix, Sacramento, San Diego, Spokane and Trenton. Also in Canada, Mexico, Central America and South America.

[2715] (MChR)—MISSIONARY SISTERS OF CHRIST THE KING FOR POLONIA (P)

Founded in Poland on Nov. 21, 1959 by Father Ignacy Posadzy, TChR. First foundation in the U.S. 1978.
General Motherhouse: Siostry Misjonarki Chrystusa Krola dla Polonii, ul. Siostr Misjonarek 10, Poznan, 50, Poland, 61-680. Sr. Ewa Kaczmarek, MChR, Supr. Gen.
Total in Congregation : 230.
Delegation Superior in the U.S: Missionary Sisters of Christ the King for Polonia, 4910 North Menard Ave., Chicago, IL 60630. Tel: 773-481-1831; Fax: 773-545-4171. Sr. Anna Blauciak, MChR, Supr.; Sr. Malgorzata Tomalka, MChR, Sec.; Sr. Katarzyna Zaremba, MChR, Treas.
Total in Congregation: 230; Professed in U.S. & Canada: 50.
Legal Title: Missionary Sisters of Christ the King for Polonia.
Ministry among Polish immigrants and people of Polish heritage.
Represented in the Archdioceses of Chicago, Detroit and Newark and in the Dioceses of Joliet and Phoenix. Also in Canada.

[2717] (M.D.P.V.M.)—MISSIONARY DAUGHTERS OF THE MOST PURE VIRGIN MARY (P)

Founded in Mexico. First foundation in the United States in the Diocese of Corpus Christi 1916.
General Motherhouse: Heroe de Nacocariz, 721 Sur Aguascalientes, Ags, Mexico, 20240. Mother Guillermina Arroyo, M.D.P.V.M., Gen. Supr.
Missionary Daughters of the Most Pure Virgin Mary: 919 N. 9th St., Kingsville, TX 78363. Tel: 361-595-1087. Sr. Consuelo Ramirez, M.D.P.V.M., Supr.; Sr. Carmen Villalpando, M.D.P.V.M., Sec.; Sr. Maximina Cruz, M.D.P.V.M., Treas.
Total in Congregation : 400; Present in U.S.A: 24.
Legal Title: Missionary Daughters of the Most Pure Virgin Mary.
Ministry in the field of Religious and Academic Education at the elementary level; Pastoral Ministry.
Represented in the Dioceses of Camden, Corpus Christi and Yakima.

[2720] (M.H.S.H.)—MISSION HELPERS OF THE SACRED HEART (P)

Founded in the United States in 1890.
Mission Helper Center: 1001 W. Joppa Rd., Baltimore, MD 21204. Tel: 410-823-8585; Fax: 410-825-6355. Sr. Elizabeth Langmead, M.H.S.H., Pres.
Total in Community: 43.
Legal Title: Institute of Mission Helpers of Baltimore City.
Represented in the Archdioceses of Baltimore, Boston, Cincinnati and in the Dioceses of Birmingham, Erie, Orlando, Pittsburgh, Rochester and Tucson. Also in Venezuela.

[2725] (M.S.E.)—MISSIONARY SISTERS OF THE EUCHARIST

Founded in Guatemala, C.A. in 1975. First foundation in the United States in 2001.
Motherhouse: San Andres Semetabaj, Solola, Guatemala Sr. Francisca Sisimit, M.S.E., Supr. Gen.
Total in Community: 54.
Visitation Convent, Magnificat Houses: 3301 San Jacinto St., Houston, TX 77004. Tel: 713-523-8831.
Mailing Address: P.O. Box 88147, Houston, TX 77288-0147. Sr. Gabina Coló, M.S.E., Local Supr. and Contact Person.
Ministry in parishes, missionary work, health care and social services.
Represented in the Archdiocese of Galveston-Houston.

[2730] (M.S.H.R.)—MISSIONARY SISTERS OF THE HOLY ROSARY (P)

Generalate (1924): 23 Cross Ave., Blackrock County, Dublin, Ireland Sr. Maureen O'Malley, Congregational Leader.
U.S. Regional Headquarters (1954): Missionary Sisters of the Holy Rosary, 741 Polo Rd., Bryn Mawr, PA 19010. Tel: 610-520-1974. Sr. Helena McNeill, Regl. Leader.
Total in Community: 349.
Represented in the Archdiocese of Philadelphia.

[2740] (M.S.SP.)—MISSION SISTERS OF THE HOLY SPIRIT (D)

Motherhouse and Novitiate: 1030 N. River Rd., Saginaw, MI 48609. Tel: 989-781-0934. Sr. Mary Lou Owczarzak, Pres.
Total in Community: 5.
Legal Title: Society of the Mission Sisters of the Holy Spirit of the Diocese of Saginaw Holy Spirit Sisters Charitable Trust, Saginaw, MI.
Ministry in Religious Education at all levels including Developmentally Disabled; Pastoral Ministry.
Represented in the Diocese of Saginaw.

[2750] (I.C.M.)—MISSIONARY SISTERS OF THE IMMACULATE HEART OF MARY (P)

Founded in India in 1897. First foundation in the United States in 1919.
Generalate: Via Filogaso 40, Rome, Italy, 00173. Sr. Lieve Stragier, I.C.M., Supr. Gen. Universal total in Congregation: 620.
American Province: 18110 Queen Palm Dr., P.O. Box 1017, Peñitas, TX 78576. Tel: 212-677-2959; Tel: 956-585-5488; Fax: 212-475-7455. Sr. Fatima Mary Santiago, I.C.M., Mission Supr.
Total in Community: 11.
Missionaries Minister in Education; Catechetical; Pastoral and Social Ministry; Health Care; Ecology; Leprosaria; International Justice and the Promotion of Human Dignity.
Represented in the Archdiocese of New York and in the Diocese of Brownsville. Also in Belgium, Brazil, Burundi, Cameroon, Guatemala, Hong Kong, India, Italy, Philippines, Taiwan, Mongolia, Caribbean Islands, Congo and Senegal.

[2760] (S.M.I.C.)—MISSIONARY SISTERS OF THE IMMACULATE CONCEPTION OF THE MOTHER OF GOD (P)

Founded in Brazil in 1910. First foundation in the United States in 1922.
Generalate: 47 Garden Ave., Woodland Park, NJ 07424. Tel: 973-279-1484. Email: smicgen@optonline.net. Sr. Livramento Melo de Oliveira, S.M.I.C., Coord. Gen.
U.S. Province (1960): Provincialate of the Immaculate Conception, 779 Broadway, Paterson, NJ 07514. Tel: 973-279-3790.
Professed Sisters: 28.
Legal Titles: Missionary Sisters of the Immaculate Conception, Inc.; Province of the Immaculate Conception, Inc.
Sisters serve and staff: Religious Education; Pastoral Ministries; Health and Social Work.
Represented in the Archdioceses of Newark and in the Dioceses of Austin, Paterson, Portland (In Maine) and San Bernardino.

[2770] (M.J.M.J.)—MISSIONARY SISTERS OF JESUS, MARY AND JOSEPH (P)

Founded in Spain in 1944. First foundation in the United States in 1956. Mother Maria Dolores de la Cruz Domingo, Foundress.
Motherhouse: Plaza Inmaculada Concepcion 1, Madrid, Spain, 28019. Sr. Luz Doñez, M.J.M.J., Supr. Gen.
Delegation Headquarters: Mount Thabor Convent, 12940 Leopard St., Corpus Christi, TX 78410. Tel: 361-241-1955; Fax: 361-241-2271. Sr. Irene Ybarra, M.J.M.J., Delegation Supr.; Sr. Gloria Rodriguez, M.J.M.J., Local Supr.
Sisters: 22.
Properties owned and/or sponsored: The Ark Assessment Center & Emergency Shelter for Youth.
Represented in the Archdiocese of San Antonio and in the Dioceses of Corpus Christi and El Paso. Also in Mexico.

[2780] (M.SS.S.)—MISSIONARY SISTERS OF THE MOST BLESSED SACRAMENT (P)

General Motherhouse: Calle Navarro Amandi, 11, Madrid, Spain, 28033. Mother Leonor Gutierreg, Mother Gen.
U.S. Foundation: Convent of Mary Immaculate, 1111 Wordin Ave., Bridgeport, CT 06605. Tel: 203-334-5681; Email: januariab@gmail.com. Sr. Marian Macias, Mother General; Sr. Januaria Beleno, Local Supr.

[2790] (M.S.B.T.)—MISSIONARY SERVANTS OF THE MOST BLESSED TRINITY (P)

Founded in the United States in 1912.
Motherhouse-Generalate-Novitiate and Candidacy: 3501 Solly Ave., Philadelphia, PA 19136. Tel: 215-335-7550. Sr. Barbara McIntyre, M.S.B.T., Gen. Custodian.
Total in Community: 97.
Properties owned and sponsored: Blessed Trinity Mother Missionary Cenacle, Philadelphia, PA; Blessed Trinity Shrine Retreat Cenacle, Holy Trinity, AL; Trinita Ecumenical Retreat Center, New Hartford, CT; Mother Boniface Spirituality Center, Philadelphia, PA.
Represented in the Archdioceses of Baltimore, Chicago, Hartford and Philadelphia and in the Dioceses of Birmingham, Camden, Charlotte, Fall River and San Bernardino. Also in Puerto Rico and Mexico.

[2800] (M.S.C.)—MISSIONARY SISTERS OF THE MOST SACRED HEART OF JESUS (OF HILTRUP) (P)

Founded in Germany in 1899. First foundation in the United States in 1908.
Generalate: Via Martiri di Via Fani, 22, Sutri (Viterbo), Italy, 01015. Sr. Barbara Winkler, M.S.C., Gen. Supr.
American Province-Motherhouse (1908): Sacred Heart Villa, 51 Seminary Ave., Reading, PA 19605. Tel: 610-929-5751. Sr. Mary Anne Bigos, M.S.C., Coordinator.
Total number in U.S. Province: 44.
Legal Title: Missionary Sisters of the Most Sacred Heart of Jesus, Inc.

Ministry in Education; Health Care; Home Health Care; Parish Ministry; Pastoral Ministry to people on the move; Prison Ministry; Counseling; Social Ministry; Spiritual Ministry; Care of the Aged.

Properties owned or sponsored: MSC Province Center; Chevalier House, Sacred Heart Villa, Reading, PA.

Represented in the Archdioceses of Atlanta, Galveston-Houston and Philadelphia and in the Dioceses of Allentown, Harrisburg, Syracuse and Venice. Also in Mexico.

MSC Province Center: 2811 Moyers Ln., Reading, PA 19605. Tel: 610-929-5944. Email: USAMSC@mscreading.org. Sr. Rosemarie Sommers, M.S.C., Prov. Supr.

[2810] (M.S.M.G.)—MISSIONARY SISTERS OF MOTHER OF GOD (D)
(Byzantine Ukrainian Rite-Philadelphia)

U.S. Province: 711 N. Franklin St., Philadelphia, PA 19132. Tel: 215-627-7808. Email: msmgnuns@gmail.com. Mother Maria Kelly, M.S.M.G., Gen. Supr.

Professed Sisters: 7.

Ministry in the field of Education.

Represented in the Ukrainian Archdiocese of Philadelphia.

[2820] (M.S.O.L.A.)—MISSIONARY SISTERS OF OUR LADY OF AFRICA (P)
(Sisters of Africa)

Founded in Algiers, N. Africa in 1869. First foundation in the United States in 1929.

General Motherhouse: Rome, Italy Sr. Carmen Sammut, Supr. Gen.

Universal total in Congregation: 640.

American Headquarters: 47 West Spring St., Winooski, VT 05404. Tel: 802-655-2395 Ext. 2240. Sr. Arlene Gates, Contact Person.

Total number in U.S: 12.

Represented in the Dioceses of Burlington and Springfield in Massachusetts.

[2830] (M.O.M.)—MISSIONARY SISTERS OF OUR LADY OF MERCY (D)

Founded in Piaui, Brazil in 1938. First foundation in the United States at Lackawanna, New York in 1955.

General Motherhouse: Salvador, Bahia, Brazil Mother Maria Ilsa Mascarenhas de Jesus, Supr. Gen.

U.S. Headquarters: Rainbow K, 388 Franklin St., Buffalo, NY 14202. Tel: 716-854-5198. Sr. Janice Benfield, M.O.M., Supr.

Total in Community: 3.

Represented in the Diocese of Buffalo.

[2840] (M.C.)—POOR CLARE MISSIONARY SISTERS (P)

Founded in Mexico by Blessed Maria Ines Teresa Arias of the Blessed Sacrament.

General Motherhouse: Via Cardinale Garampi 17, Pineta Sachetti, Rome, Italy Mother Martha G. Hernandez, Gen. Supr.

U.S. Foundation: Regional House and Novitiate, 1019 N. Newhope, Santa Ana, CA 92703. Total in Community: 42.

Ministry in Day Nurseries, Schools and Retreat House.

Represented in the Archdiocese of Los Angeles and in the Dioceses of Orange in California and Springfield-Cape Girardeau.

[2850] (C.P.S.)—MISSIONARY SISTERS OF THE PRECIOUS BLOOD (P)

Founded in South Africa on Sept. 8, 1885. First founded in the United States at Princeton, New Jersey on August 15, 1925.

Generalate: Casa Generalizia, Suore Missionarie del Preziosissimo Sangue Mariannhill, Via San Giovanni Eudes 95, Rome, Italy, I-00163.

Universal total in Congregation: 766

North American Province: Precious Blood Convent, 1094 Welsh Rd., Reading, PA 19607-9363. Tel: 610-777-1624; Fax: 610-777-3359. Sr. Monica Mary Ncube, C.P.S., Prov.

Total number in Province: 50.

Represented in the Archdiocese of Philadelphia and in the Dioceses of Allentown, Brooklyn and Lexington. Also in Canada.

[2860] (M.S.C.)—MISSIONARY SISTERS OF THE SACRED HEART OF JESUS (P)
(Cabrini Sisters)

Founded in Italy in 1880, by Saint Frances Xavier Cabrini. First foundation in the United States in 1889.

Motherhouse: Viale Cortina D'Ampezzo 269, Rome, Italy, 00135. Sr. Barbara Staley, M.S.C., Supr. Gen.

Provincial Office: 222 E. 19th St., 5B, New York, NY 10003. Sr. Pietrina Raccuglia, Prov. Supr.

Professed Sisters: 267; Total in Congregation : 286.

Ministry in the field of Education; Hospitals; Nursing Homes; Child Care; Retreat and Shrine Ministries; Parish Ministry.

Represented in the Archdioceses of Chicago, Denver, New Orleans, New York, Philadelphia and Seattle. Also in Argentina, Australia, Brazil, Central America, England, Ethiopia, Italy, Mexico, Paraguay, Siberia, Spain, Switzerland and Swaziland.

[2865] (M.S.C.GPE.)—MISSIONARIES OF THE SACRED HEART OF JESUS AND OUR LADY OF GUADALUPE (P)

National Address: 1212 E. Euclid Ave., Arlington Heights, IL 60004. Tel: 847-255-5616. Sr. Guadalupe Rosales, Local Supr.

Ministry in Schools, Nursing Homes, Seminaries and Foreign Missions.

Represented in the Archdioceses of Chicago, San Francisco and Washington and in the Diocese of Joliet.

[2880] (S.S.C.)—MISSIONARY SISTERS OF ST. COLUMBAN (P)
(Columban Sisters)

Founded in Ireland in 1922. First foundation in the United States in 1930.

General Motherhouse: Wicklow, Ireland Sr. Ann Gray, S.S.C., Congregational Leader.

U.S. Region: 73 Mapleton St., Brighton, MA 02135-2821. Tel: 617-782-5683; Tel: 617-782-1610; Fax: 617-789-3569. Sr. Virginia Mozo, S.S.C., U.S. Area Leader.

Professed Sisters: 21.

Represented in the Archdioceses of Boston and Los Angeles and in the Diocese of Buffalo. Also in Chile, China, England, Hong Kong, Ireland, Korea, Myanmar, Pakistan, Peru, Philippines and Scotland.

[2890] (M.S.S.A.)—MISSIONARY SERVANTS OF ST. ANTHONY (D)

Founded in the United States in 1929.

General Motherhouse: 100 Peter Baque Rd., San Antonio, TX 78209-1805. Tel: 210-824-4553. Sr. Mary Ann Domagalski, M.S.S.A., Supr.

Total in Community: 3.

Represented in the Archdiocese of San Antonio.

[2900] (M.S.C.S.)—MISSIONARY SISTERS OF ST. CHARLES BORROMEO (P)
(Scalabrinians)

Founded in Italy in 1895. Began its mission in the United States in 1941 which developed to be the USA Province, Our Lady of Fatima Province USA.

Motherhouse: Via Monte del Gallo 68, Rome, Italy, 00165. Sr. Neusa de Fatima Mariano, M.S.C.S., Gen. Supr.

Total in Congregation : 635.

Our Lady of Fatima Province, USA & Bishop Scalabrini Community: 1414 N. 37th Ave., Melrose Park, IL 60160. Tel: 708-343-2162; Fax: 708-343-6452. Sr. Marciana Zambiasi, M.S.C.S., Prov. Supr.; Sr. Marissonia Daltoe, M.S.C.S., First Councilor & Treas.; Sr. Elizabeth Pedernal, M.S.C.S., Councilor & Prov. Sec.; Sr. Noemie Digo, M.S.C.S., Councilor & Coord., Formation; Sr. Elisete Teresihna Signor, M.S.C.S., Councilor & Coord., Apostolate.

Total in Community: 60.

Ministry in the fields of Education; Pastoral Care of the Sick; Catechesis; Social Service; Pastoral Care of Migrants and Refugees.

Represented in the Archdioceses of Boston, Chicago, New York and Washington. Also in Canada, India, Indonesia, Mexico and the Philippines.

[2920] (M.D.)—MOTHERS OF THE HELPLESS (D)

Founded in Malaga, Spain in 1881. Founded in the United States in 1916.

General Motherhouse: Avda. San Jose de la Montana No. 15, Valencia, Spain, 46008. Mother Maria Angeles Villar, Supr. Gen.

U.S. Address: Mothers of the Helpless, 432 W. 20th St., New York, NY 10011. Mother Josefina Jiminez, Supr.

Professed Sisters in U.S: 5.

Properties owned and sponsored: Sacred Heart Residence; San Jose Day Nursery, New York, NY.

Represented in the Archdiocese of New York.

[2930] (I.H.M.)—THE CALIFORNIA INSTITUTE OF THE SISTERS OF THE MOST HOLY AND IMMACULATE HEART OF THE BLESSED VIRGIN MARY (P)

Founded in Spain in 1848. First foundation in the United States in 1871.

Pontifical Commissary: 3424 Wilshire Blvd., 5th Fl., Los Angeles, CA 90010-2241. Tel: 213-637-7534.

Professed Sisters: 3.

Represented in the Archdiocese of Los Angeles.

[2940] (M.H.S.)—SISTERS OF THE MOST HOLY SACRAMENT (P)

Founded in France in 1851. First foundation in the United States in 1872. Pontifical Approbation 1935.

Generalate: Sisters of the Most Holy Sacrament, 313 Corona Dr., Lafayette, LA 70503-4757. Tel: 337-981-8475. Sr. Ann Lacour, M.S.C., Major Supr.; Sr. Diane Dornan, M.H.S., Prov.

Total in Community: 11.

Legal Titles: St. Augustine Trust Fund, Lafayette, LA; Bethany Health Care Center, Lafayette, LA. Ministry in the field of Homes for the Aged.

Represented in the Diocese of Lafayette (LA).

[2950] (N.D.S.)—CONGREGATION OF NOTRE DAME DE SION (P)

Founded in France in 1850. First foundation in the United States in 1892.

Generalate: Rome, Italy Sr. Maureen Cusick, Supr. Gen. Universal total in Congregation: 535.

Notre Dame de Sion: 3823 Locust St., Kansas City, MO 64109. Tel: 816-531-1374.

Represented in the Archdiocese of Chicago and in the Dioceses of Brooklyn and Kansas City-St. Joseph.

[2960] (N.D.)—NOTRE DAME SISTERS (P)

Founded in Czechoslovakia, Europe in 1853. First foundation in the United States in 1910.

General Motherhouse: Hradec Kralove, Czech Republic Mother Anezka Bednarova, N.D., Supr. Gen.

U.S. Provincial Motherhouse: Notre Dame Convent, 3501 State St., Omaha, NE 68112-1709. Tel: 402-455-2994; Fax: 402-455-3974. Email: info@notredamesisters.org. Sr. Margaret Hickey, N.D., Prov.

Total in Community: 36.

Sisters serve and staff: all levels of academic education; Hispanic Ministry; Pastoral Care; Housing for low income elderly; Social Work; Religious Education; Youth Ministry; Chemical Dependency Counseling; Health Care; TEC; Adult Education; Community Administration and Services.

Represented in the Archdioceses of Denver, Dubuque and Omaha and in the Dioceses of Des Moines, Grand Island, Kansas City-St. Joseph, Pueblo and Scranton.

[2970] (S.S.N.D.)—SCHOOL SISTERS OF NOTRE DAME (P)

Founded in Germany in 1833. First foundation in the United States in 1847.

General Motherhouse: Rome, Italy Sr. Roxanne Schares, Supr. Gen.

Atlantic-Midwest Province: School Sisters of Notre Dame, 6401 N. Charles St., Baltimore, MD 21212-1099. Tel: 410-377-7774; Fax: 410-377-5363. Sr. Charmine Krohe, S.S.N.D., Prov. Leader.

Total in Community: 493.

Properties Owned and Legal Titles: School Sisters of Notre Dame in the City of Baltimore; Maria Health Care Center, Inc.; Atlantic-Midwest Province of the School Sisters of Notre Dame, Inc.; The Northeastern Province of the School Sisters of Notre Dame in the State of Connecticut; Lourdes Health Care Center, Inc.; School Sisters of Chicago Province, Inc.; Atlantic-Midwest Province Endowment Trust; SSND Service Corp.; SSND Care, Inc.; SSND Real Estate Holding Corp.; SSND Real Estate Trust; SSND Continuing Care Trust; SSND Charitable Annuity Trust.

Ministries: Teaching and Administering in the field of Academic Education at all levels; ESL and Tutoring for Women and Children; Nursing; Apostolate of the Aging; D.R.E.'s and Pastoral Associates.

Represented in the Archdioceses of Baltimore, Boston, Chicago, Hartford, Los Angeles, Newark, New York, Philadelphia and Washington and in the Dioceses of Albany, Bridgeport, Brooklyn, Charleston, El Paso, Jackson, Joliet, La Crosse, Lexington, Norwich, Oakland, Ogdensburg, Orlando, Palm Beach, Peoria, Pittsburgh, Providence, Rochester, Rockford,

Rockville Centre, St. Petersburg, Venice, Wichita and Wilmington. Also in Canada, England, Rome and South Sudan.

Sponsored Corporate Ministries: Notre Dame of Maryland University; Notre Dame Preparatory School; Institute of Notre Dame, Baltimore, MD; Academy of the Holy Angels, Demarest, NJ; The Caroline Friess Center, Inc.' Academy of Our Lady, Chicago, Inc.; Caroline House, Inc.; School Sisters of Notre Dame Educational Center, Inc.; SisterHouse; Corazon A Corazon, NFP; Notre Dame Learning Center, Inc.

Co-Sponsored Ministries: Sisters Academy of Baltimore, Inc.; Mother Seton Academy, Inc.; Marian House, Incorporated.

Chicago Office: School Sisters of Notre Dame, Atlantic Midwest-Province, P.O. Box 60762, Chicago, IL 60660. Tel: 773-867-0478. Sr. Charmine Krohe, S.S.N.D., Prov. Leader.

Ministries: Teaching and Administering in the field of Academic Education at all levels; ESL and Tutoring for Women and Children; Apostolate of the Aging; D.R.E.'s and Pastoral Associates.

Northeast Office (1957): School Sisters of Notre Dame, Atlantic-Midwest Province, 345 Belden Hill Rd., Wilton, CT 06897. Tel: 203-762-1220; Fax: 203-762-9434. Sr. Charmine Krohe, S.S.N.D., Prov. Leader.

Legal Holdings and Titles: The Northeastern Province of the School Sisters of Notre Dame in the State of Connecticut; Motherhouse and Lourdes Health Care Center, Wilton, CT; Academy of the Holy Angels, Demarest, NJ.

Ministries: Teaching and Administering in the field of Academic Education at all levels; ESL and Tutoring for Women and Children; Nursing; Apostolate of the Aging; D.R.E.'s and Pastoral Associates.

Central Pacific Province (2011): School Sisters of Notre Dame, 320 E. Ripa Ave., St. Louis, MO 63125. Tel: 314-544-0455; Fax: 314-544-6754. Sr. Mary Anne Owens, S.S.N.D., Prov. Leader.

Total in Community: 1008.

Legal Title: School Sisters of Notre Dame Central Pacific Province, Inc.; The School Sisters of Notre Dame of Dallas Charitable Trust; School Sisters of Notre Dame at Mankato, Minnesota, Inc. - Charitable Trust; School Sisters of Notre Dame Cooperative Investment Fund; School Sisters of Notre Dame at Milwaukee, Wisconsin, Inc. Charitable Trust; The School Sisters of Notre Dame of St. Louis Caroline Trust.

Ministries to the Needy and Elderly; Women and Youth; all levels of Academic Education; D.R.E.'s; Pastoral Associates.

Sponsored/Co-Sponsored Ministries: Notre Dame Education Center (NDEC), Canton, MS; Notre Dame of Dallas School; Good Counsel Learning Center, Mankato, MN; Theresa House, Mankato, MN; Notre Dame Middle School Milwaukee, WI; Milwaukee Achiever; Mount Mary University; INSPIRO, Nashotah, WI; Notre Dame High School (Guam); Progressive Education Program, Inc. (PEPI), New Iberia, LA; MORE, St. Paul, MN; East Side Learning Center, St. Paul, MN; Theresa Living Center, St. Paul, MN; Marian Middle School, St. Louis, MO; Notre Dame High School, St. Louis, MO.

Milwaukee Office: 13105 Watertown Plank Rd., Elm Grove, WI 53122-2291. Tel: 262-782-9850; Fax: 262-782-5725. Sr. Mary Anne Owens, S.S.N.D., Prov. Leader.

Total in Community: 916.

Properties owned and/or sponsored: Mount Mary College, Milwaukee, WI; Notre Dame of Elm Grove, Elm Grove, WI; Our Lady of the Angels (Co-owners).

Legal Titles: School Sisters of Notre Dame of the Central Pacific Province; School Sisters of Notre Dame at Milwaukee, Wisconsin, Inc. Charitable Trust.

Various ministries to Women, Youth, the Poor, Sick and Elderly; all levels of Academic Education; D.R.E.'s; Pastoral Associates; Volunteer Services. Represented in the Archdioceses of Agana, Chicago, Detroit, Milwaukee and Seattle and in the Dioceses of Austin, El Paso, Fort Wayne-South Bend, Gallup, Gary, Grand Rapids, Green Bay, Jefferson City, Kansas City-St. Joseph, La Crosse, Laredo, Madison, Marquette, Phoenix, Steubenville, Trenton, Tucson and Wheeling-Charleston.

Mankato Office: School Sisters of Notre Dame, 170 Good Counsel Dr., Mankato, MN 56001-3138. Tel: 507-389-4200; Fax: 507-389-4125. Sr. Mary Anne Owens, S.S.N.D., Prov. Leader.

Total in Community: 916.

Legal Titles: School Sisters of Notre Dame at Mankato, Minnesota, Inc. - Charitable Trust; School Sisters of Notre Dame Cooperative Investment Fund.

Represented in the Archdioceses of Chicago, Dubuque, New Orleans, Seattle, St. Louis, St. Paul-Minneapolis and San Francisco and in the Dioceses of Bismarck, Charleston, Charlotte, New Ulm, Phoenix, Richmond, San Jose, Superior, St. Cloud, and Winona-Rochester. Also in Nigeria, Ghana, Guatemala, Kenya and Rome.

Dallas Office: Notre Dame of Dallas - School Sisters of Notre Dame, P.O. Box 227275, Dallas, TX 75222. Tel: 214-845-7418 Fax: 214-330-9197. Sr. Mary Anne Owens, S.S.N.D., Prov. Leader.

Total in Community: 916.

Represented in the Archdioceses of Galveston-Houston, New Orleans, San Antonio and St. Louis and in the Dioceses of Amarillo, Baton Rouge, Brownsville, Dallas, Davenport, El Paso, Fort Worth, Houma-Thibodaux, Jackson, Lafayette (LA), Laredo and Tucson.

[2980] (C.N.D.)—SISTERS OF THE CONGREGATION DE NOTRE DAME (P)

Founded in Canada in 1653. First Foundation in the United States in 1860. American Novitiate established at Bourbonnais, Illinois.

Blessed Sacrament Province: 30 Highfield Rd., Wilton, CT 06897.

Generalate and Motherhouse: 2330 Sherbrooke St., W, Montreal, Canada, H3H 1G8. Sr. Agnes Campbell, C.N.D., Congregational Leader.

U.S. Province (1946): Blessed Sacrament Province, 30 Highfield Rd., Wilton, CT 06897. Tel: 203-762-4300; Fax: 203-762-4319. Sr. Patricia McCarthy, C.N.D., Prov. Leader.

Total number in the U.S. Province: 124.

Represented in the Archdioceses of Chicago, Hartford, New York and Oklahoma City and in the Dioceses of Albany, Bridgeport, Brooklyn, Charlotte, Joliet, Providence, Richmond and Scranton.

[2990] (S.N.D.)—SISTERS OF NOTRE DAME (P)

Founded in Germany in 1850. First foundation in the United States in 1874.

Generalate: Rome, Italy Sr. Mary Kristin Battles, S.N.D., Supr. Gen.

Universal total in Congregation: 1889.

Cleveland Province (1874): Notre Dame Educational Center - Provincial Center, Juniorate, & Novitiate, 13000 Auburn Rd., Chardon, OH 44024-9331. Tel: 440-286-7101; Fax: 440-286-3377. Sr. Margaret Mary Gorman, S.N.D., Prov. Supr.; Sr. M. Patricia Teckman, Prov. Sec.

Total in Community: 268.

Legal Titles: The Corporation of the Sisters of Notre Dame of Chardon, Ohio; The Sisters of Notre Dame Charitable Trust.

National and Diocesan Offices; Ministry in the field of Academic Education (preschool through college); Literacy, tutors; Special Education (K-8) for Children with Learning Disabilities; Youth, Young Adult Ministry; Parish Ministry (Pastoral Associates, Ministers, DREs); Health Care (Nurses, Chaplains, Hospice, Pastoral Care); Spiritual Direction, Speakers, Retreat work; Counseling; Foreign Mission Work, Respite Home for Children; Administration and Finance; Mission Effectiveness; Internet, Social Media Strategist; Donor Relations; Writers; Artists; Musicians; Peace and Justice Work; Outreach to the Homeless, Homebound, Marginalized, Human Trafficked, Incarcerated; Community Service.

Properties owned and sponsored: Notre Dame Cathedral Latin School, Chardon, OH; Notre Dame Elementary School, Chardon, OH; Notre Dame Pre School, Chardon, OH; Julie Billiart School, Lyndhurst, OH.

Represented in the Archdioceses of Los Angeles, and Washington and in the Dioceses of Arlington, Cleveland, Kalamazoo, Orlando, Raleigh, St. Petersburg, and Youngstown. Also in Tanzania.

Covington Province (1924): Provincial Center and Novitiate of the Sisters of Notre Dame, 1601 Dixie Hwy., (St. Joseph Heights), Covington, KY 41011. Tel: 859-291-2040; Fax: 859-291-1774. Email: info@sndky.org. Sr. Mary Ethel Parrott, S.N.D., Prov.

Total in Community: 89.

Legal Title: Sisters of Notre Dame of Covington, KY, Inc. Ministry in the field of Education; Hospital and Health Care Services; Child Care.

Properties sponsored and owned: Saint Claire Regional Medical Center, Morehead, KY; St. Charles Care Center, Inc., Covington, KY; Notre Dame Academy, Covington, KY; Notre Dame Urban Education Center, Inc., Covington, KY; Julie Learning Center, Park Hills, KY.

Represented in the Archdiocese of Cincinnati, Covington and Lexington.

Province of Toledo (1924): Sisters of Notre Dame, 3912 Sunforest Ct., Suite B, Toledo, OH 43623. Tel: 419-474-5485. Sr. Mary Delores Gatliff, S.N.D., Prov. Supr.

Total in Community: 169.

Ministry in the field of Academic Education; Foreign Mission Work; Religious Education, Pastoral Ministry, Vocational School, Health Care Ministry, Counseling Ministry, Community Service, Diocesan Offices, Spiritual Life, Hispanic and Migrant, Campus Ministries, Child Care, Care for Handicapped.

Properties owned and sponsored: Notre Dame Academy; Double ARC; Maria Early Learning Center; Lial Catholic School; Convent & Renewal Center, Whitehouse, OH; Holy Trinity Mission, Papua, New Guinea.

Represented in the Archdioceses of Detroit, Green Bay, Indianapolis and New Orleans and in the Dioceses of Charleston, Fort Wayne-South Bend, St. Augustine and Toledo.

Province of Los Angeles (1961): Sisters of Notre Dame, 1776 Hendrix Ave., Thousand Oaks, CA 91360. Tel: 805-496-3243; Fax: 805-379-3616. Sr. Mary Anncarla Costello, S.N.D., Prov. Supr.

Total number in Province: 52.

Legal Titles: Corporation of the Sisters of Notre Dame of Los Angeles; Notre Dame Academy Schools of Los Angeles; Notre Dame Center; La Reina High & Middle School, Thousand Oaks, CA; Providence House, Long Beach, CA; Notre Dame Learning Center Preschool, Thousand Oaks, CA.

Ministry in the field of Education and Parish and Social Ministry; Catechetics; Foreign Mission Work.

Represented in the Archdiocese of Los Angeles.

[3000] (S.N.D.DEN.)—SISTERS OF NOTRE DAME DE NAMUR (P)

Founded in France in 1804. First foundation in the United States in 1840.

Generalate: Suore di Nostra Signora di Namur,Via Raffaello Sardiello 20, Rome, Italy, 00165. Tel: 011-3906-6641-8704. Sr. Teresita Weind, S.N.D.deN., Gen. Mod.

U.S. Notre Dame Congregational Center: Congregational Mission Office, 30 Jeffreys Neck Rd., Ipswich, MA 01938. Tel: 978-356-2159; Fax: 978-356-2118. Sr. Lorraine Connell, S.N.D.deN., Treas.

Part of the Sisters of Notre Dame de Namur United States East-West Province: Sisters of Notre Dame de Namur, 351 Broadway, Everett, MA 02149-3425. Tel: 617-387-2500; Fax: 617-387-1303. Prov. Team: Sr. Catherine Waldron, S.N.D.deN.; Sr. Mary M. Farren, S.N.D.deN.; Sr. Barbara Barry, S.N.D.deN.; Sr. Edie Daly, S.N.D.deN; Sr. Barbara English, S.N.D.deN.; Sr. Anne Malone, S.N.D.deN.

Total in Community: 135.

Legal Title: Boston Province of the Sisters of Notre Dame de Namur, Inc.

Ministry in the field of Academic Education at all levels; Adult Education Programs; Parish Ministries; Religious Education Programs; and Social Services.

Properties owned and sponsored: Notre Dame Academy, Worcester, MA, Notre Dame Children's Class, Wenham, MA; Notre Dame Education Center, South Boston, MA; St. Patrick School and Education Center, Lowell, MA.

Represented in the Archdioceses of Boston, Hartford and Washington and in the Dioceses of Gallup, Manchester, Springfield in Massachusetts and Worcester.

Part of the Sisters of Notre Dame de Namur United States East-West Province: Sisters of Notre Dame de Namur, 30 Jeffrey's Neck Rd., Ipswich, MA 01938. Tel: 978-356-4381; Fax: 978-356-9759. Prov. Admin. Team: Sr. Catherine Waldron, S.N.D.deN.; Sr. Mary M. Farren, S.N.D.deN.; Sr. Barbara Barry, S.N.D.deN.; Sr. Edie Daly, S.N.D.deN; Sr. Barbara English, S.N.D.deN.; Sr. Anne Malone, S.N.D.deN.

Total in Community: 88.

Legal Titles: Notre Dame Training School, Inc.; The Sisters of Notre Dame de Namur, Ipswich, MA. Ministry in all fields of Education; Pastoral Ministry; Health, Social and Community Services; Retreat Work.

Properties owned and sponsored: Academy of Notre Dame, Tyngsboro, MA; Notre Dame Academy, Hingham, MA; Notre Dame Long Term Health Care Facility, Worcester, MA; Notre Dame Education Center, Lawrence, MA; Cuvilly Arts and Earth Center, Ipswich, MA; Notre Dame du Lac, Worcester, MA; St. Julie Billiart Residential Care Center, Ipswich, MA.
Represented in the Archdiocese of Boston and in the Dioceses of Gallup, Manchester and Worcester.

Part of the Sisters of Notre Dame United States East-West Province: 468 Poquonock Ave., Windsor, CT 06095-2473. Tel: 860-688-1832. Prov. Admin. Team: Sr. Catherine Waldron, S.N.D.deN.; Sr. Mary M. Farren, S.N.D.deN.; Sr. Barbara Barry, S.N.D.deN.; Sr. Edie Daly, S.N.D.deN.; Sr. Barbara English, S.N.D.deN.; Sr. Anne Malone, S.N.D.deN.
Total in Community: 43.
Legal Title: The Connecticut Province of the Sisters of Notre Dame de Namur, Inc.
Sisters serve and staff: Colleges, High Schools, Grammar Schools; Sisters Engaged in Specialized Educational Programs: Pastoral Ministry and Religious Education, Social Health and Community Services, Diocesan Offices, Spiritual Direction and Adult Basic Education.
Represented in the Archdioceses of Boston, Hartford and Washington and in the Dioceses of Bridgeport, Norwich, Providence, Scranton, Springfield in Massachusetts and Worcester.

Part of the Sisters of Notre Dame United States East-West Province: Sisters of Notre Dame de Namur Administrative Offices, 305 Cable St., Baltimore, MD 21210-2511. Tel: 410-243-1993; Fax: 410-243-2279. Prov. Team: Sr. Catherine Waldron, S.N.D.deN.; Sr. Mary M. Farren, S.N.D.deN.; Sr. Barbara Barry, S.N.D.deN.; Sr. Edie Daly, S.N.D.deN.; Sr. Barbara Ann English, S.N.D.deN.; Sr. Anne Malone, S.N.D.deN.
Total in Community: 36
Legal Title: Chesapeake Province of the Sisters of Notre Dame de Namur, Inc.
Represented in the Archdioceses of Baltimore, Miami, New York, Philadelphia and Washington and in the Dioceses of Arlington, Raleigh, and Wheeling-Charleston. Also in Brazil, Kenya and Democratic Republic of Congo.

Part of the Sisters of Notre Dame United States East-West Province: 1520 Ralston Ave., Belmont, CA 94002. Tel: 650-593-2045. Provincial Team: Sr. Catherine Waldron, S.N.D.deN.; Sr. Mary M. Farren, S.N.D.deN.; Sr. Barbara Barry, S.N.D.deN.; Sr. Edie Daly, S.N.D.deN; Sr. Barbara English, S.N.D.deN.; Sr. Anne Malone, S.N.D.deN.
Total in Community: 87.
Legal Title: Sisters of Notre Dame de Namur, California Province.
Ministries in the field of Academic Education at all levels; Adult Education Programs; Parish Ministries; Religious Education Programs; Social Services; Diocesan Administration; and Health.
Properties owned or sponsored: Notre Dame de Namur University, Belmont, CA; Moreland Notre Dame Elementary, Watsonville, CA; Notre Dame Elementary, Belmont, CA; Notre Dame High School, Belmont, CA; Notre Dame High School, San Jose, CA; Cristo Rey, Sacramento, CA. (Co-sponsored with Sisters of Mercy and Jesuits).
Represented in the Archdioceses of Los Angeles, Portland in Oregon, San Francisco and Seattle and in the Dioceses of Burlington, Monterey, Oakland, Sacramento, San Jose and Stockton.

Ohio Province (1840): Sisters of Notre Dame de Namur Provincial House, 701 E. Columbia Ave., Cincinnati, OH 45215. Tel: 513-761-7636. Sr. Carol Lichtenberg, S.N.D.deN., Prov.
Total in Community: 110.
Legal Titles: St. Mary's Educational Institute at Cincinnati; Sisters of Notre Dame de Namur - Ohio Province; Sisters of Notre Dame de Namur, Ohio Province, Charitable Trust.
Ministry in the field of Education at all levels; Pastoral Ministry; Administration and Services; Social Services; Communication; Health Care; Community Services.
Represented in the Archdioceses of Chicago, Cincinnati, Louisville and Washington and in the Dioceses of Austin, Buffalo, Columbus, Covington and Phoenix. Also in Brazil, Kenya, Nicaragua, Nigeria and Rome.

Baltimore Province (1934): Sisters of Notre Dame de Namur, Maryland Province Center, 1531 Greenspring Valley Rd., Stevenson, MD 21153. Tel: 410-486-5599.
Total in Community: 48.
Properties owned or sponsored: Maryland Province Center, Stevenson, MD; Villa Julie Residence, Stevenson, MD; Maryvale Preparatory School, Brooklandville, MD; Notre Dame Academy, Villanova, PA; Trinity School, Ellicot City, MD; Development Program, Stevenson, MD; Sisters Academy of Baltimore, Inc.
Represented in the Archdioceses of Atlanta, Baltimore, Philadelphia and Washington and in the Dioceses of Brooklyn, Rockville Centre and Wilmington.
Leadership Team: Sr. Carol Lichtenberg, S.N.D.deN., Prov.; Sr. Kathleen Harmon, S.N.D.deN.; Sr. Linda Soucek, S.N.D.deN.; Sr. Kristin Matthes, S.N.D.deN.

Base Communities Province (1989): Sisters of Notre Dame de Namur Base Communities Province Office:, 125 Michigan Ave., N.E., Washington, DC 20017-1004. Tel: 202-884-9750. Email: sndbcunit@aol.com. Communications Network: Sr. Loretta Fleming, S.N.D.deN.; Sr. Elizabeth Smoyer, S.N.D.deN.; Sr. Virginia West, S.N.D.deN.
Total in Province: 50.
Legal Title: Sisters of Notre Dame de Namur Base Communities, Inc.
Ministry in Formal Education; Health Care; Social Services/Community Development; Pastoral Ministry.
Represented in the Archdioceses of Baltimore, Boston, Cincinnati, Philadelphia and Washington and in the Dioceses of Albany, Charleston, Fort Wayne-South Bend, Harrisburg, Orlando, Richmond, Rockville Centre, St. Petersburg, San Jose, Wilmington and Worcester. Also in Brazil and Republic of Congo.

[3010] (O.S.B.S.)—OBLATE SISTERS OF THE BLESSED SACRAMENT (D)

Founded in 1935 by Rev. Sylvester Eisenman, O.S.B.
Motherhouse: St. Sylvester's Convent, 103 Church Dr., P.O. Box 204, Marty, SD 57361. Tel: 605-384-3305. Sr. Miriam Shindelar, O.S.B.S., Supr.
Total in Community: 4.
Represented in the Diocese of Sioux Falls.

[3020] (O.B.T.)—SISTERS OBLATES TO THE BLESSED TRINITY (D)

Founded in Italy in 1923. First foundation in the United States in 1987.
U.S. Generalate & Novitiate: St. Aloysius Gonzaga Novitiate, 306 Beekman Rd., P.O. Box 98, Hopewell Junction, NY 12533. Tel: 845-226-5671; Fax: 845-226-5671; Email: Jstab35097@aol.com. Mother Gloria Castro, Supr. Gen.
Total in Community: 40.
Represented in the Archdioceses of New York and San Juan and in the Dioceses of Madison and Ponce. Also in Italy and San Salvador.

[3035] (O.M.O.)—OBLATES OF THE MOTHER OF ORPHANS (P)

Founded in Italy on September 8, 1945.
General Motherhouse: via Amundsen 10, Milano, Italy Sr. Giovanna Velasquez, Gen. Supr.
Universal total in Congregation: 200.
U.S. Address: 20 E. 72nd St., New York, NY 10021. Sr. Adilia Martinez, Supr.
Total in Community: 3.
Represented in the Archdiocese of New York. Also in Cameroon, Colombia, El Salvador, Guatemala and Italy.

[3040] (O.S.P.)—OBLATE SISTERS OF PROVIDENCE (P)

Founded in the United States in 1829.
General Motherhouse: Our Lady of Mount Providence Convent, 701 Gun Rd., Baltimore, MD 21227. Tel: 410-242-8500. Sr. Rita Michelle Proctor, O.S.P., Supr. Gen.; Sr. Mary Annette Beecham, O.S.P., Asst. Supr.; Sr. Mary Crescentia Proctor, O.S.P., Sec. Gen.; Sr. Mary Sharon Young, O.S.P., Treas.
Professed Sisters: 55; Serving in Baltimore: 43.
Legal Title: The Oblate Sisters of Providence of the City of Baltimore.
Sisters serve as Pastoral Ministry-Associates; in the field of Education; Reading Center; Day Care Centers; Teaching; Counseling; Hispanic & Migrant Ministry.
Represented in the Archdioceses of Baltimore and Miami and in the Diocese of Buffalo. Also in Costa Rica.

[3050] (O.S.H.J.)—OBLATE SISTERS OF THE SACRED HEART OF JESUS (P)

Founded in 1894. First foundation in the United States in 1949.
General Motherhouse: Rome, Italy
American Headquarters: Villa Maria Teresa, 50 Warner Rd., Hubbard, OH 44425. Tel: 330-759-9329; Fax: 330-759-7290. Email: vmtoblate@aol.com. Sr. Joyce Candidi, O.S.H.J., Regl. Delegate.
Total in Community: 16; Total in Congregation : 194.
Represented in the Diocese of Youngstown.

[3060] (O.S.F.S.)—OBLATE SISTERS OF ST. FRANCIS DE SALES (P)

Founded in France in 1866. First foundation in the United States in 1951.
General Motherhouse: 4 rue des Terrasses, Troyes, France
American Headquarters: Villa Aviat Convent, 399 Childs Rd., Childs, MD 21916. Tel: 410-398-3699. Sr. Anne Elizabeth, O.S.F.S., Supr.
Total in Community: 13.
Ministry in the field of Academic and Religious Education.
Represented in the Dioceses of Arlington and Wilmington.

[3080] (R.C.D.)—SISTERS OF OUR LADY OF CHRISTIAN DOCTRINE (D)

Founded in New York in 1910 for the work of religious education and social service.
Central Office: Marydell Convent, 110 Larchdale Ave., Nyack, NY 10960. Tel: 845-512-8669. Sr. Veronica Mendez, R.C.D., Pres.
Total in Community: 16.
Ministry in the field of Religious Education and Spirituality; Social Work, Nursing and Counseling.
Represented in the Archdiocese of New York.

[3090] (C.L.H.C.)—CONGREGATION OF OUR LADY, HELP OF THE CLERGY (D)

Maryvale Sisters
Founded in the United States in 1961.
Motherhouse: Maryvale Motherhouse, 2522 June Bug Rd., Vale, NC 28168. Tel: 704-276-2626. Mother Mary Louis, Supr.
Total in Community: 4.
Represented in the Diocese of Charlotte.

[3100] (R.S.R.)—CONGREGATION OF OUR LADY OF THE HOLY ROSARY (P)

Founded in Rimouski, P.Q., Canada in 1874. First foundation in the United States in 1899.
General Motherhouse: 300 Alle du Rosaire, Rimouski, Canada, G5L 3E3. Tel: 418-724-5940. Sr. Gabrielle Cote, R.S.R., Supr. Gen.
Our Lady of the Holy Rosary Regional House: 25 Portland Ave., Old Orchard Beach, ME 04064. Tel: 207-934-0592; Tel: 207-937-3214. Sr. Jeannette Roy, R.S.R., Regl. Coord.
Total number in the Region: 8.
Ministry in the fields of Education; Diocesan Ministry; Pastoral Ministry.
Represented in the Diocese of Portland (In Maine)

[3105] (S.O.L.T.)—SISTERS OF THE SOCIETY OF OUR LADY OF THE MOST HOLY TRINITY

Founded in 1958 in New Mexico by Fr. James H. Flanagan. The family of the Society of Our Lady of the Most Holy Trinity is composed of priests, brothers, sisters, and laity. The Sisters serve on Ecclesial Teams with other SOLT members and live a Marian-Trinitarian spirituality.
Motherhouse & U.S. Regionalate: : 1200 Lantana St., Corpus Christi, TX 78407. Tel: 361-654-0054; Fax: 361-289-0087; Email: generalsisterservant@solt.net. U.S. Regionalate: Tel: 361-387-8090; Email: info@solt.net. Sr. Megan Mary Thibodeau, S.O.L.T., Gen. Sister Servant.
Total number of Sisters in Community: 117.
Professed Sisters: 117; Novices: 4; Candidates: 11.
Represented in the Archdioceses of Santa Fe and Seattle and in the Dioceses of Corpus Christi, Fargo, Kansas City-St. Joseph, Phoenix, Pueblo and Sioux City.

[3110] (R.C.)—N AMERICAN PROVINCE OF THE CONGREGATION OF OUR LADY OF THE RETREAT IN THE CENACLE (P)

Founded in France in 1826. First foundation in the United States in 1892.

Generalate: Piazza Madonna del Cenacolo, 15, Rome, Italy, 00136.

North American Province (2000): Congregation of Our Lady of the Cenacle, 513 Fullerton Pkwy., Chicago, IL 60614-6428. Tel: 773-528-6300; Fax: 773-549-0554. Province Email: cenacleprovincialate@usa.net; Web: www.cenaclesisters.org. Sr. Pamela Falkowski, R.C., Prov. Email: pamelajeanrc@gmail.com

Total in Community: 68.

Properties owned and sponsored: Cenacle Sisters, Hoschton, GA; The Cenacle Convent, Inc., Chicago, IL; Cenacle Convent, Inc., Houston, TX; Ronkonkoma Cenacle, Inc., Ronkonkoma, NY.

Represented in the Archdioceses of Atlanta, Chicago and Galveston-Houston and in the Dioceses of Green Bay, Joliet, Paterson, Rochester, Rockville Centre, St. Petersburg and Wheeling-Charleston.

[3120] (O.L.S.)—SISTERS OF OUR LADY OF SORROWS (P)

Founded in Italy in 1839. First foundation in the United States in 1947.

General Motherhouse: Viale Vaticano 90, Rome, Italy, 00165. Mother Carla Bertani, O.L.S., Supr. Gen.

American Headquarters: Sisters of Our Lady of Sorrows Convent, 9894 Norris Ferry Rd., Shreveport, LA 71106. Fax: 318-797-7003. Sr. Anna Maria Iannetti, O.L.S., USA Delegate of Supr. Gen.

Total in Community: 28; Universal total in Congregation: 280.

Ministry in the field of Education; Work with people with mental retardation; Outreach to the poor; Pastoral Ministry; CCD & Adult Education; early childhood education; afterschool art & education program.

Represented in the Dioceses of Alexandria, Lafayette in Louisiana, Las Cruces and Shreveport.

[3130] (O.L.V.M.)—OUR LADY OF VICTORY MISSIONARY SISTERS (P)

Founded in the United States in 1922.

Motherhouse: Victory Noll, 1900 West Park Dr. Huntington, IN 46750-8957. Tel: 260-200-1677; Fax: 260-356-3230; Email: victorynoll@olvm.org. Sr. Mary Jo Nelson, O.L.V.M., Pres.

Total in Community: 57.

Legal Holding: Victory Noll Sisters Community Support Trust.

Represented in the Archdioceses of Chicago, Denver, San Antonio and Santa Fe and in the Dioceses of Fort Wayne-South Bend, Phoenix, Salt Lake City, San Bernardino and San Diego.

[3140] (C.S.A.C.)—SISTERS OF THE CATHOLIC APOSTOLATE (PALLOTTINE) (P)

Founded in Italy in 1835. First foundation in the United States in 1889.

General Motherhouse: Via Caio Canuleio 162, Rome, Italy, 00174. Mother Ivete Garlet, C.S.A.C., Supr. Gen. Universal total in Congregation: 480.

Provincial Motherhouse in America: Queen of Apostles Convent, 98 Harriman Heights Rd., Monroe, NY 10950. Sr. Ann Joachim Firneno, C.S.A.C., Prov. Moderator.

Total in Community: 32.

Ministry in the field of Academic and Religious Education at Elementary and Secondary Levels; Pastoral Services; Youth Ministry - PTAF.

Represented in the Archdioceses of Newark and New York.

Provincial: 98 Harriman Heights Rd., Monroe, NY 10950. Tel: 845-492-5080.

[3150] (S.A.C.)—PALLOTTINE MISSIONARY SISTERS - QUEEN OF APOSTLES PROVINCE (P) (Missionary Sisters of the Catholic Apostolate)

Founded in Rome, Italy in 1838. First founded in the United States in 1912.

General Motherhouse: Rome, Italy Sr. Izabela Swierad, S.A.C., Supr. Gen.

American Provincialate: St. Mary's Convent, 2810 North Staunton Rd., Huntington, WV 25702. Tel: 304-522-3790; Fax: 314-526-1538. Email: provincial@pallottinesac.org. Sr. Mary Grace Barile, S.A.C., Prov.; Sr. Marian Ruth Creamer, S.A.C., Archivist.

Total in Congregation : 680; U.S. Province: 20.

Properties owned and/or sponsored: Pallottine Renewal Center, Florissant, MO; St. Mary's Convent, Huntington, WV; Convent, Buckhannon, WV; St. Vincent Pallotti Convent, High School Laurel, MD.

Sisters minister in the fields of Health Care; Education; Retreat and Renewal Ministry; Social Services; Parish and Pastoral Work.

Represented in the Archdioceses of St. Louis and Washington and in the Diocese of Wheeling-Charleston.

[3160] (P.V.M.I.)—PARISH VISITORS OF MARY IMMACULATE (P)

Founded in New York City in 1920 for family visitation and religious education. A contemplative-missionary community serving the Church by person-to-person evangelization.

Motherhouse and Novitiate: Marycrest, P.O. Box 658, Monroe, NY 10949-0658. Tel: 845-783-2251. Communications Email: marycrest@frontiernet.net.; Vocation Director Email: pvmi@frontiernet.net. Mother Maria Catherine Iannotti, Gen. Supr.; Sr. Carole Marie Troskowski, Novice Dir.

Total in Community: 61.

Ministry in evangelization, catechetics, & spiritual counseling; liaison for social services.

Represented in the Archdioceses of New York and Philadelphia and in the Dioceses of Brooklyn, Phoenix and Wilmington. Also in Nigeria and Philippines.

[3170] (C.P.)—RELIGIOUS OF THE PASSION OF JESUS CHRIST (P) (Passionist Nuns)

Founded in Italy in 1771 by St. Paul of the Cross. First foundation in the United States in 1910.

2715 Churchview Ave., Pittsburgh, PA 15227. Tel: 412-881-1155. Mother Mary Ann, C.P., Supr.

Perpetual Vows: 8.

The Religious of the Passion of Jesus Christ (Contemplative) (1926): St. Gabriel's Monastery, 631 Griffin Pond Rd., Clarks Summit, PA 18411. Tel: 570-586-2791; Fax: 570-586-8210. Sr. Teresita Kho, C.P., Supr. Professed Sisters: 7.

Sisters serve and staff: Retreats and other Programs for Women and Men of all Faiths; Clergy and Religious; Ecumenical Groups; Business and Civic Groups.

Legal Holding: St. Gabriel's Monastery and Retreat Center.

Passionist Nuns (Cloistered Contemplative) (1946): Passionist Nuns, 8564 Crisp Rd., Whitesville, KY 42378-9782. Tel: 270-233-4571. Mother John Mary Read, C.P., Supr.

Professed Nuns: 10; Temporary Vows: 4.

Passionist Nuns (Contemplative) (1947): Monastery of the Sacred Passion, 1151 Donaldson Hwy., Erlanger, KY 41018-1000. Tel: 859-371-8568. Sr. Margaret Mary, C.P., Supr.

Total in Community: 7.

Legal Title: Passionist Nuns of Covington, KY.

Passionist Nuns (Cloistered) (1948): Passionist Monastery, 15700 Clayton Rd., Ellisville, MO 63011. Tel: 636-527-6867. Mother Mary Veronica, C.P., Supr.

Total in Community: 6.

[3180] (C.P.)—SISTERS OF THE CROSS AND PASSION (P) (Passionist Sisters)

Founded in 1852. First foundation in the United States in 1924.

Generalate: Drumalis Centre, 47 Glenarm Rd., Larne BT40 1DT Northern Ireland. Tel: +44(0)2828 267005; Email: cpclt@icloud.com. Sr. Eileen Fucito, C.P., Congregational Leader.

Diversified apostolic works according to the needs of the church; catechetical, pastoral and social work; education functions; retreats; missionary work in the United States and Africa, Argentina, Australia, Bosnia, Botswana, Chile, England, Europe, Ireland, Peru, Scotland and Vietnam.

Provincial House in United States: Holy Family Convent, One Wright Ln., North Kingstown, RI 02852. Tel: 401-667-4813; 401-480-7766. Email: passcom12@gmail.com. Sr. Bernadette Hughes, C.P. Province Leader.

Professed Sisters: 29.

Sisters minister in Retreat Centers; Elementary Education; Parish Ministry; Religious Education; Social Services.

Properties owned and operated: Our Lady of Calvary Retreat, Farmington, CT.

Represented in the Archdioceses of Hartford and in the Dioceses of Providence and Rockville Centre.

[3190] (A.P.)—NUNS OF THE PERPETUAL ADORATION OF THE BLESSED SACRAMENT (P)

Founded in Rome in 1807. First foundation in the United States in 1925.

El Paso: Expiatory Shrine of Christ the King and Monastery of Perpetual Adoration, 145 N. Cotton Ave., El Paso, TX 79901. Tel: 915-533-5323; Email: mary.guadalupe@att.net. Mother Maria Zoila Flores, A.P., Supr.

Sisters: 12.

Represented in the Archdioceses of Anchorage and San Francisco and in the Dioceses of El Paso and Sioux Falls.

San Francisco: Monastery of Perpetual Adoration, 771 Ashbury St., San Francisco, CA 94117. Tel: 415-566-2743. Mother Rosalba Maria, A.P., Supr.

Sisters: 12.

Represented in the Archdiocese of San Francisco. Also in Africa, Chile, Italy, Mexico and Spain.

[3195] (A.P.G.)—SISTERS OF PERPETUAL ADORATION OF GUADALUPE, INC. (P)

U.S. Foundation: 2403 W. Travis, San Antonio, TX 78207. Tel: 210-227-5546. Mother Luz del Carmen Sanchez O., A.P.G., Gen. Counsel.

Total in Community: 10.

[3200] (SCH.P.)—SISTERS OF THE PIOUS SCHOOLS (P) (Escolapias)

Founded in Figueras, Spain in 1829.

Universal total in Congregation: 675.

General Motherhouse: Via Crescenzio 77, Rome, Italy, 00193. Mother M. Divina Garcia, Sch.P., Supr. Gen.

U.S. Headquarters (1954): 17601 Nordhoff St., Northridge, CA 91325. Tel: 818-885-6265; Fax: 818-718-6752. Sr. Guadalupe Gonzalez, Sch.P.

Total in Community: 8.

Ministry in Religious Education; Parish Schools.

Represented in the Archdiocese of Los Angeles.

[3210] (P.C.P.A.)—POOR CLARES OF PERPETUAL ADORATION (P)

Founded in France, 1854. First foundation in the United States at Cleveland, Ohio, 1921. Poor Clares of Perpetual Adoration, cloistered, contemplative, solemn vows. Object: Perpetual Adoration in spirit of Praise and Thanksgiving and Gospel living. Solemn Exposition day and night. Each monastery is autonomous.

Sancta Clara Monastery (1946): 4200 N. Market Ave., Canton, OH 44714. Tel: 330-492-1171; Web: www.poorclares.org. Mother Gertrude Espenilla, P.C.P.A., Abbess.

Total in Community: 10.

Saint Joseph Adoration Monastery (1956): 3452 Willow Oak Rd., Charlotte, NC 28209. Tel: 704-999-7895; Email: nuns@stjosephmonastery.com; Web: www.stjosephmonastery.com.

Total in Community: 7.

Legal Title: Poor Clares of Perpetual Adoration-Saint Joseph Adoration Monastery, Inc.

Adoration Monastery (1921): 4108 Euclid Ave., Cleveland, OH 44103. Tel: 216-361-0783. Email: angelspcpa@sbcglobal.net. Mother Mary James, P.C.P.A., Abbess.

Total in Community: 21.

Poor Clares of Perpetual Adoration (1954): Our Lady of the Most Blessed Sacrament Monastery, 3900 13th St., N.E., Washington, DC 20017-2699. Tel: 202-526-6808; Fax: 202-526-0678; Email: ourprayer4u@poorclareswdc.org; Web: www.poorclareswdc.org. Mother Mary Angela Perry, P.C.P.A., Abbess.

Total in Community: 5.

Our Lady of the Angels Monastery: Shrine of the Most Blessed Sacrament, 3222 County Rd. 548, Hanceville, AL 35077. Tel: 205-271-2917; Fax: 205-795-5702. Email: business@olamshrine.com. Mother Dolores Marie, P.C.P.A., Apostolic Admin. Total in Community: 12.

Legal Title: Our Lady of the Angels Monastery in Hanceville Alabama

Represented in the Diocese of Birmingham.

[3220] (P.C.J.)—SISTERS OF THE POOR CHILD JESUS (P)

Founded on February 2, 1844 in Germany. First founded in the United States on July 2, 1924 at Parkersburg, West Virginia.

General Motherhouse: Jakobstrasse 19, D-52064, Aachen, Germany Sr. Maria del Rocio, P.C.J., Supr. Gen.

Universal total in Congregation: 500.

American Region and Novitiate: In Mohun Health Care Center, 2340 Airport Dr., Columbus, OH 43219. Joseph D. Scott, Contact Person.

Ministry in the field of Healthcare and Motherhouse.

Represented in the Dioceses of Columbus and Wheeling-Charleston.

[3230] (P.H.J.C.)—POOR HANDMAIDS OF JESUS CHRIST (P) (The Ancilla Domini Sisters, Inc.)

Founded in Germany in 1851. First foundation in the United States in 1868.

General Motherhouse: Dernbach, Westerwald, Germany Sr. Gonzalo Vakasseril, P.H.J.C., Supr. Gen.

American Province-Provincialate: Convent Ancilla Domini, 9601 Union Rd., P.O. Box 1, Donaldson, IN 46513. Tel: 574-936-9936; Fax: 574-935-1785. Email: judith.diltz@poorhandmaids.org. Sr. Judith Diltz, P.H.J.C., Prov. Provincial Councilors: Sr. Michele Dvorak, P.H.J.C.; Sr. Joetta Huelsmann, P.H.J.C.; Sr. Margaret Anne Henss, P.H.J.C; Mary Hunt, Treas.; Amanda Maynard, Develop. Dir.

Professed Sisters: 67.

Ministry in the fields of Academic Education at all levels; Healthcare; Parish Ministries; Retreat Ministries; Child Care Ministry; Retirement Communities; Environmental Care and Homeless Ministries.

Properties owned or sponsored: Ancilla Domini College; Convent Ancilla Domini; Catherine Kasper Life Center, Inc.; Lindenwood Retreat & Conference Center; MoonTree Community, Donaldson, IN; Poor Handmaids of Jesus Christ Community Support Trust, Donaldson, IN; Poor Handmaids of Jesus Christ Foundation, Inc., Donaldson, IN; HealthVisions Midwest, Hammond, IN; Emmaus House, East Chicago, IN; Sojourner Truth House, Gary, IN; Ancilla Systems, Inc., Hobart, IN; St. Catherine Convent, East Chicago, IN; Annunciation Convent, Hoffman Estates, IL; St. Joseph Community Health Foundation, Ft. Wayne, IN; Catherine Kasper Place, Ft. Wayne, IN; St. Joseph Medical Center of Ft. Wayne, Inc., Ft. Wayne, IN; Nazareth Home, East Chicago, IN; Sara House, South Bend, IN.

Represented in the Archdioceses of Chicago and Cincinnati and in the Dioceses of Fort Wayne-South Bend, Gary, Lafayette in Indiana, Providence, and Savannah. Also in Africa, Brazil, Germany and Mexico.

[3240] (C.J.C.)—POOR SISTERS OF JESUS CRUCIFIED AND THE SORROWFUL MOTHER (D)

Founded in the United States in 1924.

General Motherhouse and Novitiate: Our Lady of Sorrows Convent, 261 Thatcher St., Brockton, MA 02302-3997. Sr. Mary Valliere, C.J.C., Gen. Supr.

Total in Community: 10.

Properties owned and/or sponsored: Our Lady of Sorrows Convent, Brockton, MA. Ministry in Nursing Homes; Education Center; Elementary Schools; Assisted Living facilities; and Pastoral Ministry.

Represented in the Archdiocese of Boston.

[3242] (C.S.N.)—THE CONGREGATION OF THE SISTERS OF NAZARETH (P)

Founded in England by Mother St. Basil.

Motherhouse: Hammersmith, London, England, W6 8DB. Sr. St. Hilary, Supr. Gen.

Regional Headquarters: Nazareth House, 3333 Manning Ave., Los Angeles, CA 90064. Tel: 310-839-2361. Sr. John Berchmans, Supr.

Professed Sisters: 32.

Legal Title: The Congregation of the Sisters of Nazareth Mother House U.S.A., Inc.

Represented in the Archdioceses of Los Angeles and San Francisco and in the Dioceses of Fresno, Madison and San Diego. Also in American Samoa.

[3250] (P.S.S.J.)—POOR SISTERS OF ST. JOSEPH (P)

Founded in Buenos Aires, Argentina in 1880.

U.S. Motherhouse: St. Gabriel Convent, 4319 Sano St., Alexandria, VA 22312. Tel: 703-354-0395. Email: pssjalexandria@gmail.com. Mother Maria Gonzalez.

Casa Nazareth: 532 Spruce St., Reading, PA 19602. Tel: 610-378-1947. Total in Community: 9.

General Motherhouse: Pte. Peron 734, 1663 Muñiz, Buenos Aires, Argentina Mother Raquel del Carmen Brambilla, Supr. Gen.

Represented in the Dioceses of Allentown and Arlington.

[3260] (C.PP.S.)—SISTERS OF THE PRECIOUS BLOOD (DAYTON, OHIO) (P)

Founded in Switzerland in 1834. First foundation in the United States in 1844.

C.PP.S. Administration Offices: 4000 Denlinger Rd., Dayton, OH 45426. Tel: 937-837-3302; Fax: 937-837-8825. Sr. Joyce Lehman, C.PP.S., Pres.; Sr. Nancy Kinross, C.PP.S., Councilor & Sec.; Sr. Linda Pleiman, C.PP.S., Councilor; Sr. Cecilia Taphorn, C.PP.S., Vice Pres. & Councilor; Sr. Patty Kremer, C.PP.S., Councilor; Sr. Noreen Jutte, C.PP.S., Archivist.

Total Membership: 113.

Ministry in Elementary Schools; Pastoral Ministry in Hospitals and Long-term Care Centers; Religious and Adult Education; Ethnic Minorities and Marginalized Peoples; Retreat and Music Ministry; Missionary and Volunteer Services.

Properties owned and sponsored: C.PP.S. Administration Offices, Dayton, OH; Salem Heights Convent, Dayton, OH; Maria Stein Shrine of the Holy Relics, Maria Stein, OH.

Represented in the Archdioceses of Chicago, Cincinnati, Denver and in the Dioceses of Cleveland, Columbus, Saginaw, San Bernardino, San Diego and Toledo. Also in Chile and Guatemala.

[3270] (C.PP.S.)—SISTERS OF THE MOST PRECIOUS BLOOD (O'FALLON, MO) (P)

Founded in Switzerland in 1845. First foundation in the United States in 1870.

General Administration: St. Mary's Institute of O'Fallon, 204 N. Main St., O'Fallon, MO 63366-2299. Tel: 636-240-6010; Fax: 636-272-5031. Sr. Janice Bader, C.PP.S., Supr. Gen. General Councilors: Sr. Virginia Jaskiewicz, C.PP.S., Councilor; Sr. Joni Belford, C.PP.S., Councilor & Sec.; Sr. Barbara Schlatter, C.PP.S., Councilor; Sr. Marie Fennewald, C.PP.S., Councilor; Sr. Barbara Payne, Community Archivist; Sr. Carmen Schnyder, Treas.

Total in Community: 104.

Ministry in the field of Education; Care of the Elderly; Pastoral and Parish Ministry; Foreign Missions; Social Services; Prayer/Presence. Properties owned: St. Mary's Institute of O'Fallon, O'Fallon, MO; Charitable Trust, Sisters of the Most Precious Blood of O'Fallon, MO; Centers for Professional and Pastoral Services, O'Fallon, MO.

Represented in the Archdioceses of Anchorage, St. Louis and in the Diocese of Wheeling-Charleston. Also in Bolivia, Peru, Estonia and Finland.

[3310] (P.M.)—SISTERS OF THE PRESENTATION OF MARY (P)

Founded in France in 1796. First foundation in the United States in 1873.

General Administration: Presentazionne di Maria, Viale Pio XI, 29 - C.P. 104, Castelgandolfo, Italy, 00040. Mother Angele Dion, Supr. Gen.

House of Formation: 186 Lowell Rd., Hudson, NH 03051-4908. Tel: 603-882-1347.

Provincial Administration: 209 Lawrence St., Methuen, MA 01844-3884. Tel: 978-687-1369. Sr. Helene Cote, P.M., Provincial Supr.

Total Number in Province: 149.

Properties owned and/or sponsored: Presentation of Mary Academy, Methuen, MA; Marie Joseph Spiritual Center, Biddeford, ME; Presentation of Mary Academy, Hudson, NH; St. Joseph Residence, Manchester, NH; Rivier University, Nashua, NH; Our Lady of Hope House of Prayer, New Ipswich, NH.

Represented in the Archdiocese of Boston and the Dioceses of Manchester, Portland in Maine and Providence.

[3320] (P.B.V.M.)—SISTERS OF THE PRESENTATION OF THE B.V.M. (P)

Founded in Ireland in 1775.

Represented in the United States in the following Archdioceses and Dioceses.

Dubuque (P)

Mt. Loretto Convent, Motherhouse and Novitiate: 2360 Carter Rd., Dubuque, IA 52001-2997. Tel: 563-588-2008; Fax: 563-588-4463. Sr. Julianne Brockamp, P.B.V.M., Congregational Leader.

Total in Community: 106.

Legal Title: Sisters of the Presentation of the B.V.M., Dubuque, IA.

Ministry in the field of Religious and Academic Education; Hospital Chaplaincy; Elder Care; Parish & Campus Ministries; South American Bolivian Mission; Diocesan/Metropolitan Offices; Retreat & Spiritual Direction; Hispanic Ministry; Peace and Justice; Social Services; Internal Community Ministry.

Represented in the Archdioceses of Chicago, Dubuque, Louisville, New Orleans, St. Paul-Minneapolis and Washington and in the Dioceses of Davenport, Des Moines, Jackson, Knoxville, La Crosse, Madison, Pittsburgh, Sioux City, Sioux Falls and Winona-Rochester. Also in Bolivia.

New York (P)

Mt. St. Joseph Administration Center: Sisters of the Presentation of the Blessed Virgin Mary, 84 Presentation Way, New Windsor, NY 12553. Tel: 845-564-0513; Fax: 845-567-0219. Email: administration@sistersofthepresentation.org. Sr. Patricia Anastasio, P.B.V.M., Pres.; Sr. Enid Storey, P.B.V.M., Community Archivist.

Total in Community: 98.

Ministry in the field of Academic Education at all levels; Pastoral Services; Health Care and Social Services.

Represented in the Archdioceses of New York and Washington and in the Dioceses of Brooklyn, Norwich, Paterson and Worcester.

Our Lady of the Presentation Motherhouse: 419 Woodrow Rd., Staten Island, NY 10312. Tel: 718-356-2121. Sr. Lorraine Hale, Congregational Leader.

Professed Sisters: 11.

Ministry in Elementary Schools; University; Campus Ministry; Pastoral Counseling; Adult Education; Healing & Parish Ministry.

Represented in the Archdioceses of New York and Philadelphia.

San Francisco Presentation Congregational Offices: 281 Masonic Ave., San Francisco, CA 94118. Tel: 415-422-5001. Sr. Michele Anne Murphy, P.B.V.M., Pres. Tel: 415-422-5013; Rachel Foote, Archivist.

Total in Community: 60.

Legal Title: Sisters of the Presentation.

Ministry in the field of Religious and Academic Education at all levels; Parish Ministry; Social and Health Ministry; Retreat Work; Internal Ministry.

Represented in the Archdioceses of Los Angeles, San Francisco and Washington and in the Dioceses of Monterey, Oakland, San Jose and Sioux Falls.

Albany (P)

St. Colman's Presentation Convent, Motherhouse and Novitiate: Sisters of the Presentation of the Blessed Virgin Mary P.V.B.M., 11 Haswell Rd, Watervliet, NY 12189. Tel: 518-273-4911; Fax: 518-273-3312. Mother Mary Louise Kane, P.B.V.M., Supr.

Total in Community: 19.

Ministry in the field of Special Education; Child Caring Institution; Resident/Day School for Autistic & Day School for Emotionally Challenging Children, Students with Learning Disabilities.

Represented in the Diocese of Albany.

Sioux Falls (P)

Presentation Convent, Motherhouse and Novitiate: Sisters of the Presentation of the Blessed Virgin Mary, 1500 N. Second St., Aberdeen, SD 57401. Tel: 605-229-8419. Sr. Janice Klein, P.B.V.M., Pres.; Kathleen Daly, Congregation Archivist.

Total in Community: 61.

Ministry in the field of Academic Education; Hospitals; Homes for the Aged; Parish Pastoral Ministry; Hispanic Ministry; Ministry in Zambia and Africa.

Represented in the Diocese of Sioux Falls.

Worcester (P)

Presentation Convent: 99 Church St., Leominster, MA 01453. Email: pbvmadministration@hvc.rr.com. Sr. Patricia Anastasio, P.B.V.M., Pres.

Total in Community: 103.

Sisters staff: Elementary and High School Education; Pastoral Ministry; Social Services; Nursing.

Represented in the Archdioceses of New York and Washington and in the Dioceses of Brooklyn, Norwich, Paterson and Worcester.

[3330] (P.B.V.M.)—UNION OF SISTERS OF THE PRESENTATION OF THE BLESSED VIRGIN MARY (P)

The Congregation of the Presentation was founded in Cork, Ireland, 1775. By decree of the Sacred Congregation for Religious, the Union of Sisters of the Presentation was established in Ireland in 1976. First U.S.A. Province was established in 1989.

Generalate: Monasterevan Co., Kildare, Ireland Tel: 045-525-335. Sr. Mary Deane, P.B.V.M., Supr. Gen.

Provincial Offices: P.O. Box 100785, San Antonio, TX 78201-8785. Email: sectypbvmus@yahoo.com. Sr. Joan O'Sullivan, P.B.V.M., Prov.; Sr. Francine Janousek, P.B.V.M., Asst. Prov.; Sr. Katherine Fennell, P.B.V.M., Treas.; Sr. Philippa Wall, P.B.V.M., Archivist.

Perpetual Sisters: 81

Sisters Serve and Staff: Elementary and Religious Education; Parish Ministry; Retreat Ministry; Health and Hospital Services and Social Services.

Represented in the Archdioceses of Los Angeles, Mobile, San Antonio and San Francisco and in the Dioceses of Biloxi, Fargo, Jackson, New Ulm, Orange, San Bernardino and Tucson.

Fargo (P) Sacred Heart Convent: Sisters of Presentation of the Blessed Virgin Mary P.B.V.M., 1101 32nd Ave. S., Fargo, ND 58103. Tel: 701-237-4857; Email: sistermom10@yahoo.com. Sr. Stella Olson, P.B.V.M., Local Leader; Philippa Wall, Archivist.

Total in Community: 32.

Sponsored Ministries: Presentation Prayer Center, Fargo, ND; Presentation Center, Fargo, ND; Hughes, Inc., Fargo, ND; The Presentation Sisters Foundation, Fargo, ND; Presentation Partners in Housing; Office of Peace & Justice.

[3340] (S.P.)—SISTERS OF PROVIDENCE (D)

Founded as a mission of the Sisters of Charity of the House of Providence, Kingston, Ontario, Canada in 1873. Founded as an independent diocesan foundation in 1892.

Administrative Office: 5 Gamelin St., Holyoke, MA 01040-4081. Tel: 413-536-7511; Fax: 413-536-7917; Email: sisters@sisofprov.org. Sr. Kathleen Popko, S.P., Congregation Pres.

Professed Sisters: 32.

Legal Holdings and Titles: Sisters of Providence, Inc: The Hillside at Providence, Inc. Sisters of Providence Ministry Corporation: Family Services - Providence Ministries for the Needy, Holyoke, MA; Retreat Center - Genesis Spiritual Life and Conference Center, Inc., Westfield, MA; Senior Services - Mary's Meadow at Providence Place, Inc., Holyoke, MA; Providence Place, Inc., Holyoke, MA; Mount St. Vincent Care Center, Holyoke, MA.

Represented in the Diocese of Springfield in Massachusetts.

[3350] (S.P.)—SISTERS OF PROVIDENCE (P)

Founded in Montreal in 1843. First foundation in the United States in 1856.

General Administration: 12055 rue Grenet, Montreal, Canada, H4J 2J5. Sr. Karin Dufault, S.P., Gen. Supr.

Mother Joseph Province (2000): Sisters of Providence, 1801 Lind Ave., SW, #9016, Renton, WA 98057-9016. Tel: 425-525-3012; Fax: 425-525-3386; Web: www.sistersofprovidence.net. Sr. Judith Desmarais, S.P., Prov. Supr.

Total in Community: 506; Sisters in Province: 123.

Ministry for women and children; education, healthcare, parish, aid to poor people, care for the environment; socially responsible investing; repository for history of the Catholic Church in the Northwest; skilled nursing for our senior and disabled sisters from our own and other congregations.

Properties, entities and divisions owned or operated: Sisters of Providence-Mother Joseph Province; St. Joseph Residence, Seattle, WA; Providence Archives, Seattle, WA; Sisters of Providence Retirement Trust, Renton, WA.

Represented in the Archdioceses of Los Angeles, Portland in Oregon and Seattle and in the Dioceses of Spokane and Yakima. Also in El Salvador and the Philippines.

Novitiate House: 1016 N. Superior St., #4, Spokane, WA 99202-2096. Tel: 509-487-5706. Sr. Celia Chappell, S.P., Novitiate Dir.

Vocation Office: 4800 37th Ave., S.W., Seattle, WA 98126-2724. Tel: 206-979-0577. Sr. Margarita Hernandez, S.P., Vocation Dir.

Our Lady of Province: 47 W. Spring St., Winooski, VT 05404. Tel: 802-655-2395; Fax: 802-655-3888. Sr. Carmen Proulx, S.P., Supr.

Total in Community: 10.

Emilie Gamelin Province (2005): Sisters of Providence, 47 W. Spring St., Winooski, VT 05404. Tel: 802-655-2395; Fax: 802-655-3888. Sr. Carmen Proulx, S.P., Supr.

Total in Community: 7.

[3360] (S.P.)—SISTERS OF PROVIDENCE OF SAINT MARY-OF-THE-WOODS, INDIANA (P)

Founded in France in 1806. First foundation in the United States in 1840.

General Administration: Sisters of Providence, 1 Sisters of Providence, Saint Mary-Of-The-Woods, IN 47876-1007. Tel: 812-535-4193; Web: www.sistersofprovidence.org. Sr. Dawn Tomaszewski, S.P., Gen. Supr.; Sr. Marianne Mader, S.P., Congregation Archivist; Sr. Vicki Layton, S.P., Gen. Sec.

Total number Professed Sisters: 267.

Legal Titles and Sponsored Institutions: Guerin College Preparatory High School, River Grove, IL; Saint Mary-of-the-Woods College, Saint Mary-of-the-Woods, IN; Providence Self Sufficiency Ministries, Inc., Georgetown, IN; Sisters of Providence Community Support Trust (1969-Foundation to provide support for the aged and infirm members of the Congregation) Indianapolis, IN; Providence Health Care, Inc., St. Mary-of-the-Woods, IN; Providence Cristo Rey High School, Indianapolis, IN.

Ministry in the fields of Education at all levels; Diocesan Offices; Parish and Pastoral Ministry; Health Care and Retirement Facilities; Congregation Administration; Social Services; Therapeutic/Rehabilitative/ Mental Health Services.

Represented in the Archdioceses of Baltimore, Boston, Chicago, Cincinnati, Indianapolis, Louisville, Los Angeles, San Antonio and Washington and in the Dioceses of Charlotte, Cleveland, Evansville, Joliet, Lafayette (LA), Lafayette in Indiana, Lexington, Rockford, San Bernardino, San Diego and Venice. Also in China and Taiwan.

Area of Taiwan: Providence University, 200 Taiwan Blvd., Section 7, Shalu, Taichung 43301, Taiwan, Republic of China Tel: 011-886-4-2631-1182. Sr. Norene WU, S.P., Area Rep.

Total in Community: 10.

Ministry in the field of Education; Elderly Care. Represented in the Archdiocese of Taipei and in the Dioceses of Xozhou, China, Taichung.

[3390] (R.A.)—RELIGIOUS OF THE ASSUMPTION (P)

Founded in France in 1839. Established in the United States in 1919.

Generalate: 17 rue de l'Assomption, Paris, France, 75016.

Universal total in Congregation: 1200.

Represented in 33 countries through Europe, Africa, Asia, North America, Central America and South America.

U.S. Province: Provincial House, 11 Old English Rd., Worcester, MA 01609. Tel: 508-793-1954. Sr. Mary Ann Azana, R.A., Prov. Supr.

Administrative Office: 506 Crestview Rd., Lansdale, PA 19446. Tel: 215-368-4427; Tel: 215-362-6296.

Total number in Province: 22.

Ministry in Spiritual Formation; Campus Ministry; Pastoral and Social Ministry; Education; Peace and Justice.

Represented in the Archdiocese of Philadelphia and in the Dioceses of Las Cruces and Worcester.

[3400] (R.S.C.)—RELIGIOUS SISTERS OF CHARITY (P)

Founded in Dublin, Ireland in 1815. Sisters in entire Congregation 505.

Motherhouse: Caritas, 15 Gilford Rd., Sandymount, Dublin 4, Ireland Sr. Mary Christian, Supr. Gen.

U.S. Headquarters & Novitiate (1953): Regional Residence, 10668 St. James Dr., Culver City, CA 90230. Tel: 310-559-0176; Fax: 310-559-3530. Sr. Bernadette Morgan, R.S.C., Regl. Leader.

Total in U.S. Community: 29.

Represented in the Archdiocese of Los Angeles.

[3410] (R.C.E.)—RELIGIOUS OF CHRISTIAN EDUCATION (P)

Founded in France in 1817. First foundation in the United States in 1905.

General Motherhouse: France

Provincial Residence: 444 Centre St., Milton, MA 02186. Tel: 781-894-2008; Fax: 401-349-4970. Sr. Martha Brigham, R.C.E., Pres.

Total in Community: 6.

Legal Title: Religious of Christian Education, Inc.

Represented in the Archdiocese of Boston.

[3430] (M.P.F.)—RELIGIOUS TEACHERS FILIPPINI (P)

Founded in Italy in 1692. First foundation in the United States in 1910.

General Motherhouse: Villa Maria Regina, Via Stazione Ottavia, 72, Rome, Italy Sr. Nicolina Bandiera, M.P.F., Supr. Gen.

St. Lucy Filippini Province: Villa Walsh, Morristown, NJ 07960-4928. Tel: 973-538-2886. Sr. Ascenza Tizzano, M.P.F., Prov. Supr.; Sr. Patricia Martin, M.P.F., Community Archivist.

Total in Community: 155.

Ministry in the field of Religious and Academic Education in elementary and secondary schools; Child Care Centers; Parish Ministry; Pastoral Care; Foreign Mission Work; House of Prayer; Retreat House.

Properties owned and sponsored: Villa Walsh, Morristown, NJ; Villa Victoria, Trenton, NJ; St. Joseph by The Sea, South Mantoloking, NJ; St. Joseph Convent, Bristol, CT; Villa Ferretti, Winchester Ctr, CT.

Represented in the Archdioceses of Hartford, Newark, Philadelphia and Santa Fe, and in the Dioceses of Brooklyn, Cleveland, Camden, Metuchen, Orlando, Paterson, Pittsburgh, Providence, Scranton and Trenton.

[3449] (C.V.I.)—RELIGIOUS OF THE INCARNATE WORD (P)

Founded in Lyon, France, in 1625. First foundation in the United States in 1853, in Mexico 1894.

General Motherhouse: Industria #1-Col. Toriello Guerra, Deleg., Tlalpan, Mexico, D.F. 14050. Sr. Margarita Dibildox, C.V.I., Gen. Supr.

U.S. Vice Provincial House: 153 Rainier Ct., Chula Vista, CA 91911. Tel: 619-869-7337. Sr. Camille Crabbe, C.V.I., Vice Prov.

Total in Congregation : 465.

Ministry in Parishes; Schools; Missions and Boarding for Students.

Represented in the Diocese of San Diego. Also in Africa, Argentina, El Salvador, France, Guatemala, Mexico, Spain and Uruguay.

[3450] (R.J.M.)—RELIGIOUS OF JESUS AND MARY (P)

Founded at Lyons, France, 1818. First foundation in the United States in 1877.

Motherhouse: Via Nomentana 325, Rome, Italy Sr. Monica Joseph, R.J.M., Supr. Gen. Universal total in Congregation: 1433.

United States Province: 821 Varnum St., N.E., Ste. 225, Washington, DC 20017. Tel: 202-526-3203; Email: amagner@rjmusa.org. Sr. Margaret Perron, R.J.M., Prov.

Total in Community: 71.

Legal Title: U.S. Province of the Religious of Jesus and Mary, Inc.

Ministry in the field of Academic and Religious Education; Pastoral Ministry; Social Services; Volunteer Program.

Represented in the Archdioceses of Boston, New York and Washington and in the Dioceses of Fall River, Manchester, Providence and San Diego. Also in Haiti.

[3460] (R.M.I.)—RELIGIOUS OF MARY IMMACULATE (P)

Founded in Madrid, Spain in 1876.

Mother House: Madrid, Spain Generalate: Rome, Italy

U.S. Foundation (1954): Villa Maria, 719 Augusta St., San Antonio, TX 78215. Tel: 210-226-0025; Fax: 210-226-3305. Sr. Mary Cristina Lopez G., R.M.I., Local Supr. Total in Community: 7.

Headquarters: Centro Maria, 539 West 54th St., New York, NY 10019. Tel: 212-581-5273. Sr. Hilda Ramirez, R.M.I., Local Supr.

Total in Community: 8.

Represented in the Archdioceses of New York, San Antonio and Washington.

[3465] (R.S.H.M.)—RELIGIOUS OF THE SACRED HEART OF MARY (P)

Founded in France in 1849. First foundation in the United States in 1877.

Generalate: Via Sorelle Marchisio 41, Rome, Italy, 00168. Sr. Rosamond Blanchet, R.S.H.M., Gen. Supr.

Universal total in Congregation: 627.

Eastern American Province (1907): 50 Wilson Park Dr., Tarrytown, NY 10591. Tel: 914-631-8872. Sr. Catherine Patten, R.S.H.M., Prov. Supr. Email: cpatten@rshmeap.org.

Total in Community: 119.

Legal Title: Sisters of the Sacred Heart of Mary.

Ministries including Education; Pastoral Ministry; Retreat and Spiritual Direction; Social Work.

Represented in the Archdioceses of New York and in the Dioceses of Arlington, Richmond, Rockville Centre and Venice. Also in Africa and Europe.

Western American Province (1959): Religious of the Sacred Heart of Mary R.S.H.M. Provincial Center, 441 N. Garfield Ave., Montebello, CA 90640-2901. Tel: 323-887-8821; Fax: 323-887-8952. Email: rshmwap@earthlink.net. Sr. Joan Treacy, R.S.H.M., Prov.

Total number in Province: 47.

Legal Titles or Holdings: Religious of the Sacred Heart of Mary, Western American Province, a California nonprofit corporation, Marymount School Corporation, a California nonprofit public benefit corporation.

Ministry in the field of Academic Education at all levels; Diverse Pastoral Ministries; Prison Ministry; Justice and Peace Advocacies; Youths at Risk.

Represented in the Archdiocese of Los Angeles and in the Diocese of San Bernardino. Also in Mexico.

[3470] (S.R.C.M.)—SISTERS OF REPARATION OF THE CONGREGATION OF MARY, INC. (D)

St. Zita's Villa, 50 Saddle River Rd., N., Monsey, NY 10952. Tel: 845-356-2011; Fax: 845-364-6520 Sr. Maureen Francis, S.R.C.M.

Total in Community: 2.

Represented in the Archdiocese of New York.

[3475] (S.R.)—SISTERS OF REPARATION OF THE SACRED WOUNDS OF JESUS (D)

Founded in 1954 in New York by Mother Mary Rose Therese, S.R. Established in the Diocese of San Diego in 1959. Motherhouse and Novitiate transferred to the Archdiocese of Portland in Oregon in 1973.

General Motherhouse and Novitiate: Sacred Wounds of Jesus Convent, 2120 S.E. 24th Ave., Portland, OR 97214. Tel: 503-236-4207; Fax: 503-236-3400; Email: repsrs@comcast.net; Email: MMAngels@comcast.net; Web: www.reparationsisters.org. Mother Mary of the Angels, S.R., Supr.

Sisters: 2; Donne Members: 164.

Legal Title: Sisters of Reparation of the Sacred Wounds of Jesus, Inc., Portland, OR.

Ministry in Health Care; Education; Pastoral Animation.

Represented in the Archdiocese of Portland in Oregon.

[3480] (C.R.)—SISTERS OF THE RESURRECTION (P)

Founded in Rome, Italy, in 1891. First foundation in the United States in 1900.

General Motherhouse: Via Marcantonio Colonna 52A, Rome, Italy Rev. Mother Dorota Zygmunt, C.R., Supr. Gen.

Universal total in Congregation: 385.

Western Province Provincial House and Novitiate: 7432 Talcott Ave., Chicago, IL 60631. Tel: 773-792-6363. Sr. Virginia Ann Wanzek, C.R., Prov. Supr.

Total in Community: 31.

Properties owned or sponsored: Resurrection College Prep High School.

Represented in the Archdioceses of Chicago and Milwaukee.

Eastern Province Provincial House and Novitiate: Sisters of the Resurrection, 35 Boltwood Ave., Castleton On Hudson, NY 12033. Tel: 518-732-2226; Fax: 518-732-2898; Email: crsister@resurrectionsisters.org. Sr. Dolores Stepien, C.R., Prov. Supr.

Total in Community: 30.

Legal Title: Sisters of the Resurrection, New York, Inc. Ministry in Nursing Homes; Elementary Schools; Christian Doctrine Centers; High School for Girls; Preschools; Pastoral Associates.

Represented in the Archdiocese of New York and in the Dioceses of Albany and Trenton.

[3490] (O.S.S.)—RELIGIOUS OF THE ORDER OF THE BLESSED SACRAMENT AND OF OUR LADY (P)

Founded in France in 1639. First foundation in the United States in 1912. The Sisters devote their lives to the perpetual adoration of Christ in the Eucharist.

Blessed Sacrament Monastery: 86 Dromore Rd., Scarsdale, NY 10583-1706. Tel: 914-722-1657. Sr. Mary Francis Blackmore, O.S.S., Prioress.

Professed Sisters: 5.

Monastery of Perpetual Adoration (1951): 2798 U.S. 31 N., P.O. Box 86, Conway, MI 49722. Tel: 231-347-0447. Sr. Mary Rosalie Smith, O.S.S., Prioress.

Professed Sisters: 1.

Represented in the Diocese of Gaylord.

[3499] (S.J.S.)—SISTER SERVANTS OF THE BLESSED SACRAMENT (P)

Founded in Mexico in 1904. First foundation in the United States in 1926.

General Motherhouse: Juan Bernardino 650, Guadalajara, Jalisco, Mexico, 45000. Sr. Rosa Maria Sierra Barba, S.J.S., Supr. Gen.

U.S. Province: 3173 Winnetka Dr., Bonita, CA 91902. Tel: 619-267-0720; Email: provincial@usasjs.org. Sr. Lilia M. Barba, S.J.S., Prov. Supr.

Total in Community: 46.

Legal Title: Sister Servants of the Blessed Sacrament, Inc.

Ministry in the field of Education.

Represented in the Archdiocese of Los Angeles and in the Dioceses of Fresno, Sacramento and San Diego.

Province of the Immaculate Conception.

[3500] (S.S.S.)—SERVANTS OF THE BLESSED SACRAMENT (P)

Founded in France in 1859; First foundation in the United States in 1947.

General Motherhouse: 580 Dufferin, Sherbrooke, Canada, J1H 4N1.

U.S. Address: Blessed Sacrament Convent, 101 Silver St., Waterville, ME 04901. Tel: 207-872-7072; Fax: 207-873-2317. Sr. Mary Catherine Perko, S.S.S., Local Supr.

Total in Community: 10.

Represented in the Dioceses of Portland in Maine and Pueblo.

[3510] (S.S.C.K.)—CONGREGATION OF SISTER SERVANTS OF CHRIST THE KING (D)

Founded in the United States in 1936.

General Motherhouse: Loretto Convent, N.8114Co. W.W. Calvary St., Mount Calvary, WI 53057. Tel: 920-753-1053. Sr. Stephen Bloesl, Supr.

Professed Sisters: 4.

Represented in the Archdiocese of Milwaukee and in the Diocese of Fargo.

[3520] (S.S.C.M.)—SERVANTS OF THE HOLY HEART OF MARY (P)

Founded in Paris, France in 1860. First foundation in the United States in 1889.

Generalate: 2029 rue Holy Cross, Montreal, Canada, H4E 2A4. Sr. Kathleen Mulchay, S.S.C.M., Supr. Gen.

United States Region-Holy Family Province: Provincialate, 2041 W. Rte. 113, Kankakee, IL 60901. Tel: 815-937-2380. Sr. Carol Karnitsky, S.S.C.M., Prov. Supr.

Total number in Region: 26.

Legal Title: Servants of the Holy Heart of Mary.

Ministry in Grammar Schools; Nursing Homes; Education; Pastoral Ministry; Ministry to the Aged; Spiritual Direction; Retreats and Home Missions.

Represented in the Dioceses of Joliet, Peoria and Rockford.

[3530] (S.SP.S.)—MISSIONARY SISTERS SERVANTS OF THE HOLY SPIRIT (P)

Founded in Holland in 1889. First foundation in the United States in 1901.

General Motherhouse: Convento dello Spirito Santo, Via Cassia 645, Rome, Italy, 00189. Sr. Maria Theresia Hörnemann, S.Sp.S., Congregational Leader.

Universal total in Congregation: 3,045.

American Motherhouse (1901): Convent of the Holy Spirit, 319 Waukegan Rd., Northfield, IL 60093; P.O. Box 6026, Techny, IL 60082-6026. Tel: 847-441-0126; Fax: 847-441-5587. Email: provinceleader@ssps-us.org. Sr. Monica Mabel Balbuena, S.Sp.S., Prov.

Total in Community: 80.

Legal Titles: Arnold Janssen Foundation, Techny, IL; Helena Stollenwerk Foundation, Techny, IL; The Holy Spirit Life Learning Center, Chicago, IL. Ministry in Schools; Catechetical Work; Parish Ministry & Administration.

Represented in the Archdioceses of Chicago and New York and in the Dioceses of Memphis and Dubuque.

[3540] (S.SP.S.DEA.P.)—SISTER-SERVANTS OF THE HOLY SPIRIT OF PERPETUAL ADORATION (P)

Founded in Holland in 1896. First foundation in the United States in 1915. Second foundation in the United States in 1928.

Generalate: Convent of the Most Holy Trinity, Bad Driburg, Germany Mother Maria Elizabeth, S.Sp.S.deA.P., Supr. Gen.

U.S. House of Formation: Mount Grace Convent, 1438 E. Warne Ave., Saint Louis, MO 63107-1015. Tel: 313-381-5686. Email: holyspiritvocations@gmail.com. Sr. Mary Catherine, S.Sp.S.deA.P., Supr.

Professed Sisters: 18.

Convent of Divine Love: 2212 Green St., Philadelphia, PA 19130-3197. Tel: 215-567-0123. Email: conventofdivinelove@gmail.com. Sr. Mary Amatrix, S.Sp.S.deA.P., Supr.

Professed Sisters: 21.

Blessed Sacrament Convent: 4105 Ocean Dr., Corpus Christi, TX 78411. Tel: 361-852-6212. Sr. Louise Mary Alindayu, S.Sp.S.A.P., Supr.

Professed Sisters: 8.

Adoration Convent of Christ the King Church: 1040 S. Cotner Blvd., Lincoln, NE 68510. Tel: 402-489-0765. Sr. Louise Mary, S.Sp.S.deA.P., Supr.

Professed Sisters: 9.

Represented in the Archdioceses of Lincoln.

[3550] (S.C.I.M.)—SERVANTS OF THE IMMACULATE HEART OF MARY (P)

Good Shepherd Sisters of Quebec

Founded in Canada in 1850. First foundation in the United States in 1882.

Generalate: 2550, rue Marie-Fitzbach, Canada Sr. Theresa Rounds, S.C.I.M., Supr. Gen.

Universal total in Congregation: 327.

Provincial Headquarters: St. Joseph Province, 409 Pool St., Biddeford, ME 04005. Tel: 207-282-4976; Fax: 207-282-7376. Sr. Therese Gauvin, S.C.I.M., Prov.

Total in Community: 33.

Parish Ministry; Apostolate to the Elderly; Prison/Jail Ministry; Home and Advocacy for Women in Transition; Safe House for Trafficked Women; Programs for Parenting Ministry to immigrants.

Represented in the Diocese of Portland in Maine.

[3560] (S.J.)—SERVANTS OF JESUS (P)

Founded in Detroit, Michigan in 1974.

Headquarters: Servants of Jesus, 8080 Kinmore, Dearborn Heights, MI 48127. Tel: 313-562-6156. Sr. Corinne Weiss, S.J., Pres.

Total in Community: 13.

Ministries: Diocesan Offices; Parish Ministry; Religious Education; Catholic Schools; Legal Aid; Health Care.

Represented in the Archdiocese of Detroit and in the Dioceses of Grand Rapids, Gaylord and Saginaw.

[3570] (O.S.M.)—MANTELLATE SISTERS, SERVANTS OF MARY OF BLUE ISLAND (P)

Founded in Italy in 1861. First foundation in the United States in 1916.

Generalate and Novitiate: Rome, Italy

Convent of Our Mother of Sorrows: 13811 S. Western Ave., Blue Island, IL 60406. Tel: 708-385-2103. Sr. Louise Staszewski, O.S.M., Regl. Supr.

Professed Sisters: 8.

Legal Title: Mantellate Sisters Servants of Mary Motherhouse of the Servants of Mary.

Represented in the Archdiocese of Chicago.

[3572] (O.S.M.)—MANTELLATE SISTERS SERVANTS OF MARY OF PLAINFIELD (P)

Founded October 6, 1861 in Treppio, Italy. First founded in the United States 1916.

Universal Number of Mantellate Sisters: 319.

Mantellate Sisters Servants of Mary of Plainfield (1977): 16949 S. Drauden Rd., Plainfield, IL 60586-9168. Tel: 815-436-5796. Sr. Louise Staszewski, O.S.M., Regl. Supr.

Sisters: 7.

Ministry in the field of Academic Education; Parish Ministry; Retreats; Social Work; Nursing; Homes for the Aged; Foreign Missions.
Represented in the Archdiocese of Chicago and in the Diocese of Joliet.

[3580] (O.S.M.)—SERVANTS OF MARY (P)

Founded in Italy in the 13th Century. First foundation in the United States in 1893.

Congregational Motherhouse: 1 Brownsea Ct., 160 Clarence Rd., London, England, E58EF. Sr. Marie Thèrése Connor, O.S.M., Congregational Prioress

U.S./Jamaica Community (1893) Community Motherhouse: Community Motherhouse, Convent of Our Lady of Sorrows, 7400 Military Ave., Omaha, NE 68134-3351. Tel: 402-571-2547; Fax: 402-573-6055; Web: osms.org. Sr. Mary Gehringer, O.S.M., Congregational Councilor & U.S./Jamaica Community Prioress.

Total in Community: 71.

Properties owned and/or sponsored: Marian High School, Omaha, NE; Our Lady of Sorrows Convent, Omaha, NE.

Ministry in the field of Religious and Academic Education at all levels; Parishes; Social Service Agencies; Diocesan Offices; Hospital Pastoral Care; Counseling Agencies; Campus Ministry; Hospice; Health Care Services; Medical Research; Consulting; Spiritual Direction; Retreat Work.

Represented in the Archdioceses of Detroit, Omaha and Portland in Oregon and in the Dioceses of Des Moines, Gaylord, Grand Island and Ogdensburg. Also in Jamaica.

[3590] (O.S.M.)—SERVANTS OF MARY (SERVITE SISTERS) (D)

Founded in Italy in the 13th Century. First foundation in the United States in 1912.

General Motherhouse: Servants of Mary, 1000 College Ave. W., P.O. Box 389, Ladysmith, WI 54848-0389. Tel: 715-532-3364; Fax: 715-532-6153. Email: info@servitesisters.org. Web: www.servitesisters.org. Sr. Theresa H. Sandok, O.S.M., Pres.

Total in Community: 35.

Ministry in the fields of Education, Health Care, Pastoral Ministry and Social Services.

Represented in the Archdioceses of Chicago, Milwaukee and St. Paul-Minneapolis and in the Dioceses of Joliet, La Crosse, Phoenix and Superior.

[3595] (S.S.J.)—SERVANTS OF ST. JOSEPH (P)

Founded in Spain in 1874.

Motherhouse: Salamanca, Spain

General House: Rome, Italy Mother Josefa Somoza, Supr. Gen.

U.S. Address (1957): 203 N. Spring St., Falls Church, VA 22046. Tel: 703-533-8441; Fax: 703-534-9549. Sr. Augustina Temprano.

Total in Community: 7.

Represented in the Diocese of Arlington.

[3600] (S.DEM.)—SISTERS SERVANTS OF MARY (P)

Founded in Madrid, Spain by St. Maria Soledad Torres, August 15, 1851. First foundation in the United States in 1914.

Total Membership 1,360 Sisters.

General Motherhouse: Via Antonio Musa 16, Rome, Italy, 00161. Mother Alfonsa Bellido, S.deM., Supr. Gen.

Provincial Motherhouse: 800 N. 18th St., Kansas City, KS 66102. Provincial Curia Email: mprovincialsdemkc@yahoo.com; Sr. Alicia Hermosillo, S.deM., Prov. Supr.; Sr. Bernadette Proctor, S.deM., First Provincial Counselor; Sr. Lucero Garcia, S.deM., Local Supr. Email: superiorasdemkc@gmail.com; Sr. Laura Gonzalez, S.deM., Community Archivist Email: provsecretarysdemkkc@yahoo.com; Sr. Germana Contreras, S.deM., Treas. Email: ecoprovsdemkc@gmail.com. Vocation Director Email: vocservantsmkc@yahoo.com.

Total number in Province: 198.

Represented in the Archdioceses of Kansas City in Kansas, Los Angeles, New Orleans and New York.

[3610] (S.S.M.I.)—SISTERS SERVANTS OF MARY IMMACULATE (P)

Founded in Zhuzhel, Ukraine on August 28, 1892. Approved by the Holy See, 1932. Arrived in the United States on August 15, 1935 at Stamford, Connecticut.

Generalate: Via Cassia Antica 104, Rome, Italy, 00191. Sr. Theresa Slota, S.S.M.I., Supr. Gen., Sr. Sofia Lebedowicz.

Sisters Servants of Mary Immaculate: Sisters Servants Ln., 9 Emmanuel Dr., P.O. Box 9, Sloatsburg, NY 10974-0009. Tel: 845-753-2840. Email: ssminy@aol.com. Sr. Kathleen Hutsko, S.S.M.I., Prov. Supr.

Total in Community: 23.

Properties owned and/or sponsored: Immaculate Conception Provincialate & Novitiate; St. Joseph's Home (for the aged); Saint Mary's Villa Spiritual, Cultural and Educational Center, Sloatsburg, NY.

Ministry in the field of Education; Parish and Pastoral ministry; Health Care; Administration; Retreat Ministry; Hospitality; Holy Dormition Pilgrimage; Catechetical; Seminary Library; Youth Ministry.

Represented in the Ukrainian and Byzantine Rite Catholic Dioceses of the United States.

[3615] (E.I.N.)—SERVANTS OF THE IMMACULATE CHILD MARY (ESCLAVASDE LA INMACULADA NINA) (P)

Founded in Mexico in 1901. First foundation in the United States in 1978.

Motherhouse: Mother R.M. Flor Maria Maydaleno Gonzalez, Dr. Espina #10, 28019 Madrid, Spain

Provincial House: Matamoros #100, Tlalpan D.F., Mexico, C.P. 14000. Sr. Maria del Carmen Salmeron Gutierrez.

U.S. Foundation: 5135 Dartmouth Ave., Los Angeles, CA 90032. Tel: 323-225-3279. Sr. Maria del Refugio Carlos, E.I.N.

House of Formation: 350 S. Boyle Ave., Los Angeles, CA 90033. Tel: 323-269-7786. Sr. Maria R. Carlosvaldez, E.I.N., Supr.; Sr. Maria Espindola, E.I.N.; Sr. Petra Lopez, E.I.N.; Sr. Enodina Cuovas, E.I.N.; Sr. Maria Esthola Calvillo, E.I.N.

Total number of Sisters in the U.S: 6.

Ministry in the field of religious education and adult formation in parishes.

Represented in the Archdiocese of Los Angeles.

[3620] (S.S.M.I.)—SISTERS SERVANTS OF MARY IMMACULATE (P)

First founded in Poland in 1878.

General Motherhouse: Mariowka-Opoczynska, Poland Mother Miroslawa Grunt.

Total number of Sisters in the U.S: 32; Universal total in Congregation: 740.

American Province (1935): 1220 Tugwell Dr., Catonsville, MD 21228. Tel: 410-747-1353. Sr. Danuta Zielinska, Prov. Supr.; Sr. Marianna Danko, Community Archivist.

Total in Community: 32.

Represented in the Archdioceses of Baltimore and Washington and in the Diocese of Cleveland.

[3625] S.S.V.M.—SERVANTS OF THE LORD AND VIRGIN OF MATARA, INC. (D)

Founded in Argentina in 1988.

General House: Rome, Italy

Provincial House: 28 15th St, SE, Washington, C 20003. Tel: 202-543-2064; Web: ssvmusa.org. Universal Total in Congregation: 1,305; Total in U.S: 148.

Ministry in the areas of the formation of the consciences and faith of inner city children, youth and families throughout the U.S.; assisting in after-school care for children; pastoral care in homes for the elderly and hospitals; apostolate with university students; serving as directors of religious education and as catechists in parishes and schools.

[3630] (S.S.C.J.)—SERVANTS OF THE MOST SACRED HEART OF JESUS (P)

Founded in Poland in 1894.

General Motherhouse: 24 Garncarska St., Cracow, Poland Sr. Olga Podsadnia, Supr. Gen.

Sister Servants of the Most Sacred Heart of Jesus (1959): Sacred Heart Province, 866 Cambria St., Cresson, PA 16630-1713. Tel: 814-886-4223. Email: sscjusaprovince@gmail.com; Web: sacredheartsisters.org. Mother Klara Slonina, S.S.C.J., Prov. Supr.

Total Professed: 26.

Represented in the Dioceses of Altoona-Johnstown, Harrisburg and Grand Rapids. Also in Mandeville, Jamaica.

[3640] (S.M.G.)—POOR SERVANTS OF THE MOTHER OF GOD (P)

Founded in London, England in 1869. First foundation in the United States in 1947.

General Motherhouse: Maryfield, Roehampton, London, England, S.W. 15. Sr. Rosarii O'Connor, S.M.G., Supr. Gen.

American Foundation: Maryfield Nursing Home, 1315 Greensboro Rd., High Point, NC 27260. Tel: 336-821-4000. Sr. Julia Ann Cannane.

Total in Community: 5.

Ministry in Hospitals; Nursing Homes.

Represented in the Diocese of Charlotte.

[3658] (S.S.H.J.)—SISTERS OF THE SACRED HEART OF JESUS (P)

Founded in Ragusa, Italy in 1889. First foundation in the United States in 1951.

Generalate House: Instituto Sacro Cuore di Ragusa, Via Cassia 1714, Rome, Italy, 00123. Universal total in Congregation: 610.

Motherhouse: Instituto Sacro Cuore, Via Suor Maria Schinina 2, Ragusa, Italy, 97100.

American Headquarters: Sacred Heart Villa School & Convent, 5269 Lewiston Rd., Lewiston, NY 14092. Tel: 716-284-8273.

Legal Titles: Sacred Heart Villa School & Convent, Lewiston, NY; Saint Frances Cabrini Nursery and Convent, North Haven, CT.

Ministry in the field of Religious and Academic Education at all levels; Hospitals; Homes for the Aged; Orphanages; Parish Ministry; Youth Ministry; Foreign Missions; Social Services.

Represented in the Archdiocese of Hartford and in the Diocese of Buffalo.

[3660] (S.S.H.J.P.)—SERVANTS OF THE SACRED HEART OF JESUS AND OF THE POOR (P)

Founded in Leon, Gto., Mexico in 1885. First foundation in U.S. in 1907.

Motherhouse: Apartado 92, Puebla, Pue, Mexico, 72000. Tel: 01152-2222-42-18-69. Ma. Guadalupe Cortez, S.S.H.J.P., Gen. Supr.

U.S. Address: Sacred Heart Children's Home Convent, 3310 S. Zapata Hwy., Laredo, TX 78046. Tel: 956-723-3343. Email: regionyermousa@gmail.com. Mother Maria Aurelia Mariñelarena, S.S.H.J.P., Major Supr.; Mother Magdalena Sofía Juárez, S.S.H.J.P., Supr.; Sr. Maria Isidra Valdez, S.S.H.J.P., Admin.

Professed Sisters in U.S: 38.

Ministry in academic and religious education at all levels; Children's Home.

Represented in the Dioceses of Laredo and El Paso.

[3670] (S.S.C.J.)—SISTERS OF THE SACRED HEART OF JESUS OF SAINT JACUT (P)

Founded in France in 1816. First foundation in the United States in 1903.

Generalate: Villa des Otages, No. 8 85 rue Haxo, Paris, France, 75020.

Motherhouse: St. Jacut les Pins, St. Jacut les Pins, France, 56220.

USA/Mexico Province (1916): Provincialate Offices, 11931 Radium St., San Antonio, TX 78216. Tel: 210-344-7203; Fax: 210-341-0721. Sr. Nell Marie Knezek, S.S.C.J., Prov.

Total in Community: 28.

Ministry in Education; Pastoral Work; Health Care; Mexico Missions.

Properties owned or sponsored: Mount Sacred Heart School, San Antonio, TX; Holy Spirit Convent, San Antonio, TX; Santa Maria Community, San Antonio, TX; St. Joseph's Community, San Antonio, TX; Beth Rachamim Community, San Antonio, TX; Casa Ste. Emilie, San Antonio, TX; Provincialate Community, San Antonio, TX; Firefly Residence, San Antonio, TX.

Represented in the Archdiocese San Antonio. Also in Mexico City.

[3680] (S.H.J.M.)—SISTERS OF THE SACRED HEARTS OF JESUS AND MARY (P)

Founded in France in 1866. First foundation in United States in 1953.

Motherhouse: Chigwell Convent, Essex, England

Regional House: 1607 Liberty St., El Cerrito, CA 94530. Tel: 510-234-2702; Web: sacredheartsjm.org.

Universal total in Congregation: 135; U.S. Community: 1.

Ministry in Nursing; Healthcare Management.

Represented in the Diocese of Oakland.

[3690] (SS.CC.)—CONGREGATION OF THE SACRED HEARTS AND OF PERPETUAL ADORATION (P)

Founded in France in 1800 as a Congregation of men and women. Members are consecrated to the Hearts of Jesus and Mary. Special Ministries are Perpetual Adoration, the education of youth, especially the poor, parish work and foreign missions. First Catholic missionaries to Hawaii in 1827: Sisters started Catholic Schools for girls in Hawaii 1859. First foundation in the continental United States in 1908.

Generalate: Via Aurelia 145, Scala C-Int 10-14, Rome, Italy, 00165. Sr. Emperatriz Arrobo, SS.CC., Supr. Gen.

Pacific Province: Sisters of the Sacred Hearts, 1120 Fifth Ave, Honolulu, HI 96816. Tel: 808-737-5822. Sr. Regina Mary Jenkins, SS.CC., Prov.

Total in Community: 23.

Legal Holdings and Titles: Sisters of the Sacred Hearts Corporation; Regina Pacis Convent; Sacred Hearts Academy Corporation; Saint Anthony Retreat Center Corporation; Malia O Ka Malu Community, Honolulu, HI; Paewalani Community, Honolulu, HI.

East Coast Region: Sisters of the Sacred Hearts of Jesus and Mary and of Perpetual Adoration,35 Huttleston Ave., Fairhaven, MA 02719-3154. Tel: 508-994-9341. Sr. Muriel Ann Lebeau, SS.CC., Supr.

Total in Community: 3.

Represented in the Diocese of Fall River.

[3710] (C.S.A.)—CONGREGATION OF SISTERS OF SAINT AGNES (P)

Founded in the United States in 1858.

General Motherhouse: St. Agnes Convent, 320 County Rd. K, Fond du Lac, WI 54937-8158. Tel: 920-907-2300; Fax: 920-923-3194; Email: jsteffes@csasisters.org. Sr. Jean Steffes, C.S.A., Gen. Supr.; Sr. Rhea Emmer, C.S.A., Gen. Vicar. Councilors: Sr. Susan Seeby, C.S.A.; Sr. Cynthia Nienhaus, C.S.A.

Total in Congregation : 188.

Ministry in the field of Academic and Religious Education; Parish Ministry; Foreign Missions; Social Services; Healthcare.

Properties owned or sponsored: Hazotte Ministries, Inc.; Marian University, Fond du Lac, WI.

Represented in the Archdioceses of Chicago, Milwaukee, New York and St. Paul-Minneapolis and in the Dioceses of Allentown, Columbus, Davenport, Fort Wayne-South Bend, Gallup, Gary, Jackson, Madison, Phoenix, Raleigh, Toledo, Tucson and Venice. Also in Nicaragua.

[3718] (S.S.A.)—SISTERS OF ST. ANN

Founded in Italy in 1834.

General Motherhouse: Via degli Aldobrandeschi, 100 00163 Rome, Italy. Sr. Francesca Sarcia, S.S.A., Supr. Gen.

Universal total in Congregation: 1200.

U.S. Delegation (1952): Mount St. Ann, 1120 N. Center St., P.O. Box 328, Ebensburg, PA 15931. Tel: 814-472-9354; Fax: 814-472-9354. Sr. Marykutty Vellaplamuriyil, S.S.A., Delegate; Sr. Anna Maria Lorenzon, S.S.A., Community Archivist. Total in Community: 11.

Ministry in the field of Education; Retreat Ministry; Youth Ministry, Social Service, Foreign Mission; Pastoral Ministry.

Represented in the Dioceses of Altoona-Johnstown, Brownsville and Corpus Christi.

[3720] (S.S.A.)—SISTERS OF SAINT ANNE (P)

Founded in Vaudreuil, Province of Quebec, Canada, 1850. First foundation in the United States in 1866.

Legal Title: The Community of the Sisters of St. Anne.

General Motherhouse: 1950 Provost St., H85 1P7, Lachine, Canada Sr. Rita Larivee, Congregational Leader.

Saint Marie Province (1887): 720 Boston Post Rd. E., Marlborough, MA 01752. Tel: 508-481-4934; Fax: 508-481-4939. Provincial Leaders: Sr. Yvette Dargy, S.S.A.; Sr. Pauline Laurence, S.S.A.; Sr. Joanne Dion, S.S.A.

Total number in Province: 79; Total in Community: 383.

Properties owned and/or sponsored: Saint Anne Convent; Marie Esther Health Center, Inc., Marlborough, MA; 2 Residences, Worcester, MA; 1 Residence, Ashland, MA.

Ministry in the field of Academic and Religious Education at all levels; Various Apostolates; Retreat Work; Pastoral Ministry; Ministry to the Aged, Shut-ins and the Poor; Assisted Living Nursing; Foreign Ministries.

Represented in the Archdiocese of Boston and in the Dioceses of Fall River, Providence, Springfield in Massachusetts and Worcester.

[3730] (O.S.B.M.)—SISTERS OF THE ORDER OF ST. BASIL THE GREAT (P) (International Byzantine Rite)

Founded in Cappadocia in the 4th Century by St. Basil the Great and his sister St. Macrina. First foundation in the United States in 1911.

Basilian Generalate: Via San Alessio 26, Rome, Italy, 00153. Sr. Dia Stasiuk, O.S.B.M., Gen. Supr.

Philadelphia-Ukrainian Byzantine Rite: Provincial and Motherhouse, 710 Fox Chase Rd., Jenkintown, PA 19046. Tel: 215-663-9153; Fax: 215-379-4843. Email: province@stbasils.com. Sr. Dorothy Ann Busowski, O.S.B.M., Prov. Supr.

Solemnly Professed Sisters: 29.

Sponsored Institutions: Manor College; Saint Basil Academy; Basilian Spirituality Center.

Ministry in Education at all levels; Pastoral Ministry.

Represented in the Ukrainian Archdiocese of Philadelphia and in the Ukrainian Dioceses of Chicago, Parma and Stamford.

Pittsburgh Ruthenian Byzantine Rite-Motherhouse and Novitiate: Mount St. Macrina, 500 W. Main St., P.O. Box 878, Uniontown, PA 15401. Tel: 724-438-8644. Email: osbmolph@verizon.net. Sr. Ruth Plante, O.S.B.M., Prov.

Professed Sisters: 41.

Legal Titles: Declaration of the Sisters of the Order of St. Basil the Great Endowment Trust; Declaration of Trust of the Sisters of the Order of St. Basil the Great Community Support Program; Mount St. Macrina Cemetery, Inc., Uniontown, PA.

Sisters serve in Diocesan, Parish and Religious Education Ministry; Health Care; Pastoral Ministry.

Represented in the Byzantine Archdiocese of Pittsburgh and in the Dioceses of Parma and Passaic (Byzantine).

[3735] (C.S.B.)—CONGREGATION OF ST. BRIGID (P)

Founded in Ireland in 1807.

U.S. Foundation (1953): St. Brigid's Convent, 5118 Loma Linda Dr., San Antonio, TX 78201. Tel: 210-733-0701. U.S. Team Coordinators: Sr. Teresa Carter, C.S.B.; Sr. Mary Teresa Cullen, C.S.B.; Sr. Margaret Doyle, C.S.B.

Total in Community: 12.

Properties owned and/or sponsored: Community House San Antonio and Boston.

Pastoral Ministry in Parishes, Detention Center and Education at all levels.

Represented in the Archdioceses of Boston and San Antonio.

[3740] (S.S.C.)—SISTERS OF ST. CASIMIR(P)

Founded by Venerable Servant of God, Mother Maria Kaupas in the United States in 1907.

General Motherhouse: 2601 W. Marquette Rd., Chicago, IL 60629. Tel: 773-776-1324; Fax: 773-776-8755. Email: mzalot@ssc2601.com. Sr. Regina Marie Dubickas, S.S.C., Gen. Supr.; Sr. Margaret Zalot, S.S.C., Gen. Sec.

Total in Community: 48.

Properties owned and/or sponsored: Villa Joseph Marie High School, Holland, PA.

Ministry in the field of Academic Education; Foreign Missions; Hospitals; Pastoral Ministry.

Represented in the Archdioceses of Chicago and Philadelphia. Also in Argentina.

[3750] (S.S.CH.)—SISTERS OF ST. CHRETIENNE (P)

Founded in France in 1807. First foundation in the United States in 1903.

General Motherhouse: Metz (Moselle), France, 57000.

Regional Offices: 297 Arnold St., Wrentham, MA 02093-1798. Tel: 508-384-8066; Fax: 508-507-3634. Sr. Suzanne Beaudoin, S.S.Ch., Regl. Leader.

Total number in Region: 41.

Properties owned and/or sponsored: St. Chretienne Retirement Residence, Marlborough, MA; Our Lady Thrift Shop, Marlborough, MA; St. Chretienne Residence, Wrentham, MA.

Legal Titles: St. Chretienne Educational Institute, Inc., Marlborough, MA; St. Chretienne Educational Institute Trust Wrentham, MA.

Represented in the Archdiocese of Boston and in the Dioceses of Providence, Portland in Maine and St. Petersburg.

[3760] (P.C.C.)—POOR CLARE COLETTINE
Poor Clares-Poor Clares of the Primitive Observance

Founded in Assisi, Italy in 1212. First permanent foundation in the United States in 1877.

Assisi, Italy, is called the Motherhouse of the Order, but the Abbess of said Monastery has no jurisdiction over other Communities of Poor Clares. Some Monasteries, such as those at Omaha, Evansville, New Orleans, Memphis, Jamaica Plain, Travelers Rest, Greenville, Lowell and Spokane, are subject to a Father General and to the Provincial of the Franciscan Province in which the Monastery is located. Monasteries at Cleveland, Kokomo, Los Altos Hills, Barhamsville, Rockford, Roswell and Santa Barbara.

Franciscan Monastery of St. Clare: 22625 Edgewater Rd., Omaha, NE 68022. Tel: 402-558-4916; Tel: 402-558-4916 & 402-350-6335; Fax: 402-558-5046 Web: www.omahapoorclare.org. Sr. Theresina R. Santiago, O.S.C., Abbess.

Professed Sisters: 7; Novices: 1.

Cloistered.

Monastery of St. Clare: 70 Nelson Ave., Wappingers Falls, NY 12590-1121. Tel: 845-297-1685; Fax: 845-297-7657; Web: www.poorclaresny.com.

Solemnly Professed Sisters: 7; Simply Professed: 1.

St. Clare's Monastery of the Blessed Sacrament O.S.C: 720 Henry Clay Ave., New Orleans, LA 70118. Tel: 504-895-2019. Sr. Elizabeth Mortell, O.S.C., Abbess. Total in Community: 8.

Cloistered.

Franciscan Monastery of St. Clare O.S.C: 6825 Nurrenbern Rd., Evansville, IN 47712-8518. Tel: 812-425-4396; Web: poorclare.org/evansville. Sr. Jane Marie DeLand, O.S.C., Abbess; Sr. Jeanne Maffet, O.S.C., Vicaress.

Total in Community: 8.

Monastery of St. Clare (1932): 1310 Dellwood Ave., Memphis, TN 38127. Tel: 901-357-6662. Email: memphisclares@gmail.com. Sr. Mary Marguerite, O.S.C., Abbess.

Total in Community: 5.

Solemnly Professed Cloistered.

The Franciscan Monastery of St. Clare: 920 Centre St., Jamaica Plain, MA 02130. Tel: 617-524-1760; Fax: 617-983-5205. Email: bostonpoorclares@yahoo.com. Sr. Mary Veronica McGuff, O.S.C., Abbess.

Total in Community: 14.

Monastery of St. Clare O.S.C: 150 White Pine Rd., Chesterfield, NJ 08515. Tel: 609-324-2638; Fax: 609324-2938. Sr. Miriam Varley, O.S.C., Abbess.

Total in Community: 13.

Franciscan Monastery of Saint Clare aka Monastery of St. Clare: 1271 Langhorne-Newtown Rd., Langhorne, PA 19047-1297. Tel: 215-968-5775; Fax: 215-968-6254. Email: stclare@poorclarepa.org. Sr. Patricia A. Coogan, O.S.C., Abbess.

Total in Community: 11.

Franciscan Monastery of St. Clare, Spokane, Washington: Poor Clare Nuns, 4419 N. Hawthorne St., Spokane, WA 99205. Tel: 509-327-4479. Sr. Marcia Kay LaCour, O.S.C., Abbess & Vocation Directress.

Professed Nuns: 5.

Solemn Vows, Papal Enclosure Franciscan Province of Santa Barbara. Mother Bentivoglio Federation of Poor Clares.

St. Clare's Monastery: 421 S. Fourth St., Sauk Rapids, MN 56379. Tel: 320-251-3556; Fax: 320-203-7052. Mother Marie Immaculata, O.S.C., Abbess.

Total in Community: 18.

St. Clare's Monastery of the Infant Jesus (1953): Franciscan Poor Clare Nuns, 8650 Russell Ave. S., Minneapolis, MN 55431-1998. Tel: 952-881-4766. Sr. Frances Getchell, O.S.C., Abbess.

Total in Community: 11.

Legal Title: Franciscan Poor Clare Nuns.

Monastery of Poor Clares (1877): Order of St. Clare-Poor Clare Colettine Nuns P.C.C., 3501 Rocky River Dr., Cleveland, OH 44111-2998. Tel: 216-941-2820. Mother Mary Dolores, P.C.C., Abbess.

Total in Community: 17.

Poor Clare Nuns (Colettines), observing the Primitive Rule of St. Clare. Strictly cloistered, Solemn Vows, Perpetual Exposition of the Most Blessed Sacrament.

Franciscan Monastery of St. Clare: Order of St. Clare, 1505 Miles Rd., Cincinnati, OH 45231-2427. Tel: 513-825-7177; Fax: 513-825-4071; Email: poorclareprayers@gmail.com; Web: www.poorclarescincinnati.org. Sr. Mary Pia Malaborbor, O.S.C., Abbess.
Total in Community: 8.
Solemn vows; papal enclosure.

Corpus Christi Monastery (Solemn Vows, Papal Enclosure): Poor Clare Colettines P.C.C., 2111 S. Main St., Rockford, IL 61102. Tel: 815-963-7343. Email: vicarforclergy@rockforddiocese.org. Mother Maria Dominica, P.C.C., Abbess.
Total in Community: 22.
Cloistered.

Annunciation Monastery: Poor Clare Colettines P.C.C., 6200 E. Minooka Rd., Minooka, IL 60447-9458.

Monastery of Poor Clares-P.C.C. (1928): 215 E. Los Olivos St., Santa Barbara, CA 93105. Tel: 805-682-7670. Mother Aimee Marie of the Eucharist, Abbess.
Total in Community: 15.

Monastery of St. Clare: 445 River Rd., Andover, MA 01810-4213. Tel: 978-683-7599; Fax: 978-683-6085. Sr. Therese Marie Lacroix, O.S.C., Abbess.
Total in Community: 7.
Cloistered.

Poor Clare Monastery of Our Lady of Guadalupe: 809 E. 19th St., Roswell, NM 88201. Tel: 575-622-0868. Mother M. Angela Kelly, Abbess.
Total in Community: 22.
Legal Title: The Community of Poor Clares of New Mexico, Inc.
Cloistered.

Poor Clares Immaculate Heart Monastery: 28210 Natoma Rd., Los Altos Hills, CA 94022-3220. Tel: 650-948-2947. Mother Maura, P.C.C., Abbess.
Total in Community: 25.

Monastery of St. Clare: 37 McCauley Rd., Travelers Rest, SC 29690. Tel: 864-834-8015; Fax: 864-834-5402. Email: info@poorclaresc.com; Vocation Email: vocation@poorclaresc.com. Sr. Carolyn Forgette, O.S.C., Abbess.
Total in Community: 14.
Contemplative Community.

Monastery of Poor Clares Colettine P.C.C: 5500 Holly Fork Rd., Barhamsville, VA 23011. Tel: 757-566-1684. Email: mtstfrancis@gmail.com. Mother Mary Therese, P.C.C., Abbess.
Total in Community: 26.
Solemn Vows. Cloistered.

Maria Regina Mater Monastery P.C.C: Poor Clare Nuns, 1175 N., 300 W., Kokomo, IN 46901. Tel: 765-457-5743. Mother Miriam, Abbess.
Total in Community: 11; Junior Sisters: 2.
Cloistered.

Christ the King Monastery of St. Clare O.S.C: 3900 Sherwood Blvd., Delray Beach, FL 33445. Tel: 561-498-3294. Sr. Leanna Chrostowski, O.S.C., Abbess.
Total in Community: 8.

Monastery of St. Clare of the Immaculate Conception O.S.C: Poor Clares, 200 Marycrest Dr., Saint Louis, MO 63129. Tel: 314-846-2618. Mother Mary Elizabeth Smith, O.S.C., Abbess.
Total in Community: 10.
Legal Title: Nuns of the Order of St. Clare of St. Louis.

San Damiano Monastery of St. Clare (Solemn Vows, Papal Enclosure): 6029 Estero Blvd., Fort Myers Beach, FL 33931-4325. Tel: 239-463-5599; Fax: 239463-4993. Email: saintclare@comcast.net. Sr. Mary Frances Fortin, O.S.C., Abbess.
Cloistered Sisters: 7.

Poor Clares of Montana: 3020 18th Ave., S., Great Falls, MT 59405-5167. Tel: 406-453-7891. Email: sisters@poorclaresmt.org Sr. Jane Sorenson, O.S.C., Abbess.
Sisters: 6.

Monastery of St. Clare: 4875 Shattuck Rd., Saginaw, MI 48603. Tel: 989-797-0593; Email: sisters@srsclare.com. Sr. Dianne Doughty, O.S.C., Abbess.
Solemnly Professed: 3.

[3765] (O.S.C.CAP.)—CAPUCHIN POOR CLARES (P)

Federation of Our Lady of the Angels in North America (1991): Monastery of the Blessed Sacrament, 4201 N.E. 18th St., Amarillo, TX 79107. Tel: 806-383-6771; Fax: 806-383-9877. Mother Theresa Cortes, O.S.C., Pres.

[3770] (O.S.C.)—SISTERS OF ST. CLARE (P)

St. Clare's Convent (Generalate): 63 Harold's Cross Rd., Dublin 6W, Ireland Fax: 011-353-1-496-6388. Sr. Anne Kelly, O.S.C., Abbess Gen.

Santa Clara: 1171 Via Santa Paulo, Vista, CA 92081. Tel: 760-295-0611. Sr. Madeline Fitzgerald, O.S.C., California-Pastoral Coord.; Sr. Therese Carolan, O.S.C., Regl. Supr.-Florida.
Total in Congregation: 105; Total in Guatemala & El Salvador: 22; Total in U.S: 14; Total in England: 5; Total in Ireland: 63.
Ministry in the field of Academic and Religious Education at all Levels; Pastoral & Social Ministry; Retreats; Ministry to the sick, poor and imprisoned.
Represented in the Dioceses of Orange, St. Petersburg, San Bernardino, and San Diego. Also in El Salvador, England, Guatemala and Ireland.

[3780] (SS.C.M.)—SISTERS OF SAINTS CYRIL AND METHODIUS (P)

Founded in the United States in 1909.

General Motherhouse: Villa Sacred Heart, Danville, PA 17821-1698. Tel: 570-275-3581; Fax: 570-275-5997. Sr. M. Michael Ann Orlik, SS.C.M., Gen. Supr.
Total in Community: 68.
Ministry in the field of Education; Parish Ministry and Religious Education; Retreat/Spiritual Direction; Hospital Chaplaincy; Deaf Apostolate; Homes for the Aged; Continuing Care Retirement Community.
Properties owned or sponsored: St. Cyril Preschool and Kindergarten; St. Cyril Academy Spiritual Center; Villa Sacred Heart; Maria Hall, Inc.; Maria Joseph Manor, Inc.; The Meadows at Maria Joseph Manor, Inc., Danville, PA; Villa St. Cyril, Highland Park, IL.
Represented in the Archdioceses of Chicago, New York and San Antonio and in the Dioceses of Bridgeport, Charleston, Gary, Harrisburg, Scranton and Syracuse.

[3790] (S.S.D.)—INSTITUTE OF THE SISTERS OF ST. DOROTHY (P)

Founded in Italy in 1834. First foundation in the United States in 1911.

General Motherhouse: Via del Gianicolo 4-a, Rome, Italy, 00165. Sr. Sao Ribeiro, S.S.D., Gen. Coord.

Province of United States of America (1920): Mount Saint Joseph Vice-Provincialate, 13 Monkeywrench Ln., Bristol, RI 02809-2916. Tel: 401-253-5434. Sr. Sharon A. McCarthy, S.S.D., Vice Prov. Coord.
Universal total in Congregation: 876; Total number in the U.S: 27.
Ministry in the field of Education; Spiritual Life Centers; Hospital Chaplaincies; Social work with immigrants.
Properties owned or sponsored: Villa Fatima, Taunton, MA; Mt. St. Joseph, Bristol, RI; Academy of St. Dorothy, Staten Island, NY.

[3810] (X.S.)—SOCIETY OF CATHOLIC MISSION SISTERS OF ST. FRANCIS XAVIER, INC. (D) (Xavier Sisters)

Founded in the United States in 1946.

Convent: 37179 Moravian Dr., Clinton Township, MI 48036. Tel: 586-465-5082; Fax: 586-465-1990. Email: carmelctwp@sbcglobal.net. Sr. Mary Therese, O.C.D., Prioress.
Professed Nuns: 7; Sisters in temporary vows: 3; Postulants: 5.
Represented in the Archdiocese of Detroit.

[3820] (C.S.JB.)—SISTERS OF ST. JOHN THE BAPTIST (P)

Founded in Italy in 1878. First foundation in the United States in 1906.

General Motherhouse: Rome, Italy Sr. Rosaria DiIorio, Supr. Gen.

U.S. Provincial House: 3308 Campbell Dr., Bronx, NY 10465-1358. Tel: 718-518-7820. Sr. Claudette Marie Jaszczynski, C.S.JB., Prov. Supr.
Total in Community: 69.
Legal Titles and Holdings: Mt. St. John Convent, Purchase, NY; St. John Villa Academy, Staten Island, NY; Providence Rest Nursing Home, Bronx, NY; Mt. St. John Convent, Gladstone, NJ.
Ministry in the field of Education; Health Care for Aged Women & Men; Child Day Care; Pastoral Ministry.

[3830] (C.S.J.)—SISTERS OF ST. JOSEPH

The Independent Motherhouses of the Sisters of St. Joseph are represented in the United States in the following Archdioceses and Dioceses:

[3830-01] BOSTON (D)

Motherhouse of the Congregation of the Sisters of St. Joseph of Boston-CSJ (1873): 637 Cambridge St., Brighton, MA 02135. Tel: 617-783-9090; Fax: 617-783-8246. Vocations Email: vocation.office@csjboston.org; Communications Email: communications.office@csjboston.org. Sr. Rosemary Brennan, C.S.J., Pres.; Sr. Mary Rita Grady, C.S.J., Community Archivist.
Total in Community: 251.
Legal Holdings or Titles: Motherhouse of the Sisters of Saint Joseph of Boston, Brighton, MA; Bethany Health Care Center, Inc., Framingham, MA; Bethany Hill Place, Inc.; Framingham, MA; St. Joseph Hall, Framingham, MA; Walnut Park Montessori School, Newton, MA; Jackson School, Newton, MA; Fontbonne Academy, Milton, MA; St. Joseph Preparatory High School, Brighton, MA; Regis College, Weston, MA; Corporation for the Sponsored Ministries of the Sisters of St. Joseph of Boston, Brighton, MA; The Literacy Connection, Brighton, MA.; The Women's Table, Brighton, MA; Casserly House, Roslindale, MA; Jackson Walnut Park Educational Collaborative, Inc.

[3830-03] ORANGE (P)

Sisters of St. Joseph of Orange - Motherhouse: 440 S. Batavia St., Orange, CA 92868. Tel: 714-633-8121; Fax: 717-744-3165. Sr. Jayne Helmlinger, C.S.J., Gen. Supr.; Leo Catahan, Community Archivist.
Total in Community: 110.
Legal Holdings and Titles: Sisters of St. Joseph of Orange; Sisters of St. Joseph Healthcare Foundation, Orange, CA; St. Joseph College, Orange, CA; St. Joseph Health System; St. Joseph Health System Foundation, Irvine, CA; St. Jude Hospital, Inc. (dba St. Jude Medical Center); St. Jude Memorial Foundation, Fullerton, CA; St. Joseph Hospital Orange; Yorba Linda, CA; Mission Hospital Regional Medical Center, Mission Viejo, CA; Santa Rosa Memorial Hospital, Santa Rosa, CA; St. Joseph Hospital of Eureka, Eureka, CA; Redwood Memorial Hospital, Fortuna, CA; Redwood Memorial Foundation, Fortuna, CA; Queen of the Valley Medical Center of Napa, Napa, CA; St. Mary of the Plains Hospital, Lubbock, TX; St. Mary Medical Center, Apple Valley, CA; St. Joseph Health Ministry.
Ministry in the field of Education; Health & Hospital Services; Pastoral and Social Services.
Represented in the Archdioceses of Los Angeles and San Francisco and in the Dioceses of Orange, San Diego and Santa Rosa.

[3830-05] ROCKVILLE CENTRE (D)

St. Joseph's Convent - Congregation of the Sisters of Saint Joseph of Brentwood, NY CSJ: Brentwood, NY 11717. Tel: 631-273-1187. Sr. Helen M. Kearney, C.S.J., Pres.; Virginia Dowd, Community Archivist. Total in Community: 416.
Ministry in the field of Education; Health & Hospital Services; Social Services.
Represented in the Dioceses of Brooklyn and Rockville Centre. Also in Puerto Rico.

[3830-06] BUFFALO (P)

Generalate - Congregation of the Sisters of St. Joseph SSJ: Administration, 4975 Strickler Rd., Suite A, Clarence, NY 14031. Tel: 716-759-6454. Sr. Jean Marie Zirnheld, S.S.J., Pres.; Tel: 716-759-6454, Ext. 110; Email: jmzirnheld@buffalossj.org. Sr. Eva Amadori, S.S.J., Community Archivist. Email: eamadori@buffalossj.org.
Total in Community: 61.
Ministry in the field of Education at all levels; School for Deaf; Youth Ministry; Justice Ministry; Pastoral Ministry; Hospital Chaplaincy; Spirituality Center.
Properties owned or sponsored: Administrative Office; Sisters of St. Joseph Residence.

[3830-09] ERIE (D)

Sisters of St. Joseph SSJ: 5031 W. Ridge Rd., Erie, PA 16506-1249. Tel: 814-836-4100; Fax: 814-836-4278. Sr. Mary Herrmann, S.S.J., Pres.
Total in Community: 100.
Legal Title: Sisters of St. Joseph of Northwestern PA Inc.
Ministry in the field of Education at all levels; Social Ministries; Nursing Home; Health Care; Pastoral Work and other Diocesan Ministries.
Institutions sponsored: Saint Mary's Home of Erie; Villa Maria Elementary; Sisters of St. Joseph Neighborhood Network, Inc.; St. Patrick's Haven; Erie DAWN; Bethany House; St. James Haven.

Represented in the Archdioceses of Louisville and Washington and in the Diocese of Cleveland.

[3830-12] OGDENSBURG (D)

Motherhouse of the Society of the Sisters of St. Joseph SSJ: 1425 Washington St., Watertown, NY 13601-4533. Tel: 315-782-3460; Web: www.ssjwatertown.org. Sr. Mary Eamon Lyng, S.S.J., Major Supr.; Sr. Norma Bryant, S.S.J., Community Archivist.

Total in Community: 49.

Ministry in the field of Education at all levels; Parish and Diocesan Administration.

Represented in the Dioceses of Ogdensburg and Syracuse.

[3830-13] PITTSBURGH (P)

Sisters of St. Joseph CSJ - Motherhouse: Sisters of St. Joseph: 1020 State St., Baden, PA 15005. Tel: 724-869-2151; Fax: 724-869-3336. Leadership Team: Sr. Mary Pellegrino, Congregational Mod.; Sr. Sharon Costello; Sr. Diane Cauley; Sr. Barbara Czyrnik; Kathleen Washy, Community Archivist.

Total in Community: 167.

Properties owned and/or sponsored: Motherhouse and 14 residences.

Ministry in the field of Education; Health Care; Social Services; Spiritual Development; Congregational Services.

Represented in the Archdioceses of Boston, Dubuque, Hartford, New York and Washington and in the Dioceses of Altoona-Johnstown, Buffalo, Cheyenne, Erie, Fresno, Greensburg, Jackson, Oakland, Pittsburgh, Richmond, Steubenville, and Wheeling-Charleston.

[3830-14] ROCHESTER (P)

Sisters of St. Joseph SSJ - Motherhouse: 150 French Rd., Rochester, NY 14618-3822. Tel: 585-641-8100; Fax: 585-641-8524. Sr. Sharon Bailey, S.S.J., Congregational Pres.; Kathleen Urbanic, Archivist. Email: kfleckenstein@ssjrochester.org.

Total in Community: 182.

Ministry in the field of Education PreK-6th grade; Health Care; Pastoral Ministry; Foster Care for Children; Parish and Diocesan Evangelization; College Campus Outreach; Social Service; Justice and Peace; Retreats & Spiritual Direction; Home Pastoral Care; Spirituality Programs; Domestic and Foreign Missions; Outreach and Volunteer Corps Programs.

Properties owned and/or sponsored: Nazareth Elementary; Morning Star Motherhouse Conference Center and 9 residences.

Represented in the Archdioceses of Mobile and in the Diocese of Rochester. Also in Brazil.

[3830-15] SALINA (P)

General Administration Office (1884): Sisters of St. Joseph of Concordia, 215 Court St., P.O. Box 279, Concordia, KS 66901. Tel: 785-243-2149. Email: csjcenter@csjkansas.org. Sr. Jean Rosemarynoski, C.S.J., Pres.

Motherhouse (1884): Sisters of St. Joseph of Concordia CSJ, 1300 Washington St., P.O. Box 279, Concordia, KS 66901. Tel: 785-243-2113.

Total Sisters in Community: 92.

Legal Titles: Nazareth Convent and Academy Corporation, Concordia, KS; Neighborhood Initiatives, Inc., Concordia, KS; Manna House of Prayer, Concordia, KS; Neighbor to Neighbor, Concordia, KS.

Ministry in Care for Elderly; Homeless; Education; Parish and Diocesan Evangelization; Social Services; Justice and Peace Offices; Marriage and Family Counseling; Youth Formation; Healthcare; Drug Dependency Programs; Prisons; Consultants; Refugees; Continuous Prayer.

Represented in the Archdioceses of Atlanta, Kansas City in Kansas, Omaha and St. Paul-Minneapolis and in the Dioceses of Fargo, Grand Island, Kansas City-St. Joseph, Las Cruces, Phoenix, Rockford and Salina. Also in Brazil.

[3830-16] SPRINGFIELD (MA) (D)

Motherhouse: The Congregation of the Sisters of St. Joseph of Springfield (SSJ), 577 Carew St., Springfield, MA 01104. Tel: 413-536-0853; Fax: 413-533-3275. Maxyne D. Schneider, S.S.J., Pres.; Sherry Enserro, Archivist.

Total in Community: 207.

Legal Holdings and Titles: Mont Marie Senior Residence, Inc., St. Joseph Residence at Mont Marie; The Friends of the Sisters of St. Joseph Springfield, Inc.

Ministry in the field of Religious & Academic Education; Parish Ministry; Cross-Cultural; Diocesan Administration; Chaplaincy; Health Care, Social Services; Restorative Justice; Creative Arts.

Represented in the Archdioceses of Baltimore and Boston and in the Dioceses of Bridgeport, Burlington, Fall River, Portland (ME), Providence, Springfield (MA) and Worcester.

[3832] (C.S.J.)—CONGREGATION OF THE SISTERS OF ST. JOSEPH (P)

Legal Holdings: Congregation of the Sisters of St. Joseph Ministries, Inc. d/b/a CSJ Ministries: A.B.L.E. Families, Inc.; Caregiver Companion, Inc.; Christ in the Wilderness, Inc.; Congregation of St. Joseph Ministry Against the Death Penalty, Inc.; Holy Family Childcare & Development Center, Inc.; Nazareth Academy, Inc.; People Program, Inc.; River's Edge, A Place for Reflection and Action, Inc.; St. Joseph Academy, Inc. (Cleveland, OH); St. Joseph's Academy, Inc. (Baton Rouge, LA); SJA Foundation, Inc.*; St. Joseph Adoption Referral Services, Inc. d/b/a St. Joseph Adoption Ministry; St. Joseph Health Initiative, Inc.; St. Joseph Spirituality Center, Inc.; Sisters of St. Joseph Charitable Fund, Inc./d/b/a/: Sisters Health Foundation, Inc.; Sisters of St. Joseph Dear Neighbor. Ministries, Inc.; Sisters of St. Joseph Health and Wellness Foundation, Inc.; StepStone, Inc.*; Taller de Jose, Inc.; School and Tutors on Wheels, Inc.; The Well Spirituality Center, Inc. CSJ Initiatives, Inc: Dillon Complex for Independent Living, Inc.; Sheridan Village, Inc.

Legal Title: Congregation of the Sisters of St. Joseph, Inc. d/b/a Congregation of St. Joseph. 3430 Rocky River Dr., Cleveland, OH 44111-2297. Tel: 216-252-0440; Fax: 216-941-3430; Web: www.csjoseph.org.

Total in Community: 489.

Cleveland Center: 3430 Rocky River Dr., Cleveland, OH 44111-2997. Tel: 216-252-0440; Fax: 216-941-3430.

Legal Titles: Sisters of Saint Joseph; Legal Holdings: Congregation of the Sisters of St. Joseph Charitable Trust.

Ministry in the field of Academic and Religious Education at all levels; Parish and Pastoral Ministry; Deaf Apostolate; Parish Team Member; Justice Work; Health Care; Social Services; Radio; Social Concerns; Retreat Work.

Represented in the Archdioceses of Chicago and Washington and in the Dioceses of Cleveland and Youngstown.

LaGrange Center: 1515 W. Ogden Ave., La Grange Park, IL 60526. Tel: 708-354-9200; Fax: 708-354-9573.

Legal Titles: Sisters of St. Joseph of LaGrange; Legal Holdings: Sisters of St. Joseph of LaGrange Charitable Trust.

Ministry in the field of Education; School Administration; Nursing; Pastoral Care in Hospitals; Nursing Homes; Work with the Elderly; Parish Ministry; Archdiocesan Administration; Spiritual Direction and Retreats; Administrative Services; Immigration Services.

Represented in the Archdiocese of Chicago and the Dioceses of Joliet.

Nazareth Center: 3427 Gull Rd., Nazareth, MI 49074. Tel: 269-381-6290; Fax: 269-381-4909.

Legal Titles: The Sisters of St. Joseph of Nazareth; Legal holdings: Ascension Health, Inc. (co-sponsor).

Ministry in the field of Education; Social Services; Parish and Church-related Ministries; Healthcare; Spirituality.

Represented in the Archdioceses of Detroit and Santa Fe and in the Dioceses of Grand Rapids, Kalamazoo, Lafayette in Indiana, Lansing and Saginaw.

Wheeling Center: 137 Mount St. Joseph Rd., Wheeling, WV 26003. Tel: 304-232-8160; Fax: 304-232-1404.

Legal Titles: The Sisters of St. Joseph of Wheeling, Inc.; Legal Holdings: Sisters of St. Joseph of Wheeling Foundation, Inc.

Ministry in the following areas: Parish Ministry; Pastoral Services; Health Care; Social Services; Spiritual Formation; Direction and Retreat Ministries; Diocesan, Administration and Service.

Represented in the Diocese of Lafayette, IN and Wheeling-Charleston.

Wichita Center: 3700 E. Lincoln, Wichita, KS 67218. Tel: 316-686-7171; Fax: 316-689-4056. Legal Title: Sisters of St. Joseph of Wichita, Kansas.

Ministry in the fields of Religious and Academic Education; Pro-Life Ministry to Women; Hospital and Clinical Care; Pastoral Ministry; Senior Care; Social Services; Transitional Housing; Low Income Senior Housing; Retreat Ministry.

Represented in the Archdiocese of Kansas City in Kansas and in the Dioceses of Dodge City, Grand Island, Kansas City-St. Joseph, Salina and Wichita. Also in Japan.

[3840] (C.S.J.)—SISTERS OF ST. JOSEPH OF CARONDELET (P)

Founded in France in 1650. First foundation in the United States in 1836.

Congregational Offices: 10777 Sunset Office Dr., Ste. 10, Saint Louis, MO 63127-1019. Tel: 314-394-1985; Fax: 314-735-4476. Email: congctroffice@csjcarondelet.org. Congregational Leadership Team for Provinces & Vice Provinces: Sr. Danielle Bonetti, C.S.J.; Sr. Barbara Dreher, C.S.J.; Sr. Mary Ann Leininger, C.S.J.; Sr. Mary McKay, C.S.J.; Sr. Miriam Dorothy Ukeritis, C.S.J.

Province of St. Louis (1836): St. Joseph's Provincial House, 6400 Minnesota Ave., St. Louis, MO 63111. Tel: 314-481-8800; Fax: 314-351-3111. Province Leadership Team: Sr. Marilyn Lott, C.S.J.; Sr. Mary Margaret Lazio, C.S.J.; Sr. Rita Marie Schmitz, C.S.J.; Sr. Linda Straub, C.S.J.; Sr. Maureen Freeman, C.S.J.

Total in Community: 267.

Legal Title: Sisters of St. Joseph of Carondelet, St. Louis Province.

Sponsored Institutions: Colleges 2; Academies 2; Institute for the Deaf 1; Long Term Care Facility Cosponsor 1; Health System Co-sponsor 1.

Ministries in the field of Academic Education; Pastoral Ministries; Health Care; Child Care; Geriatric Care; Foreign Missions; Social Services; Community Services.

Represented in the Archdioceses of Atlanta, Chicago, Denver, Indianapolis, Kansas City in Kansas, Mobile, St. Louis and Seattle and in the Dioceses of Belleville, Colorado Springs, Green Bay, Kansas City-St. Joseph, San Jose and Savannah.

Province of St. Paul (1851): St. Joseph's Administration Center, 1884 Randolph Ave., Saint Paul, MN 55105. Tel: 651-690-7000; Fax: 651-690-7039. Province Leadership Team: Sr. Susan Hames, C.S.J.; Sr. Suzanne Herder, C.S.J.; Sr. Cathy Steffens, C.S.J.; Sr. Michelle Hueg, C.S.J., Archivist.

Total in Community: 153.

Legal Holdings or Titles: Sisters of St. Joseph of Carondelet.

Ministry in the fields of Education; Health; Social Services; Spirituality.

Represented in the Archdioceses of Baltimore and St. Paul-Minneapolis and in the Dioceses of Fargo, New Ulm and Orlando.

Province of Albany (1858): St. Joseph's Provincial House, 385 Watervliet-Shaker Rd., Latham, NY 12110-4799. Tel: 518-783-3500; Fax: 518-783-5209; Web: www.csjalbany.org. Province Leadership Team: S. Katherine Arseneau, C.S.J.; Sr. Kathleen Eiffe, C.S.J.; Sr. Jeanne Marie Gocha, C.S.J.; Sr. Mary Anne Heenan, C.S.J., Prov. Dir.; Sr. Eileen McCann, C.S.J., First Councilor & Prov. Treas.; Sr. Sean Peters, C.S.J.; Rev. Geoffrey D. Burke, Chap.

Total in Community: 268.

Novitiate: 369 Watervliet-Shaker Rd., Latham, NY 12110. Tel: 518-785-1622.

Ministry in the fields of Academic and Special Education at all levels; Hospital and Infirmary Services; Hospital Pastoral Ministries; Parish Ministry and Religious Education; Diocesan Offices; Youth Ministry; Counseling; Retreat and Spiritual Direction; Social and Community Services; Fine Arts.

Represented in the Archdioceses of Cincinnati, Indianapolis, Los Angeles, St. Paul-Minneapolis and St. Louis and in the Dioceses of Albany, Baton Rouge, Davenport, Harrisburg, Honolulu, Rochester, Spokane and Syracuse. Also in Peru.

Province of Los Angeles (1878): St. Mary's Provincialate and Carondelet Center, 11999 Chalon Rd., Los Angeles, CA 90049-1524. Tel: 310-889-2100; Fax: 310-476-8735. Email: jawright@csjla.org. Sr. Patricia Nelson, C.S.J., Prov. Dir.; Sr. Patricia Rose Shanahan, C.S.J., Archivist. Professed Sisters: 284.

Legal Titles or Holdings: Sisters of St. Joseph in California; Sisters of St. Joseph in Arizona; Sisters of St. Joseph Ministerial Services.

Sisters serve in the fields of Education; Health Services; Social Services; Pastoral Ministry.

Represented in the Archdioceses of Los Angeles, St. Louis, San Francisco and Seattle and in the Dioceses of Boise, Fresno, Honolulu, Monterey, Oakland, Orange, San Bernardino, San Diego, San Jose, Spokane, Springfield-Cape Girardeau and Tucson. Also in Japan.

Legal Title: Sisters of St. Joseph of Carondelet-Hawaii Vice Province.

Ministries include: Elementary Schools; Services to the Elderly; Prayer & Spirituality; Religious Education Directors; Social Ministry; Adult Faith Formation; Social Justice.

Represented in the Diocese of Honolulu.

[3850] (C.S.J.)—SISTERS OF ST. JOSEPH OF CHAMBERY (P)

Founded in France in 1650. First foundation in United States in 1885.

Generalate: Via del Casaletto, 260, Rome, Italy, 00151. Sr. Sally Hodgdon, C.S.J., Supr. Gen.

Provincial House: Convent of Mary Immaculate,27 Park Rd., West Hartford, CT 06119. Tel: 860-233-5126; Tel: 860-232-8252; Fax: 860-232-4649. Sr. Susan Cunningham, C.S.J., Prov. Supr.

Total in Community: 89.

Legal Title: The Sisters of St. Joseph Corporation. Ministry in the field of Academic and Religious Education at all levels; Social Services; Pastoral and Parish Ministries; Law; Hospitals, Health Care and Prisons; Retreat work and Spiritual Direction; Theologian.

Represented in the Archdioceses of Hartford and in the Dioceses of Bridgeport, Norwich, San Jose and Springfield in Massachusetts. Also in Canada.

[3860] (S.J.C.)—SISTERS OF ST. JOSEPH OF CLUNY (P)

Founded in France in 1807.

Generalate: Paris, France Sr. Claire Houareau, S.J.C.

American Novitiate: Mary Immaculate Queen Novitiate, 853 W 7th St., San Pedro, CA 90731. Tel: 310-834-5431. Sr. Genevieve Marie Vigil, S.J.C., Local Coord.

Provincialate: 7 Restmere Ter., Middletown, RI 02842. Tel: 401-846-4757. Sr. Luke Parker, S.J.C., Prov. of U.S. & Canada.

Professed Sisters in U.S. & Canada: 17.

Legal Title: Sisters of St. Joseph of Cluny, Inc. Ministry in outreach ministry; pastoral work; retreats; healthcare; education.

Represented in the Archdioceses of Los Angeles and Newark and in the Diocese of Norwich and Providence. Also in Canada.

[3870] (C.S.J.)—SISTERS OF ST. JOSEPH OF LYONS, FRANCE (P)

Founded in France October 15, 1650. First foundation in United States in 1906 in Jackman, Maine.

General Motherhouse: Lyons, France Sr. Catherine Barange, Supr. Gen. Maine Sector: Sisters of St. Joseph, 80 Garland Rd., Winslow, ME 04901. Tel: 207-873-4512. Sr. Judith Donovan, C.S.J., Leader.

Total in Community: 22.

Ministry in Catechesis; Holistic Care; Spirituality and Ecology; Pastoral Ministry; Pastoral Care.

Represented in the Diocese of Portland (In Maine).

[3890] (C.S.J.P.)—SISTERS OF ST. JOSEPH OF PEACE (P)

Founded in England 1884. First United States foundation 1885.

Shalom Center: Sisters of St. Joseph of Peace Generalate, Inc., 399 Hudson Ter., Englewood Cliffs, NJ 07632. Tel: 201-608-5401; Fax: 201-608-5407. Email: jlinley@csjp.org. Sr. Sheila Lemieux, C.S.J.P., Congregation Leader; Sr. Margaret Shannon, C.S.J.P.; Sr. Melinda McDonald, C.S.J.P.; Sr. Susan Francois, C.S.J.P.

Total in Community: 139; Total Number in the Eastern U.S: 55.

Properties owned or sponsored: St. Joseph's Home for the Blind; St. Mary's Residence; St. Joseph's Home; The Nurturing Place; St. Joseph's School for the Blind; WATERSPIRIT; The York Street Project; St. Michael Villa; The Kenmare School; Holy Name Medical Center; Margaret Anna Cusack Center, Inc. (dba Peace Care St. Joseph's) and St. Ann's Home for the Aged (dba Peace Care St. Ann's).

Ministry in the field of Education; Health & Social Services; Religious Education; Parish Ministry, Retreat Ministry, Social & Minority Ministry.

Represented in the Archdioceses of Newark, Portland in Oregon and Seattle and in the Dioceses of Camden, Paterson, Spokane and Trenton. Also in El Salvador, Haiti and the United Kingdom.

Western U.S. (1909): St. Mary's Residence and Novitiate, 1663 Killarney Way, P.O. Box 248, Bellevue, WA 98009-0248. Tel: 425-467-5499; Fax: 425-462-9760. Sr. Sheila Lemieux, C.S.J.P., Congregation Leader.

Total Number in Western U.S: 52.

Corporate Titles: Sisters of St. Joseph of Peace; Sisters of St. Joseph of Peace Charitable Trust, Bellevue, WA.

Properties owned: St. Mary's Residence, Bellevue, WA; Prospect House, Seattle, WA; St. Therese Residence, Seattle, WA; Alicia Park House, Seattle, WA.

[3893] (S.S.J.)—SISTERS OF SAINT JOSEPH OF CHESTNUT HILL, PHILADELPHIA (P)

Founded in France in 1650. First foundation in Philadelphia in 1847.

Motherhouse (1847): Mount St. Joseph Convent, 9701 Germantown Ave., Philadelphia, PA 19118-2694. Tel: 215-248-7200; Fax: 215-248-7277; Email: msjc@ssjphila.org; Web: www.ssjphila.org. Sr. Anne Patricia Myers, S.S.J., Congregational Pres.; Sr. Patricia Annas, S.S.J., Archivist.

Total in Congregation : 706.

Legal Holdings or Titles: Saint Joseph Villa; Saint Joseph Guild; Bethlehem Retirement Village, Flour-town, PA; Academy Village, McSherrystown, PA; Saint Joseph Housing Corporation; Saint Mary by-the-Sea Convent, Cape May Point, NJ; Cecilian, Philadelphia, PA; Mount Saint Joseph Academy, Flourtown, PA; Norwood-Fontbonne Academy, Philadelphia, PA; Chestnut Hill College, Philadelphia, PA; Cecilian Village, McSherrystown, PA; SSJ Center for Spirituality, Philadelphia, PA; Saint Joseph Academy, McSherrystown, PA; The Convent of the Sisters of St. Joseph, Chestnut Hill, PA; Elizabeth House, Philadelphia, PA; Saint Joseph Village, McSherrystown, PA; Sisters of Saint Joseph Welcome Center, Philadelphia, PA.

Ministry in the field of Academic and Religious Education at all levels; Institutes for Dependent Children; Pastoral Ministry; Campus Ministry; Care of the Aged; Social Services; Prison Ministry; Health Care; Psychologists; Hospice Ministry; Hospital Chaplaincy; Spiritual Directors; Drug and Alcohol Counselors.

Represented in the Archdioceses of Baltimore, Miami, Newark, Philadelphia, San Antonio and Washington and in the Dioceses of Allentown, Arlington, Camden, Charlotte, Fort Wayne-South Bend, Harrisburg, Metuchen, Paterson, Raleigh, St. Petersburg, Savannah, Trenton, Venice, Wheeling-Charleston and Wilmington. Also in Canada.

[3900] (S.S.J.)—SISTERS OF ST. JOSEPH OF ST. AUGUSTINE, FLORIDA (D)

Founded in France in 1650. First foundation in the United States in 1866. Classified as an American Congregation in 1899.

Motherhouse (1847): St. Joseph Convent, 241 St. George St., P.O. Box 3506, St. Augustine, FL 32085. Tel: 904-824-1752; Email: srkathleencarr@ssjfl.org. Sr. Kathleen Carr, S.S.J., Gen. Supr.; Sr. Catherine Bitzer, S.S.J., Community Archivist.

Total in Community: 49.

Ministry in: Social Services; Hospital Pastoral Care; Care of Aged; Academic and Religious Education at all levels; Parish Ministry; Diocesan Office Administration; Retreat Ministry; Ministry to the Handicapped.

Represented in the Archdiocese of Miami and in the Diocese St. Augustine.

[3910] (S.J.S.M.)—SISTERS OF ST. JOSEPH OF ST. MARK (D)

Founded in France in 1845. First foundation in the United States in October, 1937.

Generalate: Colmar, France Sr. Sophie Moog, Gen. Supr. Universal total in Congregation: 249.

General Motherhouse (Cleveland) (1939): 21800 Charden Rd., Euclid, OH 44117-2199. Mother M. Raphael Gregg, Supr. Gen.

Youngstown Diocese: Sisters of St. Joseph of St. Mark, Community Center, 2300 Reno Dr., Ste. 319, Louisville, OH 44641. Tel: 330-875-7967. Sr. Edwardine Baznik, S.J.S.M., Supr.

Total number in U.S: 10.

Represented in the Dioceses of Cleveland and Youngstown.

[3920] (S.J.W.)—SISTERS OF ST. JOSEPH THE WORKER (D)

General Motherhouse: St. William Convent, 1 St. Joseph Ln., Walton, KY 41094. Mother Mary Christina Murray, S.J.W., Supr. Gen.

Total in Community: 10.

Properties owned and operated: Taylor Manor Nursing Home, Versailles, KY; 16-acre property in Walton, KY: Motherhouse Formation House; St. Joseph Academy, Walton, KY.

Represented in the Dioceses of Covington and Lexington.

[3930] (SSJ-TOSF)—SISTERS OF ST. JOSEPH OF THE THIRD ORDER OF ST. FRANCIS (P)

Founded in the United States in 1901.

Corporate Office: 1300 Maria Dr., P.O. Box 305, Stevens Point, WI 54481-0305. Tel: 715-341-8457; Fax: 715-341-8830. Sr. Marjorie White, S.S.J.-T.O.S.F., Pres.; Sr. Judith Wood, S.S.J.-T.O.S.F., Vice Pres.; Sr. Michelle Wronkowski, S.S.J.-T.O.S.F., Vice Pres.; Sr. Barb Krakora, S.S.J.-T.O.S.F., Vice Pres.

Total number in the Congregation: 196.

Sponsors: Learning Center; 2 High Schools; Health Care System.

Ministries in the following areas: Academic Education at all levels; Pastoral Ministry; Health Care Services; Ministry abroad in South America and Puerto Rico; Social Services.

Represented in the Archdioceses of Chicago, Detroit, Hartford, Milwaukee and St. Paul-Minneapolis, and in the Dioceses of Arecibo, Cleveland, Fort Wayne-South Bend, Gary, Grand Island, Green Bay, Harrisburg, Knoxville, La Crosse, Lansing, Oakland, Rockford, St. Petersburg, Superior and Toledo. Also in Peru.

[3935] (S.S.L.)—THE CONGREGATION OF THE SISTERS OF ST. LOUIS, JUILLY MONAGHAN (P)

Founded in France in 1842. First foundation in the United States in 1949.

General Motherhouse: Louisville Monaghan, Ireland Sr. Winifred Ojo, S.S.L.

Regional House: Louisville Convent, 22300 Mulholland Dr., Woodland Hills, CA 91364. Tel: 818-883-1678; Email: sslca4@sistersofsaintlouis.com (Region); Email: admin@saintlouis.ie (Institute). Sr. Judith Dieterle, S.S.L.

Finally Professed Sisters: 38.

Legal Title: Sisters of St. Louis, Juilly-Monaghan, Inc. Ministry in the field of Education; Pastoral and Social Ministries.

Represented in the Archdioceses of Los Angeles and New York. Also in Brazil.

[3950] (S.S.M.N.)—SISTERS OF SAINT MARY OF NAMUR (P)

Founded in Namur, Belgium, in 1819. First foundation in the United States in 1863.

General Motherhouse: Namur, Belgium Sr. Maureen Quinn, Gen. Supr.

Universal total in Congregation: 379; Professed: 368; Novices: 11.

Eastern Province: Provincial House, 241 Lafayette Ave., Buffalo, NY 14213-1453. Tel: 716-884-8221; Fax: 716-884-6598. Email: ssmnprov@verizon.net. Sr. Caroline Smith, S.S.M.N., Prov. Supr.

Total in Community: 65.

Legal Holdings or Titles: 6 Residences.

Ministry in the field of Religious and Academic Education; Pastoral Ministry; Community Organization; Social Services; Diocesan and Health related services; Refugee Assistance.

Represented in the Dioceses of Buffalo, Charleston and Savannah. Also in Canada.

Western Province: Provincial House - Our Lady of Victory Center, 909 W. Shaw St., Fort Worth, TX 76110. Tel: 817-923-8393. Email: ssmnamur@sbcglobal.net. Sr. Gabriela Martinez, S.S.M.N., Prov.

Total in Community: 31.

Ministry in the field of Religious and Academic Education; Pastoral Ministry; Social Services; Health Care and Missions.

Properties owned or sponsored: Our Lady of Victory Center, Fort Worth, TX; Our Lady of Victory Catholic School, Fort Worth, TX; Sisters of St. Mary of Namur, Fort Worth, TX; Mercy Convent, Wichita Falls, TX.

Represented in the Dioceses of Dallas and Fort Worth.

[3960] (S.S.M.O.)—SISTERS OF ST. MARY OF OREGON

Founded in Oregon in 1886.

General Motherhouse: Sisters of St. Mary of Oregon, 4440 S.W. 148th Ave., Beaverton, OR 97078. Tel: 503-644-9181. Email: info@ssmo.org. Sr. Charlene Herinckx, Supr. Gen.

Total in Congregation : 60.

Ministry in the field of Education; Nursing Homes; Parish Services; Social Services; and Counseling.

Properties owned or sponsored: Maryville Nursing Home; SSMO Campus Schools.

Represented in the Archdioceses of Los Angeles and Portland in Oregon.

[3980] (S.P.C)—SISTERS OF SAINT PAUL DE CHARTRES (P)

Founded in France in 1696.

General House: 193 Via della Vignaccia, Rome, Italy, 1-00163. Sr. Maria Goretti Lee, S.P.C., Supr. Gen. Universal total in Congregation: 4135.

U.S. Province: 1300 County Rd. 492, Marquette, MI 49855-9632. Tel: 906-226-3932. Sr. Estela Garcia, S.P.C., Prov.

Total in Community: 12.

Legal Holding: Bishop Noa Home for Senior Citizens, Escanaba, MI.

Ministry in the field of Academic and Religious Education; Hospital Chaplaincy; Pastoral Ministry.

Represented in the Archdiocese of Washington and in the Diocese of Marquette.

[3990] (S.S.P.C.)—MISSIONARY SISTERS OF ST. PETER CLAVER (P)

Founded in 1894. First Foundation in the United States, 1914.

General House: 16 via dell' Olmata, Rome, Italy, 00184. Sr. Maria Moryl, S.S.P.C., Supr. Gen.

Legal Title: The Sodality of St. Peter Claver for the African Missions-Missionary Sisters of St. Peter Claver.

American Headquarters: 225 Century Ave., S., Saint Paul, MN 55125-1155. Tel: 651-738-9704.

Total in Community: 17.

Represented in the Archdioceses of Chicago, St. Louis and St. Paul-Minneapolis.

[4010] (O.S.A.)—SISTERS OF ST. RITA (D)

General Motherhouse: Friedrich-Spee-Str. 32, 97072 Wurzburg, Germany Sr. Rita Maria Kaes, O.S.A., Gen.

Universal total in Congregation: 80.

U.S. Address: St. Rita's Convent, 4014 Green Bay Rd., Racine, WI 53404. Tel: 262-639-1766. Sr. Angelica Summer, O.S.A., Supr.

Represented in the Archdiocese of Milwaukee.

[4020] (S.T.J.)—SOCIETY OF ST. TERESA OF JESUS (P) (Teresian Sisters)

Founded in Spain in 1876. First foundation in the United States in 1910. Total Membership 1,307.

Generalate: Via Valcannuta, 134, Rome, Italy, 00166.

Formation House: 18080 St. Joseph's Way, Covington, LA 70435-5623. Tel: 985-893-1470; Fax: 985-893-2476. Sr. Clarice Suchy, S.T.J., Vocation Dir.; Sr. Martha L. Gonzalez, Community Archivist.

Total in Community: 27.

Properties owned and/or sponsored: Provincialate, Covington, LA; Blessed Mercedes Prat Convent, New Orleans, LA.

Ministry in the field of Academic Education at all levels; Education in underdeveloped areas; Youth Ministry; Pastoral Ministry.

Represented in the Archdioceses of Miami, New Orleans and San Antonio.

[4030] (S.S.T.V.)—CONGREGATION OF SISTERS OF SAINT THOMAS OF VILLANOVA (P)

Founded in France in 1661. First foundation in the United States in 1948.

General Motherhouse: 52 Blvd. d'Argenson, Neuilly-sur-Seine, France, 92200. Tel: 01 47 47 42 20; Fax: 01 47 47 38 00; Email: neuillystv@wanadoo.com; Web: www.congregation-stv.org.

Universal total in Congregation: 110.

Sisters of St. Thomas of Villanova Convent: 76 West Rocks Rd., Norwalk, CT 06851. Tel: 203-847-2885; Email: sstv_usa@sbcglobal.net; Web: www.saintthomasofvillanova.com. Sr. Marie Lucie Monast, S.S.T.V., Liaison.

Total in Community: 3.

Properties owned and/or sponsored: Notre Dame Convalescent Home dba Notre Dame Health & Rehabilitation Center..

Represented in the Diocese of Bridgeport.

[4040] (S.U.)—SOCIETY OF ST. URSULA (P)

Founded in Dole, France, in 1606. First foundation in the United States in 1901.

General Motherhouse: St. Cyr-Loire, France Sr. Anne Bayart, S.U., Supr. Gen.

Provincialate: 50 Linwood Rd., Rhinebeck, NY 12572. Tel: 845-876-2341. Sr. Barbara Marie Cady, S.U., Regl. Supr.

Total in Community: 23.

Legal Title: Sisters of St. Ursula of the Blessed Virgin of New York.

Ministry in the field of Education; Parish Ministry; Spiritual Direction and Retreats.

Represented in the Archdiocese of New York and in the Dioceses of Providence and Raleigh.

[4048] (F.C.J.)—SOCIETY OF THE SISTERS FAITHFUL COMPANIONS OF JESUS (P)

Founded in France in 1820. First founded in the United States in 1895.

General Motherhouse: Gumley House F.C.J., Twickenham Rd., Isleworth, England, TW7 6DN.

Provincial Office: 300 Palmerston Ave., Toronto, Canada, M6J 2J4. Tel: 416-588-1791.

U.S. Provincial Business Office: 324 Cory's Ln., Portsmouth, RI 02871. Tel: 401-683-2222. Sr. Katherine Mary O'Flynn, F.C.J., Supr. Gen.; Sr. Bonita M. Moser, Prov. Leader; Sr. Marguerite Goddard, F.C.J., Novice Dir.

Sisters: 11.

[4050] (S.D.S.H.)—SISTERS OF THE SOCIETY DEVOTED TO THE SACRED HEART (D)

Founded in Hungary in 1940.

Motherhouse (1956): 9814 Sylvia Ave., Northridge, CA 91324. Tel: 818-772-9961; Fax: 818-772-2742; Web: www.sacredheartsisters.com. Sr. Mary Tomasella, S.D.S.H., Supr. Gen.

Novitiate House: 10480 Winnetka Ave., Chatsworth, CA 91311. Tel: 818-831-9710; Fax: 818-831-0790; Web: www.sacredheartsisters.com.

Total in Community: 47.

Properties owned and/or sponsored: Sacred Heart Motherhouse, Northridge CA; Heart of Jesus Retreat Center, Santa Ana, CA; Sacred Heart Novitiate, Chatsworth, CA; Sacred Heart Retreat Camp, Big Bear, CA; Sacred Heart Convent, Los Angeles, CA.

Ministry in Parish Religious Education Centers; Catechist Formation Centers; Camp for year-round Retreats and summer Family Retreat Camps; Catechesis; Youth Leadership Programs; Day Retreat Center for Children and Adults; Catechesis in Parochial Schools and Catholic High Schools; "Sacred Heart Kids' Club" Video/DVD Catechesis; Hispanic and Chinese Catechetical Center; Catechetical Programs on Military Bases; Catechetical Missions to Dioceses; Asian Pacific Mission in Taiwan; Mission in Hungary.

Represented in the Archdiocese of Los Angeles and the Dioceses of Orange and San Bernardino. Also in Taiwan and Hungary.

[4060] (S.H.C.J.)—SOCIETY OF THE HOLY CHILD JESUS (P)

Founded in England in 1846. First foundation in the United States in 1862.

Motherhouse: Via della Maglianella 379, Rome, Italy, 00166. Sr. Veronica Openibo, S.H.C.J., Society Leader.

American Province: Provincial Offices, 1341 Montgomery Ave, Rosemont, PA 19010. Tel: 610-626-1400. Email: americanprovince@shcj.org. Sr. Carroll Juliano, S.H.C.J., Prov. Leader; Sr. Roseanne McDougall, S.H.C.J., Archivist.

Total number in Province: 116.

Ministry in a variety of Educational and Pastoral Work. Properties owned or sponsored: Connelly School of the Holy Child, Potomac, MD; Cornelia Connelly School, Anaheim, CA; Mayfield Junior School of the Holy Child Jesus; Mayfield Senior School of the Holy Child Jesus, Pasadena, CA; Oak Knoll School of the Holy Child, Summit, NJ; Old Westbury School of the Holy Child, Old Westbury, NY; Rosemont School of the Holy Child, Rosemont, PA; School of the Holy Child, Drexel Hill, PA; School of the Holy Child, Rye, NY; Providence Center, Philadelphia, PA; Cornelia Connelly Center for Education; Holy Child Middle School, New York, NY.

Represented in the Archdioceses of Boston, Chicago, Los Angeles, Milwaukee, Newark, New York, Philadelphia, Portland in Oregon and Washington DC and in the Dioceses of Orange and San Diego. Also in Chile, Dominican Republic and Santo Domingo.

[4070] (R.S.C.J.)—SOCIETY OF THE SACRED HEART (P)

Founded in France in 1800. First foundation in the United States in 1818.

Generalate: Via Tarquinio Viper, 16, Rome, Italy, 00152. Sr. Barbara Dawson, Supr. Gen.

United States-Canada Provincial House: 4120 Forest Park Ave., St. Louis, MO 63108. Tel: 314-652-1500; Fax: 314-534-6800; Email: provincialhouse@rscj.org. Sr. Sheila Hammond, R.S.C.J., Prov.; Sr. Carolyn Osiek, R.S.C.J., Prov. Archivist.

Total number in the Province: 281.

Ministry in the field of Religious and Academic Education at all levels; Adult Education; Parish, Pastoral, Social and Health Care Ministries.

Province Corporations: Society of the Sacred Heart, United States Province, Inc.; California Province of the Society of the Sacred Heart, Inc.; Society of the Sacred Heart, Chicago Province, Inc.; Religious of the Sacred Heart, Washington Province, Inc.; Religious of the Sacred Heart, New York Province, Inc.; Ladies of the Sacred Heart, MO; Religious of the Sacred Heart in Massachusetts, Inc.; Network of the Sacred Heart Schools, Inc., 700 N. Third St., St. Charles, MO 63301, Phone: 636-724-7003.

Represented in the Archdioceses of Boston, Chicago, Cincinnati, Detroit, Galveston-Houston, Louisville, Miami, Milwaukee, New Orleans, New York, Omaha, St. Louis, San Francisco, Seattle and Washington and in the Dioceses of Albany, Baton Rouge, Fall River, Fort Wayne-South Bend, Lafayette (LA), Oakland, Portland, San Bernardino, San Diego, San Jose, and Trenton.

[4080] (S.S.S.)—SISTERS OF SOCIAL SERVICE OF LOS ANGELES, INC. (P)

Founded in Hungary. Established in the United States at Los Angeles, California in 1926.

General Motherhouse: 4316 Lanai Rd., Encino, CA 91436. Tel: 818-285-3355; Fax: 818-285-3366. Sr. Michele Walsh, S.S.S., Gen. Dir.

Total in Community: 66.

Legal Titles: Sisters of Social Service of Los Angeles; Sisters of Social Service Support Trust Fund.

Social Service Work in Parishes and in Diocesan Agencies; Leadership Training of Youth and Adults; Summer Camps for Children and Families; Programs for the Elderly; Peace and Justice Work; Religious Education; Settlement Houses; Health Programs; Family Counseling Services; International houses in Mexico, Philippines and Taiwan.

Represented in the Archdioceses of Los Angeles, Portland in Oregon and San Francisco and in the Dioceses of Oakland, Sacramento and San Diego.

[4090] (S.S.S.)—SISTERS OF SOCIAL SERVICE OF BUFFALO, INC. (P)

Founded in Budapest, Hungary in 1923; Sr. Margaret Slachta, Foundress.

Generalate: H-1029, Bathori Laszlo u. 10, Budapest, Hungary

U.S. District Residence: 296 Summit Ave., Buffalo, NY 14214-1936. Tel: 716-834-0197; Fax: 716-834-6168; Email: almasy.maria@gmail.com. Sr. Maria Almasy, S.S.S., Delegate; Sr. Agnes Pataki, S.S.S., Gen. Mod.

Total number in the United States: 12.

Social Work; Parish Ministry; Ministry for Justice and Human Rights; Field of Spirituality.

Represented in the Diocese of Buffalo.

[4100] (S.S.M.)—SISTERS OF THE SORROWFUL MOTHER (THIRD ORDER OF ST. FRANCIS) (P)

Founded in Italy in 1883. First foundation in the United States in 1889.

General Motherhouse: Casa Generalizia della Suore dell'Addolorata, Via Paolo III 7-9, Rome, Italy, I-00165. Sr. Catherine Marie Hanegan, S.S.M., Gen. Supr.

SSM St. Clare of Assisi Region Administration: 815 Westhaven Dr., Ste. 100, Oshkosh, WI 54904. Tel: 920-230-2040; Fax: 920-230-2041. Email: eanderson@ssm-uscaribbean.org. Sr. M. Lois Bush, S.S.M., Regnl. Supr.

Total number in the U.S. Community: 75.
Legal Holding: Sisters of the Sorrowful Mother; St. Clare of Assisi Region
Ministry in the fields of Religious and Academic Education; Nursing Homes; Social Work; Hospitals and Hospital Administration; Clinics; Parish Ministry; Pastoral Care.
Represented in the Archdiocese of Milwaukee and in the Dioceses of Green Bay, La Crosse, Paterson, Superior, Tulsa and Wichita. Also in Trinidad, Grenada and St. Lucia and Dominican Republic.

[4110] (O.S.U.)—URSULINE NUNS (P) (Roman Union)

Founded in Italy in 1535. First foundation in the United States New Orleans, Louisiana in 1727.

Generalate: Via Nomentana 236, Rome, Italy, 00162. Mother Cecilia Wang, O.S.U., Prioress Gen.

Eastern Province of the U.S. (1900): Ursuline Provincialate, 1338 North Ave., New Rochelle, NY 10804. Tel: 914-712-0060; Fax: 914-712-3134.
Total number in the Province: 82.
Legal Titles: Ursuline Provincialate, Eastern Province of the United States, Inc.; Marian Residence Fund, New Rochelle, NY; OSU Charitable Trust, New Rochelle, NY.
Ministry in the field of Academic Education at all levels; varied Pastoral and Social Services.
Represented in the Archdioceses of New York and Washington and in the Dioceses of Bridgeport, Ogdensburg, Orlando and Wilmington.

Central Province of the U.S: Ursuline Provincialate, 353 S. Sappington Rd., Saint Louis, MO 63122. Tel: 314-821-6884; Fax: 314-821-6888. Sr. Rita Ann Bregenhorn, O.S.U., Prov. Prioress.
Total in Community: 98.
Ministry in the field of Religious and Academic Education.
Represented in the Archdioceses of Boston, New Orleans, St. Louis, St. Paul-Minneapolis and San Antonio and in the Dioceses of Dallas, Portland in Maine, Springfield-Cape Girardeau and Springfield in Illinois.

Western Province U.S. (1932): Ursuline Provincialate, 400 Angela Dr., Santa Rosa, CA 95403-1793. Tel: 707-484-7841. Mailing Address: 9248 Lakewood Drive, Windsor, CA 95492. Sr. Shirley Ann Garibaldi, O.S.U., Prov.
Total number in the Province: 15.
Ministry in the field of Elementary Education; Work with the Eskimos, American Indians, & Hispanics; Parish Ministry; Spiritual Growth Center.
Represented in the Archdioceses of Anchorage and San Francisco and in the Dioceses of Boise, Fairbanks, Great Falls-Billings and Santa Rosa.

[4120] (O.S.U.)—URSULINE NUNS (P)

Founded in Italy in 1535. First foundation in the United States in New Orleans, Louisiana in 1727.

Motherhouse (1845): Ursulines of Brown County, 20860 St. Rte. 251, Fayetteville, OH 45118-9705. Tel: 513875-2020; Fax: 513-875-2311; Web: www.ursulinesofbc.org. Sr. Phyllis Kemper, O.S.U., Congregational Min.
Total in Community: 23.
Legal Title: St. Ursula Literary Institute; Ursulines of Brown County; Ursuline Academy of Cincinnati, Chatfield College.
Ministry in the field of Academic Education at all levels; Adult Education; Catechetical Instruction; Administration; Retreats; Counseling; Organization Consultation; Senior Services; Campus and Parish Ministry; Social Services - Inner City and Rural; Social Justice; Spiritual Direction.
Represented in the Archdiocese of Cincinnati.

[4120-01] CINCINNATI (P)

Motherhouse: Ursulines of Cincinnati, St. Ursula Convent, 1339 E. McMillan St. (Walnut Hills), Cincinnati, OH 45206. Tel: 513-961-3410. Sr. Margaret Mary Efkeman, O.S.U.
Total in Community: 9.
Legal Title: Ursulines of Cincinnati.
Ministry in the field of Academic Education; Parish and Diocesan Services; Social Services; Communications; Adult Education; Social Justice.
Represented in the Archdiocese of Cincinnati.

[4120-03] LOUISVILLE (P)

Ursuline Sisters of the Immaculate Conception: 3105 Lexington Rd., Louisville, KY 40206. Tel: 502897-1811; Fax: 502-896-3913. Email: jpeterworth@ursulineslou.org. Sr. Janet Marie Peterworth, O.S.U., Pres.
Total in Community: 63.
Legal Title: Ursuline Society and Academy of Education aka Ursuline Sisters.
Ministry in the field of Academic Education; Pastoral Ministry; Social Services; Spirituality; Special Education.
Properties owned and sponsored: Sacred Heart Schools, Louisville, KY.
Represented in the Archdiocese of Louisville and in the Dioceses of Davenport, Grand Island and Lexington. Also in Peru.

[4120-04] CLEVELAND (P)

Ursuline Motherhouse and Educational Center: 2600 Lander Rd., Cleveland, OH 44124. Fax: 440-449-3588. Sr. Susan Durkin, O.S.U., Pres.; Sr. Cynthia Glavac, O.S.U., Community Archivist.
Total in Community: 136.
Legal Titles: The Ursuline Academy of Cleveland; The Ursuline Sisters of Cleveland.
Ministry in the field of Academic Education at all levels; Parish Ministry; Seminary; Social Service Agency; Hospital and Health Care Ministry; Spiritual Direction and Retreat Ministry.
Properties sponsored: Ursuline College; Beaumont High School; Villa Angela/St. Joseph High School.

[4120-05] OWENSBORO (P)

Ursuline Sisters of Mount Saint Joseph: 8001 Cummings Rd., Maple Mount, KY 42356. Tel: 270-229-4103; Fax: 270-229-4127. Sr. Amelia Stenger, O.S.U., Congregational Leader.
Total in Community: 111.
Legal Holdings and Titles: St. Joseph's Female Ursuline Academy, Inc.
Ministry in Colleges; Elementary Schools; Parishes; Retreats and Spiritual Direction; Pastoral Care; Health Care; Social Services; Hispanic Outreach; Diocesan Offices.
Represented in the Archdioceses of Kansas City in Kansas, Louisville, St. Louis and Washington and in the Dioceses of Belleville, Gallup, Owensboro, Shreveport and Springfield in Illinois. Also in Chile.

[4120-06] TOLEDO (P)

Ursuline Convent of the Sacred Heart: 4045 Indian Rd., Toledo, OH 43606. Tel: 419-536-9587. Sr. Sandra Sherman, O.S.U., Pres. & Gen. Supr.
Total in Community: 33; Associates: 137.
Legal Title: Ursuline Convent of the Sacred Heart.
Ministry in the field of Administration; Religious and Academic Education; Health Care; Counseling Services; Pastoral Ministry; Pastoral Care; Retreat Work; Spiritual Direction; Home Health Care; Volunteer Work.
Properties owned or sponsored: St. Ursula Academy, Toledo, OH.
Represented in the Archdiocese of Washington and in the Diocese of Toledo.

[4120-07] YOUNGSTOWN (P)

Motherhouse: Ursuline Motherhouse and Educational Center, 4250 Shields Rd., Canfield, OH 44406. Tel: 330-792-7636. Sr. Mary McCormick, O.S.U., Gen. Supr.
Total in Community: 43.
Properties owned and/or sponsored: Ursuline Motherhouse; Ursuline Center; Ursuline Preschool & Kindergarten; Beatitude House.
Ministry in the field of Religious and Academic Education at all levels; Parish Ministry; Social Services; Hospital Services; Single Parenting; AIDS Ministry; Preschool; Kindergarten; Nursing Home Service.
Represented in the Dioceses of Cleveland and Youngstown.

[4130] (O.S.U.)—URSULINE SISTERS OF THE CONGREGATION OF TILDONK, BELGIUM (P) International Congregation

Founded in Italy in 1535 by St. Angela Merici (Ursulines). Congregation of Tildonk founded in Belgium in 1832. First foundation in the United States in Ozone Park, New York, in 1924.

Generalate: Brussels, Belgium Sr. Bimla Minj, O.S.U., Gen. Supr.

Ursuline Provincialate: 81-15 Utopia Pkwy., Jamaica, NY 11432. Tel: 718-591-0681. Email: jcallahan@tildonkursuline.org. Sr. Joanne Callahan, O.S.U., Prov. Supr.
Total in Community: 36.
Properties owned and/or sponsored: St. Ursula Center, Blue Point, NY; Ursuline Provincialate, Jamaica NY.
Ministry in the field of Education in all its aspects; Retreat Work; Chaplaincies.
Represented in the Archdioceses of Hartford and New York and in the Dioceses of Brooklyn, Burlington and Rockville Centre.

[4140] V.D.M.F.—VERBUM DEI MISSIONARY FRATERNITY (P)

Founded in Mallorca, Spain in 1963.

Motherhouse: Rome, Italy 3365-3373 19th St., San Francisco, CA 94110.
Sisters: 20.
Ministry in the fields of retreat work; campus ministry; formation ministry.
Represented in the Archdiocese of San Francisco.

[4155] (M.T.G.)—SISTERS ADORERS OF THE HOLY CROSS (P)

Founded in 1670 in Vietnam by Bishop Pierre Lambert de la Motte. First foundation in the U.S. 1979.

General Motherhouse: 7408 S.E. Alder, Portland, OR 97215. Tel: 503-254-3284. Sr. Mary Kim Chi Bui, M.T.G., Supr.
Sisters: 30.
Represented in the Archdiocese of Portland in Oregon and in the Dioceses of Arlington and Sacramento.

[4170] (V.S.C.)—VINCENTIAN SISTERS OF CHARITY (D)

Founded in Bedford in 1928.
5900 Delhi Rd., Mount Saint Joseph, OH 45051.

[4180] (M.P.V.)—RELIGIOUS VENERINI SISTERS (P)

Founded in Italy in 1685. First foundation in the United States in 1909.

General Motherhouse: via Gioachino Belli 31, Rome, Italy Mother Eliana Massimi, Supr. Gen.
Universal total in Congregation: 381.

Provincial House for the U.S: 23 Edward St., Worcester, MA 01605. Sr. Hilda Ponte, M.P.V., Prov.
Total in Community: 19.
Legal Holdings: Venerini Academy, Worcester, MA.
Ministry in the field of Education; Health Care; Social Services; Parish and Diocesan Ministry; Foreign Missions.
Represented in the Dioceses of Albany and Worcester.

[4190] (V.H.M.)—VISITATION NUNS (P)

Founded in France in 1610. First foundation in the United States in Georgetown, Washington, DC in 1799.

First Federation of North America: Tel: 419-536-1343; Fax: 419-536-6025. Email: vhm-toledo@toast.net; Web: https://visitationsistersfirstfederation.org. Sr. Sharon Elizabeth Gworek, V.H.M., Federation Pres. Jane de Chantal Foundation Monasteries listed in the order of foundation.

Monastery of the Visitation (1833): 2300 Springhill Ave., Mobile, AL 36607-3202. Tel: 251-473-2321; Fax: 251-476-9761; Web: www.VisitationMonasteryMobile.org. Mother Rose Marie Kinsella, V.H.M., Supr.
Perpetual Vows: 12; Temporary Vows: 5; Novices: 1.

Monastery of the Visitation: 14 Beach Rd., P.O. Box 432, Tyringham, MA 01264. Tel: 413-243-3995; Fax: 413-243-3543; Email: vistyr3@aol.com; Web: www.vistyr.org. Mother Miriam Rose Niethus, Supr.
Total in Community: 15.
Legal Title: Visitation of Holy Mary.

Monastery of the Visitation: 12221 Bienvenue Rd., Rockville, VA 23146. Tel: 804-749-4885. Rev. Mother Mary Emmanuel Stahl, V.H.M., Supr.
Professed Sisters: 11.
Legal Title: Visitation of Holy Mary.

Monastery of the Visitation: 5820 City Ave., Philadelphia, PA 19131-1295. Tel: 215-473-5888. Email: viznunphil@aol.com. Mother Antoinette Marie Walker, V.H.M., Supr.
Professed Sisters Cloistered: 7; In Formation: 1.
Legal Title: Sisters of the Visitation of Philadelphia.

Monastery of the Visitation (Contemplative): 1745 Parkside Blvd., Toledo, OH 43607-1599. Tel: 419-536-1343; Fax: 419-536-6025; Email: vhm-superior@toast2.net; Web: www.toledovisitation.org. Mother Marie de Sales Kasper, V.H.M., Supr.
Professed Sisters: 14; In Formation: 5.
Legal Title: The Contemplative Order of the Visitation of Toledo, Ohio.

Monastery of the Visitation (Strictly Cloistered): 2055 Ridgedale Dr., Snellville, GA 30078. Tel: 770-972-1060. Sr. Teresa Maria Kulangara, V.H.M., Supr.

Professed Sisters: 6; Aspirants: 5.
Legal Title: Order of the Visitation of the Holy Mary.

Second Federation of North America

Monastery of the Sisters of the Visitation of Georgetown: 1500 35th St., N.W., Washington, DC 20007. Tel: 202-337-0305; Fax: 202-558-7976. Email: berchmans@visi.org. Mother Mary Berchmans Hannan, Supr.; Sr. Mada-anne Gell, Community Archivist.
Total number in the School Community: 499; Total in Community: 14.
Legal Holdings and Titles: Sisters of the Visitation of Georgetown; Georgetown Visitation Preparatory School.

Monastery of the Visitation (1833): 3020 N. Ballas Rd., St. Louis, MO 63131. Tel: 314-625-9260. Sr. Marie Therese Ruthmann, V.H.M., Supr.
Total in Community: 6.
Legal Holdings: Visitation Academy of St. Louis County; Monastery of the Visitation, St. Louis, MO.
Ministry in Education.

Monastery of the Visitation (1855): 8902 Ridge Blvd., Brooklyn, NY 11209-5716. Tel: 718-745-5151; Fax: 718-745-3680. Mother Susan Marie Kasprzak, V.H.M., Supr. Professed Sisters: 12.
Legal Title: Sisters of the Visitation of Brooklyn, NY.

Monastery of the Visitation: 2455 Visitation Dr., St. Paul, MN 55120. Tel: 651-683-1700. Email: info@vischool.org. Sr. Mary Denise Villaume, V.H.M., Supr.
Total in Community: 3.
Ministry in Prayer and Education.

[4200] (S.V.M.)—SISTERS OF THE VISITATION OF THE IMMACULATE HEART OF MARY (D)

Founded in France in 1610. First foundation in the United States in 1799.

Visitation Convent: 2950 Kaufmann Ave., Dubuque, IA 52001-1631. Tel: 563-556-2440. Email: TheSisters@sistersofthevisitationbq.org; Web: sistersofthevisitationbq.org. Sr. Patricia Clark, S.V.M., Pres.
Total in Community: 4.
Ministry in Higher Education; Adult Education; Parish Ministry.
Represented in the Archdiocese of Dubuque.

[4210] (S.D.V.)—VOCATIONIST SISTERS (P) (Sisters of the Divine Vocations)

Founded in Italy in 1921. First established in the United States in 1967.

General Motherhouse: Corso Duca D'Aosta, 22 Pianura, Naples, Italy, 80126. Sr. Antonietta Colafemina, S.D.V., Supr. Gen.

U.S. Foundation: Perpetual Help Day Nursery, 170 Broad St., Newark, NJ 07104. Tel: 973-484-3535. Sr. Perpetua Da Conceicao, S.D.V., Supr.
Total in Community: 6.
Ministry in Nursery Schools & Kindergartens; CCD Program and Parish Services.
Represented in the Archdiocese of Newark.

Sister Joanna Formation House: 88 Brooklake Rd., Florham Park, NJ 07932. Tel: 973-966-9762. Sr. Perpetua da Conceicao, Supr.; Sr. Romilda Borges, Delegate.
Total in Community: 9.
Ministry in Nursery School; Formation House; Religious Education.
Represented in the Archdiocese of Newark and in the Dioceses of Metuchen and Paterson.

[4230] (X.M.M.)—XAVERIAN MISSIONARY SOCIETY OF MARY, INC. (P)

Founded in Italy in 1945. First established in the United States in 1954.

General Motherhouse: Missionarie di Maria - Saveriane, Via Omero 4, Parma, Italy 43123. Sr. Giordana Bertacchini, X.M.M., Supr. Gen.
Total Membership: 218.

U.S. Headquarters: Xaverian Missionary Society of Mary, 242 Salisbury St., Worcester, MA 01609. Tel: 508-757-0514; Email: xavsistersusa@yahoo.com.mx.
Ministry to Hispanics; Elderly; Families; CCD Programs and Mission Education.
Represented in the Diocese of Worcester.
Sr. Rebeca Sanchez Perez, X.M.M., Supr.

DIOCESE OF BUFFALO

Chaplains of Public Institutions

BUFFALO. *Buffalo Fire Department and Erie County Emergency Services*. Vacant

Buffalo General Hospital. Revs. Richard H. Augustyn, Patrick O. Fernandes, Deacons Norman E. Foster, John M. Ruh.

Buffalo Holding Center. Deacon Miguel Santos.

Buffalo Police Department. Rev. Ross M. Syracuse, O.F.M.Conv.

Buffalo Psychiatric Center. Deacon Paul H. Bork.

Erie County Medical Center. Rev. Francis X. Mazur, Chief Trauma Chap., Deacon Ronald Walker.

Erie County Sheriff's Department. Rev. Ross M. Syracuse, O.F.M.Conv.

John R. Oishei Children's Hospital. Sr. Brenda Whelan, R.S.M., M.P.M., B.C.C.

Roswell Park Cancer Institute. Rev. Raymond G. Corbin, Deacons Carmelo Gaudioso, David R. Velasquez, William J. Walkowiak.

Veterans Hospital. Revs. Christopher Coric, O.F.M.Conv., (Croatia), Patrick Gardocki, O.F.M., (Poland).

ALDEN. *Wende Correctional Facility*. Rev. Thomas D. Doyle, Chap., Deacon Paul C. Kulczyk.

AMHERST. *Millard Fillmore Suburban Hospital*. Rev. Barry J. Allaire, Chap., (Retired), Deacons Peter J. Donnelly, Charles D. Esposito, Sr. Mary Lou Schnitzer, S.S.J.

ATTICA. *Attica Correctional Facility*. Rev. Ivan R. Trujillo, Deacon Heinz Friedman, Sr. Rosalind Rosolowski, C.S.S.F.

COLLINS. *Collins Correctional Facility*. Rev. John S. Kwiecien, Deacon John H. Burke.

CUBA. *Cuba Memorial Hospital and Adult Day Care Facility*. Deacon Michael R. Bray.

GOWANDA. *Gowanda Correctional Facility*. Deacons Terrance P. Harter, Matthew A. Hens.

JAMESTOWN. *WCA Hospital*. Deacon Michael Lennon.

NORTH TONAWANDA. *DeGraff Memorial Hospital*. Deacons David P. McDermott, John E. Steiner Jr.

OLEAN. *Olean General Hospital*. Deacon Michael L. Anderson.

WARSAW. *Warsaw Community Hospital*. Deacons Mark D. Kehl, Daniel G. McGuire.

Active Outside the Diocese:

Revs.—

Furlong, Richard V., 17 Jethol Dr., Assonet, MA 02702

Wild, Robert A., Madonna House, Combermere, ON Canada.

Inactive:

Revs.—

Kelly, John E., (Med. Leave)

Nielsen, Kenneth M.

Administrative Leave:

Rev. Msgr.—

Ryan, John M.

Revs.—

Dolinic, Louis S.

Fronczak, Dennis A.,

Gatto, Joseph C.

Giangreco, Samuel T.

Ipolito, Pascal D.

Juran, Michael P,

Maryanski, Fabian J

Mierzwa, Ronald B.

Palys, Daniel J.

Sadjak, Ronald

Salemi, Paul S.,

Sardina, John J.

Smith, Arthur J.

Stolinski, Robert A.

Venne, Samuel

Wolski, Mark J.

Yetter, Robert M.

Retired:

Rev. Msgrs.—

Becker, Vincent J., (Retired), 3532 Rte. 77, Varysburg, 14167

Belzer, Paul J., (Retired), 120 Meyer Rd. Apt. 229, Amherst, 14226

Braun, Francis, (Retired), O'Hara Residence, 69 O'Hara Rd., Tonawanda NY 14150-6227

Cahill, Richard M., (Retired), 1825 Alberta Dr., Clearwater, FL 33756

Caligiuri, Angelo M., (Retired), 69 O'Hara Rd., Tonawanda, 14150-6224

Campbell, James F., (Retired), Bishop Head Residence, 10 Rosary Ave., Lackawanna, 14218

Clody, Albert W., (Retired), 308 Edgewater Dr., Westfield, 14787

Connelly, James N., (Retired), O'Hara Residence, 69 O'Hara Rd., Apt. 3, Tonawanda, 14150-6227

Crane, Thomas E., (Retired), O'Hara Residence, 69 O'Hara Rd., Tonawanda, 14150-6227

DelVecchio, Michael E., (Retired), P.O. Box 22, Orchard Park, 14127

Dowdell, Joseph M., (Retired), 84 Pheasant Run Ln., Lancaster, 14086

Gallagher, William J., (Retired), 1223 Orchard Park Rd., West Seneca, 14224

Gallivan, David M., (Retired), P.O. Box 133, Angola, 14006

Golombek, Robert K., (Retired), 1 Gates Cir., Apt. 309, 14209-1129

Kelly, James G., (Retired), O'Hara Residence, 69 O'Hara Rd., Tonawanda, 14150-6227

Kopacz, Matthew S., (Retired), 9993 Trevett Rd., Boston, 14025-9743

Lee, David M., (Retired), 4881 Edgewood Dr., Hamburg, 14075

Leising, Frederick D., (Retired), 68 Cowing St., Depew, 14043

Lichtenthal, James J., (Retired), 9335 SE 177th Simon's Ln., The Villages, FL 32162

Lorenzetti, Dino J., (Retired), O'Hara Residence, 69 O'Hara Rd., Tonawanda, 14150-6227

Madsen, John W., (Retired), Conniff Residence, 68 Cowing St., Depew, 14043

Maloney, Thomas F., (Retired), 87 Kettering Dr., Tonawanda, 14223

McCarthy, Leo F., (Retired), 263 Claremont Ave., Kenmore, 14223

Moran, J. Thomas, (Retired), O'Hara Residence, 69 O'Hara Rd., Tonawanda, 14150

Myszka, Daniel J., (Retired), 391 Bristol St., 14206-3721

Neu, Leon M., (Retired), Bishop Head Residence, 10 Rosary Ave., Lackawanna, 14218

O'Neill, Kevin T., (Retired), Bishop Head Residence, 10 Rosary Ave., Lackawanna, 14218

Scanlan, Edward J., (Retired), McAuley Residence, 1503 Military Rd. Rm 220, Tonawanda, NY 14150

Sciera, Ronald P., (Retired), P.O. Box 553, 14240-0553

Sicari, Joseph J. (Retired), O'Hara Residence, 69 O'Hara Rd., Tonawanda NY 14150

Slubecky, David M. (Retired), Msgr. Conniff Residence, 68 Cowing St., Depew NY 14043

Sullivan, W. Jerome, J.C.D., (Retired), 68 Cowing St., Depew, 14043

Voorhes, Fred R., (Retired), 24 Forsythia Ct., Orchard Park, 14127

Wall, James E., (Retired), 711 Knox Rd., P.O. Box 607, East Aurora, 14052

Wangler, Donald R., (Retired), 193 Mill Rd., West Seneca, NY 14224

Wangler, William O., (Retired), Bishop Head Residence, 10 Rosary Ave., Lackawanna NY 14218

Weldgen, Francis G., (Retired), 6955 Maple Dr., Wheatfield, 14120

Wetter, Richard L., (Retired), O'Hara Residence, 69 O'Hara Rd., Tonawanda, 14150-6227

Williamson, Robert J., (Retired), 202 Golden Pond Estates, Akron, 14001

Yunk, Michael J., (Retired), 47 Linwood Ave., Williamsville, 14221-6501

Revs.—

Amico, Charles R., Ph.D., S.T.D., (Retired), Christ the King Seminary, P.O. Box 607, East Aurora, 14052-0607

Augustyn, James M., (Retired), 10 Rosary Ave., Lackawanna, 14218

Badding, Joseph P., (Retired), 5904 Shoreham Dr., Lake View, 14085. winter- Immaculate Conception Church, 76-5960 Mamalahoa Hwy., Holualoa, HI 96725

Bagienski, Ronald A., (Retired), 3233 N.E. 34th St., Apt. 1118, Fort Lauderdale, FL 33308

Beiter, Robert G., (Retired), Msgr. Conniff Residence, 68 Cowing St., Depew, 14043

Bigelow, William R., (Retired), 5130 Brittany Dr. S., Saint Petersburg, FL 33715. (Summer) 103 Long Ave., Hamburg, 14075

Bordonaro, Richard D., (Retired), 1229 Vista Serena Ave., Banning, CA 92220

Cilano, Richard J., (Retired), St. Matthew Rectory, 1555 Glen Ellyn Rd., Glendale Heights, IL 60139

Conoscenti, Frederick M., (Retired), 1 Fox Run Ln., Apt. 276, Orchard Park, 14127

Czarnecki, Edward R., (Retired), 211 Harding Ave. Angola, NY 14006

DiGiulio, Richard S., (Retired), Msgr. Conniff Residence, 68 Cowing St., Depew, 14043

Dobson, Gregory J., (Retired), 202 S. Union St., Olean NY 14760

Donohue, Raymond A.J., (Retired), P.O. Box 24, Fredonia, 14063

Drilling, Peter J., Th.D., (Retired), Bishop Head Residence, 10 Rosary Ave., Lackawanna NY 14218

Elis, Patrick H., (Retired), P.O. Box 1053, Buffalo, NY 14215

Enright, James C., (Retired), 15 Clark St., Auburn, 13021

Ferraro, Vincent J., (Retired), 6N. Transithill Dr., Apt. 5, Depew, 14043

Fifagrowicz, Joseph G., (Retired), Bishop Head Residence, 10 Rosary Ave., Lackawanna, 14218

Gaglione, John R., (Retired), Our Lady of the Sacred Heart, 3148 Abbott Rd., Orchard Park, NY 14127

Griffin, David G., (Retired), Bishop Head Residence, 10 Rosary Ave., Lackawanna, 14218. (Winter) 317 Mullally St., Daytona Beach, FL 32114-3105

Hassett, James F., (Retired), O'Hara Residence, 69 O'Hara Rd., Tonawanda, 14150

Herberger, Roy T., (Retired), 15 Greenwich Dr., Apt. 2, East Amherst, 14228

Hinton, Frederick M., (Retired), Kenmore Village Apts., 657 Colvin Blvd., Apt 706, Kenmore, 14217

Hora, Robert J., (Retired), 9728 Northfield St., Angola, NY 14006

Judge, James G., (Retired), 2850 Amsdell Rd., Unit 29, Hamburg, 14075

Kasinski, James J., (Retired), Msgr. Conniff Residence, 68 Cowing St., Depew, 14043

Kibler, Gary R., (Retired), 39 Cimarand Dr., Williamsville, 14221

Klos, Joseph, J.C.L., (Retired), c/o Barbara Wisniewska, Ostrowite 129, 87-522, Ostrowite, Poland

Kuhlmann, John L., (Retired), 50 Fairmont St., Jamestown, 14701

Leising, John J., (Retired), 201 Reist St., Williamsville, 14221-5341

Mahar, Raymond J., (Retired), 145 E Main St., Fredonia, NY 14063

Martin, Robert A., (Retired), Peregrine Landing, 575 Cayuga Creek Rd., Apt. B 200, Cheektowaga, NY 14227

Matuszak, Walter L., (Retired), Msgr. Conniff Residence, 68 Cowing St., Depew, 14043

McGarry, William C., (Retired), Our Lady of Peace Home, 5285 Lewiston Rd., Lewiston, 14092-1942

Measer, Donald L., (Retired), St. Amelia, 210 St. Amelia Dr., Tonawanda, 14150-7126

Mergenhagen, John J., (Retired), c/o Msgr. Paul Belzer, 120 Meyer Rd., Apt. 229, Amherst, 14226

Milby, Lawrence M., (Retired), 39 Duncan Ter., Islington, London, United Kingdom N18AL

Mitka, John J., (Retired), Msgr. Conniff Residence, 68 Cowing St., Depew, 14043

Nguyen, Andrew Tu Minh, (Retired), 348 Dewitt St., 14213

O'Connor, James C., (Retired), St Joseph Cathedral, 50 Franklin St., Buffalo, NY 14202

O'Hara, Michael D., (Retired), 15 Clough Ave., Arcade, 14009

Orszulak, Henry A., (Retired), 62 Cloister Ct., Blasdell, 14219

Quinlivan, Thomas J., (Retired), 24 Oschawa Ave., 14210

Reger, George L., (Retired), 82 Candace Ln., Depew, 14043

Reina, Richard A., M.Div., M.S.W., M.C.Sp., (Retired), 990 Hopkins Rd., Williamsville, 14221

Rodriguez, Antonio L., (Retired), Bishop Head Residence, 10 Rosary Ave., Lackawanna, 14218

Sabo, Paul P., (Retired), 81 Bogardus St., Buffalo, NY 14206
Sheedy, Edward J., Ed.D., (Retired), 1301 George Urban Blvd., Cheektowaga, 14225
Shumway, Lynn M., (Retired), 5247 Paddock Ln., Lewiston, 14092
Siracuse, Guy F., (Retired), Brothers of Mercy, 10570 Bergtold Rd., Clarence, 14031
Slomba, Eugene S., (Retired), 6425 Sherwood Dr., Lockport, 14094
Stelmach, Jerome J., (Retired), 600 Cayuga Creek Rd., Cheektowaga, 14227. (Med.)
Swiatek, Emil P., (Retired), Msgr. Conniff Residence, 68 Cowing St., Depew, 14043
Szczesniak, Harry F., (Retired), Bishop Head Residence, 10 Rosary Ave., Lackawanna, 14218
Walter, James A., (Retired), 4635 Kings Cross Rd., Clarence, 14031
Westfield, Carlton J., (Retired), 6365 Pickup Hill Rd., Cherry Creek, 14723
Wopperer, Thomas J., (Retired), 1 W. Beach Rd., Dunkirk, 14048. (Winter): 220 Argyle Rd., West Palm Beach, FL 33405
Zadora, Charles J., (Retired), Bishop Head Residence, 10 Rosary Ave., Lackawanna, 14218
Zancan, Robert D., (Retired), P.O. Box 7084, Loveland, CO 80537
Zuffoletto, Michael P., (Retired), 6799 Rivera Way, East Amherst, 14051.

Permanent Deacons:
Adamczak, Ronald D.
Amantia, Philip J. Sr.
Andelora, Gary P.
Anderson, Michael L.
Armstrong, David
Augustyniak, David M.
Badaszewski, Robert W.
Barr, Joseph M.
Bauer, Robert A.
Birmingham, Edward M.
Bochiechio, Michael G.
Bork, Paul H.
Bray, Michael R.
Brick, Daniel E. Esq.
Bringenberg, Thomas B.
Burke, John H.
Canzoneri, Michael J.
Casey, Christopher T.
Chriswell, Timothy E.
Ciezki, Robert T.
Clabeaux, David E.
Collichio, James L.
Comerford, Michael V. Jr.
Conroy, Dennis P.
Coughlin, John F.
Crimi, Victor P.
Dibb, Roy P.
Dalessandro, Michael J,
Denecke, Daniel G.
Dobmeier, Robert A.
Donnelly, Peter J.
Dulak, Michael T.
Ehrhart, David C.
Emerson, Paul C.
Eschbach, Lawrence D.
Eschrich, Paul C.
Esposito, Charles D.
Feary, Gregory L. Jr.
Ficorilli, Michael J.
Forcucci, Thomas M.
Forster, Jeffrey D.
Foster, Norman E.
Friedman, Heinz
Friedman, Thomas F.
Fudala, Walter N.
Gaudioso, Carmelo
Gaulin, John P.
Golinski, Daniel U.
Gomola, Michael A.
Griesbaum, Charles J. Jr.
Harter, Terrance P.
Harvey, David H.
Healey, Thomas R.
Hendricks, John H.
Hens, Matthew A.
Hooper, Mark J.
Hoover, Gary M.
Howard, Edward R.
Hynes, William J.
Jacobi, Robert J.
Jaworski, James J.
Jerome, David R.
Johnson, H. Wilson
Kapsiak, Dennis W.
Kedzielawa, Frank S.
Kehl, Mark D.
Kelly, John J.
Klein, George L.
Koester, Carlton M.
Kulczyk, Paul C.
Lagona, Francis J.
Leaderstorf, Marc R.
Leardon, John D.
Lemieux, Michael C.
Lennon, Michael
Licata, Thomas C.
Linnan, Neal M.
Mackiewicz, Richard F.
Maloney, Timothy J.
Manunta, Alejandro D.
Marino, Benjamin R.
Markowski, Lawrence P.
May, Thaddeus P.
McDermott, David P.
McDonnell, Thomas A.
McGuire, Daniel G.
McKeating, Michael P.
Mercurio, Joseph P.
Miranda, Roberto G.
Monaco, Kenneth R.
Moran, V. Gregory
Moscicki, Henry E.
Nowak, Mark F.
Owczarczak, John A.
Parker, Richard W.
Pasquale, Francis W. Jr.
Pasquella, Joseph A.
Pellerito, Samuel
Pijacki, Thaddeus V.
Polizzi, Frank S.
Puleo, Samuel G.
Quinn, Michael D.
Ramos, Carlos W.
Rotterman, David C.
Ruh, John M.
Santos, Miguel
Scherr, Thomas E.
Schultz, Thomas E.
Schumer, Stephen R.
Setera, John T.
Silva, Jorge L.
Slish, David P.
Smith, Kevin J.
Snyder, Paul L. III
Stachura, Richard R. Jr.
Stahl, Raymond H.
Stando, Matthew
Stankiewicz, Paul S.
Steinagle, Gordon J.
Steiner, John E. Jr.
Sullivan, Arthur T., Jr
Swinarski, Stephen J.
Szczesny, Walter T.
Terrana, Gary C.
Thomann, Bernard M.
Trzaska, James J.
Tyler, Daniel J.
Velasquez, David R.
Waggoner, James R.
Walders, Peter J.
Walker, Ronald
Walkowiak, Brian C.
Walkowiak, William J.
Walter, Paul F., Jr.
Warner, Robert G.
Watkins, Donald R. Jr.
Weigel, Donald C. Jr.
Weisenburger, Paul F.
Wlos, John J.
Zablocki, Edward M.
Zielinski, John R.
Zwack, Francis A.

DIOCESE OF FRESNO

Chaplains of Public Institutions

FRESNO. *Valley Children's Hospital,* Tel: 559-353-3000. Vacant, Chap.

Community Regional Medical Center, Fresno, Tel: 559-459-6000. Rev. Emmanuel Ogbonnya, Chap.

Fresno Heart & Surgical Hospital, Tel: 559-433-8000. Rev. Chika Kamalu, (On Call).

Kaiser Permanente Medical Center, Tel: 559-448-4500. Rev. Chika Kamalu, Chap.

VA Central California Health Care System, Tel: 559-225-6100, Ext. 5351. Rev. Abraham Kombo, Chap.

ATWATER. *United States Federal Prison,* P.O. Box 019000 Atwater, 95301 Tel: 209 386-0257

AVENAL. *Avenal State Prison,* #1 Kings Way, P.O. Box 8, Avenal, 93204. Tel: 559-386-0587; Tel: 559-386-0587, Ext. 6002; Email: Rodney.ornellas@cdcr.ca.gov. Rodney Ornellas, Chap.

BAKERSFIELD. *Bakersfield Memorial Hospital,* 420 34th St., Bakersfield, 93301. Tel: 661-327-4647.

Crossroads Juvenile Detention Camp, Tel: 661-472-4748

San Joaquin Community Hospital, 2615 Chester Ave., Bakersfield, 93301. Tel: 661-395-3000.

Juvenile Hall Lerdo Adult Facility. Contact: Deacon Scotty Bourne Tel: 661-343-3855 Contact: Sr. Elaine Elgart Tel: 209-617-2534

Mesa Verde Adult Detention Facility, 425 Golden State Ave., Bakersfield, CA Contact: Sr. Elaine Elgart Tel: 209-617-2534

Pathways Girls Rehab, Contact: Rev. Mr. Joe Lubatti Tel: 661-758-8400 Ext. 5649

CALIFORNIA CITY. *California City Correctional Center,* 22844 Virginia Blvd., California City, CA 93305. Contact: George Peate. Tel: 760-373-1764 Ext. 2284

CHINA LAKE NAWS. *China Lake.* Rev. James Dowds, C.Ss.R Chap. Tel: 760-939-3506

CHOWCHILLA. *Department of Corrections, Central California Women's Facility,* P.O. Box 1501, Chowchilla, 93610-1501. Tel: 559-665-5531, Ext. 7232. Sr. Rosa Maria Guembe, R.C.M., Chap.

Valley State Prison for Men, 21633 Ave. 24, P.O. Box 92, Chowchilla, 93610-0092. Tel: 559-665-6100, Ext. 6076.Danilo Grajales, Chap.

CLOVIS. *Clovis Community Medical Center,* Tel: 559-324-4000. Rev. Abraham Kombo.

COALINGA. *Coalinga State Hospital,* Tel: 559-935-4300. Bro. Andres Amador, O.F.M.Conv.

Pleasant Valley State Prison. Medium to high level state. 24863 W. Jayne Ave., P.O. Box 8500, Coalinga, 93210-8500. Tel: 559-935-4900, Ext. 6777; Email: edwin.peraza@cdcr.ca.gov; Web: www.cdcr.ca.gov. Edwin Peraza, Chap.

CORCORAN. *California State Prison,* 4001 King Ave., P.O. Box 8800, Corcoran, 93212. Tel: 559-992-8800, Ext. 6577; Email: charlyugwu@cdcr.ca.gov. Rev. Charles Ugwu, Chap.

California Substance Abuse Treatment Facility & State Prison - Corcoran, 900 Quebec Ave., P.O. Box 7100, Corcoran, 93212-7100. Tel: 559-992-7100, Ext. 6778 Rev. Henry Aguwa, Chap., Email: henry.aguwa@cdcr.ca.gov. Jose Ojeda, Chap. Email:jose.ojeda@cdcr.ca.gov.

DELANO. *Kern Valley State Prison,* P.O. Box 6000, Delano, 93216-6000. Tel: 661-721-6300. Rev. Francisco Diaz, Chap.

North Kern State Prison, 3737 West Cecil Ave., P.O. Box 567, Delano, 93216-0567. Tel: 661-721-2345, Ext. 5311; Email: Flordito.redulla@cdcr.ca.gov. Rev. Flordito Redulla, S.V.D., Chap.

Delano City Adult Facility. Contact: Darren Caskey. Tel: 661-333-8541

Edwards Air Force Base, 10 Park Drive Blvd 6447, Edwards Air Force Base, CA 95324 Rev. Major Philip Llanos, Chap. Tel: 661 277-2110

Fresno County Jail, 1225 "M" Street, Fresno, CA 93721 Danilo Grajales, Chap. Tel: 888 373-7011

Matthew 25 Detention Ministry, Fresno County Jail 1225 "M" St. Diocesan Liaison Jim Grant, Dir. Tel: 559 488-7463

LEMOORE. U.S. *Naval Air Station* Lemoore, CA. Rev. Richard Smith, Chap. Tel: 559 998-4618

McFarland Women's Prison. Contact: Michael Cooper. Tel: 661 282-8100

Central Valley Men's Facility. Contact: Rev. Scotty Bourne. Tel: 661 343-3855

Golden State Men's Facility. Contact: Darren Caskey. Tel: 661-333-8541

Mendota Federal Correctional Institution. Contact: Rev. Miguel Mancia. Tel: 559 655-4237

PORTERVILLE. *Porterville Developmental Center,* P.O. Box 2000, Porterville, 93258-2000. Tel: 559-782-2402, Ext. 2401. Rev. Michael A. Avila, Chap.

SHAFTER *Shafter City Adult Facility.* Contact: Uriel Payan. Tel: 661 699-0366

TAFT *Taft Correctional Institution.* P.O. Box 7000 Taft, CA 93268. Tel: 661 763-2520, ext. 1205. Contact: Deacon Scotty Bourne

Taft City Facility. Contact: Deacon Scotty Bourne. Tel: 661 343-3855

TEHACHAPI. *California Correctional Institution,* P.O. Box 1031, Tehachapi, 93581-1031. Tel: 661-822-4402, Ext. 4387. Rev. Manuel Sundaram, Chap.

WASCO. *State Prison,* 701 Scofield Ave., P.O. Box 8800, Wasco, 93280-8800. Tel: 661-758-8400, Ext. 5237; Email: joseph.lubatti@cdcr.ca.gov. Deacon Joseph Lubatti, Chap.

On Special Assignment:

Rev. Msgrs.—

Dreiling, Raymond C., V.G., Vicar General
Griesbach, John, St. Anthony Retreat Center, Dir.

Revs.—

Avila, Dan, Vocation Dir.
Del Angel, Jesus, J.C.L., Adjutant Judicial Vicar.

On Duty Outside the Diocese:

Revs.—

de la Torre, Jorge, Archdiocese of Dhaka, Bangladesh
Okorie, Onyema, Military Chap.

Retired:

Rev. Msgrs.—

Bezunartea, Herman O., (Retired)
Braun, Michael R., (Retired)
Coelho-Harguindeguy, John, (Retired)
Herrero, Nicolas, (Retired)
Janelli, Anthony, (Retired)
Lopez, Daniel, (Retired)
Marta, Raul, (Retired)
Meyer, Gilbert, (Retired)
Minhoto, Walter F., (Retired)
Shenoy, Leslie, (Retired)
Swett, Ronald, (Retired)

Revs.—

Alvernaz, Dennis, (Retired)
Amerando, Gerald, (Retired)
Azpericueta, Lucas, (Retired)
Blessing, Loren, (Retired)
Bray, Kevin, (Retired)
Bulfer, Stephen, V.F., (Retired)
Burns, John P., (Retired)
Chavez, Gerald F., (Retired)
Congdon, John, Military Chap., (Retired)
Flickenger, Don D., (Retired)
Gonzalez, Angel, (Retired)
Heffernan, Joseph A., (Retired)
Ignacio, Alejandro, (Retired)
Kudilil, James, (Retired)
Montiel, Jose, (Retired)
Norris, David J. (Retired)
Pascual, Manuel, (Retired)
Reed, David, (Retired)
Simeone, Francis, (Retired)
Varo, Jose Luis, (Retired)
Vega, Jose Luis, (Retired)

Catholic Dioceses in the United States

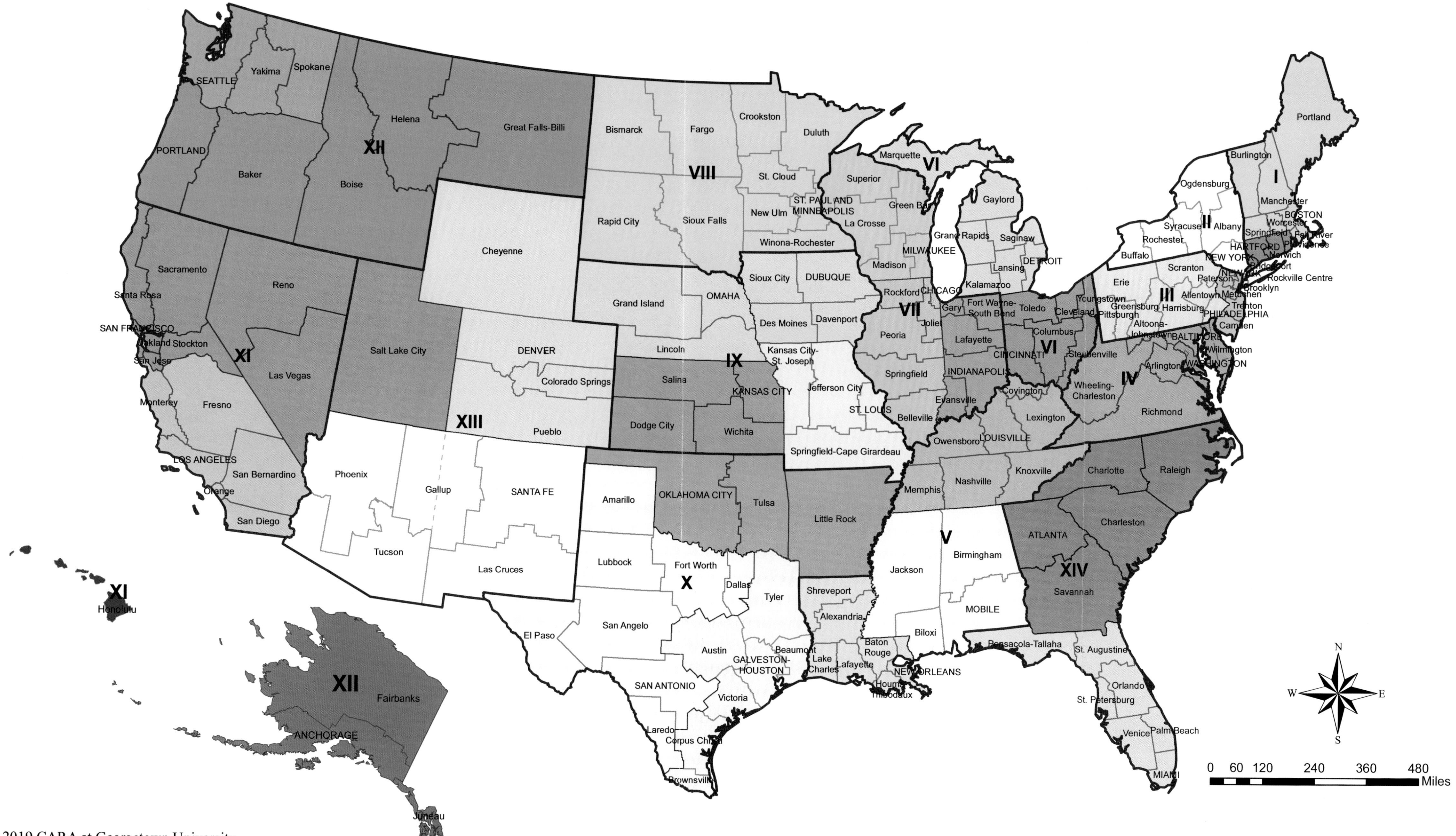

2300 Wisconsin Ave NW Suite 400A
Washington, DC 20007
cara.georgetown.edu

This map shows boundaries of the Latin Rite dioceses whose bishops belong to the United States Conference of Catholic Bishops (USCCB). Archdioceses are indicated by capital letters and Ecclesiastical Provinces are grouped by color. USCCB regions are shown within maroon lines and indicated by Roman numerals. Dashed lines show where dioceses cross state lines. This map does not show the Diocese of St. Thomas in the U.S. Virgin Islands, which is part of the Ecclesiastical Province of Washington, or the Archdiocese for the Military Services.